W9-BTA-614

The
**Princeton
Review**®

PrincetonReview.com

THE COMPLETE BOOK OF COLLEGES

WITHDRAWN FROM
SAN DIEGO COUNTY LIBRARY

2019 EDITION

Penguin
Random
House

The Princeton Review
110 East 42nd Street, 7th Floor
New York, NY 10017
editorialsupport@review.com

© 2018 by TPR Education IP Holdings, LLC.
All rights reserved.

Published in the United States by Penguin Random
House LLC, New York, and in Canada by Random
House of Canada, a division of Penguin Random
House Ltd.,Toronto. This is a revised edition of a
book first published in 1989.

All rankings, ratings, and listings are intellectual
property of TPR Education IP Holdings, LLC. No
rankings, ratings, listings, or other proprietary information in this book may be repurposed, abridged,
excerpted, combined with other data, or altered for
reproduction in any way without express permission
of TPR.

ISBN: 978-1-5247-5794-6
ISSN: 1088-8594

Production: Best Content Solutions, LLC
Production Editor: Melissa Duclos

Printed in the United States of America.

9 8 7 6 5 4 3 2 1

2019 Edition

The Princeton Review is not affiliated with Princeton
University.

Editorial

Robert Franek, Editor-in-Chief
David Soto, Director of Content Development
Stephen Koch, Student Survey Manager
Pia Aliperti, Senior Editor
Danielle Correa, Editor

Penguin Random House Publishing Team

Tom Russell, VP, Publisher
Alison Stoltzfus, Publishing Director
Ellen L. Reed, Production Manager
Amanda Yee, Associate Managing Editor
Suzanne Lee, Designer

ACKNOWLEDGMENTS

Each year we assemble an awe-inspiringly talented group of colleagues who work together to produce our guidebooks; this year is no exception. Everyone involved in this effort—authors, editors, data collectors, production specialists, and designers—gives so much more than is required to make *The Complete Book of Colleges* an exceptional student resource guide.

My sincere thanks go to the many who contributed to this tremendous project. Very special thanks go to Pia Aliperti and Danielle Correa for their editorial commitment and vision. A warm and special thank you goes to our Student Survey expert, Stephen Koch, who continues to work in partnership with school administrators and students alike. My continued thanks go to our data collection pro, David Soto, for his successful efforts in collecting and accurately representing the statistical data that appear with each college profile and to Melissa Duclos for her dedication to reading through the massive amounts of data. The enormousness of this project and its deadline constraints could not have been realized without the calm presence of our production partner, Scott Harris. Scott's many years of dedication and focus continue to delight and remind me of what a pleasure it is to work together on this project each year. Special thanks also go to publicist Jeanne Krier, for the dedicated work she continues to do on this book and the overall series since its inception. Jeanne continues to be my trusted colleague, media advisor, and friend. I would also like to make special mention of Tom Russell and Alison Stoltzfus, our Random House publishing team, for their continuous investment and faith in our ideas. Last, I thank my Princeton Review Partner Team, Andy Feld, Amy Calhoun, and Casey Cornelius, for their confidence in me and my content team and for their commitment to providing students the resources they need to find the best fit school for them. Again, to all who contributed so much to this publication, thank you for your efforts; they do not go unnoticed.

Robert Franek
Editor-in-Chief

CONTENTS

FOREWORD

Welcome. You have found the best place to begin, fine-tune, and execute the search for your perfect college. With the understanding that choosing a school wisely is a top priority for each prospective student, we have provided a significant breadth of information in this text to help you navigate the exciting, amazing, and sometimes confusing process of choosing the right college.

The design of this guidebook will allow you to narrow your search of colleges from 1,366 to a few dozen. Here you'll find all the individual college statistics you'll need to make informed choices about the competitiveness, size, location, and academic offerings of the schools available to you. In addition, you can find even more information about individual schools at The Princeton Review's website, PrincetonReview. com. The site includes college search tools, college profiles, college advice, a college majors search engine, and much more.

By using this book, you can search for, choose, and apply to colleges with the confidence of a pro—or at the very least a well-informed undergraduate hopeful! We supply the information and guidance, and you ultimately make your own decision.

The college selection, application, and interview processes can be overwhelming at times. They can also be rewarding experiences. For most, choosing a college is the first major life decision. I know it was mine. Remember that your college decision is yours alone, so arm yourself with the best available information. Badger teachers, friends, high school and college admissions counselors, brothers, sisters, and parents; ask them how they chose their colleges and why. The more you know when beginning the process, the more in control of the situation you'll feel.

Whatever it is that you choose as your path in life, your college selection will forever be your first step in that direction. The friends you make, the professors you meet, and the classes you take are all springboards to the next phase of your life.

I wish you much luck and success at whichever college you decide to attend. My sincere hope is that this publication and other Princeton Review tools will be helpful in the process.

Robert Franek
Editor-in-Chief

INTRODUCTION

Before you dive into *The Complete Book of Colleges*, we want to give you some tips for your college search—especially on how to get the most out of this book and what to do once you've made your choices and are ready to apply. Since the most important thing for you to do now is to start your search, we want to start right off by revealing the secret to getting admitted to the college of your choice.

A crucial, and often overlooked, element to getting into college is compatibility: that is, finding colleges that have the educational and social environments you're looking for, where you are well-suited academically, and have something the college is looking for in return. You have a lot more control over where you end up going to college than you might think.

Finding your college fit is a two-step process. You should begin with a thorough self-examination or personal inventory. Your personal inventory is best structured in the form of a chart, so that when you begin to consider your options, you can check off those colleges that satisfy the various needs or wants you've identified. In this way, your best college choices will gradually begin to identify themselves.

Divide your inventory into two sections. One section should be biographical, including your high school course selection, GPA, SAT and/or ACT scores, class rank, and personal information like extracurricular activities—especially those you plan to continue in college. This will help you to assess how you stack up against each college's admissions standards and student body. The second section is a listing of the characteristics you need or want in the college you'll choose to attend. This list should include anything and everything you consider important, such as location, size of the student body, availability of scholarships, dormitory options, clubs and activities, even school colors if you want. This part of your inventory should grow continuously as you become more and more aware of what is important to you in your choice of colleges.

Armed with your personal inventory, you can begin to take advantage of the numerous resources available to help you narrow your choices of where to apply. There are five sources for information and advice that have become standard for most college-bound students:

1. *College websites, social media feeds, videos, brochures, catalogs...*

If you are a junior or senior in high school, you probably know more about the information these materials should include than the people who are responsible for designing and writing them. College marketing material will give you an overview of the academic offerings and the basic admissions requirements. You will never see anything but the most appealing architecture and the best-looking students on campus, nor will you hear about the recent tuition increases that were greater than the rate of inflation. Look these materials over, but don't make any decisions based solely on what you read or see.

2. Your friends

The experts on specific colleges and universities are the students who currently attend them. Seek out any and all of your friends, offspring of your parents' friends, and recent graduates of your high school who attend colleges that you are considering. Talk to them when they come home. Arrange to stay with them when you visit their colleges. Pick their brains for everything they know. It doesn't get any more direct and honest than this.

3. Books and college guides

There are two types of books that can be helpful to you in your search: those that discuss specific aspects of going to college and college guides. A great narrative guide that stresses students' own opinions of colleges is our own annual *Best Colleges* guide. In addition, look at other guides for good second opinions. As for comprehensive guides—those that emphasize data over narrative content—you're holding the most up-to-date and useful one in your hands.

4. The Internet

Beyond a college's own website and social media presence, there are many publications and communities online dedicated to college admissions. Our site, PrincetonReview.com, provides a wide range of resources to help you research colleges, prepare for standardized tests, raise your grades, and complete your college application.

5. Your counselor

Since it's *critically* important, we'll say it again: Once you've developed some ideas about your personal inventory and college options, schedule a meeting with your school counselor. The more research you've done before you get together, the more help you're likely to get. Good advice comes out of thoughtful discussion, not from the expectation that your counselor will do your work. Many students and families opt to work with a professional college counselor, such as the expert College Admission Counselors at The Princeton Review, to supplement the support they receive from their high schools. When it comes time to file applications, look over the materials and requirements together, and allow plenty of time to craft your best application.

USING COLLEGE INFORMATION IN THE COMPLETE BOOK OF COLLEGES AND ELSEWHERE

Throughout the course of your college search, you'll confront an amazing array of statistics and other data related to every college you consider. In order for all of this information to be helpful, you need to have some sense of how to interpret it. We've included a detailed key to the college entries in this book a few pages deeper into this introduction. Almost all the statistics we've compiled are self-explanatory, but there are a few that will be more useful with some elaboration.

Let's start with **student/teacher ratio**. Don't use it to assess average class size; they are not interchangeable terms. At almost every college, the average class size is larger than its student/teacher ratio. At many big universities, it is considerably larger. What is useful about the ratio is that it can give you an idea of how accessible your professors will be outside of the classroom. Once you are in college, you'll grow to realize just how important this is.

In the same way, the **percentage of faculty that holds PhDs** is useful information. When you're paying thousands of dollars in tuition each year, there's something comforting about knowing that your professors have a considerably broader and deeper grasp of what you're studying than you do. In contrast, teaching assistants (TAs) may often be just one or two steps ahead of you.

Another interesting group of statistics deals with the **percentage of students who go on to graduate or professional school**. Never allow yourself to be swayed by such statistics, unless you've taken the time to ponder their meaning and visited the college in question. High percentages almost always mean one of two things: that the college is an intellectual enclave that inspires students onward to further their education, or that it is a pre-professional bastion of aggressive careerists. There isn't anything inherently wrong with either scenario, but neither has universal appeal to prospective students. Colleges that are exceptions to this rule are rare and precious. The most misleading figures provided to prospective students are those for medical school acceptance rates. Virtually every college in the country can boast of high acceptance rates to medical school for its graduates; pre-med programs are designed to weed out those who will not be strong candidates before they even get to apply! If you're thinking about medical school, ask colleges how many of their students apply to medical school each year. Also, try to get a sense of the attrition rate within the pre-med program.

One final piece of advice about statistics relates to the **college's acceptance rate**. Simply knowing the percentage of applicants who are admitted each year is helpful, but it is even more helpful if you also know how many applied. When you compare these figures to the first-year profile, you have the most accurate picture of just how tough it is to get in. An 80 percent acceptance rate doesn't mean there's an open door if you don't match up well to the academic achievements of the college's typical first-year. Beyond this, keep an eye out for colleges that have relatively self-selecting applicant pools. In these cases, high acceptance rates may be misleading. When evaluating highly selective public colleges as an out-of-state applicant, remember that you will likely face a more selective evaluation than state residents.

A Few Final Thoughts

Once you've narrowed down your options and decided where to apply, get to work filling out applications. The admissions process is stressful enough without putting extra pressure on yourself by waiting until the last minute. The first thing you should do when you receive the necessary forms is go over them with your school counselor. Immediately remove the recommendation forms (if they are required) and give them to the teachers and counselor(s) who will be completing them for you. They'll have a better opportunity to write a thorough and supportive recommendation if you give them enough time to complete them. This is also the time to make your request for official transcripts. Again, it takes time to do these things. Plan ahead.

As for completing the applications, organize yourself and all the materials. Keep everything in folders (physically; on your computer; or in the cloud) and accessible in case you need to speak with an admissions officer over the telephone. When essays and information on your extracurricular activities are required, do some outlining and rough draft-writing before you commit yourself to the actual forms or online tools, and make sure you ask someone you trust to proofread your work.

Paying for college requires some work on your part, too. While this book is not dedicated to the subject, it's very important that you get to work on your financial circumstances right away. Keep in mind that while college is expensive, few people pay the full "sticker price." You have to have your finances in order before you can get the most financial aid possible. Visit fafsa.gov for the latest on the Free Application for Federal Student Aid. You can also find the most exhaustive strategies for financing your education in our book *Paying for College*.

Last but not least, **don't take it easy during your senior year!** Colleges routinely request mid-year grades, and they expect you to continue taking challenging academic courses and keep your grades up throughout your high school career. Doing so takes you one step closer to getting good news. On behalf of The Princeton Review, have a good time, and good luck. See you on campus!

Nota Bene

The data reported in this book, unless otherwise noted, was collected from the profiled colleges from the fall of 2017 through the spring of 2018. In some cases, we were unable to publish the most recent data because schools did not report the necessary statistics to us in time, despite our repeated outreach efforts. Because enrollment and financial statistics as well as application and financial aid deadlines fluctuate from one year to another, we recommend that you check to make sure you have the most current information before applying. Best of luck!

HOW THE COMPLETE BOOK OF COLLEGES *IS ORGANIZED*

There are two types of profiles in this book. Not every school listed will have both. All of the 1,366 colleges and universities included in this book have their own informational profiles, and each entry follows the same basic format. Many of the institutions also have special two-page portraits located at the back of the book. These are written by the colleges and universities that wanted to present detailed descriptions of their campuses and programs.

Unless noted in the descriptions below, the Admissions Services Division of The Princeton Review collected all of the data presented in the informational profiles. As is customary with college guides, all data reflect figures for the academic year prior to publication, unless otherwise indicated. Since college offerings and demographics vary significantly from one institution to another and some colleges report data more thoroughly than others, few entries will include all of the individual data points described below.

The Heading

This section includes school name, address, telephone number, fax number, e-mail address, website, financial aid telephone number, and college code numbers for both the College Board (CEEB) and the American College Testing Program (ACT) when applicable. All website addresses were accurate and functioning at the time of publication. Check PrincetonReview.com for the most up-to-date links to colleges.

The Icons

The icons are a feature we hope will make using *The Complete Book of Colleges* easier. Icons appear under the school name for schools that are profiled in *The Best Colleges, 2019 Edition*.

The Blurb

Describes the college or university. Includes all available data that relate to the date of founding of the school, religious affiliation, whether the school is public or private, and campus size.

Ratings

This section includes the school's Fire Safety Rating, its Admissions Selectivity Rating, and its Green Rating.

Admissions Selectivity Rating

This rating measures how competitive admissions are at the school. This rating is determined by several institutionally reported factors, including: the class rank, standardized test scores, and high school GPA of entering freshmen; the percentage of students who hail from out-of-state; and the percentage of applicants accepted and those deciding to enroll. This rating is given on a scale of 60–99. Please note that if a school has an Admissions Selectivity Rating of 60* (sixty with an asterisk), it means that the school did not report to us enough of the statistics that go into the rating in order for us to accurately measure its admissions selectivity.

Fire Safety

We asked all the schools from which we collect data annually to answer several questions about their efforts to ensure fire safety for campus residents. Each school's responses to nine of those questions were considered when calculating its Fire Safety Rating. The questions were developed in consultation with the Center for Campus Fire Safety (www.campusfire.org), and they cover: 1) The percentage of student housing sleeping rooms protected by an automatic fire sprinkler system with a fire sprinkler head located in the individual sleeping rooms; 2) The percentage of student housing sleeping rooms equipped with a smoke detector connected to a supervised fire alarm system; 3) The number of malicious fire alarms that occur in student housing per year; 4) The number of unwanted fire alarms that occur in student housing per year; 5) The banning of certain hazardous items and activities in residence halls, like candles, smoking, halogen lamps, etc.; 6) The percentage of student housing building fire alarm systems that, if activated, result in a signal being transmitted to a monitored location on campus or the fire department.

Schools that did not report answers to any of the above questions receive a Fire Safety Rating of 60*. The schools have an opportunity to update their fire safety data every year and will have their fire safety ratings re-calculated and published annually.

Each individual rating places a college on a continuum for purposes of comparing all colleges within this academic year only. Though similar, these ratings are not intended to be compared directly to those that appeared on PrincetonReview.com in any prior academic year or within any Princeton Review print publication, except for *The Best Colleges, 2019 Edition*. Our ratings computations are refined and change annually.

Green

This rating, on a scale of 60–99, provides a comprehensive measure of a school's performance as an environmentally aware and prepared institution. Specifically, it includes 1) whether students have a campus quality of life that is both healthy and sustainable, 2) how well a school is preparing students for employment in the clean-energy economy of the 21st century as well as for citizenship in a world now defined by environmental concerns and opportunities and 3) how environmentally responsible a school's policies are. Colleges that did not supply answers to a sufficient number of the questions for us to fairly compare them to other schools received a Green Rating of 60*.

Students & Faculty

Enrollment

The total number of full-time undergraduates.

Student Body

The percentage of male, female, out-of-state, and international students, and the number of foreign countries represented.

Ethnic Representation

By percentage according to ethnic group. Figures may not add up to 100 percent, as student reporting of ethnicity is voluntary by law.

Retention and Graduation

The percentage of first-year undergraduate students who return for sophomore year. The percentage of last year's seniors who entered as first-years and graduated in four years. The percentage of graduates who pursue further study within one year. The percentage of graduates who pursue further study at law school. The percentage of graduates who pursue further study at business school. The percentage of graduates who pursue further study at medical school.

Faculty

The ratio of undergraduates to full-time faculty. The number of full-time instructional faculty. The percentage of faculty who hold PhDs. The percentage of faculty members who teach undergraduates.

Academics

Degrees
The types of degrees awarded to students.

Academic Requirements
Areas in which all or most students are required to complete some course work prior to graduation. Can include general education (nonspecific), arts/fine arts, computer literacy, philosophy, foreign languages, history, humanities, mathematics, English (including composition), sciences (biological or physical), social sciences, and other requirements as specified by each school.

Classes
Number of students in an average regular class and an average lab/discussion section.

Majors with Highest Enrollment
The most popular majors.

Special Study Options
May include accelerated programs, cross registration, cooperative (work-study) program, distance learning, double majors, dual enrollment, English as a Second Language, student exchange programs (domestic), external degree programs, honors programs, independent study, internships, liberal arts/career combinations, student-designed majors, study abroad, teacher certification programs, weekend college, and other options as specified by each school.

Facilities

Housing
Types of school-owned or affiliated housing available. May include coed dorms, women's dorms, men's dorms, apartments for married students, apartments for single students, special housing for disabled students, special housing for international students, fraternity/sorority housing, cooperative housing, and other options as specified by the school. The availability of assistance in finding off-campus housing. Any housing requirements that may exist, such as required on-campus residence for first-years.

Special Academic Facilities/Equipment

Other facilities and equipment of note (e.g., nuclear reactor, on-campus elementary school for student teachers, scanning electron microscopes, and so forth).

Campus Life

Activities

Standard activities available. May include campus ministries, choral groups, concert band, dance, drama/theater, international student organization, jazz band, literary magazine, Model UN, musical ensembles, musical theater, opera, pep band, radio station, student film society, student government, student newspaper, symphony orchestra, television station, and yearbook.

Organizations

Total number of registered organizations, honor societies, religious organizations, fraternities, sororities.

Athletics

Intercollegiate athletics available, listed by sex.

Admissions

Freshman Academic Profile

Average high school GPA. Class rank distribution. The percentage from public high schools. Median range of SAT (Math, Critical Reading, and Writing sections) and/or ACT composite scores. Middle 50 percent score range of SAT (Math and Evidence-Based Reading and Writing sections) and/or ACT composite scores. Test of English as a Foreign Language (TOEFL) requirements for international students.

An Important Note About SAT Scores Published in *The Complete Book of Colleges* 2019 Edition:

The SAT underwent major changes in March 2016. The test now consists of 2 sections and is scored out of 1600 points. Prior to the redesign, the test consisted of 3 sections and was scored out of 2400 points.

The admission data reported in this book reflects the entering first-year class of fall 2017, a population that submitted applications in fall 2016 subsequent to the SAT redesign. Schools reported SAT score ranges for this class on the 1600 scale using concordance information published by the College Board. For schools that did not supply updated data, SAT score ranges are reported on the old, pre-March 2016 scale. To help you convert a score out of 2400 to a score out of 1600 (or vice versa), the College Board's SAT concordance methodology and tools are available at: https://collegereadiness.collegeboard.org/educators/higher-ed/scoring/concordance.

You may also cross-reference our print profiles with our online school profiles at PrincetonReveiw.com, which list the most up-to-date data as reported by schools.

Basis for Candidate Selection
The criteria considered by the admissions committee in evaluating candidates. May include secondary school record, class rank, recommendations, standardized test scores, essay, interview, extracurricular activities, talent/ability, character/personal qualities, alumni/-ae relations, geographic residence, state residency, religious affiliation/commitment, minority status, volunteer work, work experience.

Freshman Admission Requirements
High school diploma/GED requirements. The number of academic units required or recommended in total and by academic subject. (Individual subject totals may not equal the complete sum of academic units required; in most cases, the difference is made up with electives. Check with the admissions office for any additional requirements.)

Freshman Admissions Statistics
The number of students who applied, the percentage of applicants who were accepted, and the percentage of those accepted who ultimately enrolled.

Transfer Admissions Requirements
Application requirements (may include high school transcript, college transcript, essay, interview, standardized tests, statement of good standing from prior school). Minimum high school GPA required. Minimum college GPA required. Lowest course grade transferable.

General Admissions Information
Application fee. Application deadlines. Admission notification date. "Rolling" indicates that decisions are sent to candidates as they are made, rather than held for a common notification date. Registration policy for terms other than the fall term. Common Application participation. Credit policies for College Entrance Examination Board Advanced Placement tests. Deferred admission policy.

Costs and Financial Aid

Tuition, room & board, fees, and books.

Required Forms and Deadlines

Forms that applicants for financial aid must file and their respective deadlines. May include FAFSA, institution's own financial aid form, CSS Profile, business/farm supplement, state aid form, noncustodial (divorced/separated) parent statement, and other forms specified by the school. Deadlines for filing financial aid forms.

Notification of Awards

The date that notification of financial aid awards occurs. "Rolling" indicates that notification is ongoing—the sooner you complete all of your required financial aid paperwork, the sooner you'll hear about your package.

Types of Aid

Need-based scholarships and grants may include Federal Pell, SEOG, state scholarships/grants, private scholarships, college/university gift aid from institutional funds, United Negro College Fund, Federal Nursing Scholarship, and other resources as specified by the school. Loans may include Direct Subsidized Loans, Direct Unsubsidized Loans, Direct PLUS Loans, Federal Perkins Loans, Federal Nursing Loans, state loans, college/university loans from institutional funds, and other resources as specified by the school.

Student Employment

Availability of Federal Work-Study, a federal program that is need-based and part of most financial aid packages. Availability of part-time jobs direct from the college that are not based on need. The college's own assessment of part-time employment opportunities off campus.

Financial Aid Statistics

The percentage of first-years who received some form of need-based financial aid. The percentage of undergraduates who received some form of need-based financial aid. The number of first-years and undergrads who received an athletic scholarship or grant. The average amount of first-year scholarships and grants. The average amount of first-year loans. The average income from an on-campus job.

The Best Colleges Icon

 Indicates whether the school can be found in our annual book, *The Best Colleges*. In that book, each school has a detailed profile that includes the results of our surveys regarding student opinion about many aspects of their schools and their educations.

COLLEGE DIRECTORY

ABILENE CHRISTIAN UNIVERSITY

ACU Box 29100, Abilene, TX 79699
Phone: 325-674-2650 · **Financial Aid Phone:** 325-674-2300
E-mail: info@admissions.acu.edu · **CEEB Code:** 6001
Fax: 325-674-2130 · **Website:** www.acu.edu · **ACT Code:** 4050

This private school, affiliated with the Church of Christ, was founded in 1906. It has a 208 acre campus.

RATINGS
Admissions Selectivity Rating: 84   **Fire Safety Rating:** 81   **Green Rating:** 61

STUDENTS AND FACULTY
Enrollment: 3,655. **Student Body:** 59% female, 41% male, 11% out-of-state, 4% international (39 countries represented). Asian 1%, African American 9%, Caucasian 64%, Hispanic 17%, Native American <1%, Pacific Islander <1%, Two or more races 5%, Race unknown <1%.
Retention and Graduation: 77% freshmen return for sophomore year. 47% freshmen graduate within 4 years. 60% freshmen graduate within 6 years. 30% grads go on to further study within 1 year. 22% grads pursue arts and sciences degrees. 1% grads pursue law degrees. 2% grads pursue business degrees. 2% grads pursue medical degrees. **Faculty:** Student/faculty ratio 13:1. 266 full-time faculty, 79% hold PhDs, 11% are members of minority groups, 41% are women. 1% of classes are taught by teaching assistants.

ACADEMICS
Degrees: Associate; Bachelor's; Certificate; Doctoral Other; Doctoral/Research; Master's; Post-Bachelor's certificate; Post-Master's certificate **Most popular majors:** Psychology, General; Registered Nursing/Registered Nurse; Accounting. **Special Study Options:** Cross-registration; Distance learning; Double major; Dual enrollment; English as a Second Language (ESL); Honors program; Independent study; Internships; Student-designed major; Study abroad; Teacher certification program. **Honors programs:** The Honors College offers highly motivated students extra stimulation and recognition in their course work, opportunities to work with selected faculty members and the chance to do independent projects in their major field. Ten percent of the ACU students participate. Graduating with University Honors will require numerous Honors Courses and/or Honors Projects in regular courses offered at ACU. **Disability Services offered to physically disabled students:** Note-taking services; Reader services; Tape recorders. **Career services:** Alumni network; Alumni services; Career assessment; Career/job search classes; Internships

FACILITIES
Housing: Apartments for single students; Men's dorms; Special housing for disabled student; Women's dorms 95% of campus accessible to physically diasbled. **Special Academic Facilities/Equipment:** Learning Commons, Writing Center, Speaking Center, Alpha Academic Services, AT&T learning studio, Maker Lab, Shore Art Gallery, converged media newsroom, voice institute, demonstration farm and ranch, observatory. **Computers:** 100% of classrooms, 100% of dorms, 100% of libraries, 100% of dining areas, 100% of student union, 87% of common outdoor areas have wireless network access. Students can register for classes online. Administrative functions (other than registration) can be performed online.

CAMPUS LIFE
Environment: City **Activities:** Campus Ministries; Choral groups; Concert band; Dance; Drama/theater; International Student Organization; Jazz band; Literary magazine; Marching band; Model UN; Music ensembles; Musical theater; Opera; Pep band; Radio station; Student government; Student newspaper; Symphony orchestra; Television station 108 registered organizations, 14 honor societies, 16 religious organizations. 4 fraternities, 7 sororities. **Athletics (Intercollegiate):** *Men:* baseball, basketball, cross-country, football, tennis, track/field (outdoor), track/field (indoor). *Women:* basketball, cross-country, soccer, softball, tennis, track/field (outdoor), track/field (indoor), volleyball. **On-Campus Highlights:** Student Recreation and Wellness Center, Learning Commons in Brown Library, Jacob's Dream Sculpture, World Famous Bean in McGlothlin Campus Cntr., Hunter Welcome Center **Environmental Initiatives:** Campus grounds: Bee Campus USA, Tree Campus USA, The Feral Cat Initiative.

ADMISSIONS
Freshman Academic Profile: Average high school GPA 3.6. 22% in top 10% of high school class, 54% in top 25% of high school class, 84% in top 50% of high school class. 64% from public high schools. **Test Scores:** SAT Math middle 50% range 515-600. SAT EBRW middle 50% range 510-620. ACT middle 50% range 21-26. Minimum internet-based TOEFL 80. Minimum paper TOEFL 525. **Basis for Candidate Selection:** *Very important factors considered include:* rigor of secondary school record, class rank, academic GPA,

standardized test scores. *Important factors considered include:* talent/ability, character/personal qualities. *Other factors considered include:* application essay, recommendation(s), extracurricular activities, first generation, alumni/ae relation, volunteer work, work experience, level of applicant's interest. **Freshman Admission Requirements:** High school diploma is required and GED is accepted *Academic units recommended:* 4 English, 3 math, 3 science, 2 science labs, 2 foreign language, 1 history, 1 unit from above areas or other academic areas. **Freshman Admission Statistics:** 9,827 applied, 57.8% admitted, 17% enrolled. **Transfer Admission Requirements:** High school transcript, college transcript(s), interview, Minimum college GPA of 2.0 required. Lowest grade transferable 2. **General Admission Information:** Application fee $50. Regular application deadline 2/15. Nonfall registration accepted.

COSTS AND FINANCIAL AID
Annual tuition $33,280. Room and board $10,378. Required fees $50. Average book expense $1,250. **Required Forms and Deadlines:** FAFSA. **Notification of Awards:** Applicants will be notified of awards on a rolling basis beginning 4/1. **Types of Aid:** *Need-based scholarships/grants:* College/university scholarship or grant aid from institutional funds; Federal Pell; Private scholarships; SEOG; State scholarships/grants. *Loans:* Direct PLUS loans; Direct Subsidized Stafford Loans; Direct Unsubsidized Stafford Loans. *Student Employment:* Federal Work-Study Program available. Institutional employment available. **Financial Aid Statistics:** 100% needy freshmen, 100% needy undergrads receive need-based scholarship or grant aid. 100% freshmen, 99% undergrads receive non-need-based scholarship or grant aid. 68% freshmen, 67% undergrads receive need-based self-help aid. 5% freshmen, 6% undergrads receive athletic scholarships. 100% freshmen, 94% undergrads receive any aid. **Criteria for awarding aid:** *Non-need-based:* Academics, Art, Athletics, Leadership, Minority status, Music/drama, Religious affiliation, State/district residency.

ACADEMY OF ART UNIVERSITY

79 New Montgomery St, San Francisco, CA 94105
Phone: 415-274-2222 · **Financial Aid Phone:** 800-544-2787
E-mail: info@academyart.edu
Fax: 415-618-6287 · **Website:** www.academyart.edu · **ACT Code:** 155

This proprietary school was founded in 1929. It has a 20 acre campus.

RATINGS
Admissions Selectivity Rating: 64   **Fire Safety Rating:** 91   **Green Rating:** 60*

STUDENTS AND FACULTY
Enrollment: 7,520. **Student Body:** 57% female, 43% male, 44% out-of-state, 29% international (103 countries represented). Asian 6%, African American 7%, Caucasian 18%, Hispanic 11%, Native American <1%, Pacific Islander 1%, Two or more races 3%, Race unknown 24%.
Retention and Graduation: 76% freshmen return for sophomore year. 6% freshmen graduate within 4 years. 39% freshmen graduate within 6 years. **Faculty:** Student/faculty ratio 14:1. 265 full-time faculty, 17% hold PhDs, 5% are members of minority groups, 40% are women. 0% of classes are taught by teaching assistants.

ACADEMICS
Degrees: Associate; Bachelor's; Certificate; Master's; Post-Bachelor's certificate **Classes:** Most classes have fewer than 10 students. **Most popular majors:** Animation, Interactive Technology, Video Graphics And Special Effects; Fashion/Apparel Design; Illustration. **Special Study Options:** Distance learning; English as a Second Language (ESL); Independent study; Internships; Study abroad; Teacher certification program. **Disability Services offered to physically disabled students:** Note-taking services; Reader services; Tape recorders; Tutors. **Career services:** Alumni network; Alumni services; Career assessment; Career/job search classes; Internships; Regional alumni

FACILITIES
Housing: Apartments for single students; Coed dorms; Men's dorms; Women's dorms 80% of campus accessible to physically diasbled. **Special Academic Facilities/Equipment:** 6 Art Galleries for display of student work and 1 Fashion Retail Store **Computers:** Students can register for classes online. Administrative functions (other than registration) can be performed online.

CAMPUS LIFE
Environment: Metropolis **Activities:** Choral groups; Dance; Drama/theater; International Student Organization; Model UN; Pep band; Radio station; Student government; Student newspaper; Student-run film society; Television station 27 registered organizations. **Athletics (Intercollegiate):** *Men:* baseball,

basketball, cross-country, golf, soccer, tennis, track/field (outdoor). *Women:* basketball, cross-country, golf, soccer, softball, tennis, track/field (outdoor), volleyball. Urban Knight Kafe, International/Commodore, School of Fashion building

ADMISSIONS

Freshman Admission Requirements: High school diploma is required and GED is accepted **Freshman Admission Statistics:** 2,529 applied, 100.0% admitted, 32% enrolled. **Transfer Admission Requirements:** High school transcript, college transcript(s), Minimum college GPA of 2.0 required. Lowest grade transferable C. **General Admission Information:** Application fee $50. Nonfall registration accepted. Admission may be deferred.

COSTS AND FINANCIAL AID

Annual tuition $27,510. Room and board $16,648. Required fees $300. Average book expense $1,918. **Required Forms and Deadlines:** FAFSA; Institution's own financial aid form. **Notification of Awards:** Applicants will be notified of awards on a rolling basis beginning 3/15. **Types of Aid:** *Need-based scholarships/grants:* College/university scholarship or grant aid from institutional funds; Federal Pell; Private scholarships; SEOG; State scholarships/grants. *Loans:* Direct PLUS loans; Direct Subsidized Stafford Loans; Direct Unsubsidized Stafford Loans. *Student Employment:* Federal Work-Study Program available. **Financial Aid Statistics:** 70% needy freshmen, 72% needy undergrads receive need-based scholarship or grant aid. 7% freshmen, 6% undergrads receive non-need-based scholarship or grant aid. 87% freshmen, 86% undergrads receive need-based self-help aid. 3% freshmen, 2% undergrads receive athletic scholarships. 52% freshmen, 61% undergrads receive any aid. 63% undergrads borrow to pay for school. Average cumulative indebtedness $27,020. **Criteria for awarding aid:** *Non-need-based:* Academics, Art, Athletics.

ACADIA UNIVERSITY

Admissions Office, Wolfville, NS B4P 2R6
Phone: 1-902-585-1446 · **Financial Aid Phone:** 902-585-1016
E-mail: pam.dimock@acadiau.ca
Fax: 902-585-1092 · **Website:** www.acadiau.ca

This public school was founded in 1838. It has a 200 acre campus.

RATINGS
Admissions Selectivity Rating: 72   **Fire Safety Rating:** 60*   **Green Rating:** 60*

STUDENTS AND FACULTY
Enrollment: 2,928. **Student Body:** 55% female, 45% male, 42% out-of-state, international.
Retention and Graduation: 83% freshmen return for sophomore year.
Faculty: Student/faculty ratio 10:1. 243 full-time faculty, 36% are women. 0% of classes are taught by teaching assistants.

ACADEMICS
Degrees: Bachelor's; Certificate; Diploma; Master's **Classes:** Most classes have 10-19 students. Most lab/discussion sessions have 10-19 students. **Special Study Options:** Cooperative education program; Distance learning; Double major; English as a Second Language (ESL); Exchange student program (domestic); Honors program; Independent study; Internships; Study abroad.
Career services: Career assessment; Career/job search classes; Internships

FACILITIES
Housing: Apartments for single students; Coed dorms; Men's dorms; Special housing for disabled student; Women's dorms **Computers:** Students can register for classes online. Administrative functions (other than registration) can be performed online.

CAMPUS LIFE
Environment: Rural **Activities:** Campus Ministries; Choral groups; Concert band; Dance; Drama/theater; International Student Organization; Jazz band; Literary magazine; Music ensembles; Musical theater; Opera; Pep band; Radio station; Student government; Student newspaper; Symphony orchestra; Yearbook 60 registered organizations, 3 religious organizations. **Athletics (Intercollegiate):** *Men:* basketball, cheerleading, cross-country, football, ice hockey, rugby, soccer, track/field (outdoor), volleyball. *Women:* basketball, cheerleading, cross-country, ice hockey, rugby, soccer, track/field (outdoor), volleyball. **On-Campus Highlights:** KC Irving Environmental Science Centre, The Sheldon L. Fountain Learning Commons

ADMISSIONS
Freshman Academic Profile: 80% from public high schools. **Test Scores:** Minimum paper TOEFL 550. **Basis for Candidate Selection:** *Very important factors considered include:* rigor of secondary school record, academic GPA.

Important factors considered include: recommendation(s), talent/ability. *Other factors considered include:* class rank, standardized test scores, extracurricular activities, character/personal qualities, geographical residence, volunteer work, work experience. **Freshman Admission Requirements:** High school diploma is required and GED is not accepted *Academic units required:* 1 English, 1 math, *Academic units recommended:* 1 English, 2 math, 1 science, 1 foreign language, 1 social studies, 1 history, 2 academic electives. **Freshman Admission Statistics:** 1,600 applied, 49.4% admitted, 68% enrolled. **Transfer Admission Requirements:** college transcript(s). **General Admission Information:** Application fee $25. Priority deadline 3/15. Nonfall registration accepted. Admission may be deferred.

COSTS AND FINANCIAL AID
Annual in-state tuition $8,284. Annual out-of-state tuition $8,062. Room and board $8,284. Required fees $180. Average book expense $1,200. **Notification of Awards:** Applicants will be notified of awards on or about 4/15. **Types of Aid:** *Loans:* Direct PLUS loans; Direct Subsidized Stafford Loans; Direct Unsubsidized Stafford Loans. **Criteria for awarding aid:** *Need-based:* Leadership *Non-need-based:* Academics, Leadership, Music/drama, State/district residency.

ADAMS STATE COLLEGE

208 Edgemont Boulevard, Alamosa, CO 81102
Phone: 719-587-7712 · **Financial Aid Phone:** 719-587-7306
E-mail: ascadmit@adams.edu · **CEEB Code:** 4001
Fax: 719-587-7522 · **ACT Code:** 496

This public school was founded in 1921. It has a 90 acre campus.

RATINGS
Admissions Selectivity Rating: 91   **Fire Safety Rating:** 82   **Green Rating:** 60*

STUDENTS AND FACULTY
Enrollment: 2,169. **Student Body:** 47% female, 53% male, 33% out-of-state, <1% international (10 countries represented). Asian 1%, African American 7%, Caucasian 50%, Hispanic 32%, Native American 1%, Pacific Islander <1%, Two or more races 4%, Race unknown 4%.
Retention and Graduation: 58% freshmen return for sophomore year. 0% grads go on to further study within 1 year. 0% grads pursue arts and sciences degrees. 0% grads pursue law degrees. 0% grads pursue business degrees. 0% grads pursue medical degrees. **Faculty:** Student/faculty ratio 15:1. 113 full-time faculty, 63% hold PhDs, 23% are members of minority groups, 42% are women. 0% of classes are taught by teaching assistants.

ACADEMICS
Degrees: Associate; Bachelor's; Master's **Classes:** Most classes have 10-19 students. Most lab/discussion sessions have 10-19 students. **Most popular majors:** Teacher Education, Multiple Levels; Kinesiology And Exercise Science; Business Administration And Management, General. **Special Study Options:** Accelerated program; Distance learning; Double major; Independent study; Internships; Study abroad; Teacher certification program; Weekend college. **Disability Services offered to physically disabled students:** Note-taking services; Reader services; Tutors. **Career services:** Alumni network; Career assessment; Career/job search classes; Internships

FACILITIES
Housing: Apartments for married students; Apartments for single students; Coed dorms; Men's dorms; Women's dorms 95% of campus accessible to physically disabled. **Special Academic Facilities/Equipment:** Luther Bean Museum, Hatfield Gallery, Gallery 114, Leon Memorial Music Hall, Zacheis Planetarium, Ryan Geology Museum **Computers:** 10% of classrooms, 100% of dorms, 100% of libraries, 100% of dining areas, 99% of student union, have wireless network access. Students can register for classes online. Administrative functions (other than registration) can be performed online.

CAMPUS LIFE
Environment: Village **Activities:** Campus Ministries; Choral groups; Concert band; Dance; Drama/theater; International Student Organization; Jazz band; Literary magazine; Marching band; Model UN; Music ensembles; Musical theater; Pep band; Radio station; Student government; Student newspaper; Television station 23 registered organizations, 2 religious organizations. **Athletics (Intercollegiate):** *Men:* basketball, cross-country, football, golf, soccer, track/field (outdoor), track/field (indoor), wrestling. *Women:* basketball, cross-country, golf, soccer, softball, swimming, track/field (outdoor), track/field (indoor), volleyball. **On-Campus Highlights:** Leon Memorial Concert Hall, Zacheis Planetarium, Nielson Library, Plachy Hall, Rex Activity Center

Environmental Initiatives: Establishment of EARTH (Environmental Action for Resources, Transportation, & Health) group on campus

ADMISSIONS

Freshman Academic Profile: Average high school GPA 3.1. 6% in top 10% of high school class, 25% in top 25% of high school class, 58% in top 50% of high school class. **Test Scores:** SAT Math middle 50% range 470-530. SAT EBRW middle 50% range 430-530. ACT middle 50% range 17-22. Minimum internet-based TOEFL 79. Minimum paper TOEFL 550. **Basis for Candidate Selection:** *Very important factors considered include:* rigor of secondary school record, standardized test scores. *Important factors considered include:* academic GPA. *Other factors considered include:* class rank, application essay, recommendation(s), interview, extracurricular activities, character/personal qualities, geographical residence, state residency. **Freshman Admission Requirements:** High school diploma is required and GED is accepted *Academic units recommended:* 4 English, 4 math, 3 science, 2 science labs, 1 foreign language, 2 social studies, 1 history, 2 academic electives, 0.5 unit from above areas or other academic areas. **Freshman Admission Statistics:** 2,531 applied, 18.8% admitted, 92% enrolled. **Transfer Admission Requirements:** college transcript(s), Minimum college GPA of 2.0 required. Lowest grade transferable D. **General Admission Information:** Application fee $30. Priority deadline 8/1. Nonfall registration accepted. Admission may be deferred for a maximum of 2 years.

COSTS AND FINANCIAL AID

Required Forms and Deadlines: FAFSA. **Notification of Awards:** Applicants will be notified of awards on a rolling basis beginning 3/1. **Types of Aid:** *Need-based scholarships/grants:* College/university scholarship or grant aid from institutional funds; Federal Pell; Private scholarships; SEOG; State scholarships/grants. *Loans:* Direct PLUS loans; Direct Subsidized Stafford Loans; Direct Unsubsidized Stafford Loans. *Student Employment:* Federal Work-Study Program available. Institutional employment available. **Financial Aid Statistics:** 97% needy freshmen, 92% needy undergrads receive need-based scholarship or grant aid. 0% undergrads receive non-need-based scholarship or grant aid. 66% freshmen, 76% undergrads receive need-based self-help aid. 0% freshmen, 0% undergrads receive athletic scholarships. 95% freshmen, 94% undergrads receive any aid. **Criteria for awarding aid:** *Need-based:* Academics, Alumni affiliation, Art, Athletics, Leadership, Minority status, Music/drama *Non-need-based:* Academics, Alumni affiliation, Art, Athletics, Leadership, Minority status, Music/drama, State/district residency.

ADELPHI UNIVERSITY

1 South Avenue, Garden City, NY 11530
Phone: 516-877-3050 · **Financial Aid Phone:** 516-877-3080
E-mail: admissions@adelphi.edu · **CEEB Code:** 2003
Fax: 516-877-3039 · **Website:** www.adelphi.edu · **ACT Code:** 2664

This private school was founded in 1896. It has a 75 acre campus.

RATINGS

Admissions Selectivity Rating: 78   **Fire Safety Rating:** 95   **Green Rating:** 79

STUDENTS AND FACULTY

Enrollment: 5,162. **Student Body:** 69% female, 31% male, 6% out-of-state, 3% international (46 countries represented). Asian 11%, African American 9%, Caucasian 51%, Hispanic 17%, Native American <1%, Pacific Islander <1%, Two or more races 2%, Race unknown 6%.
Retention and Graduation: 80% freshmen return for sophomore year. 55% freshmen graduate within 4 years. 68% freshmen graduate within 6 years. 31% grads go on to further study within 1 year. 1% grads pursue law degrees. 5% grads pursue business degrees. 1% grads pursue medical degrees. **Faculty:** Student/faculty ratio 12:1. 335 full-time faculty, 87% hold PhDs, 24% are members of minority groups, 54% are women. 0% of classes are taught by teaching assistants.

ACADEMICS

Degrees: Associate; Bachelor's; Certificate; Doctoral/Professional; Doctoral/Research; Master's; Post-Bachelor's certificate; Post-Master's certificate; Terminal Associate **Classes:** Most classes have 20-29 students. **Most popular majors:** Biology/Biological Sciences, General; Registered Nursing/Registered Nurse; Business/Commerce, General. **Special Study Options:** Accelerated program; Cross-registration; Distance learning; Double major; Dual enrollment; English as a Second Language (ESL); Honors program; Independent study; Internships; Liberal arts/career combination; Student-designed major; Study abroad; Teacher certification program; Weekend college. **Honors programs:** The Honors College seeks to prepare highly talented and motivated students

to face the 21st century by providing them with the intellectual perspectives and critical skills necessary to exercise responsible leadership. It involves an intense curricular and extracurricular program that asks students to view themselves and their work with integrity, passion, and seriousness. **Combined degree programs:** BA/DDS; BA/JD; BA/MA; BA/MD; BA/MEng. **Disability Services offered to physically disabled students:** Note-taking services; Reader services; Tape recorders; Tutors. **Career services:** Alumni network; Alumni services; Career assessment; Career/job search classes; Internships; Regional alumni

FACILITIES

Housing: Coed dorms; Special housing for disabled student; Theme housing 95% of campus accessible to physically diasbled. **Computers:** 90% of dorms, 99% of libraries, 99% of dining areas, 90% of student union, 75% of common outdoor areas have wireless network access. Students can register for classes online. Administrative functions (other than registration) can be performed online.

CAMPUS LIFE

Environment: Metropolis **Activities:** Campus Ministries; Choral groups; Concert band; Dance; Drama/theater; International Student Organization; Jazz band; Literary magazine; Model UN; Music ensembles; Musical theater; Opera; Radio station; Student government; Student newspaper; Student-run film society; Symphony orchestra; Yearbook 80 registered organizations, 21 honor societies, 5 religious organizations. 3 fraternities, 7 sororities. **Athletics (Intercollegiate):** *Men:* baseball, basketball, cross-country, golf, lacrosse, soccer, swimming, tennis, track/field (outdoor), track/field (indoor). *Women:* basketball, bowling, cross-country, field hockey, lacrosse, soccer, softball, swimming, tennis, track/field (outdoor), track/field (indoor), volleyball. **On-Campus Highlights:** Ruth S. Harley University Center, Underground Café, Swirbul Library, Nexus Building, Center for Recreation and Sports **Environmental Initiatives:** LEED rating for the CSPA project

ADMISSIONS

Freshman Academic Profile: Average high school GPA 3.5. 26% in top 10% of high school class, 58% in top 25% of high school class, 89% in top 50% of high school class. 75% from public high schools. **Test Scores:** SAT Math middle 50% range 530-620. SAT EBRW middle 50% range 530-600. ACT middle 50% range 22-27. Minimum internet-based TOEFL 80. Minimum paper TOEFL 550. **Basis for Candidate Selection:** *Very important factors considered include:* rigor of secondary school record. *Important factors considered include:* class rank, academic GPA, application essay, standardized test scores, recommendation(s), extracurricular activities, talent/ability, character/personal qualities, volunteer work. *Other factors considered include:* interview, first generation, alumni/ae relation, work experience, level of applicant's interest. **Freshman Admission Requirements:** High school diploma is required and GED is accepted *Academic units recommended:* 4 English, 3 math, 3 science, 2 foreign language, 4 units from above areas or other academic areas. **Freshman Admission Statistics:** 11,851 applied, 73.1% admitted, 13% enrolled. **Transfer Admission Requirements:** college transcript(s), essay or personal statement, Minimum college GPA of 2.3 required. **General Admission Information:** Application fee $40. Priority deadline 3/1. Nonfall registration accepted. Admission may be deferred.

COSTS AND FINANCIAL AID

Annual tuition $35,430. Room and board $15,500. Required fees $1,740. Average book expense $1,020. **Required Forms and Deadlines:** FAFSA; State aid form. **Notification of Awards:** Applicants will be notified of awards on a rolling basis beginning 12/15. **Types of Aid:** *Need-based scholarships/grants:* College/university scholarship or grant aid from institutional funds; Federal Pell; Private scholarships; SEOG; State scholarships/grants; United Negro College Fund. *Loans:* Direct PLUS loans; Direct Subsidized Stafford Loans; Direct Unsubsidized Stafford Loans. *Student Employment:* Federal Work-Study Program available. Institutional employment available. **Financial Aid Statistics:** 65% needy freshmen, 97% needy undergrads receive need-based scholarship or grant aid. 85% freshmen, 86% undergrads receive non-need-based scholarship or grant aid. 87% freshmen, 87% undergrads receive need-based self-help aid. 2% freshmen, 2% undergrads receive athletic scholarships. 96% freshmen, 91% undergrads receive any aid. 64% undergrads borrow to pay for school. Average cumulative indebtedness $32,558. **Criteria for awarding aid:** *Need-based:* Job skills *Non-need-based:* Academics, Alumni affiliation, Art, Athletics, Leadership, Minority status, Music/drama, Religious affiliation, State/district residency.

ADRIAN COLLEGE

110 South Madison Street, Adrian, MI 49221
Phone: 517-265-5161 · **Financial Aid Phone:** 517-265-5161
E-mail: admissions@adrian.edu · **CEEB Code:** 1001
Fax: 517-264-3331 · **Website:** www.adrian.edu · **ACT Code:** 1954

This private school, affiliated with the Methodist Church, was founded in 1859. It has a 100 acre campus.

RATINGS

Admissions Selectivity Rating: 80 **Fire Safety Rating:** 69 **Green Rating:** 60*

STUDENTS AND FACULTY

Enrollment: 1,308. **Student Body:** 47% female, 53% male, 24% out-of-state, 4% international (6 countries represented). Asian 1%, African American 4%, Caucasian 77%, Hispanic 2%, Native American <1%, Race unknown 12%. **Retention and Graduation:** 73% freshmen return for sophomore year. 25% grads go on to further study within 1 year. 51% grads pursue arts and sciences degrees. 9% grads pursue law degrees. 9% grads pursue business degrees. 22% grads pursue medical degrees. **Faculty:** Student/faculty ratio 12:1. 78 full-time faculty, 82% hold PhDs, 9% are members of minority groups, 41% are women. 0% of classes are taught by teaching assistants.

ACADEMICS

Degrees: Associate; Bachelor's; Transfer Associate **Most popular majors:** English Language And Literature, General; Kinesiology And Exercise Science; Business/Commerce, General. **Special Study Options:** Double major; Dual enrollment; Honors program; Independent study; Internships; Student-designed major; Study abroad; Teacher certification program. **Combined degree programs:** BA/MEng. **Disability Services offered to physically disabled students:** Note-taking services; Reader services; Tape recorders; Tutors. **Career services:** Alumni network; Alumni services; Career assessment; Internships; Regional alumni

FACILITIES

Housing: Apartments for single students; Coed dorms; Fraternity/sorority housing; Men's dorms; Women's dorms 50% of campus accessible to physically diasbled. **Special Academic Facilities/Equipment:** Art gallery, studio theatre, arboretum, education resource center, language lab, observatory, planetarium, solar greenhouse, nuclear magnetic resonance spectrometer, differential scanning calorimeter. **Computers:** 100% of classrooms, 100% of dorms, 100% of libraries, 100% of dining areas, 100% of student union, 100% of common outdoor areas have wireless network access. Students can register for classes online. Administrative functions (other than registration) can be performed online.

CAMPUS LIFE

Environment: Town **Activities:** Campus Ministries; Choral groups; Concert band; Dance; Drama/theater; International Student Organization; Jazz band; Literary magazine; Marching band; Music ensembles; Musical theater; Pep band; Radio station; Student government; Student newspaper; Symphony orchestra; Yearbook 68 registered organizations, 13 honor societies, 8 religious organizations. 4 fraternities, 3 sororities. **Athletics (Intercollegiate):** *Men:* baseball, basketball, cross-country, football, golf, ice hockey, lacrosse, soccer, tennis, track/field (outdoor). *Women:* basketball, bowling, cross-country, golf, ice hockey, lacrosse, soccer, softball, tennis, track/field (outdoor), volleyball. **On-Campus Highlights:** Caine Student Center, Shipman Library, Merillat Sport and Fitness Center

ADMISSIONS

Freshman Academic Profile: Average high school GPA 3.3. 17% in top 10% of high school class, 46% in top 25% of high school class, 81% in top 50% of high school class. **Test Scores:** SAT Math middle 50% range 410-535. SAT EBRW middle 50% range 430-515. ACT middle 50% range 20-25. Minimum paper TOEFL 500. **Basis for Candidate Selection:** *Very important factors considered include:* rigor of secondary school record, class rank. *Important factors considered include:* academic GPA, standardized test scores, talent/ability. *Other factors considered include:* interview, extracurricular activities, character/personal qualities, alumni/ae relation, volunteer work, work experience, level of applicant's interest. **Freshman Admission Requirements:** High school diploma is required and GED is accepted *Academic units recommended:* 4 English, 3 math, 2 science, 1 science labs, 2 foreign language, 1 social studies, 1 history, 2 academic electives. **Freshman Admission Statistics:** 3,709 applied, 64.0% admitted, 21% enrolled. **Transfer Admission Requirements:** High school transcript, college transcript(s), Minimum college GPA of 2.7 required. Lowest grade transferable C. **General Admission Information:** Priority deadline 3/15. Nonfall registration accepted. Admission may be deferred for a maximum of 1 year.

COSTS AND FINANCIAL AID

Annual tuition $23,090. Room and board $7,600. Required fees $300. Average book expense $400. **Required Forms and Deadlines:** FAFSA. **Notification of Awards:** Applicants will be notified of awards on a rolling basis beginning 3/15. **Types of Aid:** *Need-based scholarships/grants:* College/university scholarship or grant aid from institutional funds; Federal Pell; Private scholarships; SEOG; State scholarships/grants. *Student Employment:* Federal Work-Study Program available. Institutional employment available. **Financial Aid Statistics:** 87% needy freshmen, 86% needy undergrads receive need-based scholarship or grant aid. 88% freshmen, 86% undergrads receive non-need-based scholarship or grant aid. 89% freshmen, 88% undergrads receive need-based self-help aid. 0% freshmen, 0% undergrads receive athletic scholarships. 98% freshmen, 92% undergrads receive any aid. **Criteria for awarding aid:** *Non-need-based:* Academics, Alumni affiliation, Art, Leadership, Music/drama, Religious affiliation.

AGNES SCOTT COLLEGE

141 East College Avenue, Decatur, GA 30030-3770
Phone: 404-471-6285 · **Financial Aid Phone:** 404-471-6395
E-mail: https://www.agnesscott.edu/admission/index.html · **CEEB Code:** 5002
Fax: 404-471-6414 · **Website:** www.agnesscott.edu · **ACT Code:** 780

This private school, affiliated with the Presbyterian Church, was founded in 1889. It has a 100 acre campus.

RATINGS

Admissions Selectivity Rating: 86 **Fire Safety Rating:** 96 **Green Rating:** 60*

STUDENTS AND FACULTY

Enrollment: 890. **Student Body:** 100% female, 0% male, 46% out-of-state, 7% international (34 countries represented). Asian 7%, African American 30%, Caucasian 35%, Hispanic 12%, Native American <1%, Pacific Islander <1%, Two or more races 7%, Race unknown 2%. **Retention and Graduation:** 87% freshmen return for sophomore year. 62% freshmen graduate within 4 years. 67% freshmen graduate within 6 years. 20% grads go on to further study within 1 year. **Faculty:** Student/faculty ratio 10:1. 80 full-time faculty, 98% hold PhDs, 24% are members of minority groups, 66% are women. 0% of classes are taught by teaching assistants.

ACADEMICS

Degrees: Bachelor's **Classes:** Most classes have 20-29 students. **Most popular majors:** Creative Writing; Psychology, General; Business Administration And Management, General. **Special Study Options:** Accelerated program; Cross-registration; Distance learning; Double major; Dual enrollment; Exchange student program (domestic); Independent study; Internships; Liberal arts/career combination; Student-designed major; Study abroad. **Honors programs:** SUMMIT at Agnes Scott reinvents a liberal arts education for the twenty-first century by preparing every student to be an effective change agent in a global society Guided by a personal board of advisors, every student, regardless of major, designs an individualized course of study and co-curricular experiences that develop leadership abilities and an understanding of complex global dynamics. All students: • Complete a core curriculum suffused with leadership development and global learning • Kick-off their college career with a three-day leadership immersion • Participate in a faculty-led global study tour in the Spring of their first year • Build a personalized board of advisors consisting of a SUMMIT advisor, a peer advisor, a major advisor, and a career mentor to guide them in crafting their unique educational journey • Create a digital portfolio in which they collect, reflect upon and showcase their achievements • Engage a cutting edge leadership curriculum that includes coursework, practica and opportunities to meet extraordinary leaders from all walks of life and a global curriculum that builds inter-cultural understanding and grapples with global issues at home and abroad • Complete a culminating project that synthesizes and contextualizes their four years of learning at Agnes Scott College • Have the opportunity to complete a specialization in leadership development or global learning and earn a notation on their transcript Equipped with a rigorous liberal arts and sciences education, an understanding of complex global issues and the ability to lead strategically and honorably, Agnes Scott graduates are ready to scale the next SUMMIT. **Disability Services offered to physically disabled students:** Note-taking services; Reader services; Tape recorders; Tutors. **Career services:** Alumni network; Alumni services; Career assessment; Career/job search classes; Internships; Regional alumni

FACILITIES

Housing: Apartments for single students; Theme housing; Women's dorms 90% of campus accessible to physically disabled. **Special Academic Facilities/Equipment:** Art galleries,tracking LEED Gold and recently renovated Campbell Hall, collaborative learning centers, language lab, electron microscope, observatory, 30-inch Beck telescope, planetarium, interactive learning center, multimedia presentation classrooms, instructional technology center, multi-media production facility. **Computers:** 50% of classrooms, 100% of libraries, 100% of student union, 10% of common outdoor areas have wireless network access. Students can register for classes online. Administrative functions (other than registration) can be performed online.

CAMPUS LIFE

Environment: Metropolis **Activities:** Campus Ministries; Choral groups; Dance; Drama/theater; International Student Organization; Jazz band; Literary magazine; Marching band; Model UN; Music ensembles; Musical theater; Radio station; Student government; Student newspaper; Symphony orchestra; Yearbook 80 registered organizations, 12 honor societies, 12 religious organizations. **Athletics (Intercollegiate):** *Women:* basketball, lacrosse, soccer, softball, tennis, volleyball. **On-Campus Highlights:** Campbell Hall (Tracking LEED Gold, newly renovated), McCain Library, Bradley Observatory, Alston Campus Center, Evans Dining Hall **Environmental Initiatives:** Converted to campus-wide single stream recycling and composting. Agnes Scott is committed to Zero Waste and has already achieved a 62% waste diversion rate.

ADMISSIONS

Freshman Academic Profile: Average high school GPA 3.8. 30% in top 10% of high school class, 65% in top 25% of high school class, 91% in top 50% of high school class. 75% from public high schools. **Test Scores:** SAT Math middle 50% range 530-610. SAT EBRW middle 50% range 580-690. ACT middle 50% range 24-30. Minimum internet-based TOEFL 80. **Basis for Candidate Selection:** *Very important factors considered include:* rigor of secondary school record, academic GPA, talent/ability, character/personal qualities. *Important factors considered include:* application essay, standardized test scores, recommendation(s), extracurricular activities, volunteer work. *Other factors considered include:* class rank, interview, first generation, alumni/ae relation, geographical residence, state residency, work experience, level of applicant's interest. **Freshman Admission Requirements:** High school diploma is required and GED is accepted *Academic units recommended:* 4 English, 3 math, 2 science, 2 science labs, 2 foreign language, 2 social studies. **Freshman Admission Statistics:** 1,534 applied, 65.6% admitted, 25% enrolled. **Transfer Admission Requirements:** High school transcript, college transcript(s), essay or personal statement, statement of good standing from prior institution(s). Minimum college GPA of 3.0 required. Lowest grade transferable C. **General Admission Information:** Priority deadline 1/15. Regular application deadline 5/1. Nonfall registration accepted. Admission may be deferred for a maximum of 1 year.

COSTS AND FINANCIAL AID

Annual tuition $40,920. Room and board $12,330. Required fees $240. Average book expense $1,000. **Required Forms and Deadlines:** FAFSA. **Notification of Awards:** Applicants will be notified of awards on a rolling basis beginning 3/1. **Types of Aid:** *Need-based scholarships/grants:* College/university scholarship or grant aid from institutional funds; Federal Pell; Private scholarships; SEOG; State scholarships/grants. *Loans:* Direct PLUS loans; Direct Subsidized Stafford Loans; Direct Unsubsidized Stafford Loans. *Student Employment:* Federal Work-Study Program available. Institutional employment available. **Financial Aid Statistics:** 100% needy freshmen, 100% needy undergrads receive need-based scholarship or grant aid. 30% freshmen, 25% undergrads receive non-need-based scholarship or grant aid. 73% freshmen, 82% undergrads receive need-based self-help aid. 0% freshmen, 0% undergrads receive athletic scholarships. 100% freshmen, 99% undergrads receive any aid. 75% undergrads borrow to pay for school. Average cumulative indebtedness $34,022. **Criteria for awarding aid:** *Non-need-based:* Academics, Leadership, Minority status, Music/drama, Religious affiliation.

ALABAMA A&M UNIVERSITY

Box1357, Normal, AL 35762
Phone: 256-851-5245
E-mail: juan.alexander@aamu.edu • **CEEB Code:** 1003
Fax: 256-851-5249 • **ACT Code:** 2

This public school was founded in 1875. It has a 880 acre campus.

RATINGS

Admissions Selectivity Rating: 84   **Fire Safety Rating:** 60*   **Green Rating:** 60*

STUDENTS AND FACULTY

Enrollment: 4,489. **Student Body:** 52% female, 48% male, 31% out-of-state, 1% international (42 countries represented). Asian <1%, African American 96%, Caucasian 2%, Hispanic <1%, Native American <1%, Race unknown <1%.
Retention and Graduation: 77% grads go on to further study within 1 year. 40% grads pursue arts and sciences degrees. 2% grads pursue law degrees. 45% grads pursue business degrees. 11% grads pursue medical degrees. **Faculty:** Student/faculty ratio 14:1. 314 full-time faculty, 45% hold PhDs, 55% are members of minority groups, 39% are women. 1% of classes are taught by teaching assistants.

ACADEMICS

Degrees: Bachelor's; Master's; Post-Master's certificate **Classes:** Most classes have 20-29 students. Most lab/discussion sessions have 20-29 students. **Most popular majors:** Elementary Education And Teaching; Mechanical Engineering Related Technologies/Technicians, Other; Biology/Biological Sciences, General. **Special Study Options:** Accelerated program; Cooperative education program; Distance learning; Double major; Dual enrollment; Exchange student program (domestic); Honors program; Independent study; Internships; Study abroad; Teacher certification program; Weekend college. **Disability Services offered to physically disabled students:** Note-taking services; Reader services; Tape recorders; Tutors. **Career services:** Career assessment; Career/job search classes; Internships; Regional alumni

FACILITIES

Housing: Apartments for single students; Men's dorms; Women's dorms 65% of campus accessible to physically disabled. **Special Academic Facilities/Equipment:** State Black Archives **Computers:** Students can register for classes online.

CAMPUS LIFE

Environment: City **Activities:** Campus Ministries; Choral groups; Concert band; Dance; Drama/theater; International Student Organization; Jazz band; Literary magazine; Marching band; Music ensembles; Pep band; Radio station; Student government; Student newspaper; Symphony orchestra; Television station; Yearbook 76 registered organizations, 14 honor societies, 3 religious organizations. 4 fraternities, 4 sororities. **Athletics (Intercollegiate):** *Men:* baseball, basketball, cross-country, football, golf, soccer, track/field (outdoor). *Women:* basketball, cross-country, soccer, softball, track/field (outdoor), volleyball. **On-Campus Highlights:** Engineering Building, Cafeteria, Gym, Business School, Dawson Building

ADMISSIONS

Freshman Academic Profile: 90% from public high schools. **Test Scores:** SAT Math middle 50% range 380-470. SAT EBRW middle 50% range 400-470. ACT middle 50% range 16-19. Minimum paper TOEFL 550. **Basis for Candidate Selection:** *Very important factors considered include:* standardized test scores, alumni/ae relation, geographical residence, state residency. *Important factors considered include:* racial/ethnic status. *Other factors considered include:* class rank, recommendation(s). **Freshman Admission Requirements:** High school diploma is required and GED is accepted *Academic units required:* 4 English, 4 math, 4 science, 2 science labs, 4 social studies, 4 history. **Freshman Admission Statistics:** 5,697 applied, 47.3% admitted, 39% enrolled. **Transfer Admission Requirements:** High school transcript, college transcript(s), standardized test scores, statement of good standing from prior institution(s). Minimum college GPA of 2.5 required. Lowest grade transferable C. **General Admission Information:** Application fee $10. Priority deadline 4/1. Regular application deadline 7/1. Nonfall registration accepted. Admission may be deferred for a maximum of 1 year.

COSTS AND FINANCIAL AID

Annual in-state tuition $5,350. Annual out-of-state tuition $7,896. Room and board $5,350. Required fees $744. **Required Forms and Deadlines:** FAFSA; Institution's own financial aid form. **Types of Aid:** *Need-based scholarships/grants:* College/university scholarship or grant aid from institutional funds; Federal Pell; Private scholarships; SEOG; State scholarships/grants; United Negro College Fund. *Loans:* Direct PLUS loans; Direct Subsidized Stafford Loans; Direct Unsubsidized Stafford Loans.

ALASKA PACIFIC UNIVERSITY

4101 University Drive, Anchorage, AK 99508-4625
Phone: 907-564-8248 · **Financial Aid Phone:** 907-564-8341
E-mail: admissions@alaskapacific.edu · **CEEB Code:** 4201
Fax: 907-564-8317 · **Website:** http://www.alaskapacific.edu · **ACT Code:** 62

This private school, affiliated with the Methodist Church, was founded in 1957. It has a 170 acre campus.

RATINGS
Admissions Selectivity Rating: 88   **Fire Safety Rating:** 91   **Green Rating:** 60*

STUDENTS AND FACULTY
Enrollment: 455. **Student Body:** 65% female, 35% male, 32% out-of-state, <1% international (3 countries represented). Asian 2%, African American 3%, Caucasian 58%, Hispanic 3%, Native American 15%, Pacific Islander <1%, Two or more races 0%, Race unknown 18%.
Retention and Graduation: 67% freshmen return for sophomore year.
Faculty: Student/faculty ratio 10:1. 50 full-time faculty, 64% hold PhDs, 4% are members of minority groups, 58% are women. 0% of classes are taught by teaching assistants.

ACADEMICS
Degrees: Associate; Bachelor's; Certificate; Doctoral Other; Doctoral/Professional; Master's; Post-Bachelor's certificate; Terminal Associate **Classes:** Most classes have 20-29 students. Most lab/discussion sessions have 20-29 students. **Most popular majors:** Elementary Education And Teaching; Marine Biology And Biological Oceanography; Business Administration And Management, General. **Special Study Options:** Distance learning; Double major; Exchange student program (domestic); Independent study; Internships; Student-designed major; Study abroad; Teacher certification program.
Disability Services offered to physically disabled students: Note-taking services; Tape recorders; Tutors. **Career services:** Career assessment; Career/job search classes; Internships

FACILITIES
Housing: Coed dorms; Cooperative housing; Other (please specify) 75% of campus accessible to physically diasbled. **Special Academic Facilities/Equipment:** Alaskana collection; GIS lab gym with pool; Student Center with weight room and indoor climbing wall; Outdoor recreation center with classes and rental equipment; Lake for canoeing and kayaking; trails for running, skiing, hiking, biking, etc., connected to city's trail system **Computers:** 100% of classrooms, 100% of dorms, 100% of libraries, 100% of dining areas, 100% of student union, 100% of common outdoor areas have wireless network access. Students can register for classes online. Administrative functions (other than registration) can be performed online.

CAMPUS LIFE
Environment: City **Activities:** Drama/theater; Literary magazine; Music ensembles; Student government; Student newspaper; Yearbook 15 registered organizations, 1 religious organization. **On-Campus Highlights:** Student Center, Climbing wall and weight room, Pool, lounges in Grant Hall and in Carr Gottst **Environmental Initiatives:** Kellogg Farm dedicated to organic and sustainable enterprises.

ADMISSIONS
Freshman Academic Profile: Average high school GPA 3.3. 17% in top 10% of high school class, 31% in top 25% of high school class, 72% in top 50% of high school class. 95% from public high schools. **Test Scores:** SAT Math middle 50% range 470-560. SAT EBRW middle 50% range 490-600. ACT middle 50% range 21-27. Minimum internet-based TOEFL 79. Minimum paper TOEFL 550. **Basis for Candidate Selection:** *Very important factors considered include:* rigor of secondary school record, academic GPA, application essay. *Important factors considered include:* standardized test scores, recommendation(s), alumni/ae relation, level of applicant's interest. *Other factors considered include:* extracurricular activities, talent/ability, volunteer work, work experience. **Freshman Admission Requirements:** High school diploma is required and GED is accepted *Academic units recommended:* 4 English, 3 math, 2 science, 1 science labs, 2 foreign language, 1 social studies, 1 history. **Freshman Admission Statistics:** 245 applied, 48.2% admitted, 43% enrolled. **Transfer Admission Requirements:** college transcript(s), essay or personal statement, statement of good standing from prior institution(s). Minimum college GPA of 2.0 required. Lowest grade transferable C. **General Admission Information:** Application fee $25. Priority deadline 12/1. Regular application deadline 8/15. Nonfall registration accepted. Admission may be deferred for a maximum of 1 year.

COSTS AND FINANCIAL AID
Annual tuition $26,250. Room and board $9,300. Required fees $110. Average book expense $1,000. **Required Forms and Deadlines:** FAFSA.

Notification of Awards: Applicants will be notified of awards on a rolling basis beginning 2/1. **Types of Aid:** *Need-based scholarships/grants:* College/university scholarship or grant aid from institutional funds; Federal Pell; Private scholarships; SEOG; State scholarships/grants. *Loans:* Direct PLUS loans; Direct Subsidized Stafford Loans; Direct Unsubsidized Stafford Loans. *Student Employment:* Federal Work-Study Program available. Institutional employment available. **Financial Aid Statistics:** 47% needy freshmen, 55% needy undergrads receive need-based scholarship or grant aid. 100% freshmen, 48% undergrads receive non-need-based scholarship or grant aid. 68% freshmen, 42% undergrads receive need-based self-help aid. 0% freshmen, 0% undergrads receive athletic scholarships. 88% freshmen, 92% undergrads receive any aid. **Criteria for awarding aid:** *Need-based:* Academics, Alumni affiliation, Leadership, Minority status, Religious affiliation *Non-need-based:* Academics, Alumni affiliation, Leadership, Religious affiliation, State/district residency.

ALBANY COLLEGE OF PHARMACY

106 New Scotland Avenue, Albany, NY 12208
Phone: 518-694-7221 · **Financial Aid Phone:** 518-694-7256
E-mail: admissions@acp.edu · **CEEB Code:** 2013
Fax: 518-694-7322 · **Website:** www.acp.edu · **ACT Code:** 2672

This private school was founded in 1881. It has a 21 acre campus.

RATINGS
Admissions Selectivity Rating: 88   **Fire Safety Rating:** 70   **Green Rating:** 60*

STUDENTS AND FACULTY
Enrollment: 1,015. **Student Body:** 58% female, 42% male, 10% out-of-state, 8% international (6 countries represented). Asian 13%, African American 2%, Caucasian 73%, Hispanic 1%, Native American <1%, Race unknown 3%.
Retention and Graduation: 79% freshmen return for sophomore year.
Faculty: Student/faculty ratio 16:1. 82 full-time faculty, 74% hold PhDs, 12% are members of minority groups, 49% are women. 0% of classes are taught by teaching assistants.

ACADEMICS
Degrees: Bachelor's; Certificate **Classes:** Most classes have 10-19 students. Most lab/discussion sessions have 10-19 students. **Most popular majors:** Pharmacy. **Special Study Options:** Accelerated program; Cross-registration. **Combined degree programs:** BA/JD. **Disability Services offered to physically disabled students:** Tutors. **Career services:** Career assessment; Career/job search classes

FACILITIES
Housing: Apartments for single students; Coed dorms 100% of campus accessible to physically diasbled. **Special Academic Facilities/Equipment:** Throop Pharmaceutical Museum. **Computers:** Students can register for classes online. Administrative functions (other than registration) can be performed online. Undergraduates are required to own a computer.

CAMPUS LIFE
Environment: City **Activities:** Choral groups; Concert band; Dance; International Student Organization; Literary magazine; Student government; Student newspaper; Yearbook 2 honor societies, 1 religious organization. **Athletics (Intercollegiate):** *Men:* basketball, soccer. *Women:* basketball, soccer. **On-Campus Highlights:** NEW—ACP Student Center

ADMISSIONS
Freshman Academic Profile: Average high school GPA 92.0. 47% in top 10% of high school class, 86% in top 25% of high school class, 99% in top 50% of high school class. **Test Scores:** SAT Math middle 50% range 570-650. SAT EBRW middle 50% range 530-620. ACT middle 50% range 23-28. Minimum paper TOEFL 600. **Basis for Candidate Selection:** *Very important factors considered include:* academic GPA, standardized test scores. *Important factors considered include:* rigor of secondary school record, class rank. *Other factors considered include:* application essay, recommendation(s), extracurricular activities, talent/ability, character/personal qualities, alumni/ae relation, geographical residence, volunteer work, work experience, level of applicant's interest. **Freshman Admission Requirements:** High school diploma is required and GED is accepted *Academic units required:* 4 English, 4 math, 3 science, 3 science labs, 4 social studies, *Academic units recommended:* 4 science, 4 science labs, 4 foreign language. **Freshman Admission Statistics:** 1,049 applied, 61.3% admitted, 41% enrolled. **Transfer Admission Requirements:** college transcript(s), essay or personal statement, statement of good standing from prior institution(s). Minimum college GPA of 3.2 required. Lowest grade transferable B. **General Admission Information:** Application fee $75. Priority deadline 2/1. Regular application deadline 3/1. Nonfall registration accepted. Admission may be deferred for a maximum of 1 year.

COSTS AND FINANCIAL AID

Required Forms and Deadlines: FAFSA. **Notification of Awards:** Applicants will be notified of awards on a rolling basis beginning 3/25. **Types of Aid:** *Need-based scholarships/grants:* College/university scholarship or grant aid from institutional funds; Federal Pell; Private scholarships; SEOG; State scholarships/grants. **Financial Aid Statistics:** 92% needy freshmen, 80% needy undergrads receive need-based scholarship or grant aid. 12% freshmen, 6% undergrads receive non-need-based scholarship or grant aid. 84% freshmen, 92% undergrads receive need-based self-help aid. 0% freshmen, 0% undergrads receive athletic scholarships. **Criteria for awarding aid:** *Need-based:* Academics, Alumni affiliation, Leadership *Non-need-based:* Academics, Alumni affiliation, Leadership.

ALBANY STATE UNIVERSITY

504 College Drive, Albany, GA 31705
Phone: 229-430-4646 · **Financial Aid Phone:** 229-430-4650
E-mail: enrollmentservices@asurams.edu · **CEEB Code:** 5004
Fax: 229-430-4105 · **Website:** http://www.asurams.edu · **ACT Code:** 782

This public school was founded in 1903. It has a 232 acre campus.

RATINGS
Admissions Selectivity Rating: 90   **Fire Safety Rating:** 91   **Green Rating:** 60*

STUDENTS AND FACULTY
Enrollment: 4,173. **Student Body:** 66% female, 34% male, 4% out-of-state, <1% international (22 countries represented). Asian <1%, African American 83%, Caucasian 4%, Hispanic 1%, Native American <1%, Pacific Islander <1%, Two or more races <1%, Race unknown 11%.
Retention and Graduation: 65% freshmen return for sophomore year.
Faculty: Student/faculty ratio 21:1. 164 full-time faculty, 77% hold PhDs, 78% are members of minority groups, 45% are women. 0% of classes are taught by teaching assistants.

ACADEMICS
Degrees: Bachelor's; Master's; Post-Master's certificate **Classes:** Most classes have fewer than 10 students. Most lab/discussion sessions have 20-29 students. **Most popular majors:** Early Childhood Education And Teaching; Criminal Justice/Safety Studies; Business Administration And Management, General. **Special Study Options:** Cooperative education program; Cross-registration; Distance learning; Double major; Dual enrollment; Honors program; Independent study; Internships; Study abroad; Teacher certification program; Weekend college. **Honors programs:** The Velma Fudge Grant Honors Program represents a commitment made by Albany State University (ASU) to broaden and enrich educational experiences of bright, highly motivated and creative students. Honors Program students are provided opportunities for scholarships, access to special extracurricular programs, a chance to pursue independent projects and research interests, professional experience through internship programs and special service options. Through its specially designed curriculum, the University provides the opportunity for faculty to teach academically talented students in inventive, interdisciplinary, small class settings designed to fulfill core curriculum requirements, as well as in advanced or intensive classes in particular disciplines. The Honors Program is specifically designed for academic scholarship recipients, academically talented students and entering freshman and transfer students with a proven dedication to academic excellence and scholarship. The Honors Program student must reach beyond good grades for success and have the courage to demonstrate superior ethical leadership in his/her chosen field of study. **Combined degree programs:** BA/MEng. **Disability Services offered to physically disabled students:** Note-taking services; Reader services; Tape recorders; Tutors. **Career services:** Alumni network; Alumni services; Career assessment; Internships; Regional alumni

FACILITIES
Housing: Coed dorms; Men's dorms; Women's dorms 98% of campus accessible to physically disabled. **Computers:** 67% of dorms have wireless network access.

CAMPUS LIFE
Environment: City **Activities:** Choral groups; Concert band; Dance; Drama/theater; Jazz band; Marching band; Model UN; Music ensembles; Opera; Pep band; Radio station; Student government; Student newspaper; Television station; Yearbook 70 registered organizations, 10 honor societies, 6 fraternities, 4 sororities. **Athletics (Intercollegiate): Men:** baseball, basketball, cross-country, football, track/field (outdoor). *Women:* basketball, cross-country, softball, tennis, track/field (outdoor), volleyball. **On-Campus Highlights:** New Student Center, Gymnasium, Residence Halls, Stadium, The Square

---

Environmental Initiatives: 1. Hazardous Waste Labe 2. Paint shops and carpentry 3. Universal Waste

ADMISSIONS
Freshman Academic Profile: 10% in top 10% of high school class, 30% in top 25% of high school class, 67% in top 50% of high school class. **Test Scores:** SAT Math middle 50% range 390-460. SAT EBRW middle 50% range 390-450. ACT middle 50% range 16-19. Minimum paper TOEFL 523. **Basis for Candidate Selection:** *Very important factors considered include:* academic GPA, standardized test scores. *Other factors considered include:* rigor of secondary school record, class rank, application essay, recommendation(s). **Freshman Admission Requirements:** High school diploma is required and GED is accepted *Academic units required:* 4 English, 4 math, 3 science, 2 science labs, 2 foreign language, 3 social studies. **Freshman Admission Statistics:** 6,554 applied, 28.7% admitted, 57% enrolled. **Transfer Admission Requirements:** college transcript(s), Minimum college GPA of 2.0 required. Lowest grade transferable D. **General Admission Information:** Application fee $20. Priority deadline 5/1. Regular application deadline 6/1. Nonfall registration accepted. Admission may be deferred for a maximum of one year.

COSTS AND FINANCIAL AID
Required Forms and Deadlines: FAFSA; State aid form. **Notification of Awards:** Applicants will be notified of awards on a rolling basis beginning 1/7. *Student Employment:* Federal Work-Study Program available. Institutional employment available. **Criteria for awarding aid:** *Non-need-based:* Academics, Alumni affiliation, Art, Athletics.

ALBERTA COLLEGE OF ART + DESIGN

1407 14 Avenue NW, Calgary, AB T2N 4R3
Phone: 403-284-7617 · **Financial Aid Phone:** 403-284-7600
E-mail: admissions@acad.ca
Fax: 403-284-7644 · **Website:** www.acad.ca

This public school was founded in 1926.

RATINGS
Admissions Selectivity Rating: 70   **Fire Safety Rating:** 60*   **Green Rating:** 60*

STUDENTS AND FACULTY
Enrollment: 1,112. **Student Body:** 73% female, 27% male, 11% out-of-state, 5% international (49 countries represented). Asian 0%, African American 0%, Caucasian 0%, Hispanic 0%, Native American 0%, Race unknown 95%.
Retention and Graduation: 64% freshmen return for sophomore year.
Faculty: Student/faculty ratio 15:1. 46 full-time faculty,

ACADEMICS
Degrees: Bachelor's **Classes:** Most classes have 10-19 students. Most lab/discussion sessions have 10-19 students. **Most popular majors:** Drawing; Painting; Sculpture. **Special Study Options:** Cross-registration; Exchange student program (domestic); Internships; Study abroad. **Disability Services offered to physically disabled students:** Reader services; Tutors.

FACILITIES
Housing: Coed dorms; Other (please specify) 100% of campus accessible to physically diasbled. **Special Academic Facilities/Equipment:** 2 Art Galleries **Computers:** 100% of classrooms, have wireless network access. Students can register for classes online. Administrative functions (other than registration) can be performed online.

CAMPUS LIFE
Environment: Metropolis **Activities:** Student government. **Athletics (Intercollegiate):** *Men:* basketball, ice hockey, volleyball. *Women:* basketball, volleyball. **On-Campus Highlights:** Facilities, Glass Department, Graffitt Stairwell, Residence

ADMISSIONS
Freshman Academic Profile: 91% from public high schools. **Test Scores:** Minimum internet-based TOEFL 83. Minimum paper TOEFL 560. **Basis for Candidate Selection:** *Very important factors considered include:* academic GPA, application essay, talent/ability, level of applicant's interest. *Other factors considered include:* standardized test scores, recommendation(s), extracurricular activities, character/personal qualities, work experience. **Freshman Admission Requirements:** High school diploma is required and GED is accepted *Academic units required:* 4 English. **Freshman Admission Statistics:** 576 applied, 65.5% admitted, 74% enrolled. **Transfer Admission Requirements:** college transcript(s), essay or personal statement. **General Admission Information:** Application fee $85. Regular application deadline 4/1. Nonfall registration accepted.

COSTS AND FINANCIAL AID

Annual out-of-state tuition $4,435. Required fees $831. Average book expense $3,150. **Required Forms and Deadlines:** FAFSA. **Criteria for awarding aid:** *Need-based:* Academics, Art *Non-need-based:* Academics, Art.

ALBERTUS MAGNUS COLLEGE

700 Prospect Street, New Haven, CT 06511
Phone: 203-773-8501 • **Financial Aid Phone:** 203-773-8508
E-mail: admissions@albertus.edu • **CEEB Code:** 3001
Fax: 203-773-5248 • **Website:** www.albertus.edu • **ACT Code:** 549

This private school, affiliated with the Roman Catholic Church, was founded in 1925. It has a 50 acre campus.

RATINGS

Admissions Selectivity Rating: 74   **Fire Safety Rating:** 85   **Green Rating:** 60*

STUDENTS AND FACULTY

Enrollment: 1,682. **Student Body:** 68% female, 32% male, 15% out-of-state, <1% international. Asian 1%, African American 27%, Caucasian 55%, Hispanic 10%, Native American <1%, Race unknown 7%.
Retention and Graduation: 78% freshmen return for sophomore year.
Faculty: Student/faculty ratio 13:1. 42 full-time faculty, 79% hold PhDs, 43% are women. 0% of classes are taught by teaching assistants.

ACADEMICS

Degrees: Associate; Bachelor's; Certificate; Master's **Classes:** Most classes have 10-19 students. **Most popular majors:** Education, General; Psychology, General; Business/Commerce, General. **Special Study Options:** Accelerated program; Double major; Honors program; Independent study; Internships; Student-designed major; Teacher certification program. **Honors programs:** Students may apply to follow the Honors Program, which involves work in special courses designated each semester as honors courses and the development of individual projects designed in consultation with faculty mentors. Entering qualified students are assigned to special honors courses and returning students interested in such a program should consult, by the spring of their sophomore year or earlier, with their advisor and the Director of the Honors Program. **Disability Services offered to physically disabled students:** Note-taking services; Reader services; Tape recorders; Tutors. **Career services:** Alumni network; Career assessment; Career/job search classes; Internships

FACILITIES

Housing: Coed dorms; Women's dorms 70% of campus accessible to physically diasbled. **Special Academic Facilities/Equipment:** Margart McDonough Art Gallery

CAMPUS LIFE

Environment: City **Activities:** Campus Ministries; Choral groups; Dance; Drama/theater; Literary magazine; Musical theater; Student government; Yearbook 1 honor society, 1 religious organization. **Athletics (Intercollegiate):** *Men:* baseball, basketball, cross-country, lacrosse, soccer, tennis, volleyball. *Women:* basketball, cross-country, lacrosse, soccer, softball, tennis, volleyball. **On-Campus Highlights:** Center for Science, Art and Technology, Athletic Center, Library, Campus Center, Art Gallery

ADMISSIONS

Freshman Academic Profile: Average high school GPA 3.0. 10% in top 10% of high school class, 29% in top 25% of high school class, 68% in top 50% of high school class. 70% from public high schools. **Test Scores:** SAT Math middle 50% range 470-500. SAT EBRW middle 50% range 490-560. Minimum paper TOEFL 550. **Basis for Candidate Selection:** *Very important factors considered include:* rigor of secondary school record, academic GPA. *Important factors considered include:* standardized test scores, recommendation(s). *Other factors considered include:* class rank, application essay, interview, extracurricular activities, talent/ability, character/personal qualities, first generation, alumni/ae relation, volunteer work, work experience, level of applicant's interest. **Freshman Admission Requirements:** High school diploma is required and GED is accepted *Academic units required:* 4 English, 2 math, 2 science, 2 foreign language, 2 social studies, 2 history, 2 academic electives, *Academic units recommended:* 3 math, 3 science, 1 science labs, 3 foreign language, 1 social studies, 2 history. **Freshman Admission Statistics:** 556 applied, 84.2% admitted, 26% enrolled. **Transfer Admission Requirements:** college transcript(s), Minimum college GPA of 2.0 required. Lowest grade transferable C. **General Admission Information:** Application fee $35. Nonfall registration accepted. Admission may be deferred.

COSTS AND FINANCIAL AID

Annual tuition $20,166. Room and board $8,907. Required fees $908. Average book expense $920. **Required Forms and Deadlines:** FAFSA; Institution's own financial aid form. **Notification of Awards:** Applicants will be notified of awards on a rolling basis beginning 3/1. **Types of Aid:** *Need-based scholarships/grants:* College/university scholarship or grant aid from institutional funds; Federal Pell; SEOG; State scholarships/grants. *Loans:* Direct PLUS loans; Direct Subsidized Stafford Loans; Direct Unsubsidized Stafford Loans. *Student Employment:* Federal Work-Study Program available. **Financial Aid Statistics:** 89% needy freshmen, 93% needy undergrads receive need-based scholarship or grant aid. 60% freshmen, 65% undergrads receive non-need-based scholarship or grant aid. 37% freshmen, 39% undergrads receive need-based self-help aid. 87% freshmen, 75% undergrads receive any aid. **Criteria for awarding aid:** *Need-based:* Academics *Non-need-based:* Academics, Leadership, Religious affiliation.

ALBION COLLEGE

611 E. Porter Street, Albion, MI 49224
Phone: 517-629-0321 • **Financial Aid Phone:** 517-629-0440
E-mail: admission@albion.edu • **CEEB Code:** 1007
Fax: 517-629-0569 • **Website:** www.albion.edu • **ACT Code:** 1956

This private school, affiliated with the Methodist Church, was founded in 1835. It has a 585 acre campus.

RATINGS

Admissions Selectivity Rating: 81   **Fire Safety Rating:** 86   **Green Rating:** 73

STUDENTS AND FACULTY

Enrollment: 1,558. **Student Body:** 53% female, 47% male, 23% out-of-state, 2% international (15 countries represented). Asian 3%, African American 13%, Caucasian 65%, Hispanic 9%, Native American <1%, Pacific Islander <1%, Two or more races 3%, Race unknown 5%.
Retention and Graduation: 79% freshmen return for sophomore year. 46% freshmen graduate within 4 years. 71% freshmen graduate within 6 years. 30% grads go on to further study within 1 year. 17% grads pursue arts and sciences degrees. 2% grads pursue law degrees. 2% grads pursue business degrees. 4% grads pursue medical degrees. **Faculty:** Student/faculty ratio 12:1. 110 full-time faculty, 92% hold PhDs, 10% are members of minority groups, 45% are women. 0% of classes are taught by teaching assistants.

ACADEMICS

Degrees: Bachelor's **Classes:** Most classes have 10-19 students. Most lab/discussion sessions have fewer than 10 students. **Most popular majors:** Biology/Biological Sciences, General; Psychology, General; Economics, General. **Special Study Options:** Distance learning; Double major; Dual enrollment; English as a Second Language (ESL); Honors program; Independent study; Internships; Liberal arts/career combination; Student-designed major; Study abroad; Teacher certification program. **Honors programs:** The Honors Program at Albion was founded in 1976, and in August of 2004 it was renamed The Prentiss M. Brown Honors Program. We provide an exciting and unique variety of academic experiences for highly motivated and talented students. The Program's mix of small discussion classes, independent research, academic rigor, and personal attention provides Honors students with special challenges and opportunities for growth. Many of the College's finest teachers and scholars regularly contribute to the program's curriculum. **Combined degree programs:** BA/MEng. **Disability Services offered to physically disabled students:** Note-taking services; Reader services; Tape recorders; Tutors. **Career services:** Alumni network; Alumni services; Career assessment; Career/job search classes; Internships; Regional alumni

FACILITIES

Housing: Apartments for married students; Apartments for single students; Coed dorms; Cooperative housing; Fraternity/sorority housing; Special housing for disabled students 95% of campus accessible to physically diasbled. **Special Academic Facilities/Equipment:** Visual arts museum; nature center; equestrian center; science complex museum; greenhouse; geographic information systems/computer-aided mapping lab; observatory; a Dow analytical science laboratory; see website for much more, listed by department/facility: https://www.albion.edu/academics/departments/geological-sciences/campus-facilities **Computers:** 95% of classrooms, 100% of dorms, 100% of libraries, 100% of dining areas, 100% of student union, 25% of common outdoor areas have wireless network access. Students can register for classes online. Administrative functions (other than registration) can be performed online.

CAMPUS LIFE

Environment: Village **Activities:** Campus Ministries; Choral groups; Concert band; Dance; Drama/theater; International Student Organization; Jazz band; Literary magazine; Marching band; Model UN; Music ensembles; Musical theater; Opera; Radio station; Student government; Student newspaper; Symphony orchestra; Yearbook 122 registered organizations, 17 honor societies, 11 religious organizations. 6 fraternities, 7 sororities. **Athletics (Intercollegiate):** *Men:* baseball, basketball, cross-country, diving, equestrian sports, football, golf, soccer, swimming, tennis, track/field (outdoor), track/field (indoor). *Women:* basketball, cross-country, diving, equestrian sports, golf, soccer, softball, swimming, tennis, track/field (outdoor), track/field (indoor), volleyball. **On-Campus Highlights:** Kellogg Center- Student Center, Dow Recreation Center- Athletic Facility, Quad- Lawn in the center of campus, Baldwin- Dining Hall, Science Center Atrium **Environmental Initiatives:** Development of Center for Sustainability and the Environment, which fosters involvement and projects by students. Examples include establishment of residential E-House (2006-present), E.P.A. P3 grant (2006-07), two National Wildlife Federation Sustainability Fellows (2008), active "Focus the Nation" and "Step it Up" participation (2007-08), and starting a student organic farm (2010).

ADMISSIONS

Freshman Academic Profile: Average high school GPA 3.4. **Test Scores:** SAT Math middle 50% range 500-590. SAT EBRW middle 50% range 510-610. ACT middle 50% range 20-26. Minimum internet-based TOEFL 79. Minimum paper TOEFL 550. **Basis for Candidate Selection:** *Very important factors considered include:* rigor of secondary school record, academic GPA, standardized test scores. *Important factors considered include:* class rank. *Other factors considered include:* application essay, recommendation(s), interview, extracurricular activities, talent/ability, character/personal qualities, alumni/ae relation, geographical residence, state residency, racial/ethnic status, volunteer work, work experience. **Freshman Admission Requirements:** High school diploma is required and GED is accepted *Academic units recommended:* 4 English, 5 math, 3 science, 2 science labs, 2 foreign language, 2 social studies. **Freshman Admission Statistics:** 3,884 applied, 70.6% admitted, 38% enrolled. **Transfer Admission Requirements:** High school transcript, college transcript(s), essay or personal statement, interview, standardized test scores, statement of good standing from prior institution(s). Minimum college GPA of 2.5 required. Lowest grade transferable C. **General Admission Information:** Nonfall registration accepted. Admission may be deferred for a maximum of 1 year.

COSTS AND FINANCIAL AID

Required Forms and Deadlines: FAFSA. **Notification of Awards:** Applicants will be notified of awards on a rolling basis beginning 12/1. **Types of Aid:** *Need-based scholarships/grants:* College/university scholarship or grant aid from institutional funds; Federal Pell; Private scholarships; SEOG; State scholarships/grants. *Loans:* Direct PLUS loans; Direct Subsidized Stafford Loans; Direct Unsubsidized Stafford Loans. *Student Employment:* Federal Work-Study Program available. Institutional employment available. **Financial Aid Statistics:** 100% needy freshmen, 100% needy undergrads receive need-based scholarship or grant aid. 99% freshmen, 98% undergrads receive non-need-based scholarship or grant aid. 85% freshmen, 84% undergrads receive need-based self-help aid. 0% freshmen, 0% undergrads receive athletic scholarships. 100% freshmen, 99% undergrads receive any aid. 68% undergrads borrow to pay for school. Average cumulative indebtedness $38,356. **Criteria for awarding aid:** *Need-based:* Academics, Alumni affiliation, Art, Leadership, Music/drama, Religious affiliation *Non-need-based:* Academics, Alumni affiliation, Art, Leadership, Music/drama.

ALBRIGHT COLLEGE

PO Box 15234, Reading, PA 19612-5234
Phone: 610-921-7799 • **Financial Aid Phone:** 610-921-7264
E-mail: admission@albright.edu • **CEEB Code:** 2004
Fax: 610-921-7729 • **Website:** www.albright.edu • **ACT Code:** 2004

This private school, affiliated with the Methodist Church, was founded in 1856. It has a 118 acre campus.

RATINGS

Admissions Selectivity Rating: 85   **Fire Safety Rating:** 61   **Green Rating:** 60*

STUDENTS AND FACULTY

Enrollment: 1,999. **Student Body:** 59% female, 41% male, 40% out-of-state, 2% international (14 countries represented). Asian 3%, African American 21%, Caucasian 51%, Hispanic 12%, Native American 1%, Pacific Islander 0%, Two or more races 2%, Race unknown 9%.

Retention and Graduation: 69% freshmen return for sophomore year. 44% freshmen graduate within 4 years. 18% grads go on to further study within 1 year. **Faculty:** Student/faculty ratio 14:1. 103 full-time faculty, 84% hold PhDs, 17% are members of minority groups, 48% are women. 0% of classes are taught by teaching assistants.

ACADEMICS

Degrees: Bachelor's; Master's **Classes:** Most classes have 20-29 students. Most lab/discussion sessions have 10-19 students. **Most popular majors:** Sociology; Business/Commerce, General. **Special Study Options:** Accelerated program; Cross-registration; Distance learning; Double major; Exchange student program (domestic); Honors program; Independent study; Internships; Liberal arts/career combination; Student-designed major; Study abroad; Teacher certification program. **Disability Services offered to physically disabled students:** Tape recorders. **Career services:** Alumni network; Alumni services; Career assessment; Career/job search classes; Internships; Regional alumni

FACILITIES

Housing: Apartments for single students; Coed dorms; Cooperative housing; Special housing for disabled student; Theme housing; Wellness housing **Special Academic Facilities/Equipment:** Freedman Art Gallery

CAMPUS LIFE

Environment: City **Activities:** Campus Ministries; Choral groups; Concert band; Dance; Drama/theater; International Student Organization; Jazz band; Literary magazine; Music ensembles; Musical theater; Radio station; Student government; Student newspaper; Student-run film society; Symphony orchestra; Television station; Yearbook 84 registered organizations, 10 honor societies, 3 religious organizations. 4 fraternities, 3 sororities. **Athletics (Intercollegiate):** *Men:* baseball, basketball, cheerleading, cross-country, football, golf, soccer, swimming, tennis, track/field (outdoor), track/field (indoor), wrestling. *Women:* badminton, basketball, cheerleading, cross-country, field hockey, soccer, softball, swimming, tennis, track/field (outdoor), track/field (indoor), volleyball. **On-Campus Highlights:** Student Center, Jake's Place, Wachovia Theatre, Schumo Center, Natatorium

ADMISSIONS

Freshman Academic Profile: Average high school GPA 3.2. 15% in top 10% of high school class, 37% in top 25% of high school class, 73% in top 50% of high school class. 77% from public high schools. **Test Scores:** SAT Math middle 50% range 490-580. SAT EBRW middle 50% range 500-590. ACT middle 50% range 19-26. Minimum internet-based TOEFL 68. Minimum paper TOEFL 520. **Basis for Candidate Selection:** *Very important factors considered include:* rigor of secondary school record, academic GPA. *Important factors considered include:* class rank, character/personal qualities. *Other factors considered include:* application essay, standardized test scores, recommendation(s), interview, extracurricular activities, talent/ability, alumni/ae relation, volunteer work, work experience, level of applicant's interest. **Freshman Admission Requirements:** High school diploma is required and GED is accepted *Academic units required:* 4 English, 3 math, 3 science, 1 science labs, 2 foreign language, 2 social studies, 1 history, *Academic units recommended:* 4 English, 3 math, 4 science, 2 science labs, 2 foreign language, 2 social studies, 1 history, 1 academic elective. **Freshman Admission Statistics:** 8,332 applied, 50.0% admitted, 11% enrolled. **Transfer Admission Requirements:** college transcript(s), essay or personal statement, statement of good standing from prior institution(s). Minimum college GPA of 2.0 required. Lowest grade transferable C-. **General Admission Information:** Application fee $35. Priority deadline 2/1. Admission may be deferred.

COSTS AND FINANCIAL AID

Annual tuition $44,206. Required fees $1,100. Average book expense $1,000. **Required Forms and Deadlines:** FAFSA. **Notification of Awards:** Applicants will be notified of awards on a rolling basis beginning 11/15. **Types of Aid:** *Need-based scholarships/grants:* College/university scholarship or grant aid from institutional funds; Federal Pell; Private scholarships; SEOG; State scholarships/grants; United Negro College Fund. *Loans:* Direct PLUS loans; Direct Subsidized Stafford Loans; Direct Unsubsidized Stafford Loans. *Student Employment:* Federal Work-Study Program available. Institutional employment available. **Financial Aid Statistics:** 100% needy freshmen, 100% needy undergrads receive need-based scholarship or grant aid. 8% freshmen, 8% undergrads receive non-need-based scholarship or grant aid. 88% freshmen, 89% undergrads receive need-based self-help aid. 0% freshmen, 0% undergrads receive athletic scholarships. 89% undergrads borrow to pay for school. Average cumulative indebtedness $38,196. **Criteria for awarding aid:** *Non-need-based:* Academics, Art, Music/drama, Religious affiliation, State/district residency.

ALCORN STATE UNIVERSITY

1000 ASU Drive 300, Lorman, MS 39096
Phone: 601-877-6147
E-mail: ksampson@alcorn.edu • **CEEB Code:** 1008
Fax: 601-877-6347 • **Website:** www.alcorn.edu • **ACT Code:** 2176

This public school was founded in 1871. It has a 1756 acre campus.

RATINGS
Admissions Selectivity Rating: 74   **Fire Safety Rating:** 60*   **Green Rating:** 60*

STUDENTS AND FACULTY
Enrollment: 3,006. **Student Body:** 64% female, 36% male, 13% out-of-state, 1% international (14 countries represented). Asian <1%, African American 94%, Caucasian 2%, Hispanic <1%, Native American <1%, Pacific Islander <1%, Two or more races 2%,
Retention and Graduation: 76% freshmen return for sophomore year. 38% grads go on to further study within 1 year. **Faculty:** Student/faculty ratio 17:1. 163 full-time faculty, 66% hold PhDs, 80% are members of minority groups, 45% are women.

ACADEMICS
Degrees: Associate; Bachelor's; Master's; Post-Master's certificate **Classes:** Most classes have 20-29 students. **Most popular majors:** Elementary Education And Teaching; Liberal Arts And Sciences/Liberal Studies. **Special Study Options:** Accelerated program; Cooperative education program; Distance learning; Double major; Dual enrollment; Honors program; Independent study; Internships; Liberal arts/career combination; Study abroad; Teacher certification program. **Career services:** Internships

FACILITIES
Housing: Men's dorms; Women's dorms 0% of campus accessible to physically diasbled. **Special Academic Facilities/Equipment:** Honor's Resident Hall **Computers:** Students can register for classes online. Administrative functions (other than registration) can be performed online.

CAMPUS LIFE
Environment: Rural **Activities:** Choral groups; Concert band; Dance; Drama/theater; International Student Organization; Jazz band; Marching band; Music ensembles; Radio station; Student government; Student newspaper; Television station; Yearbook 120 registered organizations, 10 honor societies, 8 religious organizations. 8 fraternities, 7 sororities. **Athletics (Intercollegiate):** *Men:* baseball, basketball, cross-country, football, golf, tennis, track/field (outdoor). *Women:* basketball, cross-country, golf, soccer, softball, tennis, track/field (outdoor), volleyball.

ADMISSIONS
Freshman Academic Profile: Average high school GPA 3.0. 68% in top 50% of high school class. 99% from public high schools. **Test Scores:** SAT Math middle 50% range 405-500. SAT EBRW middle 50% range 390-485. ACT middle 50% range 16-20. Minimum paper TOEFL 525. **Basis for Candidate Selection:** *Very important factors considered include:* rigor of secondary school record, class rank, academic GPA. *Important factors considered include:* standardized test scores. *Other factors considered include:* recommendation(s), interview. **Freshman Admission Requirements:** High school diploma is required and GED is accepted *Academic units required:* 4 English, 3 math, 3 science, 2 science labs, 1 foreign language, 3 social studies, 1 academic elective, *Academic units recommended:* 4 English, 4 math, 4 science, 2 science labs, 1 foreign language, 4 social studies, 1 academic elective, 1 visual/performing arts. **Freshman Admission Statistics:** 2,078 applied, 78.4% admitted, 32% enrolled. **Transfer Admission Requirements:** college transcript(s), statement of good standing from prior institution(s). Mlnimum college GPA of 2.0 required. Lowest grade transferable C. **General Admission Information:** Nonfall registration accepted. Admission may be deferred.

COSTS AND FINANCIAL AID
Required Forms and Deadlines: FAFSA; Institution's own financial aid form. **Notification of Awards:** Applicants will be notified of awards on a rolling basis beginning 4/1. **Types of Aid:** *Need-based scholarships/grants:* College/university scholarship or grant aid from institutional funds; Federal Pell; Private scholarships; SEOG; State scholarships/grants. *Loans:* Direct PLUS loans; Direct Subsidized Stafford Loans; Direct Unsubsidized Stafford Loans. *Student Employment:* Federal Work-Study Program available. Institutional employment available. **Financial Aid Statistics:** 95% needy freshmen, 93% needy undergrads receive need-based scholarship or grant aid. 33% freshmen, 24% undergrads receive non-need-based scholarship or grant aid. 75% freshmen, 84% undergrads receive need-based self-help aid. 10% freshmen, 8% undergrads receive athletic scholarships. **Criteria for awarding aid:** *Need-based:* Academics, Alumni affiliation, Athletics, Leadership, Minority status, Music/drama *Non-need-based:* Academics, Athletics, Leadership.

ALDERSON-BROADDUS COLLEGE

101 College Hill Drive, Philippi, WV 26416
Phone: 800-263-1549 • **Financial Aid Phone:** 304-457-6354
E-mail: admissions@ab.edu • **CEEB Code:** 5005
Fax: 304-457-6239 • **Website:** www.ab.edu • **ACT Code:** 4508

This private school, affiliated with the American Baptist Church, was founded in 1871. It has a 170 acre campus.

RATINGS
Admissions Selectivity Rating: 82   **Fire Safety Rating:** 83   **Green Rating:** 60*

STUDENTS AND FACULTY
Enrollment: 1,066. **Student Body:** 46% female, 54% male, 63% out-of-state, 5% international (15 countries represented). Asian 1%, African American 16%, Caucasian 73%, Hispanic 4%, Native American <1%, Pacific Islander <1%, Two or more races 1%, Race unknown 0%.
Retention and Graduation: 55% freshmen return for sophomore year. 7% grads go on to further study within 1 year. 1% grads pursue arts and sciences degrees. 0% grads pursue law degrees. 7% grads pursue business degrees. **Faculty:** Student/faculty ratio 17:1. 62 full-time faculty, 47% hold PhDs, 6% are members of minority groups, 55% are women. 0% of classes are taught by teaching assistants.

ACADEMICS
Degrees: Associate; Bachelor's; Master's **Classes:** Most classes have 10-19 students. Most lab/discussion sessions have 10-19 students. **Most popular majors:** Biology/Biological Sciences, General; Athletic Training/Trainer; Registered Nursing/Registered Nurse. **Special Study Options:** Accelerated program; Distance learning; Double major; Honors program; Independent study; Internships; Liberal arts/career combination; Study abroad; Teacher certification program. **Disability Services offered to physically disabled students:** Note-taking services; Reader services; Tape recorders; Tutors. **Career services:** Alumni network; Career assessment; Career/job search classes; Internships

FACILITIES
Housing: Coed dorms; Special housing for disabled students 70% of campus accessible to physically diasbled. **Special Academic Facilities/Equipment:** Art Gallery in Burbick Hall. Campbell School House **Computers:** 75% of classrooms, 100% of dorms, 90% of libraries, 100% of dining areas, 100% of student union, have wireless network access. Administrative functions (other than registration) can be performed online.

CAMPUS LIFE
Environment: Rural **Activities:** Campus Ministries; Choral groups; Concert band; Dance; Drama/theater; Jazz band; Literary magazine; Marching band; Music ensembles; Musical theater; Pep band; Radio station; Student government; Student newspaper; Television station; Yearbook 49 registered organizations, 2 honor societies, 2 religious organizations. 2 fraternities, 3 sororities. **Athletics (Intercollegiate):** *Men:* baseball, basketball, cross-country, soccer, track/field (outdoor), track/field (indoor). *Women:* basketball, cross-country, soccer, softball, track/field (outdoor), track/field (indoor), volleyball. **On-Campus Highlights:** Rex Pyles Arena, Burbick Hall, EJ and Emma's at the Cave, Wilcox Chapel, Jazzman's Café & Bakery **Environmental Initiatives:** recycling efforts

ADMISSIONS
Freshman Academic Profile: Average high school GPA 3.2. 11% in top 10% of high school class, 31% in top 25% of high school class, 69% in top 50% of high school class. 97% from public high schools. **Test Scores:** SAT Math middle 50% range 450-530. SAT EBRW middle 50% range 440-510. ACT middle 50% range 19-23. Minimum paper TOEFL 500. **Basis for Candidate Selection:** *Very important factors considered include:* rigor of secondary school record, academic GPA, standardized test scores. *Important factors considered include:* application essay. *Other factors considered include:* recommendation(s), interview, talent/ability, first generation, alumni/ae relation, level of applicant's interest. **Freshman Admission Requirements:** High school diploma is required and GED is accepted *Academic units required:* 4 English, 3 math, 3 science, 1 science labs, 1 social studies, *Academic units recommended:* 3 science labs, 1 foreign language, 3 social studies. **Freshman Admission Statistics:** 4,206 applied, 53.7% admitted, 15% enrolled. **Transfer Admission Requirements:** High school transcript, college transcript(s), statement of good standing from prior institution(s). Minimum college GPA of 2.0 required. Lowest grade transferable C. **General Admission Information:** Nonfall registration accepted. Admission may be deferred for a maximum of 1 year.

COSTS AND FINANCIAL AID
Annual tuition $23,930. Room and board $7,606. Required fees $210. Average book expense $800. **Required Forms and Deadlines:** FAFSA; State aid form.

Notification of Awards: Applicants will be notified of awards on a rolling basis beginning 3/1. **Types of Aid:** *Need-based scholarships/grants:* College/university scholarship or grant aid from institutional funds; Federal Nursing Scholarships; Federal Pell; Private scholarships; SEOG; State scholarships/grants. *Loans:* Direct PLUS loans; Direct Subsidized Stafford Loans; Direct Unsubsidized Stafford Loans. *Student Employment:* Federal Work-Study Program available. **Financial Aid Statistics:** 100% needy freshmen, 99% needy undergrads receive need-based scholarship or grant aid. 10% freshmen, 13% undergrads receive non-need-based scholarship or grant aid. 96% freshmen, 84% undergrads receive need-based self-help aid. 5% freshmen, 5% undergrads receive athletic scholarships. 100% freshmen, 99% undergrads receive any aid. 88% undergrads borrow to pay for school. Average cumulative indebtedness $23,715. **Criteria for awarding aid:** *Need-based:* Academics, Athletics, Music/drama, Religious affiliation *Non-need-based:* Academics, Athletics, Music/drama.

ALFRED UNIVERSITY

One Saxon Drive, Alfred, NY 14802-1205
Phone: 607-871-2115 · **Financial Aid Phone:** 607-871-2159
E-mail: admissions@alfred.edu · **CEEB Code:** 2005
Fax: 607-871-2198 · **Website:** www.alfred.edu · **ACT Code:** 2666

This private school was founded in 1836. It has a 600 acre campus.

RATINGS
Admissions Selectivity Rating: 81   **Fire Safety Rating:** 88   **Green Rating:** 60*

STUDENTS AND FACULTY
Enrollment: 1,929. **Student Body:** 51% female, 49% male, 24% out-of-state, 3% international (4 countries represented). Asian 2%, African American 8%, Caucasian 67%, Hispanic 7%, Native American <1%, Pacific Islander 0%, Two or more races 3%, Race unknown 11%.
Retention and Graduation: 75% freshmen return for sophomore year. 30% grads go on to further study within 1 year. **Faculty:** Student/faculty ratio 12:1. 159 full-time faculty, 45% are women. 0% of classes are taught by teaching assistants.

ACADEMICS
Degrees: Bachelor's; Doctoral/Research; Master's; Post-Master's certificate **Classes:** Most classes have 20-29 students. **Most popular majors:** Psychology, General; Ceramic Arts And Ceramics; Business/Commerce, General. **Special Study Options:** Cooperative education program; Cross-registration; Double major; Exchange student program (domestic); Honors program; Independent study; Internships; Liberal arts/career combination; Student-designed major; Study abroad; Teacher certification program. **Honors programs:** The Alfred University Honors Program is designed to enrich the lives of exceptional students. It has two components: an honors seminar—meets one evening a week and the senior thesis. **Disability Services offered to physically disabled students:** Note-taking services; Tape recorders; Tutors. **Career services:** Alumni network; Alumni services; Career assessment; Internships

FACILITIES
Housing: Apartments for single students; Coed dorms; Special housing for international students; Theme housing; Wellness housing 50% of campus accessible to physically disabled. **Special Academic Facilities/Equipment:** Art museums, carillon, language labs, electron microscope, observatory, extensive engineering equipment, performing arts center. **Computers:** 90% of classrooms, 100% of dorms, 100% of libraries, 100% of student union, have wireless network access. Students can register for classes online. Administrative functions (other than registration) can be performed online.

CAMPUS LIFE
Environment: Rural **Activities:** Campus Ministries; Choral groups; Concert band; Dance; Drama/theater; International Student Organization; Jazz band; Literary magazine; Music ensembles; Musical theater; Pep band; Radio station; Student government; Student newspaper; Student-run film society; Television station; Yearbook 90 registered organizations, 13 honor societies, 3 religious organizations. **Athletics (Intercollegiate):** *Men:* basketball, cross-country, diving, equestrian sports, football, lacrosse, skiing (downhill/alpine), soccer, swimming, tennis, track/field (outdoor), track/field (indoor). *Women:* basketball, cross-country, diving, equestrian sports, lacrosse, skiing (downhill/alpine), soccer, softball, swimming, tennis, track/field (outdoor), track/field (indoor), volleyball. **On-Campus Highlights:** Powell Campus Center, Binns Merrill

Hall, Schein-Joseph International Museum of Ceramic Art, John L. Stull Observatory, Robert Turner Student Art Gallery **Environmental Initiatives:** Campus-wide recycling program (paper, glass, plastic, electronics, printer/toner cartridges)

ADMISSIONS
Freshman Academic Profile: Average high school GPA 3.2. 16% in top 10% of high school class, 43% in top 25% of high school class, 84% in top 50% of high school class. **Test Scores:** SAT Math middle 50% range 510-610. SAT EBRW middle 50% range 490-590. ACT middle 50% range 22-27. Minimum internet-based TOEFL 80. Minimum paper TOEFL 550. **Basis for Candidate Selection:** *Very important factors considered include:* rigor of secondary school record, class rank, academic GPA, extracurricular activities, character/personal qualities. *Important factors considered include:* application essay, standardized test scores, recommendation(s), volunteer work, work experience. *Other factors considered include:* interview, talent/ability, first generation, racial/ethnic status, level of applicant's interest. **Freshman Admission Requirements:** High school diploma is required and GED is accepted *Academic units required:* 4 English, *Academic units recommended:* 4 English, 4 math, 3 science, 3 science labs, 1 foreign language, 3 social studies. **Freshman Admission Statistics:** 3,417 applied, 69.8% admitted, 22% enrolled. **Transfer Admission Requirements:** college transcript(s), statement of good standing from prior institution(s). Minimum college GPA of 2.5 required. Lowest grade transferable C. **General Admission Information:** Application fee $50. Priority deadline 2/1. Regular application deadline 8/1. Nonfall registration accepted. Admission may be deferred for a maximum of 1 year.

COSTS AND FINANCIAL AID
Annual tuition $27,824. Room and board $11,618. Required fees $950. Average book expense $1,150. **Required Forms and Deadlines:** Business/Farm Supplement; FAFSA; Institution's own financial aid form; Noncustodial PROFILE; State aid form. **Notification of Awards:** Applicants will be notified of awards on a rolling basis beginning 2/15. **Types of Aid:** *Need-based scholarships/grants:* College/university scholarship or grant aid from institutional funds; Federal Pell; Private scholarships; SEOG; State scholarships/grants. *Loans:* Direct PLUS loans; Direct Subsidized Stafford Loans; Direct Unsubsidized Stafford Loans. *Student Employment:* Federal Work-Study Program available. Institutional employment available. **Financial Aid Statistics:** 100% needy freshmen, 99% needy undergrads receive need-based scholarship or grant aid. 78% freshmen, 62% undergrads receive non-need-based scholarship or grant aid. 90% freshmen, 89% undergrads receive need-based self-help aid. 0% freshmen, 0% undergrads receive athletic scholarships. 96% freshmen, 92% undergrads receive any aid. **Criteria for awarding aid:** *Need-based:* Academics, Art *Non-need-based:* Academics, Art, Leadership, Music/drama.

ALICE LLOYD COLLEGE

100 Purpose Road, Pippa Passes, KY 41844
Phone: 606-368-6036
E-mail: admissions@alc.edu · **CEEB Code:** 1098
Fax: 606-368-6215 · **Website:** www.alc.edu · **ACT Code:** 1502

This private school was founded in 1923. It has a 225 acre campus.

RATINGS
Admissions Selectivity Rating: 85   · **Fire Safety Rating:** 93   **Green Rating:** 60*

STUDENTS AND FACULTY
Enrollment: 607. **Student Body:** 51% female, 49% male, 13% out-of-state, <1% international (1 countries represented). Asian <1%, African American 1%, Caucasian 99%, Hispanic 0%, Native American 0%, Race unknown 0%.
Retention and Graduation: 63% freshmen return for sophomore year. 55% grads go on to further study within 1 year. 35% grads pursue arts and sciences degrees. 5% grads pursue law degrees. 10% grads pursue business degrees. 5% grads pursue medical degrees. **Faculty:** Student/faculty ratio 18:1. 29 full-time faculty, 59% hold PhDs, 10% are members of minority groups, 41% are women. 0% of classes are taught by teaching assistants.

ACADEMICS
Degrees: Bachelor's **Most popular majors:** Education, General; Biology/Biological Sciences, General; Business/Commerce, General. **Special Study Options:** Cooperative education program; Double major; Honors program; Independent study; Internships; Liberal arts/career combination; Study abroad; Teacher certification program. **Disability Services offered to physically disabled students:** Reader services; Tutors. **Career services:** Alumni network; Alumni services; Career assessment; Internships; Regional alumni

FACILITIES

Housing: Men's dorms; Women's dorms 90% of campus accessible to physically disabled. **Special Academic Facilities/Equipment:** Photographic archives, oral history museum, Appalachian collection, on-campus day care center, kindergarten, elementary, and secondary school. **Computers:** 100% of classrooms, 50% of dorms, 100% of libraries, 100% of dining areas, 75% of common outdoor areas have wireless network access.

CAMPUS LIFE

Environment: Rural **Activities:** Choral groups; Drama/theater; Music ensembles; Musical theater; Pep band; Radio station; Student government; Student newspaper; Yearbook 19 registered organizations, 2 honor societies, 1 religious organization. **Athletics (Intercollegiate):** *Men:* baseball, basketball, cheerleading, cross-country, golf, tennis. *Women:* basketball, cheerleading, cross-country, golf, softball, tennis. **On-Campus Highlights:** Jerry Davis Student Center, Historical Tour, Grady Nutt Athletic Center, Campbell Arts Center, Cushing Hall

ADMISSIONS

Freshman Academic Profile: Average high school GPA 3.4. 30% in top 10% of high school class, 58% in top 25% of high school class, 86% in top 50% of high school class. 90% from public high schools. **Test Scores:** SAT Math middle 50% range 480-570. SAT EBRW middle 50% range 440-590. ACT middle 50% range 17-23. Minimum paper TOEFL 550. **Basis for Candidate Selection:** *Very important factors considered include:* rigor of secondary school record, standardized test scores, character/personal qualities, geographical residence. *Important factors considered include:* class rank, recommendation(s), alumni/ae relation, state residency. *Other factors considered include:* application essay, interview, extracurricular activities, talent/ability, volunteer work, work experience. **Freshman Admission Requirements:** High school diploma is required and GED is accepted *Academic units required:* 4 English, 3 math, 2 science, 2 social studies, 1 history, *Academic units recommended:* 4 English, 3 math, 2 science, 2 foreign language, 2 social studies. **Freshman Admission Statistics:** 994 applied, 55.9% admitted, 35% enrolled. **Transfer Admission Requirements:** High school transcript, college transcript(s), standardized test scores, statement of good standing from prior institution(s). Minimum college GPA of 2.0 required. Lowest grade transferable C. **General Admission Information:** Priority deadline 6/1. Regular application deadline 5/1. Nonfall registration accepted.

COSTS AND FINANCIAL AID

Room and board $4,250. Required fees $1,300. Average book expense $850. **Required Forms and Deadlines:** FAFSA. **Notification of Awards:** Applicants will be notified of awards on a rolling basis beginning 4/1. **Types of Aid:** *Need-based scholarships/grants:* College/university scholarship or grant aid from institutional funds; Federal Pell; Private scholarships; SEOG; State scholarships/grants. *Loans: Student Employment:* Federal Work-Study Program available. Institutional employment available. **Financial Aid Statistics:** 99% needy freshmen, 99% needy undergrads receive need-based scholarship or grant aid. 11% freshmen, 16% undergrads receive non-need-based scholarship or grant aid. 89% freshmen, 84% undergrads receive need-based self-help aid. 7% freshmen, 5% undergrads receive athletic scholarships. 100% freshmen, 100% undergrads receive any aid. **Criteria for awarding aid:** *Non-need-based:* Athletics, Minority status, State/district residency.

ALLEGHENY COLLEGE

520 North Main Street, Meadville, PA 16335
Phone: 814-332-4351 · **Financial Aid Phone:** 800-835-7780
E-mail: admissions@allegheny.edu · **CEEB Code:** 2006
Fax: 814-337-0431 · **Website:** www.allegheny.edu · **ACT Code:** 3520

This private school was founded in 1815. It has a 566 acre campus.

RATINGS

Admissions Selectivity Rating: 85   **Fire Safety Rating:** 86   **Green Rating:** 89

STUDENTS AND FACULTY

Enrollment: 1,762. **Student Body:** 54% female, 46% male, 50% out-of-state, 3% international (50 countries represented). Asian 3%, African American 9%, Caucasian 70%, Hispanic 9%, Native American <1%, Pacific Islander <1%, Two or more races 4%, Race unknown 3%.
Retention and Graduation: 81% freshmen return for sophomore year. 69%

freshmen graduate within 4 years. 75% freshmen graduate within 6 years. 31% grads go on to further study within 1 year. 8% grads pursue arts and sciences degrees. 3% grads pursue law degrees. 0% grads pursue business degrees. 8% grads pursue medical degrees. **Faculty:** Student/faculty ratio 10:1. 167 full-time faculty, 93% hold PhDs, 16% are members of minority groups, 49% are women. 0% of classes are taught by teaching assistants.

ACADEMICS

Degrees: Bachelor's **Classes:** Most classes have 20-29 students. Most lab/discussion sessions have 10-19 students. **Most popular majors:** Biology/Biological Sciences, General; Psychology, General; Economics, General. **Special Study Options:** Double major; Dual enrollment; English as a Second Language (ESL); Honors program; Independent study; Internships; Student-designed major; Study abroad. **Combined degree programs:** BA/MA; BA/MEng. **Disability Services offered to physically disabled students:** Note-taking services; Tape recorders; Tutors. **Career services:** Alumni network; Alumni services; Career assessment; Career/job search classes; Internships; Regional alumni

FACILITIES

Housing: Apartments for single students; Coed dorms; Fraternity/sorority housing; Men's dorms; Special housing for disabled student; Theme housing; Wellness housing; Women's dorms 50% of campus accessible to physically disabled. **Special Academic Facilities/Equipment:** Center For Communication Arts with a trap stage and green and blue screen room; radio and television stations; state-of-the-art, nationally acclaimed science complex; video conference facilities; planetarium; observatory; GIS lab; state-of-the-art language-learning center; smart classrooms; dance studios and performance spaces; art studios & galleries; world's largest solid-volume glass sculpture grouping; 283-acre Environmental Research Reserve; 80-acre protected forest; sustainable luminescent solar concentrator roof greenhouse; alumni center; comprehensive sports and fitness center; seismographic network station; Center for Political Participation; Center for Business & Economics; environmental roof garden; Living & Learning Residential Communities; Richard J. Cook Center for Environmental Science; Allegheny Gateway: Connecting classroom learning to real-world experience; Augmented Reality Sandbox; Creek Connections; 17 acre sustainable forest; state-of-the-art neuroscience & psychology facility. **Computers:** 50% of classrooms, 100% of dorms, 100% of libraries, 100% of dining areas, 100% of student union, 100% of common outdoor areas have wireless network access. Students can register for classes online. Administrative functions (other than registration) can be performed online.

CAMPUS LIFE

Environment: Town **Activities:** Campus Ministries; Choral groups; Concert band; Dance; Drama/theater; International Student Organization; Jazz band; Literary magazine; Model UN; Music ensembles; Musical theater; Opera; Radio station; Student government; Student newspaper; Symphony orchestra; Television station; Yearbook 113 registered organizations, 15 honor societies, 8 religious organizations. 5 fraternities, 5 sororities. **Athletics (Intercollegiate):** *Men:* baseball, basketball, cross-country, diving, football, golf, soccer, swimming, tennis, track/field (outdoor), track/field (indoor). *Women:* basketball, cross-country, diving, golf, lacrosse, soccer, softball, swimming, tennis, track/field (outdoor), track/field (indoor), volleyball. **On-Campus Highlights:** Rustic Bridge, Wise Sport and Fitness Center, Henderson Campus Center, Gator Quad, Grounds for Change Coffee House **Environmental Initiatives:** Climate action plan

ADMISSIONS

Freshman Academic Profile: Average high school GPA 3.5. 33% in top 10% of high school class, 65% in top 25% of high school class, 88% in top 50% of high school class. 86% from public high schools. **Test Scores:** SAT Math middle 50% range 560-650. SAT EBRW middle 50% range 580-670. ACT middle 50% range 23-29. Minimum internet-based TOEFL 80. Minimum paper TOEFL 550. **Basis for Candidate Selection:** *Very important factors considered include:* rigor of secondary school record, class rank, academic GPA. *Important factors considered include:* recommendation(s), interview, extracurricular activities, character/personal qualities, level of applicant's interest. *Other factors considered include:* application essay, standardized test scores, talent/ability, first generation, alumni/ae relation, geographical residence, racial/ethnic status, volunteer work, work experience. **Freshman Admission Requirements:** High school diploma is required and GED is accepted *Academic units required:* 4 English, 3 math, 3 science, 2 foreign language, 3 social studies, 1 academic elective. **Freshman Admission Statistics:** 5,114 applied, 67.9% admitted, 14% enrolled. **Transfer Admission Requirements:** High school transcript, college transcript(s), essay or personal statement, standardized test scores, Minimum college GPA of 2.5 required. Lowest grade transferable C. **General Admission Information:** Regular application deadline 2/15. Nonfall registration accepted. Admission may be deferred for a maximum of 1 year.

COSTS AND FINANCIAL AID

Annual tuition $47,040. Room and board $12,140. Required fees $500. Average book expense $1,000. **Required Forms and Deadlines:** FAFSA. **Notification of Awards:** Applicants will be notified of awards on a rolling basis beginning 12/1. **Types of Aid:** *Need-based scholarships/grants:* College/university scholarship or grant aid from institutional funds; Federal Pell; Private scholarships; SEOG; State scholarships/grants. *Loans:* Direct PLUS loans; Direct Subsidized Stafford Loans; Direct Unsubsidized Stafford Loans. *Student Employment:* Federal Work-Study Program available. Institutional employment available. **Financial Aid Statistics:** 100% needy freshmen, 100% needy undergrads receive need-based scholarship or grant aid. 15% freshmen, 17% undergrads receive non-need-based scholarship or grant aid. 85% freshmen, 84% undergrads receive need-based self-help aid. 0% freshmen, 0% undergrads receive athletic scholarships. 99% freshmen, 99% undergrads receive any aid. **Criteria for awarding aid:** *Need-based:* Academics, Minority status *Non-need-based:* Academics, Leadership, Minority status, State/district residency.

See page 882.

ALLEN COLLEGE

1825 Logan Avenue, Waterloo, IA 50703
Phone: 319-226-2000 · **Financial Aid Phone:** 319-226-2000
E-mail: Admissions@AllenCollege.edu
Fax: 319-226-2051 · **Website:** www.allencollege.edu · **ACT Code:** 30691

This private school was founded in 1989.

RATINGS

Admissions Selectivity Rating: 61   **Fire Safety Rating:** 63   **Green Rating:** 60*

STUDENTS AND FACULTY

Enrollment: 329. **Student Body:** 91% female, 9% male, 7% out-of-state, 1% international (4 countries represented). Asian 1%, African American 1%, Caucasian 90%, Hispanic 1%, Native American <1%, Pacific Islander <1%, Two or more races 2%, Race unknown 5%.
Retention and Graduation: 92% freshmen return for sophomore year. 10% grads go on to further study within 1 year. 0% grads pursue arts and sciences degrees. 0% grads pursue law degrees. 0% grads pursue business degrees. 0% grads pursue medical degrees. **Faculty:** Student/faculty ratio 11:1. 42 full-time faculty, 50% hold PhDs, 2% are members of minority groups, 95% are women. 0% of classes are taught by teaching assistants.

ACADEMICS

Degrees: Associate; Bachelor's; Certificate; Doctoral; Master's; Post-Master's certificate **Classes:** Most classes have 10-19 students. Most lab/discussion sessions have 10-19 students. **Most popular majors:** Health Services/Allied Health/Health Sciences, General; Registered Nursing/Registered Nurse. **Special Study Options:** Accelerated program; Cooperative education program; Distance learning; Honors program; Independent study; Internships. **Disability Services offered to physically disabled students:** Tutors.

FACILITIES

Housing: 100% of campus accessible to physically diasbled. **Computers:** 100% of classrooms, 100% of dorms, 100% of libraries, 100% of student union, 100% of common outdoor areas have wireless network access. Administrative functions (other than registration) can be performed online.

CAMPUS LIFE

Environment: City **Activities:** Choral groups; Student government 4 registered organizations, 1 honor society, 1 religious organization.

ADMISSIONS

Basis for Candidate Selection: *Important factors considered include:* rigor of secondary school record, class rank, academic GPA, application essay, standardized test scores, recommendation(s), extracurricular activities, character/personal qualities. *Other factors considered include:* interview, talent/ability, first generation, alumni/ae relation, racial/ethnic status, volunteer work, work experience, level of applicant's interest. **Freshman Admission Requirements:** High school diploma is required and GED is accepted *Academic units required:* 8 English, 6 math, 6 science, 6 social studies. **Transfer Admission Requirements:** High school transcript, college transcript(s), essay or personal statement, standardized test scores, Minimum college GPA of 2.7 required. Lowest grade transferable C. **General Admission Information:** Application fee $50. Priority deadline 2/1. Nonfall registration accepted.

COSTS AND FINANCIAL AID

Annual tuition $16,884. Room and board $7,281. Required fees $1,342. Average book expense $1,200. **Required Forms and Deadlines:** FAFSA; Institution's own financial aid form. **Notification of Awards:** Applicants

will be notified of awards on a rolling basis beginning 4/1. **Types of Aid:** *Need-based scholarships/grants:* College/university scholarship or grant aid from institutional funds; Federal Nursing Scholarships; Federal Pell; Private scholarships; SEOG; State scholarships/grants. *Loans:* Direct PLUS loans; Direct Subsidized Stafford Loans; Direct Unsubsidized Stafford Loans. *Student Employment:* Federal Work-Study Program available. **Financial Aid Statistics:** 100% needy freshmen, 88% needy undergrads receive need-based scholarship or grant aid. 15% undergrads receive non-need-based scholarship or grant aid. 100% freshmen, 87% undergrads receive need-based self-help aid. 0% freshmen, 0% undergrads receive athletic scholarships. 100% freshmen, 99% undergrads receive any aid. 0% undergrads borrow to pay for school. **Criteria for awarding aid:** *Need-based:* Academics, Alumni affiliation, Leadership, Minority status *Non-need-based:* Academics, Alumni affiliation, Leadership, Minority status, State/district residency.

ALMA COLLEGE

614 West Superior Street, Alma, MI 48801-1599
Phone: 989-463-7139 · **Financial Aid Phone:** 989-463-7347
E-mail: admissions@alma.edu · **CEEB Code:** 1010
Fax: 989-463-7057 · **Website:** www.alma.edu · **ACT Code:** 1958

This private school, affiliated with the Presbyterian Church, was founded in 1886. It has a 125 acre campus.

RATINGS

Admissions Selectivity Rating: 82   **Fire Safety Rating:** 72   **Green Rating:** 60*

STUDENTS AND FACULTY

Enrollment: 1,392. **Student Body:** 57% female, 43% male, 9% out-of-state, 2% international (10 countries represented). Asian 1%, African American 3%, Caucasian 78%, Hispanic 5%, Native American <1%, Pacific Islander <1%, Two or more races 3%, Race unknown 7%.
Retention and Graduation: 77% freshmen return for sophomore year. 56% freshmen graduate within 4 years. 68% freshmen graduate within 6 years. 26% grads go on to further study within 1 year. **Faculty:** Student/faculty ratio 12:1. 99 full-time faculty, 83% hold PhDs, 17% are members of minority groups, 45% are women. 0% of classes are taught by teaching assistants.

ACADEMICS

Degrees: Bachelor's **Classes:** Most classes have fewer than 10 students. Most lab/discussion sessions have 10-19 students. **Most popular majors:** Education, General; Biology, General; Health And Wellness, General. **Special Study Options:** Double major; Dual enrollment; Honors program; Independent study; Internships; Student-designed major; Study abroad; Teacher certification program. **Honors programs:** Students in the Presidential Honors Program participate in special seminar opportunities and enroll in courses designed for honors scholars. **Disability Services offered to physically disabled students:** Note-taking services; Reader services; Tape recorders; Tutors. **Career services:** Alumni services; Career assessment; Internships

FACILITIES

Housing: Apartments for single students; Coed dorms; Fraternity/sorority housing; Special housing for disabled student; Special housing for international students; Theme housing; Wellness housing 75% of campus accessible to physically diasbled. **Special Academic Facilities/Equipment:** Performing arts center, art gallery, science labs, planetarium, 200-acre ecological tract **Computers:** 60% of classrooms, 100% of libraries, 100% of dining areas, 100% of student union, have wireless network access. Students can register for classes online.

CAMPUS LIFE

Environment: Village **Activities:** Campus Ministries; Choral groups; Concert band; Dance; Drama/theater; International Student Organization; Jazz band; Literary magazine; Marching band; Model UN; Music ensembles; Student government; Student newspaper; Student-run film society; Symphony orchestra; Yearbook 75 registered organizations, 20 honor societies, 4 religious organizations. 6 fraternities, 5 sororities. **Athletics (Intercollegiate):** *Men:* baseball, basketball, cross-country, diving, football, golf, soccer, swimming, tennis, track/field (outdoor). *Women:* basketball, cross-country, diving, golf, soccer, softball, swimming, tennis, track/field (outdoor), volleyball. **On-Campus Highlights:** Library, Stone Center for Recreation, Hamilton Dining Commons, Remick Heritage Center, Hogan Center **Environmental Initiatives:** The Hogan Center is the first official LEED-certified building for green construction at Alma College and Gratiot County. The renovated Hogan Center and new Art Smith Arena were awarded LEED certification at the Silver level by the U.S. Green Building Council (USGBC) and verified by the Green Building Certification Institute (GBCI). LEED is the nation's preeminent program for the design, construction and operation of high performance green buildings. The arena serves as the primary venue for commencement, convocations, major speakers, concerts, athletics and other major events.

ADMISSIONS

Freshman Academic Profile: Average high school GPA 3.5. 18% in top 10% of high school class, 25% in top 25% of high school class, 84% in top 50% of high school class. **Test Scores:** SAT Math middle 50% range 510-600. SAT EBRW middle 50% range 520-630. ACT middle 50% range 20-27. Minimum internet-based TOEFL 79. Minimum paper TOEFL 550. **Basis for Candidate Selection:** *Very important factors considered include:* academic GPA, application essay, standardized test scores. *Important factors considered include:* rigor of secondary school record. *Other factors considered include:* class rank, recommendation(s), interview, extracurricular activities, talent/ability, character/personal qualities, alumni/ae relation, volunteer work, work experience, level of applicant's interest. **Freshman Admission Requirements:** High school diploma is required and GED is accepted *Academic units required:* 4 English, 3 math, 3 science, 3 social studies, *Academic units recommended:* 2 foreign language. **Freshman Admission Statistics:** 4,728 applied, 64.0% admitted, 13% enrolled. **Transfer Admission Requirements:** High school transcript, college transcript(s), statement of good standing from prior institution(s). Minimum college GPA of 3.0 required. Lowest grade transferable C. **General Admission Information:** Application fee $25. Nonfall registration accepted. Admission may be deferred for a maximum of 1 year.

COSTS AND FINANCIAL AID

Required Forms and Deadlines: FAFSA. **Notification of Awards:** Applicants will be notified of awards on a rolling basis beginning 12/15. **Types of Aid:** *Need-based scholarships/grants:* College/university scholarship or grant aid from institutional funds; Federal Pell; Private scholarships; SEOG; State scholarships/grants. *Loans:* Direct PLUS loans; Direct Subsidized Stafford Loans; Direct Unsubsidized Stafford Loans. *Student Employment:* Federal Work-Study Program available. Institutional employment available. **Financial Aid Statistics:** 100% needy freshmen, 99% needy undergrads receive need-based scholarship or grant aid. 12% freshmen, 12% undergrads receive non-need-based scholarship or grant aid. 85% freshmen, 81% undergrads receive need-based self-help aid. 0% freshmen, 0% undergrads receive athletic scholarships. 99% freshmen, 99% undergrads receive any aid. 83% undergrads borrow to pay for school. Average cumulative indebtedness $36,046. **Criteria for awarding aid:** *Non-need-based:* Academics, Alumni affiliation, Art, Minority status, Music/drama, Religious affiliation.

ALVERNO COLLEGE

P.O. Box 343922, Milwaukee, WI 53234-3922
Phone: 414-382-6101 · **Financial Aid Phone:** 414-382-6046
E-mail: admissions@alverno.edu · **CEEB Code:** 1012
Fax: 414-382-6055 · **Website:** www.alverno.edu · **ACT Code:** 4558

This private school, affiliated with the Roman Catholic Church, was founded in 1887. It has a 47 acre campus.

RATINGS

Admissions Selectivity Rating: 75   **Fire Safety Rating:** 82   **Green Rating:** 72

STUDENTS AND FACULTY

Enrollment: 1,283. **Student Body:** 100% female, 0% male, 7% out-of-state, <1% international (7 countries represented). Asian 6%, African American 13%, Caucasian 49%, Hispanic 27%, Native American 1%, Pacific Islander <1%, Two or more races 4%, Race unknown 0%.
Retention and Graduation: 71% freshmen return for sophomore year. 12% freshmen graduate within 4 years. 45% freshmen graduate within 6 years. **Faculty:** Student/faculty ratio 10:1. 87 full-time faculty, 70% hold PhDs, 8% are members of minority groups, 79% are women. 0% of classes are taught by teaching assistants.

ACADEMICS

Degrees: Associate; Bachelor's; Doctoral/Professional; Master's; Post-Bachelor's certificate; Post-Master's certificate **Classes:** Most classes have 20-29 students. Most lab/discussion sessions have 20-29 students. **Most popular majors:** Education, General; Registered Nursing/Registered Nurse; Business Administration And Management, General. **Special Study Options:** Accelerated program; Double major; Honors program; Independent study; Internships; Student-designed major; Study abroad; Teacher certification program. **Disability Services offered to physically disabled students:** Note-taking services; Reader services; Tape recorders; Tutors. **Career services:** Alumni services; Career assessment; Career/job search classes

FACILITIES

Housing: Theme housing; Women's dorms 95% of campus accessible to physically diasbled. **Special Academic Facilities/Equipment:** Art & Culture Gallery, Career Center, Fitness center, Reiman Gymnasium, Nursing Skills Lab, Student centered multi-media production facility, Diagnostic Digital Portfolio, computer center, science labs, theatre venue **Computers:** 35% of classrooms, 100% of dorms, 100% of libraries, 100% of dining areas, 100% of student union, have wireless network access. Students can register for classes online. Administrative functions (other than registration) can be performed online.

CAMPUS LIFE

Environment: Metropolis **Activities:** Campus Ministries; Choral groups; Dance; Drama/theater; International Student Organization; Literary magazine; Model UN; Music ensembles; Radio station; Student government; Student newspaper 37 registered organizations, 1 honor society, 1 religious organization. 2 sororities. **Athletics (Intercollegiate):** *Women:* basketball, cross-country, soccer, softball, tennis, volleyball. **On-Campus Highlights:** Inferno Cafe, Alverno Library, Alexia Hall, Nursing Simulation Center, Galleria, LaVerna Commons **Environmental Initiatives:** Renovated and new construction totaling 13,000 sq ft utilizing LED lighting throughout project.

ADMISSIONS

Freshman Academic Profile: Average high school GPA 3.0. 73% from public high schools. **Test Scores:** ACT middle 50% range 17-22. Minimum internet-based TOEFL 68. Minimum paper TOEFL 520. **Basis for Candidate Selection:** *Very important factors considered include:* academic GPA, standardized test scores. *Important factors considered include:* rigor of secondary school record. *Other factors considered include:* application essay, recommendation(s), interview, extracurricular activities, talent/ability, character/personal qualities, volunteer work, work experience, level of applicant's interest. **Freshman Admission Requirements:** High school diploma is required and GED is accepted *Academic units required:* 4 English, 3 math, 3 science, 3 social studies, 4 academic electives, *Academic units recommended:* 2 foreign language. **Freshman Admission Statistics:** 610 applied, 77.9% admitted, 42% enrolled. **Transfer Admission Requirements:** High school transcript, college transcript(s), essay or personal statement, Minimum college GPA of 2.0 required. Lowest grade transferable C. **General Admission Information:** Nonfall registration accepted. Admission may be deferred for a maximum of 1 year.

COSTS AND FINANCIAL AID

Required Forms and Deadlines: FAFSA. **Notification of Awards:** Applicants will be notified of awards on a rolling basis beginning 11/1. **Types of Aid:** *Need-based scholarships/grants:* College/university scholarship or grant aid from institutional funds; Federal Pell; Private scholarships; SEOG; State scholarships/grants. *Loans:* Direct PLUS loans; Direct Subsidized Stafford Loans; Direct Unsubsidized Stafford Loans. *Student Employment:* Federal Work-Study Program available. Institutional employment available. **Financial Aid Statistics:** 100% needy freshmen, 99% needy undergrads receive need-based scholarship or grant aid. 90% freshmen, 88% undergrads receive non-need-based scholarship or grant aid. 96% freshmen, 89% undergrads receive need-based self-help aid. 0% freshmen, 0% undergrads receive athletic scholarships. 99% freshmen, 94% undergrads receive any aid. 88% undergrads borrow to pay for school. Average cumulative indebtedness $41,044. **Criteria for awarding aid:** *Non-need-based:* Academics, Alumni affiliation.

AMERICAN INTERNATIONAL COLLEGE

1000 State Street, Springfield, MA 01109-3184
Phone: 413-205-3201 · **Financial Aid Phone:** (413) 205-3270
E-mail: inquiry@aic.edu · **CEEB Code:** 3002
Fax: 413-205-3051 · **Website:** www.aic.edu · **ACT Code:** 1772

This private school was founded in 1885. It has a 58 acre campus.

RATINGS

Admissions Selectivity Rating: 72   **Fire Safety Rating:** 89   **Green Rating:** 60*

STUDENTS AND FACULTY

Enrollment: 1,478. **Student Body:** 60% female, 40% male, 39% out-of-state, 3% international (27 countries represented). Asian 1%, African American 25%, Caucasian 39%, Hispanic 14%, Native American <1%, Pacific Islander <1%, Two or more races 3%, Race unknown 14%.
Retention and Graduation: 72% freshmen return for sophomore year. 34% grads go on to further study within 1 year. **Faculty:** Student/faculty ratio 14:1. 74 full-time faculty, 64% hold PhDs, 16% are members of minority groups, 58% are women. 0% of classes are taught by teaching assistants.

ACADEMICS

Degrees: Associate; Bachelor's; Doctoral/Professional; Doctoral/Research; Master's; Post-Bachelor's certificate; Post-Master's certificate; Terminal Associate **Classes:** Most classes have 10-19 students. Most lab/discussion sessions have 10-19 students. **Most popular majors:** Psychology, General; Criminal Justice And Corrections; Registered Nursing/Registered Nurse. **Special Study Options:** Accelerated program; Cross-registration; Distance learning; Double major; Dual enrollment; Honors program; Independent study; Internships; Study abroad; Teacher certification program. **Honors programs:** Four Year Honors program open to students in any major with appropriate credentials. **Combined degree programs:** BA/MA. **Disability Services offered to physically disabled students:** Note-taking services; Reader services; Tape recorders; Tutors. **Career services:** Alumni services; Career assessment; Career/job search classes; Internships

FACILITIES

Housing: Apartments for single students; Coed dorms; Theme housing; Women's dorms 90% of campus accessible to physically diasbled. **Computers:** 100% of classrooms, 90% of dorms, 100% of libraries, 100% of dining areas, 100% of student union, 100% of common outdoor areas have wireless network access. Students can register for classes online. Administrative functions (other than registration) can be performed online.

CAMPUS LIFE

Environment: City **Activities:** Campus Ministries; Dance; Drama/theater; International Student Organization; Literary magazine; Model UN; Pep band; Student government; Student newspaper; Yearbook 45 registered organizations, 5 honor societies, 3 religious organizations. 4 fraternities, 5 sororities. **Athletics (Intercollegiate):** *Men:* baseball, basketball, cheerleading, cross-country, football, golf, ice hockey, lacrosse, soccer, tennis, track/field (outdoor), track/field (indoor), wrestling. *Women:* basketball, cheerleading, cross-country, field hockey, lacrosse, soccer, softball, tennis, track/field (outdoor), track/field (indoor), volleyball. **On-Campus Highlights:** Courniotes Hall—Health Sciences, Karen Sprague Cultural Arts Center, Butova & Metcalf Gymnasiums, Dining Commons, The Stinger

ADMISSIONS

Freshman Academic Profile: Average high school GPA 2.8. **Test Scores:** SAT Math middle 50% range 400-500. SAT EBRW middle 50% range 390-480. ACT middle 50% range 16-23. **Basis for Candidate Selection:** *Very important factors considered include:* academic GPA, standardized test scores. *Important factors considered include:* rigor of secondary school record. *Other factors considered include:* application essay, recommendation(s), extracurricular activities, talent/ability, character/personal qualities, first generation, alumni/ae relation, volunteer work, work experience, level of applicant's interest. **Freshman Admission Requirements:** High school diploma is required and GED is accepted *Academic units recommended:* 4 English, 3 math, 2 science, 2 science labs, 1 foreign language, 2 social studies, 4 academic electives. **Freshman Admission Statistics:** 1,522 applied, 86.4% admitted, 26% enrolled. **Transfer Admission Requirements:** High school transcript, college transcript(s), Minimum college GPA of 2.0 required. Lowest grade transferable C. **General Admission Information:** Nonfall registration accepted. Admission may be deferred for a maximum of 1 year.

COSTS AND FINANCIAL AID

Annual tuition $33,140. Room and board $13,590. Required fees $60. Average book expense $1,235. **Required Forms and Deadlines:** FAFSA. **Notification of Awards:** Applicants will be notified of awards on a rolling basis beginning 3/1. **Types of Aid:** *Need-based scholarships/grants:* College/university scholarship or grant aid from institutional funds; Federal Nursing Scholarships; Federal Pell; Private scholarships; SEOG; State scholarships/grants. *Loans:* Direct PLUS loans; Direct Subsidized Stafford Loans; Direct Unsubsidized Stafford Loans. *Student Employment:* Federal Work-Study Program available. Institutional employment available. **Financial Aid Statistics:** 100% needy freshmen, 100% needy undergrads receive need-based scholarship or grant aid. 10% freshmen, 10% undergrads receive non-need-based scholarship or grant aid. 89% freshmen, 89% undergrads receive need-based self-help aid. 7% freshmen, 9% undergrads receive athletic scholarships. 100% freshmen, 85% undergrads receive any aid. 91% undergrads borrow to pay for school. Average cumulative indebtedness $22,976. **Criteria for awarding aid:** *Non-need-based:* Academics, Athletics.

AMERICAN JEWISH UNIVERSITY

Familian Campus, 15600 Mulholland Drive, Bel Air, CA 90077
Phone: 310-440-1247 · **Financial Aid Phone:** 310-440-1252
E-mail: admissions@ajula.edu · **CEEB Code:** 4876
Fax: 310-471-3657 · **Website:** www.ajula.edu · **ACT Code:** 462

This private school, affiliated with the Jewish Church, was founded in 1947. It has a 28 acre campus.

RATINGS
Admissions Selectivity Rating: 73   **Fire Safety Rating:** 76   **Green Rating:** 60*

STUDENTS AND FACULTY

Enrollment: 120. **Student Body:** 49% female, 51% male, 15% out-of-state, 5% international (6 countries represented). Asian 2%, African American 2%, Caucasian 48%, Hispanic 3%, Native American 2%, Pacific Islander 0%, Two or more races 0%, Race unknown 37%.
Retention and Graduation: 58% freshmen return for sophomore year.
Faculty: Student/faculty ratio 7:1. 8 full-time faculty, 88% hold PhDs, 38% are women. 0% of classes are taught by teaching assistants.

ACADEMICS

Degrees: Bachelor's; Master's **Classes:** Most classes have 20-29 students. Most lab/discussion sessions have 20-29 students. **Most popular majors:** Political Science And Government, Other; Bioethics/Medical Ethics; Business/Commerce, General. **Special Study Options:** Cross-registration; Double major; Independent study; Internships; Student-designed major; Study abroad. **Career services:** Alumni network; Alumni services; Career assessment; Career/job search classes; Internships

FACILITIES

Housing: Apartments for married students; Apartments for single students; Coed dorms; Special housing for disabled students 90% of campus accessible to physically diasbled. **Special Academic Facilities/Equipment:** Art Gallery, Ostrow Library **Computers:** 100% of dorms, 100% of libraries, 100% of student union, 50% of common outdoor areas have wireless network access. Administrative functions (other than registration) can be performed online.

CAMPUS LIFE

Environment: Metropolis **Activities:** Choral groups; Dance; Drama/theater; Literary magazine; Student government; Student newspaper 17 registered organizations, 1 religious organization. **On-Campus Highlights:** Residence Halls, Auerbach Student Union, The Berg, our kosher dining hall, Sculpture Garden, Ostrow Library **Environmental Initiatives:** Energy Management

ADMISSIONS

Freshman Academic Profile: Average high school GPA 3.1. 0% in top 10% of high school class, 33% in top 25% of high school class, 67% in top 50% of high school class. 36% from public high schools. **Test Scores:** SAT Math middle 50% range 500-570. SAT EBRW middle 50% range 490-520. ACT middle 50% range 17-22. Minimum internet-based TOEFL 75. Minimum paper TOEFL 530. **Basis for Candidate Selection:** *Very important factors considered include:* application essay, recommendation(s), interview, extracurricular activities, talent/ability, character/personal qualities, volunteer work. *Important factors considered include:* academic GPA, standardized test scores, level of applicant's interest. *Other factors considered include:* rigor of secondary school record, class rank, alumni/ae relation, geographical residence, state residency, religious affiliation/commitment, work experience. **Freshman Admission Requirements:** High school diploma is required and GED is accepted **Freshman Admission Statistics:** 28 applied, 96.4% admitted, 48% enrolled. **Transfer Admission Requirements:** college transcript(s), essay or personal statement, Minimum college GPA of N/A required. Lowest grade transferable C. **General Admission Information:** Application fee $35. Regular application deadline 5/31. Nonfall registration accepted. Admission may be deferred for a maximum of 1 year.

COSTS AND FINANCIAL AID

Annual tuition $26,784. Room and board $14,082. Required fees $1,712. Average book expense $1,710. **Required Forms and Deadlines:** FAFSA; Institution's own financial aid form. **Notification of Awards:** Applicants will be notified of awards on a rolling basis beginning 1/1. **Types of Aid:** *Need-based scholarships/grants:* College/university scholarship or grant aid from institutional funds; Federal Pell; Private scholarships; SEOG; State scholarships/grants. *Loans:* Direct PLUS loans; Direct Subsidized Stafford Loans; Direct Unsubsidized Stafford Loans. *Student Employment:* Federal Work-Study Program available. Institutional employment available. **Financial Aid Statistics:** 27% needy freshmen, 51% needy undergrads receive need-based scholarship or grant aid. 35% freshmen, 54% undergrads receive non-need-based scholarship or grant aid. 13% freshmen, 34% undergrads receive need-based self-help aid. 0% freshmen, 0% undergrads receive athletic scholarships. **Criteria for awarding aid:** *Need-based:* Academics *Non-need-based:* Leadership, Minority status, Music/drama, State/district residency.

AMERICAN MILITARY UNIVERSITY

111 W. Congress St., Charles Town, WV 25414
Phone: (877) 777-9081 · **Financial Aid Phone:** 877-468-6268
E-mail: info@apus.edu · **Website:** www.apus.edu

This proprietary school was founded in 1991.

RATINGS
Admissions Selectivity Rating: 0   **Fire Safety Rating:** 60*   **Green Rating:** 74

STUDENTS AND FACULTY
Enrollment: 37,826. **Student Body:** 36% female, 64% male, 1% international (51 countries represented). Asian 2%, African American 17%, Caucasian 57%, Hispanic 11%, Native American 1%, Pacific Islander 1%, Two or more races 4%, Race unknown 6%.
Faculty: Student/faculty ratio 19:1. 404 full-time faculty, 54% hold PhDs, 15% are members of minority groups, 57% are women. 0% of classes are taught by teaching assistants.

ACADEMICS
Degrees: Associate; Bachelor's; Certificate; Master's; Post-Bachelor's certificate **Most popular majors:** General Studies; International/Global Studies; Business Administration And Management, General. **Special Study Options:** Distance learning; Internships; Teacher certification program. **Honors programs:** Alpha Phi Sigma Delta Mu Delta Epsilon Pi Phi Golden Key Pi Gamma Mu Sigma Beta Delta Sigma Iota Rho. **Career services:** Alumni network; Alumni services; Career assessment

CAMPUS LIFE
Environment: Rural **Environmental Initiatives:** Green building practices (all new construction built to at least USGBC LEED Silver standards and extensive adaptive reuse practices for existing [often historic] buildings on campus)

ADMISSIONS
Test Scores: Minimum paper TOEFL 520. **Freshman Admission Requirements:** High school diploma is required and GED is accepted **General Admission Information:** Nonfall registration accepted. Admission may be deferred for a maximum of 1 year.

COSTS AND FINANCIAL AID
Required fees $50. **Required Forms and Deadlines:** FAFSA; Institution's own financial aid form. **Notification of Awards:** Applicants will be notified of awards on or about 3/1. **Types of Aid:** *Need-based scholarships/grants:* College/university scholarship or grant aid from institutional funds; Federal Pell; Private scholarships. *Loans:* Direct PLUS loans; Direct Subsidized Stafford Loans; Direct Unsubsidized Stafford Loans. **Financial Aid Statistics:** 91% needy freshmen, 84% needy undergrads receive need-based scholarship or grant aid. 19% freshmen, 34% undergrads receive non-need-based scholarship or grant aid. 91% freshmen, 78% undergrads receive need-based self-help aid. 0% freshmen, 0% undergrads receive athletic scholarships. 33% undergrads borrow to pay for school. Average cumulative indebtedness $34,395.

AMERICAN PUBLIC UNIVERSITY SYSTEM

111 W Congress St, Charles Town, WV 25414
Website: www.apus.edu

This proprietary school was founded in 1991.

RATINGS
Admissions Selectivity Rating: 0   **Fire Safety Rating:** 60*   **Green Rating:** 60*

STUDENTS AND FACULTY
Enrollment: 31,670. **Student Body:** 36% female, 64% male, 1% international. Asian 2%, African American 16%, Caucasian 56%, Hispanic 12%, Native American 1%, Pacific Islander 1%, Two or more races 4%, Race unknown 7%.
Retention and Graduation: 92% freshmen return for sophomore year.
Faculty: Student/faculty ratio 20:1. 373 full-time faculty, 57% hold PhDs, 28% are members of minority groups, 57% are women.

ACADEMICS
Degrees: Associate; Bachelor's; Certificate; Doctoral/Research; Master's; Post-Bachelor's certificate **Classes:** Most classes have 10-19 students. **Special Study Options:** Distance learning; Internships. **Disability Services offered to physically disabled students:** Note-taking services; Reader services; Tape recorders. Alumni network; Alumni services; Career assessment; Internships; Regional alumni

CAMPUS LIFE
Environment: Rural

ADMISSIONS
Freshman Admission Requirements: High school diploma is required and GED is accepted

AMERICAN UNIVERSITY

4400 Massachusetts Ave., NW, Washington, DC 20016-8001
Phone: 202-885-6000 · **Financial Aid Phone:** 202-885-6500
E-mail: admissions@american.edu · **CEEB Code:** 5007
Fax: 202-885-1025 · **Website:** www.american.edu · **ACT Code:** 648

This private school, affiliated with the Methodist Church, was founded in 1893. It has a 84 acre campus.

RATINGS
Admissions Selectivity Rating: 93   **Fire Safety Rating:** 84   **Green Rating:** 99

STUDENTS AND FACULTY
Enrollment: 7,433. **Student Body:** 63% female, 37% male, 82% out-of-state, 8% international (97 countries represented). Asian 7%, African American 7%, Caucasian 57%, Hispanic 14%, Native American <1%, Pacific Islander <1%, Two or more races 4%, Race unknown 3%.
Retention and Graduation: 90% freshmen return for sophomore year. 76% freshmen graduate within 4 years. 79% freshmen graduate within 6 years. 33% grads go on to further study within 1 year. **Faculty:** Student/faculty ratio 11:1. 793 full-time faculty, 95% hold PhDs, 19% are members of minority groups, 50% are women. 0% of classes are taught by teaching assistants.

ACADEMICS
Degrees: Associate; Bachelor's; Certificate; Doctoral/Professional; Doctoral/Research; Master's; Post-Bachelor's certificate **Classes:** Most classes have fewer than 10 students. **Most popular majors:** International Relations And Affairs; Political Science And Government, General; Business/Commerce, General. **Special Study Options:** Accelerated program; Distance learning; Double major; English as a Second Language (ESL); Honors program; Independent study; Internships; Liberal arts/career combination; Student-designed major; Study abroad; Teacher certification program; Weekend college. **Honors programs:** The American University Honors Program (AU Honors) is a rigorous, hands-on, four-year program dedicated to exploring real world issues through an interdisciplinary lens. AU Honors students are dedicated, hard-working, intelligent, and committed to expanding their worldview. Enrolling small cohorts of talented students each year, the program is designed to challenge students with the desire and ability to perform at the highest level. AU Honors students receive a $30,000 undergraduate merit award each year—a $20,000 Presidential Scholarship and a $10,000 AU Honors Scholarship. **Combined degree programs:** BA/MA. **Disability Services offered to physically disabled students:** Note-taking services; Reader services; Tape recorders; Tutors. **Career services:** Alumni network; Alumni services; Career assessment; Career/job search classes; Internships; Regional alumni

FACILITIES
Housing: Coed dorms; Special housing for disabled student; Theme housing 95% of campus accessible to physically disabled. **Special Academic Facilities/Equipment:** Student-run Radio and TV Facilities, Watkins Art Gallery, Katzen Arts Center, Experimental Theater,Greenberg Theater, Friedheim Journalism Center, William I Jacobs Fitness Center, Game Lab, Kay Spiritual Life Center (interdenominational), Language Resource Center, Multimedia Center **Computers:** 100% of classrooms, 100% of dorms, 100% of libraries, 100% of dining areas, 100% of student union, 100% of common outdoor areas have wireless network access. Students can register for classes online. Administrative functions (other than registration) can be performed online.

CAMPUS LIFE

Environment: Metropolis **Activities:** Campus Ministries; Choral groups; Concert band; Dance; Drama/theater; International Student Organization; Jazz band; Literary magazine; Model UN; Music ensembles; Musical theater; Opera; Pep band; Radio station; Student government; Student newspaper; Student-run film society; Symphony orchestra; Television station; Yearbook 180 registered organizations, 15 honor societies, 15 religious organizations. 11 fraternities, 12 sororities. **Athletics (Intercollegiate):** *Men:* basketball, cross-country, diving, soccer, swimming, track/field (outdoor), track/field (indoor), wrestling. *Women:* basketball, cross-country, diving, field hockey, lacrosse, soccer, swimming, track/field (outdoor), track/field (indoor), volleyball. **On-Campus Highlights:** Mary Graydon Center (student activties hub and dining venues), Sports Center Complex and Jacobs Fitness Center, Katzen Arts Center, The Quad (large grassy area in the middle campus), Davenport Lounge (student-operated coffee shop and lounge) **Environmental Initiatives:** A Climate Action Plan which calls for achieving carbon neutrality by 2020.

ADMISSIONS

Test Scores: SAT Math middle 50% range 570-660. SAT EBRW middle 50% range 610-690. ACT middle 50% range 26-30. Minimum internet-based TOEFL 80. Minimum paper TOEFL 550. **Basis for Candidate Selection:** *Very important factors considered include:* rigor of secondary school record, academic GPA, level of applicant's interest. *Important factors considered include:* application essay, recommendation(s), extracurricular activities, talent/ability, character/personal qualities, volunteer work. *Other factors considered include:* standardized test scores, first generation, alumni/ae relation, geographical residence, racial/ethnic status, work experience. **Freshman Admission Requirements:** High school diploma is required and GED is accepted *Academic units required:* 4 English, 3 math, 3 science, 2 science labs, 2 foreign language, 2 social studies, 3 academic electives, *Academic units recommended:* 4 English, 4 math, 4 science, 3 foreign language, 4 social studies, 4 academic electives. **Freshman Admission Statistics:** 18,699 applied, 29.4% admitted, 32% enrolled. **Transfer Admission Requirements:** college transcript(s), essay or personal statement, Minimum college GPA of 2.5 required. Lowest grade transferable C. **General Admission Information:** Application fee $70. Regular application deadline 1/15. Nonfall registration accepted. Admission may be deferred for a maximum of 1 year.

COSTS AND FINANCIAL AID

Annual tuition $47,640. Room and board $14,880. Required fees $819. Average book expense $800. **Required Forms and Deadlines:** CSS/Financial Aid PROFILE; FAFSA. **Notification of Awards:** Applicants will be notified of awards on or about 4/1. **Types of Aid:** *Need-based scholarships/grants:* College/university scholarship or grant aid from institutional funds; Federal Pell; Private scholarships; SEOG. *Loans:* Direct PLUS loans; Direct Subsidized Stafford Loans; Direct Unsubsidized Stafford Loans. *Student Employment:* Federal Work-Study Program available. Institutional employment available. **Financial Aid Statistics:** 84% needy undergrads receive need-based scholarship or grant aid. 27% freshmen, 31% undergrads receive non-need-based scholarship or grant aid. 94% freshmen, 93% undergrads receive need-based self-help aid. 2% freshmen, 2% undergrads receive athletic scholarships. 89% freshmen, 71% undergrads receive any aid. 65% undergrads borrow to pay for school. Average cumulative indebtedness $32,394. **Criteria for awarding aid:** *Need-based:* Academics, Leadership *Non-need-based:* Academics, Alumni affiliation, Athletics, Leadership, Minority status, Music/drama, Religious affiliation, State/district residency.

AMERICAN UNIVERSITY IN CAIRO

AUC Avenue, P.O. Box 74 New Cairo 11835, New Cairo,
Phone: 20.2.26151459 • **Financial Aid Phone:** 2.02.2615-3865
E-mail: enrolauc@aucegypt.edu
Website: www.aucegypt.edu

This private school was founded in 1919. It has a 260 acre campus.

RATINGS

Admissions Selectivity Rating: 90   **Fire Safety Rating:** 94   **Green Rating:** 87

STUDENTS AND FACULTY

Enrollment: 5,474. **Student Body:** 54% female, 46% male, (40 countries represented).
Retention and Graduation: 93% freshmen return for sophomore year.
Faculty: Student/faculty ratio 11:1. 419 full-time faculty, 73% hold PhDs, 49% are women. 0% of classes are taught by teaching assistants.

ACADEMICS

Degrees: Bachelor's; Diploma; Doctoral; Master's **Classes:** Most classes have 10-19 students. **Most popular majors:** Mechanical Engineering; Construction Engineering; Business Administration, Management And Operations, Other. **Special Study Options:** Double major; English as a Second Language (ESL); Independent study; Internships; Liberal arts/career combination; Study abroad. **Honors programs:** Honors Program in Political Science (BA) **Combined degree programs:** BA/MA. **Disability Services offered to physically disabled students:** Note-taking services; Reader services. **Career services:** Alumni network; Alumni services; Career assessment; Career/job search classes; Internships; Regional alumni

FACILITIES

Housing: Apartments for single students; Men's dorms; Special housing for disabled student; Theme housing; Women's dorms 100% of campus accessible to physically diasbled. **Special Academic Facilities/Equipment:** Rare Books and Special Collections Library http://library.aucegypt.edu/rbscl/index.html **Computers:** 100% of classrooms, 100% of dorms, 100% of libraries, 100% of dining areas, 100% of student union, 100% of common outdoor areas have wireless network access. Students can register for classes online. Administrative functions (other than registration) can be performed online.

CAMPUS LIFE

Environment: Metropolis **Activities:** Choral groups; Concert band; Dance; Drama/theater; International Student Organization; Model UN; Music ensembles; Student government; Student newspaper; Student-run film society 62 registered organizations. **Athletics (Intercollegiate):** *Men:* basketball, boxing, fencing, football, gymnastics, handball, rugby, soccer, squash, swimming, table tennis, tennis, track/field (outdoor), volleyball, water polo, wrestling. *Women:* basketball, fencing, football, gymnastics, handball, soccer, squash, swimming, table tennis, tennis, track/field (outdoor), volleyball. **On-Campus Highlights:** Food Court, Athletic Facility, Library **Environmental Initiatives:** 1. AUC established a continuous engagement in United Nations Global Compact. The UN Global Compact is the world's largest sustainability initiative, and it calls on global organizations to align their operations with 10 principles on human rights, labor, the environment and anti-corruption. The Office of Sustainability submitted AUC's first Communication on Engagement to the United Nations Global Compact headquarters in New York City. The report is an inclusive of the state of operations of the office and future initiatives. Further details on the work of the Office of Sustainability to integrate environmental and social sustainability into the culture and structure of the University referenced in the website. (https://www.unglobalcompact.org/participation/report/cop/create-and submit/detail/281861)

ADMISSIONS

Test Scores: SAT Math middle 50% range 540-630. SAT EBRW middle 50% range 510-590. Minimum internet-based TOEFL 48. Minimum paper TOEFL 460. **Basis for Candidate Selection:** *Very important factors considered include:* academic GPA, standardized test scores. *Important factors considered include:* recommendation(s), alumni/ae relation. *Other factors considered include:* application essay, extracurricular activities, character/personal qualities, geographical residence, volunteer work, work experience. **Freshman Admission Requirements:** High school diploma is required and GED is accepted *Academic units recommended:* 3 English, 3 math, 2 science, 2 foreign language, 3 social studies. **Freshman Admission Statistics:** 2,387 applied, 53.9% admitted, 72% enrolled. **Transfer Admission Requirements:** High school transcript, college transcript(s), essay or personal statement, standardized test scores, statement of good standing from prior institution(s). Minimum college GPA of 2.0 required. Lowest grade transferable C. **General Admission Information:** Application fee $85. Regular application deadline 1/3. Nonfall registration accepted. Admission may be deferred for a maximum of One semester.

COSTS AND FINANCIAL AID

Required Forms and Deadlines: Institution's own financial aid form. **Types of Aid:** *Need-based scholarships/grants:* College/university scholarship or grant aid from institutional funds; Federal Pell; SEOG; State scholarships/grants. *Loans:* Direct PLUS loans; Direct Subsidized Stafford Loans; Direct Unsubsidized Stafford Loans. **Financial Aid Statistics:** 16% freshmen, 56% undergrads receive non-need-based scholarship or grant aid. 2% freshmen, 0% undergrads receive need-based self-help aid. 1% freshmen, 2% undergrads receive athletic scholarships. 63% freshmen, 62% undergrads receive any aid. **Criteria for awarding aid:** *Need-based:* Academics, Leadership *Non-need-based:* Academics, Athletics, Music/drama.

AMERICAN UNIVERSITY OF ROME

Via Pietro Roselli 4, Rome, RM 00153
Phone: +39.06.5833.0919
E-mail: admissions@aur.edu
Website: http://www.aur.edu/

This private school was founded in 1969.

RATINGS
Admissions Selectivity Rating: 0   Fire Safety Rating: 60*   Green Rating: 60*

STUDENTS AND FACULTY
Student Body: international (40 countries represented).
Retention and Graduation: 47% grads go on to further study within 1 year.
Faculty: 0% of classes are taught by teaching assistants.

ACADEMICS
Degrees: Associate; Bachelor's; Master's **Classes:** Most classes have 20-29 students. Most lab/discussion sessions have 20-29 students. **Most popular majors:** International Relations And Affairs; Business Administration And Management, General. **Special Study Options:** Distance learning; Double major; Internships. **Career services:** Alumni network; Alumni services; Career/job search classes; Internships

CAMPUS LIFE
Environment: Metropolis **Activities:** Model UN; Student government.

ADMISSIONS
Basis for Candidate Selection: *Important factors considered include:* academic GPA, application essay, standardized test scores, recommendation(s), interview, level of applicant's interest. *Other factors considered include:* rigor of secondary school record, class rank, extracurricular activities, talent/ability, character/personal qualities, alumni/ae relation, volunteer work, work experience. **Freshman Admission Requirements:** High school diploma is required and GED is accepted **General Admission Information:** Application fee $50. Priority deadline 3/31. Nonfall registration accepted. Admission may be deferred.

COSTS AND FINANCIAL AID
Annual tuition $13,000.

AMHERST COLLEGE

220 South Pleasant Street, Amherst, MA 01002
Phone: 413-542-2328 · **Financial Aid Phone:** 413-542-2296
E-mail: admission@amherst.edu · **CEEB Code:** 3003
Fax: 413-542-2040 · **Website:** www.amherst.edu · **ACT Code:** 1774

This private school was founded in 1821. It has a 1020 acre campus.

RATINGS
Admissions Selectivity Rating: 98   Fire Safety Rating: 60*   Green Rating: 82

STUDENTS AND FACULTY
Enrollment: 1,836. **Student Body:** 49% female, 51% male, 86% out-of-state, 9% international (58 countries represented). Asian 14%, African American 11%, Caucasian 44%, Hispanic 13%, Native American 1%, Pacific Islander <1%, Two or more races 5%, Race unknown 3%.
Retention and Graduation: 96% freshmen return for sophomore year. 90% freshmen graduate within 4 years. 95% freshmen graduate within 6 years.
Faculty: Student/faculty ratio 8:1. 223 full-time faculty, 89% hold PhDs, 23% are members of minority groups, 50% are women. 0% of classes are taught by teaching assistants.

ACADEMICS
Degrees: Bachelor's; Certificate **Classes:** Most classes have 10-19 students. **Most popular majors:** English Language And Literature, General; Psychology, General; Economics, General. **Special Study Options:** Cross-registration; Double major; Exchange student program (domestic); Independent study;

Internships; Student-designed major; Study abroad; Teacher certification program. **Honors programs:** Senior Honors Thesis: an opportunity to engage in extensive research with a professor as the student's adviser. **Career services:** Alumni network; Alumni services; Career assessment; Career/job search classes; Internships; Regional alumni

FACILITIES
Housing: Coed dorms; Cooperative housing; Theme housing; Wellness housing
Special Academic Facilities/Equipment: Mead Art Museum, Beneski Museum of Natural History, Eli Marsh Gallery, Russian Center Art Gallery, Emily Dickinson Museum, Bassett Planetarium, Wilder Observatory, Wildlife Sanctuary **Computers:** Administrative functions (other than registration) can be performed online.

CAMPUS LIFE
Environment: Town **Activities:** Campus Ministries; Choral groups; Concert band; Dance; Drama/theater; International Student Organization; Jazz band; Literary magazine; Model UN; Music ensembles; Musical theater; Opera; Pep band; Radio station; Student government; Student newspaper; Student-run film society; Symphony orchestra; Yearbook 100 registered organizations, 2 honor societies, 7 religious organizations. **Athletics (Intercollegiate):** *Men:* baseball, basketball, cross-country, diving, football, golf, ice hockey, lacrosse, soccer, squash, swimming, tennis, track/field (outdoor), track/field (indoor). *Women:* basketball, cross-country, diving, field hockey, golf, ice hockey, lacrosse, soccer, softball, squash, swimming, tennis, track/field (outdoor), track/field (indoor), volleyball. **On-Campus Highlights:** Mead Art Museum, Beneski Museum of Natural History, Russian Cultural Center, Japanese Peace Garden, Wilder Observatory

ADMISSIONS
Freshman Academic Profile: 83% in top 10% of high school class, 94% in top 25% of high school class, 100% in top 50% of high school class. 54% from public high schools. **Test Scores:** SAT Math middle 50% range 710-790. SAT EBRW middle 50% range 720-770. ACT middle 50% range 32-34. Minimum internet-based TOEFL 100. **Basis for Candidate Selection:** *Very important factors considered include:* rigor of secondary school record, academic GPA, application essay, standardized test scores, recommendation(s), extracurricular activities, talent/ability, character/personal qualities, first generation. *Important factors considered include:* class rank, volunteer work. *Other factors considered include:* alumni/ae relation, geographical residence, racial/ethnic status, work experience. **Freshman Admission Requirements:** High school diploma or equivalent is not required *Academic units recommended:* 4 English, 4 math, 3 science, 1 science labs, 3 foreign language, 2 social studies, 2 history. **Freshman Admission Statistics:** 9,285 applied, 12.9% admitted, 39% enrolled. **Transfer Admission Requirements:** High school transcript, college transcript(s), essay or personal statement, statement of good standing from prior institution(s). Minimum college GPA of 3.5 required. Lowest grade transferable C. **General Admission Information:** Application fee $65. Regular application deadline 1/1. Nonfall registration accepted. Admission may be deferred for a maximum of 2 years.

COSTS AND FINANCIAL AID
Annual tuition $53,430. Room and board $14,190. Required fees $880. Average book expense $1,000. **Required Forms and Deadlines:** CSS/Financial Aid PROFILE; FAFSA; Noncustodial PROFILE. **Notification of Awards:** Applicants will be notified of awards on or about 4/1. **Types of Aid:** *Need-based scholarships/grants:* College/university scholarship or grant aid from institutional funds; Federal Pell; Private scholarships; SEOG; State scholarships/grants. *Loans:* Direct PLUS loans; Direct Subsidized Stafford Loans; Direct Unsubsidized Stafford Loans. *Student Employment:* Federal Work-Study Program available. Institutional employment available. **Financial Aid Statistics:** 100% needy freshmen, 100% needy undergrads receive need-based scholarship or grant aid. 0% undergrads receive non-need-based scholarship or grant aid. 78% freshmen, 86% undergrads receive need-based self-help aid. 0% freshmen, 0% undergrads receive athletic scholarships. 54% freshmen, 58% undergrads receive any aid. 22% undergrads borrow to pay for school. Average cumulative indebtedness $18,662.

ANDERSON UNIVERSITY (IN)

1100 East Fifth Street, Anderson, IN 46012-3495
Phone: 765-641-4080 · **Financial Aid Phone:** 765-641-4180
E-mail: info@anderson.edu · **CEEB Code:** 1016
Fax: 765-641-4091 · **Website:** www.anderson.edu · **ACT Code:** 1174

This private school, affiliated with the Church of God, was founded in 1917. It has a 163 acre campus.

RATINGS
Admissions Selectivity Rating: 79   **Fire Safety Rating:** 85   **Green Rating:** 65

STUDENTS AND FACULTY
Enrollment: 1,506. **Student Body:** 59% female, 41% male, 24% out-of-state, 2% international (19 countries represented). Asian 1%, African American 9%, Caucasian 81%, Hispanic 2%, Native American 1%, Pacific Islander <1%, Two or more races <1%, Race unknown 2%.
Retention and Graduation: 73% freshmen return for sophomore year. 48% freshmen graduate within 4 years. 57% freshmen graduate within 6 years.
Faculty: Student/faculty ratio 10:1. 105 full-time faculty, 68% hold PhDs, 9% are members of minority groups, 45% are women. 0% of classes are taught by teaching assistants.

ACADEMICS
Degrees: Associate; Bachelor's; Doctoral; Master's **Most popular majors:** Elementary Education And Teaching; Registered Nursing/Registered Nurse; Marketing/Marketing Management, General. **Special Study Options:** Accelerated program; Cross-registration; Distance learning; Double major; Dual enrollment; Honors program; Independent study; Internships; Student-designed major; Study abroad; Teacher certification program. **Honors programs:** The Honors Program at Anderson University is devoted to fostering within its honors scholars a passionate dedication to intellectual inquiry and spiritual development so that they may serve as vibrant leaders in their professions and in their communities. **Disability Services offered to physically disabled students:** Note-taking services; Reader services; Tape recorders; Tutors. **Career services:** Alumni network; Alumni services; Career assessment; Career/job search classes; Internships

FACILITIES
Housing: Apartments for married students; Apartments for single students; Coed dorms; Men's dorms; Wellness housing; Women's dorms 95% of campus accessible to physically diasbled. **Special Academic Facilities/Equipment:** Gustav Jeeninga Museum of Bible and Near Eastern Studies, Wilson Galleries, Archives of the Church of God **Computers:** Students can register for classes online. Administrative functions (other than registration) can be performed online.

CAMPUS LIFE
Environment: Town **Activities:** Campus Ministries; Choral groups; Concert band; Dance; Drama/theater; International Student Organization; Jazz band; Literary magazine; Model UN; Music ensembles; Musical theater; Opera; Pep band; Radio station; Student government; Student newspaper; Symphony orchestra; Yearbook 33 registered organizations, 12 honor societies, 15 religious organizations. **Athletics (Intercollegiate):** *Men:* baseball, basketball, cheerleading, cross-country, football, golf, soccer, tennis, track/field (outdoor). *Women:* basketball, cheerleading, cross-country, golf, soccer, softball, tennis, track/field (outdoor); volleyball. **On-Campus Highlights:** Kardatzke Wellness Center, Mocha Joe's in the Olt Student Center, Decker Commons and Create, Reardon Auditorium, York Performance Hall **Environmental Initiatives:** recycling

ADMISSIONS
Freshman Academic Profile: Average high school GPA 3.4. 20% in top 10% of high school class, 50% in top 25% of high school class, 74% in top 50% of high school class. 95% from public high schools. **Test Scores:** SAT Math middle 50% range 460-560. SAT EBRW middle 50% range 450-550. ACT middle 50% range 19-25. Minimum internet-based TOEFL 78. Minimum paper TOEFL 547. **Basis for Candidate Selection:** *Very important factors considered include:* rigor of secondary school record, recommendation(s), religious affiliation/commitment. *Important factors considered include:* class rank, academic GPA, standardized test scores, interview, extracurricular activities, character/personal qualities, volunteer work. *Other factors considered include:* application essay, talent/ability, first generation, alumni/ae relation, racial/ethnic status, level of applicant's interest. **Freshman Admission Requirements:** High school diploma is required and GED is accepted *Academic units required:* 4 English, 3 math, 3 science, 3 science labs, 2 foreign language, 1 social studies, 1 history, *Academic units recommended:* 4 English, 4 math, 4 science, 4 science labs, 3 foreign language, 2 social studies, 2 history, 5 academic electives, 1 computer science, 1 visual/performing arts. **Freshman Admission**

Statistics: 2,236 applied, 65.3% admitted, 24% enrolled. **Transfer Admission Requirements:** High school transcript, college transcript(s), standardized test scores, statement of good standing from prior institution(s). Minimum college GPA of 2.0 required. Lowest grade transferable C-. **General Admission Information:** Application fee $25. Priority deadline 1/1. Regular application deadline 7/1. Nonfall registration accepted. Admission may be deferred for a maximum of 1 year.

COSTS AND FINANCIAL AID
Annual tuition $29,950. Required fees $500. Average book expense $1,200. **Required Forms and Deadlines:** FAFSA. **Notification of Awards:** Applicants will be notified of awards on a rolling basis beginning 2/15. **Types of Aid:** *Need-based scholarships/grants:* College/university scholarship or grant aid from institutional funds; Federal Pell; Private scholarships; SEOG; State scholarships/grants. *Loans: Student Employment:* Federal Work-Study Program available. **Financial Aid Statistics:** 100% needy freshmen, 100% needy undergrads receive need-based scholarship or grant aid. 73% freshmen, 63% undergrads receive non-need-based scholarship or grant aid. 99% freshmen, 99% undergrads receive need-based self-help aid. 0% freshmen, 0% undergrads receive athletic scholarships. **Criteria for awarding aid:** *Need-based:* Religious affiliation *Non-need-based:* Academics.

ANDERSON UNIVERSITY (SC)

316 Boulevard, Anderson, SC 29621
Phone: 864-231-2030 · **Financial Aid Phone:** 864-231-2070
E-mail: admission@andersonuniversity.edu · **CEEB Code:** 5008
Fax: 864-231-2033 · **Website:** www.andersonuniversity.edu · **ACT Code:** 3832

This private school, affiliated with the Southern Baptist Church, was founded in 1911. It has a 271 acre campus.

RATINGS
Admissions Selectivity Rating: 80   **Fire Safety Rating:** 84   **Green Rating:** 60*

STUDENTS AND FACULTY
Enrollment: 2,776. **Student Body:** 69% female, 31% male, 19% out-of-state, 1% international (29 countries represented). Asian <1%, African American 7%, Caucasian 84%, Hispanic 3%, Native American <1%, Pacific Islander <1%, Two or more races 3%, Race unknown 1%.
Retention and Graduation: 75% freshmen return for sophomore year. 52% freshmen graduate within 4 years. 57% freshmen graduate within 6 years. 40% grads go on to further study within 1 year. 13% grads pursue arts and sciences degrees. 1% grads pursue law degrees. 9% grads pursue business degrees. 3% grads pursue medical degrees. **Faculty:** Student/faculty ratio 14:1. 148 full-time faculty, 60% hold PhDs, 7% are members of minority groups, 56% are women. 0% of classes are taught by teaching assistants.

ACADEMICS
Degrees: Bachelor's; Doctoral/Professional; Master's **Classes:** Most classes have 20-29 students. Most lab/discussion sessions have 20-29 students. **Most popular majors:** Elementary Education And Teaching; Kinesiology And Exercise Science; Business Administration And Management, General. **Special Study Options:** Accelerated program; Distance learning; Double major; Dual enrollment; Honors program; Independent study; Internships; Liberal arts/career combination; Study abroad; Teacher certification program. **Disability Services offered to physically disabled students:** Note-taking services; Reader services; Tape recorders; Tutors. **Career services:** Alumni services; Career assessment; Internships; Regional alumni

FACILITIES
Housing: Men's dorms; Women's dorms **Computers:** Students can register for classes online. Administrative functions (other than registration) can be performed online.

CAMPUS LIFE
Environment: Town **Activities:** Campus Ministries; Choral groups; Concert band; Dance; Drama/theater; International Student Organization; Jazz band; Literary magazine; Music ensembles; Musical theater 27 registered organizations, 1 honor society, 6 religious organizations **Athletics (Intercollegiate):** *Men:* baseball, basketball, cross-country, equestrian sports, golf, soccer, tennis, track/field (outdoor), wrestling. *Women:* basketball, cheerleading, cross-country, equestrian sports, golf, soccer, softball, tennis, track/field (outdoor), volleyball. **On-Campus Highlights:** Java City, Food For Thought, Thrift Library, Student Center, Fitness Center

ADMISSIONS

Freshman Academic Profile: Average high school GPA 3.6. 37% in top 10% of high school class, 58% in top 25% of high school class, 85% in top 50% of high school class. **Test Scores:** SAT Math middle 50% range 470-570. SAT EBRW middle 50% range 530-620. ACT middle 50% range 21-26. Minimum paper TOEFL 550. **Basis for Candidate Selection:** *Very important factors considered include:* rigor of secondary school record. *Important factors considered include:* class rank, academic GPA, standardized test scores, character/personal qualities. *Other factors considered include:* application essay, recommendation(s), extracurricular activities, talent/ability, volunteer work. **Freshman Admission Requirements:** High school diploma is required and GED is accepted *Academic units required:* 4 English, 3 math, 3 science, 2 science labs, 2 foreign language. **Freshman Admission Statistics:** 2,322 applied, 79.1% admitted, 37% enrolled. **Transfer Admission Requirements:** college transcript(s), Minimum college GPA of 2.0 required. Lowest grade transferable C. **General Admission Information:** Application fee $25. Regular application deadline 8/1. Nonfall registration accepted. Admission may be deferred for a maximum of 1 year.

COSTS AND FINANCIAL AID

Annual tuition $24,290. Room and board $9,680. Required fees $2,680. Average book expense $2,000. **Required Forms and Deadlines:** FAFSA. **Notification of Awards:** Applicants will be notified of awards on a rolling basis beginning 3/1. **Types of Aid:** *Need-based scholarships/grants:* College/university scholarship or grant aid from institutional funds; Federal Pell; Private scholarships; SEOG; State scholarships/grants. *Loans:* Direct PLUS loans; Direct Subsidized Stafford Loans; Direct Unsubsidized Stafford Loans. *Student Employment:* Federal Work-Study Program available. Institutional employment available. **Financial Aid Statistics:** 63% needy freshmen, 71% needy undergrads receive need-based scholarship or grant aid. 100% freshmen, 100% undergrads receive non-need-based scholarship or grant aid. 73% freshmen, 72% undergrads receive need-based self-help aid. 5% freshmen, 4% undergrads receive athletic scholarships. **Criteria for awarding aid:** *Need-based:* Academics, Art, Leadership, Minority status, Music/drama *Non-need-based:* Academics, Art, Athletics, Leadership, Minority status, Music/drama, Religious affiliation, State/district residency.

ANGELO STATE UNIVERSITY

ASU Station, San Angelo, TX 76909-1014
Phone: 325-942-2041 · **Financial Aid Phone:** 325-942-2246
E-mail: admissions@angelo.edu · **CEEB Code:** 6644
Fax: 325-942-2078 · **Website:** www.angelo.edu · **ACT Code:** 4164

This public school was founded in 1928. It has a 268 acre campus.

RATINGS

Admissions Selectivity Rating: 79   **Fire Safety Rating:** 96   **Green Rating:** 82

STUDENTS AND FACULTY

Enrollment: 5,877. **Student Body:** 55% female, 45% male, 3% out-of-state, 4% international (21 countries represented). Asian 1%, African American 7%, Caucasian 49%, Hispanic 36%, Native American <1%, Pacific Islander <1%, Two or more races 3%, Race unknown <1%.
Retention and Graduation: 67% freshmen return for sophomore year. 21% freshmen graduate within 4 years. 36% freshmen graduate within 6 years. 15% grads go on to further study within 1 year. 9% grads pursue arts and sciences degrees. 4% grads pursue business degrees. **Faculty:** Student/faculty ratio 20:1. 295 full-time faculty, 80% hold PhDs, 19% are members of minority groups, 47% are women. 3% of classes are taught by teaching assistants.

ACADEMICS

Degrees: Bachelor's; Certificate; Doctoral/Professional; Master's **Classes:** Most classes have 10-19 students. **Most popular majors:** Multi-/Interdisciplinary Studies, Other; Psychology, General; Registered Nursing/Registered Nurse. **Special Study Options:** Distance learning; Double major; Dual enrollment; English as a Second Language (ESL); Honors program; Independent study; Internships; Study abroad; Teacher certification program. **Combined degree programs:** BA/MA. **Disability Services offered to physically disabled students:** Note-taking services; Reader services; Tape recorders; Tutors. **Career services:** Alumni services; Career assessment; Internships

FACILITIES

Housing: Apartments for single students; Coed dorms; Special housing for disabled students 99% of campus accessible to physically diasbled. **Special Academic Facilities/Equipment:** Global Immersion Center, combining the technology of an domed theater and a planetarium; West Texas Collection; Management, Instruction, and Research (Agricultural)Center; Food Safety and Product Development Lab. **Computers:** 100% of classrooms, 100% of dorms, 100% of libraries, 100% of dining areas, 100% of student union, 100% of common outdoor areas have wireless network access. Students can register for classes online. Administrative functions (other than registration) can be performed online.

CAMPUS LIFE

Environment: City **Activities:** Campus Ministries; Choral groups; Concert band; Dance; Drama/theater; International Student Organization; Jazz band; Literary magazine; Marching band; Music ensembles; Musical theater; Pep band; Radio station; Student government; Student newspaper; Symphony orchestra; Television station 76 registered organizations, 11 honor societies, 9 religious organizations. 4 fraternities, 2 sororities. **Athletics (Intercollegiate):** *Men:* baseball, basketball, cross-country, football, track/field (outdoor). *Women:* basketball, cross-country, golf, soccer, softball, track/field (outdoor), volleyball. **On-Campus Highlights:** Houston Harte University Center, Center for Human Performance/Rec Center, Junell Center/Stephens Arena, Global Immersion Center/Planetarium, ASU Lake House **Environmental Initiatives:** LEED Certification initiataives in all new buildings.

ADMISSIONS

Freshman Academic Profile: 10% in top 10% of high school class, 33% in top 25% of high school class, 69% in top 50% of high school class. 96% from public high schools. **Test Scores:** SAT Math middle 50% range 450-540. SAT EBRW middle 50% range 450-550. ACT middle 50% range 17-22. Minimum internet-based TOEFL 79. Minimum paper TOEFL 550. **Basis for Candidate Selection:** *Very important factors considered include:* class rank, standardized test scores. *Important factors considered include:* rigor of secondary school record. *Other factors considered include:* academic GPA, extracurricular activities, talent/ability, character/personal qualities, first generation, geographical residence, state residency, volunteer work, work experience, level of applicant's interest. **Freshman Admission Requirements:** High school diploma is required and GED is accepted *Academic units recommended:* 4 English, 4 math, 4 science, 2 foreign language, 3.5 social studies, 5.5 academic electives, 1 visual/performing arts, 2 units from above areas or other academic areas. **Freshman Admission Statistics:** 4,316 applied, 73.5% admitted, 45% enrolled. **Transfer Admission Requirements:** college transcript(s), statement of good standing from prior institution(s). Minimum college GPA of 2.0 required. Lowest grade transferable D. **General Admission Information:** Application fee $35. Regular application deadline 8/29. Nonfall registration accepted. Admission may be deferred for a maximum of 1 semester.

COSTS AND FINANCIAL AID

Annual in-state tuition $7,666. Annual out-of-state tuition $17,526. Room and board $7,666. Required fees $3,140. Average book expense $1,200. **Required Forms and Deadlines:** FAFSA. **Notification of Awards:** Applicants will be notified of awards on a rolling basis beginning 4/1. **Types of Aid:** *Need-based scholarships/grants:* College/university scholarship or grant aid from institutional funds; Federal Nursing Scholarships; Federal Pell; Private scholarships; SEOG; State scholarships/grants. *Loans:* Direct PLUS loans; Direct Subsidized Stafford Loans; Direct Unsubsidized Stafford Loans. *Student Employment:* Federal Work-Study Program available. Institutional employment available. **Financial Aid Statistics:** 79% needy freshmen, 82% needy undergrads receive need-based scholarship or grant aid. 67% freshmen, 38% undergrads receive non-need-based scholarship or grant aid. 75% freshmen, 76% undergrads receive need-based self-help aid. 6% freshmen, 6% undergrads receive athletic scholarships. 87% freshmen, 81% undergrads receive any aid. 61% undergrads borrow to pay for school. Average cumulative indebtedness $26,033. **Criteria for awarding aid:** *Need-based:* Academics *Non-need-based:* Academics, Art, Athletics, Leadership, Music/drama, State/district residency.

ANNA MARIA COLLEGE

50 Sunset Lane, Paxton, MA 01612-1198
Phone: 508-849-3360 · **Financial Aid Phone:** 508-849-3366
E-mail: admission@annamaria.edu · **CEEB Code:** 3005
Fax: 508-849-3362 · **Website:** www.annamaria.edu · **ACT Code:** 3232

This private school, affiliated with the Roman Catholic Church, was founded in 1946. It has a 190 acre campus.

RATINGS

Admissions Selectivity Rating: 72   **Fire Safety Rating:** 83   **Green Rating:** 60*

STUDENTS AND FACULTY

Enrollment: 978. **Student Body:** 56% female, 44% male, 12% out-of-state, 1% international. Asian 1%, African American 6%, Caucasian 73%, Hispanic 5%, Native American <1%, Race unknown 14%.
Retention and Graduation: 70% freshmen return for sophomore year. 47% grads go on to further study within 1 year. 19% grads pursue arts and sciences degrees. 2% grads pursue law degrees. 1% grads pursue business degrees. 0% grads pursue medical degrees. **Faculty:** Student/faculty ratio 10:1. 50 full-time faculty, 72% hold PhDs, 66% are women. 0% of classes are taught by teaching assistants.

ACADEMICS

Degrees: Associate; Bachelor's; Certificate; Master's; Post-Bachelor's certificate; Post-Master's certificate **Classes:** Most classes have 20-29 students. Most lab/discussion sessions have 20-29 students. **Most popular majors:** Criminal Justice/Safety Studies; Fire Science/Fire-Fighting; Business Administration And Management, General. **Special Study Options:** Accelerated program; Cooperative education program; Cross-registration; Double major; Independent study; Internships; Liberal arts/career combination; Student-designed major; Study abroad; Teacher certification program. **Honors programs:** The Honors Program at Anna Maria College is designed to intellectually challenge highly motivated scholastic achievers. The Program is now a member of "National Collegiate Honors Programs," the national association of Honors Programs. Each Honors Program participant will have the opportunity to engage directly in foreign culture through interesting study abroad programs, such as a semester abroad experience,or a focused Urban Seminar that meets in a city like Paris, Vienna, Rome or Berlin that is sponsored by the College and supervised by a professor who oversees the program. **Combined degree programs:** BA/MA. **Disability Services offered to physically disabled students:** Note-taking services; Reader services; Tape recorders; Tutors. **Career services:** Alumni services; Career assessment; Internships

FACILITIES

Housing: Coed dorms; Special housing for disabled student; Wellness housing **Special Academic Facilities/Equipment:** The Mondor-Eagan Library houses Anna Maria College's volumes, stacks, periodicals, study rooms, computer center, resource centers, and language laboratory. Classrooms are located in Trinity Hall, Cardinal Cushing Hall, and Foundress Hall. Foundress Hall houses the Zecco Performing Arts Center. Trinity Hall also houses the learning center. Among the other buildings are Madore Chapel, St. Joseph's Hall for sciences and Miriam Hall for music, performance, and art. **Computers:** 100% of classrooms, 100% of dorms, 100% of libraries, 100% of dining areas, 100% of student union, 100% of common outdoor areas have wireless network access. Administrative functions (other than registration) can be performed online.

CAMPUS LIFE

Environment: Rural **Activities:** Campus Ministries; Choral groups; Dance; Drama/theater; Jazz band; Pep band; Student government; Student newspaper; Yearbook 17 registered organizations, 5 honor societies, 1 religious organization. **Athletics (Intercollegiate):** *Men:* baseball, basketball, cross-country, football, golf, lacrosse, soccer, tennis. *Women:* basketball, field hockey, lacrosse, soccer, softball, tennis, volleyball. **On-Campus Highlights:** NEW: Residence Hall, NEW: Exercise / Weight Room, New Art Building w/ art gallery, Snack bar / Lounge, Student Center **Environmental Initiatives:** There is a "Green Committee" that meets regularly to discuss environmental issues and ways that the college can be be more sustainable.

ADMISSIONS

Freshman Academic Profile: Average high school GPA 2.6. 2% in top 10% of high school class, 13% in top 25% of high school class, 41% in top 50% of high school class. **Test Scores:** SAT Math middle 50% range 378-480. SAT EBRW middle 50% range 378-490. ACT middle 50% range 18-21. Minimum paper TOEFL 500. **Basis for Candidate Selection:** *Very important factors considered include:* academic GPA, standardized test scores. *Other factors considered include:* rigor of secondary school record, application essay, recommendation(s), extracurricular activities, volunteer work, work experience,

level of applicant's interest. **Freshman Admission Requirements:** High school diploma is required and GED is accepted *Academic units required:* 4 English, 3 math, 3 science, 1 science labs, 2 foreign language, 2 social studies, 2 history, 4 academic electives. **Freshman Admission Statistics:** 712 applied, 87.2% admitted, 29% enrolled. **Transfer Admission Requirements:** High school transcript, college transcript(s), essay or personal statement, statement of good standing from prior institution(s). Minimum college GPA of 2.0 required. Lowest grade transferable C. **General Admission Information:** Application fee $40. Priority deadline 3/1. Nonfall registration accepted. Admission may be deferred for a maximum of 1 year.

COSTS AND FINANCIAL AID

Annual tuition $23,500. Room and board $9,350. Required fees $2,350. Average book expense $800. **Required Forms and Deadlines:** FAFSA; State aid form. **Notification of Awards:** Applicants will be notified of awards on a rolling basis beginning 4/1. **Types of Aid:** *Need-based scholarships/grants:* College/university scholarship or grant aid from institutional funds; Federal Pell; Private scholarships; SEOG; State scholarships/grants; United Negro College Fund. *Loans: Student Employment:* Federal Work-Study Program available. **Financial Aid Statistics:** 99% needy freshmen, 98% needy undergrads receive need-based scholarship or grant aid. 99% freshmen, 98% undergrads receive non-need-based scholarship or grant aid. 92% freshmen, 92% undergrads receive need-based self-help aid. 0% freshmen, 0% undergrads receive athletic scholarships. 98% freshmen, 95% undergrads receive any aid. **Criteria for awarding aid:** *Non-need-based:* Academics, Alumni affiliation, Music/drama, Religious affiliation, State/district residency.

ANTIOCH COLLEGE

1 Morgan Place, Yellow Springs, OH 45387
Phone: 937-319-6082 · **Financial Aid Phone:** 937-319-6016
E-mail: admission@antiochcollege.edu
Fax: 937-319-6085 · **Website:** www.antiochcollege.edu · **ACT Code:** 3232

This private school was founded in 1852. It has a 1100 acre campus.

RATINGS

Admissions Selectivity Rating: 64   **Fire Safety Rating:** 91   **Green Rating:** 89

STUDENTS AND FACULTY

Enrollment: 133. **Student Body:** 62% female, 38% male, 63% out-of-state, 0% international (10 countries represented). Asian 4%, African American 10%, Caucasian 59%, Hispanic 13%, Native American 0%, Pacific Islander 1%, Two or more races 9%, Race unknown 5%.
Retention and Graduation: 53% freshmen return for sophomore year. 31% freshmen graduate within 4 years. 57% freshmen graduate within 6 years. 20% grads go on to further study within 1 year. 5% grads pursue arts and sciences degrees. 10% grads pursue law degrees. **Faculty:** Student/faculty ratio 4:1. 31 full-time faculty, 81% hold PhDs, 16% are members of minority groups, 58% are women. 0% of classes are taught by teaching assistants.

ACADEMICS

Degrees: Bachelor's **Classes:** Most classes have 10-19 students. Most lab/discussion sessions have 10-19 students. **Most popular majors:** Liberal Arts And Sciences, General Studies And Humanities, Other; Psychology, General; Political Economy. **Special Study Options:** Cooperative education program; Cross-registration; Independent study; Internships; Liberal arts/career combination; Student-designed major; Study abroad. **Disability Services offered to physically disabled students:** Note-taking services; Reader services; Tape recorders; Tutors. **Career services:** Alumni network; Alumni services; Career/job search classes; Internships; Regional alumni

FACILITIES

Housing: Coed dorms; Other (please specify) 86% of campus accessible to physically diasbled. **Special Academic Facilities/Equipment:** Glen Helen—1,000-acre nature preserve WYSO—National Public Radio station Coretta Scott King Center for Cultural and Intellectual Freedom Wellness Center with competition-length, indoor swimming pool

CAMPUS LIFE

Environment: Rural **Activities:** Literary magazine; Music ensembles; Radio station; Student government; Student newspaper; Yearbook 16 registered organizations. **On-Campus Highlights:** Wellness Center, Glen Helen Nature Preserve, Weston Hall (Student Union), 91.3 WYSO, Coretta Scott King Center **Environmental Initiatives:** Antioch College is committed to sustainable energy and building design and demonstrates this commitment in a variety of ways. Antioch College has an on-campus, five-acre solar farm of 3,300 solar panels that produces 1.2 million kilowatt hours of energy annually. This

The Princeton Review's Complete Book of Colleges

solar array provides enough power to offset the electrical consumption of the College's Central Geothermal Plant. The Central Geothermal Plant, which heats and cools campus buildings, offsets 2,900 tons of CO_2 when compared with traditional heating and cooling methods. The College tracks and monitors all energy consumption at 66% of campus buildings and provides real-time updates of that energy consumption through online data dashboards.

ADMISSIONS

Freshman Academic Profile: Average high school GPA 3.1. 68% from public high schools. **Basis for Candidate Selection:** *Very important factors considered include:* application essay, recommendation(s), character/personal qualities, level of applicant's interest. *Important factors considered include:* rigor of secondary school record, class rank, academic GPA, interview, extracurricular activities, talent/ability, volunteer work, work experience. *Other factors considered include:* standardized test scores, first generation, alumni/ae relation, geographical residence, racial/ethnic status. **Freshman Admission Requirements:** High school diploma is required and GED is accepted *Academic units recommended:* 4 English, 4 math, 4 science, 4 foreign language, 4 social studies, 4 history, 4 academic electives. **Freshman Admission Statistics:** 152 applied, 96.7% admitted, 13% enrolled. **Transfer Admission Requirements:** High school transcript, college transcript(s), essay or personal statement, statement of good standing from prior institution(s). **General Admission Information:** Priority deadline 1/15. Regular application deadline 7/1. Nonfall registration accepted. Admission may be deferred for a maximum of 1 year.

COSTS AND FINANCIAL AID

Annual tuition $34,568. Room and board $7,640. Required fees $1,150. Average book expense $1,200. **Required Forms and Deadlines:** FAFSA. **Notification of Awards:** Applicants will be notified of awards on a rolling basis beginning 11/15. **Types of Aid:** *Need-based scholarships/grants:* College/university scholarship or grant aid from institutional funds; Federal Pell; Private scholarships; State scholarships/grants. *Loans:* Direct PLUS loans; Direct Subsidized Stafford Loans; Direct Unsubsidized Stafford Loans. *Student Employment:* Institutional employment available. **Financial Aid Statistics:** 100% needy freshmen, 100% needy undergrads receive need-based scholarship or grant aid. 100% freshmen, 100% undergrads receive non-need-based scholarship or grant aid. 100% freshmen, 100% undergrads receive need-based self-help aid. 0% freshmen, 0% undergrads receive athletic scholarships. 100% freshmen, 100% undergrads receive any aid. **Criteria for awarding aid:** *Need-based:* Academics, Minority status *Non-need-based:* Academics.

ANTIOCH UNIVERSITY SANTA BARBARA

801 Garden Street, Santa Barbara, CA 93101
Phone: 805-962-8179 · **Financial Aid Phone:** 805-962-8179
E-mail: admissions@antiochsb.edu
Fax: 805-962-4786 · **Website:** www.antiochsb.edu

This private school was founded in 1852.

RATINGS

Admissions Selectivity Rating: 0   **Fire Safety Rating:** 60*   **Green Rating:** 60*

STUDENTS AND FACULTY

Enrollment: 105. **Student Body:** 75% female, 25% male, (11 countries represented).
Faculty: 16 full-time faculty, 69% are women.

ACADEMICS

Degrees: Bachelor's; Master's **Classes:** Most classes have 10-19 students. **Special Study Options:** Cross-registration; Double major; Independent study; Internships; Liberal arts/career combination; Study abroad; Teacher certification program; Weekend college.

FACILITIES

Computers: Students can register for classes online. Administrative functions (other than registration) can be performed online.

CAMPUS LIFE

Environment: City

ADMISSIONS

Freshman Admission Requirements: High school diploma is required and GED is accepted **Transfer Admission Requirements:** High school transcript, college transcript(s), essay or personal statement, interview, statement of good standing from prior institution(s). Minimum college GPA of 2.0 required. Lowest grade transferable C. **General Admission Information:** Application fee $60. Nonfall registration accepted.

COSTS AND FINANCIAL AID

Annual tuition $15,375. Required fees $26. **Required Forms and Deadlines:** FAFSA; Institution's own financial aid form. **Types of Aid:** *Need-based scholarships/grants:* College/university scholarship or grant aid from institutional funds; Federal Pell; Private scholarships; SEOG; State scholarships/grants. **Financial Aid Statistics:** 54% needy undergrads receive need-based scholarship or grant aid. 0% undergrads receive non-need-based scholarship or grant aid. 54% undergrads receive need-based self-help aid. **Criteria for awarding aid:** *Need-based:* Minority status.

APPALACHIAN STATE UNIVERSITY

Office of Admissions, Boone, NC 28608-2004
Phone: 828-262-2120 · **Financial Aid Phone:** 828-262-2190
E-mail: admissions@appstate.edu · **CEEB Code:** 5010
Fax: 828-262-3296 · **Website:** www.appstate.edu · **ACT Code:** 3062

This public school was founded in 1899. It has a 415 acre campus.

RATINGS

Admissions Selectivity Rating: 83   **Fire Safety Rating:** 95   **Green Rating:** 98

STUDENTS AND FACULTY

Enrollment: 16,891. **Student Body:** 55% female, 45% male, 8% out-of-state, <1% international (83 countries represented). Asian 2%, African American 4%, Caucasian 83%, Hispanic 6%, Native American <1%, Pacific Islander <1%, Two or more races 4%, Race unknown 1%.
Retention and Graduation: 89% freshmen return for sophomore year. 51% freshmen graduate within 4 years. 74% freshmen graduate within 6 years.
Faculty: Student/faculty ratio 16:1. 966 full-time faculty, 99% hold PhDs, 6% are members of minority groups, 48% are women. 1% of classes are taught by teaching assistants.

ACADEMICS

Degrees: Bachelor's; Doctoral/Research; Master's; Post-Bachelor's certificate; Post-Master's certificate **Classes:** Most classes have 20-29 students. Most lab/discussion sessions have 20-29 students. **Most popular majors:** Kinesiology And Exercise Science; Psychology, General; Business Administration And Management, General. **Special Study Options:** Cross-registration; Distance learning; Double major; Dual enrollment; English as a Second Language (ESL); Exchange student program (domestic); Honors program; Independent study; Internships; Liberal arts/career combination; Student-designed major; Study abroad; Teacher certification program. **Honors programs:** Heltzer Honors College offers promising and highly motivated students opportunities by providing honors classes in many fields. **Disability Services offered to physically disabled students:** Note-taking services; Reader services; Tape recorders; Tutors. **Career services:** Alumni network; Alumni services; Career assessment; Career/job search classes; Internships; Regional alumni

FACILITIES

Housing: Apartments for single students; Coed dorms; Special housing for disabled student; Theme housing; Women's dorms 100% of campus accessible to physically diasbled. **Special Academic Facilities/Equipment:** Dark Sky Observatory, Turchin Center for the Visual Arts, Living Learning Center, Beech Mountain Small Wind Research and Demonstration Site, Center for Judaic, Holocaust, and Peace Studies, Appalachian Special Collections, Biodiesel Research and Education Projects, Center for Judaic, Holocaust, and Peace Studies, Catherine J. Smith Gallery, F. Kenneth & Marjorie J. McKinney Geology Teaching Museum, Looking Glass Gallery, Outdoor Geology Lab, Rosen Outdoor Sculpture, AppalAir Meteorological Reporting Station, Solar Research and Teaching Lab, Sustainable Development Civic Garden, Language Lab **Computers:** 95% of classrooms, 70% of dorms, 90% of libraries, 90% of dining areas, 85% of student union, 5% of common outdoor areas have wireless network access. Students can register for classes online. Administrative functions (other than registration) can be performed online.

CAMPUS LIFE

Environment: Village **Activities:** Campus Ministries; Choral groups; Concert band; Dance; Drama/theater; International Student Organization; Jazz band; Literary magazine; Marching band; Model UN; Music ensembles; Musical theater; Opera; Pep band; Radio station; Student government; Student newspaper; Student-run film society; Symphony orchestra; Television station 270 registered organizations, 20 honor societies, 25 religious organizations. 18 fraternities, 11 sororities. **Athletics (Intercollegiate):** *Men:* baseball, basketball, cross-country, football, golf, soccer, tennis, track/field (outdoor), track/field (indoor), wrestling. *Women:* basketball, cross-country, field hockey, golf, soccer, softball, tennis, track/field (outdoor), track/field (indoor), volleyball.
On-Campus Highlights: Plemmons Student Union, Roess Dining Hall, Kidd Brewer Stadium "The Rock", Student Recreation Center, Sanford Mall /

Greenspace **Environmental Initiatives:** Signatory of the American College and University Presidents Climate Commitment. On track with the target requirements. Climate Action Plan completed 2010. Climate neutrality date of 2050.

ADMISSIONS

Freshman Academic Profile: Average high school GPA 4.2. 19% in top 10% of high school class, 57% in top 25% of high school class, 91% in top 50% of high school class. 93% from public high schools. **Test Scores:** SAT Math middle 50% range 540-630. SAT EBRW middle 50% range 560-640. ACT middle 50% range 23-27. Minimum internet-based TOEFL 75. **Basis for Candidate Selection:** *Very important factors considered include:* rigor of secondary school record, class rank, academic GPA, standardized test scores. *Other factors considered include:* application essay, recommendation(s), extracurricular activities, talent/ability, character/personal qualities, first generation, alumni/ae relation, racial/ethnic status, volunteer work, work experience, level of applicant's interest. **Freshman Admission Requirements:** High school diploma is required and GED is accepted *Academic units required:* 4 English, 4 math, 3 science, 1 science labs, 2 foreign language, 1 social studies, 1 history. **Freshman Admission Statistics:** 14,009 applied, 70.0% admitted, 34% enrolled. **Transfer Admission Requirements:** High school transcript, college transcript(s), Minimum college GPA of 2.0 required. Lowest grade transferable C. **General Admission Information:** Application fee $65. Priority deadline 11/15. Regular application deadline 3/15. Nonfall registration accepted. Admission may be deferred for a maximum of 2 terms.

COSTS AND FINANCIAL AID

Annual in-state tuition $8,174. Annual out-of-state tuition $18,675. Room and board $8,174. Required fees $3,061. Average book expense $700. **Required Forms and Deadlines:** FAFSA. **Notification of Awards:** Applicants will be notified of awards on a rolling basis beginning 3/15. **Types of Aid:** *Need-based scholarships/grants:* College/university scholarship or grant aid from institutional funds; Federal Pell; Private scholarships; SEOG; State scholarships/grants. *Loans:* Direct PLUS loans; Direct Subsidized Stafford Loans; Direct Unsubsidized Stafford Loans. *Student Employment:* Federal Work-Study Program available. Institutional employment available. **Financial Aid Statistics:** 67% needy freshmen, 74% needy undergrads receive need-based scholarship or grant aid. 5% freshmen, 3% undergrads receive non-need-based scholarship or grant aid. 77% freshmen, 78% undergrads receive need-based self-help aid. 1% freshmen, 1% undergrads receive athletic scholarships. 69% freshmen, 66% undergrads receive any aid. 56% undergrads borrow to pay for school. Average cumulative indebtedness $22,696. **Criteria for awarding aid:** *Non-need-based:* Academics, Alumni affiliation, Art, Athletics, Job skills, Leadership, Minority status, Music/drama, Religious affiliation, State/district residency.

AQUINAS COLLEGE

1607 Robinson Road SE, Grand Rapids, MI 49506-1799
Phone: 616-632-2900 · **Financial Aid Phone:** 616-632-2893
E-mail: admissions@aquinas.edu · **CEEB Code:** 1018
Fax: 616-732-4469 · **Website:** www.aquinas.edu · **ACT Code:** 1962

This private school was founded in 1886. It has a 107 acre campus.

RATINGS

Admissions Selectivity Rating: 72   **Fire Safety Rating:** 97   **Green Rating:** 90

STUDENTS AND FACULTY

Enrollment: 1,851. **Student Body:** 62% female, 38% male, 6% out-of-state, 1% international (8 countries represented). Asian 1%, African American 3%, Caucasian 85%, Hispanic 5%, Native American <1%, Pacific Islander 0%, Two or more races 2%, Race unknown 3%.
Retention and Graduation: 76% freshmen return for sophomore year. 17% grads go on to further study within 1 year. 7% grads pursue arts and sciences degrees. 3% grads pursue law degrees. 3% grads pursue business degrees. 2% grads pursue medical degrees. **Faculty:** 86 full-time faculty, 78% hold PhDs, 9% are members of minority groups, 44% are women.

ACADEMICS

Degrees: Associate; Bachelor's; Master's **Classes:** Most classes have 20-29 students. Most lab/discussion sessions have 10-19 students. **Most popular majors:** Liberal Arts And Sciences/Liberal Studies. **Special Study Options:** Accelerated program; Cooperative education program; Cross-registration; Distance learning; Double major; Dual enrollment; Exchange student program (domestic); Honors program; Independent study; Internships; Liberal arts/career combination; Student-designed major; Study abroad; Teacher certification program. **Honors programs:** Insignis Honors Program. **Disability

Services offered to physically disabled students: Note-taking services; Reader services; Tape recorders; Tutors. **Career services:** Alumni network; Alumni services; Career assessment; Career/job search classes; Internships

FACILITIES

Housing: Apartments for single students; Coed dorms; Theme housing; Wellness housing 95% of campus accessible to physically disabled. **Special Academic Facilities/Equipment:** Observatory and Jarecki Center for Advanced Learning featuring high-speed, two-way interactive video conferencing for courses and a virtual connection for external experts to interact with classes (sound, video, graphics) using a laptop computer equipped with a camera that is housed in a self-contained briefcase. The package includes all the technology needed to accomplish the connection through a standard phone jack. This "virtual faculty briefcase" can be shipped to a guest lecturer at another location anywhere in the world and they are able to conduct an interactive lecture or discussion with an Aquinas classroom. **Computers:** 100% of classrooms, 100% of dorms, 100% of libraries, 100% of dining areas, 100% of student union, 80% of common outdoor areas have wireless network access. Administrative functions (other than registration) can be performed online.

CAMPUS LIFE

Environment: Metropolis **Activities:** Campus Ministries; Choral groups; Dance; Drama/theater; International Student Organization; Jazz band; Literary magazine; Model UN; Music ensembles; Radio station; Student government; Student newspaper 71 registered organizations, 4 honor societies, 2 religious organizations. **Athletics (Intercollegiate):** *Men:* baseball, basketball, cheerleading, cross-country, golf, lacrosse, soccer, tennis, track/field (outdoor), track/field (indoor). *Women:* basketball, cheerleading, cross-country, golf, lacrosse, soccer, softball, tennis, track/field (outdoor), track/field (indoor), volleyball. **On-Campus Highlights:** Sturrus Sports & Fitness Center, Jarecki Center, Moose Cafe, Wege Student Center, Performing Arts Center **Environmental Initiatives:** Sustainable Business practices restore environmental quality, promote stable and healthy communities, and increase long-term profitability. The Aquinas Sustainable Business Degree program fosters ecological and social intelligence in all business decisions and is the only undergraduate program of its kind in Michigan and possibly the United States. Aquinas also offers a Master of Sustainable Business.

ADMISSIONS

Freshman Academic Profile: Average high school GPA 3.5. 19% in top 10% of high school class, 45% in top 25% of high school class, 77% in top 50% of high school class. 80% from public high schools. **Test Scores:** ACT middle 50% range 21-26. Minimum paper TOEFL 550. **Basis for Candidate Selection:** *Very important factors considered include:* rigor of secondary school record, academic GPA, standardized test scores. *Other factors considered include:* class rank, application essay, recommendation(s), interview, extracurricular activities, talent/ability, character/personal qualities, first generation, volunteer work, work experience, level of applicant's interest. **Freshman Admission Requirements:** High school diploma is required and GED is not accepted *Academic units recommended:* 4 English, 4 math, 3 science, 2 foreign language, 3 social studies. **Freshman Admission Statistics:** 1,842 applied, 100.3% admitted, 21% enrolled. **Transfer Admission Requirements:** High school transcript, college transcript(s), Minimum college GPA of 2.0 required. Lowest grade transferable D. **General Admission Information:** Priority deadline 5/1. Nonfall registration accepted. Admission may be deferred for a maximum of one year.

COSTS AND FINANCIAL AID

Annual tuition $27,332. Room and board $8,350. Required fees $394. Average book expense $800. **Required Forms and Deadlines:** FAFSA. **Notification of Awards:** Applicants will be notified of awards on a rolling basis beginning 3/1. **Types of Aid:** *Need-based scholarships/grants:* College/university scholarship or grant aid from institutional funds; Federal Pell; Private scholarships; SEOG; State scholarships/grants. *Loans:* Direct PLUS loans; Direct Subsidized Stafford Loans; Direct Unsubsidized Stafford Loans. *Student Employment:* Federal Work-Study Program available. Institutional employment available. **Financial Aid Statistics:** 100% needy freshmen, 100% needy undergrads receive need-based scholarship or grant aid. 74% freshmen, 69% undergrads receive non-need-based scholarship or grant aid. 100% freshmen, 100% undergrads receive need-based self-help aid. 2% freshmen, 6% undergrads receive athletic scholarships. 95% freshmen, 90% undergrads receive any aid. **Criteria for awarding aid:** *Non-need-based:* Academics, Alumni affiliation, Art, Athletics, Leadership, Music/drama.

ARCADIA UNIVERSITY

450 South Easton Road, Glenside, PA 19038
Phone: 215-572-2910 · **Financial Aid Phone:** 215-572-2980
E-mail: admiss@arcadia.edu · **CEEB Code:** 2039
Fax: 215-572-4049 · **Website:** www.arcadia.edu

This private school, affiliated with the Presbyterian Church, was founded in 1853. It has a 76 acre campus.

RATINGS

Admissions Selectivity Rating: 82   **Fire Safety Rating:** 60*   **Green Rating:** 60*

STUDENTS AND FACULTY

Enrollment: 2,233. **Student Body:** 69% female, 31% male, 38% out-of-state, 3% international (12 countries represented). Asian 5%, African American 9%, Caucasian 68%, Hispanic 9%, Native American <1%, Pacific Islander <1%, Two or more races 4%, Race unknown 1%.
Retention and Graduation: 78% freshmen return for sophomore year. 63% freshmen graduate within 4 years. 66% freshmen graduate within 6 years. **Faculty:** Student/faculty ratio 11:1. 179 full-time faculty, 91% hold PhDs, 14% are members of minority groups, 61% are women. 0% of classes are taught by teaching assistants.

ACADEMICS

Degrees: Bachelor's; Certificate; Doctoral/Professional; Doctoral/Research; Master's; Post-Bachelor's certificate; Post-Master's certificate **Classes:** Most classes have fewer than 10 students. Most lab/discussion sessions have 10-19 students. **Most popular majors:** English Language And Literature, General; Biology/Biological Sciences, General; Psychology, General. **Special Study Options:** Accelerated program; Cooperative education program; Cross-registration; Distance learning; Double major; Dual enrollment; Exchange student program (domestic); Honors program; Independent study; Internships; Liberal arts/career combination; Student-designed major; Study abroad; Teacher certification program. **Honors programs:** Honors program for invited students. Specialized opportunities for professional-level scholarship, co-curricular experiences, mentoring, academic service learning, and presentations are provided to ready these students for their professional careers and maximize their marketability. **Combined degree programs:** BA/MA. **Disability Services offered to physically disabled students:** Reader services; Tape recorders; Tutors. **Career services:** Alumni network; Alumni services; Career assessment; Career/job search classes; Internships

FACILITIES

Housing: Apartments for single students; Coed dorms; Special housing for disabled student; Wellness housing; Women's dorms 99% of campus accessible to physically disabled. **Special Academic Facilities/Equipment:** Art gallery, language lab, observatory. **Computers:** Students can register for classes online. Administrative functions (other than registration) can be performed online.

CAMPUS LIFE

Environment: Town **Activities:** Choral groups; Dance; Drama/theater; Literary magazine; Music ensembles; Musical theater; Pep band; Radio station; Student government; Student newspaper; Television station; Yearbook 40 registered organizations, 8 honor societies, 3 religious organizations. **Athletics (Intercollegiate):** *Men:* baseball, basketball, cheerleading, golf, soccer, swimming, tennis. *Women:* basketball, cheerleading, field hockey, lacrosse, soccer, softball, swimming, tennis, volleyball. **On-Campus Highlights:** Student Commons, Grey Towers Castle, Kuch Center, The Chat, Walk of Pride

ADMISSIONS

Freshman Academic Profile: Average high school GPA 3.6. 24% in top 10% of high school class, 55% in top 25% of high school class, 89% in top 50% of high school class. **Test Scores:** SAT Math middle 50% range 520-610. SAT EBRW middle 50% range 540-630. ACT middle 50% range 22-27. **Basis for Candidate Selection:** *Very important factors considered include:* rigor of secondary school record, academic GPA, standardized test scores, recommendation(s). *Important factors considered include:* class rank, application essay, extracurricular activities, alumni/ae relation. *Other factors considered include:* interview, talent/ability, character/personal qualities, volunteer work, work experience, level of applicant's interest. **Freshman Admission Requirements:** High school diploma is required and GED is accepted *Academic units required: Academic units recommended:* 4 English, 3 math, 3 science, 3 science labs, 2 foreign language, 2 social studies, 2 history. **Freshman Admission Statistics:** 8,931 applied, 62.3% admitted, 10% enrolled. **Transfer Admission Requirements:** college transcript(s), essay or personal statement, Minimum college GPA of 2.5 required. Lowest grade transferable C-. **General Admission Information:** Application fee $30. Priority deadline 1/15. Regular application deadline 3/1. Nonfall registration accepted. Admission may be deferred for a maximum of 1 year.

COSTS AND FINANCIAL AID

Annual tuition $41,630. Room and board $13,660. Required fees $700. Average book expense $1,500. **Required Forms and Deadlines:** FAFSA; Institution's own financial aid form. **Types of Aid:** *Need-based scholarships/grants:* College/university scholarship or grant aid from institutional funds; Federal Pell; Private scholarships; SEOG; State scholarships/grants. *Loans:* Direct PLUS loans; Direct Subsidized Stafford Loans; Direct Unsubsidized Stafford Loans. *Student Employment:* Federal Work-Study Program available. **Financial Aid Statistics:** 90% needy freshmen, 99% needy undergrads receive need-based scholarship or grant aid. 12% freshmen, 10% undergrads receive non-need-based scholarship or grant aid. 86% freshmen, 88% undergrads receive need-based self-help aid. 0% freshmen, 0% undergrads receive athletic scholarships. 97% freshmen receive any aid. **Criteria for awarding aid:** *Non-need-based:* Academics, Alumni affiliation, Art, Leadership, Music/drama.

ARIZONA STATE UNIVERSITY

Admissions Office, Tempe, AZ 85287-0112
Phone: 480-965-7788 · **Financial Aid Phone:** 855-278-5080
E-mail: admissions@asu.edu · **CEEB Code:** 4007
Fax: 480-965-3610 · **Website:** www.asu.edu · **ACT Code:** 88

This public school was founded in 1885. It has a 661 acre campus.

RATINGS

Admissions Selectivity Rating: 82   **Fire Safety Rating:** 92   **Green Rating:** 98

STUDENTS AND FACULTY

Enrollment: 42,181. **Student Body:** 43% female, 57% male, 25% out-of-state, 12% international (116 countries represented). Asian 7%, African American 4%, Caucasian 50%, Hispanic 21%, Native American 1%, Pacific Islander <1%, Two or more races 4%, Race unknown 1%.
Retention and Graduation: 87% freshmen return for sophomore year. 45% freshmen graduate within 4 years. 63% freshmen graduate within 6 years. 20% grads go on to further study within 1 year. 15% grads pursue arts and sciences degrees. 1.9% grads pursue law degrees. 2% grads pursue business degrees. 1.4% grads pursue medical degrees. **Faculty:** Student/faculty ratio 22:1. 2,135 full-time faculty, 89% hold PhDs, 27% are members of minority groups, 40% are women.

ACADEMICS

Degrees: Bachelor's; Certificate; Doctoral/Research; Master's; Post-Bachelor's certificate **Classes:** Most classes have 10-19 students. Most lab/discussion sessions have 10-19 students. **Most popular majors:** Biology/Biological Sciences, General; Psychology, General; Business, Management, Marketing, And Related Support Services, Other. **Special Study Options:** Accelerated program; Cooperative education program; Distance learning; Double major; English as a Second Language (ESL); Honors program; Independent study; Internships; Liberal arts/career combination; Student-designed major; Study abroad; Teacher certification program. **Honors programs:** Barrett, the Honors College at ASU, is a selective, residential college that recruits academically outstanding undergraduates across the nation. Students enrolled in Barrett are part of both the honors college community and an ASU disciplinary college of their choice. They may major in any field offered on any ASU campus. Honors courses are taught by honors faculty within the college and within a variety of departments and programs. **Combined degree programs:** BA/MA. **Disability Services offered to physically disabled students:** Note-taking services; Reader services; Tape recorders. **Career services:** Alumni network; Alumni services; Career assessment; Career/job search classes; Internships; Regional alumni

FACILITIES

Housing: Apartments for single students; Coed dorms; Fraternity/sorority housing; Special housing for disabled students 99% of campus accessible to physically disabled. **Special Academic Facilities/Equipment:** art, anthropology, geology, history, and sports museums, herbarium, planetarium, galleries, collections, biodesign institute, student pavilion, assorted research labs and facilities, digital labs, art, dance and development studios **Computers:** 100% of classrooms, 100% of dorms, 100% of libraries, 100% of dining areas, 100% of student union, 70% of common outdoor areas have wireless network access. Students can register for classes online. Administrative functions (other than registration) can be performed online.

CAMPUS LIFE

Environment: Metropolis **Activities:** Campus Ministries; Choral groups; Concert band; Dance; Drama/theater; International Student Organization; Jazz band; Literary magazine; Marching band; Model UN; Music ensembles; Musical theater; Opera; Pep band; Student government; Student newspaper; Student-run film society; Symphony orchestra 675 registered organizations, 16 honor societies, 51 religious organizations. 32 fraternities, 22 sororities. **Athletics (Intercollegiate):** *Men:* baseball, basketball, cross-country, diving, football, golf, swimming, track/field (outdoor), wrestling. *Women:* basketball, cross-country, diving, golf, gymnastics, soccer, softball, swimming, tennis, track/field (outdoor), volleyball, water polo. **On-Campus Highlights:** ASU Memorial Union, Grady Gammage Memorial Auditorium, Barrett Honors Complex, Hayden Library, Sun Devil Fitness Complex

ADMISSIONS

Freshman Academic Profile: Average high school GPA 3.5. 34% in top 10% of high school class, 64% in top 25% of high school class, 90% in top 50% of high school class. **Test Scores:** SAT Math middle 50% range 560-680. SAT EBRW middle 50% range 560-670. ACT middle 50% range 22-29. Minimum internet-based TOEFL 61. Minimum paper TOEFL 500. **Basis for Candidate Selection:** *Very important factors considered include:* class rank, academic GPA, standardized test scores. *Important factors considered include:* rigor of secondary school record. *Other factors considered include:* state residency. **Freshman Admission Requirements:** High school diploma is required and GED is accepted *Academic units required:* 4 English, 4 math, 3 science, 3 science labs, 2 foreign language, 1 social studies, 1 history, and 1 unit from above areas or other academic areas. **Freshman Admission Statistics:** 24,127 applied, 84.1% admitted, 39% enrolled. **Transfer Admission Requirements:** college transcript(s), standardized test scores, Minimum college GPA of 2.0 required. Lowest grade transferable C. **General Admission Information:** Application fee $50. Priority deadline 2/1. Nonfall registration accepted. Admission may be deferred for a maximum of 2 years.

COSTS AND FINANCIAL AID

Annual in-state tuition $12,209. Annual out-of-state tuition $26,684. Room and board $12,209. Required fees $688. Average book expense $1,125. **Required Forms and Deadlines:** FAFSA. **Notification of Awards:** Applicants will be notified of awards on a rolling basis beginning 3/1. **Types of Aid:** *Need-based scholarships/grants:* College/university scholarship or grant aid from institutional funds; Federal Pell; Private scholarships; SEOG; State scholarships/grants; United Negro College Fund. *Loans:* Direct PLUS loans; Direct Subsidized Stafford Loans; Direct Unsubsidized Stafford Loans. *Student Employment:* Federal Work-Study Program available. Institutional employment available. **Financial Aid Statistics:** 99% needy freshmen, 93% needy undergrads receive need-based scholarship or grant aid. 13% freshmen, 9% undergrads receive non-need-based scholarship or grant aid. 56% freshmen, 68% undergrads receive need-based self-help aid. 1% freshmen, 1% undergrads receive athletic scholarships. 90% freshmen, 83% undergrads receive any aid. 49% undergrads borrow to pay for school. Average cumulative indebtedness $22,903. **Criteria for awarding aid:** *Need-based:* Academics *Non-need-based:* Academics, Art, Athletics, Leadership, Music/drama, State/district residency.

ARIZONA STATE UNIVERSITY AT THE DOWNTOWN PHOENIX CAMPUS

Admissions Office, Tempe, AZ 85287-0112
Phone: (480) 965-7788 • **Financial Aid Phone:** 855-278-5080
E-mail: admissions@asu.edu
Fax: (480) 965-3610 • **Website:** https://campus.asu.edu/downtown/

This public school was founded in 2006. It has a 18 acre campus.

RATINGS

Admissions Selectivity Rating: 83 **Fire Safety Rating:** 92 **Green Rating:** 98

STUDENTS AND FACULTY

Enrollment: 8,898. **Student Body:** 68% female, 32% male, 27% out-of-state, 2% international (36 countries represented). Asian 5%, African American 6%, Caucasian 49%, Hispanic 31%, Native American 2%, Pacific Islander <1%, Two or more races 4%, Race unknown 1%. **Retention and Graduation:** 86% freshmen return for sophomore year. 55% freshmen graduate within 4 years. 66% freshmen graduate within 6 years. 14% grads go on to further study within 1 year. 10% grads pursue arts and sciences degrees. 1.9% grads pursue law degrees. 1% grads pursue business degrees. 0.9% grads pursue medical degrees. **Faculty:** Student/faculty ratio 19:1. 554 full-time faculty, 72% hold PhDs, 21% are members of minority groups, 62% are women.

ACADEMICS

Degrees: Bachelor's; Certificate; Doctoral/Professional; Doctoral/Research; Master's; Post-Bachelor's certificate **Classes:** Most classes have 10-19 students. Most lab/discussion sessions have fewer than 10 students. **Most popular majors:** Journalism, Other; Health and Physical Education/Fitness, Other; Criminal Justice/Law Enforcement Administration. **Special Study Options:** Accelerated program; Cooperative education program; Distance learning; Double major; Honors program; Independent study; Internships; Liberal arts/career combination; Student-designed major; Study abroad. **Honors programs:** Barrett, the Honors College at ASU, is a selective, residential college that recruits academically outstanding undergraduates across the nation. Students enrolled in Barrett are part of both the honors college community and an ASU disciplinary college of their choice. They may major in any field offered on any ASU campus. Honors courses are taught by honors faculty within the college and within a variety of departments and programs. **Disability Services offered to physically disabled students:** Note-taking services; Reader services; Tape recorders. **Career services:** Alumni network; Alumni services; Career assessment; Career/job search classes; Internships; Regional alumni

FACILITIES

Housing: Apartments for single students; Coed dorms; Special housing for disabled students 99% of campus accessible to physically diasbled. **Special Academic Facilities/Equipment:** radio station, TV station, writing labs, tutoring, research labs, instructional kitchen, news studio, news museum

CAMPUS LIFE

Environment: Metropolis **Activities:** Campus Ministries; Concert band; International Student Organization; Musical theater; Radio station; Student government; Student newspaper; Television station. Sun Devil Fitness Center, Taylor Place Residence Hall, Cronkite Edit Bays, Civic Space Park

ADMISSIONS

Freshman Academic Profile: Average high school GPA 3.6. 35% in top 10% of high school class, 72% in top 25% of high school class, 95% in top 50% of high school class. **Test Scores:** SAT Math middle 50% range 530-620. SAT EBRW middle 50% range 540-640. ACT middle 50% range 21-26. Minimum internet-based TOEFL 61. Minimum paper TOEFL 500. **Basis for Candidate Selection:** *Very important factors considered include:* class rank, academic GPA, standardized test scores. *Important factors considered include:* rigor of secondary school record. *Other factors considered include:* state residency. **Freshman Admission Requirements:** High school diploma is required and GED is accepted *Academic units required:* 4 English, 4 math, 3 science, 3 science labs, 2 foreign language, 1 social studies, 1 history, and 1 unit from above areas or other academic areas. **Freshman Admission Statistics:** 5,340 applied, 77.2% admitted, 32% enrolled. **General Admission Information:** Application fee $50. Priority deadline 2/1. Nonfall registration accepted. Admission may be deferred for a maximum of 2 years.

COSTS AND FINANCIAL AID

Annual in-state tuition $13,842. Annual out-of-state tuition $26,684. Room and board $13,842. Required fees $688. Average book expense $1,125. **Required Forms and Deadlines:** FAFSA. **Notification of Awards:** Applicants will be notified of awards on a rolling basis beginning 3/1. **Types of Aid:** *Need-based scholarships/grants:* College/university scholarship or grant aid from institutional funds; Federal Nursing Scholarships; Federal Pell; Private scholarships; SEOG; State scholarships/grants; United Negro College Fund. *Loans:* Direct PLUS loans; Direct Subsidized Stafford Loans; Direct Unsubsidized Stafford Loans. *Student Employment:* Federal Work-Study Program available. Institutional employment available. **Financial Aid Statistics:** 97% needy freshmen, 90% needy undergrads receive need-based scholarship or grant aid. 12% freshmen, 6% undergrads receive non-need-based scholarship or grant aid. 59% freshmen, 72% undergrads receive need-based self-help aid. 0% freshmen, 1% undergrads receive athletic scholarships. 97% freshmen, 89% undergrads receive any aid. 61% undergrads borrow to pay for school. Average cumulative indebtedness $25,342. **Criteria for awarding aid:** *Need-based:* Academics *Non-need-based:* Academics, Athletics, Leadership, State/district residency.

ARIZONA STATE UNIVERSITY AT THE WEST CAMPUS

Box 2418, Tempe, AZ 85287-0112
Phone: (480) 965-7788 · **Financial Aid Phone:** 855-278-5080
E-mail: admissions@asu.edu · **CEEB Code:** 4007
Fax: (480) 965-3610 · **Website:** https://campus.asu.edu/west · **ACT Code:** 880

This public school was founded in 1984. It has a 278 acre campus.

RATINGS

Admissions Selectivity Rating: 80   **Fire Safety Rating:** 92   **Green Rating:** 98

STUDENTS AND FACULTY

Enrollment: 3,563. **Student Body:** 60% female, 40% male, 14% out-of-state, 4% international (30 countries represented). Asian 5%, African American 5%, Caucasian 47%, Hispanic 33%, Native American 2%, Pacific Islander <1%, Two or more races 4%, Race unknown 1%.
Retention and Graduation: 88% freshmen return for sophomore year. 44% freshmen graduate within 4 years. 58% freshmen graduate within 6 years. 23% grads go on to further study within 1 year. 19% grads pursue arts and sciences degrees. 2.1% grads pursue law degrees. 2% grads pursue business degrees. 0% grads pursue medical degrees. **Faculty:** Student/faculty ratio 14:1. 273 full-time faculty, 79% hold PhDs, 25% are members of minority groups, 59% are women.

ACADEMICS

Degrees: Bachelor's; Certificate; Doctoral/Research; Master's; Post-Bachelor's certificate **Classes:** Most classes have 10-19 students. Most lab/discussion sessions have 10-19 students. **Most popular majors:** Speech Communication And Rhetoric; Psychology, General; Business, Management, Marketing, And Related Support Services, Other. **Special Study Options:** Accelerated program; Cooperative education program; Distance learning; Double major; English as a Second Language (ESL); Honors program; Independent study; Internships; Liberal arts/career combination; Student-designed major; Study abroad; Teacher certification program. **Honors programs:** Barrett, the Honors College at ASU, is a selective, residential college that recruits academically outstanding undergraduates across the nation. Students enrolled in Barrett are part of both the honors college community and an ASU disciplinary college of their choice. They may major in any field offered on any ASU campus. Honors courses are taught by honors faculty within the college and within a variety of departments and programs. **Combined degree programs:** BA/MA. **Disability Services offered to physically disabled students:** Note-taking services; Reader services; Tape recorders. **Career services:** Alumni network; Alumni services; Career assessment; Career/job search classes; Internships; Regional alumni

FACILITIES

Housing: Apartments for single students; Coed dorms; Special housing for disabled students 99% of campus accessible to physically diasbled. **Special Academic Facilities/Equipment:** Herberger Young Scholars Academy-school for 7th grade thru 12th grade, art collections/galleries, dance studios, Little Theatre/black box, communication assessment learning lab, research labs, digital labs, music labs, cooking labs, performing arts studios, writing labs

CAMPUS LIFE

Environment: Metropolis **Activities:** Campus Ministries; Choral groups; Dance; Drama/theater; International Student Organization; Musical theater; Student government; Student newspaper; Student-run film society. Fletcher Library, Verde Dining Pavilion, Sun Devil Fitness Center, Starbucks, Casa de Oro Residence Hall

ADMISSIONS

Freshman Academic Profile: Average high school GPA 3.5. 32% in top 10% of high school class, 66% in top 25% of high school class, 94% in top 50% of high school class. **Test Scores:** SAT Math middle 50% range 510-620. SAT EBRW middle 50% range 530-630. ACT middle 50% range 20-25. Minimum internet-based TOEFL 61. Minimum paper TOEFL 500. **Basis for Candidate Selection:** *Very important factors considered include:* class rank, academic GPA, standardized test scores. *Important factors considered include:* rigor of secondary school record. *Other factors considered include:* state residency. **Freshman Admission Requirements:** High school diploma is required and GED is accepted *Academic units required:* 4 English, 4 math, 3 science, 3 science labs, 2 foreign language, 1 social studies, 1 history, and 1 unit from above areas or other academic areas. **Freshman Admission Statistics:** 2,231 applied, 79.7% admitted, 29% enrolled. **General Admission Information:** Application fee $50. Priority deadline 2/1. Nonfall registration accepted. Admission may be deferred for a maximum of 2 years.

COSTS AND FINANCIAL AID

Annual in-state tuition $11,212. Annual out-of-state tuition $25,350. Room and board $11,212. Required fees $688. Average book expense $1,125. **Required Forms and Deadlines:** FAFSA. **Notification of Awards:** Applicants will be notified of awards on a rolling basis beginning 3/1. **Types of Aid:** *Need-based scholarships/grants:* College/university scholarship or grant aid from institutional funds; Federal Pell; Private scholarships; SEOG; State scholarships/grants; United Negro College Fund. *Loans:* Direct PLUS loans; Direct Subsidized Stafford Loans; Direct Unsubsidized Stafford Loans. *Student Employment:* Federal Work-Study Program available. Institutional employment available. **Financial Aid Statistics:** 96% needy freshmen, 92% needy undergrads receive need-based scholarship or grant aid. 5% undergrads receive non-need-based scholarship or grant aid. 72% undergrads receive need-based self-help aid. 0% freshmen, 0% undergrads receive athletic scholarships. 94% freshmen, 88% undergrads receive any aid. 56% undergrads borrow to pay for school. Average cumulative indebtedness $22,251. **Criteria for awarding aid:** *Need-based:* Academics *Non-need-based:* Academics, Athletics, Leadership, State/district residency.

ARIZONA STATE UNIVERSITY POLYTECHNIC CAMPUS

2131 Hillside Road, Tempe, AZ 85287-0112
Phone: 480-965-7788 · **Financial Aid Phone:** 855-278-5080
E-mail: admissions@asu.edu · **CEEB Code:** 4007
Fax: (480) 965-3610 · **Website:** https://campus.asu.edu/polytechnic · **ACT Code:** 88

This public school was founded in 1996. It has a 575 acre campus.

RATINGS

Admissions Selectivity Rating: 80.   **Fire Safety Rating:** 92   **Green Rating:** 98

STUDENTS AND FACULTY

Enrollment: 4,224. **Student Body:** 31% female, 69% male, 22% out-of-state, 8% international (52 countries represented). Asian 6%, African American 5%, Caucasian 53%, Hispanic 21%, Native American 1%, Pacific Islander 1%, Two or more races 5%, Race unknown 5%.
Retention and Graduation: 85% freshmen return for sophomore year. 42% freshmen graduate within 4 years. 59% freshmen graduate within 6 years. 9% grads go on to further study within 1 year. 9% grads pursue arts and sciences degrees. 0% grads pursue law degrees. 0% grads pursue business degrees. 0% grads pursue medical degrees. **Faculty:** Student/faculty ratio 21:1. 204 full-time faculty, 79% hold PhDs, 25% are members of minority groups, 43% are women.

ACADEMICS

Degrees: Bachelor's; Certificate; Doctoral/Research; Master's **Classes:** Most classes have 20-29 students. Most lab/discussion sessions have 10-19 students. **Most popular majors:** Engineering, General; Biology/Biological Sciences, General; Business, Management, Marketing, And Related Support Services, Other. **Special Study Options:** Accelerated program; Cooperative education program; Distance learning; Double major; Honors program; Independent study; Internships; Liberal arts/career combination; Student-designed major; Study abroad; Teacher certification program. **Honors programs:** Barrett, the Honors College at ASU, is a selective, residential college that recruits academically outstanding undergraduates across the nation. Students enrolled in Barrett are part of both the honors college community and an ASU disciplinary college of their choice. They may major in any field offered on any ASU campus. Honors courses are taught by honors faculty within the college and within a variety of departments and programs. **Disability Services offered to physically disabled students:** Note-taking services; Reader services; Tape recorders. **Career services:** Alumni network; Alumni services; Career assessment; Career/job search classes; Internships; Regional alumni

FACILITIES

Housing: Apartments for single students; Coed dorms; Special housing for disabled students 99% of campus accessible to physically diasbled. **Special Academic Facilities/Equipment:** variety of labs – fuel cell, perception, print and imaging, automation, technology, engineering, I3DEA, robotics, laser, photography, device and usability lab; 3-D printing technology, King Air simulator, tower simulator; altitude chamber

CAMPUS LIFE

Environment: Metropolis **Activities:** Campus Ministries; Concert band; Dance; Drama/theater; International Student Organization; Model UN; Student government; Student newspaper; Student-run film society. Sun Devil Fitness Center, Citrus Dining Facility, Engineering Studies, Start-Up Labs

ADMISSIONS

Freshman Academic Profile: Average high school GPA 3.4. 19% in top 10% of high school class, 50% in top 25% of high school class, 88% in top 50% of high school class. **Test Scores:** SAT Math middle 50% range 540-660. SAT EBRW middle 50% range 540-640. ACT middle 50% range 21-28. Minimum internet-based TOEFL 61. Minimum paper TOEFL 500. **Basis for Candidate Selection:** *Very important factors considered include:* class rank, academic GPA, standardized test scores. *Important factors considered include:* rigor of secondary school record. *Other factors considered include:* state residency. **Freshman Admission Requirements:** High school diploma is required and GED is accepted *Academic units required:* 4 English, 4 math, 3 science, 3 science labs, 2 foreign language, 1 social studies, 1 history, and 1 unit from above areas or other academic areas. **Freshman Admission Statistics:** 2,483 applied, 76.3% admitted, 31% enrolled. **General Admission Information:** Application fee $50. Priority deadline 2/1. Nonfall registration accepted. Admission may be deferred for a maximum of 2 years.

COSTS AND FINANCIAL AID

Annual in-state tuition $12,093. Annual out-of-state tuition $25,350. Room and board $12,093. Required fees $688. Average book expense $1,125. **Required Forms and Deadlines:** FAFSA. **Notification of Awards:** Applicants will be notified of awards on a rolling basis beginning 3/1. **Types of Aid:** *Need-based scholarships/grants:* College/university scholarship or grant aid from institutional funds; Federal Pell; Private scholarships; SEOG; State scholarships/grants; United Negro College Fund. *Loans:* Direct PLUS loans; Direct Subsidized Stafford Loans; Direct Unsubsidized Stafford Loans. *Student Employment:* Federal Work-Study Program available. Institutional employment available. **Financial Aid Statistics:** 97% needy freshmen, 91% needy undergrads receive need-based scholarship or grant aid. 10% freshmen, 7% undergrads receive non-need-based scholarship or grant aid. 58% freshmen, 74% undergrads receive need-based self-help aid. 0% freshmen, 0% undergrads receive athletic scholarships. 94% freshmen, 86% undergrads receive any aid. 59% undergrads borrow to pay for school. Average cumulative indebtedness $26,925. **Criteria for awarding aid:** *Need-based:* Academics *Non-need-based:* Academics, Athletics, Leadership, State/district residency.

ARKANSAS STATE UNIVERSITY

PO Box 600, State University, AR 72467
Phone: 870-972-3024 · **Financial Aid Phone:** 870-972-2310
E-mail: admissions@astate.edu · **CEEB Code:** 6011
Fax: 870-972-3406 · **Website:** www.astate.edu · **ACT Code:** 116

This public school was founded in 1909. It has a 1376 acre campus.

RATINGS

Admissions Selectivity Rating: 81   **Fire Safety Rating:** 90   **Green Rating:** 60*

STUDENTS AND FACULTY

Enrollment: 8,909. **Student Body:** 57% female, 43% male, 11% out-of-state, 6% international (50 countries represented). Asian 1%, African American 14%, Caucasian 74%, Hispanic 2%, Native American <1%, Pacific Islander <1%, Two or more races 2%, Race unknown 1%.
Retention and Graduation: 76% freshmen return for sophomore year. 22% grads go on to further study within 1 year. 15% grads pursue arts and sciences degrees. 1% grads pursue law degrees. 20% grads pursue business degrees. 24% grads pursue medical degrees. **Faculty:** Student/faculty ratio 17:1. 505 full-time faculty, 69% hold PhDs, 16% are members of minority groups, 53% are women. 4% of classes are taught by teaching assistants.

ACADEMICS

Degrees: Associate; Bachelor's; Doctoral/Professional; Doctoral/Research; Master's; Post-Bachelor's certificate; Post-Master's certificate **Classes:** Most classes have 10-19 students. Most lab/discussion sessions have 20-29 students. **Most popular majors:** Early Childhood Education And Teaching; General Studies; Registered Nursing/Registered Nurse. **Special Study Options:** Accelerated program; Distance learning; Double major; Dual enrollment; English as a Second Language (ESL); Exchange student program (domestic); Honors program; Independent study; Internships; Study abroad; Teacher certification program. **Disability Services offered to physically disabled students:** Note-taking services; Reader services; Tape recorders; Tutors. **Career services:** Alumni services; Career assessment; Career/job search classes; Internships

FACILITIES

Housing: Apartments for married students; Apartments for single students; Coed dorms; Fraternity/sorority housing; Men's dorms; Theme housing; Women's dorms 90% of campus accessible to physically diasbled. **Special**

Academic Facilities/Equipment: Art gallery, museum of Native American cultures and Arkansas artifacts. Ecotoxicology research facility, electron microscope facility, geographic information system facility. Equine center. **Computers:** Students can register for classes online. Administrative functions (other than registration) can be performed online.

CAMPUS LIFE

Environment: Town **Activities:** Campus Ministries; Choral groups; Concert band; Dance; Drama/theater; International Student Organization; Jazz band; Marching band; Model UN; Music ensembles; Musical theater; Opera; Pep band; Radio station; Student government; Student newspaper; Symphony orchestra; Television station; Yearbook 192 registered organizations, 42 honor societies, 16 religious organizations. 12 fraternities, 9 sororities. **Athletics (Intercollegiate):** *Men:* baseball, basketball, cross-country, football, golf, track/field (outdoor), track/field (indoor). *Women:* basketball, cross-country, golf, soccer, tennis, track/field (outdoor), track/field (indoor), volleyball. **On-Campus Highlights:** Student Union, Fowler Center, Convocation Center, Red Wolf Center, Centennial Bank Stadium **Environmental Initiatives:** Recycling

ADMISSIONS

Freshman Academic Profile: Average high school GPA 3.5. 27% in top 10% of high school class, 49% in top 25% of high school class, 74% in top 50% of high school class. 93% from public high schools. **Test Scores:** SAT Math middle 50% range 470-540. SAT EBRW middle 50% range 400-540. ACT middle 50% range 21-26. Minimum internet-based TOEFL 61. Minimum paper TOEFL 500. **Basis for Candidate Selection:** *Very important factors considered include:* rigor of secondary school record, standardized test scores. *Important factors considered include:* class rank. *Other factors considered include:* recommendation(s), talent/ability. **Freshman Admission Requirements:** High school diploma is required and GED is accepted *Academic units required:* 4 English, 4 math, 3 science, 3 science labs, 1 social studies, 2 history, *Academic units recommended:* 2 foreign language. **Freshman Admission Statistics:** 5,346 applied, 70.2% admitted, 42% enrolled. **Transfer Admission Requirements:** college transcript(s), Minimum college GPA of 2.0 required. Lowest grade transferable C. **General Admission Information:** Application fee $15. Regular application deadline 8/24. Nonfall registration accepted.

COSTS AND FINANCIAL AID

Annual in-state tuition $8,540. Annual out-of-state tuition $12,120. Room and board $8,540. Required fees $2,140. Average book expense $1,000. **Required Forms and Deadlines:** FAFSA; Institution's own financial aid form. **Notification of Awards:** Applicants will be notified of awards on a rolling basis beginning 6/1. **Types of Aid:** *Need-based scholarships/grants:* College/university scholarship or grant aid from institutional funds; Federal Pell; Private scholarships; SEOG; State scholarships/grants. *Loans:* Direct PLUS loans; Direct Subsidized Stafford Loans; Direct Unsubsidized Stafford Loans. *Student Employment:* Federal Work-Study Program available. Institutional employment available. **Financial Aid Statistics:** 98% needy freshmen, 96% needy undergrads receive need-based scholarship or grant aid. 46% freshmen, 55% undergrads receive non-need-based scholarship or grant aid. 53% freshmen, 65% undergrads receive need-based self-help aid. 5% freshmen, 4% undergrads receive athletic scholarships. 92% freshmen, 79% undergrads receive any aid. 67% undergrads borrow to pay for school. Average cumulative indebtedness $27,400. **Criteria for awarding aid:** *Need-based:* Academics *Non-need-based:* Academics, Alumni affiliation, Art, Athletics, Leadership, Minority status, Music/drama, State/district residency.

See page 884.

ARKANSAS TECH UNIVERSITY

ATU, Administration Building #200, Russellville, AR 72801
Phone: 479-968-0343 · **Financial Aid Phone:** 479-968-0399
E-mail: tech.enroll@atu.edu · **CEEB Code:** 6010
Fax: 479-964-0522 · **Website:** http://www.atu.edu/ · **ACT Code:** 114

This public school was founded in 1909. It has a 559 acre campus.

RATINGS

Admissions Selectivity Rating: 75   **Fire Safety Rating:** 91   **Green Rating:** 60*

STUDENTS AND FACULTY

Enrollment: 8,799. **Student Body:** 55% female, 45% male, 4% out-of-state, 4% international (36 countries represented). Asian 1%, African American 10%, Caucasian 76%, Hispanic 6%, Native American 1%, Pacific Islander <1%, Two or more races 3%, Race unknown 0%.
Retention and Graduation: 71% freshmen return for sophomore year. **Faculty:** Student/faculty ratio 19:1. 349 full-time faculty, 62% hold PhDs, 9%

are members of minority groups, 50% are women. 1% of classes are taught by teaching assistants.

ACADEMICS

Degrees: Associate; Bachelor's; Certificate; Master's; Post-Master's certificate; Terminal Associate **Classes:** Most classes have 20-29 students. Most lab/discussion sessions have 20-29 students. **Special Study Options:** Accelerated program; Distance learning; Double major; Dual enrollment; English as a Second Language (ESL); Honors program; Independent study; Internships; Study abroad; Teacher certification program; Weekend college. **Honors programs:** Arkansas Tech University's Honors Program is designed to elevate the college learning experience. To maintain a sense of community and enhance personal learning skills, honors courses are conscientiously designed to be small in size and to promote interaction, not only with peers, but with professors as well. Students admitted into the Honors program are not only educated for their university years, they are educated for life. **Disability Services offered to physically disabled students:** Note-taking services; Reader services; Tape recorders; Tutors. **Career services:** Career assessment; Career/job search classes; Internships

FACILITIES

Housing: Apartments for single students; Coed dorms; Fraternity/sorority housing; Men's dorms; Special housing for disabled student; Theme housing; Women's dorms 100% of campus accessible to physically disabled. **Special Academic Facilities/Equipment:** 1. Arkansas Center for Energy, Natural Resources, and Environmental Studies. 2. Crabaugh Communications Center. 3. Arkansas Tech Museum. 4. Technology Center **Computers:** Students can register for classes online. Administrative functions (other than registration) can be performed online.

CAMPUS LIFE

Environment: Town **Activities:** Campus Ministries; Choral groups; Concert band; Dance; Drama/theater; International Student Organization; Jazz band; Literary magazine; Marching band; Model UN; Music ensembles; Radio station; Student government; Student newspaper; Symphony orchestra; Television station 130 registered organizations, 14 honor societies, 13 religious organizations. 6 fraternities, 4 sororities. **Athletics (Intercollegiate):** *Men:* baseball, basketball, cheerleading, football, golf. *Women:* basketball, cheerleading, cross-country, golf, softball, tennis, volleyball. **On-Campus Highlights:** Ross Pendergraft Library and Technology Center, Tech Fit, Doc's Place, Tucker Coliseum, Baswell Techionery

ADMISSIONS

Freshman Academic Profile: Average high school GPA 3.2. 13% in top 10% of high school class, 34% in top 25% of high school class, 65% in top 50% of high school class. **Test Scores:** SAT Math middle 50% range 440-590. SAT EBRW middle 50% range 440-530. ACT middle 50% range 18-25. Minimum internet-based TOEFL 61. Minimum paper TOEFL 500. **Basis for Candidate Selection:** *Very important factors considered include:* academic GPA, standardized test scores. *Important factors considered include:* rigor of secondary school record. *Other factors considered include:* class rank. **Freshman Admission Requirements:** High school diploma is required and GED is accepted *Academic units required:* 4 English, 4 math, 3 science, 3 science labs, 2 foreign language, 3 social studies, 1 history, 4.5 academic electives, 0.5 visual/performing arts, and 2 units from above areas or other academic areas. **Freshman Admission Statistics:** 4,619 applied, 89.1% admitted, 49% enrolled. **Transfer Admission Requirements:** college transcript(s), Minimum college GPA of 2.0 required. Lowest grade transferable D. **General Admission Information:** Nonfall registration accepted. Admission may be deferred for a maximum of 1 semester.

COSTS AND FINANCIAL AID

Annual in-state tuition $7,098. Annual out-of-state tuition $12,900. Room and board $7,098. Required fees $1,290. Average book expense $1,410. **Required Forms and Deadlines:** FAFSA; Institution's own financial aid form. **Notification of Awards:** Applicants will be notified of awards on a rolling basis beginning 3/15. **Types of Aid:** *Need-based scholarships/grants:* Federal Pell; Private scholarships; SEOG; State scholarships/grants. *Loans:* Direct PLUS loans; Direct Subsidized Stafford Loans; Direct Unsubsidized Stafford Loans. *Student Employment:* Federal Work-Study Program available. Institutional employment available. **Financial Aid Statistics:** 84% needy freshmen, 82% needy undergrads receive need-based scholarship or grant aid. 71% freshmen, 49% undergrads receive non-need-based scholarship or grant aid. 63% freshmen, 70% undergrads receive need-based self-help aid. 4% freshmen, 3% undergrads receive athletic scholarships. **Criteria for awarding aid:** *Non-need-based:* Academics, Athletics, Leadership, Music/drama, State/district residency.

ARLINGTON BAPTIST COLLEGE

2305 West End Ave., Arlington, Tx 76012
Phone: 817-461-8741 • **Financial Aid Phone:** 817-461-8741, ext 110
E-mail: jtaylor@arlingtonbaptistcollege.edu
Fax: 817-274-1138 • **Website:** www.arlingtonbaptistcollege.edu • **ACT Code:** 4163

This private school, affiliated with the Baptist Church, was founded in 1939. It has a 35 acre campus.

RATINGS

Admissions Selectivity Rating: 66   **Fire Safety Rating:** 94   **Green Rating:** 60*

STUDENTS AND FACULTY

Enrollment: 220. **Student Body:** 45% female, 55% male, 17% out-of-state, 1% international (1 countries represented). Asian 0%, African American 18%, Caucasian 71%, Hispanic 8%, Native American 2%, Race unknown 0%. **Retention and Graduation:** 51% freshmen return for sophomore year. 15% grads go on to further study within 1 year. **Faculty:** Student/faculty ratio 16:1. 12 full-time faculty, 17% hold PhDs, 25% are women.

ACADEMICS

Degrees: Bachelor's; Certificate; Diploma; Master's **Classes:** Most classes have fewer than 10 students. Most lab/discussion sessions have fewer than 10 students. **Most popular majors:** Religious Education; Theological And Ministerial Studies, Other; Pastoral Studies/Counseling. **Special Study Options:** Distance learning; Double major; Dual enrollment; External degree program; Teacher certification program.

FACILITIES

Housing: Men's dorms; Wellness housing; Women's dorms **Special Academic Facilities/Equipment:** Heritage Collection **Computers:** 100% of classrooms, 100% of dorms, 100% of libraries, have wireless network access.

CAMPUS LIFE

Environment: Metropolis **Activities:** Campus Ministries; Choral groups; Drama/theater; Student government; Yearbook 5 religious organizations. **Athletics (Intercollegiate):** *Men:* baseball, basketball. *Women:* basketball, cheerleading, volleyball. **On-Campus Highlights:** Student Union Building, Library, Heritage Collection

ADMISSIONS

Freshman Academic Profile: Average high school GPA 2.9. 2% in top 10% of high school class, 21% in top 25% of high school class, 47% in top 50% of high school class. 80% from public high schools. **Test Scores:** Minimum paper TOEFL 550. **Basis for Candidate Selection:** *Very important factors considered include:* application essay, recommendation(s), religious affiliation/commitment. *Important factors considered include:* interview, level of applicant's interest. *Other factors considered include:* character/personal qualities. **Freshman Admission Requirements:** High school diploma is required and GED is accepted *Academic units required:* 3 English, 2 math, 1 science, 2 social studies. **Freshman Admission Statistics:** 86 applied, 100.0% admitted, 63% enrolled. **Transfer Admission Requirements:** High school transcript, college transcript(s), essay or personal statement, Lowest grade transferable C. **General Admission Information:** Application fee $15. Priority deadline 8/1. Nonfall registration accepted. Admission may be deferred for a maximum of three semesters

COSTS AND FINANCIAL AID

Annual tuition $7,100. Room and board $4,800. Required fees $740. Average book expense $750. **Required Forms and Deadlines:** FAFSA. **Notification of Awards:** Applicants will be notified of awards on a rolling basis beginning 12/1. **Types of Aid:** *Need-based scholarships/grants:* College/university scholarship or grant aid from institutional funds; Federal Pell; Private scholarships. *Loans:* Direct PLUS loans; Direct Subsidized Stafford Loans; Direct Unsubsidized Stafford Loans. *Student Employment:* Institutional employment available. **Financial Aid Statistics:** 100% needy freshmen, 100% needy undergrads receive need-based scholarship or grant aid. 0% undergrads receive non-need-based scholarship or grant aid. 0% freshmen, 0% undergrads receive need-based self-help aid. 0% freshmen, 0% undergrads receive athletic scholarships. 80% freshmen, 80% undergrads receive any aid. **Criteria for awarding aid:** *Need-based:* Academics, Alumni affiliation, Leadership, Religious affiliation *Non-need-based:* Academics, Leadership, Religious affiliation.

ART ACADEMY OF CINCINNATI

1212 Jackson Street, Cincinnati, OH 45202
Phone: 513-562-8740 · **Financial Aid Phone:** 513-562-8751
E-mail: admissions@artacademy.edu
Fax: 513-562-8778 · **Website:** www.artacademy.edu · **ACT Code:** 3011

This private school was founded in 1887.

RATINGS

Admissions Selectivity Rating: 85   **Fire Safety Rating:** 60*   **Green Rating:** 60*

STUDENTS AND FACULTY

Enrollment: 159. **Student Body:** 64% female, 36% male, 1% international (2 countries represented). Asian 1%, African American 4%, Caucasian 90%, Hispanic 1%, Native American 0%, Race unknown 2%.
Faculty: Student/faculty ratio 6:1. 14 full-time faculty, 100% hold PhDs, 7% are members of minority groups, 57% are women. 0% of classes are taught by teaching assistants.

ACADEMICS

Degrees: Associate; Bachelor's; Master's **Classes:** Most classes have fewer than 10 students. **Most popular majors:** Graphic Design; Illustration; Painting. **Special Study Options:** Cooperative education program; Cross-registration; Double major; Internships. **Disability Services offered to physically disabled students:** Note-taking services; Tape recorders; Tutors.

FACILITIES

Housing: Coed dorms

CAMPUS LIFE

Environment: Metropolis **Activities:** Literary magazine; Student government; Student-run film society; Yearbook. **On-Campus Highlights:** New Building, Dorms, Student Studios, Student Commons, Three Art Galleries **Environmental Initiatives:** Received Leadership in Energy and Environmental Design (LEED) Green Building certification by the United States Green Building Council.

ADMISSIONS

Test Scores: SAT Math middle 50% range 420-570. SAT EBRW middle 50% range 480-600. ACT middle 50% range 18-24. Minimum internet-based TOEFL 80. Minimum paper TOEFL 550. **Basis for Candidate Selection:** *Very important factors considered include:* rigor of secondary school record, interview, talent/ability. *Important factors considered include:* academic GPA, application essay. *Other factors considered include:* standardized test scores, recommendation(s), extracurricular activities, character/personal qualities. **Freshman Admission Requirements:** High school diploma is required and GED is accepted *Academic units recommended:* 4 English, 3 math, 2 science, 1 social studies. **Freshman Admission Statistics:** 192 applied, 56.8% admitted, 43% enrolled. **Transfer Admission Requirements:** High school transcript, college transcript(s), essay or personal statement, interview, Minimum college GPA of 2.0 required. Lowest grade transferable C. **General Admission Information:** Priority deadline 3/1. Regular application deadline 6/30. Nonfall registration accepted. Admission may be deferred for a maximum of one year.

COSTS AND FINANCIAL AID

Annual tuition $21,500. Required fees $380. Average book expense $1,200. **Required Forms and Deadlines:** FAFSA; State aid form. **Notification of Awards:** Applicants will be notified of awards on a rolling basis beginning 3/1. **Types of Aid:** *Need-based scholarships/grants:* College/university scholarship or grant aid from institutional funds; Federal Pell; Private scholarships; SEOG; State scholarships/grants. *Loans:* Direct PLUS loans; Direct Subsidized Stafford Loans; Direct Unsubsidized Stafford Loans. *Student Employment:* Federal Work-Study Program available. Institutional employment available. **Financial Aid Statistics:** 95% undergrads receive any aid. **Criteria for awarding aid:** *Non-need-based:* Academics, Art.

ART CENTER COLLEGE OF DESIGN

1700 Lida Street, Pasadena, CA 91103-1999
Phone: 626-396-2373 · **Financial Aid Phone:** 626-396-2215
E-mail: admissions@artcenter.edu · **CEEB Code:** 4009
Fax: 626-795-0578 · **Website:** www.artcenter.edu · **ACT Code:** 164

This private school was founded in 1930. It has a 162.62 acre campus.

RATINGS

Admissions Selectivity Rating: 0   **Fire Safety Rating:** 60*   **Green Rating:** 77

STUDENTS AND FACULTY

Enrollment: 1,974. **Student Body:** 54% female, 46% male, 31% international (51 countries represented). Asian 33%, African American 1%, Caucasian 16%, Hispanic 13%, Native American <1%, Pacific Islander <1%, Two or more races 4%, Race unknown 1%.
Retention and Graduation: 24% freshmen graduate within 4 years. 68% freshmen graduate within 6 years. **Faculty:** 0% of classes are taught by teaching assistants.

ACADEMICS

Degrees: Bachelor's; Master's **Classes:** Most classes have 10-19 students. Most lab/discussion sessions have 10-19 students. **Most popular majors:** Engineering-Related Fields, Other; Graphic Design; Illustration. **Special Study Options:** Cross-registration; Distance learning; Exchange student program (domestic); Independent study; Internships; Study abroad. **Honors programs:** Semester of study following graduation for undergraduates—project focused. **Disability Services offered to physically disabled students:** Note-taking services; Reader services; Tape recorders; Tutors. **Career services:** Alumni network; Alumni services; Career assessment; Career/job search classes; Internships; Regional alumni

FACILITIES

Housing: 98% of campus accessible to physically disabled. **Special Academic Facilities/Equipment:** Sinclair Pavilion, Williamson Gallery **Computers:** Administrative functions (other than registration) can be performed online.

CAMPUS LIFE

Environment: City **Activities:** Student government; Student-run film society 12 registered organizations. **On-Campus Highlights:** Student Gallery, Technical Skill Center, Color, Materials and Trends Exploration Lab (CMTEL), James Lemont Fogg Memorial Library, Photography and Film Stages/Equipment Room **Environmental Initiatives:** All building projects comply with CALGreen

ADMISSIONS

Test Scores: Minimum internet-based TOEFL 80. **Basis for Candidate Selection:** *Very important factors considered include:* rigor of secondary school record, application essay, talent/ability. *Important factors considered include:* class rank, academic GPA, standardized test scores, character/personal qualities. *Other factors considered include:* recommendation(s), extracurricular activities, first generation, geographical residence, volunteer work, work experience. **Freshman Admission Requirements:** High school diploma is required and GED is accepted **Transfer Admission Requirements:** college transcript(s), essay or personal statement, Lowest grade transferable c. **General Admission Information:** Application fee $50. Priority deadline 2/15. Nonfall registration accepted. Admission may be deferred for a maximum of 1 term.

COSTS AND FINANCIAL AID

Required fees $550. Average book expense $4,000. **Required Forms and Deadlines:** FAFSA; State aid form. **Notification of Awards:** Applicants will be notified of awards on a rolling basis beginning 4/1. **Types of Aid:** *Need-based scholarships/grants:* College/university scholarship or grant aid from institutional funds; Federal Pell; Private scholarships; SEOG; State scholarships/grants. *Loans:* Direct PLUS loans; Direct Subsidized Stafford Loans; Direct Unsubsidized Stafford Loans. *Student Employment:* Federal Work-Study Program available. Institutional employment available. **Criteria for awarding aid:** *Need-based:* Art *Non-need-based:* Art.

THE ART INSTITUTE OF ATLANTA

6600 Peachtree Dunwoody Road, Atlanta, GA 30328
Phone: (770) 394-8300 · **Financial Aid Phone:** 770-689-4824
E-mail: aia-admis@aii.edu
Fax: (770) 394-0008 · **Website:** http://www.artinstitutes.edu/atlanta/ · **ACT Code:** 859

This proprietary school was founded in 1949. It has a 7 acre campus.

RATINGS
Admissions Selectivity Rating: 0 **Fire Safety Rating:** 60* **Green Rating:** 60*

STUDENTS AND FACULTY
Enrollment: 3,839. **Student Body:** 44% female, 56% male, <1% international (33 countries represented). Asian 1%, African American 36%, Caucasian 30%, Hispanic 3%, Native American <1%, Race unknown 30%.
Faculty: Student/faculty ratio 21:1. 131 full-time faculty, 48% hold PhDs, 21% are members of minority groups, 45% are women.

ACADEMICS
Degrees: Associate; Bachelor's; Certificate; Diploma **Classes:** Most classes have 20-29 students. Most lab/discussion sessions have 20-29 students. **Most popular majors:** Culinary Arts/Chef Training; Commercial And Advertising Art; Interior Design. **Special Study Options:** Accelerated program; Distance learning; Dual enrollment; Honors program; Independent study; Internships; Study abroad; Weekend college. **Honors programs:** Design Honors Studio for graphic design students: students work with clients in the community. **Disability Services offered to physically disabled students:** Note-taking services; Reader services; Tape recorders; Tutors. **Career services:** Alumni network; Alumni services; Career/job search classes; Internships

FACILITIES
Housing: Coed dorms 100% of campus accessible to physically diasbled. **Special Academic Facilities/Equipment:** Art gallery, multi-camera video studio with digital and non-linear video editing suites, and an audio studio and control room featuring Protools stations. Professional photography studios with traditional and digital darkroom facilities containing high-end professional equipment such as the Imacon scanner, Cone Piezograph BandW printers, Epson 5500 printer, and Epson 10000 printer. Photographic video editing stations consist of Dual Processor G4s with cinema displays that are color managed with Greytag MacBeth equipment. Culinary facilities with five teaching kitchens and a dining lab. **Computers:** Students can register for classes online.

CAMPUS LIFE
Environment: Metropolis **Activities:** International Student Organization; Student government 16 registered organizations. **On-Campus Highlights:** Gallery, Supply Store, Coffee Bar, Snack Bar, Creations Dining Lab

ADMISSIONS
Freshman Academic Profile: 97% from public high schools. **Test Scores:** Minimum internet-based TOEFL 79-80. Minimum paper TOEFL 550. **Basis for Candidate Selection:** *Very important factors considered include:* academic GPA, application essay, standardized test scores, recommendation(s). *Important factors considered include:* interview. **Freshman Admission Requirements:** High school diploma is required and GED is accepted **Transfer Admission Requirements:** High school transcript, college transcript(s), essay or personal statement, interview, standardized test scores, statement of good standing from prior institution(s). Lowest grade transferable C. **General Admission Information:** Application fee $50. Nonfall registration accepted. Admission may be deferred for a maximum of 4 quarters.

COSTS AND FINANCIAL AID
Annual tuition $23,535. Average book expense $1,700. **Required Forms and Deadlines:** FAFSA; State aid form. **Notification of Awards:** Applicants will be notified of awards on a rolling basis beginning 3/15. **Types of Aid:** *Need-based scholarships/grants:* College/university scholarship or grant aid from institutional funds; Federal Pell; Private scholarships; SEOG; State scholarships/grants. *Loans:* Direct PLUS loans; Direct Subsidized Stafford Loans; Direct Unsubsidized Stafford Loans. *Student Employment:* Federal Work-Study Program available. Institutional employment available. **Financial Aid Statistics:** 52% needy freshmen, 72% needy undergrads receive need-based scholarship or grant aid. 39% freshmen, 8% undergrads receive non-need-based scholarship or grant aid. 100% freshmen, 100% undergrads receive need-based self-help aid. 0% freshmen, 0% undergrads receive athletic scholarships. 19% freshmen, 81% undergrads receive any aid. **Criteria for awarding aid:** *Non-need-based:* Academics, Art, State/district residency.

THE ART INSTITUTE OF BOSTON
AT LESLEY UNIVERSITY

Office of Admissions and Relations with Schools, Boston, MA 02215-2598
Phone: 617.585.6710 · **Financial Aid Phone:** 617-349-8710
E-mail: admissions@aiboston.edu · **CEEB Code:** 3777
Fax: 617.585.6720 · **Website:** aiboston.edu · **ACT Code:** 1850

This private school was founded in 1912. It has a 1 acre campus.

RATINGS
Admissions Selectivity Rating: 79 **Fire Safety Rating:** 89 **Green Rating:** 60*

STUDENTS AND FACULTY
Enrollment: 1,261. **Student Body:** 75% female, 25% male, 44% out-of-state, 3% international (15 countries represented). Asian 3%, African American 4%, Caucasian 63%, Hispanic 5%, Native American <1%, Race unknown 21%.
Retention and Graduation: 66% freshmen return for sophomore year. 0% grads pursue law degrees. 0% grads pursue business degrees. 0% grads pursue medical degrees. **Faculty:** Student/faculty ratio 10:1. 73 full-time faculty, 68% hold PhDs, 12% are members of minority groups, 55% are women. 0% of classes are taught by teaching assistants.

ACADEMICS
Degrees: Associate; Bachelor's; Master's; Post-Master's certificate **Most popular majors:** Graphic Design; Illustration; Photography. **Special Study Options:** Accelerated program; Cross-registration; Distance learning; Double major; Dual enrollment; Exchange student program (domestic); Honors program; Independent study; Internships; Liberal arts/career combination; Student-designed major; Study abroad; Teacher certification program. **Honors programs:** First year foundation students are eligible for advanced placement, foundation studio exemptions, and enrolling in Honors Studio and Honors English. **Disability Services offered to physically disabled students:** Note-taking services; Reader services; Tape recorders; Tutors. **Career services:** Alumni network; Alumni services; Career assessment; Career/job search classes; Internships; Regional alumni

FACILITIES
Housing: Coed dorms; Women's dorms 90% of campus accessible to physically diasbled. **Special Academic Facilities/Equipment:** Art Gallery with regular shows of prominant artists; art library; applied art facilities, including state of the art photo and computer labs, animation studio, ceramics studio, wood shop, metals studio, and printmaking studio **Computers:** 100% of classrooms, 10% of dorms, 100% of libraries, 100% of dining areas, 100% of student union, 25% of common outdoor areas have wireless network access. Students can register for classes online. Administrative functions (other than registration) can be performed online.

CAMPUS LIFE
Environment: Metropolis **Activities:** Campus Ministries; Choral groups; Dance; Drama/theater; International Student Organization; Literary magazine; Musical theater; Student government; Student newspaper 25 registered organizations, 2 honor societies, 2 religious organizations. **Athletics (Intercollegiate):** *Men:* basketball, cross-country, soccer, tennis, volleyball. *Women:* basketball, crew/rowing, cross-country, soccer, softball, tennis, volleyball. **On-Campus Highlights:** Gallery, Computer Labs, Animation Studio, Photo Labs, Student Lounge **Environmental Initiatives:** Continual enhancement of recycling, waste management and composting programs on campus.

ADMISSIONS
Freshman Academic Profile: Average high school GPA 3.0. 12% in top 10% of high school class, 38% in top 25% of high school class, 70% in top 50% of high school class. 84% from public high schools. **Test Scores:** SAT Math middle 50% range 460-560. SAT EBRW middle 50% range 490-600. ACT middle 50% range 19-26. Minimum internet-based TOEFL 61. Minimum paper TOEFL 500. **Basis for Candidate Selection:** *Very important factors considered include:* rigor of secondary school record, academic GPA. *Important factors considered include:* class rank, application essay, standardized test scores, recommendation(s), interview, extracurricular activities, talent/ability, character/personal qualities. *Other factors considered include:* first generation, alumni/ae relation, geographical residence, racial/ethnic status, volunteer work, work experience, level of applicant's interest. **Freshman Admission Requirements:** High school diploma is required and GED is accepted *Academic units required:* 4 English, *Academic units recommended:* 4 English, 1 math, 1 science, 1 foreign language, 2 social studies, 2 history, 2 academic electives, 2 units from above areas or other academic areas. **Freshman Admission Statistics:** 2,523 applied, 65.0% admitted, 20% enrolled. **Transfer Admission Requirements:** High school transcript, college transcript(s), essay or personal statement, interview, statement of good standing from prior institution(s). Minimum college GPA of

2.0 required. Lowest grade transferable C. **General Admission Information:** Application fee $50. Priority deadline 2/15. Nonfall registration accepted. Admission may be deferred for a maximum of 1 year.

COSTS AND FINANCIAL AID

Annual tuition $28,000. Room and board $13,250. Required fees $750. Average book expense $1,575. **Required Forms and Deadlines:** FAFSA. **Notification of Awards:** Applicants will be notified of awards on a rolling basis beginning 2/15. **Types of Aid:** *Need-based scholarships/grants:* College/ university scholarship or grant aid from institutional funds; Federal Pell; Private scholarships; SEOG; State scholarships/grants. *Loans:* Direct PLUS loans; Direct Subsidized Stafford Loans; Direct Unsubsidized Stafford Loans. *Student Employment:* Federal Work-Study Program available. Institutional employment available. **Financial Aid Statistics:** 98% needy freshmen, 96% needy undergrads receive need-based scholarship or grant aid. 19% freshmen, 38% undergrads receive non-need-based scholarship or grant aid. 73% freshmen, 70% undergrads receive need-based self-help aid. 0% freshmen, 0% undergrads receive athletic scholarships. 70% freshmen, 70% undergrads receive any aid. **Criteria for awarding aid:** *Need-based:* Academics, Art, Minority status *Non-need-based:* Academics, Art, Leadership, Minority status, State/district residency.

THE ART INSTITUTE OF LAS VEGAS

2350 Corporate Circle, Henderson, NV
Phone: 702.369.9944
E-mail: ailvadm@aii.edu
Fax: 702.992.8458 · **Website:** http://www.artinstitutes.edu/lasvegas/

This proprietary school has a 1.5 acre campus.

RATINGS

Admissions Selectivity Rating: 70   **Fire Safety Rating:** 71   **Green Rating:** 60*

STUDENTS AND FACULTY

Enrollment: 1,301. **Student Body:** 48% female, 52% male, 0% international. Asian 12%, African American 9%, Caucasian 35%, Hispanic 14%, Native American 1%, Race unknown 28%.
Retention and Graduation: 54% freshmen return for sophomore year. **Faculty:** Student/faculty ratio 17:1. 27 full-time faculty, 7% hold PhDs, 22% are women. 0% of classes are taught by teaching assistants.

ACADEMICS

Degrees: Associate; Bachelor's **Classes:** Most classes have 10-19 students. **Most popular majors:** Digital Communication And Media/Multimedia; Culinary Arts/Chef Training. **Special Study Options:** Distance learning; Independent study; Internships; Study abroad. **Disability Services offered to physically disabled students:** Note-taking services; Reader services; Tape recorders; Tutors. **Career services:** Alumni network; Alumni services; Career assessment; Career/job search classes; Internships; Regional alumni

FACILITIES

Housing: Apartments for single students; Wellness housing **Computers:**

CAMPUS LIFE

Environment: City **Activities:** Student-run film society. **On-Campus Highlights:** Student Lounge

ADMISSIONS

Freshman Academic Profile: Average high school GPA 2.6. **Test Scores:** Minimum paper TOEFL 500. **Basis for Candidate Selection:** *Very important factors considered include:* application essay, interview. *Important factors considered include:* talent/ability, level of applicant's interest. *Other factors considered include:* academic GPA, standardized test scores, character/personal qualities. **Freshman Admission Requirements:** High school diploma is required and GED is accepted **Freshman Admission Statistics:** 436 applied, 67.9% admitted, 78% enrolled. **Transfer Admission Requirements:** High school transcript, college transcript(s), essay or personal statement, interview, statement of good standing from prior institution(s). Minimum college GPA of 2.0 required. Lowest grade transferable 2. **General Admission Information:** Application fee $150. Nonfall registration accepted. Admission may be deferred.

COSTS AND FINANCIAL AID

Annual tuition $21,552. Required fees $450. **Types of Aid:** *Student Employment:* Federal Work-Study Program available.

THE ART INSTITUTES INTERNATIONAL MINNESOTA

15 South 9th Street, Minneapolis, MN 55402
Phone: 612-332-3361 · **Financial Aid Phone:** 612-332-3361
E-mail: aimadm@aii.edu
Fax: 612-332-3934 · **Website:** www.artinstitutes.edu/minneapolis

This proprietary school was founded in 1997.

RATINGS

Admissions Selectivity Rating: 61   **Fire Safety Rating:** 85   **Green Rating:** 60*

STUDENTS AND FACULTY

Enrollment: 1,974. **Student Body:** 61% female, 39% male, 20% out-of-state, international.
Retention and Graduation: 60% freshmen return for sophomore year. **Faculty:** Student/faculty ratio 20:1. 56 full-time faculty, 36% are women.

ACADEMICS

Degrees: Associate; Bachelor's; Certificate **Classes:** Most classes have 10-19 students. Most lab/discussion sessions have fewer than 10 students. **Special Study Options:** Distance learning; Independent study; Internships; Study abroad. **Disability Services offered to physically disabled students:** Note-taking services; Tape recorders; Tutors. **Career services:** Alumni network; Alumni services; Career/job search classes; Internships; Regional alumni

FACILITIES

Housing: Apartments for single students 100% of campus accessible to physically diasbled. **Computers:** 100% of classrooms, 100% of dorms, 100% of libraries, 100% of dining areas, 100% of student union, have wireless network access. Students can register for classes online. Administrative functions (other than registration) can be performed online.

CAMPUS LIFE

Environment: Metropolis **Activities:** Campus Ministries; International Student Organization; Literary magazine; Student newspaper, 16 registered organizations, 1 honor societies. **On-Campus Highlights:** School dining lab, Art galleries, Connection to the city's skyway system, New second campus

ADMISSIONS

Basis for Candidate Selection: *Very important factors considered include:* application essay, interview. *Important factors considered include:* talent/ ability. *Other factors considered include:* academic GPA, standardized test scores, extracurricular activities, character/personal qualities, level of applicant's interest. **Freshman Admission Requirements:** High school diploma is required and GED is accepted **Transfer Admission Requirements:** High school transcript, college transcript(s). **General Admission Information:** Application fee $50. Nonfall registration accepted.

COSTS AND FINANCIAL AID

Annual tuition $22,416. **Required Forms and Deadlines:** FAFSA. **Types of Aid:** *Need-based scholarships/grants:* College/university scholarship or grant aid from institutional funds; Federal Pell; Private scholarships; SEOG; State scholarships/grants; United Negro College Fund. *Loans:* Direct PLUS loans; Direct Subsidized Stafford Loans; Direct Unsubsidized Stafford Loans. *Student Employment:* Federal Work-Study Program available. Institutional employment available. **Criteria for awarding aid:** *Need-based:* Academics.

ASHLAND UNIVERSITY

401 College Avenue, Ashland, OH 44805
Phone: 419-289-5052 · **Financial Aid Phone:** 419-289-5002
E-mail: enrollme@ashland.edu · **CEEB Code:** 1021
Fax: 419-289-5999 · **Website:** www.ashland.edu · **ACT Code:** 3234

This private school, affiliated with the Church of Brethren, was founded in 1878. It has a 12 acre campus.

RATINGS

Admissions Selectivity Rating: 79   **Fire Safety Rating:** 73   **Green Rating:** 60*

STUDENTS AND FACULTY

Enrollment: 3,232. **Student Body:** 51% female, 49% male, 15% out-of-state, 2% international (16 countries represented). Asian <1%, African American

13%, Caucasian 78%, Hispanic 3%, Native American <1%, Pacific Islander <1%, Two or more races 1%, Race unknown 2%.
Retention and Graduation: 77% freshmen return for sophomore year. 13% grads go on to further study within 1 year. 2% grads pursue arts and sciences degrees. 1% grads pursue law degrees. 1% grads pursue business degrees. 1% grads pursue medical degrees. **Faculty:** Student/faculty ratio 13:1. 251 full-time faculty, 78% hold PhDs, 0% of classes are taught by teaching assistants.

ACADEMICS
Degrees: Associate; Bachelor's; Certificate; Diploma; Doctoral; Master's; Terminal Associate; Transfer Associate **Classes:** Most classes have 40-49 students. Most lab/discussion sessions have 10-19 students. **Most popular majors:** Education, General; Business/Commerce, General. **Special Study Options:** Accelerated program; Distance learning; Double major; Dual enrollment; English as a Second Language (ESL); Exchange student program (domestic); Honors program; Independent study; Internships; Student-designed major; Study abroad; Teacher certification program. **Honors programs:** Ashland University Honors Program. **Disability Services offered to physically disabled students:** Note-taking services; Reader services; Tape recorders; Tutors. **Career services:** Alumni network; Alumni services; Career assessment; Career/job search classes; Internships

FACILITIES
Housing: Apartments for single students; Coed dorms; Fraternity/sorority housing; Men's dorms; Special housing for disabled student; Special housing for international students; Theme housing; Women's.dorms 70% of campus accessible to physically diasbled. **Special Academic Facilities/Equipment:** Neumismatic Center, Patterson Technology Center, Coburn Art Gallery, Hugo Young Theatre, Studio Theatre, 33 room Radio/Television Condex, Media Center, Pre-Columbian Art Exhibit, Ashbrook Center. **Computers:** 90% of classrooms, 50% of dorms, 100% of libraries, 50% of dining areas, 100% of student union, 50% of common outdoor areas have wireless network access. Students can register for classes online. Administrative functions (other than registration) can be performed online.

CAMPUS LIFE
Environment: Town **Activities:** Campus Ministries; Choral groups; Concert band; Dance; Drama/theater; International Student Organization; Jazz band; Literary magazine; Marching band; Music ensembles; Musical theater; Opera; Pep band; Radio station; Student government; Student newspaper; Symphony orchestra; Television station; Yearbook 102 registered organizations, 18 honor societies, 9 religious organizations. 4 fraternities, 5 sororities. **Athletics (Intercollegiate):** *Men:* baseball, basketball, cross-country, diving, football, golf, soccer, swimming, track/field (outdoor), track/field (indoor), wrestling. *Women:* basketball, cheerleading, cross-country, diving, golf, soccer, softball, swimming, tennis, track/field (outdoor), track/field (indoor), volleyball.
On-Campus Highlights: Kettering Science Center, Recreation and Sport Sciences Center, Schar College of Education, Dauch College of Business and Economics, National ranked food service

ADMISSIONS
Freshman Academic Profile: Average high school GPA 3.4. 22% in top 10% of high school class, 49% in top 25% of high school class, 80% in top 50% of high school class. 89% from public high schools. **Test Scores:** SAT Math middle 50% range 490-580. SAT EBRW middle 50% range 460-560. ACT middle 50% range 20-25. Minimum internet-based TOEFL 65. Minimum paper TOEFL 500. **Basis for Candidate Selection:** *Very important factors considered include:* rigor of secondary school record, academic GPA, standardized test scores. *Important factors considered include:* class rank, extracurricular activities, level of applicant's interest. *Other factors considered include:* application essay, recommendation(s), talent/ability, character/personal qualities, first generation, alumni/ae relation, religious affiliation/commitment, volunteer work, work experience. **Freshman Admission Requirements:** High school diploma is required and GED is accepted *Academic units required:* 3 English, 3 math, 3 science, 2 social studies, 1 history, *Academic units recommended:* 4 English, 4 math, 4 science, 2 foreign language, 3 social studies, 3 history, 1 academic elective, 1 computer science. **Freshman Admission Statistics:** 3,184 applied, 71.9% admitted, 26% enrolled. **Transfer Admission Requirements:** college transcript(s), essay or personal statement, Minimum college GPA of 2.5 required. Lowest grade transferable C-. **General Admission Information:** Priority deadline 1/1. Nonfall registration accepted. Admission may be deferred for a maximum of 1 semester.

COSTS AND FINANCIAL AID
Annual tuition $29,844. Room and board $9,602. Required fees $944. Average book expense $800. **Required Forms and Deadlines:** FAFSA. **Notification of Awards:** Applicants will be notified of awards on a rolling basis beginning 3/1. **Types of Aid:** *Need-based scholarships/grants:* College/university scholarship or grant aid from institutional funds; Federal Pell; Private scholarships; SEOG; State scholarships/grants. *Loans:* Direct PLUS loans; Direct Subsidized Stafford Loans; Direct Unsubsidized Stafford Loans. *Student*

Employment: Federal Work-Study Program available. Institutional employment available. **Financial Aid Statistics:** 95% needy freshmen, 91% needy undergrads receive need-based scholarship or grant aid. 0% undergrads receive non-need-based scholarship or grant aid. 95% freshmen, 91% undergrads receive need-based self-help aid. 4% freshmen, 4% undergrads receive athletic scholarships. 99% freshmen, 98% undergrads receive any aid. **Criteria for awarding aid:** *Need-based:* Academics, Job skills, Minority status *Non-need-based:* Academics, Alumni affiliation, Art, Athletics, Job skills, Leadership, Minority status, Music/drama, Religious affiliation.

ASSUMPTION COLLEGE

500 Salisbury St., Worcester, MA 01609-1296
Financial Aid Phone: 508-767-7158
E-mail: admiss@assumption.edu • **CEEB Code:** 3009
Fax: (508) 799-4412 • **Website:** http://www.assumption.edu • **ACT Code:** 1782

This private school, affiliated with the Roman Catholic Church, was founded in 1904. It has a 180 acre campus.

RATINGS
Admissions Selectivity Rating: 77   **Fire Safety Rating:** 82   **Green Rating:** 60*

STUDENTS AND FACULTY
Enrollment: 1,929. **Student Body:** 58% female, 42% male, 35% out-of-state, 2% international (23 countries represented). Asian 3%, African American 5%, Caucasian 77%, Hispanic 7%, Native American <1%, Pacific Islander <1%, Two or more races 2%, Race unknown 4%.
Retention and Graduation: 82% freshmen return for sophomore year. 68% freshmen graduate within 4 years. 71% freshmen graduate within 6 years. 25% grads go on to further study within 1 year. 15% grads pursue arts and sciences degrees. 1.6% grads pursue law degrees. 3% grads pursue business degrees. 1% grads pursue medical degrees. **Faculty:** Student/faculty ratio 11:1. 143 full-time faculty, 91% hold PhDs, 6% are members of minority groups, 45% are women. 0% of classes are taught by teaching assistants.

ACADEMICS
Degrees: Bachelor's; Master's; Post-Bachelor's certificate; Post-Master's certificate **Classes:** Most classes have 10-19 students. Most lab/discussion sessions have fewer than 10 students. **Most popular majors:** Psychology, General; Rehabilitation And Therapeutic Professions; Accounting. **Special Study Options:** Cross-registration; Double major; Honors program; Independent study; Internships; Student-designed major; Study abroad; Teacher certification program. **Honors programs:** The Assumption College Honors Program is a selective program designed to foster academic engagement inside and outside the classroom. The program promotes intellectual friendship and discourse while providing a common, intensive learning experience in small seminar classes. **Combined degree programs:** BA/MA. **Disability Services offered to physically disabled students:** Note-taking services; Reader services; Tape recorders; Tutors. **Career services:** Alumni network; Career assessment; Career/job search classes; Internships; Regional alumni

FACILITIES
Housing: Coed dorms; Special housing for disabled student; Theme housing; Wellness housing; Women's dorms 71% of campus accessible to physically diasbled. **Special Academic Facilities/Equipment:** French Institute museum, Institute for Social and Rehabilitation Services, language lab, media center Living/Learning Center Testa Science Center Information Technology Center **Computers:** 100% of classrooms, 100% of libraries, 50% of dining areas, 100% of student union, 25% of common outdoor areas have wireless network access. Students can register for classes online. Administrative functions (other than registration) can be performed online.

CAMPUS LIFE
Environment: City **Activities:** Campus Ministries; Choral groups; Concert band; Dance; Drama/theater; Jazz band; Literary magazine; Music ensembles; Musical theater; Pep band; Student government; Student newspaper; Student-run film society; Television station; Yearbook 50 registered organizations, 12 honor societies, 1 religious organization. **Athletics (Intercollegiate):** *Men:* baseball, basketball, cross-country, football, golf, ice hockey, lacrosse, soccer, tennis, track/field (outdoor), track/field (indoor). *Women:* basketball, crew/rowing, cross-country, field hockey, lacrosse, soccer, softball, swimming, tennis, track/field (outdoor), track/field (indoor), volleyball. **On-Campus Highlights:** Testa Science Center, Living Learning Center, Plourde Recreation Center, Charlie's Cafe, D'Alzon Library

ADMISSIONS

Freshman Academic Profile: Average high school GPA 3.3. 12% in top 10% of high school class, 41% in top 25% of high school class, 80% in top 50% of high school class. 68% from public high schools. **Test Scores:** SAT Math middle 50% range 530-620. SAT EBRW middle 50% range 540-630. ACT middle 50% range 23-28. Minimum internet-based TOEFL 80. Minimum paper TOEFL 550. **Basis for Candidate Selection:** *Very important factors considered include:* academic GPA, application essay. *Important factors considered include:* rigor of secondary school record, recommendation(s), interview, volunteer work.level of applicant's interest. *Other factors considered include:* class rank, standardized test scores, extracurricular activities, talent/ability, character/ personal qualities, first generation, alumni/ae relation, racial/ethnic status. **Freshman Admission Requirements:** High school diploma is required and GED is accepted *Academic units required:* 4 English, 3 math, 2 science, 2 foreign language, 2 history, 5 academic electives. **Freshman Admission Statistics:** 4,508 applied, 79.0% admitted, 11% enrolled. **Transfer Admission Requirements:** High school transcript, college transcript(s), essay or personal statement, statement of good standing from prior institution(s). Minimum college GPA of 2.5 required. Lowest grade transferable C. **General Admission Information:** Application fee $50. Regular application deadline 2/15. Nonfall registration accepted. Admission may be deferred for a maximum of 1 year.

COSTS AND FINANCIAL AID

Annual tuition $35,510. Required fees $750. Average book expense $1,000. **Required Forms and Deadlines:** FAFSA. **Notification of Awards:** Applicants will be notified of awards on a rolling basis beginning 2/16. **Types of Aid:** *Need-based scholarships/grants:* College/university scholarship or grant aid from institutional funds; Federal Pell; Private scholarships; SEOG; State scholarships/grants. *Loans:* Direct PLUS loans; Direct Subsidized Stafford Loans; Direct Unsubsidized Stafford Loans. *Student Employment:* Federal Work-Study Program available. Institutional employment available. **Financial Aid Statistics:** 100% needy freshmen, 100% needy undergrads receive need-based scholarship or grant aid. 22% freshmen, 16% undergrads receive non-need-based scholarship or grant aid. 75% freshmen, 81% undergrads receive need-based self-help aid. 4% freshmen, 4% undergrads receive athletic scholarships. 98% freshmen, 98% undergrads receive any aid. **Criteria for awarding aid:** *Need-based:* Academics, Athletics *Non-need-based:* Academics, Athletics, Music/drama.

See page 886.

ATHABASCA UNIVERSITY

1 University Drive, Athabasca, AB T9S 3A3
Phone: 800-788-9041 • **Financial Aid Phone:** 780-675-6147
Fax: 780-675-6145 • **Website:** www.athabascau.ca

This public school was founded in 1970.

RATINGS

Admissions Selectivity Rating: 69 **Fire Safety Rating:** 60* **Green Rating:** 60*

STUDENTS AND FACULTY

Student Body: 61% out-of-state, (90 countries represented).

ACADEMICS

Degrees: Bachelor's; Certificate; Diploma; Doctoral; Master's; Post-Bachelor's certificate; Post-Master's certificate **Classes:** Most classes have 10-19 students. Most lab/discussion sessions have 10-19 students. **Most popular majors:** Elementary Education And Teaching; Criminal Justice/Safety Studies. **Special Study Options:** Accelerated program; Cross-registration; Distance learning; Double major; English as a Second Language (ESL); External degree program. **Disability Services offered to physically disabled students:** Tape recorders; Tutors.

FACILITIES

Computers: Students can register for classes online. Administrative functions (other than registration) can be performed online.

CAMPUS LIFE

Environment: Rural **Activities:** Student government.

ADMISSIONS

Freshman Admission Statistics: 38,876 applied, 100.0% admitted, 100% enrolled. **Transfer Admission Requirements:** High school transcript, college transcript(s). **General Admission Information:** Application fee $100. Nonfall registration accepted. Admission may be deferred for a maximum of 1 year.

COSTS AND FINANCIAL AID

Annual out-of-state tuition $762.

AUBURN UNIVERSITY

The Quad Center, Auburn, AL 36849-5149
Phone: 334-844-6425 • **Financial Aid Phone:** 334-844-4634
E-mail: admissions@auburn.edu • **CEEB Code:** 1005
Fax: 334-844-6436 • **Website:** www.auburn.edu • **ACT Code:** 11

This public school was founded in 1856. It has a 1875 acre campus.

RATINGS

Admissions Selectivity Rating: 83 **Fire Safety Rating:** 93 **Green Rating:** 87

STUDENTS AND FACULTY

Enrollment: 23,391. **Student Body:** 49% female, 51% male, 35% out-of-state, 3% international (59 countries represented). Asian 2%, African American 6%, Caucasian 82%, Hispanic 3%, Native American <1%, Pacific Islander <1%, Two or more races 2%, Race unknown <1%.
Retention and Graduation: 92% freshmen return for sophomore year. 49% freshmen graduate within 4 years. 77% freshmen graduate within 6 years. 42% grads go on to further study within 1 year. 9% grads pursue arts and sciences degrees. 7% grads pursue law degrees. 13% grads pursue business degrees. 30% grads pursue medical degrees. **Faculty:** Student/faculty ratio 19:1. 1,330 full-time faculty, 90% hold PhDs, 18% are members of minority groups, 39% are women.

ACADEMICS

Degrees: Bachelor's; Certificate; Doctoral; Doctoral/Professional; Doctoral/ Research; Master's; Post-Bachelor's certificate; Post-Master's certificate **Classes:** Most classes have 10-19 students. Most lab/discussion sessions have 10-19 students. **Most popular majors:** Secondary Education And Teaching; Mechanical Engineering; Business Administration And Management, General. **Special Study Options:** Accelerated program; Cooperative education program; Distance learning; Double major; Dual enrollment; English as a Second Language (ESL); Exchange student program (domestic); Honors program; Independent study; Internships; Liberal arts/career combination; Study abroad; Teacher certification program. **Honors programs:** The Auburn University's Honors College offers qualified students a unique academic experience, designed to provide many of the advantages of a small college in the midst of the many diverse opportunities available at a large university. It is designed for students capable of academic excellence. The program selects 200 entering freshmen each year, who may be enrolled in any College or School of the University which has undergraduate programs or offerings. Students already enrolled at Auburn can also qualify for the Honors College. **Disability Services offered to physically disabled students:** Note-taking services; Reader services; Tape recorders; Tutors. **Career services:** Alumni network; Alumni services; Career assessment; Career/job search classes; Internships

FACILITIES

Housing: Apartments for married students; Apartments for single students; Coed dorms; Fraternity/sorority housing; Men's dorms; Special housing for disabled student; Women's dorms 100% of campus accessible to physically diasbled. **Special Academic Facilities/Equipment:** Nuclear Science Center; Hybridoma Facility; Freeman Herbarium; Jule Collins Smith Art Museum; Hypervelocity Impact Facility; Advanced Microscopy & Imaging Laboratory; Alabama Microelectronics Science & Technology Center; Alabama Water Resources Research Institute; AU Airport with single/multi-engine aircraft and flight simulators; Center for Forest Sustainability; Center for Governmental Services; Center for Pharmacy Operations & Designs; Drug Information & Learning Resources Center; Economic & Community Development Institute; Fish Molecular Genetics & Biotechnology Laboratory; Forest Policy Center; Forest Products Development Center; Fusion Lab; Harris Early Learning Center; Dept of Psychology Health Behavior Assessment Center; Highway Research Center; Marriage & Family Therapy Center; Microfibrous Materials Manufacturing Center; Dept of Kinesiology Biomechanics Lab, and Motor Behavior Center; Plasma Sciences Lab; Veterinary Medicine Radiology Clinic, Scott-Ritchey Research Center, Southeastern Raptor Rehabilitation Center, Small & Large Animal Health Clinics **Computers:** 35% of classrooms, 100% of dorms, 95% of libraries, 50% of dining areas, 100% of student union, 30% of common outdoor areas have wireless network access. Students can register for classes online. Administrative functions (other than registration) can be performed online.

CAMPUS LIFE

Environment: Town **Activities:** Campus Ministries; Choral groups; Concert band; Dance; Drama/theater; International Student Organization; Jazz band;

Literary magazine; Marching band; Music ensembles; Musical theater; Opera; Pep band; Radio station; Student government; Student newspaper; Student-run film society; Symphony orchestra; Television station; Yearbook 300 registered organizations, 56 honor societies, 15 religious organizations. 30 fraternities, 19 sororities. **Athletics (Intercollegiate):** *Men:* baseball, basketball, cheerleading, cross-country, diving, football, golf, swimming, tennis, track/field (outdoor), track/field (indoor). *Women:* basketball, cheerleading, cross-country, diving, equestrian sports, golf, gymnastics, soccer, softball, swimming, tennis, track/field (outdoor), track/field (indoor), volleyball. **On-Campus Highlights:** Recreation and Wellness Center, Student Center, Donald E. Davis Arboretum, Ralph Draughon Library, Auburn Arena **Environmental Initiatives:** Incorporation of sustainability initiatives into university curricula, including one of the first truly interdisciplinary sustainability minors in the country.

ADMISSIONS

Freshman Academic Profile: Average high school GPA 3.9. 31% in top 10% of high school class, 63% in top 25% of high school class, 91% in top 50% of high school class. 86% from public high schools. **Test Scores:** SAT Math middle 50% range 560-660. SAT EBRW middle 50% range 570-650. ACT middle 50% range 24-30. Minimum internet-based TOEFL 79. Minimum paper TOEFL 550. **Basis for Candidate Selection:** *Very important factors considered include:* academic GPA, application essay, standardized test scores. *Important factors considered include:* rigor of secondary school record, extracurricular activities, talent/ability, character/personal qualities, first generation, alumni/ae relation, geographical residence, state residency, volunteer work, work experience, level of applicant's interest. *Other factors considered include:* recommendation(s). **Freshman Admission Requirements:** High school diploma is required and GED is accepted *Academic units required:* 4 English, 3 math, 2 science, 1 science labs, 3 social studies, *Academic units recommended:* 2 science labs, 1 foreign language, 4 social studies. **Freshman Admission Statistics:** 18,072 applied, 83.9% admitted, 32% enrolled. **Transfer Admission Requirements:** college transcript(s), Minimum college GPA of 2.5 required. Lowest grade transferable C. **General Admission Information:** Application fee $50. Priority deadline 2/1. Regular application deadline 6/1. Nonfall registration accepted.

COSTS AND FINANCIAL AID

Annual in-state tuition $13,332. Annual out-of-state tuition $28,008. Room and board $13,332. Required fees $1,632. Average book expense $1,200. **Required Forms and Deadlines:** FAFSA. **Notification of Awards:** Applicants will be notified of awards on a rolling basis beginning 10/2. **Types of Aid:** *Need-based scholarships/grants:* College/university scholarship or grant aid from institutional funds; Federal Pell; Private scholarships; SEOG; State scholarships/grants. *Loans:* Direct PLUS loans; Direct Subsidized Stafford Loans; Direct Unsubsidized Stafford Loans. *Student Employment:* Federal Work-Study Program available. Institutional employment available. **Financial Aid Statistics:** 81% needy freshmen, 72% needy undergrads receive need-based scholarship or grant aid. 14% freshmen, 9% undergrads receive non-need-based scholarship or grant aid. 64% freshmen, 77% undergrads receive need-based self-help aid. 2% freshmen, 2% undergrads receive athletic scholarships. 50% freshmen, 44% undergrads receive any aid. 41% undergrads borrow to pay for school. Average cumulative indebtedness $28,170.

AUBURN UNIVERSITY MONTGOMERY

P.O. Box 244023, Montgomery, AL 36124-4023
Phone: 334-244-3615 · **Financial Aid Phone:** (334) 244-3571
E-mail: admissions@aum.edu
Fax: 334-244-3795 · **Website:** www.aum.edu · **ACT Code:** 57

This public school was founded in 1967. It has a 500 acre campus.

RATINGS

Admissions Selectivity Rating: 74   **Fire Safety Rating:** 89   **Green Rating:** 61

STUDENTS AND FACULTY

Enrollment: 4,234. **Student Body:** 64% female, 36% male, 6% out-of-state, 4% international (34 countries represented). Asian 3%, African American 38%, Caucasian 50%, Hispanic 1%, Native American <1%, Pacific Islander <1%, Two or more races 3%, Race unknown <1%.
Retention and Graduation: 68% freshmen return for sophomore year. 9% freshmen graduate within 4 years. 28% freshmen graduate within 6 years.
Faculty: Student/faculty ratio 15:1. 207 full-time faculty, 84% hold PhDs, 21% are members of minority groups, 46% are women. 3% of classes are taught by teaching assistants.

ACADEMICS

Degrees: Bachelor's; Certificate; Doctoral/Research; Master's; Post-Bachelor's certificate; Post-Master's certificate **Classes:** Most classes have 10-19 students. Most lab/discussion sessions have 10-19 students. **Most popular majors:** Elementary Education And Teaching; Registered Nursing/Registered Nurse; Business/Commerce, General. **Special Study Options:** Accelerated program; Cross-registration; Distance learning; Double major; Dual enrollment; English as a Second Language (ESL); Honors program; Independent study; Internships; Liberal arts/career combination; Study abroad; Teacher certification program. **Honors programs:** Since 1981, the University Honors Program (UHP) has been open to qualified students in any major at AUM. The mission of the University Honors Program is to attract highly motivated AUM students and to recruit potential AUM students with qualifying ACT scores and GPAs, and to provide those students with a stimulating intellectual, scholarly, and social environment in which they can participate as part of a diverse community in which high achievement is the norm. **Disability Services offered to physically disabled students:** Note-taking services; Reader services; Tape recorders; Tutors. **Career services:** Alumni services; Career assessment; Career/job search classes; Internships

FACILITIES

Housing: Apartments for married students; Apartments for single students; Coed dorms; Special housing for international students; Theme housing 90% of campus accessible to physically diasbled. **Special Academic Facilities/Equipment:** Graphic arts center, mass communications lab, geographic information systems and computer cartography lab, multimedia television studio and other computer labs in various buildings across campus with different disciplinary areas. The Wellness Center, Warhawk Academic Success Center, Office of Global Initiatives **Computers:** Students can register for classes online. Administrative functions (other than registration) can be performed online.

CAMPUS LIFE

Environment: City **Activities:** Campus Ministries; Drama/theater; International Student Organization; Literary magazine; Music ensembles; Musical theater; Student government; Student newspaper 50 registered organizations, 10 honor societies, 7 religious organizations. 3 fraternities, 6 sororities. **Athletics (Intercollegiate):** *Men:* baseball, basketball, cheerleading, soccer, tennis. *Women:* basketball, cheerleading, soccer, softball, tennis. **On-Campus Highlights:** Wellness Center, Warhawk Academic Success Center, Taylor Center/Student Union, Warhawk Alley Lounge, The Roost **Environmental Initiatives:** Recycling

ADMISSIONS

Freshman Academic Profile: Average high school GPA 3.3. 16% in top 10% of high school class, 43% in top 25% of high school class, 75% in top 50% of high school class. 73% from public high schools. **Test Scores:** SAT Math middle 50% range 475-545. SAT EBRW middle 50% range 490-565. ACT middle 50% range 19-24. Minimum internet-based TOEFL 61. Minimum paper TOEFL 500. **Basis for Candidate Selection:** *Very important factors considered include:* rigor of secondary school record, academic GPA, standardized test scores. **Freshman Admission Requirements:** High school diploma is required and GED is accepted *Academic units recommended:* 3 English, 3 math, 2 science, 2 science labs, 2 foreign language, 2 social studies, 2 history, 2 academic electives. **Freshman Admission Statistics:** 2,474 applied, 82.5% admitted, 33% enrolled. **Transfer Admission Requirements:** college transcript(s), Minimum college GPA of 2.0 required. Lowest grade transferable D. **General Admission Information:** Regular application deadline 8/1. Nonfall registration accepted.

COSTS AND FINANCIAL AID

Annual in-state tuition $6,980. Annual out-of-state tuition $16,944. Room and board $6,980. Required fees $700. Average book expense $1,100. **Required Forms and Deadlines:** FAFSA. **Notification of Awards:** Applicants will be notified of awards on a rolling basis beginning 4/15. **Types of Aid:** *Need-based scholarships/grants:* College/university scholarship or grant aid from institutional funds; Federal Pell; SEOG; State scholarships/grants. *Loans:* Direct PLUS loans; Direct Subsidized Stafford Loans; Direct Unsubsidized Stafford Loans. *Student Employment:* Federal Work-Study Program available. Institutional employment available. **Financial Aid Statistics:** 72% needy freshmen, 74% needy undergrads receive need-based scholarship or grant aid. 35% freshmen, 23% undergrads receive non-need-based scholarship or grant aid. 97% freshmen, 96% undergrads receive need-based self-help aid. 0% freshmen, 0% undergrads receive athletic scholarships. 77% freshmen, 63% undergrads receive any aid. 69% undergrads borrow to pay for school. Average cumulative indebtedness $30,454.

AUGSBURG COLLEGE

2211 Riverside Avenue, Minneapolis, MN 55454
Phone: 612-330-1001 · Financial Aid Phone: 612-330-1046
E-mail: admissions@augsburg.edu · CEEB Code: 6014
Fax: 612-330-1590 · Website: www.augsburg.edu · ACT Code: 2080

*This private school, affiliated with the Lutheran Church, was founded in
1869. It has a 23 acre campus.*

RATINGS

Admissions Selectivity Rating: 87   **Fire Safety Rating:** 83   **Green Rating:** 60*

STUDENTS AND FACULTY

Enrollment: 3,014. **Student Body:** 55% female, 45% male, 13% out-of-state,
2% international (24 countries represented). Asian 7%, African American 9%,
Caucasian 68%, Hispanic 3%, Native American 2%, Pacific Islander <1%, Two
or more races 2%, Race unknown 6%.
Retention and Graduation: 83% freshmen return for sophomore year. 27%
grads go on to further study within 1 year. 15% grads pursue arts and sciences
degrees. 2% grads pursue law degrees. 4% grads pursue business degrees. 5%
grads pursue medical degrees. **Faculty:** Student/faculty ratio 16:1. 195 full-time
faculty, 75% hold PhDs, 8% are members of minority groups, 51% are women.
0% of classes are taught by teaching assistants.

ACADEMICS

Degrees: Bachelor's; Certificate; Doctoral/Professional; Master's **Classes:**
Most classes have 10-19 students. **Most popular majors:** Education, General;
Business/Commerce, General. **Special Study Options:** Cooperative education
program; Cross-registration; Double major; Dual enrollment; Honors program;
Independent study; Internships; Liberal arts/career combination; Student-
designed major; Study abroad; Teacher certification program; Weekend
college. **Honors programs:** First, the Honors Signature Courses, based on
the medieval divisions of knowledge, automatically satisfy all of the College's
general education requirements (except health/physical education and modern
language) in a simple sequence of challenging courses, created just for Honors
students. Second, Student-Created Courses allow students to design their own
courses—as either a replacement or supplement to the established Honors
courses. Students can learn through one-on-one tutoring, small reading groups,
or out-of-classroom experiences. Third, Honors Leadership Activities give
Honors students access to the The Augsburg Review, Honors Debate League,
Faculty/Student Research Collaboration, and the Honors Houses. Through
these activities, students can engage in travel abroad, service-learning, social
justice activities, political activism, leadership, research, and social gatherings
with their friends. **Disability Services offered to physically disabled
students:** Note-taking services; Reader services; Tape recorders; Tutors.
Career services: Alumni network; Career/job search classes; Internships;
Regional alumni

FACILITIES

Housing: Coed dorms; Special housing for disabled students 99% of campus
accessible to physically diasbled. **Special Academic Facilities/Equipment:**
Electron microscope, center for atmospheric science research, theatre, pipe
organ. **Computers:** Students can register for classes online. Administrative
functions (other than registration) can be performed online.

CAMPUS LIFE

Environment: Metropolis **Activities:** Campus Ministries; Choral groups;
Concert band; Dance; Drama/theater; International Student Organization;
Jazz band; Literary magazine; Music ensembles; Opera; Radio station; Student
government; Student newspaper; Yearbook 35 registered organizations, 1 honor
society, 1 religious organization. **Athletics (Intercollegiate):** *Men:* baseball,
basketball, cross-country, football, golf, ice hockey, soccer, tennis, track/field
(outdoor), track/field (indoor), wrestling. *Women:* basketball, cheerleading,
cross-country, golf, ice hockey, soccer, softball, swimming, tennis, track/
field (outdoor), track/field (indoor), volleyball. **On-Campus Highlights:**
Christensen Center/Starbucks Coffee Shop, Si Melby Athletic Fieldhouse,
Lindell Library, Foss Center/Atrium, Gateway Center

ADMISSIONS

Freshman Academic Profile: Average high school GPA 3.3. 11% in top 10%
of high school class, 37% in top 25% of high school class, 69% in top 50% of
high school class. **Test Scores:** SAT Math middle 50% range 500-640. SAT
EBRW middle 50% range 510-640. ACT middle 50% range 19-25. Minimum
paper TOEFL 550. **Basis for Candidate Selection:** *Very important factors
considered include:* rigor of secondary school record, class rank, academic
GPA, application essay, recommendation(s). *Important factors considered
include:* standardized test scores, extracurricular activities, alumni/ae relation,
level of applicant's interest. *Other factors considered include:* interview,

talent/ability, first generation, volunteer work, work experience. **Freshman
Admission Requirements:** High school diploma is required and GED is
accepted *Academic units required:* 4 English, 3 math, 3 science, 2 foreign
language, 2 social studies, *Academic units recommended:* 4 social studies, 2
history. **Freshman Admission Statistics:** 2,192 applied, 54.2% admitted,
35% enrolled. **Transfer Admission Requirements:** college transcript(s),
statement of good standing from prior institution(s). Minimum college GPA of
2.5 required. Lowest grade transferable B. **General Admission Information:**
Application fee $25. Priority deadline 5/1. Regular application deadline 8/15.
Nonfall registration accepted. Admission may be deferred for a maximum of 2
years.

COSTS AND FINANCIAL AID

Annual tuition $29,794. Room and board $8,072. Required fees $624.
Average book expense $1,000. **Required Forms and Deadlines:** FAFSA.
Notification of Awards: Applicants will be notified of awards on a rolling
basis beginning 3/1. **Types of Aid:** *Need-based scholarships/grants:* College/
university scholarship or grant aid from institutional funds; Federal Pell;
Private scholarships; SEOG; State scholarships/grants. *Loans:* Direct PLUS
loans; Direct Subsidized Stafford Loans; Direct Unsubsidized Stafford Loans.
Financial Aid Statistics: 99% needy freshmen, 91% needy undergrads receive
need-based scholarship or grant aid. 19% freshmen, 17% undergrads receive
non-need-based scholarship or grant aid. 94% freshmen, 92% undergrads
receive need-based self-help aid. 0% freshmen, 0% undergrads receive athletic
scholarships. 93% freshmen, 86% undergrads receive any aid. **Criteria for
awarding aid:** *Need-based:* Academics, Minority status *Non-need-based:*
Academics, Alumni affiliation, Art, Leadership, Minority status, Music/drama,
Religious affiliation.

AUGUSTANA COLLEGE (IL)

639 38th Street, Rock Island, IL 61201-2296
Phone: (309) 794-7341 · Financial Aid Phone: 309-794-7207
E-mail: admissions@augustana.edu · CEEB Code: 1025
Fax: (309) 794-7422 · Website: www.augustana.edu · ACT Code: 946

*This private school, affiliated with the Lutheran Church, was founded in
1860. It has a 115 acre campus.*

RATINGS

Admissions Selectivity Rating: 85   **Fire Safety Rating:** 94   **Green Rating:** 60*

STUDENTS AND FACULTY

Enrollment: 2,634. **Student Body:** 58% female, 42% male, 15% out-of-state,
7% international (42 countries represented). Asian 2%, African American 4%,
Caucasian 72%, Hispanic 10%, Native American <1%, Pacific Islander <1%,
Two or more races 3%, Race unknown 1%.
Retention and Graduation: 87% freshmen return for sophomore year. 71%
freshmen graduate within 4 years. 75% freshmen graduate within 6 years. 33%
grads go on to further study within 1 year. 18% grads pursue arts and sciences
degrees. 3% grads pursue law degrees. 1% grads pursue business degrees. 10%
grads pursue medical degrees. **Faculty:** Student/faculty ratio 12:1. 195 full-time
faculty, 92% hold PhDs, 14% are members of minority groups, 48% are women.
0% of classes are taught by teaching assistants.

ACADEMICS

Degrees: Bachelor's **Classes:** Most classes have 10-19 students. Most lab/
discussion sessions have 10-19 students. **Most popular majors:** Biology/
Biological Sciences, General; Psychology, General; Business Administration
And Management, General. **Special Study Options:** Double major; Honors
program; Independent study; Internships; Liberal arts/career combination;
Student-designed major; Study abroad; Teacher certification program. **Honors
programs:** Augustana has two tracks in first-year honors studies, Foundations
and Logos. The Foundations program is a challenging interdisciplinary honors
curriculum offering an intensive examination of the basic questions that have
perplexed humans for centuries, and focuses on integrated learning and the
development of critical thinking and writing skills. Logos is a challenging
interdisciplinary honors curriculum with a special focus on how science
has evolved across the centuries, how science has been used and viewed
at particular historical moments, and how we live with the fruits of science
today. **Disability Services offered to physically disabled students:** Tape
recorders; Tutors. **Career services:** Alumni network; Alumni services; Career
assessment; Career/job search classes; Internships

FACILITIES

Housing: Apartments for single students; Coed dorms; Special housing for disabled student; Wellness housing 95% of campus accessible to physically diasbled. **Special Academic Facilities/Equipment:** Educational technology building, art gallery, black culture house, Hispanic culture house, geology museum, on-campus preschool, immigration research center, scanning and transmission electron microscopes, nuclear magnetic resonance, atomic absorption, and diode array mass spectrophotometers, 3D printer, planetarium, observatory with celestron telescope, environmental field stations. **Computers:** 50% of classrooms, 30% of dorms, 100% of libraries, 100% of dining areas, 90% of student union, 25% of common outdoor areas have wireless network access. Students can register for classes online. Administrative functions (other than registration) can be performed online.

CAMPUS LIFE

Environment: City **Activities:** Campus Ministries; Choral groups; Concert band; Dance; Drama/theater; International Student Organization; Jazz band; Literary magazine; Model UN; Music ensembles; Musical theater; Opera; Pep band; Radio station; Student government; Student newspaper; Symphony orchestra 128 registered organizations, 15 honor societies, 5 religious organizations. 7 fraternities, 6 sororities. **Athletics (Intercollegiate):** *Men:* baseball, basketball, cross-country, diving, football, golf, soccer, swimming, tennis, track/field (outdoor), track/field (indoor), wrestling. *Women:* basketball, cross-country, diving, golf, lacrosse, soccer, softball, swimming, tennis, track/field (outdoor), track/field (indoor), volleyball. **On-Campus Highlights:** Gerber Center for Student Life and Thomas Tredway Libarary, Pepsico Recreation Center, Brew by the Slough-Coffee shop, F.W. Olin Center for Educational Technology, Donna and Kim Brunner Theater **Environmental Initiatives:** Recycling Program

ADMISSIONS

Freshman Academic Profile: Average high school GPA 3.3. 36% in top 10% of high school class, 64% in top 25% of high school class, 90% in top 50% of high school class. **Test Scores:** SAT Math middle 50% range 570-700. SAT EBRW middle 50% range 530-640. ACT middle 50% range 23-28. Minimum internet-based TOEFL 80. Minimum paper TOEFL 550. **Basis for Candidate Selection:** *Very important factors considered include:* rigor of secondary school record, class rank, academic GPA. *Important factors considered include:* application essay, standardized test scores, recommendation(s), interview, extracurricular activities, talent/ability, character/personal qualities, level of applicant's interest. *Other factors considered include:* alumni/ae relation, geographical residence, religious affiliation/commitment, racial/ethnic status, volunteer work, work experience. **Freshman Admission Requirements:** High school diploma is required and GED is accepted *Academic units required:* 3 English, 3 math, 3 science, 2 science labs, 1 foreign language, 1 social studies, 1 history, *Academic units recommended:* 4 English, 4 math, 4 science, 2 science labs, 2 foreign language, 2 social studies, 1 history, 4 academic electives. **Freshman Admission Statistics:** 6,750 applied, 59.0% admitted, 18% enrolled. **Transfer Admission Requirements:** High school transcript, college transcript(s), statement of good standing from prior institution(s). Minimum college GPA of 2.0 required. Lowest grade transferable D. **General Admission Information:** Priority deadline 2/1. Nonfall registration accepted. Admission may be deferred.

COSTS AND FINANCIAL AID

Annual tuition $42,135. Room and board $10,572. Average book expense $1,000. **Required Forms and Deadlines:** FAFSA; Institution's own financial aid form. **Notification of Awards:** Applicants will be notified of awards on a rolling basis beginning 3/1. **Types of Aid:** *Need-based scholarships/grants:* College/university scholarship or grant aid from institutional funds; Federal Pell; Private scholarships; SEOG; State scholarships/grants. *Loans:* Direct PLUS loans; Direct Subsidized Stafford Loans; Direct Unsubsidized Stafford Loans. *Student Employment:* Federal Work-Study Program available. Institutional employment available. **Financial Aid Statistics:** 98% needy freshmen receive need-based scholarship or grant aid. 99% freshmen, 99% undergrads receive any aid. **Criteria for awarding aid:** *Need-based:* Minority status *Non-need-based:* Academics, Alumni affiliation, Art, Leadership, Music/drama, Religious affiliation.

AUGUSTA UNIVERSITY

2500 Walton Way, Augusta, GA 30904-2200
Phone: 706-737-1632 • **Financial Aid Phone:** 706-737-1431
E-mail: admissio@aug.edu • **CEEB Code:** 5336
Fax: 706-667-4355 • **ACT Code:** 796

This public school was founded in 1925. It has a 76 acre campus.

RATINGS

Admissions Selectivity Rating: 89   **Fire Safety Rating:** 73   **Green Rating:** 60*

STUDENTS AND FACULTY

Enrollment: 5,394. **Student Body:** 64% female, 36% male, 9% out-of-state, 1% international (60 countries represented). Asian 3%, African American 28%, Caucasian 59%, Hispanic 3%, Native American <1%, Race unknown 5%. **Retention and Graduation:** 69% freshmen return for sophomore year. **Faculty:** Student/faculty ratio 18:1. 236 full-time faculty, 64% hold PhDs, 16% are members of minority groups, 51% are women. 0% of classes are taught by teaching assistants.

ACADEMICS

Degrees: Associate; Bachelor's; Master's; Post-Master's certificate; Terminal Associate; Transfer Associate **Classes:** Most classes have 10-19 students. **Most popular majors:** Elementary Education And Teaching; Biology/Biological Sciences, General; Psychology, General. **Special Study Options:** Cooperative education program; Cross-registration; Distance learning; Double major; Dual enrollment; English as a Second Language (ESL); Honors program; Independent study; Internships; Study abroad; Teacher certification program. **Honors programs:** Augusta State University's Honors Program provides about 100 of our best students with special sections of classes in the core curriculum. Those classes are usually smaller, involve much closer interaction with the professor, and encourage more independent and collaborative work than non-honors sections of these courses. In their Junior and Senior years, Honors students take two interdisciplinary courses, prepare, write, and defend a thesis, and conclude their undergraduate program with a Capstone course. **Disability Services offered to physically disabled students:** Note-taking services; Reader services; Tape recorders; Tutors. **Career services:** Alumni services

FACILITIES

Housing: Apartments for single students 90% of campus accessible to physically diasbled. **Special Academic Facilities/Equipment:** Performing Arts Theatre, Christenberry Field House, Forest Hill Golf Course **Computers:** 95% of classrooms, 5% of dorms, 100% of libraries, 100% of dining areas, 100% of student union, have wireless network access. Students can register for classes online. Administrative functions (other than registration) can be performed online.

CAMPUS LIFE

Environment: City **Activities:** Choral groups; Concert band; Drama/theater; Jazz band; Literary magazine; Pep band; Radio station; Student government; Student newspaper 60 registered organizations, 5 honor societies, 5 religious organizations. 3 fraternities, 3 sororities. **Athletics (Intercollegiate):** *Men:* baseball, basketball, golf, tennis. *Women:* basketball, golf, softball, tennis, volleyball. **On-Campus Highlights:** Allgood Hall, Christenberry Field House, University Hall, Jaguar Student Activities Center, Maxwell Performing Arts Theater

ADMISSIONS

Freshman Academic Profile: Average high school GPA 2.9. 95% from public high schools. **Test Scores:** SAT Math middle 50% range 430-540. SAT EBRW middle 50% range 440-540. ACT middle 50% range 17-21. Minimum paper TOEFL 500. **Basis for Candidate Selection:** *Important factors considered include:* rigor of secondary school record, academic GPA, standardized test scores. **Freshman Admission Requirements:** High school diploma is required and GED is accepted *Academic units required:* 4 English, 4 math, 3 science, 2 foreign language, 3 social studies. **Freshman Admission Statistics:** 2,401 applied, 52.0% admitted, 76% enrolled. **Transfer Admission Requirements:** college transcript(s), Minimum college GPA of 2.0 required. Lowest grade transferable D. **General Admission Information:** Application fee $20. Priority deadline 7/1. Nonfall registration accepted. Admission may be deferred.

COSTS AND FINANCIAL AID

Average book expense $1,000. **Required Forms and Deadlines:** FAFSA; State aid form. **Notification of Awards:** Applicants will be notified of awards on or about 6/1. **Types of Aid:** *Need-based scholarships/grants:* College/university scholarship or grant aid from institutional funds; Federal Pell; Private scholarships; SEOG; State scholarships/grants. **Financial Aid Statistics:** 73% needy freshmen, 67% needy undergrads receive need-based scholarship or grant aid. 27% freshmen, 31% undergrads receive non-need-based scholarship or grant aid. 73% freshmen, 70% undergrads receive need-based self-help aid. 0% freshmen, 2% undergrads receive athletic scholarships. **Criteria for awarding aid:** *Need-based:* Academics, Art, Leadership, Music/drama *Non-need-based:* Academics, Alumni affiliation, Art, Athletics, Job skills, Leadership, Minority status, Music/drama, State/district residency.

AUGUSTANA UNIVERSITY

2001 South Summit Avenue, Sioux Falls, SD 57197
Phone: 605-274-5516 · **Financial Aid Phone:** 605-274-5216
E-mail: admission@augie.edu · **CEEB Code:** 6015
Fax: 605-274-5518 · **Website:** www.augie.edu · **ACT Code:** 3902

This private school, affiliated with the Lutheran Church, was founded in 1860. It has a 100 acre campus.

RATINGS
Admissions Selectivity Rating: 85   **Fire Safety Rating:** 94   **Green Rating:** 86

STUDENTS AND FACULTY
Enrollment: 1,708. **Student Body:** 62% female, 38% male, 50% out-of-state, 7% international (32 countries represented). Asian 1%, African American 2%, Caucasian 85%, Hispanic 3%, Native American <1%, Pacific Islander 0%, Two or more races 2%, Race unknown <1%.
Retention and Graduation: 86% freshmen return for sophomore year. 56% freshmen graduate within 4 years. 71% freshmen graduate within 6 years. 21% grads go on to further study within 1 year. **Faculty:** Student/faculty ratio 12:1. 130 full-time faculty, 83% hold PhDs, 9% are members of minority groups, 51% are women. 0% of classes are taught by teaching assistants.

ACADEMICS
Degrees: Bachelor's; Master's **Classes:** Most classes have 20-29 students. Most lab/discussion sessions have 10-19 students. **Most popular majors:** Education, General; Registered Nursing/Registered Nurse; Business Administration, Management And Operations, Other. **Special Study Options:** Accelerated program; Cross-registration; Distance learning; Double major; Dual enrollment; Exchange student program (domestic); External degree program; Honors program; Independent study; Internships; Liberal arts/career combination; Student-designed major; Study abroad; Teacher certification program. **Honors programs:** Our campus-wide, interdisciplinary Honors program is called Civitas (citizenship). Specific majors also offer departmental honors programs for students willing to accept academic challenges that go well beyond those required for graduation. **Combined degree programs:** BA/MEng. **Disability Services offered to physically disabled students:** Note-taking services; Reader services; Tape recorders; Tutors. **Career services:** Alumni network; Alumni services; Career assessment; Career/job search classes; Internships; Regional alumni

FACILITIES
Housing: Apartments for married students; Apartments for single students; Coed dorms; Special housing for disabled student; Theme housing 85% of campus accessible to physically diasbled. **Special Academic Facilities/Equipment:** Center for Western Studies, Archeology Lab, Eide/Dalrymple Art Gallery, Center for Liturgical Art **Computers:** 25% of classrooms, 25% of dorms, 100% of libraries, 100% of dining areas, 75% of student union, have wireless network access. Students can register for classes online. Administrative functions (other than registration) can be performed online.

CAMPUS LIFE
Environment: City **Activities:** Campus Ministries; Choral groups; Concert band; Dance; Drama/theater; International Student Organization; Jazz band; Literary magazine; Music ensembles; Musical theater; Pep band; Student government; Student newspaper; Symphony orchestra; Yearbook 92 registered organizations, 13 honor societies, 9 religious organizations. **Athletics (Intercollegiate):** *Men:* baseball, basketball, cross-country, football, golf, tennis, track/field (outdoor), track/field (indoor), wrestling. *Women:* basketball, cheerleading, cross-country, golf, soccer, softball, tennis, track/field (outdoor), track/field (indoor), volleyball. **On-Campus Highlights:** Sports Complex, Morrison Commons / The Huddle, Mikkelson Library, Froiland Science Complex, Center for Visual Arts **Environmental Initiatives:** Most recent building (120,000 square feet) is at least LEED silver, the first LEED building on campus.

ADMISSIONS
Freshman Academic Profile: Average high school GPA 3.7. 35% in top 10% of high school class, 64% in top 25% of high school class, 89% in top 50% of high school class. 89% from public high schools. **Test Scores:** SAT Math middle 50% range 540-660. SAT EBRW middle 50% range 530-630. ACT middle 50%

range 23-29. Minimum internet-based TOEFL 79. Minimum paper TOEFL 550. **Basis for Candidate Selection:** *Important factors considered include:* rigor of secondary school record, academic GPA, application essay, standardized test scores, recommendation(s). *Other factors considered include:* class rank, interview, extracurricular activities, character/personal qualities, alumni/ae relation, volunteer work, work experience, level of applicant's interest. **Freshman Admission Requirements:** High school diploma is required and GED is accepted *Academic units recommended:* 4 English, 4 math, 4 science, 2 foreign language, 3 social studies, 3 visual/performing arts. **Freshman Admission Statistics:** 1,975 applied, 67.8% admitted, 36% enrolled. **Transfer Admission Requirements:** High school transcript, college transcript(s), essay or personal statement, Minimum college GPA of 2.2 required. Lowest grade transferable C-. **General Admission Information:** Priority deadline 1/15. Nonfall registration accepted. Admission may be deferred for a maximum of 1 year.

COSTS AND FINANCIAL AID
Annual tuition $31,450. Room and board $8,008. Required fees $510. Average book expense $1,000. **Required Forms and Deadlines:** FAFSA. **Notification of Awards:** Applicants will be notified of awards on a rolling basis beginning 4/1. **Types of Aid:** *Need-based scholarships/grants:* College/university scholarship or grant aid from institutional funds; Federal Pell; Private scholarships; SEOG; State scholarships/grants. *Loans:* Direct PLUS loans; Direct Subsidized Stafford Loans; Direct Unsubsidized Stafford Loans. *Student Employment:* Federal Work-Study Program available. Institutional employment available. **Financial Aid Statistics:** 100% needy freshmen, 99% needy undergrads receive need-based scholarship or grant aid. 98% freshmen, 96% undergrads receive non-need-based scholarship or grant aid. 64% freshmen, 71% undergrads receive need-based self-help aid. 22% freshmen, 19% undergrads receive athletic scholarships. 99% freshmen, 99% undergrads receive any aid. 67% undergrads borrow to pay for school. Average cumulative indebtedness $36,950. **Criteria for awarding aid:** *Need-based:* Academics, Athletics, Leadership, Minority status, Music/drama, Religious affiliation *Non-need-based:* Academics, Alumni affiliation, Art, Athletics, Leadership, Minority status, Music/drama, Religious affiliation, State/district residency.

AURORA UNIVERSITY

347 South Gladstone, Aurora, IL 60506
Phone: 630-844-5533 · **Financial Aid Phone:** 630-844-6190
E-mail: admission@aurora.edu · **CEEB Code:** 1027
Fax: 630-844-5535 · **Website:** www.aurora.edu · **ACT Code:** 950

This private school was founded in 1893. It has a 30 acre campus.

RATINGS
Admissions Selectivity Rating: 74   **Fire Safety Rating:** 91   **Green Rating:** 60*

STUDENTS AND FACULTY
Enrollment: 3,927. **Student Body:** 65% female, 35% male, 12% out-of-state, <1% international (2 countries represented). Asian 2%, African American 8%, Caucasian 50%, Hispanic 30%, Native American <1%, Pacific Islander <1%, Two or more races 3%, Race unknown 6%.
Retention and Graduation: 74% freshmen return for sophomore year. 38% freshmen graduate within 4 years. 53% freshmen graduate within 6 years. **Faculty:** Student/faculty ratio 18:1. 139 full-time faculty, 13% are members of minority groups, 53% are women. 0% of classes are taught by teaching assistants.

ACADEMICS
Degrees: Bachelor's; Doctoral/Research; Master's; Post-Master's certificate **Classes:** Most classes have fewer than 10 students. Most lab/discussion sessions have fewer than 10 students. **Most popular majors:** Elementary Education And Teaching; Nursing/Registered Nurse (Rn, Asn, Bsn, Msn); Business Administration And Management, General. **Special Study Options:** Accelerated program; Cross-registration; Distance learning; Double major; Dual enrollment; Independent study; Internships; Liberal arts/career combination; Student-designed major; Study abroad; Teacher certification program. **Honors programs:** Honors Program including honors seminars,honors section of some general education courses and a senior honors project. **Disability Services offered to physically disabled students:** Note-taking services; Reader services; Tape recorders; Tutors. **Career services:** Alumni network; Alumni services; Career assessment; Career/job search classes; Internships

FACILITIES
Housing: Coed dorms 95% of campus accessible to physically diasbled. **Special Academic Facilities/Equipment:** Schingoethe Center for Native

American Culture Downstairs Dunham Gallery Center For Faith And Action Perry Theatre in the Aurora Foundation Center for Community Education **Computers:** 100% of classrooms, 80% of dorms, 100% of libraries, 100% of dining areas, 100% of student union, 90% of common outdoor areas have wireless network access. Administrative functions (other than registration) can be performed online.

CAMPUS LIFE

Environment: City **Activities:** Campus Ministries; Choral groups; Drama/theater; Literary magazine; Model UN; Music ensembles; Musical theater; Opera; Pep band; Radio station; Student government; Student newspaper; Television station 49 registered organizations, 2 honor societies, 1 religious organization. 1 fraternity, 4 sororities. **Athletics (Intercollegiate):** *Men:* baseball, basketball, cross-country, football, golf, soccer, tennis, track/field (outdoor), track/field (indoor). *Women:* basketball, cross-country, golf, soccer, softball, tennis, track/field (outdoor), track/field (indoor), volleyball. **On-Campus Highlights:** The Spartan Spot, Fitness Center, Center for Teaching and Learning, Institute for Collaboration, Vago Stadium **Environmental Initiatives:** Campus-wide recycling

ADMISSIONS

Freshman Academic Profile: Average high school GPA 3.3. 92% from public high schools. **Test Scores:** SAT Math middle 50% range 470-560. SAT EBRW middle 50% range 480-570. ACT middle 50% range 19-23. Minimum internet-based TOEFL 79. Minimum paper TOEFL 550. **Basis for Candidate Selection:** *Very important factors considered include:* rigor of secondary school record, class rank, academic GPA, standardized test scores. *Important factors considered include:* extracurricular activities, character/personal qualities. *Other factors considered include:* application essay, recommendation(s), interview, talent/ability, first generation, alumni/ae relation, volunteer work, work experience, level of applicant's interest. **Freshman Admission Requirements:** High school diploma is required and GED is accepted *Academic units required:* 4 English, 3 math, 3 science, 3 social studies, 3 academic electives. **Freshman Admission Statistics:** 3,061 applied, 87.3% admitted, 30% enrolled. **Transfer Admission Requirements:** college transcript(s), statement of good standing from prior institution(s). Minimum college GPA of 2.0 required. Lowest grade transferable C. **General Admission Information:** Nonfall registration accepted. Admission may be deferred.

COSTS AND FINANCIAL AID

Annual tuition $24,000. Room and board $11,700. Required fees $260. Average book expense $1,000. **Required Forms and Deadlines:** FAFSA. **Notification of Awards:** Applicants will be notified of awards on a rolling basis beginning 11/15. **Types of Aid:** *Need-based scholarships/grants:* College/university scholarship or grant aid from institutional funds; Federal Pell; Private scholarships; SEOG; State scholarships/grants. *Loans:* Direct PLUS loans; Direct Subsidized Stafford Loans; Direct Unsubsidized Stafford Loans. *Student Employment:* Federal Work-Study Program available. Institutional employment available. **Financial Aid Statistics:** 78% needy freshmen, 91% needy undergrads receive need-based scholarship or grant aid. 18% freshmen, 17% undergrads receive non-need-based scholarship or grant aid. 88% freshmen, 89% undergrads receive need-based self-help aid. 0% freshmen, 0% undergrads receive athletic scholarships. 100% freshmen, 98% undergrads receive any aid. 83% undergrads borrow to pay for school. Average cumulative indebtedness $27,578. **Criteria for awarding aid:** *Need-based:* Leadership, Religious affiliation *Non-need-based:* Academics, Alumni affiliation, Art, Music/drama, Religious affiliation, State/district residency.

AUSTIN COLLEGE

900 N. Grand Avenue, Sherman, TX 75090
Phone: 903-813-3000 · **Financial Aid Phone:** 903-813-2900
E-mail: admission@austincollege.edu · **CEEB Code:** 6016
Fax: 903-813-3198 · **Website:** www.austincollege.edu · **ACT Code:** 4058

This private school, affiliated with the Presbyterian Church, was founded in 1849. It has a 70 acre campus.

RATINGS

Admissions Selectivity Rating: 88   **Fire Safety Rating:** 84   **Green Rating:** 84

STUDENTS AND FACULTY

Enrollment: 1,223. **Student Body:** 51% female, 49% male, 8% out-of-state, 3% international (15 countries represented). Asian 13%, African American 9%,

Caucasian 49%, Hispanic 21%, Native American 1%, Pacific Islander <1%, Two or more races 4%, Race unknown <1%.
Retention and Graduation: 81% freshmen return for sophomore year. 63% freshmen graduate within 4 years. 68% freshmen graduate within 6 years. 35% grads go on to further study within 1 year. 3.47% grads pursue law degrees. 0% grads pursue business degrees. 9.38% grads pursue medical degrees.
Faculty: Student/faculty ratio 13:1. 77 full-time faculty, 95% hold PhDs, 22% are members of minority groups, 38% are women. 0% of classes are taught by teaching assistants.

ACADEMICS

Degrees: Bachelor's; Master's **Classes:** Most classes have 10-19 students. **Most popular majors:** Biology/Biological Sciences, General; Psychology, General; Business/Commerce, General. **Special Study Options:** Double major; Exchange student program (domestic); Independent study; Internships; Student-designed major; Study abroad; Teacher certification program. **Disability Services offered to physically disabled students:** Tutors. **Career services:** Alumni network; Alumni services; Career assessment; Career/job search classes; Internships

FACILITIES

Housing: Apartments for single students; Men's dorms; Special housing for disabled student; Special housing for international students; Women's dorms 99% of campus accessible to physically disabled. **Special Academic Facilities/Equipment:** Idea Center, moot court program, student-managed investment fund. **Computers:** 30% of classrooms, 100% of dorms, 100% of libraries, 100% of dining areas, 100% of student union, 30% of common outdoor areas have wireless network access. Students can register for classes online. Administrative functions (other than registration) can be performed online.

CAMPUS LIFE

Environment: Town **Activities:** Campus Ministries; Choral groups; Concert band; Dance; Drama/theater; International Student Organization; Jazz band; Literary magazine; Model UN; Music ensembles; Musical theater; Pep band; Student government; Student newspaper; Symphony orchestra; Yearbook 52 registered organizations, 15 honor societies, 6 religious organizations. 6 fraternities, 6 sororities. **Athletics (Intercollegiate):** *Men:* baseball, basketball, football, soccer, swimming, tennis. *Women:* basketball, soccer, softball, swimming, tennis, volleyball. **On-Campus Highlights:** Wright Campus Center (WCC), IDEA Center (science building), Verde Dickey Fitness Pavilion in Mason Complex, Abell Library, Residence hall facilities **Environmental Initiatives:** Board approval of Climate Action Plan to reduce emissions to 0 and well established Center for Environmental Studies that offers a major and minor.

ADMISSIONS

Freshman Academic Profile: Average high school GPA 3.5. 41% in top 10% of high school class, 35% in top 25% of high school class, 96% in top 50% of high school class. 77% from public high schools. **Test Scores:** SAT Math middle 50% range 570-680. SAT EBRW middle 50% range 590-680. ACT middle 50% range 23-29. Minimum paper TOEFL 550. **Basis for Candidate Selection:** *Very important factors considered include:* rigor of secondary school record, class rank, academic GPA, application essay, standardized test scores, recommendation(s). *Important factors considered include:* interview, talent/ability, character/personal qualities, level of applicant's interest. *Other factors considered include:* extracurricular activities, first generation, alumni/ae relation, geographical residence, state residency, religious affiliation/commitment, volunteer work, work experience. **Freshman Admission Requirements:** High school diploma is required and GED is accepted *Academic units required:* 4 English, 3 math, 3 science, 1 science labs, 2 foreign language, 2 social studies, 1 history, 1 visual/performing arts, *Academic units recommended:* 4 English, 4 math, 4 science, 2 science labs, 4 foreign language, 3 social studies, 1 history, 2 visual/performing arts. **Freshman Admission Statistics:** 3,545 applied, 52.2% admitted, 18% enrolled. **Transfer Admission Requirements:** college transcript(s), essay or personal statement, statement of good standing from prior institution(s). Minimum college GPA of 3.0 required. Lowest grade transferable C. **General Admission Information:** Priority deadline 12/1. Regular application deadline 3/1. Nonfall registration accepted. Admission may be deferred.

COSTS AND FINANCIAL AID

Annual tuition $38,615. Room and board $12,334. Required fees $210. Average book expense $1,250. **Required Forms and Deadlines:** FAFSA. **Notification of Awards:** Applicants will be notified of awards on a rolling basis beginning 12/1. **Types of Aid:** *Need-based scholarships/grants:* College/university scholarship or grant aid from institutional funds; Federal Pell; Private scholarships; SEOG; State scholarships/grants. *Loans:* Direct PLUS loans; Direct Subsidized Stafford Loans; Direct Unsubsidized Stafford Loans. *Student Employment:* Federal Work-Study Program available. Institutional employment available. **Financial Aid Statistics:** 100% needy freshmen, 100% needy undergrads receive need-based scholarship or grant aid. 55% freshmen, 19% undergrads receive non-need-based scholarship or grant aid. 69% freshmen, 72% undergrads receive need-based self-help aid. 0% freshmen, 0% undergrads receive athletic scholarships. 97% freshmen, 98% undergrads receive any aid. **Criteria for awarding aid:** *Non-need-based:* Academics, Alumni affiliation, Art, Leadership, Music/drama, Religious affiliation.

AUSTIN PEAY STATE UNIVERSITY

PO Box 4675, Clarksville, TN 37044
Phone: (931) 221-7661
E-mail: admissions@apsu.edu • **CEEB Code:** 1028
Fax: (931) 221-6168 • **Website:** www.apsu.edu • **ACT Code:** 3944

This public school was founded in 1927. It has a 210 acre campus.

RATINGS

Admissions Selectivity Rating: 73   **Fire Safety Rating:** 60*   **Green Rating:** 60*

STUDENTS AND FACULTY

Enrollment: 9,090. **Student Body:** 58% female, 42% male, 11% out-of-state, <1% international (13 countries represented). Asian 2%, African American 22%, Caucasian 60%, Hispanic 7%, Native American <1%, Pacific Islander <1%, Two or more races 6%, Race unknown 2%.
Retention and Graduation: 66% freshmen return for sophomore year. 18% freshmen graduate within 4 years. 38% freshmen graduate within 6 years. **Faculty:** Student/faculty ratio 18:1. 370 full-time faculty, 14% are members of minority groups, 50% are women. 0% of classes are taught by teaching assistants.

ACADEMICS

Degrees: Associate; Bachelor's; Master's; Post-Bachelor's certificate; Post-Master's certificate; Terminal Associate; Transfer Associate **Classes:** Most classes have 10-19 students. **Special Study Options:** Accelerated program; Cooperative education program; Distance learning; Double major; Dual enrollment; English as a Second Language (ESL); Honors program; Independent study; Internships; Study abroad; Teacher certification program. **Disability Services offered to physically disabled students:** Note-taking services; Reader services; Tutors. **Career services:** Career assessment; Career/job search classes; Internships

FACILITIES

Housing: Apartments for married students; Apartments for single students; Coed dorms; Fraternity/sorority housing; Men's dorms; Special housing for disabled student; Women's dorms 100% of campus accessible to physically diasbled. **Special Academic Facilities/Equipment:** Art museum, biology museum, language lab, demonstration farm, 21st century classroom.

CAMPUS LIFE

Environment: Village **Activities:** Campus Ministries; Choral groups; Concert band; Dance; Drama/theater; International Student Organization; Jazz band; Literary magazine; Marching band; Music ensembles; Musical theater; Opera; Pep band; Radio station; Student government; Student newspaper; Student-run film society; Symphony orchestra; Television station; Yearbook 50 registered organizations, 13 honor societies, 10 religious organizations. 8 fraternities, 6 sororities. **Athletics (Intercollegiate):** *Men:* baseball, basketball, cheerleading, cross-country, football, golf, tennis. *Women:* basketball, cheerleading, cross-country, golf, riflery, soccer, softball, tennis, track/field (outdoor), volleyball. **On-Campus Highlights:** University Center, Sundquist Science Complex, Hand Village, Dunn Center

ADMISSIONS

Freshman Academic Profile: Average high school GPA 3.3. 11% in top 10% of high school class, 35% in top 25% of high school class, 70% in top 50% of high school class. 95% from public high schools. **Test Scores:** SAT Math middle 50% range 473-598. SAT EBRW middle 50% range 513-605. ACT middle 50% range 19-24. Minimum paper TOEFL 500. **Basis for Candidate Selection:** *Very important factors considered include:* academic GPA, standardized test scores. *Other factors considered include:* rigor of secondary school record. **Freshman Admission Requirements:** High school diploma is required and GED is accepted *Academic units required:* 4 English, 3 math, 2 science, 1 science labs, 2 foreign language, 1 social studies, 1 history, 1 visual/performing arts. **Freshman Admission Statistics:** 7,183 applied, 90.1% admitted, 31% enrolled. **Transfer Admission Requirements:** college transcript(s), Lowest grade transferable D. **General Admission Information:** Application fee $25. Regular application deadline 8/8. Nonfall registration accepted. Admission may be deferred for a maximum of 1 year.

COSTS AND FINANCIAL AID

Annual in-state tuition $1,529. Annual out-of-state tuition $22,692. Required fees $1,529. Average book expense $1,550. **Required Forms and Deadlines:** FAFSA. **Notification of Awards:** Applicants will be notified of awards

on a rolling basis beginning 2/1. **Types of Aid:** *Need-based scholarships/grants:* College/university scholarship or grant aid from institutional funds; Federal Pell; Private scholarships; SEOG; State scholarships/grants. *Loans:* Direct PLUS loans; Direct Subsidized Stafford Loans; Direct Unsubsidized Stafford Loans. *Student Employment:* Federal Work-Study Program available. Institutional employment available. **Financial Aid Statistics:** 80% needy freshmen, 86% needy undergrads receive need-based scholarship or grant aid. 82% freshmen, 60% undergrads receive non-need-based scholarship or grant aid. 62% freshmen, 68% undergrads receive need-based self-help aid. 2% freshmen, 1% undergrads receive athletic scholarships. 69% undergrads borrow to pay for school. Average cumulative indebtedness $23,808. **Criteria for awarding aid:** *Non-need-based:* Academics, Alumni affiliation, Art, Athletics, Leadership, Music/drama, State/district residency.

AVERETT UNIVERSITY

420 West Main Street, Danville, VA 24541
Phone: 434-791-5600 • **Financial Aid Phone:** 434-791-5890 • **CEEB Code:** 5017
Fax: 434-797-2784 • **Website:** www.averett.edu • **ACT Code:** 4338

This private school, affiliated with the Baptist General Association of Virginia Church, was founded in 1859. It has a 185 acre campus.

RATINGS

Admissions Selectivity Rating: 78   **Fire Safety Rating:** 97   **Green Rating:** 61

STUDENTS AND FACULTY

Enrollment: 911. **Student Body:** 45% female, 55% male, 39% out-of-state, 6% international (21 countries represented). Asian 1%, African American 30%, Caucasian 56%, Hispanic 5%, Native American <1%, Pacific Islander <1%, Two or more races 2%, Race unknown <1%.
Retention and Graduation: 62% freshmen return for sophomore year. 34% freshmen graduate within 4 years. 40% freshmen graduate within 6 years. 16% grads go on to further study within 1 year. 5% grads pursue arts and sciences degrees. 0% grads pursue law degrees. 4% grads pursue business degrees. 2.4% grads pursue medical degrees. **Faculty:** Student/faculty ratio 12:1. 58 full-time faculty, 64% hold PhDs, 14% are members of minority groups, 53% are women. 0% of classes are taught by teaching assistants.

ACADEMICS

Degrees: Associate; Bachelor's **Classes:** Most classes have 10-19 students. **Most popular majors:** Criminal Justice/Law Enforcement Administration; Aeronautics/Aviation/Aerospace Science And Technology, General; Pre-Medicine/Pre-Medical Studies. **Special Study Options:** Distance learning; Double major; Honors program; Independent study; Internships; Student-designed major; Study abroad; Teacher certification program. **Honors programs:** Our Honors Program gives students the opportunity to go a step beyond regular classroom study. Students explore, in-depth, selected areas of academics. Participation in the Honors Program demonstrates a commitment to scholarship and will give students an edge in graduate study or in the job market. To earn the honors distinction students would be required to complete 9 credit hours in Honors courses. [This would include one 3-credit interdisciplinary Honors course (taken in either the sophomore year or fall semester of junior year) and then the completion of an Honors project, taking place in the spring semester of one's junior year (Honors 401-3 credits) and the fall of senior year (Honors 402- 3 credits).] and have an overall GPA of 3.4 or better. Honors Program students may also participate in the Honors Association and attend conferences, social activities and cultural performances. **Disability Services offered to physically disabled students:** Note-taking services; Reader services; Tape recorders; Tutors. **Career services:** Alumni network; Alumni services; Career assessment; Career/job search classes; Internships; Regional alumni

FACILITIES

Housing: Apartments for single students; Coed dorms; Men's dorms; Women's dorms 73% of campus accessible to physically diasbled. **Special Academic Facilities/Equipment:** Averett's Flight Center located 4 miles from the main campus at Danville Regional Airport has two runways (one with ILS approach), automated weather system, and UNICOM service. Averett's facility houses aircraft, areas for ground instruction, simulator rooms, technology center. Averett's 100-acre Equestrian Center is a 15-minute drive from the main campus. It houses an indoor ring, 40 stalls with removable partitions, 3 tack rooms, wash room for horses and equipment, breeding area, offices, and a laboratory. The outdoor facilities include a round pen, riding ring, jumping area, pastures, and cross-country trails. **Computers:** 100% of libraries, 100% of dining areas, 100% of student union, have wireless network access. Students can register for classes online. Administrative functions (other than registration) can be performed online.

CAMPUS LIFE

Environment: Town **Activities:** Campus Ministries; Drama/theater; Musical theater; Pep band; Student government; Student newspaper 30 registered organizations, 4 honor societies, 4 religious organizations. 1 fraternity, 1 sorority. **Athletics (Intercollegiate):** *Men:* baseball, basketball, cheerleading, cross-country, equestrian sports, football, golf, soccer, tennis. *Women:* basketball, cheerleading, cross-country, equestrian sports, soccer, softball, tennis, volleyball. **On-Campus Highlights:** Student Center, Grant Athletic Center (North Campus), Equestrian Center, Airport Facilities, Riverview Nursing Simulation Facilities

ADMISSIONS

Freshman Academic Profile: Average high school GPA 3.2. 7% in top 10% of high school class, 24% in top 25% of high school class, 48% in top 50% of high school class. 94% from public high schools. **Test Scores:** SAT Math middle 50% range 410-500. SAT EBRW middle 50% range 420-520. ACT middle 50% range 17-22. Minimum internet-based TOEFL 61. Minimum paper TOEFL 500. **Basis for Candidate Selection:** *Very important factors considered include:* rigor of secondary school record, class rank, academic GPA, standardized test scores. *Other factors considered include:* application essay, recommendation(s), interview, extracurricular activities, character/personal qualities, alumni/ae relation, volunteer work, work experience, level of applicant's interest. **Freshman Admission Requirements:** High school diploma is required and GED is accepted *Academic units required:* 4 English, 3 math, 3 science, 2 science labs, 3 social studies, 3 history, *Academic units recommended:* 2 foreign language. **Freshman Admission Statistics:** 2,721 applied, 61.9% admitted, 17% enrolled. **Transfer Admission Requirements:** college transcript(s), statement of good standing from prior institution(s). Minimum college GPA of 2.0 required. Lowest grade transferable C. **General Admission Information:** Nonfall registration accepted. Admission may be deferred for a maximum of 2 years.

COSTS AND FINANCIAL AID

Annual tuition $33,350. Room and board $9,684. Average book expense $1,000. **Required Forms and Deadlines:** FAFSA; State aid form. **Types of Aid:** *Need-based scholarships/grants:* College/university scholarship or grant aid from institutional funds; Federal Pell; Private scholarships; SEOG; State scholarships/grants. *Loans:* Direct PLUS loans; Direct Subsidized Stafford Loans; Direct Unsubsidized Stafford Loans. *Student Employment:* Federal Work-Study Program available. Institutional employment available. **Financial Aid Statistics:** 100% needy freshmen, 100% needy undergrads receive need-based scholarship or grant aid. 11% freshmen, 12% undergrads receive non-need-based scholarship or grant aid. 84% freshmen, 82% undergrads receive need-based self-help aid. 0% freshmen, 0% undergrads receive athletic scholarships. 99% freshmen, 99% undergrads receive any aid. 81% undergrads borrow to pay for school. Average cumulative indebtedness $35,659. **Criteria for awarding aid:** *Need-based:* Academics, Art, Job skills, Leadership, Minority status, Music/drama, Religious affiliation *Non-need-based:* Academics, Alumni affiliation, Art, Job skills, Leadership, Minority status, Music/drama, Religious affiliation, State/district residency.

AZUSA PACIFIC UNIVERSITY

PO Box 7000, Azusa, CA 91702-7000
Phone: 626-812-3016 · **Financial Aid Phone:** (626) 815-2020
E-mail: admissions@apu.edu · **CEEB Code:** 4596
Fax: 626-812-3096 · **Website:** www.apu.edu · **ACT Code:** 166

This private school, affiliated with the Christian (Nondenominational) Church, was founded in 1899. It has a 105 acre campus.

RATINGS

Admissions Selectivity Rating: 74   **Fire Safety Rating:** 64   **Green Rating:** 60*

STUDENTS AND FACULTY

Enrollment: 5,762. **Student Body:** 66% female, 34% male, 19% out-of-state, 3% international. Asian 9%, African American 5%, Caucasian 41%, Hispanic 31%, Native American <1%, Pacific Islander 1%, Two or more races 8%, Race unknown 2%.
Retention and Graduation: 86% freshmen return for sophomore year.
Faculty: Student/faculty ratio 12:1. 458 full-time faculty, 63% hold PhDs, 28% are members of minority groups, 52% are women.

ACADEMICS

Degrees: Bachelor's; Certificate; Doctoral/Professional; Doctoral/Research; Master's; Post-Bachelor's certificate; Post-Master's certificate **Classes:** Most classes have fewer than 10 students. Most lab/discussion sessions have 20-29 students. **Most popular majors:** Psychology, General; Business, Management,

Marketing, And Related Support Services, Other. **Special Study Options:** Accelerated program; Cooperative education program; Distance learning; Double major; English as a Second Language (ESL); Exchange student program (domestic); Honors program; Independent study; Internships; Study abroad; Teacher certification program. **Honors programs:** Every year, Azusa Pacific University attracts increasing numbers of the country's best students seeking a rigorous academic experience grounded in the Christian faith. The university has expanded the institution's investment in academically gifted students by establishing an Honors College. Today's top-performing students are tomorrow's leaders. The Honors College telos—its aim, purpose, end—is to liberally educate the next generation of intellectually gifted Christian leaders, helping them develop the moral and intellectual virtue, the right habits of the heart and of the mind, to become global leaders. **Combined degree programs:** BA/MA. **Disability Services offered to physically disabled students:** Note-taking services; Tape recorders. **Career services:** Alumni services; Career assessment; Career/job search classes; Internships

FACILITIES

Housing: Apartments for single students; Coed dorms; Men's dorms; Theme housing; Women's dorms 100% of campus accessible to physically diasbled. **Special Academic Facilities/Equipment:** Electron microscope. **Computers:** 100% of classrooms, 100% of dorms, 100% of libraries, 100% of dining areas, 100% of student union, 100% of common outdoor areas have wireless network access. Students can register for classes online. Administrative functions (other than registration) can be performed online.

CAMPUS LIFE

Environment: Town **Activities:** Campus Ministries; Choral groups; Concert band; Dance; Drama/theater; International Student Organization; Jazz band; Literary magazine; Marching band; Music ensembles; Musical theater; Opera; Pep band; Radio station; Student government; Student newspaper; Student-run film society; Symphony orchestra; Television station; Yearbook 30 registered organizations, 7 honor societies. **Athletics (Intercollegiate):** *Men:* baseball, basketball, cross-country, football, soccer, tennis, track/field (outdoor), volleyball. *Women:* basketball, cheerleading, cross-country, diving, soccer, softball, swimming, tennis, track/field (outdoor), volleyball, water polo. **On-Campus Highlights:** Coffee Shops, Cougars' Den (Dining Facility), An Athletic Facility, Darling Library, Cougar Dome

ADMISSIONS

Freshman Academic Profile: Average high school GPA 3.7. **Test Scores:** SAT Math middle 50% range 460-580. SAT EBRW middle 50% range 470-580. ACT middle 50% range 21-26. Minimum internet-based TOEFL 68. **Basis for Candidate Selection:** *Very important factors considered include:* class rank, academic GPA, application essay, standardized test scores, character/personal qualities. *Important factors considered include:* recommendation(s), religious affiliation/commitment. *Other factors considered include:* rigor of secondary school record, interview, extracurricular activities, talent/ability, first generation, alumni/ae relation, racial/ethnic status, volunteer work, level of applicant's interest. **Freshman Admission Requirements:** High school diploma is required and GED is accepted *Academic units recommended:* 4 English, 3 math, 2 science, 3 foreign language, 1 social studies, 2 history. **Freshman Admission Statistics:** 6,605 applied, 83.5% admitted, 21% enrolled. **Transfer Admission Requirements:** college transcript(s), essay or personal statement, statement of good standing from prior institution(s). Minimum college GPA of 2.2 required. Lowest grade transferable C. **General Admission Information:** Priority deadline 2/15. Regular application deadline 6/1. Nonfall registration accepted.

COSTS AND FINANCIAL AID

Annual tuition $35,540. Required fees $580. Average book expense $1,792. *Student Employment:* Federal Work-Study Program available. Institutional employment available. **Financial Aid Statistics:** 92% needy freshmen, 98% needy undergrads receive need-based scholarship or grant aid. 10% freshmen, 7% undergrads receive non-need-based scholarship or grant aid. 71% freshmen, 78% undergrads receive need-based self-help aid. 5% freshmen, 5% undergrads receive athletic scholarships. 35% freshmen, 38% undergrads receive any aid. Average cumulative indebtedness $24,338.

BABSON COLLEGE

231 Forest Street, Babson Park, MA 02457
Phone: 781-239-5522 · **Financial Aid Phone:** 781.239.4219
E-mail: ugradadmission@babson.edu · **CEEB Code:** 2121
Fax: 781-239-4006 · **Website:** www.babson.edu · **ACT Code:** 1780

This private school was founded in 1919. It has a 370 acre campus.

RATINGS

Admissions Selectivity Rating: 95   **Fire Safety Rating:** 95   **Green Rating:** 93

STUDENTS AND FACULTY

Enrollment: 2,342. **Student Body:** 48% female, 52% male, 73% out-of-state, 28% international (77 countries represented). Asian 12%, African American 5%, Caucasian 37%, Hispanic 11%, Native American <1%, Pacific Islander <1%, Two or more races 2%, Race unknown 5%.
Retention and Graduation: 96% freshmen return for sophomore year. 90% freshmen graduate within 4 years. 92% freshmen graduate within 6 years. 4% grads go on to further study within 1 year. 1% grads pursue law degrees. 3% grads pursue business degrees. **Faculty:** Student/faculty ratio 11:1. 183 full-time faculty, 89% hold PhDs, 19% are members of minority groups, 38% are women. 0% of classes are taught by teaching assistants.

ACADEMICS

Degrees: Bachelor's; Master's; Post-Bachelor's certificate **Classes:** Most classes have 20-29 students. Most lab/discussion sessions have 10-19 students. **Most popular majors:** Business Administration And Management, General. **Special Study Options:** Accelerated program; Cross-registration; Honors program; Independent study; Internships; Study abroad. **Honors programs:** This Honors Program has three main components in which students add to their academic and personal development. This includes an Honors seminar, an Honors thesis and an international experience. **Disability Services offered to physically disabled students:** Note-taking services; Reader services; Tape recorders; Tutors. **Career services:** Alumni network; Alumni services; Career assessment; Career/job search classes; Internships; Regional alumni

FACILITIES

Housing: Coed dorms; Fraternity/sorority housing; Theme housing; Wellness housing **Special Academic Facilities/Equipment:** The Babson World Globe, Roger Babson Museum, Isaac Newton Museum, Arthur M. Blank Center for Entrepreneurship, Center for Women's Entrepreneurial Leadership, Media and Design Studio, Babson TV, Babson Radio, Stephen D. Cutler Center for Investments & Finance, Leonard A. Schlesinger Innovation Center **Computers:** 100% of classrooms, 100% of dorms, 100% of libraries, 100% of dining areas, 100% of student union, 100% of common outdoor areas have wireless network access. Students can register for classes online. Administrative functions (other than registration) can be performed online. Undergraduates are required to own a computer.

CAMPUS LIFE

Environment: Village **Activities:** Campus Ministries; Choral groups; Dance; Drama/theater; International Student Organization; Literary magazine; Model UN; Music ensembles; Musical theater; Radio station; Student government; Student newspaper; Student-run film society; Television station 78 registered organizations, 3 religious organizations. 4 fraternities, 3 sororities. **Athletics (Intercollegiate):** *Men:* baseball, basketball, cross-country, diving, golf, ice hockey, lacrosse, skiing (downhill/alpine), soccer, swimming, tennis, track/field (outdoor), track/field (indoor). *Women:* basketball, cross-country, diving, field hockey, lacrosse, skiing (downhill/alpine), soccer, softball, swimming, tennis, track/field (outdoor), track/field (indoor), volleyball. **On-Campus Highlights:** Reynolds Campus Center, Horn Library, Trim Dining Hall, Sorenson Center for the Arts, Webster Athletic Center **Environmental Initiatives:** Investment of $4 million into energy efficiency and capital improvements to save energy.

ADMISSIONS

Test Scores: SAT Math middle 50% range 620-730. SAT EBRW middle 50% range 610-680. ACT middle 50% range 27-32. Minimum internet-based TOEFL 100. Minimum paper TOEFL 600. **Basis for Candidate Selection:** *Very important factors considered include:* rigor of secondary school record, class rank, academic GPA, application essay, standardized test scores, recommendation(s), extracurricular activities, character/personal qualities. *Other factors considered include:* interview, talent/ability, first generation, alumni/ae relation, geographical residence, state residency, racial/ethnic status, volunteer work, work experience, level of applicant's interest. **Freshman**

Admission Requirements: High school diploma is required and GED is accepted *Academic units required:* 4 English, 4 math, 3 science, 4 social studies, *Academic units recommended:* 4 English, 4 math, 3 science, 4 foreign language, 4 social studies. **Freshman Admission Statistics:** 7,122 applied, 24.2% admitted, 32% enrolled. **Transfer Admission Requirements:** High school transcript, college transcript(s), essay or personal statement, statement of good standing from prior institution(s). Lowest grade transferable C. **General Admission Information:** Application fee $75. Priority deadline 11/1. Regular application deadline 1/2. Nonfall registration accepted. Admission may be deferred for a maximum of 2 years.

COSTS AND FINANCIAL AID

Annual tuition $51,104. Room and board $16,312. Average book expense $1,112. **Required Forms and Deadlines:** CSS/Financial Aid PROFILE; FAFSA; Noncustodial PROFILE. **Notification of Awards:** Applicants will be notified of awards on or about 4/1. **Types of Aid:** *Need-based scholarships/grants:* College/university scholarship or grant aid from institutional funds; Federal Pell; Private scholarships; SEOG; State scholarships/grants. *Loans:* Direct PLUS loans; Direct Subsidized Stafford Loans; Direct Unsubsidized Stafford Loans. *Student Employment:* Federal Work-Study Program available. Institutional employment available. **Financial Aid Statistics:** 89% needy freshmen, 95% needy undergrads receive need-based scholarship or grant aid. 12% freshmen, 18% undergrads receive non-need-based scholarship or grant aid. 88% freshmen, 81% undergrads receive need-based self-help aid. 0% freshmen, 0% undergrads receive athletic scholarships. 53% freshmen, 50% undergrads receive any aid. 44% undergrads borrow to pay for school. Average cumulative indebtedness $36,556. **Criteria for awarding aid:** *Non-need-based:* Academics, Leadership.

See page 888.

BAKER UNIVERSITY

PO Box 65, Baldwin City, KS 66006
Phone: 785-594-8325 · **Financial Aid Phone:** 785-594-4595
E-mail: admissions@bakeru.edu · **CEEB Code:** 6031
Fax: 785-594-8353 · **Website:** www.bakerU.edu · **ACT Code:** 1386

This private school, affiliated with the Methodist Church, was founded in 1858. It has a 36 acre campus.

RATINGS

Admissions Selectivity Rating: 75   **Fire Safety Rating:** 86   **Green Rating:** 60*

STUDENTS AND FACULTY

Enrollment: 854. **Student Body:** 50% female, 50% male, 24% out-of-state, 3% international (15 countries represented). Asian <1%, African American 10%, Caucasian 69%, Hispanic 8%, Native American 1%, Pacific Islander <1%, Two or more races 5%, Race unknown 2%.
Retention and Graduation: 68% freshmen return for sophomore year. 41% freshmen graduate within 4 years. 57% freshmen graduate within 6 years. 18% grads go on to further study within 1 year. 7% grads pursue arts and sciences degrees. 5% grads pursue law degrees. 0% grads pursue business degrees. 0% grads pursue medical degrees. **Faculty:** Student/faculty ratio 13:1. 56 full-time faculty, 86% hold PhDs, 4% are members of minority groups, 48% are women. 0% of classes are taught by teaching assistants.

ACADEMICS

Degrees: Bachelor's **Classes:** Most classes have 10-19 students. **Most popular majors:** Elementary Education And Teaching; Kinesiology And Exercise Science; Business/Commerce, General. **Special Study Options:** Accelerated program; Double major; Honors program; Independent study; Internships; Liberal arts/career combination; Student-designed major; Study abroad; Teacher certification program. **Honors programs:** Promising Scholars Honors Program, Bronston Fellows Program. **Disability Services offered to physically disabled students:** Note-taking services; Reader services; Tape recorders; Tutors. **Career services:** Alumni services; Career assessment; Career/job search classes; Internships

FACILITIES

Housing: Apartments for single students; Coed dorms; Fraternity/sorority housing; Men's dorms; Special housing for disabled student; Women's dorms 85% of campus accessible to physically diasbled. **Special Academic Facilities/Equipment:** Old Castle Museum, Quayle Bible Collection **Computers:** 95% of classrooms, 100% of dorms, 100% of libraries, 100% of dining areas, 100% of student union, have wireless network access. Students can register for classes online. Administrative functions (other than registration) can be performed online.

CAMPUS LIFE

Environment: Rural **Activities:** Campus Ministries; Choral groups; Concert band; Dance; Drama/theater; International Student Organization; Jazz band; Literary magazine; Music ensembles; Musical theater; Pep band; Radio station; Student government; Student newspaper; Symphony orchestra; Television station 60 registered organizations, 18 honor societies, 2 religious organizations. 5 fraternities, 5 sororities. **Athletics (Intercollegiate):** *Men:* baseball, basketball, cheerleading, cross-country, football, golf, soccer, tennis, track/field (outdoor), track/field (indoor), wrestling. *Women:* basketball, bowling, cheerleading, cross-country, golf, soccer, softball, tennis, track/field (outdoor), track/field (indoor), volleyball. **On-Campus Highlights:** Library, Daily Grind, Osborne Chapel, Long Student Center, Mulvane Science Hall

ADMISSIONS

Freshman Academic Profile: Average high school GPA 3.5. 18% in top 10% of high school class, 48% in top 25% of high school class, 79% in top 50% of high school class. 95% from public high schools. **Test Scores:** ACT middle 50% range 21-25. Minimum internet-based TOEFL 69. Minimum paper TOEFL 525. **Basis for Candidate Selection:** *Very important factors considered include:* rigor of secondary school record, academic GPA, standardized test scores, level of applicant's interest. *Other factors considered include:* class rank, application essay, interview, extracurricular activities, talent/ability, character/personal qualities, alumni/ae relation, geographical residence, volunteer work, work experience. **Freshman Admission Requirements:** High school diploma is required and GED is accepted *Academic units recommended:* 4 English, 3 math, 3 science, 1 science labs, 2 foreign language, 3 social studies, 1 visual/performing arts. **Freshman Admission Statistics:** 803 applied, 85.7% admitted, 37% enrolled. **Transfer Admission Requirements:** High school transcript, college transcript(s), standardized test scores, Minimum college GPA of 2.3 required. Lowest grade transferable C. **General Admission Information:** Priority deadline 3/1. Nonfall registration accepted. Admission may be deferred for a maximum of 1 year.

COSTS AND FINANCIAL AID

Annual tuition $28,430. Room and board $8,310. Required fees $450. Average book expense $1,200. **Required Forms and Deadlines:** FAFSA. **Notification of Awards:** Applicants will be notified of awards on a rolling basis beginning 1/1. **Types of Aid:** *Need-based scholarships/grants:* College/university scholarship or grant aid from institutional funds; Federal Pell; Private scholarships; SEOG; State scholarships/grants. *Loans:* Direct PLUS loans; Direct Subsidized Stafford Loans; Direct Unsubsidized Stafford Loans. *Student Employment:* Federal Work-Study Program available. Institutional employment available. **Financial Aid Statistics:** 100% needy freshmen, 91% needy undergrads receive need-based scholarship or grant aid. 100% freshmen, 100% undergrads receive non-need-based scholarship or grant aid. 98% freshmen, 77% undergrads receive need-based self-help aid. 84% freshmen, 66% undergrads receive athletic scholarships. 70% undergrads borrow to pay for school. Average cumulative indebtedness $27,627. **Criteria for awarding aid:** *Need-based:* Minority status *Non-need-based:* Academics, Alumni affiliation, Art, Athletics, Music/drama, Religious affiliation.

BALDWIN WALLACE UNIVERSITY

275 Eastland Road, Berea, OH 44017
Phone: 440-826-2222 • **Financial Aid Phone:** 440-826-2108
E-mail: admission@bw.edu • **CEEB Code:** 1050
Fax: 440-826-3830 • **Website:** www.bw.edu • **ACT Code:** 3236

This private school, affiliated with the United Methodist Church, was founded in 1845. It has a 153 acre campus.

RATINGS

Admissions Selectivity Rating: 78 **Fire Safety Rating:** 85 **Green Rating:** 77

STUDENTS AND FACULTY

Enrollment: 3,150. **Student Body:** 54% female, 46% male, 24% out-of-state, 1% international (13 countries represented). Asian 2%, African American 9%, Caucasian 78%, Hispanic 5%, Native American <1%, Pacific Islander <1%, Two or more races 5%, Race unknown <1%.
Retention and Graduation: 78% freshmen return for sophomore year. 50% freshmen graduate within 4 years. 67% freshmen graduate within 6 years.
Faculty: Student/faculty ratio 11:1. 223 full-time faculty, 73% hold PhDs, 9% are members of minority groups, 51% are women. 0% of classes are taught by teaching assistants.

ACADEMICS

Degrees: Bachelor's; Certificate; Master's **Classes:** Most classes have fewer than 10 students. Most lab/discussion sessions have fewer than 10 students.

Most popular majors: Psychology, General; Business Administration And Management, General; Accounting. **Special Study Options:** Accelerated program; Cross-registration; Distance learning; Double major; Dual enrollment; English as a Second Language (ESL); Exchange student program (domestic); Honors program; Independent study; Internships; Liberal arts/career combination; Student-designed major; Study abroad; Teacher certification program; Weekend college. **Honors programs:** The Honors Program at Baldwin Wallace University provides students with an enriched liberal arts curriculum characterized by interdisciplinary courses and an emphasis on experiential learning. Both curricular and co-curricular in nature, the Honors Program offers opportunities to live in Honors-specific housing; annual programming related to leadership development, community service, and career preparation; and numerous community-building activities that begin with a first-year student overnight orientation prior to the start of fall classes. Other special opportunities and privileges include subsidized domestic and international travel experiences; annual trips to regional Honors conferences; priority registration; and mini-scholarships to help fund study abroad, service trips, and the purchase of research supplies. **Disability Services offered to physically disabled students:** Note-taking services; Reader services; Tape recorders; Tutors. **Career services:** Alumni network; Alumni services; Career assessment; Career/job search classes; Internships

FACILITIES

Housing: Apartments for single students; Coed dorms; Fraternity/sorority housing; Special housing for disabled student; Special housing for international students; Theme housing 80% of campus accessible to physically diasbled. **Special Academic Facilities/Equipment:** Art gallery, electron microscope, observatory. **Computers:** 100% of classrooms, 100% of dorms, 100% of libraries, 100% of dining areas, 100% of student union, 100% of common outdoor areas have wireless network access. Students can register for classes online. Administrative functions (other than registration) can be performed online.

CAMPUS LIFE

Environment: Village **Activities:** Campus Ministries; Choral groups; Concert band; Dance; Drama/theater; Jazz band; Literary magazine; Marching band; Model UN; Music ensembles; Musical theater; Opera; Pep band; Radio station; Student government; Student newspaper; Student-run film society; Symphony orchestra; Television station 136 registered organizations, 25 honor societies, 7 religious organizations. 5 fraternities, 5 sororities. **Athletics (Intercollegiate):** *Men:* baseball, basketball, cross-country, diving, football, golf, soccer, swimming, tennis, track/field (outdoor), track/field (indoor), wrestling. *Women:* basketball, cross-country, diving, golf, soccer, softball, swimming, tennis, track/field (outdoor), track/field (indoor), volleyball. **On-Campus Highlights:** CyberCafe, Strosacker College Union, The S.A.C. (Student Activities Center), Conservatory/Theatre performances, Recreation Center **Environmental Initiatives:** Commitment to geo-thermal energy with all new buildings and major renovations

ADMISSIONS

Freshman Academic Profile: Average high school GPA 3.5. 22% in top 10% of high school class, 48% in top 25% of high school class, 81% in top 50% of high school class. 86% from public high schools. **Test Scores:** SAT Math middle 50% range 530-640. SAT EBRW middle 50% range 530-645. ACT middle 50% range 21-27. Minimum internet-based TOEFL 79. Minimum paper TOEFL 550. **Basis for Candidate Selection:** *Very important factors considered include:* rigor of secondary school record, academic GPA. *Important factors considered include:* class rank, application essay, standardized test scores, extracurricular activities, talent/ability, character/personal qualities. *Other factors considered include:* recommendation(s), interview, first generation, alumni/ae relation, geographical residence, state residency, racial/ethnic status, volunteer work, work experience, level of applicant's interest. **Freshman Admission Requirements:** High school diploma is required and GED is accepted *Academic units required:* 4 English, 4 math, 3 science, 2 science labs, 1 foreign language, 2 social studies, 1 history, *Academic units recommended:* 4 English, 4 math, 4 science, 2 science labs, 2 foreign language, 3 social studies, 1 history, 3 academic electives. **Freshman Admission Statistics:** 3,576 applied, 78.0% admitted, 25% enrolled. **Transfer Admission Requirements:** High school transcript, college transcript(s), statement of good standing from prior institution(s). Minimum college GPA of 2.5 required. Lowest grade transferable C. **General Admission Information:** Application fee $25. Priority deadline 3/1. Nonfall registration accepted. Admission may be deferred for a maximum of 1 year.

COSTS AND FINANCIAL AID

Annual tuition $32,586. Room and board $9,554. Average book expense $1,728. **Required Forms and Deadlines:** FAFSA. **Notification of Awards:** Applicants will be notified of awards on a rolling basis beginning 12/4. **Types of Aid:** *Need-based scholarships/grants:* College/university scholarship or grant aid from institutional funds; Federal Pell; Private scholarships; SEOG; State scholarships/grants. *Loans:* Direct PLUS loans; Direct Subsidized Stafford Loans; Direct Unsubsidized Stafford Loans. *Student Employment:* Federal

Work-Study Program available. Institutional employment available. **Financial Aid Statistics:** 100% needy freshmen, 100% needy undergrads receive need-based scholarship or grant aid. 19% freshmen, 43% undergrads receive non-need-based scholarship or grant aid. 88% freshmen, 89% undergrads receive need-based self-help aid. 0% freshmen, 0% undergrads receive athletic scholarships. 100% freshmen, 98% undergrads receive any aid. 80% undergrads borrow to pay for school. Average cumulative indebtedness $34,423. **Criteria for awarding aid:** *Need-based:* Academics, Minority status, Music/drama, Religious affiliation *Non-need-based:* Academics, Alumni affiliation, Art, Minority status, Music/drama, Religious affiliation, State/district residency.

BALL STATE UNIVERSITY

2000 W. University Avenue, Muncie, IN 47306-0855
Phone: 765-285-8300 · **Financial Aid Phone:** (765) 285-5600
E-mail: askus@bsu.edu · **CEEB Code:** 1051
Fax: 765-285-1632 · **Website:** www.bsu.edu · **ACT Code:** 1176

This public school was founded in 1918. It has a 1140 acre campus.

RATINGS
Admissions Selectivity Rating: 83   **Fire Safety Rating:** 89   **Green Rating:** 99

STUDENTS AND FACULTY
Enrollment: 15,689. **Student Body:** 59% female, 41% male, 13% out-of-state, 2% international (44 countries represented). Asian 1%, African American 7%, Caucasian 80%, Hispanic 4%, Native American <1%, Pacific Islander <1%, Two or more races 3%, Race unknown 2%.
Retention and Graduation: 82% freshmen return for sophomore year.
Faculty: Student/faculty ratio 14:1. 1,017 full-time faculty, 74% hold PhDs, 7% are members of minority groups, 47% are women.

ACADEMICS
Degrees: Associate; Bachelor's; Certificate; Doctoral; Doctoral/Professional; Doctoral/Research; Master's; Post-Bachelor's certificate; Post-Master's certificate **Classes:** Most classes have 20-29 students. **Most popular majors:** Radio And Television; Elementary Education And Teaching; General Studies. **Special Study Options:** Accelerated program; Cooperative education program; Distance learning; Double major; Dual enrollment; English as a Second Language (ESL); External degree program; Honors program; Independent study; Internships; Liberal arts/career combination; Student-designed major; Study abroad; Teacher certification program. **Honors programs:** BSU offers an Honors College which has its own curriculum, undergraduate research fellowships and study abroad programs. **Disability Services offered to physically disabled students:** Note-taking services; Reader services; Tape recorders; Tutors. **Career services:** Alumni services; Career assessment; Career/job search classes; Internships; Regional alumni

FACILITIES
Housing: Apartments for married students; Apartments for single students; Coed dorms; Fraternity/sorority housing; Men's dorms; Special housing for disabled student; Special housing for international students; Theme housing; Women's dorms 95% of campus accessible to physically diasbled. **Special Academic Facilities/Equipment:** Art gallery, museum, on-campus school (K-12), learning center, weather station, physical therapy lab, human performance lab, student wellness and recreation center including rock climbing wall, planetarium/observatory, wildlife and nature preserve. **Computers:** 100% of classrooms, 100% of dorms, 100% of libraries, 100% of dining areas, 100% of student union, 100% of common outdoor areas have wireless network access. Students can register for classes online. Administrative functions (other than registration) can be performed online. Undergraduates are required to own a computer.

CAMPUS LIFE
Environment: City **Activities:** Campus Ministries; Choral groups; Concert band; Dance; Drama/theater; International Student Organization; Jazz band; Literary magazine; Marching band; Music ensembles; Opera; Pep band; Radio station; Student government; Student newspaper; Student-run film society; Symphony orchestra; Television station 355 registered organizations, 31 honor societies, 32 religious organizations. 15 fraternities, 12 sororities. **Athletics (Intercollegiate):** *Men:* baseball, basketball, cheerleading, cross-country, diving, football, golf, swimming, tennis, volleyball. *Women:* basketball, cheerleading, cross-country, diving, field hockey, golf, gymnastics, soccer, softball, swimming, tennis, track/field (outdoor), volleyball. **On-Campus Highlights:** Student Recreation and Wellness Facility, Bracken Library, Emens Auditorium, Atrium, Letterman Communication & Media Bldg **Environmental Initiatives:** Installing a district-scale ground-source heating

and cooling system to serve all 45 campus buildings and eliminate four coal-fired boilers and reduce our GHG emissions by nearly 50%.

ADMISSIONS
Freshman Academic Profile: Average high school GPA 3.5. 19% in top 10% of high school class, 50% in top 25% of high school class, 90% in top 50% of high school class. 93% from public high schools. **Test Scores:** SAT Math middle 50% range 500-590. SAT EBRW middle 50% range 510-600. ACT middle 50% range 20-24. Minimum internet-based TOEFL 79. Minimum paper TOEFL 550. **Basis for Candidate Selection:** *Very important factors considered include:* rigor of secondary school record, academic GPA, standardized test scores. *Other factors considered include:* application essay, recommendation(s), extracurricular activities, talent/ability, volunteer work, work experience. **Freshman Admission Requirements:** High school diploma is required and GED is accepted *Academic units required:* 4 English, 3 math, 3 science, 2 science labs, 2 social studies, 1 history, *Academic units recommended:* 4 math, 3 foreign language. **Freshman Admission Statistics:** 22,147 applied, 60.5% admitted, 26% enrolled. **Transfer Admission Requirements:** college transcript(s), Minimum college GPA of 2.0 required. Lowest grade transferable C. **General Admission Information:** Application fee $55. Priority deadline 3/1. Regular application deadline 8/10. Nonfall registration accepted. Admission may be deferred.

COSTS AND FINANCIAL AID
Annual in-state tuition $9,936. Annual out-of-state tuition $24,766. Room and board $9,936. Required fees $602. Average book expense $1,320. **Required Forms and Deadlines:** FAFSA. **Notification of Awards:** Applicants will be notified of awards on a rolling basis beginning 4/1. **Types of Aid:** *Need-based scholarships/grants:* College/university scholarship or grant aid from institutional funds; Federal Pell; Private scholarships; SEOG; State scholarships/grants. *Loans:* Direct PLUS loans; Direct Subsidized Stafford Loans; Direct Unsubsidized Stafford Loans. *Student Employment:* Federal Work-Study Program available. Institutional employment available. **Financial Aid Statistics:** 63% needy freshmen, 60% needy undergrads receive need-based scholarship or grant aid. 71% freshmen, 54% undergrads receive non-need-based scholarship or grant aid. 92% freshmen, 91% undergrads receive need-based self-help aid. 2% freshmen, 2% undergrads receive athletic scholarships. 82% freshmen, 78% undergrads receive any aid. 72% undergrads borrow to pay for school. Average cumulative indebtedness $27,732. **Criteria for awarding aid:** *Need-based:* Academics, Alumni affiliation, Art, Leadership, Minority status, Music/drama *Non-need-based:* Academics, Athletics, Leadership, Minority status, Music/drama, State/district residency.

BAPTIST BIBLE COLLEGE AND SEMINARY

538 Venard Road, Clarks Summit, PA
Phone: 570-586-2400 · **Financial Aid Phone:** 570-585-9206
E-mail: admissions@SummitU.edu · **CEEB Code:** 2036
Fax: 570-585-9299 · **Website:** www.SummitU.edu · **ACT Code:** 3523

This private school, affiliated with the Baptist Church, was founded in 1932. It has a 121 acre campus.

RATINGS
Admissions Selectivity Rating: 79   **Fire Safety Rating:** 67   **Green Rating:** 60*

STUDENTS AND FACULTY
Enrollment: 668. **Student Body:** 59% female, 41% male, 68% out-of-state, 2% international (7 countries represented). Asian 1%, African American 1%, Caucasian 94%, Hispanic 2%, Native American <1%, Race unknown 1%.
Retention and Graduation: 69% freshmen return for sophomore year.
Faculty: 35 full-time faculty, 57% hold PhDs, 3% are members of minority groups, 29% are women. 0% of classes are taught by teaching assistants.

ACADEMICS
Degrees: Associate; Bachelor's; Certificate; Doctoral; Doctoral/Professional; Master's **Classes:** Most classes have 20-29 students. Most lab/discussion sessions have 10-19 students. **Most popular majors:** Elementary Education And Teaching; Theology And Religious Vocations, Other; Counseling Psychology. **Special Study Options:** Distance learning; Double major; Dual enrollment; Independent study; Internships; Study abroad; Teacher certification program. **Career services:** Alumni services; Internships

FACILITIES
Housing: Men's dorms; Women's dorms **Computers:** 100% of classrooms, 100% of libraries, 100% of dining areas, 100% of student union, 100% of common outdoor areas have wireless network access. Students can register

for classes online. Administrative functions (other than registration) can be performed online.

CAMPUS LIFE
Environment: Town **Activities:** Campus Ministries; Choral groups; Concert band; Drama/theater; Music ensembles; Student government; Yearbook. **Athletics (Intercollegiate):** *Men:* baseball, basketball, cross-country, golf, soccer. *Women:* basketball, cross-country, soccer, softball, tennis, volleyball. **On-Campus Highlights:** Underground Cafe, Residence Halls, Student Center/ Recreation Center, Jackson Hall

ADMISSIONS
Freshman Academic Profile: 40% from public high schools. **Test Scores:** SAT Math middle 50% range 430-560. SAT EBRW middle 50% range 460-570. ACT middle 50% range 20-24. Minimum paper TOEFL 500. **Basis for Candidate Selection:** *Very important factors considered include:* rigor of secondary school record, application essay, standardized test scores, recommendation(s), character/personal qualities, religious affiliation/ commitment. *Important factors considered include:* academic GPA. *Other factors considered include:* interview, extracurricular activities, talent/ability, volunteer work, work experience, level of applicant's interest. **Freshman Admission Requirements:** High school diploma is required and GED is accepted **Freshman Admission Statistics:** 452 applied, 76.1% admitted, 48% enrolled. **Transfer Admission Requirements:** High school transcript, college transcript(s), essay or personal statement, Minimum college GPA of 2 required. Lowest grade transferable 2. **General Admission Information:** Application fee $30. Priority deadline 5/1. Regular application deadline 8/15. Nonfall registration accepted. Admission may be deferred.

COSTS AND FINANCIAL AID
Annual tuition $6,840. Room and board $5,900. Required fees $468. **Required Forms and Deadlines:** FAFSA; Institution's own financial aid form. **Notification of Awards:** Applicants will be notified of awards on a rolling basis beginning 10/1. **Types of Aid:** *Need-based scholarships/grants:* College/ university scholarship or grant aid from institutional funds; Federal Pell; State scholarships/grants. *Loans:* Direct Unsubsidized Stafford Loans. *Student Employment:* Federal Work-Study Program available. Institutional employment available. **Financial Aid Statistics:** 100% freshmen, 96% undergrads receive any aid. **Criteria for awarding aid:** *Need-based:* Academics *Non-need-based:* Academics, Leadership.

BAPTIST COLLEGE OF FLORIDA

5400 College Drive, Graceville, FL 32440-1898
Phone: 850-263-3261 · **Financial Aid Phone:** 1-800-328-2660 ext. 461
E-mail: admissions@baptistcollege.edu
Fax: 850-263-9026 · **Website:** www.baptistcollege.edu · **ACT Code:** 6870

This private school, affiliated with the Southern Baptist Church, was founded in 1943. It has a 250 acre campus.

RATINGS
Admissions Selectivity Rating: 83   **Fire Safety Rating:** 81   **Green Rating:** 60*

STUDENTS AND FACULTY
Enrollment: 394. **Student Body:** 43% female, 57% male, 26% out-of-state, <1% international (1 countries represented). Asian <1%, African American 8%, Caucasian 78%, Hispanic 3%, Native American <1%, Pacific Islander 1%, Two or more races 3%, Race unknown 6%.
Retention and Graduation: 74% freshmen return for sophomore year. 26% freshmen graduate within 4 years. 46% freshmen graduate within 6 years. 50% grads go on to further study within 1 year. 0% grads pursue arts and sciences degrees. 0% grads pursue law degrees. 0% grads pursue business degrees. 0% grads pursue medical degrees. **Faculty:** Student/faculty ratio 9:1. 26 full-time faculty, 69% hold PhDs, 0% are members of minority groups, 19% are women. 0% of classes are taught by teaching assistants.

ACADEMICS
Degrees: Associate; Bachelor's; Master's **Classes:** Most classes have 20-29 students. **Most popular majors:** Religious Education; Theology/Theological Studies; Pastoral Studies/Counseling. **Special Study Options:** Distance learning; Double major; Dual enrollment; Independent study; Internships; Liberal arts/career combination. **Disability Services offered to physically disabled students:** Note-taking services; Reader services; Tape recorders; Tutors. **Career services:** Alumni services; Internships

FACILITIES
Housing: Apartments for married students; Apartments for single students; Men's dorms; Special housing for disabled student; Women's dorms 100% of campus accessible to physically disabled. **Special Academic Facilities/ Equipment:** Florida Baptist Historical Society; Heritage Village; Weight Rooms in Wellness Center. **Computers:** 100% of classrooms, 100% of dorms, 100% of libraries, 100% of dining areas, 100% of student union, 100% of common outdoor areas have wireless network access. Students can register for classes online. Administrative functions (other than registration) can be performed online.

CAMPUS LIFE
Environment: Rural **Activities:** Campus Ministries; Choral groups; Concert band; Drama/theater; Jazz band; Music ensembles; Musical theater; Radio station 3 registered organizations, 2 religious organizations. **Athletics (Intercollegiate):** *Men:* golf. *Women:* volleyball. **On-Campus Highlights:** Athletic Center, Coffee Shop, On Campus Housing, Student Center, Chapel

ADMISSIONS
Freshman Academic Profile: 90% from public high schools. **Test Scores:** SAT Math middle 50% range 400-430. SAT EBRW middle 50% range 430-440. ACT middle 50% range 17-22. Minimum paper TOEFL 500. **Basis for Candidate Selection:** *Very important factors considered include:* recommendation(s), character/personal qualities, religious affiliation/ commitment, level of applicant's interest. *Important factors considered include:* academic GPA, talent/ability, alumni/ae relation. *Other factors considered include:* rigor of secondary school record, standardized test scores, interview, extracurricular activities, volunteer work. **Freshman Admission Requirements:** High school diploma is required and GED is accepted *Academic units recommended:* 4 English, 4 math, 3 science, 1 social studies, 2 history. **Freshman Admission Statistics:** 113 applied, 61.9% admitted, 57% enrolled. **Transfer Admission Requirements:** High school transcript, college transcript(s), essay or personal statement, Minimum college GPA of 2.0 required. Lowest grade transferable C. **General Admission Information:** Application fee $25. Regular application deadline 8/15. Nonfall registration accepted. Admission may be deferred for a maximum of 2 semesters.

COSTS AND FINANCIAL AID
Annual tuition $10,200. Room and board $4,138. Required fees $900. Average book expense $950. **Required Forms and Deadlines:** Business/Farm Supplement; FAFSA; Institution's own financial aid form; State aid form. **Notification of Awards:** Applicants will be notified of awards on a rolling basis beginning 6/15. **Types of Aid:** *Need-based scholarships/grants:* Federal Pell; Private scholarships; SEOG; State scholarships/grants. *Loans:* Direct PLUS loans; Direct Subsidized Stafford Loans; Direct Unsubsidized Stafford Loans. *Student Employment:* Federal Work-Study Program available. Institutional employment available. **Financial Aid Statistics:** 61% needy freshmen, 84% needy undergrads receive need-based scholarship or grant aid. 1% undergrads receive non-need-based scholarship or grant aid. 44% freshmen, 66% undergrads receive need-based self-help aid. 0% freshmen, 0% undergrads receive athletic scholarships. 86% freshmen, 97% undergrads receive any aid. 66% undergrads borrow to pay for school. Average cumulative indebtedness $17,485. **Criteria for awarding aid:** *Need-based:* Academics, Minority status, Music/drama, Religious affiliation *Non-need-based:* Academics, Minority status, Music/drama, Religious affiliation.

BARD COLLEGE

PO Box 5000, Annandale-on-Hudson, NY 12504
Phone: 845-758-7472 · **Financial Aid Phone:** 845-758-7526
E-mail: admissions@bard.edu · **CEEB Code:** 2037
Fax: 845-758-5208 · **Website:** www.bard.edu · **ACT Code:** 2674

This private school was founded in 1860. It has a 1000 acre campus.

RATINGS
Admissions Selectivity Rating: 89   **Fire Safety Rating:** 97   **Green Rating:** 91

STUDENTS AND FACULTY
Enrollment: 1,926. **Student Body:** 58% female, 42% male, 66% out-of-state, 10% international (57 countries represented). Asian 6%, African American 8%, Caucasian 61%, Hispanic 3%, Native American 1%, Race unknown 10%.
Retention and Graduation: 86% freshmen return for sophomore year.

Faculty: Student/faculty ratio 10:1. 156 full-time faculty, 88% hold PhDs, 17% are members of minority groups, 43% are women. 0% of classes are taught by teaching assistants.

ACADEMICS

Degrees: Associate; Bachelor's; Doctoral/Research; Master's **Classes:** Most classes have 10-19 students. **Most popular majors:** English Language And Literature, General; Social Sciences, General; Visual And Performing Arts, General. **Special Study Options:** Cross-registration; Double major; Dual enrollment; English as a Second Language (ESL); Independent study; Internships; Student-designed major; Study abroad. **Combined degree programs:** BA/MA; BA/MEng. **Disability Services offered to physically disabled students:** Note-taking services; Reader services; Tape recorders; Tutors. **Career services:** Alumni network; Alumni services; Career assessment; Career/job search classes; Internships; Regional alumni

FACILITIES

Housing: Coed dorms; Cooperative housing; Special housing for disabled student; Theme housing; Wellness housing; Women's dorms 70% of campus accessible to physically disabled. **Special Academic Facilities/Equipment:** Performing arts center, gallery, art museum, collection of contemporary art, center for curatorial studies, language lab, nursery school, ecology field station, archaeology field school, economics institute. **Computers:** 5% of classrooms, 50% of dorms, 100% of libraries, 100% of dining areas, 100% of student union, have wireless network access. Students can register for classes online. Administrative functions (other than registration) can be performed online.

CAMPUS LIFE

Environment: Rural **Activities:** Campus Ministries; Choral groups; Concert band; Dance; Drama/theater; International Student Organization; Jazz band; Literary magazine; Model UN; Music ensembles; Musical theater; Opera; Radio station; Student government; Student newspaper; Student-run film society; Symphony orchestra 120 registered organizations, 5 religious organizations. **Athletics (Intercollegiate):** *Men:* basketball, cross-country, soccer, squash, tennis, track/field (outdoor), volleyball. *Women:* basketball, cross-country, soccer, tennis, track/field (outdoor), volleyball. **On-Campus Highlights:** Richard B Fisher Center for the Performing Arts, Stevenson Library, Reem-Kayden Center for Science and Computation, Museum @ Center for Curatorial Studies, Levy Economics Institute—Blithewood Mansion **Environmental Initiatives:** 40% of the total building square footages utilizes geothermal heat-exchange for space heating and cooling

ADMISSIONS

Freshman Academic Profile: 43% in top 10% of high school class, 83% in top 25% of high school class, 94% in top 50% of high school class. 58% from public high schools. **Test Scores:** SAT Math middle 50% range 550-670. SAT EBRW middle 50% range 590-700. Minimum internet-based TOEFL 100. Minimum paper TOEFL 600. **Basis for Candidate Selection:** *Very important factors considered include:* rigor of secondary school record, academic GPA, application essay, recommendation(s), extracurricular activities, talent/ability, character/personal qualities. *Important factors considered include:* volunteer work, work experience. *Other factors considered include:* class rank, standardized test scores, interview, first generation, alumni/ae relation, geographical residence, state residency, religious affiliation/commitment, racial/ethnic status, level of applicant's interest. **Freshman Admission Requirements:** High school diploma is required and GED is accepted *Academic units recommended:* 4 English, 4 math, 4 science, 3 science labs, 4 foreign language, 4 social studies, 4 history. **Freshman Admission Statistics:** 5,181 applied, 56.2% admitted, 17% enrolled. **Transfer Admission Requirements:** college transcript(s), essay or personal statement, statement of good standing from prior institution(s). Minimum college GPA of 3.0 required. Lowest grade transferable C. **General Admission Information:** Application fee $50. Regular application deadline 1/1. Nonfall registration accepted. Admission may be deferred for a maximum of 1 year.

COSTS AND FINANCIAL AID

Annual tuition $52,226. Room and board $15,066. Required fees $680. Average book expense $1,000. **Required Forms and Deadlines:** CSS/Financial Aid PROFILE; FAFSA; Noncustodial PROFILE. **Notification of Awards:** Applicants will be notified of awards on or about 4/1. **Types of Aid:** *Need-based scholarships/grants:* College/university scholarship or grant aid from institutional funds; Federal Pell; Private scholarships; SEOG; State scholarships/grants. *Loans:* Direct PLUS loans; Direct Subsidized Stafford Loans; Direct Unsubsidized Stafford Loans. *Student Employment:* Federal Work-Study Program available. Institutional employment available. **Financial Aid Statistics:** 98% needy freshmen, 97% needy undergrads receive need-based scholarship or grant aid. 0% undergrads receive non-need-based scholarship or grant aid. 85% freshmen, 82% undergrads receive need-based self-help aid. 0% freshmen, 0% undergrads receive athletic scholarships. 70% freshmen, 72% undergrads receive any aid. 54% undergrads borrow to pay for school. Average cumulative indebtedness $28,261. **Criteria for awarding aid:** *Need-based:* Academics *Non-need-based:* Academics.

BARD COLLEGE AT SIMON'S ROCK

84 Alford Road, Great Barrington, MA 01230
Financial Aid Phone: 413-528-7297
E-mail: admit@simons-rock.edu · **CEEB Code:** 3795
Fax: 413-541-0081 · **Website:** www.simons-rock.edu · **ACT Code:** 1893

This private school was founded in 1964. It has a 275 acre campus.

RATINGS

Admissions Selectivity Rating: 88   **Fire Safety Rating:** 95   **Green Rating:** 60*

STUDENTS AND FACULTY

Enrollment: 362. **Student Body:** 61% female, 39% male, 88% out-of-state, 14% international (15 countries represented). Asian 11%, African American 4%, Caucasian 56%, Hispanic 3%, Native American 1%, Pacific Islander 0%, Two or more races 3%, Race unknown 8%.
Retention and Graduation: 75% freshmen return for sophomore year.
Faculty: Student/faculty ratio 7:1. 51 full-time faculty, 90% hold PhDs, 16% are members of minority groups, 49% are women. 0% of classes are taught by teaching assistants.

ACADEMICS

Degrees: Associate; Bachelor's **Classes:** Most classes have 20-29 students. Most lab/discussion sessions have 20-29 students. **Most popular majors:** Biology/Biological Sciences, General; Political Science And Government, General; Visual And Performing Arts, General. **Special Study Options:** Double major; External degree program; Independent study; Internships; Student-designed major; Study abroad. **Disability Services offered to physically disabled students:** Note-taking services; Reader services; Tape recorders; Tutors. **Career services:** Alumni network; Alumni services; Career assessment; Career/job search classes; Internships; Regional alumni

FACILITIES

Housing: Coed dorms; Men's dorms; Special housing for disabled student; Women's dorms 75% of campus accessible to physically disabled. **Computers:** Administrative functions (other than registration) can be performed online.

CAMPUS LIFE

Environment: Village **Activities:** Choral groups; Dance; Drama/theater; International Student Organization; Jazz band; Literary magazine; Model UN; Music ensembles; Student government; Student newspaper; Yearbook 21 registered organizations, 3 religious organizations. **Athletics (Intercollegiate):** *Men:* basketball, soccer, swimming, tennis. *Women:* basketball, soccer, swimming, tennis. **On-Campus Highlights:** Fisher Science and Academic Center, Daniel Arts Center, Alumni Library, Kellogg Music Center, Kilpatrick Athletic Center

ADMISSIONS

Freshman Academic Profile: Average high school GPA 3.5. 52% in top 10% of high school class, 22% in top 25% of high school class, 18% in top 50% of high school class. 71% from public high schools. **Test Scores:** SAT Math middle 50% range 610-650. SAT EBRW middle 50% range 640-750. ACT middle 50% range 28-30. Minimum internet-based TOEFL 100. Minimum paper TOEFL 600. **Basis for Candidate Selection:** *Very important factors considered include:* rigor of secondary school record, academic GPA, application essay, interview, talent/ability. *Important factors considered include:* recommendation(s), character/personal qualities. *Other factors considered include:* class rank, standardized test scores, extracurricular activities, first generation, alumni/ae relation, volunteer work, work experience, level of applicant's interest. **Freshman Admission Requirements:** High school diploma or equivalent is not required *Academic units recommended:* 2 English, 2 math, 2 science, 2 foreign language, 2 social studies, 2 history. **Freshman Admission Statistics:** 387 applied, 67.7% admitted, 56% enrolled. **Transfer Admission Requirements:** college transcript(s), essay or personal statement, interview, Minimum college GPA of 2.0 required. Lowest grade transferable C. **General Admission Information:** Nonfall registration accepted.

COSTS AND FINANCIAL AID

Annual tuition $50,600. Room and board $14,060. Required fees $1,135. Average book expense $1,000. **Required Forms and Deadlines:** CSS/Financial Aid PROFILE; FAFSA; Noncustodial PROFILE; State aid form. **Notification of Awards:** Applicants will be notified of awards on a rolling basis beginning 1/2. **Types of Aid:** *Need-based scholarships/grants:* College/university scholarship or grant aid from institutional funds; Federal Pell; Private scholarships; SEOG; State scholarships/grants. *Loans:* Direct PLUS loans; Direct Subsidized Stafford Loans; Direct Unsubsidized Stafford Loans. *Student Employment:* Federal Work-Study Program available. Institutional employment available. **Financial Aid Statistics:** 97% needy freshmen, 99% needy undergrads receive need-based scholarship or grant aid. 0% undergrads receive non-need-based scholarship or grant aid. 69% freshmen, 71% undergrads receive need-based self-help aid. 0% freshmen, 0% undergrads receive athletic scholarships. 90% freshmen, 86% undergrads receive any aid. 61% undergrads borrow to pay for school. Average cumulative indebtedness $24,098. **Criteria for awarding aid:** *Need-based:* Academics, Minority status *Non-need-based:* Academics, Alumni affiliation, Minority status, State/district residency.

BARNARD COLLEGE

Best Colleges

3009 Broadway, New York, NY 10027
Phone: 212-854-2014 · **Financial Aid Phone:** 212-854-2154
E-mail: admissions@barnard.edu · **CEEB Code:** 2038
Fax: 212-280-8797 · **Website:** www.barnard.edu · **ACT Code:** 2718

This private school was founded in 1889. It has a 4 acre campus.

RATINGS

Admissions Selectivity Rating: 98   **Fire Safety Rating:** 79   **Green Rating:** 74

STUDENTS AND FACULTY

Enrollment: 2,600. **Student Body:** 100% female, 0% male, 73% out-of-state, 9% international (66 countries represented). Asian 15%, African American 6%, Caucasian 52%, Hispanic 12%, Native American <1%, Pacific Islander <1%, Two or more races 6%, Race unknown <1%.
Retention and Graduation: 95% freshmen return for sophomore year. 87% freshmen graduate within 4 years. 93% freshmen graduate within 6 years. 23% grads go on to further study within 1 year. **Faculty:** Student/faculty ratio 10:1. 226 full-time faculty, 93% hold PhDs, 21% are members of minority groups, 61% are women. 0% of classes are taught by teaching assistants.

ACADEMICS

Degrees: Bachelor's. **Classes:** Most classes have fewer than 10 students. Most lab/discussion sessions have 10-19 students. **Most popular majors:** English Language And Literature, General; Psychology, General; Economics, General. **Special Study Options:** Cross-registration; Double major; Dual enrollment; Exchange student program (domestic); Independent study; Internships; Student-designed major; Study abroad; Teacher certification program. **Honors programs:** The Athena Center for Leadership Studies was launched in September of 2009 and offers a range of academic courses that examines all aspects of women's leadership, sponsored lectures, mentoring and leadership opportunities and a lab which offers a wide range of workshops designed to teach practical elements of leadership to students, alums and other leaders in New York. **Combined degree programs:** BA/DDS; BA/JD; BA/MA. **Disability Services offered to physically disabled students:** Note-taking services; Reader services; Tape recorders; Tutors. **Career services:** Alumni network; Alumni services; Career assessment; Career/job search classes; Internships; Regional alumni

FACILITIES

Housing: Coed dorms; Fraternity/sorority housing; Special housing for disabled student; Women's dorms 100% of campus accessible to physically diasbled. **Special Academic Facilities/Equipment:** Black Box and full theaters, infant-toddler center, greenhouse, academic computer center, art gallery space, advanced architecture labs. **Computers:** 60% of classrooms, 80% of dorms, 80% of libraries, 100% of dining areas, 100% of student union, 100% of common outdoor areas have wireless network access. Students can register for classes online. Administrative functions (other than registration) can be performed online.

CAMPUS LIFE

Environment: Metropolis **Activities:** Campus Ministries; Choral groups; Concert band; Dance; Drama/theater; International Student Organization; Jazz band; Literary magazine; Marching band; Model UN; Music ensembles; Musical theater; Opera; Pep band; Radio station; Student government; Student newspaper; Student-run film society; Symphony orchestra; Yearbook 100 registered organizations, 1 honor societies. **Athletics (Intercollegiate):** *Women:* archery, basketball, crew/rowing, cross-country, diving, fencing, field hockey, golf, lacrosse, soccer, softball, swimming, tennis, track/field (outdoor), volleyball. **On-Campus Highlights:** Milstein Center (opening late summer 2018), Diana Center, The Quad, Lefrak Center, Liz's Place Cafe **Environmental Initiatives:** Barnard is partnered with other New York City organizations as part of Mayor deBlasio's "PlanNYC 2030 Challenge" to reduce the City's greenhouse gas footprint and improve the urban infrastructure and environment.

ADMISSIONS

Freshman Academic Profile: Average high school GPA 4.0. 84% in top 10% of high school class, 93% in top 25% of high school class, 100% in top 50% of high school class. 50% from public high schools. **Test Scores:** SAT Math middle 50% range 650-740. SAT EBRW middle 50% range 660-760. ACT middle 50% range 30-33. Minimum internet-based TOEFL 100. Minimum paper TOEFL 600. **Basis for Candidate Selection:** *Very important factors considered include:* rigor of secondary school record, academic GPA, application essay, recommendation(s), character/personal qualities. *Important factors considered include:* class rank, standardized test scores, extracurricular activities, talent/ability, volunteer work, work experience. *Other factors considered include:* interview, first generation, alumni/ae relation, geographical residence, racial/ethnic status, level of applicant's interest. **Freshman Admission Requirements:** High school diploma is required and GED is accepted *Academic units recommended:* 4 English, 3 math, 3 science, 3 foreign language, 3 history. **Freshman Admission Statistics:** 7,716 applied, 15.4% admitted, 51% enrolled. **Transfer Admission Requirements:** High school transcript, college transcript(s), essay or personal statement, standardized test scores, statement of good standing from prior institution(s). Lowest grade transferable C-. **General Admission Information:** Application fee $75. Regular application deadline 1/1. Nonfall registration accepted. Admission may be deferred for a maximum of 1 year.

COSTS AND FINANCIAL AID

Room and board $16,100. **Required Forms and Deadlines:** CSS/Financial Aid PROFILE; FAFSA; Noncustodial PROFILE; State aid form. **Notification of Awards:** Applicants will be notified of awards on or about 3/31. **Types of Aid:** *Need-based scholarships/grants:* College/university scholarship or grant aid from institutional funds; Federal Pell; Private scholarships; SEOG; State scholarships/grants. *Loans:* Direct PLUS loans; Direct Subsidized Stafford Loans; Direct Unsubsidized Stafford Loans. *Student Employment:* Federal Work-Study Program available. Institutional employment available. **Financial Aid Statistics:** 98% needy freshmen, 98% needy undergrads receive need-based scholarship or grant aid. 0% undergrads receive non-need-based scholarship or grant aid. 100% freshmen, 100% undergrads receive need-based self-help aid. 0% freshmen, 0% undergrads receive athletic scholarships. 53% freshmen, 48% undergrads receive any aid. 44% undergrads borrow to pay for school. Average cumulative indebtedness $20,008.

See page 890.

BARRY UNIVERSITY

11300 NE 2nd Avenue, Miami Shores, FL 33161-6695
Phone: 305-899-3100 · **Financial Aid Phone:** 305-899-3673
E-mail: admissions@barry.edu · **CEEB Code:** 5053
Fax: 305-899-2971 · **Website:** www.barry.edu · **ACT Code:** 718

This private school, affiliated with the Roman Catholic Church, was founded in 1940.

RATINGS

Admissions Selectivity Rating: 71   **Fire Safety Rating:** 60*   **Green Rating:** 60*

STUDENTS AND FACULTY

Enrollment: 3,459. **Student Body:** 60% female, 40% male, 20% out-of-state, 8% international (69 countries represented). Asian 1%, African American 34%, Caucasian 19%, Hispanic 34%, Native American <1%, Pacific Islander <1%, Two or more races 1%, Race unknown 1%.
Retention and Graduation: 61% freshmen return for sophomore year. 35% freshmen graduate within 6 years. **Faculty:** Student/faculty ratio 13:1. 325 full-time faculty, 32% are members of minority groups, 57% are women.

ACADEMICS

Degrees: Bachelor's; Doctoral/Professional; Doctoral/Research; Master's; Post-Master's certificate **Classes:** Most classes have 50-99 students. **Most popular majors:** Public Administration; Registered Nursing/Registered Nurse; Business Administration, Management And Operations. **Special Study Options:** Accelerated program; Distance learning; Double major; English as a Second Language (ESL); Honors program; Internships; Study abroad; Teacher certification program. **Honors programs:** Honors program—Designed to push the best and brightest toward a lifetime of learning, Barry University's Honors Program challenges, enriches, and prepares especially motivated students to pursue their fullest potential. Participants will face a rigorous curriculum, more complicated issues, and tougher questions. Those selected will benefit from exploring the entire spectrum of humanity, the competition of their brightest peers, smaller classes with fewer lectures and more discussions, individualized study (with a senior honors thesis), and hands-on learning. **Disability Services offered to physically disabled students:** Note-taking services; Reader services; Tape recorders; Tutors. **Career services:** Career assessment; Career/job search classes; Internships

FACILITIES

Housing: Coed dorms; Special housing for disabled student; Theme housing **Special Academic Facilities/Equipment:** Human performance lab, broadcasting studio, radio station, athletic training room, cell biology/biotechnology labs, Classroom of Tomorrow, Biomechanics lab,Photogrpahy lab, darkroom, and studio, Language lab, athletic training room. **Computers:** Students can register for classes online. Administrative functions (other than registration) can be performed online.

CAMPUS LIFE

Environment: Metropolis **Activities:** Campus Ministries; Dance; Drama/theater; International Student Organization; Literary magazine; Music ensembles; Musical theater; Opera; Radio station; Student government; Student newspaper; Yearbook 67 registered organizations, 20 honor societies, 5 religious organizations. 2 fraternities, 2 sororities. **Athletics (Intercollegiate):** *Men:* baseball, basketball, golf, soccer, tennis. *Women:* basketball, crew/rowing, golf, soccer, softball, tennis, volleyball. **On-Campus Highlights:** R. Kirk Landon Student Union, Health and Sports Center, Penaport Pool, Residence Halls, Shepard and Ruth K. Broad Center for the Performing Arts

ADMISSIONS

Freshman Academic Profile: Average high school GPA 3.2. **Test Scores:** SAT Math middle 50% range 500-520. SAT EBRW middle 50% range 410-440. ACT middle 50% range 17-20. Minimum internet-based TOEFL 61. Minimum paper TOEFL 500. **Basis for Candidate Selection:** *Very important factors considered include:* academic GPA, standardized test scores. *Important factors considered include:* talent/ability, character/personal qualities. *Other factors considered include:* rigor of secondary school record, class rank, recommendation(s), extracurricular activities, first generation, volunteer work, level of applicant's interest. **Freshman Admission Requirements:** High school diploma is required and GED is accepted *Academic units recommended:* 4 English, 3 math, 3 science, 3 social studies. **Freshman Admission Statistics:** 5,123 applied, 85.1% admitted, 14% enrolled. **Transfer Admission Requirements:** college transcript(s), Minimum college GPA of 2.0 required. Lowest grade transferable C. **General Admission Information:** Nonfall registration accepted. Admission may be deferred for a maximum of 1 year.

COSTS AND FINANCIAL AID

Annual tuition $29,700. Room and board $11,100. Required fees $150. Average book expense $1,500. **Required Forms and Deadlines:** FAFSA. **Notification of Awards:** Applicants will be notified of awards on or about 10/15. **Types of Aid:** *Need-based scholarships/grants:* College/university scholarship or grant aid from institutional funds; Federal Nursing Scholarships; Federal Pell; Private scholarships; SEOG; State scholarships/grants. *Loans:* Direct PLUS loans; Direct Subsidized Stafford Loans; Direct Unsubsidized Stafford Loans. *Student Employment:* Federal Work-Study Program available. Institutional employment available. **Financial Aid Statistics:** 83% needy freshmen, 79% needy undergrads receive need-based scholarship or grant aid. 93% freshmen, 93% undergrads receive non-need-based scholarship or grant aid. 80% freshmen, 82% undergrads receive need-based self-help aid. 5% freshmen, 5% undergrads receive athletic scholarships. 98% freshmen, 85% undergrads receive any aid. 68% undergrads borrow to pay for school. Average cumulative indebtedness $39,248. **Criteria for awarding aid:** *Non-need-based:* Academics, Art, Athletics, Music/drama.

BARTON COLLEGE

Box 5000, Wilson, NC 27893-7000
Phone: 252-399-6317 • **Financial Aid Phone:** 252-399-6316
E-mail: enroll@barton.edu • **CEEB Code:** 5016
Fax: 252-399-6572 • **Website:** www.barton.edu • **ACT Code:** 3066

This private school, affiliated with the Disciples of Christ Church, was founded in 1902. It has a 76 acre campus.

RATINGS

Admissions Selectivity Rating: 84   **Fire Safety Rating:** 88   **Green Rating:** 60*

STUDENTS AND FACULTY

Enrollment: 1,076. **Student Body:** 69% female, 31% male, 11% out-of-state, 3% international (8 countries represented). Asian 1%, African American 27%, Caucasian 59%, Hispanic 3%, Native American 1%, Pacific Islander <1%, Two or more races 4%, Race unknown 2%.
Retention and Graduation: 71% freshmen return for sophomore year.
Faculty: Student/faculty ratio 12:1. 69 full-time faculty, 68% hold PhDs, 13% are members of minority groups, 49% are women. 0% of classes are taught by teaching assistants.

ACADEMICS

Degrees: Bachelor's; Master's **Classes:** Most classes have 10-19 students. Most lab/discussion sessions have 10-19 students. **Most popular majors:** Elementary Education And Teaching; Nursing/Registered Nurse (Rn, Asn, Bsn, Msn); Business Administration And Management, General. **Special Study Options:** Accelerated program; Cooperative education program; Double major; Honors program; Independent study; Internships; Liberal arts/career combination; Study abroad; Teacher certification program; Weekend college. **Honors programs:** Three competitive international travel scholarships awarded to entering honors students. **Disability Services offered to physically disabled students:** Note-taking services; Reader services; Tape recorders; Tutors. **Career services:** Alumni services; Career assessment; Career/job search classes; Internships

FACILITIES

Housing: Coed dorms; Fraternity/sorority housing; Special housing for disabled student; Women's dorms 90% of campus accessible to physically diasbled. **Special Academic Facilities/Equipment:** tv station, art museum, music recording studio, greenhouse **Computers:** 90% of libraries, 90% of dining areas, have wireless network access. Administrative functions (other than registration) can be performed online.

CAMPUS LIFE

Environment: Town **Activities:** Campus Ministries; Choral groups; Dance; Drama/theater; Musical theater; Pep band; Student government; Student newspaper; Symphony orchestra 51 registered organizations, 7 honor societies, 4 religious organizations. 3 fraternities, 3 sororities. **Athletics (Intercollegiate):** *Men:* baseball, basketball, cross-country, golf, soccer, tennis. *Women:* basketball, cross-country, soccer, softball, tennis, volleyball. **On-Campus Highlights:** Hamlin Student Center, Sam and Marjorie Ragan Writing Center, Kennedy Recreation and Intramural Center, Hackney Library, Barton Art Museum

ADMISSIONS

Freshman Academic Profile: Average high school GPA 3.0. 12% in top 10% of high school class, 35% in top 25% of high school class, 73% in top 50% of high school class. 87% from public high schools. **Test Scores:** SAT Math middle 50% range 430-540. SAT EBRW middle 50% range 420-520. Minimum paper TOEFL 525. **Basis for Candidate Selection:** *Very important factors considered include:* academic GPA, standardized test scores. *Other factors considered include:* rigor of secondary school record, class rank, recommendation(s), interview, extracurricular activities, volunteer work, experience. **Freshman Admission Requirements:** High school diploma is required and GED is accepted *Academic units required:* 4 English, 3 math, 2 science, 1 science labs, 1 academic elective, *Academic units recommended:* 2 foreign language, 2 units from above areas or other academic areas. **Freshman Admission Statistics:** 3,017 applied, 44.4% admitted, 15% enrolled. **Transfer Admission Requirements:** college transcript(s), statement of good standing from prior institution(s). Minimum college GPA of 2.0 required. Lowest grade transferable C. **General Admission Information:** Application fee $25. Nonfall registration accepted. Admission may be deferred for a maximum of 1 year.

COSTS AND FINANCIAL AID

Annual tuition $22,278. Room and board $7,940. Required fees $1,902. Average book expense $1,200. **Required Forms and Deadlines:** FAFSA. **Notification of Awards:** Applicants will be notified of awards on a rolling basis beginning 2/1. **Types of Aid:** *Need-based scholarships/grants:* College/university scholarship or grant aid from institutional funds; Federal Pell; Private scholarships; SEOG; State scholarships/grants. *Loans: Student Employment:* Federal Work-Study Program available. Institutional employment available. **Financial Aid Statistics:** 99% needy freshmen, 96% needy undergrads receive need-based scholarship or grant aid. 10% freshmen, 6% undergrads receive non-need-based scholarship or grant aid. 87% freshmen, 87% undergrads receive need-based self-help aid. 9% freshmen, 6% undergrads receive athletic scholarships. 98% freshmen, 93% undergrads receive any aid. **Criteria for awarding aid:** *Need-based:* Minority status, Religious affiliation *Non-need-based:* Academics, Alumni affiliation, Art, Athletics, Leadership, Minority status, Music/drama, Religious affiliation, State/district residency.

BASTYR UNIVERSITY

VMI Office of Admissions, Kenmore, WA 98028
Phone: (425) 602-3330 · **Financial Aid Phone:** 425-602-3083
E-mail: admissions@bastyr.edu
Fax: (425) 602-3090 · **Website:** www.bastyr.edu

This private school was founded in 1978. It has a 51 acre campus.

RATINGS
Admissions Selectivity Rating: 61   **Fire Safety Rating:** 88   **Green Rating:** 60*

STUDENTS AND FACULTY
Enrollment: 227. **Student Body:** 87% female, 13% male, 5% out-of-state, 3% international (31 countries represented). Asian 8%, African American 4%, Caucasian 71%, Hispanic 5%, Native American 2%, Pacific Islander 1%, Two or more races 4%, Race unknown 3%.
Faculty: 43 full-time faculty, 19% are members of minority groups, 63% are women. 0% of classes are taught by teaching assistants.

ACADEMICS
Degrees: Bachelor's; Certificate; Doctoral/Professional; Master's; Post-Master's certificate **Classes:** Most classes have 10-19 students. Most lab/discussion sessions have 10-19 students. **Most popular majors:** Nutrition Sciences; Acupuncture And Oriental Medicine; Herbalism/Herbalist. **Special Study Options:** Double major; Independent study; Internships; Study abroad; Weekend college. **Disability Services offered to physically disabled students:** Note-taking services; Tape recorders; Tutors. **Career services:** Alumni services; Career assessment; Career/job search classes; Internships

FACILITIES
Housing: Apartments for single students; Coed dorms; Special housing for disabled students 100% of campus accessible to physically disabled. **Special Academic Facilities/Equipment:** Library, Tierney Basic Sciences Research Laboratory, Clinical Research Center

CAMPUS LIFE
Environment: Town **Activities:** Campus Ministries; Choral groups; Dance; International Student Organization; Music ensembles; Student government. **On-Campus Highlights:** Critically lauded Dining Commons, Medicinal herb garden & reflexology foot path, Spacious campus grounds and playfields, Adjacent Saint Edwards State Park (and Lake Washington), Bastyr Chapel **Environmental Initiatives:** Our 11-building Student Village has earned LEED Platinum-certification (the first student housing project on the West Coast to receive this honor) and the U.S. Green Building Council's (USGBC) Outstanding Multifamily Project in the 2010 LEED for Homes Awards. The buildings feature "butterfly" roofs to capture rainwater, high efficiency water heaters and gas boilers, energy-efficient appliances and light fixtures, low-flow plumbing, natural ventilation, radiant-heat flooring made of finished concrete, sustainable landscaping, and bicycle storage.

ADMISSIONS
Test Scores: Minimum internet-based TOEFL 79. Minimum paper TOEFL 550. **Transfer Admission Requirements:** college transcript(s), essay or personal statement, Minimum college GPA of 2.25 required. Lowest grade transferable 2. **General Admission Information:** Application fee $75. Regular application deadline 3/15. Admission may be deferred.

COSTS AND FINANCIAL AID
Annual tuition $24,273. Average book expense $2,250. **Required Forms and Deadlines:** FAFSA; Institution's own financial aid form. **Notification of Awards:** Applicants will be notified of awards on a rolling basis beginning 2/1. **Types of Aid:** *Need-based scholarships/grants:* College/university scholarship or grant aid from institutional funds; Federal Pell; Private scholarships; SEOG; State scholarships/grants. *Loans:* Direct PLUS loans; Direct Subsidized Stafford Loans; Direct Unsubsidized Stafford Loans. *Student Employment:* Federal Work-Study Program available. Institutional employment available. **Financial Aid Statistics:** 91% needy undergrads receive need-based scholarship or grant aid. 2% undergrads receive non-need-based scholarship or grant aid. 0% undergrads receive athletic scholarships. 87% undergrads receive any aid. **Criteria for awarding aid:** *Need-based:* Academics, Alumni affiliation, Job skills, Leadership *Non-need-based:* Academics, Alumni affiliation, Job skills, Leadership.

BATES COLLEGE

2 Andrews Road, Lewiston, ME 04240
Phone: 207-786-6000 · **Financial Aid Phone:** 207-786-6096
E-mail: admission@bates.edu · **CEEB Code:** 3076
Fax: 207-786-6025 · **Website:** www.bates.edu · **ACT Code:** 1634

This private school was founded in 1855. It has a 133 acre campus.

RATINGS
Admissions Selectivity Rating: 96   **Fire Safety Rating:** 98   **Green Rating:** 97

STUDENTS AND FACULTY
Enrollment: 1,787. **Student Body:** 51% female, 49% male, 7% international (71 countries represented). Asian 4%, African American 5%, Caucasian 70%, Hispanic 9%, Native American <1%, Pacific Islander <1%, Two or more races 5%, Race unknown <1%.
Retention and Graduation: 95% freshmen return for sophomore year. 89% freshmen graduate within 4 years. 92% freshmen graduate within 6 years.
Faculty: Student/faculty ratio 10:1. 179 full-time faculty, 97% hold PhDs, 17% are members of minority groups, 50% are women. 0% of classes are taught by teaching assistants.

ACADEMICS
Degrees: Bachelor's **Classes:** Most classes have 10-19 students. Most lab/discussion sessions have 10-19 students. **Most popular majors:** Psychology, General; Political Science And Government, General; History, General. **Special Study Options:** Accelerated program; Cross-registration; Double major; Exchange student program (domestic); Honors program; Independent study; Internships; Liberal arts/career combination; Student-designed major; Study abroad; Teacher certification program. **Honors programs:** The Honors Thesis Program. **Disability Services offered to physically disabled students:** Note-taking services; Reader services; Tape recorders; Tutors. **Career services:** Alumni network; Alumni services; Career assessment; Career/job search classes; Internships; Regional alumni

FACILITIES
Housing: Coed dorms; Men's dorms; Theme housing; Wellness housing; Women's dorms 60% of campus accessible to physically-disabled. **Special Academic Facilities/Equipment:** Art gallery, Edmund S. Muskie Archives, language labs, planetarium, 600-acre conservation area on seacoast for environmental studies, scanning electron microscope, Imaging Center. **Computers:** 40% of classrooms, 100% of dorms, 100% of libraries, 100% of dining areas, 100% of student union, 10% of common outdoor areas have wireless network access. Students can register for classes online. Administrative functions (other than registration) can be performed online.

CAMPUS LIFE
Environment: Town **Activities:** Campus Ministries; Choral groups; Concert band; Dance; Drama/theater; International Student Organization; Jazz band; Literary magazine; Model UN; Music ensembles; Musical theater; Radio station; Student government; Student newspaper; Student-run film society; Symphony orchestra; Yearbook 99 registered organizations, 3 honor societies, 9 religious organizations. **Athletics (Intercollegiate):** *Men:* baseball, basketball, crew/rowing, cross-country, diving, football, golf, lacrosse, skiing (downhill/alpine), skiing (nordic/cross-country), soccer, squash, swimming, tennis, track/field (outdoor), track/field (indoor). *Women:* basketball, crew/rowing, cross-country, diving, field hockey, golf, lacrosse, skiing (downhill/alpine), skiing (nordic/cross-country), soccer, softball, squash, swimming, tennis, track/field (outdoor), track/field (indoor), volleyball. **On-Campus Highlights:** Pettengill Hall, Bates College Museum of Art, Dining Commons, The George and Helen Ladd Library, Merrill Gymnasium/Underhill Arena **Environmental Initiatives:** Developing sustainable building guidelines and campus energy goals.

ADMISSIONS
Freshman Academic Profile: 63% in top 10% of high school class, 86% in top 25% of high school class, 97% in top 50% of high school class. 53% from public high schools. **Test Scores:** SAT Math middle 50% range 630-720. SAT EBRW middle 50% range 640-730. ACT middle 50% range 29-32. **Basis for Candidate Selection:** *Very important factors considered include:* rigor of secondary school record, class rank, academic GPA, application essay, recommendation(s), extracurricular activities, talent/ability, character/personal qualities, level of applicant's interest. *Important factors considered include:* first generation, geographical residence, state residency. *Other factors considered include:* standardized test scores, interview, alumni/ae relation,

racial/ethnic status, volunteer work, work experience. **Freshman Admission Requirements:** High school diploma is required and GED is not accepted *Academic units required:* 4 English, 3 math, 3 science, 2 science labs, 2 foreign language, 3 social studies, 3 history, *Academic units recommended:* 4 English, 4 math, 4 science, 3 science labs, 4 foreign language, 4 social studies, 4 history. **Freshman Admission Statistics:** 5,316 applied, 21.9% admitted, 42% enrolled. **Transfer Admission Requirements:** High school transcript, college transcript(s), essay or personal statement, statement of good standing from prior institution(s). Lowest grade transferable C. **General Admission Information:** Application fee $60. Regular application deadline 1/1. Admission may be deferred.

COSTS AND FINANCIAL AID
Annual tuition $50,310. Room and board $14,190. Average book expense $800. **Required Forms and Deadlines:** CSS/Financial Aid PROFILE; FAFSA; Noncustodial PROFILE. **Notification of Awards:** Applicants will be notified of awards on or about 4/1. **Types of Aid:** *Need-based scholarships/grants:* College/university scholarship or grant aid from institutional funds; Federal Pell; Private scholarships; SEOG; State scholarships/grants. *Loans:* Direct PLUS loans; Direct Subsidized Stafford Loans; Direct Unsubsidized Stafford Loans. *Student Employment:* Federal Work-Study Program available. Institutional employment available. **Financial Aid Statistics:** 100% needy freshmen, 100% needy undergrads receive need-based scholarship or grant aid. 0% undergrads receive non-need-based scholarship or grant aid. 98% freshmen, 99% undergrads receive need-based self-help aid. 0% freshmen, 0% undergrads receive athletic scholarships. 42% freshmen, 42% undergrads receive any aid. 34% undergrads borrow to pay for school. Average cumulative indebtedness $22,845.

BAY PATH UNIVERSITY

588 Longmeadow Street, Longmeadow, MA 01106-2292
Phone: 413-565-1331 · **Financial Aid Phone:** 413-565-1345
E-mail: admiss@baypath.edu · **CEEB Code:** 2122
Fax: 413-565-1105 · **Website:** www.baypath.edu · **ACT Code:** 1785

This private school was founded in 1897. It has a 48 acre campus.

RATINGS
Admissions Selectivity Rating: 81　　**Fire Safety Rating:** 99　　**Green Rating:** 60*

STUDENTS AND FACULTY
Enrollment: 1,947. **Student Body:** 100% female, 0% male, 42% out-of-state, 1% international (5 countries represented). Asian 2%, African American 13%, Caucasian 57%, Hispanic 19%, Native American <1%, Pacific Islander <1%, Two or more races 3%, Race unknown 5%.
Retention and Graduation: 70% freshmen return for sophomore year. 53% freshmen graduate within 4 years. 58% freshmen graduate within 6 years.
Faculty: Student/faculty ratio 13:1. 73 full-time faculty, 63% hold PhDs, 11% are members of minority groups, 78% are women. 0% of classes are taught by teaching assistants.

ACADEMICS
Degrees: Associate; Bachelor's; Certificate; Doctoral/Professional; Master's; Post-Bachelor's certificate; Post-Master's certificate **Classes:** Most classes have 10-19 students. Most lab/discussion sessions have 10-19 students. **Most popular majors:** Liberal Arts And Sciences/Liberal Studies; Psychology, General; Business Administration, Management And Operations, Other. **Special Study Options:** Accelerated program; Cooperative education program; Cross-registration; Distance learning; Double major; English as a Second Language (ESL); Exchange student program (domestic); External degree program; Honors program; Independent study; Internships; Liberal arts/career combination; Student-designed major; Study abroad; Teacher certification program; Weekend college. **Honors programs:** The Bay Path Honors Program provides academically talented and exceptionally motivated student with uniquely challenging and intellectually stimulating educational opportunities beyond the traditional curriculum. Under the guidance of faculty known for their excellence in teaching and scholarship, students investigate special topics in interdisciplinary honors seminars. The Honors Program culminates in a major independent creative or research project, or other departmental requirement. Women in Science Honors (WiSH) offers a four-year curriculum consisting of integrated and advanced study and research for dedicated future scientists. **Disability Services offered to physically disabled students:** Note-taking services; Reader services; Tape recorders; Tutors. **Career services:** Alumni network; Alumni services; Career assessment; Career/job search classes; Internships; Regional alumni

FACILITIES
Housing: Theme housing; Wellness housing; Women's dorms 50% of campus accessible to physically disabled. **Special Academic Facilities/Equipment:** Blake Student Commons, Bashevkin Academic Development Center, Breck Fitness Center, occupational therapy laboratory, physician's assistant laboratory, and D'Amour Hall for Business, Communications and Technology. **Computers:** 100% of libraries, 100% of dining areas, 100% of student union, 25% of common outdoor areas have wireless network access. Students can register for classes online. Administrative functions (other than registration) can be performed online.

CAMPUS LIFE
Environment: Village **Activities:** Choral groups; Dance; Drama/theater; International Student Organization; Model UN; Music ensembles; Musical theater; Student government 42 registered organizations, 3 honor societies, 1 religious organization. **Athletics (Intercollegiate):** *Women:* basketball, cross-country, field hockey, soccer, softball, tennis, volleyball. **On-Campus Highlights:** Carpe Diem Cafe, Toner/Helliwell Hearth and Lounge, Game Room, Breck Fitness Center, D'Amour Hall for Business, Communications and Tech. **Environmental Initiatives:** Recycling program

ADMISSIONS
Freshman Academic Profile: Average high school GPA 3.4. 19% in top 10% of high school class, 47% in top 25% of high school class, 76% in top 50% of high school class. **Test Scores:** SAT Math middle 50% range 470-580. SAT EBRW middle 50% range 500-610. ACT middle 50% range 20-25. Minimum internet-based TOEFL 76. **Basis for Candidate Selection:** *Very important factors considered include:* rigor of secondary school record, academic GPA, application essay, recommendation(s), interview. *Important factors considered include:* extracurricular activities, talent/ability, level of applicant's interest. *Other factors considered include:* class rank, standardized test scores, character/personal qualities, first generation, alumni/ae relation, geographical residence, volunteer work, work experience. **Freshman Admission Requirements:** High school diploma is required and GED is accepted *Academic units required:* 4 English, 3 math, 2 science, 2 history. **Freshman Admission Statistics:** 1,470 applied, 62.9% admitted, 16% enrolled. **Transfer Admission Requirements:** college transcript(s), Minimum college GPA of 2.0 required. Lowest grade transferable c-. **General Admission Information:** Application fee $25. Nonfall registration accepted. Admission may be deferred for a maximum of 1 year.

COSTS AND FINANCIAL AID
Required Forms and Deadlines: FAFSA. **Notification of Awards:** Applicants will be notified of awards on a rolling basis beginning 12/1. **Types of Aid:** *Need-based scholarships/grants:* College/university scholarship or grant aid from institutional funds; Federal Pell; SEOG; State scholarships/grants. *Loans:* Direct PLUS loans; Direct Subsidized Stafford Loans; Direct Unsubsidized Stafford Loans. *Student Employment:* Federal Work-Study Program available. Institutional employment available. **Financial Aid Statistics:** 100% needy freshmen, 100% needy undergrads receive need-based scholarship or grant aid. 4% freshmen, 6% undergrads receive non-need-based scholarship or grant aid. 95% freshmen, 92% undergrads receive need-based self-help aid. 0% freshmen, 0% undergrads receive athletic scholarships. 97% freshmen, 90% undergrads receive any aid. **Criteria for awarding aid:** *Non-need-based:* Academics.

BAYLOR UNIVERSITY

One Bear Place #97056, Waco, TX 76798-7056
Phone: 254-710-3435 · **Financial Aid Phone:** 254-710-2611
E-mail: admissions@baylor.edu · **CEEB Code:** 6032
Fax: 254-710-3436 · **Website:** www.baylor.edu · **ACT Code:** 4062

This private school, affiliated with the Baptist Church, was founded in 1845. It has a 1000 acre campus.

RATINGS
Admissions Selectivity Rating: 91　　**Fire Safety Rating:** 91　　**Green Rating:** 83

STUDENTS AND FACULTY
Enrollment: 14,284. **Student Body:** 59% female, 41% male, 30% out-of-state, 3% international (73 countries represented). Asian 6%, African American 6%, Caucasian 63%, Hispanic 15%, Native American <1%, Pacific Islander <1%, Two or more races 5%, Race unknown <1%.

Retention and Graduation: 90% freshmen return for sophomore year. 60% freshmen graduate within 4 years. 77% freshmen graduate within 6 years. **Faculty:** Student/faculty ratio 14:1. 1,058 full-time faculty, 83% hold PhDs, 15% are members of minority groups, 41% are women.

ACADEMICS

Degrees: Bachelor's; Doctoral/Professional; Doctoral/Research; Master's; Post-Master's certificate **Classes:** Most classes have 20-29 students. Most lab/discussion sessions have 20-29 students. **Most popular majors:** Biology/Biological Sciences, General; Registered Nursing/Registered Nurse; Accounting. **Special Study Options:** Accelerated program; Double major; Exchange student program (domestic); Honors program; Internships; Student-designed major; Study abroad; Teacher certification program. **Honors programs:** Honors Program, University Scholars Program, Great Texts Program. **Disability Services offered to physically disabled students:** Note-taking services; Reader services; Tape recorders; Tutors. **Career services:** Alumni network; Alumni services; Career assessment; Career/job search classes; Internships

FACILITIES

Housing: Apartments for married students; Apartments for single students; Coed dorms; Cooperative housing; Men's dorms; Special housing for disabled student; Special housing for international students; Theme housing; Wellness housing; Women's dorms 98% of campus accessible to physically disabled. **Special Academic Facilities/Equipment:** Baylor Research and Innovation Collaborative: Baylor Advanced Research Institute (a catalyst for creating new and emerging research clusters, interdisciplinary research programs and industrial collaborations), LAUNCH (innovative business accelerator), Baylor Institute for Air Science, Center for Astrophysics, Space Physics and Engineering Research (CASPER), Center for Spatial Research, Veterans Health Research Program of the Baylor Institute of Biomedical Studies, Quantum Optics Laboratory, Laser Spectroscopy Laboratory, and Advanced Composite Technology (ACT) Laboratory; Baylor Sciences Building (500,000-sf of classrooms, laboratories and offices); Paul L. Foster Success Center; Umphrey Law Center; Mayborn Museum Complex (includes the Jeanes Discovery Center, the Daniel Historic Village and the Strecker Museum Collection); Armstrong Browning Library; The Texas Collection; Black Gospel Music Restoration Project (Royce-Darden Collection); Allbritton Art Institute; W.R. Poage Legislative Library; Baylor University Press; Martin Museum of Art; McMullen-Connally Family Collection; J.M. Dawson Institute of Church-State Studies; Academy for Teaching and Learning; Center for Business and Economic Research; Institute for Faith and Learning; Institute for Oral History; Institute for Studies of Religion; Center for Christian Education; Center for Christian Ethics; Center for Christian Music Studies; Center for Community Learning and Enrichment; Center for Family and Community Ministries; Center for International Education; Center for Ministry Effectiveness and Educational Leadership; Center for Nonprofit Leadership and Service; Keston Center for Religion, Politics and Society; Kyle Lake Center for Effective Preaching; Institute of Biblical and Related Languages; language and environmental studies labs; high definition television; radio station **Computers:** 98% of classrooms, 10% of dorms, 95% of libraries, 95% of dining areas, 95% of student union, 50% of common outdoor areas have wireless network access. Students can register for classes online. Administrative functions (other than registration) can be performed online.

CAMPUS LIFE

Environment: City **Activities:** Campus Ministries; Choral groups; Concert band; Dance; Drama/theater; International Student Organization; Jazz band; Literary magazine; Marching band; Model UN; Music ensembles; Musical theater; Opera; Pep band; Radio station; Student government; Student newspaper; Symphony orchestra; Television station; Yearbook 222 registered organizations, 32 honor societies, 11 religious organizations. 22 fraternities, 20 sororities. **Athletics (Intercollegiate):** *Men:* baseball, basketball, cheerleading, cross-country, football, golf, tennis, track/field (outdoor), track/field (indoor). *Women:* basketball, cheerleading, cross-country, equestrian sports, golf, soccer, softball, tennis, track/field (outdoor), track/field (indoor), volleyball. **On-Campus Highlights:** Bear Habitat, Armstrong Browning Library, Baylor Sciences Building, Student Life Center, McLane Stadium **Environmental Initiatives:** Campus wide recycling, with over 700 locations on campus to recycle in which to recycle and collaboration with Athletics Department to recycle at all university sporting events.

ADMISSIONS

Freshman Academic Profile: 44% in top 10% of high school class, 75% in top 25% of high school class, 96% in top 50% of high school class. **Test Scores:** SAT Math middle 50% range 590-680. SAT EBRW middle 50% range 600-680. ACT middle 50% range 26-31. Minimum internet-based TOEFL 76. Minimum paper TOEFL 540. **Basis for Candidate Selection:** *Very important factors considered include:* rigor of secondary school record, class rank, standardized test scores. *Important factors considered include:* academic GPA. *Other factors considered include:* application essay, recommendation(s), extracurricular activities, talent/ability, character/personal qualities, alumni/ae relation, volunteer work, work experience, level of applicant's interest. **Freshman**

Admission Requirements: High school diploma is required and GED is accepted *Academic units required: Academic units recommended:* 4 English, 4 math, 4 science, 2 science labs, 2 foreign language, 2 social studies, 1 history. **Freshman Admission Statistics:** 37,083 applied, 38.9% admitted, 23% enrolled. **Transfer Admission Requirements:** college transcript(s), Minimum college GPA of 2.5 required. Lowest grade transferable C. **General Admission Information:** Regular application deadline 2/1. Nonfall registration accepted. Admission may be deferred for a maximum of 1 year.

COSTS AND FINANCIAL AID

Annual tuition $41,194. Room and board $7,800. Required fees $4,348. Average book expense $1,230. **Required Forms and Deadlines:** FAFSA. **Notification of Awards:** Applicants will be notified of awards on a rolling basis beginning 12/15. **Types of Aid:** *Need-based scholarships/grants:* College/university scholarship or grant aid from institutional funds; Federal Pell; Private scholarships; SEOG; State scholarships/grants. *Loans:* Direct PLUS loans; Direct Subsidized Stafford Loans; Direct Unsubsidized Stafford Loans. *Student Employment:* Federal Work-Study Program available. Institutional employment available. **Financial Aid Statistics:** 100% needy freshmen, 97% needy undergrads receive need-based scholarship or grant aid. 99% freshmen, 93% undergrads receive non-need-based scholarship or grant aid. 79% freshmen, 80% undergrads receive need-based self-help aid. 2% freshmen, 2% undergrads receive athletic scholarships. 98% freshmen, 93% undergrads receive any aid. 53% undergrads borrow to pay for school. Average cumulative indebtedness $44,540. **Criteria for awarding aid:** *Need-based:* Academics, Art, Athletics, Leadership, Music/drama, Religious affiliation *Non-need-based:* Academics, Art, Athletics, Leadership, Music/drama, Religious affiliation.

BEACON COLLEGE

105 E. Main Street, Leesburg, FL 34748
Phone: 352-638-9731 · **Financial Aid Phone:** 352-787-6306
E-mail: admissions@beaconcollege.edu
Fax: 352-787-0721 · **Website:** www.beaconcollege.edu · **ACT Code:** 704

This private school was founded in 1989.

RATINGS

Admissions Selectivity Rating: 67   **Fire Safety Rating:** 94   **Green Rating:** 60*

STUDENTS AND FACULTY

Enrollment: 128. **Student Body:** 38% female, 63% male, 80% out-of-state, 0% international (2 countries represented). Asian 2%, African American 10%, Caucasian 85%, Hispanic 3%, Native American 0%, Race unknown 0%. **Retention and Graduation:** 73% freshmen return for sophomore year. **Faculty:** 17 full-time faculty, 65% hold PhDs, 6% are members of minority groups, 59% are women. 0% of classes are taught by teaching assistants.

ACADEMICS

Degrees: Associate; Bachelor's **Classes:** Most classes have 20-29 students. Most lab/discussion sessions have 20-29 students. **Special Study Options:** Cooperative education program; Independent study; Internships; Study abroad. **Honors programs:** Psi Tau Omega is the academic honor society at Beacon College. **Disability Services offered to physically disabled students:** Note-taking services; Reader services; Tape recorders; Tutors.

FACILITIES

Housing: Apartments for single students; Special housing for disabled students **Computers:** 100% of classrooms, have wireless network access.

CAMPUS LIFE

Environment: Village **Activities:** Choral groups; Drama/theater; Literary magazine; Student government; Student newspaper; Yearbook 13 registered organizations, 1 honor society, 1 fraternities, 1 sorority. **On-Campus Highlights:** New Resident Apartment Complex, Student Center, Stoer Building—Office of Student Services, Beacon College Library, Administration Building

ADMISSIONS

Freshman Academic Profile: Average high school GPA 2.8. **Test Scores:** Minimum paper TOEFL 525. **Basis for Candidate Selection:** *Very important factors considered include:* recommendation(s). *Important factors considered include:* rigor of secondary school record, application essay, standardized test scores, talent/ability, character/personal qualities. *Other factors considered include:* class rank, academic GPA, interview, extracurricular activities, volunteer work, work experience. **Freshman Admission Requirements:** High school diploma is required and GED is accepted *Academic units required:* 4 English, 1 math, 1 science, 1 social studies, 2 history, 3 academic electives. **Freshman Admission Statistics:** 53 applied, 92.5% admitted, 59%

enrolled. **Transfer Admission Requirements:** High school transcript, college transcript(s), essay or personal statement, interview, Lowest grade transferable C. **General Admission Information:** Application fee $50. Priority deadline 6/1. Regular application deadline 8/1. Nonfall registration accepted.

COSTS AND FINANCIAL AID
Annual tuition $27,000. Room and board $8,150. Required fees $700. Average book expense $900. **Required Forms and Deadlines:** FAFSA; Institution's own financial aid form; State aid form. **Notification of Awards:** Applicants will be notified of awards on or about 2/1. **Types of Aid:** *Need-based scholarships/ grants:* College/university scholarship or grant aid from institutional funds; Federal Pell; Private scholarships; SEOG; State scholarships/grants. *Loans: Student Employment:* Federal Work-Study Program available. **Financial Aid Statistics:** 60% needy freshmen, 22% needy undergrads receive need-based scholarship or grant aid. 0% undergrads receive non-need-based scholarship or grant aid. 60% freshmen, 22% undergrads receive need-based self-help aid. 0% freshmen, 0% undergrads receive athletic scholarships.

BECKER COLLEGE

61 Sever Street, Worcester, MA 01609
Phone: 508-373-9400 · **Financial Aid Phone:** 508-373-9440
E-mail: admissions@becker.edu · **CEEB Code:** 3079
Fax: 508-890-1500 · **Website:** www.becker.edu · **ACT Code:** 1784

This private school was founded in 1784. It has a 100 acre campus.

RATINGS
Admissions Selectivity Rating: 78   **Fire Safety Rating:** 95   **Green Rating:** 60*

STUDENTS AND FACULTY
Enrollment: 1,797. **Student Body:** 57% female, 43% male, 38% out-of-state, 1% international (29 countries represented). Asian 2%, African American 7%, Caucasian 71%, Hispanic 8%, Native American 1%, Pacific Islander <1%, Two or more races 3%, Race unknown 6%.
Retention and Graduation: 73% freshmen return for sophomore year.
Faculty: Student/faculty ratio 14:1. 48 full-time faculty, 65% hold PhDs, 6% are members of minority groups, 60% are women. 0% of classes are taught by teaching assistants.

ACADEMICS
Degrees: Associate; Bachelor's; Certificate; Master's **Classes:** Most classes have 10-19 students. Most lab/discussion sessions have 20-29 students. **Most popular majors:** Game And Interactive Media Design; Pre-Veterinary Studies; Business Administration And Management, General. **Special Study Options:** Accelerated program; Cooperative education program; Cross-registration; Distance learning; Double major; Dual enrollment; Independent study; Internships; Liberal arts/career combination; Study abroad. **Combined degree programs:** BA/JD; BA/MA. **Disability Services offered to physically disabled students:** Note-taking services; Reader services; Tape recorders; Tutors. **Career services:** Alumni network; Alumni services; Career assessment; Career/job search classes; Internships; Regional alumni

FACILITIES
Housing: Apartments for single students; Coed dorms; Theme housing 33% of campus accessible to physically diasbled. **Special Academic Facilities/ Equipment:** Massachusetts Digital Games Institute (MassDiGI)

CAMPUS LIFE
Environment: City **Activities:** Dance; Drama/theater; International Student Organization; Music ensembles; Musical theater; Student government. Fuller Campus Center in Leicester, Weller Academic Center in Worcester, Colleen C. Barrett in Worcester, Boutin Student Center in Worcester, Lenfest Animal Clinic

ADMISSIONS
Freshman Academic Profile: Average high school GPA 3.1. 65% from public high schools. **Test Scores:** SAT Math middle 50% range 480-580. SAT EBRW middle 50% range 490-590. ACT middle 50% range 20-26. Minimum internet-based TOEFL 79/80. Minimum paper TOEFL 550. **Basis for Candidate Selection:** *Very important factors considered include:* rigor of secondary school record, academic GPA, standardized test scores. *Important factors considered include:* class rank. *Other factors considered include:* application essay, recommendation(s), interview, alumni/ae relation. **Freshman Admission Requirements:** High school diploma is required and GED is

accepted *Academic units recommended:* 4 English, 3 math, 3 science, 2 science labs, 2 foreign language, 2 social studies, 2 history. **Freshman Admission Statistics:** 4,972 applied, 69.4% admitted, 11% enrolled. **Transfer Admission Requirements:** college transcript(s), Minimum college GPA of 2.00 required. Lowest grade transferable C. **General Admission Information:** Priority deadline 2/15. Nonfall registration accepted.

COSTS AND FINANCIAL AID
Annual tuition $35,600. Room and board $13,800. Required fees $3,600. Average book expense $960. **Required Forms and Deadlines:** FAFSA. **Notification of Awards:** Applicants will be notified of awards on a rolling basis beginning 12/15. **Types of Aid:** *Need-based scholarships/grants:* College/ university scholarship or grant aid from institutional funds; Federal Pell; Private scholarships; SEOG; State scholarships/grants. *Loans:* Direct PLUS loans; Direct Subsidized Stafford Loans; Direct Unsubsidized Stafford Loans. *Student Employment:* Federal Work-Study Program available. Institutional employment available. **Financial Aid Statistics:** 75% needy freshmen, 68% needy undergrads receive need-based scholarship or grant aid. 98% freshmen, 94% undergrads receive non-need-based scholarship or grant aid. 93% freshmen, 93% undergrads receive need-based self-help aid. 0% freshmen, 0% undergrads receive athletic scholarships. 100% freshmen, 88% undergrads receive any aid. **Criteria for awarding aid:** *Non-need-based:* Academics, State/district residency.

See page 892.

BELHAVEN COLLEGE

1500 Peachtree Street, Jackson, MS 39202
Phone: 601-968-5940 · **Financial Aid Phone:** (601) 968-5920
E-mail: admission@belhaven.edu · **CEEB Code:** 1055
Fax: 601-968-8946 · **Website:** www.belhaven.edu · **ACT Code:** 2180

This private school, affiliated with the Presbyterian Church, was founded in 1883. It has a 42 acre campus.

RATINGS
Admissions Selectivity Rating: 87   **Fire Safety Rating:** 60*   **Green Rating:** 60*

STUDENTS AND FACULTY
Enrollment: 2,566. **Student Body:** 65% female, 35% male, 28% out-of-state, 2% international (21 countries represented). Asian 1%, African American 49%, Caucasian 35%, Hispanic 5%, Native American 1%, Pacific Islander <1%, Two or more races 2%, Race unknown 7%.
Retention and Graduation: 66% freshmen return for sophomore year.
Faculty: Student/faculty ratio 11:1. 101 full-time faculty, 73% hold PhDs, 44% are women. 0% of classes are taught by teaching assistants.

ACADEMICS
Degrees: Associate; Bachelor's; Certificate; Master's **Classes:** Most classes have 20-29 students. Most lab/discussion sessions have 20-29 students. **Most popular majors:** Social Sciences, General; Dance, General; Business/ Commerce, General. **Special Study Options:** Accelerated program; Distance learning; Double major; Dual enrollment; English as a Second Language (ESL); Honors program; Independent study; Internships; Student-designed major; Study abroad; Teacher certification program. **Honors programs:** Honors Program: The Honors College at Belhaven College gives academically advanced, highly motivated students a forum in which to deepen and expand their college education, both intellectually and spiritually. Enrollment in the Honors College is limited to students who demonstrate a past record of academic achievement, seriousness about their calling, and enthusiasm for challenging dialogue with students and scholars from a variety of fields. **Career services:** Internships

FACILITIES
Housing: Apartments for single students; Men's dorms; Women's dorms **Special Academic Facilities/Equipment:** Bitsy Irby art gallery **Computers:** 100% of dorms, 100% of libraries, 100% of student union, have wireless network access. Students can register for classes online. Administrative functions (other than registration) can be performed online.

CAMPUS LIFE
Environment: City **Activities:** Choral groups; Dance; Drama/theater; International Student Organization; Jazz band; Literary magazine; Marching band; Music ensembles; Musical theater; Pep band; Student government; Student newspaper; Yearbook 29 registered organizations, 5 religious organizations. **Athletics (Intercollegiate):** *Men:* baseball, basketball, cheerleading, cross-country, football, golf, soccer, tennis. *Women:* basketball, cheerleading, cross-country, golf, soccer, softball, tennis, volleyball.

ADMISSIONS

Freshman Academic Profile: Average high school GPA 3.4. **Test Scores:** SAT Math middle 50% range 450-580. SAT EBRW middle 50% range 440-610. ACT middle 50% range 20-23. Minimum internet-based TOEFL 61. Minimum paper TOEFL 500. **Basis for Candidate Selection:** *Very important factors considered include:* academic GPA, standardized test scores. *Other factors considered include:* rigor of secondary school record, application essay, recommendation(s), interview, extracurricular activities, talent/ability, character/personal qualities, alumni/ae relation, level of applicant's interest. **Freshman Admission Requirements:** High school diploma is required and GED is accepted *Academic units required:* 4 English, 2 math, 1 science, 1 history, 8 academic electives, *Academic units recommended:* 1 computer science. **Freshman Admission Statistics:** 2,474 applied, 42.6% admitted, 23% enrolled. **Transfer Admission Requirements:** college transcript(s), Minimum college GPA of 2.0 required. Lowest grade transferable D. **General Admission Information:** Application fee $25. Nonfall registration accepted. Admission may be deferred.

COSTS AND FINANCIAL AID

Annual tuition $21,626. Room and board $8,000. Required fees $190. Average book expense $1,250. **Required Forms and Deadlines:** FAFSA. **Notification of Awards:** Applicants will be notified of awards on a rolling basis beginning 2/1. **Types of Aid:** *Need-based scholarships/grants:* College/university scholarship or grant aid from institutional funds; Federal Pell; Private scholarships; SEOG; State scholarships/grants. *Loans: Student Employment:* Federal Work-Study Program available. **Financial Aid Statistics:** 100% needy freshmen receive need-based scholarship or grant aid. **Criteria for awarding aid:** *Non-need-based:* Academics, Alumni affiliation, Art, Music/drama.

BELLARMINE UNIVERSITY

2001 Newburg Road, Louisville, KY 40205
Phone: 502-272-8131 • **Financial Aid Phone:** 502-272-8124
E-mail: admissions@bellarmine.edu • **CEEB Code:** 1056
Fax: 502-272-8002 • **Website:** http://www.bellarmine.edu • **ACT Code:** 1490

This private school, affiliated with the Roman Catholic Church, was founded in 1950. It has a 144 acre campus.

RATINGS

Admissions Selectivity Rating: 76   **Fire Safety Rating:** 96   **Green Rating:** 60*

STUDENTS AND FACULTY

Enrollment: 2,474. **Student Body:** 64% female, 36% male, 30% out-of-state, 1% international (26 countries represented). Asian 2%, African American 5%, Caucasian 81%, Hispanic 4%, Native American <1%, Pacific Islander <1%, Two or more races 3%, Race unknown 3%.
Retention and Graduation: 72% freshmen return for sophomore year. 50% freshmen graduate within 4 years. 65% freshmen graduate within 6 years. 26% grads go on to further study within 1 year. **Faculty:** Student/faculty ratio 12:1. 180 full-time faculty, 83% hold PhDs, 11% are members of minority groups, 56% are women. 0% of classes are taught by teaching assistants.

ACADEMICS

Degrees: Bachelor's; Certificate; Doctoral/Professional; Doctoral/Research; Master's; Post-Bachelor's certificate **Classes:** Most classes have fewer than 10 students. Most lab/discussion sessions have 10-19 students. **Most popular majors:** Kinesiology And Exercise Science; Psychology, General; Registered Nursing/Registered Nurse. **Special Study Options:** Accelerated program; Cross-registration; Distance learning; Double major; Dual enrollment; Honors program; Independent study; Internships; Liberal arts/career combination; Student-designed major; Study abroad; Teacher certification program. **Honors programs:** Bellarmine Honors Program. **Disability Services offered to physically disabled students:** Note-taking services; Reader services; Tutors. **Career services:** Alumni network; Alumni services; Career assessment; Career/job search classes; Internships; Regional alumni

FACILITIES

Housing: Coed dorms; Fraternity/sorority housing; Men's dorms; Special housing for disabled student; Special housing for international students; Theme housing; Women's dorms **Special Academic Facilities/Equipment:** McGrath Art Gallery; Thomas Merton Center. **Computers:** 50% of classrooms, 100% of dorms, 100% of libraries, 25% of dining areas, 100% of student union, 25% of common outdoor areas have wireless network access. Students can register

for classes online. Administrative functions (other than registration) can be performed online.

CAMPUS LIFE

Environment: Metropolis **Activities:** Campus Ministries; Choral groups; Concert band; Dance; Drama/theater; International Student Organization; Jazz band; Literary magazine; Music ensembles; Musical theater; Pep band; Radio station; Student government; Student newspaper; Student-run film society; Yearbook 70 registered organizations, 3 honor societies, 6 religious organizations. 1 fraternity, 1 sorority. **Athletics (Intercollegiate):** *Men:* baseball, basketball, bowling, cross-country, golf, lacrosse, soccer, tennis, track/field (outdoor). *Women:* basketball, bowling, cheerleading, cross-country, field hockey, golf, soccer, softball, tennis, track/field (outdoor), volleyball. **On-Campus Highlights:** Norton Health Science Center, Our Lady of the Woods Chapel, Siena Halls, Owsley B. Frazier Stadium, The Thomas Merton Center **Environmental Initiatives:** Development of an on-campus fruit/vegetable garden.

ADMISSIONS

Freshman Academic Profile: Average high school GPA 3.5. 69% from public high schools. **Test Scores:** SAT Math middle 50% range 520-600. SAT EBRW middle 50% range 530-610. ACT middle 50% range 22-27. Minimum internet-based TOEFL 213. Minimum paper TOEFL 550. **Basis for Candidate Selection:** *Very important factors considered include:* rigor of secondary school record, academic GPA, standardized test scores, recommendation(s), character/personal qualities, level of applicant's interest. *Important factors considered include:* class rank, extracurricular activities. *Other factors considered include:* application essay, interview, talent/ability, first generation, alumni/ae relation, geographical residence, state residency, racial/ethnic status, volunteer work, work experience. **Freshman Admission Requirements:** High school diploma is required and GED is accepted *Academic units required:* 4 English, 3 math, 3 science, 2 science labs, 2 foreign language, 2 social studies, 1 history, 5 academic electives, *Academic units recommended:* 4 English, 4 math, 4 science, 2 science labs, 2 foreign language, 3 social studies, 2 history, 7 academic electives. **Freshman Admission Statistics:** 5,692 applied, 88.5% admitted, 14% enrolled. **Transfer Admission Requirements:** college transcript(s), Minimum college GPA of 2.0 required. Lowest grade transferable D. **General Admission Information:** Application fee $25. Priority deadline 2/1. Regular application deadline 8/15. Nonfall registration accepted. Admission may be deferred for a maximum of 1 year.

COSTS AND FINANCIAL AID

Annual tuition $40,250. Room and board $12,250. Required fees $1,550. Average book expense $788. **Required Forms and Deadlines:** FAFSA. **Notification of Awards:** Applicants will be notified of awards on a rolling basis beginning 1/31. **Types of Aid:** *Need-based scholarships/grants:* College/university scholarship or grant aid from institutional funds; Federal Pell; Private scholarships; SEOG; State scholarships/grants. *Loans:* Direct PLUS loans; Direct Subsidized Stafford Loans; Direct Unsubsidized Stafford Loans. *Student Employment:* Federal Work-Study Program available. Institutional employment available. **Financial Aid Statistics:** 100% needy freshmen, 98% needy undergrads receive need-based scholarship or grant aid. 35% freshmen, 33% undergrads receive non-need-based scholarship or grant aid. 66% freshmen, 67% undergrads receive need-based self-help aid. 5% freshmen, 7% undergrads receive athletic scholarships. 100% freshmen, 91% undergrads receive any aid. Average cumulative indebtedness $30,110. **Criteria for awarding aid:** *Non-need-based:* Academics, Alumni affiliation, Art, Athletics, Leadership, Minority status, Music/drama, Religious affiliation, State/district residency.

BELMONT ABBEY COLLEGE

100 Belmont-Mt. Holly Road, Belmont, NC 28012
Financial Aid Phone: 704-461-6718
E-mail: admissions@bac.edu • **CEEB Code:** 5055
Website: www.belmontabbeycollege.edu • **ACT Code:** 3070

This private school, affiliated with the Roman Catholic Church, was founded in 1876. It has a 650 acre campus.

RATINGS

Admissions Selectivity Rating: 78   **Fire Safety Rating:** 87   **Green Rating:** 60*

STUDENTS AND FACULTY

Enrollment: 1,545. **Student Body:** 57% female, 43% male, 28% out-of-state, 1% international (13 countries represented). Asian 1%, African American 25%, Caucasian 41%, Hispanic 1%, Native American <1%, Two or more races <1%, Race unknown 30%.
Retention and Graduation: 63% freshmen return for sophomore year.
Faculty: Student/faculty ratio 17:1. 75 full-time faculty, 69% hold PhDs, 5%

are members of minority groups, 47% are women. 0% of classes are taught by teaching assistants.

ACADEMICS

Degrees: Bachelor's **Classes:** Most classes have 20-29 students. **Most popular majors:** Education, General; Elementary Education And Teaching; Business Administration And Management, General. **Special Study Options:** Double major; Dual enrollment; Honors program; Independent study; Internships; Study abroad; Teacher certification program; Weekend college. **Honors programs:** The Hintemeyer program is designed to foster the leadership potential of a select group of Catholic men and women. The program requires exemplary character; serious commitment to the truth and life of Catholicism; exceptionally strong self-motivation, initiative, and creativity; academic diligence and accomplishment; and employment of these qualities and abilities in the service of others. Throughout their four years in the program, Hintemeyer scholars strive to grow together in faith, virtue, and knowledge, and to discern through reflection and practice the nature of authentic Catholic leadership. Central to each participant's experience will be seminars on a variety of leadership and faith topics, communal prayer and participation in the sacraments, and regular student-generated service and leadership activities on and off campus, culminating junior year in a large-scale project of the student's own design. **Disability Services offered to physically disabled students:** Note-taking services; Reader services; Tape recorders; Tutors. **Career services:** Alumni services; Career assessment; Career/job search classes; Internships; Regional alumni

FACILITIES

Housing: Apartments for single students; Coed dorms; Men's dorms; Special housing for disabled student; Women's dorms 85% of campus accessible to physically diasbled. **Special Academic Facilities/Equipment:** The Abbey Theater, Monastery, Basilica, Adoration Chapel, and Rare Book Museum. **Computers:** 10% of classrooms, 100% of libraries, 100% of dining areas, 100% of student union, have wireless network access.

CAMPUS LIFE

Environment: Village **Activities:** Campus Ministries; Choral groups; Dance; Drama/theater; International Student Organization; Literary magazine; Musical theater; Pep band; Student government; Student newspaper; Yearbook 21 registered organizations, 5 honor societies, 3 religious organizations. 5 fraternities, 4 sororities. **Athletics (Intercollegiate):** *Men:* baseball, basketball, cross-country, golf, soccer, tennis, wrestling. *Women:* basketball, cross-country, soccer, softball, tennis, volleyball. **On-Campus Highlights:** Church/Basillica, Weeler Center Athletic Center, Dining Hall, Holy Grounds Coffee Shop, Adoration Chapel

ADMISSIONS

Freshman Academic Profile: Average high school GPA 3.1. 5% in top 10% of high school class, 15% in top 25% of high school class, 61% in top 50% of high school class. **Test Scores:** SAT Math middle 50% range 450-570. SAT EBRW middle 50% range 440-550. ACT middle 50% range 18-24. Minimum internet-based TOEFL 79. Minimum paper TOEFL 550. **Basis for Candidate Selection:** *Very important factors considered include:* rigor of secondary school record, academic GPA, standardized test scores. *Important factors considered include:* class rank, interview. *Other factors considered include:* application essay, recommendation(s), extracurricular activities, talent/ability, volunteer work, work experience, level of applicant's interest. **Freshman Admission Requirements:** High school diploma is required and GED is accepted *Academic units required:* 4 English, 3 math, 2 science, 2 foreign language, 1 social studies, 1 history, 3 academic electives, *Academic units recommended:* 4 math, 3 foreign language. **Freshman Admission Statistics:** 1,950 applied, 69.2% admitted, 22% enrolled. **Transfer Admission Requirements:** college transcript(s), Minimum college GPA of 2.0 required. Lowest grade transferable C. **General Admission Information:** Application fee $35. Regular application deadline 8/1. Nonfall registration accepted. Admission may be deferred for a maximum of 2 semesters.

COSTS AND FINANCIAL AID

Annual tuition $18,500. Room and board $10,094. Average book expense $1,200. **Required Forms and Deadlines:** FAFSA. **Notification of Awards:** Applicants will be notified of awards on a rolling basis beginning 3/15. **Types of Aid:** *Need-based scholarships/grants:* College/university scholarship or grant aid from institutional funds; Federal Pell; SEOG; State scholarships/grants. *Loans:* Direct PLUS loans; Direct Subsidized Stafford Loans; Direct Unsubsidized Stafford Loans. *Student Employment:* Federal Work-Study Program available. Institutional employment available. **Financial Aid Statistics:** 99% needy freshmen, 95% needy undergrads receive need-based scholarship or grant aid. 11% freshmen, 5% undergrads receive non-need-based scholarship or grant aid. 87% freshmen, 95% undergrads receive need-based self-help aid. 13% freshmen, 7% undergrads receive athletic scholarships. 98% freshmen, 90% undergrads receive any aid. **Criteria for awarding aid:** *Need-based:* Religious affiliation *Non-need-based:* Academics, Athletics, Religious affiliation, State/district residency.

BELMONT UNIVERSITY

1900 Belmont Boulevard, Tennessee, TN Tennessee
Phone: 615-460-6785 · **Financial Aid Phone:** 615-460-6403
E-mail: admissions@belmont.edu · **CEEB Code:** 1058
Fax: 615-460-5434 · **ACT Code:** 3946

This private school, affiliated with the Christian (Nondenominational) Church, was founded in 1860. It has a 76 acre campus.

RATINGS

Admissions Selectivity Rating: 82   **Fire Safety Rating:** 91   **Green Rating:** 80

STUDENTS AND FACULTY

Enrollment: 6,444. **Student Body:** 65% female, 35% male, 70% out-of-state, 1% international (30 countries represented). Asian 2%, African American 5%, Caucasian 81%, Hispanic 5%, Native American <1%, Pacific Islander <1%, Two or more races 4%, Race unknown 2%.
Retention and Graduation: 85% freshmen return for sophomore year. 58% freshmen graduate within 4 years. 70% freshmen graduate within 6 years. 17% grads go on to further study within 1 year. **Faculty:** Student/faculty ratio 14:1. 361 full-time faculty, 88% hold PhDs, 12% are members of minority groups, 48% are women.

ACADEMICS

Degrees: Bachelor's; Doctoral/Professional; Master's **Classes:** Most classes have 10-19 students. **Most popular majors:** Music, General; Music Management; Registered Nursing/Registered Nurse. **Special Study Options:** Accelerated program; Cooperative education program; Cross-registration; Distance learning; Double major; Dual enrollment; English as a Second Language (ESL); Honors program; Independent study; Internships; Liberal arts/career combination; Student-designed major; Study abroad; Teacher certification program. **Career services:** Alumni network; Alumni services; Career assessment; Career/job search classes; Internships; Regional alumni

FACILITIES

Housing: Apartments for single students; Coed dorms; Men's dorms; Special housing for international students; Women's dorms 98% of campus accessible to physically diasbled. **Special Academic Facilities/Equipment:** Language lab, recording studio, the Belmont Mansion, The Gallery of Iconic Guitars **Computers:** 100% of classrooms, 100% of dorms, 100% of libraries, 100% of dining areas, 100% of student union, 100% of common outdoor areas have wireless network access. Students can register for classes online. Administrative functions (other than registration) can be performed online.

CAMPUS LIFE

Environment: Metropolis **Activities:** Campus Ministries; Choral groups; Concert band; Dance; Drama/theater; International Student Organization; Jazz band; Literary magazine; Marching band; Music ensembles; Musical theater; Opera; Pep band; Student government; Student newspaper; Symphony orchestra; Television station 80 registered organizations, 17 honor societies, 12 religious organizations. 3 fraternities, 4 sororities. **Athletics (Intercollegiate):** *Men:* baseball, basketball, cross-country, golf, soccer, tennis, track/field (outdoor). *Women:* basketball, cross-country, golf, soccer, softball, tennis, track/field (outdoor), volleyball. **On-Campus Highlights:** Beaman Student Life Center, Curb Event Center, Belmont Mansion, Center for Music Business Recording Studios, Massey Courtyard **Environmental Initiatives:** Recycle

ADMISSIONS

Freshman Academic Profile: Average high school GPA 3.7. 27% in top 10% of high school class, 60% in top 25% of high school class, 88% in top 50% of high school class. **Test Scores:** SAT Math middle 50% range 550-640. SAT EBRW middle 50% range 590-670. ACT middle 50% range 24-29. Minimum paper TOEFL 550. **Basis for Candidate Selection:** *Very important factors considered include:* rigor of secondary school record, academic GPA, standardized test scores. *Important factors considered include:* application essay, recommendation(s). *Other factors considered include:* class rank, extracurricular activities, talent/ability, character/personal qualities, first generation, alumni/ae relation, religious affiliation/commitment, racial/ethnic status, volunteer work, work experience. **Freshman Admission Requirements:** High school diploma is required and GED is accepted *Academic units required:* 4 English, 3 math, 3 science, 2 foreign language, 3 social studies, 3 academic electives, *Academic units recommended:* 4 English, 4 math, 4 science, 2 foreign language, 3 social studies, 3 academic electives. **Freshman Admission Statistics:** 7,737 applied, 81.2% admitted, 25% enrolled. **Transfer Admission Requirements:** High school transcript, college transcript(s), essay or personal statement, standardized test scores, Minimum college GPA of 2.0 required. Lowest grade transferable C. **General Admission Information:** Application fee $50. Priority deadline

12/1. Regular application deadline 8/1. Nonfall registration accepted. Admission may be deferred for a maximum of 1 year.

COSTS AND FINANCIAL AID
Annual tuition $31,300. Room and board $11,680. Required fees $1,520. Average book expense $1,400. **Required Forms and Deadlines:** FAFSA. **Notification of Awards:** Applicants will be notified of awards on a rolling basis beginning 3/15. **Types of Aid:** *Need-based scholarships/grants:* College/university scholarship or grant aid from institutional funds; Federal Pell; Private scholarships; SEOG; State scholarships/grants. *Loans:* Direct PLUS loans; Direct Subsidized Stafford Loans; Direct Unsubsidized Stafford Loans. *Student Employment:* Federal Work-Study Program available. **Financial Aid Statistics:** 89% needy freshmen, 88% needy undergrads receive need-based scholarship or grant aid. 13% freshmen, 10% undergrads receive non-need-based scholarship or grant aid. 81% freshmen, 84% undergrads receive need-based self-help aid. 1% freshmen, 3% undergrads receive athletic scholarships. 53% undergrads borrow to pay for school. Average cumulative indebtedness $31,020. **Criteria for awarding aid:** *Non-need-based:* Academics, Art, Athletics, Leadership, Music/drama, Religious affiliation, State/district residency.

See page 894.

BELOIT COLLEGE

Best Colleges

700 College St., Beloit, WI 53511
Phone: 608-363-2500 · **Financial Aid Phone:** (608)363-2663
E-mail: admiss@beloit.edu · **CEEB Code:** 1059
Fax: 608-363-2075 · **Website:** www.beloit.edu · **ACT Code:** 4564

This private school was founded in 1846. It has a 75 acre campus.

RATINGS
Admissions Selectivity Rating: 86   **Fire Safety Rating:** 85   **Green Rating:** 78

STUDENTS AND FACULTY
Enrollment: 1,324. **Student Body:** 52% female, 48% male, 85% out-of-state, 15% international (28 countries represented). Asian 3%, African American 7%, Caucasian 56%, Hispanic 10%, Native American <1%, Pacific Islander <1%, Two or more races 4%, Race unknown 4%.
Retention and Graduation: 85% freshmen return for sophomore year. 75% freshmen graduate within 4 years. 86% freshmen graduate within 6 years.
Faculty: Student/faculty ratio 11:1. 115 full-time faculty, 95% hold PhDs, 19% are members of minority groups, 57% are women. 0% of classes are taught by teaching assistants.

ACADEMICS
Degrees: Bachelor's **Classes:** Most classes have fewer than 10 students. Most lab/discussion sessions have fewer than 10 students. **Most popular majors:** Science, Technology And Society; Psychology, General; Anthropology. **Special Study Options:** Double major; English as a Second Language (ESL); Exchange student program (domestic); Independent study; Internships; Liberal arts/career combination; Student-designed major; Study abroad; Teacher certification program. **Combined degree programs:** BA/MEng. **Disability Services offered to physically disabled students:** Note-taking services; Reader services; Tape recorders; Tutors. **Career services:** Alumni network; Alumni services; Career assessment; Career/job search classes; Internships; Regional alumni

FACILITIES
Housing: Apartments for single students; Coed dorms; Fraternity/sorority housing; Theme housing; Women's dorms 50% of campus accessible to physically disabled. **Special Academic Facilities/Equipment:** Wright Museum of Art Logan Museum of Anthropology Center for Language Study Student Run Market Research Company (BELMARK) Alfred S. Thompson Observatory Center for Entrepreneurial Leadership (CELEB) Hendricks Center for the Arts LEED Platinum Certified Science Building **Computers:** 80% of classrooms, 10% of dorms, 100% of libraries, 100% of dining areas, 80% of student union, 4% of common outdoor areas have wireless network access. Administrative functions (other than registration) can be performed online.

CAMPUS LIFE
Environment: Town **Activities:** Campus Ministries; Choral groups; Dance; Drama/theater; International Student Organization; Jazz band; Literary magazine; Model UN; Music ensembles; Musical theater; Radio station; Student government; Student newspaper; Television station 95 registered organizations, 6 honor societies, 3 religious organizations. 3 fraternities, 3

sororities. **Athletics (Intercollegiate):** *Men:* baseball, basketball, cross-country, football, golf, soccer, swimming, tennis, track/field (outdoor), track/field (indoor). *Women:* basketball, cross-country, soccer, softball, swimming, tennis, track/field (outdoor), track/field (indoor), volleyball. **On-Campus Highlights:** Logan Museum of Anthropology, Wright Museum of Art, Center for the Sciences, Hendricks Center for the Performing Arts, Laura H. Idrich Neese Theatre Complex **Environmental Initiatives:** New Science Center has been platinum-level LEED certified, one of only three such buildings in the state

ADMISSIONS
Freshman Academic Profile: Average high school GPA 3.3. 30% in top 10% of high school class, 57% in top 25% of high school class, 92% in top 50% of high school class. 75% from public high schools. **Test Scores:** SAT Math middle 50% range 530-660. SAT EBRW middle 50% range 510-650. ACT middle 50% range 24-30. Minimum internet-based TOEFL 80. Minimum paper TOEFL 550. **Basis for Candidate Selection:** *Very important factors considered include:* rigor of secondary school record, academic GPA, application essay, recommendation(s). *Important factors considered include:* class rank, extracurricular activities, talent/ability. *Other factors considered include:* standardized test scores, interview, character/personal qualities, first generation, alumni/ae relation, racial/ethnic status, volunteer work, work experience. **Freshman Admission Requirements:** High school diploma is required and GED is accepted *Academic units recommended:* 4 English, 3 math, 3 science, 3 science labs, 2 foreign language, 3 social studies. **Freshman Admission Statistics:** 5,400 applied, 54.0% admitted, 11% enrolled. **Transfer Admission Requirements:** college transcript(s), essay or personal statement, statement of good standing from prior institution(s). Minimum college GPA of 3.00 required. Lowest grade transferable C. **General Admission Information:** Priority deadline 1/15. Nonfall registration accepted. Admission may be deferred for a maximum of 1 year.

COSTS AND FINANCIAL AID
Annual tuition $49,564. Room and board $8,830. Required fees $470. Average book expense $1,400. **Required Forms and Deadlines:** FAFSA. **Types of Aid:** *Need-based scholarships/grants:* College/university scholarship or grant aid from institutional funds; Federal Pell; Private scholarships; SEOG; State scholarships/grants. *Loans:* Direct PLUS loans; Direct Subsidized Stafford Loans; Direct Unsubsidized Stafford Loans. *Student Employment:* Federal Work-Study Program available. Institutional employment available. **Financial Aid Statistics:** 99% needy freshmen receive need-based scholarship or grant aid. 99% freshmen, 99% undergrads receive any aid. **Criteria for awarding aid:** *Need-based:* Academics *Non-need-based:* Academics, Leadership, Minority status, Music/drama.

See page 896.

BEMIDJI STATE UNIVERSITY

1500 Birchmont Drive NE, Bemidji, MN 56601
Phone: 218-755-2040 · **Financial Aid Phone:** 218-755-2034
E-mail: admissions@bemidjistate.edu · **CEEB Code:** 6676
Fax: 218-755-2390 · **Website:** http://www.bemidjistate.edu/ · **ACT Code:** 2084

This public school was founded in 1919. It has a 90 acre campus.

RATINGS
Admissions Selectivity Rating: 72   **Fire Safety Rating:** 72   **Green Rating:** 80

STUDENTS AND FACULTY
Enrollment: 4,393. **Student Body:** 57% female, 43% male, 10% out-of-state, 2% international (35 countries represented). Asian 1%, African American 2%, Caucasian 85%, Hispanic 2%, Native American 3%, Pacific Islander 0%, Two or more races 3%, Race unknown 2%.
Retention and Graduation: 66% freshmen return for sophomore year.
Faculty: Student/faculty ratio 19:1. 174 full-time faculty, 68% hold PhDs, 9% are members of minority groups, 44% are women. 5% of classes are taught by teaching assistants.

ACADEMICS
Degrees: Associate; Bachelor's; Certificate; Master's; Post-Bachelor's certificate **Classes:** Most classes have 10-19 students. **Most popular majors:** Education, General; Industrial Production Technologies/Technicians, Other; Business/Commerce, General. **Special Study Options:** Cooperative education program; Cross-registration; Distance learning; Double major; Dual enrollment; English as a Second Language (ESL); External degree program; Honors program; Independent study; Internships; Study abroad; Teacher certification program. **Honors programs:** Honors Program. **Disability Services offered to physically disabled students:** Note-taking services; Reader services; Tutors.

Career services: Alumni services; Career assessment; Career/job search classes; Internships; Regional alumni

FACILITIES
Housing: Apartments for single students; Coed dorms; Special housing for disabled student; Special housing for international students; Theme housing 95% of campus accessible to physically diasbled. **Special Academic Facilities/Equipment:** Outdoor Program Center Boathouse. C.V. Hobson Forest. American Indian Resource Center. **Computers:** 90% of classrooms, 90% of dorms, 100% of libraries, 100% of student union, have wireless network access. Students can register for classes online. Administrative functions (other than registration) can be performed online.

CAMPUS LIFE
Environment: Village **Activities:** Campus Ministries; Choral groups; Concert band; Dance; Drama/theater; International Student Organization; Jazz band; Literary magazine; Music ensembles; Musical theater; Opera; Pep band; Radio station; Student government; Student newspaper; Symphony orchestra; Television station 83 registered organizations, 1 honor society, 8 religious organizations. 2 fraternities, 1 sorority. **Athletics (Intercollegiate):** *Men:* baseball, basketball, cross-country, football, golf, ice hockey, soccer, softball, tennis, track/field (outdoor), track/field (indoor), volleyball. *Women:* basketball, cross-country, golf, ice hockey, soccer, softball, tennis, track/field (outdoor), track/field (indoor), volleyball. **On-Campus Highlights:** Recreation Center, Student Union, Library, Residence Halls, Boathouse **Environmental Initiatives:** Signature theme of Environmental Stewardship

ADMISSIONS
Freshman Academic Profile: Average high school GPA 3.1. 7% in top 10% of high school class, 23% in top 25% of high school class, 56% in top 50% of high school class. 95% from public high schools. **Test Scores:** ACT middle 50% range 19-24. Minimum internet-based TOEFL 61. Minimum paper TOEFL 500. **Basis for Candidate Selection:** *Very important factors considered include:* class rank, standardized test scores. *Important factors considered include:* rigor of secondary school record. *Other factors considered include:* academic GPA, application essay, recommendation(s), extracurricular activities, first generation. **Freshman Admission Requirements:** High school diploma is required and GED is accepted *Academic units required:* 4 English, 3 math, 3 science, 2 foreign language, 3 social studies, 1 academic elective. **Freshman Admission Statistics:** 2,566 applied, 93.8% admitted, 31% enrolled. Minimum college GPA of 2.0 required. Lowest grade transferable C. **General Admission Information:** Application fee $20. Priority deadline 2/1. Nonfall registration accepted. Admission may be deferred for a maximum of 1 year.

COSTS AND FINANCIAL AID
Annual in-state tuition $8,500. Annual out-of-state tuition $7,360. Room and board $8,500. Required fees $950. **Required Forms and Deadlines:** FAFSA; Institution's own financial aid form. **Notification of Awards:** Applicants will be notified of awards on or about 3/15. **Types of Aid:** *Need-based scholarships/grants:* College/university scholarship or grant aid from institutional funds; Federal Pell; Private scholarships; SEOG; State scholarships/grants. *Loans:* Direct PLUS loans; Direct Subsidized Stafford Loans; Direct Unsubsidized Stafford Loans. *Student Employment:* Federal Work-Study Program available. Institutional employment available. **Financial Aid Statistics:** 70% needy freshmen, 72% needy undergrads receive need-based scholarship or grant aid. 80% freshmen, 76% undergrads receive non-need-based scholarship or grant aid. 83% freshmen, 82% undergrads receive need-based self-help aid. 6% freshmen, 6% undergrads receive athletic scholarships. 62% freshmen, 65% undergrads receive any aid. **Criteria for awarding aid:** *Non-need-based:* Academics, Alumni affiliation, Art, Athletics, Job skills, Leadership, Minority status, Music/drama, Religious affiliation.

BENEDICT COLLEGE

1600 Harden St, Columbia, SC 29204
Phone: 803-705-4491
E-mail: thompso@benedict.edu
Fax: 803-253-5167 • **Website:** www.benedict.edu

This private school, affiliated with the Baptist Church, was founded in 1870. It has a 110 acre campus.

RATINGS
Admissions Selectivity Rating: 71   **Fire Safety Rating:** 60*   **Green Rating:** 60*

STUDENTS AND FACULTY
Enrollment: 2,641. **Student Body:** 51% female, 49% male, 40% out-of-state, international. Asian <1%, African American 99%, Caucasian <1%, Hispanic 1%, Native American <1%, Race unknown <1%.

Retention and Graduation: 53% freshmen return for sophomore year. **Faculty:** Student/faculty ratio 19:1. 117 full-time faculty, 65% hold PhDs, 95% are members of minority groups, 58% are women.

ACADEMICS
Degrees: Bachelor's **Classes:** Most classes have fewer than 10 students. **Special Study Options:** Accelerated program; Double major; Dual enrollment; External degree program; Honors program; Internships; Teacher certification program; Weekend college.

FACILITIES
Housing: Men's dorms; Women's dorms

CAMPUS LIFE
Environment: City **Activities:** Campus Ministries; Choral groups; Concert band; International Student Organization; Marching band; Student government; Student newspaper.

ADMISSIONS
Freshman Academic Profile: Average high school GPA 2.5. 5% in top 10% of high school class, 15% in top 25% of high school class, 39% in top 50% of high school class. 69% from public high schools. **Test Scores:** SAT Math middle 50% range 320-430. SAT EBRW middle 50% range 320-430. ACT middle 50% range 13-17. Minimum internet-based TOEFL 80. Minimum paper TOEFL 550. **Freshman Admission Requirements:** High school diploma is required and GED is accepted *Academic units recommended:* 4 English, 3 math, 2 science, 3 social studies. **Freshman Admission Statistics:** 4,624 applied, 82.9% admitted, 17% enrolled. **Transfer Admission Requirements:** High school transcript, college transcript(s), statement of good standing from prior institution(s). Minimum college GPA of 2.0 required. Lowest grade transferable C. **General Admission Information:** Application fee $25. Nonfall registration accepted. Admission may be deferred.

COSTS AND FINANCIAL AID
Annual tuition $12,516. Room and board $6,444. Required fees $1,494. Average book expense $1,000. **Required Forms and Deadlines:** FAFSA. **Types of Aid:** *Need-based scholarships/grants:* College/university scholarship or grant aid from institutional funds; Federal Pell; Private scholarships; SEOG; State scholarships/grants; United Negro College Fund. *Loans:* Direct PLUS loans; Direct Subsidized Stafford Loans; Direct Unsubsidized Stafford Loans. **Criteria for awarding aid:** *Need-based:* Academics, Alumni affiliation, Athletics, Music/drama, Religious affiliation.

BENEDICTINE COLLEGE

1020 North Second Street, Atchison, KS 66002
Phone: 800-467-5340 • **Financial Aid Phone:** 913-360-7480
E-mail: bcadmiss@benedictine.edu • **CEEB Code:** 6056
Fax: 913-367-5462 • **Website:** www.benedictine.edu • **ACT Code:** 1444

This private school, affiliated with the Roman Catholic Church, was founded in 1859. It has a 225 acre campus.

RATINGS
Admissions Selectivity Rating: 74   **Fire Safety Rating:** 64   **Green Rating:** 60*

STUDENTS AND FACULTY
Enrollment: 1,823. **Student Body:** 54% female, 46% male, 76% out-of-state, 2% international (17 countries represented). Asian 1%, African American 3%, Caucasian 79%, Hispanic 7%, Native American 1%, Pacific Islander <1%, Two or more races <1%, Race unknown 7%.
Retention and Graduation: 79% freshmen return for sophomore year. 49% freshmen graduate within 4 years. 64% freshmen graduate within 6 years. 12% grads go on to further study within 1 year. 2% grads pursue law degrees. 2% grads pursue medical degrees. **Faculty:** Student/faculty ratio 13:1. 116 full-time faculty, 71% hold PhDs, 10% are members of minority groups, 28% are women. 0% of classes are taught by teaching assistants.

ACADEMICS
Degrees: Bachelor's; Master's **Classes:** Most classes have 20-29 students. Most lab/discussion sessions have 10-19 students. **Most popular majors:** Elementary Education And Teaching; Theological And Ministerial Studies, Other; Business Administration And Management, General. **Special Study Options:** Distance learning; Double major; Dual enrollment; English as a Second Language (ESL); Honors program; Independent study; Internships; Student-designed major; Study abroad; Teacher certification program. **Honors programs:** Honors Program, Gregorian Fellows. **Disability Services offered to physically disabled students:** Note-taking services; Tape recorders; Tutors. **Career services:** Alumni network; Career assessment; Career/job search classes; Internships

FACILITIES

Housing: Apartments for single students; Men's dorms; Women's dorms 95% of campus accessible to physically diasbled. **Computers:** 60% of classrooms, 100% of dorms, 100% of libraries, 100% of dining areas, 100% of student union, 75% of common outdoor areas have wireless network access. Administrative functions (other than registration) can be performed online.

CAMPUS LIFE

Environment: Town **Activities:** Campus Ministries; Choral groups; Concert band; Dance; Drama/theater; International Student Organization; Jazz band; Literary magazine; Marching band; Music ensembles; Musical theater; Opera; Pep band; Student government; Student newspaper; Symphony orchestra; Yearbook 38 registered organizations, 14 honor societies, 4 religious organizations. **Athletics (Intercollegiate):** *Men:* baseball, basketball, cheerleading, cross-country, football, golf, soccer, tennis, track/field (outdoor), track/field (indoor). *Women:* basketball, cheerleading, cross-country, golf, soccer, softball, tennis, track/field (outdoor), track/field (indoor), volleyball. **On-Campus Highlights:** Raven Roost, Cafe 62, St. John Paul II Student Center, Monte Cassino Inn, Abbey Church & Abbey River Lookout

ADMISSIONS

Freshman Academic Profile: Average high school GPA 3.5. 19% in top 10% of high school class, 42% in top 25% of high school class, 67% in top 50% of high school class. 43% from public high schools. **Test Scores:** ACT middle 50% range 22-28. Minimum paper TOEFL 533. **Basis for Candidate Selection:** *Very important factors considered include:* rigor of secondary school record, academic GPA. *Important factors considered include:* class rank, standardized test scores. *Other factors considered include:* recommendation(s), interview, extracurricular activities, talent/ability, character/personal qualities, first generation, volunteer work, work experience. **Freshman Admission Requirements:** High school diploma is required and GED is accepted *Academic units required:* 3 math, 2 science, 2 foreign language, *Academic units recommended:* 4 English, 4 math, 4 science, 4 foreign language, 2 social studies, 1 history. **Freshman Admission Statistics:** 2,367 applied, 97.5% admitted, 19% enrolled. **Transfer Admission Requirements:** college transcript(s), Minimum college GPA of 2.0 required. Lowest grade transferable C. **General Admission Information:** Application fee $50. Nonfall registration accepted. Admission may be deferred for a maximum of 1 year.

COSTS AND FINANCIAL AID

Average book expense $1,200. **Required Forms and Deadlines:** FAFSA. **Types of Aid:** *Need-based scholarships/grants:* College/university scholarship or grant aid from institutional funds; Federal Pell; Private scholarships; SEOG; State scholarships/grants. *Loans:* Direct PLUS loans; Direct Subsidized Stafford Loans; Direct Unsubsidized Stafford Loans. *Student Employment:* Federal Work-Study Program available. Institutional employment available. **Financial Aid Statistics:** 100% needy freshmen, 100% needy undergrads receive need-based scholarship or grant aid. 18% freshmen, 16% undergrads receive non-need-based scholarship or grant aid. 76% freshmen, 77% undergrads receive need-based self-help aid. 9% freshmen, 9% undergrads receive athletic scholarships. 73% undergrads borrow to pay for school. Average cumulative indebtedness $29,602. **Criteria for awarding aid:** *Need-based:* Minority status, Religious affiliation *Non-need-based:* Academics, Alumni affiliation, Art, Athletics, Job skills, Leadership, Minority status, Music/drama, Religious affiliation, State/district residency.

BENEDICTINE UNIVERSITY

5700 College Road, Lisle, IL 60532-0900
Phone: 630-829-6300 · **Financial Aid Phone:** (630) 829-6100
E-mail: admissions@ben.edu · **CEEB Code:** 1707
Fax: 630-829-6301 · **Website:** www.ben.edu · **ACT Code:** 1132

This private school, affiliated with the Roman Catholic Church, was founded in 1887. It has a 108 acre campus.

RATINGS

Admissions Selectivity Rating: 80   **Fire Safety Rating:** 96   **Green Rating:** 60*

STUDENTS AND FACULTY

Enrollment: 2,903. **Student Body:** 58% female, 42% male, 8% out-of-state, 1% international (17 countries represented). Asian 18%, African American 8%, Caucasian 44%, Hispanic 10%, Native American <1%, Pacific Islander <1%, Two or more races 0%, Race unknown 19%.
Retention and Graduation: 74% freshmen return for sophomore year. **Faculty:** Student/faculty ratio 18:1. 128 full-time faculty, 88% hold PhDs, 16% are members of minority groups, 48% are women. 0% of classes are taught by teaching assistants.

ACADEMICS

Degrees: Associate; Bachelor's; Certificate; Doctoral/Research; Master's; Post-Bachelor's certificate; Transfer Associate **Classes:** Most classes have 10-19 students. Most lab/discussion sessions have 10-19 students. **Most popular majors:** Biology/Biological Sciences, General; Psychology, General; Organizational Behavior Studies. **Special Study Options:** Accelerated program; Cross-registration; Distance learning; Double major; Dual enrollment; English as a Second Language (ESL); Honors program; Independent study; Internships; Study abroad; Teacher certification program; Weekend college. **Honors programs:** University Scholars Program. **Disability Services offered to physically disabled students:** Note-taking services; Reader services; Tape recorders; Tutors. **Career services:** Alumni network; Alumni services; Career assessment; Career/job search classes; Internships

FACILITIES

Housing: Apartments for married students; Apartments for single students; Coed dorms; Men's dorms; Special housing for international students; Wellness housing; Women's dorms 100% of campus accessible to physically diasbled. **Special Academic Facilities/Equipment:** Natural science and history museums,http://www.ben.edu/museum/ Exercise physiology lab. **Computers:** 100% of dorms, 100% of libraries, 100% of student union, have wireless network access. Students can register for classes online. Administrative functions (other than registration) can be performed online.

CAMPUS LIFE

Environment: Town **Activities:** Campus Ministries; Choral groups; Concert band; Dance; Drama/theater; International Student Organization; Jazz band; Literary magazine; Model UN; Music ensembles; Pep band; Student government; Student newspaper; Student-run film society; Symphony orchestra; Television station 40 registered organizations, 3 religious organizations. **Athletics (Intercollegiate):** *Men:* baseball, basketball, cross-country, football, golf, soccer, track/field (outdoor), track/field (indoor). *Women:* basketball, cross-country, golf, soccer, softball, tennis, track/field (outdoor), track/field (indoor), volleyball. **On-Campus Highlights:** Jurica Nature Museum, Kindlon Hall and Benedictine Library, Birck Hall of Science, Krasa Center: Chapel, cafeteria, snack bar, The Sports Complex **Environmental Initiatives:** Energy reduction

ADMISSIONS

Freshman Academic Profile: Average high school GPA 3.4. 21% in top 10% of high school class, 48% in top 25% of high school class, 79% in top 50% of high school class. 85% from public high schools. **Test Scores:** ACT middle 50% range 20-26. Minimum internet-based TOEFL 79. Minimum paper TOEFL 550. **Basis for Candidate Selection:** *Very important factors considered include:* rigor of secondary school record, class rank, academic GPA, standardized test scores. *Other factors considered include:* application essay, recommendation(s), interview, extracurricular activities. **Freshman Admission Requirements:** High school diploma is required and GED is accepted *Academic units required:* 4 English, 3 math, 2 science, 1 science labs, 2 foreign language, 3 social studies, 1 history, *Academic units recommended:* 4 math, 3 science, 2 science labs. **Freshman Admission Statistics:** 2,108 applied, 69.5% admitted, 32% enrolled. **Transfer Admission Requirements:** college transcript(s), statement of good standing from prior institution(s). Minimum college GPA of 2.0 required. Lowest grade transferable D. **General Admission Information:** Application fee $40. Regular application deadline 8/30. Nonfall registration accepted. Admission may be deferred.

COSTS AND FINANCIAL AID

Annual tuition $25,950. Room and board $8,280. Required fees $1,000. Average book expense $1,450. **Required Forms and Deadlines:** FAFSA. **Notification of Awards:** Applicants will be notified of awards on a rolling basis beginning 2/1. **Types of Aid:** *Need-based scholarships/grants:* College/university scholarship or grant aid from institutional funds; Federal Pell; Private scholarships; SEOG; State scholarships/grants. *Loans:* Direct PLUS loans; Direct Subsidized Stafford Loans; Direct Unsubsidized Stafford Loans. *Student Employment:* Federal Work-Study Program available. Institutional employment available. **Financial Aid Statistics:** 63% needy freshmen, 62% needy undergrads receive need-based scholarship or grant aid. 98% freshmen, 85% undergrads receive non-need-based scholarship or grant aid. 76% freshmen, 90% undergrads receive need-based self-help aid. 0% freshmen, 0% undergrads receive athletic scholarships. 98% freshmen, 89% undergrads receive any aid. **Criteria for awarding aid:** *Non-need-based:* Academics, Alumni affiliation, Leadership, Music/drama, State/district residency.

BENNETT COLLEGE

900 East Washington Street, Greensboro, NC 27401
Phone: 336-370-8624 • **Financial Aid Phone:** 336-517-2220
E-mail: admiss@bennett.edu • **CEEB Code:** 5058
Fax: 336-370-8653 • **Website:** www.bennett.edu • **ACT Code:** 3072

This private school, affiliated with the Methodist Church, was founded in 1873. It has a 55 acre campus.

RATINGS
Admissions Selectivity Rating: 74   **Fire Safety Rating:** 80   **Green Rating:** 60*

STUDENTS AND FACULTY
Enrollment: 651. **Student Body:** 100% female, 0% male, 62% out-of-state, <1% international (2 countries represented). African American 94%, Caucasian <1%, Hispanic 2%, Native American <1%, Two or more races 2%, Race unknown 2%.
Retention and Graduation: 58% freshmen return for sophomore year.
Faculty: Student/faculty ratio 10:1. 61 full-time faculty, 64% hold PhDs, 70% are members of minority groups, 77% are women. 0% of classes are taught by teaching assistants.

ACADEMICS
Degrees: Bachelor's **Classes:** Most classes have 20-29 students. Most lab/discussion sessions have 10-19 students. **Most popular majors:** Communication And Media Studies, Other; Biological And Physical Sciences; Psychology, General. **Special Study Options:** Accelerated program; Cooperative education program; Cross-registration; Double major; Dual enrollment; Exchange student program (domestic); Honors program; Independent study; Internships; Student-designed major; Study abroad; Teacher certification program. **Disability Services offered to physically disabled students:** Tape recorders; Tutors. **Career services:** Alumni network; Alumni services; Career/job search classes; Internships; Regional alumni

FACILITIES
Housing: Wellness housing; Women's dorms **Special Academic Facilities/Equipment:** Intergenerational Center Global Learning Center **Computers:** Students can register for classes online.

CAMPUS LIFE
Environment: City **Activities:** Campus Ministries; Choral groups; Dance; Drama/theater; International Student Organization; Literary magazine; Model UN; Student government; Student newspaper 34 registered organizations, 5 honor societies, 1 religious organization. 4 sororities. **Athletics (Intercollegiate):** *Women:* basketball, cheerleading, cross-country, softball, swimming, tennis, track/field (outdoor), volleyball. **On-Campus Highlights:** Student Union, Chapel, Little Theathre, Holgate Library, Ida B. Goode Gym

ADMISSIONS
Freshman Academic Profile: 8% in top 10% of high school class, 12% in top 25% of high school class, 50% in top 50% of high school class. **Test Scores:** SAT Math middle 50% range 350-420. SAT EBRW middle 50% range 350-430. **Basis for Candidate Selection:** *Very important factors considered include:* rigor of secondary school record, academic GPA, recommendation(s), talent/ability. *Important factors considered include:* class rank, application essay. *Other factors considered include:* standardized test scores, interview, extracurricular activities, character/personal qualities, first generation, alumni/ae relation, geographical residence, state residency, religious affiliation/commitment, racial/ethnic status, volunteer work, work experience, level of applicant's interest. **Freshman Admission Requirements:** High school diploma is required and GED is accepted *Academic units required:* 4 English, 3 math, 2 science, 2 foreign language, 2 social studies, 5 academic electives. **Freshman Admission Statistics:** 1,433 applied, 62.8% admitted, 18% enrolled. **Transfer Admission Requirements:** college transcript(s), essay or personal statement, Minimum college GPA of 2.0 required. Lowest grade transferable C. **General Admission Information:** Application fee $35. Nonfall registration accepted. Admission may be deferred for a maximum of 1 year.

COSTS AND FINANCIAL AID
Annual tuition $14,614. Room and board $7,428. Required fees $2,180. Average book expense $1,500. **Required Forms and Deadlines:** FAFSA; Institution's own financial aid form. **Notification of Awards:** Applicants will be notified of awards on or about 7/15. **Types of Aid:** *Need-based scholarships/grants:* College/university scholarship or grant aid from institutional funds; Federal Nursing Scholarships; Federal Pell; Private scholarships; SEOG; State scholarships/grants; United Negro College Fund. *Loans:* Direct Subsidized Stafford Loans; Direct Unsubsidized Stafford Loans. *Student Employment:* Federal Work-Study Program available. **Financial Aid Statistics:** 96% needy

freshmen, 93% needy undergrads receive need-based scholarship or grant aid. 1% freshmen, 2% undergrads receive non-need-based scholarship or grant aid. 96% freshmen, 94% undergrads receive need-based self-help aid. 0% freshmen, 0% undergrads receive athletic scholarships. **Criteria for awarding aid:** *Need-based:* Academics, Alumni affiliation, Leadership, Minority status, Religious affiliation *Non-need-based:* Academics, Alumni affiliation, Leadership, Minority status, Religious affiliation, State/district residency.

BENNINGTON COLLEGE

One College Drive, Bennington, VT 05201
Phone: 802-440-4312 • **Financial Aid Phone:** 800-833-6845
E-mail: admissions@bennington.edu • **CEEB Code:** 3080
Fax: 802-440-4320 • **Website:** www.bennington.edu • **ACT Code:** 4296

This private school was founded in 1932. It has a 440 acre campus.

RATINGS
Admissions Selectivity Rating: 88   **Fire Safety Rating:** 96   **Green Rating:** 83

STUDENTS AND FACULTY
Enrollment: 742. **Student Body:** 65% female, 35% male, 98% out-of-state, 17% international (52 countries represented). Asian 2%, African American 4%, Caucasian 58%, Hispanic 10%, Native American <1%, Pacific Islander <1%, Two or more races 4%, Race unknown 4%.
Retention and Graduation: 78% freshmen return for sophomore year. 55% freshmen graduate within 4 years. 67% freshmen graduate within 6 years.
Faculty: Student/faculty ratio 10:1. 60 full-time faculty, 78% hold PhDs, 12% are members of minority groups, 53% are women.

ACADEMICS
Degrees: Bachelor's; Master's **Most popular majors:** English Language And Literature, General; Social Sciences, General; Visual And Performing Arts, General. **Special Study Options:** Cross-registration; Dual enrollment; English as a Second Language (ESL); Exchange student program (domestic); Independent study; Internships; Student-designed major; Study abroad. **Disability Services offered to physically disabled students:** Note-taking services; Reader services; Tape recorders. **Career services:** Alumni network; Alumni services; Career assessment; Career/job search classes; Internships

FACILITIES
Housing: Coed dorms 75% of campus accessible to physically diasbled. **Special Academic Facilities/Equipment:** Center for the Advancement of Public Action; observatory; student garden and greenhouse; labs for chemistry, physics, and microbiology; digital arts lab; art gallery; architecture, drawing, painting, printmaking, and sculpture studios; ceramics studio and kilns; photography darkrooms; film and video editing studio; fully equipped professional theaters; dance studios and archives; scripts library; costume shop; electronic music and sound recording studios; music practice rooms and music library; fitness center; student center with cafe and bar; greenhouse; and 440 acres of forest, ponds, wetlands, and fields for recreation and scientific study. **Computers:** 100% of classrooms, 100% of dorms, 100% of libraries, 100% of dining areas, 100% of student union, 75% of common outdoor areas have wireless network access. Administrative functions (other than registration) can be performed online.

CAMPUS LIFE
Environment: Village **Activities:** Choral groups; Dance; Drama/theater; International Student Organization; Jazz band; Literary magazine; Music ensembles; Radio station; Student government; Student newspaper; Student-run film society 21 registered organizations. **On-Campus Highlights:** Center for the Advancement of Public Action, Visual and Performing Arts Center, Edward Clark Crossett Library, Student Center, Commons Dining Hall and Lounge **Environmental Initiatives:** Converting to a campus-wide biomass heating system

ADMISSIONS
Freshman Academic Profile: 42% from public high schools. **Test Scores:** SAT Math middle 50% range 590-680. SAT EBRW middle 50% range 620-710. ACT middle 50% range 27-31. Minimum internet-based TOEFL 90-91. Minimum paper TOEFL 577. **Basis for Candidate Selection:** *Very important factors considered include:* rigor of secondary school record, academic GPA, application essay, recommendation(s), interview, talent/ability, character/

personal qualities. *Other factors considered include:* class rank, standardized test scores, extracurricular activities, volunteer work, work experience. **Freshman Admission Requirements:** High school diploma is required and GED is accepted **Freshman Admission Statistics:** 1,465 applied, 56.6% admitted, 27% enrolled. **Transfer Admission Requirements:** High school transcript, college transcript(s), essay or personal statement, statement of good standing from prior institution(s). Lowest grade transferable C. **General Admission Information:** Regular application deadline 1/15. Nonfall registration accepted. Admission may be deferred for a maximum of one year.

COSTS AND FINANCIAL AID

Annual tuition $51,240. Room and board $15,040. Required fees $680. Average book expense $1,000. **Required Forms and Deadlines:** CSS/Financial Aid PROFILE; FAFSA; Institution's own financial aid form; Noncustodial PROFILE. **Notification of Awards:** Applicants will be notified of awards on or about 3/27. **Types of Aid:** *Need-based scholarships/grants:* College/university scholarship or grant aid from institutional funds; Federal Pell; Private scholarships; SEOG; State scholarships/grants. *Loans:* Direct PLUS loans; Direct Subsidized Stafford Loans; Direct Unsubsidized Stafford Loans. *Student Employment:* Federal Work-Study Program available. Institutional employment available. **Financial Aid Statistics:** 98% needy freshmen, 99% needy undergrads receive need-based scholarship or grant aid. 8% freshmen, 8% undergrads receive non-need-based scholarship or grant aid. 89% freshmen, 89% undergrads receive need-based self-help aid. 0% freshmen, 0% undergrads receive athletic scholarships. 52% undergrads borrow to pay for school. Average cumulative indebtedness $28,648. **Criteria for awarding aid:** *Need-based:* Academics, Alumni affiliation, Art, Leadership, Minority status, Music/drama *Non-need-based:* Academics, Alumni affiliation, Art, Leadership, Minority status, Music/drama, State/district residency.

BENTLEY UNIVERSITY

175 Forest Street, Waltham, MA 02452
Phone: 781-891-2244 · **Financial Aid Phone:** 781-891-3441
E-mail: ugadmission@bentley.edu · **CEEB Code:** 3096
Fax: 781-891-3414 · **Website:** www.bentley.edu · **ACT Code:** 1783

This private school was founded in 1917. It has a 163 acre campus.

RATINGS

Admissions Selectivity Rating: 90   **Fire Safety Rating:** 99   **Green Rating:** 97

STUDENTS AND FACULTY

Enrollment: 4,203. **Student Body:** 41% female, 59% male, 58% out-of-state, 14% international (71 countries represented). Asian 8%, African American 3%, Caucasian 61%, Hispanic 7%, Native American 0%, Pacific Islander <1%, Two or more races 2%, Race unknown 4%.
Retention and Graduation: 92% freshmen return for sophomore year. 87% freshmen graduate within 4 years. 91% freshmen graduate within 6 years.
Faculty: Student/faculty ratio 11:1. 291 full-time faculty, 80% hold PhDs, 16% are members of minority groups, 40% are women. 0% of classes are taught by teaching assistants.

ACADEMICS

Degrees: Bachelor's; Doctoral/Research; Master's; Post-Bachelor's certificate; Post-Master's certificate **Classes:** Most classes have 20-29 students. Most lab/discussion sessions have 20-29 students. **Most popular majors:** Finance, General; Marketing/Marketing Management, General; Business, Management, Marketing, And Related Support Services, Other. **Special Study Options:** Accelerated program; Cross-registration; Distance learning; Double major; Exchange student program (domestic); Honors program; Independent study; Internships; Liberal arts/career combination; Student-designed major; Study abroad. **Honors programs:** The Honors Program is a four year journey that provides special challenge and fulfillment to select Bentley students. Participants typically take one or two courses each semester, first in the General Education curriculum and later in their major, that offer an extended intellectual challenge in an intimate, seminar atmosphere. **Disability Services offered to physically disabled students:** Note-taking services; Reader services; Tape recorders; Tutors. **Career services:** Alumni network; Alumni services; Career assessment; Career/job search classes; Internships; Regional alumni

FACILITIES

Housing: Apartments for single students; Coed dorms; Special housing for disabled student; Theme housing; Wellness housing 80% of campus accessible to physically diasbled. **Special Academic Facilities/Equipment:** Academic Technology Center, ACE Lab, Alliance for Ethics and Social Responsibility, Art Gallery, Bentley Library, Center for Business Ethics, Center for International Students and Scholars, Center for Languages and International Collaboration, Center for Marketing Technology, Center for Quantitative Analysis, Center for Women in Business, Cronin International Center, Cyberlaw Center, Design and Usability Center, Enterprise Risk Management Program, ESOL Center, Financial Trading Room, Hughey Center for Financial Services, Math Learning Center, Media & Culture labs and studio, Service Learning Center, Spiritual Life Center, Valente Center for Arts and Sciences, Winer Accounting Center, Writing Center **Computers:** 100% of classrooms, 100% of dorms, 100% of libraries, 100% of dining areas, 100% of student union, 100% of common outdoor areas have wireless network access. Students can register for classes online. Administrative functions (other than registration) can be performed online. Undergraduates are required to own a computer.

CAMPUS LIFE

Environment: Town **Activities:** Campus Ministries; Choral groups; Dance; Drama/theater; International Student Organization; Jazz band; Literary magazine; Model UN; Music ensembles; Musical theater; Radio station; Student government; Student newspaper; Student-run film society; Yearbook 101 registered organizations, 3 honor societies, 4 religious organizations. 5 fraternities, 4 sororities. **Athletics (Intercollegiate):** *Men:* baseball, basketball, cross-country, diving, football, golf, ice hockey, lacrosse, soccer, swimming, tennis, track/field (outdoor), track/field (indoor). *Women:* basketball, cross-country, diving, field hockey, lacrosse, soccer, softball, swimming, tennis, track/field (outdoor), track/field (indoor), volleyball. **On-Campus Highlights:** Student Center, Dana Athletic Center, Bentley Library, Green Space, Currito Burrito **Environmental Initiatives:** GHG Reduction Commitment Bentley University is committed to the following carbon footprint reduction targets (compared to a 2008 baseline): 50% by 2015, 70% by 2020 and 100% by 2030. As of January 1, 2016 we have achieved a 50% reduction in our carbon footprint.

ADMISSIONS

Freshman Academic Profile: 34% in top 10% of high school class, 74% in top 25% of high school class, 94% in top 50% of high school class. 67% from public high schools. **Test Scores:** SAT Math middle 50% range 620-710. SAT EBRW middle 50% range 590-670. ACT middle 50% range 27-31. Minimum internet-based TOEFL 90. Minimum paper TOEFL 577. **Basis for Candidate Selection:** *Very important factors considered include:* rigor of secondary school record, academic GPA, standardized test scores. *Important factors considered include:* application essay, recommendation(s), extracurricular activities, talent/ability, character/personal qualities, volunteer work.level of applicant's interest. *Other factors considered include:* class rank, interview, first generation, alumni/ae relation, geographical residence, state residency, racial/ethnic status, work experience. **Freshman Admission Requirements:** High school diploma is required and GED is accepted *Academic units required:* 4 English, 4 math, 3 science, 2 science labs, 3 foreign language, 3 social studies, *Academic units recommended:* 4 English, 4 math, 4 science, 3 science labs, 4 foreign language, 4 social studies, 2 units from above areas or other academic areas. **Freshman Admission Statistics:** 8,867 applied, 44.2% admitted, 26% enrolled. **Transfer Admission Requirements:** High school transcript, college transcript(s), essay or personal statement, statement of good standing from prior institution(s). Lowest grade transferable C. **General Admission Information:** Application fee $75. Regular application deadline 1/7. Nonfall registration accepted. Admission may be deferred for a maximum of One year.

COSTS AND FINANCIAL AID

Annual tuition $46,370. Room and board $15,720. Required fees $1,630. Average book expense $1,260. **Required Forms and Deadlines:** Business/Farm Supplement; CSS/Financial Aid PROFILE; FAFSA; Noncustodial PROFILE. **Notification of Awards:** Applicants will be notified of awards on or about 3/31. **Types of Aid:** *Need-based scholarships/grants:* College/university scholarship or grant aid from institutional funds; Federal Pell; Private scholarships; SEOG; State scholarships/grants. *Loans:* Direct PLUS loans; Direct Subsidized Stafford Loans; Direct Unsubsidized Stafford Loans. *Student Employment:* Federal Work-Study Program available. Institutional employment available. **Financial Aid Statistics:** 98% needy freshmen, 98% needy undergrads receive need-based scholarship or grant aid. 25% freshmen, 15% undergrads receive non-need-based scholarship or grant aid. 94% freshmen, 96% undergrads receive need-based self-help aid. 1% freshmen, 2% undergrads receive athletic scholarships. 73% freshmen, 66% undergrads receive any aid. 54% undergrads borrow to pay for school. Average cumulative indebtedness $29,547. **Criteria for awarding aid:** *Need-based:* Academics, Athletics, Minority status *Non-need-based:* Academics, Athletics, Leadership, Minority status.

See page 898.

BEREA COLLEGE

CPO 2182, Berea, KY 40404
Phone: 859-985-3500 · **Financial Aid Phone:** 859-985-3310
E-mail: admissions@berea.edu · **CEEB Code:** 1060
Fax: 859-985-3512 · **Website:** www.berea.edu · **ACT Code:** 1492

This private school was founded in 1855. It has a 140 acre campus.

RATINGS
Admissions Selectivity Rating: 93   **Fire Safety Rating:** 96   **Green Rating:** 92

STUDENTS AND FACULTY
Enrollment: 1,610. **Student Body:** 58% female, 42% male, 52% out-of-state, 8% international (76 countries represented). Asian 2%, African American 15%, Caucasian 56%, Hispanic 11%, Native American <1%, Pacific Islander <1%, Two or more races 7%, Race unknown 1%.
Retention and Graduation: 80% freshmen return for sophomore year. 49% freshmen graduate within 4 years. 66% freshmen graduate within 6 years. **Faculty:** Student/faculty ratio 10:1. 136 full-time faculty, 91% hold PhDs, 19% are members of minority groups, 49% are women. 0% of classes are taught by teaching assistants.

ACADEMICS
Degrees: Bachelor's **Most popular majors:** Family And Consumer Sciences/Human Sciences, General; Biology/Biological Sciences, General; Business/Commerce, General. **Special Study Options:** Double major; English as a Second Language (ESL); Exchange student program (domestic); Honors program; Independent study; Internships; Student-designed major; Study abroad; Teacher certification program. **Disability Services offered to physically disabled students:** Note-taking services; Reader services; Tape recorders. **Career services:** Alumni network; Alumni services; Career assessment; Career/job search classes; Internships

FACILITIES
Housing: Apartments for married students; Apartments for single students; Men's dorms; Women's dorms 75% of campus accessible to physically disabled. **Special Academic Facilities/Equipment:** Appalachian Gallery, Special Collections and Sound Archives in the Hutchins Library, Planetarium and Observatory, Geology Museum, The Ecovillage, the Child Development Laboratory, extensive acreage of farmland and forestland, and the Monty Saulmon Early Technology Lab. **Computers:** 33% of classrooms, 100% of libraries, 100% of dining areas, 100% of student union, 33% of common outdoor areas have wireless network access. Students can register for classes online. Administrative functions (other than registration) can be performed online. Undergraduates are required to own a computer.

CAMPUS LIFE
Environment: Village **Activities:** Campus Ministries; Choral groups; Dance; Drama/theater; International Student Organization; Jazz band; Literary magazine; Music ensembles; Pep band; Student government; Student newspaper; Yearbook 75 registered organizations, 14 honor societies, 5 religious organizations. **Athletics (Intercollegiate):** *Men:* baseball, basketball, cross-country, golf, soccer, swimming, tennis, track/field (outdoor). *Women:* basketball, cross-country, soccer, softball, swimming, tennis, track/field (outdoor), volleyball. **On-Campus Highlights:** Woods-Penn Complex (post office, cafe, etc), Alumni Building (cafeteria, lounge, gameroom), Seabury Center (gym), EcoVillage (married and single parent housing), Hutchins Library **Environmental Initiatives:** 1. Sustainability and Environmental Studies academic program

ADMISSIONS
Freshman Academic Profile: Average high school GPA 3.5. 24% in top 10% of high school class, 64% in top 25% of high school class, 93% in top 50% of high school class. **Test Scores:** SAT Math middle 50% range 490-610. SAT EBRW middle 50% range 480-590. ACT middle 50% range 22-27. Minimum internet-based TOEFL 68. Minimum paper TOEFL 520. **Basis for Candidate Selection:** *Very important factors considered include:* interview. *Important factors considered include:* rigor of secondary school record, class rank, academic GPA, application essay, standardized test scores, character/personal qualities. *Other factors considered include:* recommendation(s), extracurricular activities, talent/ability, first generation, geographical residence, state residency, racial/ethnic status, volunteer work, work experience, level of applicant's interest. **Freshman Admission Requirements:** High school diploma is required and GED is accepted *Academic units recommended:* 4 English, 3

math, 2 science, 2 science labs, 2 foreign language, 2 social studies. **Freshman Admission Statistics:** 1,744 applied, 34.4% admitted, 72% enrolled. **Transfer Admission Requirements:** High school transcript, college transcript(s), interview, Minimum college GPA of 2.0 required. Lowest grade transferable C. **General Admission Information:** Regular application deadline 4/30. Nonfall registration accepted.

COSTS AND FINANCIAL AID
Average book expense $700. **Required Forms and Deadlines:** FAFSA. **Notification of Awards:** Applicants will be notified of awards on a rolling basis beginning 11/1. **Types of Aid:** *Need-based scholarships/grants:* College/university scholarship or grant aid from institutional funds; Federal Pell; Private scholarships; SEOG; State scholarships/grants. *Loans:* Direct PLUS loans; Direct Subsidized Stafford Loans; Direct Unsubsidized Stafford Loans. *Student Employment:* Federal Work-Study Program available. **Financial Aid Statistics:** 100% needy freshmen, 100% needy undergrads receive need-based scholarship or grant aid. 0% undergrads receive non-need-based scholarship or grant aid. 100% freshmen, 100% undergrads receive need-based self-help aid. 0% freshmen, 0% undergrads receive athletic scholarships. 100% freshmen, 100% undergrads receive any aid. 65% undergrads borrow to pay for school. Average cumulative indebtedness $7,062.

BERKELEY COLLEGE

44 Rifle Camp Road, Woodland Park, NJ 07424
Phone: 1-800-446-5400 xG26
E-mail: info@berkeleycollege.edu · **CEEB Code:** 2061
ACT Code: 2576

This proprietary school was founded in 1931. It has a 25 acre campus.

RATINGS
Admissions Selectivity Rating: 61   **Fire Safety Rating:** 60*   **Green Rating:** 60*

STUDENTS AND FACULTY
Enrollment: 3,806. **Student Body:** 73% female, 27% male, 4% out-of-state, <1% international. Asian 2%, African American 21%, Caucasian 15%, Hispanic 34%, Native American <1%, Pacific Islander <1%, Race unknown 26%.
Retention and Graduation: 68% freshmen return for sophomore year. **Faculty:** Student/faculty ratio 17:1. 137 full-time faculty, 47% are members of minority groups,

ACADEMICS
Degrees: Associate; Bachelor's; Certificate; Master's; Terminal Associate; Transfer Associate **Most popular majors:** Business Administration And Management, General; Accounting; Fashion Merchandising. **Special Study Options:** Accelerated program; Distance learning; Internships; Study abroad. **Disability Services offered to physically disabled students:** Tutors.

FACILITIES
Housing: Coed dorms **Computers:** Administrative functions (other than registration) can be performed online.

CAMPUS LIFE
Environment: City **Activities:** Choral groups; Literary magazine; Student government; Student newspaper 8 registered organizations, 1 honor societies.

ADMISSIONS
Test Scores: Minimum paper TOEFL 500. **Basis for Candidate Selection:** *Very important factors considered include:* rigor of secondary school record, interview. *Important factors considered include:* standardized test scores. *Other factors considered include:* class rank, academic GPA, recommendation(s), extracurricular activities, talent/ability, character/personal qualities, volunteer work, work experience. **Freshman Admission Requirements:** High school diploma is required and GED is accepted **Transfer Admission Requirements:** college transcript(s), Lowest grade transferable C. **General Admission Information:** Application fee $50. Nonfall registration accepted. Admission may be deferred.

COSTS AND FINANCIAL AID
Annual tuition $17,400. Room and board $12,500. Required fees $750. Average book expense $1,200. **Required Forms and Deadlines:** FAFSA. **Notification of Awards:** Applicants will be notified of awards on a rolling basis beginning 3/1. **Types of Aid:** *Need-based scholarships/grants:* College/university scholarship or grant aid from institutional funds; Federal Pell; Private scholarships; SEOG; State scholarships/grants. **Financial Aid Statistics:** 85% freshmen receive any aid. **Criteria for awarding aid:** *Non-need-based:* Academics, Alumni affiliation.

BERKLEE COLLEGE OF MUSIC

1140 Boylston Street, Boston, MA 02215-3693
Phone: 617-747-2222 · **Financial Aid Phone:** 617-747-2274
E-mail: admissions@berklee.edu · **CEEB Code:** 3107
Fax: 617-747-2047 · **Website:** www.berklee.edu · **ACT Code:** 1789

This private school was founded in 1945.

RATINGS
Admissions Selectivity Rating: 82   **Fire Safety Rating:** 60*   **Green Rating:** 60*

STUDENTS AND FACULTY
Enrollment: 3,846. **Student Body:** 31% female, 69% male, 84% out-of-state, 25% international (70 countries represented). Asian 3%, African American 6%, Caucasian 45%, Hispanic 10%, Native American <1%, Pacific Islander <1%, Two or more races 3%, Race unknown 8%.
Retention and Graduation: 79% freshmen return for sophomore year.
Faculty: Student/faculty ratio 13:1. 240 full-time faculty, 15% hold PhDs, 23% are women.

ACADEMICS
Degrees: Bachelor's; Diploma; Master's **Classes:** Most classes have 10-19 students. **Most popular majors:** Music Performance, General; Music, Other. **Special Study Options:** Cooperative education program; Cross-registration; Distance learning; Double major; Dual enrollment; English as a Second Language (ESL); Internships; Student-designed major; Study abroad; Teacher certification program. **Disability Services offered to physically disabled students:** Reader services; Tape recorders; Tutors. **Career services:** Alumni services; Career/job search classes; Internships

FACILITIES
Housing: Coed dorms 80% of campus accessible to physically diasbled.
Special Academic Facilities/Equipment: Ensemble library, 10 professional recording studios, film scoring and editing studio, analog and digital music synthesis labs, 1,200-seat performance center, learning center.

CAMPUS LIFE
Environment: Metropolis **Activities:** Campus Ministries; Choral groups; Concert band; Dance; Drama/theater; International Student Organization; Jazz band; Literary magazine; Marching band; Music ensembles; Musical theater; Opera; Radio station; Student government; Student newspaper; Student-run film society; Symphony orchestra 47 registered organizations, 2 honor societies, 4 religious organizations. **On-Campus Highlights:** Student Activities Center, Berklee Performance Center, Practice Rooms, Stan Getz Media Center

ADMISSIONS
Test Scores: Minimum paper TOEFL 500. **Basis for Candidate Selection:** *Very important factors considered include:* interview, talent/ability. *Important factors considered include:* rigor of secondary school record, academic GPA, character/personal qualities, level of applicant's interest. *Other factors considered include:* class rank, application essay, standardized test scores, recommendation(s), extracurricular activities, first generation, geographical residence, volunteer work, work experience. **Freshman Admission Requirements:** High school diploma is required and GED is accepted **Freshman Admission Statistics:** 5,538 applied, 19.2% admitted, 84% enrolled. **Transfer Admission Requirements:** High school transcript, college transcript(s), essay or personal statement, interview, Lowest grade transferable C. **General Admission Information:** Application fee $150. Priority deadline 11/1. Regular application deadline 1/15. Nonfall registration accepted.1 year.

COSTS AND FINANCIAL AID
Room and board $17,200. Required fees $3,032. Average book expense $474. *Student Employment:* Federal Work-Study Program available. **Financial Aid Statistics:** 50% needy freshmen, 50% needy undergrads receive need-based scholarship or grant aid. 48% freshmen, 50% undergrads receive non-need-based scholarship or grant aid. 98% freshmen, 98% undergrads receive need-based self-help aid. 0% freshmen, 0% undergrads receive athletic scholarships. 57% freshmen, 38% undergrads receive any aid.

BERRY COLLEGE

2277 Martha Berry Hwy, NW, Mount Berry, GA 30149-0159
Phone: 706-236-2215 · **Financial Aid Phone:** 706-236-1714
E-mail: admissions@berry.edu · **CEEB Code:** 5059
Fax: 706-290-2178 · **Website:** www.berry.edu · **ACT Code:** 798

This private school was founded in 1902. It has a 27000 acre campus.

RATINGS
Admissions Selectivity Rating: 86   **Fire Safety Rating:** 95   **Green Rating:** 77

STUDENTS AND FACULTY
Enrollment: 1,963. **Student Body:** 61% female, 39% male, 32% out-of-state, 1% international (9 countries represented). Asian 2%, African American 5%, Caucasian 80%, Hispanic 7%, Native American <1%, Pacific Islander <1%, Two or more races 3%, Race unknown 2%.
Retention and Graduation: 78% freshmen return for sophomore year. 57% freshmen graduate within 4 years. 64% freshmen graduate within 6 years.
Faculty: Student/faculty ratio 11:1. 165 full-time faculty, 92% hold PhDs, 8% are members of minority groups, 48% are women.

ACADEMICS
Degrees: Bachelor's; Master's **Most popular majors:** Communication, Journalism, And Related Programs, Other; Zoology/Animal Biology; Psychology, General. **Special Study Options:** Cross-registration; Double major; Dual enrollment; Honors program; Independent study; Internships; Student-designed major; Study abroad; Teacher certification program. **Honors programs:** The Berry College Honors Program provides students with an opportunity to learn within an intellectually challenging community of peers and instructors. Honors courses familiarize students with works that have been central to our past and contemporary intellectual traditions, while encouraging them to examine issues or themes from multiple and conflicting perspectives. All Honors courses are taught as seminars that provide an ideal environment for the development of effective communication and critical-thinking skills. All Honors students also complete an Honors thesis that allows them to deeply engage with their major field or explore connections between different areas of interest. Additionally, the Berry College Honors Program offers a unique education abroad opportunity in conjunction with the University of Glasgow in Scotland and Berry College International Programs. **Disability Services offered to physically disabled students:** Note-taking services; Reader services; Tutors. **Career services:** Alumni network; Alumni services; Career assessment; Career/job search classes; Internships; Regional alumni

FACILITIES
Housing: Apartments for single students; Coed dorms; Men's dorms; Special housing for disabled student; Theme housing; Wellness housing; Women's dorms 80% of campus accessible to physically diasbled. **Special Academic Facilities/Equipment:** Gunby Equine Center, new Valhalla Stadium for football, lacrosse, and track and field, new 9,226 sq. ft. theatre featuring black-box stage with seating for 276, Memorial Library with nearly 1 million books and e-books, and over 173,000 government documents, Oak Hill and Martha Berry Museum, Child Development Center. **Computers:** 100% of classrooms, 100% of dorms, 100% of libraries, 100% of dining areas, 100% of student union, 10% of common outdoor areas have wireless network access. Students can register for classes online. Administrative functions (other than registration) can be performed online.

CAMPUS LIFE
Environment: Town **Activities:** Campus Ministries; Choral groups; Concert band; Dance; Drama/theater; International Student Organization; Jazz band; Literary magazine; Model UN; Music ensembles; Musical theater; Pep band; Student government; Student newspaper; Symphony orchestra; Yearbook 75 registered organizations, 15 honor societies, 11 religious organizations. **Athletics (Intercollegiate):** *Men:* baseball, basketball, cross-country, diving, golf, lacrosse, soccer, swimming, tennis. *Women:* basketball, cross-country, diving, equestrian sports, golf, lacrosse, soccer, softball, swimming, tennis, volleyball. **On-Campus Highlights:** 131,000 sq ft Athletic and Recreation Center, Historic Old Mill with 34 foot overshot waterwheel, Krannert Student Center with Starbucks and Chick-fil-A, Berry Reservoir, Lavender Mountain, foothills of Appalachian Mountains, English Gothic Ford Complex "the castles" **Environmental Initiatives:** Tree Campus USA award last year

ADMISSIONS
Freshman Academic Profile: Average high school GPA 3.7. 34% in top 10% of high school class, 66% in top 25% of high school class, 92% in top 50% of

high school class. 72% from public high schools. **Test Scores:** SAT Math middle 50% range 550-640. SAT EBRW middle 50% range 570-660. ACT middle 50% range 24-29. Minimum internet-based TOEFL 80. Minimum paper TOEFL 550. **Basis for Candidate Selection:** *Very important factors considered include:* rigor of secondary school record, academic GPA, standardized test scores. *Important factors considered include:* extracurricular activities. *Other factors considered include:* application essay, recommendation(s), interview, volunteer work, work experience. **Freshman Admission Requirements:** High school diploma is required and GED is accepted *Academic units required:* 4 English, 4 math, 3 science, 2 foreign language, 3 social studies, 4 academic electives. **Freshman Admission Statistics:** 3,883 applied, 61.6% admitted, 23% enrolled. **Transfer Admission Requirements:** college transcript(s), statement of good standing from prior institution(s). Minimum college GPA of 2.5 required. Lowest grade transferable C. **General Admission Information:** Priority deadline 1/15. Regular application deadline 7/20. Nonfall registration accepted.

COSTS AND FINANCIAL AID

Annual tuition $34,950. Room and board $12,260. Required fees $226. Average book expense $1,000. **Required Forms and Deadlines:** CSS/Financial Aid PROFILE; FAFSA; State aid form. **Notification of Awards:** Applicants will be notified of awards on a rolling basis beginning 11/1. **Types of Aid:** *Need-based scholarships/grants:* College/university scholarship or grant aid from institutional funds; Federal Pell; Private scholarships; SEOG. *Loans:* Direct PLUS loans; Direct Subsidized Stafford Loans; Direct Unsubsidized Stafford Loans. *Student Employment:* Federal Work-Study Program available. Institutional employment available. **Financial Aid Statistics:** 100% needy freshmen, 100% needy undergrads receive need-based scholarship or grant aid. 24% freshmen, 20% undergrads receive non-need-based scholarship or grant aid. 75% freshmen, 79% undergrads receive need-based self-help aid. 0% freshmen, 0% undergrads receive athletic scholarships. 100% freshmen, 99% undergrads receive any aid. 71% undergrads borrow to pay for school. Average cumulative indebtedness $26,449. **Criteria for awarding aid:** *Need-based:* Academics, Job skills, Leadership, Minority status, Music/drama *Non-need-based:* Academics, Art, Leadership, Minority status, Music/drama, Religious affiliation.

See page 900.

BETHANY COLLEGE (KS)

335 E Swensson, Lindsborg, KS 67456-1897
Phone: 785-227-3311 · **Financial Aid Phone:** 785-227-3311
E-mail: admissions@bethanylb.edu · **CEEB Code:** 6034
Fax: 785-227-8993 · **Website:** www.bethanylb.edu · **ACT Code:** 1388

This private school, affiliated with the Lutheran Church, was founded in 1881. It has a 62 acre campus.

RATINGS

Admissions Selectivity Rating: 80   Fire Safety Rating: 96   Green Rating: 60*

STUDENTS AND FACULTY

Enrollment: 569. **Student Body:** 48% female, 52% male, 49% out-of-state, 6% international (29 countries represented). Asian 1%, African American 11%, Caucasian 71%, Hispanic 7%, Native American 1%, Race unknown 4%. **Retention and Graduation:** 61% freshmen return for sophomore year. 20% grads go on to further study within 1 year. 1% grads pursue law degrees. 3% grads pursue medical degrees. **Faculty:** Student/faculty ratio 9:1. 44 full-time faculty, 57% hold PhDs, 5% are members of minority groups, 36% are women. 0% of classes are taught by teaching assistants.

ACADEMICS

Degrees: Bachelor's **Classes:** Most classes have 20-29 students. Most lab/discussion sessions have 20-29 students. **Most popular majors:** Elementary Education And Teaching; Biology/Biological Sciences, General; Business Administration And Management, General. **Special Study Options:** Accelerated program; Cross-registration; Double major; Dual enrollment; Exchange student program (domestic); Honors program; Independent study; Internships; Liberal arts/career combination; Student-designed major; Study abroad; Teacher certification program. **Honors programs:** Honors program offered **Combined degree programs:** BA/MEng. **Disability Services offered to physically disabled students:** Note-taking services; Reader services; Tape recorders; Tutors. **Career services:** Alumni network; Alumni services; Career assessment; Career/job search classes; Internships; Regional alumni

FACILITIES

Housing: Apartments for single students; Coed dorms; Women's dorms 80% of campus accessible to physically disabled. **Special Academic Facilities/Equipment:** Mingenback Gallery, Bethany College Archives, Plym Gallery, Sandzen Gallery.

CAMPUS LIFE

Environment: Rural **Activities:** Campus Ministries; Choral groups; Concert band; Dance; Drama/theater; International Student Organization; Jazz band; Music ensembles; Musical theater; Pep band; Student government; Student newspaper; Symphony orchestra; Yearbook 49 registered organizations, 8 honor societies, 9 religious organizations. 3 fraternities, 3 sororities. **Athletics (Intercollegiate):** *Men:* baseball, basketball, cheerleading, cross-country, football, golf, soccer, tennis, track/field (outdoor), track/field (indoor). *Women:* basketball, cheerleading, cross-country, golf, soccer, softball, tennis, track/field (outdoor), track/field (indoor), volleyball. **On-Campus Highlights:** Student Union, Walderstadt Library, Mingenback Art Gallery, Residence Halls, Athletic Fields

ADMISSIONS

Freshman Academic Profile: Average high school GPA 3.3. 15% in top 10% of high school class, 42% in top 25% of high school class, 76% in top 50% of high school class. 97% from public high schools. **Test Scores:** SAT Math middle 50% range 420-560. SAT EBRW middle 50% range 370-500. ACT middle 50% range 19-24. Minimum internet-based TOEFL 71. Minimum paper TOEFL 525. **Basis for Candidate Selection:** *Very important factors considered include:* rigor of secondary school record, academic GPA, standardized test scores. *Other factors considered include:* application essay, recommendation(s), extracurricular activities, talent/ability, character/personal qualities, racial/ethnic status, volunteer work. **Freshman Admission Requirements:** High school diploma is required and GED is accepted *Academic units recommended:* 4 English, 3 math, 3 science, 2 science labs, 2 foreign language, 3 social studies. **Freshman Admission Statistics:** 811 applied, 65.4% admitted, 34% enrolled. **Transfer Admission Requirements:** college transcript(s), statement of good standing from prior institution(s). Minimum college GPA of 2.3 required. Lowest grade transferable D. **General Admission Information:** Application fee $20. Priority deadline 2/1. Regular application deadline 7/1. Nonfall registration accepted.

COSTS AND FINANCIAL AID

Annual tuition $17,824. Room and board $5,650. Required fees $300. Average book expense $1,000. **Required Forms and Deadlines:** FAFSA. **Notification of Awards:** Applicants will be notified of awards on a rolling basis beginning 3/1. **Types of Aid:** *Need-based scholarships/grants:* College/university scholarship or grant aid from institutional funds; Federal Pell; Private scholarships; SEOG; State scholarships/grants. *Loans: Student Employment:* Federal Work-Study Program available. Institutional employment available. **Financial Aid Statistics:** 85% needy freshmen, 84% needy undergrads receive need-based scholarship or grant aid. 40% freshmen, 32% undergrads receive non-need-based scholarship or grant aid. 76% freshmen, 78% undergrads receive need-based self-help aid. 0% freshmen, 7% undergrads receive athletic scholarships. 100% freshmen, 98% undergrads receive any aid. **Criteria for awarding aid:** *Non-need-based:* Academics, Alumni affiliation, Art, Athletics, Leadership, Music/drama, Religious affiliation.

BETHANY COLLEGE (WV)

31 E Campus Dr, Bethany, WV 26032
Phone: 304-829-7611 · **Financial Aid Phone:** 304-829-7611
E-mail: enrollment@bethanywv.edu · **CEEB Code:** 5060
Fax: 304-829-7142 · **Website:** www.bethanywv.edu · **ACT Code:** 4512

This private school, affiliated with the Disciples of Christ Church, was founded in 1840. It has a 1300 acre campus.

RATINGS

Admissions Selectivity Rating: 79   Fire Safety Rating: 88   Green Rating: 60*

STUDENTS AND FACULTY

Enrollment: 716. **Student Body:** 41% female, 59% male, 68% out-of-state, 2% international (11 countries represented). Asian <1%, African American 20%, Caucasian 54%, Hispanic 4%, Native American 1%, Pacific Islander <1%, Two or more races 3%, Race unknown 16%. **Retention and Graduation:** 70% freshmen return for sophomore year. **Faculty:** Student/faculty ratio 12:1. 48 full-time faculty, 79% hold PhDs, 4% are members of minority groups, 44% are women. 0% of classes are taught by teaching assistants.

ACADEMICS

Degrees: Bachelor's; Master's **Classes:** Most classes have 10-19 students. Most lab/discussion sessions have 10-19 students. **Most popular majors:** Speech Communication And Rhetoric; Elementary Education And Teaching; Psychology, General. **Special Study Options:** Accelerated program; Distance learning; Double major; Dual enrollment; English as a Second Language (ESL); Independent study; Internships; Liberal arts/career combination; Student-designed major; Study abroad; Teacher certification program. **Combined degree programs:** BA/JD; BA/MA. **Disability Services offered to physically disabled students:** Note-taking services; Reader services; Tape recorders; Tutors. **Career services:** Alumni network; Alumni services; Career assessment; Internships; Regional alumni

FACILITIES

Housing: Apartments for married students; Apartments for single students; Coed dorms; Fraternity/sorority housing; Men's dorms; Special housing for disabled student; Women's dorms **Special Academic Facilities/Equipment:** Renner Art Gallery, outdoor classroom **Computers:** Administrative functions (other than registration) can be performed online.

CAMPUS LIFE

Environment: Rural **Activities:** Campus Ministries; Choral groups; Concert band; Dance; Drama/theater; International Student Organization; Literary magazine; Marching band; Music ensembles; Musical theater; Pep band; Radio station; Student government; Student newspaper; Television station 38 registered organizations, 16 honor societies, 3 religious organizations. 6 fraternities, 3 sororities. **Athletics (Intercollegiate):** *Men:* baseball, basketball, cross-country, diving, football, golf, soccer, swimming, tennis, track/field (outdoor), track/field (indoor). *Women:* basketball, cross-country, diving, golf, soccer, softball, swimming, tennis, track/field (outdoor), track/field (indoor), volleyball. **On-Campus Highlights:** Old Main, Athletic Facilities, Campbell Village, Bethany Beanery, Renner Art Gallery

ADMISSIONS

Freshman Academic Profile: Average high school GPA 2.9. 6% in top 10% of high school class, 20% in top 25% of high school class, 49% in top 50% of high school class. 90% from public high schools. **Test Scores:** SAT Math middle 50% range 390-490. SAT EBRW middle 50% range 370-500. ACT middle 50% range 17-23. Minimum internet-based TOEFL 90. Minimum paper TOEFL 500. **Basis for Candidate Selection:** *Very important factors considered include:* rigor of secondary school record, academic GPA, application essay, standardized test scores, recommendation(s), character/personal qualities. *Important factors considered include:* class rank, level of applicant's interest. *Other factors considered include:* interview, extracurricular activities, talent/ability, alumni/ae relation, volunteer work, work experience. **Freshman Admission Requirements:** High school diploma is required and GED is accepted *Academic units recommended:* 4 English, 3 math, 3 science, 2 foreign language, 3 social studies. **Freshman Admission Statistics:** 1,394 applied, 62.1% admitted, 28% enrolled. **Transfer Admission Requirements:** college transcript(s), essay or personal statement, statement of good standing from prior institution(s). Minimum college GPA of 2.0 required. Lowest grade transferable D°. **General Admission Information:** Priority deadline 3/1. Nonfall registration accepted. Admission may be deferred for a maximum of 1 year.

COSTS AND FINANCIAL AID

Annual tuition $24,836. Room and board $9,636. Required fees $900. Average book expense $1,200. **Required Forms and Deadlines:** FAFSA. **Notification of Awards:** Applicants will be notified of awards on a rolling basis beginning 2/15. **Types of Aid:** *Need-based scholarships/grants:* College/university scholarship or grant aid from institutional funds; Federal Pell; Private scholarships; SEOG; State scholarships/grants. *Loans:* Direct PLUS loans; Direct Subsidized Stafford Loans; Direct Unsubsidized Stafford Loans. *Student Employment:* Federal Work-Study Program available. Institutional employment available. **Financial Aid Statistics:** 80% needy freshmen, 79% needy undergrads receive need-based scholarship or grant aid. 100% freshmen, 99% undergrads receive non-need-based scholarship or grant aid. 77% freshmen, 79% undergrads receive need-based self-help aid. 0% freshmen, 0% undergrads receive athletic scholarships. 99% freshmen, 99% undergrads receive any aid. **Criteria for awarding aid:** *Need-based:* Academics, Alumni affiliation, Leadership, Music/drama, Religious affiliation *Non-need-based:* Academics, Alumni affiliation, Leadership, Music/drama, Religious affiliation, State/district residency.

See page 902.

BETHEL COLLEGE (IN)

1001 Bethel Circle, Mishawaka, IN 46545
Phone: 574-807-7600 • **Financial Aid Phone:** 574-807-7415
E-mail: admissions@bethelcollege.edu • **CEEB Code:** 1079
Fax: 574-807-7650 • **Website:** www.bethelcollege.edu • **ACT Code:** 1178

This private school, affiliated with the Missionary Church, was founded in 1947. It has a 75 acre campus.

RATINGS

Admissions Selectivity Rating: 73　　**Fire Safety Rating:** 83　　**Green Rating:** 60*

STUDENTS AND FACULTY

Enrollment: 1,254. **Student Body:** 63% female, 37% male, 27% out-of-state, 2% international (15 countries represented). Asian 2%, African American 10%, Caucasian 72%, Hispanic 9%, Native American <1%, Pacific Islander 0%, Two or more races 5%, Race unknown 1%.
Retention and Graduation: 78% freshmen return for sophomore year. 53% freshmen graduate within 4 years. 64% freshmen graduate within 6 years. 17% grads go on to further study within 1 year. **Faculty:** Student/faculty ratio 12:1. 67 full-time faculty, 61% hold PhDs, 12% are members of minority groups, 46% are women. 0% of classes are taught by teaching assistants.

ACADEMICS

Degrees: Associate; Bachelor's; Master's **Classes:** Most classes have 10-19 students. **Most popular majors:** Elementary Education And Teaching; Registered Nursing/Registered Nurse; Business Administration And Management, General. **Special Study Options:** Accelerated program; Cross-registration; Distance learning; Double major; Exchange student program (domestic); Honors program; Independent study; Internships; Liberal arts/career combination; Student-designed major; Study abroad; Teacher certification program. **Combined degree programs:** BA/MEng. **Disability Services offered to physically disabled students:** Note-taking services; Reader services; Tape recorders; Tutors. **Career services:** Alumni services; Career assessment; Career/job search classes; Internships

FACILITIES

Housing: Apartments for married students; Apartments for single students; Men's dorms; Special housing for disabled student; Theme housing; Women's dorms 90% of campus accessible to physically disabled. **Special Academic Facilities/Equipment:** Bowen Museum Weaver Gallery **Computers:** 25% of classrooms, 100% of dorms, 100% of libraries, 100% of dining areas, 100% of student union, 25% of common outdoor areas have wireless network access. Administrative functions (other than registration) can be performed online.

CAMPUS LIFE

Environment: City **Activities:** Campus Ministries; Choral groups; Concert band; Drama/theater; International Student Organization; Jazz band; Literary magazine; Music ensembles; Musical theater; Pep band; Radio station; Student government; Student newspaper; Yearbook 18 registered organizations, 1 honor society, 5 religious organizations. **Athletics (Intercollegiate):** *Men:* baseball, basketball, cheerleading, cross-country, golf, soccer, tennis, track/field (outdoor), track/field (indoor). *Women:* basketball, cheerleading, cross-country, golf, soccer, softball, tennis, track/field (outdoor), track/field (indoor), volleyball. **On-Campus Highlights:** The Acorn Snack Shop, Everst Rohrer Chapel, Sufficient Grounds Coffee House, Wiekamp Athletic Center, Dining Commons

ADMISSIONS

Freshman Academic Profile: Average high school GPA 3.4. 14% in top 10% of high school class, 41% in top 25% of high school class, 72% in top 50% of high school class. 78% from public high schools. **Test Scores:** SAT Math middle 50% range 470-570. SAT EBRW middle 50% range 480-590. ACT middle 50% range 19-25. Minimum internet-based TOEFL 76. Minimum paper TOEFL 540. **Basis for Candidate Selection:** *Very important factors considered include:* academic GPA, standardized test scores. *Important factors considered include:* rigor of secondary school record, recommendation(s), character/personal qualities. *Other factors considered include:* class rank, application essay, interview, extracurricular activities, talent/ability, alumni/ae relation, religious affiliation/commitment, racial/ethnic status, volunteer work, work experience. **Freshman Admission Requirements:** High school diploma is required and GED is accepted *Academic units recommended:* 4 English, 3 math, 1 science, 1 science labs, 2 foreign language, 1 social studies, 2 history, 3 academic electives. **Freshman Admission Statistics:** 1,065 applied, 89.8% admitted, 24% enrolled. **Transfer Admission Requirements:** High school transcript, college transcript(s), essay or personal statement, standardized test scores, statement of good standing from prior institution(s). Minimum college GPA of 2.0 required. Lowest grade transferable C-. **General Admission Information:** Priority deadline 12/1. Regular application deadline 8/15. Nonfall registration accepted. Admission may be deferred for a maximum of 1 year.

COSTS AND FINANCIAL AID

Annual tuition $28,140. Room and board $9,000. Required fees $450. Average book expense $1,230. **Required Forms and Deadlines:** FAFSA. **Notification of Awards:** Applicants will be notified of awards on a rolling basis beginning 12/1. **Types of Aid:** *Need-based scholarships/grants:* College/university scholarship or grant aid from institutional funds; Federal Nursing Scholarships; Federal Pell; Private scholarships; SEOG; State scholarships/grants. *Loans:* Direct PLUS loans; Direct Subsidized Stafford Loans; Direct Unsubsidized Stafford Loans. *Student Employment:* Federal Work-Study Program available. Institutional employment available. **Financial Aid Statistics:** 76% freshmen, 73% undergrads receive any aid. 70% undergrads borrow to pay for school. Average cumulative indebtedness $34,148. **Criteria for awarding aid:** *Non-need-based:* Academics, Art, Athletics, Leadership, Minority status, Music/drama, Religious affiliation.

BETHEL COLLEGE (KS)

300 E 27th St, North Newton, KS 67117
Phone: 316-284-5230 · **Financial Aid Phone:** 316-284-5232
E-mail: admissions@bethelks.edu · **CEEB Code:** 6037
Fax: 316-284-5870 · **Website:** www.bethelks.edu · **ACT Code:** 1390

This private school, affiliated with the Mennonite Church USA, was founded in 1887. It has a 60 acre campus.

RATINGS

Admissions Selectivity Rating: 85 **Fire Safety Rating:** 82 **Green Rating:** 60*

STUDENTS AND FACULTY

Enrollment: 484. **Student Body:** 51% female, 49% male, 38% out-of-state, 2% international (13 countries represented). Asian <1%, African American 15%, Caucasian 71%, Hispanic 10%, Native American <1%, Pacific Islander 0%, Two or more races 2%, Race unknown 0%.
Retention and Graduation: 63% freshmen return for sophomore year. **Faculty:** Student/faculty ratio 10:1. 38 full-time faculty, 66% hold PhDs, 5% are members of minority groups, 55% are women. 0% of classes are taught by teaching assistants.

ACADEMICS

Degrees: Bachelor's; Certificate **Classes:** Most classes have 10-19 students. Most lab/discussion sessions have 10-19 students. **Most popular majors:** Biology/Biological Sciences, General; Nursing/Registered Nurse (Rn, Asn, Bsn, Msn); Business/Commerce, General. **Special Study Options:** Cross-registration; Double major; Dual enrollment; Exchange student program (domestic); Independent study; Internships; Liberal arts/career combination; Student-designed major; Study abroad; Teacher certification program. **Combined degree programs:** BA/MEng. **Disability Services offered to physically disabled students:** Note-taking services; Reader services; Tape recorders; Tutors. **Career services:** Alumni network; Career assessment; Career/job search classes

FACILITIES

Housing: Coed dorms; Special housing for international students 75% of campus accessible to physically diasbled. **Special Academic Facilities/Equipment:** Art gallery, natural history and midwestern/Kansas history museums, 80 acre natural history field laboratory for biological studies, Mennonite Historical Library and Archives, Institute for Peace and Conflict Resolution, observatory **Computers:** 25% of classrooms, 75% of libraries, 100% of dining areas, 100% of student union, 50% of common outdoor areas have wireless network access. Administrative functions (other than registration) can be performed online.

CAMPUS LIFE

Environment: Village **Activities:** Campus Ministries; Choral groups; Concert band; Drama/theater; International Student Organization; Jazz band; Literary magazine; Music ensembles; Radio station; Student government; Student newspaper; Symphony orchestra; Television station; Yearbook 50 registered organizations, 2 religious organizations. **Athletics (Intercollegiate):** *Men:* basketball, cross-country, football, golf, soccer, tennis, track/field (outdoor), track/field (indoor). *Women:* basketball, cross-country, golf, soccer, tennis, track/field (outdoor), track/field (indoor), volleyball. **On-Campus Highlights:** Student Center, Krehbiel Science Center, Athletic Complex, The Green, Warkentine Court

ADMISSIONS

Freshman Academic Profile: Average high school GPA 3.4. 17% in top 10% of high school class, 38% in top 25% of high school class, 73% in top 50% of high school class. 97% from public high schools. **Test Scores:** SAT Math

middle 50% range 425-475. SAT EBRW middle 50% range 380-435. ACT middle 50% range 19-25. Minimum internet-based TOEFL 76. Minimum paper TOEFL 540. **Basis for Candidate Selection:** *Very important factors considered include:* academic GPA, standardized test scores, level of applicant's interest. *Important factors considered include:* class rank, extracurricular activities, character/personal qualities, alumni/ae relation. *Other factors considered include:* rigor of secondary school record, recommendation(s). **Freshman Admission Requirements:** High school diploma is required and GED is accepted *Academic units recommended:* 4 English, 4 math, 3 science, 2 foreign language, 3 social studies. **Freshman Admission Statistics:** 833 applied, 49.1% admitted, 27% enrolled. **Transfer Admission Requirements:** High school transcript, college transcript(s), statement of good standing from prior institution(s). Lowest grade transferable D-. **General Admission Information:** Application fee $20. Regular application deadline 8/1. Nonfall registration accepted. Admission may be deferred for a maximum of 1 year.

COSTS AND FINANCIAL AID

Annual tuition $23,500. Room and board $7,980. Average book expense $900. **Required Forms and Deadlines:** FAFSA. **Notification of Awards:** Applicants will be notified of awards on a rolling basis beginning 2/1. **Types of Aid:** *Need-based scholarships/grants:* College/university scholarship or grant aid from institutional funds; Federal Nursing Scholarships; Federal Pell; Private scholarships; SEOG; State scholarships/grants. *Loans:* Direct PLUS loans; Direct Subsidized Stafford Loans; Direct Unsubsidized Stafford Loans. *Student Employment:* Federal Work-Study Program available. Institutional employment available. **Financial Aid Statistics:** 88% needy freshmen, 85% needy undergrads receive need-based scholarship or grant aid. 100% freshmen, 100% undergrads receive non-need-based scholarship or grant aid. 89% freshmen, 90% undergrads receive need-based self-help aid. 66% freshmen, 48% undergrads receive athletic scholarships. 100% freshmen, 94% undergrads receive any aid. **Criteria for awarding aid:** *Non-need-based:* Academics, Alumni affiliation, Art, Athletics, Minority status, Music/drama, Religious affiliation, State/district residency.

BETHEL UNIVERSITY (MN)

3900 Bethel Dr, Saint Paul, MN 55112
Phone: 651-638-6242 · **Financial Aid Phone:** 651-638-6241
E-mail: undergrad-admissions@bethel.edu · **CEEB Code:** 6038
Fax: 651-635-1490 · **Website:** www.bethel.edu · **ACT Code:** 2088

This private school, affiliated with the Converge Worldwide (former Baptist General Conference) Church, was founded in 1871. It has a 289 acre campus.

RATINGS

Admissions Selectivity Rating: 77 **Fire Safety Rating:** 69 **Green Rating:** 61

STUDENTS AND FACULTY

Enrollment: 2,777. **Student Body:** 62% female, 38% male, 19% out-of-state, <1% international (8 countries represented). Asian 3%, African American 4%, Caucasian 76%, Hispanic 5%, Native American <1%, Pacific Islander <1%, Two or more races 4%, Race unknown 7%.
Retention and Graduation: 85% freshmen return for sophomore year. 61% freshmen graduate within 4 years. 70% freshmen graduate within 6 years. 27% grads go on to further study within 1 year. 10% grads pursue arts and sciences degrees. 1% grads pursue law degrees. 4% grads pursue business degrees. 3.6% grads pursue medical degrees. **Faculty:** Student/faculty ratio 11:1. 223 full-time faculty, 86% hold PhDs, 9% are members of minority groups, 50% are women. 0% of classes are taught by teaching assistants.

ACADEMICS

Degrees: Associate; Bachelor's; Certificate; Doctoral; Doctoral/Professional; Doctoral/Research; Master's; Post-Bachelor's certificate; Post-Master's certificate **Classes:** Most classes have 10-19 students. Most lab/discussion sessions have 10-19 students. **Most popular majors:** Education, General; Registered Nursing/Registered Nurse; Business Administration And Management, General. **Special Study Options:** Cross-registration; Distance learning; Double major; Dual enrollment; Exchange student program (domestic); Honors program; Independent study; Internships; Liberal arts/career combination; Student-designed major; Study abroad; Teacher certification program. **Honors programs:** The program consists of two honors courses in the freshman year, one in the sophomore year and one in the junior year. In their senior year the student will complete an Honors Senior Project. The two courses in the sophomore year and junior year, as well as the Honors Senior Project are geared toward a discipline of the students choosing. This program also consists of other Honors classes and Honors Forums throughout all four years. **Disability Services offered to physically disabled students:** Note-taking services; Reader services; Tape recorders; Tutors. **Career services:** Alumni services; Career assessment; Career/job search classes; Internships

FACILITIES

Housing: Apartments for single students; Cooperative housing; Special housing for disabled students 99% of campus accessible to physically diasbled. **Special Academic Facilities/Equipment:** Two Art galleries, media center, closed circuit TV, television studio, and radio station, cadaver lab **Computers:** 100% of classrooms, 50% of dorms, 100% of libraries, 100% of dining areas, 100% of student union, 50% of common outdoor areas have wireless network access. Students can register for classes online. Administrative functions (other than registration) can be performed online.

CAMPUS LIFE

Environment: Metropolis **Activities:** Campus Ministries; Choral groups; Concert band; Dance; Drama/theater; International Student Organization; Jazz band; Literary magazine; Music ensembles; Musical theater; Radio station; Student government; Student newspaper; Student-run film society; Symphony orchestra 55 registered organizations, 5 honor societies, 20 religious organizations. **Athletics (Intercollegiate):** *Men:* baseball, basketball, cross-country, football, golf, ice hockey, soccer, tennis, track/field (outdoor), track/field (indoor). *Women:* basketball, cross-country, golf, ice hockey, soccer, softball, tennis, track/field (outdoor), track/field (indoor), volleyball. **On-Campus Highlights:** Brushaber Commons/Student Life Building, Monson Dining Center/3900 Grill/Royal Grounds, Benson Great Hall, Student Recreation Center/Sport Fields, Nursing, Physics, Biology & Chemistry Labs **Environmental Initiatives:** Green Roof and Permeable Pavers for Brushaber Commons

ADMISSIONS

Freshman Academic Profile: Average high school GPA 3.5. 25% in top 10% of high school class, 52% in top 25% of high school class, 81% in top 50% of high school class. 76% from public high schools. **Test Scores:** ACT middle 50% range 21-27. Minimum internet-based TOEFL 70. Minimum paper TOEFL 525. **Basis for Candidate Selection:** *Very important factors considered include:* rigor of secondary school record, academic GPA, standardized test scores, character/personal qualities, alumni/ae relation, religious affiliation/commitment. *Important factors considered include:* application essay, volunteer work.level of applicant's interest. *Other factors considered include:* class rank, recommendation(s), interview, extracurricular activities, talent/ability, first generation, racial/ethnic status. **Freshman Admission Requirements:** High school diploma is required and GED is accepted *Academic units required:* 4 English, 3 math, 3 science, 2 science labs, 4 social studies, *Academic units recommended:* 2 foreign language, 2 history, 1 computer science, 1 visual/performing arts. **Freshman Admission Statistics:** 1,812 applied, 83.5% admitted, 39% enrolled. **Transfer Admission Requirements:** college transcript(s), essay or personal statement, Minimum college GPA of 2.5 required. Lowest grade transferable C. **General Admission Information:** Priority deadline 11/1. Nonfall registration accepted. Admission may be deferred for a maximum of 1 semester.

COSTS AND FINANCIAL AID

Annual tuition $37,140. Room and board $10,520. Required fees $160. Average book expense $1,240. **Required Forms and Deadlines:** FAFSA. **Notification of Awards:** Applicants will be notified of awards on a rolling basis beginning 12/9. **Types of Aid:** *Need-based scholarships/grants:* College/university scholarship or grant aid from institutional funds; Federal Pell; Private scholarships; SEOG; State scholarships/grants. *Loans:* Direct PLUS loans; Direct Subsidized Stafford Loans; Direct Unsubsidized Stafford Loans. *Student Employment:* Federal Work-Study Program available. Institutional employment available. **Financial Aid Statistics:** 100% needy freshmen, 100% needy undergrads receive need-based scholarship or grant aid. 13% freshmen, 13% undergrads receive non-need-based scholarship or grant aid. 84% freshmen, 85% undergrads receive need-based self-help aid. 0% freshmen, 0% undergrads receive athletic scholarships. 100% freshmen, 94% undergrads receive any aid. 77% undergrads borrow to pay for school. Average cumulative indebtedness $36,132. **Criteria for awarding aid:** *Need-based:* Minority status *Non-need-based:* Academics, Alumni affiliation, Art, Leadership, Music/drama, State/district residency.

BIOLA UNIVERSITY

13800 Biola Avenue, La Mirada, CA 90639
Phone: 1-800-OK-BIOLA · **Financial Aid Phone:** 562-903-4752
E-mail: admissions@biola.edu · **CEEB Code:** 4017
Fax: 562-903-4709 · **Website:** www.biola.edu · **ACT Code:** 172

This private school, affiliated with the Christian (Nondenominational) Church, was founded in 1908. It has a 95 acre campus.

RATINGS

Admissions Selectivity Rating: 82   **Fire Safety Rating:** 89   **Green Rating:** 72

STUDENTS AND FACULTY

Enrollment: 4,039. **Student Body:** 64% female, 36% male, 26% out-of-state, 3% international (40 countries represented). Asian 18%, African American 2%, Caucasian 46%, Hispanic 21%, Native American <1%, Pacific Islander <1%, Two or more races 6%, Race unknown 3%. **Retention and Graduation:** 87% freshmen return for sophomore year. 55% freshmen graduate within 4 years. 73% freshmen graduate within 6 years. **Faculty:** Student/faculty ratio 15:1. 274 full-time faculty, 84% hold PhDs, 21% are members of minority groups, 36% are women. 0% of classes are taught by teaching assistants.

ACADEMICS

Degrees: Bachelor's; Certificate; Doctoral; Doctoral Other; Doctoral/Professional; Doctoral/Research; Master's; Post-Bachelor's certificate; Post-Master's certificate **Classes:** Most classes have fewer than 10 students. Most lab/discussion sessions have 10-19 students. **Most popular majors:** Elementary Education And Teaching; Psychology, General; Business/Commerce, General. **Special Study Options:** Distance learning; Double major; English as a Second Language (ESL); Exchange student program (domestic); Honors program; Internships; Study abroad; Teacher certification program. **Honors programs:** Biola's Torrey Honors Program which is a nationally recognized great books program. **Disability Services offered to physically disabled students:** Note-taking services; Reader services; Tape recorders; Tutors. **Career services:** Alumni network; Alumni services; Career assessment; Career/job search classes; Internships; Regional alumni

FACILITIES

Housing: Apartments for married students; Apartments for single students; Coed dorms; Men's dorms; Special housing for disabled student; Women's dorms 85% of campus accessible to physically diasbled. **Special Academic Facilities/Equipment:** Art gallery, electron microscope, TV and Film Production Center, Integrated Media Room, film editing facility, media center, writing center, Student Ministry Union and tutoring services. **Computers:** 100% of dorms, 100% of libraries, 100% of student union, 75% of common outdoor areas have wireless network access. Students can register for classes online. Administrative functions (other than registration) can be performed online.

CAMPUS LIFE

Environment: Town **Activities:** Campus Ministries; Choral groups; Concert band; Dance; Drama/theater; International Student Organization; Jazz band; Music ensembles; Musical theater; Opera; Radio station; Student government; Student newspaper; Student-run film society; Symphony orchestra; Television station; Yearbook 33 registered organizations, 2 honor societies. **Athletics (Intercollegiate):** *Men:* baseball, basketball, cross-country, golf, soccer, swimming, tennis, track/field (outdoor). *Women:* basketball, cross-country, golf, soccer, softball, swimming, tennis, track/field (outdoor), volleyball. **On-Campus Highlights:** Common Grounds Coffee Shop, The Eagle's Nest Eatery, Art Gallery, The Talon Cafe, The Sub (Student Union Building) **Environmental Initiatives:** Cogen—We produce clean power on campus and use clean waste heat. A certain percentage of this is also used towards cooling purposes.

ADMISSIONS

Freshman Academic Profile: Average high school GPA 3.6. 59% from public high schools. **Test Scores:** SAT Math middle 50% range 530-630. SAT EBRW middle 50% range 520-630. ACT middle 50% range 21-28. Minimum internet-based TOEFL 100. Minimum paper TOEFL 600. **Basis for Candidate Selection:** *Very important factors considered include:* academic GPA, application essay, standardized test scores, character/personal qualities, religious affiliation/commitment. *Important factors considered include:* rigor of secondary school record, recommendation(s), interview, extracurricular activities. *Other factors considered include:* class rank, talent/ability, first generation, alumni/ae relation, geographical residence, state residency, racial/ethnic status, volunteer work, work experience. **Freshman Admission Requirements:** High school diploma is required and GED is accepted *Academic units required:* 4 English, 3 math, 2 science, 1 science labs, 4 foreign language, 1 social studies, 1 history.

Freshman Admission Statistics: 3,926 applied, 72.0% admitted, 32% enrolled. **Transfer Admission Requirements:** High school transcript, college transcript(s), essay or personal statement, statement of good standing from prior institution(s). Minimum college GPA of 2.0 required. Lowest grade transferable C. **General Admission Information:** Application fee $45. Priority deadline 3/1. Nonfall registration accepted. Admission may be deferred for a maximum of 2 years.

COSTS AND FINANCIAL AID
Annual tuition $19,224. Average book expense $1,854. **Required Forms and Deadlines:** FAFSA. **Notification of Awards:** Applicants will be notified of awards on a rolling basis beginning 11/15. **Types of Aid:** *Need-based scholarships/grants:* College/university scholarship or grant aid from institutional funds; Federal Pell; Private scholarships; SEOG; State scholarships/grants. *Loans:* Direct PLUS loans; Direct Subsidized Stafford Loans; Direct Unsubsidized Stafford Loans. *Student Employment:* Federal Work-Study Program available. Institutional employment available. **Financial Aid Statistics:** 98% needy freshmen, 97% needy undergrads receive need-based scholarship or grant aid. 6% freshmen, 3% undergrads receive non-need-based scholarship or grant aid. 77% freshmen, 82% undergrads receive need-based self-help aid. 2% freshmen, 2% undergrads receive athletic scholarships. 87% freshmen, 91% undergrads receive any aid. **Criteria for awarding aid:** *Non-need-based:* Academics, Alumni affiliation, Art, Athletics, Leadership, Minority status, Music/drama.

BIRMINGHAM-SOUTHERN COLLEGE

900 Arkadelphia Road, Birmingham, AL 35254
Phone: 205-226-4696 · **Financial Aid Phone:** 205-226-4688
E-mail: admission@bsc.edu · **CEEB Code:** 1064
Fax: 205-226-3074 · **Website:** www.bsc.edu · **ACT Code:** 1012

This private school, affiliated with the Methodist Church, was founded in 1856. It has a 196 acre campus.

RATINGS
Admissions Selectivity Rating: 83   **Fire Safety Rating:** 87   **Green Rating:** 60*

STUDENTS AND FACULTY
Enrollment: 1,226. **Student Body:** 47% female, 53% male, 41% out-of-state, 0% international (12 countries represented). Asian 4%, African American 8%, Caucasian 84%, Hispanic 3%, Native American 1%, Pacific Islander 0%, Race unknown 1%.
Retention and Graduation: 81% freshmen return for sophomore year. 42% grads go on to further study within 1 year. 27% grads pursue arts and sciences degrees. 17% grads pursue law degrees. 13% grads pursue business degrees. 24% grads pursue medical degrees. **Faculty:** Student/faculty ratio 13:1. 86 full-time faculty, 97% hold PhDs, 3% are members of minority groups, 38% are women. 0% of classes are taught by teaching assistants.

ACADEMICS
Degrees: Bachelor's **Classes:** Most classes have 10-19 students. **Most popular majors:** Biology/Biological Sciences, General; Psychology, General; Business/Commerce, General. **Special Study Options:** Accelerated program; Cross-registration; Double major; Exchange student program (domestic); Honors program; Independent study; Internships; Student-designed major; Study abroad; Teacher certification program. **Honors programs:** The Honors Program at Birmingham-Southern is designed to engage students' intellectual curiosity, enhance their oral and written communications skills, and further develop their ability to think and study independently. The importance of viewing issues from interdisciplinary perspectives and of integrating—as well as analyzing—knowledge is a special focus of the program's courses and requirements. The program addresses its mission through small, interdisciplinary seminars developed specifically for Honors students and through upper-level courses with an interdisciplinary focus. The Honors Program serves as a complementary approach to fulfilling the requirements of the College's Foundations Plan for General Education. "… Honors students are open to new ideas, aware of expanding horizons, and willing to change their own ideas to make room for the knowledge that they gain. They incorporate, embrace, and encourage differences. 'Honors' is not synonymous with straight A's and valedictorians. Ideal Honors students would participate in the program even if it did not appear on their transcripts."—Excerpted from "The Ideal Student in the Honors Program" as adopted by the Honors Committee 2002. The Honors Program component of Honors student's general education consists of five units of Honors seminars and one unit of independent study, known as the Honors Project. The specific general education requirements met by Honors courses and those met by regular courses will vary from student to student, depending on which Honors courses the student elects to take.

Students may take one January Interim Term Honors project which will count toward the five units of Honors seminars. Students who participate in study abroad programs that include interdisciplinary courses also may petition to count one such course toward their Honors requirements. Honors students' remaining general education coursework is completed in the regular curriculum of the College. The student's sixth unit in independent study is typically taken over two terms. One-half unit is taken while the project is being designed by the student, the program director, and a faculty sponsor. The project must be interdisciplinary in nature and outside the student's major. Once approved by the Honors Program Committee, the independent study is completed the next term, giving the second half-unit of credit. All Honors Senior, or independent study, projects are presented publicly as part of the program's requirements. **Combined degree programs:** BA/MEng. **Career services:** Alumni network; Alumni services; Career assessment; Career/job search classes; Internships; Regional alumni

FACILITIES
Housing: Apartments for married students; Apartments for single students; Coed dorms; Fraternity/sorority housing; Men's dorms; Special housing for disabled student; Theme housing; Women's dorms 90% of campus accessible to physically diasbled. **Special Academic Facilities/Equipment:** Theatre planetarium Environmental Center Urban Environmental Park Kennedy Art Center Ropes Course for Leadership Training **Computers:** 100% of classrooms, 100% of dorms, 100% of libraries, 100% of dining areas, 100% of student union, 90% of common outdoor areas have wireless network access. Students can register for classes online. Administrative functions (other than registration) can be performed online.

CAMPUS LIFE
Environment: Metropolis **Activities:** Campus Ministries; Choral groups; Concert band; Drama/theater; International Student Organization; Jazz band; Literary magazine; Marching band; Model UN; Music ensembles; Musical theater; Opera; Pep band; Student government; Student newspaper; Yearbook 70 registered organizations, 18 honor societies, 5 religious organizations. 6 fraternities, 6 sororities. **Athletics (Intercollegiate):** *Men:* baseball, basketball, cheerleading, cross-country, football, golf, lacrosse, soccer, tennis, track/field (outdoor), track/field (indoor). *Women:* basketball, cheerleading, cross-country, golf, lacrosse, riflery, soccer, softball, tennis, track/field (outdoor), track/field (indoor), volleyball. **On-Campus Highlights:** Urban Environmental Park, Striplin Physical Fitness Center, The Cellar—Coffee House, The Court **Environmental Initiatives:** 10 compressed natural gas operations vehicles will come on line this spring. Campus police vehicles are hybrids.

ADMISSIONS
Freshman Academic Profile: Average high school GPA 3.5. 29% in top 10% of high school class, 61% in top 25% of high school class, 82% in top 50% of high school class. 65% from public high schools. **Test Scores:** SAT Math middle 50% range 510-610. SAT EBRW middle 50% range 500-610. ACT middle 50% range 23-29. Minimum internet-based TOEFL 61. Minimum paper TOEFL 500. **Basis for Candidate Selection:** *Very important factors considered include:* academic GPA, application essay, standardized test scores, recommendation(s). *Important factors considered include:* rigor of secondary school record, class rank, extracurricular activities, character/personal qualities. *Other factors considered include:* interview, talent/ability, work experience. **Freshman Admission Requirements:** High school diploma is required and GED is accepted *Academic units required:* 4 English, *Academic units recommended:* 2 math, 2 science, 1 science labs, 2 foreign language, 2 social studies, 2 history, 2 academic electives. **Freshman Admission Statistics:** 1,846 applied, 65.1% admitted, 27% enrolled. **Transfer Admission Requirements:** High school transcript, college transcript(s), essay or personal statement, standardized test scores, statement of good standing from prior institution(s). Minimum college GPA of 2.0 required. Lowest grade transferable D. **General Admission Information:** Application fee $40. Regular application deadline 2/1. Nonfall registration accepted. Admission may be deferred for a maximum of 1 year.

COSTS AND FINANCIAL AID
Annual tuition $31,954. Room and board $11,350. Required fees $1,174. Average book expense $1,300. **Required Forms and Deadlines:** FAFSA; State aid form. **Notification of Awards:** Applicants will be notified of awards on a rolling basis beginning 3/1. **Types of Aid:** *Need-based scholarships/grants:* College/university scholarship or grant aid from institutional funds; Federal Pell; Private scholarships; SEOG; State scholarships/grants. *Loans:* Direct PLUS loans; Direct Subsidized Stafford Loans; Direct Unsubsidized Stafford Loans. *Student Employment:* Federal Work-Study Program available. Institutional employment available. **Financial Aid Statistics:** 76% needy freshmen, 82% needy undergrads receive need-based scholarship or grant aid. 92% freshmen, 89% undergrads receive non-need-based scholarship or grant aid. 99% freshmen, 82% undergrads receive need-based self-help aid. 0% freshmen, 0% undergrads receive athletic scholarships. 99% freshmen, 98% undergrads receive any aid. **Criteria for awarding aid:** *Non-need-based:* Academics, Alumni affiliation, Art, Leadership, Music/drama, Religious affiliation, State/district residency.

BLACKBURN COLLEGE

700 College Ave., Carlinville, IL 62626
Phone: 217-854-3231
E-mail: admit@blackburn.edu
Fax: 217-854-3713 • **Website:** www.blackburn.edu • **ACT Code:** 958

This private school, affiliated with the Presbyterian Church, was founded in 1837. It has a 80 acre campus.

RATINGS

Admissions Selectivity Rating: 70   **Fire Safety Rating:** 60*   **Green Rating:** 60*

STUDENTS AND FACULTY

Enrollment: 603. **Student Body:** 59% female, 41% male, (0 countries represented).
Faculty: Student/faculty ratio 17:1. 31 full-time faculty, 6% are members of minority groups, 35% are women.

ACADEMICS

Degrees: Bachelor's **Classes:** Most classes have 10-19 students. Most lab/discussion sessions have 10-19 students. **Special Study Options:** Double major; Exchange student program (domestic); Honors program; Independent study; Internships; Liberal arts/career combination; Student-designed major; Study abroad; Teacher certification program.

FACILITIES

Housing: Coed dorms; Men's dorms; Theme housing; Women's dorms
Computers:

CAMPUS LIFE

Environment: Village **Activities:** Campus Ministries; Choral groups; Dance; Drama/theater; International Student Organization; Jazz band; Literary magazine; Music ensembles; Musical theater; Radio station; Student government; Student newspaper; Student-run film society; Yearbook.

ADMISSIONS

Freshman Academic Profile: Average high school GPA 3.5. 16% in top 10% of high school class, 22% in top 25% of high school class, 37% in top 50% of high school class. 81% from public high schools. **Test Scores:** Minimum internet-based TOEFL 70. Minimum paper TOEFL 525. **Basis for Candidate Selection:** *Very important factors considered include:* rigor of secondary school record, academic GPA, standardized test scores. *Important factors considered include:* class rank, level of applicant's interest. *Other factors considered include:* application essay, recommendation(s), extracurricular activities, talent/ability, character/personal qualities, alumni/ae relation, volunteer work, work experience. **Freshman Admission Requirements:** High school diploma is required and GED is accepted *Academic units recommended:* 4 English, 3 math, 3 science, 2 foreign language, 3 social studies. **Freshman Admission Statistics:** 893 applied, 63.9% admitted, 26% enrolled. **Transfer Admission Requirements:** High school transcript, college transcript(s), standardized test scores, Minimum college GPA of 2.0 required. Lowest grade transferable C. **General Admission Information:** Nonfall registration accepted. Admission may be deferred.

COSTS AND FINANCIAL AID

Average book expense $1,000.

BLOOMFIELD COLLEGE

467 Franklin St, Bloomfield, NJ 07003
Phone: 973-748-9000 (x1230) • **Financial Aid Phone:** 973-748-9000 x1212
E-mail: admission@bloomfield.edu • **CEEB Code:** 2044
Fax: 973-748-0916 • **Website:** www.bloomfield.edu • **ACT Code:** 2540

This private school, affiliated with the Presbyterian Church, was founded in 1868. It has a 12.5 acre campus.

RATINGS

Admissions Selectivity Rating: 77   **Fire Safety Rating:** 99   **Green Rating:** 64

STUDENTS AND FACULTY

Enrollment: 1,941. **Student Body:** 62% female, 38% male, 6% out-of-state, 4% international (6 countries represented). Asian 2%, African American 50%, Caucasian 9%, Hispanic 28%, Native American <1%, Pacific Islander 1%, Two or more races 1%, Race unknown 5%.
Retention and Graduation: 65% freshmen return for sophomore year. 27% grads go on to further study within 1 year. **Faculty:** Student/faculty ratio 16:1. 70 full-time faculty, 81% hold PhDs, 24% are members of minority groups, 60% are women. 0% of classes are taught by teaching assistants.

ACADEMICS

Degrees: Bachelor's; Certificate; Master's; Post-Bachelor's certificate **Classes:** Most classes have 20-29 students. Most lab/discussion sessions have 20-29 students. **Most popular majors:** Sociology; Visual And Performing Arts, General; Business Administration And Management, General. **Special Study Options:** Accelerated program; Distance learning; Double major; Dual enrollment; English as a Second Language (ESL); Honors program; Independent study; Internships; Liberal arts/career combination; Student-designed major; Study abroad; Teacher certification program. **Honors programs:** Honors program open to new and enrolled students consisting of interdisciplinary courses, Honors seminars in the arts and sciences, special courses, and honors capstone projects. **Combined degree programs:** BA/MA. **Disability Services offered to physically disabled students:** Note-taking services; Reader services; Tape recorders; Tutors. **Career services:** Alumni network; Alumni services; Career assessment; Career/job search classes; Internships; Regional alumni

FACILITIES

Housing: Apartments for single students; Coed dorms 78% of campus accessible to physically disabled. **Computers:** 20% of classrooms, 100% of dorms, 100% of libraries, 100% of dining areas, 100% of student union, have wireless network access. Administrative functions (other than registration) can be performed online.

CAMPUS LIFE

Environment: Town **Activities:** Campus Ministries; Dance; International Student Organization; Radio station; Student government 40 registered organizations, 4 honor societies, 1 religious organization. 6 fraternities, 6 sororities. **Athletics (Intercollegiate):** *Men:* baseball, basketball, cross-country, soccer, tennis. *Women:* basketball, cross-country, soccer, softball, volleyball. **On-Campus Highlights:** Center for Technology + Creativity, Library, Talbott Hall Student Center, Learning Resource Center, Performing Arts Center **Environmental Initiatives:** Campus-wide recycling program of all materials, including cooking oil from the campus kitchen.

ADMISSIONS

Freshman Academic Profile: Average high school GPA 2.7. 7% in top 10% of high school class, 20% in top 25% of high school class, 50% in top 50% of high school class. 82% from public high schools. **Test Scores:** SAT Math middle 50% range 380-480. SAT EBRW middle 50% range 380-460. ACT middle 50% range 15-20. Minimum internet-based TOEFL 79. **Basis for Candidate Selection:** *Very important factors considered include:* rigor of secondary school record, academic GPA, recommendation(s). *Important factors considered include:* class rank, application essay, interview, extracurricular activities, volunteer work. *Other factors considered include:* standardized test scores, talent/ability, character/personal qualities, first generation, alumni/ae relation, geographical residence, state residency, work experience, level of applicant's interest. **Freshman Admission Requirements:** High school diploma is required and GED is accepted **Freshman Admission Statistics:** 3,623 applied, 61.6% admitted, 23% enrolled. **Transfer Admission Requirements:** college transcript(s), Minimum college GPA of 2.0 required. Lowest grade transferable 2. **General Admission Information:** Application fee $40. Priority deadline 3/15. Regular application deadline 8/1. Nonfall registration accepted. Admission may be deferred for a maximum of 1 year.

COSTS AND FINANCIAL AID

Annual tuition $29,300. Room and board $11,700. Average book expense $1,250. **Required Forms and Deadlines:** FAFSA. **Notification of Awards:** Applicants will be notified of awards on a rolling basis beginning 4/15. **Types of Aid:** *Need-based scholarships/grants:* College/university scholarship or grant aid from institutional funds; Federal Pell; Private scholarships; SEOG; State scholarships/grants. *Loans:* Direct PLUS loans; Direct Subsidized Stafford Loans; Direct Unsubsidized Stafford Loans. *Student Employment:* Federal Work-Study Program available. Institutional employment available. **Financial Aid Statistics:** 100% needy freshmen, 97% needy undergrads receive need-based scholarship or grant aid. 49% freshmen, 43% undergrads receive non-need-based scholarship or grant aid. 39% freshmen, 38% undergrads receive need-based self-help aid. 6% freshmen, 8% undergrads receive athletic scholarships. 98% freshmen, 94% undergrads receive any aid. 95% undergrads borrow to pay for school. Average cumulative indebtedness $46,574. **Criteria for awarding aid:** *Need-based:* Academics, Alumni affiliation, Religious affiliation *Non-need-based:* Academics, Alumni affiliation, Athletics, Leadership.

BLOOMSBURG UNIVERSITY OF PENNSYLVANIA

400 East Second Street, Bloomsburg, PA 17815
Phone: 570-389-4316 · **Financial Aid Phone:** (570) 389-4279
E-mail: www.bloomu.edu/admissions · **CEEB Code:** 2646
Fax: 570-389-4741 · **Website:** www.bloomu.edu · **ACT Code:** 3692

This public school was founded in 1839. It has a 366 acre campus.

RATINGS

Admissions Selectivity Rating: 78   **Fire Safety Rating:** 97   **Green Rating:** 60*

STUDENTS AND FACULTY

Enrollment: 8,303. **Student Body:** 57% female, 43% male, 9% out-of-state, <1% international (14 countries represented). Asian 1%, African American 9%, Caucasian 78%, Hispanic 7%, Native American <1%, Pacific Islander <1%, Two or more races 3%, Race unknown 1%.
Retention and Graduation: 74% freshmen return for sophomore year. 37% freshmen graduate within 4 years. 58% freshmen graduate within 6 years. 20% grads go on to further study within 1 year. **Faculty:** Student/faculty ratio 19:1. 419 full-time faculty, 84% hold PhDs, 13% are members of minority groups, 46% are women. 0% of classes are taught by teaching assistants.

ACADEMICS

Degrees: Bachelor's; Certificate; Doctoral Other; Doctoral/Professional; Master's; Post-Bachelor's certificate **Classes:** Most classes have 10-19 students. **Most popular majors:** Organizational Communication, General; Psychology, General; Business Administration And Management, General. **Special Study Options:** Cooperative education program; Cross-registration; Distance learning; Double major; Dual enrollment; Exchange student program (domestic); Honors program; Independent study; Internships; Liberal arts/career combination; Student-designed major; Study abroad; Teacher certification program. **Honors programs:** Bloomsburg University's Honors Program provides unique educational opportunities and experiences for academically talented students. The program challenges students to aspire to high academic standards and to achieve more professionally and personally. Students engage in various service activities that foster cooperation and altruism. Students conduct independent research in your major, become part of a community of ambitious scholars, have opportunities to explore the world, and more. » Work in your field on individual research — Choose a research topic within your field of study and, with the help of a dedicated faculty mentor, complete a written thesis and presentation to the Honors community. This independent study project allows every Honors student the opportunity to present their research at the annual meeting of the National Collegiate Honors Council, attended by students and faculty of Honors Programs across the country. Your hard work and presentation skills at this event show your dedication, commitment, and skill within your field, and your ability to work independently. » Get involved in the local community — Become involved in BU and community service projects, and make a difference with groups like the Bloomsburg Fire Department, Relay for Life, TreeFest, Balanced Care, and Habitat for Humanity. These projects enrich the community, provide a great sense of satisfaction, and help you discover other talents and skills. » Enjoy smaller classes — Smaller classes allow you to receive more attention from your professors and cover topics in greater depth and breadth. Build professional and personal relationships with your teachers so that you can create a strong network of academic references and contacts for the future. » Get settled early on campus — Move onto campus a day early and be welcomed by current Honors students. The Move-In Crew will help you ease into your dorm and get acclimated to campus, Bloomsburg, and the surrounding areas. Making immediate connections with experienced Honors students gives you an honest, inside perspective on classes, campus life, and prospective jobs after college. » Travel! — The Honors Program offers several trips for students every year. Honors students visit exciting places from other states to other countries. Expand your worldview and learn about other cultures. The Bloomsburg Honors Program plans annual trips to New York City in the fall and Washington D.C. in the spring. We are also trying to establish an annual service trip to Jamaica. **Disability Services offered to physically disabled students:** Note-taking services; Reader services; Tape recorders; Tutors. **Career services:** Alumni network; Career assessment; Career/job search classes; Internships

FACILITIES

Housing: Apartments for single students; Coed dorms; Other (please specify) 100% of campus accessible to physically disabled. **Special Academic Facilities/Equipment:** Art gallery, language lab, TV studio, radio station. **Computers:** 100% of classrooms, 100% of libraries, 100% of student union, 50% of common outdoor areas have wireless network access. Students can register for classes online. Administrative functions (other than registration) can be performed online.

CAMPUS LIFE

Environment: Village **Activities:** Campus Ministries; Choral groups; Concert band; Dance; Drama/theater; International Student Organization; Jazz band; Literary magazine; Marching band; Model UN; Music ensembles; Pep band; Radio station; Student government; Student newspaper; Symphony orchestra; Television station; Yearbook 195 registered organizations, 19 honor societies, 8 religious organizations. 15 fraternities, 13 sororities. **Athletics (Intercollegiate):** *Men:* baseball, basketball, cheerleading, cross-country, football, soccer, swimming, tennis, track/field (outdoor), track/field (indoor), wrestling. *Women:* basketball, cheerleading, cross-country, field hockey, lacrosse, soccer, softball, swimming, tennis, track/field (outdoor), track/field (indoor). **On-Campus Highlights:** Kehr Student Union, Dining Locations, Student Services Center, Recreation Center, Redman Stadium **Environmental Initiatives:** A kiosk was designed to educate the BU community about solar energy and the university's energy consumption using Lucid Design Group's Building Dashboard software. The project ultimately aims to develop energy-saving strategies for the university. The Building Dashboard touchscreen software will also allow users to take an in-depth look at energy use in five campus buildings: Hartline Science Center, Student Recreation Center, Nelson Field House, Columbia Residence Hall and Elwell Residence Hall. These buildings were chosen because they are popular with students or large consumers of energy.

ADMISSIONS

Freshman Academic Profile: Average high school GPA 3.3. 8% in top 10% of high school class, 29% in top 25% of high school class, 63% in top 50% of high school class. 87% from public high schools. **Test Scores:** SAT Math middle 50% range 480-570. SAT EBRW middle 50% range 490-580. ACT middle 50% range 19-24. Minimum internet-based TOEFL 65. Minimum paper TOEFL 500. **Basis for Candidate Selection:** *Very important factors considered include:* rigor of secondary school record, class rank, academic GPA, standardized test scores. *Other factors considered include:* application essay, recommendation(s), interview, extracurricular activities, talent/ability, character/personal qualities, geographical residence, state residency, volunteer work, work experience, level of applicant's interest. **Freshman Admission Requirements:** High school diploma is required and GED is accepted *Academic units required:* 4 English, 3 math, 3 science, 2 social studies, 2 history, 2 academic electives, and 2 units from above areas or other academic areas. *Academic units recommended:* 4 English, 4 math, 4 science, 2 foreign language, 2 social studies, 2 history, 2 academic electives, 1 computer science, 2 units from above areas or other academic areas. **Freshman Admission Statistics:** 9,683 applied, 73.3% admitted, 26% enrolled. **Transfer Admission Requirements:** High school transcript, college transcript(s), Minimum college GPA of 2.0 required. Lowest grade transferable C. **General Admission Information:** Application fee $35. Nonfall registration accepted. Admission may be deferred for a maximum of 1 year.

COSTS AND FINANCIAL AID

Annual in-state tuition $9,430. Annual out-of-state tuition $18,730. Room and board $9,430. Required fees $3,008. Average book expense $1,200. **Required Forms and Deadlines:** FAFSA. *Types of Aid: Need-based scholarships/grants:* College/university scholarship or grant aid from institutional funds; Federal Pell; Private scholarships; SEOG; State scholarships/grants. *Loans:* Direct PLUS loans; Direct Subsidized Stafford Loans; Direct Unsubsidized Stafford Loans. *Student Employment:* Federal Work-Study Program available. Institutional employment available. **Financial Aid Statistics:** 63% needy freshmen, 64% needy undergrads receive need-based scholarship or grant aid. 27% freshmen, 20% undergrads receive non-need-based scholarship or grant aid. 92% freshmen, 92% undergrads receive need-based self-help aid. 3% freshmen, 2% undergrads receive athletic scholarships. 84% undergrads receive any aid. **Criteria for awarding aid:** *Need-based:* Academics, Alumni affiliation, Leadership, Minority status *Non-need-based:* Academics, Art, Athletics, Job skills, Leadership, Minority status, Music/drama, State/district residency.

BLUE MOUNTAIN COLLEGE

PO Box 160, Blue Mountain, MS 38610
Phone: 662-685-4771 · **Financial Aid Phone:** 662-685-4771
E-mail: admissions@bmc.edu
Fax: 662-685-4776 · **Website:** bmc.edu

This private school, affiliated with the Baptist Church, was founded in 1873. It has a 44 acre campus.

RATINGS

Admissions Selectivity Rating: 88   **Fire Safety Rating:** 71   **Green Rating:** 60*

STUDENTS AND FACULTY

Enrollment: 406. **Student Body:** 64% female, 36% male, 12% out-of-state, <1% international (1 countries represented). Asian <1%, African American 12%, Caucasian 87%, Hispanic <1%, Native American 0%, Race unknown 0%. **Retention and Graduation:** 72% freshmen return for sophomore year. 14% grads go on to further study within 1 year. 14% grads pursue arts and sciences degrees. 0% grads pursue law degrees. 1% grads pursue business degrees. 2% grads pursue medical degrees. **Faculty:** Student/faculty ratio 13:1. 24 full-time faculty, 67% hold PhDs, 0% are members of minority groups, 54% are women. 0% of classes are taught by teaching assistants.

ACADEMICS

Degrees: Bachelor's; Master's **Classes:** Most classes have 20-29 students. Most lab/discussion sessions have 20-29 students. **Most popular majors:** Elementary Education And Teaching; Bible/Biblical Studies; Psychology, General. **Special Study Options:** Double major; Honors program; Internships; Teacher certification program. **Honors programs:** Academic Honors Program. **Disability Services offered to physically disabled students:** Note-taking services; Tutors.

FACILITIES

Housing: Men's dorms; Women's dorms 50% of campus accessible to physically diasbled.

CAMPUS LIFE

Environment: Rural **Activities:** Choral groups; Drama/theater; Literary magazine; Musical theater; Student government; Yearbook 28 registered organizations, 4 honor societies, 2 religious organizations. **Athletics (Intercollegiate):** *Women:* basketball, tennis. **On-Campus Highlights:** Johnnie Armstrong Gal-ry, Student Union Building, Tyler Gymnasium, Broach Hall, Fisher-Washburn Hall

ADMISSIONS

Freshman Academic Profile: Average high school GPA 3.3. 19% in top 10% of high school class, 50% in top 25% of high school class, 86% in top 50% of high school class. 73% from public high schools. **Test Scores:** ACT middle 50% range 18-23. Minimum paper TOEFL 500. **Basis for Candidate Selection:** *Important factors considered include:* rigor of secondary school record, class rank, academic GPA, standardized test scores. *Other factors considered include:* recommendation(s), character/personal qualities, alumni/ae relation. **Freshman Admission Requirements:** High school diploma is required and GED is accepted *Academic units required:* 4 English, 3 math, 3 science, 2 science labs, 2 foreign language, 1 social studies, 2 history, *Academic units recommended:* 4 English, 3 math, 3 science, 2 science labs, 2 foreign language, 1 social studies, 2 history. **Freshman Admission Statistics:** 146 applied, 46.6% admitted, 66% enrolled. **Transfer Admission Requirements:** college transcript(s), Lowest grade transferable C. **General Admission Information:** Application fee $10. Nonfall registration accepted. Admission may be deferred.

COSTS AND FINANCIAL AID

Annual tuition $6,900. Room and board $3,766. Required fees $540. Average book expense $650. **Required Forms and Deadlines:** FAFSA; Institution's own financial aid form. **Notification of Awards:** Applicants will be notified of awards on a rolling basis beginning 4/1. **Types of Aid:** *Need-based scholarships/grants:* Federal Pell; Private scholarships; SEOG; State scholarships/grants. *Student Employment:* Federal Work-Study Program available. Institutional employment available. **Financial Aid Statistics:** 81% needy freshmen, 64% needy undergrads receive need-based scholarship or grant aid. 81% freshmen, 100% undergrads receive non-need-based scholarship or grant aid. 62% freshmen, 18% undergrads receive need-based self-help aid. 8% freshmen, 6% undergrads receive athletic scholarships. 95% freshmen, 96% undergrads receive any aid. **Criteria for awarding aid:** *Need-based:* Alumni affiliation *Non-need-based:* Academics, Alumni affiliation, Athletics, Religious affiliation, State/district residency.

BLUFFTON UNIVERSITY

1 University Drive, Bluffton, OH 45817
Phone: 419-358-3257 · **Financial Aid Phone:** (419) 358-3409
E-mail: admissions@bluffton.edu · **CEEB Code:** 1067
Fax: 419-358-3081 · **Website:** www.bluffton.edu · **ACT Code:** 3238

This private school, affiliated with the Mennonite Church, was founded in 1899. It has a 65 acre campus.

RATINGS

Admissions Selectivity Rating: 83   **Fire Safety Rating:** 60*   **Green Rating:** 60*

STUDENTS AND FACULTY

Enrollment: 833. **Student Body:** 51% female, 49% male, 12% out-of-state, <1% international. Asian <1%, African American 6%, Caucasian 85%, Hispanic 4%, Native American 0%, Pacific Islander 0%, Two or more races 3%, Race unknown 2%. **Retention and Graduation:** 72% freshmen return for sophomore year. **Faculty:** Student/faculty ratio 12:1. 56 full-time faculty, 80% hold PhDs, 2% are members of minority groups, 39% are women. 0% of classes are taught by teaching assistants.

ACADEMICS

Degrees: Bachelor's; Master's; Post-Bachelor's certificate **Classes:** Most classes have 10-19 students. Most lab/discussion sessions have 10-19 students. **Most popular majors:** Early Childhood Education And Teaching; Social Work; Business Administration And Management, General. **Special Study Options:** Accelerated program; Distance learning; Double major; Dual enrollment; English as a Second Language (ESL); Honors program; Independent study; Internships; Student-designed major; Study abroad; Teacher certification program. **Disability Services offered to physically disabled students:** Note-taking services; Reader services; Tape recorders; Tutors. **Career services:** Alumni services; Career/job search classes

FACILITIES

Housing: Coed dorms; Men's dorms; Women's dorms 99% of campus accessible to physically diasbled. **Special Academic Facilities/Equipment:** Mennonite historical library, peace arts center, nature preserve.

CAMPUS LIFE

Environment: Rural **Activities:** Campus Ministries; Choral groups; Drama/theater; International Student Organization; Music ensembles; Pep band; Radio station; Student government; Student newspaper 50 registered organizations, 19 honor societies, 10 religious organizations. **Athletics (Intercollegiate):** *Men:* baseball, basketball, cheerleading, cross-country, football, golf, soccer, tennis, track/field (outdoor), track/field (indoor). *Women:* basketball, cheerleading, cross-country, golf, soccer, softball, tennis, track/field (outdoor), track/field (indoor), volleyball. **On-Campus Highlights:** Centennial Hall-academic center, Marbeck Center-student union, College Hall-administrative/classroom building, Salzman Stadium-Football Stadium, Founders Hall-gymnasium

ADMISSIONS

Freshman Academic Profile: Average high school GPA 3.2. 12% in top 10% of high school class, 25% in top 25% of high school class, 67% in top 50% of high school class. 98% from public high schools. **Test Scores:** SAT Math middle 50% range 430-560. SAT EBRW middle 50% range 410-580. ACT middle 50% range 18-23. Minimum paper TOEFL 500. **Basis for Candidate Selection:** *Very important factors considered include:* class rank, academic GPA, standardized test scores. *Other factors considered include:* interview, extracurricular activities, talent/ability, character/personal qualities. **Freshman Admission Requirements:** High school diploma is required and GED is accepted *Academic units recommended:* 4 English, 3 math, 3 science, 3 foreign language, 3 social studies. **Freshman Admission Statistics:** 1,652 applied, 53.6% admitted, 25% enrolled. **Transfer Admission Requirements:** High school transcript, college transcript(s), statement of good standing from prior institution(s). Minimum college GPA of 2.0 required. Lowest grade transferable C-. **General Admission Information:** Application fee $20. Nonfall registration accepted. Admission may be deferred for a maximum of 2 years.

COSTS AND FINANCIAL AID

Required Forms and Deadlines: FAFSA. **Notification of Awards:** Applicants will be notified of awards on a rolling basis beginning 3/1. **Types of Aid:** *Need-based scholarships/grants:* Federal Pell; Private scholarships; SEOG; State scholarships/grants. *Loans:* Direct PLUS loans; Direct Subsidized Stafford Loans; Direct Unsubsidized Stafford Loans. *Student Employment:* Federal Work-Study Program available. Institutional employment available. **Financial Aid Statistics:** 99% needy freshmen, 99% needy undergrads receive need-based scholarship or grant aid. 11% freshmen, 11% undergrads receive non-need-based scholarship or grant aid. 91% freshmen, 90% undergrads receive need-based self-help aid. 0% freshmen, 0% undergrads receive athletic scholarships. **Criteria for awarding aid:** *Need-based:* Job skills *Non-need-based:* Academics, Art, Job skills, Minority status, Music/drama, Religious affiliation, State/district residency.

BOB JONES UNIVERSITY

1700 Wade Hampton Blvd, Greenville, SC 29614
Phone: 800-252-6363 • **Financial Aid Phone:** 864-242-5100 Ext 3040
E-mail: admission@bju.edu • **CEEB Code:** 5065
Fax: 800-232-9258 • **Website:** www.bju.edu • **ACT Code:** 3836

This private school, affiliated with the Evangelical Christian Church, was founded in 1927. It has a 225 acre campus.

RATINGS
Admissions Selectivity Rating: 79   **Fire Safety Rating:** 87   **Green Rating:** 60*

STUDENTS AND FACULTY
Enrollment: 2,371. **Student Body:** 55% female, 45% male, 68% out-of-state, 7% international (45 countries represented). Asian 2%, African American 2%, Caucasian 77%, Hispanic 6%, Native American <1%, Pacific Islander 1%, Two or more races 3%, Race unknown 2%.
Retention and Graduation: 82% freshmen return for sophomore year. 68% freshmen graduate within 6 years. 23% grads go on to further study within 1 year. **Faculty:** Student/faculty ratio 13:1. 186 full-time faculty, 66% hold PhDs, 5% are members of minority groups, 37% are women. 1% of classes are taught by teaching assistants.

ACADEMICS
Degrees: Associate; Bachelor's; Doctoral; Doctoral/Professional; Master's. **Classes:** Most classes have 20-29 students. **Most popular majors:** Registered Nursing/Registered Nurse; Business Administration And Management, General; Accounting. **Special Study Options:** Distance learning; Double major; Dual enrollment; English as a Second Language (ESL); Internships; Liberal arts/career combination; Student-designed major; Teacher certification program. **Disability Services offered to physically disabled students:** Note-taking services; Reader services; Tape recorders; Tutors. **Career services:** Alumni services; Career assessment; Career/job search classes; Internships.

FACILITIES
Housing: Men's dorms; Special housing for disabled student; Women's dorms 90% of campus accessible to physically diasbled. **Special Academic Facilities/Equipment:** Alumni Building, Alumni Stadium, BJU Museum & Gallery, Davis Field House, Fremont Fitness Center, Founder's Memorial Amphitorium, Grace Haight Nursing Building, Gustafson Fine Arts Center, Howell Memorial Science Building, Performance Hall, Rodeheaver Auditorium, Sargent Art Building, Bob Jones Jr. Memorial Seminary and Graduate School of Religion, Stratton Hall, Student Center, War Memorial Chapel **Computers:** 85% of classrooms, 100% of dorms, 100% of libraries, 20% of dining areas, 100% of student union, 70% of common outdoor areas have wireless network access. Students can register for classes online. Administrative functions (other than registration) can be performed online.

CAMPUS LIFE
Environment: City **Activities:** Campus Ministries; Choral groups; Concert band; Drama/theater; International Student Organization; Music ensembles; Opera; Pep band; Radio station; Student government; Student newspaper; Symphony orchestra; Television station; Yearbook 31 registered organizations, 18 religious organizations. **On-Campus Highlights:** University Student Center, Davis Field House, Cuppa Jones (coffee shop)

ADMISSIONS
Freshman Academic Profile: Average high school GPA 3.2. 13% in top 10% of high school class, 35% in top 25% of high school class, 62% in top 50% of high school class. 4% from public high schools. **Test Scores:** ACT middle 50% range 20-27. Minimum internet-based TOEFL 61. Minimum paper TOEFL 500. **Basis for Candidate Selection:** *Very important factors considered include:* character/personal qualities, religious affiliation/commitment. *Important factors considered include:* recommendation(s). *Other factors considered include:* rigor of secondary school record, class rank, academic GPA, application essay, standardized test scores, extracurricular activities, talent/ability, volunteer work, level of applicant's interest. **Freshman Admission Requirements:** High school diploma is required and GED is accepted *Academic units required:* 3 English, 2 math, 1 science, 2 social studies, 6 academic electives, *Academic units recommended:* 2 foreign language. **Freshman Admission Statistics:** 1,062 applied, 86.2% admitted, 65% enrolled. **Transfer Admission Requirements:** college transcript(s), Minimum college GPA of 2.0 required. Lowest grade transferable D-. **General Admission Information:** Nonfall registration accepted. Admission may be deferred for a maximum of One year.

COSTS AND FINANCIAL AID
Annual tuition $17,250. Room and board $6,976. Required fees $900. Average book expense $1,200. **Required Forms and Deadlines:** FAFSA. **Notification of Awards:** Applicants will be notified of awards on a rolling basis beginning 4/1. **Types of Aid:** *Need-based scholarships/grants:* College/university scholarship or grant aid from institutional funds; Federal Pell; Private scholarships; SEOG; State scholarships/grants. *Loans:* Direct PLUS loans; Direct Subsidized Stafford Loans; Direct Unsubsidized Stafford Loans. *Student Employment:* Federal Work-Study Program available. Institutional employment available. **Financial Aid Statistics:** 100% needy undergrads receive need-based scholarship or grant aid. 39% undergrads receive non-need-based scholarship or grant aid. 58% undergrads receive need-based self-help aid. 0% undergrads receive athletic scholarships. 60% freshmen, 61% undergrads receive any aid. **Criteria for awarding aid:** *Need-based:* Academics, Alumni affiliation, Leadership *Non-need-based:* State/district residency.

BOISE STATE UNIVERSITY

1910 University Drive, Boise, ID 83725
Phone: 208-426-1156 • **Financial Aid Phone:** 208-426-1664
E-mail: bsuinfo@boisestate.edu • **CEEB Code:** 4018
Fax: 208-426-3765 • **Website:** www.boisestate.edu • **ACT Code:** 914

This public school was founded in 1932. It has a 286 acre campus.

RATINGS
Admissions Selectivity Rating: 75   **Fire Safety Rating:** 65   **Green Rating:** 62

STUDENTS AND FACULTY
Enrollment: 16,270. **Student Body:** 55% female, 45% male, 31% out-of-state, 2% international. Asian 2%, African American 2%, Caucasian 74%, Hispanic 13%, Native American <1%, Pacific Islander <1%, Two or more races 5%, Race unknown 1%.
Retention and Graduation: 80% freshmen return for sophomore year. **Faculty:** Student/faculty ratio 17:1. 757 full-time faculty, 72% hold PhDs, 11% are members of minority groups, 48% are women.

ACADEMICS
Degrees: Associate; Bachelor's; Certificate; Doctoral/Research; Master's; Post-Bachelor's certificate; Terminal Associate **Classes:** Most classes have 20-29 students. Most lab/discussion sessions have 20-29 students. **Most popular majors:** Speech Communication And Rhetoric; Registered Nursing/Registered Nurse; Business/Commerce, General. **Special Study Options:** Distance learning; Double major; Dual enrollment; Exchange student program (domestic); Honors program; Independent study; Internships; Student-designed major; Study abroad; Teacher certification program; Weekend college. **Disability Services offered to physically disabled students:** Note-taking services; Reader services; Tape recorders; Tutors. **Career services:** Alumni network; Alumni services; Career assessment; Career/job search classes; Internships

FACILITIES
Housing: Apartments for married students; Apartments for single students; Coed dorms; Other (please specify) 95% of campus accessible to physically diasbled. **Computers:** Students can register for classes online. Administrative functions (other than registration) can be performed online.

CAMPUS LIFE
Environment: City **Activities:** Choral groups; Concert band; Dance; Drama/theater; International Student Organization; Jazz band; Literary magazine; Marching band; Music ensembles; Musical theater; Pep band; Radio station; Student government; Student newspaper; Student-run film society; Symphony orchestra 180 registered organizations, 4 fraternities, 3 sororities. **Athletics (Intercollegiate):** *Men:* basketball, cheerleading, cross-country, football, golf, tennis, track/field (outdoor), track/field (indoor), wrestling. *Women:* basketball, cheerleading, cross-country, golf, gymnastics, skiing (downhill/alpine), soccer, tennis, track/field (outdoor), track/field (indoor), volleyball. Student Union Building, Albertson's Stadium, Albertson's Library, Velma V. Morrison Center, Allen Noble Hall of Fame

ADMISSIONS
Freshman Academic Profile: Average high school GPA 3.5. 15% in top 10% of high school class, 39% in top 25% of high school class, 75% in top 50% of high school class. **Test Scores:** SAT Math middle 50% range 470-580. SAT EBRW middle 50% range 470-580. ACT middle 50% range 21-26. Minimum paper TOEFL 500. **Basis for Candidate Selection:** *Other factors considered*

include: academic GPA, standardized test scores. **Freshman Admission Requirements:** High school diploma is required and GED is accepted *Academic units recommended:* 8 English, 6 math, 6 science, 2 science labs, 2 foreign language, 5 social studies, 3 units from above areas or other academic areas. **Freshman Admission Statistics:** 8,876 applied, 84.0% admitted, 37% enrolled. **Transfer Admission Requirements:** college transcript(s), Minimum college GPA of 2.0 required. Lowest grade transferable c. **General Admission Information:** Application fee $50. Regular application deadline 5/15. Nonfall registration accepted. Admission may be deferred.

COSTS AND FINANCIAL AID
Required Forms and Deadlines: FAFSA. **Notification of Awards:** Applicants will be notified of awards on a rolling basis beginning 3/15. **Types of Aid:** *Need-based scholarships/grants:* College/university scholarship or grant aid from institutional funds; Federal Nursing Scholarships; Federal Pell; Private scholarships; SEOG; State scholarships/grants. *Loans:* Direct PLUS loans; Direct Subsidized Stafford Loans; Direct Unsubsidized Stafford Loans. *Student Employment:* Federal Work-Study Program available. Institutional employment available. **Financial Aid Statistics:** 73% needy freshmen, 75% needy undergrads receive need-based scholarship or grant aid. 7% freshmen, 3% undergrads receive non-need-based scholarship or grant aid. 72% freshmen, 82% undergrads receive need-based self-help aid. 1% freshmen, 1% undergrads receive athletic scholarships. 70% freshmen, 80% undergrads receive any aid. 79% undergrads borrow to pay for school. Average cumulative indebtedness $26,772. **Criteria for awarding aid:** *Need-based:* Athletics, Music/drama *Non-need-based:* Academics, Alumni affiliation, Art, Athletics, Music/drama.

BOSTON COLLEGE

140 Commonwealth Avenue, Chestnut Hill, MA 02467-3809
Phone: 617-552-3100 • **Financial Aid Phone:** 617-552-3300 • **CEEB Code:** 3083
Fax: 617-552-0798 • **Website:** www.bc.edu • **ACT Code:** 1788

This private school, affiliated with the Roman Catholic Church, was founded in 1863. It has a 227 acre campus.

RATINGS
Admissions Selectivity Rating: 95   **Fire Safety Rating:** 98   **Green Rating:** 76

STUDENTS AND FACULTY
Enrollment: 9,358. **Student Body:** 53% female, 47% male, 74% out-of-state, 7% international (68 countries represented). Asian 10%, African American 4%, Caucasian 62%, Hispanic 11%, Native American <1%, Pacific Islander <1%, Two or more races 3%, Race unknown 4%.

Retention and Graduation: 95% freshmen return for sophomore year. 93% freshmen graduate within 6 years. 18% grads go on to further study within 1 year. 3% grads pursue arts and sciences degrees. 1.9% grads pursue law degrees. 3% grads pursue business degrees. 1.6% grads pursue medical degrees. **Faculty:** Student/faculty ratio 12:1. 821 full-time faculty, 94% hold PhDs, 17% are members of minority groups, 41% are women.

ACADEMICS
Degrees: Bachelor's; Doctoral; Doctoral Other; Doctoral/Professional; Doctoral/Research; Master's; Post-Master's certificate **Classes:** Most classes have 20-29 students. Most lab/discussion sessions have 20-29 students. **Most popular majors:** Communication And Media Studies, Other; Economics, General; Finance, General. **Special Study Options:** Accelerated program; Cross-registration; Distance learning; Double major; English as a Second Language (ESL); Exchange student program (domestic); Honors program; Independent study; Internships; Liberal arts/career combination; Student-designed major; Study abroad; Teacher certification program. **Honors programs:** In addition to BC's Presidential Scholars Program, each Undergraduate College hosts an Honors Program, and most academic Departments also offer a Departmental Honors program. **Combined degree programs:** BA/MA; BA/MD. **Disability Services offered to physically disabled students:** Note-taking services; Reader services; Tape recorders; Tutors. **Career services:** Alumni network; Alumni services; Career assessment; Career/job search classes; Internships; Regional alumni

FACILITIES
Housing: Apartments for single students; Coed dorms; Special housing for disabled student; Wellness housing; Women's dorms 95% of campus accessible

to physically disabled. **Special Academic Facilities/Equipment:** BC opened a new dorm and remodeled Art Museum in 2016. A new academic & classroom building opened in the Fall 2012, and a new recreation complex and field house started construction in 2017. BC also features a theatre arts center, state-of-the-art science facilities, and on-campus school for multihandicapped students. **Computers:** 100% of classrooms, 100% of dorms, 100% of libraries, 100% of dining areas, 100% of student union, 100% of common outdoor areas have wireless network access. Students can register for classes online. Administrative functions (other than registration) can be performed online.

CAMPUS LIFE
Environment: City **Activities:** Campus Ministries; Choral groups; Concert band; Dance; Drama/theater; International Student Organization; Jazz band; Literary magazine; Marching band; Music ensembles; Musical theater; Pep band; Radio station; Student government; Student newspaper; Student-run film society; Symphony orchestra; Television station; Yearbook 225 registered organizations, 12 honor societies, 14 religious organizations. **Athletics (Intercollegiate): Men:** baseball, basketball, cross-country, diving, fencing, football, golf, ice hockey, lacrosse, sailing, skiing (downhill/alpine), soccer, swimming, tennis, track/field (outdoor), track/field (indoor). *Women:* basketball, crew/rowing, cross-country, diving, fencing, field hockey, golf, ice hockey, lacrosse, sailing, skiing (downhill/alpine), soccer, softball, swimming, tennis, track/field (outdoor), track/field (indoor), volleyball. **On-Campus Highlights:** McMullen Museum of Art, Alumni Stadium/Conte Forum, Robsham Theater, Bapst Library, McElroy Commons/Bookstore **Environmental Initiatives:** Green Building Commitment—New Buildings to be LEED Silver, minimum.

ADMISSIONS
Freshman Academic Profile: 78% in top 10% of high school class, 95% in top 25% of high school class, 99% in top 50% of high school class. 48% from public high schools. **Test Scores:** SAT Math middle 50% range 660-730. SAT EBRW middle 50% range 660-760. ACT middle 50% range 31-33. Minimum internet-based TOEFL 100. Minimum paper TOEFL 600. **Basis for Candidate Selection:** *Very important factors considered include:* rigor of secondary school record, academic GPA, standardized test scores. *Important factors considered include:* class rank, application essay, recommendation(s), extracurricular activities, talent/ability, character/personal qualities, alumni/ae relation, religious affiliation/commitment, volunteer work. *Other factors considered include:* first generation, racial/ethnic status, work experience. **Freshman Admission Requirements:** High school diploma is required and GED is accepted *Academic units recommended:* 4 English, 4 math, 4 science, 4 science labs, 4 foreign language, 4 social studies, 4 history. **Freshman Admission Statistics:** 28,454 applied, 32.4% admitted, 26% enrolled. **Transfer Admission Requirements:** High school transcript, college transcript(s), essay or personal statement, standardized test scores, statement of good standing from prior institution(s). Minimum college GPA of 3.0 required. Lowest grade transferable C. **General Admission Information:** Application fee $80. Regular application deadline 1/1. Nonfall registration accepted. Admission may be deferred for a maximum of 2 years.

COSTS AND FINANCIAL AID
Annual tuition $52,500. Room and board $14,142. Required fees $846. Average book expense $1,250. **Required Forms and Deadlines:** Business/Farm Supplement; CSS/Financial Aid PROFILE; FAFSA; Noncustodial PROFILE. **Notification of Awards:** Applicants will be notified of awards on or about 4/1. **Types of Aid:** *Need-based scholarships/grants:* College/university scholarship or grant aid from institutional funds; Federal Pell; Private scholarships; SEOG; State scholarships/grants. *Loans:* Direct PLUS loans; Direct Subsidized Stafford Loans; Direct Unsubsidized Stafford Loans. *Student Employment:* Federal Work-Study Program available. Institutional employment available. **Financial Aid Statistics:** 88% needy freshmen, 88% needy undergrads receive need-based scholarship or grant aid. 3% freshmen, 2% undergrads receive non-need-based scholarship or grant aid. 92% freshmen, 92% undergrads receive need-based self-help aid. 3% freshmen, 3% undergrads receive athletic scholarships. 63% freshmen, 66% undergrads receive any aid. 49% undergrads borrow to pay for school. Average cumulative indebtedness $20,849. **Criteria for awarding aid:** *Need-based:* Academics *Non-need-based:* Academics, Athletics, Leadership.

BOSTON CONSERVATORY

8 The Fenway, Boston, MA 02215
Phone: 617-912-9153
E-mail: admissions@bostonconservatory.edu · **CEEB Code:** 3084
Fax: 617-247-3159 · **Website:** www.bostonconservatory.edu · **ACT Code:** 1790

This private school was founded in 1867.

RATINGS
Admissions Selectivity Rating: 71   **Fire Safety Rating:** 60*   **Green Rating:** 60*

STUDENTS AND FACULTY
Enrollment: 565. **Student Body:** 63% female, 37% male, 60% out-of-state, 9% international (26 countries represented). Asian 2%, African American 4%, Caucasian 50%, Hispanic 9%, Native American 0%, Pacific Islander 0%, Two or more races 2%, Race unknown 25%.
Faculty: Student/faculty ratio 4:1. 74 full-time faculty, 0% of classes are taught by teaching assistants.

ACADEMICS
Degrees: Bachelor's; Master's; Post-Bachelor's certificate; Post-Master's certificate **Classes:** Most classes have 10-19 students. Most lab/discussion sessions have 10-19 students. **Special Study Options:** Cross-registration; Double major; English as a Second Language (ESL); Independent study; Teacher certification program. **Career services:** Alumni services; Career assessment; Career/job search classes; Internships

FACILITIES
Housing: Coed dorms; Women's dorms

CAMPUS LIFE
Activities: International Student Organization; Literary magazine; Student government; Student newspaper 11 registered organizations, 1 honor society, 1 religious organization.

ADMISSIONS
Freshman Academic Profile: 90% from public high schools. **Basis for Candidate Selection:** *Very important factors considered include:* recommendation(s), talent/ability, character/personal qualities. *Important factors considered include:* rigor of secondary school record, class rank, academic GPA, application essay, level of applicant's interest. *Other factors considered include:* interview, extracurricular activities. **Freshman Admission Requirements:** High school diploma is required and GED is accepted *Academic units required:* 4 English, 3 math, 2 science, 2 foreign language, 2 social studies, 2 history. **Freshman Admission Statistics:** 1,216 applied, 45.9% admitted, 33% enrolled. **Transfer Admission Requirements:** High school transcript, college transcript(s), essay or personal statement, Minimum college GPA of 2.5 required. Lowest grade transferable C. **General Admission Information:** Application fee $110. Priority deadline 12/15. Nonfall registration accepted. Admission may be deferred.

COSTS AND FINANCIAL AID
Required Forms and Deadlines: FAFSA. **Notification of Awards:** Applicants will be notified of awards on or about 4/1. **Types of Aid:** *Need-based scholarships/grants:* College/university scholarship or grant aid from institutional funds; Federal Pell; Private scholarships; SEOG; State scholarships/grants. *Loans:* Direct PLUS loans; Direct Subsidized Stafford Loans; Direct Unsubsidized Stafford Loans. *Student Employment:* Federal Work-Study Program available. Institutional employment available. **Financial Aid Statistics:** 75% needy freshmen, 90% needy undergrads receive need-based scholarship or grant aid. 10% freshmen, 7% undergrads receive non-need-based scholarship or grant aid. 90% freshmen, 78% undergrads receive need-based self-help aid. 0% freshmen, 0% undergrads receive athletic scholarships. 61% undergrads borrow to pay for school. Average cumulative indebtedness $49,000. **Criteria for awarding aid:** *Need-based:* Music/drama *Non-need-based:* Music/drama.

BOSTON UNIVERSITY

One Silber Way, Boston, MA 02215
Phone: 617-353-2300 · **Financial Aid Phone:** 617-353-4176
E-mail: admissions@bu.edu; intadmis@bu.edu · **CEEB Code:** 3087
Fax: 617-353-9695 · **Website:** www.bu.edu · **ACT Code:** 1794

This private school was founded in 1839. It has a 134 acre campus.

RATINGS
Admissions Selectivity Rating: 96   **Fire Safety Rating:** 85   **Green Rating:** 87

STUDENTS AND FACULTY
Enrollment: 16,716. **Student Body:** 61% female, 39% male, 80% out-of-state, 22% international (118 countries represented). Asian 15%, African American 4%, Caucasian 40%, Hispanic 12%, Native American <1%, Pacific Islander <1%, Two or more races 4%, Race unknown 4%.
Retention and Graduation: 93% freshmen return for sophomore year. 81% freshmen graduate within 4 years. 87% freshmen graduate within 6 years.
Faculty: Student/faculty ratio 10:1. 1,839 full-time faculty, 89% hold PhDs, 15% are members of minority groups, 42% are women. 6% of classes are taught by teaching assistants.

ACADEMICS
Degrees: Bachelor's; Certificate; Doctoral/Professional; Doctoral/Research; Master's; Post-Bachelor's certificate; Post-Master's certificate **Classes:** Most classes have 10-19 students. Most lab/discussion sessions have 10-19 students. **Most popular majors:** Communication, General; Psychology, General; Business Administration And Management, General. **Special Study Options:** Accelerated program; Cooperative education program; Cross-registration; Distance learning; Double major; Dual enrollment; English as a Second Language (ESL); Exchange student program (domestic); Honors program; Internships; Liberal arts/career combination; Student-designed major; Study abroad; Teacher certification program; Weekend college. **Honors programs:** Kilachand Honors College for undergraduates, Questrom School of Business Honors Program, CAS Honors in the Major Program **Combined degree programs:** BA/MA; BA/MD. **Disability Services offered to physically disabled students:** Note-taking services; Reader services; Tape recorders; Tutors. **Career services:** Career assessment; Career/job search classes; Internships

FACILITIES
Housing: Apartments for single students; Coed dorms; Cooperative housing; Special housing for disabled student; Theme housing; Wellness housing; Women's dorms 95% of campus accessible to physically diasbled. **Special Academic Facilities/Equipment:** Center for Computational Science, Center for Advanced Biotechnology, Center for Photonics Research, art galleries, planetarium, commercial TV station, National Public Radio station, 20th century archives, professional theatre and theatre company, Center for Remote Sensing, Geddes Language Laboratory, speech, language and hearing clinic, Culinary Center, Metcalf Center for Science and Engineering, Tsai Performance Center, College of Communication Multimedia Lab, Engineering Product Innovation Center (EPIC), Joan & Edgar Booth Theatre, BUildLab student innovation center, Kilachand Center for Integrated Life Sciences & Engineering, and Yawkey Center for Student Services **Computers:** Students can register for classes online. Administrative functions (other than registration) can be performed online.

CAMPUS LIFE
Environment: Metropolis **Activities:** Campus Ministries; Choral groups; Concert band; Dance; Drama/theater; International Student Organization; Jazz band; Literary magazine; Marching band; Model UN; Music ensembles; Musical theater; Opera; Pep band; Radio station; Student government; Student newspaper; Student-run film society; Symphony orchestra; Television station; Yearbook 400 registered organizations, 11 honor societies, 26 religious organizations. 9 fraternities, 9 sororities. **Athletics (Intercollegiate):** *Men:* basketball, crew/rowing, cross-country, diving, golf, ice hockey, soccer, swimming, tennis, track/field (outdoor), track/field (indoor), wrestling. *Women:* basketball, crew/rowing, cross-country, diving, field hockey, golf, ice hockey, lacrosse, soccer, softball, swimming, tennis, track/field (outdoor), track/field (indoor). **On-Campus Highlights:** George Sherman Student Union, Yawkey Center for Student Services, Build Lab Student Innovation Center, Joan & Edgar Booth Theatre & BU Production Center, Fitness and Recreation Center **Environmental Initiatives:** Energy Efficiency Retrofits http://www.bu.edu/facilities/what-we-do/energy/

ADMISSIONS

Freshman Academic Profile: Average high school GPA 3.7. 62% in top 10% of high school class, 92% in top 25% of high school class, 99% in top 50% of high school class. 63% from public high schools. **Test Scores:** SAT Math middle 50% range 660-760. SAT EBRW middle 50% range 640-720. ACT middle 50% range 29-32. Minimum internet-based TOEFL 90-100. **Basis for Candidate Selection:** *Very important factors considered include:* rigor of secondary school record. *Important factors considered include:* class rank, academic GPA, application essay, standardized test scores, recommendation(s), extracurricular activities, character/personal qualities, alumni/ae relation, level of applicant's interest. *Other factors considered include:* first generation, geographical residence, state residency, racial/ethnic status, volunteer work, work experience. **Freshman Admission Requirements:** High school diploma is required and GED is accepted *Academic units required:* 4 English, 3 math, 3 science, 3 science labs, 2 foreign language, 3 social studies, 3 history, *Academic units recommended:* 4 English, 4 math, 4 science, 4 science labs, 4 foreign language, 4 social studies, 4 history. **Freshman Admission Statistics:** 60,825 applied, 25.1% admitted, 23% enrolled. **Transfer Admission Requirements:** High school transcript, college transcript(s), essay or personal statement, standardized test scores, statement of good standing from prior institution(s). Minimum college GPA of 3.5 required. Lowest grade transferable C. **General Admission Information:** Application fee $80. Priority deadline 11/1. Regular application deadline 1/2. Nonfall registration accepted. Admission may be deferred for a maximum of 1 year.

COSTS AND FINANCIAL AID

Annual tuition $50,980. Room and board $15,270. Required fees $1,102. Average book expense $1,000. **Required Forms and Deadlines:** CSS/Financial Aid PROFILE; FAFSA; Noncustodial PROFILE. **Notification of Awards:** Applicants will be notified of awards on a rolling basis beginning 4/1. **Types of Aid:** *Need-based scholarships/grants:* College/university scholarship or grant aid from institutional funds; Federal Pell; Private scholarships; SEOG; State scholarships/grants. *Loans:* Direct PLUS loans; Direct Subsidized Stafford Loans; Direct Unsubsidized Stafford Loans. *Student Employment:* Federal Work-Study Program available. Institutional employment available. **Financial Aid Statistics:** 100% needy freshmen, 99% needy undergrads receive need-based scholarship or grant aid. 11% freshmen, 7% undergrads receive non-need-based scholarship or grant aid. 88% freshmen, 89% undergrads receive need-based self-help aid. 2% freshmen, 2% undergrads receive athletic scholarships. 54% freshmen, 54% undergrads receive any aid. 51% undergrads borrow to pay for school. Average cumulative indebtedness $41,098. **Criteria for awarding aid:** *Need-based:* Academics, Alumni affiliation, Art, Leadership, Minority status, Music/drama, Religious affiliation *Non-need-based:* Academics, Alumni affiliation, Art, Athletics, Leadership, Music/drama, Religious affiliation, State/district residency.

See page 904.

BOWDOIN COLLEGE

255 Maine Street, Brunswick, ME 04011-8441
Phone: 207-725-3100 · **Financial Aid Phone:** (207) 725-3146
E-mail: admissions@bowdoin.edu · **CEEB Code:** 3089
Fax: 207-725-3101 · **Website:** www.bowdoin.edu · **ACT Code:** 1636

This private school was founded in 1794. It has a 207 acre campus.

RATINGS

Admissions Selectivity Rating: 98 **Fire Safety Rating:** 96 **Green Rating:** 91

STUDENTS AND FACULTY

Enrollment: 1,812. **Student Body:** 50% female, 50% male, 89% out-of-state, 5% international (35 countries represented). Asian 7%, African American 6%, Caucasian 62%, Hispanic 11%, Native American <1%, Pacific Islander <1%, Two or more races 7%, Race unknown 1%.
Retention and Graduation: 96% freshmen return for sophomore year. 91% freshmen graduate within 4 years. 95% freshmen graduate within 6 years. 16% grads go on to further study within 1 year. 11% grads pursue arts and sciences degrees. 0% grads pursue law degrees. 0% grads pursue business degrees. 2% grads pursue medical degrees. **Faculty:** Student/faculty ratio 9:1. 194 full-time faculty, 99% hold PhDs, 15% are members of minority groups, 54% are women. 0% of classes are taught by teaching assistants.

ACADEMICS

Degrees: Bachelor's **Classes:** Most classes have fewer than 10 students. **Most popular majors:** Mathematics, General; Economics, General; Political Science And Government, General. **Special Study Options:** Accelerated program; Double major; Exchange student program (domestic); Independent study; Liberal arts/career combination; Student-designed major; Study abroad; Teacher certification program. **Combined degree programs:** BA/JD; BA/MEng. **Disability Services offered to physically disabled students:** Note-taking services; Reader services; Tape recorders; Tutors. **Career services:** Alumni network; Alumni services; Career assessment; Career/job search classes; Internships; Regional alumni

FACILITIES

Housing: Apartments for single students; Coed dorms; Special housing for disabled student; Wellness housing 72% of campus accessible to physically disabled. **Special Academic Facilities/Equipment:** Bowdoin College Museum of Art; Peary-MacMillan Arctic Museum and Arctic Studies Center; Edwards Center for Art and Dance; coastal marine biology and ornithology research facility on Orr's Island; scientific station on Kent Island; Wish Theater (black box); Pickard Theater; Baldwin Program for Academic Development; Outdoor Leadership Center; Crafts Center; eight specialized libraries, including the Language Media Center; Quantitative Reasoning Program; The Writing Project; Gibson Hall of Music; Studzinski Recital Hall; Educational Technology Center; Media Commons and Telepresence Room; Environmental Studies Center; Russwurm African-American Center; Women's Resource Center; Off-Campus Study Office; Office of Health Professions Advising; Pre-Law Advising Office; McKeen Center for the Common Good; Electronic Classroom; Recording Studio; and Druckenmiller Hall, Bowdoin's science center. **Computers:** 100% of classrooms, 100% of dorms, 100% of libraries, 100% of dining areas, 100% of student union, 100% of common outdoor areas have wireless network access. Administrative functions (other than registration) can be performed online.

CAMPUS LIFE

Environment: Village **Activities:** Choral groups; Concert band; Dance; Drama/theater; International Student Organization; Jazz band; Literary magazine; Model UN; Music ensembles; Musical theater; Radio station; Student government; Student newspaper; Student-run film society; Symphony orchestra 109 registered organizations, 1 honor society, 4 religious organizations. **Athletics (Intercollegiate):** *Men:* baseball, basketball, cross-country, diving, football, golf, ice hockey, lacrosse, sailing, skiing (nordic/cross-country), soccer, squash, swimming, tennis, track/field (outdoor), track/field (indoor). *Women:* basketball, cross-country, diving, field hockey, golf, ice hockey, lacrosse, rugby, sailing, skiing (nordic/cross-country), soccer, softball, squash, swimming, tennis, track/field (outdoor), track/field (indoor), volleyball. **On-Campus Highlights:** Bowdoin College Museum of Art, Peter Buck Center for Health and Fitness, David Saul Smith Union, Schwartz Outdoor Leadership Center, The Edwards Center for Art and Dance **Environmental Initiatives:** Bowdoin has committed to becoming a carbon-neutral campus by 2020 and provided a detailed Climate Action Plan to help achieve the goal. As part of this plan, Bowdoin installed a co-generation system at its campus steam plant, along with a 1,920-square-foot solar hot water system, and most recently installed a 1.2-megawatt solar power complex that went live in fall 2014 and includes approximately 4,420 solar panels roof-mounted on three major athletic buildings along with a 654-kW ground-mount installation on three acres owned by the College at the former Naval Air Station Brunswick. These panels collectively provided about 8% of the College's electricity load annually. Combined with the electricity produced by the co-generation turbine at the heating plant, approximately 14% of the College's electricity is now generated on site from renewable or efficient sources.

ADMISSIONS

Freshman Academic Profile: 86% in top 10% of high school class, 96% in top 25% of high school class, 100% in top 50% of high school class. 53% from public high schools. **Test Scores:** SAT Math middle 50% range 640-760. SAT EBRW middle 50% range 650-750. ACT middle 50% range 30-34. Minimum internet-based TOEFL 100. Minimum paper TOEFL 600. **Basis for Candidate Selection:** *Very important factors considered include:* rigor of secondary school record, class rank, academic GPA, application essay, recommendation(s), extracurricular activities, talent/ability, character/personal qualities. *Important factors considered include:* standardized test scores. *Other factors considered include:* interview, first generation, alumni/ae relation, geographical residence, state residency, racial/ethnic status, volunteer work, work experience. **Freshman Admission Requirements:** High school diploma is required and GED is not accepted *Academic units recommended:* 4 English, 4 math, 4 science, 3 science labs, 4 foreign language, 4 social studies. **Freshman Admission Statistics:** 7,251 applied, 13.6% admitted, 51% enrolled. **Transfer Admission Requirements:** High school transcript, college transcript(s), essay or personal statement, statement of good standing from prior institution(s). Minimum college GPA of 3.0 required. Lowest grade transferable C-. **General Admission Information:** Application fee $65. Regular application deadline 1/1. Nonfall registration accepted. Admission may be deferred for a maximum of 1 year.

COSTS AND FINANCIAL AID

Annual tuition $51,344. Room and board $14,132. Required fees $504. Average book expense $840. **Required Forms and Deadlines:** Business/Farm Supplement; CSS/Financial Aid PROFILE; FAFSA; Noncustodial PROFILE. **Notification of Awards:** Applicants will be notified of awards on or about 3/25. **Types of Aid:** *Need-based scholarships/grants:* College/university scholarship or grant aid from institutional funds; Federal Pell; Private scholarships; SEOG; State scholarships/grants. *Loans:* Direct Subsidized Stafford Loans; Direct Unsubsidized Stafford Loans. *Student Employment:* Federal Work-Study Program available. Institutional employment available. **Financial Aid Statistics:** 100% needy freshmen, 100% needy undergrads receive need-based scholarship or grant aid. 0% undergrads receive non-need-based scholarship or grant aid. 95% freshmen, 96% undergrads receive need-based self-help aid. 0% freshmen, 0% undergrads receive athletic scholarships. 49% freshmen, 48% undergrads receive any aid. 27% undergrads borrow to pay for school. Average cumulative indebtedness $23,120. **Criteria for awarding aid:** *Non-need-based:* Academics, Leadership.

BOWLING GREEN STATE UNIVERSITY

200 University Hall, Bowling Green, OH 43403-0085
Phone: 419-372-2478 · **Financial Aid Phone:** 419-372-2651
E-mail: choosebgsu@bgsu.edu · **CEEB Code:** 1069
Fax: 419-372-6955 · **Website:** http://www.bgsu.edu · **ACT Code:** 3240

This public school was founded in 1910. It has a 1338 acre campus.

RATINGS

Admissions Selectivity Rating: 82   Fire Safety Rating: 91   Green Rating: 96

STUDENTS AND FACULTY

Enrollment: 13,789. **Student Body:** 56% female, 44% male, 12% out-of-state, 2% international (47 countries represented). Asian 1%, African American 9%, Caucasian 78%, Hispanic 4%, Native American <1%, Pacific Islander <1%, Two or more races 3%, Race unknown 2%.
Retention and Graduation: 77% freshmen return for sophomore year. 35% freshmen graduate within 4 years. 52% freshmen graduate within 6 years. **Faculty:** Student/faculty ratio 18:1. 744 full-time faculty, 78% hold PhDs, 16% are members of minority groups, 49% are women.

ACADEMICS

Degrees: Bachelor's; Doctoral; Master's; Post-Bachelor's certificate; Post-Master's certificate **Classes:** Most classes have 10-19 students. Most lab/discussion sessions have 10-19 students. **Most popular majors:** Education/Teaching Of Individuals In Early Childhood Special Education Programs; Education, Other; Psychology, General. **Special Study Options:** Accelerated program; Cooperative education program; Cross-registration; Distance learning; Double major; Dual enrollment; English as a Second Language (ESL); Exchange student program (domestic); Honors program; Independent study; Internships; Liberal arts/career combination; Student-designed major; Study abroad; Teacher certification program. **Disability Services offered to physically disabled students:** Note-taking services; Reader services; Tape recorders; Tutors. **Career services:** Alumni network; Alumni services; Career assessment; Career/job search classes; Internships; Regional alumni

FACILITIES

Housing: Apartments for single students; Coed dorms; Fraternity/sorority housing; Special housing for disabled students **Computers:** 99% of classrooms, 64% of dorms, 100% of libraries, 100% of dining areas, 100% of student union, 40% of common outdoor areas have wireless network access. Students can register for classes online. Administrative functions (other than registration) can be performed online.

CAMPUS LIFE

Environment: Town **Activities:** Campus Ministries; Choral groups; Concert band; Dance; Drama/theater; International Student Organization; Jazz band; Literary magazine; Marching band; Model UN; Music ensembles; Musical theater; Opera; Pep band; Radio station; Student government; Student newspaper; Student-run film society; Symphony orchestra; Television station; Yearbook 20 honor societies, 24 fraternities, 19 sororities. **Athletics (Intercollegiate):** *Men:* baseball, basketball, cross-country, football, golf, ice hockey, soccer. *Women:* basketball, cross-country, golf, gymnastics, soccer, softball, swimming, tennis, track/field (outdoor), track/field (indoor), volleyball. **On-Campus Highlights:** Bowen Thompson Student Union, Stroh Center, The Wolfe Center, College of Business Administration, New Residence Halls/New Dining Halls **Environmental Initiatives:** Completion of the Climate Action Plan by the ACUPCC Working Group, under the leadership of the

Office of Campus Sustainability, its public filing in January, 2015 and immediate reduction in electricity conservation through several very large LED lighting conversion projects.

ADMISSIONS

Freshman Academic Profile: Average high school GPA 3.4. 12% in top 10% of high school class, 36% in top 25% of high school class, 70% in top 50% of high school class. 89% from public high schools. **Test Scores:** SAT Math middle 50% range 510-610. SAT EBRW middle 50% range 510-610. ACT middle 50% range 20-25. Minimum internet-based TOEFL 71. Minimum paper TOEFL 530. **Basis for Candidate Selection:** *Very important factors considered include:* rigor of secondary school record, academic GPA, standardized test scores. *Important factors considered include:* class rank. *Other factors considered include:* application essay, recommendation(s), interview, extracurricular activities, talent/ability, character/personal qualities, first generation, alumni/ae relation, racial/ethnic status, volunteer work, work experience, level of applicant's interest. **Freshman Admission Requirements:** High school diploma is required and GED is accepted *Academic units recommended:* 4 English, 4 math, 3 science, 2 science labs, 2 foreign language, 3 social studies, 1 visual/performing arts. **Freshman Admission Statistics:** 16,739 applied, 68.3% admitted, 29% enrolled. Minimum college GPA of 2.5 required. Lowest grade transferable C. **General Admission Information:** Application fee $45. Priority deadline 2/1. Regular application deadline 7/15. Nonfall registration accepted. Admission may be deferred.

COSTS AND FINANCIAL AID

Annual in-state tuition $1,961. Annual out-of-state tuition $16,632. Required fees $1,961. Average book expense $1,010. **Required Forms and Deadlines:** FAFSA. **Notification of Awards:** Applicants will be notified of awards on a rolling basis beginning 2/1. **Types of Aid:** *Need-based scholarships/grants:* College/university scholarship or grant aid from institutional funds; Federal Pell; Private scholarships; SEOG; State scholarships/grants. *Loans:* Direct PLUS loans; Direct Subsidized Stafford Loans; Direct Unsubsidized Stafford Loans. *Student Employment:* Federal Work-Study Program available. Institutional employment available. **Financial Aid Statistics:** 90% needy freshmen, 82% needy undergrads receive need-based scholarship or grant aid. 10% freshmen, 8% undergrads receive non-need-based scholarship or grant aid. 80% freshmen, 85% undergrads receive need-based self-help aid. 3% freshmen, 3% undergrads receive athletic scholarships. 95% freshmen, 87% undergrads receive any aid. 78% undergrads borrow to pay for school. Average cumulative indebtedness $31,746. **Criteria for awarding aid:** *Need-based:* Academics, Minority status *Non-need-based:* Academics, Alumni affiliation, Art, Athletics, Leadership, Minority status, Music/drama, State/district residency.

BRADLEY UNIVERSITY

1501 W. Bradley Avenue, Peoria, IL 61625
Phone: 309-677-1000 · **Financial Aid Phone:** 309-677-3089
E-mail: admissions@bradley.edu · **CEEB Code:** 1070
Fax: 309-677-2797 · **Website:** www.bradley.edu · **ACT Code:** 960

This private school was founded in 1897. It has a 85 acre campus.

RATINGS

Admissions Selectivity Rating: 82   Fire Safety Rating: 97   Green Rating: 71

STUDENTS AND FACULTY

Enrollment: 4,643. **Student Body:** 51% female, 49% male, 18% out-of-state, 2% international (38 countries represented). Asian 4%, African American 7%, Caucasian 73%, Hispanic 10%, Native American <1%, Pacific Islander 0%, Two or more races 2%, Race unknown 2%.
Retention and Graduation: 87% freshmen return for sophomore year. 51% freshmen graduate within 4 years. 72% freshmen graduate within 6 years. **Faculty:** Student/faculty ratio 12:1. 355 full-time faculty, 80% hold PhDs, 21% are members of minority groups, 42% are women. 0% of classes are taught by teaching assistants.

ACADEMICS

Degrees: Bachelor's; Doctoral/Professional; Master's; Post-Bachelor's certificate; Post-Master's certificate **Classes:** Most classes have fewer than 10 students. Most lab/discussion sessions have fewer than 10 students. **Most popular majors:** Engineering, Other; Health Professions And Related Clinical Sciences, Other; Business, Management, Marketing, And Related Support Services, Other. **Special Study Options:** Accelerated program;

Cooperative education program; Distance learning; Double major; Honors program; Independent study; Internships; Student-designed major; Study abroad; Teacher certification program. **Honors programs:** The Honors Program is structured so that students majoring in any department are eligible to participate. The program builds progressively through a student's four years, beginning with special honors sections of Bradley Core Curriculum courses and leading to interdisciplinary seminars and possibilities for independent research. Students in the Honors Program also may select housing in a dedicated honors floor within one of our residence halls. **Disability Services offered to physically disabled students:** Note-taking services; Reader services; Tutors. **Career services:** Alumni network; Alumni services; Career assessment; Career/job search classes; Internships; Regional alumni

FACILITIES

Housing: Apartments for single students; Coed dorms; Fraternity/sorority housing; Theme housing 75% of campus accessible to physically diasbled. **Special Academic Facilities/Equipment:** Caterpillar Global Communication Center, Hartmann Center Gallery, Heuser Art Center Gallery, Hayden-Clark Alumni Center, Athletics Hall of Fame in Renaissance Coliseum **Computers:** 95% of classrooms, 5% of dorms, 100% of libraries, 80% of dining areas, 100% of student union, 30% of common outdoor areas have wireless network access. Students can register for classes online. Administrative functions (other than registration) can be performed online.

CAMPUS LIFE

Environment: City **Activities:** Campus Ministries; Choral groups; Concert band; Dance; Drama/theater; International Student Organization; Jazz band; Literary magazine; Music ensembles; Musical theater; Pep band; Radio station; Student government; Student newspaper; Student-run film society; Symphony orchestra; Television station 220 registered organizations, 31 honor societies, 17 religious organizations. 16 fraternities, 11 sororities. **Athletics (Intercollegiate):** *Men:* baseball, basketball, cross-country, golf, soccer, tennis. *Women:* basketball, cross-country, golf, softball, tennis, track/field (outdoor), track/field (indoor), volleyball. **On-Campus Highlights:** Markin Family Student Recreation Center, Caterpillar Global Communications Center, Olin Hall of Science, Michel Student Center, Renaissance Coliseum

ADMISSIONS

Freshman Academic Profile: Average high school GPA 3.6. 26% in top 10% of high school class, 60% in top 25% of high school class, 90% in top 50% of high school class. 85% from public high schools. **Test Scores:** SAT Math middle 50% range 530-650. SAT EBRW middle 50% range 550-640. ACT middle 50% range 22-28. Minimum internet-based TOEFL 79. Minimum paper TOEFL 550. **Basis for Candidate Selection:** *Very important factors considered include:* rigor of secondary school record, academic GPA. *Important factors considered include:* class rank, standardized test scores. *Other factors considered include:* application essay, recommendation(s), interview, extracurricular activities, talent/ability, character/personal qualities, first generation, alumni/ae relation, geographical residence, racial/ethnic status, volunteer work, work experience, level of applicant's interest. **Freshman Admission Requirements:** High school diploma is required and GED is accepted *Academic units required:* 4 English, 3 math, 2 science, 2 science labs, 2 social studies, *Academic units recommended:* 5 English, 4 math, 3 science, 3 science labs, 2 foreign language, 3 social studies, 2 history. **Freshman Admission Statistics:** 10,232 applied, 71.4% admitted, 17% enrolled. **Transfer Admission Requirements:** college transcript(s), statement of good standing from prior institution(s). Minimum college GPA of 2.0 required. Lowest grade transferable C. **General Admission Information:** Application fee $35. Priority deadline 2/1. Regular application deadline 5/1. Nonfall registration accepted. Admission may be deferred for a maximum of 1 year.

COSTS AND FINANCIAL AID

Annual tuition $32,540. Room and board $10,310. Required fees $390. Average book expense $1,200. **Required Forms and Deadlines:** FAFSA. **Notification of Awards:** Applicants will be notified of awards on a rolling basis beginning 9/1. **Types of Aid:** *Need-based scholarships/grants:* College/university scholarship or grant aid from institutional funds; Federal Pell; Private scholarships; SEOG; State scholarships/grants; United Negro College Fund. *Loans:* Direct PLUS loans; Direct Subsidized Stafford Loans; Direct Unsubsidized Stafford Loans. *Student Employment:* Federal Work-Study Program available. Institutional employment available. **Financial Aid Statistics:** 99% needy freshmen, 96% needy undergrads receive need-based scholarship or grant aid. 14% freshmen, 11% undergrads receive non-need-based scholarship or grant aid. 77% freshmen, 81% undergrads receive need-based self-help aid. 4% freshmen, 3% undergrads receive athletic scholarships. 95% freshmen, 88% undergrads receive any aid. **Criteria for awarding aid:** *Need-based:* Academics *Non-need-based:* Academics, Alumni affiliation, Art, Athletics, Leadership, Minority status, Music/drama.

BRANDEIS UNIVERSITY

415 South Street, Waltham, MA 02454-9110
Phone: 781-736-3500 · **Financial Aid Phone:** (781) 736-3700
E-mail: admissions@brandeis.edu · **CEEB Code:** 3092
Fax: 781-736-3536 · **Website:** http://www.brandeis.edu/ · **ACT Code:** 1802

This private school was founded in 1948. It has a 235 acre campus.

RATINGS

Admissions Selectivity Rating: 96 · **Fire Safety Rating:** 98 · **Green Rating:** 81

STUDENTS AND FACULTY

Enrollment: 3,624. **Student Body:** 59% female, 41% male, 71% out-of-state, 21% international (54 countries represented). Asian 13%, African American 5%, Caucasian 47%, Hispanic 7%, Native American <1%, Pacific Islander <1%, Two or more races 3%, Race unknown 2%.
Retention and Graduation: 94% freshmen return for sophomore year. 83% freshmen graduate within 4 years. 90% freshmen graduate within 6 years. 30% grads go on to further study within 1 year. 33% grads pursue arts and sciences degrees. 13.77% grads pursue law degrees. 12% grads pursue business degrees. 23.91% grads pursue medical degrees. **Faculty:** Student/faculty ratio 10:1. 358 full-time faculty, 95% hold PhDs, 13% are members of minority groups, 45% are women.

ACADEMICS

Degrees: Bachelor's; Doctoral; Master's; Post-Master's certificate **Classes:** Most classes have 10-19 students. Most lab/discussion sessions have 10-19 students. **Most popular majors:** Biology/Biological Sciences, General; Psychology, General; Economics, General. **Special Study Options:** Accelerated program; Cross-registration; Distance learning; Double major; Exchange student program (domestic); Independent study; Internships; Student-designed major; Study abroad; Teacher certification program. **Combined degree programs:** BA/MA. **Disability Services offered to physically disabled students:** Note-taking services; Tape recorders. **Career services:** Alumni network; Alumni services; Career assessment; Career/job search classes; Internships; Regional alumni

FACILITIES

Housing: Apartments for single students; Coed dorms; Special housing for disabled student; Theme housing 78% of campus accessible to physically diasbled. **Special Academic Facilities/Equipment:** Rose Art Museum, Spingold Theater **Computers:** 100% of classrooms, 100% of dorms, 100% of libraries, 100% of dining areas, 100% of student union, 100% of common outdoor areas have wireless network access. Students can register for classes online. Administrative functions (other than registration) can be performed online.

CAMPUS LIFE

Environment: Metropolis **Activities:** Campus Ministries; Choral groups; Concert band; Dance; Drama/theater; Jazz band; Literary magazine; Model UN; Music ensembles; Musical theater; Pep band; Radio station; Student government; Student newspaper; Television station; Yearbook 253 registered organizations, 4 honor societies, 19 religious organizations. **Athletics (Intercollegiate):** *Men:* baseball, basketball, cross-country, diving, fencing, soccer, tennis, track/field (outdoor), track/field (indoor), wrestling. *Women:* basketball, cheerleading, cross-country, diving, fencing, soccer, softball, tennis, track/field (outdoor), track/field (indoor), volleyball, wrestling. **On-Campus Highlights:** Shapiro Science Center, Mandel Center for the Humanities, Rose Art Museum, Usdan Campus Center, Gosman Sports Center **Environmental Initiatives:** In 2018, Brandeis will burn approximately of 160,000 gallons of renewable fuel oil in its central heating plant. The fuel is made from cooking oil from hundreds of restaurants, schools, hotels and food manufacturers throughout New England. The renewable fuel will displace up to 10% of our natural gas use during winter. If this pilot goes well, we hope to increase the amount we use in the future.

ADMISSIONS

Freshman Academic Profile: Average high school GPA 3.9. 65% in top 10% of high school class, 90% in top 25% of high school class, 99% in top 50% of high school class. 61% from public high schools. **Test Scores:** SAT Math middle 50% range 650-760. SAT EBRW middle 50% range 630-710. ACT middle 50% range 29-33. Minimum internet-based TOEFL 100. Minimum paper TOEFL 600. **Basis for Candidate Selection:** *Very important factors considered include:* rigor of secondary school record, class rank, academic GPA, character/personal qualities. *Important factors considered include:* application essay, recommendation(s), extracurricular activities, talent/ability, volunteer work, work experience, level of applicant's interest. *Other factors considered include:* standardized test scores, interview, first generation, alumni/ae relation, geographical residence, state residency, racial/ethnic status. **Freshman Admission Requirements:** High school diploma is required and GED is accepted *Academic units recommended:* 4 English, 4 math, 4 science, 2 science labs, 4 foreign language, 4 social studies. **Freshman Admission Statistics:** 11,721 applied, 34.2% admitted, 21% enrolled. **Transfer Admission Requirements:** High school transcript, college transcript(s), essay or personal statement, standardized test scores, statement of good standing from prior institution(s). Minimum college GPA of 3.20 required. Lowest grade transferable C-. **General Admission Information:** Application fee $80. Regular application deadline 1/1. Nonfall registration accepted. Admission may be deferred for a maximum of 1 year.

COSTS AND FINANCIAL AID

Required Forms and Deadlines: CSS/Financial Aid PROFILE; FAFSA; Noncustodial PROFILE. **Notification of Awards:** Applicants will be notified of awards on or about 4/1. **Types of Aid:** *Need-based scholarships/grants:* College/university scholarship or grant aid from institutional funds; Federal Pell; Private scholarships; SEOG; State scholarships/grants. *Loans:* Direct PLUS loans; Direct Subsidized Stafford Loans; Direct Unsubsidized Stafford Loans. *Student Employment:* Federal Work-Study Program available. Institutional employment available. **Financial Aid Statistics:** 97% needy freshmen, 94% needy undergrads receive need-based scholarship or grant aid. 7% freshmen, 5% undergrads receive non-need-based scholarship or grant aid. 88% freshmen, 93% undergrads receive need-based self-help aid. 0% freshmen, 0% undergrads receive athletic scholarships. 63% freshmen, 65% undergrads receive any aid. 55% undergrads borrow to pay for school. Average cumulative indebtedness $32,922. **Criteria for awarding aid:** *Non-need-based:* Academics.

BRENAU UNIVERSITY

500 Washington St. SE, Gainesville, GA 30501
Phone: 770-534-6100 · **Financial Aid Phone:** 770-534-6152
E-mail: admissions@brenau.edu · **CEEB Code:** 5066
Fax: 770-538-4306 · **Website:** www.brenau.edu · **ACT Code:** 800

This private school was founded in 1878. It has a 56 acre campus.

RATINGS
Admissions Selectivity Rating: 87.   **Fire Safety Rating:** 99   **Green Rating:** 64

STUDENTS AND FACULTY
Enrollment: 1,722. **Student Body:** 91% female, 9% male, 7% out-of-state, 4% international (17 countries represented). Asian 2%, African American 32%, Caucasian 46%, Hispanic 8%, Native American <1%, Pacific Islander 0%, Two or more races 3%, Race unknown 4%.
Retention and Graduation: 65% freshmen return for sophomore year. 31% freshmen graduate within 4 years. 42% freshmen graduate within 6 years. **Faculty:** Student/faculty ratio 11:1. 127 full-time faculty, 83% hold PhDs, 16% are members of minority groups, 72% are women. 0% of classes are taught by teaching assistants.

ACADEMICS
Degrees: Associate; Bachelor's; Certificate; Doctoral/Professional; Master's; Post-Bachelor's certificate; Post-Master's certificate **Classes:** Most classes have 10-19 students. Most lab/discussion sessions have 10-19 students. **Most popular majors:** Health Services/Allied Health/Health Sciences, General; Nursing Practice. **Special Study Options:** Accelerated program; Distance learning; Double major; Dual enrollment; Honors program; Independent study; Internships; Liberal arts/career combination; Study abroad; Teacher certification program; Weekend college. **Honors programs:** The Honors Program at the Women's College of Brenau University begins in the freshman year and is followed throughout the student's entire college career at Brenau. Special classes reserved for honors students are taught in an enriched manner, affording these students an approach to their general education courses which enables them to study these subjects at an advanced level. **Disability Services offered to physically disabled students:** Reader services; Tutors. **Career services:** Alumni network; Alumni services; Career assessment; Career/job search classes; Internships

FACILITIES
Housing: Apartments for single students; Fraternity/sorority housing; Men's dorms; Special housing for disabled student; Women's dorms 90% of campus accessible to physically diasbled. **Special Academic Facilities/Equipment:** Simmons Art Gallery, Wages House, Whitepath House, Natatorium Physical Fitness Center, Leo Castelli Art Gallery, Northeast Georgia History Center

Computers: Students can register for classes online. Administrative functions (other than registration) can be performed online.

CAMPUS LIFE
Environment: Town **Activities:** Choral groups; Concert band; Dance; Drama/theater; International Student Organization; Jazz band; Literary magazine; Music ensembles; Musical theater; Opera; Pep band; Radio station; Student government; Student newspaper; Yearbook 54 registered organizations, 12 honor societies, 2 religious organizations. 8 sororities. **Athletics (Intercollegiate):** *Women:* basketball, cross-country, soccer, softball, swimming, tennis, volleyball. **On-Campus Highlights:** Pearce Auditorium, Burd Center for Performing Arts, Fitness Center, Dining Hall and Tea Room, Northeast Georgia History Center

ADMISSIONS
Freshman Academic Profile: Average high school GPA 3.4. **Test Scores:** SAT Math middle 50% range 420-530. SAT EBRW middle 50% range 440-560. ACT middle 50% range 17-23. Minimum internet-based TOEFL 71. Minimum paper TOEFL 527. **Basis for Candidate Selection:** *Very important factors considered include:* academic GPA. *Important factors considered include:* rigor of secondary school record. *Other factors considered include:* class rank, application essay, standardized test scores, recommendation(s), interview, extracurricular activities, talent/ability, character/personal qualities, first generation, alumni/ae relation, volunteer work, work experience. **Freshman Admission Requirements:** High school diploma is required and GED is accepted *Academic units required:* 4 English, 4 math, 3 science, 2 foreign language, 3 social studies. **Freshman Admission Statistics:** 2,140 applied, 41.9% admitted, 35% enrolled. **Transfer Admission Requirements:** college transcript(s), Minimum college GPA of 2.0 required. Lowest grade transferable C. **General Admission Information:** Priority deadline 5/1. Nonfall registration accepted. Admission may be deferred for a maximum of 1 year.

COSTS AND FINANCIAL AID
Annual tuition $28,650. Room and board $12,418. Required fees $400. Average book expense $1,300. **Required Forms and Deadlines:** FAFSA; State aid form. **Notification of Awards:** Applicants will be notified of awards on a rolling basis beginning 3/1. **Types of Aid:** *Need-based scholarships/grants:* College/university scholarship or grant aid from institutional funds; Federal Pell; Private scholarships; SEOG; State scholarships/grants. *Loans:* Direct PLUS loans; Direct Subsidized Stafford Loans; Direct Unsubsidized Stafford Loans. *Student Employment:* Federal Work-Study Program available. Institutional employment available. **Financial Aid Statistics:** 99% needy freshmen, 0% needy undergrads receive need-based scholarship or grant aid. 0% undergrads receive non-need-based scholarship or grant aid. 0% freshmen, 0% undergrads receive need-based self-help aid. 0% freshmen, 0% undergrads receive athletic scholarships. **Criteria for awarding aid:** *Need-based:* Minority status *Non-need-based:* Academics, Art, Athletics, Leadership, Music/drama.

BRESCIA UNIVERSITY

717 Frederica Street, Owensboro, KY 42301-3023
Phone: 270-686-4241 · **Financial Aid Phone:** 1-877-BRESCIA
E-mail: admissions@brescia.edu · **CEEB Code:** 1071
Fax: 270-686-4314 · **Website:** www.brescia.edu · **ACT Code:** 14980

This private school, affiliated with the Roman Catholic Church, was founded in 1950. It has a 9 acre campus.

RATINGS
Admissions Selectivity Rating: 84   **Fire Safety Rating:** 94   **Green Rating:** 60*

STUDENTS AND FACULTY
Enrollment: 1,007. **Student Body:** 74% female, 26% male, 29% out-of-state, 1% international (17 countries represented). Asian <1%, African American 13%, Caucasian 69%, Hispanic 3%, Native American 1%, Pacific Islander 1%, Two or more races 0%, Race unknown 12%.
Retention and Graduation: 64% freshmen return for sophomore year. **Faculty:** Student/faculty ratio 13:1. 37 full-time faculty, 70% hold PhDs, 16% are members of minority groups, 51% are women. 0% of classes are taught by teaching assistants.

ACADEMICS
Degrees: Associate; Bachelor's; Master's; Post-Bachelor's certificate **Classes:** Most classes have 20-29 students. Most lab/discussion sessions have 10-19 students. **Most popular majors:** Elementary Education And Teaching; General Studies; Social Work, Other. **Special Study Options:** Accelerated program; Cross-registration; Distance learning; Double major; English as

a Second Language (ESL); Exchange student program (domestic); Honors program; Independent study; Internships; Liberal arts/career combination; Study abroad; Teacher certification program; Weekend college. **Honors programs:** The Honors Program at Brescia University is intended to challenge and recognize talented and motivated students. Through the program, students will participate in a range of multidisciplinary experiences aimed at extending their inteelectual capabilities and developing public speaking and research skills needed for personal enrichment and/or graduate study. **Disability Services offered to physically disabled students:** Note-taking services; Tape recorders; Tutors. **Career services:** Alumni services; Career assessment; Career/job search classes; Internships

FACILITIES

Housing: Apartments for single students; Coed dorms; Men's dorms; Special housing for disabled student; Theme housing; Women's dorms 87% of campus accessible to physically diasbled. **Special Academic Facilities/Equipment:** Art Gallery, computer labs, campus center, greenhouse, observatory,science building. **Computers:** 100% of classrooms, 100% of dorms, 100% of libraries, 100% of dining areas, 100% of common outdoor areas have wireless network access. Administrative functions (other than registration) can be performed online.

CAMPUS LIFE

Environment: City **Activities:** Campus Ministries; Choral groups; Drama/ theater; International Student Organization; Literary magazine; Pep band; Student government; Student newspaper 22 registered organizations, 3 honor societies, 2 religious organizations. **Athletics (Intercollegiate):** *Men:* baseball, basketball, cross-country, golf, soccer, tennis, track/field (outdoor). *Women:* basketball, cross-country, golf, soccer, softball, tennis, track/field (outdoor), volleyball. **Environmental Initiatives:** Recycling

ADMISSIONS

Freshman Academic Profile: Average high school GPA 3.3. 61% from public high schools. **Test Scores:** SAT Math middle 50% range 400-580. SAT EBRW middle 50% range 440-480. ACT middle 50% range 20-25. Minimum paper TOEFL 550. **Basis for Candidate Selection:** *Very important factors considered include:* academic GPA, standardized test scores. **Freshman Admission Requirements:** High school diploma is required and GED is accepted *Academic units recommended:* 4 English, 3 math, 2 science, 2 foreign language, 2 social studies, 2 history, 2 academic electives. **Freshman Admission Statistics:** 3,757 applied, 49.3% admitted, 9% enrolled. **Transfer Admission Requirements:** High school transcript, college transcript(s), Minimum college GPA of 2.0 required. Lowest grade transferable C. **General Admission Information:** Application fee $25. Nonfall registration accepted. Admission may be deferred for a maximum of 1 year.

COSTS AND FINANCIAL AID

Annual tuition $19,500. Room and board $8,000. Required fees $490. **Required Forms and Deadlines:** FAFSA. **Notification of Awards:** Applicants will be notified of awards on a rolling basis beginning 3/1. **Types of Aid:** *Need-based scholarships/grants:* College/university scholarship or grant aid from institutional funds; Federal Pell; Private scholarships; SEOG; State scholarships/grants. *Loans:* Direct PLUS loans; Direct Subsidized Stafford Loans; Direct Unsubsidized Stafford Loans. *Student Employment:* Federal Work-Study Program available. Institutional employment available. **Financial Aid Statistics:** 0% freshmen, 0% undergrads receive athletic scholarships. 99% freshmen, 98% undergrads receive any aid. **Criteria for awarding aid:** *Non-need-based:* Academics, Alumni affiliation, Art, Athletics, Minority status, Music/drama, Religious affiliation, State/district residency.

BREVARD COLLEGE

One Bear Place #97056, Brevard, NC 28712
Phone: 828-884-8300 · **Financial Aid Phone:** 828-884-8261
E-mail: admissions@brevard.edu · **CEEB Code:** 5067
Fax: 828-884-3790 · **ACT Code:** 3074

This private school, affiliated with the Methodist Church, was founded in 1853. It has a 120 acre campus.

RATINGS

Admissions Selectivity Rating: 85 **Fire Safety Rating:** 81 **Green Rating:** 60*

STUDENTS AND FACULTY

Enrollment: 696. **Student Body:** 42% female, 58% male, 42% out-of-state, 6% international (17 countries represented). Asian 1%, African American 10%, Caucasian 71%, Hispanic 2%, Native American 1%, Pacific Islander <1%, Two or more races 3%, Race unknown 6%.

Retention and Graduation: 59% freshmen return for sophomore year.
Faculty: Student/faculty ratio 11:1. 51 full-time faculty, 84% hold PhDs, 0% are members of minority groups, 47% are women. 0% of classes are taught by teaching assistants.

ACADEMICS

Degrees: Bachelor's **Classes:** Most classes have 10-19 students. **Most popular majors:** Multi-/Interdisciplinary Studies, Other; Parks, Recreation And Leisure Studies; Business Administration And Management, General. **Special Study Options:** Double major; Dual enrollment; Honors program; Independent study; Internships; Student-designed major; Study abroad; Teacher certification program. **Honors programs:** To complete the Honors Program, students must take a minimum of 19 s.h. in honors courses during the typical 4-year period of their enrollment at Brevard College. These hours include honors enrichment seminar courses, honors-designated sections of courses, and a senior project. The only coursework of these 19 hours that is not directly attributable to core or major requirements is 4 s.h. of ENR (Enrichment) seminars. **Disability Services offered to physically disabled students:** Note-taking services; Reader services; Tape recorders; Tutors. **Career services:** Career assessment; Career/job search classes; Internships

FACILITIES

Housing: Coed dorms; Men's dorms; Special housing for disabled student; Women's dorms 100% of campus accessible to physically diasbled. **Special Academic Facilities/Equipment:** Porter Center for Performing Arts; Sims Art Center; Morrison Playhouse; Fitness Appraisal Laboratory; Academic Enrichment Center; Center for Career, Service, and Learning; Medical Services Building; Stamey Counseling Center; 24-hour computer lab; Library with wireless connection; Moore Science Annex Building **Computers:** 25% of dorms, 100% of libraries, 100% of dining areas, 100% of student union, have wireless network access. Administrative functions (other than registration) can be performed online.

CAMPUS LIFE

Environment: Village **Activities:** Campus Ministries; Choral groups; Concert band; Dance; Drama/theater; Jazz band; Literary magazine; Music ensembles; Musical theater; Opera; Pep band; Student government; Student newspaper; Yearbook 32 registered organizations, 3 honor societies, 1 religious organization. **Athletics (Intercollegiate):** *Men:* baseball, basketball, cheerleading, cross-country, cycling, football, golf, soccer, tennis, track/field (outdoor). *Women:* basketball, cheerleading, cross-country, cycling, golf, soccer, softball, tennis, track/field (outdoor), volleyball. **On-Campus Highlights:** Food Court & Dining Hall, Porter Center for Performing Arts, Jones Library, MG Super Lab, Boshamer Gym **Environmental Initiatives:** Campus-wide recycling program

ADMISSIONS

Freshman Academic Profile: Average high school GPA 3.1. 6% in top 10% of high school class, 24% in top 25% of high school class, 62% in top 50% of high school class. 82% from public high schools. **Test Scores:** SAT Math middle 50% range 420-530. SAT EBRW middle 50% range 420-520. ACT middle 50% range 17-22. Minimum paper TOEFL 537. **Basis for Candidate Selection:** *Very important factors considered include:* rigor of secondary school record, academic GPA, level of applicant's interest. *Important factors considered include:* class rank, application essay, interview, extracurricular activities, talent/ ability, character/personal qualities, volunteer work. *Other factors considered include:* standardized test scores, recommendation(s), alumni/ae relation, work experience. **Freshman Admission Requirements:** High school diploma is required and GED is accepted *Academic units recommended:* 4 English, 3 math, 3 science, 1 science labs, 2 foreign language, 4 social studies, 1 history, 4 academic electives. **Freshman Admission Statistics:** 2,858 applied, 43.2% admitted, 18% enrolled. **Transfer Admission Requirements:** High school transcript, college transcript(s), essay or personal statement, standardized test scores, statement of good standing from prior institution(s). Minimum college GPA of 2.0 required. Lowest grade transferable C-. **General Admission Information:** Nonfall registration accepted. Admission may be deferred for a maximum of one semester.

COSTS AND FINANCIAL AID

Required Forms and Deadlines: FAFSA. **Notification of Awards:** Applicants will be notified of awards on a rolling basis beginning 2/1. **Types of Aid:** *Need-based scholarships/grants:* College/university scholarship or grant aid from institutional funds; Federal Pell; Private scholarships; SEOG; State scholarships/grants. *Loans:* Direct PLUS loans; Direct Subsidized Stafford Loans; Direct Unsubsidized Stafford Loans. *Student Employment:* Federal Work-Study Program available. Institutional employment available. **Financial Aid Statistics:** 82% needy freshmen, 80% needy undergrads receive need-based scholarship or grant aid. 100% freshmen, 60% undergrads receive non-need-based scholarship or grant aid. 82% freshmen, 80% undergrads receive need-based self-help aid. 7% freshmen, 7% undergrads receive athletic scholarships. **Criteria for awarding aid:** *Non-need-based:* Academics, Art, Athletics, Leadership, Music/drama, Religious affiliation, State/district residency.

BRIAR CLIFF UNIVERSITY

3303 Rebecca Street, Sioux City, IA 51104
Phone: 712-279-5200 • **Financial Aid Phone:** 712-279-5239
E-mail: admissions@briarcliff.edu • **CEEB Code:** 1846
Fax: 712-279-1632 • **Website:** www.briarcliff.edu • **ACT Code:** 1276

This private school, affiliated with the Roman Catholic Church, was founded in 1930. It has a 70 acre campus.

RATINGS
Admissions Selectivity Rating: 80   **Fire Safety Rating:** 88   **Green Rating:** 71

STUDENTS AND FACULTY
Enrollment: 972. **Student Body:** 55% female, 45% male, 40% out-of-state, 5% international (16 countries represented). Asian 1%, African American 9%, Caucasian 66%, Hispanic 15%, Native American 2%, Pacific Islander 1%, Two or more races 1%, Race unknown 0%.
Retention and Graduation: 79% freshmen return for sophomore year. 21% grads go on to further study within 1 year. 16% grads pursue arts and sciences degrees. 1.4% grads pursue law degrees. 2% grads pursue business degrees. 0% grads pursue medical degrees. **Faculty:** Student/faculty ratio 14:1. 64 full-time faculty, 73% hold PhDs, 8% are members of minority groups, 45% are women. 0% of classes are taught by teaching assistants.

ACADEMICS
Degrees: Associate; Bachelor's; Doctoral/Professional; Master's; Post-Bachelor's certificate; Post-Master's certificate **Classes:** Most classes have 20-29 students. Most lab/discussion sessions have 10-19 students. **Most popular majors:** Biology/Biological Sciences, General; Registered Nursing/Registered Nurse; Business Administration And Management, General. **Special Study Options:** Accelerated program; Cross-registration; Distance learning; Double major; Dual enrollment; Honors program; Independent study; Internships; Liberal arts/career combination; Student-designed major; Study abroad; Teacher certification program; Weekend college. **Honors programs:** Briar Cliff's Honor Program involves elements of leadership, service and character as well as academics, and is led by the Student Honors Executive Board. In addition to talking Honors courses with small enrollments, Honors students perform individual research work with faculty at the upper levels. **Combined degree programs:** BA/MA. **Disability Services offered to physically disabled students:** Note-taking services; Reader services; Tape recorders; Tutors. **Career services:** Alumni services; Career assessment; Career/job search classes; Internships

FACILITIES
Housing: Coed dorms; Theme housing 90% of campus accessible to physically diasbled. **Special Academic Facilities/Equipment:** Nursing Simulation Lab Integrated Multimedia Center Human Anatomy Lab Clausen Art Gallery **Computers:** 100% of classrooms, 100% of libraries, 100% of dining areas, 100% of student union, have wireless network access. Administrative functions (other than registration) can be performed online.

CAMPUS LIFE
Environment: City **Activities:** Campus Ministries; Choral groups; Dance; Drama/theater; International Student Organization; Jazz band; Literary magazine; Music ensembles; Radio station; Student government; Student newspaper; Television station 36 registered organizations, 2 honor societies, 3 religious organizations. **Athletics (Intercollegiate):** *Men:* baseball, basketball, cross-country, football, golf, soccer, tennis, track/field (outdoor), track/field (indoor), wrestling. *Women:* basketball, cross-country, golf, soccer, softball, tennis, track/field (outdoor), track/field (indoor), volleyball. **On-Campus Highlights:** Java City, Stark Student Center, Newman Flanagan Athletic Center, Bishop Mueller Library, Heelan Hall (Academics) **Environmental Initiatives:** Recycling

ADMISSIONS
Freshman Academic Profile: Average high school GPA 3.2. 11% in top 10% of high school class, 25% in top 25% of high school class, 72% in top 50% of high school class. 86% from public high schools. **Test Scores:** SAT Math middle 50% range 440-540. SAT EBRW middle 50% range 420-490. ACT middle 50% range 18-24. Minimum internet-based TOEFL 70. Minimum paper TOEFL 525. **Basis for Candidate Selection:** *Very important factors considered include:* academic GPA, standardized test scores. *Important factors considered include:* rigor of secondary school record, talent/ability, character/personal qualities. *Other factors considered include:* class rank, application essay, recommendation(s), extracurricular activities. **Freshman Admission Requirements:** High school diploma is required and GED is accepted *Academic units required:* 4 English, 4 math, 3 science, 2 foreign language, 3 social studies. **Freshman Admission Statistics:** 1,491 applied, 59.8% admitted, 24% enrolled. **Transfer Admission Requirements:** High

school transcript, college transcript(s), statement of good standing from prior institution(s). Minimum college GPA of 2.0 required. Lowest grade transferable D. **General Admission Information:** Application fee $20. Nonfall registration accepted.

COSTS AND FINANCIAL AID
Annual tuition $28,650. Room and board $9,086. Required fees $1,136. Average book expense $1,339. **Required Forms and Deadlines:** FAFSA; State aid form. **Notification of Awards:** Applicants will be notified of awards on a rolling basis beginning 2/1. **Types of Aid:** *Need-based scholarships/grants:* College/university scholarship or grant aid from institutional funds; Federal Pell; Private scholarships; SEOG; State scholarships/grants. *Loans:* Direct PLUS loans; Direct Subsidized Stafford Loans; Direct Unsubsidized Stafford Loans. *Student Employment:* Federal Work-Study Program available. Institutional employment available. **Financial Aid Statistics:** 100% needy freshmen, 99% needy undergrads receive need-based scholarship or grant aid. 24% freshmen, 24% undergrads receive non-need-based scholarship or grant aid. 82% freshmen, 86% undergrads receive need-based self-help aid. 75% freshmen, 57% undergrads receive athletic scholarships. 100% freshmen, 97% undergrads receive any aid. 92% undergrads borrow to pay for school. Average cumulative indebtedness $29,484. **Criteria for awarding aid:** *Need-based:* Academics, Minority status *Non-need-based:* Academics, Alumni affiliation, Art, Athletics, Leadership, Music/drama, Religious affiliation, State/district residency.

BRIDGEWATER COLLEGE

402 East College Street, Bridgewater, VA 22812-1599
Phone: 540-828-5375 • **Financial Aid Phone:** 540-828-5376
E-mail: admissions@bridgewater.edu • **CEEB Code:** 5069
Fax: 540-828-5481 • **Website:** www.bridgewater.edu • **ACT Code:** 4342

This private school, affiliated with the Church of Brethren, was founded in 1880. It has a 300 acre campus.

RATINGS
Admissions Selectivity Rating: 84   **Fire Safety Rating:** 91   **Green Rating:** 60*

STUDENTS AND FACULTY
Enrollment: 1,874. **Student Body:** 54% female, 46% male, 26% out-of-state, 1% international (16 countries represented). Asian 1%, African American 16%, Caucasian 66%, Hispanic 7%, Native American <1%, Pacific Islander <1%, Two or more races 5%, Race unknown 4%.
Retention and Graduation: 75% freshmen return for sophomore year. 53% freshmen graduate within 4 years. 61% freshmen graduate within 6 years. **Faculty:** Student/faculty ratio 14:1. 120 full-time faculty, 82% hold PhDs, 13% are members of minority groups, 51% are women. 0% of classes are taught by teaching assistants.

ACADEMICS
Degrees: Bachelor's; Master's **Most popular majors:** Biology/Biological Sciences, General; Health And Physical Education/Fitness, General; Business Administration And Management, General. **Special Study Options:** Distance learning; Double major; Honors program; Independent study; Internships; Liberal arts/career combination; Study abroad; Teacher certification program. **Honors programs:** The Flory Honors Program consists of stimulating and interesting opportunities both inside and outside the classroom. In the curricular element, students take a minimum of five honors designated courses, plus an honors project and capstone seminar, for a total of seven courses. Program participants may also work with faculty to build an additional honors component to a non-honors course. **Combined degree programs:** BA/MA. **Disability Services offered to physically disabled students:** Note-taking services; Reader services; Tape recorders; Tutors. **Career services:** Alumni services; Career assessment; Career/job search classes; Internships; Regional alumni

FACILITIES
Housing: Apartments for single students; Coed dorms; Men's dorms; Special housing for disabled student; Women's dorms 95% of campus accessible to physically diasbled. **Computers:** 5% of classrooms, 10% of dorms, 75% of libraries, 100% of dining areas, 100% of student union, have wireless network access. Students can register for classes online. Administrative functions (other than registration) can be performed online.

CAMPUS LIFE
Environment: Village **Activities:** Campus Ministries; Choral groups; Concert band; Dance; Drama/theater; International Student Organization; Jazz band; Literary magazine; Music ensembles; Pep band; Radio station; Student

government; Student newspaper; Yearbook 74 registered organizations, 8 honor societies, 9 religious organizations. **Athletics (Intercollegiate):** *Men:* baseball, basketball, cross-country, equestrian sports, football, golf, soccer, tennis, track/field (outdoor), track/field (indoor). *Women:* basketball, cross-country, equestrian sports, field hockey, lacrosse, soccer, softball, swimming, tennis, track/field (outdoor), track/field (indoor), volleyball. **On-Campus Highlights:** Crimson Cafe, Kline Campus Center, Funkhouser Center for Health and Wellness, Workout/game rooms **Environmental Initiatives:** Energy and water conservation

ADMISSIONS

Freshman Academic Profile: Average high school GPA 3.4. 15% in top 10% of high school class, 36% in top 25% of high school class, 72% in top 50% of high school class. 92% from public high schools. **Test Scores:** SAT Math middle 50% range 470-570. SAT EBRW middle 50% range 500-600. ACT middle 50% range 18-25. Minimum internet-based TOEFL 79. Minimum paper TOEFL 550. **Basis for Candidate Selection:** *Very important factors considered include:* rigor of secondary school record, academic GPA, standardized test scores. *Important factors considered include:* class rank, recommendation(s), interview, extracurricular activities, talent/ability, character/ personal qualities. *Other factors considered include:* geographical residence, state residency, volunteer work, work experience, level of applicant's interest. **Freshman Admission Requirements:** High school diploma is required and GED is accepted *Academic units required:* 4 English, 3 math, 3 science, 3 science labs, 4 academic electives, and 3 units from above areas or other academic areas. *Academic units recommended:* 4 English, 3 math, 3 science, 3 science labs, 2 foreign language, 4 academic electives, 3 units from above areas or other academic areas. **Freshman Admission Statistics:** 7,241 applied, 52.0% admitted, 14% enrolled. **Transfer Admission Requirements:** High school transcript, college transcript(s), standardized test scores, statement of good standing from prior institution(s). Minimum college GPA of 2.2 required. Lowest grade transferable C. **General Admission Information:** Regular application deadline 5/1. Nonfall registration accepted. Admission may be deferred for a maximum of 1 year.

COSTS AND FINANCIAL AID

Annual tuition $34,300. Room and board $12,720. Required fees $860. Average book expense $1,150. **Required Forms and Deadlines:** FAFSA; State aid form. **Notification of Awards:** Applicants will be notified of awards on a rolling basis beginning 2/1. **Types of Aid:** *Need-based scholarships/grants:* College/ university scholarship or grant aid from institutional funds; Federal Pell; Private scholarships; SEOG; State scholarships/grants. *Loans:* Direct PLUS loans; Direct Subsidized Stafford Loans; Direct Unsubsidized Stafford Loans. *Student Employment:* Federal Work-Study Program available. Institutional employment available. **Financial Aid Statistics:** 100% needy freshmen, 100% needy undergrads receive need-based scholarship or grant aid. 100% freshmen, 100% undergrads receive non-need-based scholarship or grant aid. 74% freshmen, 73% undergrads receive need-based self-help aid. 0% freshmen, 0% undergrads receive athletic scholarships. 100% freshmen, 99% undergrads receive any aid. 75% undergrads borrow to pay for school. Average cumulative indebtedness $34,035. **Criteria for awarding aid:** *Non-need-based:* Academics, Minority status, Music/drama, Religious affiliation, State/district residency.

BRIDGEWATER STATE COLLEGE

131 Summer Street, Bridgewater, MA 02325
Phone: 508-531-1237 · **Financial Aid Phone:** 508-531-1341
E-mail: admission@bridgew.edu · **CEEB Code:** 3517
Fax: 508-531-1746 · **Website:** www.bridgew.edu · **ACT Code:** 1900

This public school was founded in 1840. It has a 235 acre campus.

RATINGS

Admissions Selectivity Rating: 78   **Fire Safety Rating:** 60*   **Green Rating:** 60*

STUDENTS AND FACULTY

Enrollment: 8,310. **Student Body:** 60% female, 40% male, 5% out-of-state, 1% international (52 countries represented). Asian 2%, African American 6%, Caucasian 81%, Hispanic 2%, Native American <1%, Race unknown 8%. **Retention and Graduation:** 80% freshmen return for sophomore year. 16% grads go on to further study within 1 year. 2% grads pursue law degrees. 1% grads pursue business degrees. **Faculty:** Student/faculty ratio 19:1. 306 full-time faculty, 90% hold PhDs, 11% are members of minority groups, 48% are women. 0% of classes are taught by teaching assistants.

ACADEMICS

Degrees: Bachelor's; Master's; Post-Bachelor's certificate; Post-Master's certificate **Classes:** Most classes have 10-19 students. Most lab/discussion sessions have 10-19 students. **Most popular majors:** Elementary Education And Teaching; Psychology, General; Business/Commerce, General. **Special Study Options:** Accelerated program; Cross-registration; Distance learning; Double major; Dual enrollment; English as a Second Language (ESL); Exchange student program (domestic); Honors program; Independent study; Internships; Study abroad; Teacher certification program. **Disability Services offered to physically disabled students:** Note-taking services; Reader services; Tape recorders; Tutors. **Career services:** Alumni services; Career assessment; Career/job search classes; Internships

FACILITIES

Housing: Apartments for single students; Coed dorms; Special housing for disabled students 95% of campus accessible to physically diasbled. **Special Academic Facilities/Equipment:** On-campus school, children's physical development clinic, human performance lab, TV studio, observatory, flight simulators, electron microscope, Moakley Technology Center **Computers:** Students can register for classes online. Administrative functions (other than registration) can be performed online. Undergraduates are required to own a computer.

CAMPUS LIFE

Environment: Village **Activities:** Campus Ministries; Choral groups; Concert band; Dance; Drama/theater; International Student Organization; Jazz band; Literary magazine; Marching band; Music ensembles; Musical theater; Radio station; Student government; Student newspaper; Yearbook 67 registered organizations, 11 honor societies, 1 religious organization. **Athletics (Intercollegiate):** *Men:* baseball, basketball, cross-country, football, soccer, swimming, tennis, track/field (outdoor), wrestling. *Women:* basketball, cross-country, field hockey, lacrosse, soccer, softball, swimming, tennis, track/field (outdoor), volleyball.

ADMISSIONS

Freshman Academic Profile: Average high school GPA 3.0. 8% in top 10% of high school class, 32% in top 25% of high school class, 77% in top 50% of high school class. **Test Scores:** SAT Math middle 50% range 470-560. SAT EBRW middle 50% range 460-560. ACT middle 50% range 19-23. Minimum paper TOEFL 500. **Basis for Candidate Selection:** *Very important factors considered include:* rigor of secondary school record, academic GPA. *Important factors considered include:* class rank, standardized test scores. *Other factors considered include:* application essay, recommendation(s), extracurricular activities, talent/ability, character/personal qualities, alumni/ ae relation, racial/ethnic status, volunteer work, work experience. **Freshman Admission Requirements:** High school diploma is required and GED is accepted *Academic units required:* 4 English, 3 math, 3 science, 2 science labs, 2 foreign language, 1 social studies, 1 history, 2 academic electives, *Academic units recommended:* 4 English, 3 math, 3 science, 2 science labs, 2 foreign language, 1 social studies, 1 history, 2 academic electives. **Freshman Admission Statistics:** 6,532 applied, 71.0% admitted, 29% enrolled. **Transfer Admission Requirements:** college transcript(s), essay or personal statement, Minimum college GPA of 2.0 required. Lowest grade transferable C-. **General Admission Information:** Nonfall registration accepted. Admission may be deferred.

COSTS AND FINANCIAL AID

Annual in-state tuition $6,852. Annual out-of-state tuition $7,050. Room and board $6,852. Average book expense $1,000. **Required Forms and Deadlines:** FAFSA. **Types of Aid:** *Need-based scholarships/grants:* College/ university scholarship or grant aid from institutional funds; Federal Pell; Private scholarships; SEOG; State scholarships/grants. *Loans:* Direct PLUS loans; Direct Subsidized Stafford Loans; Direct Unsubsidized Stafford Loans. *Student Employment:* Federal Work-Study Program available. Institutional employment available. **Financial Aid Statistics:** 83% needy freshmen, 83% needy undergrads receive need-based scholarship or grant aid. 24% freshmen, 10% undergrads receive non-need-based scholarship or grant aid. 97% freshmen, 100% undergrads receive need-based self-help aid. **Criteria for awarding aid:** *Non-need-based:* Academics, Leadership, Minority status, State/district residency.

BRIERCREST COLLEGE AND SEMINARY

510 College Drive, Caronport, SK S0H 0S0
Phone: 1-800-667-5199
E-mail: admissions@briercrest.ca
Fax: 800-667-5500 · **Website:** www.briercrest.ca

This private school was founded in 1935. It has a 160 acre campus.

RATINGS
Admissions Selectivity Rating: 61   **Fire Safety Rating:** 60*   **Green Rating:** 60*

STUDENTS AND FACULTY
Student Body: 4% out-of-state, international.
Faculty: Student/faculty ratio 18:1. 31 full-time faculty.

ACADEMICS
Degrees: Associate; Bachelor's; Certificate; Master's; Post-Bachelor's certificate **Classes:** Most classes have fewer than 10 students. **Special Study Options:** Distance learning; English as a Second Language (ESL); External degree program; Independent study; Internships; Liberal arts/career combination; Study abroad. **Career services:** Alumni services; Career assessment

FACILITIES
Housing: Apartments for single students; Coed dorms; Fraternity/sorority housing; Special housing for disabled student; Special housing for international students; Theme housing; Wellness housing **Computers:** Students can register for classes online.

CAMPUS LIFE
Environment: Rural **Activities:** Campus Ministries; Choral groups; Concert band; Dance; Drama/theater; International Student Organization; Jazz band; Literary magazine; Music ensembles; Musical theater; Radio station; Student government; Student newspaper; Symphony orchestra; Yearbook. **Athletics (Intercollegiate):** *Men:* basketball, ice hockey, volleyball. *Women:* basketball, volleyball.

ADMISSIONS
Basis for Candidate Selection: *Very important factors considered include:* academic GPA, application essay, recommendation(s), character/personal qualities, religious affiliation/commitment, level of applicant's interest. *Other factors considered include:* standardized test scores, interview, volunteer work. **Freshman Admission Requirements:** High school diploma is required and GED is accepted **Transfer Admission Requirements:** High school transcript, college transcript(s), essay or personal statement. **General Admission Information:** Application fee $50. Priority deadline 4/1. Nonfall registration accepted. Admission may be deferred for a maximum of 1 year.

COSTS AND FINANCIAL AID
Annual tuition $7,470. Room and board $2,515. Required fees $250. Average book expense $500. **Required Forms and Deadlines:** Institution's own financial aid form; State aid form. **Types of Aid:** *Need-based scholarships/grants:* College/university scholarship or grant aid from institutional funds; Private scholarships.

BRIGHAM YOUNG UNIVERSITY (UT)

Brigham Young University, Provo, UT 84602-1110
Phone: 801-422-2507 · **Financial Aid Phone:** (801)378-4104
E-mail: admissions@byu.edu · **CEEB Code:** 4019
Fax: 801-422-0005 · **Website:** www.byu.edu · **ACT Code:** 4266

This private school, affiliated with the Church of Jesus Christ of Latter-day Saints, was founded in 1875. It has a 557 acre campus.

RATINGS
Admissions Selectivity Rating: 93   **Fire Safety Rating:** 76   **Green Rating:** 60*

STUDENTS AND FACULTY
Enrollment: 31,233. **Student Body:** 49% female, 51% male, 64% out-of-state, 3% international (121 countries represented). Asian 2%, African American 1%, Caucasian 82%, Hispanic 6%, Native American <1%, Pacific Islander 1%, Two or more races 4%, Race unknown 1%.
Retention and Graduation: 90% freshmen return for sophomore year. 23% freshmen graduate within 4 years. 83% freshmen graduate within 6 years.
Faculty: Student/faculty ratio 20:1. 1,256 full-time faculty, 93% hold PhDs, 6% are members of minority groups, 21% are women.

ACADEMICS
Degrees: Bachelor's; Doctoral/Professional; Doctoral/Research; Master's; Post-Bachelor's certificate; Post-Master's certificate **Classes:** Most classes have 10-19 students. Most lab/discussion sessions have 10-19 students. **Most popular majors:** Elementary Education And Teaching; Exercise Physiology; Business/Commerce, General. **Special Study Options:** Accelerated program; Cooperative education program; Cross-registration; Distance learning; Double major; English as a Second Language (ESL); External degree program; Honors program; Independent study; Internships; Liberal arts/career combination; Study abroad; Teacher certification program. **Honors programs:** The Honors Program, participation in which is open to all BYU students, complements the university's expansive educational agenda by providing the benefits of a small liberal arts learning community. These benefits include offering small classes with high-quality teaching and learning that challenge students to reach their highest potential; fostering a spirit of ongoing inquiry that includes undergraduate research in a mentored environment; and underscoring the importance of combining personal excellence, faithful discipleship, and meaningful service. **Combined degree programs:** BA/JD; BA/MA. **Disability Services offered to physically disabled students:** Note-taking services; Reader services; Tape recorders; Tutors.

FACILITIES
Housing: Apartments for married students; Apartments for single students; Men's dorms; Special housing for disabled student; Women's dorms 97% of campus accessible to physically diasbled. **Special Academic Facilities/Equipment:** Art, peoples/cultures, life science, and earth science museums, film studio, on-campus nursery school, language research center, seismography equipment, electron microscope. **Computers:** 10% of classrooms, 100% of libraries, 100% of dining areas, 100% of student union, have wireless network access. Students can register for classes online. Administrative functions (other than registration) can be performed online.

CAMPUS LIFE
Environment: City **Activities:** Choral groups; Concert band; Dance; Drama/theater; Jazz band; Literary magazine; Marching band; Music ensembles; Musical theater; Opera; Pep band; Radio station; Student government; Student newspaper; Student-run film society; Symphony orchestra; Television station 390 registered organizations, 22 honor societies, 25 religious organizations. **Athletics (Intercollegiate):** *Men:* baseball, basketball, cheerleading, cross-country, diving, football, golf, swimming, tennis, track/field (outdoor), track/field (indoor), volleyball. *Women:* basketball, cheerleading, cross-country, diving, golf, gymnastics, soccer, softball, swimming, tennis, track/field (outdoor), track/field (indoor), volleyball. **On-Campus Highlights:** Monte L. Bean Life Science Museum, The Museum of Art, Gordon B. Hinckley Alumni & Visitors Cen, Harold B. Lee Library, Wilkinson Student Center

ADMISSIONS
Freshman Academic Profile: Average high school GPA 3.8. 54% in top 10% of high school class, 85% in top 25% of high school class, 98% in top 50% of high school class. **Test Scores:** SAT Math middle 50% range 600-700. SAT EBRW middle 50% range 610-710. ACT middle 50% range 27-32. Minimum paper TOEFL 500. **Basis for Candidate Selection:** *Very important factors considered include:* rigor of secondary school record, academic GPA, application essay, standardized test scores, recommendation(s), extracurricular activities, talent/ability, character/personal qualities, religious affiliation/commitment, volunteer work, work experience. *Important factors considered include:* first generation, racial/ethnic status. *Other factors considered include:* level of applicant's interest. **Freshman Admission Requirements:** High school diploma is required and GED is accepted; High school diploma is required and GED is not accepted *Academic units recommended:* 4 English, 4 math, 3 science, 2 foreign language, 2 history. **Freshman Admission Statistics:** 12,858 applied, 52.4% admitted, 81% enrolled. **Transfer Admission Requirements:** college transcript(s), essay or personal statement, interview, Minimum college GPA of 3.0 required. Lowest grade transferable C-. **General Admission Information:** Application fee $35. Regular application deadline 12/15. Nonfall registration accepted. Admission may be deferred.

COSTS AND FINANCIAL AID
Annual tuition $5,620. **Required Forms and Deadlines:** FAFSA. **Types of Aid:** *Need-based scholarships/grants:* College/university scholarship or grant aid from institutional funds; Federal Pell; Private scholarships. *Loans:* Direct PLUS loans; Direct Subsidized Stafford Loans; Direct Unsubsidized Stafford Loans. **Financial Aid Statistics:** 57% needy freshmen, 80% needy undergrads receive need-based scholarship or grant aid. 68% freshmen, 47% undergrads receive non-need-based scholarship or grant aid. 28% freshmen, 30% undergrads receive need-based self-help aid. 3% freshmen, 2% undergrads receive athletic

scholarships. 53% freshmen, 64% undergrads receive any aid. 26% undergrads borrow to pay for school. Average cumulative indebtedness $15,158. **Criteria for awarding aid:** *Need-based:* Academics, Alumni affiliation, Minority status, Religious affiliation *Non-need-based:* Academics, Art, Athletics, Leadership, Minority status, Music/drama, Religious affiliation, State/district residency.

BRIGHAM YOUNG UNIVERSITY HAWAII

55-220 Kulanui Street, Laie, HI 96762
Phone: (808) 675- 3738 · **Financial Aid Phone:** 808-293-3530
E-mail: admissions@byuh.edu · **CEEB Code:** 4106
Fax: 808-675-3741 · **ACT Code:** 899

This private school, affiliated with the Church of Jesus Christ of Latter-day Saints, was founded in 1955. It has a 60 acre campus.

RATINGS
Admissions Selectivity Rating: 94   **Fire Safety Rating:** 73   **Green Rating:** 60*

STUDENTS AND FACULTY
Enrollment: 2,312. **Student Body:** 56% female, 44% male, 68% out-of-state, 44% international (67 countries represented). Asian 22%, African American 1%, Caucasian 29%, Hispanic 2%, Native American 1%, Race unknown 1%. **Retention and Graduation:** 57% freshmen return for sophomore year. **Faculty:** Student/faculty ratio 14:1. 122 full-time faculty, 80% hold PhDs, 23% are members of minority groups, 21% are women. 0% of classes are taught by teaching assistants.

ACADEMICS
Degrees: Bachelor's **Classes:** Most classes have 10-19 students. Most lab/discussion sessions have 10-19 students. **Most popular majors:** Information Science/Studies; Intercultural/Multicultural And Diversity Studies; International Business/Trade/Commerce. **Special Study Options:** Accelerated program; Cooperative education program; Distance learning; English as a Second Language (ESL); Exchange student program (domestic); Honors program; Independent study; Internships; Student-designed major; Teacher certification program. **Honors programs:** The University Honors Program is open to all interested students who feel they are capable of accepting the challenge of an Honors Education. You will have the opportunity to participate in a stimulating class environment with other top students and the best professors. **Disability Services offered to physically disabled students:** Note-taking services; Reader services; Tape recorders; Tutors.

FACILITIES
Housing: Apartments for married students; Men's dorms; Women's dorms 90% of campus accessible to physically diasbled. **Special Academic Facilities/Equipment:** Museum of Natural History Media Lab **Computers:** 100% of classrooms, 100% of libraries, 100% of dining areas, 100% of student union, 100% of common outdoor areas have wireless network access. Students can register for classes online. Administrative functions (other than registration) can be performed online.

CAMPUS LIFE
Environment: Village **Activities:** Choral groups; Concert band; Dance; Jazz band; Literary magazine; Music ensembles; Pep band; Student government; Student newspaper; Student-run film society 52 registered organizations, 3 honor societies. **Athletics (Intercollegiate):** *Men:* basketball, cross-country, golf, soccer, tennis. *Women:* basketball, cross-country, soccer, softball, tennis, volleyball. **On-Campus Highlights:** Joseph F. Smith Library, Cannon Activities Center, The Club Cafe, The Seasider Snackbar, Aloha Center

ADMISSIONS
Freshman Academic Profile: Average high school GPA 3.4. **Test Scores:** SAT Math middle 50% range 480-600. SAT EBRW middle 50% range 460-580. ACT middle 50% range 20-27. Minimum paper TOEFL 475. **Basis for Candidate Selection:** *Very important factors considered include:* rigor of secondary school record, application essay, standardized test scores, recommendation(s), interview, extracurricular activities, character/personal qualities, geographical residence, religious affiliation/commitment. *Important factors considered include:* class rank, talent/ability, alumni/ae relation, volunteer work, work experience. *Other factors considered include:* state residency. **Freshman Admission Requirements:** High school diploma is required and GED is not accepted *Academic units recommended:* 4 English, 2 math, 2 science, 2 science labs, 2 foreign language, 2 history. **Freshman Admission Statistics:** 2,078 applied, 18.9% admitted, 56% enrolled. **Transfer Admission Requirements:** college transcript(s), essay or personal statement, statement of good standing from prior institution(s). Minimum college GPA of

3.0 required. Lowest grade transferable C-. **General Admission Information:** Application fee $30. Regular application deadline 2/15. Nonfall registration accepted. Admission may be deferred for a maximum of 1 semester.

COSTS AND FINANCIAL AID
Annual tuition $3,600. Room and board $5,568. Average book expense $900. **Required Forms and Deadlines:** FAFSA; Institution's own financial aid form. **Notification of Awards:** Applicants will be notified of awards on or about 6/30. **Types of Aid:** *Need-based scholarships/grants:* College/university scholarship or grant aid from institutional funds; Federal Pell; Private scholarships. *Loans:* Student Employment: Institutional employment available. **Financial Aid Statistics:** 88% needy freshmen, 64% needy undergrads receive need-based scholarship or grant aid. 24% freshmen, 45% undergrads receive non-need-based scholarship or grant aid. 73% freshmen, 45% undergrads receive need-based self-help aid. 13% freshmen, 7% undergrads receive athletic scholarships. 70% freshmen, 72% undergrads receive any aid. **Criteria for awarding aid:** *Non-need-based:* Academics, Art, Athletics, Leadership, Music/drama, State/district residency.

BROCK UNIVERSITY

69 East 10th, St. Catharines, ON L2S 3A1
Phone: 905-688-5550
E-mail: admissns@brocku.ca
Fax: 905-988-5488 · **Website:** www.brocku.ca

This public school was founded in 1964. It has a 457 acre campus.

RATINGS
Admissions Selectivity Rating: 61   **Fire Safety Rating:** 85   **Green Rating:** 60*

STUDENTS AND FACULTY
Student Body: 8% out-of-state, (80 countries represented). **Faculty:** Student/faculty ratio 27:1. 577 full-time faculty, 43% are women. 0% of classes are taught by teaching assistants.

ACADEMICS
Degrees: Bachelor's; Certificate; Master's **Classes:** Most classes have 20-29 students. Most lab/discussion sessions have 10-19 students. **Most popular majors:** Education, General; Health Professions And Related Clinical Sciences, Other; Business/Commerce, General. **Special Study Options:** Cooperative education program; Double major; English as a Second Language (ESL); Exchange student program (domestic); Honors program; Internships; Liberal arts/career combination; Student-designed major; Study abroad; Teacher certification program. **Disability Services offered to physically disabled students:** Note-taking services; Reader services; Tape recorders; Tutors. **Career services:** Career/job search classes; Internships

FACILITIES
Housing: Coed dorms; Special housing for disabled student; Women's dorms 100% of campus accessible to physically diasbled. **Special Academic Facilities/Equipment:** Cool Climate Oenology and Viticulture Institute Map Library Intructional Resource Centre Rodman Hall Arts Centre Cypriote Museum **Computers:** 100% of classrooms, 100% of libraries, 100% of student union, have wireless network access. Students can register for classes online. Administrative functions (other than registration) can be performed online.

CAMPUS LIFE
Environment: City **Activities:** Campus Ministries; Choral groups; Concert band; Dance; Drama/theater; Literary magazine; Music ensembles; Musical theater; Radio station; Student government; Student newspaper; Student-run film society; Symphony orchestra; Television station; Yearbook 40 registered organizations, 6 religious organizations. **Athletics (Intercollegiate):** *Men:* baseball, basketball, cheerleading, crew/rowing, cross-country, curling, fencing, ice hockey, lacrosse, rugby, soccer, squash, swimming, wrestling. *Women:* basketball, cheerleading, crew/rowing, cross-country, curling, fencing, ice hockey, rugby, soccer, swimming, volleyball, wrestling. **On-Campus Highlights:** Residences, Walker Complex—athletic facility, Computer Commons, Isaacs, Plaza Building **Environmental Initiatives:** Our newest building earned LEED Silver Certification. The energy cost performance is almost 43 per cent better than the Model National Energy Code.

ADMISSIONS
Test Scores: Minimum internet-based TOEFL 88. **Basis for Candidate Selection:** *Very important factors considered include:* rigor of secondary school record, academic GPA. *Important factors considered include:* standardized test scores. *Other factors considered include:* class rank, recommendation(s), talent/ability. **Freshman Admission Requirements:** High school diploma

is required and GED is accepted **Freshman Admission Statistics:** 16,870 applied. **Transfer Admission Requirements:** High school transcript, college transcript(s). **General Admission Information:** Application fee $155. Regular application deadline 4/1. Nonfall registration accepted.

COSTS AND FINANCIAL AID
Annual in-state tuition $8,215. Room and board $8,215. Average book expense $900. **Required Forms and Deadlines:** Institution's own financial aid form. **Types of Aid:** *Need-based scholarships/grants:* College/university scholarship or grant aid from institutional funds. *Student Employment:* Federal Work-Study Program available. Institutional employment available. **Financial Aid Statistics:** 29% needy undergrads receive need-based scholarship or grant aid. 0% undergrads receive non-need-based scholarship or grant aid. 0% undergrads receive need-based self-help aid. 0% undergrads receive athletic scholarships. 39% undergrads receive any aid. **Criteria for awarding aid:** *Need-based:* Academics, Athletics, Leadership *Non-need-based:* Academics, Athletics, Leadership.

BROWN UNIVERSITY

One Prospect Street, Providence, RI 02912
Phone: 401-863-2378 · **Financial Aid Phone:** 401-863-2721
E-mail: admission@brown.edu · **CEEB Code:** 3094
Fax: 401-863-9300 · **Website:** www.brown.edu · **ACT Code:** 3800

This private school was founded in 1764. It has a 146 acre campus.

RATINGS
Admissions Selectivity Rating: 99   Fire Safety Rating: 91   Green Rating: 95

STUDENTS AND FACULTY
Enrollment: 6,670. **Student Body:** 53% female, 47% male, 94% out-of-state, 11% international (105 countries represented). Asian 15%, African American 6%, Caucasian 44%, Hispanic 12%, Native American <1%, Pacific Islander <1%, Two or more races 6%, Race unknown 6%. **Retention and Graduation:** 98% freshmen return for sophomore year. 86% freshmen graduate within 4 years. 95% freshmen graduate within 6 years. 21% grads go on to further study within 1 year. 10% grads pursue arts and sciences degrees. 2% grads pursue law degrees. 0% grads pursue business degrees. 5% grads pursue medical degrees. **Faculty:** Student/faculty ratio 7:1. 793 full-time faculty, 96% hold PhDs, 21% are members of minority groups, 35% are women.

ACADEMICS
Degrees: Bachelor's; Doctoral/Professional; Doctoral/Research; Master's **Classes:** Most classes have fewer than 10 students. Most lab/discussion sessions have 10-19 students. **Most popular majors:** Computer And Information Sciences, General; Applied Mathematics, General; Econometrics And Quantitative Economics. **Special Study Options:** Cross-registration; Double major; Exchange student program (domestic); Honors program; Independent study; Internships; Student-designed major; Study abroad; Teacher certification program. **Combined degree programs:** BA/MA; BA/MD. **Disability Services offered to physically disabled students:** Note-taking services; Reader services; Tape recorders; Tutors. **Career services:** Alumni network; Career assessment; Career/job search classes; Internships; Regional alumni

FACILITIES
Housing: Apartments for single students; Coed dorms; Cooperative housing; Fraternity/sorority housing; Special housing for disabled student; Theme housing; Wellness housing **Special Academic Facilities/Equipment:** List Art Center, Haffenreffer Museum of Anthropology, Language Resource Center, Child Language Lab, Infant Research Lab, Educational Technology Center, Center for Information Technology, Forbes Center for Culture and Media Studies, John Nicholas Brown Center, John Hay Library, Joukowsky Institute for Archaeology & the Ancient World, Center for Creative Arts, Ann Mary Brown Library, Brown Design Workshop, Digital Scholarship Lab, Microelectronics processing facility, Electron Microscope Central Facility, Nanotools facilities, The Cave (virtual reality studio) **Computers:** 50% of classrooms, 100% of dorms, 100% of libraries, 100% of dining areas, 100% of student union, 50% of common outdoor areas have wireless network access. Students can register for classes online. Administrative functions (other than registration) can be performed online.

CAMPUS LIFE
Environment: City **Activities:** Campus Ministries; Choral groups; Concert band; Dance; Drama/theater; International Student Organization; Jazz band; Literary magazine; Marching band; Model UN; Music ensembles; Musical theater; Opera; Pep band; Radio station; Student government; Student newspaper; Student-run film society; Symphony orchestra; Television station; Yearbook 400 registered organizations, 3 honor societies, 20 religious organizations. 8 fraternities, 2 sororities. **Athletics (Intercollegiate):** *Men:* baseball, basketball, crew/rowing, cross-country, diving, fencing, football, golf, ice hockey, lacrosse, soccer, squash, swimming, tennis, track/field (outdoor), track/field (indoor), water polo, wrestling. *Women:* basketball, crew/rowing, cross-country, diving, equestrian sports, fencing, field hockey, golf, gymnastics, ice hockey, lacrosse, skiing (downhill/alpine), soccer, softball, squash, swimming, tennis, track/field (outdoor), track/field (indoor), volleyball, water polo. **On-Campus Highlights:** The College Green (Main Green), Nelson Fitness Center, Libraries—including the John Hay Library, Orwig Music Library, Rockefeller Library, Sciences Library., Stephen Robert '62 Campus Center, Granoff Center for the Creative Arts **Environmental Initiatives:** Reduce GHG emissions to 42% (15% below 1990) below 2007 for existing buildings by 2020

ADMISSIONS
Freshman Academic Profile: 94% in top 10% of high school class, 99% in top 25% of high school class, 100% in top 50% of high school class. 57% from public high schools. **Test Scores:** SAT Math middle 50% range 700-790. SAT EBRW middle 50% range 705-780. ACT middle 50% range 31-35. **Basis for Candidate Selection:** *Very important factors considered include:* rigor of secondary school record, class rank, academic GPA, application essay, standardized test scores, recommendation(s), talent/ability, character/personal qualities. *Important factors considered include:* extracurricular activities. *Other factors considered include:* interview, first generation, alumni/ae relation, geographical residence, state residency, racial/ethnic status, volunteer work, work experience. **Freshman Admission Requirements:** High school diploma is required and GED is accepted *Academic units required:* 4 English, 3 math, 3 science, 2 science labs, 3 foreign language, 2 history, 1 academic elective, *Academic units recommended:* 4 English, 4 math, 4 science, 3 science labs, 4 foreign language, 1 social studies, 2 history, 1 academic elective, 1 visual/ performing arts. **Freshman Admission Statistics:** 32,723 applied, 8.5% admitted, 59% enrolled. **Transfer Admission Requirements:** High school transcript, college transcript(s), essay or personal statement, standardized test scores, statement of good standing from prior institution(s). Lowest grade transferable C. **General Admission Information:** Application fee $75. Regular application deadline 1/1. Nonfall registration accepted. Admission may be deferred for a maximum of 1 year.

COSTS AND FINANCIAL AID
Required Forms and Deadlines: CSS/Financial Aid PROFILE; FAFSA; Noncustodial PROFILE. **Notification of Awards:** Applicants will be notified of awards on or about 4/1. **Types of Aid:** *Need-based scholarships/ grants:* College/university scholarship or grant aid from institutional funds; Federal Pell; Private scholarships; SEOG; State scholarships/grants. *Loans:* Direct PLUS loans; Direct Subsidized Stafford Loans; Direct Unsubsidized Stafford Loans. *Student Employment:* Federal Work-Study Program available. Institutional employment available. **Financial Aid Statistics:** 96% needy freshmen, 94% needy undergrads receive need-based scholarship or grant aid. 0% undergrads receive non-need-based scholarship or grant aid. 81% freshmen, 87% undergrads receive need-based self-help aid. 0% freshmen, 0% undergrads receive athletic scholarships. 55% freshmen, 57% undergrads receive any aid. 37% undergrads borrow to pay for school. Average cumulative indebtedness $23,810.

BRYAN COLLEGE

721 Bryan Drive, Dayton, TN 37321
Phone: (423) 775-7158 · **Financial Aid Phone:** 423-775-7339
E-mail: admissions@bryan.edu · **CEEB Code:** 1908
Fax: 423-775-7199 · **Website:** www.bryan.edu · **ACT Code:** 4038

This private school, affiliated with the Christian (Nondenominational) Church, was founded in 1930. It has a 125 acre campus.

RATINGS
Admissions Selectivity Rating: 88   Fire Safety Rating: 97   Green Rating: 60*

STUDENTS AND FACULTY
Enrollment: 605. **Student Body:** 53% female, 47% male, 66% out-of-state, 5% international (22 countries represented). Asian <1%, African American 3%,

Caucasian 87%, Hispanic 3%, Native American 0%, Pacific Islander 0%, Two or more races 3%, Race unknown 0%.
Retention and Graduation: 60% freshmen return for sophomore year.
Faculty: Student/faculty ratio 15:1. 36 full-time faculty, 64% hold PhDs, 28% are women. 0% of classes are taught by teaching assistants.

ACADEMICS

Degrees: Associate; Bachelor's; Master's **Classes:** Most classes have 10-19 students. **Most popular majors:** Communication, Journalism,,And Related Programs, Other; Health And Physical Education/Fitness, General; Business Administration And Management, General. **Special Study Options:** Distance learning; Double major; Dual enrollment; Honors program; Independent study; Internships; Study abroad; Teacher certification program. **Honors programs:** Bryan Center for Undergraduate Research http://bryancollege.wpengine.com/bcur; Sigma Beta Delta Honor Society for students in business, management, and administration; Center for Leadership & Justice http://www.bryan.edu/clj. **Disability Services offered to physically disabled students:** Note-taking services; Reader services; Tape recorders; Tutors. **Career services:** Alumni network; Alumni services; Career assessment; Career/job search classes; Internships

FACILITIES

Housing: Apartments for married students; Apartments for single students; Men's dorms; Women's dorms **Special Academic Facilities/Equipment:** Willard Henning Natural History Museum **Computers:** 100% of classrooms, 100% of dorms, 100% of libraries, 100% of dining areas, 100% of student union, 80% of common outdoor areas have wireless network access. Administrative functions (other than registration) can be performed online.

CAMPUS LIFE

Environment: Town **Activities:** Campus Ministries; Choral groups; Drama/theater; International Student Organization; Music ensembles; Musical theater; Opera; Student government; Student newspaper; Yearbook. **Athletics (Intercollegiate):** *Men:* baseball, basketball, cross-country, golf, soccer, track/field (outdoor), track/field (indoor). *Women:* basketball, cross-country, golf, soccer, softball, track/field (outdoor), track/field (indoor). **On-Campus Highlights:** Student Center, Common Grounds, Gym, Mac's, Triangle/Grassy Bowl

ADMISSIONS

Freshman Academic Profile: Average high school GPA 3.6. 16% in top 10% of high school class, 48% in top 25% of high school class, 76% in top 50% of high school class. 55% from public high schools. **Test Scores:** SAT Math middle 50% range 450-580. SAT EBRW middle 50% range 450-600. ACT middle 50% range 20-26. Minimum internet-based TOEFL 75. **Basis for Candidate Selection:** *Very important factors considered include:* rigor of secondary school record, academic GPA, application essay, standardized test scores. *Important factors considered include:* recommendation(s), interview, character/personal qualities, religious affiliation/commitment, level of applicant's interest. *Other factors considered include:* class rank, extracurricular activities, talent/ability, alumni/ae relation, volunteer work. **Freshman Admission Requirements:** High school diploma is required and GED is accepted *Academic units recommended:* 4 English, 3 math, 3 science, 2 foreign language, 3 social studies. **Freshman Admission Statistics:** 760 applied, 48.4% admitted, 50% enrolled. **Transfer Admission Requirements:** college transcript(s), essay or personal statement, standardized test scores, Minimum college GPA of 2.75 required. Lowest grade transferable 2. **General Admission Information:** Application fee $35. Priority deadline 5/5. Nonfall registration accepted. Admission may be deferred.

COSTS AND FINANCIAL AID

Annual tuition $22,200. Room and board $6,550. Average book expense $1,250. **Required Forms and Deadlines:** FAFSA. **Types of Aid:** *Need-based scholarships/grants:* College/university scholarship or grant aid from institutional funds; Federal Pell; Private scholarships; SEOG; State scholarships/grants. *Loans:* Direct PLUS loans; Direct Subsidized Stafford Loans; Direct Unsubsidized Stafford Loans. *Student Employment:* Federal Work-Study Program available. Institutional employment available. **Financial Aid Statistics:** 0% freshmen, 2% undergrads receive athletic scholarships. 100% freshmen, 98% undergrads receive any aid. **Criteria for awarding aid:** *Need-based:* Academics, Minority status *Non-need-based:* Academics, Alumni affiliation, Athletics, Leadership, Minority status, Music/drama, State/district residency.

BRYANT UNIVERSITY

Best Colleges

1150 Douglas Pike, Smithfield, RI 02917-1291
Phone: 401-232-6100 · **Financial Aid Phone:** 401-232-6020
E-mail: http://www.bryant.edu/admissions/request · **CEEB Code:** 3095
Fax: 401-232-6731 · **Website:** http://www.bryant.edu/ · **ACT Code:** 3802

This private school was founded in 1863. It has a 435 acre campus.

RATINGS

Admissions Selectivity Rating: 82   **Fire Safety Rating:** 89   **Green Rating:** 75

STUDENTS AND FACULTY

Enrollment: 3,449. **Student Body:** 39% female, 61% male, 86% out-of-state, 8% international (53 countries represented). Asian 4%, African American 4%, Caucasian 75%, Hispanic 7%, Native American <1%, Pacific Islander <1%, Two or more races 1%, Race unknown 2%.
Retention and Graduation: 90% freshmen return for sophomore year. 73% freshmen graduate within 4 years. 79% freshmen graduate within 6 years. 21% grads go on to further study within 1 year. 4% grads pursue arts and sciences degrees. 1% grads pursue law degrees. 15% grads pursue business degrees. **Faculty:** Student/faculty ratio 13:1. 169 full-time faculty, 83% hold PhDs, 18% are members of minority groups, 41% are women. 0% of classes are taught by teaching assistants.

ACADEMICS

Degrees: Bachelor's; Master's; Post-Bachelor's certificate **Classes:** Most classes have 10-19 students. Most lab/discussion sessions have 10-19 students. **Most popular majors:** Accounting; Finance, General; Marketing/Marketing Management, General. **Special Study Options:** Accelerated program; Distance learning; Double major; Dual enrollment; English as a Second Language (ESL); Honors program; Independent study; Internships; Liberal arts/career combination; Study abroad; Teacher certification program. **Honors programs:** If you are a bright, driven, achievement-oriented student, Bryant's Honors Program offers you a distinctive learning opportunity that fosters research collaboration with professors who have high expectations for your personal and career development. **Disability Services offered to physically disabled students:** Note-taking services; Tape recorders; Tutors. **Career services:** Alumni network; Alumni services; Career assessment; Career/job search classes; Internships; Regional alumni

FACILITIES

Housing: Apartments for single students; Coed dorms; Special housing for disabled student; Theme housing 90% of campus accessible to physically diasbled. **Special Academic Facilities/Equipment:** George E. Bello Center for Information & Technology, C.V. Star Financial Markets Center, Heidi and Walter Stepan Grand Hall, Linday and Jerry Cerce Multi Media Wall, Douglas & Judith Krupp Library, Jane E. & Keith S. Mahre Periodical Center, Koffler Center & Communications Complex, WJMF Radio Station, TV Production Studio, Janikies Memorial Autditorium, Koffler Rotunda multimedia exhibition space, Shu Fang Zhai (replica of Beijing's Forbidden City, home to U.S.-China Institute, in planning), John H Chafee Center for International Business, Center for Global and Regional Economic Studies, Intercultural Center, Gertrude Meth Hochberg Women's Center, Ronald K. & Kati C. Machtley Interfaith Center, Center for Student Involvement, Center for Teaching & Learning, ACE (Academic Center for Excellence), Writing Center, Amica Center for Career Education, Hassenfeld Institute for Public Leadership, Executive Development Center **Computers:** 100% of classrooms, 100% of dorms, 100% of libraries, 100% of dining areas, 100% of student union, 100% of common outdoor areas have wireless network access. Students can register for classes online. Administrative functions (other than registration) can be performed online. Undergraduates are required to own a computer.

CAMPUS LIFE

Environment: Village **Activities:** Campus Ministries; Choral groups; Dance; Drama/theater; International Student Organization; Jazz band; Literary magazine; Music ensembles; Musical theater; Pep band; Radio station; Student government; Student newspaper; Television station; Yearbook 87 registered organizations, 6 honor societies, 5 religious organizations. 6 fraternities, 2 sororities. **Athletics (Intercollegiate):** *Men:* baseball, basketball, cross-country, football, golf, lacrosse, soccer, swimming, tennis, track/field (outdoor), track/field (indoor). *Women:* basketball, cross-country, field hockey, lacrosse, soccer, softball, swimming, tennis, track/field (outdoor), track/field (indoor), volleyball. **On-Campus Highlights:** Fisher Student Center, Academic Center for Innovation, Chase Athletics and Wellness Center, Bello Center for Information andTechnology, Unistructure Rotunda **Environmental Initiatives:** Recycling Program

ADMISSIONS

Freshman Academic Profile: Average high school GPA 3.4. 22% in top 10% of high school class, 52% in top 25% of high school class, 88% in top 50% of high school class. 70% from public high schools. **Test Scores:** SAT Math middle 50% range 560-650. SAT EBRW middle 50% range 560-630. ACT middle 50% range 24-29. Minimum internet-based TOEFL 80. Minimum paper TOEFL 550. **Basis for Candidate Selection:** *Very important factors considered include:* rigor of secondary school record, academic GPA. *Important factors considered include:* class rank, application essay, standardized test scores, recommendation(s). *Other factors considered include:* interview, extracurricular activities, talent/ability, character/personal qualities, first generation, alumni/ae relation, geographical residence, state residency, racial/ethnic status, volunteer work, work experience, level of applicant's interest. **Freshman Admission Requirements:** High school diploma is required and GED is accepted *Academic units required:* 4 English, 4 math, 2 science, 2 science labs, 2 foreign language, 2 history, *Academic units recommended:* 4 English, 4 math, 3 science, 2 science labs, 2 foreign language, 3 history. **Freshman Admission Statistics:** 7,242 applied, 73.0% admitted, 17% enrolled. **Transfer Admission Requirements:** High school transcript, college transcript(s), essay or personal statement, Minimum college GPA of 2.5 required. Lowest grade transferable C. **General Admission Information:** Application fee $50. Regular application deadline 2/1. Nonfall registration accepted. Admission may be deferred for a maximum of 1 year.

COSTS AND FINANCIAL AID

Annual tuition $43,076. Room and board $15,702. Required fees $897. Average book expense $1,400. **Required Forms and Deadlines:** FAFSA. **Notification of Awards:** Applicants will be notified of awards on or about 3/24. **Types of Aid:** *Need-based scholarships/grants:* College/university scholarship or grant aid from institutional funds; Federal Pell; Private scholarships; SEOG; State scholarships/grants. *Loans:* Direct PLUS loans; Direct Subsidized Stafford Loans; Direct Unsubsidized Stafford Loans. *Student Employment:* Federal Work-Study Program available. Institutional employment available. **Financial Aid Statistics:** 71% needy freshmen, 70% needy undergrads receive need-based scholarship or grant aid. 82% freshmen, 75% undergrads receive non-need-based scholarship or grant aid. 91% freshmen, 94% undergrads receive need-based self-help aid. 4% freshmen, 5% undergrads receive athletic scholarships. 79% freshmen, 87% undergrads receive any aid. 71% undergrads borrow to pay for school. Average cumulative indebtedness $44,384. **Criteria for awarding aid:** *Need-based:* Minority status *Non-need-based:* Academics, Athletics, Minority status.

See page 906.

BRYN ATHYN COLLEGE OF THE NEW CHURCH

P.O. Box 717, Bryn Athyn, PA 19009
Phone: 267-502-6000 · **Financial Aid Phone:** 267-502-6034
E-mail: admissions@brynathyn.edu · **CEEB Code:** 2002
Fax: 267-502-2593 · **Website:** www.brynathyn.edu · **ACT Code:** 3228

This private school, affiliated with the General Church of the New Jerusalem/Swedenborgian, was founded in 1877. It has a 130 acre campus.

RATINGS

Admissions Selectivity Rating: 87   **Fire Safety Rating:** 95   **Green Rating:** 60*

STUDENTS AND FACULTY

Enrollment: 273. **Student Body:** 47% female, 53% male, 41% out-of-state, 4% international (8 countries represented). Asian 3%, African American 20%, Caucasian 62%, Hispanic 10%, Native American 0%, Pacific Islander <1%, Two or more races <1%, Race unknown 1%.
Retention and Graduation: 64% freshmen return for sophomore year. 5% grads go on to further study within 1 year. 5% grads pursue arts and sciences degrees. 5% grads pursue business degrees. 10% grads pursue medical degrees. **Faculty:** Student/faculty ratio 8:1. 28 full-time faculty, 61% hold PhDs, 4% are members of minority groups, 39% are women. 0% of classes are taught by teaching assistants.

ACADEMICS

Degrees: Associate; Bachelor's; Master's **Classes:** Most classes have fewer than 10 students. **Most popular majors:** Multi-/Interdisciplinary Studies, Other; Psychology, General; Business/Commerce, General. **Special Study Options:** Accelerated program; Cooperative education program; Cross-registration; Dual enrollment; English as a Second Language (ESL); Independent study; Internships; Student-designed major; Study abroad; Teacher certification

---

program. **Disability Services offered to physically disabled students:** Tape recorders; Tutors. **Career services:** Alumni network; Alumni services; Career assessment; Internships; Regional alumni

FACILITIES

Housing: Men's dorms; Women's dorms 70% of campus accessible to physically diasbled. **Special Academic Facilities/Equipment:** Glencairn Museum Swedenborg Library Swedenborgiana Academy of the New Church Archives John Pitcairn Archives Raymond and Mildred Pitcairn Archives **Computers:** 100% of classrooms, 100% of dorms, 100% of libraries, 75% of common outdoor areas have wireless network access.

CAMPUS LIFE

Environment: Village **Activities:** Choral groups; Dance; Drama/theater; International Student Organization; Literary magazine; Music ensembles; Student government 15 registered organizations. **On-Campus Highlights:** Doering Science Center, Swedenborg Library, Brickman Center for Student Life, Asplundh Field House, Glencairn Museum **Environmental Initiatives:** Chemical purchase, storage and disposal plan, Recycling program for glass and paper in all buildings.

ADMISSIONS

Freshman Academic Profile: Average high school GPA 3.1. **Test Scores:** SAT Math middle 50% range 395-550. SAT EBRW middle 50% range 390-555. ACT middle 50% range 18-23. Minimum internet-based TOEFL 70. Minimum paper TOEFL 520. **Basis for Candidate Selection:** *Very important factors considered include:* rigor of secondary school record, academic GPA, application essay, standardized test scores, recommendation(s). *Important factors considered include:* character/personal qualities. *Other factors considered include:* interview, extracurricular activities, talent/ability, alumni/ae relation, religious affiliation/commitment, racial/ethnic status, volunteer work, work experience, level of applicant's interest. **Freshman Admission Requirements:** High school diploma is required and GED is accepted *Academic units required:* 4 English, 3 math, 3 science, 2 foreign language, 3 social studies, 3 history, *Academic units recommended:* 3 science labs. **Freshman Admission Statistics:** 439 applied, 42.1% admitted, 42% enrolled. **Transfer Admission Requirements:** High school transcript, college transcript(s), essay or personal statement, Minimum college GPA of 2.0 required. Lowest grade transferable C. **General Admission Information:** Nonfall registration accepted. Admission may be deferred for a maximum of 1 year.

COSTS AND FINANCIAL AID

Annual tuition $18,558. Room and board $11,538. Required fees $1,324. Average book expense $750. **Required Forms and Deadlines:** FAFSA; State aid form. **Notification of Awards:** Applicants will be notified of awards on a rolling basis beginning 3/1. **Types of Aid:** *Need-based scholarships/grants:* College/university scholarship or grant aid from institutional funds; Federal Pell; Private scholarships; SEOG; State scholarships/grants. *Loans:* Direct PLUS loans; Direct Subsidized Stafford Loans; Direct Unsubsidized Stafford Loans. *Student Employment:* Federal Work-Study Program available. Institutional employment available. **Financial Aid Statistics:** 88% needy freshmen, 85% needy undergrads receive need-based scholarship or grant aid. 48% freshmen, 51% undergrads receive non-need-based scholarship or grant aid. 78% freshmen, 79% undergrads receive need-based self-help aid. 0% freshmen, 0% undergrads receive athletic scholarships. 71% freshmen, 65% undergrads receive any aid. 77% undergrads borrow to pay for school. Average cumulative indebtedness $23,625. **Criteria for awarding aid:** *Non-need-based:* Academics, Religious affiliation.

BRYN MAWR COLLEGE

101 North Merion Avenue, Bryn Mawr, PA 19010-2859
Phone: 610-526-5152 · **Financial Aid Phone:** 610-526-5245
E-mail: admissions@brynmawr.edu · **CEEB Code:** 2049
Fax: 610-526-7471 · **Website:** www.brynmawr.edu · **ACT Code:** 3526

This private school was founded in 1885. It has a 111 acre campus.

RATINGS

Admissions Selectivity Rating: 94   **Fire Safety Rating:** 86   **Green Rating:** 86

STUDENTS AND FACULTY

Enrollment: 1,328. **Student Body:** 100% female, 0% male, 82% out-of-state, 23% international (58 countries represented). Asian 12%, African American 6%,

Caucasian 37%, Hispanic 9%, Native American 0%, Pacific Islander <1%, Two or more races 6%, Race unknown 7%. **Retention and Graduation:** 92% freshmen return for sophomore year. 76% freshmen graduate within 4 years. 83% freshmen graduate within 6 years. 23% grads go on to further study within 1 year. 12% grads pursue arts and sciences degrees. 1.3% grads pursue law degrees. 1% grads pursue business degrees. 1.8% grads pursue medical degrees. **Faculty:** Student/faculty ratio 8:1. 159 full-time faculty, 95% hold PhDs, 25% are members of minority groups, 59% are women. 0% of classes are taught by teaching assistants.

ACADEMICS
Degrees: Bachelor's; Doctoral/Research; Master's; Post-Bachelor's certificate **Classes:** Most classes have 20-29 students. Most lab/discussion sessions have 10-19 students. **Most popular majors:** English Language And Literature, General; Biology/Biological Sciences, General; Psychology, General. **Special Study Options:** Accelerated program; Cross-registration; Double major; Exchange student program (domestic); Independent study; Internships; Student-designed major; Study abroad; Teacher certification program. **Combined degree programs:** BA/MA. **Career services:** Alumni network; Alumni services; Career assessment; Internships; Regional alumni

FACILITIES
Housing: Apartments for single students; Coed dorms; Cooperative housing; Women's dorms **Special Academic Facilities/Equipment:** Museum of classical and Near Eastern archaeology, mineral collection, Child Study Institute, on-campus nursery school, Newfeld Collection of African Art, Language Learning Center. **Computers:** 60% of classrooms, 10% of dorms, 25% of libraries, 10% of dining areas, 100% of student union, 10% of common outdoor areas have wireless network access. Students can register for classes online. Administrative functions (other than registration) can be performed online.

CAMPUS LIFE
Environment: Metropolis **Activities:** Campus Ministries; Choral groups; Dance; Drama/theater; International Student Organization; Literary magazine; Music ensembles; Musical theater; Radio station; Student government; Student newspaper; Student-run film society 94 registered organizations, 10 religious organizations. **Athletics (Intercollegiate):** *Women:* badminton, basketball, crew/rowing, cross-country, field hockey, lacrosse, soccer, swimming, tennis, track/field (outdoor), track/field (indoor), volleyball. **On-Campus Highlights:** Great Hall (National Historic Landmark), Erdman Hall (designed by famed architect), The Cloisters (College Hall), Taft Garden, Rhys Carpenter Library

ADMISSIONS
Freshman Academic Profile: 68% in top 10% of high school class, 91% in top 25% of high school class, 97% in top 50% of high school class. 63% from public high schools. **Test Scores:** SAT Math middle 50% range 660-770. SAT EBRW middle 50% range 650-730. ACT middle 50% range 29-33. Minimum internet-based TOEFL 100. Minimum paper TOEFL 600. **Basis for Candidate Selection:** *Very important factors considered include:* rigor of secondary school record, recommendation(s). *Important factors considered include:* academic GPA, application essay, extracurricular activities, character/personal qualities. *Other factors considered include:* class rank, standardized test scores, interview, talent/ability, first generation, alumni/ae relation, geographical residence, state residency, racial/ethnic status, volunteer work, work experience. **Freshman Admission Requirements:** High school diploma is required and GED is accepted *Academic units recommended:* 4 English, 3 math, 2 science, 1 science labs, 3 foreign language, 2 social studies, 2 history, 2 academic electives. **Freshman Admission Statistics:** 2,936 applied, 38.0% admitted, 32% enrolled. **Transfer Admission Requirements:** High school transcript, college transcript(s), essay or personal statement, standardized test scores, statement of good standing from prior institution(s). Lowest grade transferable C. **General Admission Information:** Application fee $50. Regular application deadline 1/15. Nonfall registration accepted. Admission may be deferred for a maximum of 1 year.

COSTS AND FINANCIAL AID
Required Forms and Deadlines: CSS/Financial Aid PROFILE; FAFSA; Noncustodial PROFILE. **Types of Aid:** *Need-based scholarships/grants:* College/university scholarship or grant aid from institutional funds; Federal Pell; Private scholarships; SEOG; State scholarships/grants. *Loans:* Direct PLUS loans; Direct Subsidized Stafford Loans; Direct Unsubsidized Stafford Loans. *Student Employment:* Federal Work-Study Program available. Institutional employment available. **Financial Aid Statistics:** 100% needy freshmen, 98% needy undergrads receive need-based scholarship or grant aid. 6% freshmen, 5% undergrads receive non-need-based scholarship or grant aid. 94% freshmen, 94% undergrads receive need-based self-help aid. 0% freshmen, 0% undergrads receive athletic scholarships. 74% freshmen, 74% undergrads receive any aid. 52% undergrads borrow to pay for school. Average cumulative indebtedness $23,081. **Criteria for awarding aid:** *Non-need-based:* Academics, Leadership.

BUCKNELL UNIVERSITY

Best Colleges

1 Dent Drive, Lewisburg, PA 17837
Phone: 570-577-3000 • **Financial Aid Phone:** 570-577-1331
E-mail: admissions@bucknell.edu • **CEEB Code:** 2050
Fax: 570-577-3538 • **Website:** www.bucknell.edu • **ACT Code:** 3528

This private school was founded in 1846. It has a 446 acre campus.

RATINGS
Admissions Selectivity Rating: 94   **Fire Safety Rating:** 94   **Green Rating:** 97

STUDENTS AND FACULTY
Enrollment: 3,588. **Student Body:** 51% female, 49% male, 78% out-of-state, 6% international (42 countries represented). Asian 5%, African American 4%, Caucasian 74%, Hispanic 7%, Native American 0%, Pacific Islander 0%, Two or more races 4%, Race unknown <1%.
Retention and Graduation: 94% freshmen return for sophomore year. 86% freshmen graduate within 4 years. 90% freshmen graduate within 6 years. 20% grads go on to further study within 1 year. 8% grads pursue arts and sciences degrees. 1% grads pursue law degrees. 1% grads pursue business degrees. 4% grads pursue medical degrees. **Faculty:** Student/faculty ratio 9:1. 384 full-time faculty, 97% hold PhDs, 17% are members of minority groups, 41% are women. 0% of classes are taught by teaching assistants.

ACADEMICS
Degrees: Bachelor's; Master's **Classes:** Most classes have 10-19 students. Most lab/discussion sessions have fewer than 10 students. **Most popular majors:** Psychology, General; Economics, General; Accounting And Finance. **Special Study Options:** Double major; Dual enrollment; Honors program; Independent study; Internships; Liberal arts/career combination; Student-designed major; Study abroad; Teacher certification program. **Disability Services offered to physically disabled students:** Note-taking services; Reader services; Tape recorders; Tutors. **Career services:** Alumni network; Alumni services; Career assessment; Career/job search classes; Internships; Regional alumni

FACILITIES
Housing: Apartments for single students; Coed dorms; Cooperative housing; Fraternity/sorority housing; Special housing for disabled student; Special housing for international students; Theme housing; Wellness housing; Women's dorms 80% of campus accessible to physically disabled. **Special Academic Facilities/Equipment:** Art gallery, center for performing arts, poetry center, photography lab, observatory, 63-acre nature site, greenhouse, primate facility, gas chromatograph/mass spectrometer, electron microscope, herbarium, engineering structural test lab, nuclear magnetic resonance spectrometer, environmental center, 18-hole golf course, conference center, high ropes course, crafts center **Computers:** 100% of classrooms, 100% of dorms, 100% of libraries, 100% of dining areas, 100% of student union, 95% of common outdoor areas have wireless network access. Students can register for classes online. Administrative functions (other than registration) can be performed online.

CAMPUS LIFE
Environment: Village **Activities:** Campus Ministries; Choral groups; Concert band; Dance; Drama/theater; International Student Organization; Jazz band; Literary magazine; Model UN; Music ensembles; Musical theater; Opera; Pep band; Radio station; Student government; Student newspaper; Student-run film society; Symphony orchestra; Yearbook 150 registered organizations, 23 honor societies, 13 religious organizations. 12 fraternities, 8 sororities. **Athletics (Intercollegiate):** *Men:* baseball, basketball, cross-country, diving, football, golf, lacrosse, soccer, swimming, tennis, track/field (outdoor), track/field (indoor), water polo, wrestling. *Women:* basketball, crew/rowing, cross-country, diving, field hockey, golf, lacrosse, soccer, softball, swimming, tennis, track/field (outdoor), track/field (indoor), volleyball, water polo. **On-Campus Highlights:** Weis Center for the Performing Arts, Outdoor Primate Facilities, Uptown Night Club, Stadler Poetry Center, Library with Technology and Media Commons **Environmental Initiatives:** In May 2009, the Bucknell University Environmental Center (BUEC) completed a campus-wide environmental assessment of the university's operations, involving over 70 faculty, students, staff, and community members in a highly educational and collaborative project. Teams conducted research on ten indicators of sustainability, including administration/policy, education, energy, water, solid waste, hazardous materials, purchasing, dining, built environment, and landscape. The full report is available at http:www.bucknell.edu/x45647.xml.

ADMISSIONS

Freshman Academic Profile: Average high school GPA 3.6. 60% in top 10% of high school class, 89% in top 25% of high school class, 100% in top 50% of high school class. 60% from public high schools. **Test Scores:** SAT Math middle 50% range 630-720. SAT EBRW middle 50% range 620-700. ACT middle 50% range 28-31. Minimum internet-based TOEFL 100. Minimum paper TOEFL 600. **Basis for Candidate Selection:** *Very important factors considered include:* rigor of secondary school record, academic GPA, application essay, standardized test scores, talent/ability, character/personal qualities. *Important factors considered include:* recommendation(s), extracurricular activities, volunteer work, work experience. *Other factors considered include:* class rank, first generation, alumni/ae relation, geographical residence, religious affiliation/commitment, racial/ethnic status. **Freshman Admission Requirements:** High school diploma is required and GED is accepted *Academic units required:* 4 English, 3 math, 2 science, 2 foreign language, 2 social studies, 2 history, 1 academic elective, *Academic units recommended:* 4 English, 4 math, 2 science, 2 science labs, 4 foreign language, 2 social studies, 2 history, 1 academic elective. **Freshman Admission Statistics:** 10,253 applied, 31.1% admitted, 31% enrolled. **Transfer Admission Requirements:** High school transcript, college transcript(s), essay or personal statement, standardized test scores, statement of good standing from prior institution(s). Minimum college GPA of 2.5 required. Lowest grade transferable C. **General Admission Information:** Application fee $40. Regular application deadline 1/15. Nonfall registration accepted. Admission may be deferred for a maximum of 2 years.

COSTS AND FINANCIAL AID

Annual tuition $53,692. Room and board $13,150. Required fees $294. Average book expense $900. **Required Forms and Deadlines:** CSS/Financial Aid PROFILE; FAFSA. **Notification of Awards:** Applicants will be notified of awards on or about 4/1. **Types of Aid:** *Need-based scholarships/grants:* College/university scholarship or grant aid from institutional funds; Federal Pell; Private scholarships; SEOG; State scholarships/grants. *Loans:* Direct PLUS loans; Direct Subsidized Stafford Loans; Direct Unsubsidized Stafford Loans. *Student Employment:* Federal Work-Study Program available. Institutional employment available. **Financial Aid Statistics:** 89% needy freshmen, 95% needy undergrads receive need-based scholarship or grant aid. 27% freshmen, 23% undergrads receive non-need-based scholarship or grant aid. 100% freshmen, 100% undergrads receive need-based self-help aid. 4% freshmen, 5% undergrads receive athletic scholarships. 62% freshmen, 62% undergrads receive any aid. Average cumulative indebtedness $22,600. **Criteria for awarding aid:** *Need-based:* Academics, Athletics, Minority status *Non-need-based:* Academics, Art, Athletics, Leadership, Music/drama.

See page 908.

BUENA VISTA UNIVERSITY

610 West Fourth Street, Storm Lake, IA 50588-1798
Phone: 712-749-2235 · **Financial Aid Phone:** 712-749-2164
E-mail: admissions@bvu.edu · **CEEB Code:** 6047
Fax: 712-749-2035 · **Website:** www.bvu.edu · **ACT Code:** 1278

This private school, affiliated with the Presbyterian Church, was founded in 1891. It has a 60 acre campus.

RATINGS
Admissions Selectivity Rating: 80   **Fire Safety Rating:** 62   **Green Rating:** 60*

STUDENTS AND FACULTY
Enrollment: 781. **Student Body:** 51% female, 49% male, 21% out-of-state, 5% international (13 countries represented). Asian 2%, African American 3%, Caucasian 75%, Hispanic 7%, Native American 0%, Pacific Islander <1%, Two or more races 4%, Race unknown 4%.
Retention and Graduation: 73% freshmen return for sophomore year. 13% grads go on to further study within 1 year. **Faculty:** Student/faculty ratio 9:1. 82 full-time faculty, 77% hold PhDs, 9% are members of minority groups, 55% are women. 0% of classes are taught by teaching assistants.

ACADEMICS
Degrees: Bachelor's; Master's **Classes:** Most classes have 20-29 students. Most lab/discussion sessions have 10-19 students. **Most popular majors:** Elementary Education And Teaching; Biology/Biological Sciences, General; Business/Commerce, General. **Special Study Options:** Distance learning; Double major; Dual enrollment; English as a Second Language (ESL); External degree program; Honors program; Independent study; Internships; Student-designed major; Study abroad; Teacher certification program. **Disability Services offered to physically disabled students:** Note-taking services;

Reader services; Tape recorders; Tutors. **Career services:** Alumni network; Alumni services; Career assessment; Career/job search classes; Internships

FACILITIES
Housing: Coed dorms; Special housing for disabled student; Wellness housing **Special Academic Facilities/Equipment:** Art gallery, language lab, television station, radio station, satellite telecommunications system, computer labs/centers, electron microscope. **Computers:** 100% of classrooms, 100% of dorms, 100% of libraries, 100% of dining areas, 100% of common outdoor areas have wireless network access. Students can register for classes online. Administrative functions (other than registration) can be performed online.

CAMPUS LIFE
Environment: Village **Activities:** Campus Ministries; Choral groups; Concert band; Dance; Drama/theater; International Student Organization; Jazz band; Music ensembles; Musical theater; Radio station; Student government; Student newspaper; Television station 65 registered organizations, 5 honor societies, 3 religious organizations. **Athletics (Intercollegiate):** *Men:* baseball, basketball, cross-country, football, golf, soccer, tennis, track/field (outdoor), track/field (indoor), wrestling. *Women:* basketball, cross-country, golf, soccer, softball, tennis, track/field (outdoor), track/field (indoor), volleyball. **On-Campus Highlights:** Recreation Center for all your working out needs, Harold Walter Siebens Forum, our completely underground facility, Centennial Room, a huge cafe in which to hang out with friends, Suites are the biggest dorms on campus, Forum Lawn is great for playing Frisbee,

ADMISSIONS
Freshman Academic Profile: Average high school GPA 3.4. 16% in top 10% of high school class, 40% in top 25% of high school class, 79% in top 50% of high school class. 85% from public high schools. **Test Scores:** ACT middle 50% range 19-26. Minimum internet-based TOEFL 59. Minimum paper TOEFL 500. **Basis for Candidate Selection:** *Very important factors considered include:* class rank, academic GPA, standardized test scores, recommendation(s). *Important factors considered include:* extracurricular activities, character/personal qualities. *Other factors considered include:* rigor of secondary school record, application essay, interview, talent/ability, alumni/ae relation, volunteer work, work experience. **Freshman Admission Requirements:** High school diploma is required and GED is accepted *Academic units recommended:* 4 English, 4 math, 3 science, 1 science labs, 3 social studies. **Freshman Admission Statistics:** 1,256 applied, 63.7% admitted, 23% enrolled. **Transfer Admission Requirements:** college transcript(s), statement of good standing from prior institution(s). Minimum college GPA of 2.0 required. Lowest grade transferable D. **General Admission Information:** Nonfall registration accepted. Admission may be deferred for a maximum of 1 year.

COSTS AND FINANCIAL AID
Annual tuition $32,854. Room and board $9,490. Average book expense $999. **Required Forms and Deadlines:** FAFSA. **Types of Aid:** *Need-based scholarships/grants:* College/university scholarship or grant aid from institutional funds; Federal Pell; Private scholarships; SEOG; State scholarships/grants. *Loans:* Direct PLUS loans; Direct Subsidized Stafford Loans; Direct Unsubsidized Stafford Loans. *Student Employment:* Federal Work-Study Program available. Institutional employment available. **Financial Aid Statistics:** 98% needy freshmen, 99% needy undergrads receive need-based scholarship or grant aid. 15% freshmen, 17% undergrads receive non-need-based scholarship or grant aid. 90% freshmen, 90% undergrads receive need-based self-help aid. 0% freshmen, 0% undergrads receive athletic scholarships. 99% freshmen, 98% undergrads receive any aid. 86% undergrads borrow to pay for school. Average cumulative indebtedness $33,559. **Criteria for awarding aid:** *Non-need-based:* Academics, Art, Minority status, Music/drama.

BURLINGTON COLLEGE

351 North Ave, Burlington, VT 05401
Phone: 802-862-9616 x104 · **Financial Aid Phone:** 802-862-9616 ext 110
E-mail: admissions@burlington.edu · **CEEB Code:** 1119
Fax: 802/660-4331 · **Website:** www.burlington.edu · **ACT Code:** 4329

This private school was founded in 1972. It has a 32 acre campus.

RATINGS
Admissions Selectivity Rating: 73   **Fire Safety Rating:** 70   **Green Rating:** 60*

STUDENTS AND FACULTY
Enrollment: 178. **Student Body:** 48% female, 52% male, 46% out-of-state, 2% international (5 countries represented). Asian 1%, African American 1%,

Caucasian 83%, Hispanic 2%, Native American 1%, Pacific Islander 0%, Two or more races 1%, Race unknown 11%.
Retention and Graduation: 40% freshmen return for sophomore year. 16% grads go on to further study within 1 year. 10% grads pursue arts and sciences degrees. 5% grads pursue law degrees. 0% grads pursue business degrees. 0% grads pursue medical degrees. **Faculty:** Student/faculty ratio 6:1. 5 full-time faculty, 60% hold PhDs, 60% are women. 0% of classes are taught by teaching assistants.

ACADEMICS

Degrees: Associate; Bachelor's; Certificate; Master's **Classes:** Most classes have 10-19 students. Most lab/discussion sessions have 20-29 students. **Most popular majors:** English Language And Literature/Letters, Other; Multi-/Interdisciplinary Studies, General. **Special Study Options:** Cross-registration; Distance learning; Double major; Dual enrollment; Exchange student program (domestic); External degree program; Independent study; Internships; Liberal arts/career combination; Student-designed major; Study abroad. **Honors programs: Disability Services offered to physically disabled students:** Reader services; Tape recorders; Tutors. **Career services:** Career/job search classes; Internships

FACILITIES

Housing: Apartments for single students; Coed dorms; Cooperative housing; Men's dorms; Special housing for disabled student; Women's dorms 100% of campus accessible to physically diasbled. **Special Academic Facilities/Equipment:** Located in the center of City of Burlington, Vermont—Burlington College sits on 32 acres of undeveloped land on Lake Champlain. The campus is a 77,000 sq.ft. Victorian building that houses a movie theater, photography darkroom, numerous galleries, Apple Certified computer lab, student eatery, ballroom, and many activity spaces. Students have access to the YMCA for fitness and UVM's extensive library. **Computers:** 100% of classrooms, 100% of dorms, 100% of libraries, 100% of student union, have wireless network access.

CAMPUS LIFE

Environment: Town **Activities:** Literary magazine; Student government 1 registered organization. **On-Campus Highlights:** Miller Studio for film editing, Woodworking shop, Photography dark room, Library, Editing suites for film **Environmental Initiatives:** New lighting with motion sensors

ADMISSIONS

Freshman Academic Profile: Average high school GPA 2.9. 5% in top 10% of high school class, 19% in top 25% of high school class, 38% in top 50% of high school class. 72% from public high schools. **Test Scores:** SAT Math middle 50% range 425-530. SAT EBRW middle 50% range 440-575. ACT middle 50% range 18-26. Minimum internet-based TOEFL 79. Minimum paper TOEFL 550. **Basis for Candidate Selection:** *Very important factors considered include:* application essay, interview, character/personal qualities. *Important factors considered include:* academic GPA, recommendation(s), talent/ability, volunteer work.level of applicant's interest. *Other factors considered include:* rigor of secondary school record, class rank, standardized test scores, extracurricular activities, first generation, alumni/ae relation, work experience. **Freshman Admission Requirements:** High school diploma is required and GED is accepted *Academic units recommended:* 4 English, 3 math, 2 science, 2 science labs, 2 foreign language, 4 social studies, 3 history, 4 academic electives. **Freshman Admission Statistics:** 180 applied, 85.6% admitted, 25% enrolled. **Transfer Admission Requirements:** High school transcript, college transcript(s), essay or personal statement, Lowest grade transferable C. **General Admission Information:** Application fee $50. Regular application deadline 8/15. Nonfall registration accepted. Admission may be deferred for a maximum of 1 year.

COSTS AND FINANCIAL AID

Annual tuition $22,410. Required fees $135. Average book expense $1,064. **Required Forms and Deadlines:** FAFSA. **Notification of Awards:** Applicants will be notified of awards on a rolling basis beginning 2/15. **Types of Aid:** *Need-based scholarships/grants:* College/university scholarship or grant aid from institutional funds; Federal Pell; Private scholarships; SEOG; State scholarships/grants. *Loans:* Direct PLUS loans; Direct Subsidized Stafford Loans; Direct Unsubsidized Stafford Loans. *Student Employment:* Federal Work-Study Program available. **Financial Aid Statistics:** 100% needy freshmen, 95% needy undergrads receive need-based scholarship or grant aid. 0% undergrads receive non-need-based scholarship or grant aid. 86% freshmen, 96% undergrads receive need-based self-help aid. 0% freshmen, 0% undergrads receive athletic scholarships. 75% freshmen, 76% undergrads receive any aid. **Criteria for awarding aid:** *Need-based:* Academics, Leadership *Non-need-based:* Academics, Leadership.

BUTLER UNIVERSITY

4600 Sunset Avenue, Indianapolis, IN 46208
Phone: 317-940-8100 · **Financial Aid Phone:** 317-940-8200
E-mail: admission@butler.edu · **CEEB Code:** 1073
Fax: 317-940-8150 · **Website:** www.butler.edu · **ACT Code:** 1180

This private school was founded in 1855. It has a 295 acre campus.

RATINGS

Admissions Selectivity Rating: 87   **Fire Safety Rating:** 78   **Green Rating:** 60*

STUDENTS AND FACULTY

Enrollment: 4,194. **Student Body:** 60% female, 40% male, 53% out-of-state, 1% international (39 countries represented). Asian 3%, African American 4%, Caucasian 83%, Hispanic 4%, Native American <1%, Pacific Islander <1%, Two or more races 3%, Race unknown 2%.
Retention and Graduation: 89% freshmen return for sophomore year. 63% freshmen graduate within 4 years. 79% freshmen graduate within 6 years. 25% grads go on to further study within 1 year. 24% grads pursue arts and sciences degrees. 7% grads pursue law degrees. 5% grads pursue business degrees. 20% grads pursue medical degrees. **Faculty:** Student/faculty ratio 11:1. 363 full-time faculty, 80% hold PhDs, 12% are members of minority groups, 50% are women. 0% of classes are taught by teaching assistants.

ACADEMICS

Degrees: Associate; Bachelor's; Certificate; Doctoral/Professional; Master's; Post-Bachelor's certificate **Classes:** Most classes have 10-19 students. Most lab/discussion sessions have 10-19 students. **Most popular majors:** Public Relations, Advertising, And Applied Communication, Other; Finance, General; Marketing/Marketing Management, General. **Special Study Options:** Accelerated program; Cross-registration; Distance learning; Double major; Dual enrollment; Exchange student program (domestic); Honors program; Independent study; Internships; Liberal arts/career combination; Student-designed major; Study abroad; Teacher certification program. **Honors programs:** The Butler University Honors Program exists to meet the expectations of academically outstanding students in all colleges and majors who wish to develop their talents and potential to the fullest. Through a combination of honors courses, cultural events, independent study, creative activity and research, it is designed to foster a diverse and challenging intellectual environment for honors students and to enhance our academic community by adding a distinctive note of innovative thinking and interdisciplinary dialogue. **Disability Services offered to physically disabled students:** Note-taking services; Reader services; Tape recorders; Tutors. **Career services:** Alumni network; Alumni services; Career assessment; Career/job search classes; Internships; Regional alumni

FACILITIES

Housing: Apartments for single students; Coed dorms; Fraternity/sorority housing; Theme housing 100% of campus accessible to physically diasbled. **Special Academic Facilities/Equipment:** Holcomb Observatory, Clowes Memorial Hall (performing arts theatre), Schrott Center for the Arts **Computers:** 100% of classrooms, 100% of dorms, 100% of libraries, 100% of dining areas, 100% of student union, have wireless network access. Students can register for classes online. Administrative functions (other than registration) can be performed online.

CAMPUS LIFE

Environment: Metropolis **Activities:** Campus Ministries; Choral groups; Concert band; Dance; Drama/theater; International Student Organization; Jazz band; Literary magazine; Marching band; Model UN; Music ensembles; Musical theater; Opera; Pep band; Radio station; Student government; Student newspaper; Student-run film society; Symphony orchestra; Television station; Yearbook 135 registered organizations, 8 honor societies, 6 religious organizations. 7 fraternities, 9 sororities. **Athletics (Intercollegiate):** *Men:* baseball, basketball, cross-country, football, golf, soccer, tennis, track/field (outdoor), track/field (indoor). *Women:* basketball, cross-country, golf, soccer, softball, swimming, tennis, track/field (outdoor), track/field (indoor), volleyball. **On-Campus Highlights:** Starbucks in the Union, Carillon on Lake Road, Holcomb Gardens, Hinkle Fieldhouse, Atherton Union **Environmental Initiatives:** College of Pharmacy and Health Sciences building will be "Leed Certified-Silver"

ADMISSIONS

Freshman Academic Profile: Average high school GPA 3.8. 46% in top 10% of high school class, 76% in top 25% of high school class, 94% in top 50% of

high school class. **Test Scores:** SAT Math middle 50% range 570-660. SAT EBRW middle 50% range 580-660. ACT middle 50% range 25-30. Minimum internet-based TOEFL 79. Minimum paper TOEFL 550. **Basis for Candidate Selection:** *Very important factors considered include:* rigor of secondary school record, academic GPA, standardized test scores, character/personal qualities. *Important factors considered include:* application essay, recommendation(s), extracurricular activities, talent/ability, level of applicant's interest. *Other factors considered include:* class rank, first generation, alumni/ae relation, geographical residence, racial/ethnic status, volunteer work, work experience. **Freshman Admission Requirements:** High school diploma is required and GED is accepted *Academic units required:* 4 English, 3 math, 3 science, 3 science labs, 2 foreign language, 2 social studies, 2 history, *Academic units recommended:* 4 math, 4 science. **Freshman Admission Statistics:** 14,635 applied, 65.1% admitted, 11% enrolled. **Transfer Admission Requirements:** college transcript(s), essay or personal statement, statement of good standing from prior institution(s). Minimum college GPA of 2.0 required. Lowest grade transferable C. **General Admission Information:** Nonfall registration accepted. Admission may be deferred.

COSTS AND FINANCIAL AID

Annual tuition $40,160. Room and board $14,690. Required fees $960. Average book expense $1,000. **Required Forms and Deadlines:** FAFSA. **Notification of Awards:** Applicants will be notified of awards on a rolling basis beginning 1/15. **Types of Aid:** *Need-based scholarships/grants:* College/university scholarship or grant aid from institutional funds; Federal Pell; Private scholarships; SEOG; State scholarships/grants. *Loans:* Direct PLUS loans; Direct Subsidized Stafford Loans; Direct Unsubsidized Stafford Loans. *Student Employment:* Federal Work-Study Program available. Institutional employment available. **Financial Aid Statistics:** 100% needy freshmen, 98% needy undergrads receive need-based scholarship or grant aid. 17% freshmen, 13% undergrads receive non-need-based scholarship or grant aid. 73% freshmen, 76% undergrads receive need-based self-help aid. 2% freshmen, 2% undergrads receive athletic scholarships. 90% freshmen, 90% undergrads receive any aid. 63% undergrads borrow to pay for school. Average cumulative indebtedness $35,730. **Criteria for awarding aid:** *Non-need-based:* Academics, Alumni affiliation, Athletics, Leadership, Music/drama.

CABRINI UNIVERSITY

610 King of Prussia Road, Radnor, PA 19087-3698
Phone: 610-902-8552 · **Financial Aid Phone:** (610)902-8420
E-mail: admit@cabrini.edu · **CEEB Code:** 2071
Fax: 610-902-8508 · **Website:** www.cabrini.edu · **ACT Code:** 3532

This private school, affiliated with the Roman Catholic Church, was founded in 1957. It has a 112 acre campus.

RATINGS

Admissions Selectivity Rating: 73   Fire Safety Rating: 96   Green Rating: 60*

STUDENTS AND FACULTY

Enrollment: 1,820. **Student Body:** 66% female, 34% male, 34% out-of-state, 1% international (34 countries represented). Asian 2%, African American 6%, Caucasian 83%, Hispanic 3%, Native American <1%, Race unknown 6%. **Retention and Graduation:** 66% freshmen return for sophomore year. 21% grads go on to further study within 1 year. 16% grads pursue arts and sciences degrees. 1% grads pursue law degrees. 3% grads pursue business degrees. 1% grads pursue medical degrees. **Faculty:** Student/faculty ratio 16:1. 64 full-time faculty, 80% hold PhDs, 5% are members of minority groups, 55% are women. 0% of classes are taught by teaching assistants.

ACADEMICS

Degrees: Bachelor's; Certificate; Master's; Post-Bachelor's certificate **Classes:** Most classes have 10-19 students. Most lab/discussion sessions have 10-19 students. **Most popular majors:** Elementary Education And Teaching; Business, Management, Marketing, And Related Support Services, Other. **Special Study Options:** Accelerated program; Cooperative education program; Cross-registration; Double major; Honors program; Independent study; Internships; Liberal arts/career combination; Student-designed major; Study abroad; Teacher certification program. **Honors programs:** Cabrini College Honors Program; Honors in the major. **Disability Services offered to physically disabled students:** Note-taking services; Reader services; Tape recorders; Tutors. **Career services:** Alumni network; Alumni services; Career assessment; Career/job search classes; Internships

FACILITIES

Housing: Coed dorms; Special housing for disabled student; Women's dorms 97% of campus accessible to physically diasbled. **Special Academic Facilities/**

Equipment: Exercise Science Lab, Communications center (includes a graphic design lab, radio station, newsroom, and television studio.) Science Education and Technology building with state-of-the-art biology, chemistry, and physics labs, Instructional Technology labs, and research space. **Computers:** 100% of classrooms, 95% of dorms, 100% of libraries, 100% of dining areas, 100% of student union, 95% of common outdoor areas have wireless network access. Students can register for classes online. Administrative functions (other than registration) can be performed online.

CAMPUS LIFE

Environment: Town **Activities:** Campus Ministries; Choral groups; Dance; Drama/theater; International Student Organization; Literary magazine; Radio station; Student government; Student newspaper; Student-run film society; Television station; Yearbook 32 registered organizations, 18 honor societies, 1 religious organization. **Athletics (Intercollegiate):** *Men:* basketball, cross-country, golf, lacrosse, soccer, swimming, tennis, track/field (outdoor). *Women:* basketball, cross-country, field hockey, lacrosse, soccer, softball, swimming, tennis, track/field (outdoor), volleyball. **On-Campus Highlights:** Dixon Center- Athletic/Recreation facility, Jazzman's Cafe, Holy Spirit Library, Mansion, Science Technology Education Building

ADMISSIONS

Freshman Academic Profile: Average high school GPA 3.1. 6% in top 10% of high school class, 20% in top 25% of high school class, 49% in top 50% of high school class. 56% from public high schools. **Test Scores:** SAT Math middle 50% range 430-520. SAT EBRW middle 50% range 440-530. Minimum paper TOEFL 500. **Basis for Candidate Selection:** *Very important factors considered include:* academic GPA, standardized test scores. *Important factors considered include:* level of applicant's interest. *Other factors considered include:* rigor of secondary school record, class rank, application essay, recommendation(s), interview, extracurricular activities, talent/ability, character/personal qualities, alumni/ae relation, volunteer work, work experience. **Freshman Admission Requirements:** High school diploma is required and GED is accepted *Academic units required:* 4 English, 3 math, 3 science, 2 foreign language, 3 social studies, 3 history, *Academic units recommended:* 4 English, 4 math, 3 science, 2 foreign language, 3 social studies, 3 history, 2 academic electives. **Freshman Admission Statistics:** 2,374 applied, 87.4% admitted, 26% enrolled. **Transfer Admission Requirements:** college transcript(s), Minimum college GPA of 2.2 required. Lowest grade transferable C-. **General Admission Information:** Application fee $35. Priority deadline 5/1. Nonfall registration accepted. Admission may be deferred for a maximum of One year.

COSTS AND FINANCIAL AID

Average book expense $960. **Required Forms and Deadlines:** FAFSA. **Notification of Awards:** Applicants will be notified of awards on a rolling basis beginning 2/20. **Types of Aid:** *Need-based scholarships/grants:* College/university scholarship or grant aid from institutional funds; Federal Pell; Private scholarships; SEOG; State scholarships/grants. **Financial Aid Statistics:** 81% needy freshmen, 78% needy undergrads receive need-based scholarship or grant aid. 92% freshmen, 94% undergrads receive non-need-based scholarship or grant aid. 80% freshmen, 84% undergrads receive need-based self-help aid. 0% freshmen, 0% undergrads receive athletic scholarships. 98% freshmen, 97% undergrads receive any aid. **Criteria for awarding aid:** *Non-need-based:* Academics, Alumni affiliation.

See page 910.

CAIRN UNIVERSITY

200 Manor Avenue, Langhorne, PA 19047
Phone: 215-702-4235 · **Financial Aid Phone:** 215-702-4246
E-mail: admissions@cairn.edu
Fax: 215-702-4248 · **Website:** www.cairn.edu · **ACT Code:** 3658

This private school, affiliated with the Protestant Church, was founded in 1913. It has a 114 acre campus.

RATINGS

Admissions Selectivity Rating: 80   Fire Safety Rating: 82   Green Rating: 60*

STUDENTS AND FACULTY

Enrollment: 937. **Student Body:** 53% female, 47% male, 44% out-of-state, 2% international (31 countries represented). Asian 4%, African American 14%, Caucasian 72%, Hispanic 5%, Native American 1%, Pacific Islander 0%, Two or more races 2%, Race unknown 1%. **Retention and Graduation:** 78% freshmen return for sophomore year. 40% grads go on to further study within 1 year. **Faculty:** Student/faculty ratio 13:1.

50 full-time faculty, 70% hold PhDs, 18% are members of minority groups, 30% are women. 0% of classes are taught by teaching assistants.

ACADEMICS

Degrees: Bachelor's; Certificate; Master's; Post-Bachelor's certificate **Classes:** Most classes have 10-19 students. Most lab/discussion sessions have 10-19 students. **Most popular majors:** Elementary Education And Teaching; Bible/Biblical Studies; Social Work. **Special Study Options:** Accelerated program; Double major; Honors program; Internships; Study abroad; Teacher certification program. **Disability Services offered to physically disabled students:** Note-taking services; Reader services; Tape recorders; Tutors. **Career services:** Alumni network; Alumni services; Career assessment; Career/job search classes; Internships

FACILITIES

Housing: Apartments for married students; Apartments for single students; Men's dorms; Special housing for disabled student; Special housing for international students; Women's dorms 99% of campus accessible to physically diasbled. **Special Academic Facilities/Equipment:** Biblical Learning Center Museum area **Computers:** 59% of classrooms, 62% of dorms, 90% of libraries, 100% of dining areas, 100% of student union, 15% of common outdoor areas have wireless network access. Students can register for classes online. Administrative functions (other than registration) can be performed online.

CAMPUS LIFE

Environment: Village **Activities:** Campus Ministries; Choral groups; Concert band; Drama/theater; International Student Organization; Music ensembles; Musical theater; Opera; Student government; Student newspaper; Symphony orchestra; Yearbook 25 registered organizations, 4 honor societies, 3 religious organizations. **Athletics (Intercollegiate):** *Men:* baseball, basketball, cross-country, golf, soccer, volleyball. *Women:* basketball, cross-country, soccer, softball, tennis, volleyball. **On-Campus Highlights:** The Cafe, Student Lounge, Campus Walkway, Sports Fields, Heritage Hall Lounge

ADMISSIONS

Freshman Academic Profile: Average high school GPA 3.3. 18% in top 10% of high school class, 39% in top 25% of high school class, 17% in top 50% of high school class. 60% from public high schools. **Test Scores:** SAT Math middle 50% range 450-580. SAT EBRW middle 50% range 470-590. ACT middle 50% range 17-24. Minimum paper TOEFL 520. **Basis for Candidate Selection:** *Very important factors considered include:* academic GPA, standardized test scores, interview, character/personal qualities, religious affiliation/ commitment, level of applicant's interest. *Important factors considered include:* rigor of secondary school record, application essay. *Other factors considered include:* class rank, recommendation(s), extracurricular activities. **Freshman Admission Requirements:** High school diploma is required and GED is accepted *Academic units recommended:* 4 English, 1 math, 2 science, 2 foreign language, 3 social studies. **Freshman Admission Statistics:** 482 applied, 74.3% admitted, 41% enrolled. **Transfer Admission Requirements:** college transcript(s), essay or personal statement, interview, Minimum college GPA of 2.2 required. Lowest grade transferable C. **General Admission Information:** Application fee $25. Nonfall registration accepted. Admission may be deferred for a maximum of 1 year.

COSTS AND FINANCIAL AID

Annual tuition $21,500. Room and board $8,525. Required fees $205. Average book expense $1,200. **Required Forms and Deadlines:** FAFSA. **Notification of Awards:** Applicants will be notified of awards on a rolling basis beginning 2/15. **Types of Aid:** *Need-based scholarships/grants:* College/ university scholarship or grant aid from institutional funds; Federal Pell; Private scholarships; SEOG; State scholarships/grants. *Loans:* Direct PLUS loans; Direct Subsidized Stafford Loans; Direct Unsubsidized Stafford Loans. *Student Employment:* Federal Work-Study Program available. Institutional employment available. **Financial Aid Statistics:** 99% needy freshmen, 96% needy undergrads receive need-based scholarship or grant aid. 6% freshmen, 6% undergrads receive non-need-based scholarship or grant aid. 98% freshmen, 96% undergrads receive need-based self-help aid. 0% freshmen, 0% undergrads receive athletic scholarships. 84% freshmen, 82% undergrads receive any aid. **Criteria for awarding aid:** *Non-need-based:* Academics, Leadership, Music/ drama.

CALIFORNIA BAPTIST UNIVERSITY

8432 Magnolia Ave, Riverside, CA 92504
Phone: 951-343-4212 · **Financial Aid Phone:** 951-343-4236
E-mail: admissions@calbaptist.edu · **CEEB Code:** 4094
Fax: 951-343-4525 · **Website:** www.calbaptist.edu · **ACT Code:** 4094

This private school, affiliated with the Southern Baptist Church, was founded in 1950. It has a 160 acre campus.

RATINGS

Admissions Selectivity Rating: 81   **Fire Safety Rating:** 64   **Green Rating:** 60*

STUDENTS AND FACULTY

Enrollment: 6,904. **Student Body:** 63% female, 37% male, 7% out-of-state, 2% international (25 countries represented). Asian 5%, African American 8%, Caucasian 38%, Hispanic 36%, Native American 1%, Pacific Islander 1%, Two or more races 6%, Race unknown 4%.
Retention and Graduation: 75% freshmen return for sophomore year. **Faculty:** Student/faculty ratio 18:1. 315 full-time faculty, 75% hold PhDs, 29% are members of minority groups, 47% are women. 0% of classes are taught by teaching assistants.

ACADEMICS

Degrees: Associate; Bachelor's; Doctoral/Research; Master's **Classes:** Most classes have 20-29 students. Most lab/discussion sessions have 20-29 students. **Most popular majors:** Psychology, General; Registered Nursing/Registered Nurse; Business/Commerce, General. **Special Study Options:** Accelerated program; Distance learning; Double major; English as a Second Language (ESL); Exchange student program (domestic); Honors program; Internships; Liberal arts/career combination; Study abroad; Teacher certification program; Weekend college. **Honors programs:** The Honors program offers students from all major areas of study the opportunity to participate in rigorous study, requiring diligence in reading primary sources and writing original essays through 6 intensive seminars. Honors students progressively investigate a single generative idea using primary texts, drawing upon the expertise of leading faculty. These seminars may be used to fulfill elective unit requirements and specially selected general education requirements. Successful completion of the Honors Program will be posted on the academic transcript and students will be designated as Honors Program graduates at commencement. **Disability Services offered to physically disabled students:** Note-taking services; Tutors. **Career services:** Alumni network; Alumni services; Career assessment; Career/job search classes; Internships

FACILITIES

Housing: Apartments for married students; Apartments for single students; Cooperative housing; Men's dorms; Theme housing; Women's dorms 95% of campus accessible to physically diasbled. **Special Academic Facilities/ Equipment:** Metcalf Art Gallery, Annie Gabriel Library, Wallace Theater, P. Boyd Smith Hymnology Collection, Music Production and Recording Studios, Digital Design and Photography Studio, Theater Arts stage production workshop, Nie Wieder!Holocaust Collection, prayer chapel, Nursing Patient Simulation Laboratory, **Computers:** 40% of classrooms, 10% of dorms, 100% of libraries, 100% of dining areas, 100% of student union, 25% of common outdoor areas have wireless network access. Students can register for classes online. Administrative functions (other than registration) can be performed online.

CAMPUS LIFE

Environment: Metropolis **Activities:** Campus Ministries; Choral groups; Concert band; Drama/theater; International Student Organization; Jazz band; Literary magazine; Music ensembles; Musical theater; Student government; Student newspaper; Student-run film society; Symphony orchestra; Yearbook 30 registered organizations, 2 honor societies, 6 religious organizations. **Athletics (Intercollegiate):** *Men:* baseball, basketball, cheerleading, cross-country, diving, golf, soccer, swimming, volleyball, water polo, wrestling. *Women:* basketball, cheerleading, cross-country, diving, golf, soccer, softball, swimming, volleyball, water polo. **On-Campus Highlights:** Recreation Center, Campus Bookstore, Wanda's & Brisco's Coffee Shops, Van Dyne Gymnasium, Aquatic Center **Environmental Initiatives:** Energy Efficient Lighting

ADMISSIONS

Freshman Academic Profile: Average high school GPA 3.4. 15% in top 10% of high school class, 41% in top 25% of high school class, 76% in top 50% of high school class. 77% from public high schools. **Test Scores:** SAT Math middle 50% range 420-550. SAT EBRW middle 50% range 430-550. ACT middle 50% range 19-24. Minimum internet-based TOEFL 71. Minimum paper TOEFL 527. **Basis for Candidate Selection:** *Very important factors considered include:* rigor of secondary school record, academic GPA, application essay, standardized test scores, recommendation(s), character/personal qualities. *Important factors considered include:* level of applicant's interest. *Other factors considered include:* class rank, extracurricular activities, talent/ability, volunteer work. **Freshman Admission Requirements:** High school diploma is required and GED is accepted *Academic units required:* 4 English, 3 math, 2 science, 2 science labs, 2 foreign language, 2 social studies, 2 history, *Academic units recommended:* 4 English, 4 math, 3 science, 3 science labs, 3 foreign language, 2 social studies, 2 history, 3 academic electives, 1 visual/performing arts, 2 units from above areas or other academic areas. **Freshman Admission Statistics:** 4,971 applied, 64.0% admitted, 36% enrolled. **Transfer Admission Requirements:** college transcript(s), essay or personal statement, statement of good standing from prior institution(s). Minimum college GPA of 2.0 required. Lowest grade transferable C. **General Admission Information:** Application fee $45. Nonfall registration accepted. Admission may be deferred for a maximum of 1 year.

COSTS AND FINANCIAL AID

Annual tuition $30,446. Room and board $11,540. Required fees $2,120. Average book expense $1,790. **Required Forms and Deadlines:** FAFSA; State aid form. **Notification of Awards:** Applicants will be notified of awards on a rolling basis beginning 3/2. **Types of Aid:** *Need-based scholarships/grants:* College/university scholarship or grant aid from institutional funds; Federal Nursing Scholarships; Federal Pell; Private scholarships; SEOG; State scholarships/grants. *Loans:* Direct PLUS loans; Direct Subsidized Stafford Loans; Direct Unsubsidized Stafford Loans. *Student Employment:* Federal Work-Study Program available. Institutional employment available. **Financial Aid Statistics:** 90% needy freshmen, 75% needy undergrads receive need-based scholarship or grant aid. 85% freshmen, 61% undergrads receive non-need-based scholarship or grant aid. 64% freshmen, 63% undergrads receive need-based self-help aid. 5% freshmen, 4% undergrads receive athletic scholarships. 90% freshmen, 90% undergrads receive any aid. 77% undergrads borrow to pay for school. Average cumulative indebtedness $20,693. **Criteria for awarding aid:** *Need-based:* Academics, Art, Athletics, Music/drama, Religious affiliation *Non-need-based:* Academics, Art, Athletics, Music/drama, Religious affiliation.

CALIFORNIA COLLEGE OF THE ARTS

1111 Eighth Street, San Francisco, CA 94107
Phone: 415-703-9523 · **Financial Aid Phone:** 415-703-9528
E-mail: enroll@cca.edu · **CEEB Code:** 4031
Fax: 415-703-9539 · **Website:** www.cca.edu · **ACT Code:** 176

This private school was founded in 1907. It has a 12.4 acre campus.

RATINGS

Admissions Selectivity Rating: 74   Fire Safety Rating: 97   Green Rating: 90

STUDENTS AND FACULTY

Enrollment: 1,515. **Student Body:** 64% female, 36% male, 35% out-of-state, 35% international (60 countries represented). Asian 18%, African American 6%, Caucasian 23%, Hispanic 12%, Native American <1%, Pacific Islander 1%, Two or more races 0%, Race unknown 6%.
Retention and Graduation: 82% freshmen return for sophomore year. **Faculty:** 100 full-time faculty, 64% hold PhDs, 32% are members of minority groups, 48% are women. 0% of classes are taught by teaching assistants.

ACADEMICS

Degrees: Bachelor's; Master's **Classes:** Most classes have 10-19 students. **Most popular majors:** Industrial And Product Design; Graphic Design; Illustration. **Special Study Options:** Cross-registration; Double major; English as a Second Language (ESL); Exchange student program (domestic); Independent study; Internships; Student-designed major; Study abroad. **Honors programs:** The First Year Honors Program enhances student's entry-level college experience by providing additional and rigorous critique as well as an introduction to available resources at the college and throughout the Bay Area. **Disability Services offered to physically disabled students:** Note-taking services; Reader services; Tape recorders; Tutors. **Career services:** Alumni services; Career assessment; Career/job search classes; Internships

FACILITIES

Housing: Apartments for single students; Coed dorms; Special housing for disabled students 95% of campus accessible to physically disabled. **Special Academic Facilities/Equipment:** Wattis Institute for Contemporary Art **Computers:** 100% of classrooms, 60% of dorms, 100% of libraries, 100% of dining areas, 90% of common outdoor areas have wireless network access. Students can register for classes online. Administrative functions (other than registration) can be performed online.

CAMPUS LIFE

Environment: Metropolis **Activities:** International Student Organization 10 registered organizations, 1 fraternities. **On-Campus Highlights:** The Nave- San Francisco campus, The Foundry—Oakland campus, Individualized Painting Studios—SF, North/South Student Galleries—Oakland, Wattis Institute for Contemporary Art **Environmental Initiatives:** Largest solar heated facility in San Francisco, named Top Ten Green Building on Earth Day 2001.

ADMISSIONS

Freshman Academic Profile: Average high school GPA 3.3. **Test Scores:** SAT Math middle 50% range 450-620. SAT EBRW middle 50% range 445-580. ACT middle 50% range 20-27. Minimum internet-based TOEFL 80. Minimum paper TOEFL 550. **Basis for Candidate Selection:** *Very important factors considered include:* academic GPA, application essay, talent/ability. *Important factors considered include:* recommendation(s). *Other factors considered include:* rigor of secondary school record, standardized test scores, interview, extracurricular activities, character/personal qualities, first generation, alumni/ae relation, racial/ethnic status, volunteer work, work experience, level of applicant's interest. **Freshman Admission Requirements:** High school diploma is required and GED is accepted **Freshman Admission Statistics:** 1,896 applied, 80.7% admitted, 17% enrolled. **Transfer Admission Requirements:** college transcript(s), essay or personal statement, Minimum college GPA of 2.0 required. Lowest grade transferable C. **General Admission Information:** Application fee $70. Priority deadline 2/1. Nonfall registration accepted. Admission may be deferred for a maximum of one semester.

COSTS AND FINANCIAL AID

Annual tuition $44,976. Required fees $460. Average book expense $1,500. **Required Forms and Deadlines:** FAFSA; State aid form. **Notification of Awards:** Applicants will be notified of awards on a rolling basis beginning 3/15. **Types of Aid:** *Need-based scholarships/grants:* College/university scholarship or grant aid from institutional funds; Federal Pell; Private scholarships; SEOG; State scholarships/grants. *Loans:* Direct PLUS loans; Direct Subsidized Stafford Loans; Direct Unsubsidized Stafford Loans. *Student Employment:* Federal Work-Study Program available. Institutional employment available. **Financial Aid Statistics:** 100% needy freshmen, 100% needy undergrads receive need-based scholarship or grant aid. 88% freshmen, 61% undergrads receive non-need-based scholarship or grant aid. 95% freshmen, 96% undergrads receive need-based self-help aid. 0% freshmen, 0% undergrads receive athletic scholarships. **Criteria for awarding aid:** *Non-need-based:* Academics, Art.

CALIFORNIA INSTITUTE OF THE ARTS

24700 McBean Parkway, Valencia, CA 91355
Phone: 661-255-1050 · **Financial Aid Phone:** 661-253-7869
E-mail: admissions@calarts.edu · **CEEB Code:** 4049
Fax: 661-253-7710 · **Website:** www.calarts.edu · **ACT Code:** 121

This private school was founded in 1961. It has a 60 acre campus.

RATINGS

Admissions Selectivity Rating: 72   Fire Safety Rating: 76   Green Rating: 60*

STUDENTS AND FACULTY

Enrollment: 888. **Student Body:** 49% female, 51% male, 49% out-of-state, 8% international (34 countries represented). Asian 12%, African American 8%, Caucasian 58%, Hispanic 12%, Native American 1%, Race unknown 1%.
Retention and Graduation: 75% freshmen return for sophomore year. **Faculty:** Student/faculty ratio 7:1. 160 full-time faculty, 100% hold PhDs, 18% are members of minority groups, 44% are women. 0% of classes are taught by teaching assistants.

ACADEMICS

Degrees: Bachelor's; Certificate; Doctoral; Master's; Post-Bachelor's certificate **Classes:** Most classes have 10-19 students. Most lab/discussion sessions have 10-19 students. **Most popular majors:** Music Performance, General. **Special Study Options:** Independent study; Internships; Student-designed major; Study abroad. **Disability Services offered to physically disabled students:** Note-taking services; Reader services; Tape recorders; Tutors. **Career services:** Career assessment; Career/job search classes; Internships

FACILITIES

Housing: Apartments for single students; Coed dorms; Special housing for disabled students 98% of campus accessible to physically disabled. **Special Academic Facilities/Equipment:** 7 Art galleries, TV studio, Walt Disney Theater, Roy Disney Music Hall, Sharon Disney Lund Dance Theater, Bijou Film Theater **Computers:** 20% of classrooms, 100% of libraries, 100% of dining areas, 20% of common outdoor areas have wireless network access. Students can register for classes online. Administrative functions (other than registration) can be performed online.

CAMPUS LIFE

Environment: City **Activities:** Choral groups; Dance; Drama/theater; Jazz band; Literary magazine; Music ensembles; Opera; Radio station; Student government; Student newspaper; Student-run film society; Symphony orchestra; Television station 5 registered organizations. **On-Campus Highlights:** Modular Theater, Permanent Set, Gamelan Room, Main Gallery, Lund Dance Theater **Environmental Initiatives:** Recycling Program

ADMISSIONS

Test Scores: Minimum internet-based TOEFL 80. Minimum paper TOEFL 550. **Basis for Candidate Selection:** *Very important factors considered include:* application essay, talent/ability. *Important factors considered include:* recommendation(s), extracurricular activities. *Other factors considered include:* rigor of secondary school record, academic GPA, interview, character/personal qualities, level of applicant's interest. **Freshman Admission Requirements:** High school diploma is required and GED is accepted *Academic units recommended:* 4 English, 3 math, 3 science, 2 foreign language, 3 social studies, 2 academic electives, 1 computer science, 3 visual/performing arts. **Freshman Admission Statistics:** 1,186 applied, 33.5% admitted, 40% enrolled. **Transfer Admission Requirements:** High school transcript, college transcript(s), essay or personal statement, Lowest grade transferable C. **General Admission Information:** Application fee $70. Priority deadline 12/1. Regular application deadline 1/5. Nonfall registration accepted.

COSTS AND FINANCIAL AID

Annual tuition $36,166. Room and board $9,293. Required fees $576. Average book expense $1,500. **Required Forms and Deadlines:** FAFSA. **Notification of Awards:** Applicants will be notified of awards on a rolling basis beginning 4/1. **Types of Aid:** *Need-based scholarships/grants:* College/university scholarship or grant aid from institutional funds; Federal Pell; Private scholarships; SEOG; State scholarships/grants. *Loans: Student Employment:* Federal Work-Study Program available. Institutional employment available. **Financial Aid Statistics:** 92% needy freshmen, 93% needy undergrads receive need-based scholarship or grant aid. 0% undergrads receive non-need-based scholarship or grant aid. 88% freshmen, 91% undergrads receive need-based self-help aid. 0% freshmen, 0% undergrads receive athletic scholarships. 71% freshmen, 77% undergrads receive any aid. **Criteria for awarding aid:** *Need-based:* Art, Minority status, Music/drama *Non-need-based:* Art, Minority status, Music/drama.

CALIFORNIA INSTITUTE OF TECHNOLOGY

1200 East California Boulevard, Pasadena, CA 91125
Phone: 626-395-6341 · **Financial Aid Phone:** 626-395-6280
E-mail: ugadmissions@caltech.edu · **CEEB Code:** 4034
Fax: 626-683-3026 · **Website:** www.caltech.edu · **ACT Code:** 182

This private school was founded in 1891. It has a 124 acre campus.

RATINGS

Admissions Selectivity Rating: 99   **Fire Safety Rating:** 89   **Green Rating:** 60*

STUDENTS AND FACULTY

Enrollment: 961. **Student Body:** 45% female, 55% male, 66% out-of-state, 9% international (27 countries represented). Asian 43%, African American 1%, Caucasian 28%, Hispanic 12%, Native American 0%, Pacific Islander 0%, Two or more races 7%, Race unknown 0%.
Retention and Graduation: 98% freshmen return for sophomore year. 79% freshmen graduate within 4 years. 89% freshmen graduate within 6 years. 48% grads go on to further study within 1 year. **Faculty:** Student/faculty ratio 3:1. 331 full-time faculty, 98% hold PhDs, 20% are members of minority groups, 21% are women. 0% of classes are taught by teaching assistants.

ACADEMICS

Degrees: Bachelor's; Doctoral/Research; Master's; Post-Master's certificate **Classes:** Most classes have 10-19 students. Most lab/discussion sessions have 10-19 students. **Most popular majors:** Computer And Information Sciences, General; Mechanical Engineering; Physics, General. **Special Study Options:** Cooperative education program; Cross-registration; Double major; English as a Second Language (ESL); Exchange student program (domestic); Independent

study; Liberal arts/career combination; Student-designed major; Study abroad. **Disability Services offered to physically disabled students:** Note-taking services; Reader services; Tape recorders; Tutors.

FACILITIES

Housing: Apartments for married students; Apartments for single students; Coed dorms; Special housing for disabled students 95% of campus accessible to physically diasbled. **Special Academic Facilities/Equipment:** Jet Propulsion Laboratory, Palomar Observatory, Seismological Laboratory, Beckman Institute for Fundamental Research in Biology and Chemistry, Mead Chemistry Laboratory, Moore Laboratory. **Computers:** 50% of classrooms, 50% of dorms, 100% of libraries, 50% of dining areas, 100% of student union, 50% of common outdoor areas have wireless network access. Students can register for classes online. Administrative functions (other than registration) can be performed online.

CAMPUS LIFE

Environment: City **Activities:** Choral groups; Concert band; Dance; Drama/theater; International Student Organization; Jazz band; Literary magazine; Music ensembles; Musical theater; Pep band; Student government; Student newspaper; Student-run film society; Symphony orchestra; Yearbook 148 registered organizations, 2 honor societies, 6 religious organizations. **Athletics (Intercollegiate):** *Men:* baseball, basketball, cross-country, diving, fencing, soccer, swimming, tennis, track/field (outdoor), water polo. *Women:* basketball, cross-country, diving, fencing, swimming, tennis, track/field (outdoor), volleyball, water polo. **On-Campus Highlights:** Caltech Bookstore, Moore Laboratory, Mead Chemistry Laboratory, Broad Center for the Biological Sciences, Red Door Cafe **Environmental Initiatives:** Energy efficiency and retro-commissioning programs finances through the use of a green revolving loan fund (http://sustainability.caltech.edu/energy/CECIP)

ADMISSIONS

Freshman Academic Profile: 93% in top 10% of high school class, 7% in top 25% of high school class, 100% in top 50% of high school class. 70% from public high schools. **Test Scores:** SAT Math middle 50% range 780-800. SAT EBRW middle 50% range 750-790. ACT middle 50% range 34-35. Minimum internet-based TOEFL 110. **Basis for Candidate Selection:** *Very important factors considered include:* rigor of secondary school record, application essay, standardized test scores, recommendation(s), character/personal qualities. *Important factors considered include:* class rank, academic GPA, extracurricular activities. *Other factors considered include:* talent/ability, first generation, alumni/ae relation, racial/ethnic status, volunteer work, work experience. **Freshman Admission Requirements:** High school diploma or equivalent is not required *Academic units required:* 3 English, 4 math, 2 science, 1 science labs, 1 social studies, 1 history, *Academic units recommended:* 4 English, 4 science, 3 foreign language, 3 social studies, 1 history. **Freshman Admission Statistics:** 7,339 applied, 7.7% admitted, 41% enrolled. **Transfer Admission Requirements:** High school transcript, college transcript(s), essay or personal statement, statement of good standing from prior institution(s). **General Admission Information:** Application fee $75. Regular application deadline 1/3. Nonfall registration accepted. Admission may be deferred for a maximum of 2 years.

COSTS AND FINANCIAL AID

Annual tuition $48,111. Room and board $14,796. Required fees $1,797. Average book expense $1,323. **Required Forms and Deadlines:** Business/Farm Supplement; CSS/Financial Aid PROFILE; FAFSA; Institution's own financial aid form; Noncustodial PROFILE; State aid form. **Notification of Awards:** Applicants will be notified of awards on or about 4/15. **Types of Aid:** *Need-based scholarships/grants:* College/university scholarship or grant aid from institutional funds; Federal Pell; Private scholarships; SEOG; State scholarships/grants. *Loans:* Direct PLUS loans; Direct Subsidized Stafford Loans; Direct Unsubsidized Stafford Loans. *Student Employment:* Federal Work-Study Program available. Institutional employment available. **Financial Aid Statistics:** 100% needy freshmen, 100% needy undergrads receive need-based scholarship or grant aid. 1% undergrads receive non-need-based scholarship or grant aid. 62% freshmen, 68% undergrads receive need-based self-help aid. 0% freshmen, 0% undergrads receive athletic scholarships. 75% freshmen, 60% undergrads receive any aid. 33% undergrads borrow to pay for school. Average cumulative indebtedness $18,219. **Criteria for awarding aid:** *Need-based:* Academics, Leadership.

CALIFORNIA LUTHERAN UNIVERSITY

60 West Olsen Road, Thousand Oaks, CA 91360
Phone: 805-493-3135 · **Financial Aid Phone:** (805) 493-3115
E-mail: admissions@callutheran.edu · **CEEB Code:** 4088
Fax: 805-493-3645 · **Website:** www.callutheran.edu · **ACT Code:** 183

This private school, affiliated with the Lutheran Church, was founded in 1959. It has a 290 acre campus.

RATINGS

Admissions Selectivity Rating: 83   **Fire Safety Rating:** 92   **Green Rating:** 60*

STUDENTS AND FACULTY

Enrollment: 2,802. **Student Body:** 57% female, 43% male, 13% out-of-state, 3% international (52 countries represented). Asian 6%, African American 4%, Caucasian 49%, Hispanic 27%, Native American 1%, Pacific Islander 1%, Two or more races 6%, Race unknown 4%.
Retention and Graduation: 84% freshmen return for sophomore year. 28% grads go on to further study within 1 year. 35% grads pursue arts and sciences degrees. 3% grads pursue law degrees. 7% grads pursue business degrees. 4% grads pursue medical degrees. **Faculty:** Student/faculty ratio 15:1. 193 full-time faculty, 85% hold PhDs, 17% are members of minority groups, 48% are women. 0% of classes are taught by teaching assistants.

ACADEMICS

Degrees: Bachelor's; Doctoral/Professional; Master's; Post-Bachelor's certificate; Post-Master's certificate **Classes:** Most classes have 10-19 students. Most lab/discussion sessions have 10-19 students. **Most popular majors:** Liberal Arts And Sciences/Liberal Studies; Psychology, General; Business/Commerce, General. **Special Study Options:** Accelerated program; Cooperative education program; Double major; Dual enrollment; Exchange student program (domestic); Honors program; Independent study; Internships; Student-designed major; Study abroad; Teacher certification program. **Honors programs:** Honors Program. **Disability Services offered to physically disabled students:** Note-taking services; Reader services; Tape recorders; Tutors. **Career services:** Alumni network; Alumni services; Career assessment; Career/job search classes; Internships; Regional alumni

FACILITIES

Housing: Coed dorms; Special housing for disabled students 95% of campus accessible to physically disabled. **Special Academic Facilities/Equipment:** Human Performance Laboratory; bioengineering, optics and other science laboratories; radio broadcasting, TV production, multimedia and photography labs; Blackbox Theatre; Center for Economic Research and Forecasting; Center for Equality and Justice; Center for Teaching and Learning; Community Counseling & Parent-Child Study center; Community Service Center; Kwan Fong Gallery of Art and Culture; Office for Undergraduate Research; Scandinavian Center; and Segerhammar Center for Faith and Culture **Computers:** Students can register for classes online. Administrative functions (other than registration) can be performed online.

CAMPUS LIFE

Environment: Town **Activities:** Campus Ministries; Choral groups; Concert band; Dance; Drama/theater; International Student Organization; Jazz band; Literary magazine; Model UN; Music ensembles; Musical theater; Pep band; Radio station; Student government; Student newspaper; Student-run film society; Symphony orchestra; Television station 75 registered organizations, 11 honor societies, 3 religious organizations. **Athletics (Intercollegiate):** *Men:* baseball, basketball, cheerleading, cross-country, diving, football, golf, soccer, swimming, tennis, track/field (outdoor), water polo. *Women:* basketball, cheerleading, cross-country, diving, soccer, softball, swimming, tennis, track/field (outdoor), volleyball, water polo. **On-Campus Highlights:** Gilbert Sports and Fitness Center, Samuelson Chapel, Swenson Center for the Social and Behavioral Sciences, Kingsmen Park, Ullman Dining Commons

ADMISSIONS

Freshman Academic Profile: Average high school GPA 3.7. 30% in top 10% of high school class, 72% in top 25% of high school class, 93% in top 50% of high school class. 75% from public high schools. **Test Scores:** SAT Math middle 50% range 500-600. SAT EBRW middle 50% range 500-600. ACT middle 50% range 22-27. Minimum internet-based TOEFL 79. Minimum paper TOEFL 550. **Basis for Candidate Selection:** *Very important factors considered include:* rigor of secondary school record, academic GPA, application essay, standardized test scores, recommendation(s). *Important factors considered include:* class rank, extracurricular activities, talent/ability, alumni/ae relation. *Other factors considered include:* interview, character/personal qualities, first generation, geographical residence, state residency, religious affiliation/commitment, racial/ethnic status, volunteer work, work experience. **Freshman Admission Requirements:** High school diploma is required and

GED is accepted *Academic units required:* 4 English, 3 math, 3 science, 2 science labs, 2 foreign language, 2 social studies, *Academic units recommended:* 4 English, 4 math, 3 science. **Freshman Admission Statistics:** 6,569 applied, 61.6% admitted, 15% enrolled. **Transfer Admission Requirements:** college transcript(s), essay or personal statement, statement of good standing from prior institution(s). Minimum college GPA of 2.8 required. Lowest grade transferable D. **General Admission Information:** Application fee $25. Priority deadline 11/1. Regular application deadline 1/1. Nonfall registration accepted. Admission may be deferred for a maximum of 1 year.

COSTS AND FINANCIAL AID

Annual tuition $39,310. Room and board $12,740. Required fees $450. Average book expense $1,764. **Required Forms and Deadlines:** FAFSA; State aid form. **Notification of Awards:** Applicants will be notified of awards on a rolling basis beginning 2/15. **Types of Aid:** *Need-based scholarships/grants:* College/university scholarship or grant aid from institutional funds; Federal Pell; Private scholarships; SEOG; State scholarships/grants; United Negro College Fund. *Loans:* Direct PLUS loans; Direct Subsidized Stafford Loans; Direct Unsubsidized Stafford Loans. *Student Employment:* Federal Work-Study Program available. Institutional employment available. **Financial Aid Statistics:** 100% needy freshmen, 100% needy undergrads receive need-based scholarship or grant aid. 38% freshmen, 49% undergrads receive non-need-based scholarship or grant aid. 77% freshmen, 76% undergrads receive need-based self-help aid. 0% freshmen, 0% undergrads receive athletic scholarships. 96% freshmen, 95% undergrads receive any aid. 62% undergrads borrow to pay for school. Average cumulative indebtedness $28,186. **Criteria for awarding aid:** *Need-based:* Academics, Alumni affiliation, Art, Leadership, Minority status, Music/drama, Religious affiliation *Non-need-based:* Academics, Alumni affiliation, Art, Leadership, Minority status, Music/drama, Religious affiliation, State/district residency.

CALIFORNIA MARITIME ACADEMY OF CALIFORNIA STATE UNIVERSITY

200 Maritime Academy Drive, Vallejo, CA 94590-0644
Phone: 707-654-1330 · **Financial Aid Phone:** (707) 654-1276
E-mail: admission@csum.edu · **CEEB Code:** 4035
Fax: 707-654-1336 · **Website:** www.csum.edu · **ACT Code:** 184

This public school was founded in 1929. It has a 67 acre campus.

RATINGS

Admissions Selectivity Rating: 75   **Fire Safety Rating:** 60*   **Green Rating:** 60*

STUDENTS AND FACULTY

Enrollment: 1,072. **Student Body:** 15% female, 85% male, 1% international. Asian 10%, African American 2%, Caucasian 53%, Hispanic 17%, Native American <1%, Pacific Islander <1%, Two or more races 11%, Race unknown 6%.
Retention and Graduation: 82% freshmen return for sophomore year. **Faculty:** Student/faculty ratio 15:1. 64 full-time faculty, 63% hold PhDs, 6% are members of minority groups, 20% are women. 0% of classes are taught by teaching assistants.

ACADEMICS

Degrees: Bachelor's; Master's **Classes:** Most classes have fewer than 10 students. **Most popular majors:** Mechanical Engineering; International Relations And Affairs; Marine Science/Merchant Marine Officer. **Special Study Options:** Cooperative education program; Double major; Honors program; Internships. **Disability Services offered to physically disabled students:** Tutors. **Career services:** Alumni services; Career/job search classes; Internships

FACILITIES

Housing: Coed dorms; Special housing for international students; Theme housing 70% of campus accessible to physically disabled. **Special Academic Facilities/Equipment:** Bookstore, Library, Gym, Swimming Pool.

CAMPUS LIFE

Activities: Choral groups; Student government 16 registered organizations. **Athletics (Intercollegiate):** *Men:* basketball, crew/rowing, golf, sailing, soccer, water polo. *Women:* crew/rowing, sailing, volleyball.

ADMISSIONS

Freshman Academic Profile: Average high school GPA 3.3. 80% from public high schools. **Test Scores:** SAT Math middle 50% range 510-610. SAT

EBRW middle 50% range 490-600. ACT middle 50% range 21-27. Minimum paper TOEFL 550. **Basis for Candidate Selection:** *Very important factors considered include:* academic GPA, standardized test scores. *Important factors considered include:* rigor of secondary school record. *Other factors considered include:* extracurricular activities, talent/ability, geographical residence, state residency, volunteer work, work experience. **Freshman Admission Requirements:** High school diploma is required and GED is accepted *Academic units required:* 4 English, 3 math, 2 science, 2 science labs, 2 foreign language, 1 social studies, 1 history, 1 academic elective, 1 visual/performing arts, *Academic units recommended:* 4 English, 4 math, 3 science, 3 science labs, 2 foreign language, 1 social studies, 1 history, 1 academic elective, 1 visual/performing arts. **Freshman Admission Statistics:** 1,206 applied, 81.5% admitted, 23% enrolled. **Transfer Admission Requirements:** college transcript(s), statement of good standing from prior institution(s). Minimum college GPA of 2.0 required. Lowest grade transferable C. **General Admission Information:** Application fee $55. Priority deadline 11/30. Nonfall registration accepted.

COSTS AND FINANCIAL AID
Annual in-state tuition $10,544. Room and board $10,544. Required fees $1,314. Average book expense $1,336. **Required Forms and Deadlines:** FAFSA. **Notification of Awards:** Applicants will be notified of awards on a rolling basis beginning 4/15. **Types of Aid:** *Need-based scholarships/grants:* College/university scholarship or grant aid from institutional funds; Federal Pell; Private scholarships; SEOG; State scholarships/grants. *Loans:* Direct PLUS loans; Direct Subsidized Stafford Loans; Direct Unsubsidized Stafford Loans. **Financial Aid Statistics:** 84% needy undergrads receive need-based scholarship or grant aid. 0% undergrads receive non-need-based scholarship or grant aid. 80% freshmen, 17% undergrads receive need-based self-help aid. 0% freshmen, 0% undergrads receive athletic scholarships. **Criteria for awarding aid:** *Need-based:* Academics, Leadership.

CALIFORNIA POLYTECHNIC STATE UNIVERSITY

1 Grand Avenue, San Luis Obispo, CA 93407-0031
Phone: 805-756-2311 • **Financial Aid Phone:** (805) 756-2927
E-mail: admissions@calpoly.edu • **CEEB Code:** 4038
Fax: 805-756-5400 • **Website:** www.calpoly.edu • **ACT Code:** 188

This public school was founded in 1901. It has a 9678 acre campus.

RATINGS
Admissions Selectivity Rating: 93   **Fire Safety Rating:** 65   **Green Rating:** 98

STUDENTS AND FACULTY
Enrollment: 21,249. **Student Body:** 48% female, 52% male, 14% out-of-state, 2% international. Asian 13%, African American 1%, Caucasian 54%, Hispanic 17%, Native American <1%, Pacific Islander <1%, Two or more races 8%, Race unknown 5%.
Retention and Graduation: 95% freshmen return for sophomore year. 47% freshmen graduate within 4 years. 82% freshmen graduate within 6 years. **Faculty:** Student/faculty ratio 19:1. 952 full-time faculty, 76% hold PhDs, 37% are women.

ACADEMICS
Degrees: Bachelor's; Master's; Post-Bachelor's certificate **Classes:** Most classes have 10-19 students. **Special Study Options:** Cooperative education program; Distance learning; Double major; Exchange student program (domestic); Honors program; Independent study; Internships; Liberal arts/career combination; Study abroad; Teacher certification program. **Disability Services offered to physically disabled students:** Note-taking services; Reader services; Tape recorders; Tutors. **Career services:** Alumni network; Alumni services; Career assessment; Career/job search classes; Internships; Regional alumni

FACILITIES
Housing: Apartments for single students; Coed dorms; Special housing for disabled student; Special housing for international students; Theme housing **Special Academic Facilities/Equipment:** Dairy, veterinary clinic, printing museum, art gallery **Computers:** 100% of classrooms, 5% of dorms, 100% of libraries, 100% of dining areas, 100% of student union, 5% of common outdoor areas have wireless network access. Students can register for classes online. Administrative functions (other than registration) can be performed online.

CAMPUS LIFE
Environment: Town **Activities:** Campus Ministries; Choral groups; Concert band; Dance; Drama/theater; International Student Organization; Jazz band; Literary magazine; Marching band; Model UN; Music ensembles; Musical

theater; Opera; Pep band; Radio station; Student government; Student newspaper; Student-run film society; Symphony orchestra; Television station 400 registered organizations, 14 religious organizations. 25 fraternities, 14 sororities. **Athletics (Intercollegiate):** *Men:* baseball, basketball, cross-country, football, golf, soccer, swimming, tennis, track/field (outdoor), wrestling. *Women:* basketball, cross-country, golf, soccer, softball, swimming, tennis, track/field (outdoor), track/field (indoor), volleyball. **On-Campus Highlights:** Performing Arts Center, Recreation Center, Julian's Cafe Bistro, Spanos Stadium, University Union

ADMISSIONS
Freshman Academic Profile: Average high school GPA 4.0. 55% in top 10% of high school class, 86% in top 25% of high school class, 98% in top 50% of high school class. **Test Scores:** SAT Math middle 50% range 610-710. SAT EBRW middle 50% range 610-690. ACT middle 50% range 26-31. Minimum internet-based TOEFL 80. Minimum paper TOEFL 550. **Basis for Candidate Selection:** *Very important factors considered include:* rigor of secondary school record, academic GPA, standardized test scores. *Other factors considered include:* extracurricular activities, talent/ability, first generation, geographical residence, volunteer work, work experience. **Freshman Admission Requirements:** High school diploma is required and GED is accepted *Academic units required:* 4 English, 3 math, 2 science, 2 science labs, 2 foreign language, 1 social studies, 1 history, 1 academic elective, 1 visual/performing arts, *Academic units recommended:* 4 English, 4 math, 4 science, 2 science labs, 4 foreign language, 1 social studies, 1 history, 1 academic elective, 2 visual/performing arts. **Freshman Admission Statistics:** 48,588 applied, 34.6% admitted, 31% enrolled. **Transfer Admission Requirements:** college transcript(s), Minimum college GPA of 2.0 required. Lowest grade transferable D. **General Admission Information:** Application fee $55. Regular application deadline 11/30. Nonfall registration accepted.

COSTS AND FINANCIAL AID
Annual in-state tuition $13,115. Annual out-of-state tuition $264. Room and board $13,115. Required fees $3,690. Average book expense $1,884. **Required Forms and Deadlines:** FAFSA. **Notification of Awards:** Applicants will be notified of awards on a rolling basis beginning 3/15. **Types of Aid:** *Need-based scholarships/grants:* College/university scholarship or grant aid from institutional funds; Federal Pell; Private scholarships; SEOG; State scholarships/grants. *Loans:* Direct PLUS loans; Direct Subsidized Stafford Loans; Direct Unsubsidized Stafford Loans. *Student Employment:* Federal Work-Study Program available. Institutional employment available. **Financial Aid Statistics:** 92% needy freshmen, 88% needy undergrads receive need-based scholarship or grant aid. 4% freshmen, 3% undergrads receive non-need-based scholarship or grant aid. 69% freshmen, 67% undergrads receive need-based self-help aid. 2% freshmen, 2% undergrads receive athletic scholarships. 40% undergrads borrow to pay for school. Average cumulative indebtedness $22,413. **Criteria for awarding aid:** *Need-based:* Academics, Art, Job skills, Leadership, Music/drama *Non-need-based:* Academics, Alumni affiliation, Art, Athletics, Job skills, Leadership, Music/drama, State/district residency.

CALIFORNIA STATE POLYTECHNIC UNIVERSITY, POMONA

3801 W Temple Ave, Pomona, CA 91768
Phone: 909-869-5299 • **Financial Aid Phone:** 909-869-3700
E-mail: admissions@cpp.edu • **CEEB Code:** 4082
Fax: 909-869-4529 • **Website:** www.cpp.edu • **ACT Code:** 202

This public school was founded in 1938. It has a 1437 acre campus.

RATINGS
Admissions Selectivity Rating: 85   **Fire Safety Rating:** 92   **Green Rating:** 92

STUDENTS AND FACULTY
Enrollment: 24,205. **Student Body:** 46% female, 54% male, 1% out-of-state, 7% international (107 countries represented). Asian 22%, African American 3%, Caucasian 17%, Hispanic 43%, Native American <1%, Pacific Islander <1%, Two or more races 4%, Race unknown 3%.
Retention and Graduation: 87% freshmen return for sophomore year. 18% freshmen graduate within 4 years. 66% freshmen graduate within 6 years. **Faculty:** Student/faculty ratio 25:1. 607 full-time faculty, 82% hold PhDs, 40% are members of minority groups, 41% are women. 3% of classes are taught by teaching assistants.

ACADEMICS
Degrees: Bachelor's; Doctoral/Professional; Master's **Classes:** Most classes have 20-29 students. Most lab/discussion sessions have 10-19 students. **Most**

popular majors: Mechanical Engineering; Business Administration And Management, General; Hospitality Administration/Management. **Special Study Options:** Cooperative education program; Cross-registration; Distance learning; Double major; Dual enrollment; English as a Second Language (ESL); Exchange student program (domestic); External degree program; Honors program; Internships; Study abroad; Teacher certification program. **Honors programs:** See web site for complete information about The Kellogg Honors College: http://www.cpp.edu/~honorscollege/. **Disability Services offered to physically disabled students:** Note-taking services; Reader services; Tutors. **Career services:** Alumni network; Alumni services; Career assessment; Career/job search classes; Internships; Regional alumni

FACILITIES

Housing: Apartments for single students; Coed dorms; Theme housing 95% of campus accessible to physically diasbled. **Special Academic Facilities/Equipment:** Center for Hospitality Management; Restaurant at Kellogg Ranch; W. Keith & Janet Kellogg University Art Gallery; Don B. Huntley Gallery; Voorhis Ecological Reserve; John T. Lyle Center for Regenerative Studies; citrus-packing house; meat-processing building; poultry plant; feed mill; beef and sheep/swine units; W.K. Kellogg Arabian Horse Library & Arabian Horse Center; horse show arena; and aerospace wind tunnel. **Computers:** 10% of classrooms, 10% of dorms, 100% of libraries, 100% of dining areas, 100% of student union, 60% of common outdoor areas have wireless network access. Students can register for classes online. Administrative functions (other than registration) can be performed online.

CAMPUS LIFE

Environment: City **Activities:** Campus Ministries; Choral groups; Concert band; Dance; Drama/theater; International Student Organization; Jazz band; Literary magazine; Model UN; Music ensembles; Musical theater; Opera; Pep band; Student government; Student newspaper; Symphony orchestra; Yearbook 280 registered organizations, 26 honor societies, 10 religious organizations. 12 fraternities, 8 sororities. **Athletics (Intercollegiate):** *Men:* baseball, basketball, cheerleading, cross-country, soccer, tennis, track/field (outdoor). *Women:* basketball, cheerleading, cross-country, soccer, tennis, track/field (outdoor), volleyball. **On-Campus Highlights:** The Farmstore at Kellogg Ranch, Rain Bird Aquatic,Ethnobotony&Rainforest, W. K. Kellogg Arabian Horse Center, Kellogg House Pomona, John T. Lyle Center for Regenerative Studies **Environmental Initiatives:** Completed baseline inventory and updated GHG inventory for 2009.

ADMISSIONS

Freshman Academic Profile: Average high school GPA 3.5. 89% from public high schools. **Test Scores:** SAT Math middle 50% range 510-630. SAT EBRW middle 50% range 500-610. ACT middle 50% range 20-27. Minimum internet-based TOEFL 71. Minimum paper TOEFL 550. **Basis for Candidate Selection:** *Very important factors considered include:* rigor of secondary school record, academic GPA, standardized test scores. **Freshman Admission Requirements:** High school diploma is required and GED is accepted *Academic units required:* 4 English, 3 math, 2 science, 2 science labs, 2 foreign language, 1 social studies, 1 history, 1 academic elective, 1 visual/performing arts, *Academic units recommended:* 4 math. **Freshman Admission Statistics:** 36,574 applied, 55.2% admitted, 19% enrolled. **Transfer Admission Requirements:** college transcript(s), statement of good standing from prior institution(s). Minimum college GPA of 2.0 required. **General Admission Information:** Application fee $55. Priority deadline 11/30. Regular application deadline 11/30. Nonfall registration accepted.

COSTS AND FINANCIAL AID

Annual in-state tuition $14,514. Annual out-of-state tuition $17,622. Room and board $14,514. Required fees $1,555. Average book expense $1,854. **Required Forms and Deadlines:** FAFSA. **Notification of Awards:** Applicants will be notified of awards on a rolling basis beginning 4/1. **Types of Aid:** *Need-based scholarships/grants:* College/university scholarship or grant aid from institutional funds; Federal Pell; Private scholarships; SEOG; State scholarships/grants. *Loans:* Direct PLUS loans; Direct Subsidized Stafford Loans; Direct Unsubsidized Stafford Loans. *Student Employment:* Federal Work-Study Program available. Institutional employment available. **Financial Aid Statistics:** 74% needy freshmen, 73% needy undergrads receive need-based scholarship or grant aid. 9% freshmen, 6% undergrads receive non-need-based scholarship or grant aid. 47% freshmen, 49% undergrads receive need-based self-help aid. 0% freshmen, 0% undergrads receive athletic scholarships. 74% freshmen, 72% undergrads receive any aid. 53% undergrads borrow to pay for school. Average cumulative indebtedness $22,235. **Criteria for awarding aid:** *Need-based:* Academics *Non-need-based:* Academics, Alumni affiliation, Athletics, Leadership, State/district residency.

CALIFORNIA STATE UNIVERSITY, CHICO

400 West First Street, Chico, CA 95929-0722
Phone: 530-898-4428 · **Financial Aid Phone:** (530) 898-6451
E-mail: info@csuchico.edu · **CEEB Code:** 4048
Fax: 530-898-6456 · **Website:** www.csuchico.edu · **ACT Code:** 212

This public school was founded in 1887. It has a 119 acre campus.

RATINGS

Admissions Selectivity Rating: 79 **Fire Safety Rating:** 86 **Green Rating:** 98

STUDENTS AND FACULTY

Enrollment: 16,471. **Student Body:** 53% female, 47% male, 1% out-of-state, 4% international (39 countries represented). Asian 6%, African American 2%, Caucasian 44%, Hispanic 31%, Native American 1%, Pacific Islander <1%, Two or more races 5%, Race unknown 8%.
Retention and Graduation: 85% freshmen return for sophomore year.
Faculty: Student/faculty ratio 24:1. 507 full-time faculty, 85% hold PhDs, 17% are members of minority groups, 47% are women. 1% of classes are taught by teaching assistants.

ACADEMICS

Degrees: Bachelor's; Certificate; Master's; Post-Bachelor's certificate; Post-Master's certificate **Classes:** Most classes have 10-19 students. **Most popular majors:** Education, General; Engineering, General; Business Administration And Management, General. **Special Study Options:** Cooperative education program; Cross-registration; Distance learning; Double major; Dual enrollment; English as a Second Language (ESL); Exchange student program (domestic); External degree program; Honors program; Independent study; Internships; Student-designed major; Study abroad; Teacher certification program. **Honors programs:** Honors in General Education (HGE) Honors in the Major (HIM). **Disability Services offered to physically disabled students:** Note-taking services; Reader services; Tape recorders; Tutors. **Career services:** Alumni network; Alumni services; Career assessment; Internships

FACILITIES

Housing: Apartments for single students; Coed dorms; Fraternity/sorority housing; Special housing for disabled student; Special housing for international students; Theme housing 95% of campus accessible to physically diasbled. **Special Academic Facilities/Equipment:** Anthropology museum, center for intercultural studies, satellite communication dishes, biological field station, university farm, electron microscope. **Computers:** 100% of classrooms, 100% of dorms, 100% of libraries, 100% of dining areas, 100% of student union, 25% of common outdoor areas have wireless network access. Students can register for classes online. Administrative functions (other than registration) can be performed online.

CAMPUS LIFE

Environment: City **Activities:** Choral groups; Concert band; Dance; Drama/theater; International Student Organization; Jazz band; Literary magazine; Model UN; Music ensembles; Musical theater; Opera; Pep band; Radio station; Student government; Student newspaper; Student-run film society; Symphony orchestra 192 registered organizations, 18 honor societies, 12 religious organizations. 15 fraternities, 14 sororities. **Athletics (Intercollegiate):** *Men:* baseball, basketball, cross-country, golf, soccer, track/field (outdoor). *Women:* basketball, cross-country, golf, soccer, softball, track/field (outdoor), volleyball. **On-Campus Highlights:** Bell Memorial Union, Meriam Library, Trinity Commons, Humanities Gallery/University Gallery, Wildcat Recreation Center **Environmental Initiatives:** This Way to Sustainability Conference

ADMISSIONS

Freshman Academic Profile: Average high school GPA 3.3. 35% in top 10% of high school class, 76% in top 25% of high school class, 100% in top 50% of high school class. 93% from public high schools. **Test Scores:** SAT Math middle 50% range 440-550. SAT EBRW middle 50% range 440-550. ACT middle 50% range 19-24. Minimum internet-based TOEFL 79. Minimum paper TOEFL 500. **Basis for Candidate Selection:** *Very important factors considered include:* academic GPA, standardized test scores. *Important factors considered include:* geographical residence, state residency. **Freshman Admission Requirements:** High school diploma is required and GED is accepted *Academic units required:* 4 English, 3 math, 2 science, 2 science labs, 2 foreign language, 2 social studies, 1 academic elective, 1 visual/performing arts. **Freshman Admission Statistics:** 23,124 applied, 66.6% admitted, 18% enrolled. **Transfer Admission Requirements:** college transcript(s), statement of good standing from prior institution(s). Minimum college GPA of 2.0 required. Lowest grade transferable D. **General Admission Information:** Application fee $55. Priority deadline 10/1. Regular application deadline 11/30. Nonfall registration accepted. Admission may be deferred for a maximum of 1 year.

COSTS AND FINANCIAL AID

Annual in-state tuition $12,824. Annual out-of-state tuition $18,204. Room and board $12,824. Required fees $1,572. Average book expense $1,719. **Required Forms and Deadlines:** FAFSA. **Notification of Awards:** Applicants will be notified of awards on a rolling basis beginning 3/2. **Types of Aid:** *Need-based scholarships/grants:* College/university scholarship or grant aid from institutional funds; Federal Pell; Private scholarships; SEOG; State scholarships/grants. *Loans:* Direct PLUS loans; Direct Subsidized Stafford Loans; Direct Unsubsidized Stafford Loans. *Student Employment:* Federal Work-Study Program available. Institutional employment available. **Financial Aid Statistics:** 75% needy freshmen, 78% needy undergrads receive need-based scholarship or grant aid. 23% freshmen, 13% undergrads receive non-need-based scholarship or grant aid. 67% freshmen, 67% undergrads receive need-based self-help aid. 66% freshmen, 63% undergrads receive any aid. **Criteria for awarding aid:** *Need-based:* Academics, Minority status *Non-need-based:* Academics, Art, Athletics, Leadership, Minority status, Music/drama, Religious affiliation.

CALIFORNIA STATE UNIVERSITY, DOMINGUEZ HILLS

1000 East Victoria Street, Carson, CA 90747
Phone: 310-243-3645 · **Financial Aid Phone:** 310-243-3189
E-mail: info@csudh.edu · **CEEB Code:** 4098
Fax: 310-516-3609 · **Website:** www.csudh.edu · **ACT Code:** 203

This public school was founded in 1960. It has a 346 acre campus.

RATINGS

Admissions Selectivity Rating: 73   **Fire Safety Rating:** 72   **Green Rating:** 70

STUDENTS AND FACULTY

Enrollment: 12,613. **Student Body:** 63% female, 37% male, 0% out-of-state, 4% international (41 countries represented). Asian 10%, African American 13%, Caucasian 7%, Hispanic 60%, Native American <1%, Pacific Islander <1%, Two or more races 3%, Race unknown 3%.
Retention and Graduation: 82% freshmen return for sophomore year.
Faculty: Student/faculty ratio 21:1. 277 full-time faculty, 73% hold PhDs, 41% are members of minority groups, 56% are women. 0% of classes are taught by teaching assistants.

ACADEMICS

Degrees: Bachelor's; Master's; Post-Bachelor's certificate; Post-Master's certificate **Classes:** Most classes have 10-19 students. Most lab/discussion sessions have 10-19 students. **Most popular majors:** Psychology, General; Criminal Justice/Safety Studies; Business Administration And Management, General. **Special Study Options:** Accelerated program; Cross-registration; Distance learning; Double major; Dual enrollment; External degree program; Honors program; Independent study; Internships; Student-designed major; Study abroad; Teacher certification program; Weekend college. **Honors programs:** University Honors Program is currently on hiatus, while we reorganize to bring back an improved program in 2017-18. **Disability Services offered to physically disabled students:** Note-taking services; Reader services; Tape recorders; Tutors. **Career services:** Alumni services; Career assessment; Career/job search classes; Internships

FACILITIES

Housing: Apartments for married students; Apartments for single students; Special housing for disabled students 100% of campus accessible to physically diasbled. **Special Academic Facilities/Equipment:** University Art Gallery, University Library, University Theater

CAMPUS LIFE

Environment: City **Activities:** Choral groups; Concert band; Dance; Drama/theater; International Student Organization; Jazz band; Literary magazine; Music ensembles; Musical theater; Radio station; Student government; Student newspaper; Television station 65 registered organizations, 6 honor societies, 3 religious organizations. 4 fraternities, 4 sororities. **Athletics (Intercollegiate):** *Men:* baseball, basketball, golf, soccer. *Women:* basketball, cross-country, soccer, softball, tennis, track/field (outdoor), volleyball. **On-Campus Highlights:** Welch Hall, Loker Student Union, Library, Athletic Fields/Stub Hub Center, Sculpture Garden

ADMISSIONS

Freshman Academic Profile: Average high school GPA 3.1. 93% from public high schools. **Test Scores:** SAT Math middle 50% range 380-470. SAT EBRW

middle 50% range 380-470. ACT middle 50% range 15-19. Minimum internet-based TOEFL 61. Minimum paper TOEFL 500. **Basis for Candidate Selection:** *Other factors considered include:* academic GPA, standardized test scores. **Freshman Admission Requirements:** High school diploma is required and GED is accepted *Academic units required:* 4 English, 3 math, 2 science, 2 science labs, 2 foreign language, 1 social studies, 1 history, 1 academic elective, 1 visual/performing arts. **Freshman Admission Statistics:** 10,615 applied, 75.1% admitted, 16% enrolled. **Transfer Admission Requirements:** High school transcript, college transcript(s), Minimum college GPA of 2.0 required. Lowest grade transferable c. **General Admission Information:** Application fee $55. Priority deadline 11/30. Nonfall registration accepted.

COSTS AND FINANCIAL AID

Annual out-of-state tuition $16,632. Required fees $950. Average book expense $1,850. **Required Forms and Deadlines:** FAFSA. **Notification of Awards:** Applicants will be notified of awards on a rolling basis beginning 2/28. **Types of Aid:** *Need-based scholarships/grants:* College/university scholarship or grant aid from institutional funds; Federal Pell; Private scholarships; SEOG; State scholarships/grants. *Loans:* Direct PLUS loans; Direct Subsidized Stafford Loans; Direct Unsubsidized Stafford Loans. *Student Employment:* Federal Work-Study Program available. Institutional employment available. **Financial Aid Statistics:** 89% needy freshmen, 86% needy undergrads receive need-based scholarship or grant aid. 17% freshmen, 25% undergrads receive non-need-based scholarship or grant aid. 1% freshmen, 2% undergrads receive need-based self-help aid. 0% freshmen, 0% undergrads receive athletic scholarships. 87% freshmen, 81% undergrads receive any aid. 58% undergrads borrow to pay for school. Average cumulative indebtedness $16,370. **Criteria for awarding aid:** *Need-based:* Academics, Athletics *Non-need-based:* Academics, Alumni affiliation, Art, Athletics, Leadership, Music/drama.

CALIFORNIA STATE UNIVERSITY, EAST BAY

25800 Carlos Bee Boulevard, Hayward, CA 94542-3035
Phone: 510-885-2784 · **Financial Aid Phone:** 510.885.2784
E-mail: admissions@csueastbay.edu · **CEEB Code:** 4011
Fax: 510-885-3505 · **Website:** www.csueastbay.edu · **ACT Code:** 154

This public school was founded in 1957. It has a 342 acre campus.

RATINGS

Admissions Selectivity Rating: 87   **Fire Safety Rating:** 75   **Green Rating:** 60*

STUDENTS AND FACULTY

Enrollment: 9,788. **Student Body:** 60% female, 40% male, 1% out-of-state, 8% international (86 countries represented). Asian 20%, African American 10%, Caucasian 22%, Hispanic 19%, Native American <1%, Pacific Islander 3%, Two or more races 3%, Race unknown 14%.
Retention and Graduation: 76% freshmen return for sophomore year.
Faculty: Student/faculty ratio 26:1. 322 full-time faculty, 34% are members of minority groups, 49% are women. 5% of classes are taught by teaching assistants.

ACADEMICS

Degrees: Bachelor's; Certificate; Doctoral; Master's; Post-Bachelor's certificate; Post-Master's certificate **Classes:** Most classes have 30-39 students. **Special Study Options:** Cooperative education program; Cross-registration; Distance learning; Double major; Dual enrollment; English as a Second Language (ESL); Exchange student program (domestic); External degree program; Honors program; Independent study; Internships; Liberal arts/career combination; Student-designed major; Study abroad; Teacher certification program; Weekend college. **Disability Services offered to physically disabled students:** Note-taking services; Reader services; Tape recorders; Tutors. **Career services:** Alumni services; Career assessment; Career/job search classes; Internships

FACILITIES

Housing: Apartments for single students; Other (please specify) 95% of campus accessible to physically diasbled. **Special Academic Facilities/Equipment:** Anthropology museum, art gallery, scanning electron microsope facility, marine lab, ecological field station, geology summer camp. **Computers:** Students can register for classes online. Administrative functions (other than registration) can be performed online.

CAMPUS LIFE

Environment: City **Activities:** Choral groups; Concert band; Dance; Drama/theater; Jazz band; Literary magazine; Music ensembles; Musical theater; Opera; Pep band; Radio station; Student government; Student newspaper; Symphony orchestra; Television station 100 registered organizations, 2 honor societies, 2 religious organizations. 7 fraternities, 7 sororities. **Athletics (Intercollegiate):** *Men:* baseball, basketball, cross-country, golf, soccer. *Women:* basketball, cross-country, golf, soccer, softball, swimming, volleyball, water polo. **On-Campus Highlights:** University Union, Gymnasium/Pools, Warren Hall /Administration, University Theatre, University Art Gallery

ADMISSIONS

Freshman Academic Profile: Average high school GPA 3.1. **Test Scores:** SAT Math middle 50% range 400-510. SAT EBRW middle 50% range 400-500. ACT middle 50% range 16-21. Minimum paper TOEFL 525. **Basis for Candidate Selection:** *Very important factors considered include:* rigor of secondary school record, academic GPA, standardized test scores. *Other factors considered include:* recommendation(s), state residency. **Freshman Admission Requirements:** High school diploma is required and GED is accepted *Academic units required:* 4 English, 3 math, 2 science, 2 science labs, 2 foreign language, 1 social studies, 1 history, 1 academic elective, and 1 unit from above areas or other academic areas. **Freshman Admission Statistics:** 10,778 applied, 35.6% admitted, 32% enrolled. **Transfer Admission Requirements:** college transcript(s), statement of good standing from prior institution(s). Minimum college GPA of 2.0 required. Lowest grade transferable D. **General Admission Information:** Application fee $55. Priority deadline 11/30. Regular application deadline 6/30. Nonfall registration accepted. Admission may be deferred for a maximum of 2 quarters.

COSTS AND FINANCIAL AID

Annual in-state tuition $11,042. Annual out-of-state tuition $14,019. Room and board $11,042. Average book expense $1,734. **Required Forms and Deadlines:** FAFSA. **Notification of Awards:** Applicants will be notified of awards on a rolling basis beginning 3/15. **Types of Aid:** *Need-based scholarships/grants:* College/university scholarship or grant aid from institutional funds; Federal Pell; Private scholarships; SEOG; State scholarships/grants. *Loans: Student Employment:* Federal Work-Study Program available. Institutional employment available. **Financial Aid Statistics:** 83% needy freshmen, 83% needy undergrads receive need-based scholarship or grant aid. 0% undergrads receive non-need-based scholarship or grant aid. 63% freshmen, 62% undergrads receive need-based self-help aid. 0% freshmen, 0% undergrads receive athletic scholarships. 43% freshmen, 42% undergrads receive any aid. **Criteria for awarding aid:** *Need-based:* Academics *Non-need-based:* Academics.

CALIFORNIA STATE UNIVERSITY, FRESNO

5241 N. Maple Ave, Fresno, CA 93740-8026
Phone: 559-278-2261 · **Financial Aid Phone:** 559-278-2182
E-mail: admissions@csufresno.edu · **CEEB Code:** 4312
Fax: 559-278-4812 · **Website:** www.csufresno.edu · **ACT Code:** 266

This public school was founded in 1911. It has a 388 acre campus.

RATINGS

Admissions Selectivity Rating: 80   **Fire Safety Rating:** 78   **Green Rating:** 60*

STUDENTS AND FACULTY

Enrollment: 18,784. **Student Body:** 57% female, 43% male, 0% out-of-state, 3% international (116 countries represented). Asian 15%, African American 5%, Caucasian 30%, Hispanic 38%, Native American 1%, Pacific Islander <1%, Two or more races 3%, Race unknown 6%.
Retention and Graduation: 86% freshmen return for sophomore year. **Faculty:** Student/faculty ratio 22:1. 624 full-time faculty, 95% hold PhDs, 29% are members of minority groups, 42% are women. 8% of classes are taught by teaching assistants.

ACADEMICS

Degrees: Bachelor's; Doctoral/Research; Master's; Post-Bachelor's certificate; Post-Master's certificate **Classes:** Most classes have 20-29 students. Most lab/discussion sessions have 20-29 students. **Most popular majors:** Liberal Arts And Sciences/Liberal Studies; Psychology, General; Health Services/Allied Health/Health Sciences, General. **Special Study Options:** Accelerated program; Cooperative education program; Cross-registration; Distance learning; Double major; Dual enrollment; English as a Second Language (ESL); Exchange student program (domestic); Honors program; Independent study; Internships; Student-designed major; Study abroad; Teacher certification program. **Honors programs:** The Smittcamp Family Honors College (Smittcamp Honors College) was founded in the fall of 1999 to attract high-quality students to the university. These students are recruited from the entire state through solicitations of high school principals, scholarship advisers and California Scholarship Federation advisers, in addition to direct mail to high

PSAT scorers. Successful students are selected based on their grades, SAT scores, rigor of their classes, community service, awards, reference letters, and two essays. High school students satisfying any one of the following criteria are eligible to apply: 1200 SAT scores, 3.6 grade point average, or top 10% of their high school class. A large percentage of applicants who are not selected also choose to enroll at the university. Currently, there are 50 seniors, 50 juniors, 75 sophomores, and 75 freshmen in the Honors College. Classes of 75 will be selected in the future. Students in the Honors College take 36 of their 51 general education units in specifically designed honors courses, two courses in each of their first four semesters, then three upper-division general education courses. Classes go through the program as a cohort. All honors students take the Honors Colloquium for five semesters of their career. Students in the Honors College receive a four-year President's Scholarship that includes all registration fees and on-campus housing. The Residence Hall administration attempts to cluster the students in several residence halls. Students also receive free parking, special library privileges, use of a laptop computer, use of the Honors College computer lab, and use of the Honors College Office. Students must maintain escalating (3.0, 3.25, and 3.4) grade point averages during their attendance. Students perform community service as part of their status in the Honors College. **Disability Services offered to physically disabled students:** Note-taking services; Reader services; Tape recorders; Tutors.

FACILITIES

Housing: Coed dorms; Fraternity/sorority housing; Men's dorms; Women's dorms 100% of campus accessible to physically diasbled. **Special Academic Facilities/Equipment:** Marine lab, Downing Planetarium. **Computers:** 100% of classrooms, 100% of dorms, 100% of libraries, 100% of dining areas, 100% of student union, 20% of common outdoor areas have wireless network access. Students can register for classes online. Administrative functions (other than registration) can be performed online. Undergraduates are required to own a computer.

CAMPUS LIFE

Environment: Metropolis **Activities:** Choral groups; Concert band; Dance; Drama/theater; International Student Organization; Jazz band; Marching band; Music ensembles; Musical theater; Radio station; Student government; Student newspaper; Symphony orchestra; Television station; Yearbook 250 registered organizations, 21 honor societies, 11 religious organizations. 19 fraternities, 13 sororities. **Athletics (Intercollegiate):** *Men:* baseball, basketball, cheerleading, cross-country, football, golf, tennis, track/field (outdoor). *Women:* basketball, cheerleading, cross-country, diving, equestrian sports, golf, lacrosse, light weight football, soccer, softball, swimming, tennis, track/field (outdoor), volleyball. **On-Campus Highlights:** Savemart Events Center, Downing Planetarium, Kennel Bookstore, New Ciminology Center, Henry Madden Library **Environmental Initiatives:** Solar Photovoltaic Canopy Parking Structure (Lot V) This structure is a 1.1 megawatt solar system, making it the largest photovoltaic paneled parting installation at a U.S. university. Completed in the fall of 2007, the structure was estimated to provide 20% of the core campus power. The system offsets approximately 950 metric tons of carbon monoxide emissions – that is equivalent to planting over 24,300 trees or eliminating from our road systems over 200 vehicles a year!

ADMISSIONS

Freshman Academic Profile: Average high school GPA 3.3. 15% in top 10% of high school class, 80% in top 25% of high school class, 100% in top 50% of high school class. 99% from public high schools. **Test Scores:** SAT Math middle 50% range 410-530. SAT EBRW middle 50% range 400-510. ACT middle 50% range 16-22. Minimum internet-based TOEFL 61. Minimum paper TOEFL 500. **Basis for Candidate Selection:** *Very important factors considered include:* rigor of secondary school record, academic GPA, standardized test scores. **Freshman Admission Requirements:** High school diploma is required and GED is accepted *Academic units required:* 4 English, 3 math, 1 science, 1 science labs, 2 foreign language, 1 social studies, 1 history, 1 academic elective, 1 visual/performing arts. **Freshman Admission Statistics:** 15,482 applied, 60.4% admitted, 31% enrolled. **Transfer Admission Requirements:** college transcript(s), Minimum college GPA of 2.4 required. Lowest grade transferable D. **General Admission Information:** Application fee $55. Regular application deadline 11/30. Nonfall registration accepted.

COSTS AND FINANCIAL AID

Annual in-state tuition $10,550. Annual out-of-state tuition $11,160. Room and board $10,550. Required fees $790. Average book expense $1,256. **Required Forms and Deadlines:** FAFSA. **Notification of Awards:** Applicants will be notified of awards on a rolling basis beginning 4/1. **Types of Aid:** *Need-based scholarships/grants:* College/university scholarship or grant aid from institutional funds; Federal Pell; Private scholarships; SEOG; State scholarships/grants. *Loans:* Direct PLUS loans; Direct Subsidized Stafford Loans; Direct Unsubsidized Stafford Loans. *Student Employment:* Federal Work-Study Program available. Institutional employment available. **Financial Aid Statistics:** 83% needy freshmen, 80% needy undergrads receive need-based scholarship or grant aid. 2% freshmen, 9% undergrads receive non-need-based scholarship or grant aid. 69% freshmen, 82% undergrads receive need-based self-help aid. 3% freshmen, 2% undergrads receive athletic scholarships. 76% freshmen, 78% undergrads receive any aid. **Criteria for awarding aid:** *Need-based:* Academics, Athletics *Non-need-based:* Academics, Art, Athletics, Leadership, Music/drama, State/district residency.

CALIFORNIA STATE UNIVERSITY, FULLERTON

800 North State College Boulevard, Fullerton, CA 92834-6900
Phone: 657-278-7788 · **Financial Aid Phone:** 657-278-3125
E-mail: admissions@fullerton.edu · **CEEB Code:** 4589
Fax: 657-278-7699 · **Website:** www.fullerton.edu · **ACT Code:** 355

This public school was founded in 1957. It has a 240 acre campus.

RATINGS

Admissions Selectivity Rating: 86   **Fire Safety Rating:** 84   **Green Rating:** 92

STUDENTS AND FACULTY

Enrollment: 38,672. **Student Body:** 49% female, 51% male, 1% out-of-state, 6% international (77 countries represented). Asian 21%, African American 2%, Caucasian 19%, Hispanic 43%, Native American <1%, Pacific Islander <1%, Two or more races 4%, Race unknown 4%.
Retention and Graduation: 87% freshmen return for sophomore year. 22% freshmen graduate within 4 years. 66% freshmen graduate within 6 years.
Faculty: Student/faculty ratio 27:1. 981 full-time faculty, 8% are members of minority groups, 50% are women. 0% of classes are taught by teaching assistants.

ACADEMICS

Degrees: Bachelor's; Doctoral/Professional; Doctoral/Research; Master's; Post-Bachelor's certificate; Post-Master's certificate **Classes:** Most classes have fewer than 10 students. **Most popular majors:** English Language And Literature, General; Liberal Arts And Sciences/Liberal Studies; Biology/Biological Sciences, General. **Special Study Options:** Cooperative education program; Distance learning; Double major; Honors program; Internships; Study abroad. **Honors programs:** University Honors Program President's Scholars Program. **Disability Services offered to physically disabled students:** Note-taking services; Reader services; Tape recorders; Tutors. **Career services:** Alumni network; Alumni services; Career assessment; Career/job search classes; Internships; Regional alumni

FACILITIES

Housing: Apartments for single students; Fraternity/sorority housing; Theme housing; Women's dorms 100% of campus accessible to physically disabled. **Special Academic Facilities/Equipment:** W.M. Keck Foundation Center for Molecular Structure; Museum of Anthropology; Art Gallery; Fullerton Arboretum; Grand Central Art Center; Herbarium; Speech, Language/ Hearing Clinic; Titan Communications; Foreign Language Laboratory; Art Gallery; Sport and Movement Institute; Institute of Gerontology; Institute for Molecular Biology and Nutrition; Center for Molecular Structure; Center for Demographic Research; Social Science Research Center; CA Public Archeology Center. **Computers:** Students can register for classes online. Administrative functions (other than registration) can be performed online.

CAMPUS LIFE

Environment: City **Activities:** Choral groups; Concert band; Dance; Drama/ theater; International Student Organization; Jazz band; Model UN; Music ensembles; Musical theater; Radio station; Student government; Student newspaper; Symphony orchestra. **Athletics (Intercollegiate):** *Men:* baseball, basketball, cross-country, fencing, soccer, track/field (outdoor), wrestling. *Women:* basketball, cross-country, fencing, gymnastics, soccer, softball, tennis, track/field (outdoor), volleyball. **On-Campus Highlights:** Student Recreation Center, Titan Student Union, Mihaylo Hall, Fullerton Arboretum, 5 Starbucks Coffee Shops

ADMISSIONS

Freshman Academic Profile: Average high school GPA 3.6. 22% in top 10% of high school class, 68% in top 25% of high school class, 96% in top 50% of high school class. 91% from public high schools. **Test Scores:** SAT Math middle 50% range 490-590. SAT EBRW middle 50% range 457.5-570. ACT middle 50% range 19-24. Minimum internet-based TOEFL 61. Minimum paper TOEFL 500. **Basis for Candidate Selection:** *Very important factors considered include:* academic GPA, standardized test scores, geographical residence, state residency. **Freshman Admission Requirements:** High school diploma is required and GED is accepted *Academic units required:* 4 English, 3 math, 2 science, 2 science labs, 2 foreign language, 1 social studies, 1 history, 1 academic elective, 1 visual/performing arts, *Academic units recommended:* 4 English, 3 math, 2 science, 2 science labs, 3 foreign language, 1 social studies,

1 history, 1 academic elective, 1 visual/performing arts. **Freshman Admission Statistics:** 45,808 applied, 45.7% admitted, 21% enrolled. **Transfer Admission Requirements:** college transcript(s), statement of good standing from prior institution(s). Minimum college GPA of 2.0 required. Lowest grade transferable C. **General Admission Information:** Application fee $55. Priority deadline 10/30. Regular application deadline 11/30. Nonfall registration accepted.

COSTS AND FINANCIAL AID

Annual in-state tuition $15,642. Annual out-of-state tuition $16,632. Room and board $15,642. Required fees $1,108. Average book expense $1,948. **Required Forms and Deadlines:** FAFSA. *Types of Aid: Need-based scholarships/ grants:* College/university scholarship or grant aid from institutional funds; Federal Nursing Scholarships; Federal Pell; Private scholarships; SEOG; State scholarships/grants. *Loans:* Direct PLUS loans; Direct Subsidized Stafford Loans; Direct Unsubsidized Stafford Loans. *Student Employment:* Federal Work-Study Program available. Institutional employment available. **Financial Aid Statistics:** 80% needy freshmen, 76% needy undergrads receive need-based scholarship or grant aid. 14% freshmen, 9% undergrads receive non-need-based scholarship or grant aid. 28% freshmen, 33% undergrads receive need-based self-help aid. 1% freshmen, 0% undergrads receive athletic scholarships. 67% freshmen, 54% undergrads receive any aid. **Criteria for awarding aid:** *Need-based:* Academics, Art, Athletics, Music/drama *Non-need-based:* Academics, Art, Athletics, Leadership, Music/drama.

CALIFORNIA STATE UNIVERSITY, LONG BEACH

1250 Bellflower Boulevard, Long Beach, CA 90840
Phone: 562-985-5471
E-mail: eslb@csulb.edu · **CEEB Code:** 4389
Fax: 562-985-4973 · **Website:** www.csulb.edu

This public school was founded in 1949. It has a 322 acre campus.

RATINGS

Admissions Selectivity Rating: 89   **Fire Safety Rating:** 67   **Green Rating:** 88

STUDENTS AND FACULTY

Enrollment: 32,079. **Student Body:** 56% female, 44% male, 1% out-of-state, 7% international. Asian 23%, African American 4%, Caucasian 19%, Hispanic 39%, Native American <1%, Pacific Islander <1%, Two or more races 5%, Race unknown 4%.
Retention and Graduation: 91% freshmen return for sophomore year.
Faculty: Student/faculty ratio 24:1. 960 full-time faculty, 85% hold PhDs, 34% are members of minority groups, 48% are women. 8% of classes are taught by teaching assistants.

ACADEMICS

Degrees: Bachelor's; Doctoral/Professional; Doctoral/Research; Master's; Post-Bachelor's certificate **Classes:** Most classes have 20-29 students. Most lab/ discussion sessions have 10-19 students. **Most popular majors:** Psychology, General; Corrections And Criminal Justice, Other; Management Information Systems, General. **Special Study Options:** Double major; Dual enrollment; English as a Second Language (ESL); Honors program; Independent study; Internships; Student-designed major; Study abroad; Teacher certification program. **Disability Services offered to physically disabled students:** Note-taking services; Reader services. **Career services:** Alumni services; Career assessment; Internships

FACILITIES

Housing: Coed dorms; Special housing for international students 98% of campus accessible to physically disabled. **Special Academic Facilities/ Equipment:** Art and science museums, Japanese garden, special events arena with meeting facilities.

CAMPUS LIFE

Activities: Choral groups; Concert band; Dance; Drama/theater; Jazz band; Literary magazine; Music ensembles; Musical theater; Opera; Radio station; Student government; Student newspaper; Student-run film society; Symphony orchestra; Television station; Yearbook 300 registered organizations, 25 honor societies, 20 religious organizations. 16 fraternities, 15 sororities. **Athletics (Intercollegiate):** *Men:* baseball, basketball, cross-country, golf, track/field (outdoor), volleyball, water polo. *Women:* basketball, cross-country, golf, soccer, softball, tennis, track/field (outdoor), volleyball, water polo.

ADMISSIONS

Freshman Academic Profile: Average high school GPA 3.5. 82% in top 25% of high school class, 0% in top 50% of high school class. 82% from public high schools. **Test Scores:** SAT Math middle 50% range 470-600. SAT

EBRW middle 50% range 460-570. Minimum paper TOEFL 525. **Basis for Candidate Selection:** *Very important factors considered include:* academic GPA, standardized test scores, geographical residence, state residency. *Important factors considered include:* talent/ability. *Other factors considered include:* rigor of secondary school record, application essay, recommendation(s), extracurricular activities, character/personal qualities, volunteer work, work experience. **Freshman Admission Requirements:** High school diploma is required and GED is accepted *Academic units required:* 4 English, 3 math, 2 science, 2 science labs, 2 foreign language, 1 social studies, 1 history, 1 academic elective, and 1 unit from above areas or other academic areas. **Freshman Admission Statistics:** 56,975 applied, 34.5% admitted, 23% enrolled. **Transfer Admission Requirements:** college transcript(s), Minimum college GPA of 2.0 required. Lowest grade transferable C. **General Admission Information:** Regular application deadline 11/30. Nonfall registration accepted.

COSTS AND FINANCIAL AID
Annual in-state tuition $12,382. Annual out-of-state tuition $15,144. Room and board $12,382. Required fees $980. Average book expense $1,898. **Required Forms and Deadlines:** FAFSA. **Notification of Awards:** Applicants will be notified of awards on a rolling basis beginning 3/25. **Types of Aid:** *Need-based scholarships/grants:* College/university scholarship or grant aid from institutional funds; Federal Pell; Private scholarships; SEOG; State scholarships/grants. *Loans:* Direct PLUS loans; Direct Subsidized Stafford Loans; Direct Unsubsidized Stafford Loans. *Student Employment:* Federal Work-Study Program available. Institutional employment available. **Financial Aid Statistics:** 80% needy freshmen, 80% needy undergrads receive need-based scholarship or grant aid. 25% freshmen, 26% undergrads receive non-need-based scholarship or grant aid. 72% freshmen, 83% undergrads receive need-based self-help aid. 2% freshmen, 1% undergrads receive athletic scholarships. **Criteria for awarding aid:** *Need-based:* Academics, Art *Non-need-based:* Academics, Art, Athletics, Job skills, Leadership, Music/drama, State/district residency.

CALIFORNIA STATE UNIVERSITY, LOS ANGELES

5151 State University Drive, Los Angeles, CA 90032
Phone: 323-343-3901 · **Financial Aid Phone:** 323-343-6260
E-mail: admission@calstatela.edu · **CEEB Code:** 4399
Fax: 323-343-6306 · **ACT Code:** 320

This public school was founded in 1947. It has a 175 acre campus.

RATINGS
Admissions Selectivity Rating: 74   **Fire Safety Rating:** 84   **Green Rating:** 60*

STUDENTS AND FACULTY
Enrollment: 18,074. **Student Body:** 59% female, 41% male, 0% out-of-state, 4% international (121 countries represented). Asian 17%, African American 5%, Caucasian 8%, Hispanic 58%, Native American <1%, Pacific Islander <1%, Two or more races 2%, Race unknown 6%.
Retention and Graduation: 81% freshmen return for sophomore year.
Faculty: Student/faculty ratio 25:1. 533 full-time faculty, 46% hold PhDs, 44% are members of minority groups, 47% are women. 14% of classes are taught by teaching assistants.

ACADEMICS
Degrees: Bachelor's; Certificate; Master's; Post-Bachelor's certificate **Classes:** Most classes have 10-19 students. Most lab/discussion sessions have 10-19 students. **Most popular majors:** Psychology, General; Criminal Justice/Law Enforcement Administration; Business Administration And Management, General. **Special Study Options:** Accelerated program; Cooperative education program; Cross-registration; Distance learning; Double major; Dual enrollment; English as a Second Language (ESL); Exchange student program (domestic); Honors program; Independent study; Internships; Student-designed major; Study abroad; Teacher certification program. **Honors programs:** The Honors College provides an academically enriched and socially supportive environment that inspires students in all disciplines to become creative and critical thinkers as well as leaders in their fields. With core learning goals focused on knowledge creation, social innovation, and global citizenship, it prepares students to address the most pressing challenges of the 21st century. **Disability Services offered to physically disabled students:** Note-taking services; Reader services. **Career services:** Career/job search classes; Internships

FACILITIES
Housing: Apartments for single students; Fraternity/sorority housing; Special housing for disabled student; Special housing for international students 99% of campus accessible to physically diasbled. **Special Academic Facilities/Equipment:** Baroque pipe organ, bilingual center, entrepreneurship and

small business institutes, center for study of armament and disarmament, Van de Graaff accelerator. **Computers:** Administrative functions (other than registration) can be performed online.

CAMPUS LIFE
Environment: Metropolis **Activities:** Choral groups; Dance; Drama/theater; Jazz band; Literary magazine; Music ensembles; Musical theater; Opera; Student government; Student newspaper; Student-run film society; Symphony orchestra; Yearbook 130 registered organizations, 3 religious organizations. 7 fraternities, 4 sororities. **Athletics (Intercollegiate):** *Men:* baseball, basketball, cross-country, soccer, track/field (outdoor). *Women:* basketball, cross-country, soccer, tennis, track/field (outdoor), volleyball. University Student Union, Food Court, Cafe LA, King Hall, Dolcini's Cafe

ADMISSIONS
Freshman Academic Profile: Average high school GPA 3.2. **Test Scores:** SAT Math middle 50% range 390-510. SAT EBRW middle 50% range 380-480. ACT middle 50% range 15-20. Minimum paper TOEFL 550. **Basis for Candidate Selection:** *Very important factors considered include:* rigor of secondary school record, academic GPA, standardized test scores. *Other factors considered include:* state residency. **Freshman Admission Requirements:** High school diploma is required and GED is accepted *Academic units required:* 4 English, 3 math, 2 science, 2 science labs, 2 foreign language, 1 social studies, 1 history, 1 academic elective, 1 visual/performing arts, *Academic units recommended:* 4 English, 3 math, 2 science, 2 science labs, 2 foreign language, 1 social studies, 1 history, 1 academic elective, 1 visual/performing arts. **Freshman Admission Statistics:** 24,218 applied, 69.4% admitted, 15% enrolled. **Transfer Admission Requirements:** college transcript(s), Minimum college GPA of 2.0 required. Lowest grade transferable C. **General Admission Information:** Application fee $55. Regular application deadline 11/30. Nonfall registration accepted.

COSTS AND FINANCIAL AID
Annual in-state tuition $9,728. Annual out-of-state tuition $17,759. Room and board $9,728. Average book expense $1,665. **Required Forms and Deadlines:** FAFSA. **Notification of Awards:** Applicants will be notified of awards on or about 4/1. **Types of Aid:** *Need-based scholarships/grants:* College/university scholarship or grant aid from institutional funds; Federal Pell; Private scholarships; SEOG; State scholarships/grants. *Loans:* Direct Subsidized Stafford Loans; Direct Unsubsidized Stafford Loans. *Student Employment:* Federal Work-Study Program available. Institutional employment available. **Financial Aid Statistics:** 88% needy freshmen, 88% needy undergrads receive need-based scholarship or grant aid. 0% undergrads receive non-need-based scholarship or grant aid. 66% freshmen, 81% undergrads receive need-based self-help aid. 0% freshmen, 0% undergrads receive athletic scholarships. 76% freshmen, 77% undergrads receive any aid.

CALIFORNIA STATE UNIVERSITY, MONTEREY BAY

100 Campus Center, Seaside, CA 93955
Phone: 831-582-3738 · **Financial Aid Phone:** 831-582-5100
E-mail: admissions@csumb.edu · **CEEB Code:** 1945
Fax: 831-582-3738 · **Website:** https://www.csumb.edu · **ACT Code:** 321

This public school was founded in 1994. It has a 1387 acre campus.

RATINGS
Admissions Selectivity Rating: 83   **Fire Safety Rating:** 87   **Green Rating:** 94

STUDENTS AND FACULTY
Enrollment: 6,771. **Student Body:** 63% female, 37% male, 2% out-of-state, 5% international (20 countries represented). Asian 6%, African American 5%, Caucasian 29%, Hispanic 40%, Native American 1%, Pacific Islander 1%, Two or more races 8%, Race unknown 4%.
Retention and Graduation: 79% freshmen return for sophomore year. 23% freshmen graduate within 4 years. 60% freshmen graduate within 6 years.
Faculty: Student/faculty ratio 26:1. 165 full-time faculty, 92% hold PhDs, 39% are members of minority groups, 50% are women. 0% of classes are taught by teaching assistants.

ACADEMICS
Degrees: Bachelor's; Master's **Classes:** Most classes have 10-19 students. Most lab/discussion sessions have fewer than 10 students. **Most popular majors:** Health And Physical Education/Fitness, General; Psychology, General; Business Administration And Management, General. **Special Study Options:** Accelerated program; Cross-registration; Distance learning; Double major; English as a Second Language (ESL); Exchange student program (domestic);

Independent study; Internships; Student-designed major; Study abroad; Teacher certification program. **Disability Services offered to physically disabled students:** Note-taking services; Reader services; Tape recorders. **Career services:** Alumni services; Career assessment; Career/job search classes; Internships

FACILITIES

Housing: Apartments for married students; Apartments for single students; Coed dorms; Special housing for disabled student; Special housing for international students; Theme housing; Wellness housing 85% of campus accessible to physically diasbled. **Special Academic Facilities/Equipment:** Panetta Institute, Tanimura & Antle Family Memorial Library **Computers:** 100% of classrooms, 100% of dorms, 100% of libraries, 100% of dining areas, 100% of student union, 25% of common outdoor areas have wireless network access. Students can register for classes online. Administrative functions (other than registration) can be performed online.

CAMPUS LIFE

Environment: Village **Activities:** Campus Ministries; Dance; Drama/theater; International Student Organization; Radio station; Student government; Student newspaper; Student-run film society 71 registered organizations, 4 religious organizations. 5 fraternities, 8 sororities. **Athletics (Intercollegiate):** *Men:* baseball, basketball, cross-country, golf, sailing, soccer. *Women:* basketball, cross-country, golf, sailing, soccer, softball, volleyball, water polo. **On-Campus Highlights:** Black Box Cabaret, University Center, Student Center, Tanimura & Antle Library, Starbucks / Peet's Coffee **Environmental Initiatives:** We are an early signatory to the Presidents Climate Commitment

ADMISSIONS

Freshman Academic Profile: Average high school GPA 3.4. 14% in top 10% of high school class, 48% in top 25% of high school class, 89% in top 50% of high school class. 89% from public high schools. **Test Scores:** SAT Math middle 50% range 480-580. SAT EBRW middle 50% range 490-590. ACT middle 50% range 18-24. Minimum internet-based TOEFL 61. Minimum paper TOEFL 500. **Basis for Candidate Selection:** *Very important factors considered include:* academic GPA, standardized test scores. *Important factors considered include:* rigor of secondary school record, geographical residence. *Other factors considered include:* state residency. **Freshman Admission Requirements:** High school diploma is required and GED is accepted *Academic units required:* 4 English, 3 math, 2 science, 1 science labs, 2 foreign language, 1 social studies, 1 history, 1 academic elective, 1 visual/performing arts. **Freshman Admission Statistics:** 13,112 applied, 53.2% admitted, 13% enrolled. **Transfer Admission Requirements:** High school transcript, essay or personal statement, standardized test scores, Minimum college GPA of 2.5 required. Lowest grade transferable C. **General Admission Information:** Application fee $55. Priority deadline 11/30. Regular application deadline 11/30. Nonfall registration accepted.

COSTS AND FINANCIAL AID

Annual in-state tuition $12,396. Annual out-of-state tuition $17,622. Room and board $12,396. Required fees $1,301. Average book expense $1,854. **Required Forms and Deadlines:** FAFSA; State aid form. **Notification of Awards:** Applicants will be notified of awards on a rolling basis beginning 2/1. **Types of Aid:** *Need-based scholarships/grants:* College/university scholarship or grant aid from institutional funds; Federal Pell; Private scholarships; SEOG; State scholarships/grants. *Loans:* Direct PLUS loans; Direct Subsidized Stafford Loans; Direct Unsubsidized Stafford Loans. *Student Employment:* Federal Work-Study Program available. Institutional employment available. **Financial Aid Statistics:** 74% needy freshmen, 75% needy undergrads receive need-based scholarship or grant aid. 14% freshmen, 8% undergrads receive non-need-based scholarship or grant aid. 70% freshmen, 64% undergrads receive need-based self-help aid. 4% freshmen, 2% undergrads receive athletic scholarships. 49% freshmen, 59% undergrads receive any aid. 64% undergrads borrow to pay for school. Average cumulative indebtedness $20,806. **Criteria for awarding aid:** *Non-need-based:* Academics, Athletics, Leadership, State/district residency.

CALIFORNIA STATE UNIVERSITY, NORTHRIDGE

18111 Nordhoff Street, Northridge, CA 91330-8207
Phone: 818-677-3700 · **Financial Aid Phone:** 818-677-4085
E-mail: admissions.records@csun.edu · **CEEB Code:** 4707
Fax: 818-677-3766 · **Website:** www.csun.edu · **ACT Code:** 400

This public school was founded in 1956. It has a 350 acre campus.

RATINGS

Admissions Selectivity Rating: 71   **Fire Safety Rating:** 60*   **Green Rating:** 95

STUDENTS AND FACULTY

Enrollment: 36,917. **Student Body:** 54% female, 46% male, 1% out-of-state, 6% international. Asian 12%, African American 5%, Caucasian 23%, Hispanic 46%, Native American <1%, Pacific Islander <1%, Two or more races 3%, Race unknown 5%.
Retention and Graduation: 78% freshmen return for sophomore year.
Faculty: 917 full-time faculty,

ACADEMICS

Degrees: Bachelor's; Doctoral/Professional; Master's **Classes:** Most classes have 10-19 students. Most lab/discussion sessions have 10-19 students. **Most popular majors:** Psychology, General; Sociology. **Special Study Options:** Accelerated program; Double major; English as a Second Language (ESL); Exchange student program (domestic); Honors program; Independent study; Internships; Student-designed major; Study abroad; Teacher certification program; Weekend college. **Disability Services offered to physically disabled students:** Note-taking services; Reader services; Tape recorders; Tutors. **Career services:** Alumni network; Alumni services; Career/job search classes

FACILITIES

Housing: Apartments for married students; Apartments for single students; Coed dorms; Fraternity/sorority housing; Special housing for international students; Theme housing **Special Academic Facilities/Equipment:** Anthropology museum, art galleries, deafness center, urban archives, map library, cancer research/developmental biology center, planetarium, observatory.

CAMPUS LIFE

Environment: City **Activities:** Choral groups; Concert band; Dance; Drama/theater; International Student Organization; Jazz band; Literary magazine; Marching band; Music ensembles; Musical theater; Radio station; Student government; Student newspaper; Yearbook 267 registered organizations, 18 honor societies, 13 religious organizations. 24 fraternities, 12 sororities. **Athletics (Intercollegiate):** *Men:* baseball, basketball, cross-country, diving, football, golf, soccer, swimming, track/field (outdoor), track/field (indoor), volleyball. *Women:* basketball, cross-country, diving, football, golf, soccer, softball, swimming, tennis, track/field (outdoor), track/field (indoor), volleyball. Valley Performing Arts Center, Student Recreation Center, Oviatt Library, Matador Book Store

ADMISSIONS

Test Scores: Minimum paper TOEFL 500. **Basis for Candidate Selection:** *Very important factors considered include:* standardized test scores. **Freshman Admission Requirements:** High school diploma is required and GED is accepted; High school diploma is required and GED is not accepted *Academic units required:* 4 English, 3 math, 1 science, 2 science labs, 2 foreign language, 2 history, 1 academic elective, and 1 unit from above areas or other academic areas. **Freshman Admission Statistics:** 32,743 applied, 28.5% admitted, enrolled. Lowest grade transferable D. **General Admission Information:** Application fee $55. Nonfall registration accepted.

COSTS AND FINANCIAL AID

Annual in-state tuition $9,962. Annual out-of-state tuition $11,028. Room and board $9,962. Average book expense $1,860. **Required Forms and Deadlines:** FAFSA. **Types of Aid:** *Need-based scholarships/grants:* College/university scholarship or grant aid from institutional funds; Federal Nursing Scholarships; Federal Pell; Private scholarships; SEOG; State scholarships/grants. *Loans: Student Employment:* Federal Work-Study Program available. Institutional employment available.

CALIFORNIA STATE UNIVERSITY, SACRAMENTO

6000 J Street, Sacramento, CA 95819-2694
Phone: 916-278-7766 • **Financial Aid Phone:** 916-278-6554
E-mail: outreach@csus.edu • **CEEB Code:** 4671
Fax: 916-278-5603 • **Website:** www.csus.edu • **ACT Code:** 382

This public school was founded in 1947. It has a 300 acre campus.

RATINGS
Admissions Selectivity Rating: 76   **Fire Safety Rating:** 73   **Green Rating:** 99

STUDENTS AND FACULTY
Enrollment: 25,457. **Student Body:** 57% female, 43% male, 1% out-of-state, 1% international (122 countries represented). Asian 21%, African American 6%, Caucasian 39%, Hispanic 19%, Native American 1%, Pacific Islander 1%, Two or more races 4%, Race unknown 7%.
Retention and Graduation: 81% freshmen return for sophomore year.
Faculty: Student/faculty ratio 28:1. 558 full-time faculty, 87% hold PhDs, 31% are members of minority groups, 47% are women. 0% of classes are taught by teaching assistants.

ACADEMICS
Degrees: Bachelor's; Doctoral/Research; Master's **Classes:** Most classes have fewer than 10 students. Most lab/discussion sessions have fewer than 10 students. **Most popular majors:** Criminal Justice/Law Enforcement Administration; Nursing/Registered Nurse (Rn, Asn, Bsn, Msn); Business/Commerce, General. **Special Study Options:** Accelerated program; Cooperative education program; Cross-registration; Distance learning; Double major; Dual enrollment; English as a Second Language (ESL); Honors program; Independent study; Internships; Student-designed major; Study abroad; Teacher certification program. **Combined degree programs:** BA/MA. **Disability Services offered to physically disabled students:** Note-taking services; Reader services; Tape recorders; Tutors. **Career services:** Alumni network; Alumni services; Career assessment; Internships; Regional alumni

FACILITIES
Housing: Apartments for single students; Coed dorms; Special housing for disabled student; Theme housing 95% of campus accessible to physically diasbled. **Special Academic Facilities/Equipment:** CSUS Museum of Anthropology University Library Gallery (Art) Else Gallery (Art) Witt Gallery (Art) **Computers:** Students can register for classes online. Administrative functions (other than registration) can be performed online.

CAMPUS LIFE
Environment: Metropolis **Activities:** Concert band; Dance; Drama/theater; International Student Organization; Jazz band; Literary magazine; Marching band; Music ensembles; Musical theater; Opera; Pep band; Radio station; Student government; Student newspaper; Student-run film society; Symphony orchestra 222 registered organizations, 7 honor societies, 13 religious organizations. 19 fraternities, 20 sororities. **Athletics (Intercollegiate):** *Men:* baseball, basketball, cheerleading, cross-country, football, golf, soccer, tennis, track/field (outdoor). *Women:* basketball, cheerleading, crew/rowing, cross-country, golf, gymnastics, soccer, softball, tennis, track/field (outdoor), volleyball. **On-Campus Highlights:** University Union, River Front Center, Guy West Bridge, Mariposa Hall, Hornet Stadium

ADMISSIONS
Freshman Academic Profile: Average high school GPA 3.3. 100% in top 50% of high school class. 89% from public high schools. **Test Scores:** SAT Math middle 50% range 430-540. SAT EBRW middle 50% range 410-520. ACT middle 50% range 17-22. Minimum paper TOEFL 510. **Basis for Candidate Selection:** *Very important factors considered include:* academic GPA, standardized test scores. *Other factors considered include:* recommendation(s), state residency. **Freshman Admission Requirements:** High school diploma is required and GED is accepted *Academic units required:* 4 English, 3 math, 2 science, 2 science labs, 2 foreign language, 2 history, 1 academic elective, 1 visual/performing arts. **Freshman Admission Statistics:** 19,702 applied, 69.7% admitted, 23% enrolled. **Transfer Admission Requirements:** college transcript(s), statement of good standing from prior institution(s). Minimum college GPA of 2.0 required. Lowest grade transferable D. **General Admission Information:** Application fee $55. Priority deadline 10/1. Regular application deadline 11/30. Nonfall registration accepted. Admission may be deferred for a maximum of one semester.

COSTS AND FINANCIAL AID
Annual in-state tuition $1,130. Annual out-of-state tuition $16,632. Required fees $1,130. Average book expense $1,754. **Required Forms and Deadlines:** FAFSA. **Notification of Awards:** Applicants will be notified of awards on a

rolling basis beginning 4/27. **Types of Aid:** *Need-based scholarships/grants:* Federal Nursing Scholarships; Federal Pell; Private scholarships; SEOG; State scholarships/grants. *Loans:* Direct PLUS loans; Direct Subsidized Stafford Loans; Direct Unsubsidized Stafford Loans. *Student Employment:* Federal Work-Study Program available. Institutional employment available. **Financial Aid Statistics:** 77% needy freshmen, 78% needy undergrads receive need-based scholarship or grant aid. 16% freshmen, 7% undergrads receive non-need-based scholarship or grant aid. 100% freshmen, 99% undergrads receive need-based self-help aid. 0% freshmen, 0% undergrads receive athletic scholarships. 50% undergrads receive any aid.

CALIFORNIA STATE UNIVERSITY, SAN BERNARDINO

5500 University Parkway, San Bernardino, CA 92407-2397
Phone: 909-537-5188 • **Financial Aid Phone:** 909-537-5227
E-mail: moreinfo@mail.csusb.edu • **CEEB Code:** 4099
Fax: 909-537-7034 • **Website:** www.csusb.edu • **ACT Code:** 205

This public school was founded in 1965. It has a 441 acre campus.

RATINGS
Admissions Selectivity Rating: 80   **Fire Safety Rating:** 60*   **Green Rating:** 60*

STUDENTS AND FACULTY
Enrollment: 18,453. **Student Body:** 60% female, 40% male, 0% out-of-state, 7% international (78 countries represented). Asian 6%, African American 6%, Caucasian 13%, Hispanic 63%, Native American <1%, Pacific Islander <1%, Two or more races 3%, Race unknown 4%.
Retention and Graduation: 85% freshmen return for sophomore year.
Faculty: Student/faculty ratio 28:1. 458 full-time faculty, 78% hold PhDs, 33% are members of minority groups, 47% are women.

ACADEMICS
Degrees: Bachelor's; Certificate; Doctoral; Master's; Post-Bachelor's certificate **Classes:** Most classes have 10-19 students. **Most popular majors:** Psychology, General; Social Sciences, General; Business Administration And Management, General. **Special Study Options:** Accelerated program; Cooperative education program; Cross-registration; Distance learning; Double major; Dual enrollment; Exchange student program (domestic); External degree program; Honors program; Independent study; Internships; Student-designed major; Study abroad; Teacher certification program. **Honors programs:** The University Honors Program is a community of students who share a passion for learning and embrace intellectual, creative, and personal challenges as opportunities to grow. The program encourages and supports Honors students' intellectual, creative, and personal growth throughout their undergraduate education by providing challenging coursework, enriching colloquia and seminars, a diverse range of cultural events, and rigorous senior research and scholarship experiences. **Disability Services offered to physically disabled students:** Note-taking services; Reader services; Tape recorders. **Career services:** Alumni services; Career assessment; Career/job search classes; Internships

FACILITIES
Housing: Apartments for single students; Coed dorms; Special housing for disabled student; Theme housing; Women's dorms **Special Academic Facilities/Equipment:** Simulation labs, electronic music studios, language lab, desert studies center, Robert V. Fullerton Art Museum, and Anthropology Museum **Computers:** Students can register for classes online. Administrative functions (other than registration) can be performed online.

CAMPUS LIFE
Environment: City **Activities:** Campus Ministries; Choral groups; Dance; Drama/theater; International Student Organization; Jazz band; Model UN; Music ensembles; Musical theater; Radio station; Student government; Student newspaper; Television station 97 registered organizations, 3 religious organizations. 9 fraternities, 6 sororities. **Athletics (Intercollegiate):** *Men:* baseball, basketball, golf, soccer, swimming, water polo. *Women:* basketball, cross-country, soccer, softball, swimming, tennis, volleyball, water polo. **On-Campus Highlights:** Coussoulis Arena, Robert and Frances Fullerton Museum of Art, Santos Manuel Student Union, John M. Pfau Library, Student Recreation & Fitness Center Facilities

ADMISSIONS
Freshman Academic Profile: Average high school GPA 3.3. 95% from public high schools. **Test Scores:** SAT Math middle 50% range 390-490. SAT EBRW middle 50% range 390-490. ACT middle 50% range 16-20. Minimum internet-based TOEFL 61. Minimum paper TOEFL 500. **Basis for Candidate**

Selection: *Very important factors considered include:* academic GPA, standardized test scores. *Important factors considered include:* geographical residence. **Freshman Admission Requirements:** High school diploma is required and GED is accepted *Academic units required:* 4 English, 3 math, 2 science, 2 science labs, 2 foreign language, 1 social studies, 1 history, 1 academic elective, 1 visual/performing arts. **Freshman Admission Statistics:** 15,740 applied, 58.1% admitted, 30% enrolled. **Transfer Admission Requirements:** college transcript(s), Minimum college GPA of 2.0 required. Lowest grade transferable C. **General Admission Information:** Application fee $55. Priority deadline 11/30. Nonfall registration accepted.

COSTS AND FINANCIAL AID

Annual in-state tuition $12,966. Annual out-of-state tuition $11,160. Room and board $12,966. Required fees $1,129. Average book expense $1,791. **Required Forms and Deadlines:** FAFSA; State aid form. **Notification of Awards:** Applicants will be notified of awards on a rolling basis beginning 4/1. **Types of Aid:** *Need-based scholarships/grants:* College/university scholarship or grant aid from institutional funds; Federal Pell; Private scholarships; SEOG; State scholarships/grants. *Loans:* Direct PLUS loans; Direct Subsidized Stafford Loans; Direct Unsubsidized Stafford Loans. *Student Employment:* Federal Work-Study Program available. Institutional employment available. **Financial Aid Statistics:** 96% needy freshmen, 89% needy undergrads receive need-based scholarship or grant aid. 75% freshmen, 52% undergrads receive non-need-based scholarship or grant aid. 32% freshmen, 38% undergrads receive need-based self-help aid. 0% freshmen, 0% undergrads receive athletic scholarships. 66% undergrads borrow to pay for school. Average cumulative indebtedness $22,452. **Criteria for awarding aid:** *Need-based:* Academics, Alumni affiliation, Art, Athletics, Job skills, Leadership, Minority status, Music/drama, Religious affiliation.

CALIFORNIA STATE UNIVERSITY, SAN MARCOS

P.O. Box 8058, San Marcos, CA 92096-0001
Phone: 760-750-4848 · **Financial Aid Phone:** 760-750-4850
E-mail: apply@csusm.edu · **CEEB Code:** 5677
Fax: 760-750-3248 · **Website:** www.csusm.edu

This public school was founded in 1989. It has a 304 acre campus.

RATINGS

Admissions Selectivity Rating: 78   **Fire Safety Rating:** 60*   **Green Rating:** 94

STUDENTS AND FACULTY

Enrollment: 12,096. **Student Body:** 61% female, 39% male, 1% out-of-state, 2% international. Asian 10%, African American 3%, Caucasian 30%, Hispanic 42%, Native American <1%, Pacific Islander <1%, Two or more races 6%, Race unknown 5%.
Retention and Graduation: 82% freshmen return for sophomore year.
Faculty: Student/faculty ratio 25:1. 254 full-time faculty, 32% are members of minority groups, 50% are women.

ACADEMICS

Degrees: Bachelor's; Master's **Classes:** Most classes have fewer than 10 students. Most lab/discussion sessions have fewer than 10 students. **Special Study Options:** Accelerated program; Cross-registration; Distance learning; Double major; Dual enrollment; English as a Second Language (ESL); Independent study; Internships; Student-designed major; Study abroad; Teacher certification program; Weekend college. **Disability Services offered to physically disabled students:** Note-taking services; Reader services; Tape recorders; Tutors. **Career services:** Alumni services; Career assessment; Internships

FACILITIES

Housing: Apartments for single students; Other (please specify) **Computers:** Students can register for classes online.

CAMPUS LIFE

Environment: Town **Activities:** Dance; Music ensembles; Student newspaper 70 registered organizations, 5 honor societies, 2 religious organizations. 2 fraternities, 2 sororities. **Athletics (Intercollegiate):** *Men:* baseball, cross-country, golf, soccer, track/field (outdoor). *Women:* cross-country, golf, soccer, softball, track/field (outdoor).

ADMISSIONS

Freshman Academic Profile: Average high school GPA 3.3. **Test Scores:** SAT Math middle 50% range 430-530. SAT EBRW middle 50% range 420-520. Minimum paper TOEFL 550. **Basis for Candidate Selection:** *Very important factors considered include:* academic GPA, standardized test scores.

Other factors considered include: geographical residence, state residency.
Freshman Admission Requirements: High school diploma is required and GED is accepted *Academic units required:* 4 English, 3 math, 2 science, 2 science labs, 2 foreign language, 1 social studies, 1 history, 1 academic elective, 1 visual/performing arts, *Academic units recommended:* 4 English, 4 math, 2 science, 2 foreign language, 1 social studies, 1 history, 1 academic elective, 1 visual/performing arts. **Freshman Admission Statistics:** 11,560 applied, 67.0% admitted, 28% enrolled. **Transfer Admission Requirements:** college transcript(s), Minimum college GPA of 2.0 required. Lowest grade transferable C. **General Admission Information:** Application fee $55. Regular application deadline 11/30. Nonfall registration accepted.

COSTS AND FINANCIAL AID

Annual in-state tuition $13,240. Annual out-of-state tuition $14,400. Room and board $13,240. Required fees $1,792. Average book expense $1,764. **Required Forms and Deadlines:** FAFSA. **Notification of Awards:** Applicants will be notified of awards on or about 4/15. **Types of Aid:** *Need-based scholarships/grants:* College/university scholarship or grant aid from institutional funds; Federal Pell; Private scholarships; SEOG; State scholarships/grants. *Loans:* Direct PLUS loans; Direct Subsidized Stafford Loans; Direct Unsubsidized Stafford Loans. **Criteria for awarding aid:** *Need-based:* Academics, Athletics, Leadership *Non-need-based:* Academics, Athletics, Leadership, State/district residency.

CALIFORNIA STATE UNIVERSITY, STANISLAUS

Best Colleges

One University Circle, Turlock, CA 95382
Phone: 209-667-3070 · **Financial Aid Phone:** 209-667-3336
E-mail: Outreach_Help_Desk@csustan.edu · **CEEB Code:** 4713
Fax: 209-667-3788 · **Website:** www.csustan.edu · **ACT Code:** 435

This public school was founded in 1957. It has a 228 acre campus.

RATINGS

Admissions Selectivity Rating: 76   **Fire Safety Rating:** 97   **Green Rating:** 70

STUDENTS AND FACULTY

Enrollment: 8,888. **Student Body:** 65% female, 35% male, 1% out-of-state, 4% international (18 countries represented). Asian 10%, African American 2%, Caucasian 22%, Hispanic 53%, Native American <1%, Pacific Islander 1%, Two or more races 4%, Race unknown 5%.
Retention and Graduation: 81% freshmen return for sophomore year. 14% freshmen graduate within 4 years. 52% freshmen graduate within 6 years. **Faculty:** Student/faculty ratio 23:1. 341 full-time faculty, 81% hold PhDs, 27% are members of minority groups, 46% are women.

ACADEMICS

Degrees: Bachelor's; Doctoral Other; Master's **Classes:** Most classes have 10-19 students. Most lab/discussion sessions have 40-49 students. **Most popular majors:** Psychology, General; Criminal Justice/Safety Studies; Business/Commerce, General. **Special Study Options:** Accelerated program; Cooperative education program; Cross-registration; Distance learning; Double major; Dual enrollment; English as a Second Language (ESL); External degree program; Honors program; Independent study; Internships; Liberal arts/career combination; Student-designed major; Study abroad; Teacher certification program. **Honors programs:** University Honors Program. **Disability Services offered to physically disabled students:** Note-taking services; Reader services; Tape recorders; Tutors. **Career services:** Alumni network; Alumni services; Career assessment; Career/job search classes; Internships; Regional alumni

FACILITIES

Housing: Coed dorms; Theme housing 99% of campus accessible to physically diasbled. **Special Academic Facilities/Equipment:** Marine sciences station, laser lab, greenhouse, art gallery, mainstage theatre, recital hall, observatory, science building, art complex, distance learning studios, BioAg Eco building. **Computers:** 100% of classrooms, 100% of dorms, 100% of libraries, 100% of dining areas, 100% of student union, 10% of common outdoor areas have wireless network access. Students can register for classes online. Administrative functions (other than registration) can be performed online.

CAMPUS LIFE

Environment: City **Activities:** Campus Ministries; Choral groups; Drama/theater; International Student Organization; Model UN; Music ensembles; Musical theater; Opera; Radio station; Student government; Student newspaper; Student-run film society; Symphony orchestra 76 registered organizations, 11 honor societies, 4 religious organizations. 7 fraternities, 9 sororities. **Athletics (Intercollegiate):** *Men:* baseball, basketball, cross-country, golf, soccer, track/field (outdoor), track/field (indoor). *Women:* basketball, cross-country, soccer, softball, tennis, track/field (outdoor), track/field (indoor), volleyball. **On-Campus Highlights:** Naraghi Hall of Science, Nursing Department, Library, University Art Gallery, Dorms/Housing **Environmental Initiatives:** An addition of a filtration system and modifications to Central Plant chiller operations have been implemented to optimize the campus wide storm drainage/irrigation reclamation infrastructure, saving 4-5 million gallons of potable drinking water annually. The modifications also allowed for the tower blow down water to be reclaimed for irrigation purposes. Earning the California Higher Education Sustainability Conference Best practices award in Energy Efficiency and Sustainability for Water Efficiency and Site Water Quality.

ADMISSIONS

Freshman Academic Profile: Average high school GPA 3.3. 97% from public high schools. **Test Scores:** SAT Math middle 50% range 450-540. SAT EBRW middle 50% range 460-560. ACT middle 50% range 17-21. Minimum internet-based TOEFL 61. Minimum paper TOEFL 500. **Basis for Candidate Selection:** *Very important factors considered include:* rigor of secondary school record, academic GPA, standardized test scores. *Important factors considered include:* class rank. **Freshman Admission Requirements:** High school diploma is required and GED is accepted *Academic units required:* 4 English, 3 math, 2 science, 2 science labs, 2 foreign language, 1 social studies, 1 history, 1 academic elective, 1 visual/performing arts, *Academic units recommended:* 4 English, 3 math, 2 science, 2 science labs, 2 foreign language, 1 social studies, 1 history, 1 academic elective, 1 visual/performing arts. **Freshman Admission Statistics:** 8,069 applied, 77.1% admitted, 23% enrolled. **Transfer Admission Requirements:** college transcript(s), statement of good standing from prior institution(s). Minimum college GPA of 2.0 required. Lowest grade transferable D. **General Admission Information:** Application fee $55. Priority deadline 11/30. Regular application deadline 11/30. Nonfall registration accepted.

COSTS AND FINANCIAL AID

Annual in-state tuition $8,670. Annual out-of-state tuition $17,622. Room and board $8,670. Required fees $1,296. Average book expense $1,600. **Required Forms and Deadlines:** FAFSA; Institution's own financial aid form; State aid form. **Notification of Awards:** Applicants will be notified of awards on a rolling basis beginning 4/1. **Types of Aid:** *Need-based scholarships/grants:* College/university scholarship or grant aid from institutional funds; Federal Pell; Private scholarships; SEOG; State scholarships/grants. *Loans:* Direct PLUS loans; Direct Subsidized Stafford Loans; Direct Unsubsidized Stafford Loans. *Student Employment:* Federal Work-Study Program available. Institutional employment available. **Financial Aid Statistics:** 90% freshmen, 81% undergrads receive any aid. **Criteria for awarding aid:** *Need-based:* Academics, Alumni affiliation, Art, Leadership, Music/drama *Non-need-based:* Academics, Alumni affiliation, Art, Athletics, Leadership, Music/drama, State/district residency.

CALIFORNIA UNIVERSITY OF PENNSYLVANIA

250 University Avenue, California, PA 15419
Phone: 724-938-4404 · **Financial Aid Phone:** 724-938-4415
E-mail: inquiry@cup.edu · **CEEB Code:** 2647
Fax: 724-938-4564 · **Website:** www.calu.edu · **ACT Code:** 3694

This public school was founded in 1852. It has a 188 acre campus.

RATINGS

Admissions Selectivity Rating: 72   **Fire Safety Rating:** 97   **Green Rating:** 73

STUDENTS AND FACULTY

Enrollment: 5,435. **Student Body:** 53% female, 47% male, 11% out-of-state, 1% international (29 countries represented). Asian 1%, African American 13%, Caucasian 76%, Hispanic 3%, Native American <1%, Pacific Islander <1%, Two or more races 4%, Race unknown 2%.
Retention and Graduation: 73% freshmen return for sophomore year. 39% freshmen graduate within 4 years. 55% freshmen graduate within 6 years. 10% grads go on to further study within 1 year. **Faculty:** Student/faculty ratio 20:1. 252 full-time faculty, 86% hold PhDs, 13% are members of minority groups, 51% are women. 0% of classes are taught by teaching assistants.

ACADEMICS

Degrees: Associate; Bachelor's; Certificate; Doctoral Other; Master's; Post-Bachelor's certificate; Post-Master's certificate **Classes:** Most classes have 10-19 students. Most lab/discussion sessions have fewer than 10 students.
Most popular majors: Criminal Justice/Safety Studies; Registered Nursing/

Registered Nurse; Business Administration And Management, General. **Special Study Options:** Accelerated program; Cooperative education program; Cross-registration; Distance learning; Double major; Dual enrollment; English as a Second Language (ESL); Exchange student program (domestic); Honors program; Independent study; Internships; Liberal arts/career combination; Study abroad; Teacher certification program. **Disability Services offered to physically disabled students:** Note-taking services; Reader services; Tape recorders; Tutors. **Career services:** Alumni network; Alumni services; Career assessment; Career/job search classes; Internships; Regional alumni

FACILITIES

Housing: Apartments for single students; Coed dorms; Special housing for disabled student; Theme housing 90% of campus accessible to physically disabled. **Special Academic Facilities/Equipment:** Manderino Gallery of Fine Arts, hosts top 40 corporate art collection sin the world **Computers:** Students can register for classes online. Administrative functions (other than registration) can be performed online.

CAMPUS LIFE

Environment: Village **Activities:** Campus Ministries; Choral groups; Concert band; Dance; Drama/theater; International Student Organization; Jazz band; Literary magazine; Marching band; Music ensembles; Musical theater; Opera; Pep band; Radio station; Student government; Student newspaper; Symphony orchestra; Television station; Yearbook 25 honor societies, 1 religious organization. 6 fraternities, 7 sororities. **Athletics (Intercollegiate):** *Men:* baseball, basketball, cheerleading, cross-country, football, golf, rugby, soccer, softball, track/field (outdoor), track/field (indoor), volleyball. *Women:* basketball, cheerleading, cross-country, diving, golf, rugby, soccer, softball, swimming, tennis, track/field (outdoor), track/field (indoor), volleyball. **On-Campus Highlights:** Residence Halls, Student Union, Classrooms, Herron Rec Center, Library **Environmental Initiatives:** Multimillion Dollar Geothermal project plus replacing ALL residence halls in less than 5 years with Green buildings.

ADMISSIONS

Freshman Academic Profile: Average high school GPA 3.1. 7% in top 10% of high school class, 23% in top 25% of high school class, 55% in top 50% of high school class. 88% from public high schools. **Test Scores:** SAT Math middle 50% range 460-560. SAT EBRW middle 50% range 470-580. ACT middle 50% range 16-23. Minimum paper TOEFL 450. **Basis for Candidate Selection:** *Very important factors considered include:* academic GPA, standardized test scores. *Important factors considered include:* rigor of secondary school record. *Other factors considered include:* class rank, application essay, recommendation(s), interview, extracurricular activities, talent/ability, character/personal qualities, volunteer work, work experience, level of applicant's interest. **Freshman Admission Requirements:** High school diploma is required and GED is accepted *Academic units required:* **Freshman Admission Statistics:** 3,324 applied, 94.3% admitted, 32% enrolled. **Transfer Admission Requirements:** High school transcript, college transcript(s), statement of good standing from prior institution(s). Minimum college GPA of 2.3 required. Lowest grade transferable C. **General Admission Information:** Application fee $25. Priority deadline 8/21. Nonfall registration accepted. Admission may be deferred for a maximum of 3 years.

COSTS AND FINANCIAL AID

Annual in-state tuition $10,344. Annual out-of-state tuition $11,238. Room and board $10,344. Required fees $3,348. Average book expense $1,000. **Required Forms and Deadlines:** FAFSA. **Notification of Awards:** Applicants will be notified of awards on a rolling basis beginning 12/1. **Types of Aid:** *Need-based scholarships/grants:* College/university scholarship or grant aid from institutional funds; Federal Pell; Private scholarships; SEOG; State scholarships/grants. *Loans:* Direct PLUS loans; Direct Subsidized Stafford Loans; Direct Unsubsidized Stafford Loans. *Student Employment:* Federal Work-Study Program available. Institutional employment available. **Financial Aid Statistics:** 79% needy freshmen, 83% needy undergrads receive need-based scholarship or grant aid. 34% freshmen, 22% undergrads receive non-need-based scholarship or grant aid. 94% freshmen, 93% undergrads receive need-based self-help aid. 2% freshmen, 1% undergrads receive athletic scholarships. 90% freshmen receive any aid. 88% undergrads borrow to pay for school. Average cumulative indebtedness $25,683. **Criteria for awarding aid:** *Need-based:* Academics, Leadership, Minority status, Music/drama *Non-need-based:* Academics, Athletics, Leadership, Minority status, Music/drama, State/district residency.

CALVARY BIBLE COLLEGE AND THEOLOGICAL SEMINARY

15800 Calvary Rd., Kansas City, MO 64147
Phone: 816-322-3960 · **Financial Aid Phone:** 816-322-0110
E-mail: admissions@calvary.edu
Fax: 816-331-4474 · **Website:** http://www.college.calvary.edu/ · **ACT Code:** 2312

This private school, affiliated with the Christian (Nondenominational) Church, was founded in 1932. It has a 56.3 acre campus.

RATINGS

Admissions Selectivity Rating: 75　　**Fire Safety Rating:** 83　　**Green Rating:** 61

STUDENTS AND FACULTY

Enrollment: 226. **Student Body:** 50% female, 50% male, 65% out-of-state, 0% international (1 countries represented). Asian 2%, African American 11%, Caucasian 80%, Hispanic 3%, Native American 1%, Pacific Islander 0%, Two or more races 3%, Race unknown 0%.
Retention and Graduation: 69% freshmen return for sophomore year.
Faculty: Student/faculty ratio 7:1. 17 full-time faculty, 71% hold PhDs, 12% are members of minority groups, 41% are women. 0% of classes are taught by teaching assistants.

ACADEMICS

Degrees: Associate; Bachelor's; Certificate; Master's **Classes:** Most classes have 10-19 students. **Most popular majors:** Bible/Biblical Studies; Pastoral Studies/Counseling; Music, Other. **Special Study Options:** Accelerated program; Distance learning; Double major; Dual enrollment; Independent study; Internships; Teacher certification program. **Disability Services offered to physically disabled students:** Reader services; Tape recorders; Tutors.

FACILITIES

Housing: Apartments for married students; Apartments for single students; Men's dorms; Women's dorms 50% of campus accessible to physically diasbled. **Special Academic Facilities/Equipment:** The Learning Center K-Bar Cafe Gym **Computers:** 100% of dorms, 100% of libraries, 100% of student union, have wireless network access. Students can register for classes online.

CAMPUS LIFE

Environment: Metropolis **Activities:** Campus Ministries; Choral groups; Concert band; Drama/theater; Music ensembles; Musical theater; Student government. **Athletics (Intercollegiate):** *Men:* basketball, soccer. *Women:* basketball, volleyball. **On-Campus Highlights:** Student Lounge, The K-Bar Cafe, Gymnasium, The Library, The Learning Center

ADMISSIONS

Freshman Academic Profile: Average high school GPA 3.4. **Test Scores:** SAT Math middle 50% range 498-518. SAT EBRW middle 50% range 445-517.5. ACT middle 50% range 19-24. Minimum paper TOEFL 525. **Basis for Candidate Selection:** *Very important factors considered include:* academic GPA, application essay, recommendation(s), character/personal qualities, religious affiliation/commitment, level of applicant's interest. *Important factors considered include:* standardized test scores. *Other factors considered include:* class rank, interview, extracurricular activities, talent/ability, alumni/ae relation, volunteer work, work experience. **Freshman Admission Requirements:** High school diploma is required and GED is accepted **Freshman Admission Statistics:** 52 applied, 94.2% admitted, 67% enrolled. **Transfer Admission Requirements:** college transcript(s), essay or personal statement, Minimum college GPA of 2.0 required. Lowest grade transferable C-. **General Admission Information:** Nonfall registration accepted. Admission may be deferred for a maximum of One year.

COSTS AND FINANCIAL AID

Average book expense $794. **Required Forms and Deadlines:** FAFSA. **Types of Aid:** *Need-based scholarships/grants:* College/university scholarship or grant aid from institutional funds; Federal Pell; SEOG. *Loans:* Direct PLUS loans; Direct Subsidized Stafford Loans; Direct Unsubsidized Stafford Loans. *Student Employment:* Federal Work-Study Program available. Institutional employment available. **Financial Aid Statistics:** 100% needy freshmen, 91% needy undergrads receive need-based scholarship or grant aid. 19% freshmen, 10% undergrads receive non-need-based scholarship or grant aid. 100% freshmen, 88% undergrads receive need-based self-help aid. 0% freshmen, 0% undergrads receive athletic scholarships. 75% freshmen, 76% undergrads receive any aid. Average cumulative indebtedness $15,498. **Criteria for awarding aid:** *Non-need-based:* Academics, Alumni affiliation, Music/drama, Religious affiliation.

CALVIN COLLEGE

3201 Burton Street S.E., Grand Rapids, MI 49546
Phone: 616-526-6106 · **Financial Aid Phone:** 800-688-0122
E-mail: admissions@calvin.edu · **CEEB Code:** 1095
Fax: 616-526-6777 · **Website:** www.calvin.edu · **ACT Code:** 1968

This private school, affiliated with the Christian Reformed Church, was founded in 1876. It has a 400 acre campus.

RATINGS

Admissions Selectivity Rating: 81　　**Fire Safety Rating:** 83　　**Green Rating:** 76

STUDENTS AND FACULTY

Enrollment: 3,656. **Student Body:** 53% female, 47% male, 42% out-of-state, 12% international (65 countries represented). Asian 5%, African American 3%, Caucasian 70%, Hispanic 5%, Native American <1%, Pacific Islander 0%, Two or more races 3%, Race unknown 2%.
Retention and Graduation: 87% freshmen return for sophomore year. 59% freshmen graduate within 4 years. 72% freshmen graduate within 6 years. 25% grads go on to further study within 1 year. 19% grads pursue arts and sciences degrees. 1% grads pursue law degrees. 1% grads pursue business degrees. 3% grads pursue medical degrees. **Faculty:** Student/faculty ratio 13:1. 246 full-time faculty, 90% hold PhDs, 10% are members of minority groups, 34% are women. 0% of classes are taught by teaching assistants.

ACADEMICS

Degrees: Associate; Bachelor's; Certificate; Master's **Classes:** Most classes have 20-29 students. Most lab/discussion sessions have fewer than 10 students. **Most popular majors:** Engineering, General; Registered Nursing/Registered Nurse; Business Administration And Management, General. **Special Study Options:** Distance learning; Double major; Dual enrollment; Honors program; Independent study; Internships; Student-designed major; Study abroad; Teacher certification program. **Honors programs:** For almost forty years Calvin College has challenged its best students with a campus-wide Honors Program—part of our overall mission to encourage academic excellence in a Christ-centered environment. Virtually all honors students receive academic scholarships ranging from $8,000–18,000 per year. A new component of the program is the Research Fellows program, a research opportunity for students that allow them to get hands-on experience, alongside professors who are experts in their fields. This program will give the student $4000 stipend, up to $1000 voucher for Calvin's off-campus programs, and up to $500 reimbursement for travel related to research. In addition, many honors students apply to live in the Honors Living-Learning community, a residence hall floor where students develop strong relationships with peers and faculty mentors. The McGregor Sophomore Scholars Program develops targeted programming for sophomores in the Honors Program, such as one-on-one mentoring with faculty and program leaders and special events. **Combined degree programs:** BA/MA. **Disability Services offered to physically disabled students:** Note-taking services; Reader services; Tape recorders; Tutors. **Career services:** Alumni network; Alumni services; Career assessment; Career/job search classes; Internships; Regional alumni

FACILITIES

Housing: Apartments for single students; Coed dorms; Men's dorms; Special housing for disabled student; Theme housing; Wellness housing; Women's dorms 95% of campus accessible to physically diasbled. **Special Academic Facilities/Equipment:** Art gallery, observatory, ecosystem preserve, electron microscope, seismograph lab, mineralogical museum. **Computers:** 40% of classrooms, 100% of dorms, 100% of libraries, 75% of dining areas, 20% of student union, 10% of common outdoor areas have wireless network access. Students can register for classes online. Administrative functions (other than registration) can be performed online.

CAMPUS LIFE

Environment: Metropolis **Activities:** Campus Ministries; Choral groups; Concert band; Dance; Drama/theater; International Student Organization; Jazz band; Literary magazine; Music ensembles; Pep band; Student government; Student newspaper; Student-run film society; Symphony orchestra; Yearbook 60 registered organizations, 6 honor societies, 5 religious organizations. **Athletics (Intercollegiate):** *Men:* baseball, basketball, cross-country, diving, golf, soccer, swimming, tennis, track/field (outdoor). *Women:* basketball, cross-country, diving, golf, soccer, softball, swimming, tennis, track/field (outdoor), volleyball. **On-Campus Highlights:** Spoelhof Fieldhouse Complex, Johnny's Cafe, Hekman Library, DeVos Communications Building, Covenant Fine Arts Center **Environmental Initiatives:** The Calvin Energy Recovery Fund, a green revolving fund(http://www.calvin.edu/admin/development/cerf)

ADMISSIONS

Freshman Academic Profile: Average high school GPA 3.8. 28% in top 10% of high school class, 57% in top 25% of high school class, 85% in top 50% of high school class. 51% from public high schools. **Test Scores:** SAT Math middle 50% range 540-670. SAT EBRW middle 50% range 560-660. ACT middle 50% range 23-30. Minimum internet-based TOEFL 80. Minimum paper TOEFL 550. **Basis for Candidate Selection:** *Very important factors considered include:* rigor of secondary school record, academic GPA, standardized test scores, religious affiliation/commitment. *Important factors considered include:* application essay, recommendation(s), extracurricular activities, character/personal qualities. *Other factors considered include:* class rank, volunteer work, work experience, level of applicant's interest. **Freshman Admission Requirements:** High school diploma is required and GED is accepted *Academic units required:* 3 English, 3 math, 2 science, 2 social studies, 3 academic electives, *Academic units recommended:* 4 English, 3 math, 2 science, 1 science labs, 2 foreign language, 3 social studies, 3 academic electives. **Freshman Admission Statistics:** 3,221 applied, 83.5% admitted, 33% enrolled. **Transfer Admission Requirements:** High school transcript, college transcript(s), essay or personal statement, statement of good standing from prior institution(s). Minimum college GPA of 2.5 required. Lowest grade transferable C. **General Admission Information:** Application fee $35. Regular application deadline 8/15. Nonfall registration accepted. Admission may be deferred for a maximum of 1 year.

COSTS AND FINANCIAL AID

Annual tuition $33,100. Room and board $9,990. Average book expense $1,100. **Required Forms and Deadlines:** FAFSA. **Notification of Awards:** Applicants will be notified of awards on a rolling basis beginning 12/15. **Types of Aid:** *Need-based scholarships/grants:* College/university scholarship or grant aid from institutional funds; Federal Pell; Private scholarships; SEOG; State scholarships/grants. *Loans:* Direct PLUS loans; Direct Subsidized Stafford Loans; Direct Unsubsidized Stafford Loans. *Student Employment:* Federal Work-Study Program available. Institutional employment available. **Financial Aid Statistics:** 100% needy freshmen, 99% needy undergrads receive need-based scholarship or grant aid. 15% freshmen, 12% undergrads receive non-need-based scholarship or grant aid. 83% freshmen, 87% undergrads receive need-based self-help aid. 0% freshmen, 0% undergrads receive athletic scholarships. 99% freshmen, 95% undergrads receive any aid. 60% undergrads borrow to pay for school. Average cumulative indebtedness $30,998. **Criteria for awarding aid:** *Need-based:* Academics, Alumni affiliation, Leadership, Minority status *Non-need-based:* Academics, Alumni affiliation, Art, Leadership, Minority status, Music/drama, Religious affiliation, State/district residency.

CAMBRIDGE COLLEGE

1000 Massachusetts Avenue, Cambridge, MA 02138-5304
Phone: (617) 868-1000 · **Financial Aid Phone:** 800-877-4723 ext. 1440
E-mail: admit@cambridgecollege.edu
Fax: (617) 349-3561 · **Website:** www.cambridgecollege.edu

This private school was founded in 1971.

RATINGS

Admissions Selectivity Rating: 61   **Fire Safety Rating:** 60*   **Green Rating:** 60*

STUDENTS AND FACULTY

Enrollment: 1,002. **Student Body:** 75% female, 25% male, 18% out-of-state, 9% international. Asian 3%, African American 30%, Caucasian 18%, Hispanic 22%, Native American <1%, Pacific Islander <1%, Two or more races 1%, Race unknown 16%.
Retention and Graduation: 21% freshmen return for sophomore year.
Faculty: Student/faculty ratio 16:1. 19 full-time faculty, 68% hold PhDs, 26% are members of minority groups, 47% are women.

ACADEMICS

Degrees: Bachelor's; Certificate; Doctoral/Research; Master's; Post-Bachelor's certificate; Post-Master's certificate **Classes:** Most classes have 10-19 students. Most lab/discussion sessions have 10-19 students. **Special Study Options:** Accelerated program; Distance learning; Double major; Independent study; Internships; Weekend college. **Disability Services offered to physically disabled students:** Note-taking services; Reader services; Tape recorders; Tutors.

CAMPUS LIFE

Environment: Metropolis **Activities:** Student government.

ADMISSIONS

Test Scores: Minimum internet-based TOEFL 79-80. Minimum paper TOEFL 550. **Basis for Candidate Selection:** *Other factors considered include:* class rank, academic GPA, application essay, recommendation(s), interview, character/personal qualities, work experience, level of applicant's interest. **Freshman Admission Requirements:** High school diploma is required and GED is accepted **General Admission Information:** Nonfall registration accepted. Admission may be deferred for a maximum of 1 year.

COSTS AND FINANCIAL AID

Annual tuition $13,140. Required fees $140. **Required Forms and Deadlines:** FAFSA; Institution's own financial aid form. **Types of Aid:** *Need-based scholarships/grants:* College/university scholarship or grant aid from institutional funds; Federal Pell; Private scholarships; SEOG; State scholarships/grants. *Loans:* Direct PLUS loans; Direct Subsidized Stafford Loans. *Student Employment:* Federal Work-Study Program available. Institutional employment available. **Financial Aid Statistics:** 1% needy undergrads receive need-based scholarship or grant aid. 0% undergrads receive non-need-based scholarship or grant aid. 0% freshmen, 0% undergrads receive need-based self-help aid. 0% freshmen, 0% undergrads receive athletic scholarships. **Criteria for awarding aid:** *Need-based:* Academics, Religious affiliation.

CAMPBELL UNIVERSITY

P.O. Box 546, Buies Creek, NC 27506
Phone: 910-893-1200
E-mail: admissions@campbell.edu · **CEEB Code:** 5100
Website: www.campbell.edu · **ACT Code:** 3076

This private school, affiliated with the Southern Baptist Church, was founded in 1887. It has a 850 acre campus.

RATINGS

Admissions Selectivity Rating: 72   **Fire Safety Rating:** 75   **Green Rating:** 60*

STUDENTS AND FACULTY

Enrollment: 4,236. **Student Body:** 52% female, 48% male, 22% out-of-state, 2% international. Asian 2%, African American 18%, Caucasian 57%, Hispanic 7%, Native American 1%, Pacific Islander <1%, Two or more races 2%, Race unknown 11%.
Retention and Graduation: 72% freshmen return for sophomore year. 23% grads go on to further study within 1 year. 5% grads pursue arts and sciences degrees. 4% grads pursue law degrees. 7% grads pursue business degrees.
Faculty: Student/faculty ratio 14:1. 196 full-time faculty, 91% hold PhDs, 33% are women. 0% of classes are taught by teaching assistants.

ACADEMICS

Degrees: Bachelor's; Doctoral/Professional; Doctoral/Research; Master's; Post-Bachelor's certificate **Special Study Options:** Distance learning; Double major; Dual enrollment; Independent study; Internships; Study abroad; Teacher certification program. **Combined degree programs:** BA/JD; BA/MA. **Disability Services offered to physically disabled students:** Note-taking services; Tape recorders. **Career services:** Career assessment; Career/job search classes; Internships

FACILITIES

Housing: Apartments for married students; Apartments for single students; Men's dorms; Special housing for disabled student; Women's dorms 75% of campus accessible to physically disabled. **Special Academic Facilities/Equipment:** Taylor Bott-Rogers Fine Arts Bldg. Lundy-Fetterman School of Business museum and exhibit hall School of Pharmacy Clinical Research Facility

CAMPUS LIFE

Environment: Rural **Activities:** Campus Ministries; Choral groups; Concert band; Drama/theater; International Student Organization; Jazz band; Literary magazine; Music ensembles; Musical theater; Pep band; Radio station; Student government; Student newspaper; Yearbook 44 registered organizations, 14 honor societies, 20 religious organizations. **Athletics (Intercollegiate):** *Men:* baseball, basketball, cross-country, golf, soccer, tennis, track/field (outdoor), wrestling. *Women:* basketball, cheerleading, cross-country, golf, soccer, softball, swimming, tennis, track/field (outdoor), volleyball. **On-Campus Highlights:** Lundy-Fetterman School of Business, Wallace Student Center/Oasis Grill/Starbucks, Keith Hills Country Club and Golf Course, Eakes Sports Complex, D. Rich Memorial Hall

ADMISSIONS

Freshman Academic Profile: Average high school GPA 3.4. 38% in top 10% of high school class, 80% in top 25% of high school class, 92% in top 50%

of high school class. 85% from public high schools. **Test Scores:** Minimum paper TOEFL 500. **Basis for Candidate Selection:** *Very important factors considered include:* rigor of secondary school record, academic GPA, standardized test scores. *Important factors considered include:* class rank, interview, talent/ability. *Other factors considered include:* application essay, recommendation(s), extracurricular activities, character/personal qualities, alumni/ae relation, volunteer work, work experience, level of applicant's interest. **Freshman Admission Requirements:** High school diploma is required and GED is accepted *Academic units required:* 4 English, 3 math, 2 science, 1 science labs, 2 foreign language, and 2 units from above areas or other academic areas. **Freshman Admission Statistics:** 3,014 applied, 59.7% admitted, 46% enrolled. **Transfer Admission Requirements:** High school transcript, college transcript(s), standardized test scores, statement of good standing from prior institution(s). Minimum college GPA of 2.5 required. Lowest grade transferable C. **General Admission Information:** Application fee $35. Regular application deadline 8/19. Nonfall registration accepted. Admission may be deferred.

COSTS AND FINANCIAL AID
Annual tuition $19,650. Room and board $6,830. Required fees $700. Average book expense $1,100. **Required Forms and Deadlines:** FAFSA. **Notification of Awards:** Applicants will be notified of awards on a rolling basis beginning 2/1. **Types of Aid:** *Need-based scholarships/grants:* College/university scholarship or grant aid from institutional funds; Federal Pell; Private scholarships; SEOG; State scholarships/grants. *Loans:* Direct PLUS loans; Direct Subsidized Stafford Loans; Direct Unsubsidized Stafford Loans. *Student Employment:* Federal Work-Study Program available. Institutional employment available. **Financial Aid Statistics:** 69% needy freshmen, 73% needy undergrads receive need-based scholarship or grant aid. 95% freshmen, 77% undergrads receive non-need-based scholarship or grant aid. 87% freshmen, 88% undergrads receive need-based self-help aid. 4% freshmen, 3% undergrads receive athletic scholarships. 97% freshmen, 92% undergrads receive any aid. **Criteria for awarding aid:** *Non-need-based:* Academics, Athletics, Music/drama, Religious affiliation, State/district residency.

CAMPBELLSVILLE UNIVERSITY

1 University Drive, Campbellsville, KY 42718-2799
Phone: 270-789-5220 • **Financial Aid Phone:** 270-789-5013
E-mail: admissions@campbellsville.edu • **CEEB Code:** 1097
Fax: 270-789-5071 • **ACT Code:** 1500

This private school, affiliated with the Baptist Church, was founded in 1906. It has a 90 acre campus.

RATINGS
Admissions Selectivity Rating: 81   **Fire Safety Rating:** 75   **Green Rating:** 60*

STUDENTS AND FACULTY
Enrollment: 2,250. **Student Body:** 58% female, 42% male, 12% out-of-state, 7% international. Asian <1%, African American 15%, Caucasian 74%, Hispanic 1%, Native American <1%, Pacific Islander <1%, Two or more races 1%, Race unknown 2%.
Retention and Graduation: 65% freshmen return for sophomore year. 20% grads go on to further study within 1 year. 25% grads pursue arts and sciences degrees. 1% grads pursue law degrees. 15% grads pursue business degrees. 1% grads pursue medical degrees. **Faculty:** Student/faculty ratio 13:1. 146 full-time faculty, 62% hold PhDs, 10% are members of minority groups, 49% are women. 0% of classes are taught by teaching assistants.

ACADEMICS
Degrees: Associate; Bachelor's; Certificate; Master's **Classes:** Most classes have 20-29 students. **Most popular majors:** Junior High/Intermediate/Middle School Education And Teaching; Registered Nursing/Registered Nurse; Business, Management, Marketing, And Related Support Services, Other. **Special Study Options:** Cooperative education program; Distance learning; Double major; Dual enrollment; English as a Second Language (ESL); Honors program; Independent study; Internships; Liberal arts/career combination; Study abroad; Teacher certification program; Weekend college. **Disability Services offered to physically disabled students:** Tutors. **Career services:** Alumni services; Career assessment; Internships

FACILITIES
Housing: Apartments for married students; Apartments for single students; Men's dorms; Women's dorms 70% of campus accessible to physically diasbled. **Special Academic Facilities/Equipment:** Computer labs: Technology lab **Computers:** Students can register for classes online. Administrative functions (other than registration) can be performed online.

CAMPUS LIFE
Environment: Rural **Activities:** Campus Ministries; Choral groups; Concert band; Dance; Drama/theater; International Student Organization; Jazz band; Literary magazine; Marching band; Music ensembles; Musical theater; Pep band; Radio station; Student government; Student newspaper; Television station 49 registered organizations, 1 honor society, 7 religious organizations. **Athletics (Intercollegiate):** *Men:* baseball, basketball, bowling, cheerleading, cross-country, football, golf, soccer, tennis, track/field (outdoor), wrestling. *Women:* basketball, bowling, cheerleading, cross-country, golf, soccer, softball, swimming, tennis, track/field (outdoor), volleyball. **On-Campus Highlights:** Technology Center, Athletic Center, New Resident Village, Library, Fine Arts Center

ADMISSIONS
Freshman Academic Profile: Average high school GPA 3.2. 17% in top 10% of high school class, 38% in top 25% of high school class, 69% in top 50% of high school class. 90% from public high schools. **Test Scores:** SAT Math middle 50% range 430-580. SAT EBRW middle 50% range 420-590. ACT middle 50% range 18-23. Minimum paper TOEFL 500. **Basis for Candidate Selection:** *Very important factors considered include:* rigor of secondary school record. *Important factors considered include:* class rank, standardized test scores, recommendation(s), interview, character/personal qualities. *Other factors considered include:* application essay, extracurricular activities, talent/ability, alumni/ae relation, religious affiliation/commitment, volunteer work, work experience. **Freshman Admission Requirements:** High school diploma is required and GED is accepted *Academic units recommended:* 4 English, 3 math, 3 science, 1 science labs, 2 social studies, 1 history, 6 academic electives, 1 unit from above areas or other academic areas. **Freshman Admission Statistics:** 2,477 applied, 66.7% admitted, 35% enrolled. **Transfer Admission Requirements:** college transcript(s), Lowest grade transferable C. **General Admission Information:** Application fee $20. Priority deadline 4/15. Regular application deadline 8/15. Nonfall registration accepted. Admission may be deferred.

COSTS AND FINANCIAL AID
Annual tuition $21,100. Room and board $7,120. Required fees $500. Average book expense $1,000. **Required Forms and Deadlines:** FAFSA. **Notification of Awards:** Applicants will be notified of awards on a rolling basis beginning 2/15. **Types of Aid:** *Need-based scholarships/grants:* College/university scholarship or grant aid from institutional funds; Federal Pell; Private scholarships; SEOG; State scholarships/grants. *Loans: Student Employment:* Federal Work-Study Program available. Institutional employment available. **Financial Aid Statistics:** 100% needy freshmen, 97% needy undergrads receive need-based scholarship or grant aid. 14% freshmen, 11% undergrads receive non-need-based scholarship or grant aid. 74% freshmen, 78% undergrads receive need-based self-help aid. 5% freshmen, 6% undergrads receive athletic scholarships. 95% freshmen, 92% undergrads receive any aid. **Criteria for awarding aid:** *Need-based:* Academics, Art, Athletics, Leadership, Minority status, Music/drama, Religious affiliation *Non-need-based:* Academics, Art, Athletics, Leadership, Minority status, Music/drama, Religious affiliation, State/district residency.

CANISIUS COLLEGE

2001 Main Street, Buffalo, NY 14208
Phone: 716-888-2200 • **Financial Aid Phone:** (716) 888-2300
E-mail: admissions@canisius.edu • **CEEB Code:** 2073
Fax: 716-888-3230 • **Website:** http://www.canisius.edu • **ACT Code:** 2690

This private school, affiliated with the Roman Catholic-Jesuit Church, was founded in 1870. It has a 72 acre campus.

RATINGS
Admissions Selectivity Rating: 71   **Fire Safety Rating:** 89   **Green Rating:** 65

STUDENTS AND FACULTY
Enrollment: 2,325. **Student Body:** 50% female, 50% male, 4% international (19 countries represented). Asian 3%, African American 8%, Caucasian 73%, Hispanic 6%, Native American <1%, Pacific Islander <1%, Two or more races 2%, Race unknown 3%.
Retention and Graduation: 83% freshmen return for sophomore year. 62% freshmen graduate within 4 years. 69% freshmen graduate within 6 years. **Faculty:** Student/faculty ratio 11:1. 0% of classes are taught by teaching assistants.

ACADEMICS
Degrees: Associate; Bachelor's; Master's; Post-Bachelor's certificate **Classes:** Most classes have 20-29 students. **Most popular majors:** Biology/Biological Sciences, General; Psychology, General; Business Administration And

Management, General. **Special Study Options:** Cross-registration; Distance learning; Double major; Dual enrollment; English as a Second Language (ESL); Exchange student program (domestic); External degree program; Honors program; Independent study; Internships; Student-designed major; Study abroad; Teacher certification program. **Honors programs:** The All–College Honors Program is a learning community of Canisius College's top students who have excelled academically in high school and in college entrance exams. These students represent the top 10 percent of applicants to Canisius. These select students enter a program that provides a challenging and adventurous academic atmosphere that provides myriad benefits, including: A rigorous curriculum including interdisciplinary Liberal Arts courses mixed with special seminars that lead to an independent research project and thesis. Small, enriched classes of 20 or fewer students that allow for in-depth discussions between students and faculty. Close interaction with Canisius faculty in one-on-one opportunities. Out-of-classroom scholarly travel that gives students a broader "real life" view of classroom topics. **Disability Services offered to physically disabled students:** Note-taking services; Reader services; Tape recorders; Tutors. **Career services:** Alumni network; Alumni services; Career assessment; Career/job search classes; Internships; Regional alumni

FACILITIES
Housing: Apartments for single students; Special housing for disabled student; Special housing for international students; Theme housing; Wellness housing 95% of campus accessible to physically diasbled. **Special Academic Facilities/Equipment:** TV studio, electron microscope, seismograph, language lab, digital lab, human performance lab, molecular biology and physics labs, mini-planetarium. **Computers:** 100% of classrooms, 100% of dorms, 100% of libraries, 100% of dining areas, 100% of student union, 100% of common outdoor areas have wireless network access. Students can register for classes online. Administrative functions (other than registration) can be performed online.

CAMPUS LIFE
Environment: Metropolis **Activities:** Campus Ministries; Choral groups; Concert band; Dance; Drama/theater; International Student Organization; Jazz band; Literary magazine; Marching band; Model UN; Music ensembles; Musical theater; Pep band; Radio station; Student government; Student newspaper; Student-run film society; Symphony orchestra; Television station; Yearbook 102 registered organizations, 16 honor societies, 2 religious organizations. 1 fraternity, 1 sorority. **Athletics (Intercollegiate):** *Men:* baseball, basketball, cross-country, diving, golf, ice hockey, lacrosse, soccer, swimming. *Women:* basketball, cross-country, diving, lacrosse, soccer, softball, swimming, synchronized swimming, volleyball. **On-Campus Highlights:** Montante Cultural Center, Village Townhouses, Palisano Pavillion, Koessler Athletic Center, Richard E. Winter Student Center **Environmental Initiatives:** Canisius College is deeply committed to utility conservation and the sustainability of our natural resources. This is accomplished in part through our development of policies and practices which are designed to promote sound energy management, and the economic, social and environmental well-being of our students and staff. Canisius College is working with Ecology and Environment, Inc. (E & E) to develop and implement an energy conservation program. The overall goal of the program is to reduce the college's annual electric consumption by five percent, based on historical consumption during the last three academic years. A web page is being designed to explain how Canisius College conserves and supports sustainable use of our natural resources

ADMISSIONS
Freshman Academic Profile: 71% from public high schools. **Test Scores:** Minimum internet-based TOEFL 79. Minimum paper TOEFL 550. **Basis for Candidate Selection:** *Very important factors considered include:* rigor of secondary school record, academic GPA, standardized test scores. *Important factors considered include:* application essay, recommendation(s), extracurricular activities, volunteer work. *Other factors considered include:* class rank, interview, talent/ability, character/personal qualities, first generation, alumni/ae relation, work experience, level of applicant's interest. **Freshman Admission Requirements:** High school diploma is required and GED is accepted *Academic units required:* 4 English, 3 math, 3 science, 2 science labs, 2 foreign language, 4 social studies, *Academic units recommended:* 4 English, 4 math, 4 science, 2 science labs, 4 foreign language, 4 social studies, 4 academic electives. **Freshman Admission Statistics:** 4,488 applied, 78.2% admitted, 16% enrolled. **Transfer Admission Requirements:** college transcript(s), statement of good standing from prior institution(s). Minimum college GPA of 2.0 required. Lowest grade transferable C. **General Admission Information:** Nonfall registration accepted. Admission may be deferred for a maximum of 1 year.

COSTS AND FINANCIAL AID
Annual tuition $27,000. Room and board $11,300. Required fees $1,488. Average book expense $1,000. **Required Forms and Deadlines:** FAFSA; State aid form. **Notification of Awards:** Applicants will be notified of awards on a rolling basis beginning 12/20. **Types of Aid:** *Need-based scholarships/*

grants: College/university scholarship or grant aid from institutional funds; Federal Pell; Private scholarships; SEOG; State scholarships/grants; United Negro College Fund. *Loans:* Direct PLUS loans; Direct Subsidized Stafford Loans; Direct Unsubsidized Stafford Loans. *Student Employment:* Federal Work-Study Program available. Institutional employment available. **Financial Aid Statistics:** 100% needy freshmen, 99% needy undergrads receive need-based scholarship or grant aid. 26% freshmen, 23% undergrads receive non-need-based scholarship or grant aid. 74% freshmen, 76% undergrads receive need-based self-help aid. 4% freshmen, 5% undergrads receive athletic scholarships. 98% freshmen, 97% undergrads receive any aid. 74% undergrads borrow to pay for school. Average cumulative indebtedness $33,973. **Criteria for awarding aid:** *Non-need-based:* Academics, Alumni affiliation, Art, Athletics, Job skills, Music/drama.

CAPITAL UNIVERSITY

1 College and Main, Columbus, OH 43209
Phone: 614-236-6101 · **Financial Aid Phone:** 614-236-6511
E-mail: admission@capital.edu · **CEEB Code:** 1099
Fax: 614-236-6926 · **Website:** www.capital.edu · **ACT Code:** 3242

This private school, affiliated with the Lutheran Church, was founded in 1830. It has a 48 acre campus.

RATINGS
Admissions Selectivity Rating: 80   **Fire Safety Rating:** 66   **Green Rating:** 60*

STUDENTS AND FACULTY
Enrollment: 2,654. **Student Body:** 58% female, 42% male, 10% out-of-state, 2% international (18 countries represented). Asian 1%, African American 10%, Caucasian 75%, Hispanic 4%, Native American <1%, Pacific Islander 0%, Two or more races 5%, Race unknown 3%.
Retention and Graduation: 76% freshmen return for sophomore year.
Faculty: Student/faculty ratio 12:1. 159 full-time faculty, 77% hold PhDs, 9% are members of minority groups, 49% are women. 0% of classes are taught by teaching assistants.

ACADEMICS
Degrees: Bachelor's; Doctoral/Professional; Master's; Post-Bachelor's certificate **Classes:** Most classes have 10-19 students. Most lab/discussion sessions have 10-19 students. **Most popular majors:** Education, General; Registered Nursing/Registered Nurse; Business Administration And Management, General. **Special Study Options:** Accelerated program; Cooperative education program; Cross-registration; Double major; Dual enrollment; English as a Second Language (ESL); Exchange student program (domestic); External degree program; Honors program; Independent study; Internships; Liberal arts/career combination; Student-designed major; Study abroad; Teacher certification program. **Honors programs:** Capital University Honors Program. **Disability Services offered to physically disabled students:** Tape recorders; Tutors. **Career services:** Alumni network; Alumni services; Career assessment; Career/job search classes; Internships

FACILITIES
Housing: Apartments for single students; Coed dorms; Special housing for disabled student; Theme housing; Wellness housing 100% of campus accessible to physically diasbled. **Special Academic Facilities/Equipment:** Art gallery, Conservatory of Music **Computers:** Students can register for classes online. Administrative functions (other than registration) can be performed online.

CAMPUS LIFE
Environment: Metropolis **Activities:** Campus Ministries; Choral groups; Concert band; Dance; Drama/theater; International Student Organization; Jazz band; Literary magazine; Music ensembles; Musical theater; Radio station; Student government; Student newspaper; Student-run film society; Symphony orchestra; Television station 63 registered organizations, 16 honor societies, 5 religious organizations. 5 fraternities, 5 sororities. **Athletics (Intercollegiate):** *Men:* baseball, basketball, cross-country, football, golf, soccer, tennis, track/field (outdoor), track/field (indoor). *Women:* basketball, cross-country, golf, soccer, softball, tennis, track/field (outdoor), track/field (indoor), volleyball. **On-Campus Highlights:** Capital Center, College Avenue Residence Hall, Schumacher Gallery, One Main Cafe **Environmental Initiatives:** Energy management

ADMISSIONS
Freshman Academic Profile: Average high school GPA 3.5. 16% in top 10% of high school class, 47% in top 25% of high school class, 81% in top 50% of high school class. 92% from public high schools. **Test Scores:** SAT Math middle 50% range 480-580. SAT EBRW middle 50% range 480-610. ACT middle 50%

range 22-28. Minimum paper TOEFL 500. **Basis for Candidate Selection:** *Very important factors considered include:* academic GPA, standardized test scores, talent/ability. *Other factors considered include:* rigor of secondary school record, recommendation(s), interview, extracurricular activities, alumni/ae relation, geographical residence, state residency, religious affiliation/commitment, racial/ethnic status, level of applicant's interest. **Freshman Admission Requirements:** High school diploma is required and GED is accepted *Academic units recommended:* 4 English, 3 math, 3 science, 2 science labs, 2 foreign language, 3 social studies, 1 visual/performing arts. **Freshman Admission Statistics:** 3,718 applied, 72.2% admitted, 25% enrolled. **Transfer Admission Requirements:** college transcript(s), Minimum college GPA of 2.5 required. Lowest grade transferable C-. **General Admission Information:** Application fee $25. Priority deadline 12/1. Regular application deadline 5/1. Nonfall registration accepted. Admission may be deferred for a maximum of 1 year.

COSTS AND FINANCIAL AID
Annual tuition $32,630. Room and board $9,250. Required fees $200. Average book expense $1,550. **Required Forms and Deadlines:** FAFSA. **Notification of Awards:** Applicants will be notified of awards on a rolling basis beginning 3/15. **Types of Aid:** *Need-based scholarships/grants:* College/university scholarship or grant aid from institutional funds; Federal Pell; Private scholarships; SEOG; State scholarships/grants. *Loans:* Direct PLUS loans; Direct Subsidized Stafford Loans; Direct Unsubsidized Stafford Loans. *Student Employment:* Federal Work-Study Program available. Institutional employment available. **Financial Aid Statistics:** 99% needy freshmen, 95% needy undergrads receive need-based scholarship or grant aid. 98% freshmen, 93% undergrads receive non-need-based scholarship or grant aid. 75% freshmen, 78% undergrads receive need-based self-help aid. 0% freshmen, 0% undergrads receive athletic scholarships. 99% freshmen receive any aid. 82% undergrads borrow to pay for school. Average cumulative indebtedness $31,563. **Criteria for awarding aid:** *Non-need-based:* Academics, Alumni affiliation, Art, Leadership, Minority status, Music/drama, Religious affiliation, State/district residency.

CARLETON COLLEGE

One North College Street, Northfield, MN 55057
Phone: 507-222-4190 · **Financial Aid Phone:** 507-222-4138
E-mail: admissions@carleton.edu · **CEEB Code:** 6081
Fax: 507-222-4526 · **Website:** www.carleton.edu · **ACT Code:** 2092

This private school was founded in 1866. It has a 955 acre campus.

RATINGS
Admissions Selectivity Rating: 97   **Fire Safety Rating:** 97   **Green Rating:** 90

STUDENTS AND FACULTY
Enrollment: 2,023. **Student Body:** 51% female, 49% male, 85% out-of-state, 10% international (41 countries represented). Asian 8%, African American 5%, Caucasian 61%, Hispanic 8%, Native American <1%, Pacific Islander 0%, Two or more races 6%, Race unknown 2%.
Retention and Graduation: 96% freshmen return for sophomore year. 89% freshmen graduate within 4 years. 94% freshmen graduate within 6 years. 21% grads go on to further study within 1 year. **Faculty:** Student/faculty ratio 9:1. 212 full-time faculty, 98% hold PhDs, 28% are members of minority groups, 46% are women. 0% of classes are taught by teaching assistants.

ACADEMICS
Degrees: Bachelor's **Classes:** Most classes have 20-29 students. Most lab/discussion sessions have 20-29 students. **Most popular majors:** Computer And Information Sciences, General; Biology/Biological Sciences, General; Economics, General. **Special Study Options:** Accelerated program; Cross-registration; Double major; Dual enrollment; Independent study; Internships; Student-designed major; Study abroad; Teacher certification program. **Combined degree programs:** BA/JD. **Disability Services offered to physically disabled students:** Note-taking services; Reader services; Tape recorders; Tutors. **Career services:** Alumni network; Alumni services; Career assessment; Career/job search classes; Internships; Regional alumni

FACILITIES
Housing: Apartments for single students; Coed dorms; Cooperative housing; Special housing for disabled student; Theme housing; Wellness housing 39%

of campus accessible to physically diasbled. **Special Academic Facilities/Equipment:** Arboretum, greenhouse, observatory, scanning and transmission electron microscopes, refractor and reflector telescopes, nuclear magnetic resonance spectrometer, Weitz Center for Creativity **Computers:** 45% of classrooms, 15% of dorms, 85% of libraries, 50% of dining areas, 100% of student union, 15% of common outdoor areas have wireless network access. Students can register for classes online.

CAMPUS LIFE
Environment: Village **Activities:** Campus Ministries; Choral groups; Concert band; Dance; Drama/theater; International Student Organization; Jazz band; Literary magazine; Model UN; Music ensembles; Musical theater; Radio station; Student government; Student newspaper; Student-run film society; Symphony orchestra; Yearbook 132 registered organizations, 3 honor societies, 17 religious organizations. **Athletics (Intercollegiate):** *Men:* baseball, basketball, cross-country, diving, football, golf, soccer, swimming, tennis, track/field (outdoor), track/field (indoor). *Women:* basketball, cross-country, diving, golf, soccer, softball, swimming, synchronized swimming, tennis, track/field (outdoor), track/field (indoor), volleyball. **On-Campus Highlights:** Cowling Arboretum, Weitz Center for Creativity, Historic Goodsell Observatory, Japanese Garden, Recreation Center **Environmental Initiatives:** 2nd Wind Turbine provided power directly to the campus grid

ADMISSIONS
Freshman Academic Profile: 86% in top 10% of high school class, 98% in top 25% of high school class, 100% in top 50% of high school class. 60% from public high schools. **Test Scores:** SAT Math middle 50% range 680-770. SAT EBRW middle 50% range 680-760. ACT middle 50% range 31-34. Minimum paper TOEFL 600. **Basis for Candidate Selection:** *Very important factors considered include:* rigor of secondary school record, class rank, academic GPA. *Important factors considered include:* application essay, standardized test scores, recommendation(s), extracurricular activities, talent/ability, character/personal qualities, alumni/ae relation, racial/ethnic status, volunteer work, work experience. *Other factors considered include:* interview, first generation, geographical residence, state residency. **Freshman Admission Requirements:** High school diploma is required and GED is accepted *Academic units recommended:* 4 English, 3 math, 3 science, 1 science labs, 3 foreign language, 3 social studies. **Freshman Admission Statistics:** 6,499 applied, 21.2% admitted, 38% enrolled. **Transfer Admission Requirements:** High school transcript, college transcript(s), essay or personal statement, standardized test scores, statement of good standing from prior institution(s). Minimum college GPA of 2.0 required. Lowest grade transferable C-. **General Admission Information:** Application fee $30. Regular application deadline 1/15. Nonfall registration accepted. Admission may be deferred for a maximum of 1 year.

COSTS AND FINANCIAL AID
Required Forms and Deadlines: CSS/Financial Aid PROFILE; FAFSA; Noncustodial PROFILE. **Notification of Awards:** Applicants will be notified of awards on or about 3/31. **Types of Aid:** *Need-based scholarships/grants:* College/university scholarship or grant aid from institutional funds; Federal Pell; Private scholarships; SEOG; State scholarships/grants. *Loans:* Direct PLUS loans; Direct Subsidized Stafford Loans; Direct Unsubsidized Stafford Loans. *Student Employment:* Federal Work-Study Program available. Institutional employment available. **Financial Aid Statistics:** 100% needy freshmen, 100% needy undergrads receive need-based scholarship or grant aid. 14% freshmen, 16% undergrads receive non-need-based scholarship or grant aid. 98% freshmen, 99% undergrads receive need-based self-help aid. 0% freshmen, 0% undergrads receive athletic scholarships. 54% freshmen, 56% undergrads receive any aid. 41% undergrads borrow to pay for school. Average cumulative indebtedness $22,641. **Criteria for awarding aid:** *Non-need-based:* Academics.

CARLOW UNIVERSITY

3333 Fifth Avenue, Pittsburgh, PA 15213-3165
Phone: 412-578-6059
E-mail: admissions@carlow.edu · **CEEB Code:** 2421
Fax: 412-578-6321 · **Website:** www.carlow.edu · **ACT Code:** 2421

This private school, affiliated with the Roman Catholic Church, was founded in 1929. It has a 17 acre campus.

RATINGS
Admissions Selectivity Rating: 72   **Fire Safety Rating:** 72   **Green Rating:** 60*

STUDENTS AND FACULTY

Enrollment: 1,339. **Student Body:** 85% female, 15% male, 5% out-of-state, <1% international (4 countries represented). Asian 2%, African American 18%, Caucasian 67%, Hispanic 2%, Native American <1%, Pacific Islander <1%, Two or more races 4%, Race unknown 6%.

Retention and Graduation: 78% freshmen return for sophomore year. 43% freshmen graduate within 4 years. 57% freshmen graduate within 6 years. **Faculty:** Student/faculty ratio 12:1. 96 full-time faculty, 76% hold PhDs, 6% are members of minority groups, 74% are women. 0% of classes are taught by teaching assistants.

ACADEMICS

Degrees: Bachelor's; Doctoral/Professional; Master's; Post-Bachelor's certificate; Post-Master's certificate **Classes:** Most classes have 10-19 students. Most lab/discussion sessions have 10-19 students. **Most popular majors:** Biology/Biological Sciences, General; Psychology, General; Registered Nursing/Registered Nurse. **Special Study Options:** Accelerated program; Cross-registration; Distance learning; Double major; Dual enrollment; Honors program; Independent study; Internships; Liberal arts/career combination; Study abroad; Teacher certification program; Weekend college. **Career services:** Alumni network; Career assessment; Career/job search classes; Internships; Regional alumni

FACILITIES

Housing: Coed dorms; Men's dorms; Special housing for disabled student; Theme housing; Women's dorms **Special Academic Facilities/Equipment:** The A.J. Palumbo Hall of Science and Technology. features research labs, as well as a greenhouse, darkroom, biochamber, autopsy lab. Also, on-campus preschool and elementary school. **Computers:** 100% of classrooms, 100% of dorms, 100% of libraries, 100% of dining areas, 100% of student union, have wireless network access. Students can register for classes online.

CAMPUS LIFE

Environment: City **Activities:** Campus Ministries; Choral groups; Dance; Drama/theater; Literary magazine; Musical theater; Student government; Student newspaper 28 registered organizations, 5 honor societies, 1 religious organization. **Athletics (Intercollegiate):** *Women:* basketball, soccer, softball, tennis, volleyball. University Commons, St. Joseph's Gym, Commuter Lounge, AJP Atrium, The Waterfall

ADMISSIONS

Freshman Academic Profile: Average high school GPA 3.5. 16% in top 10% of high school class, 41% in top 25% of high school class, 78% in top 50% of high school class. **Test Scores:** SAT Math middle 50% range 440-520. SAT EBRW middle 50% range 460-550. ACT middle 50% range 20-24. **Basis for Candidate Selection:** *Very important factors considered include:* rigor of secondary school record, academic GPA, standardized test scores. *Other factors considered include:* class rank, application essay, recommendation(s), interview, extracurricular activities, talent/ability, character/personal qualities, first generation, alumni/ae relation, volunteer work, work experience, level of applicant's interest. **Freshman Admission Requirements:** High school diploma is required and GED is accepted *Academic units required:* 4 English, 3 math, 3 science, 2 social studies, 2 history, 4 academic electives, *Academic units recommended:* 4 math, 4 science, 2 science labs. **Freshman Admission Statistics:** 873 applied, 91.6% admitted, 30% enrolled. **Transfer Admission Requirements:** college transcript(s), Minimum college GPA of 2.0 required. Lowest grade transferable C. **General Admission Information:** Nonfall registration accepted. Admission may be deferred for a maximum of 1 year.

COSTS AND FINANCIAL AID

Required Forms and Deadlines: FAFSA; State aid form. **Notification of Awards:** Applicants will be notified of awards on a rolling basis beginning 12/1. **Types of Aid:** *Need-based scholarships/grants:* College/university scholarship or grant aid from institutional funds; Federal Pell; Private scholarships; SEOG; State scholarships/grants. *Loans:* Direct PLUS loans; Direct Subsidized Stafford Loans; Direct Unsubsidized Stafford Loans. **Financial Aid Statistics:** 100% needy freshmen, 81% needy undergrads receive need-based scholarship or grant aid. 92% freshmen, 77% undergrads receive non-need-based scholarship or grant aid. 76% freshmen, 89% undergrads receive need-based self-help aid. 17% freshmen, 12% undergrads receive athletic scholarships. **Criteria for awarding aid:** *Non-need-based:* Academics, Alumni affiliation, Art, Athletics, Job skills, State/district residency.

CARNEGIE MELLON UNIVERSITY

5000 Forbes Avenue, Pittsburgh, PA 15213
Phone: 412-268-2082 • **Financial Aid Phone:** 412-268-8186
E-mail: admission@andrew.cmu.edu • **CEEB Code:** 2074
Fax: 412-268-7838 • **Website:** www.cmu.edu • **ACT Code:** 3534

This private school was founded in 1900. It has a 152.5 acre campus.

RATINGS

Admissions Selectivity Rating: 98   **Fire Safety Rating:** 89   **Green Rating:** 98

STUDENTS AND FACULTY

Enrollment: 6,804. **Student Body:** 49% female, 51% male, 85% out-of-state, 22% international (56 countries represented). Asian 29%, African American 4%, Caucasian 26%, Hispanic 9%, Native American <1%, Pacific Islander <1%, Two or more races 4%, Race unknown 5%.

Retention and Graduation: 96% freshmen return for sophomore year. 76% freshmen graduate within 4 years. 89% freshmen graduate within 6 years. 25% grads go on to further study within 1 year. 7% grads pursue arts and sciences degrees. 0.31% grads pursue law degrees. 1% grads pursue business degrees. 1.2% grads pursue medical degrees. **Faculty:**

ACADEMICS

Degrees: Bachelor's; Doctoral/Research; Master's; Post-Bachelor's certificate; Post-Master's certificate **Classes:** Most classes have 10-19 students. Most lab/discussion sessions have 10-19 students. **Most popular majors:** Computer Science; Electrical And Electronics Engineering; Systems Science And Theory. **Special Study Options:** Accelerated program; Cooperative education program; Cross-registration; Distance learning; Double major; Independent study; Internships; Liberal arts/career combination; Student-designed major; Study abroad; Teacher certification program. **Combined degree programs:** BA/MA; BA/MEng. **Disability Services offered to physically disabled students:** Note-taking services; Reader services; Tape recorders; Tutors. **Career services:** Alumni services; Career assessment; Career/job search classes; Internships; Regional alumni

FACILITIES

Housing: Apartments for single students; Coed dorms; Fraternity/sorority housing; Men's dorms; Special housing for disabled student; Theme housing; Wellness housing; Women's dorms **Special Academic Facilities/Equipment:** Rare books collection, Entertainment Technology Center, Art galleries, Theatres, Botanical Institute, Extensive lab facilities and equipment, Recording studio, Robotics Institute, Design studios, Photo shoot studio and darkrooms, Radio station, Collaborative Innovation Center, LEED-certified green residence hall, Campo Garden, Observatory, Wood shops **Computers:** 100% of classrooms, 100% of dorms, 100% of libraries, 100% of dining areas, 100% of student union, 100% of common outdoor areas have wireless network access. Students can register for classes online. Administrative functions (other than registration) can be performed online.

CAMPUS LIFE

Environment: Metropolis **Activities:** Campus Ministries; Choral groups; Concert band; Dance; Drama/theater; International Student Organization; Literary magazine; Marching band; Model UN; Music ensembles; Musical theater; Pep band; Radio station; Student government; Student newspaper; Student-run film society; Symphony orchestra; Yearbook 225 registered organizations, 18 religious organizations. 16 fraternities, 7 sororities. **Athletics (Intercollegiate):** *Men:* basketball, cheerleading, cross-country, diving, football, golf, soccer, swimming, tennis, track/field (outdoor). *Women:* basketball, cheerleading, cross-country, diving, soccer, swimming, tennis, track/field (outdoor), volleyball. **On-Campus Highlights:** Hunt Library, Skibo Cafe, The Cut, The Underground, Cohon University Center (Student Center) **Environmental Initiatives:** 1. PRACTICE: We purchase renewable electricity certificates for 100% of our campus electricity use and, at minimum, USGBC LEED Silver, guidelines are required for all building projects and most renovations. The majority of our projects are LEED Gold Certified. The Scotty Goes Green Office Certification program promotes sustainable office practices in several administrative & academic departments.

ADMISSIONS

Freshman Academic Profile: Average high school GPA 3.8. 74% in top 10% of high school class, 94% in top 25% of high school class, 99% in top 50% of high school class. **Test Scores:** SAT Math middle 50% range 730-800. SAT EBRW middle 50% range 700-760. ACT middle 50% range 32-35. Minimum

---

internet-based TOEFL 102. **Basis for Candidate Selection:** *Very important factors considered include:* rigor of secondary school record, class rank, academic GPA, standardized test scores, extracurricular activities, volunteer work, work experience. *Important factors considered include:* application essay, recommendation(s), talent/ability, character/personal qualities, first generation, alumni/ae relation, racial/ethnic status. *Other factors considered include:* interview. **Freshman Admission Requirements:** High school diploma is required and GED is accepted *Academic units required:* 4 English, 4 math, 3 science, 2 foreign language, 3 academic electives, *Academic units recommended:* 4 English, 4 math, 3 science, 3 science labs, 2 foreign language, 3 academic electives. **Freshman Admission Statistics:** 20,497 applied, 22.2% admitted, 37% enrolled. **Transfer Admission Requirements:** High school transcript, college transcript(s), essay or personal statement, standardized test scores, statement of good standing from prior institution(s). **General Admission Information:** Application fee $75. Regular application deadline 1/1. Nonfall registration accepted. Admission may be deferred for a maximum of 1 year.

COSTS AND FINANCIAL AID
Annual tuition $54,244. Room and board $14,418. Required fees $908. Average book expense $2,400. **Required Forms and Deadlines:** CSS/ Financial Aid PROFILE; FAFSA; Noncustodial PROFILE. **Notification of Awards:** Applicants will be notified of awards on or about 4/15. **Types of Aid:** *Need-based scholarships/grants:* College/university scholarship or grant aid from institutional funds; Federal Pell; Private scholarships; SEOG; State scholarships/grants. *Loans:* Direct PLUS loans; Direct Subsidized Stafford Loans; Direct Unsubsidized Stafford Loans. *Student Employment:* Federal Work-Study Program available. Institutional employment available. **Financial Aid Statistics:** 96% needy freshmen, 95% needy undergrads receive need-based scholarship or grant aid. 9% freshmen, 9% undergrads receive non-need-based scholarship or grant aid. 87% freshmen, 87% undergrads receive need-based self-help aid. 0% freshmen, 0% undergrads receive athletic scholarships. 51% undergrads borrow to pay for school. Average cumulative indebtedness $30,866. **Criteria for awarding aid:** *Need-based:* Academics, Art, Music/drama *Non-need-based:* Academics, Art, Leadership, Minority status, Music/drama, State/district residency.

CARROLL COLLEGE (MT)

1601 North Benton Avenue, Helena, MT 59625
Phone: 406-447-4384 · **Financial Aid Phone:** 406-447-5423
E-mail: admission@carroll.edu · **CEEB Code:** 4041
Fax: 406-447-4533 · **Website:** www.carroll.edu · **ACT Code:** 2408

This private school, affiliated with the Roman Catholic Church, was founded in 1909. It has a 63 acre campus.

RATINGS
Admissions Selectivity Rating: 75   **Fire Safety Rating:** 68   **Green Rating:** 60*

STUDENTS AND FACULTY
Enrollment: 1,376. **Student Body:** 58% female, 42% male, 54% out-of-state, 1% international (15 countries represented). Asian 1%, African American 1%, Caucasian 81%, Hispanic 4%, Native American 1%, Pacific Islander <1%, Two or more races 1%, Race unknown 8%.
Retention and Graduation: 81% freshmen return for sophomore year. 22% grads go on to further study within 1 year. **Faculty:** 0% of classes are taught by teaching assistants.

ACADEMICS
Degrees: Associate; Bachelor's; Certificate; Transfer Associate **Classes:** Most classes have fewer than 10 students. **Most popular majors:** Biology/Biological Sciences, General; Psychology, General; Registered Nursing, Nursing Administration, Nursing Research And Clinical Nursing. **Special Study Options:** Cooperative education program; Double major; Dual enrollment; English as a Second Language (ESL); Exchange student program (domestic); Honors program; Independent study; Internships; Liberal arts/career combination; Student-designed major; Study abroad; Teacher certification program. **Disability Services offered to physically disabled students:** Tutors. **Career services:** Career assessment; Career/job search classes; Internships

FACILITIES
Housing: Apartments for married students; Apartments for single students; Coed dorms; Special housing for international students; Theme housing 75% of campus accessible to physically diasbled. **Special Academic Facilities/Equipment:** Arts lab, observatory, seismograph station, engineering lab.

CAMPUS LIFE
Environment: Village **Activities:** Campus Ministries; Choral groups; Dance; Drama/theater; International Student Organization; Literary magazine; Music ensembles; Musical theater; Pep band; Radio station; Student government; Student newspaper; Student-run film society; Yearbook 34 registered organizations, 10 honor societies, 4 religious organizations. **Athletics (Intercollegiate):** *Men:* basketball, cheerleading, football, golf. *Women:* basketball, cheerleading, golf, soccer, volleyball. **On-Campus Highlights:** Science and Technology Center, Nelson Stadium, Campus Center, St. Charles Chapel, Fitness Center

ADMISSIONS
Freshman Academic Profile: Average high school GPA 3.5. 25% in top 10% of high school class, 61% in top 25% of high school class, 90% in top 50% of high school class. 75% from public high schools. **Test Scores:** SAT Math middle 50% range 510-610. SAT EBRW middle 50% range 490-620. ACT middle 50% range 22-27. **Basis for Candidate Selection:** *Very important factors considered include:* rigor of secondary school record, academic GPA. *Important factors considered include:* standardized test scores, talent/ability, character/personal qualities. *Other factors considered include:* class rank, application essay, recommendation(s), interview, extracurricular activities, first generation, volunteer work, work experience, level of applicant's interest. **Freshman Admission Requirements:** High school diploma is required and GED is accepted *Academic units recommended:* 4 English, 3 math, 2 science, 1 science labs, 2 social studies, 2 history, 2 academic electives, 1 visual/performing arts. **Freshman Admission Statistics:** 13 applied, admitted, 18% enrolled. **Transfer Admission Requirements:** college transcript(s), essay or personal statement, statement of good standing from prior institution(s). Minimum college GPA of 2.5 required. Lowest grade transferable C. **General Admission Information:** Application fee $35. Priority deadline 3/1. Regular application deadline 6/1. Nonfall registration accepted. Admission may be deferred for a maximum of 1 year.

COSTS AND FINANCIAL AID
Annual tuition $27,303. Room and board $8,668. Required fees $610. Average book expense $1,000. **Required Forms and Deadlines:** FAFSA. **Notification of Awards:** Applicants will be notified of awards on a rolling basis beginning 3/1. **Types of Aid:** *Need-based scholarships/grants:* College/university scholarship or grant aid from institutional funds; Federal Pell; Private scholarships; SEOG; State scholarships/grants. *Loans: Student Employment:* Federal Work-Study Program available. Institutional employment available. **Financial Aid Statistics:** 99% needy freshmen, 99% needy undergrads receive need-based scholarship or grant aid. 17% freshmen, 14% undergrads receive non-need-based scholarship or grant aid. 81% freshmen, 85% undergrads receive need-based self-help aid. 20% freshmen, 19% undergrads receive athletic scholarships. 98% freshmen, 98% undergrads receive any aid. **Criteria for awarding aid:** *Need-based:* Academics, Art, Athletics, Minority status, Religious affiliation *Non-need-based:* Academics, Art, Athletics, Leadership, Minority status, Music/drama, Religious affiliation.

CARROLL UNIVERSITY (WI)

100 North East Avenue, Waukesha, WI 53186
Phone: 262-524-7220 · **Financial Aid Phone:** 262-524-7297 · **CEEB Code:** 1101
Fax: 262-951-3037 · **Website:** www.carrollu.edu · **ACT Code:** 4570

This private school, affiliated with the Presbyterian Church, was founded in 1846. It has a 53 acre campus.

RATINGS
Admissions Selectivity Rating: 77   **Fire Safety Rating:** 80   **Green Rating:** 60*

STUDENTS AND FACULTY
Student Body: 31% out-of-state, 2% international (39 countries represented). Asian 1%, African American 2%, Caucasian 87%, Hispanic 3%, Native American <1%, Race unknown 4%.
Retention and Graduation: 13% grads go on to further study within 1 year. **Faculty:** Student/faculty ratio 14:1. 139 full-time faculty, 0% of classes are taught by teaching assistants.

ACADEMICS
Degrees: Bachelor's; Master's; Post-Bachelor's certificate **Classes:** Most classes have 10-19 students. Most lab/discussion sessions have 10-19 students. **Most popular majors:** Biology/Biological Sciences, General; Psychology, General; Business Administration And Management, General. **Special Study Options:** Distance learning; Double major; Exchange student program (domestic); Honors program; Independent study; Internships; Liberal arts/career combination; Student-designed major; Study abroad; Teacher certification

program. **Disability Services offered to physically disabled students:** Note-taking services; Tape recorders; Tutors. **Career services:** Alumni network; Career assessment; Career/job search classes; Internships

FACILITIES

Housing: Apartments for single students; Coed dorms; Women's dorms 50% of campus accessible to physically diasbled. **Special Academic Facilities/ Equipment:** A 60 acre scientific study and conservancy area with a class 1 trout stream and associated wetland and upland habitats. **Computers:** 80% of classrooms, 100% of dorms, 100% of libraries, 100% of dining areas, 100% of student union, 90% of common outdoor areas have wireless network access. Students can register for classes online. Administrative functions (other than registration) can be performed online.

CAMPUS LIFE

Environment: Town **Activities:** Choral groups; Concert band; Dance; Drama/ theater; International Student Organization; Jazz band; Literary magazine; Music ensembles; Pep band; Radio station; Student government; Student newspaper 40 registered organizations, 2 religious organizations. 2 fraternities, 4 sororities. **Athletics (Intercollegiate):** *Men:* baseball, basketball, cross-country, football, golf, soccer, swimming, tennis, track/field (outdoor), track/field (indoor). *Women:* basketball, cross-country, golf, soccer, softball, swimming, tennis, track/field (outdoor), track/field (indoor), volleyball. **On-Campus Highlights:** Main Hall, Van Male Fieldhouse, Campus Center, Shattuck, Physical Therapy Building

ADMISSIONS

Freshman Academic Profile: 38% in top 10% of high school class, 62% in top 25% of high school class, 83% in top 50% of high school class. 87% from public high schools. **Test Scores:** ACT middle 50% range 21-26. Minimum paper TOEFL 550. **Basis for Candidate Selection:** *Very important factors considered include:* rigor of secondary school record, class rank, academic GPA. *Important factors considered include:* standardized test scores. *Other factors considered include:* application essay, recommendation(s), interview, extracurricular activities, talent/ability, character/personal qualities, alumni/ ae relation, geographical residence, state residency, racial/ethnic status, work experience. **Freshman Admission Requirements:** High school diploma is required and GED is accepted *Academic units recommended:* 4 English, 4 math, 3 science, 2 science labs, 3 social studies, 3 history. **Freshman Admission Statistics:** 2,868 applied, 83.0% admitted, enrolled. **Transfer Admission Requirements:** High school transcript, college transcript(s), Minimum college GPA of 2.0 required. Lowest grade transferable C. **General Admission Information:** Nonfall registration accepted. Admission may be deferred.

COSTS AND FINANCIAL AID

Annual tuition $27,850. Room and board $8,513. Required fees $430. **Required Forms and Deadlines:** FAFSA. **Notification of Awards:** Applicants will be notified of awards on a rolling basis beginning 2/15. **Types of Aid:** *Need-based scholarships/grants:* College/university scholarship or grant aid from institutional funds; Federal Nursing Scholarships; Federal Pell; Private scholarships; SEOG; State scholarships/grants. *Student Employment:* Federal Work-Study Program available. Institutional employment available. **Financial Aid Statistics:** 100% needy freshmen, 100% needy undergrads receive need-based scholarship or grant aid. 91% freshmen, 91% undergrads receive non-need-based scholarship or grant aid. 73% freshmen, 79% undergrads receive need-based self-help aid. 0% freshmen, 0% undergrads receive athletic scholarships. 98% freshmen, 98% undergrads receive any aid. **Criteria for awarding aid:** *Need-based:* Academics, Art, Leadership, Religious affiliation *Non-need-based:* Academics, Alumni affiliation, Art, Leadership, Minority status, Religious affiliation.

CARSON-NEWMAN UNIVERSITY

1646 Russell Avenue, Jefferson City, TN 37760
Phone: 865-471-3223 · **Financial Aid Phone:** 865-471-3247
E-mail: dmitme@cn.edu · **CEEB Code:** 1102
Fax: 865-471-4817 · **Website:** www.cn.edu · **ACT Code:** 3950

This private school, affiliated with the Baptist Church, was founded in 1851. It has a 90 acre campus.

RATINGS

Admissions Selectivity Rating: 79   **Fire Safety Rating:** 85   **Green Rating:** 60*

STUDENTS AND FACULTY

Enrollment: 1,633. **Student Body:** 58% female, 42% male, 20% out-of-state, 4% international (19 countries represented). Asian 1%, African American 8%,

Caucasian 78%, Hispanic 4%, Native American <1%, Pacific Islander 0%, Two or more races 3%, Race unknown 2%.
Retention and Graduation: 70% freshmen return for sophomore year. 37% freshmen graduate within 4 years. 25% grads go on to further study within 1 year. 20% grads pursue arts and sciences degrees. 3% grads pursue law degrees. 1% grads pursue business degrees. 2% grads pursue medical degrees. **Faculty:** Student/faculty ratio 13:1. 122 full-time faculty, 78% hold PhDs, 4% are members of minority groups, 56% are women. 0% of classes are taught by teaching assistants.

ACADEMICS

Degrees: Associate; Bachelor's; Doctoral/Research; Master's; Post-Master's certificate **Classes:** Most classes have 10-19 students. Most lab/discussion sessions have 10-19 students. **Most popular majors:** Educational, Instructional, And Curriculum Supervision; Registered Nursing/Registered Nurse; Business Administration And Management, General. **Special Study Options:** Accelerated program; Distance learning; Double major; Dual enrollment; English as a Second Language (ESL); Exchange student program (domestic); Honors program; Independent study; Internships; Liberal arts/career combination; Student-designed major; Study abroad; Teacher certification program. **Honors programs:** We have an Honors Program, though which high-ability students are given the ability to participate in specialized social and cultural activities, engage specialized coursework designed to encourage critical thinking, and write a thesis project or other special capstone project at the end of their college careers. **Disability Services offered to physically disabled students:** Note-taking services; Reader services; Tape recorders; Tutors. **Career services:** Alumni network; Alumni services; Career assessment; Career/job search classes; Internships; Regional alumni

FACILITIES

Housing: Apartments for single students; Men's dorms; Special housing for disabled student; Women's dorms 80% of campus accessible to physically diasbled. **Special Academic Facilities/Equipment:** Art galleries, Appalachian history museum, home management house, language lab and Saint Johns Bible Exhibit.

CAMPUS LIFE

Environment: Village **Activities:** Campus Ministries; Choral groups; Concert band; Dance; Drama/theater; International Student Organization; Jazz band; Literary magazine; Marching band; Music ensembles; Musical theater; Pep band; Student government; Student newspaper; Student-run film society; Symphony orchestra 45 registered organizations, 10 honor societies, 5 religious organizations. 2 fraternities, 2 sororities. **Athletics (Intercollegiate):** *Men:* baseball, basketball, cheerleading, cross-country, football, golf, soccer, tennis, track/field (outdoor), wrestling. *Women:* basketball, cheerleading, cross-country, soccer, softball, tennis, track/field (outdoor), volleyball. **On-Campus Highlights:** Maddox Student Activities Center, Chick-fil-a, Maples Cafe (coffee shop), Cafeteria, Center for Student Success

ADMISSIONS

Freshman Academic Profile: Average high school GPA 3.4. **Test Scores:** SAT Math middle 50% range 460-570. SAT EBRW middle 50% range 480-580. ACT middle 50% range 20-26. Minimum internet-based TOEFL 79. Minimum paper TOEFL 550. **Basis for Candidate Selection:** *Very important factors considered include:* academic GPA, standardized test scores, character/personal qualities. *Important factors considered include:* rigor of secondary school record, class rank, extracurricular activities. *Other factors considered include:* application essay, recommendation(s), interview, talent/ability, volunteer work. **Freshman Admission Requirements:** High school diploma is required and GED is accepted *Academic units required:* 4 English, 3 math, 3 science, 2 social studies, 1 history, 6 academic electives, and 1 unit from above areas or other academic areas. *Academic units recommended:* 2 foreign language. **Freshman Admission Statistics:** 3,294 applied, 67.4% admitted, 18% enrolled. **Transfer Admission Requirements:** college transcript(s), Minimum college GPA of 2.0 required. Lowest grade transferable d. **General Admission Information:** Nonfall registration accepted. Admission may be deferred for a maximum of 1 year.

COSTS AND FINANCIAL AID

Annual tuition $26,200. Room and board $8,630. Required fees $1,200. Average book expense $1,600. **Required Forms and Deadlines:** FAFSA. **Notification of Awards:** Applicants will be notified of awards on a rolling basis beginning 3/1. **Types of Aid:** *Need-based scholarships/grants:* College/university scholarship or grant aid from institutional funds; Federal Nursing Scholarships; Federal Pell; Private scholarships; SEOG; State scholarships/grants. *Loans:* Direct PLUS loans; Direct Subsidized Stafford Loans; Direct Unsubsidized Stafford Loans. *Student Employment:* Federal Work-Study Program available. Institutional employment available. **Financial Aid Statistics:** 99% needy freshmen, 98% needy undergrads receive need-based scholarship or grant aid. 16% freshmen, 19% undergrads receive non-need-based scholarship or grant aid. 75% freshmen, 76% undergrads receive need-based self-help aid. 6% freshmen, 6% undergrads receive athletic scholarships. 73% undergrads borrow to pay for school. Average cumulative indebtedness $27,418. **Criteria for awarding aid:** *Need-based:* Art, Music/drama, Religious affiliation *Non-need-based:* Academics, Art, Athletics, Leadership, Music/drama, Religious affiliation, State/district residency.

CARTHAGE COLLEGE

2001 Alford Park Drive, Kenosha WI, WI 53140
Phone: 262-551-6000 · **Financial Aid Phone:** 262-551-6001
E-mail: admissions@carthage.edu · **CEEB Code:** 1103
Fax: 262-551-5762 · **Website:** www.carthage.edu · **ACT Code:** 4571

This private school, affiliated with the Lutheran Church, was founded in 1847. It has a 95 acre campus.

RATINGS
Admissions Selectivity Rating: 78   **Fire Safety Rating:** 81   **Green Rating:** 60*

STUDENTS AND FACULTY
Enrollment: 2,874. **Student Body:** 54% female, 46% male, 68% out-of-state, <1% international (16 countries represented). Asian 1%, African American 5%, Caucasian 77%, Hispanic 4%, Native American <1%, Pacific Islander <1%, Two or more races 2%, Race unknown 10%.
Retention and Graduation: 78% freshmen return for sophomore year. 16% grads go on to further study within 1 year. 4% grads pursue arts and sciences degrees. 2% grads pursue law degrees. 1% grads pursue business degrees. 1% grads pursue medical degrees. **Faculty:** Student/faculty ratio 8:1. 149 full-time faculty, 91% hold PhDs, 7% are members of minority groups, 40% are women. 0% of classes are taught by teaching assistants.

ACADEMICS
Degrees: Bachelor's; Master's **Classes:** Most classes have fewer than 10 students. **Most popular majors:** Elementary Education And Teaching; Biology/Biological Sciences, General; Business Administration And Management, General. **Special Study Options:** Accelerated program; Cooperative education program; Cross-registration; Double major; Honors program; Independent study; Internships; Student-designed major; Study abroad; Teacher certification program. **Honors programs:** We offer All College Honors as well as Honors in the Major. **Combined degree programs:** BA/MA. **Disability Services offered to physically disabled students:** Note-taking services; Reader services; Tape recorders; Tutors. **Career services:** Career assessment; Career/job search classes; Internships

FACILITIES
Housing: Coed dorms; Women's dorms 99% of campus accessible to physically diasbled. **Special Academic Facilities/Equipment:** H.F. Johnson Art Gallery, Center for CHildren's Literature, planetarium, undergraduate science research lab, graphic design lab, greenhouse, computer/math research lab, physics research lab, ScienceWorks lab, A.W. Clausen Center Boardroom **Computers:** Students can register for classes online. Administrative functions (other than registration) can be performed online.

CAMPUS LIFE
Environment: City **Activities:** Campus Ministries; Choral groups; Concert band; Dance; Drama/theater; International Student Organization; Jazz band; Literary magazine; Model UN; Music ensembles; Musical theater; Pep band; Radio station; Student government; Student newspaper; Student-run film society; Symphony orchestra; Yearbook 90 registered organizations, 20 honor societies, 7 religious organizations. 8 fraternities, 7 sororities. **Athletics (Intercollegiate):** *Men:* baseball, basketball, cross-country, football, golf, soccer, swimming, tennis, track/field (outdoor), track/field (indoor), volleyball. *Women:* basketball, cross-country, golf, soccer, softball, swimming, tennis, track/field (outdoor), track/field (indoor), volleyball, water polo. **On-Campus Highlights:** Tarble Athletic and Recreation Center, Hedberg Library, A.W. Clausen Center for World Business, Oaks Residence Halls, Lake Michigan

ADMISSIONS
Freshman Academic Profile: Average high school GPA 3.3. 21% in top 10% of high school class, 44% in top 25% of high school class, 75% in top 50% of high school class. 91% from public high schools. **Test Scores:** SAT Math middle 50% range 490-620. SAT EBRW middle 50% range 480-610. ACT middle 50% range 21-27. Minimum paper TOEFL 500. **Basis for Candidate Selection:** *Very important factors considered include:* rigor of secondary school record, academic GPA, standardized test scores. *Other factors considered include:* class rank, application essay, recommendation(s), interview, extracurricular activities, talent/ability, character/personal qualities, volunteer work, work experience. **Freshman Admission Requirements:** High school diploma is required and GED is accepted *Academic units recommended:* 4 English, 3 math, 3 science, 2 foreign language, 3 social studies, 3 academic electives. **Freshman Admission**

Statistics: 7,174 applied, 70.3% admitted, 14% enrolled. **Transfer Admission Requirements:** college transcript(s), statement of good standing from prior institution(s). Minimum college GPA of 2.0 required. Lowest grade transferable C-. **General Admission Information:** Application fee $35. Nonfall registration accepted. Admission may be deferred for a maximum of one year.

COSTS AND FINANCIAL AID
Annual tuition $36,570. Room and board $9,970. Average book expense $1,600. **Required Forms and Deadlines:** FAFSA. **Notification of Awards:** Applicants will be notified of awards on a rolling basis beginning 2/1. **Types of Aid:** *Need-based scholarships/grants:* College/university scholarship or grant aid from institutional funds; Federal Pell; Private scholarships; SEOG; State scholarships/grants. *Loans:* Direct PLUS loans; Direct Subsidized Stafford Loans; Direct Unsubsidized Stafford Loans. **Financial Aid Statistics:** 100% needy freshmen, 100% needy undergrads receive need-based scholarship or grant aid. 13% freshmen, 11% undergrads receive non-need-based scholarship or grant aid. 83% freshmen, 84% undergrads receive need-based self-help aid. 0% freshmen, 0% undergrads receive athletic scholarships. 97% freshmen, 97% undergrads receive any aid. **Criteria for awarding aid:** *Need-based:* Academics, Alumni affiliation, Art, Leadership, Music/drama, Religious affiliation *Non-need-based:* Academics, Alumni affiliation, Art, Leadership, Music/drama, Religious affiliation, State/district residency.

CASCADE COLLEGE

9101 East Burnside Street, Portland, OR 97216-1515
Phone: 503-257-1202 · **Financial Aid Phone:** 503-257-1241
E-mail: admissions@cascade.edu
Fax: 503-257-1222 · **Website:** www.cascade.edu · **ACT Code:** 3459

This private school, affiliated with the Church of Christ, was founded in 1993. It has a 12 acre campus.

RATINGS
Admissions Selectivity Rating: 71   **Fire Safety Rating:** 70   **Green Rating:** 60*

STUDENTS AND FACULTY
Enrollment: 262. **Student Body:** 59% female, 41% male, 64% out-of-state, 2% international (8 countries represented). Asian 7%, African American 11%, Caucasian 64%, Hispanic 12%, Native American 1%, Race unknown 3%.
Retention and Graduation: 46% freshmen return for sophomore year. 15% grads go on to further study within 1 year. 10% grads pursue arts and sciences degrees. 2% grads pursue law degrees. 1% grads pursue business degrees. 0% grads pursue medical degrees. **Faculty:** Student/faculty ratio 12:1. 15 full-time faculty, 60% hold PhDs, 13% are members of minority groups, 27% are women. 0% of classes are taught by teaching assistants.

ACADEMICS
Degrees: Bachelor's **Classes:** Most classes have 20-29 students. Most lab/discussion sessions have 20-29 students. **Most popular majors:** Teacher Education, Multiple Levels; Psychology, General; Business/Commerce, General. **Special Study Options:** Double major; Dual enrollment; Independent study; Internships; Student-designed major; Study abroad; Teacher certification program. **Disability Services offered to physically disabled students:** Note-taking services; Reader services; Tutors.

FACILITIES
Housing: Apartments for married students; Men's dorms; Special housing for disabled student; Women's dorms 70% of campus accessible to physically diasbled. **Computers:** 100% of classrooms, 100% of dorms, 100% of libraries, 100% of dining areas, 100% of student union, 100% of common outdoor areas have wireless network access. Administrative functions (other than registration) can be performed online.

CAMPUS LIFE
Environment: Metropolis **Activities:** Choral groups; Drama/theater; Jazz band; Literary magazine; Music ensembles; Musical theater; Student government; Yearbook 16 registered organizations, 2 honor societies. **Athletics (Intercollegiate):** *Men:* basketball, cross-country, soccer, track/field (outdoor), track/field (indoor). *Women:* basketball, cross-country, soccer, track/field (outdoor), track/field (indoor), volleyball. **On-Campus Highlights:** Classrooms, Student Center, The Cabin (coffee shop), Weight room, Womack and Hamstreet Fountains

ADMISSIONS
Freshman Academic Profile: Average high school GPA 3.0. 85% from public high schools. **Test Scores:** Minimum paper TOEFL 500. **Basis for Candidate Selection:** *Other factors considered include:* academic GPA, standardized test

scores, recommendation(s). **Freshman Admission Requirements:** High school diploma is required and GED is accepted *Academic units recommended:* 4 English, 3 math, 2 science, 1 science labs, 2 foreign language, 4 social studies, 2 history, 1 computer science. **Freshman Admission Statistics:** 204 applied, 56.9% admitted, 57% enrolled. **Transfer Admission Requirements:** High school transcript, college transcript(s), Minimum college GPA of 2.0 required. Lowest grade transferable D. **General Admission Information:** Application fee $25. Nonfall registration accepted. Admission may be deferred for a maximum of 1 year.

COSTS AND FINANCIAL AID

Average book expense $900. **Required Forms and Deadlines:** FAFSA; Institution's own financial aid form. **Notification of Awards:** Applicants will be notified of awards on a rolling basis beginning 2/15. **Types of Aid:** *Need-based scholarships/grants:* College/university scholarship or grant aid from institutional funds; Federal Pell; Private scholarships; SEOG. *Loans: Student Employment:* Federal Work-Study Program available. Institutional employment available. **Financial Aid Statistics:** 100% needy freshmen, 63% needy undergrads receive need-based scholarship or grant aid. 19% freshmen, 92% undergrads receive non-need-based scholarship or grant aid. 87% freshmen, 84% undergrads receive need-based self-help aid. 48% freshmen, 36% undergrads receive athletic scholarships. 100% freshmen, 99% undergrads receive any aid. **Criteria for awarding aid:** *Need-based:* Leadership *Non-need-based:* Academics, Athletics, Leadership, Music/drama, Religious affiliation, State/district residency.

CASE WESTERN RESERVE UNIVERSITY

10900 Euclid Avenue, Cleveland, OH 44106-7055
Phone: 216-368-4450 · **Financial Aid Phone:** 216-368-4530
E-mail: admission@case.edu · **CEEB Code:** 1105
Fax: 216-368-5111 · **Website:** www.case.edu · **ACT Code:** 3244

This private school was founded in 1826. It has a 267 acre campus.

RATINGS

Admissions Selectivity Rating: 94   **Fire Safety Rating:** 88   **Green Rating:** 96

STUDENTS AND FACULTY

Enrollment: 5,020. **Student Body:** 44% female, 56% male, 72% out-of-state, 13% international (46 countries represented). Asian 21%, African American 4%, Caucasian 49%, Hispanic 7%, Native American <1%, Pacific Islander <1%, Two or more races 5%, Race unknown 2%.
Retention and Graduation: 93% freshmen return for sophomore year. 66% freshmen graduate within 4 years. 83% freshmen graduate within 6 years. 36% grads go on to further study within 1 year. 10% grads pursue arts and sciences degrees. 5% grads pursue law degrees. 6% grads pursue business degrees. 15% grads pursue medical degrees. **Faculty:** Student/faculty ratio 11:1. 789 full-time faculty, 92% hold PhDs, 19% are members of minority groups, 44% are women. 5% of classes are taught by teaching assistants.

ACADEMICS

Degrees: Bachelor's; Doctoral; Doctoral/Professional; Doctoral/Research; Master's; Post-Bachelor's certificate; Post-Master's certificate **Classes:** Most classes have 10-19 students. **Most popular majors:** Bioengineering And Biomedical Engineering; Mechanical Engineering; Biology/Biological Sciences, General. **Special Study Options:** Accelerated program; Cooperative education program; Cross-registration; Double major; Dual enrollment; English as a Second Language (ESL); Exchange student program (domestic); Honors program; Independent study; Internships; Liberal arts/career combination; Student-designed major; Study abroad; Teacher certification program. **Combined degree programs:** BA/DDS; BA/MA. **Disability Services offered to physically disabled students:** Note-taking services; Reader services; Tape recorders; Tutors. **Career services:** Alumni network; Alumni services; Career assessment; Career/job search classes; Internships; Regional alumni

FACILITIES

Housing: Apartments for married students; Apartments for single students; Coed dorms; Fraternity/sorority housing; Wellness housing 90% of campus accessible to physically disabled. **Special Academic Facilities/Equipment:** Art, natural history, and auto-aviation museums, historical society, botanical garden, biology field stations, observatory. **Computers:** 100% of classrooms,

100% of dorms, 100% of libraries, 100% of dining areas, 100% of student union, 100% of common outdoor areas have wireless network access. Students can register for classes online. Administrative functions (other than registration) can be performed online.

CAMPUS LIFE

Environment: Metropolis **Activities:** Campus Ministries; Choral groups; Concert band; Dance; Drama/theater; International Student Organization; Jazz band; Literary magazine; Marching band; Model UN; Music ensembles; Musical theater; Pep band; Radio station; Student government; Student newspaper; Student-run film society; Symphony orchestra; Yearbook 150 registered organizations, 8 honor societies, 4 religious organizations. 16 fraternities, 8 sororities. **Athletics (Intercollegiate):** *Men:* baseball, basketball, cross-country, football, soccer, swimming, tennis, track/field (outdoor), track/field (indoor), wrestling. *Women:* basketball, cross-country, soccer, softball, swimming, tennis, track/field (outdoor), track/field (indoor), volleyball. **On-Campus Highlights:** Kelvin Smith Library, Thwing Center, Jolly Scholar, Starbucks, Biomedical Research Building Dining Commons **Environmental Initiatives:** In 2008 President Barbara Snyder signed the American and College and University President's Climate Commitment, now called the Carbon Commitment which is a public declaration that CWRU will aim to be a carbon neutral campus by 2050. The commitment requires public reporting of CWRU's greenhouse gas inventory and other sustainability metrics. CWRU is proud to be a community steward and leader on this vital topic and works with the City of Cleveland and other entries to share strategies and best practices. The University is making progress towards the goal through energy efficiency investments, green buildings and behavior change campaigns.

ADMISSIONS

Freshman Academic Profile: 70% in top 10% of high school class, 95% in top 25% of high school class, 100% in top 50% of high school class. 70% from public high schools. **Test Scores:** SAT Math middle 50% range 690-780. SAT EBRW middle 50% range 650-740. ACT middle 50% range 30-33. Minimum internet-based TOEFL 90. Minimum paper TOEFL 577. **Basis for Candidate Selection:** *Very important factors considered include:* rigor of secondary school record, class rank, academic GPA, standardized test scores, extracurricular activities. *Important factors considered include:* application essay, recommendation(s), interview, talent/ability, character/personal qualities, racial/ethnic status, volunteer work. *Other factors considered include:* first generation, alumni/ae relation, work experience, level of applicant's interest. **Freshman Admission Requirements:** High school diploma is required and GED is accepted *Academic units required:* 4 English, 3 math, 3 science, 2 science labs, 2 foreign language, 3 social studies, *Academic units recommended:* 4 math, 3 science labs, 3 foreign language, 4 social studies. **Freshman Admission Statistics:** 25,380 applied, 33.1% admitted, 16% enrolled. **Transfer Admission Requirements:** High school transcript, college transcript(s), essay or personal statement, statement of good standing from prior institution(s). Minimum college GPA of 3.2 required. Lowest grade transferable C. **General Admission Information:** Application fee $70. Regular application deadline 1/15. Nonfall registration accepted. Admission may be deferred for a maximum of 1 year.

COSTS AND FINANCIAL AID

Annual tuition $47,074. Room and board $14,784. Required fees $426. Average book expense $1,200. **Required Forms and Deadlines:** CSS/Financial Aid PROFILE; FAFSA; Institution's own financial aid form; Noncustodial PROFILE. **Notification of Awards:** Applicants will be notified of awards on a rolling basis beginning 3/20. **Types of Aid:** *Need-based scholarships/grants:* College/university scholarship or grant aid from institutional funds; Federal Pell; Private scholarships; SEOG; State scholarships/grants. *Loans:* Direct PLUS loans; Direct Subsidized Stafford Loans; Direct Unsubsidized Stafford Loans. *Student Employment:* Federal Work-Study Program available. Institutional employment available. **Financial Aid Statistics:** 97% needy freshmen, 97% needy undergrads receive need-based scholarship or grant aid. 30% freshmen, 14% undergrads receive non-need-based scholarship or grant aid. 69% freshmen, 81% undergrads receive need-based self-help aid. 0% freshmen, 0% undergrads receive athletic scholarships. 83% freshmen, 87% undergrads receive any aid. 51% undergrads borrow to pay for school. Average cumulative indebtedness $30,561. **Criteria for awarding aid:** *Non-need-based:* Academics, Alumni affiliation, Art, Leadership, Music/drama.

CASTLETON STATE COLLEGE

62 Alumni Drive, Castleton, VT 05735
Phone: 802-468-1213 · **Financial Aid Phone:** 802-468-6070
E-mail: info@castleton.edu · **CEEB Code:** 3765
Fax: 802-468-1476 · **Website:** www.castleton.edu · **ACT Code:** 4314

This public school was founded in 1787. It has a 165 acre campus.

RATINGS
Admissions Selectivity Rating: 74   **Fire Safety Rating:** 87   **Green Rating:** 60*

STUDENTS AND FACULTY
Enrollment: 1,890. **Student Body:** 52% female, 48% male, 30% out-of-state, 2% international (16 countries represented). Asian 1%, African American 2%, Caucasian 85%, Hispanic 2%, Native American <1%, Pacific Islander 0%, Two or more races 2%, Race unknown 6%.
Retention and Graduation: 70% freshmen return for sophomore year.
Faculty: Student/faculty ratio 10:1. 102 full-time faculty, 93% hold PhDs, 6% are members of minority groups, 51% are women. 0% of classes are taught by teaching assistants.

ACADEMICS
Degrees: Associate; Bachelor's; Master's; Post-Master's certificate **Classes:** Most classes have 10-19 students. Most lab/discussion sessions have 10-19 students. **Most popular majors:** Psychology, General; Business/Commerce, General. **Special Study Options:** Cross-registration; Double major; Dual enrollment; English as a Second Language (ESL); Honors program; Independent study; Internships; Liberal arts/career combination; Student-designed major; Study abroad; Teacher certification program. **Honors programs:** Honors programs available in History, Literature, Psychology, and Sociology **Combined degree programs:** BA/MA. **Disability Services offered to physically disabled students:** Note-taking services; Reader services; Tape recorders; Tutors. **Career services:** Alumni network; Career assessment; Internships

FACILITIES
Housing: Coed dorms; Theme housing; Wellness housing 100% of campus accessible to physically diasbled. **Special Academic Facilities/Equipment:** Historical/medical museum **Computers:** 25% of classrooms, 100% of dorms, 100% of libraries, 100% of dining areas, 100% of student union, have wireless network access.

CAMPUS LIFE
Environment: Rural **Activities:** Campus Ministries; Choral groups; Concert band; Dance; Drama/theater; International Student Organization; Jazz band; Literary magazine; Marching band; Music ensembles; Musical theater; Pep band; Radio station; Student government; Student newspaper; Television station; Yearbook 40 registered organizations, 7 honor societies, 1 religious organization. **Athletics (Intercollegiate):** *Men:* baseball, basketball, cross-country, football, ice hockey, lacrosse, skiing (downhill/alpine), soccer, tennis. *Women:* basketball, cross-country, field hockey, ice hockey, lacrosse, skiing (downhill/alpine), soccer, softball, tennis. **On-Campus Highlights:** Fireside Cafe, Coffee Cottage, Fitness center, Library **Environmental Initiatives:** Student-driven recycling effort

ADMISSIONS
Freshman Academic Profile: Average high school GPA 3.0. 6% in top 10% of high school class, 29% in top 25% of high school class, 61% in top 50% of high school class. **Test Scores:** SAT Math middle 50% range 430-540. SAT EBRW middle 50% range 420-530. ACT middle 50% range 18-22. Minimum internet-based TOEFL 80. Minimum paper TOEFL 500. **Basis for Candidate Selection:** *Very important factors considered include:* rigor of secondary school record, class rank, academic GPA, application essay, recommendation(s), character/personal qualities. *Other factors considered include:* standardized test scores, interview, extracurricular activities, volunteer work, level of applicant's interest. **Freshman Admission Requirements:** High school diploma is required and GED is accepted *Academic units required:* 4 English, 3 math, 3 science, 2 science labs, 3 social studies, 3 history, *Academic units recommended:* 2 foreign language. **Freshman Admission Statistics:** 2,397 applied, 77.9% admitted, 20% enrolled. **Transfer Admission Requirements:** college transcript(s), essay or personal statement, Minimum college GPA of 2.0 required. Lowest grade transferable C-. **General Admission Information:** Application fee $40. Priority deadline 5/1. Nonfall registration accepted. Admission may be deferred for a maximum of 1 year.

COSTS AND FINANCIAL AID
Annual in-state tuition $9,414. Annual out-of-state tuition $24,432. Room and board $9,414. Required fees $1,004. Average book expense $1,000. **Required Forms and Deadlines:** FAFSA. **Notification of Awards:** Applicants will be notified of awards on a rolling basis beginning 2/15. **Types of Aid:** *Need-*

based scholarships/grants: College/university scholarship or grant aid from institutional funds; Federal Pell; Private scholarships; SEOG; State scholarships/grants. *Loans:* Direct PLUS loans; Direct Subsidized Stafford Loans; Direct Unsubsidized Stafford Loans. *Student Employment:* Federal Work-Study Program available. Institutional employment available. **Criteria for awarding aid:** *Need-based:* Academics, Music/drama *Non-need-based:* Academics, Alumni affiliation, Music/drama, State/district residency.

CATAWBA COLLEGE

2300 West Innes Street, Salisbury, NC 28144
Phone: 704-637-4402 · **Financial Aid Phone:** 704-637-4416
E-mail: admission@catawba.edu · **CEEB Code:** 5103
Fax: 704-637-4222 · **Website:** www.catawba.edu · **ACT Code:** 3080

This private school, affiliated with the United Church of Christ, was founded in 1851. It has a 276 acre campus.

RATINGS
Admissions Selectivity Rating: 87   **Fire Safety Rating:** 89   **Green Rating:** 97

STUDENTS AND FACULTY
Enrollment: 1,307. **Student Body:** 54% female, 46% male, 19% out-of-state, 4% international (15 countries represented). Asian 1%, African American 19%, Caucasian 65%, Hispanic 7%, Native American <1%, Pacific Islander <1%, Two or more races 3%, Race unknown <1%.
Retention and Graduation: 73% freshmen return for sophomore year. 35% freshmen graduate within 4 years. 45% freshmen graduate within 6 years.
Faculty: Student/faculty ratio 12:1. 86 full-time faculty, 78% hold PhDs, 9% are members of minority groups, 48% are women. 0% of classes are taught by teaching assistants.

ACADEMICS
Degrees: Bachelor's; Master's **Classes:** Most classes have 10-19 students. Most lab/discussion sessions have 10-19 students. **Most popular majors:** Kindergarten/Preschool Education And Teaching; Sport And Fitness Administration/Management; Business Administration And Management, General. **Special Study Options:** Cross-registration; Distance learning; Double major; Dual enrollment; Honors program; Independent study; Internships; Student-designed major; Study abroad; Teacher certification program. **Honors programs:** The Catawba Honors Program cultivates a community of academically gifted students who pursue challenging educational experiences with outstanding faculty. Through interdisciplinary, provocative, and intellectually demanding courses, e Honors Program piques the curiosity of students, encouraging them to become life-long learners whose lives are enriched by their experiences. http://www.catawba.edu/programs/honors/. **Disability Services offered to physically disabled students:** Note-taking services; Tape recorders; Tutors. **Career services:** Alumni network; Career assessment; Career/job search classes; Internships

FACILITIES
Housing: Apartments for single students; Coed dorms; Men's dorms; Women's dorms 95% of campus accessible to physically diasbled. **Special Academic Facilities/Equipment:** °189 acre Ecological Preserve °300 acre Wildlife Preserve °Center for the Environment & Environmental Programs; completed in 2000 (prior to LEED certification program), and in process of certifying through LEED for existing buildings **Computers:** 90% of classrooms, 95% of dorms, 100% of libraries, 25% of dining areas, 80% of student union, 10% of common outdoor areas have wireless network access. Administrative functions (other than registration) can be performed online.

CAMPUS LIFE
Environment: Town **Activities:** Campus Ministries; Choral groups; Concert band; Dance; Drama/theater; Literary magazine; Marching band; Music ensembles; Musical theater; Pep band; Radio station; Student government; Student newspaper; Yearbook 38 registered organizations, 9 honor societies, 4 religious organizations. **Athletics (Intercollegiate):** *Men:* baseball, basketball, cheerleading, cross-country, football, golf, lacrosse, soccer, swimming, tennis. *Women:* basketball, cheerleading, cross-country, golf, soccer, softball, swimming, tennis, volleyball. **On-Campus Highlights:** Center for the Environment, Cannon Field House, Robertson College Community Center, Ketner Hall, Cannon Student Center **Environmental Initiatives:** Center for the Environment, along with its national, regional, and community

environmental outreach. The Center for the Environment at Catawba College sets us apart from other environmental programs. We offer value-added education that goes well beyond classroom teaching, providing many real-world opportunities for our students. See: http://catawba.edu/academics/schools/arts-sciences/environmental-science-studies/ The Center for the Environment at Catawba College has assumed the leadership of the N.C. Green Schools program, a nonprofit organization that promotes sustainability in the state's schools from pre-kindergarten through 12th grade.

ADMISSIONS

Freshman Academic Profile: Average high school GPA 3.8. 13% in top 10% of high school class, 44% in top 25% of high school class, 77% in top 50% of high school class. 88% from public high schools. **Test Scores:** SAT Math middle 50% range 470-580. SAT EBRW middle 50% range 460-520. ACT middle 50% range 18-23. Minimum internet-based TOEFL 69. **Basis for Candidate Selection:** *Very important factors considered include:* academic GPA, recommendation(s), extracurricular activities, talent/ability, character/personal qualities, geographical residence. *Important factors considered include:* rigor of secondary school record, standardized test scores, volunteer work, work experience. *Other factors considered include:* class rank, application essay, interview, first generation, alumni/ae relation, state residency, religious affiliation/commitment, racial/ethnic status, level of applicant's interest. **Freshman Admission Requirements:** High school diploma is required and GED is accepted *Academic units required:* 4 English, 3 math, 3 science, 3 social studies, *Academic units recommended:* 2 foreign language. **Freshman Admission Statistics:** 3,125 applied, 42.4% admitted, 25% enrolled. **Transfer Admission Requirements:** High school transcript, college transcript(s), essay or personal statement, statement of good standing from prior institution(s). Minimum college GPA of 2.0 required. Lowest grade transferable C. **General Admission Information:** Nonfall registration accepted. Admission may be deferred for a maximum of 1 year.

COSTS AND FINANCIAL AID

Annual tuition $30,520. Room and board $10,488. Average book expense $1,400. **Required Forms and Deadlines:** FAFSA; State aid form. **Notification of Awards:** Applicants will be notified of awards on a rolling basis beginning 1/15. **Types of Aid:** *Need-based scholarships/grants:* College/university scholarship or grant aid from institutional funds; Federal Pell; Private scholarships; SEOG; State scholarships/grants. *Loans:* Direct PLUS loans; Direct Subsidized Stafford Loans; Direct Unsubsidized Stafford Loans. *Student Employment:* Federal Work-Study Program available. Institutional employment available. **Financial Aid Statistics:** 72% needy freshmen, 78% needy undergrads receive need-based scholarship or grant aid. 99% freshmen, 86% undergrads receive non-need-based scholarship or grant aid. 81% freshmen, 78% undergrads receive need-based self-help aid. 25% freshmen, 25% undergrads receive athletic scholarships. 99% freshmen, 99% undergrads receive any aid. 77% undergrads borrow to pay for school. Average cumulative indebtedness $30,490. **Criteria for awarding aid:** *Non-need-based:* Academics, Athletics, Leadership, Music/drama, Religious affiliation, State/district residency.

CATHOLIC UNIVERSITY OF AMERICA

Cardinal Station, Washington, DC 20064
Phone: 202-319-5305 · **Financial Aid Phone:** 202-319-5307
E-mail: cua-admissions@cua.edu · **CEEB Code:** 5104
Fax: 202-319-6533 · **Website:** www.catholic.edu · **ACT Code:** 654

This private school, affiliated with the Roman Catholic Church, was founded in 1887. It has a 176 acre campus.

RATINGS

Admissions Selectivity Rating: 77   **Fire Safety Rating:** 93   **Green Rating:** 86

STUDENTS AND FACULTY

Enrollment: 3,283. **Student Body:** 54% female, 46% male, 97% out-of-state, 6% international (27 countries represented). Asian 4%, African American 5%, Caucasian 65%, Hispanic 13%, Native American <1%, Pacific Islander <1%, Two or more races 5%, Race unknown 3%.
Retention and Graduation: 86% freshmen return for sophomore year. 66% freshmen graduate within 4 years. 74% freshmen graduate within 6 years. 20% grads go on to further study within 1 year. 56% grads pursue arts and sciences degrees. 15.4% grads pursue law degrees. **Faculty:** Student/faculty ratio 7:1.

400 full-time faculty, 93% hold PhDs, 14% are members of minority groups, 38% are women. 13% of classes are taught by teaching assistants.

ACADEMICS

Degrees: Associate; Bachelor's; Certificate; Doctoral; Doctoral/Professional; Doctoral/Research; Master's; Post-Bachelor's certificate; Post-Master's certificate **Most popular majors:** Architecture; Political Science And Government, General; Registered Nursing/Registered Nurse. **Special Study Options:** Accelerated program; Cross-registration; Distance learning; Double major; Dual enrollment; English as a Second Language (ESL); Honors program; Independent study; Internships; Study abroad; Teacher certification program. **Honors programs:** The University Honors Program offers classes in the classical liberal arts and contemporary social and environmental sciences to compliment students' major studies. Students take small, rigorous, discussion-based courses from offerings in philosophy, theology, history and literature, social science, environmental science, and liberal studies. Students completing any of these six tracks receive distinction at graduation. Special lectures, symposia, social events, and trips are organized for students in the program. The University Honors Program also provides a special residential community for its students. **Combined degree programs:** BA/MA. **Disability Services offered to physically disabled students:** Note-taking services; Tape recorders; Tutors. **Career services:** Alumni network; Alumni services; Career assessment; Internships; Regional alumni

FACILITIES

Housing: Apartments for single students; Men's dorms; Theme housing; Women's dorms 75% of campus accessible to physically diasbled. **Special Academic Facilities/Equipment:** Facilities available on the university campus include an art department gallery; the John K. Mullen of Denver Memorial Library, which features a rare book collection containing 65,000 volumes that range from medieval documents to first editions of 20th-century authors; the university archives, which has nearly 9,000 feet of records and manuscripts; the Vitreous State Laboratory, which engages some of the world's leading glass scientists to help research and develop methods for safe containment of disposed radioactive materials, primarily by converting nuclear waste into solid glass using vitrification techniques. In 2008, the university dedicated Opus Hall, the first LEED (Leadership in Energy and Environmental Design)-compliant residence hall among colleges and universities in Washington, D.C. The Edward J. Pryzbyla University Center includes nine meeting spaces, two separate dining facilities, a convenience store, the campus bookstore, offices, various atrium and lounge spaces and a 7,500-square-foot great room, where Pope Benedict XVI delivered a speech in April 2008. Adjacent to the campus is the Roman Catholic Basilica of the National Shrine of the Immaculate Conception, the largest church in the Western hemisphere. University Masses and commencement are held every year at the National Shrine. Directly across the street from the university is the Pope John Paul II Cultural Center, a major Catholic museum. **Computers:** 40% of classrooms, 90% of dorms, 100% of libraries, 100% of dining areas, 100% of student union, 20% of common outdoor areas have wireless network access. Students can register for classes online. Administrative functions (other than registration) can be performed online.

CAMPUS LIFE

Environment: Metropolis **Activities:** Campus Ministries; Choral groups; Concert band; Dance; Drama/theater; International Student Organization; Jazz band; Literary magazine; Model UN; Music ensembles; Musical theater; Opera; Radio station; Student government; Student newspaper; Student-run film society; Symphony orchestra; Yearbook 87 registered organizations, 16 honor societies, 4 religious organizations. 1 fraternity, 1 sorority. **Athletics (Intercollegiate):** *Men:* baseball, basketball, cross-country, football, lacrosse, soccer, swimming, tennis, track/field (outdoor), track/field (indoor). *Women:* basketball, cross-country, field hockey, lacrosse, soccer, softball, swimming, tennis, track/field (outdoor), track/field (indoor), volleyball. **On-Campus Highlights:** Edward J. Pryzbyla University Center, Eugene I. Kane Fitness Center, St. Vincent de Paul Chapel, Raymond A. DuFour Athletic Center, John K. Mullen of Denver Memorial Library **Environmental Initiatives:** LEED-NC Certified, 402 Bed Student Dormitory LEED-Silver (anticipated) Administrative Building—major renovation

ADMISSIONS

Freshman Academic Profile: Average high school GPA 3.4. 44% from public high schools. **Test Scores:** SAT Math middle 50% range 550-650. SAT EBRW middle 50% range 570-670. ACT middle 50% range 23-29. Minimum internet-based TOEFL 80. Minimum paper TOEFL 550. **Basis for Candidate Selection:** *Very important factors considered include:* rigor of secondary school record, academic GPA, recommendation(s), character/personal qualities. *Important factors considered include:* application essay, extracurricular activities, first generation. *Other factors considered include:* class rank, standardized test scores, interview, talent/ability, alumni/ae relation, geographical residence, racial/ethnic status, volunteer work, work experience, level of applicant's interest. **Freshman Admission Requirements:** High school diploma is required and GED is accepted *Academic units recommended:*

4 English, 4 math, 3 science, 2 science labs, 3 foreign language, 4 social studies. **Freshman Admission Statistics:** 6,073 applied, 82.6% admitted, 17% enrolled. **Transfer Admission Requirements:** High school transcript, college transcript(s), essay or personal statement, standardized test scores, Minimum college GPA of 2.8 required. Lowest grade transferable C. **General Admission Information:** Application fee $55. Regular application deadline 1/15. Nonfall registration accepted. Admission may be deferred for a maximum of 1 year.

COSTS AND FINANCIAL AID
Annual tuition $43,300. Room and board $14,316. Required fees $760. Average book expense $838. **Required Forms and Deadlines:** CSS/Financial Aid PROFILE; FAFSA; Noncustodial PROFILE. **Notification of Awards:** Applicants will be notified of awards on a rolling basis beginning 3/20. **Types of Aid:** *Need-based scholarships/grants:* College/university scholarship or grant aid from institutional funds; Federal Pell; Private scholarships; SEOG; State scholarships/grants. *Loans:* Direct PLUS loans; Direct Subsidized Stafford Loans; Direct Unsubsidized Stafford Loans. *Student Employment:* Federal Work-Study Program available. Institutional employment available. **Financial Aid Statistics:** 98% needy freshmen, 98% needy undergrads receive need-based scholarship or grant aid. 0% undergrads receive non-need-based scholarship or grant aid. 83% freshmen, 86% undergrads receive need-based self-help aid. 0% freshmen, 0% undergrads receive athletic scholarships. 94% freshmen, 89% undergrads receive any aid. 70% undergrads borrow to pay for school. Average cumulative indebtedness $46,779. **Criteria for awarding aid:** *Need-based:* Academics *Non-need-based:* Academics, Alumni affiliation, Music/drama, Religious affiliation.

CAZENOVIA COLLEGE

22 Sullivan St., Cazenovia, NY 13035
Phone: 315-655-7208 · **Financial Aid Phone:** 315-655-7887
E-mail: admission@cazenovia.edu
Fax: 315-655-4860 · **Website:** www.cazenovia.edu

This private school was founded in 1824. It has a 20 acre campus.

RATINGS
Admissions Selectivity Rating: 74   **Fire Safety Rating:** 99   **Green Rating:** 60*

STUDENTS AND FACULTY
Enrollment: 1,067. **Student Body:** 72% female, 28% male, 15% out-of-state, 0% international (3 countries represented). Asian 1%, African American 7%, Caucasian 67%, Hispanic 6%, Native American 1%, Pacific Islander <1%, Two or more races 4%, Race unknown 14%.
Retention and Graduation: 73% freshmen return for sophomore year. 20% grads go on to further study within 1 year. **Faculty:** Student/faculty ratio 12:1. 57 full-time faculty, 77% hold PhDs, 68% are women. 0% of classes are taught by teaching assistants.

ACADEMICS
Degrees: Associate; Bachelor's; Certificate **Classes:** Most classes have 10-19 students. Most lab/discussion sessions have fewer than 10 students. **Most popular majors:** Interior Design; Fine/Studio Arts, General; Business Administration, Management And Operations, Other. **Special Study Options:** Double major; Dual enrollment; Honors program; Independent study; Internships; Liberal arts/career combination; Study abroad; Teacher certification program. **Honors programs:** The All-College Honors Program at Cazenovia College offers to outstanding students in all majors (in the liberal arts and in the professional studies) a stimulating learning environment beyond that found in standard classroom coursework, and fosters their exceptional academic talents and intellectual curiosity. Demanding curriculum, independent research opportunities and co-curricular activities challenge students to achieve their full educational potential not only through encouraging academic excellence but also through promoting social responsibilities in the global community. An honors degree certifies that students have produced academic work that meets the highest standards of academic rigor in both general education and in their career field. **Disability Services offered to physically disabled students:** Note-taking services; Reader services; Tape recorders; Tutors. **Career services:** Alumni network; Alumni services; Career assessment; Career/job search classes; Internships; Regional alumni

FACILITIES
Housing: Apartments for single students; Coed dorms; Men's dorms; Special housing for disabled student; Theme housing; Wellness housing; Women's dorms **Special Academic Facilities/Equipment:** Reisman Hall is a state-of-the-art Art and Design facility and gallery; 243-acre Equine Education Center; historic Catherine Cummings Theatre **Computers:** Administrative functions (other than registration) can be performed online.

CAMPUS LIFE
Environment: Village **Activities:** Campus Ministries; Choral groups; Dance; Drama/theater; International Student Organization; Musical theater; Radio station; Student government; Student newspaper; Yearbook 54 registered organizations, 5 honor societies, 1 religious organization. **Athletics (Intercollegiate):** *Men:* baseball, basketball, cheerleading, crew/rowing, cross-country, equestrian sports, golf, horseback riding, lacrosse, soccer, swimming. *Women:* basketball, cheerleading, crew/rowing, cross-country, equestrian sports, horseback riding, lacrosse, soccer, softball, swimming, volleyball. **On-Campus Highlights:** Residence Halls, Academic Facilities—Art and Design Building, Equestrian Center, Athletic Facilities / Pool, Dining Hall **Environmental Initiatives:** Environmental Studies education programs; Look Again program—sustainability in fashion

ADMISSIONS
Freshman Academic Profile: Average high school GPA 3.3. 14% in top 10% of high school class, 40% in top 25% of high school class, 78% in top 50% of high school class. 90% from public high schools. **Test Scores:** SAT Math middle 50% range 430-530. SAT EBRW middle 50% range 430-540. ACT middle 50% range 19-24. Minimum paper TOEFL 550. **Basis for Candidate Selection:** *Very important factors considered include:* rigor of secondary school record, talent/ability. *Important factors considered include:* class rank, academic GPA, standardized test scores, recommendation(s), interview, extracurricular activities. *Other factors considered include:* application essay, character/personal qualities, alumni/ae relation, volunteer work, work experience, level of applicant's interest. **Freshman Admission Requirements:** High school diploma is required and GED is accepted *Academic units recommended:* 4 English, 2 math, 2 science, 4 social studies. **Freshman Admission Statistics:** 2,382 applied, 76.2% admitted, 19% enrolled. **Transfer Admission Requirements:** High school transcript, college transcript(s), Minimum college GPA of 2.0 required. Lowest grade transferable C. **General Admission Information:** Application fee $30. Priority deadline 3/1. Nonfall registration accepted. Admission may be deferred for a maximum of 1 year.

COSTS AND FINANCIAL AID
Annual tuition $30,028. Room and board $11,880. Required fees $532. **Required Forms and Deadlines:** FAFSA; State aid form. **Notification of Awards:** Applicants will be notified of awards on a rolling basis beginning 11/1. **Types of Aid:** *Need-based scholarships/grants:* College/university scholarship or grant aid from institutional funds; Federal Pell; Private scholarships; SEOG; State scholarships/grants. *Loans:* Direct PLUS loans; Direct Subsidized Stafford Loans; Direct Unsubsidized Stafford Loans. *Student Employment:* Federal Work-Study Program available. **Financial Aid Statistics:** 100% needy freshmen, 96% needy undergrads receive need-based scholarship or grant aid. 9% freshmen, 12% undergrads receive non-need-based scholarship or grant aid. 100% freshmen, 96% undergrads receive need-based self-help aid. 0% freshmen, 0% undergrads receive athletic scholarships. 92% freshmen, 91% undergrads receive any aid. **Criteria for awarding aid:** *Need-based:* Academics, Leadership *Non-need-based:* Academics, Leadership.

CEDAR CREST COLLEGE

100 College Drive, Allentown, PA 18104
Financial Aid Phone: 610-606-4602
E-mail: admissions@cedarcrest.edu · **CEEB Code:** 2079
Website: http://www.cedarcrest.edu · **ACT Code:** 3536

This private school was founded in 1867. It has a 84 acre campus.

RATINGS
Admissions Selectivity Rating: 82   **Fire Safety Rating:** 85   **Green Rating:** 60*

STUDENTS AND FACULTY
Enrollment: 1,413. **Student Body:** 88% female, 12% male, 15% out-of-state, 9% international (26 countries represented). Asian 3%, African American 9%, Caucasian 59%, Hispanic 15%, Native American <1%, Pacific Islander <1%, Two or more races 1%, Race unknown 3%.
Retention and Graduation: 82% freshmen return for sophomore year. 38% freshmen graduate within 4 years. 50% freshmen graduate within 6 years. 65% grads go on to further study within 1 year. 55% grads pursue arts and sciences degrees. 1% grads pursue law degrees. 2% grads pursue business degrees. 3% grads pursue medical degrees. **Faculty:** Student/faculty ratio 10:1. 77 full-time faculty, 71% hold PhDs, 70% are women. 0% of classes are taught by teaching assistants.

ACADEMICS

Degrees: Bachelor's; Certificate; Master's; Post-Bachelor's certificate; Post-Master's certificate **Classes:** Most classes have 20-29 students. Most lab/discussion sessions have 10-19 students. **Most popular majors:** Foods, Nutrition, And Wellness Studies, General; Social Work; Registered Nursing/Registered Nurse. **Special Study Options:** Accelerated program; Cross-registration; Distance learning; Double major; Honors program; Independent study; Internships; Liberal arts/career combination; Student-designed major; Study abroad; Teacher certification program; Weekend college. **Honors programs:** Special courses reserved for Honors Students, undergraduate research opportunities, including Honors Thesis. **Disability Services offered to physically disabled students:** Note-taking services; Reader services; Tape recorders; Tutors. **Career services:** Alumni network; Alumni services; Career assessment; Career/job search classes; Internships; Regional alumni

FACILITIES

Housing: Theme housing; Women's dorms 90% of campus accessible to physically diasbled. **Special Academic Facilities/Equipment:** Alumnae Museum **Computers:** 75% of classrooms, 85% of dorms, 100% of libraries, 85% of dining areas, 85% of student union, 50% of common outdoor areas have wireless network access. Students can register for classes online. Administrative functions (other than registration) can be performed online.

CAMPUS LIFE

Environment: City **Activities:** Choral groups; Dance; Drama/theater; International Student Organization; Literary magazine; Musical theater; Radio station; Student government; Student newspaper 18 honor societies, 4 religious organizations. **Athletics (Intercollegiate):** *Women:* basketball, cross-country, field hockey, lacrosse, soccer, softball, tennis, volleyball. **On-Campus Highlights:** Bistro, College Center, Fitness Center, Rodale Aquatic Center, DaVinci Center **Environmental Initiatives:** Recycling: participating in national Recyclemania

ADMISSIONS

Freshman Academic Profile: Average high school GPA 3.4. 20% in top 10% of high school class, 44% in top 25% of high school class, 80% in top 50% of high school class. 84% from public high schools. **Test Scores:** SAT Math middle 50% range 460-570. SAT EBRW middle 50% range 480-600. ACT middle 50% range 19-26. Minimum internet-based TOEFL 61. Minimum paper TOEFL 500. **Basis for Candidate Selection:** *Very important factors considered include:* rigor of secondary school record, class rank, academic GPA, application essay, standardized test scores, recommendation(s). *Other factors considered include:* interview, extracurricular activities, alumni/ae relation, volunteer work, work experience, level of applicant's interest. **Freshman Admission Requirements:** High school diploma is required and GED is accepted *Academic units required:* 4 English, 3 math, 2 science, 2 science labs, 2 foreign language, 3 social studies, 3 history, 3 academic electives. **Freshman Admission Statistics:** 1,208 applied, 63.3% admitted, 28% enrolled. **Transfer Admission Requirements:** High school transcript, college transcript(s), Minimum college GPA of 2.00 required. Lowest grade transferable C. **General Admission Information:** Nonfall registration accepted.

COSTS AND FINANCIAL AID

Annual tuition $38,616. Room and board $11,544. Required fees $600. Average book expense $2,000. **Required Forms and Deadlines:** FAFSA. **Notification of Awards:** Applicants will be notified of awards on a rolling basis beginning 9/15. **Types of Aid:** *Need-based scholarships/grants:* College/university scholarship or grant aid from institutional funds; Federal Pell; Private scholarships; SEOG; State scholarships/grants. *Loans:* Direct PLUS loans; Direct Subsidized Stafford Loans; Direct Unsubsidized Stafford Loans. *Student Employment:* Federal Work-Study Program available. Institutional employment available. **Financial Aid Statistics:** 100% needy freshmen, 100% needy undergrads receive need-based scholarship or grant aid. 12% freshmen, 9% undergrads receive non-need-based scholarship or grant aid. 85% freshmen, 87% undergrads receive need-based self-help aid. 0% freshmen, 0% undergrads receive athletic scholarships. 97% freshmen, 99% undergrads receive any aid. 94% undergrads borrow to pay for school. Average cumulative indebtedness $38,726. **Criteria for awarding aid:** *Non-need-based:* Academics, Alumni affiliation, Art, Music/drama.

CEDARVILLE UNIVERSITY

251 N Main Street, Cedarville, OH 45314
Phone: 937-766-7700 • **Financial Aid Phone:** 937-766-7866
E-mail: admiss@cedarville.edu • **CEEB Code:** 1151
Fax: 937-766-7575 • **Website:** www.cedarville.edu • **ACT Code:** 3245

This private school, affiliated with the Baptist Church, was founded in 1887. It has a 441 acre campus.

RATINGS

Admissions Selectivity Rating: 85   **Fire Safety Rating:** 95   **Green Rating:** 61

STUDENTS AND FACULTY

Enrollment: 3,132. **Student Body:** 53% female, 47% male, 57% out-of-state, 2% international (39 countries represented). Asian 2%, African American 1%, Caucasian 87%, Hispanic 3%, Native American <1%, Pacific Islander 0%, Two or more races 3%, Race unknown 2%. **Retention and Graduation:** 84% freshmen return for sophomore year. 60% freshmen graduate within 4 years. 72% freshmen graduate within 6 years. 19% grads go on to further study within 1 year. 2% grads pursue arts and sciences degrees. 0.3% grads pursue law degrees. 0% grads pursue business degrees. 7.2% grads pursue medical degrees. **Faculty:** Student/faculty ratio 14:1. 182 full-time faculty, 73% hold PhDs, 8% are members of minority groups, 36% are women. 0% of classes are taught by teaching assistants.

ACADEMICS

Degrees: Bachelor's; Certificate; Doctoral/Professional; Master's; Post-Bachelor's certificate; Post-Master's certificate **Classes:** Most classes have 10-19 students. Most lab/discussion sessions have 10-19 students. **Most popular majors:** Early Childhood Education And Teaching; Mechanical Engineering; Registered Nursing/Registered Nurse. **Special Study Options:** Cooperative education program; Cross-registration; Distance learning; Double major; Dual enrollment; English as a Second Language (ESL); Honors program; Independent study; Internships; Liberal arts/career combination; Student-designed major; Study abroad; Teacher certification program. **Honors programs:** Cedarville University's honors programs offer a nationally recognized curriculum, a community of inquiring minds, seminars discussing classical and innovative knowledge, and one-on-one interaction with top professors. **Disability Services offered to physically disabled students:** Note-taking services; Reader services; Tape recorders; Tutors. **Career services:** Alumni network; Alumni services; Career assessment; Career/job search classes; Internships; Regional alumni

FACILITIES

Housing: Apartments for married students; Apartments for single students; Men's dorms; Women's dorms 85% of campus accessible to physically diasbled. **Special Academic Facilities/Equipment:** Centennial Library, Observatory, Engineering Projects Laboratory, Science/Nursing/Allied Health Labs, Apple Technology Center, Computer Labs, DeVries Theatre **Computers:** 100% of classrooms, 100% of dorms, 100% of libraries, 100% of dining areas, 100% of student union, 80% of common outdoor areas have wireless network access. Students can register for classes online. Administrative functions (other than registration) can be performed online.

CAMPUS LIFE

Environment: Rural **Activities:** Campus Ministries; Choral groups; Concert band; Dance; Drama/theater; International Student Organization; Jazz band; Model UN; Music ensembles; Musical theater; Pep band; Radio station; Student government; Student newspaper; Student-run film society; Symphony orchestra; Yearbook 74 registered organizations, 4 honor societies. **Athletics (Intercollegiate):** *Men:* baseball, basketball, cheerleading, cross-country, golf, soccer, tennis, track/field (outdoor), track/field (indoor). *Women:* basketball, cheerleading, cross-country, soccer, softball, tennis, track/field (outdoor), track/field (indoor), volleyball. **On-Campus Highlights:** Fitness and Recreation Center, Stingers/Rinnova—snack shop and coffee bar, Dixon Ministry Center—daily chapel and concerts, Chucks—student cafeteria (popular hangout), Center for Biblical and Theological Studies lobby

ADMISSIONS

Freshman Academic Profile: Average high school GPA 3.7. 33% in top 10% of high school class, 62% in top 25% of high school class, 88% in top 50% of high school class. 52% from public high schools. **Test Scores:** SAT Math middle 50% range 550-670. SAT EBRW middle 50% range 580-680. ACT middle 50% range 23-29. Minimum internet-based TOEFL 80. Minimum paper TOEFL 550. **Basis for Candidate Selection:** *Very important factors considered include:* rigor of secondary school record, academic GPA, standardized test scores, recommendation(s), character/personal qualities. *Important factors considered include:* class rank, application essay, alumni/ae relation, religious affiliation/commitment, racial/ethnic status, level of applicant's interest. *Other factors considered include:* extracurricular activities, talent/ability, first generation, geographical residence, state residency, volunteer work, work experience. **Freshman Admission Requirements:** High school diploma is required and GED is accepted *Academic units recommended:* 4 English, 3 math, 3 science, 2 science labs, 3 foreign language, 2 social studies, 2 history. **Freshman Admission Statistics:** 4,039 applied, 71.5% admitted, 30% enrolled. **Transfer Admission Requirements:** High school transcript, college transcript(s), essay or personal statement, statement of good standing from prior institution(s). Minimum college GPA of 3.0 required. Lowest grade transferable C-. **General Admission Information:** Application fee $30. Priority deadline 11/1. Regular application deadline 8/1. Nonfall registration accepted. Admission may be deferred for a maximum of 1 year.

COSTS AND FINANCIAL AID

Annual tuition $30,070. Room and board $7,360. Required fees $200. Average book expense $1,248. **Required Forms and Deadlines:** FAFSA. **Notification of Awards:** Applicants will be notified of awards on a rolling basis beginning 3/1. **Types of Aid:** *Need-based scholarships/grants:* College/university scholarship or grant aid from institutional funds; Federal Nursing Scholarships; Federal Pell; Private scholarships; SEOG; State scholarships/grants. *Loans:* Direct PLUS loans; Direct Subsidized Stafford Loans; Direct Unsubsidized Stafford Loans. *Student Employment:* Federal Work-Study Program available. Institutional employment available. **Financial Aid Statistics:** 86% needy freshmen, 85% needy undergrads receive need-based scholarship or grant aid. 94% freshmen, 91% undergrads receive non-need-based scholarship or grant aid. 86% freshmen, 89% undergrads receive need-based self-help aid. 7% freshmen, 7% undergrads receive athletic scholarships. 100% freshmen, 100% undergrads receive any aid. 61% undergrads borrow to pay for school. Average cumulative indebtedness $29,454. **Criteria for awarding aid:** *Need-based:* Academics *Non-need-based:* Academics, Athletics, Minority status, Music/drama.

CENTENARY COLLEGE

400 Jefferson Street, Hackettstown, NJ 07840
Phone: 800-236-8679 · **Financial Aid Phone:** (1800) 236-8679
E-mail: admissions@centenarycollege.edu · **CEEB Code:** 2080
Fax: 908-852-3454 · **Website:** www.centenarycollege.edu · **ACT Code:** 2544

This private school, affiliated with the Methodist Church, was founded in 1867. It has a 42 acre campus.

RATINGS

Admissions Selectivity Rating: 71   **Fire Safety Rating:** 60*   **Green Rating:** 60*

STUDENTS AND FACULTY

Enrollment: 1,708. **Student Body:** 60% female, 40% male, 20% out-of-state, 5% international (17 countries represented). Asian 1%, African American 10%, Caucasian 60%, Hispanic 9%, Native American 1%, Pacific Islander 0%, Two or more races 1%, Race unknown 13%.
Retention and Graduation: 71% freshmen return for sophomore year. 18% grads go on to further study within 1 year. 8% grads pursue arts and sciences degrees. 0% grads pursue law degrees. 8% grads pursue business degrees.
Faculty: Student/faculty ratio 17:1. 79 full-time faculty, 62% hold PhDs, 8% are members of minority groups, 54% are women. 0% of classes are taught by teaching assistants.

ACADEMICS

Degrees: Associate; Bachelor's; Master's; Post-Bachelor's certificate; Terminal Associate; Transfer Associate. **Classes:** Most classes have 10-19 students. **Most popular majors:** Elementary Education And Teaching; Criminal Justice/Police Science; Business Administration And Management, General. **Special Study Options:** Accelerated program; Cross-registration; Distance learning; Double major; Dual enrollment; English as a Second Language (ESL); Independent study; Internships; Liberal arts/career combination; Student-designed major; Study abroad; Teacher certification program; Weekend college. **Disability Services offered to physically disabled students:** Note-taking services; Reader services; Tutors. **Career services:** Alumni network; Alumni services; Career assessment; Career/job search classes; Internships; Regional alumni

FACILITIES

Housing: Apartments for single students; Coed dorms 70% of campus accessible to physically disabled. **Special Academic Facilities/Equipment:** Art gallery, radio station WNTI 91.9FM, equity-status theater, equestrian center. **Computers:** 100% of classrooms, 100% of dorms, 100% of libraries, 100% of dining areas, 100% of student union, 100% of common outdoor areas have wireless network access. Students can register for classes online.

Administrative functions (other than registration) can be performed online. Undergraduates are required to own a computer.

CAMPUS LIFE

Environment: Town **Activities:** Campus Ministries; Choral groups; Dance; Drama/theater; International Student Organization; Literary magazine; Model UN; Musical theater; Radio station; Student government; Student newspaper; Student-run film society; Television station; Yearbook 30 registered organizations, 2 honor societies, 2 fraternities, 3 sororities. **Athletics (Intercollegiate):** *Men:* baseball, basketball, cross-country, golf, lacrosse, soccer, wrestling. *Women:* basketball, cross-country, golf, lacrosse, soccer, softball, volleyball. **On-Campus Highlights:** David and Carol Lackland Center, Bennett Smith Dormitory, Reeves Athletic Facility

ADMISSIONS

Freshman Academic Profile: Average high school GPA 3.0. 11% in top 10% of high school class, 28% in top 25% of high school class, 55% in top 50% of high school class. 85% from public high schools. **Test Scores:** SAT Math middle 50% range 410-550. SAT EBRW middle 50% range 410-540. ACT middle 50% range 18-23. Minimum paper TOEFL 450. **Basis for Candidate Selection:** *Very important factors considered include:* rigor of secondary school record, academic GPA, standardized test scores. *Important factors considered include:* application essay, recommendation(s), interview, extracurricular activities. *Other factors considered include:* class rank, talent/ability, character/personal qualities, alumni/ae relation, religious affiliation/commitment, volunteer work, work experience, level of applicant's interest. **Freshman Admission Requirements:** High school diploma is required and GED is accepted *Academic units required:* 4 English, 3 math, 2 science, 1 science labs, *Academic units recommended:* 4 English, 4 math, 3 science, 1 science labs, 2 foreign language, 4 social studies. **Freshman Admission Statistics:** 1,038 applied, 90.9% admitted, 22% enrolled. **Transfer Admission Requirements:** High school transcript, college transcript(s), essay or personal statement, Minimum college GPA of 2.0 required. Lowest grade transferable C-. **General Admission Information:** Application fee $30. Priority deadline 3/1. Nonfall registration accepted. Admission may be deferred for a maximum of 1 semester.

COSTS AND FINANCIAL AID

Annual tuition $15,700. Room and board $6,850. Required fees $1,100. Average book expense $666. **Required Forms and Deadlines:** FAFSA. **Notification of Awards:** Applicants will be notified of awards on a rolling basis beginning 3/15. **Types of Aid:** *Need-based scholarships/grants:* College/university scholarship or grant aid from institutional funds; Federal Pell; Private scholarships; SEOG; State scholarships/grants. **Financial Aid Statistics:** 100% needy freshmen, 99% needy undergrads receive need-based scholarship or grant aid. 10% freshmen, 7% undergrads receive non-need-based scholarship or grant aid. 90% freshmen, 92% undergrads receive need-based self-help aid. 0% freshmen, 0% undergrads receive athletic scholarships. 98% freshmen receive any aid. **Criteria for awarding aid:** *Non-need-based:* Academics, Alumni affiliation, Art, Leadership, Minority status, Music/drama, Religious affiliation, State/district residency.

CENTENARY COLLEGE OF LOUISIANA

2911 Centenary Blvd, Shreveport, LA 71104
Phone: (318) 869-5131 · **Financial Aid Phone:** 318-869-5137
E-mail: admission@centenary.edu
Fax: 318-869-5005 · **Website:** https://www.centenary.edu/ · **ACT Code:** 1576

This private school, affiliated with the United Methodist Church, was founded in 1825. It has a 65 acre campus.

RATINGS

Admissions Selectivity Rating: 85   **Fire Safety Rating:** 78   **Green Rating:** 60*

STUDENTS AND FACULTY

Enrollment: 525. **Student Body:** 57% female, 43% male, 42% out-of-state, 2% international (6 countries represented). Asian 3%, African American 16%, Caucasian 63%, Hispanic 10%, Native American 1%, Pacific Islander <1%, Two or more races 5%, Race unknown 0%.
Retention and Graduation: 78% freshmen return for sophomore year. 48% freshmen graduate within 6 years. **Faculty:** Student/faculty ratio 9:1. 55 full-time faculty, 96% hold PhDs, 5% are members of minority groups, 38% are women. 0% of classes are taught by teaching assistants.

ACADEMICS

Degrees: Bachelor's; Master's **Classes:** Most classes have 10-19 students. Most lab/discussion sessions have 20-29 students. **Most popular majors:** Biology/Biological Sciences, General; Psychology, General; Business Administration And Management, General. **Special Study Options:** Double major; Exchange student program (domestic); Honors program; Independent study; Internships; Student-designed major; Study abroad; Teacher certification program. **Disability Services offered to physically disabled students:** Note-taking services; Reader services; Tape recorders; Tutors. **Career services:** Alumni services; Career assessment; Career/job search classes; Internships

FACILITIES

Housing: Coed dorms; Fraternity/sorority housing; Special housing for disabled students 95% of campus accessible to physically diasbled. **Special Academic Facilities/Equipment:** Meadows Art Museum, Leuck Arboretum, Marjorie Lyons Playhouse, School of Music recording studio, Science Hall multimedia auditorium **Computers:** 50% of classrooms, 25% of dorms, 50% of libraries, 100% of dining areas, 50% of student union, 10% of common outdoor areas have wireless network access. Students can register for classes online. Administrative functions (other than registration) can be performed online.

CAMPUS LIFE

Environment: Metropolis **Activities:** Campus Ministries; Choral groups; Dance; Drama/theater; International Student Organization; Literary magazine; Model UN; Music ensembles; Musical theater; Radio station; Student government; Student newspaper; Student-run film society; Symphony orchestra; Yearbook 58 registered organizations, 15 honor societies, 8 religious organizations. 5 fraternities, 2 sororities. **Athletics (Intercollegiate):** *Men:* baseball, basketball, cross-country, golf, soccer, swimming, tennis. *Women:* basketball, cross-country, golf, gymnastics, soccer, softball, swimming, tennis, volleyball. **On-Campus Highlights:** Meadows Museum of Art, Dr. Ed Leuck Louisiana Academic Arboretum, Shehee Baseball Stadium, Anderson Choral Building, Gold Dome Multisport and Entertainment Complex

ADMISSIONS

Freshman Academic Profile: Average high school GPA 3.6. **Test Scores:** SAT Math middle 50% range 510-610. SAT EBRW middle 50% range 520-600. ACT middle 50% range 22-28. Minimum internet-based TOEFL 79-80. Minimum paper TOEFL 550. **Basis for Candidate Selection:** *Very important factors considered include:* rigor of secondary school record, academic GPA, application essay, standardized test scores. *Important factors considered include:* class rank, extracurricular activities, volunteer work. *Other factors considered include:* recommendation(s), interview, talent/ability, character/personal qualities, alumni/ae relation, work experience. **Freshman Admission Requirements:** High school diploma is required and GED is accepted *Academic units recommended:* 4 English, 3 math, 3 science, 2 foreign language, 3 social studies. **Freshman Admission Statistics:** 848 applied, 61.8% admitted, 33% enrolled. **Transfer Admission Requirements:** High school transcript, college transcript(s), essay or personal statement, statement of good standing from prior institution(s). Minimum college GPA of 2.0 required. Lowest grade transferable C. **General Admission Information:** Priority deadline 2/15. Regular application deadline 8/1. Nonfall registration accepted. Admission may be deferred.

COSTS AND FINANCIAL AID

Annual tuition $36,580. Room and board $13,400. Average book expense $1,300. **Required Forms and Deadlines:** FAFSA. **Notification of Awards:** Applicants will be notified of awards on a rolling basis beginning 3/15. **Types of Aid:** *Need-based scholarships/grants:* College/university scholarship or grant aid from institutional funds; Federal Pell; SEOG; State scholarships/grants. *Loans:* Direct PLUS loans; Direct Subsidized Stafford Loans; Direct Unsubsidized Stafford Loans. *Student Employment:* Federal Work-Study Program available. Institutional employment available. **Financial Aid Statistics:** 100% needy freshmen, 100% needy undergrads receive need-based scholarship or grant aid. 70% freshmen, 74% undergrads receive non-need-based scholarship or grant aid. 63% freshmen, 71% undergrads receive need-based self-help aid. 0% freshmen, 0% undergrads receive athletic scholarships. 100% freshmen, 99% undergrads receive any aid. 68% undergrads borrow to pay for school. Average cumulative indebtedness $25,770. **Criteria for awarding aid:** *Non-need-based:* Academics, Alumni affiliation, Art, Music/drama, Religious affiliation, State/district residency.

812 University Street, Pella, IA 50219-1999
Phone: 641-628-5286 • **Financial Aid Phone:** 641-628-5336
E-mail: admission@central.edu • **CEEB Code:** 6087
Fax: 641-628-5983 • **Website:** www.central.edu • **ACT Code:** 1284

This private school, affiliated with the Reformed Church, was founded in 1853. It has a 169 acre campus.

RATINGS

Admissions Selectivity Rating: 80   **Fire Safety Rating:** 89   **Green Rating:** 60*

STUDENTS AND FACULTY

Enrollment: 1,225. **Student Body:** 52% female, 48% male, 21% out-of-state, <1% international (6 countries represented). Asian 1%, African American 2%, Caucasian 87%, Hispanic 4%, Native American <1%, Pacific Islander <1%, Two or more races 1%, Race unknown 3%.
Retention and Graduation: 78% freshmen return for sophomore year. 27% grads go on to further study within 1 year. 17% grads pursue arts and sciences degrees. 2% grads pursue law degrees. 2% grads pursue business degrees. 4% grads pursue medical degrees. **Faculty:** Student/faculty ratio 12:1. 100 full-time faculty, 88% hold PhDs, 12% are members of minority groups, 45% are women. 0% of classes are taught by teaching assistants.

ACADEMICS

Degrees: Bachelor's **Classes:** Most classes have 10-19 students. **Most popular majors:** Biology/Biological Sciences, General; Exercise Physiology; Business/Commerce, General. **Special Study Options:** Cooperative education program; Distance learning; Double major; Dual enrollment; Honors program; Independent study; Internships; Student-designed major; Study abroad; Teacher certification program. **Honors programs:** The Honors Program at Central College encourages student creativity, intellectual engagement and independent thinking. The program aims to be developmental: beginning with opportunities for broad exploration, the program helps students move toward greater independence, more advanced work in a discipline, and increased opportunities for personal initiative. The centerpiece of Honors at Central College is the Emerging Scholars Program, which culminates in a Senior Honors Thesis. **Disability Services offered to physically disabled students:** Note-taking services; Reader services; Tape recorders; Tutors. **Career services:** Alumni network; Alumni services; Career assessment; Career/job search classes; Internships; Regional alumni

FACILITIES

Housing: Coed dorms; Fraternity/sorority housing; Men's dorms; Special housing for disabled student; Theme housing; Women's dorms 95% of campus accessible to physically diasbled. **Special Academic Facilities/Equipment:** Two LEED rated academic buildings: Roe Center (platinum) and Vermeer Science Center (silver); Weller Center for Business; Geisler Library with cafe, Ron Schipper Fitness Center, Lubbers Center for the Visual Arts which includes a Glass-blowing studio (only one of two in the state of Iowa). **Computers:** Students can register for classes online. Administrative functions (other than registration) can be performed online.

CAMPUS LIFE

Environment: Village **Activities:** Campus Ministries; Choral groups; Concert band; Dance; Drama/theater; Jazz band; Literary magazine; Music ensembles; Pep band; Student government; Symphony orchestra 50 registered organizations, 4 religious organizations. 4 fraternities, 2 sororities. **Athletics (Intercollegiate):** *Men:* baseball, basketball, football, golf, soccer, tennis, track/field (outdoor), track/field (indoor), wrestling. *Women:* basketball, cross-country, golf, softball, tennis, track/field (outdoor), track/field (indoor), volleyball. Geisler Cafe, Kuyper Athletic Complex, Maytag Student Activity Center, Schipper Fitness Center, Central Market Cafeteria

ADMISSIONS

Freshman Academic Profile: Average high school GPA 3.6. 23% in top 10% of high school class, 54% in top 25% of high school class, 85% in top 50% of high school class. 95% from public high schools. **Test Scores:** SAT Math middle 50% range 470-600. SAT EBRW middle 50% range 410-560. ACT middle 50% range 20-26. Minimum internet-based TOEFL 71. Minimum paper TOEFL 530. **Basis for Candidate Selection:** *Very important factors considered include:* rigor of secondary school record, academic GPA, standardized test scores. *Important factors considered include:* class rank. *Other factors considered include:* application essay, recommendation(s), interview, extracurricular activities, talent/ability, character/personal qualities, first generation, alumni/ae relation, volunteer work, work experience, level of applicant's interest. **Freshman Admission Requirements:** High school diploma is required and GED is accepted *Academic units recommended:* 4

English, 2 math, 2 science, 2 science labs, 2 foreign language, 3 social studies. **Freshman Admission Statistics:** 3,071 applied, 64.3% admitted, 16% enrolled. **Transfer Admission Requirements:** High school transcript, college transcript(s), standardized test scores, statement of good standing from prior institution(s). Minimum college GPA of 2.5 required. Lowest grade transferable C-. **General Admission Information:** Application fee $25. Regular application deadline 8/15. Nonfall registration accepted. Admission may be deferred for a maximum of 1 year.

COSTS AND FINANCIAL AID

Required Forms and Deadlines: FAFSA. **Notification of Awards:** Applicants will be notified of awards on a rolling basis beginning 3/1. **Types of Aid:** *Need-based scholarships/grants:* College/university scholarship or grant aid from institutional funds; Federal Pell; Private scholarships; SEOG; State scholarships/grants. *Loans:* Direct PLUS loans; Direct Subsidized Stafford Loans; Direct Unsubsidized Stafford Loans. *Student Employment:* Federal Work-Study Program available. Institutional employment available. **Financial Aid Statistics:** 100% needy freshmen, 100% needy undergrads receive need-based scholarship or grant aid. 83% freshmen, 12% undergrads receive non-need-based scholarship or grant aid. 100% freshmen, 89% undergrads receive need-based self-help aid. 0% freshmen, 0% undergrads receive athletic scholarships. 100% freshmen, 99% undergrads receive any aid. 78% undergrads borrow to pay for school. Average cumulative indebtedness $37,169. **Criteria for awarding aid:** *Need-based:* Academics, Minority status, Music/drama *Non-need-based:* Academics, Alumni affiliation, Art, Minority status, Music/drama, Religious affiliation, State/district residency.

CENTRAL CONNECTICUT STATE UNIVERSITY

1615 Stanley Street, New Britain, CT 06050
Phone: 860-832-2278 · **Financial Aid Phone:** 860-832-2200
E-mail: admissions@ccsu.edu · **CEEB Code:** 3898
Fax: 862-832-2295 · **Website:** www.ccsu.edu · **ACT Code:** 596

This public school was founded in 1849. It has a 314 acre campus.

RATINGS

Admissions Selectivity Rating: 80 **Fire Safety Rating:** 93 **Green Rating:** 90

STUDENTS AND FACULTY

Enrollment: 9,317. **Student Body:** 47% female, 53% male, 3% out-of-state, 1% international (30 countries represented). Asian 4%, African American 13%, Caucasian 61%, Hispanic 15%, Native American <1%, Pacific Islander <1%, Two or more races 3%, Race unknown 3%.
Retention and Graduation: 76% freshmen return for sophomore year. 24% freshmen graduate within 4 years. 52% freshmen graduate within 6 years.
Faculty: Student/faculty ratio 16:1. 448 full-time faculty, 84% hold PhDs, 22% are members of minority groups, 44% are women. 0% of classes are taught by teaching assistants.

ACADEMICS

Degrees: Bachelor's; Certificate; Doctoral/Professional; Doctoral/Research; Master's; Post-Bachelor's certificate; Post-Master's certificate **Classes:** Most classes have 10-19 students. Most lab/discussion sessions have 10-19 students. **Most popular majors:** Psychology, General; Criminology; Accounting. **Special Study Options:** Cooperative education program; Cross-registration; Distance learning; Double major; Dual enrollment; English as a Second Language (ESL); Honors program; Independent study; Internships; Student-designed major; Study abroad; Teacher certification program. **Honors programs:** Interdisciplinary writing/reading program for undergraduates with strong academic skills. Areas of study: Western Culture, Science and Society, and World Culture, capstone honors thesis in junior year. Scholarship available. **Disability Services offered to physically disabled students:** Note-taking services; Reader services; Tape recorders; Tutors. **Career services:** Alumni services; Career assessment; Career/job search classes; Internships

FACILITIES

Housing: Coed dorms; Special housing for disabled student; Theme housing; Wellness housing; Women's dorms 95% of campus accessible to physically diasbled. **Special Academic Facilities/Equipment:** Art gallery, language lab, childhood center, planetarium and space science center, center for economic education, TV studio and a Fitness Studio. **Computers:** 50% of classrooms, 100% of libraries, 100% of dining areas, 100% of student union, 50% of common outdoor areas have wireless network access. Students can register for classes online. Administrative functions (other than registration) can be performed online.

CAMPUS LIFE

Environment: Town **Activities:** Campus Ministries; Choral groups; Concert band; Dance; Drama/theater; International Student Organization; Jazz band; Literary magazine; Music ensembles; Musical theater; Radio station; Student government; Student newspaper; Student-run film society; Television station 101 registered organizations, 18 honor societies, 5 religious organizations. 1 sororities. **Athletics (Intercollegiate):** *Men:* baseball, basketball, cross-country, football, golf, soccer, track/field (outdoor), track/field (indoor). *Women:* basketball, cross-country, diving, golf, lacrosse, soccer, softball, swimming, track/field (outdoor), track/field (indoor), volleyball. **On-Campus Highlights:** Student Center, Cafeteria, Memorial Hall, Torp Theatre, Davidson Hall, Vance Academic Center, Vance Hall, Mid-Campus Residence Hall **Environmental Initiatives:** Fuel cell Class schedule for carpool ease Building use in summer

ADMISSIONS

Freshman Academic Profile: Average high school GPA 3.1. 8% in top 10% of high school class, 26% in top 25% of high school class, 65% in top 50% of high school class. 95% from public high schools. **Test Scores:** SAT Math middle 50% range 480-570. SAT EBRW middle 50% range 500-590. ACT middle 50% range 19-24. Minimum paper TOEFL 500. **Basis for Candidate Selection:** *Very important factors considered include:* rigor of secondary school record, class rank, academic GPA, standardized test scores, recommendation(s). *Other factors considered include:* application essay, interview, extracurricular activities, talent/ability, first generation, alumni/ae relation, geographical residence, state residency, racial/ethnic status, level of applicant's interest. **Freshman Admission Requirements:** High school diploma is required and GED is accepted *Academic units required:* 4 English, 3 math, 2 science, 1 science labs, 2 social studies, 1 history, *Academic units recommended:* 3 foreign language. **Freshman Admission Statistics:** 7,870 applied, 66.8% admitted, 26% enrolled. **Transfer Admission Requirements:** High school transcript, college transcript(s), statement of good standing from prior institution(s). Minimum college GPA of 2.0 required. Lowest grade transferable C. **General Admission Information:** Application fee $50. Regular application deadline 5/1. Nonfall registration accepted.

COSTS AND FINANCIAL AID

Annual in-state tuition $11,816. Annual out-of-state tuition $16,882. Room and board $11,816. Required fees $4,801. Average book expense $1,150. **Required Forms and Deadlines:** FAFSA. **Notification of Awards:** Applicants will be notified of awards on a rolling basis beginning 10/31. **Types of Aid:** *Need-based scholarships/grants:* College/university scholarship or grant aid from institutional funds; Federal Pell; Private scholarships; SEOG; State scholarships/grants. *Loans:* Direct PLUS loans; Direct Subsidized Stafford Loans; Direct Unsubsidized Stafford Loans. *Student Employment:* Federal Work-Study Program available. Institutional employment available. **Financial Aid Statistics:** 75% needy freshmen, 65% needy undergrads receive need-based scholarship or grant aid. 14% freshmen, 15% undergrads receive non-need-based scholarship or grant aid. 74% freshmen, 78% undergrads receive need-based self-help aid. 2% freshmen, 4% undergrads receive athletic scholarships. 64% freshmen, 65% undergrads receive any aid. 74% undergrads borrow to pay for school. Average cumulative indebtedness $28,016. **Criteria for awarding aid:** *Non-need-based:* Academics, Alumni affiliation, Athletics.

See page 912.

CENTRAL MICHIGAN UNIVERSITY

102 Warriner Hall, Mount Pleasant, MI 48859
Phone: 989-774-3076 · **Financial Aid Phone:** 888-392-0007
E-mail: cmuadmit@cmich.edu · **CEEB Code:** 1106
Fax: 989-774-7267 · **Website:** www.cmich.edu · **ACT Code:** 1972

This public school was founded in 1892. It has a 854 acre campus.

RATINGS

Admissions Selectivity Rating: 77 **Fire Safety Rating:** 93 **Green Rating:** 88

STUDENTS AND FACULTY

Enrollment: 19,551. **Student Body:** 56% female, 44% male, 5% out-of-state, 2% international (44 countries represented). Asian 1%, African American 9%, Caucasian 78%, Hispanic 4%, Native American 1%, Pacific Islander <1%, Two or more races 4%, Race unknown 2%.
Retention and Graduation: 77% freshmen return for sophomore year. 16% grads go on to further study within 1 year. **Faculty:** Student/faculty ratio 22:1. 608 full-time faculty, 96% hold PhDs, 23% are members of minority groups, 42% are women.

ACADEMICS

Degrees: Bachelor's; Doctoral; Doctoral Other; Doctoral/Professional; Doctoral/Research; Master's; Post-Bachelor's certificate; Post-Master's certificate **Classes:** Most classes have 20-29 students. **Most popular majors:** Kinesiology And Exercise Science; Psychology, General; Marketing/ Marketing Management, General. **Special Study Options:** Accelerated program; Distance learning; Double major; Dual enrollment; English as a Second Language (ESL); Honors program; Independent study; Internships; Student-designed major; Study abroad; Teacher certification program. **Honors programs:** The Honors Program, Centralis Program **Combined degree programs:** BA/MA. **Disability Services offered to physically disabled students:** Note-taking services; Reader services; Tape recorders; Tutors. **Career services:** Alumni network; Alumni services; Career assessment; Career/job search classes; Internships; Regional alumni

FACILITIES

Housing: Apartments for married students; Apartments for single students; Coed dorms; Special housing for disabled student; Special housing for international students; Theme housing 99% of campus accessible to physically diasbled. **Special Academic Facilities/Equipment:** Clarke Historical Library, Central Michigan University Museum of Cultural and Natural History, Gerald L. Poor School Museum, Brooks Astronomical Observatory, University Art Gallery, University Theater, Public Broadcasting, Student Activity Center, Charles V. Park Library, body scanner **Computers:** 100% of classrooms, 100% of dorms, 100% of libraries, 100% of dining areas, 100% of student union, have wireless network access. Students can register for classes online. Administrative functions (other than registration) can be performed online.

CAMPUS LIFE

Environment: Town **Activities:** Choral groups; Concert band; Dance; Drama/ theater; International Student Organization; Jazz band; Literary magazine; Marching band; Model UN; Music ensembles; Musical theater; Opera; Pep band; Radio station; Student government; Student newspaper; Student-run film society; Symphony orchestra; Television station; Yearbook 150 registered organizations, 6 honor societies, 12 religious organizations. 15 fraternities, 15 sororities. **Athletics (Intercollegiate):** *Men:* baseball, basketball, cross-country, football, track/field (outdoor), track/field (indoor), wrestling. *Women:* basketball, cross-country, field hockey, gymnastics, soccer, softball, track/field (outdoor), track/field (indoor), volleyball. **On-Campus Highlights:** CMU Events Center (2010), Education Building (2009), Student Activity Center, Bovee University Center, Park Library **Environmental Initiatives:** Campus Sustainability Advisory Committee

ADMISSIONS

Freshman Academic Profile: Average high school GPA 3.4. 14% in top 10% of high school class, 39% in top 25% of high school class, 74% in top 50% of high school class. 92% from public high schools. **Test Scores:** SAT Math middle 50% range 440-570. SAT EBRW middle 50% range 450-570. ACT middle 50% range 20-25. **Basis for Candidate Selection:** *Very important factors considered include:* rigor of secondary school record, academic GPA, standardized test scores. *Important factors considered include:* class rank, talent/ ability. *Other factors considered include:* application essay, recommendation(s), interview, extracurricular activities, character/personal qualities, alumni/ ae relation, geographical residence, volunteer work, work experience, level of applicant's interest. **Freshman Admission Requirements:** High school diploma is required and GED is accepted *Academic units recommended:* 4 English, 4 math, 4 science, 1 science labs, 2 foreign language, 2 social studies, 2 history, 1 computer science, 2 visual/performing arts. **Freshman Admission Statistics:** 18,875 applied, 72.0% admitted, 25% enrolled. **Transfer Admission Requirements:** college transcript(s), statement of good standing from prior institution(s). Minimum college GPA of 2.00 required. Lowest grade transferable C-. **General Admission Information:** Application fee $35. Priority deadline 10/1. Regular application deadline 7/1. Nonfall registration accepted. Admission may be deferred for a maximum of 1 year.

COSTS AND FINANCIAL AID

Annual in-state tuition $9,406. Annual out-of-state tuition $23,670. Room and board $9,406. Average book expense $1,000. **Required Forms and Deadlines:** FAFSA. **Notification of Awards:** Applicants will be notified of awards on a rolling basis beginning 3/31. **Types of Aid:** *Need-based scholarships/grants:* College/university scholarship or grant aid from institutional funds; Federal Pell; Private scholarships; SEOG; State scholarships/ grants. *Loans:* Direct PLUS loans; Direct Subsidized Stafford Loans; Direct Unsubsidized Stafford Loans. *Student Employment:* Federal Work-Study Program available. Institutional employment available. **Financial Aid Statistics:** 88% needy freshmen, 77% needy undergrads receive need-based scholarship or grant aid. 10% freshmen, 6% undergrads receive non-need-based scholarship or grant aid. 76% freshmen, 85% undergrads receive need-based self-help aid. 1% freshmen, 1% undergrads receive athletic scholarships. 89% freshmen, 84% undergrads receive any aid. 70% undergrads borrow to pay for school. Average cumulative indebtedness $33,480. **Criteria for awarding aid:**

Need-based: Leadership *Non-need-based:* Academics, Alumni affiliation, Art, Athletics, Leadership, Minority status, Music/drama, State/district residency.

CENTRAL OHIO TECHNICAL COLLEGE

1179 University Drive, Newark, OH 43055
Phone: 740-366-9494
E-mail: cotcadmissions@cotc.edu
Fax: 740-366-9290 • **Website:** www.cotc.edu

This is a public school.

RATINGS
Admissions Selectivity Rating: 0   **Fire Safety Rating:** 60*   **Green Rating:** 60*

STUDENTS AND FACULTY
Enrollment: 3,513. **Student Body:** 71% female, 29% male, 1% out-of-state, 0% international. Asian 1%, African American 9%, Caucasian 82%, Hispanic 1%, Native American <1%, Pacific Islander <1%, Two or more races 2%, Race unknown 4%.
Faculty:

ACADEMICS
Degrees: Associate; Certificate **Classes:** Most classes have 10-19 students. **Special Study Options:** Cooperative education program; Distance learning; Double major; Dual enrollment; English as a Second Language (ESL); Internships; Weekend college.

FACILITIES
Housing: Apartments for single students

CAMPUS LIFE
Activities: Choral groups; Drama/theater; Music ensembles; Student government; Student newspaper.

ADMISSIONS
Freshman Admission Requirements: High school diploma is required and GED is accepted **General Admission Information:** Application fee $20. Nonfall registration accepted.

COSTS AND FINANCIAL AID
Annual out-of-state tuition $6,960. Average book expense $1,800.

CENTRAL STATE UNIVERSITY

PO Box 1004, Wilberforce, OH 45384
Phone: 937-376-6348
E-mail: admissions@centralstate.edu • **CEEB Code:** 1107
Fax: 937-376-6648 • **Website:** www.centralstate.edu • **ACT Code:** 3246

This public school was founded in 1887. It has a 60 acre campus.

RATINGS
Admissions Selectivity Rating: 82   **Fire Safety Rating:** 60*   **Green Rating:** 60*

STUDENTS AND FACULTY
Enrollment: 1,701. **Student Body:** 55% female, 45% male, 45% out-of-state, 1% international. Asian <1%, African American 94%, Caucasian 1%, Hispanic 1%, Native American <1%, Pacific Islander 0%, Two or more races 1%, Race unknown 2%.
Retention and Graduation: 40% freshmen return for sophomore year. 32% grads go on to further study within 1 year. 50% grads pursue arts and sciences degrees. 7% grads pursue law degrees. 29% grads pursue business degrees. **Faculty:** Student/faculty ratio 13:1. 97 full-time faculty, 74% hold PhDs, 78% are members of minority groups, 36% are women.

ACADEMICS
Degrees: Bachelor's; Master's **Classes:** Most classes have 20-29 students. Most lab/discussion sessions have 20-29 students. **Most popular majors:** Business/ Commerce, General. **Special Study Options:** Cooperative education program; Cross-registration; Distance learning; Double major; Honors program; Independent study; Internships; Study abroad; Teacher certification program; Weekend college. **Disability Services offered to physically disabled students:** Note-taking services; Reader services; Tape recorders; Tutors.

Career services: Alumni services; Career assessment; Career/job search classes; Internships; Regional alumni

FACILITIES

Housing: Coed dorms; Men's dorms; Women's dorms 1% of campus accessible to physically diasbled. **Special Academic Facilities/Equipment:** National Afro-American Museum and Cultural Center; CJ McLin International Center for Water Resources Management; Center for Integrated Manufacturing Protocols Architectures and Logistics Laboratory; Biology Technique Laboratory; Electrochemistry Research Laboratory; Cosby Mass Communication Center; Paul Robeson Cultural and Performing Arts Center **Computers:** Administrative functions (other than registration) can be performed online.

CAMPUS LIFE

Environment: Rural **Activities:** Campus Ministries; Choral groups; Concert band; Dance; Drama/theater; Jazz band; Marching band; Music ensembles; Pep band; Radio station; Student government; Student newspaper; Television station 30 registered organizations, 3 honor societies, 4 religious organizations. 1 fraternity, 3 sororities. **Athletics (Intercollegiate):** *Men:* basketball, cheerleading, cross-country, golf, track/field (outdoor). *Women:* basketball, cheerleading, cross-country, golf, track/field (outdoor), volleyball.

ADMISSIONS

Freshman Academic Profile: Average high school GPA 2.5. 5% in top 10% of high school class, 20% in top 25% of high school class, 49% in top 50% of high school class. **Test Scores:** SAT Math middle 50% range 340-430. SAT EBRW middle 50% range 340-430. ACT middle 50% range 15-18. Minimum paper TOEFL 500. **Basis for Candidate Selection:** *Very important factors considered include:* rigor of secondary school record, academic GPA, standardized test scores. *Important factors considered include:* class rank, application essay, character/personal qualities, geographical residence, state residency. *Other factors considered include:* recommendation(s), interview, extracurricular activities, talent/ability. **Freshman Admission Requirements:** High school diploma is required and GED is accepted *Academic units recommended:* 4 English, 3 math, 3 science, 2 foreign language, 3 social studies, 1 unit from above areas or other academic areas. **Freshman Admission Statistics:** 7,669 applied, 42.0% admitted, 20% enrolled. **Transfer Admission Requirements:** college transcript(s), statement of good standing from prior institution(s). Minimum college GPA of 2.0 required. Lowest grade transferable D. **General Admission Information:** Application fee $20. Nonfall registration accepted. Admission may be deferred.

COSTS AND FINANCIAL AID

Annual in-state tuition $9,934. Annual out-of-state tuition $5,776. Room and board $9,934. Required fees $2,320. Average book expense $1,200. **Required Forms and Deadlines:** FAFSA. **Notification of Awards:** Applicants will be notified of awards on a rolling basis beginning 4/15. **Types of Aid:** *Need-based scholarships/grants:* College/university scholarship or grant aid from institutional funds; Federal Pell; Private scholarships; SEOG; State scholarships/grants. *Loans:* Direct PLUS loans; Direct Subsidized Stafford Loans; Direct Unsubsidized Stafford Loans. *Student Employment:* Federal Work-Study Program available. Institutional employment available. **Financial Aid Statistics:** 100% needy freshmen, 100% needy undergrads receive need-based scholarship or grant aid. 0% undergrads receive non-need-based scholarship or grant aid. 0% freshmen, 0% undergrads receive need-based self-help aid. 0% freshmen, 0% undergrads receive athletic scholarships. **Criteria for awarding aid:** *Need-based:* Academics *Non-need-based:* Academics, Alumni affiliation, Art, Athletics, Leadership, Music/drama.

CENTRAL WASHINGTON UNIVERSITY

400 East University Way, Ellensburg, WA 98926-7463
Phone: 509-963-1211 · **Financial Aid Phone:** 509-963-1611
E-mail: cwuadmis@cwu.edu · **CEEB Code:** 4044
Fax: 509-963-3022 · **Website:** www.cwu.edu · **ACT Code:** 4444

This public school was founded in 1891. It has a 350 acre campus.

RATINGS

Admissions Selectivity Rating: 76   **Fire Safety Rating:** 76   **Green Rating:** 60*

STUDENTS AND FACULTY

Enrollment: 9,688. **Student Body:** 51% female, 49% male, 2% out-of-state, 2% international (60 countries represented). Asian 7%, African American 3%, Caucasian 75%, Hispanic 8%, Native American 3%, Race unknown 3%. **Retention and Graduation:** 75% freshmen return for sophomore year. **Faculty:** Student/faculty ratio 20:1. 432 full-time faculty, 12% are members of minority groups, 39% are women. 3% of classes are taught by teaching assistants.

ACADEMICS

Degrees: Bachelor's; Master's; Post-Bachelor's certificate **Classes:** Most classes have 10-19 students. Most lab/discussion sessions have 10-19 students. **Most popular majors:** Elementary Education And Teaching; Social Sciences, General; Business/Commerce, General. **Special Study Options:** Cooperative education program; Distance learning; Double major; Dual enrollment; English as a Second Language (ESL); Exchange student program (domestic); Honors program; Independent study; Internships; Liberal arts/career combination; Student-designed major; Study abroad; Teacher certification program. **Honors programs:** The Douglas Honors College student is expected to maintain a grade point average above 3.0. A student will be placed on probation if the grade point average falls below 3.0, and will be dismissed from the Douglas Honors College if the cumulative grade point average is below 3.0 for two consecutive quarters. This policy does not affect academic standing as a student of Central Washington University. **Disability Services offered to physically disabled students:** Note-taking services; Reader services; Tape recorders; Tutors. **Career services:** Alumni network; Alumni services; Career assessment; Career/job search classes; Internships; Regional alumni

FACILITIES

Housing: Apartments for married students; Apartments for single students; Coed dorms; Special housing for disabled student; Special housing for international students; Theme housing; Women's dorms 100% of campus accessible to physically diasbled. **Computers:** 100% of libraries, 100% of dining areas, 100% of student union, 100% of common outdoor areas have wireless network access. Students can register for classes online. Administrative functions (other than registration) can be performed online.

CAMPUS LIFE

Environment: Village **Activities:** Campus Ministries; Choral groups; Concert band; Dance; Drama/theater; International Student Organization; Jazz band; Literary magazine; Marching band; Music ensembles; Musical theater; Opera; Pep band; Radio station; Student government; Student newspaper; Student-run film society; Symphony orchestra; Television station 96 registered organizations, 3 honor societies, 9 religious organizations. **Athletics (Intercollegiate):** *Men:* baseball, basketball, cheerleading, cross-country, football, track/field (outdoor), track/field (indoor). *Women:* basketball, cheerleading, cross-country, soccer, softball, track/field (outdoor), track/field (indoor), volleyball. **On-Campus Highlights:** Award-winning Student Union Recreation Center, Japanese Garden, Nicholson Pavilion Athletic Facilities, Chimpanzee and Human Communication Institute, Performing Arts Center **Environmental Initiatives:** Carbon Reduction

ADMISSIONS

Freshman Academic Profile: Average high school GPA 3.2. 4% in top 10% of high school class, 23% in top 25% of high school class, 65% in top 50% of high school class. **Test Scores:** SAT Math middle 50% range 440-550. SAT EBRW middle 50% range 440-540. ACT middle 50% range 18-23. Minimum paper TOEFL 525. **Basis for Candidate Selection:** *Very important factors considered include:* rigor of secondary school record, academic GPA. *Important factors considered include:* application essay, standardized test scores. *Other factors considered include:* class rank, recommendation(s), interview, extracurricular activities, talent/ability, character/personal qualities, first generation, volunteer work, work experience, level of applicant's interest. **Freshman Admission Requirements:** High school diploma is required and GED is accepted *Academic units required:* 4 English, 3 math, 2 science, 1 science labs, 2 foreign language, 3 social studies, *Academic units recommended:* 4 English, 4 math, 3 science, 2 science labs, 2 foreign language, 3 social studies. **Freshman Admission Statistics:** 5,013 applied, 79.2% admitted, 40% enrolled. **Transfer Admission Requirements:** college transcript(s), statement of good standing from prior institution(s). Minimum college GPA of 2.5 required. Lowest grade transferable D-. **General Admission Information:** Application fee $55. Regular application deadline 4/1. Nonfall registration accepted.

COSTS AND FINANCIAL AID

Annual in-state tuition $8,052. Annual out-of-state tuition $14,013. Room and board $8,052. Required fees $882. Average book expense $924. **Required Forms and Deadlines:** FAFSA. **Notification of Awards:** Applicants will be notified of awards on a rolling basis beginning 4/15. **Types of Aid:** *Need-based scholarships/grants:* College/university scholarship or grant aid from institutional funds; Federal Pell; Private scholarships; SEOG; State scholarships/grants. *Loans:* Direct PLUS loans; Direct Subsidized Stafford Loans; Direct Unsubsidized Stafford Loans. **Financial Aid Statistics:** 68% freshmen, 68% undergrads receive any aid. **Criteria for awarding aid:** *Need-based:* Academics *Non-need-based:* Academics, Alumni affiliation, Art, Athletics, Job skills, Leadership, Minority status, Music/drama, Religious affiliation, State/district residency.

CENTRAL WYOMING COLLEGE

2660 Peck Avenue, Riverton, WY 82501
Phone: 307-855-2000 • **Financial Aid Phone:** 307-855-2150
E-mail: admit@cwc.edu • **CEEB Code:** 4115
Fax: 307-855-2065 • **Website:** www.cwc.edu • **ACT Code:** 514999

This public school was founded in 1966. It has a 200 acre campus.

RATINGS

Admissions Selectivity Rating: 72   Fire Safety Rating: 84   Green Rating: 60*

STUDENTS AND FACULTY

Enrollment: 1,045. **Student Body:** 60% female, 40% male, 13% out-of-state, <1% international (6 countries represented). Asian 1%, African American 2%, Caucasian 71%, Hispanic 10%, Native American 11%, Pacific Islander <1%, Two or more races 4%, Race unknown 1%.
Retention and Graduation: 52% freshmen return for sophomore year.
Faculty: Student/faculty ratio 12:1. 58 full-time faculty, 78% hold PhDs, 5% are members of minority groups, 55% are women. 0% of classes are taught by teaching assistants.

ACADEMICS

Degrees: Associate; Certificate; Diploma; Terminal Associate; Transfer Associate **Most popular majors:** General Studies; Parks, Recreation And Leisure Facilities Management, General. **Special Study Options:** Cooperative education program; Cross-registration; Distance learning; Double major; Dual enrollment; External degree program; Honors program; Independent study; Student-designed major; Teacher certification program. **Disability Services offered to physically disabled students:** Note-taking services; Reader services; Tape recorders; Tutors. **Career services:** Career assessment; Career/job search classes; Internships

FACILITIES

Housing: Apartments for married students; Apartments for single students; Coed dorms 100% of campus accessible to physically disabled. **Special Academic Facilities/Equipment:** Fine Arts Center, Microsoft training lab, Cisco training lab, Wyoming Public Television Station and Radio station, Stewart Collection (Native American Artifacts), Sinks Canyon Center, Rodeo Arena, Library, Arts Gallery. **Computers:** Students can register for classes online. Administrative functions (other than registration) can be performed online.

CAMPUS LIFE

Environment: Village **Activities:** Choral groups; Concert band; Dance; Drama/theater; International Student Organization; Jazz band; Music ensembles; Musical theater; Radio station; Student government; Television station 16 registered organizations, 2 honor societies, 2 religious organizations. **Athletics (Intercollegiate):** *Men:* basketball, rodeo. *Women:* basketball, rodeo, volleyball. **On-Campus Highlights:** Arts Center, Stewart Collection, Student Center, Food Court, The Underground

ADMISSIONS

Freshman Academic Profile: Average high school GPA 3.1. 5% in top 10% of high school class, 17% in top 25% of high school class, 45% in top 50% of high school class. 89% from public high schools. **Test Scores:** SAT Math middle 50% range 400-490. SAT EBRW middle 50% range 400-620. ACT middle 50% range 17-22. Minimum internet-based TOEFL 60. Minimum paper TOEFL 500. **Freshman Admission Requirements:** High school diploma or equivalent is not required **Freshman Admission Statistics:** 516 applied, 100.0% admitted, 53% enrolled. **General Admission Information:** Nonfall registration accepted. Admission may be deferred.

COSTS AND FINANCIAL AID

Annual out-of-state tuition $5,976. Required fees $720. Average book expense $1,200. **Required Forms and Deadlines:** FAFSA; Institution's own financial aid form. **Notification of Awards:** Applicants will be notified of awards on a rolling basis beginning 5/1. **Types of Aid:** *Need-based scholarships/grants:* College/university scholarship or grant aid from institutional funds; Federal Pell; Private scholarships; SEOG; State scholarships/grants. *Loans:* Direct PLUS loans; Direct Subsidized Stafford Loans; Direct Unsubsidized

Stafford Loans. *Student Employment:* Federal Work-Study Program available. Institutional employment available. **Financial Aid Statistics:** 77% needy freshmen, 75% needy undergrads receive need-based scholarship or grant aid. 89% freshmen, 84% undergrads receive non-need-based scholarship or grant aid. 37% freshmen, 42% undergrads receive need-based self-help aid. 0% freshmen, 0% undergrads receive athletic scholarships. 34% freshmen, 43% undergrads receive any aid. **Criteria for awarding aid:** *Non-need-based:* Academics, Alumni affiliation, Art, Athletics, Leadership, Minority status, Music/drama, State/district residency.

CENTRE COLLEGE

Best Colleges

600 West Walnut Street, Danville, KY 40422
Phone: 859-238-5350 • **Financial Aid Phone:** 800.423.6236
E-mail: admission@centre.edu • **CEEB Code:** 1109
Fax: 859-238-5373 • **Website:** www.centre.edu • **ACT Code:** 1506

This private school, affiliated with the Presbyterian Church, was founded in 1819. It has a 160 acre campus.

RATINGS

Admissions Selectivity Rating: 89   Fire Safety Rating: 84   Green Rating: 78

STUDENTS AND FACULTY

Enrollment: 1,441. **Student Body:** 51% female, 49% male, 44% out-of-state, 7% international (15 countries represented). Asian 5%, African American 5%, Caucasian 73%, Hispanic 5%, Native American <1%, Pacific Islander <1%, Two or more races 3%, Race unknown 1%.
Retention and Graduation: 91% freshmen return for sophomore year. 80% freshmen graduate within 4 years. 82% freshmen graduate within 6 years. 36% grads go on to further study within 1 year. 26% grads pursue arts and sciences degrees. 5% grads pursue law degrees. 3% grads pursue business degrees. 2% grads pursue medical degrees. **Faculty:** Student/faculty ratio 10:1. 129 full-time faculty, 98% hold PhDs, 10% are members of minority groups, 44% are women. 0% of classes are taught by teaching assistants.

ACADEMICS

Degrees: Bachelor's **Classes:** Most classes have fewer than 10 students. Most lab/discussion sessions have 20-29 students. **Most popular majors:** Biology/Biological Sciences, General; Economics, General; Economics, Other. **Special Study Options:** Cross-registration; Double major; Honors program; Independent study; Internships; Student-designed major; Study abroad.
Honors programs: In partnership with the James Graham Brown Foundation, Centre launched the Brown Fellows Program in 2009. The initiative is the premier scholarship and enrichment program in Kentucky and is one of the nation's elite fellowship programs. Centre is the only private college in Kentucky selected for a Brown Fellows Program. The foundation has also initiated a Brown Fellows Program at the University of Louisville. The program was established as an individualized course of development in which outstanding students build leadership skills through independent study, community service, and experiential learning. Brown Fellows are awarded "full-ride-plus" scholarships and are provided four summer enrichment experiences, beginning the summer before their first year at Centre. Summer enrichment experiences in subsequent years will be organized around themes of service, research, international study, and leadership. The scholarship and enrichment program includes: Full tuition Room and board Summer enrichment programs, which allow students to focus on their areas of interest On-campus program mentors Field-based experimental learning opportunities Customized Leadership Projects that span the student's collegiate career. **Disability Services offered to physically disabled students:** Note-taking services; Reader services; Tape recorders; Tutors. **Career services:** Alumni network; Alumni services; Career assessment; Career/job search classes; Internships; Regional alumni

FACILITIES

Housing: Apartments for single students; Coed dorms; Fraternity/sorority housing; Men's dorms; Special housing for disabled student; Theme housing; Women's dorms 80% of campus accessible to physically disabled. **Special Academic Facilities/Equipment:** Arts center, physical science and math facility, electron microscope, visible and infrared mass spectroscopy equipment, visual arts center. **Computers:** Administrative functions (other than registration) can be performed online.

CAMPUS LIFE

Environment: Village **Activities:** Campus Ministries; Choral groups; Concert band; Dance; Drama/theater; International Student Organization; Jazz band; Literary magazine; Music ensembles; Musical theater; Opera; Pep band; Student government; Student newspaper; Student-run film society; Symphony orchestra 70 registered organizations, 12 honor societies, 6 religious organizations. 4 fraternities, 4 sororities. **Athletics (Intercollegiate):** *Men:* baseball, basketball, cheerleading, cross-country, diving, football, golf, soccer, swimming, tennis, track/field (outdoor). *Women:* basketball, cheerleading, cross-country, diving, field hockey, golf, soccer, softball, swimming, tennis, track/field (outdoor), volleyball. **On-Campus Highlights:** Norton Center for the Arts, College Centre, athletic and library, The Campus Center, student center, Young Hall, science facility, Glass-blowing studio **Environmental Initiatives:** All new buildings and major renovations will be designed and built to conserve energy and enhance the human environment as evaluated by LEED silver standards or equivalent. Certification through U.S.G.B.C. will be pursued as appropriate.

ADMISSIONS

Freshman Academic Profile: Average high school GPA 3.6. 64% in top 10% of high school class, 86% in top 25% of high school class, 99% in top 50% of high school class. 66% from public high schools. **Test Scores:** SAT Math middle 50% range 580-730. SAT EBRW middle 50% range 590-680. ACT middle 50% range 26-31. Minimum internet-based TOEFL 90. Minimum paper TOEFL 580. **Basis for Candidate Selection:** *Very important factors considered include:* rigor of secondary school record, academic GPA. *Important factors considered include:* class rank, application essay, standardized test scores, recommendation(s). *Other factors considered include:* interview, extracurricular activities, talent/ability, character/personal qualities, first generation, alumni/ae relation, geographical residence, racial/ethnic status, volunteer work, work experience. **Freshman Admission Requirements:** High school diploma or equivalent is not required *Academic units required:* 4 English, 3 math, 2 science, 2 science labs, 2 foreign language, 2 history, *Academic units recommended:* 4 math, 4 science, 4 foreign language, 2 social studies, 2 history, 1 visual/performing arts. **Freshman Admission Statistics:** 2,454 applied, 76.3% admitted, 21% enrolled. **Transfer Admission Requirements:** High school transcript, college transcript(s), essay or personal statement, standardized test scores, statement of good standing from prior institution(s). Lowest grade transferable C. **General Admission Information:** Regular application deadline 1/15. Nonfall registration accepted. Admission may be deferred for a maximum of 1 year.

COSTS AND FINANCIAL AID

Annual tuition $41,700. Room and board $10,480. Average book expense $1,500. **Required Forms and Deadlines:** FAFSA; Institution's own financial aid form. **Notification of Awards:** Applicants will be notified of awards on or about 1/10. **Types of Aid:** *Need-based scholarships/grants:* College/university scholarship or grant aid from institutional funds; Federal Pell; Private scholarships; SEOG; State scholarships/grants. *Loans:* Direct PLUS loans; Direct Subsidized Stafford Loans; Direct Unsubsidized Stafford Loans. *Student Employment:* Federal Work-Study Program available. Institutional employment available. **Financial Aid Statistics:** 100% needy freshmen, 99% needy undergrads receive need-based scholarship or grant aid. 0% undergrads receive non-need-based scholarship or grant aid. 60% freshmen, 65% undergrads receive need-based self-help aid. 0% freshmen, 0% undergrads receive athletic scholarships. 97% freshmen, 96% undergrads receive any aid. 48% undergrads borrow to pay for school. Average cumulative indebtedness $26,740. **Criteria for awarding aid:** *Need-based:* Academics, Leadership *Non-need-based:* Academics, Alumni affiliation, Art, Leadership, Music/drama.

CHAMINADE UNIVERSITY OF HONOLULU

3140 Waialae Avenue, Honolulu, HI 96816-1578
Phone: 808-735-8340 · **Financial Aid Phone:** 808-735-4780
E-mail: admissions@chaminade.edu · **CEEB Code:** 4105
Fax: 808-739-4647 · **Website:** www.chaminade.edu · **ACT Code:** 898

This private school, affiliated with the Roman Catholic Church, was founded in 1955. It has a 65 acre campus.

RATINGS

Admissions Selectivity Rating: 73   **Fire Safety Rating:** 62   **Green Rating:** 60*

STUDENTS AND FACULTY

Enrollment: 1,150. **Student Body:** 71% female, 29% male, 29% out-of-state, 1% international (11 countries represented). Asian 37%, African American 3%, Caucasian 14%, Hispanic 4%, Native American <1%, Pacific Islander 26%, Two or more races 10%, Race unknown 4%.

Retention and Graduation: 77% freshmen return for sophomore year. 38% freshmen graduate within 4 years. 53% freshmen graduate within 6 years. **Faculty:** Student/faculty ratio 11:1. 91 full-time faculty, 31% are members of minority groups, 47% are women. 0% of classes are taught by teaching assistants.

ACADEMICS

Degrees: Associate; Bachelor's; Master's; Post-Bachelor's certificate; Post-Master's certificate **Classes:** Most classes have 10-19 students. Most lab/discussion sessions have 20-29 students. **Most popular majors:** Psychology, General; Criminal Justice/Safety Studies; Registered Nursing/Registered Nurse. **Special Study Options:** Accelerated program; Distance learning; Double major; Dual enrollment; Exchange student program (domestic); Independent study; Internships; Study abroad; Teacher certification program. **Disability Services offered to physically disabled students:** Note-taking services; Reader services; Tape recorders. **Career services:** Alumni network; Career assessment; Career/job search classes; Internships

FACILITIES

Housing: Apartments for single students; Coed dorms; Special housing for disabled student; Women's dorms 100% of campus accessible to physically diasbled. **Special Academic Facilities/Equipment:** Montessori lab school, observatory, black box theatre. **Computers:** Students can register for classes online. Administrative functions (other than registration) can be performed online.

CAMPUS LIFE

Environment: Metropolis **Activities:** Campus Ministries; Choral groups; Drama/theater; Musical theater; Radio station; Student government; Student newspaper 38 registered organizations, 7 honor societies, 1 religious organization. **Athletics (Intercollegiate):** *Men:* basketball, cross-country, golf, tennis, water polo. *Women:* cross-country, golf, softball, tennis, volleyball. **On-Campus Highlights:** Jean E. Rolles Sculoture Center, Henry Hall Courtyard Cafe, Brother's Brew Cafe, Weigand Observatory, Vi and Paul Loo Student Center

ADMISSIONS

Freshman Academic Profile: Average high school GPA 3.4. 19% in top 10% of high school class, 46% in top 25% of high school class, 81% in top 50% of high school class. **Test Scores:** SAT Math middle 50% range 480-580. SAT EBRW middle 50% range 490-600. ACT middle 50% range 19-23. Minimum internet-based TOEFL 79. Minimum paper TOEFL 550. **Basis for Candidate Selection:** *Very important factors considered include:* academic GPA, application essay, standardized test scores. *Important factors considered include:* rigor of secondary school record, recommendation(s). *Other factors considered include:* extracurricular activities, talent/ability, character/personal qualities, volunteer work, work experience. **Freshman Admission Requirements:** High school diploma is required and GED is accepted *Academic units required:* 4 English, 3 math, 2 science, 3 social studies, and 4 units from above areas or other academic areas. *Academic units recommended:* 4 math, 4 science. **Freshman Admission Statistics:** 742 applied, 90.8% admitted, 31% enrolled. **Transfer Admission Requirements:** college transcript(s), essay or personal statement, statement of good standing from prior institution(s). Minimum college GPA of 2.0 required. Lowest grade transferable C. **General Admission Information:** Application fee $50. Nonfall registration accepted. Admission may be deferred for a maximum of 1 year.

COSTS AND FINANCIAL AID

Average book expense $1,600. **Required Forms and Deadlines:** FAFSA. **Types of Aid:** *Need-based scholarships/grants:* College/university scholarship or grant aid from institutional funds; Federal Pell; Private scholarships; SEOG. *Loans:* Direct PLUS loans; Direct Subsidized Stafford Loans; Direct Unsubsidized Stafford Loans. *Student Employment:* Federal Work-Study Program available. Institutional employment available. **Financial Aid Statistics:** 98% needy freshmen, 93% needy undergrads receive need-based scholarship or grant aid. 99% freshmen, 97% undergrads receive non-need-based scholarship or grant aid. 86% freshmen, 87% undergrads receive need-based self-help aid. 4% freshmen, 4% undergrads receive athletic scholarships. 100% freshmen, 97% undergrads receive any aid. 64% undergrads borrow to pay for school. Average cumulative indebtedness $31,145. **Criteria for awarding aid:** *Need-based:* Academics *Non-need-based:* Academics, Athletics, Minority status, Religious affiliation, State/district residency.

CHAMPLAIN COLLEGE

PO Box 670, Burlington, VT 05402-0670
Phone: 802-860-2727 · **Financial Aid Phone:** 802-860-2730
E-mail: admission@champlain.edu · **CEEB Code:** 3291
Fax: 802-860-2767 · **Website:** www.champlain.edu/ · **ACT Code:** 3291

This private school was founded in 1878. It has a 22 acre campus.

RATINGS

Admissions Selectivity Rating: 81 · **Fire Safety Rating:** 98 **Green Rating:** 95

STUDENTS AND FACULTY

Enrollment: 2,216. **Student Body:** 37% female, 63% male, 79% out-of-state, 1% international (18 countries represented). Asian 3%, African American 2%, Caucasian 75%, Hispanic 6%, Native American <1%, Pacific Islander 0%, Two or more races 3%, Race unknown 10%.
Retention and Graduation: 79% freshmen return for sophomore year. 50% freshmen graduate within 4 years. 60% freshmen graduate within 6 years.
Faculty: Student/faculty ratio 14:1. 114 full-time faculty, 71% hold PhDs, 9% are members of minority groups, 41% are women. 0% of classes are taught by teaching assistants.

ACADEMICS

Degrees: Associate; Bachelor's; Master's; Post-Bachelor's certificate **Classes:** Most classes have 10-19 students. Most lab/discussion sessions have 10-19 students. **Most popular majors:** Computer And Information Sciences And Support Services; Visual And Performing Arts; Business, Management, Marketing, And Related Support Services. **Special Study Options:** Accelerated program; Cross-registration; Distance learning; Double major; Independent study; Internships; Liberal arts/career combination; Study abroad; Teacher certification program. **Combined degree programs:** BA/MA. **Disability Services offered to physically disabled students:** Note-taking services; Reader services; Tape recorders; Tutors. **Career services:** Alumni network; Alumni services; Career assessment; Career/job search classes; Internships

FACILITIES

Housing: Apartments for single students; Coed dorms; Special housing for disabled student; Special housing for international students; Women's dorms 79% of campus accessible to physically diasbled. **Special Academic Facilities/Equipment:** Emergent Media Center Miller Information Commons Global Business Center **Computers:** Students can register for classes online. Administrative functions (other than registration) can be performed online.

CAMPUS LIFE

Environment: Town **Activities:** Choral groups; Drama/theater; International Student Organization; Literary magazine; Musical theater; Radio station; Student government; Student newspaper 40 registered organizations, 2 honor societies, 1 religious organization. **On-Campus Highlights:** Sr. Leahy Center for Digital Forenics, Center for Communication and Creative Media, Student Life Center, Emergent Media Center & Maker Lab, Miller Information Commons **Environmental Initiatives:** Green Buildings (Master Plan)

ADMISSIONS

Freshman Academic Profile: Average high school GPA 3.2. 15% in top 10% of high school class, 42% in top 25% of high school class, 66% in top 50% of high school class. **Test Scores:** SAT Math middle 50% range 530-630. SAT EBRW middle 50% range 560-670. ACT middle 50% range 23-29. Minimum internet-based TOEFL 79. **Basis for Candidate Selection:** *Very important factors considered include:* rigor of secondary school record, academic GPA, talent/ability. *Important factors considered include:* application essay, standardized test scores, recommendation(s), extracurricular activities, character/personal qualities, first generation, racial/ethnic status, level of applicant's interest. *Other factors considered include:* class rank, alumni/ae relation, volunteer work, work experience. **Freshman Admission Requirements:** High school diploma is required and GED is accepted *Academic units required:* 4 English, 3 math, 3 science, 3 science labs, 2 foreign language, 4 history, 4 academic electives, *Academic units recommended:* 4 math, 4 science, 4 foreign language. **Freshman Admission Statistics:** 5,197 applied, 75.0% admitted, 15% enrolled. **Transfer Admission Requirements:** High school transcript, college transcript(s), essay or personal statement, Minimum college GPA of 2.0 required. Lowest grade transferable C. **General Admission Information:** Regular application deadline 1/15. Nonfall registration accepted. Admission may be deferred for a maximum of 1 year.

COSTS AND FINANCIAL AID

Annual tuition $40,910. Room and board $15,354. Required fees $100. Average book expense $1,000. **Required Forms and Deadlines:** FAFSA. **Notification of Awards:** Applicants will be notified of awards on a rolling basis beginning 3/1. **Types of Aid:** *Need-based scholarships/grants:* College/university scholarship or grant aid from institutional funds; Federal Pell; Private scholarships; SEOG; State scholarships/grants. *Loans:* Direct PLUS loans; Direct Subsidized Stafford Loans; Direct Unsubsidized Stafford Loans. *Student Employment:* Federal Work-Study Program available. Institutional employment available. **Financial Aid Statistics:** 99% needy freshmen, 98% needy undergrads receive need-based scholarship or grant aid. 11% freshmen, 10% undergrads receive non-need-based scholarship or grant aid. 86% freshmen, 84% undergrads receive need-based self-help aid. 0% freshmen, 0% undergrads receive athletic scholarships. 90% freshmen, 83% undergrads receive any aid. 73% undergrads borrow to pay for school. Average cumulative indebtedness $33,236. **Criteria for awarding aid:** *Need-based:* Academics, Leadership, Minority status *Non-need-based:* Academics, Alumni affiliation, Leadership, Minority status.

CHAPMAN UNIVERSITY

One University Drive, Orange, CA 92866
Phone: 714-997-6711 · **Financial Aid Phone:** 714-997-6741
E-mail: admit@chapman.edu · **CEEB Code:** 4047
Fax: 714-997-6713 · **Website:** www.chapman.edu · **ACT Code:** 210

This private school, affiliated with the Disciples of Christ Church, was founded in 1861. It has a 78 acre campus.

RATINGS

Admissions Selectivity Rating: 88 **Fire Safety Rating:** 86 **Green Rating:** 60*

STUDENTS AND FACULTY

Enrollment: 6,740. **Student Body:** 61% female, 39% male, 31% out-of-state, 4% international (57 countries represented). Asian 12%, African American 2%, Caucasian 55%, Hispanic 15%, Native American <1%, Pacific Islander <1%, Two or more races 7%, Race unknown 6%.
Retention and Graduation: 91% freshmen return for sophomore year. 69% freshmen graduate within 4 years. 79% freshmen graduate within 6 years.
Faculty: Student/faculty ratio 14:1. 489 full-time faculty, 84% hold PhDs, 42% are women. 1% of classes are taught by teaching assistants.

ACADEMICS

Degrees: Bachelor's; Doctoral/Professional; Doctoral/Research; Master's **Classes:** Most classes have 10-19 students. Most lab/discussion sessions have 10-19 students. **Most popular majors:** Public Relations/Image Management; Cinematography And Film/Video Production; Business Administration And Management, General. **Special Study Options:** Distance learning; Double major; Dual enrollment; Honors program; Independent study; Internships; Liberal arts/career combination; Student-designed major; Study abroad; Teacher certification program. **Honors programs:** University Honors Program **Combined degree programs:** BA/MA. **Disability Services offered to physically disabled students:** Note-taking services; Reader services; Tape recorders; Tutors. **Career services:** Alumni network; Alumni services; Career assessment; Career/job search classes; Internships

FACILITIES

Housing: Apartments for married students; Apartments for single students; Coed dorms; Special housing for disabled students **Special Academic Facilities/Equipment:** Anderson Center for Economic Research, Leatherby Center for Entrepreneurship and Business Ethics, Schmid Center for International Business, Law and organizational Economics Center, Center for Cold War Studies, Henley Social Science Research Laboratory, Guggenheim Art gallery, TV studio, film and television production and digital editing studios, Waltmer Theatre, Albert Schweitzer Collection **Computers:** 100% of classrooms, 100% of dorms, 100% of libraries, 100% of dining areas, 100% of common outdoor areas have wireless network access. Students can register for classes online. Administrative functions (other than registration) can be performed online.

CAMPUS LIFE

Environment: Metropolis **Activities:** Campus Ministries; Choral groups; Concert band; Dance; Drama/theater; International Student Organization; Jazz band; Literary magazine; Model UN; Music ensembles; Musical theater; Opera; Pep band; Radio station; Student government; Student newspaper; Student-run film society; Symphony orchestra; Yearbook 84 registered organizations, 8 honor societies, 8 religious organizations. 6 fraternities, 6 sororities. **Athletics (Intercollegiate):** *Men:* baseball, basketball, cross-country, football, golf, soccer, tennis, water polo. *Women:* basketball, crew/rowing, cross-country, soccer, softball, swimming, tennis, track/field (outdoor), volleyball, water polo. **On-Campus Highlights:** Marion Knott Film Studios, Leatherby Libraries, Liberty Plaza, Beckman Hall, All-Faiths Chapel **Environmental Initiatives:** Adoption of LEED standards in new building projects.

ADMISSIONS

Freshman Academic Profile: Average high school GPA 3.7. 37% in top 10% of high school class, 78% in top 25% of high school class, 95% in top 50% of high school class. **Test Scores:** SAT Math middle 50% range 590-680. SAT EBRW middle 50% range 600-680. ACT middle 50% range 25-30. Minimum internet-based TOEFL 80. Minimum paper TOEFL 550. **Basis for Candidate Selection:** *Very important factors considered include:* rigor of secondary school record, class rank, academic GPA, application essay, standardized test scores, character/personal qualities. *Important factors considered include:* extracurricular activities, talent/ability, volunteer work. *Other factors considered include:* recommendation(s), interview, first generation, alumni/ae relation, geographical residence, state residency, racial/ethnic status, work experience. **Freshman Admission Requirements:** High school diploma is required and GED is accepted *Academic units required:* 2 English, 2 math, 2 science, 1 science labs, 2 foreign language, 3 social studies, *Academic units recommended:* 4 English, 4 math, 4 science, 2 science labs, 4 foreign language, 4 social studies. **Freshman Admission Statistics:** 13,170 applied, 57.2% admitted, 22% enrolled. **Transfer Admission Requirements:** college transcript(s), essay or personal statement, Minimum college GPA of 2.5 required. Lowest grade transferable C-. **General Admission Information:** Application fee $70. Priority deadline 11/1. Regular application deadline 1/15. Nonfall registration accepted.

COSTS AND FINANCIAL AID

Annual tuition $52,340. Room and board $15,828. Required fees $384. Average book expense $1,560. **Required Forms and Deadlines:** FAFSA; State aid form. **Notification of Awards:** Applicants will be notified of awards on a rolling basis beginning 3/15. **Types of Aid:** *Need-based scholarships/grants:* College/university scholarship or grant aid from institutional funds; Federal Pell; Private scholarships; SEOG; State scholarships/grants. *Loans:* Direct PLUS loans; Direct Subsidized Stafford Loans; Direct Unsubsidized Stafford Loans. *Student Employment:* Federal Work-Study Program available. Institutional employment available. **Financial Aid Statistics:** 86% needy freshmen, 90% needy undergrads receive need-based scholarship or grant aid. 75% freshmen, 66% undergrads receive non-need-based scholarship or grant aid. 78% freshmen, 89% undergrads receive need-based self-help aid. 0% freshmen, 0% undergrads receive athletic scholarships. 54% undergrads borrow to pay for school. Average cumulative indebtedness $25,959. **Criteria for awarding aid:** *Non-need-based:* Academics, Alumni affiliation, Art, Music/drama, Religious affiliation.

CHARTER OAK STATE COLLEGE

55 Paul Manafort Drive, New Britain, CT 06053
Phone: 860-515-3701 • **Financial Aid Phone:** 860-515-3703
E-mail: admissions@charteroak.edu
Website: www.charteroak.edu

This public school was founded in 1973.

RATINGS

Admissions Selectivity Rating: 61   **Fire Safety Rating:** 60*   **Green Rating:** 60*

STUDENTS AND FACULTY

Enrollment: 1,352. **Student Body:** 68% female, 32% male, 19% out-of-state, 1% international. Asian 2%, African American 17%, Caucasian 56%, Hispanic 16%, Native American <1%, Pacific Islander 0%, Two or more races 3%, Race unknown 5%. **Faculty:** Student/faculty ratio 12:1.

ACADEMICS

Degrees: Associate; Bachelor's; Certificate; Master's **Classes:** Most classes have 10-19 students. Most lab/discussion sessions have 10-19 students. **Special Study Options:** Accelerated program; Distance learning; Double major; External degree program; Independent study; Liberal arts/career combination; Student-designed major.

FACILITIES

Housing: 100% of campus accessible to physically diasbled. **Computers:** Students can register for classes online. Administrative functions (other than registration) can be performed online.

CAMPUS LIFE

Environment: Town **Activities:** Student government.

ADMISSIONS

Freshman Admission Requirements: High school diploma or equivalent is not required **Transfer Admission Requirements:** college transcript(s), Lowest grade transferable D. **General Admission Information:** Application fee $75. Priority deadline 7/1. Nonfall registration accepted. Admission may be deferred for a maximum of One 8-week term.

COSTS AND FINANCIAL AID

Required Forms and Deadlines: FAFSA. **Types of Aid:** *Need-based scholarships/grants:* College/university scholarship or grant aid from institutional funds; Federal Pell; Private scholarships; SEOG; State scholarships/grants. *Loans:* Direct PLUS loans; Direct Subsidized Stafford Loans; Direct Unsubsidized Stafford Loans.

CHATHAM UNIVERSITY

Woodland Road, Pittsburgh, PA 15232
Phone: 412-365-1825 • **Financial Aid Phone:** 412-365-2797
E-mail: admission@chatham.edu • **CEEB Code:** 2081
Fax: 412-365-1609 • **Website:** www.chatham.edu • **ACT Code:** 3538

This private school was founded in 1869. It has a 427 acre campus.

RATINGS

Admissions Selectivity Rating: 86   **Fire Safety Rating:** 84   **Green Rating:** 99

STUDENTS AND FACULTY

Enrollment: 981. **Student Body:** 75% female, 25% male, 21% out-of-state, 3% international (18 countries represented). Asian 3%, African American 6%, Caucasian 77%, Hispanic 4%, Native American 1%, Pacific Islander <1%, Two or more races 2%, Race unknown 4%. **Retention and Graduation:** 85% freshmen return for sophomore year. 51% freshmen graduate within 4 years. 63% freshmen graduate within 6 years. 16% grads go on to further study within 1 year. 7% grads pursue arts and sciences degrees. 17% grads pursue medical degrees. **Faculty:** Student/faculty ratio 10:1. 120 full-time faculty, 92% hold PhDs, 9% are members of minority groups, 69% are women. 0% of classes are taught by teaching assistants.

ACADEMICS

Degrees: Bachelor's; Doctoral/Professional; Master's; Post-Bachelor's certificate **Classes:** Most classes have 10-19 students. Most lab/discussion sessions have 10-19 students. **Most popular majors:** Biology/Biological Sciences, General; Registered Nursing, Nursing Administration, Nursing Research And Clinical Nursing; Business Administration And Management, General. **Special Study Options:** Accelerated program; Cooperative education program; Cross-registration; Distance learning; Double major; Dual enrollment; English as a Second Language (ESL); Exchange student program (domestic); Honors program; Independent study; Internships; Liberal arts/career combination; Student-designed major; Study abroad; Teacher certification program. **Honors programs:** The Chatham Scholars Program offers students a challenging, integrated curriculum with special opportunities for enrichment, mentoring, and networking. **Combined degree programs:** BA/MA. **Disability Services offered to physically disabled students:** Note-taking services; Reader services; Tape recorders; Tutors. **Career services:** Alumni network; Alumni services; Career assessment; Career/job search classes; Internships; Regional alumni

FACILITIES

Housing: Apartments for married students; Coed dorms; Special housing for international students; Theme housing; Wellness housing; Women's dorms 75% of campus accessible to physically diasbled. **Special Academic Facilities/Equipment:** Athletic and Fitness Center; Art and Design Center; broadcast studio; art gallery, classroom space, and coffee shop; campus arboretum and greenhouse; proscenium theater. **Computers:** 100% of classrooms, 20% of dorms, 100% of libraries, 100% of dining areas, 100% of student union, 75% of common outdoor areas have wireless network access. Students can register for classes online. Administrative functions (other than registration) can be performed online. Undergraduates are required to own a computer.

CAMPUS LIFE

Environment: Metropolis **Activities:** Campus Ministries; Choral groups; Drama/theater; International Student Organization; Literary magazine; Musical theater; Student government; Student newspaper; Student-run film society; Symphony orchestra 25 registered organizations, 10 honor societies, 6 religious organizations. **Athletics (Intercollegiate):** *Women:* basketball, cross-country, ice hockey, soccer, softball, swimming, tennis, volleyball, water polo. **On-Campus Highlights:** Cafe Rachel coffee shop and art gallery, Athletic and Fitness Center, Art and Design Center, Science Complex, The Carriage House—new student center **Environmental Initiatives:** The creation of the Falk School of Sustainability and the Environment. The Falk School provides innovative, interdisciplinary education and research opportunities for undergraduate, graduate and professional students to better prepare them to identify and solve challenges related to the environment and sustainability. The school is located at Eden Hall Campus, on a 300-acre farm with forest. Phases 1A and B of the Master Plan are constructed, and our first group of residents is in place at Orchard Hall. The Eden Hall campus is designed to be a net-zero energy campus upon completion.

ADMISSIONS

Freshman Academic Profile: Average high school GPA 3.7. 26% in top 10% of high school class, 55% in top 25% of high school class, 88% in top 50% of high school class. **Test Scores:** SAT Math middle 50% range 510-600. SAT EBRW middle 50% range 540-640. ACT middle 50% range 22-27. Minimum internet-based TOEFL 60. Minimum paper TOEFL 500. **Basis for Candidate Selection:** *Very important factors considered include:* rigor of secondary school record. *Important factors considered include:* academic GPA, application essay. *Other factors considered include:* class rank, standardized test scores, recommendation(s), interview, extracurricular activities, talent/ability, character/personal qualities, alumni/ae relation, volunteer work, work experience, level of applicant's interest. **Freshman Admission Requirements:** High school diploma is required and GED is accepted *Academic units required:* 4 English, 2 math, 2 science, and 3 units from above areas or other academic areas. *Academic units recommended:* 4 English, 3 math, 3 science, 2 foreign language, 3 social studies. **Freshman Admission Statistics:** 2,231 applied, 54.5% admitted, 23% enrolled. **Transfer Admission Requirements:** college transcript(s), essay or personal statement, Minimum college GPA of 2.0 required. Lowest grade transferable C-. **General Admission Information:** Application fee $35. Priority deadline 3/15. Regular application deadline 8/1. Nonfall registration accepted. Admission may be deferred for a maximum of 1 year.

COSTS AND FINANCIAL AID

Room and board $11,042. Required fees $1,280. Average book expense $1,000. **Required Forms and Deadlines:** FAFSA. **Notification of Awards:** Applicants will be notified of awards on a rolling basis beginning 12/1. **Types of Aid:** *Need-based scholarships/grants:* College/university scholarship or grant aid from institutional funds; Federal Pell; Private scholarships; SEOG; State scholarships/grants. *Loans:* Direct PLUS loans; Direct Subsidized Stafford Loans; Direct Unsubsidized Stafford Loans. *Student Employment:* Federal Work-Study Program available. Institutional employment available. **Financial Aid Statistics:** 88% needy freshmen, 87% needy undergrads receive need-based scholarship or grant aid. 100% freshmen, 87% undergrads receive non-need-based scholarship or grant aid. 98% freshmen, 87% undergrads receive need-based self-help aid. 0% freshmen, 0% undergrads receive athletic scholarships. 100% freshmen, 95% undergrads receive any aid. 83% undergrads borrow to pay for school. Average cumulative indebtedness $37,734. **Criteria for awarding aid:** *Need-based:* Academics *Non-need-based:* Academics, Alumni affiliation, Art, Music/drama.

CHESTNUT HILL COLLEGE

9601 Germantown Avenue, Philadelphia, PA 19118-2693
Phone: 215-248-7001 · **Financial Aid Phone:** 215-248-7182
E-mail: chcapply@chc.edu · **CEEB Code:** 2082
Fax: 215-248-7082 · **Website:** www.chc.edu · **ACT Code:** 3540

This private school, affiliated with the Roman Catholic Church, was founded in 1924. It has a 75 acre campus.

RATINGS

Admissions Selectivity Rating: 71   **Fire Safety Rating:** 91   **Green Rating:** 60*

STUDENTS AND FACULTY

Enrollment: 1,354. **Student Body:** 63% female, 37% male, 22% out-of-state, 2% international (40 countries represented). Asian 2%, African American 35%, Caucasian 40%, Hispanic 9%, Native American <1%, Pacific Islander <1%, Two or more races 4%, Race unknown 8%.
Retention and Graduation: 79% freshmen return for sophomore year. 47% freshmen graduate within 4 years. 55% freshmen graduate within 6 years. 19% grads go on to further study within 1 year. 7% grads pursue arts and sciences degrees. 2% grads pursue law degrees. 4% grads pursue business degrees. 0% grads pursue medical degrees. **Faculty:** Student/faculty ratio 10:1. 82 full-time faculty, 83% hold PhDs, 10% are members of minority groups, 67% are women. 0% of classes are taught by teaching assistants.

ACADEMICS

Degrees: Associate; Bachelor's; Certificate; Doctoral/Professional; Master's; Post-Bachelor's certificate; Post-Master's certificate; Transfer Associate **Classes:** Most classes have 10-19 students. Most lab/discussion sessions have 10-19 students. **Most popular majors:** Elementary Education And Teaching; Criminal Justice/Law Enforcement Administration; Human Services, General. **Special Study Options:** Cross-registration; Distance learning; Double major; Dual enrollment; English as a Second Language (ESL); Exchange student program (domestic); Honors program; Independent study; Internships; Student-designed major; Study abroad; Teacher certification program. **Honors programs:** Interdisciplinary Honors Program for outstanding incoming first year students offers team-taught interdisciplinary seminars which emphasize discussion and writing and which satisfy general education requirements. Departmental Honors challenges students in the junior and senior year to complete an independent research project in their major field. **Combined degree programs:** BA/MA. **Disability Services offered to physically disabled students:** Note-taking services; Reader services; Tape recorders; Tutors. **Career services:** Alumni network; Career assessment; Career/job search classes; Internships

FACILITIES

Housing: Apartments for single students; Coed dorms 80% of campus accessible to physically disabled. **Special Academic Facilities/Equipment:** Rare book collection, Irish literature collection, Religion and Science book collection, observatory, planetarium. **Computers:** 40% of classrooms, 100% of dorms, 100% of libraries, have wireless network access. Students can register for classes online. Undergraduates are required to own a computer.

CAMPUS LIFE

Environment: Metropolis **Activities:** Campus Ministries; Choral groups; Concert band; Dance; Drama/theater; International Student Organization; Jazz band; Literary magazine; Music ensembles; Musical theater; Radio station; Student government; Student newspaper; Television station; Yearbook 19 registered organizations, 14 honor societies, 1 religious organization. **Athletics (Intercollegiate):** *Men:* baseball, basketball, cross-country, golf, lacrosse, soccer, tennis. *Women:* basketball, cross-country, golf, lacrosse, soccer, softball, tennis, volleyball. **On-Campus Highlights:** McCaffrey Lounge and Snack Bar, Fitness center, Griffin's Den (casual meals), Fitzsimmons Hall (residence hall), Rotunda of Saint Joseph Hall (five floors) **Environmental Initiatives:** Recycling program

ADMISSIONS

Freshman Academic Profile: Average high school GPA 3.2. 6% in top 10% of high school class, 21% in top 25% of high school class, 60% in top 50% of high school class. 60% from public high schools. **Test Scores:** SAT Math middle 50% range 480-560. SAT EBRW middle 50% range 480-590. ACT middle 50% range 20-23. Minimum internet-based TOEFL 79. Minimum paper TOEFL 550. **Basis for Candidate Selection:** *Very important factors considered include:* academic GPA, standardized test scores. *Important factors considered include:* character/personal qualities, geographical residence, state residency, volunteer work. *Other factors considered include:* rigor of secondary school record, class rank, application essay, recommendation(s), interview, extracurricular activities, talent/ability, first generation, alumni/ae relation, level of applicant's interest. **Freshman Admission Requirements:** High school diploma is required and GED is accepted *Academic units recommended:* 4 English, 3 math, 3 science, 2 foreign language, 4 social studies, 4 history. **Freshman Admission Statistics:** 1,286 applied, 95.7% admitted, 17% enrolled. **Transfer Admission Requirements:** college transcript(s), essay or personal statement, Minimum college GPA of 2.0 required. Lowest grade transferable C. **General Admission Information:** Application fee $35. Nonfall registration accepted. Admission may be deferred for a maximum of 1 year.

COSTS AND FINANCIAL AID

Annual tuition $35,950. Room and board $11,000. Required fees $230. Average book expense $1,298. **Required Forms and Deadlines:** FAFSA; Noncustodial PROFILE; State aid form. **Notification of Awards:** Applicants will be notified of awards on a rolling basis beginning 10/1. **Types of Aid:** *Need-based scholarships/grants:* College/university scholarship or grant aid from institutional funds; Federal Pell; Private scholarships; SEOG; State scholarships/grants. *Loans:* Direct PLUS loans; Direct Subsidized Stafford Loans; Direct Unsubsidized Stafford Loans. *Student Employment:* Federal Work-Study Program available. Institutional employment available. **Financial**

Aid Statistics: 100% needy freshmen, 96% needy undergrads receive need-based scholarship or grant aid. 8% freshmen, 5% undergrads receive non-need-based scholarship or grant aid. 92% freshmen, 94% undergrads receive need-based self-help aid. 7% freshmen, 6% undergrads receive athletic scholarships. 83% freshmen, 84% undergrads receive any aid. 87% undergrads borrow to pay for school. Average cumulative indebtedness $42,058. **Criteria for awarding aid:** *Non-need-based:* Academics, Alumni affiliation, Athletics, Leadership, Music/drama.

CHEYNEY UNIVERSITY OF PENNSYLVANIA

1837 University Circle, Cheyney, PA 19319
Phone: 610-399-2275 · **Financial Aid Phone:** (610) 399-2302
E-mail: abrown@cheyney.edu · **CEEB Code:** 2648
Fax: 610-399-2099 · **Website:** www.cheyney.edu

This public school was founded in 1837. It has a 275 acre campus.

RATINGS
Admissions Selectivity Rating: 82   **Fire Safety Rating:** 98   **Green Rating:** 60*

STUDENTS AND FACULTY
Enrollment: 1,339. **Student Body:** 53% female, 47% male, 22% out-of-state, <1% international (4 countries represented). Asian <1%, African American 92%, Caucasian 1%, Hispanic 1%, Native American <1%, Race unknown 6%. **Retention and Graduation:** 60% freshmen return for sophomore year. **Faculty:** Student/faculty ratio 15:1. 75 full-time faculty, 79% are members of minority groups, 48% are women. 0% of classes are taught by teaching assistants.

ACADEMICS
Degrees: Associate; Bachelor's; Master's; Post-Bachelor's certificate **Classes:** Most classes have 10-19 students. **Most popular majors:** Speech Communication And Rhetoric; Social Sciences, General; Business Administration And Management, General. **Special Study Options:** Cooperative education program; Cross-registration; Distance learning; Double major; Honors program; Independent study; Internships; Study abroad; Teacher certification program. **Honors programs:** Keystone Honors Program. **Disability Services offered to physically disabled students:** Note-taking services; Tape recorders; Tutors. **Career services:** Alumni services; Career/job search classes; Internships

FACILITIES
Housing: Coed dorms; Men's dorms; Women's dorms 60% of campus accessible to physically disabled. **Special Academic Facilities/Equipment:** Afro-American history/culture collection, planetarium, weather station, satellite communication network. **Computers:** 60% of classrooms, 100% of libraries, 100% of student union, 20% of common outdoor areas have wireless network access. Students can register for classes online. Administrative functions (other than registration) can be performed online.

CAMPUS LIFE
Environment: Village **Activities:** Choral groups; Drama/theater; Jazz band; Marching band; Music ensembles; Radio station; Student government; Student newspaper; Student-run film society; Television station; Yearbook 30 registered organizations, 12 honor societies, 1 religious organization. 5 fraternities, 4 sororities. **Athletics (Intercollegiate):** *Men:* basketball, cross-country, football, tennis, track/field (outdoor), wrestling. *Women:* basketball, bowling, cross-country, tennis, track/field (outdoor), volleyball. **On-Campus Highlights:** Athletics, Culinary Arts, Communication Arts, Dorms, Bookstore **Environmental Initiatives:** Recycling

ADMISSIONS
Freshman Academic Profile: Average high school GPA 2.4. 6% in top 10% of high school class, 15% in top 25% of high school class, 46% in top 50% of high school class. **Test Scores:** SAT Math middle 50% range 320-410. SAT EBRW middle 50% range 330-420. ACT middle 50% range 14-21. Minimum paper TOEFL 500. **Basis for Candidate Selection:** *Very important factors considered include:* rigor of secondary school record, recommendation(s). *Important factors considered include:* class rank, application essay, standardized test scores, interview, extracurricular activities, state residency. *Other factors considered include:* talent/ability, racial/ethnic status. **Freshman Admission Requirements:** High school diploma is required and GED is accepted *Academic units required:* 4 English, 3 math, 2 science, 2 foreign language, 2 history. **Freshman Admission Statistics:** 3,298 applied, 49.6% admitted, 37% enrolled. **Transfer Admission Requirements:** college transcript(s), interview, statement of good standing from prior institution(s). Minimum college GPA of

2.0 required. Lowest grade transferable C. **General Admission Information:** Application fee $20. Priority deadline 6/15. Regular application deadline 3/31. Nonfall registration accepted. Admission may be deferred for a maximum of 1 year.

COSTS AND FINANCIAL AID
Required Forms and Deadlines: FAFSA. **Notification of Awards:** Applicants will be notified of awards on a rolling basis beginning 3/15. **Types of Aid:** *Need-based scholarships/grants:* College/university scholarship or grant aid from institutional funds; Federal Pell; Private scholarships; SEOG; State scholarships/grants. *Loans: Student Employment:* Federal Work-Study Program available. Institutional employment available. **Financial Aid Statistics:** 82% needy freshmen, 94% needy undergrads receive need-based scholarship or grant aid. 32% freshmen, 39% undergrads receive non-need-based scholarship or grant aid. 84% freshmen, 99% undergrads receive need-based self-help aid. 0% freshmen, 0% undergrads receive athletic scholarships. **Criteria for awarding aid:** *Need-based:* Academics, Alumni affiliation, Athletics, Minority status *Non-need-based:* Academics, Alumni affiliation, Athletics, Minority status.

CHRISTENDOM COLLEGE

134 Christendom Drive, Front Royal, VA 22630
Phone: 540-636-2900 · **Financial Aid Phone:** 800-877-5456
E-mail: admissions@christendom.edu · **CEEB Code:** 5691
Fax: 540-636-1655 · **Website:** www.christendom.edu · **ACT Code:** 4339

This private school, affiliated with the Roman Catholic Church, was founded in 1977. It has a 200 acre campus.

RATINGS
Admissions Selectivity Rating: 79   **Fire Safety Rating:** 62   **Green Rating:** 60*

STUDENTS AND FACULTY
Enrollment: 477. **Student Body:** 57% female, 43% male, 75% out-of-state, (4 countries represented).
Retention and Graduation: 84% freshmen return for sophomore year. 25% grads go on to further study within 1 year. 15% grads pursue arts and sciences degrees. 5% grads pursue law degrees. 5% grads pursue business degrees. 0% grads pursue medical degrees. **Faculty:** Student/faculty ratio 14:1. 26 full-time faculty, 0% are members of minority groups, 12% are women. 0% of classes are taught by teaching assistants.

ACADEMICS
Degrees: Associate; Bachelor's; Master's **Classes:** Most classes have 20-29 students. **Most popular majors:** Philosophy; Political Science And Government, General; History, General. **Special Study Options:** Double major; Honors program; Independent study; Internships; Study abroad.

FACILITIES
Housing: Men's dorms; Women's dorms

CAMPUS LIFE
Environment: Rural **Activities:** Choral groups; Dance; Drama/theater; Literary magazine; Musical theater; Radio station; Student government; Student newspaper; Student-run film society; Yearbook 5 registered organizations, 4 religious organizations. **Athletics (Intercollegiate):** *Men:* baseball, basketball, soccer. *Women:* basketball, soccer, softball, volleyball. **On-Campus Highlights:** St. John the Evangelist Library, Chapel of Christ the King, Regina Coeli Building, John Paul II Student Center, Kilian's Cafe

ADMISSIONS
Freshman Academic Profile: Average high school GPA 3.5. 0% in top 50% of high school class. 8% from public high schools. **Test Scores:** SAT Math middle 50% range 510-620. SAT EBRW middle 50% range 550-700. ACT middle 50% range 23-31. Minimum paper TOEFL 550. **Basis for Candidate Selection:** *Very important factors considered include:* academic GPA, application essay, standardized test scores, recommendation(s), character/personal qualities, religious affiliation/commitment, level of applicant's interest. *Important factors considered include:* rigor of secondary school record. *Other factors considered include:* class rank, interview, extracurricular activities, talent/ability, first generation, alumni/ae relation, volunteer work, work experience. **Freshman Admission Requirements:** High school diploma or equivalent is not required *Academic units recommended:* 4 English, 2 math, 2 science, 2 foreign language, 1 social studies, 2 history, 1 academic elective. **Freshman Admission Statistics:** 323 applied, 87.0% admitted, 42% enrolled. **Transfer Admission Requirements:** college transcript(s), essay or personal statement, Minimum college GPA of 2.8 required. Lowest grade transferable C. **General Admission Information:** Application fee $25. Priority deadline 3/1. Nonfall registration accepted.

COSTS AND FINANCIAL AID

Annual tuition $24,710. Room and board $9,976. Required fees $870. Average book expense $450. **Required Forms and Deadlines:** Institution's own financial aid form. **Notification of Awards:** Applicants will be notified of awards on a rolling basis beginning 2/1. **Types of Aid:** *Need-based scholarships/ grants:* College/university scholarship or grant aid from institutional funds; Private scholarships. *Student Employment:* Institutional employment available. **Financial Aid Statistics:** 95% needy freshmen, 100% needy undergrads receive need-based scholarship or grant aid. 3% freshmen, 3% undergrads receive non-need-based scholarship or grant aid. 96% freshmen, 96% undergrads receive need-based self-help aid. 0% freshmen, 0% undergrads receive athletic scholarships. 80% freshmen, 65% undergrads receive any aid. 69% undergrads borrow to pay for school. Average cumulative indebtedness $27,005. **Criteria for awarding aid:** *Non-need-based:* Academics.

CHRISTIAN BROTHERS UNIVERSITY

650 East Parkway South, Memphis, TN 38104-5519
Phone: 901-321-3205 · **Financial Aid Phone:** 901-321-3306
E-mail: admissions@cbu.edu · **CEEB Code:** 1121
Fax: 901-321-3202 · **Website:** www.cbu.edu · **ACT Code:** 3952

This private school, affiliated with the Roman Catholic Church, was founded in 1871. It has a 75 acre campus.

RATINGS

Admissions Selectivity Rating: 87   **Fire Safety Rating:** 63   **Green Rating:** 71

STUDENTS AND FACULTY

Enrollment: 1,295. **Student Body:** 55% female, 45% male, 20% out-of-state, 3% international (22 countries represented). Asian 5%, African American 32%, Caucasian 45%, Hispanic 7%, Native American <1%, Pacific Islander <1%, Two or more races 2%, Race unknown 5%.
Retention and Graduation: 83% freshmen return for sophomore year. 23% grads go on to further study within 1 year. 5% grads pursue arts and sciences degrees. 4% grads pursue law degrees. 5% grads pursue business degrees. 6% grads pursue medical degrees. **Faculty:** Student/faculty ratio 10:1. 104 full-time faculty, 88% hold PhDs, 12% are members of minority groups, 38% are women. 0% of classes are taught by teaching assistants.

ACADEMICS

Degrees: Associate; Bachelor's; Master's; Post-Bachelor's certificate **Classes:** Most classes have 30-39 students. Most lab/discussion sessions have 10-19 students. **Most popular majors:** Biology/Biological Sciences, General; Psychology, General; Accounting And Related Services. **Special Study Options:** Accelerated program; Distance learning; Double major; Dual enrollment; Honors program; Independent study; Internships; Student-designed major; Study abroad; Teacher certification program. **Honors programs:** The Honors Program at Christian Brothers University is designed to serve the capacities and needs of students with proven academic abilities who seek a more intensive and challenging educational experience. Students accepted into the Honors Program will be allowed each semester to take at least one special-topics course offered only to a limited number of Honors students by an instructor carefully chosen for his or her teaching expertise. These Honors courses will explore important topics in depth, often through a multi-disciplinary approach, and while the pace and the workload will demand self-motivated students, the small size of each Honors class will insure ample group discussion and individual interaction with the instructor. Besides taking honors classes, members of the Honors Program will participate in various extra-curricular activities, including outings to cultural events and regional honors conferences. **Disability Services offered to physically disabled students:** Note-taking services; Reader services; Tape recorders; Tutors. **Career services:** Alumni network; Alumni services; Career assessment; Career/job search classes; Internships

FACILITIES

Housing: Apartments for single students; Coed dorms; Men's dorms; Theme housing; Women's dorms **Special Academic Facilities/Equipment:** Art exhibits and gallery, audiovisual lab, MAC graphics lab, engineering graphics lab, Facing History and Ourselves. **Computers:** 90% of classrooms, 100% of libraries, 100% of dining areas, 25% of common outdoor areas have wireless network access. Students can register for classes online. Administrative functions (other than registration) can be performed online.

CAMPUS LIFE

Environment: Metropolis **Activities:** Campus Ministries; Choral groups; Drama/theater; International Student Organization; Literary magazine;

Student government 37 registered organizations, 10 honor societies, 3 religious organizations. 5 fraternities, 6 sororities. **Athletics (Intercollegiate): Men:** baseball, basketball, cross-country, golf, soccer, tennis. *Women:* basketball, cross-country, golf, soccer, softball, tennis, volleyball. **On-Campus Highlights:** Thomas Center (cafeteria, snack bar), Canale Arena Gymnasium, Living Learning Center, Cooper-Wilson Center for Life Sciences, Ross Art Gallery in Plough Library **Environmental Initiatives:** Building a new "green" dorm that has 90+ beds

ADMISSIONS

Freshman Academic Profile: Average high school GPA 3.7. 28% in top 10% of high school class, 60% in top 25% of high school class, 93% in top 50% of high school class. 69% from public high schools. **Test Scores:** ACT middle 50% range 21-27. Minimum internet-based TOEFL 68. Minimum paper TOEFL 520. **Basis for Candidate Selection:** *Very important factors considered include:* rigor of secondary school record, academic GPA, standardized test scores. *Important factors considered include:* class rank, application essay, recommendation(s), interview, extracurricular activities, talent/ability, alumni/ae relation, volunteer work, work experience. **Freshman Admission Requirements:** High school diploma is required and GED is accepted *Academic units recommended:* 4 English, 4 math, 4 science. **Freshman Admission Statistics:** 2,229 applied, 49.7% admitted, 32% enrolled. **Transfer Admission Requirements:** college transcript(s), Minimum college GPA of 2.5 required. Lowest grade transferable C. **General Admission Information:** Application fee $25. Priority deadline 12/1. Nonfall registration accepted. Admission may be deferred for a maximum of 1 year.

COSTS AND FINANCIAL AID

Annual tuition $29,316. Room and board $7,000. Required fees $790. Average book expense $1,000. **Required Forms and Deadlines:** FAFSA. **Notification of Awards:** Applicants will be notified of awards on a rolling basis beginning 3/1. **Types of Aid:** *Need-based scholarships/grants:* College/ university scholarship or grant aid from institutional funds; Federal Pell; Private scholarships; SEOG; State scholarships/grants. *Loans:* Direct PLUS loans; Direct Subsidized Stafford Loans; Direct Unsubsidized Stafford Loans. *Student Employment:* Federal Work-Study Program available. Institutional employment available. **Financial Aid Statistics:** 100% needy freshmen, 98% needy undergrads receive need-based scholarship or grant aid. 17% freshmen, 15% undergrads receive non-need-based scholarship or grant aid. 70% freshmen, 75% undergrads receive need-based self-help aid. 17% freshmen, 11% undergrads receive athletic scholarships. **Criteria for awarding aid:** *Need-based:* Minority status *Non-need-based:* Academics, Alumni affiliation, Athletics, Leadership, Music/drama, State/district residency.

CHRISTOPHER NEWPORT UNIVERSITY

1 Avenue of the Arts, Newport News, VA 23606-3072
Phone: 757-594-7015 · **Financial Aid Phone:** 757-594-7170
E-mail: admit@cnu.edu · **CEEB Code:** 5128
Fax: 757-594-7333 · **Website:** www.cnu.edu · **ACT Code:** 4345

This public school was founded in 1960. It has a 260 acre campus.

RATINGS

Admissions Selectivity Rating: 83   **Fire Safety Rating:** 95   **Green Rating:** 60*

STUDENTS AND FACULTY

Enrollment: 4,950. **Student Body:** 56% female, 44% male, 8% out-of-state, <1% international (34 countries represented). Asian 3%, African American 7%, Caucasian 75%, Hispanic 5%, Native American <1%, Pacific Islander <1%, Two or more races 5%, Race unknown 4%.
Retention and Graduation: 88% freshmen return for sophomore year. 63% freshmen graduate within 4 years. 75% freshmen graduate within 6 years. 28% grads go on to further study within 1 year. 9% grads pursue arts and sciences degrees. 5.1% grads pursue law degrees. 8% grads pursue business degrees. 11.5% grads pursue medical degrees. **Faculty:** Student/faculty ratio 15:1. 279 full-time faculty, 91% hold PhDs, 13% are members of minority groups, 45% are women. 0% of classes are taught by teaching assistants.

ACADEMICS

Degrees: Bachelor's; Master's **Classes:** Most classes have 10-19 students. Most lab/discussion sessions have fewer than 10 students. **Most popular majors:** Speech Communication And Rhetoric; Biology/Biological Sciences, General; Psychology, General. **Special Study Options:** Cross-registration; Double major; Dual enrollment; Honors program; Independent study; Internships; Student-designed major; Study abroad; Teacher certification program. **Honors programs:** The CNU Honors Program invites high-ability students to fashion unique academic programs to prepare for post-graduate success. **Disability Services offered to physically disabled students:** Note-taking services; Tape recorders; Tutors. **Career services:** Alumni network; Alumni services; Career assessment; Career/job search classes; Internships; Regional alumni

FACILITIES

Housing: Apartments for single students; Coed dorms; Fraternity/sorority housing; Theme housing 96% of campus accessible to physically diasbled. **Special Academic Facilities/Equipment:** Falk Art Gallery, The Freeman Center, The Ferguson Center for the Arts, Trible Library. **Computers:** 10% of classrooms, 10% of dorms, 100% of libraries, 100% of dining areas, 100% of student union, 100% of common outdoor areas have wireless network access. Students can register for classes online. Administrative functions (other than registration) can be performed online.

CAMPUS LIFE

Environment: City **Activities:** Campus Ministries; Choral groups; Concert band; Dance; Drama/theater; International Student Organization; Jazz band; Literary magazine; Marching band; Model UN; Music ensembles; Musical theater; Opera; Pep band; Radio station; Student government; Student newspaper; Student-run film society; Symphony orchestra; Television station 139 registered organizations, 23 honor societies, 12 religious organizations. 7 fraternities, 7 sororities. **Athletics (Intercollegiate):** *Men:* baseball, basketball, cheerleading, cross-country, football, golf, lacrosse, sailing, soccer, tennis, track/field (outdoor), track/field (indoor). *Women:* basketball, cheerleading, cross-country, field hockey, lacrosse, sailing, soccer, softball, tennis, track/field (outdoor), track/field (indoor), volleyball. **On-Campus Highlights:** Trible Library, Ferguson Center for the Arts, David Student Union, Christopher Newport Hall, Freeman Center

ADMISSIONS

Freshman Academic Profile: Average high school GPA 3.8. 18% in top 10% of high school class, 50% in top 25% of high school class, 84% in top 50% of high school class. 80% from public high schools. **Test Scores:** SAT Math middle 50% range 550-640. SAT EBRW middle 50% range 580-660. ACT middle 50% range 23-29. Minimum internet-based TOEFL 71. Minimum paper TOEFL 530. **Basis for Candidate Selection:** *Very important factors considered include:* rigor of secondary school record, academic GPA. *Important factors considered include:* class rank, application essay, standardized test scores, recommendation(s), interview, extracurricular activities, talent/ability, character/personal qualities, level of applicant's interest. *Other factors considered include:* first generation, alumni/ae relation, geographical residence, state residency, volunteer work, work experience. **Freshman Admission Requirements:** High school diploma is required and GED is not accepted *Academic units required:* 4 English, 4 math, 4 science, 4 science labs, 3 foreign language, 4 social studies, 2 academic electives, 1 visual/performing arts, and 4 units from above areas or other academic areas. **Freshman Admission Statistics:** 6,948 applied, 72.4% admitted, 26% enrolled. **Transfer Admission Requirements:** High school transcript, college transcript(s), statement of good standing from prior institution(s). Minimum college GPA of 3.0 required. Lowest grade transferable C. **General Admission Information:** Application fee $65. Priority deadline 2/1. Regular application deadline 2/1. Nonfall registration accepted. Admission may be deferred for a maximum of 1 year.

COSTS AND FINANCIAL AID

Required Forms and Deadlines: FAFSA. **Notification of Awards:** Applicants will be notified of awards on a rolling basis beginning 3/1. **Types of Aid:** *Need-based scholarships/grants:* College/university scholarship or grant aid from institutional funds; Federal Pell; Private scholarships; SEOG; State scholarships/grants. *Loans:* Direct PLUS loans; Direct Subsidized Stafford Loans; Direct Unsubsidized Stafford Loans. *Student Employment:* Federal Work-Study Program available. Institutional employment available. **Financial Aid Statistics:** 66% needy freshmen, 65% needy undergrads receive need-based scholarship or grant aid. 49% freshmen, 33% undergrads receive non-need-based scholarship or grant aid. 74% freshmen, 83% undergrads receive need-based self-help aid. 0% freshmen, 0% undergrads receive athletic scholarships. 71% freshmen, 59% undergrads receive any aid. 60% undergrads borrow to pay for school. Average cumulative indebtedness $30,451. **Criteria for awarding aid:** *Need-based:* Academics, Leadership *Non-need-based:* Academics, Alumni affiliation, Art, Leadership, Music/drama, State/district residency.

See page 914.

THE CITADEL, THE MILITARY COLLEGE OF SOUTH CAROLINA

171 Moultrie Street, Charleston, SC 29409
Phone: 843-953-5230 • **Financial Aid Phone:** 843-953-5187
E-mail: admissions@citadel.edu • **CEEB Code:** 5108
Fax: 843-953-7036 • **Website:** www.citadel.edu • **ACT Code:** 3838

This public school was founded in 1842. It has a 300 acre campus.

RATINGS

Admissions Selectivity Rating: 76　　**Fire Safety Rating:** 97　　**Green Rating:** 70

STUDENTS AND FACULTY

Enrollment: 2,693. **Student Body:** 9% female, 91% male, 35% out-of-state, 1% international (8 countries represented). Asian 2%, African American 9%, Caucasian 76%, Hispanic 7%, Native American 1%, Pacific Islander <1%, Two or more races 4%, Race unknown <1%.
Retention and Graduation: 85% freshmen return for sophomore year. **Faculty:** Student/faculty ratio 12:1. 193 full-time faculty, 94% hold PhDs, 15% are members of minority groups, 35% are women. 0% of classes are taught by teaching assistants.

ACADEMICS

Degrees: Bachelor's; Master's; Post-Bachelor's certificate; Post-Master's certificate **Classes:** Most classes have 20-29 students. Most lab/discussion sessions have 20-29 students. **Most popular majors:** Criminal Justice/Law Enforcement Administration; Political Science And Government, General; Business Administration And Management, General. **Special Study Options:** Cooperative education program; Distance learning; Double major; English as a Second Language (ESL); Honors program; Independent study; Internships; Study abroad; Teacher certification program. **Honors programs:** The Citadel Honors Program is a specially designed educational experience meeting the needs of students with an outstanding record of academic achievement and a sense of intellectual adventure. While pursuing any one of the more than twenty-five degree programs offered by The Citadel, Honors Students take a series of Core Curriculum Honors courses—for example, studies based in literature and writing, history, and mathematics—concentrated in their first two years, and an occasional Honors Seminar in their third and fourth years. For the qualified student, advantages of the Honors Program are clear: special program of pre-professional counseling, small classes, discussion-style teaching, tutorial session, special curriculum, fellow honors students, student advisory committee, honors faculty, special diploma seal and transcript, and emphasis on leadership. **Disability Services offered to physically disabled students:** Note-taking services; Tape recorders. **Career services:** Alumni network; Alumni services; Career assessment; Career/job search classes; Internships

FACILITIES

Housing: Coed dorms **Computers:** 5% of classrooms, 20% of dorms, 100% of libraries, 75% of student union, 10% of common outdoor areas have wireless network access. Students can register for classes online. Administrative functions (other than registration) can be performed online.

CAMPUS LIFE

Environment: City **Activities:** Campus Ministries; Choral groups; Concert band; International Student Organization; Literary magazine; Marching band; Pep band; Student government; Student newspaper; Yearbook 79 registered organizations, 12 honor societies, 16 religious organizations. **Athletics (Intercollegiate):** *Men:* baseball, basketball, cross-country, football, riflery, tennis, track/field (outdoor), track/field (indoor), wrestling. *Women:* cross-country, golf, riflery, soccer, track/field (outdoor), track/field (indoor), volleyball. **On-Campus Highlights:** Summerall Chapel, Mark Clark Hall, Daniel Library, Citadel Museum, McAlister Field House **Environmental Initiatives:** $5 Million Energy Performance Contract

ADMISSIONS

Freshman Academic Profile: Average high school GPA 3.6. 9% in top 10% of high school class, 30% in top 25% of high school class, 65% in top 50% of high school class. **Test Scores:** SAT Math middle 50% range 480-580. SAT EBRW middle 50% range 470-580. ACT middle 50% range 20-25. Minimum internet-based TOEFL 79. Minimum paper TOEFL 550. **Basis for Candidate Selection:** *Very important factors considered include:* rigor of secondary school record, academic GPA, standardized test scores, level of applicant's interest. *Important factors considered include:* extracurricular activities, talent/ability, character/personal qualities, state residency. *Other factors considered include:* class rank, recommendation(s), interview, first generation, alumni/ae relation, geographical residence, volunteer work. **Freshman Admission Requirements:** High school diploma is required and GED is accepted *Academic units required:* 4 English, 4 math, 3 science, 3 science labs, 2 foreign language, 2 social studies, 1 history, 1 academic elective, 1 visual/performing arts, and 1 unit from above areas or other academic areas. **Freshman Admission Statistics:** 2,620 applied, 82.3% admitted, 34% enrolled. **Transfer Admission Requirements:** High school transcript, college transcript(s), standardized test scores, statement of good standing from prior institution(s). Minimum college GPA of 2.0 required. Lowest grade transferable C. **General Admission Information:** Application fee $40. Nonfall registration accepted.

COSTS AND FINANCIAL AID
Average book expense $7,700. **Required Forms and Deadlines:** FAFSA. **Notification of Awards:** Applicants will be notified of awards on a rolling basis beginning 4/1. **Types of Aid:** *Need-based scholarships/grants:* College/university scholarship or grant aid from institutional funds; Federal Pell; Private scholarships; SEOG; State scholarships/grants. *Loans:* Direct PLUS loans; Direct Subsidized Stafford Loans; Direct Unsubsidized Stafford Loans. *Student Employment:* Federal Work-Study Program available. Institutional employment available. **Financial Aid Statistics:** 79% needy freshmen, 79% needy undergrads receive need-based scholarship or grant aid. 16% freshmen, 19% undergrads receive non-need-based scholarship or grant aid. 77% freshmen, 76% undergrads receive need-based self-help aid. 8% freshmen, 10% undergrads receive athletic scholarships. 78% freshmen, 81% undergrads receive any aid. 59% undergrads borrow to pay for school. Average cumulative indebtedness $27,872. **Criteria for awarding aid:** *Need-based:* Academics, Alumni affiliation, Leadership, Minority status, Religious affiliation *Non-need-based:* Academics, Alumni affiliation, Athletics, Leadership, Minority status, Music/drama, Religious affiliation, State/district residency.

CITY UNIVERSITY OF NEW YORK— BARUCH COLLEGE

One Bernard Baruch Way, New York, NY 10010
Phone: 646-312-1400 · **Financial Aid Phone:** 646-312-1390
E-mail: admissions@baruch.cuny.edu · **CEEB Code:** 2034
Fax: 646-312-1361 · **Website:** www.baruch.cuny.edu

This public school was founded in 1909. It has a 3.5 acre campus.

RATINGS
Admissions Selectivity Rating: 92   **Fire Safety Rating:** 60*   **Green Rating:** 61

STUDENTS AND FACULTY
Enrollment: 14,903. **Student Body:** 49% female, 51% male, 3% out-of-state, 11% international (168 countries represented). Asian 31%, African American 9%, Caucasian 20%, Hispanic 26%, Native American <1%, Pacific Islander <1%, Two or more races 1%, Race unknown 0%.
Retention and Graduation: 90% freshmen return for sophomore year. 41% freshmen graduate within 4 years. 70% freshmen graduate within 6 years.
Faculty: Student/faculty ratio 18:1. 499 full-time faculty, 94% hold PhDs, 40% are women. 1% of classes are taught by teaching assistants.

ACADEMICS
Degrees: Bachelor's; Master's; Post-Master's certificate **Classes:** Most classes have 10-19 students. Most lab/discussion sessions have 10-19 students. **Most popular majors:** Accounting; Finance, General. **Special Study Options:** Accelerated program; Cross-registration; Distance learning; Double major; English as a Second Language (ESL); Exchange student program (domestic); Honors program; Independent study; Internships; Liberal arts/career combination; Student-designed major; Study abroad. **Honors programs:** Macaulay Honors College, Baruch Scholar Dean's Scholar **Combined degree programs:** BA/MA. **Disability Services offered to physically disabled students:** Note-taking services; Reader services; Tape recorders; Tutors. **Career services:** Alumni network; Alumni services; Career assessment; Career/job search classes; Internships

FACILITIES
Housing: Coed dorms 100% of campus accessible to physically diasbled. **Special Academic Facilities/Equipment:** Art gallery, Subotnik Financial Services Center and Wasserman Trading Floor **Computers:** 25% of classrooms, 100% of libraries, 100% of dining areas, 100% of student union, 100% of common outdoor areas have wireless network access. Students can register for classes online. Administrative functions (other than registration) can be performed online.

CAMPUS LIFE
Environment: Metropolis **Activities:** Campus Ministries; Choral groups; Dance; Drama/theater; Literary magazine; Model UN; Musical theater; Radio station; Student government; Student newspaper; Yearbook 172 registered organizations, 9 honor societies, 7 religious organizations. 9 fraternities, 7 sororities. **Athletics (Intercollegiate):** *Men:* baseball, basketball, cross-country, soccer, swimming, tennis, volleyball. *Women:* basketball, cheerleading, cross-country, softball, swimming, tennis, volleyball. **On-Campus Highlights:** Student Club Area- Vertical Campus Build, NewMan Library, Outdoor Plaza- 25th Street, Food Court- Vertical Campus Building, College Fitness Center- Vertical Campus

ADMISSIONS
Freshman Academic Profile: Average high school GPA 3.3. 48% in top 10% of high school class, 75% in top 25% of high school class, 92% in top 50% of high school class. 87% from public high schools. **Test Scores:** SAT Math middle 50% range 610-690. SAT EBRW middle 50% range 580-660. Minimum internet-based TOEFL 80. Minimum paper TOEFL 550. **Basis for Candidate Selection:** *Very important factors considered include:* rigor of secondary school record, academic GPA, standardized test scores. *Important factors considered include:* application essay, recommendation(s). *Other factors considered include:* interview, extracurricular activities, talent/ability, character/personal qualities, work experience. **Freshman Admission Requirements:** High school diploma is required and GED is accepted *Academic units required:* 4 English, 3 math, 2 science, 2 science labs, 2 foreign language, 4 social studies, *Academic units recommended:* 2 foreign language, 1 academic elective. **Freshman Admission Statistics:** 6,268 applied, 100.0% admitted, 26% enrolled. **Transfer Admission Requirements:** High school transcript, college transcript(s), statement of good standing from prior institution(s). Minimum college GPA of 2.7 required. Lowest grade transferable C. **General Admission Information:** Application fee $65. Priority deadline 12/1. Regular application deadline 2/1. Nonfall registration accepted. Admission may be deferred.

COSTS AND FINANCIAL AID
Annual out-of-state tuition $16,800. Required fees $531. Average book expense $1,364. **Required Forms and Deadlines:** FAFSA; State aid form. **Notification of Awards:** Applicants will be notified of awards on a rolling basis beginning 4/15. **Types of Aid:** *Need-based scholarships/grants:* College/university scholarship or grant aid from institutional funds; Federal Pell; Private scholarships; SEOG; State scholarships/grants. *Loans:* Direct PLUS loans; Direct Subsidized Stafford Loans; Direct Unsubsidized Stafford Loans. *Student Employment:* Federal Work-Study Program available. Institutional employment available. **Financial Aid Statistics:** 99% needy freshmen, 100% needy undergrads receive need-based scholarship or grant aid. 6% freshmen, 2% undergrads receive non-need-based scholarship or grant aid. 15% freshmen, 27% undergrads receive need-based self-help aid. 0% freshmen, 0% undergrads receive athletic scholarships. 67% freshmen, 53% undergrads receive any aid. 30% undergrads borrow to pay for school. Average cumulative indebtedness $7,915. **Criteria for awarding aid:** *Need-based:* Academics *Non-need-based:* Academics, State/district residency.

CITY UNIVERSITY OF NEW YORK— BROOKLYN COLLEGE

2900 Bedford Avenue, Brooklyn, NY 11210
Phone: 718-951-5001 · **Financial Aid Phone:** 718-951-51
Fax: 718-951-4506 · **Website:** www.brooklyn.cuny.edu · **ACT Code:** 20169

This public school was founded in 1930. It has a 35 acre campus.

RATINGS
Admissions Selectivity Rating: 88   **Fire Safety Rating:** 60*   **Green Rating:** 60*

STUDENTS AND FACULTY
Enrollment: 13,712. **Student Body:** 57% female, 43% male, 2% out-of-state, 3% international. Asian 20%, African American 21%, Caucasian 30%, Hispanic 23%, Native American <1%, Pacific Islander <1%, Two or more races 2%, Race unknown 0%.
Retention and Graduation: 82% freshmen return for sophomore year. 28% freshmen graduate within 4 years. 58% freshmen graduate within 6 years.
Faculty: Student/faculty ratio 17:1. 538 full-time faculty, 91% hold PhDs, 25% are members of minority groups, 47% are women.

ACADEMICS

Degrees: Bachelor's; Certificate; Master's; Post-Bachelor's certificate; Post-Master's certificate **Classes:** Most classes have 20-29 students. Most lab/discussion sessions have 20-29 students. **Most popular majors:** Computer And Information Sciences, General; Psychology, General; Accounting. **Special Study Options:** Accelerated program; Distance learning; Double major; Dual enrollment; English as a Second Language (ESL); Honors program; Independent study; Internships; Liberal arts/career combination; Study abroad; Teacher certification program; Weekend college. **Honors programs:** See the URL below for more information: http://www.brooklyn.cuny.edu/pub/1654.htm **Combined degree programs:** BA/MD. **Disability Services offered to physically disabled students:** Note-taking services; Reader services; Tutors. **Career services:** Alumni network; Alumni services; Career assessment; Career/job search classes; Internships

FACILITIES

Housing: 100% of campus accessible to physically disabled. **Special Academic Facilities/Equipment:** Art museum. language lab, TV studios, speech clinic, research centers and institutes, particle accelerator, physical education and exercise labs, archeology labs, aquatic research center, theaters, music and art studios. **Computers:** 2% of classrooms, 90% of libraries, 100% of dining areas, 75% of student union, 75% of common outdoor areas have wireless network access. Students can register for classes online. Administrative functions (other than registration) can be performed online.

CAMPUS LIFE

Environment: Metropolis **Activities:** Dance; Drama/theater; International Student Organization; Literary magazine; Music ensembles; Musical theater; Radio station; Student government; Student newspaper; Student-run film society; Symphony orchestra; Television station; Yearbook 171 registered organizations, 7 honor societies, 7 fraternities, 9 sororities. **Athletics (Intercollegiate):** *Men:* basketball, cross-country, soccer, tennis, track/field (outdoor), track/field (indoor), volleyball. *Women:* basketball, cross-country, softball, tennis, track/field (outdoor), track/field (indoor), volleyball. **On-Campus Highlights:** Library, Student Center, Lily Pond, Library Cafe, Cafeteria, Dining Hall **Environmental Initiatives:** Reduce material consumption/waste

ADMISSIONS

Freshman Academic Profile: Average high school GPA 3.3. **Test Scores:** SAT Math middle 50% range 520-600. SAT EBRW middle 50% range 510-590. Minimum paper TOEFL 500. **Basis for Candidate Selection:** *Very important factors considered include:* rigor of secondary school record, academic GPA, standardized test scores. **Freshman Admission Requirements:** High school diploma is required and GED is accepted *Academic units recommended:* 4 English, 3 math, 3 science, 3 foreign language, 4 social studies, 4 academic electives. **Freshman Admission Statistics:** 20,642 applied, 40.4% admitted, 20% enrolled. **Transfer Admission Requirements:** college transcript(s), Minimum college GPA of 2.3 required. Lowest grade transferable C-. **General Admission Information:** Application fee $65. Priority deadline 2/1. Nonfall registration accepted.

COSTS AND FINANCIAL AID

Annual out-of-state tuition $17,400. Required fees $510. **Required Forms and Deadlines:** FAFSA; State aid form. **Notification of Awards:** Applicants will be notified of awards on a rolling basis beginning 5/1. **Types of Aid:** *Need-based scholarships/grants:* College/university scholarship or grant aid from institutional funds; Federal Pell; Private scholarships; SEOG; State scholarships/grants. *Loans:* Direct PLUS loans; Direct Subsidized Stafford Loans; Direct Unsubsidized Stafford Loans. *Student Employment:* Federal Work-Study Program available. Institutional employment available. **Financial Aid Statistics:** 64% needy freshmen, 82% needy undergrads receive need-based scholarship or grant aid. 26% freshmen, 27% undergrads receive non-need-based scholarship or grant aid. 77% freshmen, 89% undergrads receive need-based self-help aid. 0% freshmen, 0% undergrads receive athletic scholarships. **Criteria for awarding aid:** *Non-need-based:* Academics, Art, Leadership, Music/drama, State/district residency.

CITY UNIVERSITY OF NEW YORK— CITY COLLEGE

160 Convent Avenue, New York, NY 10031
Phone: 212 650 6977 · **Financial Aid Phone:** 212 650 5824
E-mail: admissions@ccny.cuny.edu · **CEEB Code:** 2083
Fax: 212 650 6417 · **Website:** www.ccny.cuny.edu · **ACT Code:** 2950

This public school was founded in 1847. It has a 36 acre campus.

RATINGS
Admissions Selectivity Rating: 88   **Fire Safety Rating:** 97   **Green Rating:** 95

STUDENTS AND FACULTY

Enrollment: 12,480. **Student Body:** 51% female, 49% male, 1% out-of-state, 6% international (155 countries represented). Asian 25%, African American 16%, Caucasian 16%, Hispanic 37%, Native American <1%, Pacific Islander <1%, Two or more races 2%, Race unknown 0%. **Retention and Graduation:** 92% freshmen return for sophomore year. 12% freshmen graduate within 4 years. 50% freshmen graduate within 6 years. 18% grads go on to further study within 1 year. 1.3% grads pursue law degrees. 2% grads pursue business degrees. 26.5% grads pursue medical degrees. **Faculty:** Student/faculty ratio 15:1. 504 full-time faculty, 80% hold PhDs, 14% are members of minority groups, 62% are women.

ACADEMICS

Degrees: Bachelor's; Doctoral/Professional; Doctoral/Research; Master's; Post-Master's certificate **Classes:** Most classes have fewer than 10 students. Most lab/discussion sessions have 10-19 students. **Most popular majors:** Communication And Media Studies, Other; Mechanical Engineering/Mechanical Technology/Technician; Psychology, General. **Special Study Options:** Accelerated program; Cross-registration; Double major; English as a Second Language (ESL); Honors program; Independent study; Internships; Study abroad; Teacher certification program. **Honors programs:** CUNY Macauley College and City College Honors Program. **Combined degree programs:** BA/MA; BA/MD. **Disability Services offered to physically disabled students:** Note-taking services; Reader services; Tape recorders; Tutors. **Career services:** Alumni network; Alumni services; Career assessment; Career/job search classes; Internships

FACILITIES

Special Academic Facilities/Equipment: Planetarium, NYC Structural Biological Center, Aaron Davis Hall/Harlem Stage Gatehouse, Landmark Neo-Gothic original campus buildings. **Computers:** 100% of classrooms, 100% of libraries, 100% of dining areas, 100% of common outdoor areas have wireless network access. Students can register for classes online. Administrative functions (other than registration) can be performed online.

CAMPUS LIFE

Environment: Metropolis **Activities:** Choral groups; Dance; Drama/theater; International Student Organization; Jazz band; Literary magazine; Model UN; Radio station; Student government; Student newspaper; Student-run film society; Yearbook 145 registered organizations, 8 religious organizations. 2 fraternities, 1 sorority. **Athletics (Intercollegiate):** *Men:* baseball, basketball, cross-country, soccer, tennis, track/field (outdoor), track/field (indoor), volleyball. *Women:* basketball, fencing, soccer, tennis, track/field (outdoor), track/field (indoor), volleyball. **On-Campus Highlights:** City College Center for Discovery and Innovation, Solar Roofpod—Spitzer School of Archtiecture, Wingate Hall Athletic Center, CUNY Advanced Research Center, The Towers -Residence Hall **Environmental Initiatives:** Signed on to ACUPCC and NYC Mayor's Campus 30in10 Challenge to reduce GHG emissions

ADMISSIONS

Freshman Academic Profile: 85% from public high schools. **Test Scores:** SAT Math middle 50% range 500-620. SAT EBRW middle 50% range 480-570. Minimum internet-based TOEFL 61. Minimum paper TOEFL 500. **Basis for Candidate Selection:** *Very important factors considered include:* rigor of secondary school record, academic GPA. *Important factors considered include:* standardized test scores. *Other factors considered include:* application essay, recommendation(s). **Freshman Admission Requirements:** High school diploma is required and GED is accepted *Academic units recommended:* 4 English, 3 math, 2 science, 2 science labs, 3 foreign language, 4 social studies, 1 visual/performing arts. **Freshman Admission Statistics:** 25,373 applied, 40.8% admitted, 16% enrolled. **Transfer Admission Requirements:** college transcript(s), Minimum college GPA of 2.0 required. Lowest grade transferable c. **General**

Admission Information: Application fee $65. Priority deadline 2/1. Nonfall registration accepted. Admission may be deferred for a maximum of 1 year.

COSTS AND FINANCIAL AID

Annual out-of-state tuition $17,400. Required fees $410. Average book expense $1,364. **Required Forms and Deadlines:** FAFSA; State aid form. **Notification of Awards:** Applicants will be notified of awards on a rolling basis beginning 4/1. **Types of Aid:** *Need-based scholarships/grants:* College/university scholarship or grant aid from institutional funds; Federal Pell; SEOG; State scholarships/grants. *Loans:* Direct PLUS loans; Direct Subsidized Stafford Loans; Direct Unsubsidized Stafford Loans. *Student Employment:* Federal Work-Study Program available. Institutional employment available. **Financial Aid Statistics:** 91% needy freshmen, 96% needy undergrads receive need-based scholarship or grant aid. 54% freshmen, 61% undergrads receive non-need-based scholarship or grant aid. 45% freshmen, 63% undergrads receive need-based self-help aid. 0% freshmen, 0% undergrads receive athletic scholarships. 80% freshmen, 79% undergrads receive any aid. **Criteria for awarding aid:** *Need-based:* Academics, Alumni affiliation, Art, Leadership, Minority status *Non-need-based:* Academics, Alumni affiliation, Art, Leadership, Minority status, Music/drama.

CITY UNIVERSITY OF NEW YORK— THE COLLEGE OF STATEN ISLAND

2800 Victory Boulevard, Staten Island, NY 10314
Phone: 718-982-2010 • **Financial Aid Phone:** 718-982-2030
E-mail: admissions@csi.cuny.edu • **CEEB Code:** 2778
Fax: 718-982-2500 • **Website:** www.csi.cuny.edu • **ACT Code:** 2950

This public school was founded in 1976. It has a 204 acre campus.

RATINGS

Admissions Selectivity Rating: 71   **Fire Safety Rating:** 93   **Green Rating:** 60*

STUDENTS AND FACULTY

Enrollment: 12,118. **Student Body:** 55% female, 45% male, 1% out-of-state, 3% international (117 countries represented). Asian 12%, African American 16%, Caucasian 50%, Hispanic 18%, Native American <1%, Pacific Islander 0%, Two or more races 0%, Race unknown <1%.
Retention and Graduation: 77% freshmen return for sophomore year. 20% freshmen graduate within 4 years. 47% freshmen graduate within 6 years. **Faculty:** Student/faculty ratio 18:1. 361 full-time faculty, 79% hold PhDs, 29% are members of minority groups, 47% are women.

ACADEMICS

Degrees: Associate; Bachelor's; Certificate; Doctoral/Professional; Master's; Post-Bachelor's certificate; Post-Master's certificate; Terminal Associate; Transfer Associate **Classes:** Most classes have 10-19 students. **Most popular majors:** Psychology, General; Registered Nursing/Registered Nurse; Business/Commerce, General. **Special Study Options:** Cross-registration; Double major; English as a Second Language (ESL); Honors program; Independent study; Internships; Study abroad; Teacher certification program. **Honors programs:** The University Scholars Program at the College of Staten Island, one of eight CUNY Macaulay programs, is designed to provide an outstanding educational opportunity for academically gifted students. Special features include full financial support and access to exceptional academic and cultural activities. **Combined degree programs:** BA/MA. **Disability Services offered to physically disabled students:** Note-taking services; Reader services; Tape recorders; Tutors. **Career services:** Alumni network; Alumni services; Career assessment; Career/job search classes; Internships; Regional alumni

FACILITIES

Housing: Apartments for single students; Coed dorms; Special housing for disabled students 100% of campus accessible to physically diasbled. **Special Academic Facilities/Equipment:** Art Gallery, Radio Station, Astrophysical Observatory, Archives & Special Collections, Center for Engineered Polymeric Materials, Advanced Imaging Facility, Center for the Arts, Center for Developmental Neuroscience, CUNY High Performance Computational Facility, Intelligent Robotics Lab **Computers:** 97% of classrooms, 100% of libraries, 100% of dining areas, 100% of student union, 100% of common outdoor areas have wireless network access. Students can register for classes online. Administrative functions (other than registration) can be performed online.

CAMPUS LIFE

Environment: Metropolis **Activities:** Campus Ministries; Choral groups; Dance; Drama/theater; International Student Organization; Jazz band; Literary magazine; Music ensembles; Radio station; Student government; Student newspaper; Student-run film society 47 registered organizations, 2 honor societies, 4 religious organizations. **Athletics (Intercollegiate):** *Men:* baseball, basketball, cross-country, diving, soccer, swimming, tennis. *Women:* basketball, cross-country, diving, soccer, softball, swimming, tennis, volleyball. **On-Campus Highlights:** Campus Center including cafeteria and lounge, Library, Athletics Building

ADMISSIONS

Freshman Academic Profile: Average high school GPA 3.0. 81% from public high schools. **Test Scores:** SAT Math middle 50% range 450-560. SAT EBRW middle 50% range 480-550. Minimum internet-based TOEFL 45. Minimum paper TOEFL 450. **Basis for Candidate Selection:** *Very important factors considered include:* rigor of secondary school record. *Important factors considered include:* academic GPA, standardized test scores. *Other factors considered include:* class rank, application essay, recommendation(s), interview, extracurricular activities, volunteer work, level of applicant's interest. **Freshman Admission Requirements:** High school diploma is required and GED is accepted *Academic units required:* 4 English, 2 math, 2 science, 2 foreign language, 4 social studies, 0.5 visual/performing arts, *Academic units recommended:* 4 English, 3 math, 3 science, 3 foreign language, 4 social studies, 0.5 visual/performing arts. **Freshman Admission Statistics:** 14,684 applied, 100.0% admitted, 19% enrolled. **Transfer Admission Requirements:** college transcript(s), Minimum college GPA of 2.0 required. Lowest grade transferable C. **General Admission Information:** Application fee $65. Priority deadline 2/1. Nonfall registration accepted. Admission may be deferred for a maximum of 1 year.

COSTS AND FINANCIAL AID

Required Forms and Deadlines: FAFSA; State aid form. **Notification of Awards:** Applicants will be notified of awards on a rolling basis beginning 2/15. **Types of Aid:** *Need-based scholarships/grants:* College/university scholarship or grant aid from institutional funds; Federal Pell; Private scholarships; SEOG; State scholarships/grants. *Loans:* Direct PLUS loans; Direct Subsidized Stafford Loans; Direct Unsubsidized Stafford Loans. *Student Employment:* Federal Work-Study Program available. Institutional employment available. **Financial Aid Statistics:** 63% needy freshmen, 78% needy undergrads receive need-based scholarship or grant aid. 76% freshmen, 77% undergrads receive non-need-based scholarship or grant aid. 34% freshmen, 31% undergrads receive need-based self-help aid. 0% freshmen, 0% undergrads receive athletic scholarships. **Criteria for awarding aid:** *Need-based:* Academics, Alumni affiliation, Art, Leadership, Minority status, Music/drama *Non-need-based:* Academics, Alumni affiliation, Art, Leadership, Minority status, Music/drama, State/district residency.

CITY UNIVERSITY OF NEW YORK— HUNTER COLLEGE

695 Park Ave, New York, NY 10065
Phone: 212-772-4490 • **Financial Aid Phone:** 212-772-4820
E-mail: admissions@hunter.cuny.edu • **CEEB Code:** 2301
Website: www.hunter.cuny.edu/main/

This public school was founded in 1870.

RATINGS

Admissions Selectivity Rating: 89   **Fire Safety Rating:** 97   **Green Rating:** 87

STUDENTS AND FACULTY

Enrollment: 15,820. **Student Body:** 65% female, 35% male, 3% out-of-state, 6% international (162 countries represented). Asian 30%, African American 12%, Caucasian 30%, Hispanic 22%, Native American <1%,
Retention and Graduation: 83% freshmen return for sophomore year. 24% freshmen graduate within 4 years. 52% freshmen graduate within 6 years. **Faculty:** Student/faculty ratio 14:1. 670 full-time faculty, 88% hold PhDs, 20% are members of minority groups, 52% are women.

ACADEMICS

Degrees: Bachelor's; Doctoral/Professional; Doctoral/Research; Master's; Post-Bachelor's certificate; Post-Master's certificate **Classes:** Most classes have 10-19 students. Most lab/discussion sessions have 10-19 students. **Most popular majors:** English Language And Literature, General; Chemistry, General; Psychology, General. **Special Study Options:** Accelerated program; Cross-registration; Distance learning; Double major; Dual enrollment; Exchange student program (domestic); Honors program; Independent study; Internships; Liberal arts/career combination; Student-designed major; Study abroad; Teacher certification program. **Honors programs:** Maccaulay Honors College **Combined degree programs:** BA/MA. **Disability Services offered to physically disabled students:** Note-taking services; Reader services; Tape recorders; Tutors. **Career services:** Alumni network; Alumni services; Career/job search classes; Internships

FACILITIES

Housing: Coed dorms 100% of campus accessible to physically diasbled. **Special Academic Facilities/Equipment:** Art Gallery, theatre, geology club, on-campus elementary and secondary schools. **Computers:** 70% of classrooms, have wireless network access. Students can register for classes online.

CAMPUS LIFE

Environment: Metropolis **Activities:** Choral groups; Concert band; Dance; Drama/theater; Jazz band; Literary magazine; Model UN; Music ensembles; Musical theater; Radio station; Student government; Student newspaper; Student-run film society; Symphony orchestra; Television station; Yearbook 150 registered organizations, 20 honor societies, 2 fraternities, 2 sororities. **Athletics (Intercollegiate):** *Men:* basketball, cross-country, fencing, soccer, tennis, track/field (outdoor), track/field (indoor), volleyball, wrestling. *Women:* basketball, cross-country, diving, fencing, softball, swimming, tennis, track/field (outdoor), track/field (indoor), volleyball. **On-Campus Highlights:** Over 100 Campus Clubs, CARSI Geography Lab, Television Studio, Learning Center and Computer Lab, Sports Complex **Environmental Initiatives:** Hunter has an extensive program for recycling paper, metal, glass, plastic, e-waste, and household batteries. This program is continuously being expanded.

ADMISSIONS

Freshman Academic Profile: Average high school GPA 3.4. 75% from public high schools. **Test Scores:** SAT Math middle 50% range 550-650. SAT EBRW middle 50% range 520-610. Minimum paper TOEFL 500. **Basis for Candidate Selection:** *Very important factors considered include:* rigor of secondary school record, academic GPA, standardized test scores. **Freshman Admission Requirements:** High school diploma is required and GED is accepted *Academic units required:* 2 English, 2 math, 1 science, 1 science labs, *Academic units recommended:* 4 English, 3 math, 2 science, 2 foreign language, 4 social studies, 1 academic elective, 1 visual/performing arts. **Freshman Admission Statistics:** 29,326 applied, 40.2% admitted, 20% enrolled. **Transfer Admission Requirements:** college transcript(s), Minimum college GPA of 2.3 required. Lowest grade transferable C. **General Admission Information:** Regular application deadline 2/1. Admission may be deferred.

COSTS AND FINANCIAL AID

Annual in-state tuition $450. Annual out-of-state tuition $17,400. Required fees $450. Average book expense $1,364. **Required Forms and Deadlines:** FAFSA; State aid form. **Notification of Awards:** Applicants will be notified of awards on a rolling basis beginning 5/15. **Types of Aid:** *Need-based scholarships/grants:* College/university scholarship or grant aid from institutional funds; Federal Pell; State scholarships/grants. *Loans:* Direct PLUS loans; Direct Subsidized Stafford Loans; Direct Unsubsidized Stafford Loans. *Student Employment:* Federal Work-Study Program available. Institutional employment available. **Financial Aid Statistics:** 89% needy freshmen, 86% needy undergrads receive need-based scholarship or grant aid. 84% freshmen, 39% undergrads receive non-need-based scholarship or grant aid. 8% freshmen, 17% undergrads receive need-based self-help aid. 0% freshmen, 0% undergrads receive athletic scholarships. 91% freshmen, 94% undergrads receive any aid. **Criteria for awarding aid:** *Need-based:* Academics *Non-need-based:* Academics.

CITY UNIVERSITY OF NEW YORK— KINGSBOROUGH COMMUNITY COLLEGE

2001 Oriental Blvd., Brooklyn, NY 11235
Phone: (718)368-4600 · **Financial Aid Phone:** (718) 368-4644
E-mail: info@kbcc.cuny.edu
Fax: (718) 368-5356

This public school was founded in 1963. It has a 72 acre campus.

RATINGS

Admissions Selectivity Rating: 0   **Fire Safety Rating:** 60*   **Green Rating:** 60*

STUDENTS AND FACULTY

Enrollment: 10,889. **Student Body:** 55% female, 45% male, 5% international (137 countries represented). Asian 14%, African American 32%, Caucasian 32%, Hispanic 17%, Native American <1%. **Retention and Graduation:** 70% freshmen return for sophomore year. **Faculty:** Student/faculty ratio 23:1. 333 full-time faculty, 57% hold PhDs, 28% are members of minority groups, 55% are women. 0% of classes are taught by teaching assistants.

ACADEMICS

Degrees: Associate; Certificate; Terminal Associate; Transfer Associate **Most popular majors:** Liberal Arts And Sciences/Liberal Studies; Biology/Biological Sciences, General; Business/Commerce, General. **Special Study Options:** Accelerated program; Cross-registration; Distance learning; Dual enrollment; English as a Second Language (ESL); Honors program; Independent study; Internships.

CAMPUS LIFE

Environment: Metropolis **Activities:** Musical theater; Radio station; Student government; Student newspaper.

ADMISSIONS

Test Scores: Minimum paper TOEFL 475. **Freshman Admission Requirements:** High school diploma is required and GED is accepted *Academic units recommended:* 4 English, 3 math, 2 science, 2 foreign language, 4 social studies, 1 unit from above areas or other academic areas. **Transfer Admission Requirements:** college transcript(s), essay or personal statement, interview, Lowest grade transferable C. **General Admission Information:** Application fee $65. Priority deadline 7/15. Regular application deadline 8/15. Nonfall registration accepted.

COSTS AND FINANCIAL AID

Annual out-of-state tuition $9,600. Required fees $121.

CITY UNIVERSITY OF NEW YORK— LEHMAN COLLEGE

250 Bedford Park Boulevard West, Bronx, NY 10468
Phone: 718-960-8000 · **Financial Aid Phone:** (718)960-8545
E-mail: wilkes@alpha.lehman.cuny.edu · **CEEB Code:** 2950
Fax: 718-960-8712

This public school was founded in 1968. It has a 38 acre campus.

RATINGS

Admissions Selectivity Rating: 90   **Fire Safety Rating:** 60*   **Green Rating:** 60*

STUDENTS AND FACULTY

Enrollment: 8,236. **Student Body:** 71% female, 29% male, 1% out-of-state, 5% international (123 countries represented). Asian 4%, African American 32%, Caucasian 10%, Hispanic 49%, Native American <1%, Race unknown 0%. **Retention and Graduation:** 77% freshmen return for sophomore year. **Faculty:** Student/faculty ratio 15:1. 368 full-time faculty, 75% hold PhDs, 27% are members of minority groups, 52% are women.

ACADEMICS

Degrees: Bachelor's; Certificate; Diploma; Master's **Classes:** Most classes have fewer than 10 students. **Most popular majors:** Social Work; Sociology; Nursing/Registered Nurse (Rn, Asn, Bsn, Msn). **Special Study Options:** Accelerated program; Cooperative education program; Cross-registration; Distance learning; Double major; Dual enrollment; English as a Second Language (ESL); Exchange student program (domestic); Honors program; Independent study; Internships; Student-designed major; Study abroad; Teacher certification program; Weekend college. **Honors programs:** Lehman Scholars Program. Students receive full tuition, stipends, an expense account to use for academically enriching experiences and a laptop computer. **Combined degree programs:** BA/MA. **Disability Services offered to physically disabled students:** Note-taking services; Reader services; Tape recorders; Tutors.

FACILITIES

Housing: 80% of campus accessible to physically diasbled. **Special Academic Facilities/Equipment:** Art gallery, concert hall, sports complex. **Computers:** Students can register for classes online. Administrative functions (other than registration) can be performed online.

CAMPUS LIFE

Environment: Metropolis **Activities:** Choral groups; Concert band; Dance; Drama/theater; International Student Organization; Jazz band; Literary magazine; Music ensembles; Musical theater; Opera; Radio station; Student government; Student newspaper; Student-run film society; Symphony orchestra; Television station; Yearbook 3 honor societies, 1 religious organization. 1 fraternity, 1 sorority. **Athletics (Intercollegiate):** *Men:* badminton, baseball, basketball, cross-country, diving, swimming, tennis, track/field (outdoor), volleyball. *Women:* badminton, basketball, cross-country, diving, softball, swimming, tennis, track/field (outdoor), volleyball. **On-Campus Highlights:** APEX athletic facility, Cyber Cafe, Art Gallery, Concert Hall, Information Technology Center

ADMISSIONS

Freshman Academic Profile: Average high school GPA 2.7. 74% from public high schools. **Test Scores:** SAT Math middle 50% range 400-500. SAT EBRW middle 50% range 400-490. Minimum paper TOEFL 500. **Basis for Candidate Selection:** *Very important factors considered include:* rigor of secondary school record, standardized test scores. *Important factors considered include:* academic GPA. *Other factors considered include:* application essay, recommendation(s), interview, extracurricular activities, talent/ability. **Freshman Admission Requirements:** High school diploma is required and GED is accepted *Academic units required:* 4 English, 2 math, 2 science, 1 science labs, 2 foreign language, 1 social studies, 1 history, *Academic units recommended:* 4 English, 3 math, 3 science, 2 foreign language, 2 social studies, 2 history, 1 visual/performing arts. **Freshman Admission Statistics:** 14,155 applied, 31.6% admitted, 58% enrolled. **Transfer Admission Requirements:** college transcript(s), Minimum college GPA of 2 required. Lowest grade transferable C. **General Admission Information:** Application fee $65. Priority deadline 1/15. Regular application deadline 8/15. Nonfall registration accepted. Admission may be deferred for a maximum of 1 semester.

COSTS AND FINANCIAL AID

Annual out-of-state tuition $10,800. Required fees $290. Average book expense $938. **Required Forms and Deadlines:** FAFSA; State aid form. **Notification of Awards:** Applicants will be notified of awards on a rolling basis beginning 3/1. **Types of Aid:** *Need-based scholarships/grants:* College/university scholarship or grant aid from institutional funds; Federal Pell; Private scholarships; SEOG; State scholarships/grants. *Loans:* Direct PLUS loans; Direct Subsidized Stafford Loans; Direct Unsubsidized Stafford Loans. *Student Employment:* Federal Work-Study Program available. Institutional employment available. **Financial Aid Statistics:** 88% needy freshmen, 90% needy undergrads receive need-based scholarship or grant aid. 42% freshmen, 15% undergrads receive non-need-based scholarship or grant aid. 19% freshmen, 44% undergrads receive need-based self-help aid. 0% freshmen, 0% undergrads receive athletic scholarships. 83% freshmen, 80% undergrads receive any aid. **Criteria for awarding aid:** *Need-based:* Academics *Non-need-based:* Academics.

General. **Special Study Options:** Accelerated program; Cross-registration; Distance learning; Double major; English as a Second Language (ESL); Honors program; Independent study; Internships; Study abroad; Teacher certification program; Weekend college. **Disability Services offered to physically disabled students:** Note-taking services; Reader services; Tape recorders; Tutors. **Career services:** Alumni services; Career assessment; Career/job search classes; Internships

FACILITIES

Housing: 100% of campus accessible to physically diasbled. **Computers:** 90% of classrooms, 100% of libraries, have wireless network access. Students can register for classes online. Administrative functions (other than registration) can be performed online.

CAMPUS LIFE

Environment: Metropolis **Activities:** Choral groups; Dance; Drama/theater; Jazz band; Literary magazine; Radio station; Student government; Student newspaper; Television station; Yearbook 32 registered organizations, 4 honor societies, 2 religious organizations. **Athletics (Intercollegiate):** *Men:* basketball, cross-country, soccer, swimming, track/field (outdoor), track/field (indoor), volleyball. *Women:* basketball, cheerleading, cross-country, soccer, softball, swimming, tennis, track/field (outdoor), track/field (indoor), volleyball. **On-Campus Highlights:** Amphitheater, NASA Space Center Lab, Library, Departments, AB1-New Science Building

ADMISSIONS

Freshman Academic Profile: Average high school GPA 75.2. **Test Scores:** SAT Math middle 50% range 350-430. SAT EBRW middle 50% range 380-480. Minimum paper TOEFL 475. **Basis for Candidate Selection:** *Other factors considered include:* rigor of secondary school record, academic GPA, standardized test scores. **Freshman Admission Requirements:** High school diploma is required and GED is accepted *Academic units recommended:* 4 English, 3 math, 2 science, 2 foreign language, 4 social studies, 2 academic electives. **Freshman Admission Statistics:** 10,834 applied, 100.0% admitted, 11% enrolled. **Transfer Admission Requirements:** college transcript(s), Minimum college GPA of 2.0 required. Lowest grade transferable C. **General Admission Information:** Application fee $65. Nonfall registration accepted. Admission may be deferred for a maximum of one semester.

COSTS AND FINANCIAL AID

Annual out-of-state tuition $17,400. Required fees $125. Average book expense $1,364. **Required Forms and Deadlines:** FAFSA; State aid form. **Notification of Awards:** Applicants will be notified of awards on a rolling basis beginning 5/1. **Types of Aid:** *Need-based scholarships/grants:* Federal Pell; SEOG; State scholarships/grants. *Loans:* Direct PLUS loans; Direct Subsidized Stafford Loans; Direct Unsubsidized Stafford Loans. *Student Employment:* Federal Work-Study Program available. Institutional employment available. **Criteria for awarding aid:** *Non-need-based:* Academics, Leadership.

CITY UNIVERSITY OF NEW YORK— MEDGAR EVERS COLLEGE

1650 Bedford Avenue, Brooklyn, NY 11225
Phone: 718-270-6024 · **Financial Aid Phone:** 718-270-6133
E-mail: applytomec@mec.cuny.edu
Fax: 718-270-6411 · **Website:** http://www.mec.cuny.edu/

This public school was founded in 1970. It has a 7 acre campus.

RATINGS

Admissions Selectivity Rating: 70   **Fire Safety Rating:** 60*   **Green Rating:** 60*

STUDENTS AND FACULTY

Enrollment: 6,204. **Student Body:** 72% female, 28% male, 1% out-of-state, 1% international. Asian 2%, African American 62%, Caucasian 1%, Hispanic 15%, Native American <1%, Pacific Islander 0%, Two or more races 0%, Race unknown 19%.
Faculty: Student/faculty ratio 18:1. 185 full-time faculty, 62% hold PhDs, 85% are members of minority groups, 46% are women. 0% of classes are taught by teaching assistants.

ACADEMICS

Degrees: Associate; Bachelor's; Certificate **Classes:** Most classes have fewer than 10 students. Most lab/discussion sessions have 10-19 students. **Most popular majors:** Liberal Arts And Sciences/Liberal Studies; Biology/Biological Sciences, General; Business Administration And Management,

---

CITY UNIVERSITY OF NEW YORK— NEW YORK CITY COLLEGE OF TECHNOLOGY

300 Jay Street, Brooklyn, NY 11201
Phone: (718) 260-5500 · **Financial Aid Phone:** 718-260-5700
E-mail: admissions@citytech.cuny.edu · **CEEB Code:** 2550
Fax: (718) 260-5504 · **Website:** http://www.citytech.cuny.edu/ · **ACT Code:** 2950

This public school was founded in 1946. It has a 3 acre campus.

RATINGS

Admissions Selectivity Rating: 68   **Fire Safety Rating:** 60*   **Green Rating:** 60*

STUDENTS AND FACULTY

Enrollment: 15,917. **Student Body:** 44% female, 56% male, 1% out-of-state, 5% international (106 countries represented). Asian 18%, African American 32%, Caucasian 13%, Hispanic 31%, Native American <1%, Pacific Islander <1%, Two or more races 1%,
Retention and Graduation: 77% freshmen return for sophomore year.
Faculty: Student/faculty ratio 17:1. 433 full-time faculty, 63% hold PhDs, 45% are members of minority groups, 48% are women. 0% of classes are taught by teaching assistants.

ACADEMICS

Degrees: Associate; Bachelor's; Certificate **Classes:** Most classes have 20-29 students. Most lab/discussion sessions have 20-29 students. **Most popular majors:** Information Science/Studies; Design And Visual Communications, General; Hospitality Administration/Management, General. **Special Study**

Options: Distance learning; Dual enrollment; English as a Second Language (ESL); Honors program; Independent study; Internships; Student-designed major; Study abroad; Teacher certification program; Weekend college. **Disability Services offered to physically disabled students:** Note-taking services; Reader services; Tape recorders; Tutors. **Career services:** Alumni network; Alumni services; Career assessment; Career/job search classes; Internships

FACILITIES

Housing: 100% of campus accessible to physically diasbled. **Computers:** Students can register for classes online. Administrative functions (other than registration) can be performed online.

CAMPUS LIFE

Environment: Metropolis **Activities:** Drama/theater; International Student Organization; Literary magazine; Musical theater; Student government; Student newspaper 60 registered organizations. **Athletics (Intercollegiate):** *Men:* basketball, tennis, track/field (outdoor). *Women:* basketball, tennis, track/field (outdoor). Nursing Department, Radiologic Technology & Medical Imaging Department, Hospitality Management Department, Dental Hygiene Department, Voorhees Hall **Environmental Initiatives:** reducing the amount of waste produced by our purchasing and procurement system

ADMISSIONS

Test Scores: Minimum internet-based TOEFL 61. Minimum paper TOEFL 500. **Basis for Candidate Selection:** *Important factors considered include:* rigor of secondary school record, academic GPA. *Other factors considered include:* class rank, application essay, standardized test scores, recommendation(s). **Freshman Admission Requirements:** High school diploma is required and GED is accepted *Academic units required:* 4 English, 3 math, 2 science, 2 science labs, 2 foreign language, 3 social studies, 1 visual/performing arts, *Academic units recommended:* 4 English, 4 math, 3 science, 3 science labs, 2 foreign language, 4 social studies, 1 visual/performing arts. **Freshman Admission Statistics:** 17,465 applied, 70.6% admitted, 27% enrolled. **Transfer Admission Requirements:** High school transcript, college transcript(s), statement of good standing from prior institution(s). Minimum college GPA of 2.0 required. Lowest grade transferable C. **General Admission Information:** Application fee $65. Priority deadline 2/1. Regular application deadline 2/1. Nonfall registration accepted. Admission may be deferred for a maximum of 1 semester.

COSTS AND FINANCIAL AID

Annual out-of-state tuition $15,300. Required fees $339. **Required Forms and Deadlines:** FAFSA; State aid form. **Types of Aid:** *Need-based scholarships/grants:* Federal Nursing Scholarships; Federal Pell; SEOG; State scholarships/grants. *Loans:* Direct PLUS loans; Direct Subsidized Stafford Loans; Direct Unsubsidized Stafford Loans. *Student Employment:* Federal Work-Study Program available. Institutional employment available. **Criteria for awarding aid:** *Need-based:* Academics *Non-need-based:* State/district residency.

CITY UNIVERSITY OF NEW YORK— QUEENS COLLEGE

65-30 Kissena Blvd, Queens, NY 11367
Phone: 718-997-5600 · **Financial Aid Phone:** (718) 997-5123
E-mail: vincent.angrisani@qc.cuny.edu · **CEEB Code:** 2750
Fax: (718) 997-5617 · **Website:** www.qc.cuny.edu · **ACT Code:** 20173

This public school was founded in 1937. It has a 80 acre campus.

RATINGS

Admissions Selectivity Rating: 88   **Fire Safety Rating:** 97   **Green Rating:** 91

STUDENTS AND FACULTY

Enrollment: 15,762. **Student Body:** 54% female, 46% male, 1% out-of-state, 5% international (143 countries represented). Asian 28%, African American 9%, Caucasian 26%, Hispanic 29%, Native American <1%, Pacific Islander <1%, Two or more races 1%, Race unknown 0%.
Retention and Graduation: 84% freshmen return for sophomore year. 29% freshmen graduate within 4 years. 54% freshmen graduate within 6 years. 35% grads go on to further study within 1 year. 10% grads pursue arts and sciences degrees. 2% grads pursue law degrees. 1% grads pursue business degrees. 1% grads pursue medical degrees. **Faculty:** Student/faculty ratio 15:1. 591 full-time

faculty, 86% hold PhDs, 23% are members of minority groups, 46% are women. 1% of classes are taught by teaching assistants.

ACADEMICS

Degrees: Bachelor's; Master's; Post-Bachelor's certificate; Post-Master's certificate **Classes:** Most classes have 10-19 students. Most lab/discussion sessions have 20-29 students. **Most popular majors:** Computer Science; Psychology, General; Accounting. **Special Study Options:** Accelerated program; Double major; Dual enrollment; English as a Second Language (ESL); Exchange student program (domestic); Honors program; Independent study; Internships; Liberal arts/career combination; Study abroad; Teacher certification program; Weekend college. **Honors programs:** Queens College participates in the CUNY Honors College—a highly selective program that offers a challenging curriculum and a full tuition scholarship plus other financial support. The program accepts first-time freshmen in the fall semester only. **Combined degree programs:** BA/MA. **Disability Services offered to physically disabled students:** Note-taking services; Reader services; Tape recorders; Tutors. **Career services:** Alumni network; Alumni services; Career assessment; Career/job search classes; Internships

FACILITIES

Housing: Apartments for single students; Other (please specify) 100% of campus accessible to physically diasbled. **Special Academic Facilities/Equipment:** Godwin-Ternbach Museum, Louis Armstrong House Museum & Archieves, Colden Auditorium, Kupferberg Center for the Performing Arts, Art Library **Computers:** 100% of classrooms, 100% of dorms, 100% of libraries, 100% of dining areas, 100% of student union, 100% of common outdoor areas have wireless network access. Students can register for classes online. Administrative functions (other than registration) can be performed online.

CAMPUS LIFE

Environment: Metropolis **Activities:** Campus Ministries; Choral groups; Dance; Drama/theater; International Student Organization; Jazz band; Literary magazine; Model UN; Music ensembles; Musical theater; Opera; Radio station; Student government; Student newspaper; Symphony orchestra; Yearbook 114 registered organizations, 5 honor societies, 12 religious organizations. 4 fraternities, 3 sororities. **Athletics (Intercollegiate):** *Men:* baseball, basketball, cross-country, diving, soccer, swimming, tennis, track/field (outdoor), water polo. *Women:* basketball, cross-country, diving, fencing, lacrosse, soccer, softball, swimming, tennis, track/field (outdoor), volleyball, water polo. **On-Campus Highlights:** Rosenthal Library, Student Union, The Summit, Dining Hall, Classrooms and Laboratory Facilities **Environmental Initiatives:** Retrofit and completion of mechanical upgrade 27M for the new Science Building that will significantly reduce the energy consumption

ADMISSIONS

Freshman Academic Profile: Average high school GPA 3.5. 75% from public high schools. **Test Scores:** SAT Math middle 50% range 540-620. SAT EBRW middle 50% range 520-600. Minimum internet-based TOEFL 62. Minimum paper TOEFL 500. **Basis for Candidate Selection:** *Very important factors considered include:* rigor of secondary school record, academic GPA, standardized test scores. *Other factors considered include:* application essay, recommendation(s). **Freshman Admission Requirements:** High school diploma is required and GED is accepted *Academic units required:* 4 English, 3 math, 2 science, 2 science labs, 3 foreign language, 4 social studies, *Academic units recommended:* 4 English, 3 math, 3 science, 3 science labs, 3 foreign language, 4 social studies. **Freshman Admission Statistics:** 18,180 applied, 42.7% admitted, 22% enrolled. **Transfer Admission Requirements:** High school transcript, college transcript(s), standardized test scores, Minimum college GPA of 2.25 required. Lowest grade transferable 2. **General Admission Information:** Application fee $65. Priority deadline 2/1. Nonfall registration accepted. Admission may be deferred for a maximum of 1 semester.

COSTS AND FINANCIAL AID

Annual out-of-state tuition $17,400. Room and board $15,352. Required fees $608. Average book expense $1,364. **Required Forms and Deadlines:** FAFSA; Institution's own financial aid form; State aid form. **Types of Aid:** *Need-based scholarships/grants:* College/university scholarship or grant aid from institutional funds; Federal Pell; Private scholarships; SEOG; State scholarships/grants. *Loans:* Direct PLUS loans; Direct Subsidized Stafford Loans; Direct Unsubsidized Stafford Loans. *Student Employment:* Federal Work-Study Program available. Institutional employment available. **Financial Aid Statistics:** 86% needy freshmen, 84% needy undergrads receive need-based scholarship or grant aid. 3% freshmen, 3% undergrads receive non-need-based scholarship or grant aid. 15% freshmen, 35% undergrads receive need-based self-help aid. 2% freshmen, 1% undergrads receive athletic scholarships. 85% freshmen, 53% undergrads receive any aid. 15% undergrads borrow to pay for school. Average cumulative indebtedness $15,000. **Criteria for awarding aid:** *Non-need-based:* Academics, Athletics.

See page 1000.

CLAFLIN UNIVERSITY

400 Magnolia Street, Orangeburg, SC 29115
Phone: 803-535-5340 · **Financial Aid Phone:** 803-535-5720
E-mail: admissions@claflin.edu · **CEEB Code:** 5109
Fax: 803-535-5387 · **ACT Code:** 3840

This private school, affiliated with the Methodist Church, was founded in 1869. It has a 46 acre campus.

RATINGS
Admissions Selectivity Rating: 81   **Fire Safety Rating:** 88   **Green Rating:** 84

STUDENTS AND FACULTY
Enrollment: 1,784. **Student Body:** 65% female, 35% male, 19% out-of-state, 3% international (15 countries represented). Asian 1%, African American 92%, Caucasian 1%, Hispanic 2%, Native American 1%, Pacific Islander 0%, Two or more races <1%, Race unknown 0%.
Retention and Graduation: 73% freshmen return for sophomore year.
Faculty: Student/faculty ratio 13:1. 119 full-time faculty, 84% hold PhDs, 76% are members of minority groups, 43% are women.

ACADEMICS
Degrees: Bachelor's; Master's **Classes:** Most classes have 20-29 students. Most lab/discussion sessions have 10-19 students. **Most popular majors:** Biology/Biological Sciences, General; Sociology; Business Administration And Management, General. **Special Study Options:** Accelerated program; Cooperative education program; Cross-registration; Double major; Dual enrollment; English as a Second Language (ESL); Exchange student program (domestic); Honors program; Independent study; Internships; Study abroad; Teacher certification program. **Honors programs:** The Alice Carson Tisdale Honors College. **Disability Services offered to physically disabled students:** Note-taking services. **Career services:** Career assessment; Career/job search classes; Internships

FACILITIES
Housing: Men's dorms; Women's dorms 90% of campus accessible to physically disabled. **Special Academic Facilities/Equipment:** T.V. studio, NMR Wilbur R. Gregg collection, Aruther Rose Museum. **Computers:** 33% of classrooms, 100% of libraries, 100% of dining areas, have wireless network access. Students can register for classes online. Administrative functions (other than registration) can be performed online.

CAMPUS LIFE
Environment: Village **Activities:** Choral groups; Concert band; Dance; Drama/theater; International Student Organization; Jazz band; Literary magazine; Music ensembles; Radio station; Student government; Student newspaper; Student-run film society; Television station; Yearbook 3 honor societies, 4 fraternities, 4 sororities. **Athletics (Intercollegiate):** *Men:* baseball, basketball, cross-country, track/field (outdoor), track/field (indoor). *Women:* basketball, cross-country, softball, track/field (outdoor), track/field (indoor), volleyball. **On-Campus Highlights:** Student Life Center, Computer Labs, Arthur Rose Museum, Jonas T. Kennedy Health and Physical Education Center. **Environmental Initiatives:** Recycling Program

ADMISSIONS
Freshman Academic Profile: Average high school GPA 2.7. 10% in top 10% of high school class, 26% in top 25% of high school class, 63% in top 50% of high school class. **Test Scores:** SAT Math middle 50% range 350-440. SAT EBRW middle 50% range 350-440. ACT middle 50% range 15-19. **Basis for Candidate Selection:** *Very important factors considered include:* rigor of secondary school record, class rank, academic GPA, standardized test scores, character/personal qualities, first generation. *Important factors considered include:* application essay, extracurricular activities, talent/ability, alumni/ae relation, level of applicant's interest. *Other factors considered include:* recommendation(s), state residency, volunteer work, work experience. **Freshman Admission Requirements:** High school diploma is required and GED is accepted *Academic units required:* 4 English, 3 math, 3 science, 1 foreign language, 1 social studies, 1 history, 7 academic electives, 1 computer science, and 2 units from above areas or other academic areas. **Freshman Admission Statistics:** 5,237 applied, 43.8% admitted, 17% enrolled. **Transfer Admission Requirements:** college transcript(s), statement of good standing from prior institution(s). Minimum college GPA of 2.0 required. Lowest grade transferable C. **General Admission Information:** Application fee $30. Priority deadline 1/15. Regular application deadline 8/1. Nonfall registration accepted. Admission may be deferred.

COSTS AND FINANCIAL AID
Annual tuition $14,640. Room and board $8,420. Required fees $370. Average book expense $1,750. **Required Forms and Deadlines:** FAFSA; Institution's own financial aid form. **Notification of Awards:** Applicants will be notified of awards on a rolling basis beginning 5/3. **Types of Aid:** *Need-based scholarships/grants:* College/university scholarship or grant aid from institutional funds; Federal Pell; Private scholarships; SEOG; State scholarships/grants; United Negro College Fund. *Loans: Student Employment:* Federal Work-Study Program available. Institutional employment available. **Financial Aid Statistics:** 88% needy freshmen, 95% needy undergrads receive need-based scholarship or grant aid. 7% freshmen, 6% undergrads receive non-need-based scholarship or grant aid. 75% freshmen, undergrads receive need-based self-help aid. 0% freshmen, 0% undergrads receive athletic scholarships. **Criteria for awarding aid:** *Need-based:* Academics, Alumni affiliation, Art, Athletics, Leadership, Music/drama, Religious affiliation.

CLAREMONT MCKENNA COLLEGE

500 E 9th Street, Claremont, CA 91711
Phone: (909) 621-8088 · **Financial Aid Phone:** (909) 621-8356
E-mail: admission@cmc.edu · **CEEB Code:** 4054
Fax: (909) 621-8516 · **Website:** www.claremontmckenna.edu · **ACT Code:** 224

This private school was founded in 1946. It has a 69 acre campus.

RATINGS
Admissions Selectivity Rating: 98   **Fire Safety Rating:** 88   **Green Rating:** 60*

STUDENTS AND FACULTY
Enrollment: 1,335. **Student Body:** 48% female, 52% male, 55% out-of-state, 17% international (37 countries represented). Asian 11%, African American 4%, Caucasian 41%, Hispanic 15%, Native American <1%, Pacific Islander <1%, Two or more races 6%, Race unknown 6%.
Retention and Graduation: 97% freshmen return for sophomore year. 84% freshmen graduate within 4 years. 90% freshmen graduate within 6 years. 12% grads go on to further study within 1 year. **Faculty:** Student/faculty ratio 8:1. 144 full-time faculty, 99% hold PhDs, 18% are members of minority groups, 36% are women. 0% of classes are taught by teaching assistants.

ACADEMICS
Degrees: Bachelor's; Master's **Classes:** Most classes have 10-19 students. Most lab/discussion sessions have 10-19 students. **Most popular majors:** Psychology, General; Economics, General; Political Science And Government, General. **Special Study Options:** Cross-registration; Double major; Exchange student program (domestic); Honors program; Independent study; Student-designed major; Study abroad. **Combined degree programs:** BA/MA. **Disability Services offered to physically disabled students:** Note-taking services; Reader services; Tape recorders; Tutors. **Career services:** Alumni network; Alumni services; Career assessment; Career/job search classes; Internships; Regional alumni

FACILITIES
Housing: Apartments for single students; Coed dorms; Special housing for disabled students **Computers:** 100% of classrooms, 100% of dorms, 100% of libraries, 100% of dining areas, 100% of student union, 100% of common outdoor areas have wireless network access. Administrative functions (other than registration) can be performed online.

CAMPUS LIFE
Environment: Town **Activities:** Campus Ministries; Choral groups; Concert band; Dance; Drama/theater; International Student Organization; Jazz band; Literary magazine; Model UN; Music ensembles; Musical theater; Radio station; Student government; Student newspaper; Symphony orchestra; Yearbook 280 registered organizations, 7 honor societies, 5 religious organizations. **Athletics (Intercollegiate):** *Men:* baseball, basketball, cross-country, diving, football, golf, soccer, swimming, tennis, track/field (outdoor), water polo. *Women:* basketball, cross-country, diving, golf, lacrosse, soccer, softball, swimming, tennis, track/field (outdoor), volleyball, water polo. **On-Campus Highlights:** Marian Miner Cook Athenaeum, Roberts Pavillion, Emett Student Center (The Hub), Kravis Center, Keck Science Center

ADMISSIONS
Freshman Academic Profile: 82% in top 10% of high school class, 96% in top 25% of high school class, 100% in top 50% of high school class. **Test Scores:** SAT Math middle 50% range 680-770. SAT EBRW middle 50% range 660-740. ACT middle 50% range 30-34. Minimum internet-based TOEFL 100. Minimum paper TOEFL 600. **Basis for Candidate Selection:** *Very important*

factors considered include: rigor of secondary school record, class rank, academic GPA, standardized test scores, recommendation(s), extracurricular activities, character/personal qualities. Important factors considered include: application essay, interview, talent/ability. Other factors considered include: first generation, alumni/ae relation, geographical residence, racial/ethnic status, volunteer work, work experience. **Freshman Admission Requirements:** High school diploma is required and GED is accepted Academic units required: 4 English, 3 math, 2 science, 2 science labs, 3 foreign language, 1 social studies, 1 history, Academic units recommended: 4 English, 4 math, 3 science, 3 science labs, 3 foreign language, 1 social studies, 1 history. **Freshman Admission Statistics:** 6,349 applied, 10.4% admitted, 53% enrolled. **Transfer Admission Requirements:** High school transcript, college transcript(s), essay or personal statement, statement of good standing from prior institution(s). Lowest grade transferable C. **General Admission Information:** Application fee $70. Regular application deadline 1/5. Nonfall registration accepted. Admission may be deferred for a maximum of 2 years.

COSTS AND FINANCIAL AID

Required Forms and Deadlines: Business/Farm Supplement; CSS/Financial Aid PROFILE; FAFSA; Noncustodial PROFILE; State aid form. **Notification of Awards:** Applicants will be notified of awards on or about 4/1. **Types of Aid:** Need-based scholarships/grants: College/university scholarship or grant aid from institutional funds; Federal Pell; Private scholarships; SEOG; State scholarships/grants. Loans: Direct PLUS loans; Direct Subsidized Stafford Loans; Direct Unsubsidized Stafford Loans. Student Employment: Federal Work-Study Program available. Institutional employment available. **Financial Aid Statistics:** 97% needy freshmen, 98% needy undergrads receive need-based scholarship or grant aid. 56% freshmen, 55% undergrads receive non-need-based scholarship or grant aid. 92% freshmen, 92% undergrads receive need-based self-help aid. 0% freshmen, 0% undergrads receive athletic scholarships. 43% freshmen, 45% undergrads receive any aid. 27% undergrads borrow to pay for school. Average cumulative indebtedness $23,375. **Criteria for awarding aid:** Need-based: Academics Non-need-based: Academics, Leadership.

CLARION UNIVERSITY OF PA

840 Wood St., Clarion, PA 16214
Phone: 814-393-2306 · **Financial Aid Phone:** 814-393-2315
E-mail: admissions@clarion.edu · **CEEB Code:** 2649
Fax: 814-393-2030 · **Website:** www.clarion.edu · **ACT Code:** 3698

This public school was founded in 1867. It has a 192 acre campus.

RATINGS

Admissions Selectivity Rating: 73   **Fire Safety Rating:** 93   **Green Rating:** 60*

STUDENTS AND FACULTY

Enrollment: 5,046. **Student Body:** 62% female, 38% male, 10% out-of-state, 1% international (35 countries represented). Asian <1%, African American 7%, Caucasian 88%, Hispanic 1%, Native American <1%, Pacific Islander <1%, Two or more races 2%, Race unknown 2%.
Faculty: Student/faculty ratio 20:1. 222 full-time faculty, 87% hold PhDs, 14% are members of minority groups, 49% are women. 0% of classes are taught by teaching assistants.

ACADEMICS

Degrees: Associate; Bachelor's; Certificate; Master's; Post-Bachelor's certificate; Post-Master's certificate **Classes:** Most classes have 10-19 students. Most lab/discussion sessions have 10-19 students. **Most popular majors:** Elementary Education And Teaching; Business Administration And Management, General. **Special Study Options:** Cooperative education program; Distance learning; Double major; Dual enrollment; Honors program; Independent study; Internships; Liberal arts/career combination; Student-designed major; Study abroad; Teacher certification program; Weekend college. **Honors programs:** Clarion University's Honors Program is a close-knit group of talented students preparing for the future. Honors courses satisfy general educational requirements and include field experiences. The 21-credit curriculum promotes development of essential life skills targeted for successful career outcomes. The Honors experience extends beyond the walls of the traditional classroom. Students may spend time with archaeologists in Italy, with anthropologists at a primate center, with large corporate firms and in small businesses, and with molecular biologists in laboratories. Studies have included 20th-century music, learning the art of problem solving, and pondered the ethical implications of research. Co-curricular themes prepare Honors Program students to assume leadership roles. The Honors Program is not for all students—only those individuals who desire professional success, demand

academic excellence, and expect to create the future. Each year 50 freshmen are selected for the Honors Program. Courses are taught as special topics and faculty instructors are recruited for their scholarly expertise. Honors students major in every department within the university and receive pre-professional advisement. Students take a six-credit linked English and Speech class and a three-credit Humanities course in the Freshman year. In the sophomore year, students take a three-credit mathematics or science class and a three-credit social sciences course. As juniors, students take a Junior Seminar that culminates in a project prospectus for the capstone experience. Honors 450 is the Senior Presentation delivered in a university-wide presentation. The following program standards must be maintained at the end of each academic year: Freshman Year 3.0 QPA 9 program credits Sophomore Year 3.25 QPA 15 program credits Junior Year 3.4 QPA 18 program credits Senior Year 3.4 QPA 21 program credits To be considered for Honors Program admission, entering freshman must have a minimum SAT score of 1150 or equivalent ACT scores, graduate in the top 15 percent of high school class, and successful completion of an interview. Undergraduate students already enrolled or transfer students may also apply. If a student should fail to residence at Clarion University. Candidates for graduation with an associate degree must complete a minimum of 30 credit hours in residence at the Venango Campus in Oil City, Pennsylvania. maintain the required QPA and course progression, the student will be placed on probation and have one semester to meet the requirements. A student who fails to achieve the required QPA and course progression by the end of the probationary semester will not be allowed to continue in the Honors Program or to continue to receive an Honors scholarship. **Disability Services offered to physically disabled students:** Note-taking services; Reader services; Tape recorders; Tutors. **Career services:** Career assessment; Career/job search classes; Internships

FACILITIES

Housing: Apartments for single students; Coed dorms; Men's dorms; Special housing for disabled student; Women's dorms 98% of campus accessible to physically disabled. **Special Academic Facilities/Equipment:** Planetarium. Art Gallery. **Computers:** 40% of classrooms, 100% of libraries, 50% of dining areas, 90% of student union, 10% of common outdoor areas have wireless network access. Students can register for classes online. Administrative functions (other than registration) can be performed online.

CAMPUS LIFE

Environment: Village **Activities:** Campus Ministries; Choral groups; Concert band; Dance; Drama/theater; International Student Organization; Jazz band; Literary magazine; Marching band; Music ensembles; Musical theater; Pep band; Radio station; Student government; Student newspaper; Student-run film society; Symphony orchestra; Television station 150 registered organizations, 17 honor societies, 4 religious organizations. 5 fraternities, 8 sororities. **Athletics (Intercollegiate):** Men: baseball, basketball, diving, football, golf, swimming, wrestling. Women: basketball, cross-country, diving, soccer, softball, swimming, tennis, track/field (outdoor), volleyball. **On-Campus Highlights:** Recreation Center, Carlson Library/Art Gallery, Student Center, Athletic Field, Tippin Gymnasium

ADMISSIONS

Freshman Academic Profile: Average high school GPA 3.2. 2% in top 10% of high school class, 9% in top 25% of high school class, 39% in top 50% of high school class. 87% from public high schools. **Test Scores:** SAT Math middle 50% range 420-520. SAT EBRW middle 50% range 420-510. ACT middle 50% range 17-22. Minimum paper TOEFL 500. **Basis for Candidate Selection:** Very important factors considered include: rigor of secondary school record, academic GPA, standardized test scores. Important factors considered include: class rank, application essay, recommendation(s). Other factors considered include: interview, extracurricular activities, talent/ability, character/personal qualities, first generation, racial/ethnic status, volunteer work, work experience, level of applicant's interest. **Freshman Admission Requirements:** High school diploma is required and GED is accepted Academic units required: 4 English, 3 math, 3 science, 3 social studies, Academic units recommended: 4 English, 4 math, 4 science, 1 science labs, 2 foreign language, 4 social studies, 1 history. **Freshman Admission Statistics:** 2,071 applied, 93.5% admitted, 55% enrolled. **Transfer Admission Requirements:** High school transcript, college transcript(s), statement of good standing from prior institution(s). Minimum college GPA of 2.0 required. Lowest grade transferable C. **General Admission Information:** Application fee $40. Priority deadline 2/15. Regular application deadline 8/1. Nonfall registration accepted. Admission may be deferred.

COSTS AND FINANCIAL AID

Annual in-state tuition $6,390. Annual out-of-state tuition $11,108. Room and board $6,390. Required fees $1,826. Average book expense $900. **Required Forms and Deadlines:** FAFSA; State aid form. **Notification of Awards:** Applicants will be notified of awards on a rolling basis beginning 3/30. **Types of Aid:** Need-based scholarships/grants: College/university scholarship or grant aid from institutional funds; Federal Pell; Private scholarships; SEOG; State scholarships/grants; United Negro College Fund. Loans: Direct PLUS loans; Direct Subsidized Stafford Loans; Direct Unsubsidized Stafford Loans. Student

Employment: Federal Work-Study Program available. Institutional employment available. **Financial Aid Statistics:** 78% needy freshmen, 75% needy undergrads receive need-based scholarship or grant aid. 39% freshmen, 26% undergrads receive non-need-based scholarship or grant aid. 91% freshmen, 61% undergrads receive need-based self-help aid. 4% freshmen, 3% undergrads receive athletic scholarships. 78% freshmen, 75% undergrads receive any aid. **Criteria for awarding aid:** *Need-based:* Academics, Alumni affiliation, Art, Leadership, Minority status, Music/drama *Non-need-based:* Academics, Alumni affiliation, Art, Athletics, Job skills, Leadership, Minority status, Music/drama, State/district residency.

CLARK ATLANTA UNIVERSITY

223 James P. Brawley, Dr., SW, Atlanta, GA 30314-4391
Phone: 404-880-8784 · **Financial Aid Phone:** 404-880-8992
E-mail: cauadmissions@cau.edu · **CEEB Code:** 5110
Fax: 404-880-6605 · **Website:** www.cau.edu · **ACT Code:** 804

This private school, affiliated with the Methodist Church, was founded in 1988. It has a 126 acre campus.

RATINGS
Admissions Selectivity Rating: 74   **Fire Safety Rating:** 97   **Green Rating:** 60*

STUDENTS AND FACULTY
Enrollment: 3,093. **Student Body:** 71% female, 29% male, 65% out-of-state, 4% international (10 countries represented). Asian <1%, African American 83%, Caucasian <1%, Hispanic <1%, Native American <1%, Race unknown 12%.
Retention and Graduation: 67% freshmen return for sophomore year. 27% grads go on to further study within 1 year. 24% grads pursue arts and sciences degrees. 2% grads pursue business degrees. **Faculty:** Student/faculty ratio 19:1. 176 full-time faculty, 85% hold PhDs, 90% are members of minority groups, 43% are women. 0% of classes are taught by teaching assistants.

ACADEMICS
Degrees: Bachelor's; Doctoral/Research; Master's; Post-Bachelor's certificate; Post-Master's certificate **Classes:** Most classes have 10-19 students.
Most popular majors: Radio, Television, And Digital Communication, Other; Biology/Biological Sciences, General; Business Administration And Management, General. **Special Study Options:** Accelerated program; Cooperative education program; Cross-registration; Double major; Dual enrollment; Exchange student program (domestic); Honors program; Independent study; Internships; Study abroad; Teacher certification program; Weekend college. **Combined degree programs:** BA/MA. **Disability Services offered to physically disabled students:** Note-taking services; Reader services; Tape recorders; Tutors. **Career services:** Career assessment; Career/job search classes; Internships

FACILITIES
Housing: Apartments for single students; Coed dorms; Men's dorms; Women's dorms 80% of campus accessible to physically diasbled. **Computers:** 100% of classrooms, 5% of dorms, 100% of libraries, 100% of dining areas, 100% of student union, 80% of common outdoor areas have wireless network access. Students can register for classes online. Administrative functions (other than registration) can be performed online.

CAMPUS LIFE
Environment: Metropolis **Activities:** Campus Ministries; Choral groups; Concert band; Dance; Drama/theater; International Student Organization; Marching band; Music ensembles; Musical theater; Opera; Pep band; Radio station; Student government; Student newspaper; Student-run film society; Symphony orchestra; Television station; Yearbook 80 registered organizations, 12 honor societies, 5 religious organizations. 4 fraternities, 4 sororities.
Athletics (Intercollegiate): *Men:* baseball, basketball, cross-country, football, track/field (outdoor). *Women:* basketball, cross-country, softball, tennis, track/field (outdoor), volleyball. **On-Campus Highlights:** Robert W. Woodruff Library, CAU Radio & Television Station, CAU Art Galleries, Heritage Commons Residence Hall, Henderson Student Center

ADMISSIONS
Freshman Academic Profile: Average high school GPA 3.2. 9% in top 10% of high school class, 30% in top 25% of high school class, 69% in top 50% of high school class. 90% from public high schools. **Test Scores:** SAT Math middle 50% range 400-480. SAT EBRW middle 50% range 420-490. ACT middle 50% range 18-21. Minimum paper TOEFL 500. **Basis for Candidate Selection:** *Very important factors considered include:* rigor of secondary school record, academic GPA, standardized test scores, character/personal qualities. *Important factors considered include:* application essay, recommendation(s), talent/ability.

Other factors considered include: alumni/ae relation, work experience, level of applicant's interest. **Freshman Admission Requirements:** High school diploma is required and GED is accepted *Academic units required:* 4 English, 3 math, 3 science, 1 science labs, 2 foreign language, 3 social studies, 3 academic electives. **Freshman Admission Statistics:** 10,733 applied, 71.8% admitted, 13% enrolled. **Transfer Admission Requirements:** college transcript(s), statement of good standing from prior institution(s). Minimum college GPA of 2.5 required. Lowest grade transferable C. **General Admission Information:** Application fee $35. Priority deadline 3/1. Regular application deadline 6/1. Nonfall registration accepted. Admission may be deferred for a maximum of One year.

COSTS AND FINANCIAL AID
Annual tuition $20,476. Room and board $10,878. Required fees $2,606. Average book expense $1,500. **Required Forms and Deadlines:** FAFSA; State aid form. **Notification of Awards:** Applicants will be notified of awards on a rolling basis beginning 4/1. **Types of Aid:** *Need-based scholarships/grants:* College/university scholarship or grant aid from institutional funds; Federal Pell; Private scholarships; SEOG; State scholarships/grants; United Negro College Fund. *Loans:* Direct PLUS loans; Direct Subsidized Stafford Loans; Direct Unsubsidized Stafford Loans. *Student Employment:* Federal Work-Study Program available. Institutional employment available. **Financial Aid Statistics:** 93% needy freshmen, 90% needy undergrads receive need-based scholarship or grant aid. 17% freshmen, 15% undergrads receive non-need-based scholarship or grant aid. 96% freshmen, 95% undergrads receive need-based self-help aid. 0% freshmen, 0% undergrads receive athletic scholarships. 92% freshmen, 94% undergrads receive any aid. 91% undergrads borrow to pay for school. Average cumulative indebtedness $40,393. **Criteria for awarding aid:** *Non-need-based:* Academics, Art, Athletics, Leadership, Minority status, Music/drama, Religious affiliation, State/district residency.

CLARK UNIVERSITY

950 Main Street, Worcester, MA 01610-1477
Phone: 508-793-7431 · **Financial Aid Phone:** 508-793-7478
E-mail: admissions@clarku.edu · **CEEB Code:** 3279
Fax: 508-793-8821 · **Website:** www.clarku.edu · **ACT Code:** 1808

This private school was founded in 1887. It has a 50 acre campus.

RATINGS
Admissions Selectivity Rating: 89   **Fire Safety Rating:** 98 ·   **Green Rating:** 91

STUDENTS AND FACULTY
Enrollment: 2,204. **Student Body:** 61% female, 39% male, 62% out-of-state, 14% international (65 countries represented). Asian 8%, African American 4%, Caucasian 58%, Hispanic 8%, Native American <1%, Pacific Islander 0%, Two or more races 2%, Race unknown 6%.
Retention and Graduation: 85% freshmen return for sophomore year. 77% freshmen graduate within 4 years. 83% freshmen graduate within 6 years. 42% grads go on to further study within 1 year. 25% grads pursue arts and sciences degrees. 1% grads pursue law degrees. 5% grads pursue business degrees. 1% grads pursue medical degrees. **Faculty:** Student/faculty ratio 10:1. 201 full-time faculty, 99% hold PhDs, 22% are members of minority groups, 45% are women. 1% of classes are taught by teaching assistants.

ACADEMICS
Degrees: Bachelor's; Certificate; Doctoral; Doctoral/Research; Master's; Post-Bachelor's certificate; Post-Master's certificate **Classes:** Most classes have 10-19 students. **Most popular majors:** Biology/Biological Sciences, General; Psychology, General; Political Science And Government, General. **Special Study Options:** Cross-registration; Double major; English as a Second Language (ESL); Independent study; Internships; Liberal arts/career combination; Student-designed major; Study abroad; Teacher certification program. **Combined degree programs:** BA/MA. **Disability Services offered to physically disabled students:** Note-taking services; Tape recorders. **Career services:** Alumni network; Alumni services; Career assessment; Career/job search classes; Internships; Regional alumni

FACILITIES
Housing: Apartments for single students; Coed dorms; Special housing for disabled student; Wellness housing; Women's dorms **Special Academic Facilities/Equipment:** Galleries, 3 full theatres, concert hall, machine shop, near zero lab, Kasperson enviromental library, Robert H. Goddard historical

exhibition, rare book room, rare map collection, Freud archives, craft center, music rehearsal space, map library, IDRISI GIS lab, Holocaust library & center, arboretum, herbarium, extensive darkroom facilities, radio station, satellite dish for international program reception, electron microscope, nuclear magnetic resonance spectrometer, astronomy observatory. **Computers:** 100% of classrooms, 15% of dorms, 100% of libraries, 100% of dining areas, 100% of student union, 15% of common outdoor areas have wireless network access. Students can register for classes online. Administrative functions (other than registration) can be performed online.

CAMPUS LIFE

Environment: City **Activities:** Campus Ministries; Choral groups; Concert band; Dance; Drama/theater; International Student Organization; Jazz band; Literary magazine; Marching band; Model UN; Music ensembles; Musical theater; Pep band; Radio station; Student government; Student newspaper; Student-run film society; Symphony orchestra; Television station; Yearbook 110 registered organizations, 10 honor societies, 7 religious organizations. **Athletics (Intercollegiate):** *Men:* baseball, basketball, crew/rowing, cross-country, diving, lacrosse, soccer, swimming, tennis. *Women:* basketball, crew/rowing, cross-country, diving, field hockey, soccer, softball, swimming, tennis, volleyball. **On-Campus Highlights:** Academic Commons at Goddard Library, Campus Green (in warmer months), The Bistro in the University Center, Alumni Student Engagement Center, Larger-than-life statue of Sigmund Freud in Red Square **Environmental Initiatives:** Becoming Climate Neutral—Zero Emissions—by 2030

ADMISSIONS

Freshman Academic Profile: Average high school GPA 3.6. 37% in top 10% of high school class, 75% in top 25% of high school class, 96% in top 50% of high school class. 75% from public high schools. **Test Scores:** SAT Math middle 50% range 580-680. SAT EBRW middle 50% range 600-700. ACT middle 50% range 27-31. Minimum internet-based TOEFL 80. Minimum paper TOEFL 550. **Basis for Candidate Selection:** *Very important factors considered include:* rigor of secondary school record, academic GPA, recommendation(s). *Important factors considered include:* application essay, extracurricular activities, talent/ability, character/personal qualities, volunteer work. *Other factors considered include:* class rank, standardized test scores, interview, first generation, alumni/ae relation, geographical residence, racial/ethnic status, work experience, level of applicant's interest. **Freshman Admission Requirements:** High school diploma is required and GED is accepted *Academic units recommended:* 4 English, 3 math, 3 science, 2 science labs, 2 foreign language, 2 social studies, 2 history. **Freshman Admission Statistics:** 8,355 applied, 56.3% admitted, 13% enrolled. **Transfer Admission Requirements:** High school transcript, college transcript(s), essay or personal statement, standardized test scores, statement of good standing from prior institution(s). Minimum college GPA of 2.8 required. **General Admission Information:** Application fee $60. Regular application deadline 1/15. Nonfall registration accepted. Admission may be deferred for a maximum of 1 year.

COSTS AND FINANCIAL AID

Annual tuition $44,050. Room and board $8,860. Required fees $350. Average book expense $800. **Required Forms and Deadlines:** CSS/Financial Aid PROFILE; FAFSA; Noncustodial PROFILE. **Notification of Awards:** Applicants will be notified of awards on or about 3/31. **Types of Aid:** *Need-based scholarships/grants:* College/university scholarship or grant aid from institutional funds; Federal Pell; SEOG; State scholarships/grants. *Loans:* Direct PLUS loans; Direct Subsidized Stafford Loans; Direct Unsubsidized Stafford Loans. *Student Employment:* Federal Work-Study Program available. Institutional employment available. **Financial Aid Statistics:** 98% needy freshmen, 97% needy undergrads receive need-based scholarship or grant aid. 20% freshmen, 18% undergrads receive non-need-based scholarship or grant aid. 72% freshmen, 73% undergrads receive need-based self-help aid. 0% freshmen, 0% undergrads receive athletic scholarships. 91% freshmen, 89% undergrads receive any aid. 90% undergrads borrow to pay for school. Average cumulative indebtedness $26,870. **Criteria for awarding aid:** *Non-need-based:* Academics, Leadership.

CLARKE UNIVERSITY

1550 Clarke Drive, Dubuque, IA 52001-3198
Phone: 563-588-6316
E-mail: admissions@clarke.edu • **CEEB Code:** 6099
Fax: 563-588-6789 • **Website:** www.clarke.edu • **ACT Code:** 1290

This private school, affiliated with the Roman Catholic Church, was founded in 1843. It has a 55 acre campus.

RATINGS
Admissions Selectivity Rating: 77   **Fire Safety Rating:** 60*   **Green Rating:** 60*

STUDENTS AND FACULTY
Enrollment: 933. **Student Body:** 69% female, 31% male, 38% out-of-state, 1% international (8 countries represented). Asian 1%, African American 4%, Caucasian 89%, Hispanic 5%, Native American <1%, Pacific Islander 0%, Two or more races <1%, Race unknown 0%. **Retention and Graduation:** 73% freshmen return for sophomore year. 25% grads go on to further study within 1 year. 23% grads pursue arts and sciences degrees. 0% grads pursue law degrees. 2% grads pursue business degrees. 0% grads pursue medical degrees. **Faculty:** Student/faculty ratio 10:1. 89 full-time faculty, 67% hold PhDs, 3% are members of minority groups, 67% are women. 0% of classes are taught by teaching assistants.

ACADEMICS
Degrees: Associate; Bachelor's; Doctoral/Professional; Master's **Classes:** Most classes have 10-19 students. Most lab/discussion sessions have 10-19 students. **Most popular majors:** Psychology, General; Nursing/Registered Nurse (Rn, Asn, Bsn, Msn); Business/Commerce, General. **Special Study Options:** Accelerated program; Cross-registration; Distance learning; Double major; Honors program; Independent study; Internships; Student-designed major; Study abroad; Teacher certification program. **Disability Services offered to physically disabled students:** Note-taking services; Reader services; Tape recorders; Tutors. **Career services:** Alumni services; Career assessment; Career/job search classes; Internships

FACILITIES
Housing: Apartments for single students; Coed dorms; Men's dorms; Women's dorms 90% of campus accessible to physically diasbled. **Special Academic Facilities/Equipment:** Art gallery, computer classrooms for math, biology, and computer science, computer-interfaced chemistry lab, human gross anatomy and nursing labs, electron microscope, music performance hall, foreign language lab, distance learning classroom **Computers:** Students can register for classes online. Administrative functions (other than registration) can be performed online.

CAMPUS LIFE
Environment: Town **Activities:** Campus Ministries; Choral groups; Concert band; Dance; Drama/theater; Jazz band; Literary magazine; Music ensembles; Musical theater; Radio station; Student government; Student newspaper; Yearbook 48 registered organizations, 5 honor societies, 1 religious organization. **Athletics (Intercollegiate):** *Men:* baseball, basketball, cheerleading, cross-country, golf, soccer, tennis, volleyball. *Women:* basketball, cheerleading, cross-country, golf, soccer, softball, tennis, volleyball.

ADMISSIONS
Freshman Academic Profile: Average high school GPA 3.5. 13% in top 10% of high school class, 55% in top 25% of high school class, 84% in top 50% of high school class. 81% from public high schools. **Test Scores:** SAT Math middle 50% range 475-550. SAT EBRW middle 50% range 470-530. ACT middle 50% range 20-24. Minimum paper TOEFL 527. **Basis for Candidate Selection:** *Very important factors considered include:* rigor of secondary school record, academic GPA, standardized test scores, talent/ability. *Important factors considered include:* class rank. *Other factors considered include:* interview, extracurricular activities, racial/ethnic status, volunteer work. **Freshman Admission Requirements:** High school diploma is required and GED is accepted *Academic units required:* 4 English, 3 math, 3 science, 2 science labs, 2 foreign language, 2 social studies, 4 academic electives, *Academic units recommended:* 4 math, 4 science. **Freshman Admission Statistics:** 1,359 applied, 70.5% admitted, 19% enrolled. **Transfer Admission Requirements:** High school transcript, college transcript(s), standardized test scores, statement of good standing from prior institution(s). Minimum college GPA of 2.0 required. Lowest grade transferable C. **General Admission Information:** Application fee $25. Nonfall registration accepted. Admission may be deferred for a maximum of 1 year.

COSTS AND FINANCIAL AID

Annual tuition $28,000. Room and board $8,400. Required fees $900. Average book expense $1,160. **Notification of Awards:** Applicants will be notified of awards on a rolling basis beginning 3/15. **Types of Aid:** *Need-based scholarships/grants:* College/university scholarship or grant aid from institutional funds; Federal Nursing Scholarships; Federal Pell; Private scholarships; SEOG; State scholarships/grants. *Loans:* Direct PLUS loans; Direct Subsidized Stafford Loans; Direct Unsubsidized Stafford Loans. *Student Employment:* Federal Work-Study Program available. Institutional employment available. **Financial Aid Statistics:** 100% needy freshmen, 100% needy undergrads receive need-based scholarship or grant aid. 99% freshmen, 95% undergrads receive non-need-based scholarship or grant aid. 90% freshmen, 89% undergrads receive need-based self-help aid. 41% freshmen, 33% undergrads receive athletic scholarships. **Criteria for awarding aid:** *Need-based:* Academics *Non-need-based:* Academics, Art, Athletics, Leadership, Music/drama.

CLARKSON UNIVERSITY

8 Clarkson Avenue, Potsdam, NY 13699
Phone: 315-268-6480 · **Financial Aid Phone:** 315-268-6480
E-mail: admissions@clarkson.edu · **CEEB Code:** 2084
Fax: 315-268-7647 · **Website:** http://www.clarkson.edu

This private school was founded in 1896. It has a 640 acre campus.

RATINGS

Admissions Selectivity Rating: 86   Fire Safety Rating: 96   Green Rating: 91

STUDENTS AND FACULTY

Enrollment: 2,991. **Student Body:** 30% female, 70% male, 27% out-of-state, 3% international (22 countries represented). Asian 4%, African American 2%, Caucasian 81%, Hispanic 5%, Native American <1%, Pacific Islander 0%, Two or more races 3%, Race unknown 2%.
Retention and Graduation: 87% freshmen return for sophomore year. 58% freshmen graduate within 4 years. 74% freshmen graduate within 6 years. 14% grads go on to further study within 1 year. 6% grads pursue arts and sciences degrees. 1% grads pursue law degrees. 2% grads pursue business degrees. 0% grads pursue medical degrees. **Faculty:** Student/faculty ratio 14:1. 253 full-time faculty, 87% hold PhDs, 22% are members of minority groups, 30% are women. 0% of classes are taught by teaching assistants.

ACADEMICS

Degrees: Bachelor's; Doctoral/Professional; Doctoral/Research; Master's; Post-Bachelor's certificate **Classes:** Most classes have 10-19 students. **Most popular majors:** Civil Engineering, General; Mechanical Engineering; Engineering/Industrial Management. **Special Study Options:** Accelerated program; Cooperative education program; Cross-registration; Distance learning; Double major; Dual enrollment; English as a Second Language (ESL); Honors program; Independent study; Internships; Liberal arts/career combination; Student-designed major; Study abroad. **Honors programs:** Built upon current and emerging problems in science, technology and society, the Clarkson University Honors Program offers unique academic challenges and opportunities for Clarkson's most promising students. The program is a gateway to a multitude of opportunities that include internships, research experience, fellowships, graduate schools, study abroad, and jobs. **Disability Services offered to physically disabled students:** Note-taking services; Reader services; Tape recorders; Tutors. **Career services:** Alumni network; Alumni services; Career assessment; Career/job search classes; Internships; Regional alumni

FACILITIES

Housing: Apartments for single students; Coed dorms; Fraternity/sorority housing; Men's dorms; Special housing for disabled student; Special housing for international students; Theme housing; Women's dorms 85% of campus accessible to physically diasbled. **Special Academic Facilities/Equipment:** The Student Center is a place where students can come to spend time between classes, study, and hold meetings and late night events. In it is the Forum, an innovative auditorium in the form of a stairwell equipped with a massive video wall. The Deneka Family Fitness Center offers a full workout facility with an assortment of cardiovascular machines, a weight room and classes. The Denny Brown Adirondack Lodge is home to the Outing Club and the starting point for outdoor adventures. The Outing Club also maintains the Canoe House on the Raquette River, housing canoes and kayaks for student use. Glass walkways connect all hill campus academic buildings, so students need not venture out if there is inclement weather between classes. **Computers:** 100% of classrooms, 100% of libraries, 100% of dining areas, 100% of student union, 20% of common outdoor areas have wireless network access. Students can register for classes online. Administrative functions (other than registration) can be performed online.

CAMPUS LIFE

Environment: Village **Activities:** Choral groups; Dance; Drama/theater; International Student Organization; Jazz band; Model UN; Musical theater; Pep band; Radio station; Student government; Student newspaper; Symphony orchestra; Television station; Yearbook 117 registered organizations, 7 honor societies, 3 religious organizations. 11 fraternities, 3 sororities. **Athletics (Intercollegiate):** *Men:* baseball, basketball, cross-country, diving, golf, ice hockey, lacrosse, skiing (downhill/alpine), skiing (nordic/cross-country), soccer, swimming. *Women:* basketball, cross-country, diving, ice hockey, lacrosse, skiing (downhill/alpine), skiing (nordic/cross-country), soccer, swimming, volleyball. **On-Campus Highlights:** Student Center Forum & Java City, Wooded Recreational Trails, Cheel Campus Center & Arena, Adirondack Lodge, Residence Hall Rooms **Environmental Initiatives:** Clarkson has undertaken many activities to integrate sustainability into facilities and campus life. For example, as part of a significant renovation of the Woodstock Village Apartments to increase its energy efficiency, four of the buildings were modified to create the campus' Smart Housing Project. These buildings have a high density of water, electricity and air quality sensors that are used for building energy modeling, advanced building automation and feedback to students about their utility use. Research on feedback and motivation strategies has shown significant conservation, with as much as 21% savings in electricity and hot water use.

ADMISSIONS

Freshman Academic Profile: Average high school GPA 3.6. 37% in top 10% of high school class, 74% in top 25% of high school class, 96% in top 50% of high school class. 90% from public high schools. **Test Scores:** SAT Math middle 50% range 580-680. SAT EBRW middle 50% range 563-650. ACT middle 50% range 24-29. Minimum internet-based TOEFL 80. Minimum paper TOEFL 550. **Basis for Candidate Selection:** *Very important factors considered include:* rigor of secondary school record, academic GPA. *Important factors considered include:* class rank, standardized test scores, recommendation(s), extracurricular activities, volunteer work. *Other factors considered include:* application essay, talent/ability, character/personal qualities, first generation, alumni/ae relation, work experience, level of applicant's interest. **Freshman Admission Requirements:** High school diploma is required and GED is accepted *Academic units required:* 4 English, 3 math, 1 science, and 4 units from above areas or other academic areas. *Academic units recommended:* 4 math, 4 science. **Freshman Admission Statistics:** 7,000 applied, 65.7% admitted, 15% enrolled. **Transfer Admission Requirements:** college transcript(s), Minimum college GPA of 2.75 required. Lowest grade transferable 2. **General Admission Information:** Application fee $50. Regular application deadline 1/15. Nonfall registration accepted. Admission may be deferred for a maximum of 1 year.

COSTS AND FINANCIAL AID

Annual tuition $48,194. Room and board $15,222. Required fees $1,250. Average book expense $1,446. **Required Forms and Deadlines:** FAFSA; State aid form. **Notification of Awards:** Applicants will be notified of awards on a rolling basis beginning 2/17. **Types of Aid:** *Need-based scholarships/grants:* College/university scholarship or grant aid from institutional funds; Federal Pell; Private scholarships; SEOG; State scholarships/grants. *Loans:* Direct PLUS loans; Direct Subsidized Stafford Loans; Direct Unsubsidized Stafford Loans. *Student Employment:* Federal Work-Study Program available. Institutional employment available. **Financial Aid Statistics:** 99% needy freshmen, 99% needy undergrads receive need-based scholarship or grant aid. 14% freshmen, 14% undergrads receive non-need-based scholarship or grant aid. 79% freshmen, 81% undergrads receive need-based self-help aid. 1% freshmen, 1% undergrads receive athletic scholarships. 97% freshmen, 97% undergrads receive any aid. 85% undergrads borrow to pay for school. Average cumulative indebtedness $23,500. **Criteria for awarding aid:** *Need-based:* Academics, Minority status *Non-need-based:* Academics, Alumni affiliation, Leadership, Minority status.

CLAYTON COLLEGE & STATE UNIVERSITY

2000 Clayton State Blvd., Morrow, GA 30206-0285
Phone: 678-466-4115
E-mail: ccsu-info@mail.clayton.edu
Fax: 678-466-4149 · **Website:** www.clayton.edu

This is a public school.

RATINGS

Admissions Selectivity Rating: 82   **Fire Safety Rating:** 60*   **Green Rating:** 60*

STUDENTS AND FACULTY

Enrollment: 5,661. **Student Body:** 69% female, 31% male, 5% out-of-state, 2% international. Asian 4%, African American 48%, Caucasian 43%, Hispanic 3%, Native American 1%, Race unknown 0%.
Retention and Graduation: 61% freshmen return for sophomore year. **Faculty:** Student/faculty ratio 28:1. 157 full-time faculty, 57% hold PhDs, 15% are members of minority groups, 59% are women.

ACADEMICS

Degrees: Associate; Bachelor's; Certificate; Master's; Terminal Associate; Transfer Associate **Classes:** Most classes have fewer than 10 students. Most lab/discussion sessions have 10-19 students. **Special Study Options:** Cooperative education program; Cross-registration; Distance learning; Double major; Dual enrollment; Exchange student program (domestic); Honors program; Independent study; Internships; Liberal arts/career combination; Study abroad; Teacher certification program.

FACILITIES

Housing: Apartments for single students

CAMPUS LIFE

Activities: Choral groups; Drama/theater; Jazz band; Literary magazine; Music ensembles; Musical theater; Opera; Pep band; Student government; Student newspaper.

ADMISSIONS

Freshman Academic Profile: Average high school GPA 2.9. **Test Scores:** SAT Math middle 50% range 440-550. SAT EBRW middle 50% range 450-550. ACT middle 50% range 17-21. **Basis for Candidate Selection:** *Very important factors considered include:* rigor of secondary school record, academic GPA, standardized test scores. *Other factors considered include:* class rank, extracurricular activities, talent/ability. **Freshman Admission Requirements:** High school diploma is required and GED is not accepted *Academic units required:* 4 English, 4 math, 3 science, 2 foreign language, 3 social studies. **Freshman Admission Statistics:** 2,920 applied, 71.0% admitted, 63% enrolled. **Transfer Admission Requirements:** college transcript(s), statement of good standing from prior institution(s). Minimum college GPA of 2.0 required. Lowest grade transferable D. **General Admission Information:** Application fee $40. Priority deadline 2/1. Regular application deadline 7/1. Nonfall registration accepted. Admission may be deferred.

COSTS AND FINANCIAL AID

Annual out-of-state tuition $8,848. Average book expense $1,000. **Required Forms and Deadlines:** FAFSA; State aid form. **Types of Aid:** *Need-based scholarships/grants:* College/university scholarship or grant aid from institutional funds; Federal Nursing Scholarships; Federal Pell; Private scholarships; SEOG; State scholarships/grants. **Financial Aid Statistics:** 65% needy freshmen, 67% needy undergrads receive need-based scholarship or grant aid. 76% freshmen, 45% undergrads receive non-need-based scholarship or grant aid. 45% freshmen, 64% undergrads receive need-based self-help aid. 1% freshmen, 3% undergrads receive athletic scholarships. **Criteria for awarding aid:** *Need-based:* Academics *Non-need-based:* Academics.

CLEAR CREEK BAPTIST BIBLE COLLEGE

Messikomer Hall, Pineville, KY 40977-9754
Phone: 606-337-3196 · **Financial Aid Phone:** (606)337-1457
E-mail: ccbbc@ccbbc.edu
Fax: 606-337-2372 · **Website:** www.ccbbc.edu

This private school, affiliated with the Southern Baptist Church, was founded in 1926. It has a 700 acre campus.

RATINGS

Admissions Selectivity Rating: 68   **Fire Safety Rating:** 72   **Green Rating:** 60*

STUDENTS AND FACULTY

Enrollment: 160. **Student Body:** 22% female, 78% male, 60% out-of-state, 0% international (0 countries represented). Asian 1%, African American 1%, Caucasian 95%, Hispanic 2%, Native American 0%, Race unknown 1%.
Retention and Graduation: 93% freshmen return for sophomore year. 30% grads go on to further study within 1 year. **Faculty:** Student/faculty ratio 10:1. 6 full-time faculty, 83% hold PhDs, 0% are members of minority groups, 0% are women.

ACADEMICS

Degrees: Associate; Bachelor's; Certificate **Classes:** Most classes have 10-19 students. Most lab/discussion sessions have 10-19 students. **Most popular majors:** Bible/Biblical Studies. **Special Study Options:** Distance learning; Double major; Independent study; Internships. **Career services:** Alumni network

FACILITIES

Housing: Apartments for married students; Apartments for single students; Men's dorms; Wellness housing; Women's dorms 95% of campus accessible to physically disabled. **Special Academic Facilities/Equipment:** Jerusalem model **Computers:** 10% of dorms, 100% of libraries, 5% of common outdoor areas have wireless network access. Students can register for classes online.

CAMPUS LIFE

Environment: Rural **Activities:** Campus Ministries; Choral groups; Music ensembles; Radio station; Student government; Student newspaper. **On-Campus Highlights:** Kelly Hall, Jerusalem model, Family Life Center, Creek and walking trails, Carolyn Boatman Brooks Memorial Library

ADMISSIONS

Freshman Academic Profile: 95% from public high schools. **Test Scores:** Minimum paper TOEFL 550. **Basis for Candidate Selection:** *Very important factors considered include:* application essay, recommendation(s), character/personal qualities, religious affiliation/commitment. *Important factors considered include:* interview. *Other factors considered include:* talent/ability, alumni/ae relation, level of applicant's interest. **Freshman Admission Requirements:** High school diploma is required and GED is accepted **Freshman Admission Statistics:** 14 applied, 92.9% admitted, 85% enrolled. **Transfer Admission Requirements:** High school transcript, college transcript(s), essay or personal statement, interview, Minimum college GPA of 2.0 required. Lowest grade transferable C. **General Admission Information:** Application fee $40. Priority deadline 7/15. Regular application deadline 8/2. Nonfall registration accepted. Admission may be deferred for a maximum of 2 years.

COSTS AND FINANCIAL AID

Annual tuition $5,482. Room and board $3,470. Required fees $400. Average book expense $1,200. **Required Forms and Deadlines:** FAFSA; Institution's own financial aid form. **Notification of Awards:** Applicants will be notified of awards on a rolling basis beginning 5/1. **Types of Aid:** *Need-based scholarships/grants:* College/university scholarship or grant aid from institutional funds; Federal Pell; Private scholarships; SEOG, *Loans: Student Employment:* Federal Work-Study Program available. Institutional employment available. **Financial Aid Statistics:** 100% needy freshmen, 100% needy undergrads receive need-based scholarship or grant aid. 22% freshmen, 42% undergrads receive non-need-based scholarship or grant aid. 33% freshmen, 37% undergrads receive need-based self-help aid. 0% freshmen, 0% undergrads receive athletic scholarships. 81% freshmen, 75% undergrads receive any aid. **Criteria for awarding aid:** *Need-based:* Academics, Alumni affiliation, Leadership, Religious affiliation *Non-need-based:* Academics, Leadership, Religious affiliation, State/district residency.

CLEARWATER CHRISTIAN COLLEGE

3400 Gulf-to-Bay Boulevard, Clearwater, FL 33759-4595
Phone: 727-726-1153 • **Financial Aid Phone:** (727) 726-1153
E-mail: admissions@clearwater.edu
Fax: 727-726-8597 • **Website:** www.clearwater.edu • **ACT Code:** 715

This private school, affiliated with the Christian (Nondenominational) Church, was founded in 1966. It has a 138 acre campus.

RATINGS
Admissions Selectivity Rating: 81   **Fire Safety Rating:** 96   **Green Rating:** 60*

STUDENTS AND FACULTY
Enrollment: 546. **Student Body:** 50% female, 50% male, 52% out-of-state, <1% international (2 countries represented). Asian 1%, African American 5%, Caucasian 82%, Hispanic 4%, Native American <1%, Race unknown 8%.
Retention and Graduation: 70% freshmen return for sophomore year. 26% grads go on to further study within 1 year. 16% grads pursue arts and sciences degrees. 1% grads pursue law degrees. 2% grads pursue business degrees. 4% grads pursue medical degrees. **Faculty:** 28 full-time faculty, 68% hold PhDs, 4% are members of minority groups, 32% are women. 0% of classes are taught by teaching assistants.

ACADEMICS
Degrees: Associate; Bachelor's; Certificate; Master's **Classes:** Most classes have 40-49 students. Most lab/discussion sessions have fewer than 10 students. **Most popular majors:** Elementary Education And Teaching; Kinesiology And Exercise Science; Business Administration And Management, General. **Special Study Options:** Cooperative education program; Distance learning; Double major; Dual enrollment; Honors program; Independent study; Internships; Liberal arts/career combination; Student-designed major; Study abroad; Teacher certification program. **Honors programs:** Interdisciplinary Studies, a self-designed multidisciplinary program for students with exceptional ability and focus. **Disability Services offered to physically disabled students:** Tape recorders; Tutors. **Career services:** Alumni services; Career/job search classes; Internships

FACILITIES
Housing: Men's dorms; Women's dorms **Computers:** 100% of classrooms, 100% of dorms, 100% of libraries, 100% of dining areas, have wireless network access. Administrative functions (other than registration) can be performed online.

CAMPUS LIFE
Environment: City **Activities:** Campus Ministries; Choral groups; Concert band; Drama/theater; Music ensembles; Pep band; Student government; Student newspaper; Student-run film society; Symphony orchestra; Yearbook 17 registered organizations, 1 honor society, 1 religious organization. 5 fraternities, 6 sororities. **Athletics (Intercollegiate):** *Men:* baseball, basketball, golf, soccer. *Women:* basketball, golf, soccer, softball, volleyball. **On-Campus Highlights:** the Cove, Gymnasium, Cathcart Hall Cafeteria, Easter Library

ADMISSIONS
Freshman Academic Profile: 30% from public high schools. **Test Scores:** SAT Math middle 50% range 450-530. SAT EBRW middle 50% range 470-560. ACT middle 50% range 21-23. Minimum internet-based TOEFL 84. Minimum paper TOEFL 500. **Basis for Candidate Selection:** *Very important factors considered include:* application essay, standardized test scores, recommendation(s), character/personal qualities, religious affiliation/ commitment. *Important factors considered include:* rigor of secondary school record, academic GPA, interview. *Other factors considered include:* alumni/ae relation, volunteer work, level of applicant's interest. **Freshman Admission Requirements:** High school diploma is required and GED is accepted *Academic units required:* 4 English, 3 math, 3 science, 2 foreign language, 3 social studies. **Freshman Admission Statistics:** 341 applied, 73.9% admitted, 56% enrolled. **Transfer Admission Requirements:** High school transcript, college transcript(s), essay or personal statement, standardized test scores, statement of good standing from prior institution(s). Minimum college GPA of 2.0 required. Lowest grade transferable C-. **General Admission Information:** Application fee $35. Regular application deadline 8/1. Nonfall registration accepted. Admission may be deferred for a maximum of 1 year.

COSTS AND FINANCIAL AID
Annual tuition $16,250. Required fees $95. Average book expense $1,000. **Required Forms and Deadlines:** FAFSA; Institution's own financial aid form; State aid form. **Notification of Awards:** Applicants will be notified of awards on a rolling basis beginning 3/15. **Types of Aid:** *Need-based scholarships/ grants:* College/university scholarship or grant aid from institutional funds; Federal Pell; Private scholarships; SEOG; State scholarships/grants. *Loans:*

Direct PLUS loans; Direct Subsidized Stafford Loans; Direct Unsubsidized Stafford Loans. *Student Employment:* Federal Work-Study Program available. Institutional employment available. **Financial Aid Statistics:** 100% needy freshmen, 99% needy undergrads receive need-based scholarship or grant aid. 9% freshmen, 9% undergrads receive non-need-based scholarship or grant aid. 63% freshmen, 64% undergrads receive need-based self-help aid. 0% freshmen, 0% undergrads receive athletic scholarships. 97% freshmen, 94% undergrads receive any aid. **Criteria for awarding aid:** *Need-based:* Academics, Alumni affiliation, Music/drama, Religious affiliation *Non-need-based:* Academics, Alumni affiliation, Leadership, Music/drama, Religious affiliation.

CLEMSON UNIVERSITY

105 Sikes Hall, Clemson, SC 29634-5124
Phone: 864-656-2287 • **Financial Aid Phone:** (864) 656-2280
E-mail: cuadmissions@clemson.edu • **CEEB Code:** 5111
Fax: 864-656-2464 • **Website:** www.clemson.edu • **ACT Code:** 3842

This public school was founded in 1889. It has a 17000 acre campus.

RATINGS
Admissions Selectivity Rating: 93   **Fire Safety Rating:** 97   **Green Rating:** 60*

STUDENTS AND FACULTY
Enrollment: 19,172. **Student Body:** 49% female, 51% male, 35% out-of-state, 1% international (84 countries represented). Asian 2%, African American 7%, Caucasian 83%, Hispanic 4%, Native American <1%, Pacific Islander <1%, Two or more races 3%, Race unknown <1%.
Retention and Graduation: 93% freshmen return for sophomore year. 82% freshmen graduate within 6 years. 28% grads go on to further study within 1 year. 25% grads pursue arts and sciences degrees. 5% grads pursue law degrees. 21% grads pursue business degrees. 8% grads pursue medical degrees. **Faculty:** Student/faculty ratio 16:1. 1,248 full-time faculty, 86% hold PhDs, 20% are members of minority groups, 39% are women. 7% of classes are taught by teaching assistants.

ACADEMICS
Degrees: Bachelor's; Doctoral; Master's; Post-Bachelor's certificate; Post-Master's certificate **Classes:** Most classes have 10-19 students. Most lab/ discussion sessions have 10-19 students. **Most popular majors:** Engineering, General; Biology/Biological Sciences, General; Business/Commerce, General. **Special Study Options:** Cooperative education program; Distance learning; Double major; Dual enrollment; Honors program; Independent study; Internships; Study abroad; Teacher certification program. **Honors programs:** The National Scholars Program. Please visit: http://www.clemson.edu/national_ scholars/ **Combined degree programs:** BA/MEng. **Disability Services offered to physically disabled students:** Note-taking services; Reader services; Tape recorders; Tutors. **Career services:** Alumni network; Alumni services; Career assessment; Career/job search classes; Internships; Regional alumni

FACILITIES
Housing: Apartments for single students; Coed dorms; Fraternity/sorority housing; Men's dorms; Special housing for international students; Theme housing; Wellness housing; Women's dorms **Special Academic Facilities/ Equipment:** The South Carolina Botanical Gardens, the Campbell Geology Museum, the Brooks Center for the Performing Arts, the Rudolph Lee Art Gallery, The Garrison Livestock Arena, The John C. Calhoun Home **Computers:** 75% of classrooms, 25% of dorms, 100% of libraries, 100% of dining areas, 100% of student union, 40% of common outdoor areas have wireless network access. Students can register for classes online. Administrative functions (other than registration) can be performed online. Undergraduates are required to own a computer.

CAMPUS LIFE
Environment: Village **Activities:** Choral groups; Concert band; Dance; Drama/theater; Jazz band; Literary magazine; Marching band; Music ensembles; Pep band; Radio station; Student government; Student newspaper; Television station; Yearbook 292 registered organizations, 23 honor societies, 24 religious organizations. 26 fraternities, 17 sororities. **Athletics (Intercollegiate):** *Men:* baseball, basketball, cheerleading, cross-country, diving, football, golf, soccer, swimming, tennis, track/field (outdoor), track/field (indoor). *Women:* basketball, cheerleading, crew/rowing, cross-country, diving, soccer, swimming, tennis, track/field (outdoor), track/field (indoor), volleyball.

On-Campus Highlights: SC Botanical Garden/ Discovery Center/Geology Muse, Hendrix Student Center—Clemson Ice Cream, Conference Center and Inn at Clemson/Walker Golf C, Fort Hill—John C. Calhoun House, Lee Art Gallery **Environmental Initiatives:** LEED

ADMISSIONS

Freshman Academic Profile: Average high school GPA 4.0. 62% in top 10% of high school class, 91% in top 25% of high school class, 99% in top 50% of high school class. 89% from public high schools. **Test Scores:** SAT Math middle 50% range 600-700. SAT EBRW middle 50% range 620-690. ACT middle 50% range 27-31. Minimum paper TOEFL 550. **Basis for Candidate Selection:** *Very important factors considered include:* rigor of secondary school record, class rank, academic GPA, standardized test scores, state residency. *Important factors considered include:* alumni/ae relation. *Other factors considered include:* application essay, recommendation(s), extracurricular activities, talent/ability. **Freshman Admission Requirements:** High school diploma is required and GED is accepted *Academic units required:* 4 English, 3 math, 3 science, 3 science labs, 2 foreign language, 1 social studies, 1 history, 2 academic electives, 1 computer science, 1 visual/performing arts, and 1 unit from above areas or other academic areas. *Academic units recommended:* 4 math, 4 science labs, 3 foreign language. **Freshman Admission Statistics:** 26,242 applied, 47.2% admitted, 29% enrolled. **Transfer Admission Requirements:** college transcript(s), Minimum college GPA of 2.5 required. Lowest grade transferable C. **General Admission Information:** Application fee $70. Priority deadline 12/1. Regular application deadline 5/1. Nonfall registration accepted.

COSTS AND FINANCIAL AID

Annual in-state tuition $1,132. Annual out-of-state tuition $32,738. Required fees $1,132. Average book expense $1,308. **Required Forms and Deadlines:** FAFSA. **Notification of Awards:** Applicants will be notified of awards on a rolling basis beginning 4/1. **Types of Aid:** *Need-based scholarships/ grants:* College/university scholarship or grant aid from institutional funds; Federal Nursing Scholarships; Federal Pell; Private scholarships; SEOG; State scholarships/grants. *Loans:* Direct PLUS loans; Direct Subsidized Stafford Loans; Direct Unsubsidized Stafford Loans. *Student Employment:* Federal Work-Study Program available. Institutional employment available. **Financial Aid Statistics:** 92% needy freshmen, 81% needy undergrads receive need-based scholarship or grant aid. 71% freshmen, 52% undergrads receive non-need-based scholarship or grant aid. 69% freshmen, 78% undergrads receive need-based self-help aid. 3% freshmen, 3% undergrads receive athletic scholarships. 87% freshmen, 71% undergrads receive any aid. 49% undergrads borrow to pay for school. Average cumulative indebtedness $30,270. **Criteria for awarding aid:** *Need-based:* Academics, Leadership, Minority status, Music/ drama *Non-need-based:* Academics, Art, Athletics, Leadership, Minority status, Music/drama, State/district residency.

See page 916.

CLEVELAND INSTITUTE OF ART

11610 Euclid Avenue, Cleveland, OH 44106
Phone: 216-421-7418 · **Financial Aid Phone:** 216-421-7425
E-mail: admissions@cia.edu · **CEEB Code:** 1152
Fax: 216-754-3634 · **Website:** www.cia.edu · **ACT Code:** 3243

This private school was founded in 1882. It has a 1 acre campus.

RATINGS

Admissions Selectivity Rating: 86   **Fire Safety Rating:** 95   **Green Rating:** 63

STUDENTS AND FACULTY

Enrollment: 612. **Student Body:** 65% female, 35% male, 33% out-of-state, 9% international (8 countries represented). Asian 3%, African American 9%, Caucasian 66%, Hispanic 8%, Native American <1%, Pacific Islander <1%, Two or more races 4%, Race unknown 0%.
Retention and Graduation: 90% freshmen return for sophomore year. 50% freshmen graduate within 4 years. 57% freshmen graduate within 6 years. 3% grads go on to further study within 1 year. 3% grads pursue arts and sciences degrees. 0% grads pursue law degrees. 0% grads pursue business degrees. 0% grads pursue medical degrees. **Faculty:** Student/faculty ratio 7:1. 51 full-time faculty, 67% hold PhDs, 12% are members of minority groups, 37% are women. 0% of classes are taught by teaching assistants.

ACADEMICS

Degrees: Bachelor's. **Classes:** Most classes have 10-19 students. **Most popular majors:** Animation, Interactive Technology, Video Graphics And Special Effects; Industrial And Product Design; Illustration. **Special Study Options:** Cross-registration; Distance learning; Double major; Independent

study; Internships; Study abroad. **Disability Services offered to physically disabled students:** Note-taking services; Tape recorders; Tutors. **Career services:** Alumni network; Alumni services; Career assessment; Career/job search classes; Internships

FACILITIES

Housing: Apartments for single students; Coed dorms; Fraternity/sorority housing; Special housing for disabled student; Wellness housing 100% of campus accessible to physically diasbled. **Special Academic Facilities/ Equipment:** The Reinberger Galleries **Computers:** 40% of classrooms, 100% of dorms, 100% of libraries, have wireless network access. Students can register for classes online. Administrative functions (other than registration) can be performed online.

CAMPUS LIFE

Environment: Metropolis **Activities:** Campus Ministries; International Student Organization; Marching band; Musical theater; Radio station; Student government; Student-run film society 7 registered organizations, 2 religious organizations. **On-Campus Highlights:** University Coffee Shop, Frank Gehry and Peter B. Lewis Building, Live music at Barking Spider, Cleveland Museum of Art, Reinberger Galleries **Environmental Initiatives:** Recycling

ADMISSIONS

Freshman Academic Profile: Average high school GPA 3.4. 13% in top 10% of high school class, 38% in top 25% of high school class, 68% in top 50% of high school class. **Test Scores:** SAT Math middle 50% range 490-610. SAT EBRW middle 50% range 520-660. ACT middle 50% range 20-26. Minimum internet-based TOEFL 79. Minimum paper TOEFL 550. **Basis for Candidate Selection:** *Very important factors considered include:* talent/ability. *Important factors considered include:* academic GPA, application essay, interview. *Other factors considered include:* rigor of secondary school record, standardized test scores, recommendation(s), extracurricular activities, character/personal qualities, level of applicant's interest. **Freshman Admission Requirements:** High school diploma is required and GED is accepted *Academic units recommended:* 4 English, 3 math, 3 science, 3 social studies, 6 academic electives, 3 units from above areas or other academic areas. **Freshman Admission Statistics:** 957 applied, 54.2% admitted, 30% enrolled. **Transfer Admission Requirements:** college transcript(s), essay or personal statement, Minimum college GPA of 2.0 required. Lowest grade transferable C. **General Admission Information:** Application fee $40. Priority deadline 3/1. Nonfall registration accepted. Admission may be deferred for a maximum of 1 year.

COSTS AND FINANCIAL AID

Annual tuition $39,300. Required fees $2,526. Average book expense $2,190. **Required Forms and Deadlines:** FAFSA. **Types of Aid:** *Need-based scholarships/grants:* College/university scholarship or grant aid from institutional funds; Federal Pell; Private scholarships; SEOG; State scholarships/ grants. *Loans:* Direct PLUS loans; Direct Subsidized Stafford Loans; Direct Unsubsidized Stafford Loans. *Student Employment:* Federal Work-Study Program available. Institutional employment available. **Financial Aid Statistics:** 96% needy freshmen, 100% needy undergrads receive need-based scholarship or grant aid. 5% freshmen, 5% undergrads receive non-need-based scholarship or grant aid. 95% freshmen, 95% undergrads receive need-based self-help aid. 0% freshmen, 0% undergrads receive athletic scholarships. 80% freshmen, 95% undergrads receive any aid. 88% undergrads borrow to pay for school. Average cumulative indebtedness $35,136. **Criteria for awarding aid:** *Need-based:* Academics, Art *Non-need-based:* Academics, Art.

See page 918.

CLEVELAND STATE UNIVERSITY

2121 Euclid Avenue, Cleveland, OH 44115-2214
Phone: 216-523-7416 · **Financial Aid Phone:** 216-687-5594
E-mail: admissions@csuohio.edu · **CEEB Code:** 3032
Fax: 216-687-5501 · **Website:** www.csuohio.edu · **ACT Code:** 1221

This public school was founded in 1964. It has a 85 acre campus.

RATINGS

Admissions Selectivity Rating: 72   **Fire Safety Rating:** 60*   **Green Rating:** 84

STUDENTS AND FACULTY

Enrollment: 11,669. **Student Body:** 53% female, 47% male, 4% out-of-state, 5% international (85 countries represented). Asian 3%, African American 17%, Caucasian 64%, Hispanic 5%, Native American <1%, Pacific Islander <1%, Two or more races 3%, Race unknown 2%.
Retention and Graduation: 71% freshmen return for sophomore year. **Faculty:** Student/faculty ratio 24:1. 524 full-time faculty, 89% hold PhDs, 14%

are members of minority groups, 43% are women. 1% of classes are taught by teaching assistants.

ACADEMICS

Degrees: Bachelor's; Doctoral; Doctoral/Professional; Doctoral/Research; Master's; Post-Bachelor's certificate; Post-Master's certificate **Classes:** Most classes have 10-19 students. Most lab/discussion sessions have 20-29 students. **Most popular majors:** Psychology, General; Business Administration, Management And Operations, Other; Accounting. **Special Study Options:** Accelerated program; Cooperative education program; Cross-registration; Distance learning; Double major; Dual enrollment; English as a Second Language (ESL); Exchange student program (domestic); Honors program; Independent study; Internships; Liberal arts/career combination; Study abroad; Teacher certification program; Weekend college. **Honors programs:** Each year the University Honors Program accepts a very limited number of students based on the scholarship attached to the academic program. Approximately 40 first-year college students (lower division) and 20 college juniors (upper division) enter the program each fall. The Honors Program receives anywhere from 200 to 250 applications each given year. Thus, the Honors Program is very competitive. **Disability Services offered to physically disabled students:** Note-taking services; Reader services; Tape recorders; Tutors. **Career services:** Alumni services; Career assessment; Career/job search classes; Internships

FACILITIES

Housing: Coed dorms; Special housing for disabled students 90% of campus accessible to physically diasbled. **Computers:** Students can register for classes online. Administrative functions (other than registration) can be performed online.

CAMPUS LIFE

Environment: Metropolis **Activities:** Campus Ministries; Choral groups; Concert band; Dance; Drama/theater; International Student Organization; Jazz band; Literary magazine; Model UN; Music ensembles; Radio station; Student government; Student newspaper; Symphony orchestra 10 religious organizations. 8 fraternities, 7 sororities. **Athletics (Intercollegiate):** *Men:* baseball, basketball, fencing, golf, soccer, swimming, wrestling. *Women:* basketball, cross-country, fencing, softball, swimming, tennis, track/field (outdoor), track/field (indoor), volleyball. **On-Campus Highlights:** Recreation Center, Main Classroom Atrium, Michael Schwartz Library, The Green Room, Farmer's Market

ADMISSIONS

Freshman Academic Profile: Average high school GPA 3.3. 15% in top 10% of high school class, 39% in top 25% of high school class, 71% in top 50% of high school class. **Test Scores:** SAT Math middle 50% range 450-570. SAT EBRW middle 50% range 440-570. ACT middle 50% range 19-25. Minimum internet-based TOEFL 78. Minimum paper TOEFL 550. **Basis for Candidate Selection:** *Very important factors considered include:* rigor of secondary school record, academic GPA, standardized test scores. *Important factors considered include:* class rank. **Freshman Admission Requirements:** High school diploma is required and GED is accepted *Academic units required:* 4 English, 3 math, 3 science, 3 social studies, *Academic units recommended:* 2 foreign language, 1 visual/performing arts. **Freshman Admission Statistics:** 7,544 applied, 91.1% admitted, 28% enrolled. **Transfer Admission Requirements:** college transcript(s), Minimum college GPA of 2.0 required. Lowest grade transferable D. **General Admission Information:** Application fee $30. Priority deadline 7/15. Regular application deadline 8/15. Nonfall registration accepted. Admission may be deferred for a maximum of 1 year.

COSTS AND FINANCIAL AID

Annual in-state tuition $12,500. Annual out-of-state tuition $12,878. Room and board $12,500. Average book expense $800. **Required Forms and Deadlines:** FAFSA. **Notification of Awards:** Applicants will be notified of awards on a rolling basis beginning 3/15. **Types of Aid:** *Need-based scholarships/ grants:* College/university scholarship or grant aid from institutional funds; Federal Pell; Private scholarships; SEOG; State scholarships/grants. *Loans:* Direct PLUS loans; Direct Subsidized Stafford Loans; Direct Unsubsidized Stafford Loans. *Student Employment:* Federal Work-Study Program available. Institutional employment available. **Financial Aid Statistics:** 80% needy freshmen, 75% needy undergrads receive need-based scholarship or grant aid. 5% freshmen, 3% undergrads receive non-need-based scholarship or grant aid. 74% freshmen, 81% undergrads receive need-based self-help aid. 2% freshmen, 2% undergrads receive athletic scholarships. **Criteria for awarding aid:** *Non-need-based:* Academics, Alumni affiliation, Art, Athletics, Leadership, Music/drama.

COASTAL CAROLINA UNIVERSITY

PO Box 261954, Conway, SC 29528-6054
Phone: 843-349-2170 · **Financial Aid Phone:** 843-349-2313
E-mail: admissions@coastal.edu · **CEEB Code:** 5837
Fax: 843-349-2127 · **Website:** www.coastal.edu · **ACT Code:** 3843

This public school was founded in 1954. It has a 633 acre campus.

RATINGS

Admissions Selectivity Rating: 83   **Fire Safety Rating:** 93   **Green Rating:** 80

STUDENTS AND FACULTY

Enrollment: 9,546. **Student Body:** 53% female, 47% male, 51% out-of-state, 2% international (61 countries represented). Asian 1%, African American 20%, Caucasian 67%, Hispanic 4%, Native American <1%, Pacific Islander <1%, Two or more races 5%, Race unknown 1%.
Retention and Graduation: 67% freshmen return for sophomore year. 26% freshmen graduate within 4 years. 42% freshmen graduate within 6 years. **Faculty:** Student/faculty ratio 17:1. 450 full-time faculty, 80% hold PhDs, 11% are members of minority groups, 42% are women. 0% of classes are taught by teaching assistants.

ACADEMICS

Degrees: Bachelor's; Certificate; Doctoral/Research; Master's; Post-Bachelor's certificate; Post-Master's certificate **Classes:** Most classes have 20-29 students. Most lab/discussion sessions have 20-29 students. **Most popular majors:** Marine Biology And Biological Oceanography; Kinesiology And Exercise Science; Business Administration And Management, General. **Special Study Options:** Accelerated program; Cooperative education program; Distance learning; Double major; Dual enrollment; Honors program; Independent study; Internships; Liberal arts/career combination; Student-designed major; Study abroad; Teacher certification program. **Honors programs:** The Honors Program at Coastal Carolina University is design to encourage intellectual curiosity and ability in highly motivated and academically-gifted students. Students enjoy multiple benefits for participating in the Honors Program including high levels of personal attention from faculty, priority registration, and designated housing. **Disability Services offered to physically disabled students:** Note-taking services; Reader services; Tape recorders; Tutors. **Career services:** Alumni network; Alumni services; Career assessment; Career/job search classes; Internships; Regional alumni

FACILITIES

Housing: Apartments for single students; Coed dorms; Special housing for disabled student; Special housing for international students; Theme housing; Wellness housing 98% of campus accessible to physically diasbled. **Computers:** 100% of classrooms, 100% of libraries, 100% of dining areas, 100% of student union, 83% of common outdoor areas have wireless network access. Students can register for classes online. Administrative functions (other than registration) can be performed online.

CAMPUS LIFE

Environment: Town **Activities:** Campus Ministries; Choral groups; Concert band; Dance; Drama/theater; International Student Organization; Jazz band; Literary magazine; Marching band; Model UN; Music ensembles; Musical theater; Pep band; Radio station; Student government; Student newspaper 91 registered organizations, 32 honor societies, 13 religious organizations. 9 fraternities, 7 sororities. **Athletics (Intercollegiate):** *Men:* baseball, basketball, cheerleading, cross-country, football, golf, soccer, tennis, track/field (outdoor). *Women:* basketball, cheerleading, cross-country, golf, soccer, softball, tennis, track/field (outdoor), volleyball. **On-Campus Highlights:** Swain Science Annex / Science Annex II, Star Bucks / Kimbel Library/Bryan Information Commons, Edwards Courtyard / Prince Lawn, Jackson Student Union/CINO Grille, HTC Recreation and Convocation Center **Environmental Initiatives:** Sustainable Transportation including: Zip Car, 350 in the bike sharing fleet, 2 bike fix stations, shuttles and EV stations

ADMISSIONS

Freshman Academic Profile: Average high school GPA 3.6. 11% in top 10% of high school class, 36% in top 25% of high school class, 71% in top 50% of high school class. 92% from public high schools. **Test Scores:** SAT Math middle 50% range 510-580. SAT EBRW middle 50% range 510-590. ACT middle 50% range 19-24. Minimum internet-based TOEFL 71. Minimum paper TOEFL 527. **Basis for Candidate Selection:** *Very important factors considered include:* rigor of secondary school record, academic GPA. *Important factors considered include:* class rank, standardized test scores. *Other factors considered include:* application essay, recommendation(s), extracurricular activities, talent/ability, character/personal qualities, first generation, alumni/ ae relation, geographical residence, state residency. **Freshman Admission Requirements:** High school diploma is required and GED is accepted

Academic units required: 4 English, 4 math, 3 science, 3 science labs, 2 foreign language, 2 social studies, 1 history, 1 academic elective, 1 visual/performing arts, and 1 unit from above areas or other academic areas. *Academic units recommended:* 1 computer science. **Freshman Admission Statistics:** 18,563 applied, 61.2% admitted, 21% enrolled. **Transfer Admission Requirements:** college transcript(s), statement of good standing from prior institution(s). Minimum college GPA of 2.0 required. Lowest grade transferable C-. **General Admission Information:** Application fee $45. Priority deadline 12/1. Regular application deadline 8/1. Nonfall registration accepted. Admission may be deferred for a maximum of 1 year.

COSTS AND FINANCIAL AID
Annual in-state tuition $9,140. Annual out-of-state tuition $25,692. Room and board $9,140. Required fees $180. Average book expense $1,170. **Required Forms and Deadlines:** FAFSA. **Notification of Awards:** Applicants will be notified of awards on a rolling basis beginning 3/1. **Types of Aid:** *Need-based scholarships/grants:* College/university scholarship or grant aid from institutional funds; Federal Pell; Private scholarships; SEOG; State scholarships/grants. *Loans:* Direct PLUS loans; Direct Subsidized Stafford Loans; Direct Unsubsidized Stafford Loans. *Student Employment:* Federal Work-Study Program available. Institutional employment available. **Financial Aid Statistics:** 53% needy freshmen, 54% needy undergrads receive need-based scholarship or grant aid. 45% freshmen, 31% undergrads receive non-need-based scholarship or grant aid. 93% freshmen, 93% undergrads receive need-based self-help aid. 4% freshmen, 4% undergrads receive athletic scholarships. 86% freshmen, 92% undergrads receive any aid. 77% undergrads borrow to pay for school. Average cumulative indebtedness $38,897. **Criteria for awarding aid:** *Non-need-based:* Academics, Art, Athletics, Leadership.

COE COLLEGE

1220 First Avenue NE, Cedar Rapids, IA 52402
Phone: 319-399-8500 • **Financial Aid Phone:** 319-399-8540
E-mail: admission@coe.edu • **CEEB Code:** 6101
Fax: 319-399-8816 • **Website:** www.coe.edu • **ACT Code:** 1294

This private school, affiliated with the Presbyterian Church, was founded in 1851. It has a 53 acre campus.

RATINGS
Admissions Selectivity Rating: 87   **Fire Safety Rating:** 88   **Green Rating:** 81

STUDENTS AND FACULTY
Enrollment: 1,323. **Student Body:** 57% female, 43% male, 53% out-of-state, 3% international (12 countries represented). Asian 2%, African American 7%, Caucasian 73%, Hispanic 9%, Native American <1%, Pacific Islander <1%, Two or more races 3%, Race unknown 3%.
Retention and Graduation: 75% freshmen return for sophomore year. 19% grads go on to further study within 1 year. **Faculty:** Student/faculty ratio 11:1. 96 full-time faculty, 91% hold PhDs, 7% are members of minority groups, 40% are women. 0% of classes are taught by teaching assistants.

ACADEMICS
Degrees: Bachelor's **Classes:** Most classes have 10-19 students. Most lab/discussion sessions have 10-19 students. **Most popular majors:** Biology/Biological Sciences, General; Psychology, General; Business Administration And Management, General. **Special Study Options:** Cross-registration; Double major; Dual enrollment; English as a Second Language (ESL); Exchange student program (domestic); Honors program; Independent study; Internships; Liberal arts/career combination; Student-designed major; Study abroad; Teacher certification program. **Honors programs:** College scholars program consisting of five honors seminars. **Combined degree programs:** BA/JD; BA/MEng. **Disability Services offered to physically disabled students:** Note-taking services; Tape recorders; Tutors. **Career services:** Alumni network; Alumni services; Career assessment; Career/job search classes; Internships; Regional alumni

FACILITIES
Housing: Apartments for single students; Coed dorms; Fraternity/sorority housing; Men's dorms; Special housing for disabled student; Theme housing; Wellness housing; Women's dorms 70% of campus accessible to physically disabled. **Special Academic Facilities/Equipment:** Ornithological museum, writing lab, theatre. **Computers:** 70% of classrooms, 10% of dorms, 100% of libraries, 100% of dining areas, 100% of student union, 80% of common

outdoor areas have wireless network access. Students can register for classes online.

CAMPUS LIFE
Environment: City **Activities:** Campus Ministries; Choral groups; Concert band; Dance; Drama/theater; International Student Organization; Jazz band; Literary magazine; Model UN; Music ensembles; Musical theater; Radio station; Student government; Student newspaper; Student-run film society; Symphony orchestra 60 registered organizations, 8 honor societies, 4 religious organizations. 5 fraternities, 3 sororities. **Athletics (Intercollegiate):** *Men:* baseball, basketball, cross-country, diving, football, golf, soccer, swimming, tennis, track/field (outdoor), track/field (indoor), wrestling. *Women:* basketball, cheerleading, cross-country, diving, golf, soccer, softball, swimming, tennis, track/field (outdoor), track/field (indoor), volleyball. **On-Campus Highlights:** Student Union/Coffee Shop, Dows Theatre, Library/Art Galleries, Fitness Center, Learning Commons **Environmental Initiatives:** Coe College has embarked on a $3.45m major energy reduction program that will decrease the institution's electricity use by 25 percent and natural gas consumption by almost 50 percent, and deliver approximately $220,000 in guaranteed energy and operational savings each year.

ADMISSIONS
Freshman Academic Profile: Average high school GPA 3.6. 30% in top 10% of high school class, 65% in top 25% of high school class, 89% in top 50% of high school class. **Test Scores:** SAT Math middle 50% range 510-650. SAT EBRW middle 50% range 510-620. ACT middle 50% range 22-28. Minimum internet-based TOEFL 68. Minimum paper TOEFL 520. **Basis for Candidate Selection:** *Very important factors considered include:* academic GPA, standardized test scores. *Important factors considered include:* class rank. *Other factors considered include:* rigor of secondary school record, application essay, recommendation(s), interview, extracurricular activities, talent/ability, character/personal qualities, first generation, alumni/ae relation, volunteer work, level of applicant's interest. **Freshman Admission Requirements:** High school diploma is required and GED is accepted *Academic units recommended:* 4 English, 3 math, 3 science, 1 science labs, 2 foreign language, 3 social studies, 2 academic electives. **Freshman Admission Statistics:** 6,725 applied, 49.9% admitted, 11% enrolled. **Transfer Admission Requirements:** High school transcript, college transcript(s), essay or personal statement, statement of good standing from prior institution(s). Minimum college GPA of 2.5 required. Lowest grade transferable C. **General Admission Information:** Application fee $30. Priority deadline 12/10. Regular application deadline 3/1. Nonfall registration accepted. Admission may be deferred for a maximum of 2 years.

COSTS AND FINANCIAL AID
Annual tuition $42,090. Room and board $9,140. Required fees $340. Average book expense $1,000. **Required Forms and Deadlines:** FAFSA. **Notification of Awards:** Applicants will be notified of awards on a rolling basis beginning 12/15. **Types of Aid:** *Need-based scholarships/grants:* College/university scholarship or grant aid from institutional funds; Federal Pell; Private scholarships; SEOG; State scholarships/grants. *Loans:* Direct PLUS loans; Direct Subsidized Stafford Loans; Direct Unsubsidized Stafford Loans. *Student Employment:* Federal Work-Study Program available. Institutional employment available. **Financial Aid Statistics:** 100% needy freshmen, 100% needy undergrads receive need-based scholarship or grant aid. 14% freshmen, 14% undergrads receive non-need-based scholarship or grant aid. 85% freshmen, 82% undergrads receive need-based self-help aid. 0% freshmen, 0% undergrads receive athletic scholarships. 99% freshmen, 99% undergrads receive any aid. 82% undergrads borrow to pay for school. Average cumulative indebtedness $35,782. **Criteria for awarding aid:** *Non-need-based:* Academics, Alumni affiliation, Art, Minority status, Music/drama, State/district residency.

COGSWELL COLLEGE

191 Baypointe Parkway, San Jose, CA 95134
Phone: 408-498-5160 • **Financial Aid Phone:** 408.498.5145
E-mail: admissions@cogswell.edu • **CEEB Code:** 1177
Fax: 408-747-0764 • **ACT Code:** 1177

This proprietary school was founded in 1887. It has a 5 acre campus.

RATINGS
Admissions Selectivity Rating: 86   **Fire Safety Rating:** 96   **Green Rating:** 61

STUDENTS AND FACULTY
Enrollment: 603. **Student Body:** 30% female, 70% male, 7% out-of-state, 2% international (11 countries represented). Asian 22%, African American 5%, Caucasian 35%, Hispanic 20%, Native American 1%, Pacific Islander 1%, Two or more races 7%, Race unknown 7%.

Retention and Graduation: 78% freshmen return for sophomore year. 18% freshmen graduate within 4 years. 32% freshmen graduate within 6 years. 1% grads pursue business degrees. **Faculty:** Student/faculty ratio 12:1. 20 full-time faculty, 35% hold PhDs, 0% are members of minority groups, 35% are women. 0% of classes are taught by teaching assistants.

ACADEMICS

Degrees: Bachelor's; Master's **Classes:** Most classes have 10-19 students. Most lab/discussion sessions have 10-19 students. **Most popular majors:** Animation, Interactive Technology, Video Graphics And Special Effects; Game And Interactive Media Design; Music Technology. **Special Study Options:** Cooperative education program; Distance learning; Double major; Independent study; Internships; Student-designed major. **Disability Services offered to physically disabled students:** Note-taking services; Tutors. **Career services:** Alumni network; Alumni services; Career/job search classes; Internships

FACILITIES

Housing: Apartments for single students 100% of campus accessible to physically diasbled. **Computers:** 100% of classrooms, 100% of libraries, 100% of dining areas, 100% of student union, have wireless network access. Students can register for classes online. Administrative functions (other than registration) can be performed online. Undergraduates are required to own a computer.

CAMPUS LIFE

Environment: Town **Activities:** Student government; Student newspaper 5 registered organizations. **On-Campus Highlights:** 3D Animation Studio, 3D Modeling Studio, Smart Lab, Library, Audio Recording Studio **Environmental Initiatives:** saving energy

ADMISSIONS

Test Scores: SAT Math middle 50% range 540-650. SAT EBRW middle 50% range 530-620. ACT middle 50% range 18-31. Minimum internet-based TOEFL 69. Minimum paper TOEFL 525. **Basis for Candidate Selection:** *Very important factors considered include:* academic GPA, application essay, interview, talent/ability, level of applicant's interest. *Important factors considered include:* rigor of secondary school record, recommendation(s), character/personal qualities. *Other factors considered include:* class rank, standardized test scores, extracurricular activities, volunteer work, work experience. **Freshman Admission Requirements:** High school diploma is required and GED is accepted *Academic units required:* 3 English, 3 math, 1 science, 1 science labs, *Academic units recommended:* 1 computer science, 1 visual/performing arts. **Freshman Admission Statistics:** 231 applied, 64.5% admitted, 48% enrolled. **Transfer Admission Requirements:** High school transcript, college transcript(s), essay or personal statement, Minimum college GPA of 2.5 required. Lowest grade transferable C. **General Admission Information:** Regular application deadline 8/15. Nonfall registration accepted. Admission may be deferred for a maximum of 1 year.

COSTS AND FINANCIAL AID

Annual tuition $18,648. Required fees $1,000. Average book expense $1,791. **Required Forms and Deadlines:** FAFSA. **Notification of Awards:** Applicants will be notified of awards on a rolling basis beginning 4/1. **Types of Aid:** *Need-based scholarships/grants:* College/university scholarship or grant aid from institutional funds; Federal Pell; Private scholarships; SEOG; State scholarships/grants. *Loans:* Direct PLUS loans; Direct Subsidized Stafford Loans; Direct Unsubsidized Stafford Loans. *Student Employment:* Federal Work-Study Program available. Institutional employment available. **Criteria for awarding aid:** *Need-based:* Academics, Alumni affiliation, Music/drama *Non-need-based:* Academics, Alumni affiliation, Art, Music/drama.

COKER COLLEGE

300 East College Avenue, Hartsville, SC 29550
Phone: 843-383-8050
E-mail: admissions@coker.edu
Fax: 843-383-8056 • **Website:** www.coker.edu

This is a private school.

RATINGS

Admissions Selectivity Rating: 83   **Fire Safety Rating:** 60*   **Green Rating:** 60*

STUDENTS AND FACULTY

Enrollment: 674. **Student Body:** 63% female, 37% male, 19% out-of-state, 3% international. Asian <1%, African American 27%, Caucasian 67%, Hispanic 2%, Native American 1%, Pacific Islander <1%, Two or more races 0%, Race unknown <1%.

Retention and Graduation: 71% freshmen return for sophomore year. **Faculty:** Student/faculty ratio 10:1. 58 full-time faculty, 81% hold PhDs, 12% are members of minority groups, 47% are women. 0% of classes are taught by teaching assistants.

ACADEMICS

Degrees: Bachelor's **Classes:** Most classes have 20-29 students. Most lab/discussion sessions have fewer than 10 students. **Most popular majors:** Psychology, General; Graphic Design; Business/Commerce, General. **Special Study Options:** Distance learning; Double major; Dual enrollment; Honors program; Independent study; Internships; Student-designed major; Study abroad; Teacher certification program. **Disability Services offered to physically disabled students:** Tape recorders; Tutors. **Career services:** Career assessment; Career/job search classes; Internships

FACILITIES

Housing: Coed dorms; Special housing for international students 80% of campus accessible to physically diasbled. **Special Academic Facilities/ Equipment:** Art gallery, state-of-the-art performing arts center, dark rooms, botanical gardens, graduate-level science equipment. **Computers:** Administrative functions (other than registration) can be performed online.

CAMPUS LIFE

Activities: Campus Ministries; Choral groups; Dance; Drama/theater; International Student Organization; Literary magazine; Music ensembles; Musical theater; Student government 27 registered organizations, 4 honor societies, 2 religious organizations. **Athletics (Intercollegiate):** *Men:* baseball, basketball, cheerleading, cross-country, golf, soccer, tennis. *Women:* basketball, cheerleading, cross-country, soccer, softball, tennis, volleyball. **On-Campus Highlights:** The Cobra Den, The Cobra Caf, The Student Center, The Performing Arts Center, Outdoor Volleyball Courts

ADMISSIONS

Freshman Academic Profile: Average high school GPA 3.4. 1% in top 10% of high school class, 28% in top 25% of high school class, 70% in top 50% of high school class. **Test Scores:** SAT Math middle 50% range 440-570. SAT EBRW middle 50% range 420-570. ACT middle 50% range 17-22. Minimum paper TOEFL 500. **Basis for Candidate Selection:** *Very important factors considered include:* standardized test scores. *Important factors considered include:* rigor of secondary school record, class rank, level of applicant's interest. *Other factors considered include:* application essay, recommendation(s), interview, extracurricular activities, talent/ability, character/personal qualities, alumni/ae relation, volunteer work, work experience. **Freshman Admission Requirements:** High school diploma is required and GED is accepted *Academic units required:* 4 English, 3 math, 3 science, 1 science labs, 2 foreign language, 3 social studies. **Freshman Admission Statistics:** 1,112 applied, 55.8% admitted, 25% enrolled. **Transfer Admission Requirements:** High school transcript, college transcript(s), statement of good standing from prior institution(s). Minimum college GPA of 2.0 required. Lowest grade transferable C. **General Admission Information:** Application fee $15. Priority deadline 5/1. Regular application deadline 8/1. Nonfall registration accepted. Admission may be deferred for a maximum of 1 year.

COSTS AND FINANCIAL AID

Annual tuition $22,200. Room and board $6,950. Average book expense $1,500. **Required Forms and Deadlines:** FAFSA. **Notification of Awards:** Applicants will be notified of awards on a rolling basis beginning 3/1. **Types of Aid:** *Need-based scholarships/grants:* College/university scholarship or grant aid from institutional funds; Federal Pell; Private scholarships; SEOG; State scholarships/grants. *Loans:* Direct PLUS loans; Direct Subsidized Stafford Loans; Direct Unsubsidized Stafford Loans. *Student Employment:* Federal Work-Study Program available. Institutional employment available. **Financial Aid Statistics:** 96% needy freshmen, 96% needy undergrads receive need-based scholarship or grant aid. 100% freshmen, 93% undergrads receive non-need-based scholarship or grant aid. 78% freshmen, 80% undergrads receive need-based self-help aid. 5% freshmen, 6% undergrads receive athletic scholarships. 100% freshmen, 100% undergrads receive any aid. **Criteria for awarding aid:** *Need-based:* Academics, Job skills, Minority status, Music/ drama, Religious affiliation *Non-need-based:* Academics, Alumni affiliation, Art, Athletics, Job skills, Leadership, Minority status, Music/drama, Religious affiliation, State/district residency.

COLBY COLLEGE

4000 Mayflower Hill, Waterville, ME 04901
Phone: 207-859-4828 · **Financial Aid Phone:** (207) 859-4814
E-mail: admissions@colby.edu · **CEEB Code:** 3280
Fax: 207-859-4828 · **Website:** www.colby.edu · **ACT Code:** 1638

This private school was founded in 1813. It has a 714 acre campus.

RATINGS

Admissions Selectivity Rating: 95   **Fire Safety Rating:** 98   **Green Rating:** 98

STUDENTS AND FACULTY

Student Body: 86% out-of-state, (74 countries represented).
Retention and Graduation: 29% grads go on to further study within 1 year.
20% grads pursue arts and sciences degrees. 3% grads pursue law degrees. 0%
grads pursue business degrees. 3% grads pursue medical degrees. **Faculty:**
Student/faculty ratio 9:1. 191 full-time faculty, 97% hold PhDs, 15% are
members of minority groups, 46% are women. 0% of classes are taught by
teaching assistants.

ACADEMICS

Degrees: Bachelor's **Classes:** Most classes have 10-19 students. Most lab/
discussion sessions have 10-19 students. **Most popular majors:** English
Language And Literature, General; Biology/Biological Sciences, General;
Economics, General. **Special Study Options:** Cross-registration; Double
major; Dual enrollment; Exchange student program (domestic); Honors
program; Independent study; Internships; Student-designed major; Study
abroad; Teacher certification program. **Disability Services offered to
physically disabled students:** Note-taking services; Reader services; Tape
recorders; Tutors. **Career services:** Alumni network; Alumni services; Career
assessment; Career/job search classes; Internships; Regional alumni

FACILITIES

Housing: Apartments for single students; Coed dorms; Theme housing;
Wellness housing 88% of campus accessible to physically disabled. **Special
Academic Facilities/Equipment:** Comprising five wings, nearly 8,000
works, and more than 38,000 square feet of exhibition space, the Colby
College Museum of Art is considered the finest college art museum in the
country. Additional academic spaces on campus include the Goldfarb Center
for Public Affairs and Civic Engagement, the Oak Institute for the Study of
International Human Rights, the Center for Teaching and Learning, the Center
for the Arts and Humanities, and the Pugh Center, a campus multicultural
center. Unique facilities include state-of-the-art photography and sculpture
studios, an art and music library, an electronic music center, an astronomical
observatory with a 35-cm (14-inch) telescope on a research-grade computer-
controlled mount with liquid-nitrogen cooled CCD camera, a four-capillary
genetic analyzer, a microscopy suite with multiple epifluorescence microscopes
and imaging cameras and software, a microscopy suite with Nikon E800
research grade microscope interfaced with MBF Neuroscience Neurolucida
and Stereo Investigator software systems for computerized 3-D imaging
and reconstruction of brain tissue slices in behavioral and neuroanatomical
investigations, magneto-optical trap (MOT) apparatuses, high-powered pulsed
laser systems, an astrophysics research lab, an x-ray fluorescence spectrometer,
a 500 MHz NMR, a LC-TOF mass spectrometer, an inductively coupled
plasma-atomic emissions spectrometer, a single-crystal x-ray defractometer,
a GIS lab, two high-performance Linux computer clusters for computational
research, research greenhouses, a research vessel and remote-sensing buoy for
biogeochemical lake research, and an organic garden. Most of Colby's 714-acre
campus is a wildlife sanctuary that includes the 128-acre Perkins Arboretum
and Bird Sanctuary. The College also owns a nearby kettle-hole research bog.
Comprising five wings, nearly 8,000 works, and more than 38,000 square feet
of exhibition space, the Colby College Museum of Art is considered the finest
college art museum in the country. Additional academic spaces on campus
include the Goldfarb Center for Public Affairs and Civic Engagement, the
Oak Institute for the Study of International Human Rights, the Center for
Teaching and Learning, the Center for the Arts and Humanities, and the Pugh
Center, a campus multicultural center. Unique facilities include state-of-the-
art photography and sculpture studios, an art and music library, an electronic
music center, an astronomical observatory with a 35-cm (14-inch) telescope
on a research-grade computer-controlled mount with liquid-nitrogen cooled
CCD camera, a four-capillary genetic analyzer, a microscopy suite with
multiple epifluorescence microscopes and imaging cameras and software, a

microscopy suite with Nikon E800 research grade microscope interfaced with
MBF Neuroscience Neurolucida and Stereo Investigator software systems
for computerized 3-D imaging and reconstruction of brain tissue slices in
behavioral and neuroanatomical investigations, magneto-optical trap (MOT)
apparatuses, high-powered pulsed laser systems, a confocal microscope
system, an astrophysics research lab, an x-ray fluorescence spectrometer,
a 500 MHz NMR, a LC-TOF mass spectrometer, an inductively coupled
plasma-atomic emissions spectrometer, a single-crystal x-ray defractometer,
a GIS lab, two high-performance Linux computer clusters for computational
research, research greenhouses, a research vessel and remote-sensing buoy for
biogeochemical lake research, and an organic garden. Most of Colby's 714-acre
campus is a wildlife sanctuary that includes the 128-acre Perkins Arboretum
and Bird Sanctuary. The College also owns a nearby kettle-hole research bog.
Computers: 100% of classrooms, 100% of dorms, 100% of libraries, 100%
of dining areas, 100% of student union, 10% of common outdoor areas have
wireless network access. Students can register for classes online. Administrative
functions (other than registration) can be performed online.

CAMPUS LIFE

Environment: Village **Activities:** Choral groups; Concert band; Dance;
Drama/theater; International Student Organization; Jazz band; Literary
magazine; Model UN; Music ensembles; Musical theater; Radio station;
Student government; Student newspaper; Student-run film society; Symphony
orchestra; Yearbook 91 registered organizations, 9 honor societies, 6 religious
organizations. **Athletics (Intercollegiate): Men:** baseball, basketball, crew/
rowing, cross-country, diving, football, golf, ice hockey, lacrosse, skiing
(downhill/alpine), skiing (nordic/cross-country), soccer, squash, swimming,
tennis, track/field (outdoor), track/field (indoor). **Women:** basketball, crew/
rowing, cross-country, diving, field hockey, golf, ice hockey, lacrosse, skiing
(downhill/alpine), skiing (nordic/cross-country), soccer, softball, squash,
swimming, tennis, track/field (outdoor), track/field (indoor), volleyball. **On-
Campus Highlights:** Museum of Art: lounge, sculpture terrace, evening
concerts and events, Pulver Pavilion (student center): snack bar, big-screen TV,
lounges, The Street: study lounge open 24/7 in lower level of library, Perkins
Arboretum and Bird Sanctuary: 8.5-mile Campbell Trails, Fitness center at the
athletic complex **Environmental Initiatives:** In April 2013, Colby College
became the fourth institution of higher education in the world to achieve
carbon neutrality.

ADMISSIONS

Freshman Academic Profile: 63% in top 10% of high school class, 93% in
top 25% of high school class, 97% in top 50% of high school class. 52% from
public high schools. **Test Scores:** SAT Math middle 50% range 640-740. SAT
EBRW middle 50% range 630-720. ACT middle 50% range 29-32. Minimum
internet-based TOEFL 100. **Basis for Candidate Selection:** *Very important
factors considered include:* rigor of secondary school record, academic GPA,
recommendation(s), character/personal qualities. *Important factors considered
include:* class rank, application essay, standardized test scores, extracurricular
activities, talent/ability, racial/ethnic status. *Other factors considered include:*
interview, first generation, alumni/ae relation, geographical residence, state
residency, volunteer work, work experience, level of applicant's interest.
Freshman Admission Requirements: High school diploma or equivalent
is not required *Academic units recommended:* 4 English, 3 math, 2 science,
2 science labs, 3 foreign language, 2 social studies. **Freshman Admission
Statistics:** 7,593 applied, 22.5% admitted, 30% enrolled. **Transfer Admission
Requirements:** High school transcript, college transcript(s), essay or personal
statement, standardized test scores, statement of good standing from prior
institution(s). Minimum college GPA of 3.0 required. Lowest grade transferable
C. **General Admission Information:** Regular application deadline 1/1.
Nonfall registration accepted. Admission may be deferred for a maximum of 1
year.

COSTS AND FINANCIAL AID

Annual tuition $50,890. Room and board $13,660. Required fees $2,230.
Average book expense $735. **Required Forms and Deadlines:** Business/Farm
Supplement; CSS/Financial Aid PROFILE; FAFSA. **Notification of Awards:**
Applicants will be notified of awards on or about 4/1. **Types of Aid:** *Need-
based scholarships/grants:* College/university scholarship or grant aid from
institutional funds; Federal Pell; Private scholarships; SEOG; State scholarships/
grants. *Loans:* Direct PLUS loans; Direct Subsidized Stafford Loans; Direct
Unsubsidized Stafford Loans. *Student Employment:* Federal Work-Study
Program available. Institutional employment available. **Financial Aid
Statistics:** 100% needy freshmen, 99% needy undergrads receive need-based
scholarship or grant aid. 2% freshmen, 1% undergrads receive non-need-based
scholarship or grant aid. 65% freshmen, 72% undergrads receive need-based
self-help aid. 0% freshmen, 0% undergrads receive athletic scholarships. 41%
freshmen, 43% undergrads receive any aid. Average cumulative indebtedness
$23,343.

COLBY-SAWYER COLLEGE

541 Main Street, New London, NH 03257-7835
Phone: 603-526-3700 · **Financial Aid Phone:** 603-526-3717
E-mail: admissions@colbysawyer.edu · **CEEB Code:** 3281
Fax: 603-526-3452 · **Website:** www.colby-sawyer.edu · **ACT Code:** 2506

This private school was founded in 1837. It has a 200 acre campus.

RATINGS
Admissions Selectivity Rating: 72   **Fire Safety Rating:** 75   **Green Rating:** 60*

STUDENTS AND FACULTY
Enrollment: 942. **Student Body:** 65% female, 35% male, 68% out-of-state, 1% international (11 countries represented). Asian 1%, African American 1%, Caucasian 90%, Hispanic 1%, Native American <1%, Race unknown 5%.
Retention and Graduation: 71% freshmen return for sophomore year.
Faculty: Student/faculty ratio 11:1. 60 full-time faculty, 73% hold PhDs, 2% are members of minority groups, 52% are women. 0% of classes are taught by teaching assistants.

ACADEMICS
Degrees: Associate; Bachelor's; Transfer Associate **Classes:** Most classes have 20-29 students. Most lab/discussion sessions have 20-29 students.
Most popular majors: Sport And Fitness Administration/Management; Nursing/Registered Nurse (Rn, Asn, Bsn, Msn); Business Administration And Management, General. **Special Study Options:** Accelerated program; Cross-registration; Double major; Dual enrollment; English as a Second Language (ESL); Exchange student program (domestic); Honors program; Independent study; Internships; Student-designed major; Study abroad; Teacher certification program. **Honors programs:** The Wesson Honors Program is designed to provide highly motivated students with an optional intensive experience in the liberal arts. By creating academic, cultural, and social opportunities for integrative and interdisciplinary intellectual discovery, the program challenges students not only to widen their own avenues of intellectual exploration, but to take leadership in a community of scholars and participate as catalysts for inquiry and discussion across the college. **Disability Services offered to physically disabled students:** Tape recorders; Tutors.

FACILITIES
Housing: Coed dorms; Special housing for disabled student; Women's dorms 50% of campus accessible to physically disabled. **Special Academic Facilities/Equipment:** Sawyer Fine Arts Center, Windy Hill School (pre-school- grade 3 laboratory school), Ivey Science Center, Hogan Sports Center, Video Studio and Editing Room, Radio Station (WSCS 90.9 FM)

CAMPUS LIFE
Environment: Rural **Activities:** Choral groups; Dance; Drama/theater; Literary magazine; Musical theater; Radio station; Student government; Student newspaper; Yearbook 40 registered organizations, 5 honor societies, 1 religious organization. **Athletics (Intercollegiate):** *Men:* baseball, basketball, diving, equestrian sports, skiing (downhill/alpine), soccer, swimming, tennis, track/field (outdoor). *Women:* basketball, diving, equestrian sports, lacrosse, skiing (downhill/alpine), soccer, swimming, tennis, track/field (outdoor), volleyball.
On-Campus Highlights: Dan and Kathleen Hogan Sports Center, Susan Colgate Cleveland Library/Learning Center, Lethbridge Lodge, Thornton Livingroom, Rooke Hall

ADMISSIONS
Freshman Academic Profile: Average high school GPA 3.0. 83% from public high schools. **Test Scores:** SAT Math middle 50% range 440-530. SAT EBRW middle 50% range 440-540. ACT middle 50% range 18-22. Minimum paper TOEFL 500. **Basis for Candidate Selection:** *Very important factors considered include:* rigor of secondary school record, academic GPA, interview. *Important factors considered include:* class rank, application essay, standardized test scores, recommendation(s), extracurricular activities, talent/ability, alumni/ae relation, volunteer work, work experience, level of applicant's interest. *Other factors considered include:* first generation, geographical residence, state residency. **Freshman Admission Requirements:** High school diploma is required and GED is accepted *Academic units recommended:* 4 English, 3 math, 3 science, 3 science labs, 2 foreign language, 3 social studies. **Freshman Admission Statistics:** 1,402 applied, 87.5% admitted, 18% enrolled. **Transfer Admission Requirements:** college transcript(s), essay or personal statement, Minimum college GPA of 2.0 required. Lowest grade transferable C. **General Admission Information:** Application fee $45. Regular application deadline 4/1. Nonfall registration accepted. Admission may be deferred for a maximum of 1 year.

COSTS AND FINANCIAL AID
Annual tuition $29,620. Room and board $10,340. Average book expense $750. **Required Forms and Deadlines:** FAFSA. **Notification of Awards:**

Applicants will be notified of awards on a rolling basis beginning 3/1. **Types of Aid:** *Need-based scholarships/grants:* College/university scholarship or grant aid from institutional funds; Federal Pell; Private scholarships; SEOG; State scholarships/grants. *Loans: Student Employment:* Federal Work-Study Program available. Institutional employment available. **Financial Aid Statistics:** 100% needy freshmen, 95% needy undergrads receive need-based scholarship or grant aid. 4% freshmen, 6% undergrads receive non-need-based scholarship or grant aid. 93% freshmen, 99% undergrads receive need-based self-help aid. 0% freshmen, 0% undergrads receive athletic scholarships. 83% freshmen, 83% undergrads receive any aid. **Criteria for awarding aid:** *Need-based:* Academics *Non-need-based:* Academics, Alumni affiliation, Art, Leadership, Music/drama.

COLGATE UNIVERSITY

13 Oak Drive, Hamilton, NY 13346
Phone: 315-228-7401 · **Financial Aid Phone:** 315-228-7431
E-mail: admission@colgate.edu · **CEEB Code:** 2086
Fax: 315-228-7524 · **Website:** www.colgate.edu · **ACT Code:** 2702

This private school was founded in 1819. It has a 515 acre campus.

RATINGS
Admissions Selectivity Rating: 97   **Fire Safety Rating:** 97   **Green Rating:** 98

STUDENTS AND FACULTY
Enrollment: 2,852. **Student Body:** 55% female, 45% male, 74% out-of-state, 9% international (51 countries represented). Asian 4%, African American 5%, Caucasian 65%, Hispanic 9%, Native American <1%, Pacific Islander 0%, Two or more races 4%, Race unknown 4%.
Retention and Graduation: 94% freshmen return for sophomore year. 88% freshmen graduate within 4 years. 91% freshmen graduate within 6 years. 14% grads go on to further study within 1 year. 9% grads pursue arts and sciences degrees. 1.7% grads pursue law degrees. 1% grads pursue business degrees. 2% grads pursue medical degrees. **Faculty:** Student/faculty ratio 9:1. 296 full-time faculty, 100% hold PhDs, 24% are members of minority groups, 42% are women.

ACADEMICS
Degrees: Bachelor's; Master's **Classes:** Most classes have 10-19 students. Most lab/discussion sessions have 10-19 students. **Most popular majors:** English Language And Literature, General; Economics, General; Political Science And Government, General. **Special Study Options:** Cross-registration; Double major; Independent study; Internships; Student-designed major; Study abroad; Teacher certification program. **Honors programs:** Colgate University honors top applicants in our pool as Alumni Memorial Scholars (AMS) and Benton Scholars. Acceptance to the AMS Program is the highest honor within the admission process, and an indication of an excellent match, both academically and personally, with Colgate. The cornerstone of the AMS program is the opportunity for each student to apply, at any point before graduating, for grants totaling up to $6,000 to fund independent research, attendance at academic conferences, and internships. Though not a "merit scholarship," the award does recognize academic merit and achievement combined with leadership and accomplishment in top candidates regardless of financial aid status. Selection by the admission staff is based on academic performance, demonstrated talents, and the respect a student has earned from both teachers and counselors. The Benton Scholars program infuses the curriculum of its students with an even greater focus on leadership and global themes. While Benton scholars are free to craft their own majors, courses of study, and extracurricular priorities, they receive unique opportunities to learn on and off campus, and are given the responsibility of sharing the knowledge they acquire with the greater Colgate community. **Disability Services offered to physically disabled students:** Note-taking services; Reader services; Tape recorders; Tutors. **Career services:** Alumni network; Alumni services; Career assessment; Career/job search classes; Internships

FACILITIES
Housing: Apartments for single students; Coed dorms; Cooperative housing; Fraternity/sorority housing; Special housing for disabled student; Theme housing; Wellness housing **Special Academic Facilities/Equipment:** Clifford Gallery Picker Gallery Longyear Museum of Anthropology Robert M. Linsley Geology Museum Ho Tung Visualization Laboratory Digital Learning and Media Center W.M. Keck Center for Language Study Foggy Bottom Observatory WRCU Radio Station Audio and video recording studios

Greenhouse Brehmer Theater **Computers:** Students can register for classes online. Administrative functions (other than registration) can be performed online.

CAMPUS LIFE

Environment: Rural **Activities:** Campus Ministries; Choral groups; Concert band; Dance; Drama/theater; International Student Organization; Jazz band; Literary magazine; Model UN; Music ensembles; Musical theater; Opera; Pep band; Radio station; Student government; Student newspaper; Symphony orchestra; Yearbook 160 registered organizations, 4 honor societies, 8 religious organizations. 6 fraternities, 3 sororities. **Athletics (Intercollegiate):** *Men:* basketball, crew/rowing, cross-country, diving, football, golf, ice hockey, lacrosse, soccer, swimming, tennis, track/field (outdoor). *Women:* basketball, crew/rowing, cross-country, diving, field hockey, ice hockey, lacrosse, soccer, softball, swimming, tennis, track/field (outdoor), volleyball. **On-Campus Highlights:** O'Connor Campus Center, Hieber Cafe in Case-Geyer Library, ALANA Cultural Center, Ho Tung Visualization Lab, Trudy Fitness Center **Environmental Initiatives:** All electricity used on campus is hydroelectric, with some supplemental nuclear power. Colgate's wood-chip-burning heating plant utilizes a renewable energy source to provide about 70 percent of our total requirement.

ADMISSIONS

Freshman Academic Profile: Average high school GPA 3.7. 77% in top 10% of high school class, 94% in top 25% of high school class, 99% in top 50% of high school class. 58% from public high schools. **Test Scores:** SAT Math middle 50% range 650-770. SAT EBRW middle 50% range 660-730. ACT middle 50% range 31-33. **Basis for Candidate Selection:** *Very important factors considered include:* rigor of secondary school record, class rank, academic GPA. *Important factors considered include:* application essay, standardized test scores, recommendation(s), extracurricular activities, talent/ability, character/personal qualities. *Other factors considered include:* first generation, alumni/ae relation, geographical residence, racial/ethnic status, volunteer work, work experience. **Freshman Admission Requirements:** High school diploma is required and GED is accepted *Academic units required:* 4 English, 3 math, 3 science, 2 science labs, 3 foreign language, 3 social studies, *Academic units recommended:* 4 English, 4 math, 4 science, 4 science labs, 4 foreign language, 4 social studies. **Freshman Admission Statistics:** 8,542 applied, 28.1% admitted, 32% enrolled. **Transfer Admission Requirements:** High school transcript, college transcript(s), essay or personal statement, standardized test scores, statement of good standing from prior institution(s). Minimum college GPA of 3.00 required. Lowest grade transferable C. **General Admission Information:** Application fee $60. Regular application deadline 1/15. Nonfall registration accepted. Admission may be deferred for a maximum of 1 year.

COSTS AND FINANCIAL AID

Annual tuition $53,650. Room and board $13,520. Required fees $330. Average book expense $2,360. **Required Forms and Deadlines:** CSS/Financial Aid PROFILE; FAFSA; Noncustodial PROFILE. **Notification of Awards:** Applicants will be notified of awards on or about 3/20. **Types of Aid:** *Need-based scholarships/grants:* College/university scholarship or grant aid from institutional funds; Federal Pell; SEOG. *Loans:* Direct PLUS loans; Direct Subsidized Stafford Loans; Direct Unsubsidized Stafford Loans. *Student Employment:* Federal Work-Study Program available. Institutional employment available. **Financial Aid Statistics:** 100% needy freshmen, 99% needy undergrads receive need-based scholarship or grant aid. 0% undergrads receive non-need-based scholarship or grant aid. 77% freshmen, 81% undergrads receive need-based self-help aid. 10% freshmen, 10% undergrads receive athletic scholarships. 41% freshmen, 42% undergrads receive any aid. 34% undergrads borrow to pay for school. Average cumulative indebtedness $21,427. **Criteria for awarding aid:** *Non-need-based:* Athletics.

COLLEGE FOR CREATIVE STUDIES

201 East Kirby, Detroit, MI 48202
Phone: 313-664-7425 · **Financial Aid Phone:** 313-664-7495
E-mail: admissions@collegeforcreativestudies.edu · **CEEB Code:** 1035
Fax: 313-872-2739 · **Website:** www.collegeforcreativestudies.edu · **ACT Code:** 1989

This private school was founded in 1906. It has a 11 acre campus.

RATINGS
Admissions Selectivity Rating: 89   **Fire Safety Rating:** 87   **Green Rating:** 60*

STUDENTS AND FACULTY
Student Body: 17% out-of-state, 4% international (15 countries represented). Asian 4%, African American 6%, Caucasian 71%, Hispanic 5%, Native American 1%, Race unknown 10%.

Retention and Graduation: 73% freshmen return for sophomore year. **Faculty:** Student/faculty ratio 8:1. 51 full-time faculty, 61% hold PhDs, 14% are members of minority groups, 31% are women. 0% of classes are taught by teaching assistants.

ACADEMICS
Degrees: Bachelor's; Master's; Post-Bachelor's certificate **Classes:** Most classes have fewer than 10 students. Most lab/discussion sessions have fewer than 10 students. **Most popular majors:** Commercial And Advertising Art; Industrial And Product Design; Film/Video And Photographic Arts, Other. **Special Study Options:** Cooperative education program; Double major; Dual enrollment; English as a Second Language (ESL); Exchange student program (domestic); Independent study; Internships; Study abroad; Teacher certification program. **Disability Services offered to physically disabled students:** Reader services; Tape recorders; Tutors. **Career services:** Alumni network; Alumni services; Career assessment; Career/job search classes; Internships; Regional alumni

FACILITIES
Housing: Coed dorms 95% of campus accessible to physically diasbled. **Special Academic Facilities/Equipment:** Top-of-the-line technology for design, animation and audiovisual editing. Wood and Metal shops, hot glass studio, gallery, private studios.

CAMPUS LIFE
Environment: Metropolis **Activities:** Student government 5 registered organizations. **On-Campus Highlights:** Center Galleries, U245 Student Art Gallery, Jazzman's Cafe

ADMISSIONS
Test Scores: ACT middle 50% range 18-23. Minimum paper TOEFL 525. **Basis for Candidate Selection:** *Very important factors considered include:* talent/ability. *Important factors considered include:* academic GPA, standardized test scores. *Other factors considered include:* level of applicant's interest. **Freshman Admission Requirements:** High school diploma is required and GED is accepted **Freshman Admission Statistics:** 1,260 applied, 38.7% admitted, 51% enrolled. **Transfer Admission Requirements:** High school transcript, college transcript(s), Minimum college GPA of 2.0 required. Lowest grade transferable C. **General Admission Information:** Application fee $35. Priority deadline 3/1. Regular application deadline 8/1. Nonfall registration accepted. Admission may be deferred for a maximum of 4 semesters.

COSTS AND FINANCIAL AID
Annual tuition $27,090. Required fees $1,185. Average book expense $2,500. **Required Forms and Deadlines:** FAFSA. **Notification of Awards:** Applicants will be notified of awards on a rolling basis beginning 3/15. **Types of Aid:** *Need-based scholarships/grants:* College/university scholarship or grant aid from institutional funds; Federal Pell; Private scholarships; SEOG; State scholarships/grants. **Criteria for awarding aid:** *Non-need-based:* Academics, Art, Minority status.

COLLEGE OF THE ATLANTIC

105 Eden Street, Bar Harbor, ME 04609
Phone: 207-288-5015 · **Financial Aid Phone:** 207-801-5645
E-mail: inquiry@coa.edu · **CEEB Code:** 3305
Fax: 207-288-4126 · **Website:** www.coa.edu · **ACT Code:** 1637

This private school was founded in 1969. It has a 38 acre campus.

RATINGS
Admissions Selectivity Rating: 85   **Fire Safety Rating:** 97   **Green Rating:** 99

STUDENTS AND FACULTY
Enrollment: 339. **Student Body:** 77% female, 23% male, 78% out-of-state, 22% international (40 countries represented). Asian 3%, African American 1%, Caucasian 67%, Hispanic 3%, Native American <1%, Pacific Islander 0%, Two or more races 2%, Race unknown 2%.
Retention and Graduation: 76% freshmen return for sophomore year. 53% freshmen graduate within 4 years. 66% freshmen graduate within 6 years. 25% grads go on to further study within 1 year. 25% grads pursue arts and sciences degrees. 0% grads pursue law degrees. 0% grads pursue business degrees. 0% grads pursue medical degrees. **Faculty:** Student/faculty ratio 10:1. 26 full-time faculty, 92% hold PhDs, 4% are members of minority groups, 42% are women. 0% of classes are taught by teaching assistants.

ACADEMICS

Degrees: Bachelor's; Master's **Classes:** Most classes have 10-19 students. Most lab/discussion sessions have 10-19 students. **Most popular majors:** Humanities/Humanistic Studies; Ecology; Multi-/Interdisciplinary Studies, Other. **Special Study Options:** Cross-registration; Exchange student program (domestic); Independent study; Internships; Liberal arts/career combination; Student-designed major; Study abroad; Teacher certification program. **Honors programs:** We consider all our students to be capable of honors work, which is why all students finish their time at COA with a term-long capstone, or senior project. **Disability Services offered to physically disabled students:** Note-taking services; Reader services; Tape recorders; Tutors. **Career services:** Alumni network; Alumni services; Career assessment; Internships; Regional alumni

FACILITIES

Housing: Coed dorms; Special housing for disabled student; Wellness housing 70% of campus accessible to physically diasbled. **Special Academic Facilities/Equipment:** George B. Dorr Natural History Museum, Ethel H. Blum Art Gallery, Beech Hill Farm, Peggy Rockefeller Farms, Edward McC. Blair Marine Research Station at Mount Desert Rock, Alice Eno Field Research Station at Great Duck Island, pottery studio, greenhouse, Geographic Information Systems lab, Green Media & Graphics Lab, Deering Common Community Center with cafe, organic community garden, Beatrix Farrand Gardens. Outdoor equipment includes two ocean-going vessels, sailboats, and several canoes and kayaks, bicycles for loan, plus gear for outdoor activities. We also have a protected wilderness area, the 100-acre Cox Protectorate. **Computers:** 100% of classrooms, 100% of dorms, 100% of libraries, 100% of dining areas, 100% of student union, 25% of common outdoor areas have wireless network access. Students can register for classes online. Administrative functions (other than registration) can be performed online.

CAMPUS LIFE

Environment: Rural **Activities:** Choral groups; Concert band; Dance; Drama/theater; International Student Organization; Jazz band; Literary magazine; Music ensembles; Student government; Student newspaper; Student-run film society; Yearbook. **On-Campus Highlights:** Thorndike Library, Blair Dining Hall (aka Take-A-Break, or TAB), The pier, Turrets, George B. Dorr Museum of Natural History **Environmental Initiatives:** Energy Framework: In March of 2013 the college adopted an Energy Framework that seeks to make the college fossil fuel-free by 2030. The framework includes interim goals for 2020 that the college is working on now to achieve. The framework focuses on reducing fossil fuel use and pursuing renewable sources of energy on campus and at our two nearby farms. Integral to the policy is the requirement that our students be involved in creating a fossil fuel-free campus through our hands-on curriculum. We have purchased an electric van and lease an electric Ford Focus for student transportation and have established three solar/electric charging stations for them on campus and at our two farms. These will also be used for additional electric vehicles we expect to bring into service.

ADMISSIONS

Freshman Academic Profile: Average high school GPA 3.7. 22% in top 10% of high school class, 50% in top 25% of high school class, 97% in top 50% of high school class. 52% from public high schools. **Test Scores:** SAT Math middle 50% range 550-650. SAT EBRW middle 50% range 640-700. ACT middle 50% range 26-30. Minimum internet-based TOEFL 86. Minimum paper TOEFL 567. **Basis for Candidate Selection:** *Very important factors considered include:* rigor of secondary school record, application essay, recommendation(s). *Important factors considered include:* class rank, academic GPA, interview, extracurricular activities, talent/ability, character/personal qualities, volunteer work, work experience. *Other factors considered include:* standardized test scores, first generation, alumni/ae relation, geographical residence, state residency, racial/ethnic status, level of applicant's interest. **Freshman Admission Requirements:** High school diploma is required and GED is accepted *Academic units required:* 4 English, 3 math, 2 science, 2 science labs, 2 social studies, *Academic units recommended:* 4 math, 3 science, 2 foreign language, 2 history, 1 academic elective. **Freshman Admission Statistics:** 474 applied, 67.9% admitted, 28% enrolled. **Transfer Admission Requirements:** High school transcript, college transcript(s), essay or personal statement, Minimum college GPA of 3.0 required. Lowest grade transferable C. **General Admission Information:** Application fee $50. Regular application deadline 2/1. Nonfall registration accepted. Admission may be deferred for a maximum of 1 year.

COSTS AND FINANCIAL AID

Annual tuition $42,993. Room and board $9,747. Required fees $549. Average book expense $600. **Required Forms and Deadlines:** Business/Farm Supplement; FAFSA; Institution's own financial aid form; Noncustodial PROFILE. **Notification of Awards:** Applicants will be notified of awards on or about 4/1. **Types of Aid:** *Need-based scholarships/grants:* College/university scholarship or grant aid from institutional funds; Federal Pell; Private scholarships; SEOG; State scholarships/grants. *Loans:* Direct PLUS loans; Direct Subsidized Stafford Loans; Direct Unsubsidized Stafford Loans. *Student Employment:* Federal Work-Study Program available. Institutional

employment available. **Financial Aid Statistics:** 100% needy freshmen, 99% needy undergrads receive need-based scholarship or grant aid. 1% freshmen, 1% undergrads receive non-need-based scholarship or grant aid. 96% freshmen, 99% undergrads receive need-based self-help aid. 0% freshmen, 0% undergrads receive athletic scholarships. 98% freshmen, 97% undergrads receive any aid. 57% undergrads borrow to pay for school. Average cumulative indebtedness $23,002. **Criteria for awarding aid:** *Need-based:* Academics, Art, Leadership, Music/drama *Non-need-based:* Academics, Art, Leadership, Music/drama.

COLLEGE OF CHARLESTON

66 George Street, Charleston, SC 29424
Phone: 843-953-5670 · **Financial Aid Phone:** (843) 953-5540
E-mail: admissions@cofc.edu · **CEEB Code:** 5113
Fax: 843-953-6322 · **Website:** http://cofc.edu · **ACT Code:** 3846

This public school was founded in 1770. It has a 52 acre campus.

RATINGS

Admissions Selectivity Rating: 79   **Fire Safety Rating:** 97   **Green Rating:** 87

STUDENTS AND FACULTY

Enrollment: 9,599. **Student Body:** 63% female, 37% male, 33% out-of-state, 1% international (58 countries represented). Asian 2%, African American 8%, Caucasian 78%, Hispanic 5%, Native American <1%, Pacific Islander <1%, Two or more races 4%, Race unknown 1%.
Retention and Graduation: 78% freshmen return for sophomore year. 56% freshmen graduate within 4 years. 69% freshmen graduate within 6 years. 36% grads go on to further study within 1 year. 1.1% grads pursue law degrees. 3.4% grads pursue medical degrees. **Faculty:** Student/faculty ratio 15:1. 544 full-time faculty, 92% hold PhDs, 15% are members of minority groups, 45% are women. 0% of classes are taught by teaching assistants.

ACADEMICS

Degrees: Bachelor's; Master's; Post-Bachelor's certificate; Post-Master's certificate **Classes:** Most classes have 10-19 students. Most lab/discussion sessions have 10-19 students. **Most popular majors:** Biology/Biological Sciences, General; Psychology, General; Business Administration And Management, General. **Special Study Options:** Accelerated program; Cooperative education program; Cross-registration; Distance learning; Double major; Dual enrollment; English as a Second Language (ESL); Exchange student program (domestic); Honors program; Independent study; Internships; Liberal arts/career combination; Study abroad; Teacher certification program. **Honors programs:** The Honors College at the College of Charleston began as an Honors Program in 1978 to provide a program and a community for talented and motivated students who enjoy active participation in small stimulating classes and want to be involved in a meaningful way in undergraduate research. In order to better serve the needs of the students, it became an Honors College in 2005, with new positions to provide academic advising and assistance in applying for postgraduate fellowships and additional funding to support its mission. The Honors College is dedicated to providing these students with a place where they can flourish and grow, a true learning community of teachers and students. In addition to receiving exciting and unique educational experiences, students can participate with their fellow Honors students in social, cultural, and intellectual events on the campus and in historic Charleston, SC. The Honors College challenges intellectually talented students to make the most of the opportunities available to them, to become actively involved in their own education, and to prepare themselves to excel in graduate programs, medical or law school, or in whatever comes after they complete their undergraduate education. In Honors classes, students take responsibility for their own learning through class discussions, through interaction with faculty and fellow students, and through independent research. Honors students are advised by specially chosen faculty mentors, receive priority registration, and have the opportunity to room with other Honors students in an Honors living-learning community. Classes, seminars, and student gatherings are held in the Honors Center, the historic William Aiken House built by Governor William Aiken in 1839. **Disability Services offered to physically disabled students:** Note-taking services; Reader services; Tape recorders; Tutors. **Career services:** Alumni network; Alumni services; Career assessment; Career/job search classes; Internships; Regional alumni

FACILITIES

Housing: Apartments for single students; Coed dorms; Fraternity/sorority housing; Men's dorms; Special housing for disabled student; Theme housing;

Women's dorms 70% of campus accessible to physically diasbled. **Special Academic Facilities/Equipment:** Halsey Institute of Contemporary Art, sculpture facility, Miles Early Childhood Development Center, Avery Institute for African-American History and Culture, physics and astronomy observatory, Tate Center for Entrepreneurship, Grice Marine Laboratory, Patriots Point Athletics Complex (includes softball, baseball, tennis, soccer and sailing), Natural History Museum **Computers:** 75% of classrooms, 100% of dorms, 100% of libraries, 100% of dining areas, 100% of student union, 80% of common outdoor areas have wireless network access. Students can register for classes online. Administrative functions (other than registration) can be performed online.

CAMPUS LIFE

Environment: City **Activities:** Campus Ministries; Choral groups; Dance; Drama/theater; International Student Organization; Jazz band; Literary magazine; Model UN; Music ensembles; Musical theater; Pep band; Radio station; Student government; Student newspaper; Symphony orchestra; Yearbook 120 registered organizations, 19 honor societies, 16 religious organizations. 13 fraternities, 12 sororities. **Athletics (Intercollegiate):** *Men:* baseball, basketball, cross-country, diving, golf, sailing, soccer, swimming, tennis. *Women:* basketball, cross-country, diving, equestrian sports, golf, sailing, soccer, softball, swimming, tennis, track/field (outdoor), track/field (indoor), volleyball. **On-Campus Highlights:** The Cistern Yard, TD Arena, Liberty Fresh Food Company and City Bistro, Addlestone Library / Starbucks / Rivers Green, Harbor Walk

ADMISSIONS

Freshman Academic Profile: Average high school GPA 3.9. 22% in top 10% of high school class, 53% in top 25% of high school class, 89% in top 50% of high school class. 74% from public high schools. **Test Scores:** SAT Math middle 50% range 520-600. SAT EBRW middle 50% range 550-630. ACT middle 50% range 22-27. Minimum internet-based TOEFL 80. Minimum paper TOEFL 570. **Basis for Candidate Selection:** *Very important factors considered include:* rigor of secondary school record, academic GPA, standardized test scores. *Important factors considered include:* class rank, talent/ability, character/personal qualities, first generation, state residency. *Other factors considered include:* application essay, recommendation(s), extracurricular activities, alumni/ae relation, geographical residence, racial/ethnic status, volunteer work, work experience, level of applicant's interest. **Freshman Admission Requirements:** High school diploma is required and GED is accepted *Academic units required:* 4 English, 4 math, 3 science, 3 science labs, 3 foreign language, 2 social studies, 1 history, 3 academic electives, 1 visual/performing arts, and 1 unit from above areas or other academic areas. *Academic units recommended:* 4 English, 4 math, 2 history, 1 computer science. **Freshman Admission Statistics:** 11,900 applied, 80.5% admitted, 38% enrolled. **Transfer Admission Requirements:** college transcript(s), Minimum college GPA of 2.6 required. Lowest grade transferable C. **General Admission Information:** Application fee $50. Priority deadline 2/15. Regular application deadline 2/15. Nonfall registration accepted. Admission may be deferred.

COSTS AND FINANCIAL AID

Annual out-of-state tuition $30,386. Required fees $460. Average book expense $1,159. **Required Forms and Deadlines:** FAFSA. **Notification of Awards:** Applicants will be notified of awards on a rolling basis beginning 4/10. **Types of Aid:** *Need-based scholarships/grants:* College/university scholarship or grant aid from institutional funds; Federal Pell; Private scholarships; SEOG; State scholarships/grants. *Loans:* Direct PLUS loans; Direct Subsidized Stafford Loans; Direct Unsubsidized Stafford Loans. *Student Employment:* Federal Work-Study Program available. Institutional employment available. **Financial Aid Statistics:** 71% needy freshmen, 69% needy undergrads receive need-based scholarship or grant aid. 77% freshmen, 49% undergrads receive non-need-based scholarship or grant aid. 70% freshmen, 78% undergrads receive need-based self-help aid. 1% freshmen, 1% undergrads receive athletic scholarships. 53% freshmen, 47% undergrads receive any aid. 51% undergrads borrow to pay for school. Average cumulative indebtedness $26,586. **Criteria for awarding aid:** *Non-need-based:* Academics, Alumni affiliation, Art, Athletics, Music/drama.

COLLEGE OF THE HOLY CROSS

Best Colleges

1 College Street, Worcester, MA 01610-2395
Phone: 508-793-2443 · **Financial Aid Phone:** (508) 793-2265
E-mail: admissions@holycross.edu · **CEEB Code:** 3282
Fax: 508-793-3888 · **Website:** www.holycross.edu · **ACT Code:** 1810

This private school, affiliated with the Roman Catholic Church, was founded in 1843. It has a 174 acre campus.

RATINGS

Admissions Selectivity Rating: 92   **Fire Safety Rating:** 97   **Green Rating:** 91

STUDENTS AND FACULTY

Enrollment: 3,020. **Student Body:** 52% female, 48% male, 59% out-of-state, 3% international (24 countries represented). Asian 5%, African American 4%, Caucasian 70%, Hispanic 10%, Native American <1%, Pacific Islander <1%, Two or more races 3%, Race unknown 3%.
Retention and Graduation: 95% freshmen return for sophomore year. 89% freshmen graduate within 4 years. 92% freshmen graduate within 6 years. 14% grads go on to further study within 1 year. **Faculty:** Student/faculty ratio 10:1. 278 full-time faculty, 95% hold PhDs, 13% are members of minority groups, 46% are women. 0% of classes are taught by teaching assistants.

ACADEMICS

Degrees: Bachelor's **Classes:** Most classes have fewer than 10 students. Most lab/discussion sessions have fewer than 10 students. **Most popular majors:** Psychology, General; Economics, General; Political Science And Government, General. **Special Study Options:** Accelerated program; Cross-registration; Double major; Dual enrollment; Exchange student program (domestic); Honors program; Independent study; Internships; Liberal arts/career combination; Student-designed major; Study abroad; Teacher certification program. **Honors programs:** Fenwick Scholar Program. **Disability Services offered to physically disabled students:** Note-taking services; Reader services; Tape recorders; Tutors. **Career services:** Alumni network; Alumni services; Career assessment; Career/job search classes; Internships; Regional alumni

FACILITIES

Housing: Apartments for single students; Coed dorms; Special housing for disabled student; Wellness housing 85% of campus accessible to physically diasbled. **Special Academic Facilities/Equipment:** Art gallery, Concert Hall, Taylor and Boody tracker organ, O'Callahan Science Library, Rehm Library, Multimedia Resource Center, Wellness Center; scientific equipment on par with the best research universities **Computers:** 100% of classrooms, 100% of dorms, 100% of libraries, 100% of dining areas, 100% of student union, 60% of common outdoor areas have wireless network access. Students can register for classes online. Administrative functions (other than registration) can be performed online.

CAMPUS LIFE

Environment: City **Activities:** Campus Ministries; Choral groups; Concert band; Dance; Drama/theater; International Student Organization; Jazz band; Literary magazine; Marching band; Model UN; Music ensembles; Musical theater; Pep band; Radio station; Student government; Student newspaper; Yearbook 105 registered organizations, 20 honor societies, 4 religious organizations. **Athletics (Intercollegiate):** *Men:* baseball, basketball, crew/rowing, cross-country, diving, football, golf, ice hockey, lacrosse, soccer, swimming, tennis, track/field (outdoor), track/field (indoor). *Women:* basketball, crew/rowing, cross-country, diving, field hockey, golf, ice hockey, lacrosse, soccer, softball, swimming, tennis, track/field (outdoor), track/field (indoor), volleyball. **On-Campus Highlights:** Library, Smith Hall, St. Joseph Chapel, Smith Science Labs, Hogan Campus Center **Environmental Initiatives:** The college has focused investments on energy efficiency in comparison with renewable energy generation. The college has reduced the campus energy consumption by 1,900,000 KWh/year through these investments since 2013.

ADMISSIONS

Freshman Academic Profile: 57% in top 10% of high school class, 90% in top 25% of high school class, 100% in top 50% of high school class. 50% from public high schools. **Test Scores:** SAT Math middle 50% range 640-710. SAT EBRW middle 50% range 630-700. ACT middle 50% range 28-31. Minimum internet-based TOEFL 100. Minimum paper TOEFL 600. **Basis for Candidate Selection:** *Very important factors considered include:* rigor of secondary school record, academic GPA, recommendation(s), interview. *Important factors considered include:* class rank, application essay, extracurricular activities, character/personal qualities. *Other factors considered include:* standardized test scores, talent/ability, first generation, alumni/ae relation, geographical residence, state residency, religious affiliation/commitment, racial/ethnic status, volunteer work, work experience, level of applicant's interest. **Freshman Admission Requirements:** High school diploma is required and GED is accepted *Academic units recommended:* 4 English, 4 math, 4 science, 2 science labs, 4 foreign language, 2 social studies, 2 history. **Freshman Admission Statistics:** 6,622 applied, 39.6% admitted, 31% enrolled. **Transfer Admission Requirements:** High school transcript, college transcript(s), essay or personal statement, statement of good standing from prior institution(s). Lowest grade transferable C. **General Admission Information:** Application fee $60. Regular application deadline 1/15. Nonfall registration accepted. Admission may be deferred for a maximum of 1 year.

COSTS AND FINANCIAL AID

Annual tuition $49,980. Room and board $13,690. Required fees $650. Average book expense $1,000. **Required Forms and Deadlines:** Business/Farm Supplement; CSS/Financial Aid PROFILE; FAFSA; Noncustodial PROFILE. **Types of Aid:** *Need-based scholarships/grants:* College/university scholarship or grant aid from institutional funds; Federal Pell; Private scholarships; SEOG; State scholarships/grants. *Loans:* Direct PLUS loans; Direct Subsidized Stafford Loans; Direct Unsubsidized Stafford Loans. *Student Employment:* Federal Work-Study Program available. Institutional employment available. **Financial Aid Statistics:** 85% needy freshmen, 82% needy undergrads receive need-based scholarship or grant aid. 3% freshmen, 3% undergrads receive non-need-based scholarship or grant aid. 92% freshmen, 94% undergrads receive need-based self-help aid. 8% freshmen, 6% undergrads receive athletic scholarships. 61% freshmen, 56% undergrads receive any aid. 62% undergrads borrow to pay for school. Average cumulative indebtedness $25,446. **Criteria for awarding aid:** *Need-based:* Athletics *Non-need-based:* Academics, Athletics, Music/drama, State/district residency.

THE COLLEGE OF IDAHO

2112 Cleveland Blvd, Caldwell, ID 83605-4432
Phone: 208-459-5305 · **Financial Aid Phone:** 208-459-5307
E-mail: admissions@collegeofidaho.edu · **CEEB Code:** 4060
Fax: 208-459-5757 · **Website:** www.collegeofidaho.edu · **ACT Code:** 916

This private school was founded in 1891. It has a 50 acre campus.

RATINGS

Admissions Selectivity Rating: 78 **Fire Safety Rating:** 88 **Green Rating:** 72

STUDENTS AND FACULTY

Enrollment: 936. **Student Body:** 50% female, 50% male, 66% out-of-state, 6% international (46 countries represented). Asian 2%, African American 4%, Caucasian 64%, Hispanic 14%, Native American 1%, Pacific Islander 1%, Two or more races 4%, Race unknown 4%.
Retention and Graduation: 77% freshmen return for sophomore year. 58% freshmen graduate within 4 years. 67% freshmen graduate within 6 years. 34% grads go on to further study within 1 year. 19% grads pursue arts and sciences degrees. 4% grads pursue law degrees. 6% grads pursue medical degrees. **Faculty:** Student/faculty ratio 9:1. 86 full-time faculty, 83% hold PhDs, 8% are members of minority groups, 43% are women. 0% of classes are taught by teaching assistants.

ACADEMICS

Degrees: Bachelor's; Master's **Classes:** Most classes have 10-19 students. Most lab/discussion sessions have 10-19 students. **Most popular majors:** Biology/Biological Sciences, General; Psychology, General; Business Administration And Management, General. **Special Study Options:** Cross-registration; Double major; Dual enrollment; English as a Second Language (ESL); Honors program; Independent study; Internships; Study abroad; Teacher certification program. **Honors programs:** Heritage Scholars Program Gipson Honors Program. **Disability Services offered to physically disabled students:** Note-taking services; Reader services; Tape recorders; Tutors. **Career services:** Alumni network; Alumni services; Career assessment; Career/job search classes; Internships; Regional alumni

FACILITIES

Housing: Apartments for married students; Apartments for single students; Coed dorms; Fraternity/sorority housing; Special housing for disabled student; Theme housing; Wellness housing 95% of campus accessible to physically

diasbled. **Special Academic Facilities/Equipment:** Museum of Natural History Art Gallery Planetarium Herbarium **Computers:** 100% of classrooms, 100% of dorms, 100% of libraries, 100% of dining areas, 100% of student union, 100% of common outdoor areas have wireless network access. Administrative functions (other than registration) can be performed online.

CAMPUS LIFE

Environment: Town **Activities:** Campus Ministries; Choral groups; Concert band; Dance; Drama/theater; International Student Organization; Jazz band; Literary magazine; Marching band; Model UN; Music ensembles; Musical theater; Opera; Pep band; Student government; Student newspaper; Student-run film society; Symphony orchestra; Yearbook 55 registered organizations, 4 honor societies, 3 religious organizations. 3 fraternities, 4 sororities **Athletics (Intercollegiate):** *Men:* baseball, cheerleading, cross-country, golf, skiing (downhill/alpine), skiing (nordic/cross-country), snowboarding, soccer, swimming, tennis, track/field (outdoor). *Women:* basketball, cheerleading, cross-country, golf, skiing (downhill/alpine), skiing (nordic/cross-country), snowboarding, soccer, softball, swimming, tennis, track/field (outdoor), volleyball. **On-Campus Highlights:** J.A. Albertson Activity Center, McCain Student Center, Langroise Center for Performing and Fine Arts, Centennial Amphitheater, Residence Halls **Environmental Initiatives:** Student Sustainability Steward Position

ADMISSIONS

Freshman Academic Profile: 27% in top 10% of high school class, 26% in top 25% of high school class, 50% in top 50% of high school class. **Test Scores:** SAT Math middle 50% range 360-700. SAT EBRW middle 50% range 510-620. ACT middle 50% range 21-27. Minimum internet-based TOEFL 79. Minimum paper TOEFL 550. **Basis for Candidate Selection:** *Very important factors considered include:* academic GPA. *Important factors considered include:* rigor of secondary school record, application essay, recommendation(s), character/personal qualities, alumni/ae relation. *Other factors considered include:* class rank, standardized test scores, interview, extracurricular activities, talent/ability, first generation, volunteer work, work experience, level of applicant's interest. **Freshman Admission Requirements:** High school diploma is required and GED is accepted *Academic units recommended:* 4 English, 3 math, 2 science, 2 foreign language, 2 social studies, 2 history, 4 academic electives. **Freshman Admission Statistics:** 1,665 applied, 75.9% admitted, 21% enrolled. **Transfer Admission Requirements:** college transcript(s), essay or personal statement, Minimum college GPA of 2.2 required. Lowest grade transferable D-. **General Admission Information:** Priority deadline 11/15. Regular application deadline 2/16. Nonfall registration accepted. Admission may be deferred.

COSTS AND FINANCIAL AID

Annual tuition $29,400. Room and board $9,697. Required fees $755. Average book expense $1,200. **Required Forms and Deadlines:** FAFSA. **Notification of Awards:** Applicants will be notified of awards on a rolling basis beginning 1/25. **Types of Aid:** *Need-based scholarships/grants:* College/university scholarship or grant aid from institutional funds; Federal Pell; Private scholarships; SEOG; State scholarships/grants. *Loans:* Direct PLUS loans; Direct Subsidized Stafford Loans; Direct Unsubsidized Stafford Loans. *Student Employment:* Federal Work-Study Program available. Institutional employment available. **Financial Aid Statistics:** 100% needy freshmen, 86% needy undergrads receive need-based scholarship or grant aid. 100% freshmen, 100% undergrads receive non-need-based scholarship or grant aid. 82% freshmen, 82% undergrads receive need-based self-help aid. 45% freshmen, 34% undergrads receive athletic scholarships. 99% freshmen, 100% undergrads receive any aid. 59% undergrads borrow to pay for school. Average cumulative indebtedness $7,270. **Criteria for awarding aid:** *Need-based:* Art, Athletics, Job skills, Leadership, Minority status, Music/drama, Religious affiliation *Non-need-based:* Academics, Alumni affiliation, Athletics, Job skills.

COLLEGE OF MOUNT SAINT VINCENT

6301 Riverdale Avenue, Riverdale, NY 10471
Phone: 718-405-3267 · **Financial Aid Phone:** 718-405-3349
E-mail: admissions@mountsaintvincent.edu · **CEEB Code:** 2088
Fax: 718-549-7945 · **Website:** www.mountsaintvincent.edu

This private school, affiliated with the Roman Catholic Church, was founded in 1847. It has a 70 acre campus.

RATINGS

Admissions Selectivity Rating: 71 **Fire Safety Rating:** 90 **Green Rating:** 60*

STUDENTS AND FACULTY

Enrollment: 1,683. **Student Body:** 70% female, 30% male, 12% out-of-state, 2% international (6 countries represented). Asian 9%, African American 14%,

Caucasian 25%, Hispanic 41%, Native American <1%, Pacific Islander 0%, Two or more races 4%, Race unknown 4%.
Retention and Graduation: 78% freshmen return for sophomore year.
Faculty: Student/faculty ratio 13:1. 80 full-time faculty, 90% hold PhDs, 13% are members of minority groups, 58% are women. 0% of classes are taught by teaching assistants.

ACADEMICS

Degrees: Associate; Bachelor's; Master's; Post-Master's certificate **Classes:** Most classes have fewer than 10 students. Most lab/discussion sessions have 20-29 students. **Most popular majors:** Sociology; Registered Nursing/Registered Nurse; Business/Commerce, General. **Special Study Options:** Double major; Honors program; Independent study; Internships; Liberal arts/career combination; Study abroad; Teacher certification program. **Honors programs:** The Honors Program at the College of Mount Saint Vincent provides our most competent and motivated students with a stimulating environment in which to maximize their intellectual and personal development. The Honors Curriculum is designed to challenge students through all four years of their undergraduate experience while ensuring that they are exposed to academic experiences that fit the mission of the College. The Honors Curriculum combines unique Honors Courses with select elements of the traditional core curriculum for a baccalaureate degree. The Honors Program allows students the freedom to develop an educational experience suited to their academic and intellectual interests and may be completed while pursuing any of the majors offered by the College. The program's features include small classes and innovative teaching methods (seminars, group projects, individual mentoring, field trips). **Disability Services offered to physically disabled students:** Note-taking services; Tape recorders; Tutors. **Career services:** Career assessment; Career/job search classes; Internships; Regional alumni

FACILITIES

Housing: Coed dorms; Special housing for disabled students 90% of campus accessible to physically diasbled. **Special Academic Facilities/Equipment:** Nursing lab,TV studio, radio station, Elizabeth Seton Travelling Museum, Forensic Laboratory equipment **Computers:** Students can register for classes online. Administrative functions (other than registration) can be performed online.

CAMPUS LIFE

Environment: Metropolis **Activities:** Campus Ministries; Choral groups; Dance; Drama/theater; International Student Organization; Literary magazine; Model UN; Musical theater; Radio station; Student government; Student newspaper; Television station 30 registered organizations, 15 honor societies, 2 religious organizations. **Athletics (Intercollegiate):** *Men:* baseball, basketball, cross-country, lacrosse, soccer, swimming, tennis, volleyball. *Women:* basketball, cross-country, lacrosse, soccer, softball, swimming, tennis, track/field (outdoor), volleyball. **On-Campus Highlights:** Alumnae Pavillion, Hudson Heights, Fitness Center **Environmental Initiatives:** Recycling

ADMISSIONS

Freshman Academic Profile: Average high school GPA 3.0. 8% in top 10% of high school class, 28% in top 25% of high school class, 62% in top 50% of high school class. 58% from public high schools. **Test Scores:** SAT Math middle 50% range 380-490. SAT EBRW middle 50% range 400-490. ACT middle 50% range 17-22. Minimum paper TOEFL 550. **Basis for Candidate Selection:** *Very important factors considered include:* rigor of secondary school record, academic GPA, character/personal qualities. *Important factors considered include:* application essay, standardized test scores, recommendation(s), extracurricular activities. *Other factors considered include:* class rank, interview, alumni/ae relation, geographical residence, state residency, volunteer work, work experience, level of applicant's interest. **Freshman Admission Requirements:** High school diploma is required and GED is accepted *Academic units required:* 4 English, 3 math, 3 science, 3 science labs, 2 foreign language, 2 social studies, 2 academic electives, *Academic units recommended:* 4 English, 4 math, 4 science, 4 science labs, 4 foreign language, 4 social studies, 3 academic electives. **Freshman Admission Statistics:** 2,667 applied, 92.7% admitted, 18% enrolled. **Transfer Admission Requirements:** college transcript(s), essay or personal statement, Minimum college GPA of 2.0 required. Lowest grade transferable C. **General Admission Information:** Application fee $35. Priority deadline 3/1. Nonfall registration accepted. Admission may be deferred for a maximum of 1 year.

COSTS AND FINANCIAL AID

Average book expense $1,185. **Required Forms and Deadlines:** FAFSA; State aid form. **Notification of Awards:** Applicants will be notified of awards on a rolling basis beginning 3/1. **Types of Aid:** *Need-based scholarships/grants:* College/university scholarship or grant aid from institutional funds; Federal Pell; Private scholarships; SEOG; State scholarships/grants. *Student Employment:* Federal Work-Study Program available. Institutional employment available. **Financial Aid Statistics:** 100% needy freshmen, 100% needy undergrads receive need-based scholarship or grant aid. 0% undergrads receive non-need-based scholarship or grant aid. 100% freshmen, 100% undergrads receive need-based self-help aid. 0% freshmen, 0% undergrads receive athletic

scholarships. 87% freshmen, 86% undergrads receive any aid. **Criteria for awarding aid:** *Non-need-based:* Academics, Alumni affiliation, Leadership.

THE COLLEGE OF NEW JERSEY

PO Box 7718, Ewing, NJ 08628-0718
Phone: 609-771-2131 • **Financial Aid Phone:** 609-771-2211
E-mail: tcnjinfo@tcnj.edu • **CEEB Code:** 2519
Fax: 609-637-5174 • **Website:** www.tcnj.edu • **ACT Code:** 2614

This public school was founded in 1855. It has a 289 acre campus.

RATINGS

Admissions Selectivity Rating: 89   **Fire Safety Rating:** 98   **Green Rating:** 83

STUDENTS AND FACULTY

Enrollment: 6,850. **Student Body:** 58% female, 42% male, 6% out-of-state, <1% international (32 countries represented). Asian 11%, African American 6%, Caucasian 66%, Hispanic 12%, Native American <1%, Pacific Islander <1%, Two or more races <1%, Race unknown 3%.
Retention and Graduation: 94% freshmen return for sophomore year. 73% freshmen graduate within 4 years. 1% freshmen graduate within 6 years. 25% grads go on to further study within 1 year. 16% grads pursue arts and sciences degrees. 3% grads pursue law degrees. 0% grads pursue business degrees. 3% grads pursue medical degrees. **Faculty:** Student/faculty ratio 13:1. 365 full-time faculty, 89% hold PhDs, 25% are members of minority groups, 53% are women. 0% of classes are taught by teaching assistants.

ACADEMICS

Degrees: Bachelor's; Master's; Post-Bachelor's certificate; Post-Master's certificate **Classes:** Most classes have 20-29 students. Most lab/discussion sessions have 10-19 students. **Most popular majors:** Education, General; Psychology, General; Marketing. **Special Study Options:** Accelerated program; Distance learning; Double major; Dual enrollment; English as a Second Language (ESL); Exchange student program (domestic); Honors program; Independent study; Internships; Liberal arts/career combination; Student-designed major; Study abroad; Teacher certification program. **Honors programs:** The College of New Jersey Honors Program provides a high level of challenge and stimulation to talented students who seek a broad educational experience. TCNJ College Honors is not a departmental program. It serves students in all majors in all schools of the college.Graduates of the program receive special recognition on their official transcript. Completion of the Honors Program is a mark of distinction that is valued by professional schools and graduate schools, as well as by prospective employers. **Combined degree programs:** BA/MD. **Disability Services offered to physically disabled students:** Note-taking services; Reader services; Tape recorders; Tutors. **Career services:** Alumni services; Career assessment; Career/job search classes; Internships

FACILITIES

Housing: Apartments for single students; Coed dorms; Special housing for international students; Theme housing; Wellness housing; Women's dorms 90% of campus accessible to physically diasbled. **Special Academic Facilities/Equipment:** Art gallery, concert hall, greenhouse, observatory, planetarium, nuclear magnetic resonance lab, optical spectroscopy lab, scanning and transmission electron microscopes. **Computers:** 22% of classrooms, 5% of dorms, 100% of libraries, 85% of dining areas, 70% of student union, 5% of common outdoor areas have wireless network access. Students can register for classes online. Administrative functions (other than registration) can be performed online.

CAMPUS LIFE

Environment: Town **Activities:** Campus Ministries; Choral groups; Concert band; Dance; Drama/theater; International Student Organization; Jazz band; Literary magazine; Model UN; Music ensembles; Musical theater; Opera; Pep band; Radio station; Student government; Student newspaper; Student-run film society; Television station; Yearbook 205 registered organizations, 16 honor societies, 11 religious organizations. 12 fraternities, 16 sororities. **Athletics (Intercollegiate):** *Men:* baseball, basketball, cross-country, diving, football, soccer, swimming, tennis, track/field (outdoor), track/field (indoor). *Women:* basketball, cross-country, diving, field hockey, lacrosse, soccer, softball, swimming, tennis, track/field (outdoor), track/field (indoor). **On-Campus Highlights:** New Library, New Science Complex, New Arts and Multimedia Building, Student Center, Athletic Center **Environmental Initiatives:**

Commitment to sustainability being incorporated into the curriculum at TCNJ. This may include Freshman seminars, liberal learning programs, research and possible new minor or major degrees. The College's Municipal Land Use Center is authoring the State's sustainabilty and climate neutrality plans.

ADMISSIONS

Freshman Academic Profile: 36% in top 10% of high school class, 73% in top 25% of high school class, 98% in top 50% of high school class. 70% from public high schools. **Test Scores:** SAT Math middle 50% range 580-670. SAT EBRW middle 50% range 590-660. ACT middle 50% range 25-30. Minimum internet-based TOEFL 90. Minimum paper TOEFL 550. **Basis for Candidate Selection:** *Very important factors considered include:* rigor of secondary school record, class rank, standardized test scores, extracurricular activities, volunteer work. *Important factors considered include:* application essay, recommendation(s), talent/ability, character/personal qualities, geographical residence, state residency. *Other factors considered include:* academic GPA, first generation, alumni/ae relation, racial/ethnic status, work experience, level of applicant's interest. **Freshman Admission Requirements:** High school diploma is required and GED is accepted *Academic units required:* 4 English, 4 math, 4 science, 2 science labs, 2 foreign language, 2 social studies, 2 academic electives, *Academic units recommended:* 4 English, 4 math, 4 science, 2 science labs, 2 foreign language, 2 social studies, 4 academic electives. **Freshman Admission Statistics:** 12,898 applied, 47.5% admitted, 25% enrolled. **Transfer Admission Requirements:** High school transcript, college transcript(s), essay or personal statement, standardized test scores, statement of good standing from prior institution(s). Minimum college GPA of 2.5 required. Lowest grade transferable C. **General Admission Information:** Application fee $75. Priority deadline 11/1. Regular application deadline 2/1. Nonfall registration accepted. Admission may be deferred for a maximum of 2 semesters.

COSTS AND FINANCIAL AID

Annual in-state tuition $13,200. Annual out-of-state tuition $24,061. Room and board $13,200. Required fees $3,517. Average book expense $1,200. **Required Forms and Deadlines:** FAFSA. **Notification of Awards:** Applicants will be notified of awards on a rolling basis beginning 6/1. **Types of Aid:** *Need-based scholarships/grants:* College/university scholarship or grant aid from institutional funds; Federal Pell; Private scholarships; SEOG; State scholarships/grants. *Loans:* Direct PLUS loans; Direct Subsidized Stafford Loans; Direct Unsubsidized Stafford Loans. *Student Employment:* Federal Work-Study Program available. Institutional employment available. **Financial Aid Statistics:** 37% needy freshmen, 39% needy undergrads receive need-based scholarship or grant aid. 32% freshmen, 26% undergrads receive non-need-based scholarship or grant aid. 72% freshmen, 81% undergrads receive need-based self-help aid. 0% freshmen, 0% undergrads receive athletic scholarships. 70% freshmen, 62% undergrads receive any aid. Average cumulative indebtedness $36,994. **Criteria for awarding aid:** *Need-based:* Academics *Non-need-based:* Academics, Art, Music/drama.

See page 920.

COLLEGE OF THE OZARKS

P.O. Box 17, Point Lookout, MO 65726
Phone: 417-690-2636 • **Financial Aid Phone:** (417)690-3292
E-mail: admissions@cofo.edu • **CEEB Code:** 6713
Fax: 417-690-2635 • **Website:** www.cofo.edu • **ACT Code:** 23640

This private school, affiliated with the Evangelical Christian Interdenominational, was founded in 1906. It has a 1000 acre campus.

RATINGS

Admissions Selectivity Rating: 80   Fire Safety Rating: 96   Green Rating: 60*

STUDENTS AND FACULTY

Enrollment: 1,491. **Student Body:** 55% female, 45% male, 24% out-of-state, 1% international (17 countries represented). Asian 1%, African American 1%, Caucasian 90%, Hispanic 2%, Native American <1%, Pacific Islander <1%, Two or more races 2%, Race unknown 2%.
Retention and Graduation: 73% freshmen return for sophomore year. 55% freshmen graduate within 4 years. 72% freshmen graduate within 6 years. 14% grads go on to further study within 1 year. 3% grads pursue arts and sciences degrees. 0% grads pursue law degrees. 2% grads pursue business degrees. 1% grads pursue medical degrees. **Faculty:** Student/faculty ratio 14:1. 91 full-time

faculty, 62% hold PhDs, 1% are members of minority groups, 44% are women. 0% of classes are taught by teaching assistants.

ACADEMICS

Degrees: Bachelor's **Classes:** Most classes have 10-19 students. Most lab/discussion sessions have 10-19 students. **Most popular majors:** Agriculture, Agriculture Operations, And Related Sciences; Elementary Education And Teaching; Health Professions And Related Programs. **Special Study Options:** Double major; Dual enrollment; Independent study; Internships; Student-designed major; Teacher certification program. **Combined degree programs:** BA/JD. **Disability Services offered to physically disabled students:** Note-taking services; Reader services; Tape recorders; Tutors. **Career services:** Career assessment; Career/job search classes; Internships

FACILITIES

Housing: Men's dorms; Wellness housing; Women's dorms 85% of campus accessible to physically diasbled. **Special Academic Facilities/Equipment:** The Missouri Vietnam Veterans Memorial, "Lest We Forget" 911 Memorial, The Missouri Gold Star Families Memorial, Ralph Foster Museum Edwards Mill(working grist mill) The Keeter Center(hotel and restaurant), Fruitcake and Jelly Kitchen, greenhouses, print shop, Gaetz Tractor Museum, Ozarkian room(periodicals and pictures of the Ozarks) **Computers:** 100% of dorms, 100% of libraries, 100% of dining areas, 100% of student union, have wireless network access. Students can register for classes online. Administrative functions (other than registration) can be performed online.

CAMPUS LIFE

Environment: Rural **Activities:** Campus Ministries; Choral groups; Concert band; Drama/theater; International Student Organization; Jazz band; Music ensembles; Musical theater; Pep band; Radio station; Student government; Student newspaper; Student-run film society; Yearbook 45 registered organizations, 6 honor societies, 10 religious organizations. **Athletics (Intercollegiate):** *Men:* baseball, basketball, cheerleading. *Women:* basketball, cheerleading, volleyball. **On-Campus Highlights:** Howell W. Keeter Athletic Complex, Ralph Foster Museum, Williams Memorial Chapel, The Keeter Center, Patriots Park **Environmental Initiatives:** 1. The College ensures proper management of hazardous, special and universal waste. There is campus-wide recycling: plastic bottles, corrugated cardboard, aluminum cans, tin cans, batteries, tires, light bulbs and electronic products. Light bulb reclamation (recycle of bulbs) and energy efficient lights

ADMISSIONS

Freshman Academic Profile: Average high school GPA 3.7. 25% in top 10% of high school class, 62% in top 25% of high school class, 96% in top 50% of high school class. 78% from public high schools. **Test Scores:** SAT Math middle 50% range 543-605. SAT EBRW middle 50% range 560-625. ACT middle 50% range 21-26. Minimum internet-based TOEFL 79. Minimum paper TOEFL 550. **Basis for Candidate Selection:** *Very important factors considered include:* rigor of secondary school record, class rank, interview, character/personal qualities. *Important factors considered include:* academic GPA, standardized test scores, recommendation(s), geographical residence, volunteer work, work experience, level of applicant's interest. *Other factors considered include:* extracurricular activities, talent/ability, first generation, alumni/ae relation, state residency, religious affiliation/commitment. **Freshman Admission Requirements:** High school diploma is required and GED is accepted *Academic units required:* 4 English, 3 math, 2 science, 1 science labs, 3 history, *Academic units recommended:* 2 foreign language, 3 social studies. **Freshman Admission Statistics:** 2,879 applied, 15.5% admitted, 78% enrolled. **Transfer Admission Requirements:** college transcript(s), interview, statement of good.standing from prior institution(s). Minimum college GPA of 3.0 required. Lowest grade transferable D-. **General Admission Information:** Priority deadline 12/31. Nonfall registration accepted.

COSTS AND FINANCIAL AID

Room and board $7,400. Required fees $460. Average book expense $1,100. **Required Forms and Deadlines:** FAFSA. **Notification of Awards:** Applicants will be notified of awards on or about 7/1. **Types of Aid:** *Need-based scholarships/grants:* College/university scholarship or grant aid from institutional funds; Federal Pell; Private scholarships; SEOG; State scholarships/grants. *Loans:* *Student Employment:* Federal Work-Study Program available. Institutional employment available. **Financial Aid Statistics:** 100% needy freshmen, 100% needy undergrads receive need-based scholarship or grant aid. 7% freshmen, 13% undergrads receive non-need-based scholarship or grant aid. 93% freshmen, 87% undergrads receive need-based self-help aid. 2% freshmen, 2% undergrads receive athletic scholarships. 100% freshmen, 100% undergrads receive any aid. 0% undergrads borrow to pay for school. **Criteria for awarding aid:** *Need-based:* Academics, Alumni affiliation, Leadership, Minority status *Non-need-based:* Academics, Art, Athletics, Leadership, Music/drama, State/district residency.

COLLEGE OF SAINT ELIZABETH

2 Convent Road, Morristown, NJ 07960-6989
Phone: 973-290-4700 • **Financial Aid Phone:** 973-290-4432
E-mail: apply@cse.edu • **CEEB Code:** 2090
Fax: 973-290-4710

This private school, affiliated with the Roman Catholic Church, was founded in 1899. It has a 200 acre campus.

RATINGS

Admissions Selectivity Rating: 80   **Fire Safety Rating:** 96   **Green Rating:** 60*

STUDENTS AND FACULTY

Enrollment: 852. **Student Body:** 94% female, 6% male, 4% out-of-state, 4% international (8 countries represented). Asian 2%, African American 41%, Caucasian 26%, Hispanic 20%, Native American 1%, Pacific Islander 0%, Two or more races 2%, Race unknown 4%.
Retention and Graduation: 69% freshmen return for sophomore year.
Faculty: Student/faculty ratio 12:1. 52 full-time faculty, 83% hold PhDs, 8% are members of minority groups, 65% are women. 0% of classes are taught by teaching assistants.

ACADEMICS

Degrees: Bachelor's; Certificate; Doctoral; Master's; Post-Bachelor's certificate; Post-Master's certificate **Classes:** Most classes have 10-19 students. **Most popular majors:** Psychology, General; Criminal Justice/Safety Studies; Registered Nursing/Registered Nurse. **Special Study Options:** Accelerated program; Cross-registration; Distance learning; Double major; Dual enrollment; English as a Second Language (ESL); Exchange student program (domestic); Honors program; Independent study; Internships; Student-designed major; Study abroad; Teacher certification program; Weekend college. **Combined degree programs:** BA/MA. **Disability Services offered to physically disabled students:** Note-taking services; Reader services; Tape recorders; Tutors. **Career services:** Alumni network; Career assessment; Career/job search classes; Internships

FACILITIES

Housing: Women's dorms 85% of campus accessible to physically diasbled. **Special Academic Facilities/Equipment:** Dolan Performance Hall, Greek Theater, Octagon Theater, Mahoney Library, Smart Classrooms, Hyland Lecture Hall **Computers:** 100% of classrooms, 100% of dorms, 100% of libraries, 100% of dining areas, 100% of student union, 5% of common outdoor areas have wireless network access.

CAMPUS LIFE

Environment: Town **Activities:** Campus Ministries; Choral groups; Dance; Drama/theater; International Student Organization; Literary magazine; Music ensembles; Student government; Student newspaper; Yearbook 28 registered organizations, 9 honor societies, 1 religious organization. **Athletics (Intercollegiate):** *Women:* basketball, equestrian sports, soccer, softball, swimming, tennis. **On-Campus Highlights:** St. Joesph's Hall-Student Center, Henderson Hall-Classroom Building, O'Connor Hall-Residence Hall, Anunciation Center—Dolan Performance Hall, Mahoney Library **Environmental Initiatives:** Hazardous Waste Management process exists.

ADMISSIONS

Freshman Academic Profile: 81% from public high schools. **Test Scores:** SAT Math middle 50% range 370-465. SAT EBRW middle 50% range 380-470. Minimum internet-based TOEFL 61. Minimum paper TOEFL 500. **Basis for Candidate Selection:** *Very important factors considered include:* rigor of secondary school record, class rank, academic GPA, standardized test scores, recommendation(s). *Important factors considered include:* application essay, character/personal qualities. *Other factors considered include:* interview, extracurricular activities, talent/ability, first generation, alumni/ae relation, geographical residence, volunteer work, work experience, level of applicant's interest. **Freshman Admission Requirements:** High school diploma is required and GED is accepted *Academic units required:* 3 English, 2 math, 1 science, 1 science labs, 2 foreign language, 1 history, 7 academic electives, *Academic units recommended:* 3 English, 3 math, 1 science, 2 science labs, 1 history, 8 academic electives. **Freshman Admission Statistics:** 2,496 applied, 48.4% admitted, 10% enrolled. **Transfer Admission Requirements:** college transcript(s), essay or personal statement, Minimum college GPA of 2.0 required. Lowest grade transferable C. **General Admission Information:** Application fee $35. Priority deadline 3/1. Regular application deadline 8/15. Nonfall registration accepted. Admission may be deferred for a maximum of 1 year.

COSTS AND FINANCIAL AID

Annual tuition $29,148. Room and board $12,744. Required fees $1,947. Average book expense $1,300. **Required Forms and Deadlines:** FAFSA. **Notification of Awards:** Applicants will be notified of awards on a rolling basis beginning 11/15. **Types of Aid:** *Need-based scholarships/grants:* College/university scholarship or grant aid from institutional funds; Federal Pell; Private scholarships; SEOG; State scholarships/grants. *Loans:* Direct PLUS loans; Direct Subsidized Stafford Loans; Direct Unsubsidized Stafford Loans. *Student Employment:* Federal Work-Study Program available. Institutional employment available. **Financial Aid Statistics:** 89% needy freshmen, 81% needy undergrads receive need-based scholarship or grant aid. 100% freshmen, 88% undergrads receive non-need-based scholarship or grant aid. 93% freshmen, 91% undergrads receive need-based self-help aid. 0% freshmen, 0% undergrads receive athletic scholarships. 87% freshmen, 98% undergrads receive any aid. **Criteria for awarding aid:** *Need-based:* Academics, Minority status *Non-need-based:* Academics, Alumni affiliation, Art, Leadership, Religious affiliation, State/district residency.

COLLEGE OF SAINT MARY

7000 Mercy Rd., Omaha, NE 68106
Phone: 402-399-2355 • **Financial Aid Phone:** 402-399-2415
E-mail: enroll@csm.edu • **CEEB Code:** 6106
Fax: 402-399-2412 • **Website:** www.csm.edu • **ACT Code:** 2440

This private school, affiliated with the Roman Catholic Church, was founded in 1923. It has a 40 acre campus.

RATINGS

Admissions Selectivity Rating: 84   **Fire Safety Rating:** 97   **Green Rating:** 73

STUDENTS AND FACULTY

Enrollment: 780. **Student Body:** 100% female, 0% male, 24% out-of-state, 1% international (8 countries represented). Asian 3%, African American 8%, Caucasian 70%, Hispanic 14%, Native American 1%, Pacific Islander <1%, Two or more races 3%, Race unknown 0%.
Retention and Graduation: 84% freshmen return for sophomore year. 35% freshmen graduate within 4 years. 47% freshmen graduate within 6 years. 51% grads go on to further study within 1 year. **Faculty:** Student/faculty ratio 10:1. 69 full-time faculty, 74% hold PhDs, 13% are members of minority groups, 84% are women. 0% of classes are taught by teaching assistants.

ACADEMICS

Degrees: Associate; Bachelor's; Certificate; Doctoral/Research; Master's; Post-Bachelor's certificate; Terminal Associate **Classes:** Most classes have 10-19 students. **Most popular majors:** Elementary Education And Teaching; Registered Nursing/Registered Nurse; Business Administration And Management, General. **Special Study Options:** Accelerated program; Cooperative education program; Distance learning; Double major; Dual enrollment; Honors program; Independent study; Internships; Study abroad; Teacher certification program; Weekend college. **Honors programs:** Walk Tall Honors Program. **Disability Services offered to physically disabled students:** Note-taking services; Reader services; Tape recorders; Tutors. **Career services:** Alumni services; Career assessment; Career/job search classes; Internships

FACILITIES

Housing: Special housing for disabled student; Women's dorms 100% of campus accessible to physically diasbled. **Special Academic Facilities/Equipment:** Hillmer Art Gallery Gross Auditorium **Computers:** 100% of classrooms, 100% of dorms, 100% of libraries, 100% of dining areas, 100% of student union, 100% of common outdoor areas have wireless network access. Students can register for classes online. Administrative functions (other than registration) can be performed online.

CAMPUS LIFE

Environment: Metropolis **Activities:** Campus Ministries; Choral groups; Drama/theater; Music ensembles; Student government 20 registered organizations, 2 honor societies, 1 religious organization. **Athletics (Intercollegiate):** *Women:* basketball, cross-country, soccer, softball, swimming, volleyball. **On-Campus Highlights:** Christina's Place—Coffee Shop/Deli/student gathering place, Hillmer Art Gallery—Year round exhibits, Hixson-Lied Commons—Student Center, Library, Lied Fitness Center—gym, weight rm, pool, tennis, Our Lady of Mercy Chapel—Daily Mass offered **Environmental Initiatives:** Lower temperature set points in the summer time as well as work without lights to reduce energy during peak hours.

ADMISSIONS

Freshman Academic Profile: Average high school GPA 3.4. 15% in top 10% of high school class, 40% in top 25% of high school class, 72% in top 50% of high school class. 80% from public high schools. **Test Scores:** ACT middle 50% range 18–24. Minimum internet-based TOEFL 80. **Basis for Candidate Selection:** *Very important factors considered include:* academic GPA, standardized test scores. *Important factors considered include:* class rank. *Other factors considered include:* recommendation(s), extracurricular activities. **Freshman Admission Requirements:** High school diploma is required and GED is accepted *Academic units required:* 4 English, 2 math, 2 science, 2 social studies, *Academic units recommended:* 3 math, 3 science. **Freshman Admission Statistics:** 378 applied, 56.1% admitted, 47% enrolled. **Transfer Admission Requirements:** High school transcript, college transcript(s), Minimum college GPA of 2.0 required. Lowest grade transferable C. **General Admission Information:** Application fee $30. Nonfall registration accepted. Admission may be deferred for a maximum of 1 year.

COSTS AND FINANCIAL AID

Annual tuition $20,350. Room and board $7,700. Average book expense $972. **Required Forms and Deadlines:** FAFSA. **Notification of Awards:** Applicants will be notified of awards on a rolling basis beginning 12/15. **Types of Aid:** *Need-based scholarships/grants:* College/university scholarship or grant aid from institutional funds; Federal Nursing Scholarships; Federal Pell; Private scholarships; SEOG; State scholarships/grants. *Loans:* Direct PLUS loans; Direct Subsidized Stafford Loans; Direct Unsubsidized Stafford Loans. *Student Employment:* Federal Work-Study Program available. Institutional employment available. **Financial Aid Statistics:** 100% needy freshmen, 97% needy undergrads receive need-based scholarship or grant aid. 26% freshmen, 8% undergrads receive non-need-based scholarship or grant aid. 69% freshmen, 89% undergrads receive need-based self-help aid. 15% freshmen, 7% undergrads receive athletic scholarships. 94% freshmen, 92% undergrads receive any aid. **Criteria for awarding aid:** *Non-need-based:* Academics, Athletics.

THE COLLEGE OF SAINT ROSE

432 Western Avenue, Albany, NY 12203
Phone: 518-454-5150 · **Financial Aid Phone:** 518-458-5464
E-mail: admit@strose.edu · **CEEB Code:** 2091
Fax: 518-454-2013 · **Website:** www.strose.edu · **ACT Code:** 2714

This private school was founded in 1920. It has a 49 acre campus.

RATINGS

Admissions Selectivity Rating: 73   **Fire Safety Rating:** 95   **Green Rating:** 61

STUDENTS AND FACULTY

Enrollment: 2,490. **Student Body:** 67% female, 33% male, 12% out-of-state, 2% international (32 countries represented). Asian 3%, African American 15%, Caucasian 59%, Hispanic 8%, Native American <1%, Pacific Islander <1%, Two or more races 10%, Race unknown 3%.
Retention and Graduation: 75% freshmen return for sophomore year. 46% freshmen graduate within 4 years. 59% freshmen graduate within 6 years.
Faculty: Student/faculty ratio 14:1. 170 full-time faculty, 91% hold PhDs, 12% are members of minority groups, 54% are women. 0% of classes are taught by teaching assistants.

ACADEMICS

Degrees: Bachelor's; Certificate; Master's; Post-Bachelor's certificate; Post-Master's certificate **Most popular majors:** Communication And Media Studies, Other; Elementary Education And Teaching; Business Administration And Management, General. **Special Study Options:** Accelerated program; Cross-registration; Distance learning; Double major; Dual enrollment; English as a Second Language (ESL); Exchange student program (domestic); Independent study; Internships; Liberal arts/career combination; Student-designed major; Study abroad; Teacher certification program. **Combined degree programs:** BA/JD; BA/MA. **Disability Services offered to physically disabled students:** Note-taking services; Reader services; Tape recorders; Tutors. **Career services:** Alumni network; Alumni services; Career assessment; Career/job search classes; Internships; Regional alumni

FACILITIES

Housing: Apartments for single students; Coed dorms; Men's dorms; Special housing for disabled student; Women's dorms 90% of campus accessible to physically disabled. **Special Academic Facilities/Equipment:** The Center for Art and Design houses the Saint Rose Art Gallery, the venue for student art shows and home to one of the largest screen printing facilities in the state of New York. The Esther Massry Gallery features exhibits by acclaimed visiting

artists. The College's full-scale television studio is where communications students produce three 30-minute weekly television shows aired on Time Warner Cable. The Music Center features the Saints and Sinners Sound Studio, a 16-track professional recording studio, in addition to a music library. Athletic Facilities include the College's Fitness Center, swimming pool, regulation NCAA basketball court and the Plumeri Sports Complex. The Hubbard Interfaith Sanctuary is home to Campus Ministry and hosts a variety of interfaith lectures, concerts and poetry readings. With private meditation rooms and an indoor serenity garden, this interreligious space provides a place to escape for a few minutes of quiet prayer. The Center for Cultural Diversity provides academic, social, and cultural support in an effort to enhance the quality of experiences for our diverse student population. **Computers:** 98% of classrooms, 90% of dorms, 100% of libraries, 100% of dining areas, 100% of student union, 80% of common outdoor areas have wireless network access. Students can register for classes online. Administrative functions (other than registration) can be performed online.

CAMPUS LIFE

Environment: City **Activities:** Campus Ministries; Choral groups; Concert band; Dance; Drama/theater; International Student Organization; Jazz band; Literary magazine; Marching band; Music ensembles; Musical theater; Pep band; Radio station; Student government; Student newspaper; Symphony orchestra; Television station 38 registered organizations, 6 honor societies, 2 religious organizations. **Athletics (Intercollegiate):** *Men:* baseball, basketball, cross-country, golf, soccer, swimming, track/field (outdoor). *Women:* basketball, cross-country, soccer, softball, swimming, tennis, track/field (outdoor), volleyball. **On-Campus Highlights:** Lally School of Education, Massry Center for the Fine Arts/Center for Art and Design, Events and Athletic Center, Starbucks, Student Solution Center

ADMISSIONS

Freshman Academic Profile: Average high school GPA 87.2. 8% in top 10% of high school class, 24% in top 25% of high school class, 63% in top 50% of high school class. **Test Scores:** SAT Math middle 50% range 480–560. SAT EBRW middle 50% range 490–582. ACT middle 50% range 20–25. Minimum internet-based TOEFL 80. Minimum paper TOEFL 550. **Basis for Candidate Selection:** *Very important factors considered include:* rigor of secondary school record, academic GPA. *Important factors considered include:* recommendation(s), extracurricular activities, talent/ability, character/personal qualities, first generation, level of applicant's interest. *Other factors considered include:* class rank, application essay, standardized test scores, interview, alumni/ae relation, volunteer work, work experience. **Freshman Admission Requirements:** High school diploma is required and GED is accepted *Academic units required:* 4 English, 3 math, 3 science, 2 science labs, 1 foreign language, 2 social studies, 2 history, *Academic units recommended:* 4 English, 4 math, 4 science, 2 science labs, 2 foreign language, 4 social studies, 4 history, 4 academic electives. **Freshman Admission Statistics:** 6,727 applied, 82.7% admitted, 10% enrolled. **Transfer Admission Requirements:** High school transcript, college transcript(s), statement of good standing from prior institution(s). Minimum college GPA of 2.5 required. Lowest grade transferable C-. **General Admission Information:** Priority deadline 12/1. Regular application deadline 5/1. Nonfall registration accepted. Admission may be deferred for a maximum of 1 semester.

COSTS AND FINANCIAL AID

Annual tuition $30,546. Room and board $12,356. Required fees $1,066. Average book expense $1,200. **Required Forms and Deadlines:** FAFSA; State aid form. **Notification of Awards:** Applicants will be notified of awards on a rolling basis beginning 3/1. **Types of Aid:** *Need-based scholarships/grants:* College/university scholarship or grant aid from institutional funds; Federal Pell; Private scholarships; SEOG; State scholarships/grants. *Loans:* Direct PLUS loans; Direct Subsidized Stafford Loans; Direct Unsubsidized Stafford Loans. *Student Employment:* Federal Work-Study Program available. Institutional employment available. **Financial Aid Statistics:** 90% needy freshmen, 86% needy undergrads receive need-based scholarship or grant aid. 85% undergrads receive non-need-based scholarship or grant aid. 2% freshmen, 2% undergrads receive athletic scholarships. 99% freshmen, 89% undergrads receive any aid. 88% undergrads borrow to pay for school. Average cumulative indebtedness $36,432. **Criteria for awarding aid:** *Need-based:* Academics *Non-need-based:* Academics, Alumni affiliation, Art, Athletics, Music/drama.

THE COLLEGE OF SAINT SCHOLASTICA

1200 Kenwood Avenue, Duluth, MN 55811-4199
Phone: 218-723-6046 • **Financial Aid Phone:** 218-723-6047
E-mail: admissions@css.edu • **CEEB Code:** 6107
Fax: 218-723-5991 • **Website:** www.css.edu • **ACT Code:** 2098

This private school, affiliated with the Roman Catholic Church, was founded in 1912. It has a 186 acre campus.

RATINGS
Admissions Selectivity Rating: 82   **Fire Safety Rating:** 79   **Green Rating:** 60*

STUDENTS AND FACULTY
Enrollment: 2,669. **Student Body:** 71% female, 29% male, 14% out-of-state, 2% international (34 countries represented). Asian 2%, African American 3%, Caucasian 84%, Hispanic 4%, Native American 1%, Pacific Islander <1%, Two or more races 3%, Race unknown <1%.
Retention and Graduation: 81% freshmen return for sophomore year. 58% freshmen graduate within 4 years. 67% freshmen graduate within 6 years. 29% grads go on to further study within 1 year. **Faculty:** Student/faculty ratio 14:1. 190 full-time faculty, 61% hold PhDs, 10% are members of minority groups, 69% are women. 0% of classes are taught by teaching assistants.

ACADEMICS
Degrees: Bachelor's; Certificate; Doctoral/Professional; Master's; Post-Bachelor's certificate; Post-Master's certificate **Classes:** Most classes have 10-19 students. Most lab/discussion sessions have fewer than 10 students. **Most popular majors:** Computer And Information Sciences, General; Registered Nursing/Registered Nurse; Business Administration And Management, General. **Special Study Options:** Accelerated program; Cross-registration; Distance learning; Double major; Dual enrollment; Honors program; Independent study; Internships; Liberal arts/career combination; Student-designed major; Study abroad; Teacher certification program. **Honors programs:** The Honors Program at The College of St. Scholastica was created to give honors students enriched learning experiences and to provide a community of support for learners devoted to a vigorous life of the mind. **Combined degree programs:** BA/MA. **Disability Services offered to physically disabled students:** Note-taking services; Reader services; Tape recorders; Tutors. **Career services:** Alumni network; Alumni services; Career assessment; Career/job search classes; Internships; Regional alumni

FACILITIES
Housing: Apartments for single students; Coed dorms; Special housing for disabled student; Special housing for international students; Wellness housing 95% of campus accessible to physically diasbled. **Computers:** Students can register for classes online. Administrative functions (other than registration) can be performed online.

CAMPUS LIFE
Environment: City **Activities:** Campus Ministries; Choral groups; Concert band; Dance; Drama/theater; International Student Organization; Jazz band; Literary magazine; Music ensembles; Pep band; Student government; Student newspaper; Television station 67 registered organizations, 2 honor societies, 7 religious organizations. **Athletics (Intercollegiate):** *Men:* baseball, basketball, cross-country, ice hockey, skiing (nordic/cross-country), soccer, tennis, track/field (outdoor), track/field (indoor). *Women:* basketball, cross-country, skiing (nordic/cross-country), soccer, softball, tennis, track/field (outdoor), track/field (indoor), volleyball. **On-Campus Highlights:** Wellness Center, Student Union, Storm's Den, Beakers Coffee Shop

ADMISSIONS
Freshman Academic Profile: Average high school GPA 3.5. 25% in top 10% of high school class, 55% in top 25% of high school class, 85% in top 50% of high school class. **Test Scores:** SAT Math middle 50% range 510-630. SAT EBRW middle 50% range 510-670. ACT middle 50% range 19-27. Minimum internet-based TOEFL 79. Minimum paper TOEFL 550. **Basis for Candidate Selection:** *Very important factors considered include:* academic GPA, standardized test scores. *Important factors considered include:* rigor of secondary school record, class rank. *Other factors considered include:* application essay, recommendation(s), interview. **Freshman Admission Requirements:** High school diploma is required and GED is accepted *Academic units recommended:* 4 English, 2 math, 3 science, 3 foreign language, 3 social studies, 3 history. **Freshman Admission Statistics:** 3,834 applied, 68.3% admitted, 18% enrolled. **Transfer Admission Requirements:** college transcript(s), Minimum college GPA of 1.5 required. Lowest grade transferable C. **General Admission Information:** Nonfall registration accepted. Admission may be deferred for a maximum of 1 year.

COSTS AND FINANCIAL AID
Annual tuition $35,634. Room and board $9,522. Required fees $578. Average book expense $1,150. **Required Forms and Deadlines:** FAFSA. **Notification of Awards:** Applicants will be notified of awards on a rolling basis beginning 3/1. **Types of Aid:** *Need-based scholarships/grants:* College/university scholarship or grant aid from institutional funds; Federal Pell; Private scholarships; SEOG; State scholarships/grants. *Loans:* Direct PLUS loans; Direct Subsidized Stafford Loans; Direct Unsubsidized Stafford Loans. *Student Employment:* Federal Work-Study Program available. Institutional employment available. **Financial Aid Statistics:** 76% needy freshmen, 74% needy undergrads receive need-based scholarship or grant aid. 100% freshmen, 80% undergrads receive non-need-based scholarship or grant aid. 75% freshmen, 76% undergrads receive need-based self-help aid. 0% freshmen, 0% undergrads receive athletic scholarships. 75% freshmen, 98% undergrads receive any aid. 77% undergrads borrow to pay for school. Average cumulative indebtedness $40,774. **Criteria for awarding aid:** *Non-need-based:* Academics, Alumni affiliation, Music/drama, Religious affiliation, State/district residency.

COLLEGE OF ST. BENEDICT/ SAINT JOHN'S UNIVERSITY

220 South Pleasant Street, St. Joseph, MN 56321-7155
Phone: 320-363-5060 • **Financial Aid Phone:** 320-363-5388
E-mail: admissions@csbsju.edu • **CEEB Code:** 6624
Fax: 320-363-5650 • **Website:** www.csbsju.edu • **ACT Code:** 2146

This private school, affiliated with the Roman Catholic Church, was founded in 1857. It has a 2800 acre campus.

RATINGS
Admissions Selectivity Rating: 76   **Fire Safety Rating:** 98   **Green Rating:** 81

STUDENTS AND FACULTY
Enrollment: 3,657. **Student Body:** 53% female, 47% male, 18% out-of-state, 4% international (21 countries represented). Asian 4%, African American 4%, Caucasian 79%, Hispanic 7%, Native American 1%, Pacific Islander <1%, Two or more races <1%, Race unknown 0%.
Retention and Graduation: 88% freshmen return for sophomore year. 71% freshmen graduate within 4 years. 78% freshmen graduate within 6 years. 14% grads go on to further study within 1 year. **Faculty:** Student/faculty ratio 12:1. 272 full-time faculty, 90% hold PhDs, 9% are members of minority groups, 50% are women. 0% of classes are taught by teaching assistants.

ACADEMICS
Degrees: Bachelor's; Master's **Classes:** Most classes have 10-19 students. Most lab/discussion sessions have 10-19 students. **Most popular majors:** Biology/Biological Sciences, General; Business Administration And Management, General; Accounting And Finance. **Special Study Options:** Cross-registration; Double major; Dual enrollment; English as a Second Language (ESL); Honors program; Independent study; Internships; Student-designed major; Study abroad; Teacher certification program. **Honors programs:** All departments may contribute courses to our honors program. Students in all majors may participate in the Honors Program and receive honors distinction inside the major. **Disability Services offered to physically disabled students:** Note-taking services; Reader services; Tape recorders; Tutors. **Career services:** Alumni network; Alumni services; Career assessment; Internships; Regional alumni

FACILITIES
Housing: Apartments for single students; Men's dorms; Special housing for disabled student; Theme housing; Wellness housing; Women's dorms 90% of campus accessible to physically diasbled. **Special Academic Facilities/Equipment:** Hill Museum and Manuscript Library, art galleries, natural science museum, Saint John's Outdoor University, Benedicta Arts Center, Sommers Digital Video Studio, observatory, greenhouses **Computers:** 100% of classrooms, 20% of dorms, 100% of libraries, 100% of dining areas, 100% of student union, 100% of common outdoor areas have wireless network access. Students can register for classes online. Administrative functions (other than registration) can be performed online.

CAMPUS LIFE

Environment: Village **Activities:** Campus Ministries; Choral groups; Concert band; Dance; Drama/theater; International Student Organization; Jazz band; Literary magazine; Model UN; Music ensembles; Musical theater; Opera; Pep band; Radio station; Student government; Student newspaper; Student-run film society; Symphony orchestra; Television station 85 registered organizations, 3 honor societies, 4 religious organizations. **Athletics (Intercollegiate):** *Men:* baseball, basketball, cross-country, diving, football, golf, ice hockey, skiing (nordic/cross-country), soccer, swimming, tennis, track/field (outdoor), track/field (indoor), wrestling. *Women:* basketball, cross-country, diving, golf, ice hockey, skiing (nordic/cross-country), soccer, softball, swimming, tennis, track/field (outdoor), track/field (indoor), volleyball. **On-Campus Highlights:** Gorecki Dining Center/Sexton Commons, Learning Commons at SJU, Warner Palaestra/Clemens Field House, Lake Sagatagan/Stella Maris Chapel, Clemens Perk/The Schuh Coffee shops **Environmental Initiatives:** Renewable Energy/Carbon neutrality

ADMISSIONS

Freshman Academic Profile: Average high school GPA 3.6. 25% in top 10% of high school class, 56% in top 25% of high school class, 87% in top 50% of high school class. 74% from public high schools. **Test Scores:** ACT middle 50% range 22-28. Minimum internet-based TOEFL 80. Minimum paper TOEFL 550. **Basis for Candidate Selection:** *Very important factors considered include:* rigor of secondary school record, academic GPA, standardized test scores, extracurricular activities. *Important factors considered include:* alumni/ae relation. *Other factors considered include:* application essay, recommendation(s), interview, talent/ability, character/personal qualities, first generation, geographical residence, volunteer work, work experience. **Freshman Admission Requirements:** High school diploma is required and GED is accepted *Academic units required:* 4 English, 3 math, 2 science, 2 science labs, 2 social studies, 4 academic electives, *Academic units recommended:* 4 English, 3 math, 2 science, 2 science labs, 2 foreign language, 2 social studies, 4 academic electives. **Freshman Admission Statistics:** 3,236 applied, 90.5% admitted, 34% enrolled. **Transfer Admission Requirements:** High school transcript, college transcript(s), essay or personal statement, statement of good standing from prior institution(s). Minimum college GPA of 2.75 required. Lowest grade transferable C. **General Admission Information:** Priority deadline 11/15. Nonfall registration accepted. Admission may be deferred for a maximum of one year.

COSTS AND FINANCIAL AID

Annual tuition $42,690. Room and board $10,742. Required fees $1,048. Average book expense $1,000. **Required Forms and Deadlines:** FAFSA. **Notification of Awards:** Applicants will be notified of awards on a rolling basis beginning 3/15. **Types of Aid:** *Need-based scholarships/grants:* College/university scholarship or grant aid from institutional funds; Federal Pell; Private scholarships; SEOG; State scholarships/grants. *Loans:* Direct PLUS loans; Direct Subsidized Stafford Loans; Direct Unsubsidized Stafford Loans. *Student Employment:* Federal Work-Study Program available. Institutional employment available. **Financial Aid Statistics:** 98% needy freshmen, 88% needy undergrads receive need-based scholarship or grant aid. 96% freshmen, 96% undergrads receive non-need-based scholarship or grant aid. 97% freshmen, 97% undergrads receive need-based self-help aid. 0% freshmen, 0% undergrads receive athletic scholarships. 95% freshmen, 94% undergrads receive any aid. 69% undergrads borrow to pay for school. Average cumulative indebtedness $39,904. **Criteria for awarding aid:** *Non-need-based:* Academics, Alumni affiliation, Art, Leadership, Music/drama.

COLLEGE OF ST. JOSEPH IN VERMONT

71 Clement Road, Rutland, VT 05701
Phone: 802-776-5286 · **Financial Aid Phone:** 802-776-5218
E-mail: admissions@csj.edu · **CEEB Code:** 3297
Fax: 802-776-5258 · **Website:** www.csj.edu

This private school, affiliated with the Roman Catholic Church, was founded in 1956. It has a 116 acre campus.

RATINGS

Admissions Selectivity Rating: 72   **Fire Safety Rating:** 76   **Green Rating:** 60*

STUDENTS AND FACULTY

Enrollment: 208. **Student Body:** 55% female, 45% male, 42% out-of-state, 0% international (6 countries represented). Asian 1%, African American 4%, Caucasian 89%, Hispanic 5%, Native American 1%, Race unknown 0%.
Retention and Graduation: 83% freshmen return for sophomore year.
Faculty: Student/faculty ratio 11:1. 15 full-time faculty, 47% hold PhDs, 0%

are members of minority groups, 40% are women. 0% of classes are taught by teaching assistants.

ACADEMICS

Degrees: Associate; Bachelor's; Master's **Classes:** Most classes have 20-29 students. Most lab/discussion sessions have 10-19 students. **Most popular majors:** Elementary Education And Teaching; Psychology, General; Business, Management, Marketing, And Related Support Services, Other. **Special Study Options:** Accelerated program; Double major; Dual enrollment; Independent study; Internships; Liberal arts/career combination; Teacher certification program. **Disability Services offered to physically disabled students:** Note-taking services; Reader services; Tape recorders; Tutors. **Career services:** Alumni services; Career assessment; Career/job search classes; Internships

FACILITIES

Housing: Men's dorms; Women's dorms 100% of campus accessible to physically diasbled. **Special Academic Facilities/Equipment:** Theater and Athletic Center **Computers:** 100% of libraries, have wireless network access.

CAMPUS LIFE

Environment: Village **Activities:** Campus Ministries; Choral groups; Drama/theater; Literary magazine; Student government 20 registered organizations, 6 honor societies, 1 religious organization. **Athletics (Intercollegiate):** *Men:* baseball, basketball, soccer. *Women:* basketball, soccer, softball. **On-Campus Highlights:** Tuttle Hall-Student Center, Athletic Center, Theater, Giorgetti Library, St. Joseph Hall

ADMISSIONS

Freshman Academic Profile: Average high school GPA 2.6. 0% in top 10% of high school class, 3% in top 25% of high school class, 36% in top 50% of high school class. 75% from public high schools. **Test Scores:** SAT Math middle 50% range 390-490. SAT EBRW middle 50% range 410-530. ACT middle 50% range 17-23. Minimum internet-based TOEFL 79. Minimum paper TOEFL 550. **Basis for Candidate Selection:** *Very important factors considered include:* rigor of secondary school record, academic GPA, recommendation(s). *Important factors considered include:* application essay, standardized test scores, interview, character/personal qualities. *Other factors considered include:* class rank, extracurricular activities, talent/ability, alumni/ae relation, volunteer work, level of applicant's interest. **Freshman Admission Requirements:** High school diploma is required and GED is not accepted *Academic units required:* 4 English, 3 math, 2 science, 2 social studies, 2 history, 5 academic electives, *Academic units recommended:* 2 foreign language. **Freshman Admission Statistics:** 127 applied, 89.8% admitted, 35% enrolled. **Transfer Admission Requirements:** High school transcript, college transcript(s), essay or personal statement, Minimum college GPA of 2.0 required. Lowest grade transferable C. **General Admission Information:** Application fee $25. Priority deadline 5/1. Nonfall registration accepted. Admission may be deferred for a maximum of 1 year.

COSTS AND FINANCIAL AID

Annual tuition $15,500. Room and board $7,600. Required fees $260. Average book expense $1,000. **Required Forms and Deadlines:** FAFSA; Institution's own financial aid form. **Notification of Awards:** Applicants will be notified of awards on a rolling basis beginning 3/15. **Types of Aid:** *Need-based scholarships/grants:* College/university scholarship or grant aid from institutional funds; Federal Pell; Private scholarships; SEOG; State scholarships/grants. *Loans: Student Employment:* Federal Work-Study Program available. Institutional employment available. **Financial Aid Statistics:** 100% needy freshmen, 98% needy undergrads receive need-based scholarship or grant aid. 3% undergrads receive non-need-based scholarship or grant aid. 96% freshmen, 94% undergrads receive need-based self-help aid. 0% freshmen, 0% undergrads receive athletic scholarships. 91% freshmen, 88% undergrads receive any aid. **Criteria for awarding aid:** *Need-based:* Academics, Alumni affiliation, Leadership, Religious affiliation *Non-need-based:* Academics, Music/drama.

COLLEGE OF WILLIAM AND MARY

P.O. Box 8795, Williamsburg, VA 23187-8795
Phone: 757-221-4223 · **Financial Aid Phone:** 757-221-2768
E-mail: admission@wm.edu · **CEEB Code:** 5115
Fax: 757-221-1242 · **Website:** www.wm.edu · **ACT Code:** 4344

This public school was founded in 1693. It has a 1200 acre campus.

RATINGS

Admissions Selectivity Rating: 96   **Fire Safety Rating:** 92   **Green Rating:** 81

STUDENTS AND FACULTY

Enrollment: 6,243. **Student Body:** 58% female, 42% male, 30% out-of-state, 6% international (81 countries represented). Asian 8%, African American 7%, Caucasian 59%, Hispanic 9%, Native American <1%, Pacific Islander <1%, Two or more races 5%, Race unknown 5%.
Retention and Graduation: 95% freshmen return for sophomore year. 85% freshmen graduate within 4 years. 91% freshmen graduate within 6 years. 22% grads go on to further study within 1 year. 1% grads pursue law degrees. 2% grads pursue medical degrees. **Faculty:**

ACADEMICS

Degrees: Bachelor's; Doctoral; Doctoral/Professional; Doctoral/Research; Master's; Post-Bachelor's certificate; Post-Master's certificate **Classes:** Most classes have 20-29 students. Most lab/discussion sessions have 10-19 students.
Most popular majors: Biology/Biological Sciences, General; Political Science And Government, General; Business Administration And Management, General. **Special Study Options:** Accelerated program; Distance learning; Double major; Dual enrollment; English as a Second Language (ESL); Honors program; Independent study; Internships; Student-designed major; Study abroad; Teacher certification program. **Honors programs:** 1693 Scholars This is a four-year award for approximately 8 of the College's most academically distinguished entering freshmen each year. 1693 Scholars include both Virginia residents and out-of-state students, and they all receive the full cost of education at the in-state level. They also participate in special seminars and receive funding for research projects. James Monroe Scholars About 125 academically distinguished entering freshmen are named Monroe Scholars. Another 25 are added after the conclusion of the freshman year. Monroe Scholars participate in special seminars and other activities, and receive funding for research projects. Sharpe Scholars Students are admitted as entering freshmen to the Sharpe Program. These students live together as freshmen and take specially designed seminars that integrate community projects with the seminars' curricula. **Combined degree programs:** BA/MA. **Disability Services offered to physically disabled students:** Note-taking services; Reader services; Tape recorders; Tutors. **Career services:** Alumni services; Career assessment; Internships

FACILITIES

Housing: Apartments for single students; Coed dorms; Fraternity/sorority housing; Special housing for disabled student; Special housing for international students; Theme housing 95% of campus accessible to physically diasbled.
Special Academic Facilities/Equipment: observatory, continuous beam accelerator, 3 interdisciplinary centers (humanities, international studies, writing resources), marine science institute, materials processes research center, public policy research center, health policy research center, center for geospatial analysis, center for archeological research, Institute for the Theory and Practice of International Relations, environmental field laboratory, Reves Center for International Studies, Special Collections Research Center, Charles W. Reeder Media Center, Muscarelle Museum of Art, College Woods, Lake Matoaka and Matoaka Trails (10 miles of nature trails surrounding the lake **Computers:** 100% of classrooms, 100% of dorms, 100% of libraries, 100% of dining areas, 100% of student union, 33% of common outdoor areas have wireless network access. Students can register for classes online. Administrative functions (other than registration) can be performed online. Undergraduates are required to own a computer.

CAMPUS LIFE

Environment: Town **Activities:** Campus Ministries; Choral groups; Concert band; Dance; Drama/theater; International Student Organization; Jazz band; Literary magazine; Model UN; Music ensembles; Musical theater; Opera; Pep band; Radio station; Student government; Student newspaper; Student-run film society; Symphony orchestra; Television station; Yearbook 375 registered organizations, 32 honor societies, 32 religious organizations. 18 fraternities, 11

sororities. **Athletics (Intercollegiate):** *Men:* baseball, basketball, cheerleading, cross-country, diving, football, golf, gymnastics, soccer, swimming, tennis, track/field (outdoor), track/field (indoor). *Women:* basketball, cheerleading, cross-country, diving, field hockey, golf, gymnastics, lacrosse, soccer, swimming, tennis, track/field (outdoor), track/field (indoor), volleyball. **On-Campus Highlights:** Wren Building (oldest academic building), Muscarelle Museum of Art, Lake Matoaka/College Woods, Sadler Center, Sunken Garden **Environmental Initiatives:** Adhere to LEED construction guidelines in all new construction and renovations. Three buildings have been LEED certified to date and two are in progress.

ADMISSIONS

Freshman Academic Profile: Average high school GPA 4.2. 81% in top 10% of high school class, 97% in top 25% of high school class, 100% in top 50% of high school class. 77% from public high schools. **Test Scores:** SAT Math middle 50% range 640-740. SAT EBRW middle 50% range 660-740. ACT middle 50% range 29-33. Minimum internet-based TOEFL 100. Minimum paper TOEFL 600. **Basis for Candidate Selection:** *Very important factors considered include:* rigor of secondary school record, class rank, academic GPA, application essay, standardized test scores, recommendation(s), extracurricular activities, talent/ability, character/personal qualities, state residency, volunteer work, work experience. *Other factors considered include:* interview, first generation, alumni/ae relation, geographical residence, racial/ethnic status, level of applicant's interest. **Freshman Admission Requirements:** High school diploma or equivalent is not required *Academic units recommended:* 4 English, 4 math, 4 science, 3 science labs, 4 foreign language, 4 social studies. **Freshman Admission Statistics:** 14,921 applied, 35.9% admitted, 29% enrolled. **Transfer Admission Requirements:** High school transcript, college transcript(s), essay or personal statement, statement of good standing from prior institution(s). Minimum college GPA of 3.00 required. Lowest grade transferable C. **General Admission Information:** Application fee $75. Regular application deadline 1/1. Nonfall registration accepted. Admission may be deferred for a maximum of 1 year.

COSTS AND FINANCIAL AID

Required Forms and Deadlines: CSS/Financial Aid PROFILE; FAFSA. **Notification of Awards:** Applicants will be notified of awards on or about 3/15. **Types of Aid:** *Need-based scholarships/grants:* College/university scholarship or grant aid from institutional funds; Federal Pell; Private scholarships; SEOG; State scholarships/grants. *Loans:* Direct PLUS loans; Direct Subsidized Stafford Loans; Direct Unsubsidized Stafford Loans. *Student Employment:* Federal Work-Study Program available. Institutional employment available. **Financial Aid Statistics:** 86% needy undergrads receive need-based scholarship or grant aid. 0% undergrads receive non-need-based scholarship or grant aid. 0% freshmen, 0% undergrads receive need-based self-help aid. 0% freshmen, 0% undergrads receive athletic scholarships. 54% freshmen, 53% undergrads receive any aid. **Criteria for awarding aid:** *Need-based:* Academics, Alumni affiliation, Athletics, Music/drama *Non-need-based:* Academics, Art, Athletics, Music/drama.

COLLEGE OF WOOSTER

1189 Beall Avenue, Wooster, OH 44691
Phone: 330-263-2322 · **Financial Aid Phone:** 330-263-2317
E-mail: admissions@wooster.edu · **CEEB Code:** 1134
Fax: 330-263-2621 · **Website:** www.wooster.edu · **ACT Code:** 3260

This private school, affiliated with the Presbyterian Church, was founded in 1866. It has a 240 acre campus.

RATINGS

Admissions Selectivity Rating: 89   **Fire Safety Rating:** 86   **Green Rating:** 79

STUDENTS AND FACULTY

Enrollment: 1,970. **Student Body:** 54% female, 46% male, 63% out-of-state, 13% international (37 countries represented). Asian 5%, African American 9%, Caucasian 66%, Hispanic 5%, Native American 1%, Pacific Islander 0%, Two or more races 0%, Race unknown 1%.
Retention and Graduation: 86% freshmen return for sophomore year. 70% freshmen graduate within 4 years. 77% freshmen graduate within 6 years. 23% grads go on to further study within 1 year. 28% grads pursue arts and sciences degrees. 14% grads pursue law degrees. 3% grads pursue business degrees. 11% grads pursue medical degrees. **Faculty:** Student/faculty ratio 11:1. 165 full-time

faculty, 94% hold PhDs, 18% are members of minority groups, 52% are women. 0% of classes are taught by teaching assistants.

ACADEMICS

Degrees: Bachelor's **Classes:** Most classes have 20-29 students. Most lab/discussion sessions have 10-19 students. **Most popular majors:** English Language And Literature, General; Psychology, General; History, General. **Special Study Options:** Double major; Exchange student program (domestic); Independent study; Internships; Student-designed major; Study abroad; Teacher certification program. **Combined degree programs:** BA/DDS; BA/MA; BA/MEng. **Disability Services offered to physically disabled students:** Note-taking services; Reader services; Tape recorders; Tutors. **Career services:** Alumni network; Alumni services; Career assessment; Career/job search classes; Internships; Regional alumni

FACILITIES

Housing: Apartments for single students; Coed dorms; Fraternity/sorority housing; Special housing for international students; Theme housing 95% of campus accessible to physically diasbled. **Special Academic Facilities/Equipment:** Art museum, language lab, on-campus nursery school, science library, Collaborative Research Center, Advising, Planning,& Experiential Learning Center (APEX). **Computers:** 100% of classrooms, 95% of dorms, 100% of libraries, 100% of dining areas, 100% of student union, 50% of common outdoor areas have wireless network access. Students can register for classes online. Administrative functions (other than registration) can be performed online.

CAMPUS LIFE

Environment: Town **Activities:** Campus Ministries; Choral groups; Concert band; Dance; Drama/theater; International Student Organization; Jazz band; Literary magazine; Marching band; Model UN; Music ensembles; Musical theater; Radio station; Student government; Student newspaper; Student-run film society; Symphony orchestra; Yearbook 100 registered organizations, 6 honor societies, 9 religious organizations. 5 fraternities, 6 sororities. **Athletics (Intercollegiate):** *Men:* baseball, basketball, cross-country, diving, football, golf, lacrosse, soccer, swimming, tennis, track/field (outdoor), track/field (indoor). *Women:* basketball, cross-country, diving, field hockey, lacrosse, soccer, softball, swimming, tennis, track/field (outdoor), track/field (indoor), volleyball. **On-Campus Highlights:** Kauke Hall, Scot Center, Timken Science Library, Ebert Art Center, Lowry Center **Environmental Initiatives:** Completed $5M Energy Performance Contract that reduced the College's carbon footprint by 36% through lighting and water conservation, building automation system upgrades, and the installation of two new electric chillers and a steam condensor at the Power Plant.

ADMISSIONS

Freshman Academic Profile: Average high school GPA 3.7. 45% in top 10% of high school class, 75% in top 25% of high school class, 92% in top 50% of high school class. 62% from public high schools. **Test Scores:** SAT Math middle 50% range 580-700. SAT EBRW middle 50% range 570-680. ACT middle 50% range 24-30. Minimum internet-based TOEFL 81. **Basis for Candidate Selection:** *Very important factors considered include:* rigor of secondary school record, academic GPA. *Important factors considered include:* class rank, application essay, standardized test scores, recommendation(s), interview, extracurricular activities, character/personal qualities, level of applicant's interest. *Other factors considered include:* talent/ability, first generation, alumni/ae relation, geographical residence, state residency, racial/ethnic status, volunteer work, work experience. **Freshman Admission Requirements:** High school diploma is required and GED is accepted *Academic units required:* 4 English, 3 math, 3 science, 2 science labs, 2 foreign language, 3 social studies, 1 academic elective. **Freshman Admission Statistics:** 5,615 applied, 56.4% admitted, 18% enrolled. **Transfer Admission Requirements:** High school transcript, college transcript(s), essay or personal statement, standardized test scores, statement of good standing from prior institution(s). Minimum college GPA of 2.5 required. Lowest grade transferable C. **General Admission Information:** Priority deadline 2/15. Regular application deadline 2/15. Nonfall registration accepted. Admission may be deferred for a maximum of 1 year.

COSTS AND FINANCIAL AID

Annual tuition $48,160. Room and board $11,400. Required fees $440. Average book expense $1,000. **Required Forms and Deadlines:** CSS/Financial Aid PROFILE; FAFSA; Institution's own financial aid form. **Notification of Awards:** Applicants will be notified of awards on a rolling basis beginning 3/15. **Types of Aid:** *Need-based scholarships/grants:* College/university scholarship or grant aid from institutional funds; Federal Pell; Private scholarships; SEOG; State scholarships/grants. *Loans:* Direct PLUS loans; Direct Subsidized Stafford Loans; Direct Unsubsidized Stafford Loans. *Student Employment:* Federal Work-Study Program available. Institutional employment available. **Financial Aid Statistics:** 97% needy freshmen, 97% needy undergrads receive need-based scholarship or grant aid. 18% freshmen, 13% undergrads receive non-need-based scholarship or grant aid. 80% freshmen, 83% undergrads receive need-based self-help aid. 0% freshmen receive athletic scholarships. 99% freshmen, 99% undergrads receive any aid. 61% undergrads borrow to pay for

school. Average cumulative indebtedness $29,650. **Criteria for awarding aid:** *Need-based:* Academics, Minority status *Non-need-based:* Academics, Minority status, Music/drama, Religious affiliation.

COLORADO CHRISTIAN UNIVERSITY

8787 W. Alameda Ave., Lakewood, CO 80226
Phone: 303-963-3200 • **Financial Aid Phone:** 303-963-3233
E-mail: ccuadmissions@ccu.edu • **CEEB Code:** 4659
Fax: 303-963-3201 • **Website:** www.ccu.edu • **ACT Code:** 523

This private school, affiliated with the Christian (Nondenominational) Church, was founded in 1914. It has a 26 acre campus.

RATINGS

Admissions Selectivity Rating: 78   **Fire Safety Rating:** 61   **Green Rating:** 60*

STUDENTS AND FACULTY

Enrollment: 1,849. **Student Body:** 60% female, 40% male, 56% out-of-state, 1% international. Asian 1%, African American 4%, Caucasian 76%, Hispanic 9%, Native American 1%, Race unknown 8%.
Retention and Graduation: 86% freshmen return for sophomore year.
Faculty: Student/faculty ratio 21:1. 41 full-time faculty, 68% hold PhDs, 5% are members of minority groups, 46% are women. 0% of classes are taught by teaching assistants.

ACADEMICS

Degrees: Associate; Bachelor's; Master's **Classes:** Most classes have 10-19 students. Most lab/discussion sessions have 10-19 students. **Most popular majors:** Computer/Information Technology Services Administration And Management, Other; Liberal Arts And Sciences/Liberal Studies; Management Information Systems, General. **Special Study Options:** Accelerated program; Cooperative education program; Distance learning; Double major; Honors program; Independent study; Internships; Student-designed major; Study abroad; Teacher certification program; Weekend college. **Disability Services offered to physically disabled students:** Tutors. **Career services:** Alumni services; Career assessment; Career/job search classes; Internships

FACILITIES

Housing: Apartments for single students; Coed dorms; Men's dorms; Special housing for disabled student; Women's dorms 85% of campus accessible to physically diasbled. **Special Academic Facilities/Equipment:** Music recording studio, electron microscope. **Computers:** 100% of classrooms, 100% of dorms, 100% of student union, have wireless network access. Students can register for classes online. Administrative functions (other than registration) can be performed online.

CAMPUS LIFE

Activities: Choral groups; Concert band; Drama/theater; Jazz band; Literary magazine; Music ensembles; Musical theater; Student government; Student newspaper; Symphony orchestra 21 registered organizations, 3 honor societies, 14 religious organizations. **Athletics (Intercollegiate):** *Men:* basketball, cross-country, golf, soccer, tennis. *Women:* basketball, cross-country, soccer, tennis, volleyball.

ADMISSIONS

Freshman Academic Profile: Average high school GPA 3.4. 22% in top 10% of high school class, 46% in top 25% of high school class, 79% in top 50% of high school class. **Test Scores:** SAT Math middle 50% range 480-590. SAT EBRW middle 50% range 510-630. ACT middle 50% range 20-26. Minimum paper TOEFL 500. **Basis for Candidate Selection:** *Very important factors considered include:* rigor of secondary school record, application essay, standardized test scores, talent/ability, character/personal qualities, first generation, religious affiliation/commitment. *Important factors considered include:* class rank, academic GPA, recommendation(s), extracurricular activities, racial/ethnic status, volunteer work.level of applicant's interest. *Other factors considered include:* interview, alumni/ae relation, work experience. **Freshman Admission Requirements:** High school diploma is required and GED is accepted *Academic units recommended:* 4 English, 3 math, 3 science, 2 science labs, 3 foreign language, 1 social studies, 2 history, 1 unit from above areas or other academic areas. **Freshman Admission Statistics:** 946 applied, 77.1% admitted, 33% enrolled. **Transfer Admission Requirements:** college transcript(s), essay or personal statement, statement of good standing from prior institution(s). Minimum college GPA of 2.0 required. Lowest grade transferable C. **General Admission Information:** Application fee $50. Priority deadline 3/1. Regular application deadline 8/21. Nonfall registration accepted. Admission may be deferred for a maximum of 1 year.

COSTS AND FINANCIAL AID

Annual tuition $18,850. Room and board $6,682. Required fees $150. Average book expense $1,188. **Required Forms and Deadlines:** FAFSA. **Notification of Awards:** Applicants will be notified of awards on a rolling basis beginning 4/1. **Types of Aid:** *Need-based scholarships/grants:* College/ university scholarship or grant aid from institutional funds; Federal Pell; Private scholarships; SEOG. *Student Employment:* Federal Work-Study Program available. Institutional employment available. **Financial Aid Statistics:** 97% needy freshmen, 88% needy undergrads receive need-based scholarship or grant aid. 88% freshmen, 82% undergrads receive non-need-based scholarship or grant aid. 100% freshmen, 100% undergrads receive need-based self-help aid. 14% freshmen, 7% undergrads receive athletic scholarships. **Criteria for awarding aid:** *Non-need-based:* Academics, Athletics, Leadership, Minority status.

COLORADO COLLEGE

14 East Cache la Poudre St., Colorado Springs, CO 80903
Phone: 719-389-6344 • **Financial Aid Phone:** (719) 389-6779
E-mail: admission@coloradocollege.edu • **CEEB Code:** 4072
Fax: 719-389-6816 • **Website:** www.coloradocollege.edu • **ACT Code:** 498

This private school was founded in 1874. It has a 90 acre campus.

RATINGS

Admissions Selectivity Rating: 97 **Fire Safety Rating:** 96 **Green Rating:** 91

STUDENTS AND FACULTY

Enrollment: 2,091. **Student Body:** 54% female, 46% male, 83% out-of-state, 8% international (53 countries represented). Asian 4%, African American 3%, Caucasian 66%, Hispanic 9%, Native American 1%, Pacific Islander <1%, Two or more races 9%, Race unknown 1%.
Retention and Graduation: 94% freshmen return for sophomore year. 82% freshmen graduate within 4 years. 88% freshmen graduate within 6 years.
Faculty: Student/faculty ratio 10:1. 190 full-time faculty, 99% hold PhDs, 26% are members of minority groups, 50% are women. 0% of classes are taught by teaching assistants.

ACADEMICS

Degrees: Bachelor's; Master's **Classes:** Most classes have 20-29 students. Most lab/discussion sessions have 10-19 students. **Most popular majors:** Economics, General; Political Science And Government, General; Sociology. **Special Study Options:** Double major; English as a Second Language (ESL); Exchange student program (domestic); Independent study; Internships; Liberal arts/career combination; Student-designed major; Study abroad; Teacher certification program. **Combined degree programs:** BA/MEng. **Disability Services offered to physically disabled students:** Note-taking services; Reader services; Tape recorders. **Career services:** Alumni network; Alumni services; Career assessment; Career/job search classes; Internships; Regional alumni

FACILITIES

Housing: Apartments for single students; Coed dorms; Fraternity/sorority housing; Theme housing; Wellness housing; Women's dorms **Special Academic Facilities/Equipment:** Electronic music studio, telescope dome, multimedia computer laboratory, Balinese orchestras, The Colorado Electronic music studio, Observatory, Extensive herbarium collection 4 greenhouses Environmental Science van equipped for field research Fourier transform nuclear magnetic resonance spectrometer Packard Hall, 300 seat concert/ lecture hall Photography darkrooms Drama/Dance: Armstrong Theatre, 740 seat proscenium theatre Armstrong 32, 100 seat experimental theatre 4 dance studios w/Marley, variable speed cd players Drama computer lab Geology: Petrographic microscopes X-ray diffractometer Sedimentology lab El Pomar Sports Center: Metabolic Equipment (COSMED Quark PFT Ergo) Hydrostatic Weighing Equipment Cadaver study in Sports Science Biology: Scanning electron microscope Transmission electron microscope Students amy also engage with local theater, opera, and orchestra **Computers:** 100% of classrooms, 100% of dorms, 100% of libraries, 100% of dining areas, 100% of student union, 80% of common outdoor areas have wireless network access. Students can register for classes online. Administrative functions (other than registration) can be performed online.

CAMPUS LIFE

Environment: Metropolis **Activities:** Campus Ministries; Choral groups; Concert band; Dance; Drama/theater; International Student Organization; Jazz band; Literary magazine; Music ensembles; Musical theater; Opera; Radio station; Student government; Student newspaper; Student-run film society; Symphony orchestra; Yearbook 147 registered organizations, 13 honor societies, 20 religious organizations. 1 fraternity, 3 sororities **Athletics (Intercollegiate):** *Men:* basketball, cross-country, ice hockey, lacrosse, soccer, swimming, tennis, track/field (outdoor). *Women:* basketball, cross-country, lacrosse, soccer, swimming, tennis, track/field (outdoor), track/field (indoor), volleyball. **On-Campus Highlights:** Worner Student Center, Palmer Hall, Shove Chapel, Cutler Hall—Admission, Armstrong Quad **Environmental Initiatives:** The College is committed to achieving carbon neutrality by 2020. The plan includes an efficiency target in all campus buildings that will reduce energy intensity by 30%, along with a 20% reduction target through behavior change and conservation, and a strategy to derive 100% of electricity from renewable sources.

ADMISSIONS

Freshman Academic Profile: 70% in top 10% of high school class, 94% in top 25% of high school class, 99% in top 50% of high school class. **Test Scores:** SAT Math middle 50% range 650-760. SAT EBRW middle 50% range 650-730. ACT middle 50% range 29-33. **Basis for Candidate Selection:** *Very important factors considered include:* rigor of secondary school record. *Important factors considered include:* class rank, academic GPA, application essay, standardized test scores, recommendation(s), interview, extracurricular activities. *Other factors considered include:* talent/ability, character/personal qualities, first generation, alumni/ae relation, religious affiliation/commitment, racial/ethnic status, volunteer work, work experience, level of applicant's interest. **Freshman Admission Requirements:** High school diploma or equivalent is not required *Academic units required:* 4 English, *Academic units recommended:* 4 English. **Freshman Admission Statistics:** 8,223 applied, 15.1% admitted, 44% enrolled. **Transfer Admission Requirements:** High school transcript, college transcript(s), essay or personal statement, standardized test scores, statement of good standing from prior institution(s). Lowest grade transferable C. **General Admission Information:** Application fee $60. Priority deadline 1/15. Regular application deadline 1/15. Nonfall registration accepted. Admission may be deferred for a maximum of 1 year.

COSTS AND FINANCIAL AID

Annual tuition $52,380. Required fees $438. Average book expense $1,230. **Required Forms and Deadlines:** CSS/Financial Aid PROFILE; FAFSA; Noncustodial PROFILE. **Notification of Awards:** Applicants will be notified of awards on or about 2/15. **Types of Aid:** *Need-based scholarships/grants:* College/university scholarship or grant aid from institutional funds; Federal Pell; Private scholarships; SEOG; State scholarships/grants; United Negro College Fund. *Loans:* Direct PLUS loans; Direct Subsidized Stafford Loans; Direct Unsubsidized Stafford Loans. *Student Employment:* Federal Work-Study Program available. Institutional employment available. **Financial Aid Statistics:** 97% needy freshmen, 95% needy undergrads receive need-based scholarship or grant aid. 27% freshmen, 18% undergrads receive non-need-based scholarship or grant aid. 74% freshmen, 76% undergrads receive need-based self-help aid. 2% freshmen, 2% undergrads receive athletic scholarships. 57% freshmen, 54% undergrads receive any aid. 41% undergrads borrow to pay for school. Average cumulative indebtedness $20,742. **Criteria for awarding aid:** *Non-need-based:* Academics, Athletics, Leadership.

COLORADO SCHOOL OF MINES

1500 Illinois Street, Golden, CO 80401
Phone: 303-273-3220 • **Financial Aid Phone:** (303) 273-3220
E-mail: admissions@mines.edu • **CEEB Code:** 4073
Fax: 303-273-3509 • **Website:** www.mines.edu • **ACT Code:** 500

This public school was founded in 1874. It has a 499 acre campus.

RATINGS

Admissions Selectivity Rating: 91 **Fire Safety Rating:** 92 **Green Rating:** 70

STUDENTS AND FACULTY

Enrollment: 4,757. **Student Body:** 29% female, 71% male, 39% out-of-state, 6% international (42 countries represented). Asian 5%, African American 1%, Caucasian 73%, Hispanic 8%, Native American <1%, Pacific Islander <1%, Two or more races 5%, Race unknown 1%.
Retention and Graduation: 93% freshmen return for sophomore year. 55% freshmen graduate within 4 years. 79% freshmen graduate within 6 years. 14%

grads go on to further study within 1 year. 4% grads pursue arts and sciences degrees. 1% grads pursue law degrees. 2% grads pursue business degrees. 1% grads pursue medical degrees. **Faculty:** Student/faculty ratio 15:1. 294 full-time faculty, 89% hold PhDs, 19% are members of minority groups, 28% are women. 2% of classes are taught by teaching assistants.

ACADEMICS
Degrees: Bachelor's; Doctoral/Research; Master's; Post-Master's certificate **Classes:** Most classes have 10-19 students. Most lab/discussion sessions have 10-19 students. **Most popular majors:** Chemical Engineering; Mechanical Engineering; Petroleum Engineering. **Special Study Options:** Accelerated program; Cooperative education program; Double major; Dual enrollment; Exchange student program (domestic); Honors program; Independent study; Internships; Study abroad; Teacher certification program. **Honors programs:** The THORSON FIRST YEAR HONORS EXPERIENCE: offers a gateway into the McBride Honors Program. It prepares students for success in McBride, in their major coursework, and beyond. But First Year Honors is a lot more. It offers an exciting and collaborative approach to learning that uses real-world problems to introduce students to the role of engineers and scientists in a fast-changing world. Working closely with some of the best teachers at Mines, students come to see how the global challenges of the future require innovative and creative thinking. Even better, the First Year Honors Experience includes a supportive and diverse community of students who want to be challenged and want to explore our world. In First Year Honors, professors welcome students as colleagues, they mentor and support them, and they push them to see the world differently. McBRIDE HONORS PROGRAM: instituted in 1978 through a grant from the National Endowment for the Humanities, is a 21 semester-hour program of seminars and off-campus activities that has as its primary goal: To provide a select community of Mines students the enhanced opportunity to explore the interfaces between their areas of technical expertise and the humanities and social sciences; to gain the sensitivity to project and test the moral and social implications of their future professional judgments and activities; and to foster their leadership abilities in preparation for managing change and promoting the general welfare in an evolving technological and global context. To achieve this goal, the program seeks to bring themes from the humanities and the social sciences into the engineering curriculum that will encourage in students the habits of thought necessary for effective management and enlightened leadership. **Disability Services offered to physically disabled students:** Tutors. **Career services:** Alumni services; Career assessment; Career/job search classes; Internships

FACILITIES
Housing: Apartments for married students; Apartments for single students; Coed dorms; Fraternity/sorority housing; Theme housing; Wellness housing 95% of campus accessible to physically diasbled. **Special Academic Facilities/ Equipment:** Geology Museum, US Geological Survey & Earthquake Center, Edgar Experimental Mine, Graduate Research Laboratory (GRL), Center for Technology & Learning Media which houses supercomputer "Ra,"—high performance computing (HPC) cluster that aims to be a national hub for computational inquiries aimed at the discovery of new ways to meet the world's energy demands. Estimated peak performance will be approximately 20 teraflops—This places the machine well within the top-100 fastest computers in the world. The new facility, administered by the Golden Energy Computing Organization (GECO), is dedicated to advancing energy-related science. **Computers:** 100% of classrooms, 100% of dorms, 100% of libraries, 100% of dining areas, 100% of student union, 80% of common outdoor areas have wireless network access. Students can register for classes online. Administrative functions (other than registration) can be performed online.

CAMPUS LIFE
Environment: Metropolis **Activities:** Campus Ministries; Choral groups; Concert band; Dance; Drama/theater; International Student Organization; Jazz band; Literary magazine; Marching band; Music ensembles; Musical theater; Pep band; Radio station; Student government; Student newspaper; Symphony orchestra; Yearbook 148 registered organizations, 9 honor societies, 7 religious organizations. 7 fraternities, 3 sororities. **Athletics (Intercollegiate):** *Men:* baseball, basketball, cross-country, diving, football, golf, soccer, swimming, track/field (outdoor), track/field (indoor), wrestling. *Women:* basketball, cross-country, diving, soccer, softball, swimming, track/field (outdoor), track/field (indoor), volleyball. **On-Campus Highlights:** Student Recreation Center, Student Center, Brown Hall Atrium, Marquez Hall, Computer Commons at the CTLM

ADMISSIONS
Freshman Academic Profile: Average high school GPA 3.8. 49% in top 10% of high school class, 87% in top 25% of high school class, 99% in top 50% of high school class. 81% from public high schools. **Test Scores:** SAT Math middle 50% range 670-740. SAT EBRW middle 50% range 640-710. ACT middle 50% range 28-32. Minimum internet-based TOEFL 79. Minimum paper TOEFL 550. **Basis for Candidate Selection:** *Very important factors considered include:* rigor of secondary school record, class rank, academic GPA, standardized test scores. *Other factors considered include:* application essay, recommendation(s), interview, extracurricular activities, talent/ability, character/

personal qualities, first generation, alumni/ae relation, geographical residence, state residency, racial/ethnic status, volunteer work, work experience, level of applicant's interest. **Freshman Admission Requirements:** High school diploma is required and GED is accepted *Academic units required:* 4 English, 4 math, 3 science, 3 science labs, 1 foreign language, 3 social studies, 2 academic electives. **Freshman Admission Statistics:** 10,619 applied, 55.7% admitted, 19% enrolled. **Transfer Admission Requirements:** High school transcript, college transcript(s), statement of good standing from prior institution(s). Minimum college GPA of 2.75 required. Lowest grade transferable C. **General Admission Information:** Application fee $45. Priority deadline 11/15. Regular application deadline 4/1. Nonfall registration accepted. Admission may be deferred for a maximum of 1 year.

COSTS AND FINANCIAL AID
Annual in-state tuition $11,897. Annual out-of-state tuition $35,220. Room and board $11,897. Required fees $2,216. Average book expense $1,500. **Required Forms and Deadlines:** FAFSA. **Notification of Awards:** Applicants will be notified of awards on a rolling basis beginning 3/15. **Types of Aid:** *Need-based scholarships/grants:* College/university scholarship or grant aid from institutional funds; Federal Pell; Private scholarships; SEOG; State scholarships/grants. *Loans:* Direct PLUS loans; Direct Subsidized Stafford Loans; Direct Unsubsidized Stafford Loans. *Student Employment:* Federal Work-Study Program available. Institutional employment available. **Financial Aid Statistics:** 52% needy freshmen, 56% needy undergrads receive need-based scholarship or grant aid. 87% freshmen, 67% undergrads receive non-need-based scholarship or grant aid. 86% freshmen, 91% undergrads receive need-based self-help aid. 2% freshmen, 8% undergrads receive athletic scholarships. 89% freshmen, 80% undergrads receive any aid. 58% undergrads borrow to pay for school. Average cumulative indebtedness $32,901. **Criteria for awarding aid:** *Need-based:* Academics, Alumni affiliation *Non-need-based:* Academics, Alumni affiliation, Athletics, Music/drama.

COLORADO STATE UNIVERSITY

0100 Campus Delivery, Fort Collins, CO 80523-1062
Phone: 970-491-6909 • **Financial Aid Phone:** 970-491-6321
E-mail: admissions@colostate.edu • **CEEB Code:** 4075
Fax: 970-491-7799 • **Website:** www.colostate.edu/ • **ACT Code:** 504

This public school was founded in 1870. It has a 4773 acre campus.

RATINGS
Admissions Selectivity Rating: 79   **Fire Safety Rating:** 65   **Green Rating:** 99

STUDENTS AND FACULTY
Enrollment: 24,742. **Student Body:** 51% female, 49% male, 24% out-of-state, 4% international (80 countries represented). Asian 2%, African American 2%, Caucasian 72%, Hispanic 12%, Native American <1%, Pacific Islander <1%, Two or more races 3%, Race unknown 2%.
Retention and Graduation: 84% freshmen return for sophomore year. 45% freshmen graduate within 4 years. 69% freshmen graduate within 6 years. 21% grads go on to further study within 1 year. **Faculty:** Student/faculty ratio 18:1. 1,318 full-time faculty, 15% are members of minority groups, 43% are women. 8% of classes are taught by teaching assistants.

ACADEMICS
Degrees: Bachelor's; Doctoral; Doctoral/Professional; Doctoral/Research; Master's; Post-Bachelor's certificate **Classes:** Most classes have 10-19 students. Most lab/discussion sessions have 10-19 students. **Most popular majors:** Speech Communication And Rhetoric; Human Development And Family Studies, General; Biology/Biological Sciences, General. **Special Study Options:** Accelerated program; Cooperative education program; Distance learning; Double major; Dual enrollment; English as a Second Language (ESL); Honors program; Independent study; Internships; Liberal arts/career combination; Study abroad; Teacher certification program. **Honors programs:** University Honors Program. **Disability Services offered to physically disabled students:** Note-taking services; Reader services; Tape recorders; Tutors. **Career services:** Alumni network; Alumni services; Career assessment; Career/job search classes; Internships; Regional alumni

FACILITIES
Housing: Apartments for married students; Apartments for single students; Coed dorms; Fraternity/sorority housing; Special housing for international students; Theme housing; Wellness housing 98% of campus accessible to

physically diasbled. **Special Academic Facilities/Equipment:** International Poster collection Gustafson Gallery—historic clothing Curfman Gallery— Art Student Recreation Center Ropes Course University Center for the Arts (performance hall, thrust theater,art museum) Avenir Museum of Design and Merchandising (Costumes, Textiles, Interior Artifacts) Engines and Energy Conversion Laboratory **Computers:** 100% of classrooms, 100% of dorms, 100% of libraries, 100% of dining areas, 100% of student union, 60% of common outdoor areas have wireless network access. Students can register for classes online. Administrative functions (other than registration) can be performed online.

CAMPUS LIFE

Environment: City **Activities:** Campus Ministries; Choral groups; Concert band; Dance; Drama/theater; International Student Organization; Jazz band; Literary magazine; Marching band; Music ensembles; Musical theater; Pep band; Radio station; Student government; Student newspaper; Symphony orchestra; Television station 350 registered organizations, 35 honor societies, 28 religious organizations. 21 fraternities, 14 sororities. **Athletics (Intercollegiate):** *Men:* basketball, cross-country, football, golf, track/field (outdoor), track/field (indoor). *Women:* basketball, cross-country, diving, golf, softball, swimming, tennis, track/field (outdoor), track/field (indoor), volleyball, water polo. **On-Campus Highlights:** Lory Student Center, Student Recreation Center, Morgan Library, University Center For the Arts, Colorado State Stadium **Environmental Initiatives:** Several renewable energy sources went live in the year 2010 including: a second phase of a large solar array that now totals 5,300 kilowatts on the Foothills Campus, an 18.9 kW solar array on the roof of the Engineering building, and a 12.6 kW solar array at the Academic Village residence hall, 133 kW solar array on the roof of the Lake Street Parking Garage, a 15.8 kW on the Behavioral Sciences Building and a 54 kW solar array at the Research Innovation Center. The five smaller arrays are owned and operated by the University, the larger array is owned by a third party and Colorado State serves as a site host and purchases the power produced by the panels. In addition to solar power, CSU's Foothills Campus is also home to a biomass heating plant on the Foothills Campus. This plant burns wood chips to produce hot water for building heat and displaces natural gas use.

ADMISSIONS

Freshman Academic Profile: Average high school GPA 3.6. 20% in top 10% of high school class, 47% in top 25% of high school class, 82% in top 50% of high school class. **Test Scores:** SAT Math middle 50% range 540-650. SAT EBRW middle 50% range 560-650. ACT middle 50% range 22-28. Minimum internet-based TOEFL 79. Minimum paper TOEFL 550. **Basis for Candidate Selection:** *Very important factors considered include:* rigor of secondary school record, academic GPA. *Important factors considered include:* class rank, application essay, standardized test scores, recommendation(s). *Other factors considered include:* extracurricular activities, talent/ability, character/personal qualities, first generation, alumni/ae relation, geographical residence, volunteer work, work experience. **Freshman Admission Requirements:** High school diploma is required and GED is accepted *Academic units required:* 4 English, 4 math, 3 science, 2 science labs, 1 foreign language, 3 social studies, 1 history, 2 academic electives, *Academic units recommended:* 4 English, 4 math, 3 science, 2 science labs, 2 foreign language, 3 social studies, 1 history, 2 academic electives. **Freshman Admission Statistics:** 23,137 applied, 82.6% admitted, 27% enrolled. **Transfer Admission Requirements:** college transcript(s), essay or personal statement, Minimum college GPA of 2.0 required. Lowest grade transferable C-. **General Admission Information:** Application fee $50. Priority deadline 2/1. Regular application deadline 8/1. Nonfall registration accepted. Admission may be deferred.

COSTS AND FINANCIAL AID

Annual in-state tuition $11,514. Annual out-of-state tuition $26,660. Room and board $11,514. Required fees $2,367. Average book expense $1,200. **Required Forms and Deadlines:** FAFSA; Institution's own financial aid form. **Notification of Awards:** Applicants will be notified of awards on a rolling basis beginning 3/1. **Types of Aid:** *Need-based scholarships/grants:* College/university scholarship or grant aid from institutional funds; Federal Pell; Private scholarships; SEOG; State scholarships/grants. *Loans:* Direct PLUS loans; Direct Subsidized Stafford Loans; Direct Unsubsidized Stafford Loans. *Student Employment:* Federal Work-Study Program available. Institutional employment available. **Financial Aid Statistics:** 75% needy freshmen, 68% needy undergrads receive need-based scholarship or grant aid. 28% freshmen, 12% undergrads receive non-need-based scholarship or grant aid. 76% freshmen, 80% undergrads receive need-based self-help aid. 0% freshmen, 1% undergrads receive athletic scholarships. 76% freshmen, 67% undergrads receive any aid. 54% undergrads borrow to pay for school. Average cumulative indebtedness $25,155. **Criteria for awarding aid:** *Need-based:* Academics *Non-need-based:* Academics, Alumni affiliation, Art, Athletics, Leadership, Music/drama, State/district residency.

2200 Bonforte Boulevard, Pueblo, CO 81001
Phone: 719-549-2461 · **Financial Aid Phone:** 719-549-2178
E-mail: info@colostate-pueblo.edu · **CEEB Code:** 4611
Fax: 719-549-2419 · **Website:** www.colostate-pueblo.edu · **ACT Code:** 524

This public school was founded in 1933. It has a 275 acre campus.

RATINGS

Admissions Selectivity Rating: 72   **Fire Safety Rating:** 79   **Green Rating:** 60*

STUDENTS AND FACULTY

Enrollment: 3,947. **Student Body:** 57% female, 43% male, 7% out-of-state, 2% international (27 countries represented). Asian 3%, African American 6%, Caucasian 55%, Hispanic 25%, Native American 2%, Race unknown 6%. **Retention and Graduation:** 63% freshmen return for sophomore year. **Faculty:** Student/faculty ratio 17:1. 155 full-time faculty, 17% are members of minority groups, 47% are women. 0% of classes are taught by teaching assistants.

ACADEMICS

Degrees: Bachelor's; Master's **Classes:** Most classes have 10-19 students. Most lab/discussion sessions have 10-19 students. **Most popular majors:** Liberal Arts And Sciences/Liberal Studies; Biology/Biological Sciences, General. **Special Study Options:** Accelerated program; Cooperative education program; Distance learning; Double major; Dual enrollment; English as a Second Language (ESL); External degree program; Independent study; Internships; Liberal arts/career combination; Study abroad; Teacher certification program; Weekend college. **Disability Services offered to physically disabled students:** Note-taking services; Reader services; Tape recorders; Tutors.

FACILITIES

Housing: Apartments for single students; Coed dorms; Special housing for disabled students 100% of campus accessible to physically diasbled. **Special Academic Facilities/Equipment:** Recital hall, public television and radio station. **Computers:** Students can register for classes online. Administrative functions (other than registration) can be performed online.

CAMPUS LIFE

Environment: City **Activities:** Choral groups; Concert band; Dance; Jazz band; Literary magazine; Music ensembles; Pep band; Student government; Student newspaper; Symphony orchestra; Television station 24 registered organizations, 6 honor societies, 4 religious organizations. 2 fraternities, 1 sorority. **Athletics (Intercollegiate):** *Men:* baseball, basketball, golf, soccer, tennis. *Women:* basketball, cross-country, golf, soccer, softball, tennis, volleyball. **On-Campus Highlights:** University Library, Occhiato University Center—La Cantina, Occhiato University Center—The Undergroundn, The Pavillion, The Wall

ADMISSIONS

Freshman Academic Profile: Average high school GPA 3.1. 2% in top 10% of high school class, 8% in top 25% of high school class, 36% in top 50% of high school class. 85% from public high schools. **Test Scores:** SAT Math middle 50% range 420-550. SAT EBRW middle 50% range 420-530. ACT middle 50% range 18-22. Minimum paper TOEFL 500. **Basis for Candidate Selection:** *Very important factors considered include:* rigor of secondary school record, academic GPA, standardized test scores. *Important factors considered include:* class rank. *Other factors considered include:* application essay, recommendation(s), interview, talent/ability, character/personal qualities, volunteer work, work experience, level of applicant's interest. **Freshman Admission Requirements:** High school diploma is required and GED is accepted *Academic units required:* 4 English, 3 math, 3 science, 2 science labs, 2 foreign language, 2 social studies, 1 history, *Academic units recommended:* 4 English, 3 math, 3 science, 2 science labs, 2 foreign language, 2 social studies, 1 history. **Freshman Admission Statistics:** 1,698 applied, 96.1% admitted, 41% enrolled. **Transfer Admission Requirements:** college transcript(s), Minimum college GPA of 2.3 required. Lowest grade transferable C-. **General Admission Information:** Application fee $25. Regular application deadline 8/1. Nonfall registration accepted. Admission may be deferred for a maximum of 1 semester.

COSTS AND FINANCIAL AID

Annual in-state tuition $6,300. Annual out-of-state tuition $13,543. Room and board $6,300. Required fees $996. Average book expense $1,698. **Required Forms and Deadlines:** FAFSA; Institution's own financial aid form. **Notification of Awards:** Applicants will be notified of awards on a rolling basis beginning 3/15. **Types of Aid:** *Need-based scholarships/grants:* College/university scholarship or grant aid from institutional funds; Federal Pell; Private scholarships; SEOG; State scholarships/grants. **Financial Aid Statistics:** 81% needy freshmen, 80% needy undergrads receive need-based scholarship or grant aid. 7% freshmen, 4% undergrads receive non-need-based scholarship or grant aid. 78% freshmen, 87% undergrads receive need-based self-help aid. 3% freshmen, 4% undergrads receive athletic scholarships. 81% freshmen, 86% undergrads receive any aid. **Criteria for awarding aid:** *Need-based:* Academics, Alumni affiliation, Minority status *Non-need-based:* Academics, Alumni affiliation, Art, Athletics, Leadership, Minority status, Music/drama, State/district residency.

COLORADO TECHNICAL UNIVERSITY

4435 North Chestnut Street, Colorado Springs, CO 80907-3740
Phone: 719-598-0200
E-mail: cosadmissions@coloradotech.edu
Website: http://www.coloradotech.edu/

This is a proprietary school.

RATINGS
Admissions Selectivity Rating: 0   Fire Safety Rating: 60*   Green Rating: 60*

STUDENTS AND FACULTY
Student Body: 1% international. Asian 4%, African American 8%, Caucasian 73%, Hispanic 6%, Native American <1%, Race unknown 9%.
Faculty: Student/faculty ratio 25:1. 31 full-time faculty, 52% hold PhDs, 13% are members of minority groups, 35% are women.

ACADEMICS
Degrees: Associate; Bachelor's; Certificate; Master's; Transfer Associate
Classes: Most classes have 10-19 students. Most lab/discussion sessions have 10-19 students. **Special Study Options:** Accelerated program; Double major; Independent study; Internships; Weekend college.

CAMPUS LIFE
Activities: Student government.

ADMISSIONS
Basis for Candidate Selection: *Other factors considered include:* rigor of secondary school record, class rank, standardized test scores, recommendation(s), interview, character/personal qualities, alumni/ae relation, work experience. **Freshman Admission Requirements:** *Academic units required:* 1 English, 1 math, 1 science, 1 science labs, *Academic units recommended:* 2 English, 2 math, 2 science, 1 science labs, **Transfer Admission Requirements:** college transcript(s), statement of good standing from prior institution(s). Lowest grade transferable C. **General Admission Information:** Application fee $50. Regular application deadline 10/2. Nonfall registration accepted.

COSTS AND FINANCIAL AID
Required fees $171. Average book expense $1,000. **Required Forms and Deadlines:** FAFSA; Institution's own financial aid form; State aid form. **Notification of Awards:** Applicants will be notified of awards on a rolling basis beginning 2/1.

COLUMBIA COLLEGE (MO)

1001 Rogers Street, Columbia, MO 65211
Phone: 573-875-7352 · **Financial Aid Phone:** 573-875-7390
E-mail: admissions@ccis.edu · **CEEB Code:** 6095
Fax: 573-875-7506 · **Website:** http://www.ccis.edu · **ACT Code:** 2276

This private school, affiliated with the Disciples of Christ Church, was founded in 1851. It has a 33 acre campus.

RATINGS
Admissions Selectivity Rating: 87   Fire Safety Rating: 90   Green Rating: 70

STUDENTS AND FACULTY
Enrollment: 1,028. **Student Body:** 58% female, 42% male, 12% out-of-state, 7% international (36 countries represented). Asian 1%, African American 5%, Caucasian 74%, Hispanic 4%, Native American <1%, Pacific Islander 0%, Two or more races 6%, Race unknown 3%.

Retention and Graduation: 78% freshmen return for sophomore year. 32% freshmen graduate within 4 years. 45% freshmen graduate within 6 years. 21% grads go on to further study within 1 year. 2% grads pursue arts and sciences degrees. 26% grads pursue law degrees. 2% grads pursue business degrees. 2% grads pursue medical degrees. **Faculty:** Student/faculty ratio 11:1. 74 full-time faculty, 77% hold PhDs, 11% are members of minority groups, 49% are women. 0% of classes are taught by teaching assistants.

ACADEMICS
Degrees: Associate; Bachelor's; Certificate; Master's **Classes:** Most classes have 20-29 students. Most lab/discussion sessions have 10-19 students. **Most popular majors:** Psychology, General; Criminal Justice/Law Enforcement Administration; Business Administration And Management, General. **Special Study Options:** Cooperative education program; Cross-registration; Distance learning; Double major; English as a Second Language (ESL); Exchange student program (domestic); Honors program; Independent study; Internships; Liberal arts/career combination; Student-designed major; Study abroad; Teacher certification program. **Honors programs:** The Honors Program is designed for high achieving students who are philosophers in the literal sense, i.e., lovers of wisdom. The goal of the program is to promote genuine inquiry and collaborative learning, emphasizing the dialogic nature of academic work and intellectual discovery. **Disability Services offered to physically disabled students:** Note-taking services; Reader services; Tape recorders. **Career services:** Alumni network; Alumni services; Career assessment; Career/job search classes; Internships; Regional alumni

FACILITIES
Housing: Apartments for single students; Coed dorms; Special housing for disabled student; Theme housing; Women's dorms 100% of campus accessible to physically diasbled. **Special Academic Facilities/Equipment:** Most classrooms are multimedia with SmartBoards, arts center, Larson Gallery, Jane Froman Archive, Music practice Hall, Kirkman house for Graduate Studies **Computers:** 100% of classrooms, 100% of dorms, 100% of libraries, 100% of dining areas, 100% of student union, have wireless network access. Students can register for classes online. Administrative functions (other than registration) can be performed online.

CAMPUS LIFE
Environment: City **Activities:** Campus Ministries; Choral groups; Drama/theater; International Student Organization; Model UN; Musical theater; Pep band; Student government 42 registered organizations, 16 honor societies, 2 religious organizations. **Athletics (Intercollegiate):** *Men:* basketball, soccer. *Women:* basketball, softball, volleyball. **On-Campus Highlights:** Science Building-new in Fall 2013, The newly expanded Southwell Athletic Complex, Atkins-Holman Student Commons building, Stafford Library **Environmental Initiatives:** 77% of campus building square footage is on highly efficient ground source water heat pump system.

ADMISSIONS
Freshman Academic Profile: Average high school GPA 3.4. 18% in top 10% of high school class, 38% in top 25% of high school class, 76% in top 50% of high school class. **Test Scores:** SAT Math middle 50% range 530-660. SAT EBRW middle 50% range 535-615. ACT middle 50% range 21-27. Minimum internet-based TOEFL 61. Minimum paper TOEFL 500. **Basis for Candidate Selection:** *Very important factors considered include:* class rank, academic GPA, standardized test scores. *Other factors considered include:* rigor of secondary school record, application essay, recommendation(s), interview. **Freshman Admission Requirements:** High school diploma is required and GED is accepted *Academic units recommended:* 4 English, 3 math, 3 science, 2 social studies. **Freshman Admission Statistics:** 1,589 applied, 52.3% admitted, 24% enrolled. **Transfer Admission Requirements:** college transcript(s), statement of good standing from prior institution(s). Minimum college GPA of 2.0 required. Lowest grade transferable 2. **General Admission Information:** Application fee $35. Nonfall registration accepted. Admission may be deferred.

COSTS AND FINANCIAL AID
Annual tuition $10,968. Room and board $7,632. Average book expense $1,242. **Required Forms and Deadlines:** FAFSA. **Types of Aid:** *Need-based scholarships/grants:* College/university scholarship or grant aid from institutional funds; Federal Pell; Private scholarships; SEOG; State scholarships/grants. *Loans:* Direct PLUS loans; Direct Subsidized Stafford Loans; Direct Unsubsidized Stafford Loans. *Student Employment:* Federal Work-Study Program available. Institutional employment available. **Financial Aid Statistics:** 73% needy freshmen, 74% needy undergrads receive need-based scholarship or grant aid. 100% freshmen, 85% undergrads receive non-need-based scholarship or grant aid. 72% freshmen, 71% undergrads receive need-based self-help aid. 24% freshmen, 20% undergrads receive athletic scholarships. 62% freshmen, 56% undergrads receive any aid. Average cumulative indebtedness $21,934. **Criteria for awarding aid:** *Need-based:* Academics, Art *Non-need-based:* Academics, Alumni affiliation, Art, Athletics, Job skills, Leadership, Minority status, Music/drama, Religious affiliation, State/district residency.

COLUMBIA COLLEGE (SC)

1301 Columbia College Drive, Columbia, SC 29203
Phone: 803-786-3871 · **Financial Aid Phone:** 803-786-3612
E-mail: admissions@columbiasc.edu · **CEEB Code:** 5117
Fax: 803-786-3674 · **Website:** www.columbiacollegesc.edu · **ACT Code:** 3850

This private school, affiliated with the Methodist Church, was founded in 1854. It has a 33 acre campus.

RATINGS

Admissions Selectivity Rating: 73   **Fire Safety Rating:** 86   **Green Rating:** 60*

STUDENTS AND FACULTY

Enrollment: 1,552. **Student Body:** 78% female, 22% male, 7% out-of-state, (14 countries represented).
Retention and Graduation: 62% freshmen return for sophomore year. **Faculty:** Student/faculty ratio 3:1. 79 full-time faculty, 77% hold PhDs, 18% are members of minority groups, 68% are women. 0% of classes are taught by teaching assistants.

ACADEMICS

Degrees: Bachelor's; Master's; Post-Bachelor's certificate **Classes:** Most classes have fewer than 10 students. Most lab/discussion sessions have 10-19 students. **Most popular majors:** Elementary Education And Teaching; Human Development, Family Studies, And Related Services, Other; Business Administration And Management, General. **Special Study Options:** Distance learning; Double major; Dual enrollment; Honors program; Independent study; Internships; Student-designed major; Study abroad; Teacher certification program. **Honors programs:** The Columbia College Honors Program provides enriched academic and co-curricular experiences for outstanding, motivated students committed to excellence. Offering a variety of opportunities for superior, engaged learning both within and outside the classroom, honors challenges students to reach their highest potential as scholars, individual thinkers, and leaders by emphasizing rigorous intellectual standards, risk, creativity, integrity, and dedication to service and leadership. The program is deeply active in the National Collegiate Honors Council and its regional association, regularly sponsoring numerous faculty and students at annual conferences and in executive leadership positions; honors has also earned special recognition through national and regional awards for honors faculty and students. To complete honors, students take 24 semester hours across disciplines in honors courses, including the 3 hour interdisciplinary senior seminar and the 3—4 hour mentored independent project. Students must maintain at least a 3.4 cumulative GPA to remain in honors. **Career services:** Career assessment; Career/job search classes; Internships

FACILITIES

Housing: Women's dorms 75% of campus accessible to physically diasbled. **Special Academic Facilities/Equipment:** Language lab, Alumnae Hall, Barbara Bush Center for Science and Technology, Breed Leadership Center for Women. **Computers:** 50% of libraries, 100% of dining areas, 100% of student union, 30% of common outdoor areas have wireless network access. Students can register for classes online. Administrative functions (other than registration) can be performed online.

CAMPUS LIFE

Environment: Metropolis **Activities:** Campus Ministries; Choral groups; Concert band; Dance; Drama/theater; International Student Organization; Literary magazine; Music ensembles; Musical theater; Opera; Student government; Student newspaper; Yearbook 53 registered organizations, 10 honor societies, 7 religious organizations. **Athletics (Intercollegiate):** *Women:* basketball, soccer, softball, tennis, volleyball. **On-Campus Highlights:** Leadership Center, Terrace Cafe, Student Union, Cottingham Performance Theatre, Bush Science Center **Environmental Initiatives:** Student-sponsored and initiated recycling program

ADMISSIONS

Freshman Academic Profile: Average high school GPA 3.7. 15% in top 10% of high school class, 47% in top 25% of high school class, 78% in top 50% of high school class. **Test Scores:** SAT Math middle 50% range 410-520. SAT EBRW middle 50% range 430-550. ACT middle 50% range 18-24. Minimum paper TOEFL 550. **Basis for Candidate Selection:** *Very important factors considered include:* rigor of secondary school record, standardized test scores, recommendation(s). *Important factors considered include:* class rank, character/personal qualities. *Other factors considered include:* application essay, extracurricular activities, talent/ability, alumni/ae relation, volunteer work.
Freshman Admission Requirements: High school diploma is required and GED is accepted *Academic units recommended:* 4 English, 3 math, 2 science,

2 science labs, 2 foreign language, 2 social studies, 1 history, 2 academic electives. **Freshman Admission Statistics:** 506 applied, 88.9% admitted, 41% enrolled. **Transfer Admission Requirements:** High school transcript, college transcript(s), standardized test scores, statement of good standing from prior institution(s). Minimum college GPA of 2.0 required. Lowest grade transferable C. **General Admission Information:** Application fee $25. Regular application deadline 8/1. Nonfall registration accepted. Admission may be deferred for a maximum of 1 year.

COSTS AND FINANCIAL AID

Annual tuition $28,100. Room and board $7,400. Average book expense $850. **Required Forms and Deadlines:** FAFSA. **Notification of Awards:** Applicants will be notified of awards on a rolling basis beginning 3/1. **Types of Aid:** *Need-based scholarships/grants:* College/university scholarship or grant aid from institutional funds; Federal Pell; Private scholarships; SEOG; State scholarships/grants; United Negro College Fund. *Loans: Student Employment:* Federal Work-Study Program available. Institutional employment available. **Financial Aid Statistics:** 82% needy freshmen, 94% needy undergrads receive need-based scholarship or grant aid. 18% freshmen, 15% undergrads receive non-need-based scholarship or grant aid. 76% freshmen, 78% undergrads receive need-based self-help aid. 6% freshmen, 5% undergrads receive athletic scholarships. 99% freshmen, 92% undergrads receive any aid. 90% undergrads borrow to pay for school. Average cumulative indebtedness $29,407. **Criteria for awarding aid:** *Need-based:* Academics, Alumni affiliation, Religious affiliation *Non-need-based:* Academics, Alumni affiliation, Art, Athletics, Leadership, Music/drama.

COLUMBIA COLLEGE CHICAGO (IL)

600 South Michigan Avenue, Chicago, IL 60605-1996
Phone: 1-312-369-7130 · **Financial Aid Phone:** 312-369-7831
E-mail: admissions@colum.edu · **CEEB Code:** 1135
Fax: 312-369-8024 · **Website:** www.colum.edu · **ACT Code:** 1002

This private school was founded in 1890.

RATINGS

Admissions Selectivity Rating: 75   **Fire Safety Rating:** 81   **Green Rating:** 60*

STUDENTS AND FACULTY

Enrollment: 8,929. **Student Body:** 56% female, 44% male, 40% out-of-state, 3% international (48 countries represented). Asian 3%, African American 16%, Caucasian 57%, Hispanic 10%, Native American <1%, Pacific Islander <1%, Two or more races 5%, Race unknown 6%.
Retention and Graduation: 71% freshmen return for sophomore year. 9% grads go on to further study within 1 year. 10% grads pursue arts and sciences degrees. **Faculty:** Student/faculty ratio 11:1. 374 full-time faculty, 51% hold PhDs, 17% are members of minority groups, 47% are women. 0% of classes are taught by teaching assistants.

ACADEMICS

Degrees: Bachelor's; Master's **Classes:** Most classes have 10-19 students. Most lab/discussion sessions have fewer than 10 students. **Most popular majors:** Drama And Dramatics/Theatre Arts, General; Cinematography And Film/Video Production; Photography. **Special Study Options:** Cooperative education program; Distance learning; Double major; English as a Second Language (ESL); Exchange student program (domestic); Honors program; Independent study; Internships; Liberal arts/career combination; Student-designed major; Study abroad; Teacher certification program. **Disability Services offered to physically disabled students:** Note-taking services; Reader services; Tape recorders; Tutors. **Career services:** Alumni network; Alumni services; Internships

FACILITIES

Housing: Apartments for single students; Coed dorms 90% of campus accessible to physically diasbled. **Special Academic Facilities/Equipment:** Art galleries, center for black music research, contemporary photography museum, dance center. **Computers:** Students can register for classes online. Administrative functions (other than registration) can be performed online.

CAMPUS LIFE

Environment: Metropolis **Activities:** Campus Ministries; Choral groups; Concert band; Dance; Drama/theater; International Student Organization; Jazz band; Literary magazine; Music ensembles; Musical theater; Radio station; Student government; Student newspaper; Student-run film society; Television station 64 registered organizations. **On-Campus Highlights:** Museum of Contemporary Photography, Hokin Annex and Gallery, Shop Columbia, Haus at the Quincy Wong Center **Environmental Initiatives:** Campus-wide recycling of paper, plastic, glass, techno

ADMISSIONS

Freshman Academic Profile: Average high school GPA 3.3. 8% in top 10% of high school class, 29% in top 25% of high school class, 63% in top 50% of high school class. **Test Scores:** SAT Math middle 50% range 440-570. SAT EBRW middle 50% range 485-605. ACT middle 50% range 19-25. Minimum internet-based TOEFL 80. Minimum paper TOEFL 533. **Basis for Candidate Selection:** *Very important factors considered include:* application essay. *Important factors considered include:* academic GPA, recommendation(s), character/personal qualities, level of applicant's interest. *Other factors considered include:* rigor of secondary school record, class rank, standardized test scores, extracurricular activities, talent/ability, volunteer work, work experience. **Freshman Admission Requirements:** High school diploma is required and GED is accepted **Freshman Admission Statistics:** 8,953 applied, 82.3% admitted, 25% enrolled. **Transfer Admission Requirements:** High school transcript, college transcript(s), essay or personal statement, Lowest grade transferable C. **General Admission Information:** Application fee $35. Priority deadline 5/1. Nonfall registration accepted. Admission may be deferred for a maximum of 1 year.

COSTS AND FINANCIAL AID

Annual tuition $22,884. Room and board $12,450. Required fees $660. Average book expense $1,708. **Required Forms and Deadlines:** FAFSA; Institution's own financial aid form. **Types of Aid:** *Need-based scholarships/grants:* College/university scholarship or grant aid from institutional funds; Federal Pell; Private scholarships; SEOG; State scholarships/grants. *Loans:* Direct PLUS loans; Direct Subsidized Stafford Loans; Direct Unsubsidized Stafford Loans. *Student Employment:* Federal Work-Study Program available. **Financial Aid Statistics:** 90% needy freshmen, 82% needy undergrads receive need-based scholarship or grant aid. 0% undergrads receive non-need-based scholarship or grant aid. 0% freshmen, 1% undergrads receive need-based self-help aid. 0% freshmen, 0% undergrads receive athletic scholarships. 73% freshmen, 71% undergrads receive any aid. **Criteria for awarding aid:** *Need-based:* Academics, Art, Leadership, Music/drama *Non-need-based:* Academics, Art, Leadership, Music/drama, State/district residency.

COLUMBIA INTERNATIONAL UNIVERSITY

PO Box 3122, Columbia, SC 29230-3122
Phone: 803-754-4100
E-mail: yesciu@ciu.edu
Fax: 803-786-4041 · **Website:** www.ciu.edu · **ACT Code:** 5016

This private school was founded in 1923. It has a 400 acre campus.

RATINGS

Admissions Selectivity Rating: 75   **Fire Safety Rating:** 60*   **Green Rating:** 60*

STUDENTS AND FACULTY

Enrollment: 568. **Student Body:** 54% female, 46% male, 56% out-of-state, 0% international. Asian 0%, African American 0%, Caucasian 0%, Hispanic 0%, Native American 0%, Race unknown 0%.
Retention and Graduation: 77% freshmen return for sophomore year.
Faculty: Student/faculty ratio 19:1. 19 full-time faculty, 58% hold PhDs, 11% are members of minority groups, 21% are women.

ACADEMICS

Degrees: Associate; Bachelor's; Certificate; Doctoral; Doctoral/Professional; Master's; Post-Bachelor's certificate; Terminal Associate; Transfer Associate **Classes:** Most classes have 10-19 students. Most lab/discussion sessions have 10-19 students. **Special Study Options:** Cross-registration; Distance learning; Double major; Dual enrollment; English as a Second Language (ESL); Independent study; Internships; Liberal arts/career combination; Study abroad. **Disability Services offered to physically disabled students:** Note-taking services; Reader services; Tape recorders; Tutors. **Career services:** Alumni services

FACILITIES

Housing: Apartments for single students; Men's dorms; Women's dorms

CAMPUS LIFE

Environment: Village **Activities:** Choral groups; Concert band; Drama/theater; Music ensembles; Student government; Symphony orchestra; Yearbook 4 religious organizations.

ADMISSIONS

Freshman Academic Profile: Average high school GPA 3.9. 27% in top 10% of high school class, 47% in top 25% of high school class, 75% in top 50% of high school class. **Test Scores:** SAT Math middle 50% range 490-580. SAT EBRW middle 50% range 530-630. ACT middle 50% range 20-26. Minimum

paper TOEFL 525. **Basis for Candidate Selection:** *Very important factors considered include:* academic GPA, application essay, standardized test scores, recommendation(s), character/personal qualities, religious affiliation/commitment. *Important factors considered include:* class rank, extracurricular activities, volunteer work. level of applicant's interest. *Other factors considered include:* rigor of secondary school record, interview, talent/ability, alumni/ae relation, work experience. **Freshman Admission Requirements:** High school diploma is required and GED is accepted *Academic units recommended:* 4 English, 2 math, 1 science, 2 foreign language, 2 history. **Freshman Admission Statistics:** 163 applied, 98.8% admitted, 52% enrolled. **Transfer Admission Requirements:** college transcript(s), essay or personal statement, statement of good standing from prior institution(s). Minimum college GPA of 2.0 required. Lowest grade transferable C. **General Admission Information:** Application fee $45. Priority deadline 2/28. Regular application deadline 8/1. Nonfall registration accepted. Admission may be deferred for a maximum of 1 year.

COSTS AND FINANCIAL AID

Annual tuition $8,980. Room and board $4,520. Required fees $160. Average book expense $800. **Required Forms and Deadlines:** FAFSA. **Types of Aid:** *Need-based scholarships/grants:* College/university scholarship or grant aid from institutional funds; Federal Pell; Private scholarships; SEOG; State scholarships/grants. *Student Employment:* Federal Work-Study Program available. **Financial Aid Statistics:** 75% needy freshmen, 78% needy undergrads receive need-based scholarship or grant aid. 0% freshmen, 0% undergrads receive athletic scholarships. **Criteria for awarding aid:** *Need-based:* Academics, Leadership, Minority status, Music/drama.

COLUMBIA UNION COLLEGE

7600 Flower Avenue, Takoma Park, MD 20912
Phone: 301-891-4080 · **Financial Aid Phone:** 301-891-4005
E-mail: enroll@wau.edu · **CEEB Code:** 5890
Fax: 301-891-4230 · **ACT Code:** 1687

This private school, affiliated with the Seventh Day Adventist Church, was founded in 1904. It has a 19 acre campus.

RATINGS

Admissions Selectivity Rating: 71   **Fire Safety Rating:** 60*   **Green Rating:** 60*

STUDENTS AND FACULTY

Enrollment: 986. **Student Body:** 65% female, 35% male, 57% out-of-state, (47 countries represented). Asian 6%, African American 52%, Caucasian 11%, Hispanic 11%, Native American <1%, Race unknown 20%.
Retention and Graduation: 61% freshmen return for sophomore year.
Faculty: Student/faculty ratio 14:1. 41 full-time faculty, 51% hold PhDs, 44% are members of minority groups, 51% are women. 0% of classes are taught by teaching assistants.

ACADEMICS

Degrees: Associate; Bachelor's; Certificate; Master's **Classes:** Most classes have fewer than 10 students. **Most popular majors:** Nursing/Registered Nurse (Rn, Asn, Bsn, Msn); Business/Commerce, General. **Special Study Options:** Accelerated program; Cooperative education program; Cross-registration; Distance learning; Double major; Dual enrollment; English as a Second Language (ESL); External degree program; Honors program; Independent study; Internships; Liberal arts/career combination; Student-designed major; Study abroad; Teacher certification program. **Honors programs:** The Honors Program at CUC strives to provide academically talented students the opportunity to engage and explore subject material in greater depth. This does not mean more work, it means a different kind of work, with more individual attention. The honors classes are different in design as each class explores the topic from an interdisciplinary perspective, where areas of study are combined into one course. **Disability Services offered to physically disabled students:** Reader services; Tutors. **Career services:** Career assessment; Internships

FACILITIES

Housing: Apartments for married students; Apartments for single students; Men's dorms; Women's dorms 30% of campus accessible to physically disabled. **Special Academic Facilities/Equipment:** Hospital adjacent to campus for students in health fields, performing arts at adfacent large church auditorium, learning center, radio station, playing fields and gymnasium. **Computers:** 100% of classrooms, 100% of dorms, 100% of libraries, 100% of dining areas, 100% of student union, 100% of common outdoor areas have wireless network access. Students can register for classes online. Administrative functions (other than registration) can be performed online.

CAMPUS LIFE

Environment: Metropolis **Activities:** Campus Ministries; Choral groups; Concert band; International Student Organization; Jazz band; Literary magazine; Music ensembles; Musical theater; Pep band; Radio station; Student government; Student newspaper; Symphony orchestra; Yearbook 6 honor societies. **Athletics (Intercollegiate):** *Men:* baseball, basketball, cross-country, soccer, track/field (outdoor). *Women:* basketball, cross-country, soccer, softball, track/field (outdoor).

ADMISSIONS

Freshman Academic Profile: 53% from public high schools. **Test Scores:** Minimum paper TOEFL 550. **Basis for Candidate Selection:** *Very important factors considered include:* academic GPA, standardized test scores. *Important factors considered include:* recommendation(s), character/personal qualities. *Other factors considered include:* rigor of secondary school record, application essay, talent/ability, religious affiliation/commitment. **Freshman Admission Requirements:** High school diploma is required and GED is accepted *Academic units required:* 4 English, 2 math, 2 science, 2 science labs, 4 history, 4 academic electives, *Academic units recommended:* 4 English, 4 math, 4 science, 4 science labs, 2 foreign language, 2 social studies, 4 history, 4 academic electives, 1 computer science. **Freshman Admission Statistics:** 1,293 applied, 41.1% admitted, 27% enrolled. **Transfer Admission Requirements:** college transcript(s), Minimum college GPA of 2.0 required. Lowest grade transferable C. **General Admission Information:** Application fee $25. Priority deadline 7/1. Regular application deadline 8/1. Nonfall registration accepted. Admission may be deferred for a maximum of 1 year.

COSTS AND FINANCIAL AID

Annual tuition $18,200. Room and board $7,200. Required fees $1,280. Average book expense $1,200. **Required Forms and Deadlines:** FAFSA; State aid form. **Notification of Awards:** Applicants will be notified of awards on a rolling basis beginning 5/1. **Types of Aid:** *Need-based scholarships/grants:* Federal Pell; Private scholarships; SEOG; State scholarships/grants. *Loans:* Direct PLUS loans; Direct Subsidized Stafford Loans; Direct Unsubsidized Stafford Loans. *Student Employment:* Federal Work-Study Program available. Institutional employment available. **Criteria for awarding aid:** *Non-need-based:* Academics, Athletics, Music/drama.

COLUMBIA UNIVERSITY

212 Hamilton Hall MC 2807, New York, NY 10027
Phone: 212-854-2522 · **Financial Aid Phone:** 212-854-3711
E-mail: ugrad-ask@columbia.edu · **CEEB Code:** 2116
Fax: 212-854-1209 · **Website:** www.columbia.edu · **ACT Code:** 2717

This private school was founded in 1754. It has a 36 acre campus.

RATINGS

Admissions Selectivity Rating: 99   **Fire Safety Rating:** 86   **Green Rating:** 96

STUDENTS AND FACULTY

Enrollment: 6,231. **Student Body:** 48% female, 52% male, 78% out-of-state, 16% international (90 countries represented). Asian 22%, African American 12%, Caucasian 34%, Hispanic 12%, Native American 2%, Race unknown 2%. **Retention and Graduation:** 99% freshmen return for sophomore year. 88% freshmen graduate within 4 years. 95% freshmen graduate within 6 years. **Faculty:** Student/faculty ratio 6:1. 1,476 full-time faculty, 100% hold PhDs, 24% are members of minority groups, 34% are women. 0% of classes are taught by teaching assistants.

ACADEMICS

Degrees: Bachelor's; Doctoral; Doctoral Other; Doctoral/Professional; Doctoral/Research; Master's **Classes:** Most classes have 10-19 students. **Most popular majors:** Engineering, General; Political Science And Government, General. **Special Study Options:** Accelerated program; Cooperative education program; Cross-registration; Double major; Dual enrollment; English as a Second Language (ESL); Exchange student program (domestic); Independent study; Internships; Liberal arts/career combination; Student-designed major; Study abroad; Teacher certification program. **Combined degree programs:** BA/JD. **Disability Services offered to physically disabled students:** Note-taking services; Reader services; Tape recorders; Tutors. **Career services:** Alumni network; Alumni services; Career assessment; Career/job search classes; Internships

FACILITIES

Housing: Coed dorms; Cooperative housing; Fraternity/sorority housing; Special housing for disabled student; Theme housing; Wellness housing 95% of campus accessible to physically diasbled. **Special Academic Facilities/ Equipment:** Art and Architecture Galleries, Theatres, Cinema, Observatory **Computers:** Students can register for classes online. Administrative functions (other than registration) can be performed online.

CAMPUS LIFE

Environment: Metropolis **Activities:** Campus Ministries; Choral groups; Concert band; Dance; Drama/theater; International Student Organization; Jazz band; Literary magazine; Marching band; Model UN; Music ensembles; Musical theater; Opera; Pep band; Radio station; Student government; Student newspaper; Student-run film society; Symphony orchestra; Television station; Yearbook 300 registered organizations, 17 religious organizations. 17 fraternities, 11 sororities. **Athletics (Intercollegiate):** *Men:* baseball, basketball, crew/rowing, cross-country, diving, fencing, football, golf, soccer, swimming, tennis, track/field (outdoor), track/field (indoor), wrestling. *Women:* archery, basketball, crew/rowing, cross-country, diving, fencing, field hockey, golf, lacrosse, soccer, softball, swimming, tennis, track/field (outdoor), track/field (indoor), volleyball. **On-Campus Highlights:** Low Library and Plaza, Butler Library, Postcrypt Coffee House, Ferris Booth Commons, Levien Gym **Environmental Initiatives:** Greenhouse gas reduction program targeted to meet a 30% reduction by 2017 and clean heat initiative to improve air quality and asthma rates by phasing out the use of heavy heating oils to cleaner fuels like natural gas and low-sulfur #2 oil. Columbia has also converted its entire 14 car public safety fleet to hybrid vehicles. As part of our energy efficiency initiatives, 45% of all food purchased is local and/ororganic. All honey and apples are purchased through vendors at the on-campus green market from NY farmers. Annually Dining Services contracts with a local NY farmer and canner to make all the salsa and strawberry jam for the year. In addition all milk is local and hormone free. Liquid eggs are certified humane. All coffee is roasted locally and is fair-trade, organic, shade grown and bird friendly. Tomatoes are also fair trade. All bakery items and grab and go sandwiches are purchased from local vendors. 50% of daily meals served in the dining halls are vegetarian and Meatless Mondays are run every Monday.

ADMISSIONS

Freshman Academic Profile: 56% from public high schools. **Test Scores:** SAT Math middle 50% range 730-800. SAT EBRW middle 50% range 720-780. ACT middle 50% range 32-35. Minimum internet-based TOEFL 100. Minimum paper TOEFL 600. **Basis for Candidate Selection:** *Very important factors considered include:* rigor of secondary school record, class rank, academic GPA, application essay, standardized test scores, recommendation(s), extracurricular activities, character/personal qualities. *Important factors considered include:* talent/ability. *Other factors considered include:* interview, first generation, alumni/ae relation, geographical residence, racial/ethnic status, volunteer work, work experience. **Freshman Admission Requirements:** High school diploma is required and GED is accepted *Academic units required:* 4 English, 3 math, 3 science, 3 science labs, 3 foreign language, 3 history, 3 academic electives, *Academic units recommended:* 4 English, 4 math, 4 science, 4 science labs, 4 foreign language, 4 history, 4 academic electives. **Freshman Admission Statistics:** 37,389 applied, 6.1% admitted, 62% enrolled. **Transfer Admission Requirements:** High school transcript, college transcript(s), essay or personal statement, standardized test scores, statement of good standing from prior institution(s). Lowest grade transferable C. **General Admission Information:** Application fee $85. Regular application deadline 1/1. Nonfall registration accepted. Admission may be deferred for a maximum of 2 years.

COSTS AND FINANCIAL AID

Annual tuition $54,504. Room and board $13,618. Required fees $2,704. Average book expense $1,246. **Required Forms and Deadlines:** CSS/ Financial Aid PROFILE; FAFSA; Noncustodial PROFILE. **Notification of Awards:** Applicants will be notified of awards on or about 4/1. **Types of Aid:** *Need-based scholarships/grants:* College/university scholarship or grant aid from institutional funds; Federal Pell; Private scholarships; SEOG; State scholarships/grants. *Loans:* Direct PLUS loans; Direct Subsidized Stafford Loans; Direct Unsubsidized Stafford Loans. *Student Employment:* Federal Work-Study Program available. Institutional employment available. **Financial Aid Statistics:** 96% needy freshmen, 97% needy undergrads receive need-based scholarship or grant aid. 1% freshmen, 1% undergrads receive non-need-based scholarship or grant aid. 78% freshmen, 86% undergrads receive need-based self-help aid. 0% freshmen, 0% undergrads receive athletic scholarships. 55% freshmen, 60% undergrads receive any aid. 27% undergrads borrow to pay for school. Average cumulative indebtedness $25,167.

COLUMBIA UNIVERSITY SCHOOL OF GENERAL STUDIES

408 Lewisohn Hall, Mail Code 4101, New York, NY 10027
Phone: (212) 854-2772 · **Financial Aid Phone:** (212) 854-5410
E-mail: gsdegree@columbia.edu · **CEEB Code:** 2095
Fax: (212) 854-6316 · **Website:** www.gs.columbia.edu · **ACT Code:** 2716

This private school was founded in 1947. It has a 36 acre campus.

RATINGS

Admissions Selectivity Rating: 95   **Fire Safety Rating:** 88   **Green Rating:** 60*

STUDENTS AND FACULTY

Enrollment: 2,005. **Student Body:** 41% female, 59% male, 56% out-of-state, 18% international (62 countries represented). Asian 8%, African American 5%, Caucasian 49%, Hispanic 10%, Native American <1%, Pacific Islander <1%, Two or more races <1%, Race unknown 9%.
Faculty:

ACADEMICS

Degrees: Bachelor's; Post-Bachelor's certificate **Most popular majors:** English Language And Literature, General; Economics, General; Political Science And Government, General. **Special Study Options:** Accelerated program; Cross-registration; Double major; Dual enrollment; Exchange student program (domestic); Honors program; Independent study; Internships; Student-designed major; Study abroad; Teacher certification program. **Honors programs:** Honor Society of School of General Studies **Combined degree programs:** BA/DDS; BA/JD; BA/MA; BA/MEng. **Disability Services offered to physically disabled students:** Note-taking services; Reader services; Tape recorders; Tutors. **Career services:** Alumni network; Alumni services; Career assessment; Career/job search classes; Internships; Regional alumni

FACILITIES

Housing: Apartments for married students; Apartments for single students; Coed dorms; Cooperative housing; Fraternity/sorority housing; Special housing for international students; Theme housing 100% of campus accessible to physically diasbled. **Special Academic Facilities/Equipment:** Earth Institute, Lamont-Doherty Earth Observatory University Art Collection Miller Theatre Low Memorial Library Rotunda LeRoy Neiman Center for Print Studies Music at St. Paul's Postcrypt Coffeehouse Miriam and Ira D. Wallach Art Gallery Language Houses **Computers:** 50% of classrooms, 10% of dorms, 64% of libraries, 50% of dining areas, 90% of student union, 25% of common outdoor areas have wireless network access. Students can register for classes online. Administrative functions (other than registration) can be performed online.

CAMPUS LIFE

Environment: Metropolis **Activities:** Campus Ministries; Choral groups; Concert band; Dance; Drama/theater; International Student Organization; Jazz band; Literary magazine; Marching band; Model UN; Music ensembles; Musical theater; Opera; Radio station; Student government; Student newspaper; Student-run film society; Television station; Yearbook 250 registered organizations, 2 honor societies, 21 religious organizations. **Athletics (Intercollegiate): Men:** baseball, basketball, crew/rowing, cross-country, diving, fencing, football, golf, soccer, swimming, track/field (outdoor), track/field (indoor). **Women:** archery, basketball, crew/rowing, cross-country, diving, fencing, field hockey, golf, lacrosse, soccer, softball, swimming, track/field (outdoor), track/field (indoor), volleyball. **On-Campus Highlights:** Low Memorial Library, Butler Library, Alfred Lerner Hall, Miller Theater, College Walk **Environmental Initiatives:** Greenhouse gas reduction program targeted to meet a 30% reduction by 2017 and clean heat initiative to improve air quality and asthma rates by phasing out the use of heavy heating oils to cleaner fuels like natural gas and low-sulfur #2 oil. Columbia has also converted its entire 14 car public safety fleet to hybrid vehicles. As part of our energy efficiency initiatives, 45% of all food purchased is local and/ororganic. All honey and apples are purchased through vendors at the on-campus green market from NY farmers. Annually Dining Services contracts with a local NY farmer and canner to make all the salsa and strawberry jam for the year. In addition all milk is local and hormone free. Liquid eggs are certified humane. All coffee is roasted locally and is fair-trade, organic, shade grown and bird friendly. Tomatoes are also fair trade. All bakery items and grab and go sandwiches are purchased from local vendors. 50% of daily meals served in the dining halls are vegetarian and Meatless Mondays are run every Monday.

ADMISSIONS

Freshman Academic Profile: Average high school GPA 3.7. **Test Scores:** SAT Math middle 50% range 630-740. SAT EBRW middle 50% range 630-750. ACT middle 50% range 29-32. Minimum paper TOEFL 600. **Basis for**

Candidate Selection: *Very important factors considered include:* rigor of secondary school record, academic GPA, application essay, standardized test scores, interview, character/personal qualities, first generation, work experience, level of applicant's interest. *Important factors considered include:* class rank, recommendation(s), extracurricular activities, talent/ability, racial/ethnic status. *Other factors considered include:* alumni/ae relation, geographical residence, state residency, volunteer work. **Freshman Admission Requirements:** High school diploma is required and GED is accepted **Freshman Admission Statistics:** 661 applied, 33.0% admitted, 59% enrolled. **Transfer Admission Requirements:** High school transcript, college transcript(s), Lowest grade transferable C. **General Admission Information:** Application fee $80. Priority deadline 3/1. Regular application deadline 6/1. Nonfall registration accepted. Admission may be deferred for a maximum of 2 semesters.

COSTS AND FINANCIAL AID

Annual tuition $48,900. Room and board $10,356. Required fees $2,214. Average book expense $1,400. **Required Forms and Deadlines:** FAFSA; Institution's own financial aid form. **Types of Aid:** *Need-based scholarships/grants:* College/university scholarship or grant aid from institutional funds; Federal Pell; Private scholarships; SEOG; State scholarships/grants. *Loans:* Direct PLUS loans; Direct Subsidized Stafford Loans; Direct Unsubsidized Stafford Loans. *Student Employment:* Federal Work-Study Program available. Institutional employment available. **Financial Aid Statistics:** 93% needy freshmen, 98% needy undergrads receive need-based scholarship or grant aid. 2% undergrads receive non-need-based scholarship or grant aid. 85% freshmen, 87% undergrads receive need-based self-help aid. 0% freshmen, 0% undergrads receive athletic scholarships. 70% undergrads receive any aid. **Criteria for awarding aid:** *Need-based:* Academics *Non-need-based:* Academics.

COLUMBUS COLLEGE OF ART & DESIGN

60 Cleveland Ave., Columbus, OH 43215-3875
Phone: 614-222-3261 · **Financial Aid Phone:** 614.222.3295
E-mail: admissions@ccad.edu · **CEEB Code:** 1085
Fax: 614-232-8344 · **Website:** www.ccad.edu · **ACT Code:** 3281

This private school was founded in 1879. It has a 9 acre campus.

RATINGS

Admissions Selectivity Rating: 75   **Fire Safety Rating:** 91   **Green Rating:** 60*

STUDENTS AND FACULTY

Enrollment: 1,261. **Student Body:** 62% female, 38% male, 27% out-of-state, 8% international (35 countries represented). Asian 3%, African American 8%, Caucasian 68%, Hispanic 5%, Native American <1%, Pacific Islander 0%, Two or more races 4%, Race unknown 3%.
Retention and Graduation: 78% freshmen return for sophomore year. 8% grads go on to further study within 1 year. 7% grads pursue arts and sciences degrees. 1% grads pursue medical degrees. **Faculty:** Student/faculty ratio 11:1. 72 full-time faculty, 69% hold PhDs, 7% are members of minority groups, 38% are women. 0% of classes are taught by teaching assistants.

ACADEMICS

Degrees: Bachelor's; Master's **Classes:** Most classes have 10-19 students. Most lab/discussion sessions have 10-19 students. **Most popular majors:** Graphic Design; Illustration. **Special Study Options:** Accelerated program; Cooperative education program; Cross-registration; Distance learning; Double major; English as a Second Language (ESL); Exchange student program (domestic); Honors program; Independent study; Internships; Study abroad. **Honors programs:** The CCAD Honors Program centers around seminar courses offered each semester and the creation of individualized learning contracts, culminating in a thesis/capstone project. The program activities are designed to assist students in integrating various community and academic projects with their individual creative interests within the CCAD curriculum. Benefits include honors designation on transcripts, recognition at commencement, and the opportunity to propose and implement projects that move students toward their personal, academic, and career goals. Participants in the CCAD Honors Program must maintain a cumulative GPA of at least 3.5, participate in four seminar courses during their time at CCAD, and complete a Senior Honors Thesis or Capstone Project. **Disability Services offered to physically disabled students:** Note-taking services; Reader services; Tutors. **Career services:** Alumni services; Career assessment; Career/job search classes; Internships

FACILITIES

Housing: Apartments for married students; Apartments for single students;

Coed dorms; Special housing for disabled student; Special housing for international students **Special Academic Facilities/Equipment:** Multiple art galleries, auditorium, recreation center, library, specialized studios and fabrication labs

CAMPUS LIFE

Environment: Metropolis **Activities:** International Student Organization; Literary magazine; Student government; Student-run film society 2 registered organizations, 1 religious organization. Joseph V. Canzani Center, Loann Crane Center for Design, Design Studios on Broad, CCAD MindMarket, Campus Quad

ADMISSIONS

Freshman Academic Profile: Average high school GPA 3.2. 6% in top 10% of high school class, 18% in top 25% of high school class, 59% in top 50% of high school class. **Test Scores:** SAT Math middle 50% range 450-570. SAT EBRW middle 50% range 470-610. ACT middle 50% range 19-25. Minimum internet-based TOEFL 173. Minimum paper TOEFL 500. **Basis for Candidate Selection:** *Very important factors considered include:* academic GPA, application essay, standardized test scores, recommendation(s), talent/ability. *Important factors considered include:* level of applicant's interest. *Other factors considered include:* rigor of secondary school record, interview, extracurricular activities, character/personal qualities, first generation, alumni/ae relation, geographical residence, state residency, volunteer work, work experience. **Freshman Admission Requirements:** High school diploma is required and GED is accepted *Academic units recommended:* 4 English, 2 math, 2 science, 2 foreign language. **Freshman Admission Statistics:** 666 applied, 87.4% admitted, 40% enrolled. **Transfer Admission Requirements:** High school transcript, college transcript(s), essay or personal statement, Minimum college GPA of 2.0 required. Lowest grade transferable C. **General Admission Information:** Application fee $40. Priority deadline 2/15. Regular application deadline 8/22. Nonfall registration accepted. Admission may be deferred.

COSTS AND FINANCIAL AID

Annual tuition $28,872. Room and board $7,740. Average book expense $4,000. **Required Forms and Deadlines:** FAFSA. **Notification of Awards:** Applicants will be notified of awards on a rolling basis beginning 3/15. **Types of Aid:** *Need-based scholarships/grants:* College/university scholarship or grant aid from institutional funds; Federal Pell; SEOG; State scholarships/grants. *Loans:* Direct PLUS loans; Direct Subsidized Stafford Loans; Direct Unsubsidized Stafford Loans. *Student Employment:* Federal Work-Study Program available. Institutional employment available. **Financial Aid Statistics:** 100% needy freshmen, 98% needy undergrads receive need-based scholarship or grant aid. 4% freshmen, 3% undergrads receive non-need-based scholarship or grant aid. 84% freshmen, 84% undergrads receive need-based self-help aid. 0% freshmen, 0% undergrads receive athletic scholarships. 74% freshmen, 81% undergrads receive any aid. **Criteria for awarding aid:** *Non-need-based:* Academics, Art.

COLUMBUS STATE UNIVERSITY

4225 University Avenue, Columbus, GA 31907-5645
Phone: 706-568-2035 · **Financial Aid Phone:** 706-507-8800
E-mail: admissions@colstate.edu
Fax: 706-568-5091 · **Website:** www.columbusstate.edu

This public school was founded in 1958. It has a 150 acre campus.

RATINGS

Admissions Selectivity Rating: 85   **Fire Safety Rating:** 87   **Green Rating:** 60*

STUDENTS AND FACULTY

Enrollment: 6,890. **Student Body:** 60% female, 40% male, 14% out-of-state, 1% international (67 countries represented). Asian 2%, African American 35%, Caucasian 55%, Hispanic 4%, Native American 1%, Pacific Islander <1%, Two or more races 2%, Race unknown 0%.
Retention and Graduation: 69% freshmen return for sophomore year.
Faculty: Student/faculty ratio 18:1. 279 full-time faculty, 78% hold PhDs, 23% are members of minority groups, 43% are women. 0% of classes are taught by teaching assistants.

ACADEMICS

Degrees: Bachelor's; Certificate; Doctoral; Doctoral/Research; Master's; Post-Master's certificate; Terminal Associate; Transfer Associate **Classes:** Most classes have 20-29 students. Most lab/discussion sessions have 20-29 students. **Most popular majors:** Early Childhood Education And Teaching; Nursing/Registered Nurse (Rn, Asn, Bsn, Msn); Business/Commerce, General. **Special Study Options:** Accelerated program; Cooperative education program; Distance learning; Double major; Dual enrollment; English as a Second

Language (ESL); Honors program; Independent study; Internships; Liberal arts/career combination; Study abroad; Teacher certification program. **Honors programs:** Honors Program Servant Leadership Program. **Disability Services offered to physically disabled students:** Note-taking services; Reader services; Tape recorders; Tutors. **Career services:** Alumni network; Alumni services; Career assessment; Career/job search classes; Internships; Regional alumni

FACILITIES

Housing: Apartments for married students; Apartments for single students; Fraternity/sorority housing; Special housing for disabled student; Special housing for international students; Theme housing 100% of campus accessible to physically diasbled. **Computers:** 80% of classrooms, 100% of libraries, 100% of dining areas, 100% of student union, 25% of common outdoor areas have wireless network access. Students can register for classes online. Administrative functions (other than registration) can be performed online.

CAMPUS LIFE

Environment: City **Activities:** Campus Ministries; Choral groups; Concert band; Dance; Drama/theater; International Student Organization; Jazz band; Literary magazine; Model UN; Music ensembles; Musical theater; Pep band; Student government; Student newspaper; Symphony orchestra 90 registered organizations, 22 honor societies, 10 religious organizations. 7 fraternities, 6 sororities. **Athletics (Intercollegiate):** *Men:* baseball, basketball, cheerleading, cross-country, golf, riflery, tennis. *Women:* basketball, cheerleading, cross-country, golf, riflery, soccer, softball, tennis. **On-Campus Highlights:** Einstein Bros. Bagels, RiverPark Campus, Davidson Student Center, Lumpkin Center, Coca Cola Space Science Center **Environmental Initiatives:** Green Seal Cleaning Products

ADMISSIONS

Freshman Academic Profile: Average high school GPA 3.0. **Test Scores:** SAT Math middle 50% range 420-540. SAT EBRW middle 50% range 430-550. ACT middle 50% range 17-22. Minimum internet-based TOEFL 79. Minimum paper TOEFL 550. **Basis for Candidate Selection:** *Very important factors considered include:* rigor of secondary school record. *Important factors considered include:* academic GPA, standardized test scores. *Other factors considered include:* interview, extracurricular activities, talent/ability, geographical residence. **Freshman Admission Requirements:** High school diploma is required and GED is not accepted *Academic units required:* 4 English, 4 math, 3 science, 2 science labs, 2 foreign language, 3 social studies. **Freshman Admission Statistics:** 3,454 applied, 60.1% admitted, 60% enrolled. **Transfer Admission Requirements:** college transcript(s), statement of good standing from prior institution(s). Minimum college GPA of 2.00 required. Lowest grade transferable D. **General Admission Information:** Application fee $30. Priority deadline 5/15. Regular application deadline 6/30. Nonfall registration accepted. Admission may be deferred for a maximum of One year.

COSTS AND FINANCIAL AID

Annual in-state tuition $7,280. Annual out-of-state tuition $12,669. Room and board $7,280. Required fees $1,300. Average book expense $1,072. **Required Forms and Deadlines:** FAFSA. **Notification of Awards:** Applicants will be notified of awards on a rolling basis beginning 5/15. **Types of Aid:** *Need-based scholarships/grants:* College/university scholarship or grant aid from institutional funds; Federal Pell; Private scholarships; SEOG; State scholarships/grants. *Loans:* Direct PLUS loans; Direct Subsidized Stafford Loans; Direct Unsubsidized Stafford Loans. *Student Employment:* Federal Work-Study Program available. Institutional employment available. **Financial Aid Statistics:** 71% needy freshmen, 72% needy undergrads receive need-based scholarship or grant aid. 51% freshmen, 34% undergrads receive non-need-based scholarship or grant aid. 66% freshmen, 73% undergrads receive need-based self-help aid. 4% freshmen, 4% undergrads receive athletic scholarships. 87% freshmen, 78% undergrads receive any aid. **Criteria for awarding aid:** *Need-based:* Academics, Alumni affiliation, Art, Athletics, Job skills, Leadership, Minority status, Music/drama *Non-need-based:* Academics, Alumni affiliation, Art, Athletics, Job skills, Leadership, Minority status, Music/drama.

CONCORD UNIVERSITY

1000 Vermillion Street, Athens, WV 24712
Phone: 304-384-5248 · **Financial Aid Phone:** 304-384-6069
E-mail: admissions@concord.edu · **CEEB Code:** 5120
Fax: 304-384-9044 · **Website:** www.concord.edu · **ACT Code:** 3810

This public school was founded in 1872. It has a 123 acre campus.

RATINGS
Admissions Selectivity Rating: 82   **Fire Safety Rating:** 91   **Green Rating:** 60*

STUDENTS AND FACULTY
Enrollment: 2,611. **Student Body:** 55% female, 45% male, 18% out-of-state, 0% international (16 countries represented). Asian 2%, African American 6%, Caucasian 91%, Hispanic 1%, Native American <1%, Race unknown 0%.
Retention and Graduation: 65% freshmen return for sophomore year. 33% grads go on to further study within 1 year. 8% grads pursue arts and sciences degrees. 2% grads pursue law degrees. 10% grads pursue business degrees. 3% grads pursue medical degrees. **Faculty:** Student/faculty ratio 23:1. 121 full-time faculty, 64% hold PhDs, 3% are members of minority groups, 41% are women.

ACADEMICS
Degrees: Associate; Bachelor's; Master's; Terminal Associate **Classes:** Most classes have 20-29 students. Most lab/discussion sessions have 20-29 students. **Most popular majors:** Education, General; Social Sciences, General; Business Administration And Management, General. **Special Study Options:** Cooperative education program; Double major; Dual enrollment; English as a Second Language (ESL); Honors program; Independent study; Student-designed major; Teacher certification program. **Career services:** Alumni services; Career assessment; Career/job search classes; Internships

FACILITIES
Housing: Apartments for married students; Coed dorms; Men's dorms; Special housing for disabled student; Special housing for international students; Women's dorms 100% of campus accessible to physically disabled. **Computers:** 50% of classrooms, 20% of dorms, 100% of libraries, 100% of dining areas, 100% of student union, 50% of common outdoor areas have wireless network access. Students can register for classes online. Administrative functions (other than registration) can be performed online.

CAMPUS LIFE
Environment: Rural **Activities:** Campus Ministries; Choral groups; Concert band; Drama/theater; International Student Organization; Jazz band; Marching band; Pep band; Radio station; Student government; Student newspaper; Student-run film society; Television station; Yearbook 57 registered organizations, 1 honor society, 2 religious organizations. 6 fraternities, 4 sororities. **Athletics (Intercollegiate):** *Men:* baseball, basketball, cheerleading, cross-country, football, golf, soccer, tennis, track/field (outdoor). *Women:* basketball, cheerleading, cross-country, golf, soccer, softball, tennis, track/field (outdoor), volleyball. **On-Campus Highlights:** Rahall Technology Ctr, 48 Bell Carillon, University Point, Beasley Student Ctr., Callaghan Stadium

ADMISSIONS
Freshman Academic Profile: Average high school GPA 3.2. 18% in top 10% of high school class, 45% in top 25% of high school class, 73% in top 50% of high school class. 95% from public high schools. **Test Scores:** SAT Math middle 50% range 420-520. SAT EBRW middle 50% range 420-540. ACT middle 50% range 17-25. Minimum paper TOEFL 500. **Basis for Candidate Selection:** *Very important factors considered include:* rigor of secondary school record. *Important factors considered include:* class rank, standardized test scores, extracurricular activities. *Other factors considered include:* application essay, recommendation(s), interview, talent/ability, character/personal qualities, alumni/ae relation, geographical residence, racial/ethnic status, volunteer work, work experience. **Freshman Admission Requirements:** High school diploma is required and GED is accepted *Academic units required:* 4 English, 4 math, 3 science, 3 science labs, 2 foreign language, 2 social studies, 1 history, 1 visual/performing arts. **Freshman Admission Statistics:** 2,290 applied, 60.6% admitted, 41% enrolled. **Transfer Admission Requirements:** college transcript(s), Lowest grade transferable D. **General Admission Information:** Nonfall registration accepted. Admission may be deferred for a maximum of 1 year.

COSTS AND FINANCIAL AID
Annual in-state tuition $6,962. Annual out-of-state tuition $11,050. Room and board $6,962. Average book expense $1,100. **Required Forms and Deadlines:** FAFSA; Institution's own financial aid form. **Notification of Awards:** Applicants will be notified of awards on a rolling basis beginning 4/15. **Types of Aid:** *Need-based scholarships/grants:* College/university scholarship or grant aid from institutional funds; Federal Pell; Private scholarships; SEOG;

State scholarships/grants. *Loans:* Direct PLUS loans; Direct Subsidized Stafford Loans; Direct Unsubsidized Stafford Loans. *Student Employment:* Federal Work-Study Program available. Institutional employment available. **Financial Aid Statistics:** 84% needy freshmen, 83% needy undergrads receive need-based scholarship or grant aid. 52% freshmen, 36% undergrads receive non-need-based scholarship or grant aid. 74% freshmen, 75% undergrads receive need-based self-help aid. 5% freshmen, 4% undergrads receive athletic scholarships. 90% freshmen, 77% undergrads receive any aid. **Criteria for awarding aid:** *Non-need-based:* Academics, Alumni affiliation, Art, Athletics, Job skills, Leadership, Minority status, Music/drama, State/district residency.

CONCORDIA COLLEGE (MOORHEAD, MN)

901 8th Street South, Moorhead, MN 56562
Phone: 218-299-3004 · **Financial Aid Phone:** 218.299.3010
E-mail: admissions@cord.edu · **CEEB Code:** 6113
Fax: 218-299-4720 · **Website:** https://www.concordiacollege.edu · **ACT Code:** 2104

This private school, affiliated with the Lutheran Church, was founded in 1891. It has a 120 acre campus.

RATINGS
Admissions Selectivity Rating: 83   **Fire Safety Rating:** 85   **Green Rating:** 60*

STUDENTS AND FACULTY
Enrollment: 1,967. **Student Body:** 58% female, 42% male, 29% out-of-state, 5% international (28 countries represented). Asian 2%, African American 2%, Caucasian 83%, Hispanic 2%, Native American 1%, Pacific Islander <1%, Two or more races 2%, Race unknown 4%.
Retention and Graduation: 82% freshmen return for sophomore year. 67% freshmen graduate within 4 years. 1% freshmen graduate within 6 years. 24% grads go on to further study within 1 year. 5% grads pursue arts and sciences degrees. 4% grads pursue law degrees. 3% grads pursue business degrees. 4% grads pursue medical degrees. **Faculty:** Student/faculty ratio 11:1. 166 full-time faculty, 83% hold PhDs, 7% are members of minority groups, 48% are women. 0% of classes are taught by teaching assistants.

ACADEMICS
Degrees: Bachelor's; Master's **Classes:** Most classes have greater than 100 students. **Most popular majors:** Education, General; Biology/Biological Sciences, General; Business Administration And Management, General. **Special Study Options:** Accelerated program; Cooperative education program; Cross-registration; Distance learning; Double major; Dual enrollment; English as a Second Language (ESL); Exchange student program (domestic); Honors program; Independent study; Internships; Liberal arts/career combination; Student-designed major; Study abroad; Teacher certification program. **Disability Services offered to physically disabled students:** Note-taking services; Reader services; Tape recorders; Tutors. **Career services:** Alumni network; Alumni services; Career assessment; Career/job search classes; Internships

FACILITIES
Housing: Apartments for single students; Coed dorms; Theme housing 95% of campus accessible to physically disabled. **Special Academic Facilities/Equipment:** Cyrus M. Running Gallery. **Computers:** Administrative functions (other than registration) can be performed online.

CAMPUS LIFE
Environment: City **Activities:** Campus Ministries; Choral groups; Concert band; Dance; Drama/theater; International Student Organization; Jazz band; Literary magazine; Music ensembles; Musical theater; Pep band; Radio station; Student government; Student newspaper; Symphony orchestra; Television station 80 registered organizations, 22 honor societies, 12 religious organizations. 2 fraternities, 2 sororities. **Athletics (Intercollegiate):** *Men:* baseball, basketball, cross-country, football, golf, ice hockey, soccer, tennis, track/field (outdoor), track/field (indoor), wrestling. *Women:* basketball, cross-country, diving, golf, ice hockey, soccer, softball, swimming, tennis, track/field (outdoor), track/field (indoor), volleyball. Knutson Campus Center, Offutt School of Business, Carl B. Ylvisaker Library, Coffee Stop, The Brew

ADMISSIONS
Freshman Academic Profile: Average high school GPA 3.6. 27% in top 10% of high school class, 55% in top 25% of high school class, 85% in top 50% of high school class. **Test Scores:** ACT middle 50% range 22-28. Minimum paper TOEFL 550. **Basis for Candidate Selection:** *Very important factors considered include:* rigor of secondary school record. *Important factors considered include:* academic GPA, standardized test scores. *Other factors considered include:* class rank, application essay, recommendation(s), interview,

extracurricular activities, talent/ability, character/personal qualities, first generation, alumni/ae relation, racial/ethnic status, volunteer work, work experience, level of applicant's interest. **Freshman Admission Requirements:** High school diploma is required and GED is accepted *Academic units recommended:* 4 English, 3 math, 3 science, 2 foreign language, 3 social studies, 1 computer science, 1 visual/performing arts. **Freshman Admission Statistics:** 4,539 applied, 61.4% admitted, 20% enrolled. **Transfer Admission Requirements:** college transcript(s), Minimum college GPA of 2.0 required. Lowest grade transferable C-. **General Admission Information:** Regular application deadline 9/10. Nonfall registration accepted. Admission may be deferred for a maximum of 1 year.

COSTS AND FINANCIAL AID
Annual tuition $39,650. Room and board $8,230. Required fees $228. Average book expense $1,000. **Required Forms and Deadlines:** FAFSA. **Notification of Awards:** Applicants will be notified of awards on a rolling basis beginning 12/1. **Types of Aid:** *Need-based scholarships/grants:* Federal Pell; Private scholarships; SEOG; State scholarships/grants. *Loans:* Direct PLUS loans; Direct Subsidized Stafford Loans; Direct Unsubsidized Stafford Loans. *Student Employment:* Federal Work-Study Program available. Institutional employment available. **Financial Aid Statistics:** 98% needy freshmen, 98% needy undergrads receive need-based scholarship or grant aid. 17% freshmen, 16% undergrads receive non-need-based scholarship or grant aid. 81% freshmen, 82% undergrads receive need-based self-help aid. 0% freshmen, 0% undergrads receive athletic scholarships. 100% freshmen, 96% undergrads receive any aid. Average cumulative indebtedness $39,837. **Criteria for awarding aid:** *Need-based:* Academics, Minority status *Non-need-based:* Academics, Art, Leadership, Minority status, Music/drama.

CONCORDIA COLLEGE (NY)

171 White Plains Road, Bronxville, NY 10708
Phone: 914-337-9300
E-mail: admission@concordia-ny.edu • **CEEB Code:** 2096
Fax: 914-395-4636 • **Website:** www.concordia-ny.edu • **ACT Code:** 2722

This private school, affiliated with the Lutheran Church, was founded in 1881. It has a 33 acre campus.

RATINGS
Admissions Selectivity Rating: 70   **Fire Safety Rating:** 60*   **Green Rating:** 60*

STUDENTS AND FACULTY
Student Body: 27% out-of-state, (36 countries represented). **Retention and Graduation:** 69% freshmen return for sophomore year. 40% grads go on to further study within 1 year. 30% grads pursue arts and sciences degrees. 2% grads pursue law degrees. 30% grads pursue business degrees. 10% grads pursue medical degrees. **Faculty:** Student/faculty ratio 12:1. 54 full-time faculty, 0% of classes are taught by teaching assistants.

ACADEMICS
Degrees: Associate; Bachelor's; Master's **Classes:** Most classes have fewer than 10 students. Most lab/discussion sessions have 10-19 students. **Most popular majors:** Education, General; Social Sciences, General; Business/Commerce, General. **Special Study Options:** Accelerated program; Cooperative education program; Cross-registration; Double major; English as a Second Language (ESL); Exchange student program (domestic); Honors program; Independent study; Internships; Liberal arts/career combination; Student-designed major; Study abroad; Teacher certification program. **Disability Services offered to physically disabled students:** Reader services; Tutors. **Career services:** Career assessment; Career/job search classes; Internships

FACILITIES
Housing: Men's dorms; Women's dorms 50% of campus accessible to physically disabled. **Special Academic Facilities/Equipment:** Art gallery, center for worship and performing arts, English language center, distance learning classroom

CAMPUS LIFE
Environment: Village **Activities:** Choral groups; Concert band; Dance; Drama/theater; International Student Organization; Jazz band; Literary magazine; Music ensembles; Musical theater; Student government; Student newspaper; Yearbook 35 registered organizations, 1 honor society, 3 religious organizations. **Athletics (Intercollegiate):** *Men:* baseball, basketball, soccer, tennis, volleyball. *Women:* basketball, soccer, softball, tennis, volleyball.

ADMISSIONS
Freshman Academic Profile: Average high school GPA 2.7. 60% from public high schools. **Test Scores:** SAT Math middle 50% range 415-505. SAT EBRW middle 50% range 420-500. ACT middle 50% range 16-20. Minimum paper TOEFL 550. **Basis for Candidate Selection:** *Very important factors considered include:* rigor of secondary school record. *Important factors considered include:* class rank, standardized test scores, interview, character/personal qualities. *Other factors considered include:* application essay, recommendation(s), extracurricular activities, talent/ability, alumni/ae relation, religious affiliation/commitment, volunteer work, work experience. **Freshman Admission Requirements:** High school diploma is required and GED is accepted **Transfer Admission Requirements:** High school transcript, college transcript(s), statement of good standing from prior institution(s). Minimum college GPA of 2.0 required. Lowest grade transferable C. **General Admission Information:** Application fee $50. Priority deadline 3/15. Regular application deadline 3/15. Nonfall registration accepted. Admission may be deferred.

COSTS AND FINANCIAL AID
Annual tuition $27,740. Room and board $10,265. Required fees $1,030. Average book expense $1,000. *Student Employment:* Federal Work-Study Program available. Institutional employment available.

CONCORDIA UNIVERSITY IRVINE

1530 Concordia West, Irvine, CA 92612-3299
Phone: 949-854-8002 • **Financial Aid Phone:** 949-854-8002
E-mail: admission@cui.edu
Fax: 949-854-6894 • **Website:** www.cui.edu • **ACT Code:** 227

This private school, affiliated with the Lutheran Church, was founded in 1976. It has a 70 acre campus.

RATINGS
Admissions Selectivity Rating: 82   **Fire Safety Rating:** 90   **Green Rating:** 60*

STUDENTS AND FACULTY
Enrollment: 1,203. **Student Body:** 61% female, 39% male, 17% out-of-state, 2% international (18 countries represented). Asian 4%, African American 4%, Caucasian 68%, Hispanic 13%, Native American 1%, Race unknown 7%. **Retention and Graduation:** 73% freshmen return for sophomore year. **Faculty:** Student/faculty ratio 14:1. 91 full-time faculty, 67% hold PhDs, 37% are women. 0% of classes are taught by teaching assistants.

ACADEMICS
Degrees: Associate; Bachelor's; Master's; Post-Bachelor's certificate **Classes:** Most classes have 20-29 students. Most lab/discussion sessions have 20-29 students. **Most popular majors:** Liberal Arts And Sciences/Liberal Studies; Psychology, General; Business/Commerce, General. **Special Study Options:** Accelerated program; Cross-registration; Distance learning; Double major; Dual enrollment; English as a Second Language (ESL); Exchange student program (domestic); Honors program; Independent study; Internships; Liberal arts/career combination; Student-designed major; Study abroad; Teacher certification program. **Honors programs:** General Education Honor Programs **Combined degree programs:** BA/MA. **Disability Services offered to physically disabled students:** Tutors.

FACILITIES
Housing: Men's dorms; Special housing for disabled student; Women's dorms 75% of campus accessible to physically disabled. **Special Academic Facilities/Equipment:** A hi-tech Educational/Business/Technology building, which was recently completed, houses also an art gallery. **Computers:** 60% of classrooms, 100% of dorms, 95% of libraries, 70% of dining areas, 100% of student union, 10% of common outdoor areas have wireless network access. Students can register for classes online.

CAMPUS LIFE
Environment: City **Activities:** Campus Ministries; Choral groups; Concert band; Dance; Drama/theater; Literary magazine; Music ensembles; Musical theater; Pep band; Radio station; Student government; Student newspaper; Student-run film society; Yearbook 18 registered organizations, 5 honor societies, 8 religious organizations. **Athletics (Intercollegiate):** *Men:* baseball, basketball, cross-country, golf, soccer, swimming, tennis, track/field (outdoor), water polo. *Women:* basketball, cross-country, golf, soccer, softball, swimming, tennis, track/field (outdoor), volleyball, water polo. **On-Campus Highlights:** The Gym, Student Life Center (Lounge and computer resource), Library, CU Center (Worship Center), Student Union (cafeteria)

ADMISSIONS

Freshman Academic Profile: Average high school GPA 3.5. 20% in top 10% of high school class, 54% in top 25% of high school class, 84% in top 50% of high school class. **Test Scores:** SAT Math middle 50% range 450-570. SAT EBRW middle 50% range 450-570. ACT middle 50% range 20-24. Minimum internet-based TOEFL 79-80. Minimum paper TOEFL 550. **Basis for Candidate Selection:** *Very important factors considered include:* rigor of secondary school record, class rank, academic GPA, standardized test scores, character/personal qualities. *Important factors considered include:* recommendation(s), religious affiliation/commitment. *Other factors considered include:* application essay, interview, extracurricular activities, talent/ability, alumni/ae relation, racial/ethnic status, volunteer work, work experience, level of applicant's interest. **Freshman Admission Requirements:** High school diploma is required and GED is accepted *Academic units required:* 4 English, 3 math, 3 science, 2 foreign language, 2 social studies. **Freshman Admission Statistics:** 897 applied, 65.6% admitted, 42% enrolled. **Transfer Admission Requirements:** High school transcript, college transcript(s), statement of good standing from prior institution(s). Minimum college GPA of 2.3 required. Lowest grade transferable D. **General Admission Information:** Application fee $50. Priority deadline 3/2. Nonfall registration accepted. Admission may be deferred for a maximum of 1 year.

COSTS AND FINANCIAL AID

Annual tuition $23,400. Room and board $7,650. Required fees $300. **Required Forms and Deadlines:** FAFSA; Institution's own financial aid form; State aid form. **Notification of Awards:** Applicants will be notified of awards on a rolling basis beginning 2/1. **Types of Aid:** *Need-based scholarships/grants:* College/university scholarship or grant aid from institutional funds; Federal Pell; Private scholarships; SEOG; State scholarships/grants. **Financial Aid Statistics:** 95% needy freshmen, 92% needy undergrads receive need-based scholarship or grant aid. 18% freshmen, 13% undergrads receive non-need-based scholarship or grant aid. 71% freshmen, 77% undergrads receive need-based self-help aid. 10% freshmen, 7% undergrads receive athletic scholarships. 74% freshmen, 71% undergrads receive any aid. **Criteria for awarding aid:** *Need-based:* Job skills *Non-need-based:* Academics, Art, Athletics, Leadership, Music/drama, Religious affiliation.

CONCORDIA UNIVERSITY, NEBRASKA

800 North Columbia Avenue, Seward, NE 68434-1556
Phone: 800-535-5494 · **Financial Aid Phone:** 800 535-5494
E-mail: admiss@cune.edu · **CEEB Code:** 6116
Fax: 402-643-4073 · **Website:** www.cune.edu · **ACT Code:** 2442

This private school, affiliated with the Lutheran Church, was founded in 1894. It has a 120 acre campus.

RATINGS

Admissions Selectivity Rating: 77　　**Fire Safety Rating:** 89　　**Green Rating:** 60*

STUDENTS AND FACULTY

Enrollment: 1,233. **Student Body:** 52% female, 48% male, 52% out-of-state, 2% international (9 countries represented). Asian 1%, African American 4%, Caucasian 78%, Hispanic 6%, Native American <1%, Pacific Islander <1%, Two or more races 1%, Race unknown 9%. **Retention and Graduation:** 74% freshmen return for sophomore year. 48% freshmen graduate within 4 years. 67% freshmen graduate within 6 years. 17% grads go on to further study within 1 year. 7% grads pursue arts and sciences degrees. 0.4% grads pursue law degrees. 0% grads pursue business degrees. 6% grads pursue medical degrees. **Faculty:** Student/faculty ratio 14:1. 61 full-time faculty, 77% hold PhDs, 3% are members of minority groups, 34% are women. 0% of classes are taught by teaching assistants.

ACADEMICS

Degrees: Bachelor's; Master's **Most popular majors:** Elementary Education And Teaching; Biology/Biological Sciences, General; Business/Commerce, General. **Special Study Options:** Accelerated program; Distance learning; Double major; Exchange student program (domestic); Independent study; Internships; Study abroad; Teacher certification program. **Disability Services offered to physically disabled students:** Note-taking services; Reader services; Tape recorders; Tutors. **Career services:** Alumni network; Alumni services; Career assessment; Career/job search classes; Internships; Regional alumni

FACILITIES

Housing: Apartments for married students; Apartments for single students; Men's dorms; Special housing for disabled student; Wellness housing; Women's dorms 75% of campus accessible to physically diasbled. **Special Academic**

Facilities/Equipment: Marxhausen Gallery of Art, Bartels Rock Museum, Osten Observatory, arboretum **Computers:** 40% of classrooms, 100% of dorms, 100% of libraries, 100% of student union, have wireless network access. Students can register for classes online. Administrative functions (other than registration) can be performed online.

CAMPUS LIFE

Environment: Village **Activities:** Campus Ministries; Choral groups; Concert band; Dance; Drama/theater; International Student Organization; Jazz band; Literary magazine; Music ensembles; Musical theater; Pep band; Student government; Student newspaper; Symphony orchestra; Yearbook 33 registered organizations, 1 honor society, 5 religious organizations. **Athletics (Intercollegiate):** *Men:* baseball, basketball, cross-country, football, golf, soccer, tennis, track/field (outdoor), track/field (indoor), wrestling. *Women:* basketball, cross-country, golf, soccer, softball, tennis, track/field (outdoor), track/field (indoor), volleyball. **On-Campus Highlights:** Student Center / Game Room, Coffee Shop, Marxhausen Art Gallery, Osten Observatory, Health, Human Performance & Athletic Center **Environmental Initiatives:** The committee is charged with outlining short-term and long-term plans that will render the university carbon neutral as soon as is feasible and to report progress periodically. Specific plans have not yet been formulated.

ADMISSIONS

Freshman Academic Profile: Average high school GPA 3.5. 18% in top 10% of high school class, 43% in top 25% of high school class, 72% in top 50% of high school class. **Test Scores:** SAT Math middle 50% range 440-550. SAT EBRW middle 50% range 480-550. ACT middle 50% range 21-26. **Basis for Candidate Selection:** *Very important factors considered include:* academic GPA, standardized test scores. *Important factors considered include:* rigor of secondary school record, class rank, character/personal qualities. *Other factors considered include:* application essay, recommendation(s), interview, extracurricular activities, alumni/ae relation, religious affiliation/commitment. **Freshman Admission Requirements:** High school diploma is required and GED is accepted *Academic units recommended:* 4 English, 3 math, 2 science, 1 foreign language, 3 social studies, 3 units from above areas or other academic areas. **Freshman Admission Statistics:** 1,537 applied, 75.0% admitted, 30% enrolled. **Transfer Admission Requirements:** High school transcript, college transcript(s), Minimum college GPA of 2.0 required. Lowest grade transferable D. **General Admission Information:** Priority deadline 7/1. Regular application deadline 8/1. Nonfall registration accepted. Admission may be deferred for a maximum of 1 year.

COSTS AND FINANCIAL AID

Annual tuition $31,620. Room and board $8,470. Required fees $600. Average book expense $1,000. **Required Forms and Deadlines:** FAFSA. **Notification of Awards:** Applicants will be notified of awards on a rolling basis beginning 3/1. **Types of Aid:** *Need-based scholarships/grants:* College/university scholarship or grant aid from institutional funds; Federal Pell; Private scholarships; SEOG; State scholarships/grants. *Loans:* Direct PLUS loans; Direct Subsidized Stafford Loans; Direct Unsubsidized Stafford Loans. *Student Employment:* Federal Work-Study Program available. Institutional employment available. **Financial Aid Statistics:** 100% needy freshmen, 100% needy undergrads receive need-based scholarship or grant aid. 27% freshmen, 21% undergrads receive non-need-based scholarship or grant aid. 64% freshmen, 69% undergrads receive need-based self-help aid. 14% freshmen, 14% undergrads receive athletic scholarships. 100% freshmen, 99% undergrads receive any aid. 73% undergrads borrow to pay for school. Average cumulative indebtedness $26,328. **Criteria for awarding aid:** *Need-based:* Minority status *Non-need-based:* Academics, Alumni affiliation, Art, Athletics, Leadership, Music/drama, Religious affiliation.

CONCORDIA UNIVERSITY (OR)

2811 NE Holman, Portland, OR 97211-6099
Phone: 503-280-8501 · **Financial Aid Phone:** 800-321-9371
E-mail: admissions@cu-portland.edu · **CEEB Code:** 4078
Fax: 503-280-8531 · **Website:** www.cu-portland.edu · **ACT Code:** 3458

This private school, affiliated with the Lutheran Church, was founded in 1905. It has a 12 acre campus.

RATINGS

Admissions Selectivity Rating: 83　　**Fire Safety Rating:** 60*　　**Green Rating:** 60*

STUDENTS AND FACULTY

Enrollment: 1,073. **Student Body:** 64% female, 36% male, 41% out-of-state, 1% international. Asian 6%, African American 7%, Caucasian 65%, Hispanic 6%, Native American 1%, Race unknown 14%.

Retention and Graduation: 74% freshmen return for sophomore year. **Faculty:** Student/faculty ratio 18:1. 52 full-time faculty, 67% hold PhDs, 4% are members of minority groups, 48% are women. 0% of classes are taught by teaching assistants.

ACADEMICS

Degrees: Bachelor's; Certificate; Master's; Post-Bachelor's certificate; Terminal Associate **Classes:** Most classes have 10-19 students. **Special Study Options:** Accelerated program; Cross-registration; Distance learning; Dual enrollment; English as a Second Language (ESL); Honors program; Independent study; Internships; Study abroad; Teacher certification program. **Honors programs:** Honors program features limited enrollment to 25 students create greater intellectual opportunity. **Career services:** Alumni services; Career assessment; Internships; Regional alumni

FACILITIES

Housing: Apartments for single students; Coed dorms **Computers:** Administrative functions (other than registration) can be performed online.

CAMPUS LIFE

Environment: Metropolis **Activities:** Campus Ministries; Choral groups; Drama/theater; International Student Organization; Literary magazine; Music ensembles; Student government; Student newspaper 10 registered organizations, 2 honor societies, 1 religious organization. **Athletics (Intercollegiate):** *Men:* baseball, basketball, cross-country, golf, soccer, track/field (outdoor), track/field (indoor). *Women:* basketball, cross-country, golf, soccer, softball, track/field (outdoor), track/field (indoor), volleyball.

ADMISSIONS

Freshman Academic Profile: Average high school GPA 3.4. 19% in top 10% of high school class, 45% in top 25% of high school class, 76% in top 50% of high school class. **Test Scores:** SAT Math middle 50% range 460-560. SAT EBRW middle 50% range 450-570. ACT middle 50% range 18-24. Minimum paper TOEFL 500. **Basis for Candidate Selection:** *Very important factors considered include:* rigor of secondary school record, standardized test scores, recommendation(s). *Other factors considered include:* class rank, academic GPA, application essay, interview, character/personal qualities. **Freshman Admission Requirements:** High school diploma is required and GED is accepted *Academic units recommended:* 4 English, 3 math, 3 science, 2 foreign language, 3 social studies, 3 academic electives, 1 unit from above areas or other academic areas. **Freshman Admission Statistics:** 1,002 applied, 59.5% admitted, 32% enrolled. **Transfer Admission Requirements:** college transcript(s), statement of good standing from prior institution(s). Minimum college GPA of 2.0 required. Lowest grade transferable D. **General Admission Information:** Application fee $20. Priority deadline 3/1. Regular application deadline 7/1. Nonfall registration accepted. Admission may be deferred.

COSTS AND FINANCIAL AID

Annual tuition $20,900. Room and board $6,270. Required fees $210. Average book expense $800. **Required Forms and Deadlines:** FAFSA. **Notification of Awards:** Applicants will be notified of awards on a rolling basis beginning 3/15. **Types of Aid:** *Need-based scholarships/grants:* College/university scholarship or grant aid from institutional funds; Federal Pell; SEOG; State scholarships/grants. *Loans: Student Employment:* Federal Work-Study Program available. Institutional employment available. **Financial Aid Statistics:** 83% needy freshmen, 81% needy undergrads receive need-based scholarship or grant aid. 91% freshmen, 88% undergrads receive non-need-based scholarship or grant aid. 77% freshmen, 78% undergrads receive need-based self-help aid. 28% freshmen, 27% undergrads receive athletic scholarships. 95% freshmen receive any aid. **Criteria for awarding aid:** *Need-based:* Academics *Non-need-based:* Academics, Athletics, Leadership, Music/drama, Religious affiliation.

CONCORDIA UNIVERSITY—ST PAUL

1282 Concordia Avenue, St. Paul, MN 55104-5494
Phone: 651-641-8230 · **Financial Aid Phone:** 651-603-6300
E-mail: admission@csp.edu · **CEEB Code:** 6114
Fax: 651-603-6320 · **Website:** www.csp.edu · **ACT Code:** 2106

This private school, affiliated with the Lutheran Church, was founded in 1893. It has a 37 acre campus.

RATINGS

Admissions Selectivity Rating: 82   **Fire Safety Rating:** 91   **Green Rating:** 60*

STUDENTS AND FACULTY

Enrollment: 2,556. **Student Body:** 58% female, 42% male, 26% out-of-state, 4% international (12 countries represented). Asian 8%, African American 12%, Caucasian 64%, Hispanic 5%, Native American <1%, Pacific Islander <1%, Two or more races 4%, Race unknown 3%.
Retention and Graduation: 65% freshmen return for sophomore year. 42% freshmen graduate within 4 years. 55% freshmen graduate within 6 years. 10% grads go on to further study within 1 year. **Faculty:** Student/faculty ratio 18:1. 96 full-time faculty, 77% hold PhDs, 8% are members of minority groups, 58% are women. 0% of classes are taught by teaching assistants.

ACADEMICS

Degrees: Associate; Bachelor's; Certificate; Doctoral Other; Doctoral/Professional; Master's; Post-Bachelor's certificate; Post-Master's certificate **Classes:** Most classes have 10-19 students. Most lab/discussion sessions have fewer than 10 students. **Most popular majors:** Education, Other; Kinesiology And Exercise Science; Business/Commerce, General. **Special Study Options:** Accelerated program; Cross-registration; Distance learning; Double major; Dual enrollment; Honors program; Independent study; Internships; Student-designed major; Study abroad; Teacher certification program. **Combined degree programs:** BA/MA. **Disability Services offered to physically disabled students:** Note-taking services; Reader services; Tape recorders; Tutors. **Career services:** Career assessment; Career/job search classes; Internships

FACILITIES

Housing: Apartments for married students; Apartments for single students; Coed dorms; Men's dorms; Women's dorms 90% of campus accessible to physically disabled. **Computers:** Students can register for classes online. Administrative functions (other than registration) can be performed online.

CAMPUS LIFE

Environment: Metropolis **Activities:** Campus Ministries; Choral groups; Concert band; Dance; Drama/theater; International Student Organization; Jazz band; Music ensembles; Musical theater; Pep band; Student government; Student newspaper. **Athletics (Intercollegiate):** *Men:* baseball, basketball, cross-country, football, golf, track/field (outdoor), track/field (indoor). *Women:* basketball, cross-country, golf, soccer, softball, track/field (outdoor), track/field (indoor), volleyball. **On-Campus Highlights:** Residence Life Center, Library Technology Center, Pearson Commons, Gangelhoff Athletic Center, Graebner Memorial Chapel

ADMISSIONS

Freshman Academic Profile: Average high school GPA 3.2. 92% from public high schools. ACT middle 50% range 18-24. Minimum internet-based TOEFL 65. Minimum paper TOEFL 513. **Basis for Candidate Selection:** *Very important factors considered include:* academic GPA, standardized test scores. *Important factors considered include:* rigor of secondary school record. *Other factors considered include:* class rank, application essay, recommendation(s), extracurricular activities, talent/ability, volunteer work, work experience, level of applicant's interest. **Freshman Admission Requirements:** High school diploma is required and GED is accepted *Academic units required:* 4 English, 2 math, 2 science, 2 science labs, 2 social studies, 2 history, 2 visual/performing arts, and 1 unit from above areas or other academic areas. *Academic units recommended:* 4 English, 3 math, 3 science, 1 foreign language, 2 social studies, 2 history, 2 visual/performing arts, 1 unit from above areas or other academic areas. **Freshman Admission Statistics:** 1,500 applied, 54.9% admitted, 30% enrolled. **Transfer Admission Requirements:** college transcript(s), statement of good standing from prior institution(s). Minimum college GPA of 2.0 required. Lowest grade transferable D. **General Admission Information:** Priority deadline 12/1. Regular application deadline 8/1. Nonfall registration accepted. Admission may be deferred for a maximum of 1 year.

COSTS AND FINANCIAL AID

Annual tuition $22,275. Room and board $9,000. Average book expense $2,000. **Required Forms and Deadlines:** FAFSA; State aid form. **Notification of Awards:** Applicants will be notified of awards on a rolling basis beginning 3/1. **Types of Aid:** *Need-based scholarships/grants:* College/university scholarship or grant aid from institutional funds; Federal Pell; Private scholarships; SEOG; State scholarships/grants. *Loans:* Direct PLUS loans; Direct Subsidized Stafford Loans; Direct Unsubsidized Stafford Loans. *Student Employment:* Federal Work-Study Program available. Institutional employment available. **Financial Aid Statistics:** 99% needy freshmen, 72% needy undergrads receive need-based scholarship or grant aid. 7% freshmen, 8% undergrads receive non-need-based scholarship or grant aid. 73% freshmen, 73% undergrads receive need-based self-help aid. 9% freshmen, 7% undergrads receive athletic scholarships. 92% freshmen, 73% undergrads receive any aid. 80% undergrads borrow to pay for school. Average cumulative indebtedness $33,183. **Criteria for awarding aid:** *Need-based:* Academics, Art, Athletics, Leadership, Music/drama, Religious affiliation *Non-need-based:* Academics, Art, Athletics, Music/drama, Religious affiliation.

CONCORDIA UNIVERSITY WISCONSIN

12800 North Lake Shore Drive, Mequon, WI 53097-2418
Phone: 262-243-5700 · **Financial Aid Phone:** (262) 243-4392
E-mail: admissions@cuw.edu · **CEEB Code:** 1139
Fax: (262) 243-4545 · **Website:** www.cuw.edu · **ACT Code:** 4574

This private school, affiliated with the Lutheran Church, was founded in 1881. It has a 192 acre campus.

RATINGS
Admissions Selectivity Rating: 74   **Fire Safety Rating:** 60*   **Green Rating:** 60*

STUDENTS AND FACULTY
Enrollment: 4,326. **Student Body:** 65% female, 35% male, 20% out-of-state, 1% international (23 countries represented). Asian 2%, African American 18%, Caucasian 67%, Hispanic 2%, Native American 1%, Pacific Islander <1%, Two or more races 2%, Race unknown 6%.
Retention and Graduation: 74% freshmen return for sophomore year. 28% grads go on to further study within 1 year. **Faculty:** Student/faculty ratio 14:1. 162 full-time faculty, 77% hold PhDs, 6% are members of minority groups, 49% are women. 0% of classes are taught by teaching assistants.

ACADEMICS
Degrees: Associate; Bachelor's; Certificate; Doctoral; Doctoral/Professional; Master's; Post-Master's certificate **Classes:** Most classes have fewer than 10 students. Most lab/discussion sessions have fewer than 10 students. **Most popular majors:** Education, General; Health Services/Allied Health/Health Sciences, General. **Special Study Options:** Accelerated program; Cross-registration; Distance learning; Double major; Dual enrollment; English as a Second Language (ESL); Exchange student program (domestic); Independent study; Internships; Liberal arts/career combination; Student-designed major; Study abroad; Teacher certification program. **Disability Services offered to physically disabled students:** Note-taking services; Reader services; Tape recorders; Tutors. **Career services:** Alumni network; Alumni services; Career assessment; Career/job search classes; Internships; Regional alumni

FACILITIES
Housing: Men's dorms; Women's dorms

CAMPUS LIFE
Environment: Village **Activities:** Campus Ministries; Choral groups; Concert band; Dance; Drama/theater; International Student Organization; Jazz band; Music ensembles; Musical theater; Pep band; Radio station; Student government; Student newspaper. **Athletics (Intercollegiate):** *Men:* baseball, basketball, cross-country, football, ice hockey, soccer, tennis, track/field (outdoor), volleyball, wrestling. *Women:* basketball, cross-country, ice hockey, soccer, softball, tennis, track/field (outdoor), volleyball. **On-Campus Highlights:** Coberg Residence Hall—new, Sports and Fitness Center, Field House, Books, Bagels, Altera Coffee—Rincker Library, Rincker Memorial Library—Group study area **Environmental Initiatives:** Construction of environmental education center with LEED status

ADMISSIONS
Freshman Academic Profile: Average high school GPA 3.3. 16% in top 10% of high school class, 40% in top 25% of high school class, 75% in top 50% of high school class. **Test Scores:** SAT Math middle 50% range 453-600. SAT EBRW middle 50% range 450-530. ACT middle 50% range 20-25. Minimum paper TOEFL 500. **Basis for Candidate Selection:** *Very important factors considered include:* rigor of secondary school record, academic GPA, application essay. *Important factors considered include:* standardized test scores, character/personal qualities, work experience. *Other factors considered include:* class rank, recommendation(s), interview, extracurricular activities, talent/ability, alumni/ae relation, state residency, religious affiliation/commitment, racial/ethnic status, volunteer work. **Freshman Admission Requirements:** High school diploma is required and GED is accepted *Academic units required:* 3 English, 2 math, 2 science, 2 social studies, 5 academic electives, *Academic units recommended:* 4 English, 3 math, 2 foreign language, 5 academic electives. **Freshman Admission Statistics:** 2,517 applied, 70.2% admitted, enrolled. **Transfer Admission Requirements:** college transcript(s), statement of good standing from prior institution(s). Minimum college GPA of 2.0 required. Lowest grade transferable C. **General Admission Information:** Application fee $35. Regular application deadline 8/15.

COSTS AND FINANCIAL AID
Required Forms and Deadlines: FAFSA. **Notification of Awards:** Applicants will be notified of awards on a rolling basis beginning 2/1. **Types of Aid:** *Need-based scholarships/grants:* College/university scholarship or grant aid from institutional funds; Federal Pell; Private scholarships; SEOG; State scholarships/grants. *Loans:* Direct PLUS loans; Direct Subsidized Stafford

Loans; Direct Unsubsidized Stafford Loans. **Financial Aid Statistics:** 97% needy freshmen, 93% needy undergrads receive need-based scholarship or grant aid. 22% freshmen, 16% undergrads receive non-need-based scholarship or grant aid. 82% freshmen, 84% undergrads receive need-based self-help aid. 0% freshmen, 0% undergrads receive athletic scholarships. 95% freshmen receive any aid. **Criteria for awarding aid:** *Need-based:* Academics *Non-need-based:* Academics, Art, Minority status, Music/drama.

CONNECTICUT COLLEGE

270 Mohegan Avenue, New London, CT 06320
Phone: 860-439-2200 · **Financial Aid Phone:** 860-439-2058
E-mail: admission@conncoll.edu · **CEEB Code:** 3284
Fax: 860-439-4301 · **Website:** www.conncoll.edu · **ACT Code:** 556

This private school was founded in 1911. It has a 750 acre campus.

RATINGS
Admissions Selectivity Rating: 92   **Fire Safety Rating:** 62   **Green Rating:** 89

STUDENTS AND FACULTY
Enrollment: 1,766. **Student Body:** 63% female, 37% male, 82% out-of-state, 8% international (43 countries represented). Asian 4%, African American 4%, Caucasian 71%, Hispanic 8%, Native American <1%, Pacific Islander <1%, Two or more races 3%, Race unknown 1%.
Retention and Graduation: 91% freshmen return for sophomore year. 80% freshmen graduate within 4 years. 85% freshmen graduate within 6 years. 14% grads go on to further study within 1 year. **Faculty:** Student/faculty ratio 9:1. 182 full-time faculty, 93% hold PhDs, 20% are members of minority groups, 52% are women. 0% of classes are taught by teaching assistants.

ACADEMICS
Degrees: Bachelor's **Classes:** Most classes have 10-19 students. Most lab/discussion sessions have 10-19 students. **Most popular majors:** Biology/Biological Sciences, General; Psychology, General; Economics, General. **Special Study Options:** Accelerated program; Cross-registration; Double major; Exchange student program (domestic); Independent study; Internships; Student-designed major; Study abroad; Teacher certification program. **Combined degree programs:** BA/MA. **Disability Services offered to physically disabled students:** Note-taking services; Reader services; Tape recorders; Tutors. **Career services:** Alumni network; Alumni services; Career assessment; Career/job search classes; Internships; Regional alumni

FACILITIES
Housing: Apartments for single students; Coed dorms; Theme housing; Wellness housing **Special Academic Facilities/Equipment:** Fully renovated life sciences building and main college library, Children's Program used as "lab school" for human development program, language lab, 750-acre arboretum, botanical garden, greenhouse, environment control labs, transmission and scanning electron microscope, ion accelerator, GIS lab, refracting telescope, observatory. **Computers:** 75% of classrooms, 100% of dorms, 100% of libraries, 100% of dining areas, 100% of student union, 70% of common outdoor areas have wireless network access. Students can register for classes online. Administrative functions (other than registration) can be performed online.

CAMPUS LIFE
Environment: Town **Activities:** Campus Ministries; Choral groups; Concert band; Dance; Drama/theater; International Student Organization; Jazz band; Literary magazine; Model UN; Music ensembles; Musical theater; Radio station; Student government; Student newspaper; Student-run film society; Symphony orchestra 60 registered organizations, 5 honor societies, 6 religious organizations. **Athletics (Intercollegiate):** *Men:* basketball, crew/rowing, cross-country, diving, ice hockey, lacrosse, sailing, soccer, squash, swimming, tennis, track/field (outdoor), track/field (indoor), water polo. *Women:* basketball, crew/rowing, cross-country, diving, field hockey, ice hockey, lacrosse, sailing, soccer, squash, swimming, tennis, track/field (outdoor), track/field (indoor), volleyball, water polo. **On-Campus Highlights:** College Center (Crozier-Williams), Connecticut College Arboretum, Blue Camel Cafe (in library), Athletics Center, New London Hall

ADMISSIONS
Freshman Academic Profile: 44% in top 10% of high school class, 78% in top 25% of high school class, 96% in top 50% of high school class. 50% from public high schools. **Test Scores:** SAT Math middle 50% range 630-690. SAT

EBRW middle 50% range 640-710. ACT middle 50% range 29-31. **Basis for Candidate Selection:** *Very important factors considered include:* rigor of secondary school record, class rank, academic GPA, character/personal qualities. *Important factors considered include:* application essay, recommendation(s), interview, extracurricular activities, talent/ability, racial/ethnic status, volunteer work, work experience. *Other factors considered include:* standardized test scores, first generation, alumni/ae relation, geographical residence, state residency, religious affiliation/commitment, level of applicant's interest. **Freshman Admission Requirements:** High school diploma is required and GED is accepted **Freshman Admission Statistics:** 5,434 applied, 38.0% admitted, 22% enrolled. **Transfer Admission Requirements:** High school transcript, college transcript(s), essay or personal statement, statement of good standing from prior institution(s). Lowest grade transferable C. **General Admission Information:** Regular application deadline 1/1. Nonfall registration accepted. Admission may be deferred for a maximum of 1 year.

COSTS AND FINANCIAL AID
Required Forms and Deadlines: CSS/Financial Aid PROFILE; FAFSA; Noncustodial PROFILE. **Notification of Awards:** Applicants will be notified of awards on or about 4/1. **Types of Aid:** *Need-based scholarships/grants:* College/university scholarship or grant aid from institutional funds; Federal Pell; SEOG; State scholarships/grants. *Loans:* Direct PLUS loans; Direct Subsidized Stafford Loans; Direct Unsubsidized Stafford Loans. *Student Employment:* Federal Work-Study Program available. Institutional employment available. **Financial Aid Statistics:** 96% needy freshmen, 94% needy undergrads receive need-based scholarship or grant aid. 0% undergrads receive non-need-based scholarship or grant aid. 89% freshmen, 90% undergrads receive need-based self-help aid. 0% freshmen, 0% undergrads receive athletic scholarships. 59% freshmen, 54% undergrads receive any aid. 49% undergrads borrow to pay for school. Average cumulative indebtedness $27,514. **Criteria for awarding aid:** *Need-based:* Academics, Alumni affiliation, Art, Athletics, Job skills, Leadership, Minority status, Music/drama, Religious affiliation.

CONVERSE COLLEGE

580 East Main Street, Spartanburg, SC 29302
Phone: 864-596-9040 · **Financial Aid Phone:** 864-596-9019
E-mail: admissions@converse.edu · **CEEB Code:** 5121
Fax: 864-596-9225 · **Website:** www.converse.edu · **ACT Code:** 3852

This private school was founded in 1889. It has a 70 acre campus.

RATINGS
Admissions Selectivity Rating: 85   **Fire Safety Rating:** 79   **Green Rating:** 61

STUDENTS AND FACULTY
Enrollment: 687. **Student Body:** 100% female, 0% male, 23% out-of-state, 1% international. Asian 1%, African American 8%, Caucasian 46%, Hispanic 3%, Native American <1%, Pacific Islander <1%, Two or more races 3%, Race unknown 39%.
Retention and Graduation: 76% freshmen return for sophomore year. 37% grads go on to further study within 1 year. **Faculty:** Student/faculty ratio 11:1. 76 full-time faculty, 91% hold PhDs, 7% are members of minority groups, 59% are women. 0% of classes are taught by teaching assistants.

ACADEMICS
Degrees: Bachelor's; Master's; Post-Master's certificate **Classes:** Most classes have 10-19 students. Most lab/discussion sessions have 10-19 students. **Most popular majors:** Education, General; Biology, General; Psychology, General. **Special Study Options:** Cross-registration; Double major; English as a Second Language (ESL); Honors program; Independent study; Internships; Liberal arts/career combination; Student-designed major; Study abroad; Teacher certification program. **Honors programs:** Nisbet Honors Program. **Disability Services offered to physically disabled students:** Note-taking services; Tape recorders; Tutors. **Career services:** Alumni network; Alumni services; Career assessment; Career/job search classes; Internships; Regional alumni

FACILITIES
Housing: Apartments for single students; Wellness housing; Women's dorms **Special Academic Facilities/Equipment:** Phifer Science Building, Blackman Auditorium (Music), DNA sequencer and lab. Twitchel Auditorium(Performing Arts) **Computers:** Students can register for classes online. Administrative functions (other than registration) can be performed online.

CAMPUS LIFE
Environment: City **Activities:** Campus Ministries; Choral groups; Concert band; Dance; Drama/theater; International Student Organization; Literary magazine; Model UN; Music ensembles; Musical theater; Opera; Student government; Student newspaper; Symphony orchestra; Yearbook 60 registered

organizations, 16 honor societies, 7 religious organizations. **Athletics (Intercollegiate):** *Women:* basketball, cross-country, lacrosse, soccer, swimming, tennis, volleyball. **On-Campus Highlights:** Montgomery Student Life Center, Weisiger Physical Activity Complex, Phifer Science Complex, Petrie School of Music- Twichell Auditorium, Outdoor Quad area for studying and relaxing **Environmental Initiatives:** LEED Certified new construction

ADMISSIONS
Freshman Academic Profile: 18% in top 10% of high school class, 43% in top 25% of high school class, 80% in top 50% of high school class. 80% from public high schools. **Test Scores:** SAT Math middle 50% range 460-570. SAT EBRW middle 50% range 470-600. ACT middle 50% range 20-26. Minimum internet-based TOEFL 79. Minimum paper TOEFL 550. **Basis for Candidate Selection:** *Very important factors considered include:* academic GPA, standardized test scores. *Important factors considered include:* rigor of secondary school record, class rank. *Other factors considered include:* application essay, recommendation(s), talent/ability, alumni/ae relation. **Freshman Admission Requirements:** High school diploma is required and GED is accepted *Academic units recommended:* 4 English, 3 math, 3 science, 1 science labs, 2 foreign language, 2 social studies, 2 history, 8 academic electives. **Freshman Admission Statistics:** 1,383 applied, 51.3% admitted, 26% enrolled. **Transfer Admission Requirements:** college transcript(s), statement of good standing from prior institution(s). Minimum college GPA of 2.0 required. Lowest grade transferable C. **General Admission Information:** Priority deadline 3/1. Nonfall registration accepted. Admission may be deferred for a maximum of 1 year.

COSTS AND FINANCIAL AID
Annual tuition $27,276. Room and board $8,854. Required fees $1,000. Average book expense $1,000. **Required Forms and Deadlines:** FAFSA. **Notification of Awards:** Applicants will be notified of awards on a rolling basis beginning 3/1. **Types of Aid:** *Need-based scholarships/grants:* College/university scholarship or grant aid from institutional funds; Federal Pell; Private scholarships; SEOG; State scholarships/grants. *Loans:* Direct PLUS loans; Direct Subsidized Stafford Loans; Direct Unsubsidized Stafford Loans. *Student Employment:* Federal Work-Study Program available. Institutional employment available. **Financial Aid Statistics:** 100% needy freshmen, 98% needy undergrads receive need-based scholarship or grant aid. 18% freshmen, 17% undergrads receive non-need-based scholarship or grant aid. 79% freshmen, 77% undergrads receive need-based self-help aid. 14% freshmen, 8% undergrads receive athletic scholarships. 95% freshmen, 93% undergrads receive any aid. **Criteria for awarding aid:** *Need-based:* Academics, Art, Athletics, Music/drama *Non-need-based:* Academics, Art, Athletics, Music/drama.

THE COOPER UNION FOR THE ADVANCEMENT OF SCIENCE AND ART

Best Colleges

30 Cooper Square, New York, NY 10003
Phone: 212-353-4120 · **Financial Aid Phone:** 212-353-4113
E-mail: admissions@cooper.edu · **CEEB Code:** 2097
Fax: 212-353-4342 · **Website:** cooper.edu · **ACT Code:** 2724

This private school was founded in 1859.

RATINGS
Admissions Selectivity Rating: 98   **Fire Safety Rating:** 97   **Green Rating:** 60*

STUDENTS AND FACULTY
Enrollment: 853. **Student Body:** 34% female, 66% male, 50% out-of-state, 19% international. Asian 20%, African American 3%, Caucasian 31%, Hispanic 10%, Native American 0%, Pacific Islander 0%, Two or more races 8%, Race unknown 10%.
Retention and Graduation: 95% freshmen return for sophomore year. 62% freshmen graduate within 4 years. 83% freshmen graduate within 6 years. 45% grads go on to further study within 1 year. 4% grads pursue arts and sciences degrees. 0% grads pursue law degrees. 1% grads pursue business degrees. 0% grads pursue medical degrees. **Faculty:** Student/faculty ratio 8:1. 57 full-time faculty, 75% hold PhDs, 18% are members of minority groups, 28% are women. 0% of classes are taught by teaching assistants.

ACADEMICS
Degrees: Bachelor's; Certificate; Master's **Most popular majors:** Electrical And Electronics Engineering; Mechanical Engineering; Fine And Studio Arts.

Special Study Options: Accelerated program; Cross-registration; Exchange student program (domestic); Independent study; Internships; Student-designed major; Study abroad. **Honors programs:** Cooper Union is in essence an all-honors college. **Disability Services offered to physically disabled students:** Reader services; Tape recorders; Tutors. **Career services:** Alumni network; Alumni services; Career assessment; Career/job search classes; Internships; Regional alumni

FACILITIES

Housing: Coed dorms; Other (please specify) 75% of campus accessible to physically disabled. **Special Academic Facilities/Equipment:** The Great Hall; Houghton Gallery; Institute for Sustainable Design; Center for Innovation and Applied Technology; SEA²M³; S°PROCOM²; Center for Urban Infrastructure; Institute for Urban Security; Maurice Kanbar Center for Biomedical Engineering **Computers:** 85% of classrooms, have wireless network access. Administrative functions (other than registration) can be performed online.

CAMPUS LIFE

Environment: Metropolis **Activities:** Choral groups; Concert band; Dance; Drama/theater; International Student Organization; Jazz band; Music ensembles; Musical theater; Student government; Student newspaper; Student-run film society; Symphony orchestra; Yearbook 90 registered organizations, 18 honor societies, 8 religious organizations. 2 fraternities, 1 sorority. **Athletics (Intercollegiate): Men:** baseball, basketball, cross-country, soccer, tennis, volleyball. **Women:** basketball, cross-country, soccer, tennis, volleyball. **On-Campus Highlights:** Great Hall, 41 Cooper Square, Foundation Building, Houghton and 41 Cooper Square Gallery, Frankie's Kitchen **Environmental Initiatives:** 41 Cooper Square Building please see: cooper.edu

ADMISSIONS

Freshman Academic Profile: Average high school GPA 3.6. 51% in top 10% of high school class, 85% in top 25% of high school class, 99% in top 50% of high school class. 65% from public high schools. **Test Scores:** SAT Math middle 50% range 660-790. SAT EBRW middle 50% range 650-740. ACT middle 50% range 28-34. Minimum internet-based TOEFL 100. Minimum paper TOEFL 600. **Basis for Candidate Selection:** *Very important factors considered include:* rigor of secondary school record, academic GPA, standardized test scores, recommendation(s), talent/ability, level of applicant's interest. *Important factors considered include:* application essay, interview, extracurricular activities, character/personal qualities. *Other factors considered include:* class rank, first generation, racial/ethnic status, volunteer work, work experience. **Freshman Admission Requirements:** High school diploma is required and GED is accepted *Academic units required:* 4 English, 1 math, 1 science, 1 social studies, 1 history, 8 academic electives, *Academic units recommended:* 4 English, 4 math, 4 science, 3 science labs, 2 foreign language, 4 social studies. **Freshman Admission Statistics:** 2,574 applied, 13.1% admitted, 61% enrolled. **Transfer Admission Requirements:** High school transcript, college transcript(s), essay or personal statement, standardized test scores, statement of good standing from prior institution(s). Minimum college GPA of 3.0 required. Lowest grade transferable B. **General Admission Information:** Application fee $75. Priority deadline 12/1. Regular application deadline 1/9. Nonfall registration accepted. Admission may be deferred for a maximum of 1 year.

COSTS AND FINANCIAL AID

Annual tuition $44,550. Room and board $16,638. Required fees $2,150. Average book expense $1,650. **Required Forms and Deadlines:** FAFSA. **Notification of Awards:** Applicants will be notified of awards on a rolling basis beginning 12/20. **Types of Aid:** *Need-based scholarships/grants:* College/university scholarship or grant aid from institutional funds; Federal Pell; Private scholarships; SEOG; State scholarships/grants. *Loans:* Direct PLUS loans; Direct Subsidized Stafford Loans; Direct Unsubsidized Stafford Loans. *Student Employment:* Federal Work-Study Program available. Institutional employment available. **Financial Aid Statistics:** 84% needy freshmen, 100% needy undergrads receive need-based scholarship or grant aid. 100% freshmen, 100% undergrads receive non-need-based scholarship or grant aid. 39% freshmen, 37% undergrads receive need-based self-help aid. 0% freshmen, 0% undergrads receive athletic scholarships. 100% freshmen, 100% undergrads receive any aid. 22% undergrads borrow to pay for school. Average cumulative indebtedness $21,919. **Criteria for awarding aid:** *Need-based:* Academics *Non-need-based:* Academics.

CORBAN COLLEGE

5000 Deer Park Drive SE, Salem, OR 97317
Phone: 503-375-7005 · **Financial Aid Phone:** 503-375-7030
E-mail: admissions@corban.edu
Fax: 503-585-4316 · **Website:** www.corban.edu · **ACT Code:** 477

This private school, affiliated with the Evangelical Church, was founded in 1935. It has a 145 acre campus.

RATINGS

Admissions Selectivity Rating: 87   **Fire Safety Rating:** 85   **Green Rating:** 60*

STUDENTS AND FACULTY

Enrollment: 933. **Student Body:** 60% female, 40% male, 50% out-of-state, 2% international (7 countries represented). Asian 3%, African American 1%, Caucasian 78%, Hispanic 3%, Native American 1%, Pacific Islander 1%, Two or more races 6%, Race unknown 6%. **Retention and Graduation:** 77% freshmen return for sophomore year. **Faculty:** Student/faculty ratio 14:1. 49 full-time faculty, 73% hold PhDs, 22% are women. 0% of classes are taught by teaching assistants.

ACADEMICS

Degrees: Associate; Bachelor's; Doctoral Other; Master's **Most popular majors:** Education, General; Pre-Medicine/Pre-Medical Studies; Business Administration And Management, General. **Special Study Options:** Accelerated program; Cross-registration; Distance learning; Double major; Dual enrollment; Honors program; Independent study; Internships; Liberal arts/career combination; Study abroad; Teacher certification program. **Honors programs:** In keeping with the broad educational mission of Corban University, the Honors Program is rooted in the notion that we may glorify God through our intellectual endeavors. The program provides highly motivated students with academic enrichment above and beyond the regular undergraduate curriculum, encouraging a more proficient understanding of and appreciation for the Christian worldview through the lens of classical studies, especially history, literature, philosophy, and the arts. Honors students are given the opportunity to interact with distinguished scholars at special events and to participate in at least three Honors courses while at Corban. They also may choose to work with a faculty member on a senior project. **Combined degree programs:** BA/MA. **Disability Services offered to physically disabled students:** Note-taking services; Reader services; Tape recorders; Tutors. **Career services:** Career assessment; Career/job search classes; Internships

FACILITIES

Housing: Apartments for single students; Men's dorms; Women's dorms 80% of campus accessible to physically disabled. **Special Academic Facilities/Equipment:** Prewitt-Allen Archeological Museum Psalms Performing Arts Center **Computers:** Students can register for classes online.

CAMPUS LIFE

Environment: City **Activities:** Campus Ministries; Choral groups; Concert band; Drama/theater; Jazz band; Literary magazine; Music ensembles; Musical theater; Radio station; Student government; Student newspaper; Student-run film society; Symphony orchestra; Yearbook 1 honor societies, 10 religious organizations. **Athletics (Intercollegiate): Men:** baseball, basketball, cross-country, golf, soccer, track/field (outdoor). **Women:** basketball, cross-country, golf, soccer, softball, track/field (outdoor), volleyball. **On-Campus Highlights:** Common Grounds Coffee Shop, Dining Hall, Gymnasium and Athletic Fields, Computer Lab, Book Store

ADMISSIONS

Freshman Academic Profile: Average high school GPA 3.6. 26% in top 10% of high school class, 58% in top 25% of high school class, 88% in top 50% of high school class. 60% from public high schools. **Test Scores:** SAT Math middle 50% range 440-560. SAT EBRW middle 50% range 455-580. ACT middle 50% range 18-25. Minimum paper TOEFL 500. **Basis for Candidate Selection:** *Very important factors considered include:* academic GPA, application essay, recommendation(s), religious affiliation/commitment. *Important factors considered include:* rigor of secondary school record, standardized test scores, character/personal qualities, level of applicant's interest. *Other factors considered include:* class rank, interview, extracurricular activities, alumni/ae relation. **Freshman Admission Requirements:** High school diploma is required and GED is accepted *Academic units recommended:* 4 English, 3 math, 2 science, 2 foreign language, 3 social studies. **Freshman Admission Statistics:** 2,678 applied, 37.4% admitted, 22% enrolled. **Transfer Admission Requirements:** High school transcript, college transcript(s), essay or personal statement, Minimum college GPA of 2.00 required. Lowest grade transferable C-. **General Admission Information:** Application fee $40. Priority deadline 3/1. Regular application deadline 8/1. Nonfall registration accepted. Admission may be deferred.

COSTS AND FINANCIAL AID

Annual tuition $28,980. Room and board $9,240. Required fees $660. Average book expense $900. **Required Forms and Deadlines:** FAFSA. **Notification of Awards:** Applicants will be notified of awards on a rolling basis beginning 3/1. **Types of Aid:** *Need-based scholarships/grants:* College/university scholarship or grant aid from institutional funds; Federal Pell; Private scholarships; SEOG; State scholarships/grants. *Loans:* Direct PLUS loans; Direct Subsidized Stafford Loans; Direct Unsubsidized Stafford Loans. *Student Employment:* Federal Work-Study Program available. Institutional employment available. **Financial Aid Statistics:** 98% needy freshmen receive need-based scholarship or grant aid. 13% freshmen, 12% undergrads receive non-need-based scholarship or grant aid. 76% freshmen, 74% undergrads receive need-based self-help aid. 10% freshmen, 10% undergrads receive athletic scholarships. 97% freshmen, 97% undergrads receive any aid. **Criteria for awarding aid:** *Need-based:* Academics, Alumni affiliation, Athletics, Leadership.

CORCORAN COLLEGE OF ART AND DESIGN

500 17th Street NW, Washington, DC 20006-4804
Phone: 202-639-1814 · **Financial Aid Phone:** (202) 639-1851
E-mail: admissions@corcoran.org
Fax: 202-639-1830 · **Website:** www.corcoran.edu

This private school was founded in 1890.

RATINGS

Admissions Selectivity Rating: 0   **Fire Safety Rating:** 67   **Green Rating:** 60*

STUDENTS AND FACULTY

Faculty: Student/faculty ratio 15:1. 0% of classes are taught by teaching assistants.

ACADEMICS

Degrees: Associate; Bachelor's; Certificate; Master's **Classes:** Most classes have 20-29 students. Most lab/discussion sessions have 20-29 students. **Most popular majors:** Graphic Design; Photography; Fine/Studio Arts, General. **Career services:** Alumni network; Alumni services; Career/job search classes; Internships

FACILITIES

Special Academic Facilities/Equipment: Art gallery. Student exhibition spaces **Computers:** Administrative functions (other than registration) can be performed online. Undergraduates are required to own a computer.

CAMPUS LIFE

Environment: Metropolis **On-Campus Highlights:** Corcoran Gallery, Gallery 31, Muse Cafe

ADMISSIONS

Test Scores: Minimum internet-based TOEFL 80. **Freshman Admission Requirements:** High school diploma is required and GED is accepted **Transfer Admission Requirements:** High school transcript, college transcript(s), Minimum college GPA of 2.5 required. Lowest grade transferable C. **General Admission Information:** Application fee $45.

COSTS AND FINANCIAL AID

Annual tuition $30,930.

CORNELL COLLEGE

600 First Street SW, Mount Vernon, IA 52314-1098
Phone: 319-895-4161 · **Financial Aid Phone:** 319-895-4216
E-mail: admissions@cornellcollege.edu · **CEEB Code:** 6119
Fax: 319-895-4451 · **Website:** www.cornellcollege.edu · **ACT Code:** 1296

This private school, affiliated with the Methodist Church, was founded in 1853. It has a 129 acre campus.

RATINGS

Admissions Selectivity Rating: 84   **Fire Safety Rating:** 83   **Green Rating:** 60*

STUDENTS AND FACULTY

Enrollment: 1,003. **Student Body:** 49% female, 51% male, 81% out-of-state, 5% international (16 countries represented). Asian 3%, African American 6%, Caucasian 70%, Hispanic 9%, Native American 1%, Pacific Islander 0%, Two or more races 2%, Race unknown 4%.

Retention and Graduation: 81% freshmen return for sophomore year. 65% freshmen graduate within 4 years. 71% freshmen graduate within 6 years. 17% grads go on to further study within 1 year. 16% grads pursue arts and sciences degrees. 2% grads pursue law degrees. 1% grads pursue business degrees. 0.5% grads pursue medical degrees. **Faculty:** Student/faculty ratio 11:1. 78 full-time faculty, 100% hold PhDs, 10% are members of minority groups, 51% are women. 0% of classes are taught by teaching assistants.

ACADEMICS

Degrees: Bachelor's. **Classes:** Most classes have 10-19 students. Most lab/discussion sessions have 10-19 students. **Most popular majors:** Biochemistry; Psychology, General; Economics, General. **Special Study Options:** Distance learning; Double major; Dual enrollment; Independent study; Internships; Student-designed major; Study abroad; Teacher certification program. **Combined degree programs:** BA/MA. **Disability Services offered to physically disabled students:** Note-taking services; Reader services; Tape recorders; Tutors. **Career services:** Alumni network; Alumni services; Career assessment; Career/job search classes; Internships; Regional alumni

FACILITIES

Housing: Apartments for single students; Coed dorms; Theme housing; Women's dorms 51% of campus accessible to physically disabled. **Special Academic Facilities/Equipment:** Geology center and museum, MNR machine in West Sc. Building, Luce Art Gallery. **Computers:** 100% of classrooms, 20% of dorms, 100% of libraries, 100% of dining areas, 100% of student union, 10% of common outdoor areas have wireless network access. Administrative functions (other than registration) can be performed online.

CAMPUS LIFE

Environment: Rural **Activities:** Campus Ministries; Choral groups; Concert band; Dance; Drama/theater; International Student Organization; Jazz band; Literary magazine; Music ensembles; Musical theater; Radio station; Student government; Student newspaper; Student-run film society; Symphony orchestra; Yearbook 90 registered organizations, 11 honor societies, 11 religious organizations. 8 fraternities, 7 sororities **Athletics (Intercollegiate):** *Men:* baseball, basketball, cross-country, football, golf, soccer, tennis, track/field (outdoor), track/field (indoor), wrestling. *Women:* basketball, cross-country, golf, soccer, softball, tennis, track/field (indoor), volleyball. **On-Campus Highlights:** Thomas Commons—Orange Carpet—student center, Cole Library, Small Multi-Sports Center, Kimmel Theatre—state of the art theatre, McWethy Hall **Environmental Initiatives:** Engineering study on costs of replacing current campus-side steam heat network, including specific costs and energy savings payback times for each building. Implementation of plan in two building remodels and designed into two upcoming remodel projects.

ADMISSIONS

Freshman Academic Profile: Average high school GPA 3.5. 25% in top 10% of high school class, 50% in top 25% of high school class, 83% in top 50% of high school class. **Test Scores:** SAT Math middle 50% range 550-665. SAT EBRW middle 50% range 550-675. ACT middle 50% range 23-29. Minimum internet-based TOEFL 79. Minimum paper TOEFL 550. **Basis for Candidate Selection:** *Very important factors considered include:* rigor of secondary school record, academic GPA, character/personal qualities. *Important factors considered include:* class rank, application essay, recommendation(s), extracurricular activities, talent/ability, volunteer work, work experience. *Other* factors considered include: standardized test scores, interview, first generation, alumni/ae relation, geographical residence, state residency, racial/ethnic status, level of applicant's interest. **Freshman Admission Requirements:** High school diploma is required and GED is accepted *Academic units recommended:* 4 English, 3 math, 3 science, 2 foreign language, 3 social studies, 1 academic elective. **Freshman Admission Statistics:** 2,276 applied, 65.0% admitted, 20% enrolled. **Transfer Admission Requirements:** college transcript(s), essay or personal statement, statement of good standing from prior institution(s). Lowest grade transferable C. **General Admission Information:** Application fee $30. Priority deadline 12/1. Nonfall registration accepted. Admission may be deferred for a maximum of 1 year.

COSTS AND FINANCIAL AID
Annual tuition $41,874. Room and board $9,384. Required fees $425. Average book expense $1,323. **Required Forms and Deadlines:** FAFSA. **Notification of Awards:** Applicants will be notified of awards on a rolling basis beginning 3/1. **Types of Aid:** *Need-based scholarships/grants:* College/university scholarship or grant aid from institutional funds; Federal Pell; SEOG; State scholarships/grants. *Loans:* Direct PLUS loans; Direct Subsidized Stafford Loans; Direct Unsubsidized Stafford Loans. *Student Employment:* Federal Work-Study Program available. Institutional employment available. **Financial Aid Statistics:** 100% needy freshmen, 100% needy undergrads receive need-based scholarship or grant aid. 11% freshmen, 11% undergrads receive non-need-based scholarship or grant aid. 84% freshmen, 84% undergrads receive need-based self-help aid. 0% freshmen, 0% undergrads receive athletic scholarships. 99% freshmen, 98% undergrads receive any aid. 75% undergrads borrow to pay for school. Average cumulative indebtedness $31,975. **Criteria for awarding aid:** *Non-need-based:* Academics, Alumni affiliation, Art, Leadership, Music/drama, Religious affiliation, State/district residency.

CORNELL UNIVERSITY

410 Thurston Avenue, Ithaca, NY 14850
Phone: 607-255-5241 · **Financial Aid Phone:** 607-255-5145
E-mail: admissions@cornell.edu · **CEEB Code:** 2098
Fax: 607-255-0659 · **Website:** www.cornell.edu · **ACT Code:** 2726

This private school was founded in 1865. It has a 745 acre campus.

RATINGS
Admissions Selectivity Rating: 97　　**Fire Safety Rating:** 90　　**Green Rating:** 99

STUDENTS AND FACULTY
Enrollment: 14,815. **Student Body:** 52% female, 48% male, 59% out-of-state, 10% international (88 countries represented). Asian 19%, African American 7%, Caucasian 38%, Hispanic 13%, Native American <1%, Pacific Islander <1%, Two or more races 5%, Race unknown 8%.
Retention and Graduation: 97% freshmen return for sophomore year. 85% freshmen graduate within 4 years. 93% freshmen graduate within 6 years. 24% grads go on to further study within 1 year. 2% grads pursue law degrees. 1% grads pursue business degrees. 3% grads pursue medical degrees. **Faculty:** Student/faculty ratio 9:1. 1,756 full-time faculty, 93% hold PhDs, 20% are members of minority groups, 37% are women.

ACADEMICS
Degrees: Bachelor's; Doctoral/Professional; Doctoral/Research; Master's **Classes:** Most classes have 10-19 students. Most lab/discussion sessions have 10-19 students. **Most popular majors:** Biology/Biological Sciences, General; Hotel/Motel Administration/Management; Labor And Industrial Relations. **Special Study Options:** Accelerated program; Cooperative education program; Cross-registration; Distance learning; Double major; English as a Second Language (ESL); Exchange student program (domestic); Honors program; Independent study; Internships; Liberal arts/career combination; Student-designed major; Study abroad. **Disability Services offered to physically disabled students:** Note-taking services; Reader services; Tape recorders; Tutors. **Career services:** Alumni network; Alumni services; Career assessment; Career/job search classes; Internships; Regional alumni

FACILITIES
Housing: Apartments for single students; Coed dorms; Cooperative housing; Fraternity/sorority housing; Special housing for disabled student; Special housing for international students; Theme housing; Women's dorms **Special Academic Facilities/Equipment:** Institute of Biotechnology, performing arts center, veterinary medical center, a woods sanctuary, 4 designated national

resource centers, 2 local optical observatories, Africana studies and research center, arboretum, botanical garden, particle accelerator, supercomputer, national research centers, art museum, lab of ornithology, vertebrates museum, living and learning communities, campus orchard, dairy pilot plant, mineralogical museum, animal teaching hospital, 2 agricultural experiment stations, and marine laboratory. **Computers:** 20% of classrooms, 100% of dorms, 100% of libraries, 100% of dining areas, 75% of student union, 20% of common outdoor areas have wireless network access. Students can register for classes online. Administrative functions (other than registration) can be performed online.

CAMPUS LIFE
Environment: Town **Activities:** Campus Ministries; Choral groups; Concert band; Dance; Drama/theater; International Student Organization; Jazz band; Literary magazine; Marching band; Model UN; Music ensembles; Musical theater; Pep band; Radio station; Student government; Student newspaper; Student-run film society; Symphony orchestra; Television station; Yearbook 841 registered organizations, 22 honor societies, 61 religious organizations. 50 fraternities, 19 sororities. **Athletics (Intercollegiate):** *Men:* baseball, basketball, crew/rowing, cross-country, diving, football, golf, ice hockey, lacrosse, polo, soccer, squash, swimming, tennis, track/field (outdoor), track/field (indoor), wrestling. *Women:* basketball, crew/rowing, cross-country, diving, equestrian sports, fencing, field hockey, gymnastics, ice hockey, lacrosse, polo, soccer, softball, squash, swimming, tennis, track/field (outdoor), track/field (indoor), volleyball. **On-Campus Highlights:** Lynah Rink, The Trillium, The Lindseth Climbing Wall, Ho Plaza, Willard Straight Hall **Environmental Initiatives:** Cornell works as a leader and an advocate to improve NY's distributed energy policy, tariffs and regulatory interpretation to enable development of renewable energy projects. In partnership with the New York State Energy Industries Association (NYSEIA), Cornell formed a coalition of NY solar developers and customers to reform utility interconnection practices for distributed generation of renewable energy through the Department of Public Service. Cornell has regularly engaged State leadership and moved forward the adoption of new policy, including an order known as the "Cornell Ruling" which ended a utility practice which was a major barrier to the interconnection of solar farms. More recently Cornell spear-headed the creation of the Coalition of Renewable Energy Users (CORE), including commercial and institutional leaders in NY with renewable energy and carbon reduction goals, and renewable energy developers to advocate for policies that enable continued development of voluntary renewable energy projects as part of the state's Clean Energy Standard

ADMISSIONS
Freshman Academic Profile: 86% in top 10% of high school class, 98% in top 25% of high school class, 100% in top 50% of high school class. **Test Scores:** SAT Math middle 50% range 700-790. SAT EBRW middle 50% range 690-760. ACT middle 50% range 31-34. Minimum internet-based TOEFL 100. Minimum paper TOEFL 600. **Basis for Candidate Selection:** *Very important factors considered include:* rigor of secondary school record, academic GPA, application essay, standardized test scores, recommendation(s), extracurricular activities, talent/ability, character/personal qualities. *Important factors considered include:* class rank. *Other factors considered include:* interview, first generation, alumni/ae relation, geographical residence, state residency, racial/ethnic status, volunteer work, work experience. **Freshman Admission Requirements:** High school diploma or equivalent is not required *Academic units required:* 4 English, 3 math, *Academic units recommended:* 3 science, 3 science labs, 3 foreign language, 3 social studies, 3 history. **Freshman Admission Statistics:** 27,039 applied, 22.0% admitted, 56% enrolled. **Transfer Admission Requirements:** High school transcript, college transcript(s), essay or personal statement, statement of good standing from prior institution(s). Lowest grade transferable C. **General Admission Information:** Application fee $80. Regular application deadline 1/2. Nonfall registration accepted. Admission may be deferred.

COSTS AND FINANCIAL AID
Annual tuition $52,612. Room and board $14,380. Required fees $241. Average book expense $930. **Required Forms and Deadlines:** CSS/Financial Aid PROFILE; FAFSA; Noncustodial PROFILE. **Notification of Awards:** Applicants will be notified of awards on or about 4/1. **Types of Aid:** *Need-based scholarships/grants:* College/university scholarship or grant aid from institutional funds; Federal Pell; Private scholarships; SEOG; State scholarships/grants. *Loans:* Direct PLUS loans; Direct Subsidized Stafford Loans; Direct Unsubsidized Stafford Loans. *Student Employment:* Federal Work-Study Program available. Institutional employment available. **Financial Aid Statistics:** 98% needy freshmen, 98% needy undergrads receive need-based scholarship or grant aid. 0% undergrads receive non-need-based scholarship or grant aid. 89% freshmen, 92% undergrads receive need-based self-help aid. 0% freshmen, 0% undergrads receive athletic scholarships. 60% freshmen, 57% undergrads receive any aid. 41% undergrads borrow to pay for school. Average cumulative indebtedness $23,389. **Criteria for awarding aid:** *Need-based:* Leadership.

CORNERSTONE UNIVERSITY

1001 East Beltline Avenue, NE, Grand Rapids, MI 49525-5897
Phone: 616-222-1418 · **Financial Aid Phone:** 616-949-5300
E-mail: admissions@cornerstone.edu
Fax: 616-222-1418 · **Website:** www.cornerstone.edu · **ACT Code:** 2002

This private school, affiliated with the Christian (Nondenominational) Church, was founded in 1941. It has a 130 acre campus.

RATINGS
Admissions Selectivity Rating: 79   **Fire Safety Rating:** 96   **Green Rating:** 60*

STUDENTS AND FACULTY
Enrollment: 1,741. **Student Body:** 59% female, 41% male, 16% out-of-state, 1% international (15 countries represented). Asian 1%, African American 11%, Caucasian 83%, Hispanic 4%, Native American <1%, Race unknown 0%. **Retention and Graduation:** 69% freshmen return for sophomore year. 15% grads go on to further study within 1 year. 10% grads pursue arts and sciences degrees. 1% grads pursue law degrees. 3% grads pursue business degrees. 1% grads pursue medical degrees. **Faculty:** Student/faculty ratio 13:1. 62 full-time faculty, 50% hold PhDs, 5% are members of minority groups, 32% are women. 0% of classes are taught by teaching assistants.

ACADEMICS
Degrees: Associate; Bachelor's; Certificate; Diploma; Master's; Terminal Associate **Classes:** Most classes have fewer than 10 students. Most lab/discussion sessions have fewer than 10 students. **Most popular majors:** Mass Communication/Media Studies; Elementary Education And Teaching; Youth Ministry. **Special Study Options:** Accelerated program; Distance learning; Double major; Dual enrollment; English as a Second Language (ESL); Honors program; Independent study; Internships; Liberal arts/career combination; Study abroad; Teacher certification program; Weekend college. **Honors programs:** Honors Program based on a "great books" curriculum. **Disability Services offered to physically disabled students:** Note-taking services; Reader services; Tape recorders; Tutors. **Career services:** Career assessment; Career/job search classes; Internships

FACILITIES
Housing: Apartments for married students; Apartments for single students; Men's dorms; Special housing for disabled student; Theme housing; Women's dorms 100% of campus accessible to physically disabled. **Computers:** 100% of classrooms, 100% of dorms, 100% of libraries, 100% of dining areas, 100% of student union, 100% of common outdoor areas have wireless network access. Students can register for classes online. Administrative functions (other than registration) can be performed online.

CAMPUS LIFE
Environment: City **Activities:** Campus Ministries; Choral groups; Concert band; Dance; Drama/theater; International Student Organization; Jazz band; Literary magazine; Music ensembles; Musical theater; Opera; Pep band; Radio station; Student government; Student newspaper; Student-run film society 11 registered organizations, 2 honor societies, 1 religious organization. **Athletics (Intercollegiate):** *Men:* basketball, cross-country, golf, soccer, track/field (outdoor), track/field (indoor). *Women:* basketball, cross-country, golf, soccer, softball, track/field (outdoor), track/field (indoor), volleyball. **On-Campus Highlights:** Corum Student Union, Bernice Hansen Athletic Center, Campus Bookstore Atrium, Faber Hall Seating Area, Gordon Music Hall **Environmental Initiatives:** On campus dialogue and focus on sustainability issues.

ADMISSIONS
Freshman Academic Profile: Average high school GPA 3.3. 60% from public high schools. **Test Scores:** SAT Math middle 50% range 440-540. SAT EBRW middle 50% range 360-580. ACT middle 50% range 20-25. Minimum paper TOEFL 500. **Basis for Candidate Selection:** *Very important factors considered include:* academic GPA, application essay, standardized test scores, recommendation(s), character/personal qualities, religious affiliation/commitment. *Important factors considered include:* rigor of secondary school record, class rank. *Other factors considered include:* level of applicant's interest. **Freshman Admission Requirements:** High school diploma is required and GED is accepted *Academic units recommended:* 4 English, 3 math, 2 science, 1 science labs, 2 foreign language, 3 social studies, 2 history, 4 academic electives. **Freshman Admission Statistics:** 1,109 applied, 72.9% admitted, 45% enrolled. **Transfer Admission Requirements:** High school transcript, college transcript(s), essay or personal statement, Minimum college GPA of 2.0 required. Lowest grade transferable C-. **General Admission Information:** Application fee $25. Priority deadline 7/1. Nonfall registration accepted.

COSTS AND FINANCIAL AID
Annual tuition $19,190. Room and board $6,500. Required fees $340. Average book expense $1,000. **Required Forms and Deadlines:** FAFSA. **Notification of Awards:** Applicants will be notified of awards on a rolling basis beginning 2/15. **Types of Aid:** *Need-based scholarships/grants:* College/university scholarship or grant aid from institutional funds; Federal Pell; Private scholarships; SEOG; State scholarships/grants. *Loans: Student Employment:* Federal Work-Study Program available. **Financial Aid Statistics:** 100% needy freshmen, 99% needy undergrads receive need-based scholarship or grant aid. 100% freshmen, 94% undergrads receive non-need-based scholarship or grant aid. 81% freshmen, 79% undergrads receive need-based self-help aid. 23% freshmen, 15% undergrads receive athletic scholarships. 100% freshmen, 98% undergrads receive any aid. **Criteria for awarding aid:** *Need-based:* Academics, Alumni affiliation, Minority status *Non-need-based:* Academics, Athletics, Leadership, Music/drama, State/district residency.

CORNISH COLLEGE OF THE ARTS

1000 Lenora Street, Seattle, WA 98121
Phone: 206-726-5016 · **Financial Aid Phone:** 206-726-5013
E-mail: admissions@cornish.edu · **CEEB Code:** 58
Fax: 206-720-1011 · **Website:** www.cornish.edu · **ACT Code:** 4801

This private school was founded in 1914. It has a 4 acre campus.

RATINGS
Admissions Selectivity Rating: 65   **Fire Safety Rating:** 60*   **Green Rating:** 60*

STUDENTS AND FACULTY
Enrollment: 765. **Student Body:** 64% female, 36% male, 52% out-of-state, 4% international (25 countries represented). Asian 6%, African American 4%, Caucasian 63%, Hispanic 9%, Native American 1%, Pacific Islander <1%, Two or more races 7%, Race unknown 6%. **Retention and Graduation:** 12% grads go on to further study within 1 year. 5% grads pursue arts and sciences degrees. Student/faculty ratio 8:1.

ACADEMICS
Degrees: Bachelor's; Post-Bachelor's certificate **Classes:** Most classes have 10-19 students. Most lab/discussion sessions have 10-19 students. **Most popular majors:** Design And Visual Communications, General; Drama And Dramatics/Theatre Arts, General; Music Performance, General. **Special Study Options:** Exchange student program (domestic); Independent study; Internships; Study abroad. **Disability Services offered to physically disabled students:** Note-taking services; Tape recorders. **Career services:** Internships

FACILITIES
Housing: Coed dorms 50% of campus accessible to physically disabled. **Special Academic Facilities/Equipment:** Art galleries, extensive art studio space, theatres, electronic music studio, dance studio, concert hall.

CAMPUS LIFE
Environment: Metropolis **Activities:** Choral groups; Concert band; Dance; Drama/theater; Jazz band; Literary magazine; Music ensembles; Musical theater; Opera; Radio station; Student government; Student-run film society 18 registered organizations, 6 honor societies, 1 religious organization. **On-Campus Highlights:** Raisbeck Performance Hall, Cornsh Gallery, Nellie's Cafe, Cornish Playhouse

ADMISSIONS
Freshman Academic Profile: Average high school GPA 3.2. 75% from public high schools. **Test Scores:** Minimum paper TOEFL 525. **Basis for Candidate Selection:** *Very important factors considered include:* talent/ability. *Important factors considered include:* rigor of secondary school record, application essay. *Other factors considered include:* academic GPA, standardized test scores, recommendation(s), interview, extracurricular activities. **Freshman Admission Requirements:** High school diploma is required and GED is accepted *Academic units required:* 4 English, 2 math, 2 science, 1 science labs, 3 social studies, *Academic units recommended:* 4 math, 4 science, 2 foreign language. **Freshman Admission Statistics:** 1,134 applied, 85.5% admitted, 17% enrolled. **Transfer Admission Requirements:** High school transcript, college transcript(s), essay or personal statement, interview, Minimum college GPA of 2.0 required. Lowest grade transferable C. **General Admission Information:** Application fee $40. Priority deadline 2/1. Regular application deadline 8/15. Nonfall registration accepted. Admission may be deferred for a maximum of 1 year.

COSTS AND FINANCIAL AID

Annual tuition $31,980. **Required Forms and Deadlines:** FAFSA; Institution's own financial aid form. **Notification of Awards:** Applicants will be notified of awards on or about 5/15. **Types of Aid:** *Need-based scholarships/grants:* Federal Pell; SEOG; State scholarships/grants. *Loans: Student Employment:* Federal Work-Study Program available. **Financial Aid Statistics:** 84% needy undergrads receive need-based scholarship or grant aid. 100% undergrads receive non-need-based scholarship or grant aid. 84% undergrads receive need-based self-help aid. 0% undergrads receive athletic scholarships. **Criteria for awarding aid:** *Need-based:* Academics, Art, Music/drama *Non-need-based:* Academics, Art, Music/drama.

COVENANT COLLEGE

14049 Scenic Highway, Lookout Mtn., GA 30750
Phone: 706-820-2398 · **Financial Aid Phone:** 706-419-1126
E-mail: admissions@covenant.edu · **CEEB Code:** 6124
Fax: 706-820-0893 · **Website:** www.covenant.edu · **ACT Code:** 3951

This private school, affiliated with the Presbyterian Church in America, was founded in 1955. It has a 350 acre campus.

RATINGS

Admissions Selectivity Rating: 81   **Fire Safety Rating:** 88   **Green Rating:** 60*

STUDENTS AND FACULTY

Enrollment: 986. **Student Body:** 53% female, 47% male, 70% out-of-state, 3% international (21 countries represented). Asian 1%, African American 3%, Caucasian 86%, Hispanic 3%, Native American 0%, Pacific Islander 0%, Two or more races 4%, Race unknown <1%. **Retention and Graduation:** 87% freshmen return for sophomore year. 59% freshmen graduate within 4 years. 67% freshmen graduate within 6 years. 28% grads go on to further study within 1 year. 10% grads pursue arts and sciences degrees. 1% grads pursue law degrees. 2% grads pursue business degrees. 1% grads pursue medical degrees. **Faculty:** Student/faculty ratio 13:1. 64 full-time faculty, 94% hold PhDs, 11% are members of minority groups, 22% are women. 0% of classes are taught by teaching assistants.

ACADEMICS

Degrees: Bachelor's; Master's **Classes:** Most classes have 10-19 students. Most lab/discussion sessions have 10-19 students. **Most popular majors:** Elementary Education And Teaching; English Language And Literature, General; Sociology. **Special Study Options:** Double major; Dual enrollment; English as a Second Language (ESL); Exchange student program (domestic); Independent study; Internships; Student-designed major; Study abroad; Teacher certification program. **Disability Services offered to physically disabled students:** Note-taking services; Tape recorders; Tutors. **Career services:** Alumni network; Alumni services; Career assessment; Internships

FACILITIES

Housing: Apartments for single students; Coed dorms 95% of campus accessible to physically diasbled. **Computers:** 100% of classrooms, 100% of dorms, 100% of libraries, 100% of dining areas, NA% of student union, 100% of common outdoor areas have wireless network access. Students can register for classes online. Administrative functions (other than registration) can be performed online.

CAMPUS LIFE

Environment: City **Activities:** Campus Ministries; Choral groups; Concert band; Dance; Drama/theater; International Student Organization; Jazz band; Literary magazine; Model UN; Music ensembles; Musical theater; Radio station; Student government; Student newspaper; Student-run film society; Symphony orchestra; Yearbook 40 registered organizations, 4 honor societies, 1 religious organization. **Athletics (Intercollegiate):** *Men:* baseball, basketball, cross-country, golf, soccer, tennis. *Women:* basketball, cross-country, golf, soccer, softball, tennis, volleyball. **On-Campus Highlights:** Probasco Visitor's Center, Carter Hall, The Overlook, The Chapel, Ashe Gym

ADMISSIONS

Freshman Academic Profile: Average high school GPA 3.6. 31% in top 10% of high school class, 61% in top 25% of high school class, 90% in top 50% of high school class. 55% from public high schools. **Test Scores:** SAT Math middle 50% range 540-660. SAT EBRW middle 50% range 590-690. ACT middle 50% range 24-30. Minimum internet-based TOEFL 75. **Basis for Candidate Selection:** *Very important factors considered:* rigor of secondary school record, academic GPA, application essay, standardized test scores, recommendation(s), character/personal qualities, religious affiliation/commitment. *Important factors considered:* interview. *Other factors considered:* class rank, extracurricular activities, first generation, alumni/

ae relation, racial/ethnic status, volunteer work, level of applicant's interest. **Freshman Admission Requirements:** High school diploma is required and GED is accepted *Academic units required:* 4 English, 3 math, 2 science, 2 social studies, 3 academic electives, *Academic units recommended:* 4 English, 3 math, 2 science, 2 foreign language, 2 social studies, 3 academic electives. **Freshman Admission Statistics:** 692 applied, 95.2% admitted, 40% enrolled. **Transfer Admission Requirements:** High school transcript, college transcript(s), essay or personal statement, interview, standardized test scores, statement of good standing from prior institution(s). Minimum college GPA of 2.0 required. Lowest grade transferable C-. **General Admission Information:** Application fee $35. Regular application deadline 2/1. Nonfall registration accepted. Admission may be deferred for a maximum of 1 year.

COSTS AND FINANCIAL AID

Annual tuition $33,360. Room and board $10,260. Required fees $970. Average book expense $1,170. **Required Forms and Deadlines:** FAFSA; State aid form. **Notification of Awards:** Applicants will be notified of awards on or about 3/15. **Types of Aid:** *Need-based scholarships/grants:* College/university scholarship or grant aid from institutional funds; Federal Pell; Private scholarships; SEOG; State scholarships/grants. *Loans: Student Employment:* Federal Work-Study Program available. Institutional employment available. **Financial Aid Statistics:** 99% needy freshmen, 99% needy undergrads receive need-based scholarship or grant aid. 17% freshmen, 16% undergrads receive non-need-based scholarship or grant aid. 85% freshmen, 89% undergrads receive need-based self-help aid. 0% freshmen, 0% undergrads receive athletic scholarships. 100% freshmen, 99% undergrads receive any aid. 64% undergrads borrow to pay for school. Average cumulative indebtedness $24,484. **Criteria for awarding aid:** *Need-based:* Academics, Alumni affiliation, Art, Job skills, Leadership, Minority status, Music/drama *Non-need-based:* Academics, Alumni affiliation, Art, Job skills, Leadership, Minority status, Music/drama, Religious affiliation, State/district residency.

CRANDALL UNIVERSITY

Box 6004, Moncton, NB E1C 9L7
Phone: 506-858-8970
E-mail: admissions@crandallu.ca
Fax: 506-858-9694 · **Website:** www.crandallu.ca

This is a private school.

RATINGS

Admissions Selectivity Rating: 67   **Fire Safety Rating:** 60*   **Green Rating:** 60*

STUDENTS AND FACULTY

Student Body: 11% out-of-state, international. **Retention and Graduation:** 48% freshmen return for sophomore year. **Faculty:** Student/faculty ratio 14:1. 26 full-time faculty, 81% hold PhDs, 15% are members of minority groups, 35% are women.

ACADEMICS

Degrees: Bachelor's; Certificate; Post-Bachelor's certificate **Classes:** Most classes have 10-19 students. Most lab/discussion sessions have fewer than 10 students. **Special Study Options:** Cooperative education program; Double major; Dual enrollment; English as a Second Language (ESL); Honors program; Independent study; Internships; Liberal arts/career combination; Study abroad; Teacher certification program.

FACILITIES

Housing: Men's dorms; Women's dorms

CAMPUS LIFE

Activities: Campus Ministries; Drama/theater; International Student Organization; Music ensembles; Student government; Student newspaper; Yearbook.

ADMISSIONS

Basis for Candidate Selection: *Important factors considered include:* academic GPA. **Freshman Admission Requirements:** High school diploma is required and GED is accepted **Freshman Admission Statistics:** 149 applied, 93.3% admitted, 71% enrolled. **Transfer Admission Requirements:** college transcript(s), Lowest grade transferable C-. **General Admission Information:** Application fee $35. Priority deadline 3/1. Nonfall registration accepted. Admission may be deferred for a maximum of one year.

COSTS AND FINANCIAL AID

Average book expense $1,600.

CREIGHTON UNIVERSITY

2500 California Plaza, Omaha, NE 68178
Phone: 402-280-2703 · **Financial Aid Phone:** 402-280-2731
E-mail: admissions@creighton.edu · **CEEB Code:** 6121
Fax: 402-280-2685 · **Website:** www.creighton.edu · **ACT Code:** 2444

This private school, affiliated with the Roman Catholic Church, was founded in 1878. It has a 139 acre campus.

RATINGS

Admissions Selectivity Rating: 86   **Fire Safety Rating:** 93   **Green Rating:** 86

STUDENTS AND FACULTY

Enrollment: 4,212. **Student Body:** 56% female, 44% male, 77% out-of-state, 3% international (27 countries represented). Asian 9%, African American 3%, Caucasian 71%, Hispanic 8%, Native American <1%, Pacific Islander <1%, Two or more races 5%, Race unknown 1%.
Retention and Graduation: 89% freshmen return for sophomore year. 73% freshmen graduate within 4 years. 81% freshmen graduate within 6 years. **Faculty:** Student/faculty ratio 11:1. 573 full-time faculty, 88% hold PhDs, 12% are members of minority groups, 47% are women. 0% of classes are taught by teaching assistants.

ACADEMICS

Degrees: Associate; Bachelor's; Certificate; Doctoral; Doctoral/Professional; Doctoral/Research; Master's; Post-Bachelor's certificate; Post-Master's certificate **Classes:** Most classes have 10-19 students. Most lab/discussion sessions have 20-29 students. **Most popular majors:** Biology/Biological Sciences, General; Psychology, General; Registered Nursing/Registered Nurse. **Special Study Options:** Accelerated program; Cross-registration; Distance learning; Double major; Dual enrollment; English as a Second Language (ESL); Honors program; Independent study; Internships; Liberal arts/career combination; Study abroad; Teacher certification program. **Honors programs:** Designed for talented, imaginative students desirous of participation in small, discussion-oriented classes and in courses on interdisciplinary and topical issues. For more information, visit http://www.creighton.edu/ccas/honorsprogram/ **Combined degree programs:** BA/JD. **Disability Services offered to physically disabled students:** Note-taking services; Reader services; Tape recorders; Tutors. **Career services:** Alumni network; Alumni services; Career assessment; Career/job search classes; Internships; Regional alumni

FACILITIES

Housing: Apartments for married students; Apartments for single students; Coed dorms; Special housing for disabled student; Theme housing 87% of campus accessible to physically diasbled. **Special Academic Facilities/ Equipment:** St John's Church is at the center of the Creighton University campus and serves the Omaha community as well. The Lied Art Gallery is open seven days a week and is free to the public. The University is home to a wind energy collection system and the state's largest solar array that acts as an outdoor classroom for students in the energy technology program. iJAY, an Apple Authorized Campus Store, uniquely blends commercial and educational interests by doubling as a learning center, giving students the opportunity to gain hands-on experience running a retail store as part of a practicum course. The Heider Securities Investment and Analysis Center in the business college is a state-of-the-art trading room complete with a real-time stock ticker, interactive market boards and 11 Bloomberg terminals. **Computers:** 100% of classrooms, 100% of dorms, 100% of libraries, 100% of dining areas, 100% of student union, 100% of common outdoor areas have wireless network access. Students can register for classes online. Administrative functions (other than registration) can be performed online.

CAMPUS LIFE

Environment: Metropolis **Activities:** Campus Ministries; Choral groups; Dance; Drama/theater; International Student Organization; Model UN; Music ensembles; Musical theater; Pep band; Student government; Student newspaper; Symphony orchestra 182 registered organizations, 11 honor societies, 6 religious organizations. 5 fraternities, 8 sororities. **Athletics (Intercollegiate): Men:** baseball, basketball, cross-country, golf, soccer, tennis. **Women:** basketball, crew/rowing, cross-country, golf, soccer, softball, tennis, volleyball. **On-Campus Highlights:** Heider College of Business/Harper Center, Hixson-Lied Science Building, a 100,000 square foot science facility, Morrison Soccer Stadium, nationally acclaimed collegiate soccer stadium, Wayne and Eileen Ryan Athletic Center and D.J. Sokol Arena, St. John's Church, the "heart" of campus **Environmental Initiatives:** Stewardship of

the environment has become central to the mission of Creighton University and the wider Jesuit community. The Energy Technology Program has allowed the university to become more sustainable, with 120 kW of renewable energy generated on site, including the largest solar photovoltaic array in Nebraska. Not only have these technologies reduced Creighton's environmental footprint, but they have also become the foundation for a hands-on educational platform, allowing students to work and conduct research on professional systems. The University has continued to expand renewable energy sources including solar photovoltaic and solar thermal panels, four wind turbines designed for urban environments, geothermal hearing, low voltage lighting, solar hot water, and a ground source heat pump. The presence of these technologies at Creighton exposes everyone in the community to them and concretely conveys Creighton's commitment to environmental responsibility. The Energy Technology academic program regularly connects with the community for their projects. For instance, student teams engaged with several local schools to develop a renewable energy plan for the school plus a level one energy audit for their facility. The project included a formal report and presentation to the school boards as well as teaching classes in sustainable energy related topics. Other projects have included developing a plan for solar power on a local homeless shelter and working with a hospital in Nigeria.

ADMISSIONS

Freshman Academic Profile: Average high school GPA 3.8. 33% in top 10% of high school class, 69% in top 25% of high school class, 93% in top 50% of high school class. 51% from public high schools. **Test Scores:** SAT Math middle 50% range 550-650. SAT EBRW middle 50% range 520-640. ACT middle 50% range 25-30. Minimum internet-based TOEFL 88. Minimum paper TOEFL 570. **Basis for Candidate Selection:** *Very important factors considered include:* rigor of secondary school record, academic GPA. *Important factors considered include:* application essay, standardized test scores. *Other factors considered include:* class rank, recommendation(s), extracurricular activities, talent/ability, character/personal qualities, first generation, racial/ ethnic status, volunteer work, level of applicant's interest. **Freshman Admission Requirements:** High school diploma is required and GED is accepted *Academic units required:* 4 English, 3 math, 2 science, 1 science labs, 2 foreign language, 2 social studies, 3 academic electives, *Academic units recommended:* 4 English, 4 math, 3 science, 2 science labs, 3 foreign language, 4 social studies, 3 academic electives. **Freshman Admission Statistics:** 9,727 applied, 72.0% admitted, 16% enrolled. **Transfer Admission Requirements:** High school transcript, college transcript(s), statement of good standing from prior institution(s). Minimum college GPA of 2.50 required. Lowest grade transferable C. **General Admission Information:** Application fee $40. Priority deadline 12/1. Regular application deadline 2/15. Nonfall registration accepted. Admission may be deferred.

COSTS AND FINANCIAL AID

Annual tuition $38,200. Room and board $11,036. Required fees $1,716. Average book expense $1,200. **Required Forms and Deadlines:** FAFSA; Institution's own financial aid form. **Notification of Awards:** Applicants will be notified of awards on a rolling basis beginning 2/15. **Types of Aid:** *Need-based scholarships/grants:* College/university scholarship or grant aid from institutional funds; Federal Pell; Private scholarships; SEOG; State scholarships/grants. *Loans:* Direct PLUS loans; Direct Subsidized Stafford Loans; Direct Unsubsidized Stafford Loans. *Student Employment:* Federal Work-Study Program available. Institutional employment available. **Financial Aid Statistics:** 96% needy undergrads receive need-based scholarship or grant aid. 24% freshmen, 18% undergrads receive non-need-based scholarship or grant aid. 76% freshmen, 79% undergrads receive need-based self-help aid. 4% freshmen, 4% undergrads receive athletic scholarships. 61% undergrads borrow to pay for school. Average cumulative indebtedness $35,921. **Criteria for awarding aid:** *Need-based:* Academics, Leadership *Non-need-based:* Academics, Alumni affiliation, Art, Athletics, Leadership, Minority status, Music/drama.

CROWN COLLEGE

8700 College View Drive, St. Bonifacius, MN 55375-9001
Phone: 952-446-4142 · **Financial Aid Phone:** (952) 446-4175
E-mail: info@crown.edu
Fax: 952-446-4149 · **Website:** www.crown.edu · **ACT Code:** 2152

This private school, affiliated with the Christian & Missionary Alliance Church, was founded in 1916. It has a 215 acre campus.

RATINGS

Admissions Selectivity Rating: 79   **Fire Safety Rating:** 74   **Green Rating:** 60*

STUDENTS AND FACULTY

Enrollment: 1,017. **Student Body:** 57% female, 43% male, 31% out-of-state, 1% international (21 countries represented). Asian 7%, African American 4%, Caucasian 78%, Hispanic 2%, Native American 1%, Pacific Islander <1%, Two or more races 1%, Race unknown 7%.

Retention and Graduation: 63% freshmen return for sophomore year. **Faculty:** Student/faculty ratio 14:1. 34 full-time faculty, 47% hold PhDs, 6% are members of minority groups, 26% are women. 0% of classes are taught by teaching assistants.

ACADEMICS

Degrees: Associate; Bachelor's; Certificate; Master's; Post-Bachelor's certificate **Most popular majors:** Elementary Education And Teaching; Theology And Religious Vocations, Other; Business Administration And Management, General. **Special Study Options:** Distance learning; Double major; Exchange student program (domestic); Honors program; Independent study; Internships; Study abroad; Teacher certification program. **Honors programs:** The Honors Program. **Disability Services offered to physically disabled students:** Note-taking services; Reader services; Tape recorders; Tutors. **Career services:** Alumni services; Career assessment; Career/job search classes; Internships

FACILITIES

Housing: Apartments for married students; Apartments for single students; Men's dorms; Special housing for disabled student; Women's dorms 95% of campus accessible to physically disabled. **Special Academic Facilities/ Equipment:** Peter Watne Memorial Library **Computers:** 100% of classrooms, 20% of dorms, 100% of libraries, 100% of dining areas, 100% of student union, 10% of common outdoor areas have wireless network access. Administrative functions (other than registration) can be performed online.

CAMPUS LIFE

Environment: Rural **Activities:** Campus Ministries; Choral groups; Dance; Drama/theater; International Student Organization; Jazz band; Literary magazine; Music ensembles; Musical theater; Pep band; Radio station; Student government; Student newspaper; Student-run film society; Symphony orchestra; Yearbook 19 registered organizations, 1 honor society, 6 religious organizations. **Athletics (Intercollegiate):** *Men:* baseball, basketball, cross-country, football, golf, soccer. *Women:* basketball, cross-country, golf, soccer, softball, volleyball. **On-Campus Highlights:** Storm Cafe/Student Union, Coffee Shoppe and Climbing Wall, Fireside Room, Wild Athletic Center/ Weight Room, Life Fitness Center **Environmental Initiatives:** The College recycles all cardboard and provides co-mingled recycling containers in all common areas, each classroom, and in each office. We post recycling program notes on our website from time to time and also posters throughout the building quarterly. Large amounts of metals, plastics, light bulbs, electronics, etc. are recycled each month by facilities mgmt.

ADMISSIONS

Freshman Academic Profile: Average high school GPA 3.4. 13% in top 10% of high school class, 38% in top 25% of high school class, 79% in top 50% of high school class. **Test Scores:** SAT Math middle 50% range 475-598. SAT EBRW middle 50% range 508-600. ACT middle 50% range 21-25. Minimum internet-based TOEFL 75. Minimum paper TOEFL 500. **Basis for Candidate Selection:** *Very important factors considered include:* academic GPA, application essay, standardized test scores, religious affiliation/ commitment. *Other factors considered include:* rigor of secondary school record, recommendation(s). **Freshman Admission Requirements:** High school diploma is required and GED is accepted *Academic units recommended:* 4 English, 3 math, 3 science, 2 foreign language, 3 social studies. **Freshman Admission Statistics:** 453 applied, 77.7% admitted, 45% enrolled. **Transfer Admission Requirements:** High school transcript, college transcript(s), essay or personal statement, Minimum college GPA of 2.0 required. Lowest grade transferable C. **General Admission Information:** Application fee $20. Regular application deadline 8/20. Nonfall registration accepted. Admission may be deferred for a maximum of 1 year.

COSTS AND FINANCIAL AID

Annual tuition $22,100. Room and board $7,480. Average book expense $1,140. **Required Forms and Deadlines:** FAFSA; Institution's own financial aid form. **Notification of Awards:** Applicants will be notified of awards on a rolling basis beginning 3/1. **Types of Aid:** *Need-based scholarships/grants:* College/ university scholarship or grant aid from institutional funds; Federal Pell; Private scholarships; SEOG; State scholarships/grants. *Loans:* Direct PLUS loans; Direct Subsidized Stafford Loans; Direct Unsubsidized Stafford Loans. *Student Employment:* Federal Work-Study Program available. **Financial Aid Statistics:** 84% freshmen, 83% undergrads receive any aid. **Criteria for awarding aid:** *Need-based:* Academics *Non-need-based:* Academics, Alumni affiliation, Leadership, Minority status, Music/drama, Religious affiliation.

THE CULINARY INSTITUTE OF AMERICA

1946 Campus Drive, Hyde Park, NY 12538
Phone: (845) 452-9430 · **Financial Aid Phone:** 845-451-1500
E-mail: admissions@culinary.edu · **CEEB Code:** 3301
Fax: (845) 451-1068 · **Website:** www.ciachef.edu · **ACT Code:** 2728

This private school was founded in 1946. It has a 170 acre campus.

RATINGS

Admissions Selectivity Rating: 73   **Fire Safety Rating:** 98   **Green Rating:** 60*

STUDENTS AND FACULTY

Enrollment: 3,116. **Student Body:** 50% female, 50% male, 66% out-of-state, (46 countries represented).

Faculty: Student/faculty ratio 20:1. 141 full-time faculty, 14% are members of minority groups, 28% are women. 0% of classes are taught by teaching assistants.

ACADEMICS

Degrees: Associate; Bachelor's; Certificate; Post-Bachelor's certificate **Classes:** Most classes have 10-19 students. **Most popular majors:** Culinary Science/ Culinology; Multi-/Interdisciplinary Studies, Other; Restaurant/Food Services Management. **Special Study Options:** Double major; Internships; Study abroad. **Disability Services offered to physically disabled students:** Note-taking services; Reader services; Tape recorders; Tutors. **Career services:** Alumni network; Career assessment; Career/job search classes; Internships

FACILITIES

Housing: Coed dorms

CAMPUS LIFE

Environment: Village **Activities:** International Student Organization; Student government; Student newspaper. Library Learning Commons, Student Commons, Apple Pie Bakery Cafe, The Bakery Cafe by Illy—Greystone, California Campus, Nao Latin Gastro Bar- San Antonio Campus

ADMISSIONS

Freshman Academic Profile: Average high school GPA 3.1. 9% in top 10% of high school class, 26% in top 25% of high school class, 58% in top 50% of high school class. **Test Scores:** SAT Math middle 50% range 480-580. SAT EBRW middle 50% range 500-620. ACT middle 50% range 17-24. Minimum internet-based TOEFL 80. Minimum paper TOEFL 550. **Basis for Candidate Selection:** *Important factors considered include:* rigor of secondary school record, academic GPA. *Other factors considered include:* class rank, application essay, standardized test scores, recommendation(s), extracurricular activities, talent/ability, character/personal qualities, alumni/ae relation, volunteer work, work experience, level of applicant's interest. **Freshman Admission Requirements:** High school diploma is required and GED is accepted *Academic units required:* 4 English, 3 math, 3 science, 4 social studies, *Academic units recommended:* 4 English, 3 math, 3 science, 2 foreign language, 4 social studies. **Freshman Admission Statistics:** 1,170 applied, 97.2% admitted, 38% enrolled. **General Admission Information:** Application fee $50. Nonfall registration accepted. Admission may be deferred for a maximum of 1 year.

COSTS AND FINANCIAL AID

Required Forms and Deadlines: FAFSA; State aid form. **Notification of Awards:** Applicants will be notified of awards on a rolling basis beginning 3/5. **Types of Aid:** *Need-based scholarships/grants:* College/university scholarship or grant aid from institutional funds; Federal Pell; Private scholarships; SEOG; State scholarships/grants. *Loans:* Direct PLUS loans; Direct Subsidized Stafford Loans; Direct Unsubsidized Stafford Loans. *Student Employment:* Federal Work-Study Program available. Institutional employment available. **Financial Aid Statistics:** 92% needy undergrads receive need-based scholarship or grant aid. 86% freshmen, 77% undergrads receive non-need-based scholarship or grant aid. 94% freshmen, 88% undergrads receive need-based self-help aid. 0% freshmen, 0% undergrads receive athletic scholarships. 94% freshmen, 90% undergrads receive any aid. 63% undergrads borrow to pay for school. Average cumulative indebtedness $51,200. **Criteria for awarding aid:** *Non-need-based:* Academics, Alumni affiliation, Job skills, Leadership.

CULVER-STOCKTON COLLEGE

One College Hill, Canton, MO 63435
Phone: 573-288-6331 · **Financial Aid Phone:** 573-288-6307
E-mail: admission@culver.edu · **CEEB Code:** 6123
Fax: 573-288-6618 · **ACT Code:** 2290

This private school, affiliated with the Disciples of Christ Church, was founded in 1853. It has a 139 acre campus.

RATINGS

Admissions Selectivity Rating: 83   **Fire Safety Rating:** 75   **Green Rating:** 60*

STUDENTS AND FACULTY

Enrollment: 1,028. **Student Body:** 50% female, 50% male, 46% out-of-state, 6% international (20 countries represented). Asian <1%, African American 12%, Caucasian 72%, Hispanic 6%, Native American <1%, Pacific Islander <1%, Two or more races 3%, Race unknown 0%.
Retention and Graduation: 68% freshmen return for sophomore year. 38% freshmen graduate within 4 years. 47% freshmen graduate within 6 years. 15% grads go on to further study within 1 year. 9% grads pursue arts and sciences degrees. 3% grads pursue law degrees. 3% grads pursue business degrees.
Faculty: Student/faculty ratio 15:1. 51 full-time faculty, 65% hold PhDs, 6% are members of minority groups, 47% are women. 0% of classes are taught by teaching assistants.

ACADEMICS

Degrees: Bachelor's; Master's **Classes:** Most classes have 10-19 students.
Most popular majors: Sport And Fitness Administration/Management; Criminal Justice/Law Enforcement Administration; Business Administration And Management, General. **Special Study Options:** Accelerated program; Cross-registration; Distance learning; Double major; Dual enrollment; Honors program; Independent study; Internships; Student-designed major; Study abroad; Teacher certification program. **Honors programs:** Honors Scholars are expected to complete both an academic and enrichment requirement.
Disability Services offered to physically disabled students: Note-taking services; Reader services; Tape recorders; Tutors. **Career services:** Alumni network; Alumni services; Career assessment; Career/job search classes; Internships; Regional alumni

FACILITIES

Housing: Coed dorms; Fraternity/sorority housing; Wellness housing 40% of campus accessible to physically disabled. **Special Academic Facilities/Equipment:** Phage genomics research facility with DNA sequencer, astronomy observation deck, biological research station, collegiate teaching greenhouse, fine arts multi-media editing suite and recording studio, art gallery, radio broadcasting and television studio, mock trial courtroom and legal research library **Computers:** 100% of classrooms, 100% of dorms, 100% of libraries, 100% of dining areas, 100% of student union, 100% of common outdoor areas have wireless network access. Students can register for classes online. Administrative functions (other than registration) can be performed online.

CAMPUS LIFE

Environment: Rural **Activities:** Campus Ministries; Choral groups; Concert band; Dance; Drama/theater; International Student Organization; Jazz band; Literary magazine; Music ensembles; Musical theater; Radio station; Student government; Student newspaper; Television station 44 registered organizations, 11 honor societies, 4 religious organizations. 4 fraternities, 3 sororities. **Athletics (Intercollegiate):** *Men:* baseball, basketball, cheerleading, cross-country, football, golf, soccer, track/field (outdoor), track/field (indoor). *Women:* basketball, cheerleading, cross-country, golf, soccer, softball, track/field (outdoor), track/field (indoor), volleyball. **On-Campus Highlights:** The Lab Coffee House, Cat's 'Pause', Mabee Health & Wellness Center, Joe Charles Field House, Library/TASC Center **Environmental Initiatives:** Thermostat control

ADMISSIONS

Freshman Academic Profile: Average high school GPA 3.3. 9% in top 10% of high school class, 28% in top 25% of high school class, 64% in top 50% of high school class. 95% from public high schools. **Test Scores:** SAT Math middle 50% range 470-540. SAT EBRW middle 50% range 470-540. ACT middle 50% range 18-23. Minimum internet-based TOEFL 79. Minimum paper TOEFL 550. **Basis for Candidate Selection:** *Very important factors considered include:* academic GPA, standardized test scores. *Important factors considered include:* rigor of secondary school record. *Other factors considered include:* class rank, application essay, recommendation(s), interview. **Freshman Admission Requirements:** High school diploma is required and GED is accepted *Academic units recommended:* 4 English, 2 math, 2 science, 1 foreign language, 3 social studies, 3 history. **Freshman Admission Statistics:** 3,308 applied, 54.7% admitted, 17% enrolled. **Transfer Admission Requirements:** college transcript(s), Minimum college GPA of 2.0 required. Lowest grade transferable

C-. **General Admission Information:** Regular application deadline 8/15. Nonfall registration accepted. Admission may be deferred for a maximum of 1 year.

COSTS AND FINANCIAL AID

Annual tuition $26,255. Room and board $8,520. Required fees $425. Average book expense $1,100. **Required Forms and Deadlines:** FAFSA. **Notification of Awards:** Applicants will be notified of awards on a rolling basis beginning 11/15. **Types of Aid:** *Need-based scholarships/grants:* College/university scholarship or grant aid from institutional funds; Federal Pell; Private scholarships; SEOG; State scholarships/grants. *Loans:* Direct PLUS loans; Direct Subsidized Stafford Loans; Direct Unsubsidized Stafford Loans. *Student Employment:* Federal Work-Study Program available. Institutional employment available. **Financial Aid Statistics:** 100% needy freshmen, 99% needy undergrads receive need-based scholarship or grant aid. 15% freshmen, 12% undergrads receive non-need-based scholarship or grant aid. 82% freshmen, 87% undergrads receive need-based self-help aid. 15% freshmen, 17% undergrads receive athletic scholarships. 94% freshmen, 97% undergrads receive any aid. 85% undergrads borrow to pay for school. Average cumulative indebtedness $28,605. **Criteria for awarding aid:** *Need-based:* Academics, Art, Athletics, Music/drama, Religious affiliation *Non-need-based:* Academics, Alumni affiliation, Art, Athletics, Leadership, Music/drama, Religious affiliation.

CURRY COLLEGE

1071 Blue Hill Avenue, Milton, MA 02186
Phone: 617-333-2210
E-mail: curryadm@curry.edu · **CEEB Code:** 3285
Fax: 617-333-2114 · **Website:** www.curry.edu · **ACT Code:** 1814

This private school was founded in 1879. It has a 137 acre campus.

RATINGS

Admissions Selectivity Rating: 71   **Fire Safety Rating:** 60*   **Green Rating:** 60*

STUDENTS AND FACULTY

Enrollment: 2,843. **Student Body:** 63% female, 37% male, 22% out-of-state, 1% international (20 countries represented). Asian 2%, African American 9%, Caucasian 69%, Hispanic 5%, Native American <1%, Pacific Islander 0%, Two or more races 2%, Race unknown 12%.
Retention and Graduation: 71% freshmen return for sophomore year. 17% grads go on to further study within 1 year. 10% grads pursue arts and sciences degrees. 1% grads pursue law degrees. 2% grads pursue business degrees.
Faculty: Student/faculty ratio 11:1. 122 full-time faculty, 81% hold PhDs, 7% are members of minority groups, 67% are women. 0% of classes are taught by teaching assistants.

ACADEMICS

Degrees: Bachelor's; Master's **Classes:** Most classes have 10-19 students. Most lab/discussion sessions have fewer than 10 students. **Special Study Options:** Accelerated program; Cross-registration; Double major; English as a Second Language (ESL); Honors program; Independent study; Internships; Liberal arts/career combination; Student-designed major; Study abroad; Teacher certification program. **Disability Services offered to physically disabled students:** Tape recorders; Tutors.

FACILITIES

Housing: Coed dorms; Men's dorms; Special housing for disabled student; Theme housing; Women's dorms **Special Academic Facilities/Equipment:** On-campus preschool, nursing lab, psychology lab. **Computers:** Students can register for classes online.

CAMPUS LIFE

Environment: Village **Activities:** Campus Ministries; Choral groups; Dance; Drama/theater; International Student Organization; Literary magazine; Music ensembles; Radio station; Student government; Student newspaper; Student-run film society; Television station; Yearbook 1 honor societies, 2 religious organizations. **Athletics (Intercollegiate):** *Men:* baseball, basketball, cheerleading, football, ice hockey, lacrosse, soccer, tennis. *Women:* basketball, cheerleading, cross-country, lacrosse, soccer, softball, tennis. **On-Campus Highlights:** Drapkin Student Center, Levin Library, WMLN Campus Radio Station, The Suites- New Residence Hall, Hafer Academic Center

ADMISSIONS

Freshman Academic Profile: Average high school GPA 2.8. 5% in top 10% of high school class, 18% in top 25% of high school class, 53% in top 50% of high school class. 76% from public high schools. **Test Scores:** SAT Math middle 50% range 430-520. SAT EBRW middle 50% range 420-520. ACT middle 50% range 18-21. Minimum paper TOEFL 500. **Basis for Candidate

Selection: *Very important factors considered include:* rigor of secondary school record. *Important factors considered include:* academic GPA, application essay, standardized test scores, recommendation(s), interview, extracurricular activities, character/personal qualities. *Other factors considered include:* class rank, talent/ability, alumni/ae relation, volunteer work, work experience, level of applicant's interest. **Freshman Admission Requirements:** High school diploma is required and GED is accepted *Academic units required:* 4 English, 3 math, *Academic units recommended:* 2 science, 1 science labs, 2 foreign language, 2 social studies, 2 history. **Freshman Admission Statistics:** 5,448 applied, 86.9% admitted, 14% enrolled. **Transfer Admission Requirements:** college transcript(s), essay or personal statement. Minimum college GPA of 2.0 required. Lowest grade transferable C-. **General Admission Information:** Application fee $50. Priority deadline 4/1. Nonfall registration accepted. Admission may be deferred.

COSTS AND FINANCIAL AID
Annual tuition $34,730. Room and board $13,900. Required fees $1,715. Average book expense $1,150. **Required Forms and Deadlines:** FAFSA. **Notification of Awards:** Applicants will be notified of awards on a rolling basis beginning 3/1. **Types of Aid:** *Need-based scholarships/grants:* College/university scholarship or grant aid from institutional funds; Federal Pell; Private scholarships; SEOG; State scholarships/grants. *Loans:* Direct PLUS loans; Direct Subsidized Stafford Loans; Direct Unsubsidized Stafford Loans. **Financial Aid Statistics:** 79% needy freshmen, 85% needy undergrads receive need-based scholarship or grant aid. 8% freshmen, 6% undergrads receive non-need-based scholarship or grant aid. 86% freshmen, 89% undergrads receive need-based self-help aid. 0% freshmen, 0% undergrads receive athletic scholarships. **Criteria for awarding aid:** *Non-need-based:* Academics, Alumni affiliation, Leadership.

DAEMEN COLLEGE

4380 Main Street, Amherst, NY 14226-3592
Phone: 716-839-8225 • **Financial Aid Phone:** 716-839-8254
E-mail: admissions@daemen.edu • **CEEB Code:** 2762
Fax: 716-839-8229 • **Website:** www.daemen.edu • **ACT Code:** 2874

This private school was founded in 1947. It has a 35 acre campus.

RATINGS
Admissions Selectivity Rating: 86   **Fire Safety Rating:** 90   **Green Rating:** 61

STUDENTS AND FACULTY
Enrollment: 1,884. **Student Body:** 70% female, 30% male, 5% out-of-state, 1% international (6 countries represented). Asian 2%, African American 11%, Caucasian 74%, Hispanic 7%, Native American <1%, Pacific Islander <1%, Two or more races 1%, Race unknown 2%.
Retention and Graduation: 79% freshmen return for sophomore year. **Faculty:** Student/faculty ratio 16:1. 122 full-time faculty, 76% hold PhDs, 6% are members of minority groups, 59% are women. 0% of classes are taught by teaching assistants.

ACADEMICS
Degrees: Bachelor's; Certificate; Doctoral/Professional; Master's; Post-Bachelor's certificate; Post-Master's certificate **Classes:** Most classes have 20-29 students. Most lab/discussion sessions have 10-19 students. **Most popular majors:** Elementary Education And Teaching; Natural Sciences; Registered Nursing/Registered Nurse. **Special Study Options:** Accelerated program; Cross-registration; Distance learning; Double major; Dual enrollment; Exchange student program (domestic); Honors program; Independent study; Internships; Liberal arts/career combination; Student-designed major; Study abroad; Teacher certification program; Weekend college. **Honors programs:** The Honors Program provides an enriched curriculum relying upon multiple perspectives and using primary sources rather than textbooks. Honors program students enjoy special residential accommodations, priority registration by class rank, opportunities for domestic and international travel, and unique offerings such as field trips, access to campus speakers, and research and publication opportunities. **Disability Services offered to physically disabled students:** Note-taking services; Tape recorders; Tutors. **Career services:** Alumni network; Alumni services; Career assessment; Career/job search classes; Internships; Regional alumni

FACILITIES
Housing: Coed dorms; Other (please specify) 99% of campus accessible to physically diasbled. **Special Academic Facilities/Equipment:** Research & Information Commons (RIC); Franette Goldman/Carolyn Greenfield Art Gallery; Natural and Health Sciences Research Center; Video Conferencing

Center. **Computers:** 60% of classrooms, 100% of dorms, 100% of libraries, 75% of dining areas, 50% of student union, 10% of common outdoor areas have wireless network access. Students can register for classes online. Administrative functions (other than registration) can be performed online.

CAMPUS LIFE
Environment: City **Activities:** Campus Ministries; Choral groups; Dance; Drama/theater; International Student Organization; Literary magazine; Student government; Student newspaper; Yearbook 45 registered organizations, 8 honor societies, 1 fraternities, 4 sororities. **Athletics (Intercollegiate):** *Men:* basketball, cross-country, golf, soccer. *Women:* basketball, cross-country, soccer, volleyball. **On-Campus Highlights:** Research and Information Commons, Modern Apartment-Style Residence Halls, Wick Student Center, Academic Computing Facilities, Athletic Facilities **Environmental Initiatives:** College has hosted conferences and symposia on campus: Annual Environmental Summit; Green Jobs Workshop; World on Your Plate Symposium, Focus the Nation Teach-In.

ADMISSIONS
Freshman Academic Profile: Average high school GPA 3.6. 28% in top 10% of high school class, 58% in top 25% of high school class, 89% in top 50% of high school class. **Test Scores:** SAT Math middle 50% range 470-590. SAT EBRW middle 50% range 450-570. ACT middle 50% range 21-27. Minimum internet-based TOEFL 61. Minimum paper TOEFL 500. **Basis for Candidate Selection:** *Very important factors considered include:* rigor of secondary school record, academic GPA, application essay, standardized test scores. *Important factors considered include:* recommendation(s). *Other factors considered include:* class rank, interview, talent/ability, character/personal qualities, alumni/ae relation, volunteer work, work experience, level of applicant's interest. **Freshman Admission Requirements:** High school diploma is required and GED is accepted *Academic units recommended:* 4 English, 4 math, 4 science, 1 science labs, 4 social studies. **Freshman Admission Statistics:** 3,219 applied, 52.0% admitted, 23% enrolled. **Transfer Admission Requirements:** college transcript(s), statement of good standing from prior institution(s). Minimum college GPA of 2.0 required. Lowest grade transferable C. **General Admission Information:** Application fee $25. Nonfall registration accepted. Admission may be deferred for a maximum of 1 year.

COSTS AND FINANCIAL AID
Annual tuition $21,800. Room and board $10,840. Required fees $510. Average book expense $800. **Required Forms and Deadlines:** FAFSA; State aid form. **Notification of Awards:** Applicants will be notified of awards on a rolling basis beginning 2/15. **Types of Aid:** *Need-based scholarships/grants:* College/university scholarship or grant aid from institutional funds; Federal Pell; Private scholarships; SEOG; State scholarships/grants. *Loans:* Direct PLUS loans; Direct Subsidized Stafford Loans; Direct Unsubsidized Stafford Loans. *Student Employment:* Federal Work-Study Program available. Institutional employment available. **Financial Aid Statistics:** 92% needy freshmen, 94% needy undergrads receive need-based scholarship or grant aid. 96% freshmen, 96% undergrads receive non-need-based scholarship or grant aid. 91% freshmen, 93% undergrads receive need-based self-help aid. 5% freshmen, 5% undergrads receive athletic scholarships. 99% freshmen, 84% undergrads receive any aid. **Criteria for awarding aid:** *Need-based:* Academics *Non-need-based:* Academics, Art, Athletics, Leadership.

See page 922.

DAKOTA STATE UNIVERSITY

820 N. Washington Ave., Madison, SD 57042
Phone: 605-256-5139 • **Financial Aid Phone:** (605) 256-5152
E-mail: admissions@dsu.edu • **CEEB Code:** 6247
Fax: 605-256-5020 • **Website:** www.dsu.edu • **ACT Code:** 3910

This public school was founded in 1881. It has a 62 acre campus.

RATINGS
Admissions Selectivity Rating: 78   **Fire Safety Rating:** 87   **Green Rating:** 61

STUDENTS AND FACULTY
Enrollment: 2,024. **Student Body:** 35% female, 65% male, 39% out-of-state, 1% international (34 countries represented). Asian 2%, African American 4%, Caucasian 84%, Hispanic 4%, Native American 1%, Pacific Islander <1%, Two or more races 4%, Race unknown 1%.
Retention and Graduation: 72% freshmen return for sophomore year. 18% freshmen graduate within 4 years. 35% freshmen graduate within 6 years. **Faculty:** 96 full-time faculty, 76% hold PhDs, 13% are members of minority groups, 33% are women.

ACADEMICS

Degrees: Associate; Bachelor's; Certificate; Doctoral/Research; Master's; Post-Bachelor's certificate **Classes:** Most classes have 20-29 students. **Most popular majors:** Computer And Information Sciences, General; System, Networking, And Lan/Wan Management/Manager; Computer And Information Systems Security/Information Assurance. **Special Study Options:** Cooperative education program; Cross-registration; Distance learning; Double major; Dual enrollment; Exchange student program (domestic); Honors program; Independent study; Internships; Study abroad; Teacher certification program. **Honors programs:** Center of Excellence(CEX), General Beadle Honors Program. **Disability Services offered to physically disabled students:** Note-taking services; Reader services; Tutors. **Career services:** Alumni services; Career assessment; Career/job search classes; Internships

FACILITIES

Housing: Apartments for single students; Coed dorms; Men's dorms 90% of campus accessible to physically diasbled. **Special Academic Facilities/ Equipment:** Smith Zimmerman Museum Beacom Institute of Technology The Community Center **Computers:** 100% of classrooms, 100% of dorms, 100% of libraries, 100% of dining areas, 100% of student union, 100% of common outdoor areas have wireless network access. Students can register for classes online. Administrative functions (other than registration) can be performed online. Undergraduates are required to own a computer.

CAMPUS LIFE

Environment: Village **Activities:** Choral groups; Drama/theater; International Student Organization; Jazz band; Literary magazine; Model UN; Musical theater; Radio station; Student government; Student newspaper; Student-run film society 33 registered organizations, 3 honor societies, 2 religious organizations. **Athletics (Intercollegiate):** *Men:* baseball, basketball, cheerleading, cross-country, football, track/field (outdoor), track/field (indoor). *Women:* basketball, cheerleading, cross-country, softball, track/field (outdoor), track/field (indoor), volleyball. **On-Campus Highlights:** Beacom Institute of Technology, Tunheim Classroom Building, Fieldhouse/Community Center, Caribou Coffee/Einstein's Bagels, Trojan Center/Student Union **Environmental Initiatives:** LEED Silver project in progress

ADMISSIONS

Freshman Academic Profile: Average high school GPA 3.2. **Test Scores:** SAT Math middle 50% range 460-620. SAT EBRW middle 50% range 490-620. ACT middle 50% range 19-26. Minimum internet-based TOEFL 71. Minimum paper TOEFL 525. **Basis for Candidate Selection:** *Important factors considered include:* class rank, academic GPA, standardized test scores. **Freshman Admission Requirements:** High school diploma is required and GED is accepted *Academic units recommended:* 4 English, 3 math, 3 science, 3 science labs, 3 social studies, 1 visual/performing arts. **Freshman Admission Statistics:** 972 applied, 84.4% admitted, 46% enrolled. **Transfer Admission Requirements:** High school transcript, college transcript(s), Minimum college GPA of 2.0 required. Lowest grade transferable D. **General Admission Information:** Application fee $20. Nonfall registration accepted. Admission may be deferred for a maximum of 1 semester.

COSTS AND FINANCIAL AID

Annual in-state tuition $6,720. Annual out-of-state tuition $10,121. Room and board $6,720. Required fees $1,956. Average book expense $1,200. **Required Forms and Deadlines:** FAFSA. **Notification of Awards:** Applicants will be notified of awards on a rolling basis beginning 4/1. **Types of Aid:** *Need-based scholarships/grants:* College/university scholarship or grant aid from institutional funds; Federal Pell; Private scholarships; SEOG; State scholarships/grants. *Loans:* Direct PLUS loans; Direct Subsidized Stafford Loans; Direct Unsubsidized Stafford Loans. *Student Employment:* Federal Work-Study Program available. Institutional employment available. **Financial Aid Statistics:** 62% needy freshmen, 60% needy undergrads receive need-based scholarship or grant aid. 71% freshmen, 44% undergrads receive non-need-based scholarship or grant aid. 95% freshmen, 93% undergrads receive need-based self-help aid. 21% freshmen, 13% undergrads receive athletic scholarships. 75% freshmen, 75% undergrads receive any aid. 79% undergrads borrow to pay for school. Average cumulative indebtedness $24,444. **Criteria for awarding aid:** *Need-based:* Academics, Athletics, Minority status *Non-need-based:* Academics, Alumni affiliation, Art, Athletics, Leadership, Minority status, Music/drama, State/district residency.

DALLAS BAPTIST UNIVERSITY

3000 Mountain Creek Parkway, Dallas, TX 75211-9299
Phone: 214-333-5360 • **Financial Aid Phone:** 214-333-5363
E-mail: admiss@dbu.edu • **CEEB Code:** 6159
Fax: 214-333-5447 • **Website:** http://www.dbu.edu/ • **ACT Code:** 4080

This private school, affiliated with the Baptist Church, was founded in 1898. It has a 292 acre campus.

RATINGS

Admissions Selectivity Rating: 91   **Fire Safety Rating:** 91   **Green Rating:** 60*

STUDENTS AND FACULTY

Enrollment: 3,053. **Student Body:** 59% female, 41% male, 8% out-of-state, 7% international (43 countries represented). Asian 2%, African American 13%, Caucasian 61%, Hispanic 17%, Native American 1%, Pacific Islander <1%, Two or more races 0%, Race unknown 0%.
Retention and Graduation: 70% freshmen return for sophomore year. 44% freshmen graduate within 4 years. 58% freshmen graduate within 6 years. **Faculty:** Student/faculty ratio 13:1. 134 full-time faculty, 81% hold PhDs, 10% are members of minority groups, 38% are women. 0% of classes are taught by teaching assistants.

ACADEMICS

Degrees: Associate; Bachelor's; Certificate; Doctoral/Research; Master's; Post-Bachelor's certificate; Post-Master's certificate; Transfer Associate **Most popular majors:** Multi/Interdisciplinary Studies, Other; Psychology, General; Business Administration, Management And Operations. **Special Study Options:** Accelerated program; Cross-registration; Distance learning; Double major; Dual enrollment; English as a Second Language (ESL); Exchange student program (domestic); Honors program; Internships; Study abroad; Teacher certification program; Weekend college. **Honors programs:** The University Honors Program exists to help some of our brightest and most gifted students discover the extent of their own abilities and callings. Our program with its interdisciplinary core is designed to help students make connections across their classes and to encourage a high level of critical thinking. www.dbu.edu/honors/ **Combined degree programs:** BA/MA. **Disability Services offered to physically disabled students:** Note-taking services; Reader services; Tape recorders; Tutors. **Career services:** Alumni services; Career assessment; Career/job search classes; Internships; Regional alumni

FACILITIES

Housing: Apartments for single students; Men's dorms; Special housing for disabled student; Special housing for international students; Wellness housing; Women's dorms 90% of campus accessible to physically diasbled. **Special Academic Facilities/Equipment:** Corrie ten Boom Collection; Music Recording Studio; Special University Library Collections and Archives; Decatur Collection; Lord Braine of Wheatley Archives. **Computers:** Students can register for classes online.

CAMPUS LIFE

Environment: Metropolis **Activities:** Campus Ministries; Choral groups; Dance; Drama/theater; International Student Organization; Music ensembles; Musical theater; Opera; Pep band; Student government; Yearbook 36 registered organizations, 4 honor societies, 3 religious organizations. **Athletics (Intercollegiate):** *Men:* baseball, cross-country, golf, soccer, tennis, track/field (outdoor). *Women:* cross-country, golf, soccer, tennis, track/field (outdoor), volleyball. **On-Campus Highlights:** Pilgrim Chapel, Residence Halls, The Union—Mooyah and Coffee Shop, Apartments/Townhomes/Brownstones, Fitness Center

ADMISSIONS

Freshman Academic Profile: Average high school GPA 3.5. 21% in top 10% of high school class, 48% in top 25% of high school class, 80% in top 50% of high school class. 70% from public high schools. **Test Scores:** SAT Math middle 50% range 530-610. SAT EBRW middle 50% range 560-640. ACT middle 50% range 19-24. Minimum internet-based TOEFL 71. Minimum paper TOEFL 525. **Basis for Candidate Selection:** *Very important factors considered include:* rigor of secondary school record, class rank, academic GPA, application essay, standardized test scores, talent/ability, character/personal qualities, religious affiliation/commitment. *Important factors considered include:* interview, extracurricular activities. *Other factors considered include:* recommendation(s), alumni/ae relation, volunteer work, work experience, level of applicant's interest. **Freshman Admission Requirements:** High school diploma is required and GED is accepted *Academic units recommended:* 4 English, 3 math, 2 science, 1 science labs, 2 foreign language, 3 social studies, 4 history. **Freshman Admission Statistics:** 3,770 applied, 39.4% admitted, 36% enrolled. **Transfer Admission Requirements:** college transcript(s), essay or personal statement, Minimum college GPA of 2.5 required. Lowest grade transferable C. **General Admission Information:** Application fee

$25. Priority deadline 11/1. Nonfall registration accepted. Admission may be deferred for a maximum of 1 year.

COSTS AND FINANCIAL AID
Annual tuition $27,870. Room and board $7,992. Required fees $1,000. Average book expense $1,320. **Required Forms and Deadlines:** FAFSA; Institution's own financial aid form. **Notification of Awards:** Applicants will be notified of awards on a rolling basis beginning 2/1. **Types of Aid:** *Need-based scholarships/grants:* College/university scholarship or grant aid from institutional funds; Federal Pell; Private scholarships; SEOG; State scholarships/grants. *Loans:* Direct PLUS loans; Direct Subsidized Stafford Loans; Direct Unsubsidized Stafford Loans. *Student Employment:* Federal Work-Study Program available. Institutional employment available. **Financial Aid Statistics:** 63% needy freshmen, 63% needy undergrads receive need-based scholarship or grant aid. 95% freshmen, 89% undergrads receive non-need-based scholarship or grant aid. 81% freshmen, 79% undergrads receive need-based self-help aid. 5% freshmen, 4% undergrads receive athletic scholarships. 96% freshmen, 89% undergrads receive any aid. 79% undergrads borrow to pay for school. Average cumulative indebtedness $22,568. **Criteria for awarding aid:** *Non-need-based:* Academics, Athletics, Job skills, Leadership, Music/drama, Religious affiliation.

DARTMOUTH COLLEGE

6016 McNutt Hall, Hanover, NH 03755
Phone: 603-646-2875 • **Financial Aid Phone:** (800) 443-3605
E-mail: admissions.office@dartmouth.edu • **CEEB Code:** 3351
Fax: 603-646-1216 • **Website:** www.dartmouth.edu • **ACT Code:** 2508

This private school was founded in 1769. It has a 265 acre campus.

RATINGS
Admissions Selectivity Rating: 98   **Fire Safety Rating:** 89   **Green Rating:** 90

STUDENTS AND FACULTY
Enrollment: 4,340. **Student Body:** 49% female, 51% male, 97% out-of-state, 9% international (70 countries represented). Asian 15%, African American 7%, Caucasian 50%, Hispanic 10%, Native American 2%, Pacific Islander <1%, Two or more races 5%, Race unknown 2%.
Retention and Graduation: 97% freshmen return for sophomore year. 88% freshmen graduate within 4 years. 96% freshmen graduate within 6 years. **Faculty:** Student/faculty ratio 7:1. 610 full-time faculty, 95% hold PhDs, 19% are members of minority groups, 37% are women. 1% of classes are taught by teaching assistants.

ACADEMICS
Degrees: Bachelor's; Doctoral/Professional; Doctoral/Research; Master's **Classes:** Most classes have 20-29 students. Most lab/discussion sessions have 10-19 students. **Most popular majors:** Psychology, General; Economics, General; Political Science And Government, General. **Special Study Options:** Double major; Exchange student program (domestic); Honors program; Independent study; Internships; Student-designed major; Study abroad; Teacher certification program. **Honors programs:** Presidential Scholarship Research Program; Senior Honors Thesis; Senior Fellowship. **Disability Services offered to physically disabled students:** Note-taking services; Reader services; Tape recorders; Tutors. **Career services:** Alumni network; Alumni services; Career assessment; Career/job search classes; Internships; Regional alumni

FACILITIES
Housing: Apartments for married students; Coed dorms; Cooperative housing; Fraternity/sorority housing; Special housing for international students; Theme housing; Wellness housing 75% of campus accessible to physically disabled. **Special Academic Facilities/Equipment:** Hood Museum of Art, Hopkins Center for Performing Arts, Tucker Foundation for volunteer services, observatory, centers for humanities, social science, and science. **Computers:** 100% of classrooms, 100% of dorms, 100% of libraries, 100% of dining areas, 100% of student union, 100% of common outdoor areas have wireless network access. Students can register for classes online. Administrative functions (other than registration) can be performed online. Undergraduates are required to own a computer.

CAMPUS LIFE
Environment: Village **Activities:** Campus Ministries; Choral groups; Concert band; Dance; Drama/theater; International Student Organization;

Jazz band; Literary magazine; Marching band; Model UN; Music ensembles; Musical theater; Opera; Pep band; Radio station; Student government; Student newspaper; Student-run film society; Symphony orchestra; Television station; Yearbook 330 registered organizations, 26 religious organizations. 14 fraternities, 6 sororities. **Athletics (Intercollegiate):** *Men:* baseball, basketball, crew/rowing, cross-country, diving, equestrian sports, fencing, football, golf, ice hockey, lacrosse, sailing, skiing (downhill/alpine), skiing (nordic/cross-country), soccer, squash, swimming, tennis, track/field (outdoor), track/field (indoor). *Women:* basketball, crew/rowing, cross-country, diving, equestrian sports, fencing, field hockey, golf, ice hockey, lacrosse, sailing, skiing (downhill/alpine), skiing (nordic/cross-country), soccer, softball, squash, swimming, tennis, track/field (outdoor), track/field (indoor), volleyball. **On-Campus Highlights:** Hopkins Center for Creative and Performing Arts, Hood Museum of Art, Murals by Jose Clemente Orozco, Ten library system, all open to visitors, Ledyard Canoe Club, oldest in the country **Environmental Initiatives:** As part of our commitment to reduce greenhouse gas emissions, Dartmouth commissioned an energy audit for the buildings that collectively use 75% of the energy on campus. Based on the results of this audit, the Trustees invested $12.5 million in 250 energy conservation and efficiency projects in existing buildings, which are now underway.

ADMISSIONS
Freshman Academic Profile: 93% in top 10% of high school class, 98% in top 25% of high school class, 99% in top 50% of high school class. 55% from public high schools. **Test Scores:** SAT Math middle 50% range 720-790. SAT EBRW middle 50% range 710-770. ACT middle 50% range 30-34. Minimum internet-based TOEFL 100. **Basis for Candidate Selection:** *Very important factors considered include:* rigor of secondary school record, class rank, academic GPA, application essay, standardized test scores, recommendation(s), extracurricular activities, character/personal qualities. *Important factors considered include:* talent/ability, volunteer work. *Other factors considered include:* interview, first generation, alumni/ae relation, geographical residence, racial/ethnic status. **Freshman Admission Requirements:** High school diploma or equivalent is not required *Academic units recommended:* 4 English, 4 math, 4 science, 4 foreign language, 4 social studies. **Freshman Admission Statistics:** 20,035 applied, 10.4% admitted, 58% enrolled. **Transfer Admission Requirements:** High school transcript, college transcript(s), essay or personal statement, standardized test scores, statement of good standing from prior institution(s). Lowest grade transferable B. **General Admission Information:** Application fee $80. Regular application deadline 1/1. Admission may be deferred.

COSTS AND FINANCIAL AID
Annual tuition $51,468. Room and board $15,159. Required fees $1,900. Average book expense $1,260. **Required Forms and Deadlines:** Business/Farm Supplement; CSS/Financial Aid PROFILE; FAFSA; Noncustodial PROFILE. **Notification of Awards:** Applicants will be notified of awards on or about 4/2. **Types of Aid:** *Need-based scholarships/grants:* College/university scholarship or grant aid from institutional funds; Federal Pell; Private scholarships; SEOG; State scholarships/grants. *Loans:* Direct PLUS loans; Direct Subsidized Stafford Loans; Direct Unsubsidized Stafford Loans. *Student Employment:* Federal Work-Study Program available. Institutional employment available. **Financial Aid Statistics:** 98% needy freshmen, 96% needy undergrads receive need-based scholarship or grant aid. 0% undergrads receive non-need-based scholarship or grant aid. 89% freshmen, 91% undergrads receive need-based self-help aid. 0% freshmen, 0% undergrads receive athletic scholarships. 58% freshmen, 54% undergrads receive any aid. Average cumulative indebtedness $17,849.

DAVIDSON COLLEGE

Box 5000, Davidson, NC 28035-7156
Phone: 704-894-2230
E-mail: admission@davidson.edu • **CEEB Code:** 5150
Fax: 704-894-2016 • **Website:** www.davidson.edu • **ACT Code:** 3086

This private school, affiliated with the Presbyterian Church, was founded in 1837. It has a 665 acre campus.

RATINGS
Admissions Selectivity Rating: 98   **Fire Safety Rating:** 60*   **Green Rating:** 63

STUDENTS AND FACULTY

Enrollment: 1,800. **Student Body:** 49% female, 51% male, 77% out-of-state, 7% international (42 countries represented). Asian 6%, African American 7%, Caucasian 67%, Hispanic 8%, Native American <1%, Pacific Islander <1%, Two or more races 5%, Race unknown 1%.

Retention and Graduation: 95% freshmen return for sophomore year. 21% grads go on to further study within 1 year. **Faculty:** Student/faculty ratio 9:1. 191 full-time faculty, 97% hold PhDs, 23% are members of minority groups, 45% are women. 0% of classes are taught by teaching assistants.

ACADEMICS

Degrees: Bachelor's **Classes:** Most classes have 10-19 students. Most lab/discussion sessions have 10-19 students. **Most popular majors:** Biology/Biological Sciences, General; Psychology, General; Political Science And Government, General. **Special Study Options:** Cross-registration; Double major; Exchange student program (domestic); Independent study; Internships; Student-designed major; Study abroad. **Disability Services offered to physically disabled students:** Note-taking services; Reader services; Tape recorders; Tutors. **Career services:** Alumni network; Alumni services; Career assessment; Career/job search classes; Internships

FACILITIES

Housing: Apartments for single students; Coed dorms; Cooperative housing; Theme housing; Wellness housing 90% of campus accessible to physically disabled. **Special Academic Facilities/Equipment:** Art gallery, scanning electron microscopes, UV-visible spectrometer, laser systems, Baker sports complex, Visual Arts building. **Computers:** Students can register for classes online.

CAMPUS LIFE

Environment: Village **Activities:** Campus Ministries; Choral groups; Dance; Drama/theater; International Student Organization; Jazz band; Literary magazine; Music ensembles; Musical theater; Pep band; Radio station; Student government; Student newspaper; Symphony orchestra; Yearbook 151 registered organizations, 15 honor societies, 16 religious organizations. 8 fraternities. **Athletics (Intercollegiate):** *Men:* baseball, basketball, cross-country, diving, football, golf, soccer, swimming, tennis, track/field (outdoor), wrestling. *Women:* basketball, cross-country, diving, field hockey, lacrosse, soccer, swimming, tennis, track/field (outdoor), volleyball. **On-Campus Highlights:** Belk Visual Arts Center, Baker-Watt Science Complex, Baker Sports Complex, Campus Center, Lake Campus **Environmental Initiatives:** Solar PV and solar thermal array on Baker Sports Complex

ADMISSIONS

Freshman Academic Profile: Average high school GPA 3.9. 76% in top 10% of high school class, 95% in top 25% of high school class, 99% in top 50% of high school class. 47% from public high schools. **Test Scores:** SAT Math middle 50% range 650-730. SAT EBRW middle 50% range 660-740. ACT middle 50% range 30-33. Minimum internet-based TOEFL 100. Minimum paper TOEFL 600. **Basis for Candidate Selection:** *Very important factors considered include:* rigor of secondary school record, recommendation(s), character/personal qualities, volunteer work. *Important factors considered include:* application essay, standardized test scores, extracurricular activities, talent/ability. *Other factors considered include:* class rank, academic GPA, alumni/ae relation. **Freshman Admission Requirements:** High school diploma is required and GED is not accepted *Academic units required:* 4 English, 3 math, 2 science, 2 foreign language, and 2 units from above areas or other academic areas. *Academic units recommended:* 4 math, 4 science, 4 foreign language, 4 units from above areas or other academic areas. **Freshman Admission Statistics:** 5,673 applied, 20.2% admitted, 45% enrolled. **Transfer Admission Requirements:** High school transcript, college transcript(s), essay or personal statement, standardized test scores, statement of good standing from prior institution(s). Minimum college GPA of 3.0 required. Lowest grade transferable C. **General Admission Information:** Application fee $50. Regular application deadline 1/2. Nonfall registration accepted. Admission may be deferred for a maximum of 1 year.

COSTS AND FINANCIAL AID

Annual tuition $49,454. Room and board $13,954. Required fees $495. Average book expense $1,000. **Required Forms and Deadlines:** Business/Farm Supplement; CSS/Financial Aid PROFILE; FAFSA; Noncustodial PROFILE. **Notification of Awards:** Applicants will be notified of awards on or about 4/1. **Types of Aid:** *Need-based scholarships/grants:* College/university scholarship or grant aid from institutional funds; Federal Pell; Private scholarships; SEOG; State scholarships/grants. *Loans:* Direct PLUS loans; Direct Subsidized Stafford Loans; Direct Unsubsidized Stafford Loans. *Student Employment:* Federal Work-Study Program available. Institutional employment available. **Financial Aid Statistics:** 99% needy freshmen, 98% needy undergrads receive need-based scholarship or grant aid. 34% freshmen, 27% undergrads receive non-need-based scholarship or grant aid. 63% freshmen, 66% undergrads receive need-based self-help aid. 5% freshmen, 7% undergrads receive athletic scholarships. 52% freshmen, 52% undergrads receive any aid. 26% undergrads borrow to pay for school. Average cumulative indebtedness $20,431. **Criteria**

for awarding aid: Non-need-based: Academics, Alumni affiliation, Art, Athletics, Leadership, Minority status, Music/drama.

DE SALES UNIVERSITY

2755 Station Ave., Center Valley, PA 18034
Phone: 610-282-4443 • **Financial Aid Phone:** 610-282-4443
E-mail: admiss@desales.edu • **CEEB Code:** 2021
Fax: 610-282-0131 • **Website:** www.desales.edu • **ACT Code:** 3525

This private school, affiliated with the Roman Catholic Church, was founded in 1964. It has a 500 acre campus.

RATINGS

Admissions Selectivity Rating: 79   **Fire Safety Rating:** 88   **Green Rating:** 73

STUDENTS AND FACULTY

Enrollment: 2,295. **Student Body:** 61% female, 39% male, 24% out-of-state, <1% international (5 countries represented). Asian 3%, African American 4%, Caucasian 72%, Hispanic 13%, Native American 0%, Pacific Islander <1%, Two or more races 3%, Race unknown 5%.

Retention and Graduation: 81% freshmen return for sophomore year. 62% freshmen graduate within 4 years. 70% freshmen graduate within 6 years. **Faculty:** Student/faculty ratio 12:1. 126 full-time faculty, 83% hold PhDs, 5% are members of minority groups, 52% are women. 0% of classes are taught by teaching assistants.

ACADEMICS

Degrees: Bachelor's; Certificate; Doctoral/Professional; Master's; Post-Bachelor's certificate; Post-Master's certificate **Classes:** Most classes have 10-19 students. Most lab/discussion sessions have 30-39 students. **Special Study Options:** Accelerated program; Cross-registration; Distance learning; Double major; Dual enrollment; Exchange student program (domestic); External degree program; Honors program; Independent study; Internships; Liberal arts/career combination; Student-designed major; Study abroad; Teacher certification program; Weekend college. **Honors programs:** Student participation in the Faith & Reason Honors Program is competitive, usually limited to a maximum of fifteen (15) students in each academic class. The aim of this program is to provide scholarship-level students with a unique opportunity to explore the "big questions" in life, in a small cohort of students, guided by senior-level faculty at DeSales University. Each semester, students in the Honors Program enjoy "priority pre-registration" for all their classes. Students who complete all components of the program have their participation noted on their university transcripts and receive recognition of their accomplishment at the University's commencement ceremonies. **Disability Services offered to physically disabled students:** Note-taking services; Reader services; Tape recorders; Tutors. **Career services:** Alumni network; Alumni services; Career assessment; Career/job search classes; Internships

FACILITIES

Housing: Coed dorms; Cooperative housing; Men's dorms; Special housing for disabled student; Theme housing; Women's dorms 99% of campus accessible to physically disabled. **Special Academic Facilities/Equipment:** The Gambet Center for Business and Health Care includes a replica commodities trading center and the only human gross anatomy laboratory in the region in addition to simulation labs. **Computers:** 100% of classrooms, 5% of dorms, 100% of libraries, 100% of dining areas, 5% of student union, 20% of common outdoor areas have wireless network access. Students can register for classes online. Administrative functions (other than registration) can be performed online.

CAMPUS LIFE

Environment: Town **Activities:** Campus Ministries; Choral groups; Dance; Drama/theater; International Student Organization; Jazz band; Literary magazine; Marching band; Model UN; Music ensembles; Musical theater; Pep band; Radio station; Student government; Student newspaper; Student-run film society; Television station; Yearbook 42 registered organizations, 12 honor societies, 1 religious organization. **Athletics (Intercollegiate):** *Men:* baseball, basketball, cross-country, golf, lacrosse, soccer, tennis, track/field (outdoor), track/field (indoor). *Women:* basketball, cross-country, field hockey, soccer, softball, tennis, track/field (outdoor), track/field (indoor), volleyball. **On-Campus Highlights:** Billera Athletics and Recreation Center, Hurd Science Center, Gambet Center for Business & Healthcare, University Center, Labuda Center for the Performing Arts **Environmental Initiatives:** Water reduction program—after adding one new residence hall we still reduced our water usage by 10% from 2008 to 2009.

ADMISSIONS

Freshman Academic Profile: Average high school GPA 3.3. 34% in top 10% of high school class, 52% in top 25% of high school class, 79% in top 50%

of high school class. 62% from public high schools. **Test Scores:** SAT Math middle 50% range 500-610. SAT EBRW middle 50% range 510-618. ACT middle 50% range 23-27. Minimum internet-based TOEFL 79-80. Minimum paper TOEFL 550. **Basis for Candidate Selection:** *Very important factors considered include:* rigor of secondary school record, academic GPA, character/personal qualities. *Important factors considered include:* class rank, application essay, standardized test scores, recommendation(s), interview, level of applicant's interest. *Other factors considered include:* extracurricular activities, talent/ability, first generation, volunteer work, work experience. **Freshman Admission Requirements:** High school diploma is required and GED is accepted *Academic units required:* 4 English, 3 math, 2 science, 2 science labs, 2 foreign language, 3 social studies, *Academic units recommended:* 4 English, 4 math, 3 science, 3 science labs, 4 foreign language, 3 social studies. **Freshman Admission Statistics:** 2,979 applied, 73.3% admitted, 19% enrolled. **Transfer Admission Requirements:** High school transcript, college transcript(s), statement of good standing from prior institution(s). Minimum college GPA of 2.00 required. Lowest grade transferable 2. **General Admission Information:** Priority deadline 3/1. Regular application deadline 8/1. Nonfall registration accepted. Admission may be deferred.

COSTS AND FINANCIAL AID

Required Forms and Deadlines: FAFSA. **Notification of Awards:** Applicants will be notified of awards on a rolling basis beginning 12/1. **Types of Aid:** *Need-based scholarships/grants:* College/university scholarship or grant aid from institutional funds; Federal Pell; Private scholarships; SEOG; State scholarships/grants. *Loans:* Direct PLUS loans; Direct Subsidized Stafford Loans; Direct Unsubsidized Stafford Loans. *Student Employment:* Federal Work-Study Program available. Institutional employment available. **Financial Aid Statistics:** 100% needy freshmen, 95% needy undergrads receive need-based scholarship or grant aid. 93% freshmen, 83% undergrads receive non-need-based scholarship or grant aid. 76% freshmen, 81% undergrads receive need-based self-help aid. 0% freshmen, 0% undergrads receive athletic scholarships. 81% freshmen, 77% undergrads receive any aid. 81% undergrads borrow to pay for school. Average cumulative indebtedness $15,189. **Criteria for awarding aid:** *Need-based:* Academics, Alumni affiliation *Non-need-based:* Academics, Alumni affiliation, Art, Leadership, Music/drama, Religious affiliation.

See page 924.

DEEP SPRINGS COLLEGE

HC 72 Box 45001, Dyer, NV 89010
Phone: 760-872-2000 · **Financial Aid Phone:** 760 872 2000
E-mail: apcom@deepsprings.edu · **CEEB Code:** 4281
Fax: 760-872-4466 · **Website:** www.deepsprings.edu · **ACT Code:** 252

This private school was founded in 1917. It has a 30000 acre campus.

RATINGS
Admissions Selectivity Rating: 99   **Fire Safety Rating:** 88   **Green Rating:** 60*

STUDENTS AND FACULTY
Enrollment: 28. **Student Body:** 0% female, 100% male, 82% out-of-state, 14% international (5 countries represented). Asian 14%, African American 0%, Caucasian 64%, Hispanic 4%, Native American 0%, Pacific Islander 0%, Two or more races 4%, Race unknown 0%.
Retention and Graduation: 92% freshmen return for sophomore year.
Faculty: Student/faculty ratio 4:1. 3 full-time faculty, 100% hold PhDs, 0% are members of minority groups, 67% are women. 0% of classes are taught by teaching assistants.

ACADEMICS
Degrees: Associate **Classes:** Most classes have 20-29 students. Most lab/discussion sessions have 20-29 students. **Most popular majors:** Liberal Arts And Sciences, General Studies And Humanities, Other. **Special Study Options:** Independent study; Internships.

FACILITIES
Housing: Cooperative housing; Men's dorms; Special housing for disabled student; Theme housing; Wellness housing 100% of campus accessible to physically diasbled. **Special Academic Facilities/Equipment:** Ranch- 300 cattle, 20 horses, organic farm growing hay and produce; thousands of acres of wilderness surround the college **Computers:**

CAMPUS LIFE
Environment: Rural **Activities:** Campus Ministries; Choral groups; Concert band; Dance; Drama/theater; International Student Organization; Literary magazine; Music ensembles; Musical theater; Radio station; Student government; Student newspaper; Student-run film society 1 registered organization. **On-Campus Highlights:** Boarding House, Dairy Barn, Horse Stables, The Upper Reservoir, The Druid

ADMISSIONS
Freshman Academic Profile: 100% in top 10% of high school class, 100% in top 25% of high school class, 100% in top 50% of high school class. 67% from public high schools. **Test Scores:** SAT Math middle 50% range 670-740. SAT EBRW middle 50% range 740-800. **Basis for Candidate Selection:** *Very important factors considered include:* application essay, interview, character/personal qualities, level of applicant's interest. *Important factors considered include:* rigor of secondary school record, academic GPA, extracurricular activities, volunteer work, work experience. *Other factors considered include:* class rank, standardized test scores, recommendation(s), talent/ability, first generation, racial/ethnic status. **Freshman Admission Requirements:** High school diploma or equivalent is not required **Freshman Admission Statistics:** 200 applied, 9.5% admitted, 84% enrolled. **Transfer Admission Requirements:** High school transcript, college transcript(s), essay or personal statement, interview, standardized test scores. **General Admission Information:** Regular application deadline 11/7. Nonfall registration accepted.

COSTS AND FINANCIAL AID
Average book expense $1,200. **Types of Aid: Financial Aid Statistics:** 0% freshmen, 0% undergrads receive athletic scholarships. 100% freshmen, 100% undergrads receive any aid. **Criteria for awarding aid:** *Non-need-based:* Academics, Art, Job skills, Leadership.

DEFIANCE COLLEGE

701 North Clinton Street, Defiance, OH 43512-1695
Phone: 419-783-2359 · **Financial Aid Phone:** 419-783-2458
E-mail: http://www.defiance.edu/admissions/index.html · **CEEB Code:** 1162
Fax: 419-783-2468 · **Website:** www.defiance.edu · **ACT Code:** 3264

This private school, affiliated with the United Church of Christ, was founded in 1850. It has a 150 acre campus.

RATINGS
Admissions Selectivity Rating: 80   **Fire Safety Rating:** 90   **Green Rating:** 64

STUDENTS AND FACULTY
Enrollment: 195. **Student Body:** 42% female, 58% male, 28% out-of-state, 2% international (2 countries represented). Asian 1%, African American 13%, Caucasian 74%, Hispanic 7%, Native American <1%, Pacific Islander 0%, Two or more races 3%, Race unknown 1%.
Retention and Graduation: 61% freshmen return for sophomore year.
Faculty: Student/faculty ratio 11:1. 36 full-time faculty, 61% hold PhDs, 17% are members of minority groups, 42% are women. 0% of classes are taught by teaching assistants.

ACADEMICS
Degrees: Associate; Bachelor's; Certificate; Master's **Classes:** Most classes have 10-19 students. Most lab/discussion sessions have 10-19 students. **Most popular majors:** Education, General; Criminal Justice And Corrections; Forensic Science And Technology. **Special Study Options:** Distance learning; Double major; Dual enrollment; Honors program; Independent study; Internships; Student-designed major; Study abroad; Teacher certification program. **Disability Services offered to physically disabled students:** Note-taking services; Reader services; Tape recorders; Tutors. **Career services:** Alumni network; Alumni services; Career assessment; Career/job search classes; Internships; Regional alumni

FACILITIES
Housing: Apartments for single students; Coed dorms; Theme housing; Wellness housing 100% of campus accessible to physically diasbled. **Special Academic Facilities/Equipment:** Art gallery, media center, Eisenhower archives room, curriculum resource center, Cultural Arts Center, Indian wars collection. **Computers:** 100% of classrooms, 30% of dorms, 100% of libraries, 100% of dining areas, 100% of student union, 100% of common outdoor areas have wireless network access.

CAMPUS LIFE
Environment: Village **Activities:** Campus Ministries; Choral groups; Concert band; Dance; Drama/theater; Jazz band; Literary magazine; Marching

band; Music ensembles; Musical theater; Pep band; Student government; Student newspaper 30 registered organizations, 1 honor society, 2 religious organizations. 1 fraternity, 2 sororities. **Athletics (Intercollegiate):** *Men:* baseball, basketball, cross-country, football, golf, soccer, tennis, track/field (outdoor), track/field (indoor). *Women:* basketball, cross-country, golf, soccer, softball, tennis, track/field (outdoor), track/field (indoor), volleyball. **On-Campus Highlights:** George M. Smart Athletic Center, Serrick Center, Hubbard Hall, Weaner/McMaster Center, Pilgrim Library **Environmental Initiatives:** Lowering Electrical, Gas, and Water Usage

ADMISSIONS

Freshman Academic Profile: Average high school GPA 3.1. 12% in top 10% of high school class, 29% in top 25% of high school class, 57% in top 50% of high school class. 97% from public high schools. **Test Scores:** SAT Math middle 50% range 340-470. SAT EBRW middle 50% range 360-490. ACT middle 50% range 18-22. Minimum internet-based TOEFL 79. Minimum paper TOEFL 550. **Basis for Candidate Selection:** *Very important factors considered include:* rigor of secondary school record, academic GPA, standardized test scores. *Other factors considered include:* class rank, application essay, recommendation(s), interview, extracurricular activities, character/personal qualities, volunteer work, work experience. **Freshman Admission Requirements:** High school diploma is required and GED is accepted *Academic units recommended:* 4 English, 3 math, 3 science, 2 science labs, 2 foreign language, 2 social studies, 2 visual/performing arts, 1 unit from above areas or other academic areas. **Freshman Admission Statistics:** 1,257 applied, 56.5% admitted, 21% enrolled. **Transfer Admission Requirements:** High school transcript, college transcript(s), essay or personal statement, statement of good standing from prior institution(s). Minimum college GPA of 2.0 required. Lowest grade transferable C. **General Admission Information:** Application fee $25. Nonfall registration accepted. Admission may be deferred for a maximum of one year.

COSTS AND FINANCIAL AID

Annual tuition $31,990. Room and board $10,220. Required fees $740. Average book expense $1,400. **Required Forms and Deadlines:** FAFSA. **Notification of Awards:** Applicants will be notified of awards on a rolling basis beginning 2/1. **Types of Aid:** *Need-based scholarships/grants:* College/university scholarship or grant aid from institutional funds; Federal Pell; Private scholarships; SEOG; State scholarships/grants. *Loans:* Direct PLUS loans; Direct Subsidized Stafford Loans; Direct Unsubsidized Stafford Loans. *Student Employment:* Federal Work-Study Program available. Institutional employment available. **Financial Aid Statistics:** 86% needy freshmen, 83% needy undergrads receive need-based scholarship or grant aid. 100% freshmen, 97% undergrads receive non-need-based scholarship or grant aid. 93% freshmen, 92% undergrads receive need-based self-help aid. 0% freshmen, 0% undergrads receive athletic scholarships. 100% freshmen, 99% undergrads receive any aid. **Criteria for awarding aid:** *Need-based:* Alumni affiliation, Religious affiliation *Non-need-based:* Academics, Leadership, Minority status, Music/drama.

DELAWARE VALLEY UNIVERSITY

700 East Butler Avenue, Doylestown, PA 18901-2697
Phone: 215-489-2211 · **Financial Aid Phone:** 215-489-2975
E-mail: ADMITME@delval.edu · **CEEB Code:** 2510
Fax: 215-230-2968 · **Website:** www.delval.edu · **ACT Code:** 3551

This private school was founded in 1896. It has a 571 acre campus.

RATINGS

Admissions Selectivity Rating: 80   **Fire Safety Rating:** 91   **Green Rating:** 60*

STUDENTS AND FACULTY

Enrollment: 1,890. **Student Body:** 59% female, 41% male, 37% out-of-state, 1% international (6 countries represented). Asian 1%, African American 9%, Caucasian 69%, Hispanic 8%, Native American 1%, Pacific Islander <1%, Two or more races 1%, Race unknown 10%.
Retention and Graduation: 71% freshmen return for sophomore year. 46% freshmen graduate within 4 years. 56% freshmen graduate within 6 years. 9% grads go on to further study within 1 year. 6% grads pursue arts and sciences degrees. 0.4% grads pursue law degrees. 2% grads pursue business degrees. 0.4% grads pursue medical degrees. **Faculty:** Student/faculty ratio 14:1. 92 full-time faculty, 68% hold PhDs, 12% are members of minority groups, 45% are women. 0% of classes are taught by teaching assistants.

ACADEMICS

Degrees: Associate; Bachelor's; Certificate; Doctoral/Research; Master's; Post-Bachelor's certificate **Classes:** Most classes have 10-19 students. Most lab/discussion sessions have 20-29 students. **Most popular majors:** Animal

Sciences, General; Animal Sciences, Other; Business Administration And Management, General. **Special Study Options:** Accelerated program; Distance learning; Double major; Dual enrollment; Honors program; Independent study; Internships; Study abroad; Teacher certification program. **Honors programs:** The Honors Program at DelVal is an educational enrichment program for students with exceptional promise. This four-year sequence of courses offers superior students intellectual opportunities beyond the scope of most collegiate programs: smaller discussion-based classes, direct contact with top faculty members, opportunities for international study and the freedom to pursue individualized programs with a cross-disciplinary flavor. During alternate years, the Honors Program sponsors special foreign study colloquia, which allow students the opportunity to augment their investigation of a major international city with travel to that city over spring break. Led by faculty with expertise in that particular region, these courses allow students the opportunity to explore the world around them and provide a forum for meaningful discussion of history and culture. **Combined degree programs:** BA/MA. **Disability Services offered to physically disabled students:** Note-taking services; Reader services; Tape recorders. **Career services:** Alumni services; Career assessment; Career/job search classes; Internships

FACILITIES

Housing: Coed dorms; Other (please specify) **Special Academic Facilities/Equipment:** Dairy processing plant, greenhouse and nursery lab complex, small animal science labs, poultry diagnostic lab, arboretum, equine facilities, 500+-acre farm, tissue culture lab. **Computers:** 25% of classrooms, 100% of dorms, 100% of libraries, 80% of student union, 20% of common outdoor areas have wireless network access. Students can register for classes online. Administrative functions (other than registration) can be performed online.

CAMPUS LIFE

Environment: Village **Activities:** Choral groups; Concert band; Drama/theater; Literary magazine; Music ensembles; Pep band; Student government 62 registered organizations, 2 honor societies, 2 religious organizations. 5 fraternities, 3 sororities. **Athletics (Intercollegiate):** *Men:* baseball, basketball, cross-country, football, golf, soccer, track/field (outdoor), track/field (indoor), wrestling. *Women:* basketball, cheerleading, cross-country, field hockey, soccer, softball, track/field (outdoor), track/field (indoor), volleyball. **On-Campus Highlights:** Smart Classroom, Small Animal Facility, Athletic Complex, Student Center, Equine center

ADMISSIONS

Freshman Academic Profile: Average high school GPA 3.3. 13% in top 10% of high school class, 30% in top 25% of high school class, 57% in top 50% of high school class. 98% from public high schools. **Test Scores:** SAT Math middle 50% range 480-570. SAT EBRW middle 50% range 480-595. ACT middle 50% range 19-25. Minimum internet-based TOEFL 74. Minimum paper TOEFL 537. **Basis for Candidate Selection:** *Very important factors considered include:* academic GPA, standardized test scores. *Important factors considered include:* rigor of secondary school record, interview. *Other factors considered include:* class rank, application essay, recommendation(s), extracurricular activities, talent/ability, character/personal qualities, alumni/ae relation, volunteer work, work experience, level of applicant's interest. **Freshman Admission Requirements:** High school diploma is required and GED is accepted *Academic units required:* 3 English, 2 math, 2 science, 1 science labs, 2 social studies, 6 academic electives. **Freshman Admission Statistics:** 2,405 applied, 66.4% admitted, 26% enrolled. **Transfer Admission Requirements:** High school transcript, college transcript(s), statement of good standing from prior institution(s). Minimum college GPA of 2.0 required. Lowest grade transferable C. **General Admission Information:** Application fee $50. Priority deadline 5/1. Nonfall registration accepted. Admission may be deferred for a maximum of 1 year.

COSTS AND FINANCIAL AID

Annual tuition $35,610. Room and board $13,950. Required fees $2,390. Average book expense $1,000. **Required Forms and Deadlines:** FAFSA; State aid form. **Notification of Awards:** Applicants will be notified of awards on a rolling basis beginning 1/30. **Types of Aid:** *Need-based scholarships/grants:* College/university scholarship or grant aid from institutional funds; Federal Pell; Private scholarships; SEOG; State scholarships/grants. *Loans:* Direct PLUS loans; Direct Subsidized Stafford Loans; Direct Unsubsidized Stafford Loans. *Student Employment:* Federal Work-Study Program available. Institutional employment available. **Financial Aid Statistics:** 99% needy freshmen, 99% needy undergrads receive need-based scholarship or grant aid. 9% freshmen, 8% undergrads receive non-need-based scholarship or grant aid. 83% freshmen, 80% undergrads receive need-based self-help aid. 0% freshmen, 0% undergrads receive athletic scholarships. 98% freshmen, 91% undergrads receive any aid. **Criteria for awarding aid:** *Non-need-based:* Academics, Alumni affiliation, Music/drama, State/district residency.

DENISON UNIVERSITY

100 West College Street, Granville, OH 43023
Phone: 740-587-6276 · **Financial Aid Phone:** 740-587-6279
E-mail: admissions@denison.edu · **CEEB Code:** 1164
Fax: 740-587-6306 · **Website:** denison.edu · **ACT Code:** 3266

This private school was founded in 1831. It has a 930 acre campus.

RATINGS
Admissions Selectivity Rating: 93   **Fire Safety Rating:** 96   **Green Rating:** 89

STUDENTS AND FACULTY
Enrollment: 2,321. **Student Body:** 55% female, 45% male, 74% out-of-state, 10% international (37 countries represented). Asian 4%, African American 7%, Caucasian 65%, Hispanic 9%, Native American 0%, Pacific Islander <1%, Two or more races 3%, Race unknown 2%.
Retention and Graduation: 91% freshmen return for sophomore year. 16% grads go on to further study within 1 year. 9% grads pursue arts and sciences degrees. 2% grads pursue law degrees. 2% grads pursue business degrees. 2% grads pursue medical degrees. **Faculty:** Student/faculty ratio 9:1. 218 full-time faculty, 97% hold PhDs, 22% are members of minority groups, 45% are women. 0% of classes are taught by teaching assistants.

ACADEMICS
Degrees: Bachelor's **Classes:** Most classes have 10-19 students. Most lab/discussion sessions have 10-19 students. **Most popular majors:** Biology, General; Psychology, General; Economics, General. **Special Study Options:** Double major; Independent study; Internships; Student-designed major; Study abroad. **Disability Services offered to physically disabled students:** Note-taking services; Reader services; Tape recorders; Tutors. **Career services:** Alumni network; Alumni services; Career assessment; Career/job search classes; Internships; Regional alumni

FACILITIES
Housing: Apartments for single students; Coed dorms; Cooperative housing; Men's dorms; Theme housing; Wellness housing; Women's dorms 75% of campus accessible to physically diasbled. **Special Academic Facilities/Equipment:** Burmese art collection in the Denision Museum, language lab, research station in 350-acre biological reserve, observatory, high resolution spectrometer lab, nuclear magnetic resonance spectrometer, planetarium, economics computer laboratories. **Computers:** 100% of classrooms, 100% of dorms, 100% of libraries, 100% of dining areas, 100% of student union, 100% of common outdoor areas have wireless network access. Administrative functions (other than registration) can be performed online.

CAMPUS LIFE
Environment: Village **Activities:** Campus Ministries; Choral groups; Dance; Drama/theater; International Student Organization; Jazz band; Literary magazine; Music ensembles; Musical theater; Radio station; Student government; Student newspaper; Student-run film society; Television station; Yearbook 160 registered organizations, 15 honor societies, 7 religious organizations. 8 fraternities, 6 sororities. **Athletics (Intercollegiate):** *Men:* baseball, basketball, cross-country, diving, football, golf, lacrosse, soccer, swimming, tennis, track/field (outdoor), track/field (indoor). *Women:* basketball, cross-country, diving, field hockey, golf, lacrosse, soccer, softball, swimming, tennis, track/field (outdoor), track/field (indoor), volleyball. **On-Campus Highlights:** Samson Talbot Hall of Biological Science, Bryant Arts Center, Mitchell Recreation and Athletics Center, Biological Reserve and Anderson Field Station, F.W. Olin Science Hall **Environmental Initiatives:** The signing of the ACUPCC and the development of a standing Campus Sustainability Committee as part of the campus governance system.

ADMISSIONS
Freshman Academic Profile: 65% in top 10% of high school class, 87% in top 25% of high school class, 100% in top 50% of high school class. 67% from public high schools. **Test Scores:** SAT Math middle 50% range 600-690. SAT EBRW middle 50% range 600-690. ACT middle 50% range 28-31. Minimum internet-based TOEFL 80. Minimum paper TOEFL 550. **Basis for Candidate Selection:** *Very important factors considered include:* rigor of secondary school record, academic GPA, application essay, recommendation(s). *Important factors considered include:* interview, extracurricular activities, talent/ability. *Other factors considered include:* class rank, standardized test scores, character/personal qualities, first generation, alumni/ae relation, geographical residence,

state residency, racial/ethnic status, volunteer work, work experience, level of applicant's interest. **Freshman Admission Requirements:** High school diploma is required and GED is accepted *Academic units required: Academic units recommended:* 4 English, 4 math, 4 science, 4 foreign language, 4 social studies. **Freshman Admission Statistics:** 7,540 applied, 37.2% admitted, 22% enrolled. **Transfer Admission Requirements:** High school transcript, college transcript(s), essay or personal statement, statement of good standing from prior institution(s). Minimum college GPA of 3.0 required. Lowest grade transferable C-. **General Admission Information:** Priority deadline 1/15. Regular application deadline 1/15. Nonfall registration accepted. Admission may be deferred for a maximum of 1 year.

COSTS AND FINANCIAL AID
Required Forms and Deadlines: CSS/Financial Aid PROFILE; FAFSA; Noncustodial PROFILE. **Notification of Awards:** Applicants will be notified of awards on or about 3/15. **Types of Aid:** *Need-based scholarships/grants:* College/university scholarship or grant aid from institutional funds; Federal Pell; Private scholarships; SEOG; State scholarships/grants; United Negro College Fund. *Loans:* Direct PLUS loans; Direct Subsidized Stafford Loans; Direct Unsubsidized Stafford Loans. *Student Employment:* Federal Work-Study Program available. Institutional employment available. **Financial Aid Statistics:** 100% needy freshmen, 100% needy undergrads receive need-based scholarship or grant aid. 93% freshmen, 93% undergrads receive non-need-based scholarship or grant aid. 78% freshmen, 77% undergrads receive need-based self-help aid. 0% freshmen, 0% undergrads receive athletic scholarships. 99% freshmen, 98% undergrads receive any aid. 50% undergrads borrow to pay for school. Average cumulative indebtedness $28,146. **Criteria for awarding aid:** *Need-based:* Academics, Alumni affiliation, Art, Leadership, Minority status, Music/drama *Non-need-based:* Academics, Alumni affiliation, Art, Leadership, Minority status, Music/drama, State/district residency.

DEPAUL UNIVERSITY

1 East Jackson Boulevard, Chicago, IL 60604-2287
Phone: 312-362-8300 · **Financial Aid Phone:** 312-362-8091
E-mail: admission@depaul.edu · **CEEB Code:** 001671-00
Fax: 312-362-5749 · **Website:** www.depaul.edu · **ACT Code:** 1012

This private school, affiliated with the Roman Catholic Church, was founded in 1898. It has a 38 acre campus.

RATINGS
Admissions Selectivity Rating: 82   **Fire Safety Rating:** 98   **Green Rating:** 89

STUDENTS AND FACULTY
Enrollment: 14,591. **Student Body:** 53% female, 47% male, 24% out-of-state, 3% international (95 countries represented). Asian 9%, African American 8%, Caucasian 53%, Hispanic 19%, Native American <1%, Pacific Islander <1%, Two or more races 4%, Race unknown 3%.
Retention and Graduation: 84% freshmen return for sophomore year. 59% freshmen graduate within 4 years. 71% freshmen graduate within 6 years. 14% grads go on to further study within 1 year. **Faculty:** Student/faculty ratio 16:1. 916 full-time faculty, 85% hold PhDs, 20% are members of minority groups, 46% are women.

ACADEMICS
Degrees: Bachelor's; Certificate; Doctoral; Doctoral/Professional; Doctoral/Research; Master's; Post-Bachelor's certificate; Post-Master's certificate **Classes:** Most classes have 10-19 students. Most lab/discussion sessions have 10-19 students. **Most popular majors:** Public Relations, Advertising, And Applied Communication, Other; Psychology, General; Accounting. **Special Study Options:** Accelerated program; Distance learning; Double major; English as a Second Language (ESL); Honors program; Independent study; Internships; Study abroad; Teacher certification program; Weekend college. **Honors programs:** DePaul's honors program offers small classes organized in a seminar format and taught by faculty committed to academic excellence and the attainment of lifelong learning strategies. Benefits of our scholarly community include academic advising, an Honors Lounge, a student government, peer mentoring, student-faculty dinners, newsletters, cultural outings, service activities, and many other experiences that enrich the Honors community while extending the Honors experience beyond the classroom. **Combined degree programs:** BA/JD; BA/MA. **Disability Services offered to physically disabled students:** Note-taking services; Reader services; Tape

recorders; Tutors. **Career services:** Alumni network; Alumni services; Career assessment; Career/job search classes; Internships; Regional alumni

FACILITIES

Housing: Apartments for single students; Coed dorms; Special housing for disabled student; Special housing for international students; Theme housing; Wellness housing 97% of campus accessible to physically diasbled. **Special Academic Facilities/Equipment:** LEED-certified environmental science & chemistry building with greenhouse & green roof, digital cinema laboratory with motion-capture system, green-screen studio, converged newsroom, 10 specialized computer research labs including artificial intelligence, biomedics informatics & mobile e-commerce, 1,300-seat theatre, art museum, fitness & a recreational center with pool **Computers:** 60% of classrooms, 100% of dorms, 100% of libraries, 100% of dining areas, 75% of student union, 25% of common outdoor areas have wireless network access. Students can register for classes online. Administrative functions (other than registration) can be performed online.

CAMPUS LIFE

Environment: Metropolis **Activities:** Campus Ministries; Choral groups; Concert band; Dance; Drama/theater; International Student Organization; Jazz band; Literary magazine; Model UN; Music ensembles; Musical theater; Opera; Pep band; Radio station; Student government; Student newspaper; Student-run film society; Symphony orchestra 311 registered organizations, 9 honor societies, 19 religious organizations. 9 fraternities, 13 sororities. **Athletics (Intercollegiate):** *Men:* basketball, cross-country, golf, soccer, tennis, track/field (outdoor), track/field (indoor). *Women:* basketball, cross-country, soccer, softball, tennis, track/field (outdoor), track/field (indoor), volleyball. **On-Campus Highlights:** Student Center, Lincoln Park Campus, Ray Meyer Fitness Center, The Pit, in Schmitt Academic Center (SAC), 11th floor, DePaul Center, Loop Campus, The Bean Cafe in the SAC **Environmental Initiatives:** 1. The Sustainability Initiative Task Force (SITF) created an Institutional Sustainability Plan, which can be accessed at http://mission.depaul.edu/Programs/Sustainability/Documents/SUSTAINABILITYPLANFINAL.pdf. This plan is derived from the results of a comprehensive sustainability audit conducted by five SITF Working Groups – Curriculum, Operations, Administration and Planning, Research, and Engagement—and builds on SITF Report #4 (Sustainability at DePaul University: Recommendations to the Strategic Planning Task Force) which describes the Working Groups' recommendations and attendant actionable goals for making environmental, social and economic sustainability clearly articulated strategic priorities of the next University Strategic Plan. Each Working Group was responsible for conducting the wide-ranging Sustainability Tracking, Assessment, and Rating System TM (STARS) audit. This report also influenced Vision 2018, DePaul's strategic plan, which can be accessed at the following link: http://offices.depaul.edu/president/strategic-directions/vision-2018/Pages/default.aspx.

ADMISSIONS

Freshman Academic Profile: Average high school GPA 3.6. 23% in top 10% of high school class, 53% in top 25% of high school class, 85% in top 50% of high school class. 80% from public high schools. **Test Scores:** SAT Math middle 50% range 530-640. SAT EBRW middle 50% range 550-670. ACT middle 50% range 22-28. Minimum internet-based TOEFL 80. **Basis for Candidate Selection:** *Very important factors considered include:* rigor of secondary school record, academic GPA, standardized test scores. *Important factors considered include:* class rank, recommendation(s), extracurricular activities, talent/ability, character/personal qualities, volunteer work, work experience, level of applicant's interest. *Other factors considered include:* application essay, interview, first generation, alumni/ae relation, geographical residence, state residency, religious affiliation/commitment, racial/ethnic status. **Freshman Admission Requirements:** High school diploma is required and GED is accepted *Academic units required:* 4 English, 3 math, 3 science, 2 science labs, and 2 units from above areas or other academic areas. *Academic units recommended:* 4 English, 3 math, 3 science, 2 science labs, 2 foreign language, 2 units from above areas or other academic areas. **Freshman Admission Statistics:** 22,502 applied, 68.9% admitted, 16% enrolled. **Transfer Admission Requirements:** college transcript(s), Minimum college GPA of 2.0 required. Lowest grade transferable D. **General Admission Information:** Priority deadline 11/15. Regular application deadline 2/1. Nonfall registration accepted. Admission may be deferred for a maximum of 1 year.

COSTS AND FINANCIAL AID

Annual tuition $38,410. Room and board $13,387. Required fees $600. Average book expense $1,104. **Required Forms and Deadlines:** FAFSA. **Notification of Awards:** Applicants will be notified of awards on a rolling basis beginning 12/15. **Types of Aid:** *Need-based scholarships/grants:* College/university scholarship or grant aid from institutional funds; Federal Pell; Private scholarships; SEOG; State scholarships/grants. *Loans:* Direct PLUS loans; Direct Subsidized Stafford Loans; Direct Unsubsidized Stafford Loans. *Student Employment:* Federal Work-Study Program available. Institutional employment available. **Financial Aid Statistics:** 90% needy freshmen, 85% needy undergrads receive need-based scholarship or grant aid. 86% freshmen, 67% undergrads receive non-need-based scholarship or grant aid. 73% freshmen,

78% undergrads receive need-based self-help aid. 2% freshmen, 2% undergrads receive athletic scholarships. 98% freshmen, 87% undergrads receive any aid. Average cumulative indebtedness $29,932. **Criteria for awarding aid:** *Non-need-based:* Academics, Art, Athletics, Leadership, Music/drama, State/district residency.

DEPAUW UNIVERSITY

P.O. Box 37, 313 South Locust Street, Greencastle, IN 46135
Phone: 765-658-4006 · **Financial Aid Phone:** 765-658-4030
E-mail: admission@depauw.edu · **CEEB Code:** 1166
Fax: 765-658-4007 · **Website:** www.depauw.edu · **ACT Code:** 1184

This private school, affiliated with the Methodist Church, was founded in 1837. It has a 1100 acre campus.

RATINGS

Admissions Selectivity Rating: 87   **Fire Safety Rating:** 73   **Green Rating:** 60*

STUDENTS AND FACULTY

Enrollment: 2,137. **Student Body:** 52% female, 48% male, 61% out-of-state, 10% international (34 countries represented). Asian 4%, African American 5%, Caucasian 66%, Hispanic 7%, Native American <1%, Pacific Islander 0%, Two or more races 5%, Race unknown 2%.
Retention and Graduation: 89% freshmen return for sophomore year. 76% freshmen graduate within 4 years. 81% freshmen graduate within 6 years. 23% grads go on to further study within 1 year. 15% grads pursue arts and sciences degrees. 5% grads pursue law degrees. 1% grads pursue business degrees. 2% grads pursue medical degrees. **Faculty:** Student/faculty ratio 9:1. 228 full-time faculty, 98% hold PhDs, 21% are members of minority groups, 43% are women. 0% of classes are taught by teaching assistants.

ACADEMICS

Degrees: Bachelor's **Classes:** Most classes have 10-19 students. Most lab/discussion sessions have 10-19 students. **Most popular majors:** Speech Communication And Rhetoric; Economics, General. **Special Study Options:** Double major; Dual enrollment; Exchange student program (domestic); Honors program; Independent study; Internships; Student-designed major; Study abroad. **Honors programs:** Please visit the following website for information about DePauw's **Honors programs:** http://www.depauw.edu/honors/index.asp. **Disability Services offered to physically disabled students:** Note-taking services; Reader services; Tape recorders; Tutors. **Career services:** Alumni network; Alumni services; Career assessment; Career/job search classes; Internships; Regional alumni

FACILITIES

Housing: Apartments for single students; Coed dorms; Fraternity/sorority housing; Special housing for disabled student; Special housing for international students 85% of campus accessible to physically diasbled. **Special Academic Facilities/Equipment:** Recently opened Peeler Art Center housing gallery and studio space; Center for Contemporary Media; Performing Arts Center; Anthropology Museum; Shidzuo Iikudo Museum **Computers:** Students can register for classes online. Administrative functions (other than registration) can be performed online. Undergraduates are required to own a computer.

CAMPUS LIFE

Environment: Village **Activities:** Campus Ministries; Choral groups; Concert band; Dance; Drama/theater; International Student Organization; Jazz band; Literary magazine; Music ensembles; Musical theater; Opera; Pep band; Radio station; Student government; Student newspaper; Student-run film society; Symphony orchestra; Television station 119 registered organizations, 13 honor societies, 10 religious organizations. 13 fraternities, 11 sororities. **Athletics (Intercollegiate):** *Men:* baseball, basketball, cross-country, diving, football, golf, soccer, swimming, tennis, track/field (outdoor), track/field (indoor). *Women:* basketball, cross-country, diving, field hockey, golf, soccer, softball, swimming, tennis, track/field (outdoor), track/field (indoor), volleyball. **On-Campus Highlights:** DePauw University School of Music, Roy O. West Library, Music Library, and the Prevo Science Library, Cafe Roy coffee shop, Memorial Student Union, Bowman Park **Environmental Initiatives:** LEED certified construction of the Janet Prindle Institute for Ethics.

ADMISSIONS

Freshman Academic Profile: Average high school GPA 3.8. 40% in top 10% of high school class, 70% in top 25% of high school class, 95% in top 50%

of high school class. 83% from public high schools. **Test Scores:** SAT Math middle 50% range 550-680. SAT EBRW middle 50% range 560-650. ACT middle 50% range 24-29. Minimum paper TOEFL 560. **Basis for Candidate Selection:** *Very important factors considered include:* rigor of secondary school record, academic GPA, standardized test scores. *Important factors considered include:* class rank, application essay, recommendation(s). *Other factors considered include:* interview, extracurricular activities, talent/ability, character/personal qualities, first generation, alumni/ae relation, geographical residence, state residency, volunteer work, work experience, level of applicant's interest. **Freshman Admission Requirements:** High school diploma is required and GED is accepted *Academic units recommended:* 4 English, 4 math, 3 science, 2 science labs, 2 foreign language, 2 social studies. **Freshman Admission Statistics:** 5,173 applied, 67.3% admitted, 17% enrolled. **Transfer Admission Requirements:** High school transcript, college transcript(s), essay or personal statement, statement of good standing from prior institution(s). Minimum college GPA of 3.0 required. Lowest grade transferable C. **General Admission Information:** Regular application deadline 2/1. Nonfall registration accepted. Admission may be deferred for a maximum of 1 year.

COSTS AND FINANCIAL AID

Annual tuition $47,026. Room and board $12,529. Required fees $812. Average book expense $900. **Required Forms and Deadlines:** FAFSA; Institution's own financial aid form. **Notification of Awards:** Applicants will be notified of awards on a rolling basis beginning 2/1. **Types of Aid:** *Need-based scholarships/grants:* College/university scholarship or grant aid from institutional funds; Federal Pell; Private scholarships; SEOG; State scholarships/grants. *Loans:* Direct Subsidized Stafford Loans; Direct Unsubsidized Stafford Loans. *Student Employment:* Federal Work-Study Program available. Institutional employment available. **Financial Aid Statistics:** 100% needy freshmen, 100% needy undergrads receive need-based scholarship or grant aid. 24% freshmen, 20% undergrads receive non-need-based scholarship or grant aid. 75% freshmen, 79% undergrads receive need-based self-help aid. 0% freshmen, 0% undergrads receive athletic scholarships. Average cumulative indebtedness $25,990. **Criteria for awarding aid:** *Non-need-based:* Academics, Leadership, Music/drama.

DICKINSON COLLEGE

Best Colleges

P.O. Box 1773, Carlisle, PA 17013-2896
Phone: 717-245-1231 · **Financial Aid Phone:** 717-245-1308
E-mail: admissions@dickinson.edu · **CEEB Code:** 2186
Fax: 717-245-1442 · **Website:** www.dickinson.edu/ · **ACT Code:** 3550

This private school was founded in 1783. It has a 144 acre campus.

RATINGS

Admissions Selectivity Rating: 90   **Fire Safety Rating:** 91   **Green Rating:** 99

STUDENTS AND FACULTY

Enrollment: 2,339. **Student Body:** 58% female, 42% male, 79% out-of-state, 13% international (44 countries represented). Asian 4%, African American 5%, Caucasian 66%, Hispanic 8%, Native American <1%, Pacific Islander <1%, Two or more races 4%, Race unknown 1%. **Retention and Graduation:** 90% freshmen return for sophomore year. 80% freshmen graduate within 4 years. 83% freshmen graduate within 6 years. 37% grads go on to further study within 1 year. 20% grads pursue arts and sciences degrees. 2% grads pursue law degrees. 10% grads pursue business degrees. 4% grads pursue medical degrees. **Faculty:** Student/faculty ratio 9:1. 225 full-time faculty, 92% hold PhDs, 16% are members of minority groups, 50% are women. 0% of classes are taught by teaching assistants.

ACADEMICS

Degrees: Bachelor's **Classes:** Most classes have 10-19 students. Most lab/discussion sessions have 10-19 students. **Most popular majors:** Psychology, General; Economics, General; International Business/Trade/Commerce. **Special Study Options:** Accelerated program; Cross-registration; Double major; English as a Second Language (ESL); Exchange student program (domestic); Independent study; Internships; Liberal arts/career combination; Student-designed major; Study abroad. **Combined degree programs:** BA/JD; BA/MEng. **Disability Services offered to physically disabled students:** Note-taking services; Reader services; Tape recorders; Tutors. **Career services:** Alumni network; Alumni services; Career assessment; Career/job search classes; Internships; Regional alumni

FACILITIES

Housing: Apartments for single students; Coed dorms; Fraternity/sorority housing; Special housing for disabled student; Theme housing; Wellness housing 70% of campus accessible to physically diasbled. **Special Academic Facilities/Equipment:** Old West; Rector Science Complex; Greenhouse & Center for Sustainable living; Trout Gallery; Weiss Center for the Arts; Goodyear Art Studios; planetarium; observatory; scanning electron microscope; Keck Archaeology Lab, Dog House, biogas facility, College Farm, the Hive (apiary). **Computers:** 10% of classrooms, 100% of dorms, 100% of libraries, 100% of dining areas, 100% of student union, 5% of common outdoor areas have wireless network access. Students can register for classes online. Administrative functions (other than registration) can be performed online.

CAMPUS LIFE

Environment: Town **Activities:** Choral groups; Concert band; Dance; Drama/theater; International Student Organization; Jazz band; Literary magazine; Model UN; Music ensembles; Musical theater; Radio station; Student government; Student newspaper; Student-run film society; Symphony orchestra; Yearbook 112 registered organizations, 15 honor societies, 11 religious organizations. 6 fraternities, 6 sororities. **Athletics (Intercollegiate):** *Men:* baseball, basketball, cross-country, football, golf, lacrosse, soccer, swimming, tennis, track/field (outdoor), track/field (indoor). *Women:* basketball, cross-country, field hockey, golf, lacrosse, soccer, softball, swimming, tennis, track/field (outdoor), track/field (indoor), volleyball. **On-Campus Highlights:** Old West, designed by Benjamin Latrobe, Holland Union Building, Waidner Spahr Library/Biblio Cafe, Kline Athletic Center, Rector Science Complex **Environmental Initiatives:** Integrating sustainability throughout the curriculum, supported by the Center for Sustainability Education.

ADMISSIONS

Freshman Academic Profile: 48% in top 10% of high school class, 77% in top 25% of high school class, 96% in top 50% of high school class. 55% from public high schools. **Test Scores:** SAT Math middle 50% range 610-720. SAT EBRW middle 50% range 620-700. ACT middle 50% range 27-32. Minimum internet-based TOEFL 90. **Basis for Candidate Selection:** *Very important factors considered include:* rigor of secondary school record, academic GPA, application essay, recommendation(s), extracurricular activities, talent/ability, character/personal qualities, volunteer work, level of applicant's interest. *Important factors considered include:* class rank, standardized test scores, interview, alumni/ae relation, geographical residence, state residency, racial/ethnic status, work experience. *Other factors considered include:* first generation. **Freshman Admission Requirements:** High school diploma is required and GED is accepted *Academic units required:* 4 English, 3 math, 3 science, 2 science labs, 2 foreign language, 2 social studies, 2 academic electives, *Academic units recommended:* 3 foreign language. **Freshman Admission Statistics:** 5,941 applied, 48.7% admitted, 21% enrolled. **Transfer Admission Requirements:** High school transcript, college transcript(s), essay or personal statement, statement of good standing from prior institution(s). Minimum college GPA of 2 required. Lowest grade transferable C. **General Admission Information:** Application fee $65. Regular application deadline 1/15. Nonfall registration accepted. Admission may be deferred for a maximum of 2 years.

COSTS AND FINANCIAL AID

Average book expense $1,210. **Required Forms and Deadlines:** CSS/Financial Aid PROFILE; FAFSA; Noncustodial PROFILE; State aid form. **Notification of Awards:** Applicants will be notified of awards on or about 3/23. **Types of Aid:** *Need-based scholarships/grants:* College/university scholarship or grant aid from institutional funds; Federal Pell; Private scholarships; SEOG; State scholarships/grants. *Loans:* Direct PLUS loans; Direct Subsidized Stafford Loans; Direct Unsubsidized Stafford Loans. *Student Employment:* Federal Work-Study Program available. Institutional employment available. **Financial Aid Statistics:** 98% needy freshmen, 98% needy undergrads receive need-based scholarship or grant aid. 4% freshmen, 6% undergrads receive non-need-based scholarship or grant aid. 94% freshmen, 91% undergrads receive need-based self-help aid. 0% freshmen, 0% undergrads receive athletic scholarships. 81% freshmen, 76% undergrads receive any aid. 54% undergrads borrow to pay for school. Average cumulative indebtedness $26,908. **Criteria for awarding aid:** *Need-based:* Music/drama *Non-need-based:* Academics, Leadership, Music/drama.

DICKINSON STATE UNIVERSITY

291 Campus Drive, Dickinson, ND 58601-4896
Phone: 701-483-2175 • **Financial Aid Phone:** 701-483-2371
E-mail: dsu.hawks@dsu.nodak.edu
Fax: 701-483-2409 • **Website:** www.dickinsonstate.com • **ACT Code:** 3210

This public school was founded in 1918. It has a 137 acre campus.

RATINGS
Admissions Selectivity Rating: 75   **Fire Safety Rating:** 60*   **Green Rating:** 60*

STUDENTS AND FACULTY
Enrollment: 2,669. **Student Body:** 59% female, 41% male, 34% out-of-state, 12% international (30 countries represented). Asian <1%, African American 1%, Caucasian 71%, Hispanic 1%, Native American 2%, Race unknown 12%. **Retention and Graduation:** 60% freshmen return for sophomore year. **Faculty:** Student/faculty ratio 19:1. 86 full-time faculty, 52% hold PhDs, 6% are members of minority groups, 43% are women.

ACADEMICS
Degrees: Associate; Bachelor's; Certificate; Terminal Associate; Transfer Associate **Classes:** Most classes have 20-29 students. Most lab/discussion sessions have 20-29 students. **Most popular majors:** Teacher Education, Multiple Levels; Nursing/Registered Nurse (Rn, Asn, Bsn, Msn); Business/Commerce, General. **Special Study Options:** Accelerated program; Distance learning; Double major; Dual enrollment; Honors program; Independent study; Internships; Liberal arts/career combination; Student-designed major; Study abroad; Teacher certification program. **Career services:** Alumni network; Alumni services; Career assessment; Career/job search classes; Internships

FACILITIES
Housing: Apartments for married students; Apartments for single students; Coed dorms; Men's dorms; Special housing for disabled student; Women's dorms **Special Academic Facilities/Equipment:** Art gallery, smart classrooms **Computers:** Students can register for classes online.

CAMPUS LIFE
Environment: Rural **Activities:** Choral groups; Concert band; Dance; Drama/theater; International Student Organization; Jazz band; Literary magazine; Marching band; Music ensembles; Musical theater; Pep band; Student government; Student newspaper; Student-run film society; Yearbook 51 registered organizations, 7 honor societies, 6 religious organizations. **Athletics (Intercollegiate):** *Men:* baseball, basketball, cheerleading, cross-country, football, golf, rodeo, track/field (outdoor), track/field (indoor), wrestling. *Women:* basketball, cheerleading, cross-country, golf, rodeo, softball, track/field (outdoor), track/field (indoor), volleyball. **On-Campus Highlights:** Murphy Hall, Student Center, Common Grounds Coffee Shop, Whitney Stadium

ADMISSIONS
Freshman Academic Profile: Average high school GPA 3.2. 6% in top 10% of high school class, 19% in top 25% of high school class, 53% in top 50% of high school class. 98% from public high schools. **Test Scores:** SAT Math middle 50% range 470-590. SAT EBRW middle 50% range 430-530. ACT middle 50% range 18-23. Minimum paper TOEFL 525. **Freshman Admission Requirements:** High school diploma is required and GED is accepted *Academic units required:* 4 English, 3 math, 3 science, and 3 units from above areas or other academic areas. **Freshman Admission Statistics:** 527 applied, 95.8% admitted, 71% enrolled. **Transfer Admission Requirements:** college transcript(s), Minimum college GPA of 2.0 required. Lowest grade transferable D. **General Admission Information:** Application fee $35. Nonfall registration accepted. Admission may be deferred.

COSTS AND FINANCIAL AID
Annual in-state tuition $4,076. Annual out-of-state tuition $10,222. Room and board $4,076. Required fees $945. Average book expense $900. **Required Forms and Deadlines:** FAFSA. **Notification of Awards:** Applicants will be notified of awards on a rolling basis beginning 4/30. **Types of Aid:** *Need-based scholarships/grants:* College/university scholarship or grant aid from institutional funds; Federal Pell; Private scholarships; SEOG; State scholarships/grants. *Loans: Student Employment:* Federal Work-Study Program available. Institutional employment available. **Criteria for awarding aid:** *Need-based:* Academics, Job skills, Minority status *Non-need-based:* Academics, Alumni affiliation, Art, Athletics, Job skills, Leadership, Minority status, Music/drama, State/district residency.

DIGIPEN INSTITUTE OF TECHNOLOGY

9931 Willows Road NE, Redmond, WA 98052
Phone: 425-629-5001 • **Financial Aid Phone:** 425-629-5002
E-mail: admissions@digipen.edu • **CEEB Code:** 37243
Fax: 425-558-0378 • **Website:** https://www.digipen.edu • **ACT Code:** 6659

This proprietary school was founded in 1988. It has a 2 acre campus.

RATINGS
Admissions Selectivity Rating: 90   **Fire Safety Rating:** 87   **Green Rating:** 61

STUDENTS AND FACULTY
Student Body: international (45 countries represented). **Retention and Graduation:** 81% freshmen return for sophomore year. **Faculty:** Student/faculty ratio 10:1. 77 full-time faculty, 39% hold PhDs, 25% are women. 0% of classes are taught by teaching assistants.

ACADEMICS
Degrees: Bachelor's; Master's **Classes:** Most classes have 10-19 students. Most lab/discussion sessions have fewer than 10 students. **Most popular majors:** Animation, Interactive Technology, Video Graphics And Special Effects; Modeling, Virtual Environments And Simulation; Game And Interactive Media Design. **Special Study Options:** Accelerated program; English as a Second Language (ESL); Independent study; Internships. **Disability Services offered to physically disabled students:** Note-taking services; Reader services; Tape recorders; Tutors. **Career services:** Alumni network; Alumni services; Career/job search classes; Internships

FACILITIES
Housing: Men's dorms; Special housing for disabled student; Special housing for international students; Women's dorms 100% of campus accessible to physically disabled. **Special Academic Facilities/Equipment:** a) Location: In 2010, DIT relocated to a new campus. DIT designed the space to meet the needs of our students and created an environment that would stimulate collaboration and creativity. The campus is located in Redmond, WA, over 350 game and game-related companies, granting students greater access to internships, jobs, and networking opportunities. DIT's close proximity to companies allows industry leaders to lecture and serve on DIT's program advisory committees. Because of the school's relationships with both Microsoft and Nintendo, DIT students have access to a variety of professional software development kits (SDKs) in DIT's computer labs, including those for the Nintendo Wii, the Nintendo DS, and the Microsoft Kinect. DIT's campus also has a Computer Engineering lab for electronics projects ranging from robotics research projects to the creation of proprietary game consoles, a Game Production lab with over 250 seats designed to replicate a professional game production environment, a game-testing lab, a sound lab, music practice rooms, and numerous PC labs for instruction and student use. b) Sound Lab: DIT's new Sound Lab features 27" iMac workstations with the latest Digital Audio Workstation (DAW) hardware and software for music, sound design, and soundtrack production, including Pro Tools, Logic Pro, Sibelius, Pure Data, Auralia/Musition, Boot Camp/VMWare/Windows, and more. The Lab also functions as a lecture and screening hall for demonstrations and collaboration with game and animation development teams. Music practice rooms are equipped with acoustic and electronic pianos and drums, as well as mobile recording workstations, studio microphones and preamps. c) Library and Academic Resource Center: DIT's Learning Resource Center aims to support the institute's curriculum, students, and faculty. Students have access to a variety of resources, from sound effects libraries to reference books relevant to their programs of study. The library also subscribes to a selection of major journals and magazines related to the fields of gaming, simulation, computer engineering, and animation. The library currently holds more than 4200 books, has subscriptions to over 30 different magazines and journals, over 50 board games, and over 1100 video games and videos. In addition to these curriculum-related resources, the library has a collection of career-oriented materials, including books on résumés, cover letters, and interview tips. DIT serves up a rigorous curriculum and offers free tutoring for all of its students. The campus' Academic Support Center provides individual and group tutoring sessions and is also an excellent place for students to gather to establish study groups. DIT offers short-term individual counseling services to students through the Counseling Center, and strives to ensure that all students are provided with an equal opportunity to participate in the college's programs, courses, and activities through our Disability Support Services department. d) Café: DIT's on-site food services are unique as compared to most schools. The Café was designed to encourage interaction and community on campus. DIT prepares over 1,500 meals a day, highly subsidizes the cost of meals (DIT spends $2.00 per $1.00 revenue received), and gives away more than 500 meals

a week for students and faculty to eat for free. Over the course of the past year, DIT gave away 67,826 meals and served 186,954 students, guests and staff in the Café and Bookstore. Professors are able to request free catering at events to support their academic activities and students may get free meals during their student club meetings. Just like our software, DIT prepares everything from scratch and only uses the freshest and healthiest ingredients. Next to the Café is our convenience store, which provides students with access to fresh and healthy food options to go and gives students a convenient place to purchase snacks, art supplies, and game design supplies right on-campus. 2) DIT's Singapore branch campus and Korean campus – DIT has formed a network of students, partnerships, and community on a global level. The Singapore campus and Korean campus add to the diversity of DIT's international community. In Singapore, students are able to pursue some of the same undergraduate degrees as the U.S. campus or participate in Continuing Education courses in collaboration with UbiSoft Singapore. U.S. students have the opportunity to study abroad and experience different cultures while continuing to enhance their knowledge of game development. Students participating in our Korean campus can attend the first two years of DIT's Bachelor of Science in Computer Science in Real-Time Interactive Simulation program while they are in South Korea, and then transfer to the U.S. campus to complete their degree. This international network provides students with greater access to potential employers while also expanding the game industry overseas. 3) DIT's Spain branch campus – DIT's Spain campus opened in 2011 and provides students with access to some of the same degree programs as the U.S. campus. Students at the Spain campus are helping to build the industry abroad from an international viewpoint. Similar to the campuses in Asia, students at other campuses have the opportunity to study abroad and experience different cultures while continuing to enhance their knowledge of game development. **Computers:** Students can register for classes online.

CAMPUS LIFE

Environment: Rural **Activities:** Choral groups; Concert band; Dance; Drama/theater; International Student Organization; Jazz band; Literary magazine; Marching band; Music ensembles; Musical theater; Pep band; Student government; Student newspaper; Student-run film society; Yearbook 51 registered organizations, 7 honor societies, 6 religious organizations. **Athletics (Intercollegiate):** *Men:* baseball, basketball, cheerleading, cross-country, football, golf, rodeo, track/field (outdoor), track/field (indoor), wrestling. *Women:* basketball, cheerleading, cross-country, golf, rodeo, softball, track/field (outdoor), track/field (indoor), volleyball. **On-Campus Highlights:** Murphy Hall, Student Center, Common Grounds Coffee Shop, Whitney Stadium

ADMISSIONS

Freshman Academic Profile: 98% from public high schools. **Test Scores:** SAT Math middle 50% range 570-670. SAT EBRW middle 50% range 570-680. ACT middle 50% range 25-30. Minimum paper TOEFL 525. **Freshman Admission Requirements:** High school diploma is required and GED is accepted *Academic units required:* 4 English, 3 math, 3 science, and 3 units from above areas or other academic areas. **Freshman Admission Statistics:** 742 applied, 53.4% admitted, 58% enrolled. **Transfer Admission Requirements:** college transcript(s), Minimum college GPA of 2.0 required. Lowest grade transferable D. **General Admission Information:** Application fee $35. Nonfall registration accepted. Admission may be deferred.

COSTS AND FINANCIAL AID

Annual in-state tuition $4,076. Annual out-of-state tuition $10,222. Room and board $4,076. Required fees $945. Average book expense $900. **Required Forms and Deadlines:** FAFSA. **Notification of Awards:** Applicants will be notified of awards on a rolling basis beginning 4/30. **Types of Aid:** *Need-based scholarships/grants:* College/university scholarship or grant aid from institutional funds; Federal Pell; Private scholarships; SEOG; State scholarships/grants. *Loans: Student Employment:* Federal Work-Study Program available. Institutional employment available. **Criteria for awarding aid:** *Need-based:* Academics, Job skills, Minority status *Non-need-based:* Academics, Alumni affiliation, Art, Athletics, Job skills, Leadership, Minority status, Music/drama, State/district residency.

See page 926.

DIVINE WORD COLLEGE

Newman Hall, Epworth, IA 52045
Phone: 563-876-3332
E-mail: svdvocations@dwci.edu · **CEEB Code:** 6174
Fax: 563-876-5515

This private school, affiliated with the Roman Catholic Church, was founded in 1964. It has a 30 acre campus.

RATINGS

Admissions Selectivity Rating: 67   **Fire Safety Rating:** 60*   **Green Rating:** 60*

STUDENTS AND FACULTY

Student Body: 100% out-of-state, (12 countries represented).
Faculty: Student/faculty ratio 3:1. 16 full-time faculty, 56% hold PhDs, 25% are members of minority groups, 56% are women. 0% of classes are taught by teaching assistants.

ACADEMICS

Degrees: Associate; Bachelor's **Classes:** Most classes have fewer than 10 students. Most lab/discussion sessions have 10-19 students. **Special Study Options:** Double major; English as a Second Language (ESL); Independent study; Liberal arts/career combination.

FACILITIES

Housing: Men's dorms

CAMPUS LIFE

Environment: Rural **Activities:** Campus Ministries; Choral groups; International Student Organization; Student government; Yearbook. **Athletics (Intercollegiate):** *Men:* soccer.

ADMISSIONS

Freshman Academic Profile: 0% in top 25% of high school class, **Test Scores:** Minimum paper TOEFL 550. **Basis for Candidate Selection:** *Very important factors considered include:* interview, character/personal qualities, religious affiliation/commitment, level of applicant's interest. *Important factors considered include:* academic GPA, application essay, recommendation(s). *Other factors considered include:* rigor of secondary school record, class rank, standardized test scores, extracurricular activities, talent/ability, geographical residence, volunteer work, work experience. **Freshman Admission Requirements:** High school diploma is required and GED is accepted **Freshman Admission Statistics:** 3 applied, 66.7% admitted, enrolled. **Transfer Admission Requirements:** High school transcript, college transcript(s), essay or personal statement, interview, statement of good standing from prior institution(s). **General Admission Information:** Application fee $25. Nonfall registration accepted. Admission may be deferred for a maximum of one semester.

COSTS AND FINANCIAL AID

Annual tuition $10,400. Room and board $2,700. Required fees $120. Average book expense $500. **Types of Aid:** *Need-based scholarships/grants:* College/university scholarship or grant aid from institutional funds; Federal Pell; Private scholarships; SEOG; State scholarships/grants. *Loans:* Direct Subsidized Stafford Loans; Direct Unsubsidized Stafford Loans. *Student Employment:* Federal Work-Study Program available. **Criteria for awarding aid:** *Need-based:* Academics, Leadership.

DOANE COLLEGE

1014 Boswell Avenue, Crete, NE 68333
Phone: 402-826-8222 · **Financial Aid Phone:** 402-826-8260
E-mail: admissions@doane.edu · **CEEB Code:** 6165
Fax: 402-826-8600 · **Website:** www.doane.edu · **ACT Code:** 2448

This private school, affiliated with the United Church of Christ, was founded in 1872. It has a 300 acre campus.

RATINGS

Admissions Selectivity Rating: 78   **Fire Safety Rating:** 91   **Green Rating:** 60*

STUDENTS AND FACULTY

Enrollment: 1,589. **Student Body:** 53% female, 47% male, 23% out-of-state, 1% international (8 countries represented). Asian 1%, African American 3%, Caucasian 82%, Hispanic 7%, Native American <1%, Pacific Islander <1%, Two or more races 3%, Race unknown 2%.

Retention and Graduation: 78% freshmen return for sophomore year. 58% freshmen graduate within 4 years. 63% freshmen graduate within 6 years. 32% grads go on to further study within 1 year. 16% grads pursue arts and sciences degrees. 1% grads pursue law degrees. 1% grads pursue business degrees. 5% grads pursue medical degrees. **Faculty:** Student/faculty ratio 11:1. 88 full-time faculty, 86% hold PhDs, 2% are members of minority groups, 45% are women. 0% of classes are taught by teaching assistants.

ACADEMICS
Degrees: Bachelor's; Doctoral; Master's; Post-Master's certificate **Classes:** Most classes have 20-29 students. Most lab/discussion sessions have 20-29 students. **Most popular majors:** Elementary Education And Teaching; Biological And Physical Sciences; Business Administration And Management, General. **Special Study Options:** Double major; English as a Second Language (ESL); Honors program; Independent study; Internships; Student-designed major; Study abroad; Teacher certification program. **Honors programs:** The Honors Program is designed to enrich, in a variety of ways, the educational experience of selected Doane students. Specialized, interdisciplinary, one-credit honors seminars form the intellectual core of the program. Another component is the study abroad experience undertaken during the junior or senior year. The culminating experience is a collaborative research project. **Combined degree programs:** BA/MEng. **Disability Services offered to physically disabled students:** Tutors. **Career services:** Alumni network; Career assessment; Internships

FACILITIES
Housing: Coed dorms; Theme housing 60% of campus accessible to physically diasbled. **Special Academic Facilities/Equipment:** Art gallery, language lab, communication studies facilities, electron microscope, observatory, outdoor challenge course. **Computers:** 90% of classrooms, 100% of dorms, 100% of libraries, 100% of dining areas, 100% of student union, 10% of common outdoor areas have wireless network access. Students can register for classes online. Administrative functions (other than registration) can be performed online.

CAMPUS LIFE
Environment: Rural **Activities:** Campus Ministries; Choral groups; Concert band; Dance; Drama/theater; Jazz band; Literary magazine; Marching band; Music ensembles; Musical theater; Pep band; Radio station; Student government; Student newspaper; Television station; Yearbook 50 registered organizations, 8 honor societies, 2 religious organizations. 5 fraternities, 4 sororities. **Athletics (Intercollegiate):** *Men:* baseball, basketball, cross-country, football, golf, soccer, tennis, track/field (outdoor), track/field (indoor). *Women:* basketball, cheerleading, cross-country, golf, soccer, softball, tennis, track/field (outdoor), track/field (indoor), volleyball. **On-Campus Highlights:** Tiger Inn, Perkins Library, The Quads, Fuhrer Field House, Heckman Auditorium **Environmental Initiatives:** Recycling

ADMISSIONS
Freshman Academic Profile: Average high school GPA 3.5. 15% in top 10% of high school class, 36% in top 25% of high school class, 71% in top 50% of high school class. 90% from public high schools. **Test Scores:** ACT middle 50% range 20-25. Minimum paper TOEFL 525. **Basis for Candidate Selection:** *Very important factors considered include:* academic GPA, standardized test scores. *Important factors considered include:* rigor of secondary school record, character/personal qualities, alumni/ae relation, level of applicant's interest. *Other factors considered include:* class rank, recommendation(s), interview, extracurricular activities, talent/ability, racial/ethnic status, volunteer work, work experience. **Freshman Admission Requirements:** High school diploma is required and GED is accepted *Academic units recommended:* 4 English, 3 math, 3 science, 2 foreign language, 3 social studies. **Freshman Admission Statistics:** 2,392 applied, 65.2% admitted, 19% enrolled. **Transfer Admission Requirements:** High school transcript, college transcript(s), statement of good standing from prior institution(s). Minimum college GPA of 2.0 required. Lowest grade transferable C-. **General Admission Information:** Nonfall registration accepted. Admission may be deferred for a maximum of one year.

COSTS AND FINANCIAL AID
Annual tuition $31,450. Room and board $9,090. Required fees $800. Average book expense $1,000. **Required Forms and Deadlines:** FAFSA. **Notification of Awards:** Applicants will be notified of awards on a rolling basis beginning 3/15. **Types of Aid:** *Need-based scholarships/grants:* College/university scholarship or grant aid from institutional funds; Federal Pell; SEOG; State scholarships/grants. *Loans:* Direct PLUS loans; Direct Subsidized Stafford Loans; Direct Unsubsidized Stafford Loans. *Student Employment:* Federal Work-Study Program available. Institutional employment available. **Financial Aid Statistics:** 100% needy freshmen, 100% needy undergrads receive need-based scholarship or grant aid. 22% freshmen, 17% undergrads receive non-need-based scholarship or grant aid. 77% freshmen, 82% undergrads receive need-based self-help aid. 11% freshmen, 14% undergrads receive athletic scholarships. 100% freshmen, 98% undergrads receive any aid. 78% undergrads borrow to pay for school. Average cumulative indebtedness $30,720. **Criteria**

for awarding aid: *Non-need-based:* Academics, Alumni affiliation, Athletics, Leadership, Music/drama, Religious affiliation.

DOMINICAN COLLEGE

470 Western Highway, Orangeburg, NY 10962-1210
Phone: 845-848-7901 · **Financial Aid Phone:** 845-848-7818
E-mail: admissions@dc.edu · **CEEB Code:** 2190
Fax: 845-365-3150 · **Website:** http://www.dc.edu · **ACT Code:** 2730

This private school was founded in 1952. It has a 70 acre campus.

RATINGS
Admissions Selectivity Rating: 68   **Fire Safety Rating:** 93   **Green Rating:** 60*

STUDENTS AND FACULTY
Enrollment: 1,552. **Student Body:** 66% female, 34% male, 25% out-of-state, 1% international (15 countries represented). Asian 7%, African American 17%, Caucasian 32%, Hispanic 29%, Native American 0%, Pacific Islander <1%, Two or more races 3%, Race unknown 11%.
Retention and Graduation: 71% freshmen return for sophomore year. **Faculty:** Student/faculty ratio 16:1. 73 full-time faculty, 68% hold PhDs, 15% are members of minority groups, 70% are women. 0% of classes are taught by teaching assistants.

ACADEMICS
Degrees: Associate; Bachelor's; Doctoral; Master's **Classes:** Most classes have fewer than 10 students. **Most popular majors:** Social Sciences, General; Business/Commerce, General. **Special Study Options:** Accelerated program; Cooperative education program; Distance learning; Dual enrollment; Honors program; Independent study; Internships; Liberal arts/career combination; Study abroad; Teacher certification program; Weekend college. **Disability Services offered to physically disabled students:** Note-taking services; Reader services; Tutors. **Career services:** Career assessment; Career/job search classes; Internships; Regional alumni

FACILITIES
Housing: Coed dorms; Wellness housing 100% of campus accessible to physically diasbled. **Special Academic Facilities/Equipment:** New State of the Art Prusmack Center for Health Care Programs and Science Education **Computers:** 100% of classrooms, 100% of dorms, 100% of libraries, 100% of dining areas, have wireless network access.

CAMPUS LIFE
Environment: Village **Activities:** Campus Ministries; Choral groups; Dance; Drama/theater; Literary magazine; Model UN; Musical theater; Radio station; Student government; Student newspaper; Yearbook 26 registered organizations, 8 honor societies, 1 religious organization. **Athletics (Intercollegiate):** *Men:* baseball, basketball, golf, lacrosse, soccer. *Women:* basketball, cross-country, lacrosse, soccer, softball, track/field (outdoor), volleyball. **On-Campus Highlights:** Prusmack Center for Health and Science Education, Granito Center: Book Store, Student Union, Health Services, Hennessy Athletic Center, Sullivan Library, Rosary Hall Lounge **Environmental Initiatives:** Geothermal HVAC system installed in most recently constructed academic building

ADMISSIONS
Freshman Academic Profile: Average high school GPA 3.0. 69% from public high schools. **Test Scores:** Minimum paper TOEFL 550. **Basis for Candidate Selection:** *Important factors considered include:* academic GPA, standardized test scores, recommendation(s). *Other factors considered include:* rigor of secondary school record, application essay, interview, extracurricular activities, talent/ability, character/personal qualities, volunteer work, work experience, level of applicant's interest. **Freshman Admission Requirements:** High school diploma is required and GED is accepted *Academic units required:* 4 English, 3 math, 3 science, 1 science labs, 1 foreign language, 3 social studies, 3 history, 2 academic electives, *Academic units recommended:* 4 English, 3 math, 3 science, 1 science labs, 2 foreign language, 4 social studies, 4 history, 2 academic electives. **Freshman Admission Statistics:** 1,959 applied, 71.5% admitted, 26% enrolled. **Transfer Admission Requirements:** college transcript(s), Minimum college GPA of 2.0 required. Lowest grade transferable C. **General Admission Information:** Application fee $35. Nonfall registration accepted. Admission may be deferred for a maximum of 1 year.

COSTS AND FINANCIAL AID
Annual tuition $26,578. Room and board $12,420. Required fees $860. Average book expense $1,350. **Required Forms and Deadlines:** FAFSA; State aid form. **Notification of Awards:** Applicants will be notified of awards on a rolling basis beginning 2/1. **Types of Aid:** *Need-based scholarships/grants:* College/ university scholarship or grant aid from institutional funds; Federal Pell;

Private scholarships; SEOG; State scholarships/grants. *Loans:* Direct PLUS loans; Direct Subsidized Stafford Loans; Direct Unsubsidized Stafford Loans. *Student Employment:* Federal Work-Study Program available. Institutional employment available. **Financial Aid Statistics:** 97% needy freshmen, 95% needy undergrads receive need-based scholarship or grant aid. 9% freshmen, 8% undergrads receive non-need-based scholarship or grant aid. 80% freshmen, 85% undergrads receive need-based self-help aid. 8% freshmen, 5% undergrads receive athletic scholarships. 98% freshmen, 97% undergrads receive any aid. **Criteria for awarding aid:** *Need-based:* Academics, Athletics *Non-need-based:* Academics, Athletics.

DOMINICAN SCHOOL OF PHILOSOPHY AND THEOLOGY

210 South College Ave., Berkeley, CA 94708
Phone: 510-883-2073
E-mail: admissions@dspt.edu
Fax: 510-849-1372 • **Website:** www.dspt.edu

This private school, affiliated with the Roman Catholic Church, was founded in 1932. It has a 1 acre campus.

RATINGS
Admissions Selectivity Rating: 0   **Fire Safety Rating:** 60*   **Green Rating:** 60*

STUDENTS AND FACULTY
Enrollment: 5. **Student Body:** 40% female, 60% male, 0% international (6 countries represented). Asian 40%, African American 0%, Caucasian 20%, Hispanic 40%, Native American 0%, Race unknown 0%.
Retention and Graduation: 100% freshmen return for sophomore year. 50% grads go on to further study within 1 year. 60% grads pursue arts and sciences degrees. 10% grads pursue law degrees. 0% grads pursue business degrees. 50% grads pursue medical degrees. **Faculty:** Student/faculty ratio 4:1. 12 full-time faculty, 100% hold PhDs, 0% are members of minority groups, 17% are women. 10% of classes are taught by teaching assistants.

ACADEMICS
Degrees: Bachelor's; Certificate; Master's **Classes:** Most classes have fewer than 10 students. **Special Study Options:** Cross-registration; Independent study; Study abroad.

FACILITIES
Housing: Apartments for married students; Apartments for single students; Men's dorms; Women's dorms 50% of campus accessible to physically diasbled. **Computers:** Administrative functions (other than registration) can be performed online.

CAMPUS LIFE
Environment: City **Activities:** Choral groups; Concert band; Music ensembles; Student government; Yearbook.

ADMISSIONS
Test Scores: Minimum paper TOEFL 550. **Freshman Admission Requirements:** High school diploma is required and GED is accepted **Transfer Admission Requirements:** college transcript(s), essay or personal statement, Minimum college GPA of 2.3 required. Lowest grade transferable C. **General Admission Information:** Application fee $40. Priority deadline 3/15. Nonfall registration accepted. Admission may be deferred for a maximum of 1 year.

COSTS AND FINANCIAL AID
Annual tuition $11,880. Required fees $100. Average book expense $1,113.

DOMINICAN UNIVERSITY

7900 West Division, River Forest, IL 60305
Phone: 708-524-6800 • **Financial Aid Phone:** 708-524-6950
E-mail: domadmis@dom.edu • **CEEB Code:** 1667
Fax: 708-524-6864 • **Website:** www.dom.edu • **ACT Code:** 1126

This private school, affiliated with the Roman Catholic Church, was founded in 1901. It has a 37 acre campus.

RATINGS
Admissions Selectivity Rating: 80   **Fire Safety Rating:** 96   **Green Rating:** 75

STUDENTS AND FACULTY
Enrollment: 2,155. **Student Body:** 67% female, 33% male, 6% out-of-state, 2% international (10 countries represented). Asian 3%, African American 6%, Caucasian 28%, Hispanic 43%, Native American <1%, Pacific Islander <1%, Two or more races 1%, Race unknown 2%.
Retention and Graduation: 81% freshmen return for sophomore year. 47% freshmen graduate within 4 years. 62% freshmen graduate within 6 years. 32% grads go on to further study within 1 year. **Faculty:** Student/faculty ratio 11:1. 158 full-time faculty, 87% hold PhDs, 24% are members of minority groups, 58% are women. 0% of classes are taught by teaching assistants.

ACADEMICS
Degrees: Bachelor's; Certificate; Doctoral; Master's; Post-Bachelor's certificate; Post-Master's certificate **Classes:** Most classes have fewer than 10 students. **Most popular majors:** Psychology, General; Sociology; Business/Commerce, General. **Special Study Options:** Accelerated program; Cross-registration; Distance learning; Double major; Dual enrollment; English as a Second Language (ESL); Honors program; Independent study; Internships; Liberal arts/career combination; Study abroad; Teacher certification program. **Honors programs:** Honors seminars for high ability students; Honors Program **Combined degree programs:** BA/MA. **Disability Services offered to physically disabled students:** Note-taking services; Reader services; Tape recorders; Tutors. **Career services:** Alumni network; Alumni services; Career assessment; Career/job search classes; Internships; Regional alumni

FACILITIES
Housing: Apartments for married students; Apartments for single students; Coed dorms; Special housing for disabled student; Wellness housing; Women's dorms 100% of campus accessible to physically diasbled. **Special Academic Facilities/Equipment:** Art Gallery, clinical simulation lab for nursing, Butler Children's Literature Center, cadaver lab **Computers:** 70% of classrooms, 100% of libraries, 75% of dining areas, 100% of student union, have wireless network access. Students can register for classes online. Administrative functions (other than registration) can be performed online.

CAMPUS LIFE
Environment: Metropolis **Activities:** Campus Ministries; Choral groups; Concert band; Dance; Drama/theater; International Student Organization; Literary magazine; Model UN; Musical theater; Student government; Student newspaper 76 registered organizations, 14 honor societies, 2 religious organizations. **Athletics (Intercollegiate):** *Men:* baseball, basketball, cross-country, soccer, tennis. *Women:* basketball, cross-country, soccer, softball, tennis, volleyball. **On-Campus Highlights:** Cybercafe, Parmer Hall Atrium, Noonan Reading Room, Commuter Student Lounge, Student Cafeteria **Environmental Initiatives:** Over half the surface parking lots have permeable pavers

ADMISSIONS
Freshman Academic Profile: Average high school GPA 3.7. 25% in top 10% of high school class, 55% in top 25% of high school class, 85% in top 50% of high school class. 80% from public high schools. **Test Scores:** SAT Math middle 50% range 490-590. SAT EBRW middle 50% range 530-610. ACT middle 50% range 20-25. Minimum internet-based TOEFL 79. Minimum paper TOEFL 550. **Basis for Candidate Selection:** *Very important factors considered include:* rigor of secondary school record, class rank, academic GPA, standardized test scores. *Other factors considered include:* application essay, recommendation(s), interview, extracurricular activities, talent/ability, character/personal qualities, first generation, alumni/ae relation. **Freshman Admission Requirements:** High school diploma is required and GED is accepted **Freshman Admission Statistics:** 4,697 applied, 65.0% admitted, 14% enrolled. **Transfer Admission Requirements:** college transcript(s), essay or personal statement, Minimum college GPA of 2.5 required. Lowest grade transferable C-. **General Admission Information:** Application fee $25. Nonfall registration accepted. Admission may be deferred for a maximum of 1 semester.

COSTS AND FINANCIAL AID

Annual tuition $32,964. Room and board $10,241. Required fees $470. Average book expense $1,200. **Required Forms and Deadlines:** FAFSA. **Notification of Awards:** Applicants will be notified of awards on a rolling basis beginning 2/15. **Types of Aid:** *Need-based scholarships/grants:* College/university scholarship or grant aid from institutional funds; Federal Pell; Private scholarships; SEOG; State scholarships/grants. *Loans:* Direct PLUS loans; Direct Subsidized Stafford Loans; Direct Unsubsidized Stafford Loans. *Student Employment:* Federal Work-Study Program available. Institutional employment available. **Financial Aid Statistics:** 100% needy freshmen, 99% needy undergrads receive need-based scholarship or grant aid. 6% freshmen, 8% undergrads receive non-need-based scholarship or grant aid. 91% freshmen, 90% undergrads receive need-based self-help aid. 0% freshmen, 0% undergrads receive athletic scholarships. 100% freshmen, 91% undergrads receive any aid. 88% undergrads borrow to pay for school. Average cumulative indebtedness $28,533. **Criteria for awarding aid:** *Need-based:* Academics, Alumni affiliation, Art, Minority status, Religious affiliation *Non-need-based:* Academics, Alumni affiliation, Art, Minority status, Religious affiliation.

DOMINICAN UNIVERSITY OF CALIFORNIA

50 Acacia Avenue, San Rafael, CA 94901-2298
Phone: 415-485-3204 • **Financial Aid Phone:** 415-257-1302
E-mail: enroll@dominican.edu • **CEEB Code:** 4284
Website: www.dominican.edu • **ACT Code:** 256

This private school, affiliated with the Roman Catholic Heritage, was founded in 1890. It has a 80 acre campus.

RATINGS

Admissions Selectivity Rating: 77   Fire Safety Rating: 95   Green Rating: 60*

STUDENTS AND FACULTY

Enrollment: 1,284. **Student Body:** 74% female, 26% male, 9% out-of-state, 1% international (17 countries represented). Asian 26%, African American 5%, Caucasian 32%, Hispanic 21%, Native American 1%, Pacific Islander 1%, Two or more races 8%, Race unknown 6%. **Retention and Graduation:** 86% freshmen return for sophomore year. 61% freshmen graduate within 4 years. 1% freshmen graduate within 6 years. **Faculty:** Student/faculty ratio 9:1. 106 full-time faculty, 70% hold PhDs, 15% are members of minority groups, 54% are women. 0% of classes are taught by teaching assistants.

ACADEMICS

Degrees: Bachelor's; Master's; Post-Bachelor's certificate **Classes:** Most classes have 20-29 students. Most lab/discussion sessions have fewer than 10 students. **Most popular majors:** Psychology, General; Nursing/Registered Nurse (Rn, Asn, Bsn, Msn); Business Administration And Management, General. **Special Study Options:** Accelerated program; Cross-registration; Distance learning; Double major; Dual enrollment; Exchange student program (domestic); Honors program; Independent study; Internships; Student-designed major; Study abroad; Teacher certification program; Weekend college. **Honors programs:** Honors Program Scholar in the World. **Disability Services offered to physically disabled students:** Note-taking services; Reader services; Tape recorders; Tutors. **Career services:** Alumni network; Alumni services; Career assessment; Career/job search classes; Internships; Regional alumni

FACILITIES

Housing: Coed dorms 65% of campus accessible to physically disabled. **Special Academic Facilities/Equipment:** Art Gallery, Science Lab, Computer Labs, Nursing Skills Lab **Computers:** 10% of classrooms, 5% of dorms, 100% of libraries, 100% of dining areas, 100% of student union, have wireless network access. Administrative functions (other than registration) can be performed online.

CAMPUS LIFE

Environment: Town **Activities:** Campus Ministries; Choral groups; Dance; Drama/theater; International Student Organization; Jazz band; Literary magazine; Music ensembles; Radio station; Student government; Student newspaper 19 registered organizations, 7 honor societies, 4 religious organizations. **Athletics (Intercollegiate):** *Men:* basketball, golf, lacrosse, soccer. *Women:* basketball, golf, soccer, softball, tennis, volleyball. **On-Campus Highlights:** Conlan Recreation Center, Caleruega Dining Hall, Guzman Lecture Hall, Alemany Library, Science Center **Environmental Initiatives:** We established the Dominican Center for Sustainability. The Center serves as ground central for Dominican University's numerous green activities, including educational programs, scholarships, community outreach, and national

and international partnerships. We created the Center to tap the wealth of intellectual capital in place at Dominican in order to support existing and emerging "green" programs. The Center identifies and promotes economically viable green business practices and serves as a think-tank for ongoing green projects on a community, regional, and global level.

ADMISSIONS

Freshman Academic Profile: Average high school GPA 3.7. 20% in top 10% of high school class, 57% in top 25% of high school class, 89% in top 50% of high school class. **Test Scores:** SAT Math middle 50% range 510-595. SAT EBRW middle 50% range 530-620. ACT middle 50% range 20-25. Minimum paper TOEFL 550. **Basis for Candidate Selection:** *Very important factors considered include:* rigor of secondary school record, academic GPA, application essay, standardized test scores, recommendation(s), character/personal qualities. *Important factors considered include:* class rank, interview, extracurricular activities, talent/ability, volunteer work, work experience. *Other factors considered include:* alumni/ae relation. **Freshman Admission Requirements:** High school diploma is required and GED is accepted *Academic units required:* 4 English, 2 math, 1 science, 1 science labs, 2 foreign language, 1 history, *Academic units recommended:* 3 math, 2 science, 2 history. **Freshman Admission Statistics:** 1,867 applied, 75.5% admitted, 17% enrolled. **Transfer Admission Requirements:** college transcript(s), essay or personal statement, Minimum college GPA of 2.0 required. Lowest grade transferable C. **General Admission Information:** Priority deadline 2/1. Nonfall registration accepted. Admission may be deferred for a maximum of one term.

COSTS AND FINANCIAL AID

Annual tuition $44,240. Room and board $14,650. Required fees $450. Average book expense $1,854. **Required Forms and Deadlines:** FAFSA; Institution's own financial aid form. **Notification of Awards:** Applicants will be notified of awards on a rolling basis beginning 3/15. **Types of Aid:** *Need-based scholarships/grants:* College/university scholarship or grant aid from institutional funds; Federal Pell; Private scholarships; SEOG; State scholarships/grants. *Loans:* Direct PLUS loans; Direct Subsidized Stafford Loans; Direct Unsubsidized Stafford Loans. *Student Employment:* Federal Work-Study Program available. Institutional employment available. **Financial Aid Statistics:** 100% needy freshmen, 100% needy undergrads receive need-based scholarship or grant aid. 12% freshmen, 10% undergrads receive non-need-based scholarship or grant aid. 72% freshmen, 87% undergrads receive need-based self-help aid. 1% freshmen, 2% undergrads receive athletic scholarships. 98% freshmen, 84% undergrads receive any aid. 82% undergrads borrow to pay for school. Average cumulative indebtedness $35,369. **Criteria for awarding aid:** *Need-based:* Academics, Athletics, Leadership, Minority status, Music/drama *Non-need-based:* Academics, Alumni affiliation, Athletics, Leadership, Minority status, Music/drama.

DORDT COLLEGE

498 4th Avenue Northeast, Sioux Center, IA 51250
Phone: 712-722-6080 • **Financial Aid Phone:** 712-722-6087
E-mail: admissions@dordt.edu • **CEEB Code:** 6171
Fax: 712-722-6035 • **Website:** www.dordt.edu • **ACT Code:** 1301

This private school, affiliated with the Christian Reformed Church, was founded in 1955. It has a 150 acre campus.

RATINGS

Admissions Selectivity Rating: 79   Fire Safety Rating: 89   Green Rating: 60*

STUDENTS AND FACULTY

Enrollment: 1,331. **Student Body:** 45% female, 55% male, 57% out-of-state, 8% international (21 countries represented). Asian 1%, African American 1%, Caucasian 85%, Hispanic 1%, Native American <1%, Race unknown 4%. **Retention and Graduation:** 80% freshmen return for sophomore year. 15% grads go on to further study within 1 year. 9% grads pursue arts and sciences degrees. 1% grads pursue law degrees. 3% grads pursue business degrees. 2% grads pursue medical degrees. **Faculty:** Student/faculty ratio 12:1. 81 full-time faculty, 68% hold PhDs, 1% are members of minority groups, 15% are women. 0% of classes are taught by teaching assistants.

ACADEMICS

Degrees: Associate; Bachelor's; Master's; Terminal Associate **Classes:** Most classes have 10-19 students. Most lab/discussion sessions have 10-19 students. **Most popular majors:** Education, General; Engineering, General; Business/Commerce, General. **Special Study Options:** Double major; English as a Second Language (ESL); Exchange student program (domestic); Honors program; Independent study; Internships; Student-designed major; Study abroad; Teacher certification program. **Disability Services offered to**

physically disabled students: Note-taking services; Reader services; Tape recorders; Tutors. **Career services:** Alumni network; Alumni services; Career assessment; Career/job search classes; Internships; Regional alumni

FACILITIES
Housing: Apartments for married students; Apartments for single students; Men's dorms; Special housing for disabled student; Women's dorms 100% of campus accessible to physically diasbled. **Special Academic Facilities/ Equipment:** observatories 160 acre research farm for Ag program, modern recreation facilities which include indoor track, swimming and ice arena **Computers:** 100% of classrooms, 100% of dorms, 100% of libraries, 100% of dining areas, 100% of student union, 100% of common outdoor areas have wireless network access. Students can register for classes online. Administrative functions (other than registration) can be performed online.

CAMPUS LIFE
Environment: Village **Activities:** Campus Ministries; Choral groups; Concert band; Dance; Drama/theater; International Student Organization; Jazz band; Literary magazine; Music ensembles; Musical theater; Opera; Pep band; Radio station; Student government; Student newspaper; Student-run film society; Symphony orchestra; Yearbook 40 registered organizations, 4 honor societies, 6 religious organizations. **Athletics (Intercollegiate):** *Men:* baseball, basketball, cross-country, football, golf, ice hockey, soccer, tennis, track/field (outdoor), track/field (indoor). *Women:* basketball, cross-country, soccer, softball, tennis, track/field (outdoor), track/field (indoor), volleyball. **On-Campus Highlights:** Campus Center, Recreation Center and De Witt Gymnasium, B.J. Haan Auditorium, Kuyper Apartments, 55th Ave Cafe

ADMISSIONS
Freshman Academic Profile: Average high school GPA 3.5. 21% in top 10% of high school class, 44% in top 25% of high school class, 73% in top 50% of high school class. 30% from public high schools. **Test Scores:** SAT Math middle 50% range 500-630. SAT EBRW middle 50% range 450-610. ACT middle 50% range 21-28. Minimum internet-based TOEFL 80. Minimum paper TOEFL 550. **Basis for Candidate Selection:** *Very important factors considered include:* rigor of secondary school record, academic GPA, standardized test scores, religious affiliation/commitment. *Other factors considered include:* class rank, recommendation(s), extracurricular activities, talent/ability, character/ personal qualities, first generation, alumni/ae relation, level of applicant's interest. **Freshman Admission Requirements:** High school diploma is required and GED is accepted *Academic units required:* 3 English, 2 math, 2 science, 2 foreign language, 2 history, 6 academic electives, *Academic units recommended:* 4 English, 3 math, 4 science, 3 foreign language, 1 social studies. **Freshman Admission Statistics:** 1,356 applied, 75.0% admitted, 37% enrolled. **Transfer Admission Requirements:** High school transcript, college transcript(s), standardized test scores, Minimum college GPA of 2.0 required. Lowest grade transferable C. **General Admission Information:** Priority deadline 7/1. Regular application deadline 8/1. Nonfall registration accepted. Admission may be deferred for a maximum of 1 year.

COSTS AND FINANCIAL AID
Annual tuition $26,100. Room and board $7,620. Required fees $440. Average book expense $910. **Required Forms and Deadlines:** FAFSA; Institution's own financial aid form. **Notification of Awards:** Applicants will be notified of awards on a rolling basis beginning 3/1. **Types of Aid:** *Need-based scholarships/ grants:* College/university scholarship or grant aid from institutional funds; Federal Pell; Private scholarships; SEOG; State scholarships/grants. *Loans:* Direct PLUS loans; Direct Subsidized Stafford Loans; Direct Unsubsidized Stafford Loans. **Financial Aid Statistics:** 100% needy freshmen, 100% needy undergrads receive need-based scholarship or grant aid. 14% freshmen, 14% undergrads receive non-need-based scholarship or grant aid. 99% freshmen, 100% undergrads receive need-based self-help aid. 8% freshmen, 7% undergrads receive athletic scholarships. 98% freshmen, 98% undergrads receive any aid. **Criteria for awarding aid:** *Need-based:* Academics, Alumni affiliation, Art, Athletics, Job skills, Leadership, Minority status, Music/ drama, Religious affiliation *Non-need-based:* Academics, Alumni affiliation, Art, Athletics, Job skills, Leadership, Minority status, Music/drama, Religious affiliation, State/district residency.

DOWLING COLLEGE

IdleHour Boulevard, Oakdale, NY 11769-1999
Phone: 800-369-5464 · **Financial Aid Phone:** 631-244-3220
E-mail: admissions@dowling.edu · **CEEB Code:** 2011
Fax: 631-563-3827 · **Website:** www.dowling.edu · **ACT Code:** 2665

This private school was founded in 1959. It has a 157 acre campus.

RATINGS
Admissions Selectivity Rating: 74   **Fire Safety Rating:** 81   **Green Rating:** 60*

STUDENTS AND FACULTY
Enrollment: 1,152. **Student Body:** 51% female, 49% male, 10% out-of-state, 4% international (53 countries represented). Asian 1%, African American 11%, Caucasian 32%, Hispanic 9%, Native American <1%, Pacific Islander <1%, Two or more races 0%, Race unknown 42%.
Retention and Graduation: 68% freshmen return for sophomore year. **Faculty:** Student/faculty ratio 16:1. 47 full-time faculty, 89% hold PhDs, 13% are members of minority groups, 36% are women. 0% of classes are taught by teaching assistants.

ACADEMICS
Degrees: Bachelor's; Master's; Post-Bachelor's certificate; Post-Master's certificate **Classes:** Most classes have 10-19 students. Most lab/discussion sessions have 10-19 students. **Most popular majors:** Special Education And Teaching, General; Psychology, General; Business/Commerce, General. **Special Study Options:** Accelerated program; Distance learning; Double major; English as a Second Language (ESL); Honors program; Independent study; Internships; Liberal arts/career combination; Student-designed major; Study abroad; Teacher certification program; Weekend college. **Honors programs:** The honor programs are for highly motivated, academically superior, and creative students. **Disability Services offered to physically disabled students:** Note-taking services; Reader services; Tape recorders; Tutors. **Career services:** Alumni services; Career/job search classes; Internships

FACILITIES
Housing: Coed dorms 100% of campus accessible to physically diasbled. **Special Academic Facilities/Equipment:** Art gallery, cultural study center, media center, human factors lab, meteorology lab. **Computers:** Students can register for classes online. Administrative functions (other than registration) can be performed online.

CAMPUS LIFE
Environment: Town **Activities:** Choral groups; Drama/theater; Jazz band; Literary magazine; Music ensembles; Musical theater; Student government; Student newspaper; Symphony orchestra; Yearbook 29 registered organizations, 10 honor societies, 1 religious organization. **Athletics (Intercollegiate):** *Men:* baseball, basketball, crew/rowing, golf, lacrosse, soccer, tennis. *Women:* basketball, crew/rowing, cross-country, equestrian sports, soccer, softball, tennis, volleyball. **On-Campus Highlights:** Riverside Cafe, Giordano Gallery, Loft Theatre, Connetuot River, Henry Building Atrium

ADMISSIONS
Freshman Academic Profile: Average high school GPA 2.8. 6% in top 10% of high school class, 19% in top 25% of high school class, 50% in top 50% of high school class. 89% from public high schools. **Test Scores:** SAT Math middle 50% range 410-520. SAT EBRW middle 50% range 410-520. **Basis for Candidate Selection:** *Very important factors considered include:* rigor of secondary school record. *Other factors considered include:* class rank, academic GPA, application essay, standardized test scores, recommendation(s), extracurricular activities, talent/ability, character/personal qualities, alumni/ ae relation. **Freshman Admission Requirements:** High school diploma is required and GED is accepted *Academic units recommended:* 4 English, 3 math, 2 science, 3 social studies, 4 units from above areas or other academic areas. **Freshman Admission Statistics:** 1,864 applied, 74.8% admitted, 15% enrolled. **Transfer Admission Requirements:** college transcript(s), Minimum college GPA of 2.0 required. Lowest grade transferable C. **General Admission Information:** Application fee $25. Nonfall registration accepted. Admission may be deferred for a maximum of 1 year.

COSTS AND FINANCIAL AID
Annual tuition $29,100. Room and board $11,120. Average book expense $1,000. **Required Forms and Deadlines:** FAFSA; State aid form. **Notification of Awards:** Applicants will be notified of awards on a rolling basis beginning 3/15. **Types of Aid:** *Need-based scholarships/grants:* College/ university scholarship or grant aid from institutional funds; Federal Pell; Private scholarships; SEOG; State scholarships/grants. *Loans:* Direct PLUS loans; Direct Subsidized Stafford Loans; Direct Unsubsidized Stafford Loans.

Student Employment: Federal Work-Study Program available. Institutional employment available. **Financial Aid Statistics:** 85% needy freshmen, 88% needy undergrads receive need-based scholarship or grant aid. 76% freshmen, 59% undergrads receive non-need-based scholarship or grant aid. 96% freshmen, 89% undergrads receive need-based self-help aid. 19% freshmen, 15% undergrads receive athletic scholarships. 82% freshmen, 77% undergrads receive any aid. 84% undergrads borrow to pay for school. Average cumulative indebtedness $39,540. **Criteria for awarding aid:** *Need-based:* Athletics *Non-need-based:* Academics, Alumni affiliation, Athletics.

DRAKE UNIVERSITY

2507 University Avenue, Des Moines, IA 50311-4505
Phone: 515-271-3181 · **Financial Aid Phone:** 515-271-2905
E-mail: admission@drake.edu · **CEEB Code:** 6168
Fax: 515-271-2831 · **Website:** www.drake.edu · **ACT Code:** 1302

This private school was founded in 1881. It has a 150 acre campus.

RATINGS
Admissions Selectivity Rating: 86　　**Fire Safety Rating:** 98　　**Green Rating:** 60*

STUDENTS AND FACULTY
Enrollment: 3,038. **Student Body:** 57% female, 43% male, 69% out-of-state, 5% international (43 countries represented). Asian 3%, African American 5%, Caucasian 78%, Hispanic 5%, Native American <1%, Pacific Islander 0%, Two or more races 3%, Race unknown <1%.
Retention and Graduation: 87% freshmen return for sophomore year. 73% freshmen graduate within 4 years. 79% freshmen graduate within 6 years. 22% grads go on to further study within 1 year. 9% grads pursue arts and sciences degrees. 4% grads pursue law degrees. 3% grads pursue business degrees. 4% grads pursue medical degrees. **Faculty:** Student/faculty ratio 11:1. 310 full-time faculty, 92% hold PhDs, 15% are members of minority groups, 48% are women. 0% of classes are taught by teaching assistants.

ACADEMICS
Degrees: Bachelor's; Doctoral Other; Doctoral/Professional; Doctoral/Research; Master's; Post-Bachelor's certificate; Post-Master's certificate **Classes:** Most classes have 10-19 students. Most lab/discussion sessions have 20-29 students. **Most popular majors:** Psychology, General; Pharmacy; Actuarial Science. **Special Study Options:** Accelerated program; Cooperative education program; Distance learning; Double major; Dual enrollment; English as a Second Language (ESL); Honors program; Independent study; Internships; Liberal arts/career combination; Student-designed major; Study abroad; Teacher certification program. **Honors programs:** The Honors Program is designed for motivated students who want to participate in challenging, discussion-based courses on interdisciplinary and topical issues. The program provides a unique opportunity for intellectual enrichment both in and out of the classroom. **Combined degree programs:** BA/JD. **Disability Services offered to physically disabled students:** Note-taking services; Reader services; Tape recorders; Tutors. **Career services:** Alumni network; Alumni services; Career assessment; Career/job search classes; Internships; Regional alumni

FACILITIES
Housing: Apartments for single students; Coed dorms; Fraternity/sorority housing; Theme housing 93% of campus accessible to physically diasbled. **Special Academic Facilities/Equipment:** Language lab, observatory, media service center, Anderson art gallery, Oreon E. Scott Chapel. **Computers:** 100% of classrooms, 100% of dorms, 100% of libraries, 100% of dining areas, 100% of student union, have wireless network access. Students can register for classes online. Administrative functions (other than registration) can be performed online.

CAMPUS LIFE
Environment: Metropolis **Activities:** Choral groups; Concert band; Dance; Drama/theater; International Student Organization; Jazz band; Literary magazine; Marching band; Model UN; Music ensembles; Musical theater; Pep band; Radio station; Student government; Student newspaper; Symphony orchestra 160 registered organizations, 24 honor societies, 10 religious organizations. 7 fraternities, 6 sororities. **Athletics (Intercollegiate):** *Men:* basketball, cheerleading, cross-country, football, golf, soccer, tennis, track/field (outdoor), track/field (indoor). *Women:* basketball, cheerleading, crew/rowing, cross-country, golf, soccer, softball, tennis, track/field (outdoor), track/field (indoor), volleyball. **On-Campus Highlights:** Athletic Facilities, Olmsted Center, Anderson Gallery, Helmick Commons, Residence Halls / Residence Life **Environmental Initiatives:** Sustainable building practices.

ADMISSIONS
Freshman Academic Profile: Average high school GPA 3.7. 38% in top 10% of high school class, 66% in top 25% of high school class, 94% in top 50% of high school class. **Test Scores:** SAT Math middle 50% range 560-690. SAT EBRW middle 50% range 540-660. ACT middle 50% range 24-30. Minimum internet-based TOEFL 71. Minimum paper TOEFL 530. **Basis for Candidate Selection:** *Very important factors considered include:* academic GPA, application essay, standardized test scores. *Important factors considered include:* rigor of secondary school record, recommendation(s), interview. *Other factors considered include:* class rank, extracurricular activities, talent/ability, character/personal qualities, volunteer work, work experience. **Freshman Admission Requirements:** High school diploma is required and GED is accepted *Academic units recommended:* 4 English, 3 math, 2 science, 1 science labs, 2 foreign language, 4 social studies. **Freshman Admission Statistics:** 5,574 applied, 68.8% admitted, 20% enrolled. **Transfer Admission Requirements:** college transcript(s), Minimum college GPA of 2.0 required. Lowest grade transferable C. **General Admission Information:** Priority deadline 3/1. Nonfall registration accepted. Admission may be deferred for a maximum of 1 year.

COSTS AND FINANCIAL AID
Annual tuition $41,250. Room and board $10,158. Required fees $146. Average book expense $1,100. **Required Forms and Deadlines:** FAFSA. **Notification of Awards:** Applicants will be notified of awards on a rolling basis beginning 1/1. **Types of Aid:** *Need-based scholarships/grants:* College/university scholarship or grant aid from institutional funds; Federal Pell; Private scholarships; SEOG; State scholarships/grants. *Loans:* Direct PLUS loans; Direct Subsidized Stafford Loans; Direct Unsubsidized Stafford Loans. *Student Employment:* Federal Work-Study Program available. Institutional employment available. **Financial Aid Statistics:** 99% needy freshmen, 98% needy undergrads receive need-based scholarship or grant aid. 24% freshmen, 18% undergrads receive non-need-based scholarship or grant aid. 79% freshmen, 85% undergrads receive need-based self-help aid. 3% freshmen, 4% undergrads receive athletic scholarships. 99% freshmen, 97% undergrads receive any aid. 63% undergrads borrow to pay for school. Average cumulative indebtedness $33,649. **Criteria for awarding aid:** *Need-based:* Academics *Non-need-based:* Academics, Alumni affiliation, Art, Athletics, Music/drama, State/district residency.

DREW UNIVERSITY

36 Madison Avenue, Madison, NJ 07940-1493
Phone: 973-408-3739 · **Financial Aid Phone:** 973-408-3112
E-mail: cadm@drew.edu · **CEEB Code:** 2193
Fax: 973-408-3068 · **Website:** www.drew.edu · **ACT Code:** 2550

This private school, affiliated with the Methodist Church, was founded in 1868. It has a 186 acre campus.

RATINGS
Admissions Selectivity Rating: 85　　**Fire Safety Rating:** 92　　**Green Rating:** 88

STUDENTS AND FACULTY
Enrollment: 1,404. **Student Body:** 59% female, 41% male, 35% out-of-state, 10% international (49 countries represented). Asian 5%, African American 7%, Caucasian 55%, Hispanic 13%, Native American 0%, Pacific Islander 0%, Two or more races 5%, Race unknown 5%.
Retention and Graduation: 85% freshmen return for sophomore year. 59% freshmen graduate within 4 years. 62% freshmen graduate within 6 years. 31% grads go on to further study within 1 year. 19% grads pursue arts and sciences degrees. 2% grads pursue law degrees. 1% grads pursue business degrees. 3% grads pursue medical degrees. **Faculty:** Student/faculty ratio 10:1. 148 full-time faculty, 99% hold PhDs, 20% are members of minority groups, 47% are women. 0% of classes are taught by teaching assistants.

ACADEMICS
Degrees: Bachelor's; Doctoral Other; Doctoral/Professional; Doctoral/Research; Master's; Post-Bachelor's certificate; Post-Master's certificate **Classes:** Most classes have 20-29 students. Most lab/discussion sessions have 20-29 students. **Most popular majors:** Biology/Biological Sciences, General; Psychology, General; Business Administration And Management, General. **Special Study Options:** Accelerated program; Cross-registration; Double

major; Dual enrollment; English as a Second Language (ESL); Exchange student program (domestic); Honors program; Independent study; Internships; Student-designed major; Study abroad; Teacher certification program. **Honors programs:** The Baldwin Honors program enrolls exceptional students with strong academic records who seek a special opportunity for independent learning, engagement and research. Baldwin Scholars complete a challenging set of courses beyond those in the regular undergraduate curriculum, and participate in exclusive co- and extra-curricular activities (e.g., receptions with campus speakers). The program culminates with the completion of a capstone honors thesis. **Combined degree programs:** BA/JD; BA/MA; BA/MD. **Disability Services offered to physically disabled students:** Note-taking services; Tape recorders; Tutors. **Career services:** Alumni network; Alumni services; Career assessment; Career/job search classes; Internships; Regional alumni

FACILITIES

Housing: Coed dorms; Special housing for disabled student; Special housing for international students; Theme housing; Wellness housing **Special Academic Facilities/Equipment:** The Dorothy Young Center for the Arts houses the Korn Art Gallery and a 400-seat performance hall. Drew is also home to the Zuck Arboretum, the Drew Observatory, and the New Jersey Shakespeare Festival. **Computers:** 90% of classrooms, 20% of dorms, 100% of libraries, 100% of dining areas, 100% of student union, 25% of common outdoor areas have wireless network access. Students can register for classes online. Administrative functions (other than registration) can be performed online. Undergraduates are required to own a computer.

CAMPUS LIFE

Environment: Village **Activities:** Campus Ministries; Choral groups; Dance; Drama/theater; International Student Organization; Jazz band; Literary magazine; Model UN; Music ensembles; Musical theater; Pep band; Radio station; Student government; Student newspaper; Student-run film society; Symphony orchestra; Yearbook 80 registered organizations, 17 honor societies, 9 religious organizations. **Athletics (Intercollegiate):** *Men:* baseball, basketball, cross-country, fencing, lacrosse, soccer, swimming, tennis. *Women:* basketball, cross-country, fencing, field hockey, lacrosse, soccer, softball, swimming, tennis. **On-Campus Highlights:** The Commons, Ehinger Center, Dorothy Young Center for the Arts, Simon Forum, Rose Memorial Library **Environmental Initiatives:** Newly renovated student center, Ehinger Student Center, meets USGBC Leadership in Energy and Environmental Design (LEED) Silver certification

ADMISSIONS

Freshman Academic Profile: Average high school GPA 3.5. 24% in top 10% of high school class, 60% in top 25% of high school class, 84% in top 50% of high school class. 60% from public high schools. **Test Scores:** SAT Math middle 50% range 540-640. SAT EBRW middle 50% range 560-660. ACT middle 50% range 23-28. Minimum internet-based TOEFL 80. Minimum paper TOEFL 550. **Basis for Candidate Selection:** *Very important factors considered include:* rigor of secondary school record, academic GPA, interview. *Important factors considered include:* application essay, recommendation(s), extracurricular activities, talent/ability, character/personal qualities. *Other factors considered include:* class rank, standardized test scores, alumni/ae relation, racial/ethnic status, volunteer work, work experience, level of applicant's interest. **Freshman Admission Requirements:** High school diploma is required and GED is accepted *Academic units recommended:* 4 English, 3 math, 2 science, 2 foreign language, 2 social studies, 2 history, 3 academic electives. **Freshman Admission Statistics:** 3,205 applied, 63.4% admitted, 18% enrolled. **Transfer Admission Requirements:** High school transcript, college transcript(s), essay or personal statement, statement of good standing from prior institution(s). Lowest grade transferable C. **General Admission Information:** Application fee $40. Priority deadline 11/15. Regular application deadline 2/1. Nonfall registration accepted. Admission may be deferred for a maximum of 1 year.

COSTS AND FINANCIAL AID

Annual tuition $38,668. Required fees $832. Average book expense $1,200. **Required Forms and Deadlines:** FAFSA. **Notification of Awards:** Applicants will be notified of awards on or about 3/25. **Types of Aid:** *Need-based scholarships/grants:* College/university scholarship or grant aid from institutional funds; Federal Pell; Private scholarships; SEOG; State scholarships/grants. *Loans:* Direct PLUS loans; Direct Subsidized Stafford Loans; Direct Unsubsidized Stafford Loans. *Student Employment:* Federal Work-Study Program available. Institutional employment available. **Financial Aid Statistics:** 100% needy freshmen, 100% needy undergrads receive need-based scholarship or grant aid. 10% freshmen, 9% undergrads receive non-need-based scholarship or grant aid. 84% freshmen, 82% undergrads receive need-based self-help aid. 0% freshmen, 0% undergrads receive athletic scholarships. 98% freshmen, 95% undergrads receive any aid. 67% undergrads borrow to pay for school. Average cumulative indebtedness $24,964. **Criteria for awarding aid:** *Need-based:* Academics *Non-need-based:* Academics, Art, Leadership, Minority status, Music/drama.

DREXEL UNIVERSITY

3141 Chestnut Street, Philadelphia, PA 19104
Phone: 215-895-2400 · **Financial Aid Phone:** 215-895-2537
E-mail: enroll@drexel.edu · **CEEB Code:** 2194
Fax: 215-895-1285 · **Website:** www.drexel.edu · **ACT Code:** 3556

This private school was founded in 1891. It has a 96 acre campus.

RATINGS

Admissions Selectivity Rating: 85   **Fire Safety Rating:** 97   **Green Rating:** 88

STUDENTS AND FACULTY

Enrollment: 15,409. **Student Body:** 48% female, 52% male, 51% out-of-state, 12% international (115 countries represented). Asian 16%, African American 7%, Caucasian 52%, Hispanic 6%, Native American <1%, Pacific Islander <1%, Two or more races 4%, Race unknown 2%. **Retention and Graduation:** 89% freshmen return for sophomore year. 71% freshmen graduate within 6 years. 12% grads go on to further study within 1 year. **Faculty:** Student/faculty ratio 11:1. 1,108 full-time faculty, 86% hold PhDs, 19% are members of minority groups, 46% are women.

ACADEMICS

Degrees: Bachelor's; Certificate; Doctoral; Doctoral/Professional; Doctoral/Research; Master's; Post-Bachelor's certificate; Post-Master's certificate **Classes:** Most classes have 10-19 students. Most lab/discussion sessions have 10-19 students. **Most popular majors:** Mechanical Engineering; Registered Nursing/Registered Nurse; Business/Commerce, General. **Special Study Options:** Accelerated program; Cooperative education program; Distance learning; Double major; Dual enrollment; English as a Second Language (ESL); Honors program; Independent study; Internships; Student-designed major; Study abroad; Teacher certification program; Weekend college. **Honors programs:** The Pennoni Honors College enriches the University experience for students from all majors with demonstrated academic achievement and broad intellectual interests. Established in 1991 with 33 students, the Honors Program has grown exponentially. Today, Honors Students represent nearly every major and college offered at Drexel University; Honors freshmen fill the Honors Residence Hall, and hundreds of students graduate with Honors Distinction each June. **Combined degree programs:** BA/MA; BA/MD; BA/MEng. **Disability Services offered to physically disabled students:** Note-taking services; Reader services; Tape recorders; Tutors. **Career services:** Alumni services; Career assessment; Career/job search classes; Internships

FACILITIES

Housing: Apartments for single students; Coed dorms; Fraternity/sorority housing; Special housing for disabled student; Special housing for international students 98% of campus accessible to physically diasbled. **Special Academic Facilities/Equipment:** Art museum, theatre, TV studio, recreational center, center for automation technology **Computers:** 100% of classrooms, 100% of dorms, 100% of libraries, 100% of dining areas, 100% of student union, 100% of common outdoor areas have wireless network access. Students can register for classes online. Administrative functions (other than registration) can be performed online. Undergraduates are required to own a computer.

CAMPUS LIFE

Environment: Metropolis **Activities:** Campus Ministries; Choral groups; Concert band; Dance; Drama/theater; Jazz band; Literary magazine; Model UN; Music ensembles; Musical theater; Pep band; Radio station; Student government; Student newspaper; Student-run film society; Symphony orchestra; Television station; Yearbook 136 registered organizations, 8 honor societies, 8 religious organizations. 12 fraternities, 11 sororities. **Athletics (Intercollegiate):** *Men:* basketball, cheerleading, crew/rowing, diving, golf, lacrosse, soccer, swimming, tennis, wrestling. *Women:* basketball, cheerleading, crew/rowing, diving, field hockey, lacrosse, soccer, softball, swimming, tennis, volleyball. **On-Campus Highlights:** Drexel Recreation Center, Barnes & Noble University Bookstore, Creese Student Center, Handschumacher Dining Center, The Quad **Environmental Initiatives:** Green Power: n 2002, Drexel became one of the first universities to purchase wind generated energy. In 2006, Drexel entered into a contract with PECO Wind, to purchase wind energy directly linked to the Exelon-Community Energy Wind Farms located in the PJM Interconnection, supplying Drexel with 4,000.8 MWH per year, which translated into approximately 7.92% of Drexel's total annual electric use. In 2008, Drexel entered into a contract with Community Energy, Inc. to purchase energy linked to the PJM Interconnection, which translated into 12.9% of Drexel's total annual use; the University increased its purchase to 30% of its total annual electric usage the following year. In 2010, Drexel entered into a new agreement with Community Energy to purchase Renewable Energy Certificates equal to 100% of the University's total energy use (84,268 MWH) starting in January 2011, making Drexel one of the top 50 purchasers of wind energy in the nation according to the EPA Green Power Partnership Rankings. In 2013, Drexel expanded its leadership with a renewed commitment to purchase 100% wind and solar energy from Community Energy.

ADMISSIONS

Freshman Academic Profile: Average high school GPA 3.7. 36% in top 10% of high school class, 65% in top 25% of high school class, 91% in top 50% of high school class. **Test Scores:** SAT Math middle 50% range 580-690. SAT EBRW middle 50% range 580-670. ACT middle 50% range 24-30. Minimum internet-based TOEFL 79. **Basis for Candidate Selection:** *Very important factors considered include:* rigor of secondary school record, class rank, academic GPA, standardized test scores. *Important factors considered include:* application essay, recommendation(s), character/personal qualities. *Other factors considered include:* interview, extracurricular activities, talent/ability, first generation, alumni/ae relation, volunteer work, work experience, level of applicant's interest. **Freshman Admission Requirements:** High school diploma is required and GED is accepted *Academic units required:* 3 math, 1 science, 1 science labs, *Academic units recommended:* 1 foreign language. **Freshman Admission Statistics:** 28,454 applied, 79.0% admitted, 15% enrolled. **Transfer Admission Requirements:** college transcript(s), Minimum college GPA of 2.5 required. Lowest grade transferable C. **General Admission Information:** Application fee $50. Regular application deadline 1/15. Nonfall registration accepted. Admission may be deferred.

COSTS AND FINANCIAL AID

Annual tuition $49,632. Room and board $13,890. Required fees $2,370. Average book expense $1,200. **Required Forms and Deadlines:** CSS/Financial Aid PROFILE; FAFSA. **Notification of Awards:** Applicants will be notified of awards on or about 4/1. **Types of Aid:** *Need-based scholarships/grants:* College/university scholarship or grant aid from institutional funds; Federal Pell; Private scholarships; SEOG; State scholarships/grants. *Loans:* Direct PLUS loans; Direct Subsidized Stafford Loans; Direct Unsubsidized Stafford Loans. *Student Employment:* Federal Work-Study Program available. Institutional employment available. **Financial Aid Statistics:** 100% needy freshmen, 95% needy undergrads receive need-based scholarship or grant aid. 16% freshmen, 9% undergrads receive non-need-based scholarship or grant aid. 71% freshmen, 80% undergrads receive need-based self-help aid. 2% freshmen, 1% undergrads receive athletic scholarships. **Criteria for awarding aid:** *Need-based:* Academics, Art, Athletics, Music/drama *Non-need-based:* Academics, Art, Athletics, Music/drama, State/district residency.

DRURY UNIVERSITY

900 North Benton Avenue, Springfield, MO 65802-3712
Phone: 417-873-7205 · **Financial Aid Phone:** 417-873-7312
E-mail: druryad@drury.edu · **CEEB Code:** 6169
Fax: 417-866-3873 · **Website:** www.drury.edu · **ACT Code:** 2292

This private school, affiliated with the Christian Church (Disciples of Christ), UCC, was founded in 1873. It has a 84 acre campus.

RATINGS

Admissions Selectivity Rating: 83   **Fire Safety Rating:** 80   **Green Rating:** 84

STUDENTS AND FACULTY

Enrollment: 1,420. **Student Body:** 56% female, 44% male, 25% out-of-state, 9% international (53 countries represented). Asian 2%, African American 3%, Caucasian 79%, Hispanic 3%, Native American 1%, Pacific Islander <1%, Two or more races 4%, Race unknown 0%.
Retention and Graduation: 86% freshmen return for sophomore year. 48% freshmen graduate within 4 years. 66% freshmen graduate within 6 years. 35% grads go on to further study within 1 year. 5% grads pursue arts and sciences degrees. 5% grads pursue law degrees. 9% grads pursue business degrees. 15% grads pursue medical degrees. **Faculty:** Student/faculty ratio 13:1. 110 full-time faculty, 94% hold PhDs, 6% are members of minority groups, 41% are women. 0% of classes are taught by teaching assistants.

ACADEMICS

Degrees: Associate; Bachelor's; Master's **Classes:** Most classes have 20-29 students. Most lab/discussion sessions have 10-19 students. **Most popular**

majors: Biology/Biological Sciences, General; Drama And Dramatics/Theatre Arts, General; Business Administration And Management, General. **Special Study Options:** Accelerated program; Cooperative education program; Distance learning; Double major; Dual enrollment; English as a Second Language (ESL); Honors program; Independent study; Internships; Liberal arts/career combination; Student-designed major; Study abroad; Teacher certification program. **Honors programs:** Drury Honors Program **Combined degree programs:** BA/MEng. **Disability Services offered to physically disabled students:** Note-taking services; Reader services; Tape recorders; Tutors. **Career services:** Alumni network; Alumni services; Career assessment; Career/job search classes; Internships; Regional alumni

FACILITIES

Housing: Apartments for married students; Apartments for single students; Coed dorms; Fraternity/sorority housing; Theme housing 97% of campus accessible to physically diasbled. **Special Academic Facilities/Equipment:** Science center with greenhouse and astronomical observation station, new visual art center with two galleries, TV studio, radio station, teleconference facility, language lab, electronic music lab, laser lab. **Computers:** 100% of classrooms, 30% of dorms, 100% of libraries, 100% of dining areas, 75% of student union, 20% of common outdoor areas have wireless network access. Students can register for classes online. Administrative functions (other than registration) can be performed online.

CAMPUS LIFE

Environment: Metropolis **Activities:** Campus Ministries; Choral groups; Concert band; Dance; Drama/theater; International Student Organization; Jazz band; Literary magazine; Music ensembles; Musical theater; Opera; Pep band; Radio station; Student government; Student newspaper; Student-run film society; Symphony orchestra; Television station 90 registered organizations, 11 honor societies, 7 religious organizations. 4 fraternities, 4 sororities. **Athletics (Intercollegiate):** *Men:* baseball, basketball, cheerleading, cross-country, diving, golf, soccer, softball, swimming, tennis. *Women:* basketball, cheerleading, cross-country, diving, golf, soccer, softball, swimming, tennis, volleyball. **On-Campus Highlights:** O'Reilly Family Event Center, The Quad, Findlay Student Center, Sunderland Field, Wallace Hall Lounge **Environmental Initiatives:** Energy Management strategies on buildings upgrading lighting, HVAC systems). Bicycle rentals for students to use for the semester for $25.

ADMISSIONS

Freshman Academic Profile: Average high school GPA 3.8. 34% in top 10% of high school class, 66% in top 25% of high school class, 87% in top 50% of high school class. 85% from public high schools. **Test Scores:** ACT middle 50% range 23-28. Minimum internet-based TOEFL 72. **Basis for Candidate Selection:** *Very important factors considered include:* academic GPA, standardized test scores. *Important factors considered include:* application essay. *Other factors considered include:* rigor of secondary school record, recommendation(s), interview, extracurricular activities, talent/ability, character/personal qualities, first generation, alumni/ae relation, religious affiliation/commitment, racial/ethnic status, volunteer work, work experience, level of applicant's interest. **Freshman Admission Requirements:** High school diploma is required and GED is accepted *Academic units required:* 3 math, *Academic units recommended:* 4 English, 3 math, 3 science, 2 foreign language, 3 social studies. **Freshman Admission Statistics:** 1,474 applied, 72.4% admitted, 32% enrolled. **Transfer Admission Requirements:** High school transcript, college transcript(s), essay or personal statement, Minimum college GPA of 2.0 required. Lowest grade transferable C. **General Admission Information:** Regular application deadline 8/30. Nonfall registration accepted. Admission may be deferred for a maximum of 1 year.

COSTS AND FINANCIAL AID

Annual tuition $27,350. Room and board $9,040. Required fees $1,015. Average book expense $1,200. **Required Forms and Deadlines:** FAFSA. **Notification of Awards:** Applicants will be notified of awards on a rolling basis beginning 2/15. **Types of Aid:** *Need-based scholarships/grants:* College/university scholarship or grant aid from institutional funds; Federal Pell; Private scholarships; SEOG; State scholarships/grants. *Loans:* Direct PLUS loans; Direct Subsidized Stafford Loans; Direct Unsubsidized Stafford Loans. *Student Employment:* Federal Work-Study Program available. Institutional employment available. **Financial Aid Statistics:** 100% needy freshmen, 100% needy undergrads receive need-based scholarship or grant aid. 15% freshmen, 14% undergrads receive non-need-based scholarship or grant aid. 81% freshmen, 82% undergrads receive need-based self-help aid. 13% freshmen, 11% undergrads receive athletic scholarships. 81% freshmen, 94% undergrads receive any aid. 55% undergrads borrow to pay for school. Average cumulative indebtedness $31,011. **Criteria for awarding aid:** *Need-based:* Alumni affiliation, Job skills *Non-need-based:* Academics, Alumni affiliation, Art, Athletics, Job skills, Leadership, Minority status, Music/drama, Religious affiliation.

DUKE UNIVERSITY

Chapel Drive, Durham, NC 27708-0586
Phone: 919-684-3214
E-mail: undergrad-admissions@duke.edu · **CEEB Code:** 5156
Fax: (919) 668-1661 · **Website:** www.duke.edu · **ACT Code:** 3088

This private school, affiliated with the Methodist Church, was founded in 1838. It has a 8500 acre campus.

RATINGS

Admissions Selectivity Rating: 98   **Fire Safety Rating:** 60*   **Green Rating:** 91

STUDENTS AND FACULTY

Enrollment: 6,467. **Student Body:** 49% female, 51% male, 85% out-of-state, 10% international (89 countries represented). Asian 22%, African American 10%, Caucasian 46%, Hispanic 8%, Native American 1%, Pacific Islander <1%, Two or more races 2%, Race unknown 2%.
Retention and Graduation: 38% grads go on to further study within 1 year. 14% grads pursue arts and sciences degrees. 11% grads pursue law degrees. 1% grads pursue business degrees. 12% grads pursue medical degrees. **Faculty:** Student/faculty ratio 6:1. 1,455 full-time faculty, 96% hold PhDs, 19% are members of minority groups, 39% are women. 4% of classes are taught by teaching assistants.

ACADEMICS

Degrees: Bachelor's; Doctoral/Professional; Doctoral/Research; Master's; Post-Bachelor's certificate; Post-Master's certificate **Classes:** Most classes have 10-19 students. **Most popular majors:** Psychology, General; Public Policy Analysis, General; Economics, General. **Special Study Options:** Cross-registration; Double major; Exchange student program (domestic); Independent study; Internships; Student-designed major; Study abroad; Teacher certification program. **Combined degree programs:** BA/MA; BA/MEng. **Disability Services offered to physically disabled students:** Note-taking services; Reader services; Tape recorders; Tutors. **Career services:** Alumni services; Career assessment; Career/job search classes; Internships

FACILITIES

Housing: Apartments for single students; Coed dorms; Men's dorms; Theme housing; Wellness housing; Women's dorms **Special Academic Facilities/ Equipment:** Art museum, language lab, university forest, primate center, phytotron, electron laser, nuclear magnetic resonance machine, nuclear lab. **Computers:** Students can register for classes online.

CAMPUS LIFE

Environment: City **Activities:** Campus Ministries; Choral groups; Concert band; Dance; Drama/theater; International Student Organization; Jazz band; Literary magazine; Marching band; Model UN; Music ensembles; Musical theater; Opera; Pep band; Radio station; Student government; Student newspaper; Student-run film society; Symphony orchestra; Television station 200 registered organizations, 10 honor societies, 25 religious organizations. 21 fraternities, 14 sororities. **Athletics (Intercollegiate):** *Men:* baseball, basketball, cross-country, diving, fencing, football, golf, lacrosse, soccer, swimming, tennis, track/field (outdoor), track/field (indoor), volleyball, wrestling. *Women:* basketball, crew/rowing, cross-country, diving, fencing, field hockey, golf, lacrosse, soccer, swimming, tennis, track/field (outdoor), track/ field (indoor), volleyball. **On-Campus Highlights:** Duke Chapel, Primate Center, Sarah P. Duke Gardens, Duke Forest, Levine Science Research Center **Environmental Initiatives:** Duke has signed the ACUPCC and made a commitment to make Duke a climate neutral institution.

ADMISSIONS

Freshman Academic Profile: 91% in top 10% of high school class, 97% in top 25% of high school class, 99% in top 50% of high school class. 65% from public high schools. **Test Scores:** SAT Math middle 50% range 700-800. SAT EBRW middle 50% range 680-770. ACT middle 50% range 31-34. **Basis for Candidate Selection:** *Very important factors considered include:* rigor of secondary school record, academic GPA, application essay, standardized test scores, recommendation(s), extracurricular activities, talent/ability, character/ personal qualities. *Other factors considered include:* class rank, interview, first generation, alumni/ae relation, geographical residence, state residency, religious affiliation/commitment, racial/ethnic status, volunteer work, work experience, level of applicant's interest. **Freshman Admission Requirements:** High school diploma is required and GED is not accepted *Academic units recommended:* 4 English, 3 math, 3 science, 3 foreign language, 3 social studies. **Freshman Admission Statistics:** 31,671 applied, 10.8% admitted, 50%

enrolled. **Transfer Admission Requirements:** High school transcript, college transcript(s), essay or personal statement, standardized test scores, Lowest grade transferable C. **General Admission Information:** Application fee $85. Priority deadline 12/20. Regular application deadline 1/3. Nonfall registration accepted. Admission may be deferred for a maximum of 1 year.

COSTS AND FINANCIAL AID

Annual tuition $51,720. Room and board $14,708. Required fees $1,780. Average book expense $1,300. **Required Forms and Deadlines:** Business/ Farm Supplement; CSS/Financial Aid PROFILE; FAFSA; Noncustodial PROFILE. **Notification of Awards:** Applicants will be notified of awards on or about 4/1. **Types of Aid:** *Need-based scholarships/grants:* College/ university scholarship or grant aid from institutional funds; Federal Pell; Private scholarships; SEOG; State scholarships/grants. *Loans:* Direct PLUS loans; Direct Subsidized Stafford Loans; Direct Unsubsidized Stafford Loans. *Student Employment:* Federal Work-Study Program available. Institutional employment available. **Financial Aid Statistics:** 85% needy freshmen, 94% needy undergrads receive need-based scholarship or grant aid. 13% freshmen, 10% undergrads receive non-need-based scholarship or grant aid. 83% freshmen, 87% undergrads receive need-based self-help aid. 0% freshmen, 0% undergrads receive athletic scholarships. 35% undergrads borrow to pay for school. Average cumulative indebtedness $19,104. **Criteria for awarding aid:** *Need-based:* Academics, Alumni affiliation, Leadership, Minority status, Music/drama, Religious affiliation *Non-need-based:* Academics, Alumni affiliation, Athletics, Leadership, Minority status, Music/drama, Religious affiliation, State/district residency.

DUQUESNE UNIVERSITY

600 Forbes Avenue, Pittsburgh, PA 15282
Phone: 412-396-6222 · **Financial Aid Phone:** 412-396-6607
E-mail: admissions@duq.edu
Fax: 412-396-6223 · **Website:** www.duq.edu

This private school, affiliated with the Roman Catholic Church, was founded in 1878. It has a 49.5 acre campus.

RATINGS

Admissions Selectivity Rating: 83   **Fire Safety Rating:** 98   **Green Rating:** 82

STUDENTS AND FACULTY

Enrollment: 5,930. **Student Body:** 64% female, 36% male, 28% out-of-state, 4% international (48 countries represented). Asian 3%, African American 5%, Caucasian 80%, Hispanic 4%, Native American <1%, Pacific Islander <1%, Two or more races 3%, Race unknown 1%.
Retention and Graduation: 86% freshmen return for sophomore year. 68% freshmen graduate within 4 years. 79% freshmen graduate within 6 years. 29% grads go on to further study within 1 year. 16% grads pursue arts and sciences degrees. 2% grads pursue law degrees. 6% grads pursue business degrees. 3% grads pursue medical degrees. **Faculty:** Student/faculty ratio 14:1. 502 full-time faculty, 93% hold PhDs, 9% are members of minority groups, 51% are women.

ACADEMICS

Degrees: Bachelor's; Doctoral/Professional; Doctoral/Research; Master's; Post-Bachelor's certificate; Post-Master's certificate **Classes:** Most classes have 20-29 students. Most lab/discussion sessions have 20-29 students. **Most popular majors:** Psychology, General; Pharmacy; Nursing Science. **Special Study Options:** Accelerated program; Cross-registration; Distance learning; Double major; Dual enrollment; English as a Second Language (ESL); Exchange student program (domestic); External degree program; Honors program; Independent study; Internships; Liberal arts/career combination; Student-designed major; Study abroad; Teacher certification program; Weekend college. **Honors programs:** Duquesne University offers its most qualified and outstanding freshmen the opportunity to participate in the Honors College. The Honors College works within the student's own course of study while providing enhanced opportunities for creative and critical thinking, leadership and service, education in the humanities, and global perspectives. The foundation of Duquesne's Honors College is its enhanced track of the liberal arts-based University Core Curriculum. Special honors sections of the core courses feature some of the University's most distinguished faculty and maintain small class sections, allowing close interaction and encouraging individual initiative as well as collaborative learning. Students who have completed their Honors

College Core requirements may apply to Duquesne University's Honors Fellows Program, which allows students to design and implement a research project based on their academic major and personal interests. Students are also invited to apply for an Endowed Fellowship to receive funding for travel and equipment that will contribute to the success of their Honors Fellows Project. **Combined degree programs:** BA/JD; BA/MA. **Disability Services offered to physically disabled students:** Reader services; Tape recorders; Tutors. **Career services:** Alumni network; Alumni services; Career assessment; Career/job search classes; Internships; Regional alumni

FACILITIES

Housing: Apartments for married students; Apartments for single students; Coed dorms; Fraternity/sorority housing; Men's dorms; Special housing for disabled student; Wellness housing; Women's dorms **Special Academic Facilities/Equipment:** Art Gallery, Nursing Simulation Center, Genesius Theater, Science and Pharmacy Labs **Computers:** 10% of classrooms, 100% of libraries, 85% of dining areas, 100% of student union, 100% of common outdoor areas have wireless network access. Students can register for classes online. Administrative functions (other than registration) can be performed online.

CAMPUS LIFE

Environment: Metropolis **Activities:** Campus Ministries; Choral groups; Concert band; Dance; Drama/theater; International Student Organization; Jazz band; Literary magazine; Model UN; Music ensembles; Musical theater; Opera; Pep band; Radio station; Student government; Student newspaper; Student-run film society; Symphony orchestra; Television station; Yearbook 160 registered organizations, 34 honor societies, 7 religious organizations. 10 fraternities, 7 sororities. **Athletics (Intercollegiate):** *Men:* basketball, cross-country, football, soccer, tennis, track/field (outdoor). *Women:* basketball, crew/rowing, cross-country, lacrosse, soccer, swimming, tennis, track/field (outdoor), track/field (indoor), volleyball. **On-Campus Highlights:** Genesius Theater, Power Center, Starbucks, The Red Ring, Academic Walk **Environmental Initiatives:** Duquesne University relies 100 percent on clean energy. For over 20 years, the University has produced the bulk of its own electricity with a clean-burning natural gas turbine located at the heart of campus. This cogeneration plant produces approximately 85 percent of the power used to light, heat and cool the campus with overall efficiency greater than 70 percent. It is Pennsylvania's first approved generation system for creating Alternative Energy Credits. Sustainable initiatives reached an exceptional level with the purchase of more than 14 million kilowatt hours of renewable energy credits. This combination of energy generation and renewable energy purchase led Duquesne University to rely 100 percent on clean energy.

ADMISSIONS

Freshman Academic Profile: Average high school GPA 3.7. 25% in top 10% of high school class, 56% in top 25% of high school class, 86% in top 50% of high school class. **Test Scores:** SAT Math middle 50% range 550-630. SAT EBRW middle 50% range 570-640. ACT middle 50% range 24-29. Minimum internet-based TOEFL 70. Minimum paper TOEFL 525. **Basis for Candidate Selection:** *Very important factors considered include:* rigor of secondary school record, academic GPA. *Important factors considered include:* standardized test scores. *Other factors considered include:* class rank, application essay, recommendation(s), interview, extracurricular activities, talent/ability, character/personal qualities, first generation, alumni/ae relation, racial/ethnic status, volunteer work, work experience, level of applicant's interest. **Freshman Admission Requirements:** High school diploma is required and GED is accepted *Academic units recommended:* 4 English, 2 math, 2 science, 2 foreign language, 2 social studies, 4 academic electives. **Freshman Admission Statistics:** 7,336 applied, 71.7% admitted, 30% enrolled. **Transfer Admission Requirements:** High school transcript, college transcript(s), essay or personal statement, statement of good standing from prior institution(s). Minimum college GPA of 2.5 required. Lowest grade transferable C. **General Admission Information:** Application fee $50. Priority deadline 11/1. Regular application deadline 7/1. Nonfall registration accepted. Admission may be deferred for a maximum of One academic year.

COSTS AND FINANCIAL AID

Annual tuition $36,394. Room and board $12,114. Average book expense $1,400. **Required Forms and Deadlines:** FAFSA; Institution's own financial aid form. **Notification of Awards:** Applicants will be notified of awards on a rolling basis beginning 2/1. **Types of Aid:** *Need-based scholarships/grants:* College/university scholarship or grant aid from institutional funds; Federal Pell; Private scholarships; SEOG; State scholarships/grants; United Negro College Fund. *Loans:* Direct PLUS loans; Direct Subsidized Stafford Loans; Direct Unsubsidized Stafford Loans. *Student Employment:* Federal Work-Study Program available. Institutional employment available. **Financial Aid Statistics:** 100% needy freshmen, 97% needy undergrads receive need-based scholarship or grant aid. 100% freshmen, 95% undergrads receive non-need-based scholarship or grant aid. 78% freshmen, 80% undergrads receive need-based self-help aid. 6% freshmen, 6% undergrads receive athletic scholarships. 99% freshmen, 96% undergrads receive any aid. 59% undergrads borrow to pay for school. Average cumulative indebtedness $41,272. **Criteria for awarding**

aid: *Need-based:* Academics, Athletics, Minority status *Non-need-based:* Academics, Athletics, Music/drama.

D'YOUVILLE COLLEGE

320 Porter Avenue, Buffalo, NY 14201
Phone: 716-829-7600 · **Financial Aid Phone:** 716-829-7500
E-mail: admissions@dyc.edu · **CEEB Code:** 2197
Fax: 716-829-7790 · **Website:** www.dyc.edu · **ACT Code:** 2732

This private school was founded in 1908. It has a 7 acre campus.

RATINGS

Admissions Selectivity Rating: 75   **Fire Safety Rating:** 82   **Green Rating:** 60*

STUDENTS AND FACULTY

Enrollment: 1,982. **Student Body:** 73% female, 27% male, 4% out-of-state, 7% international (55 countries represented). Asian 3%, African American 10%, Caucasian 70%, Hispanic 4%, Native American 1%, Pacific Islander 0%, Two or more races 1%, Race unknown 4%.
Retention and Graduation: 72% freshmen return for sophomore year.
Faculty: Student/faculty ratio 8:1. 180 full-time faculty, 76% hold PhDs, 8% are members of minority groups, 61% are women. 0% of classes are taught by teaching assistants.

ACADEMICS

Degrees: Bachelor's; Doctoral/Professional; Doctoral/Research; Master's; Post-Bachelor's certificate; Post-Master's certificate **Classes:** Most classes have fewer than 10 students. Most lab/discussion sessions have fewer than 10 students. **Most popular majors:** Education, General; Nursing/Registered Nurse (Rn, Asn, Bsn, Msn); Business/Commerce, General. **Special Study Options:** Accelerated program; Cooperative education program; Cross-registration; Distance learning; Double major; Dual enrollment; Honors program; Independent study; Internships; Study abroad; Teacher certification program; Weekend college. **Disability Services offered to physically disabled students:** Note-taking services; Reader services; Tape recorders; Tutors.

FACILITIES

Housing: Apartments for single students; Coed dorms; Special housing for disabled students 100% of campus accessible to physically diasbled. **Special Academic Facilities/Equipment:** Kavinoky Theatre (professional theatre) **Computers:** Students can register for classes online. Administrative functions (other than registration) can be performed online.

CAMPUS LIFE

Environment: City **Activities:** Campus Ministries; Choral groups; Drama/theater; Literary magazine; Student government; Student newspaper; Yearbook 25 registered organizations, 3 honor societies, 1 religious organization. **Athletics (Intercollegiate):** *Men:* baseball, basketball, golf, soccer, volleyball. *Women:* basketball, crew/rowing, golf, soccer, softball, volleyball. **On-Campus Highlights:** New Academic Center, New Gym, Spot Spartian Cafe, Weight Room, Gross anatomy lab

ADMISSIONS

Freshman Academic Profile: 18% in top 10% of high school class, 52% in top 25% of high school class, 87% in top 50% of high school class. 75% from public high schools. **Test Scores:** SAT Math middle 50% range 490-580. SAT EBRW middle 50% range 470-550. ACT middle 50% range 21-25. Minimum paper TOEFL 500. **Basis for Candidate Selection:** *Very important factors considered include:* rigor of secondary school record, academic GPA, standardized test scores. *Important factors considered include:* class rank. *Other factors considered include:* recommendation(s), interview, extracurricular activities, talent/ability, character/personal qualities, alumni/ae relation, volunteer work, work experience. **Freshman Admission Requirements:** High school diploma is required and GED is accepted *Academic units recommended:* 4 English, 3 math, 3 science, 3 foreign language, 3 social studies. **Freshman Admission Statistics:** 1,023 applied, 80.4% admitted, 29% enrolled. **Transfer Admission Requirements:** High school transcript, college transcript(s), Minimum college GPA of 2.0 required. Lowest grade transferable C. **General Admission Information:** Application fee $25. Nonfall registration accepted. Admission may be deferred for a maximum of 1 year.

COSTS AND FINANCIAL AID

Annual tuition $21,930. Room and board $10,250. Required fees $310. Average book expense $1,200. **Required Forms and Deadlines:** FAFSA; State aid form. **Notification of Awards:** Applicants will be notified of awards on a rolling basis beginning 4/15. **Types of Aid:** *Need-based scholarships/grants:* College/

university scholarship or grant aid from institutional funds; Federal Pell; Private scholarships; SEOG; State scholarships/grants. *Loans:* Direct PLUS loans; Direct Subsidized Stafford Loans; Direct Unsubsidized Stafford Loans. *Student Employment:* Federal Work-Study Program available. Institutional employment available. **Financial Aid Statistics:** 100% needy freshmen receive need-based scholarship or grant aid. 10% freshmen, 5% undergrads receive non-need-based scholarship or grant aid. 89% freshmen, 92% undergrads receive need-based self-help aid. 0% freshmen, 0% undergrads receive athletic scholarships. **Criteria for awarding aid:** *Need-based:* Academics, Alumni affiliation *Non-need-based:* Academics, Leadership, Religious affiliation.

EARLHAM COLLEGE

801 National Road West, Richmond, IN 47374-4095
Phone: 765-983-1600 · **Financial Aid Phone:** 765-983-1217
E-mail: admissions@earlham.edu · **CEEB Code:** 1195
Fax: 765-983-1560 · **Website:** www.earlham.edu · **ACT Code:** 1186

This private school, affiliated with the Quaker Church, was founded in 1847. It has a 800 acre campus.

RATINGS
Admissions Selectivity Rating: 89   **Fire Safety Rating:** 93   **Green Rating:** 91

STUDENTS AND FACULTY
Enrollment: 1,027. **Student Body:** 54% female, 46% male, 82% out-of-state, 22% international (76 countries represented). Asian 6%, African American 11%, Caucasian 52%, Hispanic 7%, Native American 1%, Pacific Islander <1%, Two or more races <1%, Race unknown 2%.
Retention and Graduation: 86% freshmen return for sophomore year. 58% freshmen graduate within 4 years. 68% freshmen graduate within 6 years. 18% grads go on to further study within 1 year. **Faculty:** Student/faculty ratio 10:1. 106 full-time faculty, 95% hold PhDs, 25% are members of minority groups, 52% are women. 0% of classes are taught by teaching assistants.

ACADEMICS
Degrees: Bachelor's; Master's; Post-Bachelor's certificate **Classes:** Most classes have 10-19 students. Most lab/discussion sessions have 10-19 students. **Most popular majors:** Biology/Biological Sciences, General; Multi-/Interdisciplinary Studies, Other; Psychology, General. **Special Study Options:** Accelerated program; Cross-registration; Double major; Dual enrollment; English as a Second Language (ESL); Independent study; Internships; Liberal arts/career combination; Student-designed major; Study abroad; Teacher certification program. **Combined degree programs:** BA/MA. **Disability Services offered to physically disabled students:** Note-taking services; Reader services; Tape recorders; Tutors. **Career services:** Alumni network; Alumni services; Career assessment; Career/job search classes; Internships; Regional alumni

FACILITIES
Housing: Coed dorms; Cooperative housing; Men's dorms; Special housing for disabled student; Theme housing; Wellness housing; Women's dorms 80% of campus accessible to physically diasbled. **Special Academic Facilities/Equipment:** Earlham has recently invested in a new Center for Science and Technology (CST) and a Center for the Visual and Performing Arts. Other notable facilities include the Landrum Bolling Center, which features the Center for Career and Community Engagement and the Center for Global Education, the CoLab (dedicated to collaborative learning), theme residential houses, an observatory, herbarium, and a greenhouse. **Computers:** 95% of classrooms, have wireless network access. Administrative functions (other than registration) can be performed online.

CAMPUS LIFE
Environment: Town **Activities:** Campus Ministries; Choral groups; Dance; Drama/theater; International Student Organization; Jazz band; Literary magazine; Model UN; Music ensembles; Radio station; Student government; Student newspaper; Symphony orchestra 70 registered organizations, 1 honor society, 15 religious organizations. **Athletics (Intercollegiate):** *Men:* baseball, basketball, cross-country, football, soccer, tennis, track/field (outdoor), track/field (indoor). *Women:* basketball, cross-country, field hockey, soccer, tennis, track/field (outdoor), track/field (indoor), volleyball. **On-Campus Highlights:** Center for the Visual and Performing Arts, Athletics and Wellness Center, Landrum Bolling Center—Social Sciences, Natural History Museum, Runyan

Center **Environmental Initiatives:** Earlham recently spent the 2011-12 year in a planning process leading to the Earlham Sustainability Plan, a comprehensive public document.

ADMISSIONS
Freshman Academic Profile: Average high school GPA 3.7. 36% in top 10% of high school class, 67% in top 25% of high school class, 93% in top 50% of high school class. 73% from public high schools. **Test Scores:** SAT Math middle 50% range 580-700. SAT EBRW middle 50% range 610-700. ACT middle 50% range 25-31. Minimum internet-based TOEFL 80. Minimum paper TOEFL 550. **Basis for Candidate Selection:** *Very important factors considered include:* rigor of secondary school record, academic GPA, application essay. *Important factors considered include:* recommendation(s), extracurricular activities, character/personal qualities. *Other factors considered include:* class rank, standardized test scores, interview, talent/ability, alumni/ae relation, racial/ethnic status, volunteer work, work experience. **Freshman Admission Requirements:** High school diploma is required and GED is accepted *Academic units required:* 4 English, 3 math, 3 science, 2 science labs, 2 foreign language, 2 social studies, 2 history, *Academic units recommended:* 4 English, 4 math, 4 science, 4 foreign language, 2 social studies, 2 history. **Freshman Admission Statistics:** 2,799 applied, 51.9% admitted, 20% enrolled. **Transfer Admission Requirements:** High school transcript, college transcript(s), essay or personal statement, standardized test scores, statement of good standing from prior institution(s). Minimum college GPA of 2.7 required. Lowest grade transferable C. **General Admission Information:** Priority deadline 12/1. Regular application deadline 2/15. Nonfall registration accepted. Admission may be deferred.

COSTS AND FINANCIAL AID
Annual tuition $45,500. Required fees $950. Average book expense $1,200. **Required Forms and Deadlines:** FAFSA. **Notification of Awards:** Applicants will be notified of awards on a rolling basis beginning 3/15. **Types of Aid:** *Need-based scholarships/grants:* College/university scholarship or grant aid from institutional funds; Federal Pell; Private scholarships; SEOG; State scholarships/grants. *Loans:* Direct PLUS loans; Direct Subsidized Stafford Loans; Direct Unsubsidized Stafford Loans. *Student Employment:* Federal Work-Study Program available. Institutional employment available. **Financial Aid Statistics:** 97% needy freshmen, 100% needy undergrads receive need-based scholarship or grant aid. 32% freshmen, 39% undergrads receive non-need-based scholarship or grant aid. 87% freshmen, 87% undergrads receive need-based self-help aid. 0% freshmen, 0% undergrads receive athletic scholarships. 98% freshmen, 96% undergrads receive any aid. 60% undergrads borrow to pay for school. Average cumulative indebtedness $25,784. **Criteria for awarding aid:** *Non-need-based:* Academics, Leadership, Minority status, Religious affiliation.

See page 928.

EAST CAROLINA UNIVERSITY

East 5th Street, Greenville, NC 27858-4353
Phone: 252-328-6640 · **Financial Aid Phone:** 252-328-4347
E-mail: admis@ecu.edu · **CEEB Code:** 5180
Fax: 252-328-6945 · **Website:** www.ecu.edu · **ACT Code:** 3094

This public school was founded in 1907. It has a 1600 acre campus.

RATINGS
Admissions Selectivity Rating: 78   **Fire Safety Rating:** 88   **Green Rating:** 88

STUDENTS AND FACULTY
Enrollment: 22,598. **Student Body:** 57% female, 43% male, 10% out-of-state, 1% international (54 countries represented). Asian 3%, African American 16%, Caucasian 67%, Hispanic 6%, Native American 1%, Pacific Islander <1%, Two or more races 3%, Race unknown 3%.
Retention and Graduation: 83% freshmen return for sophomore year. 36% freshmen graduate within 4 years. 61% freshmen graduate within 6 years. **Faculty:** Student/faculty ratio 19:1. 1,188 full-time faculty, 82% hold PhDs, 17% are members of minority groups, 51% are women.

ACADEMICS
Degrees: Bachelor's; Doctoral/Professional; Doctoral/Research; Master's; Post-Bachelor's certificate; Post-Master's certificate **Classes:** Most classes have 10-19 students. Most lab/discussion sessions have 20-29 students. **Most popular majors:** Speech Communication And Rhetoric; Elementary Education And Teaching; Business Administration And Management, General. **Special Study Options:** Accelerated program; Cooperative education program; Cross-registration; Distance learning; Double major; Dual enrollment; English as

a Second Language (ESL); Exchange student program (domestic); Honors program; Independent study; Internships; Student-designed major; Study abroad; Teacher certification program. **Honors programs:** The Honors College at East Carolina University is a diverse intellectual community for academically talented students of strong character. Our students engage in stimulating coursework that spans disciplines across campus, providing for a challenging and innovative curricular and co-curricular model. Honors students are provided with the opportunity to engage in immersive service-learning, undergraduate research, and pre-professional experiences throughout their undergraduate years. Students will leave the Honors College with a foundation of skills and experiences designed to make them competitive for graduate programs, scholarships, and careers following graduation. **Disability Services offered to physically disabled students:** Note-taking services; Reader services; Tape recorders; Tutors. **Career services:** Alumni network; Alumni services; Career assessment; Career/job search classes; Internships; Regional alumni

FACILITIES

Housing: Coed dorms; Fraternity/sorority housing; Theme housing; Wellness housing; Women's dorms 95% of campus accessible to physically disabled. **Special Academic Facilities/Equipment:** Wellington B. Gray Gallery, Ledonia Wright Cultural Center, A.J. Fletcher Recital Hall, Hendrix Theatre, Jenkins Fine Arts Center, McGinnis Theatre, and Mendenhall Student Center. **Computers:** 68% of classrooms, 20% of dorms, 100% of libraries, 100% of dining areas, 100% of student union, 25% of common outdoor areas have wireless network access. Students can register for classes online. Administrative functions (other than registration) can be performed online.

CAMPUS LIFE

Environment: City **Activities:** Campus Ministries; Choral groups; Concert band; Dance; Drama/theater; International Student Organization; Jazz band; Literary magazine; Marching band; Model UN; Music ensembles; Musical theater; Opera; Pep band; Radio station; Student government; Student newspaper; Student-run film society; Symphony orchestra; Television station; Yearbook 297 registered organizations, 11 honor societies, 27 religious organizations. 20 fraternities, 13 sororities. **Athletics (Intercollegiate):** *Men:* baseball, basketball, cheerleading, cross-country, diving, football, golf, swimming, tennis, track/field (outdoor). *Women:* basketball, cheerleading, cross-country, diving, golf, soccer, softball, swimming, tennis, track/field (outdoor), volleyball. **On-Campus Highlights:** Student Recreation Center, Wright Plaza, Mendenhall Student Center, Blounts Sports Complex, Science and Technology Building **Environmental Initiatives:** Water conservation

ADMISSIONS

Freshman Academic Profile: Average high school GPA 3.8. 13% in top 10% of high school class, 39% in top 25% of high school class, 78% in top 50% of high school class. **Test Scores:** SAT Math middle 50% range 510-590. SAT EBRW middle 50% range 520-590. ACT middle 50% range 20-24. Minimum internet-based TOEFL 71. Minimum paper TOEFL 500. **Basis for Candidate Selection:** *Very important factors considered include:* rigor of secondary school record, academic GPA, standardized test scores, state residency. *Important factors considered include:* class rank. *Other factors considered include:* application essay, extracurricular activities, talent/ability, character/personal qualities, first generation, alumni/ae relation, volunteer work, work experience, level of applicant's interest. **Freshman Admission Requirements:** High school diploma is required and GED is accepted *Academic units required:* 4 English, 4 math, 3 science, 1 science labs, 2 foreign language, 2 social studies, 1 history, *Academic units recommended:* 4 English, 4 math, 3 science, 1 science labs, 2 foreign language, 2 social studies, 1 history, 1 visual/performing arts. **Freshman Admission Statistics:** 16,007 applied, 78.8% admitted, 35% enrolled. **Transfer Admission Requirements:** High school transcript, college transcript(s), Minimum college GPA of 2.0 required. Lowest grade transferable C. **General Admission Information:** Application fee $75. Regular application deadline 3/1. Nonfall registration accepted. Admission may be deferred for a maximum of 1 semester.

COSTS AND FINANCIAL AID

Annual in-state tuition $9,853. Annual out-of-state tuition $20,729. Room and board $9,853. Required fees $2,691. Average book expense $1,306. **Required Forms and Deadlines:** FAFSA. **Notification of Awards:** Applicants will be notified of awards on a rolling basis beginning 4/1. **Types of Aid:** *Need-based scholarships/grants:* College/university scholarship or grant aid from institutional funds; Federal Nursing Scholarships; Federal Pell; Private scholarships; SEOG; State scholarships/grants. *Loans:* Direct PLUS loans; Direct Subsidized Stafford Loans; Direct Unsubsidized Stafford Loans. *Student Employment:* Federal Work-Study Program available. Institutional employment available. **Financial Aid Statistics:** 67% needy freshmen, 73% needy undergrads receive need-based scholarship or grant aid. 25% freshmen, 17% undergrads receive non-need-based scholarship or grant aid. 86% freshmen, 84% undergrads receive need-based self-help aid. 2% freshmen, 2% undergrads receive athletic scholarships. 70% freshmen, 70% undergrads receive any aid. Average cumulative indebtedness $27,774. **Criteria for awarding aid:** *Need-*

based: Academics *Non-need-based:* Academics, Alumni affiliation, Art, Athletics, Music/drama.

EAST STROUDSBURG UNIVERSITY OF PENNSYLVANIA

200 Prospect Street, East Stroudsburg, PA 18301-2999
Phone: 570-422-3542 · **Financial Aid Phone:** 570-422-2800
E-mail: undergrads@po-box.esu.edu · **CEEB Code:** 2650
Fax: 570-422-3933 · **Website:** www4.esu.edu · **ACT Code:** 3700

This public school was founded in 1893. It has a 213 acre campus.

RATINGS

Admissions Selectivity Rating: 79   **Fire Safety Rating:** 98   **Green Rating:** 60*

STUDENTS AND FACULTY

Enrollment: 6,274. **Student Body:** 55% female, 45% male, 25% out-of-state, 1% international (24 countries represented). Asian 1%, African American 7%, Caucasian 76%, Hispanic 7%, Native American <1%, Pacific Islander <1%, Two or more races <1%, Race unknown 8%.
Retention and Graduation: 78% freshmen return for sophomore year.
Faculty: Student/faculty ratio 17:1. 330 full-time faculty, 74% hold PhDs, 16% are members of minority groups, 51% are women. 0% of classes are taught by teaching assistants.

ACADEMICS

Degrees: Associate; Bachelor's; Master's **Classes:** Most classes have 10-19 students. Most lab/discussion sessions have 10-19 students. **Most popular majors:** Elementary Education And Teaching; Physical Education Teaching And Coaching; Business Administration And Management, General. **Special Study Options:** Accelerated program; Cross-registration; Distance learning; Double major; Dual enrollment; Exchange student program (domestic); Honors program; Independent study; Internships; Student-designed major; Study abroad; Teacher certification program. **Honors programs:** The Honors Program at ESU offers academically superior students an opportunity to challenge themselves intellectually both within and beyond the classroom setting. The focus of the Program was, and is, located in the area of the liberal arts general education curriculum. The goal of the program is to foster in the students an appreciation of the liberal arts perspective and a commitment to lifelong learning. **Disability Services offered to physically disabled students:** Note-taking services; Reader services; Tape recorders; Tutors. **Career services:** Career assessment

FACILITIES

Housing: Coed dorms 95% of campus accessible to physically disabled. **Special Academic Facilities/Equipment:** Natural history museum, human performance lab, TV production studios, 119-acre student-owned/operated recreation area and wildlife sanctuary, observatory, electron microscopes. **Computers:** 50% of classrooms, 100% of dorms, 100% of libraries, 100% of student union, 10% of common outdoor areas have wireless network access. Students can register for classes online. Administrative functions (other than registration) can be performed online.

CAMPUS LIFE

Environment: Village **Activities:** Campus Ministries; Choral groups; Concert band; Dance; Drama/theater; International Student Organization; Jazz band; Literary magazine; Marching band; Music ensembles; Musical theater; Pep band; Radio station; Student government; Student newspaper; Symphony orchestra 110 registered organizations, 28 honor societies, 3 religious organizations. 5 fraternities, 5 sororities. **Athletics (Intercollegiate):** *Men:* baseball, basketball, cross-country, football, soccer, tennis, track/field (outdoor), track/field (indoor), wrestling. *Women:* basketball, cross-country, field hockey, golf, lacrosse, soccer, softball, swimming, tennis, track/field (outdoor), track/field (indoor), volleyball. **On-Campus Highlights:** Recreation Center, Java CIty, University Center, Stoney Acres, The Quad

ADMISSIONS

Freshman Academic Profile: 7% in top 10% of high school class, 30% in top 25% of high school class, 72% in top 50% of high school class. 90% from public high schools. **Test Scores:** SAT Math middle 50% range 460-550. SAT EBRW middle 50% range 440-530. Minimum internet-based TOEFL 83. Minimum paper TOEFL 560. **Basis for Candidate Selection:** *Very important factors considered include:* rigor of secondary school record, class rank, academic GPA, standardized test scores. **Freshman Admission Requirements:** High school diploma is required and GED is accepted *Academic units recommended:* 4 English, 4 math, 3 science, 2 science labs, 2 foreign language, 3 social studies.

Freshman Admission Statistics: 7,258 applied, 62.8% admitted, 26% enrolled. **Transfer Admission Requirements:** college transcript(s), Minimum college GPA of 2.0 required. Lowest grade transferable C. **General Admission Information:** Application fee $35. Regular application deadline 4/1. Nonfall registration accepted.

COSTS AND FINANCIAL AID

Annual in-state tuition $6,658. Annual out-of-state tuition $14,510. Room and board $6,658. Required fees $1,974. Average book expense $1,200. **Required Forms and Deadlines:** FAFSA. **Notification of Awards:** Applicants will be notified of awards on or about 4/1. **Types of Aid:** *Need-based scholarships/grants:* College/university scholarship or grant aid from institutional funds; Federal Pell; Private scholarships; SEOG; State scholarships/grants. *Loans:* Direct PLUS loans; Direct Subsidized Stafford Loans; Direct Unsubsidized Stafford Loans. *Student Employment:* Federal Work-Study Program available. Institutional employment available. **Financial Aid Statistics:** 55% needy freshmen, 56% needy undergrads receive need-based scholarship or grant aid. 6% freshmen, 5% undergrads receive non-need-based scholarship or grant aid. 91% freshmen, 89% undergrads receive need-based self-help aid. 6% freshmen, 4% undergrads receive athletic scholarships. 75% freshmen, 84% undergrads receive any aid. **Criteria for awarding aid:** *Need-based:* Academics *Non-need-based:* Academics, Alumni affiliation, Art, Athletics, Leadership, Minority status, Music/drama, Religious affiliation, State/district residency.

EAST TENNESSEE STATE UNIVERSITY

1276 Gilbreath Drive, Johnson City, TN 37614
Phone: 423-439-4213 • **Financial Aid Phone:** (423) 439-4300
E-mail: go2etsu@etsu.edu • **CEEB Code:** 1198
Fax: 423-439-4630 • **Website:** www.etsu.edu • **ACT Code:** 3958

This public school was founded in 1911. It has a 366 acre campus.

RATINGS

Admissions Selectivity Rating: 76   **Fire Safety Rating:** 60*   **Green Rating:** 60*

STUDENTS AND FACULTY

Enrollment: 10,960. **Student Body:** 56% female, 44% male, 14% out-of-state, 3% international (57 countries represented). Asian 1%, African American 7%, Caucasian 82%, Hispanic 2%, Native American <1%, Pacific Islander <1%, Two or more races 3%, Race unknown 1%.
Retention and Graduation: 71% freshmen return for sophomore year. **Faculty:** Student/faculty ratio 17:1. 575 full-time faculty, 11% are members of minority groups, 47% are women.

ACADEMICS

Degrees: Bachelor's; Certificate; Doctoral; Doctoral/Professional; Doctoral/Research; Master's; Post-Bachelor's certificate; Post-Master's certificate **Classes:** Most classes have fewer than 10 students. Most lab/discussion sessions have 20-29 students. **Most popular majors:** Business Administration And Management, General. **Special Study Options:** Cooperative education program; Distance learning; Double major; Dual enrollment; English as a Second Language (ESL); Exchange student program (domestic); External degree program; Honors program; Independent study; Internships; Student-designed major; Study abroad; Teacher certification program. **Honors programs:** University Honors Program Honors-in-Discipline Programs. **Disability Services offered to physically disabled students:** Note-taking services; Reader services; Tape recorders; Tutors. **Career services:** Alumni network; Alumni services; Career assessment; Career/job search classes; Internships; Regional alumni

FACILITIES

Housing: Apartments for married students; Apartments for single students; Coed dorms; Fraternity/sorority housing; Men's dorms; Special housing for disabled student; Wellness housing; Women's dorms 75% of campus accessible to physically diasbled. **Special Academic Facilities/Equipment:** Regional history museum, art gallery, archives of Appalachia, planetarium. **Computers:** Students can register for classes online. Administrative functions (other than registration) can be performed online.

CAMPUS LIFE

Environment: Town **Activities:** Campus Ministries; Choral groups; Concert band; Drama/theater; International Student Organization; Jazz band; Literary magazine; Marching band; Music ensembles; Pep band; Radio station; Student government; Student newspaper; Television station 200 registered organizations, 19 honor societies, 13 religious organizations. 9 fraternities, 7 sororities. **Athletics (Intercollegiate):** *Men:* baseball, basketball, cheerleading, cross-country, golf, soccer, tennis, track/field (outdoor), track/field (indoor).

Women: basketball, cheerleading, cross-country, golf, soccer, softball, tennis, track/field (outdoor), track/field (indoor), volleyball. **On-Campus Highlights:** Memorial Center, New Sherrod Library, New Physical Activities Center, The Cave- a unique pizza pub located in the DP Culp Center. Built around a huge rock formation, indoors, Amphitheater- Natural stone + earth outdoor theater.

ADMISSIONS

Freshman Academic Profile: Average high school GPA 3.4. 20% in top 10% of high school class, 47% in top 25% of high school class, 75% in top 50% of high school class. 90% from public high schools. **Test Scores:** SAT Math middle 50% range 420-590. SAT EBRW middle 50% range 420-540. ACT middle 50% range 20-26. Minimum internet-based TOEFL 61. Minimum paper TOEFL 500. **Basis for Candidate Selection:** *Very important factors considered include:* rigor of secondary school record, academic GPA. *Important factors considered include:* standardized test scores. **Freshman Admission Requirements:** High school diploma is required and GED is accepted *Academic units required:* 4 English, 3 math, 2 science, 1 science labs, 2 foreign language, 1 social studies, 1 history, 1 visual/performing arts, *Academic units recommended:* 4 English, 4 math, 3 science, 1 science labs, 2 foreign language, 1 social studies, 1 history, 1 visual/performing arts. **Freshman Admission Statistics:** 8,253 applied, 79.2% admitted, 31% enrolled. **Transfer Admission Requirements:** High school transcript, college transcript(s), Minimum college GPA of 2.0 required. Lowest grade transferable D. **General Admission Information:** Application fee $25. Priority deadline 2/1. Regular application deadline 8/15. Nonfall registration accepted.

COSTS AND FINANCIAL AID

Annual in-state tuition $7,952. Annual out-of-state tuition $25,098. Room and board $7,952. Required fees $1,669. Average book expense $1,090. **Required Forms and Deadlines:** FAFSA. **Notification of Awards:** Applicants will be notified of awards on a rolling basis beginning 3/15. **Types of Aid:** *Need-based scholarships/grants:* College/university scholarship or grant aid from institutional funds; Federal Nursing Scholarships; Federal Pell; Private scholarships; SEOG; State scholarships/grants. *Loans:* Direct PLUS loans; Direct Subsidized Stafford Loans; Direct Unsubsidized Stafford Loans. *Student Employment:* Federal Work-Study Program available. Institutional employment available. **Financial Aid Statistics:** 0% freshmen, 0% undergrads receive athletic scholarships. **Criteria for awarding aid:** *Need-based:* Academics, Alumni affiliation, Art, Athletics, Job skills, Leadership, Minority status, Music/drama, Religious affiliation *Non-need-based:* Academics, Alumni affiliation, Art, Athletics, Leadership, Minority status, Music/drama, Religious affiliation, State/district residency.

EAST TEXAS BAPTIST UNIVERSITY

One Tiger Drive, Marshall, TX 75670-1498
Phone: 903-923-2000 • **Financial Aid Phone:** (903) 923-2137
E-mail: admissions@etbu.edu • **CEEB Code:** 6187
Fax: 903-923-2001 • **Website:** https://www.etbu.edu • **ACT Code:** 4086

This private school, affiliated with the Baptist Church, was founded in 1912. It has a 250 acre campus.

RATINGS

Admissions Selectivity Rating: 86   **Fire Safety Rating:** 82   **Green Rating:** 60*

STUDENTS AND FACULTY

Enrollment: 1,267. **Student Body:** 52% female, 48% male, 11% out-of-state, 1% international (7 countries represented). Asian <1%, African American 16%, Caucasian 68%, Hispanic 10%, Native American <1%, Pacific Islander <1%, Two or more races 4%, Race unknown <1%.
Retention and Graduation: 55% freshmen return for sophomore year. 19% freshmen graduate within 4 years. 31% freshmen graduate within 6 years. 35% grads go on to further study within 1 year. **Faculty:** Student/faculty ratio 15:1. 70 full-time faculty, 86% hold PhDs, 9% are members of minority groups, 39% are women. 0% of classes are taught by teaching assistants.

ACADEMICS

Degrees: Bachelor's; Certificate; Master's **Classes:** Most classes have 10-19 students. Most lab/discussion sessions have 10-19 students. **Most popular majors:** Multi-/Interdisciplinary Studies, Other; Health And Physical Education/Fitness, General; Business/Commerce, General. **Special Study Options:** Accelerated program; Distance learning; Double major; Dual enrollment; English as a Second Language (ESL); Exchange student program (domestic); Honors program; Independent study; Internships; Student-designed major; Study abroad; Teacher certification program. **Honors programs:** The mission of the ETBU Honors Program is to provide a tight-knit community of scholars in pursuit of the Christian intellectual life through the pairing of academic rigor with informed reflection for thoughtful engagement with the world. We accomplish our mission with an academic minor complementary to any major field of study offered at the university. During their first and second years, students are immersed in a rigorous study of the Western intellectual tradition, framed by Christian faith, from antiquity to the present. During their third and fourth years, students embark on an in-depth research project on a topic of their choosing, under the supervision of a faculty member in their major. Students who successfully complete both phases of the Honors Program graduate "With Distinction," receiving a stole at Commencement from the faculty member who supervised their project. For more information, see the University Scholars web page at https://www.etbu.edu/academics/university-scholars/. **Combined degree programs:** BA/MA. **Disability Services offered to physically disabled students:** Tutors. **Career services:** Alumni services; Career assessment; Career/job search classes; Internships

FACILITIES

Housing: Apartments for married students; Apartments for single students; Men's dorms; Wellness housing; Women's dorms 95% of campus accessible to physically diasbled. **Computers:** 100% of classrooms, 100% of dorms, 100% of libraries, 100% of dining areas, 100% of student union, 100% of common outdoor areas have wireless network access. Students can register for classes online. Administrative functions (other than registration) can be performed online.

CAMPUS LIFE

Environment: Town **Activities:** Campus Ministries; Choral groups; Concert band; Dance; Drama/theater; Jazz band; Marching band; Model UN; Music ensembles; Musical theater; Opera; Pep band; Student government; Symphony orchestra 38 registered organizations, 7 honor societies, 3 religious organizations. 2 fraternities, 2 sororities. **Athletics (Intercollegiate):** *Men:* baseball, basketball, cross-country, football, soccer. *Women:* basketball, cross-country, soccer, softball, volleyball. **On-Campus Highlights:** Ornelas Student Center, Bennett Student Commons, The Republic, Dean Healthplex, Ornelas Spiritual Life Center

ADMISSIONS

Freshman Academic Profile: Average high school GPA 3.4. 13% in top 10% of high school class, 38% in top 25% of high school class, 74% in top 50% of high school class. 88% from public high schools. **Test Scores:** SAT Math middle 50% range 470-560. SAT EBRW middle 50% range 490-570. ACT middle 50% range 18-23. Minimum internet-based TOEFL 61. **Basis for Candidate Selection:** *Very important factors considered include:* class rank, standardized test scores. *Important factors considered include:* academic GPA. *Other factors considered include:* character/personal qualities. **Freshman Admission Requirements:** High school diploma is required and GED is accepted **Freshman Admission Statistics:** 1,839 applied, 54.3% admitted, 42% enrolled. **Transfer Admission Requirements:** college transcript(s), statement of good standing from prior institution(s). Minimum college GPA of 2.00 required. Lowest grade transferable D. **General Admission Information:** Application fee $25. Regular application deadline 8/31. Nonfall registration accepted. Admission may be deferred for a maximum of 1 year.

COSTS AND FINANCIAL AID

Required Forms and Deadlines: FAFSA; Institution's own financial aid form. **Notification of Awards:** Applicants will be notified of awards on a rolling basis beginning 1/1. **Types of Aid:** *Need-based scholarships/grants:* College/university scholarship or grant aid from institutional funds; Federal Pell; Private scholarships; SEOG; State scholarships/grants. *Loans:* Direct PLUS loans; Direct Subsidized Stafford Loans; Direct Unsubsidized Stafford Loans. *Student Employment:* Federal Work-Study Program available. Institutional employment available. **Financial Aid Statistics:** 76% needy freshmen, 76% needy undergrads receive need-based scholarship or grant aid. 99% freshmen, 99% undergrads receive non-need-based scholarship or grant aid. 78% freshmen, 80% undergrads receive need-based self-help aid. 0% freshmen, 0% undergrads receive athletic scholarships. 99% freshmen, 99% undergrads receive any aid. 82% undergrads borrow to pay for school. Average cumulative indebtedness $34,048. **Criteria for awarding aid:** *Non-need-based:* Academics, Alumni affiliation, Leadership, Music/drama, Religious affiliation, State/district residency.

EASTERN CONNECTICUT STATE UNIVERSITY

83 Windham Street, Willimantic, CT 06226
Phone: 860-465-5286 • **Financial Aid Phone:** 860-365-5205
E-mail: admissions@easternct.edu • **CEEB Code:** 3966
Fax: 860-465-5286 • **Website:** www.easternct.edu

This public school was founded in 1889. It has a 182 acre campus.

RATINGS

Admissions Selectivity Rating: 84   **Fire Safety Rating:** 96   **Green Rating:** 94

STUDENTS AND FACULTY

Enrollment: 5,035. **Student Body:** 53% female, 47% male, 7% out-of-state, 1% international (44 countries represented). Asian 2%, African American 7%, Caucasian 79%, Hispanic 7%, Native American <1%, Pacific Islander <1%, Two or more races 2%, Race unknown 2%.
Retention and Graduation: 77% freshmen return for sophomore year. 30% grads go on to further study within 1 year. **Faculty:** Student/faculty ratio 16:1. 198 full-time faculty, 96% hold PhDs, 22% are members of minority groups, 44% are women. 0% of classes are taught by teaching assistants.

ACADEMICS

Degrees: Associate; Bachelor's; Master's **Classes:** Most classes have 20-29 students. Most lab/discussion sessions have 10-19 students. **Most popular majors:** Communication And Media Studies, Other; Psychology, General; Business/Commerce, General. **Special Study Options:** Accelerated program; Cooperative education program; Cross-registration; Distance learning; Double major; Dual enrollment; Exchange student program (domestic); Honors program; Independent study; Internships; Student-designed major; Study abroad; Teacher certification program; Weekend college. **Honors programs:** University Honor Scholars Program offers interdisciplinary and independent study opportunities. **Disability Services offered to physically disabled students:** Note-taking services; Reader services; Tape recorders; Tutors. **Career services:** Alumni network; Alumni services; Career assessment; Career/job search classes; Internships; Regional alumni

FACILITIES

Housing: Apartments for single students; Coed dorms 95% of campus accessible to physically diasbled. **Special Academic Facilities/Equipment:** Art Gallery, Arboretum, Church Farm, Family/Child Development Center (2007), Green science bldg/labs(2008), electron microscope, planetarium, Media center with TV and radio station, Sports/Fitness Center and Studios, Center for Connecticut studies, **Computers:** 100% of libraries, 100% of dining areas, 100% of student union, 100% of common outdoor areas have wireless network access. Students can register for classes online. Administrative functions (other than registration) can be performed online.

CAMPUS LIFE

Environment: Village **Activities:** Choral groups; Concert band; Dance; Drama/theater; International Student Organization; Jazz band; Literary magazine; Music ensembles; Musical theater; Radio station; Student government; Student newspaper; Television station; Yearbook 68 registered organizations, 17 honor societies, 3 religious organizations. **Athletics (Intercollegiate):** *Men:* baseball, basketball, cross-country, golf, lacrosse, soccer, track/field (outdoor), track/field (indoor). *Women:* basketball, cross-country, diving, field hockey, lacrosse, soccer, softball, swimming, track/field (outdoor), track/field (indoor), volleyball. **On-Campus Highlights:** Library, Student Center, Sports Center, Church Farm, Planetarium **Environmental Initiatives:** Education Project http://www.ctenergyeducation.com/

ADMISSIONS

Freshman Academic Profile: Average high school GPA 3.0. 7% in top 10% of high school class, 25% in top 25% of high school class, 70% in top 50% of high school class. **Test Scores:** SAT Math middle 50% range 480-580. SAT EBRW middle 50% range 470-570. Minimum paper TOEFL 550. **Basis for Candidate Selection:** *Very important factors considered include:* class rank, standardized test scores, talent/ability. *Important factors considered include:* rigor of secondary school record, academic GPA, recommendation(s), level of applicant's interest. *Other factors considered include:* applicant essay, interview, extracurricular activities, character/personal qualities, volunteer work, work experience. **Freshman Admission Requirements:** High school diploma is required and GED is accepted *Academic units required:* 4 English, 3 math, 2 science, 1 science labs, 2 foreign language, 2 social studies, 3 history, *Academic units recommended:* 4 math, 3 social studies. **Freshman Admission Statistics:** 3,493 applied, 64.5% admitted, 41% enrolled. **Transfer Admission Requirements:** High school transcript, college transcript(s), Minimum college GPA of 2.0 required. Lowest grade transferable C-. **General Admission Information:** Application fee $50. Priority deadline 5/1. Nonfall registration accepted. Admission may be deferred.

COSTS AND FINANCIAL AID

Annual in-state tuition $4,866. Annual out-of-state tuition $14,594. Required fees $4,866. Average book expense $1,554. **Required Forms and Deadlines:** FAFSA. **Types of Aid:** *Need-based scholarships/grants:* College/university scholarship or grant aid from institutional funds; Federal Pell; Private scholarships; SEOG; State scholarships/grants. *Loans: Student Employment:* Federal Work-Study Program available. Institutional employment available. **Financial Aid Statistics:** 68% needy freshmen, 66% needy undergrads receive need-based scholarship or grant aid. 4% freshmen, 1% undergrads receive non-need-based scholarship or grant aid. 92% freshmen, 93% undergrads receive need-based self-help aid. 0% freshmen, 0% undergrads receive athletic scholarships. 69% freshmen, 75% undergrads receive any aid. **Criteria for awarding aid:** *Need-based:* Academics *Non-need-based:* Academics.

EASTERN ILLINOIS UNIVERSITY

600 Lincoln Avenue, Charleston, IL 61920
Phone: 217-581-2223 · **Financial Aid Phone:** 217-581-3713
E-mail: admissions@eiu.edu · **CEEB Code:** 1199
Fax: 217-581-7060 · **Website:** https://www.eiu.edu/ · **ACT Code:** 1016

This public school was founded in 1895. It has a 320 acre campus.

RATINGS

Admissions Selectivity Rating: 84   Fire Safety Rating: 97   Green Rating: 81

STUDENTS AND FACULTY

Enrollment: 5,750. **Student Body:** 60% female, 40% male, 6% out-of-state, 2% international (30 countries represented). Asian 1%, African American 18%, Caucasian 69%, Hispanic 6%, Native American <1%, Pacific Islander <1%, Two or more races 2%, Race unknown 2%.
Retention and Graduation: 71% freshmen return for sophomore year.
Faculty: Student/faculty ratio 14:1. 419 full-time faculty, 79% hold PhDs, 15% are members of minority groups, 46% are women. 3% of classes are taught by teaching assistants.

ACADEMICS

Degrees: Bachelor's; Master's; Post-Bachelor's certificate; Post-Master's certificate **Classes:** Most classes have 10-19 students. Most lab/discussion sessions have 20-29 students. **Most popular majors:** Kinesiology And Exercise Science; Communication, General; Liberal Arts And Sciences/Liberal Studies. **Special Study Options:** Accelerated program; Distance learning; Double major; English as a Second Language (ESL); Exchange student program (domestic); Honors program; Independent study; Internships; Study abroad; Teacher certification program. **Honors programs:** Pine Honors College. **Disability Services offered to physically disabled students:** Note-taking services; Reader services; Tape recorders; Tutors. **Career services:** Alumni network; Alumni services; Career assessment; Career/job search classes; Internships; Regional alumni

FACILITIES

Housing: Apartments for married students; Apartments for single students; Coed dorms; Fraternity/sorority housing; Men's dorms; Women's dorms 80% of campus accessible to physically disabled. **Special Academic Facilities/Equipment:** Tarble Arts Center, Scanning Electron Microscope Laboratory, Observatory, Thut Greenhouse, Laboratory School Exhibit, Center for Clean Energy Research and Education. **Computers:** 100% of classrooms, 50% of dorms, 100% of libraries, 100% of dining areas, 100% of student union, have wireless network access. Students can register for classes online. Administrative functions (other than registration) can be performed online.

CAMPUS LIFE

Environment: Village **Activities:** Campus Ministries; Choral groups; Concert band; Dance; Drama/theater; International Student Organization; Jazz band; Literary magazine; Marching band; Music ensembles; Musical theater; Pep band; Radio station; Student government; Student newspaper; Student-run film society; Symphony orchestra; Television station; Yearbook 232 registered organizations, 19 honor societies, 16 religious organizations. 15 fraternities, 11 sororities. **Athletics (Intercollegiate):** *Men:* baseball, basketball, cross-country, football, golf, soccer, swimming, tennis, track/field (outdoor), track/field (indoor). *Women:* basketball, cross-country, golf, rugby, soccer, softball, swimming, tennis, track/field (outdoor), track/field (indoor), volleyball.
On-Campus Highlights: Doudna Fine Arts Center, Old Main, Martin Luther King Jr. University Union, Booth Library, Student Recreation Center **Environmental Initiatives:** Reduced campus water consumption by over 50%.

ADMISSIONS

Freshman Academic Profile: Average high school GPA 3.1. 13% in top 10% of high school class, 33% in top 25% of high school class, 69% in top 50% of high school class. **Test Scores:** ACT middle 50% range 18-24. Minimum internet-based TOEFL 61. Minimum paper TOEFL 500. **Basis for Candidate Selection:** *Very important factors considered include:* rigor of secondary school record, academic GPA, standardized test scores. *Other factors considered include:* class rank, application essay, recommendation(s), talent/ability, character/personal qualities. **Freshman Admission Requirements:** High school diploma is required and GED is accepted *Academic units required:* 4 English, 3 math, 3 science, 3 science labs, 3 social studies, 2 academic electives, *Academic units recommended:* 2 foreign language. **Freshman Admission Statistics:** 8,420 applied, 46.9% admitted, 20% enrolled. **Transfer Admission Requirements:** High school transcript, college transcript(s), standardized test scores, Minimum college GPA of 2.0 required. **General Admission Information:** Application fee $30. Regular application deadline 8/15. Nonfall registration accepted. Admission may be deferred for a maximum of 1 year.

COSTS AND FINANCIAL AID

Annual in-state tuition $9,546. Annual out-of-state tuition $10,830. Room and board $9,546. Required fees $2,910. Average book expense $150. **Required Forms and Deadlines:** FAFSA. **Notification of Awards:** Applicants will be notified of awards on a rolling basis beginning 3/1. **Types of Aid:** *Need-based scholarships/grants:* College/university scholarship or grant aid from institutional funds; Federal Pell; Private scholarships; SEOG; State scholarships/grants. *Loans:* Direct PLUS loans; Direct Subsidized Stafford Loans; Direct Unsubsidized Stafford Loans. *Student Employment:* Federal Work-Study Program available. Institutional employment available. **Financial Aid Statistics:** 74% needy freshmen, 75% needy undergrads receive need-based scholarship or grant aid. 65% freshmen, 48% undergrads receive non-need-based scholarship or grant aid. 75% freshmen, 80% undergrads receive need-based self-help aid. 3% freshmen, 3% undergrads receive athletic scholarships. 73% freshmen, 68% undergrads receive any aid. 79% undergrads borrow to pay for school. Average cumulative indebtedness $31,382. **Criteria for awarding aid:** *Need-based:* Minority status *Non-need-based:* Academics, Art, Athletics, Leadership, Music/drama.

EASTERN KENTUCKY UNIVERSITY

521 Lancaster Avenue, Richmond, KY 40475
Phone: 859-622-2106 · **Financial Aid Phone:** 859-622-2361
E-mail: admissions@eku.edu · **CEEB Code:** 1200
Fax: 859-622-8024 · **Website:** www.eku.edu · **ACT Code:** 1512

This public school was founded in 1906. It has a 675 acre campus.

RATINGS

Admissions Selectivity Rating: 77   Fire Safety Rating: 90   Green Rating: 60*

STUDENTS AND FACULTY

Enrollment: 13,333. **Student Body:** 56% female, 44% male, 13% out-of-state, (36 countries represented).
Retention and Graduation: 68% freshmen return for sophomore year.
Faculty: Student/faculty ratio 16:1. 697 full-time faculty, 68% hold PhDs, 10% are members of minority groups, 52% are women. 0% of classes are taught by teaching assistants.

ACADEMICS

Degrees: Associate; Bachelor's; Certificate; Doctoral/Professional; Master's; Post-Bachelor's certificate **Classes:** Most classes have 20-29 students. Most lab/discussion sessions have 10-19 students. **Most popular majors:** Elementary Education And Teaching; Criminal Justice/Law Enforcement Administration; Nursing/Registered Nurse (Rn, Asn, Bsn, Msn). **Special Study Options:** Cooperative education program; Distance learning; Double major; Dual enrollment; English as a Second Language (ESL); Honors program; Independent study; Internships; Student-designed major; Study abroad; Teacher certification program. **Honors programs:** Honors Program: www.honors.eku.edu. **Disability Services offered to physically disabled students:** Note-taking services; Reader services; Tape recorders; Tutors. **Career services:** Alumni network; Alumni services; Career assessment; Career/job search classes; Internships; Regional alumni

FACILITIES

Housing: Apartments for married students; Apartments for single students; Coed dorms; Fraternity/sorority housing; Men's dorms; Special housing for disabled student; Special housing for international students; Theme housing; Wellness housing; Women's dorms 90% of campus accessible to physically diasbled. **Special Academic Facilities/Equipment:** Hummel Planetarium, Giles Gallery **Computers:** Students can register for classes online. Administrative functions (other than registration) can be performed online.

CAMPUS LIFE

Environment: Town **Activities:** Campus Ministries; Choral groups; Concert band; Dance; Drama/theater; International Student Organization; Jazz band; Literary magazine; Marching band; Music ensembles; Musical theater; Pep band; Radio station; Student government; Student newspaper; Student-run film society; Symphony orchestra; Yearbook 178 registered organizations, 30 honor societies, 11 religious organizations. 16 fraternities, 13 sororities. **Athletics (Intercollegiate):** *Men:* baseball, basketball, cheerleading, cross-country, football, golf, tennis, track/field (outdoor), track/field (indoor). *Women:* basketball, cheerleading, cross-country, golf, soccer, softball, tennis, track/field (outdoor), track/field (indoor), volleyball. **On-Campus Highlights:** Student Wellness Center (New), Library Cafe (New), Student Services Building (New), First Weekend Events

ADMISSIONS

Freshman Academic Profile: Average high school GPA 3.2. 13% in top 10% of high school class, 34% in top 25% of high school class, 66% in top 50% of high school class. **Test Scores:** ACT middle 50% range 19-24. Minimum paper TOEFL 500. **Basis for Candidate Selection:** *Very important factors considered include:* rigor of secondary school record, academic GPA, standardized test scores. **Freshman Admission Requirements:** High school diploma is required and GED is accepted *Academic units required:* 4 English, 3 math, 3 science, 1 science labs, 2 foreign language, 3 social studies, 7 academic electives, and 2 units from above areas or other academic areas. **Freshman Admission Statistics:** 9,776 applied, 73.9% admitted, 38% enrolled. **Transfer Admission Requirements:** college transcript(s), Minimum college GPA of 2.0 required. Lowest grade transferable D. **General Admission Information:** Application fee $35. Regular application deadline 8/1. Nonfall registration accepted. Admission may be deferred for a maximum of 1 semester.

COSTS AND FINANCIAL AID

Annual in-state tuition $8,188. Annual out-of-state tuition $17,640. Room and board $8,188. Average book expense $1,000. **Required Forms and Deadlines:** FAFSA. **Notification of Awards:** Applicants will be notified of awards on a rolling basis beginning 4/1. **Types of Aid:** *Need-based scholarships/grants:* College/university scholarship or grant aid from institutional funds; Federal Pell; Private scholarships; SEOG; State scholarships/grants. *Loans:* Direct PLUS loans; Direct Subsidized Stafford Loans; Direct Unsubsidized Stafford Loans. *Student Employment:* Federal Work-Study Program available. Institutional employment available. **Financial Aid Statistics:** 66% needy freshmen, 66% needy undergrads receive need-based scholarship or grant aid. 91% freshmen, 61% undergrads receive non-need-based scholarship or grant aid. 81% freshmen, 83% undergrads receive need-based self-help aid. 2% freshmen, 3% undergrads receive athletic scholarships. 94% freshmen, 86% undergrads receive any aid. Average cumulative indebtedness $27,438. **Criteria for awarding aid:** *Non-need-based:* Academics, Alumni affiliation, Athletics, Leadership, Minority status, Music/drama.

EASTERN MICHIGAN UNIVERSITY

Eastern Michigan University, Ypsilanti, MI 48197
Phone: 734-487-3060 · **Financial Aid Phone:** (734) 487-0455
E-mail: admissions@emich.edu · **CEEB Code:** 1201
Fax: 734-487-1484 · **Website:** www.emich.edu · **ACT Code:** 1990

This public school was founded in 1849. It has a 460 acre campus.

RATINGS

Admissions Selectivity Rating: 77   **Fire Safety Rating:** 86   **Green Rating:** 60*

STUDENTS AND FACULTY

Enrollment: 17,256. **Student Body:** 59% female, 41% male, 10% out-of-state, 2% international (80 countries represented). Asian 2%, African American 20%, Caucasian 65%, Hispanic 5%, Native American <1%, Pacific Islander <1%, Two or more races 4%, Race unknown 2%.
Retention and Graduation: 74% freshmen return for sophomore year. **Faculty:** Student/faculty ratio 17:1. 766 full-time faculty, 81% hold PhDs, 20% are members of minority groups, 51% are women. 3% of classes are taught by teaching assistants.

ACADEMICS

Degrees: Bachelor's; Doctoral/Research; Master's; Post-Bachelor's certificate; Post-Master's certificate **Classes:** Most classes have 20-29 students. Most lab/discussion sessions have 20-29 students. **Most popular majors:** Psychology,

General; Social Work; Registered Nursing/Registered Nurse. **Special Study Options:** Accelerated program; Cooperative education program; Distance learning; Double major; Dual enrollment; English as a Second Language (ESL); External degree program; Honors program; Independent study; Internships; Student-designed major; Study abroad; Teacher certification program; Weekend college. **Combined degree programs:** BA/MA. **Disability Services offered to physically disabled students:** Note-taking services; Reader services; Tape recorders; Tutors. **Career services:** Alumni network; Alumni services; Career assessment; Career/job search classes; Internships

FACILITIES

Housing: Apartments for married students; Apartments for single students; Coed dorms; Cooperative housing; Fraternity/sorority housing; Special housing for disabled student; Special housing for international students; Theme housing; Wellness housing 80% of campus accessible to physically disabled. **Special Academic Facilities/Equipment:** Intermedia art gallery, paint research center, Sherzer observatory, Bruce T. Halle Library, Terrestial and Aquatics Ecology Research Facility, Coatings Research Institute, the John W. Porter Building housing the College of Education and the Marshall Building housing the College of Health and Human Services. **Computers:** 100% of classrooms, 25% of dorms, 100% of libraries, 100% of dining areas, 100% of student union, 15% of common outdoor areas have wireless network access. Students can register for classes online. Administrative functions (other than registration) can be performed online.

CAMPUS LIFE

Environment: City **Activities:** Campus Ministries; Choral groups; Concert band; Dance; Drama/theater; International Student Organization; Jazz band; Literary magazine; Marching band; Model UN; Music ensembles; Musical theater; Opera; Pep band; Radio station; Student government; Student newspaper; Student-run film society; Symphony orchestra; Television station 220 registered organizations, 14 honor societies, 24 religious organizations. 11 fraternities, 13 sororities. **Athletics (Intercollegiate):** *Men:* basketball, diving, football, golf, swimming, track/field (outdoor), track/field (indoor), wrestling. *Women:* basketball, crew/rowing, diving, golf, gymnastics, soccer, softball, swimming, tennis, track/field (outdoor), track/field (indoor), volleyball. **On-Campus Highlights:** New Student Center, Recreations and Intramurals Building, The Lakehouse, Halle Library, Athletic Campus **Environmental Initiatives:** Energy performance contract

ADMISSIONS

Freshman Academic Profile: Average high school GPA 3.3. 13% in top 10% of high school class, 39% in top 25% of high school class, 75% in top 50% of high school class. 85% from public high schools. **Test Scores:** SAT Math middle 50% range 450-570. SAT EBRW middle 50% range 460-550. ACT middle 50% range 19-25. Minimum paper TOEFL 500. **Basis for Candidate Selection:** *Very important factors considered include:* academic GPA, standardized test scores. *Important factors considered include:* rigor of secondary school record. *Other factors considered include:* application essay, recommendation(s). **Freshman Admission Requirements:** High school diploma is required and GED is accepted *Academic units recommended:* 4 English, 4 math, 4 science, 1 science labs, 2 foreign language, 2 social studies, 1 history, 4 academic electives. **Freshman Admission Statistics:** 14,736 applied, 73.1% admitted, 26% enrolled. **Transfer Admission Requirements:** college transcript(s), Minimum college GPA of 2.0 required. Lowest grade transferable C. **General Admission Information:** Application fee $35. Nonfall registration accepted. Admission may be deferred for a maximum of 1 year.

COSTS AND FINANCIAL AID

Annual in-state tuition $9,344. Annual out-of-state tuition $12,120. Room and board $9,344. Required fees $1,529. Average book expense $1,000. **Required Forms and Deadlines:** FAFSA. **Notification of Awards:** Applicants will be notified of awards on a rolling basis beginning 12/12. **Types of Aid:** *Need-based scholarships/grants:* College/university scholarship or grant aid from institutional funds; Federal Nursing Scholarships; Federal Pell; Private scholarships; SEOG; State scholarships/grants. *Loans: Student Employment:* Federal Work-Study Program available. Institutional employment available. **Financial Aid Statistics:** 71% needy freshmen, 74% needy undergrads receive need-based scholarship or grant aid. 77% freshmen, 47% undergrads receive non-need-based scholarship or grant aid. 72% freshmen, 78% undergrads receive need-based self-help aid. 3% freshmen, 3% undergrads receive athletic scholarships. 98% freshmen, 89% undergrads receive any aid. **Criteria for awarding aid:** *Non-need-based:* Academics, Alumni affiliation, Art, Athletics, Leadership, Music/drama.

EASTERN NEW MEXICO UNIVERSITY

Station 2, Portales, NM 88130
Phone: 575-562-2178 · **Financial Aid Phone:** 575-562-2194
E-mail: admissions@enmu.edu · **CEEB Code:** 4299
Fax: 575-562-2118 · **ACT Code:** 2636

This public school was founded in 1934. It has a 400 acre campus.

RATINGS
Admissions Selectivity Rating: 84   **Fire Safety Rating:** 92   **Green Rating:** 60*

STUDENTS AND FACULTY
Enrollment: 3,618. **Student Body:** 57% female, 43% male, 23% out-of-state, 3% international (23 countries represented). Asian 1%, African American 5%, Caucasian 54%, Hispanic 33%, Native American 3%, Pacific Islander <1%, Two or more races 2%, Race unknown 1%.
Retention and Graduation: 62% freshmen return for sophomore year.
Faculty: Student/faculty ratio 17:1. 146 full-time faculty, 76% hold PhDs, 14% are members of minority groups, 47% are women. 3% of classes are taught by teaching assistants.

ACADEMICS
Degrees: Associate; Bachelor's; Master's; Terminal Associate; Transfer Associate **Classes:** Most classes have 10-19 students. **Most popular majors:** Elementary Education And Teaching; General Studies; Business Administration And Management, General. **Special Study Options:** Accelerated program; Distance learning; Double major; Dual enrollment; English as a Second Language (ESL); Independent study; Internships; Student-designed major; Teacher certification program. **Disability Services offered to physically disabled students:** Note-taking services; Reader services; Tape recorders; Tutors. **Career services:** Alumni network; Career assessment; Internships

FACILITIES
Housing: Apartments for married students; Apartments for single students; Coed dorms; Fraternity/sorority housing; Special housing for disabled student; Women's dorms 100% of campus accessible to physically diasbled. **Special Academic Facilities/Equipment:** Natural history, mineral, and anthropology museums, performance theatre, child development center, audiovisual center, scanning electron microscope (SEM), gas chromatograph/mass spectrometer (GC/MS), nuclear magnetic resonance spectrometer (NMR), infrared spectrometer (FT/IR), UV/visible spectrometer, X-ray diffraction (XRD), X-ray fluorescence (XRF), KNEW Broadcast Center. **Computers:** Students can register for classes online. Administrative functions (other than registration) can be performed online.

CAMPUS LIFE
Environment: Village **Activities:** Campus Ministries; Choral groups; Concert band; Dance; Drama/theater; International Student Organization; Jazz band; Literary magazine; Marching band; Music ensembles; Musical theater; Radio station; Student government; Student newspaper; Student-run film society; Television station; Yearbook 55 registered organizations, 2 honor societies, 4 religious organizations. 4 fraternities, 2 sororities. **Athletics (Intercollegiate):** *Men:* baseball, basketball, cross-country, football, rodeo, soccer, track/field (outdoor). *Women:* basketball, cross-country, rodeo, soccer, softball, track/field (outdoor), volleyball. **On-Campus Highlights:** New Art/Anthropology builiding, Campus Union Building, Music Building, Library, Ground Zero (student lounge) **Environmental Initiatives:** Water savings project

ADMISSIONS
Freshman Academic Profile: Average high school GPA 3.2. 11% in top 10% of high school class, 34% in top 25% of high school class, 68% in top 50% of high school class. 98% from public high schools. **Test Scores:** SAT Math middle 50% range 430-530. SAT EBRW middle 50% range 420-525. ACT middle 50% range 17-23. Minimum paper TOEFL 500. **Basis for Candidate Selection:** *Very important factors considered include:* academic GPA, standardized test scores. **Freshman Admission Requirements:** High school diploma is required and GED is accepted *Academic units recommended:* 4 English, 4 math, 2 science, 2 social studies. **Freshman Admission Statistics:** 2,164 applied, 59.8% admitted, 48% enrolled. **Transfer Admission Requirements:** college transcript(s), statement of good standing from prior institution(s). Minimum college GPA of 2.0 required. Lowest grade transferable D. **General Admission Information:** Priority deadline 8/1. Nonfall registration accepted. Admission may be deferred for a maximum of 1 semester.

COSTS AND FINANCIAL AID
Annual in-state tuition $5,612. Annual out-of-state tuition $8,220. Room and board $5,612. Required fees $1,212. Average book expense $500. **Required Forms and Deadlines:** FAFSA. **Notification of Awards:** Applicants will

be notified of awards on a rolling basis beginning 5/1. **Types of Aid:** *Need-based scholarships/grants:* College/university scholarship or grant aid from institutional funds; Federal Pell; SEOG; State scholarships/grants. *Loans:* Direct PLUS loans; Direct Subsidized Stafford Loans; Direct Unsubsidized Stafford Loans. *Student Employment:* Federal Work-Study Program available. Institutional employment available. **Financial Aid Statistics:** 97% needy freshmen, 97% needy undergrads receive need-based scholarship or grant aid. 88% freshmen, 56% undergrads receive non-need-based scholarship or grant aid. 25% freshmen, 27% undergrads receive need-based self-help aid. 10% freshmen, 8% undergrads receive athletic scholarships. 99% freshmen, 91% undergrads receive any aid. **Criteria for awarding aid:** *Non-need-based:* Academics, Alumni affiliation, Art, Athletics, Leadership, Music/drama, State/district residency.

EASTERN OREGON UNIVERSITY

One University Blvd, La Grande, OR 97850
Phone: 1-541-962-3393 · **Financial Aid Phone:** 1 (800) 452-8639
E-mail: admissions@eou.edu · **CEEB Code:** 4300
Fax: 541-962-3418 · **Website:** www.eou.edu · **ACT Code:** 3460

This public school was founded in 1929. It has a 121 acre campus.

RATINGS
Admissions Selectivity Rating: 79   **Fire Safety Rating:** 89   **Green Rating:** 60*

STUDENTS AND FACULTY
Enrollment: 2,997. **Student Body:** 63% female, 37% male, 28% out-of-state, 2% international (20 countries represented). Asian 2%, African American 3%, Caucasian 76%, Hispanic 6%, Native American 3%, Pacific Islander 1%, Two or more races 2%, Race unknown 6%.
Retention and Graduation: 58% freshmen return for sophomore year.
Faculty: Student/faculty ratio 22:1. 106 full-time faculty, 75% hold PhDs, 8% are members of minority groups, 42% are women.

ACADEMICS
Degrees: Associate; Bachelor's; Certificate; Master's **Classes:** Most classes have fewer than 10 students. Most lab/discussion sessions have fewer than 10 students. **Most popular majors:** Education, Other; Liberal Arts And Sciences/Liberal Studies; Business Administration, Management And Operations, Other. **Special Study Options:** Cooperative education program; Cross-registration; Distance learning; Double major; Dual enrollment; Exchange student program (domestic); External degree program; Honors program; Independent study; Internships; Liberal arts/career combination; Student-designed major; Study abroad; Teacher certification program; Weekend college. **Honors programs:** Eastern Oregon University is committed to encouraging and recognizing student excellence. To this end, the Honors Program Committee is currently developing an Honors Degree. https://www.eou.edu/honors/. **Disability Services offered to physically disabled students:** Note-taking services; Reader services; Tape recorders; Tutors. **Career services:** Alumni services; Career assessment; Career/job search classes; Internships

FACILITIES
Housing: Apartments for married students; Coed dorms; Special housing for disabled students 95% of campus accessible to physically diasbled. **Special Academic Facilities/Equipment:** Art gallery, archaeological museum **Computers:** 40% of classrooms, 80% of libraries, 90% of dining areas, 90% of student union, 50% of common outdoor areas have wireless network access. Students can register for classes online.

CAMPUS LIFE
Environment: Village **Activities:** Choral groups; Concert band; Dance; Drama/theater; International Student Organization; Jazz band; Literary magazine; Music ensembles; Musical theater; Radio station; Student government; Student newspaper; Symphony orchestra 57 registered organizations, 2 honor societies, 4 religious organizations. **Athletics (Intercollegiate):** *Men:* basketball, cross-country, football, track/field (outdoor), track/field (indoor). *Women:* basketball, cross-country, soccer, softball, track/field (outdoor), track/field (indoor), volleyball. **On-Campus Highlights:** Loso Hall, Hoke Union, Community Stadium, Quinn Coliseum, Sports Practice Fields

ADMISSIONS
Freshman Academic Profile: Average high school GPA 3.2. 9% in top 10% of high school class, 36% in top 25% of high school class, 74% in top 50% of high school class. **Test Scores:** SAT Math middle 50% range 410-520. SAT EBRW middle 50% range 410-530. ACT middle 50% range 18-24. Minimum

paper TOEFL 520. **Basis for Candidate Selection:** *Very important factors considered include:* rigor of secondary school record, academic GPA. *Important factors considered include:* recommendation(s), talent/ability. *Other factors considered include:* class rank, application essay, standardized test scores, extracurricular activities, first generation, geographical residence, volunteer work, work experience, level of applicant's interest. **Freshman Admission Requirements:** High school diploma is required and GED is accepted *Academic units required:* 4 English, 3 math, 3 science, 2 foreign language, 3 social studies, *Academic units recommended:* 1 science labs. **Freshman Admission Statistics:** 1,530 applied, 64.2% admitted, 32% enrolled. **Transfer Admission Requirements:** college transcript(s), Minimum college GPA of 2.2 required. Lowest grade transferable D-. **General Admission Information:** Priority deadline 2/1. Regular application deadline 9/1. Nonfall registration accepted. Admission may be deferred for a maximum of 1 year.

COSTS AND FINANCIAL AID

Annual in-state tuition $9,642. Annual out-of-state tuition $16,110. Room and board $9,642. Required fees $1,410. Average book expense $1,425. **Required Forms and Deadlines:** FAFSA. **Notification of Awards:** Applicants will be notified of awards on a rolling basis beginning 4/1. **Types of Aid:** *Need-based scholarships/grants:* College/university scholarship or grant aid from institutional funds; Federal Pell; Private scholarships; SEOG; State scholarships/grants. *Loans:* Direct PLUS loans; Direct Subsidized Stafford Loans; Direct Unsubsidized Stafford Loans. *Student Employment:* Federal Work-Study Program available. Institutional employment available. **Financial Aid Statistics:** 69% needy freshmen, 75% needy undergrads receive need-based scholarship or grant aid. 10% freshmen, 7% undergrads receive non-need-based scholarship or grant aid. 86% freshmen, 91% undergrads receive need-based self-help aid. 13% freshmen, 9% undergrads receive athletic scholarships. **Criteria for awarding aid:** *Need-based:* Academics *Non-need-based:* Academics, Art, Leadership, Minority status, Music/drama, State/district residency.

EASTERN WASHINGTON UNIVERSITY

526 Fifth Street, Cheney, WA 99004
Phone: 509-359-6692 · **Financial Aid Phone:** 509-359-2314
E-mail: admissions@ewu.edu · **CEEB Code:** 4301
Fax: 509-359-6692 · **Website:** www.ewu.edu · **ACT Code:** 4454

This public school was founded in 1882. It has a 335 acre campus.

RATINGS

Admissions Selectivity Rating: 72   **Fire Safety Rating:** 88   **Green Rating:** 88

STUDENTS AND FACULTY

Enrollment: 10,500. **Student Body:** 53% female, 47% male, 5% out-of-state, 5% international (38 countries represented). Asian 3%, African American 3%, Caucasian 63%, Hispanic 16%, Native American 1%, Pacific Islander <1%, Two or more races 7%, Race unknown 2%.
Retention and Graduation: 76% freshmen return for sophomore year. 25% freshmen graduate within 4 years. 52% freshmen graduate within 6 years. 44% grads go on to further study within 1 year. **Faculty:** Student/faculty ratio 21:1. 483 full-time faculty, 77% hold PhDs, 18% are members of minority groups, 48% are women. 1% of classes are taught by teaching assistants.

ACADEMICS

Degrees: Bachelor's; Certificate; Doctoral Other; Master's; Post-Bachelor's certificate **Classes:** Most classes have 20-29 students. Most lab/discussion sessions have 10-19 students. **Most popular majors:** Biology/Biological Sciences, General; Psychology, General; Business Administration And Management, General. **Special Study Options:** Distance learning; Double major; Dual enrollment; English as a Second Language (ESL); Honors program; Independent study; Internships; Student-designed major; Study abroad; Teacher certification program. **Honors programs:** Honors at Eastern Washington University seeks to cultivate excellence in undergraduate education by providing enhanced educational opportunities to superior students and special teaching opportunities to outstanding faculty. Honors courses and Honors activities seek to develop thorough knowledge and appreciation of the liberal arts and sciences; cultivate excellent writing, calculation and critical thinking skills; and inspire an attitude of self-responsibility, lifelong intellectual development, and service to the world. Admission to Honors at Eastern is based entirely on demonstrated and potential intellectual and academic qualifications. **Combined degree programs:** BA/MA. **Disability Services offered to physically disabled students:** Note-taking services; Reader services; Tape recorders. **Career services:** Alumni network; Alumni services; Career assessment; Career/job search classes; Internships; Regional alumni

FACILITIES

Housing: Apartments for married students; Coed dorms; Fraternity/sorority housing; Special housing for disabled student; Theme housing; Wellness housing 77% of campus accessible to physically diasbled. **Special Academic Facilities/Equipment:** Anthropology museum, education lab, marine biology lab, ecological studies lab, wildlife refuge, planetarium, Map Library, Crime Lab, State of Washington Digital Archives **Computers:** Students can register for classes online. Administrative functions (other than registration) can be performed online.

CAMPUS LIFE

Environment: Town **Activities:** Campus Ministries; Choral groups; Concert band; Dance; Drama/theater; International Student Organization; Jazz band; Literary magazine; Marching band; Model UN; Music ensembles; Musical theater; Pep band; Radio station; Student government; Student newspaper; Student-run film society; Symphony orchestra 100 registered organizations, 14 honor societies, 10 religious organizations. 5 fraternities, 5 sororities. **Athletics (Intercollegiate):** *Men:* basketball, cross-country, football, golf, tennis, track/field (outdoor), track/field (indoor). *Women:* basketball, cross-country, golf, soccer, tennis, track/field (outdoor), track/field (indoor), volleyball. **On-Campus Highlights:** Roos Stadium: "The Inferno" red turf, URC- New Recreaton Center, JFK Library, PUB- Pence Union Building, Central Campus mall **Environmental Initiatives:** Facilities Maintenance Energy Management Program: Limiting the greenhouse gas emission

ADMISSIONS

Freshman Academic Profile: Average high school GPA 3.2. 95% from public high schools. **Test Scores:** SAT Math middle 50% range 430-560. SAT EBRW middle 50% range 440-530. ACT middle 50% range 17-24. Minimum internet-based TOEFL 71. Minimum paper TOEFL 525. **Basis for Candidate Selection:** *Very important factors considered include:* academic GPA, standardized test scores. *Important factors considered include:* rigor of secondary school record, application essay. *Other factors considered include:* recommendation(s), extracurricular activities, talent/ability, character/personal qualities, volunteer work, work experience. **Freshman Admission Requirements:** High school diploma or equivalent is not required *Academic units required:* 4 English, 3 math, 2 science, 2 science labs, 2 foreign language, 3 social studies, 1 visual/performing arts, and 1 unit from above areas or other academic areas. **Freshman Admission Statistics:** 4,444 applied, 96.2% admitted, 39% enrolled. **Transfer Admission Requirements:** college transcript(s), essay or personal statement, Minimum college GPA of 2.0 required. Lowest grade transferable D-. **General Admission Information:** Application fee $50. Priority deadline 2/15. Regular application deadline 5/15. Nonfall registration accepted. Admission may be deferred for a maximum of 1 year.

COSTS AND FINANCIAL AID

Types of Aid: *Student Employment:* Federal Work-Study Program available. Institutional employment available. **Financial Aid Statistics:** 77% needy freshmen, 74% needy undergrads receive need-based scholarship or grant aid. 54% freshmen, 28% undergrads receive non-need-based scholarship or grant aid. 69% freshmen, 80% undergrads receive need-based self-help aid. 2% freshmen, 2% undergrads receive athletic scholarships. 69% freshmen, 59% undergrads receive any aid. **Criteria for awarding aid:** *Need-based:* Academics, Alumni affiliation, Art, Athletics, Job skills, Music/drama *Non-need-based:* Academics, Alumni affiliation, Art, Athletics, Job skills, Music/drama, State/district residency.

ECKERD COLLEGE

4200 54th Avenue South, St.Petersburg, FL 33711
Phone: 727-864-8331 · **Financial Aid Phone:** 727-864-8854
E-mail: admissions@eckerd.edu
Fax: 727-866-2304 · **Website:** www.eckerd.edu · **ACT Code:** 731

This private school, affiliated with the Presbyterian Church, was founded in 1958. It has a 188 acre campus.

RATINGS

Admissions Selectivity Rating: 80   **Fire Safety Rating:** 91   **Green Rating:** 82

STUDENTS AND FACULTY

Enrollment: 1,938. **Student Body:** 66% female, 34% male, 78% out-of-state, 4% international (39 countries represented). Asian 2%, African American 3%,

Caucasian 78%, Hispanic 9%, Native American <1%, Pacific Islander <1%, Two or more races 3%, Race unknown 1%.
Retention and Graduation: 81% freshmen return for sophomore year. 63% freshmen graduate within 4 years. 70% freshmen graduate within 6 years. **Faculty:** Student/faculty ratio 12:1. 147 full-time faculty, 84% hold PhDs, 14% are members of minority groups, 48% are women. 0% of classes are taught by teaching assistants.

ACADEMICS
Degrees: Bachelor's **Classes:** Most classes have 10-19 students. Most lab/discussion sessions have 10-19 students. **Most popular majors:** Environmental Studies; Marine Biology And Biological Oceanography; Psychology, General. **Special Study Options:** Accelerated program; Double major; English as a Second Language (ESL); Honors program; Independent study; Internships; Liberal arts/career combination; Student-designed major; Study abroad. **Honors programs:** Ford Scholar program: Each year up to twenty rising Juniors are given the opportunity to participate in a two year course of study designed to prepare them for graduate school and to pursue a career in college or university teaching. Faculty select and sponsor the participants on the basis of academic achievement, intellectual promise, and a willingness to explore college teaching as career. The program involves special coursework, summer research in collaboration with a faculty sponsor, a major project during the Senior year, and supervised teaching experience. Honors program: The Honors Program at Eckerd College provides enhanced opportunities for students of outstanding ability to interact and learn from each other through class discussions and group activities. Selected students are brought together for close interaction and advanced work, such studies receiving permanent recognition on the students' transcripts. **Combined degree programs:** BA/JD. **Disability Services offered to physically disabled students:** Note-taking services. **Career services:** Alumni network; Alumni services; Career assessment; Career/job search classes; Internships

FACILITIES
Housing: Apartments for single students; Coed dorms; Special housing for disabled student; Theme housing; Wellness housing; Women's dorms 90% of campus accessible to physically disabled. **Special Academic Facilities/Equipment:** Theatre, galleries, chapel, writing center, oral communication center, marine science lab. **Computers:** 100% of classrooms, 100% of dorms, 100% of libraries, 100% of dining areas, 100% of student union, 90% of common outdoor areas have wireless network access. Students can register for classes online. Administrative functions (other than registration) can be performed online.

CAMPUS LIFE
Environment: City **Activities:** Campus Ministries; Choral groups; Concert band; Dance; Drama/theater; International Student Organization; Literary magazine; Music ensembles; Radio station; Student government; Student newspaper 74 registered organizations, 8 honor societies, 3 religious organizations. **Athletics (Intercollegiate):** *Men:* baseball, basketball, golf, sailing, soccer, tennis. *Women:* basketball, golf, sailing, soccer, softball, tennis, volleyball. **On-Campus Highlights:** the James Center for Molecular and Life Sciences, the GO Pavilion, Waterfront/South Beach, the Pub, the Center for Visual Arts **Environmental Initiatives:** The yellow bike has in recent years become a new symbol of Eckerd College. The Yellow Bike Program started in the spring of 2004, and since then it has gained national recognition. Students, faculty, staff, and even the College President can be spotted riding them. The goal of the program is to have less vehicle traffic which decreases greenhouse gas emissions and reduces our harm to the environment. The bikes on campus will help lead to a mostly walking campus, and an eco-friendly campus. The Yellow Bike Program was recognized in 2005 by the National Wildlife Federation, and it has gained local and national news attention.

ADMISSIONS
Freshman Academic Profile: Average high school GPA 3.4. **Test Scores:** SAT Math middle 50% range 520-610. SAT EBRW middle 50% range 540-650. ACT middle 50% range 23-29. Minimum internet-based TOEFL 79. Minimum paper TOEFL 550. **Basis for Candidate Selection:** *Very important factors considered include:* rigor of secondary school record, academic GPA. *Important factors considered include:* application essay, standardized test scores, recommendation(s), interview, extracurricular activities, talent/ability, character/personal qualities, volunteer work, work experience, level of applicant's interest. *Other factors considered include:* class rank, first generation, alumni/ae relation. **Freshman Admission Requirements:** High school diploma is required and GED is accepted *Academic units recommended:* 4 English, 3 math, 3 science, 2 science labs, 2 foreign language, 2 social studies, 1 history, 3 academic electives. **Freshman Admission Statistics:** 4,525 applied, 72.7% admitted, 17% enrolled. **Transfer Admission Requirements:** college transcript(s), essay or personal statement, statement of good standing from prior institution(s). Minimum college GPA of 2.5 required. Lowest grade transferable C. **General Admission Information:** Application fee $40. Nonfall registration accepted. Admission may be deferred.

COSTS AND FINANCIAL AID
Annual tuition $42,428. Room and board $12,162. Required fees $616. Average book expense $1,350. **Required Forms and Deadlines:** FAFSA. **Types of Aid:** *Need-based scholarships/grants:* College/university scholarship or grant aid from institutional funds; Federal Pell; Private scholarships; SEOG; State scholarships/grants. *Loans:* Direct PLUS loans; Direct Subsidized Stafford Loans; Direct Unsubsidized Stafford Loans. *Student Employment:* Federal Work-Study Program available. Institutional employment available. **Financial Aid Statistics:** 100% needy freshmen, 100% needy undergrads receive need-based scholarship or grant aid. 0% undergrads receive non-need-based scholarship or grant aid. 82% freshmen, 87% undergrads receive need-based self-help aid. 3% freshmen, 3% undergrads receive athletic scholarships. 97% freshmen, 95% undergrads receive any aid. 60% undergrads borrow to pay for school. Average cumulative indebtedness $32,387. **Criteria for awarding aid:** *Need-based:* Religious affiliation *Non-need-based:* Academics, Art, Athletics, Music/drama, State/district residency.

EDGEWOOD COLLEGE

1000 Edgewood College Drive, Madison, WI 53711-1997
Phone: 608-663-2294 · **Financial Aid Phone:** 608-663-4300
E-mail: admissions@edgewood.edu · **CEEB Code:** 1202
Fax: 608-663-2214 · **Website:** www.edgewood.edu · **ACT Code:** 4582

This private school, affiliated with the Roman Catholic Church, was founded in 1927. It has a 55 acre campus.

RATINGS
Admissions Selectivity Rating: 80   **Fire Safety Rating:** 94   **Green Rating:** 90

STUDENTS AND FACULTY
Enrollment: 1,521. **Student Body:** 73% female, 27% male, 8% out-of-state, 3% international (20 countries represented). Asian 3%, African American 3%, Caucasian 79%, Hispanic 6%, Native American <1%, Pacific Islander <1%, Two or more races 3%, Race unknown 3%.
Retention and Graduation: 78% freshmen return for sophomore year. 38% freshmen graduate within 4 years. 61% freshmen graduate within 6 years. **Faculty:** Student/faculty ratio 9:1. 152 full-time faculty, 71% hold PhDs, 12% are members of minority groups, 62% are women. 0% of classes are taught by teaching assistants.

ACADEMICS
Degrees: Bachelor's; Certificate; Doctoral/Professional; Doctoral/Research; Master's; Post-Bachelor's certificate **Classes:** Most classes have 10-19 students. Most lab/discussion sessions have fewer than 10 students. **Most popular majors:** Psychology, General; Registered Nursing/Registered Nurse; Business/Commerce, General. **Special Study Options:** Accelerated program; Cooperative education program; Cross-registration; Distance learning; Double major; Dual enrollment; Honors program; Independent study; Internships; Liberal arts/career combination; Student-designed major; Study abroad; Teacher certification program. **Honors programs:** We have an Honors Program for undergraduates. **Disability Services offered to physically disabled students:** Note-taking services; Reader services; Tape recorders; Tutors. **Career services:** Alumni network; Alumni services; Career assessment; Career/job search classes; Internships; Regional alumni

FACILITIES
Housing: Apartments for single students; Coed dorms; Cooperative housing; Special housing for disabled students 90% of campus accessible to physically disabled. **Special Academic Facilities/Equipment:** The Stream, and Science Exploration Center. **Computers:** 90% of classrooms, 100% of dorms, 100% of libraries, 100% of dining areas, 100% of student union, 80% of common outdoor areas have wireless network access. Students can register for classes online. Administrative functions (other than registration) can be performed online.

CAMPUS LIFE
Environment: City **Activities:** Campus Ministries; Choral groups; Concert band; Dance; Drama/theater; International Student Organization; Jazz band; Literary magazine; Model UN; Music ensembles; Musical theater; Student government; Student newspaper; Symphony orchestra 45 registered organizations, 4 honor societies, 1 religious organization. **Athletics (Intercollegiate):** *Men:* baseball, basketball, cross-country, golf, soccer, tennis, track/field (outdoor), track/field (indoor). *Women:* basketball, cross-country, golf, soccer, softball, tennis, track/field (outdoor), track/field (indoor), volleyball. **On-Campus Highlights:** Wingra Cafe, Commons, Phil's, Lake

Wingra Boardwalk, The Stream, Sonderegger Science Center **Environmental Initiatives:** The Campus Sustainability Coordinating Team has completed a Campus Sustainability Plan, components of which are incorporated into the College's Master Plan.

ADMISSIONS

Freshman Academic Profile: Average high school GPA 3.5. 17% in top 10% of high school class, 46% in top 25% of high school class, 81% in top 50% of high school class. 93% from public high schools. **Test Scores:** SAT Math middle 50% range 510-630. SAT EBRW middle 50% range 550-590. ACT middle 50% range 21-25. Minimum internet-based TOEFL 71. Minimum paper TOEFL 525. **Basis for Candidate Selection:** *Very important factors considered include:* class rank, academic GPA, standardized test scores. *Other factors considered include:* application essay, recommendation(s). **Freshman Admission Requirements:** High school diploma is required and GED is accepted *Academic units required:* 4 English, 2 math, 2 science, 1 science labs, 2 foreign language, 2 social studies, 1 history, *Academic units recommended:* 4 English, 2 math, 2 science, 1 science labs, 2 foreign language, 2 social studies, 1 history. **Freshman Admission Statistics:** 1,447 applied, 71.1% admitted, 28% enrolled. **Transfer Admission Requirements:** High school transcript, college transcript(s), Minimum college GPA of 2.0 required. Lowest grade transferable C-. **General Admission Information:** Application fee $30. Priority deadline 3/1. Regular application deadline 8/15. Nonfall registration accepted. Admission may be deferred for a maximum of 1 year.

COSTS AND FINANCIAL AID

Annual tuition $28,500. Room and board $9,870. Average book expense $800. **Required Forms and Deadlines:** FAFSA. **Notification of Awards:** Applicants will be notified of awards on a rolling basis beginning 12/15. **Types of Aid:** *Need-based scholarships/grants:* College/university scholarship or grant aid from institutional funds; Federal Pell; Private scholarships; SEOG; State scholarships/grants. *Loans:* Direct PLUS loans; Direct Subsidized Stafford Loans; Direct Unsubsidized Stafford Loans. *Student Employment:* Federal Work-Study Program available. Institutional employment available. **Financial Aid Statistics:** 99% needy freshmen, 98% needy undergrads receive need-based scholarship or grant aid. 7% freshmen, 7% undergrads receive non-need-based scholarship or grant aid. 93% freshmen, 92% undergrads receive need-based self-help aid. 0% freshmen, 0% undergrads receive athletic scholarships. 100% freshmen, 93% undergrads receive any aid. 80% undergrads borrow to pay for school. Average cumulative indebtedness $33,104. **Criteria for awarding aid:** *Need-based:* Academics, Alumni affiliation, Religious affiliation *Non-need-based:* Academics, Alumni affiliation, Art, Leadership, Music/drama, Religious affiliation.

EDINBORO UNIVERSITY OF PENNSYLVANIA

200 East Normal Street, Edinboro, PA 16444
Phone: 814-732-2761 • **Financial Aid Phone:** 814-732-3500
E-mail: eup_admissions@edinboro.edu • **CEEB Code:** 2651
Fax: 814-732-2420 • **Website:** http://www.edinboro.edu/ • **ACT Code:** 3702

This public school was founded in 1857. It has a 585 acre campus.

RATINGS

Admissions Selectivity Rating: 78 **Fire Safety Rating:** 97 **Green Rating:** 64

STUDENTS AND FACULTY

Enrollment: 6,301. **Student Body:** 56% female, 44% male, 11% out-of-state, 1% international (31 countries represented). Asian 1%, African American 9%, Caucasian 86%, Hispanic 2%, Native American <1%, Race unknown 1%. **Retention and Graduation:** 75% freshmen return for sophomore year. **Faculty:** 346 full-time faculty, 7% are members of minority groups, 46% are women. 0% of classes are taught by teaching assistants.

ACADEMICS

Degrees: Associate; Bachelor's; Master's; Post-Bachelor's certificate; Post-Master's certificate **Classes:** Most classes have 10-19 students. **Most popular majors:** Criminal Justice/Safety Studies; Fine/Studio Arts, General; Business Administration And Management, General. **Special Study Options:** Cooperative education program; Cross-registration; Distance learning; Double major; Dual enrollment; Honors program; Independent study; Internships; Liberal arts/career combination; Student-designed major; Study abroad; Teacher certification program. **Honors programs:** Admission to the Upper Division Honors Program, may be made by any full time EUP student who has completed 63 credit hours with an overall GPA of 3.4 or higher. They must also provide letters of support from two faculty members, secure approval of their academic advisor, and complete a proposal for the Senior Project in consultation

with the Honors Director, Academic Advisor and and Faculty Member who will supervise the Senior Project. **Combined degree programs:** BA/MEng. **Disability Services offered to physically disabled students:** Note-taking services; Reader services; Tape recorders; Tutors. **Career services:** Alumni services; Career assessment; Career/job search classes; Internships

FACILITIES

Housing: Coed dorms; Special housing for disabled students 98% of campus accessible to physically diasbled. **Special Academic Facilities/Equipment:** Planetarium, Solar Observatory, Bates Art Gallery, Bruce Gallery. **Computers:** 90% of classrooms, 30% of dorms, 100% of libraries, 100% of dining areas, 75% of student union, 40% of common outdoor areas have wireless network access. Students can register for classes online. Administrative functions (other than registration) can be performed online.

CAMPUS LIFE

Environment: Rural **Activities:** Campus Ministries; Choral groups; Dance; Drama/theater; International Student Organization; Jazz band; Literary magazine; Marching band; Music ensembles; Opera; Radio station; Student government; Student newspaper; Student-run film society; Television station 157 registered organizations, 13 honor societies, 4 religious organizations. 10 fraternities, 7 sororities. **Athletics (Intercollegiate):** *Men:* basketball, cross-country, football, swimming, track/field (outdoor), track/field (indoor), wheel-chair basketball, wrestling. *Women:* basketball, cross-country, lacrosse, soccer, softball, swimming, track/field (outdoor), track/field (indoor), volleyball. **On-Campus Highlights:** Tilles Center for the Performing Arts, Hillwood Commons, Pratt Recreation Center, Equestrian Center, Entrepreneurship Lab

ADMISSIONS

Freshman Academic Profile: Average high school GPA 3.2. 5% in top 10% of high school class, 20% in top 25% of high school class, 51% in top 50% of high school class. **Test Scores:** SAT Math middle 50% range 410-520. SAT EBRW middle 50% range 415-520. ACT middle 50% range 17-23. Minimum internet-based TOEFL 61. Minimum paper TOEFL 500. **Basis for Candidate Selection:** *Very important factors considered include:* rigor of secondary school record, class rank, academic GPA, standardized test scores. *Other factors considered include:* application essay, recommendation(s), interview, extracurricular activities, talent/ability, character/personal qualities, volunteer work, work experience. **Freshman Admission Requirements:** High school diploma is required and GED is accepted *Academic units recommended:* 4 English, 3 math, 3 science, 2 foreign language, 4 social studies, 1 computer science. **Freshman Admission Statistics:** 4,411 applied, 73.4% admitted, 44% enrolled. **Transfer Admission Requirements:** High school transcript, college transcript(s), statement of good standing from prior institution(s). Minimum college GPA of 2.0 required. Lowest grade transferable C-. **General Admission Information:** Application fee $30. Nonfall registration accepted. Admission may be deferred for a maximum of 1 year.

COSTS AND FINANCIAL AID

Annual in-state tuition $7,130. Annual out-of-state tuition $8,332. Room and board $7,130. Required fees $1,762. Average book expense $900. **Required Forms and Deadlines:** FAFSA. **Notification of Awards:** Applicants will be notified of awards on a rolling basis beginning 3/22. **Types of Aid:** *Need-based scholarships/grants:* College/university scholarship or grant aid from institutional funds; Federal Pell; Private scholarships; SEOG; State scholarships/grants. *Loans:* Direct Subsidized Stafford Loans; Direct Unsubsidized Stafford Loans. *Student Employment:* Federal Work-Study Program available. Institutional employment available. **Financial Aid Statistics:** 90% needy freshmen, 92% needy undergrads receive need-based scholarship or grant aid. 97% freshmen, 96% undergrads receive non-need-based scholarship or grant aid. 85% freshmen, 88% undergrads receive need-based self-help aid. 3% freshmen, 2% undergrads receive athletic scholarships. 91% freshmen, 88% undergrads receive any aid. **Criteria for awarding aid:** *Need-based:* Academics, Alumni affiliation, Art, Athletics, Job skills, Leadership, Minority status, Music/drama, Religious affiliation *Non-need-based:* Academics, Alumni affiliation, Art, Athletics, Job skills, Leadership, Minority status, Music/drama, Religious affiliation, State/district residency.

ELIZABETHTOWN COLLEGE

1 Alpha Drive, Elizabethtown, PA 17022-2298
Phone: 717-361-1400 · **Financial Aid Phone:** 717-361-1404
E-mail: admissions@etown.edu · **CEEB Code:** 2225
Fax: 717-361-1364 · **Website:** www.etown.edu · **ACT Code:** 3568

This private school, affiliated with the Church of Brethren, was founded in 1899. It has a 193 acre campus.

RATINGS

Admissions Selectivity Rating: 79   **Fire Safety Rating:** 62   **Green Rating:** 60*

STUDENTS AND FACULTY

Enrollment: 1,645. **Student Body:** 62% female, 38% male, 32% out-of-state, 2% international (17 countries represented). Asian 3%, African American 3%, Caucasian 85%, Hispanic 4%, Native American <1%, Pacific Islander <1%, Two or more races 2%, Race unknown <1%.
Retention and Graduation: 87% freshmen return for sophomore year. 69% freshmen graduate within 4 years. 75% freshmen graduate within 6 years. 20% grads go on to further study within 1 year. **Faculty:** Student/faculty ratio 11:1. 128 full-time faculty, 95% hold PhDs, 13% are members of minority groups, 47% are women. 0% of classes are taught by teaching assistants.

ACADEMICS

Degrees: Bachelor's; Master's **Classes:** Most classes have 10-19 students. Most lab/discussion sessions have 10-19 students. **Most popular majors:** Business/Commerce, General. **Special Study Options:** Distance learning; Double major; Dual enrollment; English as a Second Language (ESL); Exchange student program (domestic); Honors program; Independent study; Internships; Study abroad; Teacher certification program. **Combined degree programs:** BA/MA; BA/MD. **Disability Services offered to physically disabled students:** Tape recorders; Tutors.

FACILITIES

Housing: Apartments for single students; Coed dorms; Cooperative housing; Special housing for disabled student; Special housing for international students 75% of campus accessible to physically diasbled. **Special Academic Facilities/Equipment:** Art gallery, Mineral gallery, Meetinghouse/center for Anabaptist and Pietist studies, chapel/performance center, Fourier transform multinuclear NMR spectrometer, blood gas analyzer, scanning densitometer, PCR machine, radiometer/data logger, automated ion analyzer, computerized language lab **Computers:** Students can register for classes online. Administrative functions (other than registration) can be performed online.

CAMPUS LIFE

Environment: Village **Activities:** Campus Ministries; Choral groups; Concert band; Dance; Drama/theater; International Student Organization; Jazz band; Literary magazine; Music ensembles; Musical theater; Radio station; Student government; Student newspaper; Student-run film society; Symphony orchestra; Television station; Yearbook 80 registered organizations, 16 honor societies, 6 religious organizations. **Athletics (Intercollegiate):** *Men:* baseball, basketball, cross-country, diving, golf, lacrosse, soccer, swimming, tennis, track/field (outdoor), track/field (indoor), wrestling. *Women:* basketball, cross-country, diving, field hockey, lacrosse, soccer, softball, swimming, tennis, track/field (outdoor), track/field (indoor), volleyball. **On-Campus Highlights:** Brossman Commons Students Center, The Jay's Nest Snack Bar, The Dell, The Blue Bean Cafe, The Ira R Herr Soccer Complex

ADMISSIONS

Freshman Academic Profile: 30% in top 10% of high school class, 60% in top 25% of high school class, 88% in top 50% of high school class. 80% from public high schools. **Test Scores:** SAT Math middle 50% range 530-640. SAT EBRW middle 50% range 540-640. ACT middle 50% range 22-27. Minimum paper TOEFL 525. **Basis for Candidate Selection:** *Very important factors considered include:* rigor of secondary school record. *Important factors considered include:* class rank, academic GPA, standardized test scores, recommendation(s), interview. *Other factors considered include:* application essay, extracurricular activities, talent/ability, character/personal qualities, first generation, alumni/ae relation, geographical residence, state residency, religious affiliation/commitment, racial/ethnic status, volunteer work, work experience, level of applicant's interest. **Freshman Admission Requirements:** High school diploma is required and GED is accepted *Academic units required:* 4 English, 3 math, 2 science, 2 science labs, 2 foreign language, 2 social studies, 2 history, *Academic units recommended:* 4 English, 4 math, 4 science, 3 science labs, 2 foreign language, 2 social studies, 2 history, 2 academic electives. **Freshman Admission Statistics:** 3,033 applied, 74.0% admitted, 18% enrolled. **Transfer Admission Requirements:** High school transcript, college transcript(s), essay or personal statement, standardized test scores, statement of good standing from prior institution(s). Minimum college GPA of 2.5 required.

Lowest grade transferable C. **General Admission Information:** Application fee $30. Priority deadline 3/1. Nonfall registration accepted. Admission may be deferred for a maximum of 1 year.

COSTS AND FINANCIAL AID

Annual tuition $46,940. Room and board $11,370. Average book expense $1,100. **Required Forms and Deadlines:** FAFSA. **Notification of Awards:** Applicants will be notified of awards on a rolling basis beginning 11/1. **Types of Aid:** *Need-based scholarships/grants:* College/university scholarship or grant aid from institutional funds; Federal Pell; Private scholarships; SEOG; State scholarships/grants. *Loans:* Direct PLUS loans; Direct Subsidized Stafford Loans; Direct Unsubsidized Stafford Loans. **Financial Aid Statistics:** 100% needy freshmen, 100% needy undergrads receive need-based scholarship or grant aid. 22% freshmen, 18% undergrads receive non-need-based scholarship or grant aid. 75% freshmen, 79% undergrads receive need-based self-help aid. 0% freshmen, 0% undergrads receive athletic scholarships. 96% freshmen, 94% undergrads receive any aid. Average cumulative indebtedness $28,106. **Criteria for awarding aid:** *Need-based:* Academics, Alumni affiliation, Art, Minority status, Music/drama, Religious affiliation *Non-need-based:* Academics, Alumni affiliation, Art, Music/drama, Religious affiliation.

ELMHURST COLLEGE

190 S Prospect Avenue, Elmhurst, IL 60126
Phone: 630-617-3400 · **Financial Aid Phone:** 630-617-3075
E-mail: admit@elmhurst.edu · **CEEB Code:** 1204
Fax: 630-617-5501 · **Website:** public.elmhurst.edu · **ACT Code:** 1020

This private school, affiliated with the United Church of Christ, was founded in 1871. It has a 38 acre campus.

RATINGS

Admissions Selectivity Rating: 78   **Fire Safety Rating:** 89   **Green Rating:** 60*

STUDENTS AND FACULTY

Enrollment: 2,770. **Student Body:** 61% female, 39% male, 9% out-of-state, <1% international (25 countries represented). Asian 5%, African American 5%, Caucasian 63%, Hispanic 21%, Native American <1%, Pacific Islander <1%, Two or more races 4%, Race unknown 3%.
Retention and Graduation: 75% freshmen return for sophomore year. 53% freshmen graduate within 4 years. 64% freshmen graduate within 6 years. 17% grads go on to further study within 1 year. 0% grads pursue arts and sciences degrees. 1% grads pursue law degrees. 8% grads pursue business degrees. 2% grads pursue medical degrees. **Faculty:** 153 full-time faculty, 82% hold PhDs, 11% are members of minority groups, 61% are women. 0% of classes are taught by teaching assistants.

ACADEMICS

Degrees: Bachelor's; Master's **Classes:** Most classes have 10-19 students. Most lab/discussion sessions have 10-19 students. **Most popular majors:** Psychology, Generalhealth Services/Allied Health/Health Sciences, General. **Special Study Options:** Accelerated program; Distance learning; Double major; Dual enrollment; Honors program; Independent study; Internships; Liberal arts/career combination; Student-designed major; Study abroad; Teacher certification program. **Honors programs:** The Elmhurst College Honors program provides a challenging set of educational experiences for the most academically students featuring small, stimulating seminar courses where class discussions are lively and engaging; opportunities to conduct and present professional-level research; private receptions with distinguished guest speakers; trips to theatre and dance performances, social events, and more. **Combined degree programs:** BA/JD; BA/MEng. **Disability Services offered to physically disabled students:** Note-taking services; Reader services; Tape recorders; Tutors. **Career services:** Alumni network; Career assessment; Career/job search classes; Internships

FACILITIES

Housing: Apartments for single students; Coed dorms 95% of campus accessible to physically diasbled. **Special Academic Facilities/Equipment:** Accelerator/art space, language lab, recording studio, computer science/technology center, four electron microscopes. **Computers:** Students can register for classes online. Administrative functions (other than registration) can be performed online.

CAMPUS LIFE

Environment: Town **Activities:** Campus Ministries; Choral groups; Concert band; Dance; Drama/theater; International Student Organization; Jazz band; Literary magazine; Model UN; Music ensembles; Musical theater; Radio station; Student government; Student newspaper; Symphony orchestra; Yearbook 106 registered organizations, 15 honor societies, 6 religious organizations. 3 fraternities, 6 sororities. **Athletics (Intercollegiate):** *Men:* baseball, basketball, cross-country, football, golf, soccer, tennis, track/field (outdoor), wrestling. *Women:* basketball, bowling, cross-country, golf, soccer, softball, tennis, track/field (outdoor), volleyball. **On-Campus Highlights:** Alumni Circle, Frick Center, Library, Tyrrell Fitness Center, Circle Hall **Environmental Initiatives:** Development and execution of our Sustainability Plan. It is a living document that continues to expand as goals are achieved.

ADMISSIONS

Freshman Academic Profile: Average high school GPA 3.5. 21% in top 10% of high school class, 49% in top 25% of high school class, 77% in top 50% of high school class. 92% from public high schools. **Test Scores:** SAT Math middle 50% range 485-620. SAT EBRW middle 50% range 500-590. ACT middle 50% range 20-26. Minimum internet-based TOEFL 79. Minimum paper TOEFL 550. **Basis for Candidate Selection:** *Very important factors considered include:* rigor of secondary school record, class rank, academic GPA, standardized test scores. *Important factors considered include:* application essay, recommendation(s), interview. *Other factors considered include:* extracurricular activities, talent/ability, character/personal qualities, alumni/ ae relation. **Freshman Admission Requirements:** High school diploma is required and GED is accepted *Academic units required:* 4 English, 2 math, 2 science, 2 science labs, 1 foreign language, 2 social studies, 1 history, 4 academic electives, *Academic units recommended:* 4 English, 3 math, 3 science, 3 science labs, 2 foreign language, 3 social studies, 2 history. **Freshman Admission Statistics:** 3,645 applied, 70.5% admitted, 19% enrolled. **Transfer Admission Requirements:** High school transcript, college transcript(s), statement of good standing from prior institution(s). Minimum college GPA of 2.6 required. Lowest grade transferable C. **General Admission Information:** Priority deadline 4/15. Nonfall registration accepted. Admission may be deferred for a maximum of 2 years.

COSTS AND FINANCIAL AID

Annual tuition $36,070. Room and board $10,144. Required fees $300. Average book expense $1,000. **Required Forms and Deadlines:** FAFSA. **Notification of Awards:** Applicants will be notified of awards on a rolling basis beginning 12/1. **Types of Aid:** *Need-based scholarships/grants:* College/ university scholarship or grant aid from institutional funds; Federal Pell; Private scholarships; SEOG; State scholarships/grants. *Loans:* Direct PLUS loans; Direct Subsidized Stafford Loans; Direct Unsubsidized Stafford Loans. *Student Employment:* Federal Work-Study Program available. Institutional employment available. **Financial Aid Statistics:** 100% needy freshmen, 100% needy undergrads receive need-based scholarship or grant aid. 31% freshmen, 35% undergrads receive non-need-based scholarship or grant aid. 73% freshmen, 86% undergrads receive need-based self-help aid. 0% freshmen, 0% undergrads receive athletic scholarships. 95% freshmen, 87% undergrads receive any aid. 73% undergrads borrow to pay for school. Average cumulative indebtedness $28,383. **Criteria for awarding aid:** *Need-based:* Academics, Music/drama, Religious affiliation *Non-need-based:* Academics, Alumni affiliation, Art, Minority status, Music/drama, Religious affiliation, State/district residency.

ELMIRA COLLEGE

One Park Place, Elmira, NY 14901
Phone: 607-735-1724 · **Financial Aid Phone:** 607-735-1728
E-mail: admissions@elmira.edu · **CEEB Code:** 2226
Fax: 607-735-1718 · **Website:** www.elmira.edu · **ACT Code:** 2736

This private school was founded in 1855. It has a 55 acre campus.

RATINGS

Admissions Selectivity Rating: 73   **Fire Safety Rating:** 88   **Green Rating:** 60*

STUDENTS AND FACULTY

Enrollment: 908. **Student Body:** 71% female, 29% male, 34% out-of-state, 4% international (12 countries represented). Asian 2%, African American 5%, Caucasian 78%, Hispanic 3%, Native American 1%, Pacific Islander 0%, Two or more races 2%, Race unknown 5%.
Retention and Graduation: 76% freshmen return for sophomore year. 57% freshmen graduate within 4 years. 60% freshmen graduate within 6 years.
Faculty: Student/faculty ratio 10:1. 66 full-time faculty, 83% hold PhDs, 11% are members of minority groups, 55% are women. 0% of classes are taught by teaching assistants.

ACADEMICS

Degrees: Associate; Bachelor's; Master's; Post-Bachelor's certificate **Classes:** Most classes have 10-19 students. Most lab/discussion sessions have 10-19

students. **Most popular majors:** Education, General; Psychology, General; Business Administration And Management, General. **Special Study Options:** Accelerated program; Double major; Honors program; Independent study; Internships; Liberal arts/career combination; Student-designed major; Study abroad; Teacher certification program. **Career services:** Alumni network; Alumni services; Career assessment; Internships

FACILITIES

Housing: Apartments for single students; Coed dorms; Special housing for disabled student; Women's dorms 25% of campus accessible to physically disabled. **Special Academic Facilities/Equipment:** Center for Mark Twain Studies; Cowles Hall, Health Sciences building with state-of-the-art simulation labs.

CAMPUS LIFE

Environment: Town **Activities:** Campus Ministries; Choral groups; Concert band; Dance; Drama/theater; International Student Organization; Literary magazine; Model UN; Music ensembles; Musical theater; Radio station; Student government; Student newspaper; Yearbook 85 registered organizations, 13 honor societies, 3 religious organizations. **Athletics (Intercollegiate):** *Men:* basketball, cheerleading, golf, ice hockey, lacrosse, soccer, tennis. *Women:* basketball, cheerleading, field hockey, golf, ice hockey, lacrosse, soccer, softball, tennis, volleyball. **On-Campus Highlights:** Starbucks at the 1855 Room, Cowles Hall, Gibson Theater, Learning Commons at the Gannett-Tripp Library, The Puddle

ADMISSIONS

Freshman Academic Profile: Average high school GPA 3.2. 20% in top 10% of high school class, 45% in top 25% of high school class, 69% in top 50% of high school class. **Test Scores:** SAT Math middle 50% range 490-580. SAT EBRW middle 50% range 470-570. ACT middle 50% range 22-25. Minimum internet-based TOEFL 79. **Basis for Candidate Selection:** *Very important factors considered include:* rigor of secondary school record, academic GPA, application essay, interview, character/personal qualities. *Important factors considered include:* class rank, recommendation(s), extracurricular activities, level of applicant's interest. *Other factors considered include:* standardized test scores, talent/ability, alumni/ae relation, geographical residence, racial/ ethnic status, volunteer work, work experience. **Freshman Admission Requirements:** High school diploma is required and GED is not accepted *Academic units required:* 4 English, 3 math, 3 science, 2 science labs, 3 social studies, 1 history, 2 academic electives, *Academic units recommended:* 2 foreign language. **Freshman Admission Statistics:** 2,103 applied, 82.2% admitted, 12% enrolled. **Transfer Admission Requirements:** college transcript(s), essay or personal statement, statement of good standing from prior institution(s). Minimum college GPA of 2.0 required. Lowest grade transferable C-. **General Admission Information:** Priority deadline 2/15. Nonfall registration accepted. Admission may be deferred for a maximum of 1 year.

COSTS AND FINANCIAL AID

Annual tuition $41,900. Room and board $12,000. Average book expense $600. **Required Forms and Deadlines:** FAFSA; State aid form. **Notification of Awards:** Applicants will be notified of awards on a rolling basis beginning 12/1. **Types of Aid:** *Need-based scholarships/grants:* College/university scholarship or grant aid from institutional funds; Federal Pell; Private scholarships; SEOG; State scholarships/grants. *Loans:* Direct PLUS loans; Direct Subsidized Stafford Loans; Direct Unsubsidized Stafford Loans. *Student Employment:* Federal Work-Study Program available. Institutional employment available. **Financial Aid Statistics:** 100% needy freshmen, 100% needy undergrads receive need-based scholarship or grant aid. 17% freshmen, 14% undergrads receive non-need-based scholarship or grant aid. 81% freshmen, 80% undergrads receive need-based self-help aid. 0% freshmen, 0% undergrads receive athletic scholarships. 98% freshmen, 98% undergrads receive any aid. Average cumulative indebtedness $27,757. **Criteria for awarding aid:** *Need-based:* Academics *Non-need-based:* Academics, Leadership, State/district residency.

ELON UNIVERSITY

100 Campus Drive, Elon, NC 27244-2010
Phone: 336-278-3566 · **Financial Aid Phone:** 336-278-7640
E-mail: admissions@elon.edu · **CEEB Code:** 5183
Fax: 336-278-7699 · **Website:** www.elon.edu · **ACT Code:** 3096

This private school was founded in 1889. It has a 636 acre campus.

RATINGS
Admissions Selectivity Rating: 86   **Fire Safety Rating:** 94   **Green Rating:** 89

STUDENTS AND FACULTY
Enrollment: 6,045. **Student Body:** 60% female, 40% male, 82% out-of-state, 2% international (58 countries represented). Asian 2%, African American 5%, Caucasian 80%, Hispanic 6%, Native American <1%, Pacific Islander <1%, Two or more races 3%, Race unknown <1%.
Retention and Graduation: 89% freshmen return for sophomore year. 78% freshmen graduate within 4 years. 84% freshmen graduate within 6 years. 26% grads go on to further study within 1 year. 7% grads pursue arts and sciences degrees. 2.3% grads pursue law degrees. 2% grads pursue business degrees. 6.3% grads pursue medical degrees. **Faculty:** Student/faculty ratio 12:1. 433 full-time faculty, 86% hold PhDs, 18% are members of minority groups, 50% are women. 0% of classes are taught by teaching assistants.

ACADEMICS
Degrees: Bachelor's; Doctoral/Professional; Master's **Most popular majors:** Communication, General; Psychology, General; Business Administration And Management, General. **Special Study Options:** Accelerated program; Cross-registration; Distance learning; Double major; Dual enrollment; English as a Second Language (ESL); Exchange student program (domestic); Honors program; Independent study; Internships; Liberal arts/career combination; Student-designed major; Study abroad; Teacher certification program. **Honors programs:** Forty first-year students are selected for the Honors Fellows program, which has benefits of specialized courses, $13,500 scholarship renewable annually based on academic performance and participation in the program, $1,000 study abroad grant, development and presentation of their honors thesis, and housing options such as a living-learning community for Fellows. **Disability Services offered to physically disabled students:** Note-taking services; Reader services; Tape recorders; Tutors. **Career services:** Alumni network; Alumni services; Career assessment; Career/job search classes; Internships; Regional alumni

FACILITIES
Housing: Apartments for single students; Coed dorms; Fraternity/sorority housing; Men's dorms; Special housing for international students; Theme housing; Wellness housing; Women's dorms 85% of campus accessible to physically disabled. **Special Academic Facilities/Equipment:** Writing resource center, multi-faith center, fine arts center with recital hall, theatre, television studios, music rooms, campus center, athletic center, art gallery. **Computers:** 100% of classrooms, 100% of dorms, 100% of libraries, 100% of dining areas, 100% of student union, 25% of common outdoor areas have wireless network access. Students can register for classes online. Administrative functions (other than registration) can be performed online.

CAMPUS LIFE
Environment: Town **Activities:** Campus Ministries; Choral groups; Concert band; Dance; Drama/theater; International Student Organization; Jazz band; Literary magazine; Marching band; Model UN; Music ensembles; Musical theater; Pep band; Radio station; Student government; Student newspaper; Student-run film society; Symphony orchestra; Television station; Yearbook 150 registered organizations, 27 honor societies, 10 religious organizations. 11 fraternities, 12 sororities. **Athletics (Intercollegiate):** *Men:* baseball, basketball, cheerleading, cross-country, football, golf, soccer, tennis. *Women:* basketball, cheerleading, cross-country, golf, soccer, softball, tennis, track/field (outdoor), track/field (indoor), volleyball. **On-Campus Highlights:** Belk Library, Rhodes Football Stadium, Koury Business Center, Moseley Student Center, Koury Athletic Center **Environmental Initiatives:** Reducing greenhouse gas emissions

ADMISSIONS
Freshman Academic Profile: Average high school GPA 4.0. 21% in top 10% of high school class, 54% in top 25% of high school class, 89% in top 50% of high school class. 60% from public high schools. **Test Scores:** SAT Math middle 50% range 560-660. SAT EBRW middle 50% range 580-670. ACT

middle 50% range 25-29. Minimum internet-based TOEFL 80. Minimum paper TOEFL 550. **Basis for Candidate Selection:** *Very important factors considered include:* rigor of secondary school record, academic GPA, application essay, standardized test scores, recommendation(s). *Important factors considered include:* extracurricular activities, talent/ability, alumni/ae relation, volunteer work, work experience. *Other factors considered include:* class rank, character/personal qualities, first generation, geographical residence, state residency, racial/ethnic status, level of applicant's interest. **Freshman Admission Requirements:** High school diploma is required and GED is accepted *Academic units required:* 4 English, 3 math, 3 science, 1 science labs, 2 foreign language, 2 social studies, 1 history, *Academic units recommended:* 4 English, 4 math, 3 science, 1 science labs, 3 foreign language, 2 social studies, 1 history. **Freshman Admission Statistics:** 9,623 applied, 66.5% admitted, 25% enrolled. **Transfer Admission Requirements:** High school transcript, college transcript(s), standardized test scores, statement of good standing from prior institution(s). Minimum college GPA of 2.7 required. Lowest grade transferable C-. **General Admission Information:** Application fee $50. Priority deadline 11/10. Regular application deadline 1/10. Nonfall registration accepted. Admission may be deferred for a maximum of 1 year.

COSTS AND FINANCIAL AID
Annual tuition $33,829. Required fees $444. Average book expense $900. **Required Forms and Deadlines:** CSS/Financial Aid PROFILE; FAFSA. **Notification of Awards:** Applicants will be notified of awards on a rolling basis beginning 1/31. **Types of Aid:** *Need-based scholarships/grants:* College/university scholarship or grant aid from institutional funds; Federal Pell; Private scholarships; SEOG; State scholarships/grants; United Negro College Fund. *Loans:* Direct PLUS loans; Direct Subsidized Stafford Loans; Direct Unsubsidized Stafford Loans. *Student Employment:* Federal Work-Study Program available. Institutional employment available. **Financial Aid Statistics:** 86% needy freshmen, 90% needy undergrads receive need-based scholarship or grant aid. 44% freshmen, 46% undergrads receive non-need-based scholarship or grant aid. 79% freshmen, 80% undergrads receive need-based self-help aid. 4% freshmen, 5% undergrads receive athletic scholarships. 63% freshmen, 61% undergrads receive any aid. 42% undergrads borrow to pay for school. Average cumulative indebtedness $30,170. **Criteria for awarding aid:** *Need-based:* Religious affiliation *Non-need-based:* Academics, Alumni affiliation, Art, Athletics, Leadership, Music/drama, Religious affiliation.

EMBRY-RIDDLE AERONAUTICAL UNIVERSITY (FL)

600 South Clyde Morris Boulevard, Daytona Beach, FL 32114-3900
Phone: 386-226-6100 · **Financial Aid Phone:** 800-226-6307
E-mail: dbadmit@erau.edu · **CEEB Code:** 5190
Fax: 386-226-7070 · **Website:** https://daytonabeach.erau.edu · **ACT Code:** 725

This private school was founded in 1926. It has a 185 acre campus.

RATINGS
Admissions Selectivity Rating: 83   **Fire Safety Rating:** 94   **Green Rating:** 61

STUDENTS AND FACULTY
Enrollment: 5,689. **Student Body:** 22% female, 78% male, 64% out-of-state, 12% international (100 countries represented). Asian 5%, African American 5%, Caucasian 56%, Hispanic 7%, Native American <1%, Pacific Islander <1%, Two or more races 7%, Race unknown 7%.
Retention and Graduation: 80% freshmen return for sophomore year. 29% freshmen graduate within 4 years. 59% freshmen graduate within 6 years. 28% grads go on to further study within 1 year. 0% grads pursue arts and sciences degrees. 5% grads pursue business degrees. **Faculty:** Student/faculty ratio 15:1. 324 full-time faculty, 76% hold PhDs, 14% are members of minority groups, 26% are women. 0% of classes are taught by teaching assistants.

ACADEMICS
Degrees: Associate; Bachelor's; Doctoral/Research; Master's **Classes:** Most classes have 10-19 students. Most lab/discussion sessions have fewer than 10 students. **Most popular majors:** Aerospace, Aeronautical And Astronautical/Space Engineering; Mechanical Engineering; Airline/Commercial/Professional Pilot And Flight Crew. **Special Study Options:** Accelerated program; Cooperative education program; Double major; Dual enrollment; English as a Second Language (ESL); Exchange student program (domestic); Honors program; Internships; Student-designed major; Study abroad. **Honors programs:** The Embry-Riddle Honors Program is highly selective, offering its student members enriched educational experiences. Emphasizing Honors course work in General Education and in the majors, the Program involves

selected faculty who develop innovative courses and establish mentoring relationships with students. The Program is designed to attract and retain top students and to develop their communicative, analytical, critical, and research skills, nurturing a love of life-long learning, leadership, and service. **Disability Services offered to physically disabled students:** Reader services; Tape recorders. **Career services:** Alumni network; Alumni services; Career assessment; Career/job search classes; Internships

FACILITIES

Housing: Coed dorms 95% of campus accessible to physically diasbled. **Special Academic Facilities/Equipment:** Advanced Flight Simulation Center; Fleet Maintenance Hangar; Flight Operations Center; Next Gen Test Bed facility; Advanced Vehicles Green Garage; Eagle Flight Research Center; Wind Tunnel Laboratory; Eagle Fitness Center, Swimming Pool, ICI Center & Outdoor Sports Facilities. **Computers:** 100% of classrooms, 100% of dorms, 100% of libraries, 100% of dining areas, 100% of student union, 15% of common outdoor areas have wireless network access. Students can register for classes online. Administrative functions (other than registration) can be performed online.

CAMPUS LIFE

Environment: Town **Activities:** Campus Ministries; Choral groups; International Student Organization; Model UN; Pep band; Radio station; Student government; Student newspaper; Student-run film society 140 registered organizations, 12 honor societies, 5 religious organizations. 12 fraternities, 4 sororities. **Athletics (Intercollegiate):** *Men:* baseball, basketball, cheerleading, cross-country, golf, soccer, softball, tennis, track/field (outdoor), volleyball. *Women:* basketball, cheerleading, cross-country, golf, soccer, softball, tennis, track/field (outdoor), volleyball. **On-Campus Highlights:** Hagedorn Aviation Complex, Lehman Engineering and Technology Center, New 1-meter Ritchey-Chretien reflecting telescope (COAS), Advanced Vehicles Green Garage, ICI Center (fieldhouse) and University (Student) Ctr **Environmental Initiatives:** Embry-Riddle Opens 'Green Garage' Doors: EcoCAR Project Advances University's Environmental Commitment Daytona Beach, Fla., Dec. 10, 2009 — Embry-Riddle Aeronautical University has opened the doors of a new "green garage," where engineering students are using aerospace techniques to develop the car of tomorrow. The garage includes a rotary vehicle lift, dedicated high-voltage room, and integrated hardware-in-the-loop laboratory donated by National Instruments. It also showcases an environmental focus at Embry-Riddle's College of Engineering. Every component in the lab was chosen to reduce environmental impact, including the floor covering, which is made from recycled tires. Interior design students from Daytona State College assisted in designing the new facility. http://givingto.erau.edu/givingnews/09releases/ecocar.html

ADMISSIONS

Freshman Academic Profile: Average high school GPA 3.7. 23% in top 10% of high school class, 50% in top 25% of high school class, 83% in top 50% of high school class. **Test Scores:** SAT Math middle 50% range 540-670. SAT EBRW middle 50% range 540-650. ACT middle 50% range 22-28. Minimum internet-based TOEFL 79. Minimum paper TOEFL 550. **Basis for Candidate Selection:** *Very important factors considered include:* standardized test scores. *Important factors considered include:* rigor of secondary school record, class rank, academic GPA, application essay, recommendation(s). *Other factors considered include:* interview, extracurricular activities, alumni/ae relation, work experience. **Freshman Admission Requirements:** High school diploma is required and GED is accepted *Academic units required:* 4 English, 3 math, 2 science, 1 science labs, 3 social studies, *Academic units recommended:* 4 English, 4 math, 3 science, 1 science labs, 3 social studies. **Freshman Admission Statistics:** 4,564 applied, 74.9% admitted, 40% enrolled. **Transfer Admission Requirements:** college transcript(s), Minimum college GPA of 2.0 required. Lowest grade transferable C. **General Admission Information:** Application fee $50. Priority deadline 3/1. Nonfall registration accepted. Admission may be deferred for a maximum of 1 year.

COSTS AND FINANCIAL AID

Annual tuition $34,292. Room and board $10,826. Required fees $1,422. Average book expense $1,400. **Required Forms and Deadlines:** FAFSA. **Types of Aid:** *Need-based scholarships/grants:* College/university scholarship or grant aid from institutional funds; Federal Pell; Private scholarships; SEOG; State scholarships/grants. *Loans:* Direct PLUS loans; Direct Subsidized Stafford Loans; Direct Unsubsidized Stafford Loans. *Student Employment:* Federal Work-Study Program available. Institutional employment available. **Criteria for awarding aid:** *Need-based:* Academics, Alumni affiliation, Athletics, Leadership.

EMBRY RIDDLE AERONAUTICAL UNIVERSITY— PRESCOTT

3700 Willow Creek, Prescott, AZ 86301
Phone: (928) 777-6600 • **Financial Aid Phone:** 928-777-3765
E-mail: prescott@erau.edu • **CEEB Code:** 4305
Fax: (928) 777-6606 • **Website:** www.prescott.erau.edu • **ACT Code:** 725

This private school was founded in 1926. It has a 539 acre campus.

RATINGS

Admissions Selectivity Rating: 84   **Fire Safety Rating:** 76   **Green Rating:** 60*

STUDENTS AND FACULTY

Enrollment: 2,598. **Student Body:** 24% female, 76% male, 77% out-of-state, 7% international (31 countries represented). Asian 6%, African American 2%, Caucasian 62%, Hispanic 6%, Native American <1%, Pacific Islander 1%, Two or more races 10%, Race unknown 7%.
Retention and Graduation: 87% freshmen return for sophomore year. 32% freshmen graduate within 4 years. 60% freshmen graduate within 6 years. 21% grads go on to further study within 1 year. 3% grads pursue arts and sciences degrees. 3% grads pursue business degrees. **Faculty:** Student/faculty ratio 17:1. 120 full-time faculty, 78% hold PhDs, 13% are members of minority groups, 24% are women. 0% of classes are taught by teaching assistants.

ACADEMICS

Degrees: Bachelor's; Master's **Classes:** Most classes have 10-19 students. Most lab/discussion sessions have 10-19 students. **Most popular majors:** Aerospace, Aeronautical And Astronautical/Space Engineering; International Relations And Affairs; Airline/Commercial/Professional Pilot And Flight Crew. **Special Study Options:** Cooperative education program; Double major; Dual enrollment; English as a Second Language (ESL); Honors program; Internships; Study abroad. **Honors programs:** The Honors Program at Embry-Riddle, Prescott is highly selective, offering students an enriched educational experience focused on leadership, research, and ethics, while also giving them opportunities to enhance campus and community life for others. Honors Program students enroll in three Honors Seminars, complete Honors directed research, and participate in the Honors Student Association service, community, and professional development events. Graduates of the Honors Program are models of academic excellence and student leadership. **Disability Services offered to physically disabled students:** Reader services; Tape recorders. **Career services:** Alumni network; Alumni services; Career assessment; Career/job search classes; Internships; Regional alumni

FACILITIES

Housing: Coed dorms 80% of campus accessible to physically diasbled. **Computers:** 100% of classrooms, 100% of dorms, 100% of libraries, 100% of dining areas, 100% of student union, 80% of common outdoor areas have wireless network access. Administrative functions (other than registration) can be performed online.

CAMPUS LIFE

Environment: Town **Activities:** Campus Ministries; Choral groups; International Student Organization; Model UN; Music ensembles; Radio station; Student government; Student newspaper; Student-run film society 85 registered organizations, 5 honor societies, 2 religious organizations. 5 fraternities, 3 sororities. **Athletics (Intercollegiate):** *Men:* wrestling. **On-Campus Highlights:** Flight Line Facilities, Wind Tunnel Labs, Outdoor Pool and Racquetball,Tennis Area, The Hangar—Cafeteria, Two athletic facilities and weight room

ADMISSIONS

Freshman Academic Profile: Average high school GPA 3.7. 25% in top 10% of high school class, 55% in top 25% of high school class, 82% in top 50% of high school class. **Test Scores:** SAT Math middle 50% range 570-680. SAT EBRW middle 50% range 560-670. ACT middle 50% range 23-29. Minimum internet-based TOEFL 79. Minimum paper TOEFL 550. **Basis for Candidate Selection:** *Very important factors considered include:* standardized test scores. *Important factors considered include:* rigor of secondary school record, class rank, academic GPA, application essay, recommendation(s). *Other factors considered include:* interview, extracurricular activities, alumni/ae relation, work experience. **Freshman Admission Requirements:** High school diploma is required and GED is accepted *Academic units required:* 4 English, 3 math, 2 science, 1 science labs, 2 social studies, *Academic units recommended:* 4 English, 4 math, 3 science, 1 science labs, 2 social studies. **Freshman Admission Statistics:** 2,168 applied, 76.5% admitted, 41% enrolled. **Transfer Admission Requirements:** college transcript(s). **General Admission Information:** Application fee $50. Priority deadline 3/1. Nonfall registration accepted. Admission may be deferred for a maximum of 1 year.

COSTS AND FINANCIAL AID

Annual tuition $34,392. Room and board $11,394. Required fees $1,433. Average book expense $1,400. **Required Forms and Deadlines:** FAFSA. **Types of Aid:** *Need-based scholarships/grants:* College/university scholarship or grant aid from institutional funds; Federal Pell; Private scholarships; SEOG; State scholarships/grants. *Loans:* Direct PLUS loans; Direct Subsidized Stafford Loans; Direct Unsubsidized Stafford Loans. *Student Employment:* Federal Work-Study Program available. Institutional employment available. **Criteria for awarding aid:** *Need-based:* Academics, Athletics, Leadership.

See page 930.

EMBRY RIDDLE AERONAUTICAL UNIVERSITY—WORLDWIDE

600 S. Clyde Morris Blvd., Daytona Beach, FL 32114
E-mail: worldwide@erau.edu
Website: https://worldwide.erau.edu

This is a private school.

RATINGS

Admissions Selectivity Rating: 71   **Fire Safety Rating:** 60*   **Green Rating:** 60*

STUDENTS AND FACULTY

Enrollment: 11,433. **Student Body:** 12% female, 88% male, 3% international. Asian 4%, African American 8%, Caucasian 55%, Hispanic 9%, Native American 1%, Pacific Islander 1%, Two or more races 6%, Race unknown 14%. **Retention and Graduation:** 20% freshmen graduate within 4 years. 25% freshmen graduate within 6 years. **Faculty:** 113 full-time faculty, 78% hold PhDs, 10% are members of minority groups, 36% are women.

ACADEMICS

Degrees: Associate; Bachelor's; Certificate; Doctoral/Research; Master's **Special Study Options:** Accelerated program; Cooperative education program; Distance learning; Independent study; Study abroad; Weekend college.

ADMISSIONS

Basis for Candidate Selection: *Important factors considered include:* rigor of secondary school record, class rank, academic GPA, application essay, standardized test scores, recommendation(s). *Other factors considered include:* work experience. **Freshman Admission Requirements:** High school diploma is required and GED is accepted **Freshman Admission Statistics:** 1,225 applied, 65.1% admitted, 75% enrolled. **General Admission Information:** Application fee $50. Nonfall registration accepted. Admission may be deferred for a maximum of 1 year.

COSTS AND FINANCIAL AID

Required Forms and Deadlines: FAFSA. **Types of Aid:** *Need-based scholarships/grants:* College/university scholarship or grant aid from institutional funds; Federal Pell; Private scholarships; SEOG; State scholarships/grants. *Loans:* Direct PLUS loans; Direct Subsidized Stafford Loans; Direct Unsubsidized Stafford Loans.

EMERSON COLLEGE

Best Colleges

120 Boylston Street, Boston, MA 02116-4624
Phone: 617-824-8600 · **Financial Aid Phone:** 617-824-8655
E-mail: admission@emerson.edu · **CEEB Code:** 3367
Fax: 617-824-8609 · **Website:** www.emerson.edu · **ACT Code:** 1820

This private school was founded in 1880. It has a 10 acre campus.

RATINGS

Admissions Selectivity Rating: 90   **Fire Safety Rating:** 94   **Green Rating:** 99

STUDENTS AND FACULTY

Enrollment: 3,799. **Student Body:** 59% female, 41% male, 79% out-of-state, 9% international (60 countries represented). Asian 5%, African American 3%, Caucasian 65%, Hispanic 12%, Native American 1%, Pacific Islander 1%, Two or more races 4%, Race unknown 2%.
Retention and Graduation: 88% freshmen return for sophomore year. 77% freshmen graduate within 4 years. 81% freshmen graduate within 6 years. 10% grads go on to further study within 1 year. **Faculty:** Student/faculty ratio 13:1. 202 full-time faculty, 71% hold PhDs, 15% are members of minority groups, 43% are women. 3% of classes are taught by teaching assistants.

ACADEMICS

Degrees: Bachelor's; Master's **Classes:** Most classes have 10-19 students. Most lab/discussion sessions have 10-19 students. **Most popular majors:** Theatre/Theater; Cinematography And Film/Video Production. **Special Study Options:** Cross-registration; Double major; Honors program; Independent study; Internships; Liberal arts/career combination; Student-designed major; Study abroad; Teacher certification program. **Combined degree programs:** BA/MA. **Disability Services offered to physically disabled students:** Note-taking services; Reader services; Tape recorders; Tutors. **Career services:** Alumni network; Alumni services; Career assessment; Career/job search classes; Internships; Regional alumni

FACILITIES

Housing: Coed dorms; Theme housing; Wellness housing 90% of campus accessible to physically disabled. **Special Academic Facilities/Equipment:** The historic, 1,200-seat Cutler Majestic Theatre; 11-story Tufte Performance & Production Center (housing sound-treated television studios, makeup lab, costume shop, and theatre design/tech center); WERS-FM, Boston's oldest noncommercial radio station; Levy Marketing Suite; Journalism digital newsroom and broadcasting studio; Robbins Speech, Language & Hearing Center (one of on-campus seven facilities to observe speech and hearing therapy); and newly renovated Paramount Center (housing a 600-seat theater, scene shop, sound stage, and film screening room). **Computers:** 100% of classrooms, 100% of dorms, 100% of libraries, 100% of dining areas, 100% of student union, 100% of common outdoor areas have wireless network access. Students can register for classes online. Administrative functions (other than registration) can be performed online.

CAMPUS LIFE

Environment: Metropolis **Activities:** Campus Ministries; Choral groups; Dance; Drama/theater; International Student Organization; Literary magazine; Model UN; Music ensembles; Musical theater; Radio station; Student government; Student newspaper; Student-run film society; Television station; Yearbook 60 registered organizations, 4 honor societies, 4 religious organizations. 4 fraternities, 3 sororities. **Athletics (Intercollegiate):** *Men:* baseball, basketball, cross-country, golf, lacrosse, soccer, tennis, track/field (indoor), volleyball. *Women:* basketball, cross-country, golf, lacrosse, soccer, softball, tennis, track/field (indoor), volleyball. **On-Campus Highlights:** WERS-FM (Boston's oldest public radio), Historic Cutler Majestic Theatre, Tufte Performance and Production Center, Journalism's Integrated Digital Newsroom, Piano Row Residence Hall/College Center **Environmental Initiatives:** 3 LEED certified buildings (Colonial Building, Piano Row, and Emerson Los Angeles).

ADMISSIONS

Freshman Academic Profile: Average high school GPA 3.7. 28% in top 10% of high school class, 71% in top 25% of high school class, 95% in top 50% of high school class. **Test Scores:** SAT Math middle 50% range 580-660. SAT EBRW middle 50% range 620-700. ACT middle 50% range 26-30. Minimum internet-based TOEFL 80. Minimum paper TOEFL 550. **Basis for Candidate Selection:** *Very important factors considered include:* academic GPA, application essay. *Important factors considered include:* rigor of secondary school record, class rank, recommendation(s), extracurricular activities, talent/ability, character/personal qualities. *Other factors considered include:* standardized test scores, first generation, alumni/ae relation, geographical residence, racial/ethnic status, volunteer work, work experience. **Freshman Admission Requirements:** High school diploma is required and GED is accepted *Academic units required:* 4 English, 3 math, 3 science, 3 foreign language, 3 social studies, *Academic units recommended:* 4 English, 3 math, 3 science, 3 foreign language, 3 social studies, 4 academic electives. **Freshman Admission Statistics:** 10,360 applied, 46.1% admitted, 20% enrolled. **Transfer Admission Requirements:** High school transcript, college transcript(s), essay or personal statement, statement of good standing from prior institution(s). Minimum college GPA of 3.0 required. Lowest grade transferable C. **General Admission Information:** Application fee $65. Regular application deadline 1/15. Nonfall registration accepted. Admission may be deferred for a maximum of 1 year.

COSTS AND FINANCIAL AID

Annual tuition $46,016. Room and board $17,690. Required fees $836. Average book expense $1,150. **Required Forms and Deadlines:** Business/Farm Supplement; CSS/Financial Aid PROFILE; FAFSA; Noncustodial PROFILE. **Notification of Awards:** Applicants will be notified of awards on or about 4/1. **Types of Aid:** *Need-based scholarships/grants:* College/university scholarship or grant aid from institutional funds; Federal Pell; Private scholarships; SEOG; State scholarships/grants. *Loans:* Direct PLUS loans; Direct Subsidized Stafford Loans; Direct Unsubsidized Stafford Loans. *Student Employment:* Federal Work-Study Program available. Institutional employment available. **Financial Aid Statistics:** 91% needy freshmen, 87% needy undergrads receive need-based scholarship or grant aid. 23% freshmen, 15% undergrads receive non-need-based scholarship or grant aid. 94% freshmen, 96% undergrads receive need-based self-help aid. 0% freshmen, 0% undergrads receive athletic scholarships. **Criteria for awarding aid:** *Need-based:* Academics, Music/drama *Non-need-based:* Academics, Leadership, Music/drama, State/district residency.

EMILY CARR UNIVERSITY OF ART + DESIGN

1399 Johnston Street, Vancouver, BC V6H 3R9
Phone: 604-844-3897 · **Financial Aid Phone:** 1-604-844-3844
E-mail: admissions@ecuad.ca
Fax: 604-844-3089 · **Website:** www.ecuad.ca

This public school was founded in 1925.

RATINGS
Admissions Selectivity Rating: 71   **Fire Safety Rating:** 60*   **Green Rating:** 60*

STUDENTS AND FACULTY
Student Body: 32% out-of-state, (53 countries represented).
Retention and Graduation: 85% freshmen return for sophomore year.
Faculty: 0% of classes are taught by teaching assistants.

ACADEMICS
Degrees: Bachelor's; Master's **Classes:** Most classes have fewer than 10 students. Most lab/discussion sessions have 10-19 students. **Most popular majors:** Design And Visual Communications, General; Industrial And Product Design; Fine And Studio Arts. **Special Study Options:** Cooperative education program; Cross-registration; Distance learning; Exchange student program (domestic); External degree program; Independent study; Internships; Liberal arts/career combination; Student-designed major; Study abroad. **Disability Services offered to physically disabled students:** Note-taking services; Reader services; Tape recorders; Tutors. **Career services:** Alumni network; Alumni services; Career assessment; Career/job search classes; Internships; Regional alumni

FACILITIES
Housing: 100% of campus accessible to physically disabled. **Special Academic Facilities/Equipment:** Two Galleries A Centre for Art and Technology

CAMPUS LIFE
Environment: Metropolis **Activities:** International Student Organization; Student government; Student newspaper; Student-run film society; Yearbook 12 registered organizations.

ADMISSIONS
Freshman Academic Profile: 85% from public high schools. Minimum internet-based TOEFL 84. Minimum paper TOEFL 570. **Basis for Candidate Selection:** *Very important factors considered include:* talent/ability, character/personal qualities, level of applicant's interest. *Important factors considered include:* rigor of secondary school record, academic GPA. *Other factors considered include:* extracurricular activities, volunteer work, work experience. **Freshman Admission Requirements:** High school diploma is required and GED is not accepted *Academic units required:* 3 English, 6 academic electives, 6 visual/performing arts. **Freshman Admission Statistics:** 1,112 applied, 57.3% admitted, 65% enrolled. **Transfer Admission Requirements:** college transcript(s), essay or personal statement, statement of good standing from prior institution(s). Minimum college GPA of 2.0 required. Lowest grade transferable C. **General Admission Information:** Application fee $70. Regular application deadline 2/1. Nonfall registration accepted. Admission may be deferred for a maximum of one year.

COSTS AND FINANCIAL AID
Required fees $935. Average book expense $3,000. *Student Employment:* Institutional employment available.

EMMANUEL COLLEGE

400 The Fenway, Boston, MA 02115
Phone: 617-735-9715 · **Financial Aid Phone:** 617-735-9938
E-mail: enroll@emmanuel.edu · **CEEB Code:** 3368
Fax: 617-735-9801 · **Website:** www.emmanuel.edu · **ACT Code:** 1822

This private school, affiliated with the Roman Catholic Church, was founded in 1919. It has a 17 acre campus.

RATINGS
Admissions Selectivity Rating: 78   **Fire Safety Rating:** 99   **Green Rating:** 73

STUDENTS AND FACULTY
Enrollment: 1,848. **Student Body:** 73% female, 27% male, 42% out-of-state, 1% international (51 countries represented). Asian 4%, African American 5%, Caucasian 71%, Hispanic 10%, Native American <1%, Pacific Islander <1%, Two or more races 4%, Race unknown 4%.
Retention and Graduation: 78% freshmen return for sophomore year. 58% freshmen graduate within 4 years. 66% freshmen graduate within 6 years. 19% grads go on to further study within 1 year. **Faculty:** Student/faculty ratio 13:1. 90 full-time faculty, 88% hold PhDs, 18% are members of minority groups, 61% are women. 0% of classes are taught by teaching assistants.

ACADEMICS
Degrees: Bachelor's; Master's; Post-Bachelor's certificate; Post-Master's certificate **Classes:** Most classes have 10-19 students. Most lab/discussion sessions have 10-19 students. **Most popular majors:** Biology/Biological Sciences, General; Counseling Psychology; Business Administration And Management, General. **Special Study Options:** Accelerated program; Cross-registration; Distance learning; Double major; Honors program; Independent study; Internships; Liberal arts/career combination; Student-designed major; Study abroad; Teacher certification program. **Honors programs:** Disability **Services offered to physically disabled students:** Note-taking services; Reader services; Tape recorders; Tutors. **Career services:** Alumni network; Alumni services; Career assessment; Career/job search classes; Internships

FACILITIES
Housing: Coed dorms; Theme housing 100% of campus accessible to physically disabled. **Computers:** Students can register for classes online. Administrative functions (other than registration) can be performed online.

CAMPUS LIFE
Environment: Metropolis **Activities:** Campus Ministries; Choral groups; Dance; Drama/theater; Jazz band; Literary magazine; Model UN; Music ensembles; Musical theater; Pep band; Radio station; Student government; Student newspaper; Symphony orchestra 48 registered organizations, 11 honor societies. **Athletics (Intercollegiate):** *Men:* basketball, cross-country, golf, soccer, track/field (outdoor), track/field (indoor), volleyball. *Women:* basketball, cross-country, lacrosse, soccer, softball, tennis, track/field (outdoor), track/field (indoor), volleyball. **On-Campus Highlights:** Jean Yawkey Student Center, Cardinal Cushing Library, Roberto Clemente Field, Notre Dame Campus, Muddy River Cafe **Environmental Initiatives:** Significant reduction of the College's solid waste stream through introduction of single-stream recycling and composting programs.

ADMISSIONS
Freshman Academic Profile: Average high school GPA 3.7. 74% from public high schools. **Test Scores:** SAT Math middle 50% range 530-610. SAT EBRW middle 50% range 560-640. ACT middle 50% range 24-29. Minimum internet-based TOEFL 79. Minimum paper TOEFL 550. **Basis for Candidate Selection:** *Very important factors considered include:* rigor of secondary school record, academic GPA, application essay, recommendation(s). *Important factors considered include:* extracurricular activities, character/personal qualities, volunteer work.level of applicant's interest. *Other factors considered include:* class rank, standardized test scores, interview, talent/ability, first generation, alumni/ae relation, geographical residence, religious affiliation/commitment, work experience. **Freshman Admission Requirements:** High school diploma is required and GED is accepted *Academic units required:* 4 English, 3 math, 3 science, 2 science labs, 3 foreign language, 3 social studies. **Freshman Admission Statistics:** 5,965 applied, 73.0% admitted, 11% enrolled. **Transfer Admission Requirements:** High school transcript, college transcript(s), essay or personal statement, standardized test scores, statement of good standing from prior institution(s). Minimum college GPA of n/a required. Lowest grade transferable C. **General Admission Information:** Application fee $60. Priority deadline 11/1. Regular application deadline 2/15. Nonfall registration accepted. Admission may be deferred for a maximum of one year.

COSTS AND FINANCIAL AID
Annual tuition $39,544. Room and board $14,994. Required fees $260. Average book expense $880. **Required Forms and Deadlines:** FAFSA. **Notification of Awards:** Applicants will be notified of awards on a rolling

College Directory   **227** basis beginning 2/1. **Types of Aid:** *Need-based scholarships/grants:* College/university scholarship or grant aid from institutional funds; Federal Pell; Private scholarships; SEOG; State scholarships/grants. *Loans:* Direct PLUS loans; Direct Subsidized Stafford Loans; Direct Unsubsidized Stafford Loans. *Student Employment:* Federal Work-Study Program available. Institutional employment available. **Financial Aid Statistics:** 100% needy freshmen, 100% needy undergrads receive need-based scholarship or grant aid. 100% freshmen, 98% undergrads receive non-need-based scholarship or grant aid. 83% freshmen, 83% undergrads receive need-based self-help aid. 0% freshmen, 0% undergrads receive athletic scholarships. 99% freshmen receive any aid. 84% undergrads borrow to pay for school. Average cumulative indebtedness $36,818. **Criteria for awarding aid:** *Non-need-based:* Academics, Alumni affiliation, Leadership.

EMORY AND HENRY COLLEGE

1 Garnand Drive, Emory, VA 24327
Phone: 276-944-6133 · **Financial Aid Phone:** 866-794-0010
E-mail: ehadmiss@ehc.edu · **CEEB Code:** 5185
Fax: 276-944-6935 · **Website:** http://www.ehc.edu · **ACT Code:** 4350

This private school, affiliated with the Methodist Church, was founded in 1836. It has a 331 acre campus.

RATINGS
Admissions Selectivity Rating: 78   **Fire Safety Rating:** 60*   **Green Rating:** 60*

STUDENTS AND FACULTY
Enrollment: 900. **Student Body:** 47% female, 53% male, 36% out-of-state, 1% international (5 countries represented). Asian <1%, African American 10%, Caucasian 80%, Hispanic 2%, Native American <1%, Pacific Islander 0%, Two or more races 2%, Race unknown 4%.
Retention and Graduation: 74% freshmen return for sophomore year. 37% grads go on to further study within 1 year. 24% grads pursue arts and sciences degrees. 31% grads pursue law degrees. 23% grads pursue business degrees. 12% grads pursue medical degrees. **Faculty:** Student/faculty ratio 10:1. 72 full-time faculty, 82% hold PhDs, 10% are members of minority groups, 49% are women. 0% of classes are taught by teaching assistants.

ACADEMICS
Degrees: Bachelor's; Master's **Most popular majors:** Education, General; Pre-Medicine/Pre-Medical Studies; Business Administration And Management, General. **Special Study Options:** Accelerated program; Double major; External degree program; Honors program; Independent study; Liberal arts/career combination; Student-designed major; Study abroad; Teacher certification program. **Combined degree programs:** BA/MA. **Disability Services offered to physically disabled students:** Reader services; Tape recorders; Tutors. **Career services:** Career assessment; Career/job search classes; Internships

FACILITIES
Housing: Coed dorms; Men's dorms; Special housing for disabled student; Theme housing; Wellness housing; Women's dorms **Special Academic Facilities/Equipment:** Language lab, capillary gas chromatograph, DNA vertical slab gel electrophoretic equipment, infrared spectrophotometer. Theatre Studio, Art gallery. **Computers:** 100% of classrooms, 100% of dorms, 100% of libraries, 100% of dining areas, 100% of student union, 100% of common outdoor areas have wireless network access.

CAMPUS LIFE
Environment: Rural **Activities:** Campus Ministries; Choral groups; Concert band; Dance; Drama/theater; International Student Organization; Literary magazine; Music ensembles; Musical theater; Opera; Pep band; Radio station; Student government; Student newspaper; Television station; Yearbook 53 registered organizations, 7 honor societies, 4 religious organizations. 7 fraternities, 6 sororities. **Athletics (Intercollegiate):** *Men:* baseball, basketball, cross-country, football, golf, soccer, tennis. *Women:* basketball, cross-country, soccer, softball, swimming, tennis, volleyball. **On-Campus Highlights:** McGlothlin-Street Hall (new science buil, Memorial Chapel, Byars Hall (Arts, Music, and Theatre), King Athletic Center, Emory Mercantile (campus bookstore) **Environmental Initiatives:** Recycling is now in full swing, with a widespread distribution of recycling bins for paper, cardboard, aluminum, plastics and steel. There are thirty bins specially made for the college from sustainably-harvested local poplar. We have already reduced our trash volume significantly. We are a participant in the national Recyclemania competition, in the waste minimization category.

ADMISSIONS
Freshman Academic Profile: Average high school GPA 3.5. 20% in top 10% of high school class, 45% in top 25% of high school class, 80% in top 50% of high school class. 92% from public high schools. **Test Scores:** SAT Math middle 50% range 445-560. SAT EBRW middle 50% range 430-555. ACT middle 50% range 19-26. Minimum paper TOEFL 550. **Basis for Candidate Selection:** *Very important factors considered include:* rigor of secondary school record, academic GPA, recommendation(s), character/personal qualities, level of applicant's interest. *Important factors considered include:* application essay, standardized test scores, interview, extracurricular activities, talent/ability, geographical residence, state residency, volunteer work. *Other factors considered include:* class rank, first generation, alumni/ae relation, religious affiliation/commitment, racial/ethnic status, work experience. **Freshman Admission Requirements:** High school diploma is required and GED is accepted *Academic units required:* 4 English, 3 math, 2 science, 2 science labs, 2 foreign language, 2 social studies, *Academic units recommended:* 1 visual/performing arts. **Freshman Admission Statistics:** 1,217 applied, 72.1% admitted, 28% enrolled. **Transfer Admission Requirements:** High school transcript, college transcript(s), statement of good standing from prior institution(s). Minimum college GPA of 2.5 required. Lowest grade transferable C. **General Admission Information:** Nonfall registration accepted. Admission may be deferred for a maximum of 1 year.

COSTS AND FINANCIAL AID
Annual tuition $23,860. Room and board $7,980. Average book expense $800. **Required Forms and Deadlines:** FAFSA; State aid form. **Notification of Awards:** Applicants will be notified of awards on a rolling basis beginning 3/1. **Types of Aid:** *Need-based scholarships/grants:* College/university scholarship or grant aid from institutional funds; Federal Pell; Private scholarships; SEOG; State scholarships/grants. **Financial Aid Statistics:** 80% needy freshmen, 87% needy undergrads receive need-based scholarship or grant aid. 20% freshmen, 13% undergrads receive non-need-based scholarship or grant aid. 70% freshmen, 0% undergrads receive need-based self-help aid. 0% freshmen, 0% undergrads receive athletic scholarships. **Criteria for awarding aid:** *Non-need-based:* Academics, Art, Music/drama, Religious affiliation, State/district residency.

EMORY UNIVERSITY

201 Dowman Drive, Atlanta, GA 30322
Phone: 404-727-6036 · **Financial Aid Phone:** 404-727-6039
E-mail: admiss@emory.edu · **CEEB Code:** 5186
Fax: 404-727-4303 · **Website:** www.emory.edu · **ACT Code:** 851

This private school, affiliated with the Methodist Church, was founded in 1836. It has a 630 acre campus.

RATINGS
Admissions Selectivity Rating: 98   **Fire Safety Rating:** 83   **Green Rating:** 95

STUDENTS AND FACULTY
Enrollment: 6,776. **Student Body:** 59% female, 41% male, 78% out-of-state, 16% international (79 countries represented). Asian 20%, African American 8%, Caucasian 41%, Hispanic 9%, Native American <1%, Pacific Islander <1%, Two or more races 4%, Race unknown 2%.
Retention and Graduation: 93% freshmen return for sophomore year. 82% freshmen graduate within 4 years. 91% freshmen graduate within 6 years. 43% grads go on to further study within 1 year. 22% grads pursue arts and sciences degrees. 16% grads pursue law degrees. 0% grads pursue business degrees. 49% grads pursue medical degrees. **Faculty:** Student/faculty ratio 9:1. 1,066 full-time faculty, 96% hold PhDs, 21% are members of minority groups, 41% are women. 10% of classes are taught by teaching assistants.

ACADEMICS
Degrees: Bachelor's; Doctoral; Doctoral/Professional; Doctoral/Research; Master's; Post-Bachelor's certificate; Post-Master's certificate **Classes:** Most classes have fewer than 10 students. Most lab/discussion sessions have 10-19 students. **Most popular majors:** Biology/Biological Sciences, General; Registered Nursing/Registered Nurse; Business Administration And Management, General. **Special Study Options:** Cooperative education program; Cross-registration; Double major; Dual enrollment; English as a Second Language (ESL); Honors program; Independent study; Internships; Liberal arts/career combination; Study abroad. **Combined degree programs:**

BA/MA. **Disability Services offered to physically disabled students:** Note-taking services; Reader services; Tape recorders; Tutors. **Career services:** Alumni network; Alumni services; Career assessment; Career/job search classes; Internships; Regional alumni

FACILITIES

Housing: Apartments for single students; Coed dorms; Fraternity/sorority housing; Theme housing 90% of campus accessible to physically diasbled. **Computers:** Students can register for classes online. Administrative functions (other than registration) can be performed online.

CAMPUS LIFE

Environment: City **Activities:** Campus Ministries; Choral groups; Concert band; Dance; Drama/theater; International Student Organization; Jazz band; Literary magazine; Model UN; Music ensembles; Musical theater; Opera; Radio station; Student government; Student newspaper; Student-run film society; Symphony orchestra; Television station 51 registered organizations, 30 honor societies, 27 religious organizations. 14 fraternities, 12 sororities. **Athletics (Intercollegiate):** *Men:* baseball, basketball, cross-country, diving, golf, soccer, swimming, tennis, track/field (outdoor). *Women:* basketball, cross-country, diving, soccer, softball, swimming, tennis, track/field (outdoor), volleyball. **On-Campus Highlights:** Michael C. Carlos Museum, Lullwater Park, Clifton Health Sciences Corridor, 10th Floor of the Woodruff Library, Candler Library Reading Room **Environmental Initiatives:** Emory has among the highest number of square feet of LEED-certified space of any campus in America. Emory constructed the first LEED-certified building in the Southeast in the 1990's, the first Good LEED-EB in the U.S., and since 2001 all new and future construction must be LEED (with Silver currently the minimum). We also are auditing and retrofitting exisiting buildings—roughly 1 million square feet are currently underway with additional 1 million in planning phase.

ADMISSIONS

Freshman Academic Profile: Average high school GPA 3.8. 83% in top 10% of high school class, 97% in top 25% of high school class, 100% in top 50% of high school class. 59% from public high schools. **Test Scores:** SAT Math middle 50% range 680-780. SAT EBRW middle 50% range 670-740. ACT middle 50% range 30-33. Minimum internet-based TOEFL 100. **Basis for Candidate Selection:** *Very important factors considered include:* rigor of secondary school record, academic GPA, recommendation(s), extracurricular activities, talent/ability, character/personal qualities. *Important factors considered include:* application essay, standardized test scores, volunteer work. *Other factors considered include:* class rank, interview, first generation, alumni/ae relation, geographical residence, state residency, racial/ethnic status, work experience. **Freshman Admission Requirements:** High school diploma is required and GED is not accepted *Academic units recommended:* 4 English, 4 math, 4 science, 2 science labs, 4 foreign language, 2 social studies, 2 history, 1 computer science, 1 visual/performing arts. **Freshman Admission Statistics:** 23,747 applied, 22.0% admitted, 27% enrolled. **Transfer Admission Requirements:** High school transcript, college transcript(s), essay or personal statement, standardized test scores, statement of good standing from prior institution(s). Minimum college GPA of 3.00 required. Lowest grade transferable C. **General Admission Information:** Application fee $75. Regular application deadline 1/1. Nonfall registration accepted. Admission may be deferred for a maximum of 2 years.

COSTS AND FINANCIAL AID

Annual tuition $50,590. Room and board $14,456. Required fees $716. Average book expense $1,224. **Required Forms and Deadlines:** CSS/Financial Aid PROFILE; FAFSA; Noncustodial PROFILE. **Notification of Awards:** Applicants will be notified of awards on or about 4/1. **Types of Aid:** *Need-based scholarships/grants:* College/university scholarship or grant aid from institutional funds; Federal Pell; Private scholarships; SEOG. *Loans:* Direct PLUS loans; Direct Subsidized Stafford Loans; Direct Unsubsidized Stafford Loans. *Student Employment:* Federal Work-Study Program available. Institutional employment available. **Financial Aid Statistics:** 90% needy freshmen, 94% needy undergrads receive need-based scholarship or grant aid. 36% freshmen, 25% undergrads receive non-need-based scholarship or grant aid. 87% freshmen, 91% undergrads receive need-based self-help aid. 0% freshmen, 0% undergrads receive athletic scholarships. 55% freshmen, 54% undergrads receive any aid. 39% undergrads borrow to pay for school. Average cumulative indebtedness $29,217. **Criteria for awarding aid:** *Need-based:* Religious affiliation *Non-need-based:* Academics, Art, Leadership, Music/drama, Religious affiliation, State/district residency.

EMPORIA STATE UNIVERSITY

1 Kellogg Circle, Emporia, KS 66801-5087
Phone: 620-341-5465 · **Financial Aid Phone:** 620-341-5457
E-mail: go2esu@emporia.edu · **CEEB Code:** 6335
Fax: 620-341-5599 · **Website:** www.emporia.edu · **ACT Code:** 1430

This public school was founded in 1863. It has a 212 acre campus.

RATINGS

Admissions Selectivity Rating: 75   **Fire Safety Rating:** 77   **Green Rating:** 60*

STUDENTS AND FACULTY

Enrollment: 3,499. **Student Body:** 62% female, 38% male, 18% out-of-state, 7% international (40 countries represented). Asian 1%, African American 5%, Caucasian 71%, Hispanic 7%, Native American <1%, Pacific Islander <1%, Two or more races 8%, Race unknown 2%.
Retention and Graduation: 73% freshmen return for sophomore year. 26% freshmen graduate within 4 years. 45% freshmen graduate within 6 years. 20% grads go on to further study within 1 year. **Faculty:** Student/faculty ratio 17:1. 247 full-time faculty, 82% hold PhDs, 16% are members of minority groups, 49% are women. 9% of classes are taught by teaching assistants.

ACADEMICS

Degrees: Bachelor's; Doctoral/Research; Master's; Post-Bachelor's certificate; Post-Master's certificate **Classes:** Most classes have 20-29 students. Most lab/discussion sessions have 20-29 students. **Most popular majors:** Elementary Education And Teaching; Nursing/Registered Nurse (Rn, Asn, Bsn, Msn); Business/Commerce, General. **Special Study Options:** Distance learning; Double major; Dual enrollment; Honors program; Independent study; Internships; Liberal arts/career combination; Student-designed major; Study abroad; Teacher certification program. **Honors programs:** Honors Programs. **Disability Services offered to physically disabled students:** Note-taking services; Reader services; Tape recorders; Tutors. **Career services:** Alumni network; Alumni services; Career assessment; Internships

FACILITIES

Housing: Coed dorms; Cooperative housing; Fraternity/sorority housing; Special housing for disabled student; Special housing for international students; Theme housing; Wellness housing 100% of campus accessible to physically diasbled. **Special Academic Facilities/Equipment:** Art gallery, geology and natural history museums, Great Plains study center, planetarium. **Computers:** 25% of classrooms, 100% of libraries, 50% of student union, have wireless network access. Students can register for classes online. Administrative functions (other than registration) can be performed online.

CAMPUS LIFE

Environment: Town **Activities:** Campus Ministries; Choral groups; Concert band; Dance; Drama/theater; International Student Organization; Jazz band; Literary magazine; Marching band; Music ensembles; Musical theater; Opera; Pep band; Student government; Student newspaper; Student-run film society; Symphony orchestra; Yearbook 141 registered organizations, 15 honor societies, 11 religious organizations. 6 fraternities, 4 sororities. **Athletics (Intercollegiate):** *Men:* baseball, basketball, cheerleading, cross-country, football, tennis, track/field (outdoor), track/field (indoor). *Women:* basketball, cheerleading, cross-country, soccer, softball, tennis, track/field (outdoor), track/field (indoor), volleyball. **On-Campus Highlights:** Student Recreation Center, The Memorial Student Union, Beach Music Hall, Wooster Lake, William Allen White Library

ADMISSIONS

Freshman Academic Profile: Average high school GPA 3.4. 14% in top 10% of high school class, 38% in top 25% of high school class, 73% in top 50% of high school class. 96% from public high schools. **Test Scores:** ACT middle 50% range 19-25. Minimum internet-based TOEFL 72. Minimum paper TOEFL 530. **Basis for Candidate Selection:** *Very important factors considered include:* class rank, academic GPA, standardized test scores. *Important factors considered include:* talent/ability. *Other factors considered include:* application essay, extracurricular activities. **Freshman Admission Requirements:** High school diploma is required and GED is accepted *Academic units required:* 4 English, 3 math, 3 science, 3 social studies, 1 computer science, *Academic units recommended:* 4 English, 3 math, 3 science, 3 social studies, 1 computer science. **Freshman Admission Statistics:** 1,693 applied, 82.8% admitted, 43% enrolled. **Transfer Admission Requirements:** college transcript(s), Minimum college GPA of 2.0 required. Lowest grade transferable D. **General Admission Information:** Application fee $30. Nonfall registration accepted. Admission may be deferred for a maximum of 1 year.

COSTS AND FINANCIAL AID

Annual in-state tuition $8,681. Annual out-of-state tuition $18,600. Room and board $8,681. Required fees $1,318. Average book expense $1,000. **Required Forms and Deadlines:** FAFSA; State aid form. **Notification of Awards:** Applicants will be notified of awards on a rolling basis beginning 2/2. **Types of Aid:** *Need-based scholarships/grants:* College/university scholarship or grant aid from institutional funds; Federal Pell; Private scholarships; SEOG; State scholarships/grants. *Loans:* Direct PLUS loans; Direct Subsidized Stafford Loans; Direct Unsubsidized Stafford Loans. *Student Employment:* Federal Work-Study Program available. Institutional employment available. **Financial Aid Statistics:** 59% needy freshmen, 43% needy undergrads receive need-based scholarship or grant aid. 41% freshmen, 28% undergrads receive non-need-based scholarship or grant aid. 7% freshmen, 9% undergrads receive need-based self-help aid. 7% freshmen, 4% undergrads receive athletic scholarships. 61% freshmen, 57% undergrads receive any aid. **Criteria for awarding aid:** *Need-based:* Job skills, Minority status *Non-need-based:* Academics, Alumni affiliation, Art, Athletics, Job skills, Leadership, Minority status, Music/drama, Religious affiliation, State/district residency.

ENDICOTT COLLEGE

376 Hale Street, Beverly, MA 01915
Phone: 978-921-1000 · **Financial Aid Phone:** 978-232-2060
E-mail: admissio@endicott.edu · **CEEB Code:** 3369
Fax: 978-232-2520 · **Website:** www.endicott.edu · **ACT Code:** 1824

This private school was founded in 1939. It has a 235 acre campus.

RATINGS

Admissions Selectivity Rating: 76   **Fire Safety Rating:** 97   **Green Rating:** 91

STUDENTS AND FACULTY

Enrollment: 3,205. **Student Body:** 63% female, 37% male, 51% out-of-state, 2% international (33 countries represented). Asian 1%, African American 2%, Caucasian 83%, Hispanic 4%, Native American <1%, Pacific Islander <1%, Two or more races 2%, Race unknown 6%. **Retention and Graduation:** 84% freshmen return for sophomore year. 71% freshmen graduate within 4 years. 75% freshmen graduate within 6 years. 27% grads go on to further study within 1 year. **Faculty:** Student/faculty ratio 14:1. 105 full-time faculty, 72% hold PhDs, 14% are members of minority groups, 62% are women. 0% of classes are taught by teaching assistants.

ACADEMICS

Degrees: Associate; Bachelor's; Certificate; Doctoral; Doctoral/Research; Master's; Post-Master's certificate; Terminal Associate **Classes:** Most classes have 20-29 students. Most lab/discussion sessions have 20-29 students. **Most popular majors:** Mass Communication/Media Studies; Sport And Fitness Administration/Management; Business Administration And Management, General. **Special Study Options:** Accelerated program; Cross-registration; Distance learning; Double major; Dual enrollment; English as a Second Language (ESL); Exchange student program (domestic); Honors program; Independent study; Internships; Liberal arts/career combination; Student-designed major; Study abroad; Teacher certification program. **Honors programs:** Alpha Phi Sigma (Criminal Justice), Eta Sigma Delta (Hospitality), Iota Gamma Chi (Liberal Studies), Kappa Delta Pi (Education), Lambda Pi Eta (Communication), Mortar Board (Community Service), Phi Alpha Theta (History), Phi Epsilon Kappa (Physical education), Phi Sigma (Biological Sciences), Phi Signma Alpha (Political Science), Psi Chi (Psychology), Sigma Beta Delta (Business/Technology), Sigma Iota Rho (International Studies), Sigma Tau Delta (English), Sigma Theta Tau (Nursing), Sigma Xi (research), Endicott College Honors Program, National Honor Society for students in Senior Year. **Disability Services offered to physically disabled students:** Note-taking services; Reader services; Tape recorders; Tutors. **Career services:** Alumni network; Alumni services; Career assessment; Career/job search classes; Internships; Regional alumni

FACILITIES

Housing: Apartments for single students; Coed dorms; Special housing for disabled student; Special housing for international students; Theme housing; Wellness housing; Women's dorms 90% of campus accessible to physically disabled. **Special Academic Facilities/Equipment:** DNA Sequencing lab, Incubator, Biotech labs, Center for the Arts (galleries, theaters, specialty studios and labs); State-of-the-art television/radio station. https://www.endicott.edu/student-life/activities-events/endicott-tv-radio; Specialized Nursing lab; La Chanterelle, a student-run restaraunt https://www.endicott.edu/academics/schools/hospitality-management/la-chanterelle-restaurant, https://www.endicott.edu/academics/academic-resources-support/halle-library/endicott-archives

Computers: 100% of classrooms, 96% of dorms, 100% of libraries, 100% of dining areas, 100% of student union, have wireless network access. Students can register for classes online. Administrative functions (other than registration) can be performed online.

CAMPUS LIFE

Environment: Town **Activities:** Campus Ministries; Choral groups; Concert band; Dance; Drama/theater; International Student Organization; Jazz band; Literary magazine; Model UN; Music ensembles; Musical theater; Pep band; Radio station; Student government; Student newspaper; Student-run film society; Television station; Yearbook 47 registered organizations, 7 honor societies, 1 religious organization. **Athletics (Intercollegiate):** *Men:* baseball, basketball, cross-country, equestrian sports, football, golf, lacrosse, soccer, tennis, volleyball. *Women:* basketball, cross-country, equestrian sports, field hockey, lacrosse, soccer, softball, tennis, volleyball. **On-Campus Highlights:** Center for Life Science and Business, Center for the Arts, Post Center, Sports Complex, Lighted multi-purpose stadium, Ice Arena

ADMISSIONS

Freshman Academic Profile: Average high school GPA 3.3. 16% in top 10% of high school class, 44% in top 25% of high school class, 77% in top 50% of high school class. 80% from public high schools. **Test Scores:** SAT Math middle 50% range 520-600. SAT EBRW middle 50% range 530-610. ACT middle 50% range 22-26. Minimum internet-based TOEFL 79. Minimum paper TOEFL 550. **Basis for Candidate Selection:** *Very important factors considered include:* rigor of secondary school record, academic GPA, character/personal qualities. *Important factors considered include:* class rank, application essay, standardized test scores, extracurricular activities, talent/ability, alumni/ae relation, geographical residence, volunteer work, work experience. *Other factors considered include:* recommendation(s), interview, first generation, state residency, racial/ethnic status, level of applicant's interest. **Freshman Admission Requirements:** High school diploma is required and GED is accepted *Academic units recommended:* 4 English, 3 math, 2 science, 2 social studies, 1 history, 4 academic electives. **Freshman Admission Statistics:** 3,623 applied, 81.4% admitted, 25% enrolled. **Transfer Admission Requirements:** High school transcript, college transcript(s), essay or personal statement, standardized test scores, statement of good standing from prior institution(s). Minimum college GPA of 2.5 required. Lowest grade transferable C. **General Admission Information:** Application fee $50. Priority deadline 2/15. Regular application deadline 2/15. Nonfall registration accepted.

COSTS AND FINANCIAL AID

Annual tuition $30,612. Room and board $14,500. Required fees $700. Average book expense $1,252. **Required Forms and Deadlines:** FAFSA; Institution's own financial aid form. **Notification of Awards:** Applicants will be notified of awards on a rolling basis beginning 1/15. **Types of Aid:** *Need-based scholarships/grants:* College/university scholarship or grant aid from institutional funds; Federal Pell; Private scholarships; SEOG; State scholarships/grants. *Loans:* Direct PLUS loans; Direct Subsidized Stafford Loans; Direct Unsubsidized Stafford Loans. *Student Employment:* Federal Work-Study Program available. Institutional employment available. **Financial Aid Statistics:** 77% needy freshmen, 82% needy undergrads receive need-based scholarship or grant aid. 83% freshmen, 72% undergrads receive non-need-based scholarship or grant aid. 93% freshmen, 93% undergrads receive need-based self-help aid. 0% freshmen, 0% undergrads receive athletic scholarships. 91% freshmen, 88% undergrads receive any aid. 71% undergrads borrow to pay for school. Average cumulative indebtedness $41,901. **Criteria for awarding aid:** *Need-based:* Academics, Art, Leadership *Non-need-based:* Academics, Alumni affiliation, Art, Job skills, Leadership, Music/drama, Religious affiliation, State/district residency.

ERSKINE COLLEGE

P.O. Box 338, Due West, SC 29639
Phone: 864-379-8838 · **Financial Aid Phone:** 864-379-8832
E-mail: admissions@erskine.edu
Fax: 864-379-2172 · **Website:** www.erskine.edu

This private school, affiliated with the Presbyterian Church, was founded in 1839. It has a 90 acre campus.

RATINGS

Admissions Selectivity Rating: 80   **Fire Safety Rating:** 68   **Green Rating:** 60*

STUDENTS AND FACULTY

Enrollment: 548. **Student Body:** 53% female, 47% male, 24% out-of-state, 4% international (10 countries represented). Asian 1%, African American 8%,

Caucasian 70%, Hispanic 1%, Native American 0%, Pacific Islander 0%, Two or more races 1%, Race unknown 16%.
Retention and Graduation: 77% freshmen return for sophomore year.
Faculty: Student/faculty ratio 11:1. 41 full-time faculty, 85% hold PhDs, 7% are members of minority groups, 39% are women. 0% of classes are taught by teaching assistants.

ACADEMICS

Degrees: Bachelor's; Certificate; Doctoral/Research; Master's **Classes:** Most classes have 10-19 students. Most lab/discussion sessions have 10-19 students. **Most popular majors:** Elementary Education And Teaching; Biology/ Biological Sciences, General; Business/Commerce, General. **Special Study Options:** Double major; Independent study; Internships; Study abroad; Teacher certification program. **Disability Services offered to physically disabled students:** Tutors. **Career services:** Career/job search classes

FACILITIES

Housing: Men's dorms; Women's dorms 75% of campus accessible to physically diasbled. **Special Academic Facilities/Equipment:** Bowie Arts Center

CAMPUS LIFE

Environment: Rural **Activities:** Campus Ministries; Choral groups; Concert band; Dance; Drama/theater; Jazz band; Literary magazine; Music ensembles; Musical theater; Radio station; Student government; Student newspaper; Yearbook 51 registered organizations, 6 honor societies. **Athletics (Intercollegiate):** *Men:* baseball, basketball, cross-country, golf, soccer, tennis. *Women:* basketball, cross-country, golf, lacrosse, soccer, softball, tennis, volleyball. **On-Campus Highlights:** Java City, The Phoenix, Watkins Student Center, Bowie Arts Center

ADMISSIONS

Freshman Academic Profile: 39% in top 10% of high school class, 65% in top 25% of high school class, 87% in top 50% of high school class. 85% from public high schools. **Test Scores:** SAT Math middle 50% range 480-605. SAT EBRW middle 50% range 460-590. ACT middle 50% range 21-26. Minimum paper TOEFL 550. **Basis for Candidate Selection:** *Very important factors considered include:* rigor of secondary school record, academic GPA, application essay, standardized test scores, recommendation(s), alumni/ ae relation. *Important factors considered include:* extracurricular activities, talent/ability, character/personal qualities. *Other factors considered include:* class rank, interview, first generation, geographical residence, state residency, religious affiliation/commitment, racial/ethnic status, volunteer work, work experience, level of applicant's interest. **Freshman Admission Requirements:** High school diploma is required and GED is accepted *Academic units required:* 4 English, 2 math, 2 science, 2 science labs. **Freshman Admission Statistics:** 500 applied, 74.6% admitted, 39% enrolled. **Transfer Admission Requirements:** college transcript(s), essay or personal statement, statement of good standing from prior institution(s). Minimum college GPA of 2.0 required. Lowest grade transferable C. **General Admission Information:** Application fee $25. Nonfall registration accepted. Admission may be deferred.

COSTS AND FINANCIAL AID

Required Forms and Deadlines: FAFSA; Institution's own financial aid form; State aid form. **Notification of Awards:** Applicants will be notified of awards on a rolling basis beginning 11/1. **Types of Aid:** *Need-based scholarships/ grants:* College/university scholarship or grant aid from institutional funds; Federal Pell; Private scholarships; SEOG; State scholarships/grants. *Loans:* Direct PLUS loans; Direct Subsidized Stafford Loans; Direct Unsubsidized Stafford Loans. *Student Employment:* Federal Work-Study Program available. Institutional employment available. **Financial Aid Statistics:** 100% needy freshmen, 100% needy undergrads receive need-based scholarship or grant aid. 100% freshmen, 100% undergrads receive non-need-based scholarship or grant aid. 95% freshmen, 99% undergrads receive need-based self-help aid. 49% freshmen, 42% undergrads receive athletic scholarships. **Criteria for awarding aid:** *Need-based:* Academics, Alumni affiliation, Athletics, Leadership, Minority status, Religious affiliation *Non-need-based:* Academics, Alumni affiliation, Athletics, Leadership, Minority status, Music/drama, Religious affiliation, State/district residency.

EUGENE BIBLE COLLEGE

102 Camp Building, Eugene, OR 97405-1194
Phone: 800-322-2638 · **Financial Aid Phone:** 800-322-2638
E-mail: admissions@newhope.edu · **CEEB Code:** 4274
Fax: 541-343-5801 · **Website:** http://www.newhope.edu · **ACT Code:** 3468

This private school was founded in 1925. It has a 33 acre campus.

RATINGS

Admissions Selectivity Rating: 63   **Fire Safety Rating:** 83   **Green Rating:** 60*

STUDENTS AND FACULTY

Enrollment: 162. **Student Body:** 49% female, 51% male, 54% out-of-state, 2% international (5 countries represented). Asian 4%, African American 4%, Caucasian 61%, Hispanic 9%, Native American 1%, Pacific Islander 4%, Two or more races 9%, Race unknown 6%.
Retention and Graduation: 100% freshmen return for sophomore year. 35% grads go on to further study within 1 year. **Faculty:** Student/faculty ratio 10:1. 10 full-time faculty, 30% hold PhDs, 20% are members of minority groups, 40% are women. 0% of classes are taught by teaching assistants.

ACADEMICS

Degrees: Associate; Bachelor's; Certificate; Master's **Classes:** Most classes have 10-19 students. Most lab/discussion sessions have 10-19 students. **Most popular majors:** Bible/Biblical Studies; Pastoral Studies/Counseling; Youth Ministry. **Special Study Options:** Cooperative education program; Distance learning; Double major; Dual enrollment; Independent study; Internships; Liberal arts/career combination.

FACILITIES

Housing: Apartments for married students; Apartments for single students; Men's dorms; Women's dorms 75% of campus accessible to physically diasbled. **Special Academic Facilities/Equipment:** Music lab, computer lab **Computers:**

CAMPUS LIFE

Environment: City **Activities:** Choral groups; Drama/theater; Music ensembles; Student government; Yearbook. **Athletics (Intercollegiate):** *Men:* basketball, soccer. *Women:* soccer, volleyball. **On-Campus Highlights:** Student Center, Cafeteria, Dorm Lounges, Computer Lab, Workout Room

ADMISSIONS

Freshman Academic Profile: 90% from public high schools. **Test Scores:** Minimum paper TOEFL 500. **Basis for Candidate Selection:** *Very important factors considered include:* application essay, recommendation(s), character/ personal qualities, religious affiliation/commitment. *Important factors considered include:* rigor of secondary school record, academic GPA. *Other factors considered include:* class rank, standardized test scores, extracurricular activities, talent/ability, volunteer work, work experience, level of applicant's interest. **Freshman Admission Requirements:** High school diploma is required and GED is accepted **Freshman Admission Statistics:** 92 applied, 100.0% admitted, enrolled. **Transfer Admission Requirements:** college transcript(s), essay or personal statement, Minimum college GPA of 2.0 required. Lowest grade transferable C. **General Admission Information:** Application fee $50. Regular application deadline 9/1. Nonfall registration accepted. Admission may be deferred for a maximum of 2 years.

COSTS AND FINANCIAL AID

Annual tuition $16,500. Room and board $6,100. Required fees $801. Average book expense $800. **Required Forms and Deadlines:** FAFSA. **Notification of Awards:** Applicants will be notified of awards on a rolling basis beginning 7/15. **Types of Aid:** *Need-based scholarships/grants:* College/university scholarship or grant aid from institutional funds; Federal Pell; SEOG. *Loans:* Direct PLUS loans; Direct Subsidized Stafford Loans; Direct Unsubsidized Stafford Loans. **Financial Aid Statistics:** 100% needy freshmen, 100% needy undergrads receive need-based scholarship or grant aid. 16% freshmen, 13% undergrads receive non-need-based scholarship or grant aid. 100% freshmen, 100% undergrads receive need-based self-help aid. 36% freshmen, 49% undergrads receive athletic scholarships. **Criteria for awarding aid:** *Need-based:* Academics, Leadership, Music/drama, Religious affiliation *Non-need-based:* Academics, Alumni affiliation, Athletics, Leadership, Music/drama.

EUGENE LANG COLLEGE OF LIBERAL ARTS AT THE NEW SCHOOL

The New School/65 West 11th Street, New York, NY 10003
Phone: 212-229-510 • **Financial Aid Phone:** 212 229 8930
E-mail: lang@newschool.edu • **CEEB Code:** 2521
Website: www.newschool.edu/ • **ACT Code:** 2828

This private school was founded in 1972.

RATINGS

Admissions Selectivity Rating: 76   **Fire Safety Rating:** 89   **Green Rating:** 91

STUDENTS AND FACULTY

Enrollment: 1,717. **Student Body:** 79% female, 21% male, 74% out-of-state, 9% international (49 countries represented). Asian 6%, African American 8%, Caucasian 47%, Hispanic 17%, Native American 0%, Pacific Islander <1%, Two or more races 6%, Race unknown 7%.
Retention and Graduation: 59% freshmen graduate within 4 years. 74% freshmen graduate within 6 years. **Faculty:** Student/faculty ratio 17:1. 71 full-time faculty, 86% hold PhDs, 39% are members of minority groups, 54% are women. 0% of classes are taught by teaching assistants.

ACADEMICS

Degrees: Bachelor's **Classes:** Most classes have 10-19 students. Most lab/discussion sessions have fewer than 10 students. **Most popular majors:** Mass Communication/Media Studies; Liberal Arts And Sciences/Liberal Studies; Fine/Studio Arts, General. **Special Study Options:** Accelerated program; Cross-registration; Distance learning; Double major; Dual enrollment; English as a Second Language (ESL); Exchange student program (domestic); Independent study; Internships; Student-designed major; Study abroad. **Combined degree programs:** BA/MA. **Disability Services offered to physically disabled students:** Note-taking services; Reader services; Tape recorders. **Career services:** Career assessment; Career/job search classes; Internships

FACILITIES

Housing: Coed dorms; Special housing for disabled student; Theme housing 99% of campus accessible to physically diasbled. **Special Academic Facilities/Equipment:** Art gallery, photography gallery, extensive collections of contemporary art, concert hall, public lectures, conferences, cultural and intellectual events. **Computers:** 95% of classrooms, 100% of libraries, 100% of dining areas, na% of student union, 100% of common outdoor areas have wireless network access. Students can register for classes online. Administrative functions (other than registration) can be performed online.

CAMPUS LIFE

Environment: Metropolis **Activities:** Choral groups; Concert band; Dance; Drama/theater; International Student Organization; Jazz band; Literary magazine; Music ensembles; Musical theater; Opera; Student government; Student newspaper; Symphony orchestra 34 registered organizations. **On-Campus Highlights:** University Center, Lang Cafe, The Millimeter Reading Room, Lang Courtyard, Sheila C. Johnson Design Center **Environmental Initiatives:** Lighting Retrofits: 2W 13th St. and 66 5th Ave are in the midst of an ongoing replacement of all non-LED fixtures. The majority of the building's T8 fluorescent bulbs are being replaced with LED, stairwells are being replaced with dimming-occupancy based bi-level fixtures, and all rooms will be equiped with vacancy sensors. The main lobby and gallery spaces will also recieve significant upgrades as well. These same upgrades are being applied to 2 other large buildings, with a goal of completing the entire campus by early 2017.

ADMISSIONS

Freshman Academic Profile: Average high school GPA 3.4. 15% in top 10% of high school class, 30% in top 25% of high school class, 79% in top 50% of high school class. 52% from public high schools. **Test Scores:** SAT Math middle 50% range 480-620. SAT EBRW middle 50% range 528-663. ACT middle 50% range 24-29. Minimum internet-based TOEFL 100. **Basis for Candidate Selection:** *Very important factors considered include:* academic GPA, application essay, extracurricular activities. *Important factors considered include:* rigor of secondary school record, recommendation(s), character/personal qualities. *Other factors considered include:* class rank, standardized test scores, interview, talent/ability, volunteer work, work experience, level of applicant's interest. **Freshman Admission Requirements:** High school diploma is required and GED is accepted *Academic units required:* 4 English, *Academic units recommended:* 4 math, 4 science, 4 foreign language, 4 social studies, 4 history. **Freshman Admission Statistics:** 2,939 applied, 83.8% admitted, 19% enrolled. **Transfer Admission Requirements:** High school transcript, college transcript(s), essay or personal statement, standardized test scores, Minimum college GPA of 3.0 required. Lowest grade transferable C.
General Admission Information: Application fee $50. Priority deadline 1/15. Regular application deadline 8/1. Nonfall registration accepted. Admission may be deferred for a maximum of 1 year.

COSTS AND FINANCIAL AID

Required Forms and Deadlines: FAFSA. **Notification of Awards:** Applicants will be notified of awards on a rolling basis beginning 4/1. **Types of Aid:** *Need-based scholarships/grants:* College/university scholarship or grant aid from institutional funds; Federal Pell; Private scholarships; SEOG; State scholarships/grants. *Loans:* Direct PLUS loans; Direct Subsidized Stafford Loans; Direct Unsubsidized Stafford Loans. *Student Employment:* Federal Work-Study Program available. Institutional employment available. **Financial Aid Statistics:** 96% needy freshmen, 97% needy undergrads receive need-based scholarship or grant aid. 78% freshmen, 74% undergrads receive non-need-based scholarship or grant aid. 78% freshmen, 83% undergrads receive need-based self-help aid. 0% freshmen, 0% undergrads receive athletic scholarships. 58% freshmen, 57% undergrads receive any aid. 69% undergrads borrow to pay for school. Average cumulative indebtedness $26,583. **Criteria for awarding aid:** *Need-based:* Academics, Art, Leadership, Minority status, Music/drama *Non-need-based:* Academics, Art, Leadership, Minority status, Music/drama, State/district residency.

EVERGREEN STATE COLLEGE

2700 Evergreen Pkwy NW, Olympia, WA 98505
Phone: 360-867-6170 • **Financial Aid Phone:** 360-867-6205
E-mail: admissions@evergreen.edu • **CEEB Code:** 4292
Fax: 360-867-5114 • **Website:** www.evergreen.edu • **ACT Code:** 4457

This public school was founded in 1967. It has a 1000 acre campus.

RATINGS

Admissions Selectivity Rating: 73   **Fire Safety Rating:** 90   **Green Rating:** 60*

STUDENTS AND FACULTY

Enrollment: 3,560. **Student Body:** 58% female, 43% male, 20% out-of-state, 1% international (18 countries represented). Asian 3%, African American 5%, Caucasian 66%, Hispanic 11%, Native American 2%, Pacific Islander <1%, Two or more races 8%, Race unknown 4%.
Retention and Graduation: 61% freshmen return for sophomore year. 42% freshmen graduate within 4 years. 57% freshmen graduate within 6 years. 20% grads go on to further study within 1 year. 13% grads pursue arts and sciences degrees. 1% grads pursue law degrees. 1% grads pursue business degrees. 1% grads pursue medical degrees. **Faculty:** Student/faculty ratio 21:1. 155 full-time faculty, 92% hold PhDs, 56% are women. 0% of classes are taught by teaching assistants.

ACADEMICS

Degrees: Bachelor's; Master's **Classes:** Most classes have 10-19 students. Most lab/discussion sessions have 10-19 students. **Most popular majors:** Liberal Arts And Sciences/Liberal Studies; Natural Sciences; Social Sciences, Other. **Special Study Options:** Accelerated program; Double major; Exchange student program (domestic); Independent study; Internships; Student-designed major; Study abroad; Teacher certification program; Weekend college. **Disability Services offered to physically disabled students:** Note-taking services; Tape recorders; Tutors. **Career services:** Alumni network; Alumni services; Career assessment; Career/job search classes; Internships; Regional alumni

FACILITIES

Housing: Apartments for married students; Apartments for single students; Coed dorms; Special housing for disabled student; Special housing for international students; Theme housing; Wellness housing 85% of campus accessible to physically diasbled. **Special Academic Facilities/Equipment:** Sustainable Agriculture Lab Building; Longhouse Cultural Center; Center for Creative and Applied Media (TV studio, media engineering, sound effects studio, experimental effects lab, audio lab control room/studio, editing suites, 5.1 surround mix studio, A/V classrooms); 4 computer music labs; digital still imaging lab; color and B&W photography labs; animation studio; Media Loan equipment checkout facility; organic farm; scanning electron microscope; gas chromatography mass spectrometer; FTNMR; FTIR; scientific computing laboratory; printmaking studio; ceramics studio; wood and metal shops; weaving studio; fine metal studio; two art galleries; Evergreen Field and Ecosystem Ecology Lab. **Computers:** 100% of classrooms, 95% of dorms, 100% of libraries, 100% of dining areas, 100% of student union, 80% of common outdoor areas have wireless network access. Students can register for classes online. Administrative functions (other than registration) can be performed online.

CAMPUS LIFE

Environment: City **Activities:** Campus Ministries; Choral groups; Dance; Drama/theater; Jazz band; Literary magazine; Music ensembles; Pep band; Radio station; Student government; Student newspaper; Student-run film society; Television station 61 registered organizations, 3 religious organizations. **Athletics (Intercollegiate):** *Men:* basketball, cross-country, soccer, track/field (outdoor), track/field (indoor). *Women:* basketball, cross-country, soccer, track/field (outdoor), track/field (indoor), volleyball. **On-Campus Highlights:** College Activities Building, Trans & Queer Center, Organic Farm, The Flaming Eggplant-Student run cafe, Evergreen beach and woods **Environmental Initiatives:** We have completed the planning and begun implementation of our Climate Action Plan—Carbon Neutrality by 2020.

ADMISSIONS

Freshman Academic Profile: Average high school GPA 3.0. 9% in top 10% of high school class, 32% in top 25% of high school class, 59% in top 50% of high school class. **Test Scores:** SAT Math middle 50% range 460-560. SAT EBRW middle 50% range 500-630. ACT middle 50% range 19-27. Minimum internet-based TOEFL 79. Minimum paper TOEFL 550. **Basis for Candidate Selection:** *Very important factors considered include:* rigor of secondary school record, academic GPA, application essay. *Important factors considered include:* standardized test scores, first generation, level of applicant's interest. *Other factors considered include:* recommendation(s), interview, extracurricular activities, volunteer work, work experience. **Freshman Admission Requirements:** High school diploma is required and GED is accepted *Academic units required:* 4 English, 3 math, 2 science, 2 science labs, 2 foreign language, 3 social studies, 1 academic elective, and 1 unit from above areas or other academic areas. **Freshman Admission Statistics:** 1,772 applied, 96.3% admitted, 31% enrolled. **Transfer Admission Requirements:** college, transcript(s), Minimum college GPA of 2 required. Lowest grade transferable 2. **General Admission Information:** Application fee $50. Priority deadline 2/1. Nonfall registration accepted. Admission may be deferred for a maximum of One quarter.

COSTS AND FINANCIAL AID

Annual in-state tuition $8,681. Annual out-of-state tuition $24,138. Room and board $8,681. Required fees $738. Average book expense $750. **Required Forms and Deadlines:** FAFSA. **Notification of Awards:** Applicants will be notified of awards on a rolling basis beginning 4/1. **Types of Aid:** *Need-based scholarships/grants:* College/university scholarship or grant aid from institutional funds; Federal Pell; Private scholarships; SEOG; State scholarships/grants. *Loans:* Direct PLUS loans; Direct Subsidized Stafford Loans; Direct Unsubsidized Stafford Loans. *Student Employment:* Federal Work-Study Program available. Institutional employment available. **Financial Aid Statistics:** 85% needy freshmen, 84% needy undergrads receive need-based scholarship or grant aid. 3% freshmen, 1% undergrads receive non-need-based scholarship or grant aid. 71% freshmen, 79% undergrads receive need-based self-help aid. 1% freshmen, 1% undergrads receive athletic scholarships. 61% freshmen, 65% undergrads receive any aid. 56% undergrads borrow to pay for school. Average cumulative indebtedness $21,131. **Criteria for awarding aid:** *Non-need-based:* Academics, Art, Athletics, Leadership, State/district residency.

EXCELSIOR COLLEGE

PO Box 172190, 201 Strand Union Bldg, Albany, NY 12203-5159
Phone: 518-464-8500 · **Financial Aid Phone:** 518-464-8500
E-mail: admissions@excelsior.edu · **CEEB Code:** 759
Fax: 518-464-8777 · **Website:** https://www.excelsior.edu/ · **ACT Code:** 20214

This private school was founded in 1970.

RATINGS

Admissions Selectivity Rating: 64 **Fire Safety Rating:** 60* **Green Rating:** 60*

STUDENTS AND FACULTY

Enrollment: 32,133. **Student Body:** 58% female, 42% male, 90% out-of-state, <1% international (56 countries represented). Asian 4%, African American 17%, Caucasian 58%, Hispanic 5%, Native American 1%, Race unknown 14%.

ACADEMICS

Degrees: Associate; Bachelor's; Master's; Post-Bachelor's certificate; Post-Master's certificate **Most popular majors:** Liberal Arts And Sciences/Liberal Studies; Nursing/Registered Nurse (Rn, Asn, Bsn, Msn); Business Administration And Management, General. **Special Study Options:** Accelerated program; Distance learning; External degree program; Honors program; Independent study. **Career services:** Alumni network; Alumni services; Career assessment

FACILITIES

Computers: Students can register for classes online. Administrative functions (other than registration) can be performed online.

CAMPUS LIFE

Environment: City **Activities:** 1 honor societies. **Environmental Initiatives:** EC has a staff created and led committee that looks for opportunites to create a more 'green' environment.

ADMISSIONS

Freshman Admission Requirements: High school diploma is required and GED is accepted **Freshman Admission Statistics:** Lowest grade transferable C. **General Admission Information:** Application fee $75. Nonfall registration accepted.

COSTS AND FINANCIAL AID

Required Forms and Deadlines: FAFSA; Institution's own financial aid form. **Notification of Awards:** Applicants will be notified of awards on a rolling basis beginning 8/1. **Types of Aid:** *Need-based scholarships/grants:* College/university scholarship or grant aid from institutional funds; Federal Pell; Private scholarships; State scholarships/grants. *Loans:* Direct PLUS loans; Direct Subsidized Stafford Loans; Direct Unsubsidized Stafford Loans. **Financial Aid Statistics:** 3% undergrads receive any aid.

FAIRFIELD UNIVERSITY

1073 North Benson Road, Fairfield, CT 06824
Phone: 203-254-4100 · **Financial Aid Phone:** 203-254-4125
E-mail: admis@fairfield.edu · **CEEB Code:** 3390
Fax: 203-254-4199 · **Website:** www.fairfield.edu · **ACT Code:** 560

This private school, affiliated with the Roman Catholic-Jesuit Church, was founded in 1942. It has a 200 acre campus.

RATINGS

Admissions Selectivity Rating: 88 **Fire Safety Rating:** 98 **Green Rating:** 80

STUDENTS AND FACULTY

Enrollment: 4,023. **Student Body:** 60% female, 40% male, 71% out-of-state, 3% international (47 countries represented). Asian 2%, African American 2%, Caucasian 78%, Hispanic 8%, Native American <1%, Pacific Islander <1%, Two or more races 2%, Race unknown 5%.
Retention and Graduation: 90% freshmen return for sophomore year. 79% freshmen graduate within 4 years. 81% freshmen graduate within 6 years. 19% grads go on to further study within 1 year. 14% grads pursue arts and sciences degrees. 9.2% grads pursue law degrees. 45% grads pursue business degrees. 1.6% grads pursue medical degrees. **Faculty:** Student/faculty ratio 12:1. 270 full-time faculty, 92% hold PhDs, 8% are members of minority groups, 54% are women. 0% of classes are taught by teaching assistants.

ACADEMICS

Degrees: Bachelor's; Doctoral/Professional; Master's; Post-Bachelor's certificate; Post-Master's certificate **Classes:** Most classes have 10-19 students. **Most popular majors:** Registered Nursing/Registered Nurse; Finance, General; Marketing/Marketing Management, General. **Special Study Options:** Accelerated program; Cross-registration; Distance learning; Double major; Exchange student program (domestic); Honors program; Independent study; Internships; Liberal arts/career combination; Student-designed major; Study abroad; Teacher certification program. **Honors programs:** Brennan Fund for Global Immersion CAS Faculty/Student Research Corrigan Research Scholars (research based) Dr. Robert and Patricia Femia Science Endowment Four Year Honors Program Hardiman Research Scholars (research based) Hulseman Fund for Global Programs Ignatian Scholars Kathleen McGuinness Mentorship Program Lawrence Research Scholars (research based) Loyola Scholars Magis Scholars Mancini Family Student Research Fund Risica Family Faculty/

Student CAS History Research Fund Student Faculty Collaborative Research Xavier Scholars **Combined degree programs:** BA/MA; BA/MEng. **Disability Services offered to physically disabled students:** Note-taking services; Reader services; Tape recorders; Tutors. **Career services:** Alumni network; Alumni services; Career assessment; Career/job search classes; Internships

FACILITIES

Housing: Apartments for single students; Coed dorms; Special housing for disabled student; Theme housing; Wellness housing 95% of campus accessible to physically diasbled. **Special Academic Facilities/Equipment:** a media center, 750-seat concert hall/theater, a rehearsal and improvisation theater, a black box 150 seat theater, language learning lab, business education simulation training (BEST) classroom, SIM/simulated hospital environment and human patient simulators in the nursing facility, an art gallery and an art museum, a museum classroom and a museum educator, model interactive high technology classrooms, a resource center for core science. **Computers:** 50% of classrooms, 100% of dorms, 100% of libraries, 100% of dining areas, 100% of student union, 5% of common outdoor areas have wireless network access. Students can register for classes online. Administrative functions (other than registration) can be performed online.

CAMPUS LIFE

Environment: Town **Activities:** Campus Ministries; Choral groups; Dance; Drama/theater; International Student Organization; Jazz band; Literary magazine; Model UN; Music ensembles; Musical theater; Pep band; Radio station; Student government; Student newspaper; Student-run film society; Symphony orchestra; Television station; Yearbook 110 registered organizations, 21 honor societies, 3 religious organizations. **Athletics (Intercollegiate):** *Men:* baseball, basketball, crew/rowing, cross-country, diving, golf, lacrosse, soccer, swimming, tennis. *Women:* basketball, crew/rowing, cross-country, diving, field hockey, golf, lacrosse, soccer, softball, swimming, tennis, volleyball. **On-Campus Highlights:** Bellarmine Hall, Barone Campus Center, Leslie C. Quick, Jr. Recreation Complex, DiMenna-Nyselius Library, Regina A. Quick Center for the Arts **Environmental Initiatives:** Built a Co-generation facility providing 90% of campus electricity; 60% campus heating.

ADMISSIONS

Freshman Academic Profile: Average high school GPA 3.5. 41% in top 10% of high school class, 79% in top 25% of high school class, 98% in top 50% of high school class. 60% from public high schools. **Test Scores:** SAT Math middle 50% range 590-660. SAT EBRW middle 50% range 590-660. ACT middle 50% range 25-29. Minimum internet-based TOEFL 80. Minimum paper TOEFL 550. **Basis for Candidate Selection:** *Very important factors considered include:* rigor of secondary school record, academic GPA, application essay, recommendation(s). *Important factors considered include:* interview, extracurricular activities, talent/ability, character/personal qualities, first generation, volunteer work, work experience, level of applicant's interest. *Other factors considered include:* class rank, standardized test scores, alumni/ae relation, geographical residence, racial/ethnic status. **Freshman Admission Requirements:** High school diploma is required and GED is accepted *Academic units required:* 4 English, 3 math, 3 science, 2 science labs, 2 foreign language, 2 social studies, 2 history, *Academic units recommended:* 4 English, 4 math, 4 science, 4 foreign language, 2 social studies, 2 history. **Freshman Admission Statistics:** 11,218 applied, 60.6% admitted, 15% enrolled. **Transfer Admission Requirements:** High school transcript, college transcript(s), essay or personal statement, statement of good standing from prior institution(s). Minimum college GPA of.03 required. Lowest grade transferable C. **General Admission Information:** Application fee $60. Regular application deadline 1/15. Nonfall registration accepted. Admission may be deferred for a maximum of 1 year.

COSTS AND FINANCIAL AID

Annual tuition $46,490. Room and board $14,280. Required fees $675. Average book expense $1,150. **Required Forms and Deadlines:** Business/ Farm Supplement; CSS/Financial Aid PROFILE; FAFSA; Noncustodial PROFILE. **Notification of Awards:** Applicants will be notified of awards on or about 4/1. **Types of Aid:** *Need-based scholarships/grants:* College/university scholarship or grant aid from institutional funds; Federal Nursing Scholarships; Federal Pell; Private scholarships; SEOG; State scholarships/grants. *Loans:* Direct PLUS loans; Direct Subsidized Stafford Loans; Direct Unsubsidized Stafford Loans. *Student Employment:* Federal Work-Study Program available. Institutional employment available. **Financial Aid Statistics:** 98% needy freshmen, 85% needy undergrads receive need-based scholarship or grant aid. 92% freshmen, 88% undergrads receive non-need-based scholarship or grant aid. 83% freshmen, 82% undergrads receive need-based self-help aid. 6% freshmen, 7% undergrads receive athletic scholarships. 92% freshmen, 78% undergrads receive any aid. 66% undergrads borrow to pay for school. Average cumulative indebtedness $37,910. **Criteria for awarding aid:** *Need-based:* Academics *Non-need-based:* Academics, Alumni affiliation, Art, Athletics, Leadership, Music/drama.

FAIRLEIGH DICKINSON UNIVERSITY, COLLEGE AT FLORHAM

285 Madison Avenue, Madison, NJ 07940
Phone: 800-338-8803
E-mail: globaleducation@fdu.edu • **CEEB Code:** 226241
Fax: 973-443-8088 • **Website:** www.fdu.edu • **ACT Code:** 2554

This private school was founded in 1942. It has a 178 acre campus.

RATINGS

Admissions Selectivity Rating: 75   **Fire Safety Rating:** 91   **Green Rating:** 60*

STUDENTS AND FACULTY

Enrollment: 2,356. **Student Body:** 55% female, 45% male, 16% out-of-state, 1% international (25 countries represented). Asian 4%, African American 11%, Caucasian 62%, Hispanic 13%, Native American 1%, Pacific Islander 0%, Two or more races 1%, Race unknown 8%.
Retention and Graduation: 76% freshmen return for sophomore year.
Faculty: Student/faculty ratio 12:1. 141 full-time faculty, 45% are women.

ACADEMICS

Degrees: Bachelor's; Doctoral/Professional; Master's; Post-Bachelor's certificate; Post-Master's certificate **Classes:** Most classes have 10-19 students. Most lab/discussion sessions have 10-19 students. **Most popular majors:** Speech Communication And Rhetoric; Psychology, General; Business Administration And Management, General. **Special Study Options:** Accelerated program; Cooperative education program; Cross-registration; Distance learning; Double major; Dual enrollment; External degree program; Honors program; Independent study; Internships; Liberal arts/career combination; Student-designed major; Study abroad; Teacher certification program; Weekend college. **Combined degree programs:** BA/DDS; BA/MA; BA/MD. **Disability Services offered to physically disabled students:** Note-taking services; Reader services; Tape recorders; Tutors. **Career services:** Alumni network; Alumni services; Career assessment; Career/job search classes; Internships

FACILITIES

Housing: Coed dorms; Special housing for disabled student; Theme housing 34% of campus accessible to physically diasbled. **Computers:** 100% of classrooms, 100% of libraries, 100% of dining areas, 100% of student union, have wireless network access. Students can register for classes online. Administrative functions (other than registration) can be performed online.

CAMPUS LIFE

Environment: Village **Activities:** Campus Ministries; Choral groups; Dance; Drama/theater; International Student Organization; Literary magazine; Musical theater; Radio station; Student government; Student newspaper; Student-run film society 44 registered organizations, 9 honor societies, 3 religious organizations. 6 fraternities, 4 sororities. **Athletics (Intercollegiate):** *Men:* baseball, basketball, cross-country, football, golf, lacrosse, soccer, swimming, tennis. *Women:* basketball, cross-country, field hockey, lacrosse, soccer, softball, swimming, tennis, volleyball. **On-Campus Highlights:** Recreation Center, Bottle Hill Pub, Florham Perks, L'Orangerie of Library, Mansion gardens **Environmental Initiatives:** Recyclemania, Recycling Bins

ADMISSIONS

Freshman Academic Profile: Average high school GPA 3.1. 14% in top 10% of high school class, 36% in top 25% of high school class, 75% in top 50% of high school class. **Test Scores:** SAT Math middle 50% range 460-570. SAT EBRW middle 50% range 450-560. Minimum internet-based TOEFL 79. Minimum paper TOEFL 550. **Basis for Candidate Selection:** *Very important factors considered include:* academic GPA, standardized test scores. *Important factors considered include:* rigor of secondary school record, recommendation(s). *Other factors considered include:* class rank, application essay, interview, extracurricular activities, talent/ability, character/personal qualities, alumni/ae relation, volunteer work, level of applicant's interest. **Freshman Admission Requirements:** High school diploma is required and GED is accepted *Academic units required:* 4 English, 3 math, 2 science, 2 science labs, 2 history, 3 academic electives, *Academic units recommended:* 4 English, 3 math, 3 science, 2 science labs, 2 foreign language, 2 history, 4 academic electives. **Freshman Admission Statistics:** 3,647 applied, 77.7% admitted, 21% enrolled. **Transfer Admission Requirements:** college transcript(s), Minimum college GPA of 2.0 required. Lowest grade transferable C. **General Admission Information:** Application fee $40. Priority deadline 1/15. Nonfall registration accepted.

COSTS AND FINANCIAL AID

Annual tuition $36,386. Room and board $12,294. Required fees $958. *Student Employment:* Federal Work-Study Program available. Institutional employment available.

FAIRLEIGH DICKINSON UNIVERSITY, METROPOLITAN CAMPUS

1000 River Road, Teaneck, NJ 07666-1966
Phone: 201-692-2553
E-mail: globaleducation@fdu.edu • **CEEB Code:** 226341
Fax: 201-692-7319 • **Website:** www.fdu.edu • **ACT Code:** 2552

This private school was founded in 1942. It has a 68 acre campus.

RATINGS

Admissions Selectivity Rating: 75 **Fire Safety Rating:** 91 **Green Rating:** 60*

STUDENTS AND FACULTY

Enrollment: 4,101. **Student Body:** 57% female, 43% male, 14% out-of-state, 7% international (83 countries represented). Asian 5%, African American 14%, Caucasian 29%, Hispanic 34%, Native American <1%, Pacific Islander <1%, Two or more races 1%, Race unknown 11%.
Retention and Graduation: 70% freshmen return for sophomore year.
Faculty: Student/faculty ratio 15:1. 190 full-time faculty, 46% are women.

ACADEMICS

Degrees: Associate; Bachelor's; Certificate; Doctoral/Professional; Doctoral/Research; Master's; Post-Bachelor's certificate; Post-Master's certificate
Classes: Most classes have 10-19 students. **Most popular majors:** Psychology, General; Criminal Justice/Law Enforcement Administration; Registered Nursing/Registered Nurse. **Special Study Options:** Accelerated program; Cooperative education program; Cross-registration; Distance learning; Double major; English as a Second Language (ESL); Exchange student program (domestic); Honors program; Independent study; Internships; Liberal arts/career combination; Student-designed major; Study abroad; Teacher certification program; Weekend college. **Combined degree programs:** BA/DDS; BA/MA; BA/MD. **Disability Services offered to physically disabled students:** Note-taking services; Reader services; Tape recorders; Tutors.
Career services: Alumni network; Alumni services; Career assessment; Career/job search classes; Internships

FACILITIES

Housing: Coed dorms; Men's dorms; Theme housing; Women's dorms 41% of campus accessible to physically diasbled. **Computers:** 90% of classrooms, 100% of libraries, 100% of dining areas, 100% of student union, have wireless network access. Students can register for classes online. Administrative functions (other than registration) can be performed online.

CAMPUS LIFE

Environment: Town **Activities:** Campus Ministries; Choral groups; Dance; Drama/theater; International Student Organization; Literary magazine; Music ensembles; Musical theater; Radio station; Student government; Student newspaper; Student-run film society 72 registered organizations, 10 honor societies, 4 religious organizations. 5 fraternities, 7 sororities. **Athletics (Intercollegiate):** *Men:* baseball, basketball, cross-country, golf, soccer, tennis, track/field (indoor). *Women:* basketball, bowling, cross-country, fencing, golf, soccer, softball, tennis, track/field (indoor), volleyball. **On-Campus Highlights:** Weiner Library, Fitness Center, Jeepers (Wireless Cafe), Knight Club, Hackensack River **Environmental Initiatives:** Recyclemania, Recycling Bins

ADMISSIONS

Freshman Academic Profile: Average high school GPA 3.2. 18% in top 10% of high school class, 45% in top 25% of high school class, 83% in top 50% of high school class. **Test Scores:** SAT Math middle 50% range 450-550. SAT EBRW middle 50% range 440-530. Minimum internet-based TOEFL 79. Minimum paper TOEFL 550. **Basis for Candidate Selection:** *Very important factors considered include:* academic GPA, standardized test scores. *Important factors considered include:* rigor of secondary school record, recommendation(s). *Other factors considered include:* class rank, application essay, interview, extracurricular activities, talent/ability, character/personal qualities, alumni/ae relation, volunteer work, level of applicant's interest.
Freshman Admission Requirements: High school diploma is required and GED is accepted *Academic units required:* 4 English, 3 math, 2 science, 2 science labs, 2 history, 3 academic electives, *Academic units recommended:* 4 English, 3 math, 3 science, 2 science labs, 2 foreign language, 2 history, 4 academic electives. **Freshman Admission Statistics:** 5,193 applied, 73.4%

admitted, 20% enrolled. **Transfer Admission Requirements:** college transcript(s), Minimum college GPA of 2.0 required. Lowest grade transferable C. **General Admission Information:** Application fee $40. Priority deadline 1/15. Nonfall registration accepted.

COSTS AND FINANCIAL AID

Annual tuition $33,920. Room and board $12,742. Required fees $958. *Student Employment:* Federal Work-Study Program available.

FAIRMONT STATE UNIVERSITY, INCLUDING PIERPONT COMMUNITY & TECHNICAL COLLEGE

1201 Locust Avenue, Fairmont, WV 26554
Phone: 304-367-4892 • **Financial Aid Phone:** 304-367-4813
E-mail: admit@fairmontstate.edu • **CEEB Code:** 4520
Website: http://www.fairmontstate.edu • **ACT Code:** 4520

This public school was founded in 1865.

RATINGS

Admissions Selectivity Rating: 75 **Fire Safety Rating:** 60* **Green Rating:** 60*

STUDENTS AND FACULTY

Enrollment: 6,227. **Student Body:** 57% female, 43% male, 4% out-of-state, 1% international. Asian <1%, African American 4%, Caucasian 91%, Hispanic 1%, Native American <1%, Race unknown 3%.
Retention and Graduation: 70% freshmen return for sophomore year.
Faculty: Student/faculty ratio 18:1. 232 full-time faculty, 48% hold PhDs, 6% are members of minority groups, 45% are women. 0% of classes are taught by teaching assistants.

ACADEMICS

Degrees: Associate; Bachelor's; Certificate; Master's; Terminal Associate; Transfer Associate **Classes:** Most classes have 10-19 students. **Most popular majors:** Teacher Education And Professional Development, Specific Levels And Methods, Other; Criminal Justice/Safety Studies; Business Administration And Management, General. **Special Study Options:** Accelerated program; Cooperative education program; Cross-registration; Distance learning; Double major; Dual enrollment; English as a Second Language (ESL); Honors program; Independent study; Internships; Liberal arts/career combination; Study abroad; Teacher certification program; Weekend college. **Disability Services offered to physically disabled students:** Note-taking services; Reader services; Tutors. **Career services:** Career assessment; Career/job search classes

FACILITIES

Housing: Apartments for married students; Apartments for single students; Coed dorms; Men's dorms; Women's dorms 100% of campus accessible to physically diasbled. **Special Academic Facilities/Equipment:** Folk Life Center **Computers:** Students can register for classes online. Administrative functions (other than registration) can be performed online.

CAMPUS LIFE

Environment: Town **Activities:** Campus Ministries; Choral groups; Concert band; Dance; Drama/theater; International Student Organization; Jazz band; Literary magazine; Marching band; Music ensembles; Musical theater; Student government; Student newspaper; Symphony orchestra; Yearbook 90 registered organizations, 4 religious organizations. 4 fraternities, 3 sororities. **Athletics (Intercollegiate):** *Men:* baseball, basketball, cross-country, football, golf, swimming, tennis. *Women:* basketball, cheerleading, cross-country, golf, softball, tennis, volleyball.

ADMISSIONS

Freshman Academic Profile: Average high school GPA 3.0. 7% in top 10% of high school class, 24% in top 25% of high school class, 57% in top 50% of high school class. **Test Scores:** SAT Math middle 50% range 390-500. SAT EBRW middle 50% range 400-507.5. ACT middle 50% range 17-22. Minimum paper TOEFL 500. **Basis for Candidate Selection:** *Very important factors considered include:* academic GPA, standardized test scores. **Freshman Admission Requirements:** High school diploma is required and GED is accepted *Academic units required:* 4 English, 3 math, 3 science, 2 science labs, 3 social studies, 1 history, *Academic units recommended:* 2 foreign language. **Freshman Admission Statistics:** 3,400 applied, 79.2% admitted, 45% enrolled. **Transfer Admission Requirements:** college transcript(s), Minimum college GPA of 2.00 required. Lowest grade transferable D. **General Admission Information:** Nonfall registration accepted.

COSTS AND FINANCIAL AID

Annual in-state tuition $5,990. Annual out-of-state tuition $9,956. Room and board $5,990. Average book expense $900. *Student Employment:* Federal Work-Study Program available. Institutional employment available. **Financial Aid Statistics:** 85% freshmen, 80% undergrads receive any aid.

FAITH BAPTIST BIBLE COLLEGE AND THEOLOGICAL SEMINARY

1900 NW 4th Street, Ankeny, IA 50023
Phone: 1.888.faith.4.u · **Financial Aid Phone:** 515-964-0601
E-mail: admissions@faith.edu · **CEEB Code:** 6214
Fax: 515-964-1638 · **Website:** http://www.faith.edu/ · **ACT Code:** 1315

This private school, affiliated with the Baptist Church, was founded in 1921. It has a 52 acre campus.

RATINGS

Admissions Selectivity Rating: 86   **Fire Safety Rating:** 97   **Green Rating:** 60*

STUDENTS AND FACULTY

Enrollment: 232. **Student Body:** 55% female, 45% male, 56% out-of-state, 0% international. Asian <1%, African American 2%, Caucasian 92%, Hispanic 1%, Native American 1%, Pacific Islander 1%, Two or more races 1%, Race unknown <1%.
Retention and Graduation: 65% freshmen return for sophomore year. 23% grads go on to further study within 1 year. **Faculty:** Student/faculty ratio 13:1. 17 full-time faculty, 65% hold PhDs, 0% are members of minority groups, 12% are women. 0% of classes are taught by teaching assistants.

ACADEMICS

Degrees: Associate; Bachelor's; Master's **Classes:** Most classes have fewer than 10 students. Most lab/discussion sessions have fewer than 10 students. **Most popular majors:** Elementary Education And Teaching; Bible/Biblical Studies; Religious Education. **Special Study Options:** Distance learning; Double major; Dual enrollment; Independent study; Internships; Study abroad; Teacher certification program. **Career services:** Alumni services; Internships

FACILITIES

Housing: Apartments for married students; Apartments for single students; Men's dorms; Special housing for disabled student; Women's dorms **Computers:** 75% of classrooms, 100% of dorms, 100% of libraries, 100% of dining areas, 100% of student union, 60% of common outdoor areas have wireless network access.

CAMPUS LIFE

Environment: Town **Activities:** Campus Ministries; Choral groups; Concert band; Drama/theater; Music ensembles; Student government; Symphony orchestra 1 registered organization, 1 religious organization. **Athletics (Intercollegiate):** *Men:* basketball, soccer. *Women:* basketball, soccer, volleyball. **On-Campus Highlights:** Convocation Building, Benson Hall, Library, Gray Hall, Residence Halls

ADMISSIONS

Freshman Academic Profile: Average high school GPA 3.5. 9% in top 10% of high school class, 40% in top 25% of high school class, 60% in top 50% of high school class. 33% from public high schools. **Test Scores:** SAT Math middle 50% range 390-560. SAT EBRW middle 50% range 410-550. ACT middle 50% range 19-24. Minimum internet-based TOEFL 173. Minimum paper TOEFL 500. **Basis for Candidate Selection:** *Very important factors considered include:* religious affiliation/commitment. *Important factors considered include:* application essay. *Other factors considered include:* class rank, academic GPA, standardized test scores, recommendation(s), interview, extracurricular activities, talent/ability, character/personal qualities, volunteer work, level of applicant's interest. **Freshman Admission Requirements:** High school diploma is required and GED is accepted *Academic units recommended:* 4 English, 4 math, 2 science, 2 social studies, 2 history. **Freshman Admission Statistics:** 150 applied, 67.3% admitted, 87% enrolled. **Transfer Admission Requirements:** college transcript(s), essay or personal statement, statement of good standing from prior institution(s). Minimum college GPA of 2.0 required. Lowest grade transferable C. **General Admission Information:** Application fee $45. Nonfall registration accepted. Admission may be deferred for a maximum of 1 year.

COSTS AND FINANCIAL AID

Required Forms and Deadlines: FAFSA. **Types of Aid:** *Need-based scholarships/grants:* College/university scholarship or grant aid from

institutional funds; Federal Pell; Private scholarships; State scholarships/ grants. *Student Employment:* Institutional employment available. **Financial Aid Statistics:** 70% freshmen, 95% undergrads receive any aid. **Criteria for awarding aid:** *Need-based:* Academics, Leadership, Music/drama *Non-need-based:* Academics, Leadership, Music/drama, State/district residency.

FARMINGDALE STATE COLLEGE

2350 Broadhollow Rd, Farmingdale, NY 11735
Phone: 631-420-2200 · **Financial Aid Phone:** 631-420-2578
E-mail: admissions@farmingdale.edu · **CEEB Code:** 2526
Fax: 631-420-2633 · **Website:** www.farmingdale.edu · **ACT Code:** 2918

This public school was founded in 1912. It has a 380 acre campus.

RATINGS

Admissions Selectivity Rating: 85   **Fire Safety Rating:** 60*   **Green Rating:** 80

STUDENTS AND FACULTY

Enrollment: 9,005. **Student Body:** 43% female, 57% male, 0% out-of-state, 1% international (73 countries represented). Asian 8%, African American 10%, Caucasian 57%, Hispanic 21%, Native American <1%, Pacific Islander <1%, Two or more races 2%, Race unknown <1%.
Retention and Graduation: 83% freshmen return for sophomore year. 29% freshmen graduate within 4 years. 53% freshmen graduate within 6 years. **Faculty:** Student/faculty ratio 20:1. 239 full-time faculty, 79% hold PhDs, 49% are women. 0% of classes are taught by teaching assistants.

ACADEMICS

Degrees: Associate; Bachelor's; Certificate; Master's **Classes:** Most classes have 10-19 students. Most lab/discussion sessions have 20-29 students. **Most popular majors:** Computer And Information Sciences And Support Services, Other; Registered Nursing/Registered Nurse; Business, Management, Marketing, And Related Support Services, Other. **Special Study Options:** Cross-registration; Distance learning; Double major; Dual enrollment; Independent study; Internships; Study abroad. **Disability Services offered to physically disabled students:** Reader services; Tutors. **Career services:** Alumni services; Career assessment; Career/job search classes; Internships

FACILITIES

Housing: Coed dorms 90% of campus accessible to physically diasbled. **Computers:** Students can register for classes online. Administrative functions (other than registration) can be performed online.

CAMPUS LIFE

Environment: Village **Activities:** Dance; Drama/theater; International Student Organization; Model UN; Musical theater; Radio station; Student government; Student newspaper; Yearbook. **Athletics (Intercollegiate):** *Men:* baseball, basketball, cross-country, golf, lacrosse, soccer, track/field (outdoor), track/field (indoor). *Women:* basketball, cross-country, soccer, softball, track/ field (outdoor), track/field (indoor), volleyball. Campus Center, Memorial Gallery Hale Hall, Ornamental Horticulture Teaching Gardens, Nold Hall Athletic Facility, Greenley Library **Environmental Initiatives:** A 80 KW solar car port and the 7.2 KW wind farm.

ADMISSIONS

Freshman Academic Profile: Average high school GPA 3.2. 8% in top 10% of high school class, 30% in top 25% of high school class, 69% in top 50% of high school class. 93% from public high schools. **Test Scores:** SAT Math middle 50% range 490-570. SAT EBRW middle 50% range 490-570. ACT middle 50% range 19-23. Minimum internet-based TOEFL 79. Minimum paper TOEFL 550. **Basis for Candidate Selection:** *Very important factors considered include:* academic GPA, standardized test scores. *Important factors considered include:* rigor of secondary school record, application essay, recommendation(s). *Other factors considered include:* interview, extracurricular activities, talent/ ability, character/personal qualities, first generation, alumni/ae relation, volunteer work, work experience, level of applicant's interest. **Freshman Admission Requirements:** High school diploma is required and GED is accepted *Academic units required:* 4 English, 3 math, 3 science, 4 social studies, *Academic units recommended:* 1 foreign language. **Freshman Admission Statistics:** 6,063 applied, 59.0% admitted, 36% enrolled. **Transfer Admission Requirements:** High school transcript, college transcript(s), statement of good standing from prior institution(s). Minimum college GPA of 2.0 required. Lowest grade transferable C. **General Admission Information:** Application fee $50. Priority deadline 1/1. Regular application deadline 5/1. Nonfall registration accepted. Admission may be deferred for a maximum of 1 year.

COSTS AND FINANCIAL AID

Annual in-state tuition $12,892. Annual out-of-state tuition $16,320. Room and board $12,892. Required fees $1,406. Average book expense $1,200. **Required Forms and Deadlines:** FAFSA. **Notification of Awards:** Applicants will be notified of awards on a rolling basis beginning 3/1. **Types of Aid:** *Need-based scholarships/grants:* College/university scholarship or grant aid from institutional funds; Federal Pell; Private scholarships; SEOG; State scholarships/grants. *Loans:* Direct PLUS loans; Direct Subsidized Stafford Loans; Direct Unsubsidized Stafford Loans. *Student Employment:* Federal Work-Study Program available. Institutional employment available. **Financial Aid Statistics:** 80% needy freshmen, 81% needy undergrads receive need-based scholarship or grant aid. 8% freshmen, 6% undergrads receive non-need-based scholarship or grant aid. 43% freshmen, 52% undergrads receive need-based self-help aid. 0% freshmen, 0% undergrads receive athletic scholarships.

FAULKNER UNIVERSITY

5345 Atlanta Highway, Montgomery, AL 36109-3398
Phone: 334-386-7200 • **Financial Aid Phone:** 334-386-7195
E-mail: admissions@faulkner.edu • **CEEB Code:** 1034
Fax: 334-386-7137 • **Website:** www.faulkner.edu • **ACT Code:** 3

This private school, affiliated with the Church of Christ, was founded in 1942. It has a 78 acre campus.

RATINGS

Admissions Selectivity Rating: 82   **Fire Safety Rating:** 79   **Green Rating:** 60*

STUDENTS AND FACULTY

Enrollment: 2,282. **Student Body:** 61% female, 39% male, 14% out-of-state, 2% international (15 countries represented). Asian <1%, African American 51%, Caucasian 40%, Hispanic 2%, Native American 1%, Pacific Islander <1%, Two or more races 2%, Race unknown 2%.
Retention and Graduation: 57% freshmen return for sophomore year. 80% grads go on to further study within 1 year. 35% grads pursue arts and sciences degrees. 12% grads pursue law degrees. 32% grads pursue business degrees. 19% grads pursue medical degrees. **Faculty:** Student/faculty ratio 15:1. 120 full-time faculty, 66% hold PhDs, 10% are members of minority groups, 40% are women. 0% of classes are taught by teaching assistants.

ACADEMICS

Degrees: Associate; Bachelor's; Doctoral/Professional; Doctoral/Research; Master's **Classes:** Most classes have 20-29 students. Most lab/discussion sessions have 20-29 students. **Most popular majors:** Business/Commerce, General; Management Information Systems, General. **Special Study Options:** Cross-registration; Distance learning; Double major; Dual enrollment; Honors program; Independent study; Internships; Study abroad; Teacher certification program; Weekend college. **Honors programs:** Great Books Honors College. **Disability Services offered to physically disabled students:** Note-taking services; Reader services; Tape recorders; Tutors. **Career services:** Alumni services; Career assessment; Career/job search classes; Internships

FACILITIES

Housing: Men's dorms; Special housing for disabled student; Women's dorms 75% of campus accessible to physically disabled. **Computers:** 100% of classrooms, 100% of dorms, 100% of libraries, 100% of dining areas, 100% of student union, 100% of common outdoor areas have wireless network access. Administrative functions (other than registration) can be performed online.

CAMPUS LIFE

Environment: City **Activities:** Choral groups; Concert band; Drama/theater; International Student Organization; Literary magazine; Marching band; Music ensembles; Musical theater; Pep band; Student government; Student newspaper; Yearbook 12 registered organizations, 5 honor societies, 3 religious organizations. 5 fraternities, 5 sororities. **Athletics (Intercollegiate): Men:** baseball, basketball, cheerleading, fishing, football, golf, soccer. *Women:* cheerleading, fishing, soccer, softball, volleyball. **On-Campus Highlights:** Cafe Sienna, Student Multiplex, Dorm Lobbies, Perry Cafeteria, Dinner Theatre

ADMISSIONS

Freshman Academic Profile: Average high school GPA 3.3. 75% from public high schools. **Test Scores:** SAT Math middle 50% range 440-510. SAT EBRW middle 50% range 430-520. ACT middle 50% range 18-24. Minimum paper TOEFL 450. **Basis for Candidate Selection:** *Very important factors considered include:* academic GPA, standardized test scores. *Important factors considered include:* rigor of secondary school record, class rank, recommendation(s), interview, character/personal qualities, religious affiliation/commitment, level of applicant's interest. *Other factors considered include:*

application essay, extracurricular activities, talent/ability, first generation, alumni/ae relation, volunteer work, work experience. **Freshman Admission Requirements:** High school diploma is required and GED is accepted *Academic units required:* 3 English, 3 math, 3 science, 3 history, *Academic units recommended:* 4 English, 4 math, 4 science, 1 science labs, 1 foreign language, 2 social studies, 2 history. **Freshman Admission Statistics:** 1,712 applied, 57.3% admitted, 30% enrolled. **Transfer Admission Requirements:** High school transcript, college transcript(s), standardized test scores, statement of good standing from prior institution(s). Minimum college GPA of 2.0 required. Lowest grade transferable C. **General Admission Information:** Regular application deadline 8/1. Nonfall registration accepted. Admission may be deferred.

COSTS AND FINANCIAL AID

Annual tuition $17,500. Room and board $7,130. Required fees $1,780. Average book expense $1,800. **Required Forms and Deadlines:** FAFSA; Institution's own financial aid form; State aid form. **Notification of Awards:** Applicants will be notified of awards on or about 5/1. **Types of Aid:** *Need-based scholarships/grants:* College/university scholarship or grant aid from institutional funds; Federal Pell; Private scholarships; SEOG; State scholarships/grants. *Loans:* Direct PLUS loans; Direct Subsidized Stafford Loans; Direct Unsubsidized Stafford Loans. *Student Employment:* Federal Work-Study Program available. Institutional employment available. **Financial Aid Statistics:** 100% needy freshmen, 96% needy undergrads receive need-based scholarship or grant aid. 7% freshmen, 7% undergrads receive non-need-based scholarship or grant aid. 84% freshmen, 57% undergrads receive need-based self-help aid. 10% freshmen, 9% undergrads receive athletic scholarships. 95% freshmen, 93% undergrads receive any aid. **Criteria for awarding aid:** *Need-based:* Academics, Alumni affiliation, Art, Athletics, Leadership, Music/drama, Religious affiliation.

FERRIS STATE UNIVERSITY

1201 S. State Street, Big Rapids, MI 49307
Phone: 231-591-2100 • **Financial Aid Phone:** 231-591-2115
E-mail: admissions@ferris.edu • **CEEB Code:** 1222
Fax: 231-591-3944 • **Website:** www.ferris.edu • **ACT Code:** 1994

This public school was founded in 1884. It has a 935 acre campus.

RATINGS

Admissions Selectivity Rating: 74   **Fire Safety Rating:** 96   **Green Rating:** 72

STUDENTS AND FACULTY

Enrollment: 12,550. **Student Body:** 51% female, 49% male, 7% out-of-state, 1% international (43 countries represented). Asian 2%, African American 7%, Caucasian 80%, Hispanic 5%, Native American 1%, Pacific Islander <1%, Two or more races 3%, Race unknown 1%.
Retention and Graduation: 75% freshmen return for sophomore year. **Faculty:** Student/faculty ratio 16:1. 592 full-time faculty, 0% hold PhDs, 0% are members of minority groups, 45% are women. 0% of classes are taught by teaching assistants.

ACADEMICS

Degrees: Associate; Bachelor's; Certificate; Doctoral Other; Doctoral/Professional; Master's; Post-Bachelor's certificate **Classes:** Most classes have 10-19 students. Most lab/discussion sessions have 20-29 students. **Most popular majors:** Criminal Justice/Law Enforcement Administration; Pharmacy; Registered Nursing/Registered Nurse. **Special Study Options:** Accelerated program; Cooperative education program; Distance learning; Double major; Dual enrollment; English as a Second Language (ESL); Exchange student program (domestic); External degree program; Honors program; Independent study; Internships; Liberal arts/career combination; Student-designed major; Study abroad; Teacher certification program; Weekend college. **Honors programs:** Honors/Bachelor in Business Administration in three years. Earn MBA as a fourth year option. **Combined degree programs:** BA/MA. **Disability Services offered to physically disabled students:** Note-taking services; Reader services; Tape recorders; Tutors. **Career services:** Career assessment; Career/job search classes; Internships

FACILITIES

Housing: Apartments for married students; Apartments for single students; Coed dorms; Special housing for disabled student; Special housing for international students; Theme housing 98% of campus accessible to physically disabled. **Special Academic Facilities/Equipment:** Rankin Art Gallery, Student Recreation Center, Card Wildlife Museum, Jim Crowe Museum, Elastomer Center, FLITE **Computers:** Students can register for classes online. Administrative functions (other than registration) can be performed online.

CAMPUS LIFE

Environment: Village **Activities:** Campus Ministries; Choral groups; Concert band; Dance; Drama/theater; International Student Organization; Jazz band; Model UN; Music ensembles; Musical theater; Pep band; Student government; Student newspaper 180 registered organizations, 11 honor societies, 14 religious organizations. 8 fraternities, 6 sororities. **Athletics (Intercollegiate):** *Men:* basketball, cheerleading, cross-country, football, golf, ice hockey, tennis, track/field (outdoor). *Women:* basketball, cheerleading, cross-country, golf, soccer, softball, tennis, track/field (outdoor), volleyball. **On-Campus Highlights:** University Center, Student Recreation Center, FLITE Library, Card Wildlife Center, Ewigleben Ice Arena

ADMISSIONS

Freshman Academic Profile: Average high school GPA 3.3. **Test Scores:** ACT middle 50% range 19-25. Minimum internet-based TOEFL 61. **Basis for Candidate Selection:** *Very important factors considered include:* rigor of secondary school record. *Important factors considered include:* academic GPA, standardized test scores, character/personal qualities. *Other factors considered include:* class rank, first generation, alumni/ae relation, geographical residence, volunteer work, work experience. **Freshman Admission Requirements:** High school diploma is required and GED is accepted *Academic units recommended:* 4 English, 4 math, 3 science, 2 foreign language, 3 social studies, 1 academic elective, 1 visual/performing arts. **Freshman Admission Statistics:** 10,883 applied, 77.7% admitted, 22% enrolled. **Transfer Admission Requirements:** college transcript(s), statement of good standing from prior institution(s). Minimum college GPA of 2.0 required. Lowest grade transferable C. **General Admission Information:** Regular application deadline 8/1. Nonfall registration accepted.

COSTS AND FINANCIAL AID

Annual in-state tuition $9,652. Annual out-of-state tuition $17,640. Room and board $9,652. Average book expense $914. **Required Forms and Deadlines:** FAFSA. **Notification of Awards:** Applicants will be notified of awards on a rolling basis beginning 12/9. **Types of Aid:** *Need-based scholarships/grants:* College/university scholarship or grant aid from institutional funds; Federal Pell; Private scholarships; SEOG; State scholarships/grants. *Loans:* Direct PLUS loans; Direct Subsidized Stafford Loans; Direct Unsubsidized Stafford Loans. *Student Employment:* Federal Work-Study Program available. Institutional employment available. **Financial Aid Statistics:** 84% needy freshmen, 76% needy undergrads receive need-based scholarship or grant aid. 79% freshmen, 60% undergrads receive non-need-based scholarship or grant aid. 78% freshmen, 80% undergrads receive need-based self-help aid. 4% freshmen, 3% undergrads receive athletic scholarships. 93% freshmen, 80% undergrads receive any aid. 72% undergrads borrow to pay for school. Average cumulative indebtedness $35,710. **Criteria for awarding aid:** *Need-based:* Academics, Athletics, Job skills, Leadership, Minority status *Non-need-based:* Academics, Alumni affiliation, Art, Athletics, Job skills, Leadership, Minority status, Music/drama, State/district residency.

FISK UNIVERSITY

1000 17th Avenue N., Nasville, TN
Phone: 1-800-443-3475
Website: www.fisk.edu

This is a private school.

RATINGS
Admissions Selectivity Rating: 89   **Fire Safety Rating:** 60*   **Green Rating:** 60*

ACADEMICS

Classes: Most classes have 10-19 students. Most lab/discussion sessions have 20-29 students. **Special Study Options:** Cross-registration; Double major; Exchange student program (domestic); Honors program; Independent study; Internships; Student-designed major; Study abroad; Teacher certification program.

ADMISSIONS

Freshman Academic Profile: Average high school GPA 3.3. 10% in top 10% of high school class, 30% in top 25% of high school class, 75% in top 50% of high school class. 92% from public high schools. **Test Scores:** SAT Math middle 50% range 455-540. SAT EBRW middle 50% range 467-546. ACT middle 50% range 18-23. Minimum paper TOEFL 550. **Basis for Candidate Selection:** *Very important factors considered include:* rigor of secondary school record. *Important factors considered include:* class rank, academic GPA, application essay, standardized test scores, interview, extracurricular activities, character/personal qualities. *Other factors considered include:* recommendation(s), talent/ability, alumni/ae relation, geographical residence, volunteer work, level

of applicant's interest. **Freshman Admission Requirements:** High school diploma is required and GED is accepted *Academic units required:* 4 English, 3 math, 3 science, 2 science labs, 1 foreign language, 1 history, *Academic units recommended:* 4 English, 4 math, 3 science, 2 science labs, 2 foreign language, 1 history. **Freshman Admission Statistics:** 2,700 applied, 44.5% admitted, 51% enrolled. **Transfer Admission Requirements:** college transcript(s), essay or personal statement, statement of good standing from prior institution(s). Minimum college GPA of 2.5 required. Lowest grade transferable C. **General Admission Information:** Application fee $50. Priority deadline 3/1. Regular application deadline 3/1. Admission may be deferred for a maximum of 1 year.

COSTS AND FINANCIAL AID

Annual tuition $15,140. Room and board $7,730. Required fees $1,100. Average book expense $1,500.

FITCHBURG STATE COLLEGE

160 Pearl Street, Fitchburg, MA 01420-2697
Phone: 978-665-3144 • **Financial Aid Phone:** (978) 665-3156
E-mail: admissions@fitchburgstate.edu • **CEEB Code:** 3518
Fax: 978-665-4540 • **Website:** www.fitchburgstate.edu • **ACT Code:** 1902

This public school was founded in 1894. It has a 78 acre campus.

RATINGS
Admissions Selectivity Rating: 79   **Fire Safety Rating:** 95   **Green Rating:** 60*

STUDENTS AND FACULTY

Enrollment: 3,958. **Student Body:** 54% female, 46% male, 8% out-of-state, <1% international (6 countries represented). Asian 2%, African American 4%, Caucasian 81%, Hispanic 6%, Native American <1%, Pacific Islander <1%, Two or more races 2%, Race unknown 5%.
Retention and Graduation: 73% freshmen return for sophomore year. 10% grads go on to further study within 1 year. **Faculty:** Student/faculty ratio 16:1. 184 full-time faculty, 91% hold PhDs, 11% are members of minority groups, 46% are women. 0% of classes are taught by teaching assistants.

ACADEMICS

Degrees: Bachelor's; Certificate; Master's; Post-Bachelor's certificate; Post-Master's certificate **Classes:** Most classes have 20-29 students. Most lab/discussion sessions have 20-29 students. **Most popular majors:** Speech Communication And Rhetoric; Education, General; Business Administration And Management, General. **Special Study Options:** Cross-registration; Distance learning; Double major; Dual enrollment; Honors program; Independent study; Internships; Liberal arts/career combination; Student-designed major; Study abroad; Teacher certification program. **Honors programs:** Leadership Academy Honors Program. **Disability Services offered to physically disabled students:** Note-taking services; Reader services; Tape recorders; Tutors. **Career services:** Alumni network; Alumni services; Career assessment; Career/job search classes; Internships

FACILITIES

Housing: Apartments for single students; Coed dorms; Special housing for disabled students 90% of campus accessible to physically diasbled. **Special Academic Facilities/Equipment:** Art gallery, on-campus teacher education school, 120-acre conservation area. **Computers:** 100% of classrooms, 10% of dorms, 100% of libraries, 40% of dining areas, 100% of student union, 90% of common outdoor areas have wireless network access. Students can register for classes online. Administrative functions (other than registration) can be performed online. Undergraduates are required to own a computer.

CAMPUS LIFE

Environment: Town **Activities:** Choral groups; Concert band; Dance; Drama/theater; Jazz band; Literary magazine; Model UN; Radio station; Student government; Student newspaper; Student-run film society 60 registered organizations, 8 honor societies, 1 religious organization. 2 fraternities, 3 sororities. **Athletics (Intercollegiate):** *Men:* baseball, basketball, cross-country, football, ice hockey, soccer, track/field (outdoor), track/field (indoor). *Women:* basketball, cross-country, field hockey, lacrosse, soccer, softball, track/field (outdoor), track/field (indoor). **On-Campus Highlights:** Campus Recreation Center, Student Center Lounge, Campus Dining Hall, Commuter Cafe, Computer Labs **Environmental Initiatives:** Single stream recycling program

ADMISSIONS

Freshman Academic Profile: Average high school GPA 3.1. 90% from public high schools. **Test Scores:** SAT Math middle 50% range 460-560. SAT EBRW middle 50% range 450-560. ACT middle 50% range 19-23. Minimum internet-based TOEFL 79-80. Minimum paper TOEFL 550. **Basis for Candidate Selection:** *Very important factors considered include:* rigor of secondary school record. *Important factors considered include:* academic GPA, application essay, standardized test scores. *Other factors considered include:* recommendation(s), extracurricular activities, talent/ability, character/personal qualities, alumni/ae relation, volunteer work, work experience, level of applicant's interest. **Freshman Admission Requirements:** High school diploma is required and GED is accepted *Academic units required:* 4 English, 3 math, 3 science, 2 science labs, 2 foreign language, 1 social studies, 1 history, 2 academic electives. **Freshman Admission Statistics:** 3,104 applied, 69.7% admitted, 32% enrolled. **Transfer Admission Requirements:** college transcript(s), essay or personal statement, Minimum college GPA of 2.0 required. Lowest grade transferable C. **General Admission Information:** Application fee $25. Nonfall registration accepted. Admission may be deferred for a maximum of 1 year.

COSTS AND FINANCIAL AID
Annual in-state tuition $8,256. Annual out-of-state tuition $7,050. Room and board $8,256. Required fees $7,330. Average book expense $800. **Required Forms and Deadlines:** FAFSA. **Notification of Awards:** Applicants will be notified of awards on a rolling basis beginning 3/15. **Types of Aid:** *Need-based scholarships/grants:* College/university scholarship or grant aid from institutional funds; Federal Pell; Private scholarships; SEOG; State scholarships/grants. *Loans:* Direct PLUS loans; Direct Subsidized Stafford Loans; Direct Unsubsidized Stafford Loans. *Student Employment:* Federal Work-Study Program available. Institutional employment available. **Criteria for awarding aid:** *Need-based:* Academics, Alumni affiliation, Job skills *Non-need-based:* Academics, Alumni affiliation, Job skills, Leadership.

FIVE TOWNS COLLEGE

305 North Service Rd, Dix Hills, NY 11746
Phone: 631-656-2110 · **Financial Aid Phone:** 631-656-2164
E-mail: admissions@ftc.edu · **CEEB Code:** 3142
Fax: 631-656-2172 · **Website:** http://www.ftc.edu/

This proprietary school was founded in 1972. It has a 35 acre campus.

RATINGS
Admissions Selectivity Rating: 81   **Fire Safety Rating:** 99   **Green Rating:** 61

STUDENTS AND FACULTY
Enrollment: 630. **Student Body:** 32% female, 68% male, 8% out-of-state, 0% international (4 countries represented). Asian 4%, African American 20%, Caucasian 50%, Hispanic 15%, Native American 1%, Pacific Islander <1%, Two or more races 4%, Race unknown 5%.
Retention and Graduation: 74% freshmen return for sophomore year.
Faculty: Student/faculty ratio 15:1. 22 full-time faculty, 45% hold PhDs, 14% are members of minority groups, 36% are women. 0% of classes are taught by teaching assistants.

ACADEMICS
Degrees: Associate; Bachelor's; Doctoral; Master's **Classes:** Most classes have 10-19 students. **Most popular majors:** Recording Arts Technology/Technician; Music; Film/Cinema/Video Studies. **Special Study Options:** Distance learning; Independent study; Internships; Liberal arts/career combination; Teacher certification program. **Disability Services offered to physically disabled students:** Note-taking services; Reader services; Tape recorders; Tutors. **Career services:** Career assessment; Career/job search classes; Internships

FACILITIES
Housing: Coed dorms 100% of campus accessible to physically diasbled.
Computers: 100% of classrooms, 100% of dorms, 100% of libraries, 100% of dining areas, 100% of common outdoor areas have wireless network access. Administrative functions (other than registration) can be performed online.

CAMPUS LIFE
Environment: Town **Activities:** Choral groups; Concert band; Dance; Drama/theater; Jazz band; Music ensembles; Musical theater; Radio station; Student government; Student newspaper; Student-run film society; Yearbook.
On-Campus Highlights: Dorms, Audio Studios, Film Video Studios, Radio Station, Library

ADMISSIONS
Freshman Academic Profile: Average high school GPA 80.0. 91% from public high schools. **Test Scores:** SAT Math middle 50% range 380-490. SAT EBRW middle 50% range 390-490. ACT middle 50% range 16-24. **Basis for Candidate Selection:** *Very important factors considered include:* rigor of secondary school record, academic GPA, application essay, recommendation(s), talent/ability, character/personal qualities. *Important factors considered include:* class rank, interview, extracurricular activities, level of applicant's interest.

Other factors considered include: standardized test scores, volunteer work, work experience. **Freshman Admission Requirements:** High school diploma is required and GED is accepted *Academic units required:* 4 English, 3 math, 3 science, 2 science labs, 2 foreign language, 4 social studies, 4 academic electives, *Academic units recommended:* 4 English, 3 math, 3 science, 2 science labs, 2 foreign language, 4 social studies, 4 academic electives. **Freshman Admission Statistics:** 379 applied, 62.8% admitted, 50% enrolled. **Transfer Admission Requirements:** High school transcript, college transcript(s), essay or personal statement, statement of good standing from prior institution(s). Minimum college GPA of 2.5 required. Lowest grade transferable C. **General Admission Information:** Application fee $35. Nonfall registration accepted. Admission may be deferred for a maximum of 1 year.

COSTS AND FINANCIAL AID
Annual tuition $21,000. Room and board $12,270. Required fees $700. Average book expense $1,400. **Required Forms and Deadlines:** FAFSA; State aid form. **Notification of Awards:** Applicants will be notified of awards on a rolling basis beginning 4/30. **Types of Aid:** *Need-based scholarships/grants:* College/university scholarship or grant aid from institutional funds; Federal Pell; Private scholarships; SEOG; State scholarships/grants. *Loans:* Direct PLUS loans; Direct Subsidized Stafford Loans; Direct Unsubsidized Stafford Loans. *Student Employment:* Federal Work-Study Program available. Institutional employment available. **Financial Aid Statistics:** 73% needy freshmen, 73% needy undergrads receive need-based scholarship or grant aid. 91% freshmen, 81% undergrads receive non-need-based scholarship or grant aid. 78% freshmen, 80% undergrads receive need-based self-help aid. 0% freshmen, 0% undergrads receive athletic scholarships. 78% freshmen, 75% undergrads receive any aid. 88% undergrads borrow to pay for school. Average cumulative indebtedness $35,340. **Criteria for awarding aid:** *Need-based:* Academics, Art, Music/drama *Non-need-based:* Academics, Art, Leadership, Music/drama.

FLAGLER COLLEGE

74 King Street, St. Augustine, FL 32085-1027
Phone: 904-819-6220 · **Financial Aid Phone:** 904-819-6225
E-mail: admissions@flagler.edu · **CEEB Code:** 5235
Fax: 904-819-6466 · **Website:** www.flagler.edu · **ACT Code:** 772

This private school was founded in 1968. It has a 49 acre campus.

RATINGS
Admissions Selectivity Rating: 85   **Fire Safety Rating:** 88   **Green Rating:** 64

STUDENTS AND FACULTY
Enrollment: 2,676. **Student Body:** 65% female, 35% male, 43% out-of-state, 4% international (52 countries represented). Asian 1%, African American 4%, Caucasian 77%, Hispanic 6%, Native American <1%, Pacific Islander <1%, Two or more races 3%, Race unknown 5%.
Retention and Graduation: 72% freshmen return for sophomore year. 43% freshmen graduate within 4 years. 55% freshmen graduate within 6 years. 15% grads go on to further study within 1 year. 4% grads pursue arts and sciences degrees. 3% grads pursue law degrees. 1% grads pursue business degrees. 0% grads pursue medical degrees. **Faculty:** Student/faculty ratio 16:1. 121 full-time faculty, 74% hold PhDs, 12% are members of minority groups, 54% are women. 0% of classes are taught by teaching assistants.

ACADEMICS
Degrees: Bachelor's; Master's **Classes:** Most classes have 10-19 students. Most lab/discussion sessions have 10-19 students. **Most popular majors:** Psychology, General; Public Administration; Business Administration And Management, General. **Special Study Options:** Distance learning; Double major; Exchange student program (domestic); Honors program; Independent study; Internships; Study abroad; Teacher certification program. **Honors programs:** Only a small percentage of students (around 5% of each class of incoming freshmen) are invited to join the Honors Program each year, and other students may apply to enter the program during their sophomore, junior, or senior years. The program offers coursework and extracurricular activities that are designed to give you the highest academic challenge. Students successfully completing all elements of the Honors Program will be recognized at graduation and will have an Honors designation placed on their official academic transcripts. **Disability Services offered to physically disabled students:** Note-taking services; Reader services; Tape recorders; Tutors. **Career services:** Alumni network; Alumni services; Career assessment; Career/job search classes; Internships; Regional alumni

FACILITIES

Housing: Men's dorms; Women's dorms 95% of campus accessible to physically diasbled. **Special Academic Facilities/Equipment:** Northeast Florida Archeological Association, Crisp-Ellert Art Museum, Ponce Hall and Kenan building are on the National Register of Historic Places. **Computers:** 30% of classrooms, 100% of dorms, 100% of libraries, 100% of dining areas, 100% of student union, 80% of common outdoor areas have wireless network access. Students can register for classes online. Administrative functions (other than registration) can be performed online.

CAMPUS LIFE

Environment: Village **Activities:** Campus Ministries; Choral groups; Dance; Drama/theater; International Student Organization; Literary magazine; Model UN; Musical theater; Radio station; Student government; Student newspaper; Student-run film society 7 honor societies, 3 religious organizations. **Athletics (Intercollegiate):** *Men:* baseball, basketball, cross-country, golf, soccer, tennis. *Women:* basketball, cross-country, golf, soccer, softball, tennis, volleyball. **On-Campus Highlights:** Ringhaver Student Center, Proctor Library, Campus Courtyard, Dining Hall, Flagler College Sports Complex **Environmental Initiatives:** Chiller upgrades

ADMISSIONS

Freshman Academic Profile: Average high school GPA 3.5. **Test Scores:** SAT Math middle 50% range 430-550. SAT EBRW middle 50% range 520-610. ACT middle 50% range 21-26. Minimum internet-based TOEFL 75. Minimum paper TOEFL 550. **Basis for Candidate Selection:** *Very important factors considered include:* academic GPA, standardized test scores. *Important factors considered include:* rigor of secondary school record, application essay, recommendation(s), first generation, geographical residence. *Other factors considered include:* extracurricular activities, character/personal qualities, alumni/ae relation, volunteer work, work experience, level of applicant's interest. **Freshman Admission Requirements:** High school diploma is required and GED is accepted *Academic units recommended:* 4 English, 4 math, 3 science, 1 science labs, 2 foreign language, 1 social studies, 3 history. **Freshman Admission Statistics:** 4,921 applied, 56.6% admitted, 27% enrolled. **Transfer Admission Requirements:** college transcript(s), essay or personal statement, Minimum college GPA of 2.0 required. Lowest grade transferable C. **General Admission Information:** Application fee $50. Regular application deadline 3/1. Nonfall registration accepted. Admission may be deferred for a maximum of 1 year.

COSTS AND FINANCIAL AID

Annual tuition $18,850. Room and board $11,340. Required fees $100. Average book expense $1,100. **Required Forms and Deadlines:** FAFSA; State aid form. **Notification of Awards:** Applicants will be notified of awards on a rolling basis beginning 11/1. **Types of Aid:** *Need-based scholarships/grants:* College/ university scholarship or grant aid from institutional funds; Federal Pell; Private scholarships; SEOG; State scholarships/grants. *Loans:* Direct PLUS loans; Direct Subsidized Stafford Loans; Direct Unsubsidized Stafford Loans. *Student Employment:* Federal Work-Study Program available. Institutional employment available. **Financial Aid Statistics:** 100% needy freshmen receive need-based scholarship or grant aid. 12% freshmen, 7% undergrads receive non-need-based scholarship or grant aid. 92% undergrads receive need-based self-help aid. 3% freshmen, 4% undergrads receive athletic scholarships. 88% freshmen, 87% undergrads receive any aid. 69% undergrads borrow to pay for school. Average cumulative indebtedness $29,267. **Criteria for awarding aid:** *Need-based:* Academics, Art, Athletics, Job skills, Leadership, Minority status, Music/drama *Non-need-based:* Academics, Art, Athletics, Job skills, Leadership, Minority status, Music/drama, Religious affiliation, State/district residency.

FLORIDA A&M UNIVERSITY

Lee Hall, Tallahassee, FL 32307-3200
Phone: 850-599-3796 · **Financial Aid Phone:** 850-599-3730
E-mail: ugrdadmissions@famu.edu · **CEEB Code:** 5215
Fax: 850-599-3069 · **Website:** www.famu.edu · **ACT Code:** 726

This public school was founded in 1887. It has a 419 acre campus.

RATINGS

Admissions Selectivity Rating: 91   **Fire Safety Rating:** 99   **Green Rating:** 60*

STUDENTS AND FACULTY

Enrollment: 7,365. **Student Body:** 65% female, 35% male, 13% out-of-state, 1% international (43 countries represented). Asian 1%, African American 90%, Caucasian 3%, Hispanic 2%, Native American <1%, Pacific Islander <1%, Two or more races 3%, Race unknown 0%.

Retention and Graduation: 83% freshmen return for sophomore year. 27% grads go on to further study within 1 year. 14% grads pursue arts and sciences degrees. 0.15% grads pursue law degrees. 3% grads pursue business degrees. 2.35% grads pursue medical degrees. **Faculty:** Student/faculty ratio 15:1. 544 full-time faculty, 74% hold PhDs, 81% are members of minority groups, 46% are women. 0% of classes are taught by teaching assistants.

ACADEMICS

Degrees: Associate; Bachelor's; Doctoral/Professional; Doctoral/Research; Master's; Post-Master's certificate **Classes:** Most classes have 10-19 students. Most lab/discussion sessions have 10-19 students. **Most popular majors:** Biology/Biological Sciences, General; Criminal Justice/Safety Studies; Business Administration And Management, General. **Special Study Options:** Accelerated program; Cooperative education program; Cross-registration; Distance learning; Double major; Dual enrollment; Honors program; Independent study; Internships; Study abroad; Teacher certification program; Weekend college. **Honors programs:** Honors Program Mission The mission of the Florida Agricultural and Mechanical University Honors Program is to provide a series of challenging courses and academic enhancement experiences for undergraduate students who excel. Enhancement of academic performance should lead to consummate intellectual engagement and strong research orientation as a launch to both graduate and professional schools, as well as career paths. The program stresses four major areas of concentration: academic achievement, development of leadership potential, community service and cultural enrichment. Honors Program Objectives 1. To create an environment where academically talented students can develop and thrive. 2. To provide mentoring, nurturing and academic support to assist students in achieving their full potential. 3. To promote students' interest in international education. 4. To provide opportunities for internships and service learning involvement. **Disability Services offered to physically disabled students:** Note-taking services; Reader services; Tape recorders; Tutors. **Career services:** Alumni network; Alumni services; Career assessment; Career/job search classes; Internships; Regional alumni

FACILITIES

Housing: Apartments for married students; Apartments for single students; Coed dorms; Men's dorms; Special housing for disabled student; Theme housing; Women's dorms 90% of campus accessible to physically diasbled. **Special Academic Facilities/Equipment:** Black Archives and Resource Ctr. Coleman Memorial Library Foster Tanner Music/Art Bldg. **Computers:** 90% of classrooms, 100% of dorms, 100% of libraries, 100% of dining areas, 100% of student union, 60% of common outdoor areas have wireless network access. Students can register for classes online. Administrative functions (other than registration) can be performed online.

CAMPUS LIFE

Environment: City **Activities:** Campus Ministries; Choral groups; Concert band; Dance; Drama/theater; International Student Organization; Jazz band; Literary magazine; Marching band; Music ensembles; Musical theater; Pep band; Radio station; Student government; Student newspaper; Symphony orchestra; Television station; Yearbook 145 registered organizations, 16 honor societies, 11 religious organizations. 4 fraternities, 4 sororities. **Athletics (Intercollegiate):** *Men:* baseball, basketball, cheerleading, cross-country, football, golf, swimming, tennis, track/field (outdoor), track/field (indoor). *Women:* basketball, bowling, cheerleading, cross-country, golf, softball, swimming, tennis, track/field (outdoor), track/field (indoor), volleyball. **On-Campus Highlights:** The Black Archives, FAMU/FSU College of Engineering, Athletic Department, Army/Navy ROTC, Alfred Lawson Jr. Multipurpose Center and Teaching Gymnasium **Environmental Initiatives:** Establishment of an advisory body—the Environment & Sustainability Council to design and oversee the implementation of a sustainability strategic plan which informs and guides the various operatives on campus of the principles of sustainability as they apply specifically to the respective facets of the University—Administrative, Academic, Operations and Community

ADMISSIONS

Freshman Academic Profile: Average high school GPA 3.5. 16% in top 10% of high school class, 48% in top 25% of high school class, 85% in top 50% of high school class. 87% from public high schools. **Test Scores:** SAT Math middle 50% range 440-530. SAT EBRW middle 50% range 460-550. ACT middle 50% range 19-24. Minimum internet-based TOEFL 61. Minimum paper TOEFL 500. **Basis for Candidate Selection:** *Very important factors considered include:* rigor of secondary school record, academic GPA, application essay, standardized test scores, recommendation(s), first generation. *Important factors considered include:* extracurricular activities, talent/ability, character/personal qualities, state residency. *Other factors considered include:* alumni/ae relation, volunteer work, work experience. **Freshman Admission Requirements:** High school diploma is required and GED is accepted *Academic units required:* 4 English, 4 math, 3 science, 2 science labs, 2 foreign language, 3 social studies, 2 academic electives. **Freshman Admission Statistics:** 6,988 applied, 31.1% admitted, 50% enrolled. **Transfer Admission Requirements:** college transcript(s), Minimum college GPA of 2.0 required. Lowest grade transferable

C. **General Admission Information:** Application fee $30. Regular application deadline 5/15. Nonfall registration accepted.

COSTS AND FINANCIAL AID

Annual in-state tuition $10,058. Annual out-of-state tuition $17,585. Room and board $10,058. Required fees $140. Average book expense $1,138. **Required Forms and Deadlines:** FAFSA. **Notification of Awards:** Applicants will be notified of awards on a rolling basis beginning 4/15. **Types of Aid:** *Need-based scholarships/grants:* College/university scholarship or grant aid from institutional funds; Federal Pell; Private scholarships; SEOG; State scholarships/grants; United Negro College Fund. *Loans:* Direct PLUS loans; Direct Subsidized Stafford Loans; Direct Unsubsidized Stafford Loans. *Student Employment:* Federal Work-Study Program available. Institutional employment available. **Financial Aid Statistics:** 90% needy freshmen, 86% needy undergrads receive need-based scholarship or grant aid. 50% freshmen, 39% undergrads receive non-need-based scholarship or grant aid. 75% freshmen, 75% undergrads receive need-based self-help aid. 3% freshmen, 3% undergrads receive athletic scholarships. 96% freshmen, 70% undergrads receive any aid. **Criteria for awarding aid:** *Need-based:* Academics, Art, Leadership *Non-need-based:* Academics, Art, Athletics, Leadership, Music/drama.

FLORIDA ATLANTIC UNIVERSITY

777 Glades Road, Boca Raton, FL 33431-0991
Phone: 561-297-3040 · **Financial Aid Phone:** 561-297-3530
E-mail: admissions@fau.edu · **CEEB Code:** 5229
Fax: 561-297-2758 · **Website:** www.fau.edu · **ACT Code:** 729

This public school was founded in 1961. It has a 860 acre campus.

RATINGS

Admissions Selectivity Rating: 89   **Fire Safety Rating:** 98   **Green Rating:** 60*

STUDENTS AND FACULTY

Enrollment: 24,228. **Student Body:** 57% female, 43% male, 5% out-of-state, 2% international. Asian 4%, African American 20%, Caucasian 45%, Hispanic 25%, Native American <1%, Pacific Islander <1%, Two or more races 3%, Race unknown 1%.
Faculty: Student/faculty ratio 20:1. 730 full-time faculty, 87% hold PhDs, 26% are members of minority groups, 42% are women. 15% of classes are taught by teaching assistants.

ACADEMICS

Degrees: Associate; Bachelor's; Certificate; Doctoral; Doctoral/Professional; Doctoral/Research; Master's; Post-Master's certificate; Transfer Associate **Classes:** Most classes have 20-29 students. Most lab/discussion sessions have fewer than 10 students. **Most popular majors:** Education, General; Biology/Biological Sciences, General; Psychology, General. **Special Study Options:** Accelerated program; Cooperative education program; Cross-registration; Distance learning; Double major; Dual enrollment; English as a Second Language (ESL); Exchange student program (domestic); External degree program; Honors program; Independent study; Internships; Liberal arts/career combination; Student-designed major; Study abroad; Teacher certification program; Weekend college. **Honors programs:** The Harriet L. Wilkes Honors College of Florida Atlantic University, which opened in the Fall of 1999, is the first public honors institution to be built from the ground up in the United States. The University Honors Program is available to those students who prefer to attend the Boca Raton campus. **Combined degree programs:** BA/MEng. **Disability Services offered to physically disabled students:** Note-taking services; Reader services; Tape recorders; Tutors. **Career services:** Alumni network; Alumni services; Career assessment; Career/job search classes; Internships; Regional alumni

FACILITIES

Housing: Apartments for single students; Coed dorms; Theme housing 100% of campus accessible to physically disabled. **Special Academic Facilities/Equipment:** Art gallery, on-campus elementary school, robotics lab, marine research facilities. **Computers:** Students can register for classes online. Administrative functions (other than registration) can be performed online.

CAMPUS LIFE

Environment: City **Activities:** Campus Ministries; Choral groups; Concert band; Dance; Drama/theater; International Student Organization; Jazz band; Literary magazine; Marching band; Model UN; Music ensembles; Musical theater; Opera; Pep band; Radio station; Student government; Student newspaper; Student-run film society; Symphony orchestra; Television station 150 registered organizations, 11 honor societies, 6 religious organizations. 9 fraternities, 4 sororities. **Athletics (Intercollegiate):** *Men:* baseball, basketball,

cheerleading, cross-country, diving, football, golf, soccer, swimming, tennis. *Women:* basketball, cheerleading, cross-country, diving, golf, soccer, softball, swimming, tennis, track/field (outdoor), volleyball. **On-Campus Highlights:** Student Services Building, Student Union, Dining Hall, Breezeway, Residence Halls **Environmental Initiatives:** All new construction is designed and built to a minimum LEED silver certification level. This has been surpassed on every project to date, FAU currently has 1 platinum, 5 gold, and 2 pending gold certified buildings.

ADMISSIONS

Freshman Academic Profile: Average high school GPA 3.5. 11% in top 10% of high school class, 35% in top 25% of high school class, 78% in top 50% of high school class. **Test Scores:** SAT Math middle 50% range 490-580. SAT EBRW middle 50% range 480-570. ACT middle 50% range 21-25. Minimum internet-based TOEFL 80. Minimum paper TOEFL 550. **Basis for Candidate Selection:** *Very important factors considered include:* academic GPA, standardized test scores. *Important factors considered include:* rigor of secondary school record, class rank. *Other factors considered include:* application essay, recommendation(s), extracurricular activities, talent/ability, character/personal qualities, first generation, alumni/ae relation, volunteer work, level of applicant's interest. **Freshman Admission Requirements:** High school diploma is required and GED is accepted *Academic units required:* 4 English, 4 math, 3 science, 2 science labs, 2 foreign language, 3 social studies, 3 academic electives, *Academic units recommended:* 4 English, 4 math, 3 science, 2 science labs, 2 foreign language, 3 social studies, 3 academic electives. **Freshman Admission Statistics:** 27,888 applied, 39.0% admitted, 30% enrolled. **Transfer Admission Requirements:** college transcript(s), Minimum college GPA of 3.0 required. Lowest grade transferable D-. **General Admission Information:** Application fee $30. Priority deadline 2/15. Regular application deadline 5/1. Nonfall registration accepted. Admission may be deferred for a maximum of 3 semesters.

COSTS AND FINANCIAL AID

Annual in-state tuition $11,353. Annual out-of-state tuition $21,543. Room and board $11,353. Average book expense $1,203. **Required Forms and Deadlines:** FAFSA. **Notification of Awards:** Applicants will be notified of awards on a rolling basis beginning 5/1. **Types of Aid:** *Need-based scholarships/grants:* College/university scholarship or grant aid from institutional funds; Federal Nursing Scholarships; Federal Pell; Private scholarships; SEOG; State scholarships/grants. *Loans: Student Employment:* Federal Work-Study Program available. Institutional employment available. **Financial Aid Statistics:** 91% needy freshmen, 86% needy undergrads receive need-based scholarship or grant aid. 7% freshmen, 5% undergrads receive non-need-based scholarship or grant aid. 71% freshmen, 75% undergrads receive need-based self-help aid. 1% freshmen, 1% undergrads receive athletic scholarships. **Criteria for awarding aid:** *Need-based:* Academics *Non-need-based:* Academics, Athletics, Music/drama, State/district residency.

FLORIDA COLLEGE

110 Sproul Hall, Temple Terrace, FL 33617-5578
Phone: 813-988-5131 · **Financial Aid Phone:** (813) 988-5131
E-mail: Admissions@FloridaCollege.edu · **CEEB Code:** 1562
Fax: 813-899-6722 · **Website:** www.floridacollege.edu · **ACT Code:** 1482

This private school was founded in 1946.

RATINGS

Admissions Selectivity Rating: 82   **Fire Safety Rating:** 97   **Green Rating:** 60*

STUDENTS AND FACULTY

Enrollment: 533. **Student Body:** 51% female, 49% male, 63% out-of-state, 4% international (9 countries represented). Asian <1%, African American 6%, Caucasian 77%, Hispanic 7%, Native American 1%, Pacific Islander 0%, Two or more races 5%, Race unknown 1%.
Faculty: Student/faculty ratio 13:1. 34 full-time faculty, 44% hold PhDs, 9% are members of minority groups, 21% are women. 0% of classes are taught by teaching assistants.

ACADEMICS

Degrees: Associate; Bachelor's; Transfer Associate **Classes:** Most classes have 10-19 students. Most lab/discussion sessions have 10-19 students. **Most popular majors:** Elementary Education And Teaching; Liberal Arts And Sciences/Liberal Studies; Business Administration And Management, General. **Special Study Options:** Cross-registration; Distance learning; Double major; Independent study; Teacher certification program. **Disability Services offered to physically disabled students:** Tape recorders; Tutors.

FACILITIES

Housing: Men's dorms; Special housing for disabled student; Women's dorms

CAMPUS LIFE

Environment: Town **Activities:** Choral groups; Concert band; Drama/theater; Jazz band; Music ensembles; Musical theater; Pep band; Student government; Yearbook. **Athletics (Intercollegiate):** *Men:* basketball, cross-country, soccer. *Women:* cheerleading, cross-country, soccer, volleyball. **On-Campus Highlights:** Riverwalk, Student Center, Lobby of Boswell Hall, Sutton Hall, Conn Gymnasium

ADMISSIONS

Test Scores: SAT Math middle 50% range 460-580. SAT EBRW middle 50% range 460-630. ACT middle 50% range 20-26. Minimum paper TOEFL 550. **Basis for Candidate Selection:** *Very important factors considered include:* academic GPA, standardized test scores, recommendation(s), character/personal qualities, religious affiliation/commitment. *Important factors considered include:* rigor of secondary school record, class rank. **Freshman Admission Requirements:** High school diploma is required and GED is accepted *Academic units required:* 4 English, 3 math, 2 science, 2 science labs, 2 social studies, *Academic units recommended:* 2 foreign language, 3 social studies. **Freshman Admission Statistics:** 284 applied, 78.5% admitted, 71% enrolled. **Transfer Admission Requirements:** High school transcript, college transcript(s), standardized test scores, statement of good standing from prior institution(s). Minimum college GPA of 2.0 required. Lowest grade transferable C. **General Admission Information:** Application fee $40. Regular application deadline 8/25. Nonfall registration accepted.

COSTS AND FINANCIAL AID

Annual tuition $15,670. Room and board $8,230. Required fees $880. Average book expense $1,300. **Required Forms and Deadlines:** FAFSA; State aid form. **Notification of Awards:** Applicants will be notified of awards on a rolling basis beginning 11/1. **Types of Aid:** *Need-based scholarships/grants:* College/university scholarship or grant aid from institutional funds; Federal Pell; Private scholarships; SEOG; State scholarships/grants. **Financial Aid Statistics:** 83% needy freshmen, 86% needy undergrads receive need-based scholarship or grant aid. 94% freshmen, 92% undergrads receive non-need-based scholarship or grant aid. 76% freshmen, 77% undergrads receive need-based self-help aid. 3% freshmen, 13% undergrads receive athletic scholarships. **Criteria for awarding aid:** *Need-based:* Academics, Athletics, Music/drama *Non-need-based:* Academics, Athletics, Music/drama, State/district residency.

FLORIDA GULF COAST UNIVERSITY

10501 FGCU Blvd. South, Fort Myers, FL 33965-6565
Phone: 239-590-7878 · **Financial Aid Phone:** 239-590-7920
E-mail: admissions@fgcu.edu · **CEEB Code:** 5221
Fax: 239-590-7894 · **ACT Code:** 733

This public school was founded in 1991. It has a 760 acre campus.

RATINGS

Admissions Selectivity Rating: 81   **Fire Safety Rating:** 95   **Green Rating:** 89

STUDENTS AND FACULTY

Enrollment: 13,620. **Student Body:** 56% female, 44% male, 7% out-of-state, 2% international (89 countries represented). Asian 2%, African American 7%, Caucasian 64%, Hispanic 21%, Native American <1%, Pacific Islander <1%, Two or more races 3%, Race unknown 1%.
Retention and Graduation: 80% freshmen return for sophomore year. 22% freshmen graduate within 4 years. 48% freshmen graduate within 6 years.
Faculty: Student/faculty ratio 22:1. 465 full-time faculty, 74% hold PhDs, 17% are members of minority groups, 46% are women. 0% of classes are taught by teaching assistants.

ACADEMICS

Degrees: Associate; Bachelor's; Certificate; Doctoral/Professional; Doctoral/Research; Master's; Transfer Associate **Classes:** Most classes have 20-29 students. **Most popular majors:** Elementary Education And Teaching; Liberal Arts And Sciences/Liberal Studies; Business/Commerce, General. **Special Study Options:** Accelerated program; Cross-registration; Distance learning; Double major; Dual enrollment; Honors program; Independent study; Internships; Study abroad; Teacher certification program. **Honors programs:** The University Honors Program at Florida Gulf Coast University offers special opportunities for superior students to pursue academic work that challenges their interests and abilities. The program is university-wide, which gives students full access to the faculty and the entire range of programs at FGCU.

Since the honors program at Florida Gulf Coast University is exclusive, we have the ability to design a unique program for each individual student. Scholarship opportunities and special programs that support the honors student's educational, intellectual, and personal goals will be designed individually with the student and his or her faculty mentor. **Disability Services offered to physically disabled students:** Note-taking services; Reader services; Tape recorders; Tutors. **Career services:** Alumni network; Alumni services; Career assessment; Career/job search classes; Internships

FACILITIES

Housing: Apartments for single students; Coed dorms; Theme housing 100% of campus accessible to physically diasbled. **Special Academic Facilities/Equipment:** Art Gallery, Observatory **Computers:** Students can register for classes online. Administrative functions (other than registration) can be performed online.

CAMPUS LIFE

Environment: City **Activities:** Choral groups; Dance; Drama/theater; Literary magazine; Radio station; Student government; Student newspaper 105 registered organizations, 7 honor societies, 8 religious organizations. 4 fraternities, 4 sororities. **Athletics (Intercollegiate):** *Men:* baseball, basketball, cross-country, golf, soccer, tennis. *Women:* basketball, cross-country, diving, golf, soccer, softball, swimming, tennis, volleyball. **On-Campus Highlights:** Alico Arena, Student Union, The Quad, The Library, Baseball/Softball fields

ADMISSIONS

Freshman Academic Profile: Average high school GPA 3.3. 11% in top 10% of high school class, 36% in top 25% of high school class, 77% in top 50% of high school class. **Test Scores:** SAT Math middle 50% range 470-550. SAT EBRW middle 50% range 470-550. ACT middle 50% range 20-24. Minimum internet-based TOEFL 79. Minimum paper TOEFL 550. **Basis for Candidate Selection:** *Very important factors considered include:* rigor of secondary school record, academic GPA, standardized test scores. *Important factors considered include:* class rank. *Other factors considered include:* extracurricular activities, talent/ability. **Freshman Admission Requirements:** High school diploma is required and GED is accepted *Academic units required:* 4 English, 4 math, 3 science, 2 science labs, 2 foreign language, 3 social studies, 2 academic electives, *Academic units recommended:* 4 English, 4 math, 3 science, 2 science labs, 2 foreign language, 3 social studies, 1 history, 2 academic electives. **Freshman Admission Statistics:** 13,832 applied, 64.3% admitted, 30% enrolled. **Transfer Admission Requirements:** college transcript(s), Minimum college GPA of 2.0 required. Lowest grade transferable D. **General Admission Information:** Application fee $30. Priority deadline 2/15. Regular application deadline 5/1. Nonfall registration accepted. Admission may be deferred for a maximum of 2 semesters.

COSTS AND FINANCIAL AID

Required fees $2,834. Average book expense $1,200. **Required Forms and Deadlines:** FAFSA; Institution's own financial aid form; State aid form. **Types of Aid:** *Need-based scholarships/grants:* College/university scholarship or grant aid from institutional funds; Federal Pell; Private scholarships; SEOG; State scholarships/grants. *Loans:* Direct PLUS loans; Direct Subsidized Stafford Loans; Direct Unsubsidized Stafford Loans. **Financial Aid Statistics:** 62% needy freshmen, 64% needy undergrads receive need-based scholarship or grant aid. 67% freshmen, 31% undergrads receive non-need-based scholarship or grant aid. 61% freshmen, 66% undergrads receive need-based self-help aid. 1% freshmen, 1% undergrads receive athletic scholarships. 88% freshmen, 35% undergrads receive any aid. **Criteria for awarding aid:** *Need-based:* Academics, Athletics, Leadership, Minority status, Religious affiliation *Non-need-based:* Academics, Alumni affiliation, Athletics, Leadership, Minority status, Music/drama, Religious affiliation, State/district residency.

FLORIDA INSTITUTE OF TECHNOLOGY

150 West University Boulevard, Melbourne, FL 32901-6975
Phone: 321-674-8030 · **Financial Aid Phone:** 800-666-4348
E-mail: admission@fit.edu · **CEEB Code:** 5080
Fax: 321-674-8004 · **Website:** http://www.fit.edu · **ACT Code:** 716

This private school was founded in 1958. It has a 130 acre campus.

RATINGS

Admissions Selectivity Rating: 85   **Fire Safety Rating:** 86   **Green Rating:** 80

STUDENTS AND FACULTY

Enrollment: 3,396. **Student Body:** 29% female, 71% male, 50% out-of-state, 32% international (125 countries represented). Asian 3%, African American 6%,

Caucasian 45%, Hispanic 9%, Native American <1%, Pacific Islander <1%, Two or more races 2%, Race unknown 2%.
Retention and Graduation: 80% freshmen return for sophomore year. 46% freshmen graduate within 4 years. 62% freshmen graduate within 6 years. 32% grads go on to further study within 1 year. 8% grads pursue arts and sciences degrees. 0% grads pursue law degrees. 4% grads pursue business degrees. 1% grads pursue medical degrees. **Faculty:** Student/faculty ratio 15:1. 306 full-time faculty, 92% hold PhDs, 23% are members of minority groups, 23% are women. 0% of classes are taught by teaching assistants.

ACADEMICS
Degrees: Bachelor's; Doctoral; Doctoral/Professional; Doctoral/Research; Master's; Post-Master's certificate **Classes:** Most classes have 20-29 students. Most lab/discussion sessions have 20-29 students. **Most popular majors:** Computer Science; Aerospace, Aeronautical And Astronautical/Space Engineering; Mechanical Engineering. **Special Study Options:** Accelerated program; Cooperative education program; Cross-registration; Distance learning; Double major; Dual enrollment; English as a Second Language (ESL); Independent study; Internships; Student-designed major; Study abroad; Teacher certification program. **Disability Services offered to physically disabled students:** Note-taking services; Reader services; Tape recorders; Tutors. **Career services:** Alumni services; Career/job search classes; Internships

FACILITIES
Housing: Apartments for single students; Coed dorms; Fraternity/sorority housing 99% of campus accessible to physically diasbled. **Special Academic Facilities/Equipment:** The Emil Buehler Center for Aviation Training and Research at Melbourne International Airport. The center, valued at $5.1 million, consists of a main building and 17,600-square-foot hanger, located on eight acres at the airport. The new building houses the operations of F.I.T. Aviation. The Ruth Funk Center for Textile Arts is the only textiles center in the state of Florida. The facility is dedicated to furthering the understanding of cultural and creative achievements in the textile and fine arts. The College of Psychology and Liberal Arts opened the Scott Center for Autism Treatment. The 18,000-square-foot center provides services for individuals with autism spectrum disorder, training for parents, teachers and other professionals and research on effective treatments for autism. The Harris Center for Science and Engineering houses computer science and marine biology laboratories in two-thirds of the building, the rest is dedicated to the Harris Institute for Assured Information. The institute is already recognized for its work and numerous government and national foundation contracts. The College of Business with a gift from Nathan M. Bisk,is a leader in continuing education and online learning. The gift enhances business programs offerings and strengthens online education. Through fund-raising, the new building where they are located, was named the Nathan M. Bisk College of Business. **Computers:** 100% of classrooms, 30% of dorms, 100% of libraries, 100% of dining areas, 100% of student union, 5% of common outdoor areas have wireless network access. Students can register for classes online. Administrative functions (other than registration) can be performed online.

CAMPUS LIFE
Environment: City **Activities:** Campus Ministries; Choral groups; Concert band; Dance; Drama/theater; International Student Organization; Jazz band; Literary magazine; Music ensembles; Musical theater; Pep band; Radio station; Student government; Student newspaper; Student-run film society; Television station 106 registered organizations, 8 honor societies, 3 religious organizations. 7 fraternities, 3 sororities. **Athletics (Intercollegiate):** *Men:* baseball, basketball, cross-country, golf, soccer, tennis. *Women:* basketball, crew/rowing, cross-country, golf, soccer, softball, tennis, volleyball. **On-Campus Highlights:** Clemente Center for Sports & Recreation, Panther Dining Hall, Botanical Gardens, Library—Digital Scholarship Lab, Rathskeller **Environmental Initiatives:** 1) The university Sustainability Office with a University Sustainability Officer. This allowed us to achieve our first STARS rating, Bronze. This position also works closely with our academic Sustainability program to advance many other projects on campus.

ADMISSIONS
Freshman Academic Profile: Average high school GPA 3.7. 33% in top 10% of high school class, 60% in top 25% of high school class, 88% in top 50% of high school class. **Test Scores:** SAT Math middle 50% range 580-680. SAT EBRW middle 50% range 550-640. ACT middle 50% range 24-29. Minimum internet-based TOEFL 79+. **Basis for Candidate Selection:** *Very important factors considered include:* rigor of secondary school record, academic GPA, standardized test scores. *Important factors considered include:* level of applicant's interest. *Other factors considered include:* class rank, application essay, recommendation(s), interview, extracurricular activities, character/personal qualities, alumni/ae relation, work experience. **Freshman Admission Requirements:** High school diploma is required and GED is accepted *Academic units required:* 4 English, 3 math, 3 science, 3 science labs, 2 social studies, 2 history, 2 academic electives, *Academic units recommended:* 4 English, 4 math, 4 science, 3 science labs, 2 foreign language, 2 social studies,

2 history, 2 academic electives, 2 computer science. **Freshman Admission Statistics:** 8,898 applied, 63.5% admitted, 13% enrolled. **Transfer Admission Requirements:** college transcript(s), Minimum college GPA of 2.5 required. Lowest grade transferable C. **General Admission Information:** Priority deadline 2/1. Nonfall registration accepted. Admission may be deferred for a maximum of 1 year.

COSTS AND FINANCIAL AID
Average book expense $1,200. **Required Forms and Deadlines:** FAFSA; State aid form. **Notification of Awards:** Applicants will be notified of awards on a rolling basis beginning 12/15. **Types of Aid:** *Need-based scholarships/ grants:* College/university scholarship or grant aid from institutional funds; Federal Pell; Private scholarships; SEOG; State scholarships/grants. *Loans:* Direct PLUS loans; Direct Subsidized Stafford Loans; Direct Unsubsidized Stafford Loans. *Student Employment:* Federal Work-Study Program available. Institutional employment available. **Financial Aid Statistics:** 100% needy freshmen, 100% needy undergrads receive need-based scholarship or grant aid. 100% freshmen, 97% undergrads receive non-need-based scholarship or grant aid. 71% freshmen, 72% undergrads receive need-based self-help aid. 5% freshmen, 5% undergrads receive athletic scholarships. 97% freshmen, 85% undergrads receive any aid. 52% undergrads borrow to pay for school. Average cumulative indebtedness $36,678. **Criteria for awarding aid:** *Need-based:* Academics, Minority status *Non-need-based:* Academics, Alumni affiliation, Athletics, Music/drama, State/district residency.

FLORIDA INTERNATIONAL UNIVERSITY

11200 SW 8 st., Miami, FL 33199
Phone: 305-348-2363 · **Financial Aid Phone:** 305-348-7272
E-mail: admiss@fiu.edu · **CEEB Code:** 5206
Fax: 305-348-3648 · **Website:** www.fiu.edu · **ACT Code:** 776

This public school was founded in 1965. It has a 576 acre campus.

RATINGS
Admissions Selectivity Rating: 88   **Fire Safety Rating:** 94   **Green Rating:** 92

STUDENTS AND FACULTY
Enrollment: 41,869. **Student Body:** 56% female, 44% male, 4% out-of-state, 6% international (171 countries represented). Asian 2%, African American 12%, Caucasian 9%, Hispanic 67%, Native American <1%, Pacific Islander <1%, Two or more races 3%, Race unknown <1%.
Retention and Graduation: 89% freshmen return for sophomore year. 26% freshmen graduate within 4 years. 56% freshmen graduate within 6 years. **Faculty:** Student/faculty ratio 25:1. 1,275 full-time faculty, 87% hold PhDs, 40% are members of minority groups, 43% are women.

ACADEMICS
Degrees: Associate; Bachelor's; Doctoral/Professional; Doctoral/Research; Master's; Post-Bachelor's certificate **Classes:** Most classes have 10-19 students. Most lab/discussion sessions have 10-19 students. **Most popular majors:** Biology/Biological Sciences, General; Psychology, General; Business Administration And Management, General. **Special Study Options:** Accelerated program; Cooperative education program; Distance learning; Double major; Dual enrollment; Exchange student program (domestic); Honors program; Independent study; Internships; Study abroad; Teacher certification program; Weekend college. **Honors programs:** Please visit the honors college website at http://honors.fiu.edu/ **Combined degree programs:** BA/JD; BA/MA; BA/MEng. **Disability Services offered to physically disabled students:** Note-taking services; Reader services; Tape recorders; Tutors. **Career services:** Alumni services; Career assessment; Career/job search classes; Internships; Regional alumni

FACILITIES
Housing: Apartments for married students; Apartments for single students; Coed dorms; Fraternity/sorority housing 100% of campus accessible to physically diasbled. **Special Academic Facilities/Equipment:** The Frost Art Museum, The Wolfsonian Art Museum, Natural Preserve, Biscayne Bay Preserve **Computers:** 100% of classrooms, 100% of dorms, 1000% of libraries, 100% of dining areas, 100% of student union, 100% of common outdoor areas have wireless network access. Students can register for classes online. Administrative functions (other than registration) can be performed online.

CAMPUS LIFE
Environment: Metropolis **Activities:** Campus Ministries; Choral groups; Drama/theater; International Student Organization; Jazz band; Marching band; Model UN; Music ensembles; Opera; Radio station; Student government; Student newspaper; Symphony orchestra; Yearbook 250 registered organizations, 40 honor societies, 5 religious organizations. 21 fraternities, 17

sororities. **Athletics (Intercollegiate):** *Men:* baseball, basketball, cross-country, football, soccer, track/field (outdoor), track/field (indoor). *Women:* basketball, cross-country, diving, golf, soccer, softball, swimming, tennis, track/field (outdoor), track/field (indoor), volleyball. **On-Campus Highlights:** The Frost Museum, The Wolfsonian Museum, Steven and Dorothea Green Library, Graham University Center, Biscayne Bay Campus Library **Environmental Initiatives:** Spring 2011, FIU has officially become a smoking-free campus. Providing clean and smoke-free air to it's community.

ADMISSIONS

Freshman Academic Profile: Average high school GPA 4.0. 25% in top 10% of high school class, 58% in top 25% of high school class, 90% in top 50% of high school class. **Test Scores:** SAT Math middle 50% range 540-620. SAT EBRW middle 50% range 560-640. ACT middle 50% range 23-27. Minimum internet-based TOEFL 80. Minimum paper TOEFL 550. **Basis for Candidate Selection:** *Very important factors considered include:* rigor of secondary school record, class rank, academic GPA, standardized test scores. *Other factors considered include:* application essay, recommendation(s), extracurricular activities, talent/ability, character/personal qualities, first generation, alumni/ae relation, geographical residence, state residency, volunteer work, work experience, level of applicant's interest. **Freshman Admission Requirements:** High school diploma is required and GED is accepted *Academic units required:* 4 English, 4 math, 3 science, 2 science labs, 2 foreign language, 3 social studies, 2 academic electives. **Freshman Admission Statistics:** 14,861 applied, 51.1% admitted, 38% enrolled. **Transfer Admission Requirements:** college transcript(s), statement of good standing from prior institution(s). Minimum college GPA of 2.0 required. Lowest grade transferable D. **General Admission Information:** Application fee $30. Regular application deadline 5/1. Nonfall registration accepted. Admission may be deferred for a maximum of 1 year.

COSTS AND FINANCIAL AID

Annual in-state tuition $10,882. Annual out-of-state tuition $18,566. Room and board $10,882. Required fees $390. Average book expense $1,634. **Required Forms and Deadlines:** FAFSA. **Notification of Awards:** Applicants will be notified of awards on a rolling basis beginning 2/1. **Types of Aid:** *Need-based scholarships/grants:* College/university scholarship or grant aid from institutional funds; Federal Pell; Private scholarships; SEOG; State scholarships/grants. *Loans:* Direct PLUS loans; Direct Subsidized Stafford Loans; Direct Unsubsidized Stafford Loans. *Student Employment:* Federal Work-Study Program available. Institutional employment available. **Financial Aid Statistics:** 66% needy freshmen, 79% needy undergrads receive need-based scholarship or grant aid. 45% freshmen, 32% undergrads receive non-need-based scholarship or grant aid. 41% freshmen, 53% undergrads receive need-based self-help aid. 1% freshmen, 1% undergrads receive athletic scholarships. 50% undergrads borrow to pay for school. Average cumulative indebtedness $19,915. **Criteria for awarding aid:** *Need-based:* Academics *Non-need-based:* Academics, Art, Athletics, Minority status, Music/drama, State/district residency.

FLORIDA SOUTHERN COLLEGE

111 Lake Hollingsworth Drive, Lakeland, FL 33801
Phone: 863-680-4131 · **Financial Aid Phone:** 863-680-4140
E-mail: fscadm@flsouthern.edu · **CEEB Code:** 5218
Fax: 863-680-4120 · **Website:** www.flsouthern.edu · **ACT Code:** 732

This private school, affiliated with the Methodist Church, was founded in 1883. It has a 113 acre campus.

RATINGS

Admissions Selectivity Rating: 88   **Fire Safety Rating:** 93   **Green Rating:** 65

STUDENTS AND FACULTY

Enrollment: 2,579. **Student Body:** 65% female, 35% male, 38% out-of-state, 4% international (52 countries represented). Asian 3%, African American 5%, Caucasian 74%, Hispanic 11%, Native American 1%, Pacific Islander <1%, Two or more races 1%, Race unknown 2%.
Retention and Graduation: 80% freshmen return for sophomore year. 63% freshmen graduate within 6 years. 24% grads go on to further study within 1 year. 14% grads pursue arts and sciences degrees. 1% grads pursue law degrees. 4% grads pursue business degrees. 2% grads pursue medical degrees.
Faculty: Student/faculty ratio 15:1. 139 full-time faculty, 88% hold PhDs, 18% are members of minority groups, 50% are women. 0% of classes are taught by teaching assistants.

ACADEMICS

Degrees: Bachelor's; Doctoral Other; Master's; Post-Master's certificate
Classes: Most classes have 10-19 students. Most lab/discussion sessions have 10-19 students. **Most popular majors:** Biology/Biological Sciences, General; Registered Nursing/Registered Nurse; Business Administration And Management, General. **Special Study Options:** Accelerated program; Distance learning; Double major; Dual enrollment; External degree program; Honors program; Independent study; Internships; Student-designed major; Study abroad; Teacher certification program. **Honors programs:** The Honors Program at Florida Southern College offers dynamic and innovative academic options to talented students who seek extraordinary inter-disciplinary learning opportunities. Honors students enjoy collaborative, team-taught courses with exceptional faculty, a series of "supper seminars" that host expert speakers, and specially designated facilities—including classrooms, the Honors Suite, and special housing—which foster an enriching living-learning environment. All honor students receive priority registration and are able to take course overloads without paying additional fees. Three-year and four-year undergraduate tracks are available. **Combined degree programs:** BA/MA; BA/MD. **Career services:** Alumni network; Alumni services; Career assessment; Career/job search classes; Internships; Regional alumni

FACILITIES

Housing: Apartments for single students; Coed dorms; Fraternity/sorority housing; Men's dorms; Special housing for disabled student; Theme housing; Women's dorms 85% of campus accessible to physically diasbled. **Special Academic Facilities/Equipment:** The Rinker Technology Center; numerous computer labs across campus, and the popular TuTu's Cyber Café provide free computer access for all, in addition to the campus' free WiFi. The Christoverson Humanities Building features a film studies theater and modern language lab, and the Chatlos Communications Building offers a newly renovated television studio. The state-of-the-art, recently expanded Blanton Nursing Building houses high-tech classrooms and a clinical learning lab with a full complement of patient simulators and the latest patient information technology used in Florida hospitals. Science majors enjoy an on-site planetarium, world-class heritage rose garden, greenhouse, a citrus grove, ecological wetlands research station. The McKay Archives Center houses the College's original Frank Lloyd Wright drawings and documents, the Florida Citrus Hall of Fame, and the Center for Florida History. The Davis Performing Arts Center features the nationally renowned Branscomb Auditorium; the modern Buckner Theatre; the Melvin Art Gallery; and newly constructed facilities to house the Imperial Symphony Orchestra, a regional professional orchestra with which Florida Southern collaborates. This partnership gives FSC students the opportunity to perform with world-renowned ISO guest artists. Other special facilities for the arts include the Wynee Warden Dance Studio, opened in fall 2014, a professional-quality dance studio that features a soaring glass half-rotunda with amazing views of Lake Hollingsworth and plenty of sunshine to illuminate the rehearsal floor. For education majors, the campus is home to an on-site Preschool Learning Lab, the Roberts Center for Learning and Literacy and The Roberts Academy, a transitional school for gifted elementary-age students with dyslexia. Exciting news for business majors: the new, cutting-edge Bill '65 and Mary Ann Becker Business Building includes a simulated trading floor, high-tech classrooms, and a state-of-the-art market observation room. Finally, the new Sharp Family Tourism and Education Center celebrates the campus' architectural significance as the largest single-site collection of Frank Lloyd Wright architecture in the world, educating visitors through a film, museum, and tours. **Computers:** 20% of classrooms, 20% of dorms, 100% of libraries, 100% of dining areas, 50% of student union, 50% of common outdoor areas have wireless network access. Students can register for classes online. Administrative functions (other than registration) can be performed online.

CAMPUS LIFE

Environment: City **Activities:** Campus Ministries; Choral groups; Concert band; Dance; Drama/theater; International Student Organization; Jazz band; Literary magazine; Music ensembles; Musical theater; Opera; Pep band; Student government; Student newspaper; Symphony orchestra; Television station; Yearbook 70 registered organizations, 22 honor societies, 9 religious organizations. 7 fraternities, 7 sororities. **Athletics (Intercollegiate):** *Men:* baseball, basketball, cross-country, golf, lacrosse, soccer, swimming, tennis, track/field (outdoor). *Women:* basketball, cross-country, golf, soccer, softball, swimming, tennis, track/field (outdoor), volleyball. **On-Campus Highlights:** TuTu's Cyber Cafe, Wellness Center and Pool, Mr. George's Green – a 2-acre central campus lawn for recreation, The Buck Stop: an outdoor dining area in the center of campus, Jenkins Field House – home of our intercollegiate athletic teams **Environmental Initiatives:** Florida Southern College has installed filtered water bottle stations throughout campus that provide users with an opportunity to fill and refill reusable bottles rather than purchasing new filtered water bottles. Additionally, FSC's Student Government Association distributes refillable water bottles to each new class at Orientation, encouraging new students to make use of the stations and to be environmentally minded from the start.

ADMISSIONS

Freshman Academic Profile: Average high school GPA 3.7. 31% in top 10% of high school class, 60% in top 25% of high school class, 80% in top 50% of high school class. 78% from public high schools. **Test Scores:** SAT Math middle 50% range 530-610. SAT EBRW middle 50% range 540-640. ACT middle 50% range 24-29. Minimum internet-based TOEFL 79/80. Minimum paper TOEFL 550. **Basis for Candidate Selection:** *Very important factors considered include:* rigor of secondary school record, academic GPA. *Important factors considered include:* application essay, standardized test scores, recommendation(s), extracurricular activities, talent/ability, character/personal qualities, level of applicant's interest. *Other factors considered include:* class rank, interview, first generation, alumni/ae relation, religious affiliation/commitment, racial/ethnic status, volunteer work, work experience. **Freshman Admission Requirements:** High school diploma is required and GED is accepted *Academic units required:* 4 English, 3 math, 2 science, 2 science labs, 3 social studies, 3 history, 1 academic elective, *Academic units recommended:* 4 English, 3 math, 2 science, 2 science labs, 2 foreign language, 3 social studies, 3 history, 1 academic elective. **Freshman Admission Statistics:** 5,983 applied, 51.5% admitted, 23% enrolled. **Transfer Admission Requirements:** college transcript(s), essay or personal statement, statement of good standing from prior institution(s). Minimum college GPA of 2.0 required. Lowest grade transferable C. **General Admission Information:** Priority deadline 3/1. Nonfall registration accepted. Admission may be deferred for a maximum of 1 year.

COSTS AND FINANCIAL AID

Annual tuition $34,074. Required fees $700. Average book expense $1,250. **Required Forms and Deadlines:** FAFSA; Institution's own financial aid form. **Notification of Awards:** Applicants will be notified of awards on a rolling basis beginning 3/1. **Types of Aid:** *Need-based scholarships/grants:* College/university scholarship or grant aid from institutional funds; Federal Nursing Scholarships; Federal Pell; Private scholarships; SEOG; State scholarships/grants. *Loans:* Direct PLUS loans; Direct Subsidized Stafford Loans; Direct Unsubsidized Stafford Loans. *Student Employment:* Federal Work-Study Program available. Institutional employment available. **Financial Aid Statistics:** 100% needy freshmen, 99% needy undergrads receive need-based scholarship or grant aid. 65% freshmen, 68% undergrads receive non-need-based scholarship or grant aid. 4% freshmen, 11% undergrads receive need-based self-help aid. 4% freshmen, 6% undergrads receive athletic scholarships. 99% freshmen, 98% undergrads receive any aid. 81% undergrads borrow to pay for school. Average cumulative indebtedness $26,637. **Criteria for awarding aid:** *Need-based:* Academics, Alumni affiliation, Art, Athletics, Job skills, Leadership, Minority status, Music/drama, Religious affiliation *Non-need-based:* Academics, Alumni affiliation, Art, Athletics, Job skills, Leadership, Minority status, Music/drama, Religious affiliation, State/district residency.

See page 936.

FLORIDA STATE UNIVERSITY

PO Box 3062400, Tallahassee, FL 32306-2400
Phone: 850-644-6200 · **Financial Aid Phone:** 850-644-5716
E-mail: admissions@fsu.edu · **CEEB Code:** 5219
Fax: 850-644-0197 · **Website:** www.fsu.edu · **ACT Code:** 734

This public school was founded in 1851. It has a 474.5 acre campus.

RATINGS

Admissions Selectivity Rating: 90   **Fire Safety Rating:** 90   **Green Rating:** 60*

STUDENTS AND FACULTY

Enrollment: 32,699. **Student Body:** 56% female, 44% male, 11% out-of-state, 2% international (109 countries represented). Asian 2%, African American 8%, Caucasian 62%, Hispanic 20%, Native American <1%, Pacific Islander <1%, Two or more races 4%, Race unknown 2%.
Retention and Graduation: 94% freshmen return for sophomore year. 63% freshmen graduate within 4 years. 80% freshmen graduate within 6 years. 42% grads go on to further study within 1 year. **Faculty:** Student/faculty ratio 22:1. 1,448 full-time faculty, 93% hold PhDs, 21% are members of minority groups, 40% are women. 28% of classes are taught by teaching assistants.

ACADEMICS

Degrees: Associate; Bachelor's; Certificate; Doctoral; Doctoral/Professional; Doctoral/Research; Master's; Post-Bachelor's certificate; Post-Master's certificate; Transfer Associate **Classes:** Most classes have 10-19 students. Most

lab/discussion sessions have 20-29 students. **Most popular majors:** Psychology, General; Criminal Justice/Safety Studies; Finance, General. **Special Study Options:** Accelerated program; Cooperative education program; Cross-registration; Distance learning; Double major; Dual enrollment; English as a Second Language (ESL); Honors program; Independent study; Internships; Study abroad; Teacher certification program. **Honors programs:** The Florida State University Honors Program provides an enriched curriculum and special opportunities for exceptional, high-achieving students who are entering college for the first time. Each fall, freshmen who are admitted into this program attend the University Honors Colloquium, a weekly forum that features stimulating lectures by distinguished faculty as well as informative presentations from directors of academic programs. As they work to meet their liberal study requirements, University Honors students then have the chance to take small, honors-only courses and special topic seminars with some of the university's best researchers and teachers. With its emphasis on small classes taught by top faculty, this program provides the atmosphere of a small liberal arts college within a large research university. **Combined degree programs:** BA/MA. **Disability Services offered to physically disabled students:** Note-taking services; Reader services; Tape recorders; Tutors. **Career services:** Alumni network; Alumni services; Career assessment; Career/job search classes; Internships; Regional alumni

FACILITIES

Housing: Apartments for single students; Coed dorms; Fraternity/sorority housing; Special housing for disabled student; Theme housing 99% of campus accessible to physically diasbled. **Special Academic Facilities/Equipment:** Art gallery, museum, developmental research school, marine lab, oceanographic institute, tandem Van de Graaff accelerator, national high magnetic field lab. **Computers:** 50% of classrooms, 25% of dorms, 90% of libraries, 100% of dining areas, 90% of student union, 70% of common outdoor areas have wireless network access. Students can register for classes online. Administrative functions (other than registration) can be performed online. Undergraduates are required to own a computer.

CAMPUS LIFE

Environment: City **Activities:** Campus Ministries; Choral groups; Concert band; Dance; Drama/theater; International Student Organization; Jazz band; Literary magazine; Marching band; Model UN; Music ensembles; Musical theater; Opera; Pep band; Radio station; Student government; Student newspaper; Student-run film society; Symphony orchestra; Television station; Yearbook 520 registered organizations, 23 honor societies, 30 religious organizations. 32 fraternities, 28 sororities. **Athletics (Intercollegiate):** *Men:* baseball, basketball, cheerleading, cross-country, diving, football, golf, swimming, tennis, track/field (outdoor), track/field (indoor). *Women:* basketball, cheerleading, cross-country, diving, golf, soccer, softball, swimming, tennis, track/field (outdoor), track/field (indoor), volleyball. **On-Campus Highlights:** Suwannee Dining Hall, Bobby E. Leach Student Recreation Center, Bobby Bowden Field at Doak Campbell Stadium, National High Magnetic Field Laboratory, FSU Reservation **Environmental Initiatives:** Creation of the FSU Office of Sustainability and the hiring of a full-time Director of Campus Sustainability to help build a comprehensive sustainable campus program.

ADMISSIONS

Freshman Academic Profile: Average high school GPA 4.0. 41% in top 10% of high school class, 83% in top 25% of high school class, 99% in top 50% of high school class. 79% from public high schools. **Test Scores:** SAT Math middle 50% range 590-660. SAT EBRW middle 50% range 600-670. ACT middle 50% range 26-30. Minimum internet-based TOEFL 80. Minimum paper TOEFL 550. **Basis for Candidate Selection:** *Very important factors considered include:* rigor of secondary school record. *Important factors considered include:* academic GPA, standardized test scores, talent/ability, state residency. *Other factors considered include:* class rank, application essay, extracurricular activities, character/personal qualities, first generation, geographical residence, volunteer work, work experience. **Freshman Admission Requirements:** High school diploma is required and GED is accepted *Academic units required:* 4 English, 4 math, 3 science, 2 science labs, 2 foreign language, 1 social studies, 2 history, 3 academic electives, *Academic units recommended:* 4 English, 4 math, 4 science, 2 science labs, 4 foreign language, 2 social studies, 2 history, 3 academic electives. **Freshman Admission Statistics:** 35,334 applied, 49.2% admitted, 38% enrolled. **Transfer Admission Requirements:** college transcript(s), Minimum college GPA of 3.0 required. Lowest grade transferable D-. **General Admission Information:** Application fee $30. Regular application deadline 2/7. Nonfall registration accepted.

COSTS AND FINANCIAL AID

Annual in-state tuition $10,458. Annual out-of-state tuition $19,806. Room and board $10,458. Required fees $1,867. Average book expense $1,000. **Required Forms and Deadlines:** FAFSA; State aid form. **Notification of Awards:** Applicants will be notified of awards on a rolling basis beginning 4/5. **Types of Aid:** *Need-based scholarships/grants:* College/university scholarship or grant aid from institutional funds; Federal Pell; Private scholarships; SEOG; State scholarships/grants; United Negro College Fund. *Loans:* Direct PLUS loans; Direct Subsidized Stafford Loans; Direct Unsubsidized Stafford Loans. *Student*

Employment: Federal Work-Study Program available. Institutional employment available. **Financial Aid Statistics:** 94% needy freshmen, 89% needy undergrads receive need-based scholarship or grant aid. 74% freshmen, 77% undergrads receive non-need-based scholarship or grant aid. 54% freshmen, 82% undergrads receive need-based self-help aid. 1% freshmen, 1% undergrads receive athletic scholarships. 96% freshmen, 87% undergrads receive any aid. Average cumulative indebtedness $22,912. **Criteria for awarding aid:** *Non-need-based:* Academics, Art, Athletics, Leadership, Music/drama.

FONTBONNE UNIVERSITY

6800 Wydown Boulevard, Saint Louis, MO 63105
Phone: 314-889-1400 · **Financial Aid Phone:** 314-889-1414
E-mail: fcadmis@fontbonne.edu · **CEEB Code:** 6216
Fax: 314-889-1451 · **Website:** www.fontbonne.edu · **ACT Code:** 2298

This private school, affiliated with the Roman Catholic Church, was founded in 1917. It has a 13 acre campus.

RATINGS
Admissions Selectivity Rating: 80   **Fire Safety Rating:** 90   **Green Rating:** 60*

STUDENTS AND FACULTY
Enrollment: 1,993. **Student Body:** 72% female, 28% male, 12% out-of-state, 1% international (23 countries represented). Asian 1%, African American 34%, Caucasian 62%, Hispanic 1%, Native American <1%, Race unknown 1%. **Retention and Graduation:** 58% freshmen return for sophomore year. 25% grads go on to further study within 1 year. **Faculty:** Student/faculty ratio 16:1. 73 full-time faculty, 71% hold PhDs, 10% are members of minority groups, 68% are women. 0% of classes are taught by teaching assistants.

ACADEMICS
Degrees: Bachelor's; Certificate; Master's; Post-Bachelor's certificate **Classes:** Most classes have 20-29 students. Most lab/discussion sessions have 10-19 students. **Most popular majors:** Special Education And Teaching, General; Elementary Education And Teaching; Business Administration And Management, General. **Special Study Options:** Accelerated program; Cooperative education program; Cross-registration; Distance learning; Double major; English as a Second Language (ESL); Exchange student program (domestic); Honors program; Independent study; Internships; Liberal arts/career combination; Student-designed major; Study abroad; Teacher certification program; Weekend college. **Combined degree programs:** BA/MEng. **Disability Services offered to physically disabled students:** Note-taking services; Reader services; Tape recorders; Tutors. **Career services:** Alumni services; Career assessment; Career/job search classes; Internships

FACILITIES
Housing: Apartments for single students; Coed dorms; Special housing for international students 85% of campus accessible to physically disabled. **Special Academic Facilities/Equipment:** Art gallery. **Computers:** 75% of classrooms, 100% of dorms, 100% of libraries, 100% of dining areas, 100% of student union, 100% of common outdoor areas have wireless network access. Students can register for classes online. Administrative functions (other than registration) can be performed online.

CAMPUS LIFE
Environment: Metropolis **Activities:** Campus Ministries; Choral groups; Dance; Drama/theater; Literary magazine; Music ensembles; Radio station; Student government; Student newspaper 34 registered organizations, 7 honor societies, 4 religious organizations. **Athletics (Intercollegiate):** *Men:* baseball, basketball, cross-country, field hockey, golf, lacrosse, soccer, tennis. *Women:* basketball, bowling, cross-country, field hockey, golf, lacrosse, soccer, softball, tennis, volleyball. **On-Campus Highlights:** Ryan Hall, Dunham Student Activity Center, Library, Medaille Hall, Fine Arts Center

ADMISSIONS
Freshman Academic Profile: Average high school GPA 3.1. 7% in top 10% of high school class, 28% in top 25% of high school class, 61% in top 50% of high school class. 56% from public high schools. **Test Scores:** SAT Math middle 50% range 470-625. SAT EBRW middle 50% range 500-625. ACT middle 50% range 18-24. Minimum paper TOEFL 525. **Basis for Candidate Selection:** *Very important factors considered include:* rigor of secondary school record, class rank, academic GPA, standardized test scores, character/personal qualities. *Other factors considered include:* application essay, recommendation(s), interview, extracurricular activities, talent/ability, first generation, alumni/ae relation, volunteer work, work experience, level of applicant's interest. **Freshman Admission Requirements:** High school diploma is required and GED is accepted *Academic units required:* 4 English, 3 math, 3 science,

1 science labs, 3 social studies, 3 academic electives. **Freshman Admission Statistics:** 588 applied, 75.5% admitted, 45% enrolled. **Transfer Admission Requirements:** college transcript(s), essay or personal statement, Minimum college GPA of 2.0 required. Lowest grade transferable D. **General Admission Information:** Application fee $25. Priority deadline 1/15. Regular application deadline 8/1. Nonfall registration accepted. Admission may be deferred for a maximum of 1 year.

COSTS AND FINANCIAL AID
Annual tuition $20,860. Room and board $8,319. Required fees $440. Average book expense $650. **Required Forms and Deadlines:** FAFSA; Institution's own financial aid form. **Types of Aid:** *Need-based scholarships/grants:* College/university scholarship or grant aid from institutional funds; Federal Pell; Private scholarships; SEOG; State scholarships/grants. *Loans: Student Employment:* Federal Work-Study Program available. **Financial Aid Statistics:** 96% needy freshmen, 98% needy undergrads receive need-based scholarship or grant aid. 99% freshmen, 68% undergrads receive non-need-based scholarship or grant aid. 93% freshmen, 91% undergrads receive need-based self-help aid. 0% freshmen, 0% undergrads receive athletic scholarships. **Criteria for awarding aid:** *Need-based:* Job skills *Non-need-based:* Academics, Alumni affiliation, Art, Job skills, Leadership, Minority status, Religious affiliation.

FORDHAM UNIVERSITY

441 East Fordham Road, Bronx, NY 10458
Phone: 718-817-4000 · **Financial Aid Phone:** 718-817-3800
E-mail: enroll@fordham.edu · **CEEB Code:** 2259
Fax: 718-817-0549 · **Website:** www.fordham.edu · **ACT Code:** 2748

This private school, affiliated with the Roman Catholic Church, was founded in 1841. It has a 93 acre campus.

RATINGS
Admissions Selectivity Rating: 91   **Fire Safety Rating:** 96   **Green Rating:** 62

STUDENTS AND FACULTY
Enrollment: 9,403. **Student Body:** 57% female, 43% male, 57% out-of-state, 8% international (73 countries represented). Asian 10%, African American 4%, Caucasian 58%, Hispanic 14%, Native American <1%, Pacific Islander <1%, Two or more races 3%, Race unknown 2%. **Retention and Graduation:** 90% freshmen return for sophomore year. 74% freshmen graduate within 4 years. 80% freshmen graduate within 6 years. 17% grads go on to further study within 1 year. 6% grads pursue arts and sciences degrees. 3.4% grads pursue law degrees. 3% grads pursue business degrees. 1.5% grads pursue medical degrees. **Faculty:** Student/faculty ratio 15:1. 735 full-time faculty, 93% hold PhDs, 28% are members of minority groups, 42% are women. 8% of classes are taught by teaching assistants.

ACADEMICS
Degrees: Bachelor's; Doctoral; Doctoral/Professional; Doctoral/Research; Master's; Post-Bachelor's certificate; Post-Master's certificate **Classes:** Most classes have 20-29 students. Most lab/discussion sessions have 20-29 students. **Most popular majors:** Communication, Journalism, And Related Programs, Other; Business Administration And Management, General; Finance, General. **Special Study Options:** Accelerated program; Cross-registration; Distance learning; Double major; English as a Second Language (ESL); Exchange student program (domestic); Honors program; Independent study; Internships; Liberal arts/career combination; Student-designed major; Study abroad; Teacher certification program. **Honors programs:** Each undergraduate college has its own Honors Program. Each program offers enriched academic opportunity for qualified and interested students. Students are automatically considered for Honors programs as part of the application review process. **Combined degree programs:** BA/JD; BA/MA. **Disability Services offered to physically disabled students:** Note-taking services; Reader services; Tape recorders; Tutors. **Career services:** Alumni network; Alumni services; Career assessment; Career/job search classes; Internships; Regional alumni

FACILITIES
Housing: Apartments for single students; Coed dorms; Other (please specify) 80% of campus accessible to physically disabled. **Special Academic Facilities/Equipment:** WFUV: NPR affiliate on campus, television station, white and black box theatres, media and visual arts labs Greek and Etruscan art gallery,

seismic station, 113 acre biological field station The Louis Calder Center in Armonk, NY **Computers:** 90% of classrooms, 98% of dorms, 95% of libraries, 100% of dining areas, 80% of common outdoor areas have wireless network access. Students can register for classes online. Administrative functions (other than registration) can be performed online.

CAMPUS LIFE

Environment: Metropolis **Activities:** Campus Ministries; Choral groups; Concert band; Dance; Drama/theater; International Student Organization; Jazz band; Literary magazine; Marching band; Music ensembles; Musical theater; Pep band; Radio station; Student government; Student newspaper; Student-run film society; Symphony orchestra; Television station; Yearbook 133 registered organizations, 12 honor societies, 3 religious organizations. **Athletics (Intercollegiate):** *Men:* baseball, basketball, cross-country, diving, football, golf, soccer, squash, swimming, tennis, track/field (outdoor), track/field (indoor), water polo. *Women:* basketball, cheerleading, crew/rowing, cross-country, diving, soccer, softball, swimming, tennis, track/field (outdoor), track/field (indoor), volleyball. **On-Campus Highlights:** McKeon Hall—Lincoln Center, Hughes Hall—Gabelli School of Business at Rose Hill, William D. Walsh Family Library—Rose Hill, Edwards Parade/Keating Hall—Rose Hill, Student Center—Lincoln Center

ADMISSIONS

Freshman Academic Profile: Average high school GPA 3.7. 48% in top 10% of high school class, 78% in top 25% of high school class, 97% in top 50% of high school class. 63% from public high schools. **Test Scores:** SAT Math middle 50% range 610-710. SAT EBRW middle 50% range 620-700. ACT middle 50% range 27-31. Minimum internet-based TOEFL 90. Minimum paper TOEFL 575. **Basis for Candidate Selection:** *Very important factors considered include:* rigor of secondary school record, academic GPA, standardized test scores. *Important factors considered include:* application essay, recommendation(s), extracurricular activities, talent/ability, character/personal qualities, volunteer work. *Other factors considered include:* class rank, first generation, alumni/ae relation, geographical residence, racial/ethnic status, work experience, level of applicant's interest. **Freshman Admission Requirements:** High school diploma is required and GED is accepted *Academic units required:* 4 English, 3 math, 3 science, 2 foreign language, 3 social studies, *Academic units recommended:* 4 English, 4 math, 4 science, 4 foreign language, 4 social studies. **Freshman Admission Statistics:** 45,147 applied, 46.4% admitted, 11% enrolled. **Transfer Admission Requirements:** High school transcript, college transcript(s), essay or personal statement, statement of good standing from prior institution(s). Minimum college GPA of 3.0 required. Lowest grade transferable C. **General Admission Information:** Application fee $70. Priority deadline 11/1. Regular application deadline 1/1. Nonfall registration accepted. Admission may be deferred for a maximum of 1 year.

COSTS AND FINANCIAL AID

Annual tuition $49,645. Room and board $17,445. Required fees $956. Average book expense $1,012. **Required Forms and Deadlines:** Business/Farm Supplement; CSS/Financial Aid PROFILE; FAFSA; Noncustodial PROFILE; State aid form. **Notification of Awards:** Applicants will be notified of awards on a rolling basis beginning 3/31. **Types of Aid:** *Need-based scholarships/grants:* College/university scholarship or grant aid from institutional funds; Federal Pell; Private scholarships; SEOG; State scholarships/grants. *Loans:* Direct PLUS loans; Direct Subsidized Stafford Loans; Direct Unsubsidized Stafford Loans. *Student Employment:* Federal Work-Study Program available. Institutional employment available. **Financial Aid Statistics:** 98% needy freshmen, 96% needy undergrads receive need-based scholarship or grant aid. 23% freshmen, 19% undergrads receive non-need-based scholarship or grant aid. 66% freshmen, 69% undergrads receive need-based self-help aid. 2% freshmen, 2% undergrads receive athletic scholarships. 90% freshmen, 80% undergrads receive any aid. 60% undergrads borrow to pay for school. Average cumulative indebtedness $25,069. **Criteria for awarding aid:** *Need-based:* Academics, Athletics *Non-need-based:* Academics, Athletics.

FORT HAYS STATE UNIVERSITY

600 Park Street, Hays, KS 67601-4099
Phone: 785.628.3478 · **Financial Aid Phone:** 785-628-4408
E-mail: tigers@fhsu.edu · **CEEB Code:** 6218
Fax: 800.432.0248 · **Website:** www.fhsu.edu · **ACT Code:** 1408

This public school was founded in 1902. It has a 4160 acre campus.

RATINGS

Admissions Selectivity Rating: 72   **Fire Safety Rating:** 84   **Green Rating:** 60*

STUDENTS AND FACULTY

Enrollment: 11,503. **Student Body:** 61% female, 39% male, 31% out-of-state, 29% international. Asian 1%, African American 4%, Caucasian 57%, Hispanic 7%, Native American <1%, Pacific Islander <1%, Two or more races 2%, Race unknown 1%.
Retention and Graduation: 69% freshmen return for sophomore year. 20% grads go on to further study within 1 year. **Faculty:** Student/faculty ratio 16:1. 315 full-time faculty, 61% hold PhDs, 10% are members of minority groups, 45% are women. 1% of classes are taught by teaching assistants.

ACADEMICS

Degrees: Associate; Bachelor's; Certificate; Master's; Post-Master's certificate **Classes:** Most classes have 10-19 students. Most lab/discussion sessions have 20-29 students. **Most popular majors:** Elementary Education And Teaching; Health And Physical Education/Fitness, General; Business/Commerce, General. **Special Study Options:** Distance learning; Double major; Dual enrollment; English as a Second Language (ESL); Exchange student program (domestic); External degree program; Honors program; Independent study; Internships; Liberal arts/career combination; Student-designed major; Study abroad; Teacher certification program; Weekend college. **Combined degree programs:** BA/MEng. **Disability Services offered to physically disabled students:** Note-taking services; Reader services; Tutors. **Career services:** Alumni network; Alumni services; Career assessment; Career/job search classes; Internships

FACILITIES

Housing: Apartments for married students; Apartments for single students; Coed dorms; Fraternity/sorority housing; Men's dorms; Women's dorms 100% of campus accessible to physically diasbled. **Special Academic Facilities/Equipment:** Paleontology, natural history, visual arts and media center, farm, NMR gas analyzer, telescope (HG). **Computers:** 100% of classrooms, 100% of dorms, 100% of libraries, 100% of dining areas, 100% of student union, 100% of common outdoor areas have wireless network access.

CAMPUS LIFE

Environment: Village **Activities:** Campus Ministries; Choral groups; Concert band; Dance; Drama/theater; Jazz band; Literary magazine; Marching band; Model UN; Music ensembles; Musical theater; Opera; Pep band; Radio station; Student government; Student newspaper; Symphony orchestra; Television station 103 registered organizations, 20 honor societies, 2 religious organizations. 3 fraternities, 3 sororities. **Athletics (Intercollegiate):** *Men:* baseball, basketball, cheerleading, cross-country, football, golf, track/field (outdoor), track/field (indoor), wrestling. *Women:* basketball, cheerleading, cross-country, golf, softball, tennis, track/field (outdoor), track/field (indoor), volleyball. **On-Campus Highlights:** www.tigersportszone.com, www.fhsu.edu/sternberg/, www.fhsu.edu/tmn **Environmental Initiatives:** Clean up of Big Creek

ADMISSIONS

Freshman Academic Profile: Average high school GPA 3.4. 13% in top 10% of high school class, 32% in top 25% of high school class, 64% in top 50% of high school class. 95% from public high schools. **Test Scores:** ACT middle 50% range 18-24. Minimum internet-based TOEFL 61. Minimum paper TOEFL 500. **Basis for Candidate Selection:** *Other factors considered include:* rigor of secondary school record, class rank, academic GPA, standardized test scores. **Freshman Admission Requirements:** High school diploma is required and GED is accepted *Academic units recommended:* 4 English, 3 math, 3 science, 2 social studies, 1 history, 1 computer science. **Freshman Admission Statistics:** 2,337 applied, 85.9% admitted, 24% enrolled. **Transfer Admission Requirements:** college transcript(s), Minimum college GPA of 2.0 required. Lowest grade transferable D. **General Admission Information:** Application fee $30. Nonfall registration accepted. Admission may be deferred for a maximum of 1 year.

COSTS AND FINANCIAL AID

Required Forms and Deadlines: FAFSA; Institution's own financial aid form. **Notification of Awards:** Applicants will be notified of awards on a rolling basis beginning 3/15. **Types of Aid:** *Need-based scholarships/grants:* College/university scholarship or grant aid from institutional funds; Federal Pell; Private scholarships; SEOG; State scholarships/grants. *Loans:* Direct PLUS loans; Direct Subsidized Stafford Loans; Direct Unsubsidized Stafford Loans. *Student Employment:* Federal Work-Study Program available. **Financial Aid Statistics:** 82% needy freshmen, 80% needy undergrads receive need-based scholarship or grant aid. 3% freshmen, 3% undergrads receive non-need-based scholarship or grant aid. 85% freshmen, 10% undergrads receive need-based self-help aid. 4% freshmen, 3% undergrads receive athletic scholarships. Average cumulative indebtedness $27,462. **Criteria for awarding aid:** *Non-need-based:* Academics, Alumni affiliation, Art, Athletics, Job skills, Leadership, Minority status, Music/drama, State/district residency.

FORT LEWIS COLLEGE

1000 Rim Drive, Durango, CO 81301
Financial Aid Phone: 970-247-7142
E-mail: admisson@fortlewis.edu • **CEEB Code:** 4310
Fax: 970-247-7179 • **Website:** www.fortlewis.edu • **ACT Code:** 510

This public school was founded in 1911. It has a 362 acre campus.

RATINGS
Admissions Selectivity Rating: 71   **Fire Safety Rating:** 91   **Green Rating:** 98

STUDENTS AND FACULTY
Enrollment: 3,187. **Student Body:** 51% female, 49% male, 52% out-of-state, <1% international (14 countries represented). Asian 1%, African American 1%, Caucasian 48%, Hispanic 11%, Native American 26%, Pacific Islander <1%, Two or more races 9%, Race unknown 3%.
Retention and Graduation: 59% freshmen return for sophomore year. 21% freshmen graduate within 4 years. 40% freshmen graduate within 6 years. 14% grads go on to further study within 1 year. **Faculty:** Student/faculty ratio 15:1. 183 full-time faculty, 86% hold PhDs, 9% are members of minority groups, 51% are women. 0% of classes are taught by teaching assistants.

ACADEMICS
Degrees: Bachelor's; Certificate; Master's; Post-Bachelor's certificate **Classes:** Most classes have 20-29 students. **Most popular majors:** Biology/Biological Sciences, General; Kinesiology And Exercise Science; Business Administration And Management, General. **Special Study Options:** Accelerated program; Cooperative education program; Distance learning; Double major; Dual enrollment; English as a Second Language (ESL); Exchange student program (domestic); Honors program; Independent study; Internships; Liberal arts/career combination; Student-designed major; Study abroad; Teacher certification program. **Honors programs:** The Honors Program is a selective curriculum for high-achieving students who seek interdisciplinary academic investigations through forums, interaction with writers and scholars, cultural events, and field trips. The culmination of the Honors studies is an interdisciplinary thesis on a topic of the student's choosing, leading to a minor in the Rhetoric of Inquiry, the study of the language and arguments of the academic disciplines. To acknowledge that extra effort, qualified Honors scholars receive special recognition at Convocation and are presented a bound copy of their Honors thesis. **Combined degree programs:** BA/MA. **Disability Services offered to physically disabled students:** Note-taking services; Reader services; Tape recorders; Tutors. **Career services:** Alumni network; Alumni services; Career assessment; Career/job search classes; Internships; Regional alumni

FACILITIES
Housing: Apartments for married students; Apartments for single students; Coed dorms; Special housing for disabled student; Theme housing 100% of campus accessible to physically diasbled. **Special Academic Facilities/ Equipment:** Center for Southwest Studies **Computers:** 100% of classrooms, 100% of dorms, 100% of libraries, 100% of dining areas, 100% of student union, 10% of common outdoor areas have wireless network access. Students can register for classes online. Administrative functions (other than registration) can be performed online.

CAMPUS LIFE
Environment: Village **Activities:** Campus Ministries; Choral groups; Concert band; Dance; Drama/theater; Jazz band; Literary magazine; Musical theater; Pep band; Radio station; Student government; Student newspaper 65 registered organizations, 5 honor societies, 3 religious organizations. **Athletics (Intercollegiate):** *Men:* basketball, cross-country, football, golf, soccer. *Women:* basketball, cross-country, lacrosse, soccer, softball, volleyball. **On-Campus Highlights:** Student Union, Student Life Center, Community Concert Hall, Rim Trail, Factory Trails bicycle and disk golf course **Environmental Initiatives:** All new construction or renovation follow at minimum LEED Silver standards

ADMISSIONS
Freshman Academic Profile: Average high school GPA 3.3. 13% in top 10% of high school class, 21% in top 25% of high school class, 73% in top 50% of high school class. **Test Scores:** SAT Math middle 50% range 500-610. SAT EBRW middle 50% range 520-600. ACT middle 50% range 20-25. Minimum internet-based TOEFL 61. Minimum paper TOEFL 500. **Basis for Candidate Selection:** *Very important factors considered include:* rigor of secondary school record, class rank, academic GPA, standardized test scores. *Other factors considered include:* application essay, recommendation(s), interview, extracurricular activities, talent/ability, character/personal qualities, first generation, alumni/ae relation, level of applicant's interest. **Freshman**

Admission Requirements: High school diploma is required and GED is accepted *Academic units required:* 4 English, 4 math, 3 science, 2 science labs, 1 foreign language, 2 social studies, 1 history, 3 academic electives. **Freshman Admission Statistics:** 1,841 applied, admitted, 19% enrolled. **Transfer Admission Requirements:** college transcript(s), Minimum college GPA of 2.40 required. Lowest grade transferable C-. **General Admission Information:** Application fee $40. Regular application deadline 8/1. Nonfall registration accepted. Admission may be deferred.

COSTS AND FINANCIAL AID
Annual in-state tuition $9,658. Annual out-of-state tuition $16,872. Room and board $9,658. Required fees $1,889. Average book expense $1,250. **Required Forms and Deadlines:** FAFSA. **Notification of Awards:** Applicants will be notified of awards on a rolling basis beginning 3/1. **Types of Aid:** *Need-based scholarships/grants:* College/university scholarship or grant aid from institutional funds; Federal Pell; Private scholarships; SEOG; State scholarships/grants. *Loans:* Direct PLUS loans; Direct Subsidized Stafford Loans; Direct Unsubsidized Stafford Loans. *Student Employment:* Federal Work-Study Program available. Institutional employment available. **Financial Aid Statistics:** 90% needy freshmen, 88% needy undergrads receive need-based scholarship or grant aid. 7% freshmen, 5% undergrads receive non-need-based scholarship or grant aid. 70% freshmen, 72% undergrads receive need-based self-help aid. 10% freshmen, 8% undergrads receive athletic scholarships. 92% freshmen, 82% undergrads receive any aid. 63% undergrads borrow to pay for school. Average cumulative indebtedness $22,265. **Criteria for awarding aid:** *Need-based:* Academics, Alumni affiliation, Art, Athletics, Leadership, Music/drama *Non-need-based:* Academics, Alumni affiliation, Art, Athletics, Leadership, Music/drama, State/district residency.

FRAMINGHAM STATE UNIVERSITY

100 State Street, Framingham, MA 01701-9101
Phone: 508-626-4500 • **Financial Aid Phone:** 508-626-4534
E-mail: admissions@framingham.edu • **CEEB Code:** 3519
Fax: 508-626-4017 • **Website:** www.framingham.edu • **ACT Code:** 1904

This public school was founded in 1839. It has a 143 acre campus.

RATINGS
Admissions Selectivity Rating: 74   **Fire Safety Rating:** 98   **Green Rating:** 89

STUDENTS AND FACULTY
Enrollment: 3,963. **Student Body:** 59% female, 41% male, 6% out-of-state, 1% international (15 countries represented). Asian 3%, African American 11%, Caucasian 65%, Hispanic 14%, Native American <1%, Pacific Islander <1%, Two or more races 4%, Race unknown 2%.
Retention and Graduation: 76% freshmen return for sophomore year. 40% freshmen graduate within 4 years. 55% freshmen graduate within 6 years. 16% grads go on to further study within 1 year. **Faculty:** Student/faculty ratio 14:1. 198 full-time faculty, 19% are members of minority groups, 57% are women. 0% of classes are taught by teaching assistants.

ACADEMICS
Degrees: Bachelor's; Master's; Post-Bachelor's certificate **Classes:** Most classes have 10-19 students. Most lab/discussion sessions have 20-29 students. **Most popular majors:** Family And Consumer Sciences/Human Sciences, General; Sociology; Business/Commerce, General. **Special Study Options:** Cooperative education program; Cross-registration; Distance learning; Double major; Dual enrollment; English as a Second Language (ESL); Honors program; Independent study; Internships; Liberal arts/career combination; Student-designed major; Study abroad; Teacher certification program. **Honors programs:** The Commonwealth Honors Program at Framingham State University offers challenging courses and extracurricular activities for qualified students, and sponsors events which contribute to the intellectual life of the College community. **Combined degree programs:** BA/JD; BA/MA. **Disability Services offered to physically disabled students:** Note-taking services; Reader services; Tape recorders; Tutors. **Career services:** Alumni network; Alumni services; Career assessment; Career/job search classes; Internships

FACILITIES
Housing: Coed dorms; Special housing for disabled student; Special housing for international students; Theme housing; Wellness housing; Women's dorms 95% of campus accessible to physically diasbled. **Special Academic Facilities/ Equipment:** Mazmanian Art Gallery, McAuliffe Challenger Learning Center, Greenhouse, Early Childhood Development Lab, Education Curriculum Library,Planetarium **Computers:** 100% of classrooms, 100% of dorms, 100% of libraries, 100% of dining areas, 100% of student union, have wireless network

access. Students can register for classes online. Administrative functions (other than registration) can be performed online. Undergraduates are required to own a computer.

CAMPUS LIFE

Environment: City **Activities:** Campus Ministries; Choral groups; Concert band; Dance; Drama/theater; Literary magazine; Musical theater; Radio station; Student government; Student newspaper; Student-run film society 55 registered organizations, 11 honor societies, 4 religious organizations. **Athletics (Intercollegiate):** *Men:* baseball, basketball, cross-country, football, ice hockey, soccer. *Women:* basketball, cross-country, field hockey, lacrosse, soccer, softball, volleyball. **On-Campus Highlights:** Residence Halls, Athletic Facility, Campus Center, Academic Buildings-including new science labs, Library **Environmental Initiatives:** Conversion of our power plant from #6 oil to natural gas, decreasing our carbon footprint from the plant by 30%.

ADMISSIONS

Test Scores: SAT Math middle 50% range 470-560. SAT EBRW middle 50% range 480-570. ACT middle 50% range 19-23. Minimum internet-based TOEFL 61. Minimum paper TOEFL 500. **Basis for Candidate Selection:** *Very important factors considered include:* rigor of secondary school record, class rank, academic GPA, standardized test scores. *Other factors considered include:* application essay, recommendation(s), interview, extracurricular activities, talent/ability, character/personal qualities, first generation, alumni/ae relation, level of applicant's interest. **Freshman Admission Requirements:** High school diploma is required and GED is accepted *Academic units required:* 4 English, 4 math, 3 science, 2 science labs, 1 foreign language, 2 social studies, 1 history, 3 academic electives. **Freshman Admission Statistics:** 5,039 applied, 81.6% admitted, 19% enrolled. **Transfer Admission Requirements:** college transcript(s), Minimum college GPA of 2.40 required. Lowest grade transferable C-. **General Admission Information:** Application fee $40. Regular application deadline 8/1. Nonfall registration accepted. Admission may be deferred.

COSTS AND FINANCIAL AID

Annual in-state tuition $9,658. Annual out-of-state tuition $16,872. Room and board $9,658. Required fees $1,889. Average book expense $1,250. **Required Forms and Deadlines:** FAFSA. **Notification of Awards:** Applicants will be notified of awards on a rolling basis beginning 3/1. **Types of Aid:** *Need-based scholarships/grants:* College/university scholarship or grant aid from institutional funds; Federal Pell; Private scholarships; SEOG; State scholarships/grants. *Loans:* Direct PLUS loans; Direct Subsidized Stafford Loans; Direct Unsubsidized Stafford Loans. *Student Employment:* Federal Work-Study Program available. Institutional employment available. **Financial Aid Statistics:** 90% needy freshmen, 88% needy undergrads receive need-based scholarship or grant aid. 7% freshmen, 5% undergrads receive non-need-based scholarship or grant aid. 70% freshmen, 72% undergrads receive need-based self-help aid. 10% freshmen, 8% undergrads receive athletic scholarships. 92% freshmen, 82% undergrads receive any aid. 63% undergrads borrow to pay for school. Average cumulative indebtedness $22,265. **Criteria for awarding aid:** *Need-based:* Academics, Alumni affiliation, Art, Athletics, Leadership, Music/drama *Non-need-based:* Academics, Alumni affiliation, Art, Athletics, Leadership, Music/drama, State/district residency.

FRANCIS MARION UNIVERSITY

P.O. Box 100547, Florence, SC 29502-0547
Phone: 843-661-1231 · **Financial Aid Phone:** 843-661-1190
E-mail: admissions@fmarion.edu · **CEEB Code:** 5442
Fax: 843-661-4635 · **Website:** www.fmarion.edu · **ACT Code:** 3856

This public school was founded in 1970. It has a 400 acre campus.

RATINGS

Admissions Selectivity Rating: 82   **Fire Safety Rating:** 84   **Green Rating:** 61

STUDENTS AND FACULTY

Enrollment: 3,380. **Student Body:** 68% female, 32% male, 3% out-of-state, 1% international (19 countries represented). Asian 1%, African American 50%, Caucasian 45%, Hispanic 1%, Native American <1%, Pacific Islander <1%, Two or more races <1%, Race unknown 1%.
Retention and Graduation: 67% freshmen return for sophomore year.
Faculty: Student/faculty ratio 15:1. 204 full-time faculty, 79% hold PhDs, 11% are members of minority groups, 49% are women. 0% of classes are taught by teaching assistants.

ACADEMICS

Degrees: Bachelor's; Master's; Post-Master's certificate **Classes:** Most classes have fewer than 10 students. **Most popular majors:** Biology/Biological Sciences, General; Psychology, General; Registered Nursing/Registered Nurse. **Special Study Options:** Accelerated program; Cooperative education program; Distance learning; Double major; Dual enrollment; Honors program; Independent study; Internships; Study abroad; Teacher certification program. **Honors programs:** Link to the Honors Program web page: http://www.fmarion.edu/academics/programdescription. **Disability Services offered to physically disabled students:** Note-taking services; Reader services; Tape recorders; Tutors. **Career services:** Alumni network; Career assessment; Career/job search classes; Internships; Regional alumni

FACILITIES

Housing: Apartments for married students; Apartments for single students; Men's dorms; Special housing for disabled student; Women's dorms 100% of campus accessible to physically diasbled. **Special Academic Facilities/Equipment:** Media center, planetarium, observatory. **Computers:** Students can register for classes online.

CAMPUS LIFE

Environment: Rural **Activities:** Campus Ministries; Choral groups; Dance; Drama/theater; International Student Organization; Jazz band; Literary magazine; Model UN; Music ensembles; Student government; Student newspaper; Symphony orchestra 56 registered organizations, 13 honor societies, 5 religious organizations. 7 fraternities, 7 sororities. **Athletics (Intercollegiate):** *Men:* baseball, basketball, cross-country, golf, soccer, tennis, track/field (outdoor). *Women:* basketball, cross-country, soccer, softball, tennis, track/field (outdoor), volleyball. **On-Campus Highlights:** The Cottage, The Smith University Center, The Dooley Planetarium, The Hyman Fine Arts Center, The Hewn Timber Cabins

ADMISSIONS

Freshman Academic Profile: Average high school GPA 3.6. 15% in top 10% of high school class, 15% in top 25% of high school class, 81% in top 50% of high school class. 91% from public high schools. **Test Scores:** SAT Math middle 50% range 420-530. SAT EBRW middle 50% range 410-530. ACT middle 50% range 17-22. Minimum internet-based TOEFL 61. Minimum paper TOEFL 500. **Basis for Candidate Selection:** *Very important factors considered include:* rigor of secondary school record, academic GPA, standardized test scores. *Important factors considered include:* class rank. *Other factors considered include:* recommendation(s). **Freshman Admission Requirements:** High school diploma is required and GED is accepted *Academic units required:* 4 English, 4 math, 3 science, 3 science labs, 2 foreign language, 2 social studies, 1 history, 1 academic elective, 1 visual/performing arts, and 1 unit from above areas or other academic areas. **Freshman Admission Statistics:** 3,952 applied, 56.7% admitted, 33% enrolled. **Transfer Admission Requirements:** High school transcript, college transcript(s), statement of good standing from prior institution(s). Minimum college GPA of 2.0 required. Lowest grade transferable C. **General Admission Information:** Application fee $33. Priority deadline 7/1. Regular application deadline 8/15. Nonfall registration accepted. Admission may be deferred for a maximum of 1 year.

COSTS AND FINANCIAL AID

Annual in-state tuition $7,256. Annual out-of-state tuition $18,532. Room and board $7,256. Required fees $472. Average book expense $999. **Required Forms and Deadlines:** FAFSA. **Notification of Awards:** Applicants will be notified of awards on a rolling basis beginning 1/30. **Types of Aid:** *Need-based scholarships/grants:* College/university scholarship or grant aid from institutional funds; Federal Pell; Private scholarships; SEOG; State scholarships/grants. *Loans:* Direct PLUS loans; Direct Subsidized Stafford Loans; Direct Unsubsidized Stafford Loans. *Student Employment:* Federal Work-Study Program available. Institutional employment available. **Financial Aid Statistics:** 99% needy freshmen, 76% needy undergrads receive need-based scholarship or grant aid. 7% freshmen, 4% undergrads receive non-need-based scholarship or grant aid. 75% freshmen, 97% undergrads receive need-based self-help aid. 0% freshmen, 0% undergrads receive athletic scholarships. 88% freshmen, 82% undergrads receive any aid. **Criteria for awarding aid:** *Non-need-based:* Academics, Alumni affiliation, Art, Athletics, Job skills, Leadership, Minority status, Music/drama, Religious affiliation, State/district residency.

FRANCISCAN UNIVERSITY OF STEUBENVILLE

1235 University Boulevard, Steubenville, OH 43952-1763
Phone: 740-283-6226 · **Financial Aid Phone:** (740) 284-5216
E-mail: admissions@franciscan.edu · **CEEB Code:** 1133
Fax: 740-284-5456 · **Website:** www.franciscan.edu · **ACT Code:** 3258

This private school, affiliated with the Roman Catholic Church, was founded in 1946. It has a 235 acre campus.

RATINGS
Admissions Selectivity Rating: 82   **Fire Safety Rating:** 84   **Green Rating:** 60*

STUDENTS AND FACULTY
Enrollment: 2,038. **Student Body:** 61% female, 39% male, 80% out-of-state, 1% international (10 countries represented). Asian 2%, African American 1%, Caucasian 82%, Hispanic 11%, Native American <1%, Pacific Islander <1%, Two or more races 2%, Race unknown 2%.
Retention and Graduation: 84% freshmen return for sophomore year. 20% grads go on to further study within 1 year. 17% grads pursue arts and sciences degrees. 1% grads pursue law degrees. 1% grads pursue business degrees. 1% grads pursue medical degrees. **Faculty:** Student/faculty ratio 14:1. 127 full-time faculty, 82% hold PhDs, 2% are members of minority groups, 24% are women. 0% of classes are taught by teaching assistants.

ACADEMICS
Degrees: Associate; Bachelor's; Master's **Classes:** Most classes have 10-19 students. Most lab/discussion sessions have 10-19 students. **Most popular majors:** Theology/Theological Studies; Registered Nursing/Registered Nurse; Business Administration, Management And Operations. **Special Study Options:** Accelerated program; Distance learning; Double major; Dual enrollment; Honors program; Independent study; Internships; Study abroad; Teacher certification program. **Honors programs:** Our Great Books program is limited to 40 students in each year and prepares them for graduate school and careers in all fields. **Combined degree programs:** BA/MA. **Disability Services offered to physically disabled students:** Note-taking services; Reader services; Tape recorders; Tutors. **Career services:** Career assessment; Career/job search classes; Internships

FACILITIES
Housing: Apartments for single students; Men's dorms; Women's dorms 75% of campus accessible to physically disabled. **Special Academic Facilities/Equipment:** Art Gallery **Computers:** Students can register for classes online. Administrative functions (other than registration) can be performed online.

CAMPUS LIFE
Environment: Village **Activities:** Campus Ministries; Choral groups; Drama/theater; International Student Organization; Literary magazine; Music ensembles; Radio station; Student government; Student newspaper; Yearbook 31 registered organizations, 3 honor societies, 6 religious organizations. 1 fraternity, 1 sorority. **On-Campus Highlights:** JC Williams Student Center, Sts. Cosmas and Damian Hall-Science Building, Finnegan Fieldhouse, Christ The King Chapel, Portiuncula Chapel

ADMISSIONS
Freshman Academic Profile: Average high school GPA 3.6. 25% in top 10% of high school class, 50% in top 25% of high school class, 81% in top 50% of high school class. 37% from public high schools. **Test Scores:** SAT Math middle 50% range 500-630. SAT EBRW middle 50% range 540-670. ACT middle 50% range 22-28. Minimum internet-based TOEFL 80. Minimum paper TOEFL 550. **Basis for Candidate Selection:** *Very important factors considered include:* rigor of secondary school record, academic GPA, standardized test scores, interview, character/personal qualities. *Important factors considered include:* extracurricular activities, talent/ability. *Other factors considered include:* recommendation(s). **Freshman Admission Requirements:** High school diploma is required and GED is accepted *Academic units recommended:* 4 English, 3 math, 3 science, 3 science labs, 2 foreign language, 2 social studies, 1 history. **Freshman Admission Statistics:** 1,760 applied, 78.8% admitted, 33% enrolled. **Transfer Admission Requirements:** High school transcript, college transcript(s), essay or personal statement, Minimum college GPA of 2.2 required. Lowest grade transferable C. **General Admission Information:** Application fee $20. Nonfall registration accepted. Admission may be deferred for a maximum of one year.

COSTS AND FINANCIAL AID
Required Forms and Deadlines: FAFSA. **Notification of Awards:** Applicants will be notified of awards on a rolling basis beginning 2/15. **Types of Aid:** *Need-based scholarships/grants:* College/university scholarship or grant aid from institutional funds; Federal Pell; Private scholarships; SEOG; State scholarships/grants. *Loans:* Direct PLUS loans; Direct Subsidized

Stafford Loans; Direct Unsubsidized Stafford Loans. *Student Employment:* Federal Work-Study Program available. Institutional employment available. **Financial Aid Statistics:** 98% needy freshmen, 99% needy undergrads receive need-based scholarship or grant aid. 10% freshmen, 9% undergrads receive non-need-based scholarship or grant aid. 89% freshmen, 90% undergrads receive need-based self-help aid. 0% freshmen, 0% undergrads receive athletic scholarships. 63% freshmen, 62% undergrads receive any aid. **Criteria for awarding aid:** *Need-based:* Leadership, Religious affiliation *Non-need-based:* Academics, Alumni affiliation, Leadership, Religious affiliation.

FRANKLIN & MARSHALL COLLEGE

Best Colleges

P.O. Box 3003, Lancaster, PA 17604-3003
Phone: 717-358-3953 · **Financial Aid Phone:** 717-358-3991
E-mail: admission@fandm.edu · **CEEB Code:** 2261
Fax: 717-358-4389 · **Website:** www.fandm.edu · **ACT Code:** 3574

This private school was founded in 1787. It has a 220 acre campus.

RATINGS
Admissions Selectivity Rating: 94   **Fire Safety Rating:** 97   **Green Rating:** 95

STUDENTS AND FACULTY
Enrollment: 2,269. **Student Body:** 54% female, 46% male, 77% out-of-state, 16% international (49 countries represented). Asian 5%, African American 6%, Caucasian 57%, Hispanic 10%, Native American <1%, Pacific Islander <1%, Two or more races 2%, Race unknown 4%.
Retention and Graduation: 92% freshmen return for sophomore year. 80% freshmen graduate within 4 years. **Faculty:** Student/faculty ratio 9:1. 242 full-time faculty, 95% hold PhDs, 13% are members of minority groups, 49% are women. 0% of classes are taught by teaching assistants.

ACADEMICS
Degrees: Bachelor's **Classes:** Most classes have 30-39 students. Most lab/discussion sessions have 20-29 students. **Most popular majors:** Psychology, General; Political Science And Government, General; Business Administration, Management And Operations. **Special Study Options:** Double major; Independent study; Internships; Student-designed major; Study abroad; Teacher certification program. **Disability Services offered to physically disabled students:** Note-taking services; Reader services; Tape recorders; Tutors. **Career services:** Alumni network; Alumni services; Career assessment; Career/job search classes; Internships; Regional alumni

FACILITIES
Housing: Apartments for single students; Coed dorms; Fraternity/sorority housing; Special housing for disabled student; Special housing for international students; Theme housing; Wellness housing 80% of campus accessible to physically disabled. **Special Academic Facilities/Equipment:** Art gallery, associated with natural history museums, bronze casting foundry, retail sales complex, psychology and language labs, TV and radio station, observatory/planetarium, Writers House **Computers:** 100% of classrooms, 100% of dorms, 100% of libraries, 100% of dining areas, 100% of student union, 100% of common outdoor areas have wireless network access. Students can register for classes online. Administrative functions (other than registration) can be performed online.

CAMPUS LIFE
Environment: Town **Activities:** Campus Ministries; Choral groups; Concert band; Dance; Drama/theater; International Student Organization; Jazz band; Literary magazine; Model UN; Music ensembles; Musical theater; Pep band; Radio station; Student government; Student newspaper; Symphony orchestra; Yearbook 90 registered organizations, 13 honor societies, 8 religious organizations. 7 fraternities, 3 sororities. **Athletics (Intercollegiate):** *Men:* baseball, basketball, crew/rowing, cross-country, football, golf, lacrosse, soccer, squash, swimming, tennis, track/field (outdoor), track/field (indoor), wrestling. *Women:* basketball, crew/rowing, cross-country, field hockey, golf, lacrosse, soccer, softball, squash, swimming, tennis, track/field (outdoor), track/field (indoor), volleyball. **On-Campus Highlights:** Alumni Sport and Fitness Center, Barshinger Center in Hensel Hall, Barnes and Noble Bookstore and Blue Line Cafe, Roschel Performing Arts Center, Writers House **Environmental Initiatives:** We have established The Center for the Sustainable Environment, including a Director, student staff member, and partnership with the Millport Conservancy.

ADMISSIONS

Freshman Academic Profile: 68% in top 10% of high school class, 90% in top 25% of high school class, 100% in top 50% of high school class. 64% from public high schools. **Test Scores:** SAT Math middle 50% range 640-720. SAT EBRW middle 50% range 620-700. ACT middle 50% range 28-32. Minimum paper TOEFL 600. **Basis for Candidate Selection:** *Very important factors considered include:* rigor of secondary school record, class rank, academic GPA, character/personal qualities. *Important factors considered include:* application essay, standardized test scores, recommendation(s), interview, extracurricular activities, talent/ability, volunteer work. *Other factors considered include:* alumni/ae relation, geographical residence, racial/ethnic status, work experience, level of applicant's interest. **Freshman Admission Requirements:** High school diploma is required and GED is accepted *Academic units required:* 4 English, 3 math, 2 science, 2 science labs, 2 foreign language, 1 social studies, 2 history, 1 visual/performing arts, *Academic units recommended:* 4 math, 3 science, 3 science labs, 4 foreign language, 3 social studies, 3 history. **Freshman Admission Statistics:** 6,720 applied, 34.1% admitted, 28% enrolled. **Transfer Admission Requirements:** High school transcript, college transcript(s), essay or personal statement, interview, standardized test scores, statement of good standing from prior institution(s). Lowest grade transferable C-. **General Admission Information:** Application fee $60. Regular application deadline 1/15. Nonfall registration accepted. Admission may be deferred for a maximum of one year.

COSTS AND FINANCIAL AID

Annual tuition $54,280. Room and board $13,580. Required fees $100. Average book expense $1,200. **Required Forms and Deadlines:** CSS/Financial Aid PROFILE; FAFSA; Noncustodial PROFILE. **Notification of Awards:** Applicants will be notified of awards on or about 4/1. **Types of Aid:** *Need-based scholarships/grants:* College/university scholarship or grant aid from institutional funds; Federal Pell; Private scholarships; SEOG; State scholarships/grants. *Loans:* Direct PLUS loans; Direct Subsidized Stafford Loans; Direct Unsubsidized Stafford Loans. *Student Employment:* Federal Work-Study Program available. **Financial Aid Statistics:** 100% needy freshmen, 100% needy undergrads receive need-based scholarship or grant aid. 26% freshmen, 29% undergrads receive non-need-based scholarship or grant aid. 90% freshmen, 98% undergrads receive need-based self-help aid. 0% freshmen, 0% undergrads receive athletic scholarships. 51% freshmen, 53% undergrads receive any aid. 60% undergrads borrow to pay for school. Average cumulative indebtedness $27,133. **Criteria for awarding aid:** *Need-based:* Academics, Religious affiliation *Non-need-based:* Music/drama.

FRANKLIN COLLEGE

101 Branigin Blvd, Franklin, IN 46131-2623
Phone: 317-738-8075 • **Financial Aid Phone:** 317-738-8075
E-mail: admissions@franklincollege.edu • **CEEB Code:** 1228
Fax: 317-738-8274 • **Website:** www.franklincollege.edu • **ACT Code:** 1194

This private school, affiliated with the American Baptist Church, was founded in 1834. It has a 207 acre campus.

RATINGS

Admissions Selectivity Rating: 75   **Fire Safety Rating:** 85   **Green Rating:** 61

STUDENTS AND FACULTY

Enrollment: 977. **Student Body:** 51% female, 49% male, 8% out-of-state, 1% international (9 countries represented). Asian 1%, African American 5%, Caucasian 84%, Hispanic 3%, Native American <1%, Pacific Islander 0%, Two or more races 4%, Race unknown 2%.
Retention and Graduation: 74% freshmen return for sophomore year. 20% grads go on to further study within 1 year. 14% grads pursue arts and sciences degrees. 1.9% grads pursue law degrees. 1% grads pursue business degrees. 2.9% grads pursue medical degrees. **Faculty:** Student/faculty ratio 11:1. 78 full-time faculty, 88% hold PhDs, 13% are members of minority groups, 42% are women. 0% of classes are taught by teaching assistants.

ACADEMICS

Degrees: Bachelor's; Master's **Most popular majors:** Elementary Education And Teaching; Biology/Biological Sciences, General; Business/Commerce, General. **Special Study Options:** Cross-registration; Double major; Exchange student program (domestic); Independent study; Internships; Liberal arts/career combination; Student-designed major; Study abroad; Teacher certification program. **Honors programs:** The intercultural Honors Experience is a freshman-year program designed to attract and retain superior students and faculty to FC while internationalizing the FC community. The program is designed to help students build a solid intercultural foundation,

introduce them to interdisciplinary learning, and provide them with opportunities and incentives to study abroad. Faculty development is an integral part of the project. **Combined degree programs:** BA/MA. **Disability Services offered to physically disabled students:** Note-taking services; Reader services; Tape recorders; Tutors. **Career services:** Alumni services; Career assessment; Career/job search classes

FACILITIES

Housing: Coed dorms; Fraternity/sorority housing; Men's dorms; Special housing for disabled student; Theme housing; Women's dorms 100% of campus accessible to physically diasbled. **Special Academic Facilities/Equipment:** Pulliam School of Journalism, Dietz Center for Professional Development, Leadership Center. **Computers:** 100% of classrooms, 100% of libraries, 100% of dining areas, 100% of student union, have wireless network access. Students can register for classes online. Administrative functions (other than registration) can be performed online.

CAMPUS LIFE

Environment: Village **Activities:** Campus Ministries; Choral groups; Concert band; Dance; Drama/theater; International Student Organization; Literary magazine; Model UN; Music ensembles; Pep band; Radio station; Student government; Student newspaper 66 registered organizations, 13 honor societies, 3 religious organizations. 5 fraternities, 4 sororities. **Athletics (Intercollegiate):** *Men:* baseball, basketball, cross-country, diving, football, golf, soccer, swimming, tennis, track/field (outdoor). *Women:* basketball, cheerleading, cross-country, diving, golf, soccer, softball, swimming, tennis, track/field (outdoor), volleyball. **On-Campus Highlights:** Napolitan Student Center, Sprulock Center (athletic facility), Hamilton Library, residence halls, fraternity houses **Environmental Initiatives:** Completing green house car emissions inventory

ADMISSIONS

Freshman Academic Profile: Average high school GPA 3.5. 26% in top 10% of high school class, 54% in top 25% of high school class, 85% in top 50% of high school class. 90% from public high schools. **Test Scores:** SAT Math middle 50% range 430-550. SAT EBRW middle 50% range 420-530. ACT middle 50% range 19-25. Minimum internet-based TOEFL 79. Minimum paper TOEFL 550. **Basis for Candidate Selection:** *Very important factors considered include:* rigor of secondary school record, class rank, academic GPA, standardized test scores. *Important factors considered include:* application essay, extracurricular activities, alumni/ae relation. *Other factors considered include:* recommendation(s), interview, talent/ability, first generation, geographical residence, state residency, religious affiliation/commitment, racial/ethnic status, volunteer work, work experience, level of applicant's interest. **Freshman Admission Requirements:** High school diploma is required and GED is accepted *Academic units required:* 4 English, 4 math, 2 science, 3 social studies, *Academic units recommended:* 2 foreign language. **Freshman Admission Statistics:** 1,479 applied, 78.1% admitted, 21% enrolled. **Transfer Admission Requirements:** High school transcript, college transcript(s), essay or personal statement, statement of good standing from prior institution(s). Minimum college GPA of 2.0 required. Lowest grade transferable C-. **General Admission Information:** Priority deadline 12/1. Nonfall registration accepted. Admission may be deferred for a maximum of 1 year.

COSTS AND FINANCIAL AID

Annual tuition $29,840. Room and board $9,040. Required fees $185. Average book expense $1,200. **Required Forms and Deadlines:** FAFSA; Institution's own financial aid form. **Notification of Awards:** Applicants will be notified of awards on a rolling basis beginning 11/1. **Types of Aid:** *Need-based scholarships/grants:* College/university scholarship or grant aid from institutional funds; Federal Pell; Private scholarships; SEOG; State scholarships/grants. *Loans:* Direct PLUS loans; Direct Subsidized Stafford Loans; Direct Unsubsidized Stafford Loans. *Student Employment:* Federal Work-Study Program available. Institutional employment available. **Financial Aid Statistics:** 100% needy freshmen, 100% needy undergrads receive need-based scholarship or grant aid. 17% freshmen, 14% undergrads receive non-need-based scholarship or grant aid. 83% freshmen, 85% undergrads receive need-based self-help aid. 0% freshmen, 0% undergrads receive athletic scholarships. 100% freshmen, 96% undergrads receive any aid. 86% undergrads borrow to pay for school. Average cumulative indebtedness $34,884. **Criteria for awarding aid:** *Need-based:* Minority status, Religious affiliation *Non-need-based:* Academics, Alumni affiliation, Art, Minority status, Music/drama, Religious affiliation, State/district residency.

FRANKLIN PIERCE COLLEGE

40 University Drive, Rindge, NH 03461
Phone: 603-899-4050 · **Financial Aid Phone:** 603-899-4180
E-mail: admissions@franklinpierce.edu · **CEEB Code:** 3395
Fax: 603-889-4394 · **Website:** www.franklinpierce.edu · **ACT Code:** 2509

This private school was founded in 1962. It has a 1200 acre campus.

RATINGS
Admissions Selectivity Rating: 66   **Fire Safety Rating:** 94   **Green Rating:** 60*

STUDENTS AND FACULTY
Enrollment: 1,474. **Student Body:** 52% female, 48% male, international.
Retention and Graduation: 26% grads go on to further study within 1 year.
5% grads pursue arts and sciences degrees. 3% grads pursue law degrees. 7%
grads pursue business degrees. 1% grads pursue medical degrees. **Faculty:**
Student/faculty ratio 18:1. 100 full-time faculty, 68% hold PhDs, 1% are
members of minority groups, 45% are women. 0% of classes are taught by
teaching assistants.

ACADEMICS
Degrees: Associate; Bachelor's; Certificate; Doctoral; Master's; Post-Master's
certificate **Classes:** Most classes have 10-19 students. Most lab/discussion
sessions have 10-19 students. **Most popular majors:** Mass Communication/
Media Studies; Education, General; Criminal Justice/Safety Studies. **Special
Study Options:** Accelerated program; Double major; Dual enrollment;
English as a Second Language (ESL); Honors program; Independent study;
Internships; Liberal arts/career combination; Student-designed major; Study
abroad; Teacher certification program. **Honors programs:** Honors Program.
Disability Services offered to physically disabled students: Note-taking
services; Reader services; Tape recorders; Tutors. **Career services:** Alumni
network; Alumni services; Career assessment; Career/job search classes;
Internships; Regional alumni

FACILITIES
Housing: Apartments for single students; Coed dorms; Special housing for
disabled student; Wellness housing 67% of campus accessible to physically
diasbled. **Special Academic Facilities/Equipment:** Thoreau Art Gallery;
Flynt Center; Fitzwater Communications Center; Dance Studio; Pottery Kiln;
Glass Blowing Studio; TV Station; Radio Station; Grimshaw-Gudewicz Activities
Center: Lakeside Activity Center **Computers:** 20% of classrooms, 20% of
dorms, 100% of libraries, 80% of dining areas, 100% of student union, 50% of
common outdoor areas have wireless network access. Administrative functions
(other than registration) can be performed online.

CAMPUS LIFE
Environment: Rural **Activities:** Campus Ministries; Choral groups; Dance;
Drama/theater; Literary magazine; Music ensembles; Musical theater;
Radio station; Student government; Student newspaper; Television station
35 registered organizations, 8 honor societies, 3 religious organizations.
Athletics (Intercollegiate): *Men:* baseball, basketball, crew/rowing, golf, ice
hockey, rugby, soccer, tennis. *Women:* basketball, crew/rowing, cross-country,
field hockey, lacrosse, soccer, softball, volleyball. **On-Campus Highlights:**
Peterson Hall, The Campus Center, The Northfields Activity Center, The
Fitzwater Center for Communications, The Pub **Environmental Initiatives:**
Development of on enhanced on-campus recycling program.

ADMISSIONS
Freshman Academic Profile: Average high school GPA 2.8. 89% from
public high schools. **Test Scores:** Minimum internet-based TOEFL 61.
Minimum paper TOEFL 500. **Basis for Candidate Selection:** *Very important
factors considered include:* academic GPA, recommendation(s), character/
personal qualities. *Important factors considered include:* rigor of secondary
school record, application essay. *Other factors considered include:* class rank,
standardized test scores, interview, extracurricular activities, talent/ability,
volunteer work, work experience. **Freshman Admission Requirements:**
High school diploma is required and GED is accepted *Academic units required:*
4 English, 3 math, 2 science, 2 science labs, 3 social studies, 4 academic
electives, and 4 units from above areas or other academic areas. **Freshman
Admission Statistics:** 3,740 applied, 79.7% admitted, 16% enrolled. **Transfer
Admission Requirements:** college transcript(s), essay or personal statement,
Minimum college GPA of 2.0 required. Lowest grade transferable C-. **General
Admission Information:** Nonfall registration accepted. Admission may be
deferred for a maximum of 1 year.

COSTS AND FINANCIAL AID
Annual tuition $30,870. Room and board $12,546. Required fees $2,450.
Average book expense $1,000. **Required Forms and Deadlines:** FAFSA.

Notification of Awards: Applicants will be notified of awards on a rolling
basis beginning 2/1. **Types of Aid:** *Need-based scholarships/grants:* College/
university scholarship or grant aid from institutional funds; Federal Pell; Private
scholarships; SEOG; State scholarships/grants. *Loans: Student Employment:*
Federal Work-Study Program available. Institutional employment available.
Financial Aid Statistics: 99% needy freshmen, 99% needy undergrads receive
need-based scholarship or grant aid. 10% freshmen, 9% undergrads receive
non-need-based scholarship or grant aid. 90% freshmen, 90% undergrads
receive need-based self-help aid. 4% freshmen, 5% undergrads receive athletic
scholarships. 99% freshmen, 87% undergrads receive any aid. **Criteria for
awarding aid:** *Need-based:* Academics, Athletics *Non-need-based:* Academics,
Alumni affiliation, Athletics, Leadership, Minority status, Music/drama.

FRANKLIN UNIVERSITY

201 S Grant Ave, Columbus, OH 43215
Phone: 614-797-4700
E-mail: info@franklin.edu · **CEEB Code:** 1229
Fax: 614-224-8027 · **ACT Code:** 3275

This private school was founded in 1902. It has a 14 acre campus.

RATINGS
Admissions Selectivity Rating: 65   **Fire Safety Rating:** 60*   **Green Rating:** 60*

STUDENTS AND FACULTY
Enrollment: 5,682. **Student Body:** 55% female, 45% male, 26% out-of-state,
6% international. Asian 3%, African American 21%, Caucasian 73%, Hispanic
2%, Native American <1%, Race unknown 5%.
Retention and Graduation: 72% freshmen return for sophomore year.
Faculty: Student/faculty ratio 19:1. 36 full-time faculty, 64% hold PhDs, 6% are
members of minority groups, 44% are women.

ACADEMICS
Degrees: Associate; Bachelor's; Master's **Classes:** Most classes have 10-19
students. Most lab/discussion sessions have 10-19 students. **Most popular
majors:** Computer And Information Sciences And Support Services; Business/
Commerce, General; Accounting. **Special Study Options:** Accelerated
program; Cooperative education program; Cross-registration; Distance learning;
Double major; Dual enrollment; English as a Second Language (ESL);
Independent study; Internships; Study abroad; Weekend college. **Disability
Services offered to physically disabled students:** Note-taking services;
Reader services; Tape recorders; Tutors. **Career services:** Alumni network;
Alumni services; Internships

FACILITIES
Housing: 100% of campus accessible to physically diasbled. **Computers:**
Students can register for classes online.

CAMPUS LIFE
Activities: 6 registered organizations.

ADMISSIONS
Test Scores: Minimum paper TOEFL 430. **Freshman Admission
Requirements:** High school diploma is required and GED is accepted
Academic units recommended: 3 math. **Freshman Admission Statistics:** 262
applied, 100.0% admitted, 47% enrolled. **Transfer Admission Requirements:**
college transcript(s), Lowest grade transferable C-. **General Admission
Information:** Nonfall registration accepted. Admission may be deferred.

COSTS AND FINANCIAL AID
Annual tuition $6,990. **Required Forms and Deadlines:** FAFSA. **Types
of Aid:** *Need-based scholarships/grants:* College/university scholarship or
grant aid from institutional funds; Federal Pell; Private scholarships; SEOG;
State scholarships/grants. *Student Employment:* Federal Work-Study Program
available. Institutional employment available. **Financial Aid Statistics:** 72%
needy freshmen, 64% needy undergrads receive need-based scholarship or
grant aid. 89% freshmen, 84% undergrads receive non-need-based scholarship
or grant aid. 97% freshmen, 96% undergrads receive need-based self-help
aid. 0% freshmen, 0% undergrads receive athletic scholarships. **Criteria
for awarding aid:** *Need-based:* Academics *Non-need-based:* Academics,
Leadership, Minority status.

FRANKLIN W. OLIN COLLEGE OF ENGINEERING

1000 Olin Way, Needham, MA 02492-1200
Phone: 781-292-2222 • **Financial Aid Phone:** 781-292-2215
E-mail: info@olin.edu • **CEEB Code:** 2824
Fax: 781-292-2210 • **Website:** www.olin.edu • **ACT Code:** 1883

This private school was founded in 1997. It has a 75 acre campus.

RATINGS
Admissions Selectivity Rating: 98   **Fire Safety Rating:** 99   **Green Rating:** 70

STUDENTS AND FACULTY
Enrollment: 345. **Student Body:** 48% female, 52% male, 88% out-of-state, 8% international (11 countries represented). Asian 12%, African American 3%, Caucasian 53%, Hispanic 9%, Native American 0%, Pacific Islander 0%, Two or more races 8%, Race unknown 8%.
Retention and Graduation: 99% freshmen return for sophomore year. 79% freshmen graduate within 4 years. 91% freshmen graduate within 6 years. 9% grads go on to further study within 1 year. 9% grads pursue arts and sciences degrees. 0% grads pursue law degrees. 0% grads pursue business degrees. 0% grads pursue medical degrees. **Faculty:** Student/faculty ratio 8:1. 41 full-time faculty, 95% hold PhDs, 22% are members of minority groups, 37% are women. 0% of classes are taught by teaching assistants.

ACADEMICS
Degrees: Bachelor's **Classes:** Most classes have 10-19 students. Most lab/discussion sessions have fewer than 10 students. **Most popular majors:** Engineering, General; Electrical And Electronics Engineering; Mechanical Engineering. **Special Study Options:** Cross-registration; Exchange student program (domestic); Independent study; Internships; Student-designed major; Study abroad. **Disability Services offered to physically disabled students:** Note-taking services; Reader services; Tape recorders; Tutors. **Career services:** Alumni network; Alumni services; Career/job search classes; Internships; Regional alumni

FACILITIES
Housing: Coed dorms; Special housing for disabled students 100% of campus accessible to physically diasbled. **Computers:** 100% of classrooms, 100% of dorms, 100% of libraries, 100% of dining areas, 100% of student union, 100% of common outdoor areas have wireless network access. Students can register for classes online. Administrative functions (other than registration) can be performed online. Undergraduates are required to own a computer.

CAMPUS LIFE
Environment: Town **Activities:** Campus Ministries; Choral groups; Drama/theater; International Student Organization; Music ensembles; Student government; Student newspaper 55 registered organizations. **Environmental Initiatives:** Replacing site-wide external lighting with LEDs

ADMISSIONS
Freshman Academic Profile: Average high school GPA 3.8. **Test Scores:** SAT Math middle 50% range 740-800. SAT EBRW middle 50% range 710-770. ACT middle 50% range 33-35. **Basis for Candidate Selection:** *Very important factors considered include:* rigor of secondary school record, academic GPA, application essay, recommendation(s), interview, extracurricular activities, talent/ability, character/personal qualities, level of applicant's interest. *Important factors considered include:* class rank, standardized test scores, racial/ethnic status, volunteer work, work experience. *Other factors considered include:* first generation, alumni/ae relation, geographical residence, state residency. **Freshman Admission Requirements:** High school diploma is required and GED is accepted *Academic units recommended:* 4 English, 4 math, 4 science, 3 science labs, 2 foreign language, 2 social studies, 2 history. **Freshman Admission Statistics:** 1,062 applied, 13.4% admitted, 63% enrolled. **Transfer Admission Requirements:** college transcript(s), Minimum college GPA of 2.0 required. Lowest grade transferable C. **General Admission Information:** Application fee $85. Regular application deadline 1/1. Nonfall registration accepted. Admission may be deferred for a maximum of 2 years.

COSTS AND FINANCIAL AID
Required Forms and Deadlines: FAFSA. **Notification of Awards:** Applicants will be notified of awards on or about 3/24. **Types of Aid:** *Need-based scholarships/grants:* College/university scholarship or grant aid from institutional funds; Federal Pell; SEOG. *Loans:* Direct PLUS loans; Direct Subsidized Stafford Loans; Direct Unsubsidized Stafford Loans. *Student Employment:* Institutional employment available. **Financial Aid Statistics:**

100% needy freshmen, 100% needy undergrads receive need-based scholarship or grant aid. 100% freshmen, 100% undergrads receive non-need-based scholarship or grant aid. 81% freshmen, 88% undergrads receive need-based self-help aid. 0% freshmen, 0% undergrads receive athletic scholarships. 100% freshmen, 100% undergrads receive any aid. 43% undergrads borrow to pay for school. Average cumulative indebtedness $19,196. **Criteria for awarding aid:** *Non-need-based:* Academics, Leadership.

FREED-HARDEMAN UNIVERSITY

158 East Main Street, Henderson, TN 38340
Phone: 731-989-6651 • **Financial Aid Phone:** 731-989-6662
E-mail: jathoms1@yahoo.com • **CEEB Code:** 1230
Fax: 731-989-6047 • **Website:** web.fhu.edu • **ACT Code:** 3962

This private school, affiliated with the Church of Christ, was founded in 1869. It has a 122 acre campus.

RATINGS
Admissions Selectivity Rating: 87   **Fire Safety Rating:** 66   **Green Rating:** 60*

STUDENTS AND FACULTY
Enrollment: 1,428. **Student Body:** 55% female, 45% male, 50% out-of-state, 3% international (26 countries represented). Asian <1%, African American 4%, Caucasian 91%, Hispanic 1%, Native American <1%, Race unknown <1%.
Retention and Graduation: 74% freshmen return for sophomore year. 40% grads go on to further study within 1 year. **Faculty:** Student/faculty ratio 14:1. 108 full-time faculty, 69% hold PhDs, 5% are members of minority groups, 31% are women. 0% of classes are taught by teaching assistants.

ACADEMICS
Degrees: Bachelor's; Doctoral; Master's; Post-Bachelor's certificate; Post-Master's certificate **Classes:** Most classes have 10-19 students. Most lab/discussion sessions have fewer than 10 students. **Most popular majors:** Liberal Arts And Sciences, General Studies And Humanities, Other; Biology/Biological Sciences, General; Bible/Biblical Studies. **Special Study Options:** Accelerated program; Cooperative education program; Cross-registration; Distance learning; Double major; Dual enrollment; Honors program; Independent study; Internships; Liberal arts/career combination; Student-designed major; Study abroad; Teacher certification program. **Honors programs:** Exceptional students may be admitted to the Honors College, where he or she may graduate as an Honors College Scholar, or as an Honors College Scholar with University Honors. **Disability Services offered to physically disabled students:** Note-taking services; Reader services; Tutors. **Career services:** Alumni network; Career assessment; Internships

FACILITIES
Housing: Apartments for single students; Men's dorms; Women's dorms 70% of campus accessible to physically diasbled. **Special Academic Facilities/Equipment:** Child development lab, nursery school. **Computers:** Students can register for classes online. Administrative functions (other than registration) can be performed online.

CAMPUS LIFE
Environment: Rural **Activities:** Choral groups; Concert band; Drama/theater; Jazz band; Music ensembles; Musical theater; Pep band; Radio station; Student government; Student newspaper; Television station; Yearbook 52 registered organizations, 4 honor societies, 5 religious organizations. 6 fraternities, 6 sororities. **Athletics (Intercollegiate):** *Men:* baseball, basketball, cheerleading, soccer. *Women:* basketball, cheerleading, soccer, softball, volleyball. **On-Campus Highlights:** The Commons, The Student Center, The Sports Center, Brown-Kopel Business Center, The Library

ADMISSIONS
Freshman Academic Profile: Average high school GPA 3.4. 25% in top 10% of high school class, 51% in top 25% of high school class, 79% in top 50% of high school class. **Test Scores:** SAT Math middle 50% range 480-600. SAT EBRW middle 50% range 480-640. ACT middle 50% range 20-26. **Basis for Candidate Selection:** *Very important factors considered include:* rigor of secondary school record, academic GPA, standardized test scores. *Other factors considered include:* recommendation(s), extracurricular activities, character/personal qualities, alumni/ae relation, religious affiliation/commitment, racial/ethnic status, volunteer work, work experience. **Freshman Admission Requirements:** High school diploma is required and GED is accepted *Academic units recommended:* 4 English, 2 math, 2 science, 2 social studies, 10 academic electives. **Freshman Admission Statistics:** 1,326 applied, 54.8% admitted, 53% enrolled. **Transfer Admission Requirements:** college transcript(s), statement of good standing from prior institution(s). Lowest

grade transferable D. **General Admission Information:** Nonfall registration accepted. Admission may be deferred for a maximum of 2 years.

COSTS AND FINANCIAL AID
Annual tuition $13,192. Room and board $6,560. Average book expense $1,710. **Required Forms and Deadlines:** FAFSA. **Notification of Awards:** Applicants will be notified of awards on a rolling basis beginning 3/1. **Types of Aid:** *Need-based scholarships/grants:* College/university scholarship or grant aid from institutional funds; Federal Pell; Private scholarships; SEOG; State scholarships/grants. *Loans: Student Employment:* Federal Work-Study Program available. Institutional employment available. **Financial Aid Statistics:** 97% needy freshmen, 91% needy undergrads receive need-based scholarship or grant aid. 19% freshmen, 17% undergrads receive non-need-based scholarship or grant aid. 74% freshmen, 78% undergrads receive need-based self-help aid. 4% freshmen, 4% undergrads receive athletic scholarships. 86% freshmen receive any aid. **Criteria for awarding aid:** *Non-need-based:* Academics, Art, Athletics, Leadership, Minority status, Music/drama, State/district residency.

FRESNO PACIFIC UNIVERSITY

1717 S. Chestnut Ave, Fresno, CA 93702
Phone: 559-453-2039 · **Financial Aid Phone:** 559-453-2041
E-mail: ugadmis@fresno.edu
Fax: 559-453-2007 · **Website:** http://www.fresno.edu/

This private school, affiliated with the Mennonite Church, was founded in 1944. It has a 42 acre campus.

RATINGS
Admissions Selectivity Rating: 0   **Fire Safety Rating:** 60*   **Green Rating:** 60*

STUDENTS AND FACULTY
Enrollment: 1,459. **Student Body:** 68% female, 32% male, 2% international. Asian 4%, African American 4%, Caucasian 53%, Hispanic 26%, Native American 1%, Race unknown 10%.
Retention and Graduation: 70% freshmen return for sophomore year.

ACADEMICS
Degrees: Associate; Bachelor's; Certificate; Master's; Post-Bachelor's certificate **Classes:** Most classes have 20-29 students. Most lab/discussion sessions have 20-29 students. **Most popular majors:** Education, General; Bible/Biblical Studies; Business/Commerce, General. **Special Study Options:** Accelerated program; Cooperative education program; Cross-registration; Distance learning; Double major; English as a Second Language (ESL); Independent study; Internships; Liberal arts/career combination; Student-designed major; Study abroad; Teacher certification program. **Disability Services offered to physically disabled students:** Note-taking services; Reader services; Tutors. **Career services:** Alumni services; Career assessment; Career/job search classes; Internships

FACILITIES
Housing: Apartments for single students; Men's dorms; Special housing for disabled student; Women's dorms 100% of campus accessible to physically disabled. **Special Academic Facilities/Equipment:** English Language Training Institute

CAMPUS LIFE
Environment: Metropolis **Activities:** Campus Ministries; Choral groups; Concert band; Dance; Drama/theater; International Student Organization; Jazz band; Music ensembles; Musical theater; Pep band; Student government; Student newspaper; Yearbook 36 registered organizations, 1 honor society, 11 religious organizations. **Athletics (Intercollegiate): Men:** baseball, basketball, cross-country, soccer, tennis, track/field (outdoor). *Women:* basketball, cross-country, soccer, tennis, track/field (outdoor), volleyball. **On-Campus Highlights:** Special Events Center (Gym), Steinert Campus Center, The Green (students hang out there), Bookshop, New AIMS Building

ADMISSIONS
Basis for Candidate Selection: *Very important factors considered include:* rigor of secondary school record, standardized test scores. *Important factors considered include:* class rank, academic GPA, application essay, recommendation(s), religious affiliation/commitment. *Other factors considered include:* character/personal qualities. **Freshman Admission Requirements:** High school diploma is required and GED is accepted *Academic units required:* 4 English, 3 math, 1 science, 1 science labs, 2 foreign language, 2 social studies, *Academic units recommended:* 1 unit from above areas or other academic areas. **Transfer Admission Requirements:** High school transcript, college transcript(s), essay or personal statement, Minimum college GPA of 2.4 required. Lowest grade transferable C. **General Admission Information:**

Application fee $40. Priority deadline 12/1. Regular application deadline 7/31. Nonfall registration accepted. Admission may be deferred.

COSTS AND FINANCIAL AID
Annual tuition $24,960. Required fees $276. Average book expense $1,665. **Required Forms and Deadlines:** FAFSA. **Notification of Awards:** Applicants will be notified of awards on a rolling basis beginning 2/21. **Types of Aid:** *Need-based scholarships/grants:* College/university scholarship or grant aid from institutional funds; Federal Pell; Private scholarships; SEOG; State scholarships/grants. *Loans:* Direct PLUS loans; Direct Subsidized Stafford Loans; Direct Unsubsidized Stafford Loans. *Student Employment:* Federal Work-Study Program available. Institutional employment available. **Financial Aid Statistics:** 81% needy freshmen, 81% needy undergrads receive need-based scholarship or grant aid. 98% freshmen, 52% undergrads receive non-need-based scholarship or grant aid. 74% freshmen, 80% undergrads receive need-based self-help aid. 14% freshmen, 9% undergrads receive athletic scholarships. **Criteria for awarding aid:** *Non-need-based:* Academics, Alumni affiliation, Art, Athletics, Leadership, Minority status, Music/drama, Religious affiliation.

FRIENDS UNIVERSITY

2100 W. University Avenue, Wichita, KS 67213
Phone: 316-295-5100 · **Financial Aid Phone:** 316-295-5200
E-mail: learn@friends.edu · **CEEB Code:** 6224
Fax: 316-295-5101 · **Website:** www.friends.edu · **ACT Code:** 1918

This private school was founded in 1898. It has a 54 acre campus.

RATINGS
Admissions Selectivity Rating: 84   **Fire Safety Rating:** 89   **Green Rating:** 60*

STUDENTS AND FACULTY
Enrollment: 1,737. **Student Body:** 56% female, 44% male, 19% out-of-state, 0% international (13 countries represented). Asian 3%, African American 11%, Caucasian 71%, Hispanic 4%, Native American 2%, Pacific Islander <1%, Two or more races 5%, Race unknown 4%.
Retention and Graduation: 60% freshmen return for sophomore year.
Faculty: Student/faculty ratio 11:1. 75 full-time faculty, 71% hold PhDs, 5% are members of minority groups, 41% are women. 0% of classes are taught by teaching assistants.

ACADEMICS
Degrees: Associate; Bachelor's; Master's; Post-Bachelor's certificate **Classes:** Most classes have 10-19 students. Most lab/discussion sessions have 20-29 students. **Most popular majors:** Wildlife Biology; Psychology, General; Business Administration And Management, General. **Special Study Options:** Accelerated program; Cross-registration; Distance learning; Double major; Dual enrollment; Exchange student program (domestic); Honors program; Independent study; Internships; Student-designed major; Study abroad; Teacher certification program. **Honors programs:** The Friends University Honors Program is designed to enrich the educational experience of selected students through a process involving group interchange of ideas and independent research projects. Participating students are challenged by their peers and by faculty members to reflect upon significant contemporary issues in a number of different fields and to attempt to respond to and integrate the ideas encountered with their own personal values and faith. The experience is intended to develop powers of analysis and evaluation in an environment where encouragement is given to pursue excellence. It is also intended to deepen the appreciation of those involved for the entire range of the liberal arts. **Disability Services offered to physically disabled students:** Note-taking services; Reader services; Tape recorders; Tutors. **Career services:** Alumni network; Alumni services; Career assessment; Career/job search classes; Internships; Regional alumni

FACILITIES
Housing: Apartments for single students; Coed dorms 95% of campus accessible to physically disabled. **Special Academic Facilities/Equipment:** Davis Administration Buidling built in the 1800's and is the National Registry of Historic Places

CAMPUS LIFE
Environment: Metropolis **Activities:** Campus Ministries; Choral groups; Concert band; Dance; Drama/theater; International Student Organization; Jazz band; Literary magazine; Model UN; Music ensembles; Musical theater; Opera; Pep band; Student government; Student newspaper; Symphony orchestra; Yearbook 32 registered organizations, 4 honor societies, 3 religious

organizations. 2 fraternities, 1 sorority. **Athletics (Intercollegiate):** *Men:* baseball, basketball, cheerleading, cross-country, football, golf, soccer, tennis, track/field (outdoor). *Women:* basketball, cheerleading, cross-country, soccer, softball, tennis, track/field (outdoor), volleyball. Casado Campus Center, Green Residence Hall, Jazzman's Cafe/Sandella's Flatbread Cafe, Rose Window Plaza, Garvey Physical Education Center

ADMISSIONS

Freshman Academic Profile: Average high school GPA 3.4. 20% in top 10% of high school class, 36% in top 25% of high school class, 68% in top 50% of high school class. 84% from public high schools. **Test Scores:** SAT Math middle 50% range 400-510. SAT EBRW middle 50% range 390-515. ACT middle 50% range 18-26. Minimum internet-based TOEFL 63. Minimum paper TOEFL 500. **Basis for Candidate Selection:** *Very important factors considered include:* academic GPA, standardized test scores. *Important factors considered include:* rigor of secondary school record, class rank, extracurricular activities, talent/ability, character/personal qualities, alumni/ae relation, work experience. *Other factors considered include:* interview. **Freshman Admission Requirements:** High school diploma is required and GED is accepted *Academic units required:* 2 foreign language, 2 social studies, 2 history, *Academic units recommended:* 3 English, 3 math, 1 science, 1 science labs, 2 foreign language, 2 social studies, 2 history, 1 computer science. **Freshman Admission Statistics:** 786 applied, 58.0% admitted, 43% enrolled. **Transfer Admission Requirements:** college transcript(s), statement of good standing from prior institution(s). Minimum college GPA of 2.0 required. Lowest grade transferable C. **General Admission Information:** Application fee $35. Regular application deadline 8/28. Nonfall registration accepted.

COSTS AND FINANCIAL AID

Annual tuition $23,250. Room and board $6,800. Required fees $180. Average book expense $1,500. **Required Forms and Deadlines:** FAFSA. **Notification of Awards:** Applicants will be notified of awards on a rolling basis beginning 3/1. **Types of Aid:** *Need-based scholarships/grants:* College/ university scholarship or grant aid from institutional funds; Federal Pell; Private scholarships; SEOG; State scholarships/grants. *Loans:* Direct PLUS loans; Direct Subsidized Stafford Loans; Direct Unsubsidized Stafford Loans. *Student Employment:* Federal Work-Study Program available. Institutional employment available. **Financial Aid Statistics:** 100% needy freshmen, 84% needy undergrads receive need-based scholarship or grant aid. 24% freshmen, 13% undergrads receive non-need-based scholarship or grant aid. 78% freshmen, 89% undergrads receive need-based self-help aid. 21% freshmen, 3% undergrads receive athletic scholarships. 87% freshmen, 77% undergrads receive any aid. **Criteria for awarding aid:** *Non-need-based:* Academics, Alumni affiliation, Art, Athletics, Leadership, Music/drama, Religious affiliation.

FROSTBURG STATE UNIVERSITY

101 Braddock Rd., Frostburg, MD 21532
Phone: 301-687-4201 · **Financial Aid Phone:** 301-687-4301
E-mail: fsuadmissions@frostburg.edu · **CEEB Code:** 5402
Fax: 301-687-7074 · **Website:** www.frostburg.edu · **ACT Code:** 1714

This public school was founded in 1898. It has a 260 acre campus.

RATINGS

Admissions Selectivity Rating: 78   **Fire Safety Rating:** 87   **Green Rating:** 89

STUDENTS AND FACULTY

Enrollment: 4,486. **Student Body:** 52% female, 48% male, 7% out-of-state, 1% international (25 countries represented). Asian 2%, African American 33%, Caucasian 52%, Hispanic 6%, Native American <1%, Pacific Islander <1%, Two or more races 4%, Race unknown 1%.
Retention and Graduation: 74% freshmen return for sophomore year. 25% freshmen graduate within 4 years. 47% freshmen graduate within 6 years. **Faculty:** Student/faculty ratio 15:1. 249 full-time faculty, 78% hold PhDs, 13% are members of minority groups, 44% are women.

ACADEMICS

Degrees: Bachelor's; Doctoral/Research; Master's **Classes:** Most classes have 20-29 students. Most lab/discussion sessions have 10-19 students. **Most popular majors:** Elementary Education And Teaching; Psychology, General; Business/Commerce, General. **Special Study Options:** Distance learning; Double major; Dual enrollment; Honors program; Independent study; Internships; Study abroad; Teacher certification program. **Disability Services offered to physically disabled students:** Note-taking services; Reader services; Tape recorders; Tutors. **Career services:** Alumni network; Alumni services; Career assessment; Career/job search classes; Internships; Regional alumni

FACILITIES

Housing: Coed dorms; Men's dorms; Theme housing; Wellness housing; Women's dorms 100% of campus accessible to physically diasbled. **Special Academic Facilities/Equipment:** State-of-the-art science center, planetarium, science discovery center, art gallery. **Computers:** Students can register for classes online. Administrative functions (other than registration) can be performed online.

CAMPUS LIFE

Environment: Village **Activities:** Campus Ministries; Choral groups; Dance; Drama/theater; International Student Organization; Jazz band; Literary magazine; Marching band; Model UN; Music ensembles; Pep band; Radio station; Student government; Student newspaper; Television station; Yearbook 95 registered organizations, 18 honor societies, 6 religious organizations. 9 fraternities, 6 sororities. **Athletics (Intercollegiate):** *Men:* baseball, basketball, cross-country, diving, football, golf, soccer, swimming, tennis, track/field (outdoor), track/field (indoor). *Women:* basketball, cross-country, diving, field hockey, lacrosse, soccer, softball, swimming, tennis, track/field (outdoor), track/field (indoor), volleyball. **On-Campus Highlights:** Lane University Center, Game Room & Loft, Cordts PE Center, Performing Arts Center, Compton Science Center **Environmental Initiatives:** Adopted an energy-efficient appliance purchasing policy requiring purchase of ENERGY STAR-certified products in all areas for which such ratings exist.

ADMISSIONS

Freshman Academic Profile: Average high school GPA 3.2. 11% in top 10% of high school class, 31% in top 25% of high school class, 66% in top 50% of high school class. **Test Scores:** SAT Math middle 50% range 450-550. SAT EBRW middle 50% range 470-560. ACT middle 50% range 17-23. Minimum paper TOEFL 550. **Basis for Candidate Selection:** *Very important factors considered include:* rigor of secondary school record, academic GPA, standardized test scores. *Important factors considered include:* recommendation(s), interview. *Other factors considered include:* extracurricular activities, talent/ability, character/personal qualities, alumni/ ae relation. **Freshman Admission Requirements:** High school diploma is required and GED is accepted *Academic units required:* 4 English, 3 math, 3 science, 2 science labs, 2 foreign language, 3 history. **Freshman Admission Statistics:** 3,436 applied, 72.3% admitted, 31% enrolled. **Transfer Admission Requirements:** college transcript(s), Minimum college GPA of 2.0 required. Lowest grade transferable C. **General Admission Information:** Application fee $45. Priority deadline 6/1. Nonfall registration accepted.

COSTS AND FINANCIAL AID

Annual in-state tuition $9,210. Annual out-of-state tuition $19,816. Room and board $9,210. Required fees $2,446. Average book expense $1,400. **Required Forms and Deadlines:** FAFSA. **Notification of Awards:** Applicants will be notified of awards on a rolling basis beginning 3/15. **Types of Aid:** *Need-based scholarships/grants:* College/university scholarship or grant aid from institutional funds; Federal Pell; Private scholarships; SEOG; State scholarships/ grants. *Loans:* Direct PLUS loans; Direct Subsidized Stafford Loans; Direct Unsubsidized Stafford Loans. *Student Employment:* Federal Work-Study Program available. Institutional employment available. **Financial Aid Statistics:** 75% needy freshmen, 73% needy undergrads receive need-based scholarship or grant aid. 30% freshmen, 28% undergrads receive non-need-based scholarship or grant aid. 78% freshmen, 80% undergrads receive need-based self-help aid. 0% freshmen, 0% undergrads receive athletic scholarships. 72% freshmen, 65% undergrads receive any aid. **Criteria for awarding aid:** *Need-based:* Academics *Non-need-based:* Academics, Alumni affiliation, Art, Leadership, Music/drama, State/district residency.

FULL SAIL UNIVERSITY

3300 University Blvd, Winter Park, FL 32792
Phone: 800-226-7625
E-mail: admissions@fullsail.com
Website: http://www.fullsail.edu/

This proprietary school was founded in 1979. It has a 91 acre campus.

RATINGS

Admissions Selectivity Rating: 0   **Fire Safety Rating:** 60*   **Green Rating:** 60*

ACADEMICS

Degrees: Associate; Bachelor's; Master's; Terminal Associate **Most popular majors:** Recording Arts Technology/Technician; Animation, Interactive Technology, Video Graphics And Special Effects; Cinematography And Film/ Video Production. **Special Study Options:** Accelerated program.

CAMPUS LIFE
Environment: Metropolis

ADMISSIONS
Freshman Admission Requirements: High school diploma is required and GED is accepted **Transfer Admission Requirements:** college transcript(s), essay or personal statement, statement of good standing from prior institution(s). Minimum college GPA of 2.6 required. Lowest grade transferable c.

FURMAN UNIVERSITY

3300 Poinsett Highway, Greenville, SC 29613
Phone: 864-294-2034 · **Financial Aid Phone:** 864.294.2030
E-mail: admissions@furman.edu · **CEEB Code:** 5222
Fax: 864-294-2018 · **Website:** www.furman.edu · **ACT Code:** 3858

This private school was founded in 1826. It has a 800 acre campus.

RATINGS
Admissions Selectivity Rating: 87   **Fire Safety Rating:** 90   **Green Rating:** 92

STUDENTS AND FACULTY
Enrollment: 2,740. **Student Body:** 59% female, 41% male, 69% out-of-state, 5% international (49 countries represented). Asian 2%, African American 6%, Caucasian 76%, Hispanic 5%, Native American <1%, Pacific Islander 0%, Two or more races 3%, Race unknown 3%.
Retention and Graduation: 93% freshmen return for sophomore year. 73% freshmen graduate within 4 years. 81% freshmen graduate within 6 years. 38% grads go on to further study within 1 year. 28% grads pursue arts and sciences degrees. 3% grads pursue law degrees. 2% grads pursue business degrees. 4% grads pursue medical degrees. **Faculty:** Student/faculty ratio 10:1. 235 full-time faculty, 99% hold PhDs, 13% are members of minority groups, 38% are women. 0% of classes are taught by teaching assistants.

ACADEMICS
Degrees: Bachelor's; Master's; Post-Bachelor's certificate; Post-Master's certificate **Classes:** Most classes have fewer than 10 students. Most lab/discussion sessions have fewer than 10 students. **Most popular majors:** Political Science And Government, General; Health Professions And Related Clinical Sciences, Other; Business/Commerce, General. **Special Study Options:** Cross-registration; Double major; Independent study; Internships; Liberal arts/career combination; Student-designed major; Study abroad; Teacher certification program. **Combined degree programs:** BA/MA. **Disability Services offered to physically disabled students:** Note-taking services; Reader services; Tape recorders; Tutors. **Career services:** Alumni network; Alumni services; Career assessment; Career/job search classes; Internships

FACILITIES
Housing: Apartments for single students; Coed dorms; Men's dorms; Special housing for disabled student; Special housing for international students; Theme housing; Wellness housing; Women's dorms 98% of campus accessible to physically diasbled. **Special Academic Facilities/Equipment:** Visual arts gallery and teaching facility, language lab. Astronomical lab; Center for Engaged Learning; and Center for Collaborative Learning and Communication. **Computers:** 100% of classrooms, 100% of libraries, 100% of dining areas, 100% of student union, have wireless network access. Students can register for classes online. Administrative functions (other than registration) can be performed online.

CAMPUS LIFE
Environment: City **Activities:** Campus Ministries; Choral groups; Concert band; Dance; Drama/theater; International Student Organization; Jazz band; Literary magazine; Marching band; Model UN; Music ensembles; Musical theater; Opera; Pep band; Radio station; Student government; Student newspaper; Student-run film society; Symphony orchestra; Television station; Yearbook 143 registered organizations, 29 honor societies, 17 religious organizations. 7 fraternities, 7 sororities. **Athletics (Intercollegiate):** *Men:* baseball, basketball, cheerleading, cross-country, football, golf, soccer, tennis, track/field (outdoor), track/field (indoor). *Women:* basketball, cheerleading, cross-country, golf, soccer, softball, tennis, track/field (outdoor), track/field (indoor), volleyball. **On-Campus Highlights:** Daniel Dining Hall, Trone Student Center, Physical Activities Center, Charles Townes Science Center, Duke Library **Environmental Initiatives:** Sustainable Furman: The approval

of Sustainable Furman, the university's comprehensive sustainability master plan. The plan covers all aspects of the university; the 8 goals of Sustainable Furman address sustainability in the curriculum, co-curricular activities, campus culture, renewable energy, efficiency in operations and maintenance, transportation, sustainability service, and continuing national leadership in the sustainability arena. In addition, the plan sets out a path for the university to reach carbon neutrality by 2026.

ADMISSIONS
Freshman Academic Profile: 38% in top 10% of high school class, 71% in top 25% of high school class, 94% in top 50% of high school class. **Test Scores:** SAT Math middle 50% range 590-690. SAT EBRW middle 50% range 600-690. ACT middle 50% range 26-31. **Basis for Candidate Selection:** *Very important factors considered include:* rigor of secondary school record. *Important factors considered include:* class rank, academic GPA, application essay, extracurricular activities, character/personal qualities. *Other factors considered include:* standardized test scores, recommendation(s), interview, talent/ability, first generation, alumni/ae relation, racial/ethnic status, volunteer work, work experience, level of applicant's interest. **Freshman Admission Requirements:** High school diploma is required and GED is accepted *Academic units required:* 4 English, 3 math, 2 science, 2 science labs, 2 foreign language, 3 social studies, *Academic units recommended:* 4 English, 4 math, 3 science, 2 science labs, 3 foreign language, 4 social studies. **Freshman Admission Statistics:** 5,002 applied, 61.2% admitted, 23% enrolled. **Transfer Admission Requirements:** High school transcript, college transcript(s), essay or personal statement, standardized test scores, statement of good standing from prior institution(s). Minimum college GPA of 3.0 required. Lowest grade transferable C. **General Admission Information:** Application fee $50. Regular application deadline 1/15. Nonfall registration accepted. Admission may be deferred for a maximum of 1 year.

COSTS AND FINANCIAL AID
Annual tuition $47,968. Room and board $12,750. Required fees $380. Average book expense $1,230. **Required Forms and Deadlines:** Business/Farm Supplement; CSS/Financial Aid PROFILE; FAFSA; Noncustodial PROFILE. **Notification of Awards:** Applicants will be notified of awards on or about 4/1. **Types of Aid:** *Need-based scholarships/grants:* College/university scholarship or grant aid from institutional funds; Federal Pell; Private scholarships; SEOG; State scholarships/grants. *Loans:* Direct PLUS loans; Direct Subsidized Stafford Loans; Direct Unsubsidized Stafford Loans. *Student Employment:* Federal Work-Study Program available. Institutional employment available. **Financial Aid Statistics:** 100% needy freshmen, 100% needy undergrads receive need-based scholarship or grant aid. 100% freshmen, 100% undergrads receive non-need-based scholarship or grant aid. 71% freshmen, 69% undergrads receive need-based self-help aid. 11% freshmen, 12% undergrads receive athletic scholarships. 98% freshmen, 94% undergrads receive any aid. 35% undergrads borrow to pay for school. Average cumulative indebtedness $36,846. **Criteria for awarding aid:** *Need-based:* Academics, Alumni affiliation, Art, Athletics, Leadership, Music/drama, Religious affiliation *Non-need-based:* Academics, Alumni affiliation, Art, Athletics, Leadership, Music/drama, Religious affiliation, State/district residency.

GALLAUDET UNIVERSITY

800 Florida Avenue NE, Washington, DC 20002
Phone: 202-651-5750 · **Financial Aid Phone:** 202-651-5290
E-mail: admissions.office@gallaudet.edu · **CEEB Code:** 5240
Fax: 202-651-5744 · **Website:** http://www.gallaudet.edu/ · **ACT Code:** 662

This private school was founded in 1864. It has a 99 acre campus.

RATINGS
Admissions Selectivity Rating: 86   **Fire Safety Rating:** 92   **Green Rating:** 60*

STUDENTS AND FACULTY
Enrollment: 1,111. **Student Body:** 56% female, 44% male, 97% out-of-state, 5% international (20 countries represented). Asian 4%, African American 16%, Caucasian 51%, Hispanic 9%, Native American 1%, Pacific Islander 1%, Two or more races 4%, Race unknown 8%.
Retention and Graduation: 63% freshmen return for sophomore year. 20% freshmen graduate within 4 years. 43% freshmen graduate within 6 years. **Faculty:** Student/faculty ratio 7:1. 186 full-time faculty, 74% hold PhDs, 30% are members of minority groups, 62% are women.

ACADEMICS
Degrees: Bachelor's; Certificate; Doctoral; Doctoral Other; Doctoral/Research; Master's; Post-Bachelor's certificate; Post-Master's certificate

Classes: Most classes have 20-29 students. Most lab/discussion sessions have 10-19 students. **Most popular majors:** Ethnic, Cultural Minority, Gender, And Group Studies, Other; Psychology, General; Business Administration And Management, General. **Special Study Options:** Cross-registration; Distance learning; Double major; Dual enrollment; English as a Second Language (ESL); Honors program; Independent study; Internships; Student-designed major; Study abroad; Teacher certification program. **Honors programs:** The Gallaudet Honors Program is a Learning Community for the most academically capable and motivated students. The overall goal is to foster skills, work habits, and attitudes conducive to future achievement and lifelong learning. To this end, the Program focuses on linking rigorous, challenging, and innovative curricular offerings with co-curricular activities. It also serves as a leader in and test laboratory of curricular, co-curricular, and extracurricular innovations; successes may then be replicated for all students. **Disability Services offered to physically disabled students:** Tutors. **Career services:** Alumni network; Alumni services; Career assessment; Career/job search classes; Internships

FACILITIES

Housing: Apartments for married students; Coed dorms; Special housing for disabled students 100% of campus accessible to physically diasbled. **Special Academic Facilities/Equipment:** Kendall Demonstration Elementary School and Model Secondary School for the Deaf **Computers:** 100% of classrooms, 100% of dorms, 100% of libraries, 100% of dining areas, 100% of student union, 20% of common outdoor areas have wireless network access. Students can register for classes online. Administrative functions (other than registration) can be performed online.

CAMPUS LIFE

Environment: Metropolis **Activities:** Campus Ministries; Dance; Drama/theater; International Student Organization; Literary magazine; Student government; Student newspaper; Student-run film society; Television station; Yearbook 25 registered organizations, 1 honor society, 1 religious organization. 5 fraternities, 4 sororities. **Athletics (Intercollegiate):** *Men:* baseball, basketball, cross-country, diving, football, soccer, swimming, tennis, track/field (outdoor), wrestling. *Women:* basketball, cross-country, diving, soccer, softball, swimming, tennis, track/field (outdoor), volleyball. **On-Campus Highlights:** Rathskellar, Cafeteria, Bison Shop, Starbucks, Student Academic Center

ADMISSIONS

Freshman Academic Profile: Average high school GPA 3.2. **Test Scores:** SAT Math middle 50% range 425-545. SAT EBRW middle 50% range 380-565. ACT middle 50% range 15-19. **Basis for Candidate Selection:** *Very important factors considered include:* rigor of secondary school record, class rank, academic GPA, application essay, standardized test scores, recommendation(s). *Other factors considered include:* interview, extracurricular activities, talent/ability, character/personal qualities, first generation, alumni/ae relation, geographical residence, state residency, religious affiliation/commitment, racial/ethnic status, volunteer work, work experience, level of applicant's interest. **Freshman Admission Requirements:** High school diploma is required and GED is accepted *Academic units recommended:* 4 English, 3 math, 2 science, 2 foreign language, 2 social studies, 1 visual/performing arts, 1 unit from above areas or other academic areas. **Freshman Admission Statistics:** 588 applied, 58.7% admitted, 72% enrolled. **Transfer Admission Requirements:** college transcript(s), essay or personal statement, Lowest grade transferable C-. **General Admission Information:** Application fee $50. Nonfall registration accepted. Admission may be deferred for a maximum of 2 years.

COSTS AND FINANCIAL AID

Annual tuition $16,512. Required fees $526. Average book expense $1,600. **Required Forms and Deadlines:** FAFSA. **Notification of Awards:** Applicants will be notified of awards on a rolling basis beginning 3/1. **Types of Aid:** *Need-based scholarships/grants:* College/university scholarship or grant aid from institutional funds; Federal Pell; Private scholarships; SEOG; State scholarships/grants. *Loans:* Direct PLUS loans; Direct Subsidized Stafford Loans; Direct Unsubsidized Stafford Loans. *Student Employment:* Federal Work-Study Program available. Institutional employment available. **Financial Aid Statistics:** 99% needy freshmen, 91% needy undergrads receive need-based scholarship or grant aid. 18% freshmen, 18% undergrads receive non-need-based scholarship or grant aid. 45% freshmen, 46% undergrads receive need-based self-help aid. 0% freshmen, 0% undergrads receive athletic scholarships. 94% freshmen, 85% undergrads receive any aid. **Criteria for awarding aid:** *Need-based:* Academics *Non-need-based:* Academics.

GANNON UNIVERSITY

109 University Square, Erie, PA 16541
Phone: 814-871-7240 • **Financial Aid Phone:** 814-871-7337
E-mail: admissions@gannon.edu • **CEEB Code:** 2270
Fax: 814-871-5803 • **Website:** www.gannon.edu • **ACT Code:** 3576

This private school, affiliated with the Roman Catholic Church, was founded in 1925. It has a 52 acre campus.

RATINGS

Admissions Selectivity Rating: 75   **Fire Safety Rating:** 97   **Green Rating:** 73

STUDENTS AND FACULTY

Enrollment: 2,616. **Student Body:** 57% female, 43% male, 29% out-of-state, 9% international (39 countries represented). Asian 1%, African American 5%, Caucasian 73%, Hispanic 3%, Native American <1%, Pacific Islander <1%, Two or more races 3%, Race unknown 6%. **Retention and Graduation:** 85% freshmen return for sophomore year. 47% grads go on to further study within 1 year. 3.6% grads pursue law degrees. 4% grads pursue business degrees. 6.3% grads pursue medical degrees. **Faculty:** Student/faculty ratio 12:1. 238 full-time faculty, 78% hold PhDs, 14% are members of minority groups, 48% are women. 1% of classes are taught by teaching assistants.

ACADEMICS

Degrees: Associate; Bachelor's; Certificate; Doctoral/Professional; Doctoral/Research; Master's; Post-Bachelor's certificate; Post-Master's certificate; Terminal Associate **Classes:** Most classes have 10-19 students. Most lab/discussion sessions have 10-19 students. **Most popular majors:** Kinesiology And Exercise Science; Registered Nursing/Registered Nurse; Health Professions And Related Clinical Sciences, Other. **Special Study Options:** Accelerated program; Cooperative education program; Distance learning; Double major; Dual enrollment; English as a Second Language (ESL); Honors program; Independent study; Internships; Liberal arts/career combination; Study abroad; Teacher certification program; Weekend college. **Honors programs:** The Gannon honors program challenges and nurtures students as ethical, global leaders. Our small class sizes, reading and writing intensive courses, opportunities for travel, and service-learning engage our highly motivated students. **Combined degree programs:** BA/JD; BA/MA; BA/MD. **Disability Services offered to physically disabled students:** Note-taking services; Reader services; Tape recorders. **Career services:** Alumni network; Alumni services; Career assessment; Career/job search classes; Internships; Regional alumni

FACILITIES

Housing: Apartments for single students; Coed dorms; Fraternity/sorority housing; Special housing for disabled student; Special housing for international students; Theme housing 70% of campus accessible to physically diasbled. **Special Academic Facilities/Equipment:** Patient Simulation Center, Environaut research vessel, computer-integrated manufacturing facilities, atomic force microscope, Schuster Art Gallery, Schuster Theatres, Erie Technology Incubator **Computers:** 100% of classrooms, 100% of dorms, 100% of libraries, 100% of dining areas, 100% of student union, 100% of common outdoor areas have wireless network access. Students can register for classes online. Administrative functions (other than registration) can be performed online.

CAMPUS LIFE

Environment: City **Activities:** Campus Ministries; Choral groups; Concert band; Dance; Drama/theater; International Student Organization; Literary magazine; Model UN; Pep band; Radio station; Student government; Student newspaper 71 registered organizations, 11 honor societies, 6 religious organizations. 5 fraternities, 5 sororities. **Athletics (Intercollegiate):** *Men:* baseball, basketball, cheerleading, cross-country, football, golf, soccer, swimming, water polo, wrestling. *Women:* basketball, cheerleading, cross-country, golf, lacrosse, soccer, softball, swimming, volleyball, water polo. **On-Campus Highlights:** Waldron Campus Center, Friendship Green, Student Recreation Center, Knight Club, Hammermill Center **Environmental Initiatives:** Switching out all campus light bulbs to compact flourescent.

ADMISSIONS

Freshman Academic Profile: Average high school GPA 3.6. 22% in top 10% of high school class, 49% in top 25% of high school class, 83% in top 50% of high school class. 83% from public high schools. **Test Scores:** SAT Math middle 50% range 470-570. SAT EBRW middle 50% range 450-560. ACT middle 50% range 20-26. Minimum internet-based TOEFL 79. Minimum paper TOEFL 550. **Basis for Candidate Selection:** *Very important factors considered include:* rigor of secondary school record, academic GPA, standardized test scores. *Other factors considered include:* class rank, application essay, recommendation(s), interview, extracurricular activities, character/personal qualities, alumni/ae relation, work experience. **Freshman Admission Requirements:** High school diploma is required and GED is accepted *Academic units required:* 4 English, 2 math, 2 science, 2 science labs, 2 social studies, 1 history, 3 academic electives, *Academic units recommended:* 4 English, 4 math, 4 science, 3 science labs, 2 foreign language, 2 social studies, 1 history, 3 academic electives, 1 computer science, 1 visual/performing arts. **Freshman Admission Statistics:** 4,710 applied, 77.7% admitted, 17% enrolled. **Transfer Admission Requirements:** college transcript(s), statement of good standing from prior institution(s). Minimum college GPA of 2.0 required. Lowest grade transferable C. **General Admission Information:** Application fee $25. Nonfall registration accepted. Admission may be deferred for a maximum of 1 year.

COSTS AND FINANCIAL AID

Required Forms and Deadlines: FAFSA. **Notification of Awards:** Applicants will be notified of awards on a rolling basis beginning 11/1. **Types of Aid:** *Need-based scholarships/grants:* College/university scholarship or grant aid from institutional funds; Federal Nursing Scholarships; Federal Pell; Private scholarships; SEOG; State scholarships/grants. *Loans:* Direct PLUS loans; Direct Subsidized Stafford Loans; Direct Unsubsidized Stafford Loans. *Student Employment:* Federal Work-Study Program available. Institutional employment available. **Financial Aid Statistics:** 99% needy freshmen, 98% needy undergrads receive need-based scholarship or grant aid. 15% freshmen, 15% undergrads receive non-need-based scholarship or grant aid. 82% freshmen, 77% undergrads receive need-based self-help aid. 4% freshmen, 35% undergrads receive athletic scholarships. 98% freshmen, 96% undergrads receive any aid. **Criteria for awarding aid:** *Non-need-based:* Academics, Athletics, Leadership, Music/drama, Religious affiliation.

GARDNER-WEBB UNIVERSITY

P.O. Box 997, Boiling Springs, NC 28017
Phone: 704-406-4498 • **Financial Aid Phone:** 704-406-4243
E-mail: admissions@gardner-webb.edu • **CEEB Code:** 5242
Fax: 704-406-4488 • **Website:** www.gardner-webb.edu • **ACT Code:** 3102

This private school, affiliated with the Baptist Church, was founded in 1905. It has a 250 acre campus.

RATINGS

Admissions Selectivity Rating: 80   Fire Safety Rating: 98   Green Rating: 60*

STUDENTS AND FACULTY

Enrollment: 2,640. **Student Body:** 65% female, 35% male, 21% out-of-state, <1% international (22 countries represented). Asian <1%, African American 19%, Caucasian 72%, Hispanic 2%, Native American 1%, Race unknown 6%. **Retention and Graduation:** 74% freshmen return for sophomore year. **Faculty:** Student/faculty ratio 13:1. 140 full-time faculty, 80% hold PhDs, 4% are members of minority groups, 46% are women. 0% of classes are taught by teaching assistants.

ACADEMICS

Degrees: Associate; Bachelor's; Doctoral; Master's **Classes:** Most classes have 10-19 students. **Most popular majors:** Religion/Religious Studies; Social Sciences, Other; Business/Commerce, General. **Special Study Options:** Accelerated program; Distance learning; Double major; Dual enrollment; English as a Second Language (ESL); Honors program; Independent study; Internships; Liberal arts/career combination; Study abroad; Teacher certification program. **Honors programs:** Alpha Chi Honors Program Beta Beta Beta Delta Mu Delta Sigma Delta Pi Sigma Tau Delta Theta Alpha Kappa Pi Delta Phi Psi Chi Sigma Zeta Sigma Theta Tau Who's Who. **Disability Services offered to physically disabled students:** Note-taking services; Reader services; Tape recorders; Tutors. **Career services:** Alumni network; Career assessment; Career/job search classes; Internships

FACILITIES

Housing: Apartments for single students; Men's dorms; Special housing for disabled student; Wellness housing; Women's dorms 100% of campus accessible to physically disabled. **Special Academic Facilities/Equipment:** Williams Observatory, Millennium Playhouse, Broyhill Adventure Course, Lake Hollifield Complex and Carillon **Computers:** 100% of classrooms, 100% of dorms, 100% of libraries, 100% of dining areas, 100% of student union, 100% of common outdoor areas have wireless network access. Students can register for classes online. Administrative functions (other than registration) can be performed online.

CAMPUS LIFE

Environment: Rural **Activities:** Campus Ministries; Choral groups; Concert band; Dance; Drama/theater; International Student Organization; Jazz band;

Literary magazine; Marching band; Music ensembles; Musical theater; Opera; Pep band; Radio station; Student government; Student newspaper; Symphony orchestra; Yearbook 65 registered organizations, 12 honor societies, 11 religious organizations. **Athletics (Intercollegiate):** *Men:* baseball, basketball, cheerleading, cross-country, football, golf, soccer, swimming, tennis, track/field (outdoor), track/field (indoor), wrestling. *Women:* basketball, cheerleading, cross-country, golf, soccer, softball, swimming, tennis, track/field (outdoor), track/field (indoor), volleyball. **On-Campus Highlights:** Dover Campus Center, Suttle Wellness Center, Cafeteria, Lutz-Yelton Convocation Center, Kennel Snack Bar **Environmental Initiatives:** recycling programs

ADMISSIONS

Freshman Academic Profile: Average high school GPA 3.5. 32% in top 10% of high school class, 49% in top 25% of high school class, 72% in top 50% of high school class. 84% from public high schools. **Test Scores:** SAT Math middle 50% range 420-550. SAT EBRW middle 50% range 440-560. ACT middle 50% range 18-23. Minimum internet-based TOEFL 61. Minimum paper TOEFL 500. **Basis for Candidate Selection:** *Very important factors considered include:* rigor of secondary school record, academic GPA, standardized test scores, level of applicant's interest. *Important factors considered include:* class rank, recommendation(s), extracurricular activities, character/personal qualities. *Other factors considered include:* application essay, interview, talent/ability, volunteer work. **Freshman Admission Requirements:** High school diploma is required and GED is accepted *Academic units recommended:* 4 English, 3 math, 3 science, 2 science labs, 2 foreign language, 1 social studies, 1 history. **Freshman Admission Statistics:** 3,277 applied, 61.5% admitted, 22% enrolled. **Transfer Admission Requirements:** college transcript(s), statement of good standing from prior institution(s). Minimum college GPA of 2.25 required. Lowest grade transferable C. **General Admission Information:** Application fee $40. Nonfall registration accepted. Admission may be deferred for a maximum of 2 semesters.

COSTS AND FINANCIAL AID

Annual tuition $22,050. Room and board $7,195. Required fees $390. Average book expense $1,000. **Required Forms and Deadlines:** FAFSA; State aid form. **Notification of Awards:** Applicants will be notified of awards on a rolling basis beginning 3/1. **Types of Aid:** *Need-based scholarships/grants:* College/university scholarship or grant aid from institutional funds; Federal Pell; Private scholarships; SEOG; State scholarships/grants. *Loans: Student Employment:* Federal Work-Study Program available. Institutional employment available. **Financial Aid Statistics:** 96% needy freshmen, 34% needy undergrads receive need-based scholarship or grant aid. 77% freshmen, 70% undergrads receive non-need-based scholarship or grant aid. 66% freshmen, 75% undergrads receive need-based self-help aid. 100% freshmen receive any aid. **Criteria for awarding aid:** *Need-based:* Academics, Leadership, Minority status, Music/drama, Religious affiliation *Non-need-based:* Academics, Athletics, Leadership, Music/drama, State/district residency.

GEORGE FOX UNIVERSITY

414 N. Meridian Street, Newberg, OR 97132
Phone: 503-554-2240 • **Financial Aid Phone:** 503-554-2300
E-mail: admissions@georgefox.edu • **CEEB Code:** 4325
Fax: 503-554-3110 • **Website:** www.georgefox.edu • **ACT Code:** 3462

This private school, affiliated with the Evangelical Friends Church, was founded in 1891. It has a 108 acre campus.

RATINGS

Admissions Selectivity Rating: 79   Fire Safety Rating: 88   Green Rating: 60*

STUDENTS AND FACULTY

Enrollment: 2,358. **Student Body:** 57% female, 43% male, 35% out-of-state, 6% international (43 countries represented). Asian 4%, African American 2%, Caucasian 70%, Hispanic 7%, Native American <1%, Pacific Islander <1%, Two or more races 5%, Race unknown 4%.
Retention and Graduation: 82% freshmen return for sophomore year. 11% grads go on to further study within 1 year. 6% grads pursue arts and sciences degrees. 0% grads pursue law degrees. 2% grads pursue business degrees. 1.8% grads pursue medical degrees. **Faculty:** Student/faculty ratio 14:1. 168 full-time faculty, 76% hold PhDs, 14% are members of minority groups, 40% are women. 0% of classes are taught by teaching assistants.

ACADEMICS

Degrees: Bachelor's; Doctoral/Professional; Master's; Post-Bachelor's certificate; Post-Master's certificate **Classes:** Most classes have 20-29 students. Most lab/discussion sessions have 10-19 students. **Most popular majors:** Elementary Education And Teaching; Registered Nursing/Registered Nurse;

Business Administration And Management, General. **Special Study Options:** Accelerated program; Cross-registration; Distance learning; Double major; Dual enrollment; English as a Second Language (ESL); Exchange student program (domestic); Honors program; Independent study; Internships; Student-designed major; Study abroad; Teacher certification program. **Honors programs:** Richter Scholars, Advance Leadership Development Program, William Penn Honors Program. The William Penn Honors Program will launch in the fall of 2014 as an alternative liberal arts general education program for undergraduate students. Modeled on the Socratic tutorial style, the program is designed to hone students' critical thinking skills by exposing them to classical texts and using discussion as the primary mode of instruction. Graduates of the program will be prepared to engage their culture meaningfully at the deepest levels – and they will be able to do so in a humble and gracious manner from an orthodox Christian perspective. **Disability Services offered to physically disabled students:** Note-taking services; Reader services; Tape recorders; Tutors. **Career services:** Alumni network; Alumni services; Career assessment; Career/job search classes; Internships; Regional alumni

FACILITIES

Housing: Apartments for single students; Men's dorms; Special housing for disabled student; Theme housing; Wellness housing; Women's dorms 98% of campus accessible to physically diasbled. **Special Academic Facilities/ Equipment:** nuclear magnetic resonance spectrometer, Providence Nursing Learning Lab, language lab, electron microscope. **Computers:** 100% of classrooms, 90% of dorms, 100% of libraries, 100% of dining areas, 100% of student union, 50% of common outdoor areas have wireless network access. Students can register for classes online. Administrative functions (other than registration) can be performed online.

CAMPUS LIFE

Environment: Village **Activities:** Campus Ministries; Choral groups; Concert band; Drama/theater; International Student Organization; Jazz band; Literary magazine; Music ensembles; Musical theater; Pep band; Radio station; Student government; Student newspaper; Symphony orchestra; Yearbook 20 registered organizations, 3 honor societies, 3 religious organizations. **Athletics (Intercollegiate): Men:** baseball, basketball, cross-country, golf, soccer, tennis, track/field (outdoor). *Women:* basketball, cross-country, golf, soccer, softball, tennis, track/field (outdoor), volleyball. **On-Campus Highlights:** Bruin Den-Cafe in the Student Union Bldg, Brewin' Grounds- Student-run coffee house, The Firepit Pavillion- Student hang out, Wheeler Sports Center, The Quad **Environmental Initiatives:** LEED-certified residence hall

ADMISSIONS

Freshman Academic Profile: Average high school GPA 3.6. 27% in top 10% of high school class, 57% in top 25% of high school class, 85% in top 50% of high school class. 73% from public high schools. **Test Scores:** SAT Math middle 50% range 470-600. SAT EBRW middle 50% range 470-600. ACT middle 50% range 20-26. Minimum internet-based TOEFL 80. Minimum paper TOEFL 550. **Basis for Candidate Selection:** *Very important factors considered include:* rigor of secondary school record, academic GPA, application essay, standardized test scores, recommendation(s). *Important factors considered include:* character/personal qualities. *Other factors considered include:* class rank, interview, extracurricular activities, talent/ ability, religious affiliation/commitment, volunteer work, work experience. **Freshman Admission Requirements:** High school diploma is required and GED is accepted *Academic units recommended:* 4 English, 2 math, 2 science, 2 science labs, 2 foreign language, 3 social studies, 2 history, 1 unit from above areas or other academic areas. **Freshman Admission Statistics:** 2,431 applied, 75.3% admitted, 35% enrolled. **Transfer Admission Requirements:** college transcript(s), essay or personal statement, statement of good standing from prior institution(s). Minimum college GPA of 2.6 required. Lowest grade transferable C-. **General Admission Information:** Application fee $40. Priority deadline 2/1. Nonfall registration accepted. Admission may be deferred for a maximum of 1 year.

COSTS AND FINANCIAL AID

Annual tuition $33,370. Room and board $10,528. Required fees $360. Average book expense $950. **Required Forms and Deadlines:** FAFSA; State aid form. **Notification of Awards:** Applicants will be notified of awards on a rolling basis beginning 3/1. **Types of Aid:** *Need-based scholarships/grants:* College/ university scholarship or grant aid from institutional funds; Federal Pell; Private scholarships; SEOG; State scholarships/grants. *Loans:* Direct PLUS loans; Direct Subsidized Stafford Loans; Direct Unsubsidized Stafford Loans. *Student Employment:* Federal Work-Study Program available. Institutional employment available. **Financial Aid Statistics:** 84% needy freshmen, 96% needy undergrads receive need-based scholarship or grant aid. 7% freshmen, 6% undergrads receive non-need-based scholarship or grant aid. 87% freshmen, 88% undergrads receive need-based self-help aid. 0% freshmen, 0% undergrads receive athletic scholarships. 100% freshmen, 96% undergrads receive any aid. 79% undergrads borrow to pay for school. Average cumulative indebtedness $22,996. **Criteria for awarding aid:** *Need-based:* Minority status, Religious affiliation *Non-need-based:* Academics, Alumni affiliation, Art, Job skills, Leadership, Minority status, Music/drama, Religious affiliation.

GEORGE MASON UNIVERSITY

Best Colleges

4400 University Drive, Fairfax, VA 22030-4444
Phone: 703-993-2400 · **Financial Aid Phone:** 703-993-2353
E-mail: admissions@gmu.edu · **CEEB Code:** 5827
Fax: 703-993-4622 · **Website:** https://www2.gmu.edu · **ACT Code:** 4357

This public school was founded in 1972. It has a 817 acre campus.

RATINGS
Admissions Selectivity Rating: 79   **Fire Safety Rating:** 98   **Green Rating:** 94

STUDENTS AND FACULTY
Enrollment: 24,372. **Student Body:** 50% female, 50% male, 10% out-of-state, 5% international (106 countries represented). Asian 20%, African American 11%, Caucasian 41%, Hispanic 14%, Native American <1%, Pacific Islander <1%, Two or more races 5%, Race unknown 3%.
Retention and Graduation: 88% freshmen return for sophomore year. 49% freshmen graduate within 4 years. 71% freshmen graduate within 6 years. **Faculty:** Student/faculty ratio 17:1. 1,290 full-time faculty, 91% hold PhDs, 21% are members of minority groups, 43% are women. 7% of classes are taught by teaching assistants.

ACADEMICS
Degrees: Bachelor's; Doctoral; Doctoral/Professional; Doctoral/Research; Master's; Post-Bachelor's certificate; Post-Master's certificate **Classes:** Most classes have 20-29 students. Most lab/discussion sessions have 10-19 students. **Most popular majors:** Information Technology; Biology/Biological Sciences, General; Psychology, General. **Special Study Options:** Accelerated program; Cooperative education program; Cross-registration; Distance learning; Double major; Dual enrollment; English as a Second Language (ESL); Exchange student program (domestic); Honors program; Independent study; Internships; Liberal arts/career combination; Student-designed major; Study abroad; Teacher certification program. **Honors programs:** The Mission of the Honors College is to recruit the most highly motivated undergraduates from every background and in every field of study; to foster their capabilities to listen to, learn from, and work with people whose perspectives differ from their own; and to engage them in transformational learning experiences that prepare them to meet the challenges facing our community, our nation, and our world. Through the resources of the Honors College, the university provides students the support to excel academically and to pursue life-long goals. Included in these resources is the Honors College curriculum, which offers challenging courses that fulfill core academic requirements at Mason. Senior faculty, including Mason's Robinson Professors, teach small classes of students taking the curriculum. A select group of entering students is invited to become part of the University Scholars, a community of learners and leaders who receive Mason's most competitive merit-based scholarships. All Honors College students have direct access to the Office of Fellowships, which provides guidance and support to high-achieving Mason undergraduates and recent alumni about the application process for nationally competitive fellowships. The benefits of being part of the Honors College include participating in a diverse living-learning community. Community programs include special lectures, events, and excursions on and off campus, as well as opportunities to take advantage of internships and cultural programs in Washington, D.C. All students in the Honors College receive individualized academic advising, priority registration, and opportunities for close interaction with faculty for one-on-one mentoring and graduate and professional advising. **Combined degree programs:** BA/ MA. **Disability Services offered to physically disabled students:** Note-taking services; Reader services; Tape recorders. **Career services:** Alumni network; Alumni services; Career assessment; Career/job search classes; Internships; Regional alumni

FACILITIES
Housing: Apartments for single students; Coed dorms; Special housing for disabled student; Special housing for international students; Theme housing 95% of campus accessible to physically diasbled. **Special Academic Facilities/ Equipment:** Smithsonian-Mason School of Conservation George Mason University Observatory Point of View International Retreat and Conference Center EagleBank Arena Mason Enterprise Center/Virginia Small Business Development Center Mason Innovation Exchange Mason Trails Carty House (mock crime scene house for forensic science program) Potomac Science Center Center for the Arts Hylton Performing Arts Center Presidents Park Greenhouse Sports Medicine Assessment Research and Testing (SMART) laboratory The EDGE: Mason Center for Team and Organizational Learning **Computers:** 30% of classrooms, 100% of dorms, 100% of libraries, 100%

of dining areas, 100% of student union, 5% of common outdoor areas have wireless network access. Students can register for classes online. Administrative functions (other than registration) can be performed online.

CAMPUS LIFE

Environment: City **Activities:** Campus Ministries; Choral groups; Concert band; Dance; Drama/theater; International Student Organization; Jazz band; Literary magazine; Model UN; Music ensembles; Musical theater; Opera; Pep band; Radio station; Student government; Student newspaper; Student-run film society; Symphony orchestra; Television station; Yearbook 250 registered organizations, 7 honor societies, 29 religious organizations. 22 fraternities, 13 sororities. **Athletics (Intercollegiate):** *Men:* baseball, basketball, cheerleading, cross-country, diving, golf, soccer, swimming, tennis, track/field (outdoor), track/field (indoor), volleyball, wrestling. *Women:* basketball, cheerleading, crew/rowing, cross-country, diving, lacrosse, soccer, softball, swimming, tennis, track/field (outdoor), track/field (indoor), volleyball. **On-Campus Highlights:** Johnson Center, Aquatic and Fitness Center, Center for the Arts, Eagle Bank Arena, Hylton Performing Arts Center

ADMISSIONS

Freshman Academic Profile: Average high school GPA 3.7. 17% in top 10% of high school class, 34% in top 25% of high school class, 87% in top 50% of high school class. 74% from public high schools. **Test Scores:** SAT Math middle 50% range 540-640. SAT EBRW middle 50% range 560-650. ACT middle 50% range 24-30. Minimum internet-based TOEFL 80. Minimum paper TOEFL 570. **Basis for Candidate Selection:** *Very important factors considered include:* rigor of secondary school record, academic GPA. *Important factors considered include:* class rank, standardized test scores, talent/ability, character/personal qualities. *Other factors considered include:* application essay, recommendation(s), extracurricular activities, first generation, alumni/ae relation, geographical residence, volunteer work, work experience, level of applicant's interest. **Freshman Admission Requirements:** High school diploma is required and GED is accepted *Academic units required:* 4 English, 3 math, 2 science, 2 science labs, 2 foreign language, 3 social studies, 3 academic electives, *Academic units recommended:* 4 English, 4 math, 3 science, 3 science labs, 3 foreign language, 4 social studies, 5 academic electives. **Freshman Admission Statistics:** 18,993 applied, 81.3% admitted, 23% enrolled. **Transfer Admission Requirements:** college transcript(s), Minimum college GPA of 2.0 required. Lowest grade transferable C. **General Admission Information:** Application fee $70. Priority deadline 11/1. Regular application deadline 1/15. Nonfall registration accepted. Admission may be deferred for a maximum of 1 year.

COSTS AND FINANCIAL AID

Annual in-state tuition $11,090. Annual out-of-state tuition $31,118. Room and board $11,090. Required fees $3,252. Average book expense $1,200. **Required Forms and Deadlines:** FAFSA. **Notification of Awards:** Applicants will be notified of awards on a rolling basis beginning 4/1. **Types of Aid:** *Need-based scholarships/grants:* College/university scholarship or grant aid from institutional funds; Federal Pell; Private scholarships; SEOG; State scholarships/grants. *Loans:* Direct PLUS loans; Direct Subsidized Stafford Loans; Direct Unsubsidized Stafford Loans. *Student Employment:* Federal Work-Study Program available. Institutional employment available. **Financial Aid Statistics:** 77% needy freshmen, 78% needy undergrads receive need-based scholarship or grant aid. 38% freshmen, 19% undergrads receive non-need-based scholarship or grant aid. 79% freshmen, 79% undergrads receive need-based self-help aid. 1% freshmen, 1% undergrads receive athletic scholarships. 70% freshmen, 59% undergrads receive any aid. 56% undergrads borrow to pay for school. Average cumulative indebtedness $30,132. **Criteria for awarding aid:** *Non-need-based:* Academics, Athletics, Minority status, Music/drama.

GEORGE WASHINGTON UNIVERSITY

Best Colleges

2121 Eye Street, NW, Washington, DC 20052
Phone: 202-994-6040
E-mail: gwadm@gwu.edu • **CEEB Code:** 5246
Fax: 202-994-0325 • **Website:** www.gwu.edu • **ACT Code:** 664

This private school was founded in 1821. It has a 45 acre campus.

RATINGS

Admissions Selectivity Rating: 92   **Fire Safety Rating:** 60*   **Green Rating:** 97

STUDENTS AND FACULTY

Enrollment: 11,244. **Student Body:** 57% female, 43% male, 97% out-of-state, 11% international (122 countries represented). Asian 10%, African American 7%, Caucasian 54%, Hispanic 9%, Native American <1%, Pacific Islander <1%, Two or more races 4%, Race unknown 5%.
Retention and Graduation: 90% freshmen return for sophomore year. 22% grads go on to further study within 1 year. 48% grads pursue arts and sciences degrees. 31% grads pursue law degrees. 2% grads pursue business degrees. 18% grads pursue medical degrees. **Faculty:** Student/faculty ratio 13:1. 1,091 full-time faculty, 94% hold PhDs, 24% are members of minority groups, 44% are women. 3% of classes are taught by teaching assistants.

ACADEMICS

Degrees: Associate; Bachelor's; Certificate; Doctoral/Professional; Doctoral/Research; Master's; Post-Bachelor's certificate; Post-Master's certificate; Terminal Associate **Classes:** Most classes have 10-19 students. Most lab/discussion sessions have 10-19 students..**Most popular majors:** Psychology, General; International Relations And Affairs; Business Administration And Management, General. **Special Study Options:** Accelerated program; Cooperative education program; Cross-registration; Distance learning; Double major; Dual enrollment; Exchange student program (domestic); Honors program; Independent study; Internships; Liberal arts/career combination; Student-designed major; Study abroad. **Combined degree programs:** BA/JD; BA/MA; BA/MD. **Disability Services offered to physically disabled students:** Note-taking services; Reader services; Tape recorders; Tutors. **Career services:** Alumni network; Alumni services; Career assessment; Career/job search classes; Internships; Regional alumni

FACILITIES

Housing: Apartments for single students; Coed dorms; Fraternity/sorority housing; Theme housing; Women's dorms 95% of campus accessible to physically diasbled. **Special Academic Facilities/Equipment:** Art gallery, language lab, word processing center. **Computers:** Students can register for classes online. Administrative functions (other than registration) can be performed online.

CAMPUS LIFE

Environment: Metropolis **Activities:** Choral groups; Concert band; Dance; Drama/theater; International Student Organization; Jazz band; Literary magazine; Marching band; Model UN; Music ensembles; Musical theater; Pep band; Radio station; Student government; Student newspaper; Student-run film society; Symphony orchestra; Television station; Yearbook 220 registered organizations, 3 honor societies, 5 religious organizations. 12 fraternities, 9 sororities. **Athletics (Intercollegiate):** *Men:* baseball, basketball, crew/rowing, cross-country, diving, fencing, golf, rugby, soccer, squash, swimming, tennis, water polo. *Women:* basketball, crew/rowing, cross-country, fencing, gymnastics, soccer, swimming, tennis, volleyball. **On-Campus Highlights:** The Smith Center, The Hippo, Media and Public Affairs Building, Kogan Plaza, Gelman Library **Environmental Initiatives:** 1. GW's mission is to be the premier university on policy and governance for sustainable systems through practice, teaching, research, and outreach. The University is deploying a pan-university approach that bridges traditional disciplines. In Fall 2012 GW will offer an interdisciplinary Minor in Sustainability to all undergraduate students. The minor is a pan-university offering that provides students with inter-disciplinary teaching (with a team-taught course taught by faculty representing several schools) and experiential learning (which challenges students to apply knowledge, theory and methods learned in the classroom to analyze a real-world sustainability issue and/or practice).

ADMISSIONS

Freshman Academic Profile: 55% in top 10% of high school class, 85% in top 25% of high school class, 98% in top 50% of high school class. 70% from public high schools. **Test Scores:** SAT Math middle 50% range 600-700. SAT EBRW middle 50% range 580-690. ACT middle 50% range 27-32. Minimum paper TOEFL 550. **Basis for Candidate Selection:** *Very important factors considered include:* rigor of secondary school record, academic GPA. *Important factors considered include:* application essay, recommendation(s), extracurricular activities, talent/ability, volunteer work. *Other factors considered include:* standardized test scores, character/personal qualities, first generation, alumni/ae relation, geographical residence, racial/ethnic status, work experience, level of applicant's interest. **Freshman Admission Requirements:** High school diploma is required and GED is accepted *Academic units required:* 4 English, 2 math, 2 science, 1 science labs, 2 foreign language, 2 social studies, *Academic units recommended:* 4 English, 4 math, 4 science, 4 foreign language, 4 social studies. **Freshman Admission Statistics:** 25,488 applied, 40.2% admitted, 25% enrolled. **Transfer Admission Requirements:** High school transcript, college transcript(s), essay or personal statement, standardized test scores, Lowest grade transferable C. **General Admission Information:** Application fee $75. Priority deadline 11/1. Regular application deadline 1/1. Nonfall registration accepted. Admission may be deferred.

COSTS AND FINANCIAL AID

Annual tuition $53,435. Room and board $13,000. Required fees $83. Average book expense $1,325. **Required Forms and Deadlines:** CSS/Financial Aid PROFILE; FAFSA; Noncustodial PROFILE. **Notification of Awards:** Applicants will be notified of awards on a rolling basis beginning 3/24. **Types of Aid:** *Need-based scholarships/grants:* College/university scholarship or grant aid from institutional funds; Federal Pell; SEOG; State scholarships/grants. *Loans:* Direct PLUS loans; Direct Subsidized Stafford Loans; Direct Unsubsidized Stafford Loans. *Student Employment:* Federal Work-Study Program available. Institutional employment available. **Financial Aid Statistics:** 96% needy freshmen, 94% needy undergrads receive need-based scholarship or grant aid. 63% freshmen, 34% undergrads receive non-need-based scholarship or grant aid. 76% freshmen, 81% undergrads receive need-based self-help aid. 2% freshmen, 2% undergrads receive athletic scholarships. Average cumulative indebtedness $33,081. **Criteria for awarding aid:** *Need-based:* Minority status *Non-need-based:* Academics, Art, Athletics, Music/drama.

See page 938.

GEORGETOWN COLLEGE

400 East College Street, Georgetown, KY 40324
Phone: 502-863-8009 · **Financial Aid Phone:** 502-863-8027
E-mail: admissions@georgetowncollege.edu · **CEEB Code:** 1249
Fax: 502-868-7733 · **Website:** www.georgetowncollege.edu · **ACT Code:** 1514

This private school was founded in 1829. It has a 104 acre campus.

RATINGS

Admissions Selectivity Rating: 80   **Fire Safety Rating:** 82   **Green Rating:** 63

STUDENTS AND FACULTY

Enrollment: 942. **Student Body:** 53% female, 47% male, 23% out-of-state, 1% international (12 countries represented). Asian 1%, African American 9%, Caucasian 79%, Hispanic 1%, Native American <1%, Pacific Islander 0%, Two or more races 4%, Race unknown 5%.
Retention and Graduation: 71% freshmen return for sophomore year.
Faculty: Student/faculty ratio 11:1. 77 full-time faculty, 95% hold PhDs, 6% are members of minority groups, 47% are women. 0% of classes are taught by teaching assistants.

ACADEMICS

Degrees: Bachelor's; Master's; Post-Master's certificate **Classes:** Most classes have 10-19 students. Most lab/discussion sessions have 30-39 students. **Most popular majors:** Biology/Biological Sciences, General; Psychology, General; Athletic Training/Trainer. **Special Study Options:** Accelerated program; Cooperative education program; Distance learning; Double major; Dual enrollment; English as a Second Language (ESL); Honors program; Independent study; Internships; Liberal arts/career combination; Student-designed major; Study abroad; Teacher certification program. **Honors programs:** Academic Honors Program, Spanish Immersion Program, Equine Scholars Program. See http://www.georgetowncollege.edu/wp-content/catalog/2015-16/UGcatalog.pdf#page=26. **Disability Services offered to physically disabled students:** Note-taking services; Reader services; Tape recorders; Tutors. **Career services:** Alumni network; Alumni services; Career assessment; Career/job search classes; Internships; Regional alumni

FACILITIES

Housing: Apartments for married students; Apartments for single students; Fraternity/sorority housing; Men's dorms; Women's dorms **Special Academic Facilities/Equipment:** The Anna Ashcraft Ensor Learning Resource Center, an arboretum, three antebellum buildings, the Asher Science Center, the Anne Wright Wilson Fine Arts Building, and the Wilson Laboratory Theatre. **Computers:** 10% of classrooms, 60% of dorms, 90% of libraries, 100% of dining areas, 100% of student union, have wireless network access. Students can register for classes online. Administrative functions (other than registration) can be performed online.

CAMPUS LIFE

Environment: Town **Activities:** Campus Ministries; Choral groups; Concert band; Dance; Drama/theater; Literary magazine; Model UN; Music ensembles; Musical theater; Pep band; Radio station; Student government; Student newspaper 110 registered organizations, 20 honor societies, 8 religious organizations. 5 fraternities, 4 sororities. **Athletics (Intercollegiate):** *Men:* baseball, basketball, cross-country, football, golf, soccer, tennis, track/field (outdoor), track/field (indoor). *Women:* basketball, cheerleading, cross-country, golf, soccer, softball, tennis, track/field (outdoor), track/field (indoor), volleyball. **On-Campus Highlights:** The Ensor Learning Resource Center, Asher Science Center, Bush Campus Recreation Center, Stu Gov't Office in Cralle

Student Center, Starbucks—in the Learning Resource Center **Environmental Initiatives:** Recycling with Pepsi Co

ADMISSIONS

Freshman Academic Profile: 80% from public high schools. **Test Scores:** SAT Math middle 50% range 420-530. SAT EBRW middle 50% range 450-530. ACT middle 50% range 20-26. Minimum internet-based TOEFL 68. Minimum paper TOEFL 520. **Basis for Candidate Selection:** *Very important factors considered include:* academic GPA. *Important factors considered include:* rigor of secondary school record, standardized test scores. *Other factors considered include:* class rank, application essay, recommendation(s), interview, extracurricular activities, talent/ability, character/personal qualities, volunteer work, work experience. **Freshman Admission Requirements:** High school diploma is required and GED is accepted *Academic units recommended:* 4 English, 3 math, 3 science, 2 foreign language, 2 social studies. **Freshman Admission Statistics:** 2,127 applied, 66.5% admitted, 21% enrolled. **Transfer Admission Requirements:** High school transcript, college transcript(s), statement of good standing from prior institution(s). Minimum college GPA of 2.5 required. Lowest grade transferable C. **General Admission Information:** Application fee $30. Priority deadline 5/1. Regular application deadline 8/15. Nonfall registration accepted. Admission may be deferred for a maximum of 1 year.

COSTS AND FINANCIAL AID

Annual tuition $35,650. Room and board $9,050. Average book expense $1,250. **Required Forms and Deadlines:** FAFSA. **Notification of Awards:** Applicants will be notified of awards on a rolling basis beginning 3/1. **Types of Aid:** *Need-based scholarships/grants:* College/university scholarship or grant aid from institutional funds; Federal Pell; Private scholarships; SEOG; State scholarships/grants. *Loans:* Direct PLUS loans; Direct Subsidized Stafford Loans; Direct Unsubsidized Stafford Loans. *Student Employment:* Federal Work-Study Program available. Institutional employment available. **Financial Aid Statistics:** 100% needy freshmen, 100% needy undergrads receive need-based scholarship or grant aid. 89% freshmen, 86% undergrads receive non-need-based scholarship or grant aid. 78% freshmen, 80% undergrads receive need-based self-help aid. 3% freshmen, 3% undergrads receive athletic scholarships. 100% freshmen, 96% undergrads receive any aid. 76% undergrads borrow to pay for school. Average cumulative indebtedness $31,267. **Criteria for awarding aid:** *Need-based:* Academics, Alumni affiliation, Athletics, Leadership, Music/drama, Religious affiliation *Non-need-based:* Academics, Alumni affiliation, Art, Athletics, Leadership, Music/drama, Religious affiliation, State/district residency.

GEORGETOWN UNIVERSITY

37th and O Streets, NW, Washington, DC 20057
Phone: 202-687-3600 · **Financial Aid Phone:** 202-687-4547
E-mail: guadmiss@georgetown.edu · **CEEB Code:** 5244
Fax: 202-687-5084 · **Website:** www.georgetown.edu · **ACT Code:** 668

This private school, affiliated with the Roman Catholic Church, was founded in 1789. It has a 104 acre campus.

RATINGS

Admissions Selectivity Rating: 98   **Fire Safety Rating:** 88   **Green Rating:** 60*

STUDENTS AND FACULTY

Enrollment: 7,124. **Student Body:** 56% female, 44% male, 98% out-of-state, 13% international (138 countries represented). Asian 10%, African American 6%, Caucasian 54%, Hispanic 10%, Native American 0%, Pacific Islander <1%, Two or more races 5%, Race unknown 2%.
Retention and Graduation: 96% freshmen return for sophomore year. 90% freshmen graduate within 4 years. 95% freshmen graduate within 6 years.
Faculty: Student/faculty ratio 11:1. 1,004 full-time faculty, 83% hold PhDs, 17% are members of minority groups, 46% are women. 8% of classes are taught by teaching assistants.

ACADEMICS

Degrees: Bachelor's; Certificate; Doctoral/Professional; Doctoral/Research; Master's; Post-Bachelor's certificate; Post-Master's certificate **Classes:** Most classes have 20-29 students. Most lab/discussion sessions have 20-29 students. **Most popular majors:** English Language And Literature, General;

International Relations And Affairs; Political Science And Government, General. **Special Study Options:** Cross-registration; Distance learning; Double major; English as a Second Language (ESL); Honors program; Independent study; Internships; Student-designed major; Study abroad. **Honors programs:** The John Carroll Programs guide and support a highly selective group of academically talented and ambitious students from around the world. The Programs seek individuals who desire to make a lasting difference in the fields and communities they touch. For these young men and women, the Programs provide models and skills to help them make the most effective use of their undergraduate years, and to assists them in moving from the undergraduate experience to their post-graduate academic and professional lives. The Programs invite students to take as their own the Carroll motto, mentis vita pro vita mundi: the life of the mind for the life of the world. **Combined degree programs:** BA/MA. **Disability Services offered to physically disabled students:** Note-taking services; Reader services; Tape recorders; Tutors. **Career services:** Alumni network; Alumni services; Career assessment; Career/job search classes; Internships; Regional alumni

FACILITIES
Housing: Apartments for single students; Coed dorms; Special housing for disabled student; Wellness housing 92% of campus accessible to physically diasbled. **Special Academic Facilities/Equipment:** Language lab, seismological observatory. **Computers:** Students can register for classes online. Administrative functions (other than registration) can be performed online.

CAMPUS LIFE
Environment: Metropolis **Activities:** Campus Ministries; Choral groups; Concert band; Dance; Drama/theater; International Student Organization; Jazz band; Literary magazine; Model UN; Music ensembles; Musical theater; Pep band; Radio station; Student government; Student newspaper; Student-run film society; Symphony orchestra; Television station; Yearbook 139 registered organizations, 14 honor societies, 20 religious organizations. **Athletics (Intercollegiate):** *Men:* baseball, basketball, crew/rowing, cross-country, diving, football, golf, lacrosse, sailing, soccer, swimming, tennis, track/field (outdoor), track/field (indoor). *Women:* basketball, crew/rowing, cross-country, diving, field hockey, golf, lacrosse, sailing, soccer, softball, swimming, tennis, track/field (outdoor), track/field (indoor), volleyball. **On-Campus Highlights:** White-Gravenor, Copley Hall, The Observatory, The Quadrangle, Healy Hall **Environmental Initiatives:** Set LEED certification as the standard for new constructions & major renovations

ADMISSIONS
Freshman Academic Profile: 90% in top 10% of high school class, 97% in top 25% of high school class, 100% in top 50% of high school class. 49% from public high schools. **Test Scores:** SAT Math middle 50% range 670-760. SAT EBRW middle 50% range 680-760. ACT middle 50% range 30-34. **Basis for Candidate Selection:** *Very important factors considered include:* rigor of secondary school record, class rank, academic GPA, application essay, standardized test scores, recommendation(s), talent/ability, character/personal qualities, first generation. *Important factors considered include:* interview, extracurricular activities, volunteer work. *Other factors considered include:* alumni/ae relation, geographical residence, state residency, racial/ethnic status, work experience. **Freshman Admission Requirements:** High school diploma is required and GED is accepted *Academic units required:* 4 English, 2 math, 1 science, 2 foreign language, 2 social studies, 2 history. **Freshman Admission Statistics:** 21,462 applied, 15.7% admitted, 47% enrolled. **Transfer Admission Requirements:** High school transcript, college transcript(s), essay or personal statement, standardized test scores, statement of good standing from prior institution(s). Minimum college GPA of 3.0 required. Lowest grade transferable C. **General Admission Information:** Application fee $75. Regular application deadline 1/10. Nonfall registration accepted. Admission may be deferred.

COSTS AND FINANCIAL AID
Types of Aid: *Student Employment:* Federal Work-Study Program available. Institutional employment available. **Financial Aid Statistics:** 89% needy freshmen, 90% needy undergrads receive need-based scholarship or grant aid. 40% freshmen, 30% undergrads receive non-need-based scholarship or grant aid. 79% freshmen, 84% undergrads receive need-based self-help aid. 6% freshmen, 4% undergrads receive athletic scholarships. 38% undergrads borrow to pay for school. Average cumulative indebtedness $23,067. **Criteria for awarding aid:** *Non-need-based:* Athletics.

GEORGIA COLLEGE & STATE UNIVERSITY

Admissions, Milledgeville, GA 31061
Phone: 478-445-1283 · **Financial Aid Phone:** 478-445-5149
E-mail: admissions@gcsu.edu · **CEEB Code:** 5252
Fax: 478-445-1914 · **Website:** www.gcsu.edu · **ACT Code:** 828

This public school was founded in 1889. It has a 601.8 acre campus.

RATINGS
Admissions Selectivity Rating: 82   **Fire Safety Rating:** 99   **Green Rating:** 77

STUDENTS AND FACULTY
Enrollment: 5,857. **Student Body:** 62% female, 38% male, 1% out-of-state, <1% international (33 countries represented). Asian 2%, African American 5%, Caucasian 84%, Hispanic 5%, Native American <1%, Pacific Islander <1%, Two or more races 3%, Race unknown <1%.
Retention and Graduation: 85% freshmen return for sophomore year. 50% freshmen graduate within 4 years. 66% freshmen graduate within 6 years. **Faculty:** Student/faculty ratio 17:1. 330 full-time faculty, 82% hold PhDs, 20% are members of minority groups, 56% are women.

ACADEMICS
Degrees: Bachelor's; Doctoral/Professional; Master's; Post-Master's certificate **Classes:** Most classes have 10-19 students. Most lab/discussion sessions have 10-19 students. **Most popular majors:** Health Teacher Education; Registered Nursing/Registered Nurse; Business Administration And Management, General. **Special Study Options:** Accelerated program; Distance learning; Double major; English as a Second Language (ESL); Honors program; Independent study; Internships; Student-designed major; Study abroad; Teacher certification program. **Honors programs:** Honors Program. **Disability Services offered to physically disabled students:** Note-taking services; Reader services; Tape recorders; Tutors. **Career services:** Alumni network; Career assessment; Career/job search classes; Internships

FACILITIES
Housing: Apartments for single students; Coed dorms; Special housing for disabled student; Special housing for international students; Theme housing 90% of campus accessible to physically diasbled. **Special Academic Facilities/Equipment:** Education archives museum, old governor's mansion, Museum of Fine Arts, Natural History Museum and Planetarium **Computers:** 98% of classrooms, 98% of dorms, 100% of libraries, 98% of dining areas, 100% of student union, 100% of common outdoor areas have wireless network access. Students can register for classes online. Administrative functions (other than registration) can be performed online.

CAMPUS LIFE
Environment: Town **Activities:** Campus Ministries; Choral groups; Concert band; Dance; Drama/theater; International Student Organization; Jazz band; Literary magazine; Music ensembles; Musical theater; Pep band; Radio station; Student government; Student newspaper; Television station 238 registered organizations, 8 religious organizations. 8 fraternities, 6 sororities. **Athletics (Intercollegiate):** *Men:* baseball, basketball, cross-country, golf, tennis. *Women:* basketball, cross-country, softball, speed skating, tennis. **On-Campus Highlights:** The Wellness and Recreation Center, The Centennial Center (Gymnasium), Cafeteria, Libary and Information Technology Center **Environmental Initiatives:** recycling program

ADMISSIONS
Freshman Academic Profile: Average high school GPA 3.5. **Test Scores:** SAT Math middle 50% range 540-620. SAT EBRW middle 50% range 560-640. ACT middle 50% range 23-27. Minimum internet-based TOEFL 69. Minimum paper TOEFL 523. **Basis for Candidate Selection:** *Very important factors considered include:* rigor of secondary school record, academic GPA, application essay, standardized test scores, recommendation(s), first generation, level of applicant's interest. *Important factors considered include:* class rank, extracurricular activities, talent/ability, character/personal qualities, state residency. *Other factors considered include:* interview, alumni/ae relation, geographical residence, volunteer work, work experience. **Freshman Admission Requirements:** High school diploma is required and GED is accepted *Academic units required:* 4 English, 4 math, 4 science, 2 science labs, 2 foreign language, 3 social studies. **Freshman Admission Statistics:** 4,089 applied, 79.0% admitted, 45% enrolled. **Transfer Admission Requirements:** college transcript(s), statement of good standing from prior institution(s). Minimum college GPA of 2.0 required. **General Admission Information:** Application fee $40. Regular application deadline 4/1. Nonfall registration accepted. Admission may be deferred for a maximum of 1 year.

COSTS AND FINANCIAL AID

Annual in-state tuition $11,946. Annual out-of-state tuition $25,528. Room and board $11,946. Required fees $2,022. Average book expense $1,500. **Required Forms and Deadlines:** FAFSA. **Notification of Awards:** Applicants will be notified of awards on a rolling basis beginning 3/1. **Types of Aid:** *Need-based scholarships/grants:* College/university scholarship or grant aid from institutional funds; Federal Pell; Private scholarships; SEOG; State scholarships/grants. *Loans:* Direct PLUS loans; Direct Subsidized Stafford Loans; Direct Unsubsidized Stafford Loans. *Student Employment:* Federal Work-Study Program available. Institutional employment available. **Financial Aid Statistics:** 34% needy freshmen, 37% needy undergrads receive need-based scholarship or grant aid. 94% freshmen, 78% undergrads receive non-need-based scholarship or grant aid. 53% freshmen, 61% undergrads receive need-based self-help aid. 2% freshmen, 2% undergrads receive athletic scholarships. 96% freshmen, 86% undergrads receive any aid. 56% undergrads borrow to pay for school. Average cumulative indebtedness $24,774. **Criteria for awarding aid:** *Non-need-based:* Academics, Alumni affiliation, Art, Athletics, Leadership, Music/drama, State/district residency.

GEORGIA INSTITUTE OF TECHNOLOGY

225 North Avenue, NW, Atlanta, GA 30332-0320
Phone: 404-894-4154 · **Financial Aid Phone:** 404-894-4160
E-mail: admission@gatech.edu · **CEEB Code:** 5248
Fax: 404-894-9511 · **Website:** www.gatech.edu · **ACT Code:** 818

This public school was founded in 1885. It has a 400 acre campus.

RATINGS

Admissions Selectivity Rating: 98   **Fire Safety Rating:** 96   **Green Rating:** 97

STUDENTS AND FACULTY

Enrollment: 14,812. **Student Body:** 38% female, 62% male, 33% out-of-state, 9% international (127 countries represented). Asian 20%, African American 7%, Caucasian 49%, Hispanic 7%, Native American <1%, Pacific Islander <1%, Two or more races 4%, Race unknown 4%.

Retention and Graduation: 97% freshmen return for sophomore year. 39% freshmen graduate within 4 years. 85% freshmen graduate within 6 years. 16% grads go on to further study within 1 year. 14% grads pursue arts and sciences degrees. 0.36% grads pursue law degrees. 0% grads pursue business degrees. 1.49% grads pursue medical degrees. **Faculty:** Student/faculty ratio 22:1. 1,115 full-time faculty, 5% hold PhDs, 7% are members of minority groups, 27% are women.

ACADEMICS

Degrees: Bachelor's; Doctoral/Research; Master's **Classes:** Most classes have 20-29 students. Most lab/discussion sessions have 20-29 students. **Most popular majors:** Computer And Information Sciences, General; Mechanical Engineering; Industrial Engineering. **Special Study Options:** Accelerated program; Cooperative education program; Cross-registration; Distance learning; Dual enrollment; English as a Second Language (ESL); Honors program; Independent study; Internships; Student-designed major; Study abroad; Teacher certification program; Weekend college. **Honors programs:** The Georgia Tech Honors Program combines the challenging academic standards of one of the world's finest research universities with the closer student-faculty connections one might expect to find at smaller colleges. Our mission is to create a lively environment in which students and faculty members learn from each other through a common commitment to intellectual inquiry, careful analysis, and energetic exchange of ideas. Building on this close engagement between students and faculty in and beyond the classroom, Honors Program members benefit from unique opportunities during their years at Georgia Tech: 1) An Honors Program Residence where first-year students find a supportive living/learning community of interesting people, continue their conversations beyond the classroom, and develop connections to Georgia Tech and the surrounding community; 2) Small sections of introductory core courses designed to emphasize not just mastery of the material, but innovative inquiry and exploration within the discipline and often beyond; 3) A selection of special topic courses, each with an enrollment limit of twenty students, that encourage imaginative thinking and an interdisciplinary approach to some of the most stimulating questions; 4) Numerous informal opportunities for social interaction with faculty members from multiple disciplines across campus; and 5) A program of well-coordinated advising, regarding not only the Honors Program, but a student's overall curriculum, including co-ops, internships, study abroad,

and other extracurricular activities, as well as counseling on future pursuits after graduation. **Disability Services offered to physically disabled students:** Note-taking services; Reader services; Tape recorders; Tutors. **Career services:** Career assessment; Career/job search classes; Internships

FACILITIES

Housing: Apartments for married students; Apartments for single students; Coed dorms; Fraternity/sorority housing; Men's dorms; Special housing for disabled student; Special housing for international students; Theme housing; Women's dorms 75% of campus accessible to physically diasbled. **Special Academic Facilities/Equipment:** Clough Undergraduate Learning Commons, Nuclear Magnetic Resonance Spectroscopy Center, Georgia Tech Research Institute, Paper Museum, Mechanical Properties Research Laboratory with scanning electron microscope, Virtual Factory Laboratory, Ferris-Goldsmith Trading Floor, Klaus Advanced Computing Building, Electron Microscope, Marcus Nanotechnology Research Center, Solar Decathlon House at College of Architecture, Wind Tunnel, GT Smart House **Computers:** 100% of classrooms, 100% of dorms, 100% of libraries, 100% of dining areas, 100% of student union, 65% of common outdoor areas have wireless network access. Students can register for classes online. Administrative functions (other than registration) can be performed online. Undergraduates are required to own a computer.

CAMPUS LIFE

Environment: Metropolis **Activities:** Campus Ministries; Choral groups; Concert band; Dance; Drama/theater; International Student Organization; Jazz band; Literary magazine; Marching band; Model UN; Music ensembles; Musical theater; Pep band; Radio station; Student government; Student newspaper; Student-run film society; Symphony orchestra; Television station; Yearbook 429 registered organizations, 24 honor societies, 39 religious organizations. 38 fraternities, 14 sororities. **Athletics (Intercollegiate):** *Men:* baseball, basketball, cheerleading, cross-country, diving, football, golf, swimming, tennis, track/field (outdoor), track/field (indoor). *Women:* basketball, cheerleading, cross-country, diving, softball, swimming, tennis, track/field (outdoor), track/field (indoor), volleyball. **On-Campus Highlights:** Tech Square—Bookstore/Hotel/College of, Olympic Aquatic Center/Campus Recreation, The Hill/Tech Tower, Student Center Commons and the Library, Ferst Center for the Arts **Environmental Initiatives:** Education: Over 200 courses are offered across all of the colleges with the goal that every student who graduates has taken at least one sustainability course. Many degree programs at the undergraduate and graduate levels, and many continuing education and certificate programs focus on sustainability and major areas of sustainability. Sustainability has been included in the Institute Mission Statement and Strategic Plan since 1994. Our office updated the Sutainability Strategic Plan in 2010, and we are in the final states of finalizing and sharing the Institute Strategic Plan for Sustainable Practice in 2018. The Institute's Serve°Learn°Sustain has incorporated the UN's "Grand Challenges" in the Strategic Plan to align with, "Improving the Human Condition and a Sustainable Global Economy."

ADMISSIONS

Freshman Academic Profile: Average high school GPA 4.0. 88% in top 10% of high school class, 98% in top 25% of high school class, 99% in top 50% of high school class. **Test Scores:** SAT Math middle 50% range 720-790. SAT EBRW middle 50% range 370-730. ACT middle 50% range 30-34. **Basis for Candidate Selection:** *Very important factors considered include:* rigor of secondary school record, academic GPA, extracurricular activities. *Important factors considered include:* application essay, standardized test scores, talent/ability, character/personal qualities, geographical residence, state residency, volunteer work, work experience. *Other factors considered include:* recommendation(s), first generation, alumni/ae relation, racial/ethnic status, level of applicant's interest. **Freshman Admission Requirements:** High school diploma is required and GED is not accepted *Academic units required:* 4 English, 4 math, 4 science, 2 science labs, 2 foreign language, 3 social studies. **Freshman Admission Statistics:** 31,497 applied, 23.4% admitted, 39% enrolled. **Transfer Admission Requirements:** college transcript(s), statement of good standing from prior institution(s). Minimum college GPA of 2.7 required. Lowest grade transferable C. **General Admission Information:** Application fee $75. Priority deadline 10/15. Regular application deadline 1/1. Nonfall registration accepted. Admission may be deferred for a maximum of 1 year.

COSTS AND FINANCIAL AID

Annual out-of-state tuition $30,604. Room and board $14,126. Required fees $2,410. Average book expense $800. **Required Forms and Deadlines:** CSS/Financial Aid PROFILE; FAFSA; Institution's own financial aid form. **Notification of Awards:** Applicants will be notified of awards on or about 4/15. **Types of Aid:** *Need-based scholarships/grants:* College/university scholarship or grant aid from institutional funds; Federal Pell; Private scholarships; SEOG; State scholarships/grants. *Loans:* Direct PLUS loans; Direct Subsidized Stafford Loans; Direct Unsubsidized Stafford Loans. *Student Employment:* Federal Work-Study Program available. Institutional employment available.

Financial Aid Statistics: 86% needy freshmen, 87% needy undergrads receive need-based scholarship or grant aid. 72% freshmen, 62% undergrads receive non-need-based scholarship or grant aid. 55% freshmen, 66% undergrads receive need-based self-help aid. 1% freshmen, 1% undergrads receive athletic scholarships. 63% freshmen, 72% undergrads receive any aid. 39% undergrads borrow to pay for school. Average cumulative indebtedness $32,169. **Criteria for awarding aid:** *Need-based:* Academics, Leadership, Minority status *Non-need-based:* Academics, Athletics, Leadership, Music/drama, State/district residency.

GEORGIA SOUTHERN UNIVERSITY

P.O. Box 8126, Statesboro, GA 30460
Phone: 912-478-5391 · **Financial Aid Phone:** 912-478-5413
E-mail: admissions@georgiasouthern.edu · **CEEB Code:** 5253
Fax: 912-478-7240 · **Website:** http://www.georgiasouthern.edu/ · **ACT Code:** 830

This public school was founded in 1906. It has a 900 acre campus.

RATINGS
Admissions Selectivity Rating: 86   **Fire Safety Rating:** 97   **Green Rating:** 83

STUDENTS AND FACULTY
Enrollment: 17,062. **Student Body:** 50% female, 50% male, 5% out-of-state, 2% international (73 countries represented). Asian 2%, African American 24%, Caucasian 63%, Hispanic 6%, Native American <1%, Pacific Islander <1%, Two or more races 2%, Race unknown 1%.
Retention and Graduation: 80% freshmen return for sophomore year. 26% freshmen graduate within 4 years. 50% freshmen graduate within 6 years. 8% grads go on to further study within 1 year. **Faculty:** Student/faculty ratio 22:1. 781 full-time faculty, 85% hold PhDs, 26% are members of minority groups, 48% are women. 3% of classes are taught by teaching assistants.

ACADEMICS
Degrees: Bachelor's; Certificate; Doctoral/Research; Master's; Post-Bachelor's certificate; Post-Master's certificate **Classes:** Most classes have 10-19 students. Most lab/discussion sessions have 10-19 students. **Most popular majors:** Mechanical Engineering; General Studies; Biology/Biological Sciences, General. **Special Study Options:** Accelerated program; Cooperative education program; Distance learning; Double major; Dual enrollment; English as a Second Language (ESL); Honors program; Independent study; Internships; Student-designed major; Study abroad; Teacher certification program. **Honors programs:** The University Honors Program seeks scholars interested in research, change agents interested in engaging local and global communities, and individuals seeking to explore their curiosity and express their creativity. Honors Program students in both Statesboro and Savannah take advantage of honors sections of core courses that are seminar-based and differently designed to foster inquiry and research. During junior and senior years, students develop an honors thesis to further deepen their knowledge of their major field. Additionally, honors students engage in at least one experiential learning project each year and include study abroad, alternative break trips, research outside of coursework, leadership, and intensive volunteer experiences. **Disability Services offered to physically disabled students:** Note-taking services; Reader services; Tape recorders; Tutors. **Career services:** Alumni network; Alumni services; Career assessment; Career/job search classes; Internships

FACILITIES
Housing: Apartments for single students; Coed dorms; Special housing for disabled student; Special housing for international students; Theme housing 97% of campus accessible to physically diasbled. **Special Academic Facilities/Equipment:** bureau of business research and economic development, center for addiction recovery, center for bio-statistics and survey, center for entrepreneurial learning and leadership, center for forensic studies in accounting, center for international studies, center for Irish studies, center for retail studies, center for sustainability, center for wildlife education, child development center, graduate academic services center (GASC), institute for coastal plain science, coastlands AHEC, national youth-at-risk center (NYAR), small business development center, black box theatre, performing arts center, and botanic garden **Computers:** 80% of classrooms, 45% of dorms, 100% of libraries, 100% of dining areas, 100% of student union, 20% of common outdoor areas have wireless network access. Students can register for classes online. Administrative functions (other than registration) can be performed online.

CAMPUS LIFE
Environment: Town **Activities:** Campus Ministries; Choral groups; Concert band; Dance; Drama/theater; International Student Organization; Jazz band; Literary magazine; Marching band; Music ensembles; Musical theater; Opera;

Radio station; Student government; Student newspaper; Student-run film society; Symphony orchestra 235 registered organizations, 17 honor societies, 20 religious organizations. 20 fraternities, 9 sororities. **Athletics (Intercollegiate):** *Men:* baseball, basketball, cheerleading, football, golf, soccer, tennis. *Women:* basketball, cheerleading, cross-country, diving, soccer, softball, swimming, tennis, track/field (outdoor), volleyball. **On-Campus Highlights:** Russell Union, Recreation Activity Center, Center for Wildlife Education, Georgia Southern Museum, Paulson Stadium **Environmental Initiatives:** Georgia Southern's Student Sustainability Fee Committee has allocated > $1,000,000 in funding for 68 sustainability projects at Georgia Southern University since FY2015. The grant winners display their funded projects in a Sustainability Showcase Exhibit in the university library, viewed by thousands in the campus community during a two weeks period towards the end of each fiscal year.

ADMISSIONS
Freshman Academic Profile: Average high school GPA 3.3. 19% in top 10% of high school class, 45% in top 25% of high school class, 75% in top 50% of high school class. 86% from public high schools. **Test Scores:** SAT Math middle 50% range 540-600. SAT EBRW middle 50% range 560-630. ACT middle 50% range 22-26. Minimum internet-based TOEFL 69. **Basis for Candidate Selection:** *Very important factors considered include:* rigor of secondary school record, academic GPA, standardized test scores. *Other factors considered include:* class rank. **Freshman Admission Requirements:** High school diploma is required and GED is not accepted *Academic units required:* 4 English, 4 math, 4 science, 2 science labs, 2 foreign language, 3 social studies. **Freshman Admission Statistics:** 9,202 applied, 68.3% admitted, 56% enrolled. **Transfer Admission Requirements:** college transcript(s), statement of good standing from prior institution(s). Minimum college GPA of 2.0 required. Lowest grade transferable D. **General Admission Information:** Application fee $30. Priority deadline 4/1. Regular application deadline 5/1. Nonfall registration accepted. Admission may be deferred.

COSTS AND FINANCIAL AID
Annual in-state tuition $9,650. Annual out-of-state tuition $16,930. Room and board $9,650. Required fees $2,092. Average book expense $1,200. **Required Forms and Deadlines:** FAFSA. **Notification of Awards:** Applicants will be notified of awards on a rolling basis beginning 4/20. **Types of Aid:** *Need-based scholarships/grants:* College/university scholarship or grant aid from institutional funds; Federal Pell; Private scholarships; SEOG; State scholarships/grants. *Loans:* Direct PLUS loans; Direct Subsidized Stafford Loans; Direct Unsubsidized Stafford Loans. *Student Employment:* Federal Work-Study Program available. Institutional employment available. **Financial Aid Statistics:** 89% needy freshmen, 82% needy undergrads receive need-based scholarship or grant aid. 2% freshmen, 1% undergrads receive non-need-based scholarship or grant aid. 74% freshmen, 82% undergrads receive need-based self-help aid. 1% freshmen, 1% undergrads receive athletic scholarships. 92% freshmen, 89% undergrads receive any aid. 72% undergrads borrow to pay for school. Average cumulative indebtedness $28,098. **Criteria for awarding aid:** *Non-need-based:* Academics, Alumni affiliation, Art, Athletics, Leadership, Minority status, Music/drama, State/district residency.

GEORGIA SOUTHWESTERN STATE UNIVERSITY

800 Georgia Southwestern State Univ Dr., Americus, GA 31709-4693
Phone: 229-928-1273 · **Financial Aid Phone:** 229-928-1378
E-mail: admissions@gsw.edu · **CEEB Code:** 5250
Fax: 229-931-2983 · **Website:** www.gsw.edu · **ACT Code:** 824

This public school was founded in 1906. It has a 325 acre campus.

RATINGS
Admissions Selectivity Rating: 81   **Fire Safety Rating:** 94   **Green Rating:** 60*

STUDENTS AND FACULTY
Enrollment: 2,413. **Student Body:** 62% female, 38% male, 4% out-of-state, 2% international (29 countries represented). Asian 1%, African American 27%, Caucasian 63%, Hispanic 4%, Native American <1%, Pacific Islander <1%, Two or more races 2%, Race unknown <1%.
Retention and Graduation: 70% freshmen return for sophomore year. **Faculty:** Student/faculty ratio 18:1. 112 full-time faculty, 73% hold PhDs, 14% are members of minority groups, 51% are women. 0% of classes are taught by teaching assistants.

ACADEMICS
Degrees: Bachelor's; Master's; Post-Bachelor's certificate; Post-Master's certificate **Most popular majors:** Registered Nursing/Registered Nurse; Business Administration And Management, General; Accounting. **Special Study Options:** Accelerated program; Distance learning; Double major;

English as a Second Language (ESL); Honors program; Internships; Study abroad; Teacher certification program. **Disability Services offered to physically disabled students:** Note-taking services; Reader services; Tape recorders; Tutors.

FACILITIES

Housing: Coed dorms; Other (please specify) 99% of campus accessible to physically diasbled. **Special Academic Facilities/Equipment:** Observatory, Glass-blowing studio, Golf Course **Computers:** Students can register for classes online. Administrative functions (other than registration) can be performed online.

CAMPUS LIFE

Environment: Village **Activities:** Campus Ministries; Choral groups; Concert band; Drama/theater; International Student Organization; Jazz band; Literary magazine; Student government; Student newspaper; Television station 12 honor societies, 7 fraternities, 6 sororities. **Athletics (Intercollegiate):** *Men:* baseball, basketball, golf, soccer, tennis. *Women:* basketball, cross-country, soccer, softball, tennis. Student Success Center, Higher Grounds Café, Academic Center for Excellence, Marshall Student Center

ADMISSIONS

Freshman Academic Profile: Average high school GPA 3.3. 15% in top 10% of high school class, 42% in top 25% of high school class, 75% in top 50% of high school class. 82% from public high schools. **Test Scores:** SAT Math middle 50% range 430-520. SAT EBRW middle 50% range 440-540. ACT middle 50% range 19-23. Minimum internet-based TOEFL 70. Minimum paper TOEFL 523. **Basis for Candidate Selection:** *Very important factors considered include:* rigor of secondary school record, academic GPA, standardized test scores. *Important factors considered include:* class rank. *Other factors considered include:* application essay, recommendation(s), interview, extracurricular activities, talent/ability. **Freshman Admission Requirements:** High school diploma is required and GED is not accepted *Academic units required:* 4 English, 4 math, 4 science, 2 science labs, 2 foreign language, and 3 units from above areas or other academic areas. *Academic units recommended:* 2 academic electives. **Freshman Admission Statistics:** 1,389 applied, 68.2% admitted, 51% enrolled. **Transfer Admission Requirements:** college transcript(s), Minimum college GPA of 2.0 required. Lowest grade transferable D. **General Admission Information:** Application fee $25. Regular application deadline 7/21. Nonfall registration accepted. Admission may be deferred for a maximum of 1 year.

COSTS AND FINANCIAL AID

Annual in-state tuition $8,952. Annual out-of-state tuition $17,678. Room and board $8,952. Required fees $1,340. Average book expense $1,400. **Required Forms and Deadlines:** FAFSA; Institution's own financial aid form; State aid form. **Notification of Awards:** Applicants will be notified of awards on a rolling basis beginning 5/1. **Types of Aid:** *Need-based scholarships/grants:* College/university scholarship or grant aid from institutional funds; Federal Pell; Private scholarships; SEOG; State scholarships/grants. *Loans:* Direct PLUS loans; Direct Subsidized Stafford Loans; Direct Unsubsidized Stafford Loans. *Student Employment:* Federal Work-Study Program available. Institutional employment available. **Financial Aid Statistics:** 65% needy freshmen, 67% needy undergrads receive need-based scholarship or grant aid. 69% freshmen, 47% undergrads receive non-need-based scholarship or grant aid. 87% freshmen, 86% undergrads receive need-based self-help aid. 2% freshmen, 3% undergrads receive athletic scholarships. 76% undergrads borrow to pay for school. Average cumulative indebtedness $27,939. **Criteria for awarding aid:** *Non-need-based:* Academics, Alumni affiliation, Art, Athletics, Leadership, Music/drama, State/district residency.

GEORGIA STATE UNIVERSITY

P.O Box 3965, Atlanta, GA 30302-4009
Phone: 404-413-2500 · **Financial Aid Phone:** 404-413-2600
E-mail: admissions@gsu.edu · **CEEB Code:** 5251
Fax: 404-413-2002 · **Website:** www.gsu.edu · **ACT Code:** 826

This public school was founded in 1913. It has a 71.5 acre campus.

RATINGS

Admissions Selectivity Rating: 87   **Fire Safety Rating:** 88   **Green Rating:** 79

STUDENTS AND FACULTY

Enrollment: 25,070. **Student Body:** 59% female, 41% male, 4% out-of-state, 2% international (156 countries represented). Asian 14%, African American 42%, Caucasian 23%, Hispanic 11%, Native American <1%, Pacific Islander <1%, Two or more races 6%, Race unknown 1%.

Retention and Graduation: 77% freshmen return for sophomore year. 23% freshmen graduate within 4 years. 54% freshmen graduate within 6 years. **Faculty:** Student/faculty ratio 23:1. 1,157 full-time faculty, 92% hold PhDs, 28% are members of minority groups, 46% are women.

ACADEMICS

Degrees: Associate; Bachelor's; Certificate; Doctoral/Professional; Doctoral/Research; Master's; Post-Bachelor's certificate; Post-Master's certificate **Classes:** Most classes have 10-19 students. **Most popular majors:** Biology/Biological Sciences, General; Psychology, General; Finance, General. **Special Study Options:** Cooperative education program; Cross-registration; Distance learning; Double major; Dual enrollment; English as a Second Language (ESL); Honors program; Independent study; Internships; Study abroad; Teacher certification program. **Honors programs:** The Honors College provides the advantages of a small, highly selective college with breadth of programs and opportunities of a large research university. It is open to incoming freshmen, transfer students, and currently enrolled students who meet eligibility requirements. Honors students take small, seminar-based classes and develop close contact with outstanding faculty members. Honors sections of a number of regular courses, many of which meet core curriculum requirements, are offered throughout the academic year. In addition, students in the Honors College can enroll in special interdisciplinary courses, help design a colloquium on a topic of their choice, and, at the upper division, research and write an honors thesis. Students in the college may earn honors recognitions, which are noted on their diplomas and transcripts, and they may pursue additional opportunities to enrich the quality of their education and enhance their chances of future success. Honors students may also take advantage of dedicated facilities, priority registration, merit scholarships, graduate and professional school counseling, special travel and study abroad opportunities, and honors housing in the University Commons. **Combined degree programs:** BA/JD; BA/MA. **Disability Services offered to physically disabled students:** Note-taking services; Reader services; Tape recorders; Tutors. **Career services:** Alumni network; Alumni services; Career assessment; Career/job search classes; Internships

FACILITIES

Housing: Apartments for married students; Apartments for single students; Coed dorms; Fraternity/sorority housing; Special housing for disabled student; Special housing for international students; Theme housing 100% of campus accessible to physically diasbled. **Special Academic Facilities/Equipment:** Cartography Production Laboratory,Commuter Student Services,Cooperative Learning Laboratory,Economic Forecasting Center,Ernest G. Welch School of Art and Design Gallery, Instructional Technology Center, James M. Cox, Jr. Multi-Media Instructional Lab and Satellite Downlink Facility,Kopleff Recital Hall,Lanette L. Suttles Child Development Center,Language Acquisition and Resource Center, Mathematics Assistance Complex, Mathematics Interactive Learning Environment, Music Media Center, Rialto Center for the Performing Arts, Small Business Development Center, Visual Resource Center, Writing Studio. Digital Aquarium. **Computers:** Students can register for classes online. Administrative functions (other than registration) can be performed online.

CAMPUS LIFE

Environment: Metropolis **Activities:** Campus Ministries; Choral groups; Concert band; Dance; Drama/theater; International Student Organization; Jazz band; Literary magazine; Marching band; Model UN; Music ensembles; Musical theater; Opera; Pep band; Radio station; Student government; Student newspaper; Student-run film society; Symphony orchestra; Television station 201 registered organizations, 19 honor societies, 21 religious organizations. 9 fraternities, 15 sororities. **Athletics (Intercollegiate):** *Men:* baseball, basketball, cross-country, golf, soccer, tennis, track/field (outdoor), volleyball. *Women:* basketball, cross-country, golf, soccer, softball, tennis, track/field (outdoor), volleyball. **On-Campus Highlights:** Recreation Center, Student Housing, Aderhold Learning Center, The Rialto Center for the Performing Arts, The Student Center

ADMISSIONS

Freshman Academic Profile: Average high school GPA 3.4. 17% in top 10% of high school class, 49% in top 25% of high school class, 87% in top 50% of high school class. **Test Scores:** SAT Math middle 50% range 470-590. SAT EBRW middle 50% range 500-580. ACT middle 50% range 20-26. Minimum internet-based TOEFL 79. Minimum paper TOEFL 550. **Basis for Candidate Selection:** *Very important factors considered include:* rigor of secondary school record, academic GPA, standardized test scores. *Other factors considered include:* application essay, recommendation(s), talent/ability. **Freshman Admission Requirements:** High school diploma is required and GED is not accepted *Academic units required:* 4 English, 4 math, 4 science, 2 science labs, 2 foreign language, 3 social studies, *Academic units recommended:* 4 English, 4 math, 4 science, 2 science labs, 2 foreign language, 3 social studies. **Freshman Admission Statistics:** 18,971 applied, 52.2% admitted, 41% enrolled. **Transfer Admission Requirements:** college transcript(s), Minimum college GPA of 2.5 required. Lowest grade transferable D. **General Admission Information:** Application fee $60. Regular application deadline 3/1. Nonfall registration accepted. Admission may be deferred for a maximum of 2 terms.

COSTS AND FINANCIAL AID

Annual in-state tuition $14,392. Annual out-of-state tuition $27,304. Room and board $14,392. Required fees $2,128. Average book expense $1,600. **Required Forms and Deadlines:** FAFSA. **Notification of Awards:** Applicants will be notified of awards on a rolling basis beginning 3/1. **Types of Aid:** *Need-based scholarships/grants:* College/university scholarship or grant aid from institutional funds; Federal Pell; Private scholarships; SEOG; State scholarships/grants; United Negro College Fund. *Loans:* Direct PLUS loans; Direct Subsidized Stafford Loans; Direct Unsubsidized Stafford Loans. *Student Employment:* Federal Work-Study Program available. Institutional employment available. **Financial Aid Statistics:** 72% needy freshmen, 73% needy undergrads receive need-based scholarship or grant aid. 91% freshmen, 94% undergrads receive non-need-based scholarship or grant aid. 59% freshmen, 68% undergrads receive need-based self-help aid. 0% freshmen, 0% undergrads receive athletic scholarships. 70% undergrads borrow to pay for school. Average cumulative indebtedness $29,959. **Criteria for awarding aid:** *Non-need-based:* Academics, Alumni affiliation, Art, Athletics, Job skills, Leadership, Minority status, Music/drama, Religious affiliation, State/district residency.

GEORGIAN COURT UNIVERSITY

900 Lakewood Avenue, Lakewood, NJ 08701-2697
Phone: 732-987-2700 · **Financial Aid Phone:** 732-987-2258
E-mail: admissions@georgian.edu · **CEEB Code:** 2274
Fax: 732-987-2000 · **Website:** georgian.edu · **ACT Code:** 2562

This private school, affiliated with the Roman Catholic Church, was founded in 1908. It has a 156 acre campus.

RATINGS

Admissions Selectivity Rating: 77   **Fire Safety Rating:** 95   **Green Rating:** 60*

STUDENTS AND FACULTY

Enrollment: 1,447. **Student Body:** 74% female, 26% male, 6% out-of-state, 1% international (16 countries represented). Asian 3%, African American 12%, Caucasian 60%, Hispanic 13%, Native American <1%, Pacific Islander <1%, Two or more races 2%, Race unknown 8%.
Retention and Graduation: 72% freshmen return for sophomore year. 28% freshmen graduate within 4 years. 48% freshmen graduate within 6 years. **Faculty:** Student/faculty ratio 12:1. 87 full-time faculty, 92% hold PhDs, 25% are members of minority groups, 62% are women. 0% of classes are taught by teaching assistants.

ACADEMICS

Degrees: Bachelor's; Certificate; Master's; Post-Bachelor's certificate; Post-Master's certificate **Most popular majors:** Elementary Education And Teaching; Psychology, General; Registered Nursing/Registered Nurse. **Special Study Options:** Accelerated program; Distance learning; Double major; Dual enrollment; English as a Second Language (ESL); Honors program; Independent study; Internships; Liberal arts/career combination; Study abroad; Teacher certification program; Weekend college. **Honors programs:** Members of the University Honors Program receive an enriched academic curriculum featuring: ° Faculty chosen for their excellence as teaching-scholars ° Challenging interactive classroom format ° Emphasis on primary texts and sources ° Rigorous scholarly writing assignments and oral presentations ° Close faculty mentoring ° Preference in academic advisement and course registration ° A strong sense of belonging to a community of scholars ° Sponsorship in funding presentations at regional and national conferences ° Special advisement by faculty regarding graduate and professional school applications and prestigious fellowship opportunities ° Special recognition at commencement ceremonies. **Disability Services offered to physically disabled students:** Note-taking services; Reader services; Tape recorders; Tutors. **Career services:** Alumni network; Alumni services; Career assessment; Career/job search classes; Internships

FACILITIES

Housing: Coed dorms; Special housing for disabled students 90% of campus accessible to physically disabled. **Special Academic Facilities/Equipment:** Art gallery, arboretum, Wellness Center, NASA ERC. **Computers:** 98% of classrooms, 77% of dorms, 100% of libraries, 50% of dining areas, 100% of student union, have wireless network access. Students can register for classes online. Administrative functions (other than registration) can be performed online.

CAMPUS LIFE

Environment: Town **Activities:** Campus Ministries; Choral groups; Concert band; Dance; Drama/theater; International Student Organization; Jazz band; Literary magazine; Model UN; Music ensembles; Student government;

Student newspaper 48 registered organizations, 18 honor societies, 1 religious organization. **Athletics (Intercollegiate):** *Women:* basketball, cross-country, lacrosse, soccer, softball, tennis, track/field (outdoor), volleyball. **On-Campus Highlights:** Arboretum, Wellness Center, Art Gallery, Library, NASA Educational Resource Center **Environmental Initiatives:** We have included a sustainability commitment in our strategic plan.

ADMISSIONS

Freshman Academic Profile: Average high school GPA 3.3. 7% in top 10% of high school class, 28% in top 25% of high school class, 57% in top 50% of high school class. **Test Scores:** SAT Math middle 50% range 450-550. SAT EBRW middle 50% range 460-570. ACT middle 50% range 17-22. Minimum internet-based TOEFL 79. Minimum paper TOEFL 550. **Basis for Candidate Selection:** *Very important factors considered include:* rigor of secondary school record, academic GPA. *Important factors considered include:* standardized test scores. *Other factors considered include:* class rank, application essay, recommendation(s), interview, extracurricular activities, talent/ability, character/personal qualities, first generation, alumni/ae relation, volunteer work, work experience, level of applicant's interest. **Freshman Admission Requirements:** High school diploma is required and GED is accepted *Academic units required:* 4 English, 2 math, 1 science, 1 science labs, 2 foreign language, 1 history, 6 academic electives. **Freshman Admission Statistics:** 1,946 applied, 68.9% admitted, 16% enrolled. **Transfer Admission Requirements:** college transcript(s), Minimum college GPA of 2.0 required. Lowest grade transferable c. **General Admission Information:** Application fee $40. Regular application deadline 8/1. Nonfall registration accepted. Admission may be deferred for a maximum of 1 year.

COSTS AND FINANCIAL AID

Annual tuition $30,800. Room and board $10,808. Required fees $1,460. Average book expense $1,350. **Required Forms and Deadlines:** FAFSA. **Notification of Awards:** Applicants will be notified of awards on a rolling basis beginning 12/1. **Types of Aid:** *Need-based scholarships/grants:* College/university scholarship or grant aid from institutional funds; Federal Pell; Private scholarships; SEOG; State scholarships/grants. *Loans:* Direct PLUS loans; Direct Subsidized Stafford Loans; Direct Unsubsidized Stafford Loans. *Student Employment:* Federal Work-Study Program available. Institutional employment available. **Financial Aid Statistics:** 96% needy freshmen, 97% needy undergrads receive need-based scholarship or grant aid. 7% freshmen, 5% undergrads receive non-need-based scholarship or grant aid. 84% freshmen, 82% undergrads receive need-based self-help aid. 2% freshmen, 3% undergrads receive athletic scholarships. 99% freshmen, 95% undergrads receive any aid. Average cumulative indebtedness $40,267. **Criteria for awarding aid:** *Need-based:* Academics, Alumni affiliation, Art, Athletics, Leadership, Religious affiliation *Non-need-based:* Academics, Alumni affiliation, Art, Athletics, Leadership, Religious affiliation, State/district residency.

See page 940.

GETTYSBURG COLLEGE

300 North Washington Street, Gettysburg, PA 17325-1484
Phone: 717-337-6100 · **Financial Aid Phone:** 717-337-6611
E-mail: admiss@gettysburg.edu · **CEEB Code:** 2275
Fax: 717-337-6145 · **Website:** www.gettysburg.edu · **ACT Code:** 3580

This private school, affiliated with the Lutheran Church, was founded in 1832. It has a 200 acre campus.

RATINGS

Admissions Selectivity Rating: 92   **Fire Safety Rating:** 98   **Green Rating:** 80

STUDENTS AND FACULTY

Enrollment: 2,405. **Student Body:** 53% female, 47% male, 74% out-of-state, 7% international (38 countries represented). Asian 2%, African American 4%, Caucasian 75%, Hispanic 8%, Native American <1%, Pacific Islander 0%, Two or more races 3%, Race unknown 2%.
Retention and Graduation: 90% freshmen return for sophomore year. 79% freshmen graduate within 4 years. 84% freshmen graduate within 6 years. 21% grads go on to further study within 1 year. **Faculty:** Student/faculty ratio 9:1. 227 full-time faculty, 98% hold PhDs, 20% are members of minority groups, 44% are women. 0% of classes are taught by teaching assistants.

ACADEMICS

Degrees: Bachelor's **Classes:** Most classes have 10-19 students. Most lab/discussion sessions have fewer than 10 students. **Most popular majors:** Psychology, General; Political Science And Government, General; Business/Commerce, General. **Special Study Options:** Double major; Independent study; Internships; Student-designed major; Study abroad; Teacher certification program. **Disability Services offered to physically disabled students:** Tape recorders. **Career services:** Alumni network; Alumni services; Career assessment; Career/job search classes; Internships; Regional alumni

FACILITIES

Housing: Apartments for single students; Coed dorms; Fraternity/sorority housing; Theme housing; Women's dorms **Special Academic Facilities/Equipment:** Art gallery, language lab, child study lab, Majestic Theatre, Sunderman Conservatory, planetarium, observatory, electron microscopes, NMR spectrometer, greenhouse, organic farm, digital classrooms, wireless network, Plasma Physics labs, Science Center **Computers:** 100% of classrooms, 100% of dorms, 100% of libraries, 100% of dining areas, 100% of student union, 90% of common outdoor areas have wireless network access. Students can register for classes online. Administrative functions (other than registration) can be performed online.

CAMPUS LIFE

Environment: Village **Activities:** Campus Ministries; Choral groups; Concert band; Dance; Drama/theater; International Student Organization; Jazz band; Literary magazine; Marching band; Model UN; Music ensembles; Musical theater; Radio station; Student government; Student newspaper; Student-run film society; Symphony orchestra; Television station; Yearbook 120 registered organizations, 16 honor societies, 7 religious organizations. 10 fraternities, 6 sororities. **Athletics (Intercollegiate):** *Men:* baseball, basketball, cheerleading, cross-country, football, golf, lacrosse, soccer, swimming, tennis, track/field (outdoor), track/field (indoor), wrestling. *Women:* basketball, cheerleading, cross-country, field hockey, golf, lacrosse, soccer, softball, swimming, tennis, track/field (outdoor), track/field (indoor), volleyball. **On-Campus Highlights:** Beautiful 200-acre campus, Musselman Library, Science Center, John F. Jaeger Center for Athletics, Recreation, and Fitness, College Union Building **Environmental Initiatives:** The Center for Athletics, Recreation, and Fitness has received LEED Gold certification

ADMISSIONS

Freshman Academic Profile: 65% in top 10% of high school class, 84% in top 25% of high school class, 99% in top 50% of high school class. 70% from public high schools. **Test Scores:** SAT Math middle 50% range 630-700. SAT EBRW middle 50% range 640-710. ACT middle 50% range 26-30. **Basis for Candidate Selection:** *Very important factors considered include:* rigor of secondary school record, class rank, academic GPA, recommendation(s). *Important factors considered include:* application essay, standardized test scores, interview, extracurricular activities, talent/ability, character/personal qualities, volunteer work. *Other factors considered include:* first generation, alumni/ae relation, geographical residence, racial/ethnic status, work experience, level of applicant's interest. **Freshman Admission Requirements:** High school diploma is required and GED is accepted *Academic units required:* 4 English, 3 math, 3 science, 3 science labs, 3 foreign language, 3 social studies, 3 history, *Academic units recommended:* 4 English, 4 math, 4 science, 4 science labs, 4 foreign language, 4 social studies, 4 history. **Freshman Admission Statistics:** 6,384 applied, 45.8% admitted, 25% enrolled. **Transfer Admission Requirements:** High school transcript, college transcript(s), essay or personal statement, standardized test scores, statement of good standing from prior institution(s). Minimum college GPA of 2.5 required. Lowest grade transferable C. **General Admission Information:** Application fee $60. Priority deadline 1/15. Regular application deadline 1/15. Nonfall registration accepted. Admission may be deferred for a maximum of 1 year.

COSTS AND FINANCIAL AID

Annual tuition $52,640. Room and board $12,570. Average book expense $500. **Required Forms and Deadlines:** CSS/Financial Aid PROFILE; FAFSA. **Notification of Awards:** Applicants will be notified of awards on or about 4/1. **Types of Aid:** *Need-based scholarships/grants:* College/university scholarship or grant aid from institutional funds; Federal Pell; Private scholarships; SEOG; State scholarships/grants. *Loans:* Direct PLUS loans; Direct Subsidized Stafford Loans; Direct Unsubsidized Stafford Loans. *Student Employment:* Federal Work-Study Program available. Institutional employment available. **Financial Aid Statistics:** 96% needy freshmen, 95% needy undergrads receive need-based scholarship or grant aid. 45% freshmen, 38% undergrads receive non-need-based scholarship or grant aid. 92% freshmen, 91% undergrads receive need-based self-help aid. 0% freshmen, 0% undergrads receive athletic scholarships. 60% freshmen, 60% undergrads receive any aid. 63% undergrads borrow to pay for school. Average cumulative indebtedness $31,169. **Criteria for awarding aid:** *Need-based:* Academics, Leadership, Minority status, Music/drama *Non-need-based:* Academics, Music/drama.

GODDARD COLLEGE

123 Pitkin Road, Plainfield, VT 05667
Phone: 802-454-8311
E-mail: admissions@goddard.edu
Fax: 802-454-1029 • **Website:** www.goddard.edu

This is a private school.

RATINGS

Admissions Selectivity Rating: 70   **Fire Safety Rating:** 60*   **Green Rating:** 88

STUDENTS AND FACULTY

Enrollment: 186. **Student Body:** 70% female, 30% male, 0% out-of-state, international. Asian 0%, African American 1%, Caucasian 68%, Hispanic 2%, Native American 3%, Two or more races 5%, Race unknown 17%. **Faculty:** 16 full-time faculty, 69% are women.

ACADEMICS

Degrees: Bachelor's; Master's **Classes:** Most classes have 10-19 students. **Special Study Options:** Accelerated program; Distance learning; Dual enrollment; Independent study; Liberal arts/career combination; Student-designed major; Teacher certification program. **Combined degree programs:** BA/MA.

FACILITIES

Housing: Coed dorms; Special housing for disabled students

CAMPUS LIFE

Activities: Literary magazine; Radio station; Student government. Haybarn Theatre, Village for Learning, The Eliot Pratt Center, The Manor, Community Center **Environmental Initiatives:** Reducing emissions by 30% since 2007.

ADMISSIONS

Basis for Candidate Selection: *Very important factors considered include:* application essay, interview, character/personal qualities, level of applicant's interest. *Important factors considered include:* recommendation(s), talent/ability, volunteer work. *Other factors considered include:* rigor of secondary school record, academic GPA, extracurricular activities, first generation, alumni/ae relation, racial/ethnic status, work experience. **Freshman Admission Requirements:** High school diploma is required and GED is accepted *Academic units recommended:* 4 English, 4 math, 4 science, 3 science labs, 2 foreign language, 4 social studies. **Freshman Admission Statistics:** 5 applied, 80.0% admitted, 100% enrolled. **General Admission Information:** Application fee $40. Priority deadline 6/15. Regular application deadline 7/15. Nonfall registration accepted. Admission may be deferred for a maximum of 2 semesters.

COSTS AND FINANCIAL AID

Annual tuition $15,786. Average book expense $600. **Required Forms and Deadlines:** FAFSA. **Types of Aid:** *Need-based scholarships/grants:* College/university scholarship or grant aid from institutional funds; Federal Pell; Private scholarships; SEOG; State scholarships/grants. **Financial Aid Statistics:** 100% needy freshmen, 82% needy undergrads receive need-based scholarship or grant aid. 0% undergrads receive non-need-based scholarship or grant aid. 100% freshmen, 89% undergrads receive need-based self-help aid. 0% freshmen, 0% undergrads receive athletic scholarships.

GOLDEN GATE UNIVERSITY

536 Mission Street, San Francisco, CA 94105
Phone: 415-442-7800
E-mail: info@ggu.edu • **CEEB Code:** 4329
Fax: 415-442-7807 • **Website:** www.ggu.edu • **ACT Code:** 278

This private school was founded in 1901.

RATINGS

Admissions Selectivity Rating: 61   **Fire Safety Rating:** 60*   **Green Rating:** 60*

STUDENTS AND FACULTY

Student Body: 5% out-of-state, (61 countries represented). Asian 0%, **Retention and Graduation:** 15% grads go on to further study within 1 year. 0% grads pursue arts and sciences degrees. 30% grads pursue business degrees. 0% grads pursue medical degrees. **Faculty:** Student/faculty ratio 13:1. 81 full-time faculty, 0% of classes are taught by teaching assistants.

ACADEMICS

Degrees: Bachelor's; Certificate; Doctoral/Professional; Doctoral/Research; Master's; Post-Bachelor's certificate; Post-Master's certificate **Classes:** Most classes have fewer than 10 students. Most lab/discussion sessions have 10-19 students. **Special Study Options:** Accelerated program; Cooperative education program; Distance learning; Dual enrollment; English as a Second Language (ESL); Independent study; Internships; Weekend college. **Disability Services offered to physically disabled students:** Tape recorders. **Career services:** Alumni network; Alumni services; Career assessment; Career/job search classes; Internships

FACILITIES

Housing: 100% of campus accessible to physically diasbled. **Computers:** Students can register for classes online. Administrative functions (other than registration) can be performed online.

CAMPUS LIFE

Activities: Student government; Student newspaper 16 registered organizations, 5 honor societies.

ADMISSIONS

Freshman Academic Profile: Average high school GPA 2.7. **Test Scores:** Minimum paper TOEFL 525. **Basis for Candidate Selection:** *Very important factors considered include:* rigor of secondary school record. *Other factors considered include:* class rank, application essay, standardized test scores, recommendation(s). **Freshman Admission Requirements:** High school diploma is required and GED is accepted *Academic units recommended:* 4 English, 3 math, 2 science, 1 science labs, 2 foreign language, 1 social studies, 1 history, **Transfer Admission Requirements:** college transcript(s), Minimum college GPA of 2.0 required. Lowest grade transferable c-. **General Admission Information:** Application fee $55. Priority deadline 7/1. Nonfall registration accepted. Admission may be deferred for a maximum of 1 year.

COSTS AND FINANCIAL AID

Annual tuition $18,000. Average book expense $1,920. **Required Forms and Deadlines:** FAFSA; Institution's own financial aid form. **Notification of Awards:** Applicants will be notified of awards on a rolling basis beginning 7/15. **Types of Aid:** *Need-based scholarships/grants:* College/university scholarship or grant aid from institutional funds; Federal Pell; Private scholarships; SEOG; State scholarships/grants. *Loans:* Direct Subsidized Stafford Loans; Direct Unsubsidized Stafford Loans. *Student Employment:* Federal Work-Study Program available. Institutional employment available. **Financial Aid Statistics:** 20% needy undergrads receive need-based scholarship or grant aid. 24% undergrads receive non-need-based scholarship or grant aid. 100% undergrads receive need-based self-help aid. 0% undergrads receive athletic scholarships. **Criteria for awarding aid:** *Need-based:* Academics, Alumni affiliation, Leadership, Minority status *Non-need-based:* Academics, Alumni affiliation, Leadership.

GONZAGA UNIVERSITY

502 E Boone Avenue, Spokane, WA 99258
Phone: 509-313-6572 · **Financial Aid Phone:** 509-313-6582
E-mail: admissions@gonzaga.edu · **CEEB Code:** 4330
Fax: 509-313-5780 · **Website:** www.gonzaga.edu · **ACT Code:** 4458

This private school, affiliated with the Roman Catholic Church, was founded in 1887. It has a 152 acre campus.

RATINGS

Admissions Selectivity Rating: 88   **Fire Safety Rating:** 94   **Green Rating:** 93

STUDENTS AND FACULTY

Enrollment: 5,125. **Student Body:** 52% female, 48% male, 51% out-of-state, 1% international (29 countries represented). Asian 5%, African American 1%, Caucasian 72%, Hispanic 11%, Native American 1%, Pacific Islander <1%, Two or more races 6%, Race unknown 2%.
Retention and Graduation: 94% freshmen return for sophomore year. 78% freshmen graduate within 4 years. 87% freshmen graduate within 6 years. 19% grads go on to further study within 1 year. **Faculty:** Student/faculty ratio 12:1. 442 full-time faculty, 84% hold PhDs, 10% are members of minority groups, 46% are women. 0% of classes are taught by teaching assistants.

ACADEMICS

Degrees: Bachelor's; Doctoral/Professional; Doctoral/Research; Master's **Classes:** Most classes have 10-19 students. Most lab/discussion sessions have 10-19 students. **Most popular majors:** Engineering; Social Sciences; Business, Management, Marketing, And Related Support Services. **Special Study Options:** Cross-registration; Distance learning; Double major; Dual enrollment; English as a Second Language (ESL); Exchange student program (domestic); Honors program; Independent study; Internships; Liberal arts/ career combination; Study abroad; Teacher certification program. **Honors programs:** Hogan Entrepreneurial Leadership Program- The mission of the Hogan Entrepreneurial Leadership Program is to create the leaders the world needs most—individuals who seek out opportunities to create change by combining their passions and the power of entrepreneurship. The three-year, cross-curricular, honors-model approach identifies students who have a passion for exploring new ideas and provides them with the perspective to see the world in a new way. By connecting entrepreneurial education with service, leadership, and ethics, we prepare students to leverage their passions and abilities to create a positive difference in the Jesuit tradition. Unique features include: a three-year immersion in entrepreneurial contexts, a minor along with any major(s), hands-on experience, networking, $1,000/yr scholarship, and a rigorous personalized learning environment. Comprehensive Leadership Program (CLP)- CLP develops future leaders—women and men capable of crafting a vision for a better world. Through academic coursework leading to a Minor in Leadership Studies, reflective self-study, and co-curricular activities, this interdisciplinary, undergraduate leadership program will prepare you to be a great leaders on campus, in your community, and in your profession. **Combined degree programs:** BA/MA. **Disability Services offered to physically disabled students:** Note-taking services; Reader services; Tape recorders. **Career services:** Alumni network; Alumni services; Career assessment; Career/job search classes; Internships; Regional alumni

FACILITIES

Housing: Apartments for married students; Apartments for single students; Coed dorms; Men's dorms; Special housing for disabled student; Special housing for international students; Theme housing; Wellness housing; Women's dorms 90% of campus accessible to physically diasbled. **Special Academic Facilities/Equipment:** Art center, art museum, Bing Crosby House, language lab, finance lab, TV production center, radio station, student educational center, two electron microscopes. **Computers:** 75% of classrooms, 90% of dorms, 100% of libraries, 100% of student union, 75% of common outdoor areas have wireless network access. Students can register for classes online. Administrative functions (other than registration) can be performed online.

CAMPUS LIFE

Environment: Metropolis **Activities:** Campus Ministries; Choral groups; Concert band; Dance; Drama/theater; International Student Organization; Jazz band; Literary magazine; Model UN; Music ensembles; Musical theater; Pep band; Radio station; Student government; Student newspaper; Symphony orchestra; Television station; Yearbook 86 registered organizations, 10 honor societies, 4 religious organizations. **Athletics (Intercollegiate): Men:** baseball, basketball, crew/rowing, cross-country, golf, soccer, tennis, track/field (outdoor). **Women:** basketball, crew/rowing, cross-country, golf, soccer, tennis, track/field (outdoor), volleyball. **On-Campus Highlights:** St Aloysius Cathedral, McCarthey Athletic Center, Jundt Art Museum, Bing Crosby Museum, John J. Hemmingson Center **Environmental Initiatives:** Updating the Gonzaga University Climate Action Plan so that the strategies are measurable and actionable with clear costs and savings, prioritized in a decision matrix.

ADMISSIONS

Freshman Academic Profile: Average high school GPA 3.8. 42% in top 10% of high school class, 75% in top 25% of high school class, 96% in top 50% of high school class. 68% from public high schools. **Test Scores:** SAT Math middle 50% range 590-680. SAT EBRW middle 50% range 590-670. ACT middle 50% range 26-30. Minimum internet-based TOEFL 80. Minimum paper TOEFL 550. **Basis for Candidate Selection:** *Very important factors considered include:* rigor of secondary school record, academic GPA, character/personal qualities, first generation. *Important factors considered include:* application essay, standardized test scores, recommendation(s), extracurricular activities, talent/ability. *Other factors considered include:* interview, alumni/ae relation, racial/ethnic status, volunteer work, work experience, level of applicant's interest. **Freshman Admission Requirements:** High school diploma is required and GED is not accepted *Academic units required:* 4 English, 3 math, 3 science, 3 science labs, 2 foreign language, 2 social studies, 2 history, 2 academic electives, *Academic units recommended:* 4 English, 4 math, 4 science, 4 science labs, 3 foreign language, 3 social studies, 3 history, 3 academic electives. **Freshman Admission Statistics:** 7,613 applied, 64.8% admitted, 25% enrolled. **Transfer Admission Requirements:** college transcript(s), essay or personal statement, statement of good standing from prior institution(s). Minimum college GPA of 2.7 required. Lowest grade transferable C. **General Admission Information:** Application fee $50. Priority deadline 11/15. Regular application deadline 2/1. Nonfall registration accepted. Admission may be deferred for a maximum of 1 year.

COSTS AND FINANCIAL AID

Annual tuition $40,540. Room and board $11,550. Required fees $790. Average book expense $1,104. **Required Forms and Deadlines:** FAFSA. **Notification of Awards:** Applicants will be notified of awards on a rolling basis beginning 3/1. **Types of Aid:** *Need-based scholarships/grants:* College/university scholarship or grant aid from institutional funds; Federal Pell; Private scholarships; SEOG; State scholarships/grants. *Loans:* Direct PLUS loans; Direct Subsidized Stafford Loans; Direct Unsubsidized Stafford Loans. *Student Employment:* Federal Work-Study Program available. Institutional employment available. **Financial Aid Statistics:** 100% needy freshmen, 100% needy undergrads receive need-based scholarship or grant aid. 24% freshmen, 21% undergrads receive non-need-based scholarship or grant aid. 65% freshmen, 68% undergrads receive need-based self-help aid. 3% freshmen, 4% undergrads receive athletic scholarships. 99% freshmen, 98% undergrads receive any aid. Average cumulative indebtedness $30,700. **Criteria for awarding aid:** *Need-based:* Academics, Leadership, Minority status *Non-need-based:* Academics, Alumni affiliation, Athletics, Leadership, Minority status, Music/drama.

See page 942.

GORDON COLLEGE

255 Grapevine Road, Wenham, MA 01984-1899
Phone: 978-867-4218 · **Financial Aid Phone:** 978-867-4246
E-mail: admissions@gordon.edu · **CEEB Code:** 3417
Fax: 978-867-4682 · **Website:** www.gordon.edu · **ACT Code:** 1838

This private school, affiliated with the Multidenominational—Evangelical Church, was founded in 1889. It has a 485 acre campus.

RATINGS

Admissions Selectivity Rating: 79   **Fire Safety Rating:** 97   **Green Rating:** 86

STUDENTS AND FACULTY

Enrollment: 1,573. **Student Body:** 63% female, 37% male, 65% out-of-state, 9% international (55 countries represented). Asian 5%, African American 6%, Caucasian 68%, Hispanic 8%, Native American <1%, Pacific Islander <1%, Two or more races 3%, Race unknown 0%.
Retention and Graduation: 83% freshmen return for sophomore year. 61% freshmen graduate within 4 years. 70% freshmen graduate within 6 years. 23% grads go on to further study within 1 year. 26% grads pursue arts and sciences degrees. 4% grads pursue law degrees. 6% grads pursue business degrees. 8% grads pursue medical degrees. **Faculty:** Student/faculty ratio 11:1. 94 full-time faculty, 85% hold PhDs, 17% are members of minority groups, 41% are women. 0% of classes are taught by teaching assistants.

ACADEMICS

Degrees: Bachelor's; Master's **Classes:** Most classes have 10-19 students. Most lab/discussion sessions have 10-19 students. **Most popular majors:** Biology/Biological Sciences, General; Psychology, General; Business Administration, Management And Operations. **Special Study Options:** Cooperative education program; Cross-registration; Double major; Dual enrollment; Exchange student program (domestic); Honors program; Independent study; Internships; Liberal arts/career combination; Student-designed major; Study abroad; Teacher certification program. **Honors programs:** The Gordon Global Honors Institute provides a 4-year honors program. The Jerusalem and Athens Forum, a year-long great books honors seminar; lecture series and symposia, access to internationally recognized speakers; the Pike Scholarship program that allows students to design their own majors; The Herrmann Lectures on Faith and Science; Center for Entrepreneurial Leadership; The Great Conversation, freshman seminar exploring the Christian liberal arts through discussion, reading, and writing; Fellows and Leadership programs, apprenticeship under a senior executive leader; Faculty-student summer research fellowships.
Disability Services offered to physically disabled students: Note-taking services; Reader services; Tape recorders; Tutors. **Career services:** Alumni network; Alumni services; Career assessment; Career/job search classes; Internships; Regional alumni

FACILITIES

Housing: Apartments for married students; Apartments for single students; Coed dorms; Men's dorms; Special housing for disabled student; Women's dorms 84% of campus accessible to physically disabled. **Special Academic Facilities/Equipment:** The Barrington Center for the Arts features gallery

space and theaters. Ken Olsen Science Center is equipped with an electron microscope and gene sequencing machine; human anatomy and physiology cadaver lab; and a pre-fabrication lab. The Phillips Music center includes recital space. (include Ken O Archive). The Biomechanics Laboratory contains a 6-camera Vicon Motion Capture System and two AMTI force plates embedded into the floor of the data capture space. **Computers:** Administrative functions (other than registration) can be performed online.

CAMPUS LIFE

Environment: Village **Activities:** Campus Ministries; Choral groups; Concert band; Dance; Drama/theater; International Student Organization; Jazz band; Literary magazine; Model UN; Music ensembles; Musical theater; Radio station; Student government; Student newspaper; Student-run film society; Symphony orchestra; Yearbook 35 registered organizations, 17 honor societies, 15 religious organizations. **Athletics (Intercollegiate):** *Men:* baseball, basketball, cross-country, lacrosse, soccer, swimming, tennis, track/field (outdoor), track/field (indoor). *Women:* basketball, cross-country, field hockey, lacrosse, soccer, softball, swimming, tennis, track/field (outdoor), track/field (indoor), volleyball. **On-Campus Highlights:** Gillies Lounge/Claymore Cafe, Ken Olsen Science Center, Bennett Athletic and Recreation Center, Barrington Center for the Arts, Hiking/biking/cross country ski trails **Environmental Initiatives:** The College invested in renewable energy by purchasing 100% of its December 2016—November 2017 electricity from "green" sources (92% biomass, 8% wind-produced); these efforts have led to our recognition as an EPA Green Power Partner.

ADMISSIONS

Freshman Academic Profile: Average high school GPA 3.6. 28% in top 10% of high school class, 53% in top 25% of high school class, 82% in top 50% of high school class. 64% from public high schools. **Test Scores:** SAT Math middle 50% range 510-640. SAT EBRW middle 50% range 540-650. ACT middle 50% range 22-29. Minimum internet-based TOEFL 85. **Basis for Candidate Selection:** *Very important factors considered include:* rigor of secondary school record, academic GPA, standardized test scores, recommendation(s), interview, extracurricular activities, talent/ability, character/personal qualities, religious affiliation/commitment. *Important factors considered include:* class rank, application essay, first generation, volunteer work, work experience, level of applicant's interest. *Other factors considered include:* alumni/ae relation. **Freshman Admission Requirements:** High school diploma is required and GED is accepted *Academic units required:* 4 English, 2 math, 2 science, 1 science labs, 2 foreign language, 2 social studies, 5 academic electives, *Academic units recommended:* 4 English, 3 math, 3 science, 1 science labs, 4 foreign language, 2 social studies, 5 academic electives. **Freshman Admission Statistics:** 2,924 applied, 88.9% admitted, 16% enrolled. **Transfer Admission Requirements:** college transcript(s), essay or personal statement, interview, statement of good standing from prior institution(s). Minimum college GPA of 2.0 required. Lowest grade transferable C. **General Admission Information:** Application fee $50. Priority deadline 12/1. Regular application deadline 8/1. Nonfall registration accepted. Admission may be deferred for a maximum of 2 semesters.

COSTS AND FINANCIAL AID

Annual tuition $35,800. Room and board $11,070. Required fees $1,600. Average book expense $904. **Required Forms and Deadlines:** FAFSA. **Notification of Awards:** Applicants will be notified of awards on a rolling basis beginning 1/15. **Types of Aid:** *Need-based scholarships/grants:* College/university scholarship or grant aid from institutional funds; Federal Pell; Private scholarships; SEOG; State scholarships/grants. *Loans:* Direct PLUS loans; Direct Subsidized Stafford Loans; Direct Unsubsidized Stafford Loans. *Student Employment:* Federal Work-Study Program available. Institutional employment available. **Financial Aid Statistics:** 100% needy freshmen, 100% needy undergrads receive need-based scholarship or grant aid. 11% freshmen, 12% undergrads receive non-need-based scholarship or grant aid. 88% freshmen, 87% undergrads receive need-based self-help aid. 0% freshmen, 0% undergrads receive athletic scholarships. 99% freshmen, 99% undergrads receive any aid. 86% undergrads borrow to pay for school. Average cumulative indebtedness $36,557. **Criteria for awarding aid:** *Need-based:* Academics, Alumni affiliation, Art, Leadership, Minority status, Music/drama, Religious affiliation *Non-need-based:* Academics, Alumni affiliation, Art, Leadership, Minority status, Music/drama, State/district residency.

GOSHEN COLLEGE

1700 South Main Street, Goshen, IN 46526-4794
Phone: 574-535-7535 · **Financial Aid Phone:** 574-535-7525
E-mail: admission@goshen.edu · **CEEB Code:** 1251
Fax: 574-535-7609 · **Website:** www.goshen.edu · **ACT Code:** 1196

This private school, affiliated with the Mennonite Church, was founded in 1894. It has a 135 acre campus.

RATINGS
Admissions Selectivity Rating: 86   **Fire Safety Rating:** 97   **Green Rating:** 60*

STUDENTS AND FACULTY
Enrollment: 750. **Student Body:** 58% female, 42% male, 48% out-of-state, 9% international (25 countries represented). Asian 2%, African American 4%, Caucasian 68%, Hispanic 13%, Native American 0%, Pacific Islander 0%, Two or more races 3%, Race unknown 1%.
Retention and Graduation: 77% freshmen return for sophomore year. 15% grads go on to further study within 1 year. 13% grads pursue arts and sciences degrees. 3% grads pursue law degrees. 1% grads pursue business degrees. 3% grads pursue medical degrees. **Faculty:** Student/faculty ratio 10:1. 65 full-time faculty, 66% hold PhDs, 9% are members of minority groups, 49% are women. 0% of classes are taught by teaching assistants.

ACADEMICS
Degrees: Bachelor's; Master's **Classes:** Most classes have 20-29 students. Most lab/discussion sessions have 10-19 students. **Most popular majors:** Biology/Biological Sciences, General; Music; Registered Nursing/Registered Nurse. **Special Study Options:** Cross-registration; Double major; Dual enrollment; Independent study; Internships; Liberal arts/career combination; Student-designed major; Study abroad; Teacher certification program. **Disability Services offered to physically disabled students:** Note-taking services; Reader services; Tape recorders; Tutors. **Career services:** Alumni network; Career/job search classes; Internships; Regional alumni

FACILITIES
Housing: Apartments for married students; Apartments for single students; Coed dorms; Men's dorms; Special housing for disabled student; Wellness housing; Women's dorms 90% of campus accessible to physically diasbled. **Special Academic Facilities/Equipment:** X-ray precision lab, lab kindergarten, Mennonite Historical Library. **Computers:** 100% of classrooms, 25% of dorms, 80% of libraries, 75% of dining areas, 100% of student union, have wireless network access. Students can register for classes online. Administrative functions (other than registration) can be performed online.

CAMPUS LIFE
Environment: Town **Activities:** Campus Ministries; Choral groups; Concert band; Drama/theater; International Student Organization; Jazz band; Music ensembles; Musical theater; Opera; Pep band; Radio station; Student government; Student newspaper; Student-run film society; Symphony orchestra; Television station; Yearbook 21 registered organizations, 4 religious organizations. **Athletics (Intercollegiate):** *Men:* baseball, basketball, cross-country, golf, soccer, tennis, track/field (outdoor), track/field (indoor). *Women:* basketball, cross-country, soccer, softball, tennis, track/field (outdoor), track/field (indoor), volleyball. **On-Campus Highlights:** Music Center, Gingerich Rec-Fitness Center, Science Building, Residential Halls Connector, Good Library **Environmental Initiatives:** Built the first Platinum LEED Certified facility in Indiana at our Merry Lea Environmental Center. www.goshen.edu/merrylea

ADMISSIONS
Freshman Academic Profile: Average high school GPA 3.5. 38% in top 10% of high school class, 63% in top 25% of high school class, 85% in top 50% of high school class. 90% from public high schools. **Test Scores:** SAT Math middle 50% range 500-635. SAT EBRW middle 50% range 475-620. ACT middle 50% range 21-28. Minimum internet-based TOEFL 79. Minimum paper TOEFL 550. **Basis for Candidate Selection:** *Very important factors considered include:* academic GPA, standardized test scores. *Important factors considered include:* rigor of secondary school record, class rank. *Other factors considered include:* application essay, recommendation(s), extracurricular activities, talent/ability, character/personal qualities, first generation, alumni/ae relation, volunteer work, work experience, level of applicant's interest. **Freshman Admission Requirements:** High school diploma is required and GED is accepted *Academic units recommended:* 4 English, 2 math, 2 science, 2 foreign language, 2 history. **Freshman Admission Statistics:** 900 applied, 54.0% admitted, 33% enrolled. **Transfer Admission Requirements:** college transcript(s), essay or personal statement, statement of good standing from prior institution(s). Lowest grade transferable C. **General Admission Information:**

Application fee $25. Regular application deadline 8/15. Nonfall registration accepted. Admission may be deferred for a maximum of 1 year.

COSTS AND FINANCIAL AID
Annual tuition $29,700. Room and board $9,700. Average book expense $900. **Required Forms and Deadlines:** FAFSA. **Notification of Awards:** Applicants will be notified of awards on a rolling basis beginning 2/1. **Types of Aid:** *Need-based scholarships/grants:* College/university scholarship or grant aid from institutional funds; Federal Pell; Private scholarships; SEOG; State scholarships/grants. *Loans:* Direct PLUS loans; Direct Subsidized Stafford Loans; Direct Unsubsidized Stafford Loans. *Student Employment:* Federal Work-Study Program available. Institutional employment available. **Financial Aid Statistics:** 100% needy freshmen, 98% needy undergrads receive need-based scholarship or grant aid. 20% freshmen, 16% undergrads receive non-need-based scholarship or grant aid. 77% freshmen, 81% undergrads receive need-based self-help aid. 5% freshmen, 9% undergrads receive athletic scholarships. 100% freshmen, 99% undergrads receive any aid. **Criteria for awarding aid:** *Need-based:* Academics, Minority status, Religious affiliation *Non-need-based:* Academics, Art, Athletics, Leadership, Minority status, Music/drama.

GOUCHER COLLEGE

1021 Dulaney Valley Road, Baltimore, MD 21204-2794
Phone: 410-337-6100 · **Financial Aid Phone:** 410-337-6141
E-mail: admissions@goucher.edu · **CEEB Code:** 5257
Fax: 410-337-6354 · **Website:** www.goucher.edu · **ACT Code:** 1696

This private school was founded in 1885. It has a 287 acre campus.

RATINGS
Admissions Selectivity Rating: 80   **Fire Safety Rating:** 95   **Green Rating:** 99

STUDENTS AND FACULTY
Enrollment: 1,444. **Student Body:** 69% female, 31% male, 65% out-of-state, 3% international (27 countries represented). Asian 4%, African American 14%, Caucasian 59%, Hispanic 9%, Native American 0%, Pacific Islander <1%, Two or more races 5%, Race unknown 4%.
Retention and Graduation: 56% freshmen graduate within 4 years. 66% freshmen graduate within 6 years. 27% grads go on to further study within 1 year. 20% grads pursue arts and sciences degrees. 0% grads pursue law degrees. 1% grads pursue business degrees. 1% grads pursue medical degrees. **Faculty:** Student/faculty ratio 10:1. 133 full-time faculty, 92% hold PhDs, 17% are members of minority groups, 60% are women. 0% of classes are taught by teaching assistants.

ACADEMICS
Degrees: Bachelor's; Master's; Post-Bachelor's certificate **Classes:** Most classes have 20-29 students. Most lab/discussion sessions have 20-29 students. **Most popular majors:** English Language And Literature, General; Psychology, General; Business Administration And Management, General. **Special Study Options:** Cross-registration; Distance learning; Double major; Dual enrollment; Independent study; Internships; Student-designed major; Study abroad; Teacher certification program. **Career services:** Alumni network; Alumni services; Career assessment; Internships

FACILITIES
Housing: Apartments for single students; Coed dorms; Men's dorms; Special housing for disabled student; Theme housing; Wellness housing; Women's dorms 100% of campus accessible to physically diasbled. **Special Academic Facilities/Equipment:** The Athenaeum is the flagship building of campus, weaving together the various threads of life at Goucher under one roof. The 103,000 square foot building, open 24 hours a day during the semester, features a technologically superior library; a forum for public events; classrooms; a café; an art gallery; a center for community service programming; and spaces for exercise, conversation, and relaxation. The recently renovated 62,000-square-foot Academic Center at Julia Rogers is a place where science, humanities, and social science disciplines merge into one academic whole. The facility boasts technology-enhanced classrooms and state-of-the-art research and teaching labs, an international commons to facilitate cultural exchange, and the Welch Center for Graduate and Professional Studies. The Academic Center for Excellence offers study-skills workshops, peer-led supplemental instruction,

and yoga, meditation, and Reiki sessions. Goucher also has a TV studio, three multi-purpose performance spaces ranging in size from a few hundred to 1,000 seats, a robotics lab, a rooftop observatory providing public observing, advanced teaching labs for physics and computer science, research labs for math, physics, and psychology, a technology/learning center, international technology and media center, and centers for writing, math, and politics. Also located on Goucher's campus are equestrian stables and riding areas, a community garden, and nature trails. **Computers:** 95% of classrooms, 40% of dorms, 100% of libraries, 100% of dining areas, 100% of student union, 80% of common outdoor areas have wireless network access. Students can register for classes online. Administrative functions (other than registration) can be performed online.

CAMPUS LIFE

Environment: City **Activities:** Campus Ministries; Choral groups; Concert band; Dance; Drama/theater; International Student Organization; Jazz band; Literary magazine; Model UN; Music ensembles; Musical theater; Opera; Pep band; Radio station; Student government; Student newspaper; Student-run film society; Yearbook 60 registered organizations, 1 honor society, 8 religious organizations. **Athletics (Intercollegiate):** *Men:* basketball, cross-country, lacrosse, soccer, swimming, tennis, track/field (outdoor), track/field (indoor). *Women:* basketball, cross-country, equestrian sports, field hockey, lacrosse, soccer, swimming, tennis, track/field (outdoor), track/field (indoor), volleyball. **On-Campus Highlights:** The Library at the Athenaeum, Alice's Cafe, Sports and Recreation Center, Residential Quad, Gopher Hole **Environmental Initiatives:** Goucher ensures that every student fulfills a sustainability learning requirement regardless of their course of study.

ADMISSIONS

Freshman Academic Profile: Average high school GPA 3.1. 28% in top 10% of high school class, 54% in top 25% of high school class, 78% in top 50% of high school class. 62% from public high schools. **Test Scores:** SAT Math middle 50% range 500-600. SAT EBRW middle 50% range 550-660. ACT middle 50% range 23-29. Minimum internet-based TOEFL 79-80. Minimum paper TOEFL 550. **Basis for Candidate Selection:** *Very important factors considered include:* rigor of secondary school record, academic GPA. *Important factors considered include:* application essay, recommendation(s), extracurricular activities, talent/ability, volunteer work. *Other factors considered include:* class rank, standardized test scores, interview, character/personal qualities, first generation, alumni/ae relation, geographical residence, state residency, racial/ethnic status, work experience, level of applicant's interest. **Freshman Admission Requirements:** High school diploma is required and GED is accepted *Academic units required:* 4 English, 3 math, 2 science, 2 science labs, 2 foreign language, 3 social studies, 2 academic electives, *Academic units recommended:* 4 English, 4 math, 3 science, 3 science labs, 4 foreign language, 3 social studies, 2 academic electives. **Freshman Admission Statistics:** 3,474 applied, 78.8% admitted, 15% enrolled. **Transfer Admission Requirements:** college transcript(s), essay or personal statement, Lowest grade transferable C. **General Admission Information:** Nonfall registration accepted. Admission may be deferred.

COSTS AND FINANCIAL AID

Annual tuition $42,600. Room and board $12,670. Required fees $840. Average book expense $1,200. **Required Forms and Deadlines:** FAFSA. **Notification of Awards:** Applicants will be notified of awards on a rolling basis beginning 12/15. **Types of Aid:** *Need-based scholarships/grants:* College/ university scholarship or grant aid from institutional funds; Federal Pell; Private scholarships; SEOG; State scholarships/grants. *Loans:* Direct PLUS loans; Direct Subsidized Stafford Loans; Direct Unsubsidized Stafford Loans. *Student Employment:* Federal Work-Study Program available. Institutional employment available. **Financial Aid Statistics:** 100% needy freshmen, 100% needy undergrads receive need-based scholarship or grant aid. 19% freshmen, 15% undergrads receive non-need-based scholarship or grant aid. 82% freshmen, 83% undergrads receive need-based self-help aid. 0% freshmen, 0% undergrads receive athletic scholarships. 99% freshmen, 93% undergrads receive any aid. 62% undergrads borrow to pay for school. Average cumulative indebtedness $33,446. **Criteria for awarding aid:** *Non-need-based:* Academics, Art, Leadership, Music/drama.

GOVERNORS STATE UNIVERSITY

1 University Parkway, University Park, IL 60484
Phone: 708-534-4490 · **Financial Aid Phone:** 708-534-4480
E-mail: gsunow@govst.edu
Fax: 708-534-1640 · **Website:** www.govst.edu

This public school was founded in 1969. It has a 720 acre campus.

RATINGS
Admissions Selectivity Rating: 61   **Fire Safety Rating:** 60*   **Green Rating:** 60*

STUDENTS AND FACULTY
Enrollment: 3,103. **Student Body:** 68% female, 32% male, 3% out-of-state, <1% international (17 countries represented). Asian 2%, African American 37%, Caucasian 44%, Hispanic 10%, Native American <1%, Pacific Islander <1%, Two or more races 1%, Race unknown 7%.
Retention and Graduation: 34% grads go on to further study within 1 year. 17% grads pursue arts and sciences degrees. 1% grads pursue law degrees. 16% grads pursue business degrees. 0% grads pursue medical degrees. **Faculty:** Student/faculty ratio 11:1. 211 full-time faculty, 59% hold PhDs, 37% are members of minority groups, 59% are women. 0% of classes are taught by teaching assistants.

ACADEMICS
Degrees: Bachelor's; Doctoral Other; Doctoral/Professional; Master's; Post-Master's certificate **Classes:** Most classes have 10-19 students. Most lab/discussion sessions have 10-19 students. **Most popular majors:** Elementary Education And Teaching; Business/Commerce, General. **Special Study Options:** Cross-registration; Distance learning; Dual enrollment; External degree program; Honors program; Independent study; Internships; Student-designed major; Study abroad; Teacher certification program. **Disability Services offered to physically disabled students:** Note-taking services; Reader services; Tape recorders; Tutors. **Career services:** Alumni network; Alumni services; Career assessment; Career/job search classes; Internships

FACILITIES
Housing: 99% of campus accessible to physically diasbled. **Special Academic Facilities/Equipment:** Manilow Sculpture Park **Computers:** Students can register for classes online. Administrative functions (other than registration) can be performed online.

CAMPUS LIFE
Environment: Village **Activities:** Drama/theater; Literary magazine; Student government; Student newspaper; Student-run film society 7 honor societies.

ADMISSIONS
Transfer Admission Requirements: college transcript(s), statement of good standing from prior institution(s). Minimum college GPA of 2.0 required. Lowest grade transferable C. **General Admission Information:** Nonfall registration accepted.

COSTS AND FINANCIAL AID
Types of Aid: *Need-based scholarships/grants:* College/university scholarship or grant aid from institutional funds; Federal Nursing Scholarships; Federal Pell; Private scholarships; SEOG; State scholarships/grants. *Loans:* Direct Subsidized Stafford Loans. *Student Employment:* Federal Work-Study Program available. Institutional employment available. **Criteria for awarding aid:** *Need-based:* Academics *Non-need-based:* Academics.

GRACE COLLEGE AND SEMINARY

200 Seminary Drive, Winona Lake, IN 46590
Phone: 800-544-7223 · **Financial Aid Phone:** 574-372-5100
E-mail: enroll@grace.edu · **CEEB Code:** 1252
Fax: 574-372-5120 · **Website:** www.grace.edu · **ACT Code:** 1198

This private school, affiliated with the Fellowship of Grace Brethren Churches, was founded in 1948. It has a 150 acre campus.

RATINGS
Admissions Selectivity Rating: 74   **Fire Safety Rating:** 83   **Green Rating:** 60*

STUDENTS AND FACULTY
Enrollment: 1,482. **Student Body:** 60% female, 40% male, 31% out-of-state, 1% international (9 countries represented). Asian 1%, African American 4%,

Caucasian 84%, Hispanic 6%, Native American <1%, Pacific Islander 0%, Two or more races 3%, Race unknown 2%.

Retention and Graduation: 79% freshmen return for sophomore year. 67% freshmen graduate within 4 years. 72% freshmen graduate within 6 years.
Faculty: Student/faculty ratio 20:1. 47 full-time faculty, 81% hold PhDs, 4% are members of minority groups, 36% are women. 0% of classes are taught by teaching assistants.

ACADEMICS

Degrees: Associate; Bachelor's; Certificate; Diploma; Doctoral; Doctoral Other; Master's; Post-Bachelor's certificate **Classes:** Most classes have 10-19 students. Most lab/discussion sessions have 10-19 students. **Most popular majors:** Elementary Education And Teaching; Psychology, General; Business/Commerce, General. **Special Study Options:** Cooperative education program; Cross-registration; Distance learning; Double major; Dual enrollment; Exchange student program (domestic); Honors program; Independent study; Internships; Liberal arts/career combination; Study abroad; Teacher certification program. **Disability Services offered to physically disabled students:** Note-taking services; Reader services; Tape recorders; Tutors. **Career services:** Career assessment

FACILITIES

Housing: Apartments for single students; Men's dorms; Women's dorms 85% of campus accessible to physically diasbled. **Special Academic Facilities/Equipment:** Reneker Museum of Winona History **Computers:** 100% of classrooms, 100% of dorms, 100% of libraries, 100% of dining areas, 100% of student union, 33% of common outdoor areas have wireless network access. Students can register for classes online. Administrative functions (other than registration) can be performed online.

CAMPUS LIFE

Environment: Village **Activities:** Campus Ministries; Choral groups; Concert band; Drama/theater; Literary magazine; Music ensembles; Musical theater; Pep band; Student government; Student newspaper; Symphony orchestra; Yearbook 9 registered organizations, 1 honor society, 8 religious organizations. **Athletics (Intercollegiate):** *Men:* baseball, basketball, cheerleading, cross-country, golf, soccer, tennis, track/field (outdoor). *Women:* basketball, cheerleading, cross-country, soccer, softball, tennis, track/field (outdoor), volleyball. **On-Campus Highlights:** Gordon Recreation Center, Coffee/Sub shop

ADMISSIONS

Freshman Academic Profile: Average high school GPA 3.6. 20% in top 10% of high school class, 45% in top 25% of high school class, 78% in top 50% of high school class. 71% from public high schools. **Test Scores:** SAT Math middle 50% range 490-600. SAT EBRW middle 50% range 500-620. ACT middle 50% range 20-27. **Basis for Candidate Selection:** *Very important factors considered include:* rigor of secondary school record, application essay, standardized test scores, recommendation(s), religious affiliation/commitment. *Important factors considered include:* academic GPA, character/personal qualities. *Other factors considered include:* class rank, interview, extracurricular activities, talent/ability, alumni/ae relation. **Freshman Admission Requirements:** High school diploma is required and GED is accepted *Academic units recommended:* 4 English, 2 math, 2 science, 1 science labs, 2 foreign language, 2 social studies, 1 history. **Freshman Admission Statistics:** 4,040 applied, 81.8% admitted, 12% enrolled. **Transfer Admission Requirements:** college transcript(s), essay or personal statement, standardized test scores, Minimum college GPA of 2.0 required. Lowest grade transferable C-. **General Admission Information:** Application fee $30. Priority deadline 6/1. Regular application deadline 8/15. Nonfall registration accepted. Admission may be deferred for a maximum of 1 semester.

COSTS AND FINANCIAL AID

Annual tuition $23,930. Room and board $8,782. Average book expense $1,000. **Required Forms and Deadlines:** FAFSA. **Notification of Awards:** Applicants will be notified of awards on a rolling basis beginning 3/1. **Types of Aid:** *Need-based scholarships/grants:* College/university scholarship or grant aid from institutional funds; Federal Pell; Private scholarships; SEOG; State scholarships/grants. *Loans: Student Employment:* Federal Work-Study Program available. Institutional employment available. **Financial Aid Statistics:** 89% needy freshmen, 89% needy undergrads receive need-based scholarship or grant aid. 99% freshmen, 86% undergrads receive non-need-based scholarship or grant aid. 77% freshmen, 78% undergrads receive need-based self-help aid. 0% freshmen, 0% undergrads receive athletic scholarships. **Criteria for awarding aid:** *Need-based:* Minority status, Religious affiliation *Non-need-based:* Academics, Art, Athletics, Leadership, Music/drama.

GRACELAND UNIVERSITY

1 University Place, Lamoni, IA 50140
Phone: 641-784-5196 · **Financial Aid Phone:** 641 784 5051
E-mail: admissions@graceland.edu · **CEEB Code:** 6249
Fax: 641-784-5480 · **Website:** www.graceland.edu · **ACT Code:** 1314

This private school, affiliated with the Community of Christ Church, was founded in 1895. It has a 170 acre campus.

RATINGS
Admissions Selectivity Rating: 81   **Fire Safety Rating:** 88   **Green Rating:** 70

STUDENTS AND FACULTY
Enrollment: 1,209. **Student Body:** 56% female, 44% male, 77% out-of-state, 4% international (26 countries represented). Asian 1%, African American 11%, Caucasian 62%, Hispanic 11%, Native American <1%, Pacific Islander 1%, Two or more races 4%, Race unknown 4%.
Retention and Graduation: 62% freshmen return for sophomore year. 38% freshmen graduate within 4 years. **Faculty:** Student/faculty ratio 17:1. 63 full-time faculty, 76% hold PhDs, 17% are members of minority groups, 46% are women. 0% of classes are taught by teaching assistants.

ACADEMICS
Degrees: Bachelor's; Certificate; Doctoral Other; Master's; Post-Bachelor's certificate; Post-Master's certificate **Classes:** Most classes have 20-29 students. Most lab/discussion sessions have fewer than 10 students. **Most popular majors:** Elementary Education And Teaching; Registered Nursing/Registered Nurse; Business Administration And Management, General. **Special Study Options:** Accelerated program; Distance learning; Double major; Dual enrollment; Honors program; Independent study; Internships; Liberal arts/career combination; Student-designed major; Study abroad; Teacher certification program. **Honors programs:** The Graceland University Honors Program includes courses in Honors Discourse I & II, Honors Humanities, Jr. and Sr. Honors Seminar, and Honors Contracts to be created with instructors in any academic course the students choose. Completion of the Honors Program requires 21 hours of honors credit, completion of the Jr. and Sr. Honors Seminars, and a minimum 3.5 gpa overall and in their honors work. Honors Students with a 3.75 gpa or higher are eligible for an Honors Scholarship. Incoming students with a 3.75 gap and an ACT of 27 or higher may apply for full tuition Prestigious Honors Scholarship, which are available on a competitive basis, and require an interview. Graceland University offers an Excellent Education in a caring community. So we believe the best reason to participate in the Honors Program is the people in it, and to participate in the Honors community. **Disability Services offered to physically disabled students:** Note-taking services; Reader services; Tape recorders; Tutors. **Career services:** Alumni network; Alumni services; Internships; Regional alumni

FACILITIES
Housing: Apartments for married students; Apartments for single students; Coed dorms; Men's dorms; Special housing for disabled student; Women's dorms 95% of campus accessible to physically diasbled. **Special Academic Facilities/Equipment:** Shaw Center for the Performing Arts which includes a recital facility, outdoor amphitheatre, 500-seat auditorium, and a black box theatre. **Computers:** 100% of classrooms, 91% of dorms, 100% of libraries, 100% of dining areas, 100% of student union, 30% of common outdoor areas have wireless network access. Students can register for classes online. Administrative functions (other than registration) can be performed online.

CAMPUS LIFE
Environment: Rural **Activities:** Campus Ministries; Choral groups; Concert band; Dance; Drama/theater; International Student Organization; Jazz band; Literary magazine; Marching band; Music ensembles; Musical theater; Pep band; Radio station; Student government; Student newspaper; Symphony orchestra; Yearbook 54 registered organizations, 1 religious organization. **Athletics (Intercollegiate):** *Men:* baseball, basketball, cross-country, football, golf, soccer, tennis, track/field (outdoor), track/field (indoor), volleyball. *Women:* basketball, cross-country, golf, soccer, softball, tennis, track/field (outdoor), track/field (indoor), volleyball. **On-Campus Highlights:** Shaw Center, The Helene Center for Visual Arts, The Closson Center, Resch Science & Technology Hall, Higdon Administration Building **Environmental Initiatives:** Installation of Hoop House garden to produce vegetables for campus dining services.

ADMISSIONS
Freshman Academic Profile: Average high school GPA 3.2. 9% in top 10% of high school class, 23% in top 25% of high school class, 58% in top 50% of high school class. **Test Scores:** SAT Math middle 50% range 460-540. SAT EBRW middle 50% range 450-530. ACT middle 50% range 18-23. Minimum internet-based TOEFL 80. Minimum paper TOEFL 550. **Basis for

Candidate Selection: *Very important factors considered include:* academic GPA, standardized test scores. *Important factors considered include:* rigor of secondary school record, class rank. *Other factors considered include:* application essay, recommendation(s), interview, talent/ability. **Freshman Admission Requirements:** High school diploma is required and GED is accepted *Academic units recommended:* 4 English, 3 math, 2 science, 1 foreign language, 3 social studies. **Freshman Admission Statistics:** 2,800 applied, 56.1% admitted, 16% enrolled. **Transfer Admission Requirements:** college transcript(s), Minimum college GPA of 2.0 required. Lowest grade transferable D. **General Admission Information:** Nonfall registration accepted.

COSTS AND FINANCIAL AID
Annual tuition $28,600. Room and board $8,760. Required fees $640. Average book expense $1,320. **Required Forms and Deadlines:** FAFSA. **Notification of Awards:** Applicants will be notified of awards on a rolling basis beginning 2/1. **Types of Aid:** *Need-based scholarships/grants:* College/university scholarship or grant aid from institutional funds; Federal Pell; Private scholarships; SEOG; State scholarships/grants. *Loans:* Direct PLUS loans; Direct Subsidized Stafford Loans; Direct Unsubsidized Stafford Loans. *Student Employment:* Federal Work-Study Program available. Institutional employment available. **Financial Aid Statistics:** 100% needy freshmen, 93% needy undergrads receive need-based scholarship or grant aid. 33% freshmen, 30% undergrads receive non-need-based scholarship or grant aid. 88% freshmen, 89% undergrads receive need-based self-help aid. 14% freshmen, 13% undergrads receive athletic scholarships. 99% freshmen, 93% undergrads receive any aid. 76% undergrads borrow to pay for school. Average cumulative indebtedness $32,720. **Criteria for awarding aid:** *Need-based:* Job skills, Minority status *Non-need-based:* Academics, Alumni affiliation, Art, Athletics, Job skills, Leadership, Music/drama, Religious affiliation.

See page 944.

GRAND RAPIDS THEOLOGICAL SEMINARY

1001 E Beltline Ave. NE, Grand Rapids, MI 49525
Phone: 1-800-697-1133 · **Financial Aid Phone:** 616-949-5300
E-mail: grts@cornerstone.edu
Fax: 616-254-1623 · **Website:** http://grts.cornerstone.edu

This is a private school.

RATINGS
Admissions Selectivity Rating: 0   **Fire Safety Rating:** 96   **Green Rating:** 60*

STUDENTS AND FACULTY
Retention and Graduation: 15% grads go on to further study within 1 year. 10% grads pursue arts and sciences degrees. 1% grads pursue law degrees. 3% grads pursue business degrees. 1% grads pursue medical degrees. **Faculty:** Student/faculty ratio 17:1. 9 full-time faculty, 56% are women. 0% of classes are taught by teaching assistants.

ACADEMICS
Degrees: Certificate; Master's **Most popular majors:** Education, General; Psychology, General; Business/Commerce, General. **Special Study Options:** Distance learning; Double major; Dual enrollment; Honors program; Independent study; Internships; Study abroad. **Honors programs:** Honors Program based on a "great books" curriculum. **Disability Services offered to physically disabled students:** Note-taking services; Reader services; Tape recorders; Tutors. **Career services:** Career assessment; Career/job search classes; Internships

FACILITIES
Housing: Apartments for married students; Apartments for single students; Men's dorms; Special housing for disabled student; Women's dorms 100% of campus accessible to physically diasbled. **Computers:** Students can register for classes online. Administrative functions (other than registration) can be performed online. Undergraduates are required to own a computer.

CAMPUS LIFE
Activities: Campus Ministries; International Student Organization; Student government 11 registered organizations, 2 honor societies, 1 religious organization. **Athletics (Intercollegiate):** *Men:* basketball, cross-country, golf, soccer, track/field (outdoor), track/field (indoor). *Women:* basketball, cross-country, golf, soccer, softball, track/field (outdoor), track/field (indoor), volleyball. **On-Campus Highlights:** Corum Student Union, Bernice Hansen Athletic Center, Campus Bookstore Atrium, Faber Hall Seating Area, Gordon Music Hall **Environmental Initiatives:** On campus dialogue and focus on sustainability issues.

ADMISSIONS
Freshman Academic Profile: 60% from public high schools. **Test Scores:** Minimum paper TOEFL 500. **Basis for Candidate Selection:** *Very important factors considered include:* academic GPA, application essay, recommendation(s), religious affiliation/commitment. *Important factors considered include:* standardized test scores, extracurricular activities, character/personal qualities, volunteer work.level of applicant's interest. *Other factors considered include:* rigor of secondary school record, talent/ability, work experience. **Freshman Admission Requirements:** High school diploma is required and GED is accepted **Transfer Admission Requirements:** college transcript(s), essay or personal statement, Minimum college GPA of 2.5 required. Lowest grade transferable C.

COSTS AND FINANCIAL AID
Types of Aid: *Need-based scholarships/grants:* College/university scholarship or grant aid from institutional funds; Private scholarships; State scholarships/grants. *Loans:* Direct Subsidized Stafford Loans; Direct Unsubsidized Stafford Loans. *Student Employment:* Federal Work-Study Program available. **Financial Aid Statistics:** 100% freshmen, 98% undergrads receive any aid. **Criteria for awarding aid:** *Need-based:* Academics, Job skills, Leadership, Minority status, Religious affiliation *Non-need-based:* Academics, Job skills, Leadership, Minority status, Religious affiliation.

GRAND VALLEY STATE UNIVERSITY

1 Campus Drive, Allendale, MI 49401
Phone: 616-331-2025 · **Financial Aid Phone:** 616-331-3234
E-mail: admissions@gvsu.edu · **CEEB Code:** 1258
Fax: 616-331-2000 · **Website:** www.gvsu.edu · **ACT Code:** 2005

This public school was founded in 1960. It has a 1391 acre campus.

RATINGS
Admissions Selectivity Rating: 77   **Fire Safety Rating:** 90   **Green Rating:** 97

STUDENTS AND FACULTY
Enrollment: 21,824. **Student Body:** 59% female, 41% male, 7% out-of-state, 1% international (68 countries represented). Asian 3%, African American 5%, Caucasian 82%, Hispanic 5%, Native American <1%, Pacific Islander <1%, Two or more races 4%, Race unknown <1%. **Retention and Graduation:** 83% freshmen return for sophomore year. 34% freshmen graduate within 4 years. 66% freshmen graduate within 6 years. **Faculty:** Student/faculty ratio 17:1. 1,183 full-time faculty, 78% hold PhDs, 16% are members of minority groups, 51% are women. 0% of classes are taught by teaching assistants.

ACADEMICS
Degrees: Bachelor's; Certificate; Doctoral/Professional; Master's; Post-Bachelor's certificate; Post-Master's certificate **Classes:** Most classes have 10-19 students. Most lab/discussion sessions have 10-19 students. **Most popular majors:** Education, General; Registered Nursing/Registered Nurse; Business/Commerce, General. **Special Study Options:** Distance learning; Double major; Dual enrollment; English as a Second Language (ESL); Honors program; Independent study; Internships; Student-designed major; Study abroad; Teacher certification program. **Honors programs:** Honor's College **Combined degree programs:** BA/JD; BA/MEng. **Disability Services offered to physically disabled students:** Reader services; Tape recorders; Tutors. **Career services:** Alumni network; Alumni services; Career assessment; Career/job search classes; Internships; Regional alumni

FACILITIES
Housing: Apartments for married students; Apartments for single students; Coed dorms; Fraternity/sorority housing; Theme housing 99% of campus accessible to physically diasbled. **Special Academic Facilities/Equipment:** two Great Lakes research vessels, audio-visual center, performance/recital hall, pipe organ, physical therapy/human performance lab. **Computers:** 100% of classrooms, 63% of dorms, 100% of libraries, 100% of dining areas, 100% of student union, have wireless network access. Students·can register for classes online. Administrative functions (other than registration) can be performed online.

CAMPUS LIFE
Environment: City **Activities:** Campus Ministries; Choral groups; Concert band; Dance; Drama/theater; International Student Organization; Jazz band; Literary magazine; Marching band; Music ensembles; Musical theater; Pep band; Radio station; Student government; Student newspaper; Symphony orchestra; Television station 301 registered organizations, 20 honor societies, 20 religious organizations. 11 fraternities, 11 sororities. **Athletics (Intercollegiate):** *Men:* baseball, basketball, cross-country, diving, football, golf, swimming, tennis, track/field (outdoor), track/field (indoor). *Women:*

basketball, cross-country, diving, golf, soccer, softball, swimming, tennis, track/field (outdoor), track/field (indoor), volleyball. **On-Campus Highlights:** Living Centers, Cook DeVos Center for Health Sciences, Recreation Center and Fieldhouse, Laker Turf Building, Kirkhof Center **Environmental Initiatives:** Climate Mitigation: GVSU is a signatory to American College and University Presidents Climate Commitment and has recently completed its Climate Action Plan and set a goal of climate neutrality by 2037. The climate action plan is available online. Currently there are over 650 colleges and universities that have signed on to this agreement. LEED construction projects and bus transportation are both important climate mitigation strategies. GVSU has completed and certified 10 LEED projects with 2 more LEED projects under construction. These 12 LEED projects represent over 925,000 square feet and ~19% of total square footage. Annual bus ridership is over ~ 2MM bus rides per year for faculty and students and saves millions of dollars in annual fuel purchases and vehicle maintenance costs while reducing our carbon footprint.

ADMISSIONS

Freshman Academic Profile: Average high school GPA 3.6. 16% in top 10% of high school class, 45% in top 25% of high school class, 84% in top 50% of high school class. 78% from public high schools. **Test Scores:** SAT Math middle 50% range 530-610. SAT EBRW middle 50% range 530-620. ACT middle 50% range 21-26. Minimum paper TOEFL 550. **Basis for Candidate Selection:** *Very important factors considered include:* rigor of secondary school record, academic GPA. *Important factors considered include:* standardized test scores. *Other factors considered include:* class rank, application essay, recommendation(s), extracurricular activities, talent/ability, first generation, alumni/ae relation, volunteer work, work experience. **Freshman Admission Requirements:** High school diploma is required and GED is accepted *Academic units required:* 4 English, 3 math, 3 science, 2 science labs, 2 foreign language, 3 social studies. **Freshman Admission Statistics:** 17,509 applied, 80.9% admitted, 29% enrolled. **Transfer Admission Requirements:** college transcript(s), statement of good standing from prior institution(s). Minimum college GPA of 2.5 required. Lowest grade transferable D. **General Admission Information:** Application fee $30. Priority deadline 5/1. Nonfall registration accepted.

COSTS AND FINANCIAL AID

Annual out-of-state tuition $17,688. Room and board $9,000. Average book expense $700. **Required Forms and Deadlines:** FAFSA. **Notification of Awards:** Applicants will be notified of awards on a rolling basis beginning 1/16. **Types of Aid:** *Need-based scholarships/grants:* College/university scholarship or grant aid from institutional funds; Federal Pell; Private scholarships; SEOG; State scholarships/grants. *Loans:* Direct PLUS loans; Direct Subsidized Stafford Loans; Direct Unsubsidized Stafford Loans. *Student Employment:* Federal Work-Study Program available. Institutional employment available. **Financial Aid Statistics:** 86% needy freshmen, 84% needy undergrads receive need-based scholarship or grant aid. 6% freshmen, 4% undergrads receive non-need-based scholarship or grant aid. 86% freshmen, 88% undergrads receive need-based self-help aid. 1% freshmen, 1% undergrads receive athletic scholarships. 86% freshmen, 83% undergrads receive any aid. 74% undergrads borrow to pay for school. Average cumulative indebtedness $29,656. **Criteria for awarding aid:** *Non-need-based:* Academics, Alumni affiliation, Art, Athletics, Music/drama, State/district residency.

GRAND VIEW UNIVERSITY

1200 Grandview Avenue, Des Moines, IA 50316-1599
Phone: 515-263-2810 · **Financial Aid Phone:** 515-263-2963
E-mail: admissions@GrandView.edu · **CEEB Code:** 6251
Fax: 515-263-2974 · **Website:** www.admissions.grandview.edu · **ACT Code:** 1316

This private school, affiliated with the Lutheran Church, was founded in 1896. It has a 35 acre campus.

RATINGS
Admissions Selectivity Rating: 71   **Fire Safety Rating:** 60*   **Green Rating:** 60*

STUDENTS AND FACULTY
Enrollment: 2,079. **Student Body:** 58% female, 42% male, 13% out-of-state, 2% international (16 countries represented). Asian 3%, African American 8%, Caucasian 74%, Hispanic 3%, Native American <1%, Pacific Islander <1%, Two or more races 3%, Race unknown 7%.
Retention and Graduation: 69% freshmen return for sophomore year. **Faculty:** Student/faculty ratio 13:1. 95 full-time faculty, 68% hold PhDs, 7% are members of minority groups, 56% are women. 0% of classes are taught by teaching assistants.

ACADEMICS
Degrees: Bachelor's; Certificate; Master's; Post-Bachelor's certificate **Classes:** Most classes have 20-29 students. Most lab/discussion sessions have 20-29 students. **Most popular majors:** Education, General; Nursing/Registered Nurse (Rn, Asn, Bsn, Msn); Business/Commerce, General. **Special Study Options:** Accelerated program; Cooperative education program; Cross-registration; Distance learning; Double major; Dual enrollment; Exchange student program (domestic); Honors program; Independent study; Internships; Liberal arts/career combination; Student-designed major; Study abroad; Teacher certification program; Weekend college. **Honors programs:** Logos Honors Program.

FACILITIES
Housing: Apartments for single students; Coed dorms **Special Academic Facilities/Equipment:** Danish American Archives. **Computers:** Administrative functions (other than registration) can be performed online.

CAMPUS LIFE
Activities: Campus Ministries; Choral groups; Concert band; Dance; Drama/theater; International Student Organization; Jazz band; Literary magazine; Music ensembles; Pep band; Radio station; Student government; Student newspaper; Television station 28 registered organizations, 1 religious organization. **Athletics (Intercollegiate):** *Men:* baseball, basketball, cross-country, golf, soccer. *Women:* basketball, cross-country, golf, soccer, softball, volleyball.

ADMISSIONS
Freshman Academic Profile: Average high school GPA 3.2. 15% in top 10% of high school class, 33% in top 25% of high school class, 64% in top 50% of high school class. **Test Scores:** SAT Math middle 50% range 400-480. SAT EBRW middle 50% range 380-450. ACT middle 50% range 19-23. Minimum paper TOEFL 550. **Basis for Candidate Selection:** *Very important factors considered include:* rigor of secondary school record, class rank, academic GPA, character/personal qualities. *Important factors considered include:* standardized test scores. *Other factors considered include:* extracurricular activities, talent/ability, alumni/ae relation, volunteer work, work experience. **Freshman Admission Requirements:** High school diploma is required and GED is accepted *Academic units recommended:* 4 English, 3 math, 3 science, 2 foreign language, 3 social studies. **Freshman Admission Statistics:** 805 applied, 95.7% admitted, 39% enrolled. **Transfer Admission Requirements:** college transcript(s), Minimum college GPA of 2.0 required. Lowest grade transferable D. **General Admission Information:** Regular application deadline 8/15. Nonfall registration accepted. Admission may be deferred for a maximum of 1 semester.

COSTS AND FINANCIAL AID
Annual tuition $22,986. Room and board $7,554. Required fees $530. Average book expense $880. **Required Forms and Deadlines:** FAFSA. **Notification of Awards:** Applicants will be notified of awards on a rolling basis beginning 3/1. **Types of Aid:** *Need-based scholarships/grants:* College/university scholarship or grant aid from institutional funds; Federal Pell; Private scholarships; SEOG; State scholarships/grants. *Loans: Student Employment:* Federal Work-Study Program available. Institutional employment available. **Financial Aid Statistics:** 88% needy freshmen, 92% needy undergrads receive need-based scholarship or grant aid. 20% freshmen, 11% undergrads receive non-need-based scholarship or grant aid. 80% freshmen, 88% undergrads receive need-based self-help aid. 63% freshmen, 10% undergrads receive athletic scholarships. 97% freshmen, 99% undergrads receive any aid. **Criteria for awarding aid:** *Need-based:* Academics, Leadership *Non-need-based:* Academics, Alumni affiliation, Art, Athletics, Leadership, Music/drama.

GRANTHAM UNIVERSITY

7200 NW 86th Street, Kansas City, MO 64153
E-mail: admissions@grantham.edu
Fax: 816-595-5757 · **Website:** http://www.grantham.edu/

This is a proprietary school.

RATINGS
Admissions Selectivity Rating: 0   **Fire Safety Rating:** 60*   **Green Rating:** 60*

ACADEMICS
Degrees: Associate; Bachelor's; Master's **Classes:** Most classes have 20-29 students. **Special Study Options:** Accelerated program; Distance learning; External degree program; Independent study.

ADMISSIONS

Freshman Admission Requirements: High school diploma is required and GED is accepted **Transfer Admission Requirements:** High school transcript, college transcript(s), Minimum college GPA of 2.0 required. Lowest grade transferable C. **General Admission Information:** Nonfall registration accepted.

COSTS AND FINANCIAL AID

Annual tuition $7,500.

GREEN MOUNTAIN COLLEGE

One Brennan Circle, Poultney, VT 05764-1199
Phone: 802-287-8000 · **Financial Aid Phone:** 802-287-8209
E-mail: admiss@greenmtn.edu · **CEEB Code:** 3418

Fax: 802-287-8099 • Website: www.greenmtn.edu • ACT Code: 4302 This private school, affiliated with the Methodist Church, was founded in 1834. It has a 155 acre campus.

RATINGS

Admissions Selectivity Rating: 79   **Fire Safety Rating:** 97   **Green Rating:** 99

STUDENTS AND FACULTY

Enrollment: 457. **Student Body:** 57% female, 43% male, 82% out-of-state, 1% international (12 countries represented). Asian 1%, African American 6%, Caucasian 65%, Hispanic 4%, Native American 1%, Two or more races 2%, Race unknown 19%.
Retention and Graduation: 74% freshmen return for sophomore year. 41% freshmen graduate within 4 years. 51% freshmen graduate within 6 years.
Faculty: Student/faculty ratio 14:1. 40 full-time faculty, 93% hold PhDs, 5% are members of minority groups, 38% are women. 0% of classes are taught by teaching assistants.

ACADEMICS

Degrees: Bachelor's; Certificate; Master's **Classes:** Most classes have 20-29 students. Most lab/discussion sessions have 20-29 students. **Most popular majors:** Agroecology And Sustainable Agriculture; Environmental Studies; Parks, Recreation And Leisure Studies. **Special Study Options:** Accelerated program; Distance learning; Double major; Dual enrollment; Exchange student program (domestic); Honors program; Independent study; Internships; Liberal arts/career combination; Student-designed major; Study abroad; Teacher certification program. **Combined degree programs:** BA/JD. **Disability Services offered to physically disabled students:** Note-taking services; Reader services; Tape recorders; Tutors. **Career services:** Alumni network; Alumni services; Career assessment; Career/job search classes; Internships; Regional alumni

FACILITIES

Housing: Coed dorms; Theme housing; Wellness housing **Special Academic Facilities/Equipment:** Welsh Heritage Collection, Rare Books Room, Feick Arts Center **Computers:** Students can register for classes online. Administrative functions (other than registration) can be performed online.

CAMPUS LIFE

Environment: Rural **Activities:** Choral groups; Concert band; Drama/theater; International Student Organization; Jazz band; Literary magazine; Model UN; Music ensembles; Student government; Student newspaper; Student-run film society 25 registered organizations, 2 honor societies, 2 religious organizations. **Athletics (Intercollegiate):** *Men:* basketball, cross-country, golf, lacrosse, skiing (downhill/alpine), soccer, tennis. *Women:* basketball, cross-country, lacrosse, skiing (downhill/alpine), soccer, softball, tennis, volleyball. **On-Campus Highlights:** Griswold Library, Cerridwen Farm, Withey Student Center, Moses Coffeehouse, Poultney River **Environmental Initiatives:** 1) In 2011, Green Mountain College became the second college in the country to achieve climate neutrality under the ACUPCC agreement and the first to do it by reducing emissions by 50%. The reductions came from an integrated approach of replacing windows, upgrading to more efficient lights and appliances, and building a $5.8 million combined heat and power plant to shift the primary heat source from number six fuel oil to locally sourced woodchips, while also producing electricity with high pressure steam.

ADMISSIONS

Test Scores: SAT Math middle 50% range 475-615. SAT EBRW middle 50% range 450-560. ACT middle 50% range 21-26. Minimum internet-based TOEFL 61. Minimum paper TOEFL 500. **Basis for Candidate Selection:** *Very important factors considered include:* academic GPA, recommendation(s). *Important factors considered include:* rigor of secondary school record, class rank, application essay, standardized test scores, interview, extracurricular activities, volunteer work.level of applicant's interest. *Other factors considered include:* talent/ability, character/personal qualities, alumni/ae relation, religious affiliation/commitment, racial/ethnic status, work experience. **Freshman Admission Requirements:** High school diploma is required and GED is accepted *Academic units required:* 4 English, 3 math, 3 science, 2 science labs, 1 foreign language, 3 social studies, 1 history, 5 academic electives, *Academic units recommended:* 4 math, 4 science, 2 foreign language, 2 history. **Freshman Admission Statistics:** 677 applied, 81.8% admitted, 20% enrolled. **Transfer Admission Requirements:** High school transcript, college transcript(s), essay or personal statement, statement of good standing from prior institution(s). Minimum college GPA of 2.0 required. Lowest grade transferable C-. **General Admission Information:** Application fee $30. Priority deadline 3/1. Nonfall registration accepted. Admission may be deferred for a maximum of 1 year.

COSTS AND FINANCIAL AID

Annual tuition $35,560. Room and board $11,722. Required fees $1,442. **Required Forms and Deadlines:** FAFSA. **Notification of Awards:** Applicants will be notified of awards on a rolling basis beginning 12/16. **Types of Aid:** *Need-based scholarships/grants:* College/university scholarship or grant aid from institutional funds; Federal Pell; Private scholarships; SEOG; State scholarships/grants. *Loans:* Direct PLUS loans; Direct Subsidized Stafford Loans; Direct Unsubsidized Stafford Loans. *Student Employment:* Federal Work-Study Program available. Institutional employment available. **Financial Aid Statistics:** 100% needy freshmen, 100% needy undergrads receive need-based scholarship or grant aid. 14% freshmen, 11% undergrads receive non-need-based scholarship or grant aid. 82% freshmen, 84% undergrads receive need-based self-help aid. 0% freshmen, 0% undergrads receive athletic scholarships. 96% freshmen, 94% undergrads receive any aid. 74% undergrads borrow to pay for school. Average cumulative indebtedness $38,701. **Criteria for awarding aid:** *Need-based:* Academics, Alumni affiliation, Religious affiliation *Non-need-based:* Academics, Alumni affiliation, Religious affiliation, State/district residency.

GREENVILLE COLLEGE

315 E. College Ave., Greenville, IL 62246
Phone: 618-664-7100 · **Financial Aid Phone:** 618-664-7108
E-mail: admissions@greenville.edu · **CEEB Code:** 1256
Fax: 618-664-9841 · **Website:** www.greenville.edu · **ACT Code:** 1032

This private school, affiliated with the Free Methodist Church, was founded in 1892. It has a 40 acre campus.

RATINGS

Admissions Selectivity Rating: 80   **Fire Safety Rating:** 97   **Green Rating:** 60*

STUDENTS AND FACULTY

Enrollment: 944. **Student Body:** 49% female, 51% male, 31% out-of-state, 4% international (14 countries represented). Asian 1%, African American 14%, Caucasian 69%, Hispanic 6%, Native American <1%, Pacific Islander 0%, Two or more races 2%, Race unknown 4%.
Retention and Graduation: 73% freshmen return for sophomore year. 36% freshmen graduate within 4 years. 42% freshmen graduate within 6 years.
Faculty: Student/faculty ratio 13:1. 58 full-time faculty, 72% hold PhDs, 14% are members of minority groups, 40% are women. 0% of classes are taught by teaching assistants.

ACADEMICS

Degrees: Bachelor's; Master's **Classes:** Most classes have 10-19 students. Most lab/discussion sessions have fewer than 10 students. **Most popular majors:** Elementary Education And Teaching; Biology/Biological Sciences, General; Music Management. **Special Study Options:** Accelerated program; Cooperative education program; Cross-registration; Double major; External degree program; Honors program; Independent study; Internships; Liberal arts/career combination; Student-designed major; Study abroad; Teacher certification program. **Honors programs:** Greenville University's McAllaster Scholars Program is an academic program that was established in 1995 to provide a "value-added" dimension to the excellent, Christ-centered education students regularly receive at Greenville University. The Honors Program consists of a blend of enriched sections of several general education classes, special honors seminars, and experiential learning opportunities offered in an enhanced educational environment that strives for small class sizes to encourage total student participation, facilitate spirited discussions and promote greater student-faculty interaction. Outside the classroom, the Honors Programs offers a co-curricular program consisting of diversified cultural, social and educationally-oriented activities and events developed especially for program members. The Honors Program encourages its members to be persons with multi-dimensional interests who participate in a wide range of university sponsored events, activities, and organizations. Students admitted to The Honors Program automatically become members of The Honors Society, the student organization within the program which elects officers who assist with the planning and implementation of the aforementioned activities and other community building opportunities. The Greenville College Honors Program strives to emulate the guidelines, "Basic Characteristics of a Fully-Developed Honors Program," developed by the National Collegiate Honors Council. It, also, cooperates with member institutions of the Council of Christian Colleges and Universities by encouraging GC students to participate in one of the nearly twenty semester-long academic programs coordinated and promoted by CCCU that are offered at off-campus sites, both domestic and abroad. Locally, The Honors Program is administered by a director who is assisted by an Honors Council composed of faculty and students. To graduate with Honors Program recognition, students must fulfill the requirements of their academic major, earn a minimum of 25 credit hours of honors work, maintain a cumulative grade point average of 3.50 and complete a Departmental Honors Thesis under the supervision of a three-person faculty thesis committee. Graduates of the Honors Program are awarded a special medallion and receive special recognition at commencement. **Disability Services offered to physically disabled students:** Tutors. Career/job search classes

FACILITIES

Housing: Apartments for single students; Coed dorms; Men's dorms; Special housing for international students; Women's dorms 40% of campus accessible to physically diasbled. **Special Academic Facilities/Equipment:** Sculpture museum, sports training facility **Computers:** Administrative functions (other than registration) can be performed online.

CAMPUS LIFE

Environment: Village **Activities:** Campus Ministries; Choral groups; Concert band; Drama/theater; Jazz band; Marching band; Music ensembles; Musical theater; Pep band; Radio station; Student government; Student newspaper 25 registered organizations, 6 honor societies, 2 religious organizations. **Athletics (Intercollegiate):** *Men:* baseball, basketball, cross-country, football, soccer, tennis, track/field (outdoor), track/field (indoor). *Women:* basketball, cross-country, soccer, softball, tennis, track/field (outdoor), track/field (indoor), volleyball. **On-Campus Highlights:** Jo's Java, Sims Student Union, Fitness Training Center, Ruby E. Dare Library, Whitlock Music Center

ADMISSIONS

Test Scores: SAT Math middle 50% range 430-550. SAT EBRW middle 50% range 450-570. ACT middle 50% range 19-24. Minimum internet-based TOEFL 79. **Basis for Candidate Selection:** *Very important factors considered include:* academic GPA, standardized test scores. *Important factors considered include:* character/personal qualities, religious affiliation/commitment. **Freshman Admission Requirements:** High school diploma is required and GED is accepted *Academic units recommended:* 4 English, 2 math, 3 science, 1 science labs, 2 foreign language, 2 social studies, 1 history. **Freshman Admission Statistics:** 1,287 applied, 66.2% admitted, 26% enrolled. **Transfer Admission Requirements:** High school transcript, college transcript(s), essay or personal statement, Minimum college GPA of 2.0 required. Lowest grade transferable C. **General Admission Information:** Priority deadline 5/1. Regular application deadline 8/15. Nonfall registration accepted. Admission may be deferred for a maximum of One year.

COSTS AND FINANCIAL AID

Annual tuition $26,788. Room and board $9,048. Required fees $330. Average book expense $1,000. **Required Forms and Deadlines:** FAFSA. **Notification of Awards:** Applicants will be notified of awards on a rolling basis beginning 11/1. **Types of Aid:** *Need-based scholarships/grants:* College/university scholarship or grant aid from institutional funds; Federal Pell; Private scholarships; SEOG; State scholarships/grants. *Loans:* Direct PLUS loans; Direct Subsidized Stafford Loans; Direct Unsubsidized Stafford Loans. *Student Employment:* Federal Work-Study Program available. Institutional employment available. **Financial Aid Statistics:** 100% needy freshmen, 100% needy undergrads receive need-based scholarship or grant aid. 13% freshmen, 10% undergrads receive non-need-based scholarship or grant aid. 83% freshmen, 84% undergrads receive need-based self-help aid. 0% freshmen, 0% undergrads receive athletic scholarships. 94% freshmen, 92% undergrads receive any aid. 82% undergrads borrow to pay for school. Average cumulative indebtedness $33,083. **Criteria for awarding aid:** *Need-based:* Academics, Alumni affiliation, Leadership, Music/drama, Religious affiliation *Non-need-based:* Academics, Alumni affiliation, Leadership, Music/drama, Religious affiliation.

GRINNELL COLLEGE

1103 Park Street, Grinnell, IA 50112-1690
Phone: 641-269-3600 · **Financial Aid Phone:** 641-269-3250
E-mail: admission@grinnell.edu · **CEEB Code:** 6252
Fax: 641-269-4800 · **Website:** www.grinnell.edu · **ACT Code:** 1318

This private school was founded in 1846. It has a 120 acre campus.

RATINGS

Admissions Selectivity Rating: 95   **Fire Safety Rating:** 92   **Green Rating:** 76

STUDENTS AND FACULTY

Enrollment: 1,660. **Student Body:** 54% female, 46% male, 92% out-of-state, 20% international (51 countries represented). Asian 8%, African American 6%, Caucasian 51%, Hispanic 7%, Native American 0%, Pacific Islander 0%, Two or more races 4%, Race unknown 4%.
Retention and Graduation: 96% freshmen return for sophomore year. 84% freshmen graduate within 4 years. 87% freshmen graduate within 6 years. 19% grads go on to further study within 1 year. 12% grads pursue arts and sciences degrees. 1.5% grads pursue law degrees. 2% grads pursue business degrees. 2.8% grads pursue medical degrees. **Faculty:** Student/faculty ratio 9:1. 177 full-time faculty, 99% hold PhDs, 19% are members of minority groups, 46% are women. 0% of classes are taught by teaching assistants.

ACADEMICS

Degrees: Bachelor's **Most popular majors:** Biology/Biological Sciences, General; Economics, General; Political Science And Government, General. **Special Study Options:** Accelerated program; Double major; Dual enrollment; Independent study; Internships; Liberal arts/career combination; Student-designed major; Study abroad; Teacher certification program. **Disability Services offered to physically disabled students:** Note-taking services; Reader services; Tape recorders; Tutors. **Career services:** Alumni network; Alumni services; Career assessment; Internships; Regional alumni

FACILITIES

Housing: Coed dorms; Cooperative housing; Special housing for disabled student; Theme housing; Wellness housing 85% of campus accessible to physically diasbled. **Special Academic Facilities/Equipment:** Art galleries, language lab, Data Analysis and Social Inquiry Lab, nuclear magnetic resonance spectrometer, electron microscope, 3D printer, 24-inch reflecting telescope, 365-acre environmental research area. **Computers:** 100% of classrooms, 100% of dorms, 100% of libraries, 100% of dining areas, 100% of student union, 100% of common outdoor areas have wireless network access. Administrative functions (other than registration) can be performed online.

CAMPUS LIFE

Environment: Village **Activities:** Campus Ministries; Choral groups; Concert band; Dance; Drama/theater; International Student Organization; Jazz band; Literary magazine; Model UN; Music ensembles; Musical theater; Pep band; Radio station; Student government; Student newspaper; Student-run film society; Symphony orchestra; Yearbook 240 registered organizations, 2 honor societies, 12 religious organizations. **Athletics (Intercollegiate):** *Men:* baseball, basketball, cross-country, diving, football, golf, soccer, swimming, tennis, track/field (outdoor), track/field (indoor). *Women:* basketball, cross-country, diving, golf, soccer, softball, swimming, tennis, track/field (outdoor), track/field (indoor), volleyball. **On-Campus Highlights:** Two building on campus are listed on the National Register of Historic Places: Mears Cottage and Goodnow Hall, Faulconer Gallery, Joe Rosenfield '25 Center, Bucksbaum Center for the Arts, Charles Benson Bear '39 Recreation and Athletic Center **Environmental Initiatives:** All new buildings are LEED certified.

ADMISSIONS

Freshman Academic Profile: 69% in top 10% of high school class, 91% in top 25% of high school class, 99% in top 50% of high school class. **Test Scores:** SAT Math middle 50% range 670-770. SAT EBRW middle 50% range 640-740. ACT middle 50% range 30-34. **Basis for Candidate Selection:** *Very important factors considered include:* rigor of secondary school record, class rank, academic GPA, recommendation(s). *Important factors considered include:* application essay, standardized test scores, extracurricular activities, talent/ability. *Other factors considered include:* interview, character/personal qualities, first generation, alumni/ae relation, geographical residence, state residency, racial/ethnic status, volunteer work, work experience, level of applicant's interest. **Freshman Admission Requirements:** High school diploma is required and GED is accepted *Academic units recommended:* 4 English, 4 math, 3 science, 3 science labs, 3 foreign language, 3 social studies, 3 history. **Freshman Admission Statistics:** 5,850 applied, 28.9% admitted, 26% enrolled. **Transfer Admission Requirements:** High school transcript, college transcript(s), essay or personal statement, standardized test scores, statement of good standing from prior institution(s). Lowest grade transferable C. **General Admission Information:** Regular application deadline 1/15. Nonfall registration accepted. Admission may be deferred for a maximum of 1 year.

COSTS AND FINANCIAL AID
Annual tuition $51,924. Room and board $12,810. Required fees $468. Average book expense $900. **Required Forms and Deadlines:** CSS/Financial Aid PROFILE; FAFSA; Noncustodial PROFILE. **Notification of Awards:** Applicants will be notified of awards on or about 4/1. **Types of Aid:** *Need-based scholarships/grants:* College/university scholarship or grant aid from institutional funds; Federal Pell; Private scholarships; SEOG; State scholarships/grants. *Loans:* Direct PLUS loans; Direct Subsidized Stafford Loans; Direct Unsubsidized Stafford Loans. *Student Employment:* Federal Work-Study Program available. Institutional employment available. **Financial Aid Statistics:** 99% needy freshmen, 100% needy undergrads receive need-based scholarship or grant aid. 14% freshmen, 11% undergrads receive non-need-based scholarship or grant aid. 100% freshmen, 100% undergrads receive need-based self-help aid. 0% freshmen, 0% undergrads receive athletic scholarships. 88% freshmen, 87% undergrads receive any aid. 50% undergrads borrow to pay for school. Average cumulative indebtedness $18,780. **Criteria for awarding aid:** *Non-need-based:* Academics; State/district residency.

GROVE CITY COLLEGE

100 Campus Drive, Grove City, PA 16127-2104
Phone: 724-458-2100 · **Financial Aid Phone:** 724-458-3300
E-mail: admissions@gcc.edu · **CEEB Code:** 2277
Fax: 724-458-3395 · **Website:** www.gcc.edu · **ACT Code:** 3582

This private school was founded in 1876. It has a 180 acre campus.

RATINGS
Admissions Selectivity Rating: 86   **Fire Safety Rating:** 94   **Green Rating:** 63

STUDENTS AND FACULTY
Enrollment: 2,327. **Student Body:** 49% female, 51% male, 44% out-of-state, 1% international (13 countries represented). Asian 2%, African American 1%, Caucasian 92%, Hispanic 1%, Native American <1%, Pacific Islander 0%, Two or more races 3%, Race unknown 0%.
Retention and Graduation: 89% freshmen return for sophomore year. 78% freshmen graduate within 4 years. 83% freshmen graduate within 6 years. 12% grads go on to further study within 1 year. 9% grads pursue arts and sciences degrees. 0.8% grads pursue law degrees. 0% grads pursue business degrees. 1.3% grads pursue medical degrees. **Faculty:** Student/faculty ratio 13:1. 155 full-time faculty, 85% hold PhDs, 5% are members of minority groups, 34% are women. 0% of classes are taught by teaching assistants.

ACADEMICS
Degrees: Bachelor's **Classes:** Most classes have 10-19 students. **Most popular majors:** Speech Communication And Rhetoric; Mechanical Engineering; Biology/Biological Sciences, General. **Special Study Options:** Accelerated program; Distance learning; Double major; Dual enrollment; Independent study; Internships; Study abroad; Teacher certification program. **Career services:** Alumni network; Alumni services; Career assessment; Career/job search classes; Internships; Regional alumni

FACILITIES
Housing: Apartments for single students; Men's dorms; Wellness housing; Women's dorms 10% of campus accessible to physically disabled. **Special Academic Facilities/Equipment:** Fine arts center, language lab, on-campus preschool, technological learning center. **Computers:** 100% of classrooms, 15% of dorms, 100% of libraries, 33% of dining areas, 100% of student union, 10% of common outdoor areas have wireless network access. Students can register for classes online. Administrative functions (other than registration) can be performed online. Undergraduates are required to own a computer.

CAMPUS LIFE
Environment: Village **Activities:** Campus Ministries; Choral groups; Concert band; Dance; Drama/theater; International Student Organization; Jazz band; Literary magazine; Marching band; Music ensembles; Musical theater; Opera; Pep band; Radio station; Student government; Student newspaper; Symphony

orchestra; Television station; Yearbook 130 registered organizations, 19 honor societies, 22 religious organizations. 8 fraternities, 8 sororities. **Athletics (Intercollegiate):** *Men:* baseball, basketball, cross-country, diving, football, golf, soccer, swimming, tennis, track/field (outdoor). *Women:* basketball, cheerleading, cross-country, diving, golf, soccer, softball, swimming, tennis, track/field (outdoor), volleyball, water polo. **On-Campus Highlights:** Student Union, Chapel, Hall of Arts and Letters, Fitness Center, STEM Hall **Environmental Initiatives:** Use of high-efficiency condensing boilers in newer construction or existing retrofits.

ADMISSIONS
Freshman Academic Profile: Average high school GPA 3.7. 35% in top 10% of high school class, 84% in top 25% of high school class, 90% in top 50% of high school class. 59% from public high schools. **Test Scores:** SAT Math middle 50% range 534-662. SAT EBRW middle 50% range 537-587. ACT middle 50% range 23-32. Minimum internet-based TOEFL 79. Minimum paper TOEFL 550. **Basis for Candidate Selection:** *Very important factors considered include:* rigor of secondary school record, academic GPA, application essay, standardized test scores, interview, character/personal qualities, level of applicant's interest. *Important factors considered include:* recommendation(s), extracurricular activities. *Other factors considered include:* class rank, talent/ability, first generation, alumni/ae relation, geographical residence, state residency, religious affiliation/commitment, racial/ethnic status, volunteer work, work experience. **Freshman Admission Requirements:** High school diploma is required and GED is accepted *Academic units recommended:* 4 English, 3 math, 3 science, 2 science labs, 3 foreign language, 3 social studies, 2 history. **Freshman Admission Statistics:** 1,783 applied, 79.9% admitted, 45% enrolled. **Transfer Admission Requirements:** High school transcript, college transcript(s), essay or personal statement, standardized test scores, statement of good standing from prior institution(s). Minimum college GPA of 2.0 required. Lowest grade transferable C. **General Admission Information:** Application fee $50. Regular application deadline 1/20. Nonfall registration accepted. Admission may be deferred for a maximum of 1 year.

COSTS AND FINANCIAL AID
Average book expense $1,000. **Required Forms and Deadlines:** Institution's own financial aid form. **Notification of Awards:** Applicants will be notified of awards on a rolling basis beginning 3/1. **Types of Aid:** *Need-based scholarships/grants:* College/university scholarship or grant aid from institutional funds; Private scholarships; State scholarships/grants. *Student Employment:* Institutional employment available. **Financial Aid Statistics:** 100% needy freshmen, 98% needy undergrads receive need-based scholarship or grant aid. 12% freshmen, 9% undergrads receive non-need-based scholarship or grant aid. 58% freshmen, 66% undergrads receive need-based self-help aid. 0% freshmen, 0% undergrads receive athletic scholarships. 77% freshmen, 79% undergrads receive any aid. 54% undergrads borrow to pay for school. Average cumulative indebtedness $37,655. **Criteria for awarding aid:** *Need-based:* Academics, Art, Leadership, Minority status, Music/drama, Religious affiliation *Non-need-based:* Academics, Leadership, Music/drama.

See page 946.

GUILFORD COLLEGE

5800 West Friendly Avenue, Greensboro, NC 27410
Phone: 336-316-2100 · **Financial Aid Phone:** 336-316-2410
E-mail: admission@guilford.edu · **CEEB Code:** 5261
Fax: 336-316-2954 · **Website:** https://www.guilford.edu · **ACT Code:** 3106

This private school, affiliated with the Quaker Church, was founded in 1837. It has a 340 acre campus.

RATINGS
Admissions Selectivity Rating: 79   **Fire Safety Rating:** 94   **Green Rating:** 88

STUDENTS AND FACULTY
Enrollment: 1,493. **Student Body:** 54% female, 46% male, 29% out-of-state, 1% international (10 countries represented). Asian 3%, African American 25%, Caucasian 56%, Hispanic 9%, Native American 1%, Pacific Islander <1%, Two or more races 4%, Race unknown 1%.
Retention and Graduation: 66% freshmen return for sophomore year. 45% freshmen graduate within 4 years. 53% freshmen graduate within 6 years. 12% grads go on to further study within 1 year. 50% grads pursue arts and sciences degrees. 18% grads pursue law degrees. 5% grads pursue business degrees. 0% grads pursue medical degrees. **Faculty:** Student/faculty ratio 12:1. 101 full-time

faculty, 85% hold PhDs, 12% are members of minority groups, 52% are women. 0% of classes are taught by teaching assistants.

ACADEMICS

Degrees: Bachelor's; Master's; Post-Bachelor's certificate **Most popular majors:** Psychology, General; Criminal Justice/Safety Studies; Business Administration And Management, General. **Special Study Options:** Cross-registration; Double major; Dual enrollment; Honors program; Independent study; Internships; Student-designed major; Study abroad; Teacher certification program. **Honors programs:** The Honors Program at Guilford College provides a supportive community for students who are committed to achieving academic excellence and have demonstrated the ability to excel. The Guilford Honors Program provides a sequence of classes and research opportunities for students designed to reward, intellectually challenge students, and empower students. Honors classes are small and usually taught as discussion-style seminars. Students complete a senior thesis or project under the supervision of a faculty advisor. Students also attend professional and undergraduate research conferences where they have the opportunity to present papers. ° Guilford College is a participating member of the National Collegiate Honors Council. Membership in the NCHC means that students in the Guilford College Honors Program can participate in the NCHC Honors Semesters. These semester programs are regularly offered in different sites around the world and enable Honors students from across the country to meet and learn in unique settings. ° In recent years, Guilford College students have participated in the Study Abroad programs sponsored by Honors Programs at other colleges and universities. The University of North Carolina at Wilmington offers an Honors Semester Program at the University of Wales Swansea. For more information visit the following site: www.swan.ac.uk. Eastern Illinois University offers an Honors Summer Program at the Universite Catholique de Louvain in Belgium that features archaeological study of historic sites. For more information, one can visit: www.eiu.edu/~honprog/abroad.htm. Both these programs offer college credit courses that are transferable. **Disability Services offered to physically disabled students:** Note-taking services; Reader services; Tape recorders; Tutors. **Career services:** Alumni network; Alumni services; Career assessment; Career/job search classes; Internships; Regional alumni

FACILITIES

Housing: Coed dorms; Theme housing; Women's dorms 97% of campus accessible to physically diasbled. **Special Academic Facilities/Equipment:** ° Cline Observatory; **Computers:** 15% of classrooms, 10% of dorms, 100% of libraries, 100% of dining areas, 50% of student union, 10% of common outdoor areas have wireless network access. Students can register for classes online. Administrative functions (other than registration) can be performed online.

CAMPUS LIFE

Environment: City **Activities:** Campus Ministries; Choral groups; Drama/theater; International Student Organization; Jazz band; Music ensembles; Pep band; Radio station; Student government; Student newspaper; Student-run film society; Yearbook 47 registered organizations, 1 honor society, 8 religious organizations. **Athletics (Intercollegiate):** *Men:* baseball, basketball, cross-country, football, golf, lacrosse, rugby, soccer, tennis. *Women:* basketball, cross-country, lacrosse, rugby, soccer, softball, swimming, tennis, volleyball. **On-Campus Highlights:** Hege Library and Art Gallery, Regan Brown Field House & Physical Education Center & Mary Ragsdale Fitness, Frank Family Science Center, Founders Student Center and the new Grill 155, The Greenleaf Cafe—coffee co-op or Community Center **Environmental Initiatives:** Purchasing policy that only allows Energy Star rated appliances.

ADMISSIONS

Freshman Academic Profile: Average high school GPA 3.2. 13% in top 10% of high school class, 32% in top 25% of high school class, 66% in top 50% of high school class. 75% from public high schools. **Test Scores:** SAT Math middle 50% range 463-558. SAT EBRW middle 50% range 440-585. ACT middle 50% range 19-25. Minimum paper TOEFL 550. **Basis for Candidate Selection:** *Important factors considered include:* rigor of secondary school record, class rank, academic GPA, application essay, standardized test scores, character/personal qualities, volunteer work.level of applicant's interest. *Other factors considered include:* recommendation(s), interview, extracurricular activities, talent/ability, first generation, alumni/ae relation, geographical residence, state residency, religious affiliation/commitment, racial/ethnic status, work experience. **Freshman Admission Requirements:** High school diploma is required and GED is accepted *Academic units recommended:* 4 English, 3 math, 3 science, 2 foreign language, 3 social studies. **Freshman Admission Statistics:** 1,865 applied, 90.7% admitted, 20% enrolled. **Transfer Admission Requirements:** High school transcript, college transcript(s), essay or personal statement, standardized test scores, statement of good standing from prior institution(s). Minimum college GPA of 2.5 required. Lowest grade transferable C. **General Admission Information:** Priority deadline 11/15. Nonfall registration accepted. Admission may be deferred for a maximum of 1 year.

COSTS AND FINANCIAL AID

Required Forms and Deadlines: FAFSA. **Notification of Awards:** Applicants will be notified of awards on a rolling basis beginning 3/1. **Types of**

Aid: *Need-based scholarships/grants:* College/university scholarship or grant aid from institutional funds; Federal Pell; Private scholarships; SEOG; State scholarships/grants. *Loans:* Direct PLUS loans; Direct Subsidized Stafford Loans; Direct Unsubsidized Stafford Loans. *Student Employment:* Federal Work-Study Program available. Institutional employment available. **Financial Aid Statistics:** 91% needy freshmen, 70% needy undergrads receive need-based scholarship or grant aid. 100% freshmen, 71% undergrads receive non-need-based scholarship or grant aid. 80% freshmen, 83% undergrads receive need-based self-help aid. 0% freshmen, 0% undergrads receive athletic scholarships. 98% freshmen, 86% undergrads receive any aid. 88% undergrads borrow to pay for school. Average cumulative indebtedness $26,058. **Criteria for awarding aid:** *Need-based:* Academics *Non-need-based:* Academics.

GUSTAVUS ADOLPHUS COLLEGE

800 College Avenue, Saint Peter, MN 56082
Phone: 507-933-7676 · **Financial Aid Phone:** 507-933-7527
E-mail: admission@gustavus.edu · **CEEB Code:** 6253
Fax: 507-933-7474 · **Website:** www.gustavus.edu · **ACT Code:** 2112

This private school, affiliated with the Lutheran Church, was founded in 1862. It has a 340 acre campus.

RATINGS

Admissions Selectivity Rating: 84   **Fire Safety Rating:** 96   **Green Rating:** 60*

STUDENTS AND FACULTY

Enrollment: 2,190. **Student Body:** 56% female, 44% male, 17% out-of-state, 5% international (26 countries represented). Asian 5%, African American 2%, Caucasian 78%, Hispanic 5%, Native American <1%, Pacific Islander <1%, Two or more races 4%, Race unknown 1%.
Retention and Graduation: 88% freshmen return for sophomore year. 79% freshmen graduate within 4 years. 80% freshmen graduate within 6 years. 36% grads go on to further study within 1 year. 11% grads pursue arts and sciences degrees. 4% grads pursue law degrees. 3% grads pursue business degrees. 5% grads pursue medical degrees. **Faculty:** Student/faculty ratio 11:1. 184 full-time faculty, 91% hold PhDs, 14% are members of minority groups, 52% are women. 0% of classes are taught by teaching assistants.

ACADEMICS

Degrees: Bachelor's **Classes:** Most classes have 20-29 students. Most lab/discussion sessions have 10-19 students. **Most popular majors:** Biology/Biological Sciences, General; Psychology, General; Business/Commerce, General. **Special Study Options:** Cross-registration; Double major; Dual enrollment; Exchange student program (domestic); Honors program; Independent study; Internships; Liberal arts/career combination; Student-designed major; Study abroad; Teacher certification program. **Honors programs:** 3 Crowns Curriculum—Gustavus is unusual in having two general education choices. Both general education programs introduce students to a variety of ways of knowing. Curriculum I students choose from a list of courses to fulfill area requirements. Curriculum II, which is limited to sixty students, is an integrated sequence of courses focused on the development of the Western tradition with comparisons to non-Western cultures, the examination of values, and the theme of the individual and community. Retreats and trips to the Twin Cities for cultural events also foster a sense of community within the group. Although CII attracts some of the college's best students, it is not an honors program. We welcome all students who are intellectually curious and interested in interdisciplinary learning, the examination of values, and good discussion. If you are interested in how things connect—the past to the present, knowledge to your life—if you are interested in the big questions—How did our society come to be this way? What do I value and why? What makes for a good life?—CII may be for you! **Disability Services offered to physically disabled students:** Note-taking services; Reader services; Tape recorders; Tutors. **Career services:** Alumni network; Alumni services; Career assessment; Internships; Regional alumni

FACILITIES

Housing: Apartments for single students; Coed dorms; Special housing for disabled student; Special housing for international students; Theme housing; Wellness housing 100% of campus accessible to physically diasbled. **Special Academic Facilities/Equipment:** Art gallery, mineral museum, electron microscopes, arboretum, 14-inch computer-guided Celestron telescope, artificial intelligence laboratory, materials science laboratory, 300-MHz NMR spectrometer, five-section greenhouse. **Computers:** 100% of dorms, 100% of libraries, 100% of dining areas, 100% of student union, 50% of common outdoor areas have wireless network access. Students can register for classes online. Administrative functions (other than registration) can be performed online.

CAMPUS LIFE

Environment: Village **Activities:** Campus Ministries; Choral groups; Concert band; Dance; Drama/theater; International Student Organization; Jazz band; Literary magazine; Music ensembles; Musical theater; Pep band; Radio station; Student government; Student newspaper; Symphony orchestra; Yearbook 120 registered organizations, 11 honor societies, 8 religious organizations. 5 fraternities, 5 sororities. **Athletics (Intercollegiate):** *Men:* baseball, basketball, cross-country, diving, football, golf, ice hockey, skiing (nordic/cross-country), soccer, swimming, tennis, track/field (outdoor), track/field (indoor). *Women:* basketball, cross-country, diving, golf, gymnastics, ice hockey, skiing (nordic/cross-country), soccer, softball, swimming, tennis, track/field (outdoor), track/field (indoor), volleyball. **On-Campus Highlights:** Campus Center, Courtyard Cafe, Lund Athletic Center, Christ Chapel, Linnaeus Arboretum **Environmental Initiatives:** Seeking to acquire 5 MW of wind generator capacity

ADMISSIONS

Freshman Academic Profile: Average high school GPA 3.6. 33% in top 10% of high school class, 65% in top 25% of high school class, 93% in top 50% of high school class. 94% from public high schools. **Test Scores:** ACT middle 50% range 24-30. Minimum internet-based TOEFL 80. Minimum paper TOEFL 550. **Basis for Candidate Selection:** *Very important factors considered include:* rigor of secondary school record, academic GPA. *Important factors considered include:* class rank, application essay, recommendation(s), interview. *Other factors considered include:* standardized test scores, extracurricular activities, talent/ability, character/personal qualities, first generation, alumni/ae relation, geographical residence, state residency, religious affiliation/commitment, racial/ethnic status, volunteer work, work experience. **Freshman Admission Requirements:** High school diploma is required and GED is accepted *Academic units required:* 4 English, 3 math, 2 science, 2 science labs, 2 foreign language, 2 social studies, 2 history, *Academic units recommended:* 4 math, 3 science, 3 science labs, 3 foreign language, 2 academic electives. **Freshman Admission Statistics:** 4,834 applied, 67.8% admitted, 18% enrolled. **Transfer Admission Requirements:** High school transcript, college transcript(s), essay or personal statement, standardized test scores, statement of good standing from prior institution(s). Minimum college GPA of 2.4 required. Lowest grade transferable 2. **General Admission Information:** Regular application deadline 4/1. Nonfall registration accepted. Admission may be deferred for a maximum of 1 year.

COSTS AND FINANCIAL AID

Annual tuition $44,900. Room and board $9,910. **Required Forms and Deadlines:** FAFSA. **Notification of Awards:** Applicants will be notified of awards on a rolling basis beginning 12/15. **Types of Aid:** *Need-based scholarships/grants:* College/university scholarship or grant aid from institutional funds; Federal Pell; Private scholarships; SEOG; State scholarships/grants. *Loans:* Direct PLUS loans; Direct Subsidized Stafford Loans; Direct Unsubsidized Stafford Loans. *Student Employment:* Federal Work-Study Program available. Institutional employment available. **Financial Aid Statistics:** 100% needy freshmen, 100% needy undergrads receive need-based scholarship or grant aid. 14% freshmen, 9% undergrads receive non-need-based scholarship or grant aid. 100% freshmen, 100% undergrads receive need-based self-help aid. 0% freshmen, 0% undergrads receive athletic scholarships. 96% freshmen, 95% undergrads receive any aid. Average cumulative indebtedness $35,247. **Criteria for awarding aid:** *Need-based:* Minority status, Religious affiliation *Non-need-based:* Academics, Alumni affiliation, Art, Minority status, Music/drama, Religious affiliation.

GWYNEDD MERCY COLLEGE

1325 Sumneytown Pike, Gwynedd Valley, PA 19437-0901
Phone: 215-641-5510 · **Financial Aid Phone:** 215-646-7300
E-mail: admissions@gmercyu.edu · **CEEB Code:** 2278
Fax: 215-641-5556 · **Website:** www.gmercyu.edu · **ACT Code:** 3583

This private school, affiliated with the Roman Catholic Church, was founded in 1948. It has a 160 acre campus.

RATINGS

Admissions Selectivity Rating: 71   **Fire Safety Rating:** 82   **Green Rating:** 60*

STUDENTS AND FACULTY

Enrollment: 1,944. **Student Body:** 76% female, 24% male, 13% out-of-state, <1% international (32 countries represented). Asian 5%, African American 20%, Caucasian 50%, Hispanic 4%, Native American <1%, Pacific Islander 0%, Two or more races 0%, Race unknown 21%.

Retention and Graduation: 84% freshmen return for sophomore year. 60% grads go on to further study within 1 year. **Faculty:** Student/faculty ratio 11:1. 80 full-time faculty, 45% hold PhDs, 5% are members of minority groups, 71% are women. 0% of classes are taught by teaching assistants.

ACADEMICS

Degrees: Associate; Bachelor's; Certificate; Doctoral/Professional; Master's; Post-Bachelor's certificate; Post-Master's certificate **Classes:** Most classes have 50-99 students. Most lab/discussion sessions have 20-29 students. **Most popular majors:** Education, General; Registered Nursing, Nursing Administration, Nursing Research And Clinical Nursing; Business Administration And Management, General. **Special Study Options:** Accelerated program; Cross-registration; Distance learning; Double major; Dual enrollment; Honors program; Independent study; Internships; Liberal arts/career combination; Study abroad; Teacher certification program; Weekend college. **Honors programs:** The Honors Program in Liberal Studies consists of six interdisciplinary, team-taught courses developing the theme of "The Quest for Community and Freedom: The Individual and Society." **Disability Services offered to physically disabled students:** Reader services; Tutors. **Career services:** Alumni services; Career assessment; Internships

FACILITIES

Housing: Coed dorms 95% of campus accessible to physically diasbled. **Special Academic Facilities/Equipment:** Keiss Hall (Health and Science Center), television production room and small theater, computer labs. **Computers:** Students can register for classes online.

CAMPUS LIFE

Environment: Metropolis **Activities:** Campus Ministries; Choral groups; Dance; Literary magazine; Student government; Student newspaper 22 registered organizations, 10 honor societies, 1 religious organization. **Athletics (Intercollegiate):** *Men:* baseball, basketball, cross-country, golf, soccer, tennis, track/field (outdoor), track/field (indoor). *Women:* basketball, cross-country, field hockey, lacrosse, soccer, softball, tennis, track/field (outdoor), track/field (indoor), volleyball. **On-Campus Highlights:** Assumption Hall, The Sister Isabelle Keiss Center for Health and Sciences, The Griffin Complex Student Union and Athletic Facility, Saint Bernard Lobby and Snack Bar, Loyola Hall and Saint Brigid's Hall- Residence Halls

ADMISSIONS

Freshman Academic Profile: Average high school GPA 3.3. 7% in top 10% of high school class, 20% in top 25% of high school class, 57% in top 50% of high school class. 57% from public high schools. **Test Scores:** SAT Math middle 50% range 420-520. SAT EBRW middle 50% range 420-510. ACT middle 50% range 16-23. Minimum paper TOEFL 525. **Basis for Candidate Selection:** *Very important factors considered include:* rigor of secondary school record. *Important factors considered include:* class rank, academic GPA, standardized test scores, recommendation(s), extracurricular activities. *Other factors considered include:* application essay, interview, character/personal qualities, alumni/ae relation, volunteer work, work experience. **Freshman Admission Requirements:** High school diploma is required and GED is accepted *Academic units required:* 4 English, 3 math, 3 science, 1 history, 3 academic electives. **Freshman Admission Statistics:** 904 applied, 90.8% admitted, 27% enrolled. **Transfer Admission Requirements:** High school transcript, college transcript(s), Minimum college GPA of 2.0 required. Lowest grade transferable c. **General Admission Information:** Priority deadline 4/1. Regular application deadline 8/20. Nonfall registration accepted. Admission may be deferred for a maximum of 1 year.

COSTS AND FINANCIAL AID

Annual tuition $25,160. Room and board $9,760. Required fees $450. Average book expense $600. **Required Forms and Deadlines:** FAFSA; Institution's own financial aid form. **Notification of Awards:** Applicants will be notified of awards on a rolling basis beginning 2/15. **Types of Aid:** *Need-based scholarships/grants:* College/university scholarship or grant aid from institutional funds; Federal Pell; Private scholarships; SEOG; State scholarships/grants. *Loans:* Direct PLUS loans; Direct Subsidized Stafford Loans; Direct Unsubsidized Stafford Loans. *Student Employment:* Federal Work-Study Program available. **Financial Aid Statistics:** 97% needy freshmen, 98% needy undergrads receive need-based scholarship or grant aid. 77% freshmen, 77% undergrads receive non-need-based scholarship or grant aid. 91% freshmen, 83% undergrads receive need-based self-help aid. 0% freshmen, 0% undergrads receive athletic scholarships. 97% freshmen, 92% undergrads receive any aid. **Criteria for awarding aid:** *Need-based:* Alumni affiliation *Non-need-based:* Academics, Leadership.

HAMILTON COLLEGE

198 College Hill Road, Clinton, NY 13323
Phone: 315-859-4421 · **Financial Aid Phone:** 800-859-4413
E-mail: admission@hamilton.edu · **CEEB Code:** 2286
Fax: 315-859-4457 · **Website:** www.hamilton.edu · **ACT Code:** 2754

This private school was founded in 1812. It has a 1300 acre campus.

RATINGS
Admissions Selectivity Rating: 97   **Fire Safety Rating:** 92   **Green Rating:** 60*

STUDENTS AND FACULTY
Enrollment: 1,885. **Student Body:** 53% female, 47% male, 70% out-of-state, 6% international (45 countries represented). Asian 7%, African American 4%, Caucasian 64%, Hispanic 9%, Native American <1%, Pacific Islander 0%, Two or more races 4%, Race unknown 6%.
Retention and Graduation: 96% freshmen return for sophomore year. 90% freshmen graduate within 4 years. 94% freshmen graduate within 6 years. 9% grads go on to further study within 1 year. **Faculty:** Student/faculty ratio 9:1. 187 full-time faculty, 98% hold PhDs, 22% are members of minority groups, 51% are women. 0% of classes are taught by teaching assistants.

ACADEMICS
Degrees: Bachelor's **Classes:** Most classes have 10-19 students. **Most popular majors:** Mathematics, General; Economics, General; Political Science And Government, General. **Special Study Options:** Accelerated program; Cross-registration; Double major; English as a Second Language (ESL); Independent study; Internships; Student-designed major; Study abroad. **Combined degree programs:** BA/JD. **Disability Services offered to physically disabled students:** Note-taking services; Reader services; Tape recorders; Tutors. **Career services:** Alumni network; Alumni services; Career assessment; Career/job search classes; Internships; Regional alumni

FACILITIES
Housing: Apartments for married students; Apartments for single students; Coed dorms; Cooperative housing; Special housing for disabled student; Wellness housing **Special Academic Facilities/Equipment:** Wellin Museum of Art, language lab, cultural center, observatory, two electron microscopes. Arthur Levitt Public Affairs Center, Nesbitt-Johnston Writing Center, Jazz Archive. **Computers:** 100% of classrooms, 100% of dorms, 100% of libraries, 100% of dining areas, 100% of student union, 100% of common outdoor areas have wireless network access. Students can register for classes online. Administrative functions (other than registration) can be performed online.

CAMPUS LIFE
Environment: Rural **Activities:** Campus Ministries; Choral groups; Dance; Drama/theater; International Student Organization; Jazz band; Literary magazine; Model UN; Music ensembles; Musical theater; Radio station; Student government; Student newspaper; Student-run film society; Symphony orchestra; Television station; Yearbook 117 registered organizations, 8 honor societies, 4 religious organizations. 11 fraternities, 7 sororities. **Athletics (Intercollegiate):** *Men:* baseball, basketball, crew/rowing, cross-country, diving, football, golf, ice hockey, lacrosse, soccer, squash, swimming, tennis, track/field (outdoor), track/field (indoor). *Women:* basketball, crew/rowing, cross-country, diving, field hockey, ice hockey, lacrosse, soccer, softball, squash, swimming, tennis, track/field (outdoor), track/field (indoor), volleyball. **On-Campus Highlights:** Kennedy Center for Theatre and the Studio Arts (2014), Blood Fitness and Dance Center (2006), Wellin Museum of Art (2012), Sadove Student Center (2010), Root Glen/Outdoor Leadership Center (2006)

ADMISSIONS
Freshman Academic Profile: 77% in top 10% of high school class, 96% in top 25% of high school class, 100% in top 50% of high school class. 58% from public high schools. **Test Scores:** SAT Math middle 50% range 680-760. SAT EBRW middle 50% range 680-750. ACT middle 50% range 31-33. **Basis for Candidate Selection:** *Very important factors considered include:* rigor of secondary school record, class rank, academic GPA. *Important factors considered include:* application essay, standardized test scores, recommendation(s), interview, character/personal qualities. *Other factors considered include:* extracurricular activities, talent/ability, first generation, alumni/ae relation, geographical residence, state residency, racial/ethnic status, volunteer work, work experience, level of applicant's interest. **Freshman Admission Requirements:** High school diploma is required and GED is accepted *Academic units recommended:* 4 English, 3 math, 3 science, 3 foreign

language, 3 social studies. **Freshman Admission Statistics:** 5,678 applied, 24.2% admitted, 35% enrolled. **Transfer Admission Requirements:** High school transcript, college transcript(s), essay or personal statement, standardized test scores, statement of good standing from prior institution(s). Lowest grade transferable C. **General Admission Information:** Application fee $60. Regular application deadline 1/1. Nonfall registration accepted. Admission may be deferred.

COSTS AND FINANCIAL AID
Annual tuition $52,250. Room and board $13,400. Required fees $520. Average book expense $1,000. **Required Forms and Deadlines:** CSS/Financial Aid PROFILE; FAFSA; Institution's own financial aid form; Noncustodial PROFILE. **Notification of Awards:** Applicants will be notified of awards on or about 4/1. **Types of Aid:** *Need-based scholarships/grants:* College/university scholarship or grant aid from institutional funds; Federal Pell; Private scholarships; SEOG; State scholarships/grants. *Loans:* Direct PLUS loans; Direct Subsidized Stafford Loans; Direct Unsubsidized Stafford Loans. *Student Employment:* Federal Work-Study Program available. Institutional employment available. **Financial Aid Statistics:** 100% needy freshmen, 100% needy undergrads receive need-based scholarship or grant aid. 0% undergrads receive non-need-based scholarship or grant aid. 83% freshmen, 81% undergrads receive need-based self-help aid. 0% freshmen, 0% undergrads receive athletic scholarships. 53% freshmen, 48% undergrads receive any aid. 45% undergrads borrow to pay for school. Average cumulative indebtedness $21,491.

HAMLINE UNIVERSITY

1536 Hewitt Avenue, Saint Paul, MN 55104
Phone: 651-523-2207 · **Financial Aid Phone:** 651-523-3000
E-mail: CLA-admis@hamline.edu · **CEEB Code:** 6265
Fax: 651-523-2458 · **Website:** www.hamline.edu · **ACT Code:** 2114

This private school, affiliated with the Methodist Church, was founded in 1854. It has a 77 acre campus.

RATINGS
Admissions Selectivity Rating: 79   **Fire Safety Rating:** 89   **Green Rating:** 60*

STUDENTS AND FACULTY
Enrollment: 1,986. **Student Body:** 58% female, 42% male, 15% out-of-state, 3% international (53 countries represented). Asian 6%, African American 5%, Caucasian 75%, Hispanic 2%, Native American 1%, Race unknown 9%.
Retention and Graduation: 82% freshmen return for sophomore year. 27% grads go on to further study within 1 year. 17% grads pursue arts and sciences degrees. 4% grads pursue law degrees. 2% grads pursue business degrees. 1% grads pursue medical degrees. **Faculty:** Student/faculty ratio 14:1. 173 full-time faculty, 87% hold PhDs, 11% are members of minority groups, 49% are women. 0% of classes are taught by teaching assistants.

ACADEMICS
Degrees: Bachelor's; Master's; Post-Bachelor's certificate **Classes:** Most classes have 10-19 students. Most lab/discussion sessions have 10-19 students. **Most popular majors:** Psychology, General; Criminal Justice/Police Science; Business/Commerce, General. **Special Study Options:** Cross-registration; Double major; Dual enrollment; English as a Second Language (ESL); Exchange student program (domestic); Honors program; Independent study; Internships; Student-designed major; Study abroad; Teacher certification program. **Combined degree programs:** BA/JD; BA/MEng. **Disability Services offered to physically disabled students:** Note-taking services; Reader services; Tape recorders; Tutors. **Career services:** Alumni network; Alumni services; Career assessment; Career/job search classes; Internships; Regional alumni

FACILITIES
Housing: Apartments for married students; Apartments for single students; Coed dorms; Cooperative housing; Fraternity/sorority housing; Other (please specify) 80% of campus accessible to physically diasbled. **Special Academic Facilities/Equipment:** theatre, music hall, art gallery, science center. **Computers:** 100% of classrooms, 100% of dorms, 100% of libraries, 100% of dining areas, 100% of student union, 100% of common outdoor areas have wireless network access. Students can register for classes online. Administrative functions (other than registration) can be performed online.

CAMPUS LIFE
Environment: Metropolis **Activities:** Campus Ministries; Choral groups; Concert band; Dance; Drama/theater; International Student Organization; Jazz band; Literary magazine; Model UN; Music ensembles; Musical theater;

Pep band; Radio station; Student government; Student newspaper; Symphony orchestra; Television station; Yearbook 77 registered organizations, 11 honor societies, 9 religious organizations. 1 fraternity, 2 sororities **Athletics (Intercollegiate):** *Men:* baseball, basketball, cross-country, diving, football, ice hockey, soccer, swimming, tennis, track/field (outdoor), track/field (indoor). *Women:* basketball, cross-country, diving, gymnastics, ice hockey, soccer, softball, swimming, tennis, track/field (outdoor), track/field (indoor), volleyball. **On-Campus Highlights:** Klas Center (stadium and food service), Walker Field House, Sorin Dining Hall, Sundin Music Hall, Bush Student Center **Environmental Initiatives:** Recycling program

ADMISSIONS
Freshman Academic Profile: Average high school GPA 3.4. 20% in top 10% of high school class, 49% in top 25% of high school class, 79% in top 50% of high school class. 90% from public high schools. **Test Scores:** SAT Math middle 50% range 540-640. SAT EBRW middle 50% range 512.5-645. ACT middle 50% range 21-27. Minimum internet-based TOEFL 79-80. Minimum paper TOEFL 550. **Basis for Candidate Selection:** *Very important factors considered include:* rigor of secondary school record, class rank. *Important factors considered include:* academic GPA, application essay, standardized test scores, recommendation(s), interview, extracurricular activities, talent/ability. *Other factors considered include:* character/personal qualities, first generation, alumni/ae relation, racial/ethnic status, volunteer work, work experience. **Freshman Admission Requirements:** High school diploma is required and GED is accepted *Academic units recommended:* 4 English, 3 math, 3 science, 3 science labs, 2 foreign language, 4 social studies, 4 academic electives. **Freshman Admission Statistics:** 2,018 applied, 77.8% admitted, 29% enrolled. **Transfer Admission Requirements:** college transcript(s), essay or personal statement, Minimum college GPA of 2.0 required. Lowest grade transferable C-. **General Admission Information:** Priority deadline 5/1. Nonfall registration accepted. Admission may be deferred for a maximum of 2 years.

COSTS AND FINANCIAL AID
Annual tuition $36,888. Room and board $9,736. Required fees $998. **Required Forms and Deadlines:** FAFSA. **Notification of Awards:** Applicants will be notified of awards on a rolling basis beginning 3/15. **Types of Aid:** *Need-based scholarships/grants:* College/university scholarship or grant aid from institutional funds; Federal Pell; Private scholarships; SEOG; State scholarships/grants. *Loans:* Direct PLUS loans; Direct Subsidized Stafford Loans; Direct Unsubsidized Stafford Loans. *Student Employment:* Federal Work-Study Program available. Institutional employment available. **Financial Aid Statistics:** 100% needy freshmen, 99% needy undergrads receive need-based scholarship or grant aid. 15% freshmen, 10% undergrads receive non-need-based scholarship or grant aid. 87% freshmen, 91% undergrads receive need-based self-help aid. 0% freshmen, 0% undergrads receive athletic scholarships. 98% freshmen, 95% undergrads receive any aid. **Criteria for awarding aid:** *Need-based:* Academics, Alumni affiliation, Art, Minority status, Music/drama, Religious affiliation *Non-need-based:* Academics, Alumni affiliation, Art, Leadership, Minority status, Music/drama, Religious affiliation.

HAMPDEN-SYDNEY COLLEGE

PO Box 667, Hampden-Sydney, VA 23943-0667
Phone: 434-223-6120 · **Financial Aid Phone:** 434-223-6119
E-mail: hsapp@hsc.edu · **CEEB Code:** 5291
Fax: 434-223-6346 · **Website:** www.hsc.edu · **ACT Code:** 4356

This private school, affiliated with the Presbyterian Church, was founded in 1775. It has a 1343 acre campus.

RATINGS
Admissions Selectivity Rating: 86   **Fire Safety Rating:** 88   **Green Rating:** 65

STUDENTS AND FACULTY
Enrollment: 1,046. **Student Body:** 0% female, 100% male, 32% out-of-state, <1% international (6 countries represented). Asian <1%, African American 4%, Caucasian 86%, Hispanic 4%, Native American <1%, Pacific Islander <1%, Two or more races 3%, Race unknown 2%.
Retention and Graduation: 84% freshmen return for sophomore year. 61% freshmen graduate within 4 years. 63% freshmen graduate within 6 years. 29% grads go on to further study within 1 year. 12% grads pursue arts and sciences degrees. 8% grads pursue law degrees. 2% grads pursue business degrees. 5.7%

grads pursue medical degrees. **Faculty:** Student/faculty ratio 10:1. 95 full-time faculty, 93% hold PhDs, 7% are members of minority groups, 26% are women. 0% of classes are taught by teaching assistants.

ACADEMICS
Degrees: Bachelor's **Classes:** Most classes have fewer than 10 students. Most lab/discussion sessions have fewer than 10 students. **Most popular majors:** Economics, General; Business/Managerial Economics; History, General. **Special Study Options:** Cooperative education program; Cross-registration; Double major; Dual enrollment; Exchange student program (domestic); Honors program; Independent study; Internships; Study abroad. **Honors programs:** Student Summer Research programs, Departmental Honors, Senior Fellowship. **Disability Services offered to physically disabled students:** Note-taking services; Reader services; Tutors. **Career services:** Alumni network; Alumni services; Career assessment; Internships; Regional alumni

FACILITIES
Housing: Apartments for married students; Apartments for single students; Fraternity/sorority housing; Men's dorms; Special housing for international students; Theme housing 70% of campus accessible to physically disabled. **Special Academic Facilities/Equipment:** History museum, language lab, international communications center, observatory, Energy Research Lab. **Computers:** 15% of classrooms, 100% of libraries, 100% of dining areas, 100% of student union, 20% of common outdoor areas have wireless network access. Students can register for classes online. Administrative functions (other than registration) can be performed online.

CAMPUS LIFE
Environment: Rural **Activities:** Campus Ministries; Choral groups; Drama/theater; International Student Organization; Literary magazine; Music ensembles; Radio station; Student government; Student newspaper 45 registered organizations, 14 honor societies, 6 religious organizations. 11 fraternities. **Athletics (Intercollegiate):** *Men:* baseball, basketball, cross-country, football, golf, lacrosse, soccer, tennis. **On-Campus Highlights:** Bortz Library, Brown Student Center, Kirk Athletic Center/Hall of Fame, Kirby Fieldhouse (athletic facility), Campus Museum **Environmental Initiatives:** Electrical energy conservation.

ADMISSIONS
Freshman Academic Profile: Average high school GPA 3.4. 11% in top 10% of high school class, 30% in top 25% of high school class, 66% in top 50% of high school class. 66% from public high schools. **Test Scores:** SAT Math middle 50% range 520-630. SAT EBRW middle 50% range 530-635. ACT middle 50% range 21-27. Minimum internet-based TOEFL 100. Minimum paper TOEFL 600. **Basis for Candidate Selection:** *Very important factors considered include:* rigor of secondary school record, academic GPA, application essay, standardized test scores, recommendation(s), character/personal qualities. *Important factors considered include:* class rank, extracurricular activities. *Other factors considered include:* interview, talent/ability, first generation, alumni/ae relation, volunteer work, work experience, level of applicant's interest. **Freshman Admission Requirements:** High school diploma is required and GED is accepted *Academic units required:* 4 English, 3 math, 2 science, 1 science labs, 2 foreign language, 1 social studies, 1 history, 3 academic electives, *Academic units recommended:* 4 math, 3 science, 3 foreign language. **Freshman Admission Statistics:** 3,573 applied, 55.1% admitted, 16% enrolled. **Transfer Admission Requirements:** High school transcript, college transcript(s), essay or personal statement, standardized test scores, statement of good standing from prior institution(s). Minimum college GPA of 2.5 required. Lowest grade transferable C. **General Admission Information:** Application fee $30. Regular application deadline 3/1. Nonfall registration accepted.

COSTS AND FINANCIAL AID
Annual tuition $43,446. Room and board $13,558. Required fees $1,950. Average book expense $1,000. **Required Forms and Deadlines:** FAFSA; State aid form. **Notification of Awards:** Applicants will be notified of awards on a rolling basis beginning 12/15. **Types of Aid:** *Need-based scholarships/grants:* College/university scholarship or grant aid from institutional funds; Federal Pell; Private scholarships; SEOG; State scholarships/grants. *Loans:* Direct PLUS loans; Direct Subsidized Stafford Loans; Direct Unsubsidized Stafford Loans. *Student Employment:* Federal Work-Study Program available. Institutional employment available. **Financial Aid Statistics:** 100% needy freshmen, 100% needy undergrads receive need-based scholarship or grant aid. 26% freshmen, 18% undergrads receive non-need-based scholarship or grant aid. 73% freshmen, 75% undergrads receive need-based self-help aid. 0% freshmen, 0% undergrads receive athletic scholarships. 100% freshmen, 99% undergrads receive any aid. 68% undergrads borrow to pay for school. Average cumulative indebtedness $34,334. **Criteria for awarding aid:** *Need-based:* Academics, Leadership, Minority status, Music/drama *Non-need-based:* Academics, Leadership, Minority status, Music/drama, State/district residency.

HAMPSHIRE COLLEGE

893 West St., Amherst, MA 01002
Phone: 413-559-5471 · **Financial Aid Phone:** 413-559-5484
E-mail: admissions@hampshire.edu · **CEEB Code:** 3447
Fax: 413-559-4631 · **Website:** https://www.hampshire.edu/ · **ACT Code:** 1842

This private school was founded in 1965. It has a 850 acre campus.

RATINGS
Admissions Selectivity Rating: 69   **Fire Safety Rating:** 79   **Green Rating:** 96

STUDENTS AND FACULTY
Enrollment: 1,256. **Student Body:** 63% female, 37% male, 78% out-of-state, 5% international (31 countries represented). Asian 2%, African American 7%, Caucasian 63%, Hispanic 12%, Native American <1%, Pacific Islander 0%, Two or more races 6%, Race unknown 4%.
Retention and Graduation: 76% freshmen return for sophomore year. 10% grads go on to further study within 1 year. 8% grads pursue arts and sciences degrees. 1% grads pursue law degrees. 0% grads pursue business degrees. 1% grads pursue medical degrees. **Faculty:** Student/faculty ratio 11:1. 112 full-time faculty, 0% of classes are taught by teaching assistants.

ACADEMICS
Degrees: Bachelor's **Classes:** Most classes have 10-19 students. **Most popular majors:** Creative Writing; Cultural Studies/Critical Theory And Analysis; Film/Video And Photographic Arts, Other. **Special Study Options:** Cross-registration; Exchange student program (domestic); Independent study; Internships; Liberal arts/career combination; Student-designed major; Study abroad; Teacher certification program. **Disability Services offered to physically disabled students:** Note-taking services; Reader services. **Career services:** Alumni network; Alumni services; Career assessment; Career/job search classes; Internships; Regional alumni

FACILITIES
Housing: Apartments for single students; Coed dorms; Cooperative housing; Men's dorms; Special housing for disabled student; Theme housing; Wellness housing; Women's dorms 50% of campus accessible to physically diasbled. **Special Academic Facilities/Equipment:** Performing and visual arts center, bioshelter (integrated greenhouse/aquaculture facility), farm center, electronic music and TV production studios, extensive film and photography facilities, multimedia center. **Computers:** 100% of classrooms, 10% of dorms, 100% of libraries, 100% of dining areas, n/a% of student union, 50% of common outdoor areas have wireless network access. Students can register for classes online. Administrative functions (other than registration) can be performed online.

CAMPUS LIFE
Environment: Town **Activities:** Campus Ministries; Choral groups; Concert band; Dance; Drama/theater; International Student Organization; Literary magazine; Model UN; Music ensembles; Radio station; Student government; Student newspaper; Student-run film society 94 registered organizations, 3 religious organizations. **On-Campus Highlights:** Bridge Cafe, Bookstore, Library, Eric Carle Museum of Picture Book Art, Liebling Center—Film/Photo **Environmental Initiatives:** Constructing a new facility addition to LEED standards (minimum silver; hopefully gold); constructing a condominium community to be LEED certified.

ADMISSIONS
Freshman Academic Profile: 74% from public high schools. **Test Scores:** Minimum internet-based TOEFL 91. Minimum paper TOEFL 577. **Basis for Candidate Selection:** *Very important factors considered include:* application essay, character/personal qualities. *Important factors considered include:* rigor of secondary school record, academic GPA, recommendation(s), extracurricular activities, talent/ability. *Other factors considered include:* class rank, standardized test scores, interview, first generation, alumni/ae relation, geographical residence, racial/ethnic status, volunteer work, work experience, level of applicant's interest. **Freshman Admission Requirements:** High school diploma is required and GED is accepted *Academic units required:* 4 English, 3 math, 3 science, 2 science labs, 3 foreign language, 3 history. *Academic units recommended:* 4 English, 4 math, 4 science, 2 science labs, 4 foreign language, 4 history. **Freshman Admission Statistics:** 2,305 applied, 62.8% admitted, 23% enrolled. **Transfer Admission Requirements:** High school transcript, college transcript(s), essay or personal statement, Lowest grade transferable C. **General Admission Information:** Application fee $60. Priority deadline 11/15. Regular application deadline 1/15. Nonfall registration accepted. Admission may be deferred for a maximum of 1 year.

COSTS AND FINANCIAL AID
Annual tuition $47,620. Room and board $12,950. Required fees $1,380. Average book expense $850. **Required Forms and Deadlines:** CSS/Financial Aid PROFILE; FAFSA; Noncustodial PROFILE. **Notification**

of Awards: Applicants will be notified of awards on or about 4/1. **Types of Aid:** *Need-based scholarships/grants:* College/university scholarship or grant aid from institutional funds; Federal Pell; Private scholarships; SEOG; State scholarships/grants. *Loans:* Direct PLUS loans; Direct Subsidized Stafford Loans; Direct Unsubsidized Stafford Loans. *Student Employment:* Federal Work-Study Program available. **Financial Aid Statistics:** 97% needy freshmen, 98% needy undergrads receive need-based scholarship or grant aid. 14% freshmen, 14% undergrads receive non-need-based scholarship or grant aid. 96% freshmen, 96% undergrads receive need-based self-help aid. 0% freshmen, 0% undergrads receive athletic scholarships. 70% freshmen, 76% undergrads receive any aid. **Criteria for awarding aid:** *Non-need-based:* Academics, Art, Leadership, Music/drama.

HAMPTON UNIVERSITY

Hampton University, Hampton, VA 23668
Phone: 757-727-5328 · **Financial Aid Phone:** 757-727-5332
E-mail: admit@hamptonu.edu · **CEEB Code:** 5292
Fax: 757-727-5095 · **Website:** www.hamptonu.edu · **ACT Code:** 4358

This private school was founded in 1868. It has a 314 acre campus.

RATINGS
Admissions Selectivity Rating: 89   **Fire Safety Rating:** 72   **Green Rating:** 61

STUDENTS AND FACULTY
Enrollment: 3,799. **Student Body:** 67% female, 33% male, 73% out-of-state, 1% international (22 countries represented). Asian <1%, African American 96%, Caucasian 1%, Hispanic 1%, Native American <1%, Pacific Islander <1%, Two or more races 0%, Race unknown <1%.
Retention and Graduation: 77% freshmen return for sophomore year. 37% freshmen graduate within 4 years. 54% freshmen graduate within 6 years. 37% grads go on to further study within 1 year. 13% grads pursue arts and sciences degrees. 4% grads pursue law degrees. 6% grads pursue business degrees. 2% grads pursue medical degrees. **Faculty:** Student/faculty ratio 13:1. 288 full-time faculty, 84% hold PhDs, 83% are members of minority groups, 49% are women. 0% of classes are taught by teaching assistants.

ACADEMICS
Degrees: Associate; Bachelor's; Certificate; Doctoral/Professional; Doctoral/Research; Master's; Post-Master's certificate **Classes:** Most classes have 20-29 students. Most lab/discussion sessions have 10-19 students. **Most popular majors:** Biology, General; Psychology, General; Business Administration, Management And Operations, Other. **Special Study Options:** Accelerated program; Cooperative education program; Cross-registration; Distance learning; Double major; Dual enrollment; English as a Second Language (ESL); Honors program; Independent study; Internships; Study abroad; Teacher certification program. **Honors programs:** Honors College-Designed to augment, enhance and extend the undergraduate academic experience through community, exposure and expectations. Leadership Institute—Offers the undergraduate student a curricular option that enhances the university experience. **Disability Services offered to physically disabled students:** Note-taking services; Reader services; Tape recorders; Tutors. **Career services:** Alumni network; Alumni services; Career assessment; Career/job search classes; Internships

FACILITIES
Housing: Apartments for single students; Coed dorms; Men's dorms; Special housing for disabled student; Special housing for international students; Wellness housing; Women's dorms 90% of campus accessible to physically diasbled. **Special Academic Facilities/Equipment:** African, and Oceanic museums, and gallery. New Student Center **Computers:** 100% of classrooms, 100% of dorms, 100% of libraries, 100% of dining areas, 100% of student union, 100% of common outdoor areas have wireless network access. Students can register for classes online. Administrative functions (other than registration) can be performed online.

CAMPUS LIFE
Environment: City **Activities:** Campus Ministries; Choral groups; Concert band; Dance; Drama/theater; International Student Organization; Jazz band; Literary magazine; Marching band; Music ensembles; Musical theater; Opera; Pep band; Radio station; Student government; Student newspaper; Symphony orchestra; Television station; Yearbook 85 registered organizations, 16 honor societies, 3 religious organizations. 6 fraternities, 3 sororities. **Athletics**

(Intercollegiate): *Men:* basketball, cross-country, football, golf, sailing, tennis, track/field (outdoor), track/field (indoor). *Women:* basketball, bowling, cross-country, golf, sailing, softball, tennis, track/field (outdoor), track/field (indoor), volleyball. **On-Campus Highlights:** Emancipation Oak, Memorial Chapel, Huntington Memorial Museum, Booker T. Washington Monument, Student Center: bowling, fitness and movie

ADMISSIONS

Freshman Academic Profile: Average high school GPA 3.7. 12% in top 10% of high school class, 22% in top 25% of high school class, 71% in top 50% of high school class. 90% from public high schools. **Test Scores:** SAT Math middle 50% range 480-550. SAT EBRW middle 50% range 500-570. ACT middle 50% range 20-24. Minimum paper TOEFL 525. **Basis for Candidate Selection:** *Very important factors considered include:* rigor of secondary school record, academic GPA, application essay, character/personal qualities. *Important factors considered include:* class rank, recommendation(s). *Other factors considered include:* interview, extracurricular activities, talent/ability, volunteer work, work experience, level of applicant's interest. **Freshman Admission Requirements:** High school diploma is required and GED is accepted *Academic units required:* 4 English, 3 math, 2 science, 2 science labs, 2 social studies, 6 academic electives, *Academic units recommended:* 2 foreign language. **Freshman Admission Statistics:** 12,130 applied, 36.2% admitted, 23% enrolled. **Transfer Admission Requirements:** college transcript(s), essay or personal statement, statement of good standing from prior institution(s). Minimum college GPA of 2.3 required. Lowest grade transferable C. **General Admission Information:** Application fee $35. Priority deadline 3/1. Nonfall registration accepted. Admission may be deferred for a maximum of 1 year.

COSTS AND FINANCIAL AID

Annual tuition $22,630. Room and board $11,218. Required fees $2,562. Average book expense $1,100. **Required Forms and Deadlines:** FAFSA. **Notification of Awards:** Applicants will be notified of awards on a rolling basis beginning 4/15. **Types of Aid:** *Need-based scholarships/grants:* College/university scholarship or grant aid from institutional funds; Federal Pell; Private scholarships; SEOG; State scholarships/grants; United Negro College Fund. *Loans:* Direct PLUS loans; Direct Subsidized Stafford Loans; Direct Unsubsidized Stafford Loans. *Student Employment:* Federal Work-Study Program available. **Financial Aid Statistics:** 95% needy freshmen, 98% needy undergrads receive need-based scholarship or grant aid. 91% freshmen, 69% undergrads receive non-need-based scholarship or grant aid. 88% freshmen, 88% undergrads receive need-based self-help aid. 8% freshmen, 2% undergrads receive athletic scholarships. 39% freshmen, 43% undergrads receive any aid. 73% undergrads borrow to pay for school. Average cumulative indebtedness $1,902. **Criteria for awarding aid:** *Non-need-based:* Academics, Athletics, Job skills, Leadership, Music/drama.

HANNIBAL-LAGRANGE UNIVERSITY

2800 Palmyra Road, Hannibal, MO 63401
Phone: 573-221-3113 · **Financial Aid Phone:** 573-629-3280
E-mail: admissio@hlg.edu
Fax: 573-221-6594 · **Website:** http://www.hlg.edu/ · **ACT Code:** 2320

This private school, affiliated with the Southern Baptist Church, was founded in 1858. It has a 110 acre campus.

RATINGS

Admissions Selectivity Rating: 71   **Fire Safety Rating:** 78   **Green Rating:** 60*

STUDENTS AND FACULTY

Student Body: 23% out-of-state, (11 countries represented).
Retention and Graduation: 58% freshmen return for sophomore year.
Faculty: Student/faculty ratio 11:1. 60 full-time faculty, 28% hold PhDs, 2% are members of minority groups, 52% are women. 0% of classes are taught by teaching assistants.

ACADEMICS

Degrees: Associate; Bachelor's; Certificate; Master's **Classes:** Most classes have 10-19 students. Most lab/discussion sessions have 20-29 students. **Most popular majors:** Elementary Education And Teaching; Secondary Education And Teaching; Non-Profit/Public/Organizational Management. **Special Study Options:** Accelerated program; Distance learning; Dual enrollment; Honors program; Independent study; Internships; Liberal arts/career combination; Student-designed major; Study abroad; Teacher certification program. **Honors programs:** Honors Program qualifies a student for a semester of study at Harlaxton College, Grantham, England. **Disability Services offered to physically disabled students:** Tape recorders; Tutors. **Career services:** Career assessment; Internships

FACILITIES

Housing: Apartments for single students; Men's dorms; Special housing for disabled student; Women's dorms 98% of campus accessible to physically diasbled. **Special Academic Facilities/Equipment:** Roland Fine Arts Center, Carroll Mission Center, Nature Trail, Mabee Sport Complex **Computers:** Students can register for classes online.

CAMPUS LIFE

Environment: Village **Activities:** Campus Ministries; Choral groups; Concert band; Drama/theater; International Student Organization; Jazz band; Music ensembles; Musical theater; Student government; Student newspaper; Yearbook 22 registered organizations, 1 honor society, 3 religious organizations. **Athletics (Intercollegiate):** *Men:* baseball, basketball, cross-country, golf, soccer, swimming, track/field (outdoor), volleyball, wrestling. *Women:* basketball, cheerleading, cross-country, golf, soccer, softball, swimming, track/field (outdoor), volleyball. **On-Campus Highlights:** Fireside Cafe, Mabee Sports Complex, Student Center, Snack Shack Soup & Subs, Carroll Mission Center

ADMISSIONS

Freshman Academic Profile: 21% in top 10% of high school class, 37% in top 25% of high school class, 52% in top 50% of high school class. **Test Scores:** SAT Math middle 50% range 440-480. SAT EBRW middle 50% range 260-490. ACT middle 50% range 19-24. Minimum paper TOEFL 520. **Basis for Candidate Selection:** *Very important factors considered include:* academic GPA, standardized test scores. *Important factors considered include:* rigor of secondary school record. *Other factors considered include:* class rank, recommendation(s), extracurricular activities, talent/ability, character/personal qualities, religious affiliation/commitment, level of applicant's interest. **Freshman Admission Requirements:** High school diploma is required and GED is accepted *Academic units recommended:* 4 English, 3 math, 2 science, 1 science labs, 3 history, **Transfer Admission Requirements:** college transcript(s), Minimum college GPA of 2.0 required. Lowest grade transferable 1. **General Admission Information:** Application fee $25. Nonfall registration accepted. Admission may be deferred for a maximum of 1 semester.

COSTS AND FINANCIAL AID

Annual tuition $21,450. Room and board $8,108. Required fees $1,300. Average book expense $1,070. **Required Forms and Deadlines:** FAFSA; Institution's own financial aid form. **Types of Aid:** *Need-based scholarships/grants:* College/university scholarship or grant aid from institutional funds; Federal Pell; Private scholarships; SEOG; State scholarships/grants. *Loans:* Direct Subsidized Stafford Loans; Direct Unsubsidized Stafford Loans. *Student Employment:* Federal Work-Study Program available. Institutional employment available. **Criteria for awarding aid:** *Non-need-based:* Academics, Art, Athletics, Music/drama, Religious affiliation.

HANOVER COLLEGE

517 Ball Drive, Hanover, IN 47243-0108
Phone: 800-213-2178 · **Financial Aid Phone:** 812-866-7029
E-mail: admission@hanover.edu · **CEEB Code:** 1290
Fax: 812-866-7098 · **Website:** www.hanover.edu · **ACT Code:** 1200

This private school, affiliated with the Presbyterian Church, was founded in 1827. It has a 650 acre campus.

RATINGS

Admissions Selectivity Rating: 80   **Fire Safety Rating:** 95   **Green Rating:** 81

STUDENTS AND FACULTY

Enrollment: 1,082. **Student Body:** 54% female, 46% male, 33% out-of-state, 2% international (17 countries represented). Asian 1%, African American 5%, Caucasian 76%, Hispanic 3%, Native American 1%, Pacific Islander <1%, Two or more races 2%, Race unknown 9%.
Retention and Graduation: 79% freshmen return for sophomore year. 69% freshmen graduate within 4 years. 71% freshmen graduate within 6 years. 22% grads go on to further study within 1 year. 16% grads pursue arts and sciences degrees. 2% grads pursue law degrees. 2% grads pursue business degrees. 1% grads pursue medical degrees. **Faculty:** Student/faculty ratio 13:1. 84 full-time faculty, 93% hold PhDs, 6% are members of minority groups, 42% are women. 0% of classes are taught by teaching assistants.

ACADEMICS

Degrees: Bachelor's **Classes:** Most classes have 10-19 students. **Most popular majors:** Speech Communication And Rhetoric; Psychology, General; Economics, General. **Special Study Options:** Double major; Dual enrollment; Independent study; Internships; Student-designed major; Study abroad; Teacher certification program. **Disability Services offered to physically disabled students:** Note-taking services; Tutors. **Career services:** Alumni network; Alumni services; Career assessment; Career/job search classes; Internships; Regional alumni

FACILITIES

Housing: Apartments for single students; Coed dorms; Fraternity/sorority housing; Men's dorms; Theme housing; Wellness housing; Women's dorms 50% of campus accessible to physically diasbled. **Special Academic Facilities/ Equipment:** cadaver lab, geological museum, electronic language lab, observatory **Computers:** 80% of classrooms, 100% of dorms, 50% of libraries, 100% of dining areas, 100% of student union, 20% of common outdoor areas have wireless network access. Students can register for classes online. Administrative functions (other than registration) can be performed online.

CAMPUS LIFE

Environment: Rural **Activities:** Campus Ministries; Choral groups; Concert band; Dance; Drama/theater; International Student Organization; Jazz band; Literary magazine; Music ensembles; Musical theater; Pep band; Radio station; Student government; Student newspaper; Student-run film society; Symphony orchestra; Television station; Yearbook 60 registered organizations, 8 honor societies, 4 religious organizations. 4 fraternities, 4 sororities. **Athletics (Intercollegiate):** *Men:* baseball, basketball, cross-country, football, golf, lacrosse, soccer, tennis, track/field (outdoor). *Women:* basketball, cross-country, golf, soccer, softball, tennis, track/field (outdoor), volleyball. **On-Campus Highlights:** Science Center, Horner Health and Recreation Center (Collier Arena), Campus Center, The Shoebox, The Point-River View **Environmental Initiatives:** The College is currently developing a new strategic plan and re-evaluating our green initiatives and sustainability program as an integral component of the plan.

ADMISSIONS

Freshman Academic Profile: Average high school GPA 3.6. 32% in top 10% of high school class, 60% in top 25% of high school class, 90% in top 50% of high school class. 85% from public high schools. **Test Scores:** SAT Math middle 50% range 530-620. SAT EBRW middle 50% range 540-640. ACT middle 50% range 22-27. Minimum internet-based TOEFL 80. Minimum paper TOEFL 550. **Basis for Candidate Selection:** *Very important factors considered include:* rigor of secondary school record, class rank, academic GPA. *Important factors considered include:* standardized test scores, talent/ability, character/personal qualities. *Other factors considered include:* application essay, recommendation(s), interview, extracurricular activities, first generation, alumni/ae relation, geographical residence, state residency, racial/ethnic status, volunteer work, work experience, level of applicant's interest. **Freshman Admission Requirements:** High school diploma is required and GED is not accepted *Academic units required:* 4 English, 3 math, 3 science, 2 science labs, 2 foreign language, 2 social studies, 2 history, 2 academic electives, *Academic units recommended:* 4 English, 4 math, 4 science, 3 science labs, 4 foreign language, 3 social studies, 3 history, 3 academic electives, 1 visual/performing arts. **Freshman Admission Statistics:** 2,757 applied, 83.8% admitted, 15% enrolled. **Transfer Admission Requirements:** High school transcript, college transcript(s), essay or personal statement, standardized test scores, statement of good standing from prior institution(s). Minimum college GPA of 2.0 required. Lowest grade transferable C-. **General Admission Information:** Nonfall registration accepted. Admission may be deferred for a maximum of 1 year.

COSTS AND FINANCIAL AID

Annual tuition $36,900. Room and board $11,580. Required fees $770. Average book expense $1,200. **Required Forms and Deadlines:** FAFSA. **Notification of Awards:** Applicants will be notified of awards on or about 3/1. **Types of Aid:** *Need-based scholarships/grants:* College/university scholarship or grant aid from institutional funds; Federal Pell; Private scholarships; SEOG; State scholarships/grants. *Loans:* Direct PLUS loans; Direct Subsidized Stafford Loans; Direct Unsubsidized Stafford Loans. *Student Employment:* Federal Work-Study Program available. Institutional employment available. **Financial Aid Statistics:** 100% needy freshmen, 100% needy undergrads receive need-based scholarship or grant aid. 21% freshmen, 16% undergrads receive non-need-based scholarship or grant aid. 67% freshmen, 76% undergrads receive need-based self-help aid. 0% freshmen, 0% undergrads receive athletic scholarships. 100% freshmen, 100% undergrads receive any aid. 76% undergrads borrow to pay for school. Average cumulative indebtedness $29,745. **Criteria for awarding aid:** *Need-based:* Academics, Alumni affiliation, Art, Leadership, Minority status, Music/drama, Religious affiliation *Non-need-based:* Academics, Alumni affiliation, Art, Leadership, Minority status, Music/drama, Religious affiliation, State/district residency.

HARDING UNIVERSITY

Box 12244, Searcy, AR 72149
Phone: 501-279-4407 • **Financial Aid Phone:** 501-279-4257
E-mail: admissions@harding.edu • **CEEB Code:** 10311
Fax: 501-279-4129 • **Website:** www.harding.edu • **ACT Code:** 124

This private school, affiliated with the Church of Christ, was founded in 1924. It has a 350 acre campus.

RATINGS

Admissions Selectivity Rating: 93   **Fire Safety Rating:** 91   **Green Rating:** 60*

STUDENTS AND FACULTY

Enrollment: 4,145. **Student Body:** 55% female, 45% male, 71% out-of-state, 8% international (54 countries represented). Asian 1%, African American 4%, Caucasian 81%, Hispanic 3%, Native American <1%, Pacific Islander <1%, Two or more races 3%, Race unknown 0%.
Retention and Graduation: 83% freshmen return for sophomore year. 67% freshmen graduate within 6 years. **Faculty:** Student/faculty ratio 14:1. 302 full-time faculty, 75% hold PhDs, 5% are members of minority groups, 34% are women. 0% of classes are taught by teaching assistants.

ACADEMICS

Degrees: Bachelor's; Doctoral/Professional; Doctoral/Research; Master's; Post-Master's certificate **Classes:** Most classes have 20-29 students. **Most popular majors:** Early Childhood Education And Teaching; Business Administration And Management, General; Accounting. **Special Study Options:** Accelerated program; Cooperative education program; Distance learning; Double major; Dual enrollment; English as a Second Language (ESL); Honors program; Independent study; Internships; Liberal arts/career combination; Student-designed major; Study abroad; Teacher certification program. **Disability Services offered to physically disabled students:** Note-taking services; Reader services; Tape recorders; Tutors. **Career services:** Alumni network; Alumni services; Career assessment; Career/job search classes; Internships

FACILITIES

Housing: Apartments for married students; Apartments for single students; Men's dorms; Special housing for disabled student; Women's dorms 95% of campus accessible to physically diasbled. **Special Academic Facilities/ Equipment:** On-campus academy (prep school grades PreK-12). **Computers:** 95% of classrooms, 100% of libraries, 100% of dining areas, 100% of student union, 80% of common outdoor areas have wireless network access. Students can register for classes online. Administrative functions (other than registration) can be performed online.

CAMPUS LIFE

Environment: Village **Activities:** Campus Ministries; Choral groups; Concert band; Drama/theater; International Student Organization; Jazz band; Literary magazine; Marching band; Music ensembles; Musical theater; Pep band; Radio station; Student government; Student newspaper; Student-run film society; Symphony orchestra; Television station; Yearbook 100 registered organizations, 12 honor societies, 10 religious organizations. 14 fraternities, 15 sororities. **Athletics (Intercollegiate):** *Men:* baseball, basketball, cross-country, football, golf, soccer, tennis, track/field (outdoor). *Women:* basketball, cheerleading, cross-country, golf, soccer, tennis, track/field (outdoor), volleyball. **On-Campus Highlights:** Rhodes Memorial Field House, Front Lawn with Swings, Ganus Athletic Complex, First Security Stadium, Legacy Park and Starbucks **Environmental Initiatives:** Recycling

ADMISSIONS

Freshman Academic Profile: Average high school GPA 3.7. 25% in top 10% of high school class, 52% in top 25% of high school class, 77% in top 50% of high school class. 66% from public high schools. **Test Scores:** SAT Math middle 50% range 500-600. SAT EBRW middle 50% range 490-630. ACT middle 50% range 22-28. Minimum internet-based TOEFL 79. Minimum paper TOEFL 550. **Basis for Candidate Selection:** *Very important factors considered include:* rigor of secondary school record, standardized test scores, recommendation(s), interview, character/personal qualities. *Important factors considered include:* class rank, academic GPA, talent/ability. *Other factors considered include:* application essay, extracurricular activities, first generation, alumni/ae relation, geographical residence, state residency, volunteer work, work experience, level of applicant's interest. **Freshman Admission Requirements:** High school diploma is required and GED is accepted *Academic units required:* 4 English, 3 math, 2 science, 3 social studies, 3 academic electives, *Academic units recommended:* 4 English, 4 math, 4 science, 2 foreign language, 4 social studies, 2 academic electives. **Freshman Admission Statistics:** 2,023 applied, 47.1% admitted, 100% enrolled. **Transfer Admission Requirements:** college transcript(s), essay or personal statement, statement of good standing from prior institution(s). Minimum college GPA of

2 required. Lowest grade transferable C. **General Admission Information:** Application fee $50. Nonfall registration accepted. Admission may be deferred for a maximum of One year.

COSTS AND FINANCIAL AID

Annual tuition $18,690. Room and board $6,902. Required fees $500. Average book expense $1,200. **Required Forms and Deadlines:** FAFSA. **Notification of Awards:** Applicants will be notified of awards on a rolling basis beginning 2/15. **Types of Aid:** *Need-based scholarships/grants:* College/university scholarship or grant aid from institutional funds; Federal Pell; Private scholarships; SEOG; State scholarships/grants. *Loans:* Direct PLUS loans; Direct Subsidized Stafford Loans; Direct Unsubsidized Stafford Loans. *Student Employment:* Federal Work-Study Program available. Institutional employment available. **Financial Aid Statistics:** 98% needy freshmen, 92% needy undergrads receive need-based scholarship or grant aid. 21% freshmen, 17% undergrads receive non-need-based scholarship or grant aid. 69% freshmen, 77% undergrads receive need-based self-help aid. 4% freshmen, 4% undergrads receive athletic scholarships. 99% freshmen, 94% undergrads receive any aid. 66% undergrads borrow to pay for school. Average cumulative indebtedness $30,570. **Criteria for awarding aid:** *Need-based:* Academics, Alumni affiliation, Job skills, Minority status *Non-need-based:* Academics, Alumni affiliation, Art, Athletics, Leadership, Music/drama, Religious affiliation, State/district residency.

HARDIN-SIMMONS UNIVERSITY

Box 16000, Abilene, TX 79698
Phone: 325-670-1206 · **Financial Aid Phone:** 325-670-1217
E-mail: enroll@hsutx.edu · **CEEB Code:** 6268
Fax: 325-671-2115 · **Website:** www.hsutx.edu · **ACT Code:** 4096

This private school, affiliated with the Baptist Church, was founded in 1891. It has a 220 acre campus.

RATINGS

Admissions Selectivity Rating: 77   **Fire Safety Rating:** 76   **Green Rating:** 63

STUDENTS AND FACULTY

Enrollment: 1,671. **Student Body:** 52% female, 48% male, 3% out-of-state, 2% international (27 countries represented). Asian 1%, African American 8%, Caucasian 64%, Hispanic 19%, Native American <1%, Pacific Islander <1%, Two or more races 5%, Race unknown 1%.
Retention and Graduation: 75% freshmen return for sophomore year. 35% freshmen graduate within 4 years. 51% freshmen graduate within 6 years. 45% grads go on to further study within 1 year. 17% grads pursue arts and sciences degrees. 3% grads pursue law degrees. 2% grads pursue business degrees. 7% grads pursue medical degrees. **Faculty:** Student/faculty ratio 12:1. 134 full-time faculty, 90% hold PhDs, 4% are members of minority groups, 38% are women. 0% of classes are taught by teaching assistants.

ACADEMICS

Degrees: Bachelor's; Doctoral; Doctoral/Professional; Doctoral/Research; Master's; Post-Master's certificate **Classes:** Most classes have 10-19 students. Most lab/discussion sessions have 10-19 students. **Most popular majors:** Education, General; Registered Nursing/Registered Nurse; Business, Management, Marketing, And Related Support Services, Other. **Special Study Options:** Accelerated program; Cross-registration; Distance learning; Double major; Dual enrollment; Honors program; Independent study; Internships; Study abroad; Teacher certification program. **Honors programs:** The Hardin-Simmons University Honors Program provides an enriched educational environment for undergraduate students of exceptional promise who have a wide variety of interests and seek an enhanced learning opportunity. The Honors Program promotes creative and critical thinking skills to equip individuals for success in today's world. The Program, which serves as an integral part of the academic community, includes courses taught by selected faculty members interested in working with highly motivated students. The Honors Program expects participants to strive for excellence and assume personal accountability for their intellectual growth. **Disability Services offered to physically disabled students:** Note-taking services; Reader services; Tape recorders; Tutors. **Career services:** Alumni network; Alumni services; Career assessment; Career/job search classes; Internships; Regional alumni

FACILITIES

Housing: Apartments for married students; Apartments for single students; Men's dorms; Special housing for disabled student; Women's dorms 100% of campus accessible to physically disabled. **Special Academic Facilities/Equipment:** Art center, observatory with 14-inch telescope, rare and fine book

room, SIX WHITE HORSE facility, Holland Health Science Medical High School **Computers:** 90% of classrooms, 100% of dorms, 80% of libraries, 100% of dining areas, 100% of student union, 50% of common outdoor areas have wireless network access.

CAMPUS LIFE

Environment: City **Activities:** Campus Ministries; Choral groups; Concert band; Dance; Drama/theater; International Student Organization; Jazz band; Literary magazine; Marching band; Model UN; Music ensembles; Musical theater; Opera; Student government; Student newspaper; Symphony orchestra; Yearbook 15 honor societies, 1 religious organization. 4 fraternities, 4 sororities. **Athletics (Intercollegiate):** *Men:* baseball, basketball, cheerleading, cross-country, football, golf, soccer, tennis, track/field (outdoor). *Women:* basketball, cheerleading, cross-country, golf, soccer, softball, tennis, track/field (outdoor), volleyball. **On-Campus Highlights:** Moody Center (Student Center), The Basement, Fitness Center, Intramural Fields, The POD **Environmental Initiatives:** Estabishing a recycling program.

ADMISSIONS

Freshman Academic Profile: Average high school GPA 3.6. 18% in top 10% of high school class, 44% in top 25% of high school class, 76% in top 50% of high school class. 91% from public high schools. **Test Scores:** SAT Math middle 50% range 500-580. SAT EBRW middle 50% range 500-590. ACT middle 50% range 18-24. Minimum internet-based TOEFL 75. Minimum paper TOEFL 550. **Basis for Candidate Selection:** *Important factors considered include:* standardized test scores. *Other factors considered include:* rigor of secondary school record, class rank, academic GPA, recommendation(s), extracurricular activities, character/personal qualities, first generation, volunteer work, work experience. **Freshman Admission Requirements:** High school diploma is required and GED is accepted *Academic units required:* **Freshman Admission Statistics:** 1,673 applied, 81.8% admitted, 33% enrolled. **Transfer Admission Requirements:** college transcript(s), Minimum college GPA of 2.0 required. Lowest grade transferable C. **General Admission Information:** Nonfall registration accepted. Admission may be deferred.

COSTS AND FINANCIAL AID

Annual tuition $27,290. Room and board $8,080. Required fees $1,700. Average book expense $800. **Notification of Awards:** Applicants will be notified of awards on a rolling basis beginning 12/1. **Types of Aid:** *Need-based scholarships/grants:* College/university scholarship or grant aid from institutional funds; Federal Pell; Private scholarships; SEOG; State scholarships/grants. *Loans:* Direct PLUS loans; Direct Subsidized Stafford Loans; Direct Unsubsidized Stafford Loans. *Student Employment:* Federal Work-Study Program available. Institutional employment available. **Financial Aid Statistics:** 72% needy freshmen, 76% needy undergrads receive need-based scholarship or grant aid. 100% freshmen, 96% undergrads receive non-need-based scholarship or grant aid. 88% freshmen, 90% undergrads receive need-based self-help aid. 0% freshmen, 0% undergrads receive athletic scholarships. 99% freshmen, 98% undergrads receive any aid. 66% undergrads borrow to pay for school. Average cumulative indebtedness $39,597. **Criteria for awarding aid:** *Non-need-based:* Academics, Alumni affiliation, Art, Leadership, Minority status, Music/drama, Religious affiliation.

See page 948.

HARRISBURG UNIVERSITY OF SCIENCE AND TECHNOLOGY

326 Market Street, Harrisburg, PA 17101
Phone: 717-901-5101 · **Financial Aid Phone:** 717-901-5115
E-mail: admissions@HarrisburgU.edu · **CEEB Code:** 4511
Fax: 717-901-3101 · **Website:** www.HarrisburgU.edu · **ACT Code:** 3637

This private school was founded in 2001. It has a 2 acre campus.

RATINGS

Admissions Selectivity Rating: 84   **Fire Safety Rating:** 60*   **Green Rating:** 60*

STUDENTS AND FACULTY

Enrollment: 272. **Student Body:** 46% female, 54% male, 17% out-of-state, 1% international (3 countries represented). Asian 4%, African American 32%, Caucasian 49%, Hispanic 8%, Native American <1%, Pacific Islander 0%, Two or more races 3%, Race unknown 2%.
Retention and Graduation: 54% freshmen return for sophomore year. 10% grads go on to further study within 1 year. 10% grads pursue arts and sciences degrees. 0% grads pursue law degrees. 0% grads pursue business degrees. 0% grads pursue medical degrees. **Faculty:** Student/faculty ratio 11:1. 10 full-time

faculty, 100% hold PhDs, 40% are members of minority groups, 50% are women. 0% of classes are taught by teaching assistants.

ACADEMICS

Degrees: Bachelor's; Master's **Classes:** Most classes have fewer than 10 students. **Most popular majors:** Computer And Information Sciences, General; Biotechnology; Physical Sciences. **Special Study Options:** Dual enrollment; Internships; Student-designed major. **Career services:** Internships

FACILITIES

Housing: Coed dorms; Special housing for disabled students 100% of campus accessible to physically diasbled. **Computers:** 100% of classrooms, 100% of libraries, 100% of dining areas, 100% of student union, 100% of common outdoor areas have wireless network access. Students can register for classes online. Administrative functions (other than registration) can be performed online. Undergraduates are required to own a computer.

CAMPUS LIFE

Environment: City **On-Campus Highlights:** Conference Center

ADMISSIONS

Freshman Academic Profile: 90% from public high schools. **Test Scores:** SAT Math middle 50% range 420-550. SAT EBRW middle 50% range 440-530. ACT middle 50% range 20-24. Minimum paper TOEFL 80. **Basis for Candidate Selection:** *Very important factors considered include:* academic GPA, application essay. *Important factors considered include:* interview. *Other factors considered include:* standardized test scores, recommendation(s). **Freshman Admission Requirements:** High school diploma is required and GED is accepted **Freshman Admission Statistics:** 1,827 applied, 47.4% admitted, 15% enrolled. **General Admission Information:** Nonfall registration accepted.

COSTS AND FINANCIAL AID

Annual tuition $23,800. Average book expense $1,500. **Required Forms and Deadlines:** FAFSA. **Types of Aid:** *Need-based scholarships/grants:* College/university scholarship or grant aid from institutional funds; Federal Pell; Private scholarships; SEOG; State scholarships/grants. *Loans:* Direct PLUS loans; Direct Subsidized Stafford Loans; Direct Unsubsidized Stafford Loans. *Student Employment:* Federal Work-Study Program available. Institutional employment available. **Financial Aid Statistics:** 99% needy freshmen, 100% needy undergrads receive need-based scholarship or grant aid. 9% freshmen, 6% undergrads receive non-need-based scholarship or grant aid. 87% freshmen, 82% undergrads receive need-based self-help aid. 0% freshmen, 0% undergrads receive athletic scholarships. 98% freshmen, 94% undergrads receive any aid. **Criteria for awarding aid:** *Non-need-based:* Academics.

HARTWICK COLLEGE

PO Box 4022, Oneonta, NY 13820-4020
Phone: 607-431-4154 · **Financial Aid Phone:** 607-431-4130
E-mail: admissions@hartwick.edu · **CEEB Code:** 2288
Fax: 607-431-4102 · **Website:** www.hartwick.edu/ · **ACT Code:** 2756

This private school was founded in 1797. It has a 425 acre campus.

RATINGS

Admissions Selectivity Rating: 72   **Fire Safety Rating:** 93   **Green Rating:** 64

STUDENTS AND FACULTY

Enrollment: 1,194. **Student Body:** 59% female, 41% male, 20% out-of-state, 4% international (19 countries represented). Asian 3%, African American 8%, Caucasian 64%, Hispanic 9%, Native American 1%, Pacific Islander <1%, Two or more races 0%, Race unknown 11%.
Retention and Graduation: 70% freshmen return for sophomore year. 19% grads go on to further study within 1 year. 3% grads pursue arts and sciences degrees. 1.6% grads pursue law degrees. 2% grads pursue business degrees.
Faculty: Student/faculty ratio 11:1. 108 full-time faculty, 80% hold PhDs, 10% are members of minority groups, 45% are women. 0% of classes are taught by teaching assistants.

ACADEMICS

Degrees: Bachelor's **Classes:** Most classes have 10-19 students. Most lab/discussion sessions have 10-19 students. **Most popular majors:** Psychology, General; Registered Nursing, Nursing Administration, Nursing Research And Clinical Nursing; Business Administration And Management, General. **Special Study Options:** Accelerated program; Cross-registration; Distance learning; Double major; Honors program; Independent study; Internships;

Student-designed major; Study abroad; Teacher certification program. **Honors programs:** Requirements for the Honors Program are: Challenges—4 must be completed by graduation; Divisions—3 must be represented in Challenges; Honors Forum—a presentation of a project; Academic Excellence—a 3.50 Grade Point Average. Also, students in the Honors program can choose to live on the Honors floor in a campus residence hall. **Combined degree programs:** BA/JD; BA/MEng. **Disability Services offered to physically disabled students:** Note-taking services; Reader services; Tape recorders; Tutors. **Career services:** Alumni network; Career/job search classes; Internships

FACILITIES

Housing: Apartments for single students; Coed dorms; Fraternity/sorority housing; Theme housing 50% of campus accessible to physically diasbled. **Special Academic Facilities/Equipment:** Art and history museums, Indian artifact collection, environmental center, observatory, tissue culture lab. **Computers:** 100% of classrooms, 100% of dorms, 100% of libraries, 50% of dining areas, 50% of student union, have wireless network access. Students can register for classes online. Administrative functions (other than registration) can be performed online.

CAMPUS LIFE

Environment: Village **Activities:** Choral groups; Concert band; Dance; Drama/theater; International Student Organization; Jazz band; Literary magazine; Model UN; Music ensembles; Radio station; Student government; Student newspaper 70 registered organizations, 30 honor societies, 3 religious organizations. 3 fraternities, 3 sororities. **Athletics (Intercollegiate):** *Men:* basketball, cross-country, diving, football, lacrosse, soccer, swimming, tennis. *Women:* basketball, cheerleading, cross-country, diving, equestrian sports, field hockey, lacrosse, soccer, swimming, tennis, volleyball, water polo. **On-Campus Highlights:** Yager Museum, Stevens-German Library, Campbell Fitness Center, Elmore Soccer Field **Environmental Initiatives:** Hartwick is a signatory of the Talloires Declaration and is a member of the Association for the Advancement of Sustainability in Higher Education. In 2005, the College received a Kresge Green Building Iniative planning grant to partially fund green design of its first LEED-certified building, Golisano Hall. In keeping with Hartwick's emphasis on hands-on learning, the project provided the basis for a course entitled "Sustainable Design", taught by Richard Rittelman, FAIA principal architect and Karl Seeley, PhD. of Hartwick's economics department. The LEED-certification process for Golisano Hall is currently underway. The process involves commissioning the building's systems, which are estimated to use 75% less energy than the average building on Hartwick's campus.

ADMISSIONS

Freshman Academic Profile: Average high school GPA 86.3. 8% in top 10% of high school class, 32% in top 25% of high school class, 69% in top 50% of high school class. 86% from public high schools. **Test Scores:** SAT Math middle 50% range 460-560. SAT EBRW middle 50% range 460-540. ACT middle 50% range 21-26. Minimum internet-based TOEFL 80. Minimum paper TOEFL 550. **Basis for Candidate Selection:** *Very important factors considered include:* rigor of secondary school record, academic GPA. *Important factors considered include:* extracurricular activities, character/personal qualities, alumni/ae relation, volunteer work, work experience. *Other factors considered include:* class rank, application essay, standardized test scores, recommendation(s), interview, talent/ability, level of applicant's interest. **Freshman Admission Requirements:** High school diploma is required and GED is accepted *Academic units recommended:* 4 English, 3 math, 3 science, 2 science labs, 3 foreign language, 2 social studies, 2 history. **Freshman Admission Statistics:** 3,019 applied, 88.6% admitted, 13% enrolled. **Transfer Admission Requirements:** college transcript(s), essay or personal statement, statement of good standing from prior institution(s). Minimum college GPA of 2.0 required. Lowest grade transferable C-. **General Admission Information:** Nonfall registration accepted. Admission may be deferred for a maximum of 1 year.

COSTS AND FINANCIAL AID

Average book expense $700. **Required Forms and Deadlines:** FAFSA. **Notification of Awards:** Applicants will be notified of awards on a rolling basis beginning 12/22. **Types of Aid:** *Need-based scholarships/grants:* College/university scholarship or grant aid from institutional funds; Federal Pell; Private scholarships; SEOG; State scholarships/grants. *Loans:* Direct PLUS loans; Direct Subsidized Stafford Loans; Direct Unsubsidized Stafford Loans. *Student Employment:* Federal Work-Study Program available. Institutional employment available. **Financial Aid Statistics:** 99% needy freshmen, 99% needy undergrads receive need-based scholarship or grant aid. 14% freshmen, 12% undergrads receive non-need-based scholarship or grant aid. 86% freshmen, 86% undergrads receive need-based self-help aid. 2% freshmen, 2% undergrads receive athletic scholarships. 87% freshmen, 83% undergrads receive any aid. 71% undergrads borrow to pay for school. Average cumulative indebtedness $27,653. **Criteria for awarding aid:** *Need-based:* Music/drama *Non-need-based:* Academics, Alumni affiliation, Art, Athletics, Music/drama.

HARVARD COLLEGE

86 Brattle Street, Cambridge, MA 02138
Phone: 617-495-1551 • **Financial Aid Phone:** 617-495-1581
E-mail: college@fas.harvard.edu • **CEEB Code:** 3434
Fax: 617-495-8821 • **Website:** www.college.harvard.edu • **ACT Code:** 1840

This private school was founded in 1636. It has a 380 acre campus.

RATINGS
Admissions Selectivity Rating: 99   **Fire Safety Rating:** 60*   **Green Rating:** 97

STUDENTS AND FACULTY
Enrollment: 6,701. **Student Body:** 48% female, 52% male, 84% out-of-state, 11% international (100 countries represented). Asian 21%, African American 8%, Caucasian 40%, Hispanic 12%, Native American <1%, Pacific Islander <1%, Two or more races 7%, Race unknown 2%.
Retention and Graduation: 97% freshmen return for sophomore year. 84% freshmen graduate within 4 years. 96% freshmen graduate within 6 years.
Faculty: Student/faculty ratio 6:1. 975 full-time faculty, 86% hold PhDs, 21% are members of minority groups, 35% are women. 0% of classes are taught by teaching assistants.

ACADEMICS
Degrees: Bachelor's; Doctoral/Research; Master's **Classes:** Most classes have 20-29 students. Most lab/discussion sessions have 10-19 students. **Most popular majors:** Social Sciences, General; Economics, General; Political Science And Government, General. **Special Study Options:** Accelerated program; Cross-registration; Double major; Exchange student program (domestic); Honors program; Independent study; Student-designed major; Study abroad; Teacher certification program. **Combined degree programs:** BA/MA; BA/MEng. **Disability Services offered to physically disabled students:** Note-taking services; Reader services; Tape recorders; Tutors. **Career services:** Alumni network; Alumni services

FACILITIES
Housing: Apartments for married students; Apartments for single students; Coed dorms; Cooperative housing; Special housing for disabled students **Special Academic Facilities/Equipment:** Museums (University Arts Museums, Museums of Cultural History, many others), language labs, observatory, many science and research laboratories and facilities, new state-of-the-art computer science facility. **Computers:** 98% of classrooms, 100% of dorms, 100% of libraries, have wireless network access. Students can register for classes online. Administrative functions (other than registration) can be performed online.

CAMPUS LIFE
Environment: City **Activities:** Campus Ministries; Choral groups; Concert band; Dance; Drama/theater; International Student Organization; Jazz band; Literary magazine; Marching band; Model UN; Music ensembles; Musical theater; Opera; Pep band; Radio station; Student government; Student newspaper; Student-run film society; Symphony orchestra; Television station; Yearbook 393 registered organizations, 1 honor society, 28 religious organizations. **Athletics (Intercollegiate):** *Men:* baseball, basketball, crew/rowing, cross-country, diving, fencing, football, golf, ice hockey, lacrosse, sailing, skiing (downhill/alpine), skiing (nordic/cross-country), soccer, squash, swimming, tennis, track/field (outdoor), track/field (indoor), volleyball, water polo, wrestling. *Women:* basketball, crew/rowing, cross-country, diving, fencing, field hockey, golf, ice hockey, lacrosse, sailing, skiing (downhill/alpine), skiing (nordic/cross-country), soccer, softball, squash, swimming, tennis, track/field (outdoor), track/field (indoor), volleyball, water polo. **On-Campus Highlights:** Widener Library, Harvard Yard, Fogg Museum, Annenburg/Memorial Hall, Science Center **Environmental Initiatives:** Campus-wide Sustainability Principles that provide a broad vision to guide University operations and planning (adopted in 2004) and an established University-wide Office for Sustainability (green.harvard.edu) that oversees implementation of Harvard's GHG reduction goal and sustainability commitments. The University has had a formal sustainability office for a decade initially created by a faculty and staff initiative with strong student involvement.

ADMISSIONS
Freshman Academic Profile: Average high school GPA 4.2. 95% in top 10% of high school class, 99% in top 25% of high school class, 100% in top 50% of high school class. 58% from public high schools. **Test Scores:** SAT Math middle 50% range 730-800. SAT EBRW middle 50% range 730-790. ACT middle 50% range 32-35. **Basis for Candidate Selection:** *Other factors considered include:* rigor of secondary school record, academic GPA, application essay, standardized test scores, recommendation(s), interview, extracurricular activities, talent/ability, character/personal qualities, first generation, alumni/ae relation, geographical residence, racial/ethnic status, volunteer work, work experience. **Freshman Admission Requirements:** High school diploma or equivalent is not required *Academic units recommended:* 4 English, 4 math, 4 science, 4 foreign language, 3 social studies, 2 history. **Freshman Admission Statistics:** 39,506 applied, 5.2% admitted, 83% enrolled. **General Admission Information:** Application fee $75. Regular application deadline 1/1. Nonfall registration accepted. Admission may be deferred for a maximum of 1 year.

COSTS AND FINANCIAL AID
Annual tuition $44,990. Room and board $16,660. Required fees $3,959. Average book expense $1,000. **Required Forms and Deadlines:** Business/Farm Supplement; CSS/Financial Aid PROFILE; FAFSA; Noncustodial PROFILE. **Notification of Awards:** Applicants will be notified of awards on or about 4/1. **Types of Aid:** *Need-based scholarships/grants:* College/university scholarship or grant aid from institutional funds; Federal Pell; Private scholarships; SEOG; State scholarships/grants. *Loans:* Direct PLUS loans; Direct Subsidized Stafford Loans; Direct Unsubsidized Stafford Loans. *Student Employment:* Federal Work-Study Program available. Institutional employment available. **Financial Aid Statistics:** 100% needy freshmen, 100% needy undergrads receive need-based scholarship or grant aid. 0% undergrads receive non-need-based scholarship or grant aid. 70% freshmen, 85% undergrads receive need-based self-help aid. 0% freshmen, 0% undergrads receive athletic scholarships. 54% freshmen, 56% undergrads receive any aid. 23% undergrads borrow to pay for school. Average cumulative indebtedness $16,702.

HARVEY MUDD COLLEGE

301 Platt Boulevard, Claremont, CA 91711
Phone: 909-621-8011 • **Financial Aid Phone:** 909-621-8055
E-mail: admission@hmc.edu • **CEEB Code:** 4341
Fax: 909-607-7046 • **Website:** www.hmc.edu

This private school was founded in 1955. It has a 33 acre campus.

RATINGS
Admissions Selectivity Rating: 98   **Fire Safety Rating:** 84   **Green Rating:** 60*

STUDENTS AND FACULTY
Enrollment: 844. **Student Body:** 48% female, 52% male, 57% out-of-state, 10% international (26 countries represented). Asian 17%, African American 4%, Caucasian 34%, Hispanic 18%, Native American <1%, Pacific Islander <1%, Two or more races 11%, Race unknown 5%.
Retention and Graduation: 98% freshmen return for sophomore year. 86% freshmen graduate within 4 years. 96% freshmen graduate within 6 years.
Faculty: Student/faculty ratio 8:1. 106 full-time faculty, 100% hold PhDs, 27% are members of minority groups, 42% are women. 0% of classes are taught by teaching assistants.

ACADEMICS
Degrees: Bachelor's **Classes:** Most classes have 10-19 students. **Most popular majors:** Computer And Information Sciences, General; Engineering, General; Mathematics, General. **Special Study Options:** Cross-registration; Double major; Dual enrollment; Exchange student program (domestic); Independent study; Internships; Student-designed major; Study abroad. **Disability Services offered to physically disabled students:** Note-taking services; Reader services; Tape recorders; Tutors. **Career services:** Alumni network; Alumni services; Career assessment; Internships

FACILITIES
Housing: Apartments for married students; Apartments for single students; Coed dorms 90% of campus accessible to physically diasbled. **Computers:** 100% of classrooms, 100% of dorms, 100% of libraries, 100% of dining areas, 100% of student union, 75% of common outdoor areas have wireless network access. Students can register for classes online. Administrative functions (other than registration) can be performed online.

CAMPUS LIFE
Environment: Town **Activities:** Campus Ministries; Choral groups; Concert band; Dance; Drama/theater; International Student Organization;

Jazz band; Literary magazine; Music ensembles; Radio station; Student government; Student newspaper; Symphony orchestra; Yearbook 109 registered organizations, 4 honor societies, 6 religious organizations. **Athletics (Intercollegiate):** *Men:* baseball, basketball, cross-country, diving, football, golf, soccer, swimming, tennis, track/field (outdoor), water polo. *Women:* basketball, cross-country, diving, golf, lacrosse, soccer, softball, swimming, tennis, track/field (outdoor), volleyball, water polo. **On-Campus Highlights:** Dorm Lounges, Platt Campus Center Living Room, Hoch Shanahan Dining Hall, Jay's Pizza Place, Linde Student Activities Center **Environmental Initiatives:** In February 2008 Harvey Mudd College President Maria Klawe signed the American College & University Presidents Climate Commitment and Harvey Mudd College Board of Trustees adopted HMC Sustainability Policy Statement. Additionally, the Board of Trustees passed a resolution where the standard for new buildings will be at least U.S. Green Building Council LEED Silver standard or equivalent and premium rated or ENERGY STAR certified products are purchased for use on campus where possible.

ADMISSIONS

Freshman Academic Profile: 90% in top 10% of high school class, 100% in top 25% of high school class, 100% in top 50% of high school class. 65% from public high schools. **Test Scores:** SAT Math middle 50% range 750-800. SAT EBRW middle 50% range 720-770. ACT middle 50% range 33-35. Minimum internet-based TOEFL 100. Minimum paper TOEFL 600. **Basis for Candidate Selection:** *Very important factors considered include:* rigor of secondary school record, academic GPA, application essay, recommendation(s), talent/ability, character/personal qualities. *Important factors considered include:* class rank, standardized test scores, extracurricular activities. *Other factors considered include:* interview, first generation, alumni/ae relation, geographical residence, state residency, racial/ethnic status, volunteer work, work experience. **Freshman Admission Requirements:** High school diploma or equivalent is not required *Academic units required:* 4 English, 4 math, 3 science, 1 history, *Academic units recommended:* 4 English, 4 math, 4 science, 2 science labs, 2 foreign language, 2 social studies, 2 history, 2 academic electives. **Freshman Admission Statistics:** 4,078 applied, 15.4% admitted, 36% enrolled. **Transfer Admission Requirements:** High school transcript, college transcript(s), essay or personal statement, statement of good standing from prior institution(s). Minimum college GPA of 3.0 required. Lowest grade transferable C. **General Admission Information:** Application fee $70. Regular application deadline 1/5. Nonfall registration accepted. Admission may be deferred.

COSTS AND FINANCIAL AID

Annual tuition $54,347. Room and board $17,592. Required fees $289. Average book expense $800. **Required Forms and Deadlines:** Business/Farm Supplement; CSS/Financial Aid PROFILE; FAFSA; Noncustodial PROFILE; State aid form. **Notification of Awards:** Applicants will be notified of awards on or about 4/1. **Types of Aid:** *Need-based scholarships/grants:* College/university scholarship or grant aid from institutional funds; Federal Pell; Private scholarships; SEOG; State scholarships/grants. *Loans:* Direct PLUS loans; Direct Subsidized Stafford Loans; Direct Unsubsidized Stafford Loans. *Student Employment:* Federal Work-Study Program available. Institutional employment available. **Financial Aid Statistics:** 98% needy freshmen, 95% needy undergrads receive need-based scholarship or grant aid. 26% freshmen, 16% undergrads receive non-need-based scholarship or grant aid. 62% freshmen, 73% undergrads receive need-based self-help aid. 0% freshmen, 0% undergrads receive athletic scholarships. 84% freshmen, 76% undergrads receive any aid. 42% undergrads borrow to pay for school. Average cumulative indebtedness $25,412. **Criteria for awarding aid:** *Non-need-based:* Academics.

HASTINGS COLLEGE

710 N. Turner Avenue, Hastings, NE 68901
Phone: 402-461-7403 • **Financial Aid Phone:** 402-461-7431
E-mail: mmolliconi@hastings.edu • **CEEB Code:** 6270
Fax: 402-461-7490 • **Website:** www.hastings.edu • **ACT Code:** 2456

This private school, affiliated with the Presbyterian Church, was founded in 1882. It has a 109 acre campus.

RATINGS

Admissions Selectivity Rating: 76   **Fire Safety Rating:** 79   **Green Rating:** 60*

STUDENTS AND FACULTY

Enrollment: 1,067. **Student Body:** 46% female, 54% male, 28% out-of-state, 1% international (7 countries represented). Asian 1%, African American 2%, Caucasian 92%, Hispanic 3%, Native American <1%, Race unknown 1%. **Retention and Graduation:** 76% freshmen return for sophomore year. 24% grads go on to further study within 1 year. 16% grads pursue arts and sciences

degrees. 2% grads pursue law degrees. 1% grads pursue business degrees. 1% grads pursue medical degrees. **Faculty:** Student/faculty ratio 11:1. 87 full-time faculty, 71% hold PhDs, 1% are members of minority groups, 34% are women. 0% of classes are taught by teaching assistants.

ACADEMICS

Degrees: Bachelor's; Master's **Classes:** Most classes have 20-29 students. Most lab/discussion sessions have 20-29 students. **Most popular majors:** Education, General; Psychology, General; Business/Commerce, General. **Special Study Options:** Double major; Exchange student program (domestic); Independent study; Internships; Student-designed major; Study abroad; Teacher certification program. **Disability Services offered to physically disabled students:** Note-taking services; Reader services; Tape recorders; Tutors. **Career services:** Alumni network; Alumni services; Career assessment; Career/job search classes; Internships; Regional alumni

FACILITIES

Housing: Apartments for single students; Coed dorms; Men's dorms; Women's dorms 90% of campus accessible to physically disabled. **Special Academic Facilities/Equipment:** center for communication arts, glass-blowing studio, observatory, art gallery **Computers:** 95% of classrooms, 100% of libraries, 100% of dining areas, 100% of student union, have wireless network access. Administrative functions (other than registration) can be performed online.

CAMPUS LIFE

Environment: Village **Activities:** Campus Ministries; Choral groups; Concert band; Dance; Drama/theater; Jazz band; Literary magazine; Marching band; Music ensembles; Musical theater; Pep band; Radio station; Student government; Student newspaper; Symphony orchestra; Television station; Yearbook 85 registered organizations, 13 honor societies, 10 religious organizations. 4 fraternities, 4 sororities. **Athletics (Intercollegiate):** *Men:* baseball, basketball, cross-country, football, golf, soccer, tennis, track/field (outdoor), track/field (indoor), wrestling. *Women:* basketball, cheerleading, cross-country, golf, soccer, softball, tennis, track/field (outdoor), track/field (indoor), volleyball. **On-Campus Highlights:** Fleharty Educational Center and weight room, Hazelrigg Student Union, Perkins Library, Gray Center of Communication Arts, Dorm lounges

ADMISSIONS

Freshman Academic Profile: Average high school GPA 3.2. 16% in top 10% of high school class, 40% in top 25% of high school class, 65% in top 50% of high school class. 88% from public high schools. **Test Scores:** SAT Math middle 50% range 490-605. SAT EBRW middle 50% range 500-600. ACT middle 50% range 20-26. Minimum paper TOEFL 600. **Basis for Candidate Selection:** *Very important factors considered include:* rigor of secondary school record, class rank, academic GPA, standardized test scores, recommendation(s). *Important factors considered include:* extracurricular activities, talent/ability, character/personal qualities. *Other factors considered include:* application essay, interview, alumni/ae relation, racial/ethnic status, level of applicant's interest. **Freshman Admission Requirements:** High school diploma is required and GED is accepted *Academic units required:* 3 English, 3 math, 3 science, 3 science labs, 4 social studies, 3 history, *Academic units recommended:* 4 English, 4 math, 4 science, 4 science labs, 2 foreign language, 4 social studies, 4 history. **Freshman Admission Statistics:** 1,210 applied, 81.4% admitted, 26% enrolled. **Transfer Admission Requirements:** High school transcript, college transcript(s), statement of good standing from prior institution(s). Minimum college GPA of 2.0 required. Lowest grade transferable C. **General Admission Information:** Application fee $20. Nonfall registration accepted.

COSTS AND FINANCIAL AID

Annual tuition $27,300. Room and board $8,080. Average book expense $730. **Required Forms and Deadlines:** FAFSA; Institution's own financial aid form. **Notification of Awards:** Applicants will be notified of awards on a rolling basis beginning 3/1. **Types of Aid:** *Need-based scholarships/grants:* College/university scholarship or grant aid from institutional funds; Federal Pell; Private scholarships; SEOG; State scholarships/grants. *Loans: Student Employment:* Federal Work-Study Program available. Institutional employment available. **Financial Aid Statistics:** 100% needy freshmen, 98% needy undergrads receive need-based scholarship or grant aid. 20% freshmen, 16% undergrads receive non-need-based scholarship or grant aid. 73% freshmen, 79% undergrads receive need-based self-help aid. 23% freshmen, 16% undergrads receive athletic scholarships. 97% freshmen, 98% undergrads receive any aid. **Criteria for awarding aid:** *Need-based:* Academics, Art, Athletics, Leadership, Music/drama *Non-need-based:* Academics, Art, Athletics, Leadership, Music/drama.

HAVERFORD COLLEGE

370 Lancaster Avenue, Haverford, PA 19041
Phone: 610-896-1350 · **Financial Aid Phone:** (610)896-1350
E-mail: http://www.haverford.edu/admission/ · **CEEB Code:** 2289
Fax: 610-896-1338 · **Website:** www.haverford.edu · **ACT Code:** 3409

This private school was founded in 1833. It has a 200 acre campus.

RATINGS
Admissions Selectivity Rating: 98   **Fire Safety Rating:** 89   **Green Rating:** 82

STUDENTS AND FACULTY
Enrollment: 1,291. **Student Body:** 52% female, 48% male, 86% out-of-state, 9% international (36 countries represented). Asian 12%, African American 7%, Caucasian 57%, Hispanic 10%, Native American 0%, Pacific Islander 0%, Two or more races 3%, Race unknown 3%.
Retention and Graduation: 97% freshmen return for sophomore year. 87% freshmen graduate within 4 years. 93% freshmen graduate within 6 years. 20% grads go on to further study within 1 year. 13% grads pursue arts and sciences degrees. 1% grads pursue law degrees. 1% grads pursue business degrees. 3% grads pursue medical degrees. **Faculty:** Student/faculty ratio 9:1. 137 full-time faculty, 99% hold PhDs, 18% are members of minority groups, 50% are women. 0% of classes are taught by teaching assistants.

ACADEMICS
Degrees: Bachelor's **Classes:** Most classes have 20-29 students. Most lab/discussion sessions have 10-19 students. **Most popular majors:** English Language And Literature, General; Biology/Biological Sciences, General; Psychology, General. **Special Study Options:** Cross-registration; Double major; Exchange student program (domestic); Independent study; Student-designed major; Study abroad; Teacher certification program. **Combined degree programs:** BA/MEng. **Disability Services offered to physically disabled students:** Note-taking services; Tape recorders. **Career services:** Alumni network; Alumni services; Career assessment; Internships; Regional alumni

FACILITIES
Housing: Apartments for single students; Coed dorms; Men's dorms; Special housing for disabled student; Theme housing; Women's dorms 66% of campus accessible to physically diasbled. **Special Academic Facilities/Equipment:** Art gallery, arboretum, observatory, foundry. **Computers:** 75% of classrooms, 75% of libraries, 100% of dining rooms, 100% of student union, 80% of common outdoor areas have wireless network access. Students can register for classes online. Administrative functions (other than registration) can be performed online.

CAMPUS LIFE
Environment: Town **Activities:** Campus Ministries; Choral groups; Dance; Drama/theater; International Student Organization; Literary magazine; Music ensembles; Musical theater; Student government; Student newspaper; Yearbook 144 registered organizations, 1 honor society, 6 religious organizations. **Athletics (Intercollegiate):** *Men:* baseball, basketball, cross-country, fencing, lacrosse, soccer, squash, tennis, track/field (outdoor), track/field (indoor). *Women:* basketball, cross-country, fencing, field hockey, lacrosse, soccer, softball, squash, tennis, track/field (outdoor), track/field (indoor), volleyball. **On-Campus Highlights:** Integrated Natural Sciences Center, John Whitehead Campus Center, Cantor Fitzgerald Gallery, Arboreteum, Douglas B. Gardner Athletic Center **Environmental Initiatives:** The athletic center is the 1st gold LEED certified recreation center in the US (opened in 2005).

ADMISSIONS
Freshman Academic Profile: 96% in top 10% of high school class, 99% in top 25% of high school class, 100% in top 50% of high school class. 60% from public high schools. **Test Scores:** SAT Math middle 50% range 690-770. SAT EBRW middle 50% range 700-760. ACT middle 50% range 31-34. Minimum internet-based TOEFL 100. **Basis for Candidate Selection:** *Very important factors considered include:* rigor of secondary school record, academic GPA, application essay, recommendation(s), extracurricular activities, character/personal qualities. *Important factors considered include:* class rank, standardized test scores, talent/ability, volunteer work, work experience. *Other factors considered include:* interview, first generation, alumni/ae relation, geographical residence, racial/ethnic status, level of applicant's interest.
Freshman Admission Requirements: High school diploma is required and GED is accepted *Academic units recommended:* 4 English, 3 math, 3 science,

3 science labs, 3 foreign language, 3 social studies. **Freshman Admission Statistics:** 4,408 applied, 20.1% admitted, 39% enrolled. **Transfer Admission Requirements:** college transcript(s), essay or personal statement, standardized test scores, statement of good standing from prior institution(s). Minimum college GPA of 3.0 required. Lowest grade transferable C. **General Admission Information:** Application fee $65. Regular application deadline 1/15. Nonfall registration accepted. Admission may be deferred for a maximum of 1 year.

COSTS AND FINANCIAL AID
Annual tuition $52,278. Room and board $15,958. Required fees $476.
Required Forms and Deadlines: Business/Farm Supplement; CSS/Financial Aid PROFILE; FAFSA; Noncustodial PROFILE. **Notification of Awards:** Applicants will be notified of awards on or about 3/25. **Types of Aid:** *Need-based scholarships/grants:* College/university scholarship or grant aid from institutional funds; Federal Pell; SEOG; State scholarships/grants. *Loans:* Direct PLUS loans; Direct Subsidized Stafford Loans; Direct Unsubsidized Stafford Loans. *Student Employment:* Federal Work-Study Program available. Institutional employment available. **Financial Aid Statistics:** 98% needy freshmen, 100% needy undergrads receive need-based scholarship or grant aid. 0% undergrads receive non-need-based scholarship or grant aid. 94% freshmen, 93% undergrads receive need-based self-help aid. 0% freshmen, 0% undergrads receive athletic scholarships. 51% freshmen, 51% undergrads receive any aid. 29% undergrads borrow to pay for school. Average cumulative indebtedness $18,932.

HAWAI'I PACIFIC UNIVERSITY

1 Aloha Tower Drive, Honolulu, HI 96813
Phone: 808-544-0238 · **Financial Aid Phone:** 808-544-0253
E-mail: admissions@hpu.edu · **CEEB Code:** 4352
Fax: 808-544-1136 · **Website:** www.hpu.edu · **ACT Code:** 4352

This private school was founded in 1965. It has a 135 acre campus.

RATINGS
Admissions Selectivity Rating: 76   **Fire Safety Rating:** 92   **Green Rating:** 60*

STUDENTS AND FACULTY
Enrollment: 3,236. **Student Body:** 59% female, 41% male, 42% out-of-state, 11% international (62 countries represented). Asian 16%, African American 6%, Caucasian 27%, Hispanic 16%, Native American 1%, Pacific Islander 2%, Two or more races 17%, Race unknown 4%.
Retention and Graduation: 64% freshmen return for sophomore year. **Faculty:** Student/faculty ratio 12:1. 140 full-time faculty, 74% hold PhDs, 30% are members of minority groups, 49% are women. 0% of classes are taught by teaching assistants.

ACADEMICS
Degrees: Associate; Bachelor's; Certificate; Doctoral/Professional; Master's; Post-Bachelor's certificate; Post-Master's certificate **Classes:** Most classes have 10-19 students. **Special Study Options:** Accelerated program; Cooperative education program; Distance learning; Double major; Dual enrollment; English as a Second Language (ESL); Exchange student program (domestic); Honors program; Independent study; Internships; Liberal arts/career combination; Student-designed major; Study abroad; Teacher certification program. **Honors programs:** The Residential Honors Program at Hawai'i Pacific University is designed for exceptionally capable and motivated students to help get the most out of their college experience. Through a myriad of challenging coursework, meaningful research, creative endeavors, and an international study abroad experience, it gives students the tools and opportunities to excel intellectually and academically. For more information visit our website: https://hpu.edu/honorsprogram/index.html#howToApply. **Combined degree programs:** BA/MA.

FACILITIES
Housing: Apartments for married students; Apartments for single students; Coed dorms; Theme housing; Wellness housing **Special Academic Facilities/Equipment:** Hawaii Pacific University Art Gallery, Hawaii Pacific University Theatre **Computers:** Students can register for classes online. Administrative functions (other than registration) can be performed online.

CAMPUS LIFE
Environment: Metropolis **Activities:** Campus Ministries; Choral groups; Concert band; Dance; Drama/theater; International Student Organization; Jazz band; Literary magazine; Model UN; Music ensembles; Musical theater; Pep band; Student government; Student newspaper; Student-run film society; Symphony orchestra 80 registered organizations, 18 honor societies, 3

religious organizations. **Athletics (Intercollegiate):** *Men:* baseball, basketball, cheerleading, cross-country, golf, tennis. *Women:* cheerleading, cross-country, golf, softball, tennis, volleyball.

ADMISSIONS

Freshman Academic Profile: Average high school GPA 3.4. **Test Scores:** SAT Math middle 50% range 490-590. SAT EBRW middle 50% range 510-608. ACT middle 50% range 20-25. Minimum internet-based TOEFL 80. Minimum paper TOEFL 550. **Basis for Candidate Selection:** *Very important factors considered include:* rigor of secondary school record, academic GPA. *Important factors considered include:* application essay, standardized test scores, extracurricular activities. *Other factors considered include:* recommendation(s), interview, talent/ability, character/personal qualities, first generation, volunteer work, work experience. **Freshman Admission Requirements:** High school diploma is required and GED is accepted *Academic units recommended:* 4 English, 3 math, 3 science, 1 science labs, 2 foreign language, 2 social studies, 2 history. **Freshman Admission Statistics:** 6,551 applied, 74.7% admitted, 10% enrolled. **Transfer Admission Requirements:** college transcript(s), Minimum college GPA of 2.0 required. Lowest grade transferable C. **General Admission Information:** Application fee $50. Nonfall registration accepted. Admission may be deferred for a maximum of 2 years.

COSTS AND FINANCIAL AID

Annual tuition $25,630. Room and board $14,204. Required fees $350. Average book expense $1,200. **Required Forms and Deadlines:** FAFSA. **Notification of Awards:** Applicants will be notified of awards on or about 3/15. **Types of Aid:** *Need-based scholarships/grants:* College/university scholarship or grant aid from institutional funds; Federal Nursing Scholarships; Federal Pell; Private scholarships; SEOG; State scholarships/grants. *Loans:* Direct PLUS loans; Direct Subsidized Stafford Loans; Direct Unsubsidized Stafford Loans. **Financial Aid Statistics:** 68% needy undergrads receive need-based scholarship or grant aid. 100% freshmen, 83% undergrads receive non-need-based scholarship or grant aid. 96% freshmen, 98% undergrads receive need-based self-help aid. 8% freshmen, 7% undergrads receive athletic scholarships. 59% undergrads borrow to pay for school. Average cumulative indebtedness $26,216. **Criteria for awarding aid:** *Non-need-based:* Academics, Alumni affiliation, Athletics, Job skills, Leadership, Music/drama, Religious affiliation.

HEIDELBERG COLLEGE

310 East Market Street, Tiffin, OH 44883
Phone: 419-448-2330 · **Financial Aid Phone:** 419-448-2293
E-mail: adminfo@heidelberg.edu · **CEEB Code:** 1292
Fax: 419-448-2334 · **Website:** www.heidelberg.edu · **ACT Code:** 3278

This private school, affiliated with the United Church of Christ, was founded in 1850. It has a 120 acre campus.

RATINGS

Admissions Selectivity Rating: 78   **Fire Safety Rating:** 63   **Green Rating:** 60*

STUDENTS AND FACULTY

Enrollment: 1,089. **Student Body:** 48% female, 52% male, 15% out-of-state, 1% international. Asian 1%, African American 7%, Caucasian 78%, Hispanic 2%, Native American <1%, Pacific Islander 0%, Two or more races 2%, Race unknown 9%.
Retention and Graduation: 61% freshmen return for sophomore year. 25% grads go on to further study within 1 year. 15% grads pursue arts and sciences degrees. 2% grads pursue law degrees. 5% grads pursue business degrees. 3% grads pursue medical degrees. **Faculty:** Student/faculty ratio 12:1. 50 full-time faculty, 86% hold PhDs, 6% are members of minority groups, 46% are women. 0% of classes are taught by teaching assistants.

ACADEMICS

Degrees: Bachelor's; Master's **Classes:** Most classes have fewer than 10 students. Most lab/discussion sessions have fewer than 10 students. **Most popular majors:** Education, General; Biological And Physical Sciences; Business/Commerce, General. **Special Study Options:** Cross-registration; Double major; Dual enrollment; English as a Second Language (ESL); Exchange student program (domestic); Honors program; Independent study; Internships; Liberal arts/career combination; Student-designed major; Study abroad; Teacher certification program. **Honors programs:** The Honors Program, entitled "The Life of the Mind," integrates learning and life experiences, stems from the mission of the University. It features extensive contact with the fundamental values that underpin self-worth and integrity, free inquiry, and intellectual rigor, an understanding of other cultures and traditions, and a lifelong habit of commitment to the community and concern for social

responsibility. **Disability Services offered to physically disabled students:** Tutors. **Career services:** Alumni network; Career assessment; Internships

FACILITIES

Housing: Apartments for married students; Apartments for single students; Coed dorms; Cooperative housing; Fraternity/sorority housing; Special housing for disabled student; Theme housing; Women's dorms 65% of campus accessible to physically diasbled. **Special Academic Facilities/Equipment:** Forest research lots, water quality lab, Center for Historic and Military Archaeology **Computers:** 80% of classrooms, 70% of dorms, 100% of libraries, 100% of dining areas, 100% of student union, have wireless network access. Students can register for classes online. Administrative functions (other than registration) can be performed online.

CAMPUS LIFE

Environment: Village **Activities:** Campus Ministries; Choral groups; Concert band; Dance; Drama/theater; International Student Organization; Jazz band; Literary magazine; Model UN; Music ensembles; Musical theater; Pep band; Radio station; Student government; Student newspaper; Student-run film society; Television station; Yearbook 75 registered organizations, 6 honor societies, 3 religious organizations. 5 fraternities, 4 sororities. **Athletics (Intercollegiate):** *Men:* baseball, basketball, cheerleading, cross-country, football, golf, soccer, tennis, track/field (outdoor), track/field (indoor), wrestling. *Women:* basketball, cheerleading, cross-country, golf, soccer, softball, tennis, track/field (outdoor), track/field (indoor), volleyball. **On-Campus Highlights:** Gillmor Science Center, Campus Center, Seiberling Gymnasium, Education Center

ADMISSIONS

Freshman Academic Profile: Average high school GPA 3.2. 14% in top 10% of high school class, 33% in top 25% of high school class, 62% in top 50% of high school class. 61% from public high schools. **Test Scores:** SAT Math middle 50% range 420-570. SAT EBRW middle 50% range 420-590. ACT middle 50% range 19-25. Minimum paper TOEFL 550. **Basis for Candidate Selection:** *Very important factors considered include:* rigor of secondary school record, academic GPA, standardized test scores, interview, talent/ability, character/personal qualities. *Important factors considered include:* class rank, application essay, extracurricular activities, level of applicant's interest. *Other factors considered include:* recommendation(s), first generation, alumni/ae relation, geographical residence, volunteer work, work experience. **Freshman Admission Requirements:** High school diploma is required and GED is accepted *Academic units recommended:* 4 English, 3 math, 3 science, 1 science labs, 2 foreign language, 3 social studies, 2 history, 3 academic electives. **Freshman Admission Statistics:** 1,726 applied, 71.0% admitted, 29% enrolled. **Transfer Admission Requirements:** High school transcript, college transcript(s), standardized test scores, statement of good standing from prior institution(s). Minimum college GPA of 2.0 required. Lowest grade transferable C-. **General Admission Information:** Application fee $25. Priority deadline 1/1. Regular application deadline 8/1. Nonfall registration accepted. Admission may be deferred for a maximum of 3 years.

COSTS AND FINANCIAL AID

Average book expense $1,500. **Required Forms and Deadlines:** FAFSA. **Notification of Awards:** Applicants will be notified of awards on a rolling basis beginning 3/1. **Types of Aid:** *Need-based scholarships/grants:* College/university scholarship or grant aid from institutional funds; Federal Pell; Private scholarships; SEOG; State scholarships/grants. *Loans:* Direct PLUS loans; Direct Subsidized Stafford Loans; Direct Unsubsidized Stafford Loans. *Student Employment:* Federal Work-Study Program available. Institutional employment available. **Financial Aid Statistics:** 100% needy freshmen, 100% needy undergrads receive need-based scholarship or grant aid. 89% freshmen, 70% undergrads receive non-need-based scholarship or grant aid. 89% freshmen, 89% undergrads receive need-based self-help aid. 0% freshmen, 0% undergrads receive athletic scholarships. 99% freshmen, 97% undergrads receive any aid. **Criteria for awarding aid:** *Non-need-based:* Academics, Music/drama, Religious affiliation, State/district residency.

HELLENIC COLLEGE

50 Goddard Avenue, Brookline, MA 02445
Phone: 617-850-1260 · **Financial Aid Phone:** 617-850-1239
E-mail: admissions@hchc.edu · **CEEB Code:**
Fax: 617-850-1460 · **Website:** www.hchc.edu · **ACT Code:** 1843

This private school, affiliated with the Greek Orthodox Church, was founded in 1937. It has a 52 acre campus.

RATINGS
Admissions Selectivity Rating: 65   **Fire Safety Rating:** 99   **Green Rating:** 60*

STUDENTS AND FACULTY
Enrollment: 78. **Student Body:** 42% female, 58% male, 86% out-of-state, 5% international (9 countries represented). Asian 0%, African American 1%, Caucasian 75%, Hispanic 6%, Native American 1%, Pacific Islander 0%, Two or more races 1%, Race unknown 11%.
Retention and Graduation: 80% freshmen return for sophomore year. 24% grads go on to further study within 1 year. 24% grads pursue arts and sciences degrees. 2% grads pursue law degrees. 5% grads pursue business degrees. 0% grads pursue medical degrees. **Faculty:** Student/faculty ratio 8:1. 21 full-time faculty, 95% hold PhDs, 0% are members of minority groups, 29% are women.

ACADEMICS
Degrees: Bachelor's; Master's **Classes:** Most classes have 10-19 students. Most lab/discussion sessions have 10-19 students. **Most popular majors:** Religion/Religious Studies; Psychology, General; Business/Commerce, General. **Special Study Options:** Accelerated program; Cross-registration; Exchange student program (domestic); Honors program; Independent study; Internships; Liberal arts/career combination; Study abroad; Teacher certification program. **Honors programs:** Interdisciplinary Honors Program with rigorous Thesis direction. **Disability Services offered to physically disabled students:** Tutors. **Career services:** Alumni network; Alumni services; Career assessment; Career/job search classes; Internships; Regional alumni

FACILITIES
Housing: Apartments for married students; Apartments for single students; Men's dorms; Women's dorms 20% of campus accessible to physically diasbled. **Computers:** 100% of dorms, have wireless network access.

CAMPUS LIFE
Environment: City **Activities:** Campus Ministries; Choral groups; Literary magazine; Student government; Student newspaper; Yearbook. **Athletics (Intercollegiate):** *Men:* basketball. *Women:* tennis.

ADMISSIONS
Freshman Academic Profile: Average high school GPA 3.3. 97% from public high schools. **Test Scores:** Minimum internet-based TOEFL 80. **Basis for Candidate Selection:** *Very important factors considered include:* academic GPA, application essay, recommendation(s). *Important factors considered include:* rigor of secondary school record, class rank, standardized test scores, interview, character/personal qualities. *Other factors considered include:* extracurricular activities, first generation, alumni/ae relation, religious affiliation/commitment, volunteer work, work experience, level of applicant's interest. **Freshman Admission Requirements:** High school diploma is required and GED is accepted *Academic units required:* 4 English, 2 math, 2 science, 2 foreign language, 2 social studies, 2 history. **Freshman Admission Statistics:** 20 applied, 100.0% admitted, 45% enrolled. **Transfer Admission Requirements:** college transcript(s), essay or personal statement, interview, Minimum college GPA of 2.0 required. Lowest grade transferable C+. **General Admission Information:** Priority deadline 2/1. Regular application deadline 8/15. Nonfall registration accepted. Admission may be deferred.

COSTS AND FINANCIAL AID
Annual tuition $21,940. Room and board $12,142. Required fees $550. Average book expense $600. **Required Forms and Deadlines:** FAFSA; Institution's own financial aid form. **Notification of Awards:** Applicants will be notified of awards on a rolling basis beginning 4/1. **Types of Aid:** *Need-based scholarships/grants:* College/university scholarship or grant aid from institutional funds; Federal Pell; Private scholarships; SEOG; State scholarships/grants. *Loans:* Direct PLUS loans; Direct Subsidized Stafford Loans; Direct Unsubsidized Stafford Loans. *Student Employment:* Federal Work-Study Program available. Institutional employment available. **Financial Aid Statistics:** 100% needy freshmen, 100% needy undergrads receive need-based scholarship or grant aid. 0% undergrads receive non-need-based scholarship or grant aid. 100% freshmen, 100% undergrads receive need-based self-help aid. 0% freshmen, 0% undergrads receive athletic scholarships. 98% freshmen, 96% undergrads receive any aid. 100% undergrads borrow to pay for school. Average cumulative indebtedness $15,500. **Criteria for awarding aid:** *Need-based:* Academics,

Leadership, Religious affiliation *Non-need-based:* Academics, Alumni affiliation, Religious affiliation.

HENDERSON STATE UNIVERSITY

1100 Henderson Street, Arkadelphia, AR 71999-0001
Phone: 870-230-5028 · **Financial Aid Phone:** 870-230-5148
E-mail: admissions@hsu.edu · **CEEB Code:** 6272
Fax: 870-230-5066 · **ACT Code:** 126

This public school was founded in 1890. It has a 151 acre campus.

RATINGS
Admissions Selectivity Rating: 83   **Fire Safety Rating:** 89   **Green Rating:** 60*

STUDENTS AND FACULTY
Enrollment: 3,048. **Student Body:** 57% female, 43% male, 14% out-of-state, 1% international (26 countries represented). Asian 1%, African American 23%, Caucasian 66%, Hispanic 4%, Native American <1%, Pacific Islander <1%, Two or more races 3%, Race unknown <1%.
Retention and Graduation: 60% freshmen return for sophomore year. **Faculty:** Student/faculty ratio 16:1. 174 full-time faculty, 76% hold PhDs, 19% are members of minority groups, 46% are women. 0% of classes are taught by teaching assistants.

ACADEMICS
Degrees: Associate; Bachelor's; Certificate; Master's; Post-Bachelor's certificate; Post-Master's certificate **Classes:** Most classes have 10-19 students. Most lab/discussion sessions have fewer than 10 students. **Most popular majors:** Elementary Education And Teaching; Biology/Biological Sciences, General; Business/Commerce, General. **Special Study Options:** Cross-registration; Distance learning; Dual enrollment; Honors program; Internships; Teacher certification program. **Honors programs:** The overarching purpose of the Honors College is summed up in the single ancient Greek word, aretĀ© (highest excellence), which the students and faculty of the College have taken as their motto. In working to achieve this purpose, the Honors College shares the university's goal "to excel in undergraduate education, always striving to enrich the quality of learning and teaching." The program is directly involved in "actively recruiting, challenging, and supporting those students" who are among the most "highly motivated toward achieving academic success." **Disability Services offered to physically disabled students:** Note-taking services; Tutors. **Career services:** Alumni services; Career assessment; Internships

FACILITIES
Housing: Coed dorms; Men's dorms; Special housing for international students; Theme housing; Women's dorms 95% of campus accessible to physically diasbled. **Special Academic Facilities/Equipment:** closed-circuit TV studio, Planetarium **Computers:** Students can register for classes online. Administrative functions (other than registration) can be performed online.

CAMPUS LIFE
Environment: Rural **Activities:** Choral groups; Concert band; Dance; Drama/theater; International Student Organization; Jazz band; Literary magazine; Marching band; Music ensembles; Pep band; Radio station; Student government; Student newspaper; Television station; Yearbook 80 registered organizations, 11 honor societies, 7 religious organizations. 9 fraternities, 6 sororities. **Athletics (Intercollegiate):** *Men:* baseball, basketball, cross-country, football, golf, swimming. *Women:* basketball, cross-country, golf, softball, swimming, tennis, volleyball. **On-Campus Highlights:** HSU Planetarium, New Reddie Athletic Center, Newly Renovated Arkansas Hall, Henderson House Bed and Breakfast, Starbucks **Environmental Initiatives:** Recycling paper, cans and bottles on campus.

ADMISSIONS
Freshman Academic Profile: Average high school GPA 3.2. 15% in top 10% of high school class, 36% in top 25% of high school class, 69% in top 50% of high school class. 92% from public high schools. **Test Scores:** SAT Math middle 50% range 440-590. SAT EBRW middle 50% range 430-580. ACT middle 50% range 19-25. Minimum internet-based TOEFL 61. Minimum paper TOEFL 500. **Basis for Candidate Selection:** *Very important factors considered include:* rigor of secondary school record, academic GPA, standardized test scores. *Important factors considered include:* class rank. **Freshman Admission Requirements:** High school diploma is required and GED is accepted *Academic units required:* 4 English, 4 math, 3 science, 2 social studies, 1 history, and 8 units from above areas or other academic areas. *Academic units recommended:* 4 English, 4 math, 4 science, 2 foreign language, 2 social studies, 2 history, 8 units from above areas or other academic areas. **Freshman Admission Statistics:** 3,388 applied, 62.2% admitted, 35% enrolled. **Transfer

Admission Requirements: college transcript(s), Lowest grade transferable C. **General Admission Information:** Regular application deadline 7/15. Nonfall registration accepted. Admission may be deferred.

COSTS AND FINANCIAL AID
Required Forms and Deadlines: FAFSA; Institution's own financial aid form. **Notification of Awards:** Applicants will be notified of awards on a rolling basis beginning 3/1. **Types of Aid:** *Need-based scholarships/grants:* College/university scholarship or grant aid from institutional funds; Federal Pell; Private scholarships; SEOG; State scholarships/grants. *Loans:* Direct PLUS loans; Direct Subsidized Stafford Loans; Direct Unsubsidized Stafford Loans. *Student Employment:* Federal Work-Study Program available. **Financial Aid Statistics:** 69% needy freshmen, 69% needy undergrads receive need-based scholarship or grant aid. 87% freshmen, 72% undergrads receive non-need-based scholarship or grant aid. 63% freshmen, 71% undergrads receive need-based self-help aid. 8% freshmen, 8% undergrads receive athletic scholarships. **Criteria for awarding aid:** *Non-need-based:* Academics, Alumni affiliation, Art, Athletics, Leadership, Minority status, Music/drama.

HENDRIX COLLEGE

1600 Washington Avenue, Conway, AR 72032
Phone: 501-450-1362 · **Financial Aid Phone:** 501-450-1368
E-mail: adm@hendrix.edu · **CEEB Code:** 6273
Fax: 501-450-3843 · **Website:** www.hendrix.edu · **ACT Code:** 128

This private school, affiliated with the Methodist Church, was founded in 1876. It has a 160 acre campus.

RATINGS
Admissions Selectivity Rating: 80   **Fire Safety Rating:** 81   **Green Rating:** 61

STUDENTS AND FACULTY
Enrollment: 1,303. **Student Body:** 53% female, 47% male, 52% out-of-state, 3% international (13 countries represented). Asian 5%, African American 5%, Caucasian 78%, Hispanic 5%, Native American 1%, Pacific Islander <1%, Two or more races 3%, Race unknown 1%.
Retention and Graduation: 79% freshmen return for sophomore year. 63% grads go on to further study within 1 year. 43% grads pursue arts and sciences degrees. 10% grads pursue law degrees. 3% grads pursue business degrees. 6% grads pursue medical degrees. **Faculty:** Student/faculty ratio 11:1. 107 full-time faculty, 93% hold PhDs, 13% are members of minority groups, 44% are women. 0% of classes are taught by teaching assistants.

ACADEMICS
Degrees: Bachelor's; Master's **Classes:** Most classes have 20-29 students. Most lab/discussion sessions have 20-29 students. **Most popular majors:** Biology/Biological Sciences, General; Psychology, General. **Special Study Options:** Cooperative education program; Double major; English as a Second Language (ESL); Independent study; Internships; Student-designed major; Study abroad; Teacher certification program. **Combined degree programs:** BA/MEng. **Disability Services offered to physically disabled students:** Note-taking services; Tape recorders. **Career services:** Alumni network; Alumni services; Career assessment; Career/job search classes; Internships

FACILITIES
Housing: Apartments for married students; Apartments for single students; Coed dorms; Men's dorms; Special housing for disabled student; Special housing for international students; Theme housing; Wellness housing; Women's dorms 49% of campus accessible to physically diasbled. **Special Academic Facilities/Equipment:** Herbarium, Wilbur A. Mills Library. **Computers:** 100% of classrooms, 100% of dorms, 100% of libraries, 100% of dining areas, 100% of student union, 100% of common outdoor areas have wireless network access. Students can register for classes online. Administrative functions (other than registration) can be performed online.

CAMPUS LIFE
Environment: Town **Activities:** Campus Ministries; Choral groups; Concert band; Dance; Drama/theater; International Student Organization; Jazz band; Literary magazine; Marching band; Model UN; Music ensembles; Musical theater; Radio station; Student government; Student newspaper; Student-run film society; Symphony orchestra; Yearbook 80 registered organizations, 6 honor societies, 5 religious organizations. **Athletics (Intercollegiate):** *Men:* baseball, basketball, cross-country, diving, golf, lacrosse, soccer, swimming, tennis, track/field (outdoor). *Women:* basketball, cross-country, diving, field hockey, golf, soccer, softball, swimming, tennis, track/field (outdoor), volleyball. **On-Campus Highlights:** Student Life & Technology Center, Village at Hendrix, Wellness & Athletic Center, Charles D. Morgan Center for Physical Sc, D.W. Reynolds

building for the life scie **Environmental Initiatives:** Reduction in paper utilization

ADMISSIONS
Freshman Academic Profile: Average high school GPA 3.9. 48% in top 10% of high school class, 96% in top 50% of high school class. 77% from public high schools. **Test Scores:** SAT Math middle 50% range 580-660. SAT EBRW middle 50% range 640-680. ACT middle 50% range 25-32. Minimum internet-based TOEFL 79. Minimum paper TOEFL 550. **Basis for Candidate Selection:** *Very important factors considered include:* rigor of secondary school record, academic GPA, application essay, standardized test scores. *Important factors considered include:* class rank, recommendation(s), interview, extracurricular activities. *Other factors considered include:* talent/ability, racial/ethnic status, volunteer work. **Freshman Admission Requirements:** High school diploma is required and GED is accepted *Academic units recommended:* 4 English, 3 math, 2 science, 2 foreign language, 3 social studies. **Freshman Admission Statistics:** 1,656 applied, 83.0% admitted, 27% enrolled. **Transfer Admission Requirements:** college transcript(s), essay or personal statement, statement of good standing from prior institution(s). Minimum college GPA of 2.5 required. Lowest grade transferable C. **General Admission Information:** Application fee $40. Priority deadline 2/1. Regular application deadline 6/1. Nonfall registration accepted.

COSTS AND FINANCIAL AID
Required Forms and Deadlines: FAFSA. **Notification of Awards:** Applicants will be notified of awards on a rolling basis beginning 3/1. **Types of Aid:** *Need-based scholarships/grants:* College/university scholarship or grant aid from institutional funds; Federal Pell; Private scholarships; SEOG; State scholarships/grants. *Loans:* Direct PLUS loans; Direct Subsidized Stafford Loans; Direct Unsubsidized Stafford Loans. *Student Employment:* Federal Work-Study Program available. Institutional employment available. **Financial Aid Statistics:** 100% needy freshmen, 100% needy undergrads receive need-based scholarship or grant aid. 31% freshmen, 34% undergrads receive non-need-based scholarship or grant aid. 69% freshmen, 65% undergrads receive need-based self-help aid. 0% freshmen, 0% undergrads receive athletic scholarships. 100% freshmen, 100% undergrads receive any aid. Average cumulative indebtedness $30,213. **Criteria for awarding aid:** *Non-need-based:* Academics, Art, Leadership, Music/drama, State/district residency.

HIGH POINT UNIVERSITY

One University Parkway, High Point, NC 27268
Phone: 336-841-9216 · **Financial Aid Phone:** 336-841-9124
E-mail: admiss@highpoint.edu · **CEEB Code:** 5293
Fax: 336-888-6382 · **Website:** www.highpoint.edu · **ACT Code:** 3108

This private school, affiliated with the Methodist Church, was founded in 1924. It has a 430 acre campus.

RATINGS
Admissions Selectivity Rating: 78   **Fire Safety Rating:** 89   **Green Rating:** 61

STUDENTS AND FACULTY
Enrollment: 4,407. **Student Body:** 59% female, 41% male, 78% out-of-state, 2% international (30 countries represented). Asian 2%, African American 5%, Caucasian 77%, Hispanic 5%, Native American <1%, Pacific Islander <1%, Two or more races 7%, Race unknown 2%.
Retention and Graduation: 79% freshmen return for sophomore year. 59% freshmen graduate within 4 years. 63% freshmen graduate within 6 years. 19% grads go on to further study within 1 year. 50% grads pursue arts and sciences degrees. 7% grads pursue law degrees. 9% grads pursue business degrees. 13% grads pursue medical degrees. **Faculty:** Student/faculty ratio 14:1. 305 full-time faculty, 81% hold PhDs, 11% are members of minority groups, 47% are women. 0% of classes are taught by teaching assistants.

ACADEMICS
Degrees: Bachelor's; Doctoral/Professional; Doctoral/Research; Master's; Post-Bachelor's certificate **Classes:** Most classes have 20-29 students. **Most popular majors:** Communication, General; Biology/Biological Sciences, General; Business Administration And Management, General. **Special Study Options:** Accelerated program; Cooperative education program; Cross-registration; Double major; Dual enrollment; English as a Second Language (ESL); Honors

program; Independent study; Internships; Liberal arts/career combination; Student-designed major; Study abroad; Teacher certification program. **Honors programs:** With a commitment to the rich traditions of the liberal arts, the High Point University Honors Scholar Program takes a multidisciplinary, holistic approach to higher education, empowering students to cultivate contemplative selves and to build meaningful public lives. Believing a liberal education transcends the sum of its parts, the program challenges students to connect diverse ways of comprehending their world, to approach problems and questions intellectual rigor and adaptability. Its graduates have prepared themselves for leadership on a global stage, their lives deepened by intellectual curiosity, broadened by cultural and academic diversity, and strengthened by empathy and self-awareness. They distinguish themselves by their abilities to synthesize information, create new knowledge, render sound judgments, and communicate effectively. **Combined degree programs:** BA/MA; BA/MEng. **Disability Services offered to physically disabled students:** Note-taking services; Reader services; Tape recorders; Tutors. **Career services:** Alumni network; Alumni services; Career assessment; Career/job search classes; Internships; Regional alumni

FACILITIES

Housing: Apartments for single students; Coed dorms; Fraternity/sorority housing; Men's dorms; Special housing for disabled student; Theme housing; Wellness housing; Women's dorms 98% of campus accessible to physically diasbled. **Special Academic Facilities/Equipment:** Campus Facilities: Brand new or recently renovated, state-of-the-art residence halls (with cable TV and wireless Internet connection in each student room). Excellent classroom, library and laboratory space. Athletic/Convocation center with arena, indoor 25 meter competition pool, racquetball courts, sports medicine center, tennis courts. Facilities include TV station, internet radio station, computer laboratories including MAC design labs, Linux labs and CAD labs, tutoring center, newly renovated chapel, Slane Student Center, the R.G. Wanek University Center, Hayworth Fine Arts Center and the Norton International Home Furnishings Center. New Construction: The campus of High Point University is currently experiencing the greatest period of growth in our 90+ year history. Congdon Hall was built in 2017 and is a four-story, 224,000-square-foot complex that is home to the Congdon School of Health Sciences and the Fred Wilson School of Pharmacy. The facility offers advanced biomedical research facilities, a cadaver lab, standardized client space, medical simulation rooms, a biomechanics lab, and vivariums. Cottrell Hall opened fall of 2015 and is located at the intersection of Founders Street and Alumni Avenue behind the R.G. Wanek Center complex and supported by $22 million in gifts from HPU parents. Cottrell Hall serves as a hub of activity for students seeking career preparation and skill diversification. The two story, 43,000-square-foot, LEED-certified building houses the Office of Career and Professional Development, the Internship Resource Center, the Office of Study Abroad, the Center for Entrepreneurship, Undergraduate Research and Creative Works, the Flanagan Center for Student Success, the Student Employment Program, and the Center for Selling Excellence. In addition, a new alumni amphitheater just outside this building seats about 1,000 people and serves as a connecting point between Cottrell Hall and the new residential Centennial Square II complex. The School of Education opened its doors in 2012 featuring a Georgian-style structure that houses the education and psychology faculty in technologically advanced classrooms, computer labs and offices. This 29,000-square foot facility has its own resource center, library, and study lounge. It's also constructed to meet LEED (Leadership in Energy and Environmental and Design) certification, which is a rating system for "green" buildings. The R. G. Wanek Center is situated on Panther Drive, across from the Millis Athletic/Convocation Center. The $65 million, 277,000 square feet building functions as a one-stop shop of sorts– it includes residential space for 580 students, as well as multiple dining venues, a cinema house, a convenience store and an entire floor of study areas – all under one roof. Among the dining facilities is The Point Sports Grille, an interactive sports entertainment restaurant and community gaming center, similar to an ESPN Zone© concept. In addition to the sports and entertainment venue, the University Center has the Great Day Bakery, where students are able to dine on fresh-baked breads, sandwiches, Panini, fresh salads and pastries. 1924 Prime Steakhouse serves steaks, in addition to fresh fish and poultry entrees and unique vegetarian options. The Plato S. Wilson Family School of Commerce is a $16 million, 60,000-square-foot building named in honor of Plato S. Wilson. It was made possible in large part by a financial gift from Wilson, a 40-year furniture sales and manufacturer's representative for companies including Heritage, Henredon and Henkel-Harris. The new building contains several spaces dedicated to business endeavors, such as a New York Stock Exchange-style investment trading room, complete with a real stock ticker and Reuters trading software, as well as a Center for Entrepreneurship and Innovation. The state-of-the-art Nido R. Qubein School of Communication houses the University's seven communication-based majors including Electronic Media Production, Games and Interactive Media Design, Journalism, Media and Popular Culture Studies, Strategic Communication, Sport and Event Management, and Sport Communication. Curriculum housed in the 60,000-square-foot school blends traditional liberal arts education and hands-on technical instruction with the latest communication technologies,

taking academics far beyond the textbook and into the "real world." The facility is equipped with an incredible array of high-tech instructional equipment and spaces including two high-definition TV production studios, computer labs, a multi-track audio recording studio, observation decks, 12 editing suites with Final Cut Pro and Pro Tools editing systems, a games/interactive communication development studio, classrooms and faculty offices, a library lounge with rare first-edition books, and the HPU internet radio station. Blessing Residence Hall is a $10 million facility made possible by the generous lead gift of one anonymous donor who requested we call it the "Blessing" residence hall. It is loaded with amenities that make it a prototype for 21st-century college residence halls. It offers 240 fully furnished, private bedrooms arranged in suites with living rooms, kitchens and dining areas. Residents enjoy spacious common areas, computer lounges, conference areas, laundry rooms and elevators. Slane Student Center is a centerpiece of campus. This $6.5 million, 45,000-square-foot building connects to the original Slane Student Center via a two-story atrium and features a high-performance aerobics room, elevated running track, fully equipped weight room, food court, dramatic inside and outside basketball courts, outdoor swimming pool, sand volleyball courts, and a grand student atrium with several restaurant locations and sitting areas. The Earl N. Phillips School of Business is a 27,000-square-foot building that is the home for the more than 1,100 undergraduate students pursuing a degree in one of High Point University's 6 undergraduate majors and Master of Business Administration graduate degree. The facility features a 200-seat, tiered lecture hall, four smaller lecture rooms, traditional classrooms, a spacious auditorium, private study rooms, computer labs and faculty offices. The Jerry & Kitty Steele Sports Center is a $5 million, two-story, 27,000-square-foot facility featuring training and weight rooms, a hospitality/conference room, locker rooms and an academic services room. In addition, another $5 million has been invested in a new soccer stadium, baseball stadium and eight-lane track. High Point University also has a university park and it is an extraordinary outdoor experience. Featuring a network of trails and bridges, spectacular waterfalls, a 15-foot overhead trellis, multilevel reflecting pools, and an amphitheater, this park is the perfect place for an outdoor class, receptions, plays and programs. **Computers:** 100% of classrooms, 100% of dorms, 100% of libraries, 100% of dining areas, 100% of student union, 100% of common outdoor areas have wireless network access. Students can register for classes online. Administrative functions (other than registration) can be performed online.

CAMPUS LIFE

Environment: City **Activities:** Campus Ministries; Choral groups; Concert band; Dance; Drama/theater; International Student Organization; Jazz band; Literary magazine; Model UN; Music ensembles; Musical theater; Opera; Pep band; Radio station; Student government; Student newspaper; Student-run film society; Symphony orchestra; Television station; Yearbook 109 registered organizations, 14 honor societies, 8 religious organizations. 4 fraternities, 5 sororities. **Athletics (Intercollegiate):** *Men:* baseball, basketball, cheerleading, cross-country, golf, soccer, tennis, track/field (outdoor), track/field (indoor). *Women:* basketball, cheerleading, cross-country, golf, soccer, tennis, track/field (outdoor), track/field (indoor), volleyball. **On-Campus Highlights:** Wanek University Center, Slane Student Center, Cottrell Hall- Flanagan Center for Student Success, Hayworth Fine Arts Center, Smith Library **Environmental Initiatives:** Arboreatum and Tree Campus USA

ADMISSIONS

Freshman Academic Profile: Average high school GPA 3.3. 18% in top 10% of high school class, 47% in top 25% of high school class, 78% in top 50% of high school class. 64% from public high schools. **Test Scores:** SAT Math middle 50% range 520-620. SAT EBRW middle 50% range 530-620. ACT middle 50% range 21-27. Minimum internet-based TOEFL 79. **Basis for Candidate Selection:** *Very important factors considered include:* academic GPA, standardized test scores. *Important factors considered include:* rigor of secondary school record, application essay, recommendation(s), interview, extracurricular activities, talent/ability, character/personal qualities, volunteer work, work experience, level of applicant's interest. *Other factors considered include:* first generation, alumni/ae relation. **Freshman Admission Requirements:** High school diploma is required and GED is accepted *Academic units required:* 4 English, 3 math, 3 science, 1 science labs, 2 foreign language, 3 social studies, *Academic units recommended:* 4 English, 4 math, 3 science, 1 science labs, 3 foreign language, 3 social studies. **Freshman Admission Statistics:** 8,936 applied, 80.7% admitted, 15% enrolled. **Transfer Admission Requirements:** High school transcript, college transcript(s), standardized test scores, statement of good standing from prior institution(s). Minimum college GPA of 2.0 required. Lowest grade transferable C. **General Admission Information:** Application fee $50. Priority deadline 3/15. Regular application deadline 3/15. Nonfall registration accepted. Admission may be deferred for a maximum of 1 year.

COSTS AND FINANCIAL AID

Annual tuition $29,800. Room and board $13,350. Required fees $4,205. Average book expense $1,500. **Required Forms and Deadlines:** FAFSA; State aid form. **Notification of Awards:** Applicants will be notified of awards on a rolling basis beginning 4/1. **Types of Aid:** *Need-based scholarships/*

grants: College/university scholarship or grant aid from institutional funds; Federal Pell; Private scholarships; SEOG; State scholarships/grants. Loans: Direct PLUS loans; Direct Subsidized Stafford Loans; Direct Unsubsidized Stafford Loans. Student Employment: Federal Work-Study Program available. Institutional employment available. **Financial Aid Statistics:** 96% needy freshmen, 69% needy undergrads receive need-based scholarship or grant aid. 83% freshmen, 79% undergrads receive non-need-based scholarship or grant aid. 70% freshmen, 78% undergrads receive need-based self-help aid. 5% freshmen, 6% undergrads receive athletic scholarships. 85% freshmen, 77% undergrads receive any aid. 58% undergrads borrow to pay for school. Average cumulative indebtedness $35,897. **Criteria for awarding aid:** Non-need-based: Academics, Alumni affiliation, Art, Athletics, Leadership, Music/drama, Religious affiliation, State/district residency.

See page 950.

HILBERT COLLEGE

5200 South Park Avenue, Hamburg, NY 14075-1597
Phone: 716-649-7900 • **Financial Aid Phone:** 716-649-7900
E-mail: admissions@hilbert.edu • **CEEB Code:** 2334
Fax: 716-649-0702 • **Website:** www.hilbert.edu • **ACT Code:** 2759

This private school, affiliated with the Roman Catholic Church, was founded in 1957. It has a 40 acre campus.

RATINGS

Admissions Selectivity Rating: 73 **Fire Safety Rating:** 93 **Green Rating:** 60*

STUDENTS AND FACULTY

Enrollment: 998. **Student Body:** 60% female, 40% male, 10% out-of-state, <1% international (4 countries represented). Asian <1%, African American 6%, Caucasian 82%, Hispanic 2%, Native American 2%, Race unknown 7%. **Retention and Graduation:** 70% freshmen return for sophomore year. 15% grads go on to further study within 1 year. 4% grads pursue arts and sciences degrees. 4% grads pursue law degrees. 4% grads pursue business degrees. 0% grads pursue medical degrees. **Faculty:** Student/faculty ratio 13:1. 48 full-time faculty, 50% hold PhDs, 2% are members of minority groups, 48% are women. 0% of classes are taught by teaching assistants.

ACADEMICS

Degrees: Associate; Bachelor's; Certificate; Terminal Associate **Classes:** Most classes have fewer than 10 students. Most lab/discussion sessions have 20-29 students. **Most popular majors:** Criminal Justice/Law Enforcement Administration; Forensic Science And Technology; Business/Commerce, General. **Special Study Options:** Cross-registration; Distance learning; Dual enrollment; Honors program; Independent study; Internships; Study abroad. **Honors programs:** About the Honors Program The Hilbert Honors Program will give you more from your college experience. You will enroll in regular classes and fulfill honors credit requirements by doing advanced work, or in lieu of projects. These special projects allow you to work one-on-one with Hilbert's outstanding honors faculty in your major and in other academic areas. As an honors student, you will also have a student mentor for your first semester and personal faculty advisement. **Disability Services offered to physically disabled students:** Note-taking services; Reader services; Tape recorders; Tutors. **Career services:** Alumni network; Alumni services; Career assessment; Internships

FACILITIES

Housing: Apartments for single students; Coed dorms 95% of campus accessible to physically disabled. **Special Academic Facilities/Equipment:** Honors Lounge, Institute for Law and Justice, Center for Creative Media, **Computers:** 100% of classrooms, 100% of dorms, 100% of libraries, 100% of dining areas, 100% of student union, 100% of common outdoor areas have wireless network access. Students can register for classes online. Administrative functions (other than registration) can be performed online.

CAMPUS LIFE

Environment: Village **Activities:** Campus Ministries; Choral groups; Drama/theater; Literary magazine; Student government; Student newspaper 20 registered organizations, 5 honor societies, 1 religious organization. **Athletics (Intercollegiate):** Men: baseball, basketball, cross-country, golf, soccer, volleyball. Women: basketball, cross-country, golf, soccer, softball, volleyball. **On-Campus Highlights:** Hafner Recreation Center, Franciscan Hall Atrium, Campus Apartments, Swan Auditorium, Paczesny Hall

ADMISSIONS

Freshman Academic Profile: Average high school GPA 2.8. 2% in top 10% of high school class, 13% in top 25% of high school class, 40% in top 50% of high

school class. 85% from public high schools. **Test Scores:** SAT Math middle 50% range 400-510. SAT EBRW middle 50% range 400-510. ACT middle 50% range 17-22. Minimum paper TOEFL 500. **Basis for Candidate Selection:** Very important factors considered include: rigor of secondary school record, academic GPA. Important factors considered include: recommendation(s). Other factors considered include: application essay, interview, extracurricular activities, talent/ability, character/personal qualities, volunteer work, work experience. **Freshman Admission Requirements:** High school diploma is required and GED is accepted Academic units required: 4 English, 2 math, 2 science, 1 science labs, 2 social studies, 2 history, 4 academic electives, Academic units recommended: 4 English, 3 math, 3 science, 1 foreign language, 3 social studies, 3 history, 3 academic electives. **Freshman Admission Statistics:** 726 applied, 84.7% admitted, 35% enrolled. **Transfer Admission Requirements:** High school transcript, college transcript(s), Minimum college GPA of 2.0 required. Lowest grade transferable C. **General Admission Information:** Application fee $20. Priority deadline 6/30. Regular application deadline 9/1. Nonfall registration accepted. Admission may be deferred for a maximum of 1 year.

COSTS AND FINANCIAL AID

Annual tuition $16,000. Room and board $6,600. Required fees $600. Average book expense $700. **Required Forms and Deadlines:** FAFSA; State aid form. **Notification of Awards:** Applicants will be notified of awards on a rolling basis beginning 3/1. **Types of Aid:** Need-based scholarships/grants: College/university scholarship or grant aid from institutional funds; Federal Pell; Private scholarships; SEOG; State scholarships/grants. Loans: Student Employment: Federal Work-Study Program available. Institutional employment available. **Financial Aid Statistics:** 99% needy freshmen, 98% needy undergrads receive need-based scholarship or grant aid. 4% freshmen, 5% undergrads receive non-need-based scholarship or grant aid. 90% freshmen, 88% undergrads receive need-based self-help aid. 0% freshmen, 0% undergrads receive athletic scholarships. 92% freshmen, 87% undergrads receive any aid. **Criteria for awarding aid:** Non-need-based: Academics, Leadership, Minority status.

HILLSDALE COLLEGE

33 East College Street, Hillsdale, MI 49242
Phone: 517-607-2327 • **Financial Aid Phone:** 517-607-2350
E-mail: admissions@hillsdale.edu • **CEEB Code:** 1295
Fax: 517-607-2223 • **Website:** www.hillsdale.edu • **ACT Code:** 2010

This private school, affiliated with the Christian (Nondenominational) Church, was founded in 1844. It has a 400 acre campus.

RATINGS

Admissions Selectivity Rating: 93 **Fire Safety Rating:** 91 **Green Rating:** 62

STUDENTS AND FACULTY

Enrollment: 1,502. **Student Body:** 49% female, 51% male, 65% out-of-state, (14 countries represented). **Retention and Graduation:** 92% freshmen return for sophomore year. 71% freshmen graduate within 4 years. 85% freshmen graduate within 6 years. 22% grads go on to further study within 1 year. 14% grads pursue arts and sciences degrees. 2% grads pursue law degrees. 1% grads pursue business degrees. 2% grads pursue medical degrees. **Faculty:** Student/faculty ratio 10:1. 137 full-time faculty, 95% hold PhDs, 24% are women. 0% of classes are taught by teaching assistants.

ACADEMICS

Degrees: Bachelor's; Doctoral; Master's **Classes:** Most classes have 20-29 students. Most lab/discussion sessions have 10-19 students. **Most popular majors:** English Language And Literature, General; Economics, General; History, General. **Special Study Options:** Double major; Dual enrollment; Honors program; Independent study; Internships; Student-designed major; Study abroad. **Honors programs:** The Collegiate Scholars program provides highly motivated students, who have demonstrated academic excellence at Hillsdale College, with an enhanced program of study that reinforces the highest ideals of the college's core curriculum. Students selected to be Collegiate Scholars benefit from small, interdisciplinary seminars giving close attention to the authors and works covered more generally in the core. These scholars serve the campus community by reaching beyond specialization to help bind the campus together within a common conversation about liberal arts education and the life of the mind. Foreign travel after the junior year widens the experience even further, and a senior thesis provides exceptional experience in crafting a well-researched, well-written argument defended before a faculty committee and a college audience. **Disability Services offered to physically disabled students:** Tape recorders; Tutors. **Career services:** Alumni network; Alumni services; Career assessment; Internships; Regional alumni

FACILITIES

Housing: Apartments for single students; Cooperative housing; Fraternity/ sorority housing; Men's dorms; Women's dorms 85% of campus accessible to physically diasbled. **Special Academic Facilities/Equipment:** Greenhouse, Sage Center for the Arts, Howard Music Hall, media center, K-8 private academy,Slayton Arboretum, rare books library, shooting range, Herbert Henry Dow Science Building, Daniel M. Fisk Museum of Natural History, Strosaker Science Center, Mary Randall Preschool, Hayden Park **Computers:** 100% of classrooms, 85% of dorms, 100% of libraries, 100% of dining areas, 100% of student union, 100% of common outdoor areas have wireless network access.

CAMPUS LIFE

Environment: Village **Activities:** Campus Ministries; Choral groups; Concert band; Dance; Drama/theater; International Student Organization; Jazz band; Literary magazine; Music ensembles; Musical theater; Opera; Pep band; Radio station; Student government; Student newspaper; Student-run film society; Symphony orchestra; Yearbook 50 registered organizations, 26 honor societies, 4 religious organizations. 3 fraternities, 3 sororities. **Athletics (Intercollegiate):** *Men:* baseball, basketball, cheerleading, cross-country, football, track/field (outdoor), track/field (indoor). *Women:* basketball, cheerleading, cross-country, diving, equestrian sports, softball, swimming, track/field (outdoor), track/field (indoor), volleyball. **On-Campus Highlights:** Student Union, Classrooms/ Labs, Sage Center for the Arts, Howard Music Hall, Sports Complex

ADMISSIONS

Freshman Academic Profile: Average high school GPA 3.9. 45% from public high schools. **Test Scores:** SAT Math middle 50% range 620-710. SAT EBRW middle 50% range 660-730. ACT middle 50% range 28-32. **Basis for Candidate Selection:** *Very important factors considered include:* rigor of secondary school record, academic GPA, application essay, standardized test scores, interview, extracurricular activities, character/personal qualities, level of applicant's interest. *Important factors considered include:* recommendation(s), volunteer work, work experience. *Other factors considered include:* talent/ ability, alumni/ae relation. **Freshman Admission Requirements:** High school diploma is required and GED is accepted *Academic units required:* 4 English, 3 math, 3 science, 2 social studies, 3 history, *Academic units recommended:* 4 English, 4 math, 4 science, 2 science labs, 3 foreign language, 4 social studies, 4 history. **Freshman Admission Statistics:** 2,080 applied, 41.5% admitted, 43% enrolled. **Transfer Admission Requirements:** High school transcript, college transcript(s), essay or personal statement, standardized test scores, statement of good standing from prior institution(s). Minimum college GPA of 3.25 required. Lowest grade transferable C. **General Admission Information:** Application fee $35. Priority deadline 1/1. Regular application deadline 4/1. Nonfall registration accepted.

COSTS AND FINANCIAL AID

Required Forms and Deadlines: Institution's own financial aid form. **Notification of Awards:** Applicants will be notified of awards on a rolling basis beginning 12/1. **Types of Aid:** *Need-based scholarships/grants:* College/ university scholarship or grant aid from institutional funds; Private scholarships. *Loans: Student Employment:* Institutional employment available. **Financial Aid Statistics:** 65% needy freshmen, 64% needy undergrads receive need-based scholarship or grant aid. 91% freshmen, 93% undergrads receive non-need-based scholarship or grant aid. 63% freshmen, 72% undergrads receive need-based self-help aid. 21% freshmen, 16% undergrads receive athletic scholarships. 97% freshmen, 98% undergrads receive any aid. **Criteria for awarding aid:** *Non-need-based:* Academics, Alumni affiliation, Art, Athletics, Leadership, Music/drama.

See page 952.

HIRAM COLLEGE

P.O. Box 67, Hiram, OH 44234
Phone: 330-569-5169 · **Financial Aid Phone:** (330) 569-5107
E-mail: admission@hiram.edu · **CEEB Code:** 1297
Fax: 330-569-5944 · **Website:** www.hiram.edu · **ACT Code:** 3280

This private school, affiliated with the Disciples of Christ Church, was founded in 1850. It has a 110 acre campus.

RATINGS

Admissions Selectivity Rating: 80   **Fire Safety Rating:** 60*   **Green Rating:** 60*

STUDENTS AND FACULTY

Enrollment: 967. **Student Body:** 53% female, 47% male, 18% out-of-state, 1% international (12 countries represented). Asian 1%, African American 16%, Caucasian 64%, Hispanic 4%, Pacific Islander <1%, Two or more races 3%, Race unknown 9%.

Retention and Graduation: 70% freshmen return for sophomore year. 50% freshmen graduate within 4 years. 56% freshmen graduate within 6 years. **Faculty:** Student/faculty ratio 10:1. 79 full-time faculty, 95% hold PhDs, 58% are women. 0% of classes are taught by teaching assistants.

ACADEMICS

Degrees: Bachelor's; Master's **Classes:** Most classes have 10-19 students. Most lab/discussion sessions have 20-29 students. **Most popular majors:** Registered Nursing/Registered Nurse; Business Administration And Management, General; Accounting And Finance. **Special Study Options:** Accelerated program; Cross-registration; Distance learning; Double major; Dual enrollment; English as a Second Language (ESL); Exchange student program (domestic); Honors program; Independent study; Internships; Liberal arts/career combination; Student-designed major; Study abroad; Teacher certification program; Weekend college. **Honors programs:** The Hiram College Eclectic Scholars Program aims to serve committed, self-motivated, intellectually curious students with an enriched undergraduate liberal arts education. Toward this end, it provides opportunities for creative, interdisciplinary scholarship; intimate interactions with renowned scholars in Hiram's Centers of Distinction; and professional career development. **Disability Services offered to physically disabled students:** Note-taking services; Tutors. **Career services:** Alumni network; Alumni services; Career assessment; Career/job search classes; Internships

FACILITIES

Housing: Apartments for single students; Coed dorms; Theme housing; Wellness housing; Women's dorms 55% of campus accessible to physically diasbled. **Special Academic Facilities/Equipment:** James H. Barrow Field Station, Northwoods Field Station, Stephens Memorial Observatory **Computers:**

CAMPUS LIFE

Environment: Rural **Activities:** Campus Ministries; Choral groups; Dance; Drama/theater; International Student Organization; Literary magazine; Music ensembles; Musical theater; Student government; Yearbook 55 registered organizations, 7 honor societies, 6 religious organizations. 3 fraternities, 3 sororities. **Athletics (Intercollegiate):** *Men:* baseball, basketball, cheerleading, cross-country, diving, football, golf, soccer, swimming, tennis, track/field (outdoor), track/field (indoor). *Women:* basketball, cheerleading, cross-country, diving, golf, soccer, softball, swimming, tennis, track/field (outdoor), track/ field (indoor), volleyball. **On-Campus Highlights:** James H. Barrow Field Station, The Hiram College Library, Kennedy Center(Food Court, Bookstore, ballroom,and other facilities), Koritansky Hall, Stevens Memorial Observatory

ADMISSIONS

Freshman Academic Profile: Average high school GPA 3.4. 11% in top 10% of high school class, 30% in top 25% of high school class, 70% in top 50% of high school class. **Test Scores:** SAT Math middle 50% range 460-590. SAT EBRW middle 50% range 480-610. ACT middle 50% range 18-24. Minimum internet-based TOEFL 79. Minimum paper TOEFL 550. **Basis for Candidate Selection:** *Very important factors considered include:* rigor of secondary school record, academic GPA, character/personal qualities, level of applicant's interest. *Important factors considered include:* application essay, recommendation(s), interview, extracurricular activities, talent/ability. *Other factors considered include:* class rank, standardized test scores, alumni/ae relation, volunteer work, work experience. **Freshman Admission Requirements:** High school diploma is required and GED is accepted *Academic units required:* 4 English, 4 math, 3 science, 1 science labs, 1 foreign language, 1 social studies, 1 history, 1 academic elective, *Academic units recommended:* 4 English, 4 math, 3 science, 1 science labs, 2 foreign language, 1 social studies, 1 history, 2 academic electives. **Freshman Admission Statistics:** 2,761 applied, 63.5% admitted, 15% enrolled. **General Admission Information:** Application fee $25. Priority deadline 12/15. Nonfall registration accepted. Admission may be deferred for a maximum of 1 year.

COSTS AND FINANCIAL AID

Average book expense $800. **Required Forms and Deadlines:** FAFSA. **Types of Aid:** *Need-based scholarships/grants:* College/university scholarship or grant aid from institutional funds; Federal Pell; Private scholarships; SEOG; State scholarships/grants. *Loans:* Direct PLUS loans; Direct Subsidized Stafford Loans; Direct Unsubsidized Stafford Loans. *Student Employment:* Federal Work-Study Program available. Institutional employment available. **Criteria for awarding aid:** *Non-need-based:* Academics, Alumni affiliation, Art, Music/ drama, Religious affiliation.

HOBART AND WILLIAM SMITH COLLEGES

300 Pulteney Street, Geneva, NY 14456
Phone: 315-781-3622 • **Financial Aid Phone:** (315) 781-3315
E-mail: admissions@hws.edu • **CEEB Code:** 2294
Fax: 315-781-3914 • **Website:** www.hws.edu • **ACT Code:** 2758

This private school was founded in 1822. It has a 320 acre campus.

RATINGS
Admissions Selectivity Rating: 87   **Fire Safety Rating:** 96   **Green Rating:** 95

STUDENTS AND FACULTY
Enrollment: 2,220. **Student Body:** 51% female, 49% male, 60% out-of-state, 6% international (34 countries represented). Asian 3%, African American 6%, Caucasian 75%, Hispanic 5%, Native American <1%, Pacific Islander <1%, Two or more races 0%, Race unknown 5%.
Retention and Graduation: 86% freshmen return for sophomore year. 75% freshmen graduate within 4 years. 81% freshmen graduate within 6 years. **Faculty:** Student/faculty ratio 10:1. 221 full-time faculty, 98% hold PhDs, 18% are members of minority groups, 49% are women. 0% of classes are taught by teaching assistants.

ACADEMICS
Degrees: Bachelor's; Master's **Classes:** Most classes have 10-19 students. Most lab/discussion sessions have 20-29 students. **Most popular majors:** Environmental Studies; Mass Communication/Media Studies; Economics. **Special Study Options:** Double major; English as a Second Language (ESL); Honors program; Independent study; Internships; Student-designed major; Study abroad; Teacher certification program. **Honors programs:** The Honors Program at Hobart and William Smith Colleges makes possible the most sustained and sophisticated work available for juniors and seniors in the HWS curriculum. It affords students the opportunity to pursue skills and interests at the advanced level and grow in self-knowledge as their project develops. It also can greatly assist students in pursuing their professional ambitions after graduation. **Combined degree programs:** BA/MA. **Disability Services offered to physically disabled students:** Note-taking services; Reader services; Tape recorders; Tutors. **Career services:** Alumni network; Alumni services; Career assessment; Career/job search classes; Internships; Regional alumni

FACILITIES
Housing: Apartments for married students; Apartments for single students; Coed dorms; Cooperative housing; Fraternity/sorority housing; Men's dorms; Special housing for disabled student; Special housing for international students; Theme housing; Wellness housing; Women's dorms 69% of campus accessible to physically disabled. **Special Academic Facilities/Equipment:** The Gearan Center for the Performing Arts, Davis Gallery at Houghton House, William Scandling research vessel, Melly Academic Center, Rosenberg science center, Finger Lakes Institute, Centennial Center for Leadership, Richard S. Perkin Observatory (a teaching and outreach facility), 100 acre Hanley Nature Preserve, HWS solar farms and the HWS Fribolin Farm. **Computers:** Students can register for classes online. Administrative functions (other than registration) can be performed online.

CAMPUS LIFE
Environment: Village **Activities:** Campus Ministries; Choral groups; Concert band; Dance; Drama/theater; International Student Organization; Jazz band; Literary magazine; Music ensembles; Radio station; Student government; Student newspaper; Student-run film society; Yearbook 77 registered organizations, 12 honor societies, 4 religious organizations. 5 fraternities. **Athletics (Intercollegiate):** *Men:* basketball, crew/rowing, cross-country, football, golf, ice hockey, lacrosse, sailing, soccer, squash, tennis. *Women:* basketball, crew/rowing, cross-country, diving, field hockey, golf, lacrosse, sailing, soccer, squash, swimming, tennis. **On-Campus Highlights:** Scandling Campus Center, The Katherine D. Elliott Studio Arts Center, Stern Hall, Caird Center for Sports and Recreation, Rosensweig Learning Commons **Environmental Initiatives:** Integrating the Colleges' Sustainability "living laboratory" approach in the Climate Action Plan. The living laboratory approach is exemplified through student projects—class, independent study or volunteer that directly effect the Colleges' impact on the environment and culture of environmental sustainability. For example, The Finger Lakes Institute's renovation was directed by a first year Energy class project that identified specific environmental parameters to be incorporated into the building. These students' vision and project qualified the Finger Lakes Institute for the Energy

Star Small Business Award. This living laboratory, student oriented learning approach is at the core of the Colleges Sustainability Program and enhanced by the Colleges Climate Action Plan.

ADMISSIONS
Freshman Academic Profile: Average high school GPA 3.4. 33% in top 10% of high school class, 59% in top 25% of high school class, 83% in top 50% of high school class. 61% from public high schools. **Test Scores:** SAT Math middle 50% range 600-680. SAT EBRW middle 50% range 610-680. ACT middle 50% range 27-31. Minimum internet-based TOEFL 80. Minimum paper TOEFL 550. **Basis for Candidate Selection:** *Very important factors considered include:* rigor of secondary school record, academic GPA. *Important factors considered include:* application essay, recommendation(s), interview, extracurricular activities, character/personal qualities, volunteer work, work experience. *Other factors considered include:* class rank, standardized test scores, talent/ability, first generation, alumni/ae relation, geographical residence, state residency, racial/ethnic status, level of applicant's interest. **Freshman Admission Requirements:** High school diploma is required and GED is accepted *Academic units required:* 4 English, 3 math, 3 science, 2 science labs, 2 foreign language, 2 social studies, 2 academic electives, *Academic units recommended:* 3 foreign language, 3 social studies, 4 academic electives. **Freshman Admission Statistics:** 4,409 applied, 61.1% admitted, 24% enrolled. **Transfer Admission Requirements:** High school transcript, college transcript(s), essay or personal statement, standardized test scores, Minimum college GPA of 2.5 required. Lowest grade transferable C. **General Admission Information:** Regular application deadline 2/1. Nonfall registration accepted. Admission may be deferred for a maximum of 1 year.

COSTS AND FINANCIAL AID
Annual tuition $52,345. Room and board $13,525. Required fees $1,180. Average book expense $1,300. **Required Forms and Deadlines:** CSS/Financial Aid PROFILE; FAFSA; Noncustodial PROFILE; State aid form. **Notification of Awards:** Applicants will be notified of awards on or about 4/1. **Types of Aid:** *Need-based scholarships/grants:* College/university scholarship or grant aid from institutional funds; Federal Pell; Private scholarships; SEOG; State scholarships/grants. *Loans:* Direct PLUS loans; Direct Subsidized Stafford Loans; Direct Unsubsidized Stafford Loans. *Student Employment:* Federal Work-Study Program available. Institutional employment available. **Financial Aid Statistics:** 99% needy freshmen, 99% needy undergrads receive need-based scholarship or grant aid. 20% freshmen, 18% undergrads receive non-need-based scholarship or grant aid. 81% freshmen, 81% undergrads receive need-based self-help aid. 0% freshmen, 0% undergrads receive athletic scholarships. 90% freshmen, 88% undergrads receive any aid. Average cumulative indebtedness $34,935. **Criteria for awarding aid:** *Need-based:* Academics, Alumni affiliation, Art, Leadership, Music/drama, Religious affiliation *Non-need-based:* Academics, Alumni affiliation, Art, Leadership, Music/drama, Religious affiliation.

HOFSTRA UNIVERSITY

100 Hofstra University, Hempstead, NY 11549
Phone: 516-463-6700 • **Financial Aid Phone:** 516-463-8000
E-mail: admission@hofstra.edu • **CEEB Code:** 2295
Fax: 516-463-5100 • **Website:** http://www.hofstra.edu • **ACT Code:** 2760

This private school was founded in 1935. It has a 244 acre campus.

RATINGS
Admissions Selectivity Rating: 85   **Fire Safety Rating:** 98   **Green Rating:** 77

STUDENTS AND FACULTY
Enrollment: 6,783. **Student Body:** 55% female, 45% male, 38% out-of-state, 6% international (76 countries represented). Asian 10%, African American 9%, Caucasian 56%, Hispanic 13%, Native American <1%, Pacific Islander 1%, Two or more races 3%, Race unknown 3%.
Retention and Graduation: 81% freshmen return for sophomore year. 53% freshmen graduate within 4 years. 63% freshmen graduate within 6 years. 31% grads go on to further study within 1 year. 5% grads pursue arts and sciences degrees. 3% grads pursue law degrees. 6% grads pursue business degrees. 4% grads pursue medical degrees. **Faculty:** Student/faculty ratio 13:1. 493 full-time faculty, 91% hold PhDs, 20% are members of minority groups, 45% are women. 0% of classes are taught by teaching assistants.

ACADEMICS

Degrees: Bachelor's; Certificate; Doctoral; Doctoral/Professional; Doctoral/Research; Master's; Post-Bachelor's certificate; Post-Master's certificate
Classes: Most classes have 10-19 students. Most lab/discussion sessions have fewer than 10 students. **Most popular majors:** Biology/Biological Sciences, General; Psychology, General; Finance, General. **Special Study Options:** Accelerated program; Cooperative education program; Cross-registration; Distance learning; Double major; Dual enrollment; English as a Second Language (ESL); External degree program; Honors program; Independent study; Internships; Liberal arts/career combination; Student-designed major; Study abroad; Teacher certification program. **Honors programs:** Hofstra University's Honors College (HUHC) is the leading edge of Hofstra's pursuit of academic excellence by enriching the education of exceptional students both inside the classroom and beyond. HUHC promotes intellectual engagement, creativity, conversation, leadership, civic responsibility and global reach. In short, HUHC serves and challenges students in ways that radiate throughout the entire Hofstra community. HUHC's highly flexible curriculum is tailored to the specific interests of individual students. It includes a unique sequence of first year courses (called Culture and Expression), small, discussion-based honors seminars, and the opportunity to turn any regular course into an honors experience via our Honors Option Program. As a result of this curricular flexibility, HUHC students are diverse both in personal background and in their intellectual interests, coming from every major and school at Hofstra. Beyond the classroom, HUHC faculty mentors sponsor a rich array of cultural and social experiences, including opportunities to enjoy regular trips to New York City to visit museums, Broadway shows, concerts, lectures, and major league sporting events. Many HUHC students opt to live in honors housing, where they enjoy an even greater sense of community and an exceptional level of support from a professional staff and student leaders. HUHC students are student government leaders, newspaper editors, and champions of social and political causes. They are committed to the arts and to sports (including some 45 Division I athletes in a variety of sports) and can be found in leadership roles in just about every student club or program imaginable. They come from all across the United States, and increasingly, from abroad as well. Most of all, they are curious about one another and the wider world. HUHC graduates have won grants and fellowships such as the Fulbright, the National Science Fellowship, and the Jack Kent Cooke Fellowship. In 2012 an HUHC student was Hofstra's second finalist for the prestigious Rhodes Scholarship. HUHC students are regularly admitted to the most competitive law, medical, graduate and other professional schools. In recent years 80% of HUHC students undertake one or more internships before graduation, many of which lead directly into full-time positions after graduation. Among our 2015-2016 Honors College graduates who earned a Bachelor's degree, 98% of the respondents report that within one year of graduation they were employed (91%) or attending/plan to attend graduate school (42%). Outcomes are based on the 81% of 2015-2016 Hofstra University Honors College undergraduate degree recipients who responded to a survey or for whom data was gathered from LinkedIn within one year of graduation. All HUHC students receive merit-based scholarships. All students who qualify for admission to HUHC will also be recipients of Hofstra's Merit-Based Presidential Scholarships of approximately $20,000 or more depending on their high school record. Students whose achievements place them among the top 5% of applicants may be named Trustee Scholars. Trustee Scholars receive full tuition and additional privileges. In addition, outside of Honors College (HUHC), each academic department has a listing for a capstone course that allows a student with a minimum GPA of 3.5 in the major and 3.4 overall to pursue Departmental Honors through the completion under supervision of an advanced research or creative project and its subsequent presentation (or 'defense') before the department of committee, which can then award departmental Honors or High Honors. The awarded designation is noted on the transcript and at commencement. This form of capstone project for Departmental Honors is central to the Undergraduate Research program at Hofstra, though it does not at all encompass all of undergraduate research, which might also be done in other discrete courses, with topical or research listings, or as an independent study. Further, individual disciplines support Hofstra chapters of national honor societies. These honor organizations sponsor events which include lectures, seminars, workshops, social events, open meetings, department activities, group discussions, field trips, exhibitions, and demonstrations. **Combined degree programs:** BA/JD; BA/MA; BA/MD. **Disability Services offered to physically disabled students:** Note-taking services; Reader services; Tape recorders; Tutors. **Career services:** Alumni network; Alumni services; Career assessment; Career/job search classes; Internships; Regional alumni

FACILITIES

Housing: Apartments for single students; Coed dorms; Special housing for disabled student; Theme housing; Wellness housing 100% of campus accessible to physically disabled. **Special Academic Facilities/Equipment:** Big Data Lab, Hofstra Museum, Biology Collaboratorium, Robotics Lab, 4K Ultra High Definition Cameras (School of Communication television studio), Occupational Therapy Lab, Center for Innovation, Joan & Donald Schaeffer Black Box Theater, Shakespearean Globe Theatre Stage located in the recently renovated and expanded playhouse, Professional Film Audio Editing/Mixing Suite, Film Screening Room/Theater, The Martin B. Greenberg Trading Room — access and analyze a vast array of financial and economic data, apply analytical methods, School of Medicine Structural/Anatomy Lab, Center for Entrepreneurship: IdeaHUb & Start-Up NY Site, Center for Academic Excellence Student Learning Hub, new state of the art Zarb School of Business building (opening January 2019), WRHU Radio Station building. **Computers:** 57% of classrooms, 100% of dorms, 100% of libraries, 100% of dining areas, 100% of student union, 60% of common outdoor areas have wireless network access. Students can register for classes online. Administrative functions (other than registration) can be performed online.

CAMPUS LIFE

Environment: City **Activities:** Campus Ministries; Choral groups; Concert band; Dance; Drama/theater; International Student Organization; Jazz band; Literary magazine; Model UN; Music ensembles; Musical theater; Opera; Pep band; Radio station; Student government; Student newspaper; Student-run film society; Symphony orchestra; Television station; Yearbook 135 registered organizations, 32 honor societies, 9 religious organizations. 13 fraternities, 12 sororities. **Athletics (Intercollegiate):** *Men:* baseball, basketball, cross-country, golf, lacrosse, soccer, tennis, wrestling. *Women:* basketball, cross-country, field hockey, golf, lacrosse, soccer, softball, tennis, volleyball. 1. Mack Student Center – home of the newly renovated Commuter Lounge and Pride Den (the campus living room), is the focal point of campus community life where students meet for meals, socializing, club and organizational events, a large game room, the bookstore and diverse dining venues including vegan, organic and ethnic food and a late night pizza and salad station. 2. The Fitness Center—The Fitness Center has an indoor track, six basketball courts, three group exercise studios for Cycling, Zumba, Yoga, and other wellness programs as well as cardio and strength training machines, including ADA certified equipment. When not working out, students enjoy computer kiosks, a Wi-Fi accessible lounge area, healthy snacks, and intramural sports programs. 3. Lawrence Herbert School of Communication – Home of the WRHU Radio Station, the largest noncommercial TV studio on the east coast, and a multi-media converged newsroom. 4. "Hof USA"—A multi-functional entertainment center located in the center of residential and student life on campus. The complex includes a billiards and game area, casual dining, a large performance and dance area, Smashburger and Dutch Treats—open around the clock—with grab and go sandwiches and salads, grocery, and sundries. Hof USA is a favorite evening and weekend destination on campus. 5. David S. Mack Sports and Exhibition Complex – serves as the site for Hofstra's men's and women's Division I basketball team competitions, career and internship fairs, numerous national association exhibitions and shows, three Presidential debates, and is where Hofstra students and their families begin their college journey during Welcome Week and conclude the journey four years later during the commencement program. **Environmental Initiatives:** New construction complies with LEED standards where feasible. The new School of Business Building will be built to obtain LEED Silver Certification. The approximate 52,500 sq. ft building is expected to open in 2018.

ADMISSIONS

Freshman Academic Profile: Average high school GPA 3.6. 28% in top 10% of high school class, 62% in top 25% of high school class, 90% in top 50% of high school class. **Test Scores:** SAT Math middle 50% range 560-650. SAT EBRW middle 50% range 570-660. ACT middle 50% range 24-29. Minimum internet-based TOEFL 80. Minimum paper TOEFL 550. **Basis for Candidate Selection:** *Very important factors considered include:* rigor of secondary school record, class rank, academic GPA, application essay, recommendation(s). *Important factors considered include:* interview, extracurricular activities, talent/ability, character/personal qualities. *Other factors considered include:* standardized test scores, first generation, alumni/ae relation, geographical residence, racial/ethnic status, volunteer work, work experience, level of applicant's interest. **Freshman Admission Requirements:** High school diploma is required and GED is accepted *Academic units required:* 4 English, 3 math, 3 science, 1 science labs, 2 foreign language, 3 social studies, *Academic units recommended:* 4 math, 4 science, 2 science labs, 3 foreign language, 4 social studies. **Freshman Admission Statistics:** 26,808 applied, 63.9% admitted, 10% enrolled. **Transfer Admission Requirements:** college transcript(s), statement of good standing from prior institution(s). Lowest grade transferable C-. **General Admission Information:** Application fee $70. Nonfall registration accepted. Admission may be deferred for a maximum of 1 year.

COSTS AND FINANCIAL AID

Annual tuition $42,900. Room and board $14,930. Required fees $1,060. Average book expense $1,000. **Required Forms and Deadlines:** FAFSA; State aid form. **Notification of Awards:** Applicants will be notified of awards on a rolling basis beginning 1/15. **Types of Aid:** *Need-based scholarships/grants:* College/university scholarship or grant aid from institutional funds; Federal Pell; Private scholarships; SEOG; State scholarships/grants; United Negro College Fund. *Loans:* Direct PLUS loans; Direct Subsidized Stafford Loans; Direct Unsubsidized Stafford Loans. *Student Employment:* Federal Work-Study Program available. Institutional employment available. **Financial**

Aid Statistics: 96% needy freshmen, 94% needy undergrads receive need-based scholarship or grant aid. 22% freshmen, 16% undergrads receive non-need-based scholarship or grant aid. 81% freshmen, 76% undergrads receive need-based self-help aid. 1% freshmen, 1% undergrads receive athletic scholarships. 96% freshmen, 91% undergrads receive any aid. 69% undergrads borrow to pay for school. **Criteria for awarding aid:** *Need-based:* Academics, Alumni affiliation, Art, Leadership, Music/drama *Non-need-based:* Academics, Alumni affiliation, Art, Athletics, Leadership, Minority status, Music/drama, State/district residency.

See page 954.

HOLLINS UNIVERSITY

7916 Williamson Road, Roanoke, VA 24020-1707
Phone: 540-362-6401 · **Financial Aid Phone:** 540-362-6332
E-mail: huadm@hollins.edu · **CEEB Code:** 5294
Fax: 540-362-6218 · **Website:** www.hollins.edu · **ACT Code:** 4360

This private school was founded in 1842. It has a 475 acre campus.

RATINGS

Admissions Selectivity Rating: 87   **Fire Safety Rating:** 84   **Green Rating:** 79

STUDENTS AND FACULTY

Enrollment: 628. **Student Body:** 100% female, 0% male, 47% out-of-state, 5% international (20 countries represented). Asian 2%, African American 12%, Caucasian 66%, Hispanic 6%, Native American 1%, Pacific Islander <1%, Two or more races 6%, Race unknown 3%.
Retention and Graduation: 78% freshmen return for sophomore year. 58% freshmen graduate within 4 years. 62% freshmen graduate within 6 years. 23% grads go on to further study within 1 year. 17% grads pursue arts and sciences degrees. 1% grads pursue law degrees. 1% grads pursue business degrees.
Faculty: Student/faculty ratio 10:1. 70 full-time faculty, 99% hold PhDs, 13% are members of minority groups, 61% are women. 1% of classes are taught by teaching assistants.

ACADEMICS

Degrees: Bachelor's; Master's; Post-Master's certificate **Classes:** Most classes have 10-19 students. Most lab/discussion sessions have fewer than 10 students. **Most popular majors:** English Language And Literature, General; Biology, General; Business/Commerce, General. **Special Study Options:** Accelerated program; Cross-registration; Double major; Dual enrollment; Exchange student program (domestic); Honors program; Independent study; Internships; Student-designed major; Study abroad; Teacher certification program. **Honors programs:** A number of university departments offer honors programs. The specific nature of departmental honors varies from department to department. The programs, which are undertaken for at least the full senior year, may involve research, theses, oral or written examinations, seminars, reading programs, or any combination thereof. **Disability Services offered to physically disabled students:** Reader services; Tape recorders. **Career services:** Alumni network; Alumni services; Career assessment; Career/job search classes; Internships; Regional alumni

FACILITIES

Housing: Apartments for single students; Theme housing; Wellness housing; Women's dorms 44% of campus accessible to physically diasbled. **Special Academic Facilities/Equipment:** Athletic complex, a writing center, language labs, campus-wide computer network, scientific equipment and instrumentation, art museum, and a state-of-the-art library. **Computers:** 90% of classrooms, 100% of dorms, 100% of libraries, 100% of dining areas, 100% of student union, 100% of common outdoor areas have wireless network access. Students can register for classes online. Administrative functions (other than registration) can be performed online.

CAMPUS LIFE

Environment: City **Activities:** Campus Ministries; Choral groups; Dance; Drama/theater; International Student Organization; Literary magazine; Model UN; Music ensembles; Musical theater; Student government; Student-run film society 28 registered organizations, 15 honor societies, 5 religious organizations. **Athletics (Intercollegiate):** *Women:* basketball, equestrian sports, golf, lacrosse, soccer, swimming, tennis. **On-Campus Highlights:** Front Quadrangle, Wetherill Visual Arts Center and Wilson Museum, Wyndham Robertson Library, Moody Center, Gymnasium, Northern Swim Cntr, Tayloe Fitness Cntr **Environmental Initiatives:** Signing the President's Climate Agreement

ADMISSIONS

Freshman Academic Profile: Average high school GPA 3.8. 29% in top 10% of high school class, 66% in top 25% of high school class, 89% in top 50% of high school class. 80% from public high schools. **Test Scores:** SAT Math middle 50% range 530-615. SAT EBRW middle 50% range 580-680. ACT middle 50% range 23-28. Minimum internet-based TOEFL 80. Minimum paper TOEFL 550. **Basis for Candidate Selection:** *Very important factors considered include:* academic GPA, standardized test scores. *Important factors considered include:* rigor of secondary school record, application essay, recommendation(s). *Other factors considered include:* class rank, interview, extracurricular activities, talent/ability, character/personal qualities, first generation, alumni/ae relation, volunteer work, work experience, level of applicant's interest. **Freshman Admission Requirements:** High school diploma is required and GED is accepted *Academic units required:* 4 English, 3 math, 3 science, 3 social studies, *Academic units recommended:* 3 foreign language. **Freshman Admission Statistics:** 2,842 applied, 48.4% admitted, 11% enrolled. **Transfer Admission Requirements:** High school transcript, college transcript(s), essay or personal statement, Minimum college GPA of 2.5 required. Lowest grade transferable C. **General Admission Information:** Priority deadline 2/1. Nonfall registration accepted. Admission may be deferred for a maximum of 1 year.

COSTS AND FINANCIAL AID

Annual tuition $37,650. Room and board $13,120. Required fees $635. Average book expense $600. **Required Forms and Deadlines:** FAFSA; State aid form. **Notification of Awards:** Applicants will be notified of awards on a rolling basis beginning 3/1. **Types of Aid:** *Need-based scholarships/grants:* College/university scholarship or grant aid from institutional funds; Federal Pell; Private scholarships; SEOG; State scholarships/grants. *Loans:* Direct PLUS loans; Direct Subsidized Stafford Loans; Direct Unsubsidized Stafford Loans. *Student Employment:* Federal Work-Study Program available. Institutional employment available. **Financial Aid Statistics:** 100% needy freshmen, 100% needy undergrads receive need-based scholarship or grant aid. 100% freshmen, 100% undergrads receive non-need-based scholarship or grant aid. 70% freshmen, 73% undergrads receive need-based self-help aid. 0% freshmen, 0% undergrads receive athletic scholarships. 99% freshmen, 96% undergrads receive any aid. 76% undergrads borrow to pay for school. Average cumulative indebtedness $34,414. **Criteria for awarding aid:** *Need-based:* Academics, Alumni affiliation, Art, Leadership, Minority status, Music/drama *Non-need-based:* Academics, Alumni affiliation, Art, Leadership, Music/drama, State/district residency.

HOLY FAMILY UNIVERSITY

9801 Frankford Avenue, Philadelphia, PA 19114-2009
Phone: 215-637-7700 · **Financial Aid Phone:** 267-341-3234
E-mail: admissions@holyfamily.edu gradstudy@holyfamily.edu · **CEEB Code:** 2297
Fax: 215-281-1022 · **Website:** www.holyfamily.edu · **ACT Code:** 3592

This private school, affiliated with the Roman Catholic Church, was founded in 1954. It has a 46 acre campus.

RATINGS

Admissions Selectivity Rating: 78   **Fire Safety Rating:** 99   **Green Rating:** 61

STUDENTS AND FACULTY

Enrollment: 1,766. **Student Body:** 74% female, 26% male, 14% out-of-state, <1% international (8 countries represented). Asian 5%, African American 12%, Caucasian 62%, Hispanic 6%, Native American <1%, Pacific Islander <1%, Two or more races 0%, Race unknown 15%.
Retention and Graduation: 76% freshmen return for sophomore year.
Faculty: Student/faculty ratio 13:1. 76 full-time faculty, 82% hold PhDs, 13% are members of minority groups, 71% are women. 0% of classes are taught by teaching assistants.

ACADEMICS

Degrees: Associate; Bachelor's; Certificate; Doctoral; Master's; Post-Bachelor's certificate; Post-Master's certificate **Classes:** Most classes have 20-29 students. Most lab/discussion sessions have 20-29 students. **Most popular majors:** Education, General; Registered Nursing/Registered Nurse; Business Administration And Management, General. **Special Study Options:** Accelerated program; Cooperative education program; Cross-registration; Distance learning; English as a Second Language (ESL); Honors program; Independent study; Internships; Liberal arts/career combination; Study abroad; Teacher certification program; Weekend college. **Honors programs:** Honor's Program. Honor's classes in the core curriculum. **Combined degree**

programs: BA/MA. **Disability Services offered to physically disabled students:** Note-taking services; Reader services; Tape recorders; Tutors. **Career services:** Alumni services; Career assessment; Career/job search classes; Internships

FACILITIES

Housing: Apartments for single students; Coed dorms; Special housing for disabled students **Special Academic Facilities/Equipment:** On-campus nursery school, art gallery. **Computers:** 100% of classrooms, 100% of dorms, 100% of libraries, 100% of dining areas, 100% of student union, 100% of common outdoor areas have wireless network access. Students can register for classes online. Administrative functions (other than registration) can be performed online.

CAMPUS LIFE

Environment: Metropolis **Activities:** Campus Ministries; Choral groups; Dance; Drama/theater; International Student Organization; Literary magazine; Musical theater; Student government; Student newspaper; Television station; Yearbook 15 registered organizations, 14 honor societies, 1 religious organization. **Athletics (Intercollegiate):** *Men:* basketball, cross-country, golf, soccer, track/field (outdoor), track/field (indoor). *Women:* basketball, cross-country, lacrosse, soccer, softball, tennis, track/field (outdoor), track/field (indoor), volleyball. **On-Campus Highlights:** Campus Center, Education / Technology Center, Library, Student Residence Halls, Nurse Education Building

ADMISSIONS

Freshman Academic Profile: Average high school GPA 3.1. 10% in top 10% of high school class, 25% in top 25% of high school class, 62% in top 50% of high school class. 60% from public high schools. **Test Scores:** SAT Math middle 50% range 410-520. SAT EBRW middle 50% range 420-510. Minimum internet-based TOEFL 79-80. Minimum paper TOEFL 550. **Basis for Candidate Selection:** *Very important factors considered include:* academic GPA. *Important factors considered include:* standardized test scores. *Other factors considered include:* rigor of secondary school record, class rank, application essay, recommendation(s), interview, extracurricular activities, character/personal qualities, alumni/ae relation, volunteer work. **Freshman Admission Requirements:** High school diploma is required and GED is accepted *Academic units required:* 4 English, 3 math, 2 science, 2 foreign language, 2 history, 3 academic electives. **Freshman Admission Statistics:** 1,441 applied, 68.5% admitted, 35% enrolled. **Transfer Admission Requirements:** High school transcript, college transcript(s), essay or personal statement, statement of good standing from prior institution(s). Minimum college GPA of 2.5 required. Lowest grade transferable C. **General Admission Information:** Application fee $25. Nonfall registration accepted. Admission may be deferred for a maximum of 1 year.

COSTS AND FINANCIAL AID

Annual tuition $29,338. Room and board $13,576. Required fees $1,008. Average book expense $1,090. **Required Forms and Deadlines:** FAFSA. **Notification of Awards:** Applicants will be notified of awards on a rolling basis beginning 3/15. **Types of Aid:** *Need-based scholarships/grants:* College/ university scholarship or grant aid from institutional funds; Federal Pell; Private scholarships; SEOG; State scholarships/grants. *Loans:* Direct PLUS loans; Direct Subsidized Stafford Loans; Direct Unsubsidized Stafford Loans. *Student Employment:* Federal Work-Study Program available. **Financial Aid Statistics:** 100% needy freshmen, 94% needy undergrads receive need-based scholarship or grant aid. 99% freshmen, 92% undergrads receive non-need-based scholarship or grant aid. 96% freshmen, 93% undergrads receive need-based self-help aid. 14% freshmen, 9% undergrads receive athletic scholarships. 83% freshmen, 97% undergrads receive any aid. 86% undergrads borrow to pay for school. Average cumulative indebtedness $39,664. **Criteria for awarding aid:** *Need-based:* Academics *Non-need-based:* Academics, Athletics, Leadership.

HOOD COLLEGE

401 Rosemont Avenue, Frederick, MD 21701
Phone: 301-696-3400 · **Financial Aid Phone:** 301-696-3411
E-mail: admission@hood.edu · **CEEB Code:** 5296
Fax: 301-696-3819 · **Website:** www.hood.edu · **ACT Code:** 1702

This private school, affiliated with the United Church of Christ, was founded in 1893. It has a 50 acre campus.

RATINGS

Admissions Selectivity Rating: 75   **Fire Safety Rating:** 96   **Green Rating:** 61

STUDENTS AND FACULTY

Enrollment: 1,108. **Student Body:** 62% female, 38% male, 24% out-of-state, 2% international (11 countries represented). Asian 3%, African American 17%, Caucasian 58%, Hispanic 11%, Native American <1%, Pacific Islander <1%, Two or more races 6%, Race unknown 4%.
Retention and Graduation: 78% freshmen return for sophomore year. 54% freshmen graduate within 4 years. 61% freshmen graduate within 6 years. 36% grads go on to further study within 1 year. 18% grads pursue arts and sciences degrees. 5% grads pursue law degrees. 16% grads pursue business degrees. 0% grads pursue medical degrees. **Faculty:** Student/faculty ratio 10:1. 105 full-time faculty, 93% hold PhDs, 21% are members of minority groups, 61% are women. 0% of classes are taught by teaching assistants.

ACADEMICS

Degrees: Bachelor's; Certificate; Doctoral/Research; Master's; Post-Bachelor's certificate **Classes:** Most classes have 10-19 students. Most lab/discussion sessions have 20-29 students. **Most popular majors:** Biology/Biological Sciences, General; Psychology, General; Business Administration, Management And Operations. **Special Study Options:** Double major; Dual enrollment; Honors program; Independent study; Internships; Liberal arts/career combination; Student-designed major; Study abroad; Teacher certification program. **Honors programs:** Our award-winning program offers exceptional undergraduate students four years of exciting coursework and co-curriuclar activities. Classes are small, discussion oriented, and enhanced by guest speakers and field trips. Interdisciplinary in approach, students are encouraged to engage in personal and intellectual development in the context of community memebership and service. **Combined degree programs:** BA/MA. **Disability Services offered to physically disabled students:** Note-taking services; Reader services; Tape recorders; Tutors. **Career services:** Alumni network; Alumni services; Career assessment; Career/job search classes; Internships; Regional alumni

FACILITIES

Housing: Coed dorms; Special housing for disabled students 50% of campus accessible to physically diasbled. **Special Academic Facilities/Equipment:** Art gallery, child development lab, language lab, observatory, science labs, nursing lab, Hood History Museum, Financial trading room, Mock trial courtroom **Computers:** 100% of classrooms, 100% of dorms, 100% of libraries, 100% of dining areas, 100% of student union, 100% of common outdoor areas have wireless network access. Students can register for classes online. Administrative functions (other than registration) can be performed online.

CAMPUS LIFE

Environment: Town **Activities:** Campus Ministries; Choral groups; Dance; Drama/theater; International Student Organization; Literary magazine; Model UN; Music ensembles; Musical theater; Radio station; Student government; Student newspaper 92 registered organizations, 14 honor societies, 6 religious organizations. **Athletics (Intercollegiate):** *Men:* basketball, cross-country, golf, lacrosse, soccer, swimming, tennis, track/field (outdoor). *Women:* basketball, cross-country, field hockey, golf, lacrosse, soccer, softball, swimming, tennis, track/field (outdoor), volleyball. **On-Campus Highlights:** Ronald J. Volpe Athletic Complex, Whitaker Campus Center, Hodson Science and Technology Building, Coblentz Dining Hall, Beneficial-Hodson Library **Environmental Initiatives:** Reduction of natural gas consumption through the use of new decentralized building heating boilers and software controls programming.

ADMISSIONS

Freshman Academic Profile: Average high school GPA 3.5. 15% in top 10% of high school class, 34% in top 25% of high school class, 76% in top 50% of high school class. 79% from public high schools. **Test Scores:** SAT Math middle 50% range 480-600. SAT EBRW middle 50% range 500-620. ACT middle 50% range 18-23. Minimum internet-based TOEFL 79. Minimum paper TOEFL 550. **Basis for Candidate Selection:** *Very important factors considered include:* rigor of secondary school record, academic GPA. *Important factors considered include:* application essay, recommendation(s), interview, extracurricular activities, character/personal qualities, alumni/ae relation. *Other factors considered include:* class rank, standardized test scores, talent/ability, volunteer work, work experience, level of applicant's interest. **Freshman Admission Requirements:** High school diploma is required and GED is accepted *Academic units required:* 4 English, 3 math, 3 science, 2 science labs, 2 foreign language, 3 social studies, 1 academic elective, *Academic units recommended:* 4 English, 4 math, 3 science, 2 science labs, 3 foreign language, 3 social studies, 2 academic electives. **Freshman Admission Statistics:** 1,431 applied, 81.1% admitted, 22% enrolled. **Transfer Admission Requirements:** college transcript(s), Minimum college GPA of 2.5 required. Lowest grade transferable C-. **General Admission Information:** Priority deadline 4/15. Nonfall registration accepted.

COSTS AND FINANCIAL AID

Annual tuition $38,910. Room and board $12,700. Required fees $582. Average book expense $1,226. **Required Forms and Deadlines:** FAFSA; Institution's own financial aid form. **Notification of Awards:** Applicants will be notified of awards on or about 3/1. **Types of Aid:** *Need-based scholarships/grants:* College/university scholarship or grant aid from institutional funds; Federal Pell; Private scholarships; SEOG; State scholarships/grants. *Loans:* Direct PLUS loans; Direct Subsidized Stafford Loans; Direct Unsubsidized Stafford Loans. *Student Employment:* Federal Work-Study Program available. Institutional employment available. **Financial Aid Statistics:** 100% needy freshmen, 100% needy undergrads receive need-based scholarship or grant aid. 15% freshmen, 17% undergrads receive non-need-based scholarship or grant aid. 81% freshmen, 79% undergrads receive need-based self-help aid. 0% freshmen, 0% undergrads receive athletic scholarships. 98% freshmen, 97% undergrads receive any aid. 71% undergrads borrow to pay for school. Average cumulative indebtedness $30,554. **Criteria for awarding aid:** *Need-based:* Leadership, Minority status, Music/drama, Religious affiliation *Non-need-based:* Academics, Alumni affiliation, Leadership, Minority status, Music/drama, Religious affiliation, State/district residency.

HOPE COLLEGE

69 East 10th, Holland, MI 49422-9000
Phone: 616-395-7850 · **Financial Aid Phone:** 616-395-7765
E-mail: admissions@hope.edu · **CEEB Code:** 1301
Fax: 616-395-7130 · **Website:** www.hope.edu · **ACT Code:** 2012

This private school, affiliated with the Reformed Church, was founded in 1862. It has a 120 acre campus.

RATINGS
Admissions Selectivity Rating: 88   **Fire Safety Rating:** 89   **Green Rating:** 85

STUDENTS AND FACULTY
Enrollment: 3,028. **Student Body:** 61% female, 39% male, 28% out-of-state, 2% international (35 countries represented). Asian 2%, African American 3%, Caucasian 83%, Hispanic 8%, Native American 0%, Pacific Islander 0%, Two or more races 2%, Race unknown <1%.
Retention and Graduation: 88% freshmen return for sophomore year. 67% freshmen graduate within 4 years. 80% freshmen graduate within 6 years. 24% grads go on to further study within 1 year. 17% grads pursue arts and sciences degrees. 2% grads pursue law degrees. 6% grads pursue business degrees. 4% grads pursue medical degrees. **Faculty:** Student/faculty ratio 11:1. 246 full-time faculty, 79% hold PhDs, 16% are members of minority groups, 46% are women. 0% of classes are taught by teaching assistants.

ACADEMICS
Degrees: Bachelor's **Classes:** Most classes have 10-19 students. Most lab/discussion sessions have 20-29 students. **Most popular majors:** Education; Social Work; Business/Commerce, General. **Special Study Options:** Double major; Dual enrollment; Exchange student program (domestic); Independent study; Internships; Student-designed major; Study abroad; Teacher certification program. **Disability Services offered to physically disabled students:** Note-taking services; Reader services; Tape recorders; Tutors. **Career services:** Alumni network; Alumni services; Career assessment; Career/job search classes; Internships; Regional alumni

FACILITIES
Housing: Apartments for married students; Coed dorms; Fraternity/sorority housing; Men's dorms; Special housing for disabled student; Special housing for international students; Theme housing; Women's dorms 95% of campus accessible to physically disabled. **Special Academic Facilities/Equipment:** Art gallery, particle accelerator, computational chemistry lab, electron microscopes, spectrometers, ultracentrifuge, observatory, new $38M science building. **Computers:** 70% of classrooms, 100% of libraries, 34% of dining areas, 100% of student union, 40% of common outdoor areas have wireless network access. Students can register for classes online. Administrative functions (other than registration) can be performed online.

CAMPUS LIFE
Environment: Town **Activities:** Campus Ministries; Choral groups; Concert band; Dance; Drama/theater; International Student Organization; Jazz band; Literary magazine; Music ensembles; Radio station; Student government; Student newspaper; Yearbook 67 registered organizations, 22 honor societies, 6 religious organizations. 6 fraternities, 7 sororities. **Athletics (Intercollegiate):** *Men:* baseball, basketball, cheerleading, cross-country, diving, football, golf, soccer, swimming, tennis, track/field (outdoor), track/field (indoor). *Women:* basketball, cheerleading, cross-country, diving, golf, soccer, softball, swimming, tennis, track/field (outdoor), track/field (indoor), volleyball. **On-Campus Highlights:** DeWitt Student Center, Martha Miller Center for

Global Communic, Library, Paul A Schaap Science Center, DeVos Fieldhouse **Environmental Initiatives:** electrical use reduction

ADMISSIONS
Freshman Academic Profile: Average high school GPA 3.9. 55% in top 10% of high school class, 98% in top 25% of high school class, 93% in top 50% of high school class. 88% from public high schools. **Test Scores:** SAT Math middle 50% range 540-660. SAT EBRW middle 50% range 550-660. ACT middle 50% range 24-29. Minimum internet-based TOEFL 80. **Basis for Candidate Selection:** *Important factors considered include:* rigor of secondary school record, academic GPA, standardized test scores. *Other factors considered include:* class rank, application essay, recommendation(s), extracurricular activities, talent/ability, alumni/ae relation, geographical residence. **Freshman Admission Requirements:** High school diploma is required and GED is accepted *Academic units recommended:* 4 English, 4 math, 4 science, 2 science labs, 4 foreign language, 4 social studies, 4 history. **Freshman Admission Statistics:** 4,377 applied, 73.6% admitted, 23% enrolled. **Transfer Admission Requirements:** High school transcript, college transcript(s), essay or personal statement, standardized test scores, statement of good standing from prior institution(s). Minimum college GPA of 2.5 required. Lowest grade transferable C. **General Admission Information:** Application fee $35. Priority deadline 11/1. Nonfall registration accepted. Admission may be deferred for a maximum of 1 year.

COSTS AND FINANCIAL AID
Annual tuition $32,490. Room and board $10,000. Required fees $290. Average book expense $920. **Required Forms and Deadlines:** FAFSA; Institution's own financial aid form. **Notification of Awards:** Applicants will be notified of awards on a rolling basis beginning 3/15. **Types of Aid:** *Need-based scholarships/grants:* College/university scholarship or grant aid from institutional funds; Federal Pell; Private scholarships; SEOG; State scholarships/grants. *Loans:* Direct PLUS loans; Direct Subsidized Stafford Loans; Direct Unsubsidized Stafford Loans. *Student Employment:* Federal Work-Study Program available. Institutional employment available. **Financial Aid Statistics:** 87% needy freshmen, 88% needy undergrads receive need-based scholarship or grant aid. 81% freshmen, 73% undergrads receive non-need-based scholarship or grant aid. 77% freshmen, 82% undergrads receive need-based self-help aid. 0% freshmen, 0% undergrads receive athletic scholarships. 95% freshmen, 95% undergrads receive any aid. Average cumulative indebtedness $32,188. **Criteria for awarding aid:** *Need-based:* Academics, Minority status *Non-need-based:* Academics, Art, Minority status, Music/drama, Religious affiliation.

HOPE INTERNATIONAL UNIVERSITY

2500 East Nutwood Avenue, Fullerton, CA 92831
Phone: 866-722-4673 · **Financial Aid Phone:** (714)879-3901
E-mail: pccadmissions@hiu.edu
Fax: 714-681-7423 · **Website:** www.hiu.edu · **ACT Code:** 356

This private school, affiliated with the Church of Christ, was founded in 1928. It has a 18 acre campus.

RATINGS
Admissions Selectivity Rating: 91   **Fire Safety Rating:** 70   **Green Rating:** 60*

STUDENTS AND FACULTY
Enrollment: 521. **Student Body:** 60% female, 40% male, 24% out-of-state, 2% international. Asian 5%, African American 5%, Caucasian 63%, Hispanic 16%, Native American 1%, Race unknown 7%.
Retention and Graduation: 71% freshmen return for sophomore year. **Faculty:** Student/faculty ratio 15:1. 32 full-time faculty, 59% hold PhDs, 6% are members of minority groups, 25% are women. 0% of classes are taught by teaching assistants.

ACADEMICS
Degrees: Associate; Bachelor's; Certificate; Master's; Post-Bachelor's certificate **Classes:** Most classes have 20-29 students. Most lab/discussion sessions have 10-19 students. **Most popular majors:** Teacher Education, Multiple Levels; Youth Ministry; Psychology, General. **Special Study Options:** Accelerated program; Cross-registration; Distance learning; Double major; Dual enrollment; English as a Second Language (ESL); Independent study; Internships; Liberal arts/career combination; Student-designed major; Study abroad; Teacher certification program. **Disability Services offered to physically disabled students:** Note-taking services; Tape recorders; Tutors.

FACILITIES
Housing: Men's dorms; Women's dorms 95% of campus accessible to physically disabled.

CAMPUS LIFE
Environment: City **Activities:** Choral groups; Drama/theater; Jazz band; Music ensembles; Musical theater; Student government; Student newspaper; Yearbook. **Athletics (Intercollegiate):** *Men:* basketball, soccer, tennis, volleyball. *Women:* basketball, soccer, softball, tennis, volleyball. **On-Campus Highlights:** Lawson-Fulton Student Center, Darling Library, Lambda Lounge, Auditorium, The Commons

ADMISSIONS
Freshman Academic Profile: Average high school GPA 3.3. 20% in top 10% of high school class, 37% in top 25% of high school class, 77% in top 50% of high school class. 95% from public high schools. **Test Scores:** SAT Math middle 50% range 420-530. SAT EBRW middle 50% range 440-540. ACT middle 50% range 18-21. Minimum paper TOEFL 500. **Basis for Candidate Selection:** *Very important factors considered include:* rigor of secondary school record, class rank, academic GPA, application essay, standardized test scores, recommendation(s). *Important factors considered include:* level of applicant's interest. *Other factors considered include:* interview, extracurricular activities, talent/ability, character/personal qualities, religious affiliation/commitment, volunteer work. **Freshman Admission Requirements:** High school diploma is required and GED is accepted *Academic units recommended:* 4 English, 2 math, 1 science, 1 science labs, 1 foreign language, 1 social studies, 1 history, 3 academic electives. **Freshman Admission Statistics:** 413 applied, 32.4% admitted, 62% enrolled. **Transfer Admission Requirements:** college transcript(s), essay or personal statement, statement of good standing from prior institution(s). Minimum college GPA of 2.5 required. Lowest grade transferable C. **General Admission Information:** Application fee $40. Nonfall registration accepted. Admission may be deferred.

COSTS AND FINANCIAL AID
Annual tuition $21,560. Room and board $6,940. Required fees $325. Average book expense $1,386. **Required Forms and Deadlines:** FAFSA; Institution's own financial aid form. **Notification of Awards:** Applicants will be notified of awards on a rolling basis beginning 3/15. **Types of Aid:** *Need-based scholarships/grants:* College/university scholarship or grant aid from institutional funds; Federal Pell; Private scholarships; SEOG; State scholarships/grants. *Loans:* Direct PLUS loans; Direct Subsidized Stafford Loans; Direct Unsubsidized Stafford Loans. *Student Employment:* Federal Work-Study Program available. Institutional employment available. **Financial Aid Statistics:** 98% needy freshmen, 96% needy undergrads receive need-based scholarship or grant aid. 19% freshmen, 15% undergrads receive non-need-based scholarship or grant aid. 74% freshmen, 79% undergrads receive need-based self-help aid. 0% freshmen, 0% undergrads receive athletic scholarships. 67% freshmen, 73% undergrads receive any aid. **Criteria for awarding aid:** *Need-based:* Academics, Alumni affiliation, Athletics, Job skills, Leadership, Music/drama, Religious affiliation *Non-need-based:* Academics, Alumni affiliation, Athletics, Leadership, Music/drama, Religious affiliation.

HOUGHTON COLLEGE

1 Willard Ave, Houghton, NY 14744
Phone: 585-567-9353 · **Financial Aid Phone:** 585-567-9328
E-mail: admission@houghton.edu · **CEEB Code:** 2299
Fax: 716-567-9522 · **Website:** www.houghton.edu · **ACT Code:** 2766

This private school, affiliated with the Wesleyan Church, was founded in 1883. It has a 1300 acre campus.

RATINGS
Admissions Selectivity Rating: 77   **Fire Safety Rating:** 82   **Green Rating:** 75

STUDENTS AND FACULTY
Enrollment: 1,021. **Student Body:** 62% female, 38% male, 35% out-of-state, 10% international (31 countries represented). Asian 4%, African American 4%, Caucasian 73%, Hispanic 2%, Native American <1%, Pacific Islander <1%, Two or more races 5%, Race unknown 5%.
Retention and Graduation: 80% freshmen return for sophomore year. 67% freshmen graduate within 4 years. 73% freshmen graduate within 6 years. 18% grads go on to further study within 1 year. 11% grads pursue arts and sciences degrees. 0.4% grads pursue law degrees. 1% grads pursue business degrees. 0.8% grads pursue medical degrees. **Faculty:** Student/faculty ratio 12:1. 65 full-time faculty, 94% hold PhDs, 38% are women. 0% of classes are taught by teaching assistants.

ACADEMICS
Degrees: Associate; Bachelor's; Master's **Classes:** Most classes have 10-19 students. **Most popular majors:** Digital Communication And Media/Multimedia; Biology/Biological Sciences, General; Business Administration And

Management, General. **Special Study Options:** Accelerated program; Cross-registration; Distance learning; Double major; Dual enrollment; Exchange student program (domestic); Honors program; Independent study; Internships; Liberal arts/career combination; Student-designed major; Study abroad; Teacher certification program. **Honors programs:** Three honors programs for first-year students: two programs involving studying abroad in London or Eastern Europe as well as a hands-on science honors program. **Disability Services offered to physically disabled students:** Note-taking services; Reader services; Tape recorders; Tutors. **Career services:** Alumni network; Alumni services; Career assessment; Career/job search classes; Internships; Regional alumni

FACILITIES
Housing: Apartments for married students; Apartments for single students; Cooperative housing; Men's dorms; Special housing for disabled student; Women's dorms 80% of campus accessible to physically disabled. **Special Academic Facilities/Equipment:** Electron microscope, Art Gallery, Greenhouse. **Computers:** 100% of classrooms, 100% of dorms, 100% of libraries, 100% of dining areas, 100% of student union, 50% of common outdoor areas have wireless network access. Students can register for classes online. Administrative functions (other than registration) can be performed online.

CAMPUS LIFE
Environment: Rural **Activities:** Campus Ministries; Choral groups; Concert band; Dance; Drama/theater; International Student Organization; Jazz band; Literary magazine; Music ensembles; Musical theater; Opera; Pep band; Student government; Student newspaper; Symphony orchestra; Yearbook 34 registered organizations, 2 honor societies, 9 religious organizations. **Athletics (Intercollegiate):** *Men:* basketball, cross-country, soccer, track/field (outdoor), track/field (indoor). *Women:* basketball, cross-country, field hockey, soccer, track/field (outdoor), track/field (indoor), volleyball. **On-Campus Highlights:** Campus Center, Wesley Chapel, Nielsen Physical Education Center, Center for the Arts, Chamberlain Center **Environmental Initiatives:** Achieving carbon neutrality by 2050.

ADMISSIONS
Freshman Academic Profile: Average high school GPA 3.5. 26% in top 10% of high school class, 54% in top 25% of high school class, 80% in top 50% of high school class. 66% from public high schools. **Test Scores:** SAT Math middle 50% range 520-650. SAT EBRW middle 50% range 540-670. ACT middle 50% range 22-29. Minimum internet-based TOEFL 80. Minimum paper TOEFL 550. **Basis for Candidate Selection:** *Very important factors considered include:* class rank, academic GPA, religious affiliation/commitment. *Important factors considered include:* rigor of secondary school record, application essay, recommendation(s), character/personal qualities. *Other factors considered include:* standardized test scores, interview, extracurricular activities, talent/ability, first generation, alumni/ae relation, racial/ethnic status, volunteer work, work experience, level of applicant's interest. **Freshman Admission Requirements:** High school diploma is required and GED is accepted *Academic units recommended:* 4 English, 3 math, 2 science, 2 science labs, 2 foreign language, 1 social studies, 3 history. **Freshman Admission Statistics:** 821 applied, 91.4% admitted, 29% enrolled. **Transfer Admission Requirements:** college transcript(s), essay or personal statement, Lowest grade transferable C-. **General Admission Information:** Application fee $40. Priority deadline 3/1. Nonfall registration accepted. Admission may be deferred for a maximum of 2 years.

COSTS AND FINANCIAL AID
Annual tuition $31,040. Room and board $9,018. Required fees $500. Average book expense $1,000. **Required Forms and Deadlines:** FAFSA; State aid form. **Notification of Awards:** Applicants will be notified of awards on a rolling basis beginning 3/1. **Types of Aid:** *Need-based scholarships/grants:* College/university scholarship or grant aid from institutional funds; Federal Pell; Private scholarships; SEOG; State scholarships/grants. *Loans:* Direct PLUS loans; Direct Subsidized Stafford Loans; Direct Unsubsidized Stafford Loans. *Student Employment:* Federal Work-Study Program available. Institutional employment available. **Financial Aid Statistics:** 90% needy freshmen, 88% needy undergrads receive need-based scholarship or grant aid. 76% freshmen, 76% undergrads receive non-need-based scholarship or grant aid. 90% freshmen, 89% undergrads receive need-based self-help aid. 0% freshmen, 5% undergrads receive athletic scholarships. 100% freshmen, 98% undergrads receive any aid. **Criteria for awarding aid:** *Need-based:* Academics, Leadership, Minority status, Religious affiliation *Non-need-based:* Academics, Alumni affiliation, Art, Music/drama, Religious affiliation, State/district residency.

HOUSTON BAPTIST UNIVERSITY

7502 Fondren Road, Houston, TX 77074
Phone: 281-649-3211 • **Financial Aid Phone:** 281-649-3749
E-mail: admissions@hbu.edu • **CEEB Code:** 6282
Fax: 281-649-3217 • **Website:** www.hbu.edu • **ACT Code:** 4101

This private school, affiliated with the Southern Baptist Church, was founded in 1960. It has a 100 acre campus.

RATINGS
Admissions Selectivity Rating: 78   **Fire Safety Rating:** 60*   **Green Rating:** 60*

STUDENTS AND FACULTY
Enrollment: 2,302. **Student Body:** 64% female, 36% male, 3% out-of-state, 3% international (28 countries represented). Asian 9%, African American 19%, Caucasian 24%, Hispanic 35%, Native American <1%, Pacific Islander <1%, Two or more races 4%, Race unknown 6%.
Retention and Graduation: 72% freshmen return for sophomore year. 29% freshmen graduate within 4 years. **Faculty:** Student/faculty ratio 14:1. 151 full-time faculty, 81% hold PhDs, 20% are members of minority groups, 46% are women. 0% of classes are taught by teaching assistants.

ACADEMICS
Degrees: Bachelor's; Doctoral/Research; Master's **Classes:** Most classes have 10-19 students. Most lab/discussion sessions have 10-19 students. **Most popular majors:** Biology/Biological Sciences, General; Kinesiology And Exercise Science; Registered Nursing/Registered Nurse. **Special Study Options:** Accelerated program; Distance learning; Double major; Dual enrollment; Honors program; Independent study; Internships; Teacher certification program. **Honors programs:** The Honors College provides students with an interdisciplinary curriculum rooted in the Christian faith that cultivates knowledge, character, and wisdom by examining the great works of Western civilization and exploring timeless questions. **Disability Services offered to physically disabled students:** Note-taking services; Reader services; Tape recorders; Tutors. **Career services:** Career assessment; Career/job search classes; Internships

FACILITIES
Housing: Apartments for married students; Apartments for single students; Coed dorms; Men's dorms; Special housing for disabled student; Theme housing; Women's dorms **Special Academic Facilities/Equipment:** Dunham Bible Museum, Museum of Southern History, Lyceum, Academic Success Center **Computers:** Students can register for classes online.

CAMPUS LIFE
Environment: Metropolis **Activities:** Campus Ministries; Choral groups; Dance; Drama/theater; International Student Organization; Marching band; Music ensembles; Student government; Student newspaper 36 registered organizations, 9 honor societies, 3 religious organizations, 2 fraternities, 2 sororities. **Athletics (Intercollegiate): Men:** baseball, basketball, cheerleading. *Women:* basketball, cheerleading, softball, volleyball. **On-Campus Highlights:** MD Anderson Student Center, Moody Library, Baugh Center, Hinton Center, HODO Residence Hall

ADMISSIONS
Freshman Academic Profile: Average high school GPA 3.4. 22% in top 10% of high school class, 51% in top 25% of high school class, 78% in top 50% of high school class. **Test Scores:** SAT Math middle 50% range 520-590. SAT EBRW middle 50% range 510-600. ACT middle 50% range 20-25. Minimum internet-based TOEFL 80. **Basis for Candidate Selection:** *Important factors considered include:* class rank, academic GPA, standardized test scores. *Other factors considered include:* rigor of secondary school record, recommendation(s), extracurricular activities, religious affiliation/commitment. **Freshman Admission Requirements:** High school diploma is required and GED is accepted *Academic units required:* 4 English, 3 math, 3 science, 3 science labs, 3 social studies, 3 history, 1.5 academic electives, 1.5 computer science, and 2 units from above areas or other academic areas. *Academic units recommended:* 4 English, 4 math, 4 science, 4 science labs, 2 foreign language, 4 social studies, 3 history, 1.5 academic electives, 1.5 computer science, 1 visual/performing arts, 2 units from above areas or other academic areas. **Freshman Admission Statistics:** 6,461 applied, 69.0% admitted, 12% enrolled. **Transfer Admission Requirements:** college transcript(s), essay or personal statement, statement of good standing from prior institution(s). Minimum college GPA of 2.0 required. Lowest grade transferable C. **General Admission Information:** Nonfall registration accepted. Admission may be deferred for a maximum of 1 year.

COSTS AND FINANCIAL AID
Annual tuition $30,480. Required fees $2,050. Average book expense $1,000. **Required Forms and Deadlines:** FAFSA. **Notification of Awards:**

Applicants will be notified of awards on a rolling basis beginning 3/1. **Types of Aid:** *Need-based scholarships/grants:* College/university scholarship or grant aid from institutional funds; Federal Pell; SEOG; State scholarships/grants. *Loans:* Direct PLUS loans; Direct Subsidized Stafford Loans; Direct Unsubsidized Stafford Loans. *Student Employment:* Federal Work-Study Program available. Institutional employment available. **Financial Aid Statistics:** 99% needy freshmen, 99% needy undergrads receive need-based scholarship or grant aid. 100% freshmen, 93% undergrads receive non-need-based scholarship or grant aid. 84% freshmen, 82% undergrads receive need-based self-help aid. 10% freshmen, 14% undergrads receive athletic scholarships. 66% undergrads borrow to pay for school. Average cumulative indebtedness $32,027. **Criteria for awarding aid:** *Need-based:* Religious affiliation *Non-need-based:* Academics, Alumni affiliation, Art, Athletics, Leadership, Music/drama.

HOWARD UNIVERSITY

2400 Sixth Street, NW, Washington, DC 20059
Phone: 202-806-2755 • **Financial Aid Phone:** (202) 806-2840
E-mail: admission@howard.edu • **CEEB Code:** 5297
Fax: (202) 806-4465 • **Website:** www.howard.edu • **ACT Code:** 674

This private school was founded in 1867. It has a 258 acre campus.

RATINGS
Admissions Selectivity Rating: 87   **Fire Safety Rating:** 98   **Green Rating:** 60*

STUDENTS AND FACULTY
Enrollment: 6,961. **Student Body:** 67% female, 33% male, 95% out-of-state, 4% international (86 countries represented). Asian 2%, African American 91%, Caucasian 1%, Hispanic <1%, Native American 1%, Pacific Islander <1%, Two or more races 0%, Race unknown 0%.
Retention and Graduation: 85% freshmen return for sophomore year. 60% grads go on to further study within 1 year. 42% grads pursue arts and sciences degrees. 12% grads pursue law degrees. 15% grads pursue business degrees. 11% grads pursue medical degrees. **Faculty:** Student/faculty ratio 10:1. 1,094 full-time faculty, 87% are members of minority groups, 42% are women.

ACADEMICS
Degrees: Bachelor's; Certificate; Doctoral; Doctoral/Professional; Doctoral/Research; Master's; Post-Master's certificate **Classes:** Most classes have 10-19 students. Most lab/discussion sessions have 10-19 students. **Most popular majors:** Biology/Biological Sciences, General. **Special Study Options:** Accelerated program; Cooperative education program; Distance learning; Double major; English as a Second Language (ESL); Exchange student program (domestic); Honors program; Independent study; Internships; Study abroad; Teacher certification program. **Combined degree programs:** BA/DDS; BA/MD. **Disability Services offered to physically disabled students:** Note-taking services; Reader services. **Career services:** Career assessment; Career/job search classes; Internships

FACILITIES
Housing: Apartments for married students; Apartments for single students; Coed dorms; Men's dorms; Women's dorms 100% of campus accessible to physically disabled. **Special Academic Facilities/Equipment:** Moorland-Spingarn Research Center; Ralph J Bunche Center; Afro-American Resource Center; Patent/TM Resource Center; Channing Pollock Theater Collection **Computers:** 10% of classrooms, 100% of dorms, 100% of libraries, 10% of dining areas, 50% of student union, 10% of common outdoor areas have wireless network access. Students can register for classes online. Administrative functions (other than registration) can be performed online.

CAMPUS LIFE
Environment: Metropolis **Activities:** Campus Ministries; Choral groups; Concert band; Dance; Drama/theater; International Student Organization; Jazz band; Marching band; Music ensembles; Musical theater; Opera; Pep band; Radio station; Student government; Student newspaper; Student-run film society; Symphony orchestra; Television station; Yearbook 150 registered organizations, 15 honor societies, 3 religious organizations. 10 fraternities, 8 sororities. **Athletics (Intercollegiate): Men:** basketball, cheerleading, cross-country, diving, football, soccer, swimming, tennis, track/field (outdoor). *Women:* basketball, bowling, boxing, cheerleading, cross-country, diving, lacrosse, soccer, softball, swimming, tennis, track/field (outdoor), volleyball. **On-Campus Highlights:** Founders Library, Rankin Chapel, Punchout, Ira Aldridge Theatre, Burr Gymnasium

ADMISSIONS

Freshman Academic Profile: Average high school GPA 3.3. 26% in top 10% of high school class, 55% in top 25% of high school class, 86% in top 50% of high school class. 80% from public high schools. **Test Scores:** SAT Math middle 50% range 490-610. SAT EBRW middle 50% range 500-610. ACT middle 50% range 21-27. Minimum paper TOEFL 550. **Basis for Candidate Selection:** *Very important factors considered include:* rigor of secondary school record, class rank, academic GPA, standardized test scores. *Other factors considered include:* application essay, recommendation(s), extracurricular activities, talent/ability, first generation, alumni/ae relation, volunteer work, work experience, level of applicant's interest. **Freshman Admission Requirements:** High school diploma is required and GED is accepted *Academic units required:* 4 English, 3 math, 2 science, 2 science labs, 2 foreign language, 2 social studies, 4 academic electives. **Freshman Admission Statistics:** 13,760 applied, 48.4% admitted, 22% enrolled. **Transfer Admission Requirements:** college transcript(s), statement of good standing from prior institution(s). Minimum college GPA of 2.5 required. Lowest grade transferable C. **General Admission Information:** Application fee $45. Priority deadline 2/15. Regular application deadline 2/15. Nonfall registration accepted. Admission may be deferred for a maximum of 1 semester.

COSTS AND FINANCIAL AID

Annual tuition $22,737. Room and board $13,814. Required fees $1,233. Average book expense $3,000. **Required Forms and Deadlines:** FAFSA. **Notification of Awards:** Applicants will be notified of awards on a rolling basis beginning 2/16. **Types of Aid:** *Need-based scholarships/grants:* College/university scholarship or grant aid from institutional funds; Federal Nursing Scholarships; Federal Pell; Private scholarships; SEOG; State scholarships/grants. *Loans:* Direct PLUS loans; Direct Subsidized Stafford Loans; Direct Unsubsidized Stafford Loans. *Student Employment:* Federal Work-Study Program available. Institutional employment available. **Financial Aid Statistics:** 62% needy freshmen, 63% needy undergrads receive need-based scholarship or grant aid. 57% freshmen, 47% undergrads receive non-need-based scholarship or grant aid. 72% freshmen, 77% undergrads receive need-based self-help aid. 3% freshmen, 4% undergrads receive athletic scholarships. 96% freshmen, 96% undergrads receive any aid. **Criteria for awarding aid:** *Need-based:* Academics, Leadership, Music/drama *Non-need-based:* Academics, Art, Athletics, Leadership, Music/drama.

HULT INTERNATIONAL BUSINESS SCHOOL

1355 Sansome St, San Francisco, CA 94111
Phone: +1 415 869 2900 • **Financial Aid Phone:** 617-619-1097
E-mail: bachelor@hult.edu
Website: http://www.hult.edu/ • **ACT Code:** 1835

This private school was founded in 1964.

RATINGS

Admissions Selectivity Rating: 85   **Fire Safety Rating:** 96   **Green Rating:** 64

STUDENTS AND FACULTY

Enrollment: 1,147. **Student Body:** 38% female, 62% male, 70% out-of-state, international.
Retention and Graduation: 86% freshmen return for sophomore year.
Faculty: Student/faculty ratio 15:1. 49 full-time faculty, 61% hold PhDs, 2% are members of minority groups, 22% are women. 0% of classes are taught by teaching assistants.

ACADEMICS

Degrees: Bachelor's; Diploma; Doctoral/Professional; Master's **Classes:** Most classes have 30-39 students. **Most popular majors:** Business Administration And Management, General; Entrepreneurship/Entrepreneurial Studies; Marketing. **Special Study Options:** Accelerated program; Double major; English as a Second Language (ESL); Honors program; Independent study; Internships; Study abroad. **Honors programs:** Deans List Students who achieve a GPA of 3.60 or higher for a given semester are recognized on the Dean's List for the subsequent semester. To be eligible for the Dean's List a student must earn at least 12 credits during Fall or Spring Semester, and at least 6 credits during Summer 1 or Summer 2 terms. Qualifying participants receive notification from the Dean with appropriate recording in the student's permanent academic record. The Dean's List is published each semester, including the names of all qualifying students who consent to their name being published. Academic Excellence At Hult, the most academically talented students graduate with Distinction (final cumulative GPA of 3.60 or higher). Students who achieve a cumulative 3.60 GPA at Hult, having completed a minimum of 12 credits at Hult, are automatically added to the Academic Excellence Track. For as long as they maintain this level of academic excellence,

students are entitled to the following privileges: • Accelerated degree progression. Students on the Academic Excellence Track are entitled to take one extra course in the Fall and Spring Semesters. (Note: Students, including those on Academic Excellence, who take more than 30 credits per year will be charged for additional credits on a pro rata basis.) • Exclusive elective classes. The School runs a number of elective classes to provide additional challenges for top undergraduate students. • Each campus holds dedicated events for its Academic Excellence students, which may include speakers, networking events, and social activities. The privileges of Academic Excellence are awarded on a rolling basis to any student whose cumulative GPA is 3.60 or higher, and are awarded for a single semester to any student who is on the Dean's List that semester. **Disability Services offered to physically disabled students:** Tutors. Alumni network; Alumni services; Career assessment; Career/job search classes; Internships; Regional alumni

FACILITIES

Housing: Apartments for married students; Apartments for single students; Coed dorms; Other (please specify) 92% of campus accessible to physically diasbled.

CAMPUS LIFE

Environment: Metropolis **Activities:** Drama/theater; International Student Organization; Model UN; Music ensembles; Student government; Student newspaper; Yearbook. Benugo Cafe & The Warehouse—Pizzeria & Bar, 1st Floor Social Area, Library, and Free Coffee Kart, 1st and 2nd Floor Terraces, Multi-Faith Room, 1st and 2nd Floor Study Areas

ADMISSIONS

Freshman Academic Profile: Average high school GPA 3.0. **Test Scores:** SAT Math middle 50% range 440-600. SAT EBRW middle 50% range 415-547. **Basis for Candidate Selection:** *Very important factors considered include:* academic GPA, application essay, extracurricular activities, volunteer work, work experience. *Important factors considered include:* rigor of secondary school record, interview, talent/ability, character/personal qualities, level of applicant's interest. *Other factors considered include:* class rank, standardized test scores, recommendation(s). **Freshman Admission Requirements:** High school diploma is required and GED is accepted **Freshman Admission Statistics:** 3,206 applied, 50.2% admitted, 23% enrolled. **General Admission Information:** Application fee $75. Nonfall registration accepted. Admission may be deferred for a maximum of 1 year.

COSTS AND FINANCIAL AID

Annual tuition $38,450. Required fees $3,100. Average book expense $1,000. **Required Forms and Deadlines:** Institution's own financial aid form. **Types of Aid:** *Need-based scholarships/grants:* College/university scholarship or grant aid from institutional funds; Federal Pell; Private scholarships. *Loans:* Direct PLUS loans; Direct Subsidized Stafford Loans; Direct Unsubsidized Stafford Loans. *Student Employment:* Institutional employment available. **Financial Aid Statistics:** 100% needy freshmen receive need-based scholarship or grant aid. 74% freshmen, 77% undergrads receive any aid. **Criteria for awarding aid:** *Need-based:* Academics, Leadership *Non-need-based:* Academics, Leadership, State/district residency.

HUMBOLDT STATE UNIVERSITY

1 Harpst Street, Arcata, CA 95521-8299
Phone: 707-826-4402 • **Financial Aid Phone:** 707-826-4321
E-mail: hsuinfo@humboldt.edu • **CEEB Code:** 4345
Fax: 707-826-6190 • **Website:** www.humboldt.edu • **ACT Code:** 286

This public school was founded in 1913. It has a 161 acre campus.

RATINGS

Admissions Selectivity Rating: 82   **Fire Safety Rating:** 95   **Green Rating:** 93

STUDENTS AND FACULTY

Enrollment: 7,758. **Student Body:** 57% female, 43% male, 1% international (45 countries represented). Asian 3%, African American 4%, Caucasian 42%, Hispanic 35%, Native American 1%, Pacific Islander <1%, Two or more races 7%, Race unknown 7%.
Retention and Graduation: 68% freshmen return for sophomore year. 7% freshmen graduate within 4 years. 49% freshmen graduate within 6 years. **Faculty:** Student/faculty ratio 22:1. 258 full-time faculty, 98% hold PhDs, 18% are members of minority groups, 47% are women.

ACADEMICS

Degrees: Bachelor's; Master's; Post-Bachelor's certificate **Most popular majors:** Biology/Biological Sciences, General; Psychology, General; Business Administration And Management, General. **Special Study Options:** Distance learning; Double major; English as a Second Language (ESL); Exchange student program (domestic); Independent study; Internships; Study abroad; Teacher certification program. **Disability Services offered to physically disabled students:** Note-taking services; Reader services; Tape recorders; Tutors. **Career services:** Alumni services; Career assessment; Career/job search classes; Internships; Regional alumni

FACILITIES

Housing: Coed dorms; Theme housing 85% of campus accessible to physically diasbled. **Special Academic Facilities/Equipment:** Art and geology museums, marine research lab, fish hatchery, wildlife game pen, observatory, First Street Gallery **Computers:** 85% of classrooms, 100% of dorms, 100% of libraries, 100% of dining areas, 100% of student union, 80% of common outdoor areas have wireless network access. Students can register for classes online. Administrative functions (other than registration) can be performed online.

CAMPUS LIFE

Environment: Village **Activities:** Choral groups; Concert band; Dance; Drama/theater; International Student Organization; Jazz band; Literary magazine; Model UN; Music ensembles; Musical theater; Pep band; Radio station; Student government; Student newspaper; Student-run film society; Symphony orchestra 160 registered organizations, 6 honor societies, 8 religious organizations. 2 fraternities, 4 sororities. **Athletics (Intercollegiate):** *Men:* basketball, cross-country, football, soccer, track/field (outdoor). *Women:* basketball, crew/rowing, cross-country, soccer, softball, track/field (outdoor), volleyball. **On-Campus Highlights:** Founders Hall, Campus Center for Appropriate Technology, University Center, Redwood Bowl, University Library **Environmental Initiatives:** Campus Center for Appropriate Technology (CCAT): For 35 years, the Campus Center for Appropriate Technology's live-in demonstration home for sustainability annually exposes over 2,000 students, faculty, staff, and visitors through tours, student-taught courses, workshops, presentations and hands-on projects. The first of its kind, CCAT has been the inspiration for similar projects on college campuses across the nation. http://www.humboldt.edu/~ccat/

ADMISSIONS

Freshman Academic Profile: Average high school GPA 3.2. 13% in top 10% of high school class, 46% in top 25% of high school class, 80% in top 50% of high school class. 90% from public high schools. **Test Scores:** SAT Math middle 50% range 470-570. SAT EBRW middle 50% range 490-600. Minimum internet-based TOEFL 71. Minimum paper TOEFL 525. **Basis for Candidate Selection:** *Very important factors considered include:* rigor of secondary school record, academic GPA. *Important factors considered include:* geographical residence, state residency. *Other factors considered include:* standardized test scores. **Freshman Admission Requirements:** High school diploma is required and GED is accepted *Academic units required:* 4 English, 3 math, 2 science, 2 science labs, 2 foreign language, 1 social studies, 1 history, 1 academic elective, 1 visual/performing arts. **Freshman Admission Statistics:** 11,562 applied, 58.1% admitted, 14% enrolled. **Transfer Admission Requirements:** college transcript(s), statement of good standing from prior institution(s). Minimum college GPA of 2.00 required. Lowest grade transferable D-. **General Admission Information:** Application fee $55. Priority deadline 11/30. Regular application deadline 11/30. Nonfall registration accepted. Admission may be deferred for a maximum of 1 year.

COSTS AND FINANCIAL AID

Annual in-state tuition $13,056. Annual out-of-state tuition $17,622. Room and board $13,056. Required fees $1,750. Average book expense $1,726. **Required Forms and Deadlines:** FAFSA. **Notification of Awards:** Applicants will be notified of awards on a rolling basis beginning 4/15. **Types of Aid:** *Need-based scholarships/grants:* College/university scholarship or grant aid from institutional funds; Federal Pell; Private scholarships; SEOG; State scholarships/grants. *Loans:* Direct PLUS loans; Direct Subsidized Stafford Loans; Direct Unsubsidized Stafford Loans. *Student Employment:* Federal Work-Study Program available. Institutional employment available. **Financial Aid Statistics:** 93% needy freshmen, 93% needy undergrads receive need-based scholarship or grant aid. 2% freshmen, 2% undergrads receive non-need-based scholarship or grant aid. 77% freshmen, 73% undergrads receive need-based self-help aid. 1% freshmen, 1% undergrads receive athletic scholarships. 72% freshmen, 74% undergrads receive any aid. 73% undergrads borrow to pay for school. Average cumulative indebtedness $23,834. **Criteria for awarding aid:** *Non-need-based:* Academics, Alumni affiliation, Athletics, Leadership, Minority status, State/district residency.

HUMPHREYS COLLEGE

6650 Inglewood Ave., Stockton, CA 95207
Phone: 209-478-0800 · **Financial Aid Phone:** 209-478-0800
E-mail: slopez@humphreys.edu
Fax: 209-478-0800 · **Website:** http://www.humphreys.edu/

This private school was founded in 1896. It has a 10 acre campus.

RATINGS

Admissions Selectivity Rating: 70 **Fire Safety Rating:** 60* **Green Rating:** 60*

STUDENTS AND FACULTY

Enrollment: 692. **Student Body:** 85% female, 15% male, 0% out-of-state, <1% international. Asian 13%, African American 17%, Caucasian 29%, Hispanic 37%, Native American 1%, Race unknown 2%.
Retention and Graduation: 64% freshmen return for sophomore year. 54% grads go on to further study within 1 year. 20% grads pursue arts and sciences degrees. 30% grads pursue law degrees. 40% grads pursue business degrees. 1% grads pursue medical degrees. **Faculty:** Student/faculty ratio 18:1. 18 full-time faculty, 17% hold PhDs, 6% are members of minority groups, 67% are women. 0% of classes are taught by teaching assistants.

ACADEMICS

Degrees: Associate; Bachelor's; Certificate **Classes:** Most classes have 10-19 students. Most lab/discussion sessions have 10-19 students. **Special Study Options:** Distance learning; Double major; Dual enrollment; Independent study; Internships. **Career services:** Alumni services; Internships

FACILITIES

Housing: Apartments for single students 100% of campus accessible to physically diasbled.

CAMPUS LIFE

Environment: Village **Activities:** Literary magazine; Student newspaper 3 registered organizations.

ADMISSIONS

Freshman Academic Profile: Average high school GPA 3.0. 0% in top 10% of high school class, 0% in top 25% of high school class, 15% in top 50% of high school class. 95% from public high schools. **Test Scores:** Minimum paper TOEFL 450. **Basis for Candidate Selection:** *Very important factors considered include:* interview. *Important factors considered include:* character/personal qualities. *Other factors considered include:* level of applicant's interest. **Freshman Admission Requirements:** High school diploma is required and GED is accepted **Freshman Admission Statistics:** 143 applied, 81.1% admitted, 100% enrolled. **Transfer Admission Requirements:** High school transcript, college transcript(s), interview, Minimum college GPA of 2.0 required. Lowest grade transferable C-. **General Admission Information:** Application fee $35. Nonfall registration accepted. Admission may be deferred.

COSTS AND FINANCIAL AID

Required Forms and Deadlines: FAFSA. **Types of Aid:** *Need-based scholarships/grants:* Federal Pell; Private scholarships; SEOG; State scholarships/grants. **Financial Aid Statistics:** 100% needy freshmen, 100% needy undergrads receive need-based scholarship or grant aid. 0% undergrads receive non-need-based scholarship or grant aid. 23% freshmen, 7% undergrads receive need-based self-help aid. 0% freshmen, 0% undergrads receive athletic scholarships. 98% freshmen, 98% undergrads receive any aid. **Criteria for awarding aid:** *Need-based:* Academics.

HUNTINGDON COLLEGE

1500 East Fairview Avenue, Montgomery, AL 36106-2148
Phone: 334-833-4497 · **Financial Aid Phone:** 334-833-4428
E-mail: admiss@huntingdon.edu · **CEEB Code:** 1303
Fax: 334-833-4347 · **Website:** www.huntingdon.edu · **ACT Code:** 18

This private school, affiliated with the Methodist Church, was founded in 1854. It has a 71 acre campus.

RATINGS

Admissions Selectivity Rating: 85 **Fire Safety Rating:** 85 **Green Rating:** 60*

STUDENTS AND FACULTY

Enrollment: 1,099. **Student Body:** 52% female, 48% male, 30% out-of-state, <1% international (4 countries represented). Asian <1%, African American 21%, Caucasian 64%, Hispanic 6%, Native American 1%, Pacific Islander <1%, Two or more races 5%, Race unknown 3%.

Retention and Graduation: 65% freshmen return for sophomore year. 27% freshmen graduate within 4 years. **Faculty:** Student/faculty ratio 15:1. 47 full-time faculty, 74% hold PhDs, 4% are members of minority groups, 47% are women. 0% of classes are taught by teaching assistants.

ACADEMICS

Degrees: Bachelor's **Classes:** Most classes have 10-19 students. Most lab/discussion sessions have fewer than 10 students. **Most popular majors:** Biology/Biological Sciences, General; Kinesiology And Exercise Science; Business/Commerce, General. **Special Study Options:** Cross-registration; Distance learning; Double major; Honors program; Independent study; Internships; Liberal arts/career combination; Student-designed major; Study abroad; Teacher certification program. **Honors programs:** The Joyce and Truman Hobbs Honors Program at Huntingdon College encourages students to embrace the social nature of knowledge through enriched classroom experiences and challenging civic service. Asked to commit to the high ideals of "faith, wisdom, and service," honors students will better understand their responsibility to humankind in Montgomery and around the world. Some specific advantages to the students participating in the Honors Program include classes designed specifically for Honors students, recognition at graduation and on the student's transcript, and enriching experiences outside the classroom (honors colloquia, etc.) Departmental Honors—An outstanding student in a particular major has the opportunity to create an individualized honors project within the major to meet a particular need and interest. **Disability Services offered to physically disabled students:** Reader services; Tape recorders; Tutors. **Career services:** Alumni network; Alumni services; Career assessment; Career/job search classes; Internships

FACILITIES

Housing: Coed dorms; Fraternity/sorority housing; Men's dorms; Special housing for disabled student; Women's dorms 85% of campus accessible to physically disabled. **Special Academic Facilities/Equipment:** The Bowman Ecological Center, a place where students collect and study samples of plants, trees, and aquatic life. Sybil Smith Hall, a fully equipped music facility with recital hall, reception hall, faculty offices and an extensive music collection. The Dr. Laurie Jean Weil Center for Human Performance, adjacent to the College's main training/fitness facility for athletes. The Methodist Archives Center, the central depository for the archival and historical records of the Alabama-West Florida Conference of the United Methodist Church and of Huntingdon College, located in Huntingdon College's Houghton Memorial Library. Leo J. Drum Jr. Theater, a theater with 246 retractable seats, theatrical lighting, glassed-in control room, and sound system, housed in the historic auditorium where treasured architectural details from the building's original Cloverdale construction have been preserved. Roland Band Hall, a new space recently renovated to include offices, instrument storage, lockers, and a work room, as well as a large rehearsal room. **Computers:** 40% of classrooms, 33% of dorms, 100% of libraries, 100% of dining areas, 100% of student union, have wireless network access. Administrative functions (other than registration) can be performed online. Undergraduates are required to own a computer.

CAMPUS LIFE

Environment: City **Activities:** Campus Ministries; Choral groups; Concert band; Dance; Drama/theater; Jazz band; Literary magazine; Marching band; Music ensembles; Pep band; Student government 50 registered organizations, 15 honor societies, 3 religious organizations. 4 fraternities, 4 sororities. **Athletics (Intercollegiate):** *Men:* baseball, basketball, cross-country, football, golf, soccer, tennis. *Women:* basketball, cross-country, golf, soccer, softball, tennis, volleyball. **On-Campus Highlights:** Roland Student Center (Hawk's Nest, Fitness Center, Massey Beach), Houghton Memorial Library, The Coffee House, The Green, Samford Stadium

ADMISSIONS

Freshman Academic Profile: Average high school GPA 3.4. 13% in top 10% of high school class, 27% in top 25% of high school class, 69% in top 50% of high school class. 82% from public high schools. **Test Scores:** SAT Math middle 50% range 500-580. SAT EBRW middle 50% range 490-595. ACT middle 50% range 19-24. Minimum internet-based TOEFL 45. Minimum paper TOEFL 500. **Basis for Candidate Selection:** *Very important factors considered include:* rigor of secondary school record, academic GPA, standardized test scores. *Other factors considered include:* class rank, application essay, recommendation(s), interview. **Freshman Admission Requirements:** High school diploma is required and GED is accepted *Academic units recommended:* 4 English, 3 math, 2 science, 2 foreign language, 3 social studies, 3 history. **Freshman Admission Statistics:** 2,074 applied, 56.0% admitted, 25% enrolled. **Transfer Admission Requirements:** High school transcript, college transcript(s), statement of good standing from prior institution(s). Minimum college GPA of 2.25 required. Lowest grade transferable C. **General**

Admission Information: Nonfall registration accepted. Admission may be deferred for a maximum of 1 semester.

COSTS AND FINANCIAL AID

Required Forms and Deadlines: FAFSA. **Notification of Awards:** Applicants will be notified of awards on a rolling basis beginning 3/1. **Types of Aid:** *Need-based scholarships/grants:* College/university scholarship or grant aid from institutional funds; Federal Pell; SEOG; State scholarships/grants. *Loans:* Direct PLUS loans; Direct Subsidized Stafford Loans; Direct Unsubsidized Stafford Loans. *Student Employment:* Federal Work-Study Program available. Institutional employment available. **Financial Aid Statistics:** 100% needy freshmen, 100% needy undergrads receive need-based scholarship or grant aid. 11% freshmen, 11% undergrads receive non-need-based scholarship or grant aid. 82% freshmen, 81% undergrads receive need-based self-help aid. 0% freshmen, 0% undergrads receive athletic scholarships. 100% freshmen, 100% undergrads receive any aid. 81% undergrads borrow to pay for school. Average cumulative indebtedness $33,503. **Criteria for awarding aid:** *Need-based:* Art, Music/drama, Religious affiliation *Non-need-based:* Academics, Alumni affiliation, Leadership, Music/drama, Religious affiliation, State/district residency.

HUNTINGTON UNIVERSITY

2303 College Avenue, Huntington, IN 46750
Phone: (260) 359-4000 · **Financial Aid Phone:** 800-642-6493
E-mail: admissions@huntington.edu · **CEEB Code:** 1304
Fax: (260) 358-3699 · **Website:** www.huntington.edu · **ACT Code:** 1202

This private school, affiliated with the Protestant Church, was founded in 1897. It has a 170 acre campus.

RATINGS

Admissions Selectivity Rating: 74   **Fire Safety Rating:** 96   **Green Rating:** 60*

STUDENTS AND FACULTY

Enrollment: 968. **Student Body:** 57% female, 43% male, 35% out-of-state, 4% international (20 countries represented). Asian <1%, African American 2%, Caucasian 88%, Hispanic 3%, Native American <1%, Pacific Islander <1%, Two or more races 1%, Race unknown 0%.

Retention and Graduation: 79% freshmen return for sophomore year. 14% grads go on to further study within 1 year. 13% grads pursue arts and sciences degrees. 0% grads pursue law degrees. 0% grads pursue business degrees. 1% grads pursue medical degrees. **Faculty:** Student/faculty ratio 13:1. 55 full-time faculty, 87% hold PhDs, 2% are members of minority groups, 38% are women. 0% of classes are taught by teaching assistants.

ACADEMICS

Degrees: Associate; Bachelor's; Doctoral; Master's **Classes:** Most classes have 10-19 students. Most lab/discussion sessions have 10-19 students. **Most popular majors:** Animation, Interactive Technology, Video Graphics And Special Effects; Cinematography And Film/Video Production; Practical Nursing, Vocational Nursing And Nursing Assistants, Other. **Special Study Options:** Accelerated program; Distance learning; Double major; Dual enrollment; Honors program; Independent study; Internships; Study abroad; Teacher certification program. **Honors programs:** Our honors program pushing students beyond their typical academic classes. Students will work through the "Great Books" curriculum and have opportunities for seminars and field trips. Learn more at http://www.huntington.edu/honors/. **Disability Services offered to physically disabled students:** Note-taking services; Reader services; Tutors. **Career services:** Alumni network; Alumni services; Career assessment; Career/job search classes; Internships; Regional alumni

FACILITIES

Housing: Apartments for married students; Apartments for single students; Men's dorms; Special housing for disabled student; Theme housing; Women's dorms 61% of campus accessible to physically disabled. **Special Academic Facilities/Equipment:** Thornhill Nature Preserve, Herbarium, BOD POD, greenhouse **Computers:** 100% of classrooms, 100% of dorms, 100% of libraries, 100% of dining areas, 100% of student union, have wireless network access. Students can register for classes online. Administrative functions (other than registration) can be performed online.

CAMPUS LIFE

Environment: Town **Activities:** Campus Ministries; Choral groups; Concert band; Dance; Drama/theater; International Student Organization; Literary magazine; Music ensembles; Musical theater; Radio station; Student government; Student newspaper; Student-run film society; Television station 6 honor societies, 4 religious organizations. **Athletics (Intercollegiate):** *Men:*

baseball, basketball, cheerleading, cross-country, golf, soccer, tennis, track/field (outdoor), track/field (indoor). *Women:* basketball, cheerleading, cross-country, golf, soccer, softball, tennis, track/field (outdoor), track/field (indoor), volleyball. **On-Campus Highlights:** Residence Halls-lounges, Habecker Dining Commons, Norm's Place (student union), Merillat Complex (athletic facility), Merillat Centre for the Arts **Environmental Initiatives:** Campus recycling program

ADMISSIONS

Freshman Academic Profile: Average high school GPA 3.5. 26% in top 10% of high school class, 53% in top 25% of high school class, 80% in top 50% of high school class. 81% from public high schools. **Test Scores:** SAT Math middle 50% range 440-560. SAT EBRW middle 50% range 440-570. ACT middle 50% range 21-27. Minimum internet-based TOEFL 65. Minimum paper TOEFL 525. **Basis for Candidate Selection:** *Very important factors considered include:* academic GPA, standardized test scores. *Important factors considered include:* rigor of secondary school record, class rank, application essay. *Other factors considered include:* recommendation(s), interview, extracurricular activities, talent/ability, character/personal qualities, first generation, alumni/ae relation, geographical residence, state residency, religious affiliation/commitment, racial/ethnic status, volunteer work, work experience, level of applicant's interest. **Freshman Admission Requirements:** High school diploma is required and GED is accepted *Academic units recommended:* 4 English, 2 math, 3 social studies. **Freshman Admission Statistics:** 780 applied, 97.3% admitted, 30% enrolled. **Transfer Admission Requirements:** college transcript(s), essay or personal statement, Minimum college GPA of 2.0 required. Lowest grade transferable C. **General Admission Information:** Application fee $20. Priority deadline 3/1. Regular application deadline 8/1. Nonfall registration accepted. Admission may be deferred for a maximum of 1 year.

COSTS AND FINANCIAL AID

Annual tuition $23,976. Room and board $8,306. Required fees $795. Average book expense $1,000. **Required Forms and Deadlines:** FAFSA. **Notification of Awards:** Applicants will be notified of awards on a rolling basis beginning 2/15. **Types of Aid:** *Need-based scholarships/grants:* College/university scholarship or grant aid from institutional funds; Federal Pell; Private scholarships; SEOG; State scholarships/grants. *Loans:* Direct PLUS loans; Direct Subsidized Stafford Loans; Direct Unsubsidized Stafford Loans. *Student Employment:* Federal Work-Study Program available. Institutional employment available. **Financial Aid Statistics:** 94% needy freshmen, 94% needy undergrads receive need-based scholarship or grant aid. 22% freshmen, 17% undergrads receive non-need-based scholarship or grant aid. 88% freshmen, 90% undergrads receive need-based self-help aid. 6% freshmen, 5% undergrads receive athletic scholarships. 98% freshmen, 94% undergrads receive any aid. **Criteria for awarding aid:** *Need-based:* Minority status, Religious affiliation *Non-need-based:* Academics, Alumni affiliation, Art, Athletics, Leadership, Minority status, Music/drama, Religious affiliation.

HUSSON UNIVERSITY

1 College Circle, Bangor, ME 04401
Phone: 207-941-7100 · **Financial Aid Phone:** 207-973-1090
E-mail: admit@husson.edu · **CEEB Code:** 3440
Fax: 207-941-7935 · **Website:** www.husson.edu · **ACT Code:** 1646

This private school was founded in 1898. It has a 208 acre campus.

RATINGS

Admissions Selectivity Rating: 74   **Fire Safety Rating:** 99   **Green Rating:** 87

STUDENTS AND FACULTY

Enrollment: 2,724. **Student Body:** 54% female, 46% male, 22% out-of-state, 3% international (19 countries represented). Asian 1%, African American 4%, Caucasian 86%, Hispanic 2%, Native American 1%, Pacific Islander <1%, Two or more races 2%, Race unknown 2%.
Retention and Graduation: 76% freshmen return for sophomore year. 20% grads go on to further study within 1 year. 1% grads pursue arts and sciences degrees. 1% grads pursue law degrees. 10% grads pursue business degrees. 1% grads pursue medical degrees. **Faculty:** Student/faculty ratio 14:1. 147 full-time faculty, 46% hold PhDs, 6% are members of minority groups, 48% are women. 0% of classes are taught by teaching assistants.

ACADEMICS

Degrees: Associate; Bachelor's; Certificate; Doctoral/Professional; Master's; Post-Bachelor's certificate; Post-Master's certificate; Transfer Associate **Classes:** Most classes have 10-19 students. Most lab/discussion sessions have 10-19 students. **Most popular majors:** Criminal Justice/Law Enforcement

Administration; Registered Nursing/Registered Nurse; Business/Commerce, General. **Special Study Options:** Accelerated program; Distance learning; Double major; Dual enrollment; English as a Second Language (ESL); Internships; Liberal arts/career combination; Student-designed major; Study abroad; Teacher certification program; Weekend college. **Disability Services offered to physically disabled students:** Note-taking services; Tape recorders; Tutors. **Career services:** Alumni network; Alumni services; Career assessment; Career/job search classes; Internships; Regional alumni

FACILITIES

Housing: Apartments for single students; Coed dorms; Special housing for disabled students 100% of campus accessible to physically disabled. **Special Academic Facilities/Equipment:** White Art Gallery Dahl Anatomy Lab Kenduskeag Research Institute Gracie Theater **Computers:** 100% of classrooms, 100% of dorms, 100% of libraries, 100% of student union, have wireless network access. Students can register for classes online. Administrative functions (other than registration) can be performed online.

CAMPUS LIFE

Environment: Town **Activities:** Campus Ministries; Choral groups; Drama/theater; International Student Organization; Literary magazine; Pep band; Radio station; Student government; Yearbook 30 registered organizations, 1 honor society, 2 religious organizations. 2 fraternities, 3 sororities. **Athletics (Intercollegiate):** *Men:* baseball, basketball, football, golf, lacrosse, soccer. *Women:* basketball, field hockey, lacrosse, soccer, softball, swimming, tennis, volleyball. **On-Campus Highlights:** Swan Fitness Center, Campus Center, Student Lounge, Newman Gym, Gracie Theater and Atrium **Environmental Initiatives:** Green Cleaning Supplies

ADMISSIONS

Freshman Academic Profile: Average high school GPA 3.3. 10% in top 10% of high school class, 39% in top 25% of high school class, 77% in top 50% of high school class. 90% from public high schools. **Test Scores:** SAT Math middle 50% range 430-540. SAT EBRW middle 50% range 430-530. ACT middle 50% range 17-23. Minimum internet-based TOEFL 75. Minimum paper TOEFL 500. **Basis for Candidate Selection:** *Very important factors considered include:* rigor of secondary school record, academic GPA. *Important factors considered include:* class rank, application essay, standardized test scores, recommendation(s), interview, extracurricular activities, talent/ability, character/personal qualities. *Other factors considered include:* alumni/ae relation, volunteer work, work experience, level of applicant's interest. **Freshman Admission Requirements:** High school diploma is required and GED is accepted *Academic units recommended:* 4 English, 3 math, 3 science, 2 science labs, 1 social studies, 1 history. **Freshman Admission Statistics:** 2,460 applied, 80.2% admitted, 32% enrolled. **Transfer Admission Requirements:** High school transcript, college transcript(s), essay or personal statement, Minimum college GPA of 2.0 required. Lowest grade transferable C. **General Admission Information:** Application fee $40. Priority deadline 3/1. Regular application deadline 8/15. Nonfall registration accepted. Admission may be deferred for a maximum of 1 year.

COSTS AND FINANCIAL AID

Annual tuition $16,530. Room and board $9,498. Required fees $480. Average book expense $1,150. **Required Forms and Deadlines:** FAFSA. **Notification of Awards:** Applicants will be notified of awards on a rolling basis beginning 12/1. **Types of Aid:** *Need-based scholarships/grants:* College/university scholarship or grant aid from institutional funds; Federal Pell; Private scholarships; SEOG; State scholarships/grants. *Loans:* Direct PLUS loans; Direct Subsidized Stafford Loans; Direct Unsubsidized Stafford Loans. *Student Employment:* Federal Work-Study Program available. **Financial Aid Statistics:** 94% needy freshmen, 84% needy undergrads receive need-based scholarship or grant aid. 98% freshmen, 79% undergrads receive non-need-based scholarship or grant aid. 93% freshmen, 93% undergrads receive need-based self-help aid. 0% freshmen, 0% undergrads receive athletic scholarships. 85% freshmen, 86% undergrads receive any aid. 88% undergrads borrow to pay for school. Average cumulative indebtedness $9,088. **Criteria for awarding aid:** *Need-based:* Academics, Leadership *Non-need-based:* Academics, Leadership.

HUSTON-TILLOTSON UNIVERSITY

900 Chicon Street, Austin, TX 78702
Phone: 512-505-3028 • **Financial Aid Phone:** 512.505.3028
E-mail: admission@htu.edu • **CEEB Code:** 6280
Fax: 512-505-3192 • **Website:** www.htu.edu./ • **ACT Code:** 4104

This private school was founded in 1875. It has a 23 acre campus.

RATINGS

Admissions Selectivity Rating: 71   **Fire Safety Rating:** 60*   **Green Rating:** 60*

STUDENTS AND FACULTY

Enrollment: 889. **Student Body:** 51% female, 49% male, 3% out-of-state, 3% international (11 countries represented). African American 72%, Caucasian 5%, Hispanic 19%, Two or more races <1%,
Retention and Graduation: 50% freshmen return for sophomore year.
Faculty: Student/faculty ratio 15:1. 47 full-time faculty, 70% hold PhDs, 57% are members of minority groups, 53% are women. 0% of classes are taught by teaching assistants.

ACADEMICS

Degrees: Bachelor's; Post-Bachelor's certificate **Classes:** Most classes have fewer than 10 students. Most lab/discussion sessions have 10-19 students.
Most popular majors: Computer And Information Sciences And Support Services; Education, General; Business, Management, Marketing, And Related Support Services. **Special Study Options:** Cooperative education program; Cross-registration; Distance learning; Double major; Dual enrollment; External degree program; Honors program; Independent study; Internships; Liberal arts/career combination; Study abroad; Teacher certification program. **Honors programs:** W.E.B. DuBois Honors Program.

FACILITIES

Housing: Men's dorms; Wellness housing; Women's dorms

CAMPUS LIFE

Environment: Metropolis **Activities:** Campus Ministries; Choral groups; Dance; Drama/theater; International Student Organization; Jazz band; Literary magazine; Model UN; Music ensembles; Student government; Student-run film society 17 registered organizations, 5 honor societies, 5 religious organizations. **Athletics (Intercollegiate):** *Men:* baseball, basketball, soccer, track/field (outdoor). *Women:* basketball, track/field (outdoor), volleyball.

ADMISSIONS

Freshman Academic Profile: Average high school GPA 2.8. 6% in top 10% of high school class, 12% in top 25% of high school class, 53% in top 50% of high school class. **Test Scores:** SAT Math middle 50% range 360-460. SAT EBRW middle 50% range 350-460. ACT middle 50% range 14-19. Minimum internet-based TOEFL 61. Minimum paper TOEFL 500. **Basis for Candidate Selection:** *Very important factors considered include:* rigor of secondary school record, academic GPA. *Important factors considered include:* class rank, standardized test scores, interview. *Other factors considered include:* application essay, recommendation(s), extracurricular activities, talent/ability, first generation, alumni/ae relation, work experience. **Freshman Admission Requirements:** High school diploma is required and GED is accepted *Academic units required:* 4 English, 3 math, 2 science, 3 social studies, 1 computer science, and 2 units from above areas or other academic areas. *Academic units recommended:* 2 foreign language. **Freshman Admission Statistics:** 652 applied, 96.3% admitted, 43% enrolled. **Transfer Admission Requirements:** college transcript(s), essay or personal statement, Minimum college GPA of 2.0 required. Lowest grade transferable C. **General Admission Information:** Application fee $25. Priority deadline 3/15. Regular application deadline 7/1. Nonfall registration accepted. Admission may be deferred for a maximum of 1 semester.

COSTS AND FINANCIAL AID

Annual tuition $10,396. Room and board $6,946. Required fees $2,034. Average book expense $600. **Required Forms and Deadlines:** FAFSA. **Notification of Awards:** Applicants will be notified of awards on a rolling basis beginning 3/1. **Types of Aid:** *Need-based scholarships/grants:* College/university scholarship or grant aid from institutional funds; Federal Pell; Private scholarships; SEOG; State scholarships/grants; United Negro College Fund. *Loans:* Direct PLUS loans; Direct Subsidized Stafford Loans; Direct Unsubsidized Stafford Loans. *Student Employment:* Federal Work-Study Program available. **Financial Aid Statistics:** 25% needy freshmen, 33% needy undergrads receive need-based scholarship or grant aid. 33% freshmen, 35% undergrads receive non-need-based scholarship or grant aid. 100% freshmen, 100% undergrads receive need-based self-help aid. 15% freshmen, 14% undergrads receive athletic scholarships. 97% undergrads receive any aid. **Criteria for awarding aid:** *Non-need-based:* Academics, Alumni affiliation,

Art, Athletics, Job skills, Leadership, Minority status, Music/drama, Religious affiliation, State/district residency.

IDAHO STATE UNIVERSITY

921 South 8th Avenue, Pocatello, ID 83209-8270
Phone: 208-282-2475 • **Financial Aid Phone:** 208-282-2981
E-mail: admiss@isu.edu • **CEEB Code:** 4355
Fax: 208-282-4511 • **Website:** www.isu.edu • **ACT Code:** 918

This public school was founded in 1901. It has a 1100 acre campus.

RATINGS

Admissions Selectivity Rating: 89   **Fire Safety Rating:** 73   **Green Rating:** 60*

STUDENTS AND FACULTY

Enrollment: 8,974. **Student Body:** 50% female, 50% male, 8% out-of-state, 14% international (63 countries represented). Asian 1%, African American 1%, Caucasian 67%, Hispanic 10%, Native American 1%, Pacific Islander <1%, Two or more races 3%, Race unknown 2%.
Retention and Graduation: 71% freshmen return for sophomore year.
Faculty: Student/faculty ratio 15:1. 585 full-time faculty, 51% hold PhDs, 9% are members of minority groups, 45% are women.

ACADEMICS

Degrees: Associate; Bachelor's; Certificate; Doctoral; Doctoral/Professional; Doctoral/Research; Master's; Post-Bachelor's certificate; Post-Master's certificate **Classes:** Most classes have 20-29 students. **Most popular majors:** Elementary Education And Teaching; Secondary Education And Teaching; Biology/Biological Sciences, General. **Special Study Options:** Accelerated program; Cooperative education program; Cross-registration; Distance learning; Double major; Dual enrollment; English as a Second Language (ESL); Exchange student program (domestic); Honors program; Independent study; Internships; Liberal arts/career combination; Student-designed major; Study abroad; Teacher certification program; Weekend college. **Honors programs:** Honors courses are offered in small classes and deal with interdisciplinary issues and confront some aspect of the human condition. Innovative teaching and assignments are encourages and interaction with faculty and class members is lively. **Disability Services offered to physically disabled students:** Note-taking services; Reader services; Tape recorders; Tutors. **Career services:** Career assessment; Career/job search classes

FACILITIES

Housing: Apartments for married students; Apartments for single students; Coed dorms; Men's dorms; Special housing for disabled student; Women's dorms 100% of campus accessible to physically disabled. **Special Academic Facilities/Equipment:** Museum of Natural History, Idaho Accelerator Center, Rendezvous Center **Computers:** Students can register for classes online. Administrative functions (other than registration) can be performed online.

CAMPUS LIFE

Environment: Town **Activities:** Campus Ministries; Choral groups; Concert band; Dance; Drama/theater; International Student Organization; Jazz band; Marching band; Music ensembles; Musical theater; Opera; Pep band; Radio station; Student government; Student newspaper; Symphony orchestra; Television station; Yearbook 134 registered organizations, 8 honor societies, 7 religious organizations. 2 fraternities, 3 sororities. **Athletics (Intercollegiate):** *Men:* basketball, cheerleading, cross-country, football, golf, tennis, track/field (outdoor). *Women:* basketball, cheerleading, cross-country, golf, soccer, softball, tennis, track/field (outdoor), volleyball. **On-Campus Highlights:** Idaho Museum of Natural History, Rock Climbing Wall at Reed Gym, L.E. and Thelma E Stephens performing Ar, Rendezvous Center, Particle Accelerator

ADMISSIONS

Freshman Academic Profile: Average high school GPA 3.2. 11% in top 10% of high school class, 30% in top 25% of high school class, 59% in top 50% of high school class. **Test Scores:** SAT Math middle 50% range 420-530. SAT EBRW middle 50% range 420-540. ACT middle 50% range 19-25. Minimum internet-based TOEFL 61. Minimum paper TOEFL 500. **Basis for Candidate Selection:** *Other factors considered include:* academic GPA, standardized test scores. **Freshman Admission Requirements:** High school diploma is required and GED is accepted *Academic units required:* 4 English, 3 math, 3 science, 1 science labs, 1 foreign language, 2.5 social studies, and 1.5 units from above areas or other academic areas. *Academic units recommended:* 4 math. **Freshman Admission Statistics:** 3,057 applied, 53.3% admitted, 90% enrolled. **Transfer Admission Requirements:** High school transcript, college transcript(s), standardized test scores, Minimum college GPA of 2.0 required. Lowest grade transferable D. **General Admission Information:**

Application fee $50. Nonfall registration accepted. Admission may be deferred for a maximum of 3 years.

COSTS AND FINANCIAL AID

Annual in-state tuition $6,338. Annual out-of-state tuition $18,504. Room and board $6,338. Required fees $1,678. Average book expense $1,000. **Required Forms and Deadlines:** FAFSA. **Notification of Awards:** Applicants will be notified of awards on a rolling basis beginning 4/1. **Types of Aid:** *Need-based scholarships/grants:* College/university scholarship or grant aid from institutional funds; Federal Nursing Scholarships; Federal Pell; Private scholarships; SEOG; State scholarships/grants. *Loans:* Direct PLUS loans; Direct Subsidized Stafford Loans; Direct Unsubsidized Stafford Loans. *Student Employment:* Federal Work-Study Program available. Institutional employment available. **Financial Aid Statistics:** 77% needy freshmen, 77% needy undergrads receive need-based scholarship or grant aid. 56% freshmen, 31% undergrads receive non-need-based scholarship or grant aid. 72% freshmen, 79% undergrads receive need-based self-help aid. 3% freshmen, 3% undergrads receive athletic scholarships. 73% freshmen, 74% undergrads receive any aid. 69% undergrads borrow to pay for school. Average cumulative indebtedness $29,983. **Criteria for awarding aid:** *Non-need-based:* Academics, Alumni affiliation, Art, Athletics, Leadership, Minority status, Music/drama, State/district residency.

ILLINOIS COLLEGE

1101 West College Ave., Jacksonville, IL 62650
Phone: 217-245-3030
E-mail: admissions@mail.ic.edu • **CEEB Code:** 1315
Fax: 217-245-3034 • **Website:** www.ic.edu • **ACT Code:** 1034

This private school, affiliated with the Presbyterian Church, was founded in 1829. It has a 62 acre campus.

RATINGS

Admissions Selectivity Rating: 83   **Fire Safety Rating:** 60*   **Green Rating:** 60*

STUDENTS AND FACULTY

Enrollment: 947. **Student Body:** 51% female, 49% male, 14% out-of-state, 5% international. Asian 1%, African American 11%, Caucasian 71%, Hispanic 9%, Native American <1%, Pacific Islander <1%, Two or more races 3%, Race unknown 0%.
Retention and Graduation: 77% freshmen return for sophomore year. 55% freshmen graduate within 4 years. 60% freshmen graduate within 6 years. 22% grads go on to further study within 1 year. 13% grads pursue arts and sciences degrees. 5% grads pursue law degrees. 2% grads pursue business degrees. 4% grads pursue medical degrees. **Faculty:** Student/faculty ratio 12:1. 75 full-time faculty, 85% hold PhDs, 7% are members of minority groups, 37% are women.

ACADEMICS

Degrees: Bachelor's; Master's **Classes:** Most classes have fewer than 10 students. Most lab/discussion sessions have 20-29 students. **Special Study Options:** Cross-registration; Double major; Dual enrollment; English as a Second Language (ESL); Honors program; Independent study; Internships; Liberal arts/career combination; Student-designed major; Study abroad; Teacher certification program. **Career services:** Career assessment; Career/job search classes; Internships

FACILITIES

Housing: Apartments for single students; Coed dorms; Men's dorms; Theme housing; Women's dorms **Special Academic Facilities/Equipment:** Art gallery, language lab.

CAMPUS LIFE

Environment: Rural **Activities:** Campus Ministries; Choral groups; Concert band; Dance; Drama/theater; International Student Organization; Jazz band; Literary magazine; Model UN; Music ensembles; Pep band; Radio station; Student government; Student newspaper; Symphony orchestra; Yearbook 72 registered organizations, 12 honor societies, 3 religious organizations. 4 fraternities, 3 sororities. **Athletics (Intercollegiate):** *Men:* baseball, basketball, cross-country, football, golf, soccer, tennis, track/field (outdoor), track/field (indoor), wrestling. *Women:* basketball, cheerleading, cross-country, golf, soccer, softball, tennis, track/field (outdoor), track/field (indoor), volleyball.

ADMISSIONS

Freshman Academic Profile: Average high school GPA 3.5. 14% in top 10% of high school class, 41% in top 25% of high school class, 80% in top 50% of high school class. 80% from public high schools. **Test Scores:** SAT Math middle 50% range 510-620. SAT EBRW middle 50% range 470-610. ACT middle 50% range 19-25. Minimum paper TOEFL 550. **Basis for Candidate**

Selection: *Very important factors considered include:* rigor of secondary school record, academic GPA, character/personal qualities. *Important factors considered include:* class rank, application essay, recommendation(s), interview, extracurricular activities, talent/ability. *Other factors considered include:* standardized test scores, first generation, alumni/ae relation, geographical residence, racial/ethnic status, volunteer work, work experience, level of applicant's interest. **Freshman Admission Requirements:** High school diploma is required and GED is accepted *Academic units required:* 4 English, 3 math, 2 science, 2 science labs, 1 social studies, 1 history, 3 academic electives, *Academic units recommended:* 4 English, 3 math, 3 science, 3 science labs, 2 foreign language, 1 social studies, 1 history, 3 academic electives. **Freshman Admission Statistics:** 4,121 applied, 54.9% admitted, 11% enrolled. **Transfer Admission Requirements:** High school transcript, college transcript(s), Minimum college GPA of 2.50 required. Lowest grade transferable C. **General Admission Information:** Nonfall registration accepted. Admission may be deferred for a maximum of 1 year.

COSTS AND FINANCIAL AID

Annual tuition $32,540. Room and board $9,280. Required fees $550. **Required Forms and Deadlines:** FAFSA. **Notification of Awards:** Applicants will be notified of awards on a rolling basis beginning 12/15. **Types of Aid:** *Need-based scholarships/grants:* College/university scholarship or grant aid from institutional funds; Federal Pell; Private scholarships; SEOG; State scholarships/grants. *Loans:* Direct PLUS loans; Direct Subsidized Stafford Loans; Direct Unsubsidized Stafford Loans. *Student Employment:* Federal Work-Study Program available. Institutional employment available. **Financial Aid Statistics:** 100% needy freshmen, 100% needy undergrads receive need-based scholarship or grant aid. 11% freshmen, 12% undergrads receive non-need-based scholarship or grant aid. 89% freshmen, 87% undergrads receive need-based self-help aid. 0% freshmen, 0% undergrads receive athletic scholarships. 78% undergrads borrow to pay for school. Average cumulative indebtedness $32,000. **Criteria for awarding aid:** *Non-need-based:* Academics, Art, Music/drama.

ILLINOIS INSTITUTE OF TECHNOLOGY

10 West 35th Street, Chicago, IL 60616
Phone: 312-567-3025 • **Financial Aid Phone:** 312-567-7219
E-mail: admission@iit.edu • **CEEB Code:** 1318
Fax: 312-567-6939 • **Website:** http://www.iit.edu/ • **ACT Code:** 1040

This private school was founded in 1892. It has a 120 acre campus.

RATINGS

Admissions Selectivity Rating: 88   **Fire Safety Rating:** 83   **Green Rating:** 61

STUDENTS AND FACULTY

Enrollment: 2,722. **Student Body:** 31% female, 69% male, 26% out-of-state, 21% international (94 countries represented). Asian 14%, African American 6%, Caucasian 33%, Hispanic 16%, Native American <1%, Pacific Islander <1%, Two or more races 3%, Race unknown 7%.
Retention and Graduation: 93% freshmen return for sophomore year. 32% freshmen graduate within 4 years. 72% freshmen graduate within 6 years. **Faculty:** Student/faculty ratio 12:1. 413 full-time faculty, 97% hold PhDs, 21% are members of minority groups, 27% are women. 0% of classes are taught by teaching assistants.

ACADEMICS

Degrees: Bachelor's; Doctoral/Professional; Doctoral/Research; Master's; Post-Bachelor's certificate; Post-Master's certificate **Classes:** Most classes have 10-19 students. Most lab/discussion sessions have 10-19 students. **Most popular majors:** Architecture; Computer And Information Sciences, General; Mechanical Engineering. **Special Study Options:** Cooperative education program; Cross-registration; Distance learning; Double major; Dual enrollment; English as a Second Language (ESL); Independent study; Internships; Liberal arts/career combination; Study abroad; Teacher certification program. **Combined degree programs:** BA/JD; BA/MA. **Disability Services offered to physically disabled students:** Note-taking services; Reader services; Tape recorders; Tutors. **Career services:** Alumni network; Alumni services; Career assessment; Career/job search classes; Internships; Regional alumni

FACILITIES

Housing: Apartments for married students; Apartments for single students; Coed dorms; Fraternity/sorority housing; Other (please specify) 90% of campus accessible to physically diasbled. **Special Academic Facilities/Equipment:** The Center for Accelerator and Particle Physics (CAPP), The Center for Complex Systems and Dynamics (CCSD), The Center for Digital Design and Manufacturing (CDDM), The Center for Electrochemical Science and Engineering, The Center for Excellence in Polymer Science and Engineering, The Center for Integrative Neuroscience and Neuroengineering Research, The Center for the Management of Medical Technology (CMMT), The Center for Molecular Study of Soft Condensed Matter (CMS2), The Center for Strategic Competitiveness (CSC), The Center for the Study of Ethics in the Professions (CSEP), The Center for Synchrotron Radiation Research and Instrumentation, The Center for Work Zone Safety and Mobility (CWZSM), Electric Power and Power Electronics Center (EPPEC), Energy + Power Center, Energy and Sustainability Institute, The Engineering Center For Diabetes Research and Education (ECDRE), The Fluid Dynamics Research Center, The High Performance Computing Center (HPCC), IIT Research Institute (IITRI), The International Center for Sensor Science and Engineering (ICSSE), The International Center for Sustainable New Cities (ICSNC), The Medical Imaging Research Center (MIRC), The National Center for Food Safety and Technology (NCFST), The Particle Technology and Crystallization Center (PTCC), The Pritzker Institute of Biomedical Science and Engineering, The Thermal Processing Technology Center (TPTC), The Wireless Network and Communications Research Center (WiNCom), Main Campus design by Ludwig Mies van der Rohe, McCormick Tribune Campus Center (MTCC) design by Rem Koolhaas, residence hall designed by Helmut Jahn, IIT Research Institute (IITRI), University Technology Park At IIT (UTP), Kemper Room Art Gallery, Illinois Tech Model Railroad (ITMR) **Computers:** 100% of classrooms, 100% of dorms, 100% of libraries, 100% of dining areas, 100% of student union, have wireless network access. Students can register for classes online. Administrative functions (other than registration) can be performed online.

CAMPUS LIFE

Environment: Metropolis **Activities:** Campus Ministries; Choral groups; Concert band; Dance; Drama/theater; International Student Organization; Literary magazine; Music ensembles; Musical theater; Radio station; Student government; Student newspaper; Student-run film society; Television station 100 registered organizations, 4 honor societies, 10 religious organizations. 7 fraternities, 3 sororities. **Athletics (Intercollegiate):** *Men:* baseball, cross-country, diving, soccer, swimming. *Women:* cross-country, diving, soccer, swimming, volleyball. **On-Campus Highlights:** S.R. Crown Hall (Architecture Building), McCormick Tribune Center, Keating Athletic Center, Hermann Hall, State Street Village **Environmental Initiatives:** Creation of an Office of Campus Energy and Sustainability and the Wanger Institute of Sustainable Energy Research bringing students, faculty, staff, and alumni together to address complex sustainability issues.

ADMISSIONS

Freshman Academic Profile: 87% from public high schools. **Test Scores:** SAT Math middle 50% range 650-730. SAT EBRW middle 50% range 580-680. ACT middle 50% range 25-31. Minimum internet-based TOEFL 70. **Basis for Candidate Selection:** *Very important factors considered include:* rigor of secondary school record, academic GPA, standardized test scores. *Important factors considered include:* class rank, recommendation(s). *Other factors considered include:* application essay, interview, extracurricular activities, talent/ability, character/personal qualities, first generation, alumni/ae relation, volunteer work, work experience, level of applicant's interest. **Freshman Admission Requirements:** High school diploma is required and GED is accepted *Academic units required:* 4 English, 4 math, 3 science, 2 science labs, 2 foreign language, 2 social studies, *Academic units recommended:* 4 English, 4 math, 3 science, 2 science labs, 2 foreign language, 2 social studies, 2 history, 1 computer science, 1 visual/performing arts. **Freshman Admission Statistics:** 4,708 applied, 54.1% admitted, 19% enrolled. **Transfer Admission Requirements:** college transcript(s), essay or personal statement, statement of good standing from prior institution(s). Minimum college GPA of 3.0 required. Lowest grade transferable C. **General Admission Information:** Priority deadline 12/1. Regular application deadline 8/1. Nonfall registration accepted. Admission may be deferred.

COSTS AND FINANCIAL AID

Required Forms and Deadlines: FAFSA. **Notification of Awards:** Applicants will be notified of awards on a rolling basis beginning 2/15. **Types of Aid:** *Need-based scholarships/grants:* College/university scholarship or grant aid from institutional funds; Federal Pell; Private scholarships; SEOG; State scholarships/grants. *Loans:* Direct PLUS loans; Direct Subsidized Stafford Loans; Direct Unsubsidized Stafford Loans. *Student Employment:* Federal Work-Study Program available. Institutional employment available. **Financial Aid Statistics:** 100% needy freshmen receive need-based scholarship or grant aid. 100% freshmen, 99% undergrads receive any aid. **Criteria for awarding aid:** *Non-need-based:* Academics, Alumni affiliation, Leadership.

ILLINOIS STATE UNIVERSITY

Admissions, Normal, IL 61790-2200
Phone: 309-438-2181 · **Financial Aid Phone:** 309-438-2231
E-mail: admissions@illinoisstate.edu · **CEEB Code:** 1319
Fax: 309-438-3932 · **Website:** www.ilstu.edu · **ACT Code:** 1042

This public school was founded in 1857. It has a 1100 acre campus.

RATINGS

Admissions Selectivity Rating: 74   **Fire Safety Rating:** 91   **Green Rating:** 89

STUDENTS AND FACULTY

Enrollment: 18,571. **Student Body:** 55% female, 45% male, 2% out-of-state, <1% international (35 countries represented). Asian 2%, African American 8%, Caucasian 76%, Hispanic 10%, Native American <1%, Pacific Islander <1%, Two or more races 3%, Race unknown <1%. **Retention and Graduation:** 81% freshmen return for sophomore year. **Faculty:** Student/faculty ratio 18:1. 882 full-time faculty, 82% hold PhDs, 16% are members of minority groups, 52% are women.

ACADEMICS

Degrees: Bachelor's; Doctoral/Professional; Doctoral/Research; Master's; Post-Bachelor's certificate; Post-Master's certificate **Classes:** Most classes have 10-19 students. Most lab/discussion sessions have 10-19 students. **Most popular majors:** Special Education And Teaching, General; Elementary Education And Teaching; Business Administration And Management, General. **Special Study Options:** Accelerated program; Cooperative education program; Distance learning; Double major; Dual enrollment; English as a Second Language (ESL); Exchange student program (domestic); Honors program; Independent study; Internships; Student-designed major; Study abroad; Teacher certification program. **Honors programs:** The Honors Program at Illinois State University promotes exceptional learning for exceptional learners by enriching students' learning experiences at Illinois State University. This is done by providing opportunities, resources, and support for Honors students to customize their learning in ways that are valuable to them in General Education and across all disciplines. **Combined degree programs:** BA/MA. **Disability Services offered to physically disabled students:** Note-taking services; Reader services; Tape recorders; Tutors. **Career services:** Alumni services; Career assessment; Internships

FACILITIES

Housing: Apartments for married students; Apartments for single students; Coed dorms; Fraternity/sorority housing; Special housing for disabled student; Special housing for international students; Theme housing; Wellness housing 100% of campus accessible to physically diasbled. **Special Academic Facilities/Equipment:** Art gallery, cultural museums, on-campus elementary and secondary schools, greenhouse, farm, planetarium **Computers:** 100% of classrooms, 100% of dorms, 100% of libraries, 100% of dining areas, 100% of student union, have wireless network access. Students can register for classes online. Administrative functions (other than registration) can be performed online. Undergraduates are required to own a computer.

CAMPUS LIFE

Environment: City **Activities:** Campus Ministries; Choral groups; Concert band; Dance; Drama/theater; International Student Organization; Jazz band; Literary magazine; Marching band; Model UN; Music ensembles; Musical theater; Opera; Pep band; Radio station; Student government; Student newspaper; Student-run film society; Symphony orchestra; Television station 270 registered organizations, 23 honor societies, 22 religious organizations. 21 fraternities, 17 sororities. **Athletics (Intercollegiate):** *Men:* baseball, basketball, cheerleading, cross-country, football, golf, tennis, track/field (outdoor), track/field (indoor). *Women:* basketball, cheerleading, cross-country, diving, golf, gymnastics, soccer, softball, swimming, tennis, track/field (outdoor), track/field (indoor), volleyball. **On-Campus Highlights:** Student Fitness Center, Hancock Stadium, Bone Student Center, Redbird Arena, State Farm Hall of Business **Environmental Initiatives:** Establishing a formal Office of Sustainability with 2 full time staff, 1 graduate assistant and multiple interns.

ADMISSIONS

Freshman Academic Profile: Average high school GPA 3.4. 86% from public high schools. **Test Scores:** ACT middle 50% range 21-26. Minimum internet-based TOEFL 79. Minimum paper TOEFL 550. **Basis for Candidate Selection:** *Very important factors considered include:* academic GPA, standardized test scores. *Other factors considered include:* rigor of secondary school record, application essay, talent/ability. **Freshman Admission Requirements:** High school diploma is required and GED is accepted *Academic units required:* 4 English, 3 math, 2 science, 2 science labs, 2 foreign language, 2 social studies, 2 academic electives. **Freshman Admission**

Statistics: 12,078 applied, 88.9% admitted, 34% enrolled. **Transfer Admission Requirements:** college transcript(s), essay or personal statement, Minimum college GPA of 3.0 required. Lowest grade transferable D. **General Admission Information:** Application fee $50. Priority deadline 11/15. Regular application deadline 4/1. Nonfall registration accepted. Admission may be deferred for a maximum of 2 semesters.

COSTS AND FINANCIAL AID
Annual in-state tuition $9,948. Annual out-of-state tuition $22,215. Room and board $9,948. Required fees $2,953. Average book expense $942. **Required Forms and Deadlines:** FAFSA. **Notification of Awards:** Applicants will be notified of awards on a rolling basis beginning 4/1. *Types of Aid: Need-based scholarships/grants:* College/university scholarship or grant aid from institutional funds; Federal Nursing Scholarships; Federal Pell; Private scholarships; SEOG; State scholarships/grants. *Loans:* Direct PLUS loans; Direct Subsidized Stafford Loans; Direct Unsubsidized Stafford Loans. *Student Employment:* Federal Work-Study Program available. Institutional employment available. **Criteria for awarding aid:** *Need-based:* Academics, Art, Music/drama *Non-need-based:* Academics, Art, Athletics, Music/drama.

ILLINOIS WESLEYAN UNIVERSITY

PO Box 2900, Bloomington, IL 61702-2900
Phone: 309-556-3031 · **Financial Aid Phone:** 309-556-3096
E-mail: iwuadmit@iwu.edu · **CEEB Code:** 1320
Fax: 309-556-3820 · **Website:** www.iwu.edu · **ACT Code:** 1044

This private school was founded in 1850. It has a 82 acre campus.

RATINGS
Admissions Selectivity Rating: 85   **Fire Safety Rating:** 94   **Green Rating:** 64

STUDENTS AND FACULTY
Enrollment: 1,642. **Student Body:** 55% female, 45% male, 14% out-of-state, 8% international (23 countries represented). Asian 6%, African American 5%, Caucasian 69%, Hispanic 8%, Native American 0%, Pacific Islander <1%, Two or more races 2%, Race unknown 1%.
Retention and Graduation: 89% freshmen return for sophomore year. 71% freshmen graduate within 4 years. 78% freshmen graduate within 6 years. 25% grads go on to further study within 1 year. **Faculty:** Student/faculty ratio 10:1. 142 full-time faculty, 96% hold PhDs, 14% are members of minority groups, 42% are women. 0% of classes are taught by teaching assistants.

ACADEMICS
Degrees: Bachelor's **Classes:** Most classes have 10-19 students. Most lab/discussion sessions have 20-29 students. **Most popular majors:** Nursing/Registered Nurse (Rn, Asn, Bsn, Msn); Business/Commerce, General; Accounting. **Special Study Options:** Double major; Exchange student program (domestic); Honors program; Independent study; Internships; Student-designed major; Study abroad; Teacher certification program. **Honors programs:** IWU offers a research honors designation to eligible senior students who successfully complete and defend an intensive, advanced research or creative project under the direction of an interdisciplinary faculty committee. Performance Honors designations are also available in the Art, Music, and Theatre Arts. **Disability Services offered to physically disabled students:** Note-taking services; Reader services; Tape recorders; Tutors. **Career services:** Alumni network; Alumni services; Career assessment; Career/job search classes; Internships; Regional alumni

FACILITIES
Housing: Apartments for single students; Coed dorms; Fraternity/sorority housing; Special housing for disabled student; Special housing for international students 80% of campus accessible to physically diasbled. **Special Academic Facilities/Equipment:** observatory, computerized music lab, graphic design studio, Ames Library archives and special collections, visual anthropology lab, social science lab **Computers:** 60% of classrooms, 100% of libraries, 100% of dining areas, 100% of student union, have wireless network access. Students can register for classes online. Administrative functions (other than registration) can be performed online.

CAMPUS LIFE
Environment: City **Activities:** Campus Ministries; Choral groups; Concert band; Dance; Drama/theater; International Student Organization; Jazz band; Literary magazine; Model UN; Music ensembles; Musical theater; Opera; Pep band; Radio station; Student government; Student newspaper; Student-run

film society; Symphony orchestra; Television station; Yearbook 165 registered organizations, 29 honor societies, 15 religious organizations. 6 fraternities, 5 sororities. **Athletics (Intercollegiate):** *Men:* baseball, basketball, cross-country, diving, football, golf, soccer, swimming, tennis, track/field (outdoor), track/field (indoor). *Women:* basketball, cross-country, diving, golf, soccer, softball, swimming, tennis, track/field (outdoor), track/field (indoor), volleyball. **On-Campus Highlights:** The Ames Library, Hansen Student Center, Shirk Center for Athletics and Wellness, Center for Natural Science, The Dugout (snack bar and coffee shop) **Environmental Initiatives:** IWU has a commitment to environmental sustainability in its mission statement.

ADMISSIONS
Freshman Academic Profile: Average high school GPA 3.7. 39% in top 10% of high school class, 72% in top 25% of high school class, 95% in top 50% of high school class. 74% from public high schools. **Test Scores:** ACT middle 50% range 24-29. Minimum internet-based TOEFL 80. Minimum paper TOEFL 550. **Basis for Candidate Selection:** *Very important factors considered include:* rigor of secondary school record, academic GPA, interview. *Important factors considered include:* class rank, application essay, standardized test scores, extracurricular activities, talent/ability, character/personal qualities. *Other factors considered include:* recommendation(s), first generation, alumni/ae relation, geographical residence, state residency, racial/ethnic status, volunteer work, work experience, level of applicant's interest. **Freshman Admission Requirements:** High school diploma is required and GED is accepted *Academic units recommended:* 4 English, 3 math, 3 science, 2 science labs, 3 foreign language, 2 social studies. **Freshman Admission Statistics:** 3,697 applied, 60.9% admitted, 17% enrolled. **Transfer Admission Requirements:** High school transcript, college transcript(s), essay or personal statement, standardized test scores, Minimum college GPA of 2.0 required. Lowest grade transferable C-. **General Admission Information:** Nonfall registration accepted. Admission may be deferred for a maximum of 1 year.

COSTS AND FINANCIAL AID
Annual tuition $45,654. Room and board $10,574. Average book expense $800. **Required Forms and Deadlines:** FAFSA; Institution's own financial aid form. **Notification of Awards:** Applicants will be notified of awards on a rolling basis beginning 3/1. *Types of Aid: Need-based scholarships/grants:* College/university scholarship or grant aid from institutional funds; Federal Pell; Private scholarships; SEOG; State scholarships/grants. *Loans:* Direct PLUS loans; Direct Subsidized Stafford Loans; Direct Unsubsidized Stafford Loans. *Student Employment:* Federal Work-Study Program available. Institutional employment available. **Financial Aid Statistics:** 100% needy freshmen, 100% needy undergrads receive need-based scholarship or grant aid. 19% freshmen, 12% undergrads receive non-need-based scholarship or grant aid. 72% freshmen, 81% undergrads receive need-based self-help aid. 0% freshmen, 0% undergrads receive athletic scholarships. 100% freshmen, 100% undergrads receive any aid. 73% undergrads borrow to pay for school. Average cumulative indebtedness $34,999. **Criteria for awarding aid:** *Need-based:* Academics, Art, Music/drama *Non-need-based:* Academics, Art, Music/drama.

IMMACULATA UNIVERSITY

1145 King Road, Immaculata, PA 19345-0642
Phone: (610)647-4400 x3060 · **Financial Aid Phone:** 610-647-4400
E-mail: admiss@immaculata.edu · **CEEB Code:** 2320
Fax: 610-640-0836 · **Website:** www.immaculata.edu · **ACT Code:** 3596

This private school, affiliated with the Roman Catholic Church, was founded in 1920. It has a 373 acre campus.

RATINGS
Admissions Selectivity Rating: 73   **Fire Safety Rating:** 60*   **Green Rating:** 60*

STUDENTS AND FACULTY
Enrollment: 1,383. **Student Body:** 75% female, 25% male, 27% out-of-state, 1% international. Asian 2%, African American 16%, Caucasian 71%, Hispanic 7%, Native American <1%, Pacific Islander <1%, Two or more races 2%, Race unknown 1%.
Retention and Graduation: 78% freshmen return for sophomore year. 48% freshmen graduate within 4 years. 62% freshmen graduate within 6 years. **Faculty:** Student/faculty ratio 9:1. 85 full-time faculty, 85% hold PhDs, 69% are women. 0% of classes are taught by teaching assistants.

ACADEMICS
Degrees: Associate; Bachelor's; Certificate; Doctoral/Professional; Doctoral/Research; Master's **Classes:** Most classes have 10-19 students. **Most popular majors:** Kinesiology And Exercise Science; Registered Nursing/Registered

Nurse; Fashion Merchandising. **Special Study Options:** Accelerated program; Cross-registration; Distance learning; Double major; Dual enrollment; Honors program; Independent study; Internships; Study abroad; Teacher certification program. **Honors programs:** Please see website for a description of the honors program: http://www.immaculata.edu/academics/cus/honors. **Disability Services offered to physically disabled students:** Note-taking services; Reader services; Tape recorders; Tutors. **Career services:** Alumni network; Alumni services; Career assessment; Career/job search classes; Internships

FACILITIES

Housing: Apartments for single students; Coed dorms; Men's dorms; Special housing for disabled student; Theme housing; Wellness housing; Women's dorms 100% of campus accessible to physically diasbled. **Computers:** Administrative functions (other than registration) can be performed online.

CAMPUS LIFE

Environment: Town **Activities:** Campus Ministries; Choral groups; Concert band; Dance; Drama/theater; International Student Organization; Jazz band; Literary magazine; Music ensembles; Musical theater; Student government; Student newspaper; Symphony orchestra 28 registered organizations, 14 honor societies, 1 religious organization. **Athletics (Intercollegiate):** *Men:* basketball, golf, soccer, tennis. *Women:* basketball, cross-country, field hockey, golf, lacrosse, soccer, softball, tennis, volleyball. **On-Campus Highlights:** Gabriele Library, Draper Walsh Stadium, Alumnae Hall Fitness Center and Pool, ImmacuLatte Coffee Shop, The Underground (student space)

ADMISSIONS

Freshman Academic Profile: Average high school GPA 3.3. 13% in top 10% of high school class, 32% in top 25% of high school class, 60% in top 50% of high school class. **Test Scores:** SAT Math middle 50% range 470-570. SAT EBRW middle 50% range 480-600. ACT middle 50% range 17-23. Minimum internet-based TOEFL 65. Minimum paper TOEFL 513. **Basis for Candidate Selection:** *Very important factors considered include:* rigor of secondary school record, academic GPA. *Important factors considered include:* class rank, application essay, recommendation(s), first generation. *Other factors considered include:* standardized test scores, interview, extracurricular activities, talent/ability, character/personal qualities, alumni/ae relation, religious affiliation/commitment, volunteer work, work experience, level of applicant's interest. **Freshman Admission Requirements:** High school diploma is required and GED is accepted *Academic units required:* 4 English, 2 math, 2 science, 1 science labs, 2 foreign language, 2 social studies, and 4 units from above areas or other academic areas. **Freshman Admission Statistics:** 1,550 applied, 83.4% admitted, 17% enrolled. **Transfer Admission Requirements:** High school transcript, college transcript(s), Minimum college GPA of 2.0 required. Lowest grade transferable C. **General Admission Information:** Application fee $35. Nonfall registration accepted. Admission may be deferred.

COSTS AND FINANCIAL AID

Annual tuition $26,500. Room and board $12,620. Required fees $850. Average book expense $2,166. **Required Forms and Deadlines:** FAFSA. **Notification of Awards:** Applicants will be notified of awards on a rolling basis beginning 10/1. **Types of Aid:** *Need-based scholarships/grants:* College/university scholarship or grant aid from institutional funds; Federal Pell; Private scholarships; SEOG; State scholarships/grants; United Negro College Fund. *Loans:* Direct PLUS loans; Direct Subsidized Stafford Loans; Direct Unsubsidized Stafford Loans. *Student Employment:* Federal Work-Study Program available. Institutional employment available. **Financial Aid Statistics:** 34% undergrads receive any aid.

INDIANA STATE UNIVERSITY

200 North 7th Street, Terre Haute, IN 47809
Phone: 812-237-2121 · **Financial Aid Phone:** 812-237-2215
E-mail: http://www.indstate.edu/admissions · **CEEB Code:** 1322
Fax: 812-237-8023 · **Website:** www.indstate.edu · **ACT Code:** 1206

This public school was founded in 1865. It has a 435 acre campus.

RATINGS

Admissions Selectivity Rating: 74   **Fire Safety Rating:** 92   **Green Rating:** 89

STUDENTS AND FACULTY

Enrollment: 10,818. **Student Body:** 54% female, 46% male, 20% out-of-state, 4% international (69 countries represented). Asian 1%, African American 19%, Caucasian 65%, Hispanic 4%, Native American <1%, Pacific Islander <1%, Two or more races 4%, Race unknown 1%.
Retention and Graduation: 68% freshmen return for sophomore year. 19% freshmen graduate within 4 years. 38% freshmen graduate within 6 years.

Faculty: Student/faculty ratio 21:1. 460 full-time faculty, 81% hold PhDs, 15% are members of minority groups, 47% are women. 4% of classes are taught by teaching assistants.

ACADEMICS

Degrees: Bachelor's; Certificate; Doctoral Other; Doctoral/Professional; Doctoral/Research; Master's; Post-Bachelor's certificate; Post-Master's certificate **Most popular majors:** Psychology, General; Criminology; Registered Nursing/Registered Nurse. **Special Study Options:** Accelerated program; Cooperative education program; Distance learning; Double major; Dual enrollment; English as a Second Language (ESL); Honors program; Independent study; Internships; Study abroad; Teacher certification program. **Honors programs:** University Honors Program. **Disability Services offered to physically disabled students:** Note-taking services; Tape recorders; Tutors. **Career services:** Alumni network; Alumni services; Career assessment; Internships; Regional alumni

FACILITIES

Housing: Apartments for married students; Apartments for single students; Coed dorms; Fraternity/sorority housing; Men's dorms; Special housing for disabled student; Theme housing; Women's dorms 98% of campus accessible to physically diasbled. **Special Academic Facilities/Equipment:** Music hall, art gallery, civic center, museum,flight simulator, audio-visual center, observatory, theaters. **Computers:** 100% of classrooms, 100% of dorms, 100% of libraries, 100% of dining areas, 100% of student union, have wireless network access. Students can register for classes online. Administrative functions (other than registration) can be performed online. Undergraduates are required to own a computer.

CAMPUS LIFE

Environment: Town **Activities:** Campus Ministries; Choral groups; Concert band; Dance; Drama/theater; International Student Organization; Jazz band; Literary magazine; Marching band; Music ensembles; Musical theater; Pep band; Radio station; Student government; Student newspaper; Student-run film society; Symphony orchestra; Yearbook 130 registered organizations, 19 honor societies, 13 religious organizations. 11 fraternities, 10 sororities. **Athletics (Intercollegiate):** *Men:* baseball, basketball, cross-country, football, track/field (outdoor), track/field (indoor). *Women:* basketball, cross-country, golf, soccer, softball, track/field (outdoor), track/field (indoor), volleyball. **On-Campus Highlights:** Hulman Memorial Student Union, Student Recreation Center, John C. Hook's Memorial Observatory, Cunningham Memorial Library, Three Art Galleries **Environmental Initiatives:** The signing of the American Colleges & Universities President's Climate Commitment that resulted in the development of a Climate Action Plan and three rounds of carbon footprint analyses.

ADMISSIONS

Freshman Academic Profile: Average high school GPA 3.1. 10% in top 10% of high school class, 28% in top 25% of high school class, 63% in top 50% of high school class. **Test Scores:** SAT Math middle 50% range 440-550. SAT EBRW middle 50% range 460-560. ACT middle 50% range 17-23. Minimum internet-based TOEFL 61. Minimum paper TOEFL 500. **Basis for Candidate Selection:** *Very important factors considered include:* rigor of secondary school record, class rank, academic GPA. *Important factors considered include:* application essay, standardized test scores, recommendation(s). *Other factors considered include:* interview, extracurricular activities, talent/ability, character/personal qualities. **Freshman Admission Requirements:** High school diploma is required and GED is accepted *Academic units recommended:* 4 English, 4 math, 3 science, 3 science labs, 1 foreign language, 2 social studies, 1 history, 2 academic electives, 2 units from above areas or other academic areas. **Freshman Admission Statistics:** 11,720 applied, 84.5% admitted, 27% enrolled. **Transfer Admission Requirements:** college transcript(s), Minimum college GPA of 2.0 required. Lowest grade transferable C. **General Admission Information:** Application fee $25. Priority deadline 7/1. Regular application deadline 8/15. Nonfall registration accepted. Admission may be deferred for a maximum of 1 year.

COSTS AND FINANCIAL AID

Annual in-state tuition $9,883. Annual out-of-state tuition $19,252. Room and board $9,883. Required fees $200. Average book expense $1,200. **Required Forms and Deadlines:** FAFSA. **Notification of Awards:** Applicants will be notified of awards on a rolling basis beginning 3/15. **Types of Aid:** *Need-based scholarships/grants:* College/university scholarship or grant aid from institutional funds; Federal Pell; Private scholarships; SEOG; State scholarships/grants. *Loans:* Direct PLUS loans; Direct Subsidized Stafford Loans; Direct Unsubsidized Stafford Loans. *Student Employment:* Federal Work-Study Program available. Institutional employment available. **Financial Aid Statistics:** 68% needy freshmen, 64% needy undergrads receive need-based scholarship or grant aid. 70% freshmen, 56% undergrads receive non-need-based scholarship or grant aid. 75% freshmen, 78% undergrads receive need-based self-help aid. 3% freshmen, 3% undergrads receive athletic scholarships. 76% freshmen, 69% undergrads receive any aid. Average cumulative indebtedness $27,457. **Criteria for awarding aid:** *Need-based:*

Academics *Non-need-based:* Academics, Alumni affiliation, Art, Athletics, Minority status, Music/drama, State/district residency.

INDIANA UNIVERSITY—BLOOMINGTON

107 South Indiana Avenue, Bloomington, IN 47405-1106
Phone: 812-855-0661 · **Financial Aid Phone:** (812) 855-6500
E-mail: iuadmit@indiana.edu · **CEEB Code:** 1324
Fax: 812-855-5102 · **Website:** www.iub.edu · **ACT Code:** 1210

This public school was founded in 1820. It has a 1939 acre campus.

RATINGS

Admissions Selectivity Rating: 85   **Fire Safety Rating:** 93   **Green Rating:** 97

STUDENTS AND FACULTY

Enrollment: 33,104. **Student Body:** 49% female, 51% male, 34% out-of-state, 10% international (122 countries represented). Asian 5%, African American 4%, Caucasian 70%, Hispanic 6%, Native American <1%, Pacific Islander <1%, Two or more races 4%, Race unknown <1%.
Retention and Graduation: 91% freshmen return for sophomore year. 60% freshmen graduate within 4 years. 76% freshmen graduate within 6 years. **Faculty:** Student/faculty ratio 17:1. 2,114 full-time faculty, 84% hold PhDs, 20% are members of minority groups, 39% are women.

ACADEMICS

Degrees: Bachelor's; Certificate; Doctoral; Doctoral/Professional; Doctoral/Research; Master's; Post-Bachelor's certificate; Terminal Associate **Classes:** Most classes have 10-19 students. Most lab/discussion sessions have 10-19 students. **Most popular majors:** Informatics; Public Administration; Business/Commerce, General. **Special Study Options:** Accelerated program; Cooperative education program; Distance learning; Double major; Dual enrollment; English as a Second Language (ESL); External degree program; Honors program; Independent study; Internships; Liberal arts/career combination; Student-designed major; Study abroad; Teacher certification program. **Honors programs:** Hutton Honors College and the Hudson/Holland Scholar Programs. **Disability Services offered to physically disabled students:** Note-taking services; Reader services; Tape recorders; Tutors. **Career services:** Alumni network; Alumni services; Career assessment; Career/job search classes; Internships

FACILITIES

Housing: Apartments for married students; Apartments for single students; Coed dorms; Cooperative housing; Fraternity/sorority housing; Men's dorms; Special housing for disabled student; Special housing for international students; Theme housing; Women's dorms 95% of campus accessible to physically disabled. **Special Academic Facilities/Equipment:** Art Gallery, Folklore, Radio station, Natural history museum, TV station, Art Museum, Mathers Museum of World Cultures, Kirkwood Observatory, Hilltop Garden and Nature Center, Arboretum, Student Recreational Sports and Aquatic Center, Auditorium, Beck Chapel, Golf Driving Range, Musical Arts Center, Health Physical Education and Recreation facilities, Indoor swimming, Outdoor swimming, Wildermuth Intramural Center, Cyclotron, Lilly Library, and more than 70 research centers. **Computers:** Students can register for classes online. Administrative functions (other than registration) can be performed online.

CAMPUS LIFE

Environment: City **Activities:** Campus Ministries; Choral groups; Concert band; Dance; Drama/theater; International Student Organization; Jazz band; Literary magazine; Marching band; Music ensembles; Musical theater; Opera; Pep band; Radio station; Student government; Student newspaper; Symphony orchestra; Television station; Yearbook 9 religious organizations. **Athletics (Intercollegiate):** *Men:* baseball, basketball, cheerleading, cross-country, diving, football, golf, soccer, swimming, tennis, track/field (outdoor), wrestling. *Women:* basketball, cheerleading, cross-country, diving, field hockey, golf, soccer, softball, swimming, tennis, track/field (outdoor), volleyball, water polo. **On-Campus Highlights:** Indiana Memorial Union, Art Museum, Lilly Library, Assembly Hall, Student Recreational Sports Center **Environmental Initiatives:** The Bicentennial Strategic Plan (IU turns 200 in 2020) was adopted by the Board of Trustees in December establishing Core Value 7: "Sustainability, stewardship and accountability for the natural, human, and economic resources and relationships entrusted to IU." Bicentennial Priority 3: Support innovative campus "living laboratory" initiatives that provide opportunities to integrate campus operations, faculty and student

research, education, student life, and community engagement to applied, solutions-oriented sustainability research. Bicentennial Priority 8: Building for Excellence—IU has also become a leader in high-quality environmentally conscious design, and leads the Big Ten in LEED-certified green buildings with twelve certified to date, including four at the gold level (platinum is the highest certification). This strategy pays dividends for the life of each building in terms of occupant health and productivity, resource efficiency, life cycle cost savings and retention of human capital. Bicentennial Action Item 3: IU will implement plans to solidify IU's Focus on efficient and environmentally conscious campus design and operation by: a. Completing and implementing pedestrian, transportation, and bicycle sub-master plans on each campus. b. Certifying all major new buildings with the LEED Green Building Certification System and elevate the minimum certification level to Gold. c. Continuing to explore and research a variety of energy and utility supply and delivery options that reflect changes in economies, demand, and climate variables. d. Achieving the goals for energy efficiency and emissions reductions called for in the Campus Master Plan and the Integrated Energy Master Plan for the IU Bloomington campus; expand that analysis to all campuses. e. Increasing energy and utility system efficiency while reducing demand and consumption. Continuing Priorities Give special emphasis on all campuses to improving traffic flow, making them more "pedestrian and bicycle friendly," and to improving parking and alternative modes of transportation for students, faculty, and staff. Expand efforts to make all IU campuses more energy efficient and sustainable.

ADMISSIONS

Freshman Academic Profile: Average high school GPA 3.7. 36% in top 10% of high school class, 70% in top 25% of high school class, 95% in top 50% of high school class. **Test Scores:** SAT Math middle 50% range 570-680. SAT EBRW middle 50% range 570-670. ACT middle 50% range 25-31. Minimum internet-based TOEFL 79. Minimum paper TOEFL 550. **Basis for Candidate Selection:** *Very important factors considered include:* rigor of secondary school record, class rank, academic GPA, standardized test scores. *Important factors considered include:* application essay. *Other factors considered include:* recommendation(s), interview, extracurricular activities, talent/ability, character/personal qualities, first generation, alumni/ae relation, geographical residence, state residency, racial/ethnic status, volunteer work, work experience. **Freshman Admission Requirements:** High school diploma is required and GED is accepted *Academic units required:* 4 English, 3.5 math, 3 science, 2 science labs, 2 foreign language, 3 social studies, 1.5 academic electives. **Freshman Admission Statistics:** 41,939 applied, 76.0% admitted, 25% enrolled. **Transfer Admission Requirements:** college transcript(s), Minimum college GPA of 2.0 required. Lowest grade transferable C. **General Admission Information:** Application fee $65. Priority deadline 2/1. Nonfall registration accepted. Admission may be deferred for a maximum of 1 year.

COSTS AND FINANCIAL AID

Annual in-state tuition $10,258. Annual out-of-state tuition $33,522. Room and board $10,258. Required fees $1,323. Average book expense $1,034. **Required Forms and Deadlines:** FAFSA. **Notification of Awards:** Applicants will be notified of awards on a rolling basis beginning 2/15. **Types of Aid:** *Need-based scholarships/grants:* College/university scholarship or grant aid from institutional funds; Federal Pell; Private scholarships; SEOG; State scholarships/grants. *Loans:* Direct PLUS loans; Direct Subsidized Stafford Loans; Direct Unsubsidized Stafford Loans. *Student Employment:* Federal Work-Study Program available. Institutional employment available. **Financial Aid Statistics:** 77% needy freshmen, 80% needy undergrads receive need-based scholarship or grant aid. 19% freshmen, 16% undergrads receive non-need-based scholarship or grant aid. 62% freshmen, 65% undergrads receive need-based self-help aid. 1% freshmen, 1% undergrads receive athletic scholarships. 72% freshmen, 75% undergrads receive any aid. 44% undergrads borrow to pay for school. Average cumulative indebtedness $28,039. **Criteria for awarding aid:** *Need-based:* Academics, Alumni affiliation, Art, Athletics, Leadership, Minority status, Music/drama *Non-need-based:* Academics, Art, Athletics, Leadership, Minority status, Music/drama, Religious affiliation.

INDIANA UNIVERSITY EAST

2325 Chester Boulevard, Richmond, IN 47374-1289
Phone: 765-973-8208 · **Financial Aid Phone:** 765-973-8206
E-mail: applynow@iue.edu · **CEEB Code:** 1194
Fax: 765-973-8209 · **Website:** www.iue.edu · **ACT Code:** 1216

This public school was founded in 1971. It has a 182 acre campus.

RATINGS
Admissions Selectivity Rating: 82   **Fire Safety Rating:** 60*   **Green Rating:** 60*

STUDENTS AND FACULTY
Enrollment: 2,969. **Student Body:** 64% female, 36% male, 24% out-of-state, 1% international (40 countries represented). Asian 1%, African American 5%, Caucasian 85%, Hispanic 4%, Native American <1%, Pacific Islander <1%, Two or more races 3%, Race unknown 1%.
Retention and Graduation: 66% freshmen return for sophomore year. 14% freshmen graduate within 4 years. 32% freshmen graduate within 6 years.
Faculty: Student/faculty ratio 14:1. 117 full-time faculty, 76% hold PhDs, 15% are members of minority groups, 62% are women.

ACADEMICS
Degrees: Bachelor's; Certificate; Master's; Post-Bachelor's certificate **Most popular majors:** Psychology, General; Registered Nursing/Registered Nurse; Business/Commerce, General. **Special Study Options:** Accelerated program; Cooperative education program; Cross-registration; Distance learning; Double major; Dual enrollment; External degree program; Honors program; Independent study; Internships; Study abroad; Teacher certification program; Weekend college. **Honors programs:** Any existing college level course may be offered with an Honors (H) option. Instructors may integrate this option into their courses or offer Honors-only sections; or you, as an Honors student, may request an H-option from your instructor during priority registration. In your junior or early senior year, you will enroll in H499, a one-semester independent study, to complete your Honors Project. This scholarly, creative, or service learning project is completed under the guidance of a faculty mentor. It will be submitted as part of your honors portfolio and must be accepted by the Honors Committee in order to graduate from the Honors Program. **Disability Services offered to physically disabled students:** Note-taking services; Reader services; Tape recorders; Tutors. **Career services:** Alumni network; Alumni services; Career assessment; Career/job search classes; Internships; Regional alumni

FACILITIES
Computers: Students can register for classes online. Administrative functions (other than registration) can be performed online.

CAMPUS LIFE
Environment: Town **Activities:** Drama/theater; Literary magazine; Music ensembles; Pep band; Student government; Student newspaper; Television station. **Athletics (Intercollegiate):** *Men:* basketball, golf. *Women:* volleyball. Graf Recreation Center, Bear Creek Coffee, Internet Cafe bar

ADMISSIONS
Freshman Academic Profile: Average high school GPA 3.2. 8% in top 10% of high school class, 30% in top 25% of high school class, 71% in top 50% of high school class. **Test Scores:** SAT Math middle 50% range 470-548. SAT EBRW middle 50% range 470-570. ACT middle 50% range 18-23. Minimum internet-based TOEFL 79. Minimum paper TOEFL 550. **Basis for Candidate Selection:** *Very important factors considered include:* rigor of secondary school record, class rank, standardized test scores. *Important factors considered include:* academic GPA. *Other factors considered include:* recommendation(s), geographical residence, state residency. **Freshman Admission Requirements:** High school diploma is required and GED is accepted *Academic units required:* 4 English, 3 math, 3 science, 3 science labs, 3 social studies, 4 academic electives. **Freshman Admission Statistics:** 1,279 applied, 69.7% admitted, 44% enrolled. **Transfer Admission Requirements:** college transcript(s), Minimum college GPA of 2.0 required. Lowest grade transferable C. **General Admission Information:** Application fee $35. Priority deadline 5/1. Nonfall registration accepted. Admission may be deferred.

COSTS AND FINANCIAL AID
Annual out-of-state tuition $18,432. Required fees $606. **Required Forms and Deadlines:** FAFSA; Institution's own financial aid form. **Notification of Awards:** Applicants will be notified of awards on a rolling basis beginning 5/1. **Types of Aid:** *Need-based scholarships/grants:* College/university scholarship or grant aid from institutional funds; Federal Pell; Private scholarships; SEOG; State scholarships/grants. *Loans:* Direct PLUS loans; Direct Subsidized Stafford Loans; Direct Unsubsidized Stafford Loans. *Student Employment:* Federal Work-Study Program available. Institutional employment available.

Financial Aid Statistics: 91% needy freshmen, 84% needy undergrads receive need-based scholarship or grant aid. 18% freshmen, 9% undergrads receive non-need-based scholarship or grant aid. 41% freshmen, 66% undergrads receive need-based self-help aid. 5% freshmen, 3% undergrads receive athletic scholarships. 96% freshmen, 82% undergrads receive any aid. 78% undergrads borrow to pay for school. Average cumulative indebtedness $27,379. **Criteria for awarding aid:** *Need-based:* Academics, Alumni affiliation, Leadership *Non-need-based:* Academics, Alumni affiliation, Leadership.

INDIANA UNIVERSITY—KOKOMO

2300 South Washington Street, Kokomo, IN 46902-9003
Phone: 765-455-9217 · **Financial Aid Phone:** (765) 455-9216
E-mail: iuadmis@iuk.edu · **CEEB Code:** 1337
Fax: 765-455-9537 · **Website:** www.iuk.edu · **ACT Code:** 1219

This public school was founded in 1945. It has a 52 acre campus.

RATINGS
Admissions Selectivity Rating: 73   **Fire Safety Rating:** 60*   **Green Rating:** 60*

STUDENTS AND FACULTY
Enrollment: 2,746. **Student Body:** 65% female, 35% male, 2% out-of-state, 1% international (28 countries represented). Asian 1%, African American 4%, Caucasian 83%, Hispanic 6%, Native American <1%, Pacific Islander <1%, Two or more races 3%, Race unknown 1%.
Retention and Graduation: 60% freshmen return for sophomore year. 17% freshmen graduate within 4 years. 39% freshmen graduate within 6 years.
Faculty: Student/faculty ratio 16:1. 123 full-time faculty, 61% hold PhDs, 16% are members of minority groups, 64% are women.

ACADEMICS
Degrees: Associate; Bachelor's; Certificate; Master's; Post-Bachelor's certificate **Classes:** Most classes have fewer than 10 students. Most lab/discussion sessions have 10-19 students. **Most popular majors:** Liberal Arts And Sciences, General Studies And Humanities, Other; Registered Nursing/Registered Nurse; Business/Commerce, General. **Special Study Options:** Accelerated program; Cross-registration; Distance learning; Double major; Dual enrollment; English as a Second Language (ESL); External degree program; Honors program; Independent study; Internships; Liberal arts/career combination; Study abroad; Teacher certification program; Weekend college. **Honors programs:** The Indiana University Kokomo Honors Program offers unique educational and cultural opportunities for bright, highly motivated and creative students like you. Honors Courses and other activities are specially designed to cultivate academic excellence in different disciplines and challenge you to reach your full potential. The Honors Program is committed to guiding you in different disciplines, leading to self-improvement, and preparing you to make important contributions to society. http://www.iuk.edu/honors/index.php. **Disability Services offered to physically disabled students:** Note-taking services; Reader services; Tutors. **Career services:** Alumni network; Alumni services; Career assessment; Career/job search classes; Internships

FACILITIES
Special Academic Facilities/Equipment: Observatory, Art Gallery **Computers:** Students can register for classes online. Administrative functions (other than registration) can be performed online.

CAMPUS LIFE
Environment: Town **Activities:** Campus Ministries; Choral groups; Dance; Drama/theater; International Student Organization; Literary magazine; Musical theater; Student government; Student newspaper. Kelley Student Center, KC Commons, Kresge Auditorium, MILT and Jean Cole Family Wellness and Fitness Center, Havens Auditorium

ADMISSIONS
Freshman Academic Profile: Average high school GPA 3.2. 8% in top 10% of high school class, 28% in top 25% of high school class, 70% in top 50% of high school class. **Test Scores:** SAT Math middle 50% range 470-550. SAT EBRW middle 50% range 480-570. ACT middle 50% range 17-22. Minimum internet-based TOEFL 65. Minimum paper TOEFL 513. **Basis for Candidate Selection:** *Very important factors considered include:* rigor of secondary school record, class rank, standardized test scores. *Important factors considered include:* academic GPA. *Other factors considered include:* recommendation(s). **Freshman Admission Requirements:** High school diploma is required and GED is accepted *Academic units required:* 4 English, 3 math, 3 science, 3 science labs, 3 social studies, 7 academic electives, *Academic units recommended:* 2 foreign language. **Freshman Admission Statistics:** 1,170 applied, admitted, 49% enrolled. **Transfer Admission Requirements:** college

transcript(s), Minimum college GPA of 2.0 required. Lowest grade transferable C. **General Admission Information:** Application fee $35. Priority deadline 3/1. Nonfall registration accepted. Admission may be deferred for a maximum of 1 year.

COSTS AND FINANCIAL AID
Annual out-of-state tuition $18,432. Required fees $606. **Required Forms and Deadlines:** FAFSA. **Notification of Awards:** Applicants will be notified of awards on a rolling basis beginning 1/10. **Types of Aid:** *Need-based scholarships/grants:* College/university scholarship or grant aid from institutional funds; Federal Pell; Private scholarships; SEOG; State scholarships/grants. *Loans:* Direct PLUS loans; Direct Subsidized Stafford Loans; Direct Unsubsidized Stafford Loans. *Student Employment:* Federal Work-Study Program available. Institutional employment available. **Financial Aid Statistics:** 84% needy freshmen, 82% needy undergrads receive need-based scholarship or grant aid. 9% freshmen, 5% undergrads receive non-need-based scholarship or grant aid. 50% freshmen, 64% undergrads receive need-based self-help aid. 1% freshmen, 1% undergrads receive athletic scholarships. 89% freshmen, 85% undergrads receive any aid. 74% undergrads borrow to pay for school. Average cumulative indebtedness $25,675. **Criteria for awarding aid:** *Need-based:* Academics, Athletics, Leadership *Non-need-based:* Academics, Athletics, Leadership.

INDIANA UNIVERSITY NORTHWEST

3400 Broadway, Gary, IN 46408-1197
Phone: 219-980-6991 • **Financial Aid Phone:** (219) 980-6778
E-mail: admit@iun.edu • **CEEB Code:** 1338
Fax: 219-981-4219 • **Website:** www.iun.edu • **ACT Code:** 1218

This public school was founded in 1963. It has a 43 acre campus.

RATINGS
Admissions Selectivity Rating: 79　　**Fire Safety Rating:** 60*　　**Green Rating:** 60*

STUDENTS AND FACULTY
Enrollment: 3,549. **Student Body:** 70% female, 30% male, 3% out-of-state, <1% international (37 countries represented). Asian 3%, African American 17%, Caucasian 53%, Hispanic 23%, Native American <1%, Pacific Islander 0%, Two or more races 3%, Race unknown 1%.
Retention and Graduation: 69% freshmen return for sophomore year. 7% freshmen graduate within 4 years. 23% freshmen graduate within 6 years.
Faculty: Student/faculty ratio 14:1. 165 full-time faculty, 73% hold PhDs, 29% are members of minority groups, 53% are women.

ACADEMICS
Degrees: Associate; Bachelor's; Certificate; Master's; Post-Bachelor's certificate **Classes:** Most classes have 10-19 students. Most lab/discussion sessions have 10-19 students. **Most popular majors:** Liberal Arts And Sciences, General Studies And Humanities, Other; Registered Nursing/Registered Nurse; Business/Commerce, General. **Special Study Options:** Accelerated program; Cooperative education program; Distance learning; Double major; Dual enrollment; External degree program; Honors program; Independent study; Internships; Liberal arts/career combination; Student-designed major; Study abroad; Teacher certification program; Weekend college. **Disability Services offered to physically disabled students:** Note-taking services; Reader services; Tape recorders; Tutors. **Career services:** Alumni network; Alumni services; Career assessment; Career/job search classes; Internships

FACILITIES
Computers: Students can register for classes online. Administrative functions (other than registration) can be performed online.

CAMPUS LIFE
Environment: Metropolis **Activities:** Campus Ministries; Drama/theater; International Student Organization; Literary magazine; Musical theater; Radio station; Student government; Student newspaper; Student-run film society 60 registered organizations, 4 honor societies, 2 religious organizations. 2 fraternities, 3 sororities. **Athletics (Intercollegiate):** *Men:* baseball, basketball, cheerleading, golf. *Women:* basketball, cheerleading, volleyball. The Savannah Center, The RedHawk Cafe, Arts On Grant, Sculpture Garden

ADMISSIONS
Freshman Academic Profile: Average high school GPA 3.0. 11% in top 10% of high school class, 32% in top 25% of high school class, 69% in top 50% of high school class. **Test Scores:** SAT Math middle 50% range 440-540. SAT EBRW middle 50% range 450-553. ACT middle 50% range 17-22. Minimum internet-based TOEFL 71. Minimum paper TOEFL 530. **Basis for Candidate**

Selection: *Very important factors considered include:* rigor of secondary school record, academic GPA, standardized test scores. *Important factors considered include:* class rank. *Other factors considered include:* recommendation(s).
Freshman Admission Requirements: High school diploma is required and GED is accepted *Academic units required:* 4 English, 3 math, 3 science, 3 science labs, 2 social studies, 1 history, 7 academic electives, *Academic units recommended:* 2 foreign language. **Freshman Admission Statistics:** 1,749 applied, 74.4% admitted, 47% enrolled. **Transfer Admission Requirements:** High school transcript, college transcript(s), Minimum college GPA of 2.0 required. Lowest grade transferable C. **General Admission Information:** Application fee $35. Priority deadline 7/1. Nonfall registration accepted. Admission may be deferred for a maximum of 1 year.

COSTS AND FINANCIAL AID
Annual out-of-state tuition $18,432. Required fees $606. **Required Forms and Deadlines:** FAFSA. **Notification of Awards:** Applicants will be notified of awards on a rolling basis beginning 4/15. **Types of Aid:** *Need-based scholarships/grants:* College/university scholarship or grant aid from institutional funds; Federal Nursing Scholarships; Federal Pell; Private scholarships; SEOG; State scholarships/grants; United Negro College Fund. *Loans:* Direct PLUS loans; Direct Subsidized Stafford Loans; Direct Unsubsidized Stafford Loans. *Student Employment:* Federal Work-Study Program available. Institutional employment available. **Financial Aid Statistics:** 78% needy freshmen, 78% needy undergrads receive need-based scholarship or grant aid. 7% freshmen, 4% undergrads receive non-need-based scholarship or grant aid. 48% freshmen, 63% undergrads receive need-based self-help aid. 1% freshmen, 0% undergrads receive athletic scholarships. 82% freshmen, 79% undergrads receive any aid. 68% undergrads borrow to pay for school. Average cumulative indebtedness $29,701. **Criteria for awarding aid:** *Need-based:* Academics, Minority status *Non-need-based:* Academics, Athletics.

INDIANA UNIVERSITY OF PENNSYLVANIA

1011 South Drive, Indiana, PA 15705
Phone: 724-357-2230 • **Financial Aid Phone:** 724-357-2218
E-mail: admissions-inquiry@iup.edu • **CEEB Code:** 2652
Fax: 724-357-6281 • **Website:** www.iup.edu • **ACT Code:** 3704

This public school was founded in 1875. It has a 374 acre campus.

RATINGS
Admissions Selectivity Rating: 73　　**Fire Safety Rating:** 97　　**Green Rating:** 60*

STUDENTS AND FACULTY
Enrollment: 9,849. **Student Body:** 57% female, 43% male, 5% out-of-state, 3% international (32 countries represented). Asian 1%, African American 12%, Caucasian 74%, Hispanic 4%, Native American <1%, Pacific Islander <1%, Two or more races 4%, Race unknown 1%.
Retention and Graduation: 71% freshmen return for sophomore year. 37% freshmen graduate within 4 years. 54% freshmen graduate within 6 years.
Faculty: Student/faculty ratio 16:1. 569 full-time faculty, 15% are members of minority groups, 48% are women. 0% of classes are taught by teaching assistants.

ACADEMICS
Degrees: Associate; Bachelor's; Certificate; Doctoral/Professional; Doctoral/Research; Master's; Post-Bachelor's certificate; Post-Master's certificate **Classes:** Most classes have 20-29 students. **Most popular majors:** Criminology; Registered Nursing/Registered Nurse; Marketing/Marketing Management, General. **Special Study Options:** Accelerated program; Cooperative education program; Cross-registration; Distance learning; Double major; Dual enrollment; English as a Second Language (ESL); Exchange student program (domestic); External degree program; Honors program; Independent study; Internships; Liberal arts/career combination; Student-designed major; Study abroad; Teacher certification program; Weekend college. **Honors programs:** Cook Honors College **Combined degree programs:** BA/MA. **Disability Services offered to physically disabled students:** Note-taking services; Reader services; Tape recorders. **Career services:** Alumni services; Career assessment; Career/job search classes; Internships

FACILITIES
Housing: Apartments for single students; Coed dorms; Fraternity/sorority housing; Special housing for disabled student; Special housing for international students; Theme housing; Wellness housing 99% of campus accessible to

The Princeton Review's Complete Book of Colleges

physically diasbled. **Special Academic Facilities/Equipment:** Art museum, lodge, farm, co-generation plant, ski slope, sailing base. **Computers:** 90% of classrooms, 60% of dorms, 100% of libraries, 100% of dining areas, 80% of student union, 100% of common outdoor areas have wireless network access. Students can register for classes online. Administrative functions (other than registration) can be performed online.

CAMPUS LIFE

Environment: Village **Activities:** Campus Ministries; Choral groups; Concert band; Dance; Drama/theater; International Student Organization; Jazz band; Literary magazine; Marching band; Model UN; Music ensembles; Musical theater; Opera; Pep band; Radio station; Student government; Student newspaper; Student-run film society; Symphony orchestra; Television station 210 registered organizations, 23 honor societies, 18 religious organizations. 18 fraternities, 14 sororities. **Athletics (Intercollegiate):** *Men:* baseball, basketball, cross-country, diving, football, golf, swimming, track/field (outdoor), track/field (indoor). *Women:* basketball, cross-country, diving, field hockey, lacrosse, soccer, softball, swimming, tennis, track/field (outdoor), track/field (indoor), volleyball. **On-Campus Highlights:** Housing Quad, Oak Grove, Hadley Union Building Fitness Center/Food Court, Stapleton Library/Java City, Kovalchick Convention and Athletic Complex

ADMISSIONS

Freshman Academic Profile: 8% in top 10% of high school class, 27% in top 25% of high school class, 59% in top 50% of high school class. **Test Scores:** SAT Math middle 50% range 450-540. SAT EBRW middle 50% range 460-560. Minimum internet-based TOEFL 61. Minimum paper TOEFL 500. **Basis for Candidate Selection:** *Very important factors considered include:* academic GPA. *Important factors considered include:* rigor of secondary school record, standardized test scores. *Other factors considered include:* class rank, application essay, recommendation(s), interview, extracurricular activities, talent/ability, character/personal qualities, first generation. **Freshman Admission Requirements:** High school diploma is required and GED is accepted *Academic units required:* 4 English, 3 math, 3 science, 2 science labs, *Academic units recommended:* 2 foreign language, 3 social studies. **Freshman Admission Statistics:** 9,880 applied, 90.8% admitted, 27% enrolled. **Transfer Admission Requirements:** High school transcript, college transcript(s), statement of good standing from prior institution(s). Minimum college GPA of 2.0 required. Lowest grade transferable C-. **General Admission Information:** Application fee $25. Nonfall registration accepted. Admission may be deferred for a maximum of 1 year.

COSTS AND FINANCIAL AID

Annual in-state tuition $12,488. Annual out-of-state tuition $12,736. Room and board $12,488. Required fees $3,146. Average book expense $1,100. **Required Forms and Deadlines:** FAFSA; State aid form. **Notification of Awards:** Applicants will be notified of awards on a rolling basis beginning 12/15. **Types of Aid:** *Need-based scholarships/grants:* College/university scholarship or grant aid from institutional funds; Federal Pell; Private scholarships; SEOG; State scholarships/grants; United Negro College Fund. *Loans:* Direct PLUS loans; Direct Subsidized Stafford Loans; Direct Unsubsidized Stafford Loans. *Student Employment:* Federal Work-Study Program available. Institutional employment available. **Financial Aid Statistics:** 67% needy freshmen, 67% needy undergrads receive need-based scholarship or grant aid. 51% freshmen, 27% undergrads receive non-need-based scholarship or grant aid. 92% freshmen, 92% undergrads receive need-based self-help aid. 3% freshmen, 3% undergrads receive athletic scholarships. 80% freshmen, 81% undergrads receive any aid. 83% undergrads borrow to pay for school. Average cumulative indebtedness $36,514. **Criteria for awarding aid:** *Need-based:* Academics, Alumni affiliation, Art, Job skills, Leadership, Music/drama *Non-need-based:* Academics, Alumni affiliation, Art, Athletics, Job skills, Leadership, Music/drama, State/district residency.

INDIANA UNIVERSITY— PURDUE UNIVERSITY FORT WAYNE

2101 Coliseum Boulevard East, Fort Wayne, IN 46805-1499
Phone: 260-481-6812
E-mail: ipfwadms@ipfw.edu • **CEEB Code:** 1336
Fax: 260-481-6880 • **Website:** www.ipfw.edu • **ACT Code:** 1217

This public school was founded in 1917. It has a 565 acre campus.

RATINGS

Admissions Selectivity Rating: 74   **Fire Safety Rating:** 60*   **Green Rating:** 60*

STUDENTS AND FACULTY

Enrollment: 10,587. **Student Body:** 58% female, 42% male, 5% out-of-state, 2% international (71 countries represented). Asian 2%, African American 5%, Caucasian 87%, Hispanic 2%, Native American <1%, Race unknown 2%. **Retention and Graduation:** 60% freshmen return for sophomore year. **Faculty:** Student/faculty ratio 19:1. 329 full-time faculty, 83% hold PhDs, 13% are members of minority groups, 37% are women. 1% of classes are taught by teaching assistants.

ACADEMICS

Degrees: Associate; Bachelor's; Certificate; Master's; Post-Bachelor's certificate; Post-Master's certificate; Terminal Associate; Transfer Associate **Classes:** Most classes have 10-19 students. Most lab/discussion sessions have fewer than 10 students. **Most popular majors:** Elementary Education And Teaching; Nursing/Registered Nurse (Rn, Asn, Bsn, Msn); Business/Commerce, General. **Special Study Options:** Cooperative education program; Distance learning; Double major; English as a Second Language (ESL); Exchange student program (domestic); Honors program; Independent study; Internships; Liberal arts/career combination; Student-designed major; Study abroad; Teacher certification program; Weekend college. **Disability Services offered to physically disabled students:** Note-taking services; Reader services; Tape recorders; Tutors. **Career services:** Alumni network; Alumni services; Career assessment; Career/job search classes; Internships; Regional alumni

FACILITIES

Housing: Coed dorms 100% of campus accessible to physically diasbled. **Special Academic Facilities/Equipment:** Williams theatre. recital hall anthropology and geology exhibits art gallery **Computers:** Students can register for classes online. Administrative functions (other than registration) can be performed online.

CAMPUS LIFE

Environment: Village **Activities:** Choral groups; Concert band; Dance; Drama/theater; Jazz band; Literary magazine; Music ensembles; Musical theater; Opera; Pep band; Student government; Student newspaper; Symphony orchestra; Television station 65 registered organizations, 7 honor societies, 3 religious organizations. 2 fraternities, 3 sororities. **Athletics (Intercollegiate):** *Men:* baseball, basketball, cross-country, soccer, tennis, track/field (outdoor), volleyball. *Women:* basketball, cross-country, soccer, softball, tennis, track/field (outdoor), volleyball.

ADMISSIONS

Freshman Academic Profile: Average high school GPA 2.6. 7% in top 10% of high school class, 24% in top 25% of high school class, 57% in top 50% of high school class. **Test Scores:** SAT Math middle 50% range 430-550. SAT EBRW middle 50% range 420-540. ACT middle 50% range 17-23. Minimum paper TOEFL 550. **Basis for Candidate Selection:** *Very important factors considered include:* rigor of secondary school record, class rank, standardized test scores. *Other factors considered include:* recommendation(s), state residency. **Freshman Admission Requirements:** High school diploma is required and GED is accepted *Academic units required:* 4 English, 3 math, 1 science, 1 foreign language, 1 social studies, *Academic units recommended:* 3 science, 1 science labs, 3 foreign language, 3 social studies. **Freshman Admission Statistics:** 2,471 applied, 96.9% admitted, 71% enrolled. **Transfer Admission Requirements:** High school transcript, college transcript(s), Minimum college GPA of 2.0 required. Lowest grade transferable C-. **General Admission Information:** Application fee $30. Priority deadline 3/1. Regular application deadline 8/1. Nonfall registration accepted.

COSTS AND FINANCIAL AID

Annual out-of-state tuition $7,728. Required fees $384. Average book expense $800. **Required Forms and Deadlines:** FAFSA. **Notification of Awards:** Applicants will be notified of awards on or about 4/30. **Types of Aid:** *Need-based scholarships/grants:* Federal Nursing Scholarships; Federal Pell; Private scholarships; SEOG; State scholarships/grants. *Loans: Student Employment:* Federal Work-Study Program available. Institutional employment available.

Financial Aid Statistics: 56% needy freshmen, 69% needy undergrads receive need-based scholarship or grant aid. 28% freshmen, 23% undergrads receive non-need-based scholarship or grant aid. 46% freshmen, 50% undergrads receive need-based self-help aid. 3% freshmen, 3% undergrads receive athletic scholarships. **Criteria for awarding aid:** *Need-based:* Athletics, Job skills *Non-need-based:* Academics, Alumni affiliation, Art, Athletics.

INDIANA UNIVERSITY—
PURDUE UNIVERSITY INDIANAPOLIS

420 University Boulevard, Indianapolis, IN 46202
Phone: 317-274-4591 • **Financial Aid Phone:** (317) 274-4162
E-mail: apply@iupui.edu • **CEEB Code:** 1325
Fax: 317-278-1862 • **Website:** www.iupui.edu • **ACT Code:** 1214

This public school was founded in 1969. It has a 534 acre campus.

RATINGS
Admissions Selectivity Rating: 80   **Fire Safety Rating:** 90   **Green Rating:** 95

STUDENTS AND FACULTY
Enrollment: 20,870. **Student Body:** 56% female, 44% male, 4% out-of-state, 4% international (133 countries represented). Asian 4%, African American 9%, Caucasian 70%, Hispanic 7%, Native American <1%, Pacific Islander <1%, Two or more races 4%, Race unknown 1%.
Retention and Graduation: 75% freshmen return for sophomore year. 19% freshmen graduate within 4 years. 47% freshmen graduate within 6 years.
Faculty: Student/faculty ratio 17:1. 2,414 full-time faculty, 85% hold PhDs, 24% are members of minority groups, 43% are women.

ACADEMICS
Degrees: Associate; Bachelor's; Certificate; Doctoral; Doctoral/Professional; Doctoral/Research; Master's; Post-Bachelor's certificate; Post-Master's certificate **Classes:** Most classes have 10-19 students. **Most popular majors:** Liberal Arts And Sciences, General Studies And Humanities, Other; Registered Nursing/Registered Nurse; Business/Commerce, General. **Special Study Options:** Accelerated program; Cooperative education program; Cross-registration; Distance learning; Double major; Dual enrollment; English as a Second Language (ESL); Exchange student program (domestic); External degree program; Honors program; Independent study; Internships; Liberal arts/career combination; Student-designed major; Study abroad; Teacher certification program. **Honors programs:** Honors College offers a dynamic academic experience to high ability students seeking a unique experience in an urban research environment, and links students to world-class faculty engaged in cutting edge and translational research, creating a community of scholars which will make a difference. **Combined degree programs:** BA/MEng. **Disability Services offered to physically disabled students:** Note-taking services; Reader services; Tape recorders; Tutors. **Career services:** Alumni network; Alumni services; Career assessment; Career/job search classes; Internships; Regional alumni

FACILITIES
Housing: Apartments for married students; Apartments for single students; Coed dorms; Special housing for disabled student; Special housing for international students; Theme housing; Wellness housing 90% of campus accessible to physically diasbled. **Special Academic Facilities/Equipment:** Inlow Hall-Law School Eskenazi Hall-Herron School of Art and Design Cavanaugh Hall-School of Liberal Arts and IUPUI Enrollment Center University Library-Most high tech library in North America IUPUI Sport Complex-host of 11 Olympic Team Trails White River State Park-Indianapolis' version of the mall in Washington, D.C. **Computers:** 100% of classrooms, 100% of dorms, 100% of libraries, 100% of dining areas, 100% of student union, 100% of common outdoor areas have wireless network access. Students can register for classes online. Administrative functions (other than registration) can be performed online.

CAMPUS LIFE
Environment: Metropolis **Activities:** Campus Ministries; Choral groups; Dance; Drama/theater; International Student Organization; Jazz band; Literary magazine; Model UN; Music ensembles; Pep band; Student government; Student newspaper; Student-run film society 154 registered organizations, 9 honor societies, 10 religious organizations. 2 fraternities, 1 sorority. **Athletics (Intercollegiate):** *Men:* basketball, cross-country, diving, golf, soccer, swimming, tennis. *Women:* basketball, cross-country, diving, golf, soccer, softball, swimming, tennis, volleyball. **On-Campus Highlights:** IUPUI Sport Complex, University College, Cavanaugh Hall, University Library, Eskenazi Hall

ADMISSIONS
Freshman Academic Profile: Average high school GPA 3.5. 15% in top 10% of high school class, 43% in top 25% of high school class, 84% in top 50% of high school class. **Test Scores:** SAT Math middle 50% range 500-590. SAT EBRW middle 50% range 500-600. ACT middle 50% range 19-26. Minimum internet-based TOEFL 60. **Basis for Candidate Selection:** *Very important factors considered include:* rigor of secondary school record, academic GPA, standardized test scores. *Other factors considered include:* class rank, application essay, character/personal qualities, first generation, volunteer work, work experience. **Freshman Admission Requirements:** High school diploma is required and GED is accepted *Academic units required:* 4 English, 3 math, 3 science, 3 science labs, 3 social studies, 7 academic electives. **Freshman Admission Statistics:** 11,091 applied, 79.7% admitted, 46% enrolled. **Transfer Admission Requirements:** college transcript(s), Minimum college GPA of 2.0 required. Lowest grade transferable C. **General Admission Information:** Application fee $65. Regular application deadline 5/1. Nonfall registration accepted.

COSTS AND FINANCIAL AID
Annual in-state tuition $8,745. Annual out-of-state tuition $28,727. Room and board $8,745. Required fees $1,079. Average book expense $1,176. **Required Forms and Deadlines:** FAFSA. **Notification of Awards:** Applicants will be notified of awards on a rolling basis beginning 4/1. **Types of Aid:** *Need-based scholarships/grants:* College/university scholarship or grant aid from institutional funds; Federal Pell; Private scholarships; SEOG; State scholarships/grants. *Loans:* Direct PLUS loans; Direct Subsidized Stafford Loans; Direct Unsubsidized Stafford Loans. *Student Employment:* Federal Work-Study Program available. Institutional employment available. **Financial Aid Statistics:** 83% needy freshmen, 80% needy undergrads receive need-based scholarship or grant aid. 14% freshmen, 10% undergrads receive non-need-based scholarship or grant aid. 56% freshmen, 67% undergrads receive need-based self-help aid. 0% freshmen, 1% undergrads receive athletic scholarships. 89% freshmen, 83% undergrads receive any aid. 70% undergrads borrow to pay for school. Average cumulative indebtedness $28,951. **Criteria for awarding aid:** *Need-based:* Academics *Non-need-based:* Academics, Alumni affiliation, Art, Athletics, Leadership, State/district residency.

INDIANA UNIVERSITY SOUTH BEND

1700 Mishawaka Avenue, South Bend, IN 46634-7111
Phone: 574-520-4839 • **Financial Aid Phone:** (574) 520-4357
E-mail: admissions@iusb.edu • **CEEB Code:** 1339
Fax: 574-520-4834 • **Website:** www.iusb.edu • **ACT Code:** 1225

This public school was founded in 1922. It has a 104 acre campus.

RATINGS
Admissions Selectivity Rating: 78   **Fire Safety Rating:** 98   **Green Rating:** 64

STUDENTS AND FACULTY
Enrollment: 4,790. **Student Body:** 62% female, 38% male, 5% out-of-state, 3% international (64 countries represented). Asian 2%, African American 8%, Caucasian 71%, Hispanic 11%, Native American <1%, Pacific Islander <1%, Two or more races 4%, Race unknown 1%.
Retention and Graduation: 66% freshmen return for sophomore year. 7% freshmen graduate within 4 years. 28% freshmen graduate within 6 years.
Faculty: Student/faculty ratio 13:1. 258 full-time faculty, 78% hold PhDs, 21% are members of minority groups, 49% are women.

ACADEMICS
Degrees: Associate; Bachelor's; Certificate; Diploma; Master's; Post-Bachelor's certificate **Classes:** Most classes have 10-19 students. **Most popular majors:** Liberal Arts And Sciences, General Studies And Humanities, Other; Registered Nursing/Registered Nurse; Business/Commerce, General. **Special Study Options:** Accelerated program; Cross-registration; Distance learning; Double major; Dual enrollment; English as a Second Language (ESL); External degree program; Honors program; Independent study; Internships; Liberal arts/career combination; Study abroad; Teacher certification program; Weekend college. **Honors programs:** The Honors Program at IU South Bend provides many opportunities, challenges, and rewards for outstanding undergraduate students. The Freshman Honors Colloquium, Honors sections of general education courses, special interdisciplinary Honors courses, topical Honors seminars, and individual Senior Honors Projects enable students to enhance their learning experience in a "small college atmosphere" within a major university. Students taking part in the Honors Program will benefit from: • Opportunities to receive generous Honors Scholarships. • Small Honors classes (no more than 15 students and often fewer). • Instruction by experienced faculty known for excellence in the classroom as well as in their academic fields. • Special

Honors advising by the Honors Program director and discipline-specific faculty members. • Interaction with other outstanding students in a supportive environment. • The Freshman Honors Colloquium, which introduces students to the academic offerings at IU South Bend. • Honors Program awards, transcript designations, and the special Honors degree diploma as well as a graduation medallion. **Disability Services offered to physically disabled students:** Note-taking services; Reader services; Tape recorders; Tutors. **Career services:** Alumni network; Alumni services; Career assessment; Career/job search classes; Internships

FACILITIES

Housing: Apartments for single students; Coed dorms; Special housing for international students **Computers:** Students can register for classes online. Administrative functions (other than registration) can be performed online.

CAMPUS LIFE

Environment: City **Activities:** Choral groups; Dance; Drama/theater; Literary magazine; Music ensembles; Musical theater; Opera; Pep band; Student government; Student newspaper; Student-run film society; Symphony orchestra 30 registered organizations, 1 religious organization. 2 fraternities, 1 sorority. **Athletics (Intercollegiate):** *Men:* basketball. *Women:* basketball. Student Activities Center, Schurz Library, Auditorium and Recital Hall, University Grill

ADMISSIONS

Freshman Academic Profile: Average high school GPA 3.1. 7% in top 10% of high school class, 25% in top 25% of high school class, 66% in top 50% of high school class. **Test Scores:** SAT Math middle 50% range 460-550. SAT EBRW middle 50% range 470-570. ACT middle 50% range 18-24. Minimum internet-based TOEFL 71. Minimum paper TOEFL 530. **Basis for Candidate Selection:** *Very important factors considered include:* rigor of secondary school record. *Important factors considered include:* academic GPA, standardized test scores. *Other factors considered include:* recommendation(s), interview, extracurricular activities, geographical residence, state residency. **Freshman Admission Requirements:** High school diploma is required and GED is accepted *Academic units required:* 4 English, 3 math, 3 science, 3 science labs, 3 social studies, 7 academic electives, *Academic units recommended:* 2 foreign language. **Freshman Admission Statistics:** 2,580 applied, 77.7% admitted, 49% enrolled. **Transfer Admission Requirements:** college transcript(s), Minimum college GPA of 2.0 required. Lowest grade transferable C. **General Admission Information:** Application fee $35. Priority deadline 8/1. Nonfall registration accepted. Admission may be deferred.

COSTS AND FINANCIAL AID

Annual out-of-state tuition $18,432. Required fees $606. Average book expense $1,176. **Required Forms and Deadlines:** FAFSA; Institution's own financial aid form. **Notification of Awards:** Applicants will be notified of awards on a rolling basis beginning 5/1. **Types of Aid:** *Need-based scholarships/ grants:* College/university scholarship or grant aid from institutional funds; Federal Pell; Private scholarships; SEOG; State scholarships/grants. *Loans:* Direct PLUS loans; Direct Subsidized Stafford Loans; Direct Unsubsidized Stafford Loans. *Student Employment:* Federal Work-Study Program available. Institutional employment available. **Financial Aid Statistics:** 86% needy freshmen, 82% needy undergrads receive need-based scholarship or grant aid. 6% freshmen, 6% undergrads receive non-need-based scholarship or grant aid. 49% freshmen, 63% undergrads receive need-based self-help aid. 6% freshmen, 2% undergrads receive athletic scholarships. 90% freshmen, 82% undergrads receive any aid. 76% undergrads borrow to pay for school. Average cumulative indebtedness $27,306. **Criteria for awarding aid:** *Need-based:* Academics, Alumni affiliation, Art, Athletics, Job skills, Leadership, Minority status *Non-need-based:* Academics, Athletics.

INDIANA UNIVERSITY SOUTHEAST

4201 Grant Line Road, New Albany, IN 47150
Phone: 812-941-2212 • **Financial Aid Phone:** (812) 941-2246
E-mail: admissions@ius.edu • **CEEB Code:** 1314
Fax: 812-941-2595 • **Website:** www.ius.edu • **ACT Code:** 1229

This public school was founded in 1941. It has a 180 acre campus.

RATINGS

Admissions Selectivity Rating: 76   **Fire Safety Rating:** 95   **Green Rating:** 63

STUDENTS AND FACULTY

Enrollment: 4,722. **Student Body:** 60% female, 40% male, 31% out-of-state, 1% international (43 countries represented). Asian 1%, African American 7%, Caucasian 83%, Hispanic 4%, Native American <1%, Pacific Islander <1%, Two or more races 3%, Race unknown 1%.

Retention and Graduation: 59% freshmen return for sophomore year. 12% freshmen graduate within 4 years. 31% freshmen graduate within 6 years. **Faculty:** Student/faculty ratio 14:1. 214 full-time faculty, 79% hold PhDs, 18% are members of minority groups, 53% are women.

ACADEMICS

Degrees: Associate; Bachelor's; Certificate; Master's; Post-Bachelor's certificate **Classes:** Most classes have 10-19 students. **Most popular majors:** Psychology, General; Registered Nursing/Registered Nurse; Business/Commerce, General. **Special Study Options:** Accelerated program; Cross-registration; Distance learning; Double major; Dual enrollment; English as a Second Language (ESL); External degree program; Honors program; Independent study; Internships; Student-designed major; Study abroad; Teacher certification program; Weekend college. **Honors programs:** The Indiana University Southeast Honors Program (IUSHP) is designed to promote a rigorous and nurturing academic program for talented, motivated, and highly curious students. The IUSHP reflects the mutual commitment of both students and faculty to achieve the following goals: • To create an atmosphere of intellectual inquiry with an emphasis on scholarly interdependence and self-reliance; • To foster an environment of intellectual flexibility and creativity; • To encourage academic and personal camaraderie among all participants; • To nurture the intellectual and personal development of all participants; • To benefit the entire campus through mentorship,service learning and applied learning, campus and community citizenship, leadership, and outreach activities. https://www.ius.edu/honors-program/. **Disability Services offered to physically disabled students:** Note-taking services; Reader services; Tape recorders; Tutors. **Career services:** Alumni network; Alumni services; Career assessment; Career/job search classes; Internships

FACILITIES

Housing: Apartments for single students 95% of campus accessible to physically diasbled. **Special Academic Facilities/Equipment:** Paul W. Ogle Center, Concert Hall, Theatre, Recital Hall, Japanese Cultural Center, Ronald L. Barr Art Gallery **Computers:** Students can register for classes online. Administrative functions (other than registration) can be performed online.

CAMPUS LIFE

Environment: Town **Activities:** Campus Ministries; Choral groups; Concert band; Dance; Drama/theater; International Student Organization; Jazz band; Literary magazine; Marching band; Model UN; Music ensembles; Musical theater; Pep band; Radio station; Student government; Student newspaper; Symphony orchestra 76 registered organizations, 1 religious organization. 2 fraternities, 4 sororities. **Athletics (Intercollegiate):** *Men:* baseball, basketball, cross-country, tennis. *Women:* basketball, cross-country, softball, tennis, volleyball. Paul W. Ogle Cultural & Community Center, Fitness Center, Food Court, University Grounds Coffee Shop **Environmental Initiatives:** Single stream waste recycling

ADMISSIONS

Freshman Academic Profile: Average high school GPA 3.2. 9% in top 10% of high school class, 32% in top 25% of high school class, 70% in top 50% of high school class. **Test Scores:** SAT Math middle 50% range 470-550. SAT EBRW middle 50% range 480-570. ACT middle 50% range 17-22. Minimum internet-based TOEFL 75. Minimum paper TOEFL 530. **Basis for Candidate Selection:** *Very important factors considered include:* rigor of secondary school record, academic GPA. *Other factors considered include:* standardized test scores. **Freshman Admission Requirements:** High school diploma is required and GED is accepted *Academic units required:* 4 English, 3 math, 3 science, 3 science labs, 3 social studies, 7 academic electives, *Academic units recommended:* 2 foreign language. **Freshman Admission Statistics:** 2,273 applied, 82.8% admitted, 49% enrolled. **Transfer Admission Requirements:** college transcript(s), Lowest grade transferable C. **General Admission Information:** Application fee $35. Priority deadline 8/17. Nonfall registration accepted. Admission may be deferred for a maximum of one calendar year.

COSTS AND FINANCIAL AID

Annual out-of-state tuition $18,432. Required fees $606. Average book expense $1,176. **Required Forms and Deadlines:** FAFSA. **Notification of Awards:** Applicants will be notified of awards on a rolling basis beginning 2/10. **Types of Aid:** *Need-based scholarships/grants:* College/university scholarship or grant aid from institutional funds; Federal Pell; Private scholarships; SEOG; State scholarships/grants. *Loans:* Direct PLUS loans; Direct Subsidized Stafford Loans; Direct Unsubsidized Stafford Loans. *Student Employment:* Federal Work-Study Program available. Institutional employment available. **Financial Aid Statistics:** 83% needy freshmen, 81% needy undergrads receive need-based scholarship or grant aid. 6% freshmen, 5% undergrads receive non-need-based scholarship or grant aid. 50% freshmen, 63% undergrads receive need-based self-help aid. 1% freshmen, 1% undergrads receive athletic scholarships. 90% freshmen, 78% undergrads receive any aid. 71% undergrads borrow to pay for school. Average cumulative indebtedness $22,612. **Criteria for awarding aid:** *Need-based:* Academics, Alumni affiliation, Art, Athletics, Leadership, Minority status *Non-need-based:* Academics, Art, Athletics, Leadership, Minority status, Music/drama.

INDIANA WESLEYAN UNIVERSITY

4201 South Washington Street, Marion, IN 46953
Phone: 765-677-2138 · **Financial Aid Phone:** 765-677-2116
E-mail: admissions@indwes.edu · **CEEB Code:** 1446
Fax: 765-677-2333 · **Website:** www.indwes.edu · **ACT Code:** 1226

This private school, affiliated with the Wesleyan Church, was founded in 1920. It has a 300 acre campus.

RATINGS
Admissions Selectivity Rating: 80   **Fire Safety Rating:** 96   **Green Rating:** 60*

STUDENTS AND FACULTY
Enrollment: 2,683. **Student Body:** 65% female, 35% male, 46% out-of-state, 1% international (21 countries represented). Asian 1%, African American 4%, Caucasian 84%, Hispanic 4%, Native American <1%, Pacific Islander <1%, Two or more races 4%, Race unknown 2%.
Retention and Graduation: 82% freshmen return for sophomore year.
Faculty: Student/faculty ratio 13:1. 163 full-time faculty, 75% hold PhDs, 9% are members of minority groups, 44% are women. 0% of classes are taught by teaching assistants.

ACADEMICS
Degrees: Associate; Bachelor's; Doctoral; Doctoral/Research; Master's; Post-Bachelor's certificate; Post-Master's certificate **Most popular majors:** Psychology, General; Registered Nursing/Registered Nurse; Business Administration And Management, General. **Special Study Options:** Accelerated program; Cross-registration; Distance learning; Double major; Honors program; Independent study; Internships; Study abroad; Teacher certification program. **Honors programs:** John Wesley Honors College. **Disability Services offered to physically disabled students:** Note-taking services; Reader services; Tape recorders; Tutors. **Career services:** Alumni network; Alumni services; Career assessment; Career/job search classes; Internships; Regional alumni

FACILITIES
Housing: Apartments for married students; Apartments for single students; Men's dorms; Theme housing; Women's dorms 99% of campus accessible to physically diasbled. **Special Academic Facilities/Equipment:** Lee Howard art collection (European artists) Lewis Jackson Library (2003) Tom and Joanne Phillippe Performing Arts Center (1998) Bronze statues from Israel (1998-2002) Williams chapel—medieval replica (2001) Burns Hall of Science and Nursing (2000) Luckey Recreation and Wellness Center (2001) John Maxwell Business Center (1999) **Computers:** 100% of classrooms, 100% of dorms, 100% of libraries, 100% of dining areas, 100% of student union, 100% of common outdoor areas have wireless network access. Students can register for classes online. Administrative functions (other than registration) can be performed online.

CAMPUS LIFE
Environment: Town **Activities:** Campus Ministries; Choral groups; Concert band; Dance; Drama/theater; International Student Organization; Jazz band; Literary magazine; Model UN; Music ensembles; Musical theater; Opera; Pep band; Radio station; Student government; Student newspaper; Student-run film society; Symphony orchestra; Television station 35 registered organizations, 1 honor society, 5 religious organizations. **Athletics (Intercollegiate):** *Men:* baseball, basketball, cheerleading, cross-country, golf, soccer, tennis, track/field (outdoor), track/field (indoor). *Women:* basketball, cheerleading, cross-country, soccer, softball, tennis, track/field (outdoor), track/field (indoor), volleyball. **On-Campus Highlights:** McConn Coffee Shop, Recreation and Wellness Center, Globe Theater, The 1920 Art Gallery, Williams Chapel **Environmental Initiatives:** Creation of a multi-disciplinary Task Force for Campus Sustainabilty

ADMISSIONS
Freshman Academic Profile: Average high school GPA 3.6. 3% in top 10% of high school class, 57% in top 25% of high school class, 88% in top 50% of high school class. **Test Scores:** SAT Math middle 50% range 480-590. SAT EBRW middle 50% range 460-570. ACT middle 50% range 21-26. Minimum internet-based TOEFL 79. Minimum paper TOEFL 550. **Basis for Candidate Selection:** *Very important factors considered include:* academic GPA, standardized test scores. *Important factors considered include:* application essay, recommendation(s). *Other factors considered include:* rigor of secondary school record, class rank, interview, extracurricular activities, talent/ability, character/personal qualities, first generation, alumni/ae relation, religious affiliation/commitment, racial/ethnic status, volunteer work, work experience, level of applicant's interest. **Freshman Admission Requirements:** High school diploma is required and GED is accepted *Academic units recommended:* 4 English, 3 math, 3 science, 2 foreign language, 3 social studies, 5 academic

electives, 1 unit from above areas or other academic areas. **Freshman Admission Statistics:** 3,796 applied, 72.0% admitted, 34% enrolled. **Transfer Admission Requirements:** college transcript(s), statement of good standing from prior institution(s). Minimum college GPA of 2.0 required. Lowest grade transferable C. **General Admission Information:** Nonfall registration accepted.

COSTS AND FINANCIAL AID
Annual tuition $25,980. Average book expense $1,386. **Required Forms and Deadlines:** FAFSA; Institution's own financial aid form. **Types of Aid:** *Need-based scholarships/grants:* College/university scholarship or grant aid from institutional funds; Federal Nursing Scholarships; Federal Pell; Private scholarships; SEOG; State scholarships/grants. *Loans:* Direct PLUS loans; Direct Subsidized Stafford Loans; Direct Unsubsidized Stafford Loans. *Student Employment:* Federal Work-Study Program available. Institutional employment available. **Financial Aid Statistics:** 100% needy freshmen, 83% needy undergrads receive need-based scholarship or grant aid. 92% freshmen, 88% undergrads receive non-need-based scholarship or grant aid. 86% freshmen, 88% undergrads receive need-based self-help aid. 10% freshmen, 8% undergrads receive athletic scholarships. 94% freshmen, 95% undergrads receive any aid. Average cumulative indebtedness $28,907. **Criteria for awarding aid:** *Need-based:* Alumni affiliation, Minority status, Religious affiliation *Non-need-based:* Academics, Alumni affiliation, Art, Athletics, Music/drama, State/district residency.

INTERNATIONAL COLLEGE

2655 Northbrooke Drive, Naples, FL 34119
Phone: 239-513-1122 · **Financial Aid Phone:** 239-513-1122
E-mail: admit@internationalcollege.edu · **CEEB Code:** 7113
Fax: 239-598-6254 · **Website:** www.hodges.edu · **ACT Code:** 4775

This private school was founded in 1990.

RATINGS
Admissions Selectivity Rating: 70   **Fire Safety Rating:** 60*   **Green Rating:** 60*

STUDENTS AND FACULTY
Enrollment: 1,475. **Student Body:** 68% female, 32% male, 0% out-of-state, <1% international (40 countries represented). Asian 2%, African American 16%, Caucasian 55%, Hispanic 24%, Native American <1%, Race unknown 2%. **Faculty:** Student/faculty ratio 17:1. 61 full-time faculty, 66% hold PhDs, 8% are members of minority groups, 33% are women. 0% of classes are taught by teaching assistants.

ACADEMICS
Degrees: Associate; Bachelor's; Certificate; Master's **Most popular majors:** Multi-/Interdisciplinary Studies, Other; Health Professions And Related Clinical Sciences, Other; Business, Management, Marketing, And Related Support Services, Other. **Special Study Options:** Accelerated program; Cooperative education program; Distance learning; Double major; English as a Second Language (ESL); Independent study; Internships; Weekend college. **Career services:** Alumni services; Career assessment; Career/job search classes

FACILITIES
Housing: Coed dorms 100% of campus accessible to physically diasbled. **Computers:** 100% of classrooms, 100% of libraries, have wireless network access. Students can register for classes online. Administrative functions (other than registration) can be performed online.

CAMPUS LIFE
Environment: City **Activities:** Dance; Drama/theater; International Student Organization; Model UN; Musical theater; Radio station; Student government; Student newspaper; Yearbook 1 honor societies. **Environmental Initiatives:** Reduction in energy usage

ADMISSIONS
Test Scores: Minimum paper TOEFL 500. **Basis for Candidate Selection:** *Important factors considered include:* interview, level of applicant's interest. **Freshman Admission Requirements:** High school diploma is required and GED is accepted **Freshman Admission Statistics:** 210 applied, 79.0% admitted, 94% enrolled. **Transfer Admission Requirements:** High school transcript, essay or personal statement, Lowest grade transferable C. **General Admission Information:** Application fee $20. Nonfall registration accepted. Admission may be deferred for a maximum of 1 year.

COSTS AND FINANCIAL AID
Required Forms and Deadlines: FAFSA. **Types of Aid:** *Need-based*

scholarships/grants: College/university scholarship or grant aid from institutional funds; Federal Pell; Private scholarships; SEOG; State scholarships/grants. *Student Employment:* Federal Work-Study Program available. Institutional employment available. **Financial Aid Statistics:** 90% needy freshmen, 94% needy undergrads receive need-based scholarship or grant aid. 41% freshmen, 66% undergrads receive non-need-based scholarship or grant aid. 87% freshmen, 91% undergrads receive need-based self-help aid. 0% freshmen, 0% undergrads receive athletic scholarships. **Criteria for awarding aid:** *Non-need-based:* Academics, Leadership.

IONA COLLEGE

715 North Avenue, New Rochelle, NY 10801
Phone: 914-633-2502 · **Financial Aid Phone:** 914-633-2497
E-mail: admissions@iona.edu · **CEEB Code:** 2324
Fax: 914-633-2182 · **Website:** www.iona.edu · **ACT Code:** 2770

This private school, affiliated with the Roman Catholic Church, was founded in 1940. It has a 45 acre campus.

Admissions Selectivity Rating: 72	Fire Safety Rating: 92	Green Rating: 71

STUDENTS AND FACULTY

Enrollment: 2,989. **Student Body:** 51% female, 49% male, 24% out-of-state, 3% international (38 countries represented). Asian 2%, African American 10%, Caucasian 56%, Hispanic 24%, Native American <1%, Pacific Islander <1%, Two or more races 2%, Race unknown 3%.
Retention and Graduation: 75% freshmen return for sophomore year. 59% freshmen graduate within 4 years. 64% freshmen graduate within 6 years.
Faculty: Student/faculty ratio 15:1. 171 full-time faculty, 93% hold PhDs, 19% are members of minority groups, 46% are women. 0% of classes are taught by teaching assistants.

ACADEMICS

Degrees: Bachelor's; Certificate; Master's; Post-Bachelor's certificate; Post-Master's certificate **Classes:** Most classes have fewer than 10 students. Most lab/discussion sessions have fewer than 10 students. **Most popular majors:** Mass Communication/Media Studies; Psychology, General; Business Administration And Management, General. **Special Study Options:** Accelerated program; Distance learning; Double major; Dual enrollment; English as a Second Language (ESL); External degree program; Honors program; Independent study; Internships; Liberal arts/career combination; Student-designed major; Study abroad; Teacher certification program; Weekend college. **Honors programs:** The Iona College Honors Degree Program is designed to meet the educational needs of the ablest and most highly motivated students at Iona. Grounded in a challenging curriculum, the program offers gifted students the resources and opportunities to develop their talents and to perform at the peak of their capabilities. The course of study is designed to develop intellectual curiosity, analytic abilities, and awareness of ethical and civic responsibilities. The program encourages the development of a nucleus of independent learners able to inspire each other academically and fosters a sense of self-respect in students, encouraging them to stretch their abilities in pursuit of lifelong learning, independent thinking, and personal fulfillment. The Honors Degree Program seeks to establish a core academic community that enriches and serves the wider college community. The program endeavors to create an intellectual atmosphere to attract and challenge superior students and faculty and to enhance the public image of the College by promoting the concept of excellence in education. The curriculum promotes an appreciation and understanding of the interrelatedness of knowledge and culture by providing a wide range of interdisciplinary courses and opportunities to study abroad. Students in the program take specially designed honors courses and advanced courses in other areas, and engage in independent research under the guidance of faculty mentors. Small class sizes encourage student participation and promote a close student-faculty relationship. Students are offered close individual guidance, both academically and in terms of career preparation. There is a faculty committee that works with students interested in applying for competitive grants and fellowships and advises them regarding graduate and professional studies. A career mentoring program affords students a unique chance to explore career opportunities by matching them with an appropriate alumnus/alumna or corporate liaison. **Combined degree programs:** BA/MA. **Disability Services offered to physically disabled students:** Note-taking services; Reader services; Tape recorders; Tutors. **Career services:** Alumni network; Alumni services; Career assessment; Career/job search classes; Internships; Regional alumni

FACILITIES

Housing: Apartments for single students; Coed dorms; Special housing for disabled student; Special housing for international students; Theme housing;

Wellness housing 70% of campus accessible to physically diasbled. **Special Academic Facilities/Equipment:** Iona College Arts Center, Br. Kenneth Chapman Gallery, Murphy Science and Technology Center, Advanced Computer Laboratory, TV Production Studio, LaPenta Student Union, Hynes Athletic Center, Rowing tank, Arrigoni Center, Blessed Edmund Ignatius Rice Chapel **Computers:** 100% of classrooms, 100% of dorms, 100% of libraries, 100% of dining areas, 100% of student union, 100% of common outdoor areas have wireless network access. Students can register for classes online. Administrative functions (other than registration) can be performed online.

CAMPUS LIFE

Environment: City **Activities:** Campus Ministries; Choral groups; Concert band; Dance; Drama/theater; International Student Organization; Literary magazine; Model UN; Music ensembles; Musical theater; Pep band; Radio station; Student government; Student newspaper; Student-run film society; Television station; Yearbook 65 registered organizations, 9 honor societies, 4 religious organizations. 4 fraternities, 6 sororities. **Athletics (Intercollegiate):** *Men:* baseball, basketball, crew/rowing, cross-country, diving, golf, soccer, swimming, track/field (outdoor), track/field (indoor), water polo. *Women:* basketball, crew/rowing, cross-country, diving, lacrosse, soccer, softball, swimming, track/field (outdoor), track/field (indoor), volleyball, water polo. **On-Campus Highlights:** Lapenta Student Union, Hynes Athletics Center, Ryan Library, Residence Halls, Starbucks

ADMISSIONS

Freshman Academic Profile: Average high school GPA 3.0. 7% in top 10% of high school class, 21% in top 25% of high school class, 51% in top 50% of high school class. 61% from public high schools. **Test Scores:** SAT Math middle 50% range 480-590. SAT EBRW middle 50% range 500-590. ACT middle 50% range 20-25. Minimum internet-based TOEFL 80. Minimum paper TOEFL 550. **Basis for Candidate Selection:** *Very important factors considered include:* rigor of secondary school record, academic GPA. *Important factors considered include:* application essay, standardized test scores, character/personal qualities, level of applicant's interest. *Other factors considered include:* class rank, recommendation(s), interview, extracurricular activities, talent/ability, first generation, alumni/ae relation, geographical residence, volunteer work, work experience. **Freshman Admission Requirements:** High school diploma is required and GED is accepted *Academic units required:* 4 English, 3 math, 3 science, 2 science labs, 2 foreign language, 2 social studies, 1 history, 1 academic elective, *Academic units recommended:* 4 math, 2 history, 3 academic electives. **Freshman Admission Statistics:** 10,304 applied, 92.2% admitted, 9% enrolled. **Transfer Admission Requirements:** High school transcript, college transcript(s), essay or personal statement, Minimum college GPA of 2.5 required. Lowest grade transferable C. **General Admission Information:** Application fee $50. Priority deadline 2/15. Regular application deadline 2/15. Nonfall registration accepted. Admission may be deferred for a maximum of 1 year.

COSTS AND FINANCIAL AID

Annual tuition $35,482. Room and board $14,832. Required fees $2,200. Average book expense $1,500. **Required Forms and Deadlines:** FAFSA; State aid form. **Notification of Awards:** Applicants will be notified of awards on a rolling basis beginning 1/1. **Types of Aid:** *Need-based scholarships/grants:* College/university scholarship or grant aid from institutional funds; Federal Pell; Private scholarships; SEOG; State scholarships/grants. *Loans:* Direct PLUS loans; Direct Subsidized Stafford Loans; Direct Unsubsidized Stafford Loans. *Student Employment:* Federal Work-Study Program available. Institutional employment available. **Financial Aid Statistics:** 42% needy freshmen, 41% needy undergrads receive need-based scholarship or grant aid. 100% freshmen, 99% undergrads receive non-need-based scholarship or grant aid. 73% freshmen, 74% undergrads receive need-based self-help aid. 6% freshmen, 7% undergrads receive athletic scholarships. 99% freshmen, 96% undergrads receive any aid. 76% undergrads borrow to pay for school. Average cumulative indebtedness $34,199. **Criteria for awarding aid:** *Non-need-based:* Academics, Alumni affiliation, Athletics.

IOWA STATE UNIVERSITY

100 Enrollment Services Center, Ames, IA 50011-2011
Phone: 515-294-5836 · **Financial Aid Phone:** 515-294-2223
E-mail: admissions@iastate.edu · **CEEB Code:** 6306
Fax: 515-294-2592 · **Website:** www.iastate.edu · **ACT Code:** 1320

This public school was founded in 1858. It has a 1813 acre campus.

RATINGS
Admissions Selectivity Rating: 78　　**Fire Safety Rating:** 92　　**Green Rating:** 98

STUDENTS AND FACULTY
Enrollment: 29,957. **Student Body:** 42% female, 58% male, 35% out-of-state, 7% international (128 countries represented). Asian 3%, African American 3%, Caucasian 74%, Hispanic 5%, Native American <1%, Pacific Islander <1%, Two or more races 2%, Race unknown 5%.
Retention and Graduation: 88% freshmen return for sophomore year. 45% freshmen graduate within 4 years. 73% freshmen graduate within 6 years. 16% grads go on to further study within 1 year. 4% grads pursue arts and sciences degrees. 1% grads pursue law degrees. 1% grads pursue business degrees. 2% grads pursue medical degrees. **Faculty:** Student/faculty ratio 19:1. 1,561 full-time faculty, 93% hold PhDs, 22% are members of minority groups, 37% are women.

ACADEMICS
Degrees: Bachelor's; Doctoral/Professional; Doctoral/Research; Master's; Post-Bachelor's certificate; Post-Master's certificate **Classes:** Most classes have 20-29 students. Most lab/discussion sessions have 10-19 students. **Special Study Options:** Accelerated program; Cooperative education program; Cross-registration; Distance learning; Double major; Dual enrollment; English as a Second Language (ESL); Exchange student program (domestic); External degree program; Honors program; Independent study; Internships; Student-designed major; Study abroad; Teacher certification program.
Honors programs: ISU offers both a University Honors Program and a Freshman Honors Program. Each program promotes an enhanced academic environment for students of high ability and emphasizes the development of an enriched, individualized program study that meets each student's particular needs, interests and abilities. Honors gives students a supportive community in which to pursue their goals and stretch their horizons. Benefits include unique courses, small class sizes, research opportunities and funding, access to graduate-level courses, and priority registration. **Combined degree programs:** BA/MEng. **Disability Services offered to physically disabled students:** Note-taking services; Reader services; Tape recorders; Tutors. **Career services:** Alumni network; Alumni services; Career assessment; Career/job search classes; Internships

FACILITIES
Housing: Apartments for married students; Apartments for single students; Coed dorms; Fraternity/sorority housing; Men's dorms; Special housing for disabled student; Special housing for international students; Theme housing; Women's dorms 96% of campus accessible to physically diasbled. **Special Academic Facilities/Equipment:** Brunnier art museum, Farm House museum, observatory, numerous institutes, research centers, College of Design Gallery, Virtual Reality Application Center, Pappajohn Center for Entrepreneurship **Computers:** 100% of classrooms, 75% of dorms, 100% of libraries, 100% of dining areas, 100% of student union, 40% of common outdoor areas have wireless network access. Students can register for classes online. Administrative functions (other than registration) can be performed online.

CAMPUS LIFE
Environment: Town **Activities:** Campus Ministries; Choral groups; Concert band; Dance; Drama/theater; International Student Organization; Jazz band; Literary magazine; Marching band; Model UN; Music ensembles; Musical theater; Pep band; Radio station; Student government; Student newspaper; Student-run film society; Symphony orchestra; Television station 799 registered organizations, 43 honor societies, 34 religious organizations. 34 fraternities, 19 sororities. **Athletics (Intercollegiate):** *Men:* basketball, cross-country, football, golf, track/field (outdoor), track/field (indoor), wrestling. *Women:* basketball, cross-country, diving, golf, gymnastics, soccer, softball, swimming, tennis, track/field (outdoor), track/field (indoor), volleyball. **On-Campus Highlights:** Union Drive Community Center (dining center), Reiman Gardens, Lied Recreation Center, Memorial Union, Virtual Reality Lab (available to visitors also) **Environmental Initiatives:** Establishment of the Live Green Initiative (http://

www.livegreen.iastate.edu/about/)that has included: 1. Hiring of a Director of Sustainability (http://www.iastate.edu/Inside/2008/1212/rankin.shtml) 2. Creation of a 13 member (students, staff, and faculty) President's Advisory Committee on Energy Conservation and Global Climate Change (http://www.committees.iastate.edu/comm-info.php?id=136) 3. Creation of a Live Green Loan Fund for energy conservation and sustainability projects (http://www.livegreen.iastate.edu/loan/) 4. Completion of an annual Symposium on Sustainability (http://www.livegreen.iastate.edu/symposium/archive/)

ADMISSIONS
Freshman Academic Profile: Average high school GPA 3.5. 25% in top 10% of high school class, 57% in top 25% of high school class, 92% in top 50% of high school class. **Test Scores:** SAT Math middle 50% range 545-680. ACT middle 50% range 22-28. Minimum internet-based TOEFL 71. Minimum paper TOEFL 530. **Basis for Candidate Selection:** *Very important factors considered include:* rigor of secondary school record, class rank, academic GPA, standardized test scores. *Other factors considered include:* application essay, recommendation(s), interview, extracurricular activities, talent/ability, character/personal qualities, geographical residence, state residency, volunteer work, work experience. **Freshman Admission Requirements:** High school diploma is required and GED is accepted *Academic units required:* 4 English, 3 math, 3 science, 2 science labs, 2 foreign language, 2 social studies, *Academic units recommended:* 4 English, 4 math, 4 science, 3 science labs, 3 foreign language, 4 social studies. **Freshman Admission Statistics:** 19,262 applied, 89.3% admitted, 35% enrolled. **Transfer Admission Requirements:** college transcript(s), statement of good standing from prior institution(s). Minimum college GPA of 2.0 required. Lowest grade transferable D. **General Admission Information:** Application fee $40. Nonfall registration accepted. Admission may be deferred for a maximum of 1 year.

COSTS AND FINANCIAL AID
Annual in-state tuition $8,546. Annual out-of-state tuition $21,292. Room and board $8,546. Required fees $1,180. Average book expense $994. **Required Forms and Deadlines:** FAFSA. **Notification of Awards:** Applicants will be notified of awards on a rolling basis beginning 1/30. **Types of Aid:** *Need-based scholarships/grants:* College/university scholarship or grant aid from institutional funds; Federal Pell; SEOG; State scholarships/grants. *Loans:* Direct PLUS loans; Direct Subsidized Stafford Loans; Direct Unsubsidized Stafford Loans. *Student Employment:* Federal Work-Study Program available. Institutional employment available. **Financial Aid Statistics:** 98% needy freshmen, 97% needy undergrads receive need-based scholarship or grant aid. 48% freshmen, 46% undergrads receive non-need-based scholarship or grant aid. 62% freshmen, 74% undergrads receive need-based self-help aid. 1% freshmen, 1% undergrads receive athletic scholarships. 88% freshmen, 79% undergrads receive any aid. Average cumulative indebtedness $28,617. **Criteria for awarding aid:** *Need-based:* Academics, Minority status *Non-need-based:* Academics, Alumni affiliation, Art, Athletics, Leadership, Minority status, Music/drama, State/district residency.

ITHACA COLLEGE

953 Danby Road, Ithaca, NY 14850-7002
Phone: (607) 274-3124 · **Financial Aid Phone:** 607-274-3131
E-mail: admission@ithaca.edu · **CEEB Code:** 2325
Fax: (607) 274-1900 · **Website:** www.ithaca.edu · **ACT Code:** 2772

This private school was founded in 1892. It has a 669 acre campus.

RATINGS
Admissions Selectivity Rating: 83　　**Fire Safety Rating:** 93　　**Green Rating:** 89

STUDENTS AND FACULTY
Enrollment: 6,021. **Student Body:** 58% female, 42% male, 56% out-of-state, 2% international (52 countries represented). Asian 4%, African American 6%, Caucasian 73%, Hispanic 8%, Native American <1%, Pacific Islander <1%, Two or more races 3%, Race unknown 4%.
Retention and Graduation: 83% freshmen return for sophomore year. 69% freshmen graduate within 4 years. 76% freshmen graduate within 6 years. 23% grads go on to further study within 1 year. 15% grads pursue arts and sciences degrees. 1% grads pursue law degrees. 1% grads pursue business degrees. 1% grads pursue medical degrees. **Faculty:** Student/faculty ratio 10:1. 517 full-time faculty, 80% hold PhDs, 12% are members of minority groups, 49% are women. 2% of classes are taught by teaching assistants.

ACADEMICS

Degrees: Bachelor's; Certificate; Doctoral/Professional; Master's **Classes:** Most classes have 10-19 students. Most lab/discussion sessions have 10-19 students. **Most popular majors:** Radio And Television; Music, General; Business Administration, Management And Operations. **Special Study Options:** Accelerated program; Cross-registration; Distance learning; Double major; Dual enrollment; Honors program; Independent study; Internships; Liberal arts/career combination; Student-designed major; Study abroad; Teacher certification program. **Honors programs:** The Ithaca College Honors Program provides students with a highly enhanced, integrated, and comprehensive liberal arts program that emphasizes critical thinking, intellectual curiosity, and lifelong learning. The Honors Program supports an innovative community of faculty and students and encourages a culture of intellectual engagement through curricular, co-curricular and extracurricular opportunities. Honors seminars are unique to the Honors Program and the program offers a variety of three-credit and one-credit courses to feed student's curiosity, challenge their thinking, and expand their intellect. Often, professors and the program supplement classroom education with out-of-class activities such as trips or speakers. In order to graduate with Ithaca College honors, students must demonstrate by portfolio that they have experienced significant involvement in five important areas: academic challenge, global citizenship, cultural engagement, scholarly achievement, and civic engagement. To a greater extent than other students, honors students are held personally responsible for their learning and are expected to incorporate into the portfolio artifacts and reflections demonstrating their learning in each area. Honors is open to any qualified student in any school or department at Ithaca College. The Honors Program does not conflict with departmental honors programs; qualified students can complete both. **Disability Services offered to physically disabled students:** Note-taking services; Reader services; Tape recorders. **Career services:** Alumni network; Alumni services; Career assessment; Career/job search classes; Internships; Regional alumni

FACILITIES

Housing: Apartments for single students; Coed dorms; Fraternity/sorority housing; Special housing for disabled student; Theme housing **Special Academic Facilities/Equipment:** The Dorothy D. and Roy H. Park Center for Business and Sustainable Enterprise, and the Peggy Ryan Williams Center are both Platinum LEED-certified buildings. In addition, the LINK Connector between Job Hall and Dillingham Center for the Performing Arts has been certified LEED Gold. The new Athletics and Events Center was certified LEED Gold. The Handwerker Gallery provides an outlet for creative work and intellectual discourse for students and faculty in diverse programs across campus. **Computers:** 50% of classrooms, 100% of dorms, 100% of libraries, 100% of dining areas, 100% of student union, have wireless network access. Students can register for classes online. Administrative functions (other than registration) can be performed online.

CAMPUS LIFE

Environment: Town **Activities:** Campus Ministries; Choral groups; Concert band; Dance; Drama/theater; International Student Organization; Jazz band; Literary magazine; Model UN; Music ensembles; Musical theater; Opera; Pep band; Radio station; Student government; Student newspaper; Student-run film society; Symphony orchestra; Television station 180 registered organizations, 28 honor societies, 8 religious organizations. 3 fraternities, 1 sorority. **Athletics (Intercollegiate):** *Men:* baseball, basketball, crew/rowing, cross-country, diving, football, lacrosse, soccer, swimming, tennis, track/field (outdoor), wrestling. *Women:* basketball, crew/rowing, cross-country, diving, field hockey, golf, gymnastics, lacrosse, soccer, softball, swimming, tennis, track/field (outdoor), volleyball. **On-Campus Highlights:** IC Square and Food Court, Handwerker Gallery, Fitness Center, Business School Atrium, Athletics & Events Center **Environmental Initiatives:** Sustainability Initiative that spurs and chronicles progress in three separate but highly inter-related areas: development of curriculum to infuse considerations of sustainability and applied research opportunities to study and solve sustainability challenges; modification of campus operations to incorporate more sustainable decision-making; and campus in-reach and community outreach to share our experiences as a learning organization seeking to become more sustainable.

ADMISSIONS

Freshman Academic Profile: 21% in top 10% of high school class, 55% in top 25% of high school class, 88% in top 50% of high school class. 83% from public high schools. **Test Scores:** SAT Math middle 50% range 560-660. SAT EBRW middle 50% range 590-670. ACT middle 50% range 25-29. Minimum internet-based TOEFL 80. Minimum paper TOEFL 550. **Basis for Candidate Selection:** *Very important factors considered include:* rigor of secondary school record, academic GPA, level of applicant's interest. *Important factors considered include:* application essay, recommendation(s), extracurricular activities, talent/ability, character/personal qualities. *Other factors considered include:* class rank, standardized test scores, interview, first generation, alumni/ae relation, volunteer work, work experience. **Freshman**

Admission Requirements: High school diploma is required and GED is accepted *Academic units required:* 4 English, 3 math, 3 science, 2 foreign language, 3 social studies, 1 academic elective, *Academic units recommended:* 4 English, 4 math, 4 science, 3 foreign language, 4 social studies, 1 academic elective. **Freshman Admission Statistics:** 14,152 applied, 70.5% admitted, 16% enrolled. **Transfer Admission Requirements:** High school transcript, college transcript(s), essay or personal statement, statement of good standing from prior institution(s). Minimum college GPA of 2.75 required. Lowest grade transferable C-. **General Admission Information:** Application fee $60. Regular application deadline 2/1. Nonfall registration accepted. Admission may be deferred for a maximum of 1 year.

COSTS AND FINANCIAL AID

Annual tuition $43,978. Room and board $15,562. Average book expense $1,200. **Required Forms and Deadlines:** CSS/Financial Aid PROFILE; FAFSA. **Types of Aid:** *Need-based scholarships/grants:* College/university scholarship or grant aid from institutional funds; Federal Pell; Private scholarships; SEOG; State scholarships/grants. *Loans:* Direct PLUS loans; Direct Subsidized Stafford Loans; Direct Unsubsidized Stafford Loans. *Student Employment:* Federal Work-Study Program available. Institutional employment available. **Financial Aid Statistics:** 97% needy freshmen, 98% needy undergrads receive need-based scholarship or grant aid. 33% freshmen, 16% undergrads receive non-need-based scholarship or grant aid. 88% freshmen, 89% undergrads receive need-based self-help aid. 0% freshmen, 0% undergrads receive athletic scholarships. 96% freshmen, 93% undergrads receive any aid. 70% undergrads borrow to pay for school. Average cumulative indebtedness $40,595. **Criteria for awarding aid:** *Need-based:* Academics, Minority status, Music/drama *Non-need-based:* Academics, Alumni affiliation, Leadership, Minority status, Music/drama.

JACKSON STATE UNIVERSITY

1400 J.R. Lynch Street, Jackson, MS 39217
Phone: (601) 979-2100 • **Financial Aid Phone:** 601-979-2227
E-mail: admappl@jsums.edu • **CEEB Code:** 1341
Fax: 601-979-3445 • **Website:** www.jsums.edu • **ACT Code:** 2204

This public school was founded in 1877. It has a 175 acre campus.

RATINGS
Admissions Selectivity Rating: 73   **Fire Safety Rating:** 89   **Green Rating:** 60*

STUDENTS AND FACULTY

Enrollment: 6,844. **Student Body:** 62% female, 38% male, 17% out-of-state, 2% international (35 countries represented). Asian <1%, African American 93%, Caucasian 3%, Hispanic <1%, Native American <1%, Two or more races 1%, Race unknown 0%.
Retention and Graduation: 78% freshmen return for sophomore year. **Faculty:** Student/faculty ratio 17:1. 378 full-time faculty, 81% hold PhDs, 81% are members of minority groups, 46% are women.

ACADEMICS

Degrees: Bachelor's; Doctoral; Master's; Post-Master's certificate **Classes:** Most classes have 20-29 students. Most lab/discussion sessions have 20-29 students. **Most popular majors:** Elementary Education And Teaching; Biology/Biological Sciences, General; Criminal Justice/Safety Studies. **Special Study Options:** Distance learning; Double major; Dual enrollment; English as a Second Language (ESL); Honors program; Independent study; Internships; Study abroad; Teacher certification program; Weekend college. **Honors programs:** Honors College. **Disability Services offered to physically disabled students:** Note-taking services; Reader services; Tape recorders; Tutors. **Career services:** Career assessment; Career/job search classes; Internships

FACILITIES

Housing: Men's dorms; Women's dorms 100% of campus accessible to physically disabled. **Special Academic Facilities/Equipment:** Research center,science observatory,e-center. **Computers:** Students can register for classes online. Administrative functions (other than registration) can be performed online.

CAMPUS LIFE

Environment: Metropolis **Activities:** Campus Ministries; Choral groups; Concert band; Dance; Drama/theater; International Student Organization; Jazz band; Literary magazine; Marching band; Music ensembles; Opera; Radio station; Student government; Student newspaper; Student-run film society; Symphony orchestra; Television station; Yearbook 150 registered organizations, 20 honor societies, 11 religious organizations. 4 fraternities, 4 sororities.

Athletics (Intercollegiate): *Men:* baseball, basketball, cross-country, football, golf, soccer, tennis, track/field (outdoor), track/field (indoor), volleyball. *Women:* basketball, cross-country, golf, soccer, softball, tennis, track/field (outdoor), track/field (indoor), volleyball. Student Center, Walter Payton Wellness Center, H.T. Sampson Library, Gibbs-Green Plaza, National Research Center

ADMISSIONS

Freshman Academic Profile: Average high school GPA 2.9. 85% from public high schools. **Test Scores:** ACT middle 50% range 17-20. Minimum paper TOEFL 525. **Basis for Candidate Selection:** *Very important factors considered include:* rigor of secondary school record, academic GPA, standardized test scores. *Important factors considered include:* level of applicant's interest. **Freshman Admission Requirements:** High school diploma is required and GED is accepted *Academic units required:* 4 English, 3 math, 3 science, 3 social studies, 2 academic electives, 0.5 computer science. **Freshman Admission Statistics:** 7,265 applied, 74.5% admitted, 19% enrolled. **Transfer Admission Requirements:** High school transcript, college transcript(s), Minimum college GPA of 2.0 required. Lowest grade transferable C. **General Admission Information:** Priority deadline 8/1. Regular application deadline 8/1. Nonfall registration accepted.

COSTS AND FINANCIAL AID

Annual in-state tuition $6,494. Annual out-of-state tuition $13,494. Room and board $6,494. Average book expense $800. **Required Forms and Deadlines:** FAFSA; Institution's own financial aid form; State aid form. **Notification of Awards:** Applicants will be notified of awards on a rolling basis beginning 2/15. **Types of Aid:** *Need-based scholarships/grants:* College/university scholarship or grant aid from institutional funds; Federal Pell; Private scholarships; SEOG; State scholarships/grants. *Loans: Student Employment:* Federal Work-Study Program available. Institutional employment available. **Criteria for awarding aid:** *Need-based:* Academics.

JACKSONVILLE UNIVERSITY

2800 University Boulevard North, Jacksonville, FL 32211
Phone: 904-256-7000 • **Financial Aid Phone:** 800-558-3467
E-mail: admissions@ju.edu • **CEEB Code:** 5331
Website: http://www.ju.edu/ • **ACT Code:** 740

This private school was founded in 1934. It has a 198 acre campus.

RATINGS

Admissions Selectivity Rating: 87   **Fire Safety Rating:** 82   **Green Rating:** 60*

STUDENTS AND FACULTY

Enrollment: 3,122. **Student Body:** 59% female, 41% male, 29% out-of-state, 1% international (50 countries represented). Asian 4%, African American 19%, Caucasian 60%, Hispanic 7%, Native American 1%, Pacific Islander <1%, Two or more races 8%.
Retention and Graduation: 60% freshmen return for sophomore year. 22% grads go on to further study within 1 year. **Faculty:** Student/faculty ratio 13:1. 180 full-time faculty, 79% hold PhDs, 9% are members of minority groups, 43% are women. 0% of classes are taught by teaching assistants.

ACADEMICS

Degrees: Bachelor's; Master's; Post-Master's certificate **Classes:** Most classes have 10-19 students. Most lab/discussion sessions have fewer than 10 students. **Most popular majors:** Aviation/Airway Management And Operations; Nursing/Registered Nurse (Rn, Asn, Bsn, Msn); Business/Commerce, General. **Special Study Options:** Accelerated program; Cooperative education program; Distance learning; Double major; Dual enrollment; Honors program; Independent study; Internships; Liberal arts/career combination; Student-designed major; Study abroad; Teacher certification program. **Honors programs:** University Honors Program. **Disability Services offered to physically disabled students:** Note-taking services; Reader services; Tutors.

FACILITIES

Housing: Apartments for single students; Coed dorms; Fraternity/sorority housing; Men's dorms; Special housing for disabled student; Wellness housing; Women's dorms **Special Academic Facilities/Equipment:** Art museum, dance pavilion, concert hall, on-campus pre-school. **Computers:** Students can register for classes online. Administrative functions (other than registration) can be performed online.

CAMPUS LIFE

Environment: Metropolis **Activities:** Campus Ministries; Choral groups; Concert band; Dance; Drama/theater; International Student Organization; Jazz band; Literary magazine; Marching band; Music ensembles; Musical theater;

Pep band; Radio station; Student government; Student newspaper; Symphony orchestra; Television station; Yearbook 60 registered organizations, 16 honor societies, 9 fraternities, 6 sororities. **Athletics (Intercollegiate):** *Men:* baseball, basketball, crew/rowing, cross-country, football, golf, soccer, tennis. *Women:* basketball, crew/rowing, cross-country, golf, soccer, softball, tennis, track/field (outdoor), track/field (indoor), volleyball. **On-Campus Highlights:** Alexander Brest Fine Arts Museum, Davis College of Business/ Jazzman's Cafe (New), JU Baseball Complex, Lazzara Health Sciences Center (New), Residential Apartment Village (New)

ADMISSIONS

Freshman Academic Profile: Average high school GPA 3.5. **Test Scores:** SAT Math middle 50% range 480-570. SAT EBRW middle 50% range 470-560. ACT middle 50% range 20-26. Minimum paper TOEFL 540. **Basis for Candidate Selection:** *Very important factors considered include:* academic GPA, standardized test scores. *Important factors considered include:* rigor of secondary school record, talent/ability. *Other factors considered include:* application essay, recommendation(s), interview, extracurricular activities, character/personal qualities, volunteer work, work experience. **Freshman Admission Requirements:** High school diploma is required and GED is accepted *Academic units required:* 4 English, 3 math, 3 science, 2 science labs, 3 social studies, *Academic units recommended:* 4 English, 4 math, 3 science, 2 science labs, 2 foreign language, 3 social studies. **Freshman Admission Statistics:** 8,096 applied, 41.6% admitted, 16% enrolled. **Transfer Admission Requirements:** college transcript(s), essay or personal statement, statement of good standing from prior institution(s). Minimum college GPA of 2.0 required. Lowest grade transferable C. **General Admission Information:** Application fee $30. Priority deadline 3/1. Nonfall registration accepted. Admission may be deferred.

COSTS AND FINANCIAL AID

Required Forms and Deadlines: FAFSA; Institution's own financial aid form; State aid form. **Notification of Awards:** Applicants will be notified of awards on a rolling basis beginning 2/15. **Types of Aid:** *Need-based scholarships/grants:* College/university scholarship or grant aid from institutional funds; Federal Pell; Private scholarships; SEOG; State scholarships/grants. **Financial Aid Statistics:** 98% needy freshmen, 99% needy undergrads receive need-based scholarship or grant aid. 1% freshmen, 1% undergrads receive non-need-based scholarship or grant aid. 62% freshmen, 69% undergrads receive need-based self-help aid. 2% freshmen, 4% undergrads receive athletic scholarships. 97% freshmen, 87% undergrads receive any aid. **Criteria for awarding aid:** *Need-based:* Job skills, Leadership *Non-need-based:* Academics, Art, Athletics, Job skills, Leadership, Music/drama, State/district residency.

JAMES MADISON UNIVERSITY

Best Colleges

800 South Main Street, Harrisonburg, VA 22807
Phone: 540-568-5681 • **Financial Aid Phone:** 540-568-7820
E-mail: admissions@jmu.edu • **CEEB Code:** 5392
Fax: 540-568-3332 • **Website:** www.jmu.edu • **ACT Code:** 4370

This public school was founded in 1908. It has a 785 acre campus.

RATINGS

Admissions Selectivity Rating: 81   **Fire Safety Rating:** 85   **Green Rating:** 89

STUDENTS AND FACULTY

Enrollment: 19,666. **Student Body:** 59% female, 41% male, 23% out-of-state, 2% international (70 countries represented). Asian 5%, African American 5%, Caucasian 75%, Hispanic 7%, Native American <1%, Pacific Islander <1%, Two or more races 4%, Race unknown 3%.
Retention and Graduation: 90% freshmen return for sophomore year. 58% freshmen graduate within 4 years. 83% freshmen graduate within 6 years. 29% grads go on to further study within 1 year. 14% grads pursue arts and sciences degrees. 1.26% grads pursue law degrees. 2% grads pursue business degrees. 0.57% grads pursue medical degrees. **Faculty:** Student/faculty ratio 16:1. 1,044 full-time faculty, 78% hold PhDs, 13% are members of minority groups, 49% are women. 1% of classes are taught by teaching assistants.

ACADEMICS

Degrees: Bachelor's; Doctoral/Professional; Doctoral/Research; Master's **Classes:** Most classes have 10-19 students. Most lab/discussion sessions have 10-19 students. **Most popular majors:** Speech Communication And Rhetoric;

Psychology, General; Community Health Services/Liaison/Counseling. **Special Study Options:** Accelerated program; Distance learning; Double major; Dual enrollment; Honors program; Independent study; Internships; Study abroad; Teacher certification program. **Honors programs:** Academic honors program, honors scholars (3.25 or above),honors courses, and senior honors project (3.25). **Disability Services offered to physically disabled students:** Note-taking services; Reader services; Tape recorders. **Career services:** Alumni network; Alumni services; Career assessment; Career/job search classes; Internships; Regional alumni

FACILITIES

Housing: Apartments for single students; Coed dorms; Fraternity/sorority housing; Special housing for disabled student; Theme housing; Wellness housing 90% of campus accessible to physically diasbled. **Special Academic Facilities/Equipment:** language lab, music and fine arts buildings, herbarium, university farm, planetarium, arboretum,mineral museum,Science on a Sphere. **Computers:** 25% of classrooms, 100% of dorms, 100% of libraries, 50% of dining areas, 100% of student union, 25% of common outdoor areas have wireless network access. Students can register for classes online. Administrative functions (other than registration) can be performed online.

CAMPUS LIFE

Environment: Town **Activities:** Campus Ministries; Choral groups; Concert band; Dance; Drama/theater; International Student Organization; Jazz band; Literary magazine; Marching band; Music ensembles; Musical theater; Opera; Pep band; Radio station; Student government; Student newspaper; Student-run film society; Symphony orchestra; Yearbook 298 registered organizations, 28 honor societies, 28 religious organizations. 15 fraternities, 9 sororities. **Athletics (Intercollegiate):** *Men:* baseball, basketball, cheerleading, football, golf, soccer, tennis. *Women:* basketball, cheerleading, cross-country, diving, field hockey, golf, lacrosse, soccer, softball, swimming, tennis, track/field (outdoor), volleyball. **On-Campus Highlights:** Quad, Taylor Down Under, University Recreation Center, East Campus Dining Hall, Student Success Center **Environmental Initiatives:** Development of student learning outcomes for environmental literacy and an assessment.

ADMISSIONS

Freshman Academic Profile: 16% in top 10% of high school class, 51% in top 25% of high school class, 94% in top 50% of high school class. 60% from public high schools. **Test Scores:** SAT Math middle 50% range 540-620. SAT EBRW middle 50% range 560-640. ACT middle 50% range 23-28. Minimum internet-based TOEFL 80-81. Minimum paper TOEFL 550. **Basis for Candidate Selection:** *Very important factors considered include:* rigor of secondary school record, academic GPA. *Other factors considered include:* application essay, standardized test scores, recommendation(s), extracurricular activities, talent/ability, character/personal qualities, first generation, alumni/ae relation, geographical residence, state residency, racial/ethnic status, volunteer work, work experience. **Freshman Admission Requirements:** High school diploma is required and GED is accepted *Academic units required:* 4 English, 4 math, 3 science, 3 foreign language, 2 social studies, 3 history, *Academic units recommended:* 4 English, 4 math, 3 science, 3 foreign language, 2 social studies, 3 history. **Freshman Admission Statistics:** 21,099 applied, 75.2% admitted, 29% enrolled. **Transfer Admission Requirements:** High school transcript, college transcript(s), Minimum college GPA of 2.0 required. Lowest grade transferable C. **General Admission Information:** Application fee $70. Regular application deadline 1/15. Nonfall registration accepted. Admission may be deferred for a maximum of 1 year.

COSTS AND FINANCIAL AID

Annual in-state tuition $9,822. Annual out-of-state tuition $22,614. Room and board $9,822. Required fees $4,580. Average book expense $1,016. **Required Forms and Deadlines:** FAFSA. **Notification of Awards:** Applicants will be notified of awards on a rolling basis beginning 4/1. **Types of Aid:** *Need-based scholarships/grants:* College/university scholarship or grant aid from institutional funds; Federal Pell; Private scholarships; SEOG; State scholarships/grants. *Loans:* Direct PLUS loans; Direct Subsidized Stafford Loans; Direct Unsubsidized Stafford Loans. *Student Employment:* Federal Work-Study Program available. Institutional employment available. **Financial Aid Statistics:** 53% needy freshmen, 51% needy undergrads receive need-based scholarship or grant aid. 8% freshmen, 9% undergrads receive non-need-based scholarship or grant aid. 88% freshmen, 86% undergrads receive need-based self-help aid. 2% freshmen, 2% undergrads receive athletic scholarships. 59% freshmen, 56% undergrads receive any aid. 52% undergrads borrow to pay for school. Average cumulative indebtedness $28,407. **Criteria for awarding aid:** *Need-based:* Academics, Leadership, Minority status, Religious affiliation *Non-need-based:* Academics, Alumni affiliation, Art, Athletics, Leadership, Minority status, Music/drama, State/district residency.

JARVIS CHRISTIAN COLLEGE

P.O. Box 1470, Hawkins, TX 75765-1470
Phone: 903-769-5730 · **Financial Aid Phone:** 903-769-5740
E-mail: felecia_tyiska@jarvis.edu
Fax: 903-769-1282 · **Website:** http://www.jarvis.edu/ · **ACT Code:** 4110

This private school, affiliated with the Disciples of Christ Church, was founded in 1912. It has a 243 acre campus.

RATINGS

Admissions Selectivity Rating: 65   **Fire Safety Rating:** 92   **Green Rating:** 60*

STUDENTS AND FACULTY

Enrollment: 547. **Student Body:** 60% female, 40% male, 15% out-of-state, <1% international (2 countries represented). Asian 0%, African American 95%, Caucasian 1%, Hispanic 3%, Native American <1%, Race unknown 0%. **Retention and Graduation:** 41% freshmen return for sophomore year. 2% grads go on to further study within 1 year. 1% grads pursue business degrees. 0% grads pursue medical degrees. **Faculty:** Student/faculty ratio 13:1. 35 full-time faculty, 46% hold PhDs, 63% are members of minority groups, 49% are women. 0% of classes are taught by teaching assistants.

ACADEMICS

Degrees: Bachelor's **Classes:** Most classes have 10-19 students. Most lab/discussion sessions have fewer than 10 students. **Most popular majors:** Biology/Biological Sciences, General; Health And Physical Education/Fitness, General; Criminal Justice/Law Enforcement Administration. **Special Study Options:** Cross-registration; Distance learning; Double major; Dual enrollment; English as a Second Language (ESL); Honors program; Independent study; Internships; Liberal arts/career combination; Student-designed major; Teacher certification program. **Honors programs:** JETS Honors Program. **Disability Services offered to physically disabled students:** Reader services; Tutors. **Career services:** Alumni network; Alumni services

FACILITIES

Housing: Apartments for married students; Apartments for single students; Men's dorms; Special housing for disabled student; Women's dorms 95% of campus accessible to physically diasbled. **Special Academic Facilities/Equipment:** Archives. **Computers:** 100% of classrooms, 100% of dorms, 100% of libraries, 100% of dining areas, 100% of student union, 20% of common outdoor areas have wireless network access. Students can register for classes online.

CAMPUS LIFE

Environment: Rural **Activities:** Choral groups; Drama/theater; International Student Organization; Music ensembles; Pep band; Student government 33 registered organizations, 6 honor societies, 5 religious organizations. 4 fraternities, 4 sororities. **Athletics (Intercollegiate):** *Men:* baseball, basketball. *Women:* basketball, volleyball. **On-Campus Highlights:** E. W. Rand Health, Physical Education, and Recreat, J. N. Ervin Religion Center, Walk of Fame, Community and Technology Center, Meyer Science and Mathematics Center

ADMISSIONS

Freshman Academic Profile: Average high school GPA 2.6. 0% in top 10% of high school class, 6% in top 25% of high school class, 23% in top 50% of high school class. 99% from public high schools. **Test Scores:** Minimum paper TOEFL 500. **Basis for Candidate Selection:** *Other factors considered include:* rigor of secondary school record, class rank, academic GPA, standardized test scores, extracurricular activities, talent/ability, character/personal qualities. **Freshman Admission Requirements:** High school diploma is required and GED is accepted *Academic units required:* 3 English, 2 math, 1 science, 3 social studies, 7 academic electives, *Academic units recommended:* 3 English, 2 math, 1 science, 3 social studies, 7 academic electives. **Freshman Admission Statistics:** 525 applied, 92.4% admitted, 25% enrolled. **Transfer Admission Requirements:** High school transcript, college transcript(s), standardized test scores, Lowest grade transferable F. **General Admission Information:** Application fee $50. Priority deadline 5/1. Nonfall registration accepted. Admission may be deferred for a maximum of one year.

COSTS AND FINANCIAL AID

Annual tuition $8,528. Room and board $6,715. Required fees $1,080. Average book expense $1,000. **Required Forms and Deadlines:** FAFSA; Institution's own financial aid form; State aid form. **Notification of Awards:** Applicants will be notified of awards on a rolling basis beginning 5/1. **Types of Aid:** *Need-based scholarships/grants:* College/university scholarship or grant aid from institutional funds; Federal Pell; Private scholarships; SEOG; State scholarships/grants; United Negro College Fund. *Loans:* Direct PLUS loans;

Direct Subsidized Stafford Loans; Direct Unsubsidized Stafford Loans. *Student Employment:* Federal Work-Study Program available. **Financial Aid Statistics:** 94% needy freshmen, 100% needy undergrads receive need-based scholarship or grant aid. 41% freshmen, 23% undergrads receive non-need-based scholarship or grant aid. 79% freshmen, 89% undergrads receive need-based self-help aid. 3% freshmen, 6% undergrads receive athletic scholarships. 98% freshmen, 98% undergrads receive any aid. **Criteria for awarding aid:** *Non-need-based:* Academics, Athletics, Religious affiliation, State/district residency.

JEWISH THEOLOGICAL SEMINARY, ALBERT A. LIST COLLEGE

3080 Broadway, New York, NY 10027
Phone: 212-678-8832 · **Financial Aid Phone:** 212-678-8007
E-mail: lcadmissions@jtsa.edu · **CEEB Code:** 2339
Fax: 212-280-6022 · **Website:** www.jtsa.edu · **ACT Code:** 2776

This private school, affiliated with the Jewish Church, was founded in 1886. It has a 1 acre campus.

RATINGS
Admissions Selectivity Rating: 92   **Fire Safety Rating:** 60*   **Green Rating:** 60*

STUDENTS AND FACULTY
Enrollment: 177. **Student Body:** 54% female, 46% male, 84% out-of-state, 3% international (10 countries represented). Asian 0%, African American 0%, Caucasian 94%, Hispanic 1%, Native American 0%, Race unknown 2%. **Retention and Graduation:** 89% freshmen return for sophomore year. 15% grads go on to further study within 1 year. 6% grads pursue arts and sciences degrees. 6% grads pursue law degrees. 0% grads pursue business degrees. 3% grads pursue medical degrees. **Faculty:** Student/faculty ratio 6:1. 52 full-time faculty, 0% are members of minority groups, 29% are women. 0% of classes are taught by teaching assistants.

ACADEMICS
Degrees: Bachelor's; Doctoral/Professional; Doctoral/Research; Master's. **Classes:** Most classes have 10-19 students. Most lab/discussion sessions have 10-19 students. **Most popular majors:** Jewish/Judaic Studies; Bible/Biblical Studies; Talmudic Studies. **Special Study Options:** Cross-registration; Distance learning; Double major; Exchange student program (domestic); Honors program; Independent study; Internships; Liberal arts/career combination; Student-designed major; Study abroad. **Combined degree programs:** BA/MA. **Disability Services offered to physically disabled students:** Tape recorders; Tutors. **Career services:** Alumni network; Alumni services; Career/job search classes; Internships

FACILITIES
Housing: Apartments for married students; Apartments for single students; Coed dorms **Special Academic Facilities/Equipment:** The Jewish Museum and the Rare Book Room of the Library **Computers:** 100% of classrooms, 100% of dorms, 80% of libraries, 100% of dining areas, 50% of common outdoor areas have wireless network access. Students can register for classes online. Administrative functions (other than registration) can be performed online.

CAMPUS LIFE
Environment: Metropolis **Activities:** Choral groups; Concert band; Dance; Drama/theater; Jazz band; Literary magazine; Music ensembles; Musical theater; Radio station; Student government; Student newspaper; Yearbook 1 religious organizations. **Athletics (Intercollegiate):** *Men:* baseball, basketball, crew/rowing, soccer, tennis, track/field (outdoor), volleyball. *Women:* baseball, basketball, crew/rowing, soccer, tennis, track/field (outdoor), volleyball. **On-Campus Highlights:** The Library of the Jewish Theological Seminary **Environmental Initiatives:** 4-Day work week to save on electricity

ADMISSIONS
Freshman Academic Profile: Average high school GPA 3.7. **Test Scores:** SAT Math middle 50% range 620-660. SAT EBRW middle 50% range 640-700. ACT middle 50% range 30-32. Minimum paper TOEFL 600. **Basis for Candidate Selection:** *Very important factors considered include:* rigor of secondary school record, academic GPA, standardized test scores. *Important factors considered include:* class rank, application essay, recommendation(s), interview. *Other factors considered include:* extracurricular activities, talent/ability, character/personal qualities, first generation, alumni/ae relation, religious affiliation/commitment, volunteer work, level of applicant's interest. **Freshman Admission Requirements:** High school diploma is required and GED is not accepted *Academic units recommended:* 4 English, 4 math, 4 science, 4 foreign language, 1 social studies, 3 history, 4 academic electives. **Freshman Admission Statistics:** 102 applied, 61.8% admitted, 65% enrolled. **Transfer Admission Requirements:** High school transcript, college transcript(s), essay or personal statement, standardized test scores, statement of good standing from prior institution(s). **General Admission Information:** Application fee $65. Priority deadline 1/15. Regular application deadline 2/15. Nonfall registration accepted. Admission may be deferred.

COSTS AND FINANCIAL AID
Annual tuition $14,200. Required fees $800. Average book expense $500. **Required Forms and Deadlines:** Business/Farm Supplement; CSS/Financial Aid PROFILE; FAFSA; Institution's own financial aid form; Noncustodial PROFILE; State aid form. **Notification of Awards:** Applicants will be notified of awards on a rolling basis beginning 4/1. **Types of Aid:** *Need-based scholarships/grants:* College/university scholarship or grant aid from institutional funds; Private scholarships. *Loans:* Direct Subsidized Stafford Loans; Direct Unsubsidized Stafford Loans. *Student Employment:* Federal Work-Study Program available. Institutional employment available. **Financial Aid Statistics:** 100% needy freshmen, 100% needy undergrads receive need-based scholarship or grant aid. 50% freshmen, 41% undergrads receive non-need-based scholarship or grant aid. 86% freshmen, 97% undergrads receive need-based self-help aid. 0% freshmen, 0% undergrads receive athletic scholarships. **Criteria for awarding aid:** *Non-need-based:* Academics, Alumni affiliation, Leadership.

JOHN BROWN UNIVERSITY

2000 W. University Street, Siloam Springs, AR 72761
Phone: 479-524-7454 · **Financial Aid Phone:** 479-524-7424
E-mail: jbuinfo@jbu.edu · **CEEB Code:** 6321
Fax: 479-524-4196 · **Website:** www.jbu.edu · **ACT Code:** 130

This private school was founded in 1919. It has a 200 acre campus.

RATINGS
Admissions Selectivity Rating: 81   **Fire Safety Rating:** 88   **Green Rating:** 72

STUDENTS AND FACULTY
Enrollment: 1,608. **Student Body:** 59% female, 41% male, 49% out-of-state, 6% international (40 countries represented). Asian 1%, African American 2%, Caucasian 74%, Hispanic 6%, Native American 2%, Pacific Islander <1%, Two or more races 4%, Race unknown 4%. **Retention and Graduation:** 82% freshmen return for sophomore year. 59% freshmen graduate within 4 years. 73% freshmen graduate within 6 years. 18% grads go on to further study within 1 year. **Faculty:** Student/faculty ratio 14:1. 87 full-time faculty, 76% hold PhDs, 13% are members of minority groups, 32% are women. 0% of classes are taught by teaching assistants.

ACADEMICS
Degrees: Associate; Bachelor's; Master's; Post-Master's certificate **Classes:** Most classes have fewer than 10 students. **Most popular majors:** Engineering, General; Graphic Design; Registered Nursing/Registered Nurse. **Special Study Options:** Accelerated program; Distance learning; Double major; Dual enrollment; English as a Second Language (ESL); Exchange student program (domestic); Honors program; Independent study; Internships; Liberal arts/career combination; Student-designed major; Study abroad; Teacher certification program. **Honors programs:** The Honors Scholars Program consists of enriched Core Curriculum courses developed especially for gifted and highly motivated students. Emphasizing the use of primary texts, instructors challenge students through individual research, critical reflection, incisive discussion, interactive projects, and professional presentations. **Disability Services offered to physically disabled students:** Note-taking services; Reader services; Tutors. **Career services:** Alumni network; Career assessment; Career/job search classes

FACILITIES
Housing: Apartments for married students; Apartments for single students; Coed dorms; Men's dorms; Special housing for disabled student; Women's dorms 90% of campus accessible to physically diasbled. **Special Academic Facilities/Equipment:** Art Gallery, Human Anatomy Lab, TV Studio, Radio Station, Outdoor Learning Center, Center for Relationship Enrichment, Soderquist Center for Business and Ethics **Computers:** 100% of classrooms, 100% of dorms, 100% of libraries, 100% of dining areas, 100% of student union, 30% of common outdoor areas have wireless network access. Students can register for classes online. Administrative functions (other than registration) can be performed online.

CAMPUS LIFE

Environment: Village **Activities:** Campus Ministries; Choral groups; Concert band; Dance; Drama/theater; International Student Organization; Jazz band; Literary magazine; Music ensembles; Musical theater; Pep band; Radio station; Student government; Student newspaper; Student-run film society; Television station; Yearbook 20 registered organizations, 3 honor societies. **Athletics (Intercollegiate):** *Men:* basketball, golf, soccer, tennis. *Women:* basketball, soccer, swimming, tennis, volleyball. **On-Campus Highlights:** Walker Student Center, California Cafe, Chapel, Walton Lifetime Health Complex, Intramural Sports

ADMISSIONS

Freshman Academic Profile: Average high school GPA 3.7. 29% in top 10% of high school class, 58% in top 25% of high school class, 83% in top 50% of high school class. **Test Scores:** SAT Math middle 50% range 530-630. SAT EBRW middle 50% range 550-680. ACT middle 50% range 24-29. Minimum internet-based TOEFL 85. Minimum paper TOEFL 560. **Basis for Candidate Selection:** *Very important factors considered include:* academic GPA, standardized test scores, recommendation(s). *Important factors considered include:* class rank, application essay, interview, character/personal qualities, religious affiliation/commitment. *Other factors considered include:* rigor of secondary school record, extracurricular activities, talent/ability, first generation, alumni/ae relation, level of applicant's interest. **Freshman Admission Requirements:** High school diploma is required and GED is accepted *Academic units recommended:* 4 English, 3 math, 2 science, 1 science labs, 2 foreign language, 2 social studies, 1 history. **Freshman Admission Statistics:** 1,198 applied, 75.8% admitted, 36% enrolled. **Transfer Admission Requirements:** High school transcript, college transcript(s), essay or personal statement, Minimum college GPA of 2.5 required. Lowest grade transferable C. **General Admission Information:** Application fee $25. Priority deadline 5/1. Nonfall registration accepted. Admission may be deferred for a maximum of 1 year.

COSTS AND FINANCIAL AID

Annual tuition $25,000. Room and board $9,040. Required fees $1,144. Average book expense $800. **Required Forms and Deadlines:** FAFSA; Institution's own financial aid form; State aid form. **Notification of Awards:** Applicants will be notified of awards on a rolling basis beginning 3/1. **Types of Aid:** *Need-based scholarships/grants:* College/university scholarship or grant aid from institutional funds; Federal Pell; Private scholarships; SEOG; State scholarships/grants. *Loans:* Direct PLUS loans; Direct Subsidized Stafford Loans; Direct Unsubsidized Stafford Loans. *Student Employment:* Federal Work-Study Program available. Institutional employment available. **Financial Aid Statistics:** 90% needy freshmen, 91% needy undergrads receive need-based scholarship or grant aid. 89% freshmen, 69% undergrads receive non-need-based scholarship or grant aid. 81% freshmen, 59% undergrads receive need-based self-help aid. 7% freshmen, 5% undergrads receive athletic scholarships. 90% freshmen, 91% undergrads receive any aid. 59% undergrads borrow to pay for school. Average cumulative indebtedness $26,651. **Criteria for awarding aid:** *Non-need-based:* Academics, Alumni affiliation, Art, Athletics, Leadership, Music/drama.

JOHN CARROLL UNIVERSITY

1 John Carroll Boulevard, University Heights, OH 44118-4581
Phone: 216-397-4294 · **Financial Aid Phone:** 216-397-4270 · **CEEB Code:** 1342
Fax: 216-397-4981 · **Website:** http://sites.jcu.edu/ · **ACT Code:** 3282

This private school, affiliated with the Roman Catholic Church, was founded in 1886. It has a 62 acre campus.

RATINGS

Admissions Selectivity Rating: 75 **Fire Safety Rating:** 85 **Green Rating:** 76

STUDENTS AND FACULTY

Enrollment: 3,081. **Student Body:** 47% female, 53% male, 31% out-of-state, 2% international (23 countries represented). Asian 2%, African American 4%, Caucasian 85%, Hispanic 3%, Native American <1%, Pacific Islander 0%, Two or more races 2%, Race unknown 1%.
Retention and Graduation: 85% freshmen return for sophomore year. 28% grads go on to further study within 1 year. 48% grads pursue arts and sciences degrees. 7% grads pursue law degrees. 28% grads pursue business degrees. 9% grads pursue medical degrees. **Faculty:** Student/faculty ratio 13:1. 190 full-time faculty, 98% hold PhDs, 17% are members of minority groups, 43% are women. 1% of classes are taught by teaching assistants.

ACADEMICS

Degrees: Bachelor's; Certificate; Master's; Post-Bachelor's certificate; Post-Master's certificate **Classes:** Most classes have fewer than 10 students. **Most popular majors:** Speech Communication And Rhetoric; Psychology, General; Marketing/Marketing Management, General. **Special Study Options:** Accelerated program; Cooperative education program; Cross-registration; Double major; Dual enrollment; Exchange student program (domestic); Honors program; Independent study; Internships; Liberal arts/career combination; Student-designed major; Study abroad; Teacher certification program. **Honors programs:** JCU's Honors Program provides a framework of opportunities for academically outstanding students. Students have access to funds to attend one or more cultural events each semester. The program also includes opportunities to engage in faculty and student dialogue through academic seminars and social events. **Combined degree programs:** BA/MA. **Disability Services offered to physically disabled students:** Note-taking services; Reader services; Tape recorders; Tutors. **Career services:** Alumni network; Alumni services; Career assessment; Career/job search classes; Internships; Regional alumni

FACILITIES

Housing: Coed dorms; Fraternity/sorority housing; Special housing for disabled student; Wellness housing 94% of campus accessible to physically diasbled. **Special Academic Facilities/Equipment:** The first known handwritten and illuminated Bible in more than 500 years is on permanent display in The Grasselli Library and Breen Learning Center at John Carroll University. **Computers:** 100% of classrooms, 100% of dorms, 100% of libraries, 100% of dining areas, 100% of student union, 100% of common outdoor areas have wireless network access. Students can register for classes online. Administrative functions (other than registration) can be performed online.

CAMPUS LIFE

Environment: Metropolis **Activities:** Campus Ministries; Choral groups; Concert band; Dance; Drama/theater; International Student Organization; Jazz band; Literary magazine; Music ensembles; Musical theater; Pep band; Radio station; Student government; Student newspaper; Student-run film society; Television station; Yearbook 95 registered organizations, 12 honor societies, 2 religious organizations. 4 fraternities, 5 sororities. **Athletics (Intercollegiate):** *Men:* baseball, basketball, cross-country, diving, football, golf, soccer, swimming, tennis, track/field (outdoor), track/field (indoor), wrestling. *Women:* basketball, cheerleading, cross-country, diving, golf, soccer, softball, swimming, tennis, track/field (outdoor), track/field (indoor), volleyball. **On-Campus Highlights:** Einstein Bros. Bagels, Dolan Center for Science and Technology, Inn-Between Cafe (Tweener), Grasselli Library (Learning Commons), Student Center Atrium **Environmental Initiatives:** Reuse building materials on campus or divert from landfills

ADMISSIONS

Freshman Academic Profile: Average high school GPA 3.5. 20% in top 10% of high school class, 44% in top 25% of high school class, 79% in top 50% of high school class. 57% from public high schools. **Test Scores:** SAT Math middle 50% range 500-610. SAT EBRW middle 50% range 500-590. ACT middle 50% range 22-27. Minimum internet-based TOEFL 79. Minimum paper TOEFL 550. **Basis for Candidate Selection:** *Very important factors considered include:* rigor of secondary school record, academic GPA. *Important factors considered include:* application essay, standardized test scores, extracurricular activities, talent/ability, character/personal qualities, volunteer work. *Other factors considered include:* class rank, recommendation(s), interview, first generation, alumni/ae relation, geographical residence, work experience, level of applicant's interest. **Freshman Admission Requirements:** High school diploma is required and GED is accepted *Academic units required:* 4 English, 3 math, 2 science, 2 science labs, 2 foreign language, 2 history, 3 academic electives, and 2 units from above areas or other academic areas. *Academic units recommended:* 4 English, 4 math, 3 science, 3 science labs, 3 foreign language, 4 history, 4 units from above areas or other academic areas. **Freshman Admission Statistics:** 3,873 applied, 82.9% admitted, 25% enrolled. **Transfer Admission Requirements:** High school transcript, college transcript(s), essay or personal statement, standardized test scores, statement of good standing from prior institution(s). Lowest grade transferable 2. **General Admission Information:** Priority deadline 12/1. Regular application deadline 2/1. Nonfall registration accepted. Admission may be deferred for a maximum of 1 year.

COSTS AND FINANCIAL AID

Annual tuition $35,930. Room and board $10,920. Required fees $1,250. Average book expense $1,000. **Required Forms and Deadlines:** FAFSA. **Notification of Awards:** Applicants will be notified of awards on a rolling basis beginning 2/15. **Types of Aid:** *Need-based scholarships/grants:* College/university scholarship or grant aid from institutional funds; Federal Pell; Private scholarships; SEOG; State scholarships/grants. *Loans:* Direct PLUS loans; Direct Subsidized Stafford Loans; Direct Unsubsidized Stafford Loans. *Student Employment:* Federal Work-Study Program available. Institutional employment available. **Financial Aid Statistics:** 92% needy freshmen, 98% needy undergrads receive need-based scholarship or grant aid. 99% freshmen, 99% undergrads receive non-need-based scholarship or grant aid. 82% freshmen,

85% undergrads receive need-based self-help aid. 0% freshmen, 0% undergrads receive athletic scholarships. 100% freshmen, 95% undergrads receive any aid. **Criteria for awarding aid:** *Non-need-based:* Academics, Leadership.

JOHNS HOPKINS UNIVERSITY

3400 North Charles Street, Baltimore, MD 21218
Phone: 410-516-8171 · **Financial Aid Phone:** 410-516-8028
E-mail: gotojhu@jhu.edu · **CEEB Code:** 5332
Fax: 410-516-6025 · **Website:** www.jhu.edu

This private school was founded in 1876. It has a 140 acre campus.

RATINGS
Admissions Selectivity Rating: 99   **Fire Safety Rating:** 98   **Green Rating:** 92

STUDENTS AND FACULTY
Enrollment: 5,421. **Student Body:** 51% female, 49% male, 89% out-of-state, 9% international (65 countries represented). Asian 26%, African American 6%, Caucasian 33%, Hispanic 14%, Native American <1%, Pacific Islander <1%, Two or more races 5%, Race unknown 5%.
Retention and Graduation: 97% freshmen return for sophomore year. 88% freshmen graduate within 4 years. 94% freshmen graduate within 6 years. 35% grads go on to further study within 1 year. 11% grads pursue arts and sciences degrees. 1% grads pursue law degrees. 2% grads pursue business degrees. 5.7% grads pursue medical degrees. **Faculty:** Student/faculty ratio 8:1. 637 full-time faculty, 94% hold PhDs, 20% are members of minority groups, 34% are women.

ACADEMICS
Degrees: Bachelor's; Certificate; Diploma; Doctoral/Research; Master's; Post-Bachelor's certificate **Classes:** Most classes have 20-29 students. Most lab/discussion sessions have 10-19 students. **Most popular majors:** Bioengineering And Biomedical Engineering; Neuroscience; Public Health, General. **Special Study Options:** Cross-registration; Double major; Independent study; Internships; Student-designed major; Study abroad. **Combined degree programs:** BA/MA; BA/MEng. **Disability Services offered to physically disabled students:** Note-taking services; Reader services; Tape recorders; Tutors. **Career services:** Alumni network; Alumni services; Career assessment; Career/job search classes; Internships; Regional alumni

FACILITIES
Housing: Apartments for single students; Coed dorms; Special housing for disabled student; Wellness housing **Special Academic Facilities/Equipment:** Baltimore Museum of Art, on-campus Digital Media Center, art gallery, electron microscope, Space Telescope Science Institute, four major research centers **Computers:** 95% of classrooms, 100% of dorms, 100% of libraries, 90% of dining areas, 100% of student union, 50% of common outdoor areas have wireless network access. Students can register for classes online. Administrative functions (other than registration) can be performed online.

CAMPUS LIFE
Environment: Metropolis **Activities:** Campus Ministries; Choral groups; Concert band; Dance; Drama/theater; International Student Organization; Jazz band; Literary magazine; Model UN; Music ensembles; Musical theater; Opera; Pep band; Radio station; Student government; Student newspaper; Student-run film society; Symphony orchestra; Yearbook 250 registered organizations, 17 honor societies, 20 religious organizations. 12 fraternities, 7 sororities.
Athletics (Intercollegiate): *Men:* baseball, basketball, cross-country, diving, fencing, football, lacrosse, soccer, swimming, tennis, track/field (outdoor), track/field (indoor), water polo, wrestling. *Women:* basketball, cross-country, diving, fencing, field hockey, lacrosse, soccer, swimming, tennis, track/field (outdoor), track/field (indoor), volleyball. **On-Campus Highlights:** Brody Learning Commons, Gilman Hall, Undergraduate Teaching Labs, Ralph S. O'Connor Recreation Center, Mason Hall Visitor Center **Environmental Initiatives:** Comprehensive climate commitment includes reaching a 51% reduction in GHG by 2025, investing over $73 million in GHG reduction projects, and seed grants for climate researchers.

ADMISSIONS
Freshman Academic Profile: Average high school GPA 3.9. 93% in top 10% of high school class, 99% in top 25% of high school class, 100% in top 50% of high school class. 57% from public high schools. **Test Scores:** SAT Math middle 50% range 740-800. SAT EBRW middle 50% range 720-780. ACT middle 50%

range 33-35. Minimum paper TOEFL 600. **Basis for Candidate Selection:** *Very important factors considered include:* rigor of secondary school record, academic GPA, application essay, standardized test scores, recommendation(s), character/personal qualities. *Important factors considered include:* class rank, extracurricular activities, talent/ability. *Other factors considered include:* interview, first generation, alumni/ae relation, geographical residence, state residency, racial/ethnic status, volunteer work, work experience. **Freshman Admission Requirements:** High school diploma or equivalent is not required *Academic units recommended:* 4 English, 4 math, 4 science, 4 foreign language, 2 social studies, 2 history. **Freshman Admission Statistics:** 26,578 applied, 12.2% admitted, 40% enrolled. **Transfer Admission Requirements:** High school transcript, college transcript(s), essay or personal statement, statement of good standing from prior institution(s). Minimum college GPA of 3.0 required. Lowest grade transferable C. **General Admission Information:** Application fee $70. Regular application deadline 1/1. Nonfall registration accepted. Admission may be deferred for a maximum of 2 years.

COSTS AND FINANCIAL AID
Required Forms and Deadlines: CSS/Financial Aid PROFILE; FAFSA; Noncustodial PROFILE. **Notification of Awards:** Applicants will be notified of awards on or about 4/1. **Types of Aid:** *Need-based scholarships/grants:* College/university scholarship or grant aid from institutional funds; Federal Pell; Private scholarships; SEOG; State scholarships/grants. *Loans:* Direct PLUS loans; Direct Subsidized Stafford Loans; Direct Unsubsidized Stafford Loans. *Student Employment:* Federal Work-Study Program available. Institutional employment available. **Financial Aid Statistics:** 93% needy freshmen, 92% needy undergrads receive need-based scholarship or grant aid. 33% freshmen, 20% undergrads receive non-need-based scholarship or grant aid. 80% freshmen, 84% undergrads receive need-based self-help aid. 1% freshmen, 1% undergrads receive athletic scholarships. 42% undergrads borrow to pay for school. Average cumulative indebtedness $24,702. **Criteria for awarding aid:** *Need-based:* Academics, Leadership *Non-need-based:* Academics, Athletics, Leadership, State/district residency.

See page 956.

JOHNSON & WALES UNIVERSITY
AT CHARLOTTE

801 W. Trade Street, Charlotte, NC
Phone: 980-598-1100
E-mail: clt@admissions.jwu.edu
Fax: 980-598-1111 · **Website:** https://www1.jwu.edu/charlotte/

This is a private school.

RATINGS
Admissions Selectivity Rating: 67   **Fire Safety Rating:** 60*   **Green Rating:** 60*

STUDENTS AND FACULTY
Enrollment: 2,218. **Student Body:** 66% female, 34% male, 62% out-of-state, 1% international. Asian 1%, African American 37%, Caucasian 43%, Hispanic 6%, Native American <1%, Pacific Islander 0%, Two or more races 7%, Race unknown 5%.
Retention and Graduation: 76% freshmen return for sophomore year. **Faculty:** Student/faculty ratio 23:1. 83 full-time faculty,

ACADEMICS
Degrees: Associate; Bachelor's **Classes:** Most classes have fewer than 10 students. **Special Study Options:** Accelerated program; Cooperative education program; Dual enrollment; English as a Second Language (ESL); Exchange student program (domestic); Honors program; Independent study; Internships; Study abroad.

FACILITIES
Housing: Apartments for single students; Coed dorms; Special housing for disabled student; Wellness housing

CAMPUS LIFE
Activities: Campus Ministries; Dance; International Student Organization; Student government; Student newspaper; Yearbook.

ADMISSIONS
Freshman Academic Profile: Average high school GPA 3.5. **Basis for Candidate Selection:** *Very important factors considered include:* rigor of secondary school record, class rank, academic GPA. *Important factors considered include:* application essay, interview, extracurricular activities. *Other*

factors considered include: standardized test scores, recommendation(s), talent/ability, character/personal qualities, alumni/ae relation, volunteer work, work experience, level of applicant's interest. **Freshman Admission Requirements:** High school diploma is required and GED is accepted *Academic units required:* 4 English, 3 math, 3 science, 2 social studies. **Freshman Admission Statistics:** 4,537 applied, 72.4% admitted, 20% enrolled. **General Admission Information:** Nonfall registration accepted. Admission may be deferred.

COSTS AND FINANCIAL AID

Annual tuition $30,396. Average book expense $1,500.

JOHNSON & WALES UNIVERSITY AT NORTH MIAMI

Mitchell Building, North Miami, FL 33181
Phone: 1-866-598-3567
E-mail: mia@admissions.jwu.edu
Fax: 305-892-7020 • **Website:** http://admissions.jwu.edu

This is a private school.

RATINGS

Admissions Selectivity Rating: 67 **Fire Safety Rating:** 60* **Green Rating:** 60*

STUDENTS AND FACULTY

Enrollment: 1,752. **Student Body:** 63% female, 37% male, 53% out-of-state, 10% international. Asian <1%, African American 31%, Caucasian 24%, Hispanic 23%, Native American <1%, Pacific Islander <1%, Two or more races 8%, Race unknown 5%.
Retention and Graduation: 69% freshmen return for sophomore year.
Faculty: Student/faculty ratio 25:1. 57 full-time faculty,

ACADEMICS

Degrees: Associate; Bachelor's **Classes:** Most classes have 20-29 students. Most lab/discussion sessions have 20-29 students. **Special Study Options:** Accelerated program; Cooperative education program; Dual enrollment; English as a Second Language (ESL); Exchange student program (domestic); Honors program; Independent study; Internships; Study abroad.

FACILITIES

Housing: Apartments for single students; Coed dorms; Theme housing; Wellness housing

CAMPUS LIFE

Activities: Campus Ministries; Dance; International Student Organization; Music ensembles; Pep band; Student government; Student newspaper.

ADMISSIONS

Freshman Academic Profile: Average high school GPA 3.2. **Basis for Candidate Selection:** *Very important factors considered include:* rigor of secondary school record, class rank, academic GPA. *Important factors considered include:* application essay, interview, extracurricular activities. *Other factors considered include:* standardized test scores, recommendation(s), talent/ability, character/personal qualities, alumni/ae relation, volunteer work, work experience, level of applicant's interest. **Freshman Admission Requirements:** High school diploma is required and GED is accepted *Academic units required:* 4 English, 3 math, 3 science, 2 social studies. **Freshman Admission Statistics:** 4,049 applied, 75.8% admitted, 14% enrolled. **Transfer Admission Requirements:** High school transcript, college transcript(s), Minimum college GPA of 2.0 required. Lowest grade transferable C. **General Admission Information:** Nonfall registration accepted. Admission may be deferred for a maximum of 1 year.

COSTS AND FINANCIAL AID

Annual tuition $30,396. Room and board $8,268. Average book expense $1,500. **Required Forms and Deadlines:** FAFSA. **Notification of Awards:** Applicants will be notified of awards on a rolling basis beginning 3/1. **Types of Aid:** *Need-based scholarships/grants:* College/university scholarship or grant aid from institutional funds; Federal Pell; Private scholarships; SEOG; State scholarships/grants. **Financial Aid Statistics:** 94% needy undergrads receive need-based scholarship or grant aid. 72% freshmen, 63% undergrads receive non-need-based scholarship or grant aid. 98% freshmen, 97% undergrads receive need-based self-help aid. 0% freshmen, 0% undergrads receive athletic scholarships. **Criteria for awarding aid:** *Need-based:* Academics *Non-need-based:* Academics, Alumni affiliation, Job skills, Leadership, State/district residency.

JOHNSON AND WALES UNIVERSITY—DENVER

7150 Montview Boulevard, Denver, CO 80220
Phone: 303-256-9300
E-mail: den@admissions.jwu.edu
Fax: 303-256-9333 • **Website:** http://www.jwu.edu/denver

This private school was founded in 1914.

RATINGS

Admissions Selectivity Rating: 66 **Fire Safety Rating:** 60* **Green Rating:** 60*

STUDENTS AND FACULTY

Enrollment: 1,356. **Student Body:** 59% female, 41% male, 63% out-of-state, 1% international. Asian 2%, African American 9%, Caucasian 54%, Hispanic 19%, Native American <1%, Pacific Islander <1%, Two or more races 8%, Race unknown 6%.
Retention and Graduation: 75% freshmen return for sophomore year.
Faculty: Student/faculty ratio 16:1. 52 full-time faculty,

ACADEMICS

Degrees: Associate; Bachelor's; Master's **Classes:** Most classes have 10-19 students. Most lab/discussion sessions have 10-19 students. **Most popular majors:** Business/Commerce, General; Hotel/Motel Administration/Management; Restaurant/Food Services Management. **Special Study Options:** Accelerated program; Cooperative education program; Dual enrollment; English as a Second Language (ESL); Exchange student program (domestic); Honors program; Independent study; Internships; Study abroad.

FACILITIES

Housing: Apartments for single students; Coed dorms; Special housing for disabled student; Wellness housing

CAMPUS LIFE

Activities: Campus Ministries; Dance; International Student Organization; Student government; Student newspaper; Yearbook.

ADMISSIONS

Freshman Academic Profile: Average high school GPA 3.2. **Basis for Candidate Selection:** *Very important factors considered include:* rigor of secondary school record, class rank, academic GPA. *Important factors considered include:* application essay, interview, extracurricular activities. *Other factors considered include:* standardized test scores, recommendation(s), talent/ability, character/personal qualities, alumni/ae relation, volunteer work, work experience, level of applicant's interest. **Freshman Admission Requirements:** High school diploma is required and GED is accepted *Academic units required:* 4 English, 3 math, 3 science, 2 social studies. **Freshman Admission Statistics:** 2,319 applied, 81.2% admitted, 18% enrolled. **Transfer Admission Requirements:** High school transcript, college transcript(s), Minimum college GPA of 2.0 required. Lowest grade transferable C. **General Admission Information:** Nonfall registration accepted. Admission may be deferred.

COSTS AND FINANCIAL AID

Annual tuition $30,396. Average book expense $1,500. **Required Forms and Deadlines:** FAFSA. **Notification of Awards:** Applicants will be notified of awards on a rolling basis beginning 3/1. **Types of Aid:** *Need-based scholarships/grants:* College/university scholarship or grant aid from institutional funds; Federal Pell; Private scholarships; SEOG; State scholarships/grants. **Financial Aid Statistics:** 91% needy freshmen, 84% needy undergrads receive need-based scholarship or grant aid. 85% freshmen, 75% undergrads receive non-need-based scholarship or grant aid. 90% freshmen, 94% undergrads receive need-based self-help aid. 0% freshmen, 0% undergrads receive athletic scholarships. **Criteria for awarding aid:** *Need-based:* Academics *Non-need-based:* Academics, Alumni affiliation, Job skills, Leadership, State/district residency.

JOHNSON AND WALES UNIVERSITY— PROVIDENCE CAMPUS

8 Abbott Park Place, Providence, RI
Phone: 1-401-598-1000
E-mail: pvd@admissions.jwu.edu
Website: http://admissions.jwu.edu/ • **ACT Code:** 3804

This private school was founded in 1914. It has a 50 acre campus.

RATINGS
Admissions Selectivity Rating: 66   **Fire Safety Rating:** 60*   **Green Rating:** 60*

STUDENTS AND FACULTY
Enrollment: 8,718. **Student Body:** 60% female, 40% male, 81% out-of-state, 9% international. Asian 1%, African American 11%, Caucasian 56%, Hispanic 11%, Native American <1%, Pacific Islander <1%, Two or more races 8%, Race unknown 4%.
Retention and Graduation: 78% freshmen return for sophomore year.
Faculty: Student/faculty ratio 20:1. 294 full-time faculty.

ACADEMICS
Degrees: Associate; Bachelor's; Certificate; Diploma; Doctoral/Research; Master's **Classes:** Most classes have fewer than 10 students. Most lab/discussion sessions have fewer than 10 students. **Special Study Options:** Accelerated program; Cooperative education program; Dual enrollment; English as a Second Language (ESL); Exchange student program (domestic); Honors program; Independent study; Internships; Study abroad.

FACILITIES
Housing: Apartments for single students; Coed dorms; Special housing for disabled student; Wellness housing **Special Academic Facilities/Equipment:** Culinary Archives and Museum. **Computers:** Students can register for classes online. Administrative functions (other than registration) can be performed online.

CAMPUS LIFE
Environment: City **Activities:** Campus Ministries; Dance; International Student Organization; Student government; Student newspaper; Yearbook. **Athletics (Intercollegiate):** *Men:* baseball, basketball, cheerleading, cross-country, equestrian sports, golf, ice hockey, soccer, tennis, volleyball, wrestling. *Women:* basketball, cheerleading, cross-country, equestrian sports, golf, ice hockey, soccer, softball, tennis, volleyball.

ADMISSIONS
Freshman Academic Profile: Average high school GPA 3.1. **Basis for Candidate Selection:** *Very important factors considered include:* rigor of secondary school record, class rank, academic GPA. *Important factors considered include:* application essay, interview, extracurricular activities. *Other factors considered include:* standardized test scores, recommendation(s), talent/ability, character/personal qualities, alumni/ae relation, volunteer work, work experience, level of applicant's interest. **Freshman Admission Requirements:** High school diploma is required and GED is accepted *Academic units required:* 4 English, 3 math, 3 science, 2 social studies. **Freshman Admission Statistics:** 11,971 applied, 81.9% admitted, 20% enrolled. **Transfer Admission Requirements:** High school transcript, college transcript(s), Minimum college GPA of 2.0 required. Lowest grade transferable C. **General Admission Information:** Nonfall registration accepted. Admission may be deferred.

COSTS AND FINANCIAL AID
Annual tuition $30,396. Average book expense $1,500. **Required Forms and Deadlines:** FAFSA. **Notification of Awards:** Applicants will be notified of awards on a rolling basis beginning 3/1. **Types of Aid:** *Need-based scholarships/grants:* College/university scholarship or grant aid from institutional funds; Federal Pell; Private scholarships; SEOG; State scholarships/grants. **Financial Aid Statistics:** 90% needy freshmen, 84% needy undergrads receive need-based scholarship or grant aid. 71% freshmen, 59% undergrads receive non-need-based scholarship or grant aid. 94% freshmen, 95% undergrads receive need-based self-help aid. 0% freshmen, 0% undergrads receive athletic scholarships. **Criteria for awarding aid:** *Need-based:* Academics *Non-need-based:* Academics, Alumni affiliation, Job skills, Leadership, State/district residency.

JOHNSON BIBLE COLLEGE

7900 Johnson Drive, Knoxville, TN 37998
Phone: 800-827-2122 • **Financial Aid Phone:** 865-251-2303
E-mail: http://www.johnsonu.edu/ • **CEEB Code:** 1345
Fax: 865-251-2336 • **Website:** http://www.johnsonu.edu/ • **ACT Code:** 3968

This private school, affiliated with the Christian (Nondenominational) Church, was founded in 1893. It has a 350 acre campus.

RATINGS
Admissions Selectivity Rating: 75   **Fire Safety Rating:** 81   **Green Rating:** 60*

STUDENTS AND FACULTY
Student Body: 78% out-of-state, 2% international (12 countries represented). Asian 1%, African American 2%, Caucasian 90%, Hispanic 2%, Native American 1%, Two or more races 2%, Race unknown 0%.
Retention and Graduation: 73% freshmen return for sophomore year.
Faculty: Student/faculty ratio 21:1. 30 full-time faculty, 63% hold PhDs, 0% are members of minority groups, 17% are women. 0% of classes are taught by teaching assistants.

ACADEMICS
Degrees: Associate; Bachelor's; Certificate; Master's **Classes:** Most classes have 10-19 students. **Special Study Options:** Accelerated program; Cooperative education program; Distance learning; Double major; English as a Second Language (ESL); Honors program; Independent study; Internships; Teacher certification program. **Disability Services offered to physically disabled students:** Reader services; Tape recorders.

FACILITIES
Housing: Apartments for married students; Men's dorms; Women's dorms **Computers:** Students can register for classes online. Administrative functions (other than registration) can be performed online.

CAMPUS LIFE
Environment: Rural **Activities:** Choral groups; Music ensembles; Musical theater; Radio station; Student government; Yearbook 3 honor societies, 3 religious organizations. **Athletics (Intercollegiate):** *Men:* baseball, basketball, cheerleading, soccer. *Women:* basketball, cheerleading, volleyball. **On-Campus Highlights:** women's residence hall, men's residence hall, global-education-tech building

ADMISSIONS
Freshman Academic Profile: Average high school GPA 3.0. 21% in top 10% of high school class, 48% in top 25% of high school class, 78% in top 50% of high school class. **Test Scores:** SAT Math middle 50% range 470-560. SAT EBRW middle 50% range 480-612. ACT middle 50% range 20-26. Minimum paper TOEFL 500. **Basis for Candidate Selection:** *Very important factors considered include:* rigor of secondary school record, class rank, standardized test scores, recommendation(s), character/personal qualities, religious affiliation/commitment. *Important factors considered include:* application essay, interview. *Other factors considered include:* extracurricular activities, talent/ability, alumni/ae relation, volunteer work. **Freshman Admission Requirements:** High school diploma is required and GED is accepted **Freshman Admission Statistics:** 296 applied, 94.6% admitted, 57% enrolled. **Transfer Admission Requirements:** High school transcript, college transcript(s), essay or personal statement, statement of good standing from prior institution(s). Lowest grade transferable C. **General Admission Information:** Application fee $35. Regular application deadline 7/1. Nonfall registration accepted. Admission may be deferred for a maximum of one year.

COSTS AND FINANCIAL AID
Annual tuition $7,000. Room and board $4,890. Required fees $770. Average book expense $1,300. **Required Forms and Deadlines:** FAFSA; Institution's own financial aid form. **Notification of Awards:** Applicants will be notified of awards on or about 3/30. **Types of Aid:** *Need-based scholarships/grants:* College/university scholarship or grant aid from institutional funds; Federal Pell; Private scholarships; SEOG; State scholarships/grants. *Loans: Student Employment:* Federal Work-Study Program available. Institutional employment available. **Financial Aid Statistics:** 97% needy freshmen, 98% needy undergrads receive need-based scholarship or grant aid. 24% freshmen, 26% undergrads receive non-need-based scholarship or grant aid. 59% freshmen, 58% undergrads receive need-based self-help aid. 0% freshmen, 0% undergrads receive athletic scholarships. 97% undergrads receive any aid. **Criteria for awarding aid:** *Non-need-based:* Academics, Minority status, Music/drama, Religious affiliation, State/district residency.

JOHNSON STATE COLLEGE

337 College Hill, Johnson, VT 05656-9408
Phone: 802-635-1219 • **Financial Aid Phone:** 802-635-1380
E-mail: jscadmissions@jsc.edu • **CEEB Code:** 3766
Fax: 802-635-1230 • **Website:** www.jsc.edu • **ACT Code:** 4316

This public school was founded in 1828. It has a 350 acre campus.

RATINGS

Admissions Selectivity Rating: 76   **Fire Safety Rating:** 80   **Green Rating:** 60*

STUDENTS AND FACULTY

Enrollment: 1,640. **Student Body:** 62% female, 38% male, 28% out-of-state, <1% international (2 countries represented). Asian 1%, African American 3%, Caucasian 85%, Hispanic 1%, Native American 1%, Pacific Islander 0%, Two or more races 0%, Race unknown 8%.
Retention and Graduation: 64% freshmen return for sophomore year.
Faculty: Student/faculty ratio 16:1. 50 full-time faculty, 98% hold PhDs, 4% are members of minority groups, 36% are women. 0% of classes are taught by teaching assistants.

ACADEMICS

Degrees: Associate; Bachelor's; Master's; Post-Bachelor's certificate; Terminal Associate **Classes:** Most classes have 10-19 students. Most lab/discussion sessions have 10-19 students. **Most popular majors:** Elementary Education And Teaching; Visual And Performing Arts, Other; Tourism And Travel Services Management. **Special Study Options:** Cross-registration; Double major; Dual enrollment; English as a Second Language (ESL); Exchange student program (domestic); External degree program; Honors program; Independent study; Internships; Study abroad; Teacher certification program. **Disability Services offered to physically disabled students:** Note-taking services; Reader services; Tape recorders; Tutors. **Career services:** Alumni network; Alumni services; Career assessment; Career/job search classes; Internships; Regional alumni

FACILITIES

Housing: Apartments for married students; Apartments for single students; Coed dorms; Theme housing; Wellness housing 80% of campus accessible to physically diasbled. **Special Academic Facilities/Equipment:** Art gallery, visual arts center, child development center, human performance lab, 1,000-acre nature preserve, snowboard terrain park, dance studio **Computers:** Students can register for classes online. Administrative functions (other than registration) can be performed online.

CAMPUS LIFE

Environment: Rural **Activities:** Choral groups; Concert band; Dance; Drama/theater; Jazz band; Literary magazine; Music ensembles; Musical theater; Radio station; Student government; Student newspaper; Yearbook 30 registered organizations, 1 honor society, 4 religious organizations. **Athletics (Intercollegiate):** *Men:* basketball, cross-country, golf, lacrosse, soccer, tennis. *Women:* basketball, cross-country, soccer, softball, tennis, volleyball. **On-Campus Highlights:** Dibden Center For the Arts, Snowboarding Hill, Movie Cinema, Disc Golf Course, SHAPE Athletic Facility **Environmental Initiatives:** We compose.

ADMISSIONS

Freshman Academic Profile: 34% in top 10% of high school class, 66% in top 25% of high school class, 68% in top 50% of high school class. **Test Scores:** SAT Math middle 50% range 430-550. SAT EBRW middle 50% range 430-550. ACT middle 50% range 20-28. Minimum internet-based TOEFL 61. Minimum paper TOEFL 500. **Basis for Candidate Selection:** *Very important factors considered include:* rigor of secondary school record, standardized test scores. *Important factors considered include:* class rank, academic GPA, application essay, recommendation(s), talent/ability, character/personal qualities. *Other factors considered include:* interview, extracurricular activities, volunteer work, work experience. **Freshman Admission Requirements:** High school diploma is required and GED is accepted *Academic units required:* 4 English, 2 math, 2 science, 1 science labs, 3 social studies, 2 history, *Academic units recommended:* 4 English, 3 math, 3 science, 2 science labs, 1 foreign language, 3 social studies, 3 history. **Freshman Admission Statistics:** 973 applied, 86.6% admitted, 34% enrolled. **Transfer Admission Requirements:** High school transcript, college transcript(s), essay or personal statement, statement of good standing from prior institution(s). Minimum college GPA of 2.0 required. Lowest grade transferable C-. **General Admission Information:** Application fee $40. Priority deadline 3/1. Nonfall registration accepted. Admission may be deferred for a maximum of 1 year.

COSTS AND FINANCIAL AID

Annual in-state tuition $8,446. Annual out-of-state tuition $19,008. Room and board $8,446. Required fees $1,113. Average book expense $1,000. **Required Forms and Deadlines:** FAFSA; State aid form. **Notification of Awards:** Applicants will be notified of awards on a rolling basis beginning 4/1. **Types of Aid:** *Need-based scholarships/grants:* College/university scholarship or grant aid from institutional funds; Federal Pell; Private scholarships; SEOG; State scholarships/grants. *Loans:* Direct PLUS loans; Direct Subsidized Stafford Loans; Direct Unsubsidized Stafford Loans. *Student Employment:* Federal Work-Study Program available. Institutional employment available. **Financial Aid Statistics:** 93% needy freshmen, 89% needy undergrads receive need-based scholarship or grant aid. 4% freshmen, 3% undergrads receive non-need-based scholarship or grant aid. 95% freshmen, 95% undergrads receive need-based self-help aid. 0% freshmen, 0% undergrads receive athletic scholarships. 87% freshmen, 82% undergrads receive any aid. **Criteria for awarding aid:** *Need-based:* Academics, Alumni affiliation, Art, Leadership, Music/drama *Non-need-based:* Academics, Art, Leadership, Music/drama, State/district residency.

JONES INTERNATIONAL UNIVERSITY

9697 E. Mineral Avenue, Centennial, CO 80112
Phone: 800-811-5663
E-mail: admissions@international.edu
Fax: 303-799-0966 • **Website:** www.jonesinternational.edu

This is a private school.

RATINGS

Admissions Selectivity Rating: 68   **Fire Safety Rating:** 60*   **Green Rating:** 60*

STUDENTS AND FACULTY

Enrollment: 22. **Student Body:** 50% female, 50% male, international.
Retention and Graduation: 97% freshmen return for sophomore year.
Faculty:

ACADEMICS

Degrees: Bachelor's; Certificate; Master's **Special Study Options:** Accelerated program; Distance learning; External degree program.

ADMISSIONS

Freshman Admission Requirements: High school diploma is required and GED is accepted **Freshman Admission Statistics:** 22 applied, 100.0% admitted, 86% enrolled. **Transfer Admission Requirements:** High school transcript, college transcript(s), Lowest grade transferable C. **General Admission Information:** Application fee $75. Nonfall registration accepted. Admission may be deferred for a maximum of 1 year.

COSTS AND FINANCIAL AID

Annual tuition $835. Required fees $75. Average book expense $100.

JUDSON COLLEGE (AL)

302 Bibb Street, Marion, AL 36756
Phone: 334-683-5110 • **Financial Aid Phone:** 334-683-5157
E-mail: admissions@judson.edu • **CEEB Code:** 1349
Fax: 334-683-5282 • **Website:** www.judson.edu • **ACT Code:** 22

This private school, affiliated with the Baptist Church, was founded in 1838. It has a 80 acre campus.

RATINGS

Admissions Selectivity Rating: 76   **Fire Safety Rating:** 75   **Green Rating:** 60*

STUDENTS AND FACULTY

Enrollment: 315. **Student Body:** 97% female, 3% male, 29% out-of-state, 1% international (3 countries represented). Asian 0%, African American 12%, Caucasian 83%, Hispanic 1%, Native American 1%, Race unknown 1%.
Retention and Graduation: 61% freshmen return for sophomore year. 15% grads go on to further study within 1 year. 83% grads pursue arts and sciences degrees. 0% grads pursue law degrees. 0% grads pursue business degrees. 17% grads pursue medical degrees. **Faculty:** Student/faculty ratio 11:1. 18 full-time faculty, 83% hold PhDs, 0% are members of minority groups, 39% are women. 0% of classes are taught by teaching assistants.

ACADEMICS

Degrees: Bachelor's **Classes:** Most classes have 10-19 students. Most lab/discussion sessions have 10-19 students. **Most popular majors:** Elementary Education And Teaching; Biology/Biological Sciences, General; Psychology, General. **Special Study Options:** Accelerated program; Cross-registration; Distance learning; Double major; Dual enrollment; Independent study; Internships; Student-designed major; Study abroad; Teacher certification program. **Disability Services offered to physically disabled students:** Tutors. **Career services:** Alumni services; Career assessment; Internships

FACILITIES

Housing: Women's dorms 50% of campus accessible to physically diasbled. **Special Academic Facilities/Equipment:** Alabama Women's Hall of Fame. **Computers:** 50% of classrooms, 100% of dorms, 100% of libraries, 100% of student union, have wireless network access.

CAMPUS LIFE

Environment: Rural **Activities:** Campus Ministries; Choral groups; Drama/theater; Literary magazine; Marching band; Music ensembles; Student government; Student newspaper; Yearbook 23 registered organizations, 8 honor societies, 1 religious organization. **Athletics (Intercollegiate):** *Women:* basketball, equestrian sports, soccer, softball, volleyball. **On-Campus Highlights:** Residence Hall Lobbies, Gym, Computer Labs, Club House, Student Center

ADMISSIONS

Freshman Academic Profile: Average high school GPA 3.4. 32% in top 10% of high school class, 22% in top 25% of high school class, 84% in top 50% of high school class. 78% from public high schools. **Test Scores:** SAT Math middle 50% range 470-590. SAT EBRW middle 50% range 540-590. ACT middle 50% range 19-26. Minimum paper TOEFL 500. **Basis for Candidate Selection:** *Very important factors considered include:* class rank, academic GPA, standardized test scores. *Other factors considered include:* rigor of secondary school record, recommendation(s), extracurricular activities, talent/ability, character/personal qualities, alumni/ae relation, level of applicant's interest. **Freshman Admission Requirements:** High school diploma is required and GED is accepted *Academic units required:* 4 English, 2 math, 2 science, 3 social studies, 5 academic electives, *Academic units recommended:* 4 English, 4 math, 4 science, 2 foreign language, 4 social studies, 2 history. **Freshman Admission Statistics:** 306 applied, 83.7% admitted, 38% enrolled. **Transfer Admission Requirements:** college transcript(s), Minimum college GPA of 2.0 required. Lowest grade transferable C-. **General Admission Information:** Application fee $35. Nonfall registration accepted. Admission may be deferred for a maximum of 1 year.

COSTS AND FINANCIAL AID

Annual tuition $12,327. Room and board $7,969. Required fees $220. Average book expense $1,200. **Required Forms and Deadlines:** FAFSA; Institution's own financial aid form; State aid form. **Notification of Awards:** Applicants will be notified of awards on a rolling basis beginning 11/15. **Types of Aid:** *Need-based scholarships/grants:* College/university scholarship or grant aid from institutional funds; Federal Pell; Private scholarships; SEOG; State scholarships/grants. *Loans:* Student Employment: Federal Work-Study Program available. Institutional employment available. **Financial Aid Statistics:** 97% needy freshmen, 97% needy undergrads receive need-based scholarship or grant aid. 11% freshmen, 12% undergrads receive non-need-based scholarship or grant aid. 75% freshmen, 86% undergrads receive need-based self-help aid. 12% freshmen, 12% undergrads receive athletic scholarships. 99% freshmen, 96% undergrads receive any aid. **Criteria for awarding aid:** *Need-based:* Academics, Alumni affiliation, Art, Athletics, Leadership, Music/drama *Non-need-based:* Academics, Alumni affiliation, Art, Athletics, Music/drama, Religious affiliation, State/district residency.

THE JUILLIARD SCHOOL

60 Lincoln Center Plaza, New York, NY 10023-6588
Phone: 212-799-2000 ext.223 · **Financial Aid Phone:** 212-799-5000
E-mail: admissions@juilliard.edu · **CEEB Code:** 2340
Fax: 212-769-6420 · **Website:** www.juilliard.edu

This private school was founded in 1905.

RATINGS

Admissions Selectivity Rating: 84   **Fire Safety Rating:** 69   **Green Rating:** 60*

STUDENTS AND FACULTY

Enrollment: 499. **Student Body:** 49% female, 51% male, 89% out-of-state, 26% international (40 countries represented). Asian 14%, African American 5%,

Caucasian 40%, Hispanic 7%, Native American 0%, Pacific Islander 0%, Two or more races 6%, Race unknown 1%.
Faculty: Student/faculty ratio 4:1. 136 full-time faculty, 15% are members of minority groups, 39% are women.

ACADEMICS

Degrees: Bachelor's; Diploma; Doctoral; Doctoral/Research; Master's; Post-Bachelor's certificate; Post-Master's certificate **Classes:** Most classes have 20-29 students. **Most popular majors:** Keyboard Instruments; Voice And Opera; Stringed Instruments. **Special Study Options:** Accelerated program; Double major.

FACILITIES

Housing: Coed dorms **Special Academic Facilities/Equipment:** 2 recital halls, 1 theater (1000 ppl), 1 drama theater (200 ppl), 15 two-story studios, 35 private teaching studios, 106 practice rooms, organ studios, 200+ pianos, recording studio, The Peter Jay Sharp Special Collections Room. **Computers:** Students can register for classes online. Administrative functions (other than registration) can be performed online.

CAMPUS LIFE

Environment: Metropolis **Activities:** Dance; Drama/theater; International Student Organization; Jazz band; Music ensembles; Musical theater; Opera; Student government; Student newspaper; Symphony orchestra 5 registered organizations, 2 religious organizations. **On-Campus Highlights:** Lila Acheson Wallace Library, Lincoln Center, Rose Building—cafeteria, Juilliard Bookstore

ADMISSIONS

Test Scores: Minimum paper TOEFL 533. **Basis for Candidate Selection:** *Very important factors considered include:* interview, talent/ability. *Other factors considered include:* academic GPA, application essay, recommendation(s), extracurricular activities, character/personal qualities. **Freshman Admission Requirements:** High school diploma is required and GED is accepted *Academic units recommended:* 4 visual/performing arts. **Freshman Admission Statistics:** 2,533 applied, 6.6% admitted, 65% enrolled. **Transfer Admission Requirements:** college transcript(s), essay or personal statement, interview, Lowest grade transferable C. **General Admission Information:** Application fee $110. Priority deadline 12/1. Regular application deadline 12/1. Nonfall registration accepted.

COSTS AND FINANCIAL AID

Annual tuition $41,310. Required fees $100. Average book expense $580. **Required Forms and Deadlines:** CSS/Financial Aid PROFILE; FAFSA. **Notification of Awards:** Applicants will be notified of awards on or about 4/1. **Types of Aid:** *Need-based scholarships/grants:* College/university scholarship or grant aid from institutional funds; Federal Pell; Private scholarships; SEOG; State scholarships/grants. *Loans:* Direct PLUS loans; Direct Subsidized Stafford Loans; Direct Unsubsidized Stafford Loans. **Financial Aid Statistics:** 94% needy freshmen, 97% needy undergrads receive need-based scholarship or grant aid. 7% freshmen, 2% undergrads receive non-need-based scholarship or grant aid. 100% freshmen, 100% undergrads receive need-based self-help aid. 0% freshmen, 0% undergrads receive athletic scholarships. Average cumulative indebtedness $32,493. **Criteria for awarding aid:** *Need-based:* Music/drama *Non-need-based:* Music/drama.

JUNIATA COLLEGE

1700 Moore Street, Huntingdon, PA 16652
Phone: 814-641-3420 · **Financial Aid Phone:** 814-641-3144
E-mail: admissions@juniata.edu · **CEEB Code:** 2341
Fax: 814-641-3100 · **Website:** www.juniata.edu · **ACT Code:** 3600

This private school was founded in 1876. It has a 800 acre campus.

RATINGS

Admissions Selectivity Rating: 83   **Fire Safety Rating:** 87   **Green Rating:** 70

STUDENTS AND FACULTY

Enrollment: 1,371. **Student Body:** 55% female, 45% male, 34% out-of-state, 8% international (37 countries represented). Asian 4%, African American 3%, Caucasian 75%, Hispanic 5%, Native American <1%, Pacific Islander 0%, Two or more races 3%, Race unknown 2%.
Retention and Graduation: 81% freshmen return for sophomore year. 80% freshmen graduate within 4 years. 84% freshmen graduate within 6 years. 28% grads go on to further study within 1 year. 35% grads pursue arts and sciences

degrees. 0% grads pursue law degrees. 6% grads pursue business degrees. 15% grads pursue medical degrees. **Faculty:** Student/faculty ratio 11:1. 118 full-time faculty, 92% hold PhDs, 8% are members of minority groups, 45% are women. 0% of classes are taught by teaching assistants.

ACADEMICS

Degrees: Bachelor's; Master's **Classes:** Most classes have 10-19 students. Most lab/discussion sessions have fewer than 10 students. **Most popular majors:** Biology/Biological Sciences, General; Physical Sciences; Business/Commerce, General. **Special Study Options:** Distance learning; Double major; Dual enrollment; English as a Second Language (ESL); Exchange student program (domestic); Honors program; Independent study; Internships; Student-designed major; Study abroad; Teacher certification program. **Honors programs:** Entire college is considered to be an honors program. **Combined degree programs:** BA/DDS; BA/JD; BA/MA; BA/MD; BA/MEng. **Disability Services offered to physically disabled students:** Reader services; Tape recorders; Tutors. **Career services:** Alumni network; Alumni services; Career assessment; Career/job search classes; Internships

FACILITIES

Housing: Apartments for single students; Coed dorms; Special housing for international students; Women's dorms 75% of campus accessible to physically diasbled. **Special Academic Facilities/Equipment:** Environmental Studies Field Station,Juniata Museum of Art, Early Childhood Education Center, Ceramics studio and Anagama Kiln, Nature preserve and Peace Chapel, Observatory, Electron microscopes, Nuclear magnetic resonance spectrometers, Human Interaction Lab. three story, free form theater. **Computers:** 100% of classrooms, 100% of dorms, 100% of libraries, 100% of dining areas, 100% of student union, 100% of common outdoor areas have wireless network access. Students can register for classes online. Administrative functions (other than registration) can be performed online. Undergraduates are required to own a computer.

CAMPUS LIFE

Environment: Village **Activities:** Campus Ministries; Choral groups; Concert band; Dance; Drama/theater; International Student Organization; Jazz band; Music ensembles; Musical theater; Radio station; Student government; Student newspaper; Student-run film society; Symphony orchestra 94 registered organizations, 12 honor societies, 7 religious organizations. **Athletics (Intercollegiate):** *Men:* baseball, basketball, cross-country, football, soccer, tennis, track/field (outdoor), track/field (indoor), volleyball. *Women:* basketball, cross-country, field hockey, soccer, softball, swimming, tennis, track/field (outdoor), track/field (indoor), volleyball. **On-Campus Highlights:** von Liebig Science Center, Founders Hall, The Quad, Eagles Landing, Kepple Hall, Juniata's Integrated Media and Studio Arts Building **Environmental Initiatives:** 60% today and 75% by 2012 Electric in Wind RECS

ADMISSIONS

Freshman Academic Profile: Average high school GPA 3.7. 31% in top 10% of high school class, 64% in top 25% of high school class, 91% in top 50% of high school class. 70% from public high schools. **Test Scores:** SAT Math middle 50% range 540-640. SAT EBRW middle 50% range 540-650. ACT middle 50% range 22-29. Minimum internet-based TOEFL 79. Minimum paper TOEFL 550. **Basis for Candidate Selection:** *Very important factors considered include:* rigor of secondary school record, academic GPA, application essay, standardized test scores, recommendation(s), character/personal qualities. *Important factors considered include:* interview, extracurricular activities, talent/ability, first generation, volunteer work. *Other factors considered include:* alumni/ae relation, geographical residence, state residency, racial/ethnic status, level of applicant's interest. **Freshman Admission Requirements:** High school diploma is required and GED is accepted *Academic units required:* 4 English, 3 math, 3 science, 2 science labs, 1 social studies, 3 history. **Freshman Admission Statistics:** 2,289 applied, 70.8% admitted, 21% enrolled. **Transfer Admission Requirements:** High school transcript, college transcript(s), essay or personal statement, Minimum college GPA of 2.5 required. Lowest grade transferable C-. **General Admission Information:** Priority deadline 11/15. Regular application deadline 2/15. Nonfall registration accepted. Admission may be deferred for a maximum of 1 year.

COSTS AND FINANCIAL AID

Annual tuition $44,772. Room and board $12,521. Required fees $825. Average book expense $1,000. **Required Forms and Deadlines:** FAFSA. **Types of Aid:** *Need-based scholarships/grants:* College/university scholarship or grant aid from institutional funds; Federal Pell; Private scholarships; SEOG; State scholarships/grants. *Loans:* Direct PLUS loans; Direct Subsidized Stafford Loans; Direct Unsubsidized Stafford Loans. *Student Employment:* Federal Work-Study Program available. Institutional employment available. **Financial Aid Statistics:** 99% needy freshmen, 98% needy undergrads receive need-based scholarship or grant aid. 97% freshmen, 100% undergrads receive non-need-based scholarship or grant aid. 86% freshmen, 89% undergrads receive need-based self-help aid. 0% freshmen receive athletic scholarships. 100% freshmen, 100% undergrads receive any aid. 73% undergrads borrow to pay

for school. Average cumulative indebtedness $36,338. **Criteria for awarding aid:** *Need-based:* Academics, Minority status, Music/drama *Non-need-based:* Academics, Alumni affiliation, Art, Minority status, Music/drama.

KALAMAZOO COLLEGE

1200 Academy Street, Kalamazoo, MI 49006
Phone: 269-337-7166 · **Financial Aid Phone:** 269-337-7192
E-mail: admission@kzoo.edu · **CEEB Code:** 1365
Fax: 269-337-7390 · **Website:** www.kzoo.edu · **ACT Code:** 2018

This private school was founded in 1833. It has a 60 acre campus.

RATINGS
Admissions Selectivity Rating: 88   **Fire Safety Rating:** 83   **Green Rating:** 60*

STUDENTS AND FACULTY

Enrollment: 1,415. **Student Body:** 57% female, 43% male, 33% out-of-state, 6% international (32 countries represented). Asian 8%, African American 8%, Caucasian 57%, Hispanic 13%, Native American 0%, Pacific Islander <1%, Two or more races 4%, Race unknown 3%.
Retention and Graduation: 90% freshmen return for sophomore year. 82% freshmen graduate within 4 years. 86% freshmen graduate within 6 years.
Faculty: Student/faculty ratio 13:1. 100 full-time faculty, 96% hold PhDs, 27% are members of minority groups, 52% are women. 0% of classes are taught by teaching assistants.

ACADEMICS

Degrees: Bachelor's **Classes:** Most classes have fewer than 10 students. Most lab/discussion sessions have 10-19 students. **Most popular majors:** English Language And Literature, General; Psychology, General; Economics, General. **Special Study Options:** Accelerated program; Cross-registration; Double major; Dual enrollment; English as a Second Language (ESL); Exchange student program (domestic); Independent study; Internships; Student-designed major; Study abroad. **Disability Services offered to physically disabled students:** Note-taking services; Tape recorders; Tutors. **Career services:** Alumni network; Alumni services; Career assessment; Career/job search classes; Internships; Regional alumni

FACILITIES

Housing: Coed dorms; Theme housing; Wellness housing 25% of campus accessible to physically diasbled. **Special Academic Facilities/Equipment:** Science center, Rare book room **Computers:** 100% of classrooms, 70% of dorms, 100% of libraries, 100% of dining areas, 100% of student union, have wireless network access. Students can register for classes online. Administrative functions (other than registration) can be performed online.

CAMPUS LIFE

Environment: City **Activities:** Campus Ministries; Choral groups; Concert band; Dance; Drama/theater; International Student Organization; Jazz band; Literary magazine; Model UN; Music ensembles; Musical theater; Radio station; Student government; Student newspaper; Symphony orchestra; Television station; Yearbook 50 registered organizations, 3 honor societies, 5 religious organizations. **Athletics (Intercollegiate):** *Men:* baseball, basketball, cross-country, diving, football, golf, soccer, swimming, tennis. *Women:* basketball, cross-country, diving, golf, soccer, softball, swimming, tennis, volleyball. **On-Campus Highlights:** Upjohn Library Commons, The Quad, Coffee Shop, Hicks Student Center, Dorm Lounges in Residence Halls **Environmental Initiatives:** The College is currently involved in a LEED registered expansion and renovation of Hicks Student Center. The project is expected to receive Silver certification when completed in summer 2008.

ADMISSIONS

Freshman Academic Profile: Average high school GPA 3.8. 50% in top 10% of high school class, 87% in top 25% of high school class, 99% in top 50% of high school class. 80% from public high schools. **Test Scores:** SAT Math middle 50% range 580-690. SAT EBRW middle 50% range 600-690. ACT middle 50% range 26-30. Minimum internet-based TOEFL 84. Minimum paper TOEFL 550. **Basis for Candidate Selection:** *Very important factors considered include:* rigor of secondary school record, academic GPA, extracurricular activities. *Important factors considered include:* application essay, recommendation(s). *Other factors considered include:* standardized test scores, interview, talent/ability, character/personal qualities, first generation, alumni/ae relation, geographical residence, state residency, racial/ethnic status, volunteer work, work experience, level of applicant's interest. **Freshman Admission Requirements:** High school diploma is required and GED is accepted *Academic units required:* 4 English, 3 math, 3 science, 3 foreign language, 2 social studies, 2 history, *Academic units recommended:* 4 English, 4 math, 4 science, 4 foreign language, 2 social studies, 2 history. **Freshman Admission Statistics:** 3,434 applied, 73.4% admitted, 18% enrolled. **Transfer Admission Requirements:** High school transcript, college transcript(s), essay or personal statement, standardized test scores, statement of good standing from prior institution(s). Lowest grade transferable C. **General Admission Information:** Priority deadline 11/15. Regular application deadline 1/15. Nonfall registration accepted. Admission may be deferred for a maximum of 1 year.

COSTS AND FINANCIAL AID
Annual tuition $42,510. Room and board $8,886. Required fees $336. Average book expense $720. **Required Forms and Deadlines:** FAFSA. **Notification of Awards:** Applicants will be notified of awards on a rolling basis beginning 1/15. **Types of Aid:** *Need-based scholarships/grants:* College/ university scholarship or grant aid from institutional funds; Federal Pell; Private scholarships; SEOG; State scholarships/grants. *Loans:* Direct PLUS loans; Direct Subsidized Stafford Loans; Direct Unsubsidized Stafford Loans. *Student Employment:* Federal Work-Study Program available. Institutional employment available. **Financial Aid Statistics:** 97% needy freshmen, 99% needy undergrads receive need-based scholarship or grant aid. 23% freshmen, 17% undergrads receive non-need-based scholarship or grant aid. 79% freshmen, 82% undergrads receive need-based self-help aid. 0% freshmen, 0% undergrads receive athletic scholarships. 98% freshmen, 97% undergrads receive any aid. 61% undergrads borrow to pay for school. Average cumulative indebtedness $27,653. **Criteria for awarding aid:** *Need-based:* Academics *Non-need-based:* Academics, Alumni affiliation, Art, Leadership, Music/drama.

KANSAS CITY ART INSTITUTE

4415 Warwick Boulevard, Kansas City, MO 64111
Phone: 800-522-5224 · **Financial Aid Phone:** 816-802-3337
E-mail: admiss@kcai.edu · **CEEB Code:** 6330
Fax: 816-802-3309 · **Website:** www.kcai.edu · **ACT Code:** 2277

This private school was founded in 1885. It has a 15 acre campus.

RATINGS
Admissions Selectivity Rating: 80   **Fire Safety Rating:** 71   **Green Rating:** 60*

STUDENTS AND FACULTY
Enrollment: 671. **Student Body:** 55% female, 45% male, 62% out-of-state, 1% international (6 countries represented). Asian 4%, African American 3%, Caucasian 80%, Hispanic 6%, Native American 1%, Race unknown 6%. **Retention and Graduation:** 78% freshmen return for sophomore year. 40% grads go on to further study within 1 year. **Faculty:** Student/faculty ratio 12:1. 51 full-time faculty, 84% hold PhDs, 2% are members of minority groups, 37% are women. 0% of classes are taught by teaching assistants.

ACADEMICS
Degrees: Bachelor's **Classes:** Most classes have fewer than 10 students. Most lab/discussion sessions have 20-29 students. **Most popular majors:** Design And Visual Communications, General; Film/Video And Photographic Arts, Other; Painting. **Special Study Options:** Cross-registration; Double major; Exchange student program (domestic); Independent study; Internships; Student-designed major; Study abroad. **Disability Services offered to physically disabled students:** Tape recorders; Tutors. **Career services:** Alumni network; Alumni services; Career assessment; Career/job search classes; Internships; Regional alumni

FACILITIES
Housing: Apartments for single students; Coed dorms **Special Academic Facilities/Equipment:** H and R Block Art Space **Computers:** Students can register for classes online. Administrative functions (other than registration) can be performed online.

CAMPUS LIFE
Environment: Metropolis **Activities:** Student government. **On-Campus Highlights:** Dodge Painting Building, Cafe Nerman, Jannes Library-Learning Center, H&R Block Artspace, Green space in center of campus

ADMISSIONS
Freshman Academic Profile: Average high school GPA 3.2. 11% in top 10% of high school class, 39% in top 25% of high school class, 73% in top 50% of high school class. 80% from public high schools. **Test Scores:** SAT Math middle 50% range 430-590. SAT EBRW middle 50% range 430-580. ACT middle 50% range 20-25. Minimum internet-based TOEFL 79. Minimum paper TOEFL

550. **Basis for Candidate Selection:** *Very important factors considered include:* recommendation(s). *Important factors considered include:* rigor of secondary school record, academic GPA, application essay, standardized test scores. *Other factors considered include:* interview, extracurricular activities, talent/ability, character/personal qualities, first generation, volunteer work, work experience, level of applicant's interest. **Freshman Admission Requirements:** High school diploma is required and GED is accepted *Academic units recommended:* 3 social studies, 3 academic electives, 4 units from above areas or other academic areas. **Freshman Admission Statistics:** 603 applied, 72.3% admitted, 44% enrolled. **Transfer Admission Requirements:** High school transcript, college transcript(s), essay or personal statement, statement of good standing from prior institution(s). Minimum college GPA of 2.5 required. Lowest grade transferable C. **General Admission Information:** Application fee $35. Priority deadline 1/15. Nonfall registration accepted. Admission may be deferred.

COSTS AND FINANCIAL AID
Annual tuition $27,220. Room and board $8,294. Average book expense $1,500. **Required Forms and Deadlines:** FAFSA. **Notification of Awards:** Applicants will be notified of awards on a rolling basis beginning 4/1. **Types of Aid:** *Need-based scholarships/grants:* College/university scholarship or grant aid from institutional funds; Federal Pell; SEOG; State scholarships/grants. *Loans: Student Employment:* Federal Work-Study Program available. Institutional employment available. **Financial Aid Statistics:** 100% needy freshmen, 100% needy undergrads receive need-based scholarship or grant aid. 15% freshmen, 9% undergrads receive non-need-based scholarship or grant aid. 78% freshmen, 87% undergrads receive need-based self-help aid. 0% freshmen, 0% undergrads receive athletic scholarships. 99% freshmen, 95% undergrads receive any aid. **Criteria for awarding aid:** *Need-based:* Academics, Art *Non-need-based:* Academics, Art.

KANSAS STATE UNIVERSITY

110 Anderson Hall, Manhattan, KS 66506
Phone: 785-532-6250 · **Financial Aid Phone:** 785-532-6420
E-mail: k-state@k-state.edu · **CEEB Code:** 6334
Fax: 785-532-6393 · **Website:** www.k-state.edu · **ACT Code:** 1428

This public school was founded in 1863. It has a 668 acre campus.

RATINGS
Admissions Selectivity Rating: 76   **Fire Safety Rating:** 88   **Green Rating:** 64

STUDENTS AND FACULTY
Enrollment: 18,171. **Student Body:** 47% female, 53% male, 18% out-of-state, 5% international (107 countries represented). Asian 1%, African American 3%, Caucasian 78%, Hispanic 7%, Native American <1%, Pacific Islander <1%, Two or more races 4%, Race unknown 1%. **Retention and Graduation:** 84% freshmen return for sophomore year. 33% freshmen graduate within 4 years. 63% freshmen graduate within 6 years. 22% grads go on to further study within 1 year. **Faculty:** Student/faculty ratio 18:1. 1,092 full-time faculty, 85% hold PhDs, 17% are members of minority groups, 43% are women. 17% of classes are taught by teaching assistants.

ACADEMICS
Degrees: Associate; Bachelor's; Certificate; Doctoral/Professional; Doctoral/ Research; Master's; Post-Bachelor's certificate **Classes:** Most classes have 20-29 students. Most lab/discussion sessions have 10-19 students. **Most popular majors:** Animal Sciences, General; Mechanical Engineering; Business Administration And Management, General. **Special Study Options:** Cooperative education program; Distance learning; Double major; Dual enrollment; English as a Second Language (ESL); Exchange student program (domestic); Honors program; Independent study; Internships; Liberal arts/career combination; Study abroad; Teacher certification program. **Honors programs:** The University Honors Program is an opportunity for undergraduate students from all colleges to enhance their education with special classes and opportunities for personal growth. **Disability Services offered to physically disabled students:** Note-taking services; Reader services; Tape recorders; Tutors. **Career services:** Alumni services; Career assessment; Career/job search classes

FACILITIES
Housing: Apartments for married students; Apartments for single students; Coed dorms; Cooperative housing; Fraternity/sorority housing; Men's dorms;

Special housing for international students; Women's dorms 75% of campus accessible to physically diasbled. **Special Academic Facilities/Equipment:** South Asian area study center, education communications center, center for cancer research, planetarium, nuclear reactor/accelerator, Beach Art museum. **Computers:** 85% of classrooms, 100% of dorms, 100% of libraries, 100% of dining areas, 100% of student union, 10% of common outdoor areas have wireless network access. Students can register for classes online. Administrative functions (other than registration) can be performed online.

CAMPUS LIFE

Environment: Town **Activities:** Campus Ministries; Choral groups; Concert band; Dance; Drama/theater; International Student Organization; Jazz band; Marching band; Music ensembles; Musical theater; Pep band; Radio station; Student government; Student newspaper; Symphony orchestra; Television station; Yearbook 594 registered organizations, 36 honor societies, 37 religious organizations. 28 fraternities, 16 sororities. **Athletics (Intercollegiate):** *Men:* baseball, basketball, cheerleading, cross-country, football, golf, track/field (outdoor), track/field (indoor). *Women:* basketball, cheerleading, crew/rowing, cross-country, equestrian sports, golf, tennis, track/field (outdoor), track/field (indoor), volleyball. **On-Campus Highlights:** Peters Recreation Complex; Sports Complexes: Wagner Field, Bramlage Coliseum, K-State Student Union, Ahearn Fieldhouse, Beach Museum of Art **Environmental Initiatives:** A university-wide task force for long-term visioning and planning in all areas of the university, including campus operations, curriculum, research, and external relations/outreach.

ADMISSIONS

Freshman Academic Profile: Average high school GPA 3.5. 25% in top 10% of high school class, 51% in top 25% of high school class, 80% in top 50% of high school class. 80% from public high schools. **Test Scores:** ACT middle 50% range 22-28. **Basis for Candidate Selection:** *Very important factors considered include:* rigor of secondary school record, class rank, academic GPA, standardized test scores. *Important factors considered include:* level of applicant's interest. *Other factors considered include:* recommendation(s). **Freshman Admission Requirements:** High school diploma is required and GED is accepted *Academic units required:* 4 English, 3 math, 3 science, 3 social studies, 3 academic electives. **Freshman Admission Statistics:** 8,310 applied, 94.6% admitted, 43% enrolled. **Transfer Admission Requirements:** college transcript(s), Minimum college GPA of 2.0 required. Lowest grade transferable C. **General Admission Information:** Application fee $40. Nonfall registration accepted.

COSTS AND FINANCIAL AID

Required Forms and Deadlines: FAFSA. **Notification of Awards:** Applicants will be notified of awards on a rolling basis beginning 4/1. **Types of Aid:** *Need-based scholarships/grants:* College/university scholarship or grant aid from institutional funds; Federal Pell; Private scholarships; SEOG; State scholarships/grants. *Loans:* Direct PLUS loans; Direct Subsidized Stafford Loans; Direct Unsubsidized Stafford Loans. *Student Employment:* Federal Work-Study Program available. Institutional employment available. **Financial Aid Statistics:** 54% needy freshmen, 56% needy undergrads receive need-based scholarship or grant aid. 77% freshmen, 52% undergrads receive non-need-based scholarship or grant aid. 66% freshmen, 75% undergrads receive need-based self-help aid. 2% freshmen, 2% undergrads receive athletic scholarships. 57% undergrads borrow to pay for school. Average cumulative indebtedness $27,198. **Criteria for awarding aid:** *Non-need-based:* Academics, Alumni affiliation, Art, Athletics, Leadership, Music/drama, State/district residency.

KANSAS WESLEYAN UNIVERSITY

100 E. Claflin, Salina, KS 67401
Financial Aid Phone: 785-827-5541
Fax: 785-827-0927 · **Website:** www.kwu.edu · **ACT Code:** 1434

This private school, affiliated with the Methodist Church, was founded in 1886. It has a 28 acre campus.

RATINGS

Admissions Selectivity Rating: 84   **Fire Safety Rating:** 80   **Green Rating:** 60*

STUDENTS AND FACULTY

Enrollment: 742. **Student Body:** 57% female, 43% male, 29% out-of-state, 2% international (8 countries represented). Asian 1%, African American 9%, Caucasian 77%, Hispanic 9%, Native American 1%, Race unknown 0%. **Retention and Graduation:** 53% freshmen return for sophomore year. 30% grads go on to further study within 1 year. 24% grads pursue arts and sciences

degrees. **Faculty:** Student/faculty ratio 15:1. 42 full-time faculty, 67% hold PhDs, 38% are women. 0% of classes are taught by teaching assistants.

ACADEMICS

Degrees: Associate; Bachelor's; Master's **Classes:** Most classes have fewer than 10 students. Most lab/discussion sessions have 10-19 students. **Special Study Options:** Cross-registration; Double major; Honors program; Independent study; Internships; Student-designed major; Study abroad; Teacher certification program. **Honors programs:** Alpha Chi Beta Beta Beta Sigma Pi Sigma Alpha Psi Omega Phi Alpha Theta. **Career services:** Alumni services; Career assessment; Internships; Regional alumni

FACILITIES

Housing: Apartments for married students; Apartments for single students; Coed dorms; Men's dorms; Special housing for disabled student; Women's dorms 95% of campus accessible to physically diasbled. **Computers:**

CAMPUS LIFE

Environment: Town **Activities:** Campus Ministries; Choral groups; Concert band; Dance; Drama/theater; International Student Organization; Jazz band; Literary magazine; Model UN; Music ensembles; Musical theater; Pep band; Student government; Student newspaper; Symphony orchestra; Yearbook 20 registered organizations, 5 honor societies, 3 religious organizations. **Athletics (Intercollegiate):** *Men:* baseball, basketball, cheerleading, cross-country, football, golf, racquetball, soccer, tennis, track/field (outdoor). *Women:* basketball, cheerleading, cross-country, golf, racquetball, soccer, softball, tennis, track/field (outdoor), volleyball. **On-Campus Highlights:** NEW Student Center & Gym, Sam's Chapel, dorms, library, Science Hall

ADMISSIONS

Freshman Academic Profile: Average high school GPA 3.2. 9% in top 10% of high school class, 32% in top 25% of high school class, 62% in top 50% of high school class. **Test Scores:** SAT Math middle 50% range 500-590. SAT EBRW middle 50% range 420-520. ACT middle 50% range 22-. **Basis for Candidate Selection:** *Very important factors considered include:* academic GPA, standardized test scores. **Freshman Admission Requirements:** High school diploma is required and GED is accepted **Freshman Admission Statistics:** 442 applied, 60.6% admitted, 43% enrolled. **Transfer Admission Requirements:** college transcript(s), Minimum college GPA of 2.0 required. Lowest grade transferable D. **General Admission Information:** Application fee $20. Nonfall registration accepted. Admission may be deferred.

COSTS AND FINANCIAL AID

Annual tuition $18,200. Room and board $6,400. Average book expense $800. **Required Forms and Deadlines:** FAFSA. **Types of Aid:** *Need-based scholarships/grants:* College/university scholarship or grant aid from institutional funds; Federal Pell; Private scholarships; SEOG; State scholarships/grants. *Loans:* Direct PLUS loans; Direct Subsidized Stafford Loans; Direct Unsubsidized Stafford Loans. *Student Employment:* Federal Work-Study Program available. **Financial Aid Statistics:** 0% undergrads receive non-need-based scholarship or grant aid. 0% freshmen, 0% undergrads receive need-based self-help aid. 0% freshmen, 0% undergrads receive athletic scholarships. 75% undergrads receive any aid. **Criteria for awarding aid:** *Need-based:* Academics, Alumni affiliation, Art, Athletics, Music/drama *Non-need-based:* Academics, Alumni affiliation, Art, Athletics, Music/drama.

KEAN UNIVERSITY

1000 Morris Ave, PO Box 411, Union, NJ 07083-0411
Phone: 908-737-7100 · **Financial Aid Phone:** 908-737-3190
E-mail: admitme@kean.edu · **CEEB Code:** 2517
Fax: 908-737-7105 · **Website:** www.kean.edu · **ACT Code:** 2582

This public school was founded in 1855. It has a 185 acre campus.

RATINGS

Admissions Selectivity Rating: 73   **Fire Safety Rating:** 98   **Green Rating:** 73

STUDENTS AND FACULTY

Enrollment: 11,761. **Student Body:** 60% female, 40% male, 2% out-of-state, 3% international (43 countries represented). Asian 5%, African American 20%, Caucasian 33%, Hispanic 28%, Native American <1%, Pacific Islander <1%, Two or more races 2%, Race unknown 8%. **Retention and Graduation:** 76% freshmen return for sophomore year. 21% freshmen graduate within 4 years. 50% freshmen graduate within 6 years. **Faculty:** Student/faculty ratio 17:1. 333 full-time faculty, 81% hold PhDs, 31% are members of minority groups, 55% are women.

ACADEMICS

Degrees: Bachelor's; Doctoral; Doctoral/Professional; Doctoral/Research; Master's; Post-Master's certificate **Classes:** Most classes have 10-19 students. **Most popular majors:** Psychology, General; Criminal Justice/Law Enforcement Administration; Business Administration And Management, General. **Special Study Options:** Accelerated program; Cooperative education program; Cross-registration; Distance learning; Double major; Dual enrollment; English as a Second Language (ESL); Exchange student program (domestic); External degree program; Honors program; Independent study; Internships; Study abroad; Teacher certification program. **Honors programs:** Please see our online Undergraduate Catalog available at: www.kean.edu **Combined degree programs:** BA/MA. **Disability Services offered to physically disabled students:** Note-taking services; Tape recorders; Tutors. **Career services:** Alumni network; Alumni services; Career assessment; Career/job search classes; Internships

FACILITIES

Housing: Apartments for single students; Coed dorms; Special housing for disabled student; Special housing for international students 100% of campus accessible to physically diasbled. **Special Academic Facilities/Equipment:** Liberty Hall Museum, Holocaust Resource Center, Harwood Arena, Human Rights Institute, Wynona Moore Lipman Ethnic Studies Center, Planetarium **Computers:** 100% of classrooms, 100% of dorms, 100% of libraries, 100% of dining areas, 100% of student union, 100% of common outdoor areas have wireless network access. Students can register for classes online. Administrative functions (other than registration) can be performed online.

CAMPUS LIFE

Environment: City **Activities:** Campus Ministries; Choral groups; Concert band; Dance; Drama/theater; International Student Organization; Jazz band; Literary magazine; Music ensembles; Musical theater; Pep band; Radio station; Student government; Student newspaper; Student-run film society; Symphony orchestra; Television station; Yearbook 143 registered organizations, 23 honor societies, 6 religious organizations. 16 fraternities, 17 sororities. **Athletics (Intercollegiate):** *Men:* baseball, basketball, football, lacrosse, soccer, track/field (outdoor). *Women:* basketball, field hockey, lacrosse, soccer, softball, tennis, track/field (outdoor), volleyball. **On-Campus Highlights:** University (Student) Center, Harwood Arena Sports Complex, Green Lane Academic Bldg, New Jersey Center for Science, Technology & Mathematics, Maxine and Jack Lane Center for Academic Success (CAS) **Environmental Initiatives:** Creation of a bachelor of science degree in sustainability.

ADMISSIONS

Freshman Academic Profile: Average high school GPA 3.0. **Test Scores:** SAT Math middle 50% range 440-530. SAT EBRW middle 50% range 440-540. ACT middle 50% range 16-22. Minimum internet-based TOEFL 79. Minimum paper TOEFL 550. **Basis for Candidate Selection:** *Very important factors considered include:* rigor of secondary school record, academic GPA. *Important factors considered include:* standardized test scores. *Other factors considered include:* application essay, recommendation(s), interview, extracurricular activities, talent/ability, character/personal qualities, alumni/ae relation, volunteer work, work experience. **Freshman Admission Requirements:** High school diploma is required and GED is accepted *Academic units required:* 4 English, 3 math, 2 science, 2 science labs, 2 history, 5 academic electives, *Academic units recommended:* 4 English, 3 math, 2 science, 2 science labs, 2 foreign language, 2 social studies, 2 history, 5 academic electives. **Freshman Admission Statistics:** 8,851 applied, 82.2% admitted, 25% enrolled. **Transfer Admission Requirements:** college transcript(s), statement of good standing from prior institution(s). Minimum college GPA of 2.0 required. Lowest grade transferable C. **General Admission Information:** Application fee $75. Priority deadline 4/30. Regular application deadline 8/15. Nonfall registration accepted. Admission may be deferred for a maximum of 1 semester.

COSTS AND FINANCIAL AID

Required Forms and Deadlines: FAFSA. **Notification of Awards:** Applicants will be notified of awards on a rolling basis beginning 11/1. **Types of Aid:** *Need-based scholarships/grants:* College/university scholarship or grant aid from institutional funds; Federal Pell; Private scholarships; SEOG; State scholarships/grants. *Loans:* Direct PLUS loans; Direct Subsidized Stafford Loans; Direct Unsubsidized Stafford Loans. *Student Employment:* Federal Work-Study Program available. Institutional employment available. **Financial Aid Statistics:** 67% needy freshmen, 70% needy undergrads receive need-based scholarship or grant aid. 17% freshmen, 11% undergrads receive non-need-based scholarship or grant aid. 98% freshmen, 97% undergrads receive need-based self-help aid. 0% freshmen, 0% undergrads receive athletic scholarships. 82% freshmen, 74% undergrads receive any aid. 75% undergrads borrow to pay for school. Average cumulative indebtedness $33,693. **Criteria for awarding aid:** *Non-need-based:* Academics, Art, Leadership, Music/drama.

KEENE STATE COLLEGE

229 Main Street, Keene, NH 03435-2604
Phone: 603-358-2276 · **Financial Aid Phone:** 603-358-2283
E-mail: admissions@keene.edu · **CEEB Code:** 3472
Fax: 603-358-2767 · **Website:** www.keene.edu · **ACT Code:** 2510

This public school was founded in 1909. It has a 150 acre campus.

RATINGS

Admissions Selectivity Rating: 73   **Fire Safety Rating:** 93   **Green Rating:** 93

STUDENTS AND FACULTY

Enrollment: 3,688. **Student Body:** 55% female, 45% male, 57% out-of-state, <1% international (9 countries represented). Asian 2%, African American 2%, Caucasian 86%, Hispanic 4%, Native American <1%, Pacific Islander <1%, Two or more races 2%, Race unknown 4%.
Retention and Graduation: 71% freshmen return for sophomore year. 53% freshmen graduate within 4 years. 62% freshmen graduate within 6 years.
Faculty: 0% of classes are taught by teaching assistants.

ACADEMICS

Degrees: Bachelor's; Certificate; Master's; Post-Bachelor's certificate; Post-Master's certificate **Classes:** Most classes have 10-19 students. Most lab/discussion sessions have 20-29 students. **Most popular majors:** Elementary Education And Teaching; Occupational Safety And Health Technology/Technician; Psychology, General. **Special Study Options:** Accelerated program; Cooperative education program; Distance learning; Double major; Exchange student program (domestic); Honors program; Independent study; Internships; Liberal arts/career combination; Student-designed major; Study abroad; Teacher certification program. **Honors programs:** The Keene State College Honors Program provides exceptional students with intellectual stimulation and academically rich experiences for personal and professional growth. National Society of Collegiate Scholars. **Disability Services offered to physically disabled students:** Note-taking services; Reader services; Tape recorders; Tutors. **Career services:** Alumni network; Alumni services; Career assessment; Career/job search classes; Internships

FACILITIES

Housing: Apartments for single students; Coed dorms; Fraternity/sorority housing; Theme housing; Wellness housing; Women's dorms 98% of campus accessible to physically diasbled. **Special Academic Facilities/Equipment:** Thorne-Sagendorph Art gallery, Redfern Arts Center, Recreational Center, Science Center, Mason Library, Media Arts Center, Cohen Center for Holocaust Studies, Center for Writing, Child Development Center, Alumni Center **Computers:** 10% of classrooms, 100% of libraries, 50% of dining areas, 80% of student union, have wireless network access. Students can register for classes online. Administrative functions (other than registration) can be performed online.

CAMPUS LIFE

Environment: Village **Activities:** Campus Ministries; Choral groups; Concert band; Dance; Drama/theater; International Student Organization; Jazz band; Literary magazine; Music ensembles; Musical theater; Radio station; Student government; Student newspaper; Student-run film society; Television station; Yearbook 100 registered organizations, 21 honor societies, 4 religious organizations. 4 fraternities, 5 sororities. **Athletics (Intercollegiate):** *Men:* baseball, basketball, cheerleading, cross-country, diving, lacrosse, soccer, swimming, track/field (outdoor), track/field (indoor). *Women:* basketball, cheerleading, cross-country, diving, field hockey, lacrosse, soccer, softball, swimming, track/field (outdoor), track/field (indoor), volleyball. **On-Campus Highlights:** Technology, Design, and Safety Center, Mason Library, Young Student Center, Night Owl Cafe, Arts Center on Brickyard Pond, Science Center **Environmental Initiatives:** LEED Silver residence hall (awarded 2008)

ADMISSIONS

Freshman Academic Profile: Average high school GPA 3.0. 6% in top 10% of high school class, 21% in top 25% of high school class, 55% in top 50% of high school class. **Test Scores:** SAT Math middle 50% range 450-560. SAT EBRW middle 50% range 480-580. ACT middle 50% range 18-24. Minimum internet-based TOEFL 61. Minimum paper TOEFL 550. **Basis for Candidate Selection:** *Important factors considered include:* rigor of secondary school record, academic GPA, application essay, recommendation(s). *Other factors considered include:* class rank, standardized test scores, extracurricular activities, talent/ability, character/personal qualities, first generation, alumni/ae relation, racial/ethnic status, volunteer work, work experience, level of applicant's interest. **Freshman Admission Requirements:** High school diploma is required and GED is accepted *Academic units required:* 4 English, 3 math, 3 science, 2 social studies, 2 academic electives. **Freshman Admission**

Statistics: 5,580 applied, 82.7% admitted, 20% enrolled. **Transfer Admission Requirements:** High school transcript, college transcript(s), essay or personal statement, statement of good standing from prior institution(s). Minimum college GPA of 2.0 required. Lowest grade transferable C. **General Admission Information:** Application fee $50. Regular application deadline 4/1. Nonfall registration accepted. Admission may be deferred for a maximum of 1 year.

COSTS AND FINANCIAL AID
Annual out-of-state tuition $19,352. Room and board $10,390. Required fees $2,645. Average book expense $900. **Required Forms and Deadlines:** FAFSA. **Types of Aid:** *Need-based scholarships/grants:* College/university scholarship or grant aid from institutional funds; Federal Pell; Private scholarships; SEOG; State scholarships/grants. *Loans:* Direct PLUS loans; Direct Subsidized Stafford Loans; Direct Unsubsidized Stafford Loans. *Student Employment:* Federal Work-Study Program available. Institutional employment available. **Financial Aid Statistics:** 70% needy freshmen, 70% needy undergrads receive need-based scholarship or grant aid. 65% freshmen, 50% undergrads receive non-need-based scholarship or grant aid. 89% freshmen, 91% undergrads receive need-based self-help aid. 0% freshmen, 0% undergrads receive athletic scholarships. 94% freshmen, 89% undergrads receive any aid. 84% undergrads borrow to pay for school. Average cumulative indebtedness $41,016. **Criteria for awarding aid:** *Need-based:* Alumni affiliation *Non-need-based:* Academics, Alumni affiliation, Art, Music/drama.

KENDALL COLLEGE OF ART AND DESIGN OF FERRIS STATE UNIVERSITY

17 Fountain Street NW, Grand Rapids, MI 49503-3002
Phone: 616-451-2787 · **Financial Aid Phone:** 616-451-2787
E-mail: brittons@ferris.edu · **CEEB Code:** 1983
Fax: 616-831-9689 · **Website:** www.kcad.edu · **ACT Code:** 1983

This public school was founded in 1928. It has a 2 acre campus.

RATINGS
Admissions Selectivity Rating: 70 **Fire Safety Rating:** 60* **Green Rating:** 60*

STUDENTS AND FACULTY
Student Body: 13% out-of-state, (15 countries represented).
Retention and Graduation: 12% grads go on to further study within 1 year. 12% grads pursue arts and sciences degrees. **Faculty:** Student/faculty ratio 15:1. 50 full-time faculty, 6% hold PhDs, 4% are members of minority groups, 0% of classes are taught by teaching assistants.

ACADEMICS
Degrees: Bachelor's; Master's **Classes:** Most classes have 10-19 students. Most lab/discussion sessions have 10-19 students. **Most popular majors:** Interior Design; Graphic Design; Illustration. **Special Study Options:** Cooperative education program; Double major; Dual enrollment; Independent study; Internships; Liberal arts/career combination; Study abroad; Teacher certification program. **Disability Services offered to physically disabled students:** Note-taking services; Reader services; Tape recorders; Tutors. **Career services:** Alumni network; Alumni services; Career/job search classes; Internships; Regional alumni

FACILITIES
Housing: Apartments for married students; Apartments for single students; Other (please specify) 100% of campus accessible to physically diasbled. **Computers:** 100% of classrooms, 100% of libraries, 100% of student union, have wireless network access. Students can register for classes online. Administrative functions (other than registration) can be performed online. Undergraduates are required to own a computer.

CAMPUS LIFE
Environment: Metropolis **Activities:** 12 registered organizations, 1 religious organization. **On-Campus Highlights:** Studio Spaces, Studio Class Rooms, Library, Student Commons, Labs

ADMISSIONS
Freshman Academic Profile: Average high school GPA 3.1. 10% in top 10% of high school class, 20% in top 25% of high school class, 75% in top 50% of high school class. **Test Scores:** Minimum internet-based TOEFL 61. Minimum paper TOEFL 500. **Basis for Candidate Selection:** *Very important factors considered include:* rigor of secondary school record, academic GPA, application essay, standardized test scores, talent/ability. *Important factors considered include:* interview, character/personal qualities. *Other factors considered*

include: class rank, recommendation(s), extracurricular activities. **Freshman Admission Requirements:** High school diploma is required and GED is accepted **Freshman Admission Statistics:** 338 applied, 78.1% admitted, 91% enrolled. **Transfer Admission Requirements:** High school transcript, college transcript(s), essay or personal statement, Lowest grade transferable C. **General Admission Information:** Application fee $30. Nonfall registration accepted. Admission may be deferred for a maximum of one semester.

COSTS AND FINANCIAL AID
Annual out-of-state tuition $19,220. Required fees $420. Average book expense $3,604. **Required Forms and Deadlines:** FAFSA. **Notification of Awards:** Applicants will be notified of awards on a rolling basis beginning 4/1. **Types of Aid:** *Need-based scholarships/grants:* College/university scholarship or grant aid from institutional funds; Federal Pell; Private scholarships; SEOG; State scholarships/grants. *Loans:* Direct PLUS loans; Direct Subsidized Stafford Loans; Direct Unsubsidized Stafford Loans. *Student Employment:* Federal Work-Study Program available. Institutional employment available. **Criteria for awarding aid:** *Non-need-based:* Academics, Alumni affiliation, Art.

KENNESAW STATE UNIVERSITY

1000 Chastain Road, Kennesaw, GA 30144-5591
Phone: 770-423-6300 · **Financial Aid Phone:** 770-423-6074
E-mail: ksuadmit@kennesaw.edu · **CEEB Code:** 5359
Fax: 470-578-9169 · **Website:** http://www.kennesaw.edu · **ACT Code:** 833

This public school was founded in 1963. It has a 602 acre campus.

RATINGS
Admissions Selectivity Rating: 88 **Fire Safety Rating:** 92 **Green Rating:** 96

STUDENTS AND FACULTY
Enrollment: 32,312. **Student Body:** 47% female, 53% male, 12% out-of-state, 2% international (134 countries represented). Asian 5%, African American 21%, Caucasian 56%, Hispanic 10%, Native American <1%, Pacific Islander <1%, Two or more races 5%, Race unknown 2%.
Retention and Graduation: 78% freshmen return for sophomore year. 12% freshmen graduate within 4 years. 42% freshmen graduate within 6 years. **Faculty:** Student/faculty ratio 20:1. 1,151 full-time faculty, 78% hold PhDs, 25% are members of minority groups, 50% are women. 0% of classes are taught by teaching assistants.

ACADEMICS
Degrees: Bachelor's; Certificate; Doctoral/Research; Master's; Post-Bachelor's certificate; Post-Master's certificate **Classes:** Most classes have fewer than 10 students. Most lab/discussion sessions have 10-19 students. **Most popular majors:** Biology/Biological Sciences, General; Psychology, General; Registered Nursing/Registered Nurse. **Special Study Options:** Cooperative education program; Cross-registration; Distance learning; Double major; Dual enrollment; English as a Second Language (ESL); Exchange student program (domestic); Honors program; Internships; Study abroad; Teacher certification program; Weekend college. **Honors programs:** Honors College: The Honors College houses the University Honors Program, including the President's Emerging Global Scholars cohort and the Great Books cohort, available to entering first-year students. the University Honors Program provides more challenging educational experiences for eligible students eager to broaden themselves intellectually, enhance the critical thinking skills essential to most careers, and join an intimate community of like-minded peers. The mission of the President's Emerging Global Scholars (PEGS) program is to accelerate the personal, professional, and academic development of exceptional Honors students. professional, and academic development of exceptional Honors students. The objective of PEGS is to prepare our students to actively engage in their communities, develop global competencies, and grow as exceptional scholars. The Great Books program is a select cohort within the University Honors Program. The cohort is limited to twenty (20) students who are chosen by the Great Books Steering Committee. **Disability Services offered to physically disabled students:** Note-taking services; Reader services; Tape recorders; Tutors. **Career services:** Alumni network; Alumni services; Career assessment; Career/job search classes; Internships

FACILITIES
Housing: Apartments for single students; Theme housing 100% of campus accessible to physically diasbled. **Special Academic Facilities/Equipment:** Museum of History and Holocaust Education; Zuckerman Museum of Art; Bentley Rare Book Collection; Dr. Bobbie Bailey & Family Performance Center **Computers:** 100% of classrooms, 100% of libraries, 100% of dining areas, 100% of student union, 5% of common outdoor areas have wireless

network access. Students can register for classes online. Administrative functions (other than registration) can be performed online.

CAMPUS LIFE

Environment: Town **Activities:** Campus Ministries; Choral groups; Concert band; Dance; Drama/theater; International Student Organization; Jazz band; Literary magazine; Marching band; Music ensembles; Musical theater; Opera; Pep band; Radio station; Student government; Student newspaper; Symphony orchestra 151 registered organizations, 20 honor societies, 18 religious organizations. 10 fraternities, 8 sororities. **Athletics (Intercollegiate):** *Men:* baseball, basketball, cross-country, golf, tennis, track/field (outdoor), track/field (indoor). *Women:* basketball, cheerleading, cross-country, golf, soccer, softball, tennis, track/field (outdoor), track/field (indoor), volleyball. **On-Campus Highlights:** The Commons (Student Culinary Center), Housing, Brand New Academic Buildings; Nursing, Social Sciences, and Business, Student Recreation and Wellness Center, Campus Green **Environmental Initiatives:** Commitment by former KSU President Daniel S. Papp to reduce the university's carbon footprint, in line with a national coalition of college and university presidents.

ADMISSIONS

Freshman Academic Profile: Average high school GPA 3.3. 21% in top 10% of high school class, 53% in top 25% of high school class, 81% in top 50% of high school class. **Test Scores:** SAT Math middle 50% range 530-610. SAT EBRW middle 50% range 550-630. ACT middle 50% range 21-26. Minimum internet-based TOEFL 79. Minimum paper TOEFL 550. **Basis for Candidate Selection:** *Very important factors considered include:* academic GPA, standardized test scores. **Freshman Admission Requirements:** High school diploma is required and GED is not accepted *Academic units required:* 4 English, 4 math, 4 science, 2 science labs, 2 foreign language, 1 social studies, 2 history, *Academic units recommended:* 4 English, 4 math, 4 science, 2 science labs, 2 foreign language, 1 social studies, 2 history. **Freshman Admission Statistics:** 13,998 applied, 60.6% admitted, 62% enrolled. **Transfer Admission Requirements:** college transcript(s), Minimum college GPA of 2.0 required. Lowest grade transferable D. **General Admission Information:** Application fee $40. Priority deadline 11/1. Regular application deadline 4/1. Nonfall registration accepted.

COSTS AND FINANCIAL AID

Student Employment: Federal Work-Study Program available. Institutional employment available. **Financial Aid Statistics:** 58% needy undergrads receive need-based scholarship or grant aid. 77% freshmen, 50% undergrads receive non-need-based scholarship or grant aid. 73% freshmen, 77% undergrads receive need-based self-help aid. 0% freshmen, 0% undergrads receive athletic scholarships. 63% undergrads borrow to pay for school. Average cumulative indebtedness $25,123. **Criteria for awarding aid:** *Need-based:* Academics, Art, Athletics, Job skills, Leadership, Minority status *Non-need-based:* Academics, Alumni affiliation, Art, Athletics, Job skills, Leadership, Minority status, Music/drama, State/district residency.

KENT STATE UNIVERSITY—KENT CAMPUS

PO Box 5190, Kent, OH 44242-0001
Phone: 330-672-2444 · **Financial Aid Phone:** 330-672-6000
E-mail: kentadm@kent.edu · **CEEB Code:** 1367
Fax: 330-672-2499 · **Website:** http://www.kent.edu · **ACT Code:** 3284

This public school was founded in 1910. It has a 946 acre campus.

RATINGS

Admissions Selectivity Rating: 75   **Fire Safety Rating:** 92   **Green Rating:** 79

STUDENTS AND FACULTY

Enrollment: 22,403. **Student Body:** 61% female, 39% male, 15% out-of-state, 5% international (90 countries represented). Asian 2%, African American 9%, Caucasian 75%, Hispanic 4%, Native American <1%, Pacific Islander <1%, Two or more races 4%, Race unknown 3%.
Retention and Graduation: 80% freshmen return for sophomore year. 34% freshmen graduate within 4 years. 57% freshmen graduate within 6 years. 21% grads go on to further study within 1 year. **Faculty:** Student/faculty ratio 20:1. 1,010 full-time faculty, 13% are members of minority groups, 53% are women. 6% of classes are taught by teaching assistants.

ACADEMICS

Degrees: Bachelor's; Certificate; Doctoral; Doctoral/Professional; Doctoral/Research; Master's; Post-Bachelor's certificate; Post-Master's certificate
Classes: Most classes have 20-29 students. Most lab/discussion sessions have

20-29 students. **Most popular majors:** Psychology, General; Registered Nursing/Registered Nurse; Fashion Merchandising. **Special Study Options:** Accelerated program; Cooperative education program; Cross-registration; Distance learning; Double major; Dual enrollment; English as a Second Language (ESL); Exchange student program (domestic); Honors program; Independent study; Internships; Liberal arts/career combination; Student-designed major; Study abroad; Teacher certification program. **Honors programs:** The Kent State University Honors College is an institutional member of the National Collegiate Honors Council and the Mid-East Honors Association. The Honors College is open to all majors and provides talented and motivated undergraduate students a small liberal arts experience with the opportunities of a large public research university. This mission is carried out through the offering of smaller sections of courses, individualized interaction with faculty through research and other projects, the option of living in our learning community in the Stopher-Johnson complex, community service opportunities, personal advising, and several other educational opportunities and enhancements The Honors College is guided by two basic principles: the responsibility to provide academic work that offers intellectual challenge that demands the best efforts of students, and the belief that all students should be liberally educated, regardless of degree program. Our goal is to help students find the opportunities that will enrich their Kent State educations and empower them in directing their talents for a successful future. **Combined degree programs:** BA/MA; BA/MD. **Disability Services offered to physically disabled students:** Note-taking services; Reader services; Tape recorders; Tutors. **Career services:** Alumni network; Alumni services; Career assessment; Career/job search classes; Internships; Regional alumni

FACILITIES

Housing: Apartments for married students; Apartments for single students; Coed dorms; Cooperative housing; Fraternity/sorority housing; Men's dorms; Special housing for disabled student; Special housing for international students; Theme housing; Wellness housing; Women's dorms 95% of campus accessible to physically disabled. **Special Academic Facilities/Equipment:** May 4th visitors center, fashion museum, herbarium, liquid crystal institute, planetarium, airport. **Computers:** 90% of classrooms, 20% of dorms, 40% of libraries, 70% of dining areas, 100% of student union, 10% of common outdoor areas have wireless network access. Students can register for classes online. Administrative functions (other than registration) can be performed online.

CAMPUS LIFE

Environment: Town **Activities:** Campus Ministries; Choral groups; Concert band; Dance; Drama/theater; International Student Organization; Jazz band; Literary magazine; Marching band; Model UN; Music ensembles; Musical theater; Opera; Pep band; Radio station; Student government; Student newspaper; Symphony orchestra; Television station 214 registered organizations, 10 honor societies, 15 religious organizations. 17 fraternities, 6 sororities. **Athletics (Intercollegiate):** *Men:* baseball, basketball, cheerleading, cross-country, football, golf, track/field (outdoor), track/field (indoor), wrestling. *Women:* basketball, cheerleading, cross-country, field hockey, football, golf, gymnastics, soccer, softball, track/field (outdoor), track/field (indoor), volleyball. **On-Campus Highlights:** Student Recreation and Wellness Center, University Library, Kent Student Center and Plaza, New College of Architecture and Environmental Design, May 4 Visitors Center **Environmental Initiatives:** Kent State's focus on energy includes ongoing energy efficiency retrofits which have reduced consumption by over 15% to date, a combined heat and power plant on campus which is about twice as efficient as a utility power plant, and a half-megawatt solar array installed in spring 2012 as part of our renewable energy master plan.

ADMISSIONS

Freshman Academic Profile: Average high school GPA 3.4. 15% in top 10% of high school class, 39% in top 25% of high school class, 78% in top 50% of high school class. **Test Scores:** SAT Math middle 50% range 510-600. SAT EBRW middle 50% range 530-620. ACT middle 50% range 21-25. Minimum internet-based TOEFL 71. Minimum paper TOEFL 525. **Basis for Candidate Selection:** *Very important factors considered include:* academic GPA, standardized test scores. *Important factors considered include:* rigor of secondary school record. *Other factors considered include:* application essay, recommendation(s), interview, talent/ability, level of applicant's interest. **Freshman Admission Requirements:** High school diploma is required and GED is accepted *Academic units recommended:* 4 English, 4 math, 3 science, 2 science labs, 2 foreign language, 3 social studies, 1 visual/performing arts. **Freshman Admission Statistics:** 15,538 applied, 87.5% admitted, 32% enrolled. **Transfer Admission Requirements:** college transcript(s), Minimum college GPA of 2.0 required. Lowest grade transferable C. **General Admission Information:** Application fee $50. Priority deadline 3/1. Regular application deadline 5/1. Admission may be deferred for a maximum of 1 year.

COSTS AND FINANCIAL AID

Required Forms and Deadlines: FAFSA. **Notification of Awards:** Applicants will be notified of awards on a rolling basis beginning 1/15. **Types**

of Aid: *Need-based scholarships/grants:* College/university scholarship or grant aid from institutional funds; Federal Pell; Private scholarships; SEOG; State scholarships/grants. *Loans:* Direct PLUS loans; Direct Subsidized Stafford Loans; Direct Unsubsidized Stafford Loans. *Student Employment:* Federal Work-Study Program available. Institutional employment available. **Financial Aid Statistics:** 52% needy freshmen, 54% needy undergrads receive need-based scholarship or grant aid. 74% freshmen, 55% undergrads receive non-need-based scholarship or grant aid. 80% freshmen, 83% undergrads receive need-based self-help aid. 1% freshmen, 1% undergrads receive athletic scholarships. 76% undergrads borrow to pay for school. Average cumulative indebtedness $33,234. **Criteria for awarding aid:** *Need-based:* Academics, Alumni affiliation, Athletics, Leadership, Minority status *Non-need-based:* Academics, Alumni affiliation, Art, Athletics, Leadership, Minority status, Music/drama, State/district residency.

KENTUCKY STATE UNIVERSITY

400 East Main Street, Frankfort, KY 40601
Phone: 502-597-6813 · **Financial Aid Phone:** 502-597-5959
E-mail: admissions@kysu.edu · **CEEB Code:** 1368
Fax: 502-597-5814 · **Website:** www.kysu.edu · **ACT Code:** 1516

This public school was founded in 1886. It has a 916.03 acre campus.

RATINGS
Admissions Selectivity Rating: 83   **Fire Safety Rating:** 97   **Green Rating:** 75

STUDENTS AND FACULTY
Enrollment: 1,349. **Student Body:** 58% female, 42% male, 31% out-of-state, 1% international (9 countries represented). Asian 1%, African American 63%, Caucasian 24%, Hispanic 3%, Native American 1%, Pacific Islander 0%, Two or more races 4%, Race unknown 5%.
Retention and Graduation: 59% freshmen return for sophomore year. 34% grads go on to further study within 1 year. 18% grads pursue arts and sciences degrees. 1.5% grads pursue law degrees. 2% grads pursue business degrees. 2.9% grads pursue medical degrees. **Faculty:** Student/faculty ratio 11:1. 106 full-time faculty, 69% hold PhDs, 43% are members of minority groups, 48% are women. 0% of classes are taught by teaching assistants.

ACADEMICS
Degrees: Associate; Bachelor's; Certificate; Doctoral/Professional; Master's; Terminal Associate; Transfer Associate **Classes:** Most classes have 20-29 students. Most lab/discussion sessions have 10-19 students. **Most popular majors:** Criminal Justice/Safety Studies; Registered Nursing/Registered Nurse; Business Administration And Management, General. **Special Study Options:** Cooperative education program; Distance learning; Double major; Dual enrollment; Honors program; Independent study; Internships; Liberal arts/career combination; Student-designed major; Study abroad; Teacher certification program. **Honors programs:** The Honors Program is an integrated liberal arts program that emphasizes student discussion of excellent books. Honors students can complete the core general studies requirements through the Honors Program and then go on to major in any field. Honors students may also major or minor in Liberal Studies. The Honors Program features small classes with fifteen or fewer students, a challenging interdisciplinary and multicultural curriculum, a faculty devoted to undergraduate education, and a community spirit among faculty and students. It also offers scholarships, opportunities for study abroad, internships, and participation in state, regional and national honors conferences. **Disability Services offered to physically disabled students:** Note-taking services; Reader services; Tape recorders; Tutors. **Career services:** Alumni network; Alumni services; Career assessment; Career/job search classes; Internships; Regional alumni

FACILITIES
Housing: Coed dorms; Men's dorms; Women's dorms 100% of campus accessible to physically diasbled. **Special Academic Facilities/Equipment:** Art gallery, nutrition lab, agriculture research building, research farm, fish hatchery, electron microscope. **Computers:** 100% of classrooms, 100% of dorms, 100% of libraries, 100% of dining areas, 100% of student union, 60% of common outdoor areas have wireless network access. Students can register for classes online. Administrative functions (other than registration) can be performed online.

CAMPUS LIFE
Environment: Town **Activities:** Campus Ministries; Choral groups; Concert band; Dance; Drama/theater; International Student Organization; Jazz band; Marching band; Music ensembles; Musical theater; Pep band;

Student government; Student newspaper 30 registered organizations, 5 honor societies, 4 religious organizations. 6 fraternities, 5 sororities. **Athletics (Intercollegiate):** *Men:* baseball, basketball, cross-country, football, golf, track/field (outdoor), track/field (indoor). *Women:* basketball, cross-country, softball, track/field (outdoor), track/field (indoor), volleyball. **On-Campus Highlights:** Jackson Hall, Carl Hill Student Center, William Exum Building, Whitney Young Residence Hall, Hume Hall **Environmental Initiatives:** Energy efficient fixtures for Power & water

ADMISSIONS
Freshman Academic Profile: Average high school GPA 2.8. **Test Scores:** SAT Math middle 50% range 400-510. SAT EBRW middle 50% range 418-500. ACT middle 50% range 16-21. Minimum internet-based TOEFL 70. Minimum paper TOEFL 525. **Basis for Candidate Selection:** *Very important factors considered include:* academic GPA, standardized test scores. *Important factors considered include:* rigor of secondary school record, class rank. *Other factors considered include:* application essay, recommendation(s), interview, extracurricular activities, talent/ability, character/personal qualities, first generation, alumni/ae relation, geographical residence, state residency, level of applicant's interest. **Freshman Admission Requirements:** High school diploma is required and GED is accepted *Academic units required:* 4 English, 3 math, 3 science, 2 foreign language, 3 social studies, 3 history, 7 academic electives, 1 visual/performing arts, and 0.5 unit from above areas or other academic areas. *Academic units recommended:* 1 unit from above areas or other academic areas. **Freshman Admission Statistics:** 2,078 applied, 45.3% admitted, 14% enrolled. **Transfer Admission Requirements:** college transcript(s), Minimum college GPA of 2.0 required. Lowest grade transferable C. **General Admission Information:** Application fee $30. Priority deadline 2/15. Regular application deadline 7/31. Nonfall registration accepted. Admission may be deferred.

COSTS AND FINANCIAL AID
Annual in-state tuition $6,690. Annual out-of-state tuition $18,314. Room and board $6,690. Required fees $390. Average book expense $650. **Required Forms and Deadlines:** FAFSA. **Notification of Awards:** Applicants will be notified of awards on a rolling basis beginning 3/15. **Types of Aid:** *Need-based scholarships/grants:* College/university scholarship or grant aid from institutional funds; Federal Pell; Private scholarships; SEOG; State scholarships/grants; United Negro College Fund. *Loans:* Direct PLUS loans; Direct Subsidized Stafford Loans; Direct Unsubsidized Stafford Loans. *Student Employment:* Federal Work-Study Program available. Institutional employment available. **Financial Aid Statistics:** 95% needy freshmen, 89% needy undergrads receive need-based scholarship or grant aid. 4% freshmen, 3% undergrads receive non-need-based scholarship or grant aid. 69% freshmen, 76% undergrads receive need-based self-help aid. 3% freshmen, 2% undergrads receive athletic scholarships. 94% freshmen, 83% undergrads receive any aid. 66% undergrads borrow to pay for school. Average cumulative indebtedness $32,813. **Criteria for awarding aid:** *Non-need-based:* Academics, Alumni affiliation, Art, Athletics, Leadership, Music/drama.

KENTUCKY WESLEYAN COLLEGE

3000 Frederica Street, Owensboro, KY 42301
Phone: 270-852-3120 · **Financial Aid Phone:** 270-852-3130
E-mail: http://www.kwc.edu/page.php?page=353 · **CEEB Code:** 1369
Fax: 270-852-3133 · **Website:** www.kwc.edu · **ACT Code:** 1518

This private school, affiliated with the Methodist Church, was founded in 1858. It has a 52 acre campus.

RATINGS
Admissions Selectivity Rating: 78   **Fire Safety Rating:** 85   **Green Rating:** 60*

STUDENTS AND FACULTY
Enrollment: 657. **Student Body:** 48% female, 52% male, 28% out-of-state, 2% international (8 countries represented). Asian <1%, African American 12%, Caucasian 74%, Hispanic 2%, Native American <1%, Pacific Islander 0%, Two or more races 0%, Race unknown 10%.
Retention and Graduation: 54% freshmen return for sophomore year. 25% grads go on to further study within 1 year. **Faculty:** Student/faculty ratio 12:1. 48 full-time faculty, 71% hold PhDs, 6% are members of minority groups, 48% are women. 0% of classes are taught by teaching assistants.

ACADEMICS
Degrees: Bachelor's **Classes:** Most classes have fewer than 10 students. Most lab/discussion sessions have 10-19 students. **Most popular majors:** Biology/Biological Sciences, General; Criminal Justice/Safety Studies; Business/

Commerce, General. **Special Study Options:** Distance learning; Double major; Dual enrollment; Independent study; Internships; Liberal arts/career combination; Student-designed major; Study abroad; Teacher certification program. **Disability Services offered to physically disabled students:** Note-taking services; Reader services; Tape recorders; Tutors. **Career services:** Alumni network; Alumni services; Career assessment; Career/job search classes; Internships; Regional alumni

FACILITIES
Housing: Apartments for married students; Apartments for single students; Coed dorms; Fraternity/sorority housing; Men's dorms; Special housing for disabled student; Women's dorms 100% of campus accessible to physically diasbled. **Special Academic Facilities/Equipment:** President's Hall/Library Learning Center Ralph Center for Fine Arts. Woodward Health and Recreation Center. Yu Hak Hahn Center for the Sciences. **Computers:** 100% of classrooms, 100% of dorms, 100% of libraries, 100% of dining areas, 100% of student union, have wireless network access. Students can register for classes online. Administrative functions (other than registration) can be performed online.

CAMPUS LIFE
Environment: City **Activities:** Campus Ministries; Choral groups; Concert band; Dance; Drama/theater; Literary magazine; Marching band; Music ensembles; Musical theater; Pep band; Radio station; Student government; Student newspaper; Yearbook 42 registered organizations, 6 honor societies, 6 religious organizations. 3 fraternities, 2 sororities. **Athletics (Intercollegiate):** *Men:* baseball, basketball, cheerleading, cross-country, football, golf, soccer. *Women:* basketball, cheerleading, cross-country, golf, soccer, softball, tennis, volleyball. **On-Campus Highlights:** Winchester Center-New Campus Center, Ralph Fine Arts Center, Yu Hak Hahn Center for the Sciences, Woodward Health and Recreation Center, The Quad

ADMISSIONS
Freshman Academic Profile: Average high school GPA 3.2. 20% in top 10% of high school class, 44% in top 25% of high school class, 68% in top 50% of high school class. 90% from public high schools. **Test Scores:** SAT Math middle 50% range 410-555. SAT EBRW middle 50% range 410-540. ACT middle 50% range 19-25. Minimum paper TOEFL 500. **Basis for Candidate Selection:** *Very important factors considered include:* academic GPA, standardized test scores. *Important factors considered include:* rigor of secondary school record, interview, extracurricular activities. *Other factors considered include:* class rank, recommendation(s), talent/ability, character/personal qualities, alumni/ae relation, volunteer work, work experience, level of applicant's interest. **Freshman Admission Requirements:** High school diploma is required and GED is accepted *Academic units required:* 4 English, 3 math, 3 science, 3 social studies, *Academic units recommended:* 2 foreign language. **Freshman Admission Statistics:** 1,006 applied, 67.1% admitted, 24% enrolled. **Transfer Admission Requirements:** college transcript(s), Minimum college GPA of 2.0 required. Lowest grade transferable C. **General Admission Information:** Nonfall registration accepted. Admission may be deferred for a maximum of 1 year.

COSTS AND FINANCIAL AID
Annual tuition $21,400. Room and board $7,800. Required fees $600. Average book expense $1,400. **Required Forms and Deadlines:** FAFSA. **Notification of Awards:** Applicants will be notified of awards on a rolling basis beginning 2/15. **Types of Aid:** *Need-based scholarships/grants:* College/university scholarship or grant aid from institutional funds; Federal Pell; Private scholarships; SEOG; State scholarships/grants. *Loans:* Direct PLUS loans; Direct Subsidized Stafford Loans; Direct Unsubsidized Stafford Loans. *Student Employment:* Federal Work-Study Program available. Institutional employment available. **Financial Aid Statistics:** 99% needy freshmen, 98% needy undergrads receive need-based scholarship or grant aid. 8% freshmen, 11% undergrads receive non-need-based scholarship or grant aid. 81% freshmen, 77% undergrads receive need-based self-help aid. 0% freshmen, 0% undergrads receive athletic scholarships. 99% freshmen, 85% undergrads receive any aid. **Criteria for awarding aid:** *Need-based:* Academics, Alumni affiliation, Art, Athletics, Leadership, Music/drama, Religious affiliation *Non-need-based:* Academics, Alumni affiliation, Art, Athletics, Leadership, Music/drama, Religious affiliation, State/district residency.

KENYON COLLEGE

Ransom Hall, 106 College Park Street, Gambier, OH 43022-9623
Phone: 740-427-5776 · **Financial Aid Phone:** 740-427-5240
E-mail: admissions@kenyon.edu · **CEEB Code:** 1370
Fax: 740-427-5770 · **Website:** www.kenyon.edu · **ACT Code:** 3286

This private school, affiliated with the Episcopal Church, was founded in 1824. It has a 1000 acre campus.

RATINGS
Admissions Selectivity Rating: 95   **Fire Safety Rating:** 89   **Green Rating:** 80

STUDENTS AND FACULTY
Enrollment: 1,661. **Student Body:** 56% female, 44% male, 85% out-of-state, 6% international (49 countries represented). Asian 3%, African American 3%, Caucasian 72%, Hispanic 6%, Native American 0%, Pacific Islander 0%, Two or more races 7%, Race unknown 3%.
Retention and Graduation: 93% freshmen return for sophomore year. 86% freshmen graduate within 4 years. 91% freshmen graduate within 6 years. 19% grads go on to further study within 1 year. **Faculty:** Student/faculty ratio 9:1. 167 full-time faculty, 91% hold PhDs, 27% are members of minority groups, 44% are women. 0% of classes are taught by teaching assistants.

ACADEMICS
Degrees: Bachelor's **Classes:** Most classes have 20-29 students. Most lab/discussion sessions have 20-29 students. **Most popular majors:** English Language And Literature, General; Psychology, General; Economics, General. **Special Study Options:** Double major; Honors program; Independent study; Internships; Student-designed major; Study abroad. **Honors programs:** Honors programs are offered by all departmental and interdepartmental majors. **Disability Services offered to physically disabled students:** Note-taking services; Reader services; Tape recorders; Tutors. **Career services:** Alumni network; Alumni services; Career assessment; Career/job search classes; Internships; Regional alumni

FACILITIES
Housing: Apartments for single students; Coed dorms; Fraternity/sorority housing; Special housing for disabled student; Special housing for international students; Theme housing; Wellness housing; Women's dorms 70% of campus accessible to physically diasbled. **Special Academic Facilities/Equipment:** Gund Art Gallery; Bolton and Hill theaters; Rosse and Storer halls for music; Science quadrangle; greenhouse; observatory; environmental center; new Lentz House (English), $70-million fitness, recreation, and athletics facility; new studio art building. **Computers:** 100% of classrooms, 100% of dorms, 100% of libraries, 100% of dining areas, NA% of student union, 33% of common outdoor areas have wireless network access. Administrative functions (other than registration) can be performed online.

CAMPUS LIFE
Environment: Rural **Activities:** Campus Ministries; Choral groups; Concert band; Dance; Drama/theater; International Student Organization; Jazz band; Literary magazine; Model UN; Music ensembles; Musical theater; Opera; Radio station; Student government; Student newspaper; Student-run film society; Symphony orchestra 140 registered organizations, 5 honor societies, 6 religious organizations. 8 fraternities, 4 sororities. **Athletics (Intercollegiate):** *Men:* baseball, basketball, cross-country, diving, football, golf, lacrosse, soccer, swimming, tennis, track/field (outdoor), track/field (indoor). *Women:* basketball, cross-country, diving, field hockey, lacrosse, soccer, softball, swimming, tennis, track/field (outdoor), track/field (indoor), volleyball. **On-Campus Highlights:** Kenyon College Bookstore, Kenyon Athletic Center, Gund Gallery, Brown Family Environmental Center, Peirce Hall **Environmental Initiatives:** 1 Food for Thought (purchase of local foods for dining hall and building a county-wide sustainable food system) http://rurallife.kenyon.edu

ADMISSIONS
Freshman Academic Profile: Average high school GPA 3.9. 63% in top 10% of high school class, 86% in top 25% of high school class, 100% in top 50% of high school class. 50% from public high schools. **Test Scores:** SAT Math middle 50% range 623-730. SAT EBRW middle 50% range 640-730. ACT middle 50% range 29-33. Minimum internet-based TOEFL 100. **Basis for Candidate Selection:** *Very important factors considered include:* rigor of secondary school record, academic GPA, application essay, recommendation(s). *Important factors considered include:* class rank, standardized test scores, interview, extracurricular activities, talent/ability, character/personal qualities, level of

applicant's interest. *Other factors considered include:* first generation, alumni/ae relation, geographical residence, state residency, racial/ethnic status, volunteer work, work experience. **Freshman Admission Requirements:** High school diploma is required and GED is accepted *Academic units required:* 4 English, 4 math, 3 science, 3 science labs, 3 foreign language, 3 social studies, 3 academic electives, *Academic units recommended:* 4 English, 4 math, 4 science, 3 science labs, 4 foreign language, 3 social studies, 3 academic electives, 1 unit from above areas or other academic areas. **Freshman Admission Statistics:** 5,603 applied, 33.8% admitted, 24% enrolled. **Transfer Admission Requirements:** High school transcript, college transcript(s), essay or personal statement, standardized test scores, statement of good standing from prior institution(s). Minimum college GPA of 3.0 required. Lowest grade transferable C. **General Admission Information:** Priority deadline 1/15. Regular application deadline 1/15. Nonfall registration accepted. Admission may be deferred for a maximum of 1 year.

COSTS AND FINANCIAL AID
Required Forms and Deadlines: CSS/Financial Aid PROFILE; FAFSA; Noncustodial PROFILE. **Types of Aid:** *Need-based scholarships/grants:* College/university scholarship or grant aid from institutional funds; Federal Pell; Private scholarships; SEOG; State scholarships/grants. *Loans:* Direct PLUS loans; Direct Subsidized Stafford Loans; Direct Unsubsidized Stafford Loans. *Student Employment:* Federal Work-Study Program available. Institutional employment available. **Financial Aid Statistics:** 97% needy freshmen, 98% needy undergrads receive need-based scholarship or grant aid. 30% freshmen, 21% undergrads receive non-need-based scholarship or grant aid. 90% freshmen, 87% undergrads receive need-based self-help aid. 0% freshmen, 0% undergrads receive athletic scholarships. 53% freshmen, 42% undergrads receive any aid. 36% undergrads borrow to pay for school. Average cumulative indebtedness $26,746. **Criteria for awarding aid:** *Non-need-based:* Academics, Art, Minority status, Music/drama.

KETTERING UNIVERSITY

1700 University Avenue, Flint, MI 48504-6214
Phone: 810-762-9500 • **Financial Aid Phone:** 810-762-7859 • **CEEB Code:** 1246
Website: www.kettering.edu • **ACT Code:** 1998

This private school was founded in 1919. It has a 85 acre campus.

RATINGS
Admissions Selectivity Rating: 83   **Fire Safety Rating:** 78   **Green Rating:** 61

STUDENTS AND FACULTY
Enrollment: 1,850. **Student Body:** 19% female, 81% male, 15% out-of-state, 4% international (21 countries represented). Asian 4%, African American 3%, Caucasian 76%, Hispanic 5%, Native American <1%, Pacific Islander 0%, Two or more races 3%, Race unknown 5%.
Retention and Graduation: 93% freshmen return for sophomore year. 9% freshmen graduate within 4 years. 62% freshmen graduate within 6 years. **Faculty:** Student/faculty ratio 15:1. 114 full-time faculty, 87% hold PhDs, 25% are members of minority groups, 29% are women. 0% of classes are taught by teaching assistants.

ACADEMICS
Degrees: Bachelor's; Master's; Post-Bachelor's certificate **Classes:** Most classes have 10-19 students. Most lab/discussion sessions have fewer than 10 students. **Most popular majors:** Chemical Engineering; Electrical And Electronics Engineering; Mechanical Engineering. **Special Study Options:** Cooperative education program; Distance learning; Double major; Dual enrollment; English as a Second Language (ESL); Honors program; Independent study; Internships; Liberal arts/career combination; Study abroad. **Disability Services offered to physically disabled students:** Note-taking services; Reader services; Tape recorders; Tutors.

FACILITIES
Housing: Coed dorms; Fraternity/sorority housing; Men's dorms; Special housing for disabled student; Theme housing; Women's dorms 100% of campus accessible to physically disabled. **Special Academic Facilities/Equipment:** Humanities Art Museum Factory 1 5 D Spaces 1 TSpace **Computers:** 100% of classrooms, 100% of libraries, 100% of dining areas, have wireless network access. Students can register for classes online. Administrative functions (other than registration) can be performed online.

CAMPUS LIFE
Environment: City **Activities:** Campus Ministries; Concert band; Dance; International Student Organization; Jazz band; Model UN; Radio station; Student government; Student newspaper 43 registered organizations, 13 honor societies, 1 religious organization. 13 fraternities, 6 sororities. **On-Campus**

Highlights: CS Mott Engineering and Science Center, Connie and Jim John Recreation Center, Frances Wilson Thompson Residence Hall, Academic Building, Einstein Bros. Bagels

ADMISSIONS
Freshman Academic Profile: Average high school GPA 3.7. 32% in top 10% of high school class, 60% in top 25% of high school class, 91% in top 50% of high school class. 82% from public high schools. **Test Scores:** SAT Math middle 50% range 610-690. SAT EBRW middle 50% range 580-660. ACT middle 50% range 24-29. Minimum internet-based TOEFL 79. Minimum paper TOEFL 550. **Basis for Candidate Selection:** *Very important factors considered include:* rigor of secondary school record, academic GPA, standardized test scores. *Important factors considered include:* extracurricular activities. *Other factors considered include:* class rank, application essay, recommendation(s), talent/ability, racial/ethnic status, volunteer work, work experience, level of applicant's interest. **Freshman Admission Requirements:** High school diploma is required and GED is accepted *Academic units required:* 3 English, 3.5 math, 2 science, 2 science labs, *Academic units recommended:* 4 English, 4 math, 3 science, 3 science labs, 2 social studies, 2 history, 1 academic elective. **Freshman Admission Statistics:** 1,931 applied, 70.3% admitted, 27% enrolled. **Transfer Admission Requirements:** college transcript(s), Minimum college GPA of 3.0 required. Lowest grade transferable C. **General Admission Information:** Admission may be deferred for a maximum of 1 year.

COSTS AND FINANCIAL AID
Required Forms and Deadlines: FAFSA. **Notification of Awards:** Applicants will be notified of awards on or about 3/1. **Types of Aid:** *Need-based scholarships/grants:* College/university scholarship or grant aid from institutional funds; Federal Pell; Private scholarships; SEOG; State scholarships/grants; United Negro College Fund. *Loans:* Direct PLUS loans; Direct Subsidized Stafford Loans; Direct Unsubsidized Stafford Loans. *Student Employment:* Federal Work-Study Program available. Institutional employment available. **Financial Aid Statistics:** 100% needy freshmen, 100% needy undergrads receive need-based scholarship or grant aid. 12% freshmen, 9% undergrads receive non-need-based scholarship or grant aid. 73% freshmen, 68% undergrads receive need-based self-help aid. 99% freshmen, 88% undergrads receive any aid. **Criteria for awarding aid:** *Non-need-based:* Academics, Leadership.

See page 958.

KEUKA COLLEGE

141 Central Ave., Keuka Park, NY 14478-0098
Phone: 315-279-5254 • **Financial Aid Phone:** 315-279-5646
E-mail: admissions@mail.keuka.edu • **CEEB Code:** 2744
Fax: 315-536-5386 • **Website:** www.keuka.edu • **ACT Code:** 2782

This private school, affiliated with the American Baptist Church, was founded in 1890. It has a 203 acre campus.

RATINGS
Admissions Selectivity Rating: 72   **Fire Safety Rating:** 87   **Green Rating:** 60*

STUDENTS AND FACULTY
Enrollment: 1,738. **Student Body:** 76% female, 24% male, 6% out-of-state, 0% international (3 countries represented). Asian 1%, African American 8%, Caucasian 84%, Hispanic <1%, Native American 1%, Pacific Islander <1%, Two or more races 1%, Race unknown 6%.
Retention and Graduation: 72% freshmen return for sophomore year. 28% grads go on to further study within 1 year. **Faculty:** Student/faculty ratio 15:1. 90 full-time faculty, 70% hold PhDs, 18% are members of minority groups, 61% are women. 0% of classes are taught by teaching assistants.

ACADEMICS
Degrees: Bachelor's; Master's **Classes:** Most classes have 10-19 students. **Most popular majors:** Special Education And Teaching, General; Occupational Therapy/Therapist; Business Administration And Management, General. **Special Study Options:** Accelerated program; Cooperative education program; Cross-registration; Double major; Dual enrollment; Independent study; Internships; Student-designed major; Study abroad; Teacher certification program. **Disability Services offered to physically disabled students:** Note-taking services; Reader services; Tape recorders; Tutors. **Career services:** Alumni network; Alumni services; Career assessment; Career/job search classes; Internships; Regional alumni

FACILITIES
Housing: Coed dorms; Cooperative housing; Men's dorms; Special housing for disabled student; Women's dorms 61% of campus accessible to physically

diasbled. **Special Academic Facilities/Equipment:** Bird Museum, Lightner Gallery

CAMPUS LIFE

Environment: Rural **Activities:** Choral groups; Concert band; Dance; Drama/theater; Literary magazine; Musical theater; Radio station; Student government; Student newspaper; Student-run film society; Yearbook 32 registered organizations, 7 honor societies, 2 religious organizations. **Athletics (Intercollegiate):** *Men:* baseball, basketball, cross-country, golf, lacrosse, soccer, tennis. *Women:* basketball, cross-country, golf, lacrosse, soccer, softball, synchronized swimming, tennis, volleyball. **On-Campus Highlights:** The Weed Physical Arts Center (Gym, pool, fitness rooms, coaches offices), Dahstrom Student Center (bookstore, club offices, student affairs), Ostrander Field (soccer, lacrosse games), Hegeman Hall (classes, faculty offices), Jephson Hall (sciences, greenhouse, labs, electronic classroom).

ADMISSIONS

Freshman Academic Profile: Average high school GPA 3.1. 7% in top 10% of high school class, 27% in top 25% of high school class, 75% in top 50% of high school class. 96% from public high schools. **Test Scores:** SAT Math middle 50% range 430-530. SAT EBRW middle 50% range 430-520. ACT middle 50% range 18-23. Minimum paper TOEFL 500. **Basis for Candidate Selection:** *Very important factors considered include:* rigor of secondary school record, standardized test scores. *Important factors considered include:* class rank, academic GPA, application essay, recommendation(s), interview, extracurricular activities. *Other factors considered include:* talent/ability, alumni/ae relation, volunteer work, work experience, level of applicant's interest. **Freshman Admission Requirements:** High school diploma is required and GED is accepted *Academic units recommended:* 4 English, 3 math, 3 science, 2 science labs, 3 foreign language, 3 social studies, 2 history. **Freshman Admission Statistics:** 1,371 applied, 82.9% admitted, 19% enrolled. **Transfer Admission Requirements:** college transcript(s), essay or personal statement, Minimum college GPA of 2.0 required. Lowest grade transferable C. **General Admission Information:** Application fee $50. Nonfall registration accepted. Admission may be deferred.

COSTS AND FINANCIAL AID

Annual tuition $26,490. Room and board $10,590. Required fees $790. Average book expense $1,500. **Required Forms and Deadlines:** FAFSA. **Notification of Awards:** Applicants will be notified of awards on a rolling basis beginning 3/1. **Types of Aid:** *Need-based scholarships/grants:* College/university scholarship or grant aid from institutional funds; Federal Pell; SEOG; State scholarships/grants. *Loans:* Direct PLUS loans; Direct Subsidized Stafford Loans; Direct Unsubsidized Stafford Loans. **Financial Aid Statistics:** 91% needy freshmen, 80% needy undergrads receive need-based scholarship or grant aid. 83% freshmen, 58% undergrads receive non-need-based scholarship or grant aid. 97% freshmen, 93% undergrads receive need-based self-help aid. 0% freshmen, 0% undergrads receive athletic scholarships. 92% freshmen, 93% undergrads receive any aid. **Criteria for awarding aid:** *Need-based:* Academics, Alumni affiliation, Leadership, Minority status, Religious affiliation *Non-need-based:* Academics, Alumni affiliation, Leadership, Minority status, Religious affiliation.

KEYSTONE COLLEGE

One College Green, La Plume, PA 18440
Phone: 570-945-8111 · **Financial Aid Phone:** 570-945-8132
E-mail: admissions@keystone.edu · **CEEB Code:** 2351
Fax: 570-945-7916 · **Website:** www.keystone.edu · **ACT Code:** 2602

This private school was founded in 1868. It has a 270 acre campus.

RATINGS

Admissions Selectivity Rating: 77   **Fire Safety Rating:** 97   **Green Rating:** 60*

STUDENTS AND FACULTY

Enrollment: 1,647. **Student Body:** 60% female, 40% male, 13% out-of-state, 1% international (9 countries represented). Asian 1%, African American 5%, Caucasian 72%, Hispanic 3%, Native American <1%, Pacific Islander <1%, Two or more races 2%, Race unknown 16%.
Retention and Graduation: 61% freshmen return for sophomore year. 25% grads go on to further study within 1 year. 1% grads pursue arts and sciences degrees. 0.5% grads pursue law degrees. 1% grads pursue business degrees. 1% grads pursue medical degrees. **Faculty:** Student/faculty ratio 11:1. 68 full-time faculty, 49% hold PhDs, 1% are members of minority groups, 63% are women. 0% of classes are taught by teaching assistants.

ACADEMICS

Degrees: Associate; Bachelor's; Certificate; Post-Bachelor's certificate **Classes:** Most classes have 10-19 students. Most lab/discussion sessions have 10-19 students. **Most popular majors:** Education, General; Homeland Security, Law Enforcement, Firefighting And Related Protective Services, Other; Business Administration And Management, General. **Special Study Options:** Distance learning; Double major; Dual enrollment; Honors program; Independent study; Internships; Study abroad; Teacher certification program; Weekend college. **Honors programs:** Freshmen Honor's Program. **Disability Services offered to physically disabled students:** Note-taking services; Reader services; Tutors. **Career services:** Alumni network; Alumni services; Career assessment; Career/job search classes; Internships; Regional alumni

FACILITIES

Housing: Apartments for single students; Coed dorms; Men's dorms; Special housing for disabled student; Theme housing; Women's dorms 80% of campus accessible to physically diasbled. **Special Academic Facilities/Equipment:** Linder Art Gallery; Cupillari Astronomical Observatory; Willary Water Resource Center **Computers:** 100% of classrooms, 50% of dorms, 100% of libraries, 100% of dining areas, 100% of student union, 50% of common outdoor areas have wireless network access. Students can register for classes online. Administrative functions (other than registration) can be performed online.

CAMPUS LIFE

Environment: Rural **Activities:** Campus Ministries; Choral groups; Drama/ theater; International Student Organization; Literary magazine; Pep band; Radio station; Student government; Student newspaper 22 registered organizations, 1 religious organization. **Athletics (Intercollegiate):** *Men:* baseball, basketball, cross-country, golf, soccer, tennis, track/field (outdoor), track/field (indoor). *Women:* basketball, cross-country, field hockey, soccer, softball, tennis, track/field (outdoor), track/field (indoor), volleyball. **On-Campus Highlights:** Lindner Art Gallery in Miller Library, 270 acre Woodlands campus (nature trails), Gambal Athletic Center, Giants' Den, Giant's Grill **Environmental Initiatives:** A recycling program

ADMISSIONS

Test Scores: SAT Math middle 50% range 400-500. SAT EBRW middle 50% range 400-500. ACT middle 50% range 17-22. Minimum internet-based TOEFL 80. Minimum paper TOEFL 550. **Basis for Candidate Selection:** *Very important factors considered include:* rigor of secondary school record, academic GPA, interview, talent/ability. *Important factors considered include:* application essay, standardized test scores, extracurricular activities, character/ personal qualities, volunteer work, work experience. *Other factors considered include:* class rank, recommendation(s), first generation, alumni/ae relation, level of applicant's interest. **Freshman Admission Requirements:** High school diploma is required and GED is accepted *Academic units required:* 4 English, 3 math, 2 science, 1 science labs, 2 social studies, 4 academic electives, *Academic units recommended:* 4 English, 3 math, 3 science, 1 science labs, 2 foreign language, 2 social studies, 2 history, 4 academic electives, 1 computer science, 1 visual/performing arts. **Freshman Admission Statistics:** 1,192 applied, 70.2% admitted, 43% enrolled. **Transfer Admission Requirements:** college transcript(s), essay or personal statement, standardized test scores, statement of good standing from prior institution(s). Minimum college GPA of 2 required. Lowest grade transferable 2. **General Admission Information:** Application fee $30. Priority deadline 4/1. Regular application deadline 6/1. Nonfall registration accepted. Admission may be deferred for a maximum of 1 year.

COSTS AND FINANCIAL AID

Annual tuition $20,300. Room and board $9,800. Required fees $900. Average book expense $1,900. **Required Forms and Deadlines:** FAFSA; State aid form. **Notification of Awards:** Applicants will be notified of awards on or about 3/1. **Types of Aid:** *Need-based scholarships/grants:* College/university scholarship or grant aid from institutional funds; Federal Pell; Private scholarships; SEOG; State scholarships/grants. *Loans:* Direct PLUS loans; Direct Subsidized Stafford Loans; Direct Unsubsidized Stafford Loans. *Student Employment:* Federal Work-Study Program available. Institutional employment available. **Financial Aid Statistics:** 100% needy freshmen, 99% needy undergrads receive need-based scholarship or grant aid. 76% freshmen, 72% undergrads receive non-need-based scholarship or grant aid. 90% freshmen, 91% undergrads receive need-based self-help aid. 0% freshmen, 0% undergrads receive athletic scholarships. 88% freshmen, 91% undergrads receive any aid. **Criteria for awarding aid:** *Non-need-based:* Academics, Alumni affiliation, Art.

KING UNIVERSITY

1350 King College Road, Bristol, TN 37620-2699
Phone: 423-652-4861 · **Financial Aid Phone:** 423-652-4728
E-mail: admissions@king.edu · **CEEB Code:** 1371
Fax: 423-652-4727 · **Website:** www.king.edu · **ACT Code:** 3970

This private school, affiliated with the Presbyterian Church, was founded in 1867. It has a 135 acre campus.

RATINGS
Admissions Selectivity Rating: 83   **Fire Safety Rating:** 95   **Green Rating:** 60*

STUDENTS AND FACULTY
Enrollment: 1,736. **Student Body:** 61% female, 39% male, 40% out-of-state, 3% international (26 countries represented). Asian 1%, African American 7%, Caucasian 80%, Hispanic 4%, Native American <1%, Pacific Islander <1%, Two or more races 2%, Race unknown 3%.
Retention and Graduation: 69% freshmen return for sophomore year. 38% freshmen graduate within 4 years. 52% freshmen graduate within 6 years. 14% grads go on to further study within 1 year. 4% grads pursue arts and sciences degrees. 1% grads pursue law degrees. 5% grads pursue business degrees. 1% grads pursue medical degrees. **Faculty:** Student/faculty ratio 13:1. 98 full-time faculty, 66% hold PhDs, 56% are women. 0% of classes are taught by teaching assistants.

ACADEMICS
Degrees: Associate; Bachelor's; Doctoral/Professional; Master's; Post-Master's certificate **Classes:** Most classes have 10-19 students. Most lab/discussion sessions have 10-19 students. **Most popular majors:** Psychology; Health Professions And Related Programs; Business, Management, Marketing, And Related Support Services. **Special Study Options:** Distance learning; Double major; Dual enrollment; Honors program; Independent study; Internships; Liberal arts/career combination; Student-designed major; Study abroad; Teacher certification program. **Honors programs:** The Jack E. Snider Honors Center allows students to interact with other students and faculty of diverse interests. Participants take selected courses that stimulate thinking and allow for creative response while engaging in special opportunities such as meeting with faculty members and outside guests. Other courses may allow honors students, for extra credit, to develop more extensive research projects. The honors seminars also examine ideas from a variety of academic disciplines. Participants serve both the campus and the larger community by tutoring and mentoring and are encouraged to explore other perspectives through study abroad experiences. **Disability Services offered to physically disabled students:** Note-taking services; Reader services; Tape recorders; Tutors. **Career services:** Career assessment; Career/job search classes; Internships

FACILITIES
Housing: Men's dorms; Women's dorms 53% of campus accessible to physically diasbled. **Special Academic Facilities/Equipment:** Electron microscope, Burke Observatory, Sign of the George Press, Nuclear Physics Lab.

CAMPUS LIFE
Environment: Town **Activities:** Campus Ministries; Choral groups; Concert band; Dance; Drama/theater; International Student Organization; Jazz band; Literary magazine; Music ensembles; Musical theater; Pep band; Student government; Student newspaper 35 registered organizations, 5 honor societies, 9 religious organizations. **Athletics (Intercollegiate):** *Men:* baseball, basketball, bowling, cheerleading, cross-country, cycling, diving, golf, soccer, swimming, tennis, track/field (outdoor), track/field (indoor), wrestling. *Women:* basketball, bowling, cheerleading, cross-country, cycling, diving, golf, soccer, softball, swimming, tennis, track/field (outdoor), track/field (indoor), volleyball, wrestling. **On-Campus Highlights:** Student Center/Athletic Complex, Campus oval, Library, Residence hall lobbies, Entrance way and sporting fields

ADMISSIONS
Freshman Academic Profile: Average high school GPA 3.5. 23% in top 10% of high school class, 50% in top 25% of high school class, 80% in top 50% of high school class. 87% from public high schools. **Test Scores:** SAT Math middle 50% range 436-634. SAT EBRW middle 50% range 421-624. ACT middle 50% range 18-28. Minimum internet-based TOEFL 84. Minimum paper TOEFL 563. **Basis for Candidate Selection:** *Very important factors considered include:* academic GPA. *Important factors considered include:* rigor of secondary school record. *Other factors considered include:* application essay, recommendation(s). **Freshman Admission Requirements:** High school diploma is required and GED is accepted *Academic units required:* 4 English, 3 math, 2 science, 2 science labs, 2 foreign language, 1 social studies, 1 history, 4 academic electives, *Academic units recommended:* 4 English, 4 math, 4 science, 4 science labs, 2 foreign language, 2 social studies, 2 history, 2 academic electives. **Freshman Admission Statistics:** 1,152 applied, 59.3% admitted,

25% enrolled. **Transfer Admission Requirements:** college transcript(s), Minimum college GPA of 2.0 required. Lowest grade transferable C-. **General Admission Information:** Nonfall registration accepted. Admission may be deferred.

COSTS AND FINANCIAL AID
Annual tuition $27,024. Room and board $8,424. Required fees $1,548. Average book expense $1,440. **Required Forms and Deadlines:** FAFSA. **Notification of Awards:** Applicants will be notified of awards on a rolling basis beginning 12/15. **Types of Aid:** *Need-based scholarships/grants:* College/university scholarship or grant aid from institutional funds; Federal Pell; Private scholarships; SEOG; State scholarships/grants. *Loans:* Direct PLUS loans; Direct Subsidized Stafford Loans; Direct Unsubsidized Stafford Loans. *Student Employment:* Federal Work-Study Program available. Institutional employment available. **Financial Aid Statistics:** 95% needy freshmen, 80% needy undergrads receive need-based scholarship or grant aid. 13% freshmen, 7% undergrads receive non-need-based scholarship or grant aid. 87% freshmen, 93% undergrads receive need-based self-help aid. 20% freshmen, 6% undergrads receive athletic scholarships. 98% freshmen, 94% undergrads receive any aid. Average cumulative indebtedness $23,950. **Criteria for awarding aid:** *Need-based:* Alumni affiliation *Non-need-based:* Academics, Art, Athletics, Job skills, Music/drama, State/district residency.

KING'S COLLEGE (PA)

133 North River Street, Wilkes-Barre, PA 18711
Phone: 570-208-5858 · **Financial Aid Phone:** 570-208-5868
E-mail: admissions@kings.edu · **CEEB Code:** 2353
Fax: 570-208-5971 · **Website:** www.kings.edu · **ACT Code:** 3604

This private school, affiliated with the Roman Catholic Church, was founded in 1946. It has a 48 acre campus.

RATINGS
Admissions Selectivity Rating: 78   **Fire Safety Rating:** 96   **Green Rating:** 63

STUDENTS AND FACULTY
Enrollment: 2,064. **Student Body:** 45% female, 55% male, 30% out-of-state, 8% international (5 countries represented). Asian 2%, African American 4%, Caucasian 72%, Hispanic 7%, Native American <1%, Pacific Islander <1%, Two or more races 3%, Race unknown 4%.
Retention and Graduation: 73% freshmen return for sophomore year. 62% freshmen graduate within 4 years. 67% freshmen graduate within 6 years. 30% grads go on to further study within 1 year. 6% grads pursue arts and sciences degrees. 2% grads pursue law degrees. 8% grads pursue business degrees. 1% grads pursue medical degrees. **Faculty:** Student/faculty ratio 13:1. 135 full-time faculty, 89% hold PhDs, 3% are members of minority groups, 50% are women. 0% of classes are taught by teaching assistants.

ACADEMICS
Degrees: Bachelor's; Master's; Post-Bachelor's certificate **Classes:** Most classes have 10-19 students. **Most popular majors:** Criminal Justice/Safety Studies; Physician Assistant; Accounting. **Special Study Options:** Accelerated program; Cross-registration; Distance learning; Double major; Dual enrollment; English as a Second Language (ESL); Honors program; Independent study; Internships; Student-designed major; Study abroad; Teacher certification program; Weekend college. **Disability Services offered to physically disabled students:** Note-taking services; Reader services; Tape recorders; Tutors. **Career services:** Alumni network; Alumni services; Career assessment; Career/job search classes; Internships; Regional alumni

FACILITIES
Housing: Apartments for single students; Coed dorms; Men's dorms; Special housing for disabled student; Women's dorms 99% of campus accessible to physically diasbled. **Special Academic Facilities/Equipment:** Electron microscope, rooftop greenhouse, molecular biology lab, computer graphics lab **Computers:** 50% of classrooms, 25% of dorms, 100% of libraries, 100% of dining areas, 100% of student union, 100% of common outdoor areas have wireless network access. Students can register for classes online. Administrative functions (other than registration) can be performed online.

CAMPUS LIFE
Environment: City **Activities:** Campus Ministries; Choral groups; Dance; Drama/theater; International Student Organization; Literary magazine; Music ensembles; Pep band; Radio station; Student government; Student newspaper 50 registered organizations, 15 honor societies, 2 religious organizations. **Athletics (Intercollegiate):** *Men:* baseball, basketball, cheerleading, cross-country, football, golf, lacrosse, soccer, swimming,

tennis, wrestling. *Women:* basketball, cheerleading, cross-country, field hockey, lacrosse, soccer, softball, swimming, tennis, volleyball. **On-Campus Highlights:** Sheehy-Farmer Campus Center, McGowan School of Business, Scandlon Physical Education Center, Betzler Fields (Athletic Complex), Thomas J. O'Hara Hall

ADMISSIONS

Freshman Academic Profile: Average high school GPA 3.4. 18% in top 10% of high school class, 42% in top 25% of high school class, 72% in top 50% of high school class. 77% from public high schools. **Test Scores:** SAT Math middle 50% range 490-600. SAT EBRW middle 50% range 490-590. ACT middle 50% range 21-25. Minimum internet-based TOEFL 69. Minimum paper TOEFL 520. **Basis for Candidate Selection:** *Very important factors considered include:* rigor of secondary school record, class rank, academic GPA. *Important factors considered include:* application essay, standardized test scores, character/personal qualities. *Other factors considered include:* recommendation(s), interview, extracurricular activities, alumni/ae relation, volunteer work, work experience. **Freshman Admission Requirements:** High school diploma is required and GED is accepted *Academic units required:* 4 English, 3 math, 3 science, 2 science labs, 2 foreign language, 3 social studies, 1 history, *Academic units recommended:* 4 English, 4 math, 4 science, 2 science labs, 4 foreign language, 3 social studies, 1 history, 2 academic electives, 2 computer science. **Freshman Admission Statistics:** 4,354 applied, 70.7% admitted, 20% enrolled. **Transfer Admission Requirements:** High school transcript, college transcript(s), essay or personal statement, Minimum college GPA of 2.0 required. Lowest grade transferable C. **General Admission Information:** Application fee $30. Nonfall registration accepted. Admission may be deferred for a maximum of 1 year.

COSTS AND FINANCIAL AID

Required Forms and Deadlines: FAFSA. **Notification of Awards:** Applicants will be notified of awards on a rolling basis beginning 3/1. **Types of Aid:** *Need-based scholarships/grants:* College/university scholarship or grant aid from institutional funds; Federal Pell; Private scholarships; SEOG; State scholarships/grants. *Loans:* Direct PLUS loans; Direct Subsidized Stafford Loans; Direct Unsubsidized Stafford Loans. *Student Employment:* Federal Work-Study Program available. Institutional employment available. **Financial Aid Statistics:** 97% needy freshmen, 100% needy undergrads receive need-based scholarship or grant aid. 15% freshmen, 14% undergrads receive non-need-based scholarship or grant aid. 82% freshmen, 83% undergrads receive need-based self-help aid. 0% freshmen, 0% undergrads receive athletic scholarships. 98% freshmen, 96% undergrads receive any aid. 86% undergrads borrow to pay for school. Average cumulative indebtedness $37,874. **Criteria for awarding aid:** *Non-need-based:* Academics, Leadership.

See page 960.

KNOX COLLEGE

2 East South Street, Galesburg, IL 61401
Phone: 309-341-7100 • **Financial Aid Phone:** 309-341-7149
E-mail: admission@knox.edu • **CEEB Code:** 1372
Fax: 309-341-7070 • **Website:** www.knox.edu • **ACT Code:** 1052

This private school was founded in 1837. It has a 82 acre campus.

RATINGS

Admissions Selectivity Rating: 85   **Fire Safety Rating:** 92   **Green Rating:** 92

STUDENTS AND FACULTY

Enrollment: 1,341. **Student Body:** 57% female, 43% male, 55% out-of-state, 17% international (46 countries represented). Asian 5%, African American 8%, Caucasian 47%, Hispanic 15%, Native American 0%, Pacific Islander <1%, Two or more races 6%, Race unknown 2%.
Retention and Graduation: 87% freshmen return for sophomore year. 72% freshmen graduate within 4 years. 76% freshmen graduate within 6 years. 15% grads go on to further study within 1 year. 9% grads pursue arts and sciences degrees. **Faculty:** Student/faculty ratio 11:1. 110 full-time faculty, 95% hold PhDs, 15% are members of minority groups, 43% are women. 0% of classes are taught by teaching assistants.

ACADEMICS

Degrees: Bachelor's **Classes:** Most classes have 20-29 students. Most lab/discussion sessions have 20-29 students. **Most popular majors:** Creative

Writing; Psychology, General; Economics, General. **Special Study Options:** Cooperative education program; Double major; English as a Second Language (ESL); Honors program; Independent study; Internships; Student-designed major; Study abroad; Teacher certification program. **Honors programs:** Specialized independent research, scholarship, and creative work are supported by our nationally recognized Honors Program, which was cited as one of two model programs in the nation by the federal Fund for the Improvement of Postsecondary Education. Honors may be undertaken as early as junior year, though most projects are conducted during the senior year. Candidates for Honors obtain the endorsement from their department and complete advanced study under the supervision and guidance of an interdisciplinary faculty committee. At the end of their year-long research projects, which comprise fully a third of the student's coursework during the year, students defend their thesis or creative project or have it critiqued before a qualified outside examiner, modeling the dissertation defense of many grad programs. Often, the Honors experience can jump-start a meaningful career or admission into a top-notch graduate program. **Disability Services offered to physically disabled students:** Note-taking services; Reader services; Tape recorders; Tutors. **Career services:** Alumni network; Alumni services; Career assessment; Career/job search classes; Internships; Regional alumni

FACILITIES

Housing: Apartments for single students; Coed dorms; Fraternity/sorority housing; Men's dorms; Special housing for disabled student; Women's dorms 55% of campus accessible to physically diasbled. **Special Academic Facilities/Equipment:** The Umbeck Science-Mathematics Center is home to an electron microscopy lab, a greenhouse, and a science makerspace that includes a 3-D printer, laser cutter, and computer-controlled milling machine. The Ford Center for Fine Arts houses a black-box studio theatre, a large-scale production theatre that includes a revolving stage, and two recital halls. The Whitcomb Art Center, Knox's new art and art history building, opened in January 2017. The center includes studios for painting, printmaking, design, sculpture, ceramics, drawing, and digital art, as well as metalworking and woodworking shops, a seminar room, and dedicated studio space for seniors working on capstone projects. A two-floor critique hall offers a gallery-like setting in which to evaluate works. Green Oaks Biological Field Station, located 20 miles from the main Knox campus, is 700 acres of tallgrass prairie, old growth oaks, second-growth oak-hickory forest, lakes, and streams. The facility is used by faculty and student for research and is home to Green Oaks Term, an interdisciplinary exploration of life in a community that is fully integrated into its natural surroundings. The Knox Farm features two high tunnels and a community garden that is used for academic purposes and provides local produce for campus use. The recently renovated Alumni Hall, a LEED-certified space for students, faculty, staff, and visitors, recognizes the key role that experiential learning plays in the education of every Knox student by bringing together all of the centers that support experiential learning: the Vovis Center for Research and Advanced Study, the Stellyes Center for Global Studies, the Kleine Center for Community Service, and the Bastian Family Career Center. It also houses the Offices of Admission & Financial Aid and Alumni Relations and the Whitcomb Heritage Center. **Computers:** 100% of classrooms, 100% of dorms, 100% of libraries, 100% of dining areas, 100% of student union, 90% of common outdoor areas have wireless network access. Students can register for classes online. Administrative functions (other than registration) can be performed online.

CAMPUS LIFE

Environment: Town **Activities:** Choral groups; Dance; Drama/theater; International Student Organization; Jazz band; Literary magazine; Model UN; Music ensembles; Radio station; Student government; Student newspaper; Symphony orchestra 102 registered organizations, 8 honor societies, 6 religious organizations. 5 fraternities, 3 sororities. **Athletics (Intercollegiate):** *Men:* baseball, basketball, cross-country, football, golf, soccer, swimming, tennis, track/field (outdoor), track/field (indoor), wrestling. *Women:* basketball, cross-country, golf, soccer, softball, swimming, tennis, track/field (outdoor), track/field (indoor), volleyball. **On-Campus Highlights:** Taylor Lounge & Games Room, Gizmo (snack bar), Andrew Fitness Center, Whitcomb Art Center **Environmental Initiatives:** WASTE REDUCTION: Knox continues to make great strides in waste recovery. This is exemplified by the sharing culture on Knox' campus. Initiatives include a car-share program, a student-run bike share, and the institutionalization of the campus Share Shop and Office Supply Share, a place to donate gently used clothes and goods for other students to be able to take without charge. These initiatives find a new home for items that might have been destined for the landfill and encourage alternative transportation options to students, faculty, and staff. Move out at Knox features the "There's No Away" campaign that collects donations from students as they are packing to leave for the summer. This past year we collected more than 6 tons of still-good items that were donated to local thrift stores, properly disposed of or recycled, or sorted into the campus Share Shop and Office Supply Share. Knox also finds ways to divert other items from the landfill. The non-traditional recycling program collects hard to recycle items, from batteries to toothbrushes, and has found places that collect them for recycling. Food waste is also combated. Last year the Knox chapter of the Food Recovery Network diverted and donated more than 13,700 pounds of food to local organizations. Also, the annual zero waste lunch at Commencement continues to be a success. In 2017 the event served 1500 guests and created less than a pound of landfill-only waste.

ADMISSIONS

Freshman Academic Profile: Average high school GPA 3.4. 34% in top 10% of high school class, 66% in top 25% of high school class, 94% in top 50% of high school class. 81% from public high schools. **Test Scores:** SAT Math middle 50% range 580-695. SAT EBRW middle 50% range 560-670. ACT middle 50% range 23-30. Minimum internet-based TOEFL 80. Minimum paper TOEFL 550. **Basis for Candidate Selection:** *Very important factors considered include:* rigor of secondary school record, academic GPA. *Important factors considered include:* class rank, application essay, recommendation(s). *Other factors considered include:* standardized test scores, interview, extracurricular activities, talent/ability, character/personal qualities, first generation, alumni/ae relation, geographical residence, state residency, racial/ethnic status, volunteer work, work experience, level of applicant's interest. **Freshman Admission Requirements:** High school diploma is required and GED is accepted *Academic units recommended:* 4 English, 4 math, 3 science, 2 science labs, 3 foreign language, 2 social studies, 1 history. **Freshman Admission Statistics:** 3,222 applied, 71.5% admitted, 15% enrolled. **Transfer Admission Requirements:** High school transcript, college transcript(s), essay or personal statement, statement of good standing from prior institution(s). Minimum college GPA of 3.0 required. Lowest grade transferable C. **General Admission Information:** Application fee $50. Priority deadline 1/15. Nonfall registration accepted. Admission may be deferred for a maximum of 1 year.

COSTS AND FINANCIAL AID

Annual tuition $45,783. Room and board $9,870. Required fees $771. Average book expense $900. **Required Forms and Deadlines:** FAFSA; Institution's own financial aid form. **Notification of Awards:** Applicants will be notified of awards on a rolling basis beginning 12/1. **Types of Aid:** *Need-based scholarships/grants:* College/university scholarship or grant aid from institutional funds; Federal Pell; Private scholarships; SEOG; State scholarships/grants. *Loans:* Direct PLUS loans; Direct Subsidized Stafford Loans; Direct Unsubsidized Stafford Loans. *Student Employment:* Federal Work-Study Program available. Institutional employment available. **Financial Aid Statistics:** 99% needy freshmen, 98% needy undergrads receive need-based scholarship or grant aid. 11% freshmen, 9% undergrads receive non-need-based scholarship or grant aid. 85% freshmen, 87% undergrads receive need-based self-help aid. 0% freshmen, 0% undergrads receive athletic scholarships. 99% freshmen, 98% undergrads receive any aid. 64% undergrads borrow to pay for school. Average cumulative indebtedness $30,638. **Criteria for awarding aid:** *Non-need-based:* Academics, Art, Leadership, Music/drama.

See page 962.

KUTZTOWN UNIVERSITY OF PENNSYLVANIA

PO Box 730, Kutztown, PA 19530-0730
Phone: 610-683-4060 · **Financial Aid Phone:** 610-683-4032
E-mail: admissions@kutztown.edu · **CEEB Code:** 2653
Fax: 610-683-1375 · **Website:** www.kutztown.edu · **ACT Code:** 3706

This public school was founded in 1866. It has a 289 acre campus.

RATINGS

Admissions Selectivity Rating: 78   **Fire Safety Rating:** 98   **Green Rating:** 60*

STUDENTS AND FACULTY

Enrollment: 7,443. **Student Body:** 53% female, 47% male, 12% out-of-state, 1% international (29 countries represented). Asian 1%, African American 7%, Caucasian 76%, Hispanic 9%, Native American <1%, Pacific Islander <1%, Two or more races 3%, Race unknown 1%.
Retention and Graduation: 74% freshmen return for sophomore year. 35% freshmen graduate within 4 years. 53% freshmen graduate within 6 years. 12% grads go on to further study within 1 year. **Faculty:** Student/faculty ratio 18:1. 388 full-time faculty, 86% hold PhDs, 21% are members of minority groups, 50% are women. 0% of classes are taught by teaching assistants.

ACADEMICS

Degrees: Bachelor's; Doctoral/Research; Master's; Post-Bachelor's certificate; Post-Master's certificate **Classes:** Most classes have fewer than 10 students. Most lab/discussion sessions have 10-19 students. **Most popular majors:** Communication, Journalism, And Related Programs; Education; English Language And Literature, General. **Special Study Options:** Cross-registration; Distance learning; Double major; Dual enrollment; Honors program; Independent study; Internships; Liberal arts/career combination; Student-designed major; Study abroad; Teacher certification program. **Honors programs:** 1)University Honors Program 2)Various Honor Societies. **Disability Services offered to physically disabled students:** Note-taking services; Reader services; Tape recorders; Tutors. **Career services:** Alumni network; Alumni services; Career assessment; Career/job search classes; Internships; Regional alumni

FACILITIES

Housing: Apartments for married students; Apartments for single students; Coed dorms; Cooperative housing; Women's dorms 90% of campus accessible to physically disabled. **Special Academic Facilities/Equipment:** Art Gallery, German Cultural Heritage Center, Early Childhood Learning Center, Cartography Lab, Observatory, Planetarium, Daycare Center **Computers:** 25% of classrooms, 95% of dorms, 100% of libraries, 75% of dining areas, 100% of student union, 65% of common outdoor areas have wireless network access. Students can register for classes online. Administrative functions (other than registration) can be performed online.

CAMPUS LIFE

Environment: Rural **Activities:** Campus Ministries; Choral groups; Concert band; Dance; Drama/theater; International Student Organization; Jazz band; Literary magazine; Marching band; Model UN; Music ensembles; Musical theater; Radio station; Student government; Student newspaper; Student-run film society; Symphony orchestra; Television station; Yearbook 218 registered organizations, 15 honor societies, 11 religious organizations. 9 fraternities, 8 sororities. **Athletics (Intercollegiate):** *Men:* baseball, basketball, cross-country, football, tennis, track/field (outdoor), track/field (indoor), wrestling. *Women:* basketball, bowling, cross-country, field hockey, golf, lacrosse, soccer, softball, swimming, tennis, track/field (outdoor), track/field (indoor), volleyball. **On-Campus Highlights:** Taylor and Burnes Gourmet Coffee, Student Rec Center, Alumni Plaza-new walkway with outdoor amphitheater, Pennsylvania German Cultural Heritage Center, Academic Forum **Environmental Initiatives:** Recycling program

ADMISSIONS

Freshman Academic Profile: Average high school GPA 3.2. 7% in top 10% of high school class, 24% in top 25% of high school class, 55% in top 50% of high school class. 91% from public high schools. **Test Scores:** SAT Math middle 50% range 480-560. SAT EBRW middle 50% range 490-580. ACT middle 50% range 18-24. Minimum internet-based TOEFL 79. Minimum paper TOEFL 550. **Basis for Candidate Selection:** *Very important factors considered include:* rigor of secondary school record, class rank, standardized test scores. *Other factors considered include:* academic GPA, recommendation(s), talent/ability. **Freshman Admission Requirements:** High school diploma is required and GED is accepted *Academic units required:* 4 English, 3 math, 3 science, 2 science labs, 3 social studies. **Freshman Admission Statistics:** 8,073 applied, 73.9% admitted, 27% enrolled. **Transfer Admission Requirements:** college transcript(s), statement of good standing from prior institution(s). Minimum college GPA of 2.0 required. Lowest grade transferable C-. **General Admission Information:** Application fee $35. Priority deadline 12/1. Nonfall registration accepted. Admission may be deferred for a maximum of 1 year.

COSTS AND FINANCIAL AID

Annual in-state tuition $10,282. Annual out-of-state tuition $11,238. Room and board $10,282. Required fees $2,495. Average book expense $1,684. **Required Forms and Deadlines:** FAFSA. **Notification of Awards:** Applicants will be notified of awards on a rolling basis beginning 3/30. **Types of Aid:** *Need-based scholarships/grants:* College/university scholarship or grant aid from institutional funds; Federal Pell; Private scholarships; SEOG; State scholarships/grants. *Loans:* Direct PLUS loans; Direct Subsidized Stafford Loans; Direct Unsubsidized Stafford Loans. *Student Employment:* Federal Work-Study Program available. Institutional employment available. **Financial Aid Statistics:** 62% needy freshmen, 62% needy undergrads receive need-based scholarship or grant aid. 67% freshmen, 27% undergrads receive non-need-based scholarship or grant aid. 89% freshmen, 90% undergrads receive need-based self-help aid. 5% freshmen, 4% undergrads receive athletic scholarships. 88% freshmen, 82% undergrads receive any aid. 80% undergrads borrow to pay for school. Average cumulative indebtedness $39,230. **Criteria for awarding aid:** *Need-based:* Academics *Non-need-based:* Academics, Art, Athletics, Leadership, Minority status, Music/drama.

LA ROCHE COLLEGE

9000 Babcock Boulevard, Pittsburgh, PA 15237
Phone: 412-536-1271 • **Financial Aid Phone:** 412-536-1120
E-mail: admissions@laroche.edu • **CEEB Code:** 2379
Fax: 412-847-1820 • **Website:** www.laroche.edu • **ACT Code:** 3607

This private school, affiliated with the Roman Catholic Church, was founded in 1963. It has a 43 acre campus.

RATINGS

Admissions Selectivity Rating: 71   **Fire Safety Rating:** 93   **Green Rating:** 60*

STUDENTS AND FACULTY

Enrollment: 1,315. **Student Body:** 54% female, 46% male, 10% out-of-state, 15% international (27 countries represented). Asian 2%, African American 10%, Caucasian 63%, Hispanic 3%, Native American <1%, Pacific Islander <1%, Two or more races 2%, Race unknown 4%.
Retention and Graduation: 68% freshmen return for sophomore year. 35% freshmen graduate within 4 years. 51% freshmen graduate within 6 years. **Faculty:** Student/faculty ratio 12:1. 65 full-time faculty, 83% hold PhDs, 14% are members of minority groups, 57% are women. 0% of classes are taught by teaching assistants.

ACADEMICS

Degrees: Associate; Bachelor's; Certificate; Doctoral/Professional; Master's; Post-Bachelor's certificate; Post-Master's certificate; Terminal Associate **Classes:** Most classes have 10-19 students. Most lab/discussion sessions have 10-19 students. **Most popular majors:** Psychology, General; Criminal Justice/Safety Studies; Accounting. **Special Study Options:** Accelerated program; Cross-registration; Distance learning; Double major; Dual enrollment; English as a Second Language (ESL); Honors program; Independent study; Internships; Student-designed major; Study abroad. **Honors programs:** The Honors Institute at La Roche College is designed to recognize and promote academic excellence and focuses on those academically gifted students who are searching for a challenge. With a program designed specifically for honors-level students executed by fine scholars in their field and coupled with exclusive co-curricular activities, housing and study areas specifically for Honors Institute students, the program is tailored to exemplary students who are looking for an outstanding educational opportunity that will serve as the pathway for a successful future. **Combined degree programs:** BA/MA. **Disability Services offered to physically disabled students:** Note-taking services; Reader services; Tutors. **Career services:** Career assessment; Career/job search classes; Internships; Regional alumni

FACILITIES

Housing: Coed dorms 100% of campus accessible to physically diasbled. **Special Academic Facilities/Equipment:** Cantellopes Art Gallery; Huber Academic Center has state of the art smart classrooms **Computers:** 100% of classrooms, 10% of dorms, 100% of libraries, 100% of dining areas, 100% of student union, 25% of common outdoor areas have wireless network access. Students can register for classes online. Administrative functions (other than registration) can be performed online.

CAMPUS LIFE

Environment: City **Activities:** Campus Ministries; Dance; International Student Organization; Literary magazine; Radio station; Student government; Student newspaper; Student-run film society 40 registered organizations, 4 honor societies, 2 religious organizations. **Athletics (Intercollegiate):** *Men:* baseball, basketball, cross-country, golf, lacrosse, soccer. *Women:* basketball, cheerleading, cross-country, soccer, softball, tennis, volleyball. **On-Campus Highlights:** Sports and Fitness Center, College bookstore, Magdalen Chapel, Huber Academic Center caontains state of the art smart classrooms, Newly renovated library

ADMISSIONS

Freshman Academic Profile: Average high school GPA 3.3. 8% in top 10% of high school class, 17% in top 25% of high school class, 71% in top 50% of high school class. 83% from public high schools. **Test Scores:** SAT Math middle 50% range 470-550. SAT EBRW middle 50% range 480-590. ACT middle 50% range 18-23. **Basis for Candidate Selection:** *Very important factors considered include:* rigor of secondary school record, academic GPA. *Important factors considered include:* standardized test scores. *Other factors considered include:* class rank, application essay, recommendation(s), interview, extracurricular activities, talent/ability, character/personal qualities, first generation, alumni/ae relation, volunteer work, work experience, level of applicant's interest. **Freshman Admission Requirements:** High school diploma is required and GED is accepted *Academic units required:* 4 English, 2 math, 3 science, 2 science labs, 2 social studies, 2 history, 2 academic electives, *Academic units*

recommended: 4 English, 3 math, 4 science, 3 science labs, 2 foreign language, 2 social studies, 2 history, 3 academic electives, 1 computer science. **Freshman Admission Statistics:** 1,197 applied, 96.6% admitted, 20% enrolled. **Transfer Admission Requirements:** college transcript(s), essay or personal statement, Minimum college GPA of 2.0 required. Lowest grade transferable C. **General Admission Information:** Application fee $50. Nonfall registration accepted. Admission may be deferred for a maximum of 1 year.

COSTS AND FINANCIAL AID

Annual tuition $27,720. Room and board $11,220. Required fees $800. Average book expense $1,200. **Required Forms and Deadlines:** FAFSA. **Notification of Awards:** Applicants will be notified of awards on a rolling basis beginning 11/1. **Types of Aid:** *Need-based scholarships/grants:* College/university scholarship or grant aid from institutional funds; Federal Pell; Private scholarships; SEOG; State scholarships/grants. *Loans:* Direct PLUS loans; Direct Subsidized Stafford Loans; Direct Unsubsidized Stafford Loans. *Student Employment:* Federal Work-Study Program available. **Financial Aid Statistics:** 98% needy freshmen, 80% needy undergrads receive need-based scholarship or grant aid. 100% freshmen, 92% undergrads receive non-need-based scholarship or grant aid. 82% freshmen, 74% undergrads receive need-based self-help aid. 0% freshmen, 0% undergrads receive athletic scholarships. 91% freshmen, 91% undergrads receive any aid. 79% undergrads borrow to pay for school. Average cumulative indebtedness $34,992. **Criteria for awarding aid:** *Non-need-based:* Academics, Religious affiliation.

LA SALLE UNIVERSITY

1900 West Olney Avenue, Philadelphia, PA 19141-1199
Phone: 215-951-1500 • **Financial Aid Phone:** 215-951-1070
E-mail: admiss@lasalle.edu • **CEEB Code:** 2363
Fax: 215-951-1656 • **Website:** http://www.lasalle.edu • **ACT Code:** 3608

This private school, affiliated with the Roman Catholic Church, was founded in 1863. It has a 133 acre campus.

RATINGS

Admissions Selectivity Rating: 75   **Fire Safety Rating:** 87   **Green Rating:** 63

STUDENTS AND FACULTY

Enrollment: 3,705. **Student Body:** 61% female, 39% male, 31% out-of-state, 2% international (31 countries represented). Asian 5%, African American 20%, Caucasian 50%, Hispanic 18%, Native American <1%, Pacific Islander <1%, Two or more races 3%, Race unknown 2%.
Retention and Graduation: 76% freshmen return for sophomore year. 59% freshmen graduate within 4 years. 67% freshmen graduate within 6 years. 18% grads go on to further study within 1 year. **Faculty:** Student/faculty ratio 11:1. 220 full-time faculty, 76% hold PhDs, 12% are members of minority groups, 56% are women. 0% of classes are taught by teaching assistants.

ACADEMICS

Degrees: Associate; Bachelor's; Doctoral/Professional; Master's; Post-Bachelor's certificate; Post-Master's certificate **Classes:** Most classes have 10-19 students. Most lab/discussion sessions have 10-19 students. **Most popular majors:** Communication And Media Studies; Registered Nursing/Registered Nurse; Marketing/Marketing Management, General. **Special Study Options:** Accelerated program; Cooperative education program; Cross-registration; Distance learning; Double major; Dual enrollment; English as a Second Language (ESL); Exchange student program (domestic); Honors program; Independent study; Internships; Student-designed major; Study abroad; Teacher certification program. **Honors programs:** Business Scholars Co-op Program, graduate in 4-years with two full-time co-op work experiences; La Salle University Honors Program, similarly-talented peers, meeting in small seminar settings with faculty dedicated to undergraduate teaching is but one of the hallmarks of the La Salle Honors community. You will be participating in a Program which has as its specific objective the challenge of educating the superior student. **Combined degree programs:** BA/MA. **Disability Services offered to physically disabled students:** Note-taking services; Reader services; Tape recorders; Tutors. **Career services:** Alumni network; Alumni services; Career assessment; Career/job search classes; Internships; Regional alumni

FACILITIES

Housing: Apartments for single students; Coed dorms; Special housing for disabled students; Theme housing; Wellness housing 95% of campus accessible to physically diasbled. **Special Academic Facilities/Equipment:** Hugh and Nancy Devlin Science and Technology Center, West Campus School of Nursing and Health Science (formally Germantown Hospital), Art Museum, Japanese tea house, language lab, and child development center. **Computers:** Students can register for classes online. Administrative functions (other than registration) can be performed online.

CAMPUS LIFE

Environment: Metropolis **Activities:** Campus Ministries; Choral groups; Dance; Drama/theater; International Student Organization; Jazz band; Literary magazine; Music ensembles; Musical theater; Pep band; Radio station; Student government; Student newspaper; Student-run film society; Television station; Yearbook 100 registered organizations, 10 honor societies, 4 religious organizations. 7 fraternities, 5 sororities. **Athletics (Intercollegiate):** *Men:* baseball, basketball, cheerleading, crew/rowing, cross-country, diving, football, golf, soccer, swimming, tennis, track/field (outdoor), wrestling. *Women:* basketball, cheerleading, crew/rowing, cross-country, diving, field hockey, golf, lacrosse, soccer, softball, swimming, tennis, track/field (outdoor), volleyball. **On-Campus Highlights:** Hayman Center (sports facility), Connelly Library, Founders' Hall (New School of Business Building), Hugh and Nancy Devlin Science and Technology Center, La Salle University Art Museum

ADMISSIONS

Freshman Academic Profile: Average high school GPA 3.3. 14% in top 10% of high school class, 36% in top 25% of high school class, 64% in top 50% of high school class. 59% from public high schools. **Test Scores:** SAT Math middle 50% range 480-580. SAT EBRW middle 50% range 500-590. ACT middle 50% range 19-25. Minimum internet-based TOEFL 76. Minimum paper TOEFL 540. **Basis for Candidate Selection:** *Very important factors considered include:* rigor of secondary school record, academic GPA. *Important factors considered include:* extracurricular activities. *Other factors considered include:* application essay, standardized test scores, recommendation(s), interview, talent/ability, character/personal qualities, alumni/ae relation, volunteer work, work experience. **Freshman Admission Requirements:** High school diploma is required and GED is accepted *Academic units required:* 4 English, 3 math, 1 science, 1 science labs, 2 foreign language, 1 history, 5 academic electives. **Freshman Admission Statistics:** 6,566 applied, 79.3% admitted, 20% enrolled. **Transfer Admission Requirements:** High school transcript, college transcript(s), essay or personal statement, standardized test scores, statement of good standing from prior institution(s). Minimum college GPA of 2.5 required. Lowest grade transferable C. **General Admission Information:** Nonfall registration accepted. Admission may be deferred for a maximum of 1 year.

COSTS AND FINANCIAL AID

Annual tuition $28,800. Room and board $14,690. Required fees $700. Average book expense $500. **Required Forms and Deadlines:** FAFSA. **Notification of Awards:** Applicants will be notified of awards on a rolling basis beginning 2/1. **Types of Aid:** *Need-based scholarships/grants:* College/university scholarship or grant aid from institutional funds; Federal Nursing Scholarships; Federal Pell; Private scholarships; SEOG; State scholarships/grants. *Loans:* Direct PLUS loans; Direct Subsidized Stafford Loans; Direct Unsubsidized Stafford Loans. *Student Employment:* Federal Work-Study Program available. Institutional employment available. **Financial Aid Statistics:** 99% needy freshmen, 97% needy undergrads receive need-based scholarship or grant aid. 7% freshmen, 7% undergrads receive non-need-based scholarship or grant aid. 77% freshmen, 81% undergrads receive need-based self-help aid. 4% freshmen, 5% undergrads receive athletic scholarships. 97% freshmen, 93% undergrads receive any aid. 77% undergrads borrow to pay for school. Average cumulative indebtedness $36,907. **Criteria for awarding aid:** *Need-based:* Academics *Non-need-based:* Academics, Athletics.

LA SIERRA UNIVERSITY

4500 Riverwalk Parkway, Riverside, CA 92515
Phone: 951-785-2176
E-mail: admissions@lasierra.edu
Fax: (951) 785-2477 · **Website:** www.lasierra.edu · **ACT Code:** 294

This private school, affiliated with the Seventh Day Adventist Church, was founded in 1922. It has a 100 acre campus.

RATINGS

Admissions Selectivity Rating: 85　　**Fire Safety Rating:** 60*　　**Green Rating:** 60*

STUDENTS AND FACULTY

Enrollment: 2,060. **Student Body:** 58% female, 42% male, 6% out-of-state, 12% international. Asian 16%, African American 7%, Caucasian 16%, Hispanic 42%, Native American <1%, Pacific Islander 2%, Two or more races 4%, Race unknown <1%.
Retention and Graduation: 76% freshmen return for sophomore year.

Faculty: Student/faculty ratio 14:1. 103 full-time faculty, 95% hold PhDs, 32% are members of minority groups, 44% are women.

ACADEMICS

Degrees: Bachelor's; Certificate; Doctoral/Research; Master's; Post-Bachelor's certificate; Post-Master's certificate **Classes:** Most classes have fewer than 10 students. Most lab/discussion sessions have 10-19 students. **Special Study Options:** Cross-registration; Distance learning; Double major; Dual enrollment; English as a Second Language (ESL); Honors program; Independent study; Internships; Student-designed major; Study abroad; Teacher certification program.

FACILITIES

Housing: Apartments for married students; Apartments for single students; Men's dorms; Special housing for international students; Wellness housing; Women's dorms

CAMPUS LIFE

Environment: City **Activities:** Campus Ministries; Choral groups; Concert band; Drama/theater; International Student Organization; Jazz band; Literary magazine; Music ensembles; Student government; Student newspaper; Symphony orchestra; Yearbook.

ADMISSIONS

Freshman Academic Profile: Average high school GPA 3.3. 10% in top 10% of high school class, 41% in top 25% of high school class, 63% in top 50% of high school class. **Test Scores:** SAT Math middle 50% range 410-530. SAT EBRW middle 50% range 400-510. ACT middle 50% range 17-22. Minimum paper TOEFL 525. **Basis for Candidate Selection:** *Very important factors considered include:* rigor of secondary school record, academic GPA, standardized test scores, character/personal qualities. *Important factors considered include:* application essay, recommendation(s), religious affiliation/commitment, level of applicant's interest. **Freshman Admission Requirements:** High school diploma is required and GED is accepted *Academic units required:* 4 English, 3 math, 2 science, 2 science labs, 2 foreign language, 2 social studies, 1 visual/performing arts, and 1 unit from above areas or other academic areas. *Academic units recommended:* 4 math, 3 science, 3 science labs, 3 foreign language. **Freshman Admission Statistics:** 3,479 applied, 46.8% admitted, 29% enrolled. **General Admission Information:** Application fee $30. Regular application deadline 8/15. Nonfall registration accepted. Admission may be deferred.

COSTS AND FINANCIAL AID

Annual tuition $27,972. Room and board $7,500. Required fees $1,131. Average book expense $1,710.

LAFAYETTE COLLEGE

730 High Street, Easton, PA 18042
Phone: 610-330-5100 · **Financial Aid Phone:** 610 330-5055
E-mail: admissions@lafayette.edu · **CEEB Code:** 2361
Fax: 610-330-5355 · **Website:** http://www.lafayette.edu/

This private school was founded in 1826. It has a 340 acre campus.

RATINGS

Admissions Selectivity Rating: 95　　**Fire Safety Rating:** 91　　**Green Rating:** 79

STUDENTS AND FACULTY

Enrollment: 2,567. **Student Body:** 52% female, 48% male, 81% out-of-state, 10% international (61 countries represented). Asian 4%, African American 5%, Caucasian 66%, Hispanic 7%, Native American 0%, Pacific Islander <1%, Two or more races 2%, Race unknown 6%.
Retention and Graduation: 95% freshmen return for sophomore year. 85% freshmen graduate within 4 years. 89% freshmen graduate within 6 years. 16% grads go on to further study within 1 year. 2% grads pursue law degrees. 2% grads pursue medical degrees. **Faculty:** Student/faculty ratio 10:1. 237 full-time faculty, 98% hold PhDs, 19% are members of minority groups, 40% are women. 0% of classes are taught by teaching assistants.

ACADEMICS

Degrees: Bachelor's **Classes:** Most classes have 10-19 students. Most lab/discussion sessions have 20-29 students. **Most popular majors:** Mechanical Engineering; Biology/Biological Sciences, General; Economics, General.

Special Study Options: Cross-registration; Double major; Dual enrollment; Exchange student program (domestic); Honors program; Independent study; Internships; Student-designed major; Study abroad. Disability Services offered to physically disabled students: Tutors. Career services: Alumni network; Alumni services; Career assessment; Career/job search classes; Internships; Regional alumni

FACILITIES

Housing: Apartments for single students; Coed dorms; Fraternity/sorority housing; Men's dorms; Special housing for disabled student; Theme housing; Wellness housing; Women's dorms Special Academic Facilities/Equipment: Art and geological museums, center for the arts, engineering labs, INSTRON materials testing machine, electron microscopes, transform nuclear magnetic resonance spectrometer, computerized gas chromatograph/mass spectrometer. Computers: Students can register for classes online. Administrative functions (other than registration) can be performed online.

CAMPUS LIFE

Environment: City Activities: Campus Ministries; Choral groups; Concert band; Dance; Drama/theater; International Student Organization; Jazz band; Literary magazine; Model UN; Music ensembles; Musical theater; Pep band; Radio station; Student government; Student newspaper; Student-run film society; Symphony orchestra; Yearbook 250 registered organizations, 14 honor societies, 7 religious organizations. 7 fraternities, 6 sororities. Athletics (Intercollegiate): Men: baseball, basketball, cheerleading, crew/rowing, cross-country, diving, equestrian sports, fencing, football, golf, gymnastics, ice hockey, lacrosse, soccer, softball, swimming, tennis, track/field (outdoor), track/field (indoor), volleyball, wrestling. Women: basketball, cheerleading, crew/rowing, cross-country, diving, equestrian sports, fencing, field hockey, golf, gymnastics, softball, swimming, tennis, track/field (outdoor), track/field (indoor), volleyball. On-Campus Highlights: Skillman and Kirby Libraries, Farinon College Center, Williams Center for the Arts, Kirby Sports Center, Williams Visual Arts Building Environmental Initiatives: In addition to signing American College and University Presidents Climate Commitment, three undertakings summarize the College's efforts towards responsible stewardship of the Environment: 1. Waste Reduction—Recycling, including composting.—Purchases of materials/goods made from recycled materials and/or virgin material that is recyclable and produced from renewable sources.

ADMISSIONS

Freshman Academic Profile: Average high school GPA 3.5. 60% in top 10% of high school class, 91% in top 25% of high school class, 99% in top 50% of high school class. 61% from public high schools. Test Scores: SAT Math middle 50% range 630-730. SAT EBRW middle 50% range 630-710. ACT middle 50% range 28-31. Minimum internet-based TOEFL 80. Minimum paper TOEFL 550. Basis for Candidate Selection: Very important factors considered include: rigor of secondary school record, academic GPA. Important factors considered include: class rank, application essay, standardized test scores, recommendation(s), interview, extracurricular activities, talent/ability, character/personal qualities. Other factors considered include: first generation, alumni/ae relation, geographical residence, racial/ethnic status, volunteer work, work experience, level of applicant's interest. Freshman Admission Requirements: High school diploma or equivalent is not required Academic units recommended: 4 English, 3 math, 2 science, 2 science labs, 2 foreign language, 5 academic electives. Freshman Admission Statistics: 8,469 applied, 30.8% admitted, 25% enrolled. Transfer Admission Requirements: High school transcript, college transcript(s), essay or personal statement, statement of good standing from prior institution(s). Lowest grade transferable C. General Admission Information: Application fee $65. Regular application deadline 1/15. Nonfall registration accepted. Admission may be deferred for a maximum of 1 year.

COSTS AND FINANCIAL AID

Annual tuition $52,415. Room and board $14,470. Required fees $465. Average book expense $1,000. Required Forms and Deadlines: CSS/Financial Aid PROFILE; FAFSA; Noncustodial PROFILE. Notification of Awards: Applicants will be notified of awards on or about 4/1. Types of Aid: Need-based scholarships/grants: College/university scholarship or grant aid from institutional funds; Federal Pell; Private scholarships; SEOG; State scholarships/grants. Loans: Direct PLUS loans; Direct Subsidized Stafford Loans; Direct Unsubsidized Stafford Loans. Student Employment: Federal Work-Study Program available. Institutional employment available. Financial Aid Statistics: 95% needy freshmen, 94% needy undergrads receive need-based scholarship or grant aid. 26% freshmen, 21% undergrads receive non-need-based scholarship or grant aid. 88% freshmen, 92% undergrads receive need-based self-help aid. 10% freshmen, 9% undergrads receive athletic scholarships. 61% freshmen, 58% undergrads receive any aid. 48% undergrads borrow to pay for school. Average cumulative indebtedness $29,324. Criteria for awarding aid: Need-based: Academics, Athletics, Leadership Non-need-based: Academics, Athletics, Leadership.

LAGRANGE COLLEGE

601 Broad Street, LaGrange, GA 30240
Phone: 706-880-8005 · Financial Aid Phone: 888-253-9918
E-mail: lgcadmis@lagrange.edu · CEEB Code: 5362
Fax: 706-880-8010 · Website: www.lagrange.edu · ACT Code: 834

This private school, affiliated with the Methodist Church, was founded in 1831. It has a 120 acre campus.

RATINGS

Admissions Selectivity Rating: 80   Fire Safety Rating: 60*   Green Rating: 60*

STUDENTS AND FACULTY

Enrollment: 860. Student Body: 55% female, 45% male, 11% out-of-state, 2% international (10 countries represented). Asian 1%, African American 22%, Caucasian 72%, Hispanic 2%, Native American <1%, Race unknown 1%. Retention and Graduation: 71% freshmen return for sophomore year. Faculty: Student/faculty ratio 10:1. 65 full-time faculty, 83% hold PhDs, 48% are women. 0% of classes are taught by teaching assistants.

ACADEMICS

Degrees: Associate; Bachelor's; Master's Classes: Most classes have 10-19 students. Most popular majors: Teacher Education, Multiple Levels; Business Administration And Management, General; Organizational Behavior Studies. Special Study Options: Double major; Dual enrollment; Independent study; Internships; Liberal arts/career combination; Study abroad; Teacher certification program. Career services: Alumni network; Alumni services; Career assessment; Career/job search classes; Internships

FACILITIES

Housing: Apartments for single students; Coed dorms; Fraternity/sorority housing; Men's dorms; Theme housing; Women's dorms 75% of campus accessible to physically disabled. Special Academic Facilities/Equipment: Lamar Dodd Art Center, Price Theater, Callaway Auditorium Computers: Students can register for classes online. Administrative functions (other than registration) can be performed online.

CAMPUS LIFE

Environment: Village Activities: Campus Ministries; Choral groups; Drama/theater; International Student Organization; Literary magazine; Music ensembles; Musical theater; Pep band; Student government; Student newspaper; Symphony orchestra; Yearbook 49 registered organizations, 11 honor societies, 8 religious organizations. 3 fraternities, 6 sororities. Athletics (Intercollegiate): Men: baseball, basketball, cross-country, football, golf, soccer, swimming, tennis. Women: basketball, cheerleading, cross-country, soccer, softball, swimming, tennis, volleyball. On-Campus Highlights: Turner Student Center, Smith Hall, Academic Quadrangle, Smith Patio, Callaway Sports Facilities Environmental Initiatives: Building a LEED library

ADMISSIONS

Freshman Academic Profile: Average high school GPA 3.5. 25% in top 10% of high school class, 54% in top 25% of high school class, 92% in top 50% of high school class. Test Scores: SAT Math middle 50% range 460-570. SAT EBRW middle 50% range 460-570. ACT middle 50% range 20-25. Minimum paper TOEFL 500. Basis for Candidate Selection: Very important factors considered include: academic GPA, standardized test scores, character/personal qualities. Important factors considered include: class rank, recommendation(s), extracurricular activities, level of applicant's interest. Other factors considered include: rigor of secondary school record, application essay, interview, talent/ability, alumni/ae relation, geographical residence, volunteer work. Freshman Admission Requirements: High school diploma is required and GED is accepted Academic units required: 4 English, 4 math, 3 science, 3 social studies, Academic units recommended: 4 English, 4 math, 3 science, 2 foreign language, 3 social studies. Freshman Admission Statistics: 1,342 applied, 64.8% admitted, 27% enrolled. Transfer Admission Requirements: college transcript(s), statement of good standing from prior institution(s). Minimum college GPA of 2.0 required. Lowest grade transferable 1. General Admission Information: Application fee $30. Priority deadline 3/1. Nonfall registration accepted. Admission may be deferred for a maximum of one term.

COSTS AND FINANCIAL AID

Annual tuition $19,900. Room and board $8,168. Required Forms and Deadlines: FAFSA; State aid form. Notification of Awards: Applicants will be notified of awards on a rolling basis beginning 3/15. Types of Aid: Need-based scholarships/grants: College/university scholarship or grant aid from institutional funds; Federal Pell; Private scholarships; SEOG; State scholarships/grants. Loans: Student Employment: Federal Work-Study Program available. Institutional employment available. Financial Aid Statistics: 100% needy freshmen, 100% needy undergrads receive need-based scholarship or grant aid. 24% freshmen, 17% undergrads receive non-need-based scholarship or grant aid. 69% freshmen, 77% undergrads receive need-based self-help aid. 0% freshmen, 0% undergrads receive athletic scholarships. **Criteria for awarding aid:** *Need-based:* Minority status, Religious affiliation *Non-need-based:* Academics, Art, Leadership, Music/drama, Religious affiliation, State/district residency.

LAKE ERIE COLLEGE

391 West Washington Street, Painesville, OH 44077-3389
Phone: (440) 375-7050 · **Financial Aid Phone:** 440-375-7100
E-mail: admissions@lec.edu · **CEEB Code:** 1391
Fax: (440) 375-7005 · **Website:** www.lec.edu · **ACT Code:** 3288

This private school was founded in 1856. It has a 48 acre campus.

RATINGS
Admissions Selectivity Rating: 78   **Fire Safety Rating:** 93   **Green Rating:** 60*

STUDENTS AND FACULTY
Enrollment: 750. **Student Body:** 48% female, 52% male, 26% out-of-state, 4% international. Asian 1%, African American 14%, Caucasian 72%, Hispanic 2%, Native American 1%, Two or more races 3%, Race unknown 3%. **Retention and Graduation:** 70% freshmen return for sophomore year. 23% grads go on to further study within 1 year. **Faculty:** Student/faculty ratio 14:1. 42 full-time faculty, 74% hold PhDs, 64% are women. 0% of classes are taught by teaching assistants.

ACADEMICS
Degrees: Bachelor's; Master's; Post-Bachelor's certificate **Classes:** Most classes have 10-19 students. Most lab/discussion sessions have fewer than 10 students. **Most popular majors:** Biology/Biological Sciences, General; Psychology, General; Business Administration And Management, General. **Special Study Options:** Accelerated program; Cross-registration; Double major; Dual enrollment; Honors program; Independent study; Internships; Liberal arts/career combination; Student-designed major; Study abroad; Teacher certification program. **Honors programs:** Mortar Board. **Disability Services offered to physically disabled students:** Tape recorders; Tutors. **Career services:** Alumni network; Alumni services; Career assessment; Career/job search classes; Internships

FACILITIES
Housing: Apartments for married students; Apartments for single students; Coed dorms; Men's dorms; Women's dorms 90% of campus accessible to physically diasbled. **Special Academic Facilities/Equipment:** Pheasant Run Airport, Equestrian Facility **Computers:** Students can register for classes online. Administrative functions (other than registration) can be performed online.

CAMPUS LIFE
Environment: Town **Activities:** Choral groups; Dance; Drama/theater; International Student Organization; Music ensembles; Student government 15 registered organizations, 3 honor societies, 1 sorority. **Athletics (Intercollegiate):** *Men:* baseball, basketball, cross-country, equestrian sports, football, golf, soccer. *Women:* basketball, cross-country, equestrian sports, soccer, softball, volleyball. College Hall, Austin Science Center, Jerome T. Osborne Family Athletic & Wellness Center, EQ Facilities, Residence Halls **Environmental Initiatives:** Recent initiation of Sustainability committee.

ADMISSIONS
Freshman Academic Profile: Average high school GPA 3.1. 91% from public high schools. **Test Scores:** SAT Math middle 50% range 420-510. SAT EBRW middle 50% range 420-510. ACT middle 50% range 18-22. Minimum internet-based TOEFL 79. Minimum paper TOEFL 550. **Basis for Candidate Selection:** *Very important factors considered include:* rigor of secondary school record, academic GPA, recommendation(s), interview, character/personal qualities. *Important factors considered include:* class rank, application essay, standardized test scores, extracurricular activities, talent/ability. *Other factors considered include:* alumni/ae relation, volunteer work, work experience, level of applicant's interest. **Freshman Admission Requirements:** High school diploma is required and GED is accepted *Academic units required:* 4 English, 3 math, 3 science, 2 science labs, 2 foreign language, 3 social studies. *Academic units recommended:* 4 English, 3 math, 3 science, 2 science labs, 2 foreign language, 3 social studies. **Freshman Admission Statistics:** 1,485 applied, 63.1% admitted, 23% enrolled. **Transfer Admission Requirements:** High school transcript, college transcript(s), statement of good standing from prior institution(s). Minimum college GPA of 2.0 required. Lowest grade transferable

C. General Admission Information: Application fee $30. Priority deadline 5/1. Regular application deadline 8/1. Nonfall registration accepted. Admission may be deferred for a maximum of 1 year.

COSTS AND FINANCIAL AID
Annual tuition $29,426. Room and board $9,132. Required fees $1,436. Average book expense $1,100. **Required Forms and Deadlines:** FAFSA. **Notification of Awards:** Applicants will be notified of awards on a rolling basis beginning 2/15. **Types of Aid:** *Need-based scholarships/grants:* College/university scholarship or grant aid from institutional funds; Federal Pell; Private scholarships; SEOG; State scholarships/grants. *Loans:* Direct PLUS loans; Direct Subsidized Stafford Loans; Direct Unsubsidized Stafford Loans. *Student Employment:* Federal Work-Study Program available. Institutional employment available. **Financial Aid Statistics:** 100% needy freshmen, 100% needy undergrads receive need-based scholarship or grant aid. 7% freshmen, 12% undergrads receive non-need-based scholarship or grant aid. 92% freshmen, 87% undergrads receive need-based self-help aid. 8% freshmen, 11% undergrads receive athletic scholarships. 100% freshmen, 99% undergrads receive any aid. **Criteria for awarding aid:** *Need-based:* Academics, Athletics, Leadership *Non-need-based:* Academics, Art, Athletics, Leadership, Music/drama, State/district residency.

LAKE FOREST COLLEGE

555 North Sheridan Road, Lake Forest, IL 60045
Phone: 847-735-5000 · **Financial Aid Phone:** 847-725-5103
E-mail: admissions@lakeforest.edu · **CEEB Code:** 1392
Fax: 847-735-6271 · **Website:** www.lakeforest.edu · **ACT Code:** 1054

This private school was founded in 1857. It has a 107 acre campus.

RATINGS
Admissions Selectivity Rating: 86   **Fire Safety Rating:** 89   **Green Rating:** 60*

STUDENTS AND FACULTY
Enrollment: 1,483. **Student Body:** 57% female, 43% male, 38% out-of-state, 8% international (71 countries represented). Asian 6%, African American 6%, Caucasian 58%, Hispanic 15%, Native American <1%, Pacific Islander 0%, Two or more races 4%, Race unknown 4%. **Retention and Graduation:** 85% freshmen return for sophomore year. 66% freshmen graduate within 4 years. 72% freshmen graduate within 6 years. **Faculty:** Student/faculty ratio 12:1. 99 full-time faculty, 96% hold PhDs, 18% are members of minority groups, 44% are women. 0% of classes are taught by teaching assistants.

ACADEMICS
Degrees: Bachelor's; Master's; Post-Bachelor's certificate **Classes:** Most classes have fewer than 10 students. Most lab/discussion sessions have 10-19 students. **Most popular majors:** Psychology, General; Business/Commerce, General; Finance, General. **Special Study Options:** Accelerated program; Double major; Honors program; Independent study; Internships; Liberal arts/career combination; Student-designed major; Study abroad; Teacher certification program. **Honors programs:** The Richter Scholar Summer Research Program provides students, early in their academic careers, with the opportunity to conduct independent, individual research with Lake Forest College faculty. In the summer between their first and second year, each student in the Richter Program is employed for a ten week period and works one-on-one with a faculty member, doing independent research in a particular field. As the Richter Apprentice Scholars live and work together and participate in a weekly colloquium, they become a community of peers providing encouragement and support for each others present and future intellectual and research endeavors. **Combined degree programs:** BA/JD; BA/MA. **Disability Services offered to physically disabled students:** Note-taking services; Reader services; Tape recorders; Tutors. **Career services:** Alumni network; Alumni services; Career assessment; Career/job search classes; Internships; Regional alumni

FACILITIES
Housing: Apartments for single students; Coed dorms; Special housing for disabled student; Theme housing; Wellness housing 75% of campus accessible to physically diasbled. **Special Academic Facilities/Equipment:** Center for Chicago Programs, art galleries, language labs, technology resource center, speech and video production room, "smart" classrooms, music/recording studio with synthesizers, public access computer labs, electron microscope, computer molecular modeling equipment, high-resolution FT-IR, NMR spectrometer,

neutron howitzer, digital storage oscilloscopes, flourescence microscope **Computers:** 90% of classrooms, 100% of dorms, 100% of libraries, 75% of dining areas, 100% of student union, 10% of common outdoor areas have wireless network access. Administrative functions (other than registration) can be performed online.

CAMPUS LIFE

Environment: Village **Activities:** Campus Ministries; Choral groups; Concert band; Dance; Drama/theater; International Student Organization; Jazz band; Literary magazine; Model UN; Music ensembles; Musical theater; Opera; Pep band; Radio station; Student government; Student newspaper; Symphony orchestra 80 registered organizations, 12 honor societies, 6 religious organizations. 2 fraternities, 4 sororities. **Athletics (Intercollegiate):** *Men:* basketball, cross-country, diving, football, handball, ice hockey, soccer, swimming, tennis. *Women:* basketball, cross-country, diving, handball, ice hockey, soccer, softball, swimming, tennis, volleyball. **On-Campus Highlights:** Donnelley and Lee Library, Mohr Student Center, Sports and Recreation Center, Center for Chicago Programs, Career Advancement Center **Environmental Initiatives:** The organic campus garden provides internship opportunities for students and it supplies the campus cafeteria with food during the summer and fall.

ADMISSIONS

Freshman Academic Profile: 38% in top 10% of high school class, 67% in top 25% of high school class, 93% in top 50% of high school class. **Test Scores:** SAT Math middle 50% range 530-640. SAT EBRW middle 50% range 470-660. ACT middle 50% range 24-29. Minimum internet-based TOEFL 83. Minimum paper TOEFL 550. **Basis for Candidate Selection:** *Very important factors considered include:* rigor of secondary school record, application essay, interview, extracurricular activities, talent/ability, character/personal qualities. *Important factors considered include:* academic GPA. *Other factors considered include:* class rank, standardized test scores, recommendation(s), first generation, alumni/ae relation, geographical residence, volunteer work, work experience, level of applicant's interest. **Freshman Admission Requirements:** High school diploma is required and GED is accepted *Academic units required:* 4 English, 3 math, 3 science, 3 science labs, 2 foreign language, 2 social studies, 2 history, 3 academic electives, *Academic units recommended:* 4 English, 4 math, 4 science, 4 science labs, 4 foreign language, 2 social studies, 2 history, 3 academic electives, 1 unit from above area or other academic areas. **Freshman Admission Statistics:** 4,303 applied, 53.0% admitted, 16% enrolled. **Transfer Admission Requirements:** High school transcript, college transcript(s), essay or personal statement, Minimum college GPA of 2.5 required. Lowest grade transferable C-. **General Admission Information:** Regular application deadline 2/15. Nonfall registration accepted. Admission may be deferred for a maximum of 1 year.

COSTS AND FINANCIAL AID

Annual tuition $46,320. Room and board $10,390. Required fees $744. Average book expense $1,000. **Required Forms and Deadlines:** FAFSA. **Notification of Awards:** Applicants will be notified of awards on a rolling basis beginning 3/1. **Types of Aid:** *Need-based scholarships/grants:* College/ university scholarship or grant aid from institutional funds; Federal Pell; Private scholarships; SEOG; State scholarships/grants. *Loans:* Direct PLUS loans; Direct Subsidized Stafford Loans; Direct Unsubsidized Stafford Loans. *Student Employment:* Federal Work-Study Program available. Institutional employment available. **Financial Aid Statistics:** 100% needy freshmen, 100% needy undergrads receive need-based scholarship or grant aid. 0% undergrads receive non-need-based scholarship or grant aid. 90% freshmen, 88% undergrads receive need-based self-help aid. 0% freshmen, 0% undergrads receive athletic scholarships. 94% freshmen, 95% undergrads receive any aid. **Criteria for awarding aid:** *Non-need-based:* Academics, Alumni affiliation, Art, Leadership, Music/drama.

See page 964.

LAKE REGION STATE COLLEGE

1801 College Drive N, Devils Lake, ND 58301-1598
Phone: 701-662-1514 · **Financial Aid Phone:** 701-662-1516
E-mail: lrsc.admissions@lrsc.edu
Fax: 701-662-1581 · **Website:** www.lrsc.edu · **ACT Code:** 3198

This public school was founded in 1941. It has a 120 acre campus.

RATINGS

Admissions Selectivity Rating: 77   **Fire Safety Rating:** 96   **Green Rating:** 60*

STUDENTS AND FACULTY

Enrollment: 696. **Student Body:** 53% female, 47% male, 12% out-of-state, 3% international (14 countries represented). Asian 2%, African American 4%, Caucasian 82%, Hispanic 2%, Native American 5%, Race unknown 3%. **Faculty:** Student/faculty ratio 13:1. 35 full-time faculty, 14% hold PhDs, 3% are members of minority groups, 51% are women. 0% of classes are taught by teaching assistants.

ACADEMICS

Degrees: Associate; Certificate; Diploma; Terminal Associate; Transfer Associate **Classes:** Most classes have 10-19 students. Most lab/discussion sessions have 20-29 students. **Most popular majors:** Liberal Arts And Sciences/Liberal Studies; Criminal Justice/Police Science; Business Administration And Management, General. **Special Study Options:** Cooperative education program; Cross-registration; Distance learning; Dual enrollment; English as a Second Language (ESL); Internships; Liberal arts/ career combination. **Disability Services offered to physically disabled students:** Note-taking services; Reader services; Tape recorders; Tutors. **Career services:** Career/job search classes; Internships

FACILITIES

Housing: Apartments for married students; Apartments for single students; Men's dorms; Special housing for disabled student; Women's dorms 100% of campus accessible to physically diasbled. **Special Academic Facilities/ Equipment:** Paul Hoghaug Library and Law Library **Computers:** 100% of classrooms, 100% of dorms, 100% of libraries, 100% of dining areas, 100% of student union, have wireless network access. Students can register for classes online. Administrative functions (other than registration) can be performed online.

CAMPUS LIFE

Environment: Village **Activities:** Drama/theater; Literary magazine; Musical theater; Student government; Symphony orchestra 12 registered organizations, 1 religious organization. **Athletics (Intercollegiate):** *Men:* basketball. *Women:* basketball. **On-Campus Highlights:** Student Union, Computer Lab, Recreational Area, Library, Gymnasium

ADMISSIONS

Freshman Academic Profile: 98% from public high schools. **Test Scores:** ACT middle 50% range 18-25. Minimum internet-based TOEFL 65. Minimum paper TOEFL 510. **Freshman Admission Requirements:** High school diploma is required and GED is accepted *Academic units recommended:* 4 English, 3 math, 3 science, 2 science labs, 2 foreign language, 3 social studies. **Freshman Admission Statistics:** 233 applied, 98.7% admitted, 95% enrolled. **Transfer Admission Requirements:** High school transcript, college transcript(s), statement of good standing from prior institution(s). Minimum college GPA of 2.0 required. Lowest grade transferable D. **General Admission Information:** Application fee $35. Nonfall registration accepted. Admission may be deferred for a maximum of one semester.

COSTS AND FINANCIAL AID

Annual in-state tuition $5,230. Annual out-of-state tuition $3,065. Room and board $5,230. Required fees $843. Average book expense $900. **Required Forms and Deadlines:** FAFSA. **Notification of Awards:** Applicants will be notified of awards on a rolling basis beginning 5/15. **Types of Aid:** *Need-based scholarships/grants:* College/university scholarship or grant aid from institutional funds; Federal Pell; Private scholarships; SEOG; State scholarships/grants. *Loans:* Student Employment:* Federal Work-Study Program available. Institutional employment available. **Financial Aid Statistics:** 93% needy freshmen, 87% needy undergrads receive need-based scholarship or grant aid. 1% freshmen, 0% undergrads receive non-need-based scholarship or grant aid. 86% freshmen, 90% undergrads receive need-based self-help aid. 6% freshmen, 6% undergrads receive athletic scholarships. 80% undergrads receive any aid. **Criteria for awarding aid:** *Need-based:* Academics, Athletics, Minority status *Non-need-based:* Academics, Athletics, Leadership, Minority status, Music/drama.

LAKE SUPERIOR STATE UNIVERSITY

650 West Easterday Avenue, Sault Ste. Marie, MI 49783-1699
Phone: 906-635-2231 · **Financial Aid Phone:** 906-635-2678
E-mail: admissions@lssu.edu · **CEEB Code:** 1421
Fax: 906-635-6669 · **ACT Code:** 2031

This public school was founded in 1946. It has a 115 acre campus.

RATINGS

Admissions Selectivity Rating: 73   **Fire Safety Rating:** 60*   **Green Rating:** 60*

STUDENTS AND FACULTY

Enrollment: 2,440. **Student Body:** 50% female, 50% male, 5% out-of-state, 7% international. Asian 1%, African American 1%, Caucasian 79%, Hispanic 2%, Native American 8%, Pacific Islander 0%, Two or more races <1%, Race unknown 2%.

Retention and Graduation: 70% freshmen return for sophomore year. **Faculty:** Student/faculty ratio 17:1. 114 full-time faculty, 53% hold PhDs, 5% are members of minority groups, 46% are women. 0% of classes are taught by teaching assistants.

ACADEMICS

Degrees: Associate; Bachelor's; Certificate; Master's **Classes:** Most classes have 10-19 students. Most lab/discussion sessions have 10-19 students. **Special Study Options:** Cooperative education program; Distance learning; Double major; Dual enrollment; Honors program; Independent study; Internships; Student-designed major; Study abroad; Teacher certification program. **Disability Services offered to physically disabled students:** Note-taking services; Reader services; Tape recorders; Tutors.

FACILITIES

Housing: Apartments for single students; Coed dorms; Men's dorms; Women's dorms 90% of campus accessible to physically disabled. **Special Academic Facilities/Equipment:** Natural science, Michigan history, and Great Lakes shipping museums, planetarium, industrial robots, atomic absorption/flame emission spectrophotometer. **Computers:** Students can register for classes online.

CAMPUS LIFE

Environment: City **Activities:** Campus Ministries; Choral groups; Dance; Drama/theater; International Student Organization; Literary magazine; Model UN; Pep band; Radio station; Student government; Student newspaper 60 registered organizations, 4 fraternities, 4 sororities. **Athletics (Intercollegiate):** *Men:* basketball, cross-country, ice hockey, tennis, track/field (outdoor), track/field (indoor). *Women:* basketball, cross-country, softball, tennis, track/field (outdoor), track/field (indoor), volleyball.

ADMISSIONS

Freshman Academic Profile: Average high school GPA 3.3. 14% in top 10% of high school class, 40% in top 25% of high school class, 75% in top 50% of high school class. **Test Scores:** ACT middle 50% range 20-25. Minimum paper TOEFL 550. **Basis for Candidate Selection:** *Very important factors considered include:* rigor of secondary school record, academic GPA, standardized test scores. *Other factors considered include:* class rank, recommendation(s), interview, geographical residence. **Freshman Admission Requirements:** High school diploma is required and GED is accepted *Academic units recommended:* 4 English, 3 math, 3 science, 3 science labs, 2 foreign language, 2 social studies, 1 history. **Freshman Admission Statistics:** 1,425 applied, 89.7% admitted, 34% enrolled. **Transfer Admission Requirements:** college transcript(s), Minimum college GPA of 2.0 required. Lowest grade transferable C-. **General Admission Information:** Application fee $35. Priority deadline 3/1. Nonfall registration accepted. Admission may be deferred for a maximum of 1 year.

COSTS AND FINANCIAL AID

Annual in-state tuition $8,481. Annual out-of-state tuition $14,410. Room and board $8,481. Required fees $100. Average book expense $1,200. **Required Forms and Deadlines:** FAFSA. **Notification of Awards:** Applicants will be notified of awards on a rolling basis beginning 10/11. **Types of Aid:** *Need-based scholarships/grants:* College/university scholarship or grant aid from institutional funds; Federal Nursing Scholarships; Federal Pell; Private scholarships; SEOG; State scholarships/grants. *Loans:* Direct PLUS loans; Direct Subsidized Stafford Loans; Direct Unsubsidized Stafford Loans. **Financial Aid Statistics:** 75% needy freshmen, 75% needy undergrads receive need-based scholarship or grant aid. 61% freshmen, 40% undergrads receive non-need-based scholarship or grant aid. 82% freshmen, 90% undergrads receive need-based self-help aid. 10% freshmen, 9% undergrads receive athletic scholarships. 83% undergrads receive any aid. **Criteria for awarding aid:** *Need-based:* Academics, Alumni affiliation, Athletics, Job skills, Leadership, Minority status *Non-need-based:* Academics, Athletics, State/district residency.

LAKEHEAD UNIVERSITY

955 Oliver Road, Thunder Bay, ON P7B 5E1
Phone: (807) 343-8500 · **Financial Aid Phone:** (807) 343-8206
E-mail: admissions@lakeheadu.ca · **CEEB Code:**
Fax: (807) 766-7209 · **Website:** www.lakeheadu.ca · **ACT Code:**

This public school was founded in 1965. It has a 288 acre campus.

RATINGS

Admissions Selectivity Rating: 0   **Fire Safety Rating:** 60*   **Green Rating:** 60*

STUDENTS AND FACULTY

Student Body: international.
Retention and Graduation: 85% freshmen return for sophomore year.
Faculty: Student/faculty ratio 24:1.

ACADEMICS

Degrees: Bachelor's; Certificate; Diploma; Master's **Classes:** Most classes have 10-19 students. **Most popular majors:** Forestry, General; Engineering, General; Business Administration And Management, General.

FACILITIES

Housing: Apartments for single students; Coed dorms; Special housing for disabled student; Wellness housing **Computers:** Students can register for classes online.

CAMPUS LIFE

Environment: City **Activities:** Campus Ministries; Choral groups; Concert band; Dance; Drama/theater; International Student Organization; Jazz band; Literary magazine; Model UN; Music ensembles; Musical theater; Radio station; Student government; Student newspaper. **Athletics (Intercollegiate):** *Men:* basketball, cross-country, ice hockey, skiing (nordic/cross-country), track/field (outdoor), track/field (indoor), wrestling. *Women:* basketball, cross-country, skiing (nordic/cross-country), track/field (outdoor), track/field (indoor), volleyball, wrestling.

ADMISSIONS

Freshman Admission Requirements: High school diploma is required and GED is accepted **General Admission Information:** Application fee $105. Priority deadline 6/1. Regular application deadline 9/24. Nonfall registration accepted. Admission may be deferred for a maximum of one year.

COSTS AND FINANCIAL AID

Annual out-of-state tuition $4,670. Required fees $825.

LAMAR UNIVERSITY

Lamar Station, Beaumont, TX 77710
Phone: 409-880-8888
E-mail: admissions@hal.lamar.edu · **CEEB Code:** 6360
Fax: 409-880-8463 · **Website:** www.lamar.edu · **ACT Code:** 4114

This public school was founded in 1923. It has a 200 acre campus.

RATINGS

Admissions Selectivity Rating: 64   **Fire Safety Rating:** 60*   **Green Rating:** 60*

STUDENTS AND FACULTY

Enrollment: 9,057. **Student Body:** 55% female, 45% male, 1% out-of-state, 1% international. Asian 3%, African American 21%, Caucasian 70%, Hispanic 4%, Native American 1%, Race unknown 0%.
Faculty:

ACADEMICS

Degrees: Bachelor's; Master's **Classes:** Most classes have 20-29 students. Most lab/discussion sessions have 10-19 students. **Special Study Options:** Cooperative education program; Distance learning; Double major; Dual enrollment; English as a Second Language (ESL); Honors program; Internships; Study abroad; Teacher certification program. **Disability Services offered to physically disabled students:** Note-taking services; Reader services; Tape recorders; Tutors. **Career services:** Alumni services; Career assessment; Career/job search classes

FACILITIES

Housing: Apartments for single students; Coed dorms; Fraternity/sorority housing; Men's dorms; Women's dorms **Special Academic Facilities/Equipment:** Museum.

CAMPUS LIFE

Environment: Village **Activities:** Student government; Student newspaper 145 registered organizations, 11 fraternities, 8 sororities. **Athletics (Intercollegiate):** *Men:* baseball, basketball, cross-country, golf, tennis, track/field (outdoor). *Women:* basketball, cross-country, golf, tennis, track/field (outdoor), volleyball.

ADMISSIONS

Freshman Academic Profile: 10% in top 10% of high school class, 27% in top 25% of high school class, 90% in top 50% of high school class. 96% from public high schools. **Test Scores:** Minimum paper TOEFL 500. **Freshman Admission Requirements:** High school diploma is required and GED is accepted; High school diploma is required and GED is not accepted *Academic units recommended:* 4 English, 3 math, 2 science, 2 social studies, 2 academic electives. **Freshman Admission Statistics:** Minimum college GPA of 2.0 required. Lowest grade transferable D. **General Admission Information:** Regular application deadline 8/1. Nonfall registration accepted.

COSTS AND FINANCIAL AID

Annual in-state tuition $3,040. Annual out-of-state tuition $5,976. Room and board $3,040. Required fees $840. **Required Forms and Deadlines:** FAFSA; Institution's own financial aid form; State aid form. *Student Employment:* Federal Work-Study Program available. Institutional employment available.

LAMBUTH UNIVERSITY

705 Lambuth Boulevard, Jackson, TN 38301-5296
Phone: 731-425-3223 · **Financial Aid Phone:** 731-425-3332
E-mail: admit@lambuth.edu · **CEEB Code:** 1394
Fax: 731-425-3496 · **Website:** www.lambuth.edu · **ACT Code:** 3974

This private school, affiliated with the Methodist Church, was founded in 1843. It has a 50 acre campus.

RATINGS

Admissions Selectivity Rating: 85   **Fire Safety Rating:** 87   **Green Rating:** 60*

STUDENTS AND FACULTY

Enrollment: 765. **Student Body:** 47% female, 53% male, 21% out-of-state, (9 countries represented).
Retention and Graduation: 60% freshmen return for sophomore year. 20% grads go on to further study within 1 year. 5% grads pursue arts and sciences degrees. 5% grads pursue law degrees. 5% grads pursue business degrees. 5% grads pursue medical degrees. **Faculty:** Student/faculty ratio 12:1. 51 full-time faculty, 78% hold PhDs, 2% are members of minority groups, 41% are women. 0% of classes are taught by teaching assistants.

ACADEMICS

Degrees: Bachelor's **Classes:** Most classes have 10-19 students. Most lab/discussion sessions have 10-19 students. **Most popular majors:** Health And Physical Education/Fitness, General; Psychology, General; Business/Commerce, General. **Special Study Options:** Cross-registration; Double major; Honors program; Independent study; Internships; Student-designed major; Study abroad; Teacher certification program. **Honors programs:** University Honors is a 3 semester sequence of courses designed to offer more in-depth study of classic literature and themes. Various topics are considered including art, psychology, ecology, history, ethics, politics, science, sociology, business, religion, and literature. Honors study is available in most disciplines and consists of an 8 hour sequence of research over the last 3 semesters of study in a particular discipline. **Disability Services offered to physically disabled students:** Tape recorders; Tutors. **Career services:** Alumni network; Alumni services; Career assessment; Career/job search classes; Internships; Regional alumni

FACILITIES

Housing: Apartments for single students; Coed dorms; Fraternity/sorority housing; Men's dorms; Special housing for disabled student; Women's dorms 80% of campus accessible to physically diasbled. **Special Academic Facilities/Equipment:** Academic Support Center, Interior Design lab, M.D. Anderson Planetarium, Oxley Biological Field Station **Computers:** 40% of classrooms, 10% of dorms, 100% of libraries, 100% of dining areas, 100% of student union, 50% of common outdoor areas have wireless network access.

CAMPUS LIFE

Environment: City **Activities:** Campus Ministries; Choral groups; Concert band; Dance; Drama/theater; International Student Organization; Jazz band; Literary magazine; Model UN; Music ensembles; Musical theater; Student government; Student newspaper; Yearbook 41 registered organizations, 6

honor societies, 3 religious organizations. 3 fraternities, 3 sororities. **Athletics (Intercollegiate):** *Men:* baseball, basketball, football, golf, soccer, tennis. *Women:* basketball, golf, soccer, softball, tennis. **On-Campus Highlights:** Eagle's Nest Bistro, E/MI Studio, The Quadrangle, Eickoff Plaza, M.D. Anderson Planetarium

ADMISSIONS

Freshman Academic Profile: Average high school GPA 3.3. 21% in top 10% of high school class, 42% in top 25% of high school class, 71% in top 50% of high school class. 85% from public high schools. **Test Scores:** SAT Math middle 50% range 460-570. SAT EBRW middle 50% range 440-570. ACT middle 50% range 20-25. Minimum paper TOEFL 425. **Basis for Candidate Selection:** *Very important factors considered include:* rigor of secondary school record, academic GPA, standardized test scores. *Important factors considered include:* application essay, recommendation(s), interview, extracurricular activities, level of applicant's interest. *Other factors considered include:* class rank, talent/ability, first generation, alumni/ae relation, geographical residence, state residency, religious affiliation/commitment, volunteer work, work experience. **Freshman Admission Requirements:** High school diploma is required and GED is accepted *Academic units recommended:* 4 English, 3 math, 3 science, 1 foreign language, 2 social studies, 1 history. **Freshman Admission Statistics:** 1,042 applied, 52.7% admitted, 30% enrolled. **Transfer Admission Requirements:** college transcript(s), essay or personal statement, statement of good standing from prior institution(s). Minimum college GPA of 2.0 required. Lowest grade transferable D. **General Admission Information:** Application fee $25. Nonfall registration accepted. Admission may be deferred for a maximum of one year.

COSTS AND FINANCIAL AID

Annual tuition $17,000. Room and board $7,160. Required fees $400. Average book expense $1,200. **Required Forms and Deadlines:** FAFSA; Institution's own financial aid form. **Notification of Awards:** Applicants will be notified of awards on a rolling basis beginning 2/15. **Types of Aid:** *Need-based scholarships/grants:* College/university scholarship or grant aid from institutional funds; Federal Pell; Private scholarships; SEOG; State scholarships/grants. *Loans: Student Employment:* Federal Work-Study Program available. Institutional employment available. **Financial Aid Statistics:** 98% needy freshmen, 97% needy undergrads receive need-based scholarship or grant aid. 24% freshmen, 22% undergrads receive non-need-based scholarship or grant aid. 66% freshmen, 69% undergrads receive need-based self-help aid. 9% freshmen, 9% undergrads receive athletic scholarships. 99% freshmen, 99% undergrads receive any aid. **Criteria for awarding aid:** *Need-based:* Academics, Alumni affiliation, Art, Athletics, Job skills, Leadership, Music/drama, Religious affiliation *Non-need-based:* Academics, Alumni affiliation, Art, Athletics, Job skills, Leadership, Music/drama, Religious affiliation.

LANCASTER BIBLE COLLEGE

901 Eden Rd, Lancaster, PA 17601-5036
Phone: 717-560-8271 · **Financial Aid Phone:** 717-560-8254
E-mail: admissions@lbc.edu · **CEEB Code:** 2388
Fax: 717-560-8213 · **Website:** www.lbc.edu · **ACT Code:** 3707

This private school was founded in 1933. It has a 100 acre campus.

RATINGS

Admissions Selectivity Rating: 65   **Fire Safety Rating:** 77   **Green Rating:** 60*

STUDENTS AND FACULTY

Enrollment: 702. **Student Body:** 47% female, 53% male, 26% out-of-state, 1% international. Asian 1%, African American 3%, Caucasian 73%, Hispanic 1%, Native American <1%, Race unknown 20%.
Retention and Graduation: 77% freshmen return for sophomore year. **Faculty:** Student/faculty ratio 10:1. 48 full-time faculty, 52% hold PhDs, 2% are members of minority groups, 25% are women. 0% of classes are taught by teaching assistants.

ACADEMICS

Degrees: Associate; Bachelor's; Certificate; Master's; Post-Bachelor's certificate **Classes:** Most classes have 10-19 students. Most lab/discussion sessions have fewer than 10 students. **Most popular majors:** Elementary Education And Teaching; Bible/Biblical Studies; Theology And Religious Vocations, Other. **Special Study Options:** Accelerated program; Double major; Independent study; Internships; Study abroad; Teacher certification program. **Disability Services offered to physically disabled students:** Note-taking services; Reader services; Tape recorders; Tutors. **Career services:** Alumni network; Internships

FACILITIES

Housing: Men's dorms; Women's dorms 80% of campus accessible to physically diasbled.

CAMPUS LIFE

Environment: Village **Activities:** Choral groups; Concert band; Drama/theater; Music ensembles; Musical theater; Student government; Student newspaper; Yearbook 20 registered organizations. **Athletics (Intercollegiate):** *Men:* baseball, basketball, cheerleading, soccer, volleyball. *Women:* basketball, cheerleading, lacrosse, soccer, volleyball.

ADMISSIONS

Freshman Academic Profile: 60% from public high schools. **Test Scores:** Minimum paper TOEFL 550. **Basis for Candidate Selection:** *Very important factors considered include:* rigor of secondary school record, application essay, standardized test scores, recommendation(s), character/personal qualities, religious affiliation/commitment. *Important factors considered include:* extracurricular activities. *Other factors considered include:* interview, talent/ability, volunteer work. **Freshman Admission Requirements:** High school diploma is required and GED is accepted **Freshman Admission Statistics:** 314 applied, 96.8% admitted, 44% enrolled. **Transfer Admission Requirements:** High school transcript, college transcript(s), essay or personal statement, standardized test scores, statement of good standing from prior institution(s). Minimum college GPA of 2.0 required. Lowest grade transferable C. **General Admission Information:** Application fee $25. Priority deadline 8/1. Nonfall registration accepted. Admission may be deferred for a maximum of 1 year.

COSTS AND FINANCIAL AID

Annual tuition $15,930. Room and board $7,110. Required fees $630. Average book expense $1,000. **Required Forms and Deadlines:** FAFSA; State aid form. **Notification of Awards:** Applicants will be notified of awards on a rolling basis beginning 3/1. **Types of Aid:** *Need-based scholarships/grants:* College/university scholarship or grant aid from institutional funds; Federal Pell; Private scholarships; SEOG; State scholarships/grants. *Student Employment:* Federal Work-Study Program available. Institutional employment available. **Financial Aid Statistics:** 98% needy freshmen, 94% needy undergrads receive need-based scholarship or grant aid. 97% freshmen, 79% undergrads receive non-need-based scholarship or grant aid. 83% freshmen, 88% undergrads receive need-based self-help aid. 0% freshmen, 0% undergrads receive athletic scholarships. **Criteria for awarding aid:** *Non-need-based:* Academics, Alumni affiliation, Leadership, Music/drama.

LANDMARK COLLEGE

P.O. Box 820, Putney, VT 05346-0820
Phone: 802-387-6718 · **Financial Aid Phone:** 802-387-6736
E-mail: admissions@landmark.edu
Fax: 802-387-6868 · **Website:** http://www.landmark.edu/ · **ACT Code:** 4317

This private school was founded in 1984. It has a 128 acre campus.

RATINGS

Admissions Selectivity Rating: 71 **Fire Safety Rating:** 84 **Green Rating:** 60*

STUDENTS AND FACULTY

Enrollment: 487. **Student Body:** 32% female, 68% male, 95% out-of-state, 3% international (14 countries represented). Asian 1%, African American 5%, Caucasian 70%, Hispanic 0%, Native American 0%, Pacific Islander 1%, Two or more races 3%, Race unknown 14%.
Retention and Graduation: 95% grads go on to further study within 1 year. **Faculty:** Student/faculty ratio 6:1. 86 full-time faculty, 1% are members of minority groups, 64% are women. 0% of classes are taught by teaching assistants.

ACADEMICS

Degrees: Associate; Terminal Associate; Transfer Associate **Classes:** Most classes have 10-19 students. **Special Study Options:** Internships; Study abroad. **Honors programs:** Phi Theta Kappa.

FACILITIES

Housing: Coed dorms; Special housing for disabled student; Wellness housing 65% of campus accessible to physically diasbled.

CAMPUS LIFE

Environment: Rural **Activities:** Choral groups; Dance; Drama/theater; Jazz band; Literary magazine; Music ensembles; Radio station; Student government; Student newspaper.

ADMISSIONS

Freshman Academic Profile: 70% from public high schools. **Test Scores:** Minimum paper TOEFL 200. **Basis for Candidate Selection:** *Very important factors considered include:* recommendation(s), interview. *Important factors considered include:* character/personal qualities, level of applicant's interest. *Other factors considered include:* rigor of secondary school record, class rank, academic GPA, application essay, standardized test scores, extracurricular activities, talent/ability. **Freshman Admission Requirements:** High school diploma is required and GED is accepted *Academic units recommended:* 4 English, 3 math, 3 science, 1 foreign language, 3 social studies, 3 history, 1 academic elective, 1 visual/performing arts. **Freshman Admission Statistics:** 395 applied, 53.7% admitted, 54% enrolled. **Transfer Admission Requirements:** High school transcript, college transcript(s), essay or personal statement, interview, Lowest grade transferable C-. **General Admission Information:** Application fee $75. Priority deadline 5/15. Nonfall registration accepted. Admission may be deferred for a maximum of 1 year.

COSTS AND FINANCIAL AID

Annual tuition $48,210. Room and board $8,620. Required fees $500. Average book expense $1,200. **Required Forms and Deadlines:** FAFSA. **Notification of Awards:** Applicants will be notified of awards on a rolling basis beginning 3/15. **Types of Aid:** *Need-based scholarships/grants:* College/university scholarship or grant aid from institutional funds; Federal Pell; Private scholarships; SEOG; State scholarships/grants. *Loans:* Direct PLUS loans; Direct Subsidized Stafford Loans; Direct Unsubsidized Stafford Loans. *Student Employment:* Federal Work-Study Program available. Institutional employment available. **Financial Aid Statistics:** 100% needy undergrads receive need-based scholarship or grant aid. 4% undergrads receive non-need-based scholarship or grant aid. 100% undergrads receive need-based self-help aid. 0% undergrads receive athletic scholarships. 35% freshmen, 42% undergrads receive any aid. **Criteria for awarding aid:** *Non-need-based:* Academics, Art, Athletics, Leadership, Minority status, Music/drama.

LANE COLLEGE

545 Lane Avenue, Jackson, TN 38301
Phone: 731-426-7533 · **Financial Aid Phone:** (731) 426-7536
E-mail: admissions@lanecollege.edu
Fax: 731-426-7559 · **Website:** www.lanecollege.edu · **ACT Code:** 3976

This private school, affiliated with the Methodist Church, was founded in 1882. It has a 25 acre campus.

RATINGS

Admissions Selectivity Rating: 75 **Fire Safety Rating:** 95 **Green Rating:** 60*

STUDENTS AND FACULTY

Enrollment: 1,427. **Student Body:** 47% female, 53% male, 40% out-of-state, <1% international (1 countries represented). Asian <1%, African American 90%, Caucasian <1%, Hispanic <1%, Native American <1%, Pacific Islander 0%, Two or more races 1%, Race unknown 8%.
Retention and Graduation: 62% freshmen return for sophomore year. 35% grads go on to further study within 1 year. 37% grads pursue arts and sciences degrees. 6% grads pursue law degrees. 10% grads pursue business degrees. 7% grads pursue medical degrees. **Faculty:** Student/faculty ratio 19:1. 65 full-time faculty, 65% hold PhDs, 57% are members of minority groups, 38% are women. 0% of classes are taught by teaching assistants.

ACADEMICS

Degrees: Associate; Bachelor's **Classes:** Most classes have 20-29 students. Most lab/discussion sessions have 20-29 students. **Most popular majors:** Biology/Biological Sciences, General; Criminal Justice/Law Enforcement Administration; Business/Commerce, General. **Special Study Options:** Dual enrollment; Honors program; Independent study; Internships; Study abroad. **Disability Services offered to physically disabled students:** Tutors. **Career services:** Alumni services; Career assessment; Career/job search classes; Internships

FACILITIES

Housing: Coed dorms; Men's dorms; Women's dorms 98% of campus accessible to physically diasbled. **Special Academic Facilities/Equipment:** The Grand Student Center The Cyber Cafe **Computers:** 50% of classrooms, 100% of libraries, 100% of student union, 25% of common outdoor areas have wireless network access.

CAMPUS LIFE

Environment: Town **Activities:** Campus Ministries; Choral groups; Concert band; Dance; Drama/theater; Jazz band; Marching band; Music ensembles; Pep band; Radio station; Student government; Student newspaper; Student-run film society 21 registered organizations, 6 honor societies, 4 religious organizations. 4 fraternities, 4 sororities. **Athletics (Intercollegiate):** *Men:* baseball, basketball, cross-country, football, tennis, track/field (outdoor). *Women:* basketball, cheerleading, cross-country, softball, tennis, track/field (outdoor), volleyball. **On-Campus Highlights:** Pond at the Plain, Williams/Boyd Campus Center, The Cyber Cafe, Phillips Dining Hall, The Grand

ADMISSIONS

Freshman Academic Profile: Average high school GPA 2.6. 5% in top 10% of high school class, 17% in top 25% of high school class, 52% in top 50% of high school class. 96% from public high schools. **Test Scores:** ACT middle 50% range 14-16. Minimum paper TOEFL 339. **Basis for Candidate Selection:** *Very important factors considered include:* rigor of secondary school record, recommendation(s), first generation. *Important factors considered include:* academic GPA, standardized test scores. *Other factors considered include:* class rank, interview, extracurricular activities, character/personal qualities, alumni/ae relation, religious affiliation/commitment, level of applicant's interest. **Freshman Admission Requirements:** High school diploma is required and GED is accepted *Academic units recommended:* 4 English, 2 math, 2 science, 2 foreign language, 2 social studies. **Freshman Admission Statistics:** 5,311 applied, 50.3% admitted, 15% enrolled. **Transfer Admission Requirements:** college transcript(s), standardized test scores, statement of good standing from prior institution(s). Lowest grade transferable C. **General Admission Information:** Nonfall registration accepted. Admission may be deferred for a maximum of 2 semesters.

COSTS AND FINANCIAL AID

Annual tuition $9,000. Required fees $1,690. Average book expense $1,300. **Required Forms and Deadlines:** FAFSA. **Notification of Awards:** Applicants will be notified of awards on a rolling basis beginning 3/1. **Types of Aid:** *Need-based scholarships/grants:* College/university scholarship or grant aid from institutional funds; Federal Pell; Private scholarships; SEOG; State scholarships/grants; United Negro College Fund. *Loans:* Direct PLUS loans; Direct Subsidized Stafford Loans; Direct Unsubsidized Stafford Loans. *Student Employment:* Federal Work-Study Program available. Institutional employment available. **Financial Aid Statistics:** 98% needy freshmen, 94% needy undergrads receive need-based scholarship or grant aid. 87% freshmen, 85% undergrads receive non-need-based scholarship or grant aid. 96% freshmen, 92% undergrads receive need-based self-help aid. 12% freshmen, 10% undergrads receive athletic scholarships. 96% freshmen, 98% undergrads receive any aid. **Criteria for awarding aid:** *Need-based:* Academics, Athletics, Religious affiliation *Non-need-based:* Academics, Athletics, Religious affiliation.

LASALLE COLLEGE VANCOUVER

2665 Renfrew Street, Vancouver, BC V5M0A7
Phone: 604-683-2006
E-mail: admissions@lasallecollegevancouver.com
Fax: 604-684-8839 · **Website:** http://lasallecollegevancouver.com

This is a proprietary school.

RATINGS
Admissions Selectivity Rating: 0   **Fire Safety Rating:** 60*   **Green Rating:** 60*

STUDENTS AND FACULTY
Enrollment: 245. **Student Body:** 52% female, 48% male, international. **Faculty:** Student/faculty ratio 13:1.

ACADEMICS
Degrees: Bachelor's; Certificate; Diploma **Special Study Options:** Cooperative education program; Distance learning; Independent study; Internships; Study abroad.

FACILITIES
Computers:

CAMPUS LIFE
Activities: Music ensembles; Student government; Student-run film society.

ADMISSIONS
Basis for Candidate Selection: *Very important factors considered include:* application essay, interview, level of applicant's interest. *Other factors considered include:* rigor of secondary school record, class rank, academic GPA, standardized test scores, recommendation(s), extracurricular activities, talent/ability, character/personal qualities, volunteer work, work experience.

Freshman Admission Requirements: High school diploma is required and GED is accepted **General Admission Information:** Application fee $50. Admission may be deferred.

LASELL COLLEGE

1844 Commonwealth Avenue, Newton, MA 02466
Phone: 617-243-2225 · **Financial Aid Phone:** 617-243-2227
E-mail: info@lasell.edu · **CEEB Code:** 3481
Fax: 617-243-2380 · **Website:** www.lasell.edu · **ACT Code:** 1848

This private school was founded in 1851. It has a 55 acre campus.

RATINGS
Admissions Selectivity Rating: 74   **Fire Safety Rating:** 78   **Green Rating:** 63

STUDENTS AND FACULTY
Enrollment: 1,696. **Student Body:** 64% female, 36% male, 42% out-of-state, 7% international (22 countries represented). Asian 2%, African American 7%, Caucasian 69%, Hispanic 9%, Native American <1%, Pacific Islander <1%, Two or more races 2%, Race unknown 4%.
Retention and Graduation: 73% freshmen return for sophomore year. 50% freshmen graduate within 4 years. 54% freshmen graduate within 6 years. 13% grads go on to further study within 1 year. 6% grads pursue arts and sciences degrees. 1.2% grads pursue law degrees. 5% grads pursue business degrees. 0% grads pursue medical degrees. **Faculty:** Student/faculty ratio 13:1. 93 full-time faculty, 81% hold PhDs, 18% are members of minority groups, 66% are women. 0% of classes are taught by teaching assistants.

ACADEMICS
Degrees: Bachelor's; Master's **Classes:** Most classes have 10-19 students. **Most popular majors:** Sport And Fitness Administration/Management; Psychology, General; Fashion/Apparel Design. **Special Study Options:** Accelerated program; Cross-registration; Distance learning; Double major; Dual enrollment; English as a Second Language (ESL); Exchange student program (domestic); Honors program; Independent study; Internships; Liberal arts/career combination; Student-designed major; Study abroad; Teacher certification program. **Honors programs:** Lasell College Honor's Program. **Disability Services offered to physically disabled students:** Note-taking services; Reader services; Tape recorders; Tutors. **Career services:** Alumni services; Career assessment; Career/job search classes; Internships

FACILITIES
Housing: Coed dorms; Special housing for disabled student; Theme housing; Wellness housing; Women's dorms **Special Academic Facilities/Equipment:** Center for Public Service—Yamawaki Art/Cultural Center **Computers:**

CAMPUS LIFE
Environment: City **Activities:** Campus Ministries; Choral groups; Dance; Drama/theater; International Student Organization; Literary magazine; Music ensembles; Musical theater; Radio station; Student government; Student newspaper; Yearbook 30 registered organizations, 1 honor societies. **Athletics (Intercollegiate):** *Men:* basketball, cross-country, lacrosse, soccer, volleyball. *Women:* basketball, cross-country, field hockey, lacrosse, soccer, softball, volleyball. **On-Campus Highlights:** Science and Technology Center, Arnow Campus Center, Grellier Field, Arnow Quad, Edwards Student Center

ADMISSIONS
Freshman Academic Profile: Average high school GPA 2.9. 80% from public high schools. **Test Scores:** SAT Math middle 50% range 480-580. SAT EBRW middle 50% range 500-580. ACT middle 50% range 19-23. Minimum internet-based TOEFL 71. Minimum paper TOEFL 525. **Basis for Candidate Selection:** *Very important factors considered include:* rigor of secondary school record, academic GPA, interview. *Important factors considered include:* application essay, recommendation(s), extracurricular activities, volunteer work, work experience. *Other factors considered include:* standardized test scores, talent/ability, character/personal qualities, alumni/ae relation, level of applicant's interest. **Freshman Admission Requirements:** High school diploma is required and GED is accepted *Academic units required:* 4 English, 3 math, 2 science, 2 science labs, 1 social studies, 1 history, *Academic units recommended:* 4 English, 4 math, 3 science, 3 science labs, 2 foreign language, 2 social studies, 2 history. **Freshman Admission Statistics:** 3,466 applied, 81.5% admitted, 15% enrolled. **Transfer Admission Requirements:** college transcript(s), standardized test scores, statement of good standing from prior institution(s). Minimum college GPA of 2.3 required. Lowest grade transferable C. **General Admission Information:** Application fee $40. Priority deadline 11/15. Nonfall registration accepted. Admission may be deferred for a maximum of 1 year.

COSTS AND FINANCIAL AID

Annual tuition $34,700. Room and board $15,400. Required fees $1,300. Average book expense $1,000. **Required Forms and Deadlines:** FAFSA. **Notification of Awards:** Applicants will be notified of awards on a rolling basis beginning 12/1. **Types of Aid:** *Need-based scholarships/grants:* College/university scholarship or grant aid from institutional funds; Federal Pell; Private scholarships; SEOG; State scholarships/grants. *Loans:* Direct PLUS loans; Direct Subsidized Stafford Loans; Direct Unsubsidized Stafford Loans. *Student Employment:* Federal Work-Study Program available. Institutional employment available. **Financial Aid Statistics:** 100% needy freshmen receive need-based scholarship or grant aid. 87% freshmen, 85% undergrads receive any aid. **Criteria for awarding aid:** *Need-based:* Academics, Alumni affiliation, Leadership *Non-need-based:* Academics, Alumni affiliation, Leadership.

LAWRENCE TECHNOLOGICAL UNIVERSITY

21000 West Ten Mile Road, Southfield, MI 48075-1058
Phone: 248-204-3160 · **Financial Aid Phone:** 248-204-2280
E-mail: admissions@ltu.edu · **CEEB Code:** 1399
Fax: 248-204-3188 · **Website:** www.ltu.edu · **ACT Code:** 2020

This private school was founded in 1932. It has a 107 acre campus.

RATINGS

Admissions Selectivity Rating: 86   **Fire Safety Rating:** 95   **Green Rating:** 77

STUDENTS AND FACULTY

Enrollment: 1,978. **Student Body:** 26% female, 74% male, 8% out-of-state, 15% international (49 countries represented). Asian 3%, African American 6%, Caucasian 65%, Hispanic 3%, Native American <1%, Pacific Islander 0%, Two or more races 2%, Race unknown 6%.
Retention and Graduation: 82% freshmen return for sophomore year. 42% freshmen graduate within 4 years. 73% freshmen graduate within 6 years. 10% grads go on to further study within 1 year. **Faculty:** Student/faculty ratio 11:1. 127 full-time faculty, 25% are members of minority groups, 31% are women. 0% of classes are taught by teaching assistants.

ACADEMICS

Degrees: Associate; Bachelor's; Certificate; Doctoral; Doctoral/Research; Master's; Post-Bachelor's certificate **Classes:** Most classes have 10-19 students. **Most popular majors:** Architecture; Mechanical Engineering; Business Administration And Management, General. **Special Study Options:** Cooperative education program; Cross-registration; Distance learning; English as a Second Language (ESL); Honors program; Independent study; Internships; Study abroad. **Honors programs:** The LTU Honors Program is designed for highly qualified students who want an educational experience that will take full advantage of the challenging curricula offered at Lawrence Tech. **Combined degree programs:** BA/MEng. **Disability Services offered to physically disabled students:** Note-taking services; Reader services; Tape recorders; Tutors. **Career services:** Alumni services; Career assessment; Internships

FACILITIES

Housing: Apartments for married students; Apartments for single students; Special housing for disabled students 97% of campus accessible to physically disabled. **Special Academic Facilities/Equipment:** Albert Kahn Library Center for Innovative Materials Research; Applied Research Center; Environmental Scanning Electron Microscope; Confocal Microscope; Center for Innovative Materials Research; Robotics Lab; **Computers:** 100% of classrooms, 100% of dorms, 100% of libraries, 100% of dining areas, 100% of student union, 75% of common outdoor areas have wireless network access. Students can register for classes online. Administrative functions (other than registration) can be performed online. Undergraduates are required to own a computer.

CAMPUS LIFE

Environment: City **Activities:** Drama/theater; Literary magazine; Music ensembles; Student government; Student newspaper 54 registered organizations, 7 honor societies, 1 religious organization. 6 fraternities, 3 sororities. **On-Campus Highlights:** Atrium, Field House, Engineering Lounge, Einstein Bros. Bagels, Housing **Environmental Initiatives:** Reuss Hall and Taubman Complex were both designed to environmental management without consideration of submittal and LEED recognition.

ADMISSIONS

Freshman Academic Profile: Average high school GPA 3.5. 38% in top 10% of high school class, 54% in top 25% of high school class, 100% in top 50% of high school class. **Test Scores:** SAT Math middle 50% range 530-

660. SAT EBRW middle 50% range 530-620. ACT middle 50% range 21-28. Minimum internet-based TOEFL 79. Minimum paper TOEFL 550. **Basis for Candidate Selection:** *Very important factors considered include:* rigor of secondary school record, academic GPA, standardized test scores. *Other factors considered include:* application essay, recommendation(s). **Freshman Admission Requirements:** High school diploma is required and GED is accepted *Academic units required:* 4 English, 3 math, 2 science, 3 social studies, *Academic units recommended:* 4 English, 4 math, 4 science, 2 science labs, 2 history. **Freshman Admission Statistics:** 2,173 applied, 59.6% admitted, 29% enrolled. **Transfer Admission Requirements:** High school transcript, college transcript(s), Minimum college GPA of 2.2 required. Lowest grade transferable C. **General Admission Information:** Application fee $30. Nonfall registration accepted. Admission may be deferred for a maximum of 3 years.

COSTS AND FINANCIAL AID

Annual tuition $32,370. Room and board $9,950. Required fees $1,200. Average book expense $1,506. **Required Forms and Deadlines:** FAFSA. **Notification of Awards:** Applicants will be notified of awards on a rolling basis beginning 4/1. **Types of Aid:** *Need-based scholarships/grants:* College/university scholarship or grant aid from institutional funds; Federal Pell; Private scholarships; SEOG; State scholarships/grants. *Loans:* Direct PLUS loans; Direct Subsidized Stafford Loans; Direct Unsubsidized Stafford Loans. *Student Employment:* Federal Work-Study Program available. Institutional employment available. **Financial Aid Statistics:** 99% needy freshmen, 97% needy undergrads receive need-based scholarship or grant aid. 91% freshmen, 83% undergrads receive non-need-based scholarship or grant aid. 81% freshmen, 85% undergrads receive need-based self-help aid. 15% freshmen, 13% undergrads receive athletic scholarships. 94% freshmen, 54% undergrads receive any aid. 66% undergrads borrow to pay for school. Average cumulative indebtedness $35,810. **Criteria for awarding aid:** *Non-need-based:* Academics, Alumni affiliation, Athletics, Leadership, Minority status, State/district residency.

See page 966.

LAWRENCE UNIVERSITY

711 East Boldt Way, Appleton, WI 54911-5699
Phone: 920-832-6500 · **Financial Aid Phone:** 920-832-6583
E-mail: admissions@lawrence.edu · **CEEB Code:** 1398
Fax: 920-832-6782 · **Website:** www.lawrence.edu · **ACT Code:** 4596

This private school was founded in 1847. It has a 84 acre campus.

RATINGS

Admissions Selectivity Rating: 88   **Fire Safety Rating:** 86   **Green Rating:** 89

STUDENTS AND FACULTY

Enrollment: 1,441. **Student Body:** 54% female, 46% male, 71% out-of-state, 12% international (52 countries represented). Asian 5%, African American 5%, Caucasian 65%, Hispanic 9%, Native American <1%, Pacific Islander <1%, Two or more races 4%, Race unknown 1%.
Retention and Graduation: 88% freshmen return for sophomore year. 65% freshmen graduate within 4 years. 80% freshmen graduate within 6 years. 23% grads go on to further study within 1 year. 46% grads pursue arts and sciences degrees. 5% grads pursue law degrees. 0% grads pursue business degrees. 2% grads pursue medical degrees. **Faculty:** Student/faculty ratio 8:1. 174 full-time faculty, 91% hold PhDs, 16% are members of minority groups, 44% are women. 0% of classes are taught by teaching assistants.

ACADEMICS

Degrees: Bachelor's **Classes:** Most classes have 10-19 students. Most lab/discussion sessions have fewer than 10 students. **Most popular majors:** Biology/Biological Sciences, General; Psychology, General; Music Performance, General. **Special Study Options:** Double major; Independent study; Internships; Student-designed major; Study abroad; Teacher certification program. **Disability Services offered to physically disabled students:** Note-taking services; Reader services; Tape recorders; Tutors. **Career services:** Alumni network; Alumni services; Career assessment; Career/job search classes; Internships; Regional alumni

FACILITIES

Housing: Apartments for married students; Apartments for single students; Coed dorms; Cooperative housing; Fraternity/sorority housing; Men's dorms;

Special housing for disabled student; Theme housing; Wellness housing; Women's dorms 95% of campus accessible to physically diasbled. **Special Academic Facilities/Equipment:** Film production studio, sound stage, editing rooms, screening rooms, cinema; music studios; baroque instrument collection; gamelan; art galleries, anthropology collection, 425-acre estate on Lake Michigan hosting retreats and seminars for students, electron microscope, laser physics lab, physics/computational graphics lab, nuclear magnetic resonance spectrometer, Wriston Art Center, Mudd Gallery, Teekwood Room, The Maker Space with 3D Printer, Chapel-Organ **Computers:** 100% of classrooms, 20% of dorms, 100% of libraries, 100% of dining areas, 100% of student union, have wireless network access. Students can register for classes online. Administrative functions (other than registration) can be performed online.

CAMPUS LIFE

Environment: City **Activities:** Campus Ministries; Choral groups; Concert band; Dance; Drama/theater; International Student Organization; Jazz band; Literary magazine; Model UN; Music ensembles; Musical theater; Opera; Pep band; Radio station; Student government; Student newspaper; Student-run film society; Symphony orchestra 90 registered organizations, 5 honor societies, 3 religious organizations. 5 fraternities, 3 sororities. **Athletics (Intercollegiate):** *Men:* baseball, basketball, cross-country, diving, fencing, football, golf, ice hockey, soccer, swimming, tennis, track/field (outdoor), track/field (indoor), wrestling. *Women:* basketball, cross-country, diving, fencing, soccer, softball, swimming, tennis, track/field (outdoor), track/field (indoor), volleyball. **On-Campus Highlights:** Warch Campus Center, Memorial Chapel, Alexander Gymnasium, Seeley G. Mudd Library, Hurvis Center Film Studies **Environmental Initiatives:** Construction of LEED certified Student Center—Gold!

ADMISSIONS

Freshman Academic Profile: Average high school GPA 3.5. 38% in top 10% of high school class, 68% in top 25% of high school class, 94% in top 50% of high school class. **Test Scores:** SAT Math middle 50% range 600-730. SAT EBRW middle 50% range 620-730. ACT middle 50% range 25-32. Minimum internet-based TOEFL 90. Minimum paper TOEFL 577. **Basis for Candidate Selection:** *Very important factors considered include:* rigor of secondary school record, class rank, academic GPA, talent/ability, character/personal qualities. *Important factors considered include:* application essay, recommendation(s), interview, extracurricular activities. *Other factors considered include:* standardized test scores, first generation, alumni/ae relation, geographical residence, racial/ethnic status, volunteer work, work experience, level of applicant's interest. **Freshman Admission Requirements:** High school diploma is required and GED is accepted *Academic units recommended:* 4 English, 3 math, 3 science, 2 foreign language, 2 social studies, 2 history. **Freshman Admission Statistics:** 3,612 applied, 61.4% admitted, 16% enrolled. **Transfer Admission Requirements:** High school transcript, college transcript(s), essay or personal statement, Minimum college GPA of 2.75 required. Lowest grade transferable C-. **General Admission Information:** Regular application deadline 1/15. Nonfall registration accepted. Admission may be deferred for a maximum of 1 year.

COSTS AND FINANCIAL AID

Annual tuition $45,801. Room and board $10,032. Required fees $300. Average book expense $900. **Required Forms and Deadlines:** CSS/Financial Aid PROFILE; FAFSA; Noncustodial PROFILE. **Notification of Awards:** Applicants will be notified of awards on or about 1/15. **Types of Aid:** *Need-based scholarships/grants:* College/university scholarship or grant aid from institutional funds; Federal Pell; Private scholarships; SEOG; State scholarships/grants. *Loans:* Direct PLUS loans; Direct Subsidized Stafford Loans; Direct Unsubsidized Stafford Loans. *Student Employment:* Federal Work-Study Program available. Institutional employment available. **Financial Aid Statistics:** 96% needy freshmen, 99% needy undergrads receive need-based scholarship or grant aid. 0% undergrads receive non-need-based scholarship or grant aid. 80% freshmen, 80% undergrads receive need-based self-help aid. 0% freshmen, 0% undergrads receive athletic scholarships. 97% freshmen, 97% undergrads receive any aid. 62% undergrads borrow to pay for school. Average cumulative indebtedness $33,343. **Criteria for awarding aid:** *Need-based:* Academics, Music/drama *Non-need-based:* Academics, Alumni affiliation, Leadership, Minority status, Music/drama.

LE MOYNE COLLEGE

1419 Salt Springs Rd., Syracuse, NY 13214-1301
Phone: 315-445-4300 · **Financial Aid Phone:** 315-445-4400
E-mail: admission@lemoyne.edu · **CEEB Code:** 2366
Fax: 315-445-4711 · **Website:** www.lemoyne.edu · **ACT Code:** 2790

This private school, affiliated with the Roman Catholic Church, was founded in 1946. It has a 161 acre campus.

RATINGS
Admissions Selectivity Rating: 83   **Fire Safety Rating:** 91   **Green Rating:** 78

STUDENTS AND FACULTY
Enrollment: 2,676. **Student Body:** 60% female, 40% male, 6% out-of-state, 1% international (45 countries represented). Asian 3%, African American 6%, Caucasian 78%, Hispanic 5%, Native American <1%, Pacific Islander <1%, Two or more races 2%, Race unknown 4%.
Retention and Graduation: 84% freshmen return for sophomore year. 64% freshmen graduate within 4 years. 74% freshmen graduate within 6 years. 18% grads go on to further study within 1 year. 7% grads pursue arts and sciences degrees. 1% grads pursue law degrees. 2% grads pursue business degrees. 4% grads pursue medical degrees. **Faculty:** Student/faculty ratio 12:1. 166 full-time faculty, 89% hold PhDs, 16% are members of minority groups, 45% are women. 0% of classes are taught by teaching assistants.

ACADEMICS
Degrees: Bachelor's; Master's; Post-Bachelor's certificate; Post-Master's certificate **Classes:** Most classes have 10-19 students. Most lab/discussion sessions have 10-19 students. **Most popular majors:** Biology/Biological Sciences, General; Psychology, General; Accounting. **Special Study Options:** Accelerated program; Cross-registration; Distance learning; Double major; Dual enrollment; Honors program; Independent study; Internships; Study abroad; Teacher certification program. **Honors programs:** Students in the program complete a 21-hour sequence of interdisciplinary humanities courses that replaces the standard core requirements in English, history, philosophy, and religious studies. Seniors complete an honors project working in close collaboration with a faculty advisor. **Combined degree programs:** BA/DDS; BA/JD; BA/MA; BA/MD; BA/MEng. **Disability Services offered to physically disabled students:** Note-taking services; Reader services; Tape recorders; Tutors. **Career services:** Alumni network; Alumni services; Career assessment; Career/job search classes; Internships; Regional alumni

FACILITIES
Housing: Apartments for single students; Coed dorms; Special housing for disabled student; Theme housing 98% of campus accessible to physically diasbled. **Special Academic Facilities/Equipment:** W.Carroll Coyne Center for the Performing Arts, Wilson Art Gallery, Audio Visual Center, electron microscopes, Le Moyne College Archives, Media Center, NMR Room, Student Wellness Center, Student Success Center. **Computers:** 100% of classrooms, 75% of dorms, 100% of libraries, 100% of dining areas, 100% of student union, 100% of common outdoor areas have wireless network access. Students can register for classes online. Administrative functions (other than registration) can be performed online.

CAMPUS LIFE
Environment: City **Activities:** Campus Ministries; Choral groups; Concert band; Dance; Drama/theater; International Student Organization; Jazz band; Literary magazine; Model UN; Music ensembles; Musical theater; Radio station; Student government; Student newspaper; Student-run film society; Symphony orchestra; Television station; Yearbook 70 registered organizations, 14 honor societies, 11 religious organizations. **Athletics (Intercollegiate):** *Men:* baseball, basketball, cross-country, diving, golf, lacrosse, soccer, swimming, tennis. *Women:* basketball, cross-country, diving, golf, lacrosse, soccer, softball, swimming, tennis, volleyball. **On-Campus Highlights:** The Thomas J. Niland Athletic Complex, Campus Center, The W.Carroll Coyne Center for the Performing Arts, Panasci Family Chapel, Noreen Reale Falcone Library **Environmental Initiatives:** LEED GOLD certification on new science building.

ADMISSIONS
Freshman Academic Profile: Average high school GPA 3.5. 23% in top 10% of high school class, 51% in top 25% of high school class, 88% in top 50% of high school class. 82% from public high schools. **Test Scores:** SAT Math middle 50% range 540-620. SAT EBRW middle 50% range 540-620. ACT

middle 50% range 22–27. Minimum internet-based TOEFL 79. Minimum paper TOEFL 550. **Basis for Candidate Selection:** *Very important factors considered include:* rigor of secondary school record, academic GPA. *Important factors considered include:* class rank, application essay, recommendation(s), interview, extracurricular activities, talent/ability, work experience. *Other factors considered include:* standardized test scores, character/personal qualities, alumni/ae relation, geographical residence, state residency, volunteer work, level of applicant's interest. **Freshman Admission Requirements:** High school diploma is required and GED is accepted *Academic units required:* 4 English, 3 math, 3 science, 3 foreign language, 4 social studies, *Academic units recommended:* 4 math, 4 science, 3 science labs. **Freshman Admission Statistics:** 7,429 applied, 64.0% admitted, 11% enrolled. **Transfer Admission Requirements:** college transcript(s), essay or personal statement, Minimum college GPA of 2.6 required. Lowest grade transferable C-. **General Admission Information:** Priority deadline 2/1. Nonfall registration accepted. Admission may be deferred for a maximum of 1 year.

COSTS AND FINANCIAL AID

Annual tuition $32,840. Room and board $13,400. Required fees $1,065. Average book expense $1,300. **Required Forms and Deadlines:** FAFSA; State aid form. **Notification of Awards:** Applicants will be notified of awards on or about 2/15. **Types of Aid:** *Need-based scholarships/grants:* College/university scholarship or grant aid from institutional funds; Federal Pell; Private scholarships; SEOG; State scholarships/grants. *Loans:* Direct PLUS loans; Direct Subsidized Stafford Loans; Direct Unsubsidized Stafford Loans. *Student Employment:* Federal Work-Study Program available. Institutional employment available. **Financial Aid Statistics:** 100% needy freshmen, 100% needy undergrads receive need-based scholarship or grant aid. 16% freshmen, 14% undergrads receive non-need-based scholarship or grant aid. 78% freshmen, 80% undergrads receive need-based self-help aid. 3% freshmen, 3% undergrads receive athletic scholarships. 88% freshmen, 91% undergrads receive any aid. 84% undergrads borrow to pay for school. Average cumulative indebtedness $37,337. **Criteria for awarding aid:** *Non-need-based:* Academics, Alumni affiliation, Athletics, Leadership, Minority status.

See page 968.

LEBANON VALLEY COLLEGE

101 North College Avenue, Annville, PA 17003-1400
Phone: 717-867-6181 • **Financial Aid Phone:** 717-867-6126
E-mail: admission@lvc.edu • **CEEB Code:** 2364
Fax: 717-867-6026 • **Website:** www.lvc.edu • **ACT Code:** 3610

This private school, affiliated with the Methodist Church, was founded in 1866. It has a 357 acre campus.

RATINGS
Admissions Selectivity Rating: 79   **Fire Safety Rating:** 94   **Green Rating:** 86

STUDENTS AND FACULTY
Enrollment: 1,658. **Student Body:** 55% female, 45% male, 20% out-of-state, 1% international (9 countries represented). Asian 2%, African American 3%, Caucasian 83%, Hispanic 6%, Native American <1%, Pacific Islander <1%, Two or more races 3%, Race unknown 2%.
Retention and Graduation: 81% freshmen return for sophomore year. 69% freshmen graduate within 4 years. 73% freshmen graduate within 6 years. 42% grads go on to further study within 1 year. 19% grads pursue arts and sciences degrees. 0.6% grads pursue law degrees. 1% grads pursue business degrees. 2.4% grads pursue medical degrees. **Faculty:** Student/faculty ratio 10:1. 118 full-time faculty, 90% hold PhDs, 10% are members of minority groups, 42% are women. 0% of classes are taught by teaching assistants.

ACADEMICS
Degrees: Bachelor's; Doctoral/Professional; Master's; Post-Bachelor's certificate **Classes:** Most classes have 10-19 students. **Most popular majors:** Early Childhood Education And Teaching; Health Services/Allied Health/Health Sciences, General. **Special Study Options:** Accelerated program; Cooperative education program; Distance learning; Double major; Dual enrollment; English as a Second Language (ESL); Independent study; Internships; Liberal arts/career combination; Student-designed major; Study abroad; Teacher certification program. **Disability Services offered to physically disabled students:** Note-taking services; Reader services; Tape recorders; Tutors. **Career services:** Alumni network; Alumni services; Internships

FACILITIES
Housing: Apartments for single students; Coed dorms; Special housing for disabled student; Theme housing; Wellness housing 80% of campus accessible to physically diasbled. **Special Academic Facilities/Equipment:** Major-specific computer labs and resource libraries; animal behaviors labs; genetic testing equipment; psychology tests for personality and intelligence; bio-feedback equipment; technology, equipment, and materials for gene isolation, amplification, quantitation, mutation, including a Real-Time PCR machine; technology, equipment, and materials for recombinant protein production, purification, and analysis; mass spectrometers such as the MALDI-TOF MS and an ESI-Triple quad LC-MS; UV, visible, and fluorescent spectrophotometers, including a SpectraMax Plus 384 Absorbance UV/Vis Microplate Reader for use in biochemical and immunological assays such as ELISAs; tissue culture facility; animal facility; analytical and preparative liquid chromatography and electrophoresis systems for biomolecules; 20 acres of woodland dedicated to field studies in ecology, animal behavior, and plant science; game cameras to remotely sample wildlife populations; two greenhouse for botanical collection and experimentation; oversized Morris water maze, video camera, and Smart Maze software for behavioral studies; scanning electron microscope; transmission electron microscope; Thermo Scientific cryostat; biotechnology suite with a new RT-PCR instrument; sound recording studios; optics, atomic/nuclear, electronics, advanced physics, atomic force microscopy, and computational physics laboratories; physical therapy wellness pool and center; and more. **Computers:** 100% of classrooms, 100% of dorms, 100% of libraries, 100% of dining areas, 100% of student union, 90% of common outdoor areas have wireless network access. Students can register for classes online. Administrative functions (other than registration) can be performed online.

CAMPUS LIFE
Environment: Rural **Activities:** Campus Ministries; Choral groups; Concert band; Dance; Drama/theater; Jazz band; Literary magazine; Marching band; Music ensembles; Musical theater; Student government; Student newspaper; Symphony orchestra 79 registered organizations, 6 honor societies, 14 religious organizations. 4 fraternities, 4 sororities. **Athletics (Intercollegiate):** *Men:* baseball, basketball, cross-country, football, golf, ice hockey, lacrosse, soccer, swimming, tennis, track/field (outdoor), track/field (indoor). *Women:* basketball, cross-country, field hockey, lacrosse, soccer, softball, swimming, tennis, track/field (outdoor), track/field (indoor), volleyball. **On-Campus Highlights:** Peace Garden, Jeanne and Edward H. Arnold Health Professions Pavilion, Center for Student Engagement, Office of Intercultural Affairs & Inclusive Programming, LVC Sports Center **Environmental Initiatives:** energy conservation

ADMISSIONS
Freshman Academic Profile: Average high school GPA 3.7. 28% in top 10% of high school class, 55% in top 25% of high school class, 85% in top 50% of high school class. **Test Scores:** SAT Math middle 50% range 530-630. SAT EBRW middle 50% range 533-620. ACT middle 50% range 22-26. Minimum internet-based TOEFL 80. Minimum paper TOEFL 550. **Basis for Candidate Selection:** *Very important factors considered include:* rigor of secondary school record, class rank, academic GPA. *Important factors considered include:* interview, extracurricular activities, talent/ability, character/personal qualities, level of applicant's interest. *Other factors considered include:* application essay, standardized test scores, recommendation(s), first generation, alumni/ae relation, geographical residence, state residency, racial/ethnic status, volunteer work, work experience. **Freshman Admission Requirements:** High school diploma is required and GED is accepted *Academic units required:* 4 English, 3 math, 3 science, 2 foreign language, 3 social studies, and 1 unit from above areas or other academic areas. *Academic units recommended:* 2 science labs, 3 foreign language, 2 history. **Freshman Admission Statistics:** 2,833 applied, 72.9% admitted, 23% enrolled. **Transfer Admission Requirements:** High school transcript, college transcript(s), essay or personal statement, statement of good standing from prior institution(s). Minimum college GPA of 2.0 required. Lowest grade transferable C-. **General Admission Information:** Regular application deadline 2/15. Nonfall registration accepted.

COSTS AND FINANCIAL AID
Annual tuition $42,420. Room and board $11,860. Required fees $1,230. **Required Forms and Deadlines:** FAFSA. **Notification of Awards:** Applicants will be notified of awards on a rolling basis beginning 12/5. **Types of Aid:** *Need-based scholarships/grants:* College/university scholarship or grant aid from institutional funds; Federal Pell; Private scholarships; SEOG; State scholarships/grants. *Loans:* Direct PLUS loans; Direct Subsidized Stafford Loans; Direct Unsubsidized Stafford Loans. *Student Employment:* Federal Work-Study Program available. Institutional employment available. **Financial Aid Statistics:** 100% needy freshmen, 99% needy undergrads receive need-based scholarship or grant aid. 12% freshmen, 11% undergrads receive non-need-based scholarship or grant aid. 86% freshmen, 84% undergrads receive need-based self-help aid. 0% freshmen, 0% undergrads receive athletic scholarships. 99% freshmen, 99% undergrads receive any aid. Average cumulative indebtedness $46,346. **Criteria for awarding aid:** *Need-based:* Academics, Minority status *Non-need-based:* Academics, Alumni affiliation, Music/drama.

LEE UNIVERSITY

P.O. Box 3450, Cleveland, TN 37320-3450
Phone: 423-614-8500 · **Financial Aid Phone:** 423-614-8300
E-mail: admissions@leeuniversity.edu · **CEEB Code:** 1401
Fax: 423-614-8533 · **Website:** www.leeuniversity.edu · **ACT Code:** 3978

This private school, affiliated with the Church of God, was founded in 1918. It has a 120 acre campus.

RATINGS

Admissions Selectivity Rating: 78   **Fire Safety Rating:** 89   **Green Rating:** 61

STUDENTS AND FACULTY

Enrollment: 4,265. **Student Body:** 62% female, 38% male, 55% out-of-state, 3% international (51 countries represented). Asian 1%, African American 5%, Caucasian 81%, Hispanic 2%, Native American 1%, Pacific Islander <1%, Two or more races 3%, Race unknown 4%.
Retention and Graduation: 81% freshmen return for sophomore year. 37% freshmen graduate within 4 years. 52% freshmen graduate within 6 years.
Faculty: Student/faculty ratio 16:1. 184 full-time faculty, 77% hold PhDs, 11% are members of minority groups, 35% are women. 0% of classes are taught by teaching assistants.

ACADEMICS

Degrees: Bachelor's; Master's; Post-Master's certificate **Classes:** Most classes have 10-19 students. **Most popular majors:** Digital Communication And Media/Multimedia; Elementary Education And Teaching; Liberal Arts And Sciences/Liberal Studies. **Special Study Options:** Distance learning; Double major; Dual enrollment; English as a Second Language (ESL); External degree program; Honors program; Independent study; Internships; Student-designed major; Study abroad; Teacher certification program. **Honors programs:** The Kairos Scholars Honors Program. Also, several academic subject honors societies like Psychology, Business, Music and Pre-Med. **Disability Services offered to physically disabled students:** Note-taking services; Reader services; Tape recorders; Tutors. **Career services:** Alumni network; Alumni services; Career assessment; Internships

FACILITIES

Housing: Apartments for married students; Apartments for single students; Men's dorms; Women's dorms 76.32% of campus accessible to physically diasbled. **Special Academic Facilities/Equipment:** Curriculum Library in the College of Education. **Computers:** 80% of classrooms, 50% of dorms, 100% of libraries, 100% of dining areas, 100% of student union, 50% of common outdoor areas have wireless network access. Students can register for classes online. Administrative functions (other than registration) can be performed online.

CAMPUS LIFE

Environment: Town **Activities:** Campus Ministries; Choral groups; Concert band; Drama/theater; International Student Organization; Jazz band; Literary magazine; Model UN; Music ensembles; Musical theater; Opera; Pep band; Student government; Student newspaper; Symphony orchestra; Yearbook 72 registered organizations, 16 honor societies, 10 religious organizations. 5 fraternities, 4 sororities. **Athletics (Intercollegiate):** *Men:* baseball, basketball, cheerleading, cross-country, golf, soccer, tennis. *Women:* basketball, cheerleading, cross-country, soccer, softball, tennis, volleyball. **On-Campus Highlights:** Paul Conn Student Union-Bookstore, Chick-fil-a, Conn Center-Home of Chapels, Concerts, etc., Dixon Center plays, recitals, community events, De Vos Recreaction Center, Dunkin Donuts, Einstein Bros., Subway

ADMISSIONS

Freshman Academic Profile: Average high school GPA 3.6. 24% in top 10% of high school class, 50% in top 25% of high school class, 79% in top 50% of high school class. **Test Scores:** SAT Math middle 50% range 490-610. SAT EBRW middle 50% range 510-630. ACT middle 50% range 21-28. Minimum internet-based TOEFL 45. Minimum paper TOEFL 450. **Basis for Candidate Selection:** *Very important factors considered include:* rigor of secondary school record, academic GPA, standardized test scores. *Important factors considered include:* class rank, character/personal qualities, level of applicant's interest. *Other factors considered include:* application essay, recommendation(s), interview, extracurricular activities, talent/ability, first generation, alumni/ae relation. **Freshman Admission Requirements:** High school diploma is required and GED is accepted *Academic units required:* 4 English, 3 math, 2 science, 1 foreign language, 2 social studies, 1 history, *Academic units recommended:* 4 English, 3 math, 2 science, 1 foreign language, 2 social studies, 1 history, 1 computer science. **Freshman Admission Statistics:** 2,387 applied, 85.0% admitted, 44% enrolled. **Transfer Admission Requirements:** college transcript(s), Minimum college GPA of 2.0 required. Lowest grade transferable

D. **General Admission Information:** Application fee $25. Priority deadline 4/15. Nonfall registration accepted. Admission may be deferred for a maximum of 1 semester.

COSTS AND FINANCIAL AID

Annual tuition $17,040. Room and board $8,300. Required fees $650. Average book expense $1,600. **Required Forms and Deadlines:** FAFSA. **Notification of Awards:** Applicants will be notified of awards on a rolling basis beginning 2/1. **Types of Aid:** *Need-based scholarships/grants:* College/university scholarship or grant aid from institutional funds; Federal Pell; Private scholarships; SEOG; State scholarships/grants. *Loans:* Direct PLUS loans; Direct Subsidized Stafford Loans; Direct Unsubsidized Stafford Loans. *Student Employment:* Federal Work-Study Program available. Institutional employment available. **Financial Aid Statistics:** 95% needy freshmen, 89% needy undergrads receive need-based scholarship or grant aid. 40% freshmen, 14% undergrads receive non-need-based scholarship or grant aid. 59% freshmen, 80% undergrads receive need-based self-help aid. 5% freshmen, 4% undergrads receive athletic scholarships. 95% freshmen, 85% undergrads receive any aid. 60% undergrads borrow to pay for school. Average cumulative indebtedness $31,630. **Criteria for awarding aid:** *Non-need-based:* Academics, Alumni affiliation, Athletics, Leadership, Minority status, Music/drama, Religious affiliation, State/district residency.

LEHIGH UNIVERSITY

27 Memorial Drive West, Bethlehem, PA 18015
Phone: 610-758-3100 · **Financial Aid Phone:** 610-758-3181
E-mail: admissions@lehigh.edu · **CEEB Code:** 2365
Fax: 610-758-4361 · **Website:** www.lehigh.edu · **ACT Code:** 3612

This private school was founded in 1865. It has a 2355 acre campus.

RATINGS

Admissions Selectivity Rating: 95   **Fire Safety Rating:** 97   **Green Rating:** 93

STUDENTS AND FACULTY

Enrollment: 5,057. **Student Body:** 45% female, 55% male, 73% out-of-state, 9% international (62 countries represented). Asian 8%, African American 4%, Caucasian 64%, Hispanic 9%, Native American <1%, Pacific Islander <1%, Two or more races 3%, Race unknown 4%.
Retention and Graduation: 96% freshmen return for sophomore year. 76% freshmen graduate within 4 years. 86% freshmen graduate within 6 years. 25% grads go on to further study within 1 year. 20% grads pursue arts and sciences degrees. 7% grads pursue law degrees. 15% grads pursue business degrees. 11% grads pursue medical degrees. **Faculty:** Student/faculty ratio 9:1. 542 full-time faculty, 96% hold PhDs, 22% are members of minority groups, 35% are women.

ACADEMICS

Degrees: Bachelor's; Doctoral; Doctoral/Research; Master's; Post-Bachelor's certificate; Post-Master's certificate **Classes:** Most classes have 10-19 students. Most lab/discussion sessions have 10-19 students. **Most popular majors:** Mechanical Engineering; Accounting; Finance, General. **Special Study Options:** Accelerated program; Cooperative education program; Cross-registration; Distance learning; Double major; English as a Second Language (ESL); Exchange student program (domestic); External degree program; Honors program; Independent study; Internships; Liberal arts/career combination; Study abroad. **Honors programs:** Integrated Business and Engineering (IBE) Honors Program, program description available at https://ibe.lehigh.edu **Combined degree programs:** BA/DDS; BA/MD. **Disability Services offered to physically disabled students:** Note-taking services; Reader services; Tape recorders; Tutors. **Career services:** Alumni network; Alumni services; Career assessment; Career/job search classes; Internships; Regional alumni

FACILITIES

Housing: Apartments for married students; Apartments for single students; Coed dorms; Fraternity/sorority housing; Special housing for disabled student; Special housing for international students; Theme housing; Wellness housing **Special Academic Facilities/Equipment:** Art Museum, Zoellner Arts Center Electron optical labs STEPS Building **Computers:** 70% of classrooms, 100% of dorms, 100% of libraries, 100% of dining areas, 75% of student union, 80% of common outdoor areas have wireless network access. Students can register for classes online. Administrative functions (other than registration) can be performed online.

CAMPUS LIFE

Environment: City **Activities:** Campus Ministries; Choral groups; Concert band; Dance; Drama/theater; International Student Organization; Jazz band; Literary magazine; Marching band; Model UN; Music ensembles; Musical theater; Pep band; Radio station; Student government; Student newspaper; Student-run film society; Symphony orchestra; Yearbook 18 honor societies, 10 religious organizations. 21 fraternities, 9 sororities. **Athletics (Intercollegiate):** *Men:* baseball, basketball, cross-country, diving, football, golf, lacrosse, soccer, swimming, tennis, track/field (outdoor), track/field (indoor), wrestling. *Women:* basketball, crew/rowing, cross-country, diving, field hockey, golf, lacrosse, soccer, softball, swimming, tennis, track/field (outdoor), track/field (indoor), volleyball. **On-Campus Highlights:** Linderman Library, University Center, STEPS Building, Taylor Gymnasium, Zoellner Arts Center

ADMISSIONS

Freshman Academic Profile: 63% in top 10% of high school class, 89% in top 25% of high school class, 99% in top 50% of high school class. **Test Scores:** SAT Math middle 50% range 650-730. SAT EBRW middle 50% range 620-700. ACT middle 50% range 29-32. Minimum internet-based TOEFL 90. Minimum paper TOEFL 570. **Basis for Candidate Selection:** *Very important factors considered include:* rigor of secondary school record, academic GPA, recommendation(s), extracurricular activities, character/personal qualities. *Important factors considered include:* application essay, standardized test scores, talent/ability, volunteer work.level of applicant's interest. *Other factors considered include:* class rank, interview, first generation, alumni/ae relation, geographical residence, racial/ethnic status, work experience. **Freshman Admission Requirements:** High school diploma is required and GED is accepted *Academic units required:* 4 English, 3 math, 2 science, 2 science labs, 2 foreign language, 2 social studies, 3 academic electives, *Academic units recommended:* 4 math, 4 science, 2 science labs. **Freshman Admission Statistics:** 13,871 applied, 25.2%.admitted, 35% enrolled. **Transfer Admission Requirements:** High school transcript, college transcript(s), essay or personal statement, statement of good standing from prior institution(s). Minimum college GPA of 3.25 required. **General Admission Information:** Application fee $70. Regular application deadline 1/1. Nonfall registration accepted. Admission may be deferred for a maximum of 1 year.

COSTS AND FINANCIAL AID

Annual tuition $50,320. Room and board $13,120. Required fees $420. Average book expense $1,000. **Required Forms and Deadlines:** Business/Farm Supplement; CSS/Financial Aid PROFILE; FAFSA; Noncustodial PROFILE. **Notification of Awards:** Applicants will be notified of awards on or about 3/30. **Types of Aid:** *Need-based scholarships/grants:* College/university scholarship or grant aid from institutional funds; Federal Pell; Private scholarships; SEOG; State scholarships/grants. *Loans:* Direct PLUS loans; Direct Subsidized Stafford Loans; Direct Unsubsidized Stafford Loans. *Student Employment:* Federal Work-Study Program available. Institutional employment available. **Financial Aid Statistics:** 96% needy freshmen, 98% needy undergrads receive need-based scholarship or grant aid. 20% freshmen, 17% undergrads receive non-need-based scholarship or grant aid. 93% freshmen, 94% undergrads receive need-based self-help aid. 6% freshmen, 5% undergrads receive athletic scholarships. 57% freshmen, 62% undergrads receive any aid. 53% undergrads borrow to pay for school. Average cumulative indebtedness $34,215. **Criteria for awarding aid:** *Need-based:* Academics, Athletics, Minority status, Religious affiliation *Non-need-based:* Academics, Art, Athletics, Leadership, Music/drama.

LENOIR-RHYNE UNIVERSITY

635 North 7th Avenue, Hickory, NC 28603
Phone: 828.328.7300 • **Financial Aid Phone:** (828) 328-7356
E-mail: admission@lr.edu • **CEEB Code:** 5365
Website: www.lr.edu • **ACT Code:** 2941

This private school, affiliated with the Lutheran Church, was founded in 1891. It has a 100 acre campus.

RATINGS

Admissions Selectivity Rating: 76   **Fire Safety Rating:** 85   **Green Rating:** 70

STUDENTS AND FACULTY

Enrollment: 1,573. **Student Body:** 60% female, 40% male, 19% out-of-state, 3% international (19 countries represented). Asian 2%, African American 13%, Caucasian 67%, Hispanic 7%, Native American <1%, Pacific Islander 0%, Two or more races 4%, Race unknown 4%. **Retention and Graduation:** 73% freshmen return for sophomore year. 32% freshmen graduate within 4 years. 43% freshmen graduate within 6 years. 22% grads go on to further study within 1 year. **Faculty:** Student/faculty ratio 13:1.

130 full-time faculty, 88% hold PhDs, 9% are members of minority groups, 53% are women. 0% of classes are taught by teaching assistants.

ACADEMICS

Degrees: Bachelor's; Doctoral Other; Master's; Post-Bachelor's certificate **Classes:** Most classes have 10-19 students. Most lab/discussion sessions have 10-19 students. **Most popular majors:** Health And Physical Education/Fitness, General; Health And Wellness, General; Registered Nursing/Registered Nurse. **Special Study Options:** Accelerated program; Cross-registration; Distance learning; Double major; Dual enrollment; Honors program; Independent study; Internships; Study abroad; Teacher certification program. **Combined degree programs:** BA/MEng. **Disability Services offered to physically disabled students:** Note-taking services; Reader services; Tape recorders; Tutors. **Career services:** Alumni network; Alumni services; Career assessment; Career/job search classes; Internships; Regional alumni

FACILITIES

Housing: Coed dorms; Fraternity/sorority housing; Theme housing 75% of campus accessible to physically diasbled.

CAMPUS LIFE

Environment: Town **Activities:** Campus Ministries; Choral groups; Concert band; Dance; Drama/theater; International Student Organization; Jazz band; Literary magazine; Marching band; Model UN; Music ensembles; Musical theater; Pep band; Radio station; Student government; Student newspaper; Student-run film society; Symphony orchestra; Yearbook 54 registered organizations, 10 honor societies, 6 religious organizations. 4 fraternities, 4 sororities. **Athletics (Intercollegiate):** *Men:* baseball, basketball, cheerleading, cross-country, football, golf, soccer. *Women:* basketball, cheerleading, cross-country, golf, soccer, softball, volleyball. **On-Campus Highlights:** McCrorie Center, Cromer College Center, Shuford Physical Education Complex, Alex and Lee George Hall, Grace Chapel

ADMISSIONS

Freshman Academic Profile: Average high school GPA 3.3. 87% from public high schools. **Test Scores:** SAT Math middle 50% range 490-590. SAT EBRW middle 50% range 480-580. Minimum internet-based TOEFL 79. Minimum paper TOEFL 500. **Basis for Candidate Selection:** *Very important factors considered include:* academic GPA, standardized test scores. *Important factors considered include:* rigor of secondary school record, class rank, application essay, recommendation(s), extracurricular activities, character/personal qualities, volunteer work, work experience. **Freshman Admission Requirements:** High school diploma is required and GED is accepted *Academic units required:* 4 English, 3 math, 1 science, 1 science labs, 2 foreign language, 1 history, *Academic units recommended:* 4 English, 4 math, 2 science, 1 science labs, 3 foreign language, 2 history. **Freshman Admission Statistics:** 6,300 applied, 70.1% admitted, 9% enrolled. **Transfer Admission Requirements:** college transcript(s), statement of good standing from prior institution(s). Minimum college GPA of 2.5 required. Lowest grade transferable C. **General Admission Information:** Application fee $35. Nonfall registration accepted. Admission may be deferred for a maximum of 1 year.

COSTS AND FINANCIAL AID

Annual tuition $35,350. Room and board $12,150. Average book expense $1,160. **Required Forms and Deadlines:** FAFSA. **Types of Aid:** *Need-based scholarships/grants:* College/university scholarship or grant aid from institutional funds; Federal Pell; Private scholarships; SEOG; State scholarships/grants. *Loans:* Direct PLUS loans; Direct Subsidized Stafford Loans; Direct Unsubsidized Stafford Loans. *Student Employment:* Federal Work-Study Program available. Institutional employment available. **Financial Aid Statistics:** 100% needy freshmen, 99% needy undergrads receive need-based scholarship or grant aid. 16% freshmen, 12% undergrads receive non-need-based scholarship or grant aid. 81% freshmen, 85% undergrads receive need-based self-help aid. 15% freshmen, 12% undergrads receive athletic scholarships. 99% freshmen, 88% undergrads receive any aid. Average cumulative indebtedness $28,104. **Criteria for awarding aid:** *Need-based:* Academics, Alumni affiliation, Athletics, Leadership, Minority status, Music/drama, Religious affiliation *Non-need-based:* Academics, Alumni affiliation, Athletics, Leadership, Religious affiliation.

LESLEY UNIVERSITY

29 Everett St., Cambridge, MA 02140
Phone: 617-349-8800 · **Financial Aid Phone:** 617-349-8710
E-mail: admissions@lesley.edu · **CEEB Code:** 3483
Fax: 617-349-8810 · **Website:** www.lesley.edu · **ACT Code:** 1850

This private school was founded in 1909. It has a 1 acre campus.

RATINGS
Admissions Selectivity Rating: 78   **Fire Safety Rating:** 91   **Green Rating:** 60*

STUDENTS AND FACULTY
Enrollment: 1,418. **Student Body:** 75% female, 25% male, 57% out-of-state, 2% international (30 countries represented). Asian 4%, African American 4%, Caucasian 71%, Hispanic 10%, Native American <1%, Pacific Islander <1%, Two or more races 4%, Race unknown 5%.
Retention and Graduation: 78% freshmen return for sophomore year.
Faculty: Student/faculty ratio 9:1. 80 full-time faculty, 80% hold PhDs, 16% are members of minority groups, 50% are women. 0% of classes are taught by teaching assistants.

ACADEMICS
Degrees: Associate; Bachelor's; Certificate; Doctoral/Research; Master's; Post-Bachelor's certificate; Post-Master's certificate **Most popular majors:** Elementary Education And Teaching; Counseling Psychology; Marketing/Marketing Management, General. **Special Study Options:** Accelerated program; Cross-registration; Distance learning; Double major; Dual enrollment; Exchange student program (domestic); Honors program; Independent study; Internships; Liberal arts/career combination; Student-designed major; Study abroad; Teacher certification program. **Combined degree programs:** BA/MA. **Disability Services offered to physically disabled students:** Note-taking services; Reader services; Tape recorders; Tutors. **Career services:** Alumni network; Alumni services; Career assessment; Career/job search classes; Internships; Regional alumni

FACILITIES
Housing: Coed dorms; Theme housing; Wellness housing; Women's dorms 85% of campus accessible to physically diasbled. **Special Academic Facilities/Equipment:** Kresge Center for Teaching Resources and Educational Software Collection, Marran Art Gallery, Porter Exchange Gallery, AIB Main Gallery **Computers:** 100% of classrooms, 100% of libraries, 100% of dining areas, 100% of student union, 20% of common outdoor areas have wireless network access. Students can register for classes online. Administrative functions (other than registration) can be performed online.

CAMPUS LIFE
Environment: Metropolis **Activities:** Campus Ministries; Choral groups; Dance; Drama/theater; International Student Organization; Literary magazine; Musical theater; Student government; Student newspaper 25 registered organizations, 2 honor societies, 2 religious organizations **Athletics (Intercollegiate):** *Men:* basketball, cross-country, soccer, tennis, volleyball. *Women:* basketball, crew/rowing, cross-country, soccer, softball, tennis, volleyball. **On-Campus Highlights:** Student Center, Ludke Library, Porter Exchange Building, Stebbins Fitness Room, Kresge Center for Teaching Resources **Environmental Initiatives:** The continual enhancement of recycling, waste management and composting programs on campus.

ADMISSIONS
Freshman Academic Profile: Average high school GPA 3.3. 15% in top 10% of high school class, 44% in top 25% of high school class, 80% in top 50% of high school class. 83% from public high schools. **Test Scores:** SAT Math middle 50% range 460-570. SAT EBRW middle 50% range 490-600. ACT middle 50% range 21-25. Minimum internet-based TOEFL 61. Minimum paper TOEFL 500. **Basis for Candidate Selection:** *Very important factors considered include:* rigor of secondary school record, academic GPA, interview. *Important factors considered include:* class rank, application essay, standardized test scores, recommendation(s), extracurricular activities, talent/ability, character/personal qualities, volunteer work.level of applicant's interest. *Other factors considered include:* first generation, alumni/ae relation, racial/ethnic status, work experience. **Freshman Admission Requirements:** High school diploma is required and GED is accepted *Academic units required:* 4 English, 3 math, 3 science, 2 science labs, 1 social studies, 1 history, 4 academic electives, *Academic units recommended:* 4 English, 4 math, 4 science, 2 science labs, 2 foreign language, 2 social studies, 2 history, 2 units from above areas or other academic areas. **Freshman Admission Statistics:** 3,115 applied, 68.5% admitted, 18% enrolled. **Transfer Admission Requirements:** High school transcript, college transcript(s), essay or personal statement, statement of good standing from prior institution(s). Minimum college GPA of 2.5 required. Lowest grade transferable C. **General Admission Information:** Priority

deadline 2/15. Nonfall registration accepted. Admission may be deferred for a maximum of 1 year.

COSTS AND FINANCIAL AID
Annual tuition $25,500. Room and board $15,300. **Required Forms and Deadlines:** FAFSA. **Notification of Awards:** Applicants will be notified of awards on a rolling basis beginning 2/1. **Types of Aid:** *Need-based scholarships/grants:* College/university scholarship or grant aid from institutional funds; Federal Pell; Private scholarships; SEOG; State scholarships/grants. *Loans:* Direct PLUS loans; Direct Subsidized Stafford Loans; Direct Unsubsidized Stafford Loans. *Student Employment:* Federal Work-Study Program available. Institutional employment available. **Financial Aid Statistics:** 96% needy freshmen, 97% needy undergrads receive need-based scholarship or grant aid. 8% freshmen, 5% undergrads receive non-need-based scholarship or grant aid. 86% freshmen, 91% undergrads receive need-based self-help aid. 0% freshmen, 0% undergrads receive athletic scholarships. 70% freshmen, 70% undergrads receive any aid. 75% undergrads borrow to pay for school. Average cumulative indebtedness $2,300.

LETOURNEAU UNIVERSITY

P.O. Box 7001, Longview, TX 75607-7001
Phone: 903-233-4300
E-mail: admissions@letu.edu · **CEEB Code:** 6365
Fax: 903-233-4301 · **Website:** www.letu.edu · **ACT Code:** 4120

This private school, affiliated with the Nondenominational Christian Church, was founded in 1946. It has a 162 acre campus.

RATINGS
Admissions Selectivity Rating: 89   **Fire Safety Rating:** 60*   **Green Rating:** 60*

STUDENTS AND FACULTY
Enrollment: 1,802. **Student Body:** 43% female, 57% male, 35% out-of-state, 3% international (29 countries represented). Asian 1%, African American 10%, Caucasian 64%, Hispanic 8%, Native American <1%, Pacific Islander <1%, Two or more races 6%, Race unknown 7%.
Retention and Graduation: 81% freshmen return for sophomore year. 50% freshmen graduate within 4 years. 59% freshmen graduate within 6 years.
Faculty: Student/faculty ratio 15:1. 83 full-time faculty, 80% hold PhDs, 12% are members of minority groups, 22% are women.

ACADEMICS
Degrees: Associate; Bachelor's; Master's **Classes:** Most classes have 10-19 students. **Most popular majors:** Education; Engineering; Business, Management, Marketing, And Related Support Services. **Special Study Options:** Accelerated program; Cooperative education program; Cross-registration; Distance learning; Double major; Dual enrollment; English as a Second Language (ESL); Exchange student program (domestic); Honors program; Independent study; Internships; Study abroad; Teacher certification program. **Disability Services offered to physically disabled students:** Tutors. **Career services:** Alumni network; Alumni services; Career assessment; Career/job search classes; Internships

FACILITIES
Housing: Apartments for married students; Apartments for single students; Fraternity/sorority housing; Men's dorms; Special housing for disabled student; Special housing for international students; Theme housing; Women's dorms **Computers:** Students can register for classes online. Administrative functions (other than registration) can be performed online.

CAMPUS LIFE
Environment: Town **Activities:** Campus Ministries; Choral groups; Drama/theater; International Student Organization; Jazz band; Student government; Student newspaper; Yearbook 44 registered organizations, 4 honor societies, 10 religious organizations. **Athletics (Intercollegiate):** *Men:* baseball, basketball, cross-country, golf, soccer, tennis. *Women:* basketball, cross-country, golf, soccer, softball, tennis, volleyball.

ADMISSIONS
Freshman Academic Profile: Average high school GPA 3.6. 25% in top 10% of high school class, 52% in top 25% of high school class, 84% in top 50% of high school class. **Test Scores:** SAT Math middle 50% range 530-660. SAT EBRW middle 50% range 530-650. ACT middle 50% range 21-28. Minimum internet-based TOEFL 80. Minimum paper TOEFL 525. **Basis for Candidate Selection:** *Very important factors considered include:* rigor of secondary school record, academic GPA, standardized test scores, character/personal qualities. *Important factors considered include:* religious affiliation/commitment. *Other factors considered include:* class rank, interview, extracurricular activities, talent/

ability, first generation, alumni/ae relation, volunteer work, work experience, level of applicant's interest. **Freshman Admission Requirements:** High school diploma is required and GED is accepted **Freshman Admission Statistics:** 1,780 applied, 47.1% admitted, 38% enrolled. **Transfer Admission Requirements:** college transcript(s), essay or personal statement, Minimum college GPA of 2.0 required. Lowest grade transferable C. **General Admission Information:** Nonfall registration accepted. Admission may be deferred for a maximum of 2 semesters.

COSTS AND FINANCIAL AID
Annual tuition $29,630. Room and board $9,970. Required fees $580. Average book expense $1,580. **Required Forms and Deadlines:** FAFSA. **Notification of Awards:** Applicants will be notified of awards on a rolling basis beginning 11/30. **Types of Aid:** *Need-based scholarships/grants:* College/university scholarship or grant aid from institutional funds; Federal Pell; Private scholarships; SEOG; State scholarships/grants; United Negro College Fund. *Loans:* Direct PLUS loans; Direct Subsidized Stafford Loans; Direct Unsubsidized Stafford Loans. *Student Employment:* Federal Work-Study Program available. Institutional employment available. **Financial Aid Statistics:** 100% needy freshmen, 96% needy undergrads receive need-based scholarship or grant aid. 18% freshmen, 9% undergrads receive non-need-based scholarship or grant aid. 75% freshmen, 84% undergrads receive need-based self-help aid. 0% freshmen, 0% undergrads receive athletic scholarships. 69% undergrads borrow to pay for school. Average cumulative indebtedness $38,988. **Criteria for awarding aid:** *Need-based:* Academics, Alumni affiliation, Leadership, Minority status, Religious affiliation *Non-need-based:* Academics, Alumni affiliation, Leadership, Minority status, Religious affiliation, State/district residency.

LEWIS & CLARK COLLEGE

0615 S.W. Palatine Hill Road, Portland, OR 97219-7899
Phone: 503-768-7040 • **Financial Aid Phone:** 503-768-7090
E-mail: admissions@lclark.edu • **CEEB Code:** 4384
Fax: 503-768-7055 • **Website:** www.lclark.edu • **ACT Code:** 3464

This private school was founded in 1867. It has a 137 acre campus.

RATINGS
Admissions Selectivity Rating: 83   **Fire Safety Rating:** 87   **Green Rating:** 98

STUDENTS AND FACULTY
Enrollment: 2,021. **Student Body:** 59% female, 41% male, 88% out-of-state, 5% international (72 countries represented). Asian 6%, African American 3%, Caucasian 64%, Hispanic 12%, Native American 1%, Pacific Islander <1%, Two or more races 5%, Race unknown 4%.
Retention and Graduation: 83% freshmen return for sophomore year. 75% freshmen graduate within 4 years. 80% freshmen graduate within 6 years.
Faculty: Student/faculty ratio 12:1. 212 full-time faculty, 92% hold PhDs, 21% are members of minority groups, 54% are women. 0% of classes are taught by teaching assistants.

ACADEMICS
Degrees: Bachelor's; Doctoral/Professional; Master's; Post-Master's certificate **Classes:** Most classes have 10-19 students. **Most popular majors:** Biology/Biological Sciences, General; Psychology, General; Sociology And Anthropology. **Special Study Options:** Cross-registration; Double major; Dual enrollment; English as a Second Language (ESL); Honors program; Independent study; Internships; Student-designed major; Study abroad. **Honors programs:** Honors are designated by each department. **Disability Services offered to physically disabled students:** Note-taking services; Reader services; Tape recorders; Tutors. **Career services:** Alumni network; Alumni services; Career assessment; Career/job search classes; Internships; Regional alumni

FACILITIES
Housing: Apartments for single students; Coed dorms; Theme housing; Wellness housing; Women's dorms 85% of campus accessible to physically disabled. **Special Academic Facilities/Equipment:** Art gallery, observatory, world music room, 85 Rank Casavant organ, renovated greenhouse. **Computers:** 50% of classrooms, 20% of dorms, 100% of libraries, 25% of common outdoor areas have wireless network access. Students can register for classes online. Administrative functions (other than registration) can be performed online.

CAMPUS LIFE
Environment: Metropolis **Activities:** Campus Ministries; Choral groups; Concert band; Dance; Drama/theater; International Student Organization; Jazz band; Literary magazine; Model UN; Music ensembles; Musical theater; Pep band; Radio station; Student government; Student newspaper; Symphony orchestra 70 registered organizations, 5 honor societies, 9 religious organizations. **Athletics (Intercollegiate):** *Men:* baseball, basketball, crew/rowing, cross-country, football, golf, swimming, tennis, track/field (outdoor). *Women:* basketball, crew/rowing, cross-country, golf, soccer, softball, swimming, tennis, track/field (outdoor), volleyball. **On-Campus Highlights:** Aubrey Watzek Library, Templeton Student Center, Pamplin Sports Center, Estate Gardens, Maggies Coffee Shop **Environmental Initiatives:** Our undergraduate students voluntary contribute to the purchase of renewable energy and greenhouse gas offsets to account for 100% of our carbon footprint.

ADMISSIONS
Freshman Academic Profile: Average high school GPA 3.9. 77% from public high schools. **Test Scores:** SAT Math middle 50% range 590-680. SAT EBRW middle 50% range 620-710. ACT middle 50% range 27-31. Minimum internet-based TOEFL 91. Minimum paper TOEFL 575. **Basis for Candidate Selection:** *Very important factors considered include:* rigor of secondary school record, academic GPA. *Important factors considered include:* application essay, standardized test scores, recommendation(s), extracurricular activities, talent/ability, character/personal qualities, volunteer work, work experience. *Other factors considered include:* class rank, interview, first generation, alumni/ae relation, geographical residence, racial/ethnic status, level of applicant's interest. **Freshman Admission Requirements:** High school diploma is required and GED is accepted *Academic units recommended:* 4 English, 4 math, 3 science, 2 science labs, 2 foreign language, 3 social studies, 1 visual/performing arts. **Freshman Admission Statistics:** 6,305 applied, 71.4% admitted, 12% enrolled. **Transfer Admission Requirements:** High school transcript, college transcript(s), essay or personal statement, statement of good standing from prior institution(s). Minimum college GPA of 2.0 required. Lowest grade transferable C. **General Admission Information:** Priority deadline 1/15. Regular application deadline 1/15. Nonfall registration accepted. Admission may be deferred for a maximum of One year.

COSTS AND FINANCIAL AID
Annual tuition $48,628. Room and board $11,996. Required fees $360. Average book expense $1,050. **Required Forms and Deadlines:** CSS/Financial Aid PROFILE; FAFSA. **Notification of Awards:** Applicants will be notified of awards on a rolling basis beginning 1/30. **Types of Aid:** *Need-based scholarships/grants:* College/university scholarship or grant aid from institutional funds; Federal Pell; Private scholarships; SEOG; State scholarships/grants. *Loans:* Direct PLUS loans; Direct Subsidized Stafford Loans; Direct Unsubsidized Stafford Loans. *Student Employment:* Federal Work-Study Program available. Institutional employment available. **Financial Aid Statistics:** 98% needy freshmen, 99% needy undergrads receive need-based scholarship or grant aid. 16% freshmen, 8% undergrads receive non-need-based scholarship or grant aid. 91% freshmen, 92% undergrads receive need-based self-help aid. 0% freshmen, 0% undergrads receive athletic scholarships. 94% freshmen, 91% undergrads receive any aid. 55% undergrads borrow to pay for school. Average cumulative indebtedness $29,913. **Criteria for awarding aid:** *Need-based:* Academics *Non-need-based:* Academics, Leadership, Music/drama.

See page.970

LEWIS UNIVERSITY

One University Parkway, Romeoville, IL 60446
Phone: (815) 836-5250 • **Financial Aid Phone:** (815) 836-5263
E-mail: admissions@lewisu.edu • **CEEB Code:** 1404
Fax: (815) 836-5002 • **Website:** www.lewisu.edu • **ACT Code:** 1058

This private school, affiliated with the Roman Catholic Church, was founded in 1932. It has a 410 acre campus.

RATINGS
Admissions Selectivity Rating: 85   **Fire Safety Rating:** 97   **Green Rating:** 73

STUDENTS AND FACULTY
Enrollment: 4,372. **Student Body:** 53% female, 47% male, 9% out-of-state, 2% international (26 countries represented). Asian 4%, African American 5%, Caucasian 59%, Hispanic 20%, Native American <1%, Pacific Islander <1%, Two or more races 3%, Race unknown 7%.
Retention and Graduation: 80% freshmen return for sophomore year. 48% freshmen graduate within 4 years. 67% freshmen graduate within 6 years.
Faculty: Student/faculty ratio 13:1. 223 full-time faculty, 80% hold PhDs, 14%

are members of minority groups, 47% are women. 0% of classes are taught by teaching assistants.

ACADEMICS

Degrees: Associate; Bachelor's; Certificate; Doctoral Other; Doctoral/ Research; Master's; Post-Bachelor's certificate; Post-Master's certificate **Classes:** Most classes have 10-19 students. Most lab/discussion sessions have 10-19 students. **Most popular majors:** Criminal Justice/Safety Studies; Registered Nursing/Registered Nurse; Business Administration And Management, General. **Special Study Options:** Accelerated program; Distance learning; Double major; Dual enrollment; English as a Second Language (ESL); Honors program; Independent study; Internships; Liberal arts/career combination; Student-designed major; Study abroad; Teacher certification program; Weekend college. **Honors programs:** Lewis' Honors Program provides exclusive intellectual opportunities for academically gifted undergraduate students guided by four pillars—Inquiry, Integration, Dialogue, and Service. For information on our Scholars Academy use the following url: http://www.lewisu.edu/academics/scholars/index.htm **Combined degree programs:** BA/MA. **Disability Services offered to physically disabled students:** Tape recorders; Tutors. **Career services:** Alumni network; Alumni services; Career assessment; Career/job search classes; Internships; Regional alumni

FACILITIES

Housing: Coed dorms; Special housing for disabled student; Theme housing 90% of campus accessible to physically diasbled. **Special Academic Facilities/ Equipment:** ° The Lewis University aviation program continues to provide hard-working students with top-of-the-line equipment and state-of-the-art facilities. Lewis' aviation facilities include: An airplane hangar and machine shops includes a Snap-on Tools partnership, Flight simulators, a Boeing 737 for maintenance training, Seven Cessna 152's, 13 Cessna 172's, four Cessna 182's and one Piper Seminole and the Harold E. White Aviation Center. Located adjacent to the main campus is the Lewis University Airport which serves as a reliever airport for O'Hare International. ° The Oremus Fine Arts Center is one of the most highly-used buildings on campus and home of the Philip Lynch Theatre, Lewis' largest auditorium and meeting space, the Oremus Fine Arts Center hosts hundreds of student performances, concerts, community events and lectures each year and is visited by more than 28,000 patrons from surrounding communities. ° JFK Student Recreation and Fitness Center houses: an aerobics studio with a suspended floor where you can take classes such as Pilates and spinning, a fitness center with weights and cardiovascular machines, a 25 yard, 8-lane collegiate size swimming pool, a field house that features four playing courts used primarily for basketball, volleyball, tennis, and floor hockey, Surrounded by a 200-meter track and the Neil Carey Arena where indoor varsity athletics are played. °The Andrew Center for Electronic Media, Lewis' state-of-the-art multimedia facility, provides students with the tools, technology and environment to assemble an impressive portfolio of work. Another multimedia lab features the latest Macs, equipped for animation, desktop publishing, podcasting, web design, video-editing and more. **Computers:** 100% of classrooms, 100% of dorms, 100% of libraries, 100% of dining areas, 100% of student union, 100% of common outdoor areas have wireless network access. Students can register for classes online. Administrative functions (other than registration) can be performed online.

CAMPUS LIFE

Environment: City **Activities:** Campus Ministries; Choral groups; Dance; Drama/theater; International Student Organization; Jazz band; Literary magazine; Model UN; Music ensembles; Musical theater; Pep band; Radio station; Student government; Student newspaper; Symphony orchestra; Television station 45 registered organizations, 10 honor societies, 7 religious organizations. 7 fraternities, 6 sororities. **Athletics (Intercollegiate):** *Men:* baseball, basketball, cheerleading, cross-country, golf, soccer, swimming, tennis, track/field (outdoor), track/field (indoor), volleyball. *Women:* basketball, cheerleading, cross-country, golf, soccer, softball, swimming, tennis, track/field (outdoor), track/field (indoor), volleyball. **On-Campus Highlights:** Harold E. White Aviation Center, Main Quad & Flyers Den, Student Recreation and Fitness Center, College of Nursing & College of Business, Science Building **Environmental Initiatives:** The Lewis University Environment and Energy Conservation Council sponsors annual events such as an Earth Day event in spring where we clear out Buckthorn (an invasive plant species) from the nature trail here on campus and the Arbor Day Initiative in which we plant an assortment of native trees back into the University nature trail.

ADMISSIONS

Freshman Academic Profile: Average high school GPA 3.5. 20% in top 10% of high school class, 49% in top 25% of high school class, 77% in top 50% of high school class. **Test Scores:** SAT Math middle 50% range 470-630. SAT EBRW middle 50% range 470-600. ACT middle 50% range 21-26. Minimum internet-based TOEFL 79. Minimum paper TOEFL 550. **Basis for Candidate Selection:** *Very important factors considered include:* rigor of secondary school record, academic GPA, standardized test scores. *Important factors considered include:* application essay. *Other factors considered include:* class rank, recommendation(s), interview, extracurricular activities, talent/ability,

character/personal qualities, first generation, alumni/ae relation, geographical residence, racial/ethnic status, volunteer work, work experience, level of applicant's interest. **Freshman Admission Requirements:** High school diploma is required and GED is accepted *Academic units required:* 3 English, 2 math, 2 science, 1 science labs, 2 social studies, 1 history, 8 academic electives, *Academic units recommended:* 4 English, 3 math, 2 science, 1 science labs, 2 foreign language, 2 social studies, 1 history, 8 academic electives. **Freshman Admission Statistics:** 5,447 applied, 53.8% admitted, 21% enrolled. **Transfer Admission Requirements:** college transcript(s), Minimum college GPA of 2.0 required. Lowest grade transferable D. **General Admission Information:** Application fee $40. Priority deadline 4/15. Nonfall registration accepted. Admission may be deferred for a maximum of 1 year.

COSTS AND FINANCIAL AID

Annual tuition $32,300. Room and board $10,578. Required fees $150. Average book expense $1,500. **Required Forms and Deadlines:** FAFSA. **Notification of Awards:** Applicants will be notified of awards on a rolling basis beginning 11/1. **Types of Aid:** *Need-based scholarships/grants:* College/university scholarship or grant aid from institutional funds; Federal Nursing Scholarships; Federal Pell; Private scholarships; SEOG; State scholarships/grants. *Loans:* Direct PLUS loans; Direct Subsidized Stafford Loans; Direct Unsubsidized Stafford Loans. *Student Employment:* Federal Work-Study Program available. Institutional employment available. **Financial Aid Statistics:** 100% needy freshmen, 95% needy undergrads receive need-based scholarship or grant aid. 15% freshmen, 11% undergrads receive non-need-based scholarship or grant aid. 86% freshmen, 90% undergrads receive need-based self-help aid. 4% freshmen, 2% undergrads receive athletic scholarships. 99% freshmen, 88% undergrads receive any aid. 81% undergrads borrow to pay for school. Average cumulative indebtedness $36,073. **Criteria for awarding aid:** *Non-need-based:* Academics, Alumni affiliation, Art, Athletics, Music/drama, Religious affiliation.

LEWIS-CLARK STATE COLLEGE

500 Eighth Avenue, Lewiston, ID 83501
Phone: 208-792-2210 • **Financial Aid Phone:** 208-792-2224
E-mail: admissions@lcsc.edu • **CEEB Code:** 4385
Fax: 208-792-2876 • **Website:** www.lcsc.edu • **ACT Code:** 920

This public school was founded in 1893. It has a 44 acre campus.

RATINGS

Admissions Selectivity Rating: 73   **Fire Safety Rating:** 78   **Green Rating:** 60*

STUDENTS AND FACULTY

Enrollment: 3,172. **Student Body:** 61% female, 39% male, 20% out-of-state, 4% international (32 countries represented). Asian 1%, African American 1%, Caucasian 82%, Hispanic 6%, Native American 2%, Pacific Islander <1%, Two or more races 2%, Race unknown 2%.
Retention and Graduation: 61% freshmen return for sophomore year. 7% grads go on to further study within 1 year. **Faculty:** Student/faculty ratio 18:1. 159 full-time faculty, 47% hold PhDs, 4% are members of minority groups, 53% are women. 0% of classes are taught by teaching assistants.

ACADEMICS

Degrees: Associate; Bachelor's; Certificate; Terminal Associate; Transfer Associate **Classes:** Most classes have 10-19 students. Most lab/discussion sessions have 10-19 students. **Most popular majors:** Elementary Education And Teaching; Nursing/Registered Nurse (Rn, Asn, Bsn, Msn); Business/ Commerce, General. **Special Study Options:** Accelerated program; Cooperative education program; Distance learning; Double major; Dual enrollment; Independent study; Internships; Liberal arts/career combination; Student-designed major; Study abroad; Teacher certification program. **Disability Services offered to physically disabled students:** Note-taking services; Reader services; Tape recorders; Tutors.

FACILITIES

Housing: Apartments for married students; Apartments for single students; Coed dorms; Special housing for international students; Theme housing 95% of campus accessible to physically diasbled. **Special Academic Facilities/ Equipment:** Museum/art gallery, Media Services **Computers:** Students can register for classes online. Administrative functions (other than registration) can be performed online.

CAMPUS LIFE

Environment: Town **Activities:** Campus Ministries; Drama/theater; International Student Organization; Jazz band; Literary magazine; Radio station; Student government; Student newspaper 52 registered organizations,

1 honor society, 3 religious organizations. **Athletics (Intercollegiate):** *Men:* baseball, basketball, cross-country, golf, tennis. *Women:* basketball, cross-country, golf, tennis, volleyball. **On-Campus Highlights:** Information Commons in the Library, Student Union Building, Athletic Center which is under construction, Centennial Mall, Yo Espresso or Jitterz

ADMISSIONS

Freshman Academic Profile: Average high school GPA 3.1. 5% in top 10% of high school class, 18% in top 25% of high school class, 46% in top 50% of high school class. 99% from public high schools. **Test Scores:** SAT Math middle 50% range 400-520. SAT EBRW middle 50% range 410-510. ACT middle 50% range 17-22. Minimum paper TOEFL 500. **Basis for Candidate Selection:** *Other factors considered include:* academic GPA, standardized test scores. **Freshman Admission Requirements:** High school diploma is required and GED is accepted *Academic units required:* 4 English, 3 math, 3 science, 1 science labs, 2.5 social studies, 1.5 academic electives, and 1 unit from above areas or other academic areas. **Freshman Admission Statistics:** 852 applied, 99.1% admitted, 61% enrolled. **Transfer Admission Requirements:** college transcript(s), Minimum college GPA of 2.0 required. Lowest grade transferable D. **General Admission Information:** Regular application deadline 8/8. Nonfall registration accepted. Admission may be deferred for a maximum of 1 year.

COSTS AND FINANCIAL AID

Annual in-state tuition $6,194. Room and board $6,194. Required fees $2,724. **Required Forms and Deadlines:** FAFSA. **Notification of Awards:** Applicants will be notified of awards on a rolling basis beginning 4/15. **Types of Aid:** *Need-based scholarships/grants:* College/university scholarship or grant aid from institutional funds; Federal Pell; Private scholarships; SEOG; State scholarships/grants. *Loans: Student Employment:* Federal Work-Study Program available. Institutional employment available. **Financial Aid Statistics:** 58% needy freshmen, 66% needy undergrads receive need-based scholarship or grant aid. 55% freshmen, 24% undergrads receive non-need-based scholarship or grant aid. 77% freshmen, 82% undergrads receive need-based self-help aid. 5% freshmen, 8% undergrads receive athletic scholarships. 85% freshmen, 76% undergrads receive any aid. **Criteria for awarding aid:** *Need-based:* Academics, Alumni affiliation, Minority status *Non-need-based:* Academics, Alumni affiliation, Art, Athletics, Leadership, Minority status, Music/drama.

LIBERTY UNIVERSITY

1971 University Boulevard, Lynchburg, VA 24515
Phone: 434-582-2000 · **Financial Aid Phone:** 434-582-2270
E-mail: admissions@liberty.edu · **CEEB Code:** 5385
Fax: 800-628-7977 · **Website:** https://www.liberty.edu/ · **ACT Code:** 4364

This private school, affiliated with the Baptist Church, was founded in 1971. It has a 4400 acre campus.

RATINGS

Admissions Selectivity Rating: 91   **Fire Safety Rating:** 84   **Green Rating:** 60*

STUDENTS AND FACULTY

Enrollment: 13,748. **Student Body:** 54% female, 46% male, 61% out-of-state, 5% international (125 countries represented). Asian 2%, African American 4%, Caucasian 66%, Hispanic 5%, Native American <1%, Pacific Islander <1%, Two or more races 3%, Race unknown 14%.
Retention and Graduation: 86% freshmen return for sophomore year. 38% freshmen graduate within 4 years. 60% freshmen graduate within 6 years.
Faculty: 0% of classes are taught by teaching assistants.

ACADEMICS

Degrees: Associate; Bachelor's; Certificate; Doctoral; Doctoral/Professional; Doctoral/Research; Master's; Post-Bachelor's certificate; Post-Master's certificate; Terminal Associate **Classes:** Most classes have fewer than 10 students. Most lab/discussion sessions have 10-19 students. **Most popular majors:** Religion/Religious Studies; Psychology, General; Business/Commerce, General. **Special Study Options:** Accelerated program; Cooperative education program; Distance learning; Double major; Dual enrollment; External degree program; Honors program; Independent study; Internships; Student-designed major; Study abroad; Teacher certification program. **Honors programs:** An early class registration period, smaller class size (15:1) for general education Honors seminars, and a generous scholarship based on grade point average are just a few of the benefits enjoyed by our Honors students. Once Honors students reach junior status, they petition one Honors course per semester in their desired major field of study. **Disability Services offered to physically disabled students:** Tutors. **Career services:** Career assessment; Internships

FACILITIES

Housing: Apartments for single students; Men's dorms; Special housing for disabled student; Women's dorms 98% of campus accessible to physically diasbled. **Special Academic Facilities/Equipment:** Displays from the Museum of Life and Earth History are located in the Library. The Jerry Falwell Museum located in the main lobby of DeMoss Hall. **Computers:** 90% of classrooms, have wireless network access. Students can register for classes online. Administrative functions (other than registration) can be performed online.

CAMPUS LIFE

Environment: Town **Activities:** Campus Ministries; Choral groups; Concert band; Drama/theater; Literary magazine; Marching band; Music ensembles; Musical theater; Pep band; Radio station; Student government; Student newspaper; Symphony orchestra; Television station; Yearbook 25 registered organizations, 8 honor societies, 10 religious organizations. **Athletics (Intercollegiate):** *Men:* baseball, basketball, cheerleading, cross-country, football, golf, soccer, tennis, track/field (outdoor), track/field (indoor), wrestling. *Women:* basketball, cheerleading, cross-country, soccer, softball, tennis, track/field (outdoor), track/field (indoor), volleyball. **On-Campus Highlights:** LaHaye Student Center, Bookstore, Hangar (Food Court), ILRC Computer Lab, LaHaye Ice Center (Ice Arena)

ADMISSIONS

Freshman Academic Profile: Average high school GPA 3.5. 20% in top 10% of high school class, 44% in top 25% of high school class, 78% in top 50% of high school class. **Test Scores:** SAT Math middle 50% range 510-600. SAT EBRW middle 50% range 530-640. ACT middle 50% range 21-28. Minimum internet-based TOEFL 60. Minimum paper TOEFL 500. **Basis for Candidate Selection:** *Very important factors considered include:* rigor of secondary school record, academic GPA. *Important factors considered include:* standardized test scores, character/personal qualities. *Other factors considered include:* class rank, application essay, recommendation(s), extracurricular activities, talent/ability, level of applicant's interest. **Freshman Admission Requirements:** High school diploma is required and GED is accepted *Academic units recommended:* 4 English, 3 math, 2 science, 2 science labs, 2 foreign language, 2 social studies, 4 academic electives. **Freshman Admission Statistics:** 14,567 applied, 39.4% admitted, 49% enrolled. **Transfer Admission Requirements:** High school transcript, college transcript(s), essay or personal statement, statement of good standing from prior institution(s). Minimum college GPA of 2.0 required. Lowest grade transferable C. **General Admission Information:** Application fee $50. Priority deadline 1/31. Nonfall registration accepted. Admission may be deferred for a maximum of 1 year.

COSTS AND FINANCIAL AID

Annual tuition $22,000. Room and board $9,306. Required fees $1,020. Average book expense $1,700. **Required Forms and Deadlines:** FAFSA; State aid form. **Notification of Awards:** Applicants will be notified of awards on a rolling basis beginning 3/15. **Types of Aid:** *Need-based scholarships/grants:* College/university scholarship or grant aid from institutional funds; Federal Pell; Private scholarships; SEOG; State scholarships/grants. *Loans:* Direct PLUS loans; Direct Subsidized Stafford Loans; Direct Unsubsidized Stafford Loans. **Financial Aid Statistics:** 99% needy freshmen receive need-based scholarship or grant aid. 95% freshmen, 87% undergrads receive any aid. **Criteria for awarding aid:** *Non-need-based:* Academics, Alumni affiliation, Athletics, Leadership, Music/drama, Religious affiliation, State/district residency.

LIFE UNIVERSITY

1269 Barclay Circle, Marietta, GA 30060
Phone: 770.426.2884 · **Financial Aid Phone:** 770.426.2667
E-mail: admissions@life.edu
Website: http://www.life.edu/

This private school was founded in 1974. It has a 104 acre campus.

RATINGS

Admissions Selectivity Rating: 70   **Fire Safety Rating:** 60*   **Green Rating:** 60*

STUDENTS AND FACULTY

Enrollment: 811. **Student Body:** 48% female, 52% male, (31 countries represented). Asian 3%, African American 25%, Caucasian 34%, Hispanic 8%, Native American 1%, Race unknown 29%.
Faculty: Student/faculty ratio 17:1. 124 full-time faculty, 86% hold PhDs, 44% are women.

ACADEMICS

Degrees: Associate; Bachelor's; Certificate; Doctoral; Master's **Classes:** Most classes have 10-19 students. **Special Study Options:** Accelerated program;

Double major; English as a Second Language (ESL); Independent study; Internships; Study abroad. **Career services:** Alumni network; Internships; Regional alumni

FACILITIES

Housing: Apartments for married students; Apartments for single students; Coed dorms; Other (please specify)

CAMPUS LIFE

Environment: Metropolis **Activities:** International Student Organization; Student government; Student newspaper. Socrates Cafe, Ian Grassam Treehouse, Wellness Center, CCE Building, SHS Building

ADMISSIONS

Basis for Candidate Selection: *Important factors considered include:* academic GPA, extracurricular activities, talent/ability, alumni/ae relation. *Other factors considered include:* rigor of secondary school record, class rank, character/personal qualities, work experience. **Freshman Admission Requirements:** High school diploma is required and GED is accepted **Freshman Admission Statistics:** 259 applied, 67.6% admitted, 43% enrolled. **General Admission Information:** Application fee $50. Regular application deadline 9/1. Nonfall registration accepted. Admission may be deferred.

COSTS AND FINANCIAL AID

Annual tuition $9,874. Room and board $12,480. Required fees $747. **Required Forms and Deadlines:** FAFSA. **Types of Aid:** *Need-based scholarships/grants:* Federal Pell; SEOG. *Loans:* Direct PLUS loans; Direct Subsidized Stafford Loans; Direct Unsubsidized Stafford Loans. **Financial Aid Statistics:** 74% needy freshmen, 66% needy undergrads receive need-based scholarship or grant aid. 85% freshmen, 70% undergrads receive non-need-based scholarship or grant aid. 91% freshmen, 90% undergrads receive need-based self-help aid. 32% freshmen, 16% undergrads receive athletic scholarships. **Criteria for awarding aid:** *Non-need-based:* Academics, Alumni affiliation, Athletics, Leadership, State/district residency.

LIM COLLEGE

12 East 53rd Street, New York, NY 10022
Phone: 212-310-0639 • **Financial Aid Phone:** 212-752-1530
E-mail: admissions@limcollege.edu • **CEEB Code:** 2380
Website: www.limcollege.edu • **ACT Code:** 4807

This proprietary school was founded in 1939.

RATINGS

Admissions Selectivity Rating: 75　　**Fire Safety Rating:** 81　　**Green Rating:** 60*

STUDENTS AND FACULTY

Enrollment: 1,402. **Student Body:** 91% female, 9% male, 65% out-of-state, 6% international (13 countries represented). Asian 8%, African American 15%, Caucasian 53%, Hispanic 8%, Native American 1%, Pacific Islander <1%, Two or more races 0%, Race unknown 8%.
Retention and Graduation: 67% freshmen return for sophomore year. 47% freshmen graduate within 4 years. 55% freshmen graduate within 6 years. **Faculty:** Student/faculty ratio 8:1. 27 full-time faculty, 0% of classes are taught by teaching assistants.

ACADEMICS

Degrees: Associate; Bachelor's; Certificate; Master's; Post-Bachelor's certificate **Classes:** Most classes have 10-19 students. Most lab/discussion sessions have 10-19 students. **Most popular majors:** Marketing/Marketing Management, General; Fashion Merchandising. **Special Study Options:** Distance learning; Honors program; Internships; Study abroad. **Disability Services offered to physically disabled students:** Tape recorders; Tutors. **Career services:** Alumni network; Alumni services; Career assessment; Career/job search classes; Internships

FACILITIES

Housing: Coed dorms 100% of campus accessible to physically diasbled. **Computers:** 100% of classrooms, 100% of dorms, 100% of libraries, 100% of dining areas, 100% of student union, have wireless network access. Students can register for classes online. Administrative functions (other than registration) can be performed online.

CAMPUS LIFE

Environment: Metropolis **Activities:** Dance; International Student Organization; Literary magazine; Student government 12 registered organizations, 1 honor societies. **On-Campus Highlights:** Library, Cafe 45, Cyber Lounge, 1760 Third Ave.

ADMISSIONS

Freshman Academic Profile: Average high school GPA 3.0. 73% from public high schools. **Test Scores:** SAT Math middle 50% range 420-580. SAT EBRW middle 50% range 440-600. ACT middle 50% range 16-26. Minimum internet-based TOEFL 80. Minimum paper TOEFL 550. **Basis for Candidate Selection:** *Very important factors considered include:* rigor of secondary school record, academic GPA. *Important factors considered include:* application essay, recommendation(s), level of applicant's interest. *Other factors considered include:* class rank, interview, extracurricular activities, talent/ability, character/personal qualities, alumni/ae relation, volunteer work, work experience. **Freshman Admission Requirements:** High school diploma is required and GED is accepted **Freshman Admission Statistics:** 1,340 applied, 78.4% admitted, 24% enrolled. **Transfer Admission Requirements:** High school transcript, college transcript(s), essay or personal statement, Minimum college GPA of 2.0 required. Lowest grade transferable D-. **General Admission Information:** Application fee $40. Nonfall registration accepted. Admission may be deferred for a maximum of 1 semester.

COSTS AND FINANCIAL AID

Annual tuition $26,210. Room and board $20,350. Required fees $820. Average book expense $900. **Required Forms and Deadlines:** FAFSA; Institution's own financial aid form. **Types of Aid:** *Need-based scholarships/grants:* College/university scholarship or grant aid from institutional funds; Federal Pell; Private scholarships; SEOG; State scholarships/grants. *Loans:* Direct PLUS loans; Direct Subsidized Stafford Loans; Direct Unsubsidized Stafford Loans. *Student Employment:* Federal Work-Study Program available. Institutional employment available. **Financial Aid Statistics:** 76% needy freshmen, 74% needy undergrads receive need-based scholarship or grant aid. 60% freshmen, 50% undergrads receive non-need-based scholarship or grant aid. 77% freshmen, 90% undergrads receive need-based self-help aid. 0% freshmen, 0% undergrads receive athletic scholarships. 85% freshmen, 85% undergrads receive any aid. 75% undergrads borrow to pay for school. Average cumulative indebtedness $37,238. **Criteria for awarding aid:** *Need-based:* Academics, Alumni affiliation, Minority status *Non-need-based:* Academics, Leadership, State/district residency.

See page 972.

LIMESTONE COLLEGE

1115 College Drive, Gaffney, SC 29340-3799
Phone: 864-488-4549 • **Financial Aid Phone:** 864-488-8800
E-mail: admiss@limestone.edu • **CEEB Code:** 5366
Fax: 864-487-8706 • **Website:** www.limestone.edu • **ACT Code:** 3862

This private school was founded in 1845. It has a 119 acre campus.

RATINGS

Admissions Selectivity Rating: 85　　**Fire Safety Rating:** 81　　**Green Rating:** 60*

STUDENTS AND FACULTY

Enrollment: 1,052. **Student Body:** 38% female, 62% male, 42% out-of-state, 9% international. Asian <1%, African American 29%, Caucasian 54%, Hispanic 4%, Native American <1%, Two or more races 2%, Race unknown 1%.
Retention and Graduation: 57% freshmen return for sophomore year. **Faculty:** Student/faculty ratio 13:1. 75 full-time faculty, 80% hold PhDs, 5% are members of minority groups, 51% are women. 0% of classes are taught by teaching assistants.

ACADEMICS

Degrees: Bachelor's; Master's; Transfer Associate **Classes:** Most classes have 10-19 students. Most lab/discussion sessions have 10-19 students. **Most popular majors:** Elementary Education And Teaching; Health And Physical Education/Fitness, Other; Business/Managerial Economics. **Special Study Options:** Accelerated program; Distance learning; Double major; Dual enrollment; Honors program; Independent study; Internships; Liberal arts/career combination; Student-designed major; Teacher certification program. **Honors programs:** The Honors Program was established at Limestone College in 1983 to create a challenging academic environment for gifted and special ability students. **Disability Services offered to physically disabled students:** Note-taking services; Tape recorders; Tutors. **Career services:** Alumni services; Career assessment

FACILITIES

Housing: Apartments for single students; Men's dorms; Women's dorms 90% of campus accessible to physically diasbled. **Special Academic Facilities/Equipment:** Computer graphic arts lab; Museum of Limestone College

History in Winnie Davis Hall **Computers:** 20% of classrooms, 20% of dorms, 100% of libraries, 100% of student union, 5% of common outdoor areas have wireless network access. Students can register for classes online. Administrative functions (other than registration) can be performed online.

CAMPUS LIFE
Environment: Town **Activities:** Campus Ministries; Choral groups; Concert band; Drama/theater; Jazz band; Literary magazine; Marching band; Music ensembles; Musical theater; Pep band; Student government; Yearbook 2 religious organizations. **Athletics (Intercollegiate):** *Men:* baseball, basketball, cross-country, golf, lacrosse, soccer, swimming, tennis, track/field (outdoor), volleyball, wrestling. *Women:* basketball, cross-country, field hockey, golf, lacrosse, soccer, softball, swimming, tennis, track/field (outdoor), volleyball. **On-Campus Highlights:** Dixie Lodge Student Center, Stephenson Dining Hall, Timken Gym and Pool, Eastwood Library, Curtis Administration Building **Environmental Initiatives:** Community Garden

ADMISSIONS
Freshman Academic Profile: Average high school GPA 3.2. 3% in top 10% of high school class, 19% in top 25% of high school class, 51% in top 50% of high school class. 90% from public high schools. **Test Scores:** SAT Math middle 50% range 480-560. SAT EBRW middle 50% range 450-530. Minimum internet-based TOEFL 75. Minimum paper TOEFL 500. **Basis for Candidate Selection:** *Very important factors considered include:* rigor of secondary school record, academic GPA, standardized test scores. *Important factors considered include:* class rank. *Other factors considered include:* recommendation(s), interview. **Freshman Admission Requirements:** High school diploma is required and GED is accepted *Academic units required:* 4 English, 3 math, 2 science, 2 science labs, 3 social studies. **Freshman Admission Statistics:** 2,318 applied, 53.7% admitted, 33% enrolled. **Transfer Admission Requirements:** college transcript(s), statement of good standing from prior institution(s). Minimum college GPA of 2.0 required. Lowest grade transferable C. **General Admission Information:** Application fee $25. Priority deadline 6/1. Regular application deadline 8/25. Nonfall registration accepted. Admission may be deferred for a maximum of 18 months.

COSTS AND FINANCIAL AID
Annual tuition $23,000. Room and board $7,800. Average book expense $2,304. **Required Forms and Deadlines:** FAFSA. **Notification of Awards:** Applicants will be notified of awards on a rolling basis beginning 1/15. **Types of Aid:** *Need-based scholarships/grants:* College/university scholarship or grant aid from institutional funds; Federal Pell; Private scholarships; SEOG; State scholarships/grants. *Loans:* Direct PLUS loans; Direct Subsidized Stafford Loans; Direct Unsubsidized Stafford Loans. *Student Employment:* Federal Work-Study Program available. Institutional employment available. **Financial Aid Statistics:** 100% needy freshmen, 100% needy undergrads receive need-based scholarship or grant aid. 8% freshmen, 10% undergrads receive non-need-based scholarship or grant aid. 86% freshmen, 85% undergrads receive need-based self-help aid. 12% freshmen, 16% undergrads receive athletic scholarships. 98% freshmen, 98% undergrads receive any aid. **Criteria for awarding aid:** *Need-based:* Academics, Art, Athletics, Leadership, Music/drama *Non-need-based:* Academics, Art, Athletics, Leadership, Music/drama, State/district residency.

LINCOLN CHRISTIAN UNIVERSITY

201 Criser Hall, Lincoln, IL 62656-2167
Phone: 2177323168 x:2251 · **Financial Aid Phone:** (217) 732-3168
E-mail: coladmis@lccs.edu
Fax: (217) 732-4199 · **Website:** www.lccs.edu · **ACT Code:** 1060

This private school, affiliated with the Church of Christ, was founded in 1944. It has a 100 acre campus.

RATINGS
Admissions Selectivity Rating: 78   **Fire Safety Rating:** 84   **Green Rating:** 60*

STUDENTS AND FACULTY
Enrollment: 601. **Student Body:** 51% female, 49% male, 40% out-of-state, 0% international (19 countries represented). Asian <1%, African American 5%, Caucasian 91%, Hispanic 2%, Native American <1%, Race unknown 1%. **Retention and Graduation:** 66% freshmen return for sophomore year. 17% grads go on to further study within 1 year. **Faculty:** Student/faculty ratio 15:1. 44 full-time faculty, 45% hold PhDs, 5% are members of minority groups, 18% are women. 0% of classes are taught by teaching assistants.

ACADEMICS
Degrees: Associate; Bachelor's; Certificate; Master's **Classes:** Most classes have 20-29 students. **Special Study Options:** Distance learning; Double major;

Honors program; Independent study; Internships; Study abroad; Teacher certification program; Weekend college. **Honors programs:** Students with at least sophomore standing and a cumulative grade average of 3.5 or higher may apply for acceptance into an honors degree program. The honors degree requires 5 additional semester hours of study under a mentoring professor and the completion of a capstone project. The additional work may be completed in the area of the student's ministry specialization or in an area of interest outside the specialization. Since the program is funded by memorial gifts, honors degree students do not pay tuition for the additional 5 hours. For students who complet the honors degree requirements, special recognition will be given at the Commencement service, and an honors designation will be included on the academic transcript. **Disability Services offered to physically disabled students:** Reader services; Tape recorders; Tutors.

FACILITIES
Housing: Apartments for married students; Men's dorms; Women's dorms 80% of campus accessible to physically diasbled. **Computers:** 90% of classrooms, 100% of dorms, 80% of libraries, have wireless network access. Students can register for classes online. Administrative functions (other than registration) can be performed online.

CAMPUS LIFE
Environment: Village **Activities:** Campus Ministries; Choral groups; Drama/theater; International Student Organization; Music ensembles; Musical theater; Student government; Student newspaper 7 registered organizations. **Athletics (Intercollegiate):** *Men:* baseball, basketball, soccer. *Women:* basketball, softball, volleyball. **On-Campus Highlights:** The Warehouse, The CoffeeShop

ADMISSIONS
Freshman Academic Profile: 19% in top 10% of high school class, 45% in top 25% of high school class, 76% in top 50% of high school class. **Test Scores:** ACT middle 50% range 19-25. Minimum internet-based TOEFL 75. Minimum paper TOEFL 550. **Basis for Candidate Selection:** *Very important factors considered include:* rigor of secondary school record, application essay, standardized test scores, state residency, religious affiliation/commitment, level of applicant's interest. *Important factors considered include:* class rank, academic GPA, extracurricular activities, character/personal qualities, alumni/ae relation, geographical residence, racial/ethnic status, volunteer work. *Other factors considered include:* recommendation(s), interview, talent/ability, work experience. **Freshman Admission Requirements:** High school diploma is required and GED is accepted *Academic units recommended:* 4 English, 3 math, 2 science, 2 foreign language, 3 social studies, 3 history. **Freshman Admission Statistics:** 195 applied, 84.1% admitted, 65% enrolled. **Transfer Admission Requirements:** High school transcript, college transcript(s), essay or personal statement, Minimum college GPA of 2.0 required. Lowest grade transferable 2. **General Admission Information:** Application fee $25. Nonfall registration accepted. Admission may be deferred for a maximum of 1 semester.

COSTS AND FINANCIAL AID
Annual tuition $11,790. Room and board $5,355. **Required Forms and Deadlines:** FAFSA. **Notification of Awards:** Applicants will be notified of awards on a rolling basis beginning 3/1. **Types of Aid:** *Need-based scholarships/ grants:* Federal Pell; SEOG; State scholarships/grants. *Loans: Student Employment:* Federal Work-Study Program available. Institutional employment available. **Financial Aid Statistics:** 55% needy freshmen, 64% needy undergrads receive need-based scholarship or grant aid. 84% freshmen, 79% undergrads receive non-need-based scholarship or grant aid. 67% freshmen, 72% undergrads receive need-based self-help aid. 0% freshmen, 0% undergrads receive athletic scholarships. 80% freshmen, 80% undergrads receive any aid. **Criteria for awarding aid:** *Non-need-based:* Academics.

LINCOLN MEMORIAL UNIVERSITY

6965 Cumberland Gap Parkway, Harrogate, TN 37752
Phone: 423-869-6280 · **Financial Aid Phone:** 423.869.6465
E-mail: admissions@lmunet.edu · **CEEB Code:** 1408
Fax: 423-869-6444 · **Website:** www.lmunet.edu · **ACT Code:** 3982

This private school was founded in 1897. It has a 1000 acre campus.

RATINGS
Admissions Selectivity Rating: 82   **Fire Safety Rating:** 60*   **Green Rating:** 60*

STUDENTS AND FACULTY
Enrollment: 1,749. **Student Body:** 73% female, 27% male, 36% out-of-state, 2% international (32 countries represented). Asian 1%, African American 4%, Caucasian 80%, Hispanic 2%, Native American <1%, Pacific Islander 0%, Two or more races <1%, Race unknown 10%.

Retention and Graduation: 66% freshmen return for sophomore year. **Faculty:** Student/faculty ratio 13:1. 256 full-time faculty, 97% hold PhDs, 8% are members of minority groups, 53% are women. 0% of classes are taught by teaching assistants.

ACADEMICS

Degrees: Associate; Bachelor's; Doctoral; Doctoral/Professional; Doctoral/Research; Master's; Post-Bachelor's certificate; Post-Master's certificate; Transfer Associate **Classes:** Most classes have 10-19 students. Most lab/discussion sessions have 10-19 students. **Most popular majors:** Veterinary/Animal Health Technology/Technician And Veterinary Assistant; Athletic Training/Trainer; Osteopathic Medicine/Osteopathy. **Special Study Options:** Distance learning; Double major; Dual enrollment; English as a Second Language (ESL); Honors program; Independent study; Internships; Study abroad; Teacher certification program. **Disability Services offered to physically disabled students:** Note-taking services; Reader services; Tutors. **Career services:** Alumni services; Career assessment; Career/job search classes; Internships

FACILITIES

Housing: Apartments for married students; Apartments for single students; Coed dorms; Men's dorms; Special housing for disabled student; Women's dorms 80% of campus accessible to physically diasbled. **Special Academic Facilities/Equipment:** Civil War museum, including Abraham Lincoln memorabilia collection of over 6,000 books, paintings, and manuscripts.

CAMPUS LIFE

Environment: Rural **Activities:** Campus Ministries; Choral groups; Dance; Drama/theater; International Student Organization; Literary magazine; Music ensembles; Musical theater; Pep band; Radio station; Student government; Television station; Yearbook 26 registered organizations, 5 honor societies, 3 religious organizations. 3 fraternities, 3 sororities. **Athletics (Intercollegiate):** *Men:* baseball, basketball, cross-country, golf, soccer, tennis. *Women:* basketball, cross-country, golf, soccer, softball, tennis, volleyball. College of Osteopathic Medicine, School of Math and Science, Abraham Lincoln Museum

ADMISSIONS

Freshman Academic Profile: Average high school GPA 3.4. 90% from public high schools. **Test Scores:** SAT Math middle 50% range 430-560. SAT EBRW middle 50% range 420-550. ACT middle 50% range 20-25. Minimum paper TOEFL 500. **Basis for Candidate Selection:** *Very important factors considered include:* rigor of secondary school record, academic GPA, standardized test scores. *Important factors considered include:* class rank, character/personal qualities, alumni/ae relation. *Other factors considered include:* extracurricular activities, first generation, religious affiliation/commitment, racial/ethnic status, volunteer work. **Freshman Admission Requirements:** High school diploma is required and GED is accepted *Academic units required:* 4 English, 3 math, 2 science, 2 foreign language, 1 social studies, 1 history, 1 visual/performing arts, *Academic units recommended:* 4 English, 4 math, 2 science labs, 2 social studies, 7 academic electives. **Freshman Admission Statistics:** 984 applied, 65.2% admitted, 39% enrolled. **Transfer Admission Requirements:** High school transcript, college transcript(s), standardized test scores, Minimum college GPA of 2.0 required. Lowest grade transferable C. **General Admission Information:** Application fee $25. Priority deadline 6/1. Nonfall registration accepted.

COSTS AND FINANCIAL AID

Room and board $7,770. Required fees $530. Average book expense $1,250. **Required Forms and Deadlines:** FAFSA. **Notification of Awards:** Applicants will be notified of awards on a rolling basis beginning 11/10. **Types of Aid:** *Need-based scholarships/grants:* College/university scholarship or grant aid from institutional funds; Federal Pell; Private scholarships; SEOG; State scholarships/grants. *Loans: Student Employment:* Federal Work-Study Program available. **Financial Aid Statistics:** 100% needy freshmen, 97% needy undergrads receive need-based scholarship or grant aid. 17% freshmen, 9% undergrads receive non-need-based scholarship or grant aid. 42% freshmen, 59% undergrads receive need-based self-help aid. 2% freshmen, 1% undergrads receive athletic scholarships. **Criteria for awarding aid:** *Non-need-based:* Academics, Alumni affiliation, Athletics, Leadership, Music/drama.

LINCOLN UNIVERSITY (CA)

104 Kerr Administration Building, Oakland, CA 94612
Phone: 510-628-8010 · **Financial Aid Phone:** 510-628-8023
E-mail: admissions@lincolnuca.edu
Fax: 510-628-8012 · **Website:** www.lincolnuca.edu

This private school was founded in 1919.

RATINGS

Admissions Selectivity Rating: 67   **Fire Safety Rating:** 60*   **Green Rating:** 60*

STUDENTS AND FACULTY

Enrollment: 91. **Student Body:** 57% female, 43% male, international. **Faculty:** 11 full-time faculty, 82% hold PhDs, 9% are women.

ACADEMICS

Degrees: Bachelor's; Certificate; Doctoral; Master's **Classes:** Most classes have 10-19 students. Most lab/discussion sessions have 10-19 students. **Most popular majors:** Education, General; Bible/Biblical Studies; Youth Ministry. **Special Study Options:** Cross-registration; Double major; English as a Second Language (ESL); Internships; Student-designed major. **Career services:** Alumni network; Internships

CAMPUS LIFE

Environment: Metropolis **Activities:** Student government.

ADMISSIONS

Minimum paper TOEFL 500. **Basis for Candidate Selection:** *Very important factors considered include:* rigor of secondary school record. *Important factors considered include:* academic GPA. *Other factors considered include:* class rank, standardized test scores. **Freshman Admission Requirements:** High school diploma is required and GED is accepted **Freshman Admission Statistics:** 130 applied, 81.5% admitted, 40% enrolled. **Transfer Admission Requirements:** college transcript(s), Minimum college GPA of 2.0 required. Lowest grade transferable C. **General Admission Information:** Application fee $75. Nonfall registration accepted. Admission may be deferred.

COSTS AND FINANCIAL AID

Annual tuition $9,600. Required fees $400. Average book expense $400. **Types of Aid:** *Need-based scholarships/grants:* Federal Pell.

LINCOLN UNIVERSITY (MO)

820 Chestnut Street, Jefferson City, MO 65101
Phone: 573-681-5102 · **Financial Aid Phone:** 573-681-6156
E-mail: admissions@lincolnu.edu
Fax: 573-681-5889 · **Website:** www.lincolnu.edu · **ACT Code:** 2322

This public school was founded in 1866. It has a 174 acre campus.

RATINGS

Admissions Selectivity Rating: 80   **Fire Safety Rating:** 91   **Green Rating:** 75

STUDENTS AND FACULTY

Enrollment: 2,045. **Student Body:** 57% female, 43% male, 30% out-of-state, 2% international (4 countries represented). Asian 1%, African American 57%, Caucasian 29%, Hispanic 2%, Native American <1%, Pacific Islander <1%, Two or more races 3%, Race unknown 5%.
Retention and Graduation: 53% freshmen return for sophomore year. 7% freshmen graduate within 4 years. 14% freshmen graduate within 6 years. **Faculty:** Student/faculty ratio 17:1. 105 full-time faculty, 62% hold PhDs, 29% are members of minority groups, 48% are women.

ACADEMICS

Degrees: Associate; Bachelor's; Master's; Post-Bachelor's certificate **Classes:** Most classes have 10-19 students. Most lab/discussion sessions have 10-19 students. **Most popular majors:** Criminal Justice/Law Enforcement Administration; Registered Nursing/Registered Nurse. **Special Study Options:** Accelerated program; Cooperative education program; Cross-registration; Distance learning; Double major; Dual enrollment; Exchange student program (domestic); Honors program; Independent study; Internships; Study abroad; Teacher certification program. **Honors programs:** Lincoln University offers a 18-credit-hour Honors Program which features small classes, unique academic challenges, individual attention from Honors faculty, and association with other like-minded students. An Honors student has opportunities to compete for summer mentorships, work closely with a faculty member on a research or creative project; to do sustained research or creative work leading to a thesis in the student's major; and to present his/her work at regional, national, and international conferences. These students also qualify for Honors housing, certain restricted courses, and other activities. **Disability Services offered to physically disabled students:** Note-taking services; Reader services; Tape recorders; Tutors. **Career services:** Alumni network; Alumni services; Career assessment; Career/job search classes; Internships

FACILITIES

Housing: Coed dorms; Men's dorms; Women's dorms 100% of campus accessible to physically disabled. **Special Academic Facilities/Equipment:** University Archives/Ethnic Studies Center Media Center Academic Support Services Agriculture and Extension Information Center Education Curriculum Library **Computers:** 100% of classrooms, 100% of dorms, 100% of libraries, 100% of dining areas, 100% of student union, have wireless network access. Students can register for classes online. Administrative functions (other than registration) can be performed online.

CAMPUS LIFE

Environment: Town **Activities:** Campus Ministries; Choral groups; Concert band; Dance; International Student Organization; Jazz band; Literary magazine; Marching band; Model UN; Music ensembles; Radio station; Student government; Student newspaper; Television station 24 registered organizations, 6 honor societies, 2 religious organizations. 4 fraternities, 2 sororities. **Athletics (Intercollegiate):** *Men:* baseball, basketball, football, golf, track/field (outdoor). *Women:* basketball, cheerleading, cross-country, golf, softball, tennis, track/field (outdoor). **On-Campus Highlights:** Clifford G. Scruggs University Center (SUC), Inman E. Page Library, The LINC, Richardson Fine Arts Center, Dwight T. Reed Stadium **Environmental Initiatives:** Environmental Health & Safety Management provides resources and services to ensure the proper management and disposal of hazardous materials around campus.

ADMISSIONS

Freshman Academic Profile: Average high school GPA 2.6. 5% in top 10% of high school class, 15% in top 25% of high school class, 39% in top 50% of high school class. **Test Scores:** SAT Math middle 50% range 355-490. SAT EBRW middle 50% range 420-470. ACT middle 50% range 14-19. Minimum internet-based TOEFL 61. Minimum paper TOEFL 500. **Basis for Candidate Selection:** *Other factors considered include:* rigor of secondary school record, academic GPA, standardized test scores, state residency. **Freshman Admission Requirements:** High school diploma is required and GED is accepted *Academic units required:* 4 English, 3 math, 3 science, 1 science labs, 3 social studies, 3 academic electives, 1 visual/performing arts, *Academic units recommended:* 4 English, 3 math, 3 science, 1 science labs, 2 foreign language, 3 social studies, 3 academic electives, 1 visual/performing arts. **Freshman Admission Statistics:** 3,423 applied, 52.5% admitted, 26% enrolled. **Transfer Admission Requirements:** college transcript(s), Minimum college GPA of 2.0 required. Lowest grade transferable C. **General Admission Information:** Nonfall registration accepted. Admission may be deferred for a maximum of 1 semester.

COSTS AND FINANCIAL AID

Required Forms and Deadlines: FAFSA; Institution's own financial aid form. **Notification of Awards:** Applicants will be notified of awards on a rolling basis beginning 1/15. **Types of Aid:** *Need-based scholarships/grants:* College/university scholarship or grant aid from institutional funds; Federal Pell; Private scholarships; SEOG; State scholarships/grants. *Loans:* Direct PLUS loans; Direct Subsidized Stafford Loans; Direct Unsubsidized Stafford Loans. *Student Employment:* Federal Work-Study Program available. Institutional employment available. **Financial Aid Statistics:** 91% needy freshmen, 88% needy undergrads receive need-based scholarship or grant aid. 48% freshmen, 40% undergrads receive non-need-based scholarship or grant aid. 100% freshmen, 95% undergrads receive need-based self-help aid. 1% freshmen, 1% undergrads receive athletic scholarships. 95% freshmen, 82% undergrads receive any aid. Average cumulative indebtedness $32,691. **Criteria for awarding aid:** *Need-based:* Alumni affiliation *Non-need-based:* Academics, Art, Athletics, Job skills, Leadership, Minority status, Music/drama, State/district residency.

LINCOLN UNIVERSITY (PA)

1570 Baltimore Pike, Lincoln University, PA 19352
Phone: 484-365-8000 • **Financial Aid Phone:** (800) 561-2606 • **CEEB Code:** 2367
Fax: 484-365-8109 • **Website:** www.lincoln.edu • **ACT Code:** 3614

This public school was founded in 1854. It has a 422 acre campus.

RATINGS

Admissions Selectivity Rating: 74   **Fire Safety Rating:** 77   **Green Rating:** 61

STUDENTS AND FACULTY

Enrollment: 1,994. **Student Body:** 66% female, 34% male, 54% out-of-state, 3% international (13 countries represented). Asian <1%, African American 84%, Caucasian 1%, Hispanic 3%, Native American <1%, Pacific Islander 0%, Two or more races 2%, Race unknown 6%.
Retention and Graduation: 68% freshmen return for sophomore year. 30% freshmen graduate within 4 years. 34% grads go on to further study within 1 year. 15% grads pursue arts and sciences degrees. 1% grads pursue law degrees. 9% grads pursue business degrees. 0.5% grads pursue medical degrees.
Faculty: Student/faculty ratio 15:1. 97 full-time faculty, 84% hold PhDs, 58% are members of minority groups, 40% are women. 0% of classes are taught by teaching assistants.

ACADEMICS

Degrees: Bachelor's; Master's **Classes:** Most classes have 20-29 students. Most lab/discussion sessions have 20-29 students. **Most popular majors:** Criminal Justice/Safety Studies; Human Services, General; Health Services/Allied Health/Health Sciences, General. **Special Study Options:** Double major; Dual enrollment; Exchange student program (domestic); Honors program; Independent study; Internships; Study abroad; Teacher certification program; Weekend college. **Honors programs:** The Horace Mann Bond Honors Program is designed to encourage academically talented students to become problem solvers and more responsive to the needs of the human community. It does so by combining excellence in Liberal Arts education with traditional virtues of adult accountability: reason, respect, reverence, reciprocity, restraint, reliability and responsibility. **Disability Services offered to physically disabled students:** Note-taking services; Reader services; Tape recorders; Tutors. **Career services:** Alumni services; Career assessment; Career/job search classes; Internships

FACILITIES

Housing: Apartments for single students; Coed dorms; Men's dorms; Special housing for disabled student; Special housing for international students; Women's dorms **Special Academic Facilities/Equipment:** The Student Union Building (SUB): houses two television studios, and a radio studio. Danjuma African Art Center: houses select installations of the university's extensive collection of African art and artifacts. International Cultural Center: houses a 1,049-seat theater, conference facility and art gallery. Wright Hall: houses the Learning Resource Center and planetarium. Langston Hughes Memorial Library: contains areas for microforms, periodicals, computer labs, reading lounges, individual and group study rooms, special collections and the University archives. Ware Fine Arts Center: houses a ceramic studio, 2D/3D design studio, printmaking studio, graphic arts studio, painting/drawing studio, clavinova labs and an auditorium, fully equipped for digital recording and transmission.

CAMPUS LIFE

Environment: Rural **Activities:** Campus Ministries; Choral groups; Concert band; Dance; Drama/theater; International Student Organization; Jazz band; Marching band; Music ensembles; Musical theater; Opera; Pep band; Radio station; Student government; Student newspaper; Symphony orchestra; Television station; Yearbook 30 registered organizations, 9 honor societies, 4 fraternities, 3 sororities. **Athletics (Intercollegiate):** *Men:* baseball, basketball, cross-country, soccer, tennis, track/field (outdoor), track/field (indoor). *Women:* basketball, cross-country, soccer, tennis, track/field (outdoor), track/field (indoor), volleyball. **On-Campus Highlights:** Langston Hughes Memorial Library, Thurgood Marshall Living and Learning Center, Health and Wellness Center, Student Union Building, Ivory V. Nelson Science Center

ADMISSIONS

Freshman Academic Profile: Average high school GPA 3.1. 15% in top 10% of high school class, 34% in top 25% of high school class, 60% in top 50% of high school class. **Test Scores:** SAT Math middle 50% range 430-530. SAT EBRW middle 50% range 440-540. ACT middle 50% range 16-21. Minimum internet-based TOEFL 71. Minimum paper TOEFL 500. **Basis for Candidate Selection:** *Very important factors considered include:* academic GPA, standardized test scores, level of applicant's interest. *Important factors* considered include: talent/ability. *Other factors considered include:* rigor of secondary school record, class rank, application essay, interview, character/ personal qualities, geographical residence, state residency. **Freshman Admission Requirements:** High school diploma is required and GED is accepted *Academic units required:* 4 English, 4 math, 3 science, 3 social studies, 1 history, *Academic units recommended:* 4 English, 4 math, 3 science, 3 social studies, 1 history. **Freshman Admission Statistics:** 3,587 applied, 79.7% admitted, 23% enrolled. **Transfer Admission Requirements:** college transcript(s), essay or personal statement, statement of good standing from prior institution(s). Minimum college GPA of 2.0 required. Lowest grade transferable C. **General Admission Information:** Priority deadline 3/1. Regular application deadline 5/1. Nonfall registration accepted. Admission may be deferred for a maximum of 1 year.

COSTS AND FINANCIAL AID
Required Forms and Deadlines: FAFSA. **Notification of Awards:** Applicants will be notified of awards on or about 2/20. **Types of Aid:** *Need-based scholarships/grants:* College/university scholarship or grant aid from institutional funds; Federal Pell; Private scholarships; SEOG; State scholarships/grants; United Negro College Fund. *Loans:* Direct PLUS loans; Direct Subsidized Stafford Loans; Direct Unsubsidized Stafford Loans. *Student Employment:* Federal Work-Study Program available. Institutional employment available. **Financial Aid Statistics:** 0% undergrads receive non-need-based scholarship or grant aid. 89% freshmen, 88% undergrads receive need-based self-help aid. 0% freshmen, 0% undergrads receive athletic scholarships. 99% freshmen, 93% undergrads receive any aid. **Criteria for awarding aid:** *Need-based:* Academics, Leadership *Non-need-based:* Academics, Alumni affiliation, Leadership, Music/drama.

LINDENWOOD UNIVERSITY

209 South Kingshighway, Saint Charles, MO 63301-1695
Phone: 314-949-4949 · **Financial Aid Phone:** 636-949-4923
E-mail: admissions@lindenwood.edu · **CEEB Code:** 6367
Fax: 314-949-4989 · **Website:** www.lindenwood.edu · **ACT Code:** 2324

This private school, affiliated with the Presbyterian Church, was founded in 1827. It has a 550 acre campus.

RATINGS
Admissions Selectivity Rating: 80 **Fire Safety Rating:** 73 **Green Rating:** 61

STUDENTS AND FACULTY
Enrollment: 6,807. **Student Body:** 54% female, 46% male, 39% out-of-state, 12% international (99 countries represented). Asian 1%, African American 12%, Caucasian 50%, Hispanic 4%, Native American <1%, Pacific Islander <1%, Two or more races 2%, Race unknown 18%.
Retention and Graduation: 73% freshmen return for sophomore year. 32% freshmen graduate within 4 years. 50% freshmen graduate within 6 years. **Faculty:** Student/faculty ratio 13:1. 292 full-time faculty, 83% hold PhDs, 12% are members of minority groups, 51% are women. 0% of classes are taught by teaching assistants.

ACADEMICS
Degrees: Bachelor's; Certificate; Doctoral/Research; Master's; Post-Bachelor's certificate; Post-Master's certificate **Classes:** Most classes have fewer than 10 students. **Most popular majors:** Education, Other; Criminology; Business Administration And Management, General. **Special Study Options:** Accelerated program; Cross-registration; Distance learning; Double major; Dual enrollment; English as a Second Language (ESL); External degree program; Honors program; Independent study; Internships; Student-designed major; Study abroad; Teacher certification program. **Honors programs:** Honors College. **Disability Services offered to physically disabled students:** Reader services; Tutors. **Career services:** Alumni services; Career assessment; Career/job search classes; Internships

FACILITIES
Housing: Apartments for married students; Apartments for single students; Coed dorms; Fraternity/sorority housing; Men's dorms; Women's dorms **Special Academic Facilities/Equipment:** University archives.

CAMPUS LIFE
Environment: Town **Activities:** Campus Ministries; Choral groups; Concert band; Dance; Drama/theater; International Student Organization; Literary magazine; Marching band; Music ensembles; Musical theater; Pep band; Radio station; Student government; Student newspaper; Symphony orchestra; Television station 72 registered organizations, 8 honor societies, 13 religious organizations. 1 fraternity, 1 sorority. **Athletics (Intercollegiate):** Men:

baseball, basketball, cheerleading, cross-country, diving, football, golf, ice hockey, lacrosse, riflery, soccer, swimming, tennis, track/field (outdoor), track/field (indoor), volleyball, water polo, wrestling. *Women:* basketball, cheerleading, cross-country, diving, field hockey, golf, ice hockey, lacrosse, riflery, soccer, softball, swimming, tennis, track/field (outdoor), track/field (indoor), volleyball, water polo. J. Scheidegger Center, Evans Commons, Spellman Center, Student-Athlete Center, Butler Library **Environmental Initiatives:** Paper recycling

ADMISSIONS
Freshman Academic Profile: Average high school GPA 3.2. 18% in top 10% of high school class, 46% in top 25% of high school class, 79% in top 50% of high school class. **Test Scores:** SAT Math middle 50% range 500-590. SAT EBRW middle 50% range 480-580. ACT middle 50% range 20-25. Minimum internet-based TOEFL 61. Minimum paper TOEFL 500. **Basis for Candidate Selection:** *Very important factors considered include:* academic GPA, standardized test scores. *Important factors considered include:* rigor of secondary school record, application essay, recommendation(s). *Other factors considered include:* class rank, interview, extracurricular activities, talent/ability, volunteer work. **Freshman Admission Requirements:** High school diploma is required and GED is accepted *Academic units recommended:* 4 English, 3 math, 3 science, 1 science labs, 2 foreign language, 3 social studies, 1 history, 1 visual/performing arts. **Freshman Admission Statistics:** 2,895 applied, 73.7% admitted, 43% enrolled. **Transfer Admission Requirements:** college transcript(s), Minimum college GPA of 2.0 required. Lowest grade transferable D. **General Admission Information:** Application fee $30. Nonfall registration accepted. Admission may be deferred for a maximum of 1 year.

COSTS AND FINANCIAL AID
Annual tuition $15,672. Room and board $8,800. Required fees $660. Average book expense $1,200. **Required Forms and Deadlines:** FAFSA. **Types of Aid:** *Need-based scholarships/grants:* College/university scholarship or grant aid from institutional funds; Federal Pell; Private scholarships; SEOG; State scholarships/grants. *Loans:* Direct PLUS loans; Direct Subsidized Stafford Loans; Direct Unsubsidized Stafford Loans. *Student Employment:* Federal Work-Study Program available. Institutional employment available. **Financial Aid Statistics:** 94% needy freshmen, 83% needy undergrads receive need-based scholarship or grant aid. 66% freshmen, 51% undergrads receive non-need-based scholarship or grant aid. 89% freshmen, 91% undergrads receive need-based self-help aid. 6% freshmen, 4% undergrads receive athletic scholarships. 98% freshmen, 86% undergrads receive any aid. 70% undergrads borrow to pay for school. Average cumulative indebtedness $33,182. **Criteria for awarding aid:** *Non-need-based:* Academics, Art, Athletics, Leadership, Minority status, Music/drama, Religious affiliation, State/district residency.

LINFIELD COLLEGE

900 South East Baker Street, McMinnville, OR 97128-6894
Phone: 503-883-2213 · **Financial Aid Phone:** 503-883-2269
E-mail: admission@linfield.edu · **CEEB Code:** 4387
Fax: 503-883-2472 · **Website:** www.linfield.edu · **ACT Code:** 3466

This private school, affiliated with the American Baptist Church, was founded in 1858. It has a 189 acre campus.

RATINGS
Admissions Selectivity Rating: 80 **Fire Safety Rating:** 97 **Green Rating:** 94

STUDENTS AND FACULTY
Enrollment: 1,503. **Student Body:** 60% female, 40% male, 42% out-of-state, 3% international (24 countries represented). Asian 5%, African American 2%, Caucasian 59%, Hispanic 17%, Native American 1%, Pacific Islander 1%, Two or more races 10%, Race unknown 3%.
Retention and Graduation: 81% freshmen return for sophomore year. 65% freshmen graduate within 4 years. 78% freshmen graduate within 6 years. 14% grads go on to further study within 1 year. 4% grads pursue arts and sciences degrees. 1% grads pursue law degrees. 1% grads pursue business degrees. 1% grads pursue medical degrees. **Faculty:** Student/faculty ratio 10:1. 123 full-time faculty, 95% hold PhDs, 14% are members of minority groups, 52% are women. 0% of classes are taught by teaching assistants.

ACADEMICS
Degrees: Bachelor's **Classes:** Most classes have 20-29 students. Most lab/ discussion sessions have 20-29 students. **Most popular majors:** Kinesiology And Exercise Science; Psychology, General; Registered Nursing/Registered Nurse. **Special Study Options:** Cross-registration; Distance learning; Double major; Dual enrollment; English as a Second Language (ESL); External degree program; Independent study; Internships; Liberal arts/career combination;

Student-designed major; Study abroad; Teacher certification program.
Disability Services offered to physically disabled students: Note-taking services; Reader services; Tape recorders; Tutors. **Career services:** Alumni network; Alumni services; Career assessment; Career/job search classes; Internships; Regional alumni

FACILITIES

Housing: Apartments for single students; Coed dorms; Fraternity/sorority housing; Men's dorms; Special housing for disabled student; Wellness housing; Women's dorms 80% of campus accessible to physically diasbled. **Special Academic Facilities/Equipment:** student-run garden, pristine concert hall, Steinway concert grand piano, student-run radio station, anthropology museum, cadaver lab, music technology lab, field house for spring training, student-run bicycle rental and repair shop **Computers:** 90% of classrooms, 90% of dorms, 100% of libraries, have wireless network access. Students can register for classes online. Administrative functions (other than registration) can be performed online.

CAMPUS LIFE

Environment: Town **Activities:** Campus Ministries; Choral groups; Concert band; Dance; Drama/theater; International Student Organization; Jazz band; Literary magazine; Marching band; Model UN; Music ensembles; Musical theater; Opera; Pep band; Radio station; Student government; Student newspaper; Symphony orchestra 41 registered organizations, 18 honor societies, 5 religious organizations. 4 fraternities, 4 sororities. **Athletics (Intercollegiate):** *Men:* baseball, basketball, cross-country, football, golf, soccer, swimming, tennis, track/field (outdoor). *Women:* basketball, cross-country, golf, lacrosse, soccer, softball, swimming, tennis, track/field (outdoor), volleyball. **On-Campus Highlights:** Nicholson Library, Modern language rooms (Walker Hall, 3rd floor), Elkinton and Terrell Halls, Dining and coffee shop, Athletic complex **Environmental Initiatives:** Signatory on ACUPCC

ADMISSIONS

Freshman Academic Profile: Average high school GPA 3.6. 30% in top 10% of high school class, 67% in top 25% of high school class, 93% in top 50% of high school class. 90% from public high schools. **Test Scores:** SAT Math middle 50% range 510-600. SAT EBRW middle 50% range 510-610. ACT middle 50% range 20-26. Minimum internet-based TOEFL 80. Minimum paper TOEFL 550. **Basis for Candidate Selection:** *Very important factors considered include:* rigor of secondary school record, academic GPA, standardized test scores. *Important factors considered include:* class rank, application essay, recommendation(s). *Other factors considered include:* extracurricular activities, talent/ability, character/personal qualities, first generation, alumni/ae relation, geographical residence, racial/ethnic status, volunteer work, work experience, level of applicant's interest. **Freshman Admission Requirements:** High school diploma is required and GED is accepted *Academic units recommended:* 4 English, 4 math, 3 science, 2 foreign language, 3 social studies. **Freshman Admission Statistics:** 2,325 applied, 81.2% admitted, 21% enrolled. **Transfer Admission Requirements:** college transcript(s), essay or personal statement, Lowest grade transferable C. **General Admission Information:** Priority deadline 2/1. Nonfall registration accepted. Admission may be deferred for a maximum of 1 year.

COSTS AND FINANCIAL AID

Annual tuition $41,100. Room and board $11,770. Required fees $476. Average book expense $900. **Required Forms and Deadlines:** FAFSA. **Notification of Awards:** Applicants will be notified of awards on a rolling basis beginning 4/15. **Types of Aid:** *Need-based scholarships/grants:* College/university scholarship or grant aid from institutional funds; Federal Pell; Private scholarships; SEOG; State scholarships/grants. *Loans:* Direct PLUS loans; Direct Subsidized Stafford Loans; Direct Unsubsidized Stafford Loans. *Student Employment:* Federal Work-Study Program available. Institutional employment available. **Financial Aid Statistics:** 84% needy freshmen, 80% needy undergrads receive need-based scholarship or grant aid. 96% freshmen, 94% undergrads receive non-need-based scholarship or grant aid. 100% freshmen, 100% undergrads receive need-based self-help aid. 0% freshmen, 0% undergrads receive athletic scholarships. 99% freshmen, 95% undergrads receive any aid. 70% undergrads borrow to pay for school. Average cumulative indebtedness $34,320. **Criteria for awarding aid:** *Need-based:* Academics, Minority status, Music/drama *Non-need-based:* Academics, Leadership, Minority status, Music/drama.

One University Park Dr., Nashville, TN 37204-3951
Phone: 615-966-1776 • **Financial Aid Phone:** 615-966-1791
E-mail: admissions@lipscomb.edu • **CEEB Code:** 1161
Fax: 615-966-1804 • **Website:** http://www.lipscomb.edu • **ACT Code:** 3956

This private school, affiliated with the Church of Christ, was founded in 1891. It has a 88.5 acre campus.

RATINGS
Admissions Selectivity Rating: 85   **Fire Safety Rating:** 97   **Green Rating:** 78

STUDENTS AND FACULTY
Enrollment: 2,973. **Student Body:** 61% female, 39% male, 34% out-of-state, 3% international (45 countries represented). Asian 3%, African American 7%, Caucasian 76%, Hispanic 7%, Native American <1%, Pacific Islander <1%, Two or more races 3%, Race unknown 1%.
Retention and Graduation: 79% freshmen return for sophomore year. 46% freshmen graduate within 4 years. 59% freshmen graduate within 6 years. 30% grads go on to further study within 1 year. **Faculty:** Student/faculty ratio 14:1. 213 full-time faculty, 84% hold PhDs, 8% are members of minority groups, 40% are women. 0% of classes are taught by teaching assistants.

ACADEMICS
Degrees: Associate; Bachelor's; Certificate; Doctoral/Professional; Doctoral/Research; Master's; Post-Bachelor's certificate **Classes:** Most classes have 20-29 students. Most lab/discussion sessions have 20-29 students. **Most popular majors:** Biology/Biological Sciences, General; Registered Nursing/Registered Nurse; Business Administration And Management, General. **Special Study Options:** Accelerated program; Cross-registration; Distance learning; Double major; Dual enrollment; English as a Second Language (ESL); Honors program; Independent study; Internships; Student-designed major; Study abroad; Teacher certification program. **Honors programs:** The Honors College at Lipscomb University seeks to provide students with a significant enhancement to their university education through a challenging academic program, through cultural and entertainment opportunities, and through planning and mentoring for the future. Courses within the program offer more student participation, a deeper exploration of key ideas, and an opportunity for students to develop critical thinking, problem-solving, and project management skills. In addition to a strong academic challenge, students in The Honors College explore different cultural ideas and events by attending Broadway plays which come to Nashville, foreign films, and ethnic dining experiences. We sponsor a Masquerade Ball each year and have several other social functions designed to strengthen the friendships established in classes with other honors students. Finally all students receive mentoring in planning their careers at Lipscomb University and beyond, including information and advice on major national competitive scholarships like the U. S. Fulbright Scholar, he Goldwater Scholarship, and the Truman Scholarship and on appropriate study abroad and internship possibilities. The program seeks students who have a lot of ambition, who are creative, and who are willing to take some risks to create an outstanding educational experience at Lipscomb University. **Disability Services offered to physically disabled students:** Note-taking services; Reader services; Tape recorders; Tutors. **Career services:** Alumni network; Alumni services; Career assessment; Career/job search classes; Internships

FACILITIES
Housing: Apartments for single students; Men's dorms; Women's dorms 100% of campus accessible to physically diasbled. **Special Academic Facilities/Equipment:** On-campus elementary, middle, and secondary schools. **Computers:** 100% of classrooms, 100% of dorms, 100% of libraries, 100% of dining areas, 100% of student union, 100% of common outdoor areas have wireless network access. Students can register for classes online. Administrative functions (other than registration) can be performed online.

CAMPUS LIFE
Environment: Metropolis **Activities:** Campus Ministries; Choral groups; Concert band; Dance; Drama/theater; International Student Organization; Jazz band; Music ensembles; Musical theater; Pep band; Radio station; Student government; Student newspaper; Yearbook 65 registered organizations. **Athletics (Intercollegiate):** *Men:* baseball, basketball, cross-country, golf, soccer, tennis, track/field (outdoor). *Women:* basketball, cheerleading, cross-country, soccer, softball, tennis, track/field (outdoor), track/field (indoor), volleyball. **On-Campus Highlights:** Bennett Campus Center, SAC—Student Activity Center, Allen Arena, Willard Collins Alumni Auditorium, Bison Square **Environmental Initiatives:** Academic: First and only comprehensive sustainability academic program in the SE US;

ADMISSIONS

Freshman Academic Profile: Average high school GPA 3.6. 29% in top 10% of high school class, 54% in top 25% of high school class, 80% in top 50% of high school class. 53% from public high schools. **Test Scores:** SAT Math middle 50% range 520-660. SAT EBRW middle 50% range 540-670. ACT middle 50% range 23-29. Minimum internet-based TOEFL 80. Minimum paper TOEFL 550. **Basis for Candidate Selection:** *Very important factors considered include:* class rank, standardized test scores. *Important factors considered include:* rigor of secondary school record, academic GPA, recommendation(s). *Other factors considered include:* application essay, extracurricular activities, talent/ability, character/personal qualities, first generation, volunteer work, work experience. **Freshman Admission Requirements:** High school diploma is required and GED is accepted **Freshman Admission Statistics:** 3,581 applied, 60.4% admitted, 30% enrolled. **Transfer Admission Requirements:** college transcript(s), interview, statement of good standing from prior institution(s). Minimum college GPA of 2.0 required. Lowest grade transferable C. **General Admission Information:** Application fee $50. Nonfall registration accepted. Admission may be deferred for a maximum of 1 year.

COSTS AND FINANCIAL AID

Annual tuition $29,676. Room and board $12,652. Required fees $2,468. Average book expense $1,500. **Required Forms and Deadlines:** FAFSA. **Notification of Awards:** Applicants will be notified of awards on a rolling basis beginning 3/1. **Types of Aid:** *Need-based scholarships/grants:* College/university scholarship or grant aid from institutional funds; Federal Pell; Private scholarships; SEOG; State scholarships/grants. *Loans:* Direct PLUS loans; Direct Subsidized Stafford Loans; Direct Unsubsidized Stafford Loans. *Student Employment:* Federal Work-Study Program available. Institutional employment available. **Financial Aid Statistics:** 43% needy freshmen, 98% needy undergrads receive need-based scholarship or grant aid. 100% freshmen, 87% undergrads receive non-need-based scholarship or grant aid. 76% freshmen, 78% undergrads receive need-based self-help aid. 3% freshmen, 3% undergrads receive athletic scholarships. 99% freshmen, 73% undergrads receive any aid. 55% undergrads borrow to pay for school. Average cumulative indebtedness $31,082. **Criteria for awarding aid:** *Need-based:* Leadership *Non-need-based:* Academics, Art, Athletics, Job skills, Leadership, Minority status, Music/drama, Religious affiliation, State/district residency.

LOCK HAVEN UNIVERSITY OF PENNSYLVANIA

401 North Fairview Street, Lock Haven, PA 17745
Phone: 570-484-2027
E-mail: admissions@lhup.edu • **CEEB Code:** 2654
Fax: 570-484-2201 • **Website:** www.lhup.edu • **ACT Code:** 3708

This public school was founded in 1870. It has a 175 acre campus.

RATINGS

Admissions Selectivity Rating: 73   **Fire Safety Rating:** 62   **Green Rating:** 60*

STUDENTS AND FACULTY

Enrollment: 3,425. **Student Body:** 58% female, 42% male, 5% out-of-state, 1% international (39 countries represented). Asian 1%, African American 10%, Caucasian 81%, Hispanic 2%, Native American 1%, Pacific Islander <1%, Two or more races 1%, Race unknown 4%.
Retention and Graduation: 70% freshmen return for sophomore year. 35% freshmen graduate within 4 years. 55% freshmen graduate within 6 years.
Faculty: Student/faculty ratio 17:1. 203 full-time faculty, 88% hold PhDs, 15% are members of minority groups, 49% are women. 0% of classes are taught by teaching assistants.

ACADEMICS

Degrees: Associate; Bachelor's; Master's **Classes:** Most classes have fewer than 10 students. **Most popular majors:** Elementary Education And Teaching; Health And Physical Education/Fitness, Other; Health Professions And Related Clinical Sciences, Other. **Special Study Options:** Accelerated program; Cross-registration; Distance learning; Double major; Dual enrollment; Honors program; Independent study; Internships; Student-designed major; Study abroad; Teacher certification program. **Honors programs:** The University Honors Program provides students and faculty opportunities for creative intellectual engagement through a mix of special curricular and co-curricular opportunities. Students may apply for entry as a first-year freshman or after completing 1-4 semesters of college-level work. Entry as a first-year freshman may be either directly into the University Honors or through the First Year Excellence Program. Students successfully completing the First Year Excellence Program receive certificate recognition. Students completing the University Honors Program receive recognition on their transcript, on their diploma and at commencement. Students in both the First Year Excellence and University Honors programs must participate in co-curricular activities and community service in addition to their curriculum. Engaging activity groups and Speaker Series allow students in the Honors Program to bond together and learn from each other, creating a community of both friends and scholars. **Disability Services offered to physically disabled students:** Note-taking services; Reader services; Tape recorders; Tutors. **Career services:** Alumni network; Alumni services; Career assessment; Career/job search classes; Internships; Regional alumni

FACILITIES

Housing: Apartments for single students; Coed dorms 98% of campus accessible to physically diasbled. **Special Academic Facilities/Equipment:** Planetarium, Sloan Art Gallery, Library Archives **Computers:** Students can register for classes online. Administrative functions (other than registration) can be performed online. Undergraduates are required to own a computer.

CAMPUS LIFE

Environment: Village **Activities:** Campus Ministries; Choral groups; Concert band; Dance; Drama/theater; International Student Organization; Jazz band; Literary magazine; Marching band; Music ensembles; Musical theater; Pep band; Radio station; Student government; Student newspaper; Symphony orchestra; Television station; Yearbook 96 registered organizations, 10 honor societies, 7 religious organizations. 6 fraternities, 4 sororities. **Athletics (Intercollegiate):** *Men:* baseball, basketball, football, soccer, track/field (outdoor), track/field (indoor), wrestling. *Women:* basketball, field hockey, lacrosse, soccer, softball, swimming, track/field (outdoor), track/field (indoor), volleyball. **On-Campus Highlights:** Student Recreation Center, Parsons Union Building, Library, Residence Halls, Bentley Dining Hall

ADMISSIONS

Freshman Academic Profile: Average high school GPA 3.3. 8% in top 10% of high school class, 27% in top 25% of high school class, 58% in top 50% of high school class. **Test Scores:** SAT Math middle 50% range 450-550. SAT EBRW middle 50% range 460-560. ACT middle 50% range 16-22. Minimum paper TOEFL 550. **Basis for Candidate Selection:** *Very important factors considered include:* rigor of secondary school record, class rank, academic GPA, talent/ability, character/personal qualities. *Important factors considered include:* standardized test scores, racial/ethnic status. *Other factors considered include:* application essay, recommendation(s), interview, extracurricular activities, first generation, volunteer work, work experience, level of applicant's interest. **Freshman Admission Requirements:** High school diploma is required and GED is accepted *Academic units required:* 4 English, 3 math, 3 science, 2 science labs, 2 social studies, 2 history, *Academic units recommended:* 4 English, 4 math, 4 science, 3 science labs, 2 foreign language, 2 social studies, 2 history. **Freshman Admission Statistics:** 3,020 applied, 89.0% admitted, 29% enrolled. **Transfer Admission Requirements:** college transcript(s), statement of good standing from prior institution(s). Minimum college GPA of 2.0 required. Lowest grade transferable C. **General Admission Information:** Application fee $25. Nonfall registration accepted. Admission may be deferred for a maximum of 1 year.

COSTS AND FINANCIAL AID

Annual in-state tuition $9,968. Annual out-of-state tuition $16,730. Room and board $9,968. Required fees $3,084. Average book expense $1,700. **Required Forms and Deadlines:** FAFSA; State aid form. **Notification of Awards:** Applicants will be notified of awards on a rolling basis beginning 4/10. **Types of Aid:** *Need-based scholarships/grants:* College/university scholarship or grant aid from institutional funds; Federal Pell; Private scholarships; SEOG; State scholarships/grants. *Loans:* Direct PLUS loans; Direct Subsidized Stafford Loans; Direct Unsubsidized Stafford Loans. *Student Employment:* Federal Work-Study Program available. Institutional employment available. **Financial Aid Statistics:** 70% needy freshmen, 87% needy undergrads receive need-based scholarship or grant aid. 31% freshmen, 19% undergrads receive non-need-based scholarship or grant aid. 87% freshmen, 88% undergrads receive need-based self-help aid. 6% freshmen, 4% undergrads receive athletic scholarships. 87% undergrads borrow to pay for school. Average cumulative indebtedness $31,806. **Criteria for awarding aid:** *Need-based:* Academics, Athletics, Leadership *Non-need-based:* Academics, Art, Athletics, Leadership, Minority status, Music/drama, State/district residency.

LONG ISLAND UNIVERSITY—C.W. POST

720 Northern Blvd., Brookville, NY 11548
Phone: 516-299-2900 · **Financial Aid Phone:** 516-299-2553
E-mail: post-enroll@liu.edu · **CEEB Code:** 2070
Fax: 516-299-2137 · **Website:** www.liu.edu/post · **ACT Code:** 2687

This private school was founded in 1954. It has a 308 acre campus.

RATINGS

Admissions Selectivity Rating: 74   **Fire Safety Rating:** 98   **Green Rating:** 78

STUDENTS AND FACULTY

Enrollment: 3,133. **Student Body:** 61% female, 39% male, 9% out-of-state, 6% international (27 countries represented). Asian 4%, African American 11%, Caucasian 48%, Hispanic 15%, Native American <1%, Pacific Islander <1%, Two or more races 2%, Race unknown 14%.
Retention and Graduation: 78% freshmen return for sophomore year. 29% freshmen graduate within 4 years. 48% freshmen graduate within 6 years. 24% grads go on to further study within 1 year. 31% grads pursue arts and sciences degrees. 4% grads pursue law degrees. 9% grads pursue business degrees. 16% grads pursue medical degrees. **Faculty:** Student/faculty ratio 14:1. 260 full-time faculty, 89% hold PhDs, 17% are members of minority groups, 54% are women.

ACADEMICS

Degrees: Associate; Bachelor's; Doctoral/Research; Master's; Post-Bachelor's certificate; Post-Master's certificate **Classes:** Most classes have 10-19 students. Most lab/discussion sessions have 10-19 students. **Most popular majors:** Education, General; Health Professions And Related Programs; Business, Management, Marketing, And Related Support Services. **Special Study Options:** Accelerated program; Cooperative education program; Distance learning; Double major; Dual enrollment; English as a Second Language (ESL); Exchange student program (domestic); Honors program; Independent study; Internships; Liberal arts/career combination; Student-designed major; Study abroad; Teacher certification program. **Honors programs:** LIU Post has a separate Honors College. **Combined degree programs:** BA/JD; BA/MA. **Disability Services offered to physically disabled students:** Note-taking services; Reader services; Tape recorders; Tutors. **Career services:** Alumni network; Alumni services; Career assessment; Career/job search classes; Internships; Regional alumni

FACILITIES

Housing: Coed dorms; Fraternity/sorority housing; Special housing for disabled student; Special housing for international students; Theme housing 80% of campus accessible to physically disabled. **Special Academic Facilities/Equipment:** Tilles Center for the Performing Arts, a concert hall that features a wide range of dance, music, and theater events, where students in the School of Visual and Performing Arts are able to perform alongside world-renowned performers and engage in live stage productions. Student-Run Businesses: These fully functional business operations afford students unique experiential learning opportunities as they make executive-level decisions. They include: Browse: A high-tech, Apple-licensed technology store, with "Genius Bar" inspired customer service that employs students; Post Marketing and PR Agency: A full-service agency managed by students; The Student Body Boutique: A trendy clothing boutique that sells the latest fashions at an affordable price; Eateries that include: Hutton & Post, which offers traditional snacks in addition to healthy options; End Zone, a lounge that offers a full menu and HD televisions for watching sports and other entertainment; and Time Out Smoothie Bar, a juice bar that sells nutritious offerings for students on the go Wall Street Trading Floor: Featuring Bloomberg terminals and other business technology, this simulated trading floor empowers students to utilize the latest financial tools and learn in a real-time trading environment; home to the University's student-run LIU-iF Investment Fund Student Innovation Incubator: A physical and virtual workspace for students to launch startup businesses and collaborate with successful entrepreneurs Equestrian Stables: North Shore Equestrian Center houses the LIU Post Equine Studies program, offering a large indoor arena and two spacious outdoor rings. On-campus nursery school, Psychobiology Lab, marine station and fleet of research vessels, Silicon Graphics Computer Lab.

CAMPUS LIFE

Environment: Metropolis **Activities:** Campus Ministries; Choral groups; Concert band; Dance; Drama/theater; International Student Organization; Literary magazine; Marching band; Model UN; Musical theater; Pep band; Radio station; Student government; Student newspaper; Student-run film society; Television station; Yearbook. Tilles Center for the Performing Arts, Hillwood Commons, Pratt Recreation Center, Equestrian Center, Entrepreneurship Lab

ADMISSIONS

Freshman Academic Profile: Average high school GPA 3.2. 10% in top 10% of high school class, 33% in top 25% of high school class, 65% in top 50% of high school class. 79% from public high schools. **Test Scores:** SAT Math middle 50% range 525-620. SAT EBRW middle 50% range 530-620. ACT middle 50% range 21-26. Minimum internet-based TOEFL 75. Minimum paper TOEFL 550. **Basis for Candidate Selection:** *Very important factors considered include:* rigor of secondary school record, academic GPA, standardized test scores. *Important factors considered include:* application essay, recommendation(s), extracurricular activities, talent/ability, character/personal qualities, first generation, volunteer work, work experience, level of applicant's interest. *Other factors considered include:* class rank, interview, alumni/ae relation. **Freshman Admission Requirements:** High school diploma is required and GED is accepted *Academic units recommended:* 4 English, 3 math, 3 science, 3 science labs, 2 foreign language, 4 social studies. **Freshman Admission Statistics:** 6,951 applied, 82.7% admitted, 12% enrolled. **General Admission Information:** Application fee $50. Priority deadline 12/1. Nonfall registration accepted. Admission may be deferred for a maximum of one semester.

COSTS AND FINANCIAL AID

Annual tuition $35,038. Room and board $13,720. Required fees $1,940. Average book expense $2,000. **Required Forms and Deadlines:** FAFSA; State aid form. **Notification of Awards:** Applicants will be notified of awards on a rolling basis beginning 12/20. **Types of Aid:** *Need-based scholarships/grants:* College/university scholarship or grant aid from institutional funds; Federal Pell; Private scholarships; SEOG; State scholarships/grants; United Negro College Fund. *Loans:* Direct PLUS loans; Direct Subsidized Stafford Loans; Direct Unsubsidized Stafford Loans. *Student Employment:* Federal Work-Study Program available. Institutional employment available. **Financial Aid Statistics:** 64% needy undergrads receive need-based scholarship or grant aid. 24% freshmen, 73% undergrads receive non-need-based scholarship or grant aid. 66% freshmen, 62% undergrads receive need-based self-help aid. 15% freshmen, 10% undergrads receive athletic scholarships.

LONGWOOD UNIVERSITY

201 High Street, Farmville, VA 23909
Phone: 434-395-2060 · **Financial Aid Phone:** 800-281-4677
E-mail: admissions@longwood.edu · **CEEB Code:** 5368
Fax: 434-395-2332 · **Website:** www.whylongwood.com · **ACT Code:** 4366

This public school was founded in 1839. It has a 160 acre campus.

RATINGS

Admissions Selectivity Rating: 77   **Fire Safety Rating:** 97   **Green Rating:** 60*

STUDENTS AND FACULTY

Enrollment: 4,185. **Student Body:** 66% female, 34% male, 3% out-of-state, 1% international (46 countries represented). Asian 1%, African American 7%, Caucasian 81%, Hispanic 4%, Native American <1%, Pacific Islander <1%, Two or more races 3%, Race unknown 3%.
Retention and Graduation: 79% freshmen return for sophomore year. **Faculty:** Student/faculty ratio 18:1. 222 full-time faculty, 85% hold PhDs, 8% are members of minority groups, 48% are women. 0% of classes are taught by teaching assistants.

ACADEMICS

Degrees: Bachelor's; Master's; Post-Bachelor's certificate; Post-Master's certificate **Classes:** Most classes have 20-29 students. Most lab/discussion sessions have 20-29 students. **Most popular majors:** Elementary Education And Teaching; Psychology, General; Business/Commerce, General. **Special Study Options:** Accelerated program; Cross-registration; Distance learning; Double major; Dual enrollment; Honors program; Independent study; Internships; Study abroad; Teacher certification program. **Honors programs:** The Cormier Honors College at Longwood University is designed to meet the needs of academically gifted and talented undergraduate students. Challenging courses with high academic standards enable students to expand their intellectual and creative horizons. The Honors Program focuses on the exchange of ideas and the enrichment of students' educational and cultural experiences. Learning takes place not only in the classroom, but also through cultural events, conferences, field trips, and study abroad. In keeping with the University's mission, the Longwood Honors Program strives to develop citizens who are committed to using their learning to provide service to their local communities as well as to the larger national and global communities. The concept of linking learning with the practice of citizenship is the distinctive feature of our Program. **Combined degree programs:** BA/MA. **Disability**

Services offered to physically disabled students: Note-taking services; Reader services; Tape recorders; Tutors. **Career services:** Alumni network; Career assessment; Career/job search classes; Internships

FACILITIES

Housing: Apartments for single students; Coed dorms; Fraternity/sorority housing; Special housing for disabled student; Women's dorms 100% of campus accessible to physically diasbled. **Special Academic Facilities/Equipment:** Longwood Center for the Visual Arts **Computers:** 100% of classrooms, 100% of libraries, 100% of dining areas, 100% of student union, have wireless network access. Students can register for classes online. Administrative functions (other than registration) can be performed online. Undergraduates are required to own a computer.

CAMPUS LIFE

Environment: Village **Activities:** Campus Ministries; Choral groups; Concert band; Dance; Drama/theater; Jazz band; Music ensembles; Pep band; Radio station; Student government; Student newspaper 129 registered organizations, 17 honor societies, 11 religious organizations. 9 fraternities, 12 sororities. **Athletics (Intercollegiate):** *Men:* baseball, basketball, cheerleading, cross-country, golf, soccer, tennis. *Women:* basketball, cheerleading, cross-country, field hockey, golf, lacrosse, soccer, softball, tennis. **On-Campus Highlights:** Brock Commons, Lankford Student Union, Health and Fitness Center, Greenwood Library, Dorrill Dining Hall

ADMISSIONS

Freshman Academic Profile: Average high school GPA 3.4. 12% in top 10% of high school class, 39% in top 25% of high school class, 79% in top 50% of high school class. 92% from public high schools. **Test Scores:** SAT Math middle 50% range 470-560. SAT EBRW middle 50% range 480-570. ACT middle 50% range 20-24. Minimum internet-based TOEFL 79. Minimum paper TOEFL 550. **Basis for Candidate Selection:** *Very important factors considered include:* rigor of secondary school record, academic GPA, application essay, standardized test scores. *Important factors considered include:* class rank, extracurricular activities, talent/ability, character/personal qualities, first generation, alumni/ae relation, geographical residence, racial/ethnic status, volunteer work. *Other factors considered include:* recommendation(s), state residency. **Freshman Admission Requirements:** High school diploma is required and GED is accepted *Academic units required:* 4 English, 3 math, 3 science, 2 science labs, 2 foreign language, 2 social studies, 2 history, 1 visual/performing arts, and 2 units from above areas or other academic areas. *Academic units recommended:* 4 English, 4 math, 4 science, 3 science labs, 4 foreign language, 2 social studies, 2 history, 1 visual/performing arts, 2 units from above areas or other academic areas. **Freshman Admission Statistics:** 4,166 applied, 77.6% admitted, 32% enrolled. **Transfer Admission Requirements:** High school transcript, college transcript(s), essay or personal statement, Minimum college GPA of 2.50 required. Lowest grade transferable C-. **General Admission Information:** Application fee $50. Priority deadline 3/1. Nonfall registration accepted. Admission may be deferred for a maximum of 1 year.

COSTS AND FINANCIAL AID

Annual in-state tuition $9,584. Annual out-of-state tuition $24,210. Room and board $9,584. Required fees $4,890. Average book expense $1,000. **Required Forms and Deadlines:** FAFSA. **Notification of Awards:** Applicants will be notified of awards on a rolling basis beginning 2/4. **Types of Aid:** *Need-based scholarships/grants:* College/university scholarship or grant aid from institutional funds; Federal Pell; Private scholarships; SEOG; State scholarships/grants. *Loans:* Direct PLUS loans; Direct Subsidized Stafford Loans; Direct Unsubsidized Stafford Loans. *Student Employment:* Federal Work-Study Program available. Institutional employment available. **Financial Aid Statistics:** 85% needy freshmen, 79% needy undergrads receive need-based scholarship or grant aid. 2% freshmen, 2% undergrads receive non-need-based scholarship or grant aid. 87% freshmen, 86% undergrads receive need-based self-help aid. 3% freshmen, 3% undergrads receive athletic scholarships. 60% freshmen receive any aid. **Criteria for awarding aid:** *Non-need-based:* Academics, Alumni affiliation, Art, Athletics, Leadership, Music/drama, State/district residency.

LORAS COLLEGE

1450 Alta Vista, Dubuque, IA 52001
Phone: 563-588-7236 · **Financial Aid Phone:** 563-588-7136
E-mail: admission@loras.edu · **CEEB Code:** 6370
Fax: 563-588-7119 · **Website:** www.loras.edu · **ACT Code:** 1328

This private school, affiliated with the Roman Catholic Church, was founded in 1839. It has a 64 acre campus.

RATINGS

Admissions Selectivity Rating: 73   **Fire Safety Rating:** 96   **Green Rating:** 70

STUDENTS AND FACULTY

Enrollment: 1,362. **Student Body:** 48% female, 52% male, 58% out-of-state, 2% international (9 countries represented). Asian 1%, African American 2%, Caucasian 82%, Hispanic 8%, Native American <1%, Pacific Islander <1%, Two or more races 2%, Race unknown 3%.
Retention and Graduation: 76% freshmen return for sophomore year. 57% freshmen graduate within 4 years. 68% freshmen graduate within 6 years. 21% grads go on to further study within 1 year. 3% grads pursue arts and sciences degrees. 2.2% grads pursue law degrees. 3% grads pursue business degrees. 2.2% grads pursue medical degrees. **Faculty:** Student/faculty ratio 12:1. 101 full-time faculty, 91% hold PhDs, 5% are members of minority groups, 40% are women. 0% of classes are taught by teaching assistants.

ACADEMICS

Degrees: Associate; Bachelor's; Master's; Post-Bachelor's certificate **Classes:** Most classes have 20-29 students. **Most popular majors:** Sport And Fitness Administration/Management; Accounting; Marketing/Marketing Management, General. **Special Study Options:** Cross-registration; Distance learning; Double major; Dual enrollment; Honors program; Independent study; Internships; Student-designed major; Study abroad; Teacher certification program. **Honors programs:** The Loras College Honors Program offers academically challenging, experiential, and interdisciplinary courses taken with a peer group of active learners. We encourage students to employ analytical and creative thinking as they explore the various disciplines that comprise the liberal arts. A key component of the Honors Program is a long-term, interdisciplinary group project that emphasizes community engagement and research in collaboration with a faculty mentor. The Honors Program curriculum focuses on real-world problem solving and cultivates essential skills for professional success, graduate education, and meaningful contributions to the community. **Disability Services offered to physically disabled students:** Note-taking services; Reader services; Tape recorders; Tutors. **Career services:** Alumni network; Alumni services; Career assessment; Career/job search classes; Internships

FACILITIES

Housing: Apartments for single students; Coed dorms 63% of campus accessible to physically diasbled. **Special Academic Facilities/Equipment:** Planetarium, observatory, regional history archive, residential arts complex, television studio **Computers:** Students can register for classes online. Administrative functions (other than registration) can be performed online. Undergraduates are required to own a computer.

CAMPUS LIFE

Environment: Town **Activities:** Campus Ministries; Choral groups; Concert band; Dance; Drama/theater; International Student Organization; Jazz band; Literary magazine; Music ensembles; Pep band; Radio station; Student government; Student newspaper; Television station; Yearbook 71 registered organizations, 710 honor societies, 5 religious organizations. 2 fraternities, 2 sororities. **Athletics (Intercollegiate):** *Men:* baseball, basketball, cross-country, diving, football, golf, soccer, swimming, tennis, track/field (outdoor), track/field (indoor), wrestling. *Women:* basketball, cross-country, diving, golf, soccer, softball, swimming, tennis, track/field (outdoor), track/field (indoor), volleyball. **On-Campus Highlights:** Academic Resource Center, Alumni Campus Center, Rock Bowl Stadium, Athletic and Wellness Center, Center for Dubuque History **Environmental Initiatives:** Petal Certification through the Petal Project, a Dubuque-area green business initiative.

ADMISSIONS

Freshman Academic Profile: Average high school GPA 3.4. 17% in top 10% of high school class, 46% in top 25% of high school class, 73% in top 50% of high school class. 69% from public high schools. **Test Scores:** SAT Math middle 50% range 530-605. SAT EBRW middle 50% range 515-575. ACT middle 50% range 20-26. Minimum internet-based TOEFL 79. Minimum paper TOEFL 550. **Basis for Candidate Selection:** *Very important factors considered include:* rigor of secondary school record, academic GPA, standardized test scores. *Other factors considered include:* class rank, application essay, recommendation(s), interview, extracurricular activities, character/personal qualities, racial/ethnic status, volunteer work, work experience, level of applicant's interest. **Freshman Admission Requirements:** High school diploma is required and GED is accepted *Academic units recommended:* 4 English, 4 math, 3 science, 2 science labs, 3 social studies, 2 academic electives. **Freshman Admission Statistics:** 1,159 applied, 95.1% admitted, 31% enrolled. **Transfer Admission Requirements:** High school transcript, college transcript(s), standardized test scores, Minimum college GPA of 2.0 required. Lowest grade transferable C. **General Admission Information:** Nonfall registration accepted. Admission may be deferred for a maximum of 1 year.

COSTS AND FINANCIAL AID

Annual tuition $32,524. Room and board $8,275. Required fees $1,660. Average book expense $1,100. **Required Forms and Deadlines:** FAFSA. **Types of Aid:** *Need-based scholarships/grants:* College/university scholarship or grant aid from institutional funds; Federal Pell; Private scholarships; SEOG; State scholarships/grants. *Loans:* Direct PLUS loans; Direct Subsidized Stafford Loans; Direct Unsubsidized Stafford Loans. *Student Employment:* Federal Work-Study Program available. Institutional employment available. **Financial Aid Statistics:** 100% needy freshmen, 100% needy undergrads receive need-based scholarship or grant aid. 47% freshmen, 58% undergrads receive non-need-based scholarship or grant aid. 66% freshmen, 70% undergrads receive need-based self-help aid. 0% freshmen, 0% undergrads receive athletic scholarships. 100% freshmen, 100% undergrads receive any aid. 71% undergrads borrow to pay for school. Average cumulative indebtedness $31,418. **Criteria for awarding aid:** *Non-need-based:* Academics, Art.

LOUISIANA COLLEGE

1140 College Drive, Pineville, LA 71359-0566
Phone: 318-487-7259 • **Financial Aid Phone:** 318-487-7387
E-mail: admissions@lacollege.edu • **CEEB Code:** 6371
Website: www.lacollege.edu • **ACT Code:** 1586

This private school, affiliated with the Southern Baptist Church, was founded in 1906. It has a 81 acre campus.

RATINGS

Admissions Selectivity Rating: 85   Fire Safety Rating: 86   Green Rating: 60*

STUDENTS AND FACULTY

Enrollment: 937. **Student Body:** 45% female, 55% male, 10% out-of-state, 3% international (12 countries represented). Asian 1%, African American 25%, Caucasian 64%, Hispanic 3%, Native American 1%, Pacific Islander <1%, Two or more races 2%, Race unknown 1%.
Retention and Graduation: 55% freshmen return for sophomore year. **Faculty:** Student/faculty ratio 12:1. 72 full-time faculty, 78% hold PhDs, 11% are members of minority groups, 60% are women. 0% of classes are taught by teaching assistants.

ACADEMICS

Degrees: Associate; Bachelor's; Certificate; Master's **Classes:** Most classes have 10-19 students. Most lab/discussion sessions have 10-19 students. **Most popular majors:** Education, General; Health And Physical Education/Fitness, General; Registered Nursing, Nursing Administration, Nursing Research And Clinical Nursing, Other. **Special Study Options:** Distance learning; Double major; Dual enrollment; English as a Second Language (ESL); Honors program; Independent study; Internships; Liberal arts/career combination; Student-designed major; Teacher certification program. **Disability Services offered to physically disabled students:** Note-taking services; Reader services; Tutors. **Career services:** Career assessment; Career/job search classes; Internships

FACILITIES

Housing: Apartments for married students; Apartments for single students; Men's dorms; Wellness housing; Women's dorms 95% of campus accessible to physically diasbled. **Special Academic Facilities/Equipment:** Art gallery, radio station, performing arts center, theater

CAMPUS LIFE

Environment: Town **Activities:** Campus Ministries; Choral groups; Concert band; Drama/theater; International Student Organization; Jazz band; Marching band; Music ensembles; Musical theater; Opera; Pep band; Radio station; Student government; Symphony orchestra; Yearbook. Healthplex/Wellness Center, Hixon Student Center/Granberry, Martin Performing Arts Center, Weathersby Fine Arts Building, Alexandria Hall

ADMISSIONS

Freshman Academic Profile: Average high school GPA 3.2. 13% in top 10% of high school class, 30% in top 25% of high school class, 61% in top 50% of high school class. **Test Scores:** SAT Math middle 50% range 490-650. SAT EBRW middle 50% range 560-580. ACT middle 50% range 19-24. Minimum internet-based TOEFL 60. Minimum paper TOEFL 500. **Basis for Candidate Selection:** *Very important factors considered include:* academic GPA, standardized test scores. *Other factors considered include:* rigor of secondary school record, application essay, extracurricular activities, talent/ability, character/personal qualities, religious affiliation/commitment. **Freshman Admission Requirements:** High school diploma is required and GED is accepted *Academic units required:* 4 English, 4 math, 3 science, 2 science labs, 3 social studies, and 8 units from above areas or other academic areas. **Freshman Admission Statistics:** 780 applied, 71.9% admitted, 55% enrolled. **General Admission Information:** Application fee $25. Regular application deadline 8/15. Nonfall registration accepted.

COSTS AND FINANCIAL AID

Annual tuition $16,000. Room and board $5,274. Average book expense $1,200. **Required Forms and Deadlines:** FAFSA; Institution's own financial aid form. **Notification of Awards:** Applicants will be notified of awards on a rolling basis beginning 1/1. **Types of Aid:** *Need-based scholarships/grants:* College/ university scholarship or grant aid from institutional funds; Federal Pell; SEOG; State scholarships/grants. *Loans:* Direct PLUS loans; Direct Subsidized Stafford Loans; Direct Unsubsidized Stafford Loans. *Student Employment:* Federal Work-Study Program available. Institutional employment available.

LOUISIANA STATE UNIVERSITY—BATON ROUGE

1146 Pleasant Hall, Baton Rouge, LA 70803
Phone: 225-578-1175 • **Financial Aid Phone:** 225-578-3103
E-mail: admissions@lsu.edu • **CEEB Code:** 6373
Fax: 225-578-4433 • **Website:** www.lsu.edu • **ACT Code:** 1590

This public school was founded in 1860. It has a 2000 acre campus.

RATINGS

Admissions Selectivity Rating: 82   Fire Safety Rating: 98   Green Rating: 90

STUDENTS AND FACULTY

Enrollment: 24,904. **Student Body:** 52% female, 48% male, 17% out-of-state, 2% international (66 countries represented). Asian 4%, African American 8%, Caucasian 76%, Hispanic 6%, Native American <1%, Pacific Islander <1%, Two or more races 2%, Race unknown <1%.
Retention and Graduation: 85% freshmen return for sophomore year. **Faculty:** Student/faculty ratio 23:1. 1,278 full-time faculty, 88% hold PhDs, 18% are members of minority groups, 35% are women. 7% of classes are taught by teaching assistants.

ACADEMICS

Degrees: Bachelor's; Certificate; Doctoral; Doctoral/Professional; Doctoral/ Research; Master's; Post-Bachelor's certificate; Post-Master's certificate **Classes:** Most classes have 20-29 students. **Most popular majors:** Mass Communication/Media Studies; Physical Education Teaching And Coaching; Biology/Biological Sciences, General. **Special Study Options:** Accelerated program; Cooperative education program; Cross-registration; Distance learning; Double major; Dual enrollment; English as a Second Language (ESL); Exchange student program (domestic); Honors program; Independent study; Internships; Student-designed major; Study abroad; Teacher certification program. **Honors programs:** Admissions to the Honors College. **Disability Services offered to physically disabled students:** Note-taking services; Reader services; Tape recorders. **Career services:** Alumni services; Career assessment; Career/job search classes; Internships; Regional alumni

FACILITIES

Housing: Apartments for married students; Apartments for single students; Coed dorms; Fraternity/sorority housing; Men's dorms; Special housing for disabled student; Theme housing; Women's dorms 75% of campus accessible to physically diasbled. **Special Academic Facilities/Equipment:** Art Museum, Natural Science Museum, Rural Life Museum, Lichen/Bryophyte Mycological and Vascular Plant herbariums, on campus K-12 schools, geoscience and mycological museums, electron microscope, nuclear science center and civil war center. **Computers:** 100% of classrooms, 100% of dorms, 100% of libraries, 90% of dining areas, 100% of student union, 90% of common outdoor areas have wireless network access. Students can register for classes online. Administrative functions (other than registration) can be performed online.

CAMPUS LIFE

Environment: City **Activities:** Campus Ministries; Choral groups; Concert band; Dance; Drama/theater; International Student Organization; Jazz band; Literary magazine; Marching band; Music ensembles; Musical theater; Opera; Pep band; Radio station; Student government; Student newspaper; Student-run film society; Symphony orchestra; Television station; Yearbook 300 registered organizations, 32 honor societies, 25 religious organizations. 23 fraternities, 15 sororities. **Athletics (Intercollegiate):** *Men:* baseball, basketball, cheerleading, cross-country, diving, football, golf, swimming, tennis, track/field (outdoor), track/field (indoor). *Women:* basketball, cheerleading, cross-country, diving, golf, gymnastics, soccer, softball, swimming, tennis, track/field (outdoor), track/field (indoor), volleyball. **On-Campus Highlights:** LSU Student Union, Mike VI Tiger Habitat, Parade Grounds, Tiger Stadium, Alex Box Stadium **Environmental Initiatives:** Goal to increase recycling rate to 50%.

ADMISSIONS

Freshman Academic Profile: Average high school GPA 3.4. 26% in top 10% of high school class, 52% in top 25% of high school class, 82% in top 50% of high school class. 58% from public high schools. **Test Scores:** SAT Math middle 50% range 510-640. SAT EBRW middle 50% range 510-620. ACT middle 50% range 23-28. Minimum internet-based TOEFL 79. Minimum paper TOEFL 550. **Basis for Candidate Selection:** *Very important factors considered include:* rigor of secondary school record, academic GPA, standardized test scores. *Important factors considered include:* talent/ability. *Other factors considered include:* class rank, application essay, recommendation(s), interview, extracurricular activities, first generation, alumni/ae relation, level of applicant's interest. **Freshman Admission Requirements:** High school diploma is required and GED is accepted *Academic units required:* 4 English, 4 math, 4 science, 2 foreign language, 3 social studies, 1 history, 1 visual/performing arts. **Freshman Admission Statistics:** 17,429 applied, 77.3% admitted, 42% enrolled. **Transfer Admission Requirements:** college transcript(s), Minimum college GPA of 2.5 required. Lowest grade transferable D. **General Admission Information:** Application fee $40. Priority deadline 11/15. Regular application deadline 4/15. Nonfall registration accepted. Admission may be deferred for a maximum of 1 academic year.

COSTS AND FINANCIAL AID

Annual in-state tuition $11,750. Annual out-of-state tuition $24,715. Room and board $11,750. Required fees $3,336. Average book expense $1,160. **Required Forms and Deadlines:** FAFSA; Institution's own financial aid form. **Notification of Awards:** Applicants will be notified of awards on a rolling basis beginning 11/15. **Types of Aid:** *Need-based scholarships/grants:* College/university scholarship or grant aid from institutional funds; Federal Pell; Private scholarships; SEOG; State scholarships/grants. *Loans:* Direct PLUS loans; Direct Subsidized Stafford Loans; Direct Unsubsidized Stafford Loans. *Student Employment:* Federal Work-Study Program available. Institutional employment available. **Financial Aid Statistics:** 95% needy freshmen, 84% needy undergrads receive need-based scholarship or grant aid. 4% freshmen, 3% undergrads receive non-need-based scholarship or grant aid. 66% freshmen, 73% undergrads receive need-based self-help aid. 2% freshmen, 2% undergrads receive athletic scholarships. 95% freshmen, 81% undergrads receive any aid. Average cumulative indebtedness $24,509. **Criteria for awarding aid:** *Need-based:* Academics *Non-need-based:* Academics, Athletics, Music/drama.

LOUISIANA TECH UNIVERSITY

PO Box 3168, Ruston, LA 71272
Phone: 318-257-3036
E-mail: bulldog@latech.edu
Fax: 318-257-2499 • **Website:** www.latech.edu

This is a public school.

RATINGS
Admissions Selectivity Rating: 82   **Fire Safety Rating:** 60*   **Green Rating:** 60*

STUDENTS AND FACULTY
Enrollment: 7,047. **Student Body:** 43% female, 57% male, 10% out-of-state, 4% international. Asian 1%, African American 15%, Caucasian 68%, Hispanic 1%, Native American <1%, Pacific Islander <1%, Two or more races 1%, Race unknown 8%.
Retention and Graduation: 79% freshmen return for sophomore year.
Faculty: Student/faculty ratio 23:1. 352 full-time faculty, 79% hold PhDs, 39% are women.

ACADEMICS
Degrees: Associate; Bachelor's; Doctoral/Professional; Doctoral/Research; Master's; Post-Bachelor's certificate; Post-Master's certificate **Classes:** Most classes have 20-29 students. Most lab/discussion sessions have 20-29 students. **Special Study Options:** Distance learning; Double major; Dual enrollment; Honors program; Independent study; Internships; Study abroad; Teacher certification program. **Career services:** Alumni network; Alumni services; Career assessment; Career/job search classes; Internships; Regional alumni

FACILITIES
Housing: Apartments for married students; Apartments for single students; Men's dorms; Special housing for disabled student; Theme housing; Women's dorms

CAMPUS LIFE
Activities: Campus Ministries; Choral groups; Concert band; Dance; Drama/theater; International Student Organization; Jazz band; Marching band; Music ensembles; Musical theater; Pep band; Radio station; Student government; Student newspaper; Student-run film society; Television station; Yearbook.

ADMISSIONS
Freshman Academic Profile: Average high school GPA 3.4. 24% in top 10% of high school class, 51% in top 25% of high school class, 80% in top 50% of high school class. 77% from public high schools. **Test Scores:** SAT Math middle 50% range 490-600. SAT EBRW middle 50% range 450-590. ACT middle 50% range 21-26. Minimum internet-based TOEFL 80. Minimum paper TOEFL 570. **Basis for Candidate Selection:** *Very important factors considered include:* rigor of secondary school record, class rank, academic GPA, standardized test scores. *Important factors considered include:* talent/ability, level of applicant's interest. *Other factors considered include:* recommendation(s), extracurricular activities, first generation, alumni/ae relation. **Freshman Admission Requirements:** High school diploma is required and GED is not accepted *Academic units required:* 4 English, 4 math, 4 science, 2 foreign language, 4 social studies, 1 visual/performing arts. **Freshman Admission Statistics:** 5,077 applied, 67.4% admitted, 45% enrolled. **General Admission Information:** Application fee $20. Nonfall registration accepted.

COSTS AND FINANCIAL AID
Required Forms and Deadlines: FAFSA; Institution's own financial aid form. **Notification of Awards:** Applicants will be notified of awards on a rolling basis beginning 4/1. **Types of Aid:** *Need-based scholarships/grants:* College/university scholarship or grant aid from institutional funds; Federal Pell; Private scholarships; SEOG; State scholarships/grants. *Loans:* Direct PLUS loans; Direct Subsidized Stafford Loans; Direct Unsubsidized Stafford Loans. **Financial Aid Statistics:** 94% needy freshmen, 89% needy undergrads receive need-based scholarship or grant aid. 18% freshmen, 15% undergrads receive non-need-based scholarship or grant aid. 51% freshmen, 61% undergrads receive need-based self-help aid. 1% freshmen, 2% undergrads receive athletic scholarships. **Criteria for awarding aid:** *Non-need-based:* Academics, Alumni affiliation, Art, Athletics, Job skills, Leadership, Music/drama, State/district residency.

LOURDES COLLEGE

6832 Convent Boulevard, Sylvania, OH 43560-2898
Phone: 419-885-5291 • **Financial Aid Phone:** 419-824-3732
E-mail: AdmissionsLCAdmits@lourdes.edu • **CEEB Code:** 1427
Fax: 419-824-3916 • **Website:** www.lourdes.edu • **ACT Code:** 3598

This private school, affiliated with the Roman Catholic Church, was founded in 1958. It has a 113 acre campus.

RATINGS
Admissions Selectivity Rating: 76   **Fire Safety Rating:** 85   **Green Rating:** 61

STUDENTS AND FACULTY
Enrollment: 1,666. **Student Body:** 71% female, 29% male, 14% out-of-state, <1% international. Asian 1%, African American 18%, Caucasian 72%, Hispanic 6%, Native American <1%, Pacific Islander 0%, Two or more races 2%, Race unknown 2%.
Retention and Graduation: 63% freshmen return for sophomore year.
Faculty: Student/faculty ratio 10:1. 100 full-time faculty, 59% hold PhDs, 10% are members of minority groups, 67% are women. 2% of classes are taught by teaching assistants.

ACADEMICS
Degrees: Associate; Bachelor's; Certificate; Master's; Post-Bachelor's certificate; Post-Master's certificate **Classes:** Most classes have 10-19 students.

Most lab/discussion sessions have 10-19 students. **Most popular majors:** Social Work; Registered Nursing/Registered Nurse; Business Administration And Management, General. **Special Study Options:** Distance learning; Double major; Dual enrollment; Independent study; Internships; Liberal arts/career combination; Student-designed major; Study abroad; Teacher certification program. **Disability Services offered to physically disabled students:** Note-taking services; Reader services; Tape recorders; Tutors. **Career services:** Career assessment; Career/job search classes

FACILITIES

Housing: Apartments for single students; Coed dorms **Special Academic Facilities/Equipment:** Planetarium **Computers:** 100% of classrooms, 100% of libraries, 100% of dining areas, 100% of student union, have wireless network access. Students can register for classes online. Administrative functions (other than registration) can be performed online.

CAMPUS LIFE

Environment: Village **Activities:** Campus Ministries; Choral groups; Drama/theater; Literary magazine; Student government 25 registered organizations, 2 honor societies. **Athletics (Intercollegiate):** *Men:* basketball, golf. *Women:* golf, volleyball. **On-Campus Highlights:** Delp Hall, Ebied Center, Lourdes Dining Hall, Academic Support Center

ADMISSIONS

Freshman Academic Profile: Average high school GPA 3.0. 8% in top 10% of high school class, 27% in top 25% of high school class, 59% in top 50% of high school class. **Test Scores:** SAT Math middle 50% range 350-500. SAT EBRW middle 50% range 410-540. ACT middle 50% range 17-22. Minimum internet-based TOEFL 173. Minimum paper TOEFL 500. **Basis for Candidate Selection:** *Very important factors considered include:* academic GPA, standardized test scores. *Other factors considered include:* interview. **Freshman Admission Requirements:** High school diploma is required and GED is accepted *Academic units recommended:* 4 English, 3 math, 3 science, 2 foreign language, 3 social studies, 1 visual/performing arts, 1 unit from above areas or other academic areas. **Freshman Admission Statistics:** 1,296 applied, 68.0% admitted, 29% enrolled. **Transfer Admission Requirements:** college transcript(s), Minimum college GPA of 2.0 required. Lowest grade transferable C. **General Admission Information:** Application fee $25. Nonfall registration accepted. Admission may be deferred for a maximum of 4 years.

COSTS AND FINANCIAL AID

Annual tuition $17,455. Room and board $8,400. Required fees $200. Average book expense $1,275. **Required Forms and Deadlines:** FAFSA. **Notification of Awards:** Applicants will be notified of awards on a rolling basis beginning 3/1. **Types of Aid:** *Need-based scholarships/grants:* College/university scholarship or grant aid from institutional funds; Federal Pell; Private scholarships; SEOG; State scholarships/grants. *Loans:* Direct PLUS loans; Direct Subsidized Stafford Loans; Direct Unsubsidized Stafford Loans. *Student Employment:* Federal Work-Study Program available. Institutional employment available. **Financial Aid Statistics:** 88% needy freshmen, 82% needy undergrads receive need-based scholarship or grant aid. 89% freshmen, 63% undergrads receive non-need-based scholarship or grant aid. 92% freshmen, 91% undergrads receive need-based self-help aid. 28% freshmen, 18% undergrads receive athletic scholarships. 96% freshmen, 84% undergrads receive any aid. **Criteria for awarding aid:** *Need-based:* Academics, Alumni affiliation, Art, Leadership, Minority status, Religious affiliation *Non-need-based:* Academics, Art, Athletics, Minority status, Music/drama, Religious affiliation, State/district residency.

LOYOLA MARYMOUNT UNIVERSITY

1 LMU Drive, Los Angeles, CA 90045-8350
Phone: 310-338-2750 · **Financial Aid Phone:** 310-338-2753
E-mail: admissions@lmu.edu · **CEEB Code:** 4403
Fax: 310-338-2797 · **Website:** www.lmu.edu · **ACT Code:** 326

This private school, affiliated with the Roman Catholic Church, was founded in 1911. It has a 142 acre campus.

RATINGS

Admissions Selectivity Rating: 89   **Fire Safety Rating:** 89   **Green Rating:** 99

STUDENTS AND FACULTY

Enrollment: 6,257. **Student Body:** 56% female, 44% male, 29% out-of-state, 10% international (80 countries represented). Asian 10%, African American 7%,

Caucasian 44%, Hispanic 21%, Native American <1%, Pacific Islander <1%, Two or more races 7%, Race unknown 0%.
Retention and Graduation: 91% freshmen return for sophomore year. 70% freshmen graduate within 4 years. 79% freshmen graduate within 6 years. 20% grads go on to further study within 1 year. **Faculty:** 1% of classes are taught by teaching assistants.

ACADEMICS

Degrees: Bachelor's; Doctoral/Professional; Doctoral/Research; Master's; Post-Bachelor's certificate; Post-Master's certificate **Most popular majors:** Speech Communication And Rhetoric; Psychology, General; Marketing/Marketing Management, General. **Special Study Options:** Accelerated program; Cross-registration; Distance learning; Double major; Dual enrollment; English as a Second Language (ESL); Exchange student program (domestic); Honors program; Independent study; Internships; Liberal arts/career combination; Student-designed major; Study abroad; Teacher certification program; Weekend college. **Honors programs:** University Honors Program **Combined degree programs:** BA/MEng. **Disability Services offered to physically disabled students:** Note-taking services; Reader services; Tape recorders; Tutors. **Career services:** Alumni network; Alumni services; Career assessment; Career/job search classes; Internships; Regional alumni

FACILITIES

Housing: Apartments for single students; Coed dorms; Men's dorms; Special housing for disabled student; Special housing for international students; Theme housing; Women's dorms 95% of campus accessible to physically diasbled. **Special Academic Facilities/Equipment:** Art gallery, theater, TV production labs, computer graphics lab, radio station. **Computers:** Students can register for classes online. Administrative functions (other than registration) can be performed online.

CAMPUS LIFE

Environment: Town **Activities:** Campus Ministries; Choral groups; Dance; Drama/theater; International Student Organization; Literary magazine; Model UN; Music ensembles; Opera; Pep band; Radio station; Student government; Student newspaper; Student-run film society; Television station; Yearbook 120 registered organizations, 12 honor societies, 2 religious organizations. 6 fraternities, 8 sororities. **Athletics (Intercollegiate):** *Men:* baseball, basketball, crew/rowing, cross-country, golf, soccer, tennis, water polo. *Women:* basketball, crew/rowing, cross-country, soccer, softball, swimming, tennis, volleyball, water polo. Wm. H. Hannon Library, Malone Student Center, Burns Recreation Center, Lion's Den and Living Room, Life Sciences Building **Environmental Initiatives:** LEED Building Program: LMU's new LEED Gold Life Science Building is a 120,000 GSF building is designed with state-of-the-art laboratory technologies, collaborative research space, and energy efficiency features, complementing our 5 other LEED-certified campus buildings and signifying LMU's commitment to continued leadership in environmental stewardship. The building will also act as a 'living lab' for students studying with a 200,000 kwh Solar Array and a green roof with research functionality. the building also houses 9,000 SF of faculty research lab space, 24 teaching labs, lab support spaces, vivarium, faculty offices, classrooms, shared public spaces, conference rooms, and a 292-fixed seat auditorium.

ADMISSIONS

Freshman Academic Profile: Average high school GPA 3.8. 41% in top 10% of high school class, 75% in top 25% of high school class, 95% in top 50% of high school class. 49% from public high schools. **Test Scores:** SAT Math middle 50% range 580-680. SAT EBRW middle 50% range 600-680. ACT middle 50% range 26-31. Minimum internet-based TOEFL 80. Minimum paper TOEFL 550. **Basis for Candidate Selection:** *Very important factors considered include:* academic GPA. *Important factors considered include:* rigor of secondary school record, application essay, standardized test scores, talent/ability, character/personal qualities. *Other factors considered include:* class rank, recommendation(s), extracurricular activities, first generation, alumni/ae relation, volunteer work, work experience. **Freshman Admission Requirements:** High school diploma is required and GED is accepted *Academic units recommended:* 4 English, 3 math, 2 science, 2 science labs, 3 foreign language, 3 social studies, 1 academic elective. **Freshman Admission Statistics:** 15,381 applied, 52.5% admitted, 18% enrolled. **Transfer Admission Requirements:** college transcript(s), essay or personal statement, statement of good standing from prior institution(s). Minimum college GPA of 2.8 required. Lowest grade transferable C. **General Admission Information:** Application fee $60. Regular application deadline 1/15. Nonfall registration accepted. Admission may be deferred for a maximum of 1 year.

COSTS AND FINANCIAL AID

Required Forms and Deadlines: FAFSA. **Types of Aid:** *Need-based scholarships/grants:* College/university scholarship or grant aid from institutional funds; Federal Pell; Private scholarships; SEOG; State scholarships/grants. *Loans:* Direct PLUS loans; Direct Subsidized Stafford Loans; Direct Unsubsidized Stafford Loans. *Student Employment:* Federal Work-Study Program available. Institutional employment available. **Financial Aid Statistics:** 97% needy freshmen, 95% needy undergrads receive need-based scholarship or grant aid. 14% freshmen, 11% undergrads receive non-need-based scholarship or grant aid. 76% freshmen, 78% undergrads receive need-based self-help aid. 3% freshmen, 3% undergrads receive athletic scholarships. 92% freshmen, 87% undergrads receive any aid. 54% undergrads borrow to pay for school. Average cumulative indebtedness $30,698. **Criteria for awarding aid:** *Need-based:* Academics, Leadership, Minority status, Religious affiliation *Non-need-based:* Academics, Alumni affiliation, Art, Athletics, Music/drama, Religious affiliation.

LOYOLA UNIVERSITY MARYLAND

4501 North Charles Street, Baltimore, MD 21212
Phone: 410-617-5012 · **Financial Aid Phone:** 410-617-2576
E-mail: admissions@loyola.edu · **CEEB Code:** 5370
Fax: 410-617-2176 · **Website:** www.loyola.edu

This private school, affiliated with the Roman Catholic Church, was founded in 1852. It has a 89 acre campus.

RATINGS

Admissions Selectivity Rating: 85   **Fire Safety Rating:** 94   **Green Rating:** 73

STUDENTS AND FACULTY

Enrollment: 3,903. **Student Body:** 58% female, 42% male, 82% out-of-state, 1% international (53 countries represented). Asian 4%, African American 5%, Caucasian 78%, Hispanic 10%, Native American <1%, Pacific Islander <1%, Two or more races 3%, Race unknown <1%.
Retention and Graduation: 85% freshmen return for sophomore year. 3% freshmen graduate within 4 years. 85% freshmen graduate within 6 years. 21% grads go on to further study within 1 year. 53% grads pursue arts and sciences degrees. 10% grads pursue law degrees. 4% grads pursue business degrees. 7% grads pursue medical degrees. **Faculty:** Student/faculty ratio 11:1. 368 full-time faculty, 86% hold PhDs, 20% are members of minority groups, 50% are women. 0% of classes are taught by teaching assistants.

ACADEMICS

Degrees: Bachelor's; Doctoral/Professional; Doctoral/Research; Master's; Post-Bachelor's certificate; Post-Master's certificate **Classes:** Most classes have 20-29 students. Most lab/discussion sessions have 10-19 students. **Most popular majors:** Communication And Media Studies; Social Sciences, Other; Business Administration And Management, General. **Special Study Options:** Cross-registration; Double major; Exchange student program (domestic); Honors program; Independent study; Internships; Liberal arts/career combination; Study abroad; Teacher certification program. **Disability Services offered to physically disabled students:** Note-taking services; Reader services; Tape recorders; Tutors. **Career services:** Alumni network; Alumni services; Career assessment; Career/job search classes; Internships; Regional alumni

FACILITIES

Housing: Coed dorms; Theme housing; Wellness housing 100% of campus accessible to physically disabled. **Special Academic Facilities/Equipment:** Art gallery, advanced biology lab, humanities building, speech pathology lab and audiology center, black box theater **Computers:** 75% of classrooms, 80% of dorms, 100% of libraries, 100% of dining areas, 50% of student union, 50% of common outdoor areas have wireless network access. Students can register for classes online. Administrative functions (other than registration) can be performed online.

CAMPUS LIFE

Environment: Metropolis **Activities:** Campus Ministries; Choral groups; Dance; Drama/theater; International Student Organization; Jazz band; Literary magazine; Music ensembles; Musical theater; Radio station; Student government; Student newspaper; Student-run film society; Television station; Yearbook 185 registered organizations, 25 honor societies, 4 religious organizations. **Athletics (Intercollegiate):** *Men:* basketball, crew/rowing, cross-country, diving, golf, lacrosse, soccer, swimming, tennis. *Women:* basketball, crew/rowing, cross-country, diving, lacrosse, soccer, swimming, tennis, track/field (outdoor), track/field (indoor), volleyball. **On-Campus Highlights:** Reverend Harold Ridley, S.J., Athletic Complex, Loyola/Notre Dame Library, The Loyola University Art Gallery, Fitness and Aquatic Center, Boulder Garden Cafe/Primo's: New Marketplace **Environmental Initiatives:** Our commitment responsible building can be seen in our 100,000 sq. ft. green residential hall that was built in 2007. In 2010 we completed construction of an athletic facility that was built on a landfill and is considered an example of smart growth.

ADMISSIONS

Freshman Academic Profile: Average high school GPA 3.5. 29% in top 10% of high school class, 68% in top 25% of high school class, 95% in top 50% of high school class. **Test Scores:** SAT Math middle 50% range 560-650. SAT EBRW middle 50% range 580-660. ACT middle 50% range 25-30. Minimum internet-based TOEFL 79. Minimum paper TOEFL 550. **Basis for Candidate Selection:** *Very important factors considered include:* rigor of secondary school record, academic GPA, application essay, recommendation(s), character/personal qualities. *Important factors considered include:* extracurricular activities, talent/ability, volunteer work. *Other factors considered include:* class rank, standardized test scores, first generation, alumni/ae relation, geographical residence, racial/ethnic status, work experience, level of applicant's interest. **Freshman Admission Requirements:** High school diploma is required and GED is accepted *Academic units required:* 4 English, 3 math, 3 science, 3 foreign language, 2 social studies, 2 history, *Academic units recommended:* 4 English, 4 math, 4 science, 4 foreign language, 3 social studies, 3 history, 1 computer science, 1 visual/performing arts. **Freshman Admission Statistics:** 11,600 applied, 75.3% admitted, 12% enrolled. **Transfer Admission Requirements:** High school transcript, college transcript(s), essay or personal statement, statement of good standing from prior institution(s). Minimum college GPA of 2.7 required. Lowest grade transferable C. **General Admission Information:** Application fee $60. Priority deadline 11/1. Regular application deadline 1/15. Nonfall registration accepted. Admission may be deferred for a maximum of 1 year.

COSTS AND FINANCIAL AID

Required Forms and Deadlines: CSS/Financial Aid PROFILE; FAFSA; Noncustodial PROFILE. **Notification of Awards:** Applicants will be notified of awards on or about 3/15. **Types of Aid:** *Need-based scholarships/grants:* College/university scholarship or grant aid from institutional funds; Federal Pell; Private scholarships; SEOG; State scholarships/grants. *Loans:* Direct PLUS loans; Direct Subsidized Stafford Loans; Direct Unsubsidized Stafford Loans. *Student Employment:* Federal Work-Study Program available. Institutional employment available. **Financial Aid Statistics:** 89% needy freshmen, 89% needy undergrads receive need-based scholarship or grant aid. 33% freshmen, 29% undergrads receive non-need-based scholarship or grant aid. 96% freshmen, 95% undergrads receive need-based self-help aid. 3% freshmen, 3% undergrads receive athletic scholarships. 75% freshmen, 70% undergrads receive any aid. 61% undergrads borrow to pay for school. Average cumulative indebtedness $34,375. **Criteria for awarding aid:** *Non-need-based:* Academics, Athletics.

LOYOLA UNIVERSITY NEW ORLEANS

6363 St. Charles Avenue, New Orleans, LA 70118-6195
Phone: 504-865-3240 · **Financial Aid Phone:** 504-865-3231
E-mail: admit@loyno.edu · **CEEB Code:** 6374
Fax: 504-865-3383 · **Website:** www.loyno.edu · **ACT Code:** 1592

This private school, affiliated with the Roman Catholic-Jesuit Church, was founded in 1912. It has a 26 acre campus.

RATINGS

Admissions Selectivity Rating: 84   **Fire Safety Rating:** 98   **Green Rating:** 85

STUDENTS AND FACULTY

Enrollment: 2,534. **Student Body:** 62% female, 38% male, 57% out-of-state, 2% international (42 countries represented). Asian 3%, African American 15%, Caucasian 51%, Hispanic 16%, Native American <1%, Pacific Islander <1%, Two or more races 5%, Race unknown 6%.
Retention and Graduation: 80% freshmen return for sophomore year. 47% freshmen graduate within 4 years. 56% freshmen graduate within 6 years. 14% grads go on to further study within 1 year. **Faculty:** Student/faculty ratio 11:1. 241 full-time faculty, 90% hold PhDs, 21% are members of minority groups, 45% are women. 0% of classes are taught by teaching assistants.

ACADEMICS

Degrees: Bachelor's; Certificate; Doctoral Other; Doctoral/Professional; Master's; Post-Bachelor's certificate; Post-Master's certificate **Classes:** Most classes have 10-19 students. Most lab/discussion sessions have 20-29 students. **Most popular majors:** Public Relations, Advertising, And

Applied Communication; Research And Experimental Psychology, Other; Music Management. **Special Study Options:** Accelerated program; Cross-registration; Distance learning; Double major; Dual enrollment; English as a Second Language (ESL); Exchange student program (domestic); External degree program; Honors program; Independent study; Internships; Liberal arts/career combination; Student-designed major; Study abroad; Teacher certification program. **Honors programs:** The Loyola University Honors Program offers the opportunity for academically superior, highly motivated students to take challenging Honors courses and to participate in special cultural and intellectual enrichment activities. The University Honors Program is open to qualified students of all undergraduate colleges and majors. The Honors courses replace other required courses, and therefore do not add to the number of requirements for graduation. **Disability Services offered to physically disabled students:** Note-taking services; Reader services; Tape recorders; Tutors. **Career services:** Alumni network; Alumni services; Career assessment; Career/job search classes; Internships; Regional alumni

FACILITIES

Housing: Apartments for single students; Coed dorms; Special housing for disabled student; Theme housing; Wellness housing 95% of campus accessible to physically diasbled. **Special Academic Facilities/Equipment:** Monroe Hall, complete with a 3-D printing machine, state-of-the-art 3,000-square-foot greenhouse, specialized science labs and exhibit spaces; multimedia classrooms throughout campus; The Maroon newsroom, complete with in-house TV studio and digital communications laboratory; Carlos F. Ayala Stock Trading Room in the College of Business; Collins C. Diboll Art Gallery; The Brand Lab in the School of Mass Communication; Shawn M. Donnelley Center for Nonprofit Communications; audio recording/video editing studio; Center for International Education; University Sports Complex with suspended pool; Career Development Center; Jesuit Social Research Institute; Business Portfolio Program; Office of Service Learning; the Pan-American Life Student Success Center; Louis J. Roussel Hall and Nunemaker Auditorium used for performances. **Computers:** 50% of classrooms, 100% of dorms, 100% of libraries, 100% of dining areas, 100% of student union, 100% of common outdoor areas have wireless network access. Students can register for classes online. Administrative functions (other than registration) can be performed online.

CAMPUS LIFE

Environment: Metropolis **Activities:** Campus Ministries; Choral groups; Concert band; Dance; Drama/theater; International Student Organization; Jazz band; Literary magazine; Music ensembles; Musical theater; Opera; Pep band; Radio station; Student government; Student newspaper; Student-run film society; Symphony orchestra; Television station; Yearbook 90 registered organizations, 13 honor societies, 4 religious organizations. 7 fraternities, 7 sororities. **Athletics (Intercollegiate):** *Men:* baseball, basketball, cross-country, track/field (outdoor), track/field (indoor). *Women:* basketball, cross-country, track/field (outdoor), track/field (indoor), volleyball. **On-Campus Highlights:** J. Edgar and Louise S. Monroe Library, Danna Student Center, University Sports Complex, Peace Quad, Residential Quad **Environmental Initiatives:** Formation of a committee that has representatives from important units on campus, including SGA and other student organizations. Full support of the Administration, starting with the President and Provost.

ADMISSIONS

Freshman Academic Profile: Average high school GPA 3.6. 31% in top 10% of high school class, 60% in top 25% of high school class, 87% in top 50% of high school class. 55% from public high schools. **Test Scores:** SAT Math middle 50% range 520-620. SAT EBRW middle 50% range 560-650. ACT middle 50% range 22-28. Minimum internet-based TOEFL 79. Minimum paper TOEFL 550. **Basis for Candidate Selection:** *Very important factors considered include:* rigor of secondary school record, academic GPA, standardized test scores. *Important factors considered include:* application essay, recommendation(s), extracurricular activities, talent/ability. *Other factors considered include:* class rank, interview, character/personal qualities, alumni/ae relation, geographical residence, volunteer work, work experience, level of applicant's interest. **Freshman Admission Requirements:** High school diploma is required and GED is accepted *Academic units required:* 4 English, 2 math, 2 science, 2 social studies, *Academic units recommended:* 4 English, 3 math, 3 science, 1 science labs, 2 foreign language, 2 social studies, 2 history. **Freshman Admission Statistics:** 5,112 applied, 69.1% admitted, 23% enrolled. **Transfer Admission Requirements:** college transcript(s), essay or personal statement, statement of good standing from prior institution(s). Minimum college GPA of 2.25 required. Lowest grade transferable C. **General Admission Information:** Priority deadline 11/15. Nonfall registration accepted. Admission may be deferred for a maximum of 1 year.

COSTS AND FINANCIAL AID

Annual tuition $38,126. Room and board $13,380. Required fees $1,566. Average book expense $1,276. **Required Forms and Deadlines:** FAFSA. **Notification of Awards:** Applicants will be notified of awards on a rolling basis beginning 3/1. **Types of Aid:** *Need-based scholarships/grants:* College/

university scholarship or grant aid from institutional funds; Federal Pell; Private scholarships; SEOG; State scholarships/grants; United Negro College Fund. *Loans:* Direct PLUS loans; Direct Subsidized Stafford Loans; Direct Unsubsidized Stafford Loans. *Student Employment:* Federal Work-Study Program available. Institutional employment available. **Financial Aid Statistics:** 100% needy freshmen, 99% needy undergrads receive need-based scholarship or grant aid. 13% freshmen, 11% undergrads receive non-need-based scholarship or grant aid. 85% freshmen, 84% undergrads receive need-based self-help aid. 3% freshmen, 3% undergrads receive athletic scholarships. 92% freshmen, 92% undergrads receive any aid. **Criteria for awarding aid:** *Need-based:* Academics, Alumni affiliation *Non-need-based:* Academics, Alumni affiliation, Art, Athletics, Music/drama.

LOYOLA UNIVERSITY CHICAGO

1032 W. Sheridan Rd., Chicago, IL 60611
Phone: 312-915-6500 · **Financial Aid Phone:** 773-508-7704
E-mail: admission@luc.edu · **CEEB Code:** 1412
Fax: 312-915-7216 · **Website:** www.luc.edu/

This private school, affiliated with the Roman Catholic-Jesuit Church, was founded in 1870. It has a 105 acre campus.

RATINGS

Admissions Selectivity Rating: 85   **Fire Safety Rating:** 97   **Green Rating:** 98

STUDENTS AND FACULTY

Enrollment: 11,193. **Student Body:** 66% female, 34% male, 35% out-of-state, 5% international (103 countries represented). Asian 12%, African American 6%, Caucasian 55%, Hispanic 16%, Native American <1%, Pacific Islander <1%, Two or more races 4%, Race unknown 1%.
Retention and Graduation: 83% freshmen return for sophomore year. 69% freshmen graduate within 4 years. 77% freshmen graduate within 6 years.
Faculty: Student/faculty ratio 14:1. 827 full-time faculty, 93% hold PhDs, 17% are members of minority groups, 48% are women. 0% of classes are taught by teaching assistants.

ACADEMICS

Degrees: Associate; Bachelor's; Certificate; Doctoral/Professional; Doctoral/Research; Master's; Post-Bachelor's certificate; Post-Master's certificate **Most popular majors:** Biology/Biological Sciences, General; Psychology, General; Registered Nursing/Registered Nurse. **Special Study Options:** Accelerated program; Distance learning; Double major; Dual enrollment; English as a Second Language (ESL); External degree program; Honors program; Independent study; Internships; Liberal arts/career combination; Study abroad; Teacher certification program. **Honors programs:** Loyola University Chicago offers an Interdisciplinary Honors Program that integrates a challenging academic program with service-learning opportunities. Taking a series of team-taught, interdisciplinary courses, students learn to perceive unexpected convergences among discrete facts, to synthesize information from many sources, and to use their knowledge to benefit society. **Combined degree programs:** BA/JD; BA/MA. **Disability Services offered to physically disabled students:** Note-taking services; Reader services; Tape recorders. **Career services:** Alumni network; Alumni services; Career assessment; Career/job search classes; Internships; Regional alumni

FACILITIES

Housing: Apartments for single students; Coed dorms; Special housing for disabled student; Special housing for international students 90% of campus accessible to physically diasbled. **Special Academic Facilities/Equipment:** theaters, art museums, digital media labs, convergence media studio, language learning resource center, neuroscience labs, clean energy lab, mock trial room, performance and specialized fine arts rooms, clinical simulation nursing laboratory, histology lab, geothermal system, ecodome greenhouse, aquaponics system showcase, artificial stream research facility, retreat and ecology campus **Computers:** 75% of classrooms, 60% of dorms, 95% of libraries, 50% of dining areas, 100% of student union, 40% of common outdoor areas have wireless network access. Students can register for classes online. Administrative functions (other than registration) can be performed online.

CAMPUS LIFE

Environment: Metropolis **Activities:** Campus Ministries; Choral groups; Concert band; Dance; Drama/theater; International Student Organization; Jazz band; Literary magazine; Model UN; Music ensembles; Musical theater; Pep band; Literary magazine; Model UN; Music ensembles; Musical theater; Pep band; Radio station; Student government; Student newspaper; Student-run film society; Television station 185 registered organizations, 11 honor societies, 9 religious organizations. 6 fraternities, 9 sororities. **Athletics (Intercollegiate):** *Men:* basketball, cheerleading, cross-country, golf, soccer, track/field (outdoor), track/field (indoor), volleyball. *Women:* basketball, cheerleading, cross-country, golf, soccer, softball, track/field (outdoor), track/field (indoor), volleyball. **On-Campus Highlights:** Damen Student center, Klarchek Information Commons, Institute of Environmental Sustainability, Halas Recreation Center, Madonna della Strada Chapel **Environmental Initiatives:** Carbon Neutral by 2025: Climate Acton Plan sets out goals for energy and conservation, clean energy and green transportation: Adopt green building design standards for all new construction. 30% reduction in greenhouse gas emissions since 2008. Lighting, heating/cooling retrofits, largest geothermal installation in Chicago. Biodiesel production from dining hall's waster vegetable oil used in campus shuttles. (www.luc.edu/biodiesel) Transportation: walk-to-work program, bicycle program, electric vehicles, public transit passes for students, car sharing program.

ADMISSIONS

Freshman Academic Profile: Average high school GPA 3.7. 37% in top 10% of high school class, 70% in top 25% of high school class, 93% in top 50% of high school class. 66% from public high schools. **Test Scores:** SAT Math middle 50% range 550-650. SAT EBRW middle 50% range 570-660. ACT middle 50% range 24-29. Minimum internet-based TOEFL 79. Minimum paper TOEFL 550. **Basis for Candidate Selection:** *Very important factors considered include:* rigor of secondary school record, academic GPA, standardized test scores. *Important factors considered include:* application essay, recommendation(s), extracurricular activities, character/personal qualities, volunteer work.level of applicant's interest. *Other factors considered include:* class rank, interview, talent/ability, first generation, alumni/ae relation, geographical residence, state residency, work experience. **Freshman Admission Requirements:** High school diploma is required and GED is accepted *Academic units required:* 4 English, 3 math, 3 science, 2 foreign language, 2 social studies, 1 history, *Academic units recommended:* 4 English, 4 math, 3 science, 2 foreign language, 2 social studies, 2 history, 3 academic electives. **Freshman Admission Statistics:** 23,571 applied, 70.6% admitted, 16% enrolled. **Transfer Admission Requirements:** college transcript(s), Minimum college GPA of 2.0 required. Lowest grade transferable C. **General Admission Information:** Priority deadline 12/1. Nonfall registration accepted.

COSTS AND FINANCIAL AID

Annual tuition $42,690. Room and board $14,480. Required fees $1,358. Average book expense $1,200. **Required Forms and Deadlines:** FAFSA. **Notification of Awards:** Applicants will be notified of awards on a rolling basis beginning 2/15. **Types of Aid:** *Need-based scholarships/grants:* College/university scholarship or grant aid from institutional funds; Federal Pell; Private scholarships; SEOG; State scholarships/grants. *Loans:* Direct PLUS loans; Direct Subsidized Stafford Loans; Direct Unsubsidized Stafford Loans. *Student Employment:* Institutional employment available. **Financial Aid Statistics:** 98% needy freshmen, 95% needy undergrads receive need-based scholarship or grant aid. 11% freshmen, 9% undergrads receive non-need-based scholarship or grant aid. 83% freshmen, 83% undergrads receive need-based self-help aid. 1% freshmen, 1% undergrads receive athletic scholarships. 97% freshmen, 88% undergrads receive any aid. 71% undergrads borrow to pay for school. Average cumulative indebtedness $31,750. **Criteria for awarding aid:** *Non-need-based:* Academics, Art, Athletics, Leadership, Music/drama, Religious affiliation.

LUBBOCK CHRISTIAN UNIVERSITY

5601 19th Street, Lubbock, TX 79407
Phone: 800-720-7151 · **Financial Aid Phone:** 806-720-7176
E-mail: admissions@lcu.edu · **CEEB Code:** 6378
Fax: 806-720-7162 · **Website:** www.lcu.edu · **ACT Code:** 4123

This private school, affiliated with the Church of Christ, was founded in 1957. It has a 120 acre campus.

RATINGS

Admissions Selectivity Rating: 72   **Fire Safety Rating:** 72   **Green Rating:** 61

STUDENTS AND FACULTY

Enrollment: 1,496. **Student Body:** 59% female, 41% male, 9% out-of-state, 2% international (21 countries represented). Asian 1%, African American 5%, Caucasian 66%, Hispanic 25%, Native American 1%, Pacific Islander <1%, Two or more races 0%, Race unknown 0%.

Retention and Graduation: 73% freshmen return for sophomore year. 16% grads go on to further study within 1 year. 0% grads pursue arts and sciences degrees. 14% grads pursue law degrees. 7% grads pursue business degrees. 0% grads pursue medical degrees. **Faculty:** Student/faculty ratio 13:1. 99 full-time faculty, 73% hold PhDs, 4% are members of minority groups, 43% are women. 0% of classes are taught by teaching assistants.

ACADEMICS

Degrees: Associate; Bachelor's; Master's **Classes:** Most classes have fewer than 10 students. Most lab/discussion sessions have fewer than 10 students. **Special Study Options:** Distance learning; Double major; Dual enrollment; Honors program; Internships; Liberal arts/career combination; Study abroad; Teacher certification program. **Honors programs:** Honors program available to all majors. **Disability Services offered to physically disabled students:** Tape recorders; Tutors. **Career services:** Alumni services; Career assessment; Career/job search classes; Internships

FACILITIES

Housing: Apartments for married students; Apartments for single students; Men's dorms; Women's dorms 78% of campus accessible to physically diasbled. **Special Academic Facilities/Equipment:** Pioneer Gallery, Rhodes Perrin Rec Center. **Computers:** Students can register for classes online.

CAMPUS LIFE

Environment: City **Activities:** Campus Ministries; Choral groups; Concert band; Drama/theater; International Student Organization; Jazz band; Music ensembles; Musical theater; Pep band; Radio station; Student government; Student newspaper; Yearbook 24 registered organizations, 3 honor societies, 4 fraternities, 4 sororities. **Athletics (Intercollegiate):** *Men:* baseball, basketball, cheerleading, golf. *Women:* basketball, cheerleading, golf, volleyball. **On-Campus Highlights:** Student Union Building, Rhodes Perrin Fitness Center, Rip Griffin Athletic Center, Library, Starbucks

ADMISSIONS

Freshman Academic Profile: Average high school GPA 3.5. 19% in top 10% of high school class, 43% in top 25% of high school class, 74% in top 50% of high school class. 83% from public high schools. **Test Scores:** SAT Math middle 50% range 430-555. SAT EBRW middle 50% range 440-550. ACT middle 50% range 19-25. Minimum internet-based TOEFL 71. Minimum paper TOEFL 525. **Basis for Candidate Selection:** *Very important factors considered include:* standardized test scores. *Other factors considered include:* rigor of secondary school record, class rank, academic GPA, recommendation(s), extracurricular activities, talent/ability, character/personal qualities, first generation, alumni/ae relation, volunteer work, work experience, level of applicant's interest. **Freshman Admission Requirements:** High school diploma is required and GED is accepted *Academic units recommended:* 4 English, 3 math, 3 science, 2 science labs, 2 foreign language, 1 social studies, 2 history, 2 academic electives, 1 computer science, 1 visual/performing arts. **Freshman Admission Statistics:** 867 applied, 96.1% admitted, 33% enrolled. **Transfer Admission Requirements:** college transcript(s), statement of good standing from prior institution(s). Lowest grade transferable C. **General Admission Information:** Application fee $25. Regular application deadline 6/1. Nonfall registration accepted.

COSTS AND FINANCIAL AID

Annual tuition $20,360. Room and board $6,070. Average book expense $1,100. **Required Forms and Deadlines:** FAFSA; Institution's own financial aid form. **Notification of Awards:** Applicants will be notified of awards on a rolling basis beginning 3/1. **Types of Aid:** *Need-based scholarships/grants:* Federal Pell; SEOG; State scholarships/grants. *Loans:* Direct PLUS loans; Direct Subsidized Stafford Loans; Direct Unsubsidized Stafford Loans. *Student Employment:* Federal Work-Study Program available. **Financial Aid Statistics:** 99% needy freshmen, 97% needy undergrads receive need-based scholarship or grant aid. 9% freshmen, 10% undergrads receive non-need-based scholarship or grant aid. 90% freshmen, 89% undergrads receive need-based self-help aid. 8% freshmen, 6% undergrads receive athletic scholarships. 98% freshmen, 83% undergrads receive any aid. **Criteria for awarding aid:** *Non-need-based:* Academics, Athletics, Leadership, Music/drama, Religious affiliation.

LUTHER COLLEGE

700 College Drive, Decorah, IA 52101-1042
Phone: 563-387-1287 • **Financial Aid Phone:** (563) 387-1018
E-mail: admissions@luther.edu • **CEEB Code:** 6375
Fax: 563-387-2159 • **Website:** www.luther.edu • **ACT Code:** 1330

This private school, affiliated with the Lutheran Church, was founded in 1861. It has a 200 acre campus.

RATINGS

Admissions Selectivity Rating: 84   **Fire Safety Rating:** 74   **Green Rating:** 94

STUDENTS AND FACULTY

Enrollment: 2,008. **Student Body:** 55% female, 45% male, 71% out-of-state, 8% international (73 countries represented). Asian 1%, African American 2%, Caucasian 81%, Hispanic 5%, Native American <1%, Pacific Islander <1%, Two or more races 2%, Race unknown 0%.
Retention and Graduation: 83% freshmen return for sophomore year. 71% freshmen graduate within 4 years. 80% freshmen graduate within 6 years. 16% grads go on to further study within 1 year. 10% grads pursue arts and sciences degrees. 5% grads pursue law degrees. 2% grads pursue business degrees. 16% grads pursue medical degrees. **Faculty:** Student/faculty ratio 11:1. 168 full-time faculty, 95% hold PhDs, 11% are members of minority groups, 48% are women. 0% of classes are taught by teaching assistants.

ACADEMICS

Degrees: Bachelor's **Classes:** Most classes have 10-19 students. Most lab/discussion sessions have 10-19 students. **Most popular majors:** Biology/Biological Sciences, General; Psychology, General; Music, General. **Special Study Options:** Double major; Dual enrollment; Honors program; Independent study; Internships; Student-designed major; Study abroad; Teacher certification program. **Honors programs:** The Scholars Program at Luther has the following goals? to challenge intellectually talented students to excel academically, to encourage them to develop a wide-ranging interest in the conversation of ideas and to engage in independent and self-motivated learning, to offer them opportunities to enrich the cultural life of the community, to enable them to become attractive candidates for graduate and professional school and professional employment, and to prepare them for exceptional achievement and service. **Disability Services offered to physically disabled students:** Note-taking services; Reader services; Tutors. **Career services:** Alumni network; Career assessment; Career/job search classes; Internships; Regional alumni

FACILITIES

Housing: Apartments for married students; Apartments for single students; Coed dorms; Special housing for disabled student; Wellness housing 95% of campus accessible to physically diasbled. **Special Academic Facilities/Equipment:** Natural history museum, Norwegian-American museum, five art galleries, planetarium, live animal center, archaeological research center, computer music lab, two electron microscopes, wind turbine. **Computers:** 90% of classrooms, 75% of dorms, 90% of libraries, 90% of dining areas, 90% of student union, 25% of common outdoor areas have wireless network access. Students can register for classes online. Administrative functions (other than registration) can be performed online.

CAMPUS LIFE

Environment: Village **Activities:** Campus Ministries; Choral groups; Concert band; Dance; Drama/theater; International Student Organization; Jazz band; Literary magazine; Model UN; Music ensembles; Musical theater; Opera; Pep band; Radio station; Student government; Student newspaper; Symphony orchestra 83 registered organizations, 13 honor societies, 8 religious organizations. 1 fraternity, 3 sororities. **Athletics (Intercollegiate):** *Men:* baseball, basketball, cross-country, diving, football, golf, soccer, swimming, tennis, track/field (outdoor), track/field (indoor), wrestling. *Women:* basketball, cross-country, diving, golf, soccer, softball, swimming, tennis, track/field (outdoor), track/field (indoor), volleyball. **On-Campus Highlights:** Marty's Cyber Cafe, Legends Fitness Center, The Cafeteria, Residence Hall Lounges, Sunnyside Cafe in the Center for the Arts **Environmental Initiatives:** Energy audit and efficiency upgrades totaling $1.5 million and has reduced campus carbon footprint by 15%

ADMISSIONS

Freshman Academic Profile: Average high school GPA 3.7. 26% in top 10% of high school class, 54% in top 25% of high school class, 86% in top 50% of high school class. 90% from public high schools. **Test Scores:** SAT Math middle 50% range 520-665. SAT EBRW middle 50% range 503-640. ACT middle 50% range 23-28. Minimum internet-based TOEFL 80. Minimum paper TOEFL 550. **Basis for Candidate Selection:** *Very important factors considered include:* rigor of secondary school record, class rank, academic GPA, standardized test scores, recommendation(s). *Important factors considered*

include: extracurricular activities, talent/ability, character/personal qualities. *Other factors considered include:* application essay, interview, first generation, alumni/ae relation, racial/ethnic status, volunteer work, level of applicant's interest. **Freshman Admission Requirements:** High school diploma is required and GED is accepted *Academic units recommended:* 4 English, 3 math, 2 science, 1 science labs, 2 foreign language, 3 social studies. **Freshman Admission Statistics:** 4,288 applied, 65.1% admitted, 19% enrolled. **Transfer Admission Requirements:** High school transcript, college transcript(s), essay or personal statement, standardized test scores, Minimum college GPA of 2.50 required. Lowest grade transferable C. **General Admission Information:** Nonfall registration accepted. Admission may be deferred for a maximum of 1 year.

COSTS AND FINANCIAL AID

Annual tuition $41,950. Required fees $340. Average book expense $1,040. **Required Forms and Deadlines:** FAFSA; Institution's own financial aid form. **Notification of Awards:** Applicants will be notified of awards on a rolling basis beginning 3/15. **Types of Aid:** *Need-based scholarships/grants:* College/university scholarship or grant aid from institutional funds; Federal Pell; Private scholarships; SEOG; State scholarships/grants. *Loans:* Direct PLUS loans; Direct Subsidized Stafford Loans; Direct Unsubsidized Stafford Loans. *Student Employment:* Federal Work-Study Program available. Institutional employment available. **Financial Aid Statistics:** 100% needy freshmen, 100% needy undergrads receive need-based scholarship or grant aid. 26% freshmen, 18% undergrads receive non-need-based scholarship or grant aid. 73% freshmen, 81% undergrads receive need-based self-help aid. 0% freshmen, 0% undergrads receive athletic scholarships. 98% freshmen, 97% undergrads receive any aid. 69% undergrads borrow to pay for school. Average cumulative indebtedness $35,642. **Criteria for awarding aid:** *Non-need-based:* Academics, Alumni affiliation, Art, Minority status, Music/drama.

LYCOMING COLLEGE

Best Colleges

700 College Place, Williamsport, PA 17701
Phone: 570-321-4026 • **Financial Aid Phone:** 570-321-4040
E-mail: admissions@lycoming.edu • **CEEB Code:** 2372
Fax: 570-321-4317 • **Website:** www.lycoming.edu • **ACT Code:** 3622

This private school, affiliated with the Methodist Church, was founded in 1812. It has a 39 acre campus.

RATINGS

Admissions Selectivity Rating: 82   **Fire Safety Rating:** 87   **Green Rating:** 77

STUDENTS AND FACULTY

Enrollment: 1,192. **Student Body:** 50% female, 50% male, 41% out-of-state, 5% international (21 countries represented). Asian 1%, African American 12%, Caucasian 63%, Hispanic 10%, Native American <1%, Pacific Islander <1%, Two or more races 3%, Race unknown 5%.
Retention and Graduation: 80% freshmen return for sophomore year. 59% freshmen graduate within 4 years. 67% freshmen graduate within 6 years. 13% grads go on to further study within 1 year. **Faculty:** Student/faculty ratio 12:1. 89 full-time faculty, 94% hold PhDs, 4% are members of minority groups, 46% are women. 0% of classes are taught by teaching assistants.

ACADEMICS

Degrees: Bachelor's **Classes:** Most classes have 10-19 students. Most lab/discussion sessions have 10-19 students. **Most popular majors:** Biology/Biological Sciences, General; Psychology, General; Business Administration And Management, General. **Special Study Options:** Accelerated program; Cooperative education program; Cross-registration; Double major; Dual enrollment; Exchange student program (domestic); Honors program; Independent study; Internships; Student-designed major; Study abroad; Teacher certification program. **Honors programs:** Scholars Program offered to students through admissions process; each major also provides an Honors major option for students who wish to graduate with honors within their field of study. **Disability Services offered to physically disabled students:** Note-taking services; Reader services; Tutors. **Career services:** Alumni network; Alumni services; Career assessment; Career/job search classes; Internships; Regional alumni

FACILITIES

Housing: Apartments for single students; Coed dorms; Fraternity/sorority housing; Special housing for disabled student; Theme housing; Women's dorms

Special Academic Facilities/Equipment: Language lab, tissue culture lab, TV studio, planetarium, video conferencing. **Computers:** 100% of classrooms, 100% of dorms, 100% of libraries, 100% of dining areas, 100% of student union, 100% of common outdoor areas have wireless network access. Students can register for classes online. Administrative functions (other than registration) can be performed online.

CAMPUS LIFE

Environment: Town **Activities:** Campus Ministries; Choral groups; Concert band; Dance; Drama/theater; International Student Organization; Jazz band; Literary magazine; Music ensembles; Musical theater; Pep band; Radio station; Student government; Student newspaper; Student-run film society; Symphony orchestra; Yearbook 78 registered organizations, 20 honor societies, 3 religious organizations. 5 fraternities, 5 sororities. **Athletics (Intercollegiate):** *Men:* basketball, cross-country, football, golf, lacrosse, soccer, swimming, tennis, wrestling. *Women:* basketball, cross-country, golf, lacrosse, soccer, softball, swimming, tennis, volleyball. **On-Campus Highlights:** Lynn Science Center, Quad, Jack's Place, Cafe 1812 & Penny's Plaza, Recreation Center **Environmental Initiatives:** The College has a Sustainability Committee that is comprised of faculty, administrators and students. Several initiatives have emerged from this group including using the grease waste from campus dining and converting it into biodiesel.

ADMISSIONS

Freshman Academic Profile: Average high school GPA 3.4. 14% in top 10% of high school class, 33% in top 25% of high school class, 69% in top 50% of high school class. 90% from public high schools. **Test Scores:** SAT Math middle 50% range 498-600. SAT EBRW middle 50% range 490-600. ACT middle 50% range 21-25. Minimum internet-based TOEFL 70. Minimum paper TOEFL 525. **Basis for Candidate Selection:** *Very important factors considered include:* rigor of secondary school record, recommendation(s). *Important factors considered include:* class rank, academic GPA, application essay, standardized test scores, interview, racial/ethnic status. *Other factors considered include:* extracurricular activities, talent/ability, character/personal qualities, first generation, alumni/ae relation, geographical residence, state residency, volunteer work, work experience, level of applicant's interest. **Freshman Admission Requirements:** High school diploma is required and GED is accepted *Academic units required:* 4 English, 3 math, 3 science, 2 foreign language, 3 social studies, 2 academic electives, *Academic units recommended:* 4 English, 4 math, 3 science, 3 foreign language, 4 social studies, 3 academic electives. **Freshman Admission Statistics:** 1,924 applied, 64.0% admitted, 23% enrolled. **Transfer Admission Requirements:** college transcript(s), statement of good standing from prior institution(s). Minimum college GPA of 2.0 required. Lowest grade transferable C-. **General Admission Information:** Priority deadline 12/1. Nonfall registration accepted. Admission may be deferred for a maximum of 1 year.

COSTS AND FINANCIAL AID

Annual tuition $37,888. Room and board $11,980. Required fees $730. Average book expense $1,200. **Required Forms and Deadlines:** FAFSA. **Notification of Awards:** Applicants will be notified of awards on a rolling basis beginning 3/1. **Types of Aid:** *Need-based scholarships/grants:* College/university scholarship or grant aid from institutional funds; Federal Pell; Private scholarships; SEOG; State scholarships/grants. *Loans:* Direct PLUS loans; Direct Subsidized Stafford Loans; Direct Unsubsidized Stafford Loans. *Student Employment:* Federal Work-Study Program available. Institutional employment available. **Financial Aid Statistics:** 100% needy freshmen, 100% needy undergrads receive need-based scholarship or grant aid. 11% freshmen, 13% undergrads receive non-need-based scholarship or grant aid. 80% freshmen, 85% undergrads receive need-based self-help aid. 0% freshmen, 0% undergrads receive athletic scholarships. 100% freshmen, 100% undergrads receive any aid. **Criteria for awarding aid:** *Need-based:* Academics, Minority status *Non-need-based:* Academics, Art, Minority status, Music/drama.

LYME ACADEMY COLLEGE OF FINE ARTS

84 Lyme Street, Old Lyme, CT 06371
Phone: 860-434-3571 x118 · **Financial Aid Phone:** 860-434-5232
E-mail: admissions@lymeacademy.edu · **CEEB Code:** 1971
Fax: 860-434-8725 · **Website:** http://www.lymeacademy.edu/

This private school was founded in 1976. It has a 47 acre campus.

RATINGS

Admissions Selectivity Rating: 81   **Fire Safety Rating:** 60*   **Green Rating:** 60*

STUDENTS AND FACULTY

Enrollment: 92. **Student Body:** 63% female, 37% male, 47% out-of-state, 0% international (0 countries represented). Asian 1%, African American 4%, Caucasian 88%, Hispanic 1%, Native American 3%, Pacific Islander 1%, Two or more races 3%, Race unknown 0%.
Retention and Graduation: 89% freshmen return for sophomore year. 10% grads go on to further study within 1 year. **Faculty:** Student/faculty ratio 14:1. 8 full-time faculty, 75% hold PhDs, 0% are members of minority groups, 38% are women. 0% of classes are taught by teaching assistants.

ACADEMICS

Degrees: Bachelor's; Certificate; Post-Bachelor's certificate **Classes:** Most classes have 10-19 students. Most lab/discussion sessions have fewer than 10 students. **Most popular majors:** Illustration; Painting; Sculpture. **Special Study Options:** Independent study.

FACILITIES

Housing: 95% of campus accessible to physically disabled. **Special Academic Facilities/Equipment:** Sill House Gallery, Chauncey Stillman Gallery, Academy Wood Shop, Sculpture Casting rooms **Computers:** 20% of classrooms, 100% of libraries, 100% of dining areas, 100% of student union, 40% of common outdoor areas have wireless network access.

CAMPUS LIFE

Environment: Village **Activities:** Literary magazine; Student government; Student-run film society. **On-Campus Highlights:** Chauncey Stillman Art Gallery, Cafe, Student Commons, Library, Sill House Art Gallery

ADMISSIONS

Freshman Academic Profile: Average high school GPA 3.2. 85% from public high schools. **Test Scores:** SAT Math middle 50% range 395-555. SAT EBRW middle 50% range 440-650. Minimum paper TOEFL 550. **Basis for Candidate Selection:** *Very important factors considered include:* academic GPA, interview, talent/ability, character/personal qualities, level of applicant's interest. *Important factors considered include:* rigor of secondary school record, application essay, recommendation(s). *Other factors considered include:* standardized test scores, racial/ethnic status. **Freshman Admission Requirements:** High school diploma is required and GED is accepted **Freshman Admission Statistics:** 82 applied, 68.3% admitted, 43% enrolled. **Transfer Admission Requirements:** college transcript(s), essay or personal statement, interview, Minimum college GPA of 2.0 required. Lowest grade transferable C. **General Admission Information:** Application fee $55. Nonfall registration accepted. Admission may be deferred for a maximum of 1 year.

COSTS AND FINANCIAL AID

Annual tuition $25,248. Required fees $1,536. Average book expense $1,500. **Required Forms and Deadlines:** FAFSA. **Notification of Awards:** Applicants will be notified of awards on a rolling basis beginning 3/1. **Types of Aid:** *Need-based scholarships/grants:* College/university scholarship or grant aid from institutional funds; Federal Pell; Private scholarships; SEOG; State scholarships/grants. *Loans:* Direct PLUS loans; Direct Subsidized Stafford Loans; Direct Unsubsidized Stafford Loans. *Student Employment:* Federal Work-Study Program available. Institutional employment available. **Financial Aid Statistics:** 0% freshmen, 0% undergrads receive athletic scholarships. 88% freshmen, 84% undergrads receive any aid. **Criteria for awarding aid:** *Need-based:* Alumni affiliation, Art, Job skills, Minority status *Non-need-based:* Academics, Art, Leadership.

LYNN UNIVERSITY

3601 North Military Trail, Boca Raton, FL 33431-5598
Phone: 561-237-7900 · **Financial Aid Phone:** (561) 237-7973
E-mail: admission@lynn.edu · **CEEB Code:** 5437
Fax: 561-237-7100 · **Website:** www.lynn.edu · **ACT Code:** 706

This private school was founded in 1962. It has a 123 acre campus.

RATINGS
Admissions Selectivity Rating: 73   **Fire Safety Rating:** 98   **Green Rating:** 93

STUDENTS AND FACULTY
Enrollment: 2,182. **Student Body:** 48% female, 52% male, 41% out-of-state, 17% international (94 countries represented). Asian 1%, African American 11%, Caucasian 44%, Hispanic 15%, Native American <1%, Pacific Islander 0%, Two or more races 1%, Race unknown 10%.
Retention and Graduation: 69% freshmen return for sophomore year. 44% freshmen graduate within 4 years. 51% freshmen graduate within 6 years. **Faculty:** Student/faculty ratio 17:1. 127 full-time faculty, 61% hold PhDs, 13% are members of minority groups, 41% are women. 0% of classes are taught by teaching assistants.

ACADEMICS
Degrees: Associate; Bachelor's; Doctoral; Master's; Post-Bachelor's certificate; Post-Master's certificate **Classes:** Most classes have 10-19 students. Most lab/discussion sessions have 10-19 students. **Most popular majors:** Sport And Fitness Administration/Management; Entrepreneurship/Entrepreneurial Studies; International Business/Trade/Commerce. **Special Study Options:** Accelerated program; Distance learning; Double major; Dual enrollment; English as a Second Language (ESL); Independent study; Internships; Student-designed major; Study abroad; Teacher certification program. **Combined degree programs:** BA/JD. **Disability Services offered to physically disabled students:** Tape recorders; Tutors. **Career services:** Alumni network; Alumni services; Career assessment; Career/job search classes; Internships; Regional alumni

FACILITIES
Housing: Coed dorms; Special housing for disabled students 99% of campus accessible to physically diasbled. **Special Academic Facilities/Equipment:** 3D Printer, IBC, Lynn Library **Computers:** Students can register for classes online. Administrative functions (other than registration) can be performed online.

CAMPUS LIFE
Environment: City **Activities:** Campus Ministries; Dance; Drama/theater; International Student Organization; Literary magazine; Model UN; Music ensembles; Musical theater; Radio station; Student government; Student newspaper; Student-run film society; Symphony orchestra; Television station 25 registered organizations, 4 honor societies, 4 religious organizations. 2 fraternities, 1 sorority. **Athletics (Intercollegiate):** *Men:* baseball, basketball, golf, soccer, tennis. *Women:* basketball, golf, soccer, softball, tennis, volleyball. **On-Campus Highlights:** The International Business Center, The Wold Performing Arts Center, The Eugene M. and Christine E. Lynn Library, Elmore Dining Commons, Bobby Campbell Stadium **Environmental Initiatives:** Lynn's Going Green initiatives include a complete campus retrofit of water fixtures and lighting equipment (over 7,500 light bulbs changed out in 2012). These projects also include building a new Central Energy Plant, complete retrofit of campus A/C equipment, boilers and hot water heaters, as well as other measures to save energy. This project was completed in January of 2015.

ADMISSIONS
Freshman Academic Profile: Average high school GPA 3.0. **Test Scores:** ACT middle 50% range 19-24. Minimum internet-based TOEFL 71. Minimum paper TOEFL 525. **Basis for Candidate Selection:** *Very important factors considered include:* rigor of secondary school record, academic GPA, application essay. *Important factors considered include:* class rank, standardized test scores, recommendation(s), interview, extracurricular activities, character/personal qualities, volunteer work, work experience. *Other factors considered include:* level of applicant's interest. **Freshman Admission Requirements:** High school diploma is required and GED is accepted *Academic units recommended:* 4 English, 4 math, 4 science, 2 social studies, 2 history. **Freshman Admission Statistics:** 3,003 applied, 84.6% admitted, 19% enrolled. **Transfer Admission Requirements:** college transcript(s), essay or personal statement, statement of good standing from prior institution(s). Minimum college GPA of 2.0 required. Lowest grade transferable C. **General Admission Information:** Application fee $45. Priority deadline 3/1. Regular application deadline 8/1. Nonfall registration accepted. Admission may be deferred.

COSTS AND FINANCIAL AID
Annual tuition $35,960. Room and board $12,170. Required fees $2,250. Average book expense $800. **Required Forms and Deadlines:** FAFSA. **Notification of Awards:** Applicants will be notified of awards on a rolling basis beginning 11/1. **Types of Aid:** *Need-based scholarships/grants:* College/university scholarship or grant aid from institutional funds; Federal Pell; Private scholarships; SEOG; State scholarships/grants. *Loans:* Direct PLUS loans; Direct Subsidized Stafford Loans; Direct Unsubsidized Stafford Loans. *Student Employment:* Federal Work-Study Program available. Institutional employment available. **Financial Aid Statistics:** 84% needy freshmen, 84% needy undergrads receive need-based scholarship or grant aid. 96% freshmen, 88% undergrads receive non-need-based scholarship or grant aid. 80% freshmen, 76% undergrads receive need-based self-help aid. 12% freshmen, 7% undergrads receive athletic scholarships. 95% freshmen, 80% undergrads receive any aid. 30% undergrads borrow to pay for school. Average cumulative indebtedness $33,689. **Criteria for awarding aid:** *Need-based:* Leadership *Non-need-based:* Academics, Alumni affiliation, Athletics, Leadership, Music/drama.

LYON COLLEGE

PO Box 2317, Batesville, AR 72503-2317
Phone: 870-307-7250 · **Financial Aid Phone:** 870-307-7257
E-mail: admissions@lyon.edu · **CEEB Code:** 1088
Website: www.lyon.edu · **ACT Code:** 112

This private school, affiliated with the Presbyterian Church, was founded in 1872. It has a 136 acre campus.

RATINGS
Admissions Selectivity Rating: 82   **Fire Safety Rating:** 83   **Green Rating:** 60*

STUDENTS AND FACULTY
Enrollment: 664. **Student Body:** 45% female, 55% male, 32% out-of-state, 4% international (12 countries represented). Asian 3%, African American 7%, Caucasian 70%, Hispanic 8%, Native American 2%, Pacific Islander 0%, Two or more races 0%, Race unknown 6%.
Retention and Graduation: 62% freshmen return for sophomore year. 48% freshmen graduate within 4 years. 1% freshmen graduate within 6 years. 26% grads go on to further study within 1 year. **Faculty:** Student/faculty ratio 14:1. 43 full-time faculty, 98% hold PhDs, 5% are members of minority groups, 33% are women. 0% of classes are taught by teaching assistants.

ACADEMICS
Degrees: Bachelor's **Classes:** Most classes have 20-29 students. Most lab/discussion sessions have 20-29 students. **Most popular majors:** English Language And Literature, General; Biology/Biological Sciences, General; Psychology, General. **Special Study Options:** Double major; Dual enrollment; English as a Second Language (ESL); Honors program; Independent study; Internships; Student-designed major; Study abroad; Teacher certification program. **Combined degree programs:** BA/MEng. **Disability Services offered to physically disabled students:** Tape recorders. **Career services:** Alumni network; Alumni services; Career assessment; Career/job search classes; Internships; Regional alumni

FACILITIES
Housing: Apartments for married students; Apartments for single students; Coed dorms; Theme housing 80% of campus accessible to physically diasbled. **Special Academic Facilities/Equipment:** Ozark Regional Studies Center **Computers:** 100% of classrooms, 100% of dorms, 100% of libraries, 100% of dining areas, 100% of student union, 100% of common outdoor areas have wireless network access. Students can register for classes online. Administrative functions (other than registration) can be performed online.

CAMPUS LIFE
Environment: Village **Activities:** Campus Ministries; Choral groups; Dance; Drama/theater; International Student Organization; Jazz band; Marching band; Model UN; Pep band; Student government; Student newspaper; Student-run film society 44 registered organizations, 9 honor societies, 7 religious organizations. 3 fraternities, 2 sororities. **Athletics (Intercollegiate):** *Men:* baseball, basketball, cheerleading, cross-country, golf, soccer. *Women:* basketball, cheerleading, cross-country, golf, soccer, softball, volleyball. **On-Campus Highlights:** Derby Center for Science and Mathematics, Becknell Gymnasium, Holloway Theater, Edwards Commons / Bookstore, Mabee Simpson Library

ADMISSIONS

Freshman Academic Profile: Average high school GPA 3.6. 27% in top 10% of high school class, 49% in top 25% of high school class, 82% in top 50% of high school class. **Test Scores:** SAT Math middle 50% range 520-633. SAT EBRW middle 50% range 510-603. ACT middle 50% range 22-28. Minimum internet-based TOEFL 79. Minimum paper TOEFL 550. **Basis for Candidate Selection:** *Very important factors considered include:* academic GPA, standardized test scores. **Freshman Admission Requirements:** High school diploma is required and GED is accepted *Academic units required:* **Freshman Admission Statistics:** 1,652 applied, 64.3% admitted, 18% enrolled. **Transfer Admission Requirements:** college transcript(s), statement of good standing from prior institution(s). Minimum college GPA of 2.75 required. Lowest grade transferable C. **General Admission Information:** Nonfall registration accepted. Admission may be deferred for a maximum of 1 fall term.

COSTS AND FINANCIAL AID

Annual tuition $28,200. Room and board $9,130. Required fees $590. Average book expense $1,500. **Required Forms and Deadlines:** FAFSA; State aid form. **Notification of Awards:** Applicants will be notified of awards on a rolling basis beginning 12/1. **Types of Aid:** *Need-based scholarships/grants:* College/university scholarship or grant aid from institutional funds; Federal Pell; Private scholarships; SEOG; State scholarships/grants. *Loans:* Direct PLUS loans; Direct Subsidized Stafford Loans; Direct Unsubsidized Stafford Loans. *Student Employment:* Federal Work-Study Program available. Institutional employment available. **Financial Aid Statistics:** 100% needy freshmen, 100% needy undergrads receive need-based scholarship or grant aid. 22% freshmen, 20% undergrads receive non-need-based scholarship or grant aid. 70% freshmen, 73% undergrads receive need-based self-help aid. 11% freshmen, 15% undergrads receive athletic scholarships. 100% freshmen, 99% undergrads receive any aid. 72% undergrads borrow to pay for school. **Criteria for awarding aid:** *Non-need-based:* Academics, Alumni affiliation, Art, Athletics, Music/drama, Religious affiliation, State/district residency.

MACALESTER COLLEGE

1600 Grand Avenue, St. Paul, MN 55105
Phone: 651-696-6357 · **Financial Aid Phone:** 651-696-6214
E-mail: admissions@macalester.edu · **CEEB Code:** 6390
Fax: 651-696-6724 · **Website:** www.macalester.edu · **ACT Code:** 2122

This private school was founded in 1874. It has a 53 acre campus.

RATINGS

Admissions Selectivity Rating: 93   **Fire Safety Rating:** 98   **Green Rating:** 95

STUDENTS AND FACULTY

Enrollment: 2,101. **Student Body:** 60% female, 40% male, 83% out-of-state, 15% international (90 countries represented). Asian 7%, African American 3%, Caucasian 61%, Hispanic 8%, Native American <1%, Pacific Islander <1%, Two or more races 6%, Race unknown <1%.
Retention and Graduation: 93% freshmen return for sophomore year. 85% freshmen graduate within 4 years. 87% freshmen graduate within 6 years. 14% grads go on to further study within 1 year. **Faculty:** Student/faculty ratio 10:1. 184 full-time faculty, 93% hold PhDs, 23% are members of minority groups, 53% are women. 0% of classes are taught by teaching assistants.

ACADEMICS

Degrees: Bachelor's **Most popular majors:** Biology/Biological Sciences, General; Mathematics, General; Political Science And Government, General. **Special Study Options:** Cross-registration; Double major; Honors program; Independent study; Internships; Student-designed major; Study abroad. **Honors programs:** The Honors Program is designed to enable seniors with demonstrated ability to undertake substantial independent work that culminates in a project of exceptionally high quality. **Disability Services offered to physically disabled students:** Note-taking services; Reader services; Tape recorders. **Career services:** Alumni network; Alumni services; Career assessment; Internships; Regional alumni

FACILITIES

Housing: Apartments for single students; Coed dorms; Cooperative housing; Special housing for disabled student; Theme housing; Wellness housing 90% of campus accessible to physically diasbled. **Special Academic Facilities/Equipment:** Digital Resource Center, econometrics lab, cartography lab, 250-

acre nature preserve, observatory and planetarium, two electron microscopes, nuclear magnetic resonance spectrometer, laser spectroscopy lab, X-ray diffractometer, Center for Study Away, Center for Scholarship and Teaching, Ethnographic lab, GIS lab, state-of-the-art science labs, fine arts gallery **Computers:** 100% of classrooms, 98% of dorms, 100% of libraries, 100% of dining areas, 100% of student union, 90% of common outdoor areas have wireless network access. Students can register for classes online. Administrative functions (other than registration) can be performed online.

CAMPUS LIFE

Environment: Metropolis **Activities:** Campus Ministries; Choral groups; Concert band; Dance; Drama/theater; International Student Organization; Jazz band; Literary magazine; Model UN; Music ensembles; Musical theater; Radio station; Student government; Student newspaper; Symphony orchestra 80 registered organizations, 15 honor societies, 10 religious organizations. **Athletics (Intercollegiate):** *Men:* baseball, basketball, cross-country, diving, football, golf, soccer, swimming, tennis, track/field (outdoor), track/field (indoor). *Women:* basketball, cross-country, diving, golf, soccer, softball, swimming, tennis, track/field (outdoor), track/field (indoor), volleyball, water polo. **On-Campus Highlights:** Idea Lab in DeWitt Wallace Library, Janet Wallace Fine Arts Center, Leonard Center (athletic facility), Bateman Plaza (our front patio), Shaw Field **Environmental Initiatives:** Developed a comprehensive sustainability plan.

ADMISSIONS

Freshman Academic Profile: 67% in top 10% of high school class, 91% in top 25% of high school class, 100% in top 50% of high school class. 65% from public high schools. **Test Scores:** SAT Math middle 50% range 640-740. SAT EBRW middle 50% range 660-740. ACT middle 50% range 29-32. **Basis for Candidate Selection:** *Very important factors considered include:* rigor of secondary school record, academic GPA. *Important factors considered include:* application essay, standardized test scores, recommendation(s), extracurricular activities, character/personal qualities. *Other factors considered include:* class rank, interview, talent/ability, first generation, alumni/ae relation, racial/ethnic status, volunteer work, work experience. **Freshman Admission Requirements:** High school diploma or equivalent is not required *Academic units recommended:* 4 English, 3 math, 3 science, 3 science labs, 3 foreign language, 3 social studies. **Freshman Admission Statistics:** 5,900 applied, 40.6% admitted, 23% enrolled. **Transfer Admission Requirements:** High school transcript, college transcript(s), essay or personal statement, standardized test scores, statement of good standing from prior institution(s). Lowest grade transferable C-. **General Admission Information:** Application fee $40. Regular application deadline 1/15. Nonfall registration accepted. Admission may be deferred for a maximum of 1 year.

COSTS AND FINANCIAL AID

Annual tuition $52,234. Required fees $230. Average book expense $1,145. **Required Forms and Deadlines:** CSS/Financial Aid PROFILE; FAFSA; Noncustodial PROFILE. **Notification of Awards:** Applicants will be notified of awards on or about 4/1. **Types of Aid:** *Need-based scholarships/grants:* College/university scholarship or grant aid from institutional funds; Federal Pell; Private scholarships; SEOG; State scholarships/grants. *Loans:* Direct PLUS loans; Direct Subsidized Stafford Loans; Direct Unsubsidized Stafford Loans. *Student Employment:* Federal Work-Study Program available. Institutional employment available. **Financial Aid Statistics:** 99% needy freshmen, 99% needy undergrads receive need-based scholarship or grant aid. 6% freshmen, 4% undergrads receive non-need-based scholarship or grant aid. 91% freshmen, 93% undergrads receive need-based self-help aid. 0% freshmen, 0% undergrads receive athletic scholarships. 79% freshmen, 79% undergrads receive any aid. 63% undergrads borrow to pay for school. Average cumulative indebtedness $23,875. **Criteria for awarding aid:** *Non-need-based:* Academics, Minority status.

MACMURRAY COLLEGE

447 East College, Jacksonville, IL 62650
Phone: 217-479-7056 · **Financial Aid Phone:** 217-479-7041
E-mail: admissions@mac.edu · **CEEB Code:** 1435
Fax: 217-291-0702 · **Website:** www.mac.edu · **ACT Code:** 1068

This private school, affiliated with the Methodist Church, was founded in 1846. It has a 60 acre campus.

RATINGS

Admissions Selectivity Rating: 82   **Fire Safety Rating:** 72   **Green Rating:** 60*

STUDENTS AND FACULTY

Enrollment: 581. **Student Body:** 66% female, 34% male, 11% out-of-state, <1% international (2 countries represented). Asian 1%, African American 13%, Caucasian 73%, Hispanic 3%, Native American 0%, Race unknown 10%. **Retention and Graduation:** 72% freshmen return for sophomore year. 25% grads go on to further study within 1 year. 9% grads pursue arts and sciences degrees. 1% grads pursue law degrees. 12% grads pursue business degrees. 1% grads pursue medical degrees. **Faculty:** Student/faculty ratio 14:1. 35 full-time faculty, 63% hold PhDs, 3% are members of minority groups, 74% are women. 0% of classes are taught by teaching assistants.

ACADEMICS

Degrees: Associate; Bachelor's **Classes:** Most classes have 20-29 students. Most lab/discussion sessions have 20-29 students. **Most popular majors:** Special Education And Teaching, General; Nursing/Registered Nurse (Rn, Asn, Bsn, Msn); Business, Management, Marketing, And Related Support Services. **Special Study Options:** Cooperative education program; Double major; Dual enrollment; Independent study; Internships; Liberal arts/career combination; Student-designed major; Study abroad; Teacher certification program. **Combined degree programs:** BA/MEng. **Disability Services offered to physically disabled students:** Note-taking services; Reader services; Tape recorders; Tutors. **Career services:** Alumni network; Alumni services; Career assessment; Career/job search classes; Internships; Regional alumni

FACILITIES

Housing: Coed dorms; Special housing for disabled student; Women's dorms 50% of campus accessible to physically diasbled. **Special Academic Facilities/Equipment:** Art gallery, language lab, music hall, nursing labs.

CAMPUS LIFE

Environment: Village **Activities:** Campus Ministries; Choral groups; Dance; Drama/theater; Literary magazine; Student government; Yearbook 37 registered organizations, 2 honor societies, 2 religious organizations. 2 fraternities, 1 sorority. **Athletics (Intercollegiate):** *Men:* baseball, basketball, football, golf, soccer, wrestling. *Women:* basketball, golf, soccer, softball, volleyball. **On-Campus Highlights:** Gamble Campus, Education Complex, Jane Hall, Putnam Center for the Arts, McClelland Dining Hall

ADMISSIONS

Freshman Academic Profile: Average high school GPA 2.8. 4% in top 10% of high school class, 28% in top 25% of high school class, 55% in top 50% of high school class. 75% from public high schools. **Test Scores:** SAT Math middle 50% range 430-500. SAT EBRW middle 50% range 370-470. ACT middle 50% range 17-23. Minimum paper TOEFL 550. **Basis for Candidate Selection:** *Very important factors considered include:* rigor of secondary school record, academic GPA, standardized test scores. *Important factors considered include:* class rank, extracurricular activities, character/personal qualities. *Other factors considered include:* application essay, recommendation(s), interview, volunteer work, work experience. **Freshman Admission Requirements:** High school diploma is required and GED is accepted *Academic units recommended:* 4 English, 3 math, 3 science, 2 science labs, 2 foreign language, 2 social studies, 3 history. **Freshman Admission Statistics:** 1,004 applied, 56.1% admitted, 31% enrolled. **Transfer Admission Requirements:** college transcript(s), Minimum college GPA of 2.0 required. Lowest grade transferable C. **General Admission Information:** Application fee $25. Priority deadline 5/1. Nonfall registration accepted. Admission may be deferred.

COSTS AND FINANCIAL AID

Annual tuition $15,500. Room and board $5,998. Required fees $250. Average book expense $775. **Required Forms and Deadlines:** FAFSA. **Notification of Awards:** Applicants will be notified of awards on a rolling basis beginning 2/1. **Types of Aid:** *Need-based scholarships/grants:* College/university scholarship or grant aid from institutional funds; Federal Nursing Scholarships; Federal Pell; Private scholarships; SEOG; State scholarships/grants. *Loans: Student Employment:* Federal Work-Study Program available. Institutional employment available. **Financial Aid Statistics:** 100% needy freshmen, 100% needy undergrads receive need-based scholarship or grant aid. 9% freshmen, 7% undergrads receive non-need-based scholarship or grant aid. 79% freshmen, 86% undergrads receive need-based self-help aid. 0% freshmen, 0% undergrads receive athletic scholarships. 95% freshmen, 97% undergrads receive any aid. **Criteria for awarding aid:** *Need-based:* Academics, Alumni affiliation, Art, Music/drama *Non-need-based:* Academics, Alumni affiliation, Art, Leadership, Music/drama, Religious affiliation.

MAHARISHI UNIVERSITY OF MANAGEMENT

1000 North Fourth Street, Fairfield, IA 52557
Phone: 641-472-1110 • **Financial Aid Phone:** 641-472-1156
E-mail: admissions@mum.edu
Fax: 641-472-1179 • **Website:** www.mum.edu • **ACT Code:** 1317

This private school was founded in 1971. It has a 242 acre campus.

RATINGS

Admissions Selectivity Rating: 66   **Fire Safety Rating:** 60*   **Green Rating:** 60*

STUDENTS AND FACULTY

Enrollment: 320. **Student Body:** 56% female, 44% male, 76% out-of-state, 6% international. Asian 3%, African American 7%, Caucasian 34%, Hispanic 8%, Native American 1%, Pacific Islander 1%, Two or more races 4%, Race unknown 37%. **Retention and Graduation:** 70% freshmen return for sophomore year. 84% grads go on to further study within 1 year. **Faculty:** 107 full-time faculty, 32% hold PhDs, 29% are members of minority groups, 26% are women. 0% of classes are taught by teaching assistants.

ACADEMICS

Degrees: Bachelor's; Certificate; Doctoral; Master's; Post-Bachelor's certificate **Classes:** Most classes have 10-19 students. Most lab/discussion sessions have fewer than 10 students. **Most popular majors:** Environmental Studies; Fine/Studio Arts, General; Business/Commerce, General. **Special Study Options:** Distance learning; Double major; English as a Second Language (ESL); Independent study; Internships; Student-designed major; Study abroad.

FACILITIES

Housing: Apartments for married students; Men's dorms; Special housing for disabled student; Women's dorms 80% of campus accessible to physically diasbled. **Special Academic Facilities/Equipment:** art gallery; scanning electron microscope; real-time cell-imaging computer system; DNA synthesizer; rock-climbing wall

CAMPUS LIFE

Environment: Village **Activities:** Choral groups; International Student Organization; Radio station; Student government; Student newspaper; Student-run film society; Yearbook 25 registered organizations, 3 honor societies, 1 religious organization. **Athletics (Intercollegiate):** *Men:* golf. *Women:* golf. **On-Campus Highlights:** Sustainable Living Center, Golden Domes, 60,000 sq. ft. Recreation Center, Student Cafe, Vedic Organic Greenhouses **Environmental Initiatives:** Four-year bachelors of Science degree offered in Sustainable Living.

ADMISSIONS

Freshman Academic Profile: Average high school GPA 3.6. 0% in top 10% of high school class, 0% in top 25% of high school class, 80% in top 50% of high school class. **Test Scores:** Minimum paper TOEFL 550. **Basis for Candidate Selection:** *Very important factors considered include:* application essay, recommendation(s), interview, level of applicant's interest. *Important factors considered include:* rigor of secondary school record, academic GPA, talent/ability, character/personal qualities. *Other factors considered include:* standardized test scores, extracurricular activities, alumni/ae relation, volunteer work, work experience. **Freshman Admission Requirements:** High school diploma is required and GED is accepted *Academic units recommended:* 4 English, 3 math, 2 science, 1 science labs, 1 social studies, 1 computer science. **Freshman Admission Statistics:** 83 applied, 89.2% admitted, 31% enrolled. **Transfer Admission Requirements:** High school transcript, college transcript(s), essay or personal statement, interview, Minimum college GPA of 2.5 required. Lowest grade transferable 2. **General Admission Information:** Application fee $20. Nonfall registration accepted. Admission may be deferred for a maximum of one semester.

COSTS AND FINANCIAL AID

Annual tuition $27,000. Room and board $7,400. Required fees $530. Average book expense $800. **Required Forms and Deadlines:** FAFSA. **Notification of Awards:** Applicants will be notified of awards on a rolling basis beginning 3/1. **Types of Aid:** *Need-based scholarships/grants:* College/university scholarship or grant aid from institutional funds; Federal Pell; Private scholarships; SEOG; State scholarships/grants. *Student Employment:* Federal Work-Study Program available. **Financial Aid Statistics:** 100% needy freshmen, 100% needy undergrads receive need-based scholarship or grant aid. 7% undergrads receive non-need-based scholarship or grant aid. 100% freshmen, 100% undergrads receive need-based self-help aid. 0% freshmen, 0% undergrads receive athletic scholarships. 93% freshmen, 98% undergrads receive any aid. **Criteria for awarding aid:** *Need-based:* Academics, Minority status, Music/drama *Non-need-based:* Academics, Alumni affiliation, Music/drama, State/district residency.

MALONE UNIVERSITY

2600 Cleveland Avenue NW, Canton, OH 44709
Phone: 330-471-8145 · **Financial Aid Phone:** 330-471-8161
E-mail: admissions@malone.edu · **CEEB Code:** 1439
Fax: 330-471-8149 · **Website:** www.malone.edu · **ACT Code:** 3289

This private school, affiliated with the Evangelical Friends Church— Eastern Region, was founded in 1892. It has a 96 acre campus.

RATINGS
Admissions Selectivity Rating: 78   **Fire Safety Rating:** 86   **Green Rating:** 61

STUDENTS AND FACULTY
Enrollment: 1,496. **Student Body:** 58% female, 42% male, 14% out-of-state, 1% international (17 countries represented). Asian 1%, African American 8%, Caucasian 84%, Hispanic 2%, Native American <1%, Pacific Islander <1%, Two or more races 2%, Race unknown <1%.
Retention and Graduation: 70% freshmen return for sophomore year. **Faculty:** Student/faculty ratio 12:1. 95 full-time faculty, 78% hold PhDs, 4% are members of minority groups, 52% are women. 0% of classes are taught by teaching assistants.

ACADEMICS
Degrees: Bachelor's; Master's; Post-Master's certificate **Classes:** Most classes have 10-19 students. Most lab/discussion sessions have fewer than 10 students. **Most popular majors:** Early Childhood Education And Teaching; Registered Nursing, Nursing Administration, Nursing Research And Clinical Nursing; Business/Commerce, General. **Special Study Options:** Accelerated program; Cross-registration; Distance learning; Double major; Dual enrollment; Exchange student program (domestic); Honors program; Independent study; Internships; Student-designed major; Study abroad; Teacher certification program. **Honors programs:** The purpose of the Malone University Honors Program is to support the university's intellectually gifted and highly motivated students, to create a community of students and faculty engaged in serious, substantive, and sustained critical inquiry, and to underscore the university's commitment to academic excellence. The Honors Program fulfills this purpose through pursuit of the following goals: 1. Challenging students to fulfill their intellectual and personal potential through enriching and stimulating experiences in and out of the classroom. 2. Cultivating an esprit de corps, committed to an earnest, cooperative, free, and open pursuit of truth. 3. Developing students' understanding of the unity of knowledge and the interrelationship of the academic disciplines. 4. Providing students the occasion for mentoring relationships with faculty. 5. Preparing students for the pursuit of original and advanced research, scholarship, and performance. 6. Equipping students for outstanding leadership in service to God, their communities, and the world. **Disability Services offered to physically disabled students:** Note-taking services; Reader services; Tape recorders; Tutors. **Career services:** Alumni network; Alumni services; Career assessment; Career/job search classes; Internships

FACILITIES
Housing: Men's dorms; Special housing for disabled student; Theme housing; Women's dorms **Computers:** 100% of classrooms, 85% of dorms, 100% of libraries, 100% of dining areas, 100% of student union, 40% of common outdoor areas have wireless network access. Students can register for classes online. Administrative functions (other than registration) can be performed online.

CAMPUS LIFE
Environment: City **Activities:** Campus Ministries; Choral groups; Concert band; Drama/theater; International Student Organization; Jazz band; Literary magazine; Marching band; Music ensembles; Musical theater; Opera; Radio station; Student government; Student newspaper; Student-run film society; Television station 53 registered organizations, 11 honor societies, 9 religious organizations. **Athletics (Intercollegiate):** *Men:* baseball, basketball, cheerleading, cross-country, diving, football, golf, soccer, swimming, tennis, track/field (outdoor), track/field (indoor). *Women:* basketball, cheerleading, cross-country, diving, golf, soccer, softball, swimming, tennis, track/field (outdoor), track/field (indoor), volleyball. **On-Campus Highlights:** Hoover Dining Commons—Brehme Centennial Center, Randall Campus Center, Wellness Center, Froggy's Cafe, Regula Cafe **Environmental Initiatives:** Recycling

ADMISSIONS
Freshman Academic Profile: Average high school GPA 3.3. 18% in top 10% of high school class, 44% in top 25% of high school class, 76% in top 50% of high school class. 80% from public high schools. **Test Scores:** SAT Math middle 50% range 473-570. SAT EBRW middle 50% range 430-570. ACT middle 50% range 20-25. Minimum internet-based TOEFL 79. Minimum paper TOEFL 550. **Basis for Candidate Selection:** *Very important factors considered include:* rigor of secondary school record, academic GPA, standardized test scores, character/personal qualities. *Important factors considered include:* class rank, talent/ability, religious affiliation/commitment. *Other factors considered include:* application essay, recommendation(s), interview, extracurricular activities, alumni/ae relation, racial/ethnic status, volunteer work, level of applicant's interest. **Freshman Admission Requirements:** High school diploma is required and GED is accepted *Academic units required:* 4 English, 3 math, 3 science, 1 science labs, 2 foreign language, 2 social studies, 1 history, 2 academic electives, 1 visual/performing arts. **Freshman Admission Statistics:** 1,327 applied, 71.7% admitted, 33% enrolled. **Transfer Admission Requirements:** High school transcript, college transcript(s), statement of good standing from prior institution(s). Minimum college GPA of 2.0 required. **General Admission Information:** Application fee $20. Nonfall registration accepted. Admission may be deferred for a maximum of 2 years.

COSTS AND FINANCIAL AID
Annual tuition $26,456. Room and board $9,266. Required fees $984. Average book expense $1,200. **Required Forms and Deadlines:** FAFSA. **Notification of Awards:** Applicants will be notified of awards on a rolling basis beginning 3/1. **Types of Aid:** *Need-based scholarships/grants:* College/university scholarship or grant aid from institutional funds; Federal Pell; Private scholarships; SEOG; State scholarships/grants. *Loans:* Direct PLUS loans; Direct Subsidized Stafford Loans; Direct Unsubsidized Stafford Loans. *Student Employment:* Federal Work-Study Program available. Institutional employment available. **Financial Aid Statistics:** 100% needy freshmen, 98% needy undergrads receive need-based scholarship or grant aid. 13% freshmen, 13% undergrads receive non-need-based scholarship or grant aid. 82% freshmen, 81% undergrads receive need-based self-help aid. 12% freshmen, 10% undergrads receive athletic scholarships. 100% freshmen, 95% undergrads receive any aid. **Criteria for awarding aid:** *Need-based:* Academics, Athletics, Leadership, Music/drama, Religious affiliation *Non-need-based:* Academics, Athletics, Leadership, Music/drama, Religious affiliation.

MANCHESTER UNIVERSITY

604 E. College Avenue, North Manchester, IN 46962
Phone: 260-982-5055 · **Financial Aid Phone:** 260-982-5066
E-mail: admitinfo@manchester.edu · **CEEB Code:** 1440
Fax: 260-982-5239 · **Website:** www.manchester.edu · **ACT Code:** 1222

This private school, affiliated with the Church of Brethren, was founded in 1889. It has a 125 acre campus.

RATINGS
Admissions Selectivity Rating: 79   **Fire Safety Rating:** 84   **Green Rating:** 60*

STUDENTS AND FACULTY
Enrollment: 1,254. **Student Body:** 52% female, 48% male, 12% out-of-state, 4% international (19 countries represented). Asian 2%, African American 7%, Caucasian 77%, Hispanic 6%, Native American <1%, Pacific Islander 0%, Two or more races 4%, Race unknown 1%.
Retention and Graduation: 69% freshmen return for sophomore year. 14% grads go on to further study within 1 year. 9% grads pursue arts and sciences degrees. 1.6% grads pursue law degrees. 0% grads pursue business degrees. 3% grads pursue medical degrees. **Faculty:** Student/faculty ratio 14:1. 82 full-time faculty, 87% hold PhDs, 10% are members of minority groups, 46% are women. 0% of classes are taught by teaching assistants.

ACADEMICS
Degrees: Associate; Bachelor's; Doctoral/Professional; Master's **Classes:** Most classes have fewer than 10 students. **Most popular majors:** Education, General; Health Services/Allied Health/Health Sciences, General. **Special Study Options:** Accelerated program; Distance learning; Double major; Dual enrollment; Exchange student program (domestic); Honors program; Independent study; Internships; Liberal arts/career combination; Student-designed major; Study abroad; Teacher certification program. **Honors programs:** An Honors Program for top students. **Disability Services offered to physically disabled students:** Reader services; Tape recorders; Tutors. **Career services:** Alumni network; Alumni services; Career assessment; Career/job search classes; Internships; Regional alumni

FACILITIES
Housing: Coed dorms; Special housing for disabled students **Special Academic Facilities/Equipment:** Observatory, environmental center and labs. **Computers:** 50% of classrooms, 100% of libraries, 100% of dining areas,

100% of student union, 5% of common outdoor areas have wireless network access. Students can register for classes online. Administrative functions (other than registration) can be performed online.

CAMPUS LIFE

Environment: Rural **Activities:** Campus Ministries; Choral groups; Concert band; Dance; Drama/theater; International Student Organization; Jazz band; Literary magazine; Model UN; Music ensembles; Opera; Pep band; Radio station; Student government; Student newspaper; Symphony orchestra; Yearbook 47 registered organizations, 3 honor societies, 5 religious organizations. **Athletics (Intercollegiate):** *Men:* baseball, basketball, cheerleading, cross-country, football, golf, soccer, tennis, track/field (outdoor), wrestling. *Women:* basketball, cheerleading, cross-country, golf, soccer, softball, tennis, track/field (outdoor), volleyball. **On-Campus Highlights:** Athletic Facilities, Residence Halls, College Union, Petersime Chapel, Science Center **Environmental Initiatives:** Over 25 years of active recyling on campus

ADMISSIONS

Freshman Academic Profile: Average high school GPA 3.3. 13% in top 10% of high school class, 34% in top 25% of high school class, 75% in top 50% of high school class. **Test Scores:** SAT Math middle 50% range 435-550. SAT EBRW middle 50% range 430-540. ACT middle 50% range 18-30. Minimum internet-based TOEFL 79. Minimum paper TOEFL 550. **Basis for Candidate Selection:** *Very important factors considered include:* rigor of secondary school record, class rank, academic GPA, recommendation(s). *Important factors considered include:* extracurricular activities, talent/ability, character/personal qualities. *Other factors considered include:* application essay, standardized test scores, interview, alumni/ae relation, volunteer work, work experience, level of applicant's interest. **Freshman Admission Requirements:** High school diploma is required and GED is accepted *Academic units required:* 4 English, 2 math, 2 science, 2 science labs, 1 social studies, 1 history, 2 academic electives, *Academic units recommended:* 4 English, 3 math, 3 science, 2 science labs, 2 foreign language, 2 social studies, 2 history, 2 academic electives, 1 computer science, 1 visual/performing arts. **Freshman Admission Statistics:** 2,431 applied, 70.5% admitted, 23% enrolled. **Transfer Admission Requirements:** High school transcript, college transcript(s), statement of good standing from prior institution(s). Minimum college GPA of 2.0 required. **General Admission Information:** Application fee $25. Priority deadline 12/31. Nonfall registration accepted. Admission may be deferred for a maximum of 1 year.

COSTS AND FINANCIAL AID

Annual tuition $30,450. Room and board $9,880. Required fees $1,210. Average book expense $1,000. **Required Forms and Deadlines:** FAFSA. **Notification of Awards:** Applicants will be notified of awards on a rolling basis beginning 3/18. **Types of Aid:** *Need-based scholarships/grants:* College/university scholarship or grant aid from institutional funds; Federal Pell; Private scholarships; SEOG; State scholarships/grants. *Loans:* Direct PLUS loans; Direct Subsidized Stafford Loans; Direct Unsubsidized Stafford Loans. *Student Employment:* Federal Work-Study Program available. Institutional employment available. **Financial Aid Statistics:** 100% needy freshmen, 99% needy undergrads receive need-based scholarship or grant aid. 11% freshmen, 12% undergrads receive non-need-based scholarship or grant aid. 89% freshmen, 88% undergrads receive need-based self-help aid. 0% freshmen, 0% undergrads receive athletic scholarships. 100% freshmen, 99% undergrads receive any aid. 87% undergrads borrow to pay for school. Average cumulative indebtedness $33,011. **Criteria for awarding aid:** *Non-need-based:* Academics, Alumni affiliation, Leadership, Minority status, Music/drama, Religious affiliation.

MANHATTAN COLLEGE

Manhattan College Parkway, Riverdale, NY 10471
Phone: 718-862-7200 · **Financial Aid Phone:** 718-862-7100
E-mail: admit@manhattan.edu · **CEEB Code:** 2395
Fax: 718-862-8019 · **Website:** www.manhattan.edu

This private school, affiliated with the Roman Catholic Church, was founded in 1853. It has a 22 acre campus.

RATINGS
Admissions Selectivity Rating: 79   **Fire Safety Rating:** 83   **Green Rating:** 65

STUDENTS AND FACULTY

Enrollment: 3,664. **Student Body:** 45% female, 55% male, 31% out-of-state, 3% international (46 countries represented). Asian 5%, African American 5%, Caucasian 55%, Hispanic 22%, Native American <1%, Pacific Islander <1%, Two or more races 2%, Race unknown 8%.
Retention and Graduation: 85% freshmen return for sophomore year. 71% freshmen graduate within 6 years. 28% grads go on to further study within 1 year. 0.5% grads pursue law degrees. 2% grads pursue business degrees. 0.5% grads pursue medical degrees. **Faculty:** Student/faculty ratio 13:1. 240 full-time faculty, 97% hold PhDs, 16% are members of minority groups, 45% are women. 0% of classes are taught by teaching assistants.

ACADEMICS

Degrees: Associate; Bachelor's; Master's; Post-Master's certificate **Classes:** Most classes have fewer than 10 students. **Most popular majors:** Special Education And Teaching, Other; Civil Engineering, General; Marketing/Marketing Management, General. **Special Study Options:** Distance learning; English as a Second Language (ESL); Independent study; Internships; Study abroad; Teacher certification program. **Honors programs:** Honors Enrichment Program **Combined degree programs:** BA/MA; BA/MEng. **Disability Services offered to physically disabled students:** Note-taking services; Reader services; Tape recorders; Tutors. **Career services:** Alumni network; Alumni services; Career assessment; Career/job search classes; Internships

FACILITIES

Housing: Apartments for married students; Apartments for single students; Coed dorms; Special housing for disabled student; Special housing for international students; Theme housing 100% of campus accessible to physically diasbled. **Special Academic Facilities/Equipment:** Research and learning center; 24-hour Internet cafe; Holocaust, Genocide and Interfaith Education Center, Center for Academic Success. **Computers:** 100% of classrooms, 50% of dorms, 100% of libraries, 100% of dining areas, 100% of student union, 100% of common outdoor areas have wireless network access. Students can register for classes online. Administrative functions (other than registration) can be performed online.

CAMPUS LIFE

Environment: Metropolis **Activities:** Campus Ministries; Choral groups; Concert band; Dance; Drama/theater; International Student Organization; Jazz band; Literary magazine; Model UN; Music ensembles; Musical theater; Pep band; Radio station; Student government; Student newspaper; Student-run film society; Symphony orchestra; Television station; Yearbook 64 registered organizations, 30 honor societies, 2 religious organizations. 2 fraternities, 2 sororities. **Athletics (Intercollegiate):** *Men:* baseball, basketball, cross-country, golf, lacrosse, soccer, tennis, track/field (outdoor), track/field (indoor). *Women:* basketball, cross-country, lacrosse, soccer, softball, swimming, tennis, track/field (outdoor), track/field (indoor), volleyball. **On-Campus Highlights:** Quadrangle, O'Malley Library, Internet Cafe, Draddy Gymnasium, Thomas Hall

ADMISSIONS

Freshman Academic Profile: Average high school GPA 89.6. 23% in top 10% of high school class, 54% in top 25% of high school class, 79% in top 50% of high school class. 57% from public high schools. **Test Scores:** SAT Math middle 50% range 520-620. SAT EBRW middle 50% range 530-623. ACT middle 50% range 23-28. Minimum internet-based TOEFL 80. Minimum paper TOEFL 550. **Basis for Candidate Selection:** *Very important factors considered include:* rigor of secondary school record, class rank, academic GPA, standardized test scores. *Important factors considered include:* application essay, recommendation(s). *Other factors considered include:* interview, extracurricular activities, talent/ability, character/personal qualities, first generation, alumni/ae relation, geographical residence, volunteer work, work experience, level of applicant's interest. **Freshman Admission Requirements:** High school diploma is required and GED is accepted *Academic units required:* 4 English, 3 math, 2 science, 2 science labs, 2 foreign language, 3 social studies, 2 academic electives, *Academic units recommended:* 4 English, 4 math, 4 science, 4 science labs, 3 foreign language, 4 social studies. **Freshman Admission Statistics:** 7,622 applied, 75.4% admitted, 13% enrolled. **Transfer Admission Requirements:** High school transcript, college transcript(s), standardized test scores, statement of good standing from prior institution(s). Minimum college GPA of 2.5 required. Lowest grade transferable C. **General Admission Information:** Application fee $75. Priority deadline 3/1. Nonfall registration accepted. Admission may be deferred for a maximum of 1 year.

COSTS AND FINANCIAL AID

Required Forms and Deadlines: FAFSA. **Notification of Awards:** Applicants will be notified of awards on a rolling basis beginning 2/15. **Types of Aid:** *Need-based scholarships/grants:* College/university scholarship or grant aid from institutional funds; Federal Pell; Private scholarships; SEOG; State scholarships/grants. *Loans:* Direct PLUS loans; Direct Subsidized Stafford Loans; Direct Unsubsidized Stafford Loans. *Student Employment:* Federal Work-Study Program available. Institutional employment available. **Financial Aid Statistics:** 80% needy undergrads receive need-based scholarship or grant aid. 14% freshmen, 11% undergrads receive non-need-based scholarship or grant aid. 56% freshmen, 58% undergrads receive need-based self-help aid. 3% freshmen, 3% undergrads receive athletic scholarships. 88% freshmen, 86% undergrads receive any aid. 97% undergrads borrow to pay for school. Average cumulative indebtedness $46,498. **Criteria for awarding aid:** *Need-based:* Academics, Music/drama *Non-need-based:* Academics, Athletics, State/district residency.

See page 976.

MANHATTANVILLE COLLEGE

2900 Purchase Street, Purchase, NY 10577
Phone: 914-323-5464 · **Financial Aid Phone:** 914-323-5357
E-mail: admissions@mville.edu · **CEEB Code:** 2397
Fax: 914-694-1732 · **Website:** www.mville.edu · **ACT Code:** 2800

This private school was founded in 1841. It has a 100 acre campus.

RATINGS
Admissions Selectivity Rating: 74   **Fire Safety Rating:** 98   **Green Rating:** 74

STUDENTS AND FACULTY
Enrollment: 1,674. **Student Body:** 63% female, 37% male, 27% out-of-state, 7% international (47 countries represented). Asian 2%, African American 9%, Caucasian 47%, Hispanic 25%, Native American <1%, Pacific Islander <1%, Two or more races 2%, Race unknown 7%.
Retention and Graduation: 74% freshmen return for sophomore year. 49% freshmen graduate within 4 years. 55% freshmen graduate within 6 years. 21% grads go on to further study within 1 year. 31% grads pursue arts and sciences degrees. 5.9% grads pursue law degrees. 16% grads pursue business degrees. 1.5% grads pursue medical degrees. **Faculty:** Student/faculty ratio 11:1. 118 full-time faculty, 86% hold PhDs, 16% are members of minority groups, 52% are women. 0% of classes are taught by teaching assistants.

ACADEMICS
Degrees: Bachelor's; Doctoral/Research; Master's; Post-Bachelor's certificate; Post-Master's certificate **Classes:** Most classes have 10-19 students. **Most popular majors:** Communication, General; Psychology, General; Business/Commerce, General. **Special Study Options:** Accelerated program; Cross-registration; Double major; Dual enrollment; Exchange student program (domestic); Honors program; Independent study; Internships; Liberal arts/career combination; Student-designed major; Study abroad; Teacher certification program; Weekend college. **Honors programs:** The Castle Scholars Honors Program offers students of exceptional ability a broader and more intensive program of study than the usual college curriculum. It provides motivated students in any major field with challenging, cross-disciplinary courses that encourage their academic and personal growth. Participation in the Castle Scholars Program encourages intellectual exchange among students and faculty and fosters independent initiative in academic and creative realms. Castle Scholars are well prepared for success in graduate and professional schools, as well as in the professional world. Castle Scholars build relationships with each other and with the college's faculty in specially-designed Honors Seminars and other unique academic opportunities, as well as in a host of social events throughout the year. Through their studies, research, and service, the Scholars contribute to the intellectual and social life of the college. Studies are augmented by participation in the wider New York City community. Privileges accorded to Castle Scholars include priority registration, the ability to register for 21 credits per semester without a financial penalty (after the first year), and access to research or travel funds in their junior and senior year. To remain in good standing, Castle Scholars must maintain a GPA of 3.6. The Castle Scholars Honors Program complements a student's chosen major and is distinct from honors options within the major. Castle Scholars are recognized annually at college-wide awards receptions, and honors courses are noted on student academic transcripts. Successful completion of the program will be noted on the final transcript as well as on printed graduation materials. **Combined degree programs:** BA/MA. **Disability Services offered to physically disabled students:** Note-taking services; Reader services; Tape recorders; Tutors. **Career services:** Alumni network; Alumni services; Career assessment; Career/job search classes; Internships; Regional alumni

FACILITIES
Housing: Coed dorms; Special housing for disabled student; Wellness housing 90% of campus accessible to physically diasbled. **Special Academic Facilities/**

Equipment: Westchester office of the New York State Small Business Development Center (SBDC), Rose Institute for Literacy and Learning, art gallery, art and music studios, Environmental Lab, English Language Institute, Heritage Hall, two electron microscopes, library **Computers:** Students can register for classes online. Administrative functions (other than registration) can be performed online.

CAMPUS LIFE
Environment: Town **Activities:** Campus Ministries; Choral groups; Concert band; Dance; Drama/theater; International Student Organization; Jazz band; Literary magazine; Model UN; Music ensembles; Musical theater; Opera; Radio station; Student government; Student newspaper; Student-run film society 46 registered organizations, 2 honor societies, 5 religious organizations. **Athletics (Intercollegiate):** *Men:* baseball, basketball, golf, ice hockey, lacrosse, soccer, tennis. *Women:* basketball, cheerleading, field hockey, ice hockey, lacrosse, soccer, softball, tennis, volleyball. **On-Campus Highlights:** The Castle, Library Cafe, Richard Berman Student Center, Kennedy Gymnasium, Quad **Environmental Initiatives:** The LEED Gold-Rated Berman Student Center

ADMISSIONS
Freshman Academic Profile: Average high school GPA 3.1. 5% in top 10% of high school class, 27% in top 25% of high school class, 63% in top 50% of high school class. **Test Scores:** SAT Math middle 50% range 430-625. ACT middle 50% range 17-27. Minimum internet-based TOEFL 80. Minimum paper TOEFL 550. **Basis for Candidate Selection:** *Very important factors considered include:* academic GPA, application essay, recommendation(s), extracurricular activities, talent/ability, character/personal qualities, alumni/ae relation. *Important factors considered include:* rigor of secondary school record, standardized test scores, interview, first generation, geographical residence, volunteer work. level of applicant's interest. *Other factors considered include:* class rank, state residency, work experience. **Freshman Admission Requirements:** High school diploma is required and GED is accepted *Academic units required:* 4 English, 3 math, 2 science, 2 social studies, 5 academic electives. **Freshman Admission Statistics:** 3,841 applied, 82.1% admitted, 13% enrolled. **Transfer Admission Requirements:** college transcript(s), statement of good standing from prior institution(s). Minimum college GPA of 2.5 required. Lowest grade transferable C. **General Admission Information:** Application fee $50. Priority deadline 3/1. Nonfall registration accepted. Admission may be deferred for a maximum of 1 year.

COSTS AND FINANCIAL AID
Annual tuition $37,370. Room and board $14,520. Required fees $1,450. Average book expense $800. **Required Forms and Deadlines:** FAFSA; State aid form. **Notification of Awards:** Applicants will be notified of awards on a rolling basis beginning 1/1. **Types of Aid:** *Need-based scholarships/grants:* College/university scholarship or grant aid from institutional funds; Federal Pell; Private scholarships; SEOG; State scholarships/grants. *Loans:* Direct PLUS loans; Direct Subsidized Stafford Loans; Direct Unsubsidized Stafford Loans. *Student Employment:* Federal Work-Study Program available. Institutional employment available. **Financial Aid Statistics:** 69% needy freshmen, 85% needy undergrads receive need-based scholarship or grant aid. 99% freshmen, undergrads receive non-need-based scholarship or grant aid. 72% freshmen, 79% undergrads receive need-based self-help aid. 0% freshmen, 0% undergrads receive athletic scholarships. 97% freshmen, 94% undergrads receive any aid. 69% undergrads borrow to pay for school. Average cumulative indebtedness $32,212. **Criteria for awarding aid:** *Non-need-based:* Academics, Alumni affiliation, Art, Leadership, Music/drama.

MANSFIELD UNIVERSITY

Academy Street, Mansfield, PA 16933
Phone: 570-662-4243 · **Financial Aid Phone:** 570-664-4129
E-mail: admissions@mansfield.edu · **CEEB Code:** 2655
Fax: 570-662-4121 · **Website:** mansfield.edu · **ACT Code:** 3710

This public school was founded in 1857. It has a 174 acre campus.

RATINGS
Admissions Selectivity Rating: 79   **Fire Safety Rating:** 79   **Green Rating:** 60*

STUDENTS AND FACULTY
Enrollment: 1,771. **Student Body:** 59% female, 41% male, 17% out-of-state, 1% international (15 countries represented). Asian 1%, African American 10%, Caucasian 81%, Hispanic 4%, Native American <1%, Pacific Islander <1%, Two or more races 2%, Race unknown 2%.
Retention and Graduation: 71% freshmen return for sophomore year. 19% freshmen graduate within 4 years. 57% freshmen graduate within 6 years. 23%

grads go on to further study within 1 year. **Faculty:** Student/faculty ratio 15:1. 100 full-time faculty, 85% hold PhDs, 52% are members of minority groups, 48% are women. 0% of classes are taught by teaching assistants.

ACADEMICS

Degrees: Associate; Bachelor's; Master's; Post-Bachelor's certificate **Classes:** Most classes have 20-29 students. Most lab/discussion sessions have 10-19 students. **Most popular majors:** Music Teacher Education; Psychology, General; Criminal Justice/Law Enforcement Administration. **Special Study Options:** Cross-registration; Distance learning; Double major; Dual enrollment; English as a Second Language (ESL); Exchange student program (domestic); Honors program; Independent study; Internships; Liberal arts/career combination; Student-designed major; Study abroad; Teacher certification program. **Honors programs:** The program includes a 22-credit curriculum that fits within most General Education and Degree program requirements. These courses include the following core principles of an Honors Education: Discussion-based instruction and small class-sizes; Critical thinking through speaking and writing; Experiential learning and interdisciplinary integration. The curriculum culminates in a Senior Honors Project, in which students choose a topic of interest and work individually with a faculty mentor to complete their project. These projects are presented to the community at large, and students are encouraged to apply their findings to create real-world solutions within the university, local, or regional communities. In addition to the curriculum, the Honors Program also includes extracurricular events, both educational and social. The majority of extracurricular activities are created, programmed, and executed by our Honors students, primarily through the Honors Association (a student government group) and the MOHBs (Mansfield Outstanding Honors Buddy system). All first-year students are assigned a MOHB, led by an upper-class Honors student (the MOHB Boss), which meets 8-10 times a semester. The MOHBs create social events, provide study skills workshops, registration advice, workshop student papers, and carry out service projects. **Disability Services offered to physically disabled students:** Note-taking services; Reader services; Tape recorders; Tutors. **Career services:** Career assessment; Career/job search classes; Internships

FACILITIES

Housing: Coed dorms; Fraternity/sorority housing 90% of campus accessible to physically diasbled. **Special Academic Facilities/Equipment:** Science museum, two art galleries, animal collection, planetarium, solar collector. **Computers:** Students can register for classes online.

CAMPUS LIFE

Environment: Rural **Activities:** Campus Ministries; Choral groups; Concert band; Dance; Drama/theater; International Student Organization; Jazz band; Literary magazine; Marching band; Music ensembles; Musical theater; Pep band; Radio station; Student government; Student newspaper; Student-run film society; Symphony orchestra; Television station; Yearbook 108 registered organizations, 10 honor societies, 4 religious organizations. 6 fraternities, 4 sororities. **Athletics (Intercollegiate):** *Men:* baseball, basketball, cross-country, football, track/field (outdoor), track/field (indoor). *Women:* basketball, cheerleading, cross-country, diving, field hockey, soccer, softball, swimming, track/field (outdoor), track/field (indoor). **On-Campus Highlights:** North Hall Library, Fitness Center, Student Union

ADMISSIONS

Freshman Academic Profile: Average high school GPA 3.4. 8% in top 10% of high school class, 29% in top 25% of high school class, 70% in top 50% of high school class. **Test Scores:** SAT Math middle 50% range 470-560. SAT EBRW middle 50% range 480-570. Minimum internet-based TOEFL 61. Minimum paper TOEFL 500. **Basis for Candidate Selection:** *Very important factors considered include:* rigor of secondary school record, class rank, academic GPA, standardized test scores. *Other factors considered include:* application essay, recommendation(s), interview, extracurricular activities, talent/ability, character/personal qualities, first generation, alumni/ae relation, geographical residence, volunteer work, work experience, level of applicant's interest. **Freshman Admission Requirements:** High school diploma is required and GED is accepted *Academic units required:* 4 English, 3 math, 2 science, 2 science labs, 2 foreign language, 4 history, 6 academic electives, *Academic units recommended:* 4 English, 4 math, 3 science, 3 science labs, 4 foreign language. **Freshman Admission Statistics:** 2,501 applied, 68.1% admitted, 22% enrolled. **Transfer Admission Requirements:** college transcript(s), Minimum college GPA of 2.0 required. Lowest grade transferable D. **General Admission Information:** Application fee $25. Priority deadline 11/30. Admission may be deferred.

COSTS AND FINANCIAL AID

Annual in-state tuition $11,928. Annual out-of-state tuition $18,900. Room and board $11,928. Required fees $2,866. Average book expense $2,000. **Required Forms and Deadlines:** FAFSA; State aid form. **Types of Aid:** *Need-based scholarships/grants:* College/university scholarship or grant aid from institutional funds; Federal Pell; Private scholarships; SEOG; State scholarships/grants. *Loans:* Direct PLUS loans; Direct Subsidized Stafford

Loans; Direct Unsubsidized Stafford Loans. *Student Employment:* Federal Work-Study Program available. Institutional employment available. **Financial Aid Statistics:** 69% needy freshmen, 69% needy undergrads receive need-based scholarship or grant aid. 46% freshmen, 36% undergrads receive non-need-based scholarship or grant aid. 91% freshmen, 90% undergrads receive need-based self-help aid. 0% freshmen, 1% undergrads receive athletic scholarships. 90% freshmen, 90% undergrads receive any aid. 80% undergrads borrow to pay for school. Average cumulative indebtedness $41,816. **Criteria for awarding aid:** *Need-based:* Academics *Non-need-based:* Academics, Alumni affiliation, Art, Athletics, Job skills, Leadership, Minority status, Music/drama, Religious affiliation, State/district residency.

MARIAN COLLEGE

3200 Cold Spring Rd., Indianapolis, IN 46222-1997
Phone: 317-955-6300 • **Financial Aid Phone:** 317.955.6040
E-mail: admissions@marian.edu • **CEEB Code:** 1442
Fax: 317-955-6401 • **Website:** www.marian.edu • **ACT Code:** 1224

This private school, affiliated with the Roman Catholic Church, was founded in 1851. It has a 114 acre campus.

RATINGS

Admissions Selectivity Rating: 84   **Fire Safety Rating:** 82   **Green Rating:** 61

STUDENTS AND FACULTY

Enrollment: 2,173. **Student Body:** 62% female, 38% male, 23% out-of-state, 1% international (18 countries represented). Asian 2%, African American 11%, Caucasian 74%, Hispanic 5%, Native American <1%, Pacific Islander <1%, Two or more races 3%, Race unknown 3%.
Retention and Graduation: 78% freshmen return for sophomore year. 35% freshmen graduate within 4 years. 52% freshmen graduate within 6 years. 22% grads go on to further study within 1 year. 6% grads pursue arts and sciences degrees. 1.4% grads pursue law degrees. 1% grads pursue business degrees. 2.3% grads pursue medical degrees. **Faculty:** Student/faculty ratio 14:1. 151 full-time faculty, 70% hold PhDs, 12% are members of minority groups, 55% are women. 0% of classes are taught by teaching assistants.

ACADEMICS

Degrees: Associate; Bachelor's; Doctoral/Professional; Master's **Classes:** Most classes have 10-19 students. Most lab/discussion sessions have 20-29 students. **Most popular majors:** Education; Registered Nursing/Registered Nurse; Business, Management, Marketing, And Related Support Services. **Special Study Options:** Accelerated program; Cooperative education program; Cross-registration; Distance learning; Double major; Dual enrollment; Honors program; Independent study; Internships; Liberal arts/career combination; Study abroad; Teacher certification program. **Honors programs:** The Honors Academy is a distinguished living & learning community of undergraduate scholars devoted to inquiry, discovery, innovation and the life of the engaged mind. The Academy advances scholarly leadership and achievement through a unique cohort of cornerstone-to-capstone experiences from deep-learning and international immersion to civic service and creative research. **Disability Services offered to physically disabled students:** Note-taking services; Reader services; Tape recorders; Tutors. **Career services:** Alumni network; Alumni services; Career assessment; Career/job search classes; Internships; Regional alumni

FACILITIES

Housing: Apartments for married students; Apartments for single students; Coed dorms; Cooperative housing; Special housing for disabled student; Theme housing; Wellness housing 95% of campus accessible to physically diasbled. **Computers:** 15% of classrooms, 100% of dorms, 100% of libraries, 100% of dining areas, 100% of student union, 50% of common outdoor areas have wireless network access. Administrative functions (other than registration) can be performed online.

CAMPUS LIFE

Environment: Metropolis **Activities:** Campus Ministries; Choral groups; Concert band; Dance; Drama/theater; International Student Organization; Jazz band; Literary magazine; Marching band; Model UN; Music ensembles; Musical theater; Pep band; Student government; Student newspaper; Yearbook. **Athletics (Intercollegiate):** *Men:* baseball, basketball, cheerleading, cross-country, cycling, football, golf, tennis, track/field (outdoor), track/field (indoor). *Women:* basketball, cheerleading, cross-country, cycling, golf, softball, tennis, track/field (outdoor), track/field (indoor), volleyball. Evans Center, Alumni Hall Student Center, New Dining and PE Center, St. Vincent Field (stadium), Drew Hall, University Hall **Environmental Initiatives:** Recycling

ADMISSIONS

Freshman Academic Profile: Average high school GPA 3.5. 18% in top 10% of high school class, 44% in top 25% of high school class, 80% in top 50% of high school class. 78% from public high schools. **Test Scores:** SAT Math middle 50% range 500-600. SAT EBRW middle 50% range 500-600. ACT middle 50% range 19-25. Minimum internet-based TOEFL 69. Minimum paper TOEFL 523. **Basis for Candidate Selection:** *Very important factors considered include:* academic GPA, standardized test scores. *Important factors considered include:* rigor of secondary school record, class rank, recommendation(s). *Other factors considered include:* application essay, interview, extracurricular activities, talent/ability, character/personal qualities, alumni/ae relation, volunteer work, level of applicant's interest. **Freshman Admission Requirements:** High school diploma is required and GED is accepted *Academic units required:* 4 English, 2 math, 2 science, 2 science labs, 1 social studies, 1 history, 9 academic electives, *Academic units recommended:* 4 English, 3 math, 3 science, 2 science labs, 2 foreign language, 1 social studies, 1 history, 8 academic electives. **Freshman Admission Statistics:** 2,246 applied, 58.8% admitted, 26% enrolled. **Transfer Admission Requirements:** college transcript(s), Minimum college GPA of 2 required. Lowest grade transferable C-. **General Admission Information:** Application fee $35. Priority deadline 3/1. Regular application deadline 8/1. Nonfall registration accepted. Admission may be deferred for a maximum of 1 year.

COSTS AND FINANCIAL AID

Annual tuition $34,000. Room and board $10,640. Average book expense $1,200. **Required Forms and Deadlines:** FAFSA. **Notification of Awards:** Applicants will be notified of awards on a rolling basis beginning 3/20. **Types of Aid:** *Need-based scholarships/grants:* College/university scholarship or grant aid from institutional funds; Federal Pell; Private scholarships; SEOG; State scholarships/grants. *Loans:* Direct PLUS loans; Direct Subsidized Stafford Loans; Direct Unsubsidized Stafford Loans. *Student Employment:* Federal Work-Study Program available. Institutional employment available. **Criteria for awarding aid:** *Need-based:* Minority status *Non-need-based:* Academics, Alumni affiliation, Art, Athletics, Leadership, Music/drama, Religious affiliation.

MARIAN UNIVERSITY

45 South National Avenue, Fond du Lac, WI 54935
Phone: 920-923-7650 · **Financial Aid Phone:** 920-923-7614
E-mail: admissions@marianuniversity.edu · **CEEB Code:** 1443
Fax: 920-923-8755 · **Website:** www.marianuniversity.edu · **ACT Code:** 4606

This private school, affiliated with the Roman Catholic Church, was founded in 1936. It has a 100 acre campus.

RATINGS

Admissions Selectivity Rating: 73   **Fire Safety Rating:** 66   **Green Rating:** 60*

STUDENTS AND FACULTY

Enrollment: 1,903. **Student Body:** 75% female, 25% male, 7% out-of-state, 1% international (13 countries represented). Asian 1%, African American 5%, Caucasian 88%, Hispanic 2%, Native American 1%, Race unknown 1%. **Retention and Graduation:** 71% freshmen return for sophomore year. 16% grads go on to further study within 1 year. **Faculty:** Student/faculty ratio 12:1. 83 full-time faculty, 60% hold PhDs, 6% are members of minority groups, 55% are women. 0% of classes are taught by teaching assistants.

ACADEMICS

Degrees: Bachelor's; Master's **Classes:** Most classes have 10-19 students. **Most popular majors:** Teacher Education And Professional Development, Specific Levels And Methods, Other; Nursing/Registered Nurse (Rn, Asn, Bsn, Msn); Business/Commerce, General. **Special Study Options:** Accelerated program; Cooperative education program; Distance learning; Double major; Dual enrollment; Honors program; Independent study; Internships; Liberal arts/career combination; Student-designed major; Study abroad; Teacher certification program. **Honors programs:** Honors. **Disability Services offered to physically disabled students:** Note-taking services; Reader services; Tape recorders; Tutors. **Career services:** Career assessment; Career/job search classes; Internships

FACILITIES

Housing: Apartments for single students; Coed dorms; Fraternity/sorority housing; Special housing for disabled students 95% of campus accessible to physically diasbled. **Special Academic Facilities/Equipment:** On-campus child-care center, electron microscope. **Computers:** Students can register for classes online. Administrative functions (other than registration) can be performed online.

CAMPUS LIFE

Environment: Town **Activities:** Campus Ministries; Choral groups; Concert band; Dance; Drama/theater; Jazz band; Literary magazine; Model UN; Music ensembles; Pep band; Student government; Student newspaper; Symphony orchestra 40 registered organizations, 6 honor societies, 1 religious organization. 1 fraternity, 2 sororities. **Athletics (Intercollegiate):** *Men:* baseball, basketball, cross-country, golf, ice hockey, soccer, tennis. *Women:* basketball, cross-country, golf, ice hockey, soccer, softball, tennis, volleyball. **On-Campus Highlights:** Housing, Coffee House, Student Center, Stayer Center, Library and Academic buildings

ADMISSIONS

Freshman Academic Profile: Average high school GPA 3.0. 9% in top 10% of high school class, 30% in top 25% of high school class, 66% in top 50% of high school class. 87% from public high schools. **Test Scores:** ACT middle 50% range 18-22. Minimum paper TOEFL 525. **Basis for Candidate Selection:** *Very important factors considered include:* rigor of secondary school record, class rank, academic GPA, standardized test scores. *Important factors considered include:* interview, character/personal qualities, level of applicant's interest. *Other factors considered include:* application essay, recommendation(s), extracurricular activities, talent/ability, alumni/ae relation, volunteer work, work experience. **Freshman Admission Requirements:** High school diploma is required and GED is accepted *Academic units required:* 4 English, 2 math, 1 science, 1 science labs, 1 history, *Academic units recommended:* 3 math, 2 science, 2 foreign language. **Freshman Admission Statistics:** 754 applied, 84.6% admitted, 38% enrolled. **Transfer Admission Requirements:** High school transcript, college transcript(s), Minimum college GPA of 2.0 required. Lowest grade transferable C. **General Admission Information:** Application fee $20. Priority deadline 4/1. Nonfall registration accepted. Admission may be deferred.

COSTS AND FINANCIAL AID

Annual tuition $19,590. Room and board $5,380. Required fees $350. Average book expense $700. **Required Forms and Deadlines:** FAFSA; Institution's own financial aid form. **Notification of Awards:** Applicants will be notified of awards on a rolling basis beginning 3/1. **Types of Aid:** *Need-based scholarships/grants:* College/university scholarship or grant aid from institutional funds; Federal Pell; Private scholarships; SEOG; State scholarships/grants. *Loans: Student Employment:* Federal Work-Study Program available. Institutional employment available. **Financial Aid Statistics:** 100% needy freshmen, 97% needy undergrads receive need-based scholarship or grant aid. 91% freshmen, 85% undergrads receive non-need-based scholarship or grant aid. 89% freshmen, 91% undergrads receive need-based self-help aid. 0% freshmen, 0% undergrads receive athletic scholarships. 99% freshmen, 94% undergrads receive any aid. **Criteria for awarding aid:** *Need-based:* Academics, Alumni affiliation, Art, Leadership, Music/drama, Religious affiliation *Non-need-based:* Academics, State/district residency.

MARIETTA COLLEGE

215 Fifth Street, Marietta, OH 45750
Phone: 740-376-4600 · **Financial Aid Phone:** 740-376-4712
E-mail: admit@marietta.edu · **CEEB Code:** 1444
Fax: 740-376-8888 · **Website:** www.marietta.edu · **ACT Code:** 3290

This private school was founded in 1835. It has a 90 acre campus.

RATINGS

Admissions Selectivity Rating: 80   **Fire Safety Rating:** 88   **Green Rating:** 63

STUDENTS AND FACULTY

Enrollment: 1,470. **Student Body:** 43% female, 57% male, 36% out-of-state, 12% international (15 countries represented). Asian 1%, African American 6%, Caucasian 71%, Hispanic 2%, Native American <1%, Pacific Islander 0%, Two or more races 1%, Race unknown 6%. **Retention and Graduation:** 75% freshmen return for sophomore year. 20% grads go on to further study within 1 year. 9% grads pursue arts and sciences degrees. 3% grads pursue law degrees. 2% grads pursue business degrees. 2% grads pursue medical degrees. **Faculty:** Student/faculty ratio 12:1. 110 full-time faculty, 89% hold PhDs, 7% are members of minority groups, 45% are women. 0% of classes are taught by teaching assistants.

ACADEMICS

Degrees: Associate; Bachelor's; Certificate; Master's **Classes:** Most classes have fewer than 10 students. **Most popular majors:** Education, General; Petroleum Engineering; Athletic Training/Trainer. **Special Study Options:** Double major; Dual enrollment; English as a Second Language (ESL); Exchange student program (domestic); Honors program; Independent study; Internships; Liberal arts/career combination; Student-designed major; Study abroad; Teacher certification program. **Honors programs:** Four Year Program for Top Scholarship Winners **Combined degree programs:** BA/MA. **Disability Services offered to physically disabled students:** Note-taking services; Reader services; Tape recorders; Tutors. **Career services:** Alumni network; Alumni services; Career assessment; Career/job search classes; Internships; Regional alumni

FACILITIES

Housing: Apartments for single students; Coed dorms; Fraternity/sorority housing; Men's dorms; Special housing for disabled student; Theme housing; Wellness housing; Women's dorms 90% of campus accessible to physically diasbled. **Special Academic Facilities/Equipment:** Mass media building, fine arts center, natural science field camp, observatory, special collections in library **Computers:** 100% of classrooms, 100% of dorms, 100% of libraries, 100% of dining areas, 100% of student union, have wireless network access. Students can register for classes online. Administrative functions (other than registration) can be performed online.

CAMPUS LIFE

Environment: Town **Activities:** Campus Ministries; Choral groups; Concert band; Dance; Drama/theater; International Student Organization; Jazz band; Literary magazine; Model UN; Music ensembles; Musical theater; Radio station; Student government; Student newspaper; Television station; Yearbook 80 registered organizations, 23 honor societies, 2 religious organizations. 3 fraternities, 3 sororities. **Athletics (Intercollegiate):** *Men:* baseball, basketball, crew/rowing, cross-country, football, soccer, tennis, track/field (outdoor), track/field (indoor). *Women:* basketball, crew/rowing, cross-country, soccer, softball, tennis, track/field (outdoor), track/field (indoor), volleyball. **On-Campus Highlights:** Gathering Place, new Upper Class Residence Hall, Legacy Library, Hermann Fine Arts Center, Dyson Baudo Recreation Center **Environmental Initiatives:** Added Sustainable Energy Minor under the Petroleum Engineering Program.

ADMISSIONS

Freshman Academic Profile: Average high school GPA 3.5. 30% in top 10% of high school class, 56% in top 25% of high school class, 84% in top 50% of high school class. 89% from public high schools. **Test Scores:** SAT Math middle 50% range 490-610. SAT EBRW middle 50% range 480-610. ACT middle 50% range 21-26. Minimum internet-based TOEFL 79. Minimum paper TOEFL 550. **Basis for Candidate Selection:** *Very important factors considered include:* rigor of secondary school record, class rank, academic GPA, standardized test scores. *Important factors considered include:* application essay, recommendation(s), interview, character/personal qualities. *Other factors considered include:* extracurricular activities, talent/ability, first generation, alumni/ae relation, geographical residence, state residency, racial/ethnic status, volunteer work, work experience, level of applicant's interest. **Freshman Admission Requirements:** High school diploma is required and GED is accepted *Academic units required:* 4 English, 3 math, 3 science, 2 science labs, 2 foreign language, 2 social studies, 2 history. **Freshman Admission Statistics:** 4,157 applied, 67.6% admitted, 14% enrolled. **Transfer Admission Requirements:** college transcript(s), essay or personal statement, statement of good standing from prior institution(s). Minimum college GPA of 2.3 required. Lowest grade transferable C. **General Admission Information:** Application fee $25. Priority deadline 3/1. Nonfall registration accepted. Admission may be deferred for a maximum of 1 year.

COSTS AND FINANCIAL AID

Annual tuition $30,090. Room and board $9,560. Required fees $850. Average book expense $1,136. **Required Forms and Deadlines:** FAFSA. **Notification of Awards:** Applicants will be notified of awards on a rolling basis beginning 3/15. **Types of Aid:** *Need-based scholarships/grants:* College/university scholarship or grant aid from institutional funds; Federal Pell; Private scholarships; SEOG; State scholarships/grants. *Loans:* Direct PLUS loans; Direct Subsidized Stafford Loans; Direct Unsubsidized Stafford Loans. *Student Employment:* Federal Work-Study Program available. Institutional employment available. **Financial Aid Statistics:** 98% needy freshmen, 97% needy undergrads receive need-based scholarship or grant aid. 71% freshmen, 87% undergrads receive non-need-based scholarship or grant aid. 86% freshmen, 88% undergrads receive need-based self-help aid. 0% freshmen, 0% undergrads receive athletic scholarships. 98% freshmen, 94% undergrads receive any aid. **Criteria for awarding aid:** *Need-based:* Academics, Leadership *Non-need-based:* Academics, Alumni affiliation, Art, Leadership, Minority status, Music/drama, State/district residency.

MARIST COLLEGE

3399 North Road, Poughkeepsie, NY 12601-1387
Phone: 845-575-3226 • **Financial Aid Phone:** 845-575-3230
E-mail: Admission@Marist.edu • **CEEB Code:** 2400
Fax: 845-575-3215 • **Website:** http://www.Marist.edu/ • **ACT Code:** 2804

This private school was founded in 1929. It has a 210 acre campus.

RATINGS

Admissions Selectivity Rating: 89   **Fire Safety Rating:** 97   **Green Rating:** 75

STUDENTS AND FACULTY

Enrollment: 5,404. **Student Body:** 58% female, 42% male, 47% out-of-state, 2% international (61 countries represented). Asian 3%, African American 4%, Caucasian 77%, Hispanic 10%, Native American <1%, Pacific Islander <1%, Two or more races 2%, Race unknown 1%.
Retention and Graduation: 89% freshmen return for sophomore year. 75% freshmen graduate within 4 years. 83% freshmen graduate within 6 years. 25% grads go on to further study within 1 year. **Faculty:** Student/faculty ratio 16:1. 243 full-time faculty, 74% hold PhDs, 19% are members of minority groups, 54% are women. 0% of classes are taught by teaching assistants.

ACADEMICS

Degrees: Bachelor's; Certificate; Doctoral/Professional; Master's; Post-Bachelor's certificate **Classes:** Most classes have 20-29 students. Most lab/discussion sessions have 20-29 students. **Most popular majors:** Communication, General; Psychology, General; Business Administration And Management, General. **Special Study Options:** Accelerated program; Cross-registration; Distance learning; Double major; Dual enrollment; English as a Second Language (ESL); Honors program; Independent study; Internships; Liberal arts/career combination; Study abroad; Teacher certification program; Weekend college. **Honors programs:** The Marist College Honors Program brings together talented students with some of the College's best faculty in honors-enriched classes that often coordinate with co-curricular activities such as field trips and lectures. The Program encourages undergraduate research, civic engagement, and ethical leadership. The Program encourages students to move beyond standard curricula and engage in a broader range of ideas and experiences consonant with their interests. **Combined degree programs:** BA/MA. **Disability Services offered to physically disabled students:** Note-taking services; Reader services; Tape recorders; Tutors. **Career services:** Alumni network; Alumni services; Career assessment; Career/job search classes; Internships; Regional alumni

FACILITIES

Housing: Apartments for single students; Coed dorms; Special housing for disabled student; Theme housing 95% of campus accessible to physically diasbled. **Special Academic Facilities/Equipment:** Art gallery, language lab, estuarine and environmental studies lab, public opinion institute, audiovisual/TV center, communications center, high tech classroom, digital state of the art library. **Computers:** 100% of classrooms, 100% of dorms, 100% of libraries, 100% of dining areas, 100% of student union, 57% of common outdoor areas have wireless network access. Students can register for classes online. Administrative functions (other than registration) can be performed online.

CAMPUS LIFE

Environment: Town **Activities:** Campus Ministries; Choral groups; Concert band; Dance; Drama/theater; International Student Organization; Jazz band; Literary magazine; Marching band; Model UN; Music ensembles; Musical theater; Pep band; Radio station; Student government; Student newspaper; Symphony orchestra; Television station 86 registered organizations, 16 honor societies, 6 religious organizations. 3 fraternities, 4 sororities. **Athletics (Intercollegiate):** *Men:* baseball, basketball, crew/rowing, cross-country, diving, football, lacrosse, soccer, swimming, tennis, track/field (outdoor). *Women:* basketball, crew/rowing, cross-country, diving, lacrosse, soccer, softball, swimming, tennis, track/field (outdoor), volleyball, water polo. **On-Campus Highlights:** James A Cannavino Library, James J McCann Recreation Center, Hancock Center, Murray Student Center and Dining Hall, Newly Built Music Department **Environmental Initiatives:** Sustainable food purchases

ADMISSIONS

Freshman Academic Profile: Average high school GPA 3.3. 22% in top 10% of high school class, 51% in top 25% of high school class, 87% in top 50% of high school class. 67% from public high schools. **Test Scores:** SAT Math middle 50% range 550-660. SAT EBRW middle 50% range 570-660. ACT

middle 50% range 24-29. Minimum internet-based TOEFL 80. Minimum paper TOEFL 550. **Basis for Candidate Selection:** *Very important factors considered include:* rigor of secondary school record, academic GPA. *Important factors considered include:* class rank, application essay, recommendation(s), extracurricular activities, talent/ability, character/personal qualities, geographical residence, state residency, volunteer work, work experience. *Other factors considered include:* standardized test scores, first generation, alumni/ae relation, racial/ethnic status, level of applicant's interest. **Freshman Admission Requirements:** High school diploma is required and GED is accepted *Academic units required:* 4 English, 3 math, 3 science, 2 science labs, 2 foreign language, 2 social studies, 1 history, 2 academic electives, *Academic units recommended:* 4 math, 4 science, 3 science labs, 3 foreign language. **Freshman Admission Statistics:** 11,376 applied, 42.6% admitted, 27% enrolled. **Transfer Admission Requirements:** High school transcript, college transcript(s), essay or personal statement, Minimum college GPA of 2.8 required. Lowest grade transferable 2. **General Admission Information:** Application fee $50. Regular application deadline 2/1. Nonfall registration accepted. Admission may be deferred for a maximum of 1 year.

COSTS AND FINANCIAL AID

Annual tuition $36,100. Room and board $16,650. Required fees $580. Average book expense $1,000. **Required Forms and Deadlines:** FAFSA. **Notification of Awards:** Applicants will be notified of awards on or about 3/31. **Types of Aid:** *Need-based scholarships/grants:* College/university scholarship or grant aid from institutional funds; Federal Pell; Private scholarships; SEOG; State scholarships/grants. *Loans:* Direct PLUS loans; Direct Subsidized Stafford Loans; Direct Unsubsidized Stafford Loans. *Student Employment:* Federal Work-Study Program available. Institutional employment available. **Financial Aid Statistics:** 72% needy freshmen, 71% needy undergrads receive need-based scholarship or grant aid. 87% undergrads receive non-need-based scholarship or grant aid. 80% freshmen, 83% undergrads receive need-based self-help aid. 6% freshmen, 6% undergrads receive athletic scholarships. 66% freshmen, 64% undergrads receive any aid. 66% undergrads borrow to pay for school. Average cumulative indebtedness $39,584. **Criteria for awarding aid:** *Need-based:* Academics, Alumni affiliation, Art, Leadership, Minority status, Music/drama *Non-need-based:* Academics, Athletics, Music/drama, State/district residency.

MARLBORO COLLEGE

PO Box A, Marlboro, VT 05344-0300
Phone: 802-258-9236 · **Financial Aid Phone:** 802-258-9312
E-mail: admissions@marlboro.edu · **CEEB Code:** 3509
Fax: 802-451-7555 · **Website:** www.marlboro.edu · **ACT Code:** 4304

This private school was founded in 1946. It has a 350 acre campus.

RATINGS

Admissions Selectivity Rating: 75   **Fire Safety Rating:** 82   **Green Rating:** 60*

STUDENTS AND FACULTY

Enrollment: 174. **Student Body:** 53% female, 47% male, 11% out-of-state, 2% international (4 countries represented). Asian 1%, African American 4%, Caucasian 78%, Hispanic 3%, Native American 1%, Pacific Islander 0%, Two or more races 5%, Race unknown 7%.
Retention and Graduation: 85% freshmen return for sophomore year. 24% grads go on to further study within 1 year. **Faculty:** Student/faculty ratio 5:1. 32 full-time faculty, 91% hold PhDs, 6% are members of minority groups, 53% are women. 0% of classes are taught by teaching assistants.

ACADEMICS

Degrees: Bachelor's; Certificate; Master's; Post-Bachelor's certificate **Classes:** Most classes have 10-19 students. **Most popular majors:** English Language And Literature, General; Social Sciences, General; Visual And Performing Arts, Other. **Special Study Options:** Cross-registration; Double major; Dual enrollment; English as a Second Language (ESL); Exchange student program (domestic); Independent study; Internships; Student-designed major; Study abroad. **Combined degree programs:** BA/MA. **Disability Services offered to physically disabled students:** Note-taking services; Reader services; Tape recorders; Tutors. **Career services:** Alumni network; Alumni services; Career assessment; Career/job search classes; Internships; Regional alumni

FACILITIES

Housing: Apartments for married students; Apartments for single students; Coed dorms; Cooperative housing; Special housing for disabled student; Theme housing; Wellness housing; Women's dorms 80% of campus accessible to physically diasbled. **Special Academic Facilities/Equipment:** Serkin Center for the Performing Arts, Drury art gallery, theater, dance studio, observatory, darkroom, art studios, music practice and performance spaces. **Computers:** 80% of classrooms, 85% of dorms, 100% of libraries, 100% of dining areas, 100% of student union, 80% of common outdoor areas have wireless network access. Students can register for classes online. Administrative functions (other than registration) can be performed online.

CAMPUS LIFE

Environment: Rural **Activities:** Choral groups; Dance; Drama/theater; Jazz band; Literary magazine; Music ensembles; Radio station; Student government; Student newspaper; Student-run film society 22 registered organizations. **On-Campus Highlights:** The Rice-Aron Library, Whittemore Theatre, Gander World Studies Center, Serkin Center for the Performing Arts, Persons Auditorium **Environmental Initiatives:** Energy audits of all campus buildings in preparation for efficiency upgrades.

ADMISSIONS

Freshman Academic Profile: Average high school GPA 3.1. 0% in top 10% of high school class, 0% in top 25% of high school class, 0% in top 50% of high school class. 66% from public high schools. **Test Scores:** SAT Math middle 50% range 550-630. SAT EBRW middle 50% range 600-710. ACT middle 50% range 24-32. Minimum internet-based TOEFL 90. Minimum paper TOEFL 577. **Basis for Candidate Selection:** *Very important factors considered include:* application essay, interview. *Important factors considered include:* rigor of secondary school record, academic GPA, recommendation(s), extracurricular activities, talent/ability, character/personal qualities, level of applicant's interest. *Other factors considered include:* standardized test scores, volunteer work, work experience. **Freshman Admission Requirements:** High school diploma is required and GED is accepted *Academic units recommended:* 4 English, 3 math, 3 science, 2 foreign language, 2 social studies, 2 history. **Freshman Admission Statistics:** 120 applied, 96.7% admitted, 24% enrolled. **Transfer Admission Requirements:** High school transcript, college transcript(s), essay or personal statement, interview, Minimum college GPA of 2.0 required. Lowest grade transferable C-. **General Admission Information:** Application fee $50. Priority deadline 3/1. Nonfall registration accepted. Admission may be deferred for a maximum of 2 semesters.

COSTS AND FINANCIAL AID

Annual tuition $39,870. Room and board $12,385. Required fees $970. Average book expense $1,200. **Required Forms and Deadlines:** FAFSA. **Notification of Awards:** Applicants will be notified of awards on a rolling basis beginning 3/1. **Types of Aid:** *Need-based scholarships/grants:* College/university scholarship or grant aid from institutional funds; Federal Pell; Private scholarships; SEOG; State scholarships/grants. *Loans:* Direct PLUS loans; Direct Subsidized Stafford Loans; Direct Unsubsidized Stafford Loans. *Student Employment:* Federal Work-Study Program available. Institutional employment available. **Financial Aid Statistics:** 100% needy freshmen, 98% needy undergrads receive need-based scholarship or grant aid. 72% freshmen, 77% undergrads receive non-need-based scholarship or grant aid. 100% freshmen, 99% undergrads receive need-based self-help aid. 0% freshmen, 0% undergrads receive athletic scholarships. 98% freshmen, 94% undergrads receive any aid. 77% undergrads borrow to pay for school. Average cumulative indebtedness $31,747. **Criteria for awarding aid:** *Non-need-based:* Academics, Art, Leadership, Music/drama.

See page 978.

MARQUETTE UNIVERSITY

P.O. Box 1881, Milwaukee, WI 53201-1881
Phone: 414-288-7302 · **Financial Aid Phone:** 414-288-7390
E-mail: admissions@Marquette.edu · **CEEB Code:** 1448
Fax: 414-288-3764 · **Website:** www.marquette.edu · **ACT Code:** 4610

This private school, affiliated with the Roman Catholic-Jesuit Church, was founded in 1881. It has a 107 acre campus.

RATINGS
Admissions Selectivity Rating: 79   **Fire Safety Rating:** 98   **Green Rating:** 79

STUDENTS AND FACULTY
Enrollment: 8,093. **Student Body:** 53% female, 47% male, 69% out-of-state, 3% international (60 countries represented). Asian 7%, African American 4%, Caucasian 70%, Hispanic 12%, Native American <1%, Pacific Islander <1%, Two or more races 4%, Race unknown <1%.
Retention and Graduation: 89% freshmen return for sophomore year. 89% freshmen graduate within 4 years. 81% freshmen graduate within 6 years.
Faculty: Student/faculty ratio 14:1. 646 full-time faculty, 91% hold PhDs, 16% are members of minority groups, 44% are women.

ACADEMICS
Degrees: Bachelor's; Doctoral; Doctoral/Professional; Doctoral/Research; Master's; Post-Bachelor's certificate; Post-Master's certificate **Classes:** Most classes have 10-19 students. Most lab/discussion sessions have 10-19 students.
Most popular majors: Mechanical Engineering; Biomedical Sciences, General; Registered Nursing/Registered Nurse. **Special Study Options:** Accelerated program; Cooperative education program; Cross-registration; Distance learning; Double major; English as a Second Language (ESL); Honors program; Independent study; Internships; Student-designed major; Study abroad; Teacher certification program; Weekend college. **Honors programs:** Pre-Dental Scholars Program Pre-Law Scholars Program **Combined degree programs:** BA/DDS; BA/JD; BA/MA. **Disability Services offered to physically disabled students:** Note-taking services; Reader services; Tutors. **Career services:** Alumni network; Alumni services; Career assessment; Career/job search classes; Internships; Regional alumni

FACILITIES
Housing: Apartments for married students; Apartments for single students; Coed dorms; Cooperative housing; Fraternity/sorority housing; Men's dorms; Special housing for disabled student; Special housing for international students; Theme housing; Wellness housing; Women's dorms 90% of campus accessible to physically diasbled. **Special Academic Facilities/Equipment:** Haggerty Museum of Art, Helfaer Theatre, Al McGuire Center Broadcast Facilities, Dental School/Clinic **Computers:** 30% of classrooms, 100% of dorms, 100% of libraries, 100% of dining areas, 100% of student union, 10% of common outdoor areas have wireless network access. Students can register for classes online. Administrative functions (other than registration) can be performed online.

CAMPUS LIFE
Environment: Metropolis **Activities:** Campus Ministries; Choral groups; Concert band; Dance; Drama/theater; International Student Organization; Jazz band; Literary magazine; Model UN; Music ensembles; Musical theater; Pep band; Radio station; Student government; Student newspaper; Symphony orchestra; Television station; Yearbook 230 registered organizations, 21 honor societies, 11 religious organizations. 11 fraternities, 11 sororities. **Athletics (Intercollegiate):** *Men:* basketball, cheerleading, cross-country, golf, soccer, tennis, track/field (outdoor), track/field (indoor). *Women:* basketball, cheerleading, cross-country, soccer, tennis, track/field (outdoor), track/field (indoor), volleyball. **On-Campus Highlights:** The Raynor Memorial Library and the Law, Gesu Church, Haggerty Museum of Art, Al McGuire Center, Helfaer Recreation Center **Environmental Initiatives:** President Lovell signed the St Francis Pledge in April 2015. "Taking the St. Francis Pledge commits you or your organization to respond to the moral call for action on climate change. By pledging, you commit to praying, acting, and advocating to solve climate change."

ADMISSIONS
Freshman Academic Profile: 34% in top 10% of high school class, 64% in top 25% of high school class, 93% in top 50% of high school class. 60% from public high schools. **Test Scores:** SAT Math middle 50% range 560-650. SAT EBRW middle 50% range 570-660. ACT middle 50% range 24-29. Minimum internet-based TOEFL 78. Minimum paper TOEFL 530. **Basis for Candidate**

Selection: *Very important factors considered include:* rigor of secondary school record, academic GPA. *Important factors considered include:* application essay, standardized test scores, extracurricular activities, volunteer work. *Other factors considered include:* class rank, recommendation(s), talent/ability, character/personal qualities, first generation, alumni/ae relation, racial/ethnic status, work experience. **Freshman Admission Requirements:** High school diploma is required and GED is accepted *Academic units required:* 4 English, 2 math, 2 science, 2 science labs, 2 social studies, 2 academic electives, *Academic units recommended:* 4 English, 4 math, 4 science, 3 science labs, 2 foreign language, 3 social studies, 2 history, 5 academic electives. **Freshman Admission Statistics:** 12,957 applied, 89.3% admitted, 17% enrolled. **Transfer Admission Requirements:** High school transcript, college transcript(s), essay or personal statement, Lowest grade transferable C. **General Admission Information:** Priority deadline 12/1. Regular application deadline 12/1. Nonfall registration accepted. Admission may be deferred for a maximum of 1 semester.

COSTS AND FINANCIAL AID
Annual tuition $41,290. Room and board $11,890. Required fees $580. Average book expense $912. **Required Forms and Deadlines:** FAFSA. **Notification of Awards:** Applicants will be notified of awards on a rolling basis beginning 1/9. **Types of Aid:** *Need-based scholarships/grants:* College/university scholarship or grant aid from institutional funds; Federal Pell; Private scholarships; SEOG; State scholarships/grants. *Loans:* Direct PLUS loans; Direct Subsidized Stafford Loans; Direct Unsubsidized Stafford Loans. *Student Employment:* Federal Work-Study Program available. Institutional employment available. **Financial Aid Statistics:** 98% needy freshmen, 98% needy undergrads receive need-based scholarship or grant aid. 14% freshmen, 12% undergrads receive non-need-based scholarship or grant aid. 79% freshmen, 81% undergrads receive need-based self-help aid. 2% freshmen, 2% undergrads receive athletic scholarships. 100% freshmen, 99% undergrads receive any aid. 56% undergrads borrow to pay for school. Average cumulative indebtedness $35,421. **Criteria for awarding aid:** *Need-based:* Minority status *Non-need-based:* Academics, Athletics, Leadership, Music/drama.

MARSHALL UNIVERSITY

One John Marshall Drive, Huntington, WV 25755
Phone: 304-696-3160 · **Financial Aid Phone:** (304) 696-3162
E-mail: admissions@marshall.edu · **CEEB Code:** 5396
Fax: 304-696-3135 · **Website:** www.marshall.edu · **ACT Code:** 4526

This public school was founded in 1837. It has a 70 acre campus.

RATINGS
Admissions Selectivity Rating: 74   **Fire Safety Rating:** 67   **Green Rating:** 60*

STUDENTS AND FACULTY
Enrollment: 8,554. **Student Body:** 57% female, 43% male, 20% out-of-state, 1% international. Asian 1%, African American 6%, Caucasian 84%, Hispanic 2%, Native American <1%, Pacific Islander <1%, Two or more races 3%, Race unknown 1%.
Retention and Graduation: 72% freshmen return for sophomore year. 29% freshmen graduate within 4 years. 49% freshmen graduate within 6 years. 27% grads go on to further study within 1 year. **Faculty:** Student/faculty ratio 19:1. 486 full-time faculty, 80% hold PhDs, 19% are members of minority groups, 48% are women.

ACADEMICS
Degrees: Associate; Bachelor's; Certificate; Doctoral/Professional; Doctoral/Research; Master's; Post-Bachelor's certificate; Post-Master's certificate **Classes:** Most classes have 10-19 students. **Most popular majors:** Elementary Education And Teaching; Psychology, General; Business/Commerce, General. **Special Study Options:** Accelerated program; Cooperative education program; Cross-registration; Distance learning; Double major; Dual enrollment; English as a Second Language (ESL); Exchange student program (domestic); Honors program; Independent study; Internships; Study abroad; Teacher certification program. **Honors programs:** John Marshall Scholars, Society of Yeager Scholars. **Disability Services offered to physically disabled students:** Note-taking services; Reader services; Tutors. **Career services:** Alumni network; Alumni services; Career assessment; Career/job search classes; Internships; Regional alumni

FACILITIES
Housing: Coed dorms; Special housing for disabled student; Theme housing; Women's dorms 100% of campus accessible to physically diasbled. **Special Academic Facilities/Equipment:** Art gallery, audiovisual center, language lab, superconducting nuclear magnetic resonance spectrometer. **Computers:** Students can register for classes online. Administrative functions (other than

registration) can be performed online.

CAMPUS LIFE

Environment: Town **Activities:** Campus Ministries; Choral groups; Concert band; Dance; Drama/theater; International Student Organization; Jazz band; Literary magazine; Marching band; Model UN; Music ensembles; Musical theater; Opera; Pep band; Radio station; Student government; Student newspaper; Symphony orchestra; Television station 100 registered organizations, 11 honor societies, 10 religious organizations. 12 fraternities, 7 sororities. **Athletics (Intercollegiate):** *Men:* baseball, basketball, cross-country, football, golf, soccer, track/field (outdoor). *Women:* basketball, cross-country, golf, soccer, softball, swimming, tennis, track/field (outdoor), volleyball. **On-Campus Highlights:** Memorial Student Center Plaza, Drinko Library, Marshall Stadium, Henderson Center, Buskirk Field

ADMISSIONS

Freshman Academic Profile: Average high school GPA 3.5. **Test Scores:** SAT Math middle 50% range 470-560. SAT EBRW middle 50% range 490-608. ACT middle 50% range 19-25. Minimum paper TOEFL 500. **Basis for Candidate Selection:** *Very important factors considered include:* academic GPA, standardized test scores. *Other factors considered include:* rigor of secondary school record. **Freshman Admission Requirements:** High school diploma is required and GED is accepted *Academic units required: Academic units recommended:* 4 English, 4 math, 3 science, 3 science labs, 2 foreign language, 3 social studies, 1 visual/performing arts. **Freshman Admission Statistics:** 5,026 applied, 90.2% admitted, 42% enrolled. **Transfer Admission Requirements:** college transcript(s). **General Admission Information:** Application fee $40. Nonfall registration accepted. Admission may be deferred for a maximum of 1 year.

COSTS AND FINANCIAL AID

Annual in-state tuition $9,254. Annual out-of-state tuition $16,734. Room and board $9,254. Required fees $1,122. Average book expense $1,100. **Required Forms and Deadlines:** FAFSA; State aid form. **Notification of Awards:** Applicants will be notified of awards on a rolling basis beginning 4/1. **Types of Aid:** *Need-based scholarships/grants:* College/university scholarship or grant aid from institutional funds; Federal Nursing Scholarships; Federal Pell; Private scholarships; SEOG; State scholarships/grants. *Loans:* Direct PLUS loans; Direct Subsidized Stafford Loans; Direct Unsubsidized Stafford Loans. **Financial Aid Statistics:** 77% needy freshmen, 76% needy undergrads receive need-based scholarship or grant aid. 61% freshmen, 47% undergrads receive non-need-based scholarship or grant aid. 68% freshmen, 73% undergrads receive need-based self-help aid. 5% freshmen, 5% undergrads receive athletic scholarships. 69% undergrads borrow to pay for school. Average cumulative indebtedness $27,121. **Criteria for awarding aid:** *Non-need-based:* Academics, Alumni affiliation, Art, Athletics, Minority status, Music/drama, State/district residency.

MARY BALDWIN COLLEGE

PO Box 1500, Staunton, VA 24402
Phone: 540-887-7019 · **Financial Aid Phone:** 540-887-7022
E-mail: admit@marybaldwin.edu · **CEEB Code:** 5397
Fax: 540-887-7292 · **Website:** www.marybaldwin.edu · **ACT Code:** 4374

This private school, affiliated with the Presbyterian Church, was founded in 1842. It has a 58.5 acre campus.

RATINGS

Admissions Selectivity Rating: 73   **Fire Safety Rating:** 88   **Green Rating:** 60*

STUDENTS AND FACULTY

Enrollment: 1,059. **Student Body:** 93% female, 7% male, 23% out-of-state, 1% international (6 countries represented). Asian 2%, African American 21%, Caucasian 58%, Hispanic 7%, Native American 1%, Pacific Islander <1%, Two or more races 4%, Race unknown 5%.
Retention and Graduation: 65% freshmen return for sophomore year. 41% freshmen graduate within 4 years. 45% freshmen graduate within 6 years. 24% grads go on to further study within 1 year. **Faculty:** Student/faculty ratio 8:1. 97 full-time faculty, 81% hold PhDs, 15% are members of minority groups, 72% are women.

ACADEMICS

Degrees: Bachelor's; Certificate; Doctoral/Professional; Master's; Post-Bachelor's certificate **Classes:** Most classes have 10-19 students. Most lab/discussion sessions have 10-19 students. **Most popular majors:** Liberal Arts And Sciences/Liberal Studies; Psychology, General; Business Administration And Management, General. **Special Study Options:** Accelerated program;

Distance learning; Double major; Dual enrollment; Exchange student program (domestic); Honors program; Independent study; Internships; Student-designed major; Study abroad; Teacher certification program. **Combined degree programs:** BA/MEng. **Disability Services offered to physically disabled students:** Note-taking services; Reader services; Tape recorders; Tutors. **Career services:** Alumni services; Career assessment; Career/job search classes; Internships

FACILITIES

Housing: Coed dorms; Special housing for international students; Women's dorms 75% of campus accessible to physically disabled. **Special Academic Facilities/Equipment:** Audiovisual center, TV studio, communications lab, electron microscope, gas chromatoscope, greenhouse. **Computers:** 100% of classrooms, 100% of dorms, 100% of libraries, 100% of common outdoor areas have wireless network access. Students can register for classes online. Administrative functions (other than registration) can be performed online.

CAMPUS LIFE

Environment: Town **Activities:** Choral groups; Dance; Drama/theater; International Student Organization; Literary magazine; Marching band; Music ensembles; Musical theater; Student government; Television station; Yearbook 34 registered organizations, 9 honor societies, 4 religious organizations. **Athletics (Intercollegiate):** *Women:* basketball, field hockey, soccer, softball, swimming, tennis, volleyball. **On-Campus Highlights:** Spencer Center for Civic and Global Engagement, University Cafe, Grafton Library, Physical Activities Center, Staunton Military Academy/VWIL Museum

ADMISSIONS

Freshman Academic Profile: Average high school GPA 3.6. 18% in top 10% of high school class, 55% in top 25% of high school class, 77% in top 50% of high school class. **Test Scores:** SAT Math middle 50% range 460-580. SAT EBRW middle 50% range 490-620. ACT middle 50% range 19-26. Minimum paper TOEFL 500. **Basis for Candidate Selection:** *Very important factors considered include:* rigor of secondary school record, academic GPA. *Important factors considered include:* standardized test scores, character/personal qualities. *Other factors considered include:* class rank, application essay, recommendation(s), interview, extracurricular activities, talent/ability, first generation, alumni/ae relation, volunteer work, work experience, level of applicant's interest. **Freshman Admission Requirements:** High school diploma is required and GED is accepted *Academic units required:* 4 English, 3 math, 2 science, 2 science labs, 2 foreign language, 1 social studies, 2 history, *Academic units recommended:* 4 English, 3 math, 2 science, 2 science labs, 2 foreign language, 1 social studies, 2 history, 2 academic electives. **Freshman Admission Statistics:** 1,397 applied, 94.7% admitted, 8% enrolled. **Transfer Admission Requirements:** High school transcript, college transcript(s), statement of good standing from prior institution(s). Minimum college GPA of 2.0 required. Lowest grade transferable c-. **General Admission Information:** Nonfall registration accepted. Admission may be deferred for a maximum of 1 year.

COSTS AND FINANCIAL AID

Annual tuition $30,690. Room and board $9,410. Required fees $395. Average book expense $900. **Required Forms and Deadlines:** FAFSA; State aid form. **Notification of Awards:** Applicants will be notified of awards on a rolling basis beginning 3/15. **Types of Aid:** *Need-based scholarships/grants:* College/university scholarship or grant aid from institutional funds; Federal Pell; Private scholarships; SEOG; State scholarships/grants. *Loans:* Direct PLUS loans; Direct Subsidized Stafford Loans; Direct Unsubsidized Stafford Loans. *Student Employment:* Federal Work-Study Program available. Institutional employment available. **Financial Aid Statistics:** 98% needy freshmen, 99% needy undergrads receive need-based scholarship or grant aid. 7% freshmen, 7% undergrads receive non-need-based scholarship or grant aid. 87% freshmen, 88% undergrads receive need-based self-help aid. 0% freshmen, 0% undergrads receive athletic scholarships. 90% freshmen, 95% undergrads receive any aid. **Criteria for awarding aid:** *Need-based:* Academics, Leadership *Non-need-based:* Academics, Leadership, State/district residency.

MARYLAND INSTITUTE COLLEGE OF ART

1300 West Mount Royal Avenue, Baltimore, MD 21217
Phone: 410-225-2222 · **Financial Aid Phone:** 410-225-2285
E-mail: admissions@mica.edu · **CEEB Code:** 5399
Fax: 410-225-2337 · **Website:** www.mica.edu · **ACT Code:** 1710

This private school was founded in 1826. It has a 16 acre campus.

RATINGS

Admissions Selectivity Rating: 84   **Fire Safety Rating:** 93   **Green Rating:** 65

STUDENTS AND FACULTY

Enrollment: 1,688. **Student Body:** 75% female, 25% male, 74% out-of-state, 24% international (62 countries represented). Asian 11%, African American 7%, Caucasian 41%, Hispanic 3%, Native American <1%, Pacific Islander <1%, Two or more races 12%, Race unknown 1%.

Retention and Graduation: 86% freshmen return for sophomore year. 67% freshmen graduate within 4 years. 72% freshmen graduate within 6 years. **Faculty:** Student/faculty ratio 8:1. 162 full-time faculty, 0% of classes are taught by teaching assistants.

ACADEMICS

Degrees: Bachelor's; Master's; Post-Bachelor's certificate **Classes:** Most classes have fewer than 10 students. **Most popular majors:** Graphic Design; Illustration; Painting. **Special Study Options:** Accelerated program; Cross-registration; Distance learning; Double major; Dual enrollment; Exchange student program (domestic); Independent study; Internships; Liberal arts/career combination; Student-designed major; Study abroad; Teacher certification program. **Combined degree programs:** BA/MA. **Disability Services offered to physically disabled students:** Note-taking services; Tape recorders; Tutors. **Career services:** Alumni network; Alumni services; Career assessment; Career/job search classes; Internships; Regional alumni

FACILITIES

Housing: Apartments for single students; Coed dorms; Special housing for disabled student; Special housing for international students; Theme housing; Wellness housing 85% of campus accessible to physically diasbled. **Special Academic Facilities/Equipment:** There are seven art galleries open to the public year-round featuring work by MICA faculty, students, and nationally/internationally known artists; a nature library; and an extensive slide library containing over 215,000 slides. **Computers:** 100% of libraries, 100% of dining areas, 80% of common outdoor areas have wireless network access. Students can register for classes online. Administrative functions (other than registration) can be performed online.

CAMPUS LIFE

Environment: Metropolis **Activities:** Campus Ministries; Choral groups; Dance; Drama/theater; International Student Organization; Literary magazine; Music ensembles; Musical theater; Radio station; Student government; Student-run film society 50 registered organizations, 3 religious organizations. **On-Campus Highlights:** Founders Green, our new dormitory, The Gateway dormitory, The Brown Center, our Digital Arts center, The Meyerhoff House dormitory & dining, Various on-campus galleries/exhibitiions **Environmental Initiatives:** Single-Stream recycling of recyclable waste.

ADMISSIONS

Freshman Academic Profile: Average high school GPA 3.5. 70% from public high schools. **Test Scores:** SAT Math middle 50% range 520-630. SAT EBRW middle 50% range 540-660. ACT middle 50% range 24-29. Minimum internet-based TOEFL 80. Minimum paper TOEFL 550. **Basis for Candidate Selection:** *Very important factors considered include:* rigor of secondary school record, academic GPA, talent/ability, level of applicant's interest. *Important factors considered include:* class rank, application essay, standardized test scores, interview, extracurricular activities. *Other factors considered include:* recommendation(s), character/personal qualities, alumni/ae relation, racial/ethnic status, volunteer work. **Freshman Admission Requirements:** High school diploma is required and GED is accepted *Academic units required:* 4 English, 2 math, 2 science, 1 science labs, 4 social studies, 3 history, 6 academic electives, and 2 units from above areas or other academic areas. *Academic units recommended:* 4 English, 3 math, 3 science, 4 social studies, 4 history, 5 units from above areas or other academic areas. **Freshman Admission Statistics:** 3,636 applied, 61.6% admitted, 19% enrolled. **Transfer Admission Requirements:** High school transcript, college transcript(s), essay or personal statement, Minimum college GPA of 2.8 required. Lowest grade transferable C. **General Admission Information:** Application fee $70. Regular application deadline 2/1. Nonfall registration accepted. Admission may be deferred for a maximum of 1 year.

COSTS AND FINANCIAL AID

Annual tuition $45,290. Room and board $12,860. Required fees $1,700. Average book expense $1,500. **Required Forms and Deadlines:** FAFSA; Institution's own financial aid form. **Notification of Awards:** Applicants will be notified of awards on or about 4/2. **Types of Aid:** *Need-based scholarships/grants:* College/university scholarship or grant aid from institutional funds; Federal Pell; Private scholarships; SEOG; State scholarships/grants. *Loans:* Direct PLUS loans; Direct Subsidized Stafford Loans; Direct Unsubsidized Stafford Loans. *Student Employment:* Federal Work-Study Program available. Institutional employment available. **Criteria for awarding aid:** *Need-based:* Academics, Art *Non-need-based:* Academics, Art.

MARYLHURST UNIVERSITY

PO BOX 261, Marylhurst, OR 97036
Phone: 503-699-6268 · **Financial Aid Phone:** 503-699-6253
E-mail: admissions@marylhurst.edu · **CEEB Code:** 440
Fax: 503-636-9526 · **Website:** www.marylhurst.edu · **ACT Code:** 3470

This private school, affiliated with the Roman Catholic Church, was founded in 1893. It has a 68 acre campus.

RATINGS

Admissions Selectivity Rating: 69   **Fire Safety Rating:** 60*   **Green Rating:** 63

STUDENTS AND FACULTY

Enrollment: 503. **Student Body:** 73% female, 27% male, 25% out-of-state, 3% international (10 countries represented). Asian 3%, African American 3%, Caucasian 70%, Hispanic 7%, Native American 1%, Pacific Islander <1%, Two or more races 3%, Race unknown 11%.

Retention and Graduation: 67% freshmen return for sophomore year. **Faculty:** 0% of classes are taught by teaching assistants.

ACADEMICS

Degrees: Bachelor's; Certificate; Master's; Post-Bachelor's certificate; Post-Master's certificate **Classes:** Most classes have 10-19 students. Most lab/discussion sessions have 10-19 students. **Most popular majors:** Multi-/Interdisciplinary Studies, Other; Psychology, General; Business Administration And Management, General. **Special Study Options:** Accelerated program; Distance learning; Double major; Dual enrollment; Independent study; Internships; Student-designed major; Study abroad; Teacher certification program; Weekend college. **Disability Services offered to physically disabled students:** Note-taking services; Reader services; Tape recorders; Tutors. **Career services:** Career/job search classes; Internships

FACILITIES

Housing: 90% of campus accessible to physically diasbled. **Special Academic Facilities/Equipment:** Art Gym Art Gallery Streff Gallery **Computers:** Students can register for classes online. Administrative functions (other than registration) can be performed online.

CAMPUS LIFE

Environment: City **Activities:** Campus Ministries; Choral groups; Jazz band; Literary magazine; Music ensembles; Musical theater; Student government; Student-run film society 6 registered organizations, 1 honor societies.

ADMISSIONS

Freshman Admission Requirements: High school diploma is required and GED is accepted **Freshman Admission Statistics:** 5 applied, 100.0% admitted, 100% enrolled. **Transfer Admission Requirements:** High school transcript, college transcript(s), Minimum college GPA of 2.0 required. Lowest grade transferable C-. **General Admission Information:** Application fee $50. Nonfall registration accepted. Admission may be deferred for a maximum of 1 year.

COSTS AND FINANCIAL AID

Annual tuition $20,835. **Required Forms and Deadlines:** FAFSA; Institution's own financial aid form. **Notification of Awards:** Applicants will be notified of awards on a rolling basis beginning 4/1. **Types of Aid:** *Need-based scholarships/grants:* College/university scholarship or grant aid from institutional funds; Federal Pell; Private scholarships; SEOG; State scholarships/grants. *Loans:* Direct PLUS loans; Direct Subsidized Stafford Loans; Direct Unsubsidized Stafford Loans. **Financial Aid Statistics:** 100% needy freshmen, 96% needy undergrads receive need-based scholarship or grant aid. 0% undergrads receive non-need-based scholarship or grant aid. 100% freshmen, 91% undergrads receive need-based self-help aid. 0% freshmen, 0% undergrads receive athletic scholarships. **Criteria for awarding aid:** *Need-based:* Academics, Art, Minority status, Music/drama *Non-need-based:* Academics, Art, Music/drama.

MARYMOUNT COLLEGE

30800 Palos Verdes Drive East, Rancho Palos Verdes, CA 90275
Phone: 310-377-5501 · **Financial Aid Phone:** (310) 303-7311
E-mail: admissions@marymountcalifornia.edu · **CEEB Code:** 4515
Fax: 310-265-0962 · **Website:** http://www.marymountcalifornia.edu/ · **ACT Code:** 316

This private school, affiliated with the Roman Catholic Church, was founded in 1932. It has a 22 acre campus.

RATINGS
Admissions Selectivity Rating: 81   **Fire Safety Rating:** 93   **Green Rating:** 60*

STUDENTS AND FACULTY
Enrollment: 1,034. **Student Body:** 55% female, 45% male, 5% out-of-state, 14% international (42 countries represented). Asian 5%, African American 8%, Caucasian 25%, Hispanic 36%, Native American <1%, Pacific Islander 1%, Two or more races 4%, Race unknown 6%.
Retention and Graduation: 68% freshmen return for sophomore year.
Faculty: Student/faculty ratio 17:1. 28 full-time faculty, 68% hold PhDs, 18% are members of minority groups, 43% are women. 0% of classes are taught by teaching assistants.

ACADEMICS
Degrees: Associate; Bachelor's; Master's **Most popular majors:** Liberal Arts And Sciences, General Studies And Humanities, Other; Psychology, Other; Business, Management, Marketing, And Related Support Services, Other. **Special Study Options:** Distance learning; Double major; Dual enrollment; English as a Second Language (ESL); Honors program; Internships; Liberal arts/career combination; Study abroad. **Honors programs:** Marymount Honors Program Phi Theta Kappa Delta Epsilon Sigma **Combined degree programs:** BA/MA. **Disability Services offered to physically disabled students:** Note-taking services; Reader services; Tape recorders; Tutors. **Career services:** Alumni network; Alumni services; Career assessment; Internships; Regional alumni

FACILITIES
Housing: Apartments for single students; Coed dorms; Special housing for disabled students 100% of campus accessible to physically diasbled. **Computers:** 100% of classrooms, 100% of dorms, 100% of libraries, 100% of dining areas, 100% of student union, 75% of common outdoor areas have wireless network access. Administrative functions (other than registration) can be performed online.

CAMPUS LIFE
Environment: Town **Activities:** Campus Ministries; Choral groups; Dance; Drama/theater; International Student Organization; Jazz band; Literary magazine; Musical theater; Student government; Student-run film society 2 honor societies, 2 religious organizations. **Athletics (Intercollegiate):** *Men:* soccer. *Women:* soccer.

ADMISSIONS
Freshman Academic Profile: Average high school GPA 3.0. 30% from public high schools. **Test Scores:** SAT Math middle 50% range 390-520. SAT EBRW middle 50% range 410-520. ACT middle 50% range 16-22. Minimum internet-based TOEFL 61. **Basis for Candidate Selection:** *Very important factors considered include:* rigor of secondary school record, academic GPA. *Other factors considered include:* class rank, application essay, standardized test scores, recommendation(s), interview, extracurricular activities, talent/ability, character/personal qualities, alumni/ae relation, volunteer work, level of applicant's interest. **Freshman Admission Requirements:** High school diploma is required and GED is accepted *Academic units recommended:* 4 English, 3 math, 2 science, 2 foreign language, 2 social studies, 2 history, 1 academic elective. **Freshman Admission Statistics:** 1,612 applied, 59.4% admitted, 30% enrolled. **Transfer Admission Requirements:** High school transcript, college transcript(s), Lowest grade transferable C-. **General Admission Information:** Application fee $50. Priority deadline 3/1. Nonfall registration accepted. Admission may be deferred for a maximum of 1 year.

COSTS AND FINANCIAL AID
Required Forms and Deadlines: FAFSA. **Notification of Awards:** Applicants will be notified of awards on or about 3/1. **Types of Aid:** *Need-based scholarships/grants:* College/university scholarship or grant aid from institutional funds; Federal Pell; Private scholarships; SEOG; State scholarships/grants. *Loans:* Direct PLUS loans; Direct Subsidized Stafford Loans; Direct Unsubsidized Stafford Loans. *Student Employment:* Federal Work-Study Program available. Institutional employment available. **Financial Aid Statistics:** 100% needy freshmen, 100% needy undergrads receive need-based scholarship or grant aid. 86% freshmen, 88% undergrads receive non-need-based scholarship or grant aid. 1% freshmen, 6% undergrads receive need-

based self-help aid. 5% freshmen, 5% undergrads receive athletic scholarships. 84% freshmen, 74% undergrads receive any aid. **Criteria for awarding aid:** *Need-based:* Academics *Non-need-based:* Academics, Art, Athletics.

MARYMOUNT MANHATTAN COLLEGE

221 East 71st Street, New York, NY 10021
Phone: 212-517-0430 · **Financial Aid Phone:** 212-517-0500
E-mail: admissions@mmm.edu · **CEEB Code:** 2405
Fax: 212-517-0448 · **Website:** www.mmm.edu · **ACT Code:** 2810

This private school was founded in 1936. It has a 1 acre campus.

RATINGS
Admissions Selectivity Rating: 73   **Fire Safety Rating:** 60*   **Green Rating:** 60*

STUDENTS AND FACULTY
Enrollment: 1,875. **Student Body:** 77% female, 23% male, 59% out-of-state, 5% international (66 countries represented). Asian 4%, African American 10%, Caucasian 57%, Hispanic 18%, Native American 1%, Pacific Islander <1%, Two or more races 1%, Race unknown 5%.
Retention and Graduation: 74% freshmen return for sophomore year.
Faculty: Student/faculty ratio 11:1. 94 full-time faculty, 95% hold PhDs, 10% are members of minority groups, 62% are women. 0% of classes are taught by teaching assistants.

ACADEMICS
Degrees: Associate; Bachelor's **Classes:** Most classes have 20-29 students. Most lab/discussion sessions have fewer than 10 students. **Most popular majors:** Communication And Media Studies, Other; Psychology, General; Visual And Performing Arts, General. **Special Study Options:** Accelerated program; Cross-registration; Distance learning; Double major; Exchange student program (domestic); Honors program; Independent study; Internships; Liberal arts/career combination; Student-designed major; Study abroad. **Honors programs:** The College Honors Program described in detail at http://www.mmm.edu/academics/college-honors-program.php. **Disability Services offered to physically disabled students:** Note-taking services; Reader services; Tape recorders; Tutors. **Career services:** Alumni network; Alumni services; Career assessment; Career/job search classes; Internships; Regional alumni

FACILITIES
Housing: Coed dorms; Other (please specify) **Special Academic Facilities/Equipment:** Gallery, communications and learning center, theatre, media center, college skills center, mathematics lab, Samuel Freeman science center,Comm Arts multimedia suite. **Computers:** 40% of classrooms, 100% of libraries, have wireless network access. Students can register for classes online. Administrative functions (other than registration) can be performed online.

CAMPUS LIFE
Environment: Metropolis **Activities:** Campus Ministries; Choral groups; Dance; Drama/theater; International Student Organization; Musical theater; Radio station; Student government; Student newspaper; Yearbook 30 registered organizations, 7 honor societies, 2 religious organizations. **On-Campus Highlights:** Theresa Lang Theatre, Hewitt Gallery of Art, Science Laboratories, 55th Street Residence Hall, Shanahan Library **Environmental Initiatives:** purchase of renewable energy

ADMISSIONS
Freshman Academic Profile: Average high school GPA 3.3. **Test Scores:** SAT Math middle 50% range 440-550. SAT EBRW middle 50% range 470-590. ACT middle 50% range 20-26. Minimum internet-based TOEFL 80. **Basis for Candidate Selection:** *Very important factors considered include:* rigor of secondary school record, academic GPA, standardized test scores. *Important factors considered include:* application essay, recommendation(s), talent/ability, character/personal qualities, level of applicant's interest. *Other factors considered include:* interview, extracurricular activities, first generation, alumni/ae relation, geographical residence, state residency, volunteer work, work experience. **Freshman Admission Requirements:** High school diploma is required and GED is accepted *Academic units required:* 4 English, 3 math, 3 science, 3 social studies, 4 academic electives, *Academic units recommended:* 2 science labs, 2 foreign language. **Freshman Admission Statistics:** 4,459 applied, 83.8% admitted, 14% enrolled. **Transfer Admission Requirements:** High school transcript, college transcript(s), essay or personal statement, statement of good standing from prior institution(s). Minimum college GPA of 2.5 required. Lowest grade transferable C-. **General Admission Information:** Application fee $60. Priority deadline 8/1. Nonfall registration accepted. Admission may be deferred.

COSTS AND FINANCIAL AID

Annual tuition $28,870. Room and board $15,990. Required fees $1,420. Average book expense $1,000. **Required Forms and Deadlines:** FAFSA; State aid form. **Notification of Awards:** Applicants will be notified of awards on a rolling basis beginning 3/15. **Types of Aid:** *Need-based scholarships/grants:* College/university scholarship or grant aid from institutional funds; Federal Pell; Private scholarships; SEOG; State scholarships/grants. *Loans:* Direct PLUS loans; Direct Subsidized Stafford Loans; Direct Unsubsidized Stafford Loans. *Student Employment:* Federal Work-Study Program available. Institutional employment available. **Financial Aid Statistics:** 99% needy undergrads receive need-based scholarship or grant aid. 0% undergrads receive non-need-based scholarship or grant aid. 73% freshmen, 79% undergrads receive need-based self-help aid. 0% freshmen, 0% undergrads receive athletic scholarships. Average cumulative indebtedness $30,159. **Criteria for awarding aid:** *Need-based:* Academics *Non-need-based:* Academics, Art, Leadership, Music/drama, State/district residency.

MARYMOUNT UNIVERSITY

2807 North Glebe Road, Arlington, VA 22207
Phone: 703-284-1500 · **Financial Aid Phone:** 703-284-1530
E-mail: admissions@marymount.edu · **CEEB Code:** 5405
Fax: 703-522-0349 · **Website:** http://www.marymount.edu · **ACT Code:** 4378

This private school, affiliated with the Roman Catholic Church, was founded in 1950. It has a 21 acre campus.

RATINGS

Admissions Selectivity Rating: 74   **Fire Safety Rating:** 86   **Green Rating:** 60*

STUDENTS AND FACULTY

Enrollment: 2,199. **Student Body:** 75% female, 25% male, 42% out-of-state, 6% international (70 countries represented). Asian 8%, African American 15%, Caucasian 46%, Hispanic 12%, Native American 1%, Race unknown 13%. **Retention and Graduation:** 71% freshmen return for sophomore year. **Faculty:** Student/faculty ratio 14:1. 138 full-time faculty, 89% hold PhDs, 5% are members of minority groups, 74% are women. 0% of classes are taught by teaching assistants.

ACADEMICS

Degrees: Bachelor's; Certificate; Doctoral; Master's; Post-Bachelor's certificate; Post-Master's certificate **Classes:** Most classes have fewer than 10 students. **Most popular majors:** Biology/Biological Sciences, General; Fashion/Apparel Design; Business Administration And Management, General. **Special Study Options:** Accelerated program; Cross-registration; Distance learning; Double major; English as a Second Language (ESL); Honors program; Independent study; Internships; Student-designed major; Study abroad; Teacher certification program. **Honors programs:** The Honors Program at Marymount University. **Disability Services offered to physically disabled students:** Note-taking services; Reader services; Tape recorders; Tutors. **Career services:** Alumni network; Career/job search classes; Internships

FACILITIES

Housing: Coed dorms; Men's dorms; Women's dorms 75% of campus accessible to physically disabled. **Special Academic Facilities/Equipment:** Art gallery, learning resource center, audiovisual center, studio, and computer labs **Computers:** Students can register for classes online. Administrative functions (other than registration) can be performed online.

CAMPUS LIFE

Environment: City **Activities:** Campus Ministries; Choral groups; Dance; Drama/theater; International Student Organization; Literary magazine; Student government; Student newspaper; Yearbook 33 registered organizations, 11 honor societies, 2 religious organizations. **Athletics (Intercollegiate):** *Men:* basketball, cross-country, golf, lacrosse, soccer, swimming. *Women:* basketball, cross-country, lacrosse, soccer, swimming, volleyball. **On-Campus Highlights:** Student Center, Gym, Bernie's Cafe, Turf field, Ballston campus **Environmental Initiatives:** Recycling program

ADMISSIONS

Freshman Academic Profile: Average high school GPA 3.1. 15% in top 10% of high school class, 41% in top 25% of high school class, 81% in top 50% of high school class. 68% from public high schools. **Test Scores:** SAT Math middle 50% range 450-550. SAT EBRW middle 50% range 450-560. ACT middle 50% range 18-24. Minimum internet-based TOEFL 79. Minimum paper TOEFL 550. **Basis for Candidate Selection:** *Very important factors considered*

include: rigor of secondary school record, academic GPA, standardized test scores. *Important factors considered include:* class rank, recommendation(s), interview, talent/ability. *Other factors considered include:* application essay, extracurricular activities, character/personal qualities, first generation, alumni/ae relation, volunteer work, work experience, level of applicant's interest. **Freshman Admission Requirements:** High school diploma is required and GED is accepted *Academic units recommended:* 4 English, 3 math, 2 science, 3 foreign language, 3 social studies. **Freshman Admission Statistics:** 1,904 applied, 80.9% admitted, 26% enrolled. **Transfer Admission Requirements:** college transcript(s), statement of good standing from prior institution(s). Minimum college GPA of 2.0 required. Lowest grade transferable C. **General Admission Information:** Application fee $40. Priority deadline 5/1. Nonfall registration accepted. Admission may be deferred for a maximum of 1 year.

COSTS AND FINANCIAL AID

Annual tuition $23,700. Room and board $8,705. Required fees $220. Average book expense $800. **Required Forms and Deadlines:** FAFSA. **Notification of Awards:** Applicants will be notified of awards on a rolling basis beginning 3/15. **Types of Aid:** *Need-based scholarships/grants:* College/university scholarship or grant aid from institutional funds; Federal Pell; Private scholarships; SEOG; State scholarships/grants. *Loans:* Direct Subsidized Stafford Loans; Direct Unsubsidized Stafford Loans. *Student Employment:* Federal Work-Study Program available. Institutional employment available. **Financial Aid Statistics:** 83% needy freshmen, 74% needy undergrads receive need-based scholarship or grant aid. 80% freshmen, 73% undergrads receive non-need-based scholarship or grant aid. 78% freshmen, 83% undergrads receive need-based self-help aid. 0% freshmen, 0% undergrads receive athletic scholarships. 92% freshmen, 84% undergrads receive any aid. **Criteria for awarding aid:** *Need-based:* Academics, Religious affiliation *Non-need-based:* Academics, Alumni affiliation, Leadership, State/district residency.

MARYVILLE COLLEGE

502 East Lamar Alexander Parkway, Maryville, TN 37804-5907
Phone: 865-981-8092 · **Financial Aid Phone:** 865-981-8100
E-mail: admissions@maryvillecollege.edu · **CEEB Code:** 1454
Fax: 865-981-8005 · **Website:** www.maryvillecollege.edu · **ACT Code:** 3988

This private school, affiliated with the Presbyterian Church, was founded in 1819. It has a 370 acre campus.

RATINGS

Admissions Selectivity Rating: 80   **Fire Safety Rating:** 92   **Green Rating:** 77

STUDENTS AND FACULTY

Enrollment: 1,114. **Student Body:** 55% female, 45% male, 24% out-of-state, 4% international (20 countries represented). Asian 1%, African American 5%, Caucasian 86%, Hispanic 2%, Native American <1%, Race unknown 2%. **Retention and Graduation:** 67% freshmen return for sophomore year. 28% grads go on to further study within 1 year. 0% grads pursue arts and sciences degrees. 0% grads pursue law degrees. 0% grads pursue business degrees. 0% grads pursue medical degrees. **Faculty:** Student/faculty ratio 12:1. 79 full-time faculty, 76% hold PhDs, 4% are members of minority groups, 54% are women. 0% of classes are taught by teaching assistants.

ACADEMICS

Degrees: Bachelor's **Classes:** Most classes have 10-19 students. Most lab/discussion sessions have 10-19 students. **Most popular majors:** Education, General; Biology/Biological Sciences, General; Business/Commerce, General. **Special Study Options:** Double major; English as a Second Language (ESL); Honors program; Independent study; Internships; Liberal arts/career combination; Student-designed major; Study abroad; Teacher certification program. **Honors programs:** Presidential and Deans scholars participate in honors courses and honors tutorial practicum. Most courses may be taken with "honors" status. **Disability Services offered to physically disabled students:** Note-taking services; Reader services; Tape recorders; Tutors. **Career services:** Alumni network; Alumni services; Career assessment; Career/job search classes; Internships; Regional alumni

FACILITIES

Housing: Apartments for single students; Coed dorms; Men's dorms; Special housing for disabled student; Women's dorms 90% of campus accessible to physically disabled. **Special Academic Facilities/Equipment:** Art gallery, theatre, greenhouse, College Woods **Computers:** 100% of classrooms, 100% of dorms, 100% of libraries, 100% of dining areas, 100% of student union, 50% of common outdoor areas have wireless network access. Students can register for classes online. Administrative functions (other than registration) can be performed online.

CAMPUS LIFE

Environment: Town **Activities:** Campus Ministries; Choral groups; Concert band; Dance; Drama/theater; Jazz band; Literary magazine; Music ensembles; Musical theater; Student government; Student newspaper; Symphony orchestra; Yearbook 63 registered organizations, 15 honor societies, 5 religious organizations. **Athletics (Intercollegiate):** *Men:* baseball, basketball, cross-country, equestrian sports, football, soccer, tennis. *Women:* basketball, cross-country, equestrian sports, soccer, softball, tennis, volleyball. **On-Campus Highlights:** Isaacs Student Center, Mountain Challenge, Lloyd Beach, New Lloyd Residence Hall, Center for Calling and Career **Environmental Initiatives:** Steam plant boiler is fueled by recycled wood products

ADMISSIONS

Freshman Academic Profile: Average high school GPA 3.6. 34% in top 10% of high school class, 65% in top 25% of high school class, 89% in top 50% of high school class. 91% from public high schools. **Test Scores:** SAT Math middle 50% range 480-610. SAT EBRW middle 50% range 470-630. ACT middle 50% range 21-28. Minimum paper TOEFL 525. **Basis for Candidate Selection:** *Very important factors considered include:* rigor of secondary school record, class rank, standardized test scores. *Important factors considered include:* academic GPA, recommendation(s), interview, extracurricular activities. *Other factors considered include:* application essay, talent/ability, character/personal qualities, first generation, alumni/ae relation, volunteer work, level of applicant's interest. **Freshman Admission Requirements:** High school diploma is required and GED is accepted *Academic units required:* 4 English, 3 math, 2 science, 1 science labs, 2 foreign language, 2 social studies, 1 academic elective, *Academic units recommended:* 1 history. **Freshman Admission Statistics:** 1,291 applied, 77.7% admitted, 30% enrolled. **Transfer Admission Requirements:** college transcript(s), statement of good standing from prior institution(s). Minimum college GPA of 2.0 required. Lowest grade transferable C. **General Admission Information:** Priority deadline 1/15. Nonfall registration accepted. Admission may be deferred for a maximum of 1 year.

COSTS AND FINANCIAL AID

Annual tuition $26,272. Room and board $8,240. Required fees $675. Average book expense $880. **Required Forms and Deadlines:** FAFSA. **Types of Aid:** *Need-based scholarships/grants:* College/university scholarship or grant aid from institutional funds; Federal Pell; Private scholarships; SEOG; State scholarships/grants. *Loans:* Direct PLUS loans; Direct Subsidized Stafford Loans; Direct Unsubsidized Stafford Loans. *Student Employment:* Federal Work-Study Program available. **Financial Aid Statistics:** 75% needy freshmen, 98% needy undergrads receive need-based scholarship or grant aid. 31% freshmen, 25% undergrads receive non-need-based scholarship or grant aid. 78% freshmen, 61% undergrads receive need-based self-help aid. 0% freshmen, 0% undergrads receive athletic scholarships. 100% freshmen, 98% undergrads receive any aid. **Criteria for awarding aid:** *Need-based:* Academics, Art, Leadership, Minority status, Music/drama, Religious affiliation *Non-need-based:* Academics, Art, Leadership, Minority status, Music/drama, Religious affiliation, State/district residency.

MARYVILLE UNIVERSITY OF SAINT LOUIS

650 Maryville University Drive, St. Louis, MO 63141-7299
Phone: 314-529-9350 · **Financial Aid Phone:** 314-529-9360
E-mail: admissions@maryville.edu · **CEEB Code:** 6399
Fax: 314-529-9927 · **ACT Code:** 2326

This private school was founded in 1872. It has a 130 acre campus.

RATINGS

Admissions Selectivity Rating: 77   **Fire Safety Rating:** 93   **Green Rating:** 70

STUDENTS AND FACULTY

Enrollment: 3,112. **Student Body:** 66% female, 34% male, 49% out-of-state, 4% international (42 countries represented). Asian 3%, African American 8%, Caucasian 72%, Hispanic 4%, Native American <1%, Pacific Islander <1%, Two or more races 3%, Race unknown 5%.
Retention and Graduation: 83% freshmen return for sophomore year. 54% freshmen graduate within 4 years. 72% freshmen graduate within 6 years.
Faculty: Student/faculty ratio 14:1. 149 full-time faculty, 75% hold PhDs, 16% are members of minority groups, 62% are women. 0% of classes are taught by teaching assistants.

ACADEMICS

Degrees: Bachelor's; Certificate; Doctoral/Research; Master's; Post-Bachelor's certificate; Post-Master's certificate **Most popular majors:** Psychology; Physical Therapy/Therapist; Registered Nursing/Registered Nurse. **Special**

Study Options: Accelerated program; Cooperative education program; Cross-registration; Distance learning; Double major; Dual enrollment; External degree program; Honors program; Independent study; Internships; Liberal arts/career combination; Student-designed major; Study abroad; Teacher certification program; Weekend college. **Honors programs:** Bascom Honors Program. **Disability Services offered to physically disabled students:** Note-taking services; Reader services; Tape recorders; Tutors. **Career services:** Alumni services; Career assessment; Career/job search classes; Internships

FACILITIES

Housing: Apartments for single students; Coed dorms; Theme housing; Wellness housing 100% of campus accessible to physically diasbled. **Special Academic Facilities/Equipment:** University Center, art galleries, auditorium, chapel, observatory, teaching lab, clinical labs, art and design labs, Apple Distinguished University. **Computers:** 100% of classrooms, 100% of dorms, 100% of libraries, 100% of dining areas, 100% of student union, 100% of common outdoor areas have wireless network access. Students can register for classes online. Administrative functions (other than registration) can be performed online.

CAMPUS LIFE

Environment: Metropolis **Activities:** Campus Ministries; Choral groups; Dance; International Student Organization; Literary magazine; Music ensembles; Pep band; Student government; Student newspaper; Symphony orchestra 40 registered organizations, 3 honor societies, 4 religious organizations. **Athletics (Intercollegiate):** *Men:* baseball, basketball, cheerleading, cross-country, golf, soccer, tennis. *Women:* basketball, cheerleading, cross-country, golf, soccer, softball, tennis, volleyball. Gander Dining Hall, Walker Hall-Health Professions Bldg., Buder Commons, Donius University Center, Kaldi's Coffee House

ADMISSIONS

Freshman Academic Profile: Average high school GPA 3.6. 28% in top 10% of high school class, 59% in top 25% of high school class, 85% in top 50% of high school class. 77% from public high schools. **Test Scores:** SAT EBRW middle 50% range 485-615. ACT middle 50% range 22-27. Minimum internet-based TOEFL 61. Minimum paper TOEFL 500. **Basis for Candidate Selection:** *Very important factors considered include:* academic GPA, standardized test scores. *Important factors considered include:* rigor of secondary school record, extracurricular activities. *Other factors considered include:* class rank, application essay, recommendation(s), interview, talent/ability, character/personal qualities. **Freshman Admission Requirements:** High school diploma is required and GED is accepted *Academic units required:* 4 English, 3 math, 2 science, 2 social studies, and 3 units from above areas or other academic areas. **Freshman Admission Statistics:** 2,241 applied, 91.9% admitted, 29% enrolled. **Transfer Admission Requirements:** college transcript(s), Minimum college GPA of 2.0 required. Lowest grade transferable C-. **General Admission Information:** Priority deadline 12/15. Regular application deadline 8/15. Nonfall registration accepted. Admission may be deferred for a maximum of 1 year.

COSTS AND FINANCIAL AID

Annual tuition $26,070. Room and board $10,088. Required fees $2,400. **Required Forms and Deadlines:** FAFSA. **Notification of Awards:** Applicants will be notified of awards on a rolling basis beginning 2/22. **Types of Aid:** *Need-based scholarships/grants:* College/university scholarship or grant aid from institutional funds; Federal Pell; Private scholarships; SEOG; State scholarships/grants; United Negro College Fund. *Loans:* Direct PLUS loans; Direct Subsidized Stafford Loans; Direct Unsubsidized Stafford Loans. *Student Employment:* Federal Work-Study Program available. Institutional employment available. **Financial Aid Statistics:** 98% needy freshmen, 97% needy undergrads receive need-based scholarship or grant aid. 15% freshmen, 9% undergrads receive non-need-based scholarship or grant aid. 59% freshmen, 71% undergrads receive need-based self-help aid. 10% freshmen, 7% undergrads receive athletic scholarships. 72% freshmen, 65% undergrads receive any aid. 84% undergrads borrow to pay for school. Average cumulative indebtedness $19,266. **Criteria for awarding aid:** *Need-based:* Academics, Art, Minority status, Music/drama *Non-need-based:* Academics, Art, Athletics, Job skills, Leadership, Minority status, Music/drama, State/district residency.

MARYWOOD UNIVERSITY

2300 Adams Avenue, Scranton, PA 18509
Phone: 570-348-6234 · **Financial Aid Phone:** 866-279-9663
E-mail: yourfuture@marywood.edu · **CEEB Code:** 2407
Fax: 570-961-4763 · **Website:** www.marywood.edu · **ACT Code:** 3626

This private school, affiliated with the Roman Catholic Church, was founded in 1915. It has a 122.7 acre campus.

RATINGS

Admissions Selectivity Rating: 77   **Fire Safety Rating:** 95   **Green Rating:** 60*

STUDENTS AND FACULTY

Enrollment: 1,817. **Student Body:** 68% female, 32% male, 30% out-of-state, 1% international (8 countries represented). Asian 2%, African American 2%, Caucasian 79%, Hispanic 6%, Native American <1%, Pacific Islander <1%, Two or more races 2%, Race unknown 8%. **Retention and Graduation:** 83% freshmen return for sophomore year. 40% grads go on to further study within 1 year. 6% grads pursue arts and sciences degrees. 0.4% grads pursue law degrees. 1% grads pursue business degrees. 1% grads pursue medical degrees. **Faculty:** Student/faculty ratio 11:1. 160 full-time faculty, 91% hold PhDs, 14% are members of minority groups, 56% are women. 0% of classes are taught by teaching assistants.

ACADEMICS

Degrees: Bachelor's; Certificate; Doctoral/Professional; Doctoral/Research; Master's; Post-Bachelor's certificate; Post-Master's certificate **Classes:** Most classes have 20-29 students. Most lab/discussion sessions have 10-19 students. **Most popular majors:** Psychology, General; Audiology/Audiologist And Speech-Language Pathology/Pathologist; Registered Nursing/Registered Nurse. **Special Study Options:** Cross-registration; Distance learning; Double major; Dual enrollment; English as a Second Language (ESL); Honors program; Independent study; Internships; Student-designed major; Study abroad; Teacher certification program; Weekend college. **Honors programs:** Open Honors program focused on both scholarship and research. **Combined degree programs:** BA/MA. **Disability Services offered to physically disabled students:** Note-taking services; Reader services; Tape recorders; Tutors. **Career services:** Alumni network; Alumni services; Career assessment; Career/job search classes; Internships; Regional alumni

FACILITIES

Housing: Apartments for single students; Coed dorms; Special housing for disabled student; Women's dorms 98% of campus accessible to physically disabled. **Special Academic Facilities/Equipment:** Academic excellence center; student counseling center; human physiology lab; human development (counseling, psychology) laboratories; biotechnology lab; communication sciences and disorders clinic; nutrition and dietetics lab; assistive technology center; outpatient mental health clinic; multiple "smart" classrooms; multiple computer labs; full-service library; television studio and editing suites; radio station and studio; 60,000-square-foot, studio art center (including ceramic, painting, drawing/foundation, sculpture, glass, metal, clay, wood, photography, fabric, jewelry, and printmaking studios); 15,000-square foot visual arts center (including graphic design and interior architecture computer labs, two art exhibit galleries; Maslow Collection of Contemporary Art; and Maslow Study Gallery); 1,100-seat performance theater; black box theater; 1,500-seat athletics arena (2,500 seats for events); 5,000-square-foot fitness center; NCAA regulation pool and Aquatics Center; additional basketball courts; exterior tennis courts; 1,200-square foot dance/aerobic studio; hydro-therapy room, separate team and student locker facilities; Center for Architectural Studies studios, arboretum **Computers:** 75% of classrooms, 75% of dorms, 100% of libraries, 100% of dining areas, 100% of student union, 75% of common outdoor areas have wireless network access. Students can register for classes online. Administrative functions (other than registration) can be performed online.

CAMPUS LIFE

Environment: Town **Activities:** Campus Ministries; Choral groups; Concert band; Dance; Drama/theater; International Student Organization; Jazz band; Literary magazine; Music ensembles; Musical theater; Opera; Radio station; Student government; Student newspaper; Symphony orchestra; Television station 43 registered organizations, 31 honor societies, 1 religious organization. 1 sororities. **Athletics (Intercollegiate):** *Men:* baseball, basketball, cross-country, diving, lacrosse, soccer, swimming, tennis. *Women:* basketball, cross-country, diving, field hockey, lacrosse, soccer, softball, swimming, tennis, volleyball. **On-Campus Highlights:** Center for Athletics and Wellness, School of Architecture, New Learning Commons, Cafe Ritazza/Main Dining Room, Nazareth Student Center **Environmental Initiatives:** Purchase of renewable fuel sources; wind and solar power $28,800 annually.

ADMISSIONS

Freshman Academic Profile: Average high school GPA 3.5. 13% in top 10% of high school class, 48% in top 25% of high school class, 80% in top 50% of high school class. 89% from public high schools. **Test Scores:** SAT Math middle 50% range 470-560. SAT EBRW middle 50% range 460-560. Minimum internet-based TOEFL 71. Minimum paper TOEFL 530. **Basis for Candidate Selection:** *Very important factors considered include:* rigor of secondary school record, class rank, academic GPA, standardized test scores, interview, character/personal qualities. *Important factors considered include:* application essay, recommendation(s), extracurricular activities, talent/ability. *Other factors considered include:* volunteer work, work experience, level of applicant's interest. **Freshman Admission Requirements:** High school diploma is required and GED is accepted *Academic units required:* 4 English, 2 math, 1 science, 1 science labs, 3 social studies, 6 academic electives. **Freshman Admission Statistics:** 2,273 applied, 70.5% admitted, 23% enrolled. **Transfer Admission Requirements:** High school transcript, college transcript(s), Minimum college GPA of 2.25 required. Lowest grade transferable C. **General Admission Information:** Application fee $35. Nonfall registration accepted. Admission may be deferred for a maximum of 1 year.

COSTS AND FINANCIAL AID

Annual tuition $30,942. Room and board $13,900. Required fees $1,750. Average book expense $1,000. **Required Forms and Deadlines:** FAFSA; State aid form. **Notification of Awards:** Applicants will be notified of awards on a rolling basis beginning 3/15. **Types of Aid:** *Need-based scholarships/grants:* College/university scholarship or grant aid from institutional funds; Federal Pell; Private scholarships; SEOG; State scholarships/grants. *Loans:* Direct PLUS loans; Direct Subsidized Stafford Loans; Direct Unsubsidized Stafford Loans. *Student Employment:* Federal Work-Study Program available. **Financial Aid Statistics:** 100% needy freshmen, 99% needy undergrads receive need-based scholarship or grant aid. 16% freshmen, 12% undergrads receive non-need-based scholarship or grant aid. 79% freshmen, 84% undergrads receive need-based self-help aid. 0% freshmen, 0% undergrads receive athletic scholarships. 99% freshmen, 99% undergrads receive any aid. 83% undergrads borrow to pay for school. Average cumulative indebtedness $29,064. **Criteria for awarding aid:** *Need-based:* Academics, Art, Leadership, Music/drama *Non-need-based:* Academics, Alumni affiliation, Art, Leadership, Music/drama.

MASSACHUSETTS COLLEGE OF ART AND DESIGN

621 Huntington Avenue, Boston, MA 02115
Phone: 617-879-7222 · **Financial Aid Phone:** 617.879.7850
E-mail: admissions@massart.edu · **CEEB Code:** 3516
Fax: 617-879-7250 · **ACT Code:** 1846

This public school was founded in 1873. It has a 5 acre campus.

RATINGS

Admissions Selectivity Rating: 66   **Fire Safety Rating:** 90   **Green Rating:** 60*

STUDENTS AND FACULTY

Enrollment: 1,813. **Student Body:** 71% female, 29% male, 32% out-of-state, 4% international. Asian 9%, African American 5%, Caucasian 65%, Hispanic 11%, Native American <1%, Pacific Islander <1%, Two or more races 2%, Race unknown 4%. **Retention and Graduation:** 87% freshmen return for sophomore year. 57% freshmen graduate within 4 years. 73% freshmen graduate within 6 years. **Faculty:** Student/faculty ratio 9:1. 111 full-time faculty, 82% hold PhDs, 14% are members of minority groups, 51% are women. 0% of classes are taught by teaching assistants.

ACADEMICS

Degrees: Bachelor's; Certificate; Master's; Post-Bachelor's certificate **Most popular majors:** Graphic Design; Illustration; Painting. **Special Study Options:** Cross-registration; Double major; Exchange student program (domestic); Independent study; Internships; Liberal arts/career combination; Student-designed major; Study abroad; Teacher certification program. **Disability Services offered to physically disabled students:** Note-taking services; Reader services; Tutors. **Career services:** Alumni network; Alumni services; Career assessment; Career/job search classes; Internships

FACILITIES

Housing: Apartments for single students; Coed dorms; Other (please specify) 95% of campus accessible to physically disabled. **Special Academic Facilities/Equipment:** Ten art galleries, foundry, glass furnaces, ceramic kilns, video and film studios, performance spaces, Polaroid 20x24 camera, individual studio spaces, design research unit, printmaking facilities, video and photography equipment and facilities, specialized computer labs, specialized equipment and facilities for all art and design programs and levels. **Computers:** 100% of classrooms, 100% of dorms, 100% of libraries, 100% of dining areas, 100% of student union, 100% of common outdoor areas have wireless network access. Students can register for classes online. Administrative functions (other than registration) can be performed online.

CAMPUS LIFE

Environment: Metropolis **Activities:** Dance; Drama/theater; Music ensembles; Radio station; Student government; Student newspaper; Student-run film society; Television station; Yearbook 30 registered organizations, 1 honor society, 3 religious organizations. **Athletics (Intercollegiate):** *Men:* baseball, basketball, cross-country, golf, lacrosse, soccer, softball, tennis, volleyball. *Women:* basketball, cross-country, golf, lacrosse, soccer, softball, tennis, volleyball. **On-Campus Highlights:** 10 art galleries, student studios, courtyard, cafes, student center **Environmental Initiatives:** http://inside.massart.edu/Administration/Administration_and_Finance/Facilities/Sustainability.html

ADMISSIONS

Freshman Academic Profile: Average high school GPA 3.5. **Test Scores:** Minimum internet-based TOEFL 85. Minimum paper TOEFL 530. **Basis for Candidate Selection:** *Very important factors considered include:* rigor of secondary school record, academic GPA, application essay, talent/ability. *Important factors considered include:* state residency. *Other factors considered include:* recommendation(s), extracurricular activities, character/personal qualities, geographical residence, volunteer work, work experience. **Freshman Admission Requirements:** High school diploma is required and GED is accepted *Academic units required:* 4 English, 2 math, 2 science, 2 science labs, 2 foreign language, 2 social studies, 2 academic electives, and 2 units from above areas or other academic areas. *Academic units recommended:* 1 history. **Freshman Admission Statistics:** 2,082 applied, 81.0% admitted, 25% enrolled. **Transfer Admission Requirements:** college transcript(s), essay or personal statement, statement of good standing from prior institution(s). Minimum college GPA of 2.5 required. Lowest grade transferable C. **General Admission Information:** Application fee $70. Regular application deadline 2/1. Nonfall registration accepted. Admission may be deferred for a maximum of 1 year.

COSTS AND FINANCIAL AID

Annual in-state tuition $13,500. Annual out-of-state tuition $34,400. Room and board $13,500. Average book expense $2,100. **Required Forms and Deadlines:** FAFSA. **Types of Aid:** *Need-based scholarships/grants:* College/university scholarship or grant aid from institutional funds; Federal Pell; Private scholarships; SEOG; State scholarships/grants. *Loans:* Direct PLUS loans; Direct Subsidized Stafford Loans; Direct Unsubsidized Stafford Loans. *Student Employment:* Federal Work-Study Program available. Institutional employment available. **Financial Aid Statistics:** 85% needy freshmen, 74% needy undergrads receive need-based scholarship or grant aid. 27% freshmen, 21% undergrads receive non-need-based scholarship or grant aid. 89% freshmen, 91% undergrads receive need-based self-help aid. 0% freshmen, 0% undergrads receive athletic scholarships. **Criteria for awarding aid:** *Need-based:* Academics, Leadership *Non-need-based:* Academics, Art, Leadership, State/district residency.

MASSACHUSETTS COLLEGE OF PHARMACY AND HEALTH SCIENCE

179 Longwood Avenue, Boston, MA 02115
Phone: 617-732-2850 · **Financial Aid Phone:** 617-732-2864
E-mail: admissions@mcphs.edu · **CEEB Code:** 3512
Fax: 617-732-2118 · **Website:** www.mcphs.edu · **ACT Code:** 1860

This private school was founded in 1823. It has a 3 acre campus.

RATINGS

Admissions Selectivity Rating: 73 **Fire Safety Rating:** 97 **Green Rating:** 60*

STUDENTS AND FACULTY

Enrollment: 3,791. **Student Body:** 71% female, 29% male, 42% out-of-state, 13% international (32 countries represented). Asian 23%, African American 7%, Caucasian 41%, Hispanic 6%, Native American <1%, Pacific Islander <1%, Two or more races 2%, Race unknown 7%.
Retention and Graduation: 85% freshmen return for sophomore year.

Faculty: 309 full-time faculty, 91% hold PhDs, 0% of classes are taught by teaching assistants.

ACADEMICS

Degrees: Bachelor's; Certificate; Doctoral/Professional; Doctoral/Research; Master's; Post-Bachelor's certificate; Post-Master's certificate **Classes:** Most classes have 10-19 students. Most lab/discussion sessions have 10-19 students. **Most popular majors:** Pre-Medicine/Pre-Medical Studies; Nursing/Registered Nurse (Rn, Asn, Bsn, Msn); Pharmacy. **Special Study Options:** Accelerated program; Cross-registration; Distance learning; Double major; Study abroad. **Disability Services offered to physically disabled students:** Note-taking services; Reader services; Tape recorders; Tutors. **Career services:** Alumni network; Alumni services; Regional alumni

FACILITIES

Housing: Apartments for single students; Coed dorms; Special housing for disabled student; Theme housing; Wellness housing 100% of campus accessible to physically disabled. **Special Academic Facilities/Equipment:** Museum of Fine Arts and Isabella Stewart Gardner museum next door. **Computers:** 100% of classrooms, 100% of dorms, 100% of libraries, 100% of dining areas, 100% of student union, 100% of common outdoor areas have wireless network access. Students can register for classes online. Administrative functions (other than registration) can be performed online.

CAMPUS LIFE

Environment: Metropolis **Activities:** Campus Ministries; Choral groups; Dance; Drama/theater; International Student Organization; Jazz band; Student government; Student newspaper 66 registered organizations, 5 honor societies, 2 religious organizations. **On-Campus Highlights:** New Building, residence hall, labs, Pharmacy Laboratory, Dental Hygiene Clinic, Cafeteria (located in Mass. College of Art), Student Lounge

ADMISSIONS

Freshman Academic Profile: Average high school GPA 3.5. **Test Scores:** SAT Math middle 50% range 490-620. SAT EBRW middle 50% range 460-560. ACT middle 50% range 21-27. Minimum internet-based TOEFL 79. Minimum paper TOEFL 550. **Basis for Candidate Selection:** *Very important factors considered include:* rigor of secondary school record, academic GPA, standardized test scores. *Other factors considered include:* class rank, application essay, recommendation(s), interview, extracurricular activities, talent/ability, character/personal qualities, first generation, alumni/ae relation, volunteer work, work experience, level of applicant's interest. **Freshman Admission Requirements:** High school diploma is required and GED is accepted *Academic units required:* 4 English, 3 math, 2 science, 2 science labs, 1 social studies, 1 history, 5 academic electives. **Freshman Admission Statistics:** 5,530 applied, 84.4% admitted, 12% enrolled. **Transfer Admission Requirements:** college transcript(s), essay or personal statement, Minimum college GPA of 2.5 required. Lowest grade transferable C. **General Admission Information:** Nonfall registration accepted. Admission may be deferred.

COSTS AND FINANCIAL AID

Annual tuition $30,600. Room and board $15,834. Required fees $1,070. Average book expense $1,028. **Required Forms and Deadlines:** FAFSA. **Notification of Awards:** Applicants will be notified of awards on a rolling basis beginning 2/15. **Types of Aid:** *Need-based scholarships/grants:* College/university scholarship or grant aid from institutional funds; Federal Pell; SEOG; State scholarships/grants. *Loans:* Direct PLUS loans; Direct Subsidized Stafford Loans; Direct Unsubsidized Stafford Loans. *Student Employment:* Federal Work-Study Program available. **Financial Aid Statistics:** 99% needy freshmen, 93% needy undergrads receive need-based scholarship or grant aid. 0% undergrads receive non-need-based scholarship or grant aid. 89% freshmen, 90% undergrads receive need-based self-help aid. 0% freshmen, 0% undergrads receive athletic scholarships. 90% freshmen, 90% undergrads receive any aid. **Criteria for awarding aid:** *Non-need-based:* Academics.

MASSACHUSETTS INSTITUTE OF TECHNOLOGY

Best Colleges

77 Massachusetts Avenue, Cambridge, MA 02139
Phone: 617-253-3400 · **Financial Aid Phone:** 617-258-8600
E-mail: admissions@mit.edu · **CEEB Code:** 3514
Fax: 617-258-8304 · **Website:** web.mit.edu · **ACT Code:** 1858

This private school was founded in 1861. It has a 168 acre campus.

RATINGS
Admissions Selectivity Rating: 99   **Fire Safety Rating:** 91   **Green Rating:** 60*

STUDENTS AND FACULTY
Enrollment: 4,489. **Student Body:** 46% female, 54% male, 90% out-of-state, 10% international (107 countries represented). Asian 27%, African American 6%, Caucasian 34%, Hispanic 14%, Native American <1%, Pacific Islander 0%, Two or more races 7%, Race unknown 1%.
Retention and Graduation: 99% freshmen return for sophomore year. 85% freshmen graduate within 4 years. 94% freshmen graduate within 6 years. 39% grads go on to further study within 1 year. 26% grads pursue arts and sciences degrees. 1% grads pursue law degrees. 0% grads pursue business degrees. 13% grads pursue medical degrees. **Faculty:** Student/faculty ratio 3:1. 1,283 full-time faculty, 92% hold PhDs, 18% are members of minority groups, 26% are women.

ACADEMICS
Degrees: Bachelor's; Doctoral/Research; Master's **Most popular majors:** Computer Science; Mechanical Engineering; Mathematics, General. **Special Study Options:** Cooperative education program; Cross-registration; Double major; Internships; Study abroad; Teacher certification program. **Disability Services offered to physically disabled students:** Note-taking services; Reader services; Tape recorders. **Career services:** Alumni network; Alumni services; Career assessment; Career/job search classes; Internships; Regional alumni

FACILITIES
Housing: Apartments for married students; Apartments for single students; Coed dorms; Cooperative housing; Fraternity/sorority housing; Special housing for disabled student; Theme housing; Women's dorms **Special Academic Facilities/Equipment:** List Visual Arts Center; MIT Museum; Ray and Maria Stata Center for Computer, Information and Intelligence Sciences; numerous labs and centers **Computers:** 100% of classrooms, 100% of dorms, 100% of libraries, 100% of dining areas, 100% of student union, 80-98% of common outdoor areas have wireless network access. Administrative functions (other than registration) can be performed online.

CAMPUS LIFE
Environment: City **Activities:** Campus Ministries; Choral groups; Concert band; Dance; Drama/theater; International Student Organization; Jazz band; Literary magazine; Marching band; Model UN; Music ensembles; Musical theater; Radio station; Student government; Student newspaper; Student-run film society; Symphony orchestra; Television station; Yearbook 400 registered organizations, 10 honor societies, 29 religious organizations. 27 fraternities, 6 sororities. **Athletics (Intercollegiate):** *Men:* baseball, basketball, crew/rowing, cross-country, diving, fencing, football, golf, gymnastics, lacrosse, pistol, riflery, sailing, skiing (downhill/alpine), skiing (nordic/cross-country), soccer, squash, swimming, tennis, track/field (outdoor), track/field (indoor), volleyball, water polo, wrestling. *Women:* basketball, crew/rowing, cross-country, diving, fencing, field hockey, gymnastics, ice hockey, lacrosse, pistol, riflery, sailing, skiing (downhill/alpine), skiing (nordic/cross-country), soccer, softball, swimming, tennis, track/field (outdoor), track/field (indoor), volleyball. **On-Campus Highlights:** Ray and Maria Stata Center, Zesiger Sports and Fitness Center, Killian Court, The Infinite Corridor, The Student Center (W20) **Environmental Initiatives:** In 2013, MIT created a new Office of Sustainability reporting directly to our Executive Vice President, which is the highest administrative for operations office. This creates an office at the highest level with a new director to scale up MIT's already robust sustainability programs. MIT has also launched a new Sustainability Executive Committee (comprised of the Provost, Directors of MIT's top sustainability research programs, Chancellor, and Vice President for Research) and a Campus Sustainability Task Force (comprised of respresentatives of all 5 schools, and key operational areas and students) to coordinate implementation of MIT's sustainability plans.

ADMISSIONS
Freshman Academic Profile: 98% in top 10% of high school class, 100% in top 25% of high school class, 100% in top 50% of high school class. 67% from public high schools. **Test Scores:** SAT Math middle 50% range 770-800. SAT EBRW middle 50% range 720-770. ACT middle 50% range 33-35. Minimum internet-based TOEFL 90. **Basis for Candidate Selection:** *Very important factors considered include:* character/personal qualities. *Important factors considered include:* rigor of secondary school record, academic GPA, application essay, standardized test scores, recommendation(s), interview, extracurricular activities, talent/ability. *Other factors considered include:* class rank, first generation, geographical residence, racial/ethnic status, volunteer work, work experience. **Freshman Admission Requirements:** High school diploma or equivalent is not required *Academic units recommended:* 4 English, 4 math, 4 science, 2 foreign language, 2 social studies. **Freshman Admission Statistics:** 20,247 applied, 7.2% admitted, 76% enrolled. **Transfer Admission Requirements:** High school transcript, college transcript(s), essay or personal statement, standardized test scores, statement of good standing from prior institution(s). Lowest grade transferable B. **General Admission Information:** Application fee $75. Regular application deadline 1/1. Nonfall registration accepted. Admission may be deferred for a maximum of 2 years.

COSTS AND FINANCIAL AID
Annual tuition $51,520. Room and board $15,510. Required fees $312. Average book expense $1,000. **Required Forms and Deadlines:** CSS/Financial Aid PROFILE; FAFSA; Noncustodial PROFILE. **Notification of Awards:** Applicants will be notified of awards on or about 3/15. **Types of Aid:** *Need-based scholarships/grants:* College/university scholarship or grant aid from institutional funds; Federal Pell; Private scholarships; SEOG; State scholarships/grants; United Negro College Fund. *Loans:* Direct PLUS loans; Direct Subsidized Stafford Loans; Direct Unsubsidized Stafford Loans. *Student Employment:* Federal Work-Study Program available. Institutional employment available. **Financial Aid Statistics:** 96% needy freshmen, 96% needy undergrads receive need-based scholarship or grant aid. 5% freshmen, 2% undergrads receive non-need-based scholarship or grant aid. 71% freshmen, 77% undergrads receive need-based self-help aid. 0% freshmen, 0% undergrads receive athletic scholarships. 86% freshmen, 76% undergrads receive any aid. 27% undergrads borrow to pay for school. Average cumulative indebtedness $24,954.

MASSACHUSETTS MARITIME ACADEMY

101 Academy Drive, Buzzards Bay, MA 02532
Phone: 800-544-3411 · **Financial Aid Phone:** 508-830-5087
E-mail: admissions@maritime.edu · **CEEB Code:** 3515
Fax: 508-830-5077 · **Website:** https://www.maritime.edu

This public school was founded in 1891. It has a 54 acre campus.

RATINGS
Admissions Selectivity Rating: 80   **Fire Safety Rating:** 60*   **Green Rating:** 60*

STUDENTS AND FACULTY
Enrollment: 1,627. **Student Body:** 12% female, 88% male, 20% out-of-state, 1% international (3 countries represented). Asian 1%, African American 1%, Caucasian 88%, Hispanic 3%, Native American <1%, Pacific Islander 0%, Two or more races 3%, Race unknown 3%.
Retention and Graduation: 88% freshmen return for sophomore year. 58% freshmen graduate within 4 years. 75% freshmen graduate within 6 years. **Faculty:** Student/faculty ratio 16:1. 87 full-time faculty, 66% hold PhDs, 18% are members of minority groups, 31% are women.

ACADEMICS
Degrees: Bachelor's; Master's **Classes:** Most classes have fewer than 10 students. **Special Study Options:** Cooperative education program; Double major; Dual enrollment; Internships; Study abroad. **Disability Services offered to physically disabled students:** Note-taking services; Tape recorders; Tutors. Alumni network; Alumni services; Career/job search classes; Internships

FACILITIES
Housing: Coed dorms; Wellness housing

CAMPUS LIFE
Environment: Rural **Activities:** Concert band; Drama/theater; International Student Organization; Jazz band; Literary magazine; Marching band; Music ensembles; Pep band; Student government; Yearbook

ADMISSIONS

Test Scores: SAT Math middle 50% range 520-600. SAT EBRW middle 50% range 520-600. ACT middle 50% range 21-25. Minimum internet-based TOEFL 75. Minimum paper TOEFL 530. **Basis for Candidate Selection:** *Very important factors considered include:* rigor of secondary school record, academic GPA, application essay, standardized test scores, recommendation(s). *Important factors considered include:* interview, extracurricular activities, level of applicant's interest. *Other factors considered include:* class rank, talent/ability, character/personal qualities, first generation, alumni/ae relation, racial/ethnic status, volunteer work, work experience. **Freshman Admission Requirements:** High school diploma is required and GED is accepted *Academic units required:* 4 English, 4 math, 3 science, 3 science labs, 2 foreign language, 1 social studies, 1 history, 2 academic electives, *Academic units recommended:* 4 English, 4 math, 4 science, 3 science labs, 2 foreign language, 1 social studies, 1 history, 2 academic electives. **Freshman Admission Statistics:** 838 applied, 83.2% admitted, 56% enrolled. **General Admission Information:** Application fee $50. Nonfall registration accepted. Admission may be deferred for a maximum of 1 year.

COSTS AND FINANCIAL AID

Average book expense $1,500. **Required Forms and Deadlines:** FAFSA. **Notification of Awards:** Applicants will be notified of awards on a rolling basis beginning 1/15. **Types of Aid:** *Need-based scholarships/grants:* College/university scholarship or grant aid from institutional funds; Federal Pell; Private scholarships; SEOG; State scholarships/grants. *Loans:* Direct PLUS loans; Direct Subsidized Stafford Loans; Direct Unsubsidized Stafford Loans. *Student Employment:* Federal Work-Study Program available. Institutional employment available.

THE MASTER'S COLLEGE

21726 Placerita Canyon Road, Santa Clarita, CA 91321
Phone: (661) 362-2363 · **Financial Aid Phone:** 661-362-2293
E-mail: admissions@masters.edu · **CEEB Code:** 4411
Fax: (661) 362-2718 · **Website:** www.masters.edu · **ACT Code:** 303

This private school, affiliated with the Nondenominational Christian, was founded in 1927. It has a 110 acre campus.

RATINGS

Admissions Selectivity Rating: 85   **Fire Safety Rating:** 85   **Green Rating:** 60*

STUDENTS AND FACULTY

Enrollment: 1,166. **Student Body:** 44% female, 56% male, 36% out-of-state, 4% international (25 countries represented). Asian 5%, African American 2%, Caucasian 65%, Hispanic 11%, Native American <1%, Pacific Islander <1%, Two or more races 6%, Race unknown 6%.
Retention and Graduation: 85% freshmen return for sophomore year. 44% freshmen graduate within 4 years. 50% freshmen graduate within 6 years.
Faculty: Student/faculty ratio 12:1. 51 full-time faculty, 75% hold PhDs, 8% are members of minority groups, 20% are women. 0% of classes are taught by teaching assistants.

ACADEMICS

Degrees: Bachelor's; Diploma; Doctoral; Doctoral Other; Doctoral/Professional; Doctoral/Research; Master's **Classes:** Most classes have 10-19 students. Most lab/discussion sessions have fewer than 10 students. **Most popular majors:** Communication And Media Studies; Bible/Biblical Studies; Business/Commerce, General. **Special Study Options:** Accelerated program; Distance learning; Double major; Dual enrollment; Independent study; Internships; Liberal arts/career combination; Study abroad; Teacher certification program. **Disability Services offered to physically disabled students:** Note-taking services; Reader services; Tape recorders; Tutors. **Career services:** Alumni services; Career assessment; Career/job search classes; Internships

FACILITIES

Housing: Apartments for married students; Apartments for single students; Men's dorms; Women's dorms 95% of campus accessible to physically diasbled. **Computers:** 100% of classrooms, 100% of dorms, 100% of libraries, 100% of dining areas, 100% of student union, 95% of common outdoor areas have wireless network access. Students can register for classes online. Administrative functions (other than registration) can be performed online. Undergraduates are required to own a computer.

CAMPUS LIFE

Environment: City **Activities:** Campus Ministries; Choral groups; Concert band; Drama/theater; International Student Organization; Music ensembles;

Musical theater; Opera; Pep band; Student government; Student newspaper; Symphony orchestra 15 registered organizations, 1 honor society, 11 religious organizations. **Athletics (Intercollegiate):** *Men:* baseball, basketball, cross-country, golf, soccer, track/field (outdoor). *Women:* basketball, cross-country, soccer, tennis, track/field (outdoor), volleyball. **On-Campus Highlights:** MacArthur Center (chapel and gym), Mustang Grill and Student Center, Canyon Cafe, Under the Oaks, Fitness Center

ADMISSIONS

Freshman Academic Profile: Average high school GPA 3.7. 31% in top 10% of high school class, 69% in top 25% of high school class, 90% in top 50% of high school class. 40% from public high schools. **Test Scores:** SAT Math middle 50% range 510-600. SAT EBRW middle 50% range 520-640. ACT middle 50% range 20-23. Minimum internet-based TOEFL 80. **Basis for Candidate Selection:** *Very important factors considered include:* academic GPA, application essay, standardized test scores, recommendation(s), character/personal qualities, religious affiliation/commitment. *Important factors considered include:* rigor of secondary school record. *Other factors considered include:* extracurricular activities, talent/ability, alumni/ae relation, level of applicant's interest. **Freshman Admission Requirements:** High school diploma is required and GED is accepted *Academic units required:* 4 English, 3 math, 2 science, 2 history, *Academic units recommended:* 3 academic electives. **Freshman Admission Statistics:** 617 applied, 65.8% admitted, 40% enrolled. **Transfer Admission Requirements:** High school transcript, college transcript(s), essay or personal statement, interview, statement of good standing from prior institution(s). Minimum college GPA of 2.5 required. Lowest grade transferable C. **General Admission Information:** Application fee $40. Priority deadline 3/2. Nonfall registration accepted. Admission may be deferred for a maximum of 2 semesters.

COSTS AND FINANCIAL AID

Annual tuition $24,950. Room and board $11,200. Required fees $440. Average book expense $1,792. **Required Forms and Deadlines:** FAFSA; Institution's own financial aid form. **Notification of Awards:** Applicants will be notified of awards on a rolling basis beginning 2/18. **Types of Aid:** *Need-based scholarships/grants:* College/university scholarship or grant aid from institutional funds; Federal Pell; Private scholarships; SEOG; State scholarships/grants. *Loans:* Direct PLUS loans; Direct Subsidized Stafford Loans; Direct Unsubsidized Stafford Loans. *Student Employment:* Federal Work-Study Program available. Institutional employment available. **Financial Aid Statistics:** 88% needy freshmen, 97% needy undergrads receive need-based scholarship or grant aid. 13% freshmen, 10% undergrads receive non-need-based scholarship or grant aid. 78% freshmen, 82% undergrads receive need-based self-help aid. 5% freshmen, 4% undergrads receive athletic scholarships. 95% freshmen, 90% undergrads receive any aid. **Criteria for awarding aid:** *Need-based:* Job skills *Non-need-based:* Academics, Alumni affiliation, Art, Athletics, Music/drama.

MAYNOOTH UNIVERSITY

Maynooth, Co Kildare, IR Co Kildare
Phone: +353 1 708 3868
E-mail: international.office@nuim.ie
Fax: 353 1 628 9063 · **Website:** www.maynoothuniversity.ie · **ACT Code:** 5483

This public school was founded in 1997. It has a 100 acre campus.

RATINGS

Admissions Selectivity Rating: 81   **Fire Safety Rating:** 93   **Green Rating:** 73

STUDENTS AND FACULTY

Enrollment: 9,144. **Student Body:** 55% female, 45% male, (90 countries represented).
Retention and Graduation: 88% freshmen return for sophomore year.
Faculty: Student/faculty ratio 28:1. 381 full-time faculty, 0% of classes are taught by teaching assistants.

ACADEMICS

Degrees: Bachelor's; Diploma; Doctoral; Doctoral Other; Doctoral/Professional; Doctoral/Research; Master's; Post-Bachelor's certificate; Post-Master's certificate **Classes:** Most classes have greater than 100 students. **Most popular majors:** Liberal Arts And Sciences, General Studies And Humanities; Multi/Interdisciplinary Studies; Multi-/Interdisciplinary Studies, General. **Special Study Options:** Distance learning; Double major; Dual enrollment; English as a Second Language (ESL); Exchange student program (domestic); Honors program; Independent study; Internships; Liberal arts/career combination; Study abroad; Teacher certification program. **Honors programs:** Geography; International Development; Anthropology; Music (performance is particularly strong); Electronic Engineering; Media Studies; Law. **Disability Services offered to physically disabled students:** Note-taking services; Reader services; Tape recorders. **Career services:** Alumni network; Career/job search classes; Internships; Regional alumni

FACILITIES

Housing: Coed dorms; Special housing for disabled student; Special housing for international students 75% of campus accessible to physically diasbled. **Special Academic Facilities/Equipment:** The National Science Museum of Ireland is located on the South Campus. We offer two libraries—our main library has access to 16 types of study spaces and over 45,000 materials and our Rare books and Manuscripts library contains materials from the 11th century on. The South Campus is home to several medieval buildings dating from the 1800s, including some designed by the famous architect Augustus Pugin, and the chapel on the south campus is a beautiful building. The Science facilities include laboratories for Biology, Chemistry, Pharmacy, and Physics and are all only 15 years old, so are home to very modern facilities. Eight Research Institutes are housed on campus: Hamilton Institute, Institute of Immunology, Callan Institute, National Centre for Geocomputation, Innovation Value Institute, National Institute for Regional and Spatial Analysis, An Foras Feasa, and Edward M Kennedy Centre for Conflict Resolution and Mediation

CAMPUS LIFE

Environment: Village **Activities:** Campus Ministries; Choral groups; Concert band; Dance; Drama/theater; International Student Organization; Jazz band; Literary magazine; Music ensembles; Musical theater; Radio station; Student government; Student newspaper; Student-run film society; Symphony orchestra. St Joseph's Square and Chapel (19th century), MSU—Maynooth Students Union Bar and Venue, Russell Library / Main Library—new building, The Phoenix—new Student Restaurant and Sports Center, South Campus walks and secret garden **Environmental Initiatives:** To provide and co-ordinate the travel strategy at Maynooth University to enable a lasting and maintained shift to sustainable travel in line with the University's vision of becoming a sustainable campus by providing the best range of travel options to staff, students and visitors.

ADMISSIONS

Freshman Academic Profile: Average high school GPA 3.2. **Test Scores:** Minimum internet-based TOEFL 90. Minimum paper TOEFL 550. **Basis for Candidate Selection:** *Very important factors considered include:* rigor of secondary school record, academic GPA, standardized test scores. *Important factors considered include:* class rank. *Other factors considered include:* talent/ability, character/personal qualities, level of applicant's interest. **Freshman Admission Requirements:** High school diploma is required and GED is not accepted *Academic units required:* **Freshman Admission Statistics:** 14,112 applied, 23.0% admitted, 90% enrolled. **General Admission Information:** Regular application deadline 7/31. Nonfall registration accepted. Admission may be deferred for a maximum of 1 year.

COSTS AND FINANCIAL AID

Room and board $8,500. Required fees $15,300. Average book expense $600. **Required Forms and Deadlines:** FAFSA. **Notification of Awards:** Applicants will be notified of awards on a rolling basis beginning 3/1. **Types of Aid:** *Need-based scholarships/grants:* Federal Pell. *Loans:* Direct PLUS loans; Direct Subsidized Stafford Loans; Direct Unsubsidized Stafford Loans. **Criteria for awarding aid:** *Need-based:* Academics *Non-need-based:* Academics.

See page 980.

MAYVILLE STATE UNIVERSITY

330 Third Street Northeast, Mayville, ND 58257-1299
Phone: 701-788-4842 • **Financial Aid Phone:** 701-788-4767
E-mail: MaSU.admissions@mayvillestate.edu • **CEEB Code:** 6478
Fax: 701-788-4656 • **Website:** www.mayvillestate.edu • **ACT Code:** 3212

This public school was founded in 1889. It has a 55 acre campus.

RATINGS

Admissions Selectivity Rating: 87   **Fire Safety Rating:** 81   **Green Rating:** 60*

STUDENTS AND FACULTY

Enrollment: 819. **Student Body:** 56% female, 44% male, 43% out-of-state, 3% international (7 countries represented). Asian <1%, African American 8%, Caucasian 78%, Hispanic 5%, Native American 1%, Pacific Islander 1%, Two or more races 3%, Race unknown 1%.
Retention and Graduation: 49% freshmen return for sophomore year. 12% grads go on to further study within 1 year. 1% grads pursue arts and sciences

degrees. 0% grads pursue law degrees. 4% grads pursue business degrees. 0% grads pursue medical degrees. **Faculty:** Student/faculty ratio 13:1. 49 full-time faculty, 41% hold PhDs, 2% are members of minority groups, 49% are women. 0% of classes are taught by teaching assistants.

ACADEMICS

Degrees: Bachelor's; Transfer Associate **Classes:** Most classes have 10-19 students. Most lab/discussion sessions have 20-29 students. **Most popular majors:** Elementary Education And Teaching; Physical Education Teaching And Coaching; Business/Commerce, General. **Special Study Options:** Accelerated program; Cooperative education program; Distance learning; Double major; Dual enrollment; Independent study; Internships; Student-designed major; Teacher certification program. **Disability Services offered to physically disabled students:** Note-taking services; Tape recorders; Tutors. **Career services:** Alumni network; Alumni services; Career assessment; Career/job search classes; Internships; Regional alumni

FACILITIES

Housing: Apartments for married students; Apartments for single students; Coed dorms; Men's dorms; Women's dorms 80% of campus accessible to physically diasbled. **Computers:** 100% of classrooms, 25% of dorms, 100% of libraries, 100% of dining areas, 100% of student union, 25% of common outdoor areas have wireless network access. Students can register for classes online. Administrative functions (other than registration) can be performed online. Undergraduates are required to own a computer.

CAMPUS LIFE

Environment: Rural **Activities:** Choral groups; Concert band; Drama/theater; International Student Organization; Jazz band; Music ensembles; Musical theater; Radio station; Student government; Student newspaper 118 registered organizations, 1 honor society, 2 religious organizations. **Athletics (Intercollegiate):** *Men:* baseball, basketball, football. *Women:* basketball, softball, volleyball. **On-Campus Highlights:** Lewy Lee Fieldhouse, Campus Center, Agassiz Hall, Library, Education/Science/Library complex

ADMISSIONS

Freshman Academic Profile: Average high school GPA 3.0. 95% from public high schools. **Test Scores:** ACT middle 50% range 17-22. Minimum internet-based TOEFL 68. Minimum paper TOEFL 520. **Basis for Candidate Selection:** *Very important factors considered include:* rigor of secondary school record, academic GPA. *Important factors considered include:* standardized test scores. *Other factors considered include:* interview, character/personal qualities. **Freshman Admission Requirements:** High school diploma is required and GED is accepted *Academic units required:* 4 English, 3 math, 3 science, 3 science labs, 3 social studies, *Academic units recommended:* 2 foreign language. **Freshman Admission Statistics:** 336 applied, 53.6% admitted, 76% enrolled. **Transfer Admission Requirements:** college transcript(s), statement of good standing from prior institution(s). Minimum college GPA of 2.0 required. Lowest grade transferable d. **General Admission Information:** Application fee $35. Nonfall registration accepted. Admission may be deferred.

COSTS AND FINANCIAL AID

Annual in-state tuition $5,904. Annual out-of-state tuition $7,395. Room and board $5,904. Required fees $1,450. Average book expense $1,000. **Required Forms and Deadlines:** FAFSA. **Notification of Awards:** Applicants will be notified of awards on a rolling basis beginning 5/1. **Types of Aid:** *Need-based scholarships/grants:* College/university scholarship or grant aid from institutional funds; Federal Pell; Private scholarships; SEOG; State scholarships/grants. *Loans:* Direct PLUS loans; Direct Subsidized Stafford Loans; Direct Unsubsidized Stafford Loans. *Student Employment:* Federal Work-Study Program available. Institutional employment available. **Financial Aid Statistics:** 94% needy freshmen, 88% needy undergrads receive need-based scholarship or grant aid. 9% freshmen, 6% undergrads receive non-need-based scholarship or grant aid. 79% freshmen, 83% undergrads receive need-based self-help aid. 8% freshmen, 8% undergrads receive athletic scholarships. 83% freshmen, 78% undergrads receive any aid. 71% undergrads borrow to pay for school. Average cumulative indebtedness $32,424. **Criteria for awarding aid:** *Need-based:* Academics, Athletics, Leadership, Minority status, Music/drama *Non-need-based:* Academics, Athletics, Leadership, Minority status, Music/drama, State/district residency.

MCDANIEL COLLEGE

2 College Hill, Westminster, MD 21157
Phone: 410-857-2230 • **Financial Aid Phone:** 410-857-2233
E-mail: admissions@mcdaniel.edu • **CEEB Code:** 5898
Website: www.mcdaniel.edu • **ACT Code:** 1756

This private school was founded in 1867. It has a 160 acre campus.

RATINGS
Admissions Selectivity Rating: 76   **Fire Safety Rating:** 88   **Green Rating:** 60*

STUDENTS AND FACULTY
Enrollment: 1,549. **Student Body:** 51% female, 49% male, 34% out-of-state, 4% international (36 countries represented). Asian 3%, African American 14%, Caucasian 65%, Hispanic 6%, Native American <1%, Pacific Islander <1%, Two or more races 4%, Race unknown 4%.
Retention and Graduation: 81% freshmen return for sophomore year. 59% freshmen graduate within 4 years. 68% freshmen graduate within 6 years.
Faculty: Student/faculty ratio 11:1. 133 full-time faculty, 89% hold PhDs, 11% are members of minority groups, 54% are women. 0% of classes are taught by teaching assistants.

ACADEMICS
Degrees: Bachelor's; Master's; Post-Bachelor's certificate **Most popular majors:** Health And Physical Education/Fitness, General; Psychology, General; Business Administration And Management, General. **Special Study Options:** Accelerated program; Distance learning; Double major; Dual enrollment; Exchange student program (domestic); Honors program; Independent study; Internships; Student-designed major; Study abroad; Teacher certification program. **Honors programs:** Honors Program allows students to be a part of a community of scholars who are dedicated to academic rigor and the pursuit of liberal arts in the classroom and beyond. McDaniel is also one of only 280 U.S. colleges and universities with a Phi Beta Kappa chapter. Additionally, there are numerous other honorary societies on campus. Three societies oriented toward general accomplishment are Omicron Delta Kappa, a national society recognizing leadership qualities; Alpha Lambda Delta, a national honor society for first-year students; and the Trumpeters, a local society honoring senior students dedicated to service. National and international honor societies which recognize academic accomplishment in specific fields are Beta Beta Beta (Biology), Gamma Sigma Epsilon (Chemistry), Lambda Pi Eta (Communication), Omicron Delta Epsilon (Economics), Kappa Delta Pi (Education), Phi Alpha Theta (History), Lambda Iota Tau (Literature), Phi Sigma Iota (Foreign Languages), Kappa Mu Epsilon (Mathematics), Omicron Psi (Nontraditional Students), Phi Sigma Tau (Philosophy), Sigma Pi Sigma (Physics), Pi Sigma Alpha (Political Science), Psi Chi (Psychology), Pi Gamma Mu (Social Sciences), Phi Alpha (Social Work), and Alpha Psi Omega (Theatre Arts). **Disability Services offered to physically disabled students:** Note-taking services; Reader services; Tape recorders; Tutors. **Career services:** Alumni network; Alumni services; Career assessment; Career/job search classes; Internships; Regional alumni

FACILITIES
Housing: Apartments for single students; Coed dorms; Fraternity/sorority housing; Special housing for disabled student; Theme housing 85% of campus accessible to physically diasbled. **Special Academic Facilities/Equipment:** Rice Art Gallery, Human Performance Lab, Merritt Fitness Center, video production lab, Writing Center, 9-hole golf course, photo studio, graphics lab, observatory, student research science labs, radio station, TV station **Computers:** Students can register for classes online. Administrative functions (other than registration) can be performed online.

CAMPUS LIFE
Environment: Town **Activities:** Campus Ministries; Choral groups; Concert band; Dance; Drama/theater; International Student Organization; Jazz band; Literary magazine; Model UN; Music ensembles; Musical theater; Pep band; Radio station; Student government; Student newspaper; Student-run film society; Television station; Yearbook 136 registered organizations, 22 honor societies, 5 religious organizations. 6 fraternities, 4 sororities. **Athletics (Intercollegiate):** *Men:* baseball, basketball, cross-country, football, golf, lacrosse, soccer, swimming, tennis, track/field (outdoor), track/field (indoor), volleyball, wrestling. *Women:* basketball, cross-country, field hockey, golf, lacrosse, soccer, softball, swimming, tennis, track/field (outdoor), track/field (indoor), volleyball. **On-Campus Highlights:** The Hoover Library & Caseys' Corner, Merritt Fitness Center, Decker College Center, Gill Stadium, Golf Course

ADMISSIONS
Freshman Academic Profile: Average high school GPA 3.5. 26% in top 10% of high school class, 51% in top 25% of high school class, 84% in top 50% of high school class. **Test Scores:** SAT Math middle 50% range 520-610. SAT EBRW middle 50% range 540-620. ACT middle 50% range 21-28. Minimum internet-based TOEFL 80. Minimum paper TOEFL 550. **Basis for Candidate Selection:** *Very important factors considered include:* rigor of secondary school record, academic GPA. *Important factors considered include:* application essay, standardized test scores, recommendation(s). *Other factors considered include:* class rank, interview, extracurricular activities, talent/ability, character/personal qualities, first generation, alumni/ae relation, volunteer work, work experience, level of applicant's interest. **Freshman Admission Requirements:** High school diploma is required and GED is accepted *Academic units required:* 4 English, 3 math, 3 science, 3 science labs, 3 foreign language, 3 social studies, *Academic units recommended:* 4 English, 4 math, 4 science, 4 foreign language, 3 social studies. **Freshman Admission Statistics:** 2,814 applied, 85.0% admitted, 19% enrolled. **General Admission Information:** Application fee $50. Priority deadline 2/1. Regular application deadline 4/1. Nonfall registration accepted. Admission may be deferred for a maximum of 1 year.

COSTS AND FINANCIAL AID
Required Forms and Deadlines: FAFSA. **Notification of Awards:** Applicants will be notified of awards on a rolling basis beginning 3/15. **Types of Aid:** *Need-based scholarships/grants:* College/university scholarship or grant aid from institutional funds; Federal Pell; Private scholarships; SEOG; State scholarships/grants. *Loans:* Direct PLUS loans; Direct Subsidized Stafford Loans; Direct Unsubsidized Stafford Loans. *Student Employment:* Federal Work-Study Program available. Institutional employment available. **Financial Aid Statistics:** 100% needy freshmen, 100% needy undergrads receive need-based scholarship or grant aid. 22% freshmen, 16% undergrads receive non-need-based scholarship or grant aid. 82% freshmen, 85% undergrads receive need-based self-help aid. 0% freshmen, 0% undergrads receive athletic scholarships. 100% freshmen, 98% undergrads receive any aid. 71% undergrads borrow to pay for school. Average cumulative indebtedness $35,397. **Criteria for awarding aid:** *Non-need-based:* Academics, State/district residency.

MCGILL UNIVERSITY

845 Sherbrooke Street West, Montreal, QC H3A 0C8
Phone: 514-398-7878 · **Financial Aid Phone:** 514-398-6013 · **CEEB Code:** 935
Fax: 514-398-5544 · **Website:** http://www.mcgill.ca/admissions/ · **ACT Code:** 5231

This public school was founded in 1821. It has a 80 acre campus.

RATINGS
Admissions Selectivity Rating: 89   **Fire Safety Rating:** 79   **Green Rating:** 60*

STUDENTS AND FACULTY
Student Body: 37% out-of-state, (136 countries represented).
Faculty: Student/faculty ratio 16:1.

ACADEMICS
Degrees: Bachelor's; Certificate; Diploma; Doctoral; Master's; Post-Bachelor's certificate **Classes:** Most classes have 20-29 students. Most lab/discussion sessions have 20-29 students. **Most popular majors:** Psychology, General; Political Science And Government, General; Business/Commerce, General. **Special Study Options:** Accelerated program; Cooperative education program; Cross-registration; Distance learning; Double major; English as a Second Language (ESL); Exchange student program (domestic); Honors program; Independent study; Internships; Study abroad; Teacher certification program. **Honors programs:** McGill's Faculties of Arts, Science, and Engineering, the Desautels Faculty of Management, and the McGill School of Environment offer many outstanding honours and joint honours programs. Honours programs offer specialization and research in one academic discipline while joint honours programs offer specialization and research in a combination of disciplines. **Disability Services offered to physically disabled students:** Note-taking services; Reader services; Tape recorders; Tutors. **Career services:** Career assessment; Career/job search classes

FACILITIES
Housing: Apartments for single students; Coed dorms; Special housing for disabled student; Women's dorms 90% of campus accessible to physically diasbled. **Special Academic Facilities/Equipment:** McCord Museum of Canadian History, Redpath Museum of Natural History, Lyman Entomological Museum and Research Laboratory, Ecomuseum, Rutherford Museum, Lawrence Lande Collection of Canadiana, Canadian Architecture Collection, Morgan Arboretum, Gault Nature Reserve, Herbarium, McGill Archives

(Canadian History), Islamic Studies Library, Bellairs Research Institute, McConnell Brain Imaging Centre, McConnell Winter Arena, McGill Sports Centre Gymnasiums, Percival Molson Stadium, Memorial Pool, Richard Tomlinson Fieldhouse, Outdoor Tennis Courts, McGill Arctic Research Station, McGill Subarctic Research Station, Phytotron, Schulich School of Music (world-class sound stage, recording studio), McGill Centre for Interdisciplinary Research in Music, Media and Technology, Research Greenhouse, J. S. Marshall Weather Radar Observatory, Mountain and Glen Campuses (McGill University Health Centre Teaching Hospitals), McGill Medical Simulation Centre, McGill Reproductive Centre, McGill University and Genome Quebec Innovation Centre. **Computers:** 100% of classrooms, 100% of dorms, 100% of libraries, 100% of dining areas, 100% of student union, 100% of common outdoor areas have wireless network access. Students can register for classes online. Administrative functions (other than registration) can be performed online.

CAMPUS LIFE

Environment: Metropolis **Activities:** Choral groups; Concert band; Dance; Drama/theater; International Student Organization; Jazz band; Literary magazine; Marching band; Music ensembles; Musical theater; Opera; Pep band; Radio station; Student government; Student newspaper; Student-run film society; Symphony orchestra; Television station; Yearbook 250 registered organizations, 2 honor societies, 10 religious organizations. 8 fraternities, 4 sororities. **Athletics (Intercollegiate):** *Men:* badminton, baseball, basketball, cheerleading, crew/rowing, cross-country, curling, cycling, fencing, football, golf, ice hockey, lacrosse, rugby, sailing, skiing (downhill/alpine), skiing (nordic/cross-country), soccer, squash, swimming, tennis, track/field (indoor), ultimate frisbee, volleyball, wrestling. *Women:* badminton, basketball, cheerleading, crew/rowing, cross-country, curling, cycling, fencing, field hockey, golf, ice hockey, lacrosse, rugby, sailing, skiing (downhill/alpine), skiing (nordic/cross-country), soccer, squash, swimming, synchronized swimming, tennis, track/field (indoor), ultimate frisbee, volleyball, wrestling. **On-Campus Highlights:** Arts Building, Schulich School of Music, McGill Bookstore, MacDonald Campus, Redpath Museum **Environmental Initiatives:** Excellence in environmental research and teaching (e.g. School of Environment, GEC3, Brace, VERT, etc.)

ADMISSIONS

Test Scores: SAT Math middle 50% range 650-720. SAT EBRW middle 50% range 640-740. ACT middle 50% range 29-32. Minimum internet-based TOEFL 90. Minimum paper TOEFL 577. **Basis for Candidate Selection:** *Very important factors considered include:* rigor of secondary school record, academic GPA, standardized test scores. *Important factors considered include:* class rank. *Other factors considered include:* recommendation(s). **Freshman Admission Requirements:** High school diploma is required and GED is not accepted *Academic units recommended:* 4 English, 4 math, 3 science, 3 science labs, 3 foreign language, 2 social studies, 2 history. **Freshman Admission Statistics:** 24,901 applied, 56.1% admitted, 35% enrolled. **Transfer Admission Requirements:** High school transcript, college transcript(s), Minimum college GPA of 3.00 required. Lowest grade transferable C. **General Admission Information:** Application fee $102.2. Regular application deadline 1/15. Nonfall registration accepted. Admission may be deferred for a maximum of 1 year.

COSTS AND FINANCIAL AID

Annual out-of-state tuition $7,031. Required fees $2,552. Average book expense $1,000. **Required Forms and Deadlines:** Institution's own financial aid form. **Notification of Awards:** Applicants will be notified of awards on a rolling basis beginning 3/1. **Types of Aid:** *Need-based scholarships/grants:* College/university scholarship or grant aid from institutional funds; Private scholarships. *Loans: Student Employment:* Institutional employment available. **Financial Aid Statistics:** 63% needy undergrads receive need-based scholarship or grant aid. 31% undergrads receive non-need-based scholarship or grant aid. 89% undergrads receive need-based self-help aid. 0% undergrads receive athletic scholarships. 28% undergrads receive any aid. **Criteria for awarding aid:** *Need-based:* Academics, Alumni affiliation, Leadership, Minority status *Non-need-based:* Academics, Art, Athletics, Leadership, Music/drama, State/district residency.

MCMURRY UNIVERSITY

1 McMurry University, Abilene, TX 79697
Phone: 325-793-4700 • **Financial Aid Phone:** 325-793-4713
E-mail: admissions@mcm.edu • **CEEB Code:** 3591
Fax: 325-793-4701 • **Website:** ww2.mcm.edu • **ACT Code:** 4130

This private school, affiliated with the United Methodist Church, was founded in 1923. It has a 52 acre campus.

RATINGS
Admissions Selectivity Rating: 87　　**Fire Safety Rating:** 87　　**Green Rating:** 61

STUDENTS AND FACULTY
Enrollment: 1,031. **Student Body:** 49% female, 51% male, 5% out-of-state, 6% international (10 countries represented). Asian 1%, African American 15%, Caucasian 47%, Hispanic 26%, Native American 1%, Pacific Islander <1%, Two or more races 3%, Race unknown 1%.
Retention and Graduation: 62% freshmen return for sophomore year. 28% freshmen graduate within 4 years. 36% freshmen graduate within 6 years. 32% grads go on to further study within 1 year. 27% grads pursue arts and sciences degrees. 1% grads pursue law degrees. 1% grads pursue business degrees. 3% grads pursue medical degrees. **Faculty:** Student/faculty ratio 11:1. 78 full-time faculty, 77% hold PhDs, 44% are women. 0% of classes are taught by teaching assistants.

ACADEMICS
Degrees: Bachelor's; Master's **Special Study Options:** Accelerated program; Cross-registration; Distance learning; Double major; Dual enrollment; English as a Second Language (ESL); Honors program; Internships; Liberal arts/career combination; Student-designed major; Study abroad; Teacher certification program. **Honors programs:** The McMurry University Honors Program is a four-year honors track designed to enrich the academic experience of our most outstanding students. More information is available at http://academics.mcm.edu/Honors/index.html **Combined degree programs:** BA/DDS. **Disability Services offered to physically disabled students:** Note-taking services; Tutors. **Career services:** Alumni services; Career assessment; Internships

FACILITIES
Housing: Apartments for single students; Coed dorms; Men's dorms; Special housing for disabled student; Wellness housing; Women's dorms 85% of campus accessible to physically diasbled.

CAMPUS LIFE
Environment: City **Activities:** Campus Ministries; Choral groups; Concert band; Drama/theater; Jazz band; Literary magazine; Marching band; Model UN; Music ensembles; Musical theater; Student government; Student newspaper; Yearbook. Garrison Campus Center, Java City / Library, Activity Center, Wellness Center, Cafeteria / Dining Hall **Environmental Initiatives:** Effluent water—The University uses effluent water for all landscape irrigation.

ADMISSIONS
Freshman Academic Profile: Average high school GPA 3.5. 12% in top 10% of high school class, 33% in top 25% of high school class, 73% in top 50% of high school class. 93% from public high schools. **Test Scores:** SAT Math middle 50% range 470-560. SAT EBRW middle 50% range 460-550. ACT middle 50% range 17-22. Minimum internet-based TOEFL 68. Minimum paper TOEFL 520. **Basis for Candidate Selection:** *Very important factors considered include:* rigor of secondary school record, class rank, academic GPA, standardized test scores. *Important factors considered include:* application essay, interview, extracurricular activities, talent/ability, character/personal qualities, volunteer work. *Other factors considered include:* recommendation(s), first generation, alumni/ae relation, geographical residence, state residency, religious affiliation/commitment, work experience, level of applicant's interest. **Freshman Admission Requirements:** High school diploma is required and GED is accepted *Academic units required: Academic units recommended:* 4 English, 4 math, 4 science, 2 foreign language, 4 social studies. **Freshman Admission Statistics:** 1,843 applied, 43.4% admitted, 31% enrolled. **General Admission Information:** Application fee $25. Priority deadline 3/1. Regular application deadline 8/15. Nonfall registration accepted. Admission may be deferred for a maximum of 1 year.

COSTS AND FINANCIAL AID
Annual tuition $26,622. Room and board $8,324. Required fees $90. Average book expense $1,200. **Required Forms and Deadlines:** FAFSA; Institution's own financial aid form. **Notification of Awards:** Applicants will be notified of awards on a rolling basis beginning 11/1. **Types of Aid:** *Need-based scholarships/grants:* College/university scholarship or grant aid from institutional funds; Federal Nursing Scholarships; Federal Pell; Private scholarships; SEOG; State scholarships/grants. *Loans:* Direct PLUS loans;

Direct Subsidized Stafford Loans; Direct Unsubsidized Stafford Loans. *Student Employment:* Federal Work-Study Program available. Institutional employment available. **Financial Aid Statistics:** 100% needy freshmen, 99% needy undergrads receive need-based scholarship or grant aid. 6% freshmen, 9% undergrads receive non-need-based scholarship or grant aid. 93% freshmen, 91% undergrads receive need-based self-help aid. 0% freshmen, 2% undergrads receive athletic scholarships. 100% freshmen, 90% undergrads receive any aid. 69% undergrads borrow to pay for school. Average cumulative indebtedness $39,362. **Criteria for awarding aid:** *Need-based:* Minority status, Religious affiliation *Non-need-based:* Academics, Art, Athletics, Job skills, Leadership, Music/drama, Religious affiliation.

MCNEESE STATE UNIVERSITY

4205 Ryan Street, Lake Charles, LA 70609
Phone: 337-475-5504 · **Financial Aid Phone:** 337 475-5065
E-mail: admissions@mcneese.edu
Fax: 337-475-5151 · **Website:** www.mcneese.edu · **ACT Code:** 1594

This public school was founded in 1939.

RATINGS
Admissions Selectivity Rating: 78   Fire Safety Rating: 60*   Green Rating: 60*

STUDENTS AND FACULTY
Enrollment: 6,598. **Student Body:** 60% female, 40% male, 8% out-of-state, 7% international (53 countries represented). Asian 2%, African American 18%, Caucasian 68%, Hispanic 3%, Native American 1%, Pacific Islander <1%, Two or more races 2%, Race unknown <1%.
Retention and Graduation: 67% freshmen return for sophomore year.
Faculty: Student/faculty ratio 20:1. 256 full-time faculty, 65% hold PhDs, 47% are women.

ACADEMICS
Degrees: Associate; Bachelor's; Master's; Post-Bachelor's certificate; Post-Master's certificate **Classes:** Most classes have fewer than 10 students.

CAMPUS LIFE
Environment: City **Activities:** Campus Ministries; Choral groups; Concert band; Drama/theater; International Student Organization; Jazz band; Marching band; Musical theater; Pep band; Student government; Student newspaper; Yearbook.

ADMISSIONS
Freshman Academic Profile: 18% in top 10% of high school class, 41% in top 25% of high school class, 73% in top 50% of high school class. **Test Scores:** SAT Math middle 50% range 470-580. SAT EBRW middle 50% range 440-530. ACT middle 50% range 20-24. Minimum internet-based TOEFL 61. Minimum paper TOEFL 500. **Freshman Admission Statistics:** 3,002 applied, 82.0% admitted, 58% enrolled. **Transfer Admission Requirements:** college transcript(s), statement of good standing from prior institution(s). Minimum college GPA of 2.00 required. Lowest grade transferable C.

MCPHERSON COLLEGE

P.O. Box 1402, McPherson, KS 67460
Phone: 620-241-0731 · **Financial Aid Phone:** 800-365-7402
E-mail: admiss@mcpherson.edu · **CEEB Code:** 6404
Fax: 620-241-8443 · **ACT Code:** 1440

This private school, affiliated with the Church of Brethren, was founded in 1887. It has a 23 acre campus.

RATINGS
Admissions Selectivity Rating: 72   Fire Safety Rating: 60*   Green Rating: 60*

STUDENTS AND FACULTY
Enrollment: 573. **Student Body:** 43% female, 57% male, 5% out-of-state, 1% international. Asian 2%, African American 10%, Caucasian 77%, Hispanic 7%, Native American 3%, Race unknown 0%.
Retention and Graduation: 67% freshmen return for sophomore year. 9% grads go on to further study within 1 year. 9% grads pursue medical degrees.
Faculty: Student/faculty ratio 15:1. 34 full-time faculty, 82% hold PhDs, 12%

are members of minority groups, 32% are women. 0% of classes are taught by teaching assistants.

ACADEMICS
Degrees: Bachelor's **Classes:** Most classes have 10-19 students. Most lab/ discussion sessions have 10-19 students. **Special Study Options:** Cross-registration; Double major; Dual enrollment; English as a Second Language (ESL); Independent study; Internships; Student-designed major; Study abroad; Teacher certification program.

FACILITIES
Housing: Coed dorms; Men's dorms; Special housing for disabled student; Women's dorms **Special Academic Facilities/Equipment:** Natural history museum.

CAMPUS LIFE
Environment: Village **Activities:** Campus Ministries; Choral groups; Concert band; Dance; Drama/theater; Jazz band; Music ensembles; Musical theater; Pep band; Student government; Student newspaper; Yearbook. **Athletics (Intercollegiate):** *Women:* basketball, cross-country, golf, tennis, track/field (outdoor), volleyball.

ADMISSIONS
Freshman Academic Profile: Average high school GPA 3.2. 9% in top 10% of high school class, 25% in top 25% of high school class, 60% in top 50% of high school class. 99% from public high schools. **Test Scores:** SAT Math middle 50% range 450-563. SAT EBRW middle 50% range 448-560. ACT middle 50% range 19-24. Minimum internet-based TOEFL 79-80. Minimum paper TOEFL 550. **Basis for Candidate Selection:** *Very important factors considered include:* rigor of secondary school record, academic GPA, standardized test scores. *Other factors considered include:* class rank, recommendation(s), interview, extracurricular activities, talent/ability, character/personal qualities, first generation, volunteer work, work experience, level of applicant's interest. **Freshman Admission Requirements:** High school diploma is required and GED is accepted **Freshman Admission Statistics:** 474 applied, 86.7% admitted, 13% enrolled. **Transfer Admission Requirements:** High school transcript, college transcript(s), statement of good standing from prior institution(s). Minimum college GPA of 2.0 required. Lowest grade transferable C. **General Admission Information:** Application fee $25. Priority deadline 3/1. Nonfall registration accepted. Admission may be deferred.

COSTS AND FINANCIAL AID
Annual tuition $17,900. Room and board $6,910. Required fees $500. Average book expense $1,170. **Required Forms and Deadlines:** FAFSA; State aid form. **Notification of Awards:** Applicants will be notified of awards on a rolling basis beginning 3/1. **Types of Aid:** *Need-based scholarships/grants:* College/ university scholarship or grant aid from institutional funds; Federal Pell; Private scholarships; SEOG; State scholarships/grants; United Negro College Fund. *Student Employment:* Federal Work-Study Program available. Institutional employment available. **Financial Aid Statistics:** 85% needy freshmen, 85% needy undergrads receive need-based scholarship or grant aid. 95% freshmen, 98% undergrads receive non-need-based scholarship or grant aid. 86% freshmen, 88% undergrads receive need-based self-help aid. 66% freshmen, 38% undergrads receive athletic scholarships. **Criteria for awarding aid:** *Non-need-based:* Academics, Alumni affiliation, Art, Athletics, Music/drama, Religious affiliation, State/district residency.

MEDCENTER ONE COLLEGE OF NURSING

101 Wilder Tower, Bismarck, ND 58501
Phone: 701-323-6271 · **Financial Aid Phone:** 701-323-6270
E-mail: msmith@mohs.org
Fax: 701-323-6289 · **Website:** www.medcenterone.com/collegeofnursing · **ACT Code:** 3197

This private school was founded in 1988.

RATINGS
Admissions Selectivity Rating: 61   Fire Safety Rating: 60*   Green Rating: 60*

STUDENTS AND FACULTY
Enrollment: 91. **Student Body:** 91% female, 9% male, 6% out-of-state, 0% international (0 countries represented). Asian 1%, African American 4%, Caucasian 90%, Hispanic 1%, Native American 0%, Two or more races 3%, Race unknown 0%.
Faculty: Student/faculty ratio 8:1. 10 full-time faculty, 10% hold PhDs, 100% are women. 0% of classes are taught by teaching assistants.

ACADEMICS

Degrees: Bachelor's **Classes:** Most classes have 10-19 students. **Most popular majors:** Nursing/Registered Nurse (Rn, Asn, Bsn, Msn). **Special Study Options:** Independent study; Internships.

FACILITIES

Special Academic Facilities/Equipment: Alumni Corner **Computers:** 100% of classrooms, 100% of libraries, 100% of common outdoor areas have wireless network access.

CAMPUS LIFE

Environment: Rural **Activities:** Student government 2 registered organizations, 1 honor societies. **On-Campus Highlights:** Simulation Lab

ADMISSIONS

Freshman Admission Requirements: High school diploma is required and GED is accepted **Transfer Admission Requirements:** High school transcript, college transcript(s), essay or personal statement, interview, Minimum college GPA of 2.5 required. Lowest grade transferable C. **General Admission Information:** Application fee $40. Priority deadline 11/1.

COSTS AND FINANCIAL AID

Annual tuition $9,720. Required fees $889. Average book expense $1,169. **Notification of Awards:** Applicants will be notified of awards on a rolling basis beginning 6/1. **Types of Aid:** *Need-based scholarships/grants:* College/university scholarship or grant aid from institutional funds; Federal Pell; Private scholarships; SEOG; State scholarships/grants. *Loans: Student Employment:* Federal Work-Study Program available. **Financial Aid Statistics:** 78% needy undergrads receive need-based scholarship or grant aid. 29% undergrads receive non-need-based scholarship or grant aid. 77% undergrads receive need-based self-help aid. 0% undergrads receive athletic scholarships. 0% freshmen receive any aid. **Criteria for awarding aid:** *Need-based:* Academics, Alumni affiliation, Leadership *Non-need-based:* Academics, Alumni affiliation, Leadership.

MEDICAL UNIVERSITY OF SOUTH CAROLINA

179 Ashley Avenue, Charleston, SC 29425-0203
Phone: 843-792-3281 · **Financial Aid Phone:** (843)792-2536
E-mail: oesadmis@musc.edu
Fax: 843-792-6615 · **Website:** www.musc.edu · **ACT Code:** 6440

This public school was founded in 1824. It has a 82 acre campus.

RATINGS

Admissions Selectivity Rating: 61   **Fire Safety Rating:** 60*   **Green Rating:** 60*

STUDENTS AND FACULTY

Enrollment: 198. **Student Body:** 79% female, 21% male, 12% out-of-state, 0% international (26 countries represented). Asian 3%, African American 11%, Caucasian 73%, Hispanic 6%, Native American 1%, Two or more races 1%, Race unknown 5%.
Faculty: Student/faculty ratio 2:1. 153 full-time faculty, 92% hold PhDs, 10% are members of minority groups, 56% are women. 0% of classes are taught by teaching assistants.

ACADEMICS

Degrees: Bachelor's; Doctoral; Doctoral/Professional; Doctoral/Research; Master's; Post-Bachelor's certificate; Post-Master's certificate **Classes:** Most classes have 10-19 students. Most lab/discussion sessions have 10-19 students. **Most popular majors:** Registered Nursing/Registered Nurse. **Special Study Options:** Cross-registration; Distance learning. **Disability Services offered to physically disabled students:** Note-taking services; Reader services; Tape recorders; Tutors. **Career services:** Internships

FACILITIES

Housing: 97% of campus accessible to physically diasbled. **Special Academic Facilities/Equipment:** Dental Museum, Medical Museum, Pharmacy Museum, and Waring Historical Library. **Computers:** 100% of classrooms, n/a% of dorms, 100% of libraries, 100% of dining areas, n/a% of student union, 100% of common outdoor areas have wireless network access. Students can register for classes online. Administrative functions (other than registration) can be performed online.

CAMPUS LIFE

Environment: City **Activities:** Campus Ministries; Choral groups; International Student Organization; Literary magazine; Music ensembles; Student government 77 registered organizations, 4 honor societies. **On-Campus Highlights:** Student Activity and Fitness Center, Library, Various

---

Student Lounges, Classroom and Laboratories **Environmental Initiatives:** Installed ground source heat pump as first renewable energy project

ADMISSIONS

Test Scores: Minimum internet-based TOEFL 80. Minimum paper TOEFL 550. **Freshman Admission Requirements:** High school diploma is required and GED is accepted **General Admission Information:** Application fee $95. Regular application deadline 6/30. Admission may be deferred.

COSTS AND FINANCIAL AID

Annual in-state tuition $1,140. Annual out-of-state tuition $23,824. Required fees $1,140. **Required Forms and Deadlines:** FAFSA; Institution's own financial aid form. **Types of Aid:** *Need-based scholarships/grants:* College/university scholarship or grant aid from institutional funds; Federal Nursing Scholarships; Federal Pell; Private scholarships; SEOG; State scholarships/grants. *Loans: Student Employment:* Federal Work-Study Program available. **Financial Aid Statistics:** 49% needy undergrads receive need-based scholarship or grant aid. 23% undergrads receive non-need-based scholarship or grant aid. 99% undergrads receive need-based self-help aid. 0% undergrads receive athletic scholarships. 0% freshmen, 75% undergrads receive any aid. **Criteria for awarding aid:** *Need-based:* Academics, Alumni affiliation, Minority status *Non-need-based:* Academics, Alumni affiliation, Minority status, State/district residency.

MEMPHIS COLLEGE OF ART

NULL, Memphis, TN
Financial Aid Phone: 901-272-5136 · **CEEB Code:** 1511
ACT Code: 3991

This private school was founded in 1936.

RATINGS

Admissions Selectivity Rating: 72   **Fire Safety Rating:** 82   **Green Rating:** 60*

STUDENTS AND FACULTY

Enrollment: 337. **Student Body:** 66% female, 34% male, 55% out-of-state, <1% international (13 countries represented). Asian 1%, African American 33%, Caucasian 54%, Hispanic 7%, Native American 1%, Pacific Islander 0%, Two or more races 3%, Race unknown 1%.
Retention and Graduation: 78% freshmen return for sophomore year. 10% grads go on to further study within 1 year. **Faculty:** Student/faculty ratio 10:1. 27 full-time faculty, 85% hold PhDs, 19% are members of minority groups, 59% are women. 0% of classes are taught by teaching assistants.

ACADEMICS

Classes: Most classes have 10-19 students. Most lab/discussion sessions have 10-19 students. **Special Study Options:** Cross-registration; Double major; Dual enrollment; Exchange student program (domestic); Independent study; Internships; Study abroad; Teacher certification program. **Disability Services offered to physically disabled students:** Note-taking services; Reader services; Tape recorders; Tutors. **Career services:** Alumni network; Alumni services; Career/job search classes; Internships; Regional alumni

FACILITIES

Housing: Apartments for single students; Coed dorms 100% of campus accessible to physically diasbled. **Special Academic Facilities/Equipment:** Art museum, numerous galleries for student exhibition. Computer writing lab. **Computers:** 100% of classrooms, 100% of dorms, 100% of libraries, 100% of dining areas, have wireless network access.

CAMPUS LIFE

Environment: Metropolis **Activities:** Student government; Student newspaper. Metz & Fogelman Hall Student Residences

ADMISSIONS

Freshman Academic Profile: Average high school GPA 3.2. 80% from public high schools. **Test Scores:** Minimum paper TOEFL 500. **Basis for Candidate Selection:** *Very important factors considered include:* academic GPA, talent/ability. *Important factors considered include:* rigor of secondary school record, standardized test scores, interview. *Other factors considered include:* class rank, application essay, recommendation(s), extracurricular activities, character/personal qualities, volunteer work, work experience, level of applicant's interest. **Freshman Admission Requirements:** High school diploma is required and GED is accepted *Academic units recommended:* 4 visual/performing arts. **Freshman Admission Statistics:** 390 applied, 40.8% admitted, 48% enrolled. **Transfer Admission Requirements:** college transcript(s), Minimum college GPA of 2.0 required. Lowest grade transferable C. **General Admission Information:** Priority deadline 3/31. Nonfall registration accepted. Admission may be deferred for a maximum of 1 year.

COSTS AND FINANCIAL AID

Annual tuition $32,400. Room and board $8,890. Required fees $730. Average book expense $1,650. **Required Forms and Deadlines:** FAFSA. **Notification of Awards:** Applicants will be notified of awards on a rolling basis beginning 1/15. **Types of Aid:** *Need-based scholarships/grants:* College/university scholarship or grant aid from institutional funds; Federal Pell; Private scholarships; SEOG; State scholarships/grants. *Loans:* Direct PLUS loans; Direct Subsidized Stafford Loans; Direct Unsubsidized Stafford Loans. *Student Employment:* Federal Work-Study Program available. **Financial Aid Statistics:** 58% needy freshmen, 64% needy undergrads receive need-based scholarship or grant aid. 97% freshmen, 97% undergrads receive non-need-based scholarship or grant aid. 71% freshmen, 71% undergrads receive need-based self-help aid. 0% freshmen, 0% undergrads receive athletic scholarships. 95% freshmen, 95% undergrads receive any aid. **Criteria for awarding aid:** *Non-need-based:* Academics, Art.

MENLO COLLEGE

1000 El Camino Real, Atherton, CA 94027
Phone: 650-543-3753 · **Financial Aid Phone:** 650-543-3880
E-mail: admissions@menlo.edu · **CEEB Code:** 1236
Fax: 650-543-4103 · **Website:** www.menlo.edu · **ACT Code:** 330

This private school was founded in 1927. It has a 45 acre campus.

RATINGS

Admissions Selectivity Rating: 71　　**Fire Safety Rating:** 78　　**Green Rating:** 60*

STUDENTS AND FACULTY

Enrollment: 774. **Student Body:** 45% female, 55% male, 19% out-of-state, 14% international (35 countries represented). Asian 10%, African American 6%, Caucasian 26%, Hispanic 23%, Native American 1%, Pacific Islander 2%, Two or more races 9%, Race unknown 10%.
Retention and Graduation: 77% freshmen return for sophomore year. **Faculty:** Student/faculty ratio 14:1. 30 full-time faculty, 87% hold PhDs, 33% are members of minority groups, 53% are women. 0% of classes are taught by teaching assistants.

ACADEMICS

Degrees: Bachelor's **Classes:** Most classes have 20-29 students. Most lab/discussion sessions have 20-29 students. **Most popular majors:** Sport And Fitness Administration/Management; Accounting; Marketing/Marketing Management, General. **Special Study Options:** Accelerated program; Double major; English as a Second Language (ESL); Independent study; Internships; Student-designed major; Study abroad. **Disability Services offered to physically disabled students:** Note-taking services; Reader services; Tape recorders; Tutors. **Career services:** Alumni network; Alumni services; Career assessment; Career/job search classes; Internships; Regional alumni

FACILITIES

Housing: Coed dorms; Men's dorms; Special housing for disabled student; Women's dorms 95% of campus accessible to physically diasbled. **Computers:** 33% of classrooms, 100% of libraries, 100% of dining areas, 100% of student union, have wireless network access. Students can register for classes online. Administrative functions (other than registration) can be performed online.

CAMPUS LIFE

Environment: Town **Activities:** Dance; International Student Organization; Student government; Student newspaper; Student-run film society 30 registered organizations, 2 honor societies. **Athletics (Intercollegiate):** *Men:* baseball, basketball, cross-country, football, golf, soccer, wrestling. *Women:* basketball, cross-country, soccer, softball, volleyball, wrestling. **On-Campus Highlights:** Brawner Hall, Library, Student Union, Dining commons **Environmental Initiatives:** Plastic bottle and styrofoam cups free campus.

ADMISSIONS

Freshman Academic Profile: Average high school GPA 3.2. 80% from public high schools. **Test Scores:** Minimum internet-based TOEFL 74. Minimum paper TOEFL 537. **Basis for Candidate Selection:** *Very important factors considered include:* rigor of secondary school record, academic GPA, standardized test scores. *Important factors considered include:* class rank, application essay, recommendation(s), character/personal qualities, volunteer work. *Other factors considered include:* interview, alumni/ae relation, work experience, level of applicant's interest. **Freshman Admission Requirements:** High school diploma is required and GED is accepted *Academic units recommended:* 4 English, 3 math, 3 science, 2 foreign language, 3 social studies. **Freshman Admission Statistics:** 2,195 applied, 40.9% admitted, 18% enrolled. **Transfer Admission Requirements:** college transcript(s), essay

or personal statement, statement of good standing from prior institution(s). Minimum college GPA of 2.0 required. Lowest grade transferable C-. **General Admission Information:** Application fee $40. Priority deadline 2/1. Regular application deadline 4/1. Nonfall registration accepted. Admission may be deferred for a maximum of 2 semesters.

COSTS AND FINANCIAL AID

Annual tuition $40,625. Room and board $13,680. Required fees $725. Average book expense $550. **Required Forms and Deadlines:** FAFSA; State aid form. **Notification of Awards:** Applicants will be notified of awards on a rolling basis beginning 12/15. **Types of Aid:** *Need-based scholarships/grants:* College/university scholarship or grant aid from institutional funds; Federal Pell; SEOG; State scholarships/grants. *Loans:* Direct PLUS loans; Direct Subsidized Stafford Loans; Direct Unsubsidized Stafford Loans. *Student Employment:* Federal Work-Study Program available. Institutional employment available. **Financial Aid Statistics:** 100% needy freshmen, 100% needy undergrads receive need-based scholarship or grant aid. 14% freshmen, 9% undergrads receive non-need-based scholarship or grant aid. 83% freshmen, 88% undergrads receive need-based self-help aid. 12% freshmen, 16% undergrads receive athletic scholarships. 97% freshmen, 96% undergrads receive any aid. 65% undergrads borrow to pay for school. Average cumulative indebtedness $30,145. **Criteria for awarding aid:** *Need-based:* Academics, Athletics *Non-need-based:* Academics, Athletics.

MERCER UNIVERSITY

1501 Mercer University Drive, Macon, GA 31207-0001
Phone: 478-301-2650 · **Financial Aid Phone:** 478-301-2670
E-mail: admissions@mercer.edu · **CEEB Code:** 5409
Fax: 478-301-2828 · **Website:** www.mercer.edu · **ACT Code:** 838

This private school was founded in 1833. It has a 150 acre campus.

RATINGS

Admissions Selectivity Rating: 86　　**Fire Safety Rating:** 89　　**Green Rating:** 60*

STUDENTS AND FACULTY

Enrollment: 3,215. **Student Body:** 53% female, 47% male, 18% out-of-state, 3% international (38 countries represented). Asian 9%, African American 19%, Caucasian 56%, Hispanic 6%, Native American <1%, Pacific Islander <1%, Two or more races 4%, Race unknown 3%.
Retention and Graduation: 86% freshmen return for sophomore year. 47% freshmen graduate within 4 years. 64% freshmen graduate within 6 years. 38% grads go on to further study within 1 year. **Faculty:** Student/faculty ratio 13:1. 384 full-time faculty, 92% hold PhDs, 25% are members of minority groups, 51% are women. 0% of classes are taught by teaching assistants.

ACADEMICS

Degrees: Bachelor's; Certificate; Doctoral Other; Doctoral/Professional; Doctoral/Research; Master's; Post-Master's certificate **Classes:** Most classes have 10-19 students. **Most popular majors:** Engineering, General; Biology/Biological Sciences, General; Business/Commerce, General. **Special Study Options:** Accelerated program; Cross-registration; Double major; Dual enrollment; English as a Second Language (ESL); Honors program; Independent study; Internships; Liberal arts/career combination; Student-designed major; Study abroad; Teacher certification program. **Honors programs:** The University Honors Program provides academically advanced students with supportive environment needed to pursue their intellectual interests through research within distinctive paths of enrichment. The honors program offers several different tracks including: research, service, international studies, engineering, and business. For more information please see the Mercer Catalog. **Combined degree programs:** BA/MEng. **Disability Services offered to physically disabled students:** Note-taking services; Reader services; Tape recorders; Tutors. **Career services:** Alumni network; Alumni services; Career assessment; Career/job search classes; Internships; Regional alumni

FACILITIES

Housing: Apartments for married students; Apartments for single students; Coed dorms; Fraternity/sorority housing; Men's dorms; Special housing for disabled student; Special housing for international students; Theme housing; Women's dorms 85% of campus accessible to physically diasbled. **Special Academic Facilities/Equipment:** McCorkle Music Building **Computers:**

100% of classrooms, 100% of dorms, 100% of libraries, 100% of dining areas, 100% of student union, 100% of common outdoor areas have wireless network access. Students can register for classes online. Administrative functions (other than registration) can be performed online.

CAMPUS LIFE

Environment: City **Activities:** Campus Ministries; Choral groups; Concert band; Drama/theater; International Student Organization; Jazz band; Literary magazine; Marching band; Music ensembles; Musical theater; Opera; Pep band; Radio station; Student government; Student newspaper; Symphony orchestra; Television station 115 registered organizations, 18 honor societies, 7 religious organizations. 9 fraternities, 7 sororities. **Athletics (Intercollegiate):** *Men:* baseball, basketball, cross-country, golf, riflery, soccer, tennis. *Women:* basketball, cross-country, golf, soccer, softball, tennis, volleyball. **On-Campus Highlights:** University Center, Connell Student Center, Greek Village, Porter Patch, Spearman C. Godsey Science Center **Environmental Initiatives:** We have long-standing community partnerships to improve and rehabilitate housing and commerical stock in Macon proper, which has significant positive impact on the sustability of the community.

ADMISSIONS

Freshman Academic Profile: Average high school GPA 3.9. 36% in top 10% of high school class, 71% in top 25% of high school class, 93% in top 50% of high school class. **Test Scores:** SAT Math middle 50% range 580-670. SAT EBRW middle 50% range 590-670. ACT middle 50% range 25-30. Minimum internet-based TOEFL 80. Minimum paper TOEFL 550. **Basis for Candidate Selection:** *Very important factors considered include:* rigor of secondary school record, academic GPA, standardized test scores, level of applicant's interest. *Important factors considered include:* application essay, recommendation(s), extracurricular activities, talent/ability, character/personal qualities, volunteer work. *Other factors considered include:* class rank, interview, alumni/ae relation, work experience. **Freshman Admission Requirements:** High school diploma is required and GED is accepted *Academic units required:* 4 English, 4 math, 4 science, 3 science labs, 2 foreign language, 1 social studies, 2 history. **Freshman Admission Statistics:** 4,749 applied, 73.3% admitted, 14% enrolled. **Transfer Admission Requirements:** college transcript(s), statement of good standing from prior institution(s). Minimum college GPA of 2.5 required. Lowest grade transferable C. **General Admission Information:** Application fee $50. Priority deadline 3/1. Regular application deadline 7/1. Nonfall registration accepted. Admission may be deferred for a maximum of 1 year.

COSTS AND FINANCIAL AID

Annual tuition $35,700. Room and board $12,153. Required fees $300. Average book expense $1,200. **Required Forms and Deadlines:** FAFSA. **Notification of Awards:** Applicants will be notified of awards on a rolling basis beginning 3/15. **Types of Aid:** *Need-based scholarships/grants:* College/university scholarship or grant aid from institutional funds; Federal Nursing Scholarships; Federal Pell; SEOG; State scholarships/grants. *Loans:* Direct PLUS loans; Direct Subsidized Stafford Loans; Direct Unsubsidized Stafford Loans. *Student Employment:* Federal Work-Study Program available. Institutional employment available. **Financial Aid Statistics:** 100% needy freshmen, 99% needy undergrads receive need-based scholarship or grant aid. 31% freshmen, 28% undergrads receive non-need-based scholarship or grant aid. 58% freshmen, 55% undergrads receive need-based self-help aid. 4% freshmen, 6% undergrads receive athletic scholarships. 99% freshmen, 97% undergrads receive any aid. 64% undergrads borrow to pay for school. Average cumulative indebtedness $28,194. **Criteria for awarding aid:** *Need-based:* Job skills *Non-need-based:* Academics, Art, Athletics, Job skills, Leadership, Music/drama, State/district residency.

MERCY COLLEGE

555 Broadway, Dobbs Ferry, NY 10522
Phone: (877) 637-2946 · **Financial Aid Phone:** 1-888-464-6737
E-mail: admissions@mercy.edu · **CEEB Code:** 2409
Fax: 914-674-7382 · **Website:** www.mercy.edu · **ACT Code:** 2814

This private school was founded in 1950. It has a 66 acre campus.

RATINGS

Admissions Selectivity Rating: 69   **Fire Safety Rating:** 97   **Green Rating:** 64

STUDENTS AND FACULTY

Enrollment: 6,410. **Student Body:** 69% female, 31% male, 7% out-of-state, 1% international (48 countries represented). Asian 4%, African American 23%, Caucasian 27%, Hispanic 35%, Native American <1%, Pacific Islander <1%, Two or more races 1%, Race unknown 7%.

Retention and Graduation: 76% freshmen return for sophomore year. **Faculty:** Student/faculty ratio 17:1. 198 full-time faculty, 86% hold PhDs, 23% are members of minority groups, 62% are women. 0% of classes are taught by teaching assistants.

ACADEMICS

Degrees: Associate; Bachelor's; Certificate; Doctoral/Professional; Master's; Post-Bachelor's certificate **Classes:** Most classes have 20-29 students. Most lab/discussion sessions have 20-29 students. **Most popular majors:** Psychology, General; Social Sciences, General; Business Administration And Management, General. **Special Study Options:** Accelerated program; Cooperative education program; Distance learning; Double major; Dual enrollment; Honors program; Independent study; Internships; Study abroad; Teacher certification program; Weekend college. **Honors programs:** The Honors Program activities are selected to expand students' awareness of the cultural, social, and historical diversity of the world. Honors students are invited to participate in exclusive seminar opportunities with world leaders, academic scholars, and industry executives. Students in the Honors Program take Honors versions of General Education courses (e.g., English, speech, and math) in classes that average less than 20 students and complete an individualized Honors project in connection with their major for a total of 24 Honors credits. Honors students also receive a Laptop Computer and are given registration priority. **Combined degree programs:** BA/MA. **Disability Services offered to physically disabled students:** Note-taking services; Reader services; Tape recorders; Tutors. **Career services:** Alumni network; Alumni services; Career assessment; Career/job search classes; Internships; Regional alumni

FACILITIES

Housing: Coed dorms 75% of campus accessible to physically diasbled. **Special Academic Facilities/Equipment:** Students, faculty and the community are further enriched by a number of centers including the Center for Global Engagement, Cybersecurity Education Center, Speech and Hearing Center, and Centers of Excellence within the Business School including Strategic Consulting Institute, Center for Entrepreneurship, Center for Business Communication, Center for International Business, Women's Leadership Institute and Lifepath Coaching Institute. The college has a range of specialized academic areas from the School of Business 525 sq. foot trading room that replicates Wall Street to the state-of-the-art Roy Disney Studio for Animation Studies; Exercise Science Facility; music and recording studios; and STEM biological research labs. **Computers:** 40% of classrooms, 100% of dorms, 60% of libraries, 60% of dining areas, 60% of student union, have wireless network access. Students can register for classes online. Administrative functions (other than registration) can be performed online.

CAMPUS LIFE

Environment: Town **Activities:** Campus Ministries; Dance; International Student Organization; Model UN; Student government; Student newspaper 20 registered organizations, 1 religious organization. **Athletics (Intercollegiate):** *Men:* baseball, basketball, cross-country, lacrosse, soccer, tennis, track/field (outdoor). *Women:* basketball, cross-country, lacrosse, soccer, softball, track/field (outdoor), volleyball. **On-Campus Highlights:** Waterfront campus on the Hudson River, New State-of-the-Art Library, Victory Café, Music and Recording Studio, Roy Disney Center for Computer Animation **Environmental Initiatives:** Updated Central Heating Plant

ADMISSIONS

Freshman Academic Profile: Average high school GPA 84.8. **Test Scores:** Minimum internet-based TOEFL 71. Minimum paper TOEFL 550. **Basis for Candidate Selection:** *Very important factors considered include:* academic GPA, extracurricular activities, talent/ability, character/personal qualities, volunteer work. *Important factors considered include:* rigor of secondary school record, application essay, recommendation(s), interview, level of applicant's interest. *Other factors considered include:* class rank, alumni/ae relation, work experience. **Freshman Admission Requirements:** High school diploma is required and GED is accepted *Academic units required:* 4 English, 4 math, 3 science, 1 science labs, 3 foreign language, 2 social studies, 2 history, 3 academic electives, *Academic units recommended:* 4 English, 4 math, 3 science, 1 science labs, 3 foreign language, 2 social studies, 2 history, 3 academic electives. **Freshman Admission Statistics:** 5,573 applied, 65.7% admitted, 26% enrolled. **Transfer Admission Requirements:** college transcript(s), Minimum college GPA of 2.0 required. Lowest grade transferable C. **General Admission Information:** Application fee $40. Nonfall registration accepted. Admission may be deferred for a maximum of 1 year.

COSTS AND FINANCIAL AID

Annual tuition $17,466. Room and board $13,700. Required fees $610. Average book expense $1,492. **Required Forms and Deadlines:** FAFSA; State aid form. **Notification of Awards:** Applicants will be notified of awards on a rolling basis beginning 2/20. **Types of Aid:** *Need-based scholarships/grants:* College/university scholarship or grant aid from institutional funds; Federal Pell; Private scholarships; SEOG; State scholarships/grants. *Loans:* Direct PLUS loans; Direct Subsidized Stafford Loans; Direct Unsubsidized Stafford Loans. *Student Employment:* Federal Work-Study Program available. Institutional employment available. **Financial Aid Statistics:** 90% needy freshmen, 89% needy undergrads receive need-based scholarship or grant aid. 52% freshmen, 29% undergrads receive non-need-based scholarship or grant aid. 72% freshmen, 82% undergrads receive need-based self-help aid. 8% freshmen, 4% undergrads receive athletic scholarships. 82% freshmen, 82% undergrads receive any aid. Average cumulative indebtedness $26,100. **Criteria for awarding aid:** *Non-need-based:* Academics, Athletics.

MERCYHURST UNIVERSITY

501 E. 38th Street, Erie, PA 16546
Phone: 814-824-2202 · **Financial Aid Phone:** 814 824 2288
E-mail: admissions@mercyhurst.edu · **CEEB Code:** 2410
Fax: 814-824-2071 · **Website:** www.mercyhurst.edu · **ACT Code:** 3629

This private school, affiliated with the Roman Catholic Church, was founded in 1926. It has a 75 acre campus.

RATINGS
Admissions Selectivity Rating: 77   **Fire Safety Rating:** 91   **Green Rating:** 95

STUDENTS AND FACULTY
Enrollment: 2,680. **Student Body:** 56% female, 44% male, 48% out-of-state, 8% international. Asian 1%, African American 4%, Caucasian 77%, Hispanic 2%, Native American <1%, Pacific Islander 0%, Two or more races 0%, Race unknown 7%.
Retention and Graduation: 79% freshmen return for sophomore year. **Faculty:** Student/faculty ratio 14:1. 164 full-time faculty, 68% hold PhDs, 9% are members of minority groups, 44% are women. 0% of classes are taught by teaching assistants.

ACADEMICS
Degrees: Bachelor's; Doctoral; Master's; Post-Bachelor's certificate **Classes:** Most classes have 20-29 students. Most lab/discussion sessions have 20-29 students. **Most popular majors:** Elementary Education And Teaching; International/Global Studies; Business Administration And Management, General. **Special Study Options:** Cross-registration; Distance learning; Double major; Honors program; Independent study; Internships; Liberal arts/career combination; Student-designed major; Study abroad; Teacher certification program. **Disability Services offered to physically disabled students:** Note-taking services; Reader services; Tape recorders; Tutors. **Career services:** Alumni network; Alumni services; Career assessment; Career/job search classes; Internships

FACILITIES
Housing: Apartments for single students; Coed dorms; Men's dorms; Theme housing; Women's dorms **Special Academic Facilities/Equipment:** Art gallery, college-owned restaurant for hotel/restaurant management department, observatory, archaeology lab. **Computers:** Students can register for classes online. Administrative functions (other than registration) can be performed online.

CAMPUS LIFE
Environment: City **Activities:** Campus Ministries; Choral groups; Dance; Drama/theater; International Student Organization; Jazz band; Literary magazine; Model UN; Music ensembles; Musical theater; Pep band; Radio station; Student government; Student newspaper; Television station; Yearbook 9 honor societies, 2 religious organizations. **Athletics (Intercollegiate):** *Men:* baseball, basketball, cheerleading, crew/rowing, cross-country, football, golf, ice hockey, lacrosse, soccer, tennis, volleyball, water polo, wrestling. *Women:* basketball, cheerleading, crew/rowing, cross-country, field hockey, golf, ice hockey, lacrosse, soccer, softball, tennis, volleyball, water polo. **On-Campus Highlights:** Performing Arts Center, Mercyhurst Athletic Center, Library, Student Union, Ice Rink **Environmental Initiatives:** Sustainability Studies academic program

ADMISSIONS
Freshman Academic Profile: Average high school GPA 3.4. 21% in top 10% of high school class, 29% in top 25% of high school class, 87% in top 50% of high school class. 55% from public high schools. **Test Scores:** SAT Math middle 50% range 470-570. SAT EBRW middle 50% range 470-580. ACT middle 50% range 21-26. Minimum internet-based TOEFL 79. Minimum paper TOEFL 550. **Basis for Candidate Selection:** *Very important factors considered include:* rigor of secondary school record, class rank, academic GPA, standardized test scores. *Important factors considered include:* application essay, recommendation(s), interview, extracurricular activities, talent/ability, character/personal qualities. *Other factors considered include:* alumni/ae relation, geographical residence, state residency, religious affiliation/commitment, racial/

ethnic status, volunteer work, work experience, level of applicant's interest.
Freshman Admission Requirements: High school diploma is required and GED is accepted *Academic units required:* 4 English, 3 math, 2 science, 1 science labs, 2 foreign language, 5 social studies, *Academic units recommended:* 4 English, 3 math, 3 science, 2 science labs, 2 foreign language, 5 social studies. **Freshman Admission Statistics:** 2,938 applied, 75.4% admitted, 27% enrolled. **Transfer Admission Requirements:** High school transcript, college transcript(s), standardized test scores, Minimum college GPA of 2.0 required. Lowest grade transferable C. **General Admission Information:** Application fee $30. Priority deadline 5/1. Nonfall registration accepted. Admission may be deferred for a maximum of 1 year.

COSTS AND FINANCIAL AID
Annual tuition $29,600. Room and board $10,800. Required fees $1,885. Average book expense $1,000. **Notification of Awards:** Applicants will be notified of awards on a rolling basis beginning 2/15. **Types of Aid:** *Need-based scholarships/grants:* College/university scholarship or grant aid from institutional funds; Federal Pell; Private scholarships; SEOG; State scholarships/grants. *Loans:* Direct PLUS loans; Direct Subsidized Stafford Loans; Direct Unsubsidized Stafford Loans. *Student Employment:* Federal Work-Study Program available. Institutional employment available. **Financial Aid Statistics:** 95% needy freshmen, 94% needy undergrads receive need-based scholarship or grant aid. 75% freshmen, 66% undergrads receive non-need-based scholarship or grant aid. 82% freshmen, 87% undergrads receive need-based self-help aid. 5% freshmen, 5% undergrads receive athletic scholarships. 93% freshmen receive any aid. **Criteria for awarding aid:** *Need-based:* Academics, Alumni affiliation, Art, Athletics, Leadership, Music/drama, Religious affiliation *Non-need-based:* Academics, Alumni affiliation, Art, Athletics, Leadership, Music/drama, Religious affiliation.

MEREDITH COLLEGE

3800 Hillsborough Street, Raleigh, NC
Financial Aid Phone: 919-760-8565 · **CEEB Code:** 5410
Website: www.meredith.edu • **ACT Code:** 3126

This private school was founded in 1891. It has a 225 acre campus.

RATINGS
Admissions Selectivity Rating: 82   **Fire Safety Rating:** 71   **Green Rating:** 64

STUDENTS AND FACULTY
Enrollment: 1,638. **Student Body:** 100% female, 0% male, 12% out-of-state, 2% international (24 countries represented). Asian 3%, African American 8%, Caucasian 71%, Hispanic 8%, Native American 1%, Pacific Islander <1%, Two or more races 4%, Race unknown 4%.
Retention and Graduation: 80% freshmen return for sophomore year. 52% freshmen graduate within 4 years. 61% freshmen graduate within 6 years. **Faculty:** Student/faculty ratio 12:1. 131 full-time faculty, 88% hold PhDs, 9% are members of minority groups, 69% are women. 0% of classes are taught by teaching assistants.

ACADEMICS
Degrees: Bachelor's; Master's; Post-Bachelor's certificate **Classes:** Most classes have 20-29 students. Most lab/discussion sessions have 20-29 students. **Most popular majors:** Biology/Biological Sciences, General; Psychology, General; Business/Commerce, General. **Special Study Options:** Accelerated program; Cooperative education program; Cross-registration; Double major; Dual enrollment; Honors program; Independent study; Internships; Student-designed major; Study abroad; Teacher certification program. **Honors programs:** Meredith offers an enriched academic and co-curricular Honors Program that spans the four years and involves honors courses in general education, in the major field, and a thesis or equivalent project. Interdisciplinary honors courses and weekend trips/programs enrich the experience, and a Focus on Excellence series offers a variety of outings to cultural/intellectual/entertainment venues. Scholarships are provided for Honors Program participants. **Disability Services offered to physically disabled students:** Note-taking services; Reader services; Tape recorders; Tutors. **Career services:** Alumni network; Alumni services; Career assessment; Career/job search classes; Internships

FACILITIES
Housing: Apartments for single students; Women's dorms 80% of campus accessible to physically disabled. **Special Academic Facilities/Equipment:** Art gallery, amphitheatre, child-care lab, learning center and fitness center. Experimental and clinical psychology labs including an autism lab. A new Science and Mathematics Building provides a roof top telescope platform for astronomy observations, an electron microscope suite, greenhouse, and 15

student/faculty research labs. **Computers:** Students can register for classes online. Administrative functions (other than registration) can be performed online.

CAMPUS LIFE
Environment: Metropolis **Activities:** Campus Ministries; Choral groups; Dance; Drama/theater; International Student Organization; Literary magazine; Model UN; Music ensembles; Musical theater; Student government; Student newspaper; Symphony orchestra; Yearbook 91 registered organizations, 22 honor societies, 7 religious organizations. **Athletics (Intercollegiate):** *Women:* basketball, cross-country, soccer, softball, tennis, volleyball. **On-Campus Highlights:** Science and Math Building, Cate Student Center/Bee Hive (snack bar), Lowery Fitness Center, Elizabeth Triplett Beam Fountain Plaza

ADMISSIONS
Freshman Academic Profile: Average high school GPA 3.4. 17% in top 10% of high school class, 45% in top 25% of high school class, 85% in top 50% of high school class. **Test Scores:** SAT Math middle 50% range 490-585. SAT EBRW middle 50% range 510-610. ACT middle 50% range 20-25. Minimum paper TOEFL 500. **Basis for Candidate Selection:** *Very important factors considered include:* academic GPA, application essay, recommendation(s), character/personal qualities. *Important factors considered include:* rigor of secondary school record, class rank, standardized test scores, interview, extracurricular activities, talent/ability, volunteer work.level of applicant's interest. *Other factors considered include:* first generation, alumni/ae relation, work experience. **Freshman Admission Requirements:** High school diploma is required and GED is not accepted *Academic units required:* 4 English, 3 math, 3 science, 2 foreign language, 1 academic elective. **Freshman Admission Statistics:** 1,737 applied, 68.9% admitted, 33% enrolled. **Transfer Admission Requirements:** High school transcript, college transcript(s), statement of good standing from prior institution(s). Minimum college GPA of 2.0 required. Lowest grade transferable C. **General Admission Information:** Application fee $40. Priority deadline 11/1. Nonfall registration accepted. Admission may be deferred.

COSTS AND FINANCIAL AID
Annual tuition $35,816. Room and board $10,718. Required fees $100. Average book expense $850. **Required Forms and Deadlines:** FAFSA. **Notification of Awards:** Applicants will be notified of awards on a rolling basis beginning 12/10. **Types of Aid:** *Need-based scholarships/grants:* College/university scholarship or grant aid from institutional funds; Federal Pell; Private scholarships; SEOG; State scholarships/grants. **Financial Aid Statistics:** 100% needy freshmen, 100% needy undergrads receive need-based scholarship or grant aid. 0% undergrads receive non-need-based scholarship or grant aid. 83% freshmen, 83% undergrads receive need-based self-help aid. 0% freshmen, 0% undergrads receive athletic scholarships. 69% undergrads borrow to pay for school. Average cumulative indebtedness $33,993. **Criteria for awarding aid:** *Need-based:* Academics, Art, Leadership, Minority status, Music/drama, Religious affiliation *Non-need-based:* Academics, Art, Leadership, Minority status, Music/drama, Religious affiliation, State/district residency.

MERRIMACK COLLEGE

315 Turnpike Street, North Andover, MA 01845
Phone: 978-837-5100 · **Financial Aid Phone:** 978-837-5186
E-mail: admission@merrimack.edu · **CEEB Code:** 3525
Fax: 978-837-5133 · **Website:** www.merrimack.edu

This private school, affiliated with the Roman Catholic Church, was founded in 1947. It has a 220 acre campus.

RATINGS
Admissions Selectivity Rating: 66 **Fire Safety Rating:** 98 **Green Rating:** 63

STUDENTS AND FACULTY
Enrollment: 2,118. **Student Body:** 22% female, 78% male, 29% out-of-state, 2% international (27 countries represented). Asian 1%, African American 4%, Caucasian 77%, Hispanic 7%, Native American <1%, Pacific Islander <1%, Two or more races 1%, Race unknown 6%.
Retention and Graduation: 80% freshmen return for sophomore year. 63% freshmen graduate within 4 years. 1% freshmen graduate within 6 years. **Faculty:** Student/faculty ratio 14:1. 186 full-time faculty, 88% hold PhDs, 13% are members of minority groups, 50% are women. 0% of classes are taught by teaching assistants.

ACADEMICS
Degrees: Bachelor's; Master's; Post-Master's certificate **Classes:** Most classes have 20-29 students. Most lab/discussion sessions have 20-29 students.

Most popular majors: Human Development And Family Studies, General; Accounting; Marketing. **Special Study Options:** Accelerated program; Cooperative education program; Cross-registration; Double major; Dual enrollment; Honors program; Independent study; Internships; Liberal arts/career combination; Student-designed major; Study abroad; Teacher certification program. **Honors programs:** The Honors Program offers students with strong academic credentials, class standing, and leadership qualities the opportunity to study with other exceptional students in smaller and more challenging classes. It is an innovative and exciting approach to fulfilling the college's general education requirements and includes a variety of social and co-curricular activities. **Disability Services offered to physically disabled students:** Note-taking services; Reader services; Tape recorders; Tutors. **Career services:** Alumni network; Alumni services; Career assessment; Career/job search classes; Internships; Regional alumni

FACILITIES
Housing: Apartments for single students; Coed dorms; Special housing for disabled student; Theme housing 95% of campus accessible to physically disabled. **Special Academic Facilities/Equipment:** The Writers House, The Markets Lab, Astronomy Dome and Telescope, Rogers Center for the Arts, Diversity Education Center, Center for Augustinian Study & Legacy, Center for Student Research in the Life Sciences, Center for the Study of Jewish-Christian-Muslim Relations, Center for Engaged Democracy, RFID (Radio Frequency Identification) Technology Lab, Center for Campus Ministry, Center for Excellence in Teaching & Learning, Service Learning Center, Memory & Sleep Lab **Computers:** 100% of classrooms, 100% of libraries, 100% of dining areas, 100% of student union, have wireless network access. Students can register for classes online. Administrative functions (other than registration) can be performed online.

CAMPUS LIFE
Environment: Town **Activities:** Campus Ministries; Choral groups; Dance; Drama/theater; International Student Organization; Jazz band; Model UN; Music ensembles; Musical theater; Pep band; Radio station; Student government; Student newspaper; Student-run film society; Television station; Yearbook 47 registered organizations, 3 honor societies, 5 religious organizations. 2 fraternities, 3 sororities. **Athletics (Intercollegiate):** *Men:* baseball, basketball, cross-country, football, ice hockey, lacrosse, soccer, tennis. *Women:* basketball, cross-country, field hockey, lacrosse, soccer, softball, tennis, volleyball. **On-Campus Highlights:** The Sanctuary Coffeehouse, Mendel Pond, Merrimack Stadium, -McQuade Library (Academic Success Center & Zyme)?, Fitness Center **Environmental Initiatives:** Roll-out of the new interdisciplinary Environmental Studies and Sustainability Major in fall 2011. The new major has an integrated curriculum across the College's four Schools, Science and Engineering, Liberal Arts, Business, and Education.

ADMISSIONS
Freshman Academic Profile: Average high school GPA 3.1. 74% from public high schools. **Test Scores:** Minimum internet-based TOEFL 79. **Basis for Candidate Selection:** *Very important factors considered include:* rigor of secondary school record, academic GPA, application essay. *Important factors considered include:* class rank, recommendation(s), interview, extracurricular activities, talent/ability, character/personal qualities, volunteer work, work experience, level of applicant's interest. *Other factors considered include:* standardized test scores, first generation, alumni/ae relation, geographical residence, religious affiliation/commitment, racial/ethnic status. **Freshman Admission Requirements:** High school diploma is required and GED is accepted *Academic units required:* 4 English, 3 math, 2 science, 2 foreign language, 2 history. **Freshman Admission Statistics:** 8,656 applied, 81.5% admitted, 12% enrolled. **Transfer Admission Requirements:** college transcript(s), essay or personal statement, Minimum college GPA of 2.5 required. Lowest grade transferable C. **General Admission Information:** Regular application deadline 2/15. Nonfall registration accepted. Admission may be deferred for a maximum of 1 year.

COSTS AND FINANCIAL AID
Required Forms and Deadlines: FAFSA. **Notification of Awards:** Applicants will be notified of awards on a rolling basis beginning 3/15. **Types of Aid:** *Need-based scholarships/grants:* College/university scholarship or grant aid from institutional funds; Federal Pell; Private scholarships; SEOG; State scholarships/grants. *Loans:* Direct PLUS loans; Direct Subsidized Stafford Loans; Direct Unsubsidized Stafford Loans. *Student Employment:* Federal Work-Study Program available. Institutional employment available. **Financial Aid Statistics:** 100% needy freshmen, 99% needy undergrads receive need-based scholarship or grant aid. 10% freshmen, 11% undergrads receive non-need-based scholarship or grant aid. 86% freshmen, 86% undergrads receive need-based self-help aid. 6% freshmen, 7% undergrads receive athletic scholarships. **Criteria for awarding aid:** *Need-based:* Athletics *Non-need-based:* Academics, Alumni affiliation, Athletics, Leadership, Music/drama, Religious affiliation.

MESSIAH COLLEGE

One College Avenue, Mechanicsburg, PA 17055
Phone: (717) 691-6000 · **Financial Aid Phone:** (717) 691-6007
E-mail: admissions@messiah.edu · **CEEB Code:** 2411
Fax: 717-691-2307 · **Website:** www.messiah.edu · **ACT Code:** 3630

This private school, affiliated with the Interdenominational Christian, was founded in 1909. It has a 471 acre campus.

RATINGS
Admissions Selectivity Rating: 84   **Fire Safety Rating:** 86   **Green Rating:** 79

STUDENTS AND FACULTY
Enrollment: 2,670. **Student Body:** 60% female, 40% male, 36% out-of-state, 5% international (32 countries represented). Asian 2%, African American 2%, Caucasian 81%, Hispanic 5%, Native American <1%, Pacific Islander <1%, Two or more races 4%, Race unknown 1%.
Retention and Graduation: 88% freshmen return for sophomore year. 76% freshmen graduate within 4 years. 81% freshmen graduate within 6 years. 14% grads go on to further study within 1 year. 27% grads pursue arts and sciences degrees. 2% grads pursue law degrees. 5% grads pursue business degrees. 21% grads pursue medical degrees. **Faculty:** Student/faculty ratio 12:1. 197 full-time faculty, 85% hold PhDs, 9% are members of minority groups, 41% are women. 0% of classes are taught by teaching assistants.

ACADEMICS
Degrees: Bachelor's; Doctoral/Professional; Master's; Post-Bachelor's certificate; Post-Master's certificate **Classes:** Most classes have 20-29 students. Most lab/discussion sessions have 10-19 students. **Most popular majors:** Engineering, General; Health Services/Allied Health/Health Sciences, General; Business Administration And Management, General. **Special Study Options:** Accelerated program; Double major; Dual enrollment; English as a Second Language (ESL); Exchange student program (domestic); Honors program; Independent study; Internships; Student-designed major; Study abroad; Teacher certification program. **Honors programs:** The College Honors Program is designed for students who demonstrate high scholarly ability early in their academic career. The program provides a series of interdisciplinary honors courses which satisfy selected general education requirements. Participation in the program culminates in an honors research project, typically during the senior year. In addition, various campus activities are designed each semester for participants in the College Honors Program. Admission to the program is highly competitive and students selected for the College Honors Program receive either full tuition or partial tuition scholarships. **Disability Services offered to physically disabled students:** Note-taking services; Reader services; Tape recorders; Tutors. **Career services:** Alumni network; Alumni services; Career assessment; Internships; Regional alumni

FACILITIES
Housing: Apartments for single students; Coed dorms; Men's dorms; Special housing for disabled student; Special housing for international students; Theme housing; Women's dorms 80% of campus accessible to physically disabled. .
Special Academic Facilities/Equipment: Ernest L. Boyer Center; Brethren in Christ Historical Society and Archives; Oakes Museum of Natural History.
Computers: 100% of classrooms, 100% of dorms, 100% of libraries, 100% of dining areas, 100% of student union, have wireless network access. Students can register for classes online. Administrative functions (other than registration) can be performed online.

CAMPUS LIFE
Environment: Village **Activities:** Campus Ministries; Choral groups; Concert band; Dance; Drama/theater; International Student Organization; Jazz band; Literary magazine; Music ensembles; Musical theater; Pep band; Radio station; Student government; Student newspaper; Student-run film society; Symphony orchestra; Yearbook 71 registered organizations, 7 honor societies, 10 religious organizations. **Athletics (Intercollegiate):** *Men:* baseball, basketball, cross-country, golf, lacrosse, soccer, swimming, tennis, track/field (outdoor), track/field (indoor), ultimate frisbee, wrestling. *Women:* basketball, cross-country, field hockey, lacrosse, soccer, softball, swimming, tennis, track/field (outdoor), track/field (indoor), volleyball. **On-Campus Highlights:** Boyer Hall (Schools of Humanities, Ed. and Soc. Sci.), Eisenhower Campus Center/Sollenberger Sports Cent, Oakes Museum of Natural History, Stoner Covered Bridge, Starry Athletic Complex

ADMISSIONS
Freshman Academic Profile: Average high school GPA 3.8. 33% in top 10% of high school class, 63% in top 25% of high school class, 90% in top 50% of high school class. 71% from public high schools. **Test Scores:** SAT Math middle 50% range 540-650. SAT EBRW middle 50% range 560-660. ACT middle 50% range 22-29. Minimum internet-based TOEFL 80. Minimum

paper TOEFL 550. **Basis for Candidate Selection:** *Very important factors considered include:* rigor of secondary school record, class rank, academic GPA, standardized test scores, extracurricular activities, talent/ability, character/personal qualities, religious affiliation/commitment. *Important factors considered include:* application essay, volunteer work. *Other factors considered include:* recommendation(s), alumni/ae relation, racial/ethnic status, work experience, level of applicant's interest. **Freshman Admission Requirements:** High school diploma is required and GED is accepted *Academic units required:* 4 English, 2 math, 2 science, 2 science labs, 2 foreign language, 2 social studies, 4 academic electives, *Academic units recommended:* 4 English, 3 math, 3 science, 3 science labs, 2 foreign language, 2 social studies, 2 history, 4 academic electives. **Freshman Admission Statistics:** 2,558 applied, 77.0% admitted, 34% enrolled. **Transfer Admission Requirements:** college transcript(s), essay or personal statement, statement of good standing from prior institution(s). Minimum college GPA of 2.5 required. Lowest grade transferable C. **General Admission Information:** Application fee $50. Nonfall registration accepted.

COSTS AND FINANCIAL AID
Annual tuition $34,320. Room and board $10,520. Required fees $840. Average book expense $1,280. **Required Forms and Deadlines:** FAFSA. **Notification of Awards:** Applicants will be notified of awards on a rolling basis beginning 12/1. **Types of Aid:** *Need-based scholarships/grants:* College/university scholarship or grant aid from institutional funds; Federal Nursing Scholarships; Federal Pell; Private scholarships; SEOG; State scholarships/grants. *Loans:* Direct PLUS loans; Direct Subsidized Stafford Loans; Direct Unsubsidized Stafford Loans. *Student Employment:* Federal Work-Study Program available. Institutional employment available. **Financial Aid Statistics:** 99% needy freshmen, 99% needy undergrads receive need-based scholarship or grant aid. 14% freshmen, 12% undergrads receive non-need-based scholarship or grant aid. 79% freshmen, 79% undergrads receive need-based self-help aid. 0% freshmen, 0% undergrads receive athletic scholarships. 100% freshmen, 96% undergrads receive any aid. 70% undergrads borrow to pay for school. Average cumulative indebtedness $39,617. **Criteria for awarding aid:** *Need-based:* Academics *Non-need-based:* Academics, Art, Leadership, Music/drama, Religious affiliation.

METHODIST UNIVERSITY

5400 Ramsey Street, Fayetteville, NC 28311
Phone: 910-630-7027 · **Financial Aid Phone:** 910-630-7192
E-mail: admissions@methodist.edu · **CEEB Code:** 5426
Fax: 910-630-7285 · **Website:** www.methodist.edu · **ACT Code:** 3127

This private school, affiliated with the Methodist Church, was founded in 1956. It has a 620 acre campus.

RATINGS
Admissions Selectivity Rating: 80   **Fire Safety Rating:** 79   **Green Rating:** 60*

STUDENTS AND FACULTY
Enrollment: 2,226. **Student Body:** 48% female, 52% male, 30% out-of-state, 5% international (53 countries represented). Asian 1%, African American 24%, Caucasian 48%, Hispanic 6%, Native American 1%, Pacific Islander <1%, Two or more races 5%, Race unknown 10%.
Retention and Graduation: 62% freshmen return for sophomore year. 38% grads go on to further study within 1 year. 8% grads pursue arts and sciences degrees. 1% grads pursue law degrees. 12% grads pursue business degrees. 7% grads pursue medical degrees. **Faculty:** Student/faculty ratio 13:1. 142 full-time faculty, 69% hold PhDs, 13% are members of minority groups, 49% are women. 0% of classes are taught by teaching assistants.

ACADEMICS
Degrees: Associate; Bachelor's; Master's; Terminal Associate **Classes:** Most classes have 20-29 students. Most lab/discussion sessions have 10-19 students. **Most popular majors:** Secondary Education And Teaching; Cell/Cellular And Molecular Biology; Business/Commerce, General. **Special Study Options:** Cooperative education program; Distance learning; Double major; Dual enrollment; English as a Second Language (ESL); Honors program; Independent study; Internships; Liberal arts/career combination; Student-designed major; Study abroad; Teacher certification program; Weekend college. **Honors programs:** The Methodist College Honors Program is based on the "Great Books" and is an outstanding opportunity for high acheiving students. **Disability Services offered to physically disabled students:** Note-taking services; Reader services; Tape recorders; Tutors. **Career services:** Career assessment; Career/job search classes; Internships

FACILITIES

Housing: Apartments for single students; Fraternity/sorority housing; Men's dorms; Wellness housing; Women's dorms 80% of campus accessible to physically disabled. **Special Academic Facilities/Equipment:** Art gallery, Nature Trail, 18 hole golf course with practice facilities for PGM students, Academic Developement Center **Computers:** Administrative functions (other than registration) can be performed online.

CAMPUS LIFE

Environment: City **Activities:** Campus Ministries; Choral groups; Concert band; Dance; Drama/theater; International Student Organization; Jazz band; Literary magazine; Marching band; Model UN; Music ensembles; Musical theater; Opera; Pep band; Radio station; Student government; Student newspaper; Symphony orchestra; Yearbook 72 registered organizations, 15 honor societies, 8 religious organizations. 3 fraternities, 2 sororities. **Athletics (Intercollegiate):** *Men:* baseball, basketball, cheerleading, cross-country, football, golf, soccer, tennis, track/field (outdoor). *Women:* basketball, cheerleading, cross-country, golf, lacrosse, soccer, softball, tennis, track/field (outdoor), volleyball.

ADMISSIONS

Freshman Academic Profile: Average high school GPA 3.3. 9% in top 10% of high school class, 34% in top 25% of high school class, 73% in top 50% of high school class. 86% from public high schools. **Test Scores:** SAT Math middle 50% range 450-550. SAT EBRW middle 50% range 430-520. ACT middle 50% range 17-23. Minimum paper TOEFL 500. **Basis for Candidate Selection:** *Very important factors considered include:* rigor of secondary school record, academic GPA. *Important factors considered include:* class rank, standardized test scores, interview. *Other factors considered include:* application essay, recommendation(s), extracurricular activities, talent/ability, character/personal qualities, first generation, alumni/ae relation. **Freshman Admission Requirements:** High school diploma is required and GED is accepted *Academic units required:* 4 English, 3 math, 3 science, 1 science labs, 1 social studies, 2 history, 4 academic electives, *Academic units recommended:* 4 English, 4 math, 4 science, 1 science labs, 2 foreign language, 2 social studies, 2 history. **Freshman Admission Statistics:** 3,823 applied, 60.6% admitted, 21% enrolled. **Transfer Admission Requirements:** High school transcript, college transcript(s), statement of good standing from prior institution(s). Minimum college GPA of 2.0 required. Lowest grade transferable C. **General Admission Information:** Application fee $25. Nonfall registration accepted. Admission may be deferred for a maximum of 1 academic year.

COSTS AND FINANCIAL AID

Annual tuition $25,160. Room and board $9,521. Required fees $465. Average book expense $1,200. **Required Forms and Deadlines:** FAFSA. **Notification of Awards:** Applicants will be notified of awards on a rolling basis beginning 3/1. **Types of Aid:** *Need-based scholarships/grants:* College/university scholarship or grant aid from institutional funds; Federal Pell; Private scholarships; SEOG; State scholarships/grants. *Loans: Student Employment:* Federal Work-Study Program available. **Financial Aid Statistics:** 96% needy freshmen, 90% needy undergrads receive need-based scholarship or grant aid. 71% freshmen, 79% undergrads receive non-need-based scholarship or grant aid. 92% freshmen, 87% undergrads receive need-based self-help aid. 0% freshmen, 0% undergrads receive athletic scholarships. 90% freshmen, 86% undergrads receive any aid. **Criteria for awarding aid:** *Need-based:* Academics, Alumni affiliation, Leadership, Music/drama, Religious affiliation *Non-need-based:* Academics, Alumni affiliation, Leadership, Music/drama, Religious affiliation, State/district residency.

METROPOLITAN STATE UNIVERSITY

700 E. 7th Street, St. Paul, MN
Website: Http://www.metrostate.edu

This public school was founded in 1971.

RATINGS

Admissions Selectivity Rating: 0   **Fire Safety Rating:** 60*   **Green Rating:** 60*

ACADEMICS

Degrees: Bachelor's; Certificate; Master's

CAMPUS LIFE

Environment: City **Activities:** Student government; Student newspaper.

ADMISSIONS

Freshman Admission Requirements: High school diploma is required and GED is accepted **Transfer Admission Requirements:** High school transcript, college transcript(s), essay or personal statement, standardized test scores,

Lowest grade transferable C. **General Admission Information:** Application fee $20.

COSTS AND FINANCIAL AID

Annual out-of-state tuition $5,670.

MIAMI UNIVERSITY

501 E. High Street, Oxford, OH 45056
Phone: 513-529-2531 · **Financial Aid Phone:** 513-529-0001
E-mail: admission@miamioh.edu · **CEEB Code:** 1463
Fax: 513-529-1550 · **Website:** http://www.miamioh.edu/ · **ACT Code:** 3294

This public school was founded in 1809. It has a 2100 acre campus.

RATINGS

Admissions Selectivity Rating: 87   **Fire Safety Rating:** 95   **Green Rating:** 88

STUDENTS AND FACULTY

Enrollment: 16,816. **Student Body:** 50% female, 50% male, 36% out-of-state, 14% international (89 countries represented). Asian 2%, African American 3%, Caucasian 72%, Hispanic 5%, Native American <1%, Pacific Islander <1%, Two or more races 3%, Race unknown <1%.
Retention and Graduation: 91% freshmen return for sophomore year. 67% freshmen graduate within 4 years. 79% freshmen graduate within 6 years. **Faculty:** Student/faculty ratio 17:1. 973 full-time faculty, 85% hold PhDs, 20% are members of minority groups, 44% are women. 5% of classes are taught by teaching assistants.

ACADEMICS

Degrees: Bachelor's; Certificate; Doctoral/Research; Master's; Post-Master's certificate **Classes:** Most classes have 20-29 students. **Most popular majors:** Biology/Biological Sciences, General; Finance, General; Marketing/Marketing Management, General. **Special Study Options:** Cooperative education program; Cross-registration; Distance learning; Double major; Dual enrollment; English as a Second Language (ESL); Exchange student program (domestic); Honors program; Independent study; Internships; Liberal arts/career combination; Student-designed major; Study abroad; Teacher certification program. **Honors programs:** Miami has a University Honors Program. Students selected to participate receive a renewable scholarship, priority registration, and other special opportunities. **Combined degree programs:** BA/MA. **Disability Services offered to physically disabled students:** Note-taking services; Reader services; Tape recorders; Tutors. **Career services:** Alumni network; Alumni services; Career assessment; Career/job search classes; Internships; Regional alumni

FACILITIES

Housing: Apartments for married students; Apartments for single students; Coed dorms; Cooperative housing; Fraternity/sorority housing; Men's dorms; Special housing for disabled student; Special housing for international students; Theme housing; Wellness housing; Women's dorms 100% of campus accessible to physically disabled. **Special Academic Facilities/Equipment:** Geology, art, anthropology, and zoology museums, performing arts center, herbarium, ecology research center, 400-acre nature preserve, electron microscope center. **Computers:** 100% of classrooms, 100% of dorms, 100% of libraries, 100% of dining areas, 100% of student union, 65% of common outdoor areas have wireless network access. Students can register for classes online. Administrative functions (other than registration) can be performed online.

CAMPUS LIFE

Environment: Village **Activities:** Campus Ministries; Choral groups; Concert band; Dance; Drama/theater; International Student Organization; Jazz band; Literary magazine; Marching band; Model UN; Music ensembles; Musical theater; Opera; Pep band; Radio station; Student government; Student newspaper; Student-run film society; Symphony orchestra; Television station; Yearbook 304 registered organizations, 38 honor societies, 22 religious organizations. 32 fraternities, 23 sororities. **Athletics (Intercollegiate):** *Men:* baseball, basketball, cross-country, diving, football, golf, ice hockey, swimming, track/field (outdoor). *Women:* basketball, cross-country, diving, field hockey, soccer, softball, swimming, tennis, track/field (outdoor), volleyball. **On-Campus Highlights:** Farmer School of Business, McGuffey Museum, Center for the Performing Arts, Recreational Sports Center, Peabody Hall (National Historical Landmark)

ADMISSIONS

Freshman Academic Profile: Average high school GPA 3.8. 39% in top 10% of high school class, 66% in top 25% of high school class, 94% in top 50% of high school class. 68% from public high schools. **Test Scores:** SAT Math middle 50% range 610-710. SAT EBRW middle 50% range 580-670. ACT middle 50% range 26-31. Minimum internet-based TOEFL 80. Minimum paper TOEFL 550. **Basis for Candidate Selection:** *Very important factors considered include:* rigor of secondary school record, class rank, academic GPA, application essay, standardized test scores, recommendation(s), talent/ability, character/personal qualities. *Other factors considered include:* extracurricular activities, first generation, alumni/ae relation, geographical residence, state residency, volunteer work, work experience. **Freshman Admission Requirements:** High school diploma is required and GED is accepted *Academic units recommended:* 4 English, 4 math, 3 science, 2 foreign language, 2 social studies, 1 history, 1 visual/performing arts. **Freshman Admission Statistics:** 33,255 applied, 62.1% admitted, 19% enrolled. **Transfer Admission Requirements:** High school transcript, college transcript(s), essay or personal statement, statement of good standing from prior institution(s). Minimum college GPA of 2.0 required. Lowest grade transferable C. **General Admission Information:** Application fee $50. Regular application deadline 2/1. Nonfall registration accepted. Admission may be deferred.

COSTS AND FINANCIAL AID

Annual in-state tuition $12,725. Annual out-of-state tuition $31,962. Room and board $12,725. Required fees $806. Average book expense $1,216. **Required Forms and Deadlines:** FAFSA. **Notification of Awards:** Applicants will be notified of awards on a rolling basis beginning 3/20. **Types of Aid:** *Need-based scholarships/grants:* College/university scholarship or grant aid from institutional funds; Federal Pell; Private scholarships; SEOG; State scholarships/grants. *Loans:* Direct PLUS loans; Direct Subsidized Stafford Loans; Direct Unsubsidized Stafford Loans. *Student Employment:* Federal Work-Study Program available. Institutional employment available. **Financial Aid Statistics:** 88% needy freshmen, 85% needy undergrads receive need-based scholarship or grant aid. 21% freshmen, 14% undergrads receive non-need-based scholarship or grant aid. 63% freshmen, 72% undergrads receive need-based self-help aid. 2% freshmen, 2% undergrads receive athletic scholarships. 53% undergrads borrow to pay for school. Average cumulative indebtedness $30,015. **Criteria for awarding aid:** *Need-based:* Academics, Art, Athletics, Leadership, Minority status, Music/drama *Non-need-based:* Academics, Art, Athletics, Leadership, Minority status, Music/drama, State/district residency.

MICHIGAN STATE UNIVERSITY

426 Auditorium Rd., East Lansing, MI 48824
Phone: 517-355-8332 • **Financial Aid Phone:** 517-353-5940
E-mail: admis@msu.edu • **CEEB Code:** 1465
Fax: 517-353-1647 • **Website:** www.msu.edu • **ACT Code:** 2032

This public school was founded in 1855. It has a 5200 acre campus.

RATINGS

Admissions Selectivity Rating: 85 | **Fire Safety Rating:** 60* | **Green Rating:** 95

STUDENTS AND FACULTY

Enrollment: 38,770. **Student Body:** 51% female, 49% male, 13% out-of-state, 12% international (102 countries represented). Asian 5%, African American 7%, Caucasian 67%, Hispanic 4%, Native American <1%, Pacific Islander <1%, Two or more races 3%, Race unknown 1%.
Retention and Graduation: 91% freshmen return for sophomore year. 52% freshmen graduate within 4 years. 79% freshmen graduate within 6 years. 27% grads go on to further study within 1 year. 6% grads pursue law degrees. 1% grads pursue business degrees. **Faculty:** Student/faculty ratio 16:1. 2,519 full-time faculty, 90% hold PhDs, 23% are members of minority groups, 41% are women.

ACADEMICS

Degrees: Bachelor's; Certificate; Doctoral/Professional; Doctoral/Research; Master's; Post-Bachelor's certificate; Post-Master's certificate **Classes:** Most classes have 20-29 students. Most lab/discussion sessions have 20-29 students. **Special Study Options:** Accelerated program; Cooperative education program; Distance learning; Double major; Dual enrollment; English as a Second Language (ESL); Exchange student program (domestic); Honors

program; Independent study; Internships; Liberal arts/career combination; Student-designed major; Study abroad; Teacher certification program; Weekend college. **Honors programs:** MSU's Honors College embodies MSU's long-standing commitment to provide programs of study that attract and challenge unusually talented undergraduates utilizing carefully planned, highly individualized programs of study that will meet the needs of academically talented students. **Combined degree programs:** BA/MA. **Disability Services offered to physically disabled students:** Note-taking services; Reader services; Tape recorders; Tutors. **Career services:** Alumni network; Alumni services; Career assessment; Career/job search classes; Internships; Regional alumni

FACILITIES

Housing: Apartments for married students; Apartments for single students; Coed dorms; Cooperative housing; Fraternity/sorority housing; Special housing for disabled student; Special housing for international students; Theme housing; Women's dorms **Special Academic Facilities/Equipment:** Eli & Edythe Broad Art Museum, natural history, Michigan history, anthropology museums, art center, on-campus preschool and elementary school, biological station, experimental farms, botanical garden, planetarium, two superconducting cyclotrons, observatory **Computers:** Students can register for classes online. Administrative functions (other than registration) can be performed online. Undergraduates are required to own a computer.

CAMPUS LIFE

Environment: City **Activities:** Campus Ministries; Choral groups; Concert band; Dance; Drama/theater; International Student Organization; Jazz band; Literary magazine; Marching band; Model UN; Music ensembles; Musical theater; Opera; Pep band; Radio station; Student government; Student newspaper; Student-run film society; Symphony orchestra; Television station; Yearbook 500 registered organizations, 47 honor societies, 50 religious organizations. 31 fraternities, 19 sororities. **Athletics (Intercollegiate):** *Men:* baseball, basketball, cheerleading, cross-country, diving, football, golf, ice hockey, soccer, swimming, tennis, track/field (outdoor), track/field (indoor), wrestling. *Women:* basketball, cheerleading, crew/rowing, cross-country, diving, field hockey, golf, gymnastics, soccer, softball, swimming, tennis, track/field (outdoor), track/field (indoor), volleyball. **On-Campus Highlights:** MSU Student Union, Jack Breslin Student Events Center, MSU Main Library and Cyber Cafe, International Center, Wharton Center for the Performing Arts **Environmental Initiatives:** Chicago Climate Exchange

ADMISSIONS

Freshman Academic Profile: Average high school GPA 3.7. 30% in top 10% of high school class, 67% in top 25% of high school class, 95% in top 50% of high school class. **Test Scores:** SAT Math middle 50% range 550-670. SAT EBRW middle 50% range 550-650. ACT middle 50% range 23-28. Minimum internet-based TOEFL 79. Minimum paper TOEFL 550. **Basis for Candidate Selection:** *Very important factors considered include:* academic GPA, application essay, standardized test scores. *Important factors considered include:* rigor of secondary school record, level of applicant's interest. *Other factors considered include:* class rank, extracurricular activities, talent/ability, character/personal qualities, first generation, geographical residence, state residency, volunteer work. **Freshman Admission Requirements:** High school diploma is required and GED is accepted *Academic units required:* 4 English, 3 math, 3 science, 1 science labs, 2 foreign language, 3 social studies, *Academic units recommended:* 4 English, 4 math, 3 science, 1 science labs, 2 foreign language, 3 social studies. **Freshman Admission Statistics:** 36,143 applied, 71.5% admitted, 32% enrolled. **Transfer Admission Requirements:** college transcript(s), essay or personal statement, statement of good standing from prior institution(s). Minimum college GPA of 2.0 required. Lowest grade transferable C. **General Admission Information:** Application fee $65. Priority deadline 11/1. Nonfall registration accepted. Admission may be deferred for a maximum of 1 semester.

COSTS AND FINANCIAL AID

Annual in-state tuition $16,290. Annual out-of-state tuition $40,643. Room and board $9,976. Average book expense $1,084. **Required Forms and Deadlines:** FAFSA. **Notification of Awards:** Applicants will be notified of awards on a rolling basis beginning 1/1. **Types of Aid:** *Need-based scholarships/grants:* College/university scholarship or grant aid from institutional funds; Federal Pell; Private scholarships; SEOG; State scholarships/grants; United Negro College Fund. *Loans:* Direct PLUS loans; Direct Subsidized Stafford Loans; Direct Unsubsidized Stafford Loans. *Student Employment:* Federal Work-Study Program available. Institutional employment available. **Financial Aid Statistics:** 71% needy freshmen, 74% needy undergrads receive need-based scholarship or grant aid. 43% freshmen, 29% undergrads receive non-need-based scholarship or grant aid. 79% freshmen, 82% undergrads receive need-based self-help aid. 1% freshmen, 1% undergrads receive athletic scholarships. 48% freshmen, 46% undergrads receive any aid. **Criteria for awarding aid:** *Need-based:* Academics *Non-need-based:* Academics, Alumni affiliation, Art, Athletics, Leadership, Music/drama, State/district residency.

MICHIGAN TECHNOLOGICAL UNIVERSITY

1400 Townsend Drive, Houghton, MI 49931
Phone: 906-487-2335 · **Financial Aid Phone:** (906) 487-2622
E-mail: mtu4u@mtu.edu · **CEEB Code:** 1464
Fax: 906-487-2125 · **Website:** www.mtu.edu · **ACT Code:** 2030

This public school was founded in 1885. It has a 925 acre campus.

RATINGS
Admissions Selectivity Rating: 84   **Fire Safety Rating:** 96   **Green Rating:** 74

STUDENTS AND FACULTY
Enrollment: 5,854. **Student Body:** 27% female, 73% male, 22% out-of-state, 3% international (35 countries represented). Asian 1%, African American 1%, Caucasian 88%, Hispanic 2%, Native American <1%, Pacific Islander <1%, Two or more races 3%, Race unknown 2%.
Retention and Graduation: 83% freshmen return for sophomore year. 28% freshmen graduate within 4 years. 67% freshmen graduate within 6 years.
Faculty: Student/faculty ratio 12:1. 416 full-time faculty, 89% hold PhDs, 20% are members of minority groups, 29% are women. 7% of classes are taught by teaching assistants.

ACADEMICS
Degrees: Associate; Bachelor's; Certificate; Doctoral/Research; Master's; Post-Bachelor's certificate; Terminal Associate **Classes:** Most classes have 10-19 students. Most lab/discussion sessions have fewer than 10 students. **Most popular majors:** Chemical Engineering; Civil Engineering, General; Mechanical Engineering. **Special Study Options:** Accelerated program; Cooperative education program; Distance learning; Double major; Dual enrollment; English as a Second Language (ESL); Honors program; Independent study; Internships; Study abroad; Teacher certification program. **Honors programs:** The Pavlis Honors College at Michigan Technological University is a vibrant community of scholars and leaders committed to education in and out of the classroom. Our mission is to serve all of Michigan Tech's highly motivated students, regardless of GPA, by providing countless (and unexpected) ways to enhance the college experience. Learn more at www.mtu.edu/honors. **Disability Services offered to physically disabled students:** Note-taking services; Reader services; Tape recorders; Tutors. **Career services:** Alumni network; Alumni services; Career assessment; Career/job search classes; Internships; Regional alumni

FACILITIES
Housing: Apartments for married students; Apartments for single students; Coed dorms; Fraternity/sorority housing; Special housing for disabled student; Special housing for international students; Theme housing; Wellness housing 80% of campus accessible to physically diasbled. **Special Academic Facilities/Equipment:** A. E. Seaman Mineral Museum, which is the official mineral museum of Michigan; Rozsa Center for the Performing Arts, 1,100-seat, state-of-the-art theater; Ford Center with 4,000-acre Ford Forest; newly renovated MacInnes Student Ice Arena with suites; Cosmic Ray Observatory; X-ray Fluorescence Spectrometer; Unit Operations Lab and Process Simulation and Control Center; Earth, Planetary and Space Sciences Institute; Computer-aided Engineering Lab; Microfabrication Facility; and the Great Lakes Research Center. **Computers:** 93% of classrooms, 10% of dorms, 100% of libraries, 100% of dining areas, 100% of student union, 10% of common outdoor areas have wireless network access. Students can register for classes online. Administrative functions (other than registration) can be performed online.

CAMPUS LIFE
Environment: Village **Activities:** Campus Ministries; Choral groups; Concert band; Dance; Drama/theater; International Student Organization; Jazz band; Literary magazine; Music ensembles; Musical theater; Pep band; Radio station; Student government; Student newspaper; Student-run film society; Symphony orchestra 210 registered organizations, 16 honor societies, 16 religious organizations. 13 fraternities, 8 sororities. **Athletics (Intercollegiate):** *Men:* basketball, cross-country, football, ice hockey, skiing (nordic/cross-country), tennis, track/field (outdoor). *Women:* basketball, cross-country, skiing (nordic/cross-country), tennis, track/field (outdoor), volleyball. **On-Campus Highlights:** Student Development Complex, Rozsa Center for the Performing Arts, Mont Ripley Ski Hill, Portage Lake Golf Course, Van Pelt and Opie Library **Environmental Initiatives:** Emphasis on multidisciplinary sustainability research (http://www.sfi.mtu.edu/research.php/), education (http://www.sfi.mtu.edu/education.php), and outreach, such as Sustainable Futures Institute, Center for Water and Society, Environmentally Responsible Design

and Manufacturing Research Group, National Institute for Climatic Change Research (Midwestern Region), Advanced Power Systems Research Center, Materials in Sustainable Transportation Infrastructure, Power and Energy Research Center, International Sustainable Engineering Initiative, IGERT for Sustainable Futures, Graduate Certificate in Sustainability, D80 Center, Peace Corps Masters International Program, International Sustainable Development Engineering Certificate, International Senior Design Programs, Sustainability Research Experience for Undergraduates, Wood-to-Wheels Graduate Enterprise, sustainability-based undergraduate Enterprise Programs (Challenge X, Clean Snowmobile, Alternative Fuels Group, Aqua Terra Tech, Efficiency Through Engineering and Construction), Undergraduate and Graduate Colloquium in Sustainability, Sustainable Futures 1 and 2 courses.

ADMISSIONS
Freshman Academic Profile: Average high school GPA 3.7. 32% in top 10% of high school class, 65% in top 25% of high school class, 91% in top 50% of high school class. **Test Scores:** SAT Math middle 50% range 590-680. SAT EBRW middle 50% range 570-660. ACT middle 50% range 25-30. Minimum internet-based TOEFL 79. Minimum paper TOEFL 550. **Basis for Candidate Selection:** *Very important factors considered include:* academic GPA, standardized test scores. *Important factors considered include:* rigor of secondary school record. *Other factors considered include:* class rank, application essay, recommendation(s), extracurricular activities, talent/ability, character/personal qualities, volunteer work. **Freshman Admission Requirements:** High school diploma is required and GED is accepted *Academic units required:* 3 English, 3 math, 2 science, *Academic units recommended:* 4 English, 4 math, 3 science, 2 foreign language, 3 social studies, 2 academic electives, 1 computer science. **Freshman Admission Statistics:** 5,469 applied, 74.5% admitted, 32% enrolled. **Transfer Admission Requirements:** college transcript(s), statement of good standing from prior institution(s). Minimum college GPA of 2.75 required. Lowest grade transferable C. **General Admission Information:** Priority deadline 1/15. Nonfall registration accepted. Admission may be deferred for a maximum of 1 year.

COSTS AND FINANCIAL AID
Required Forms and Deadlines: FAFSA. **Notification of Awards:** Applicants will be notified of awards on a rolling basis beginning 2/1. **Types of Aid:** *Need-based scholarships/grants:* College/university scholarship or grant aid from institutional funds; Federal Pell; Private scholarships; SEOG; State scholarships/grants. *Loans:* Direct PLUS loans; Direct Subsidized Stafford Loans; Direct Unsubsidized Stafford Loans. *Student Employment:* Federal Work-Study Program available. Institutional employment available. **Financial Aid Statistics:** 85% needy freshmen, 79% needy undergrads receive need-based scholarship or grant aid. 82% freshmen, 74% undergrads receive non-need-based scholarship or grant aid. 77% freshmen, 85% undergrads receive need-based self-help aid. 5% freshmen, 5% undergrads receive athletic scholarships. 97% freshmen, 91% undergrads receive any aid. 68% undergrads borrow to pay for school. Average cumulative indebtedness $34,942. **Criteria for awarding aid:** *Need-based:* Academics *Non-need-based:* Academics, Alumni affiliation, Athletics, Job skills, Leadership, State/district residency.

See page 982.

MIDAMERICA NAZARENE UNIVERSITY

2030 E. College Way, Olathe, KS 66062
Phone: 913-791-3380 · **Financial Aid Phone:** 913-971-3298
E-mail: admissions@mnu.edu · **CEEB Code:** 6437
Fax: 913-791-3481 · **Website:** www.mnu.edu · **ACT Code:** 1445

This private school, affiliated with the Nazarene Church, was founded in 1966. It has a 105 acre campus.

RATINGS
Admissions Selectivity Rating: 85   **Fire Safety Rating:** 81   **Green Rating:** 60*

STUDENTS AND FACULTY
Enrollment: 1,224. **Student Body:** 58% female, 42% male, 42% out-of-state, 0% international (12 countries represented). Asian 2%, African American 12%, Caucasian 74%, Hispanic 2%, Native American 1%, Pacific Islander <1%, Two or more races 1%, Race unknown 8%.
Retention and Graduation: 68% freshmen return for sophomore year.
Faculty: Student/faculty ratio 17:1. 81 full-time faculty, 64% hold PhDs, 47% are women. 0% of classes are taught by teaching assistants.

ACADEMICS

Degrees: Associate; Bachelor's; Master's; Post-Bachelor's certificate; Post-Master's certificate; Terminal Associate **Classes:** Most classes have 10-19 students. **Most popular majors:** Elementary Education And Teaching; Business/Commerce, General. **Special Study Options:** Accelerated program; Cross-registration; Distance learning; Double major; Dual enrollment; Exchange student program (domestic); Honors program; Independent study; Internships; Student-designed major; Study abroad; Teacher certification program; Weekend college. **Disability Services offered to physically disabled students:** Note-taking services; Reader services; Tape recorders; Tutors.

FACILITIES

Housing: Apartments for single students; Men's dorms; Special housing for disabled student; Wellness housing; Women's dorms 90% of campus accessible to physically diasbled. **Computers:** Students can register for classes online. Administrative functions (other than registration) can be performed online.

CAMPUS LIFE

Environment: City **Activities:** Campus Ministries; Choral groups; Concert band; Drama/theater; International Student Organization; Jazz band; Literary magazine; Music ensembles; Musical theater; Pep band; Radio station; Student government; Student newspaper; Symphony orchestra; Television station; Yearbook 43 registered organizations, 6 honor societies, 4 religious organizations. **Athletics (Intercollegiate):** *Men:* baseball, basketball, cheerleading, cross-country, football, soccer, track/field (outdoor), track/field (indoor). *Women:* basketball, cheerleading, cross-country, soccer, softball, track/field (outdoor), track/field (indoor), volleyball. **On-Campus Highlights:** Cook Center, Land Memorial Gym, Fitness Center, Campus Center, Bell Cultural Events Center

ADMISSIONS

Freshman Academic Profile: Average high school GPA 3.2. 88% from public high schools. **Test Scores:** ACT middle 50% range 18-25. Minimum paper TOEFL 550. **Basis for Candidate Selection:** *Important factors considered include:* character/personal qualities. *Other factors considered include:* rigor of secondary school record, class rank, academic GPA, standardized test scores, recommendation(s), interview, extracurricular activities, talent/ability, alumni/ae relation, religious affiliation/commitment, volunteer work, level of applicant's interest. **Freshman Admission Requirements:** High school diploma is required and GED is accepted *Academic units recommended:* 4 English, 3 math, 3 science, 1 foreign language, 3 social studies. **Freshman Admission Statistics:** 1,077 applied, 51.8% admitted, 32% enrolled. **Transfer Admission Requirements:** college transcript(s), Minimum college GPA of 2.0 required. Lowest grade transferable D. **General Admission Information:** Priority deadline 3/1. Regular application deadline 8/1. Nonfall registration accepted. Admission may be deferred.

COSTS AND FINANCIAL AID

Annual tuition $29,170. Required fees $500. Average book expense $1,490. **Required Forms and Deadlines:** FAFSA. **Notification of Awards:** Applicants will be notified of awards on a rolling basis beginning 2/1. **Types of Aid:** *Need-based scholarships/grants:* College/university scholarship or grant aid from institutional funds; Federal Pell; Private scholarships; SEOG; State scholarships/grants. *Loans:* Direct Subsidized Stafford Loans; Direct Unsubsidized Stafford Loans. *Student Employment:* Federal Work-Study Program available. Institutional employment available. **Financial Aid Statistics:** 77% needy freshmen, 94% needy undergrads receive need-based scholarship or grant aid. 53% freshmen, 41% undergrads receive non-need-based scholarship or grant aid. 75% freshmen, 79% undergrads receive need-based self-help aid. 46% freshmen, 36% undergrads receive athletic scholarships. 98% undergrads receive any aid. **Criteria for awarding aid:** *Need-based:* Athletics, Job skills, Leadership, Minority status, Music/drama, Religious affiliation *Non-need-based:* Academics, Athletics, Leadership, Minority status, Music/drama, Religious affiliation, State/district residency.

MIDDLE TENNESSEE STATE UNIVERSITY

1301 E Main Street, Murfressboro, TN 37132
Phone: 615-898-2111 · **Financial Aid Phone:** 615-898-2111
E-mail: admissions@mtsu.edu · **CEEB Code:** 1466
Fax: 615-898-5478 · **Website:** www.mtsu.edu · **ACT Code:** 3994

This public school was founded in 1911. It has a 500 acre campus.

RATINGS

Admissions Selectivity Rating: 85   **Fire Safety Rating:** 95   **Green Rating:** 60*

STUDENTS AND FACULTY

Enrollment: 18,600. **Student Body:** 53% female, 47% male, 4% international (65 countries represented). Asian 3%, African American 21%, Caucasian 63%, Hispanic 5%, Native American <1%, Pacific Islander <1%, Two or more races 3%, Race unknown <1%.
Retention and Graduation: 77% freshmen return for sophomore year. 20% freshmen graduate within 4 years. 44% freshmen graduate within 6 years.
Faculty: Student/faculty ratio 18:1. 932 full-time faculty, 75% hold PhDs, 19% are members of minority groups, 48% are women.

ACADEMICS

Degrees: Bachelor's; Certificate; Doctoral/Research; Master's; Post-Bachelor's certificate; Post-Master's certificate **Classes:** Most classes have 10-19 students. Most lab/discussion sessions have 10-19 students. **Most popular majors:** Communication And Media Studies; Audiovisual Communications Technologies/Technicians; Psychology, General. **Special Study Options:** Distance learning; Double major; Dual enrollment; Honors program; Independent study; Internships; Student-designed major; Study abroad; Teacher certification program. **Honors programs:** Honors College **Combined degree programs:** BA/MA. **Disability Services offered to physically disabled students:** Note-taking services; Reader services; Tape recorders; Tutors. Alumni network; Alumni services; Career assessment; Career/job search classes; Internships

FACILITIES

Housing: Apartments for married students; Apartments for single students; Coed dorms; Fraternity/sorority housing; Men's dorms; Special housing for disabled student; Special housing for international students; Theme housing; Women's dorms

CAMPUS LIFE

Environment: City **Activities:** Campus Ministries; Choral groups; Concert band; Dance; Drama/theater; International Student Organization; Jazz band; Literary magazine; Marching band; Model UN; Music ensembles; Musical theater; Pep band; Radio station; Student government; Student newspaper; Student-run film society; Symphony orchestra; Television station. Student Union, Recreation Center, Library, Bragg Building (Recording Industry), Science Building

ADMISSIONS

Freshman Academic Profile: Average high school GPA 3.5. **Test Scores:** SAT Math middle 50% range 470-590. ACT middle 50% range 20-25. Minimum internet-based TOEFL 173. Minimum paper TOEFL 500. **Basis for Candidate Selection:** *Very important factors considered include:* academic GPA, standardized test scores. *Other factors considered include:* rigor of secondary school record, application essay, recommendation(s), extracurricular activities, talent/ability, character/personal qualities, volunteer work, work experience, level of applicant's interest. **Freshman Admission Requirements:** High school diploma is required and GED is accepted *Academic units required:* 4 English, 4 math, 3 science, 1 science labs, 2 foreign language, 1 social studies, 1 history, 1 visual/performing arts. **Freshman Admission Statistics:** 9,938 applied, 59.3% admitted, 51% enrolled. **Transfer Admission Requirements:** college transcript(s), Minimum college GPA of 2.0 required. Lowest grade transferable D. **General Admission Information:** Application fee $25. Nonfall registration accepted.

COSTS AND FINANCIAL AID

Annual out-of-state tuition $25,806. Room and board $9,154. Required fees $1,772. **Required Forms and Deadlines:** FAFSA. **Notification of Awards:** Applicants will be notified of awards on a rolling basis beginning 2/6. **Types of Aid:** *Need-based scholarships/grants:* College/university scholarship or grant aid from institutional funds; Federal Pell; Private scholarships; SEOG; State scholarships/grants. *Loans:* Direct PLUS loans; Direct Subsidized Stafford Loans; Direct Unsubsidized Stafford Loans. *Student Employment:* Federal Work-Study Program available. Institutional employment available. **Financial Aid Statistics:** 67% needy undergrads receive need-based scholarship or grant aid. 87% freshmen, 59% undergrads receive non-need-based scholarship or grant aid. 59% freshmen, 66% undergrads receive need-based self-help aid. 2% freshmen, 2% undergrads receive athletic scholarships. 64% undergrads borrow to pay for school. Average cumulative indebtedness $25,452. **Criteria for awarding aid:** *Need-based:* Academics, Athletics *Non-need-based:* Academics, Leadership, Minority status, Music/drama.

MIDDLEBURY COLLEGE

Best Colleges

The Emma Willard House, Middlebury, VT 05753-6002
Phone: 802-443-3000 • **Financial Aid Phone:** 802-443-5158
E-mail: admissions@middlebury.edu • **CEEB Code:** 3526
Fax: 802-443-2056 • **Website:** www.middlebury.edu • **ACT Code:** 4306

This private school was founded in 1800. It has a 350 acre campus.

RATINGS
Admissions Selectivity Rating: 97   **Fire Safety Rating:** 96   **Green Rating:** 99

STUDENTS AND FACULTY
Enrollment: 2,531. **Student Body:** 52% female, 48% male, 94% out-of-state, 10% international (74 countries represented). Asian 6%, African American 4%, Caucasian 64%, Hispanic 10%, Native American <1%, Pacific Islander <1%, Two or more races 5%, Race unknown 2%.
Retention and Graduation: 96% freshmen return for sophomore year. 86% freshmen graduate within 4 years. 95% freshmen graduate within 6 years. 12% grads go on to further study within 1 year. **Faculty:** Student/faculty ratio 8:1. 293 full-time faculty, 96% hold PhDs, 18% are members of minority groups, 47% are women. 0% of classes are taught by teaching assistants.

ACADEMICS
Degrees: Bachelor's; Doctoral/Research; Master's **Classes:** Most classes have 20-29 students. Most lab/discussion sessions have 20-29 students. **Most popular majors:** Environmental Studies; Economics, General; Political Science And Government, General. **Special Study Options:** Accelerated program; Double major; Exchange student program (domestic); Honors program; Independent study; Internships; Student-designed major; Study abroad; Teacher certification program. **Disability Services offered to physically disabled students:** Note-taking services; Reader services; Tape recorders; Tutors. **Career services:** Alumni network; Alumni services; Career assessment; Career/job search classes; Internships; Regional alumni

FACILITIES
Housing: Apartments for single students; Coed dorms; Special housing for disabled student; Theme housing 65% of campus accessible to physically disabled. **Special Academic Facilities/Equipment:** Art museum, theaters, language lab, observatory, electron microscope, mountain campus, downhill and cross-country ski areas, golf course, Franklin Environmental Center, organic garden. **Computers:** Students can register for classes online. Administrative functions (other than registration) can be performed online.

CAMPUS LIFE
Environment: Village **Activities:** Campus Ministries; Choral groups; Dance; Drama/theater; International Student Organization; Jazz band; Literary magazine; Model UN; Music ensembles; Musical theater; Pep band; Radio station; Student government; Student newspaper; Student-run film society; Symphony orchestra; Yearbook 100 registered organizations. **Athletics (Intercollegiate):** *Men:* baseball, basketball, cross-country, diving, football, golf, ice hockey, lacrosse, skiing (downhill/alpine), skiing (nordic/cross-country), soccer, swimming, tennis, track/field (outdoor), track/field (indoor). *Women:* basketball, cross-country, diving, field hockey, golf, ice hockey, lacrosse, skiing (downhill/alpine), skiing (nordic/cross-country), soccer, softball, squash, swimming, tennis, track/field (outdoor), track/field (indoor), volleyball. **On-Campus Highlights:** Science—Bicentennial Hall, The Center for the Arts, Athletic Facilities, The Commons System, Middlebury College Snow Bowl (Ski Area) **Environmental Initiatives:** Student initiated effort that led to Trustees resolution in 2007 charging the entire college community to work together to achieve carbon neutrality by 2016. A similar effort modeled on this one is also in progress with regard to divesting the college endowment from fossil fuel related companies. Thus far, it has led to new proxy voting policies in support of open and transparent governance and environmental and social responsibility, a student member of the Advisory Committee on Socially Responsible Investing has been appointed to the Investment Committee of the Board, and the question of divesting from fossil fuels is currently being given full and open consideration by the Trustees with significant community involvement in the discussion.

ADMISSIONS
Test Scores: SAT Math middle 50% range 660-760. SAT EBRW middle 50% range 660-750. ACT middle 50% range 30-34. **Basis for Candidate Selection:** *Very important factors considered include:* rigor of secondary school record, class rank, academic GPA, extracurricular activities, talent/ability, character/personal qualities. *Important factors considered include:* application essay, standardized test scores, recommendation(s), racial/ethnic status. *Other factors considered include:* interview, first generation, alumni/ae relation, geographical residence, volunteer work, work experience, level of applicant's interest. **Freshman Admission Requirements:** High school diploma or equivalent is not required *Academic units recommended:* 4 English, 4 math, 3 science, 3 science labs, 4 foreign language, 3 social studies. **Freshman Admission Statistics:** 8,909 applied, 17.1% admitted, 42% enrolled. **Transfer Admission Requirements:** High school transcript, college transcript(s), essay or personal statement, statement of good standing from prior institution(s). Minimum college GPA of 3.0 required. Lowest grade transferable C-. **General Admission Information:** Application fee $65. Regular application deadline 1/1. Nonfall registration accepted. Admission may be deferred.

COSTS AND FINANCIAL AID
Average book expense $1,000. **Required Forms and Deadlines:** CSS/Financial Aid PROFILE; FAFSA; Institution's own financial aid form; Noncustodial PROFILE. **Notification of Awards:** Applicants will be notified of awards on or about 4/1. **Types of Aid:** *Need-based scholarships/grants:* College/university scholarship or grant aid from institutional funds; Federal Pell; Private scholarships; SEOG; State scholarships/grants. *Loans:* Direct PLUS loans; Direct Subsidized Stafford Loans; Direct Unsubsidized Stafford Loans. *Student Employment:* Federal Work-Study Program available. Institutional employment available. **Financial Aid Statistics:** 100% needy freshmen, 98% needy undergrads receive need-based scholarship or grant aid. 0% undergrads receive non-need-based scholarship or grant aid. 90% freshmen, 94% undergrads receive need-based self-help aid. 0% freshmen, 0% undergrads receive athletic scholarships. 48% freshmen, 42% undergrads receive any aid. 45% undergrads borrow to pay for school. Average cumulative indebtedness $18,736.

MIDWAY COLLEGE

512 East Stephens Street, Midway, KY 40347-1120
Phone: 859-846-5347 • **Financial Aid Phone:** 859-846-5410
E-mail: admissions@midway.edu • **CEEB Code:** 1975
Fax: 859-846-5787 • **Website:** www.midway.edu • **ACT Code:** 1528

This private school, affiliated with the Disciples of Christ Church, was founded in 1847. It has a 105 acre campus.

RATINGS
Admissions Selectivity Rating: 79   **Fire Safety Rating:** 66   **Green Rating:** 60*

STUDENTS AND FACULTY
Enrollment: 1,395. **Student Body:** 91% female, 9% male, 9% out-of-state, <1% international (1 countries represented). Asian 1%, African American 9%, Caucasian 85%, Hispanic 2%, Native American 1%, Race unknown 3%.
Retention and Graduation: 76% freshmen return for sophomore year. **Faculty:** Student/faculty ratio 15:1. 41 full-time faculty, 46% hold PhDs, 39% are women. 0% of classes are taught by teaching assistants.

ACADEMICS
Degrees: Associate; Bachelor's; Master's **Classes:** Most classes have 10-19 students. Most lab/discussion sessions have fewer than 10 students. **Most popular majors:** Elementary Education And Teaching; Nursing/Registered Nurse (Rn, Asn, Bsn, Msn). **Special Study Options:** Accelerated program; Distance learning; Double major; Dual enrollment; Honors program; Study abroad; Teacher certification program; Weekend college. **Honors programs:** Ruth Slack Roach Leadership, President's Ambassadors, Gamma Beta Phi, Tri Beta. **Disability Services offered to physically disabled students:** Note-taking services; Reader services; Tape recorders; Tutors.

FACILITIES
Housing: Women's dorms 75% of campus accessible to physically disabled.

CAMPUS LIFE
Environment: Rural **Activities:** Choral groups; Music ensembles; Student government; Student newspaper; Yearbook. **Athletics (Intercollegiate):** *Women:* basketball, cross-country, equestrian sports, soccer, softball, tennis, volleyball. **On-Campus Highlights:** Anne Hart Raymond Center, Little Memorial Library, Equestrian Center, McManus Student Center, Piper Dining Hall

ADMISSIONS
Freshman Academic Profile: Average high school GPA 3.2. 12% in top 10% of high school class, 25% in top 25% of high school class, 64% in top 50% of

high school class. **Test Scores:** SAT Math middle 50% range 400-560. SAT EBRW middle 50% range 420-560. ACT middle 50% range 18-22. Minimum paper TOEFL 500. **Basis for Candidate Selection:** *Very important factors considered include:* rigor of secondary school record, standardized test scores. *Important factors considered include:* alumni/ae relation. *Other factors considered include:* class rank, application essay, recommendation(s), interview, extracurricular activities, talent/ability, character/personal qualities, volunteer work, work experience. **Freshman Admission Requirements:** High school diploma is required and GED is accepted *Academic units required:* 4 English, *Academic units recommended:* 3 math, 2 science, 1 foreign language, 1 social studies. **Freshman Admission Statistics:** 399 applied, 76.9% admitted, 52% enrolled. **Transfer Admission Requirements:** High school transcript, college transcript(s), Minimum college GPA of 2.0 required. Lowest grade transferable c. **General Admission Information:** Application fee $25. Priority deadline 4/1. Nonfall registration accepted. Admission may be deferred.

COSTS AND FINANCIAL AID

Annual tuition $15,750. Room and board $6,000. Required fees $150. Average book expense $1,200. **Required Forms and Deadlines:** FAFSA; Institution's own financial aid form. **Types of Aid:** *Need-based scholarships/ grants:* College/university scholarship or grant aid from institutional funds; Federal Pell; Private scholarships; SEOG; State scholarships/grants. *Loans: Student Employment:* Federal Work-Study Program available. Institutional employment available. **Financial Aid Statistics:** 100% needy freshmen, 93% needy undergrads receive need-based scholarship or grant aid. 8% freshmen, 8% undergrads receive non-need-based scholarship or grant aid. 81% freshmen, 90% undergrads receive need-based self-help aid. 1% freshmen, 1% undergrads receive athletic scholarships. 85% freshmen, 81% undergrads receive any aid. **Criteria for awarding aid:** *Need-based:* Academics, Alumni affiliation, Athletics *Non-need-based:* Academics, Alumni affiliation, Athletics, Leadership, Religious affiliation.

MILLERSVILLE UNIVERSITY OF PENNSYLVANIA

P.O. Box 1002, Millersville, PA 17551-0302
Phone: 717-871-4625 · **Financial Aid Phone:** 717-871-5100
E-mail: admissions@millersville.edu · **CEEB Code:** 2656
Fax: 717-871-2147 · **Website:** www.millersville.edu · **ACT Code:** 3712

This public school was founded in 1855. It has a 250 acre campus.

RATINGS

Admissions Selectivity Rating: 75   **Fire Safety Rating:** 95   **Green Rating:** 86

STUDENTS AND FACULTY

Enrollment: 6,613. **Student Body:** 57% female, 43% male, 6% out-of-state, 1% international (57 countries represented). Asian 3%, African American 9%, Caucasian 74%, Hispanic 11%, Native American <1%, Pacific Islander <1%, Two or more races 2%, Race unknown 1%.
Retention and Graduation: 77% freshmen return for sophomore year. 36% freshmen graduate within 4 years. 62% freshmen graduate within 6 years. **Faculty:** Student/faculty ratio 18:1. 308 full-time faculty, 94% hold PhDs, 19% are members of minority groups, 47% are women. 0% of classes are taught by teaching assistants.

ACADEMICS

Degrees: Associate; Bachelor's; Certificate; Doctoral Other; Master's; Post-Bachelor's certificate; Post-Master's certificate **Classes:** Most classes have 30-39 students. Most lab/discussion sessions have fewer than 10 students. **Most popular majors:** Speech Communication And Rhetoric; Psychology, General; Business Administration And Management, General. **Special Study Options:** Accelerated program; Cooperative education program; Cross-registration; Distance learning; Double major; Dual enrollment; English as a Second Language (ESL); Exchange student program (domestic); Honors program; Independent study; Internships; Student-designed major; Study abroad; Teacher certification program. **Honors programs:** Honors College. **Disability Services offered to physically disabled students:** Note-taking services; Reader services; Tape recorders; Tutors. **Career services:** Alumni network; Alumni services; Career assessment; Career/job search classes; Internships

FACILITIES

Housing: Apartments for single students; Coed dorms; Special housing for disabled student; Special housing for international students; Theme housing; Wellness housing 85% of campus accessible to physically diasbled. **Special Academic Facilities/Equipment:** Art galleries, Radio station, TV station, Other—Recording studio, Teleconferencing center, Weather information

center, Foreign language lab, Two performing arts centers—Winter and Ware, Atmospheric Research and Aerostat Facility, Center for Disaster Research & Education, Foucault Pendulum, Chincoteague Bay Field Station at the Marine Science Consortium, Servicemembers Opportunity Colleges Consortium (SOCC), Aircraft flight simulators, Safety engineering and training modules **Computers:** 100% of classrooms, 100% of dorms, 100% of libraries, 100% of dining areas, 100% of student union, 100% of common outdoor areas have wireless network access. Students can register for classes online. Administrative functions (other than registration) can be performed online.

CAMPUS LIFE

Environment: Village **Activities:** Campus Ministries; Choral groups; Concert band; Dance; Drama/theater; International Student Organization; Jazz band; Literary magazine; Marching band; Music ensembles; Musical theater; Radio station; Student government; Student newspaper; Student-run film society; Symphony orchestra; Television station 120 registered organizations, 11 honor societies, 12 religious organizations. 9 fraternities, 10 sororities. **Athletics (Intercollegiate):** *Men:* baseball, basketball, cross-country, football, golf, soccer, tennis, track/field (outdoor), track/field (indoor), wrestling. *Women:* basketball, cheerleading, cross-country, field hockey, lacrosse, soccer, softball, swimming, tennis, track/field (outdoor), track/field (indoor), volleyball. **On-Campus Highlights:** Student Memorial Center, The Francine G. McNairy Library and Learning Forum, Roddy and Caputo Science and Technology Buildings, Biemesderfer Executive Center, Gordinier Dining Hall **Environmental Initiatives:** Currently constructing a net zero energy building

ADMISSIONS

Freshman Academic Profile: Average high school GPA 3.3. 10% in top 10% of high school class, 28% in top 25% of high school class, 65% in top 50% of high school class. **Test Scores:** SAT Math middle 50% range 480-570. SAT EBRW middle 50% range 490-590. ACT middle 50% range 19-24. Minimum internet-based TOEFL 70. Minimum paper TOEFL 550. **Basis for Candidate Selection:** *Very important factors considered include:* rigor of secondary school record, class rank, academic GPA. *Important factors considered include:* application essay, standardized test scores, talent/ability, character/personal qualities. *Other factors considered include:* recommendation(s), extracurricular activities, first generation, racial/ethnic status, volunteer work, work experience, level of applicant's interest. **Freshman Admission Requirements:** High school diploma is required and GED is accepted *Academic units required:* 4 English, 3 math, 3 science, 2 science labs, 3 social studies, 2 history, *Academic units recommended:* 4 English, 3 math, 3 science, 2 science labs, 2 foreign language, 3 social studies, 2 history, 4 academic electives. **Freshman Admission Statistics:** 6,717 applied, 79.5% admitted, 25% enrolled. **Transfer Admission Requirements:** High school transcript, college transcript(s), statement of good standing from prior institution(s). Minimum college GPA of 2.0 required. Lowest grade transferable C. **General Admission Information:** Application fee $50. Nonfall registration accepted. Admission may be deferred for a maximum of 1 year.

COSTS AND FINANCIAL AID

Annual in-state tuition $13,440. Annual out-of-state tuition $18,730. Room and board $13,440. Required fees $2,588. Average book expense $1,000. **Required Forms and Deadlines:** FAFSA. **Notification of Awards:** Applicants will be notified of awards on a rolling basis beginning 3/19. **Types of Aid:** *Need-based scholarships/grants:* College/university scholarship or grant aid from institutional funds; Federal Pell; Private scholarships; SEOG; State scholarships/grants. *Loans:* Direct PLUS loans; Direct Subsidized Stafford Loans; Direct Unsubsidized Stafford Loans. *Student Employment:* Federal Work-Study Program available. Institutional employment available. **Financial Aid Statistics:** 81% needy freshmen, 71% needy undergrads receive need-based scholarship or grant aid. 15% freshmen, 11% undergrads receive non-need-based scholarship or grant aid. 91% freshmen, 89% undergrads receive need-based self-help aid. 1% freshmen, 1% undergrads receive athletic scholarships. 87% freshmen, 82% undergrads receive any aid. Average cumulative indebtedness $29,481. **Criteria for awarding aid:** *Need-based:* Academics, Art, Minority status *Non-need-based:* Academics, Athletics, Minority status.

MILLIGAN COLLEGE

P.O. Box 500, Milligan College, TN 37682
Phone: 423-461-8730 · **Financial Aid Phone:** 423-461-8968
E-mail: admissions@milligan.edu · **CEEB Code:** 1469
Fax: 423-461-8982 · **Website:** http://www.milligan.edu/ · **ACT Code:** 3996

This private school, affiliated with the Christian Churches/Churches of Christ (independent, was founded in 1866. It has a 181 acre campus.

RATINGS
Admissions Selectivity Rating: 85   **Fire Safety Rating:** 88   **Green Rating:** 71

STUDENTS AND FACULTY
Enrollment: 806. **Student Body:** 56% female, 44% male, 36% out-of-state, 5% international (17 countries represented). Asian 2%, African American 4%, Caucasian 83%, Hispanic 5%, Native American 0%, Pacific Islander <1%, Two or more races 2%, Race unknown 0%.
Retention and Graduation: 76% freshmen return for sophomore year. 60% freshmen graduate within 4 years. 64% freshmen graduate within 6 years. 29% grads go on to further study within 1 year. 21% grads pursue arts and sciences degrees. 1% grads pursue law degrees. 2% grads pursue business degrees. 2% grads pursue medical degrees. **Faculty:** Student/faculty ratio 9:1. 84 full-time faculty, 83% hold PhDs, 5% are members of minority groups, 50% are women. 0% of classes are taught by teaching assistants.

ACADEMICS
Degrees: Bachelor's; Doctoral/Professional; Master's **Classes:** Most classes have fewer than 10 students. Most lab/discussion sessions have 10-19 students. **Most popular majors:** Bible/Biblical Studies; Registered Nursing/Registered Nurse; Business Administration And Management, General. **Special Study Options:** Cooperative education program; Distance learning; Double major; Dual enrollment; Honors program; Independent study; Internships; Student-designed major; Study abroad; Teacher certification program. **Honors programs:** Interdisciplinary Honors Major. **Disability Services offered to physically disabled students:** Note-taking services; Tape recorders; Tutors. **Career services:** Alumni services; Career assessment; Career/job search classes; Internships; Regional alumni

FACILITIES
Housing: Apartments for married students; Apartments for single students; Men's dorms; Women's dorms 80% of campus accessible to physically diasbled. **Special Academic Facilities/Equipment:** Gregory Liberal Arts Center, Seeger Chapel **Computers:** 95% of classrooms, 95% of dorms, 100% of libraries, 100% of dining areas, 100% of student union, 25% of common outdoor areas have wireless network access. Students can register for classes online. Administrative functions (other than registration) can be performed online.

CAMPUS LIFE
Environment: Town **Activities:** Campus Ministries; Choral groups; Dance; Drama/theater; International Student Organization; Model UN; Music ensembles; Musical theater; Radio station; Student government; Student newspaper; Symphony orchestra; Television station; Yearbook 36 registered organizations, 5 honor societies, 5 religious organizations. **Athletics (Intercollegiate):** *Men:* baseball, basketball, cross-country, golf, mountain biking, soccer, swimming, tennis, track/field (outdoor), track/field (indoor). *Women:* basketball, cross-country, soccer, softball, swimming, tennis, track/field (outdoor), track/field (indoor), volleyball. **On-Campus Highlights:** The Gregory Center, Student Center, Residence Halls/ Dining Hall, Seeger Chapel, Gilliam Wellness Center **Environmental Initiatives:** Campuswide recycling

ADMISSIONS
Freshman Academic Profile: Average high school GPA 3.7. 80% from public high schools. **Test Scores:** SAT Math middle 50% range 500-590. SAT EBRW middle 50% range 500-630. ACT middle 50% range 23-27. Minimum internet-based TOEFL 79. Minimum paper TOEFL 550. **Basis for Candidate Selection:** *Very important factors considered include:* rigor of secondary school record, academic GPA, standardized test scores. *Important factors considered include:* application essay, recommendation(s), character/personal qualities. *Other factors considered include:* class rank, interview, extracurricular activities, talent/ability, first generation, alumni/ae relation, volunteer work, work experience, level of applicant's interest. **Freshman Admission Requirements:** High school diploma is required and GED is accepted *Academic units recommended:* 4 English, 4 math, 3 science, 3 science labs, 2 foreign language, 3 social studies, 3 academic electives, 1 visual/performing arts. **Freshman Admission Statistics:** 621 applied, 67.1% admitted, 47% enrolled. **Transfer Admission Requirements:** college transcript(s), essay or personal statement, Minimum college GPA of 2.0 required. Lowest grade transferable C-. **General Admission Information:** Application fee $30. Regular application deadline 8/16. Nonfall registration accepted. Admission may be deferred for a maximum of 1 year.

COSTS AND FINANCIAL AID
Annual tuition $32,500. Room and board $7,100. Required fees $1,200. Average book expense $1,300. **Required Forms and Deadlines:** FAFSA. **Notification of Awards:** Applicants will be notified of awards on a rolling basis beginning 12/1. **Types of Aid:** *Need-based scholarships/grants:* College/university scholarship or grant aid from institutional funds; Federal Pell; Private scholarships; SEOG; State scholarships/grants. *Loans:* Direct PLUS loans; Direct Subsidized Stafford Loans; Direct Unsubsidized Stafford Loans. *Student Employment:* Federal Work-Study Program available. Institutional employment available. **Financial Aid Statistics:** 100% needy freshmen, 99% needy undergrads receive need-based scholarship or grant aid. 31% freshmen, 24% undergrads receive non-need-based scholarship or grant aid. 58% freshmen, 66% undergrads receive need-based self-help aid. 32% freshmen, 20% undergrads receive athletic scholarships. 97% freshmen, 92% undergrads receive any aid. 67% undergrads borrow to pay for school. Average cumulative indebtedness $27,146. **Criteria for awarding aid:** *Need-based:* Alumni affiliation *Non-need-based:* Academics, Athletics, Job skills, Leadership, Minority status, Music/drama, Religious affiliation, State/district residency.

MILLIKIN UNIVERSITY

1184 West Main Street, Decatur, IL 62522-2084
Phone: 217-424-6210 · **Financial Aid Phone:** 217-424-6317
E-mail: admis@millikin.edu · **CEEB Code:** 1470
Fax: 217-425-4669 · **Website:** www.millikin.edu · **ACT Code:** 1080

This private school, affiliated with the Presbyterian Church, was founded in 1901. It has a 75 acre campus.

RATINGS
Admissions Selectivity Rating: 84   **Fire Safety Rating:** 98   **Green Rating:** 63

STUDENTS AND FACULTY
Enrollment: 1,883. **Student Body:** 57% female, 43% male, 17% out-of-state, 2% international (24 countries represented). Asian 1%, African American 15%, Caucasian 69%, Hispanic 7%, Native American <1%, Pacific Islander <1%, Two or more races 4%, Race unknown 1%.
Retention and Graduation: 76% freshmen return for sophomore year. 48% freshmen graduate within 4 years. 60% freshmen graduate within 6 years. 22% grads go on to further study within 1 year. 4% grads pursue arts and sciences degrees. 2% grads pursue law degrees. 5% grads pursue business degrees. 2% grads pursue medical degrees. **Faculty:** Student/faculty ratio 10:1. 150 full-time faculty, 80% hold PhDs, 8% are members of minority groups, 52% are women. 0% of classes are taught by teaching assistants.

ACADEMICS
Degrees: Bachelor's; Certificate; Doctoral/Professional; Master's; Post-Master's certificate **Classes:** Most classes have 10-19 students. Most lab/discussion sessions have 10-19 students. **Most popular majors:** Biology/Biological Sciences, General; Drama And Dramatics/Theatre Arts, General; Registered Nursing/Registered Nurse. **Special Study Options:** Accelerated program; Distance learning; Double major; Dual enrollment; English as a Second Language (ESL); Exchange student program (domestic); Honors program; Independent study; Internships; Student-designed major; Study abroad; Teacher certification program. **Honors programs:** Millikin's honors programs are described at https://millikin.edu/honors. **Disability Services offered to physically disabled students:** Note-taking services; Reader services; Tape recorders; Tutors. **Career services:** Alumni network; Alumni services; Career assessment; Career/job search classes; Internships

FACILITIES
Housing: Apartments for married students; Coed dorms; Fraternity/sorority housing; Special housing for disabled students 66% of campus accessible to physically diasbled. **Special Academic Facilities/Equipment:** Art galleries, art museum, fitness/wellness center, recording studio, indoor sports center, greenhouse, observatory, 2000 seat performance center **Computers:** 75% of classrooms, 75% of dorms, 100% of libraries, 100% of dining areas, 100% of student union, 5% of common outdoor areas have wireless network access. Students can register for classes online. Administrative functions (other than registration) can be performed online.

CAMPUS LIFE
Environment: City **Activities:** Choral groups; Concert band; Dance; Drama/theater; International Student Organization; Jazz band; Literary magazine; Model UN; Music ensembles; Musical theater; Opera; Radio station; Student

government; Student newspaper; Student-run film society; Symphony orchestra 96 registered organizations, 7 honor societies, 2 religious organizations. 5 fraternities, 4 sororities. **Athletics (Intercollegiate):** *Men:* baseball, basketball, cheerleading, cross-country, football, golf, soccer, swimming, track/field (outdoor), track/field (indoor). *Women:* basketball, cheerleading, cross-country, golf, soccer, softball, swimming, tennis, track/field (outdoor), track/field (indoor), volleyball. **On-Campus Highlights:** University Commons, ADM-Scovill Hall, Perkinson Music Center, Albert Taylor Theatre, Decatur Indoor Sports Center

ADMISSIONS

Freshman Academic Profile: Average high school GPA 3.4. 13% in top 10% of high school class, 38% in top 25% of high school class, 71% in top 50% of high school class. 91% from public high schools. **Test Scores:** SAT Math middle 50% range 530-620. SAT EBRW middle 50% range 550-640. ACT middle 50% range 19-26. Minimum internet-based TOEFL 76. Minimum paper TOEFL 550. **Basis for Candidate Selection:** *Very important factors considered include:* rigor of secondary school record. *Important factors considered include:* class rank, academic GPA, standardized test scores, recommendation(s), interview. *Other factors considered include:* extracurricular activities, talent/ability, character/personal qualities, alumni/ae relation, volunteer work, work experience, level of applicant's interest. **Freshman Admission Requirements:** High school diploma is required and GED is accepted *Academic units recommended:* 4 English, 3 math, 3 science, 2 foreign language, 2 social studies, 2 history. **Freshman Admission Statistics:** 3,431 applied, 64.6% admitted, 21% enrolled. **Transfer Admission Requirements:** High school transcript, college transcript(s), Minimum college GPA of 2.0 required. Lowest grade transferable C-. **General Admission Information:** Priority deadline 5/1. Nonfall registration accepted. Admission may be deferred for a maximum of 1 year.

COSTS AND FINANCIAL AID

Annual tuition $32,274. Room and board $11,082. Required fees $792. Average book expense $1,000. **Required Forms and Deadlines:** FAFSA. **Notification of Awards:** Applicants will be notified of awards on a rolling basis beginning 1/15. **Types of Aid:** *Need-based scholarships/grants:* College/university scholarship or grant aid from institutional funds; Federal Pell; Private scholarships; SEOG; State scholarships/grants. *Loans:* Direct PLUS loans; Direct Subsidized Stafford Loans; Direct Unsubsidized Stafford Loans. *Student Employment:* Federal Work-Study Program available. Institutional employment available. **Financial Aid Statistics:** 92% needy freshmen, 89% needy undergrads receive need-based scholarship or grant aid. 100% freshmen, 92% undergrads receive non-need-based scholarship or grant aid. 79% freshmen, 81% undergrads receive need-based self-help aid. 0% freshmen, 0% undergrads receive athletic scholarships. 100% freshmen, 99% undergrads receive any aid. 81% undergrads borrow to pay for school. Average cumulative indebtedness $32,924. **Criteria for awarding aid:** *Need-based:* Academics *Non-need-based:* Academics, Alumni affiliation, Art, Leadership, Minority status, Music/drama.

MILLS COLLEGE

5000 MacArthur Boulevard, Oakland, CA 94613
Phone: 510-430-2135 · **Financial Aid Phone:** (510) 430-3264
E-mail: admission@mills.edu · **CEEB Code:** 4485
Fax: 510-430-3314 · **Website:** www.mills.edu · **ACT Code:** 4485

This private school was founded in 1852. It has a 135 acre campus.

RATINGS

Admissions Selectivity Rating: 77   **Fire Safety Rating:** 78   **Green Rating:** 87

STUDENTS AND FACULTY

Enrollment: 757. **Student Body:** 100% female, 0% male, 1% international (4 countries represented). Asian 10%, African American 9%, Caucasian 41%, Hispanic 28%, Native American <1%, Pacific Islander <1%, Two or more races 9%, Race unknown 1%.
Retention and Graduation: 77% freshmen return for sophomore year. 57% freshmen graduate within 4 years. 64% freshmen graduate within 6 years. 29% grads go on to further study within 1 year. 22% grads pursue arts and sciences degrees. 1% grads pursue law degrees. 2% grads pursue business degrees. 2% grads pursue medical degrees. **Faculty:** Student/faculty ratio 10:1. 82 full-time faculty, 85% hold PhDs, 40% are members of minority groups, 73% are women. 0% of classes are taught by teaching assistants.

ACADEMICS

Degrees: Bachelor's; Certificate; Doctoral/Research; Master's; Post-Bachelor's certificate **Classes:** Most classes have 10-19 students. **Most popular majors:** English Language And Literature, General; Biology/Biological Sciences, General; Psychology, General. **Special Study Options:** Accelerated program; Cooperative education program; Cross-registration; Double major; Exchange student program (domestic); Independent study; Internships; Student-designed major; Study abroad; Teacher certification program. **Combined degree programs:** BA/MA; BA/MEng. **Disability Services offered to physically disabled students:** Note-taking services; Reader services; Tape recorders; Tutors. **Career services:** Alumni network; Alumni services; Career assessment; Career/job search classes; Internships; Regional alumni

FACILITIES

Housing: Apartments for married students; Apartments for single students; Coed dorms; Cooperative housing; Men's dorms; Special housing for disabled student; Theme housing; Wellness housing; Women's dorms 100% of campus accessible to physically diasbled. **Special Academic Facilities/Equipment:** Art Museum, Center for Contemporary Music, Campus Farm, Mills Elementary School (Laboratory School), Botanical Gardens, LEED rated Natural Sciences Building and Lorry I. Lokey Graduate School of Business. **Computers:** 100% of classrooms, 100% of dorms, 100% of libraries, 100% of dining areas, 100% of student union, 100% of common outdoor areas have wireless network access. Students can register for classes online. Administrative functions (other than registration) can be performed online.

CAMPUS LIFE

Environment: Metropolis **Activities:** Campus Ministries; Choral groups; Dance; Drama/theater; International Student Organization; Literary magazine; Model UN; Music ensembles; Student government; Student newspaper; Yearbook 47 registered organizations, 2 honor societies, 4 religious organizations. **Athletics (Intercollegiate):** *Women:* crew/rowing, cross-country, soccer, swimming, tennis, track/field (outdoor), volleyball. **On-Campus Highlights:** The Mills College Art Museum, Haas Pavilion & Trefethen Aquatic Center, Rothwell Student Center, Lorry I. Lokey Graduate School of Business, Littlefield Concert Hall **Environmental Initiatives:** Mills recycles, composts and reuses all consumer materials to the extent possible. www.mills.edu/green/recycling Mills students, staff and faculty participate in Recycle Mania.

ADMISSIONS

Freshman Academic Profile: Average high school GPA 3.6. 11% in top 10% of high school class, 24% in top 25% of high school class, 96% in top 50% of high school class. 81% from public high schools. **Test Scores:** SAT EBRW middle 50% range 530-670. ACT middle 50% range 29-29. Minimum internet-based TOEFL 80. Minimum paper TOEFL 550. **Basis for Candidate Selection:** *Very important factors considered include:* rigor of secondary school record. *Important factors considered include:* class rank, academic GPA, application essay, recommendation(s), extracurricular activities, character/personal qualities. *Other factors considered include:* interview, talent/ability, first generation, alumni/ae relation, geographical residence, state residency, racial/ethnic status, volunteer work, work experience. **Freshman Admission Requirements:** High school diploma is required and GED is accepted *Academic units required:* 4 English, 3 math, 2 science, 2 science labs, 2 foreign language, 2 social studies, 2 history, *Academic units recommended:* 4 English, 4 math, 4 science, 2 science labs, 4 foreign language, 4 social studies, 4 history, 2 visual/performing arts. **Freshman Admission Statistics:** 965 applied, 92.0% admitted, 20% enrolled. **Transfer Admission Requirements:** High school transcript, college transcript(s), essay or personal statement, Lowest grade transferable C-. **General Admission Information:** Application fee $50. Priority deadline 1/15. Nonfall registration accepted. Admission may be deferred for a maximum of 1 semester.

COSTS AND FINANCIAL AID

Annual tuition $28,765. Room and board $13,448. Required fees $1,492. Average book expense $1,611. **Required Forms and Deadlines:** FAFSA; Noncustodial PROFILE. **Notification of Awards:** Applicants will be notified of awards on a rolling basis beginning 2/15. **Types of Aid:** *Need-based scholarships/grants:* College/university scholarship or grant aid from institutional funds; Federal Pell; Private scholarships; SEOG; State scholarships/grants. *Loans:* Direct PLUS loans; Direct Subsidized Stafford Loans; Direct Unsubsidized Stafford Loans. *Student Employment:* Federal Work-Study Program available. Institutional employment available. **Financial Aid Statistics:** 91% needy freshmen, 92% needy undergrads receive need-based scholarship or grant aid. 99% freshmen, 98% undergrads receive non-need-based scholarship or grant aid. 87% freshmen, 85% undergrads receive need-based self-help aid. 0% freshmen, 0% undergrads receive athletic scholarships. 100% freshmen, 95% undergrads receive any aid. 76% undergrads borrow to pay for school. Average cumulative indebtedness $33,327. **Criteria for awarding aid:** *Non-need-based:* Academics, Leadership, Music/drama.

MILLSAPS COLLEGE

1701 North State Street, Jackson, MS 39210
Phone: 601-974-1050 · **Financial Aid Phone:** 800-352-1050
E-mail: admissions@millsaps.edu · **CEEB Code:** 1471
Fax: 601-974-1059 · **Website:** www.millsaps.edu · **ACT Code:** 2212

This private school, affiliated with the Methodist Church, was founded in 1890. It has a 100 acre campus.

RATINGS
Admissions Selectivity Rating: 87   **Fire Safety Rating:** 90   **Green Rating:** 71

STUDENTS AND FACULTY
Enrollment: 802. **Student Body:** 49% female, 51% male, 56% out-of-state, 5% international (16 countries represented). Asian 3%, African American 17%, Caucasian 66%, Hispanic 5%, Native American 1%, Pacific Islander <1%, Two or more races 0%, Race unknown 2%.
Retention and Graduation: 75% freshmen return for sophomore year. 62% freshmen graduate within 4 years. 67% freshmen graduate within 6 years. 44% grads go on to further study within 1 year. 15% grads pursue arts and sciences degrees. 6% grads pursue law degrees. 9% grads pursue business degrees. 5% grads pursue medical degrees. **Faculty:** Student/faculty ratio 9:1. 85 full-time faculty, 95% hold PhDs, 13% are members of minority groups, 49% are women. 0% of classes are taught by teaching assistants.

ACADEMICS
Degrees: Bachelor's; Master's **Classes:** Most classes have fewer than 10 students. Most lab/discussion sessions have 10-19 students. **Most popular majors:** Biology/Biological Sciences, General; Psychology, General; Business Administration, Management And Operations. **Special Study Options:** Accelerated program; Double major; Honors program; Independent study; Internships; Liberal arts/career combination; Student-designed major; Study abroad; Teacher certification program; Weekend college. **Honors programs:** The Honors Program, Ford Teaching Fellows program (research and internships for students interested in college teaching), Weiner Pre-Medical Fellows Program (summer research), Lilly Fellows Faith and Work Initiative (connecting individual passions with learning, meaning, service, and career). **Disability Services offered to physically disabled students:** Note-taking services; Reader services; Tutors. **Career services:** Alumni network; Alumni services; Career assessment; Internships; Regional alumni

FACILITIES
Housing: Coed dorms; Fraternity/sorority housing; Men's dorms; Special housing for disabled student; Theme housing; Women's dorms 90% of campus accessible to physically diasbled. **Special Academic Facilities/Equipment:** Millsaps' W.M. Keck Center for Instrumental and Biochemical Comparative Archaeology is the only undergraduate facility of its kind in the world. The new multi-disciplinary research laboratory provides undergraduate students with the opportunity to explore complex archeological questions using advanced bioanalytical and biochemical techniques. 4-6 Keck Fellows assist each year in gathering the artifacts studied in the lab from the College's archaeological field programs in YucatÃn, Mexico, and northern Albania. The lab houses an inductively-coupled plasma spectrometer with laser ablation, a gas-chromotography spectrometer, a liquid-chromotography spectrometer, and a portable x-ray fluorescence spectrometer. In addition, the college's other labs include a unique array of spectrometers for measuring atomic absorption, infrared transitional modes, nuclear magnetic resonance, and other forms of energy; high performance chromatographs for separation and identification of compounds; electrophoresis instruments for analyzing biomolecules and other biological materials; and an inert atmosphere reaction chamber. Other facilities include a state-of-the-art molecular biology/functional genomics research laboratory; a fluorescence microscopy suite and imaging facility; a GIS workstation with Rockware and Arcview 9.1 GIS Software; a specially-designed automated 24-hour food monitoring system for rats; a microsurgical lab for animal surgeries; an on-campus hydrogeologic monitoring station to measure the water table and water levels in four on-campus wells; and a computational modeling lab for math, chemistry and physics students which provides numerical and graphical solutions in three dimensions. The College Sorbent and Environmental Laboratory provides undergraduates with opportunities for oil spill and stormwater remediation research. **Computers:** 100% of classrooms, 100% of dorms, 100% of libraries, 100% of dining areas, 100% of student union, 100% of common outdoor areas have wireless network access. Students can register for classes online. Administrative functions (other than registration) can be performed online.

CAMPUS LIFE
Environment: Metropolis **Activities:** Campus Ministries; Choral groups; Dance; Drama/theater; International Student Organization; Literary magazine; Model UN; Music ensembles; Musical theater; Student government; Student newspaper; Yearbook 85 registered organizations, 28 honor societies, 12 religious organizations. 6 fraternities, 6 sororities. **Athletics (Intercollegiate):** *Men:* baseball, basketball, cross-country, football, golf, lacrosse, soccer, tennis, track/field (outdoor). *Women:* basketball, cross-country, golf, lacrosse, soccer, softball, tennis, track/field (outdoor), volleyball. **On-Campus Highlights:** Hall Activities Center (fitness/athletic facility), Campbell College Center (student activities), The Bowl (outdoor green space/campus center), Millsaps Wilson Library (study center), Fraternity Row **Environmental Initiatives:** The College supports the Center for Research and Learning at the H. Moyers Biocultural Reserve operated by Kaxil Kiuic, YucatÃn, Mexico. The Center is an off the grid facility built using sustainable design and technology. Applied Ecological Design, taught by Millsaps faculty at the Center, focuses on topics critical to planning, designing, and creating a sustainable home including sustainable construction, solar power, energy efficiency, water supply, waste and wastewater management, and agriculture/ permaculture; coursework includes on-site project experimentation, design, and construction.

ADMISSIONS
Freshman Academic Profile: Average high school GPA 3.7. 55% from public high schools. **Test Scores:** SAT Math middle 50% range 550-660. SAT EBRW middle 50% range 560-660. ACT middle 50% range 22-28. Minimum internet-based TOEFL 80. Minimum paper TOEFL 550. **Basis for Candidate Selection:** *Very important factors considered include:* rigor of secondary school record, academic GPA, standardized test scores, character/ personal qualities. *Important factors considered include:* class rank, application essay, recommendation(s), extracurricular activities, talent/ability. *Other factors considered include:* interview, volunteer work, work experience. **Freshman Admission Requirements:** High school diploma is required and GED is accepted *Academic units required:* 4 English, 3 math, 3 science, 2 science labs, 1 foreign language, 2 social studies, 2 history, 1 academic elective, *Academic units recommended:* 4 English, 4 math, 4 science, 2 science labs, 2 foreign language, 2 social studies, 2 history, 2 academic electives. **Freshman Admission Statistics:** 4,276 applied, 48.9% admitted, 11% enrolled. **Transfer Admission Requirements:** college transcript(s), essay or personal statement, standardized test scores, statement of good standing from prior institution(s). Minimum college GPA of 2.75 required. Lowest grade transferable C. **General Admission Information:** Priority deadline 2/1. Regular application deadline 7/1. Nonfall registration accepted. Admission may be deferred for a maximum of 1 year.

COSTS AND FINANCIAL AID
Annual tuition $37,290. Room and board $13,730. Required fees $2,620. Average book expense $1,200. **Required Forms and Deadlines:** FAFSA. **Notification of Awards:** Applicants will be notified of awards on a rolling basis beginning 3/15. **Types of Aid:** *Need-based scholarships/grants:* College/ university scholarship or grant aid from institutional funds; Federal Pell; Private scholarships; SEOG; State scholarships/grants. *Loans:* Direct PLUS loans; Direct Subsidized Stafford Loans; Direct Unsubsidized Stafford Loans. *Student Employment:* Federal Work-Study Program available. Institutional employment available. **Financial Aid Statistics:** 100% needy freshmen, 100% needy undergrads receive need-based scholarship or grant aid. 26% freshmen, 20% undergrads receive non-need-based scholarship or grant aid. 70% freshmen, 76% undergrads receive need-based self-help aid. 0% freshmen, 0% undergrads receive athletic scholarships. 100% freshmen, 98% undergrads receive any aid. **Criteria for awarding aid:** *Need-based:* Minority status, Religious affiliation *Non-need-based:* Academics, Art, Leadership, Music/drama, Religious affiliation.

MILWAUKEE SCHOOL OF ENGINEERING

1025 North Broadway, Milwaukee, WI 53202-3109
Phone: 414-277-6763 · **Financial Aid Phone:** 800-778-7223
E-mail: explore@msoe.edu · **CEEB Code:** 1476
Fax: 414-277-7475 · **Website:** www.msoe.edu · **ACT Code:** 4616

This private school was founded in 1903. It has a 22 acre campus.

RATINGS
Admissions Selectivity Rating: 86   **Fire Safety Rating:** 98   **Green Rating:** 73

STUDENTS AND FACULTY
Enrollment: 2,605. **Student Body:** 27% female, 73% male, 34% out-of-state, 10% international (29 countries represented). Asian 4%, African American 2%, Caucasian 67%, Hispanic 6%, Native American <1%, Pacific Islander <1%, Two or more races 3%, Race unknown 8%.

Retention and Graduation: 85% freshmen return for sophomore year. 42% freshmen graduate within 4 years. 67% freshmen graduate within 6 years. 8% grads go on to further study within 1 year. 0% grads pursue arts and sciences degrees. 1% grads pursue law degrees. 3% grads pursue business degrees. 1% grads pursue medical degrees. **Faculty:** Student/faculty ratio 16:1. 139 full-time faculty, 83% hold PhDs, 10% are members of minority groups, 32% are women. 0% of classes are taught by teaching assistants.

ACADEMICS

Degrees: Bachelor's; Master's **Classes:** Most classes have 20-29 students. Most lab/discussion sessions have 20-29 students. **Most popular majors:** Architectural Engineering; Electrical And Electronics Engineering; Mechanical Engineering. **Special Study Options:** Accelerated program; Double major; Dual enrollment; English as a Second Language (ESL); Honors program; Independent study; Internships; Study abroad. **Honors programs:** The University Scholars program encourages independent, collaborative and cooperative learning. The benefits of participating in the USP include having classes with like-minded students; having greater opportunities to pursue individual interests; experiencing an enriched academic environment; the integration of diverse topics into the classroom, with more in-depth preparation for graduate school; the ability to hone your leadership skills through project work, professional presentations and interaction with regional leaders in various fields. **Combined degree programs:** BA/MEng. **Disability Services offered to physically disabled students:** Note-taking services; Reader services; Tape recorders; Tutors. **Career services:** Alumni network; Alumni services; Career assessment; Career/job search classes; Internships; Regional alumni

FACILITIES

Housing: Apartments for married students; Apartments for single students; Coed dorms; Fraternity/sorority housing; Special housing for disabled student; Wellness housing 95% of campus accessible to physically disabled. **Special Academic Facilities/Equipment:** Grohmann Museum, Kern Center Health, Wellness, Fitness and Recreation Facility, Rader School of Business, Johnson Controls Software Engineering Lab, Fluid Power Institute, Rapid Prototyping Center, Applied Technology Center, Center for BioMolecular Modeling, Ruehlow Nursing Complex, Harley Davidson Design Lab, Johnson Controls Environmental Systems Lab **Computers:** 100% of classrooms, 10% of dorms, 100% of libraries, 100% of dining areas, 100% of student union, 100% of common outdoor areas have wireless network access. Students can register for classes online. Administrative functions (other than registration) can be performed online. Undergraduates are required to own a computer.

CAMPUS LIFE

Environment: Metropolis **Activities:** Campus Ministries; Choral groups; Concert band; Dance; Drama/theater; International Student Organization; Jazz band; Literary magazine; Pep band; Radio station; Student government; Student-run film society; Symphony orchestra 61 registered organizations, 6 honor societies, 4 religious organizations. 3 fraternities, 3 sororities. **Athletics (Intercollegiate):** *Men:* baseball, basketball, cheerleading, crew/rowing, cross-country, golf, ice hockey, lacrosse, soccer, tennis, track/field (outdoor), track/field (indoor), volleyball, wrestling. *Women:* basketball, cheerleading, cross-country, golf, soccer, softball, tennis, track/field (outdoor), track/field (indoor), volleyball. **On-Campus Highlights:** Kern Center and Viets Field, Campus Center, Grohmann Museum, Rapid Prototyping Center, Ruehlow Nursing Complex **Environmental Initiatives:** In the Fall of 2010, MSOE initiated a compostable service ware program in the school's cafe. It included replacing hot and cold beverage cups, plates and soup bowls. At the time, there was also a dedicated collection stream setup to help divert an estimated 150 cubic yards of waste per year from going into local landfills. Efforts have been made to increase MSOE's recycling rate from 10% in 6/09 to over 60% in 1/11.

ADMISSIONS

Freshman Academic Profile: Average high school GPA 3.7. 92% from public high schools. **Test Scores:** SAT Math middle 50% range 603-710. SAT EBRW middle 50% range 550-650. ACT middle 50% range 25-30. Minimum internet-based TOEFL 82. Minimum paper TOEFL 550. **Basis for Candidate Selection:** *Very important factors considered include:* academic GPA, standardized test scores. *Important factors considered include:* rigor of secondary school record, extracurricular activities, talent/ability. *Other factors considered include:* character/personal qualities, alumni/ae relation. **Freshman Admission Requirements:** High school diploma is required and GED is accepted *Academic units required:* 4 English, 4 math, 4 science, *Academic units recommended:* 3 science labs. **Freshman Admission Statistics:** 2,893 applied, 62.8% admitted, 31% enrolled. **Transfer Admission Requirements:** college transcript(s), Minimum college GPA of 2.5 required. Lowest grade transferable C. **General Admission Information:** Priority deadline 1/1. Regular application deadline 9/1. Nonfall registration accepted. Admission may be deferred for a maximum of 2 years.

COSTS AND FINANCIAL AID

Annual tuition $39,040. Required fees $1,710. Average book expense $1,000. **Required Forms and Deadlines:** FAFSA. **Notification of Awards:** Applicants will be notified on a rolling basis beginning 1/15. **Types**

of Aid: *Need-based scholarships/grants:* College/university scholarship or grant aid from institutional funds; Federal Pell; Private scholarships; SEOG; State scholarships/grants. *Loans:* Direct PLUS loans; Direct Subsidized Stafford Loans; Direct Unsubsidized Stafford Loans. *Student Employment:* Federal Work-Study Program available. Institutional employment available. **Financial Aid Statistics:** 100% needy freshmen, 100% needy undergrads receive need-based scholarship or grant aid. 18% freshmen, 15% undergrads receive non-need-based scholarship or grant aid. 77% freshmen, 82% undergrads receive need-based self-help aid. 0% freshmen, 0% undergrads receive athletic scholarships. 100% freshmen, 90% undergrads receive any aid. 76% undergrads borrow to pay for school. Average cumulative indebtedness $38,745. **Criteria for awarding aid:** *Non-need-based:* Academics.

MINERVA SCHOOLS AT KGI

1145 Market Street, San Francisco, CA 94103
Phone: (415) 649-7658
E-mail: admissions@minerva.kgi.edu
Fax: 415.520.0517 • **Website:** www.minerva.kgi.edu

This is a private school.

RATINGS

Admissions Selectivity Rating: 84 **Fire Safety Rating:** 72 **Green Rating:** 60*

STUDENTS AND FACULTY

Enrollment: 111. **Student Body:** 48% female, 52% male, 78% international. Race unknown 22%.
Retention and Graduation: 90% freshmen return for sophomore year. **Faculty:** Student/faculty ratio 10:1. 12 full-time faculty, 100% hold PhDs, 17% are members of minority groups, 50% are women. 0% of classes are taught by teaching assistants.

ACADEMICS

Degrees: Bachelor's; Master's **Classes:** Most classes have 10-19 students. **Special Study Options:** Distance learning; Double major; Independent study; Internships; Study abroad. **Career services:** Career assessment; Career/job search classes; Internships

FACILITIES

Housing: Apartments for single students; Coed dorms

CAMPUS LIFE

Environment: Metropolis **Activities:** Drama/theater; International Student Organization; Music ensembles; Student government; Student newspaper; Student-run film society.

ADMISSIONS

Freshman Academic Profile: 0% in top 10% of high school class. **Basis for Candidate Selection:** *Very important factors considered include:* rigor of secondary school record, class rank, academic GPA, interview, extracurricular activities, talent/ability, character/personal qualities. *Important factors considered include:* volunteer work, work experience. **Freshman Admission Statistics:** 9,032 applied, 2.1% admitted, 53% enrolled. **General Admission Information:** Regular application deadline 1/17. Nonfall registration accepted. Admission may be deferred.

COSTS AND FINANCIAL AID

Annual tuition $10,000. Required fees $1,450. Average book expense $1,000. **Required Forms and Deadlines:** CSS/Financial Aid PROFILE; Noncustodial PROFILE. **Notification of Awards:** Applicants will be notified of awards on or about 3/25. **Types of Aid:** *Need-based scholarships/grants:* College/university scholarship or grant aid from institutional funds. *Loans:* *Student Employment:* Institutional employment available. **Financial Aid Statistics:** 100% needy undergrads receive need-based scholarship or grant aid. 0% undergrads receive non-need-based scholarship or grant aid. 11% undergrads receive need-based self-help aid. 0% undergrads receive athletic scholarships.

MINNEAPOLIS COLLEGE OF ART AND DESIGN

2501 Stevens Avenue South, Minneapolis, MN 55404
Phone: 612-874-3760 • **Financial Aid Phone:** 612-874-3782
E-mail: admissions@mcad.edu • **CEEB Code:** 6411
Fax: 612-874-3701 • **Website:** www.mcad.edu • **ACT Code:** 2130

This private school was founded in 1886. It has a 3 acre campus.

RATINGS
Admissions Selectivity Rating: 83   **Fire Safety Rating:** 60*   **Green Rating:** 60*

STUDENTS AND FACULTY
Enrollment: 594. **Student Body:** 61% female, 39% male, 36% out-of-state, 1% international (10 countries represented). Asian 6%, African American 2%, Caucasian 69%, Hispanic 6%, Native American 1%, Race unknown 15%. **Retention and Graduation:** 70% freshmen return for sophomore year. 10% grads go on to further study within 1 year. 10% grads pursue arts and sciences degrees. **Faculty:** Student/faculty ratio 13:1. 42 full-time faculty, 100% hold PhDs, 31% are women. 0% of classes are taught by teaching assistants.

ACADEMICS
Degrees: Bachelor's; Master's; Post-Bachelor's certificate **Classes:** Most classes have 20-29 students. Most lab/discussion sessions have 20-29 students. **Special Study Options:** Cooperative education program; Cross-registration; Distance learning; Independent study; Internships; Study abroad. **Disability Services offered to physically disabled students:** Note-taking services; Reader services; Tape recorders; Tutors. **Career services:** Alumni services; Career assessment; Internships

FACILITIES
Housing: Apartments for single students; Coed dorms 95% of campus accessible to physically diasbled. **Special Academic Facilities/Equipment:** Art gallery.

CAMPUS LIFE
Environment: Metropolis **Activities:** Student government; Student-run film society. **On-Campus Highlights:** Main gallery, Student Center

ADMISSIONS
Freshman Academic Profile: Average high school GPA 3.3. 89% from public high schools. **Test Scores:** SAT Math middle 50% range 430-604. SAT EBRW middle 50% range 503-680. ACT middle 50% range 21-27. Minimum paper TOEFL 550. **Basis for Candidate Selection:** *Very important factors considered include:* academic GPA, application essay, standardized test scores, recommendation(s), talent/ability. *Important factors considered include:* interview, character/personal qualities. *Other factors considered include:* rigor of secondary school record. **Freshman Admission Requirements:** High school diploma is required and GED is accepted *Academic units recommended:* 4 English, 4 social studies, 4 history, 4 visual/performing arts. **Freshman Admission Statistics:** 406 applied, 63.5% admitted, 33% enrolled. **Transfer Admission Requirements:** High school transcript, college transcript(s), essay or personal statement, standardized test scores, Minimum college GPA of 2.5 required. Lowest grade transferable C-. **General Admission Information:** Application fee $50. Priority deadline 2/15. Regular application deadline 5/1. Nonfall registration accepted.

COSTS AND FINANCIAL AID
Annual tuition $31,450. Required fees $200. Average book expense $2,724. **Required Forms and Deadlines:** FAFSA. **Notification of Awards:** Applicants will be notified of awards on a rolling basis beginning 3/1. **Types of Aid:** *Need-based scholarships/grants:* College/university scholarship or grant aid from institutional funds; Federal Pell; Private scholarships; SEOG; State scholarships/grants. *Loans:* Direct PLUS loans; Direct Subsidized Stafford Loans; Direct Unsubsidized Stafford Loans. *Student Employment:* Federal Work-Study Program available. Institutional employment available. **Financial Aid Statistics:** 99% needy freshmen, 96% needy undergrads receive need-based scholarship or grant aid. 3% freshmen, 4% undergrads receive non-need-based scholarship or grant aid. 97% freshmen, 96% undergrads receive need-based self-help aid. 0% freshmen, 0% undergrads receive athletic scholarships. **Criteria for awarding aid:** *Need-based:* Academics, Art, Leadership, Minority status *Non-need-based:* Academics, Alumni affiliation, Art, Leadership.

MINNESOTA STATE UNIVERSITY, MANKATO

205 South Street, Mankato, MN 56001
Phone: 507-389-1822 • **Financial Aid Phone:** 507-389-5124
E-mail: admissions@mnsu.edu • **CEEB Code:** 6677
Fax: 507-389-1511 • **Website:** www.mnsu.edu • **ACT Code:** 2126

This public school was founded in 1868. It has a 354 acre campus.

RATINGS
Admissions Selectivity Rating: 82   **Fire Safety Rating:** 73   **Green Rating:** 60*

STUDENTS AND FACULTY
Enrollment: 11,942. **Student Body:** 52% female, 48% male, 14% out-of-state, 9% international (84 countries represented). Asian 4%, African American 6%, Caucasian 73%, Hispanic 4%, Native American <1%, Pacific Islander <1%, Two or more races 3%, Race unknown 1%. **Retention and Graduation:** 74% freshmen return for sophomore year. **Faculty:** Student/faculty ratio 24:1. 454 full-time faculty, 93% hold PhDs, 19% are members of minority groups, 48% are women.

ACADEMICS
Degrees: Associate; Bachelor's; Certificate; Doctoral/Professional; Doctoral/Research; Master's; Post-Bachelor's certificate; Post-Master's certificate **Classes:** Most classes have 20-29 students. **Most popular majors:** Psychology, General; Registered Nursing/Registered Nurse; Business Administration And Management, General. **Special Study Options:** Cross-registration; Distance learning; Double major; Dual enrollment; English as a Second Language (ESL); Exchange student program (domestic); Honors program; Independent study; Internships; Study abroad; Teacher certification program. **Disability Services offered to physically disabled students:** Note-taking services; Reader services; Tape recorders. **Career services:** Alumni network; Alumni services; Career assessment; Career/job search classes; Internships; Regional alumni

FACILITIES
Housing: Apartments for single students; Coed dorms; Special housing for disabled student; Theme housing 90% of campus accessible to physically diasbled. **Special Academic Facilities/Equipment:** Two art galleries, day care facility, two astronomy observ- atories, main stage and studio theatres **Computers:** 100% of classrooms, 10% of dorms, 100% of libraries, 100% of dining areas, 100% of student union, 80% of common outdoor areas have wireless network access. Students can register for classes online. Administrative functions (other than registration) can be performed online.

CAMPUS LIFE
Environment: Town **Activities:** Campus Ministries; Choral groups; Concert band; Dance; Drama/theater; International Student Organization; Jazz band; Marching band; Music ensembles; Musical theater; Pep band; Radio station; Student government; Student newspaper; Symphony orchestra 178 registered organizations, 18 honor societies, 15 religious organizations. 7 fraternities, 4 sororities. **Athletics (Intercollegiate):** *Men:* baseball, basketball, cross-country, diving, football, golf, ice hockey, swimming, tennis, track/field (outdoor), track/field (indoor), wrestling. *Women:* basketball, bowling, cross-country, diving, golf, ice hockey, soccer, softball, swimming, tennis, track/field (outdoor), track/field (indoor), volleyball. **On-Campus Highlights:** Student Union, Myers Field House, Campus Recreation Center, Preska Residence Hall, Memorial Library **Environmental Initiatives:** Energy retrofit of building for lighting and motors

ADMISSIONS
Freshman Academic Profile: Average high school GPA 3.3. 7% in top 10% of high school class, 27% in top 25% of high school class, 67% in top 50% of high school class. **Test Scores:** ACT middle 50% range 20-24. Minimum internet-based TOEFL 61. Minimum paper TOEFL 500. **Basis for Candidate Selection:** *Very important factors considered include:* class rank, standardized test scores. *Other factors considered include:* academic GPA, recommendation(s). **Freshman Admission Requirements:** High school diploma is required and GED is accepted *Academic units required:* 4 English, 3 math, 3 science, 3 science labs, 2 foreign language, 3 social studies, and 1 unit from above areas or other academic areas. **Freshman Admission Statistics:** 11,689 applied, 61.0% admitted, 32% enrolled. **Transfer Admission Requirements:** college transcript(s), statement of good standing from prior institution(s). Minimum college GPA of 2.0 required. Lowest grade transferable D. **General Admission Information:** Application fee $20. Nonfall registration accepted. Admission may be deferred.

COSTS AND FINANCIAL AID
Annual in-state tuition $9,096. Annual out-of-state tuition $15,230. Room and board $9,096. Required fees $986. Average book expense $1,022. **Required**

Forms and Deadlines: FAFSA. **Notification of Awards:** Applicants will be notified of awards on a rolling basis beginning 3/30. **Types of Aid:** *Need-based scholarships/grants:* College/university scholarship or grant aid from institutional funds; Federal Pell; Private scholarships; SEOG; State scholarships/grants. *Loans:* Direct PLUS loans; Direct Subsidized Stafford Loans; Direct Unsubsidized Stafford Loans. *Student Employment:* Federal Work-Study Program available. Institutional employment available. **Financial Aid Statistics:** 68% needy freshmen, 67% needy undergrads receive need-based scholarship or grant aid. 38% freshmen, 24% undergrads receive non-need-based scholarship or grant aid. 98% freshmen, 96% undergrads receive need-based self-help aid. 1% freshmen, 0% undergrads receive athletic scholarships. 89% freshmen, 80% undergrads receive any aid. 74% undergrads borrow to pay for school. Average cumulative indebtedness $31,117. **Criteria for awarding aid:** *Need-based:* Academics, Minority status *Non-need-based:* Academics, Art, Athletics, Leadership, Minority status, Music/drama.

MINNESOTA STATE UNIVERSITY MOORHEAD

1104 Seventh Avenue South, Moorhead, MN 56563
Phone: 218-477-2161 · **Financial Aid Phone:** 218-477-2251
E-mail: admissions@mnstate.edu · **CEEB Code:** 6678
Fax: 218-477-4374 · **Website:** www.mnstate.edu · **ACT Code:** 2134

This public school was founded in 1887. It has a 140 acre campus.

RATINGS
Admissions Selectivity Rating: 75   **Fire Safety Rating:** 60*   **Green Rating:** 60*

STUDENTS AND FACULTY
Enrollment: 5,025. **Student Body:** 60% female, 40% male, 33% out-of-state, 7% international (56 countries represented). Asian 1%, African American 3%, Caucasian 78%, Hispanic 3%, Native American 1%, Pacific Islander <1%, Two or more races 3%, Race unknown 5%.
Retention and Graduation: 73% freshmen return for sophomore year.
Faculty: Student/faculty ratio 17:1. 274 full-time faculty, 62% hold PhDs, 9% are members of minority groups, 49% are women.

ACADEMICS
Degrees: Associate; Bachelor's; Certificate; Master's; Post-Bachelor's certificate; Post-Master's certificate **Classes:** Most classes have 10-19 students. Most lab/discussion sessions have 20-29 students. **Most popular majors:** Mass Communication/Media Studies; Elementary Education And Teaching; Business Administration And Management, General. **Special Study Options:** Cross-registration; Distance learning; Double major; Dual enrollment; Exchange student program (domestic); Honors program; Independent study; Internships; Student-designed major; Study abroad; Teacher certification program. **Honors programs:** Honors Program to reward and encourage superior academic achievement. **Disability Services offered to physically disabled students:** Note-taking services; Reader services; Tape recorders; Tutors. **Career services:** Career assessment; Career/job search classes; Internships

FACILITIES
Housing: Apartments for married students; Apartments for single students; Coed dorms; Men's dorms; Theme housing; Women's dorms 95% of campus accessible to physically diasbled. **Special Academic Facilities/Equipment:** Art and biology museums on-campus, planetarium, regional science center, Center for Business, new Science Building, Center for Business, new Wellness Center. **Computers:** Students can register for classes online. Administrative functions (other than registration) can be performed online.

CAMPUS LIFE
Environment: City **Activities:** Campus Ministries; Choral groups; Concert band; Dance; Drama/theater; International Student Organization; Jazz band; Literary magazine; Model UN; Music ensembles; Musical theater; Pep band; Radio station; Student government; Student newspaper; Student-run film society; Television station 109 registered organizations, 6 honor societies, 11 religious organizations. 2 sororities. **Athletics (Intercollegiate): Men:** basketball, cross-country, football, track/field (outdoor), track/field (indoor), wrestling. *Women:* basketball, cross-country, golf, soccer, softball, swimming, tennis, track/field (outdoor), track/field (indoor), volleyball. **On-Campus Highlights:** Underground Night Club, Comstock Memorial Student Union, Regional Science Center, Nemzek Athletic Complex, Planetarium

ADMISSIONS
Freshman Academic Profile: 10% in top 10% of high school class, 35% in top 25% of high school class, 74% in top 50% of high school class. **Test Scores:** SAT Math middle 50% range 480-570. SAT EBRW middle 50%

range 445-520. ACT middle 50% range 20-25. Minimum paper TOEFL 500.
Basis for Candidate Selection: *Very important factors considered include:* class rank, academic GPA, standardized test scores. *Other factors considered include:* rigor of secondary school record, application essay, recommendation(s).
Freshman Admission Requirements: High school diploma is required and GED is accepted *Academic units required:* 4 English, 3 math, 3 science, 1 science labs, 2 foreign language, 3 social studies, and 1 unit from above areas or other academic areas. **Freshman Admission Statistics:** 2,610 applied, 82.1% admitted, 34% enrolled. **Transfer Admission Requirements:** college transcript(s), statement of good standing from prior institution(s). Minimum college GPA of 2.0 required. Lowest grade transferable D. **General Admission Information:** Application fee $20. Regular application deadline 6/15. Nonfall registration accepted. Admission may be deferred for a maximum of one semester.

COSTS AND FINANCIAL AID
Annual in-state tuition $7,398. Annual out-of-state tuition $13,796. Room and board $7,398. Required fees $940. Average book expense $800. **Required Forms and Deadlines:** FAFSA; State aid form. **Types of Aid:** *Need-based scholarships/grants:* College/university scholarship or grant aid from institutional funds; Private scholarships; State scholarships/grants. *Loans:* Direct PLUS loans; Direct Subsidized Stafford Loans; Direct Unsubsidized Stafford Loans. *Student Employment:* Federal Work-Study Program available. Institutional employment available. **Financial Aid Statistics:** 66% needy freshmen, 67% needy undergrads receive need-based scholarship or grant aid. 58% freshmen, 30% undergrads receive non-need-based scholarship or grant aid. 93% freshmen, 94% undergrads receive need-based self-help aid. 0% freshmen, 0% undergrads receive athletic scholarships. 75% freshmen, 58% undergrads receive any aid. **Criteria for awarding aid:** *Non-need-based:* Academics, Athletics.

MISERICORDIA UNIVERSITY

301 Lake Street, Dallas, PA 18612
Phone: 570-674-6264 · **Financial Aid Phone:** 570-674-6222
E-mail: admiss@misericordia.edu · **CEEB Code:** 2087
Fax: 570-675-2441 · **Website:** www.misericordia.edu · **ACT Code:** 3539

This private school, affiliated with the Roman Catholic Church, was founded in 1924. It has a 123 acre campus.

RATINGS
Admissions Selectivity Rating: 78   **Fire Safety Rating:** 96   **Green Rating:** 60*

STUDENTS AND FACULTY
Enrollment: 2,100. **Student Body:** 67% female, 33% male, 27% out-of-state, <1% international (4 countries represented). Asian 1%, African American 3%, Caucasian 87%, Hispanic 3%, Native American <1%, Pacific Islander <1%, Two or more races 3%, Race unknown 2%.
Retention and Graduation: 85% freshmen return for sophomore year. 71% freshmen graduate within 4 years. 76% freshmen graduate within 6 years. 33% grads go on to further study within 1 year. 25% grads pursue arts and sciences degrees. 0% grads pursue law degrees. 8% grads pursue business degrees. 0% grads pursue medical degrees. **Faculty:** Student/faculty ratio 12:1. 139 full-time faculty, 78% hold PhDs, 10% are members of minority groups, 60% are women. 0% of classes are taught by teaching assistants.

ACADEMICS
Degrees: Bachelor's; Certificate; Doctoral/Professional; Master's; Post-Bachelor's certificate; Post-Master's certificate **Classes:** Most classes have 20-29 students. **Most popular majors:** Health/Health Care Administration/Management; Registered Nursing/Registered Nurse; Business Administration And Management, General. **Special Study Options:** Accelerated program; Cross-registration; Distance learning; Double major; Dual enrollment; Honors program; Independent study; Internships; Student-designed major; Study abroad; Teacher certification program; Weekend college. **Honors programs:** The Honors Program is an interdisciplinary learning community based in a common sequence of enriched and intensified core curriculum courses which honors students take in place of the regular core offerings. Honors courses emphasize discussion over lecture, use writing as an integrative feature of learning, are highly interdisciplinary, and provide a very interactive relationship between student and faculty. Honors courses are not intended to be more difficult, but do approach topics in different ways then traditional core courses. **Disability Services offered to physically disabled students:** Tape recorders; Tutors. **Career services:** Alumni network; Alumni services; Career assessment; Career/job search classes; Internships; Regional alumni

FACILITIES

Housing: Coed dorms; Other (please specify) 100% of campus accessible to physically diasbled. **Computers:** 5% of classrooms, 100% of libraries, 100% of dining areas, 100% of student union, 10% of common outdoor areas have wireless network access. Students can register for classes online. Administrative functions (other than registration) can be performed online.

CAMPUS LIFE

Environment: Town **Activities:** Campus Ministries; Choral groups; Dance; Drama/theater; Jazz band; Literary magazine; Music ensembles; Radio station; Student government; Student newspaper; Television station; Yearbook 27 registered organizations, 1 honor society, 1 religious organization. **Athletics (Intercollegiate):** *Men:* baseball, basketball, cross-country, golf, lacrosse, soccer, swimming, tennis, track/field (outdoor). *Women:* basketball, cheerleading, cross-country, field hockey, lacrosse, soccer, softball, swimming, tennis, track/field (outdoor), volleyball. **On-Campus Highlights:** Anderson Sports and Health Center, Banks Student Life Center, Mangelsdorf Field, Bevevino Library, Insalaco Hall.

ADMISSIONS

Freshman Academic Profile: Average high school GPA 3.4. 18% in top 10% of high school class, 51% in top 25% of high school class, 80% in top 50%. of high school class. 82% from public high schools. **Test Scores:** SAT Math middle 50% range 510-595. SAT EBRW middle 50% range 520-610. ACT middle 50% range 22-26. Minimum paper TOEFL 500. **Basis for Candidate Selection:** *Very important factors considered include:* rigor of secondary school record, academic GPA, standardized test scores, character/personal qualities. *Important factors considered include:* class rank, extracurricular activities, talent/ability, volunteer work. *Other factors considered include:* application essay, recommendation(s), interview, first generation, alumni/ae relation, work experience, level of applicant's interest. **Freshman Admission Requirements:** High school diploma is required and GED is accepted *Academic units required:* 4 English, 4 math, 4 science, 4 social studies. **Freshman Admission Statistics:** 1,740 applied, 78.8% admitted, 32% enrolled. **Transfer Admission Requirements:** college transcript(s), Minimum college GPA of 2.0 required. Lowest grade transferable C. **General Admission Information:** Nonfall registration accepted. Admission may be deferred for a maximum of 1 year.

COSTS AND FINANCIAL AID

Annual tuition $31,530. Room and board $13,960. Required fees $1,710. Average book expense $1,250. **Required Forms and Deadlines:** FAFSA. **Notification of Awards:** Applicants will be notified of awards on a rolling basis beginning 3/15. **Types of Aid:** *Need-based scholarships/grants:* College/university scholarship or grant aid from institutional funds; Federal Nursing Scholarships; Federal Pell; Private scholarships; SEOG; State scholarships/grants. *Loans:* Direct PLUS loans; Direct Subsidized Stafford Loans; Direct Unsubsidized Stafford Loans. *Student Employment:* Federal Work-Study Program available. Institutional employment available. **Financial Aid Statistics:** 99% needy freshmen, 100% needy undergrads receive need-based scholarship or grant aid. 18% freshmen, 17% undergrads receive non-need-based scholarship or grant aid. 80% freshmen, 79% undergrads receive need-based self-help aid. 0% freshmen, 0% undergrads receive athletic scholarships. 99% freshmen, 99% undergrads receive any aid. 84% undergrads borrow to pay for school. Average cumulative indebtedness $42,686. **Criteria for awarding aid:** *Need-based:* Minority status *Non-need-based:* Academics, Alumni affiliation, Leadership, Minority status, State/district residency.

MISSISSIPPI COLLEGE

Box 4001, Clinton, MS 39058-0001
Phone: 601-925-3800 • **Financial Aid Phone:** (601) 925-3212
E-mail: enrollment-services@mc.edu • **CEEB Code:** 1477
Fax: 601-925-3950 • **Website:** http://www.mc.edu • **ACT Code:** 2214

This private school, affiliated with the Southern Baptist Church, was founded in 1826. It has a 474 acre campus.

RATINGS

Admissions Selectivity Rating: 85   **Fire Safety Rating:** 96   **Green Rating:** 60*

STUDENTS AND FACULTY

Enrollment: 3,030. **Student Body:** 61% female, 39% male, 24% out-of-state, 3% international (21 countries represented). Asian 1%, African American 24%, Caucasian 67%, Hispanic 2%, Native American 1%, Pacific Islander 0%, Two or more races 1%, Race unknown 2%.
Retention and Graduation: 73% freshmen return for sophomore year. **Faculty:** Student/faculty ratio 15:1. 205 full-time faculty, 78% hold PhDs, 9%

are members of minority groups, 48% are women. 0% of classes are taught by teaching assistants.

ACADEMICS

Degrees: Bachelor's; Doctoral/Professional; Doctoral/Research; Master's; Post-Bachelor's certificate; Post-Master's certificate **Classes:** Most classes have 10-19 students. Most lab/discussion sessions have 10-19 students. **Most popular majors:** Elementary Education And Teaching; Biomedical Sciences, General; Business Administration And Management, General. **Special Study Options:** Accelerated program; Distance learning; Double major; Dual enrollment; English as a Second Language (ESL); Honors program; Independent study; Internships; Study abroad; Teacher certification program. **Honors programs:** Honors programs open to freshmen, sophomores, juniors, and seniors and administered by the Honors Council. Freshmen who have a high ACT score (established each year) are invited to participate in a program of study called Freshman Honors Seminar (IDS161), it is an interdisciplinary study dealing with contemporary issues and interests. Upperclassmen who maintain a high GPA may also participate in Sophomore and Senior Honors Seminars (IDS 261, 461). Successful completion of the Junior-Senior Honors Program leads to a degree "With Honors" or "With High Honors." **Combined degree programs:** BA/JD. **Disability Services offered to physically disabled students:** Note-taking services; Reader services; Tape recorders; Tutors. **Career services:** Alumni services; Career assessment; Career/job search classes; Internships

FACILITIES

Housing: Apartments for single students; Men's dorms; Special housing for disabled student; Wellness housing; Women's dorms 100% of campus accessible to physically diasbled. **Special Academic Facilities/Equipment:** Samuel Marshall Gore Art Gallery New Science Building with Cadaver Lab Healthplex **Computers:** 60% of classrooms, 100% of dorms, 100% of libraries, 100% of dining areas, 60% of common outdoor areas have wireless network access. Students can register for classes online. Administrative functions (other than registration) can be performed online.

CAMPUS LIFE

Environment: City **Activities:** Campus Ministries; Choral groups; Concert band; Dance; Drama/theater; International Student Organization; Jazz band; Literary magazine; Marching band; Music ensembles; Musical theater; Opera; Radio station; Student government; Student newspaper; Yearbook 66 registered organizations, 22 honor societies, 6 religious organizations. 5 fraternities. 4 sororities. **Athletics (Intercollegiate):** *Men:* baseball, basketball, cross-country, football, golf, soccer, tennis, track/field (outdoor). *Women:* basketball, cheerleading, cross-country, equestrian sports, soccer, softball, tennis, track/field (outdoor), volleyball. **On-Campus Highlights:** Samuel Marshall Gore Art Gallery, Healthplex, Men's Rotunda and New Women's Residence Hall, Provine Chapel, Anderson Hall in BCR Student Center

ADMISSIONS

Freshman Academic Profile: Average high school GPA 3.4. 33% in top 10% of high school class, 57% in top 25% of high school class, 74% in top 50% of high school class. **Test Scores:** SAT Math middle 50% range 470-580. SAT EBRW middle 50% range 470-613. ACT middle 50% range 20-27. Minimum internet-based TOEFL 69. **Basis for Candidate Selection:** *Very important factors considered include:* standardized test scores. *Important factors considered include:* rigor of secondary school record, extracurricular activities, character/personal qualities, level of applicant's interest. *Other factors considered include:* class rank, academic GPA, recommendation(s), interview, talent/ability, alumni/ae relation, volunteer work, work experience. **Freshman Admission Requirements:** High school diploma is required and GED is accepted *Academic units recommended:* 4 English, 4 math, 4 science, 2 science labs, 1 foreign language, 2 social studies, 2 history, 3.5 academic electives, 0.5 computer science, 1 visual/performing arts, 2 units from above areas or other academic areas. **Freshman Admission Statistics:** 2,178 applied, 58.1% admitted, 38% enrolled. **Transfer Admission Requirements:** college transcript(s), essay or personal statement, statement of good standing from prior institution(s). Minimum college GPA of 2.0 required. Lowest grade transferable C. **General Admission Information:** Application fee $25. Priority deadline 5/1. Nonfall registration accepted. Admission may be deferred for a maximum of 1 year.

COSTS AND FINANCIAL AID

Annual tuition $14,120. Room and board $7,150. Required fees $748. Average book expense $1,100. **Required Forms and Deadlines:** FAFSA; State aid form. **Notification of Awards:** Applicants will be notified of awards on a rolling basis beginning 3/1. **Types of Aid:** *Need-based scholarships/grants:* College/university scholarship or grant aid from institutional funds; Federal Pell; Private scholarships; SEOG; State scholarships/grants. *Loans:* Direct PLUS loans; Direct Subsidized Stafford Loans; Direct Unsubsidized Stafford Loans. *Student Employment:* Federal Work-Study Program available. Institutional employment available. **Financial Aid Statistics:** 89% needy freshmen, 86% needy undergrads receive need-based scholarship or grant aid. 96% freshmen, 86% undergrads receive non-need-based scholarship or grant aid. 81% freshmen, 85% undergrads receive need-based self-help aid. 0% freshmen, 0% undergrads receive athletic scholarships. 98% freshmen, 94% undergrads receive any aid. **Criteria for awarding aid:** *Non-need-based:* Academics, Alumni affiliation, Art, Leadership, Music/drama, Religious affiliation.

MISSISSIPPI STATE UNIVERSITY

P.O. Box 6018, Mississippi State, MS 39762
Phone: 662-325-2224 · **Financial Aid Phone:** 662-325-2450
E-mail: admit@msstate.edu · **CEEB Code:** 1480
Fax: 662-325-1MSU · **Website:** www.msstate.edu · **ACT Code:** 2220

This public school was founded in 1878. It has a 4200 acre campus.

RATINGS

Admissions Selectivity Rating: 80   **Fire Safety Rating:** 91   **Green Rating:** 60*

STUDENTS AND FACULTY

Enrollment: 17,723. **Student Body:** 50% female, 50% male, 30% out-of-state, 1% international (77 countries represented). Asian 1%, African American 20%, Caucasian 72%, Hispanic 3%, Native American <1%, Pacific Islander <1%, Two or more races 2%, Race unknown <1%.
Retention and Graduation: 79% freshmen return for sophomore year. 32% freshmen graduate within 4 years. 60% freshmen graduate within 6 years.
Faculty: Student/faculty ratio 20:1. 970 full-time faculty, 80% hold PhDs, 19% are members of minority groups, 41% are women.

ACADEMICS

Degrees: Bachelor's; Doctoral; Doctoral/Professional; Doctoral/Research; Master's; Post-Master's certificate **Classes:** Most classes have 20-29 students. Most lab/discussion sessions have 10-19 students. **Most popular majors:** Physical Education Teaching And Coaching; Geology/Earth Science, General; Business Administration And Management, General. **Special Study Options:** Cooperative education program; Cross-registration; Distance learning; Double major; Dual enrollment; English as a Second Language (ESL); Exchange student program (domestic); Honors program; Independent study; Internships; Liberal arts/career combination; Student-designed major; Study abroad; Teacher certification program; Weekend college. **Honors programs:** University Honors Program and the Montgomery Leadership Program.
Disability Services offered to physically disabled students: Note-taking services; Reader services; Tape recorders; Tutors. **Career services:** Alumni network; Alumni services; Career assessment; Career/job search classes; Internships; Regional alumni

FACILITIES

Housing: Fraternity/sorority housing; Men's dorms; Special housing for disabled student; Theme housing; Women's dorms 95% of campus accessible to physically diasbled. **Special Academic Facilities/Equipment:** Geology, archeology, music, entomological museums; art gallery; flight research lab.
Computers: 100% of classrooms, 100% of dorms, 100% of libraries, 100% of dining areas, 100% of student union, 100% of common outdoor areas have wireless network access. Students can register for classes online. Administrative functions (other than registration) can be performed online.

CAMPUS LIFE

Environment: Town **Activities:** Campus Ministries; Choral groups; Concert band; Dance; Drama/theater; International Student Organization; Jazz band; Literary magazine; Marching band; Model UN; Music ensembles; Musical theater; Opera; Pep band; Radio station; Student government; Student newspaper; Student-run film society; Symphony orchestra; Television station 326 registered organizations, 42 honor societies, 30 religious organizations. 17 fraternities, 11 sororities. **Athletics (Intercollegiate):** *Men:* baseball, basketball, cheerleading, cross-country, football, golf, tennis, track/field (outdoor). *Women:* basketball, cheerleading, cross-country, golf, soccer, softball, tennis, track/field (outdoor), volleyball. **On-Campus Highlights:** Scott Field Stadium, Dudy Noble Field, Humphrey Coliseum, Barnes and Noble Campus Bookstore, Sanderson Student Recreation Center **Environmental Initiatives:** Recycling

ADMISSIONS

Freshman Academic Profile: Average high school GPA 3.4. 25% in top 10% of high school class, 54% in top 25% of high school class, 82% in top 50% of high school class. **Test Scores:** ACT middle 50% range 21-28. Minimum internet-based TOEFL 71. Minimum paper TOEFL 525. **Basis for Candidate Selection:** *Very important factors considered include:* academic GPA, standardized test scores. *Important factors considered include:* class rank. *Other factors considered include:* rigor of secondary school record, state residency.
Freshman Admission Requirements: High school diploma is required and GED is accepted *Academic units required:* 4 English, 3 math, 3 science, 2

science labs, 1 foreign language, 1 social studies, 2 history, 1 academic elective, 0.5 computer science, 1 visual/performing arts, *Academic units recommended:* 4 English, 4 math, 4 science, 2 science labs, 1 foreign language, 2 social studies, 2 history, 1 academic elective, 0.5 computer science, 1 visual/performing arts. **Freshman Admission Statistics:** 13,817 applied, 73.4% admitted, 36% enrolled. **Transfer Admission Requirements:** college transcript(s), statement of good standing from prior institution(s). Minimum college GPA of 2.0 required. Lowest grade transferable D. **General Admission Information:** Application fee $40. Nonfall registration accepted.

COSTS AND FINANCIAL AID

Annual in-state tuition $9,570. Annual out-of-state tuition $22,358. Room and board $9,570. Average book expense $1,200. **Required Forms and Deadlines:** FAFSA; State aid form. **Notification of Awards:** Applicants will be notified of awards on a rolling basis beginning 12/1. **Types of Aid:** *Need-based scholarships/grants:* College/university scholarship or grant aid from institutional funds; Federal Pell; Private scholarships; SEOG; State scholarships/grants; United Negro College Fund. *Loans:* Direct PLUS loans; Direct Subsidized Stafford Loans; Direct Unsubsidized Stafford Loans. *Student Employment:* Federal Work-Study Program available. Institutional employment available. **Financial Aid Statistics:** 91% needy freshmen, 87% needy undergrads receive need-based scholarship or grant aid. 14% freshmen, 8% undergrads receive non-need-based scholarship or grant aid. 69% freshmen, 77% undergrads receive need-based self-help aid. 3% freshmen, 3% undergrads receive athletic scholarships. 57% undergrads borrow to pay for school. Average cumulative indebtedness $30,659. **Criteria for awarding aid:** *Need-based:* Academics, Alumni affiliation, Leadership, Minority status, Music/drama *Non-need-based:* Academics, Alumni affiliation, Art, Athletics, Job skills, Leadership, Minority status, Music/drama, State/district residency.

MISSISSIPPI VALLEY STATE UNIVERSITY

14000 Highway 82 West, Itta Bena, MS 38941-1400
Phone: 662-254-3344 · **Financial Aid Phone:** 662-254-3338
E-mail: nbtaylor@mvsu.edu · **CEEB Code:** 1482
Fax: 662-254-3759 · **Website:** www.mvsu.edu · **ACT Code:** 2224

This public school was founded in 1950. It has a 250 acre campus.

RATINGS

Admissions Selectivity Rating: 86   **Fire Safety Rating:** 84   **Green Rating:** 60*

STUDENTS AND FACULTY

Enrollment: 2,357. **Student Body:** 62% female, 38% male, 11% out-of-state, 0% international (2 countries represented). Asian <1%, African American 93%, Caucasian 4%, Hispanic 1%, Native American <1%, Race unknown 2%.
Retention and Graduation: 55% freshmen return for sophomore year.
Faculty: Student/faculty ratio 21:1. 133 full-time faculty, 58% hold PhDs, 30% are members of minority groups, 46% are women. 0% of classes are taught by teaching assistants.

ACADEMICS

Degrees: Bachelor's; Master's **Classes:** Most classes have 10-19 students. **Most popular majors:** Kindergarten/Preschool Education And Teaching; Social Work; Business, Management, Marketing, And Related Support Services, Other. **Special Study Options:** Cooperative education program; Distance learning; Double major; Honors program; Internships; Teacher certification program; Weekend college. **Disability Services offered to physically disabled students:** Tape recorders; Tutors. **Career services:** Alumni services

FACILITIES

Housing: Apartments for married students; Apartments for single students; Men's dorms; Women's dorms **Computers:** Students can register for classes online.

CAMPUS LIFE

Environment: Rural **Activities:** Choral groups; Concert band; Drama/ theater; Marching band; Radio station; Student government; Student newspaper; Yearbook 35 registered organizations, 19 honor societies, 4 religious organizations. 4 fraternities, 2 sororities. **Athletics (Intercollegiate):** *Men:* baseball, basketball, cross-country, football, golf, tennis, track/field (outdoor). *Women:* basketball, cross-country, golf, soccer, softball, tennis, track/field (outdoor), volleyball. **On-Campus Highlights:** Student Union, Student Pavillion, Administration Building, Library

ADMISSIONS

Freshman Academic Profile: Average high school GPA 2.6. 0% in top 10% of high school class, 96% from public high schools. **Test Scores:** ACT middle 50%

range 15-19. Minimum paper TOEFL 525. **Basis for Candidate Selection:** *Very important factors considered include:* rigor of secondary school record, class rank, standardized test scores, state residency. *Other factors considered include:* recommendation(s), interview, extracurricular activities, talent/ability. **Freshman Admission Requirements:** High school diploma is required and GED is accepted *Academic units required:* 4 English, 3 math, 3 science, 2 science labs, 1 foreign language, 3 social studies, 2 academic electives, and 1 unit from above areas or other academic areas. *Academic units recommended:* 1 foreign language. **Freshman Admission Statistics:** 6,086 applied, 29.5% admitted, 23% enrolled. **Transfer Admission Requirements:** college transcript(s), Minimum college GPA of 2.0 required. Lowest grade transferable C. **General Admission Information:** Nonfall registration accepted.

COSTS AND FINANCIAL AID
Annual in-state tuition $5,081. Annual out-of-state tuition $11,410. Room and board $5,081. Required fees $25. Average book expense $1,400. **Required Forms and Deadlines:** FAFSA; Institution's own financial aid form. **Notification of Awards:** Applicants will be notified of awards on or about 7/15. **Types of Aid:** *Need-based scholarships/grants:* College/university scholarship or grant aid from institutional funds; Federal Pell; Private scholarships; SEOG; State scholarships/grants. *Loans:* Direct PLUS loans; Direct Unsubsidized Stafford Loans. *Student Employment:* Federal Work-Study Program available. **Financial Aid Statistics:** 95% freshmen, 95% undergrads receive any aid.

MISSOURI UNIVERSITY OF SCIENCE AND TECHNOLOGY

1870 Miner Circle, Rolla, MO 65409-1060
Phone: 573-341-4165 · **Financial Aid Phone:** 573-341-4282
E-mail: admissions@mst.edu · **CEEB Code:** 6876
Fax: 573-341-4082 · **Website:** www.mst.edu · **ACT Code:** 2398

This public school was founded in 1870. It has a 284 acre campus.

RATINGS
Admissions Selectivity Rating: 85 | **Fire Safety Rating:** 88 | **Green Rating:** 85

STUDENTS AND FACULTY
Enrollment: 6,872. **Student Body:** 24% female, 76% male, 17% out-of-state, 3% international (60 countries represented). Asian 4%, African American 3%, Caucasian 81%, Hispanic 4%, Native American <1%, Pacific Islander <1%, Two or more races 3%, Race unknown 2%.
Retention and Graduation: 23% freshmen graduate within 4 years. 64% freshmen graduate within 6 years. **Faculty:** Student/faculty ratio 19:1. 375 full-time faculty, 92% hold PhDs, 36% are members of minority groups, 27% are women. 15% of classes are taught by teaching assistants.

ACADEMICS
Degrees: Bachelor's; Certificate; Doctoral/Research; Master's; Post-Bachelor's certificate **Classes:** Most classes have 10-19 students. Most lab/discussion sessions have 10-19 students. **Most popular majors:** Civil Engineering, General; Electrical And Electronics Engineering; Mechanical Engineering. **Special Study Options:** Accelerated program; Cooperative education program; Distance learning; Double major; Dual enrollment; English as a Second Language (ESL); Honors program; Independent study; Internships; Study abroad; Teacher certification program. **Honors programs:** Honors Academy and Master Student Fellowship Programs- http://academicsupport.mst.edu/ **Combined degree programs:** BA/MEng. **Disability Services offered to physically disabled students:** Note-taking services; Reader services; Tape recorders; Tutors. **Career services:** Alumni network; Alumni services; Career assessment; Career/job search classes; Internships; Regional alumni

FACILITIES
Housing: Apartments for married students; Apartments for single students; Coed dorms; Fraternity/sorority housing; Special housing for disabled student; Theme housing; Wellness housing 95% of campus accessible to physically disabled. **Special Academic Facilities/Equipment:** Writing Center, Student Design Center, Nuclear Reactor, Observatory, Explosives Testing Lab, Underground Mine, Museum of Rocks, Minerals, and Gemstones, Centers for Environmental Research, Water Resources, Industrial Research, and Rock Mechanics Research, Geophysical Observatory, Computerized Manufacturing

System, Millennium Arch, and Stonehenge. **Computers:** 100% of classrooms, 100% of dorms, 100% of libraries, 66% of dining areas, 100% of student union, 80% of common outdoor areas have wireless network access. Students can register for classes online. Administrative functions (other than registration) can be performed online.

CAMPUS LIFE
Environment: Village **Activities:** Campus Ministries; Choral groups; Concert band; Dance; Drama/theater; International Student Organization; Jazz band; Literary magazine; Marching band; Model UN; Music ensembles; Musical theater; Pep band; Radio station; Student government; Student newspaper; Student-run film society; Symphony orchestra; Yearbook 202 registered organizations, 29 honor societies, 13 religious organizations. 21 fraternities, 4 sororities. **Athletics (Intercollegiate):** *Men:* baseball, basketball, cross-country, football, soccer, swimming, track/field (outdoor), track/field (indoor). *Women:* basketball, cross-country, soccer, softball, track/field (outdoor), track/field (indoor), volleyball. **On-Campus Highlights:** Havener Student Center, Residential College, Student Design Team Center, Castleman Performing Arts Center, Student Recreation Center **Environmental Initiatives:** Reducing amount of paper being consumed.

ADMISSIONS
Freshman Academic Profile: Average high school GPA 3.6. 39% in top 10% of high school class, 72% in top 25% of high school class, 94% in top 50% of high school class. 85% from public high schools. **Test Scores:** SAT Math middle 50% range 580-700. SAT EBRW middle 50% range 520-640. ACT middle 50% range 25-31. Minimum internet-based TOEFL 79. Minimum paper TOEFL 550. **Basis for Candidate Selection:** *Very important factors considered include:* rigor of secondary school record, class rank, academic GPA, standardized test scores. *Important factors considered include:* recommendation(s). *Other factors considered include:* application essay, interview, extracurricular activities, talent/ability, character/personal qualities, volunteer work, work experience, level of applicant's interest. **Freshman Admission Requirements:** High school diploma is required and GED is accepted *Academic units required:* 4 English, 4 math, 3 science, 1 science labs, 2 foreign language, 3 social studies, 1 visual/performing arts. **Freshman Admission Statistics:** 3,876 applied, 83.5% admitted, 44% enrolled. **Transfer Admission Requirements:** college transcript(s), Minimum college GPA of 2.5 required. **General Admission Information:** Application fee $50. Priority deadline 12/1. Regular application deadline 7/1. Admission may be deferred.

COSTS AND FINANCIAL AID
Required Forms and Deadlines: FAFSA. **Notification of Awards:** Applicants will be notified of awards on a rolling basis beginning 4/1. **Types of Aid:** *Need-based scholarships/grants:* College/university scholarship or grant aid from institutional funds; Federal Pell; Private scholarships; SEOG; State scholarships/grants. *Loans: Student Employment:* Federal Work-Study Program available. Institutional employment available. **Financial Aid Statistics:** 95% needy freshmen, 92% needy undergrads receive need-based scholarship or grant aid. 33% freshmen, 36% undergrads receive non-need-based scholarship or grant aid. 100% freshmen, 100% undergrads receive need-based self-help aid. 5% freshmen, 5% undergrads receive athletic scholarships. 91% freshmen, 85% undergrads receive any aid. 75% undergrads borrow to pay for school. Average cumulative indebtedness $28,259. **Criteria for awarding aid:** *Need-based:* Job skills, Minority status *Non-need-based:* Academics, Alumni affiliation, Athletics, Job skills, Leadership, Minority status, Music/drama, Religious affiliation, State/district residency.

MISSOURI VALLEY COLLEGE

500 East College, Marshall, MO 65340
Phone: 660-831-4114
E-mail: admissions@moval.edu
Fax: 660-831-4233 · **Website:** www.moval.edu · **ACT Code:** 2330

This private school, affiliated with the Presbyterian Church, was founded in 1889. It has a 150 acre campus.

RATINGS
Admissions Selectivity Rating: 70 | **Fire Safety Rating:** 62 | **Green Rating:** 60*

STUDENTS AND FACULTY
Enrollment: 1,329. **Student Body:** 39% female, 61% male, 53% out-of-state, 16% international (43 countries represented). Asian 1%, African American 20%, Caucasian 46%, Hispanic 10%, Native American 1%, Pacific Islander 1%, Two or more races 4%, Race unknown 2%.
Retention and Graduation: 45% freshmen return for sophomore year. 15% freshmen graduate within 4 years. 20% grads go on to further study within 1 year. **Faculty:** Student/faculty ratio 14:1. 87 full-time faculty, 38% hold PhDs,

3% are members of minority groups, 47% are women. 0% of classes are taught by teaching assistants.

ACADEMICS

Degrees: Associate; Bachelor's; Master's **Classes:** Most classes have 10-19 students. Most lab/discussion sessions have fewer than 10 students. **Most popular majors:** Elementary Education And Teaching; Criminal Justice/Law Enforcement Administration; Business/Commerce, General. **Special Study Options:** Distance learning; Double major; Dual enrollment; English as a Second Language (ESL); Honors program; Independent study; Internships; Liberal arts/career combination; Student-designed major; Study abroad; Teacher certification program. **Disability Services offered to physically disabled students:** Reader services; Tutors. **Career services:** Internships

FACILITIES

Housing: Apartments for single students; Fraternity/sorority housing; Men's dorms; Women's dorms

CAMPUS LIFE

Environment: Village **Activities:** Campus Ministries; Dance; Drama/theater; International Student Organization; Jazz band; Musical theater; Radio station; Student government; Student newspaper; Television station 28 registered organizations, 8 honor societies, 7 religious organizations. 4 fraternities, 2 sororities. **Athletics (Intercollegiate):** *Men:* baseball, basketball, cheerleading, cross-country, football, golf, rodeo, soccer, tennis, track/field (outdoor), track/field (indoor), volleyball, wrestling. *Women:* basketball, cheerleading, cross-country, golf, rodeo, soccer, softball, tennis, track/field (outdoor), track/field (indoor), volleyball, wrestling. **On-Campus Highlights:** Burns Gym, Eckilson-Mabee Theater, Black Box Theater, The Malcolm Center for Student Life, Tech Center Computer Lab

ADMISSIONS

Freshman Academic Profile: Average high school GPA 2.9. 3% in top 10% of high school class, 16% in top 25% of high school class, 31% in top 50% of high school class. **Test Scores:** Minimum paper TOEFL 450. **Basis for Candidate Selection:** *Very important factors considered include:* academic GPA, standardized test scores. *Important factors considered include:* class rank. *Other factors considered include:* rigor of secondary school record, recommendation(s), talent/ability, character/personal qualities, first generation, alumni/ae relation. **Freshman Admission Requirements:** High school diploma is required and GED is accepted **Freshman Admission Statistics:** 2,300 applied, 53.7% admitted, 32% enrolled. **Transfer Admission Requirements:** High school transcript, college transcript(s), standardized test scores, Minimum college GPA of 2.0 required. Lowest grade transferable C. **General Admission Information:** Regular application deadline 9/1. Nonfall registration accepted.

COSTS AND FINANCIAL AID

Annual tuition $19,300. Room and board $9,150. Required fees $1,300. Average book expense $2,890. **Required Forms and Deadlines:** FAFSA. **Notification of Awards:** Applicants will be notified of awards on a rolling basis beginning 10/30. **Types of Aid:** *Need-based scholarships/grants:* College/university scholarship or grant aid from institutional funds; Federal Pell; Private scholarships; SEOG; State scholarships/grants. *Loans:* Direct PLUS loans; Direct Subsidized Stafford Loans; Direct Unsubsidized Stafford Loans. *Student Employment:* Federal Work-Study Program available. Institutional employment available. **Financial Aid Statistics:** 100% needy freshmen, 100% needy undergrads receive need-based scholarship or grant aid. 100% freshmen, 100% undergrads receive non-need-based scholarship or grant aid. 87% freshmen, 87% undergrads receive need-based self-help aid. 0% freshmen, 0% undergrads receive athletic scholarships. 98% freshmen, 92% undergrads receive any aid.

MITCHELL COLLEGE

437 Pequot Ave., New London, CT 06320
Phone: 860-701-5011 · **Financial Aid Phone:** 800-443-2811
E-mail: admissions@mitchell.edu · **CEEB Code:** 3528
Fax: 860-444-1209 · **Website:** http://www.mitchell.edu/ · **ACT Code:** 572

This private school was founded in 1938. It has a 68 acre campus.

RATINGS

Admissions Selectivity Rating: 70　　**Fire Safety Rating:** 72　　**Green Rating:** 60*

STUDENTS AND FACULTY

Enrollment: 785. **Student Body:** 47% female, 53% male, 42% out-of-state, <1% international. Asian 2%, African American 11%, Caucasian 68%, Hispanic 13%, Native American 1%, Two or more races 4%, Race unknown 2%.
Retention and Graduation: 57% freshmen return for sophomore year. 0%

---

grads pursue arts and sciences degrees. 0% grads pursue law degrees. 0% grads pursue business degrees. 0% grads pursue medical degrees. **Faculty:** Student/faculty ratio 14:1. 35 full-time faculty, 74% hold PhDs, 51% are women. 0% of classes are taught by teaching assistants.

ACADEMICS

Degrees: Associate; Bachelor's **Classes:** Most classes have 20-29 students. Most lab/discussion sessions have 10-19 students. **Special Study Options:** Independent study; Internships; Liberal arts/career combination; Student-designed major; Teacher certification program. **Disability Services offered to physically disabled students:** Note-taking services; Reader services; Tape recorders; Tutors. **Career services:** Career assessment

FACILITIES

Housing: Apartments for single students; Coed dorms; Special housing for disabled student; Theme housing 50% of campus accessible to physically diasbled.

CAMPUS LIFE

Environment: Town **Activities:** Dance; Drama/theater; Radio station; Student government 30 registered organizations, 2 honor societies, 2 religious organizations. **Athletics (Intercollegiate):** *Men:* baseball, basketball, cross-country, golf, lacrosse, soccer, tennis. *Women:* basketball, cross-country, golf, soccer, softball, tennis, volleyball.

ADMISSIONS

Freshman Academic Profile: Average high school GPA 2.7. **Test Scores:** Minimum paper TOEFL 500. **Basis for Candidate Selection:** *Very important factors considered include:* academic GPA, interview. *Important factors considered include:* rigor of secondary school record, application essay, recommendation(s), extracurricular activities, character/personal qualities, volunteer work.level of applicant's interest. *Other factors considered include:* standardized test scores, talent/ability, alumni/ae relation, work experience. **Freshman Admission Requirements:** High school diploma is required and GED is accepted *Academic units recommended:* 4 English, 3 math, 3 science, 2 social studies, 2 history, 2 academic electives. **Freshman Admission Statistics:** 1,041 applied, 59.7% admitted, 24% enrolled. **Transfer Admission Requirements:** High school transcript, college transcript(s), essay or personal statement, standardized test scores, Minimum college GPA of 2.0 required. Lowest grade transferable C-. **General Admission Information:** Application fee $30. Priority deadline 4/1. Nonfall registration accepted. Admission may be deferred for a maximum of 1 year.

COSTS AND FINANCIAL AID

Annual tuition $26,774. Room and board $12,492. Required fees $1,720. Average book expense $1,500. **Required Forms and Deadlines:** FAFSA. **Notification of Awards:** Applicants will be notified of awards on a rolling basis beginning 3/1. **Types of Aid:** *Need-based scholarships/grants:* College/university scholarship or grant aid from institutional funds; Federal Pell; Private scholarships; SEOG; State scholarships/grants. *Loans:* Direct PLUS loans; Direct Subsidized Stafford Loans; Direct Unsubsidized Stafford Loans. *Student Employment:* Federal Work-Study Program available. Institutional employment available. **Financial Aid Statistics:** 100% needy freshmen, 99% needy undergrads receive need-based scholarship or grant aid. 93% freshmen, 87% undergrads receive non-need-based scholarship or grant aid. 93% freshmen, 95% undergrads receive need-based self-help aid. 0% freshmen, 0% undergrads receive athletic scholarships. **Criteria for awarding aid:** *Non-need-based:* Academics, Alumni affiliation, Art, Leadership.

MOLLOY COLLEGE

1000 Hempstead Avenue, Rockville Centre, NY 11570
Phone: 516-323-4000 · **Financial Aid Phone:** 516.323.4209
E-mail: admissions@molloy.edu · **CEEB Code:** 2415
Website: http://www.molloy.edu/ · **ACT Code:** 2820

This private school was founded in 1955. It has a 35 acre campus.

RATINGS

Admissions Selectivity Rating: 77　　**Fire Safety Rating:** 91　　**Green Rating:** 60*

STUDENTS AND FACULTY

Enrollment: 3,505. **Student Body:** 75% female, 25% male, 4% out-of-state, <1% international (10 countries represented). Asian 8%, African American 11%, Caucasian 60%, Hispanic 17%, Native American <1%, Pacific Islander <1%, Two or more races 2%, Race unknown 1%.
Retention and Graduation: 88% freshmen return for sophomore year. 51% freshmen graduate within 4 years. 72% freshmen graduate within 6 years. **Faculty:** Student/faculty ratio 10:1. 194 full-time faculty, 81% hold PhDs, 20%

are members of minority groups, 73% are women. 0% of classes are taught by teaching assistants.

ACADEMICS

Degrees: Associate; Bachelor's; Doctoral/Research; Master's; Post-Bachelor's certificate; Post-Master's certificate **Classes:** Most classes have 10-19 students. Most lab/discussion sessions have fewer than 10 students. **Most popular majors:** Psychology, General; Registered Nursing/Registered Nurse; Accounting. **Special Study Options:** Distance learning; Double major; English as a Second Language (ESL); Honors program; Independent study; Internships; Liberal arts/career combination; Student-designed major; Study abroad; Teacher certification program. **Disability Services offered to physically disabled students:** Note-taking services; Reader services; Tape recorders; Tutors. **Career services:** Alumni network; Alumni services; Internships; Regional alumni

FACILITIES

Housing: Coed dorms 100% of campus accessible to physically diasbled. **Special Academic Facilities/Equipment:** dance studio, Institute for Interfaith Dialogue, Institute of Gerontology,television studio **Computers:** 100% of classrooms, 100% of libraries, 100% of dining areas, 100% of student union, 100% of common outdoor areas have wireless network access. Students can register for classes online. Administrative functions (other than registration) can be performed online.

CAMPUS LIFE

Environment: Village **Activities:** Campus Ministries; Choral groups; Dance; Drama/theater; Jazz band; Literary magazine; Music ensembles; Student government; Student newspaper; Yearbook 21 registered organizations, 18 honor societies, 1 religious organization. **Athletics (Intercollegiate):** *Men:* baseball, basketball, cross-country, lacrosse, soccer, track/field (outdoor), track/field (indoor). *Women:* basketball, cross-country, lacrosse, soccer, softball, tennis, track/field (outdoor), track/field (indoor), volleyball. **On-Campus Highlights:** Hagan Center for Nursing, Public Square, Office of Student Affairs, Anselma Room, Library **Environmental Initiatives:** The Sustainability Institute at Molloy College http://www.molloy.edu/si/index.asp

ADMISSIONS

Freshman Academic Profile: Average high school GPA 3.0. 19% in top 10% of high school class, 54% in top 25% of high school class, 89% in top 50% of high school class. 55% from public high schools. **Test Scores:** SAT Math middle 50% range 530-600. SAT EBRW middle 50% range 530-610. ACT middle 50% range 21-27. Minimum internet-based TOEFL 79. Minimum paper TOEFL 550. **Basis for Candidate Selection:** *Very important factors considered include:* rigor of secondary school record, academic GPA, standardized test scores. *Other factors considered include:* class rank, application essay, recommendation(s), interview, extracurricular activities, talent/ability, volunteer work, work experience. **Freshman Admission Requirements:** High school diploma is required and GED is accepted *Academic units required:* 4 English, 3 math, 3 science, 3 foreign language, 4 social studies, 3.5 academic electives, *Academic units recommended:* 4 English, 4 math, 4 science, 3 foreign language, 4 social studies, 1.5 academic electives. **Freshman Admission Statistics:** 4,188 applied, 76.0% admitted, 16% enrolled. **Transfer Admission Requirements:** college transcript(s), Minimum college GPA of 2.0 required. Lowest grade transferable c. **General Admission Information:** Application fee $40. Nonfall registration accepted. Admission may be deferred for a maximum of 1 year.

COSTS AND FINANCIAL AID

Annual tuition $29,110. Room and board $14,712. Required fees $1,200. Average book expense $1,470. **Required Forms and Deadlines:** FAFSA; State aid form. **Notification of Awards:** Applicants will be notified of awards on a rolling basis beginning 1/20. **Types of Aid:** *Need-based scholarships/grants:* College/university scholarship or grant aid from institutional funds; Federal Nursing Scholarships; Federal Pell; Private scholarships; SEOG; State scholarships/grants. *Loans:* Direct PLUS loans; Direct Subsidized Stafford Loans; Direct Unsubsidized Stafford Loans. *Student Employment:* Federal Work-Study Program available. **Financial Aid Statistics:** 97% needy freshmen, 93% needy undergrads receive need-based scholarship or grant aid. 7% freshmen, 6% undergrads receive non-need-based scholarship or grant aid. 88% freshmen, 85% undergrads receive need-based self-help aid. 1% freshmen, 2% undergrads receive athletic scholarships. 97% freshmen, 79% undergrads receive any aid. 76% undergrads borrow to pay for school. Average cumulative indebtedness $34,078. **Criteria for awarding aid:** *Non-need-based:* Academics, Alumni affiliation, Art, Athletics, Leadership, Music/drama, Religious affiliation.

See page 984.

MONMOUTH COLLEGE

700 East Broadway, Monmouth, IL 61462
Phone: 309-457-2131 • **Financial Aid Phone:** 309-457-2129
E-mail: admissions@monmouthcollege.edu • **CEEB Code:** 1484
Fax: 309-457-2141 • **Website:** www.monmouthcollege.edu • **ACT Code:** 1084

This private school, affiliated with the Presbyterian Church, was founded in 1853. It has a 112 acre campus.

RATINGS

Admissions Selectivity Rating: 80   **Fire Safety Rating:** 92   **Green Rating:** 82

STUDENTS AND FACULTY

Enrollment: 1,174. **Student Body:** 52% female, 48% male, 9% out-of-state, 6% international (35 countries represented). Asian 2%, African American 10%, Caucasian 63%, Hispanic 12%, Native American 1%, Pacific Islander 0%, Two or more races 2%, Race unknown 5%.
Retention and Graduation: 74% freshmen return for sophomore year. 15% grads go on to further study within 1 year. 10% grads pursue arts and sciences degrees. 1% grads pursue law degrees. 0% grads pursue business degrees. 1% grads pursue medical degrees. **Faculty:** Student/faculty ratio 11:1. 92 full-time faculty, 88% hold PhDs, 5% are members of minority groups, 42% are women. 0% of classes are taught by teaching assistants.

ACADEMICS

Degrees: Bachelor's **Classes:** Most classes have 20-29 students. Most lab/discussion sessions have 10-19 students. **Most popular majors:** Speech Communication And Rhetoric; Psychology, General; Business Administration And Management, General. **Special Study Options:** Double major; English as a Second Language (ESL); Exchange student program (domestic); Honors program; Independent study; Internships; Student-designed major; Study abroad; Teacher certification program. **Honors programs:** The Monmouth College Honors Program is intended for a select group of academically well-prepared and intellectually ambitious students. Acceptance into the program is determined competitively, normally occurring at the end of the first semester of the freshman year. The program consists of three levels: exploration of the history of the liberal arts as a field of inquiry, in-depth seminars upon historically significant persons, events, movements and ideas, and a senior capstone course. **Disability Services offered to physically disabled students:** Note-taking services; Reader services; Tape recorders; Tutors. **Career services:** Alumni network; Alumni services; Career assessment; Career/job search classes; Internships; Regional alumni

FACILITIES

Housing: Apartments for single students; Coed dorms; Fraternity/sorority housing; Men's dorms; Special housing for disabled student; Special housing for international students; Theme housing; Women's dorms 98% of campus accessible to physically diasbled. **Special Academic Facilities/Equipment:** Shields Art & Antiquities Collection, Wackerle Career & Leadership Center, the Teaching & Learning Center, MC-TV (student-run television station), WMCR (student-run radio station), Adolphson Observatory, LeSuer Nature Preserve **Computers:** 100% of classrooms, 100% of dorms, 100% of libraries, 100% of dining areas, 100% of student union, 80% of common outdoor areas have wireless network access. Students can register for classes online. Administrative functions (other than registration) can be performed online.

CAMPUS LIFE

Environment: Village **Activities:** Campus Ministries; Choral groups; Concert band; Dance; Drama/theater; International Student Organization; Jazz band; Literary magazine; Marching band; Music ensembles; Musical theater; Radio station; Student government; Student newspaper; Student-run film society; Symphony orchestra; Television station 67 registered organizations, 16 honor societies, 6 religious organizations. 4 fraternities, 3 sororities. **Athletics (Intercollegiate):** *Men:* baseball, basketball, cross-country, diving, football, golf, soccer, swimming, tennis, track/field (outdoor), track/field (indoor). *Women:* basketball, cross-country, diving, golf, soccer, softball, swimming, tennis, track/field (outdoor), track/field (indoor), volleyball. **On-Campus Highlights:** The Mellinger Commons in the Center for Science and Business, Hewes Library (including Einstein's Bagel Shop), Huff Athletic Center, The Educational Garden and Farm, The Center for Science and Business (a new academic building) **Environmental Initiatives:** The College has a comprehensive recycling and waste diversion program. Recycling receptacles are provided for paper, glass, plastic and aluminum in every office and every bedroom in all academic buildings and residence halls, with a recycling center for electronics, flourescent lights and cell phones in the Stockdale Center (the student center). All cardboard generated at the dining service is recycled. A fleet of 5 hybrid cars are used by Monmouth faculty and staff for college purposes.

ADMISSIONS

Freshman Academic Profile: Average high school GPA 3.3. 13% in top 10% of high school class, 36% in top 25% of high school class, 70% in top 50% of high school class. 80% from public high schools. **Test Scores:** ACT middle 50% range 20-26. Minimum internet-based TOEFL 79. Minimum paper TOEFL 550. **Basis for Candidate Selection:** *Very important factors considered include:* rigor of secondary school record. *Important factors considered include:* class rank, academic GPA, standardized test scores. *Other factors considered include:* application essay, recommendation(s), interview, extracurricular activities, talent/ability, character/personal qualities, alumni/ae relation, volunteer work, level of applicant's interest. **Freshman Admission Requirements:** High school diploma is required and GED is accepted *Academic units required:* 4 English, 2 math, 2 science, 1 science labs, 1 social studies, 1 history, *Academic units recommended:* 4 English, 4 math, 3 science, 2 science labs, 2 foreign language, 1 social studies, 2 history, 2 academic electives, 2 visual/performing arts. **Freshman Admission Statistics:** 2,657 applied, 62.4% admitted, 16% enrolled. **Transfer Admission Requirements:** college transcript(s), Minimum college GPA of 2.5 required. Lowest grade transferable C-. **General Admission Information:** Nonfall registration accepted. Admission may be deferred for a maximum of 1 year.

COSTS AND FINANCIAL AID

Annual tuition $35,300. Room and board $8,300. Average book expense $1,200. **Required Forms and Deadlines:** FAFSA. **Notification of Awards:** Applicants will be notified of awards on a rolling basis beginning 2/15. **Types of Aid:** *Need-based scholarships/grants:* College/university scholarship or grant aid from institutional funds; Federal Pell; Private scholarships; SEOG; State scholarships/grants. *Loans:* Direct PLUS loans; Direct Subsidized Stafford Loans; Direct Unsubsidized Stafford Loans. *Student Employment:* Federal Work-Study Program available. Institutional employment available. **Financial Aid Statistics:** 100% needy freshmen, 100% needy undergrads receive need-based scholarship or grant aid. 14% freshmen, 13% undergrads receive non-need-based scholarship or grant aid. 83% freshmen, 80% undergrads receive need-based self-help aid. 0% freshmen, 0% undergrads receive athletic scholarships. 99% freshmen, 99% undergrads receive any aid. 83% undergrads borrow to pay for school. Average cumulative indebtedness $33,646. **Criteria for awarding aid:** *Need-based:* Academics *Non-need-based:* Academics, Art, Leadership, Music/drama, Religious affiliation.

MONMOUTH UNIVERSITY (NJ)

400 Cedar Avenue, West Long Branch, NJ 07764-1898
Phone: 732-571-3456 · **Financial Aid Phone:** 732-571-3463
E-mail: admission@monmouth.edu · **CEEB Code:** 2416
Fax: 732-263-5166 · **Website:** www.monmouth.edu · **ACT Code:** 2571

This private school was founded in 1933. It has a 158.6 acre campus.

RATINGS

Admissions Selectivity Rating: 78   **Fire Safety Rating:** 99   **Green Rating:** 78

STUDENTS AND FACULTY

Enrollment: 4,683. **Student Body:** 58% female, 42% male, 16% out-of-state, 1% international (42 countries represented). Asian 3%, African American 5%, Caucasian 72%, Hispanic 14%, Native American <1%, Pacific Islander 0%, Two or more races 2%, Race unknown 4%.
Retention and Graduation: 79% freshmen return for sophomore year. 57% freshmen graduate within 4 years. 70% freshmen graduate within 6 years. 33% grads go on to further study within 1 year. **Faculty:** Student/faculty ratio 13:1. 310 full-time faculty, 75% hold PhDs, 15% are members of minority groups, 57% are women. 0% of classes are taught by teaching assistants.

ACADEMICS

Degrees: Associate; Bachelor's; Certificate; Doctoral/Professional; Master's; Post-Bachelor's certificate; Post-Master's certificate **Classes:** Most classes have 10-19 students. Most lab/discussion sessions have 20-29 students.
Most popular majors: Speech Communication And Rhetoric; Education, General; Business Administration And Management, General. **Special Study Options:** Accelerated program; Cooperative education program; Cross-registration; Distance learning; Double major; Dual enrollment; Honors program; Independent study; Internships; Liberal arts/career combination; Student-designed major; Study abroad; Teacher certification program. **Honors programs:** The Honors School is committed to providing motivated students

with a unique learning environment in a community of scholars. By supporting both disciplinary and interdisciplinary approaches to education, the Honors School seeks to help students develop not only depth within their intended field of study, but also an appreciation for how that knowledge is embedded within a broader context of intellectual inquiry. The Honors School also is dedicated to raising students' level of cultural, ethical, and societal awareness as its participants develop into well-rounded scholars and citizens within a global community. **Combined degree programs:** BA/MA; BA/MD. **Disability Services offered to physically disabled students:** Note-taking services; Reader services; Tape recorders; Tutors. **Career services:** Alumni network; Alumni services; Career assessment; Career/job search classes; Internships; Regional alumni

FACILITIES

Housing: Apartments for single students; Coed dorms; Theme housing 95% of campus accessible to physically disabled. **Special Academic Facilities/ Equipment:** Art galleries, instructional media center with TV and Radio stations, theatre, greenhouse, Financial Markets lab, community garden **Computers:** 100% of classrooms, 100% of dorms, 100% of libraries, 100% of dining areas, 100% of student union, 90% of common outdoor areas have wireless network access. Students can register for classes online. Administrative functions (other than registration) can be performed online.

CAMPUS LIFE

Environment: Village **Activities:** Campus Ministries; Choral groups; Concert band; Dance; Drama/theater; International Student Organization; Jazz band; Literary magazine; Model UN; Music ensembles; Musical theater; Pep band; Radio station; Student government; Student newspaper; Television station; Yearbook 67 registered organizations, 19 honor societies, 3 religious organizations. 7 fraternities, 6 sororities. **Athletics (Intercollegiate):** *Men:* baseball, basketball, cross-country, football, golf, soccer, tennis, track/field (outdoor), track/field (indoor). *Women:* basketball, cross-country, field hockey, golf, lacrosse, soccer, softball, tennis, track/field (outdoor), track/field (indoor). **On-Campus Highlights:** Rebecca Stafford Student Center, OceanFirst Bank Center, Magill Commons residential restuarant, Pollak Theatre, Dunkin' Donuts **Environmental Initiatives:** Monmouth University was the first private institution of higher education in New Jersey to enter into a voluntary Memorandum of Understanding (MOU) with the US Environmental Protection Agency (EPA). The MOU documents Monmouth's commitment as an environmental steward that has pledged to reduce its carbon footprint and to contribute to a better living environment. Monmouth University uses the EPA's environmental stewardship programs to develop policies, practices and specifications for environmental efficiency standards; to increase its stewardship awareness; to remain current with EPA regulations and guidelines; and to increase the involvement and recognition of Monmouth's stakeholders in environmental sustainability programs. Monmouth University has pledged to partner with local government on environmental initiatives and addressing environmental concerns swiftly. Monmouth recognizes EPA's program requirements for outreach and involvement, data collecting and reporting, and strives to become a recognized leader and a candidate for EPA environmental stewardship awards

ADMISSIONS

Freshman Academic Profile: Average high school GPA 3.4. 12% in top 10% of high school class, 37% in top 25% of high school class, 76% in top 50% of high school class. 85% from public high schools. **Test Scores:** SAT Math middle 50% range 480-590. SAT EBRW middle 50% range 490-600. ACT middle 50% range 19-26. Minimum internet-based TOEFL 79. Minimum paper TOEFL 550. **Basis for Candidate Selection:** *Very important factors considered include:* rigor of secondary school record, academic GPA, standardized test scores. *Important factors considered include:* application essay, recommendation(s), extracurricular activities, volunteer work, work experience. *Other factors considered include:* character/personal qualities, alumni/ae relation. **Freshman Admission Requirements:** High school diploma is required and GED is accepted *Academic units required:* 4 English, 3 math, 2 science, 1 science labs, 2 history, 5 academic electives, *Academic units recommended:* 2 foreign language, 2 social studies. **Freshman Admission Statistics:** 9,261 applied, 73.9% admitted, 16% enrolled. **Transfer Admission Requirements:** college transcript(s), statement of good standing from prior institution(s). Minimum college GPA of 2.25 required. Lowest grade transferable C. **General Admission Information:** Application fee $50. Priority deadline 12/1. Regular application deadline 3/1. Nonfall registration accepted. Admission may be deferred for a maximum of 2 semesters.

COSTS AND FINANCIAL AID

Average book expense $1,234. **Required Forms and Deadlines:** FAFSA. **Notification of Awards:** Applicants will be notified of awards on a rolling basis beginning 12/22. **Types of Aid:** *Need-based scholarships/grants:* College/university scholarship or grant aid from institutional funds; Federal Pell; Private scholarships; SEOG; State scholarships/grants. *Loans:* Direct PLUS loans; Direct Subsidized Stafford Loans; Direct Unsubsidized Stafford Loans. *Student Employment:* Federal Work-Study Program available. Institutional employment available. **Financial Aid Statistics:** 68% needy freshmen, 57% needy undergrads receive need-based scholarship or grant aid. 97% freshmen, 95% undergrads receive non-need-based scholarship or grant aid. 83% freshmen, 84% undergrads receive need-based self-help aid. 8% freshmen, 8% undergrads receive athletic scholarships. 99% freshmen, 96% undergrads receive any aid. 75% undergrads borrow to pay for school. Average cumulative indebtedness $47,794. **Criteria for awarding aid:** *Non-need-based:* Academics, Alumni affiliation, Art, Athletics, State/district residency.

See page 986.

MONROE COLLEGE

2501 Jerome Ave., Bronx, NY 10468
Phone: 718-933-6700
E-mail: cpatrick@monroecollege.edu
Fax: 718-364-3552 • **Website:** http://www.monroecollege.edu/

This is a proprietary school.

RATINGS
Admissions Selectivity Rating: 71   **Fire Safety Rating:** 60*   **Green Rating:** 60*

STUDENTS AND FACULTY
Enrollment: 6,713. **Student Body:** 64% female, 36% male, 2% out-of-state, 5% international. Asian 1%, African American 46%, Caucasian 2%, Hispanic 42%, Native American <1%, Race unknown 5%.
Retention and Graduation: 75% freshmen return for sophomore year. **Faculty:** Student/faculty ratio 21:1. 70 full-time faculty, 40% hold PhDs, 57% are members of minority groups, 44% are women.

ACADEMICS
Degrees: Associate; Bachelor's; Certificate; Master's **Classes:** Most classes have 20-29 students. Most lab/discussion sessions have 20-29 students. **Special Study Options:** Distance learning; Honors program; Independent study; Internships; Weekend college.

FACILITIES
Housing: Coed dorms

CAMPUS LIFE
Activities: Literary magazine.

ADMISSIONS
Basis for Candidate Selection: *Very important factors considered include:* interview. *Important factors considered include:* application essay. *Other factors considered include:* rigor of secondary school record, class rank, standardized test scores, recommendation(s), extracurricular activities, talent/ability, character/personal qualities, alumni/ae relation, geographical residence, state residency, religious affiliation/commitment, racial/ethnic status, volunteer work, work experience. **Freshman Admission Requirements:** High school diploma or equivalent is not required **Freshman Admission Statistics:** 2,108 applied, 67.5% admitted, 95% enrolled. **General Admission Information:** Application fee $35. Nonfall registration accepted.

COSTS AND FINANCIAL AID
Annual tuition $11,744. Room and board $11,660. Required fees $800. Average book expense $900. **Required Forms and Deadlines:** FAFSA. **Notification of Awards:** Applicants will be notified of awards on or about 7/1. **Types of Aid:** *Need-based scholarships/grants:* College/university scholarship or grant aid from institutional funds; Federal Pell. *Loans:* Direct PLUS loans; Direct Subsidized Stafford Loans; Direct Unsubsidized Stafford Loans. **Financial Aid Statistics:** 97% needy freshmen, 100% needy undergrads receive need-based scholarship or grant aid. 1% freshmen, 1% undergrads receive non-need-based scholarship or grant aid. 41% freshmen, 43% undergrads receive need-based self-help aid. 1% freshmen, 0% undergrads receive athletic scholarships. **Criteria for awarding aid:** *Need-based:* Academics.

MONTANA STATE UNIVERSITY

PO Box 172190, 201 Strand Union Bldg, Bozeman, MT 59717-2190
Phone: 406-994-2452 • **Financial Aid Phone:** 406-994-2845
E-mail: admissions@montana.edu • **CEEB Code:** 4488
Fax: 406-994-1923 • **Website:** http://www.montana.edu • **ACT Code:** 2420

This public school was founded in 1893. It has a 1850 acre campus.

RATINGS
Admissions Selectivity Rating: 76   **Fire Safety Rating:** 94   **Green Rating:** 63

STUDENTS AND FACULTY
Enrollment: 14,445. **Student Body:** 45% female, 55% male, 38% out-of-state, 3% international (55 countries represented). Asian 1%, African American <1%, Caucasian 80%, Hispanic 4%, Native American 84%, Pacific Islander 1%, Two or more races <1%, Race unknown 4%.
Retention and Graduation: 24% freshmen graduate within 4 years. 52% freshmen graduate within 6 years. 31% grads go on to further study within 1 year. 20% grads pursue business degrees. 9% grads pursue medical degrees. **Faculty:** Student/faculty ratio 19:1. 602 full-time faculty, 79% hold PhDs, 10% are members of minority groups, 43% are women. 6% of classes are taught by teaching assistants.

ACADEMICS
Degrees: Associate; Bachelor's; Certificate; Doctoral/Professional; Doctoral/Research; Master's; Post-Bachelor's certificate; Terminal Associate; Transfer Associate **Classes:** Most classes have 20-29 students. **Most popular majors:** Liberal Arts And Sciences/Liberal Studies; Registered Nursing/Registered Nurse; Marketing/Marketing Management, General. **Special Study Options:** Cooperative education program; Cross-registration; Distance learning; Double major; Dual enrollment; English as a Second Language (ESL); Exchange student program (domestic); Honors program; Independent study; Internships; Student-designed major; Study abroad; Teacher certification program. **Combined degree programs:** BA/MEng. **Disability Services offered to physically disabled students:** Note-taking services; Reader services; Tape recorders; Tutors. **Career services:** Alumni network; Alumni services; Career assessment; Career/job search classes; Internships

FACILITIES
Housing: Apartments for married students; Apartments for single students; Coed dorms; Fraternity/sorority housing; Men's dorms; Special housing for disabled student; Special housing for international students; Theme housing; Wellness housing; Women's dorms 90% of campus accessible to physically disabled. **Special Academic Facilities/Equipment:** 1. Blackstone Business Launchpad: http://montana.thelaunchpad.org/ 2. Museum of the Rockies: http://www.museumoftherockies.org/ 3. Jake Jabs College of Business and Entrepreneurship Center for Entrepreneurship: http://www.montana.edu/us/pdc/projects/allPrjs/JabsHall/ 4. Nursing Simulation Laboratory with 3G Mannequin: http://www.montana.edu/nursing/undergraduate/sim.html 5. Space Science Engineering Lab (Physics & Engineering): https://www.ssel.montana.edu/ 6. Subzero Science and Engineering Research Facility: http://www.coe.montana.edu/ce/subzero/ 7. Optical Technology Center (OpTeC): http://www.optics.montana.edu/ **Computers:** Students can register for classes online. Administrative functions (other than registration) can be performed online.

CAMPUS LIFE
Environment: Town **Activities:** Campus Ministries; Choral groups; Concert band; Dance; Drama/theater; International Student Organization; Jazz band; Literary magazine; Marching band; Model UN; Music ensembles; Musical theater; Opera; Pep band; Radio station; Student government; Student newspaper; Student-run film society; Symphony orchestra; Television station 140 registered organizations, 18 honor societies, 12 religious organizations. 9 fraternities, 4 sororities. **Athletics (Intercollegiate):** *Men:* basketball, cheerleading, cross-country, football, rodeo, skiing (downhill/alpine), skiing (nordic/cross-country), tennis, track/field (outdoor), track/field (indoor). *Women:* basketball, cheerleading, cross-country, golf, rodeo, skiing (downhill/alpine), skiing (nordic/cross-country), tennis, track/field (outdoor), track/field (indoor), volleyball. **On-Campus Highlights:** Museum of the Rockies, Planetarium, Fitness Center ($11.7 million student funded renovation completed in 2008, Burns Telecommunications Center, Chemistry & Biochemistry Research Facility **Environmental Initiatives:** 1) Building Lighting Retrofit projects;

ADMISSIONS
Freshman Academic Profile: Average high school GPA 3.4. 20% in top 10% of high school class, 44% in top 25% of high school class, 76% in top 50% of high school class. **Test Scores:** SAT Math middle 50% range 540-650. SAT EBRW middle 50% range 550-650. ACT middle 50% range 21-28. Minimum internet-based TOEFL 71. Minimum paper TOEFL 525. **Basis for Candidate Selection:** *Very important factors considered include:* rigor of

secondary school record, class rank, academic GPA, standardized test scores. **Freshman Admission Requirements:** High school diploma is required and GED is accepted *Academic units required:* 4 English, 3 math, 2 science, 2 science labs, 3 social studies. **Freshman Admission Statistics:** 16,769 applied, 83.1% admitted, 22% enrolled. **Transfer Admission Requirements:** college transcript(s), standardized test scores, statement of good standing from prior institution(s). Minimum college GPA of 2.0 required. Lowest grade transferable D-. **General Admission Information:** Application fee $30. Nonfall registration accepted: Admission may be deferred for a maximum of one year.

COSTS AND FINANCIAL AID

Annual in-state tuition $9,250. Annual out-of-state tuition $22,194. Room and board $9,250. Required fees $1,733. Average book expense $1,350. **Required Forms and Deadlines:** FAFSA. **Notification of Awards:** Applicants will be notified of awards on a rolling basis beginning 4/1. **Types of Aid:** *Need-based scholarships/grants:* Federal Nursing Scholarships; Federal Pell; Private scholarships; SEOG; State scholarships/grants. *Loans:* Direct PLUS loans; Direct Subsidized Stafford Loans; Direct Unsubsidized Stafford Loans. *Student Employment:* Institutional employment available. **Financial Aid Statistics:** 75% needy freshmen, 71% needy undergrads receive need-based scholarship or grant aid. 6% freshmen, 3% undergrads receive non-need-based scholarship or grant aid. 77% freshmen, 84% undergrads receive need-based self-help aid. 1% freshmen, 2% undergrads receive athletic scholarships. 76% freshmen, 75% undergrads receive any aid. 57% undergrads borrow to pay for school. Average cumulative indebtedness $27,672. **Criteria for awarding aid:** *Need-based:* Academics, Art, Job skills, Minority status *Non-need-based:* Academics, Alumni affiliation, Art, Athletics, Job skills, Leadership, Minority status, Music/drama, State/district residency.

MONTANA STATE UNIVERSITY-BILLINGS

1500 University Drive, Billings, MT 59101
Phone: 406-657-2158 · **Financial Aid Phone:** 406-657-1617 · **CEEB Code:** 4298
Fax: 406-657-2302 · **Website:** www.msubillings.edu · **ACT Code:** 2416

This public school was founded in 1927. It has a 92 acre campus.

RATINGS

Admissions Selectivity Rating: 71   Fire Safety Rating: 82   Green Rating: 60*

STUDENTS AND FACULTY

Enrollment: 3,570. **Student Body:** 61% female, 39% male, 9% out-of-state, 2% international (21 countries represented). Asian 1%, African American 1%, Caucasian 81%, Hispanic 6%, Native American 4%, Pacific Islander <1%, Two or more races 3%, Race unknown 1%.
Retention and Graduation: 55% freshmen return for sophomore year. 10% grads go on to further study within 1 year. 70% grads pursue arts and sciences degrees. 14% grads pursue business degrees. 1% grads pursue medical degrees. **Faculty:** Student/faculty ratio 17:1. 174 full-time faculty, 59% hold PhDs, 7% are members of minority groups, 44% are women. 0% of classes are taught by teaching assistants.

ACADEMICS

Degrees: Associate; Bachelor's; Certificate; Master's **Classes:** Most classes have fewer than 10 students. **Most popular majors:** Elementary Education And Teaching; Liberal Arts And Sciences/Liberal Studies; Business/Commerce, General. **Special Study Options:** Accelerated program; Cooperative education program; Cross-registration; Distance learning; Double major; Dual enrollment; English as a Second Language (ESL); External degree program; Honors program; Independent study; Internships; Liberal arts/career combination; Student-designed major; Study abroad; Teacher certification program. **Honors programs:** The MSU-Billings University Honors Program is designed for curious students who are eager to participate actively in their education. Classes in the University Honors Program tend to be smaller than other classes and emphasize class discussion. Often these classes are interdisciplinary in nature; this helps students study issues from several perspectives. Some classes are team-taught, which also enriches the discussion. **Disability Services offered to physically disabled students:** Note-taking services; Reader services; Tape recorders; Tutors. **Career services:** Career assessment; Career/job search classes; Internships

FACILITIES

Housing: Apartments for married students; Coed dorms; Special housing for disabled students 99% of campus accessible to physically diasbled. **Special Academic Facilities/Equipment:** Montana Center for Disabilities, Business Enterprise, Small Business Institute, Urban Institute, Public Radio, Applied Economic Research, Biological Station, Northern Plains Studies Center, Montana Business Connections, Information Commons, Academic

Support Center, Advising Center, TRIO Programs, SOS Programs, Northcutt Steele Gallery, Cisel Recital Hall, Petro Theatre, MSU-Billings Downtown **Computers:** 30% of classrooms, 100% of dorms, 100% of libraries, 100% of dining areas, 100% of student union, have wireless network access. Students can register for classes online. Administrative functions (other than registration) can be performed online.

CAMPUS LIFE

Environment: City **Activities:** Campus Ministries; Choral groups; Concert band; Drama/theater; International Student Organization; Jazz band; Literary magazine; Music ensembles; Musical theater; Pep band; Radio station; Student government; Student newspaper; Symphony orchestra 53 registered organizations, 10 honor societies, 8 religious organizations. **Athletics (Intercollegiate):** *Men:* baseball, basketball, cross-country, golf, soccer, tennis, track/field (outdoor), track/field (indoor). *Women:* basketball, cross-country, golf, soccer, softball, tennis, track/field (outdoor), track/field (indoor), volleyball. **On-Campus Highlights:** Alterowitz Gym, Stingers Bistro, SUB Coffee Shop, Liberal Arts Coffee Shop, Library

ADMISSIONS

Freshman Academic Profile: Average high school GPA 3.1. 10% in top 10% of high school class, 27% in top 25% of high school class, 63% in top 50% of high school class. 96% from public high schools. **Test Scores:** SAT Math middle 50% range 420-500. SAT EBRW middle 50% range 430-520. ACT middle 50% range 18-22. Minimum internet-based TOEFL 68. Minimum paper TOEFL 515. **Basis for Candidate Selection:** *Very important factors considered include:* rigor of secondary school record, class rank, academic GPA, standardized test scores. *Other factors considered include:* character/personal qualities, work experience. **Freshman Admission Requirements:** High school diploma is required and GED is accepted *Academic units required:* 4 English, 3 math, 2 science, 2 science labs, 3 social studies, and 2 units from above areas or other academic areas. **Freshman Admission Statistics:** 1,478 applied, 99.9% admitted, 45% enrolled. **Transfer Admission Requirements:** college transcript(s), statement of good standing from prior institution(s). Minimum college GPA of 2.0 required. Lowest grade transferable C-. **General Admission Information:** Application fee $30. Priority deadline 3/1. Nonfall registration accepted.

COSTS AND FINANCIAL AID

Annual in-state tuition $7,510. Annual out-of-state tuition $16,662. Room and board $7,510. Required fees $1,429. Average book expense $1,460. **Required Forms and Deadlines:** FAFSA. **Notification of Awards:** Applicants will be notified of awards on a rolling basis beginning 3/1. **Types of Aid:** *Need-based scholarships/grants:* College/university scholarship or grant aid from institutional funds; Federal Pell; Private scholarships; SEOG; State scholarships/grants. *Loans:* Direct PLUS loans; Direct Subsidized Stafford Loans; Direct Unsubsidized Stafford Loans. *Student Employment:* Federal Work-Study Program available. Institutional employment available. **Financial Aid Statistics:** 91% needy freshmen, 85% needy undergrads receive need-based scholarship or grant aid. 3% freshmen, 2% undergrads receive non-need-based scholarship or grant aid. 75% freshmen, 83% undergrads receive need-based self-help aid. 4% freshmen, 5% undergrads receive athletic scholarships. 66% undergrads borrow to pay for school. Average cumulative indebtedness $28,546. **Criteria for awarding aid:** *Need-based:* Academics, Alumni affiliation, Art, Job skills, Leadership, Minority status, Music/drama *Non-need-based:* Academics, Alumni affiliation, Art, Athletics, Job skills, Leadership, Minority status, Music/drama, State/district residency.

MONTANA TECH OF THE UNIVERSITY OF MONTANA

1300 West Park Street, Butte, MT 59701
Phone: 406-496-4256 · **Financial Aid Phone:** 406-496-4213
E-mail: enrollment@mtech.edu · **CEEB Code:** 4487
Fax: 406-496-4710 · **Website:** www.mtech.edu · **ACT Code:** 24180

This public school was founded in 1893. It has a 176 acre campus.

RATINGS

Admissions Selectivity Rating: 78   Fire Safety Rating: 98   Green Rating: 60*

STUDENTS AND FACULTY

Enrollment: 2,096. **Student Body:** 36% female, 64% male, 14% out-of-state, 10% international (10 countries represented). Asian 1%, African American 1%, Caucasian 78%, Hispanic 2%, Native American 2%, Two or more races <1%, Race unknown 6%.

Retention and Graduation: 77% freshmen return for sophomore year. 44% freshmen graduate within 6 years. 15% grads go on to further study within 1 year. 5% grads pursue arts and sciences degrees. 0% grads pursue law degrees. 0% grads pursue business degrees. 0.55% grads pursue medical degrees. **Faculty:** Student/faculty ratio 13:1. 150 full-time faculty, 59% hold PhDs, 7% are members of minority groups, 35% are women.

ACADEMICS

Degrees: Associate; Bachelor's; Certificate; Doctoral; Master's; Post-Bachelor's certificate **Classes:** Most classes have 20-29 students. Most lab/discussion sessions have 10-19 students. **Most popular majors:** Engineering, General; Petroleum Engineering; Management Information Systems And Services, Other. **Special Study Options:** Cooperative education program; Cross-registration; Distance learning; Double major; Dual enrollment; External degree program; Honors program; Independent study; Internships; Teacher certification program. **Honors programs:** In order to fulfill requirements for the Montana Tech Honors program, students will complete the following by her or his graduation: 1.Six Semesters of Honors Seminar—Fall and Spring Semesters-1 credits each 2.Undergraduate Research—1-6 credits (A higher minimum number of credits may be established by accrediting agency for a particular degree program.) 3.Thesis—1 credit (Topic to be agreed upon by student, department head from student's major and the Honor's Committee. These could be a co-requirement with a particular department; however, the student could not receive credit twice for the same thesis.) 4.Twelve Credits of Honors Courses—Students may choose established honors courses, augment current non-honors courses, or create new honors courses in cooperation with faculty. **Combined degree programs:** BA/MA. **Disability Services offered to physically disabled students:** Note-taking services; Reader services; Tape recorders; Tutors. **Career services:** Alumni network; Alumni services; Career assessment; Career/job search classes; Internships; Regional alumni

FACILITIES

Housing: Apartments for married students; Apartments for single students; Coed dorms; Special housing for disabled students 75% of campus accessible to physically diasbled. **Special Academic Facilities/Equipment:** Mineral Museum World Museum of Mining **Computers:** 30% of classrooms, 100% of libraries, 100% of dining areas, 100% of student union, have wireless network access. Students can register for classes online. Administrative functions (other than registration) can be performed online.

CAMPUS LIFE

Environment: Town **Activities:** Campus Ministries; Choral groups; International Student Organization; Pep band; Radio station; Student government; Student newspaper 58 registered organizations, 2 honor societies, 3 religious organizations. **Athletics (Intercollegiate):** *Men:* basketball, football, golf. *Women:* basketball, golf, volleyball. **On-Campus Highlights:** Mineral Museum, Mill Building (student lounge & activity area), HPER (athletic facility), Student Union, Mall area (outdoor center of campus)

ADMISSIONS

Freshman Academic Profile: Average high school GPA 3.6. 25% in top 10% of high school class, 56% in top 25% of high school class, 87% in top 50% of high school class. **Test Scores:** SAT Math middle 50% range 575-670. SAT EBRW middle 50% range 540-630. ACT middle 50% range 22-27. Minimum internet-based TOEFL 71. Minimum paper TOEFL 525. **Basis for Candidate Selection:** *Very important factors considered include:* class rank, academic GPA, standardized test scores. **Freshman Admission Requirements:** High school diploma is required and GED is accepted *Academic units required:* 4 English, 3 math, 2 science, 2 science labs, 3 social studies, and 2 units from above areas or other academic areas. *Academic units recommended:* 4 math. **Freshman Admission Statistics:** 981 applied, 91.5% admitted, 43% enrolled. **Transfer Admission Requirements:** college transcript(s), Minimum college GPA of 2.0 required. Lowest grade transferable C. **General Admission Information:** Application fee $30. Nonfall registration accepted. Admission may be deferred for a maximum of 1 semester.

COSTS AND FINANCIAL AID

Annual in-state tuition $9,350. Annual out-of-state tuition $21,969. Room and board $9,350. Average book expense $1,100. **Required Forms and Deadlines: FAFSA. **Notification of Awards:** Applicants will be notified of awards on a rolling basis beginning 3/15. **Types of Aid:** *Need-based scholarships/grants:* College/university scholarship or grant aid from institutional funds; Federal Pell; Private scholarships; SEOG; State scholarships/grants. *Loans:* Direct PLUS loans; Direct Subsidized Stafford Loans; Direct Unsubsidized Stafford Loans. *Student Employment:* Federal Work-Study Program available. Institutional employment available. **Financial Aid

Statistics: 90% needy freshmen, 89% needy undergrads receive need-based scholarship or grant aid. 10% freshmen, 5% undergrads receive non-need-based scholarship or grant aid. 73% freshmen, 80% undergrads receive need-based self-help aid. 4% freshmen, 3% undergrads receive athletic scholarships. 72% freshmen, 67% undergrads receive any aid. **Criteria for awarding aid:** *Need-based:* Academics, Athletics, Leadership, Minority status *Non-need-based:* Academics, Alumni affiliation, Athletics, Leadership, Minority status, Music/drama, Religious affiliation, State/district residency.

MONTCLAIR STATE UNIVERSITY

One Normal Avenue, Montclair, NJ 07043-1624
Phone: 973-655-4444 · **Financial Aid Phone:** 973-655-4461
E-mail: undergraduate.admissions@montclair.edu · **CEEB Code:** 2520
Fax: 973-655-7700 · **Website:** www.montclair.edu/ · **ACT Code:** 2572

This public school was founded in 1908. It has a 275 acre campus.

RATINGS

Admissions Selectivity Rating: 79   **Fire Safety Rating:** 98   **Green Rating:** 90

STUDENTS AND FACULTY

Enrollment: 16,673. **Student Body:** 61% female, 39% male, 3% out-of-state, 1% international (106 countries represented). Asian 6%, African American 13%, Caucasian 41%, Hispanic 28%, Native American <1%, Pacific Islander <1%, Two or more races 3%, Race unknown 7%.

Retention and Graduation: 81% freshmen return for sophomore year. 42% freshmen graduate within 4 years. 65% freshmen graduate within 6 years. 21% grads go on to further study within 1 year. **Faculty:** Student/faculty ratio 17:1. 636 full-time faculty, 89% hold PhDs, 25% are members of minority groups, 50% are women.

ACADEMICS

Degrees: Bachelor's; Certificate; Doctoral; Doctoral/Professional; Doctoral/Research; Master's; Post-Bachelor's certificate **Special Study Options:** Cooperative education program; Double major; English as a Second Language (ESL); Honors program; Independent study; Internships; Study abroad; Teacher certification program. **Combined degree programs:** BA/MA. **Disability Services offered to physically disabled students:** Note-taking services; Reader services; Tape recorders; Tutors. **Career services:** Alumni network; Alumni services; Career assessment; Internships; Regional alumni

FACILITIES

Housing: Apartments for married students; Apartments for single students; Coed dorms; Special housing for disabled student; Special housing for international students; Theme housing; Women's dorms 90% of campus accessible to physically diasbled. **Special Academic Facilities/Equipment:** The Dumont Television Center, Yogi Berra Museum and Stadium,Floyd Hall Arena, Cali School of Music, Kasser Theater, George Segal Gallery **Computers:** 70% of classrooms, 20% of dorms, 100% of libraries, 75% of dining areas, 50% of student union, 10% of common outdoor areas have wireless network access. Students can register for classes online. Administrative functions (other than registration) can be performed online.

CAMPUS LIFE

Environment: Town **Activities:** Campus Ministries; Choral groups; Concert band; Dance; Drama/theater; International Student Organization; Jazz band; Literary magazine; Marching band; Music ensembles; Musical theater; Opera; Pep band; Radio station; Student government; Student newspaper; Student-run film society; Symphony orchestra; Television station; Yearbook 121 registered organizations, 28 honor societies, 8 religious organizations. 13 fraternities, 16 sororities. **Athletics (Intercollegiate):** *Men:* baseball, basketball, diving, football, lacrosse, soccer, swimming, track/field (outdoor). *Women:* basketball, diving, field hockey, lacrosse, soccer, softball, swimming, track/field (outdoor), volleyball. **On-Campus Highlights:** Living Communities, The Heights, John J. Cali School of Music, CELS, Kasser Theater **Environmental Initiatives:** Recycling Program—campus-wide New Cogen Plant to begin operation for April 2013 New Peaker/Migrogrid 2018 New LEED Building—College Hall

ADMISSIONS

Freshman Academic Profile: Average high school GPA 3.2. 10% in top 10% of high school class, 34% in top 25% of high school class, 76% in top 50% of high school class. **Test Scores:** SAT Math middle 50% range 490-570. SAT EBRW middle 50% range 500-580. Minimum internet-based TOEFL 80. Minimum paper TOEFL 550. **Basis for Candidate Selection:** *Very important factors considered include:* rigor of secondary school record, academic GPA, recommendation(s). *Important factors considered include:* application essay. *Other factors considered include:* class rank, standardized test scores, extracurricular activities, talent/ability, character/personal qualities, religious affiliation/commitment, work experience. **Freshman Admission Requirements:** High school diploma is required and GED is accepted *Academic units required:* 4 English, 3 math, 2 science, 2 science labs, 2 foreign language, 2 social studies, 3 academic electives. **Freshman Admission Statistics:** 13,384 applied, 70.7% admitted, 32% enrolled. **Transfer Admission Requirements:** college transcript(s), statement of good standing from prior institution(s). Minimum college GPA of 2.0 required. Lowest grade transferable C-. **General Admission Information:** Application fee $65. Priority deadline 12/15. Regular application deadline 3/1. Nonfall registration accepted. Admission may be deferred for a maximum of 1 semester.

COSTS AND FINANCIAL AID

Annual in-state tuition $13,466. Annual out-of-state tuition $18,920. Room and board $13,466. Required fees $1,647. Average book expense $1,300. **Required Forms and Deadlines:** FAFSA; State aid form. **Notification of Awards:** Applicants will be notified of awards on a rolling basis beginning 2/15. **Types of Aid:** *Need-based scholarships/grants:* College/university scholarship or grant aid from institutional funds; Federal Pell; Private scholarships; SEOG; State scholarships/grants. *Loans:* Direct PLUS loans; Direct Subsidized Stafford Loans; Direct Unsubsidized Stafford Loans. *Student Employment:* Federal Work-Study Program available. Institutional employment available. **Financial Aid Statistics:** 58% needy freshmen, 62% needy undergrads receive need-based scholarship or grant aid. 7% freshmen, 6% undergrads receive non-need-based scholarship or grant aid. 81% freshmen, 84% undergrads receive need-based self-help aid. 0% freshmen, 0% undergrads receive athletic scholarships. 67% freshmen, 58% undergrads receive any aid. **Criteria for awarding aid:** *Need-based:* Leadership *Non-need-based:* Academics, Alumni affiliation, Art, Leadership, Minority status, Music/drama, Religious affiliation, State/district residency.

MOORE COLLEGE OF ART AND DESIGN

20th Street and the Parkway, Philadelphia, PA 19103-1179
Phone: 215-965-4017 · **Financial Aid Phone:** 215-965-4042
E-mail: enroll@moore.edu · **CEEB Code:** 2417
Fax: 215-568-3547 · **Website:** www.moore.edu · **ACT Code:** 2417

This private school was founded in 1848.

RATINGS
Admissions Selectivity Rating: 84   **Fire Safety Rating:** 97   **Green Rating:** 60*

STUDENTS AND FACULTY
Enrollment: 482. **Student Body:** 100% female, 0% male, 42% out-of-state, 3% international (15 countries represented). Asian 4%, African American 16%, Caucasian 65%, Hispanic 5%, Native American 1%, Pacific Islander 1%, Two or more races 5%, Race unknown 1%.
Retention and Graduation: 73% freshmen return for sophomore year.
Faculty: Student/faculty ratio 9:1. 24 full-time faculty, 50% hold PhDs, 8% are members of minority groups, 67% are women. 0% of classes are taught by teaching assistants.

ACADEMICS
Degrees: Bachelor's; Master's; Post-Bachelor's certificate **Classes:** Most classes have 10-19 students. Most lab/discussion sessions have 20-29 students. **Most popular majors:** Fashion/Apparel Design; Illustration; Fine/Studio Arts, General. **Special Study Options:** Double major; Exchange student program (domestic); Independent study; Internships; Study abroad; Teacher certification program. **Disability Services offered to physically disabled students:** Tape recorders; Tutors. **Career services:** Alumni services; Internships; Regional alumni

FACILITIES
Housing: Women's dorms **Special Academic Facilities/Equipment:** Paley, Graham and Levy Galleries **Computers:** 100% of classrooms, 100% of dorms, 100% of libraries, 100% of dining areas, have wireless network access. Students can register for classes online. Administrative functions (other than registration) can be performed online. Undergraduates are required to own a computer.

CAMPUS LIFE
Environment: Metropolis **Activities:** Student government; Yearbook 8 registered organizations. **On-Campus Highlights:** Three art galleries, Outdoor coffee shop, Internships, Leadership Fellowships, Locks Career Center

ADMISSIONS
Freshman Academic Profile: Average high school GPA 3.2. **Test Scores:** SAT Math middle 50% range 420-520. SAT EBRW middle 50% range 450-560. ACT middle 50% range 17-22. Minimum paper TOEFL 527. **Basis for**

Candidate Selection: *Very important factors considered include:* rigor of secondary school record, academic GPA, standardized test scores, interview, talent/ability, character/personal qualities, level of applicant's interest. *Important factors considered include:* application essay, recommendation(s), extracurricular activities. *Other factors considered include:* class rank, volunteer work, work experience. **Freshman Admission Requirements:** High school diploma is required and GED is accepted *Academic units recommended:* 4 English, 2 math, 2 science, 2 foreign language, 4 social studies, 3 visual/performing arts, 1 unit from above areas or other academic areas. **Freshman Admission Statistics:** 607 applied, 54.4% admitted, 33% enrolled. **Transfer Admission Requirements:** High school transcript, college transcript(s), essay or personal statement, statement of good standing from prior institution(s). Minimum college GPA of 2.5 required. Lowest grade transferable C. **General Admission Information:** Application fee $40. Priority deadline 3/1. Regular application deadline 8/15. Nonfall registration accepted. Admission may be deferred for a maximum of 1 year.

COSTS AND FINANCIAL AID

Annual tuition $31,654. Room and board $12,298. Required fees $1,084. Average book expense $2,000. **Required Forms and Deadlines:** FAFSA. **Notification of Awards:** Applicants will be notified of awards on a rolling basis beginning 2/15. **Types of Aid:** *Need-based scholarships/grants:* College/university scholarship or grant aid from institutional funds; Federal Pell; Private scholarships; SEOG; State scholarships/grants. *Loans: Student Employment:* Federal Work-Study Program available. **Financial Aid Statistics:** 97% undergrads receive any aid. **Criteria for awarding aid:** *Need-based:* Academics, Art, Leadership, Minority status *Non-need-based:* Academics, Art, Leadership.

MORAVIAN COLLEGE

1200 Main Street, Bethlehem, PA 18018
Phone: 610-861-1320 · **Financial Aid Phone:** (610) 861-1330
E-mail: admission@moravian.edu · **CEEB Code:** 3301
Fax: 610-625-7930 · **Website:** www.moravian.edu · **ACT Code:** 3634

This private school, affiliated with the Moravian Church, was founded in 1742. It has a 85 acre campus.

RATINGS
Admissions Selectivity Rating: 78   **Fire Safety Rating:** 93   **Green Rating:** 77

STUDENTS AND FACULTY
Enrollment: 1,952. **Student Body:** 59% female, 41% male, 31% out-of-state, 6% international (19 countries represented). Asian 2%, African American 5%, Caucasian 70%, Hispanic 10%, Native American <1%, Pacific Islander 0%, Two or more races 2%, Race unknown 1%.
Retention and Graduation: 82% freshmen return for sophomore year. 59% freshmen graduate within 4 years. 63% freshmen graduate within 6 years. 20% grads go on to further study within 1 year. 7% grads pursue arts and sciences degrees. 1% grads pursue law degrees. 1% grads pursue business degrees. 1% grads pursue medical degrees. **Faculty:** Student/faculty ratio 11:1. 141 full-time faculty, 91% hold PhDs, 12% are members of minority groups, 60% are women. 0% of classes are taught by teaching assistants.

ACADEMICS
Degrees: Bachelor's; Doctoral/Professional; Master's; Post-Bachelor's certificate; Post-Master's certificate **Classes:** Most classes have 10-19 students. Most lab/discussion sessions have 10-19 students. **Most popular majors:** Psychology, General; Registered Nursing/Registered Nurse; Registered Nursing, Nursing Administration, Nursing Research And Clinical Nursing, Other. **Special Study Options:** Accelerated program; Cooperative education program; Cross-registration; Distance learning; Double major; Dual enrollment; Honors program; Independent study; Internships; Student-designed major; Study abroad; Teacher certification program. **Honors programs:** Students can do honors projects within their selected major. **Disability Services offered to physically disabled students:** Note-taking services; Reader services; Tape recorders; Tutors. **Career services:** Alumni network; Alumni services; Career assessment; Career/job search classes; Internships; Regional alumni

FACILITIES
Housing: Apartments for single students; Coed dorms; Fraternity/sorority

housing; Men's dorms; Special housing for disabled student; Special housing for international students; Theme housing; Women's dorms **Special Academic Facilities/Equipment:** Payne [art] Gallery, Deputy Field Center for Environmental and Biological Sciences, Foy [concert] Hall, greenhouse, student art studios, observation room for psychology classes, Center for Leadership and Service, Sally Breidegam Miksiewicz Center for Health Sciences **Computers:** 80% of classrooms, 100% of libraries, 100% of dining areas, 100% of student union, 25% of common outdoor areas have wireless network access. Administrative functions (other than registration) can be performed online.

CAMPUS LIFE

Environment: City **Activities:** Campus Ministries; Choral groups; Concert band; Dance; Drama/theater; International Student Organization; Jazz band; Literary magazine; Marching band; Model UN; Music ensembles; Opera; Pep band; Radio station; Student government; Student newspaper; Symphony orchestra; Yearbook 80 registered organizations, 16 honor societies, 4 religious organizations. 3 fraternities, 4 sororities. **Athletics (Intercollegiate):** *Men:* baseball, basketball, cross-country, football, golf, lacrosse, soccer, tennis, track/field (outdoor), track/field (indoor). *Women:* basketball, cross-country, field hockey, lacrosse, soccer, softball, tennis, track/field (outdoor), track/field (indoor), volleyball. **On-Campus Highlights:** Haupert Union Building, Priscilla Payne Hurd Academic Complex, Breidegam Miksiewicz Center for Health Sciences/DeLight's Cafe, Fitness Center, The Quad **Environmental Initiatives:** The Moravian College Green Hounds Fund (GHF) is a sustainability revolving loan fund established in 2017 to provide a formalized method for funding campus-based projects that advance operational efficiency and reduce the College's environmental impact.

ADMISSIONS

Freshman Academic Profile: Average high school GPA 3.5. 18% in top 10% of high school class, 48% in top 25% of high school class, 85% in top 50% of high school class. 90% from public high schools. **Test Scores:** SAT Math middle 50% range 500-600. SAT EBRW middle 50% range 510-610. ACT middle 50% range 21-27. Minimum internet-based TOEFL 85. **Basis for Candidate Selection:** *Very important factors considered include:* rigor of secondary school record, extracurricular activities, character/personal qualities. *Important factors considered include:* class rank, academic GPA, application essay, recommendation(s), talent/ability, volunteer work.level of applicant's interest. *Other factors considered include:* standardized test scores, interview, first generation, alumni/ae relation, work experience. **Freshman Admission Requirements:** High school diploma is required and GED is accepted *Academic units required:* 4 English, 3 math, 3 science, 2 science labs, 2 foreign language, 4 social studies, *Academic units recommended:* 4 math. **Freshman Admission Statistics:** 3,059 applied, 76.0% admitted, 21% enrolled. **Transfer Admission Requirements:** High school transcript, college transcript(s), essay or personal statement, statement of good standing from prior institution(s). Minimum college GPA of 3.0 required. Lowest grade transferable C. **General Admission Information:** Priority deadline 3/1. Regular application deadline 3/1. Nonfall registration accepted. Admission may be deferred for a maximum of 1 year.

COSTS AND FINANCIAL AID

Annual tuition $41,905. Room and board $13,378. Required fees $1,731. Average book expense $1,200. **Required Forms and Deadlines:** FAFSA. **Notification of Awards:** Applicants will be notified of awards on a rolling basis beginning 11/20. **Types of Aid:** *Need-based scholarships/grants:* College/university scholarship or grant aid from institutional funds; Federal Nursing Scholarships; Federal Pell; Private scholarships; SEOG; State scholarships/grants; United Negro College Fund. *Loans:* Direct PLUS loans; Direct Subsidized Stafford Loans; Direct Unsubsidized Stafford Loans. *Student Employment:* Federal Work-Study Program available. Institutional employment available. **Financial Aid Statistics:** 100% needy freshmen, 100% needy undergrads receive need-based scholarship or grant aid. 12% freshmen, 10% undergrads receive non-need-based scholarship or grant aid. 89% freshmen, 90% undergrads receive need-based self-help aid. 0% freshmen, 0% undergrads receive athletic scholarships. 99% freshmen, 98% undergrads receive any aid. Average cumulative indebtedness $33,377. **Criteria for awarding aid:** *Need-based:* Academics *Non-need-based:* Academics, Alumni affiliation, Art, Leadership, Music/drama, Religious affiliation, State/district residency.

MOREHEAD STATE UNIVERSITY

University Boulevard, Morehead, KY 40351
Phone: 606-783-2000 · **Financial Aid Phone:** 606-783-2011
E-mail: admissions@moreheadstate.edu
Fax: 606-783-5038 · **Website:** http://www.moreheadstate.edu/ · **ACT Code:** 1530

This public school was founded in 1922. It has a 1016 acre campus.

RATINGS

Admissions Selectivity Rating: 74   **Fire Safety Rating:** 88   **Green Rating:** 60*

STUDENTS AND FACULTY

Enrollment: 7,212. **Student Body:** 60% female, 40% male, 14% out-of-state, 1% international (35 countries represented). Asian <1%, African American 4%, Caucasian 90%, Hispanic 1%, Native American <1%, Pacific Islander <1%, Two or more races 1%, Race unknown 1%.
Retention and Graduation: 69% freshmen return for sophomore year. **Faculty:** Student/faculty ratio 18:1. 359 full-time faculty, 7% are members of minority groups, 48% are women.

ACADEMICS

Degrees: Associate; Bachelor's; Certificate; Doctoral Other; Master's; Post-Bachelor's certificate; Post-Master's certificate **Classes:** Most classes have 10-19 students. **Most popular majors:** Elementary Education And Teaching; General Studies; Nursing/Registered Nurse (Rn, Asn, Bsn, Msn). **Special Study Options:** Accelerated program; Cooperative education program; Cross-registration; Distance learning; Double major; Dual enrollment; English as a Second Language (ESL); Exchange student program (domestic); Honors program; Independent study; Internships; Student-designed major; Study abroad; Teacher certification program; Weekend college. **Disability Services offered to physically disabled students:** Note-taking services; Reader services; Tutors. **Career services:** Alumni network; Alumni services; Career assessment; Career/job search classes; Internships

FACILITIES

Housing: Apartments for single students; Coed dorms; Fraternity/sorority housing; Special housing for disabled student; Special housing for international students 90% of campus accessible to physically disabled. **Special Academic Facilities/Equipment:** Ky. Folk Art Center, 320-acre agricultural complex, Space Science Center, Ky. Center for Traditional Music **Computers:** 100% of classrooms, 20% of dorms, 100% of libraries, 100% of dining areas, 100% of student union, 100% of common outdoor areas have wireless network access. Students can register for classes online. Administrative functions (other than registration) can be performed online.

CAMPUS LIFE

Environment: Village **Activities:** Campus Ministries; Choral groups; Concert band; Dance; Drama/theater; International Student Organization; Jazz band; Literary magazine; Marching band; Music ensembles; Musical theater; Opera; Pep band; Radio station; Student government; Student newspaper; Symphony orchestra; Television station 101 registered organizations, 11 honor societies, 7 religious organizations. 10 fraternities, 9 sororities. **Athletics (Intercollegiate):** *Men:* baseball, basketball, cheerleading, cross-country, football, golf, riflery, tennis, track/field (outdoor). *Women:* basketball, cheerleading, cross-country, golf, riflery, soccer, softball, tennis, track/field (outdoor), track/field (indoor), volleyball. **On-Campus Highlights:** Adron Doran University Center, Eagle Lake, MSU Wellness Center, Laughlin Health Building **Environmental Initiatives:** Environmental Education Center: Organizes educational workshops, Earth Day Activities, and community outreach.

ADMISSIONS

Freshman Academic Profile: Average high school GPA 3.3. 17% in top 10% of high school class, 42% in top 25% of high school class, 76% in top 50% of high school class. **Test Scores:** SAT Math middle 50% range 450-560. SAT EBRW middle 50% range 450-535. ACT middle 50% range 19-25. Minimum paper TOEFL 500. **Basis for Candidate Selection:** *Very important factors considered include:* rigor of secondary school record, academic GPA, standardized test scores. *Other factors considered include:* recommendation(s). **Freshman Admission Requirements:** High school diploma is required and GED is accepted *Academic units required:* 4 English, 3 math, 3 science, 1 science labs, 2 foreign language, 3 social studies, 5 academic electives, 1 visual/performing arts, and 1 unit from above areas or other academic areas. *Academic units recommended:* 1 computer science. **Freshman Admission Statistics:** 5,236 applied, 84.5% admitted, 34% enrolled. **Transfer Admission Requirements:** college transcript(s), statement of good standing from prior institution(s). Minimum college GPA of 2.0 required. Lowest grade transferable C. **General Admission Information:** Application fee $30. Nonfall registration accepted. Admission may be deferred for a maximum of one semester.

COSTS AND FINANCIAL AID

Average book expense $1,200. **Required Forms and Deadlines:** FAFSA; Institution's own financial aid form. **Types of Aid:** *Need-based scholarships/grants:* College/university scholarship or grant aid from institutional funds; Federal Pell; Private scholarships; SEOG; State scholarships/grants. *Loans:* Direct PLUS loans; Direct Subsidized Stafford Loans; Direct Unsubsidized Stafford Loans. *Student Employment:* Federal Work-Study Program available. Institutional employment available. **Financial Aid Statistics:** 67% needy freshmen, 69% needy undergrads receive need-based scholarship or grant aid. 45% freshmen, 63% undergrads receive non-need-based scholarship or grant aid. 66% freshmen, 74% undergrads receive need-based self-help aid. 6% freshmen, 5% undergrads receive athletic scholarships. **Criteria for awarding aid:** *Non-need-based:* Academics, Alumni affiliation, Art, Athletics, Leadership, Minority status, Music/drama, State/district residency.

MOREHOUSE COLLEGE

830 Westview Drive SW, Atlanta, GA 30314
Phone: 470-639-0391 • **Financial Aid Phone:** (844) 512-6672
E-mail: admissions@morehouse.edu • **CEEB Code:** 5415
Website: www.morehouse.edu • **ACT Code:** 792

This private school was founded in 1867. It has a 61 acre campus.

RATINGS

Admissions Selectivity Rating: 79   **Fire Safety Rating:** 60*   **Green Rating:** 60*

STUDENTS AND FACULTY

Enrollment: 2,199. **Student Body:** 0% female, 100% male, 73% out-of-state, 1% international. Asian <1%, African American 94%, Caucasian <1%, Hispanic 1%, Native American <1%, Pacific Islander 0%, Two or more races 2%, Race unknown 1%.
Retention and Graduation: 80% freshmen return for sophomore year. 42% freshmen graduate within 4 years. 55% freshmen graduate within 6 years. 22% grads go on to further study within 1 year. **Faculty:** Student/faculty ratio 11:1. 177 full-time faculty, 78% are members of minority groups, 37% are women.

ACADEMICS

Degrees: Bachelor's **Classes:** Most classes have 10-19 students. **Most popular majors:** Computer And Information Sciences, General; Business/Commerce, General. **Special Study Options:** Cooperative education program; Cross-registration; Double major; Dual enrollment; Exchange student program (domestic); Honors program; Independent study; Internships; Study abroad; Teacher certification program. **Honors programs:** The Morehouse College Honors Program is a four-year comprehensive program providing special learning opportunities for students of outstanding intellectual ability, high motivation, and broad interests. The Program has majors from 14 of the College's 16 academic departments and emphasizes leadership and social outreach systematically in classes and in co-curricular activities from freshman year to graduation. The Program has established a record of actively supporting the College's internationalization focus by introducing its students at the freshman level, in classes and in external meetings – to active interest and participation in global studies and study-abroad commitments to balance the students' academic pursuits. **Combined degree programs:** BA/MEng. **Disability Services offered to physically disabled students:** Reader services; Tape recorders; Tutors. Career assessment; Career/job search classes; Internships

FACILITIES

Housing: Apartments for single students; Men's dorms; Special housing for international students **Special Academic Facilities/Equipment:** Three chapels, a meditation room, and an arena that was built by and used for the Olympic games in 1996.

CAMPUS LIFE

Activities: Campus Ministries; Choral groups; Concert band; Dance; Drama/theater; International Student Organization; Jazz band; Literary magazine; Marching band; Model UN; Music ensembles; Pep band; Student government; Student newspaper; Student-run film society; Symphony orchestra; Yearbook. Forbes Arena, Martin Luther King International Chapel, Kilgore Student Center, Walter E. Massey Leadership Center, Ray Charles Performing Arts Center

ADMISSIONS

Freshman Academic Profile: Average high school GPA 3.2. 12% in top 10% of high school class, 36% in top 25% of high school class, 66% in top 50% of high school class. **Test Scores:** SAT Math middle 50% range 470-570. SAT EBRW middle 50% range 480-590. ACT middle 50% range 18-23. Minimum

internet-based TOEFL 75. **Basis for Candidate Selection:** *Very important factors considered include:* rigor of secondary school record, academic GPA, application essay, standardized test scores, interview, volunteer work, level of applicant's interest. *Important factors considered include:* class rank, recommendation(s), extracurricular activities, character/personal qualities. *Other factors considered include:* talent/ability, first generation, alumni/ae relation, work experience. **Freshman Admission Requirements:** High school diploma is required and GED is accepted *Academic units required:* 4 English, 3 math, 2 science, 2 social studies, *Academic units recommended:* 4 English, 3 math, 2 science, 2 foreign language, 2 social studies, 3 academic electives. **Freshman Admission Statistics:** 2,349 applied, 74.4% admitted, 35% enrolled. **General Admission Information:** Application fee $50. Priority deadline 11/1. Regular application deadline 2/15. Nonfall registration accepted. Admission may be deferred for a maximum of 1 year.

COSTS AND FINANCIAL AID

Annual tuition $25,055. Required fees $2,223. Average book expense $2,088. **Required Forms and Deadlines:** CSS/Financial Aid PROFILE; FAFSA; Institution's own financial aid form; State aid form. **Notification of Awards:** Applicants will be notified of awards on a rolling basis beginning 3/1. **Types of Aid:** *Need-based scholarships/grants:* College/university scholarship or grant aid from institutional funds; Federal Pell; Private scholarships; SEOG; State scholarships/grants; United Negro College Fund. *Loans:* Direct PLUS loans; Direct Subsidized Stafford Loans; Direct Unsubsidized Stafford Loans. *Student Employment:* Federal Work-Study Program available. Institutional employment available.

MORGAN STATE UNIVERSITY

Cold Spring Lane and Hillen Road, Baltimore, MD
Phone: 800-332-6674
E-mail: tjenness@moac.morgan.edu • **CEEB Code:** 5416
Fax: 410-319-3684 • **Website:** www.morgan.edu • **ACT Code:** 1722

This public school was founded in 1867. It has a 122 acre campus.

RATINGS

Admissions Selectivity Rating: 67   **Fire Safety Rating:** 60*   **Green Rating:** 60*

STUDENTS AND FACULTY

Student Body: 40% out-of-state, 2% international. Asian 2%, African American 92%, Caucasian 2%, Hispanic 1%, Native American 1%, Race unknown 0%.
Retention and Graduation: 76% freshmen return for sophomore year.

ACADEMICS

Degrees: Bachelor's; Master's **Classes:** Most classes have 20-29 students. **Special Study Options:** Cooperative education program. **Disability Services offered to physically disabled students:** Tutors. **Career services:** Career assessment; Career/job search classes; Internships

FACILITIES

Housing: Apartments for single students; Coed dorms; Men's dorms; Women's dorms **Special Academic Facilities/Equipment:** African-American collection, new science complex and school of engineering.

CAMPUS LIFE

Activities: Radio station; Student government; Student newspaper; Television station; Yearbook 250 registered organizations, 1 religious organization. 4 fraternities, 4 sororities. **Athletics (Intercollegiate):** *Men:* basketball, cross-country, football, tennis, track/field (outdoor), volleyball. *Women:* basketball, cross-country, tennis, track/field (outdoor), volleyball. **On-Campus Highlights:** Fine Arts Center, Hughes Stadium, Mitchell Building, Research Facility, University Museum

ADMISSIONS

Freshman Academic Profile: 10% in top 10% of high school class, 80% in top 25% of high school class, 96% in top 50% of high school class. 77% from public high schools. **Test Scores:** Minimum internet-based TOEFL 80. Minimum paper TOEFL 570. **Freshman Admission Requirements:** High school diploma is required and GED is accepted; High school diploma is required and GED is not accepted *Academic units recommended:* 4 English, 3 math, 3 science, 2 foreign language, 3 social studies, 2 history. **Freshman Admission Statistics:** Lowest grade transferable C. **General Admission Information:** Regular application deadline 4/15. Nonfall registration accepted.

COSTS AND FINANCIAL AID

Annual in-state tuition $5,296. Annual out-of-state tuition $4,405. Room and board $5,296. Required fees $762. Average book expense $1,500. **Required**

Forms and Deadlines: FAFSA; Institution's own financial aid form; State aid form. Types of Aid: *Need-based scholarships/grants:* State scholarships/grants; United Negro College Fund. *Loans: Student Employment:* Federal Work-Study Program available. Institutional employment available.

MORNINGSIDE COLLEGE

1501 Morningside Avenue, Sioux City, IA 51106-1751
Phone: 712-274-5511 · **Financial Aid Phone:** 712-274-5159
E-mail: mscadm@morningside.edu · **CEEB Code:** 6415
Fax: 712-274-5101 · **Website:** www.morningside.edu · **ACT Code:** 1338

This private school, affiliated with the Methodist Church, was founded in 1894. It has a 68 acre campus.

RATINGS

Admissions Selectivity Rating: 73 **Fire Safety Rating:** 70 **Green Rating:** 60*

STUDENTS AND FACULTY

Enrollment: 1,180. **Student Body:** 54% female, 46% male, 32% out-of-state, 1% international (4 countries represented). Asian 2%, African American 1%, Caucasian 84%, Hispanic 3%, Native American 1%, Race unknown 9%. **Retention and Graduation:** 70% freshmen return for sophomore year. 11% grads go on to further study within 1 year. 48% grads pursue arts and sciences degrees. 10% grads pursue law degrees. 0% grads pursue business degrees. 0% grads pursue medical degrees. **Faculty:** Student/faculty ratio 17:1. 69 full-time faculty, 77% hold PhDs, 3% are members of minority groups, 45% are women. 0% of classes are taught by teaching assistants.

ACADEMICS

Degrees: Bachelor's; Master's **Classes:** Most classes have 20-29 students. Most lab/discussion sessions have 20-29 students. **Most popular majors:** Elementary Education And Teaching; Biology/Biological Sciences, General; Business Administration And Management, General. **Special Study Options:** Distance learning; Double major; Dual enrollment; English as a Second Language (ESL); Honors program; Independent study; Internships; Liberal arts/career combination; Student-designed major; Study abroad; Teacher certification program. **Combined degree programs:** BA/MA. **Disability Services offered to physically disabled students:** Note-taking services; Reader services; Tape recorders; Tutors. **Career services:** Alumni network; Alumni services; Career assessment; Career/job search classes; Internships; Regional alumni

FACILITIES

Housing: Apartments for married students; Apartments for single students; Coed dorms; Fraternity/sorority housing 50% of campus accessible to physically diasbled. **Special Academic Facilities/Equipment:** media-enhanced "smart classroom", high-speed campus internet connection, art gallery, theatre, totally renovated science facility **Computers:** 100% of classrooms, 100% of dorms, 100% of libraries, 100% of dining areas, 100% of student union, 100% of common outdoor areas have wireless network access. Students can register for classes online. Administrative functions (other than registration) can be performed online. Undergraduates are required to own a computer.

CAMPUS LIFE

Environment: City **Activities:** Campus Ministries; Choral groups; Concert band; Dance; Drama/theater; International Student Organization; Jazz band; Literary magazine; Marching band; Music ensembles; Musical theater; Pep band; Radio station; Student government; Student newspaper; Television station; Yearbook 40 registered organizations, 15 honor societies, 10 religious organizations. 2 fraternities, 1 sorority. **Athletics (Intercollegiate):** *Men:* baseball, basketball, cheerleading, cross-country, football, golf, soccer, swimming, tennis, track/field (outdoor), track/field (indoor), wrestling. *Women:* basketball, cheerleading, cross-country, golf, soccer, softball, swimming, tennis, track/field (outdoor), track/field (indoor), volleyball. **On-Campus Highlights:** New Student Apartments, Health-Fitness Center, Eppley Auditorium, Olsen Student Center, Walker Science Center

ADMISSIONS

Freshman Academic Profile: Average high school GPA 3.4. 15% in top 10% of high school class, 42% in top 25% of high school class, 78% in top 50% of high school class. 94% from public high schools. **Test Scores:** ACT middle 50% range 20-25. Minimum paper TOEFL 450. **Basis for Candidate Selection:** *Very important factors considered include:* rigor of secondary school record, class rank, academic GPA, standardized test scores, recommendation(s). *Important factors considered include:* interview, extracurricular activities, talent/ability. *Other factors considered include:* application essay. **Freshman Admission Requirements:** High school diploma is required and GED is accepted *Academic units recommended:* 3 English, 2 math, 2 science, 3 social studies. **Freshman Admission Statistics:** 1,240 applied, 89.5% admitted, 30% enrolled. **Transfer Admission Requirements:** High school transcript, college transcript(s), statement of good standing from prior institution(s). Minimum college GPA of 2.25 required. Lowest grade transferable C-. **General Admission Information:** Application fee $25. Priority deadline 8/15. Nonfall registration accepted. Admission may be deferred.

COSTS AND FINANCIAL AID

Annual tuition $21,116. Room and board $6,729. Required fees $1,130. Average book expense $800. **Required Forms and Deadlines:** FAFSA. **Notification of Awards:** Applicants will be notified of awards on a rolling basis beginning 3/31. **Types of Aid:** *Need-based scholarships/grants:* College/university scholarship or grant aid from institutional funds; Federal Pell; Private scholarships; SEOG; State scholarships/grants. *Loans: Student Employment:* Federal Work-Study Program available. Institutional employment available. **Financial Aid Statistics:** 73% needy freshmen, 76% needy undergrads receive need-based scholarship or grant aid. 83% freshmen, 86% undergrads receive need-based self-help aid. 56% freshmen, 45% undergrads receive athletic scholarships. 100% freshmen, 100% undergrads receive any aid. **Criteria for awarding aid:** *Need-based:* Job skills *Non-need-based:* Academics, Alumni affiliation, Art, Athletics, Job skills, Leadership, Music/drama, Religious affiliation, State/district residency.

MORRIS COLLEGE

100 West College Street, Sumter, SC 29150
Phone: 803-934-3225 · **Financial Aid Phone:** (803)934-3238
E-mail: gscriven@morris.edu · **CEEB Code:** 5418
Fax: 803-773-8241 · **Website:** http://www.morris.edu/ · **ACT Code:** 3868

This private school, affiliated with the Baptist Church, was founded in 1908. It has a 41 acre campus.

RATINGS

Admissions Selectivity Rating: 66 **Fire Safety Rating:** 85 **Green Rating:** 60*

STUDENTS AND FACULTY

Enrollment: 733. **Student Body:** 55% female, 45% male, 17% out-of-state, 0% international (0 countries represented). Asian <1%, African American 98%, Caucasian <1%, Hispanic 1%, Native American <1%, Two or more races 1%. **Retention and Graduation:** 49% freshmen return for sophomore year. 16% grads go on to further study within 1 year. 6% grads pursue arts and sciences degrees. 0% grads pursue law degrees. 6% grads pursue business degrees. 0% grads pursue medical degrees. **Faculty:** Student/faculty ratio 13:1. 38 full-time faculty, 68% hold PhDs, 71% are members of minority groups, 50% are women.

ACADEMICS

Degrees: Bachelor's **Classes:** Most classes have 10-19 students. **Most popular majors:** Biology/Biological Sciences, General; Criminal Justice/Law Enforcement Administration; Business Administration And Management, General. **Special Study Options:** Accelerated program; Cooperative education program; Double major; Honors program; Internships; Liberal arts/career combination; Study abroad; Teacher certification program. **Career services:** Alumni network; Alumni services; Career assessment; Career/job search classes; Internships

FACILITIES

Housing: Men's dorms; Women's dorms 90% of campus accessible to physically diasbled. **Special Academic Facilities/Equipment:** WMMC-640AM Student Radio Station Forensics Center (Forensics-laboratories for ballistics, DNA, arson, and fingerprint) **Computers:** 100% of classrooms, 100% of dorms, 100% of libraries, 100% of dining areas, 100% of student union, 95% of common outdoor areas have wireless network access. Administrative functions (other than registration) can be performed online.

CAMPUS LIFE

Environment: Town **Activities:** Campus Ministries; Choral groups; Dance; Drama/theater; Radio station; Student government; Student newspaper; Yearbook 55 registered organizations, 7 honor societies, 2 religious organizations. 4 fraternities, 4 sororities. **Athletics (Intercollegiate):** *Men:* baseball, basketball, cheerleading, cross-country, golf, tennis, track/field (outdoor). *Women:* basketball, cheerleading, cross-country, softball, tennis, track/field (outdoor), volleyball. **On-Campus Highlights:** Student Center, Library, Human Development Center, Outdoor Basketball Court, Student Health and Wellness Center

ADMISSIONS

Freshman Academic Profile: Average high school GPA 2.6. 0% in top 10% of high school class, 0% in top 25% of high school class, 26% in top 50% of high school class. 98% from public high schools. **Test Scores:** Minimum paper TOEFL 500. **Basis for Candidate Selection:** *Very important factors considered include:* academic GPA. *Important factors considered include:* class rank, standardized test scores. **Freshman Admission Requirements:** High school diploma is required and GED is accepted *Academic units required:* 4 English, 4 math, 3 science, 1 foreign language, 1 social studies, 1 history, 7 academic electives, 1 computer science, and 2 units from above areas or other academic areas. *Academic units recommended:* 2 foreign language. **Freshman Admission Statistics:** 2,616 applied, 79.4% admitted, 11% enrolled. **Transfer Admission Requirements:** High school transcript, college transcript(s), standardized test scores, statement of good standing from prior institution(s). Minimum college GPA of 2.0 required. Lowest grade transferable C. **General Admission Information:** Application fee $20. Priority deadline 7/1. Nonfall registration accepted. Admission may be deferred for a maximum of 1 semester.

COSTS AND FINANCIAL AID

Annual tuition $12,100. Room and board $5,737. Required fees $1,358. Average book expense $3,000. **Required Forms and Deadlines:** FAFSA; Institution's own financial aid form. **Notification of Awards:** Applicants will be notified of awards on a rolling basis beginning 4/30. **Types of Aid:** *Need-based scholarships/grants:* College/university scholarship or grant aid from institutional funds; Federal Pell; Private scholarships; SEOG; State scholarships/grants; United Negro College Fund. *Loans:* Direct PLUS loans; Direct Subsidized Stafford Loans; Direct Unsubsidized Stafford Loans. *Student Employment:* Federal Work-Study Program available. **Financial Aid Statistics:** 98% needy freshmen, 95% needy undergrads receive need-based scholarship or grant aid. 24% freshmen, 21% undergrads receive non-need-based scholarship or grant aid. 93% freshmen, 96% undergrads receive need-based self-help aid. 7% freshmen, 8% undergrads receive athletic scholarships. 99% freshmen, 98% undergrads receive any aid. 99% undergrads borrow to pay for school. Average cumulative indebtedness $31,500. **Criteria for awarding aid:** *Non-need-based:* Academics, Athletics, State/district residency.

MOUNT ALLISON UNIVERSITY

65 York Street, Sackville, NB E4L1E4
Phone: 506-364-2269 · **Financial Aid Phone:** 506 364 2258
E-mail: admissions@mta.ca
Fax: 506-364-2272 · **Website:** www.mta.ca

This public school was founded in 1839. It has a 25 acre campus.

RATINGS

Admissions Selectivity Rating: 68   **Fire Safety Rating:** 93   **Green Rating:** 60*

STUDENTS AND FACULTY

Enrollment: 2,521. **Student Body:** 58% female, 42% male, 43% out-of-state, (40 countries represented).
Retention and Graduation: 82% freshmen return for sophomore year. 30% grads go on to further study within 1 year. 10% grads pursue arts and sciences degrees. 3% grads pursue law degrees. 5% grads pursue business degrees. 12% grads pursue medical degrees. **Faculty:** Student/faculty ratio 15:1. 132 full-time faculty, 92% hold PhDs, 43% are women. 0% of classes are taught by teaching assistants.

ACADEMICS

Degrees: Bachelor's; Master's **Classes:** Most classes have 10-19 students. Most lab/discussion sessions have 10-19 students. **Most popular majors:** English Literature (British And Commonwealth); Chemistry, General; Geography. **Special Study Options:** Distance learning; Double major; English as a Second Language (ESL); Exchange student program (domestic); Honors program; Independent study; Internships; Student-designed major; Study abroad. **Disability Services offered to physically disabled students:** Reader services; Tutors. **Career services:** Career/job search classes

FACILITIES

Housing: Coed dorms; Cooperative housing; Special housing for disabled student; Special housing for international students; Wellness housing; Women's dorms 80% of campus accessible to physically diasbled. **Special Academic Facilities/Equipment:** Art gallery **Computers:** 100% of classrooms, 100% of dorms, 100% of libraries, 100% of dining areas, 100% of student union, 85% of common outdoor areas have wireless network access. Students can register for classes online. Administrative functions (other than registration) can be performed online.

CAMPUS LIFE

Environment: Rural **Activities:** Campus Ministries; Choral groups; Concert band; Dance; Drama/theater; International Student Organization; Jazz band; Music ensembles; Musical theater; Radio station; Student government; Student newspaper; Symphony orchestra; Yearbook 106 registered organizations. **Athletics (Intercollegiate):** *Men:* badminton, basketball, football, rugby, soccer, swimming. *Women:* badminton, basketball, rugby, soccer, swimming, volleyball. **On-Campus Highlights:** Ownes Art Gallery, Jenings Dinning Hall, Library, Student Center **Environmental Initiatives:** Residence Climate Change Challenge expanded this year to include academic and administrative buildings—buildings reduced their consumption of utilities during the month of February from 10 to 25%

ADMISSIONS

Freshman Academic Profile: 99% from public high schools. **Test Scores:** Minimum paper TOEFL 550. **Basis for Candidate Selection:** *Very important factors considered include:* rigor of secondary school record, academic GPA, interview, extracurricular activities, talent/ability. *Important factors considered include:* recommendation(s), character/personal qualities, volunteer work. *Other factors considered include:* class rank, application essay, standardized test scores, work experience. **Freshman Admission Requirements:** High school diploma is required and GED is accepted **Freshman Admission Statistics:** 1,789 applied, 84.8% admitted, 49% enrolled. **Transfer Admission Requirements:** High school transcript, college transcript(s), essay or personal statement, statement of good standing from prior institution(s). Lowest grade transferable c-. **General Admission Information:** Application fee $50. Priority deadline 3/15. Nonfall registration accepted. Admission may be deferred.

COSTS AND FINANCIAL AID

Annual in-state tuition $9,595. Annual out-of-state tuition $7,465. Room and board $9,595. Required fees $545. Average book expense $1,200. **Required Forms and Deadlines:** FAFSA; Institution's own financial aid form. **Types of Aid:** *Need-based scholarships/grants:* College/university scholarship or grant aid from institutional funds; Private scholarships. **Financial Aid Statistics:** 100% needy freshmen, 100% needy undergrads receive need-based scholarship or grant aid. 0% undergrads receive non-need-based scholarship or grant aid. 0% freshmen, 0% undergrads receive need-based self-help aid. 0% freshmen, 0% undergrads receive athletic scholarships. **Criteria for awarding aid:** *Need-based:* Academics, Alumni affiliation, Art, Athletics, Job skills, Leadership, Minority status, Music/drama, Religious affiliation *Non-need-based:* Academics, Alumni affiliation, Art, Athletics, Job skills, Leadership, Minority status, Music/drama, State/district residency.

MOUNT ALOYSIUS COLLEGE

7373 Admiral Peary Highway, Cresson, PA 16630
Phone: 814-886-6383 · **Financial Aid Phone:** 814-886-6463
E-mail: admissions@mtaloy.edu · **CEEB Code:** 2420
Fax: 814-886-6441 · **Website:** www.mtaloy.edu · **ACT Code:** 3635

This private school, affiliated with the Roman Catholic Church, was founded in 1853. It has a 193 acre campus.

RATINGS

Admissions Selectivity Rating: 81   **Fire Safety Rating:** 60*   **Green Rating:** 60*

STUDENTS AND FACULTY

Enrollment: 1,185. **Student Body:** 71% female, 29% male, 6% out-of-state, 6% international. Asian 1%, African American 3%, Caucasian 77%, Hispanic 1%, Native American <1%, Race unknown 12%.
Faculty: Student/faculty ratio 11:1. 71 full-time faculty, 3% are members of minority groups, 75% are women. 0% of classes are taught by teaching assistants.

ACADEMICS

Degrees: Associate; Bachelor's; Certificate; Master's; Terminal Associate **Most popular majors:** Medical Radiologic Technology/Science Radiation Therapist; Registered Nursing/Registered Nurse; Business Administration And Management, General. **Special Study Options:** Accelerated program; Distance learning; Double major; Dual enrollment; Honors program; Independent study; Internships; Student-designed major; Study abroad; Teacher certification program. **Career services:** Alumni services; Career assessment; Career/job search classes; Internships

FACILITIES

Housing: Coed dorms **Computers:** 100% of classrooms, 100% of dorms, 100% of libraries, 100% of dining areas, 100% of student union, 100% of common outdoor areas have wireless network access.

CAMPUS LIFE

Environment: Rural **Activities:** Campus Ministries; Choral groups; Dance; Drama/theater; International Student Organization; Student government; Student newspaper 16 registered organizations, 2 honor societies, 1 religious organization. **Athletics (Intercollegiate):** *Men:* basketball, golf, soccer. *Women:* basketball, soccer, volleyball.

ADMISSIONS

Freshman Academic Profile: Average high school GPA 3.4. **Test Scores:** SAT Math middle 50% range 470-560. SAT EBRW middle 50% range 470-560. ACT middle 50% range 18-22. **Basis for Candidate Selection:** *Very important factors considered include:* rigor of secondary school record, academic GPA, interview, extracurricular activities, talent/ability, character/personal qualities, first generation, volunteer work. *Important factors considered include:* class rank, standardized test scores, recommendation(s), level of applicant's interest. *Other factors considered include:* application essay. **Freshman Admission Requirements:** High school diploma is required and GED is accepted *Academic units required:* 4 English, 3 math, 3 science, 3 social studies, 3 academic electives, *Academic units recommended:* 2 foreign language, 3 history. **Freshman Admission Statistics:** 1,748 applied, 60.9% admitted, 25% enrolled. **Transfer Admission Requirements:** High school transcript, college transcript(s), Minimum college GPA of 2.0 required. Lowest grade transferable C. **General Admission Information:** Application fee $30. Nonfall registration accepted. Admission may be deferred.

COSTS AND FINANCIAL AID

Required Forms and Deadlines: FAFSA. **Notification of Awards:** Applicants will be notified of awards on a rolling basis beginning 2/15. **Types of Aid:** *Need-based scholarships/grants:* Federal Pell; Private scholarships; SEOG; State scholarships/grants. *Loans:* Direct PLUS loans; Direct Subsidized Stafford Loans; Direct Unsubsidized Stafford Loans. *Student Employment:* Federal Work-Study Program available. Institutional employment available. **Financial Aid Statistics:** 100% needy freshmen, 100% needy undergrads receive need-based scholarship or grant aid. 30% freshmen, 20% undergrads receive non-need-based scholarship or grant aid. 100% freshmen, 100% undergrads receive need-based self-help aid. 0% freshmen, 0% undergrads receive athletic scholarships. **Criteria for awarding aid:** *Non-need-based:* Academics, Art, Leadership, Music/drama, Religious affiliation.

See page 988.

MOUNT HOLYOKE COLLEGE

50 College Street, South Hadley, MA 01075
Phone: 413-538-2023 • **Financial Aid Phone:** 413-538-2291
E-mail: admission@mtholyoke.edu • **CEEB Code:** 3529
Fax: 413-538-2409 • **Website:** www.mtholyoke.edu • **ACT Code:** 1866

This private school was founded in 1837. It has a 800 acre campus.

RATINGS

Admissions Selectivity Rating: 93   **Fire Safety Rating:** 91   **Green Rating:** 91

STUDENTS AND FACULTY

Enrollment: 2,186. **Student Body:** 100% female, 0% male, 53% out-of-state, 27% international (69 countries represented). Asian 10%, African American 5%, Caucasian 45%, Hispanic 7%, Native American <1%, Pacific Islander <1%, Two or more races 4%, Race unknown 1%.
Retention and Graduation: 91% freshmen return for sophomore year. 81% freshmen graduate within 4 years. 86% freshmen graduate within 6 years. 17% grads go on to further study within 1 year. 12% grads pursue arts and sciences degrees. 1% grads pursue law degrees. 1% grads pursue business degrees. 2% grads pursue medical degrees. **Faculty:** Student/faculty ratio 9:1. 213 full-time faculty, 91% hold PhDs, 23% are members of minority groups, 55% are women. 0% of classes are taught by teaching assistants.

ACADEMICS

Degrees: Bachelor's; Master's; Post-Bachelor's certificate **Classes:** Most classes have 10-19 students. **Most popular majors:** Biology/Biological Sciences, General; Psychology, General; Social Sciences, General. **Special Study Options:** Cross-registration; Distance learning; Double major; Exchange student program (domestic); Independent study; Internships; Liberal arts/career combination; Student-designed major; Study abroad; Teacher

---

certification program. **Disability Services offered to physically disabled students:** Note-taking services; Reader services; Tape recorders; Tutors. **Career services:** Alumni network; Alumni services; Career assessment; Career/job search classes; Internships; Regional alumni

FACILITIES

Housing: Apartments for single students; Special housing for disabled student; Theme housing; Wellness housing; Women's dorms **Special Academic Facilities/Equipment:** Art and historical museums, bronze-casting foundry, child study center, audio-visual center, language learning center, greenhouse, Japanese meditation garden, equestrian center, observatory, linear accelerator, electron microscope, refracting telescope, nuclear magnetic resonance equipment, McCulloch Center for Global Initiatives, Weissman Center for Leadership and the Liberal Arts, Miller Worley Center for the Environment. **Computers:** 20% of classrooms, 100% of dorms, 100% of libraries, 100% of dining areas, 100% of student union, 4% of common outdoor areas have wireless network access. Students can register for classes online. Administrative functions (other than registration) can be performed online.

CAMPUS LIFE

Environment: Town **Activities:** Campus Ministries; Choral groups; Dance; Drama/theater; International Student Organization; Jazz band; Literary magazine; Model UN; Music ensembles; Radio station; Student government; Student newspaper; Student-run film society; Symphony orchestra 150 registered organizations, 4 honor societies, 12 religious organizations **Athletics (Intercollegiate):** *Women:* basketball, crew/rowing, cross-country, diving, equestrian sports, field hockey, golf, horseback riding, lacrosse, soccer, squash, swimming, tennis, track/field (outdoor), track/field (indoor), volleyball. **On-Campus Highlights:** Blanchard Community Center, Kendall Sports and Dance Complex, The Equestrian Center, Science Center, Williston Memorial Library **Environmental Initiatives:** The College's recently completed strategic Plan, The Plan for Mount Holyoke 2021, directs the community to amplify and promote environmental efforts to fulfill our responsibility to the future of our campus and the planet. Toward that end, the President has appointed a task force with broad representation to develop a sustainability plan to identify opportunities to pursue more aggressive action related to campus sustainability and the environmental curriculum.

ADMISSIONS

Freshman Academic Profile: Average high school GPA 3.8. 54% in top 10% of high school class, 91% in top 25% of high school class, 98% in top 50% of high school class. 65% from public high schools. **Test Scores:** SAT Math middle 50% range 630-750. SAT EBRW middle 50% range 640-713. ACT middle 50% range 29-33. Minimum internet-based TOEFL 100. **Basis for Candidate Selection:** *Very important factors considered include:* rigor of secondary school record, academic GPA, application essay, recommendation(s). *Important factors considered include:* class rank, interview, extracurricular activities, talent/ability, character/personal qualities; volunteer work, work experience. *Other factors considered include:* standardized test scores, first generation, alumni/ae relation, geographical residence, racial/ethnic status, level of applicant's interest. **Freshman Admission Requirements:** High school diploma is required and GED is accepted *Academic units recommended:* 4 English, 3 math, 3 science, 3 science labs, 3 foreign language, 3 history, 1 academic elective. **Freshman Admission Statistics:** 3,446 applied, 50.8% admitted, 30% enrolled. **Transfer Admission Requirements:** High school transcript, college transcript(s), essay or personal statement, statement of good standing from prior institution(s). Minimum college GPA of 3.0 required. Lowest grade transferable C-. **General Admission Information:** Application fee $60. Regular application deadline 1/15. Nonfall registration accepted. Admission may be deferred for a maximum of 2 semesters.

COSTS AND FINANCIAL AID

Annual tuition $47,740. Room and board $14,060. Required fees $200. Average book expense $950. **Required Forms and Deadlines:** CSS/Financial Aid PROFILE; FAFSA; Noncustodial PROFILE. **Notification of Awards:** Applicants will be notified of awards on or about 4/1. **Types of Aid:** *Need-based scholarships/grants:* College/university scholarship or grant aid from institutional funds; Federal Pell; Private scholarships; SEOG; State scholarships/grants. *Loans:* Direct PLUS loans; Direct Subsidized Stafford Loans; Direct Unsubsidized Stafford Loans. *Student Employment:* Federal Work-Study Program available. Institutional employment available. **Financial Aid Statistics:** 100% needy freshmen, 99% needy undergrads receive need-based scholarship or grant aid. 23% freshmen, 21% undergrads receive non-need-based scholarship or grant aid. 78% freshmen, 84% undergrads receive need-based self-help aid. 0% freshmen, 0% undergrads receive athletic scholarships. 81% freshmen, 80% undergrads receive any aid. 60% undergrads borrow to pay for school. Average cumulative indebtedness $23,872. **Criteria for awarding aid:** *Non-need-based:* Academics, Leadership.

MOUNT IDA COLLEGE

777 Dedham Street, Newton, MA 02459
Phone: 617-928-4553 · **Financial Aid Phone:** 617-928-4785
E-mail: admissions@mountida.edu · **CEEB Code:** 3530
Fax: 617-928-4507 · **Website:** www.mountida.edu · **ACT Code:** 1868

This private school was founded in 1899. It has a 72 acre campus.

RATINGS
Admissions Selectivity Rating: 78   **Fire Safety Rating:** 60*   **Green Rating:** 60*

STUDENTS AND FACULTY
Enrollment: 1,317. **Student Body:** 67% female, 33% male, 34% out-of-state, 8% international (32 countries represented). Asian 2%, African American 9%, Caucasian 63%, Hispanic 10%, Native American 0%, Pacific Islander <1%, Two or more races 2%, Race unknown 5%.
Retention and Graduation: 57% freshmen return for sophomore year. **Faculty:** Student/faculty ratio 14:1. 55 full-time faculty, 5% are members of minority groups, 62% are women. 0% of classes are taught by teaching assistants.

ACADEMICS
Degrees: Associate; Bachelor's; Certificate; Master's; Terminal Associate; Transfer Associate **Classes:** Most classes have 20-29 students. Most lab/discussion sessions have fewer than 10 students. **Special Study Options:** Distance learning; Double major; English as a Second Language (ESL); Honors program; Internships; Study abroad. **Honors programs:** Honors Program. **Disability Services offered to physically disabled students:** Tape recorders; Tutors. **Career services:** Alumni network; Alumni services; Career assessment; Internships

FACILITIES
Housing: Coed dorms; Special housing for disabled student; Theme housing **Special Academic Facilities/Equipment:** Mount Ida College Art Gallery

CAMPUS LIFE
Environment: Village **Activities:** Choral groups; Dance; Drama/theater; International Student Organization; Literary magazine; Student government; Student newspaper; Yearbook 22 registered organizations, 6 honor societies. **Athletics (Intercollegiate):** *Men:* basketball, football, lacrosse, soccer, volleyball. *Women:* basketball, cheerleading, cross-country, equestrian sports, soccer, softball, volleyball.

ADMISSIONS
Freshman Academic Profile: Average high school GPA 3.0. **Test Scores:** SAT Math middle 50% range 400-500. SAT EBRW middle 50% range 400-510. ACT middle 50% range 16-22. Minimum internet-based TOEFL 70. Minimum paper TOEFL 525. **Basis for Candidate Selection:** *Very important factors considered include:* rigor of secondary school record, academic GPA, standardized test scores, recommendation(s). *Important factors considered include:* application essay. *Other factors considered include:* interview, extracurricular activities, talent/ability, character/personal qualities, volunteer work, work experience. **Freshman Admission Requirements:** High school diploma is required and GED is accepted *Academic units recommended:* 4 English, 3 math, 3 science, 2 foreign language, 2 social studies. **Freshman Admission Statistics:** 2,319 applied, 63.3% admitted, 30% enrolled. **Transfer Admission Requirements:** High school transcript, college transcript(s), essay or personal statement, statement of good standing from prior institution(s). Minimum college GPA of 2.0 required. Lowest grade transferable C. **General Admission Information:** Priority deadline 5/1. Nonfall registration accepted. Admission may be deferred for a maximum of 1 year.

COSTS AND FINANCIAL AID
Annual tuition $32,300. Room and board $13,000. Required fees $1,520. Average book expense $1,000. **Required Forms and Deadlines:** FAFSA. **Notification of Awards:** Applicants will be notified of awards on a rolling basis beginning 3/1. **Types of Aid:** *Need-based scholarships/grants:* College/university scholarship or grant aid from institutional funds; Federal Pell; Private scholarships; SEOG; State scholarships/grants. *Loans: Student Employment:* Federal Work-Study Program available. Institutional employment available. **Financial Aid Statistics:** 99% needy freshmen, 85% needy undergrads receive need-based scholarship or grant aid. 100% freshmen, 99% undergrads receive non-need-based scholarship or grant aid. 90% freshmen, 89% undergrads receive need-based self-help aid. 0% freshmen, 0% undergrads receive athletic scholarships. **Criteria for awarding aid:** *Need-based:* Academics, Art, Leadership *Non-need-based:* Academics, Art, Leadership.

MOUNT MARY UNIVERSITY

2900 North Menomonee River Parkway, Milwaukee, WI 53222-4597
Phone: 414-930-3024 · **Financial Aid Phone:** 414-930-3163
E-mail: mmu-admiss@mtmary.edu · **CEEB Code:** 1490
Fax: 414-930-3708 · **Website:** http://www.mtmary.edu/ · **ACT Code:** 4620

This private school, affiliated with the Roman Catholic Church, was founded in 1913. It has a 80 acre campus.

RATINGS
Admissions Selectivity Rating: 82   **Fire Safety Rating:** 86   **Green Rating:** 60*

STUDENTS AND FACULTY
Enrollment: 789. **Student Body:** 100% female, 0% male, 7% out-of-state, 2% international (15 countries represented). Asian 8%, African American 17%, Caucasian 52%, Hispanic 16%, Native American <1%, Pacific Islander 0%, Two or more races 4%, Race unknown <1%.
Retention and Graduation: 77% freshmen return for sophomore year. **Faculty:** Student/faculty ratio 12:1. 61 full-time faculty, 79% hold PhDs, 85% are women. 0% of classes are taught by teaching assistants.

ACADEMICS
Degrees: Bachelor's; Doctoral/Professional; Master's; Post-Bachelor's certificate; Post-Master's certificate **Classes:** Most classes have 10-19 students. Most lab/discussion sessions have 20-29 students. **Most popular majors:** Fashion/Apparel Design; Occupational Therapy/Therapist; Fashion Merchandising. **Special Study Options:** Accelerated program; Double major; Honors program; Independent study; Internships; Liberal arts/career combination; Student-designed major; Study abroad; Teacher certification program. **Honors programs:** The purpose of the Mount Mary University Honors Program is to reward superior scholarly achievement and to provide special challenges to serious students who wish to achieve maximum benefit from their college education. Students completing the program receive the diploma citation, "Graduation in the Honors Program." **Disability Services offered to physically disabled students:** Note-taking services; Reader services; Tape recorders; Tutors. **Career services:** Career assessment; Career/job search classes; Internships

FACILITIES
Housing: Women's dorms 90% of campus accessible to physically disabled. **Special Academic Facilities/Equipment:** Haggerty Library, Marian Art Gallery, Walter and Olive Steimke Memorial Hall and Conference Center. **Computers:** 100% of dorms, have wireless network access. Students can register for classes online. Administrative functions (other than registration) can be performed online.

CAMPUS LIFE
Environment: Metropolis **Activities:** Campus Ministries; Choral groups; Dance; International Student Organization; Model UN; Music ensembles; Student government; Student newspaper 42 registered organizations, 14 honor societies, 1 religious organization. **Athletics (Intercollegiate):** *Women:* basketball, cross-country, soccer, softball, tennis, volleyball. **On-Campus Highlights:** Cyber Cafe, Gerhardinger Science and Technology Center, Haggerty Library, Notre Dame Hall, Bloechl Recreation Center **Environmental Initiatives:** The university collaborates with our food service provider, FSI, to compost all food preparation materials, plant waste and coffee grounds. The efforts, which began in 2009, produce eight, 18 gallon totes of compost each week during the school year.

ADMISSIONS
Freshman Academic Profile: Average high school GPA 3.2. 23% in top 10% of high school class, 51% in top 25% of high school class, 84% in top 50% of high school class. **Test Scores:** ACT middle 50% range 18-23. Minimum internet-based TOEFL 61. Minimum paper TOEFL 500. **Basis for Candidate Selection:** *Very important factors considered include:* rigor of secondary school record, academic GPA. *Important factors considered include:* standardized test scores, talent/ability, character/personal qualities. *Other factors considered include:* class rank, application essay, recommendation(s), extracurricular activities, volunteer work, work experience. **Freshman Admission Requirements:** High school diploma is required and GED is accepted *Academic units required:* 4 English, 2 math, 4 science, 2 science labs, 2 social studies, 2 history, 2 academic electives, *Academic units recommended:* 4 English, 3 math, 5 science, 2 science labs, 2 foreign language, 2 social studies, 2 history, 2 academic electives. **Freshman Admission Statistics:** 689 applied, 56.3% admitted, 30% enrolled. **Transfer Admission Requirements:** High school transcript, college transcript(s), Minimum college GPA of 2.0 required. Lowest grade transferable C. **General Admission Information:** Nonfall registration accepted. Admission may be deferred for a maximum of 1 year.

COSTS AND FINANCIAL AID

Annual tuition $28,940. Room and board $8,530. Required fees $570. Average book expense $1,400. **Required Forms and Deadlines:** FAFSA. **Notification of Awards:** Applicants will be notified of awards on a rolling basis beginning 3/1. **Types of Aid:** *Need-based scholarships/grants:* College/university scholarship or grant aid from institutional funds; Federal Pell; Private scholarships; SEOG; State scholarships/grants. *Loans:* Direct PLUS loans; Direct Subsidized Stafford Loans; Direct Unsubsidized Stafford Loans. *Student Employment:* Federal Work-Study Program available. Institutional employment available. **Financial Aid Statistics:** 100% needy freshmen, 100% needy undergrads receive need-based scholarship or grant aid. 8% freshmen, 7% undergrads receive non-need-based scholarship or grant aid. 86% freshmen, 91% undergrads receive need-based self-help aid. 0% freshmen, 0% undergrads receive athletic scholarships. 100% freshmen, 95% undergrads receive any aid. Average cumulative indebtedness $26,237. **Criteria for awarding aid:** *Non-need-based:* Academics, Alumni affiliation, Art, Leadership, Music/drama.

MOUNT MERCY UNIVERSITY

1330 Elmhurst Drive NE, Cedar Rapids, IA 52402-4797
Phone: 319-368-6460 • **Financial Aid Phone:** (319) 363-8213
E-mail: admission@mtmercy.edu
Fax: 319-363-5270 • **Website:** www.mtmercy.edu • **ACT Code:** 1340

This private school, affiliated with the Reformed Church, was founded in 1928. It has a 40 acre campus.

RATINGS

Admissions Selectivity Rating: 85   **Fire Safety Rating:** 60*   **Green Rating:** 61

STUDENTS AND FACULTY

Enrollment: 1,417. **Student Body:** 71% female, 29% male, 6% out-of-state, 3% international (27 countries represented). Asian 1%, African American 4%, Caucasian 84%, Hispanic 2%, Native American <1%, Pacific Islander <1%, Two or more races 2%, Race unknown 4%.
Retention and Graduation: 81% freshmen return for sophomore year. 17% grads go on to further study within 1 year. **Faculty:** Student/faculty ratio 14:1. 84 full-time faculty, 54% hold PhDs, 10% are members of minority groups, 65% are women. 0% of classes are taught by teaching assistants.

ACADEMICS

Degrees: Bachelor's; Master's **Classes:** Most classes have 10-19 students. Most lab/discussion sessions have 10-19 students. **Most popular majors:** Education, General; Registered Nursing/Registered Nurse; Business/Commerce, General. **Special Study Options:** Accelerated program; Cooperative education program; Cross-registration; Double major; Dual enrollment; Honors program; Independent study; Internships; Liberal arts/career combination; Student-designed major; Study abroad; Teacher certification program; Weekend college. **Disability Services offered to physically disabled students:** Note-taking services; Reader services; Tape recorders; Tutors. **Career services:** Alumni network; Alumni services; Career assessment; Career/job search classes; Internships; Regional alumni

FACILITIES

Housing: Apartments for single students; Coed dorms; Theme housing 95% of campus accessible to physically diasbled.

CAMPUS LIFE

Environment: City **Activities:** Choral groups; Drama/theater; Literary magazine; Pep band; Student government; Student newspaper 35 registered organizations, 16 honor societies, 7 religious organizations. **Athletics (Intercollegiate):** *Men:* baseball, basketball, cross-country, golf, soccer, track/field (outdoor). *Women:* basketball, cross-country, golf, soccer, softball, track/field (outdoor), volleyball. **On-Campus Highlights:** Lundy Commons: Game Room, TV Room, Convenience Store, Bookstore, Lounges, Hilltop Grill and Dining Hall, Busse Library, Andrea's House-144 bed, suite style campus residence, Entire campus is connected by underground tunnels

ADMISSIONS

Freshman Academic Profile: Average high school GPA 3.4. 10% in top 10% of high school class, 38% in top 25% of high school class, 72% in top 50% of high school class. 83% from public high schools. **Test Scores:** ACT middle 50% range 19-25. Minimum paper TOEFL 550. **Basis for Candidate Selection:** *Very important factors considered include:* rigor of secondary school record, class rank, standardized test scores. *Important factors considered include:* application essay, recommendation(s), extracurricular activities. *Other factors considered include:* interview, talent/ability, character/personal qualities, volunteer

work. **Freshman Admission Requirements:** High school diploma is required and GED is accepted *Academic units recommended:* 4 English, 4 math, 3 science, 2 foreign language, 2 social studies, 2 history. **Freshman Admission Statistics:** 695 applied, 56.8% admitted, 42% enrolled. **Transfer Admission Requirements:** college transcript(s), statement of good standing from prior institution(s). Minimum college GPA of 2.5 required. Lowest grade transferable D. **General Admission Information:** Application fee $20. Regular application deadline 8/30. Nonfall registration accepted. Admission may be deferred for a maximum of 1 year.

COSTS AND FINANCIAL AID

Annual tuition $28,226. Room and board $8,600. Average book expense $1,200. **Required Forms and Deadlines:** FAFSA. **Notification of Awards:** Applicants will be notified of awards on a rolling basis beginning 3/15. **Types of Aid:** *Need-based scholarships/grants:* College/university scholarship or grant aid from institutional funds; Federal Pell; SEOG; State scholarships/grants. *Loans:* Direct PLUS loans; Direct Subsidized Stafford Loans; Direct Unsubsidized Stafford Loans. *Student Employment:* Federal Work-Study Program available. Institutional employment available. **Financial Aid Statistics:** 100% needy freshmen, 99% needy undergrads receive need-based scholarship or grant aid. 14% freshmen, 12% undergrads receive non-need-based scholarship or grant aid. 82% freshmen, 85% undergrads receive need-based self-help aid. 16% freshmen, 9% undergrads receive athletic scholarships. 100% freshmen receive any aid. **Criteria for awarding aid:** *Non-need-based:* Academics, Art, Leadership, Music/drama.

MOUNT OLIVE COLLEGE

634 Henderson Street, Mount Olive, NC 28365
Phone: 919-658-2502
E-mail: admissions@moc.edu • **CEEB Code:** 5435
Fax: 919-658-9816 • **Website:** www.moc.edu • **ACT Code:** 3131

This private school, affiliated with the Baptist Church, was founded in 1951. It has a 138 acre campus.

RATINGS

Admissions Selectivity Rating: 85   **Fire Safety Rating:** 60*   **Green Rating:** 60*

STUDENTS AND FACULTY

Enrollment: 3,305. **Student Body:** 68% female, 32% male, 4% out-of-state, international. Asian 1%, African American 36%, Caucasian 52%, Hispanic 3%, Native American <1%, Race unknown 7%.
Retention and Graduation: 68% freshmen return for sophomore year. 20% grads go on to further study within 1 year. **Faculty:** Student/faculty ratio 26:1. 80 full-time faculty, 96% hold PhDs, 15% are members of minority groups, 35% are women.

ACADEMICS

Degrees: Associate; Bachelor's; Terminal Associate; Transfer Associate **Classes:** Most classes have 10-19 students. Most lab/discussion sessions have 20-29 students. **Special Study Options:** Accelerated program; Cooperative education program; Distance learning; Double major; Dual enrollment; External degree program; Honors program; Independent study; Internships; Liberal arts/career combination; Teacher certification program. **Disability Services offered to physically disabled students:** Tutors. **Career services:** Alumni services; Career assessment; Career/job search classes; Internships

FACILITIES

Housing: Apartments for single students; Men's dorms; Women's dorms 95% of campus accessible to physically diasbled.

CAMPUS LIFE

Environment: Rural **Activities:** Campus Ministries; Choral groups; Concert band; International Student Organization; Music ensembles; Musical theater; Student government 33 registered organizations, 4 honor societies, 6 religious organizations. **Athletics (Intercollegiate):** *Men:* baseball, basketball, cross-country, golf, soccer, tennis. *Women:* basketball, cross-country, soccer, softball, tennis, volleyball.

ADMISSIONS

Freshman Academic Profile: Average high school GPA 3.1. 9% in top 10% of high school class, 26% in top 25% of high school class, 59% in top 50% of high school class. **Test Scores:** SAT Math middle 50% range 420-520. SAT EBRW middle 50% range 410-490. ACT middle 50% range 15-20. Minimum paper TOEFL 500. **Basis for Candidate Selection:** *Very important factors considered include:* rigor of secondary school record, academic GPA, character/personal qualities. *Important factors considered include:* class rank, standardized test scores, interview, extracurricular activities, talent/ability, level of applicant's interest. *Other factors considered include:* recommendation(s), alumni/ae relation, geographical residence. **Freshman Admission Requirements:** High school diploma is required and GED is accepted *Academic units required:* 4 English, 3 math, 3 science, 1 science labs, 3 social studies, 3 academic electives. **Freshman Admission Statistics:** 1,838 applied, 49.8% admitted, 37% enrolled. **Transfer Admission Requirements:** High school transcript, college transcript(s), Minimum college GPA of 2.0 required. **General Admission Information:** Application fee $20. Regular application deadline 8/18. Nonfall registration accepted. Admission may be deferred for a maximum of 1 year.

COSTS AND FINANCIAL AID

Annual tuition $7,223. Room and board $2,775. Average book expense $656. **Required Forms and Deadlines:** FAFSA; State aid form. **Notification of Awards:** Applicants will be notified of awards on a rolling basis beginning 2/14. **Types of Aid:** *Need-based scholarships/grants:* College/university scholarship or grant aid from institutional funds; Federal Pell; Private scholarships; SEOG; State scholarships/grants. *Loans:* Direct PLUS loans; Direct Subsidized Stafford Loans; Direct Unsubsidized Stafford Loans. *Student Employment:* Federal Work-Study Program available. **Financial Aid Statistics:** 97% needy freshmen, 93% needy undergrads receive need-based scholarship or grant aid. 5% freshmen, 4% undergrads receive non-need-based scholarship or grant aid. 84% freshmen, 87% undergrads receive need-based self-help aid. 7% freshmen, 2% undergrads receive athletic scholarships. **Criteria for awarding aid:** *Need-based:* Art, Athletics, Music/drama, Religious affiliation *Non-need-based:* Academics, Art, Athletics, Leadership, Music/drama, Religious affiliation.

MOUNT SAINT MARY COLLEGE

330 Powell Avenue, Newburgh, NY 12550
Phone: 845-569-3488 · **Financial Aid Phone:** 845-569-3298
E-mail: admissions@msmc.edu · **CEEB Code:** 2423
Fax: 845-569-3520 · **Website:** www.msmc.edu · **ACT Code:** 2819

This private school, affiliated with the Roman Catholic Church, was founded in 1959. It has a 86 acre campus.

RATINGS

Admissions Selectivity Rating: 72   **Fire Safety Rating:** 97   **Green Rating:** 60*

STUDENTS AND FACULTY

Enrollment: 2,030. **Student Body:** 70% female, 30% male, 12% out-of-state, 1% international (9 countries represented). Asian 2%, African American 7%, Caucasian 61%, Hispanic 17%, Native American 1%, Pacific Islander <1%, Two or more races 9%, Race unknown 9%.
Retention and Graduation: 78% freshmen return for sophomore year. 43% freshmen graduate within 4 years. 54% freshmen graduate within 6 years. 31% grads go on to further study within 1 year. 16% grads pursue arts and sciences degrees. 1% grads pursue law degrees. 5% grads pursue business degrees. 1% grads pursue medical degrees. **Faculty:** Student/faculty ratio 13:1. 89 full-time faculty, 83% hold PhDs, 11% are members of minority groups, 56% are women. 0% of classes are taught by teaching assistants.

ACADEMICS

Degrees: Bachelor's; Certificate; Master's; Post-Master's certificate **Classes:** Most classes have 20-29 students. Most lab/discussion sessions have 10-19 students. **Most popular majors:** Teacher Education And Professional Development, Specific Levels And Methods, Other; Registered Nursing/Registered Nurse; Business Administration And Management, General. **Special Study Options:** Accelerated program; Cooperative education program; Cross-registration; Distance learning; Double major; Dual enrollment; Exchange student program (domestic); Honors program; Independent study; Internships; Liberal arts/career combination; Student-designed major; Study abroad; Teacher certification program. **Honors programs:** The Honors Program comprises academic, cultural, and social activities, each of which complements and reinforces the others. **Combined degree programs:** BA/MA. **Disability Services offered to physically disabled students:** Tape recorders; Tutors. **Career services:** Alumni network; Alumni services; Career assessment; Career/job search classes; Internships

FACILITIES

Housing: Coed dorms; Men's dorms; Special housing for disabled student; Women's dorms 95% of campus accessible to physically diasbled. **Special Academic Facilities/Equipment:** On-campus elementary school, television studio, and radio station. Multi-media lab. **Computers:** 100% of classrooms, 100% of dorms, 100% of libraries, 100% of dining areas, 100% of student union, 40% of common outdoor areas have wireless network access. Students can register for classes online. Administrative functions (other than registration) can be performed online.

CAMPUS LIFE

Environment: Town **Activities:** Campus Ministries; Choral groups; Concert band; Dance; Drama/theater; Literary magazine; Music ensembles; Musical theater; Radio station; Student government; Student newspaper; Student-run film society; Yearbook 30 registered organizations, 12 honor societies, 1 religious organization. **Athletics (Intercollegiate):** *Men:* baseball, basketball, cross-country, lacrosse, soccer, swimming, tennis. *Women:* basketball, cross-country, lacrosse, soccer, softball, swimming, tennis, volleyball. **On-Campus Highlights:** Athletic Center with indoor pool, cardio/weight rm, Knight Court Cyber Cafe', Library with wireless internet access, Multi-media production laboratory, Theater with student productions/music events **Environmental Initiatives:** Use of high efficiency boilers.

ADMISSIONS

Freshman Academic Profile: Average high school GPA 3.3. 9% in top 10% of high school class, 29% in top 25% of high school class, 69% in top 50% of high school class. 80% from public high schools. **Test Scores:** SAT Math middle 50% range 500-570. SAT EBRW middle 50% range 500-590. ACT middle 50% range 19-24. Minimum internet-based TOEFL 79. Minimum paper TOEFL 550. **Basis for Candidate Selection:** *Very important factors considered include:* rigor of secondary school record, academic GPA. *Important factors considered include:* class rank, application essay, standardized test scores, recommendation(s), interview, talent/ability, character/personal qualities. *Other factors considered include:* extracurricular activities, first generation, alumni/ae relation, volunteer work, work experience, level of applicant's interest. **Freshman Admission Requirements:** High school diploma is required and GED is accepted *Academic units recommended:* 4 English, 3 math, 3 science, 3 foreign language, 4 social studies, 3.5 academic electives. **Freshman Admission Statistics:** 3,824 applied, 93.4% admitted, 11% enrolled. **Transfer Admission Requirements:** High school transcript, college transcript(s), standardized test scores, statement of good standing from prior institution(s). Minimum college GPA of 2.0 required. Lowest grade transferable C. **General Admission Information:** Application fee $45. Regular application deadline 8/15. Nonfall registration accepted. Admission may be deferred for a maximum of 1 year.

COSTS AND FINANCIAL AID

Annual tuition $30,046. Room and board $15,108. Required fees $1,072. Average book expense $1,300. **Required Forms and Deadlines:** FAFSA. **Notification of Awards:** Applicants will be notified of awards on a rolling basis beginning 3/1. **Types of Aid:** *Need-based scholarships/grants:* College/university scholarship or grant aid from institutional funds; Federal Nursing Scholarships; Federal Pell; Private scholarships; SEOG; State scholarships/grants. *Loans:* Direct PLUS loans; Direct Subsidized Stafford Loans; Direct Unsubsidized Stafford Loans. *Student Employment:* Federal Work-Study Program available. Institutional employment available. **Financial Aid Statistics:** 100% needy freshmen, 97% needy undergrads receive need-based scholarship or grant aid. 14% freshmen, 10% undergrads receive non-need-based scholarship or grant aid. 86% freshmen, 89% undergrads receive need-based self-help aid. 0% freshmen, 0% undergrads receive athletic scholarships. 99% freshmen, 93% undergrads receive any aid. 80% undergrads borrow to pay for school. Average cumulative indebtedness $26,773. **Criteria for awarding aid:** *Non-need-based:* Academics, Alumni affiliation, Leadership, State/district residency.

MOUNT SAINT MARY'S UNIVERSITY

12001 Chalon Road, Los Angeles, CA 90049-1597
Financial Aid Phone: 310-954-4190
E-mail: admissions@msmu.edu · **CEEB Code:** 4493
Fax: 310-954-4259 · **Website:** www.msmu.edu · **ACT Code:** 338

This private school, affiliated with the Roman Catholic Church, was founded in 1925. It has a 72 acre campus.

RATINGS

Admissions Selectivity Rating: 72   **Fire Safety Rating:** 99   **Green Rating:** 62

STUDENTS AND FACULTY

Enrollment: 2,789. **Student Body:** 94% female, 6% male, 2% out-of-state, 1% international (7 countries represented). Asian 15%, African American 6%, Caucasian 9%, Hispanic 63%, Native American <1%, Pacific Islander 1%, Two or more races 2%, Race unknown 3%.
Retention and Graduation: 79% freshmen return for sophomore year.
Faculty: Student/faculty ratio 11:1. 126 full-time faculty, 75% hold PhDs, 29% are members of minority groups, 73% are women. 0% of classes are taught by teaching assistants.

ACADEMICS

Degrees: Associate; Bachelor's; Doctoral/Professional; Master's; Post-Bachelor's certificate; Post-Master's certificate **Classes:** Most classes have 20-29 students. Most lab/discussion sessions have 20-29 students. **Most popular majors:** Sociology; Registered Nursing/Registered Nurse; Business Administration And Management, General. **Special Study Options:** Accelerated program; Cooperative education program; Cross-registration; Distance learning; Double major; Exchange student program (domestic); Honors program; Independent study; Internships; Student-designed major; Study abroad; Teacher certification program; Weekend college. **Honors programs:** Honors program is available to qualifying incoming freshmen and college students meeting eligibility requirements. **Disability Services offered to physically disabled students:** Note-taking services; Reader services; Tape recorders; Tutors. **Career services:** Alumni services; Career assessment; Career/job search classes; Internships

FACILITIES

Housing: Men's dorms; Theme housing; Women's dorms 100% of campus accessible to physically diasbled. **Special Academic Facilities/Equipment:** Drudis-Biada Art Gallery **Computers:** 100% of classrooms, 100% of dorms, 100% of libraries, 100% of dining areas, have wireless network access. Students can register for classes online. Administrative functions (other than registration) can be performed online.

CAMPUS LIFE

Environment: Metropolis **Activities:** Campus Ministries; Choral groups; Dance; Music ensembles; Student government; Student-run film society; Symphony orchestra; Yearbook 29 registered organizations, 3 honor societies, 1 religious organization. 3 sororities. **On-Campus Highlights:** Starbucks Coffee, Fitness Center, Chapel, Circle (Patio) **Environmental Initiatives:** Water Conservation: Bottled water deliveries virtually canceled on both campuses. Activated Carbon Water filters added to bottle-free water dispensers on both campuses.

ADMISSIONS

Freshman Academic Profile: Average high school GPA 3.3. 11% in top 10% of high school class, 35% in top 25% of high school class, 76% in top 50% of high school class. 56% from public high schools. **Test Scores:** SAT Math middle 50% range 420-510. SAT EBRW middle 50% range 410-510. ACT middle 50% range 17-22. Minimum internet-based TOEFL 79. Minimum paper TOEFL 530. **Basis for Candidate Selection:** *Very important factors considered include:* rigor of secondary school record, academic GPA, application essay, standardized test scores, recommendation(s). *Other factors considered include:* class rank, interview, extracurricular activities, talent/ability, character/personal qualities, first generation, alumni/ae relation, volunteer work, work experience, level of applicant's interest. **Freshman Admission Requirements:** High school diploma is required and GED is accepted *Academic units recommended:* 4 English, 3 math, 2 science, 1 science labs, 2 foreign language, 3 social studies, 2 history, 1 academic elective. **Freshman Admission Statistics:** 2,486 applied, 85.9% admitted, 25% enrolled. **Transfer Admission Requirements:** college transcript(s), essay or personal statement, statement of good standing from prior institution(s). Minimum college GPA of 2.4 required. Lowest grade transferable D. **General Admission Information:** Application fee $50. Priority deadline 12/1. Regular application deadline 8/1. Nonfall registration accepted.

COSTS AND FINANCIAL AID

Annual tuition $36,682. Room and board $11,451. Required fees $1,040. Average book expense $1,900. **Required Forms and Deadlines:** FAFSA. **Notification of Awards:** Applicants will be notified of awards on a rolling basis beginning 3/1. **Types of Aid:** *Need-based scholarships/grants:* College/university scholarship or grant aid from institutional funds; Federal Pell; Private scholarships; SEOG; State scholarships/grants. *Loans:* Direct PLUS loans; Direct Subsidized Stafford Loans; Direct Unsubsidized Stafford Loans. *Student Employment:* Federal Work-Study Program available. Institutional employment available. **Financial Aid Statistics:** 99% needy freshmen, 80% needy undergrads receive need-based scholarship or grant aid. 98% freshmen, 96% undergrads receive non-need-based scholarship or grant aid. 98% freshmen, 97% undergrads receive need-based self-help aid. 0% freshmen, 0% undergrads receive athletic scholarships. 94% freshmen, 68% undergrads receive any aid. 86% undergrads borrow to pay for school. Average cumulative indebtedness $32,805. **Criteria for awarding aid:** *Non-need-based:* Academics, Alumni affiliation, Music/drama.

5701 Delhi Road, Cincinnati, OH 45233
Phone: 513-244-4531 · **Financial Aid Phone:** 513-244-4418
E-mail: admissions@msj.edu · **CEEB Code:** 1129
Fax: 513-244-4629 · **Website:** www.msj.edu · **ACT Code:** 3254

This private school, affiliated with the Roman Catholic Church, was founded in 1920. It has a 92 acre campus.

RATINGS

Admissions Selectivity Rating: 80   **Fire Safety Rating:** 99   **Green Rating:** 60*

STUDENTS AND FACULTY

Enrollment: 1,177. **Student Body:** 57% female, 43% male, 81% out-of-state, <1% international (3 countries represented). Asian 1%, African American 13%, Caucasian 78%, Hispanic 1%, Native American <1%, Pacific Islander <1%, Two or more races 5%, Race unknown 2%.
Retention and Graduation: 72% freshmen return for sophomore year. 44% freshmen graduate within 4 years. 61% freshmen graduate within 6 years. 17% grads go on to further study within 1 year. 12% grads pursue arts and sciences degrees. 0.4% grads pursue law degrees. 4% grads pursue business degrees. 0% grads pursue medical degrees. **Faculty:** Student/faculty ratio 11:1. 94 full-time faculty, 66% hold PhDs, 6% are members of minority groups, 64% are women. 0% of classes are taught by teaching assistants.

ACADEMICS

Degrees: Associate; Bachelor's; Certificate; Doctoral/Professional; Master's; Post-Bachelor's certificate **Classes:** Most classes have 20-29 students. Most lab/discussion sessions have 20-29 students. **Most popular majors:** Sport And Fitness Administration/Management; Registered Nursing, Nursing Administration, Nursing Research And Clinical Nursing; Business Administration And Management, General. **Special Study Options:** Accelerated program; Cooperative education program; Cross-registration; Distance learning; Double major; Dual enrollment; Honors program; Independent study; Internships; Liberal arts/career combination; Student-designed major; Study abroad; Teacher certification program. **Honors programs:** Honors program—designed to meet the interests of highly motivated students who are able to take responsibility for their own learning under the guidance of experienced faculty members. **Disability Services offered to physically disabled students:** Note-taking services; Reader services; Tape recorders; Tutors. **Career services:** Alumni services; Career assessment; Career/job search classes; Internships

FACILITIES

Housing: Coed dorms; Fraternity/sorority housing; Men's dorms; Special housing for disabled student; Theme housing; Women's dorms 95% of campus accessible to physically diasbled. **Special Academic Facilities/Equipment:** Art studio/gallery, Student Scholar Center, Computer Labs, Theatre. **Computers:** 100% of classrooms, 100% of dorms, 100% of libraries, 100% of dining areas, 100% of common outdoor areas have wireless network access. Students can register for classes online. Administrative functions (other than registration) can be performed online.

CAMPUS LIFE

Environment: Metropolis **Activities:** Campus Ministries; Choral groups; Concert band; Dance; Drama/theater; Jazz band; Literary magazine; Musical theater; Pep band; Student government; Student newspaper 35 registered organizations, 10 honor societies, 1 religious organization. **Athletics (Intercollegiate):** *Men:* baseball, basketball, cross-country, football, golf, lacrosse, soccer, tennis, track/field (outdoor), track/field (indoor), volleyball, wrestling. *Women:* basketball, cheerleading, cross-country, golf, lacrosse, soccer, softball, tennis, track/field (outdoor), track/field (indoor), volleyball. **On-Campus Highlights:** Harrington Student Center/Sports Complex, Food Court, Residential Suites, Computer Learning Center, Sports Complex / Schueler Field **Environmental Initiatives:** New green roof installed on Library (2008)

ADMISSIONS

Freshman Academic Profile: Average high school GPA 3.5. 13% in top 10% of high school class, 36% in top 25% of high school class, 79% in top 50% of high school class. 70% from public high schools. **Test Scores:** SAT Math middle 50% range 490-578. SAT EBRW middle 50% range 490-578. ACT middle 50% range 20-24. Minimum internet-based TOEFL 64. Minimum paper TOEFL 510. **Basis for Candidate Selection:** *Very important factors considered include:* rigor of secondary school record, academic GPA, standardized test scores. *Important factors considered include:* extracurricular activities, volunteer work, work experience, level of applicant's interest. *Other factors considered include:* class rank, application essay, recommendation(s), interview, talent/ability, character/personal qualities. **Freshman Admission Requirements:** High school diploma is required and GED is accepted *Academic units required:* 4 English, 3 math, 2 science, 2 science labs, 2 foreign language, 1 visual/performing arts,

Academic units recommended: 3 social studies, 3 history. **Freshman Admission Statistics:** 983 applied, 73.2% admitted, 38% enrolled. **Transfer Admission Requirements:** college transcript(s), Minimum college GPA of 2.0 required. Lowest grade transferable C. **General Admission Information:** Application fee $25. Priority deadline 3/3. Regular application deadline 8/18. Nonfall registration accepted. Admission may be deferred for a maximum of 1 year.

COSTS AND FINANCIAL AID

Required Forms and Deadlines: FAFSA. **Types of Aid:** *Need-based scholarships/grants:* College/university scholarship or grant aid from institutional funds; Federal Pell; Private scholarships; SEOG; State scholarships/grants. *Loans:* Direct PLUS loans; Direct Subsidized Stafford Loans; Direct Unsubsidized Stafford Loans. *Student Employment:* Federal Work-Study Program available. Institutional employment available. **Financial Aid Statistics:** 100% needy freshmen, 99% needy undergrads receive need-based scholarship or grant aid. 15% freshmen, 13% undergrads receive non-need-based scholarship or grant aid. 90% freshmen, 92% undergrads receive need-based self-help aid. 0% freshmen, 0% undergrads receive athletic scholarships. 99% freshmen, 83% undergrads receive any aid. **Criteria for awarding aid:** *Need-based:* Academics *Non-need-based:* Academics, Alumni affiliation, Art, Leadership, Music/drama, State/district residency.

MOUNT ST. MARY'S UNIVERSITY

16300 Old Emmitsburg Road, Emmitsburg, MD 21727
Phone: 301-447-5214 · **Financial Aid Phone:** 301-447-5207
E-mail: admissions@msmary.edu · **CEEB Code:** 5421
Fax: 301-447-5860 · **Website:** www.msmary.edu · **ACT Code:** 1726

This private school, affiliated with the Roman Catholic Church, was founded in 1808. It has a 1500 acre campus.

RATINGS

Admissions Selectivity Rating: 80   **Fire Safety Rating:** 99   **Green Rating:** 77

STUDENTS AND FACULTY

Enrollment: 1,785. **Student Body:** 52% female, 48% male, 43% out-of-state, 1% international (10 countries represented). Asian 3%, African American 17%, Caucasian 63%, Hispanic 11%, Native American 1%, Pacific Islander <1%, Two or more races 4%, Race unknown 1%.
Retention and Graduation: 76% freshmen return for sophomore year. 58% freshmen graduate within 4 years. 63% freshmen graduate within 6 years. 30% grads go on to further study within 1 year. 10% grads pursue arts and sciences degrees. 2% grads pursue law degrees. 6% grads pursue business degrees. 2% grads pursue medical degrees. **Faculty:** Student/faculty ratio 13:1. 129 full-time faculty, 87% hold PhDs, 9% are members of minority groups, 40% are women. 0% of classes are taught by teaching assistants.

ACADEMICS

Degrees: Bachelor's; Master's; Post-Bachelor's certificate; Post-Master's certificate **Classes:** Most classes have fewer than 10 students. Most lab/discussion sessions have 10-19 students. **Most popular majors:** Criminology; Business/Commerce, General; Accounting. **Special Study Options:** Accelerated program; Cross-registration; Double major; Dual enrollment; Honors program; Independent study; Internships; Liberal arts/career combination; Student-designed major; Study abroad; Teacher certification program; Weekend college.
Honors programs: The Honors Program offers talented and motivated students an educational experience that integrates curricular, co-curricular, and extra-curricular learning in both interdisciplinary and major areas of study.
Disability Services offered to physically disabled students: Note-taking services; Reader services; Tape recorders; Tutors. **Career services:** Alumni network; Alumni services; Career assessment; Career/job search classes; Internships; Regional alumni

FACILITIES

Housing: Apartments for single students; Coed dorms; Special housing for disabled student; Theme housing; Wellness housing 85% of campus accessible to physically diasbled. **Special Academic Facilities/Equipment:** Historical art collection reflecting Catholic history in America and Marylandia. **Computers:** 100% of classrooms, 100% of dorms, 100% of libraries, 100% of dining areas, 100% of student union, 50% of common outdoor areas have wireless network access. Students can register for classes online. Administrative functions (other than registration) can be performed online.

CAMPUS LIFE

Environment: Rural **Activities:** Campus Ministries; Choral groups; Concert band; Dance; Drama/theater; International Student Organization; Jazz band; Literary magazine; Music ensembles; Musical theater; Pep band; Radio station; Student government; Student newspaper 68 registered organizations, 19 honor societies, 8 religious organizations. **Athletics (Intercollegiate):** *Men:* baseball, basketball, cross-country, golf, lacrosse, soccer, tennis, track/field (outdoor), track/field (indoor). *Women:* basketball, cross-country, golf, lacrosse, soccer, softball, swimming, tennis, track/field (outdoor), track/field (indoor). **On-Campus Highlights:** McGowan Student Center—Patriot Hall, Knott Athletic Recreation Convocation Complex, Knott Academic Center, Phillips Library, National Shrine Grotto of Lourdes **Environmental Initiatives:** We have 1.6 MW photovoltaic panels installed that provide a substantial fraction of electricity needs.

ADMISSIONS

Freshman Academic Profile: Average high school GPA 3.3. 8% in top 10% of high school class, 30% in top 25% of high school class, 64% in top 50% of high school class. 63% from public high schools. **Test Scores:** SAT Math middle 50% range 470-590. SAT EBRW middle 50% range 500-600. ACT middle 50% range 19-24. Minimum internet-based TOEFL 83. Minimum paper TOEFL 550. **Basis for Candidate Selection:** *Very important factors considered include:* academic GPA. *Important factors considered include:* rigor of secondary school record, application essay, standardized test scores, recommendation(s), extracurricular activities, talent/ability, character/personal qualities, level of applicant's interest. *Other factors considered include:* class rank, interview, volunteer work, work experience. **Freshman Admission Requirements:** High school diploma is required and GED is accepted *Academic units required:* 4 English, 3 math, 3 science, 2 science labs, 2 foreign language, 3 social studies, 1 history. **Freshman Admission Statistics:** 6,130 applied, 64.2% admitted, 13% enrolled. **Transfer Admission Requirements:** college transcript(s), statement of good standing from prior institution(s). Minimum college GPA of 2.0 required. Lowest grade transferable C. **General Admission Information:** Application fee $45. Priority deadline 12/1. Regular application deadline 3/1. Nonfall registration accepted. Admission may be deferred for a maximum of 1 year.

COSTS AND FINANCIAL AID

Annual tuition $39,200. Room and board $13,075. Required fees $1,375. Average book expense $1,300. **Required Forms and Deadlines:** FAFSA. **Notification of Awards:** Applicants will be notified of awards on a rolling basis beginning 1/15. **Types of Aid:** *Need-based scholarships/grants:* College/university scholarship or grant aid from institutional funds; Federal Pell; Private scholarships; SEOG; State scholarships/grants. *Loans:* Direct PLUS loans; Direct Subsidized Stafford Loans; Direct Unsubsidized Stafford Loans. *Student Employment:* Federal Work-Study Program available. Institutional employment available. **Financial Aid Statistics:** 100% needy freshmen, 99% needy undergrads receive need-based scholarship or grant aid. 24% freshmen, 19% undergrads receive non-need-based scholarship or grant aid. 73% freshmen, 77% undergrads receive need-based self-help aid. 10% freshmen, 8% undergrads receive athletic scholarships. 100% freshmen, 97% undergrads receive any aid. 77% undergrads borrow to pay for school. Average cumulative indebtedness $33,894. **Criteria for awarding aid:** *Need-based:* Job skills *Non-need-based:* Academics, Art, Athletics, Leadership.

MOUNT VERNON NAZARENE UNIVERSITY

800 Martinsburg Road, Mount Vernon, OH 43050
Phone: 740-392-6868 · **Financial Aid Phone:** 866-686-8243
E-mail: admissions@mvnu.edu · **CEEB Code:** 1531
Fax: 740-393-0511 · **Website:** www.mvnu.edu · **ACT Code:** 3372

This private school, affiliated with the Nazarene Church, was founded in 1964. It has a 332 acre campus.

RATINGS

Admissions Selectivity Rating: 78   **Fire Safety Rating:** 82   **Green Rating:** 61

STUDENTS AND FACULTY

Enrollment: 1,623. **Student Body:** 63% female, 37% male, 8% out-of-state, <1% international (12 countries represented). Asian 1%, African American 2%, Caucasian 85%, Hispanic 2%, Native American <1%, Pacific Islander <1%, Two or more races 3%, Race unknown 6%.
Retention and Graduation: 79% freshmen return for sophomore year. 58% freshmen graduate within 4 years. 63% freshmen graduate within 6 years. 17% grads go on to further study within 1 year. 1% grads pursue law degrees. 3% grads pursue business degrees. 2% grads pursue medical degrees. **Faculty:** Student/faculty ratio 14:1. 75 full-time faculty, 73% hold PhDs, 9% are members of minority groups, 43% are women. 0% of classes are taught by teaching assistants.

ACADEMICS

Degrees: Associate; Bachelor's; Master's **Most popular majors:** Education, General; Registered Nursing/Registered Nurse; Business Administration And Management, General. **Special Study Options:** Cross-registration; Distance learning; Double major; Dual enrollment; Honors program; Independent study; Internships; Liberal arts/career combination; Study abroad; Teacher certification program. **Honors programs:** The MVNU Honors Program is not about having gifted students simply do more work; instead, the program exists to enrich the academic and cultural experience for gifted students by offering unique and challenging courses, special extracurricular opportunities, and a supportive environment in which students can excel. The Honors Program adds depth to students' academic development and allows them to have input in designing their own curriculum by proposing study topics for Honors courses and by developing independent projects. Students will work closely with a faculty mentor to complete an Honors Project in their major. There are also opportunities for off-campus cultural enrichment and entertainment, as well as travel-study and experiential learning seminars. **Disability Services offered to physically disabled students:** Note-taking services; Reader services; Tape recorders; Tutors. **Career services:** Alumni services; Career assessment; Career/job search classes

FACILITIES

Housing: Apartments for married students; Apartments for single students; Coed dorms; Men's dorms; Special housing for disabled student; Women's dorms 95% of campus accessible to physically diasbled. **Special Academic Facilities/Equipment:** Buchwald Art Center, nature reserve. **Computers:** 95% of classrooms, 5% of dorms, 100% of libraries, 100% of dining areas, 100% of student union, 10% of common outdoor areas have wireless network access. Administrative functions (other than registration) can be performed online.

CAMPUS LIFE

Environment: Village **Activities:** Campus Ministries; Choral groups; Concert band; Drama/theater; International Student Organization; Jazz band; Literary magazine; Music ensembles; Musical theater; Pep band; Radio station; Student government; Student newspaper; Yearbook 26 registered organizations, 4 honor societies, 16 religious organizations. **Athletics (Intercollegiate):** *Men:* baseball, basketball, cross-country, golf, soccer. *Women:* basketball, cross-country, soccer, softball, volleyball. **On-Campus Highlights:** Ariel Arena, The Prince Student Union, The Chapel, Happy Bean, The Grove **Environmental Initiatives:** Campus-wide recycling program

ADMISSIONS

Freshman Academic Profile: Average high school GPA 3.5. 22% in top 10% of high school class, 43% in top 25% of high school class, 79% in top 50% of high school class. **Test Scores:** SAT Math middle 50% range 470-570. SAT EBRW middle 50% range 490-580. ACT middle 50% range 19-28. Minimum internet-based TOEFL 70. Minimum paper TOEFL 525. **Basis for Candidate Selection:** *Very important factors considered include:* academic GPA, standardized test scores. *Important factors considered include:* rigor of secondary school record. *Other factors considered include:* class rank, application essay, recommendation(s). **Freshman Admission Requirements:** High school diploma is required and GED is accepted *Academic units required:* 2 foreign language, *Academic units recommended:* 4 English, 4 math, 3 science, 3 science labs, 3 foreign language, 3 social studies, 2 academic electives, 1 visual/performing arts, 1 unit from above areas or other academic areas. **Freshman Admission Statistics:** 1,187 applied, 76.7% admitted, 36% enrolled. **Transfer Admission Requirements:** High school transcript, college transcript(s), essay or personal statement, statement of good standing from prior institution(s). Minimum college GPA of 2.0 required. Lowest grade transferable C-. **General Admission Information:** Application fee $25. Priority deadline 4/15. Regular application deadline 7/15. Nonfall registration accepted. Admission may be deferred for a maximum of 1 year.

COSTS AND FINANCIAL AID

Annual tuition $28,944. Room and board $8,170. Required fees $250. Average book expense $1,400. **Required Forms and Deadlines:** FAFSA. **Notification of Awards:** Applicants will be notified of awards on a rolling basis beginning 12/1. **Types of Aid:** *Need-based scholarships/grants:* College/university scholarship or grant aid from institutional funds; Federal Pell; Private scholarships; SEOG; State scholarships/grants. *Loans:* Direct PLUS loans; Direct Subsidized Stafford Loans; Direct Unsubsidized Stafford Loans. *Student Employment:* Federal Work-Study Program available. Institutional employment available. **Financial Aid Statistics:** 98% needy freshmen, 99% needy undergrads receive need-based scholarship or grant aid. 35% freshmen, 42% undergrads receive non-need-based scholarship or grant aid. 75% freshmen, 73% undergrads receive need-based self-help aid. 10% freshmen, 3% undergrads receive athletic scholarships. 82% undergrads borrow to pay for school. Average cumulative indebtedness $21,564. **Criteria for awarding aid:** *Need-based:* Academics *Non-need-based:* Academics, Art, Athletics, Minority status, Music/drama, Religious affiliation, State/district residency.

MUHLENBERG COLLEGE

2400 West Chew Street, Allentown, PA 18104-5596
Phone: 484-664-3200 · **Financial Aid Phone:** 484-664-3175
E-mail: admissions@muhlenberg.edu · **CEEB Code:** 2424
Fax: 484-664-3032 · **Website:** www.muhlenberg.edu · **ACT Code:** 3640

This private school, affiliated with the Lutheran Church, was founded in 1848. It has a 81 acre campus.

RATINGS

Admissions Selectivity Rating: 89 **Fire Safety Rating:** 97 **Green Rating:** 82

STUDENTS AND FACULTY

Enrollment: 2,375. **Student Body:** 60% female, 40% male, 76% out-of-state, 3% international (17 countries represented). Asian 3%, African American 3%, Caucasian 75%, Hispanic 7%, Native American <1%, Pacific Islander <1%, Two or more races 1%, Race unknown 6%.
Retention and Graduation: 90% freshmen return for sophomore year. 22% grads go on to further study within 1 year. 14% grads pursue arts and sciences degrees. 3.3% grads pursue law degrees. 1% grads pursue business degrees. 5% grads pursue medical degrees. **Faculty:** Student/faculty ratio 11:1. 186 full-time faculty, 89% hold PhDs, 10% are members of minority groups, 52% are women. 0% of classes are taught by teaching assistants.

ACADEMICS

Degrees: Associate; Bachelor's; Certificate **Classes:** Most classes have 20-29 students. Most lab/discussion sessions have 10-19 students. **Most popular majors:** Psychology, General; Drama And Dramatics/Theatre Arts, General; Business/Commerce, General. **Special Study Options:** Accelerated program; Cross-registration; Double major; Exchange student program (domestic); Honors program; Independent study; Internships; Student-designed major; Study abroad; Teacher certification program; Weekend college. **Honors programs:** Muhlenberg Scholar, Dana Associate, R.J. Fellow (each provides a $4,000 annual stipend, dedicated freshman seminar, and mentored research) **Combined degree programs:** BA/DDS; BA/MD. **Disability Services offered to physically disabled students:** Note-taking services; Tutors. **Career services:** Alumni network; Alumni services; Career assessment; Career/job search classes; Internships; Regional alumni

FACILITIES

Housing: Apartments for single students; Coed dorms; Fraternity/sorority housing; Special housing for disabled student; Special housing for international students; Women's dorms 95% of campus accessible to physically diasbled. **Special Academic Facilities/Equipment:** Martin art gallery, biology museum, Graver arboretum, greenhouse, mainstage theatre, recital hall, 20-foot boat for marine studies, 40-acre Raker environmental field station, two electron microscopes, dance studios, experimental theatres, proscenium theatres. **Computers:** 10% of classrooms, 20% of dorms, 100% of libraries, 100% of dining areas, 100% of student union, 10% of common outdoor areas have wireless network access. Students can register for classes online. Administrative functions (other than registration) can be performed online.

CAMPUS LIFE

Environment: City **Activities:** Campus Ministries; Choral groups; Concert band; Dance; Drama/theater; International Student Organization; Jazz band; Literary magazine; Music ensembles; Musical theater; Pep band; Radio station; Student government; Student newspaper; Student-run film society; Symphony orchestra; Yearbook 100 registered organizations, 12 honor societies, 7 religious organizations. 4 fraternities, 4 sororities. **Athletics (Intercollegiate):** *Men:* baseball, basketball, cheerleading, cross-country, football, golf, lacrosse, soccer, tennis, track/field (outdoor), track/field (indoor), wrestling. *Women:* basketball, cheerleading, cross-country, field hockey, golf, lacrosse, soccer, softball, tennis, track/field (outdoor), track/field (indoor), volleyball. **On-Campus Highlights:** Seegers Union by fireplace & Java Joe's, The Life Sports Center-Athletic Facility, Parents Plaza-Outdoor Courtyard, The Wood Dining Common & GQ, Seegers Union, Trexler Pavilion for Threatre & Dance

ADMISSIONS

Freshman Academic Profile: Average high school GPA 3.3. 36% in top 10% of high school class, 71% in top 25% of high school class, 93% in top 50% of high school class. 69% from public high schools. **Test Scores:** SAT Math middle 50% range 570-660. SAT EBRW middle 50% range 560-660. ACT middle 50% range 26-30. Minimum internet-based TOEFL 79. Minimum paper TOEFL 550. **Basis for Candidate Selection:** *Very important factors considered include:* rigor of secondary school record, academic GPA, character/

personal qualities. *Important factors considered include:* class rank, application essay, standardized test scores, recommendation(s), interview, extracurricular activities, talent/ability, volunteer work, work experience. *Other factors considered include:* first generation, alumni/ae relation, geographical residence, racial/ethnic status, level of applicant's interest. **Freshman Admission Requirements:** High school diploma is required and GED is accepted *Academic units required:* 4 English, 3 math, 2 science, 2 science labs, 2 foreign language, 2 history, 1 academic elective, *Academic units recommended:* 4 English, 4 math, 3 science, 3 science labs, 4 foreign language, 2 social studies, 2 history, 1 academic elective. **Freshman Admission Statistics:** 4,862 applied, 48.3% admitted, 25% enrolled. **Transfer Admission Requirements:** High school transcript, college transcript(s), essay or personal statement, interview, standardized test scores, statement of good standing from prior institution(s). Minimum college GPA of 2.5 required. Lowest grade transferable C. **General Admission Information:** Application fee $50. Priority deadline 2/15. Regular application deadline 2/15. Nonfall registration accepted. Admission may be deferred for a maximum of 1 year.

COSTS AND FINANCIAL AID

Annual tuition $50,095. Required fees $735. Average book expense $1,300. **Required Forms and Deadlines:** CSS/Financial Aid PROFILE; FAFSA; Institution's own financial aid form; Noncustodial PROFILE. **Notification of Awards:** Applicants will be notified of awards on or about 4/1. **Types of Aid:** *Need-based scholarships/grants:* College/university scholarship or grant aid from institutional funds; Federal Pell; Private scholarships; SEOG; State scholarships/grants. *Loans:* Direct PLUS loans; Direct Subsidized Stafford Loans; Direct Unsubsidized Stafford Loans. *Student Employment:* Federal Work-Study Program available. Institutional employment available. **Financial Aid Statistics:** 90% needy freshmen, 97% needy undergrads receive need-based scholarship or grant aid. 24% freshmen, 17% undergrads receive non-need-based scholarship or grant aid. 70% freshmen, 75% undergrads receive need-based self-help aid. 0% freshmen, 0% undergrads receive athletic scholarships. 89% freshmen, 88% undergrads receive any aid. 58% undergrads borrow to pay for school. Average cumulative indebtedness $31,063. **Criteria for awarding aid:** *Non-need-based:* Academics, Art, Leadership, Religious affiliation.

MULTNOMAH BIBLE COLLEGE AND BIBLICAL SEMINARY

8435 Northeast Glisan Street, Portland, OR 97220-5898
Phone: 503-251-6485 · **Financial Aid Phone:** 503-251-5337
E-mail: admiss@multnomah.edu
Fax: 503-254-1268 · **Website:** http://www.multnomah.edu/

This private school, affiliated with the Christian (Nondenominational) Church, was founded in 1936. It has a 25 acre campus.

RATINGS

Admissions Selectivity Rating: 85   **Fire Safety Rating:** 63   **Green Rating:** 61

STUDENTS AND FACULTY

Enrollment: 383. **Student Body:** 47% female, 53% male, 57% out-of-state, 0% international (1 countries represented). Asian 2%, African American 3%, Caucasian 74%, Hispanic 8%, Native American 2%, Pacific Islander 1%, Two or more races 8%, Race unknown 2%.
Retention and Graduation: 63% freshmen return for sophomore year. **Faculty:** Student/faculty ratio 10:1. 27 full-time faculty, 78% hold PhDs, 30% are women. 0% of classes are taught by teaching assistants.

ACADEMICS

Degrees: Bachelor's; Doctoral Other; Master's; Post-Bachelor's certificate **Classes:** Most classes have 10-19 students. Most lab/discussion sessions have 10-19 students. **Most popular majors:** Bible/Biblical Studies; Psychology, General; Business Administration And Management, General. **Special Study Options:** Double major. **Disability Services offered to physically disabled students:** Note-taking services; Reader services; Tape recorders; Tutors. **Career services:** Career assessment; Career/job search classes; Internships

FACILITIES

Housing: Apartments for married students; Apartments for single students; Men's dorms; Women's dorms 90% of campus accessible to physically diasbled. **Computers:** 100% of classrooms, 100% of dorms, 100% of libraries, 100% of dining areas, 30% of common outdoor areas have wireless network access. Students can register for classes online. Administrative functions (other than registration) can be performed online.

CAMPUS LIFE

Environment: Metropolis **Activities:** Choral groups; Music ensembles; Student government. **Athletics (Intercollegiate):** *Men:* basketball. *Women:* volleyball. **On-Campus Highlights:** Roger's Cafe, JCA Commons, The Den, Cafeteria, Commuter Lounge

ADMISSIONS

Freshman Academic Profile: Average high school GPA 3.2. 24% in top 10% of high school class, 34% in top 25% of high school class, 57% in top 50% of high school class. 53% from public high schools. **Test Scores:** ACT middle 50% range 20-28. Minimum paper TOEFL 550. **Basis for Candidate Selection:** *Very important factors considered include:* academic GPA, application essay, recommendation(s), character/personal qualities, religious affiliation/commitment. *Important factors considered include:* rigor of secondary school record, standardized test scores. *Other factors considered include:* class rank, interview, extracurricular activities, talent/ability, first generation, alumni/ae relation, geographical residence, volunteer work, work experience, level of applicant's interest. **Freshman Admission Requirements:** High school diploma is required and GED is accepted *Academic units recommended:* 4 English, 3 math, 2 science, 1 science labs, 3 social studies, 2 academic electives. **Freshman Admission Statistics:** 205 applied, 64.4% admitted, 51% enrolled. **Transfer Admission Requirements:** college transcript(s), essay or personal statement, statement of good standing from prior institution(s). Minimum college GPA of 2.0 required. Lowest grade transferable C-. **General Admission Information:** Application fee $40. Priority deadline 3/1. Nonfall registration accepted. Admission may be deferred for a maximum of one semester.

COSTS AND FINANCIAL AID

Annual tuition $24,100. Room and board $8,560. Required fees $580. Average book expense $1,000. **Required Forms and Deadlines:** FAFSA. **Notification of Awards:** Applicants will be notified of awards on a rolling basis beginning 3/1. **Types of Aid:** *Need-based scholarships/grants:* College/university scholarship or grant aid from institutional funds; Federal Pell; Private scholarships; SEOG. *Loans:* Direct PLUS loans; Direct Subsidized Stafford Loans; Direct Unsubsidized Stafford Loans. *Student Employment:* Federal Work-Study Program available. Institutional employment available. **Financial Aid Statistics:** 89% needy freshmen, 98% needy undergrads receive need-based scholarship or grant aid. 12% freshmen, 4% undergrads receive non-need-based scholarship or grant aid. 90% freshmen, 97% undergrads receive need-based self-help aid. 10% freshmen, 4% undergrads receive athletic scholarships. 100% freshmen, 93% undergrads receive any aid. Average cumulative indebtedness $14,758. **Criteria for awarding aid:** *Need-based:* Minority status *Non-need-based:* Academics, Alumni affiliation, Athletics.

MURRAY STATE UNIVERSITY

102 Curris Center, Murray, KY 42071-0009
Phone: 270-809-3741 · **Financial Aid Phone:** (270) 809-2546
E-mail: msu.admissions@murraystate.edu · **CEEB Code:** 1494
Fax: 270-809-3780 · **Website:** www.murraystate.edu · **ACT Code:** 1532

This public school was founded in 1922. It has a 253 acre campus.

RATINGS

Admissions Selectivity Rating: 75   **Fire Safety Rating:** 94   **Green Rating:** 71

STUDENTS AND FACULTY

Enrollment: 7,290. **Student Body:** 58% female, 42% male, 33% out-of-state, 3% international (43 countries represented). Asian 1%, African American 6%, Caucasian 82%, Hispanic 2%, Native American <1%, Pacific Islander <1%, Two or more races 3%, Race unknown 2%.
Retention and Graduation: 75% freshmen return for sophomore year. 28% freshmen graduate within 4 years. 49% freshmen graduate within 6 years. **Faculty:** Student/faculty ratio 15:1. 455 full-time faculty, 75% hold PhDs, 17% are members of minority groups, 47% are women.

ACADEMICS

Degrees: Associate; Bachelor's; Certificate; Doctoral Other; Doctoral/Professional; Master's; Post-Bachelor's certificate; Post-Master's certificate **Classes:** Most classes have 10-19 students. Most lab/discussion sessions have fewer than 10 students. **Most popular majors:** Agriculture, Agriculture Operations, And Related Sciences, Other; Veterinary/Animal Health Technology/Technician And Veterinary Assistant; Registered Nursing/Registered Nurse. **Special Study Options:** Accelerated program; Cooperative education program; Cross-registration; Distance learning; Double major; Dual enrollment; English as a Second Language (ESL); Exchange student program (domestic); External degree program; Honors program; Independent study; Internships; Liberal arts/career combination; Student-designed major; Study abroad; Teacher certification program; Weekend college. **Honors programs:** Our undergraduate honors college has been designed to provide future social and professional leaders with exceptional thinking and communication skills, an appropriate breadth and depth of knowledge, and a sense of cultural and social responsibility. The Honors Sequence is a curriculum that includes dedicated Honors seminars, competency courses (language, math, and science), study abroad, and the Honors thesis. **Disability Services offered to physically disabled students:** Note-taking services; Reader services; Tape recorders; Tutors. **Career services:** Alumni network; Alumni services; Career assessment; Career/job search classes; Internships; Regional alumni

FACILITIES

Housing: Apartments for married students; Apartments for single students; Coed dorms; Special housing for disabled student; Women's dorms **Special Academic Facilities/Equipment:** Arboretum, Biological Research Station, Watershed Studies Institute, Mid-America Remote Sensing Center, Wrather Museum (museum and cultural events center), Lovett Auditorium and CFSB Center (used for musical and theater productions, concerts, and lectures), Price Doyle Fine Arts Center (for performances and exhibitions), State Farm Financial Services Center (applied learning for students in Finance and Economics), 4 agricultural research farms, Breathitt Veterinary Center (veterinary research center), Cherry Agricultural Exposition Center, use of federal Land Between the Lakes for research and field work, state center of excellence for telecommunications systems management **Computers:** 95% of classrooms, 90% of dorms, 100% of libraries, 100% of dining areas, 100% of student union, have wireless network access. Students can register for classes online. Administrative functions (other than registration) can be performed online.

CAMPUS LIFE

Environment: Village **Activities:** Campus Ministries; Choral groups; Concert band; Dance; Drama/theater; International Student Organization; Jazz band; Literary magazine; Marching band; Model UN; Music ensembles; Musical theater; Opera; Pep band; Radio station; Student government; Student newspaper; Student-run film society; Symphony orchestra; Television station 175 registered organizations, 30 honor societies, 15 religious organizations. 15 fraternities, 7 sororities. **Athletics (Intercollegiate):** *Men:* baseball, basketball, bowling, cheerleading, cross-country, equestrian sports, football, golf, horseback riding, riflery, rodeo, tennis. *Women:* basketball, cheerleading, cross-country, equestrian sports, golf, horseback riding, riflery, rodeo, soccer, softball, tennis, track/field (outdoor), volleyball. **On-Campus Highlights:** Susan E. Bauernfeind Student Recreation and Wellness Center, Curris Student Center, CFSB Center (Special Events and Basketball Arena), William B. Cherry Expo Center (Rodeos and other events), Lovett Auditorium (historic theater: concerts, plays, public speakers)

ADMISSIONS

Freshman Academic Profile: Average high school GPA 3.6. 25% in top 10% of high school class, 52% in top 25% of high school class, 80% in top 50% of high school class. **Test Scores:** SAT Math middle 50% range 518-593. SAT EBRW middle 50% range 478-560. ACT middle 50% range 21-27. Minimum internet-based TOEFL 71. Minimum paper TOEFL 527. **Basis for Candidate Selection:** *Very important factors considered include:* rigor of secondary school record, class rank, academic GPA, standardized test scores. **Freshman Admission Requirements:** High school diploma is required and GED is accepted *Academic units required:* 4 English, 3 math, 3 science, 1 science labs, 2 foreign language, 3 social studies, 3 history, 5 academic electives, and 1 unit from above areas or other academic areas. *Academic units recommended:* 4 math, 4 science, 1 computer science. **Freshman Admission Statistics:** 6,899 applied, 86.7% admitted, 24% enrolled. **Transfer Admission Requirements:** college transcript(s), statement of good standing from prior institution(s). Minimum college GPA of 2.0 required. Lowest grade transferable d. **General Admission Information:** Application fee $40. Nonfall registration accepted. Admission may be deferred for a maximum of 1 year.

COSTS AND FINANCIAL AID

Average book expense $1,265. **Required Forms and Deadlines:** FAFSA. **Notification of Awards:** Applicants will be notified of awards on a rolling basis beginning 12/15. **Types of Aid:** *Need-based scholarships/grants:* College/university scholarship or grant aid from institutional funds; Federal Pell; Private scholarships; SEOG; State scholarships/grants. *Loans:* Direct PLUS loans; Direct Subsidized Stafford Loans; Direct Unsubsidized Stafford Loans. *Student Employment:* Federal Work-Study Program available. Institutional employment available. **Financial Aid Statistics:** 92% needy freshmen, 86% needy undergrads receive need-based scholarship or grant aid. 10% freshmen, 7% undergrads receive non-need-based scholarship or grant aid. 69% freshmen, 78% undergrads receive need-based self-help aid. 3% freshmen, 3% undergrads receive athletic scholarships. 94% freshmen, 86% undergrads receive any aid. 50% undergrads borrow to pay for school. Average cumulative indebtedness $26,598. **Criteria for awarding aid:** *Need-based:* Academics, Alumni affiliation, Job skills, Minority status, Music/drama *Non-need-based:* Academics, Alumni affiliation, Art, Athletics, Job skills, Leadership, Minority status, Music/drama, State/district residency.

MUSKINGUM COLLEGE

163 Stormont Street, New Concord, OH 43762
Phone: 740-826-8137 · **Financial Aid Phone:** 740-826-8137
E-mail: ssoba@muskingum.edu · **CEEB Code:** 1496
Fax: 614-826-8100 · **ACT Code:** 3305

This private school, affiliated with the Presbyterian Church, was founded in 1837. It has a 245 acre campus.

RATINGS

Admissions Selectivity Rating: 77   **Fire Safety Rating:** 60*   **Green Rating:** 60*

STUDENTS AND FACULTY

Enrollment: 1,524. **Student Body:** 56% female, 44% male, 8% out-of-state, 4% international (9 countries represented). Asian 1%, African American 5%, Caucasian 79%, Hispanic 3%, Native American <1%, Pacific Islander 0%, Two or more races 4%, Race unknown 5%. **Retention and Graduation:** 74% freshmen return for sophomore year. 34% freshmen graduate within 4 years. 48% freshmen graduate within 6 years. 25% grads go on to further study within 1 year. 5% grads pursue arts and sciences degrees. 3% grads pursue law degrees. 4% grads pursue business degrees. 2% grads pursue medical degrees. **Faculty:** Student/faculty ratio 14:1. 95 full-time faculty, 93% hold PhDs, 12% are members of minority groups, 47% are women. 0% of classes are taught by teaching assistants.

ACADEMICS

Degrees: Bachelor's; Master's **Most popular majors:** Early Childhood Education And Teaching; Registered Nursing/Registered Nurse; Business Administration And Management, General. **Special Study Options:** Accelerated program; Distance learning; Double major; Dual enrollment; English as a Second Language (ESL); Exchange student program (domestic); Independent study; Internships; Liberal arts/career combination; Student-designed major; Study abroad; Teacher certification program; Weekend college. **Combined degree programs:** BA/MEng. **Disability Services offered to physically disabled students:** Note-taking services; Reader services; Tape recorders; Tutors. **Career services:** Alumni network; Alumni services; Career assessment; Internships; Regional alumni

FACILITIES

Housing: Apartments for single students; Coed dorms; Fraternity/sorority housing; Men's dorms; Theme housing; Women's dorms 50% of campus accessible to physically disabled. **Special Academic Facilities/Equipment:** Art gallery, on-campus nursery school, electron microscope, 57-acre biology field station and mobile biology lab. **Computers:** 15% of classrooms, 100% of libraries, 33% of dining areas, 100% of student union, 10% of common outdoor areas have wireless network access. Students can register for classes online. Administrative functions (other than registration) can be performed online.

CAMPUS LIFE

Environment: Rural **Activities:** Campus Ministries; Choral groups; Concert band; Dance; Drama/theater; International Student Organization; Jazz band; Literary magazine; Marching band; Model UN; Music ensembles; Musical theater; Pep band; Radio station; Student government; Student newspaper; Symphony orchestra; Television station 95 registered organizations, 16 honor societies, 4 religious organizations. 5 fraternities, 5 sororities. **Athletics (Intercollegiate):** *Men:* baseball, basketball, cheerleading, cross-country, football, golf, soccer, tennis, track/field (outdoor), track/field (indoor), wrestling. *Women:* basketball, cheerleading, cross-country, golf, soccer, softball, tennis, track/field (outdoor), track/field (indoor), volleyball. **On-Campus Highlights:** Philip and Betsey Caldwell Hall, Boyd Science Center, Rec Center, Otto and Fran Walter Hall, Walter K. Chess Student Center

ADMISSIONS

Freshman Academic Profile: Average high school GPA 3.2. 20% in top 10% of high school class, 40% in top 25% of high school class, 70% in top 50% of high school class. 92% from public high schools. **Test Scores:** SAT Math middle 50% range 460-530. SAT EBRW middle 50% range 463-578. ACT middle 50% range 18-24. Minimum internet-based TOEFL 79. Minimum paper TOEFL 550. **Basis for Candidate Selection:** *Very important factors considered include:* rigor of secondary school record, academic GPA. *Important factors considered include:* class rank, standardized test scores. *Other factors considered include:* application essay, recommendation(s), interview, extracurricular activities, talent/ability, character/personal qualities, alumni/ae relation, geographical residence, racial/ethnic status, work experience. **Freshman Admission Requirements:** High school diploma is required and GED is accepted *Academic units required:* 4 English, 2 math, 2 science, 1 science labs, 2 foreign language, 2 social studies, *Academic units recommended:* 4 English, 3 math, 3 science, 2 science labs, 2 foreign language, 3 social studies. **Freshman**

Admission Statistics: 1,850 applied, 74.4% admitted, 28% enrolled. **Transfer Admission Requirements:** High school transcript, college transcript(s), Minimum college GPA of 2.0 required. Lowest grade transferable C. **General Admission Information:** Priority deadline 3/1. Regular application deadline 8/1. Nonfall registration accepted. Admission may be deferred for a maximum of 1 year.

COSTS AND FINANCIAL AID

Annual tuition $26,900. Room and board $11,040. Required fees $912. Average book expense $1,100. **Required Forms and Deadlines:** FAFSA. **Notification of Awards:** Applicants will be notified of awards on a rolling basis beginning 12/15. **Types of Aid:** *Need-based scholarships/grants:* College/university scholarship or grant aid from institutional funds; Federal Pell; Private scholarships; SEOG; State scholarships/grants. *Loans:* Direct PLUS loans; Direct Subsidized Stafford Loans; Direct Unsubsidized Stafford Loans. *Student Employment:* Federal Work-Study Program available. Institutional employment available. **Financial Aid Statistics:** 100% needy freshmen, 99% needy undergrads receive need-based scholarship or grant aid. 89% freshmen, 88% undergrads receive non-need-based scholarship or grant aid. 91% freshmen, 88% undergrads receive need-based self-help aid. 0% freshmen, 0% undergrads receive athletic scholarships. 98% freshmen, 98% undergrads receive any aid. 81% undergrads borrow to pay for school. Average cumulative indebtedness $36,062. **Criteria for awarding aid:** *Need-based:* Academics, Leadership, Minority status *Non-need-based:* Academics, Alumni affiliation, Art, Leadership, Minority status, Music/drama, Religious affiliation, State/district residency.

NAROPA UNIVERSITY

219 Student Union, Boulder, CO 80302
Phone: 303-546-3572 • **Financial Aid Phone:** (303) 546-3534
E-mail: admissions@naropa.edu • **CEEB Code:** 908
Fax: 303-546-3583 • **Website:** www.naropa.edu/ • **ACT Code:** 4853

This private school was founded in 1974. It has a 12 acre campus.

RATINGS

Admissions Selectivity Rating: 66   **Fire Safety Rating:** 61   **Green Rating:** 60*

STUDENTS AND FACULTY

Enrollment: 464. **Student Body:** 61% female, 39% male, 74% out-of-state, 3% international (24 countries represented). Asian 3%, African American 2%, Caucasian 75%, Hispanic 4%, Native American 3%, Race unknown 11%. **Retention and Graduation:** 64% freshmen return for sophomore year. **Faculty:** Student/faculty ratio 9:1. 51 full-time faculty, 51% hold PhDs, 12% are members of minority groups, 57% are women. 0% of classes are taught by teaching assistants.

ACADEMICS

Degrees: Bachelor's; Certificate; **Master's Classes:** Most classes have 10-19 students. **Most popular majors:** English Language And Literature, General; Psychology, General; Visual And Performing Arts, General. **Special Study Options:** Double major; Independent study; Internships; Student-designed major; Study abroad. **Disability Services offered to physically disabled students:** Note-taking services; Reader services; Tape recorders; Tutors.

FACILITIES

Housing: Apartments for married students; Apartments for single students; Other (please specify) 85% of campus accessible to physically disabled. **Special Academic Facilities/Equipment:** Maitri Rooms, meditation halls, Allen Ginsberg library and a preschool **Computers:** 100% of classrooms, 100% of dorms, 100% of libraries, 100% of dining areas, 100% of student union, 100% of common outdoor areas have wireless network access. Students can register for classes online. Administrative functions (other than registration) can be performed online.

CAMPUS LIFE

Environment: City **Activities:** Choral groups; Dance; Drama/theater; Jazz band; Literary magazine; Music ensembles; Student government 20 registered organizations, 2 religious organizations. **On-Campus Highlights:** Lincoln Building, Nalanda Event Center, Meditation Hall, Naropa Cafe, Visual Arts Studio **Environmental Initiatives:** We compost all of our paper towels in public restrooms diverting 25% of our landfill waste into compost.

ADMISSIONS

Freshman Academic Profile: Average high school GPA 3.0. **Test Scores:** Minimum paper TOEFL 550. **Basis for Candidate Selection:** *Very important factors considered include:* rigor of secondary school record, academic GPA, application essay, recommendation(s), interview. *Important factors considered*

include: extracurricular activities, talent/ability, character/personal qualities, volunteer work. *Other factors considered include:* first generation, alumni/ae relation, racial/ethnic status, work experience. **Freshman Admission Requirements:** High school diploma is required and GED is accepted *Academic units recommended:* 4 English, 3 math, 3 science, 2 science labs, 3 foreign language, 3 social studies, 3 history, 2 academic electives, 2 units from above areas or other academic areas. **Freshman Admission Statistics:** 139 applied, 92.8% admitted, 53% enrolled. **Transfer Admission Requirements:** college transcript(s), essay or personal statement, interview, Lowest grade transferable C. **General Admission Information:** Application fee $50. Priority deadline 1/15. Nonfall registration accepted. Admission may be deferred for a maximum of 1 year.

COSTS AND FINANCIAL AID

Annual tuition $23,420. Room and board $8,478. Required fees $100. Average book expense $1,200. **Required Forms and Deadlines:** FAFSA. **Notification of Awards:** Applicants will be notified of awards on a rolling basis beginning 3/1. **Types of Aid:** *Need-based scholarships/grants:* College/university scholarship or grant aid from institutional funds; Federal Pell; Private scholarships; SEOG. *Student Employment:* Federal Work-Study Program available. **Financial Aid Statistics:** 87% needy freshmen, 88% needy undergrads receive need-based scholarship or grant aid. 0% undergrads receive non-need-based scholarship or grant aid. 94% freshmen, 91% undergrads receive need-based self-help aid. 0% freshmen, 0% undergrads receive athletic scholarships. 71% freshmen, 71% undergrads receive any aid. **Criteria for awarding aid:** *Need-based:* Academics, Job skills, Leadership, Minority status, Music/drama, Religious affiliation.

NATIONAL UNIVERSITY OF HEALTH SCIENCES

200 E. Roosevelt Road, Lombard, IL 60148
Phone: 630-889-6566 • **Financial Aid Phone:** 630-889-6700
E-mail: admissions@nuhs.edu
Fax: 630-889-6554 • **Website:** www.nuhs.edu

This private school was founded in 1906. It has a 32 acre campus.

RATINGS

Admissions Selectivity Rating: 63   **Fire Safety Rating:** 60*   **Green Rating:** 60*

STUDENTS AND FACULTY

Enrollment: 74. **Student Body:** 16% female, 84% male, 70% out-of-state, 4% international (9 countries represented). Asian 5%, African American 16%, Caucasian 63%, Hispanic 5%, Native American 0%, Race unknown 7%. **Retention and Graduation:** 90% freshmen return for sophomore year. **Faculty:** Student/faculty ratio 6:1. 46 full-time faculty, 93% hold PhDs, 17% are women.

ACADEMICS

Degrees: Bachelor's; Certificate; Doctoral/Professional; **Master's Classes:** Most classes have 10-19 students. Most lab/discussion sessions have 30-39 students. **Most popular majors:** Biomedical Sciences, General; Massage Therapy/Therapeutic Massage. **Special Study Options:** Internships.

FACILITIES

Housing: Apartments for married students; Apartments for single students; Coed dorms; Men's dorms; Women's dorms **Special Academic Facilities/Equipment:** Museum Fitness Center Learning Resource Center Health Care Clinic **Computers:** 88% of classrooms, 100% of libraries, 100% of common outdoor areas have wireless network access. Students can register for classes online.

CAMPUS LIFE

Environment: Town **Activities:** Student government; Student newspaper; Yearbook 24 registered organizations, 1 religious organization. 2 fraternities, 1 sorority. **On-Campus Highlights:** Janse Hall, Student Center, Clinic, Learning Resource Center, Dormitories

ADMISSIONS

Test Scores: Minimum internet-based TOEFL 79. Minimum paper TOEFL 550. **Freshman Admission Requirements:** High school diploma is required and GED is accepted **Transfer Admission Requirements:** college transcript(s), statement of good standing from prior institution(s). Minimum college GPA of 2.5 required. Lowest grade transferable C. **General Admission Information:** Application fee $55. Nonfall registration accepted. Admission may be deferred.

444   *The Princeton Review's* Complete Book of Colleges

COSTS AND FINANCIAL AID

Types of Aid: *Need-based scholarships/grants:* College/university scholarship or grant aid from institutional funds; Federal Pell; Private scholarships; SEOG; State scholarships/grants. *Student Employment:* Federal Work-Study Program available. Institutional employment available. **Financial Aid Statistics:** 62% needy undergrads receive need-based scholarship or grant aid. 10% undergrads receive non-need-based scholarship or grant aid. 62% undergrads receive need-based self-help aid.

NAZARETH COLLEGE

4245 East Avenue, Rochester, NY 14618-3790
Phone: 585-389-2860 • **Financial Aid Phone:** 585-389-2310
E-mail: admissions@naz.edu • **CEEB Code:** 2511
Fax: 585-389-2826 • **Website:** www.naz.edu • **ACT Code:** 2826

This private school was founded in 1924. It has a 150 acre campus.

RATINGS

Admissions Selectivity Rating: 83   **Fire Safety Rating:** 93   **Green Rating:** 73

STUDENTS AND FACULTY

Enrollment: 2,175. **Student Body:** 74% female, 26% male, 10% out-of-state, 1% international (34 countries represented). Asian 3%, African American 6%, Caucasian 79%, Hispanic 6%, Native American <1%, Pacific Islander <1%, Two or more races 2%, Race unknown 3%.
Retention and Graduation: 79% freshmen return for sophomore year. 56% freshmen graduate within 4 years. 1% freshmen graduate within 6 years. **Faculty:** Student/faculty ratio 9:1. 175 full-time faculty, 81% hold PhDs, 14% are members of minority groups, 63% are women. 0% of classes are taught by teaching assistants.

ACADEMICS

Degrees: Bachelor's; Doctoral/Professional; **Master's Classes:** Most classes have 20-29 students. Most lab/discussion sessions have 10-19 students. **Most popular majors:** Education, General; Physical Therapy/Therapist; Business Administration, Management And Operations, Other. **Special Study Options:** Accelerated program; Cross-registration; Distance learning; Double major; Dual enrollment; English as a Second Language (ESL); Exchange student program (domestic); Honors program; Independent study; Internships; Liberal arts/career combination; Study abroad; Teacher certification program. **Disability Services offered to physically disabled students:** Note-taking services; Reader services; Tape recorders; Tutors. **Career services:** Alumni network; Alumni services; Career assessment; Career/job search classes; Internships; Regional alumni

FACILITIES

Housing: Apartments for single students; Coed dorms; Other (please specify) 80% of campus accessible to physically diasbled. **Special Academic Facilities/Equipment:** Arts Center, speech/hearing/language clinics, reading clinic, psychology center, Center for Civic Engagement, Center for Service Learning, Center for Teaching Excellence, Center for Spirituality, and Center for International Education. **Computers:** Students can register for classes online.

CAMPUS LIFE

Environment: Village **Activities:** Campus Ministries; Choral groups; Concert band; Dance; Drama/theater; International Student Organization; Jazz band; Literary magazine; Music ensembles; Musical theater; Opera; Pep band; Radio station; Student government; Student newspaper; Symphony orchestra; Yearbook 50 registered organizations, 19 honor societies, 5 religious organizations. **Athletics (Intercollegiate):** *Men:* basketball, cross-country, diving, equestrian sports, golf, lacrosse, soccer, swimming, tennis, track/field (outdoor), track/field (indoor), volleyball. *Women:* basketball, cross-country, diving, equestrian sports, field hockey, golf, lacrosse, soccer, softball, swimming, tennis, track/field (outdoor), track/field (indoor), volleyball. **On-Campus Highlights:** Nazareth College Arts Center, York Wellness Rehabilitation Center, Shults Community Center, Peckham Hall, Library

ADMISSIONS

Freshman Academic Profile: Average high school GPA 90.1. 26% in top 10% of high school class, 60% in top 25% of high school class, 89% in top 50% of high school class. 90% from public high schools. **Test Scores:** SAT Math middle 50% range 530-620. SAT EBRW middle 50% range 540-630. ACT

middle 50% range 22-27. Minimum internet-based TOEFL 79. Minimum paper TOEFL 550. **Basis for Candidate Selection:** *Very important factors considered include:* rigor of secondary school record, class rank, academic GPA, application essay, recommendation(s). *Important factors considered include:* interview, extracurricular activities, talent/ability, character/personal qualities, geographical residence, state residency, racial/ethnic status, volunteer work, work experience, level of applicant's interest. *Other factors considered include:* standardized test scores, first generation, alumni/ae relation. **Freshman Admission Requirements:** High school diploma is required and GED is accepted *Academic units required:* 3 English, 3 math, 3 science, 3 foreign language, 3 social studies, *Academic units recommended:* 4 English, 4 math, 4 science, 4 foreign language, 4 social studies. **Freshman Admission Statistics:** 4,494 applied, 62.6% admitted, 20% enrolled. **Transfer Admission Requirements:** college transcript(s), essay or personal statement, Minimum college GPA of 2.5 required. Lowest grade transferable C. **General Admission Information:** Application fee $45. Priority deadline 12/1. Regular application deadline 2/1. Nonfall registration accepted. Admission may be deferred for a maximum of 1 year.

COSTS AND FINANCIAL AID

Required Forms and Deadlines: FAFSA; State aid form. **Notification of Awards:** Applicants will be notified of awards on a rolling basis beginning 2/1. **Types of Aid:** *Need-based scholarships/grants:* College/university scholarship or grant aid from institutional funds; Federal Pell; Private scholarships; SEOG; State scholarships/grants. *Loans:* Direct PLUS loans; Direct Subsidized Stafford Loans; Direct Unsubsidized Stafford Loans. *Student Employment:* Federal Work-Study Program available. Institutional employment available. **Financial Aid Statistics:** 100% needy freshmen, 100% needy undergrads receive need-based scholarship or grant aid. 49% freshmen, 35% undergrads receive non-need-based scholarship or grant aid. 95% freshmen, 94% undergrads receive need-based self-help aid. 0% freshmen, 0% undergrads receive athletic scholarships. Average cumulative indebtedness $40,567. **Criteria for awarding aid:** *Need-based:* Alumni affiliation *Non-need-based:* Academics, Art, Minority status, Music/drama.

See page 990.

NEBRASKA METHODIST COLLEGE

105 Sikes Hall, Omaha, NE 68114
Phone: 402-354-7200 • **Financial Aid Phone:** 402-354-7225
E-mail: admissions@methodistcollege.edu • **CEEB Code:** 6510
Fax: 402-354-7020 • **ACT Code:** 2465

This private school, affiliated with the Methodist Church, was founded in 1891. It has a 6 acre campus.

RATINGS

Admissions Selectivity Rating: 84   **Fire Safety Rating:** 68   **Green Rating:** 60*

STUDENTS AND FACULTY

Enrollment: 504. **Student Body:** 92% female, 8% male, 35% out-of-state, 0% international (3 countries represented). Asian 3%, African American 3%, Caucasian 87%, Hispanic 1%, Native American 1%, Race unknown 5%.
Retention and Graduation: 81% freshmen return for sophomore year. 10% grads go on to further study within 1 year. 10% grads pursue arts and sciences degrees. **Faculty:** Student/faculty ratio 10:1. 43 full-time faculty, 28% hold PhDs, 7% are members of minority groups, 91% are women. 0% of classes are taught by teaching assistants.

ACADEMICS

Degrees: Associate; Bachelor's; Certificate; Master's; Post-Master's certificate **Classes:** Most classes have fewer than 10 students. Most lab/discussion sessions have fewer than 10 students. **Most popular majors:** Diagnostic Medical Sonography/Sonographer And Ultrasound Technician; Radiologic Technology/Science, Radiographer; Nursing/Registered Nurse (Rn, Asn, Bsn, Msn). **Special Study Options:** Accelerated program; Distance learning; Independent study. **Disability Services offered to physically disabled students:** Note-taking services; Reader services; Tape recorders; Tutors. **Career services:** Alumni network; Alumni services; Career/job search classes

FACILITIES

Housing: Apartments for single students 90% of campus accessible to physically diasbled. **Computers:** 100% of classrooms, 100% of libraries, 100% of dining areas, 100% of student union, have wireless network access. Students can register for classes online. Administrative functions (other than registration) can be performed online.

CAMPUS LIFE

Environment: City **Activities:** Student government 11 registered organizations, 2 honor societies. **On-Campus Highlights:** Student Center, Library, Human Cadaver Lab, Chapel

ADMISSIONS

Freshman Academic Profile: Average high school GPA 3.3. 11% in top 10% of high school class, 11% in top 25% of high school class, 50% in top 50% of high school class. 90% from public high schools. **Test Scores:** ACT middle 50% range 19-23. Minimum internet-based TOEFL 80. Minimum paper TOEFL 550. **Basis for Candidate Selection:** *Very important factors considered include:* rigor of secondary school record, academic GPA, standardized test scores. *Important factors considered include:* class rank, application essay, recommendation(s), interview, character/personal qualities. *Other factors considered include:* first generation, alumni/ae relation, geographical residence, state residency, racial/ethnic status, volunteer work, work experience, level of applicant's interest. **Freshman Admission Requirements:** High school diploma is required and GED is accepted *Academic units required:* 4 English, 3 math, 2 science, 2 science labs, 2 social studies. **Freshman Admission Statistics:** 64 applied, 60.9% admitted, 59% enrolled. **Transfer Admission Requirements:** High school transcript, college transcript(s), essay or personal statement, interview, statement of good standing from prior institution(s). Minimum college GPA of 2.5 required. Lowest grade transferable C. **General Admission Information:** Application fee $25. Priority deadline 1/1. Regular application deadline 3/1. Nonfall registration accepted. Admission may be deferred for a maximum of 1 year.

COSTS AND FINANCIAL AID

Annual tuition $12,840. Required fees $600. Average book expense $1,300. **Required Forms and Deadlines:** FAFSA; Institution's own financial aid form. **Notification of Awards:** Applicants will be notified of awards on a rolling basis beginning 3/1. **Types of Aid:** *Need-based scholarships/grants:* College/university scholarship or grant aid from institutional funds; Federal Pell; Private scholarships; SEOG; State scholarships/grants. *Loans: Student Employment:* Federal Work-Study Program available. Institutional employment available. **Financial Aid Statistics:** 38% needy freshmen, 51% needy undergrads receive need-based scholarship or grant aid. 8% freshmen, 7% undergrads receive non-need-based scholarship or grant aid. 92% freshmen, 89% undergrads receive need-based self-help aid. 0% freshmen, 0% undergrads receive athletic scholarships. 85% freshmen, 69% undergrads receive any aid. **Criteria for awarding aid:** *Need-based:* Minority status *Non-need-based:* Academics, Minority status, Religious affiliation.

NEBRASKA WESLEYAN UNIVERSITY

5000 Saint Paul Avenue, Lincoln, NE 68504
Phone: 402-465-2218 • **Financial Aid Phone:** 402-465-2212
E-mail: admissions@nebrwesleyan.edu • **CEEB Code:** 6470
Fax: 402-465-2177 • **Website:** http://www.nebrwesleyan.edu • **ACT Code:** 2474

This private school, affiliated with the Methodist Church, was founded in 1887. It has a 50 acre campus.

RATINGS

Admissions Selectivity Rating: 78   **Fire Safety Rating:** 83   **Green Rating:** 60*

STUDENTS AND FACULTY

Enrollment: 1,788. **Student Body:** 61% female, 39% male, 13% out-of-state, 1% international (20 countries represented). Asian 2%, African American 2%, Caucasian 84%, Hispanic 5%, Native American <1%, Pacific Islander <1%, Two or more races 2%, Race unknown 3%.
Retention and Graduation: 79% freshmen return for sophomore year. **Faculty:** Student/faculty ratio 12:1. 106 full-time faculty, 92% hold PhDs, 2% are members of minority groups, 54% are women. 0% of classes are taught by teaching assistants.

ACADEMICS

Degrees: Bachelor's; Certificate; Master's; Post-Bachelor's certificate; Post-Master's certificate **Classes:** Most classes have 20-29 students. **Most popular majors:** Biology/Biological Sciences, General; Psychology, General; Business Administration And Management, General. **Special Study Options:** Double major; Dual enrollment; Independent study; Internships; Liberal arts/career combination; Student-designed major; Study abroad; Teacher certification program; Weekend college. **Disability Services offered to physically disabled students:** Note-taking services; Reader services; Tape recorders; Tutors. **Career services:** Alumni network; Alumni services; Career assessment; Career/job search classes; Internships; Regional alumni

FACILITIES

Housing: Apartments for single students; Coed dorms; Fraternity/sorority housing; Special housing for disabled student; Theme housing; Women's dorms **Special Academic Facilities/Equipment:** Art galleries, observatory and planetarium, green house, laboratory theatre, herbarium, nuclear magnetic resonance laboratory **Computers:** Students can register for classes online. Administrative functions (other than registration) can be performed online.

CAMPUS LIFE

Environment: City **Activities:** Campus Ministries; Choral groups; Concert band; Dance; Drama/theater; International Student Organization; Jazz band; Literary magazine; Marching band; Model UN; Music ensembles; Musical theater; Opera; Pep band; Radio station; Student government; Student newspaper; Symphony orchestra 80 registered organizations, 18 honor societies, 5 religious organizations. 3 fraternities, 4 sororities. **Athletics (Intercollegiate):** *Men:* baseball, basketball, cross-country, football, golf, soccer, tennis, track/field (outdoor), track/field (indoor). *Women:* basketball, cross-country, golf, soccer, softball, tennis, track/field (outdoor), track/field (indoor), volleyball. **On-Campus Highlights:** Weary Center for Health and Fitness, Wesleyan Coffee House, Old Main, Roy G Story Student Center, Great Hall, Smith-Curtis **Environmental Initiatives:** Completed light inventory; retrofitted 80% of all lights.

ADMISSIONS

Freshman Academic Profile: Average high school GPA 3.6. 18% in top 10% of high school class, 50% in top 25% of high school class, 84% in top 50% of high school class. **Test Scores:** SAT Math middle 50% range 510-600. SAT EBRW middle 50% range 430-590. ACT middle 50% range 22-27. Minimum internet-based TOEFL 71. Minimum paper TOEFL 525. **Basis for Candidate Selection:** *Very important factors considered include:* academic GPA, standardized test scores. *Important factors considered include:* rigor of secondary school record, class rank, extracurricular activities, talent/ability, character/personal qualities. *Other factors considered include:* application essay, recommendation(s), interview, first generation, alumni/ae relation, geographical residence, state residency, racial/ethnic status, volunteer work, level of applicant's interest. **Freshman Admission Requirements:** High school diploma is required and GED is accepted *Academic units recommended:* 4 English, 4 math, 3 science, 3 science labs, 3 foreign language, 3 social studies. **Freshman Admission Statistics:** 1,689 applied, 78.8% admitted, 33% enrolled. **Transfer Admission Requirements:** college transcript(s), statement of good standing from prior institution(s). Minimum college GPA of 2.0 required. Lowest grade transferable C-. **General Admission Information:** Priority deadline 5/1. Regular application deadline 8/15. Nonfall registration accepted. Admission may be deferred for a maximum of 1 year.

COSTS AND FINANCIAL AID

Annual tuition $29,200. Room and board $8,340. Required fees $600. Average book expense $1,000. **Required Forms and Deadlines:** FAFSA. **Notification of Awards:** Applicants will be notified of awards on a rolling basis beginning 2/1. **Types of Aid:** *Need-based scholarships/grants:* College/university scholarship or grant aid from institutional funds; Federal Pell; Private scholarships; SEOG; State scholarships/grants. *Loans:* Direct PLUS loans; Direct Subsidized Stafford Loans; Direct Unsubsidized Stafford Loans. *Student Employment:* Federal Work-Study Program available. Institutional employment available. **Financial Aid Statistics:** 99% needy freshmen, 98% needy undergrads receive need-based scholarship or grant aid. 19% freshmen, 12% undergrads receive non-need-based scholarship or grant aid. 76% freshmen, 83% undergrads receive need-based self-help aid. 0% freshmen, 0% undergrads receive athletic scholarships. 99% freshmen, 96% undergrads receive any aid. 78% undergrads borrow to pay for school. Average cumulative indebtedness $29,136. **Criteria for awarding aid:** *Need-based:* Academics, Leadership, Minority status, Religious affiliation *Non-need-based:* Academics, Alumni affiliation, Art, Leadership, Music/drama.

NEUMANN UNIVERSITY

One Neumann Drive, Aston, PA 19014-1298
Phone: 610-558-5616 • **Financial Aid Phone:** 610-558-5521
E-mail: neumann@neumann.edu • **CEEB Code:** 2628
Fax: 610-361-2548 • **Website:** www.neumann.edu • **ACT Code:** 3649

This private school, affiliated with the Roman Catholic Church, was founded in 1965. It has a 68 acre campus.

RATINGS

Admissions Selectivity Rating: 71   **Fire Safety Rating:** 95   **Green Rating:** 63

STUDENTS AND FACULTY

Enrollment: 1,997. **Student Body:** 66% female, 34% male, 31% out-of-state, 1% international (9 countries represented). Asian 1%, African American 24%, Caucasian 53%, Hispanic 6%, Native American <1%, Pacific Islander <1%, Two or more races 2%, Race unknown 12%.

Retention and Graduation: 77% freshmen return for sophomore year. 38% freshmen graduate within 4 years. 57% freshmen graduate within 6 years. **Faculty:** Student/faculty ratio 15:1. 96 full-time faculty, 80% hold PhDs, 61% are women. 0% of classes are taught by teaching assistants.

ACADEMICS

Degrees: Associate; Bachelor's; Doctoral; Doctoral/Professional; Doctoral/Research; Master's; Post-Bachelor's certificate; Post-Master's certificate **Classes:** Most classes have 10-19 students. Most lab/discussion sessions have 10-19 students. **Most popular majors:** Elementary Education And Teaching; Liberal Arts And Sciences/Liberal Studies; Registered Nursing, Nursing Administration, Nursing Research And Clinical Nursing, Other. **Special Study Options:** Accelerated program; Cooperative education program; Cross-registration; Distance learning; Double major; Dual enrollment; Honors program; Independent study; Internships; Liberal arts/career combination; Study abroad; Teacher certification program. Honors programs: The Neumann University Honors Program is based upon the belief that students who have demonstrated the motivation for learning, a desire to excel, and the capability for leadership should have the opportunity to further develop these abilities. The Honors Program is a two-tiered program consisting of a Freshman Honors Program and a University Honors Program for sophomores, juniors, and seniors. Students who complete the University Honors Program will receive a Certificate of Completion and medallion at the Academic Awards Convocation, and recognition in the Commencement Program. **Disability Services offered to physically disabled students:** Note-taking services; Reader services; Tape recorders; Tutors. **Career services:** Alumni network; Alumni services; Career assessment; Career/job search classes; Internships

FACILITIES

Housing: Apartments for single students; Coed dorms; Special housing for disabled students 100% of campus accessible to physically disabled. **Special Academic Facilities/Equipment:** The Mirenda Center for Sport, Spirituality and Character Development; the Neumann Institute for Franciscan Studies; The Institute for Sport, Spirituality and Character Development; and the John J. Mullen Communication Center **Computers:** 100% of classrooms, 100% of libraries, have wireless network access. Administrative functions (other than registration) can be performed online.

CAMPUS LIFE

Environment: Metropolis **Activities:** Campus Ministries; Choral groups; Dance; Drama/theater; Jazz band; Literary magazine; Music ensembles; Musical theater; Pep band; Radio station; Student government; Student newspaper; Symphony orchestra; Television station 14 registered organizations, 4 honor societies, 2 religious organizations. **Athletics (Intercollegiate):** *Men:* baseball, basketball, cross-country, golf, ice hockey, lacrosse, soccer, tennis. *Women:* basketball, cross-country, field hockey, ice hockey, lacrosse, soccer, softball, tennis, volleyball. **On-Campus Highlights:** Neumann Media Radio Station, Knight's Cafe, Library, Mirenda Center, Residence Halls

ADMISSIONS

Freshman Academic Profile: Average high school GPA 3.1. 73% from public high schools. **Test Scores:** SAT Math middle 50% range 440-530. SAT EBRW middle 50% range 450-550. ACT middle 50% range 15-20. Minimum internet-based TOEFL 70. Minimum paper TOEFL 550. **Basis for Candidate Selection:** *Very important factors considered include:* rigor of secondary school record, academic GPA, standardized test scores. *Important factors considered include:* interview. *Other factors considered include:* application essay, recommendation(s), extracurricular activities, talent/ability, character/personal qualities, first generation, alumni/ae relation, volunteer work, work experience, level of applicant's interest. **Freshman Admission Requirements:** High school diploma is required and GED is accepted *Academic units required:* 4 English, 2 math, 2 science, 2 foreign language, 2 social studies, 4 academic electives, *Academic units recommended:* 4 English, 2 math, 3 science, 2 science labs, 2 foreign language, 2 social studies, 4 academic electives. **Freshman Admission Statistics:** 1,505 applied, 96.3% admitted, 25% enrolled. **Transfer Admission Requirements:** college transcript(s), Minimum college GPA of 2.0 required. Lowest grade transferable C. **General Admission Information:** Application fee $35. Nonfall registration accepted. Admission may be deferred for a maximum of 2 semesters.

COSTS AND FINANCIAL AID

Annual tuition $28,710. Room and board $12,520. Required fees $1,340. Average book expense $1,488. **Required Forms and Deadlines:** FAFSA; State aid form. **Notification of Awards:** Applicants will be notified of awards on a rolling basis beginning 3/1. **Types of Aid:** *Need-based scholarships/grants:* College/university scholarship or grant aid from institutional funds; Federal Pell; Private scholarships; SEOG; State scholarships/grants. *Loans:*

Direct PLUS loans; Direct Subsidized Stafford Loans; Direct Unsubsidized Stafford Loans. *Student Employment:* Federal Work-Study Program available. **Financial Aid Statistics:** 88% needy freshmen, 83% needy undergrads receive need-based scholarship or grant aid. 100% freshmen, 96% undergrads receive non-need-based scholarship or grant aid. 91% freshmen, 94% undergrads receive need-based self-help aid. 0% freshmen, 0% undergrads receive athletic scholarships. 100% freshmen, 100% undergrads receive any aid. **Criteria for awarding aid:** *Need-based:* Academics *Non-need-based:* Academics.

NEUMONT UNIVERSITY

143 South Main Street, Salt Lake City, UT 84111
Phone: 888-638-6668 · **Financial Aid Phone:** 801 302 2873
E-mail: admissions@neumont.edu
Fax: 801-302-2811 • **Website:** www.neumont.edu

This proprietary school was founded in 2003.

RATINGS

Admissions Selectivity Rating: 75   **Fire Safety Rating:** 60*   **Green Rating:** 60*

STUDENTS AND FACULTY

Enrollment: 429. **Student Body:** 10% female, 90% male, 88% out-of-state, 0% international. Asian 3%, African American 5%, Caucasian 49%, Hispanic 10%, Native American 1%, Pacific Islander <1%, Two or more races 6%, Race unknown 25%.

Retention and Graduation: 85% freshmen return for sophomore year. **Faculty:** Student/faculty ratio 21:1. 15 full-time faculty, 13% hold PhDs, 7% are members of minority groups, 0% are women.

ACADEMICS

Degrees: Bachelor's; **Master's Classes:** Most classes have 10-19 students. Most lab/discussion sessions have 10-19 students. **Special Study Options:** Accelerated program; Cooperative education program; Internships. **Disability Services offered to physically disabled students:** Note-taking services; Reader services; Tape recorders; Tutors. **Career services:** Alumni network; Career assessment; Career/job search classes; Internships

FACILITIES

Housing: Apartments for single students; Men's dorms; Women's dorms 100% of campus accessible to physically disabled. **Computers:** 100% of classrooms, 100% of libraries, 100% of dining areas, 100% of student union, have wireless network access. Students can register for classes online. Undergraduates are required to own a computer.

CAMPUS LIFE

Environment: Metropolis **Activities:** Student government 8 registered organizations.

ADMISSIONS

Freshman Academic Profile: Average high school GPA 3.2. **Test Scores:** SAT Math middle 50% range 455-640. SAT EBRW middle 50% range 445-615. ACT middle 50% range 20-29. Minimum paper TOEFL 79. **Basis for Candidate Selection:** *Very important factors considered include:* academic GPA, application essay, standardized test scores. *Important factors considered include:* interview, extracurricular activities, talent/ability, character/personal qualities, volunteer work, work experience, level of applicant's interest. *Other factors considered include:* rigor of secondary school record, class rank, recommendation(s). **Freshman Admission Requirements:** High school diploma is required and GED is accepted **Freshman Admission Statistics:** 727 applied, 82.9% admitted, 28% enrolled. **General Admission Information:** Application fee $35. Nonfall registration accepted. Admission may be deferred for a maximum of 1 year.

COSTS AND FINANCIAL AID

Annual tuition $22,950. Required fees $1,500. Average book expense $1,200. **Required Forms and Deadlines:** FAFSA; Institution's own financial aid form. **Notification of Awards:** Applicants will be notified of awards on a rolling basis beginning 11/23. **Types of Aid:** *Need-based scholarships/grants:* College/university scholarship or grant aid from institutional funds; Federal Pell; Private scholarships; SEOG. *Loans:* Direct PLUS loans; Direct Subsidized Stafford Loans; Direct Unsubsidized Stafford Loans. **Financial Aid Statistics:** 96% needy freshmen, 88% needy undergrads receive need-based scholarship or grant aid. 79% freshmen, 57% undergrads receive non-need-based scholarship or grant aid. 0% freshmen, 0% undergrads receive need-based self-help aid. 0% freshmen, 0% undergrads receive athletic scholarships. 91% undergrads borrow to pay for school. Average cumulative indebtedness $39,623. **Criteria for awarding aid:** *Need-based:* Academics *Non-need-based:* Academics, Job skills, Leadership, State/district residency.

NEW COLLEGE OF FLORIDA

5800 Bay Shore Rd, Sarasota, FL 34243-2109
Phone: 941-487-5000 • **Financial Aid Phone:** 941-487-5000
E-mail: admissions@ncf.edu • **CEEB Code:** 39574
Fax: 941-487-5001 • **Website:** www.ncf.edu • **ACT Code:** 750

This public school was founded in 1960. It has a 118.6 acre campus.

RATINGS
Admissions Selectivity Rating: 87   **Fire Safety Rating:** 91   **Green Rating:** 71

STUDENTS AND FACULTY
Enrollment: 835. **Student Body:** 63% female, 37% male, 18% out-of-state, 2% international (20 countries represented). Asian 3%, African American 3%, Caucasian 69%, Hispanic 18%, Native American 0%, Pacific Islander 0%, Two or more races 3%, Race unknown 2%.
Retention and Graduation: 79% freshmen return for sophomore year. 57% freshmen graduate within 4 years. 65% freshmen graduate within 6 years. 29% grads go on to further study within 1 year. 17% grads pursue arts and sciences degrees. 3% grads pursue law degrees. 0% grads pursue business degrees. 5% grads pursue medical degrees. **Faculty:** Student/faculty ratio 10:1. 79 full-time faculty, 97% hold PhDs, 15% are members of minority groups, 57% are women. 0% of classes are taught by teaching assistants.

ACADEMICS
Degrees: Bachelor's; **Master's Classes:** Most classes have 10-19 students. Most lab/discussion sessions have fewer than 10 students. **Most popular majors:** Biology/Biological Sciences, General; Chemistry, General; Psychology, General. **Special Study Options:** Accelerated program; Cross-registration; Double major; Exchange student program (domestic); Honors program; Independent study; Internships; Student-designed major; Study abroad. Honors programs: New College of Florida is the state's officially-designated "honors college for the liberal arts." **Disability Services offered to physically disabled students:** Note-taking services; Reader services; Tape recorders. **Career services:** Alumni network; Alumni services; Career assessment; Career/job search classes; Internships; Regional alumni

FACILITIES
Housing: Apartments for single students; Coed dorms; Special housing for disabled student; Special housing for international students; Theme housing; Wellness housing 80% of campus accessible to physically diasbled. **Special Academic Facilities/Equipment:** Anthropology and psychology labs. Electronic music lab. Individual studio space for senior art students. Marine biology research center with Living Ecosystem Teaching and Research Aquarium, wet lab, and seawater on tap. NMR, scanning electron microscope, inert atmosphere glovebox, transparent fume hoods, greenhouse. **Computers:** 95% of classrooms, 100% of dorms, 100% of libraries, 100% of dining areas, 100% of student union, 20% of common outdoor areas have wireless network access. Students can register for classes online. Administrative functions (other than registration) can be performed online.

CAMPUS LIFE
Environment: Town **Activities:** Campus Ministries; Choral groups; Dance; Drama/theater; International Student Organization; Jazz band; Literary magazine; Music ensembles; Musical theater; Radio station; Student government; Student newspaper; Student-run film society 90 registered organizations, 5 religious organizations. **Athletics (Intercollegiate):** *Men:* sailing. *Women:* sailing. **On-Campus Highlights:** Pritzker Marine Biology Research Center, Four Winds Cafe—student-run vegetarian coffeehouse, College Hall (Charles Ringling's mansion- visit center), Bayfront behind College Hall—sunset watching, Caples Fine Arts Complex—concerts and exhibits **Environmental Initiatives:** We've had an environmental studies program since 1972.

ADMISSIONS
Freshman Academic Profile: Average high school GPA 4.0. 37% in top 10% of high school class, 71% in top 25% of high school class, 95% in top 50% of high school class. 82% from public high schools. **Test Scores:** SAT Math middle 50% range 570-670. SAT EBRW middle 50% range 620-710. ACT middle 50% range 25-30. Minimum internet-based TOEFL 83. Minimum paper TOEFL 560. **Basis for Candidate Selection:** *Very important factors considered include:* rigor of secondary school record, academic GPA, application essay. *Important factors considered include:* class rank, standardized test scores, recommendation(s), extracurricular activities, character/personal qualities, volunteer work, work experience, level of applicant's interest. *Other factors considered include:* talent/ability, first generation, alumni/

ae relation, geographical residence, state residency. **Freshman Admission Requirements:** High school diploma is required and GED is accepted *Academic units required:* 4 English, 4 math, 3 science, 2 science labs, 2 foreign language, 3 social studies, 2 academic electives, *Academic units recommended:* 4 English, 4 math, 4 science, 2 science labs, 4 foreign language, 4 social studies, 4 academic electives. **Freshman Admission Statistics:** 1,353 applied, 69.0% admitted, 21% enrolled. **Transfer Admission Requirements:** college transcript(s), essay or personal statement, Minimum college GPA of 2.0 required. Lowest grade transferable C. **General Admission Information:** Application fee $30. Priority deadline 11/1. Regular application deadline 4/15. Nonfall registration accepted. Admission may be deferred for a maximum of 1 year.

COSTS AND FINANCIAL AID
Annual in-state tuition $9,370. Annual out-of-state tuition $29,944. Room and board $9,370. Average book expense $1,200. **Required Forms and Deadlines:** FAFSA. **Notification of Awards:** Applicants will be notified of awards on a rolling basis beginning 2/1. **Types of Aid:** *Need-based scholarships/ grants:* College/university scholarship or grant aid from institutional funds; Federal Pell; Private scholarships; SEOG; State scholarships/grants. *Loans:* Direct PLUS loans; Direct Subsidized Stafford Loans; Direct Unsubsidized Stafford Loans. *Student Employment:* Federal Work-Study Program available. Institutional employment available. **Financial Aid Statistics:** 91% needy freshmen, 92% needy undergrads receive need-based scholarship or grant aid. 16% freshmen, 12% undergrads receive non-need-based scholarship or grant aid. 79% freshmen, 84% undergrads receive need-based self-help aid. 0% freshmen, 0% undergrads receive athletic scholarships. 100% freshmen, 98% undergrads receive any aid. 48% undergrads borrow to pay for school. Average cumulative indebtedness $14,929. **Criteria for awarding aid:** *Need-based:* Academics *Non-need-based:* Academics, State/district residency.

NEW ENGLAND COLLEGE

15 Main Street, Henniker, NH 03242
Phone: 603-428-2223 • **Financial Aid Phone:** 603-428-2226
E-mail: admission@nec.edu • **CEEB Code:** 3657
Fax: 603-428-3155 • **Website:** www.nec.edu • **ACT Code:** 2513

This private school was founded in 1946. It has a 225 acre campus.

RATINGS
Admissions Selectivity Rating: 71   **Fire Safety Rating:** 98   **Green Rating:** 74

STUDENTS AND FACULTY
Enrollment: 1,816. **Student Body:** 60% female, 40% male, 80% out-of-state, 4% international. Asian 2%, African American 23%, Caucasian 50%, Hispanic 9%, Native American 1%, Pacific Islander <1%, Two or more races 2%, Race unknown 10%.
Retention and Graduation: 51% freshmen return for sophomore year. 35% freshmen graduate within 4 years. 45% freshmen graduate within 6 years. 22% grads go on to further study within 1 year. 10% grads pursue arts and sciences degrees. 0% grads pursue law degrees. 6% grads pursue business degrees. 0% grads pursue medical degrees. **Faculty:** Student/faculty ratio 13:1. 39 full-time faculty, 64% hold PhDs, 3% are members of minority groups, 56% are women. 0% of classes are taught by teaching assistants.

ACADEMICS
Degrees: Associate; Bachelor's; Doctoral; Master's; Post-Master's certificate **Classes:** Most classes have fewer than 10 students. Most lab/discussion sessions have 10-19 students. **Most popular majors:** Elementary Education And Teaching; Sport And Fitness Administration/Management; Business/ Commerce, General. **Special Study Options:** Accelerated program; Cross-registration; Distance learning; Double major; English as a Second Language (ESL); External degree program; Honors program; Independent study; Internships; Liberal arts/career combination; Student-designed major; Study abroad; Teacher certification program. Honors programs: Honors Program Combined degree programs: BA/JD. **Disability Services offered to physically disabled students:** Note-taking services; Tape recorders; Tutors. **Career services:** Alumni network; Career assessment; Career/job search classes; Internships; Regional alumni

FACILITIES
Housing: Apartments for single students; Coed dorms; Theme housing; Wellness housing 75% of campus accessible to physically diasbled. **Special Academic Facilities/Equipment:** New England Art Gallery, Graphic Design and Imaging Lab Center for Educational Innovation (High Tech Building) We have the John Lyons Center (Business) and the Putnam Fine Arts Center under construction. **Computers:** 100% of classrooms, 100% of dorms, 100%

of libraries, 100% of dining areas, 100% of student union, 75% of common outdoor areas have wireless network access. Students can register for classes online. Administrative functions (other than registration) can be performed online.

CAMPUS LIFE

Environment: Rural **Activities:** Drama/theater; International Student Organization; Literary magazine; Radio station; Student government; Student newspaper 26 registered organizations, 2 honor societies, 1 religious organization. 2 fraternities, 2 sororities. **Athletics (Intercollegiate):** *Men:* baseball, basketball, cross-country, ice hockey, lacrosse, soccer. *Women:* basketball, cheerleading, cross-country, field hockey, ice hockey, lacrosse, soccer, softball. **On-Campus Highlights:** Simon Center (Student Center), Center of Education Innovation, Fitness Center, Gilmore Dining Hall, Coffee House **Environmental Initiatives:** Addition of sustainability to the mission statement. A complete overhaul of lighting at the College for energy efficiency. Completion of a campus wide facilities plan.

ADMISSIONS

Freshman Academic Profile: Average high school GPA 2.9. 5% in top 10% of high school class, 31% in top 25% of high school class, 41% in top 50% of high school class. 90% from public high schools. **Test Scores:** SAT Math middle 50% range 420-530. SAT EBRW middle 50% range 430-550. Minimum internet-based TOEFL 13. Minimum paper TOEFL 550. **Basis for Candidate Selection:** *Very important factors considered include:* academic GPA. *Important factors considered include:* volunteer work, work experience, level of applicant's interest. *Other factors considered include:* rigor of secondary school record, class rank, application essay, recommendation(s), extracurricular activities, talent/ability, character/personal qualities, alumni/ae relation. **Freshman Admission Requirements:** High school diploma is required and GED is accepted *Academic units required: Academic units recommended:* 4 English, 3 math, 3 science, 1 science labs, 3 social studies. **Freshman Admission Statistics:** 9,214 applied, 99.6% admitted, 5% enrolled. **Transfer Admission Requirements:** High school transcript, college transcript(s), essay or personal statement, statement of good standing from prior institution(s). Lowest grade transferable C-. **General Admission Information:** Application fee $30. Nonfall registration accepted. Admission may be deferred for a maximum of 1 year.

COSTS AND FINANCIAL AID

Annual tuition $35,858. Room and board $12,550. Required fees $1,096. Average book expense $1,000. **Required Forms and Deadlines:** CSS/Financial Aid PROFILE; FAFSA. **Notification of Awards:** Applicants will be notified of awards on a rolling basis beginning 2/1. **Types of Aid:** *Need-based scholarships/grants:* College/university scholarship or grant aid from institutional funds; Federal Pell; Private scholarships; SEOG; State scholarships/grants. *Loans:* Direct PLUS loans; Direct Subsidized Stafford Loans; Direct Unsubsidized Stafford Loans. *Student Employment:* Federal Work-Study Program available. Institutional employment available. **Financial Aid Statistics:** 98% needy freshmen, 84% needy undergrads receive need-based scholarship or grant aid. 5% freshmen, 4% undergrads receive non-need-based scholarship or grant aid. 92% freshmen, 92% undergrads receive need-based self-help aid. 0% freshmen, 0% undergrads receive athletic scholarships. 93% freshmen, 86% undergrads receive any aid. 88% undergrads borrow to pay for school. Average cumulative indebtedness $35,230. **Criteria for awarding aid:** *Need-based:* Academics, Alumni affiliation, Art, Job skills, Leadership, Music/drama *Non-need-based:* Academics, Alumni affiliation, Art, Job skills, Leadership, Music/drama.

NEW JERSEY CITY UNIVERSITY

2039 Kennedy Boulevard, Jersey City, NJ 07305
Phone: 888-441-6528 • **Financial Aid Phone:** 201-200-3378
E-mail: admissions@njcu.edu • **CEEB Code:** 2316
Fax: 201-200-2044 • **Website:** www.njcu.edu

This public school was founded in 1927. It has a 17 acre campus.

RATINGS

Admissions Selectivity Rating: 71   **Fire Safety Rating:** 85   **Green Rating:** 61

STUDENTS AND FACULTY

Enrollment: 6,357. **Student Body:** 59% female, 41% male, 9% out-of-state, 1% international (15 countries represented). Asian 8%, African American 23%, Caucasian 21%, Hispanic 40%, Native American <1%, Pacific Islander 1%, Two or more races 2%, Race unknown 4%.

Retention and Graduation: 77% freshmen return for sophomore year.
Faculty: Student/faculty ratio 15:1. 253 full-time faculty, 0% of classes are taught by teaching assistants.

ACADEMICS

Degrees: Bachelor's; Certificate; Doctoral/Research; Master's; Post-Bachelor's certificate; Post-Master's certificate **Classes:** Most classes have fewer than 10 students. Most lab/discussion sessions have 10-19 students. **Most popular majors:** Psychology, General; Corrections And Criminal Justice, Other; Registered Nursing/Registered Nurse. **Special Study Options:** Accelerated program; Cooperative education program; Cross-registration; Distance learning; Double major; Dual enrollment; English as a Second Language (ESL); Exchange student program (domestic); Honors program; Independent study; Internships; Study abroad; Teacher certification program. Combined degree programs: BA/MA. **Disability Services offered to physically disabled students:** Note-taking services; Reader services; Tape recorders; Tutors. **Career services:** Career assessment; Internships

FACILITIES

Housing: Coed dorms; Special housing for disabled students 90% of campus accessible to physically diasbled. **Special Academic Facilities/Equipment:** NJCU is located on a 51.46-acre site in Jersey City. The University's 27 buildings house a total of 180 classrooms, including 46 labs, 19 studios, three performance art spaces, three art galleries, two athletic training facilities, a 25-meter swimming pool, two dance studios, a media arts facility, two auditoriums, The Peter G. Mangin Real Estate Institute, and Margaret Williams Theatre. NJCU also maintains the A. Harry Moore School for Special Education and the University Academy Charter High School. **Computers:** Students can register for classes online. Administrative functions (other than registration) can be performed online.

CAMPUS LIFE

Environment: City **Activities:** Campus Ministries; Choral groups; Concert band; Dance; Drama/theater; Jazz band; Literary magazine; Music ensembles; Musical theater; Opera; Radio station; Student government; Student newspaper; Symphony orchestra; Yearbook 50 registered organizations, 2 religious organizations. 7 fraternities, 5 sororities. **Athletics (Intercollegiate):** *Men:* baseball, basketball, cross-country, soccer, track/field (outdoor), track/field (indoor), volleyball. *Women:* basketball, bowling, cross-country, soccer, softball, track/field (outdoor), track/field (indoor), volleyball. **On-Campus Highlights:** Student Union Building, Physical fitness center, Library, Cafeteria, Dunkin Donuts

ADMISSIONS

Freshman Academic Profile: Average high school GPA 3.0. 11% in top 10% of high school class, 28% in top 25% of high school class, 61% in top 50% of high school class. **Test Scores:** SAT Math middle 50% range 440-540. SAT EBRW middle 50% range 430-540. Minimum internet-based TOEFL 79. **Basis for Candidate Selection:** *Very important factors considered include:* rigor of secondary school record, academic GPA, standardized test scores. *Important factors considered include:* class rank. *Other factors considered include:* application essay, recommendation(s), interview, extracurricular activities, talent/ability, character/personal qualities, volunteer work, level of applicant's interest. **Freshman Admission Requirements:** High school diploma is required and GED is accepted *Academic units required:* 4 English, 4 math, 4 science, 2 science labs, 4 social studies, *Academic units recommended:* 4 English, 4 math, 4 science, 3 science labs, 2 foreign language, 4 social studies. **Freshman Admission Statistics:** 2,631 applied, admitted, 25% enrolled. **Transfer Admission Requirements:** college transcript(s), Minimum college GPA of 2.0 required. Lowest grade transferable C. **General Admission Information:** Application fee $50. Nonfall registration accepted. Admission may be deferred.

COSTS AND FINANCIAL AID

Annual in-state tuition $3,315. Annual out-of-state tuition $17,142. Required fees $3,315. Average book expense $1,000. **Required Forms and Deadlines:** FAFSA. **Notification of Awards:** Applicants will be notified of awards on or about 5/15. **Types of Aid:** *Need-based scholarships/grants:* College/university scholarship or grant aid from institutional funds; Federal Pell; SEOG; State scholarships/grants. *Loans:* Direct PLUS loans; Direct Subsidized Stafford Loans; Direct Unsubsidized Stafford Loans. *Student Employment:* Federal Work-Study Program available. Institutional employment available. **Financial Aid Statistics:** 84% needy freshmen, 80% needy undergrads receive need-based scholarship or grant aid. 17% freshmen, 13% undergrads receive non-need-based scholarship or grant aid. 46% freshmen, 69% undergrads receive need-based self-help aid. 0% freshmen, 0% undergrads receive athletic scholarships. **Criteria for awarding aid:** *Need-based:* Academics *Non-need-based:* Academics.

NEW JERSEY INSTITUTE OF TECHNOLOGY

Best Colleges

323 Dr. MLK Jr. Blvd, Newark, NJ 07102
Phone: 973-596-3300 • **Financial Aid Phone:** 973-596-3479
E-mail: admissions@njit.edu • **CEEB Code:** 2580
Fax: 973-596-3461 • **Website:** www.njit.edu • **ACT Code:** 2513

This public school was founded in 1881. It has a 48 acre campus.

RATINGS

Admissions Selectivity Rating: 87   **Fire Safety Rating:** 99   **Green Rating:** 60*

STUDENTS AND FACULTY

Enrollment: 7,489. **Student Body:** 22% female, 78% male, 3% out-of-state, 5% international (65 countries represented). Asian 22%, African American 8%, Caucasian 35%, Hispanic 21%, Native American <1%, Pacific Islander <1%, Two or more races 3%, Race unknown 6%.
Retention and Graduation: 88% freshmen return for sophomore year. 25% freshmen graduate within 4 years. 61% freshmen graduate within 6 years. 17% grads go on to further study within 1 year. 1% grads pursue arts and sciences degrees. 1% grads pursue business degrees. **Faculty:** Student/faculty ratio 17:1. 439 full-time faculty, 92% hold PhDs, 27% are members of minority groups, 21% are women. 0% of classes are taught by teaching assistants.

ACADEMICS

Degrees: Bachelor's; Doctoral; Master's; Post-Bachelor's certificate **Classes:** Most classes have 10-19 students. Most lab/discussion sessions have 20-29 students. **Most popular majors:** Architecture; Information Technology; Mechanical Engineering. **Special Study Options:** Accelerated program; Cooperative education program; Cross-registration; Distance learning; Double major; Dual enrollment; English as a Second Language (ESL); Honors program; Independent study; Internships; Study abroad; Teacher certification program; Weekend college. Honors programs: The Albert Dorman Honors College at the New Jersey Institute of Technology (NJIT) enrolls over 500 exceptional students who excel in the fields of engineering, architecture, computing sciences, management, and the sciences. Combined degree programs: BA/MA; BA/MD. **Disability Services offered to physically disabled students:** Note-taking services; Reader services; Tape recorders; Tutors. **Career services:** Alumni network; Alumni services; Career assessment; Career/job search classes; Internships; Regional alumni

FACILITIES

Housing: Coed dorms 100% of campus accessible to physically disabled. **Special Academic Facilities/Equipment:** New Jersey Literary Hall of Fame and more than 50 research centers and sponsored research laboratories, including computer chip manufacturing center, manufacturing systems center, and many others **Computers:** 100% of classrooms, 100% of dorms, 100% of libraries, 100% of dining areas, 100% of student union, 100% of common outdoor areas have wireless network access. Students can register for classes online. Administrative functions (other than registration) can be performed online. Undergraduates are required to own a computer.

CAMPUS LIFE

Environment: Metropolis **Activities:** Concert band; Dance; Drama/theater; International Student Organization; Jazz band; Music ensembles; Musical theater; Pep band; Radio station; Student government; Student newspaper; Student-run film society; Yearbook 70 registered organizations, 10 honor societies, 5 religious organizations. 15 fraternities, 7 sororities. **Athletics (Intercollegiate):** *Men:* baseball, basketball, cheerleading, cross-country, fencing, soccer, swimming, tennis, track/field (outdoor), track/field (indoor), volleyball. *Women:* basketball, cheerleading, cross-country, fencing, soccer, swimming, tennis, track/field (outdoor), track/field (indoor), volleyball. **On-Campus Highlights:** Campus Center, Van Houten Library, Zoom Fleisher Athletic Center, Fenster Hall—Admissions, Student Mall **Environmental Initiatives:** Recycling

ADMISSIONS

Freshman Academic Profile: Average high school GPA 3.6. 40% in top 10% of high school class, 66% in top 25% of high school class, 89% in top 50% of high school class. 85% from public high schools. **Test Scores:** SAT Math middle 50% range 610-700. SAT EBRW middle 50% range 580-670. ACT middle 50% range 24-30. Minimum internet-based TOEFL 79. Minimum paper TOEFL 550. **Basis for Candidate Selection:** *Very important factors considered include:* rigor of secondary school record, class rank, standardized test scores. *Important factors considered include:* academic GPA. *Other factors considered include:* application essay, recommendation(s), interview, extracurricular

activities, talent/ability, character/personal qualities, alumni/ae relation, geographical residence, state residency, religious affiliation/commitment, racial/ethnic status, volunteer work, work experience, level of applicant's interest.
Freshman Admission Requirements: High school diploma is required and GED is accepted *Academic units required:* 4 English, 4 math, 2 science, 2 science labs, *Academic units recommended:* 2 foreign language, 1 social studies, 1 history, 2 academic electives. **Freshman Admission Statistics:** 7,248 applied, 61.4% admitted, 25% enrolled. **Transfer Admission Requirements:** college transcript(s), Minimum college GPA of 2.0 required. Lowest grade transferable C. **General Admission Information:** Application fee $75. Regular application deadline 3/1. Nonfall registration accepted. Admission may be deferred for a maximum of 1 year.

COSTS AND FINANCIAL AID

Annual in-state tuition $13,300. Annual out-of-state tuition $28,926. Room and board $13,300. Required fees $2,992. Average book expense $2,600. **Required Forms and Deadlines:** FAFSA. **Notification of Awards:** Applicants will be notified of awards on a rolling basis beginning 12/15. **Types of Aid:** *Need-based scholarships/grants:* College/university scholarship or grant aid from institutional funds; Federal Pell; Private scholarships; SEOG; State scholarships/grants; United Negro College Fund. *Loans:* Direct PLUS loans; Direct Subsidized Stafford Loans; Direct Unsubsidized Stafford Loans. *Student Employment:* Federal Work-Study Program available. Institutional employment available. **Financial Aid Statistics:** 88% needy freshmen, 96% needy undergrads receive need-based scholarship or grant aid. 61% freshmen, 35% undergrads receive non-need-based scholarship or grant aid. 63% freshmen, 76% undergrads receive need-based self-help aid. 2% freshmen, 2% undergrads receive athletic scholarships. 87% freshmen, 72% undergrads receive any aid. 64% undergrads borrow to pay for school. Average cumulative indebtedness $40,967. **Criteria for awarding aid:** *Need-based:* Academics, Alumni affiliation, Art, Athletics, Job skills, Leadership, Minority status, Music/drama, Religious affiliation *Non-need-based:* Academics, Alumni affiliation, Art, Athletics, Job skills, Leadership, Minority status, Music/drama, Religious affiliation, State/district residency.

NEW MEXICO INSTITUTE OF MINING & TECHNOLOGY

Campus Station, Socorro, NM 87801
Phone: 575-835-5424 • **Financial Aid Phone:** 575-835-5333
E-mail: admission@nmt.edu • **CEEB Code:** 4533
Fax: 575-835-5989 • **Website:** www.nmt.edu • **ACT Code:** 2642

This public school was founded in 1889. It has a 320 acre campus.

RATINGS

Admissions Selectivity Rating: 97   **Fire Safety Rating:** 60*   **Green Rating:** 60*

STUDENTS AND FACULTY

Enrollment: 1,358. **Student Body:** 27% female, 73% male, 11% out-of-state, 2% international. Asian 4%, African American 2%, Caucasian 52%, Hispanic 30%, Native American 4%, Pacific Islander <1%, Two or more races 5%, Race unknown 1%.
Retention and Graduation: 74% freshmen return for sophomore year. **Faculty:** Student/faculty ratio 11:1. 132 full-time faculty, 27% are members of minority groups, 23% are women.

ACADEMICS

Degrees: Bachelor's; Doctoral/Research; Master's; Post-Bachelor's certificate; Terminal Associate **Classes:** Most classes have 10-19 students. Most lab/discussion sessions have fewer than 10 students. **Most popular majors:** Computer And Information Sciences, General; Electrical And Electronics Engineering; Mechanical Engineering. **Special Study Options:** Accelerated program; Cooperative education program; Distance learning; Double major; Dual enrollment; Exchange student program (domestic); Independent study; Internships; Student-designed major; Teacher certification program. **Disability Services offered to physically disabled students:** Note-taking services; Reader services; Tape recorders; Tutors. **Career services:** Career assessment; Career/job search classes; Internships

FACILITIES

Housing: Apartments for married students; Apartments for single students; Coed dorms; Men's dorms; Women's dorms **Special Academic Facilities/Equipment:** Mineral museum, observatory, radio telescope, seismic observatory and library, explosives labs **Computers:** Students can register for classes online. Administrative functions (other than registration) can be performed online.

CAMPUS LIFE

Environment: Village **Activities:** Choral groups; Concert band; Dance; Drama/theater; International Student Organization; Jazz band; Music ensembles; Musical theater; Radio station; Student government; Student newspaper 60 registered organizations, 7 honor societies, 3 religious organizations. **On-Campus Highlights:** Fidel Student Center, Skeen Library, Workman Center

ADMISSIONS

Freshman Academic Profile: Average high school GPA 3.7. 35% in top 10% of high school class, 68% in top 25% of high school class, 87% in top 50% of high school class. 80% from public high schools. **Test Scores:** SAT Math middle 50% range 550-690. SAT EBRW middle 50% range 610-780. ACT middle 50% range 23-29. Minimum paper TOEFL 540. **Basis for Candidate Selection:** *Very important factors considered include:* rigor of secondary school record, academic GPA, standardized test scores. *Other factors considered include:* class rank, extracurricular activities, talent/ability. **Freshman Admission Requirements:** High school diploma is required and GED is accepted *Academic units required:* 4 English, 3 math, 2 science, 2 science labs, 2 social studies, 1 history, 3 academic electives, *Academic units recommended:* 4 English, 4 math, 4 science, 3 science labs, 2 foreign language, 3 social studies, 1 history. **Freshman Admission Statistics:** 1,513 applied, 21.7% admitted, 73% enrolled. **Transfer Admission Requirements:** High school transcript, college transcript(s), statement of good standing from prior institution(s). Minimum college GPA of 2.0 required. Lowest grade transferable D. **General Admission Information:** Application fee $15. Priority deadline 3/1. Regular application deadline 8/1. Nonfall registration accepted. Admission may be deferred for a maximum of 1 year.

COSTS AND FINANCIAL AID

Annual in-state tuition $8,202. Annual out-of-state tuition $19,941. Room and board $8,202. Required fees $1,050. Average book expense $1,106. **Required Forms and Deadlines:** FAFSA. **Notification of Awards:** Applicants will be notified of awards on a rolling basis beginning 5/1. **Types of Aid:** *Need-based scholarships/grants:* College/university scholarship or grant aid from institutional funds; Federal Pell; Private scholarships; SEOG; State scholarships/grants. *Loans:* Direct PLUS loans; Direct Subsidized Stafford Loans; Direct Unsubsidized Stafford Loans. *Student Employment:* Federal Work-Study Program available. Institutional employment available. **Financial Aid Statistics:** 88% needy freshmen, 68% needy undergrads receive need-based scholarship or grant aid. 96% freshmen, 72% undergrads receive non-need-based scholarship or grant aid. 57% freshmen, 64% undergrads receive need-based self-help aid. 0% freshmen, 0% undergrads receive athletic scholarships. 45% undergrads borrow to pay for school. Average cumulative indebtedness $22,355. **Criteria for awarding aid:** *Need-based:* Minority status *Non-need-based:* Academics, Alumni affiliation, Minority status, State/district residency.

NEW MEXICO STATE UNIVERSITY

PO Box 30001, Las Cruces, NM 88003-8001
Phone: 575-646-3121 • **Financial Aid Phone:** 575-646-4105
E-mail: admissions@nmsu.edu • **CEEB Code:** 4531
Fax: 575-646-6330 • **Website:** www.nmsu.edu • **ACT Code:** 2638

This public school was founded in 1888. It has a 900 acre campus.

RATINGS

Admissions Selectivity Rating: 83 **Fire Safety Rating:** 71 **Green Rating:** 60*

STUDENTS AND FACULTY

Enrollment: 11,173. **Student Body:** 54% female, 46% male, 26% out-of-state, 4% international (54 countries represented). Asian 1%, African American 3%, Caucasian 27%, Hispanic 59%, Native American 2%, Pacific Islander <1%, Two or more races 2%, Race unknown 1%.
Retention and Graduation: 74% freshmen return for sophomore year. 18% freshmen graduate within 4 years. 46% freshmen graduate within 6 years. **Faculty:** Student/faculty ratio 16:1. 639 full-time faculty, 88% hold PhDs, 32% are members of minority groups, 44% are women.

ACADEMICS

Degrees: Associate; Bachelor's; Doctoral/Professional; Doctoral/Research; Master's; Post-Bachelor's certificate; Post-Master's certificate **Classes:** Most classes have fewer than 10 students. Most lab/discussion sessions have fewer than 10 students. **Most popular majors:** Kinesiology And Exercise Science; Criminal Justice/Safety Studies; Registered Nursing/Registered Nurse. **Special Study Options:** Cooperative education program; Distance learning; Double major; Dual enrollment; English as a Second Language (ESL); Exchange student program (domestic); Honors program; Independent study; Internships;

Student-designed major; Study abroad; Teacher certification program. Combined degree programs: BA/MA. **Disability Services offered to physically disabled students:** Note-taking services; Reader services; Tutors. **Career services:** Alumni services; Career assessment; Career/job search classes; Internships

FACILITIES

Housing: Apartments for married students; Apartments for single students; Coed dorms; Fraternity/sorority housing; Special housing for international students 95% of campus accessible to physically diasbled. **Special Academic Facilities/Equipment:** University and art department museums, theatre, horse farm, sports medicine training clinic, observatory, electron microscope, CRAY supercomputer. **Computers:** Students can register for classes online. Administrative functions (other than registration) can be performed online.

CAMPUS LIFE

Environment: City **Activities:** Campus Ministries; Choral groups; Concert band; Dance; Drama/theater; International Student Organization; Jazz band; Literary magazine; Marching band; Model UN; Music ensembles; Musical theater; Opera; Pep band; Radio station; Student government; Student newspaper; Symphony orchestra; Television station 263 registered organizations, 24 honor societies, 23 religious organizations. 14 fraternities, 5 sororities. **Athletics (Intercollegiate):** *Men:* baseball, basketball, cross-country, football, golf, tennis. *Women:* basketball, cross-country, golf, softball, swimming, tennis, track/field (outdoor), volleyball. Corbett Center Student Union, Zhul Library, Barnes and Noble, Activity Center, Frenger Food Court

ADMISSIONS

Freshman Academic Profile: Average high school GPA 3.5. 21% in top 10% of high school class, 51% in top 25% of high school class, 83% in top 50% of high school class. **Test Scores:** SAT Math middle 50% range 460-580. SAT EBRW middle 50% range 450-580. ACT middle 50% range 18-23. Minimum internet-based TOEFL 68. Minimum paper TOEFL 520. **Basis for Candidate Selection:** *Very important factors considered include:* academic GPA, standardized test scores. *Other factors considered include:* rigor of secondary school record, class rank. **Freshman Admission Requirements:** High school diploma is required and GED is accepted *Academic units required:* 4 English, 4 math, 2 science, 2 science labs, 1 foreign language. **Freshman Admission Statistics:** 8,192 applied, 63.8% admitted, 39% enrolled. **Transfer Admission Requirements:** college transcript(s), Minimum college GPA of 2.0 required. Lowest grade transferable C. **General Admission Information:** Application fee $20. Nonfall registration accepted.

COSTS AND FINANCIAL AID

Required Forms and Deadlines: FAFSA. **Notification of Awards:** Applicants will be notified of awards on a rolling basis beginning 1/1. **Types of Aid:** *Need-based scholarships/grants:* College/university scholarship or grant aid from institutional funds; Federal Pell; Private scholarships; SEOG; State scholarships/grants. *Loans:* Direct PLUS loans; Direct Subsidized Stafford Loans; Direct Unsubsidized Stafford Loans. *Student Employment:* Federal Work-Study Program available. Institutional employment available. **Financial Aid Statistics:** 91% needy freshmen, 95% needy undergrads receive need-based scholarship or grant aid. 9% freshmen, 6% undergrads receive non-need-based scholarship or grant aid. 45% freshmen, 62% undergrads receive need-based self-help aid. 3% freshmen, 2% undergrads receive athletic scholarships. 56% undergrads borrow to pay for school. Average cumulative indebtedness $21,402. **Criteria for awarding aid:** *Need-based:* Academics, Athletics, Minority status, Music/drama *Non-need-based:* Academics, Alumni affiliation, Athletics, Leadership, Minority status, Music/drama, State/district residency.

THE NEW SCHOOL COLLEGE OF PERFORMING ARTS

The New School/55 West 13th Street, New York, NY 10003
Phone: 212.580.0210x4862 • **Financial Aid Phone:** 212 229 8930
E-mail: performingarts@newschool.edu • **CEEB Code:** 2398
Website: http://www.newschool.edu/performing-arts/ • **ACT Code:** 2828

This private school was founded in 1916.

RATINGS

Admissions Selectivity Rating: 88 **Fire Safety Rating:** 89 **Green Rating:** 91

STUDENTS AND FACULTY

Enrollment: 594. **Student Body:** 44% female, 56% male, 79% out-of-state, 30% international (47 countries represented). Asian 4%, African American 9%, Caucasian 39%, Hispanic 9%, Native American <1%, Pacific Islander <1%, Two or more races 5%, Race unknown 4%.

Retention and Graduation: 84% freshmen return for sophomore year. 53% freshmen graduate within 4 years. 64% freshmen graduate within 6 years. **Faculty:** Student/faculty ratio 5:1. 16 full-time faculty, 75% hold PhDs, 13% are members of minority groups, 50% are women. 0% of classes are taught by teaching assistants.

ACADEMICS

Degrees: Bachelor's; Diploma; **Master's Classes:** Most classes have 20-29 students. Most lab/discussion sessions have 10-19 students. **Special Study Options:** Accelerated program; Cross-registration; Double major; English as a Second Language (ESL); Independent study; Internships. **Disability Services offered to physically disabled students:** Note-taking services; Reader services; Tape recorders; Tutors. **Career services:** Career assessment; Career/job search classes; Internships

FACILITIES

Housing: Coed dorms; Special housing for disabled student; Theme housing 99% of campus accessible to physically diasbled. **Special Academic Facilities/Equipment:** Art gallery, photography gallery, extensive collections of contemporary art, concert hall, public lectures, conferences, cultural and intellectual events. **Computers:** 95% of classrooms, 100% of libraries, 100% of dining areas, na% of student union, 100% of common outdoor areas have wireless network access. Students can register for classes online. Administrative functions (other than registration) can be performed online.

CAMPUS LIFE

Environment: Metropolis **Activities:** Choral groups; Concert band; Dance; Drama/theater; International Student Organization; Jazz band; Literary magazine; Music ensembles; Musical theater; Opera; Student government; Student newspaper; Student-run film society 39 registered organizations. **On-Campus Highlights:** Mannes Concert Hall, University Welcome Center, The University Center, John L. Tishman Auditorium, Sheila C. Johnson Design Center **Environmental Initiatives:** Lighting Retrofits: 2W 13th St. and 66 5th Ave are in the midst of an ongoing replacement of all non-LED fixtures. The majority of the building's T8 fluorescent bulbs are being replaced with LED, stairwells are being replaced with dimming-occupancy based bi-level fixtures, and all rooms will be equiped with vacancy sensors. The main lobby and gallery spaces will also recieve significant upgrades as well. These same upgrades are being applied to 2 other large buildings, with a goal of completing the entire campus by early 2017.

ADMISSIONS

Freshman Academic Profile: Average high school GPA 3.3. 9% in top 10% of high school class, 28% in top 25% of high school class, 59% in top 50% of high school class. 72% from public high schools. **Test Scores:** SAT Math middle 50% range 490-630. SAT EBRW middle 50% range 560-630. ACT middle 50% range 25-30. Minimum internet-based TOEFL 100. **Basis for Candidate Selection:** *Very important factors considered include:* academic GPA, application essay, extracurricular activities. *Important factors considered include:* rigor of secondary school record, recommendation(s), character/personal qualities. *Other factors considered include:* class rank, standardized test scores, interview, talent/ability, volunteer work, work experience, level of applicant's interest. **Freshman Admission Requirements:** High school diploma is required and GED is accepted *Academic units required:* 4 English, *Academic units recommended:* 4 math, 4 science, 4 foreign language, 4 social studies, 4 history. **Freshman Admission Statistics:** 1,259 applied, 51.2% admitted, 26% enrolled. **Transfer Admission Requirements:** college transcript(s), essay or personal statement, Minimum college GPA of 2.0 required. Lowest grade transferable C. **General Admission Information:** Application fee $50. Priority deadline 1/15. Regular application deadline 8/1. Nonfall registration accepted. Admission may be deferred for a maximum of 1 year.

COSTS AND FINANCIAL AID

Required Forms and Deadlines: FAFSA. **Notification of Awards:** Applicants will be notified of awards on a rolling basis beginning 4/1. **Types of Aid:** *Need-based scholarships/grants:* College/university scholarship or grant aid from institutional funds; Federal Pell; Private scholarships; SEOG; State scholarships/grants. *Loans:* Direct PLUS loans; Direct Subsidized Stafford Loans; Direct Unsubsidized Stafford Loans. *Student Employment:* Federal Work-Study Program available. Institutional employment available. **Financial Aid Statistics:** 80% needy freshmen, 81% needy undergrads receive need-based scholarship or grant aid. 51% freshmen, 52% undergrads receive non-need-based scholarship or grant aid. 86% freshmen, 85% undergrads receive need-based self-help aid. 0% freshmen, 0% undergrads receive athletic scholarships. 64% freshmen, 44% undergrads receive any aid. 68% undergrads borrow to pay for school. Average cumulative indebtedness $20,736. **Criteria for awarding aid:** *Need-based:* Academics, Art, Leadership, Minority status, Music/drama *Non-need-based:* Academics, Art, Leadership, Minority status, Music/drama, State/district residency.

NEW YORK SCHOOL OF INTERIOR DESIGN

1146 Pleasant Hall, New York, NY 10021
Phone: 212-472-1500 • **Financial Aid Phone:** 212-472-1500 x212
E-mail: admissions@nysid.edu • **CEEB Code:** 333
Fax: 212-472-1867 • **ACT Code:** 2829

This private school was founded in 1916.

RATINGS

Admissions Selectivity Rating: 71   **Fire Safety Rating:** 60*   **Green Rating:** 60*

STUDENTS AND FACULTY

Enrollment: 353. **Student Body:** 87% female, 13% male, 15% international. Asian 6%, African American 3%, Caucasian 48%, Hispanic 9%, Native American 0%, Two or more races 2%, Race unknown 16%. **Retention and Graduation:** 0% grads go on to further study within 1 year. 0% grads pursue arts and sciences degrees. 0% grads pursue law degrees. 0% grads pursue business degrees. 0% grads pursue medical degrees. **Faculty:** 8 full-time faculty, 88% hold PhDs, 50% are women. 0% of classes are taught by teaching assistants.

ACADEMICS

Degrees: Associate; Bachelor's; Certificate; Master's; Transfer Associate **Classes:** Most classes have 10-19 students. **Most popular majors:** Interior Design. **Special Study Options:** Independent study; Internships; Study abroad. **Disability Services offered to physically disabled students:** Tutors. **Career services:** Alumni network; Alumni services; Internships

FACILITIES

Housing: 100% of campus accessible to physically diasbled. **Special Academic Facilities/Equipment:** Three galleries, lighting laboratory, student atelier.

CAMPUS LIFE

Environment: Metropolis **Activities:** 1 registered organization.

ADMISSIONS

Test Scores: Minimum internet-based TOEFL 79. Minimum paper TOEFL 550. **Basis for Candidate Selection:** *Very important factors considered include:* rigor of secondary school record, application essay, talent/ability. *Important factors considered include:* academic GPA, recommendation(s), level of applicant's interest. *Other factors considered include:* class rank, standardized test scores, interview, extracurricular activities, character/personal qualities, alumni/ae relation, work experience. **Freshman Admission Requirements:** High school diploma is required and GED is accepted *Academic units recommended:* 4 English, 2 math, 2 science, 2 foreign language, 2 social studies, 2 history. **Freshman Admission Statistics:** 178 applied, 45.5% admitted, 33% enrolled. **Transfer Admission Requirements:** High school transcript, college transcript(s), essay or personal statement, Minimum college GPA of 3.0 required. Lowest grade transferable C. **General Admission Information:** Application fee $60. Priority deadline 2/1. Nonfall registration accepted. Admission may be deferred for a maximum of 1 year.

COSTS AND FINANCIAL AID

Annual tuition $30,195. Required fees $570. Average book expense $1,000. **Required Forms and Deadlines:** FAFSA; Institution's own financial aid form; State aid form. **Notification of Awards:** Applicants will be notified of awards on a rolling basis beginning 2/1. **Types of Aid:** *Need-based scholarships/grants:* College/university scholarship or grant aid from institutional funds; Federal Pell; SEOG; State scholarships/grants. *Loans: Student Employment:* Federal Work-Study Program available. **Criteria for awarding aid:** *Need-based:* Academics, Art.

NEW YORK UNIVERSITY

70 Washington Square South, New York, NY 10012
Phone: 212-998-4500 • **Financial Aid Phone:** 212-998-4444
E-mail: admissions@nyu.edu • **CEEB Code:** 2562
Fax: 212-995-4902 • **Website:** www.nyu.edu • **ACT Code:** 2838

This private school was founded in 1831.

RATINGS

Admissions Selectivity Rating: 95   **Fire Safety Rating:** 98   **Green Rating:** 83

STUDENTS AND FACULTY

Enrollment: 26,055. **Student Body:** 57% female, 43% male, 66% out-of-state, 19% international (140 countries represented). Asian 20%, African American 6%, Caucasian 31%, Hispanic 14%, Native American <1%, Pacific Islander <1%, Two or more races 5%, Race unknown 6%.

Retention and Graduation: 93% freshmen return for sophomore year. 82% freshmen graduate within 4 years. 84% freshmen graduate within 6 years. 13% grads go on to further study within 1 year. 31% grads pursue arts and sciences degrees. 14% grads pursue law degrees. 10% grads pursue business degrees. 14% grads pursue medical degrees. **Faculty:** Student/faculty ratio 10:1. 2,965 full-time faculty, 93% hold PhDs, 21% are members of minority groups, 43% are women.

ACADEMICS

Degrees: Associate; Bachelor's; Certificate; Diploma; Doctoral; Doctoral Other; Doctoral/Professional; Doctoral/Research; Master's; Post-Bachelor's certificate; Post-Master's certificate; Terminal Associate; Transfer Associate **Classes:** Most classes have 10-19 students. Most lab/discussion sessions have 10-19 students. **Most popular majors:** Liberal Arts And Sciences/Liberal Studies; Drama And Dramatics/Theatre Arts, General; Business/Commerce, General. **Special Study Options:** Accelerated program; Cooperative education program; Cross-registration; Distance learning; Double major; English as a Second Language (ESL); Exchange student program (domestic); External degree program; Honors program; Independent study; Internships; Liberal arts/career combination; Student-designed major; Study abroad; Teacher certification program. Honors programs: There are various honors programs in the different Schools and Colleges. Combined degree programs: BA/DDS. **Disability Services offered to physically disabled students:** Note-taking services; Reader services; Tape recorders. **Career services:** Alumni network; Alumni services; Career assessment; Career/job search classes; Internships; Regional alumni

FACILITIES

Housing: Apartments for single students; Coed dorms; Fraternity/sorority housing; Special housing for disabled students; Special housing for international students; Theme housing; Wellness housing 90% of campus accessible to physically diasbled. **Special Academic Facilities/Equipment:** Bobst Library and study center; Grey Art Gallery and study center; Special academic facilities for arts, business, culture, education, international relations, language, law, media, music, public service, research, and social policy, and Skirball Center for Performing Arts. **Computers:** 70% of classrooms, 100% of libraries, 100% of dining areas, 100% of student union, 50% of common outdoor areas have wireless network access. Students can register for classes online. Administrative functions (other than registration) can be performed online.

CAMPUS LIFE

Environment: Metropolis **Activities:** Campus Ministries; Choral groups; Concert band; Dance; Drama/theater; International Student Organization; Jazz band; Literary magazine; Model UN; Music ensembles; Musical theater; Opera; Pep band; Radio station; Student government; Student newspaper; Student-run film society; Symphony orchestra; Television station; Yearbook 407 registered organizations, 3 honor societies, 31 religious organizations. 14 fraternities, 10 sororities. **Athletics (Intercollegiate):** *Men:* basketball, cross-country, diving, fencing, golf, soccer, swimming, tennis, track/field (outdoor), track/field (indoor), volleyball, wrestling. *Women:* basketball, cross-country, diving, fencing, golf, soccer, swimming, tennis, track/field (outdoor), track/field (indoor), volleyball. **On-Campus Highlights:** Kimmel Center for Student Life, Coles Athletic Center, Palladium Athletic Facility, Skirball Center for the Performing Arts, Center for Spiritual Life **Environmental Initiatives:** NYU achieved its first carbon goal of reducing emissions 30% from a 2006 baseline five years ahead of schedule. NYU than committed to an aggressive 50% emissions reduction goal by 2025.

ADMISSIONS

Freshman Academic Profile: Average high school GPA 3.7. 57% from public high schools. **Test Scores:** SAT Math middle 50% range 640-760. SAT EBRW middle 50% range 650-730. ACT middle 50% range 29-33. Minimum internet-based TOEFL 100. **Basis for Candidate Selection:** *Very important factors considered include:* rigor of secondary school record, class rank, academic GPA, standardized test scores, talent/ability. *Important factors considered include:* application essay, recommendation(s), extracurricular activities, character/personal qualities. *Other factors considered include:* interview, first generation, alumni/ae relation, geographical residence, racial/ethnic status, volunteer work, work experience, level of applicant's interest. **Freshman Admission Requirements:** High school diploma is required and GED is accepted *Academic units required:* 4 English, 3 math, 3 science, 3 science labs, 3 foreign language, 3 social studies, 3 history, *Academic units recommended:* 4 English, 4 math, 4 science, 4 science labs, 4 foreign language, 4 social studies, 4 history. **Freshman Admission Statistics:** 64,007 applied, 27.7% admitted, 34% enrolled. **Transfer Admission Requirements:** High school transcript, college transcript(s), essay or personal statement, statement of good standing from prior institution(s). Lowest grade transferable C. **General Admission Information:** Application fee $80. Regular application deadline 1/1. Nonfall registration accepted. Admission may be deferred for a maximum of 1-2 years.

COSTS AND FINANCIAL AID

Annual tuition $47,942. Room and board $17,664. Required fees $2,522. Average book expense $904. **Required Forms and Deadlines:** CSS/Financial Aid PROFILE; FAFSA; Noncustodial PROFILE. **Notification of Awards:** Applicants will be notified of awards on or about 4/1. **Types of Aid:** *Need-based scholarships/grants:* College/university scholarship or grant aid from institutional funds; Federal Nursing Scholarships; Federal Pell; Private scholarships; SEOG; State scholarships/grants. *Loans:* Direct PLUS loans; Direct Subsidized Stafford Loans; Direct Unsubsidized Stafford Loans. *Student Employment:* Federal Work-Study Program available. Institutional employment available. **Financial Aid Statistics:** 90% needy freshmen, 89% needy undergrads receive need-based scholarship or grant aid. 0% freshmen, 0% undergrads receive non-need-based scholarship or grant aid. 82% freshmen, 84% undergrads receive need-based self-help aid. 0% freshmen, 0% undergrads receive athletic scholarships. 49% undergrads borrow to pay for school. Average cumulative indebtedness $30,480. **Criteria for awarding aid:** *Need-based:* Academics, Art, Leadership, Music/drama *Non-need-based:* Music/drama.

See page 992.

NIAGARA UNIVERSITY

5795 Lewiston Road, Niagara University, NY 14109
Phone: 716-286-8700 • **Financial Aid Phone:** 716-286-8669
E-mail: admissions@niagara.edu • **CEEB Code:** 2558
Fax: 716-286-8710 • **Website:** www.niagara.edu • **ACT Code:** 2842

This private school, affiliated with the Roman Catholic Church, was founded in 1856. It has a 160 acre campus.

RATINGS

Admissions Selectivity Rating: 75   **Fire Safety Rating:** 82   **Green Rating:** 90

STUDENTS AND FACULTY

Enrollment: 2,902. **Student Body:** 62% female, 38% male, 8% out-of-state, 13% international (42 countries represented). Asian 2%, African American 5%, Caucasian 71%, Hispanic 4%, Native American 1%, Pacific Islander 0%, Two or more races 3%, Race unknown 2%.

Retention and Graduation: 83% freshmen return for sophomore year. 60% freshmen graduate within 4 years. 68% freshmen graduate within 6 years. 26% grads go on to further study within 1 year. 2% grads pursue arts and sciences degrees. 1% grads pursue law degrees. 5% grads pursue business degrees. 1% grads pursue medical degrees. **Faculty:** Student/faculty ratio 11:1. 166 full-time faculty, 94% hold PhDs, 13% are members of minority groups, 41% are women. 0% of classes are taught by teaching assistants.

ACADEMICS

Degrees: Associate; Bachelor's; Certificate; Doctoral/Research; Master's; Post-Bachelor's certificate; Post-Master's certificate **Classes:** Most classes have 20-29 students. Most lab/discussion sessions have 10-19 students. **Most popular majors:** Teacher Education, Multiple Levels; Business/Commerce, General. **Special Study Options:** Accelerated program; Cooperative education program; Cross-registration; Distance learning; Double major; Dual enrollment; English as a Second Language (ESL); Exchange student program (domestic); Honors program; Independent study; Internships; Liberal arts/career combination; Study abroad; Teacher certification program. Combined degree programs: BA/MA. **Disability Services offered to physically disabled students:** Note-taking services; Reader services; Tape recorders; Tutors. **Career services:** Alumni network; Alumni services; Career assessment; Career/job search classes; Internships; Regional alumni

FACILITIES

Housing: Apartments for single students; Coed dorms; Special housing for international students; Theme housing 75% of campus accessible to physically diasbled. **Special Academic Facilities/Equipment:** Castellani Art Museum **Computers:** Students can register for classes online.

CAMPUS LIFE

Environment: Town **Activities:** Campus Ministries; Choral groups; Dance; Drama/theater; International Student Organization; Literary magazine; Model UN; Music ensembles; Musical theater; Pep band; Radio station; Student government; Student newspaper 70 registered organizations, 14 honor societies, 2 religious organizations. 3 fraternities, 2 sororities. **Athletics (Intercollegiate):** *Men:* baseball, basketball, cross-country, diving, golf, ice hockey, soccer, swimming, tennis. *Women:* basketball, cross-country, diving, golf, ice hockey, lacrosse, soccer, softball, swimming, tennis, volleyball. **On-Campus Highlights:** Gallagher Center, St. Vincent's Hall, Castellani Art Museum, Golisano Center for Integrated Sciences, Dwyer Arena **Environmental Initiatives:** 50000 sq. ft. science complex opened in Fall 2013 earned LEED Gold Certification. Installed (4) electric car charging stations (Summer 2017) on campus for students, employees and visitors.

ADMISSIONS

Freshman Academic Profile: Average high school GPA 89.0. 17% in top 10% of high school class, 42% in top 25% of high school class, 75% in top 50% of high school class. **Test Scores:** SAT Math middle 50% range 510-600. SAT EBRW middle 50% range 510-600. ACT middle 50% range 21-26. Minimum internet-based TOEFL 79. Minimum paper TOEFL 550. **Basis for Candidate Selection:** *Very important factors considered include:* rigor of secondary school record, class rank, academic GPA. *Important factors considered include:* standardized test scores, recommendation(s), interview. *Other factors considered include:* application essay, extracurricular activities, talent/ability, character/personal qualities, alumni/ae relation, volunteer work, work experience, level of applicant's interest. **Freshman Admission Requirements:** High school diploma is required and GED is accepted *Academic units required:* 4 English, 2 math, 2 science, 2 foreign language, 2 social studies, 4 academic electives. **Freshman Admission Statistics:** 3,101 applied, 84.2% admitted, 23% enrolled. **Transfer Admission Requirements:** High school transcript, college transcript(s), Minimum college GPA of 2.0 required. Lowest grade transferable C. **General Admission Information:** Regular application deadline 8/30. Nonfall registration accepted. Admission may be deferred for a maximum of 1 year.

COSTS AND FINANCIAL AID

Annual tuition $30,500. Room and board $12,950. Required fees $1,450. Average book expense $1,050. **Required Forms and Deadlines:** FAFSA; State aid form. **Notification of Awards:** Applicants will be notified of awards on a rolling basis beginning 3/1. **Types of Aid:** *Need-based scholarships/grants:* College/university scholarship or grant aid from institutional funds; Federal Pell; Private scholarships; SEOG; State scholarships/grants. *Loans:* Direct PLUS loans; Direct Subsidized Stafford Loans; Direct Unsubsidized Stafford Loans. *Student Employment:* Federal Work-Study Program available. **Financial Aid Statistics:** 99% needy freshmen, 98% needy undergrads receive need-based scholarship or grant aid. 84% freshmen, 80% undergrads receive non-need-based scholarship or grant aid. 84% freshmen, 79% undergrads receive need-based self-help aid. 7% freshmen, 4% undergrads receive athletic scholarships. 97% freshmen, 94% undergrads receive any aid. 74% undergrads borrow to pay for school. Average cumulative indebtedness $32,251. **Criteria for awarding aid:** *Need-based:* Academics, Athletics, Music/drama *Non-need-based:* Academics, Athletics, Music/drama.

See page 994.

NICHOLLS STATE UNIVERSITY

P.O.Box 2009 Univ. Station, Thibodaux, LA 70310
Phone: 985-448-4507 • **Financial Aid Phone:** (985) 448-4048
E-mail: nicholls@nicholls.edu • **CEEB Code:** 6221
Fax: 985-448-4929 • **Website:** www.nicholls.edu • **ACT Code:** 1580

This public school was founded in 1948. It has a 210 acre campus.

RATINGS

Admissions Selectivity Rating: 75   **Fire Safety Rating:** 85   **Green Rating:** 60*

STUDENTS AND FACULTY

Enrollment: 6,246. **Student Body:** 61% female, 39% male, 4% out-of-state, 2% international (40 countries represented). Asian 1%, African American 18%, Caucasian 73%, Hispanic 1%, Native American 2%, Race unknown 2%. **Retention and Graduation:** 66% freshmen return for sophomore year. **Faculty:** Student/faculty ratio 20:1. 295 full-time faculty, 54% hold PhDs, 11% are members of minority groups, 51% are women. 1% of classes are taught by teaching assistants.

ACADEMICS

Degrees: Associate; Bachelor's; Certificate; Master's; Post-Master's certificate **Classes:** Most classes have 10-19 students. Most lab/discussion sessions have fewer than 10 students. **Most popular majors:** General Studies; Nursing/Registered Nurse (Rn, Asn, Bsn, Msn); Business Administration And Management, General. **Special Study Options:** Cooperative education program; Cross-registration; Distance learning; Dual enrollment; Honors program; Independent study; Internships; Study abroad; Teacher certification

program. Honors programs: You can learn advanced material in small classes taught by outstanding professors. You can enrich your college experience through intellectually stimulating courses that allow you to reach your potential. The Honors Program invites all academically talented and intellectually curious students to participate. By joining the program you can become a select member of the campus community and associate with students who share similar goals and interests. The Program is designed to meet students' needs and interests. Therefore, students in the program determine their degree of involvement. You may take as many honors courses as you choose or simply successfully complete one-three hour honors course each year. And because honors classes fit degree requirements for all majors, participants graduate on time. Combined degree programs: BA/MA. **Disability Services offered to physically disabled students:** Note-taking services; Reader services; Tape recorders; Tutors. **Career services:** Alumni network; Alumni services; Career assessment; Career/job search classes; Internships

FACILITIES

Housing: Apartments for married students; Apartments for single students; Men's dorms; Special housing for disabled student; Special housing for international students; Wellness housing; Women's dorms **Special Academic Facilities/Equipment:** Ameen Art Gallery **Computers:** 100% of classrooms, 100% of dorms, 100% of libraries, 100% of dining areas, 100% of student union, 100% of common outdoor areas have wireless network access. Students can register for classes online. Administrative functions (other than registration) can be performed online.

CAMPUS LIFE

Environment: Village **Activities:** Choral groups; Concert band; Dance; Drama/theater; Jazz band; Literary magazine; Marching band; Music ensembles; Musical theater; Radio station; Student government; Student newspaper; Student-run film society; Television station; Yearbook 121 registered organizations, 24 honor societies, 6 religious organizations. 10 fraternities, 5 sororities. **Athletics (Intercollegiate):** *Men:* baseball, basketball, cross-country, football, golf, tennis. *Women:* basketball, cross-country, golf, soccer, softball, tennis, track/field (outdoor), track/field (indoor), volleyball. **On-Campus Highlights:** Admissions Office, Student Union, Ellender Memorial Library, Guidry Stadium

ADMISSIONS

Freshman Academic Profile: Average high school GPA 3.2. 18% in top 10% of high school class, 43% in top 25% of high school class, 73% in top 50% of high school class. 68% from public high schools. **Test Scores:** ACT middle 50% range 24-20. Minimum internet-based TOEFL 61. Minimum paper TOEFL 500. **Basis for Candidate Selection:** *Very important factors considered include:* rigor of secondary school record. *Important factors considered include:* standardized test scores. *Other factors considered include:* class rank, academic GPA, talent/ability. **Freshman Admission Requirements:** High school diploma is required and GED is accepted *Academic units required:* 4 English, 3 math, 3 science, 2 foreign language, 1 social studies, 2 history, 2 academic electives. **Freshman Admission Statistics:** 2,075 applied, 87.5% admitted, 62% enrolled. **Transfer Admission Requirements:** college transcript(s), Minimum college GPA of 2.0 required. Lowest grade transferable D. **General Admission Information:** Application fee $20. Priority deadline 8/15. Nonfall registration accepted. Admission may be deferred for a maximum of 1 semester.

COSTS AND FINANCIAL AID

Annual in-state tuition $4,556. Annual out-of-state tuition $7,679. Room and board $4,556. Required fees $1,364. Average book expense $1,200. **Required Forms and Deadlines:** FAFSA; Institution's own financial aid form; Noncustodial PROFILE; State aid form. **Types of Aid:** *Need-based scholarships/grants:* College/university scholarship or grant aid from institutional funds; Federal Pell; Private scholarships; SEOG; State scholarships/grants. *Loans: Student Employment:* Federal Work-Study Program available. Institutional employment available. **Financial Aid Statistics:** 93% needy freshmen, 86% needy undergrads receive need-based scholarship or grant aid. 69% freshmen, 33% undergrads receive non-need-based scholarship or grant aid. 51% freshmen, 70% undergrads receive need-based self-help aid. 3% freshmen, 3% undergrads receive athletic scholarships. 77% freshmen, 74% undergrads receive any aid. **Criteria for awarding aid:** *Need-based:* Academics *Non-need-based:* Academics, Athletics, State/district residency.

NICHOLS COLLEGE

PO Box 5000, Dudley, MA 01571-5000
Phone: 508-213-2203 • **Financial Aid Phone:** 508-213-2340
E-mail: admissions@nichols.edu • **CEEB Code:** 3666
Fax: 508-943-9885 • **Website:** www.nichols.edu • **ACT Code:** 1878

This private school was founded in 1815. It has a 200 acre campus.

RATINGS
Admissions Selectivity Rating: 71   **Fire Safety Rating:** 97   **Green Rating:** 64

STUDENTS AND FACULTY
Enrollment: 1,273. **Student Body:** 37% female, 63% male, 40% out-of-state, 2% international (12 countries represented). Asian 1%, African American 8%, Caucasian 78%, Hispanic 8%, Two or more races 4%,
Retention and Graduation: 76% freshmen return for sophomore year. 47% freshmen graduate within 4 years. 51% freshmen graduate within 6 years. 9% grads go on to further study within 1 year. 2% grads pursue business degrees.
Faculty: Student/faculty ratio 17:1. 54 full-time faculty, 72% hold PhDs, 9% are members of minority groups, 41% are women. 0% of classes are taught by teaching assistants.

ACADEMICS
Degrees: Associate; Bachelor's; **Master's Classes:** Most classes have 10-19 students. Most lab/discussion sessions have 10-19 students. **Most popular majors:** Sport And Fitness Administration/Management; Criminal Justice/Law Enforcement Administration; Business/Commerce, General. **Special Study Options:** Accelerated program; Distance learning; Double major; Dual enrollment; Honors program; Independent study; Internships; Study abroad. Honors programs: Students with high academic promise should declare Honors Scholar candidacy during summer orientations for new students or during the Add/Drop periods at the beginning of the first, second, or at the latest, third semester of study. Throughout the program experience, all Honors candidates are required to maintain high standards of academic work and personal integrity as well as to meet all academic performance requirements. **Disability Services offered to physically disabled students:** Note-taking services; Reader services; Tape recorders; Tutors. **Career services:** Alumni network; Alumni services; Career assessment; Career/job search classes; Internships

FACILITIES
Housing: Apartments for single students; Coed dorms; Men's dorms; Special housing for disabled student; Wellness housing; Women's dorms 80% of campus accessible to physically diasbled. **Computers:** 10% of classrooms, 100% of libraries, 100% of dining areas, have wireless network access. Students can register for classes online. Administrative functions (other than registration) can be performed online.

CAMPUS LIFE
Environment: Village **Activities:** Campus Ministries; Dance; International Student Organization; Literary magazine; Model UN; Radio station; Student government 25 registered organizations, 5 honor societies, 1 religious organization. **Athletics (Intercollegiate):** *Men:* baseball, basketball, football, golf, ice hockey, lacrosse, soccer, tennis. *Women:* basketball, field hockey, golf, ice hockey, lacrosse, soccer, softball, tennis. **On-Campus Highlights:** Athletic and Recreation Complex, The Currier Center, Fels Student Center, Davis Cafe, WNRC Radio Station

ADMISSIONS
Freshman Academic Profile: Average high school GPA 2.9. 3% in top 10% of high school class, 17% in top 25% of high school class, 47% in top 50% of high school class. 85% from public high schools. **Test Scores:** SAT Math middle 50% range 450-550. SAT EBRW middle 50% range 460-560. ACT middle 50% range 18-23. Minimum internet-based TOEFL 72. **Basis for Candidate Selection:** *Very important factors considered include:* academic GPA. *Important factors considered include:* rigor of secondary school record, application essay, standardized test scores, recommendation(s), interview, extracurricular activities, character/personal qualities. *Other factors considered include:* class rank, alumni/ae relation, volunteer work, work experience, level of applicant's interest. **Freshman Admission Requirements:** High school diploma is required and GED is accepted *Academic units required:* 4 English, 3 math, 3 science, 2 social studies, 1 history. **Freshman Admission Statistics:** 2,161 applied, 92.5% admitted, 19% enrolled. **Transfer Admission Requirements:** High school transcript, college transcript(s), essay or personal statement, Minimum college GPA of 2.0 required. Lowest grade transferable C. **General Admission Information:** Nonfall registration accepted. Admission may be deferred for a maximum of 1 year.

COSTS AND FINANCIAL AID
Annual tuition $33,600. Room and board $13,800. Required fees $400. Average book expense $1,400. **Required Forms and Deadlines:** FAFSA. **Notification of Awards:** Applicants will be notified of awards on a rolling basis beginning 12/1. **Types of Aid:** *Need-based scholarships/grants:* College/university scholarship or grant aid from institutional funds; Federal Pell; Private scholarships; SEOG; State scholarships/grants. *Loans:* Direct PLUS loans; Direct Subsidized Stafford Loans; Direct Unsubsidized Stafford Loans. *Student Employment:* Federal Work-Study Program available. Institutional employment available. **Financial Aid Statistics:** 100% needy undergrads receive need-based scholarship or grant aid. 8% freshmen, 13% undergrads receive non-need-based scholarship or grant aid. 96% freshmen, 96% undergrads receive need-based self-help aid. 0% freshmen, 0% undergrads receive athletic scholarships. 87% undergrads borrow to pay for school. Average cumulative indebtedness $35,392. **Criteria for awarding aid:** *Need-based:* Academics *Non-need-based:* Academics.

NORTH CAROLINA A&T STATE UNIVERSITY

1601 East Market Street, Greensboro, NC 27411
Phone: 336-334-7946
E-mail: uadmit@ncat.edu
Fax: 336-334-7478 • **Website:** www.ncat.edu

This is a public school.

RATINGS
Admissions Selectivity Rating: 79   **Fire Safety Rating:** 60*   **Green Rating:** 60*

STUDENTS AND FACULTY
Enrollment: 8,921. **Student Body:** 54% female, 46% male, 16% out-of-state, 1% international. Asian 1%, African American 89%, Caucasian 4%, Hispanic 2%, Native American <1%, Pacific Islander <1%, Two or more races <1%, Race unknown 3%.
Retention and Graduation: 74% freshmen return for sophomore year.
Faculty: 532 full-time faculty, 77% hold PhDs, 73% are members of minority groups, 44% are women.

ACADEMICS
Degrees: Bachelor's; Doctoral/Research; **Master's Classes:** Most classes have 10-19 students. Most lab/discussion sessions have fewer than 10 students. **Special Study Options:** Accelerated program; Cooperative education program; Cross-registration; Distance learning; Double major; Dual enrollment; Honors program; Internships; Liberal arts/career combination; Study abroad; Teacher certification program.

FACILITIES
Housing: Coed dorms; Men's dorms; Women's dorms

CAMPUS LIFE
Activities: Campus Ministries; Choral groups; Concert band; Dance; Drama/theater; International Student Organization; Jazz band; Marching band; Music ensembles; Pep band; Radio station; Student government; Student newspaper; Television station; Yearbook.

ADMISSIONS
Freshman Academic Profile: Average high school GPA 3.1. 0% in top 10% of high school class, 6% in top 25% of high school class, 34% in top 50% of high school class. 77% from public high schools. **Test Scores:** SAT Math middle 50% range 410-500. SAT EBRW middle 50% range 390-480. ACT middle 50% range 17-21. Minimum internet-based TOEFL 80. Minimum paper TOEFL 570. **Basis for Candidate Selection:** *Very important factors considered include:* rigor of secondary school record, academic GPA. *Important factors considered include:* class rank, standardized test scores. *Other factors considered include:* extracurricular activities, talent/ability, character/personal qualities, geographical residence, state residency, volunteer work, work experience, level of applicant's interest. **Freshman Admission Requirements:** High school diploma is required and GED is accepted *Academic units required:* 4 English, 4 math, 3 science, 1 science labs, 2 foreign language, 1 social studies, 1 history, 4 academic electives. **Freshman Admission Statistics:** 6,692 applied, 66.4% admitted, 42% enrolled. **Transfer Admission Requirements:** High school transcript, Minimum college GPA of 2.0 required. Lowest grade transferable C. **General Admission Information:** Application fee $45. Priority deadline 2/15. Nonfall registration accepted. Admission may be deferred for a maximum of 1 year.

COSTS AND FINANCIAL AID
Annual in-state tuition $7,225. Annual out-of-state tuition $12,425. Room and board $7,225. Required fees $1,877. Average book expense $1,400. **Required**

Forms and Deadlines: FAFSA. **Notification of Awards:** Applicants will be notified of awards on or about 4/15. **Types of Aid:** *Need-based scholarships/grants:* College/university scholarship or grant aid from institutional funds; Federal Pell; Private scholarships; SEOG; State scholarships/grants. *Loans:* Direct PLUS loans; Direct Subsidized Stafford Loans; Direct Unsubsidized Stafford Loans. **Financial Aid Statistics:** 78% needy freshmen, 75% needy undergrads receive need-based scholarship or grant aid. 92% freshmen, 85% undergrads receive non-need-based scholarship or grant aid. 85% freshmen, 86% undergrads receive need-based self-help aid. 3% freshmen, 2% undergrads receive athletic scholarships. **Criteria for awarding aid:** *Non-need-based:* Academics.

NORTH CAROLINA STATE UNIVERSITY

Box 7001, Raleigh, NC 27695
Phone: 919-515-2434 • **Financial Aid Phone:** 919-515-2421
E-mail: undergrad-admissions@ncsu.edu • **CEEB Code:** 5496
Fax: 919-515-5039 • **Website:** http://www.ncsu.edu/ • **ACT Code:** 3164

This public school was founded in 1887. It has a 2100 acre campus.

RATINGS

Admissions Selectivity Rating: 90   **Fire Safety Rating:** 97   **Green Rating:** 96

STUDENTS AND FACULTY

Enrollment: 22,755. **Student Body:** 45% female, 55% male, 10% out-of-state, 5% international (102 countries represented). Asian 6%, African American 6%, Caucasian 71%, Hispanic 5%, Native American <1%, Pacific Islander <1%, Two or more races 4%, Race unknown 3%.
Retention and Graduation: 94% freshmen return for sophomore year. 50% freshmen graduate within 4 years. 79% freshmen graduate within 6 years. 17% grads go on to further study within 1 year. 7% grads pursue arts and sciences degrees. 1.5% grads pursue law degrees. 2% grads pursue business degrees. 4.7% grads pursue medical degrees. **Faculty:** Student/faculty ratio 13:1. 2,245 full-time faculty, 93% hold PhDs, 17% are members of minority groups, 38% are women. 16% of classes are taught by teaching assistants.

ACADEMICS

Degrees: Bachelor's; Doctoral; Doctoral/Professional; Doctoral/Research; Master's; Post-Bachelor's certificate; Post-Master's certificate; Terminal Associate **Classes:** Most classes have 10-19 students. Most lab/discussion sessions have 20-29 students. **Most popular majors:** Engineering, General; Biology/Biological Sciences, General; Business Administration And Management, General. **Special Study Options:** Accelerated program; Cooperative education program; Cross-registration; Distance learning; Double major; Dual enrollment; English as a Second Language (ESL); Exchange student program (domestic); Honors program; Independent study; Internships; Liberal arts/career combination; Student-designed major; Study abroad; Teacher certification program. Honors programs: The University Honors Program recruits and provides programmatic support for a diverse group of nationally outstanding students, ensuring that they benefit fully from the resources of a major land-grant, research university and the Research Triangle by emphasizing inquiry-, creativity-, and discovery-based learning. The program offers interdisciplinary seminars and a variety of credit-earning opportunites for out-of-classroom experiences. The program emphasizes participation in research by students from all disciplines. Entering students may instead choose to participate in the University Scholars program, which emphasizes enrichment activities and leadership development. There are over 30 honors programs located in the colleges or departments that invite students in their sophomore or junior years. These programs include honors sections of courses, honors seminars, and honors research. Some programs require a senior honor thesis. Combined degree programs: BA/MA. **Disability Services offered to physically disabled students:** Note-taking services; Reader services; Tape recorders. **Career services:** Alumni services; Career assessment; Career/job search classes; Internships

FACILITIES

Housing: Apartments for married students; Apartments for single students; Coed dorms; Fraternity/sorority housing; Men's dorms; Special housing for disabled student; Special housing for international students; Theme housing; Wellness housing; Women's dorms 81% of campus accessible to physically disabled. **Special Academic Facilities/Equipment:** Art museum, arts/crafts center, innovation "sandbox," world-renowned technology library, research

farms and forests, Phytotron with controlled atmosphere growth chambers, pulp/paper and wood products labs, processing equipment for fiber, fabric, and garment manufacture, electron microscopes, nuclear reactor, stable isotope lab, Clean Technology Center, Cellular and Molecular Imaging Facility, Genomic Science Laboratory, Nanofabrication Facility, Analytical Instrumentation Facility, and a Molecular Education, Technology and Research Innovation Center. **Computers:** 94% of classrooms, 100% of libraries, 92% of dining areas, 100% of student union, 52% of common outdoor areas have wireless network access. Students can register for classes online. Administrative functions (other than registration) can be performed online.

CAMPUS LIFE

Environment: Metropolis **Activities:** Campus Ministries; Choral groups; Concert band; Dance; Drama/theater; International Student Organization; Jazz band; Literary magazine; Marching band; Model UN; Music ensembles; Musical theater; Pep band; Radio station; Student government; Student newspaper; Student-run film society; Symphony orchestra; Yearbook 560 registered organizations, 26 honor societies, 25 religious organizations. 33 fraternities, 17 sororities. **Athletics (Intercollegiate):** *Men:* baseball, basketball, cheerleading, cross-country, diving, football, golf, riflery, soccer, swimming, tennis, track/field (outdoor), track/field (indoor), wrestling. *Women:* basketball, cheerleading, cross-country, diving, golf, gymnastics, riflery, soccer, softball, swimming, tennis, track/field (outdoor), track/field (indoor), volleyball. **On-Campus Highlights:** Hunt Library, Gregg Museum of Art and Design, Carter Finley Stadium / PNC Center, Talley Student Union, University Theatre **Environmental Initiatives:** NC State students become leaders in sustainability through the NC State Stewards campus sustainability ambassadors, the Social Innovation Fellows entrepreneurial leaders program and the B Corp Clinic, which pairs student consultants with local businesses seeking to improve sustainability.

ADMISSIONS

Freshman Academic Profile: Average high school GPA 3.7. 46% in top 10% of high school class, 88% in top 25% of high school class, 99% in top 50% of high school class. 87% from public high schools. **Test Scores:** SAT Math middle 50% range 620-710. SAT EBRW middle 50% range 610-680. ACT middle 50% range 27-31. **Basis for Candidate Selection:** *Very important factors considered include:* rigor of secondary school record, class rank, academic GPA, standardized test scores. *Other factors considered include:* application essay, extracurricular activities, talent/ability, character/personal qualities, first generation, alumni/ae relation, geographical residence, state residency, racial/ethnic status, volunteer work, work experience. **Freshman Admission Requirements:** High school diploma is required and GED is accepted *Academic units required:* 4 English, 4 math, 3 science, 1 science labs, 2 foreign language, 1 social studies, 1 history, *Academie units recommended:* 4 English, 4 math, 3 science, 1 science labs, 2 foreign language, 1 social studies, 1 history. **Freshman Admission Statistics:** 26,859 applied, 51.0% admitted, 34% enrolled. **Transfer Admission Requirements:** college transcript(s), Minimum college GPA of 2.0 required. Lowest grade transferable C-. **General Admission Information:** Application fee $85. Priority deadline 10/15. Regular application deadline 1/15. Nonfall registration accepted. Admission may be deferred for a maximum of 1 year.

COSTS AND FINANCIAL AID

Annual in-state tuition $11,078. Annual out-of-state tuition $25,879. Room and board $11,078. Required fees $2,565. Average book expense $1,082. **Required Forms and Deadlines:** FAFSA. **Notification of Awards:** Applicants will be notified of awards on a rolling basis beginning 4/1. **Types of Aid:** *Need-based scholarships/grants:* College/university scholarship or grant aid from institutional funds; Federal Pell; Private scholarships; SEOG; State scholarships/grants; United Negro College Fund. *Loans:* Direct PLUS loans; Direct Subsidized Stafford Loans; Direct Unsubsidized Stafford Loans. *Student Employment:* Federal Work-Study Program available. Institutional employment available. **Financial Aid Statistics:** 93% needy freshmen, 91% needy undergrads receive need-based scholarship or grant aid. 21% freshmen, 13% undergrads receive non-need-based scholarship or grant aid. 68% freshmen, 73% undergrads receive need-based self-help aid. 2% freshmen, 2% undergrads receive athletic scholarships. 75% freshmen, 68% undergrads receive any aid. 54% undergrads borrow to pay for school. Average cumulative indebtedness $21,509. **Criteria for awarding aid:** *Need-based:* Academics, Alumni affiliation, Leadership *Non-need-based:* Academics, Alumni affiliation, Athletics, Leadership, State/district residency.

NORTH CENTRAL COLLEGE

PO Box 3063, Naperville, IL 60566-7063
Phone: 630-637-5800 • **Financial Aid Phone:** 630-637-5600
E-mail: admissions@noctrl.edu • **CEEB Code:** 1555
Fax: 630-637-5819 • **Website:** www.northcentralcollege.edu • **ACT Code:** 1096

This private school, affiliated with the Methodist Church, was founded in 1861. It has a 63.5 acre campus.

RATINGS
Admissions Selectivity Rating: 84   **Fire Safety Rating:** 95   **Green Rating:** 78

STUDENTS AND FACULTY
Enrollment: 2,688. **Student Body:** 55% female, 45% male, 7% out-of-state, 3% international (38 countries represented). Asian 3%, African American 4%, Caucasian 65%, Hispanic 15%, Native American <1%, Pacific Islander <1%, Two or more races 4%, Race unknown 7%.
Retention and Graduation: 79% freshmen return for sophomore year. 61% freshmen graduate within 4 years. 68% freshmen graduate within 6 years.
Faculty: Student/faculty ratio 14:1. 151 full-time faculty, 91% hold PhDs, 16% are members of minority groups, 48% are women. 0% of classes are taught by teaching assistants.

ACADEMICS
Degrees: Bachelor's; Master's; Post-Bachelor's certificate **Most popular majors:** Psychology, General; Business Administration, Management And Operations, Other; Marketing/Marketing Management, General. **Special Study Options:** Accelerated program; Cross-registration; Double major; Dual enrollment; English as a Second Language (ESL); Exchange student program (domestic); Honors program; Independent study; Internships; Liberal arts/career combination; Student-designed major; Study abroad; Teacher certification program. Honors programs: The College Scholars is a comprehensive four year integrative program culminating in a senior honors thesis. The program is open to students from all academic disciplines. Combined degree programs: BA/MA. **Disability Services offered to physically disabled students:** Note-taking services; Reader services; Tape recorders; Tutors. **Career services:** Alumni network; Alumni services; Career assessment; Career/job search classes; Internships; Regional alumni

FACILITIES
Housing: Apartments for single students; Coed dorms; Special housing for disabled student; Wellness housing; Women's dorms 95% of campus accessible to physically disabled. **Computers:** 50% of classrooms, 30% of dorms, 100% of libraries, 100% of dining areas, 100% of student union, 100% of common outdoor areas have wireless network access. Students can register for classes online. Administrative functions (other than registration) can be performed online.

CAMPUS LIFE
Environment: City **Activities:** Campus Ministries; Choral groups; Concert band; Dance; Drama/theater; International Student Organization; Jazz band; Literary magazine; Marching band; Model UN; Music ensembles; Musical theater; Opera; Pep band; Radio station; Student government; Student newspaper 54 registered organizations, 14 honor societies, 6 religious organizations. **Athletics (Intercollegiate):** *Men:* baseball, basketball, cross-country, football, golf, soccer, swimming, tennis, track/field (outdoor), track/field (indoor), wrestling. *Women:* basketball, cheerleading, cross-country, golf, lacrosse, soccer, softball, swimming, tennis, track/field (outdoor), track/field (indoor), volleyball. **On-Campus Highlights:** Old Main—historic home of North Central College, Benedtti-Wehrli Stadium, Res/Rec Center, Fine Arts Center & Wentz Concert Hall, Oesterle Library **Environmental Initiatives:** The College created a green revolving fund, the Cardinal Sustainability Fund, committing a portion of the unrestricted endowment for sustainability initiatives.

ADMISSIONS
Freshman Academic Profile: Average high school GPA 3.7. 28% in top 10% of high school class, 55% in top 25% of high school class, 85% in top 50% of high school class. 89% from public high schools. **Test Scores:** ACT middle 50% range 22-27. Minimum internet-based TOEFL 68. Minimum paper TOEFL 520. **Basis for Candidate Selection:** *Very important factors considered include:* rigor of secondary school record, academic GPA, standardized test scores, character/personal qualities. *Important factors considered include:* extracurricular activities, talent/ability, volunteer work. *Other factors considered include:* application essay, recommendation(s), interview, first generation, alumni/ae relation, work experience, level of applicant's interest. **Freshman Admission Requirements:** High school diploma is required and GED is accepted *Academic units required:* 4 English, 3 math, 3 science, 2 science labs, 2 social studies, 1 history, 3 academic electives, *Academic units recommended:*

3 science labs, 3 foreign language. **Freshman Admission Statistics:** 7,220 applied, 54.4% admitted, 15% enrolled. **Transfer Admission Requirements:** college transcript(s), Minimum college GPA of 2.25 required. Lowest grade transferable D. **General Admission Information:** Application fee $25. Priority deadline 4/15. Nonfall registration accepted. Admission may be deferred for a maximum of 1 year.

COSTS AND FINANCIAL AID
Annual tuition $37,569. Room and board $10,089. Required fees $180. Average book expense $1,200. **Required Forms and Deadlines:** FAFSA. **Notification of Awards:** Applicants will be notified of awards on a rolling basis beginning 12/1. **Types of Aid:** *Need-based scholarships/grants:* College/university scholarship or grant aid from institutional funds; Federal Pell; Private scholarships; SEOG; State scholarships/grants. *Loans:* Direct PLUS loans; Direct Subsidized Stafford Loans; Direct Unsubsidized Stafford Loans. *Student Employment:* Federal Work-Study Program available. Institutional employment available. **Financial Aid Statistics:** 100% needy freshmen, 99% needy undergrads receive need-based scholarship or grant aid. 12% freshmen, 11% undergrads receive non-need-based scholarship or grant aid. 82% freshmen, 84% undergrads receive need-based self-help aid. 0% freshmen, 0% undergrads receive athletic scholarships. 100% freshmen, 98% undergrads receive any aid. 99% undergrads borrow to pay for school. Average cumulative indebtedness $34,809. **Criteria for awarding aid:** *Need-based:* Academics, Religious affiliation *Non-need-based:* Academics, Art, Leadership, Minority status, Music/drama, Religious affiliation, State/district residency.

NORTH DAKOTA STATE UNIVERSITY

PO Box 6050, Fargo, ND 58108
Phone: 701-231-8643 • **Financial Aid Phone:** 800-726-3188
E-mail: ndsu.admission@ndsu.edu • **CEEB Code:** 6474
Fax: 701-231-8802 • **Website:** www.ndsu.edu • **ACT Code:** 3202

This public school was founded in 1890. It has a 2100 acre campus.

RATINGS
Admissions Selectivity Rating: 76   **Fire Safety Rating:** 81   **Green Rating:** 60*

STUDENTS AND FACULTY
Enrollment: 11,609. **Student Body:** 45% female, 55% male, 57% out-of-state, 2% international (38 countries represented). Asian 1%, African American 3%, Caucasian 87%, Hispanic 2%, Native American 1%, Pacific Islander <1%, Two or more races 2%, Race unknown 2%.
Retention and Graduation: 78% freshmen return for sophomore year.
Faculty: Student/faculty ratio 17:1. 712 full-time faculty, 86% hold PhDs, 17% are members of minority groups, 40% are women.

ACADEMICS
Degrees: Bachelor's; Certificate; Doctoral; Doctoral/Professional; Master's; Post-Bachelor's certificate; Post-Master's certificate **Classes:** Most classes have 20-29 students. Most lab/discussion sessions have 10-19 students. **Most popular majors:** Civil Engineering, General; Mechanical Engineering; Business, Management, Marketing, And Related Support Services, Other. **Special Study Options:** Accelerated program; Cooperative education program; Cross-registration; Distance learning; Double major; Dual enrollment; English as a Second Language (ESL); Exchange student program (domestic); Honors program; Independent study; Internships; Student-designed major; Study abroad; Teacher certification program. Honors programs: Scholars Program. **Disability Services offered to physically disabled students:** Note-taking services; Reader services; Tape recorders; Tutors. **Career services:** Career/job search classes; Internships

FACILITIES
Housing: Apartments for married students; Apartments for single students; Coed dorms; Men's dorms; Special housing for disabled student; Special housing for international students; Wellness housing; Women's dorms **Computers:** Students can register for classes online. Administrative functions (other than registration) can be performed online.

CAMPUS LIFE
Environment: City **Activities:** Campus Ministries; Choral groups; Concert band; Dance; Drama/theater; International Student Organization; Jazz band; Marching band; Model UN; Music ensembles; Musical theater; Opera; Pep band; Radio station; Student government; Student newspaper; Symphony orchestra; Television station 218 registered organizations, 22 honor societies, 18 religious organizations. 10 fraternities, 5 sororities. **Athletics (Intercollegiate):** *Men:* baseball, basketball, cross-country, football, golf, track/field (outdoor), track/field (indoor), wrestling. *Women:* basketball, cross-country, golf, soccer,

softball, track/field (outdoor), track/field (indoor), volleyball. **On-Campus Highlights:** Wellness Center, Memorial Union, Fargo Dome, STEM Classroom and Lab Building, Quentin Burdick Building

ADMISSIONS

Freshman Academic Profile: Average high school GPA 3.4. 15% in top 10% of high school class, 41% in top 25% of high school class, 71% in top 50% of high school class. **Test Scores:** SAT Math middle 50% range 500-630. SAT EBRW middle 50% range 480-630. ACT middle 50% range 21-26. Minimum internet-based TOEFL 71. Minimum paper TOEFL 525. **Basis for Candidate Selection:** *Very important factors considered include:* academic GPA, standardized test scores. **Freshman Admission Requirements:** High school diploma is required and GED is accepted *Academic units required:* 4 English, 3 math, 3 science, 3 science labs, 3 social studies. **Freshman Admission Statistics:** 5,311 applied, 93.7% admitted, 51% enrolled. **Transfer Admission Requirements:** college transcript(s), Minimum college GPA of 2.0 required. Lowest grade transferable D. **General Admission Information:** Application fee $35. Regular application deadline 8/1. Nonfall registration accepted. Admission may be deferred for a maximum of 3 years.

COSTS AND FINANCIAL AID

Annual in-state tuition $7,502. Annual out-of-state tuition $18,056. Room and board $7,502. Required fees $1,216. Average book expense $1,100. **Required Forms and Deadlines:** FAFSA. **Notification of Awards:** Applicants will be notified of awards on a rolling basis beginning 4/1. **Types of Aid:** *Need-based scholarships/grants:* College/university scholarship or grant aid from institutional funds; Federal Pell; Private scholarships; SEOG; State scholarships/grants. *Loans:* Direct PLUS loans; Direct Subsidized Stafford Loans; Direct Unsubsidized Stafford Loans. *Student Employment:* Federal Work-Study Program available. Institutional employment available. **Financial Aid Statistics:** 77% needy freshmen, 71% needy undergrads receive need-based scholarship or grant aid. 8% freshmen, 5% undergrads receive non-need-based scholarship or grant aid. 82% freshmen, 83% undergrads receive need-based self-help aid. 2% freshmen, 1% undergrads receive athletic scholarships. 69% undergrads borrow to pay for school. Average cumulative indebtedness $30,740. **Criteria for awarding aid:** *Need-based:* Academics, Alumni affiliation, Art, Athletics, Leadership, Minority status, Music/drama *Non-need-based:* Academics, Alumni affiliation, Art, Athletics, Leadership, Minority status, Music/drama, State/district residency.

NORTH GEORGIA COLLEGE AND STATE UNIVERSITY

82 College Circle, Dahlonega, GA 30503
Phone: 706-864-1800 • **Financial Aid Phone:** 706-864-1412
E-mail: admissions@ung.edu • **CEEB Code:** 5497
Fax: 706-864-1478 • **Website:** www.ung.edu • **ACT Code:** 848

This public school was founded in 1873. It has a 781 acre campus.

RATINGS

Admissions Selectivity Rating: 85   **Fire Safety Rating:** 95   **Green Rating:** 60*

STUDENTS AND FACULTY

Enrollment: 17,089. **Student Body:** 56% female, 44% male, 29% out-of-state, 2% international (94 countries represented). Asian 3%, African American 4%, Caucasian 74%, Hispanic 12%, Native American <1%, Pacific Islander <1%, Two or more races 3%, Race unknown 1%.
Retention and Graduation: 81% freshmen return for sophomore year. 28% freshmen graduate within 4 years. 54% freshmen graduate within 6 years.
Faculty: Student/faculty ratio 19:1. 678 full-time faculty, 69% hold PhDs, 24% are members of minority groups, 49% are women. 0% of classes are taught by teaching assistants.

ACADEMICS

Degrees: Associate; Bachelor's; Certificate; Doctoral/Professional; Doctoral/Research; Master's; Post-Bachelor's certificate; Post-Master's certificate
Classes: Most classes have 10-19 students. Most lab/discussion sessions have 20-29 students. **Most popular majors:** Biology/Biological Sciences, General; Business Administration And Management, General. **Special Study Options:** Accelerated program; Cooperative education program; Distance learning; Double major; Dual enrollment; English as a Second Language (ESL); Honors program; Internships; Liberal arts/career combination; Study abroad; Teacher certification program. Honors programs: UNG's Honors Program provides selected students the opportunity to obtain an education designed to foster maximum intellectual growth while, at the same time, encouraging the development of the whole person. Honors Program students take courses

designed to expand such capabilities as writing, speaking, quantitative reasoning, ethical reasoning, critical and creative thinking, and the ability to engage technology. The program emphasizes independent learning, teamwork, initiative, responsibility, and respect for all persons. **Disability Services offered to physically disabled students:** Note-taking services; Reader services; Tape recorders; Tutors. **Career services:** Alumni services; Career assessment; Career/job search classes; Internships

FACILITIES

Housing: Apartments for single students; Men's dorms; Theme housing; Women's dorms **Special Academic Facilities/Equipment:** Planetarium; 2 Art galleries; Hall of fame; North Georgia museum **Computers:** Students can register for classes online. Administrative functions (other than registration) can be performed online.

CAMPUS LIFE

Environment: Village **Activities:** Campus Ministries; Choral groups; Concert band; Dance; Drama/theater; International Student Organization; Jazz band; Literary magazine; Marching band; Model UN; Music ensembles; Musical theater; Radio station; Student government; Student newspaper; Student-run film society; Symphony orchestra 60 registered organizations, 8 honor societies, 5 religious organizations. 6 fraternities, 4 sororities. **Athletics (Intercollegiate):** *Men:* baseball, basketball, cross-country, football, golf, riflery, soccer, table tennis, tennis, track/field (outdoor), volleyball, water polo. *Women:* basketball, cheerleading, cross-country, golf, riflery, soccer, softball, table tennis, tennis, track/field (outdoor), volleyball, water polo. **On-Campus Highlights:** Library Technology Center, Drill Field, North Georgia Suites, Rec Center, Dining Hall

ADMISSIONS

Freshman Academic Profile: Average high school GPA 3.6. 23% in top 10% of high school class, 62% in top 25% of high school class, 92% in top 50% of high school class. **Test Scores:** SAT Math middle 50% range 510-590. SAT EBRW middle 50% range 520-590. ACT middle 50% range 23-27. Minimum internet-based TOEFL 79. Minimum paper TOEFL 550. **Basis for Candidate Selection:** *Very important factors considered include:* rigor of secondary school record, academic GPA, standardized test scores. **Freshman Admission Requirements:** High school diploma is required and GED is accepted *Academic units required:* 4 English, 4 math, 4 science, 2 science labs, 2 foreign language, 3 social studies, *Academic units recommended:* 4 English, 4 math, 4 science, 2 science labs, 2 foreign language, 3 social studies. **Freshman Admission Statistics:** 4,392 applied, 65.2% admitted, 52% enrolled. **Transfer Admission Requirements:** college transcript(s), statement of good standing from prior institution(s). Minimum college GPA of 2.0 required. Lowest grade transferable C. **General Admission Information:** Application fee $30. Regular application deadline 2/15. Nonfall registration accepted. Admission may be deferred.

COSTS AND FINANCIAL AID

Annual in-state tuition $10,800. Annual out-of-state tuition $19,657. Room and board $10,800. Required fees $1,826. Average book expense $1,420. **Required Forms and Deadlines:** FAFSA. **Notification of Awards:** Applicants will be notified of awards on a rolling basis beginning 4/1. **Types of Aid:** *Need-based scholarships/grants:* College/university scholarship or grant aid from institutional funds; Federal Pell; Private scholarships; SEOG; State scholarships/grants. *Loans:* Direct PLUS loans; Direct Subsidized Stafford Loans; Direct Unsubsidized Stafford Loans. *Student Employment:* Federal Work-Study Program available. Institutional employment available. **Financial Aid Statistics:** 59% needy freshmen, 58% needy undergrads receive need-based scholarship or grant aid. 68% undergrads receive non-need-based scholarship or grant aid. 88% freshmen, 92% undergrads receive need-based self-help aid. 2% freshmen, 2% undergrads receive athletic scholarships. **Criteria for awarding aid:** *Need-based:* Academics, Leadership, Religious affiliation *Non-need-based:* Academics, Alumni affiliation, Art, Athletics, Leadership, Music/drama, State/district residency.

NORTH PARK UNIVERSITY

3225 West Foster Avenue, Chicago, IL 60625-4895
Phone: 773-244-5500 • **Financial Aid Phone:** 773-244-5506
E-mail: admission@northpark.edu • **CEEB Code:** 1556
Fax: 773-244-5243 • **Website:** www.northpark.edu • **ACT Code:** 1098

This private school, affiliated with the Evangelical Covenant Church, was founded in 1891. It has a 30 acre campus.

RATINGS

Admissions Selectivity Rating: 82   **Fire Safety Rating:** 75   **Green Rating:** 60*

The Princeton Review's Complete Book of Colleges

STUDENTS AND FACULTY

Enrollment: 2,188. **Student Body:** 63% female, 37% male, 31% out-of-state, 4% international (31 countries represented). Asian 7%, African American 9%, Caucasian 60%, Hispanic 10%, Native American <1%, Race unknown 10%. **Retention and Graduation:** 71% freshmen return for sophomore year. 15% grads go on to further study within 1 year. 15% grads pursue arts and sciences degrees. 2% grads pursue law degrees. 10% grads pursue business degrees. 3% grads pursue medical degrees. **Faculty:** Student/faculty ratio 14:1. 125 full-time faculty, 88% hold PhDs, 17% are members of minority groups, 50% are women. 0% of classes are taught by teaching assistants.

ACADEMICS

Degrees: Bachelor's; Master's; Post-Bachelor's certificate **Classes:** Most classes have 10-19 students. Most lab/discussion sessions have 10-19 students. **Most popular majors:** Education, General; Biology/Biological Sciences, General; Business Administration And Management, General. **Special Study Options:** Accelerated program; Distance learning; Double major; English as a Second Language (ESL); Honors program; Independent study; Internships; Liberal arts/career combination; Student-designed major; Study abroad; Teacher certification program. Honors programs: The North Park University Honors Congress brings together students of high academic ability with faculty in a learning community designed to promote academic excellence, rigorous intellectual development, community involvement, service to others, and vocational direction. As Honors Congress Scholars, students of promise are provided opportunities to excel during their first two years of undergraduate study. Honors courses during the second two years are offered in individual departments. We strive to take the words of Jesus, "To whom much is given, much is required," and give them special consideration in the Honors Congress. Our philosophy is simply this: The Honors Congress gives students of high intellectual ability an array of learning experiences from which to choose, places them sideby-side with faculty mentors who care, and offers them guidance and encouragement along the way. **Disability Services offered to physically disabled students:** Note-taking services; Reader services; Tape recorders; Tutors. **Career services:** Alumni network; Career assessment; Career/job search classes; Internships

FACILITIES

Housing: Apartments for single students; Men's dorms; Special housing for disabled student; Women's dorms **Special Academic Facilities/Equipment:** Art gallery, language lab, Swedish Historical Society Archives. **Computers:** 100% of libraries, 25% of dining areas, have wireless network access. Students can register for classes online. Administrative functions (other than registration) can be performed online.

CAMPUS LIFE

Environment: Metropolis **Activities:** Campus Ministries; Choral groups; Concert band; Drama/theater; International Student Organization; Jazz band; Literary magazine; Music ensembles; Musical theater; Opera; Pep band; Student government; Student newspaper; Symphony orchestra; Yearbook 4 honor societies, 1 religious organization. **Athletics (Intercollegiate):** *Men:* baseball, basketball, cross-country, football, golf, soccer, track/field (outdoor), track/field (indoor). *Women:* basketball, crew/rowing, cross-country, golf, soccer, softball, track/field (outdoor), track/field (indoor), volleyball. **On-Campus Highlights:** Helwig Recreation Center, Brandel Library, Holmgren Athletic Complex, Central Campus Greenspace, Diverse neighborhood

ADMISSIONS

Freshman Academic Profile: Average high school GPA 3.1. 11% in top 10% of high school class, 35% in top 25% of high school class, 66% in top 50% of high school class. 80% from public high schools. **Test Scores:** SAT Math middle 50% range 460-590. SAT EBRW middle 50% range 470-580. ACT middle 50% range 19-24. Minimum paper TOEFL 550. **Basis for Candidate Selection:** *Very important factors considered include:* rigor of secondary school record, class rank, academic GPA, application essay, standardized test scores, recommendation(s), talent/ability, character/personal qualities. *Important factors considered include:* interview, extracurricular activities, first generation, racial/ethnic status, volunteer work. *Other factors considered include:* alumni/ae relation, geographical residence, work experience, level of applicant's interest. **Freshman Admission Requirements:** High school diploma is required and GED is accepted *Academic units recommended:* 4 English, 3 math, 3 science, 2 foreign language, 1 social studies, 1 history. **Freshman Admission Statistics:** 1,304 applied, 69.8% admitted, 41% enrolled. **Transfer Admission Requirements:** college transcript(s), essay or personal statement, statement of good standing from prior institution(s). Minimum college GPA of 2.0 required. Lowest grade transferable D. **General Admission Information:** Application fee $40. Priority deadline 4/1. Regular application deadline 7/1. Nonfall registration accepted. Admission may be deferred for a maximum of 1 year.

COSTS AND FINANCIAL AID

Annual tuition $23,290. Room and board $8,600. Average book expense $1,000. **Required Forms and Deadlines:** FAFSA. **Notification of Awards:** Applicants will be notified of awards on a rolling basis beginning 3/15. **Types of Aid:** *Need-based scholarships/grants:* College/university scholarship or grant

aid from institutional funds; Federal Nursing Scholarships; Federal Pell; Private scholarships; SEOG; State scholarships/grants. *Loans:* Direct PLUS loans; Direct Subsidized Stafford Loans; Direct Unsubsidized Stafford Loans. *Student Employment:* Federal Work-Study Program available. Institutional employment available. **Financial Aid Statistics:** 70% needy freshmen receive need-based scholarship or grant aid. 42% freshmen, undergrads receive non-need-based scholarship or grant aid. 64% freshmen, undergrads receive need-based self-help aid. 0% freshmen, 0% undergrads receive athletic scholarships. 90% freshmen, 90% undergrads receive any aid. **Criteria for awarding aid:** *Non-need-based:* Academics, Art, Music/drama, Religious affiliation, State/district residency.

NORTHEASTERN ILLINOIS UNIVERSITY

5500 North St. Louis Avenue, Chicago, IL 60625-4699
Phone: 773-442-4000 • **Financial Aid Phone:** 773-442-5009
E-mail: admrec@neiu.edu • **CEEB Code:** 1090
Fax: 773-442-4020 • **Website:** www.neiu.edu • **ACT Code:** 993

This public school was founded in 1867. It has a 67 acre campus.

RATINGS

Admissions Selectivity Rating: 75   **Fire Safety Rating:** 60*   **Green Rating:** 76

STUDENTS AND FACULTY

Enrollment: 7,979. **Student Body:** 56% female, 44% male, 1% out-of-state, 4% international (91 countries represented). Asian 9%, African American 10%, Caucasian 33%, Hispanic 37%, Native American <1%, Pacific Islander <1%, Two or more races 2%, Race unknown 3%. **Retention and Graduation:** 61% freshmen return for sophomore year. **Faculty:** Student/faculty ratio 14:1. 374 full-time faculty, 82% hold PhDs, 30% are members of minority groups, 53% are women.

ACADEMICS

Degrees: Bachelor's; Certificate; **Master's Classes:** Most classes have 20-29 students. Most lab/discussion sessions have 20-29 students. **Most popular majors:** Biology/Biological Sciences, General; Psychology, General; Social Work. **Special Study Options:** Distance learning; Double major; Dual enrollment; English as a Second Language (ESL); Honors program; Independent study; Internships; Liberal arts/career combination; Student-designed major; Study abroad; Teacher certification program; Weekend college. Honors programs: The University Honors Program is a four-year university wide program providing a challenging educational experience to qualified students. The program serves as a laboratory for academic innovation that will improve undergraduate education, and provide a place for students to discover the best in themselves. Through small classes emphasizing writing and critical thinking skills and close, continual academic advisement, the Honors Program seeks to provide access to excellent education for its students. **Disability Services offered to physically disabled students:** Note-taking services; Reader services; Tape recorders; Tutors. **Career services:** Alumni network; Alumni services; Career assessment; Career/job search classes; Internships

FACILITIES

Housing: 98% of campus accessible to physically diasbled. **Special Academic Facilities/Equipment:** Art gallery, learning center with audiovisual, TV, multimedia, film, photography, graphic arts, and electronic instructional equipment, listening room. **Computers:** 50% of classrooms, n/a% of dorms, 100% of libraries, 80% of dining areas, 100% of student union, 50% of common outdoor areas have wireless network access. Students can register for classes online. Administrative functions (other than registration) can be performed online.

CAMPUS LIFE

Environment: Metropolis **Activities:** Campus Ministries; Choral groups; Concert band; Dance; Drama/theater; International Student Organization; Jazz band; Literary magazine; Model UN; Music ensembles; Musical theater; Opera; Radio station; Student government; Student newspaper; Student-run film society; Symphony orchestra 42 registered organizations, 12 honor societies, 6 religious organizations. 3 fraternities, 3 sororities. **On-Campus Highlights:** Angelina Pedroso Center, Fine Arts Building/ Art Gallery, Ensemble Dance Company, Health and Wellness Center, Library **Environmental Initiatives:** Recycling

ADMISSIONS

Freshman Academic Profile: Average high school GPA 2.8. 3% in top 10% of high school class, 13% in top 25% of high school class, 44% in top 50% of high school class. 87% from public high schools. **Test Scores:** ACT middle 50% range 16-20. Minimum paper TOEFL 500. **Basis for Candidate Selection:** *Very important factors considered include:* class rank, academic GPA, standardized test scores. **Freshman Admission Requirements:** High school diploma is required and GED is accepted *Academic units required:* 4 English, 3 math, 3 science, 3 social studies, 2 visual/performing arts, *Academic units recommended:* 4 English, 3 math, 3 science, 3 social studies, 2 visual/performing arts. **Freshman Admission Statistics:** 4,499 applied, 67.0% admitted, 25% enrolled. **Transfer Admission Requirements:** college transcript(s), statement of good standing from prior institution(s). Minimum college GPA of 2.0 required. Lowest grade transferable D. **General Admission Information:** Application fee $30. Regular application deadline 7/1. Nonfall registration accepted. Admission may be deferred.

COSTS AND FINANCIAL AID
Annual in-state tuition $11,100. Annual out-of-state tuition $14,596. Room and board $11,100. Required fees $3,322. **Required Forms and Deadlines:** FAFSA. **Notification of Awards:** Applicants will be notified of awards on a rolling basis beginning 3/15. **Types of Aid:** *Need-based scholarships/ grants:* College/university scholarship or grant aid from institutional funds; Federal Pell; Private scholarships; SEOG; State scholarships/grants. *Loans:* Direct PLUS loans; Direct Subsidized Stafford Loans; Direct Unsubsidized Stafford Loans. *Student Employment:* Federal Work-Study Program available. Institutional employment available. **Financial Aid Statistics:** 84% needy freshmen, 78% needy undergrads receive need-based scholarship or grant aid. 9% freshmen, 17% undergrads receive non-need-based scholarship or grant aid. 18% freshmen, 41% undergrads receive need-based self-help aid. 0% freshmen, 0% undergrads receive athletic scholarships. 59% freshmen, 55% undergrads receive any aid. Average cumulative indebtedness $15,713. **Criteria for awarding aid:** *Non-need-based:* Academics, Art, Leadership, Music/drama.

NORTHEASTERN STATE UNIVERSITY

600 North Grand Ave, Tahlequah, OK 74464-2399
Phone: 918-444-2200 • **Financial Aid Phone:** 918-444-3456
E-mail: nsuinfo@nsuok.edu • **CEEB Code:** 6485
Fax: 918-458-2342 • **ACT Code:** 3408

This public school was founded in 1846. It has a 200 acre campus.

RATINGS
Admissions Selectivity Rating: 74   **Fire Safety Rating:** 60*   **Green Rating:** 60*

STUDENTS AND FACULTY
Enrollment: 7,036. **Student Body:** 61% female, 39% male, 6% out-of-state, 2% international (41 countries represented). Asian 2%, African American 4%, Caucasian 49%, Hispanic 5%, Native American 20%, Pacific Islander <1%, Two or more races 17%, Race unknown 2%.
Retention and Graduation: 62% freshmen return for sophomore year.
Faculty: Student/faculty ratio 17:1. 306 full-time faculty, 77% hold PhDs, 21% are members of minority groups, 51% are women.

ACADEMICS
Degrees: Bachelor's; Master's; Post-Bachelor's certificate; Post-Master's certificate **Classes:** Most classes have 20-29 students. Most lab/discussion sessions have 20-29 students. **Most popular majors:** Elementary Education And Teaching; Psychology, General; Accounting. **Special Study Options:** Distance learning; Double major; Dual enrollment; English as a Second Language (ESL); Honors program; Independent study; Internships; Student-designed major; Study abroad; Teacher certification program; Weekend college. Honors programs: NSU Honors Program: The Honors Program at Northeastern State University is a challenging educational option for academically talented students who enjoy learning. Honor students work with distinguished faculty members and peers in enhanced courses, pursue independent research, and participate in co-curricular cultural experiences. NSU President's Leadership Class: The President's Leadership Class is a unique leadership/scholarship program designed to cultivate outstanding potential in proven student leaders. Applicants for the PLC should display outstanding leadership capabilities, and must have an exceptionally strong academic record. **Disability Services offered to physically disabled students:** Note-taking services; Reader services; Tape recorders; Tutors. **Career services:** Alumni services; Career assessment; Career/job search classes

FACILITIES
Housing: Apartments for married students; Apartments for single students; Coed dorms; Fraternity/sorority housing; Special housing for disabled student; Theme housing; Women's dorms **Computers:** Administrative functions (other than registration) can be performed online.

CAMPUS LIFE
Environment: Village **Activities:** Campus Ministries; Choral groups; Concert band; Dance; Drama/theater; International Student Organization; Jazz band; Marching band; Model UN; Music ensembles; Pep band; Student government; Student newspaper; Symphony orchestra; Television station 77 registered organizations, 9 honor societies, 5 religious organizations. 7 fraternities, 6 sororities. **Athletics (Intercollegiate):** *Men:* baseball, basketball, football, golf, soccer. *Women:* basketball, golf, soccer, softball, tennis. **On-Campus Highlights:** Seminary Hall, University Center, Science Lab Building, NET Building, Seminary Suites

ADMISSIONS
Freshman Academic Profile: Average high school GPA 3.4. 20% in top 10% of high school class, 47% in top 25% of high school class, 83% in top 50% of high school class. 95% from public high schools. **Test Scores:** ACT middle 50% range 19-23. Minimum paper TOEFL 500. **Basis for Candidate Selection:** *Very important factors considered include:* rigor of secondary school record, class rank, academic GPA, standardized test scores. *Other factors considered include:* interview, extracurricular activities, first generation, geographical residence, state residency, level of applicant's interest. **Freshman Admission Requirements:** High school diploma is required and GED is accepted *Academic units required:* 4 English, 3 math, 3 science, 3 science labs, 2 social studies, 1 history, and 2 units from above areas or other academic areas. **Freshman Admission Statistics:** 1,512 applied, 91.8% admitted, 58% enrolled. **Transfer Admission Requirements:** college transcript(s), Minimum college GPA of 2.0 required. Lowest grade transferable D. **General Admission Information:** Application fee $25. Nonfall registration accepted. Admission may be deferred.

COSTS AND FINANCIAL AID
Annual in-state tuition $1,122. Annual out-of-state tuition $11,775. Required fees $1,122. Average book expense $1,200. **Required Forms and Deadlines:** FAFSA. **Notification of Awards:** Applicants will be notified of awards on a rolling basis beginning 3/1. **Types of Aid:** *Need-based scholarships/ grants:* College/university scholarship or grant aid from institutional funds; Federal Pell; Private scholarships; SEOG; State scholarships/grants. *Loans:* Direct PLUS loans; Direct Subsidized Stafford Loans; Direct Unsubsidized Stafford Loans. *Student Employment:* Federal Work-Study Program available. Institutional employment available. **Financial Aid Statistics:** 94% needy freshmen, 86% needy undergrads receive need-based scholarship or grant aid. 31% freshmen, 15% undergrads receive non-need-based scholarship or grant aid. 80% freshmen, 89% undergrads receive need-based self-help aid. 4% freshmen, 3% undergrads receive athletic scholarships. 63% freshmen, 62% undergrads receive any aid. Average cumulative indebtedness $21,055. **Criteria for awarding aid:** *Non-need-based:* Academics, Alumni affiliation, Art, Athletics, Leadership, Minority status, Music/drama, Religious affiliation, State/district residency.

NORTHEASTERN UNIVERSITY

360 Huntington Avenue, Boston, MA 02115
Phone: 617-373-2200 • **Financial Aid Phone:** 617-373-3190
E-mail: admissions@northeastern.edu • **CEEB Code:** 3667
Fax: 617-373-8780 • **Website:** www.northeastern.edu • **ACT Code:** 1880

This private school was founded in 1898. It has a 73 acre campus.

RATINGS
Admissions Selectivity Rating: 96   **Fire Safety Rating:** 94   **Green Rating:** 93

STUDENTS AND FACULTY
Enrollment: 18,109. **Student Body:** 51% female, 49% male, 73% out-of-state, 18% international (139 countries represented). Asian 13%, African American 4%, Caucasian 47%, Hispanic 8%, Native American <1%, Pacific Islander <1%, Two or more races 4%, Race unknown 6%.
Retention and Graduation: 97% freshmen return for sophomore year. 87% freshmen graduate within 6 years. **Faculty:** Student/faculty ratio 14:1. 1,310 full-time faculty, 94% hold PhDs, 18% are members of minority groups, 42% are women.

ACADEMICS
Degrees: Bachelor's; Doctoral/Professional; Doctoral/Research; Master's; Post-Master's certificate **Classes:** Most classes have 10-19 students. **Most popular**

majors: Engineering, General; Health Services/Allied Health/Health Sciences, General. **Special Study Options:** Accelerated program; Cooperative education program; Cross-registration; Distance learning; Double major; English as a Second Language (ESL); Exchange student program (domestic); Honors program; Independent study; Internships; Liberal arts/career combination; Student-designed major; Study abroad; Teacher certification program. Honors programs: The University Honors Program at Northeastern offers exceptionally motivated students an opportunity to elevate their educational experience through deeper academic exploration, a higher level of engagement with faculty, and special options for service and leadership. Honors Program students are invited to choose one of several Living and Learning Communities (LLCs) proposed by the students each year. Combined degree programs: BA/JD; BA/MA; BA/MEng. **Disability Services offered to physically disabled students:** Note-taking services; Reader services; Tape recorders. **Career services:** Alumni network; Alumni services; Career assessment; Career/job search classes; Internships; Regional alumni

FACILITIES

Housing: Apartments for single students; Coed dorms; Theme housing; Wellness housing 95% of campus accessible to physically diasbled. **Special Academic Facilities/Equipment:** 'Gallery 360,' state-of-the-art homeland security research facility; complex network research, drug recovery, high-rate non-manufacturing, subsurface sensing and imaging systems, and urban and regional policy centers; chemical and biological analysis, information assurance, urban health research, African-American, race and justice, and global innovation institutes. John D. O'Bryant African-American Institute, Egan Science/Engineering Center, Behrakis Health Sciences Center, Marine Science Center, Center for Subsurfacing Sensing and Imaging Systems (CenSSIS), Barnett Institute of Chemical and Biological Analysis, Research Vessel MYSIS, Badger-Rosen Squashbusters Center **Computers:** 100% of classrooms, 20% of dorms, 100% of libraries, 75% of dining areas, 100% of student union, 100% of common outdoor areas have wireless network access. Students can register for classes online. Administrative functions (other than registration) can be performed online.

CAMPUS LIFE

Environment: Metropolis **Activities:** Choral groups; Concert band; Dance; Drama/theater; International Student Organization; Jazz band; Literary magazine; Model UN; Music ensembles; Musical theater; Pep band; Radio station; Student government; Student newspaper; Student-run film society; Symphony orchestra; Television station; Yearbook 225 registered organizations, 15 honor societies, 20 religious organizations. 9 fraternities, 8 sororities. **Athletics (Intercollegiate):** *Men:* baseball, basketball, crew/rowing, cross-country, ice hockey, soccer, track/field (outdoor), track/field (indoor). *Women:* basketball, crew/rowing, cross-country, diving, field hockey, ice hockey, soccer, swimming, track/field (outdoor), track/field (indoor), volleyball. **On-Campus Highlights:** Curry Student Center, Marino Health and Fitness Center, Cyber Cafe, International Village, Levine Marketplace **Environmental Initiatives:** ACUPCC Presidents Climate Committee

ADMISSIONS

Freshman Academic Profile: 75% in top 10% of high school class, 93% in top 25% of high school class, 99% in top 50% of high school class. **Test Scores:** SAT Math middle 50% range 690-770. SAT EBRW middle 50% range 680-750. ACT middle 50% range 32-34. Minimum internet-based TOEFL 92. **Basis for Candidate Selection:** *Very important factors considered include:* rigor of secondary school record, academic GPA, application essay, standardized test scores, recommendation(s). *Important factors considered include:* extracurricular activities, talent/ability, character/personal qualities, volunteer work, work experience. *Other factors considered include:* class rank, first generation, geographical residence, racial/ethnic status, level of applicant's interest. **Freshman Admission Requirements:** High school diploma is required and GED is accepted *Academic units required:* 4 English, 3 math, 3 science, 2 science labs, 2 foreign language, 3 social studies, 2 history, *Academic units recommended:* 4 math, 4 science. **Freshman Admission Statistics:** 54,209 applied, 27.4% admitted, 21% enrolled. **Transfer Admission Requirements:** college transcript(s), essay or personal statement, statement of good standing from prior institution(s). Minimum college GPA of 2.0 required. Lowest grade transferable C. **General Admission Information:** Application fee $75. Regular application deadline 1/1. Nonfall registration accepted. Admission may be deferred.

COSTS AND FINANCIAL AID

Average book expense $1,000. **Required Forms and Deadlines:** CSS/Financial Aid PROFILE; FAFSA; Noncustodial PROFILE. **Notification of Awards:** Applicants will be notified of awards on or about 4/1. **Types of Aid:** *Need-based scholarships/grants:* College/university scholarship or grant aid from institutional funds; Federal Pell; Private scholarships; SEOG; State scholarships/grants. *Loans:* Direct PLUS loans; Direct Subsidized Stafford Loans; Direct Unsubsidized Stafford Loans. *Student Employment:* Federal Work-Study Program available. Institutional employment available. **Financial Aid Statistics:** 98% needy freshmen, 91% needy undergrads receive need-based scholarship or grant aid. 45% freshmen, 37% undergrads receive

non-need-based scholarship or grant aid. 89% freshmen, 88% undergrads receive need-based self-help aid. 2% freshmen, 1% undergrads receive athletic scholarships. **Criteria for awarding aid:** *Non-need-based:* Academics, Athletics, Leadership.

See page 996.

NORTHERN ARIZONA UNIVERSITY

PO Box 4084, Flagstaff, AZ 86011-4084
Phone: 928-523-5511 • **Financial Aid Phone:** 855.628.6333
E-mail: admissions@nau.edu • **CEEB Code:** 4006
Fax: 928-523-6023 • **Website:** www.nau.edu • **ACT Code:** 86

This public school was founded in 1899. It has a 683 acre campus.

RATINGS
Admissions Selectivity Rating: 76   **Fire Safety Rating:** 91   **Green Rating:** 97

STUDENTS AND FACULTY
Enrollment: 26,974. **Student Body:** 60% female, 40% male, 29% out-of-state, 4% international (70 countries represented). Asian 2%, African American 3%, Caucasian 57%, Hispanic 24%, Native American 2%, Pacific Islander <1%, Two or more races 6%, Race unknown 1%.
Retention and Graduation: 76% freshmen return for sophomore year. 40% freshmen graduate within 4 years. 55% freshmen graduate within 6 years. 18% grads go on to further study within 1 year. **Faculty:** Student/faculty ratio 19:1. 1,132 full-time faculty, 15% are members of minority groups, 51% are women.

ACADEMICS
Degrees: Bachelor's; Certificate; Doctoral; Doctoral/Professional; Doctoral/Research; Master's; Post-Bachelor's certificate; Post-Master's certificate **Classes:** Most classes have 20-29 students. Most lab/discussion sessions have 20-29 students. **Most popular majors:** Biomedical Sciences, General; Criminology; Registered Nursing/Registered Nurse. **Special Study Options:** Accelerated program; Cooperative education program; Distance learning; Double major; Dual enrollment; English as a Second Language (ESL); Exchange student program (domestic); Honors program; Independent study; Internships; Liberal arts/career combination; Student-designed major; Study abroad; Teacher certification program. Honors programs: Our rigorous, personalized program of study with honors-distinguished coursework challenges students' intellect and stimulates their love of learning. Upon graduation students will receive special honors distinction on their transcripts and diploma, helping graduates gain a competitive edge early in their chosen career Combined degree programs: BA/JD; BA/MA; BA/MEng. **Disability Services offered to physically disabled students:** Note-taking services; Reader services; Tape recorders; Tutors. **Career services:** Alumni services; Career assessment; Career/job search classes; Internships

FACILITIES
Housing: Apartments for married students; Apartments for single students; Coed dorms; Fraternity/sorority housing; Special housing for disabled student; Special housing for international students; Theme housing 90% of campus accessible to physically diasbled. **Special Academic Facilities/Equipment:** Health and Learning Center, Native American Cultural Center, art gallery, art and music studios, observatory, multi-disciplinary research center, 4,000-acre experimental forest. **Computers:** 100% of classrooms, 100% of dorms, 100% of libraries, 100% of dining areas, 100% of student union, 25% of common outdoor areas have wireless network access. Students can register for classes online. Administrative functions (other than registration) can be performed online.

CAMPUS LIFE
Environment: Town **Activities:** Campus Ministries; Choral groups; Concert band; Dance; Drama/theater; International Student Organization; Jazz band; Marching band; Model UN; Music ensembles; Musical theater; Opera; Pep band; Radio station; Student government; Student newspaper; Symphony orchestra; Television station 193 registered organizations, 20 honor societies, 7 religious organizations. 14 fraternities, 9 sororities. **Athletics (Intercollegiate):** *Men:* basketball, cheerleading, cross-country, football, tennis, track/field (outdoor). *Women:* basketball, cheerleading, cross-country, diving, golf, soccer, swimming, tennis, track/field (outdoor), volleyball. **On-Campus Highlights:** University Union, Historic Main Quadrangle, Health and Learning Center, Cline Library, NAU Skydome **Environmental Initiatives:** Green Building commitment

ADMISSIONS
Freshman Academic Profile: Average high school GPA 3.6. 21% in top 10% of high school class, 51% in top 25% of high school class, 82% in top 50% of

high school class. **Test Scores:** SAT Math middle 50% range 510-610. SAT EBRW middle 50% range 520-620. ACT middle 50% range 20-25. Minimum internet-based TOEFL 70. Minimum paper TOEFL 525. **Basis for Candidate Selection:** *Very important factors considered include:* rigor of secondary school record, academic GPA. *Important factors considered include:* class rank, standardized test scores. **Freshman Admission Requirements:** High school diploma is required and GED is accepted *Academic units required:* 4 English, 4 math, 3 science, 3 science labs, 2 foreign language, 1 social studies, 1 history, and 1 unit from above areas or other academic areas. **Freshman Admission Statistics:** 36,875 applied, 80.8% admitted, 20% enrolled. Minimum college GPA of 2.0 required. Lowest grade transferable C. **General Admission Information:** Application fee $25. Nonfall registration accepted. Admission may be deferred.

COSTS AND FINANCIAL AID

Average book expense $1,000. **Required Forms and Deadlines:** FAFSA. **Notification of Awards:** Applicants will be notified of awards on a rolling basis beginning 2/1. **Types of Aid:** *Need-based scholarships/grants:* College/university scholarship or grant aid from institutional funds; Federal Nursing Scholarships; Federal Pell; Private scholarships; SEOG; State scholarships/grants. *Loans:* Direct PLUS loans; Direct Subsidized Stafford Loans; Direct Unsubsidized Stafford Loans. *Student Employment:* Federal Work-Study Program available. Institutional employment available. **Financial Aid Statistics:** 67% needy freshmen, 69% needy undergrads receive need-based scholarship or grant aid. 77% freshmen, 54% undergrads receive non-need-based scholarship or grant aid. 60% freshmen, 67% undergrads receive need-based self-help aid. 1% freshmen, 1% undergrads receive athletic scholarships. 84% freshmen, 75% undergrads receive any aid. 63% undergrads borrow to pay for school. Average cumulative indebtedness $29,311. **Criteria for awarding aid:** *Need-based:* Academics, Art, Leadership, Minority status, Music/drama *Non-need-based:* Academics, Alumni affiliation, Art, Athletics, Leadership, Minority status, Music/drama, State/district residency.

NORTHERN ILLINOIS UNIVERSITY

NULL, DeKalb, IL
Financial Aid Phone: 815-753-1395 • **CEEB Code:** 1559
ACT Code: 1102

This public school was founded in 1895. It has a 546 acre campus.

RATINGS

Admissions Selectivity Rating: 84   **Fire Safety Rating:** 60*   **Green Rating:** 61

STUDENTS AND FACULTY

Enrollment: 14,036. **Student Body:** 49% female, 51% male, 3% out-of-state, 2% international. Asian 5%, African American 16%, Caucasian 56%, Hispanic 17%, Native American <1%, Pacific Islander <1%, Two or more races 4%, Race unknown 1%.
Retention and Graduation: 73% freshmen return for sophomore year. 16% grads pursue arts and sciences degrees. 3% grads pursue law degrees. 51% grads pursue business degrees. 1% grads pursue medical degrees. **Faculty:** Student/faculty ratio 15:1. 832 full-time faculty, 82% hold PhDs; 14% are members of minority groups, 46% are women.

ACADEMICS

Classes: Most classes have 20-29 students. Most lab/discussion sessions have 10-19 students. **Special Study Options:** Cooperative education program; Distance learning; Double major; Dual enrollment; External degree program; Honors program; Independent study; Internships; Student-designed major; Study abroad; Teacher certification program. Combined degree programs: BA/JD. **Disability Services offered to physically disabled students:** Note-taking services; Reader services; Tape recorders. **Career services:** Alumni network; Alumni services; Career/job search classes; Internships; Regional alumni

FACILITIES

Housing: Apartments for married students; Coed dorms; Fraternity/sorority housing; Men's dorms; Special housing for disabled student; Special housing for international students; Women's dorms 90% of campus accessible to physically disabled. **Special Academic Facilities/Equipment:** Art and anthropology museums, plant molecular biology center. **Computers:** Students can register for classes online.

CAMPUS LIFE

Environment: Village **Activities:** Campus Ministries; Choral groups; Concert band; Dance; Drama/theater; International Student Organization;

Jazz band; Marching band; Model UN; Music ensembles; Musical theater; Opera; Pep band; Radio station; Student government; Student newspaper; Student-run film society; Symphony orchestra; Television station 200 registered organizations, 13 religious organizations. 22 fraternities, 14 sororities. **Athletics (Intercollegiate):** *Men:* baseball, basketball, diving, football, golf, soccer, swimming, tennis, wrestling. *Women:* basketball, cross-country, golf, gymnastics, soccer, softball, swimming, tennis, volleyball. **On-Campus Highlights:** Barsema Hall, Convocation Center, Holmes Student Center, Campus Life Building, Recreation Center

ADMISSIONS

Freshman Academic Profile: 12% in top 10% of high school class, 36% in top 25% of high school class, 71% in top 50% of high school class. **Test Scores:** ACT middle 50% range 19-25. Minimum paper TOEFL 525. **Basis for Candidate Selection:** *Very important factors considered include:* rigor of secondary school record, class rank, standardized test scores. *Other factors considered include:* application essay, recommendation(s), interview, extracurricular activities, talent/ability, racial/ethnic status. **Freshman Admission Requirements:** High school diploma is required and GED is accepted *Academic units required:* 4 English, 2 math, 2 science, 1 science labs, 1 foreign language, 2 social studies, 1 history, *Academic units recommended:* 4 math, 4 science, 2 science labs, 2 foreign language, 3 social studies. **Freshman Admission Statistics:** 14,980 applied, 51.8% admitted, 23% enrolled. **Transfer Admission Requirements:** college transcript(s), Minimum college GPA of 2.0 required. Lowest grade transferable c. **General Admission Information:** Application fee $40. Priority deadline 3/1. Regular application deadline 8/1. Nonfall registration accepted.

COSTS AND FINANCIAL AID

Room and board $9,670. Required fees $2,758. Average book expense $1,400. **Required Forms and Deadlines:** FAFSA; Institution's own financial aid form; Noncustodial PROFILE. **Notification of Awards:** Applicants will be notified of awards on a rolling basis beginning 3/1. **Types of Aid:** *Need-based scholarships/grants:* College/university scholarship or grant aid from institutional funds; Federal Nursing Scholarships; Federal Pell; Private scholarships; SEOG; State scholarships/grants. *Loans: Student Employment:* Federal Work-Study Program available. Institutional employment available. **Financial Aid Statistics:** 99% needy freshmen, 83% needy undergrads receive need-based scholarship or grant aid. 6% freshmen, 3% undergrads receive non-need-based scholarship or grant aid. 87% freshmen, 92% undergrads receive need-based self-help aid. 2% freshmen, 2% undergrads receive athletic scholarships. 81% freshmen, 70% undergrads receive any aid. 78% undergrads borrow to pay for school. Average cumulative indebtedness $34,713. **Criteria for awarding aid:** *Need-based:* Academics *Non-need-based:* Academics, Alumni affiliation, Art, Athletics, Leadership, Music/drama.

NORTHERN KENTUCKY UNIVERSITY

Nunn Drive, Highland Heights, KY 41099
Phone: 859-572-5220 • **Financial Aid Phone:** 859-572-5143
E-mail: beanorse@nku.edu • **CEEB Code:** 1574
Fax: 859-572-6665 • **Website:** www.nku.edu • **ACT Code:** 1566

This public school was founded in 1968. It has a 400 acre campus.

RATINGS

Admissions Selectivity Rating: 74   **Fire Safety Rating:** 85   **Green Rating:** 76

STUDENTS AND FACULTY

Enrollment: 10,746. **Student Body:** 56% female, 44% male, 32% out-of-state, 3% international (61 countries represented). Asian 1%, African American 7%, Caucasian 81%, Hispanic 3%, Native American <1%, Pacific Islander <1%, Two or more races 3%, Race unknown 1%.
Retention and Graduation: 71% freshmen return for sophomore year. 16% freshmen graduate within 4 years. 40% freshmen graduate within 6 years. **Faculty:** Student/faculty ratio 19:1. 568 full-time faculty, 69% hold PhDs, 14% are members of minority groups, 53% are women. 0% of classes are taught by teaching assistants.

ACADEMICS

Degrees: Associate; Bachelor's; Certificate; Doctoral; Doctoral Other; Doctoral/Professional; Master's; Post-Bachelor's certificate; Post-Master's certificate **Classes:** Most classes have 10-19 students. **Most popular majors:** Biology/Biological Sciences, General; Registered Nursing/Registered Nurse; Organizational Behavior Studies. **Special Study Options:** Accelerated program; Cooperative education program; Cross-registration; Distance learning; Double major; Dual enrollment; English as a Second Language (ESL); Honors

The Princeton Review's Complete Book of Colleges

program; Independent study; Internships; Liberal arts/career combination; Student-designed major; Study abroad; Teacher certification program. Honors programs: The NKU Honors Program provides qualified students a 21-hour minor, which includes 15 semester hours of seminars, each having a maximum enrollment of 15 students, plus 6 semester hours for completing the Honors Thesis. At the core of the Honors experience, the seminars emphasize discussion and discovery of ideas. NKU's Honors Program is university-wide. The program showcases open-ended seminars not conforming to the boundaries traditionally dividing fields of expertise. Honors learning affords the intellectual challenges of interdisciplinary education. Combined degree programs: BA/JD. **Disability Services offered to physically disabled students:** Note-taking services; Reader services; Tape recorders; Tutors. **Career services:** Alumni services; Career assessment; Career/job search classes; Internships

FACILITIES

Housing: Apartments for single students; Coed dorms; Fraternity/sorority housing; Special housing for disabled student; Special housing for international students; Theme housing 100% of campus accessible to physically diasbled. **Special Academic Facilities/Equipment:** Art gallery, The Museum of Anthropology, US Bank/Ralph V. Haile Planetarium, George and Ellen Rieveschl Digitorium **Computers:** Students can register for classes online. Administrative functions (other than registration) can be performed online.

CAMPUS LIFE

Environment: Village **Activities:** Campus Ministries; Choral groups; Dance; Drama/theater; International Student Organization; Literary magazine; Marching band; Model UN; Music ensembles; Musical theater; Opera; Pep band; Radio station; Student government; Student newspaper; Student-run film society; Television station 125 registered organizations, 14 honor societies, 9 religious organizations. 8 fraternities, 8 sororities. **Athletics (Intercollegiate):** *Men:* baseball, basketball, cheerleading, cross-country, golf, soccer, tennis. *Women:* basketball, cheerleading, cross-country, golf, soccer, softball, tennis, volleyball. **On-Campus Highlights:** Student Union, Starbucks Cafe, Campus Recreation Center, BB&T Arena, Norse Tech Bar **Environmental Initiatives:** In an effort to reduce greenhouse gas emissions from commuting, NKU is committed to providing alternative transportation options to the campus community. Students, faculty, and staff can take advantage of the University's free bike share program, free access to all TANK buses, and the ZipCar car-sharing service.

ADMISSIONS

Freshman Academic Profile: Average high school GPA 3.4. 12% in top 10% of high school class, 34% in top 25% of high school class, 68% in top 50% of high school class. **Test Scores:** ACT middle 50% range 20-26. Minimum internet-based TOEFL 61. Minimum paper TOEFL 500. **Basis for Candidate Selection:** *Very important factors considered include:* rigor of secondary school record, academic GPA, standardized test scores. *Important factors considered include:* class rank. *Other factors considered include:* recommendation(s), talent/ability. **Freshman Admission Requirements:** High school diploma is required and GED is accepted *Academic units required:* 4 English, 3 math, 3 science, 1 science labs, 2 foreign language, 3 social studies, *Academic units recommended:* 1 history, 5 academic electives, 1 computer science, 1 visual/performing arts. **Freshman Admission Statistics:** 5,852 applied, 90.4% admitted, 41% enrolled. **Transfer Admission Requirements:** college transcript(s), Minimum college GPA of 2.0 required. Lowest grade transferable D. **General Admission Information:** Application fee $40. Priority deadline 5/1. Regular application deadline 8/22. Nonfall registration accepted. Admission may be deferred for a maximum of 1 year.

COSTS AND FINANCIAL AID

Required Forms and Deadlines: FAFSA. **Notification of Awards:** Applicants will be notified of awards on a rolling basis beginning 3/15. **Types of Aid:** *Need-based scholarships/grants:* College/university scholarship or grant aid from institutional funds; Federal Pell; Private scholarships; SEOG; State scholarships/grants. *Loans:* Direct PLUS loans; Direct Subsidized Stafford Loans; Direct Unsubsidized Stafford Loans. *Student Employment:* Federal Work-Study Program available. Institutional employment available. **Financial Aid Statistics:** 58% needy freshmen, 59% needy undergrads receive need-based scholarship or grant aid. 75% freshmen, 57% undergrads receive non-need-based scholarship or grant aid. 88% freshmen, 90% undergrads receive need-based self-help aid. 3% freshmen, 3% undergrads receive athletic scholarships. 69% undergrads borrow to pay for school. Average cumulative indebtedness $27,285. **Criteria for awarding aid:** *Non-need-based:* Academics, Alumni affiliation, Art, Athletics, Leadership, Music/drama, State/district residency.

NORTHERN MICHIGAN UNIVERSITY

1401 Presque Isle Avenue, Marquette, MI 49855
Phone: 906-227-2650 • **Financial Aid Phone:** 800-682-9797
E-mail: admissions@nmu.edu • **CEEB Code:** 1560
Fax: 906-227-1747 • **Website:** www.nmu.edu • **ACT Code:** 2038

This public school was founded in 1899. It has a 350 acre campus.

RATINGS
Admissions Selectivity Rating: 77   **Fire Safety Rating:** 75   **Green Rating:** 71

STUDENTS AND FACULTY
Enrollment: 6,618. **Student Body:** 54% female, 46% male, 19% out-of-state, 1% international (30 countries represented). Asian 1%, African American 2%, Caucasian 86%, Hispanic 3%, Native American 1%, Pacific Islander <1%, Two or more races 5%, Race unknown 1%.
Retention and Graduation: 78% freshmen return for sophomore year. 27% freshmen graduate within 4 years. 53% freshmen graduate within 6 years.
Faculty: Student/faculty ratio 20:1. 288 full-time faculty, 65% hold PhDs, 11% are members of minority groups, 45% are women.

ACADEMICS
Degrees: Associate; Bachelor's; Certificate; Doctoral/Professional; Master's; Post-Bachelor's certificate; Post-Master's certificate; Terminal Associate; Transfer Associate **Classes:** Most classes have 10-19 students. **Most popular majors:** Criminal Justice/Safety Studies; Art/Art Studies, General; Nursing Science. **Special Study Options:** Accelerated program; Distance learning; Double major; Dual enrollment; English as a Second Language (ESL); Honors program; Independent study; Internships; Student-designed major; Study abroad; Teacher certification program. Honors programs: Honors Program for eligible freshmen and transfer students. **Disability Services offered to physically disabled students:** Note-taking services; Reader services; Tape recorders; Tutors. **Career services:** Alumni network; Career/job search classes; Internships

FACILITIES
Housing: Apartments for married students; Apartments for single students; Coed dorms; Men's dorms; Special housing for disabled student; Women's dorms 100% of campus accessible to physically diasbled. **Special Academic Facilities/Equipment:** Seaborg Science Center, New Science facility, new and remodeled Music and Art and Design instructional rooms, DeVos Art Gallery. **Computers:** 100% of classrooms, 100% of dorms, 100% of libraries, 100% of dining areas, 100% of student union, 100% of common outdoor areas have wireless network access. Students can register for classes online. Administrative functions (other than registration) can be performed online.

CAMPUS LIFE
Environment: Village **Activities:** Campus Ministries; Choral groups; Concert band; Dance; Drama/theater; International Student Organization; Jazz band; Literary magazine; Marching band; Model UN; Music ensembles; Musical theater; Opera; Pep band; Radio station; Student government; Student newspaper; Student-run film society; Symphony orchestra; Television station 308 registered organizations, 11 honor societies, 19 religious organizations. 3 fraternities, 4 sororities. **Athletics (Intercollegiate):** *Men:* basketball, football, golf, ice hockey, skiing (nordic/cross-country). *Women:* basketball, cross-country, diving, skiing (nordic/cross-country), soccer, swimming, track/field (outdoor), track/field (indoor), volleyball. **On-Campus Highlights:** Hedgcock Student Service Center, Superior Dome, New Science Facility, Market Place Dining Facility, De Vos Art Galleries **Environmental Initiatives:** Northern is a member of the Association for the Advancement of Sustainability in Higher Education and USGBC.

ADMISSIONS
Freshman Academic Profile: Average high school GPA 3.2. **Test Scores:** SAT Math middle 50% range 460-560. SAT EBRW middle 50% range 480-590. ACT middle 50% range 20-26. Minimum internet-based TOEFL 61. Minimum paper TOEFL 500. **Basis for Candidate Selection:** *Very important factors considered include:* academic GPA, standardized test scores. **Freshman Admission Requirements:** High school diploma is required and GED is accepted *Academic units recommended:* 4 English, 4 math, 4 science, 2 foreign language, 4 social studies. **Freshman Admission Statistics:** 6,173 applied, 74.4% admitted, 18% enrolled. **Transfer Admission Requirements:** college transcript(s), statement of good standing from prior institution(s). Minimum college GPA of 2.0 required. Lowest grade transferable C-. **General Admission Information:** Application fee $35. Nonfall registration accepted. Admission may be deferred for a maximum of 1 year.

COSTS AND FINANCIAL AID
Annual in-state tuition $10,328. Annual out-of-state tuition $15,024. Room and board $10,328. Required fees $712. Average book expense $800. **Required**

Forms and Deadlines: FAFSA. Notification of Awards: Applicants will be notified of awards on a rolling basis beginning 12/15. Types of Aid: *Need-based scholarships/grants:* College/university scholarship or grant aid from institutional funds; Federal Pell; Private scholarships; SEOG; State scholarships/grants. *Loans:* Direct PLUS loans; Direct Subsidized Stafford Loans; Direct Unsubsidized Stafford Loans. *Student Employment:* Federal Work-Study Program available. Institutional employment available. Financial Aid Statistics: 60% needy freshmen, 61% needy undergrads receive need-based scholarship or grant aid. 46% freshmen, 37% undergrads receive non-need-based scholarship or grant aid. 79% freshmen, 86% undergrads receive need-based self-help aid. 1% freshmen, 0% undergrads receive athletic scholarships. Criteria for awarding aid: *Non-need-based:* Academics, Art, Athletics, Leadership, Minority status, Music/drama, Religious affiliation, State/district residency.

NORTHERN STATE UNIVERSITY

1200 South Jay Street, Aberdeen, SD 57401-7198
Phone: 605-626-2544 • **Financial Aid Phone:** 605-626-2640
E-mail: admission2@northern.edu • **CEEB Code:** 6487
Fax: 605-626-2531 • **Website:** www.northern.edu • **ACT Code:** 3916

This public school was founded in 1901. It has a 72 acre campus.

RATINGS
Admissions Selectivity Rating: 74   Fire Safety Rating: 79   Green Rating: 60*

STUDENTS AND FACULTY
Enrollment: 1,693. **Student Body:** 57% female, 43% male, 18% out-of-state, 4% international (35 countries represented). Asian 1%, African American 2%, Caucasian 84%, Hispanic 3%, Native American 2%, Pacific Islander <1%, Two or more races 2%, Race unknown <1%.
Retention and Graduation: 67% freshmen return for sophomore year. 33% grads go on to further study within 1 year. **Faculty:** Student/faculty ratio 21:1. 90 full-time faculty, 86% hold PhDs, 8% are members of minority groups, 37% are women. 0% of classes are taught by teaching assistants.

ACADEMICS
Degrees: Associate; Bachelor's; Certificate; Master's; Post-Bachelor's certificate **Classes:** Most classes have 20-29 students. Most lab/discussion sessions have 10-19 students. **Most popular majors:** Elementary Education And Teaching; Sociology; Business/Commerce, General. **Special Study Options:** Accelerated program; Cooperative education program; Cross-registration; Distance learning; Double major; Dual enrollment; English as a Second Language (ESL); Exchange student program (domestic); Honors program; Independent study; Internships; Liberal arts/career combination; Student-designed major; Study abroad; Teacher certification program. Honors programs: Honors Program. **Disability Services offered to physically disabled students:** Note-taking services; Reader services; Tape recorders; Tutors. **Career services:** Alumni network; Alumni services; Career assessment; Career/job search classes; Internships; Regional alumni

FACILITIES
Housing: Apartments for married students; Apartments for single students; Coed dorms; Special housing for disabled student; Special housing for international students 90% of campus accessible to physically diasbled. **Special Academic Facilities/Equipment:** State-Wide E-Learning Center; Art galleries. **Computers:** 100% of classrooms, 100% of dorms, 100% of libraries, 100% of dining areas, 100% of student union, have wireless network access. Students can register for classes online. Administrative functions (other than registration) can be performed online.

CAMPUS LIFE
Environment: Town **Activities:** Campus Ministries; Choral groups; Concert band; Dance; Drama/theater; International Student Organization; Jazz band; Literary magazine; Marching band; Music ensembles; Musical theater; Pep band; Student government; Student newspaper; Symphony orchestra; Television station 100 registered organizations, 5 honor societies, 6 religious organizations. **Athletics (Intercollegiate):** *Men:* baseball, basketball, cheerleading, cross-country, football, golf, track/field (outdoor), track/field (indoor), wrestling. *Women:* basketball, cheerleading, cross-country, golf, soccer, softball, swimming, tennis, track/field (outdoor), track/field (indoor), volleyball. **On-Campus Highlights:** NSU Student Center, NSU State-Wide E-Learning Center, NSU Barnett Athletic Center, NSU Johnson Fine Arts Center, NSU International Center of Excellence

ADMISSIONS
Freshman Academic Profile: Average high school GPA 3.3. 7% in top 10% of high school class, 20% in top 25% of high school class, 60% in top 50% of

high school class. **Test Scores:** SAT Math middle 50% range 370-580. SAT EBRW middle 50% range 420-540. ACT middle 50% range 19-25. Minimum internet-based TOEFL 61. Minimum paper TOEFL 525. **Basis for Candidate Selection:** *Very important factors considered include:* rigor of secondary school record, class rank, standardized test scores. *Other factors considered include:* recommendation(s), interview, extracurricular activities, talent/ability, character/personal qualities. **Freshman Admission Requirements:** High school diploma is required and GED is accepted *Academic units required:* 4 English, 3 math, 3 science, 3 science labs, 3 social studies. **Freshman Admission Statistics:** 1,379 applied, 82.9% admitted, 32% enrolled. **Transfer Admission Requirements:** High school transcript, college transcript(s), statement of good standing from prior institution(s). Minimum college GPA of 2.0 required. Lowest grade transferable C. **General Admission Information:** Application fee $20. Nonfall registration accepted. Admission may be deferred.

COSTS AND FINANCIAL AID
Annual in-state tuition $6,942. Annual out-of-state tuition $5,992. Room and board $6,942. Required fees $4,050. Average book expense $1,200. **Required Forms and Deadlines:** FAFSA. **Notification of Awards:** Applicants will be notified of awards on a rolling basis beginning 4/15. **Types of Aid:** *Need-based scholarships/grants:* Federal Pell; SEOG; State scholarships/grants. *Loans:* Direct PLUS loans; Direct Subsidized Stafford Loans; Direct Unsubsidized Stafford Loans. *Student Employment:* Federal Work-Study Program available. Institutional employment available. **Financial Aid Statistics:** 92% needy freshmen, 83% needy undergrads receive need-based scholarship or grant aid. 8% freshmen, 6% undergrads receive non-need-based scholarship or grant aid. 86% freshmen, 88% undergrads receive need-based self-help aid. 12% freshmen, 9% undergrads receive athletic scholarships. **Criteria for awarding aid:** *Need-based:* Minority status *Non-need-based:* Academics, Art, Athletics, Leadership, Minority status, Music/drama.

NORTHLAND COLLEGE

1411 Ellis Avenue, Ashland, WI 54806-3999
Phone: 715-682-1224 • **Financial Aid Phone:** 715-682-1255
E-mail: admit@northland.edu • **CEEB Code:** 1561
Fax: 715-682-1258 • **Website:** www.northland.edu • **ACT Code:** 4624

This private school, affiliated with the United Church of Christ, was founded in 1892. It has a 130 acre campus.

RATINGS
Admissions Selectivity Rating: 82   Fire Safety Rating: 80   Green Rating: 95

STUDENTS AND FACULTY
Enrollment: 602. **Student Body:** 53% female, 47% male, 50% out-of-state, 4% international (4 countries represented). Asian 1%, African American 3%, Caucasian 80%, Hispanic 5%, Native American 2%, Pacific Islander 0%, Two or more races 3%, Race unknown 2%.
Retention and Graduation: 73% freshmen return for sophomore year. 55% freshmen graduate within 4 years. 64% freshmen graduate within 6 years. **Faculty:** Student/faculty ratio 11:1. 50 full-time faculty, 88% hold PhDs, 2% are members of minority groups, 38% are women. 0% of classes are taught by teaching assistants.

ACADEMICS
Degrees: Bachelor's **Classes:** Most classes have 20-29 students. Most lab/discussion sessions have 10-19 students. **Most popular majors:** Natural Resources And Conservation, Other; Teacher Education, Multiple Levels; Biology/Biological Sciences, General. **Special Study Options:** Cross-registration; Double major; Dual enrollment; Exchange student program (domestic); Independent study; Internships; Student-designed major; Study abroad; Teacher certification program. **Disability Services offered to physically disabled students:** Note-taking services; Reader services; Tape recorders; Tutors. **Career services:** Alumni network; Internships

FACILITIES
Housing: Apartments for single students; Coed dorms; Special housing for disabled student; Theme housing; Women's dorms **Special Academic Facilities/Equipment:** Sigurd Olson Environmental Institute, Mary Griggs Burke Center for Freshwater Innovation, Center for Rural Communities, Indigenous Cultures Center **Computers:** 20% of classrooms, 20% of dorms, 100% of libraries, 100% of dining areas, 100% of student union, 75% of common outdoor areas have wireless network access. Students can register for classes online. Administrative functions (other than registration) can be performed online.

CAMPUS LIFE

Environment: Village **Activities:** Campus Ministries; Choral groups; Concert band; Dance; Drama/theater; International Student Organization; Jazz band; Literary magazine; Music ensembles; Radio station; Student government; Student newspaper; Symphony orchestra; Yearbook 30 registered organizations, 1 honor society, 2 religious organizations. **Athletics (Intercollegiate):** *Men:* baseball, basketball, cross-country, ice hockey, skiing (nordic/cross-country), soccer. *Women:* basketball, cross-country, skiing (nordic/cross-country), soccer, softball, volleyball. **On-Campus Highlights:** Campus Center, Science Center, The Fire Ring, The Environmental Living and Learning Center, The Ravine **Environmental Initiatives:** Extensive local food systems work including an 80% local food purchasing goal; a new Food Systems Facility began operations on July 15, 2017 that is used to process and store local fruits and vegetables to help meet this 80% goal, provide work experience to students and community in food processing, and bolster sustainable food networks for rural communities; and the creation of a sophisticated new composting infrastructure as part of the Food Systems Facility to advance our ability to process up to a ton of compost a day from a variety of community and institutional sources.

ADMISSIONS

Freshman Academic Profile: Average high school GPA 3.3. 16% in top 10% of high school class, 41% in top 25% of high school class, 75% in top 50% of high school class. **Test Scores:** ACT middle 50% range 20-26. Minimum paper TOEFL 525. **Basis for Candidate Selection:** *Very important factors considered include:* class rank, academic GPA. *Important factors considered include:* rigor of secondary school record, standardized test scores, character/ personal qualities, first generation. *Other factors considered include:* interview, extracurricular activities, volunteer work, work experience. **Freshman Admission Requirements:** High school diploma is required and GED is accepted *Academic units required:* 4 English, 3 math, 3 science, 1 science labs, 3 social studies, 3 academic electives. **Freshman Admission Statistics:** 1,625 applied, 61.2% admitted, 19% enrolled. **Transfer Admission Requirements:** High school transcript, college transcript(s), essay or personal statement, statement of good standing from prior institution(s). Minimum college GPA of 2.0 required. Lowest grade transferable C-. **General Admission Information:** Nonfall registration accepted. Admission may be deferred for a maximum of 2 years.

COSTS AND FINANCIAL AID

Annual tuition $34,666. Room and board $9,176. Required fees $1,517. Average book expense $800. **Required Forms and Deadlines:** FAFSA. **Notification of Awards:** Applicants will be notified of awards on a rolling basis beginning 3/1. **Types of Aid:** *Need-based scholarships/grants:* College/ university scholarship or grant aid from institutional funds; Federal Pell; Private scholarships; SEOG; State scholarships/grants. *Loans:* Direct PLUS loans; Direct Subsidized Stafford Loans; Direct Unsubsidized Stafford Loans. *Student Employment:* Federal Work-Study Program available. Institutional employment available. **Financial Aid Statistics:** 100% needy freshmen, 96% needy undergrads receive need-based scholarship or grant aid. 15% freshmen, 14% undergrads receive non-need-based scholarship or grant aid. 75% freshmen, 71% undergrads receive need-based self-help aid. 0% freshmen, 0% undergrads receive athletic scholarships. 98% freshmen, 99% undergrads receive any aid. 83% undergrads borrow to pay for school. Average cumulative indebtedness $34,144. **Criteria for awarding aid:** *Need-based:* Academics, Job skills, Minority status, Music/drama *Non-need-based:* Academics, Alumni affiliation, Art, Job skills, Leadership, Minority status, Music/drama, Religious affiliation, State/district residency.

NORTHWEST NAZARENE UNIVERSITY

623 S. University Blvd., Nampa, ID 83686
Phone: 208-467-8000 • **Financial Aid Phone:** 208-467-8641
E-mail: admissions@nnu.edu • **CEEB Code:** 4544
Fax: 208-467-8645 • **Website:** www.nnu.edu • **ACT Code:** 924

This private school, affiliated with the Nazarene Church, was founded in 1913. It has a 85 acre campus.

RATINGS

Admissions Selectivity Rating: 83   **Fire Safety Rating:** 70   **Green Rating:** 60*

STUDENTS AND FACULTY

Enrollment: 1,263. **Student Body:** 59% female, 41% male, 51% out-of-state, 2% international (20 countries represented). Asian 2%, African American 1%, Caucasian 75%, Hispanic 7%, Native American 1%, Pacific Islander <1%, Two or more races 1%, Race unknown 12%.

Faculty: Student/faculty ratio 14:1. 103 full-time faculty, 73% hold PhDs, 6% are members of minority groups, 45% are women. 0% of classes are taught by teaching assistants.

ACADEMICS

Degrees: Bachelor's; Doctoral/Professional; Master's; Post-Master's certificate **Classes:** Most classes have 10-19 students. **Most popular majors:** Education, General; Nursing/Registered Nurse (Rn, Asn, Bsn, Msn); Business/Commerce, General. **Special Study Options:** Accelerated program; Cooperative education program; Cross-registration; Distance learning; Double major; Dual enrollment; English as a Second Language (ESL); Exchange student program (domestic); Honors program; Independent study; Internships; Liberal arts/career combination; Student-designed major; Study abroad; Teacher certification program. **Disability Services offered to physically disabled students:** Reader services; Tape recorders; Tutors. **Career services:** Alumni network; Career/job search classes; Internships; Regional alumni

FACILITIES

Housing: Apartments for married students; Apartments for single students; Coed dorms; Men's dorms; Women's dorms 70% of campus accessible to physically disabled. **Computers:** 100% of classrooms, have wireless network access. Administrative functions (other than registration) can be performed online.

CAMPUS LIFE

Environment: City **Activities:** Campus Ministries; Choral groups; Concert band; Drama/theater; International Student Organization; Jazz band; Literary magazine; Music ensembles; Musical theater; Opera; Pep band; Student government; Student newspaper; Student-run film society; Symphony orchestra; Yearbook 21 registered organizations, 6 honor societies, 8 religious organizations. **Athletics (Intercollegiate):** *Men:* baseball, basketball, cross-country, golf, soccer, track/field (outdoor), track/field (indoor). *Women:* basketball, cross-country, soccer, softball, track/field (outdoor), track/field (indoor), volleyball. **On-Campus Highlights:** Helstrom Business Center, The Brandt Center, Ford Hall, Johnson Sports Center, Thomas Family Health & Science Center

ADMISSIONS

Freshman Academic Profile: Average high school GPA 3.5. 29% in top 10% of high school class, 52% in top 25% of high school class, 81% in top 50% of high school class. **Test Scores:** SAT Math middle 50% range 470-620. SAT EBRW middle 50% range 470-600. ACT middle 50% range 21-27. Minimum paper TOEFL 500. **Basis for Candidate Selection:** *Very important factors considered include:* class rank, academic GPA, standardized test scores, character/personal qualities. *Other factors considered include:* rigor of secondary school record, recommendation(s), extracurricular activities, talent/ability, alumni/ae relation, religious affiliation/commitment. **Freshman Admission Requirements:** High school diploma is required and GED is accepted *Academic units recommended:* 4 English, 3 math, 3 science, 2 foreign language, 3 history. **Freshman Admission Statistics:** 984 applied, 69.0% admitted, 41% enrolled. **Transfer Admission Requirements:** college transcript(s), Minimum college GPA of 2.0 required. Lowest grade transferable C-. **General Admission Information:** Application fee $25. Priority deadline 3/1. Regular application deadline 8/15. Nonfall registration accepted. Admission may be deferred.

COSTS AND FINANCIAL AID

Annual tuition $26,150. Room and board $6,400. Required fees $400. Average book expense $1,160. **Required Forms and Deadlines:** FAFSA. **Notification of Awards:** Applicants will be notified of awards on a rolling basis beginning 4/1. **Types of Aid:** *Need-based scholarships/grants:* College/ university scholarship or grant aid from institutional funds; Federal Pell; Private scholarships; SEOG; State scholarships/grants. *Loans:* Direct PLUS loans; Direct Subsidized Stafford Loans; Direct Unsubsidized Stafford Loans. *Student Employment:* Federal Work-Study Program available. Institutional employment available. **Financial Aid Statistics:** 100% needy freshmen, 95% needy undergrads receive need-based scholarship or grant aid. 14% freshmen, 8% undergrads receive non-need-based scholarship or grant aid. 72% freshmen, 79% undergrads receive need-based self-help aid. 9% freshmen, 9% undergrads receive athletic scholarships. **Criteria for awarding aid:** *Need-based:* Athletics, Leadership, Religious affiliation *Non-need-based:* Academics, Alumni affiliation, Art, Athletics, Leadership, Minority status, Music/drama, Religious affiliation.

NORTHWESTERN COLLEGE (IA)

101 7th St. SW, Orange City, IA 51041
Phone: 712-707-7130 • **Financial Aid Phone:** 712-707-7131
E-mail: admissions@nwciowa.edu • **CEEB Code:** 6490
Fax: 712-707-7164 • **Website:** www.nwciowa.edu • **ACT Code:** 1346

This private school, affiliated with the Reformed Church, was founded in 1882. It has a 100 acre campus.

RATINGS
Admissions Selectivity Rating: 82   **Fire Safety Rating:** 96   **Green Rating:** 60*

STUDENTS AND FACULTY
Enrollment: 1,013. **Student Body:** 56% female, 44% male, 42% out-of-state, 3% international (24 countries represented). Asian 1%, African American 1%, Caucasian 83%, Hispanic 4%, Native American <1%, Pacific Islander 0%, Two or more races 2%, Race unknown 5%.
Retention and Graduation: 77% freshmen return for sophomore year. 57% freshmen graduate within 4 years. 68% freshmen graduate within 6 years. 16% grads go on to further study within 1 year. 5% grads pursue arts and sciences degrees. 1% grads pursue law degrees. 1% grads pursue business degrees. 6% grads pursue medical degrees. **Faculty:** Student/faculty ratio 11:1. 82 full-time faculty, 89% hold PhDs, 5% are members of minority groups, 39% are women. 0% of classes are taught by teaching assistants.

ACADEMICS
Degrees: Bachelor's; Master's; Post-Bachelor's certificate **Classes:** Most classes have 10-19 students. Most lab/discussion sessions have 10-19 students. **Most popular majors:** Education, General; Registered Nursing/Registered Nurse; Business/Commerce, General. **Special Study Options:** Distance learning; Double major; Dual enrollment; English as a Second Language (ESL); Honors program; Independent study; Internships; Liberal arts/career combination; Student-designed major; Study abroad; Teacher certification program. Honors programs: Honors Program: Affords students an interdisciplinary approach to understanding perennial and contemporary issues, such as technology, war and peace, gender roles, work and calling, and humor. Affords students th eopportunity to delve more deeply into a topic of their choice, workinh with selected faculty members to complete a project that goes beyond the normal upper-division work at the college. Encourages graduate education by sponsoring trips to regional graduate schools and financially supporting graduate school applications. **Disability Services offered to physically disabled students:** Note-taking services; Reader services; Tape recorders; Tutors. **Career services:** Alumni network; Alumni services; Career assessment; Career/job search classes; Internships

FACILITIES
Housing: Apartments for single students; Men's dorms; Special housing for disabled student; Women's dorms 90% of campus accessible to physically diasbled. **Special Academic Facilities/Equipment:** DeWitt Learning Commons and Library, Christ Chapel and DeWitt Music Hall, DeWitt Theatre Arts Center, Korver Visual Arts Center, Te Paske Art Gallery, Ramaker Center **Computers:** 75% of classrooms, 30% of dorms, 100% of libraries, 100% of dining areas, 100% of student union, 30% of common outdoor areas have wireless network access. Students can register for classes online. Administrative functions (other than registration) can be performed online.

CAMPUS LIFE
Environment: Rural **Activities:** Campus Ministries; Choral groups; Concert band; Dance; Drama/theater; International Student Organization; Jazz band; Literary magazine; Music ensembles; Musical theater; Student government; Student newspaper; Symphony orchestra; Television station; Yearbook 30 registered organizations, 2 honor societies, 5 religious organizations. **Athletics (Intercollegiate):** *Men:* baseball, basketball, cheerleading, cross-country, football, golf, soccer, track/field (outdoor), track/field (indoor), wrestling. *Women:* basketball, cheerleading, cross-country, golf, soccer, softball, track/field (outdoor), track/field (indoor), volleyball. **On-Campus Highlights:** DeWitt Learning Commons, Rowenhorst Student Center, Bultman Center Gymnasium, Christ Chapel, Ramaker Center

ADMISSIONS
Freshman Academic Profile: Average high school GPA 3.6. 25% in top 10% of high school class, 59% in top 25% of high school class, 83% in top 50% of high school class. 75% from public high schools. **Test Scores:** SAT Math middle 50% range 510-640. SAT EBRW middle 50% range 490-590. ACT middle 50% range 21-27. Minimum internet-based TOEFL 79. Minimum paper TOEFL 550. **Basis for Candidate Selection:** *Very important factors considered include:* rigor of secondary school record, standardized test scores. *Important factors considered include:* class rank, academic GPA, recommendation(s), interview, talent/ability, character/personal qualities, first

generation, religious affiliation/commitment, level of applicant's interest. *Other factors considered include:* application essay, extracurricular activities, alumni/ae relation. **Freshman Admission Requirements:** High school diploma is required and GED is accepted *Academic units recommended:* 4 English, 3 math, 3 science, 3 foreign language, 3 social studies. **Freshman Admission Statistics:** 1,959 applied, 68.1% admitted, 21% enrolled. **Transfer Admission Requirements:** college transcript(s), Minimum college GPA of 2.2 required. Lowest grade transferable C. **General Admission Information:** Priority deadline 6/1. Nonfall registration accepted. Admission may be deferred for a maximum of 4 years.

COSTS AND FINANCIAL AID
Annual tuition $30,900. Room and board $9,200. Required fees $200. Average book expense $1,300. **Required Forms and Deadlines:** FAFSA. **Notification of Awards:** Applicants will be notified of awards on a rolling basis beginning 12/1. **Types of Aid:** *Need-based scholarships/grants:* College/ university scholarship or grant aid from institutional funds; Federal Pell; Private scholarships; SEOG; State scholarships/grants; United Negro College Fund. *Loans:* Direct PLUS loans; Direct Subsidized Stafford Loans; Direct Unsubsidized Stafford Loans. *Student Employment:* Federal Work-Study Program available. Institutional employment available. **Financial Aid Statistics:** 100% needy freshmen, 96% needy undergrads receive need-based scholarship or grant aid. 97% freshmen, 99% undergrads receive non-need-based scholarship or grant aid. 70% freshmen, 76% undergrads receive need-based self-help aid. 20% freshmen, 15% undergrads receive athletic scholarships. 100% freshmen, 99% undergrads receive any aid. 78% undergrads borrow to pay for school. Average cumulative indebtedness $28,501. **Criteria for awarding aid:** *Non-need-based:* Academics, Alumni affiliation, Art, Athletics, Music/drama, Religious affiliation.

NORTHWESTERN STATE UNIVERSITY

University Parkway, Natchitoches, LA 71497
Phone: 318-357-4078 • **Financial Aid Phone:** 800-823-3008
E-mail: applications@nsula.edu • **CEEB Code:** 6492
Fax: 318-357-4660 • **Website:** www.nsula.edu • **ACT Code:** 1600

This public school was founded in 1884. It has a 916 acre campus.

RATINGS
Admissions Selectivity Rating: 76   **Fire Safety Rating:** 88   **Green Rating:** 60*

STUDENTS AND FACULTY
Enrollment: 7,333. **Student Body:** 68% female, 32% male, 9% out-of-state, 1% international (34 countries represented). Asian 1%, African American 30%, Caucasian 57%, Hispanic 3%, Native American 1%, Pacific Islander <1%, Two or more races 3%, Race unknown 4%.
Retention and Graduation: 71% freshmen return for sophomore year. **Faculty:** Student/faculty ratio 19:1. 291 full-time faculty, 60% hold PhDs, 8% are members of minority groups, 55% are women. 1% of classes are taught by teaching assistants.

ACADEMICS
Degrees: Associate; Bachelor's; Master's; Post-Bachelor's certificate; Post-Master's certificate **Classes:** Most classes have 20-29 students. Most lab/discussion sessions have 10-19 students. **Most popular majors:** General Studies; Nursing/Registered Nurse (Rn, Asn, Bsn, Msn); Business Administration And Management, General. **Special Study Options:** Cooperative education program; Distance learning; Double major; Dual enrollment; Honors program; Independent study; Internships; Study abroad; Teacher certification program. Honors programs: The Louisiana Scholar's College is a special institution at Northwestern that enrolls students in a strong liberal arts program while simultaneously letting them take part in the other great areas of NSU. **Disability Services offered to physically disabled students:** Note-taking services; Reader services; Tape recorders; Tutors. **Career services:** Alumni services; Career assessment; Career/job search classes; Internships

FACILITIES
Housing: Apartments for married students; Apartments for single students; Coed dorms; Fraternity/sorority housing; Special housing for disabled student; Theme housing 96% of campus accessible to physically diasbled. **Special Academic Facilities/Equipment:** Cammie G. Henry Research Center; Louisiana Creole Heritage Center; Louisiana Folklife Center; Louisiana Regional Folklife Center; The Space Science Group; Williamson Museum **Computers:** 50% of classrooms, 100% of dorms, 100% of libraries, 50% of dining areas, 100% of student union, 75% of common outdoor areas have

wireless network access. Students can register for classes online. Administrative functions (other than registration) can be performed online.

CAMPUS LIFE

Environment: Village **Activities:** Campus Ministries; Choral groups; Concert band; Dance; Drama/theater; International Student Organization; Jazz band; Literary magazine; Marching band; Music ensembles; Musical theater; Opera; Pep band; Radio station; Student government; Student newspaper; Symphony orchestra; Television station; Yearbook 109 registered organizations, 11 honor societies, 6 religious organizations. 10 fraternities, 7 sororities. **Athletics (Intercollegiate):** *Men:* baseball, basketball, cheerleading, cross-country, football, soccer, track/field (outdoor), track/field (indoor). *Women:* basketball, cheerleading, cross-country, soccer, softball, tennis, track/field (outdoor), track/field (indoor), volleyball. **On-Campus Highlights:** Wellness, Recreation, and Activity Center, Student Union, University Place Apartments, University Columns Apartments, BCM/CSO/Wellesley Foundation **Environmental Initiatives:** NSU student groups and organizations participate in recycling, liter-abatement, campus beautification, and related 'Green' service (and service-learning) activities.

ADMISSIONS

Freshman Academic Profile: Average high school GPA 3.2. 16% in top 10% of high school class, 39% in top 25% of high school class, 72% in top 50% of high school class. **Test Scores:** SAT Math middle 50% range 435-555. SAT EBRW middle 50% range 435-550. ACT middle 50% range 19-23. Minimum internet-based TOEFL 61. Minimum paper TOEFL 500. **Basis for Candidate Selection:** *Very important factors considered include:* rigor of secondary school record, standardized test scores. *Important factors considered include:* class rank, academic GPA. *Other factors considered include:* extracurricular activities, talent/ability, alumni/ae relation, geographical residence, state residency. **Freshman Admission Requirements:** High school diploma is required and GED is accepted *Academic units required:* 4 English, 3 math, 3 science, 3 science labs, 2 foreign language, 1 social studies, 2 history, 0.5 computer science, 1 visual/performing arts, and 1 unit from above areas or other academic areas. **Freshman Admission Statistics:** 2,633 applied, 83.2% admitted, 51% enrolled. **Transfer Admission Requirements:** college transcript(s), statement of good standing from prior institution(s). Minimum college GPA of 2.0 required. Lowest grade transferable D. **General Admission Information:** Application fee $20. Regular application deadline 7/6. Nonfall registration accepted. Admission may be deferred for a maximum of 3 semesters.

COSTS AND FINANCIAL AID

Required Forms and Deadlines: FAFSA; Institution's own financial aid form. **Notification of Awards:** Applicants will be notified of awards on a rolling basis beginning 5/1. **Types of Aid:** *Need-based scholarships/grants:* College/university scholarship or grant aid from institutional funds; Federal Nursing Scholarships; Federal Pell; Private scholarships; SEOG; State scholarships/grants; United Negro College Fund. *Loans:* Direct PLUS loans; Direct Subsidized Stafford Loans; Direct Unsubsidized Stafford Loans. *Student Employment:* Federal Work-Study Program available. Institutional employment available. **Financial Aid Statistics:** 64% needy freshmen, 65% needy undergrads receive need-based scholarship or grant aid. 68% freshmen, 47% undergrads receive non-need-based scholarship or grant aid. 57% freshmen, 66% undergrads receive need-based self-help aid. 6% freshmen, 5% undergrads receive athletic scholarships. 91% freshmen, 82% undergrads receive any aid. **Criteria for awarding aid:** *Non-need-based:* Academics, Alumni affiliation, Art, Athletics, Job skills, Leadership, Minority status, Music/drama, Religious affiliation, State/district residency.

NORTHWESTERN UNIVERSITY

633 Clark Street, Evanston, IL 60204
Phone: 847-491-7271 • **Financial Aid Phone:** (847) 491-7400
E-mail: ug-admission@northwestern.edu • **CEEB Code:** 1565
Website: www.northwestern.edu • **ACT Code:** 1106

This private school was founded in 1851. It has a 240 acre campus.

RATINGS

Admissions Selectivity Rating: 98   **Fire Safety Rating:** 83   **Green Rating:** 96

STUDENTS AND FACULTY

Enrollment: 8,271. **Student Body:** 50% female, 50% male, 68% out-of-state, 9% international (77 countries represented). Asian 17%, African American 6%,

Caucasian 46%, Hispanic 13%, Native American <1%, Pacific Islander 0%, Two or more races 5%, Race unknown 3%. **Retention and Graduation:** 98% freshmen return for sophomore year. 84% freshmen graduate within 4 years. 94% freshmen graduate within 6 years. 23% grads go on to further study within 1 year. 7% grads pursue arts and sciences degrees. 3% grads pursue law degrees. 1% grads pursue business degrees. 7% grads pursue medical degrees. **Faculty:** Student/faculty ratio 6:1. 1,491 full-time faculty, 100% hold PhDs, 18% are members of minority groups, 38% are women. 2% of classes are taught by teaching assistants.

ACADEMICS

Degrees: Bachelor's; Certificate; Doctoral/Professional; Doctoral/Research; Master's; Post-Master's certificate **Classes:** Most classes have 10-19 students. Most lab/discussion sessions have 20-29 students. **Most popular majors:** Journalism; Engineering, General; Economics, General. **Special Study Options:** Accelerated program; Cooperative education program; Double major; Honors program; Independent study; Internships; Liberal arts/career combination; Student-designed major; Study abroad; Teacher certification program. Honors programs: Honors Program in Medical Education (HPME), Integrated Science Program (ISP), MENU, MMSS Combined degree programs: BA/MA; BA/MD. **Disability Services offered to physically disabled students:** Note-taking services; Reader services; Tape recorders; Tutors. **Career services:** Alumni network; Alumni services; Career assessment; Career/job search classes; Internships; Regional alumni

FACILITIES

Housing: Coed dorms; Fraternity/sorority housing; Men's dorms; Theme housing; Wellness housing; Women's dorms 100% of campus accessible to physically diasbled. **Special Academic Facilities/Equipment:** Art gallery, learning sciences institute, communicative disorders and materials and life sciences buildings, catalysis center, astronomical research center. Ford Motor Company Engineering Design Center for engineering students. **Computers:** 100% of classrooms, 100% of dorms, 100% of libraries, 100% of dining areas, 100% of student union, 100% of common outdoor areas have wireless network access. Students can register for classes online.

CAMPUS LIFE

Environment: City **Activities:** Campus Ministries; Choral groups; Concert band; Dance; Drama/theater; International Student Organization; Jazz band; Literary magazine; Marching band; Model UN; Music ensembles; Musical theater; Opera; Pep band; Radio station; Student government; Student newspaper; Student-run film society; Symphony orchestra; Television station; Yearbook 415 registered organizations, 23 honor societies, 29 religious organizations. 17 fraternities, 19 sororities. **Athletics (Intercollegiate):** *Men:* baseball, basketball, cheerleading, diving, football, golf, soccer, swimming, tennis, wrestling. *Women:* basketball, cheerleading, cross-country, diving, fencing, field hockey, golf, lacrosse, soccer, softball, swimming, tennis, volleyball. **On-Campus Highlights:** Shakespeare Garden, Dearborn Observatory, Norris Student Center, Henry Crown Sports Pavilion and Acquatic Center, The lakefill on Lake Michigan **Environmental Initiatives:** The development of a Strategic Plan for sustainability that will detail the long-term sustainability vision and goals for Northwestern University as well as putting in place the governance and accountability for the implementation of that plan and communicating our progress to stakeholders at all levels.

ADMISSIONS

Freshman Academic Profile: 91% in top 10% of high school class, 100% in top 25% of high school class, 100% in top 50% of high school class. 65% from public high schools. **Test Scores:** SAT Math middle 50% range 710-800. SAT EBRW middle 50% range 680-760. ACT middle 50% range 32-34. **Basis for Candidate Selection:** *Very important factors considered include:* rigor of secondary school record, class rank, academic GPA, standardized test scores. *Important factors considered include:* application essay, recommendation(s), extracurricular activities, talent/ability, character/personal qualities. *Other factors considered include:* interview, first generation, alumni/ae relation, racial/ethnic status, volunteer work, work experience, level of applicant's interest. **Freshman Admission Requirements:** High school diploma is required and GED is accepted *Academic units recommended:* 4 English, 3 math, 2 science, 2 science labs, 2 foreign language, 2 social studies, 2 history, 1 academic elective. **Freshman Admission Statistics:** 37,259 applied, 9.2% admitted, 55% enrolled. **Transfer Admission Requirements:** High school transcript, college transcript(s), essay or personal statement, standardized test scores, statement of good standing from prior institution(s). Minimum college GPA of 3.0 required. Lowest grade transferable C. **General Admission Information:** Application fee $75. Regular application deadline 1/1. Nonfall registration accepted. Admission may be deferred for a maximum of 1 year.

COSTS AND FINANCIAL AID

Annual tuition $50,424. Room and board $15,489. Required fees $431. Average book expense $1,620. **Required Forms and Deadlines:** CSS/Financial Aid PROFILE; FAFSA; Noncustodial PROFILE. **Notification of Awards:** Applicants will be notified of awards on or about 4/15. **Types of Aid:** *Need-based scholarships/grants:* College/university scholarship or grant aid from institutional funds; Federal Pell; SEOG; State scholarships/grants. *Loans:* Direct PLUS loans; Direct Subsidized Stafford Loans; Direct Unsubsidized Stafford Loans. *Student Employment:* Federal Work-Study Program available. Institutional employment available. **Financial Aid Statistics:** 98% needy freshmen, 98% needy undergrads receive need-based scholarship or grant aid. 0% undergrads receive non-need-based scholarship or grant aid. 54% freshmen, 65% undergrads receive need-based self-help aid. 4% freshmen, 5% undergrads receive athletic scholarships. 42% undergrads borrow to pay for school. Average cumulative indebtedness $33,369. **Criteria for awarding aid:** *Non-need-based:* Athletics, Music/drama.

NORTHWOOD UNIVERSITY

4000 Whiting Drive, Midland, MI 48640
Phone: 989-837-4273 • **Financial Aid Phone:** 989-837-4320
E-mail: miadmit@northwood.edu • **CEEB Code:** 1568
Fax: 989-837-4273 • **Website:** www.northwood.edu • **ACT Code:** 2041

This private school was founded in 1959. It has a 434 acre campus.

RATINGS
Admissions Selectivity Rating: 82   **Fire Safety Rating:** 85   **Green Rating:** 60*

STUDENTS AND FACULTY
Enrollment: 1,318. **Student Body:** 34% female, 66% male, 13% out-of-state, 8% international (26 countries represented). Asian <1%, African American 2%, Caucasian 79%, Hispanic 4%, Native American <1%, Pacific Islander 1%, Two or more races 3%, Race unknown 4%.
Retention and Graduation: 73% freshmen return for sophomore year. 44% freshmen graduate within 4 years. 63% freshmen graduate within 6 years.
Faculty: Student/faculty ratio 28:1. 35 full-time faculty, 37% hold PhDs, 20% are members of minority groups, 40% are women. 0% of classes are taught by teaching assistants.

ACADEMICS
Degrees: Associate; Bachelor's; **Master's Classes:** Most classes have 10-19 students. **Most popular majors:** Sport And Fitness Administration/Management; Business Administration And Management, General. **Special Study Options:** Accelerated program; Distance learning; Double major; Dual enrollment; English as a Second Language (ESL); Exchange student program (domestic); Honors program; Independent study; Internships; Study abroad; Weekend college. Honors programs: An Honors Program began in Fall Term, 1991. In it, honors sections of six critically important courses are offered. The best instructors and the most demanding material and expectations are used. Additionally, special one credit hour seminars, which include outside speakers, are offered to sophomores and juniors. **Disability Services offered to physically disabled students:** Tutors. **Career services:** Alumni network; Alumni services; Career assessment; Career/job search classes; Internships

FACILITIES
Housing: Apartments for single students; Coed dorms; Men's dorms; Special housing for disabled student; Women's dorms **Special Academic Facilities/Equipment:** Hach Student Life Center, Gerstacker Student Union **Computers:** 100% of classrooms, 100% of dorms, 100% of libraries, 100% of dining areas, 100% of student union, have wireless network access. Students can register for classes online. Administrative functions (other than registration) can be performed online.

CAMPUS LIFE
Environment: Town **Activities:** Campus Ministries; Drama/theater; International Student Organization; Model UN; Student government; Student newspaper 42 registered organizations, 2 honor societies, 2 religious organizations. 9 fraternities, 3 sororities. **Athletics (Intercollegiate):** *Men:* baseball, basketball, cheerleading, cross-country, football, golf, soccer, tennis, track/field (outdoor), track/field (indoor). *Women:* basketball, cheerleading, cross-country, golf, soccer, softball, tennis, track/field (outdoor), track/field (indoor), volleyball. **On-Campus Highlights:** Hach Student Life Center, Mid—Caf @ Northwood, Bennett Sports Center

ADMISSIONS
Freshman Academic Profile: Average high school GPA 3.3. 8% in top 10% of high school class, 30% in top 25% of high school class, 67% in top 50% of high school class. 70% from public high schools. **Test Scores:** SAT Math middle 50% range 500-580. SAT EBRW middle 50% range 500-580. ACT middle 50% range 20-25. Minimum paper TOEFL 500. **Basis for Candidate Selection:** *Very important factors considered include:* academic GPA, standardized test scores, level of applicant's interest. *Important factors considered include:* rigor of secondary school record, class rank, application essay, recommendation(s),

interview, extracurricular activities. *Other factors considered include:* talent/ability, alumni/ae relation, volunteer work, work experience. **Freshman Admission Requirements:** High school diploma is required and GED is accepted *Academic units recommended:* 4 English, 3 math, 3 science, 2 science labs, 1 foreign language, 3 social studies, 1 academic elective. **Freshman Admission Statistics:** 1,819 applied, 69.3% admitted, 35% enrolled. **Transfer Admission Requirements:** college transcript(s), Minimum college GPA of 2.0 required. Lowest grade transferable C. **General Admission Information:** Application fee $30. Regular application deadline 8/1. Nonfall registration accepted. Admission may be deferred for a maximum of 1 year.

COSTS AND FINANCIAL AID
Annual tuition $25,710. Room and board $10,480. Required fees $1,530. Average book expense $1,220. **Required Forms and Deadlines:** FAFSA. **Notification of Awards:** Applicants will be notified of awards on a rolling basis beginning 1/1. **Types of Aid:** *Need-based scholarships/grants:* College/university scholarship or grant aid from institutional funds; Federal Pell; Private scholarships; SEOG; State scholarships/grants. *Loans:* Direct PLUS loans; Direct Subsidized Stafford Loans; Direct Unsubsidized Stafford Loans. *Student Employment:* Federal Work-Study Program available. Institutional employment available. **Financial Aid Statistics:** 82% needy freshmen, 84% needy undergrads receive need-based scholarship or grant aid. 43% freshmen, 41% undergrads receive non-need-based scholarship or grant aid. 86% freshmen, 88% undergrads receive need-based self-help aid. 12% freshmen, 9% undergrads receive athletic scholarships. 75% undergrads borrow to pay for school. Average cumulative indebtedness $26,815. **Criteria for awarding aid:** *Non-need-based:* Academics, Alumni affiliation, Athletics, Leadership, Minority status, State/district residency.

NORTHWOOD UNIVERSITY, FLORIDA CAMPUS

2600 North Military Trail, West Palm Beach, FL 33409-2911
Phone: (561) 478-5500 • **Financial Aid Phone:** 561-478-5590
E-mail: fladmit@northwood.edu • **CEEB Code:** 4072
Fax: 561-681-7901 • **Website:** northwood.edu • **ACT Code:** 6736

This private school was founded in 1982. It has a 90 acre campus.

RATINGS
Admissions Selectivity Rating: 84   **Fire Safety Rating:** 85   **Green Rating:** 60*

STUDENTS AND FACULTY
Enrollment: 490. **Student Body:** 36% female, 64% male, 37% out-of-state, 39% international (40 countries represented). Asian 1%, African American 10%, Caucasian 25%, Hispanic 11%, Native American 1%, Two or more races <1%, Race unknown 13%.
Retention and Graduation: 60% freshmen return for sophomore year.
Faculty: Student/faculty ratio 20:1. 16 full-time faculty, 38% hold PhDs, 38% are women. 0% of classes are taught by teaching assistants.

ACADEMICS
Degrees: Associate; Bachelor's; Master's **Most popular majors:** Banking And Financial Support Services; Marketing/Marketing Management, General. **Special Study Options:** Accelerated program; Distance learning; Double major; Dual enrollment; External degree program; Honors program; Internships; Study abroad; Weekend college. Honors programs: An Honors Program began in fall term 1991. In it, honors sections of a variety of critically important courses are offered. The best instructors and the most demanding material and expectations are used. Additionally, special one-credit-hour seminars, which include outside speakers, are offered to sophomores and juniors. Honor students having completed 17 credit hours in honors courses may apply for honors admission to Term in Europe, Term in Asia, or Term in Northern Europe and are eligible for a partial scholarship to support these travel abroad programs. This also provides a powerful incentive for students to successfully compete in the Honors Program. **Disability Services offered to physically disabled students:** Note-taking services. **Career services:** Alumni network; Alumni services; Career assessment; Career/job search classes; Internships

FACILITIES
Housing: Coed dorms; Special housing for disabled students **Special Academic Facilities/Equipment:** Art Gallery **Computers:** 100% of classrooms, 100% of dorms, 100% of libraries, 100% of dining areas, 100% of student union, have wireless network access. Students can register for classes online. Administrative functions (other than registration) can be performed online.

CAMPUS LIFE

Environment: City **Activities:** Dance; Drama/theater; Musical theater; Student government; Student-run film society 23 registered organizations, 1 honor societies. **Athletics (Intercollegiate):** *Men:* baseball, basketball, golf, soccer, tennis. *Women:* basketball, golf, soccer, softball, tennis, volleyball. **On-Campus Highlights:** Countess de Hoernle Student Life Center **Environmental Initiatives:** We keep use of paper to a minimum (e-mail attachments/files, Blackboard portal).

ADMISSIONS

Freshman Academic Profile: Average high school GPA 3.2. 13% in top 10% of high school class, 27% in top 25% of high school class, 57% in top 50% of high school class. 70% from public high schools. **Test Scores:** SAT Math middle 50% range 440-550. SAT EBRW middle 50% range 430-510. ACT middle 50% range 18-21. Minimum paper TOEFL 500. **Basis for Candidate Selection:** *Very important factors considered include:* rigor of secondary school record, class rank, academic GPA, application essay, standardized test scores, recommendation(s), interview, extracurricular activities, character/personal qualities, level of applicant's interest. *Important factors considered include:* talent/ability, volunteer work, work experience. *Other factors considered include:* first generation, alumni/ae relation. **Freshman Admission Requirements:** High school diploma is required and GED is accepted *Academic units recommended:* 4 math, 3 science. **Freshman Admission Statistics:** 628 applied, 54.0% admitted, 31% enrolled. **Transfer Admission Requirements:** High school transcript, college transcript(s), Minimum college GPA of 2.0 required. Lowest grade transferable C. **General Admission Information:** Application fee $25. Regular application deadline 8/1. Nonfall registration accepted. Admission may be deferred for a maximum of 1 year.

COSTS AND FINANCIAL AID

Required Forms and Deadlines: FAFSA; State aid form. **Notification of Awards:** Applicants will be notified of awards on a rolling basis beginning 3/1. **Types of Aid:** *Need-based scholarships/grants:* College/university scholarship or grant aid from institutional funds; Federal Pell; Private scholarships; SEOG; State scholarships/grants. **Financial Aid Statistics:** 87% needy freshmen, 86% needy undergrads receive need-based scholarship or grant aid. 27% freshmen, 21% undergrads receive non-need-based scholarship or grant aid. 84% freshmen, 90% undergrads receive need-based self-help aid. 20% freshmen, 19% undergrads receive athletic scholarships. **Criteria for awarding aid:** *Non-need-based:* Academics, Athletics, Leadership, Minority status.

NORTHWOOD UNIVERSITY, TEXAS CAMPUS

1114 West FM 1382, Cedar Hill, TX 75104-1204
Financial Aid Phone: 972-293-5430 • **CEEB Code:** 6499
Website: northwood.edu • **ACT Code:** 4135

This private school was founded in 1966. It has a 360 acre campus.

RATINGS

Admissions Selectivity Rating: 85   **Fire Safety Rating:** 71   **Green Rating:** 60*

STUDENTS AND FACULTY

Enrollment: 531. **Student Body:** 42% female, 58% male, 25% international (18 countries represented). Asian 2%, African American 14%, Caucasian 19%, Hispanic 24%, Native American <1%, Two or more races <1%, Race unknown 15%.
Retention and Graduation: 58% freshmen return for sophomore year.
Faculty: Student/faculty ratio 19:1. 20 full-time faculty, 25% hold PhDs, 15% are members of minority groups, 45% are women. 0% of classes are taught by teaching assistants.

ACADEMICS

Degrees: Associate; Bachelor's; **Master's Classes:** Most classes have 20-29 students. Most lab/discussion sessions have 20-29 students. **Most popular majors:** Entrepreneurship/Entrepreneurial Studies; International Business/Trade/Commerce; Marketing/Marketing Management, General. **Special Study Options:** Accelerated program; Distance learning; Double major; Dual enrollment; External degree program; Honors program; Internships; Study abroad; Weekend college. Honors programs: An Honors Program begain in Fall Term, 1991. In it, honors sections of six critically important courses are offered. The best instructors and the most demanding material and expectations are used. Additionally, special one credit hour seminars, which include outside speakers, are offered to sophomores and juniors. **Disability Services offered to physically disabled students:** Tutors. **Career services:** Alumni network; Alumni services; Career assessment; Internships

FACILITIES

Housing: Apartments for single students; Coed dorms; Men's dorms; Wellness housing **Special Academic Facilities/Equipment:** Butler Gallery, Hopkins Display Cases, Hach Library **Computers:** 100% of classrooms, 100% of dorms, 100% of libraries, 100% of dining areas, 100% of student union, have wireless network access. Students can register for classes online. Administrative functions (other than registration) can be performed online.

CAMPUS LIFE

Environment: Village **Activities:** Campus Ministries; Choral groups; Dance; Drama/theater; International Student Organization; Student newspaper 17 registered organizations, 1 honor society, 2 religious organizations. 1 fraternity, 1 sorority. **Athletics (Intercollegiate):** *Men:* baseball, cross-country, golf, soccer, track/field (outdoor), track/field (indoor). *Women:* cross-country, golf, soccer, softball, track/field (outdoor), track/field (indoor). **Environmental Initiatives:** Paper recycling. We have two large bins in one of the parking lots. The paper is collected twice a week from offices and common areas.

ADMISSIONS

Freshman Academic Profile: Average high school GPA 3.3. 8% in top 10% of high school class, 27% in top 25% of high school class, 65% in top 50% of high school class. 90% from public high schools. **Test Scores:** SAT Math middle 50% range 420-520. SAT EBRW middle 50% range 390-500. ACT middle 50% range 17-22. Minimum paper TOEFL 500. **Basis for Candidate Selection:** *Very important factors considered include:* rigor of secondary school record, academic GPA, standardized test scores, interview, extracurricular activities, character/personal qualities, level of applicant's interest. *Important factors considered include:* class rank, talent/ability, volunteer work, work experience. *Other factors considered include:* application essay, recommendation(s), first generation, alumni/ae relation. **Freshman Admission Requirements:** High school diploma is required and GED is accepted *Academic units recommended:* 4 English, 3 math, 3 science, 2 science labs, 1 foreign language, 3 social studies, 1 computer science. **Freshman Admission Statistics:** 452 applied, 58.6% admitted, 65% enrolled. **Transfer Admission Requirements:** High school transcript, college transcript(s), essay or personal statement, Minimum college GPA of 2.0 required. Lowest grade transferable C. **General Admission Information:** Application fee $25. Regular application deadline 8/1. Nonfall registration accepted. Admission may be deferred for a maximum of 1 year.

COSTS AND FINANCIAL AID

Required Forms and Deadlines: FAFSA. **Notification of Awards:** Applicants will be notified of awards on a rolling basis beginning 3/1. **Types of Aid:** *Need-based scholarships/grants:* Federal Pell; Private scholarships; SEOG. **Financial Aid Statistics:** 92% needy freshmen, 89% needy undergrads receive need-based scholarship or grant aid. 24% freshmen, 22% undergrads receive non-need-based scholarship or grant aid. 90% freshmen, 91% undergrads receive need-based self-help aid. 11% freshmen, 12% undergrads receive athletic scholarships. **Criteria for awarding aid:** *Non-need-based:* Academics, Alumni affiliation, Athletics, Leadership, Minority status.

NORWICH UNIVERSITY

158 Harmon Drive, Northfield, VT 05663
Phone: 802-485-2001
E-mail: nuadm@norwich.edu
Fax: 802-485-2032 • **Website:** www.norwich.edu

This private school was founded in 1819. It has a 1125 acre campus.

RATINGS

Admissions Selectivity Rating: 74   **Fire Safety Rating:** 60*   **Green Rating:** 60*

STUDENTS AND FACULTY

Enrollment: 2,201. **Student Body:** 26% female, 74% male, 84% out-of-state, 2% international. Asian 2%, African American 3%, Caucasian 72%, Hispanic 4%, Native American 1%, Pacific Islander <1%, Two or more races 2%, Race unknown 15%.
Retention and Graduation: 85% freshmen return for sophomore year. 10% grads go on to further study within 1 year. 2% grads pursue arts and sciences degrees. 2% grads pursue law degrees. 2% grads pursue business degrees. 1% grads pursue medical degrees. **Faculty:** Student/faculty ratio 14:1. 140 full-time faculty, 9% are members of minority groups, 36% are women. 0% of classes are taught by teaching assistants.

ACADEMICS

Degrees: Bachelor's; Master's; Post-Bachelor's certificate **Classes:** Most classes have 10-19 students. **Most popular majors:** Liberal Arts And Sciences/

Liberal Studies; Criminal Justice/Law Enforcement Administration. **Special Study Options:** Distance learning; Double major; Dual enrollment; English as a Second Language (ESL); Exchange student program (domestic); Honors program; Internships; Study abroad; Teacher certification program. **Disability Services offered to physically disabled students:** Tutors. **Career services:** Career/job search classes

FACILITIES
Housing: Coed dorms 95% of campus accessible to physically diasbled. **Special Academic Facilities/Equipment:** museum, architecture and art building w/galery, new library.

CAMPUS LIFE
Environment: Rural **Activities:** Campus Ministries; Dance; Drama/theater; International Student Organization; Jazz band; Marching band; Model UN; Radio station; Student government; Student newspaper; Yearbook 40 registered organizations, 8 honor societies, 4 religious organizations **Athletics (Intercollegiate):** *Men:* baseball, basketball, cross-country, diving, football, ice hockey, lacrosse, riflery, rugby, soccer, swimming, track/field (outdoor), volleyball, wrestling. *Women:* basketball, cross-country, diving, riflery, rugby, soccer, softball, swimming, track/field (outdoor), volleyball.

ADMISSIONS
Freshman Academic Profile: Average high school GPA 3.1. 11% in top 10% of high school class, 37% in top 25% of high school class, 74% in top 50% of high school class. **Test Scores:** SAT Math middle 50% range 500-640. SAT EBRW middle 50% range 480-580. ACT middle 50% range 21-26. Minimum internet-based TOEFL 75. Minimum paper TOEFL 550. **Basis for Candidate Selection:** *Very important factors considered include:* rigor of secondary school record, academic GPA, standardized test scores. *Other factors considered include:* class rank, application essay, recommendation(s), interview, extracurricular activities, talent/ability, character/personal qualities, alumni/ae relation, volunteer work, work experience. **Freshman Admission Requirements:** High school diploma is required and GED is accepted *Academic units recommended:* 4 English, 4 math, 4 science, 3 science labs, 2 foreign language, 3 social studies, 3 history. **Freshman Admission Statistics:** 1,473 applied, 91.0% admitted, 37% enrolled. **Transfer Admission Requirements:** High school transcript, college transcript(s), Lowest grade transferable c-. **General Admission Information:** Application fee $35. Priority deadline 2/1. Nonfall registration accepted. Admission may be deferred for a maximum of 1 term.

COSTS AND FINANCIAL AID
Annual tuition $30,048. Room and board $10,976. Required fees $1,734. Average book expense $1,000. **Required Forms and Deadlines:** FAFSA. **Notification of Awards:** Applicants will be notified of awards on a rolling basis beginning 2/15. **Types of Aid:** *Need-based scholarships/grants:* College/ university scholarship or grant aid from institutional funds; Federal Pell; Private scholarships; SEOG; State scholarships/grants. *Loans:* Direct PLUS loans; Direct Subsidized Stafford Loans; Direct Unsubsidized Stafford Loans. *Student Employment:* Federal Work-Study Program available. Institutional employment available. **Financial Aid Statistics:** 100% needy freshmen, 100% needy undergrads receive need-based scholarship or grant aid. 18% freshmen, 17% undergrads receive non-need-based scholarship or grant aid. 79% freshmen, 79% undergrads receive need-based self-help aid. 0% freshmen, 0% undergrads receive athletic scholarships. **Criteria for awarding aid:** *Need-based:* Academics *Non-need-based:* Academics.

NOTRE DAME DE NAMUR UNIVERSITY

1500 Ralston Avenue, Belmont, CA 94002-1908
Phone: 650-508-3600 • **Financial Aid Phone:** 650-508-3600
E-mail: admiss@ndnu.edu • **CEEB Code:** 4063
Fax: 650-508-3426 • **Website:** www.ndnu.edu • **ACT Code:** 236

This private school, affiliated with the Roman Catholic Church, was founded in 1851. It has a 80 acre campus.

RATINGS
Admissions Selectivity Rating: 73   **Fire Safety Rating:** 60*   **Green Rating:** 60*

STUDENTS AND FACULTY
Enrollment: 1,177. **Student Body:** 67% female, 33% male, 6% out-of-state, 3% international. Asian 12%, African American 6%, Caucasian 25%, Hispanic 37%, Native American 1%, Pacific Islander 3%, Two or more races 4%, Race unknown 9%.
Retention and Graduation: 75% freshmen return for sophomore year.
Faculty: Student/faculty ratio 11:1. 60 full-time faculty, 95% hold PhDs, 22%

are members of minority groups, 55% are women. 0% of classes are taught by teaching assistants.

ACADEMICS
Degrees: Bachelor's; Doctoral/Research; Master's; Post-Bachelor's certificate **Classes:** Most classes have 10-19 students. **Most popular majors:** Psychology, General; Human Services, General. **Special Study Options:** Accelerated program; Double major; Dual enrollment; English as a Second Language (ESL); Exchange student program (domestic); Independent study; Internships; Liberal arts/career combination; Student-designed major; Study abroad; Teacher certification program. **Disability Services offered to physically disabled students:** Note-taking services; Reader services; Tape recorders; Tutors. **Career services:** Alumni network; Career assessment; Career/job search classes; Internships

FACILITIES
Housing: Coed dorms; Theme housing; Wellness housing **Special Academic Facilities/Equipment:** Wiegand Gallery, theatre.

CAMPUS LIFE
Environment: Town **Activities:** Campus Ministries; Dance; Drama/theater; International Student Organization; Music ensembles; Musical theater; Student government; Student newspaper 15 registered organizations, 3 honor societies, 1 religious organization **Athletics (Intercollegiate):** *Men:* basketball, cheerleading, soccer, tennis, track/field (outdoor). *Women:* basketball, cheerleading, cross-country, soccer, softball, tennis, track/field (outdoor), volleyball.

ADMISSIONS
Freshman Academic Profile: Average high school GPA 3.2. 13% in top 10% of high school class, 35% in top 25% of high school class, 76% in top 50% of high school class. 62% from public high schools. **Test Scores:** SAT Math middle 50% range 420-520. SAT EBRW middle 50% range 430-520. ACT middle 50% range 17-21. Minimum internet-based TOEFL 61. Minimum paper TOEFL 500. **Basis for Candidate Selection:** *Very important factors considered include:* rigor of secondary school record, academic GPA. *Important factors considered include:* class rank, application essay, standardized test scores, recommendation(s), extracurricular activities, talent/ability, character/ personal qualities, level of applicant's interest. *Other factors considered include:* interview, first generation, alumni/ae relation, religious affiliation/commitment, racial/ethnic status, volunteer work, work experience. **Freshman Admission Requirements:** High school diploma is required and GED is accepted *Academic units required:* 4 English, 2 math, 1 science, 1 science labs, 2 foreign language, 2 social studies, 1 history, 3 academic electives, *Academic units recommended:* 4 English, 3 math, 2 science, 1 science labs, 3 foreign language, 2 social studies, 1 history, 3 academic electives. **Freshman Admission Statistics:** 2,167 applied, 77.7% admitted, 11% enrolled. **Transfer Admission Requirements:** college transcript(s), essay or personal statement, statement of good standing from prior institution(s). Minimum college GPA of 2.0 required. Lowest grade transferable C. **General Admission Information:** Application fee $50. Priority deadline 2/1. Nonfall registration accepted. Admission may be deferred for a maximum of 1 year.

COSTS AND FINANCIAL AID
Annual tuition $32,208. Required fees $400. Average book expense $1,790. **Required Forms and Deadlines:** FAFSA. **Notification of Awards:** Applicants will be notified of awards on a rolling basis beginning 2/15. **Types of Aid:** *Need-based scholarships/grants:* College/university scholarship or grant aid from institutional funds; Federal Pell; Private scholarships; SEOG; State scholarships/grants. *Loans:* Direct PLUS loans; Direct Subsidized Stafford Loans; Direct Unsubsidized Stafford Loans. *Student Employment:* Federal Work-Study Program available. Institutional employment available. **Financial Aid Statistics:** 100% needy freshmen, 100% needy undergrads receive need-based scholarship or grant aid. 5% freshmen, 3% undergrads receive non-need-based scholarship or grant aid. 87% freshmen, 80% undergrads receive need-based self-help aid. 3% freshmen, 1% undergrads receive athletic scholarships. **Criteria for awarding aid:** *Need-based:* Academics, Alumni affiliation, Athletics *Non-need-based:* Academics, Art, Athletics, Leadership, Music/drama, Religious affiliation.

NOVA SOUTHEASTERN UNIVERSITY

3301 College Avenue, Fort Lauderdale, FL 33314
Phone: 954-262-8000 • **Financial Aid Phone:** 954-262-7456
E-mail: admissions@nova.edu • **CEEB Code:** 5514
Fax: 954-262-3811 • **Website:** www.nova.edu • **ACT Code:** 6706

This private school was founded in 1964. It has a 300 acre campus.

RATINGS
Admissions Selectivity Rating: 84 **Fire Safety Rating:** 92 **Green Rating:** 60*

STUDENTS AND FACULTY
Enrollment: 6,246. **Student Body:** 71% female, 29% male, 16% out-of-state, 4% international. Asian 6%, African American 24%, Caucasian 28%, Hispanic 32%, Native American <1%, Pacific Islander <1%, Two or more races 1%, Race unknown 4%.
Retention and Graduation: 70% freshmen return for sophomore year.
Faculty: Student/faculty ratio 20:1. 814 full-time faculty, 88% hold PhDs, 30% are members of minority groups, 49% are women. 0% of classes are taught by teaching assistants.

ACADEMICS
Degrees: Associate; Bachelor's; Doctoral; Doctoral Other; Doctoral/Professional; Doctoral/Research; Master's; Post-Bachelor's certificate; Post-Master's certificate **Classes:** Most classes have 10-19 students. Most lab/discussion sessions have fewer than 10 students. **Most popular majors:** Biology/Biological Sciences, General; Psychology, General; Business Administration And Management, General. **Special Study Options:** Distance learning; Double major; Honors program; Independent study; Internships; Study abroad; Teacher certification program. Combined degree programs: BA/DDS; BA/JD; BA/MA. **Disability Services offered to physically disabled students:** Note-taking services; Reader services; Tape recorders; Tutors. **Career services:** Alumni services; Career assessment; Internships; Regional alumni

FACILITIES
Housing: Apartments for married students; Apartments for single students; Coed dorms; Special housing for disabled student; Theme housing **Special Academic Facilities/Equipment:** Institute for Early Childhood Studies, University School for pre-kindergarten to grade 12, Oceanographic Center and Lab, Biofeedback and Learning Technology Labs, Audiology and Speech Language Pathology, and Psychology Clinics **Computers:** 100% of classrooms, 100% of dorms, 100% of libraries, 80% of dining areas, 100% of student union, 70% of common outdoor areas have wireless network access. Students can register for classes online. Administrative functions (other than registration) can be performed online.

CAMPUS LIFE
Environment: City **Activities:** Campus Ministries; Choral groups; Dance; Drama/theater; International Student Organization; Literary magazine; Radio station; Student government; Student newspaper; Television station 292 registered organizations. **Athletics (Intercollegiate):** *Men:* baseball, basketball, cross-country, golf, soccer, track/field (outdoor). *Women:* basketball, cheerleading, crew/rowing, cross-country, golf, soccer, softball, tennis, track/field (outdoor), volleyball. **On-Campus Highlights:** Don Taft Univeristy Center, Alvin Sherman Library, Research & Inform, The Shark Tank Arena, Health Professions Division Museum, Miniaci Performing Arts Center

ADMISSIONS
Test Scores: SAT Math middle 50% range 470-590. SAT EBRW middle 50% range 460-570. ACT middle 50% range 20-25. Minimum paper TOEFL 550. **Basis for Candidate Selection:** *Very important factors considered include:* academic GPA, standardized test scores. *Important factors considered include:* rigor of secondary school record. *Other factors considered include:* application essay, recommendation(s), interview, extracurricular activities, talent/ability, character/personal qualities, volunteer work. **Freshman Admission Requirements:** High school diploma is required and GED is accepted *Academic units recommended:* 4 English, 3 math, 3 science, 3 social studies. **Freshman Admission Statistics:** 3,780 applied, 57.7% admitted, 31% enrolled. **Transfer Admission Requirements:** college transcript(s), statement of good standing from prior institution(s). Minimum college GPA of 2.50 required. Lowest grade transferable D. **General Admission Information:** Application fee $50. Regular application deadline 8/1. Nonfall registration accepted. Admission may be deferred for a maximum of 1 year.

COSTS AND FINANCIAL AID
Annual tuition $21,600. Room and board $9,086. Required fees $550. Average book expense $1,500. **Required Forms and Deadlines:** FAFSA; State aid form. **Notification of Awards:** Applicants will be notified of awards on a rolling

basis beginning 3/15. **Types of Aid:** *Need-based scholarships/grants:* College/university scholarship or grant aid from institutional funds; Federal Pell; Private scholarships; SEOG; State scholarships/grants. *Loans:* Direct PLUS loans; Direct Subsidized Stafford Loans; Direct Unsubsidized Stafford Loans. *Student Employment:* Federal Work-Study Program available. Institutional employment available. **Financial Aid Statistics:** 97% needy freshmen, 96% needy undergrads receive need-based scholarship or grant aid. 100% freshmen, 100% undergrads receive non-need-based scholarship or grant aid. 83% freshmen, 88% undergrads receive need-based self-help aid. 12% freshmen, 7% undergrads receive athletic scholarships. 92% freshmen, 83% undergrads receive any aid. **Criteria for awarding aid:** *Need-based:* Academics *Non-need-based:* Academics, Athletics, Leadership, Music/drama.

OAK HILLS CHRISTIAN COLLEGE

220 Main Building, Bemidji, MN 56601
Phone: 218-751-8670 • **Financial Aid Phone:** 218-751-8670
E-mail: admissions@oakhills.edu
Fax: 218-751-8825 • **Website:** www.oakhills.edu • **ACT Code:** 2167

This private school was founded in 1946. It has a 180 acre campus.

RATINGS
Admissions Selectivity Rating: 86 **Fire Safety Rating:** 71 **Green Rating:** 60*

STUDENTS AND FACULTY
Enrollment: 131. **Student Body:** 53% female, 47% male, 33% out-of-state, 1% international (1 countries represented). Asian 2%, African American 1%, Caucasian 95%, Native American 1%,
Retention and Graduation: 55% freshmen return for sophomore year.
Faculty: Student/faculty ratio 13:1. 6 full-time faculty, 67% hold PhDs, 0% are members of minority groups, 33% are women. 0% of classes are taught by teaching assistants.

ACADEMICS
Degrees: Associate; Bachelor's; Certificate **Classes:** Most classes have 10-19 students. **Most popular majors:** Bible/Biblical Studies; Pastoral Studies/Counseling; Youth Ministry. **Special Study Options:** Cooperative education program; Double major; Independent study; Internships. **Disability Services offered to physically disabled students:** Note-taking services; Reader services; Tape recorders; Tutors. **Career services:** Alumni network; Career assessment; Career/job search classes; Internships

FACILITIES
Housing: Apartments for married students; Apartments for single students; Men's dorms; Special housing for disabled student; Women's dorms 20% of campus accessible to physically diasbled. **Special Academic Facilities/Equipment:** American Indian Resource Center **Computers:** 50% of classrooms, 100% of dorms, 100% of libraries, 100% of student union, 50% of common outdoor areas have wireless network access. Students can register for classes online. Administrative functions (other than registration) can be performed online.

CAMPUS LIFE
Environment: Village **Activities:** Campus Ministries; Choral groups; Music ensembles; Student government. **Athletics (Intercollegiate):** *Men:* basketball. *Women:* basketball, volleyball. **On-Campus Highlights:** The Fellowship Center Lounge, Schreiber Activity Center (SAC) Gym, Library, Chapel, Lake Front

ADMISSIONS
Freshman Academic Profile: 5% in top 10% of high school class, 5% in top 25% of high school class, 47% in top 50% of high school class. 79% from public high schools. **Test Scores:** ACT middle 50% range 16-21. Minimum paper TOEFL 500. **Basis for Candidate Selection:** *Important factors considered include:* rigor of secondary school record, class rank, academic GPA, application essay, recommendation(s), character/personal qualities. *Other factors considered include:* standardized test scores, interview, alumni/ae relation, religious affiliation/commitment. **Freshman Admission Requirements:** High school diploma is required and GED is accepted **Freshman Admission Statistics:** 70 applied, 55.7% admitted, 79% enrolled. **Transfer Admission Requirements:** High school transcript, college transcript(s), essay or personal statement, Minimum college GPA of 2.0 required. Lowest grade transferable C. **General Admission Information:** Application fee $25. Nonfall registration accepted. Admission may be deferred for a maximum of 2 years.

COSTS AND FINANCIAL AID
Annual tuition $14,420. Room and board $5,180. Average book expense $990. **Required Forms and Deadlines:** FAFSA; Institution's own financial aid

form. **Notification of Awards:** Applicants will be notified of awards on a rolling basis beginning 3/1. **Types of Aid:** *Need-based scholarships/grants:* College/university scholarship or grant aid from institutional funds; Federal Pell; Private scholarships; SEOG; State scholarships/grants. *Loans: Student Employment:* Federal Work-Study Program available. Institutional employment available. **Financial Aid Statistics:** 100% needy freshmen, 100% needy undergrads receive need-based scholarship or grant aid. 0% undergrads receive non-need-based scholarship or grant aid. 75% freshmen, 86% undergrads receive need-based self-help aid. 0% freshmen, 0% undergrads receive athletic scholarships. 100% freshmen, 100% undergrads receive any aid. **Criteria for awarding aid:** *Non-need-based:* Academics, Alumni affiliation.

OAKLAND CITY UNIVERSITY

138 N. Lucretia Street, Oakland City, IN 47660
Phone: 812-749-1221
E-mail: ocuadmit@oak.edu
Fax: 812-749-1433 • **Website:** http://www.oak.edu

This is a private school.

RATINGS
Admissions Selectivity Rating: 89   **Fire Safety Rating:** 60*   **Green Rating:** 60*

STUDENTS AND FACULTY
Enrollment: 1,492. **Student Body:** 53% female, 47% male, 17% out-of-state, 1% international. Asian 1%, African American 11%, Caucasian 84%, Hispanic <1%, Native American <1%, Race unknown 3%.
Retention and Graduation: 66% freshmen return for sophomore year.
Faculty: Student/faculty ratio 15:1. 58 full-time faculty, 0% are members of minority groups, 47% are women.

ACADEMICS
Degrees: Associate; Bachelor's; Certificate; Doctoral; Doctoral/Professional; **Master's Classes:** Most classes have 20-29 students. Most lab/discussion sessions have 20-29 students. **Special Study Options:** Distance learning; Double major; Dual enrollment; Independent study; Internships; Teacher certification program.

FACILITIES
Housing: Apartments for married students; Apartments for single students; Men's dorms; Women's dorms

CAMPUS LIFE
Activities: Campus Ministries; Choral groups; Drama/theater; Pep band; Student government; Student newspaper; Yearbook.

ADMISSIONS
Freshman Academic Profile: Average high school GPA 3.2. 9% in top 10% of high school class, 16% in top 25% of high school class, 41% in top 50% of high school class. **Test Scores:** SAT Math middle 50% range 420-530. SAT EBRW middle 50% range 400-510. ACT middle 50% range 17-23. **Basis for Candidate Selection:** *Very important factors considered include:* rigor of secondary school record, academic GPA, standardized test scores. *Other factors considered include:* class rank, interview, character/personal qualities, alumni/ae relation, level of applicant's interest. **Freshman Admission Requirements:** High school diploma is required and GED is accepted *Academic units recommended:* 4 English, 3 math, 3 science, 2 social studies. **Freshman Admission Statistics:** 620 applied, 56.3% admitted, 100% enrolled. **Transfer Admission Requirements:** High school transcript, college transcript(s), standardized test scores, Minimum college GPA of 2.0 required. Lowest grade transferable C. **General Admission Information:** Application fee $35. Regular application deadline 9/5. Nonfall registration accepted. Admission may be deferred.

COSTS AND FINANCIAL AID
Annual tuition $15,200. Room and board $6,000. Required fees $360. Average book expense $1,500. **Required Forms and Deadlines:** FAFSA. **Notification of Awards:** Applicants will be notified of awards on a rolling basis beginning 5/1. **Types of Aid:** *Need-based scholarships/grants:* College/university scholarship or grant aid from institutional funds; Federal Pell; Private scholarships; SEOG; State scholarships/grants. **Financial Aid Statistics:** 0% freshmen, 0% undergrads receive athletic scholarships. **Criteria for awarding aid:** *Non-need-based:* Academics, Alumni affiliation, Art, Athletics, Minority status, Music/drama, Religious affiliation.

OAKLAND UNIVERSITY

2200 N. Squirrel Rd., Rochester, MI 48309-4454
Phone: 248-370-3360 • **Financial Aid Phone:** 248-370-2550
E-mail: visit@oakland.edu • **CEEB Code:** 1497
Website: http://www.oakland.edu • **ACT Code:** 2033

This public school was founded in 1957. It has a 1444 acre campus.

RATINGS
Admissions Selectivity Rating: 76   **Fire Safety Rating:** 89   **Green Rating:** 72

STUDENTS AND FACULTY
Enrollment: 15,864. **Student Body:** 56% female, 44% male, 1% out-of-state, 2% international (45 countries represented). Asian 5%, African American 7%, Caucasian 75%, Hispanic 4%, Native American <1%, Pacific Islander <1%, Two or more races 3%, Race unknown 4%.
Retention and Graduation: 77% freshmen return for sophomore year. 19% freshmen graduate within 4 years. 46% freshmen graduate within 6 years.
Faculty: Student/faculty ratio 21:1. 582 full-time faculty, 93% hold PhDs, 23% are members of minority groups, 47% are women. 1% of classes are taught by teaching assistants.

ACADEMICS
Degrees: Bachelor's; Doctoral; Doctoral/Professional; Doctoral/Research; Master's; Post-Bachelor's certificate; Post-Master's certificate **Most popular majors:** Biology/Biological Sciences, General; Psychology, General; Health Professions And Related Clinical Sciences, Other. **Special Study Options:** Accelerated program; Cooperative education program; Cross-registration; Distance learning; Double major; Dual enrollment; English as a Second Language (ESL); Exchange student program (domestic); Honors program; Independent study; Internships; Liberal arts/career combination; Student-designed major; Study abroad; Teacher certification program. Honors programs: Honors College. **Disability Services offered to physically disabled students:** Note-taking services; Reader services; Tape recorders; Tutors. **Career services:** Alumni network; Alumni services; Career assessment; Career/job search classes; Internships

FACILITIES
Housing: Apartments for single students; Coed dorms; Fraternity/sorority housing; Special housing for disabled student; Special housing for international students; Theme housing 90% of campus accessible to physically diasbled. **Special Academic Facilities/Equipment:** Art gallery, robotics lab, Eye Research institute, Professional theater, Meadowbrook Hall, Meadowbrook Music Festival, two golf courses, Pawley Learning center, Lowry Early Childhood Education Center, Jack's Place for Autism at OU. **Computers:** Students can register for classes online. Administrative functions (other than registration) can be performed online.

CAMPUS LIFE
Environment: Town **Activities:** Campus Ministries; Choral groups; Concert band; Dance; Drama/theater; International Student Organization; Jazz band; Literary magazine; Model UN; Music ensembles; Musical theater; Opera; Pep band; Radio station; Student government; Student newspaper; Student-run film society; Symphony orchestra; Television station 170 registered organizations, 9 honor societies, 12 religious organizations. 6 fraternities, 6 sororities. **Athletics (Intercollegiate):** *Men:* baseball, basketball, cross-country, diving, golf, soccer, swimming, track/field (outdoor). *Women:* basketball, cross-country, diving, golf, soccer, softball, swimming, tennis, track/field (outdoor), volleyball. **On-Campus Highlights:** Recreation Center, Pawley Hall, Oakland Center, Kresge Library, Oak View Hall-home of the Honors College **Environmental Initiatives:** $8 million Facility upgrade from 1998 to save on energy costs

ADMISSIONS
Freshman Academic Profile: Average high school GPA 3.4. 20% in top 10% of high school class, 46% in top 25% of high school class, 79% in top 50% of high school class. 90% from public high schools. **Test Scores:** SAT Math middle 50% range 500-610. SAT EBRW middle 50% range 510-620. ACT middle 50% range 21-27. Minimum internet-based TOEFL 79. Minimum paper TOEFL 550. **Basis for Candidate Selection:** *Very important factors considered include:* rigor of secondary school record, academic GPA. *Important factors considered include:* standardized test scores. *Other factors considered include:* class rank, application essay, recommendation(s), interview, extracurricular activities, talent/ability, character/personal qualities, volunteer work, work experience. **Freshman Admission Requirements:** High school diploma is required and GED is accepted *Academic units required:* 4 English, 4 math, 3 science, 3 social studies, *Academic units recommended:* 2 foreign language. **Freshman Admission Statistics:** 10,362 applied, 84.3% admitted, 28%

enrolled. **Transfer Admission Requirements:** college transcript(s), statement of good standing from prior institution(s). Minimum college GPA of 2.50 required. Lowest grade transferable C. **General Admission Information:** Regular application deadline 8/1. Nonfall registration accepted. Admission may be deferred.

COSTS AND FINANCIAL AID
Annual in-state tuition $9,910. Annual out-of-state tuition $24,735. Room and board $9,910. Average book expense $764. **Required Forms and Deadlines:** FAFSA. **Types of Aid:** *Need-based scholarships/grants:* College/university scholarship or grant aid from institutional funds; Federal Pell; Private scholarships; SEOG; State scholarships/grants. *Loans:* Direct PLUS loans; Direct Subsidized Stafford Loans; Direct Unsubsidized Stafford Loans. *Student Employment:* Federal Work-Study Program available. Institutional employment available. **Criteria for awarding aid:** *Need-based:* Academics *Non-need-based:* Academics, Art, Athletics, Leadership, Music/drama, State/district residency.

OBERLIN COLLEGE

70 North Professor Street, Oberlin, OH 44074
Phone: 440-775-8411 • **Financial Aid Phone:** 440-775-8142
E-mail: college.admissions@oberlin.edu • **CEEB Code:** 1587
Fax: 440-775-6905 • **Website:** www.oberlin.edu • **ACT Code:** 3304

This private school was founded in 1833. It has a 452 acre campus.

RATINGS
Admissions Selectivity Rating: 94   Fire Safety Rating: 89   Green Rating: 99

STUDENTS AND FACULTY
Enrollment: 2,827. **Student Body:** 58% female, 42% male, 94% out-of-state, 10% international. Asian 4%, African American 5%, Caucasian 64%, Hispanic 8%, Native American <1%, Pacific Islander <1%, Two or more races 8%, Race unknown 1%.
Retention and Graduation: 91% freshmen return for sophomore year. 75% freshmen graduate within 4 years. 86% freshmen graduate within 6 years. 22% grads go on to further study within 1 year. **Faculty:** Student/faculty ratio 10:1. 331 full-time faculty, 0% of classes are taught by teaching assistants.

ACADEMICS
Degrees: Bachelor's; Diploma; Master's; Post-Bachelor's certificate **Classes:** Most classes have 10-19 students. **Most popular majors:** Environmental Studies; Economics; Political Science And Government. **Special Study Options:** Double major; English as a Second Language (ESL); Independent study; Student-designed major; Study abroad; Teacher certification program. Honors programs: Students with proven independence and high academic ability may achieve an Honors designation at graduation by completing an Honors project within their major during their senior year. Honors projects vary, but always involve independent work supervised by a faculty advisor. Projects may be completed in seminars or private readings, in research, or in the preparation of a thesis, exhibition, or performance. Every honors candidate must also pass an examination at the end of the senior year—oral or written or both. **Disability Services offered to physically disabled students:** Note-taking services; Reader services; Tape recorders; Tutors. **Career services:** Alumni network; Alumni services; Career assessment; Career/job search classes; Internships; Regional alumni

FACILITIES
Housing: Apartments for single students; Coed dorms; Cooperative housing; Special housing for disabled student; Theme housing; Wellness housing; Women's dorms 90% of campus accessible to physically diasbled. **Special Academic Facilities/Equipment:** Allen Memorial Art museum (one of the top ranked in the US), Theaters, music performance halls, observatory, environmental studies building that helped launch the green building movement, arboretum, high performance computer cluster **Computers:** Students can register for classes online. Administrative functions (other than registration) can be performed online.

CAMPUS LIFE
Environment: Village **Activities:** Campus Ministries; Choral groups; Concert band; Dance; Drama/theater; International Student Organization; Jazz band; Literary magazine; Marching band; Music ensembles; Musical theater; Opera; Pep band; Radio station; Student government; Student newspaper; Student-run film society; Symphony orchestra; Yearbook 125 registered organizations,

3 honor societies, 10 religious organizations. **Athletics (Intercollegiate):** *Men:* baseball, basketball, cross-country, diving, football, golf, lacrosse, soccer, swimming, tennis, track/field (outdoor), track/field (indoor). *Women:* basketball, cross-country, diving, field hockey, golf, lacrosse, soccer, softball, swimming, tennis, track/field (outdoor), track/field (indoor), volleyball. **On-Campus Highlights:** Allen Memorial Art Museum, Oberlin College Science Center, Adam Joseph Lewis Center for Environmental Studies, Arboretum, Jesse Philips Recreational Center **Environmental Initiatives:** Development of Campus Resource Monitoring System. oberlin.edu/dormenergy

ADMISSIONS
Freshman Academic Profile: Average high school GPA 3.6. 58% in top 10% of high school class, 79% in top 25% of high school class, 97% in top 50% of high school class. 66% from public high schools. **Test Scores:** SAT Math middle 50% range 630-730. SAT EBRW middle 50% range 650-720. ACT middle 50% range 28-33. Minimum internet-based TOEFL 100. Minimum paper TOEFL 600. **Basis for Candidate Selection:** *Very important factors considered include:* rigor of secondary school record, class rank, academic GPA, standardized test scores. *Important factors considered include:* extracurricular activities, talent/ability, character/personal qualities, first generation. *Other factors considered include:* application essay, recommendation(s), interview, alumni/ae relation, racial/ethnic status, volunteer work, work experience, level of applicant's interest. **Freshman Admission Requirements:** High school diploma is required and GED is not accepted *Academic units required:* 4 English, 3 math, 3 science, 3 foreign language, 3 social studies, *Academic units recommended:* 4 science. **Freshman Admission Statistics:** 7,762 applied, 33.7% admitted, 29% enrolled. **Transfer Admission Requirements:** High school transcript, college transcript(s), essay or personal statement, standardized test scores, statement of good standing from prior institution(s). Minimum college GPA of 3.0 required. Lowest grade transferable C-. **General Admission Information:** Priority deadline 1/15. Regular application deadline 1/15. Nonfall registration accepted. Admission may be deferred for a maximum of 1 year.

COSTS AND FINANCIAL AID
Annual tuition $52,762. Room and board $15,212. Required fees $698. Average book expense $1,958. **Required Forms and Deadlines:** Business/Farm Supplement; CSS/Financial Aid PROFILE; FAFSA; Institution's own financial aid form; Noncustodial PROFILE. **Notification of Awards:** Applicants will be notified of awards on or about 4/1. **Types of Aid:** *Need-based scholarships/grants:* College/university scholarship or grant aid from institutional funds; Federal Pell; Private scholarships; SEOG; State scholarships/grants. *Loans:* Direct PLUS loans; Direct Subsidized Stafford Loans; Direct Unsubsidized Stafford Loans. *Student Employment:* Federal Work-Study Program available. Institutional employment available. **Financial Aid Statistics:** 96% needy freshmen, 99% needy undergrads receive need-based scholarship or grant aid. 81% freshmen, 79% undergrads receive non-need-based scholarship or grant aid. 87% freshmen, 88% undergrads receive need-based self-help aid. 0% freshmen, 0% undergrads receive athletic scholarships. 61% freshmen, 60% undergrads receive any aid. 43% undergrads borrow to pay for school. Average cumulative indebtedness $27,144. **Criteria for awarding aid:** *Non-need-based:* Academics, Music/drama.

OCCIDENTAL COLLEGE

1600 Campus Road, Los Angeles, CA 90041-3314
Phone: 800-825-5262 • **Financial Aid Phone:** 323-259-2548
E-mail: admission@oxy.edu • **CEEB Code:** 4581
Fax: 323-341-4875 • **Website:** www.oxy.edu • **ACT Code:** 350

This private school was founded in 1887. It has a 120 acre campus.

RATINGS
Admissions Selectivity Rating: 93   Fire Safety Rating: 81   Green Rating: 87

STUDENTS AND FACULTY
Enrollment: 2,041. **Student Body:** 58% female, 42% male, 51% out-of-state, 6% international (29 countries represented). Asian 14%, African American 5%, Caucasian 51%, Hispanic 14%, Native American <1%, Pacific Islander <1%, Two or more races 8%, Race unknown 2%.
Retention and Graduation: 91% freshmen return for sophomore year. 80% freshmen graduate within 4 years. 84% freshmen graduate within 6 years. 21% grads go on to further study within 1 year. **Faculty:** Student/faculty ratio 9:1.

188 full-time faculty, 97% hold PhDs, 30% are members of minority groups, 51% are women. 0% of classes are taught by teaching assistants.

ACADEMICS

Degrees: Bachelor's; **Master's Classes:** Most classes have 10-19 students. Most lab/discussion sessions have 10-19 students. **Most popular majors:** Biology/Biological Sciences, General; Economics, General; International Relations And Affairs. **Special Study Options:** Cross-registration; Double major; Exchange student program (domestic); Honors program; Independent study; Internships; Student-designed major; Study abroad. Combined degree programs: BA/JD. **Disability Services offered to physically disabled students:** Note-taking services; Reader services; Tape recorders. **Career services:** Alumni network; Alumni services; Career/job search classes; Internships; Regional alumni

FACILITIES

Housing: Coed dorms; Fraternity/sorority housing; Theme housing; Women's dorms 65% of campus accessible to physically diasbled. **Special Academic Facilities/Equipment:** Keck Theater; Mullin Studio and Art Gallery; Moore Ornithology Collection; Cosman Shell Collection; Smiley Geological Collection; Morse Collection of Astronomical Instruments; superconducting magnet; paleomagnetic lab; vivarium **Computers:** 100% of classrooms, 100% of dorms, 90% of libraries, 100% of dining areas, 80% of student union, 50% of common outdoor areas have wireless network access. Students can register for classes online. Administrative functions (other than registration) can be performed online.

CAMPUS LIFE

Environment: Metropolis **Activities:** Campus Ministries; Choral groups; Concert band; Dance; Drama/theater; International Student Organization; Jazz band; Literary magazine; Music ensembles; Pep band; Student government; Student newspaper; Yearbook 8 honor societies, 5 religious organizations. 4 fraternities, 4 sororities. **Athletics (Intercollegiate):** Men: baseball, basketball, cross-country, diving, football, golf, soccer, swimming, tennis, track/field (outdoor), water polo. Women: basketball, cross-country, diving, golf, lacrosse, soccer, softball, swimming, tennis, track/field (outdoor), volleyball, water polo. **On-Campus Highlights:** Green Bean Coffee Lounge, Clapp Library, Samuelson Pavilion (The Cooler), The Quad, Alumni Gymnasium Fitness Center **Environmental Initiatives:** Sustainability coordinator

ADMISSIONS

Freshman Academic Profile: Average high school GPA 3.6. 62% in top 10% of high school class, 86% in top 25% of high school class, 99% in top 50% of high school class. 58% from public high schools. **Test Scores:** SAT Math middle 50% range 630-720. SAT EBRW middle 50% range 650-720. ACT middle 50% range 27-32. Minimum paper TOEFL 600. **Basis for Candidate Selection:** Very important factors considered include: rigor of secondary school record, academic GPA, application essay. Important factors considered include: class rank, standardized test scores, recommendation(s), extracurricular activities, character/personal qualities, volunteer work, work experience. Other factors considered include: interview, talent/ability, first generation, alumni/ae relation, geographical residence, racial/ethnic status, level of applicant's interest. **Freshman Admission Requirements:** High school diploma is required and GED is accepted Academic units recommended: 4 English, 3 math, 3 science, 3 foreign language, 2 social studies, 3 history. **Freshman Admission Statistics:** 6,775 applied, 41.8% admitted, 20% enrolled. **Transfer Admission Requirements:** High school transcript, college transcript(s), essay or personal statement, statement of good standing from prior institution(s). Minimum college GPA of 3.0 required. Lowest grade transferable D. **General Admission Information:** Application fee $65. Regular application deadline 1/15. Nonfall registration accepted. Admission may be deferred for a maximum of 1 year.

COSTS AND FINANCIAL AID

Annual tuition $52,260. Room and board $14,968. Required fees $578. Average book expense $1,230. **Required Forms and Deadlines:** CSS/Financial Aid PROFILE; FAFSA; Noncustodial PROFILE; State aid form. **Notification of Awards:** Applicants will be notified of awards on or about 3/25. **Types of Aid:** Need-based scholarships/grants: College/university scholarship or grant aid from institutional funds; Federal Pell; Private scholarships; SEOG; State scholarships/grants. Loans: Direct PLUS loans; Direct Subsidized Stafford Loans; Direct Unsubsidized Stafford Loans. Student Employment: Federal Work-Study Program available. Institutional employment available. **Financial Aid Statistics:** 90% needy freshmen, 99% needy undergrads receive need-based scholarship or grant aid. 56% freshmen, 50% undergrads receive non-need-based scholarship or grant aid. 83% freshmen, 86% undergrads receive need-based self-help aid. 0% freshmen, 0% undergrads receive athletic scholarships. 72% freshmen, 74% undergrads receive any aid. Average cumulative indebtedness $29,940. **Criteria for awarding aid:** Non-need-based: Academics, Leadership, Music/drama, State/district residency.

See page 998.

OGLETHORPE UNIVERSITY

4484 Peachtree Road N.E., Atlanta, GA 30319
Phone: 404-364-8307 • **Financial Aid Phone:** 404-364-8356
E-mail: admission@oglethorpe.edu • **CEEB Code:** 5521
Fax: 404-364-8491 • **Website:** www.oglethorpe.edu • **ACT Code:** 850

This private school was founded in 1835. It has a 102 acre campus.

RATINGS

Admissions Selectivity Rating: 77   **Fire Safety Rating:** 83   **Green Rating:** 60*

STUDENTS AND FACULTY

Enrollment: 1,125. **Student Body:** 58% female, 42% male, 23% out-of-state, 7% international (24 countries represented). Asian 3%, African American 18%, Caucasian 33%, Hispanic 10%, Native American <1%, Pacific Islander <1%, Two or more races 3%, Race unknown 26%.
Retention and Graduation: 73% freshmen return for sophomore year. 40% grads go on to further study within 1 year. 19% grads pursue arts and sciences degrees. 9% grads pursue law degrees. 10% grads pursue business degrees. 2% grads pursue medical degrees. **Faculty:** Student/faculty ratio 15:1. 59 full-time faculty, 92% hold PhDs, 15% are members of minority groups, 39% are women. 0% of classes are taught by teaching assistants.

ACADEMICS

Degrees: Bachelor's **Classes:** Most classes have 10-19 students. Most lab/discussion sessions have 20-29 students. **Most popular majors:** English Language And Literature, General; Psychology, General; Business/Commerce, General. **Special Study Options:** Accelerated program; Cooperative education program; Cross-registration; Double major; Dual enrollment; English as a Second Language (ESL); Exchange student program (domestic); Honors program; Independent study; Internships; Liberal arts/career combination; Student-designed major; Study abroad. **Disability Services offered to physically disabled students:** Note-taking services; Tutors. **Career services:** Alumni services; Career assessment; Career/job search classes; Internships

FACILITIES

Housing: Coed dorms; Fraternity/sorority housing; Theme housing 60% of campus accessible to physically diasbled. **Special Academic Facilities/Equipment:** Art museum, scanning electron microscope. **Computers:** 100% of classrooms, 100% of dorms, 100% of libraries, 100% of student union, 25% of common outdoor areas have wireless network access. Administrative functions (other than registration) can be performed online.

CAMPUS LIFE

Environment: Metropolis **Activities:** Campus Ministries; Choral groups; Concert band; Dance; Drama/theater; International Student Organization; Literary magazine; Music ensembles; Musical theater; Pep band; Radio station; Student government; Student newspaper; Yearbook 57 registered organizations, 10 honor societies, 5 religious organizations. 4 fraternities, 3 sororities. **Athletics (Intercollegiate):** Men: baseball, basketball, cross-country, golf, lacrosse, soccer, tennis, track/field (outdoor). Women: basketball, cheerleading, cross-country, golf, lacrosse, soccer, tennis, track/field (outdoor), volleyball. **On-Campus Highlights:** Oglethorpe University Museum, Phillip Weltner Library, Conant Performing Arts Center, Hermance Stadium, New Residence Halls **Environmental Initiatives:** New buildings are built according to LEED requiesments

ADMISSIONS

Freshman Academic Profile: Average high school GPA 3.5. 79% from public high schools. **Test Scores:** SAT Math middle 50% range 510-610. SAT EBRW middle 50% range 530-630. ACT middle 50% range 22-28. Minimum paper TOEFL 550. **Basis for Candidate Selection:** Very important factors considered include: rigor of secondary school record, academic GPA, standardized test scores. Important factors considered include: class rank, application essay, recommendation(s), interview, extracurricular activities, volunteer work.level of applicant's interest. Other factors considered include: talent/ability, character/personal qualities, first generation, alumni/ae relation, work experience. **Freshman Admission Requirements:** High school diploma is required and GED is accepted Academic units required: 4 English, 3 math, 2 science, 3 social studies, Academic units recommended: 2 foreign language. **Freshman Admission Statistics:** 2,768 applied, 78.5% admitted, 20% enrolled. **Transfer Admission Requirements:** college transcript(s), statement of good standing from prior institution(s). Minimum college GPA of 2.8 required. Lowest grade transferable C. **General Admission Information:** Application fee $50. Priority deadline 11/15. Nonfall registration accepted. Admission may be deferred for a maximum of 1 semester.

COSTS AND FINANCIAL AID

Annual tuition $35,000. Room and board $12,710. Required fees $425. Average book expense $1,100. **Required Forms and Deadlines:** FAFSA. **Notification of Awards:** Applicants will be notified of awards on a rolling basis beginning 3/1. **Types of Aid:** *Need-based scholarships/grants:* College/university scholarship or grant aid from institutional funds; Federal Pell; Private scholarships; SEOG; State scholarships/grants; United Negro College Fund. *Loans:* Direct Subsidized Stafford Loans; Direct Unsubsidized Stafford Loans. *Student Employment:* Federal Work-Study Program available. Institutional employment available. **Financial Aid Statistics:** 100% needy freshmen, 99% needy undergrads receive need-based scholarship or grant aid. 16% freshmen, 13% undergrads receive non-need-based scholarship or grant aid. 75% freshmen, 80% undergrads receive need-based self-help aid. 0% freshmen, 0% undergrads receive athletic scholarships. 95% freshmen, 95% undergrads receive any aid. 68% undergrads borrow to pay for school. Average cumulative indebtedness $23,212. **Criteria for awarding aid:** *Need-based:* Academics, Leadership, Minority status, Music/drama *Non-need-based:* Academics, Art, Leadership, Minority status, Music/drama, State/district residency.

OHIO DOMINICAN UNIVERSITY

1216 Sunbury Road, Columbus, OH 42319-2099
Phone: 614-251-4500 • **Financial Aid Phone:** 614-251-4778
E-mail: admissions@ohiodominican.edu • **CEEB Code:** 1131
Fax: 614-251-0156 • **Website:** http://www.ohiodominican.edu • **ACT Code:** 3256

This private school, affiliated with the Roman Catholic Church, was founded in 1911. It has a 75 acre campus.

RATINGS

Admissions Selectivity Rating: 77   **Fire Safety Rating:** 91   **Green Rating:** 70

STUDENTS AND FACULTY

Enrollment: 1,072. **Student Body:** 54% female, 46% male, 5% out-of-state, 2% international (10 countries represented). Asian 1%, African American 22%, Caucasian 56%, Hispanic 4%, Native American <1%, Pacific Islander 0%, Two or more races 5%, Race unknown 10%. **Retention and Graduation:** 62% freshmen return for sophomore year. 38% freshmen graduate within 4 years. 47% freshmen graduate within 6 years. 13% grads go on to further study within 1 year. **Faculty:** Student/faculty ratio 14:1. 60 full-time faculty, 95% hold PhDs, 10% are members of minority groups, 47% are women. 0% of classes are taught by teaching assistants.

ACADEMICS

Degrees: Associate; Bachelor's; Certificate; Master's; Post-Bachelor's certificate **Classes:** Most classes have 20-29 students. Most lab/discussion sessions have fewer than 10 students. **Most popular majors:** Biology/Biological Sciences, General; Kinesiology And Exercise Science; Business Administration And Management, General. **Special Study Options:** Accelerated program; Cross-registration; Distance learning; Double major; English as a Second Language (ESL); Honors program; Independent study; Internships; Liberal arts/career combination; Student-designed major; Study abroad; Teacher certification program. Honors programs: The Honors Program is designed for high-ability, motivated students. Honors-designed courses will be offered to specifically challenge and engage students in the program. **Disability Services offered to physically disabled students:** Note-taking services; Reader services; Tape recorders; Tutors. **Career services:** Alumni network; Alumni services; Career assessment; Career/job search classes; Internships; Regional alumni

FACILITIES

Housing: Coed dorms 98% of campus accessible to physically diasbled. **Special Academic Facilities/Equipment:** Wehrle Art Gallery, Student Center (w/eating facilities,bookstore, games and TV), Athletic Facilities and Fitness Center. **Computers:** 90% of classrooms, 100% of libraries, 100% of dining areas, na% of student union, 5% of common outdoor areas have wireless network access. Students can register for classes online. Administrative functions (other than registration) can be performed online.

CAMPUS LIFE

Environment: Metropolis **Activities:** Campus Ministries; Choral groups; Concert band; Drama/theater; International Student Organization; Literary magazine; Marching band; Model UN; Music ensembles; Musical theater; Pep band; Radio station; Student government; Student newspaper 40 registered organizations, 2 honor societies, 1 religious organization. **Athletics (Intercollegiate):** *Men:* baseball, basketball, cross-country, football, golf, soccer, tennis. *Women:* basketball, cross-country, golf, soccer, softball, tennis,

volleyball. **On-Campus Highlights:** Bishop James A. Griffin Student Center, Alumni Hall Fitness Center, Alumni Hall Gymnasium, Wehrle Hall, Griffin Center Grill & Deli

ADMISSIONS

Freshman Academic Profile: Average high school GPA 3.3. 15% in top 10% of high school class, 43% in top 25% of high school class, 76% in top 50% of high school class. **Test Scores:** SAT Math middle 50% range 510-610. SAT EBRW middle 50% range 460-600. ACT middle 50% range 19-24. Minimum internet-based TOEFL 79. Minimum paper TOEFL 550. **Basis for Candidate Selection:** *Very important factors considered include:* rigor of secondary school record, academic GPA, standardized test scores. *Other factors considered include:* class rank, application essay, recommendation(s), interview, extracurricular activities, talent/ability, character/personal qualities, volunteer work, work experience, level of applicant's interest. **Freshman Admission Requirements:** High school diploma is required and GED is accepted *Academic units recommended:* 4 English, 4 math, 4 science, 3 foreign language, 3 social studies. **Freshman Admission Statistics:** 1,238 applied, 77.2% admitted, 26% enrolled. **Transfer Admission Requirements:** college transcript(s), Lowest grade transferable C. **General Admission Information:** Priority deadline 12/2. Nonfall registration accepted. Admission may be deferred.

COSTS AND FINANCIAL AID

Annual tuition $30,500. Room and board $10,948. Required fees $580. Average book expense $1,100. *Student Employment:* Federal Work-Study Program available. Institutional employment available. **Financial Aid Statistics:** 0% freshmen, 0% undergrads receive athletic scholarships. 100% freshmen, 66% undergrads receive any aid. **Criteria for awarding aid:** *Non-need-based:* Academics, Athletics, Music/drama.

OHIO NORTHERN UNIVERSITY

525 South Main Street, Ada, OH 45810
Phone: 419-772-2260 • **Financial Aid Phone:** 419-772-2272
E-mail: admissions-ug@onu.edu • **CEEB Code:** 1591
Fax: 419-772-2313 • **Website:** www.onu.edu • **ACT Code:** 3310

This private school, affiliated with the Methodist Church, was founded in 1871. It has a 342 acre campus.

RATINGS

Admissions Selectivity Rating: 83   **Fire Safety Rating:** 62   **Green Rating:** 60*

STUDENTS AND FACULTY

Enrollment: 2,116. **Student Body:** 44% female, 56% male, 17% out-of-state, 4% international (17 countries represented). Asian 1%, African American 3%, Caucasian 84%, Hispanic 1%, Native American <1%, Pacific Islander 0%, Two or more races 3%, Race unknown 3%. **Retention and Graduation:** 86% freshmen return for sophomore year. **Faculty:** Student/faculty ratio 11:1. 211 full-time faculty, 84% hold PhDs, 14% are members of minority groups, 41% are women. 0% of classes are taught by teaching assistants.

ACADEMICS

Degrees: Bachelor's; Certificate; Doctoral/Professional; Master's; Post-Bachelor's certificate **Classes:** Most classes have 20-29 students. Most lab/discussion sessions have 20-29 students. **Most popular majors:** Mechanical Engineering; Biology/Biological Sciences, General; Registered Nursing/Registered Nurse. **Special Study Options:** Cooperative education program; Distance learning; Double major; Dual enrollment; English as a Second Language (ESL); Exchange student program (domestic); Honors program; Independent study; Internships; Liberal arts/career combination; Study abroad; Teacher certification program. Honors programs: Honors Program consists of a First-Year Honors Seminar and 3 additional Honors Seminars, 2 "contract" courses and a final Honors project under the quarter system; ONU is switching to semesters for Fall 2011. Combined degree programs: BA/JD. **Disability Services offered to physically disabled students:** Note-taking services; Reader services; Tape recorders; Tutors. **Career services:** Alumni network; Alumni services; Career assessment; Career/job search classes; Internships

FACILITIES

Housing: Apartments for married students; Apartments for single students; Coed dorms; Fraternity/sorority housing; Men's dorms; Special housing for disabled student; Theme housing; Women's dorms 95% of campus accessible to physically disabled. **Special Academic Facilities/Equipment:** Art gallery, performing arts center, language lab, sports center, pharmacy museum. **Computers:** 100% of classrooms, 100% of dorms, 100% of libraries, 100% of dining areas, 100% of student union, have wireless network access. Students can register for classes online. Administrative functions (other than registration) can be performed online.

CAMPUS LIFE

Environment: Village **Activities:** Campus Ministries; Choral groups; Concert band; Dance; Drama/theater; International Student Organization; Jazz band; Literary magazine; Marching band; Model UN; Music ensembles; Musical theater; Pep band; Radio station; Student government; Student newspaper; Symphony orchestra; Television station; Yearbook 200 registered organizations, 40 honor societies, 27 religious organizations. 6 fraternities, 4 sororities. **Athletics (Intercollegiate):** *Men:* baseball, basketball, cross-country, diving, football, golf, soccer, swimming, tennis, track/field (outdoor), track/field (indoor), wrestling. *Women:* basketball, cross-country, diving, golf, soccer, softball, swimming, tennis, track/field (outdoor), track/field (indoor), volleyball. **On-Campus Highlights:** ONU Sports Center, Mathile Natural Sciences Center, Performing Arts Center, New Student Apartments, James F. Dicke Hall

ADMISSIONS

Freshman Academic Profile: Average high school GPA 3.6. 32% in top 10% of high school class, 60% in top 25% of high school class, 85% in top 50% of high school class. **Test Scores:** SAT Math middle 50% range 530-640. SAT EBRW middle 50% range 480-600. ACT middle 50% range 23-28. Minimum internet-based TOEFL 54. Minimum paper TOEFL 480. **Basis for Candidate Selection:** *Very important factors considered include:* rigor of secondary school record, academic GPA, standardized test scores. *Important factors considered include:* class rank, interview, extracurricular activities. *Other factors considered include:* application essay, recommendation(s), talent/ability, character/personal qualities, first generation, alumni/ae relation, volunteer work, level of applicant's interest. **Freshman Admission Requirements:** High school diploma is required and GED is accepted *Academic units required:* 4 English, 2 math, 2 science, 2 science labs, 2 social studies, 2 history, 4 academic electives, *Academic units recommended:* 4 English, 4 math, 3 science, 2 science labs, 2 foreign language, 3 social studies, 2 history, 4 academic electives, 1 computer science, 1 visual/performing arts. **Freshman Admission Statistics:** 3,108 applied, 69.0% admitted, 27% enrolled. **Transfer Admission Requirements:** High school transcript, college transcript(s), statement of good standing from prior institution(s). Minimum college GPA of 2.0 required. Lowest grade transferable C. **General Admission Information:** Priority deadline 12/1. Regular application deadline 8/15. Nonfall registration accepted. Admission may be deferred.

COSTS AND FINANCIAL AID

Annual tuition $30,120. Room and board $11,270. Required fees $870. Average book expense $1,800. **Required Forms and Deadlines:** FAFSA. **Notification of Awards:** Applicants will be notified of awards on a rolling basis beginning 12/1. **Types of Aid:** *Need-based scholarships/grants:* College/university scholarship or grant aid from institutional funds; Federal Pell; Private scholarships; SEOG; State scholarships/grants. *Loans:* Direct PLUS loans; Direct Subsidized Stafford Loans; Direct Unsubsidized Stafford Loans. *Student Employment:* Federal Work-Study Program available. Institutional employment available. **Criteria for awarding aid:** *Non-need-based:* Academics, Alumni affiliation, Art, Leadership, Minority status, Music/drama, State/district residency.

THE OHIO STATE UNIVERSITY AT LIMA

Student Academic Service Building, Columbus, OH 45804-3596
Phone: 614-292-3980 • **Financial Aid Phone:** (614) 292-0300
E-mail: askabuckeye@osu.edu • **CEEB Code:** 1541
Fax: 614-292-3980 • **Website:** http://www.osu.edu • **ACT Code:** 3312

This public school was founded in 1960. It has a 562 acre campus.

RATINGS
Admissions Selectivity Rating: 72   **Fire Safety Rating:** 60*   **Green Rating:** 81

STUDENTS AND FACULTY
Enrollment: 927. **Student Body:** 56% female, 44% male, 1% out-of-state, <1% international (1 countries represented). Asian 2%, African American 5%, Caucasian 83%, Hispanic 4%, Native American 0%, Pacific Islander 0%, Two or more races 4%, Race unknown 3%.
Retention and Graduation: 65% freshmen return for sophomore year. 18% freshmen graduate within 4 years. 38% freshmen graduate within 6 years.

Faculty: Student/faculty ratio 19:1. 32 full-time faculty, 9% are members of minority groups, 41% are women. 0% of classes are taught by teaching assistants.

ACADEMICS
Degrees: Associate; Bachelor's; **Master's Classes:** Most classes have fewer than 10 students. Most lab/discussion sessions have 10-19 students. **Special Study Options:** Accelerated program; Cooperative education program; Cross-registration; Distance learning; Double major; Dual enrollment; English as a Second Language (ESL); Exchange student program (domestic); Honors program; Independent study; Internships; Liberal arts/career combination; Student-designed major; Study abroad; Teacher certification program; Weekend college. Honors programs: The University Honors Program is dedicated to promoting the intellectual and personal development of high-performing students. It strives to promote a more active and enriching relationship between Honors students and the University by connecting them with resources and opportunities that will encourage them to maximize their potential. **Disability Services offered to physically disabled students:** Note-taking services; Tape recorders; Tutors. **Career services:** Alumni network; Alumni services; Career assessment; Career/job search classes; Internships

FACILITIES
Housing: Special housing for disabled students 100% of campus accessible to physically disabled. **Special Academic Facilities/Equipment:** Geological Museum Observatory **Computers:** 75% of classrooms, 100% of libraries, 100% of dining areas, 100% of student union, 100% of common outdoor areas have wireless network access. Students can register for classes online. Administrative functions (other than registration) can be performed online.

CAMPUS LIFE
Environment: Town **Activities:** Campus Ministries; Choral groups; Dance; Drama/theater; Literary magazine; Music ensembles; Musical theater; Student government 32 registered organizations, 1 honor society, 2 religious organizations.

ADMISSIONS
Freshman Academic Profile: 8% in top 10% of high school class, 34% in top 25% of high school class, 73% in top 50% of high school class. 95% from public high schools. **Test Scores:** SAT Math middle 50% range 498-658. SAT EBRW middle 50% range 498-608. ACT middle 50% range 20-26. **Basis for Candidate Selection:** *Other factors considered include:* standardized test scores. **Freshman Admission Requirements:** High school diploma is required and GED is accepted *Academic units required:* 4 English, 3 math, 3 science, 3 science labs, 2 foreign language, 2 social studies, 1 academic elective, 1 visual/performing arts, *Academic units recommended:* 4 English, 4 math, 3 science, 3 science labs, 3 foreign language, 3 social studies, 1 academic elective, 1 visual/performing arts. **Freshman Admission Statistics:** 1,294 applied, 99.1% admitted, 25% enrolled. **Transfer Admission Requirements:** college transcript(s), Minimum college GPA of 2.0 required. Lowest grade transferable C-. **General Admission Information:** Application fee $60. Regular application deadline 6/1. Nonfall registration accepted.

COSTS AND FINANCIAL AID
Annual out-of-state tuition $26,244. Average book expense $1,168. **Required Forms and Deadlines:** FAFSA. **Notification of Awards:** Applicants will be notified of awards on or about 3/15. **Types of Aid:** *Need-based scholarships/grants:* College/university scholarship or grant aid from institutional funds; Federal Pell; Private scholarships; SEOG; State scholarships/grants. *Loans:* Direct PLUS loans; Direct Subsidized Stafford Loans; Direct Unsubsidized Stafford Loans. *Student Employment:* Federal Work-Study Program available. Institutional employment available. **Financial Aid Statistics:** 79% needy freshmen, 75% needy undergrads receive need-based scholarship or grant aid. 2% freshmen, 1% undergrads receive non-need-based scholarship or grant aid. 85% freshmen, 90% undergrads receive need-based self-help aid. 0% freshmen, 0% undergrads receive athletic scholarships. 94% freshmen, 87% undergrads receive any aid. **Criteria for awarding aid:** *Need-based:* Academics, Alumni affiliation, Art, Athletics, Job skills, Leadership, Minority status, Music/drama *Non-need-based:* Academics, Alumni affiliation, Art, Athletics, Job skills, Leadership, Minority status, Music/drama, State/district residency.

THE OHIO STATE UNIVERSITY AT MANSFIELD

Student Academic Services Building, Columbus, OH 43210
Phone: 614-292-3980 • **Financial Aid Phone:** (614) 292-0330
E-mail: askabuckeye@osu.edu • **CEEB Code:** 744
Website: www.osu.edu • **ACT Code:** 3312

This public school was founded in 1958. It has a 620 acre campus.

RATINGS
Admissions Selectivity Rating: 72   **Fire Safety Rating:** 64   **Green Rating:** 80

STUDENTS AND FACULTY
Enrollment: 962. **Student Body:** 51% female, 49% male, 1% out-of-state, <1% international (1 countries represented). Asian 2%, African American 9%, Caucasian 78%, Hispanic 4%, Native American <1%, Two or more races 3%, Race unknown 3%.
Retention and Graduation: 68% freshmen return for sophomore year. 21% freshmen graduate within 4 years. 44% freshmen graduate within 6 years.
Faculty: Student/faculty ratio 18:1. 37 full-time faculty, 8% are members of minority groups, 43% are women.

ACADEMICS
Degrees: Associate; Bachelor's; **Master's Classes:** Most classes have 10-19 students. Most lab/discussion sessions have 10-19 students. **Special Study Options:** Accelerated program; Cooperative education program; Cross-registration; Distance learning; Double major; Dual enrollment; English as a Second Language (ESL); Exchange student program (domestic); Honors program; Independent study; Internships; Liberal arts/career combination; Student-designed major; Study abroad; Teacher certification program; Weekend college. Honors programs: The University Honors Program is dedicated to promoting the intellectual and personal development of high-performing students. It strives to promote a more active and enriching relationship between Honors students and the University by connecting them with resources and opportunities that will encourage them to maximize their potential. **Disability Services offered to physically disabled students:** Note-taking services; Reader services; Tape recorders; Tutors. **Career services:** Alumni network; Alumni services; Career assessment; Career/job search classes; Internships; Regional alumni

FACILITIES
Housing: Coed dorms 90% of campus accessible to physically diasbled. **Computers:** 100% of classrooms, 100% of dorms, 100% of libraries, 100% of dining areas, 100% of student union, 50% of common outdoor areas have wireless network access. Students can register for classes online. Administrative functions (other than registration) can be performed online.

CAMPUS LIFE
Environment: Town **Activities:** Campus Ministries; Choral groups; Drama/theater; Musical theater 16 registered organizations, 2 honor societies, 2 religious organizations. **Athletics (Intercollegiate):** *Men:* baseball, basketball, soccer. *Women:* basketball, cheerleading, volleyball.

ADMISSIONS
Freshman Academic Profile: 7% in top 10% of high school class, 29% in top 25% of high school class, 64% in top 50% of high school class. 89% from public high schools. **Test Scores:** SAT Math middle 50% range 468-630. SAT EBRW middle 50% range 500-633. ACT middle 50% range 20-25. **Basis for Candidate Selection:** *Other factors considered include:* standardized test scores. **Freshman Admission Requirements:** High school diploma is required and GED is accepted *Academic units required:* 4 English, 3 math, 3 science, 3 science labs, 2 foreign language, 2 social studies, 1 academic elective, 1 visual/performing arts, *Academic units recommended:* 4 English, 4 math, 3 science, 3 science labs, 3 foreign language, 3 social studies, 1 academic elective, 1 visual/performing arts. **Freshman Admission Statistics:** 1,770 applied, 99.3% admitted, 25% enrolled. **Transfer Admission Requirements:** college transcript(s), Minimum college GPA of 2.0 required. Lowest grade transferable C-. **General Admission Information:** Application fee $60. Regular application deadline 6/1. Nonfall registration accepted.

COSTS AND FINANCIAL AID
Annual out-of-state tuition $26,244. Room and board $7,976. Average book expense $1,168. **Required Forms and Deadlines:** FAFSA. **Notification of Awards:** Applicants will be notified of awards on or about 3/15. **Types of Aid:** *Need-based scholarships/grants:* College/university scholarship or grant aid from institutional funds; Federal Pell; Private scholarships; SEOG; State scholarships/grants. *Loans:* Direct PLUS loans; Direct Subsidized Stafford Loans; Direct Unsubsidized Stafford Loans. *Student Employment:* Federal Work-Study Program available. Institutional employment available. **Financial Aid Statistics:** 83% needy freshmen, 81% needy undergrads receive need-based scholarship or grant aid. 1% freshmen, 1% undergrads receive non-need-based scholarship or grant aid. 93% freshmen, 92% undergrads receive need-based self-help aid. 0% freshmen, 0% undergrads receive athletic scholarships. 93% freshmen, 87% undergrads receive any aid. **Criteria for awarding aid:** *Need-based:* Academics, Alumni affiliation, Art, Athletics, Job skills, Leadership, Minority status, Music/drama *Non-need-based:* Academics, Alumni affiliation, Art, Athletics, Job skills, Leadership, Minority status, Music/drama, State/district residency.

THE OHIO STATE UNIVERSITY AT MARION

Student Academic Services Building, Columbus, OH 43210
Phone: 614-292-3980 • **Financial Aid Phone:** (614) 292-0300
E-mail: askabuckeye@osu.edu • **CEEB Code:** 752
Fax: 614-292-3980 • **Website:** http://osu.edu/ • **ACT Code:** 3312

This public school was founded in 1957. It has a 188 acre campus.

RATINGS
Admissions Selectivity Rating: 73   **Fire Safety Rating:** 60*   **Green Rating:** 85

STUDENTS AND FACULTY
Enrollment: 1,097. **Student Body:** 52% female, 48% male, 1% out-of-state, <1% international (3 countries represented). Asian 4%, African American 4%, Caucasian 81%, Hispanic 4%, Native American 1%, Pacific Islander <1%, Two or more races 3%, Race unknown 3%.
Retention and Graduation: 70% freshmen return for sophomore year. 16% freshmen graduate within 4 years. 42% freshmen graduate within 6 years.
Faculty: Student/faculty ratio 19:1. 36 full-time faculty, 14% are members of minority groups, 50% are women. 0% of classes are taught by teaching assistants.

ACADEMICS
Degrees: Associate; Bachelor's **Classes:** Most classes have 20-29 students. Most lab/discussion sessions have 20-29 students. **Most popular majors:** Elementary And Middle School Administration/Principalship; Elementary Education And Teaching; Junior High/Intermediate/Middle School Education And Teaching. **Special Study Options:** Accelerated program; Cooperative education program; Cross-registration; Distance learning; Double major; Dual enrollment; English as a Second Language (ESL); Exchange student program (domestic); Honors program; Independent study; Internships; Liberal arts/career combination; Student-designed major; Study abroad; Teacher certification program; Weekend college. Honors programs: The University Honors Program is dedicated to promoting the intellectual and personal development of high-performing students. It strives to promote a more active and enriching relationship between Honors students and the University by connecting them with resources and opportunities that will encourage them to maximize their potential. **Disability Services offered to physically disabled students:** Note-taking services; Reader services; Tape recorders; Tutors. **Career services:** Alumni network; Alumni services; Career assessment; Career/job search classes; Internships; Regional alumni

FACILITIES
Housing: 100% of campus accessible to physically diasbled. **Special Academic Facilities/Equipment:** Kuhn Art Gallery **Computers:** 100% of classrooms, 100% of libraries, have wireless network access. Students can register for classes online. Administrative functions (other than registration) can be performed online.

CAMPUS LIFE
Environment: Town **Activities:** Campus Ministries; Choral groups; Drama/theater; International Student Organization; Marching band; Musical theater; Student government 33 registered organizations, 1 honor society, 3 religious organizations. **Athletics (Intercollegiate):** *Men:* basketball, gymnastics, volleyball. *Women:* gymnastics. Kuhn Fine Arts Gallery, Yoder Prairie Learning Laboratory

ADMISSIONS
Freshman Academic Profile: 8% in top 10% of high school class, 30% in top 25% of high school class, 73% in top 50% of high school class. 98% from public high schools. **Test Scores:** SAT Math middle 50% range 515-640. SAT EBRW middle 50% range 535-625. ACT middle 50% range 19-25. **Basis for Candidate Selection:** *Other factors considered include:* standardized test scores. **Freshman Admission Requirements:** High school diploma is required and GED is accepted *Academic units required:* 4 English, 3 math, 3 science, 3 science labs, 2 foreign language, 2 social studies, 1 academic elective, 1 visual/performing arts, *Academic units recommended:* 4 English, 4 math, 3 science, 3 science labs, 3 foreign language, 3 social studies, 1 academic elective, 1 visual/performing arts. **Freshman Admission Statistics:** 1,025 applied,

98.7% admitted, 43% enrolled. **Transfer Admission Requirements:** college transcript(s), Minimum college GPA of 2.0 required. Lowest grade transferable C-. **General Admission Information:** Application fee $60. Regular application deadline 6/1. Nonfall registration accepted.

COSTS AND FINANCIAL AID

Annual out-of-state tuition $26,244. Average book expense $1,168. **Required Forms and Deadlines:** FAFSA. **Notification of Awards:** Applicants will be notified of awards on or about 3/15. **Types of Aid:** *Need-based scholarships/ grants:* College/university scholarship or grant aid from institutional funds; Federal Pell; Private scholarships; SEOG; State scholarships/grants. *Loans:* Direct PLUS loans; Direct Subsidized Stafford Loans; Direct Unsubsidized Stafford Loans. *Student Employment:* Federal Work-Study Program available. Institutional employment available. **Financial Aid Statistics:** 85% needy freshmen, 83% needy undergrads receive need-based scholarship or grant aid. 2% freshmen, 1% undergrads receive non-need-based scholarship or grant aid. 91% freshmen, 91% undergrads receive need-based self-help aid. 0% freshmen, 0% undergrads receive athletic scholarships. 94% freshmen, 88% undergrads receive any aid. **Criteria for awarding aid:** *Need-based:* Academics, Alumni affiliation, Art, Athletics, Job skills, Leadership, Minority status, Music/drama *Non-need-based:* Academics, Alumni affiliation, Art, Athletics, Job skills, Leadership, Minority status, Music/drama, State/district residency.

OHIO STATE UNIVERSITY—COLUMBUS

Student Academic Services Building, Columbus, OH 43210
Phone: 614-292-3980 • **Financial Aid Phone:** 614-292-0300
E-mail: askabuckeye@osu.edu • **CEEB Code:** 1592
Fax: 614-292-3980 • **Website:** www.osu.edu • **ACT Code:** 3312

This public school was founded in 1870. It has a 1665 acre campus.

RATINGS

Admissions Selectivity Rating: 91   **Fire Safety Rating:** 87   **Green Rating:** 94

STUDENTS AND FACULTY

Enrollment: 23,709. **Student Body:** 91% female, 9% male, 19% out-of-state, 8% international (66 countries represented). Asian 7%, African American 6%, Caucasian 69%, Hispanic 4%, Native American <1%, Pacific Islander <1%, Two or more races 3%, Race unknown 3%.
Retention and Graduation: 94% freshmen return for sophomore year. 59% freshmen graduate within 4 years. 83% freshmen graduate within 6 years. **Faculty:** Student/faculty ratio 19:1. 3,992 full-time faculty, 99% hold PhDs, 26% are members of minority groups, 41% are women. 12% of classes are taught by teaching assistants.

ACADEMICS

Degrees: Associate; Bachelor's; Certificate; Diploma; Doctoral; Doctoral/ Professional; Doctoral/Research; Master's; Post-Bachelor's certificate; Post-Master's certificate **Classes:** Most classes have fewer than 10 students. Most lab/discussion sessions have 10-19 students. **Most popular majors:** Communication, General; Psychology, General; Finance, General. **Special Study Options:** Accelerated program; Cooperative education program; Cross-registration; Distance learning; Double major; Dual enrollment; English as a Second Language (ESL); Exchange student program (domestic); Honors program; Independent study; Internships; Liberal arts/career combination; Student-designed major; Study abroad; Teacher certification program; Weekend college. Honors programs: The University Honors Program promotes intellectual and personal development of undergraduate students through an enriched academic experience and integration of curricular and co-curricular programming. The Ohio State Scholars Program offers students the chance to live and learn with other students who share similar interests through 17 specialized communities?. Each of the Scholars programs is centered around a unique theme, ranging from academic and professional pursuits to critical issues and leadership development. **Disability Services offered to physically disabled students:** Note-taking services. **Career services:** Alumni network; Alumni services; Career assessment; Career/job search classes; Internships; Regional alumni

FACILITIES

Housing: Apartments for married students; Apartments for single students; Coed dorms; Cooperative housing; Fraternity/sorority housing; Special housing for disabled student; Theme housing; Wellness housing; Women's dorms 100%

of campus accessible to physically diasbled. **Special Academic Facilities/ Equipment:** Wexner Center for the Arts Zoology Museum Geology Museum Art and Photography Galleries Nuclear Research Reactor Electrosciences Lab Biomedical Engineering Center Cartoon Art Museum **Computers:** 100% of dorms, 90% of libraries, 100% of dining areas, 100% of student union, 4% of common outdoor areas have wireless network access. Students can register for classes online. Administrative functions (other than registration) can be performed online.

CAMPUS LIFE

Environment: Metropolis **Activities:** Campus Ministries; Choral groups; Concert band; Dance; Drama/theater; International Student Organization; Jazz band; Literary magazine; Marching band; Model UN; Music ensembles; Musical theater; Opera; Pep band; Radio station; Student government; Student newspaper; Student-run film society; Symphony orchestra; Television station 950 registered organizations, 39 honor societies, 93 religious organizations. 42 fraternities, 25 sororities. **Athletics (Intercollegiate):** *Men:* baseball, basketball, cheerleading, cross-country, diving, fencing, football, golf, gymnastics, ice hockey, lacrosse, pistol, riflery, soccer, swimming, tennis, track/ field (outdoor), track/field (indoor), volleyball, wrestling. *Women:* baseball, basketball, cheerleading, crew/rowing, cross-country, diving, fencing, field hockey, golf, gymnastics, ice hockey, lacrosse, pistol, riflery, soccer, softball, swimming, synchronized swimming, tennis, track/field (outdoor), track/ field (indoor), volleyball. **On-Campus Highlights:** Hale Cultural Center, Chadwick Arboretum, Jack Nicklaus Golf Museum, Schottenstein Center and Value City Arena, Wexner Center for the Arts 0 **Environmental Initiatives:** 1. Comprehensive Goal Establishment Ohio State has developed an holistic approach to sustainability endeavors through the establishment of university-wide sustainability goals that encompass the university's mission and physical operations. These include goals for Teaching and Learning, Research and Innovation, Outreach and Engagement, and Resource Stewardship. The goals have been embedded throughout the university to ensure widespread participation and achievement towards the goals. The goals can be found here: http://oee.osu.edu/assets/uploads/Sustainability_Goals_2017.pdf

ADMISSIONS

Freshman Academic Profile: 64% in top 10% of high school class, 95% in top 25% of high school class, 99% in top 50% of high school class. 84% from public high schools. **Test Scores:** SAT Math middle 50% range 650-750. SAT EBRW middle 50% range 610-700. ACT middle 50% range 27-31. Minimum internet-based TOEFL 79. Minimum paper TOEFL 550. **Basis for Candidate Selection:** *Very important factors considered include:* rigor of secondary school record, class rank, academic GPA, standardized test scores. *Important factors considered include:* application essay, extracurricular activities, talent/ability, first generation, volunteer work, work experience. *Other factors considered include:* recommendation(s), character/personal qualities, geographical residence, state residency, racial/ethnic status. **Freshman Admission Requirements:** High school diploma is required and GED is accepted *Academic units required:* 4 English, 3 math, 3 science, 3 science labs, 2 foreign language, 2 social studies, 1 academic elective, 1 visual/performing arts, *Academic units recommended:* 4 English, 4 math, 3 science, 3 science labs, 3 foreign language, 3 social studies, 1 academic elective, 1 visual/performing arts. **Freshman Admission Statistics:** 47,782 applied, 48.1% admitted, 31% enrolled. **Transfer Admission Requirements:** college transcript(s), Minimum college GPA of 2.0 required. Lowest grade transferable C-. **General Admission Information:** Application fee $60. Regular application deadline 2/1. Nonfall registration accepted. Admission may be deferred for a maximum of 1 year.

COSTS AND FINANCIAL AID

Annual in-state tuition $12,998. Annual out-of-state tuition $29,141. Room and board $12,998. Average book expense $1,168. **Required Forms and Deadlines:** FAFSA. **Types of Aid:** *Need-based scholarships/grants:* College/ university scholarship or grant aid from institutional funds; Federal Pell; Private scholarships; SEOG; State scholarships/grants. *Loans:* Direct PLUS loans; Direct Subsidized Stafford Loans; Direct Unsubsidized Stafford Loans. *Student Employment:* Federal Work-Study Program available. Institutional employment available. **Financial Aid Statistics:** 90% needy freshmen, 83% needy undergrads receive need-based scholarship or grant aid. 9% freshmen, 5% undergrads receive non-need-based scholarship or grant aid. 77% freshmen, 88% undergrads receive need-based self-help aid. 1% freshmen, 1% undergrads receive athletic scholarships. 90% freshmen, 79% undergrads receive any aid. 55% undergrads borrow to pay for school. Average cumulative indebtedness $27,400. **Criteria for awarding aid:** *Need-based:* Academics, Alumni affiliation, Art, Athletics, Job skills, Leadership, Minority status, Music/ drama *Non-need-based:* Academics, Alumni affiliation, Art, Athletics, Job skills, Leadership, Minority status, Music/drama, State/district residency.

OHIO STATE UNIVERSITY—NEWARK

Student Academic Services Building, Columbus, OH 43210
Phone: 614-292-39890 • **Financial Aid Phone:** 614-292-0300
E-mail: askabuckeye@osu.edu • **CEEB Code:** 752
Fax: 740-364-9645 • **Website:** http://www.osu.edu • **ACT Code:** 3312

This public school was founded in 1957. It has a 111 acre campus.

RATINGS
Admissions Selectivity Rating: 73   **Fire Safety Rating:** 82   **Green Rating:** 77

STUDENTS AND FACULTY
Enrollment: 2,518. **Student Body:** 51% female, 49% male, 1% out-of-state, <1% international (1 countries represented). Asian 4%, African American 15%, Caucasian 69%, Hispanic 3%, Native American <1%, Pacific Islander <1%, Two or more races 4%, Race unknown 4%.
Retention and Graduation: 68% freshmen return for sophomore year. 15% freshmen graduate within 4 years. 37% freshmen graduate within 6 years. **Faculty:** Student/faculty ratio 28:1. 47 full-time faculty, 21% are members of minority groups, 36% are women. 0% of classes are taught by teaching assistants.

ACADEMICS
Degrees: Associate; Bachelor's; **Master's Classes:** Most classes have 10-19 students. Most lab/discussion sessions have 20-29 students. **Most popular majors:** Elementary And Middle School Administration/Principalship; Elementary Education And Teaching; Junior High/Intermediate/Middle School Education And Teaching. **Special Study Options:** Accelerated program; Cooperative education program; Cross-registration; Distance learning; Double major; Dual enrollment; English as a Second Language (ESL); Exchange student program (domestic); Honors program; Independent study; Internships; Liberal arts/career combination; Student-designed major; Study abroad; Teacher certification program; Weekend college. Honors programs: The Honors program promotes the intellectual and personal development of high-ability undergraduate students both inside and outside the classroom. Along with admission to Honors classes and the opportunity to graduate with Honors distinction, Honors students receive priority scheduling, access to free printing in the Honors lounge, and invitations to special outings through the Laurel Collegiate Society, the social club for high-achieving students (with 3.4 GPA and above). Honors students are given first priority in study abroad courses and many are recognized at the Ohio State Newark Salute to Undergraduate Achievement dinner every spring. **Disability Services offered to physically disabled students:** Note-taking services; Reader services; Tape recorders. **Career services:** Alumni services; Career assessment; Career/job search classes; Internships; Regional alumni

FACILITIES
Housing: Apartments for single students; Coed dorms; Special housing for disabled students 100% of campus accessible to physically diasbled. **Computers:** 100% of classrooms, 100% of dorms, 100% of libraries, 100% of dining areas, 100% of student union, have wireless network access. Students can register for classes online. Administrative functions (other than registration) can be performed online.

CAMPUS LIFE
Environment: Town **Activities:** Campus Ministries; Choral groups; Drama/theater; International Student Organization; Literary magazine; Student government 33 registered organizations, 2 honor societies, 2 religious organizations. **Athletics (Intercollegiate):** *Men:* basketball, golf, soccer. *Women:* basketball, soccer, softball, volleyball.

ADMISSIONS
Freshman Academic Profile: 4% in top 10% of high school class, 27% in top 25% of high school class, 63% in top 50% of high school class. 91% from public high schools. **Test Scores:** SAT Math middle 50% range 520-600. SAT EBRW middle 50% range 510-610. ACT middle 50% range 20-25. **Basis for Candidate Selection:** *Other factors considered include:* standardized test scores. **Freshman Admission Requirements:** High school diploma is required and GED is accepted *Academic units required:* 4 English, 3 math, 3 science, 3 science labs, 2 foreign language, 2 social studies, 1 academic elective, 1 visual/performing arts, *Academic units recommended:* 4 English, 4 math, 3 science, 3 science labs, 3 foreign language, 3 social studies, 1 academic elective, 1 visual/performing arts. **Freshman Admission Statistics:** 3,665 applied, 99.1% admitted, 38% enrolled. **Transfer Admission Requirements:** college transcript(s), Minimum college GPA of 2.0 required. Lowest grade transferable C-. **General Admission Information:** Application fee $60. Regular application deadline 6/1. Nonfall registration accepted.

COSTS AND FINANCIAL AID
Annual out-of-state tuition $26,244. Room and board $9,132. Average book expense $1,168. **Required Forms and Deadlines:** FAFSA. **Notification of Awards:** Applicants will be notified of awards on or about 3/15. **Types of Aid:** *Need-based scholarships/grants:* College/university scholarship or grant aid from institutional funds; Federal Pell; Private scholarships; SEOG; State scholarships/grants. *Loans:* Direct PLUS loans; Direct Subsidized Stafford Loans; Direct Unsubsidized Stafford Loans. *Student Employment:* Federal Work-Study Program available. Institutional employment available. **Financial Aid Statistics:** 67% needy freshmen, 69% needy undergrads receive need-based scholarship or grant aid. 1% freshmen, 1% undergrads receive non-need-based scholarship or grant aid. 94% freshmen, 94% undergrads receive need-based self-help aid. 0% freshmen, 0% undergrads receive athletic scholarships. 86% freshmen, 80% undergrads receive any aid. **Criteria for awarding aid:** *Need-based:* Academics, Alumni affiliation, Art, Athletics, Job skills, Leadership, Minority status, Music/drama *Non-need-based:* Academics, Alumni affiliation, Art, Athletics, Job skills, Leadership, Minority status, Music/drama, State/district residency.

OHIO UNIVERSITY—ATHENS

1 Ohio University, Athens, OH 45701
Phone: 740-593-4100 • **Financial Aid Phone:** 740-593-4141
E-mail: admissions@ohio.edu • **CEEB Code:** 1593
Fax: 740-593-0560 • **Website:** www.ohio.edu • **ACT Code:** 3314

This public school was founded in 1804. It has a 1774 acre campus.

RATINGS
Admissions Selectivity Rating: 81   **Fire Safety Rating:** 89   **Green Rating:** 98

STUDENTS AND FACULTY
Enrollment: 23,084. **Student Body:** 60% female, 40% male, 15% out-of-state, 2% international (66 countries represented). Asian 1%, African American 6%, Caucasian 83%, Hispanic 3%, Native American <1%, Pacific Islander <1%, Two or more races 4%, Race unknown 2%.
Retention and Graduation: 80% freshmen return for sophomore year. 44% freshmen graduate within 4 years. 64% freshmen graduate within 6 years. 29% grads go on to further study within 1 year. 8% grads pursue arts and sciences degrees. 2% grads pursue law degrees. 1% grads pursue business degrees. 3% grads pursue medical degrees. **Faculty:** Student/faculty ratio 17:1. 997 full-time faculty, 79% hold PhDs, 15% are members of minority groups, 42% are women. 11% of classes are taught by teaching assistants.

ACADEMICS
Degrees: Associate; Bachelor's; Certificate; Doctoral/Professional; Doctoral/Research; **Master's Classes:** Most classes have 10-19 students. **Most popular majors:** Speech Communication And Rhetoric; Liberal Arts And Sciences, General Studies And Humanities, Other; Registered Nursing/Registered Nurse. **Special Study Options:** Accelerated program; Cooperative education program; Cross-registration; Distance learning; Double major; Dual enrollment; English as a Second Language (ESL); External degree program; Honors program; Independent study; Internships; Liberal arts/career combination; Student-designed major; Study abroad; Teacher certification program. Honors programs: Honors Tutorial College: The most selective of Ohio University's nine undergraduate colleges, the Honor's Tutorial College (HTC) is the oldest, largest, and most academically diverse degree-granting tutorial college in the country. Based on the Oxbridge system of tutorial education developed in Great Britain, HTC offers highly motivated, talented students the opportunity to receive a substantial part of their education through tutorials (one-on-one classes or small seminars). There are generally 275 students in the Honors Tutorial College spread across 36 programs of study. To preserve the tutorial experience, HTC enrolls about 80 new students each year, and admission is highly competitive. **Disability Services offered to physically disabled students:** Note-taking services; Tape recorders; Tutors. **Career services:** Alumni network; Alumni services; Career assessment; Career/job search classes; Internships; Regional alumni

FACILITIES
Housing: Coed dorms; Special housing for disabled student; Special housing for international students; Theme housing; Wellness housing; Women's dorms 89% of campus accessible to physically diasbled. **Special Academic

Facilities/Equipment: Museum of American Art, Innovation Center, Nuclear Accelerator, Electron Microscope, Biotech Center, Kennedy Museum of Art, Trisolini Gallery, Art Gallery in Multicultural Programs, Voinovich Center, & Academic & Research Center, Greenhouse, Ridges Land Lab, Cartography & Meteorology Centers, Contemporary History Institute, Maker Space and 3d Printer. **Computers:** 100% of classrooms, 100% of dorms, 100% of libraries, 100% of dining areas, 100% of student union, 100% of common outdoor areas have wireless network access. Students can register for classes online. Administrative functions (other than registration) can be performed online.

CAMPUS LIFE

Environment: Town **Activities:** Campus Ministries; Choral groups; Concert band; Dance; Drama/theater; International Student Organization; Jazz band; Literary magazine; Marching band; Music ensembles; Musical theater; Opera; Pep band; Radio station; Student government; Student newspaper; Student-run film society; Symphony orchestra; Television station; Yearbook 323 registered organizations, 16 honor societies, 27 religious organizations. 17 fraternities, 12 sororities. **Athletics (Intercollegiate):** *Men:* baseball, basketball, cheerleading, cross-country, football, golf, wrestling. *Women:* basketball, cheerleading, cross-country, diving, field hockey, golf, soccer, softball, swimming, track/field (outdoor), volleyball. **On-Campus Highlights:** Charles J. Ping Recreation Center, Kennedy Museum of Art, Templeton-Blackburn Memorial Auditorium, Convocation Center, Alden Library **Environmental Initiatives:** Between FY12 and FY17, Ohio University has reduced net greenhouse gas emissions by 25%.

ADMISSIONS

Freshman Academic Profile: Average high school GPA 3.5. 18% in top 10% of high school class, 46% in top 25% of high school class, 82% in top 50% of high school class. 83% from public high schools. **Test Scores:** SAT Math middle 50% range 530-620. SAT EBRW middle 50% range 550-640. ACT middle 50% range 22-26. Minimum internet-based TOEFL 71. Minimum paper TOEFL 525. **Basis for Candidate Selection:** *Very important factors considered include:* rigor of secondary school record, academic GPA, standardized test scores. *Important factors considered include:* class rank, application essay, first generation. *Other factors considered include:* recommendation(s), interview, extracurricular activities, talent/ability, character/personal qualities, alumni/ae relation, geographical residence, state residency, volunteer work, work experience. **Freshman Admission Requirements:** High school diploma is required and GED is accepted *Academic units required:* 4 English, 4 math, 3 science, 2 foreign language, 3 social studies, 4 academic electives, and 1 unit from above areas or other academic areas. *Academic units recommended:* 1 visual/performing arts. **Freshman Admission Statistics:** 26,263 applied, 73.9% admitted, 21% enrolled. **Transfer Admission Requirements:** college transcript(s), Minimum college GPA of 2.0 required. Lowest grade transferable C-. **General Admission Information:** Application fee $50. Priority deadline 12/1. Regular application deadline 2/1. Nonfall registration accepted. Admission may be deferred for a maximum of 1 year.

COSTS AND FINANCIAL AID

Annual in-state tuition $10,734. Annual out-of-state tuition $19,566. Room and board $10,734. Average book expense $1,034. **Required Forms and Deadlines:** FAFSA. **Notification of Awards:** Applicants will be notified of awards on or about 2/1. **Types of Aid:** *Need-based scholarships/grants:* College/university scholarship or grant aid from institutional funds; Federal Pell; Private scholarships; SEOG; State scholarships/grants. *Loans:* Direct PLUS loans; Direct Subsidized Stafford Loans; Direct Unsubsidized Stafford Loans. *Student Employment:* Federal Work-Study Program available. Institutional employment available. **Financial Aid Statistics:** 93% needy freshmen, 77% needy undergrads receive need-based scholarship or grant aid. 13% freshmen, 17% undergrads receive non-need-based scholarship or grant aid. 99% freshmen, 99% undergrads receive need-based self-help aid. 1% freshmen, 1% undergrads receive athletic scholarships. 92% freshmen, 75% undergrads receive any aid. 67% undergrads borrow to pay for school. Average cumulative indebtedness $27,880. **Criteria for awarding aid:** *Non-need-based:* Academics, Art, Athletics, Minority status, Music/drama, Religious affiliation.

OHIO WESLEYAN UNIVERSITY

61 South Sandusky Street, Delaware, OH 43015
Phone: 740-368-3020 • **Financial Aid Phone:** (740) 368-3050
E-mail: owuadmit@owu.edu • **CEEB Code:** 1594
Fax: 740-368-3314 • **Website:** www.owu.edu • **ACT Code:** 3316

This private school, affiliated with the Methodist Church, was founded in 1842. It has a 200 acre campus.

RATINGS

Admissions Selectivity Rating: 80   **Fire Safety Rating:** 86   **Green Rating:** 60*

STUDENTS AND FACULTY

Enrollment: 1,554. **Student Body:** 53% female, 47% male, 54% out-of-state, 5% international (41 countries represented). Asian 3%, African American 10%, Caucasian 69%, Hispanic 6%, Native American <1%, Pacific Islander <1%, Two or more races 5%, Race unknown 2%.
Retention and Graduation: 78% freshmen return for sophomore year. 62% freshmen graduate within 4 years. 60% freshmen graduate within 6 years. **Faculty:** Student/faculty ratio 9:1. 137 full-time faculty, 100% hold PhDs, 6% are members of minority groups, 39% are women. 0% of classes are taught by teaching assistants.

ACADEMICS

Degrees: Bachelor's **Classes:** Most classes have 10-19 students. Most lab/discussion sessions have 10-19 students. **Most popular majors:** Zoology/Animal Biology; Psychology, General; Economics, General. **Special Study Options:** Double major; Dual enrollment; Exchange student program (domestic); Honors program; Independent study; Internships; Student-designed major; Study abroad; Teacher certification program. Honors programs: The Leland F. and Helen Schubert Honors Program recognizes the most talented students among Ohio Wesleyan's community of scholars and challenges them through Honors Tutorials, Honors Seminars, and Honors Scholarships. Combined degree programs: BA/MEng. **Disability Services offered to physically disabled students:** Note-taking services; Tape recorders; Tutors. **Career services:** Alumni network; Alumni services; Career assessment

FACILITIES

Housing: Apartments for single students; Coed dorms; Fraternity/sorority housing; Special housing for international students; Theme housing; Women's dorms 60% of campus accessible to physically diasbled. **Special Academic Facilities/Equipment:** Perkins and Student Observatories Woltemade Center for Economics, Business and Entrepreneurship Ross Art Museum Schimmel/Conrades Science Center 150,000 square foot science center with state-of-the art classrooms and equipment, including a new Scanning transmission electron microscope for undergraduate studies, Wireless campus. **Computers:** 10% of classrooms, 100% of libraries, 10% of dining areas, 10% of common outdoor areas have wireless network access. Administrative functions (other than registration) can be performed online.

CAMPUS LIFE

Environment: Town **Activities:** Campus Ministries; Choral groups; Dance; Drama/theater; International Student Organization; Jazz band; Literary magazine; Model UN; Music ensembles; Musical theater; Opera; Pep band; Radio station; Student government; Student newspaper; Symphony orchestra; Yearbook 86 registered organizations, 26 honor societies, 10 religious organizations. 11 fraternities, 7 sororities. **Athletics (Intercollegiate):** *Men:* baseball, basketball, cross-country, diving, football, golf, lacrosse, sailing, soccer, swimming, tennis, track/field (outdoor), track/field (indoor). *Women:* basketball, cross-country, diving, field hockey, lacrosse, sailing, soccer, softball, swimming, tennis, track/field (outdoor), track/field (indoor), volleyball. **On-Campus Highlights:** Schimmel/Conrades Science Center, Hamilton Williams Campus Center, Selby Stadium, R.W. Corns Building, Merrick Hall **Environmental Initiatives:** Waste reduction

ADMISSIONS

Freshman Academic Profile: Average high school GPA 3.4. 22% in top 10% of high school class, 47% in top 25% of high school class, 78% in top 50% of high school class. 77% from public high schools. **Test Scores:** SAT Math middle 50% range 510-630. SAT EBRW middle 50% range 530-640. ACT middle 50% range 22-28. Minimum paper TOEFL 550. **Basis for Candidate Selection:** *Very important factors considered include:* rigor of secondary school record, academic GPA, application essay, recommendation(s), interview, character/personal qualities. *Important factors considered include:*

class rank, standardized test scores, extracurricular activities, talent/ability. *Other factors considered include:* first generation, alumni/ae relation, geographical residence, volunteer work, work experience, level of applicant's interest. **Freshman Admission Requirements:** High school diploma is required and GED is accepted *Academic units required:* 4 English, 3 math, 3 science, 2 foreign language, 3 social studies, *Academic units recommended:* 4 English, 4 math, 4 science, 3 foreign language, 4 social studies. **Freshman Admission Statistics:** 4,160 applied, 71.4% admitted, 15% enrolled. **Transfer Admission Requirements:** High school transcript, college transcript(s), essay or personal statement, statement of good standing from prior institution(s). Minimum college GPA of 2.5 required. Lowest grade transferable C-. **General Admission Information:** Priority deadline 1/15. Regular application deadline 3/1. Nonfall registration accepted. Admission may be deferred.

COSTS AND FINANCIAL AID

Required Forms and Deadlines: FAFSA. **Types of Aid:** *Need-based scholarships/grants:* College/university scholarship or grant aid from institutional funds; Federal Pell; Private scholarships; SEOG; State scholarships/grants. *Loans:* Direct PLUS loans; Direct Subsidized Stafford Loans; Direct Unsubsidized Stafford Loans. *Student Employment:* Federal Work-Study Program available. Institutional employment available. **Financial Aid Statistics:** 100% needy freshmen, 100% needy undergrads receive need-based scholarship or grant aid. 15% freshmen, 19% undergrads receive non-need-based scholarship or grant aid. 89% freshmen, 85% undergrads receive need-based self-help aid. 0% freshmen, 0% undergrads receive athletic scholarships. 65% undergrads borrow to pay for school. Average cumulative indebtedness $34,666. **Criteria for awarding aid:** *Non-need-based:* Academics, Alumni affiliation, Art, Minority status, Music/drama, Religious affiliation, State/district residency.

OKLAHOMA BAPTIST UNIVERSITY

500 West University, Shawnee, OK 74804
Phone: 800-654-3285 • **Financial Aid Phone:** 405-878-2016
E-mail: admissions@okbu.edu • **CEEB Code:** 6541
Fax: 405-585-5017 • **Website:** www.okbu.edu • **ACT Code:** 3414

This private school, affiliated with the Southern Baptist Church, was founded in 1910. It has a 200 acre campus.

RATINGS
Admissions Selectivity Rating: 75   **Fire Safety Rating:** 83   **Green Rating:** 60*

STUDENTS AND FACULTY
Enrollment: 1,930. **Student Body:** 59% female, 41% male, 49% out-of-state, 4% international (35 countries represented). Asian 1%, African American 5%, Caucasian 67%, Hispanic 2%, Native American 5%, Pacific Islander <1%, Two or more races 12%, Race unknown 4%.
Retention and Graduation: 68% freshmen return for sophomore year. 14% grads go on to further study within 1 year. 8% grads pursue arts and sciences degrees. 0.7% grads pursue law degrees. 2.8% grads pursue medical degrees.
Faculty: Student/faculty ratio 12:1. 127 full-time faculty, 63% hold PhDs, 11% are members of minority groups, 0% of classes are taught by teaching assistants.

ACADEMICS
Degrees: Associate; Bachelor's; Certificate; **Master's Classes:** Most classes have 10-19 students. Most lab/discussion sessions have 10-19 students.
Most popular majors: Education, General; Bible/Biblical Studies; Health Services/Allied Health/Health Sciences, General. **Special Study Options:** Accelerated program; Cooperative education program; Double major; Dual enrollment; English as a Second Language (ESL); Exchange student program (domestic); Honors program; Independent study; Internships; Liberal arts/career combination; Student-designed major; Study abroad; Teacher certification program. Honors programs: The OBU Honors Program is a curricular program designed to enhance the undergraduate study experience for certain exceptionally well-qualified students. Students completing all of the requirements for gradulation in the Honors Program earn the designation "with Honors" on their OBU diplomas. Combined degree programs: BA/MA.
Disability Services offered to physically disabled students: Note-taking services; Reader services; Tape recorders; Tutors. **Career services:** Alumni network; Alumni services; Career assessment; Career/job search classes; Internships.

FACILITIES
Housing: Apartments for married students; Apartments for single students; Men's dorms; Wellness housing; Women's dorms 100% of campus accessible to physically diasbled. **Special Academic Facilities/Equipment:** planetarium, Baptist Historical Society Archives, Avery T. Willis Center for Global Outreach **Computers:** Students can register for classes online. Administrative functions (other than registration) can be performed online.

CAMPUS LIFE
Environment: Town **Activities:** Campus Ministries; Choral groups; Concert band; Dance; Drama/theater; International Student Organization; Jazz band; Literary magazine; Marching band; Model UN; Music ensembles; Musical theater; Opera; Pep band; Student government; Student newspaper; Symphony orchestra; Television station; Yearbook 80 registered organizations, 15 honor societies, 5 religious organizations. 5 fraternities, 5 sororities. **Athletics (Intercollegiate):** *Men:* baseball, basketball, cheerleading, cross-country, golf, soccer, tennis, track/field (outdoor), track/field (indoor). *Women:* basketball, cheerleading, cross-country, golf, soccer, softball, tennis, track/field (outdoor), track/field (indoor), volleyball. **On-Campus Highlights:** Geiger Center (Student Building), Recreation and Wellness Center, Noble Complex (athletics), Mabee Learning Center (Library), Intramural Field

ADMISSIONS
Freshman Academic Profile: 23% in top 10% of high school class, 49% in top 25% of high school class, 90% in top 50% of high school class. 79% from public high schools. **Test Scores:** SAT Math middle 50% range 470-560. SAT EBRW middle 50% range 490-590. ACT middle 50% range 20-26. Minimum paper TOEFL 500. **Basis for Candidate Selection:** *Very important factors considered include:* class rank, academic GPA, application essay. *Important factors considered include:* rigor of secondary school record, extracurricular activities, level of applicant's interest. *Other factors considered include:* standardized test scores, interview, talent/ability, character/personal qualities, first generation, alumni/ae relation, religious affiliation/commitment, volunteer work, work experience. **Freshman Admission Requirements:** High school diploma is required and GED is accepted *Academic units recommended:* 4 English, 3 math, 3 science, 2 science labs, 2 foreign language, 2 social studies, 1 history, 2 academic electives, 2 visual/performing arts. **Freshman Admission Statistics:** 4,119 applied, 87.2% admitted, 16% enrolled. **Transfer Admission Requirements:** college transcript(s), Minimum college GPA of 2.5 required. Lowest grade transferable D. **General Admission Information:** Priority deadline 4/1. Regular application deadline 8/1. Nonfall registration accepted. Admission may be deferred.

COSTS AND FINANCIAL AID
Annual tuition $25,138. Room and board $7,350. Required fees $3,120. Average book expense $1,300. **Required Forms and Deadlines:** FAFSA. **Notification of Awards:** Applicants will be notified of awards on a rolling basis beginning 2/1. **Types of Aid:** *Need-based scholarships/grants:* College/university scholarship or grant aid from institutional funds; Federal Nursing Scholarships; Federal Pell; Private scholarships; SEOG; State scholarships/grants. *Loans:* Direct PLUS loans; Direct Subsidized Stafford Loans; Direct Unsubsidized Stafford Loans. *Student Employment:* Federal Work-Study Program available. Institutional employment available. **Financial Aid Statistics:** 79% needy freshmen, 85% needy undergrads receive need-based scholarship or grant aid. 98% freshmen, 97% undergrads receive non-need-based scholarship or grant aid. 75% freshmen, 76% undergrads receive need-based self-help aid. 22% freshmen, 24% undergrads receive athletic scholarships. 100% freshmen, 98% undergrads receive any aid. 58% undergrads borrow to pay for school. Average cumulative indebtedness $24,451. **Criteria for awarding aid:** *Need-based:* Academics, Leadership, Minority status *Non-need-based:* Academics, Art, Athletics, Leadership, Minority status, Music/drama, Religious affiliation.

OKLAHOMA CHRISTIAN UNIVERSITY

Box 11000, Oklahoma City, OK 73136-1100
Phone: 405-425-5050 • **Financial Aid Phone:** 405-425-5190
E-mail: info@oc.edu
Fax: 405-425-5069 • **Website:** www.oc.edu • **ACT Code:** 3415

This private school, affiliated with the Church of Christ, was founded in 1950. It has a 240 acre campus.

RATINGS
Admissions Selectivity Rating: 89   **Fire Safety Rating:** 82   **Green Rating:** 60*

STUDENTS AND FACULTY
Enrollment: 1,910. **Student Body:** 49% female, 51% male, 63% out-of-state, 11% international (38 countries represented). Asian 1%, African American 3%, Caucasian 63%, Hispanic 3%, Native American 4%, Race unknown 14%.
Retention and Graduation: 73% freshmen return for sophomore year.

Faculty: Student/faculty ratio 13:1. 116 full-time faculty, 73% hold PhDs, 30% are women. 0% of classes are taught by teaching assistants.

ACADEMICS

Degrees: Bachelor's; **Master's Classes:** Most classes have 10-19 students. Most lab/discussion sessions have 10-19 students. **Most popular majors:** Elementary Education And Teaching; Liberal Arts And Sciences/Liberal Studies; Registered Nursing/Registered Nurse. **Special Study Options:** Cross-registration; Distance learning; Double major; English as a Second Language (ESL); Honors program; Independent study; Internships; Student-designed major; Study abroad; Teacher certification program. Honors programs: The Honors Program is designed for good thinkers who value knowledge for its intrinsic worth and its enabling power. • Honors students have had strong academic experiences in high school. • Honors students accept intellectual challenges to understand and perform at the highest possible level. • Honors students are majoring in many disciplines, bringing their diverse insights to their work with other honors students. A detailed description of the OC Honors Program, and contact information, can be found at www.oc.edu/academics/honors. **Career services:** Alumni network; Alumni services; Career assessment; Career/job search classes; Internships

FACILITIES

Housing: Apartments for married students; Apartments for single students; Men's dorms; Special housing for disabled student; Women's dorms **Special Academic Facilities/Equipment:** Art Museum Art Gallery **Computers:** 100% of classrooms, 100% of dorms, 100% of libraries, 100% of dining areas, 100% of student union, 95% of common outdoor areas have wireless network access. Students can register for classes online. Administrative functions (other than registration) can be performed online.

CAMPUS LIFE

Environment: Metropolis **Activities:** Campus Ministries; Choral groups; Concert band; Drama/theater; International Student Organization; Jazz band; Literary magazine; Music ensembles; Musical theater; Opera; Pep band; Student government; Student newspaper; Symphony orchestra; Television station; Yearbook 20 registered organizations, 5 honor societies, 2 religious organizations. 6 fraternities, 6 sororities. **Athletics (Intercollegiate):** *Men:* baseball, basketball, cross-country, golf, soccer, tennis, track/field (outdoor). *Women:* basketball, cheerleading, cross-country, soccer, softball, tennis, track/field (outdoor). **On-Campus Highlights:** Gaylord University Center, University House Commons, Lawson Commons, Payne Athletic & Fitness Center, Mabee Learning Center **Environmental Initiatives:** Trayless Cafeteria

ADMISSIONS

Freshman Academic Profile: Average high school GPA 3.6. 30% in top 10% of high school class, 54% in top 25% of high school class, 80% in top 50% of high school class. **Test Scores:** SAT Math middle 50% range 470-640. SAT EBRW middle 50% range 440-620. ACT middle 50% range 21-28. Minimum internet-based TOEFL 61. Minimum paper TOEFL 500. **Basis for Candidate Selection:** *Very important factors considered include:* character/personal qualities. *Important factors considered include:* academic GPA, standardized test scores. *Other factors considered include:* rigor of secondary school record, class rank, recommendation(s), interview, extracurricular activities, talent/ability, religious affiliation/commitment, volunteer work, work experience, level of applicant's interest. **Freshman Admission Requirements:** High school diploma is required and GED is accepted *Academic units required:* 4 English, 4 math, 4 science, *Academic units recommended:* 3 science labs, 2 foreign language, 3 social studies. **Freshman Admission Statistics:** 2,156 applied, 44.7% admitted, 47% enrolled. **Transfer Admission Requirements:** High school transcript, college transcript(s), standardized test scores, statement of good standing from prior institution(s). Lowest grade transferable D. **General Admission Information:** Application fee $25. Priority deadline 5/1. Nonfall registration accepted. Admission may be deferred for a maximum of 1 year.

COSTS AND FINANCIAL AID

Annual tuition $18,800. Room and board $6,775. Average book expense $1,000. **Required Forms and Deadlines:** FAFSA. **Notification of Awards:** Applicants will be notified of awards on a rolling basis beginning 2/15. **Types of Aid:** *Need-based scholarships/grants:* College/university scholarship or grant aid from institutional funds; Federal Pell; Private scholarships; SEOG; State scholarships/grants. *Loans:* Direct PLUS loans; Direct Subsidized Stafford Loans; Direct Unsubsidized Stafford Loans. *Student Employment:* Federal Work-Study Program available. Institutional employment available. **Financial Aid Statistics:** 58% needy freshmen, 58% needy undergrads receive need-based scholarship or grant aid. 82% freshmen, 77% undergrads receive non-need-based scholarship or grant aid. 60% freshmen, 42% undergrads receive need-based self-help aid. 9% freshmen, 9% undergrads receive athletic scholarships. 100% freshmen, 98% undergrads receive any aid. **Criteria for awarding aid:** *Need-based:* Academics, Art, Athletics, Music/drama *Non-need-based:* Religious affiliation.

OKLAHOMA CITY UNIVERSITY

2501 North Blackwelder, Oklahoma City, OK 73106
Phone: 405-208-5055 • **Financial Aid Phone:** 405-208-5848
E-mail: uadmissions@okcu.edu • **CEEB Code:** 6543
Fax: 405-208-5916 • **Website:** www.okcu.edu • **ACT Code:** 3416

This private school, affiliated with the Methodist Church, was founded in 1904. It has a 104 acre campus.

RATINGS

Admissions Selectivity Rating: 84   **Fire Safety Rating:** 95   **Green Rating:** 60*

STUDENTS AND FACULTY

Enrollment: 1,670. **Student Body:** 68% female, 32% male, 50% out-of-state, 11% international (35 countries represented). Asian 2%, African American 5%, Caucasian 63%, Hispanic 9%, Native American 2%, Pacific Islander 0%, Two or more races 8%, Race unknown 0%.
Retention and Graduation: 82% freshmen return for sophomore year. 49% freshmen graduate within 4 years. 63% freshmen graduate within 6 years. 10% grads go on to further study within 1 year. **Faculty:** Student/faculty ratio 11:1. 194 full-time faculty, 66% hold PhDs, 18% are members of minority groups, 49% are women. 0% of classes are taught by teaching assistants.

ACADEMICS

Degrees: Bachelor's; Doctoral; Doctoral/Professional; Doctoral/Research; **Master's Classes:** Most classes have 10-19 students. Most lab/discussion sessions have 10-19 students. **Most popular majors:** Dance, General; Nursing Practice; Business/Commerce, General. **Special Study Options:** Accelerated program; Cooperative education program; Distance learning; Double major; Dual enrollment; English as a Second Language (ESL); Exchange student program (domestic); External degree program; Honors program; Independent study; Internships; Student-designed major; Study abroad; Teacher certification program. Honors programs: University Honors Program: The mission of the University Honors program is to provide an enhanced learning environment for academically gifted undergraduate students. Each new class of Honors students at OCU will be a spcial community of scholars. Students will have the opportunity to become acquainted with one another and the Honors program in the Honors Colloquium, a course required for all new honors students during their first semester in the program. Honors students will have the opportunities to meet with visiting scholars and participate in special events. As part of a network of honors programs through the National Collegiate Honors Council and the Great Plains Honors Council, students may present research at national and regional honors conferences and participate in exciting summer and semester programs. Combined degree programs: BA/JD; BA/MA. **Disability Services offered to physically disabled students:** Reader services; Tutors. **Career services:** Alumni network; Alumni services; Career assessment; Career/job search classes; Internships; Regional alumni

FACILITIES

Housing: Apartments for married students; Apartments for single students; Coed dorms; Fraternity/sorority housing; Men's dorms; Special housing for disabled student; Special housing for international students; Theme housing; Women's dorms 95% of campus accessible to physically diasbled. **Special Academic Facilities/Equipment:** Art museum, audiovisual center, language lab. **Computers:** 100% of classrooms, 100% of dorms, 100% of libraries, 100% of dining areas, 100% of student union, 90% of common outdoor areas have wireless network access. Students can register for classes online. Administrative functions (other than registration) can be performed online.

CAMPUS LIFE

Environment: Metropolis **Activities:** Campus Ministries; Choral groups; Concert band; Dance; Drama/theater; International Student Organization; Jazz band; Literary magazine; Music ensembles; Musical theater; Opera; Pep band; Student government; Student newspaper; Symphony orchestra; Television station; Yearbook 64 registered organizations, 14 honor societies, 6 religious organizations. 2 fraternities, 4 sororities. **Athletics (Intercollegiate):** *Men:* baseball, basketball, cheerleading, crew/rowing, golf, soccer, track/field (outdoor), wrestling. *Women:* basketball, cheerleading, crew/rowing, golf, soccer, softball, track/field (outdoor), volleyball, wrestling. **On-Campus Highlights:** Tom and Brenda McDaniel Univ Center, Henry J Freede Wellness and Activity Center, Meinders' School of Business, Walker Center for Arts and Sciences, Norick Art Center **Environmental Initiatives:** Computer recycling program, community garden

ADMISSIONS

Freshman Academic Profile: Average high school GPA 3.8. 31% in top 10% of high school class, 61% in top 25% of high school class, 82% in top 50%

of high school class. 88% from public high schools. **Test Scores:** SAT Math middle 50% range 540-630. SAT EBRW middle 50% range 570-650. ACT middle 50% range 23-28. Minimum internet-based TOEFL 80. Minimum paper TOEFL 550. **Basis for Candidate Selection:** *Very important factors considered include:* rigor of secondary school record, talent/ability. *Important factors considered include:* academic GPA, application essay, standardized test scores, character/personal qualities. *Other factors considered include:* class rank, recommendation(s), interview, extracurricular activities, volunteer work, work experience, level of applicant's interest. **Freshman Admission Requirements:** High school diploma is required and GED is accepted *Academic units required:* 4 English, 3 math, 3 science, 2 science labs, 2 foreign language, 2 social studies, 2 history, 3 academic electives, *Academic units recommended:* 4 English, 4 math, 4 science, 3 science labs, 2 foreign language, 3 social studies, 1 history, 3 academic electives. **Freshman Admission Statistics:** 1,820 applied, 71.7% admitted, 23% enrolled. **Transfer Admission Requirements:** college transcript(s), essay or personal statement, statement of good standing from prior institution(s). Minimum college GPA of 2.0 required. Lowest grade transferable C-. **General Admission Information:** Application fee $55. Priority deadline 3/1. Nonfall registration accepted. Admission may be deferred for a maximum of 1 year.

COSTS AND FINANCIAL AID

Annual tuition $27,276. Room and board $10,796. Required fees $3,750. Average book expense $1,500. **Required Forms and Deadlines:** FAFSA. **Notification of Awards:** Applicants will be notified of awards on a rolling basis beginning 3/1. **Types of Aid:** *Need-based scholarships/grants:* College/university scholarship or grant aid from institutional funds; Federal Pell; Private scholarships; SEOG; State scholarships/grants. *Loans:* Direct PLUS loans; Direct Subsidized Stafford Loans; Direct Unsubsidized Stafford Loans. *Student Employment:* Federal Work-Study Program available. Institutional employment available. **Financial Aid Statistics:** 99% needy freshmen, 93% needy undergrads receive need-based scholarship or grant aid. 16% freshmen, 14% undergrads receive non-need-based scholarship or grant aid. 64% freshmen, 72% undergrads receive need-based self-help aid. 4% freshmen, 3% undergrads receive athletic scholarships. 97% freshmen, 87% undergrads receive any aid. 57% undergrads borrow to pay for school. Average cumulative indebtedness $26,329. **Criteria for awarding aid:** *Non-need-based:* Academics, Art, Athletics, Leadership, Music/drama, Religious affiliation.

OKLAHOMA STATE UNIVERSITY

219 Student Union, Stillwater, OK 74078
Phone: 405-744-5358 • **Financial Aid Phone:** 405-744-6604
E-mail: admissions@okstate.edu • **CEEB Code:** 6546
Fax: 405-744-7092 • **Website:** http://go.okstate.edu • **ACT Code:** 3424

This public school was founded in 1890. It has a 840 acre campus.

RATINGS

Admissions Selectivity Rating: 84   **Fire Safety Rating:** 93   **Green Rating:** 89

STUDENTS AND FACULTY

Enrollment: 20,736. **Student Body:** 49% female, 51% male, 27% out-of-state, 4% international (67 countries represented). Asian 2%, African American 5%, Caucasian 68%, Hispanic 8%, Native American 5%, Pacific Islander <1%, Two or more races 10%, Race unknown <1%.
Retention and Graduation: 81% freshmen return for sophomore year. 39% freshmen graduate within 4 years. 63% freshmen graduate within 6 years. **Faculty:** Student/faculty ratio 20:1. 1,021 full-time faculty, 91% hold PhDs, 20% are members of minority groups, 36% are women. 23% of classes are taught by teaching assistants.

ACADEMICS

Degrees: Bachelor's; Doctoral; Doctoral/Professional; Doctoral/Research; Master's; Post-Bachelor's certificate; Post-Master's certificate **Classes:** Most classes have 10-19 students. Most lab/discussion sessions have 10-19 students. **Most popular majors:** Animal Sciences, General; Mechanical Engineering; Business Administration And Management, General. **Special Study Options:** Accelerated program; Cross-registration; Distance learning; Double major; Dual enrollment; English as a Second Language (ESL); Exchange student program (domestic); Honors program; Independent study; Internships; Student-designed major; Study abroad; Teacher certification program. Honors programs: OSU has an Honors College that students across undergraduate disciplines can be a part of. For more information see https://honors.okstate. edu/ Combined degree programs: BA/MA. **Disability Services offered to physically disabled students:** Note-taking services; Reader services; Tape recorders; Tutors. **Career services:** Alumni network; Alumni services; Career

assessment; Career/job search classes; Internships; Regional alumni

FACILITIES

Housing: Apartments for married students; Apartments for single students; Coed dorms; Fraternity/sorority housing; Men's dorms; Special housing for disabled student; Theme housing; Wellness housing; Women's dorms 97% of campus accessible to physically diasbled. **Special Academic Facilities/Equipment:** Art, history, and natural science museums, wellness center, laser research center, Henry Bellmon Research center **Computers:** 80% of classrooms, 80% of dorms, 100% of libraries, 80% of student union, have wireless network access. Students can register for classes online. Administrative functions (other than registration) can be performed online.

CAMPUS LIFE

Environment: Town **Activities:** Campus Ministries; Choral groups; Concert band; Dance; Drama/theater; International Student Organization; Jazz band; Literary magazine; Marching band; Music ensembles; Musical theater; Opera; Pep band; Radio station; Student government; Student newspaper; Symphony orchestra; Television station 300 registered organizations. **Athletics (Intercollegiate):** *Men:* baseball, basketball, cross-country, football, golf, tennis, track/field (outdoor), wrestling. *Women:* basketball, cross-country, equestrian sports, golf, soccer, softball, tennis, track/field (outdoor). **On-Campus Highlights:** Colvin Recreational Center, Gallagher/Iba Arena and Museum, Student Union Building, Edmon Low Library, ConocoPhillips Alumni Center **Environmental Initiatives:** The OSU Energy Management program focuses on behavior change to conserve energy across campus. This program has saved nearly $38 million for the OSU Stillwater campus since 2007.

ADMISSIONS

Freshman Academic Profile: Average high school GPA 3.6. 27% in top 10% of high school class, 54% in top 25% of high school class, 85% in top 50% of high school class. **Test Scores:** SAT Math middle 50% range 530-630. SAT EBRW middle 50% range 540-630. ACT middle 50% range 22-28. Minimum internet-based TOEFL 61. Minimum paper TOEFL 500. **Basis for Candidate Selection:** *Very important factors considered include:* class rank, academic GPA, standardized test scores. *Important factors considered include:* application essay. *Other factors considered include:* recommendation(s). **Freshman Admission Requirements:** High school diploma is required and GED is accepted *Academic units required:* 4 English, 3 math, 3 science, 3 science labs, 2 social studies, 1 history. **Freshman Admission Statistics:** 13,635 applied, 71.4% admitted, 43% enrolled. **Transfer Admission Requirements:** college transcript(s), Minimum college GPA of 2.25 required. Lowest grade transferable D. **General Admission Information:** Application fee $40. Nonfall registration accepted. Admission may be deferred.

COSTS AND FINANCIAL AID

Annual in-state tuition $8,558. Annual out-of-state tuition $20,228. Room and board $8,558. Required fees $3,548. Average book expense $1,270. **Required Forms and Deadlines:** FAFSA. **Types of Aid:** *Need-based scholarships/grants:* College/university scholarship or grant aid from institutional funds; Federal Pell; Private scholarships; SEOG; State scholarships/grants. *Loans:* Direct PLUS loans; Direct Subsidized Stafford Loans; Direct Unsubsidized Stafford Loans. *Student Employment:* Federal Work-Study Program available. Institutional employment available. **Financial Aid Statistics:** 80% needy freshmen, 76% needy undergrads receive need-based scholarship or grant aid. 10% freshmen, 6% undergrads receive non-need-based scholarship or grant aid. 55% freshmen, 66% undergrads receive need-based self-help aid. 1% freshmen, 1% undergrads receive athletic scholarships. 88% freshmen, 84% undergrads receive any aid. 50% undergrads borrow to pay for school. Average cumulative indebtedness $24,252. **Criteria for awarding aid:** *Need-based:* Academics, Minority status *Non-need-based:* Academics, Alumni affiliation, Art, Athletics, Leadership, Minority status, Music/drama, State/district residency.

OLD DOMINION UNIVERSITY

5115 Hampton Boulevard, Norfolk, VA 23529-0050
Phone: 757-683-3685 • **Financial Aid Phone:** 757-683-3683
E-mail: admissions@odu.edu • **CEEB Code:** 5126
Fax: 757-683-3255 • **Website:** www.odu.edu • **ACT Code:**

This public school was founded in 1930. It has a 251 acre campus.

RATINGS

Admissions Selectivity Rating: 75   **Fire Safety Rating:** 91   **Green Rating:** 79

STUDENTS AND FACULTY

Enrollment: 19,364. **Student Body:** 55% female, 45% male, 8% out-of-state, 2% international (87 countries represented). Asian 5%, African American 31%,

Caucasian 45%, Hispanic 9%, Native American <1%, Pacific Islander <1%, Two or more races 7%, Race unknown 3%.
Retention and Graduation: 80% freshmen return for sophomore year. 27% freshmen graduate within 4 years. 54% freshmen graduate within 6 years. 26% grads go on to further study within 1 year. 9% grads pursue arts and sciences degrees. 1% grads pursue law degrees. 2% grads pursue business degrees. 1% grads pursue medical degrees. **Faculty:** Student/faculty ratio 18:1. 840 full-time faculty, 82% hold PhDs, 23% are members of minority groups, 45% are women.

ACADEMICS
Degrees: Bachelor's; Certificate; Doctoral; Doctoral/Professional; Doctoral/Research; Master's; Post-Bachelor's certificate; Post-Master's certificate **Classes:** Most classes have 10-19 students. **Most popular majors:** Psychology, General; Criminology; Mental And Social Health Services And Allied Professions, Other. **Special Study Options:** Accelerated program; Cooperative education program; Cross-registration; Distance learning; Double major; Dual enrollment; English as a Second Language (ESL); Exchange student program (domestic); Honors program; Independent study; Internships; Liberal arts/career combination; Student-designed major; Study abroad; Teacher certification program. Honors programs: Honors College. The Honors College was established to further the University's commitment to excellence in education. With an emphasis on teaching, innovation, and small classes, the college offers the experience of a small liberal arts college within the framework of the large university. The four-year experience offers specially designed, low-enrollment courses to honors students and selected juniors and seniors. Several out-of-class and off-campus experiences are often part of these courses – at no extra cost to students. A one credit honors tutorial is required in the junior year, and a senior honors colloquium is taken in the final year of study. All Honors College students are awarded an annual honors stipend. Combined degree programs: BA/MA; BA/MEng. **Disability Services offered to physically disabled students:** Note-taking services; Reader services; Tape recorders; Tutors. **Career services:** Alumni network; Alumni services; Career assessment; Career/job search classes; Internships; Regional alumni

FACILITIES
Housing: Apartments for single students; Coed dorms; Special housing for disabled student; Special housing for international students; Theme housing; Women's dorms 100% of campus accessible to physically diasbled. **Special Academic Facilities/Equipment:** Student art gallery, laser optics lab, robotics lab, sub-/super-sonic wind tunnels, centers for urban research/service, economic education, and child study, planetarium, marine science research vessel, random wave pool. **Computers:** 100% of classrooms, 100% of dorms, 100% of libraries, 100% of dining areas, 100% of student union, 20% of common outdoor areas have wireless network access. Students can register for classes online. Administrative functions (other than registration) can be performed online.

CAMPUS LIFE
Environment: Metropolis **Activities:** Campus Ministries; Choral groups; Concert band; Dance; Drama/theater; International Student Organization; Jazz band; Marching band; Model UN; Music ensembles; Musical theater; Pep band; Radio station; Student government; Student newspaper; Student-run film society; Symphony orchestra 155 registered organizations, 16 honor societies, 25 religious organizations. 14 fraternities, 10 sororities. **Athletics (Intercollegiate):** *Men:* baseball, basketball, diving, football, golf, sailing, soccer, tennis, wrestling. *Women:* basketball, crew/rowing, diving, field hockey, golf, lacrosse, sailing, soccer, tennis. **On-Campus Highlights:** Webb Student Center, Student Recreation Center, University Village, Constant Convocation Center, Kaufman Mall **Environmental Initiatives:** All new contruction and major renovations are designed to LEED Silver standards at a minimum. We completed two projects this year, one new construction and one renovation.

ADMISSIONS
Freshman Academic Profile: Average high school GPA 3.3. 9% in top 10% of high school class, 31% in top 25% of high school class, 69% in top 50% of high school class. 93% from public high schools. **Test Scores:** SAT Math middle 50% range 480-590. SAT EBRW middle 50% range 500-610. ACT middle 50% range 19-26. Minimum internet-based TOEFL 79. Minimum paper TOEFL 550. **Basis for Candidate Selection:** *Very important factors considered include:* rigor of secondary school record, academic GPA, standardized test scores. *Important factors considered include:* application essay, recommendation(s), extracurricular activities, volunteer work, work experience. *Other factors considered include:* class rank, talent/ability, character/personal qualities, first generation, alumni/ae relation, level of applicant's interest. **Freshman Admission Requirements:** High school diploma is required and GED is accepted *Academic units required:* 4 English, 3 math, 3 science, 3 foreign language, 3 social studies, *Academic units recommended:* 4 English, 4 math, 3 science, 3 foreign language, 3 social studies. **Freshman Admission Statistics:** 11,159 applied, 85.7% admitted, 31% enrolled. **Transfer Admission Requirements:** college transcript(s), Minimum college GPA of 2.2 required. Lowest grade transferable c. **General Admission Information:** Application fee $50. Priority deadline 12/1. Regular application deadline 2/1. Nonfall registration accepted. Admission may be deferred for a maximum of 1 year.

COSTS AND FINANCIAL AID
Annual in-state tuition $11,268. Annual out-of-state tuition $27,900. Room and board $11,268. Required fees $300. Average book expense $1,000. **Required Forms and Deadlines:** FAFSA. **Notification of Awards:** Applicants will be notified of awards on a rolling basis beginning 3/1. **Types of Aid:** *Need-based scholarships/grants:* College/university scholarship or grant aid from institutional funds; Federal Nursing Scholarships; Federal Pell; Private scholarships; SEOG; State scholarships/grants; United Negro College Fund. *Loans:* Direct PLUS loans; Direct Subsidized Stafford Loans; Direct Unsubsidized Stafford Loans. *Student Employment:* Federal Work-Study Program available. Institutional employment available. **Financial Aid Statistics:** 75% needy freshmen, 76% needy undergrads receive need-based scholarship or grant aid. 38% freshmen, 21% undergrads receive non-need-based scholarship or grant aid. 80% freshmen, 81% undergrads receive need-based self-help aid. 3% freshmen, 2% undergrads receive athletic scholarships. 85% freshmen, 72% undergrads receive any aid. 70% undergrads borrow to pay for school. Average cumulative indebtedness $30,410. **Criteria for awarding aid:** *Non-need-based:* Academics, Alumni affiliation, Art, Athletics, Leadership, Music/drama, State/district residency.

ORAL ROBERTS UNIVERSITY

7777 S. Lewis Avenue, Tulsa, OK 74171
Phone: 918-495-6518 • **Financial Aid Phone:** (918) 495-6510
E-mail: admissions@oru.edu • **CEEB Code:** 6552
Fax: 918-495-6222 • **Website:** www.oru.edu • **ACT Code:** 3427

This private school, affiliated with the Interdenominational, was founded in 1963. It has a 263 acre campus.

RATINGS
Admissions Selectivity Rating: 79   **Fire Safety Rating:** 98   **Green Rating:** 60*

STUDENTS AND FACULTY
Enrollment: 3,098. **Student Body:** 60% female, 40% male, 56% out-of-state, 10% international (100 countries represented). Asian 2%, African American 13%, Caucasian 44%, Hispanic 13%, Native American 3%, Pacific Islander 0%, Two or more races 5%, Race unknown 10%.
Retention and Graduation: 84% freshmen return for sophomore year. 47% freshmen graduate within 4 years. 57% freshmen graduate within 6 years. 16% grads go on to further study within 1 year. 18% grads pursue arts and sciences degrees. 2.3% grads pursue law degrees. 27% grads pursue business degrees. 9.3% grads pursue medical degrees. **Faculty:** Student/faculty ratio 14:1. 156 full-time faculty, 71% hold PhDs, 23% are members of minority groups, 41% are women. 0% of classes are taught by teaching assistants.

ACADEMICS
Degrees: Bachelor's; Certificate; Diploma; Doctoral/Research; **Master's Classes:** Most classes have 10-19 students. **Most popular majors:** Theology/Theological Studies; Marketing/Marketing Management, General. **Special Study Options:** Accelerated program; Distance learning; Double major; Dual enrollment; English as a Second Language (ESL); Exchange student program (domestic); Honors program; Independent study; Internships; Student-designed major; Study abroad; Teacher certification program. Honors programs: ORU Honors Program includes "Scholars" and "Fellows" — Highly selective Includes Beta Gamma Phi and other Honor Societies. **Disability Services offered to physically disabled students:** Note-taking services; Reader services; Tape recorders; Tutors. Alumni network; Alumni services; Career assessment; Career/job search classes; Internships; Regional alumni

FACILITIES
Housing: Men's dorms; Special housing for disabled student; Women's dorms 100% of campus accessible to physically diasbled. **Special Academic Facilities/Equipment:** Elsing Museum, Global Learning Center

CAMPUS LIFE
Environment: Metropolis **Activities:** Campus Ministries; Choral groups; Concert band; Dance; Drama/theater; International Student Organization; Jazz band; Literary magazine; Model UN; Music ensembles; Musical theater; Opera; Pep band; Radio station; Student government; Student newspaper; Symphony orchestra; Television station; Yearbook. **Athletics (Intercollegiate):** *Men:* baseball, basketball, cheerleading, cross-country, soccer, swimming, tennis, track/field (outdoor). *Women:* basketball, cheerleading, cross-country, soccer, swimming, tennis, track/field (outdoor), volleyball. **On-Campus Highlights:** Hammer Student Center, Global Learning Center, Prayer Tower, Mabee Center (Multi-purpose Event Complex), Aerobics Center

ADMISSIONS

Freshman Academic Profile: Average high school GPA 3.6. 22% in top 10% of high school class, 46% in top 25% of high school class, 80% in top 50% of high school class. 75% from public high schools. **Test Scores:** SAT Math middle 50% range 490-590. SAT EBRW middle 50% range 500-623. ACT middle 50% range 20-26. Minimum paper TOEFL 500. **Basis for Candidate Selection:** *Very important factors considered include:* academic GPA, standardized test scores. **Freshman Admission Requirements:** High school diploma is required and GED is accepted *Academic units recommended:* 4 English, 3 math, 3 science, 1 science labs, 2 foreign language, 2 social studies, 3 history, 8 academic electives. **Freshman Admission Statistics:** 2,433 applied, 93.3% admitted, 27% enrolled. **Transfer Admission Requirements:** High school transcript, college transcript(s), essay or personal statement, Minimum college GPA of 2.0 required. Lowest grade transferable 2. **General Admission Information:** Application fee $35. Nonfall registration accepted. Admission may be deferred for a maximum of 1 year.

COSTS AND FINANCIAL AID

Annual tuition $26,700. Room and board $9,450. Required fees $1,028. Average book expense $1,848. **Required Forms and Deadlines:** FAFSA. **Notification of Awards:** Applicants will be notified of awards on a rolling basis beginning 12/1. **Types of Aid:** *Need-based scholarships/grants:* College/university scholarship or grant aid from institutional funds; Federal Pell; Private scholarships; SEOG; State scholarships/grants. *Loans:* Direct PLUS loans; Direct Subsidized Stafford Loans; Direct Unsubsidized Stafford Loans. *Student Employment:* Federal Work-Study Program available. Institutional employment available. **Financial Aid Statistics:** 99% needy freshmen, 98% needy undergrads receive need-based scholarship or grant aid. 28% freshmen, 37% undergrads receive non-need-based scholarship or grant aid. 92% freshmen, 93% undergrads receive need-based self-help aid. 5% freshmen, 4% undergrads receive athletic scholarships. Average cumulative indebtedness $32,970. **Criteria for awarding aid:** *Non-need-based:* Academics, Alumni affiliation, Art, Athletics, Job skills, Leadership, Music/drama.

OREGON COLLEGE OF ART AND CRAFT

8245 Southwest Barnes Road, Portland, OR 97225
Phone: 971-255-4192 • **Financial Aid Phone:** 971-255-4224
E-mail: admissions@ocac.edu • **CEEB Code:** 4236
Fax: 503-297-9651 • **Website:** www.ocac.edu • **ACT Code:** 3471

This private school was founded in 1907. It has a 10 acre campus.

RATINGS

Admissions Selectivity Rating: 70   **Fire Safety Rating:** 68   **Green Rating:** 60*

STUDENTS AND FACULTY

Enrollment: 151. **Student Body:** 73% female, 27% male, 18% out-of-state, 0% international (2 countries represented). Asian 2%, African American 0%, Caucasian 70%, Hispanic 5%, Native American 3%, Pacific Islander 2%, Two or more races 8%, Race unknown 11%.
Retention and Graduation: 65% freshmen return for sophomore year. 9% grads pursue arts and sciences degrees. **Faculty:** Student/faculty ratio 7:1. 10 full-time faculty, 90% hold PhDs, 10% are members of minority groups, 50% are women. 0% of classes are taught by teaching assistants.

ACADEMICS

Degrees: Bachelor's; Certificate; Post-Bachelor's certificate **Classes:** Most classes have 20-29 students. **Most popular majors:** Fine Arts And Art Studies, Other. **Special Study Options:** Cross-registration; Exchange student program (domestic); Independent study; Internships; Study abroad. **Disability Services offered to physically disabled students:** Tutors. **Career services:** Alumni network; Career/job search classes; Internships

FACILITIES

Housing: Coed dorms **Special Academic Facilities/Equipment:** Hoffman Gallery, Centrum Gallery, and 7 specialized studios for artmaking.

CAMPUS LIFE

Environment: Metropolis **Activities:** Student government; Student newspaper 1 registered organization. **On-Campus Highlights:** Hands On Cafe, Centrum Art Gallery, Thesis Studios, Library, Computer Lab **Environmental Initiatives:** Public Transportation

ADMISSIONS

Freshman Academic Profile: Average high school GPA 3.0. 20% in top 10% of high school class, 20% in top 25% of high school class, 60% in top 50% of

high school class. **Test Scores:** Minimum internet-based TOEFL 80. Minimum paper TOEFL 550. **Basis for Candidate Selection:** *Very important factors considered include:* academic GPA, application essay, talent/ability. *Important factors considered include:* rigor of secondary school record, standardized test scores, recommendation(s), interview. *Other factors considered include:* class rank, extracurricular activities, character/personal qualities, alumni/ae relation, volunteer work, work experience, level of applicant's interest. **Freshman Admission Requirements:** High school diploma is required and GED is accepted *Academic units recommended:* 4 English, 3 math, 3 science, 2 foreign language, 1 social studies, 3 history, 4 visual/performing arts. **Freshman Admission Statistics:** 60 applied, 75.0% admitted, 58% enrolled. **Transfer Admission Requirements:** High school transcript, college transcript(s), essay or personal statement, Minimum college GPA of 2.0 required. Lowest grade transferable C. **General Admission Information:** Application fee $35. Nonfall registration accepted. Admission may be deferred for a maximum of 1 year.

COSTS AND FINANCIAL AID

Annual tuition $22,614. Required fees $1,657. Average book expense $1,000. **Required Forms and Deadlines:** FAFSA. **Notification of Awards:** Applicants will be notified of awards on a rolling basis beginning 3/15. **Types of Aid:** *Need-based scholarships/grants:* College/university scholarship or grant aid from institutional funds; Federal Pell; Private scholarships; SEOG; State scholarships/grants. *Loans:* Direct PLUS loans; Direct Subsidized Stafford Loans; Direct Unsubsidized Stafford Loans. *Student Employment:* Federal Work-Study Program available. Institutional employment available. **Financial Aid Statistics:** 100% needy freshmen, 84% needy undergrads receive need-based scholarship or grant aid. 88% freshmen, 82% undergrads receive non-need-based scholarship or grant aid. 94% freshmen, 95% undergrads receive need-based self-help aid. 0% freshmen, 0% undergrads receive athletic scholarships. 90% freshmen, 93% undergrads receive any aid. **Criteria for awarding aid:** *Need-based:* Academics, Art *Non-need-based:* Academics, Art.

OREGON HEALTH SCIENCES UNIVERSITY

3181 SW Sam Jackson Park Rd, Portland, OR 97239
Phone: 503-494-2998 • **Financial Aid Phone:** (503) 494-7800
E-mail: proginfo@ohsu.edu • **CEEB Code:** 4900
Fax: 503-494-3400 • **Website:** www.ohsu.edu

This public school was founded in 1867. It has a 120 acre campus.

RATINGS

Admissions Selectivity Rating: 61   **Fire Safety Rating:** 60*   **Green Rating:** 60*

STUDENTS AND FACULTY

Enrollment: 591. **Student Body:** 84% female, 16% male, 10% out-of-state, 1% international. Asian 5%, African American 1%, Caucasian 79%, Hispanic 5%, Native American 2%, Race unknown 6%.
Faculty: 1,290 full-time faculty,

ACADEMICS

Degrees: Associate; Bachelor's; Master's; Post-Bachelor's certificate; Post-Master's certificate **Classes:** Most classes have 20-29 students. Most lab/discussion sessions have 10-19 students. **Most popular majors:** Emergency Medical Technology/Technician (Emt Paramedic); Clinical Laboratory Science/Medical Technology/Technologist; Nursing/Registered Nurse (Rn, Asn, Bsn, Msn). **Special Study Options:** Accelerated program; Distance learning.

FACILITIES

Computers: Students can register for classes online.

CAMPUS LIFE

Environment: Metropolis **Activities:** Student government; Student newspaper; Yearbook. **On-Campus Highlights:** Portland Aerial Tram, Center for Health and Healing Cafe, Marquam Hill Hiking Trails

ADMISSIONS

Freshman Admission Requirements: High school diploma is required and GED is accepted **Transfer Admission Requirements:** college transcript(s), essay or personal statement, standardized test scores, statement of good standing from prior institution(s). Lowest grade transferable C. **General Admission Information:** Application fee $120. Regular application deadline 1/15. Admission may be deferred.

COSTS AND FINANCIAL AID

Annual out-of-state tuition $20,176. **Types of Aid:** *Need-based scholarships/grants:* College/university scholarship or grant aid from institutional funds; Federal Pell; Private scholarships; SEOG; State scholarships/grants. *Loans:* Direct PLUS loans; Direct Subsidized Stafford Loans; Direct Unsubsidized

Stafford Loans. *Student Employment:* Federal Work-Study Program available. Institutional employment available. **Financial Aid Statistics:** 49% needy undergrads receive need-based scholarship or grant aid. 1% undergrads receive non-need-based scholarship or grant aid. 100% undergrads receive need-based self-help aid. 0% undergrads receive athletic scholarships. 70% undergrads receive any aid. **Criteria for awarding aid:** *Need-based:* Academics, Minority status *Non-need-based:* Academics, Minority status, State/district residency.

OREGON STATE UNIVERSITY

104 Kerr Administration Building, Corvallis, OR 97331-2106
Phone: 541-737-4411 • **Financial Aid Phone:** 541-737-2241
E-mail: osuadmit@oregonstate.edu • **CEEB Code:** 3210
Fax: 541-737-2482 • **Website:** http://oregonstate.edu/ • **ACT Code:** 3482

This public school was founded in 1868. It has a 421 acre campus.

RATINGS
Admissions Selectivity Rating: 81   **Fire Safety Rating:** 92   **Green Rating:** 93

STUDENTS AND FACULTY
Enrollment: 24,921. **Student Body:** 46% female, 54% male, 32% out-of-state, 7% international (81 countries represented). Asian 7%, African American 1%, Caucasian 65%, Hispanic 9%, Native American 1%, Pacific Islander <1%, Two or more races 7%, Race unknown 2%.
Retention and Graduation: 85% freshmen return for sophomore year. 33% freshmen graduate within 4 years. 65% freshmen graduate within 6 years. 19% grads go on to further study within 1 year. **Faculty:** Student/faculty ratio 18:1. 1,184 full-time faculty, 86% hold PhDs, 18% are members of minority groups, 39% are women. 9% of classes are taught by teaching assistants.

ACADEMICS
Degrees: Bachelor's; Certificate; Doctoral; Doctoral/Professional; Doctoral/Research; Master's; Post-Bachelor's certificate **Classes:** Most classes have 10-19 students. Most lab/discussion sessions have 10-19 students. **Most popular majors:** Computer Science; Mechanical Engineering; Business Administration And Management, General. **Special Study Options:** Accelerated program; Cooperative education program; Cross-registration; Distance learning; Double major; Dual enrollment; English as a Second Language (ESL); Exchange student program (domestic); Honors program; Independent study; Internships; Liberal arts/career combination; Student-designed major; Study abroad; Teacher certification program. Honors programs: As a small degree-granting college within Oregon State University, the UHC offers OSU's most prestigious degree, the Honors Baccalaureate Degree in any undergraduate major. The UHC Features: Challenging and creative curricula for students of all majors Unique honors classes, typically limited to 12 or 20 students Courses that complement, not complicate, other course work OSU's finest professors, often hand-picked by UHC students One-on-one mentoring by faculty members while preparing the Honors Thesis. **Disability Services offered to physically disabled students:** Note-taking services; Reader services; Tape recorders; Tutors. **Career services:** Alumni network; Alumni services; Career assessment; Career/job search classes; Internships; Regional alumni

FACILITIES
Housing: Apartments for married students; Apartments for single students; Coed dorms; Fraternity/sorority housing; Special housing for disabled student; Special housing for international students; Theme housing; Wellness housing 86% of campus accessible to physically disabled. **Special Academic Facilities/Equipment:** Museums, galleries, collections, exhibits of cultural and scientific materials, language lab. **Computers:** 100% of classrooms, 2% of dorms, 100% of libraries, 50% of dining areas, 100% of student union, 2% of common outdoor areas have wireless network access. Students can register for classes online. Administrative functions (other than registration) can be performed online.

CAMPUS LIFE
Environment: Town **Activities:** Campus Ministries; Choral groups; Concert band; Dance; Drama/theater; International Student Organization; Jazz band; Literary magazine; Marching band; Model UN; Music ensembles; Musical theater; Opera; Pep band; Radio station; Student government; Student newspaper; Student-run film society; Symphony orchestra; Television station; Yearbook 350 registered organizations, 29 honor societies, 23 religious organizations. 24 fraternities, 13 sororities. **Athletics (Intercollegiate):** *Men:*

baseball, basketball, crew/rowing, football, golf, soccer, wrestling. *Women:* basketball, crew/rowing, cross-country, golf, gymnastics, soccer, softball, swimming, track/field (outdoor), volleyball. **On-Campus Highlights:** Memorial Union, Valley Library, Kelly Engineering Center, Dixon Recreation Center, Reser Stadium **Environmental Initiatives:** OSU sustainability related research has impacts state- and nation-wide. Standout research occurs at the Oregon Climate Change Research Institute and within the colleges of Earth, Atmospheric and Oceanic Sciences, Agricultural Sciences and Engineering. More info at http://senergi.oregonstate.edu/home

ADMISSIONS
Freshman Academic Profile: 26% in top 10% of high school class, 58% in top 25% of high school class, 91% in top 50% of high school class. **Test Scores:** SAT Math middle 50% range 530-650. SAT EBRW middle 50% range 540-650. ACT middle 50% range 22-28. Minimum internet-based TOEFL 80. **Basis for Candidate Selection:** *Very important factors considered include:* academic GPA. *Important factors considered include:* rigor of secondary school record, application essay, talent/ability, character/personal qualities, volunteer work, work experience. *Other factors considered include:* class rank, standardized test scores, recommendation(s), extracurricular activities, level of applicant's interest. **Freshman Admission Requirements:** High school diploma is required and GED is accepted *Academic units required:* 4 English, 3 math, 3 science, 2 science labs, 2 foreign language, 3 social studies, *Academic units recommended:* 3 science labs. **Freshman Admission Statistics:** 14,888 applied, 78.8% admitted, 33% enrolled. **Transfer Admission Requirements:** college transcript(s), essay or personal statement, statement of good standing from prior institution(s). Minimum college GPA of 2.25 required. Lowest grade transferable D. **General Admission Information:** Application fee $60. Priority deadline 2/1. Regular application deadline 9/1. Nonfall registration accepted. Admission may be deferred for a maximum of 1 year.

COSTS AND FINANCIAL AID
Required Forms and Deadlines: FAFSA. **Notification of Awards:** Applicants will be notified of awards on a rolling basis beginning 4/1. **Types of Aid:** *Need-based scholarships/grants:* College/university scholarship or grant aid from institutional funds; Federal Pell; Private scholarships; SEOG; State scholarships/grants. *Loans:* Direct PLUS loans; Direct Subsidized Stafford Loans; Direct Unsubsidized Stafford Loans. *Student Employment:* Federal Work-Study Program available. Institutional employment available. **Financial Aid Statistics:** 81% needy freshmen, 77% needy undergrads receive need-based scholarship or grant aid. 2% freshmen, 2% undergrads receive non-need-based scholarship or grant aid. 96% freshmen, 97% undergrads receive need-based self-help aid. 2% freshmen, 2% undergrads receive athletic scholarships. 74% freshmen, 71% undergrads receive any aid. 61% undergrads borrow to pay for school. Average cumulative indebtedness $26,400. **Criteria for awarding aid:** *Need-based:* Academics, Alumni affiliation, Athletics, Job skills, Leadership, Minority status *Non-need-based:* Academics, Alumni affiliation, Athletics, Job skills, Leadership, Minority status, State/district residency.

OTIS COLLEGE OF ART AND DESIGN

9045 Lincoln Boulevard, Los Angeles, CA 90045
Phone: 310-665-6820 • **Financial Aid Phone:** 310-665-6880
E-mail: admissions@otis.edu • **CEEB Code:** 4394
Fax: 310-665-6821 • **Website:** www.otis.edu • **ACT Code:** 359

This private school was founded in 1918. It has a 5 acre campus.

RATINGS
Admissions Selectivity Rating: 72   **Fire Safety Rating:** 60*   **Green Rating:** 61

STUDENTS AND FACULTY
Enrollment: 1,088. **Student Body:** 67% female, 33% male, 22% international. Asian 29%, African American 4%, Caucasian 24%, Hispanic 10%, Native American 1%, Pacific Islander <1%, Two or more races 6%, Race unknown 4%. **Retention and Graduation:** 79% freshmen return for sophomore year. 80% grads pursue arts and sciences degrees. **Faculty:** Student/faculty ratio 4:1. 55 full-time faculty, 53% hold PhDs, 20% are members of minority groups, 55% are women. 0% of classes are taught by teaching assistants.

ACADEMICS
Degrees: Bachelor's; **Master's Classes:** Most classes have 10-19 students. Most lab/discussion sessions have 20-29 students. **Most popular majors:** Animation, Interactive Technology, Video Graphics And Special Effects; Fashion/Apparel Design; Graphic Design. **Special Study Options:** Honors program; Independent study; Internships; Liberal arts/career combination; Study abroad. Honors programs: We have an honors program for qualified

enrolled students. **Disability Services offered to physically disabled students:** Note-taking services; Reader services; Tape recorders; Tutors. **Career services:** Alumni network; Alumni services; Career assessment; Career/job search classes; Internships; Regional alumni

FACILITIES

Housing: Apartments for single students 100% of campus accessible to physically diasbled. **Special Academic Facilities/Equipment:** Art gallery, student gallery, Woodshop, Metal Shop, Photo lab, Digital Media lab, Printmaking lab, letterpress lab **Computers:** Administrative functions (other than registration) can be performed online.

CAMPUS LIFE

Environment: Metropolis **Activities:** Literary magazine; Student government; Student newspaper 7 registered organizations.

ADMISSIONS

Freshman Academic Profile: Average high school GPA 3.2. **Test Scores:** SAT Math middle 50% range 440-590. SAT EBRW middle 50% range 430-560. ACT middle 50% range 18-25. Minimum internet-based TOEFL 79. Minimum paper TOEFL 550. **Basis for Candidate Selection:** *Very important factors considered include:* rigor of secondary school record, academic GPA, standardized test scores, talent/ability. *Important factors considered include:* application essay, level of applicant's interest. *Other factors considered include:* interview, extracurricular activities, character/personal qualities, alumni/ae relation, volunteer work, work experience. **Freshman Admission Requirements:** High school diploma is required and GED is accepted *Academic units required:* 4 English, 3 math, 2 science, 1 science labs, 1 social studies, 2 history, *Academic units recommended:* 4 English, 4 math, 4 science, 4 science labs, 2 foreign language, 2 social studies, 3 history. **Freshman Admission Statistics:** 1,160 applied, 90.8% admitted, 27% enrolled. **Transfer Admission Requirements:** High school transcript, college transcript(s), essay or personal statement, statement of good standing from prior institution(s). Minimum college GPA of 2.5 required. Lowest grade transferable C. **General Admission Information:** Application fee $60. Priority deadline 2/15. Nonfall registration accepted.

COSTS AND FINANCIAL AID

Annual tuition $37,380. Room and board $11,800. Required fees $2,050. Average book expense $1,400. **Required Forms and Deadlines:** FAFSA; State aid form. **Notification of Awards:** Applicants will be notified of awards on a rolling basis beginning 3/1. **Types of Aid:** *Need-based scholarships/grants:* College/university scholarship or grant aid from institutional funds; Federal Pell; Private scholarships; SEOG; State scholarships/grants. *Loans:* Direct PLUS loans; Direct Subsidized Stafford Loans; Direct Unsubsidized Stafford Loans. *Student Employment:* Federal Work-Study Program available. Institutional employment available. **Financial Aid Statistics:** 100% needy freshmen, 99% needy undergrads receive need-based scholarship or grant aid. 38% freshmen, 28% undergrads receive non-need-based scholarship or grant aid. 82% freshmen, 87% undergrads receive need-based self-help aid. 0% freshmen, 0% undergrads receive athletic scholarships. **Criteria for awarding aid:** *Need-based:* Academics, Art, Leadership *Non-need-based:* Academics, Art.

OTTERBEIN COLLEGE

One Otterbein College, Westerville, OH 43081
Phone: 614-823-1500 • **Financial Aid Phone:** 614-823-1502
E-mail: uotterb@otterbein.edu • **CEEB Code:** 1597
Fax: 614-823-1200 • **Website:** www.otterbein.edu • **ACT Code:** 3318

This private school, affiliated with the Methodist Church, was founded in 1847. It has a 140 acre campus.

RATINGS

Admissions Selectivity Rating: 75   **Fire Safety Rating:** 60*   **Green Rating:** 60*

STUDENTS AND FACULTY

Student Body: 10% out-of-state, 2% international (12 countries represented). Asian 1%, African American 6%, Caucasian 83%, Hispanic 1%, Native American <1%, Race unknown 5%.
Retention and Graduation: 92% freshmen return for sophomore year.
Faculty: Student/faculty ratio 12:1. 161 full-time faculty, 93% hold PhDs, 11% are members of minority groups, 55% are women. 0% of classes are taught by teaching assistants.

ACADEMICS

Degrees: Bachelor's; **Master's Classes:** Most classes have 20-29 students. Most lab/discussion sessions have 10-19 students. **Most popular majors:** Education, General; Nursing/Registered Nurse (Rn, Asn, Bsn, Msn);

Business/Commerce, General. **Special Study Options:** Accelerated program; Cooperative education program; Cross-registration; Double major; Dual enrollment; Exchange student program (domestic); Honors program; Independent study; Internships; Liberal arts/career combination; Student-designed major; Study abroad; Teacher certification program; Weekend college. Honors programs: The Honors Program at Otterbein College is designed to provide intellectual stimulation and challenge for students with high academic ability and motivation. The four-year program provides the opportunity to participate in a community of students and faculty who have shared scholarly and creative interests. As part of that community students develop and complete their own Honors research and creative projects. Through the Honors seminars and Honors project, students develop advanced knowledge in their disciplinary fields and acquire the skills for independent work in their own areas of academic and professional interest. The Honors Program at Otterbein College is designed to provide intellectual stimulation and challenge for students with high academic ability and motivation. The four-year program provides the opportunity to participate in a community of students and faculty who have shared scholarly and creative interests. As part of that community students develop and complete their own Honors research and creative projects. Through the Honors seminars and Honors project, students develop advanced knowledge in their disciplinary fields and acquire the skills for independent work in their own areas of academic and professional interest. **Disability Services offered to physically disabled students:** Note-taking services; Reader services; Tape recorders; Tutors. **Career services:** Alumni network; Alumni services; Career assessment; Career/job search classes; Internships; Regional alumni

FACILITIES

Housing: Apartments for single students; Coed dorms; Fraternity/sorority housing; Men's dorms; Women's dorms **Special Academic Facilities/Equipment:** Language lab, horse stable, observatory and planetarium, Celestron 8-inch and 14-inch telescopes, 3 art galleries. **Computers:** Students can register for classes online. Administrative functions (other than registration) can be performed online.

CAMPUS LIFE

Environment: Town **Activities:** Choral groups; Concert band; Dance; Drama/theater; International Student Organization; Jazz band; Literary magazine; Marching band; Music ensembles; Musical theater; Opera; Pep band; Radio station; Student government; Student newspaper; Symphony orchestra; Television station; Yearbook 100 registered organizations, 7 fraternities, 6 sororities. **Athletics (Intercollegiate):** *Men:* baseball, basketball, cheerleading, cross-country, equestrian sports, football, golf, soccer, tennis, track/field (outdoor), track/field (indoor). *Women:* basketball, cheerleading, cross-country, equestrian sports, golf, soccer, softball, tennis, track/field (outdoor), track/field (indoor), volleyball. **On-Campus Highlights:** Clements Recreation Center, Cowen Hall- Theatre, Campus Center, Art Galleries/Art Building

ADMISSIONS

Freshman Academic Profile: Average high school GPA 3.3. 24% in top 10% of high school class, 55% in top 25% of high school class, 85% in top 50% of high school class. **Test Scores:** SAT Math middle 50% range 480-590. SAT EBRW middle 50% range 470-600. ACT middle 50% range 20-25. Minimum paper TOEFL 500. **Basis for Candidate Selection:** *Important factors considered include:* rigor of secondary school record, class rank, standardized test scores. *Other factors considered include:* application essay, recommendation(s), interview, extracurricular activities, talent/ability, character/personal qualities, alumni/ae relation, racial/ethnic status, volunteer work, work experience. **Freshman Admission Requirements:** High school diploma is required and GED is accepted *Academic units recommended:* 4 English, 3 math, 3 science, 2 foreign language, 3 social studies, 2 units from above areas or other academic areas. **Freshman Admission Statistics:** 3,381 applied, 82.0% admitted, 24% enrolled. **Transfer Admission Requirements:** college transcript(s), Minimum college GPA of 2.5 required. Lowest grade transferable c-. **General Admission Information:** Application fee $25. Priority deadline 3/1. Nonfall registration accepted. Admission may be deferred.

COSTS AND FINANCIAL AID

Annual tuition $26,319. Room and board $7,461. Average book expense $700. **Required Forms and Deadlines:** FAFSA. **Types of Aid:** *Need-based scholarships/grants:* College/university scholarship or grant aid from institutional funds; Federal Pell; Private scholarships; SEOG; State scholarships/grants. *Loans:* Direct PLUS loans; Direct Subsidized Stafford Loans; Direct Unsubsidized Stafford Loans. *Student Employment:* Federal Work-Study Program available. Institutional employment available. **Criteria for awarding aid:** *Non-need-based:* Academics, Alumni affiliation, Art, Leadership, Minority status, Music/drama, Religious affiliation.

OUACHITA BAPTIST UNIVERSITY

410 Ouachita St, Arkadelphia, AR 71998-0001
Phone: 870-245-5110 • **Financial Aid Phone:** 870-245-5587
E-mail: admissions@alpha.obu.edu • **CEEB Code:** 6549
Fax: 870-245-5500 • **Website:** www.obu.edu • **ACT Code:** 134

This private school, affiliated with the Arkansas Baptist State Convention Church, was founded in 1886. It has a 200 acre campus.

RATINGS
Admissions Selectivity Rating: 84   **Fire Safety Rating:** 94   **Green Rating:** 60*

STUDENTS AND FACULTY
Enrollment: 1,513. **Student Body:** 55% female, 45% male, 32% out-of-state, 2% international (36 countries represented). Asian <1%, African American 8%, Caucasian 82%, Hispanic 5%, Native American <1%, Pacific Islander <1%, Two or more races 2%, Race unknown 0%.
Retention and Graduation: 79% freshmen return for sophomore year. 54% freshmen graduate within 4 years. 64% freshmen graduate within 6 years. 44% grads go on to further study within 1 year. 22% grads pursue arts and sciences degrees. 2% grads pursue law degrees. 2% grads pursue business degrees. 13% grads pursue medical degrees. **Faculty:** Student/faculty ratio 12:1. 99 full-time faculty, 91% hold PhDs, 4% are members of minority groups, 36% are women. 0% of classes are taught by teaching assistants.

ACADEMICS
Degrees: Associate; Bachelor's **Most popular majors:** Mass Communication/Media Studies; Biology/Biological Sciences, General; Business Administration And Management, General. **Special Study Options:** Cross-registration; Distance learning; Double major; English as a Second Language (ESL); Honors program; Independent study; Internships; Study abroad; Teacher certification program. Honors programs: The Carl Goodson Honors Program involves 7-8 percent of all students in ongoing writing and research activities. **Disability Services offered to physically disabled students:** Note-taking services; Reader services; Tape recorders; Tutors. **Career services:** Alumni network; Alumni services; Career assessment; Career/job search classes; Internships

FACILITIES
Housing: Apartments for married students; Apartments for single students; Men's dorms; Special housing for disabled student; Women's dorms 95% of campus accessible to physically disabled. **Special Academic Facilities/Equipment:** Historical archives, Senator John McClellan collection, language lab, TV studio. **Computers:** 100% of classrooms, 100% of dorms, 100% of libraries, 100% of dining areas, 100% of student union, 50% of common outdoor areas have wireless network access. Administrative functions (other than registration) can be performed online.

CAMPUS LIFE
Environment: Village **Activities:** Campus Ministries; Choral groups; Concert band; Dance; Drama/theater; International Student Organization; Jazz band; Literary magazine; Marching band; Model UN; Music ensembles; Musical theater; Opera; Pep band; Student government; Student newspaper; Television station; Yearbook 60 registered organizations, 8 honor societies, 4 religious organizations. 5 fraternities, 5 sororities. **Athletics (Intercollegiate):** *Men:* baseball, basketball, diving, football, golf, soccer, swimming, tennis, wrestling. *Women:* basketball, cross-country, diving, golf, soccer, softball, swimming, tennis, volleyball. **On-Campus Highlights:** Starbuck's, Chick-fil-A, Commons (dining), Food Court, Evans Student Center **Environmental Initiatives:** Employment of Energy Management Director

ADMISSIONS
Freshman Academic Profile: Average high school GPA 3.6. 36% in top 10% of high school class, 64% in top 25% of high school class, 86% in top 50% of high school class. 86% from public high schools. **Test Scores:** SAT Math middle 50% range 480-620. SAT EBRW middle 50% range 540-640. ACT middle 50% range 21-28. Minimum internet-based TOEFL 80. Minimum paper TOEFL 550. **Basis for Candidate Selection:** *Very important factors considered include:* rigor of secondary school record, academic GPA, standardized test scores. *Other factors considered include:* talent/ability, character/personal qualities. **Freshman Admission Requirements:** High school diploma is required and GED is accepted *Academic units required:* 4 English, 2 math, 2 science, 1 social studies, 2 history, 4 academic electives, *Academic units recommended:* 4 English, 3 math, 3 science, 2 foreign language, 1 social studies, 2 history, 4 academic electives. **Freshman Admission Statistics:** 1,786 applied, 70.9% admitted, 37% enrolled. **Transfer Admission Requirements:** college transcript(s), statement of good standing from prior institution(s). Minimum college GPA of 2.0 required. Lowest grade transferable C. **General Admission Information:** Priority deadline 12/1. Nonfall registration accepted. Admission may be deferred for a maximum of 1 year.

COSTS AND FINANCIAL AID
Annual tuition $26,200. Room and board $7,880. Required fees $590. Average book expense $1,100. **Required Forms and Deadlines:** FAFSA; State aid form. **Notification of Awards:** Applicants will be notified of awards on a rolling basis beginning 11/1. **Types of Aid:** *Need-based scholarships/grants:* College/university scholarship or grant aid from institutional funds; Federal Pell; Private scholarships; SEOG; State scholarships/grants. *Loans:* Direct PLUS loans; Direct Subsidized Stafford Loans; Direct Unsubsidized Stafford Loans. *Student Employment:* Federal Work-Study Program available. **Financial Aid Statistics:** 99% needy freshmen, 98% needy undergrads receive need-based scholarship or grant aid. 22% freshmen, 23% undergrads receive non-need-based scholarship or grant aid. 83% freshmen, 71% undergrads receive need-based self-help aid. 8% freshmen, 8% undergrads receive athletic scholarships. 98% freshmen, 96% undergrads receive any aid. 51% undergrads borrow to pay for school. Average cumulative indebtedness $26,648. **Criteria for awarding aid:** *Non-need-based:* Academics, Alumni affiliation, Art, Athletics, Job skills, Leadership, Minority status, Music/drama, Religious affiliation, State/district residency.

OUR LADY OF THE LAKE UNIVERSITY (OLLU)

411 S.W. 24th Street, San Antonio, TX 78207-4689
Phone: 210-431-3961 • **Financial Aid Phone:** 800-324-4310
E-mail: webmaster@ollusa.edu • **CEEB Code:** 6550
Fax: 210-431-4036 • **Website:** www.ollusa.edu • **ACT Code:** 4140

This private school, affiliated with the Roman Catholic Church, was founded in 1895. It has a 75 acre campus.

RATINGS
Admissions Selectivity Rating: 84   **Fire Safety Rating:** 64   **Green Rating:** 60*

STUDENTS AND FACULTY
Enrollment: 1,554. **Student Body:** 73% female, 27% male, 2% out-of-state, 1% international. Asian 1%, African American 8%, Caucasian 17%, Hispanic 63%, Native American 1%, Pacific Islander <1%, Two or more races 1%, Race unknown 8%.
Retention and Graduation: 60% freshmen return for sophomore year. 30% grads go on to further study within 1 year. **Faculty:** Student/faculty ratio 15:1. 101 full-time faculty, 80% hold PhDs, 35% are members of minority groups, 60% are women. 0% of classes are taught by teaching assistants.

ACADEMICS
Degrees: Bachelor's; Doctoral/Professional; Doctoral/Research; Master's; Post-Bachelor's certificate; Post-Master's certificate **Classes:** Most classes have 20-29 students. **Most popular majors:** Biology/Biological Sciences, General; Psychology, General; Business Administration And Management, General. **Special Study Options:** Accelerated program; Cooperative education program; Cross-registration; Distance learning; Double major; Dual enrollment; Exchange student program (domestic); Honors program; Independent study; Internships; Study abroad; Teacher certification program; Weekend college. **Disability Services offered to physically disabled students:** Note-taking services; Reader services; Tape recorders; Tutors. **Career services:** Alumni services; Career assessment; Internships

FACILITIES
Housing: Coed dorms; Men's dorms; Theme housing; Women's dorms 99% of campus accessible to physically disabled. **Special Academic Facilities/Equipment:** Lab school for children with language and learning disabilities, elementary demonstration school, intercultural institute for training and research, language lab. **Computers:**

CAMPUS LIFE
Activities: Campus Ministries; Choral groups; Dance; Drama/theater; International Student Organization; Jazz band; Literary magazine; Music ensembles; Musical theater; Pep band; Student government; Student newspaper; Student-run film society; Symphony orchestra; Television station; Yearbook. Main Building, Flores Cyber Cafe, Constantineau Chapel, Lake Elmendorf, Sister Elizabeth Anne Sueltenfuss Library

ADMISSIONS
Freshman Academic Profile: Average high school GPA 3.3. 22% in top 10% of high school class, 49% in top 25% of high school class, 82% in top 50% of high school class. **Test Scores:** SAT Math middle 50% range 410-513. SAT EBRW middle 50% range 400-500. ACT middle 50% range 17-21. Minimum internet-based TOEFL 79. Minimum paper TOEFL 650. **Basis for Candidate Selection:** *Other factors considered include:* rigor of secondary school record, class rank, academic GPA, application essay, standardized test

scores, recommendation(s), talent/ability, volunteer work, work experience. **Freshman Admission Requirements:** High school diploma is required and GED is accepted *Academic units required:* 4 English, 3 math, 2 science, 3 social studies, and 2 units from above areas or other academic areas. **Freshman Admission Statistics:** 2,109 applied, 48.6% admitted, 29% enrolled. **Transfer Admission Requirements:** college transcript(s), Minimum college GPA of 2.0 required. Lowest grade transferable D. **General Admission Information:** Application fee $25. Nonfall registration accepted. Admission may be deferred for a maximum of 1 year.

COSTS AND FINANCIAL AID
Annual tuition $22,256. Room and board $7,327. Required fees $456. Average book expense $1,200. **Required Forms and Deadlines:** FAFSA; Institution's own financial aid form. **Notification of Awards:** Applicants will be notified of awards on a rolling basis beginning 3/31. **Types of Aid:** *Need-based scholarships/grants:* College/university scholarship or grant aid from institutional funds; Federal Pell; Private scholarships; SEOG; State scholarships/grants. *Loans:* Direct PLUS loans; Direct Subsidized Stafford Loans; Direct Unsubsidized Stafford Loans. *Student Employment:* Federal Work-Study Program available. Institutional employment available. **Financial Aid Statistics:** 99% needy freshmen, 96% needy undergrads receive need-based scholarship or grant aid. 3% freshmen, 6% undergrads receive non-need-based scholarship or grant aid. 71% freshmen, 84% undergrads receive need-based self-help aid. 5% freshmen, 7% undergrads receive athletic scholarships. 91% freshmen, 89% undergrads receive any aid. **Criteria for awarding aid:** *Non-need-based:* Academics, Alumni affiliation, Art, Leadership, Music/drama.

PACE UNIVERSITY

1 Pace Plaza, New York, NY 10038
Phone: 212-346-1323 • **Financial Aid Phone:** 212-346-1309
E-mail: ugnyc@pace.edu • **CEEB Code:** 2635
Fax: 212-346-1040 • **Website:** www.pace.edu • **ACT Code:** 2852

This private school was founded in 1906.

RATINGS
Admissions Selectivity Rating: 76   **Fire Safety Rating:** 91   **Green Rating:** 65

STUDENTS AND FACULTY
Enrollment: 8,456. **Student Body:** 61% female, 39% male, 41% out-of-state, 10% international (98 countries represented). Asian 8%, African American 11%, Caucasian 51%, Hispanic 13%, Native American <1%, Pacific Islander <1%, Two or more races 4%, Race unknown 2%.
Retention and Graduation: 80% freshmen return for sophomore year. 39% freshmen graduate within 4 years. 54% freshmen graduate within 6 years. 11% grads go on to further study within 1 year. **Faculty:** Student/faculty ratio 14:1. 518 full-time faculty, 85% hold PhDs, 22% are members of minority groups, 52% are women. 0% of classes are taught by teaching assistants.

ACADEMICS
Degrees: Associate; Bachelor's; Certificate; Doctoral; Doctoral/Professional; Doctoral/Research; Master's; Post-Bachelor's certificate; Post-Master's certificate **Classes:** Most classes have 10-19 students. Most lab/discussion sessions have 10-19 students. **Most popular majors:** Registered Nursing/Registered Nurse; Accounting; Finance, General. **Special Study Options:** Accelerated program; Cooperative education program; Cross-registration; Distance learning; Double major; Dual enrollment; English as a Second Language (ESL); Honors program; Independent study; Internships; Study abroad; Teacher certification program. Honors programs: Pforzheimer Honors College for incoming freshmen. Combined degree programs: BA/JD; BA/MA. **Disability Services offered to physically disabled students:** Note-taking services; Reader services; Tape recorders. **Career services:** Alumni network; Alumni services; Career assessment; Career/job search classes; Internships; Regional alumni

FACILITIES
Housing: Apartments for single students; Coed dorms; Theme housing; Wellness housing 80% of campus accessible to physically diasbled. **Special Academic Facilities/Equipment:** Schimmel Center at Pace University, Laboratory Theatre, Communication Center, Language Center, Art Galleries,

Environmental Center, English Language Institute. **Computers:** 20% of classrooms, 10% of dorms, 100% of libraries, 100% of dining areas, 100% of student union, have wireless network access. Students can register for classes online. Administrative functions (other than registration) can be performed online.

CAMPUS LIFE
Environment: Metropolis **Activities:** Choral groups; Dance; Drama/theater; International Student Organization; Literary magazine; Model UN; Musical theater; Radio station; Student government; Student newspaper; Student-run film society; Television station; Yearbook 79 registered organizations, 25 honor societies, 4 religious organizations. 11 fraternities, 9 sororities. **Athletics (Intercollegiate):** *Men:* baseball, basketball, cross-country, football, golf, lacrosse, swimming, tennis, track/field (outdoor), track/field (indoor). *Women:* basketball, cheerleading, cross-country, equestrian sports, soccer, softball, swimming, tennis, track/field (outdoor), track/field (indoor), volleyball. **On-Campus Highlights:** Student Union, Fitness Center, Theater, Library, Residence Halls **Environmental Initiatives:** Environmental Law Program—Pace Law School

ADMISSIONS
Freshman Academic Profile: Average high school GPA 3.3. 16% in top 10% of high school class, 42% in top 25% of high school class, 75% in top 50% of high school class. 75% from public high schools. **Test Scores:** SAT Math middle 50% range 510-600. SAT EBRW middle 50% range 530-620. ACT middle 50% range 21-27. Minimum internet-based TOEFL 80. Minimum paper TOEFL 550. **Basis for Candidate Selection:** *Very important factors considered include:* rigor of secondary school record, application essay, standardized test scores. *Important factors considered include:* class rank, academic GPA, recommendation(s). *Other factors considered include:* interview, extracurricular activities, talent/ability, character/personal qualities, alumni/ae relation, volunteer work, work experience. **Freshman Admission Requirements:** High school diploma is required and GED is accepted *Academic units required:* 4 English, 3 math, 2 science labs, 2 foreign language, 3 history, 2 academic electives. **Freshman Admission Statistics:** 20,944 applied, 79.6% admitted, 12% enrolled. **Transfer Admission Requirements:** college transcript(s), statement of good standing from prior institution(s). Minimum college GPA of 2.5 required. Lowest grade transferable C. **General Admission Information:** Application fee $50. Priority deadline 2/15. Nonfall registration accepted. Admission may be deferred for a maximum of 1 year.

COSTS AND FINANCIAL AID
Annual tuition $42,354. Room and board $18,002. Required fees $1,632. Average book expense $800. **Required Forms and Deadlines:** FAFSA. **Notification of Awards:** Applicants will be notified of awards on a rolling basis beginning 12/1. **Types of Aid:** *Need-based scholarships/grants:* College/university scholarship or grant aid from institutional funds; Federal Nursing Scholarships; Federal Pell; Private scholarships; SEOG; State scholarships/grants. *Loans:* Direct PLUS loans; Direct Subsidized Stafford Loans; Direct Unsubsidized Stafford Loans. *Student Employment:* Federal Work-Study Program available. Institutional employment available. **Financial Aid Statistics:** 100% needy freshmen, 99% needy undergrads receive need-based scholarship or grant aid. 13% freshmen, 10% undergrads receive non-need-based scholarship or grant aid. 80% freshmen, 80% undergrads receive need-based self-help aid. 0% freshmen, 0% undergrads receive athletic scholarships. 92% freshmen, 85% undergrads receive any aid. 75% undergrads borrow to pay for school. Average cumulative indebtedness $33,749. **Criteria for awarding aid:** *Need-based:* Academics *Non-need-based:* Academics, Alumni affiliation, Athletics, Music/drama.

PACIFIC LUTHERAN UNIVERSITY

1010 S 122nd St, Tacoma, WA 98447
Phone: 253-535-7151 • **Financial Aid Phone:** 253-535-7134
E-mail: admissions@plu.edu • **CEEB Code:** 4597
Fax: 253-536-5136 • **Website:** www.plu.edu • **ACT Code:** 4597

This private school, affiliated with the Lutheran Church, was founded in 1890. It has a 156 acre campus.

RATINGS
Admissions Selectivity Rating: 78   **Fire Safety Rating:** 93   **Green Rating:** 60*

STUDENTS AND FACULTY
Enrollment: 2,676. **Student Body:** 63% female, 37% male, 22% out-of-state, 3% international (21 countries represented). Asian 10%, African American 3%, Caucasian 63%, Hispanic 9%, Native American 1%, Pacific Islander 1%, Two or more races 9%, Race unknown 1%.

Retention and Graduation: 83% freshmen return for sophomore year. 56% freshmen graduate within 4 years. 70% freshmen graduate within 6 years. 14% grads go on to further study within 1 year. **Faculty:** Student/faculty ratio 11:1. 223 full-time faculty, 91% hold PhDs, 17% are members of minority groups, 52% are women. 0% of classes are taught by teaching assistants.

ACADEMICS

Degrees: Bachelor's; Doctoral/Professional; Master's; Post-Bachelor's certificate; Post-Master's certificate **Classes:** Most classes have 10-19 students. Most lab/discussion sessions have 10-19 students. **Most popular majors:** Social Sciences, General; Registered Nursing/Registered Nurse; Business Administration And Management, General. **Special Study Options:** Cooperative education program; Cross-registration; Distance learning; Double major; Dual enrollment; English as a Second Language (ESL); Exchange student program (domestic); Honors program; Independent study; Internships; Liberal arts/career combination; Student-designed major; Study abroad; Teacher certification program. Honors programs: International Honors Program Combined degree programs: BA/MEng. **Disability Services offered to physically disabled students:** Note-taking services; Reader services; Tape recorders; Tutors. **Career services:** Alumni network; Alumni services; Career assessment; Career/job search classes; Internships; Regional alumni

FACILITIES

Housing: Apartments for married students; Apartments for single students; Coed dorms; Special housing for disabled student; Special housing for international students; Theme housing; Women's dorms 90% of campus accessible to physically diasbled. **Special Academic Facilities/Equipment:** Mary Baker Russell Music Center Wekell Art Gallery Keck Observatory Carol Sheffels Quigg Greenhouse Rieke Science Center Scandinavian Cultural Center Morken Center for Learning and Technology Karen Hille Phillips Center for the Performing Arts **Computers:** 25% of classrooms, 25% of dorms, 100% of libraries, 100% of dining areas, 100% of student union, 25% of common outdoor areas have wireless network access. Students can register for classes online.

CAMPUS LIFE

Environment: City **Activities:** Campus Ministries; Choral groups; Concert band; Dance; Drama/theater; International Student Organization; Jazz band; Literary magazine; Model UN; Music ensembles; Musical theater; Opera; Pep band; Radio station; Student government; Student newspaper; Student-run film society; Symphony orchestra; Television station 67 registered organizations, 6 honor societies, 8 religious organizations. **Athletics (Intercollegiate):** *Men:* baseball, basketball, cheerleading, crew/rowing, cross-country, football, golf, soccer, swimming, tennis, track/field (outdoor), track/field (indoor). *Women:* basketball, cheerleading, crew/rowing, cross-country, golf, soccer, softball, swimming, tennis, track/field (outdoor), track/field (indoor), volleyball. **On-Campus Highlights:** Keck Observatory, Rieke Science Center, Mary Baker Russell Music Center, Wekell Art Gallery, Karen Hille Phillips Center for the Performing Arts **Environmental Initiatives:** Successfully building a community commitment to sustainability that encompasses students, faculty and staff in part through sustainability fellowships.

ADMISSIONS

Freshman Academic Profile: Average high school GFA 3.7. **Test Scores:** SAT Math middle 50% range 520-630. SAT EBRW middle 50% range 520-640. ACT middle 50% range 21-27. **Basis for Candidate Selection:** *Very important factors considered include:* rigor of secondary school record, application essay. *Important factors considered include:* class rank, academic GPA, standardized test scores, recommendation(s), extracurricular activities, talent/ability, character/personal qualities, volunteer work. *Other factors considered include:* interview, first generation, alumni/ae relation, geographical residence, state residency, religious affiliation/commitment, racial/ethnic status, work experience. **Freshman Admission Requirements:** High school diploma is required and GED is accepted *Academic units required:* 2 math, 2 foreign language, *Academic units recommended:* 4 English, 3 math, 2 science, 2 science labs, 2 foreign language, 2 social studies, 3 academic electives, 1 visual/performing arts. **Freshman Admission Statistics:** 3,629 applied, 75.4% admitted, 23% enrolled. **Transfer Admission Requirements:** High school transcript, college transcript(s), essay or personal statement, statement of good standing from prior institution(s). Minimum college GPA of 2.5 required. Lowest grade transferable C-. **General Admission Information:** Application fee $40. Priority deadline 2/1. Nonfall registration accepted. Admission may be deferred for a maximum of 2 years.

COSTS AND FINANCIAL AID

Annual tuition $41,696. Room and board $10,790. Required fees $370. Average book expense $870. **Required Forms and Deadlines:** FAFSA. **Notification of Awards:** Applicants will be notified of awards on a rolling basis beginning 12/16. **Types of Aid:** *Need-based scholarships/grants:* College/university scholarship or grant aid from institutional funds; Federal Nursing Scholarships; Federal Pell; Private scholarships; SEOG; State scholarships/grants. *Loans:* Direct PLUS loans; Direct Subsidized Stafford Loans; Direct Unsubsidized

Stafford Loans. *Student Employment:* Federal Work-Study Program available. Institutional employment available. **Financial Aid Statistics:** 99% needy freshmen, 99% needy undergrads receive need-based scholarship or grant aid. 87% freshmen, 87% undergrads receive non-need-based scholarship or grant aid. 78% freshmen, 85% undergrads receive need-based self-help aid. 0% freshmen, 0% undergrads receive athletic scholarships. 99% freshmen, 97% undergrads receive any aid. 74% undergrads borrow to pay for school. Average cumulative indebtedness $32,862. **Criteria for awarding aid:** *Need-based:* Academics *Non-need-based:* Academics, Alumni affiliation, Art, Leadership, Music/drama, Religious affiliation, State/district residency.

PACIFIC STATES UNIVERSITY

3450 Wilshire blvd, Los Angeles, CA 90010
Phone: 323-731-2383 EXT:203
E-mail: admissions@psuca.edu
Fax: 323-731-7276 • **Website:** www.psuca.edu

This private school was founded in 1928.

RATINGS

Admissions Selectivity Rating: 69   **Fire Safety Rating:** 60*   **Green Rating:** 60*

STUDENTS AND FACULTY

Enrollment: 14. **Student Body:** 29% female, 71% male, 5% out-of-state, 57% international. Asian 14%, African American 7%, Caucasian 7%, Hispanic 0%, Native American 0%, Race unknown 14%.
Retention and Graduation: 100% freshmen return for sophomore year.
Faculty: Student/faculty ratio 6:1. 7 full-time faculty, 43% hold PhDs, 29% are women.

ACADEMICS

Degrees: Bachelor's; Doctoral/Research; Master's; Post-Bachelor's certificate **Classes:** Most classes have 10-19 students. **Special Study Options:** Distance learning; Double major; English as a Second Language (ESL); Independent study.

FACILITIES

Housing: Coed dorms

CAMPUS LIFE

Environment: Metropolis **Activities:** International Student Organization; Television station; Yearbook.

ADMISSIONS

Basis for Candidate Selection: *Important factors considered include:* standardized test scores. *Other factors considered include:* rigor of secondary school record, academic GPA, application essay, level of applicant's interest. **Freshman Admission Requirements:** High school diploma is required and GED is accepted **Freshman Admission Statistics:** applied, admitted, 100% enrolled. **Transfer Admission Requirements:** college transcript(s), Minimum college GPA of 2.5 required. Lowest grade transferable C. **General Admission Information:** Application fee $100. Nonfall registration accepted.

COSTS AND FINANCIAL AID

Annual tuition $14,055. Required fees $540. Average book expense $1,800. **Required Forms and Deadlines:** FAFSA. **Types of Aid:** *Need-based scholarships/grants:* Federal Pell. *Loans:* Direct Subsidized Stafford Loans; Direct Unsubsidized Stafford Loans.

PACIFIC UNION COLLEGE

One Angwin Avenue, Angwin, CA 94508
Phone: 707-965-6336 • **Financial Aid Phone:** 707-965-7200
E-mail: enroll@puc.edu • **CEEB Code:** 4600
Fax: 707-965-6671 • **Website:** www.puc.edu • **ACT Code:** 362

This private school, affiliated with the Seventh Day Adventist Church, was founded in 1882. It has a 200 acre campus.

RATINGS

Admissions Selectivity Rating: 85   **Fire Safety Rating:** 89   **Green Rating:** 60*

STUDENTS AND FACULTY

Enrollment: 1,508. **Student Body:** 58% female, 42% male, 14% out-of-state, 3% international (21 countries represented). Asian 19%, African American 9%, Caucasian 26%, Hispanic 28%, Native American <1%, Pacific Islander 2%, Two or more races 7%, Race unknown 5%.

Retention and Graduation: 77% freshmen return for sophomore year. **Faculty:** Student/faculty ratio 14:1. 94 full-time faculty, 52% hold PhDs, 26% are members of minority groups, 50% are women. 0% of classes are taught by teaching assistants.

ACADEMICS

Degrees: Associate; Bachelor's; Certificate; Master's; Terminal Associate; Transfer Associate **Classes:** Most classes have 10-19 students. Most lab/discussion sessions have 20-29 students. **Most popular majors:** Biology/Biological Sciences, General; Registered Nursing/Registered Nurse; Business/Commerce, General. **Special Study Options:** Cooperative education program; Double major; Honors program; Independent study; Internships; Liberal arts/career combination; Study abroad; Teacher certification program. Honors programs: The Honors Program offers an alternative general-education program for academically motivated students. There are no other general education requirements. Students fulfilling the Honors Program graduate "With Honors." **Disability Services offered to physically disabled students:** Note-taking services; Reader services; Tape recorders; Tutors. **Career services:** Alumni network; Career assessment; Career/job search classes; Internships

FACILITIES

Housing: Apartments for married students; Men's dorms; Wellness housing; Women's dorms 80% of campus accessible to physically disabled. **Special Academic Facilities/Equipment:** Flight training facility, observatory, art gallery, natural history collection, Pitcairn Island studies center, on-campus elementary and high schools, airport. **Computers:** Students can register for classes online. Administrative functions (other than registration) can be performed online.

CAMPUS LIFE

Environment: Rural **Activities:** Campus Ministries; Choral groups; Concert band; Drama/theater; Jazz band; Literary magazine; Music ensembles; Student government; Student newspaper; Student-run film society; Symphony orchestra; Yearbook 24 registered organizations, 8 honor societies. **Athletics (Intercollegiate):** Men: basketball, cross-country, volleyball. Women: basketball, cross-country, volleyball. **On-Campus Highlights:** Campus Center, Learning Commons, Pacific Auditorium (Gym), Paulin Auditorium (Music), 1500 acres of hiking/biking land **Environmental Initiatives:** Buy Locally (50%)

ADMISSIONS

Freshman Academic Profile: Average high school GPA 3.3. 31% from public high schools. **Test Scores:** SAT Math middle 50% range 430-570. SAT EBRW middle 50% range 420-560. ACT middle 50% range 18-23. Minimum internet-based TOEFL 70. Minimum paper TOEFL 525. **Basis for Candidate Selection:** Very important factors considered include: academic GPA, recommendation(s). Important factors considered include: rigor of secondary school record, standardized test scores, character/personal qualities, level of applicant's interest. Other factors considered include: class rank, interview, extracurricular activities, talent/ability, religious affiliation/commitment. **Freshman Admission Requirements:** High school diploma is required and GED is accepted Academic units required: 4 English, 2 math, 2 science, 2 history, Academic units recommended: 4 English, 3 math, 3 science, 2 foreign language, 2 history, 1 computer science, 1 unit from above areas or other academic areas. **Freshman Admission Statistics:** 2,041 applied, 45.2% admitted, 27% enrolled. **Transfer Admission Requirements:** High school transcript, college transcript(s), Minimum college GPA of 2.0 required. Lowest grade transferable C-. **General Admission Information:** Application fee $30. Nonfall registration accepted. Admission may be deferred for a maximum of 1 year.

COSTS AND FINANCIAL AID

Annual tuition $27,999. Room and board $7,695. Required fees $315. Average book expense $1,764. **Required Forms and Deadlines:** FAFSA; Institution's own financial aid form. **Notification of Awards:** Applicants will be notified of awards on a rolling basis beginning 4/1. **Types of Aid:** Need-based scholarships/grants: College/university scholarship or grant aid from institutional funds; Federal Pell; Private scholarships; SEOG; State scholarships/grants. Loans: Direct PLUS loans; Direct Subsidized Stafford Loans; Direct Unsubsidized Stafford Loans. Student Employment: Federal Work-Study Program available. Institutional employment available. **Financial Aid Statistics:** 100% needy freshmen, 100% needy undergrads receive need-based scholarship or grant aid. 39% freshmen, 31% undergrads receive non-need-based scholarship or grant aid. 95% freshmen, 97% undergrads receive need-based self-help aid. 2% freshmen, 0% undergrads receive athletic scholarships. **Criteria for awarding aid:** Need-based: Academics Non-need-based: Academics, Art, Athletics, Leadership, Music/drama, Religious affiliation.

PACIFIC UNIVERSITY

2043 College Way, Forest Grove, OR 97116
Phone: 503-352-2218 • **Financial Aid Phone:** (503) 352-2222
E-mail: admissions@pacificu.edu • **CEEB Code:** 4601
Fax: 503-352-2975 • **Website:** www.pacificu.edu

This private school was founded in 1849. It has a 60 acre campus.

RATINGS

Admissions Selectivity Rating: 76   **Fire Safety Rating:** 82   **Green Rating:** 60*

STUDENTS AND FACULTY

Enrollment: 1,884. **Student Body:** 60% female, 40% male, 55% out-of-state, 2% international (32 countries represented). Asian 12%, African American 2%, Caucasian 52%, Hispanic 13%, Native American 1%, Pacific Islander 3%, Two or more races 12%, Race unknown 4%.

Retention and Graduation: 77% freshmen return for sophomore year. 24% grads go on to further study within 1 year. 11% grads pursue arts and sciences degrees. 4% grads pursue law degrees. 2% grads pursue business degrees. 2% grads pursue medical degrees. **Faculty:** Student/faculty ratio 10:1. 216 full-time faculty, 87% hold PhDs, 13% are members of minority groups, 51% are women. 0% of classes are taught by teaching assistants.

ACADEMICS

Degrees: Bachelor's; Doctoral; Doctoral/Professional; Doctoral/Research; Master's; Post-Bachelor's certificate; Post-Master's certificate **Classes:** Most classes have 20-29 students. **Most popular majors:** Biology/Biological Sciences, General; Kinesiology And Exercise Science; Business Administration And Management, General. **Special Study Options:** Accelerated program; Cross-registration; Distance learning; Double major; Dual enrollment; English as a Second Language (ESL); Independent study; Internships; Study abroad; Teacher certification program. **Disability Services offered to physically disabled students:** Note-taking services; Reader services; Tape recorders; Tutors. **Career services:** Alumni network; Alumni services; Career assessment; Career/job search classes; Internships; Regional alumni

FACILITIES

Housing: Apartments for single students; Coed dorms; Special housing for disabled students **Special Academic Facilities/Equipment:** State history museum, performing arts center, media center, humanitarian center, Holocaust resource center, politics/law forum, Berglund Center for Internet Studies, electron microscopes. **Computers:** 100% of classrooms, 100% of dorms, 100% of libraries, 100% of dining areas, 100% of student union, 90% of common outdoor areas have wireless network access. Administrative functions (other than registration) can be performed online.

CAMPUS LIFE

Environment: Village **Activities:** Campus Ministries; Choral groups; Concert band; Dance; Drama/theater; International Student Organization; Jazz band; Literary magazine; Music ensembles; Pep band; Radio station; Student government; Student newspaper; Student-run film society; Symphony orchestra 58 registered organizations, 2 honor societies, 4 religious organizations. 3 fraternities, 4 sororities. **Athletics (Intercollegiate):** Men: baseball, basketball, cross-country, golf, soccer, swimming, tennis, track/field (outdoor), wrestling. Women: basketball, cross-country, golf, lacrosse, soccer, softball, swimming, tennis, track/field (outdoor), volleyball, wrestling. **On-Campus Highlights:** Pacific Athletic Center, Pacific Library (New Library), Marsh Hall, Old College Hall, New Bookstore/Vera's Cafe **Environmental Initiatives:** Sustainability Committee

ADMISSIONS

Freshman Academic Profile: Average high school GPA 3.6. 88% from public high schools. **Test Scores:** SAT Math middle 50% range 500-600. SAT EBRW middle 50% range 490-590. ACT middle 50% range 21-26. Minimum paper TOEFL 550. **Basis for Candidate Selection:** Very important factors considered include: rigor of secondary school record, academic GPA, standardized test scores, recommendation(s), extracurricular activities, character/personal qualities, volunteer work, level of applicant's interest. Important factors considered include: class rank, application essay, talent/ability. Other factors considered include: first generation, alumni/ae relation, work experience. **Freshman Admission Requirements:** High school diploma is required and GED is accepted Academic units recommended: 4 English, 3 math, 3 science, 1 science labs, 2 foreign language, 3 social studies, 1 history, 4 academic electives. **Freshman Admission Statistics:** 3,004 applied, 79.0% admitted, 20% enrolled. **Transfer Admission Requirements:** college transcript(s), essay or personal statement, statement of good standing from prior institution(s). Minimum college GPA of 2.70 required. Lowest grade transferable C-. **General Admission Information:** Application fee $40. Priority deadline 2/15. Regular application deadline 8/15. Nonfall registration accepted. Admission may be deferred for a maximum of 2 years.

COSTS AND FINANCIAL AID

Annual tuition $40,120. Room and board $11,822. Required fees $934. Average book expense $1,050. **Required Forms and Deadlines:** FAFSA. **Notification of Awards:** Applicants will be notified of awards on a rolling basis beginning 3/15. **Types of Aid:** *Need-based scholarships/grants:* College/university scholarship or grant aid from institutional funds; Federal Pell; Private scholarships; SEOG; State scholarships/grants. *Loans:* Direct PLUS loans; Direct Subsidized Stafford Loans; Direct Unsubsidized Stafford Loans. *Student Employment:* Federal Work-Study Program available. Institutional employment available. **Financial Aid Statistics:** 97% needy freshmen, 72% needy undergrads receive need-based scholarship or grant aid. 97% freshmen, 92% undergrads receive non-need-based scholarship or grant aid. 84% freshmen, 84% undergrads receive need-based self-help aid. 0% freshmen, 0% undergrads receive athletic scholarships. 93% freshmen, 93% undergrads receive any aid. 79% undergrads borrow to pay for school. Average cumulative indebtedness $30,081. **Criteria for awarding aid:** *Need-based:* Academics, Leadership *Non-need-based:* Academics, Alumni affiliation, Art, Music/drama.

PALM BEACH ATLANTIC UNIVERSITY

PO Box 24708, West Palm Beach, FL 33416-4708
Phone: 561-803-2100 • **Financial Aid Phone:** 561-803-2126
E-mail: admit@pba.edu • **CEEB Code:** 5553
Fax: 561-803-2115 • **Website:** www.pba.edu • **ACT Code:** 739

This private school, affiliated with the Christian (Nondenominational) Church, was founded in 1968. It has a 25 acre campus.

RATINGS

Admissions Selectivity Rating: 73   **Fire Safety Rating:** 60*   **Green Rating:** 60*

STUDENTS AND FACULTY

Enrollment: 2,475. **Student Body:** 65% female, 35% male, 34% out-of-state, 3% international (28 countries represented). Asian 2%, African American 11%, Caucasian 62%, Hispanic 16%, Native American <1%, Pacific Islander <1%, Two or more races 3%, Race unknown 2%.
Retention and Graduation: 76% freshmen return for sophomore year. 43% freshmen graduate within 4 years. 54% freshmen graduate within 6 years.
Faculty: Student/faculty ratio 12:1. 171 full-time faculty, 81% hold PhDs, 15% are members of minority groups, 44% are women. 0% of classes are taught by teaching assistants.

ACADEMICS

Degrees: Bachelor's; Doctoral/Professional; **Master's Classes:** Most classes have 20-29 students. Most lab/discussion sessions have 10-19 students. **Most popular majors:** Education, General; Psychology, General; Accounting And Business/Management. **Special Study Options:** Accelerated program; Distance learning; Double major; Dual enrollment; Honors program; Independent study; Internships; Student-designed major; Study abroad; Teacher certification program. Honors programs: The Frederick M. Supper Honors Program exists to establish a community of scholars. The program encourages students to develop a thoughtful and insightful Christian worldview through enduring conversation to enable students to live the examined life and to facilitate character formation. **Career services:** Alumni network; Alumni services; Career assessment; Career/job search classes; Internships

FACILITIES

Housing: Apartments for single students; Coed dorms; Men's dorms; Theme housing; Women's dorms **Special Academic Facilities/Equipment:** DeSantis Family Chapel; Greene Sports Complex (Cafe); Helen K.Persson Recital Hall **Computers:** Students can register for classes online. Administrative functions (other than registration) can be performed online.

CAMPUS LIFE

Environment: Metropolis **Activities:** Campus Ministries; Choral groups; Concert band; Dance; Drama/theater; International Student Organization; Jazz band; Literary magazine; Music ensembles; Musical theater; Pep band; Student government; Student newspaper; Symphony orchestra 56 registered organizations, 29 honor societies, 6 religious organizations. **Athletics (Intercollegiate):** *Men:* baseball, basketball, cross-country, soccer, tennis. *Women:* basketball, cross-country, soccer, softball, tennis, volleyball. **On-Campus Highlights:** DeSantis Family Chapel, Greene Complex (athletics, snack shop), Vera Lea Rinker Music Building

ADMISSIONS

Freshman Academic Profile: Average high school GPA 3.6. **Test Scores:** SAT Math middle 50% range 480-590. SAT EBRW middle 50% range 500-610. ACT middle 50% range 20-26. Minimum paper TOEFL 550. **Basis for**

Candidate Selection: *Very important factors considered include:* academic GPA, application essay, standardized test scores, character/personal qualities, religious affiliation/commitment. *Important factors considered include:* rigor of secondary school record, recommendation(s), interview, extracurricular activities, talent/ability. *Other factors considered include:* class rank, alumni/ae relation, volunteer work, level of applicant's interest. **Freshman Admission Requirements:** High school diploma is required and GED is accepted *Academic units required:* 4 English, 3 math, 3 science, 3 science labs, 5 academic electives, *Academic units recommended:* 4 English, 3 math, 3 science, 1 science labs, 2 foreign language. **Freshman Admission Statistics:** 1,380 applied, 97.4% admitted, 40% enrolled. **Transfer Admission Requirements:** college transcript(s), essay or personal statement, Minimum college GPA of 2.5 required. Lowest grade transferable C. **General Admission Information:** Application fee $50. Nonfall registration accepted. Admission may be deferred for a maximum of 1 semester.

COSTS AND FINANCIAL AID

Annual tuition $30,990. Room and board $10,130. Required fees $460. Average book expense $1,058. **Required Forms and Deadlines:** FAFSA; State aid form. **Notification of Awards:** Applicants will be notified of awards on a rolling basis beginning 10/15. **Types of Aid:** *Loans:* Direct PLUS loans; Direct Subsidized Stafford Loans; Direct Unsubsidized Stafford Loans. *Student Employment:* Federal Work-Study Program available. Institutional employment available. **Financial Aid Statistics:** 100% needy freshmen, 100% needy undergrads receive need-based scholarship or grant aid. 20% freshmen, 15% undergrads receive non-need-based scholarship or grant aid. 61% freshmen, 68% undergrads receive need-based self-help aid. 5% freshmen, 5% undergrads receive athletic scholarships. 100% freshmen, 100% undergrads receive any aid. 63% undergrads borrow to pay for school. Average cumulative indebtedness $28,862. **Criteria for awarding aid:** *Need-based:* Academics, Alumni affiliation *Non-need-based:* Academics, Alumni affiliation, Art, Athletics, Leadership, Music/drama, State/district residency.

PARK UNIVERSITY

8700 NW River Park Drive, Parkville, MO 64152
Phone: 816-584-6213 • **Financial Aid Phone:** 816-548-6290
E-mail: admissions@mail.park.edu • **CEEB Code:** 6574
Fax: 816-741-4462 • **ACT Code:** 2340

This private school was founded in 1875. It has a 700 acre campus.

RATINGS

Admissions Selectivity Rating: 78   **Fire Safety Rating:** 75   **Green Rating:** 60*

STUDENTS AND FACULTY

Enrollment: 1,672. **Student Body:** 56% female, 44% male, 20% out-of-state, 19% international (93 countries represented). Asian <1%, African American 10%, Caucasian 61%, Hispanic 5%, Native American 1%, Pacific Islander <1%, Two or more races 3%, Race unknown 0%.
Retention and Graduation: 61% freshmen return for sophomore year. 7% grads go on to further study within 1 year. 6% grads pursue arts and sciences degrees. 1% grads pursue business degrees. **Faculty:** Student/faculty ratio 12:1. 82 full-time faculty, 66% hold PhDs, 4% are members of minority groups, 38% are women. 0% of classes are taught by teaching assistants.

ACADEMICS

Degrees: Associate; Bachelor's; Certificate; Master's; Post-Bachelor's certificate **Most popular majors:** Computer And Information Sciences, General; Education, General; Business Administration And Management, General. **Special Study Options:** Accelerated program; Cross-registration; Distance learning; Double major; Dual enrollment; English as a Second Language (ESL); Honors program; Independent study; Internships; Student-designed major; Study abroad; Teacher certification program; Weekend college. **Disability Services offered to physically disabled students:** Note-taking services; Reader services; Tape recorders; Tutors.

FACILITIES

Housing: Apartments for married students; Coed dorms 90% of campus accessible to physically diasbled. **Computers:** Students can register for classes online. Administrative functions (other than registration) can be performed online.

CAMPUS LIFE

Environment: Town **Activities:** Choral groups; Drama/theater; Literary magazine; Radio station; Student government; Student newspaper; Symphony orchestra; Yearbook 15 registered organizations, 4 honor societies, 13 religious organizations. **Athletics (Intercollegiate):** *Men:* baseball, basketball, cross-country, soccer, track/field (outdoor), track/field (indoor), volleyball. *Women:* basketball, cross-country, golf, soccer, softball, track/field (outdoor), track/field (indoor), volleyball. **On-Campus Highlights:** Gym, Cafeteria, Classrooms (Underground), Library, Bookstore

ADMISSIONS

Freshman Academic Profile: Average high school GPA 3.3. 14% in top 10% of high school class, 37% in top 25% of high school class, 68% in top 50% of high school class. 80% from public high schools. **Test Scores:** ACT middle 50% range 17-23. Minimum paper TOEFL 500. **Basis for Candidate Selection:** *Very important factors considered include:* rigor of secondary school record, class rank, standardized test scores. *Other factors considered include:* application essay, recommendation(s). **Freshman Admission Requirements:** High school diploma is required and GED is accepted *Academic units recommended:* 3 English, 2 math, 2 science, 1 science labs, 2 foreign language, 3 social studies, 1 history, 6 academic electives. **Freshman Admission Statistics:** 778 applied, 69.3% admitted, 39% enrolled. **Transfer Admission Requirements:** High school transcript, college transcript(s), Minimum college GPA of 2.0 required. Lowest grade transferable C. **General Admission Information:** Application fee $25. Priority deadline 4/15. Regular application deadline 7/1. Nonfall registration accepted. Admission may be deferred.

COSTS AND FINANCIAL AID

Annual tuition $10,380. Required fees $100. Average book expense $1,800. **Required Forms and Deadlines:** FAFSA; Institution's own financial aid form. **Notification of Awards:** Applicants will be notified of awards on a rolling basis beginning 2/15. **Types of Aid:** *Need-based scholarships/grants:* Federal Pell; Private scholarships; SEOG; State scholarships/grants. *Loans:* Direct PLUS loans; Direct Subsidized Stafford Loans; Direct Unsubsidized Stafford Loans. *Student Employment:* Federal Work-Study Program available. Institutional employment available. **Financial Aid Statistics:** 78% needy freshmen, 73% needy undergrads receive need-based scholarship or grant aid. 75% freshmen, 53% undergrads receive non-need-based scholarship or grant aid. 56% freshmen, 71% undergrads receive need-based self-help aid. 17% freshmen, 11% undergrads receive athletic scholarships. 78% freshmen receive any aid. **Criteria for awarding aid:** *Non-need-based:* Academics, Alumni affiliation, Art, Athletics, Job skills, State/district residency.

PARSONS THE NEW SCHOOL FOR DESIGN

66 Fifth Avenue, New York, NY 10003
Phone: 212-229-5150 • **Financial Aid Phone:** 212.229.8930
E-mail: thinkparsons@newschool.edu • **CEEB Code:** 2638
Website: www.newschool.edu/parsons • **ACT Code:** 2854

This private school was founded in 1896.

RATINGS
Admissions Selectivity Rating: 89 **Fire Safety Rating:** 89 **Green Rating:** 88

STUDENTS AND FACULTY
Enrollment: 4,275. **Student Body:** 78% female, 22% male, 75% out-of-state, 44% international (95 countries represented). Asian 13%, African American 4%, Caucasian 24%, Hispanic 10%, Native American <1%, Pacific Islander <1%, Two or more races 3%, Race unknown 3%.
Retention and Graduation: 58% freshmen graduate within 4 years. 75% freshmen graduate within 6 years. **Faculty:** Student/faculty ratio 11:1. 159 full-time faculty, 65% hold PhDs, 31% are members of minority groups, 53% are women. 0% of classes are taught by teaching assistants.

ACADEMICS
Degrees: Associate; Bachelor's; Certificate; **Master's Classes:** Most classes have 10-19 students. Most lab/discussion sessions have 10-19 students. **Most popular majors:** Fashion/Apparel Design; Graphic Design; Fine And Studio Arts Management. **Special Study Options:** Accelerated program; Cooperative education program; Cross-registration; Distance learning; Double major; English as a Second Language (ESL); Honors program; Independent study; Internships; Student-designed major; Study abroad; Teacher certification program. **Disability Services offered to physically disabled students:** Note-taking services; Reader services; Tape recorders. **Career services:** Career assessment; Career/job search classes; Internships

FACILITIES
Housing: Coed dorms; Special housing for disabled student; Theme housing 99% of campus accessible to physically diasbled. **Special Academic Facilities/Equipment:** Art gallery, photography gallery, extensive collections of contemporary art, concert hall, public lectures, conferences, cultural and intellectual events. **Computers:** 95% of classrooms, 100% of libraries, 100%

of dining areas, na% of student union, 100% of common outdoor areas have wireless network access. Students can register for classes online. Administrative functions (other than registration) can be performed online.

CAMPUS LIFE
Environment: Metropolis **Activities:** Choral groups; Concert band; Dance; Drama/theater; International Student Organization; Jazz band; Literary magazine; Music ensembles; Musical theater; Opera; Student government; Student newspaper; Student-run film society; Symphony orchestra 34 registered organizations. **On-Campus Highlights:** Sheila Johnson Design Center, Schwartz Fashion Center, University Welcome Center, University Center, Project Runway Studio **Environmental Initiatives:** Lighting Retrofits: 2W 13th St. and 66 5th Ave are in the midst of an ongoing replacement of all non-LED fixtures. The majority of the building's T8 fluorescent bulbs are being replaced with LED, stairwells are being replaced with dimming-occupancy based bi-level fixtures, and all rooms will be equiped with vacancy sensors. The main lobby and gallery spaces will also recieve significant upgrades as well. These same upgrades are being applied to 2 other large buildings, with a goal of completing the entire campus by early 2017.

ADMISSIONS
Freshman Academic Profile: Average high school GPA 3.4. 17% in top 10% of high school class, 31% in top 25% of high school class, 82% in top 50% of high school class. 39% from public high schools. **Test Scores:** SAT Math middle 50% range 555-700. SAT EBRW middle 50% range 530-630. Minimum internet-based TOEFL 92. **Basis for Candidate Selection:** *Very important factors considered include:* academic GPA, application essay, extracurricular activities. *Important factors considered include:* rigor of secondary school record, recommendation(s), character/personal qualities. *Other factors considered include:* class rank, standardized test scores, interview, talent/ability, volunteer work, work experience, level of applicant's interest. **Freshman Admission Requirements:** High school diploma is required and GED is accepted *Academic units required:* 4 English, *Academic units recommended:* 4 math, 4 science, 4 foreign language, 4 social studies, 4 history. **Freshman Admission Statistics:** 4,825 applied, 50.7% admitted, 38% enrolled. **Transfer Admission Requirements:** college transcript(s), Minimum college GPA of 2.0 required. Lowest grade transferable C. **General Admission Information:** Application fee $50. Priority deadline 1/15. Regular application deadline 8/1. Nonfall registration accepted. Admission may be deferred for a maximum of 1 year.

COSTS AND FINANCIAL AID
Required Forms and Deadlines: FAFSA. **Notification of Awards:** Applicants will be notified of awards on a rolling basis beginning 4/1. **Types of Aid:** *Need-based scholarships/grants:* College/university scholarship or grant aid from institutional funds; Federal Pell; Private scholarships; SEOG; State scholarships/grants. *Loans:* Direct PLUS loans; Direct Subsidized Stafford Loans; Direct Unsubsidized Stafford Loans. *Student Employment:* Federal Work-Study Program available. Institutional employment available. **Financial Aid Statistics:** 95% needy freshmen, 98% needy undergrads receive need-based scholarship or grant aid. 71% freshmen, 63% undergrads receive non-need-based scholarship or grant aid. 80% freshmen, 83% undergrads receive need-based self-help aid. 0% freshmen, 0% undergrads receive athletic scholarships. 38% freshmen, 40% undergrads receive any aid. 52% undergrads borrow to pay for school. Average cumulative indebtedness $30,659. **Criteria for awarding aid:** *Need-based:* Academics, Art, Leadership, Minority status, Music/drama *Non-need-based:* Academics, Art, Leadership, Minority status, Music/drama, State/district residency.

PATRICK HENRY COLLEGE

10 Patrick Henry Circle, Purcellville, VA 20132
Financial Aid Phone: 540-441-8142
E-mail: admissions@phc.edu • **CEEB Code:** 2804
Fax: 540-441-8119 • **Website:** www.phc.edu • **ACT Code:** 4383

This private school, affiliated with the Christian (Nondenominational) Church, was founded in 2000. It has a 106 acre campus.

RATINGS
Admissions Selectivity Rating: 89 **Fire Safety Rating:** 90 **Green Rating:** 60*

STUDENTS AND FACULTY
Enrollment: 263. **Student Body:** 46% female, 54% male, 80% out-of-state, international. Asian 3%, African American <1%, Caucasian 82%, Hispanic 5%, Pacific Islander <1%, Race unknown 10%.
Retention and Graduation: 83% freshmen return for sophomore year. 10% grads go on to further study within 1 year. 23% grads pursue law degrees.

Faculty: Student/faculty ratio 10:1. 19 full-time faculty, 89% hold PhDs, 5% are women. 0% of classes are taught by teaching assistants.

ACADEMICS

Degrees: Bachelor's **Classes:** Most classes have 10-19 students. Most lab/discussion sessions have 20-29 students. **Most popular majors:** Journalism; Political Science And Government, General; Business/Managerial Economics. **Special Study Options:** Cooperative education program; Cross-registration; Distance learning; Double major; Independent study; Internships; Liberal arts/career combination. **Disability Services offered to physically disabled students:** Tutors. **Career services:** Alumni network; Alumni services; Career assessment; Career/job search classes; Internships

FACILITIES

Housing: Men's dorms; Women's dorms 100% of campus accessible to physically diasbled. **Computers:** 100% of classrooms, 100% of dorms, 100% of libraries, 100% of dining areas, 100% of student union, 100% of common outdoor areas have wireless network access. Students can register for classes online. Administrative functions (other than registration) can be performed online. Undergraduates are required to own a computer.

CAMPUS LIFE

Environment: Village **Activities:** Campus Ministries; Choral groups; Dance; Drama/theater; Literary magazine; Model UN; Music ensembles; Student government; Student newspaper; Symphony orchestra. **Athletics (Intercollegiate):** *Men:* basketball, soccer. *Women:* basketball, soccer. **On-Campus Highlights:** Student Coffee Lounge, Workout facilities, Raquetball courts, Chapel, Classrooms **Environmental Initiatives:** water conservation

ADMISSIONS

Freshman Academic Profile: Average high school GPA 3.8. 20% from public high schools. **Test Scores:** SAT Math middle 50% range 523-625. SAT EBRW middle 50% range 593-738. ACT middle 50% range 25-31. **Basis for Candidate Selection:** *Very important factors considered include:* application essay, interview, character/personal qualities, religious affiliation/commitment. *Important factors considered include:* rigor of secondary school record, academic GPA, standardized test scores. *Other factors considered include:* class rank, recommendation(s), extracurricular activities, talent/ability, volunteer work, work experience, level of applicant's interest. **Freshman Admission Requirements:** High school diploma is required and GED is not accepted *Academic units required:* 4 English, 3 math, 2 science, 2 science labs, 1 foreign language, 2 history, 5 academic electives, *Academic units recommended:* 4 English, 3 math, 3 science, 3 science labs, 2 foreign language, 2 history, 5 academic electives. **Freshman Admission Statistics:** 244 applied, 52.5% admitted, 40% enrolled. **Transfer Admission Requirements:** High school transcript, college transcript(s), essay or personal statement, interview, standardized test scores, statement of good standing from prior institution(s). Lowest grade transferable C. **General Admission Information:** Application fee $40. Nonfall registration accepted. Admission may be deferred for a maximum of One year.

COSTS AND FINANCIAL AID

Annual tuition $27,922. Room and board $10,728. Required fees $200. Average book expense $1,000. **Required Forms and Deadlines:** CSS/Financial Aid PROFILE. **Notification of Awards:** Applicants will be notified of awards on a rolling basis beginning 3/1. **Types of Aid:** *Need-based scholarships/grants:* College/university scholarship or grant aid from institutional funds; Private scholarships. *Loans: Student Employment:* Institutional employment available. **Financial Aid Statistics:** 100% needy freshmen, 100% needy undergrads receive need-based scholarship or grant aid. 87% freshmen, 86% undergrads receive non-need-based scholarship or grant aid. 100% freshmen, 100% undergrads receive need-based self-help aid. 0% freshmen, 0% undergrads receive athletic scholarships. 94% freshmen, 94% undergrads receive any aid. 39% undergrads borrow to pay for school. **Criteria for awarding aid:** *Non-need-based:* Academics, Leadership, Music/drama.

THE PENNSYLVANIA ACADEMY OF THE FINE ARTS

128 North Broad Street, Philadelphia, PA 19102
Phone: 215-972-7625 • **Financial Aid Phone:** 215-972-2019
E-mail: admissions@pafa.edu
Fax: 215-972-0839 • **Website:** www.pafa.edu

This private school was founded in 1804.

RATINGS

Admissions Selectivity Rating: 61   **Fire Safety Rating:** 60*   **Green Rating:** 60*

STUDENTS AND FACULTY

Enrollment: 169. **Student Body:** 66% female, 34% male, 25% out-of-state, 5% international (19 countries represented). Asian 6%, African American 7%, Caucasian 59%, Hispanic 7%, Native American 1%, Two or more races 4%, Race unknown 12%.
Faculty: Student/faculty ratio 13:1. 0% of classes are taught by teaching assistants.

ACADEMICS

Degrees: Bachelor's; Certificate; Master's; Post-Bachelor's certificate **Most popular majors:** Fine/Studio Arts, General; Painting. **Special Study Options:** Dual enrollment; Exchange student program (domestic); Independent study; Internships.

FACILITIES

Special Academic Facilities/Equipment: PAFA's museum is the first art museum in the country, and one of the most important collections of American Art in the world. **Computers:**

CAMPUS LIFE

Environment: Metropolis **Activities:** Student government; Student-run film society 4 registered organizations. **On-Campus Highlights:** Museum of American Art, World Famous Cast Hall

ADMISSIONS

Test Scores: Minimum internet-based TOEFL 100. Minimum paper TOEFL 600. **Transfer Admission Requirements:** High school transcript, essay or personal statement, Lowest grade transferable C. **General Admission Information:** Application fee $60. Priority deadline 12/1. Regular application deadline 2/15.

COSTS AND FINANCIAL AID

Annual tuition $32,960. Room and board $10,815. Required fees $1,450. Average book expense $1,511. **Required Forms and Deadlines:** FAFSA. **Notification of Awards:** Applicants will be notified of awards on a rolling basis beginning 3/1. **Types of Aid:** *Need-based scholarships/grants:* College/university scholarship or grant aid from institutional funds; Federal Pell; Private scholarships; SEOG; State scholarships/grants. *Loans:* Direct PLUS loans; Direct Subsidized Stafford Loans; Direct Unsubsidized Stafford Loans. *Student Employment:* Federal Work-Study Program available. Institutional employment available. **Financial Aid Statistics:** 80% freshmen, 80% undergrads receive any aid. **Criteria for awarding aid:** *Non-need-based:* Academics, Art.

PENNSYLVANIA COLLEGE OF TECHNOLOGY

One College Avenue, Williamsport, PA 17701
Phone: (570) 327-4761 • **Financial Aid Phone:** 570-327-4761
E-mail: admissions@pct.edu
Fax: (570) 321-5551 • **Website:** www.pct.edu

This public school was founded in 1989. It has a 994 acre campus.

RATINGS

Admissions Selectivity Rating: 65   **Fire Safety Rating:** 60*   **Green Rating:** 60*

STUDENTS AND FACULTY

Enrollment: 5,416. **Student Body:** 36% female, 64% male, 10% out-of-state, international.
Retention and Graduation: 75% freshmen return for sophomore year.
Faculty: Student/faculty ratio 18:1. 293 full-time faculty, 5% are members of minority groups, 31% are women. 0% of classes are taught by teaching assistants.

ACADEMICS

Degrees: Associate; Bachelor's; Certificate **Special Study Options:** Accelerated program; Cooperative education program; Cross-registration; Distance learning; Dual enrollment; English as a Second Language (ESL); Exchange student program (domestic); Honors program; Independent study; Internships; Student-designed major; Study abroad; Weekend college. **Disability Services offered to physically disabled students:** Note-taking services; Reader services; Tape recorders; Tutors. **Career services:** Alumni services; Career assessment; Career/job search classes

FACILITIES

Housing: Apartments for single students; Coed dorms; Wellness housing 100% of campus accessible to physically diasbled. **Computers:** Students can register for classes online. Administrative functions (other than registration) can be performed online.

CAMPUS LIFE

Environment: Town **Activities:** Campus Ministries; Dance; International Student Organization; Student government 50 registered organizations, 3 honor societies, 4 religious organizations. 3 fraternities. **Athletics (Intercollegiate):** *Men:* archery, baseball, basketball, bowling, cross-country, golf, soccer, tennis, volleyball. *Women:* archery, basketball, bowling, cross-country, golf, soccer, softball, tennis, volleyball. **On-Campus Highlights:** Academic Facilities and Labs, Madigan Library and The Gallery, Campus Center, Student & Administrative Services Center, Academic Center

ADMISSIONS

Freshman Academic Profile: 4% in top 10% of high school class, 16% in top 25% of high school class, 48% in top 50% of high school class. **Test Scores:** Minimum paper TOEFL 500. **Freshman Admission Requirements:** High school diploma is required and GED is accepted **Freshman Admission Statistics:** 3,144 applied, 85.0% admitted, enrolled. **Transfer Admission Requirements:** High school transcript, college transcript(s), Minimum college GPA of 2.5 required. Lowest grade transferable C. **General Admission Information:** Application fee $50. Regular application deadline 7/1. Nonfall registration accepted. Admission may be deferred for a maximum of 1 year.

COSTS AND FINANCIAL AID

Annual in-state tuition $11,108. Annual out-of-state tuition $19,980. Room and board $11,108. Required fees $2,490. Average book expense $1,400. **Required Forms and Deadlines:** FAFSA; Institution's own financial aid form. **Notification of Awards:** Applicants will be notified of awards on a rolling basis beginning 6/1. **Types of Aid:** *Need-based scholarships/grants:* Federal Pell; Private scholarships; SEOG; State scholarships/grants. *Student Employment:* Federal Work-Study Program available. Institutional employment available.

PENNSYLVANIA STATE UNIVERSITY— ABINGTON

1600 Woodland Road, Abington, PA 19001
Phone: 215-881-7600
E-mail: abingtonadmissions@psu.edu
Fax: 215-881-7655 • **Website:** http://www.abington.psu.edu

This public school was founded in 1950. It has a 45 acre campus.

RATINGS

Admissions Selectivity Rating: 74   **Fire Safety Rating:** 60*   **Green Rating:** 60*

STUDENTS AND FACULTY

Enrollment: 3,490. **Student Body:** 51% female, 49% male, 7% out-of-state, 5% international. Asian 17%, African American 13%, Caucasian 50%, Hispanic 10%, Native American <1%, Pacific Islander <1%, Two or more races 2%, Race unknown 3%.
Retention and Graduation: 80% freshmen return for sophomore year.
Faculty: Student/faculty ratio 18:1. 136 full-time faculty, 65% hold PhDs, 17% are members of minority groups, 50% are women.

ACADEMICS

Degrees: Associate; Bachelor's; Certificate; Post-Bachelor's certificate **Classes:** Most classes have 20-29 students. Most lab/discussion sessions have fewer than 10 students. **Special Study Options:** Accelerated program; Cooperative education program; Distance learning; Double major; Dual enrollment; English as a Second Language (ESL); Exchange student program (domestic); External degree program; Honors program; Independent study; Internships; Liberal arts/career combination; Student-designed major; Study abroad; Teacher certification program; Weekend college.

CAMPUS LIFE

Environment: Village **Activities:** Campus Ministries; Choral groups; Dance; Drama/theater; International Student Organization; Jazz band; Literary magazine; Music ensembles; Student government; Student newspaper; Student-run film society. **Athletics (Intercollegiate):** *Men:* basketball, soccer, softball, tennis. *Women:* basketball, field hockey, softball, tennis, volleyball.

ADMISSIONS

Freshman Academic Profile: Average high school GPA 3.1. 8% in top 10% of high school class, 27% in top 25% of high school class, 64% in top 50% of high school class. **Test Scores:** SAT Math middle 50% range 430-570. SAT EBRW middle 50% range 420-520. ACT middle 50% range 19-25. Minimum paper TOEFL 550. **Basis for Candidate Selection:** *Very important factors considered include:* academic GPA, standardized test scores. *Important factors considered include:* rigor of secondary school record. *Other factors considered include:* class rank, application essay, extracurricular activities, talent/ability, character/personal qualities, alumni/ae relation, geographical residence, state residency, volunteer work, work experience. **Freshman Admission Requirements:** High school diploma is required and GED is accepted *Academic units required:* 4 English, 3 math, 3 science, 2 foreign language, 3 social studies, *Academic units recommended:* 3 foreign language. **Freshman Admission Statistics:** 3,946 applied, 82.4% admitted, 27% enrolled. **Transfer Admission Requirements:** High school transcript, college transcript(s), Lowest grade transferable C. **General Admission Information:** Application fee $50. Priority deadline 11/30. Nonfall registration accepted. Admission may be deferred for a maximum of One year.

COSTS AND FINANCIAL AID

Annual out-of-state tuition $20,324. Required fees $942. **Required Forms and Deadlines:** FAFSA. **Types of Aid:** *Need-based scholarships/grants:* College/university scholarship or grant aid from institutional funds; Federal Pell; Private scholarships; SEOG; State scholarships/grants. *Loans:* Direct PLUS loans; Direct Subsidized Stafford Loans; Direct Unsubsidized Stafford Loans. **Financial Aid Statistics:** 77% needy freshmen, 80% needy undergrads receive need-based scholarship or grant aid. 36% freshmen, 29% undergrads receive non-need-based scholarship or grant aid. 71% freshmen, 81% undergrads receive need-based self-help aid. 0% freshmen, 0% undergrads receive athletic scholarships. 82% undergrads borrow to pay for school. Average cumulative indebtedness $35,013. **Criteria for awarding aid:** *Need-based:* Academics, Alumni affiliation *Non-need-based:* Academics, Alumni affiliation.

PENNSYLVANIA STATE UNIVERSITY—ALTOONA

3000 Ivyside Park, Altoona, PA 16601-3760
Phone: 814-949-5466
E-mail: aaadmit@psu.edu
Fax: 814-949-5564 • **Website:** www.altoona.psu.edu

This public school was founded in 1929.

RATINGS

Admissions Selectivity Rating: 72   **Fire Safety Rating:** 60*   **Green Rating:** 60*

STUDENTS AND FACULTY

Enrollment: 3,772. **Student Body:** 44% female, 56% male, 17% out-of-state, 5% international. Asian 3%, African American 7%, Caucasian 77%, Hispanic 6%, Native American <1%, Pacific Islander <1%, Two or more races 2%, Race unknown 1%.
Retention and Graduation: 84% freshmen return for sophomore year.
Faculty: Student/faculty ratio 16:1. 203 full-time faculty, 67% hold PhDs, 12% are members of minority groups, 50% are women.

ACADEMICS

Degrees: Associate; Bachelor's; Certificate **Classes:** Most classes have 20-29 students. Most lab/discussion sessions have 10-19 students. **Special Study Options:** Accelerated program; Cooperative education program; Cross-registration; Distance learning; Double major; Dual enrollment; English as a Second Language (ESL); Exchange student program (domestic); External degree program; Honors program; Independent study; Internships; Liberal arts/career combination; Student-designed major; Study abroad; Teacher certification program; Weekend college.

FACILITIES

Housing: Coed dorms; Special housing for disabled student; Theme housing; Wellness housing

CAMPUS LIFE

Environment: Village **Activities:** Campus Ministries; Choral groups; Dance; Drama/theater; International Student Organization; Jazz band; Literary magazine; Music ensembles; Musical theater; Pep band; Student government; Student newspaper; Student-run film society; Yearbook. **Athletics (Intercollegiate):** *Men:* basketball, diving, skiing (downhill/alpine), soccer, swimming, tennis, volleyball. *Women:* basketball, diving, skiing (downhill/alpine), swimming, tennis, volleyball.

ADMISSIONS

Freshman Academic Profile: Average high school GPA 3.1. 6% in top 10% of high school class, 24% in top 25% of high school class, 67% in top 50% of high school class. **Test Scores:** SAT Math middle 50% range 450-550. SAT EBRW middle 50% range 440-540. ACT middle 50% range 20-24. **Basis for Candidate Selection:** *Very important factors considered include:* academic GPA, standardized test scores. *Important factors considered include:* rigor of secondary school record. *Other factors considered include:* class rank, application essay, extracurricular activities, talent/ability, character/personal qualities, alumni/ae relation, geographical residence, state residency, volunteer work, work experience. **Freshman Admission Requirements:** High school diploma is required and GED is accepted *Academic units required:* 4 English, 3 math, 3 science, 2 foreign language, 3 social studies, *Academic units recommended:* 3 foreign language. **Freshman Admission Statistics:** 5,738 applied, 89.4% admitted, 27% enrolled. **Transfer Admission Requirements:** High school transcript, college transcript(s), Lowest grade transferable C. **General Admission Information:** Application fee $50. Priority deadline 11/30. Nonfall registration accepted. Admission may be deferred for a maximum of One year.

COSTS AND FINANCIAL AID

Annual in-state tuition $10,920. Annual out-of-state tuition $21,392. Room and board $10,920. Required fees $952. Average book expense $1,840. **Required Forms and Deadlines:** FAFSA. **Types of Aid:** *Need-based scholarships/grants:* College/university scholarship or grant aid from institutional funds; Federal Pell; Private scholarships; SEOG; State scholarships/grants. *Loans:* Direct PLUS loans; Direct Subsidized Stafford Loans; Direct Unsubsidized Stafford Loans. **Financial Aid Statistics:** 58% needy freshmen, 62% needy undergrads receive need-based scholarship or grant aid. 51% freshmen, 46% undergrads receive non-need-based scholarship or grant aid. 83% freshmen, 86% undergrads receive need-based self-help aid. 0% freshmen, 0% undergrads receive athletic scholarships. 76% undergrads borrow to pay for school. Average cumulative indebtedness $39,091. **Criteria for awarding aid:** *Need-based:* Academics, Alumni affiliation *Non-need-based:* Academics, Alumni affiliation.

PENNSYLVANIA STATE UNIVERSITY—BEAVER

100 University Drive, Monaca, PA 15061-2799
Phone: (877) 564-6778
E-mail: br-admissions@psu.edu
Fax: (724)773-3769 • **Website:** http://beaver.psu.edu

This is a public school.

RATINGS

Admissions Selectivity Rating: 73   **Fire Safety Rating:** 60*   **Green Rating:** 60*

STUDENTS AND FACULTY

Enrollment: 639. **Student Body:** 39% female, 61% male, 9% out-of-state, 3% international. Asian 3%, African American 9%, Caucasian 75%, Hispanic 5%, Native American <1%, Pacific Islander <1%, Two or more races 2%, Race unknown 1%.
Retention and Graduation: 78% freshmen return for sophomore year.
Faculty: Student/faculty ratio 16:1. 32 full-time faculty, 66% hold PhDs, 22% are members of minority groups, 59% are women.

ACADEMICS

Degrees: Bachelor's; Certificate **Classes:** Most classes have 20-29 students. **Special Study Options:** Cross-registration; Distance learning; Double major; Dual enrollment; Honors program; Independent study; Internships; Study abroad.

FACILITIES

Housing: Coed dorms; Special housing for disabled students

CAMPUS LIFE

Activities: Campus Ministries; Choral groups; Drama/theater; International Student Organization; Radio station; Student government; Student newspaper; Student-run film society.

ADMISSIONS

Freshman Academic Profile: Average high school GPA 3.1. 7% in top 10% of high school class, 31% in top 25% of high school class, 73% in top 50% of high school class. **Test Scores:** SAT Math middle 50% range 450-570. SAT EBRW middle 50% range 430-550. ACT middle 50% range 18-24. **Basis for Candidate Selection:** *Very important factors considered include:* academic GPA, standardized test scores. *Important factors considered include:* rigor of secondary school record. *Other factors considered include:* class rank, application essay, extracurricular activities, talent/ability, character/personal qualities, alumni/ae relation, geographical residence, state residency, volunteer work, work experience. **Freshman Admission Requirements:** High school diploma is required and GED is accepted *Academic units required:* 4 English, 3 math, 3 science, 2 foreign language, 3 social studies, *Academic units recommended:* 3 foreign language. **Freshman Admission Statistics:** 653 applied, 94.9% admitted, 34% enrolled. **General Admission Information:** Application fee $50. Priority deadline 11/30. Nonfall registration accepted. Admission may be deferred for a maximum of One year.

COSTS AND FINANCIAL AID

Annual in-state tuition $10,920. Annual out-of-state tuition $19,404. Room and board $10,920. Required fees $942. Average book expense $1,840. **Required Forms and Deadlines:** FAFSA. **Types of Aid:** *Need-based scholarships/grants:* College/university scholarship or grant aid from institutional funds; Federal Pell; Private scholarships; SEOG; State scholarships/grants. *Loans:* Direct PLUS loans; Direct Subsidized Stafford Loans; Direct Unsubsidized Stafford Loans. **Financial Aid Statistics:** 70% needy freshmen, 75% needy undergrads receive need-based scholarship or grant aid. 69% freshmen, 57% undergrads receive non-need-based scholarship or grant aid. 85% freshmen, 87% undergrads receive need-based self-help aid. 0% freshmen, 0% undergrads receive athletic scholarships. 86% undergrads borrow to pay for school. Average cumulative indebtedness $37,485. **Criteria for awarding aid:** *Need-based:* Academics, Alumni affiliation *Non-need-based:* Academics, Alumni affiliation.

PENNSYLVANIA STATE UNIVERSITY—BERKS

Tulpehocken Road, Reading, PA 19610-6009
Phone: 610-396-6060
E-mail: admissionsbk@psu.edu
Fax: 610-396-6077 • **Website:** http://berks.psu.edu

This public school was founded in 1924. It has a 241 acre campus.

RATINGS

Admissions Selectivity Rating: 74   **Fire Safety Rating:** 60*   **Green Rating:** 60*

STUDENTS AND FACULTY

Enrollment: 2,778. **Student Body:** 43% female, 57% male, 8% out-of-state, 3% international. Asian 5%, African American 9%, Caucasian 68%, Hispanic 11%, Native American <1%, Pacific Islander <1%, Two or more races 2%, Race unknown 1%.
Retention and Graduation: 82% freshmen return for sophomore year.
Faculty: Student/faculty ratio 17:1. 136 full-time faculty, 70% hold PhDs, 15% are members of minority groups, 50% are women.

ACADEMICS

Degrees: Associate; Bachelor's; Certificate; Post-Bachelor's certificate **Classes:** Most classes have 10-19 students. Most lab/discussion sessions have 10-19 students. **Special Study Options:** Accelerated program; Cooperative education program; Cross-registration; Distance learning; Dual enrollment; English as a Second Language (ESL); Honors program; Independent study; Internships; Study abroad; Teacher certification program.

FACILITIES

Housing: Coed dorms; Special housing for disabled students

CAMPUS LIFE

Environment: Village **Activities:** Campus Ministries; Choral groups; Dance; Drama/theater; Literary magazine; Radio station; Student government; Student newspaper; Student-run film society. **Athletics (Intercollegiate):** *Men:* baseball, basketball, fencing, soccer, tennis, volleyball. *Women:* fencing, softball, tennis, volleyball.

ADMISSIONS

Freshman Academic Profile: Average high school GPA 3.1. 8% in top 10% of high school class, 29% in top 25% of high school class, 66% in top 50% of high school class. **Test Scores:** SAT Math middle 50% range 430-560. SAT EBRW middle 50% range 420-540. ACT middle 50% range 18-25. Minimum paper TOEFL 550. **Basis for Candidate Selection:** *Very important factors* considered include: academic GPA, standardized test scores. Important factors considered include: rigor of secondary school record. Other factors considered include: class rank, application essay, extracurricular activities, talent/ability, character/personal qualities, alumni/ae relation, geographical residence, state residency, volunteer work, work experience. **Freshman Admission Requirements:** High school diploma is required and GED is accepted Academic units required: 4 English, 3 math, 3 science, 2 foreign language, 3 social studies, Academic units recommended: 3 foreign language. **Freshman Admission Statistics:** 2,413 applied, 84.9% admitted, 39% enrolled. **Transfer Admission Requirements:** High school transcript, college transcript(s), Lowest grade transferable C. **General Admission Information:** Application fee $50. Priority deadline 11/30. Nonfall registration accepted. Admission may be deferred for a maximum of One year.

COSTS AND FINANCIAL AID
Annual in-state tuition $11,950. Annual out-of-state tuition $21,392. Room and board $11,950. Required fees $952. Average book expense $1,840. **Required Forms and Deadlines:** FAFSA. **Types of Aid:** Need-based scholarships/grants: College/university scholarship or grant aid from institutional funds; Federal Pell; Private scholarships; SEOG; State scholarships/grants. Loans: Direct PLUS loans; Direct Subsidized Stafford Loans; Direct Unsubsidized Stafford Loans. **Financial Aid Statistics:** 66% needy freshmen, 70% needy undergrads receive need-based scholarship or grant aid. 38% freshmen, 33% undergrads receive non-need-based scholarship or grant aid. 85% freshmen, 87% undergrads receive need-based self-help aid. 0% freshmen, 0% undergrads receive athletic scholarships. 80% undergrads borrow to pay for school. Average cumulative indebtedness $35,853. **Criteria for awarding aid:** Need-based: Academics, Alumni affiliation Non-need-based: Academics, Alumni affiliation.

PENNSYLVANIA STATE UNIVERSITY— DELAWARE COUNTY

25 Yearsley Mill Road, Media, PA 19063
Phone: (610)892-1200
E-mail: bwadmissions@psu.edu
Fax: (610)892-1320 • **Website:** brandywine.psu.edu

This is a public school.

RATINGS
Admissions Selectivity Rating: 60*   Fire Safety Rating: 60*

STUDENTS AND FACULTY
Enrollment: 1,291. **Student Body:** 44% female, 56% male, 5% out-of-state, 1% international. Asian 11%, African American 15%, Caucasian 63%, Hispanic 5%, Native American <1%, Pacific Islander <1%, Two or more races 2%, Race unknown 2%.
Retention and Graduation: 74% freshmen return for sophomore year.
Faculty: Student/faculty ratio 15:1. 68 full-time faculty, 71% hold PhDs, 15% are members of minority groups, 53% are women.

ACADEMICS
Degrees: Associate; Bachelor's; Certificate **Classes:** Most classes have 20-29 students. **Special Study Options:** Accelerated program; Distance learning; Double major; Dual enrollment; English as a Second Language (ESL); Honors program; Independent study; Internships; Study abroad.

CAMPUS LIFE
Activities: Literary magazine; Student government; Student newspaper.

ADMISSIONS
Freshman Academic Profile: Average high school GPA 3.0. 4% in top 10% of high school class, 18% in top 25% of high school class, 56% in top 50% of high school class. **Test Scores:** SAT Math middle 50% range 440-550. SAT EBRW middle 50% range 420-520. ACT middle 50% range 18-26. **Basis for Candidate Selection:** Very important factors considered include: academic GPA, standardized test scores. Important factors considered include: rigor of secondary school record. Other factors considered include: class rank, application essay, extracurricular activities, talent/ability, character/personal qualities, alumni/ae relation, geographical residence, state residency, volunteer work, work experience. **Freshman Admission Requirements:** High school diploma is required and GED is accepted Academic units required: 4 English, 3 math, 3 science, 2 foreign language, 3 social studies, Academic units recommended: 3 foreign language. **Freshman Admission Statistics:** 1,265 applied, 83.1% admitted, 36% enrolled. **General Admission Information:** Application fee $50. Priority deadline 11/30. Nonfall registration accepted. Admission may be deferred for a maximum of One year.

COSTS AND FINANCIAL AID
Annual out-of-state tuition $20,206. Required fees $952. **Required Forms and Deadlines:** FAFSA. **Types of Aid:** Need-based scholarships/grants: College/university scholarship or grant aid from institutional funds; Federal Pell; Private scholarships; SEOG; State scholarships/grants. Loans: Direct PLUS loans; Direct Subsidized Stafford Loans; Direct Unsubsidized Stafford Loans. **Financial Aid Statistics:** 75% needy freshmen, 76% needy undergrads receive need-based scholarship or grant aid. 41% freshmen, 32% undergrads receive non-need-based scholarship or grant aid. 80% freshmen, 83% undergrads receive need-based self-help aid. 0% freshmen, 0% undergrads receive athletic scholarships. 78% undergrads borrow to pay for school. Average cumulative indebtedness $34,962. **Criteria for awarding aid:** Need-based: Academics, Alumni affiliation Non-need-based: Academics, Alumni affiliation.

PENNSYLVANIA STATE UNIVERSITY DUBOIS

1 College Place, DuBois, PA 15801-3199
Phone: (814)375-4720
E-mail: duboisinfo@psu.edu
Fax: (814)375-4784 • **Website:** http://dubois.psu.edu

This is a public school.

RATINGS
Admissions Selectivity Rating: 74   Fire Safety Rating: 60*   Green Rating: 60*

STUDENTS AND FACULTY
Enrollment: 512. **Student Body:** 44% female, 56% male, 3% out-of-state, <1% international. Asian 1%, African American 2%, Caucasian 94%, Hispanic 2%, Native American 0%, Pacific Islander <1%, Two or more races <1%, Race unknown 1%.
Retention and Graduation: 87% freshmen return for sophomore year.
Faculty: Student/faculty ratio 11:1. 42 full-time faculty, 57% hold PhDs, 19% are members of minority groups, 60% are women.

ACADEMICS
Degrees: Associate; Bachelor's; Certificate **Classes:** Most classes have 10-19 students. Most lab/discussion sessions have fewer than 10 students. **Special Study Options:** Accelerated program; Cross-registration; Distance learning; Double major; Dual enrollment; Honors program; Independent study; Internships; Student-designed major; Study abroad.

CAMPUS LIFE
Activities: Campus Ministries; Choral groups; Student government; Student-run film society.

ADMISSIONS
Freshman Academic Profile: Average high school GPA 3.1. 9% in top 10% of high school class, 33% in top 25% of high school class, 68% in top 50% of high school class. **Test Scores:** SAT Math middle 50% range 420-560. SAT EBRW middle 50% range 420-530. ACT middle 50% range 21-25. **Basis for Candidate Selection:** Very important factors considered include: academic GPA, standardized test scores. Important factors considered include: rigor of secondary school record. Other factors considered include: class rank, application essay, extracurricular activities, talent/ability, character/personal qualities, alumni/ae relation, geographical residence, state residency, volunteer work, work experience. **Freshman Admission Requirements:** High school diploma is required and GED is accepted Academic units required: 4 English, 3 math, 3 science, 2 foreign language, 3 social studies, Academic units recommended: 3 foreign language. **Freshman Admission Statistics:** 394 applied, 85.0% admitted, 49% enrolled. **General Admission Information:** Application fee $50. Priority deadline 11/30. Nonfall registration accepted. Admission may be deferred for a maximum of 1 year.

COSTS AND FINANCIAL AID
Annual out-of-state tuition $19,404. Required fees $828. **Required Forms and Deadlines:** FAFSA. **Types of Aid:** Need-based scholarships/grants: College/university scholarship or grant aid from institutional funds; Federal Pell; Private scholarships; SEOG; State scholarships/grants. Loans: Direct PLUS loans; Direct Subsidized Stafford Loans; Direct Unsubsidized Stafford Loans. **Financial Aid Statistics:** 87% needy freshmen, 89% needy undergrads receive need-based scholarship or grant aid. 48% freshmen, 37% undergrads receive non-need-based scholarship or grant aid. 81% freshmen, 87% undergrads receive need-based self-help aid. 0% freshmen, 0% undergrads receive athletic scholarships. 88% undergrads borrow to pay for school. Average cumulative indebtedness $43,504. **Criteria for awarding aid:** Need-based: Academics, Alumni affiliation Non-need-based: Academics, Alumni affiliation.

PENNSYLVANIA STATE UNIVERSITY ERIE, THE BEHREND COLLEGE

4701 College Drive, Erie, PA 16563-0105
Phone: 814-898-6100
E-mail: behrend.admissions@psu.edu
Fax: 814-898-6044 • **Website:** http://psbehrend.psu.edu/ • **ACT Code:** 3656

This public school was founded in 1948. It has a 732 acre campus.

RATINGS
Admissions Selectivity Rating: 74   **Fire Safety Rating:** 60*   **Green Rating:** 60*

STUDENTS AND FACULTY
Enrollment: 4,092. **Student Body:** 35% female, 65% male, 10% out-of-state, 9% international. Asian 3%, African American 4%, Caucasian 79%, Hispanic 2%, Native American <1%, Pacific Islander <1%, Two or more races 2%, Race unknown 1%.
Retention and Graduation: 85% freshmen return for sophomore year.
Faculty: Student/faculty ratio 15:1. 260 full-time faculty, 67% hold PhDs, 12% are members of minority groups, 37% are women. 0% of classes are taught by teaching assistants.

ACADEMICS
Degrees: Associate; Bachelor's; Certificate; **Master's Classes:** Most classes have 10-19 students. **Special Study Options:** Accelerated program; Cooperative education program; Distance learning; Double major; Dual enrollment; Honors program; Independent study; Internships; Liberal arts/career combination; Study abroad; Teacher certification program. **Disability Services offered to physically disabled students:** Note-taking services; Reader services; Tape recorders; Tutors. **Career services:** Alumni services; Career assessment; Career/job search classes; Internships

FACILITIES
Housing: Apartments for single students; Coed dorms; Men's dorms; Special housing for disabled student; Women's dorms **Special Academic Facilities/Equipment:** Observatory, plastics lab. **Computers:** Students can register for classes online. Administrative functions (other than registration) can be performed online.

CAMPUS LIFE
Environment: Village **Activities:** Campus Ministries; Choral groups; Concert band; Dance; Drama/theater; International Student Organization; Jazz band; Literary magazine; Model UN; Music ensembles; Pep band; Radio station; Student government; Student newspaper; Student-run film society 75 registered organizations, 46 honor societies, 26 religious organizations. 6 fraternities, 4 sororities. **Athletics (Intercollegiate):** *Men:* baseball, basketball, cheerleading, cross-country, golf, soccer, swimming, tennis, track/field (outdoor), water polo, wrestling. *Women:* basketball, cheerleading, cross-country, golf, soccer, softball, swimming, tennis, track/field (outdoor), volleyball, water polo. **On-Campus Highlights:** Junker Athletic Center, Logan House, Smith Chapel and Carillon, Bruno's Caf, Reen Union Building, Historic Behrend Farmhouse

ADMISSIONS
Freshman Academic Profile: Average high school GPA 3.3. 13% in top 10% of high school class, 42% in top 25% of high school class, 80% in top 50% of high school class. **Test Scores:** SAT Math middle 50% range 480-610. SAT EBRW middle 50% range 460-560. ACT middle 50% range 20-25. Minimum paper TOEFL 550. **Basis for Candidate Selection:** *Very important factors considered include:* academic GPA, standardized test scores. *Important factors considered include:* rigor of secondary school record. *Other factors considered include:* class rank, application essay, extracurricular activities, talent/ability, character/personal qualities, alumni/ae relation, geographical residence, state residency, volunteer work, work experience. **Freshman Admission Requirements:** High school diploma is required and GED is accepted *Academic units required:* 4 English, 3 math, 3 science, 2 foreign language, 3 social studies, *Academic units recommended:* 3 foreign language. **Freshman Admission Statistics:** 4,079 applied, 87.1% admitted, 33% enrolled. **Transfer Admission Requirements:** High school transcript, college transcript(s), Lowest grade transferable C. **General Admission Information:** Application fee $50. Priority deadline 11/30. Nonfall registration accepted. Admission may be deferred for a maximum of One year.

COSTS AND FINANCIAL AID
Annual in-state tuition $10,920. Annual out-of-state tuition $21,392. Room and board $10,920. Required fees $952. Average book expense $1,840. **Required Forms and Deadlines:** FAFSA. **Types of Aid:** *Need-based scholarships/grants:* College/university scholarship or grant aid from institutional funds; Federal Pell; Private scholarships; SEOG; State scholarships/grants. *Loans:*

Direct PLUS loans; Direct Subsidized Stafford Loans; Direct Unsubsidized Stafford Loans. *Student Employment:* Federal Work-Study Program available. Institutional employment available. **Financial Aid Statistics:** 63% needy freshmen, 64% needy undergrads receive need-based scholarship or grant aid. 46% freshmen, 39% undergrads receive non-need-based scholarship or grant aid. 87% freshmen, 89% undergrads receive need-based self-help aid. 0% freshmen, 0% undergrads receive athletic scholarships. 81% undergrads borrow to pay for school. Average cumulative indebtedness $39,346. **Criteria for awarding aid:** *Need-based:* Academics, Alumni affiliation *Non-need-based:* Academics, Alumni affiliation.

PENNSYLVANIA STATE UNIVERSITY FAYETTE, THE EBERLY CAMPUS

2201 University Drive, Lemont Furnace, PA 15456
Phone: (724)430-4130
E-mail: feadm@psu.edu
Fax: (724)430-4175 • **Website:** fe.psu.edu

This is a public school.

RATINGS
Admissions Selectivity Rating: 73   **Fire Safety Rating:** 60*   **Green Rating:** 60*

STUDENTS AND FACULTY
Enrollment: 671. **Student Body:** 59% female, 41% male, 5% out-of-state, 2% international. Asian <1%, African American 4%, Caucasian 89%, Hispanic 2%, Native American <1%, Pacific Islander 0%, Two or more races 3%, Race unknown 1%.
Retention and Graduation: 77% freshmen return for sophomore year.
Faculty: Student/faculty ratio 12:1. 44 full-time faculty, 48% hold PhDs, 2% are members of minority groups, 45% are women.

ACADEMICS
Degrees: Associate; Bachelor's; Certificate **Special Study Options:** Accelerated program; Cross-registration; Distance learning; Double major; Dual enrollment; Honors program; Independent study; Internships; Student-designed major; Study abroad.

CAMPUS LIFE
Activities: Campus Ministries; Choral groups; Drama/theater; Literary magazine; Musical theater; Student government; Student newspaper.

ADMISSIONS
Freshman Academic Profile: Average high school GPA 3.2. 10% in top 10% of high school class, 35% in top 25% of high school class, 73% in top 50% of high school class. **Test Scores:** SAT Math middle 50% range 410-520. SAT EBRW middle 50% range 390-510. ACT middle 50% range 17-22. **Basis for Candidate Selection:** *Very important factors considered include:* academic GPA, standardized test scores. *Important factors considered include:* rigor of secondary school record. *Other factors considered include:* class rank, application essay, extracurricular activities, talent/ability, character/personal qualities, alumni/ae relation, geographical residence, state residency, volunteer work, work experience. **Freshman Admission Requirements:** High school diploma is required and GED is accepted *Academic units required:* 4 English, 3 math, 3 science, 2 foreign language, 3 social studies, *Academic units recommended:* 3 foreign language. **Freshman Admission Statistics:** 659 applied, 80.9% admitted, 36% enrolled. **General Admission Information:** Application fee $50. Priority deadline 11/30. Nonfall registration accepted. Admission may be deferred for a maximum of One year.

COSTS AND FINANCIAL AID
Annual out-of-state tuition $19,404. Required fees $890. **Required Forms and Deadlines:** FAFSA. **Types of Aid:** *Need-based scholarships/grants:* College/university scholarship or grant aid from institutional funds; Federal Pell; Private scholarships; SEOG; State scholarships/grants. *Loans:* Direct PLUS loans; Direct Subsidized Stafford Loans; Direct Unsubsidized Stafford Loans. **Financial Aid Statistics:** 80% needy freshmen, 82% needy undergrads receive need-based scholarship or grant aid. 55% freshmen, 44% undergrads receive non-need-based scholarship or grant aid. 74% freshmen, 81% undergrads receive need-based self-help aid. 0% freshmen, 0% undergrads receive athletic scholarships. 87% undergrads borrow to pay for school. Average cumulative indebtedness $37,338. **Criteria for awarding aid:** *Need-based:* Academics, Alumni affiliation *Non-need-based:* Academics, Alumni affiliation.

PENNSYLVANIA STATE UNIVERSITY— GREATER ALLEGHENY

4000 University Drive, McKeesport, PA 15132-7698
Phone: (412)675-9010
E-mail: psuga@psu.edu
Fax: (412)675-9056 • **Website:** http://ga.psu.edu

This is a public school.

RATINGS
Admissions Selectivity Rating: 76   **Fire Safety Rating:** 60*   **Green Rating:** 60*

STUDENTS AND FACULTY
Enrollment: 532. **Student Body:** 41% female, 59% male, 7% out-of-state, 4% international. Asian 5%, African American 19%, Caucasian 61%, Hispanic 7%, Native American 0%, Pacific Islander 0%, Two or more races 3%, Race unknown 1%.
Retention and Graduation: 80% freshmen return for sophomore year.
Faculty: Student/faculty ratio 11:1. 34 full-time faculty, 74% hold PhDs, 29% are members of minority groups, 59% are women.

ACADEMICS
Degrees: Associate; Bachelor's; Certificate; Master's **Special Study Options:** Cross-registration; Distance learning; Double major; Dual enrollment; English as a Second Language (ESL); Honors program; Independent study; Internships; Liberal arts/career combination; Student-designed major; Study abroad.

FACILITIES
Housing: Special housing for disabled student; Wellness housing

CAMPUS LIFE
Activities: Campus Ministries; Choral groups; Dance; Drama/theater; Literary magazine; Music ensembles; Radio station; Student government; Student newspaper; Television station.

ADMISSIONS
Freshman Academic Profile: Average high school GPA 3.1. 6% in top 10% of high school class, 22% in top 25% of high school class, 64% in top 50% of high school class. **Test Scores:** SAT Math middle 50% range 400-540. SAT EBRW middle 50% range 390-540. ACT middle 50% range 20-25. **Basis for Candidate Selection:** *Very important factors considered include:* academic GPA, standardized test scores. *Important factors considered include:* rigor of secondary school record. *Other factors considered include:* class rank, application essay, extracurricular activities, talent/ability, character/personal qualities, alumni/ae relation, geographical residence, state residency, volunteer work, work experience. **Freshman Admission Requirements:** High school diploma is required and GED is accepted *Academic units required:* 4 English, 3 math, 3 science, 2 foreign language, 3 social studies, *Academic units recommended:* 3 foreign language. **Freshman Admission Statistics:** 594 applied, 78.8% admitted, 34% enrolled. **General Admission Information:** Application fee $50. Priority deadline 11/30. Nonfall registration accepted. Admission may be deferred for a maximum of One year.

COSTS AND FINANCIAL AID
Annual in-state tuition $10,920. Annual out-of-state tuition $19,404. Room and board $10,920. Required fees $942. Average book expense $1,840. **Required Forms and Deadlines:** FAFSA. **Types of Aid:** *Need-based scholarships/grants:* College/university scholarship or grant aid from institutional funds; Federal Pell; Private scholarships; SEOG; State scholarships/grants. *Loans:* Direct PLUS loans; Direct Subsidized Stafford Loans; Direct Unsubsidized Stafford Loans. **Financial Aid Statistics:** 86% needy freshmen, 84% needy undergrads receive need-based scholarship or grant aid. 71% freshmen, 52% undergrads receive non-need-based scholarship or grant aid. 77% freshmen, 84% undergrads receive need-based self-help aid. 0% freshmen, 0% undergrads receive athletic scholarships. 81% undergrads borrow to pay for school. Average cumulative indebtedness $38,931. **Criteria for awarding aid:** *Need-based:* Academics, Alumni affiliation *Non-need-based:* Academics, Alumni affiliation.

PENNSYLVANIA STATE UNIVERSITY— HARRISBURG

777 West Harrisburg Pike, Middletown, PA 17057-4898
Phone: 717-948-6250
E-mail: hbgadmit@psu.edu
Fax: 717-948-6325 • **Website:** www.harrisburg.psu.edu

This public school was founded in 1966.

RATINGS
Admissions Selectivity Rating: 74   **Fire Safety Rating:** 60*   **Green Rating:** 60*

STUDENTS AND FACULTY
Enrollment: 3,740. **Student Body:** 39% female, 61% male, 16% out-of-state, 10% international. Asian 9%, African American 11%, Caucasian 59%, Hispanic 6%, Native American <1%, Pacific Islander <1%, Two or more races 3%, Race unknown 2%.
Retention and Graduation: 87% freshmen return for sophomore year.
Faculty: Student/faculty ratio 15:1. 229 full-time faculty, 85% hold PhDs, 20% are members of minority groups, 41% are women.

ACADEMICS
Degrees: Associate; Bachelor's; Certificate; Doctoral/Research; Master's; Post-Bachelor's certificate **Classes:** Most classes have 10-19 students. Most lab/discussion sessions have 10-19 students. **Special Study Options:** Cooperative education program; Cross-registration; Distance learning; Double major; Dual enrollment; Honors program; Independent study; Internships; Student-designed major; Study abroad; Teacher certification program.

FACILITIES
Housing: Apartments for single students; Special housing for disabled students

CAMPUS LIFE
Environment: Village **Activities:** Choral groups; Dance; Drama/theater; Literary magazine; Music ensembles; Radio station; Student government; Student newspaper 2 honor societies, 1 religious organization. **Athletics (Intercollegiate):** *Men:* basketball, skiing (downhill/alpine), soccer, tennis, track/field (outdoor), volleyball. *Women:* skiing (downhill/alpine), soccer, track/field (outdoor), volleyball.

ADMISSIONS
Freshman Academic Profile: Average high school GPA 3.1. 9% in top 10% of high school class, 33% in top 25% of high school class, 72% in top 50% of high school class. **Test Scores:** SAT Math middle 50% range 470-610. SAT EBRW middle 50% range 440-560. ACT middle 50% range 20-26. **Basis for Candidate Selection:** *Very important factors considered include:* academic GPA, standardized test scores. *Important factors considered include:* rigor of secondary school record. *Other factors considered include:* class rank, application essay, extracurricular activities, talent/ability, character/personal qualities, alumni/ae relation, geographical residence, state residency, volunteer work, work experience. **Freshman Admission Requirements:** High school diploma is required and GED is accepted *Academic units required:* 4 English, 3 math, 3 science, 2 foreign language, 3 social studies, *Academic units recommended:* 3 foreign language. **Freshman Admission Statistics:** 3,938 applied, 84.9% admitted, 26% enrolled. **Transfer Admission Requirements:** High school transcript, college transcript(s), Lowest grade transferable C. **General Admission Information:** Application fee $50. Priority deadline 11/30. Nonfall registration accepted. Admission may be deferred for a maximum of One year.

COSTS AND FINANCIAL AID
Annual in-state tuition $12,450. Annual out-of-state tuition $21,392. Room and board $12,450. Required fees $952. Average book expense $1,840. **Required Forms and Deadlines:** FAFSA. **Types of Aid:** *Need-based scholarships/grants:* College/university scholarship or grant aid from institutional funds; Federal Pell; Private scholarships; SEOG; State scholarships/grants. *Loans:* Direct PLUS loans; Direct Subsidized Stafford Loans; Direct Unsubsidized Stafford Loans. **Financial Aid Statistics:** 62% needy freshmen, 66% needy undergrads receive need-based scholarship or grant aid. 70% freshmen, 46% undergrads receive non-need-based scholarship or grant aid. 77% freshmen, 83% undergrads receive need-based self-help aid. 0% freshmen, 0% undergrads receive athletic scholarships. 76% undergrads borrow to pay for school. Average cumulative indebtedness $40,639. **Criteria for awarding aid:** *Need-based:* Academics, Alumni affiliation *Non-need-based:* Academics, Alumni affiliation.

PENNSYLVANIA STATE UNIVERSITY— HAZLETON

76 University Drive, Hazleton, PA 18202-1291
Phone: (570)450-3142
E-mail: hn-admissions@psu.edu
Website: http://hazleton.psu.edu/

This is a public school.

RATINGS
Admissions Selectivity Rating: 74   **Fire Safety Rating:** 60*   **Green Rating:** 60*

STUDENTS AND FACULTY
Enrollment: 753. **Student Body:** 42% female, 58% male, 19% out-of-state, 2% international. Asian 3%, African American 12%, Caucasian 60%, Hispanic 19%, Native American <1%, Pacific Islander <1%, Two or more races 3%, Race unknown 1%.
Retention and Graduation: 79% freshmen return for sophomore year.
Faculty: Student/faculty ratio 13:1. 50 full-time faculty, 66% hold PhDs, 12% are members of minority groups, 38% are women.

ACADEMICS
Degrees: Associate; Bachelor's; Certificate; Post-Bachelor's certificate **Special Study Options:** Accelerated program; Cross-registration; Distance learning; Double major; Dual enrollment; English as a Second Language (ESL); Honors program; Independent study; Internships; Student-designed major; Study abroad.

FACILITIES
Housing: Coed dorms; Theme housing

CAMPUS LIFE
Activities: Choral groups; Dance; Drama/theater; Literary magazine; Student government; Student newspaper.

ADMISSIONS
Freshman Academic Profile: Average high school GPA 3.1. 11% in top 10% of high school class, 36% in top 25% of high school class, 77% in top 50% of high school class. **Test Scores:** SAT Math middle 50% range 430-540. SAT EBRW middle 50% range 410-520. ACT middle 50% range 17-25. **Basis for Candidate Selection:** *Very important factors considered include:* academic GPA, standardized test scores. *Important factors considered include:* rigor of secondary school record. *Other factors considered include:* class rank, application essay, extracurricular activities, talent/ability, character/personal qualities, alumni/ae relation, geographical residence, state residency, volunteer work, work experience. **Freshman Admission Requirements:** High school diploma is required and GED is accepted *Academic units required:* 4 English, 3 math, 3 science, 2 foreign language, 3 social studies, *Academic units recommended:* 3 foreign language. **Freshman Admission Statistics:** 763 applied, 83.9% admitted, 41% enrolled. **General Admission Information:** Application fee $50. Priority deadline 11/30. Nonfall registration accepted. Admission may be deferred for a maximum of One year.

COSTS AND FINANCIAL AID
Annual in-state tuition $10,920. Annual out-of-state tuition $20,206. Room and board $10,920. Required fees $890. Average book expense $1,840. **Required Forms and Deadlines:** FAFSA. **Types of Aid:** *Need-based scholarships/grants:* College/university scholarship or grant aid from institutional funds; Federal Pell; Private scholarships; SEOG; State scholarships/grants. *Loans:* Direct PLUS loans; Direct Subsidized Stafford Loans; Direct Unsubsidized Stafford Loans. **Financial Aid Statistics:** 72% needy freshmen, 76% needy undergrads receive need-based scholarship or grant aid. 60% freshmen, 50% undergrads receive non-need-based scholarship or grant aid. 81% freshmen, 86% undergrads receive need-based self-help aid. 0% freshmen, 0% undergrads receive athletic scholarships. 83% undergrads borrow to pay for school. Average cumulative indebtedness $45,582. **Criteria for awarding aid:** *Need-based:* Academics, Alumni affiliation *Non-need-based:* Academics, Alumni affiliation.

PENNSYLVANIA STATE UNIVERSITY— LEHIGH VALLEY

2809 Saucon Valley Road, Center Valley, PA 18034-8447
Phone: 610-285-5035
E-mail: admissions-lv@psu.edu
Fax: 610-285-5220 • **Website:** www.lv.psu.edu

This public school was founded in 1912. It has a 42 acre campus.

RATINGS
Admissions Selectivity Rating: 74   **Fire Safety Rating:** 60*   **Green Rating:** 60*

STUDENTS AND FACULTY
Enrollment: 773. **Student Body:** 48% female, 52% male, 3% out-of-state, <1% international. Asian 10%, African American 6%, Caucasian 64%, Hispanic 16%, Native American 0%, Pacific Islander <1%, Two or more races 2%, Race unknown 1%.
Retention and Graduation: 78% freshmen return for sophomore year.
Faculty: Student/faculty ratio 14:1. 43 full-time faculty, 60% hold PhDs, 9% are members of minority groups, 65% are women.

ACADEMICS
Degrees: Associate; Bachelor's; Certificate; Post-Bachelor's certificate **Classes:** Most classes have fewer than 10 students. **Special Study Options:** Cooperative education program; Cross-registration; Distance learning; Double major; Dual enrollment; Honors program; Independent study; Internships; Liberal arts/career combination; Study abroad; Teacher certification program.

CAMPUS LIFE
Activities: Choral groups; Dance; Drama/theater; Literary magazine; Student government; Student newspaper; Student-run film society. **Athletics (Intercollegiate):** *Men:* basketball, cross-country, golf, soccer, tennis, volleyball. *Women:* basketball, golf, tennis, volleyball.

ADMISSIONS
Freshman Academic Profile: Average high school GPA 3.0. 8% in top 10% of high school class, 33% in top 25% of high school class, 69% in top 50% of high school class. **Test Scores:** SAT Math middle 50% range 450-580. SAT EBRW middle 50% range 440-560. ACT middle 50% range 19-27. Minimum paper TOEFL 550. **Basis for Candidate Selection:** *Very important factors considered include:* academic GPA, standardized test scores. *Important factors considered include:* rigor of secondary school record. *Other factors considered include:* class rank, application essay, extracurricular activities, talent/ability, character/personal qualities, alumni/ae relation, geographical residence, state residency, volunteer work, work experience. **Freshman Admission Requirements:** High school diploma is required and GED is accepted *Academic units required:* 4 English, 3 math, 3 science, 2 foreign language, 3 social studies, *Academic units recommended:* 3 foreign language. **Freshman Admission Statistics:** 543 applied, 86.4% admitted, 29% enrolled. **Transfer Admission Requirements:** High school transcript, college transcript(s), Lowest grade transferable C. **General Admission Information:** Application fee $50. Priority deadline 11/30. Nonfall registration accepted. Admission may be deferred for a maximum of 1 year.

COSTS AND FINANCIAL AID
Annual out-of-state tuition $20,206. Required fees $952. **Required Forms and Deadlines:** FAFSA. **Types of Aid:** *Need-based scholarships/grants:* College/university scholarship or grant aid from institutional funds; Federal Pell; Private scholarships; SEOG; State scholarships/grants. *Loans:* Direct PLUS loans; Direct Subsidized Stafford Loans; Direct Unsubsidized Stafford Loans. **Financial Aid Statistics:** 74% needy freshmen, 80% needy undergrads receive need-based scholarship or grant aid. 46% freshmen, 30% undergrads receive non-need-based scholarship or grant aid. 72% freshmen, 82% undergrads receive need-based self-help aid. 0% freshmen, 0% undergrads receive athletic scholarships. 79% undergrads borrow to pay for school. Average cumulative indebtedness $35,803. **Criteria for awarding aid:** *Need-based:* Academics, Alumni affiliation *Non-need-based:* Academics, Alumni affiliation.

PENNSYLVANIA STATE UNIVERSITY— MONT ALTO

1 Campus Drive, Mont Alto, PA 17237-9703
Phone: 717-749-6130
E-mail: psuma@psu.edu
Fax: 717-749-6132 • **Website:** http://www.montalto.psu.edu

This public school was founded in 1929. It has a 62 acre campus.

RATINGS
Admissions Selectivity Rating: 76   **Fire Safety Rating:** 60*   **Green Rating:** 60*

STUDENTS AND FACULTY
Enrollment: 809. **Student Body:** 58% female, 42% male, 12% out-of-state, <1% international. Asian 2%, African American 8%, Caucasian 80%, Hispanic 5%, Native American 0%, Pacific Islander <1%, Two or more races 3%, Race unknown 1%.
Retention and Graduation: 77% freshmen return for sophomore year. 22% grads go on to further study within 1 year. **Faculty:** Student/faculty ratio 11:1. 56 full-time faculty, 46% hold PhDs, 11% are members of minority groups, 52% are women.

ACADEMICS
Degrees: Associate; Bachelor's; Certificate **Classes:** Most classes have 10-19 students. Most lab/discussion sessions have 10-19 students. **Special Study Options:** Accelerated program; Cross-registration; Distance learning; Double major; Dual enrollment; Honors program; Independent study; Internships; Liberal arts/career combination; Student-designed major; Study abroad; Weekend college. Honors programs: The Schreyer Honors College is widely recognized as one of the best and most comprehensive undergraduate honors programs in the United States. http://www.scholars.psu.edu/index.cfm Combined degree programs: BA/MD; BA/MEng. **Disability Services offered to physically disabled students:** Note-taking services; Reader services; Tape recorders; Tutors.

FACILITIES
Housing: Coed dorms; Special housing for disabled students 99% of campus accessible to physically disabled.

CAMPUS LIFE
Environment: Village **Activities:** Choral groups; Dance; Drama/theater; Jazz band; Student government; Student newspaper. **Athletics (Intercollegiate):** *Men:* basketball, soccer, tennis. *Women:* basketball, tennis.

ADMISSIONS
Freshman Academic Profile: Average high school GPA 3.1. 6% in top 10% of high school class, 36% in top 25% of high school class, 77% in top 50% of high school class. **Test Scores:** SAT Math middle 50% range 425-535. SAT EBRW middle 50% range 420-530. ACT middle 50% range 17-24. **Basis for Candidate Selection:** *Very important factors considered include:* academic GPA, standardized test scores. *Important factors considered include:* rigor of secondary school record. *Other factors considered include:* class rank, application essay, extracurricular activities, talent/ability, character/personal qualities, alumni/ae relation, geographical residence, state residency, volunteer work, work experience. **Freshman Admission Requirements:** High school diploma is required and GED is accepted *Academic units required:* 4 English, 3 math, 3 science, 2 foreign language, 3 social studies, *Academic units recommended:* 3 foreign language. **Freshman Admission Statistics:** 688 applied, 79.4% admitted, 45% enrolled. **Transfer Admission Requirements:** High school transcript, college transcript(s), Lowest grade transferable C. **General Admission Information:** Application fee $50. Priority deadline 11/30. Nonfall registration accepted. Admission may be deferred for a maximum of One year.

COSTS AND FINANCIAL AID
Annual in-state tuition $10,920. Annual out-of-state tuition $19,404. Room and board $10,920. Required fees $952. Average book expense $1,840. **Required Forms and Deadlines:** FAFSA. **Types of Aid:** *Need-based scholarships/grants:* College/university scholarship or grant aid from institutional funds; Federal Pell; Private scholarships; SEOG; State scholarships/grants. *Loans:* Direct PLUS loans; Direct Subsidized Stafford Loans; Direct Unsubsidized Stafford Loans. **Financial Aid Statistics:** 71% needy freshmen, 75% needy undergrads receive need-based scholarship or grant aid. 56% freshmen, 48% undergrads receive non-need-based scholarship or grant aid. 82% freshmen, 86% undergrads receive need-based self-help aid. 0% freshmen, 0% undergrads receive athletic scholarships. 87% undergrads borrow to pay for school. Average cumulative indebtedness $46,030. **Criteria for awarding aid:** *Need-based:* Academics, Alumni affiliation, Minority status *Non-need-based:* Academics, Alumni affiliation, Minority status.

PENNSYLVANIA STATE UNIVERSITY— NEW KENSINGTON

3550 7th Street Road, New Kensington, PA 15068-1765
Phone: (724)334-5466
E-mail: nkadmissions@psu.edu
Fax: (724)334-6111 • **Website:** http://nk.psu.edu

This is a public school.

RATINGS
Admissions Selectivity Rating: 77   **Fire Safety Rating:** 60*   **Green Rating:** 60*

STUDENTS AND FACULTY
Enrollment: 598. **Student Body:** 41% female, 59% male, 2% out-of-state, 2% international. Asian 2%, African American 5%, Caucasian 87%, Hispanic 2%, Native American <1%, Pacific Islander 0%, Two or more races 1%, Race unknown 1%.
Retention and Graduation: 67% freshmen return for sophomore year. **Faculty:** Student/faculty ratio 12:1. 35 full-time faculty, 63% hold PhDs, 20% are members of minority groups, 43% are women.

ACADEMICS
Degrees: Associate; Bachelor's; Certificate **Classes:** Most classes have fewer than 10 students. **Special Study Options:** Cross-registration; Distance learning; Double major; Dual enrollment; External degree program; Honors program; Independent study; Internships; Study abroad.

CAMPUS LIFE
Activities: Dance; Drama/theater; Jazz band; Literary magazine; Musical theater; Student government; Student newspaper.

ADMISSIONS
Freshman Academic Profile: Average high school GPA 3.1. 10% in top 10% of high school class, 29% in top 25% of high school class, 68% in top 50% of high school class. **Test Scores:** SAT Math middle 50% range 440-550. SAT EBRW middle 50% range 440-530. ACT middle 50% range 19-23. **Basis for Candidate Selection:** *Very important factors considered include:* academic GPA, standardized test scores. *Important factors considered include:* rigor of secondary school record. *Other factors considered include:* class rank, application essay, extracurricular activities, talent/ability, character/personal qualities, alumni/ae relation, geographical residence, state residency, volunteer work, work experience, level of applicant's interest. **Freshman Admission Requirements:** High school diploma is required and GED is accepted *Academic units required:* 4 English, 3 math, 3 science, 2 foreign language, 3 social studies, *Academic units recommended:* 3 foreign language. **Freshman Admission Statistics:** 508 applied, 79.1% admitted, 44% enrolled. **General Admission Information:** Application fee $50. Priority deadline 11/30. Nonfall registration accepted. Admission may be deferred for a maximum of One year.

COSTS AND FINANCIAL AID
Annual out-of-state tuition $19,404. Required fees $890. **Required Forms and Deadlines:** FAFSA. **Types of Aid:** *Need-based scholarships/grants:* College/university scholarship or grant aid from institutional funds; Federal Pell; Private scholarships; SEOG; State scholarships/grants. *Loans:* Direct PLUS loans; Direct Subsidized Stafford Loans; Direct Unsubsidized Stafford Loans. **Financial Aid Statistics:** 81% needy freshmen, 77% needy undergrads receive need-based scholarship or grant aid. 62% freshmen, 40% undergrads receive non-need-based scholarship or grant aid. 65% freshmen, 81% undergrads receive need-based self-help aid. 0% freshmen, 0% undergrads receive athletic scholarships. 93% undergrads borrow to pay for school. Average cumulative indebtedness $33,237. **Criteria for awarding aid:** *Need-based:* Academics, Alumni affiliation *Non-need-based:* Academics, Alumni affiliation.

PENNSYLVANIA STATE UNIVERSITY—SCHUYLKILL

200 University Drive, Schuykill Haven, PA 17972-2208
Phone: 570-385-6252
E-mail: sl-admissions@psu.edu
Fax: 570-385-3672 • **Website:** http://www.sl.psu.edu

This public school was founded in 1934. It has a 42 acre campus.

RATINGS
Admissions Selectivity Rating: 78   **Fire Safety Rating:** 60*   **Green Rating:** 60*

STUDENTS AND FACULTY
Enrollment: 720. **Student Body:** 60% female, 40% male, 12% out-of-state, 1% international. Asian 1%, African American 18%, Caucasian 69%, Hispanic 7%, Native American <1%, Pacific Islander <1%, Two or more races 1%, Race unknown 2%.
Retention and Graduation: 76% freshmen return for sophomore year.
Faculty: Student/faculty ratio 13:1. 43 full-time faculty, 77% hold PhDs, 2% are members of minority groups, 40% are women.

ACADEMICS
Degrees: Associate; Bachelor's; Certificate **Classes:** Most classes have 10-19 students. Most lab/discussion sessions have 10-19 students. **Special Study Options:** Accelerated program; Distance learning; Double major; Dual enrollment; English as a Second Language (ESL); Honors program; Independent study; Internships; Study abroad.

FACILITIES
Housing: Apartments for single students; Special housing for disabled student; Theme housing

CAMPUS LIFE
Activities: Campus Ministries; Choral groups; Dance; Drama/theater; International Student Organization; Musical theater; Radio station; Student government. **Athletics (Intercollegiate):** *Men:* basketball, cross-country, softball, tennis, volleyball. *Women:* basketball, cross-country, softball, tennis, volleyball.

ADMISSIONS
Freshman Academic Profile: Average high school GPA 2.9. 5% in top 10% of high school class, 24% in top 25% of high school class, 51% in top 50% of high school class. **Test Scores:** SAT Math middle 50% range 420-510. SAT EBRW middle 50% range 410-520. ACT middle 50% range 16-19. Minimum paper TOEFL 550. **Basis for Candidate Selection:** *Very important factors considered include:* academic GPA, standardized test scores. *Important factors considered include:* rigor of secondary school record. *Other factors considered include:* class rank, application essay, extracurricular activities, talent/ability, character/personal qualities, alumni/ae relation, geographical residence, state residency, volunteer work, work experience. **Freshman Admission Requirements:** High school diploma is required and GED is accepted *Academic units required:* 4 English, 3 math, 3 science, 2 foreign language, 3 social studies, *Academic units recommended:* 3 foreign language. **Freshman Admission Statistics:** 690 applied, 73.0% admitted, 44% enrolled. **Transfer Admission Requirements:** High school transcript, college transcript(s), Lowest grade transferable C. **General Admission Information:** Application fee $50. Priority deadline 11/30. Nonfall registration accepted. Admission may be deferred for a maximum of 1 year.

COSTS AND FINANCIAL AID
Annual in-state tuition $8,060. Annual out-of-state tuition $20,206. Room and board $8,060. Required fees $890. Average book expense $1,840. **Required Forms and Deadlines:** FAFSA. **Types of Aid:** *Need-based scholarships/grants:* College/university scholarship or grant aid from institutional funds; Federal Pell; Private scholarships; SEOG; State scholarships/grants. *Loans:* Direct PLUS loans; Direct Subsidized Stafford Loans; Direct Unsubsidized Stafford Loans. **Financial Aid Statistics:** 84% needy freshmen, 83% needy undergrads receive need-based scholarship or grant aid. 78% freshmen, 57% undergrads receive non-need-based scholarship or grant aid. 85% freshmen, 89% undergrads receive need-based self-help aid. 0% freshmen, 0% undergrads receive athletic scholarships. 92% undergrads borrow to pay for school. Average cumulative indebtedness $38,822. **Criteria for awarding aid:** *Need-based:* Academics, Alumni affiliation *Non-need-based:* Academics, Alumni affiliation.

PENNSYLVANIA STATE UNIVERSITY—SHENANGO

147 Shenango Ave, Sharon, PA 16146-1597
Phone: (724)983-2803
E-mail: psushenango@psu.edu
Fax: (724)983-2820 • **Website:** http://shenango.psu.edu

This is a public school.

RATINGS
Admissions Selectivity Rating: 81   **Fire Safety Rating:** 60*   **Green Rating:** 60*

STUDENTS AND FACULTY
Enrollment: 436. **Student Body:** 73% female, 27% male, 22% out-of-state, 0% international. Asian 1%, African American 7%, Caucasian 85%, Hispanic 2%, Native American 0%, Pacific Islander 0%, Two or more races 3%, Race unknown 3%.
Retention and Graduation: 66% freshmen return for sophomore year.
Faculty: Student/faculty ratio 11:1. 28 full-time faculty, 50% hold PhDs, 7% are members of minority groups, 68% are women.

ACADEMICS
Degrees: Associate; Bachelor's; Certificate **Classes:** Most classes have 20-29 students. Most lab/discussion sessions have fewer than 10 students. **Special Study Options:** Accelerated program; Cross-registration; Distance learning; Double major; Dual enrollment; Honors program; Independent study; Internships; Student-designed major; Study abroad.

CAMPUS LIFE
Activities: Choral groups; Drama/theater; Student government.

ADMISSIONS
Freshman Academic Profile: Average high school GPA 3.0. 1% in top 10% of high school class, 35% in top 25% of high school class, 72% in top 50% of high school class. **Test Scores:** SAT Math middle 50% range 410-520. SAT EBRW middle 50% range 410-530. ACT middle 50% range 19-22. **Basis for Candidate Selection:** *Very important factors considered include:* academic GPA, standardized test scores. *Important factors considered include:* rigor of secondary school record. *Other factors considered include:* class rank, application essay, extracurricular activities, talent/ability, character/personal qualities, alumni/ae relation, geographical residence, state residency, volunteer work, work experience. **Freshman Admission Requirements:** High school diploma is required and GED is accepted *Academic units required:* 4 English, 3 math, 3 science, 2 foreign language, 3 social studies, *Academic units recommended:* 3 foreign language. **Freshman Admission Statistics:** 154 applied, 68.2% admitted, 54% enrolled. **General Admission Information:** Application fee $50. Priority deadline 11/30. Nonfall registration accepted. Admission may be deferred for a maximum of One year.

COSTS AND FINANCIAL AID
Annual out-of-state tuition $19,030. Required fees $880. **Required Forms and Deadlines:** FAFSA. **Types of Aid:** *Need-based scholarships/grants:* College/university scholarship or grant aid from institutional funds; Federal Pell; Private scholarships; SEOG; State scholarships/grants. *Loans:* Direct PLUS loans; Direct Subsidized Stafford Loans; Direct Unsubsidized Stafford Loans. **Financial Aid Statistics:** 81% needy freshmen, 85% needy undergrads receive need-based scholarship or grant aid. 66% freshmen, 54% undergrads receive non-need-based scholarship or grant aid. 75% freshmen, 87% undergrads receive need-based self-help aid. 0% freshmen, 0% undergrads receive athletic scholarships. 80% undergrads borrow to pay for school. Average cumulative indebtedness $35,187. **Criteria for awarding aid:** *Need-based:* Academics, Alumni affiliation *Non-need-based:* Academics, Alumni affiliation.

PENNSYLVANIA STATE UNIVERSITY— UNIVERSITY PARK

Best Colleges

201 Old Main, University Park, PA 16802
Phone: 814-865-5471 • **Financial Aid Phone:** 814-865-6301
E-mail: admissions@psu.edu • **CEEB Code:** 2660
Fax: 814-863-7590 • **Website:** www.psu.edu • **ACT Code:** 3656

This public school was founded in 1855. It has a 7958 acre campus.

RATINGS
Admissions Selectivity Rating: 88   **Fire Safety Rating:** 97   **Green Rating:** 92

STUDENTS AND FACULTY
Enrollment: 40,552. **Student Body:** 47% female, 53% male, 34% out-of-state, 12% international (105 countries represented). Asian 6%, African American 4%, Caucasian 66%, Hispanic 7%, Native American <1%, Pacific Islander <1%, Two or more races 3%, Race unknown 2%.
Retention and Graduation: 93% freshmen return for sophomore year. 67% freshmen graduate within 4 years. 85% freshmen graduate within 6 years. 17% grads go on to further study within 1 year. **Faculty:** Student/faculty ratio 16:1. 2,679 full-time faculty, 82% hold PhDs, 19% are members of minority groups, 40% are women.

ACADEMICS
Degrees: Associate; Bachelor's; Certificate; Doctoral/Professional; Doctoral/Research; Master's; Post-Bachelor's certificate **Classes:** Most classes have 10-19 students. Most lab/discussion sessions have 10-19 students. **Most popular majors:** Communication, Journalism, And Related Programs, Other; Engineering, Other; Business, Management, Marketing, And Related Support Services, Other. **Special Study Options:** Accelerated program; Cooperative education program; Cross-registration; Distance learning; Double major; Dual enrollment; English as a Second Language (ESL); Exchange student program (domestic); External degree program; Honors program; Independent study; Internships; Liberal arts/career combination; Student-designed major; Study abroad; Teacher certification program; Weekend college. Honors programs: The Schreyer Honors College is widely recognized as one of the best and most comprehensive undergraduate honors program in the United States. http://shc.psu.edu/ Combined degree programs: BA/MA; BA/MD. **Disability Services offered to physically disabled students:** Note-taking services; Reader services; Tape recorders. **Career services:** Alumni network; Alumni services; Career assessment; Career/job search classes; Internships; Regional alumni

FACILITIES
Housing: Apartments for married students; Apartments for single students; Coed dorms; Fraternity/sorority housing; Special housing for disabled student; Theme housing; Wellness housing; Women's dorms 95% of campus accessible to physically disabled. **Special Academic Facilities/Equipment:** The EMS Museum & Art Gallery, Frost Entomological Museum, Matson Museum of Anthropology, Palmer Museum of Art, Pasto Agricultural Museum, All-Sports Museum, Special Collections Library Exhibit Gallery, the Arboretum at Penn State, and Shaver's Creek Environmental Center. In addition, the campus features theaters, language labs, a weather station and a nuclear reactor. **Computers:** 83% of classrooms, 50% of dorms, 100% of libraries, 100% of dining areas, 100% of student union, 25% of common outdoor areas have wireless network access. Students can register for classes online. Administrative functions (other than registration) can be performed online.

CAMPUS LIFE
Environment: Town **Activities:** Campus Ministries; Choral groups; Concert band; Dance; Drama/theater; International Student Organization; Jazz band; Literary magazine; Marching band; Model UN; Music ensembles; Musical theater; Opera; Pep band; Radio station; Student government; Student newspaper; Student-run film society; Symphony orchestra; Television station; Yearbook 784 registered organizations, 34 honor societies, 49 religious organizations. 58 fraternities, 32 sororities. **Athletics (Intercollegiate):** *Men:* baseball, basketball, cheerleading, cross-country, diving, fencing, football, golf, gymnastics, lacrosse, soccer, swimming, tennis, track/field (outdoor), track/field (indoor), volleyball, wrestling. *Women:* basketball, cheerleading, cross-country, diving, fencing, field hockey, golf, gymnastics, lacrosse, soccer, softball, swimming, tennis, track/field (outdoor), track/field (indoor), volleyball. **On-Campus Highlights:** Hetzel Union Building, Pattee/Paterno Library, The Creamery, Old Main, The Lion Shrine **Environmental Initiatives:** To address the issue of climate change, Penn State established the goal of reducing greenhouse gas emissions to 17.5% below FY05/06 levels by 2012. This goal was

achieved, and the university subsequently set a more ambitious goal of reducing emissions by an additional 17.5%, for a total 35% reduction by 2020. In 2014, Penn State joined the U.S. Department of Energy's Better Buildings Challenge and pledged to reduce its building portfolio's energy use by 20 percent over the next decade. With a commitment of 28 million square feet (all campuses except Hershey Medical & Pennsylvania College of Technology), Penn State becomes the largest university in the program.

ADMISSIONS
Freshman Academic Profile: Average high school GPA 3.6. 35% in top 10% of high school class, 73% in top 25% of high school class, 96% in top 50% of high school class. **Test Scores:** SAT Math middle 50% range 580-680. SAT EBRW middle 50% range 580-660. ACT middle 50% range 25-30. Minimum internet-based TOEFL 80. Minimum paper TOEFL 550. **Basis for Candidate Selection:** *Very important factors considered include:* academic GPA, standardized test scores. *Important factors considered include:* rigor of secondary school record. *Other factors considered include:* class rank, application essay, extracurricular activities, talent/ability, character/personal qualities, alumni/ae relation, geographical residence, state residency, volunteer work, work experience. **Freshman Admission Requirements:** High school diploma is required and GED is accepted *Academic units required:* 4 English, 3 math, 3 science, 2 foreign language, 3 social studies, *Academic units recommended:* 3 foreign language. **Freshman Admission Statistics:** 56,114 applied, 50.3% admitted, 28% enrolled. **Transfer Admission Requirements:** High school transcript, college transcript(s), Lowest grade transferable C. **General Admission Information:** Application fee $65. Priority deadline 11/30. Nonfall registration accepted. Admission may be deferred for a maximum of One year.

COSTS AND FINANCIAL AID
Annual in-state tuition $11,280. Annual out-of-state tuition $32,644. Room and board $11,280. Required fees $1,020. Average book expense $1,840. **Required Forms and Deadlines:** FAFSA. *Types of Aid: Need-based scholarships/grants:* College/university scholarship or grant aid from institutional funds; Federal Pell; Private scholarships; SEOG; State scholarships/grants. *Loans:* Direct PLUS loans; Direct Subsidized Stafford Loans; Direct Unsubsidized Stafford Loans. *Student Employment:* Federal Work-Study Program available. Institutional employment available. **Financial Aid Statistics:** 43% needy freshmen, 50% needy undergrads receive need-based scholarship or grant aid. 54% freshmen, 40% undergrads receive non-need-based scholarship or grant aid. 77% freshmen, 85% undergrads receive need-based self-help aid. 2% freshmen, 2% undergrads receive athletic scholarships. 66% freshmen, 67% undergrads receive any aid. 54% undergrads borrow to pay for school. Average cumulative indebtedness $37,213. **Criteria for awarding aid:** *Need-based:* Academics, Alumni affiliation, Athletics *Non-need-based:* Academics, Alumni affiliation, Athletics.

PENNSYLVANIA STATE UNIVERSITY— WILKES-BARRE

Old Route 115, Lehman, PA 18627-0217
Phone: 570-675-9238
E-mail: wbadmissions@psu.edu
Fax: 570-675-9113 • **Website:** http://www.wb.psu.edu

This is a public school.

RATINGS
Admissions Selectivity Rating: 73   **Fire Safety Rating:** 60*   **Green Rating:** 60*

STUDENTS AND FACULTY
Enrollment: 460. **Student Body:** 33% female, 67% male, 5% out-of-state, <1% international. Asian 1%, African American 3%, Caucasian 88%, Hispanic 5%, Native American <1%, Pacific Islander 0%, Two or more races 2%, Race unknown 1%.
Retention and Graduation: 84% freshmen return for sophomore year. **Faculty:** Student/faculty ratio 13:1. 30 full-time faculty, 63% hold PhDs, 23% are members of minority groups, 33% are women.

ACADEMICS
Degrees: Associate; Bachelor's; Certificate; Post-Bachelor's certificate **Classes:** Most classes have fewer than 10 students. **Special Study Options:** Accelerated program; Cross-registration; Distance learning; Double major; Dual enrollment; Honors program; Independent study; Internships; Student-designed major; Study abroad.

CAMPUS LIFE

Activities: Dance; Radio station; Student government; Student newspaper.

ADMISSIONS

Freshman Academic Profile: Average high school GPA 3.1. 8% in top 10% of high school class, 30% in top 25% of high school class, 74% in top 50% of high school class. **Test Scores:** SAT Math middle 50% range 440-550. SAT EBRW middle 50% range 430-540. ACT middle 50% range 18-26. **Basis for Candidate Selection:** *Very important factors considered include:* academic GPA, standardized test scores. *Important factors considered include:* rigor of secondary school record. *Other factors considered include:* class rank, application essay, extracurricular activities, talent/ability, character/personal qualities, alumni/ae relation, geographical residence, state residency, volunteer work, work experience. **Freshman Admission Requirements:** High school diploma is required and GED is accepted *Academic units required:* 4 English, 3 math, 3 science, 2 foreign language, 3 social studies, *Academic units recommended:* 3 foreign language. **Freshman Admission Statistics:** 411 applied, 87.6% admitted, 40% enrolled. **General Admission Information:** Application fee $50. Priority deadline 11/30. Nonfall registration accepted. Admission may be deferred for a maximum of 1 year.

COSTS AND FINANCIAL AID

Annual out-of-state tuition $19,404. Required fees $880. **Required Forms and Deadlines:** FAFSA. **Types of Aid:** *Need-based scholarships/grants:* College/university scholarship or grant aid from institutional funds; Federal Pell; Private scholarships; SEOG; State scholarships/grants. *Loans:* Direct PLUS loans; Direct Subsidized Stafford Loans; Direct Unsubsidized Stafford Loans. **Financial Aid Statistics:** 75% needy freshmen, 74% needy undergrads receive need-based scholarship or grant aid. 56% freshmen, 45% undergrads receive non-need-based scholarship or grant aid. 82% freshmen, 81% undergrads receive need-based self-help aid. 0% freshmen, 0% undergrads receive athletic scholarships. 85% undergrads borrow to pay for school. Average cumulative indebtedness $38,387. **Criteria for awarding aid:** *Need-based:* Academics, Alumni affiliation *Non-need-based:* Academics, Alumni affiliation.

PENNSYLVANIA STATE UNIVERSITY— WORTHINGTON SCRANTON

120 Ridge View Drive, Dunmore, PA 18512-1602
Phone: (570)963-2500
E-mail: wsadmissions@psu.edu
Fax: (570)963-2524 • **Website:** http://worthingtonscranton.psu.edu/

This is a public school.

RATINGS

Admissions Selectivity Rating: 75   **Fire Safety Rating:** 60*   **Green Rating:** 60*

STUDENTS AND FACULTY

Enrollment: 967. **Student Body:** 53% female, 47% male, 1% out-of-state, <1% international. Asian 5%, African American 3%, Caucasian 81%, Hispanic 6%, Native American 0%, Pacific Islander 0%, Two or more races 2%, Race unknown 2%.
Retention and Graduation: 75% freshmen return for sophomore year.
Faculty: Student/faculty ratio 14:1. 50 full-time faculty, 64% hold PhDs, 10% are members of minority groups, 52% are women.

ACADEMICS

Degrees: Associate; Bachelor's; Certificate **Special Study Options:** Accelerated program; Cooperative education program; Cross-registration; Distance learning; Double major; Dual enrollment; Honors program; Independent study; Internships; Liberal arts/career combination; Study abroad.

FACILITIES

Housing: Apartments for single students; Coed dorms

CAMPUS LIFE

Activities: Choral groups; Drama/theater; Jazz band; Literary magazine; Music ensembles; Student government; Student newspaper.

ADMISSIONS

Freshman Academic Profile: Average high school GPA 3.0. 10% in top 10% of high school class, 30% in top 25% of high school class, 70% in top 50% of high school class. **Test Scores:** SAT Math middle 50% range 430-540. SAT EBRW middle 50% range 420-530. ACT middle 50% range 17-21. **Basis for Candidate Selection:** *Very important factors considered include:* academic GPA, standardized test scores. *Important factors considered include:* rigor of secondary school record. *Other factors considered include:* class rank,

application essay, extracurricular activities, talent/ability, character/personal qualities, alumni/ae relation, geographical residence, state residency, volunteer work, work experience. **Freshman Admission Requirements:** High school diploma is required and GED is accepted *Academic units required:* 4 English, 3 math, 3 science, 2 foreign language, 3 social studies, *Academic units recommended:* 3 foreign language. **Freshman Admission Statistics:** 733 applied, 80.6% admitted, 39% enrolled. **General Admission Information:** Application fee $50. Priority deadline 11/30. Nonfall registration accepted. Admission may be deferred for a maximum of One year.

COSTS AND FINANCIAL AID

Annual out-of-state tuition $20,206. Required fees $890. **Required Forms and Deadlines:** FAFSA. **Types of Aid:** *Need-based scholarships/grants:* College/university scholarship or grant aid from institutional funds; Federal Pell; Private scholarships; SEOG; State scholarships/grants. *Loans:* Direct PLUS loans; Direct Subsidized Stafford Loans; Direct Unsubsidized Stafford Loans. **Financial Aid Statistics:** 76% needy freshmen, 80% needy undergrads receive need-based scholarship or grant aid. 34% freshmen, 25% undergrads receive non-need-based scholarship or grant aid. 80% freshmen, 86% undergrads receive need-based self-help aid. 0% freshmen, 0% undergrads receive athletic scholarships. 76% undergrads borrow to pay for school. Average cumulative indebtedness $42,128. **Criteria for awarding aid:** *Need-based:* Academics, Alumni affiliation *Non-need-based:* Academics, Alumni affiliation.

PENNSYLVANIA STATE UNIVERSITY—YORK

1031 Edgecomb Ave, York, PA 17403-3398
Phone: (717)771-4040
E-mail: ykadmission@psu.edu
Fax: (717)771-4005 • **Website:** http://www.yk.psu.edu

This is a public school.

RATINGS

Admissions Selectivity Rating: 74   **Fire Safety Rating:** 60*   **Green Rating:** 60*

STUDENTS AND FACULTY

Enrollment: 935. **Student Body:** 43% female, 57% male, 9% out-of-state, 15% international. Asian 5%, African American 6%, Caucasian 63%, Hispanic 6%, Native American <1%, Pacific Islander <1%, Two or more races 3%, Race unknown 2%.
Retention and Graduation: 80% freshmen return for sophomore year.
Faculty: Student/faculty ratio 15:1. 50 full-time faculty, 72% hold PhDs, 16% are members of minority groups, 48% are women.

ACADEMICS

Degrees: Associate; Bachelor's; Certificate; Master's; Post-Bachelor's certificate
Special Study Options: Accelerated program; Cross-registration; Distance learning; Double major; Dual enrollment; English as a Second Language (ESL); Honors program; Independent study; Internships; Study abroad; Weekend college.

CAMPUS LIFE

Activities: International Student Organization; Literary magazine; Student government.

ADMISSIONS

Freshman Academic Profile: Average high school GPA 3.1. 8% in top 10% of high school class, 27% in top 25% of high school class, 64% in top 50% of high school class. **Test Scores:** SAT Math middle 50% range 470-630. SAT EBRW middle 50% range 430-560. ACT middle 50% range 21-26. **Basis for Candidate Selection:** *Very important factors considered include:* academic GPA, standardized test scores. *Important factors considered include:* rigor of secondary school record. *Other factors considered include:* class rank, application essay, extracurricular activities, talent/ability, character/personal qualities, alumni/ae relation, geographical residence, state residency, volunteer work, work experience. **Freshman Admission Requirements:** High school diploma is required and GED is accepted *Academic units required:* 4 English, 3 math, 3 science, 2 foreign language, 3 social studies, *Academic units recommended:* 3 foreign language. **Freshman Admission Statistics:** 1,397 applied, 85.6% admitted, 27% enrolled. **General Admission Information:** Application fee $50. Priority deadline 11/30. Nonfall registration accepted. Admission may be deferred for a maximum of One year.

COSTS AND FINANCIAL AID

Annual out-of-state tuition $20,206. Required fees $952. **Required Forms and Deadlines:** FAFSA. **Types of Aid:** *Need-based scholarships/grants:* College/university scholarship or grant aid from institutional funds; Federal Pell;

Private scholarships; SEOG; State scholarships/grants. *Loans:* Direct PLUS loans; Direct Subsidized Stafford Loans; Direct Unsubsidized Stafford Loans. **Financial Aid Statistics:** 77% needy freshmen, 79% needy undergrads receive need-based scholarship or grant aid. 54% freshmen, 49% undergrads receive non-need-based scholarship or grant aid. 83% freshmen, 84% undergrads receive need-based self-help aid. 0% freshmen, 0% undergrads receive athletic scholarships. 75% undergrads borrow to pay for school. Average cumulative indebtedness $39,770. **Criteria for awarding aid:** *Need-based:* Academics, Alumni affiliation *Non-need-based:* Academics, Alumni affiliation.

PEPPERDINE UNIVERSITY

24255 Pacific Coast Highway, Malibu, CA 90263
Phone: 310-506-4392 • **Financial Aid Phone:** (310) 506-4301
E-mail: admission-seaver@pepperdine.edu • **CEEB Code:** 4630
Fax: 310-506-4861 • **Website:** www.pepperdine.edu • **ACT Code:** 373

This private school, affiliated with the Church of Christ, was founded in 1937. It has a 830 acre campus.

RATINGS

Admissions Selectivity Rating: 92   **Fire Safety Rating:** 86   **Green Rating:** 76

STUDENTS AND FACULTY

Enrollment: 3,594. **Student Body:** 59% female, 41% male, 45% out-of-state, 11% international (72 countries represented). Asian 10%, African American 4%, Caucasian 51%, Hispanic 14%, Native American <1%, Pacific Islander <1%, Two or more races 6%, Race unknown 3%.
Retention and Graduation: 90% freshmen return for sophomore year. 72% freshmen graduate within 4 years. 80% freshmen graduate within 6 years. 18% grads go on to further study within 1 year. 10% grads pursue arts and sciences degrees. 2% grads pursue law degrees. 2% grads pursue business degrees. 3% grads pursue medical degrees. **Faculty:** Student/faculty ratio 13:1. 394 full-time faculty, 89% hold PhDs, 20% are members of minority groups, 40% are women. 0% of classes are taught by teaching assistants.

ACADEMICS

Degrees: Bachelor's; Doctoral/Professional; Doctoral/Research; **Master's Classes:** Most classes have 10-19 students. Most lab/discussion sessions have fewer than 10 students. **Most popular majors:** Law; Clinical Psychology; Business Administration And Management, General. **Special Study Options:** Distance learning; Double major; Honors program; Independent study; Internships; Student-designed major; Study abroad; Teacher certification program. **Disability Services offered to physically disabled students:** Note-taking services; Reader services; Tape recorders; Tutors. **Career services:** Alumni network; Alumni services; Career assessment; Career/job search classes; Internships; Regional alumni

FACILITIES

Housing: Apartments for married students; Apartments for single students; Men's dorms; Special housing for disabled student; Women's dorms **Special Academic Facilities/Equipment:** Weisman Art Museum, Smothers Theater, Ahmanson Music Building **Computers:** 100% of classrooms, 100% of dorms, 100% of libraries, 100% of dining areas, 100% of student union, 100% of common outdoor areas have wireless network access. Students can register for classes online. Administrative functions (other than registration) can be performed online.

CAMPUS LIFE

Environment: City **Activities:** Campus Ministries; Choral groups; Concert band; Dance; Drama/theater; International Student Organization; Jazz band; Literary magazine; Model UN; Music ensembles; Musical theater; Opera; Pep band; Radio station; Student government; Student newspaper; Student-run film society; Symphony orchestra; Television station; Yearbook 50 registered organizations, 5 honor societies, 8 religious organizations. 5 fraternities, 7 sororities. **Athletics (Intercollegiate):** *Men:* baseball, basketball, cross-country, golf, tennis, volleyball, water polo. *Women:* basketball, cheerleading, cross-country, golf, soccer, swimming, tennis, track/field (outdoor), volleyball. **On-Campus Highlights:** Weisman Art Museum, Smother'sTheatre, The Sandbar, Alumni Park, Heroes Garden **Environmental Initiatives:** Pepperdine University has conserved billions of gallons of drinking water annually dating back to 1972. Pepperdine uses recycled water to irrigate over 99% of the

University's managed grounds. The University carefully monitors irrigation practices and uses an automated irrigation program based upon historical trends and current climactic conditions to conserve water and reduce runoff.

ADMISSIONS

Freshman Academic Profile: Average high school GPA 3.6. 49% in top 10% of high school class, 80% in top 25% of high school class, 97% in top 50% of high school class. **Test Scores:** SAT Math middle 50% range 600-700. SAT EBRW middle 50% range 600-690. ACT middle 50% range 25-30. Minimum internet-based TOEFL 80. Minimum paper TOEFL 550. **Basis for Candidate Selection:** *Very important factors considered include:* rigor of secondary school record, academic GPA, application essay, extracurricular activities, talent/ability, character/personal qualities, religious affiliation/commitment. *Important factors considered include:* standardized test scores, recommendation(s), volunteer work. *Other factors considered include:* first generation, alumni/ae relation, racial/ethnic status, work experience. **Freshman Admission Requirements:** High school diploma is required and GED is accepted **Freshman Admission Statistics:** 11,704 applied, 39.8% admitted, 18% enrolled. **Transfer Admission Requirements:** High school transcript, college transcript(s), essay or personal statement, Minimum college GPA of 3.00 required. Lowest grade transferable C. **General Admission Information:** Application fee $65. Regular application deadline 1/5. Nonfall registration accepted.

COSTS AND FINANCIAL AID

Required Forms and Deadlines: FAFSA. **Notification of Awards:** Applicants will be notified of awards on or about 4/15. **Types of Aid:** *Need-based scholarships/grants:* College/university scholarship or grant aid from institutional funds; Federal Pell; Private scholarships; SEOG; State scholarships/grants; United Negro College Fund. *Loans:* Direct PLUS loans; Direct Subsidized Stafford Loans; Direct Unsubsidized Stafford Loans. *Student Employment:* Federal Work-Study Program available. Institutional employment available. **Financial Aid Statistics:** 99% needy freshmen, 98% needy undergrads receive need-based scholarship or grant aid. 0% undergrads receive non-need-based scholarship or grant aid. 70% freshmen, 70% undergrads receive need-based self-help aid. 4% freshmen, 3% undergrads receive athletic scholarships. 94% freshmen, 81% undergrads receive any aid. Average cumulative indebtedness $29,640. **Criteria for awarding aid:** *Need-based:* Alumni affiliation, Job skills, Minority status *Non-need-based:* Academics, Art, Athletics, Leadership, Music/drama, Religious affiliation.

PHILADELPHIA UNIVERSITY

School House Lane and Henry Avenue, Philadelphia, PA 19144-5497
Phone: 215-951-2800 • **Financial Aid Phone:** 215-951-2940
E-mail: admissions@philau.edu • **CEEB Code:** 2666
Fax: 215-951-2907 • **Website:** www.PhilaU.edu • **ACT Code:** 3668

This private school was founded in 1884. It has a 100 acre campus.

RATINGS

Admissions Selectivity Rating: 81   **Fire Safety Rating:** 60*   **Green Rating:** 60*

STUDENTS AND FACULTY

Enrollment: 2,885. **Student Body:** 66% female, 34% male, 42% out-of-state, 4% international (30 countries represented). Asian 5%, African American 14%, Caucasian 59%, Hispanic 7%, Native American <1%, Pacific Islander <1%, Two or more races 2%, Race unknown 8%.
Retention and Graduation: 79% freshmen return for sophomore year. 19% grads go on to further study within 1 year. 8% grads pursue arts and sciences degrees. 1% grads pursue law degrees. 10% grads pursue business degrees. 1% grads pursue medical degrees. **Faculty:** Student/faculty ratio 13:1. 123 full-time faculty, 76% hold PhDs, 13% are members of minority groups, 46% are women. 0% of classes are taught by teaching assistants.

ACADEMICS

Degrees: Associate; Bachelor's; Certificate; Doctoral/Research; Master's; Post-Bachelor's certificate; Post-Master's certificate **Classes:** Most classes have 10-19 students. Most lab/discussion sessions have 10-19 students. **Most popular majors:** Architecture; Industrial And Product Design; Fashion/Apparel Design. **Special Study Options:** Accelerated program; Distance learning; Double major; Honors program; Independent study; Internships; Liberal arts/career combination; Study abroad. Honors programs: University Honors Program. **Disability Services offered to physically disabled students:** Note-taking services; Reader services; Tape recorders; Tutors. **Career services:** Alumni services; Career assessment; Career/job search classes; Internships

FACILITIES

Housing: Apartments for single students; Coed dorms; Special housing for disabled student; Women's dorms 63% of campus accessible to physically disabled. **Special Academic Facilities/Equipment:** The Design Center, Industrial Design Studios, Graphic Design Studios, Architecture Design Studios, CAD Labs in fashion design, interior design and architecture. **Computers:** Students can register for classes online. Administrative functions (other than registration) can be performed online.

CAMPUS LIFE

Environment: Metropolis **Activities:** Campus Ministries; Choral groups; Dance; Drama/theater; International Student Organization; Student government; Student newspaper; Yearbook 32 registered organizations, 3 religious organizations. 1 fraternity, 1 sorority. **Athletics (Intercollegiate):** *Men:* baseball, basketball, crew/rowing, cross-country, golf, soccer, tennis. *Women:* basketball, crew/rowing, cross-country, field hockey, lacrosse, soccer, softball, tennis, volleyball. **On-Campus Highlights:** Kanbar Campus Center, Athletic and Recreation Center, Gutman Library, SEED Center, The Design Center

ADMISSIONS

Freshman Academic Profile: Average high school GPA 3.5. 17% in top 10% of high school class, 46% in top 25% of high school class, 78% in top 50% of high school class. 80% from public high schools. **Test Scores:** SAT Math middle 50% range 490-600. SAT EBRW middle 50% range 480-580. ACT middle 50% range 20-26. Minimum paper TOEFL 500. **Basis for Candidate Selection:** *Very important factors considered include:* rigor of secondary school record, academic GPA, standardized test scores. *Important factors considered include:* class rank, application essay, recommendation(s). *Other factors considered include:* interview, extracurricular activities. **Freshman Admission Requirements:** High school diploma is required and GED is accepted *Academic units required:* 4 English, 3 math, 3 science, 2 science labs, 2 social studies, 1 history, 2 academic electives, *Academic units recommended:* 4 English, 4 math, 4 science, 2 foreign language, 3 social studies, 2 history. **Freshman Admission Statistics:** 4,767 applied, 63.9% admitted, 22% enrolled. **Transfer Admission Requirements:** college transcript(s), Minimum college GPA of 2.5 required. Lowest grade transferable C. **General Admission Information:** Application fee $40. Nonfall registration accepted. Admission may be deferred for a maximum of 1 year.

COSTS AND FINANCIAL AID

Average book expense $1,600. **Required Forms and Deadlines:** FAFSA. **Notification of Awards:** Applicants will be notified of awards on a rolling basis beginning 3/1. **Types of Aid:** *Need-based scholarships/grants:* College/university scholarship or grant aid from institutional funds; Federal Pell; Private scholarships; SEOG; State scholarships/grants. *Loans:* Direct PLUS loans; Direct Subsidized Stafford Loans; Direct Unsubsidized Stafford Loans. *Student Employment:* Federal Work-Study Program available. Institutional employment available. **Financial Aid Statistics:** 100% needy freshmen, 100% needy undergrads receive need-based scholarship or grant aid. 24% freshmen, 10% undergrads receive non-need-based scholarship or grant aid. 77% freshmen, 88% undergrads receive need-based self-help aid. 1% freshmen, 3% undergrads receive athletic scholarships. 99% freshmen, 97% undergrads receive any aid. **Criteria for awarding aid:** *Need-based:* Academics *Non-need-based:* Academics, Athletics.

PIEDMONT COLLEGE

P.O. Box 10, Demorest, GA 30535
Phone: 706-776-0103 • **Financial Aid Phone:** 706-778-3000
E-mail: ugrad@piedmont.edu • **CEEB Code:** 5537
Fax: 706-776-6635 • **Website:** www.piedmont.edu • **ACT Code:** 853

This private school, affiliated with the National Association of Congregational Christian Churches and United Church of Christ, was founded in 1897. It has a 186 acre campus.

RATINGS

Admissions Selectivity Rating: 85   **Fire Safety Rating:** 60*   **Green Rating:** 60*

STUDENTS AND FACULTY

Enrollment: 1,284. **Student Body:** 66% female, 34% male, 9% out-of-state, 1% international (4 countries represented). Asian 1%, African American 9%, Caucasian 71%, Hispanic 5%, Native American <1%, Pacific Islander <1%, Two or more races 2%, Race unknown 10%.
Retention and Graduation: 63% freshmen return for sophomore year.

Faculty: Student/faculty ratio 11:1. 128 full-time faculty, 74% hold PhDs, 55% are women. 0% of classes are taught by teaching assistants.

ACADEMICS

Degrees: Bachelor's; Doctoral/Research; Master's; Post-Master's certificate **Classes:** Most classes have 10-19 students. Most lab/discussion sessions have 10-19 students. **Most popular majors:** Elementary Education And Teaching; Nursing Practice; Business/Commerce, General. **Special Study Options:** Accelerated program; Distance learning; Double major; Dual enrollment; Honors program; Independent study; Internships; Student-designed major; Study abroad; Teacher certification program. **Career services:** Alumni network; Career assessment; Career/job search classes; Regional alumni

FACILITIES

Housing: Apartments for single students; Coed dorms; Men's dorms; Special housing for disabled student; Women's dorms 98% of campus accessible to physically disabled. **Special Academic Facilities/Equipment:** Art Gallery; Swanson Center, Johnny Mize Athletic Center, Student Commons **Computers:** Administrative functions (other than registration) can be performed online.

CAMPUS LIFE

Environment: Rural **Activities:** Campus Ministries; Choral groups; Concert band; Drama/theater; Music ensembles; Musical theater; Opera; Pep band; Radio station; Student government; Student newspaper; Student-run film society; Television station; Yearbook 20 registered organizations, 7 honor societies, 1 religious organization. **Athletics (Intercollegiate):** *Men:* baseball, basketball, cross-country, golf, soccer, tennis. *Women:* basketball, cross-country, golf, soccer, softball, tennis, volleyball. **On-Campus Highlights:** Johnny Mize Athletic Center, Student Center, Stewart Hall & Swanson Center, Center for Music and Worship, Arrendale Library

ADMISSIONS

Freshman Academic Profile: Average high school GPA 3.4. **Test Scores:** SAT Math middle 50% range 440-550. SAT EBRW middle 50% range 430-550. ACT middle 50% range 19-24. Minimum paper TOEFL 550. **Basis for Candidate Selection:** *Very important factors considered include:* rigor of secondary school record, academic GPA, standardized test scores. *Important factors considered include:* class rank, application essay, recommendation(s), interview, extracurricular activities, talent/ability, character/personal qualities, first generation. *Other factors considered include:* alumni/ae relation, geographical residence, state residency, volunteer work, work experience, level of applicant's interest. **Freshman Admission Requirements:** High school diploma is required and GED is accepted *Academic units recommended:* 4 English, 4 math, 4 science, 2 foreign language, 1 social studies, 3 history. **Freshman Admission Statistics:** 1,135 applied, 57.0% admitted, 43% enrolled. **Transfer Admission Requirements:** college transcript(s), statement of good standing from prior institution(s). Minimum college GPA of 2.0 required. Lowest grade transferable C. **General Admission Information:** Regular application deadline 7/1. Nonfall registration accepted. Admission may be deferred.

COSTS AND FINANCIAL AID

Annual tuition $21,990. Room and board $9,050. Average book expense $1,400. **Required Forms and Deadlines:** FAFSA; Institution's own financial aid form; State aid form. **Notification of Awards:** Applicants will be notified of awards on a rolling basis beginning 2/1. **Types of Aid:** *Need-based scholarships/grants:* College/university scholarship or grant aid from institutional funds; Federal Pell; Private scholarships; SEOG; State scholarships/grants. *Loans:* Direct PLUS loans; Direct Subsidized Stafford Loans; Direct Unsubsidized Stafford Loans. *Student Employment:* Federal Work-Study Program available. Institutional employment available. **Financial Aid Statistics:** 100% needy freshmen, 100% needy undergrads receive need-based scholarship or grant aid. 19% freshmen, 12% undergrads receive non-need-based scholarship or grant aid. 56% freshmen, 73% undergrads receive need-based self-help aid. 0% freshmen, 0% undergrads receive athletic scholarships. 99% freshmen, 99% undergrads receive any aid. 80% undergrads borrow to pay for school. Average cumulative indebtedness $29,289. **Criteria for awarding aid:** *Need-based:* Academics, Leadership *Non-need-based:* Academics, Alumni affiliation, Art, Leadership, Music/drama, Religious affiliation, State/district residency.

PITTSBURG STATE UNIVERSITY

1701 South Broadway, Pittsburg, KS 66762
Phone: 620-235-4251 • **Financial Aid Phone:** 800-854-7488 • **CEEB Code:** 6336
Fax: 620-235-6003 • **Website:** www.pittstate.edu • **ACT Code:** 1449

This public school was founded in 1903. It has a 630 acre campus.

RATINGS
Admissions Selectivity Rating: 75   **Fire Safety Rating:** 91   **Green Rating:** 79

STUDENTS AND FACULTY
Enrollment: 5,536. **Student Body:** 47% female, 53% male, 30% out-of-state, 3% international (42 countries represented). Asian 1%, African American 4%, Caucasian 79%, Hispanic 5%, Native American 1%, Pacific Islander <1%, Two or more races 6%, Race unknown <1%.
Retention and Graduation: 74% freshmen return for sophomore year.
Faculty: Student/faculty ratio 17:1. 323 full-time faculty, 80% hold PhDs, 10% are members of minority groups, 43% are women. 2% of classes are taught by teaching assistants.

ACADEMICS
Degrees: Associate; Bachelor's; Certificate; Doctoral/Professional; Master's; Post-Bachelor's certificate; Post-Master's certificate **Classes:** Most classes have 10-19 students. **Most popular majors:** Education, General; Engineering Technology, General. **Special Study Options:** Accelerated program; Distance learning; Double major; Dual enrollment; Honors program; Independent study; Internships; Student-designed major; Study abroad; Teacher certification program. Honors programs: Honors College. **Disability Services offered to physically disabled students:** Note-taking services; Reader services; Tape recorders; Tutors. **Career services:** Alumni services; Career assessment; Career/job search classes; Internships

FACILITIES
Housing: Apartments for married students; Coed dorms; Special housing for disabled student; Theme housing; Wellness housing 90% of campus accessible to physically disabled. **Special Academic Facilities/Equipment:** planetarium, observatory, field biology reserve, nature reach, herbarium, technology center, mammal collection, greenhouse, art gallery, polymer research center, cadaver lab, Veterans Memorial Amphitheater, broadcasting lab, public radio station **Computers:** 100% of classrooms, 100% of dorms, 100% of libraries, 100% of dining areas, 100% of student union, 80% of common outdoor areas have wireless network access. Students can register for classes online. Administrative functions (other than registration) can be performed online.

CAMPUS LIFE
Environment: Village **Activities:** Campus Ministries; Choral groups; Concert band; Drama/theater; International Student Organization; Jazz band; Literary magazine; Marching band; Music ensembles; Opera; Radio station; Student government; Student newspaper; Television station; Yearbook 150 registered organizations, 8 fraternities, 3 sororities. **Athletics (Intercollegiate):** *Men:* baseball, basketball, cheerleading, cross-country, football, golf, track/field (outdoor), track/field (indoor). *Women:* basketball, cheerleading, cross-country, softball, track/field (outdoor), track/field (indoor), volleyball. **On-Campus Highlights:** Planetarium, Veterans Memorial Amphitheater, Gorilla Village, Brandenburg Field/Carnie Smith Stadium, Timmons Chapel **Environmental Initiatives:** Addition of Sustainability as a goal in the university strategic plan.

ADMISSIONS
Freshman Academic Profile: Average high school GPA 3.4. 31% in top 10% of high school class, 46% in top 25% of high school class, 74% in top 50% of high school class. **Test Scores:** ACT middle 50% range 19-24. Minimum internet-based TOEFL 68. Minimum paper TOEFL 520. **Basis for Candidate Selection:** *Very important factors considered include:* rigor of secondary school record, class rank, academic GPA, standardized test scores. **Freshman Admission Requirements:** High school diploma is required and GED is accepted *Academic units required:* 4 English, 4 math, 3 science, 3 social studies, 3 academic electives. **Freshman Admission Statistics:** 2,593 applied, 84.3% admitted, 45% enrolled. **Transfer Admission Requirements:** college transcript(s), Minimum college GPA of 2.0 required. Lowest grade transferable D. **General Admission Information:** Application fee $30. Nonfall registration accepted. Admission may be deferred for a maximum of 3 semesters.

COSTS AND FINANCIAL AID
Annual in-state tuition $6,734. Annual out-of-state tuition $16,978. Room and board $6,734. Required fees $1,196. Average book expense $1,000. **Required Forms and Deadlines:** FAFSA; State aid form. **Notification of Awards:** Applicants will be notified of awards on a rolling basis beginning 3/1. **Types of Aid:** *Need-based scholarships/grants:* College/university scholarship or grant

aid from institutional funds; Federal Pell; Private scholarships; SEOG; State scholarships/grants. *Loans:* Direct PLUS loans; Direct Subsidized Stafford Loans; Direct Unsubsidized Stafford Loans. *Student Employment:* Federal Work-Study Program available. Institutional employment available. **Financial Aid Statistics:** 64% needy freshmen receive need-based scholarship or grant aid. 72% freshmen, 57% undergrads receive non-need-based scholarship or grant aid. 48% freshmen, 55% undergrads receive need-based self-help aid. 0% freshmen, 0% undergrads receive athletic scholarships. 91% freshmen, 85% undergrads receive any aid. 70% undergrads borrow to pay for school. Average cumulative indebtedness $24,384. **Criteria for awarding aid:** *Non-need-based:* Academics, Alumni affiliation, Art, Athletics, Leadership, Minority status, Music/drama.

PITZER COLLEGE

1050 North Mills Avenue, Claremont, CA 91711-6101
Phone: 909-621-8129 • **Financial Aid Phone:** 909-621-8208
E-mail: admission@pitzer.edu • **CEEB Code:** 4619
Fax: 909-621-8770 • **Website:** www.pitzer.edu • **ACT Code:** 363

This private school was founded in 1963. It has a 35 acre campus.

RATINGS
Admissions Selectivity Rating: 97   **Fire Safety Rating:** 60*   **Green Rating:** 96

STUDENTS AND FACULTY
Enrollment: 1,074. **Student Body:** 54% female, 46% male, 55% out-of-state, 9% international (33 countries represented). Asian 10%, African American 6%, Caucasian 47%, Hispanic 15%, Native American <1%, Pacific Islander <1%, Two or more races 7%, Race unknown 5%.
Retention and Graduation: 95% freshmen return for sophomore year. 83% freshmen graduate within 4 years. 88% freshmen graduate within 6 years.
Faculty: Student/faculty ratio 11:1. 82 full-time faculty, 100% hold PhDs, 46% are members of minority groups, 55% are women. 0% of classes are taught by teaching assistants.

ACADEMICS
Degrees: Bachelor's **Classes:** Most classes have 10-19 students. Most lab/discussion sessions have 10-19 students. **Most popular majors:** Biological And Physical Sciences; Psychology, General; Political Science And Government, General. **Special Study Options:** Cooperative education program; Cross-registration; Double major; English as a Second Language (ESL); Exchange student program (domestic); Honors program; Independent study; Internships; Liberal arts/career combination; Student-designed major; Study abroad. Combined degree programs: BA/MA. **Disability Services offered to physically disabled students:** Note-taking services; Reader services; Tape recorders; Tutors. **Career services:** Alumni network; Career assessment; Career/job search classes; Internships

FACILITIES
Housing: Coed dorms; Special housing for disabled students 95% of campus accessible to physically disabled. **Special Academic Facilities/Equipment:** Theatre arts center, Black, Asian American and Chicano Study centers; film, TV, and videotape studios; arboretum; biological field station; student health services, Gold Student Center **Computers:** 95% of classrooms, 100% of dorms, 95% of libraries, have wireless network access. Students can register for classes online. Administrative functions (other than registration) can be performed online.

CAMPUS LIFE
Environment: Town **Activities:** Campus Ministries; Choral groups; Dance; Drama/theater; International Student Organization; Literary magazine; Model UN; Music ensembles; Musical theater; Radio station; Student government; Student newspaper; Student-run film society; Symphony orchestra 120 registered organizations, 1 honor societies. **Athletics (Intercollegiate):** *Men:* baseball, basketball, cross-country, diving, football, golf, soccer, swimming, tennis, track/field (outdoor), water polo. *Women:* basketball, cross-country, diving, soccer, softball, swimming, tennis, track/field (outdoor), volleyball, water polo. **On-Campus Highlights:** Grove House, McConnell Center, Gloria and Peter Gold Student Center, Marquis Library, The Mounds **Environmental Initiatives:** New 'Green' dorms

ADMISSIONS

Freshman Academic Profile: Average high school GPA 3.9. 63% in top 10% of high school class, 88% in top 25% of high school class, 100% in top 50% of high school class. **Test Scores:** SAT Math middle 50% range 670-750. SAT EBRW middle 50% range 640-740. ACT middle 50% range 29-32. Minimum internet-based TOEFL 70. Minimum paper TOEFL 190. **Basis for Candidate Selection:** *Very important factors considered include:* rigor of secondary school record, academic GPA, application essay, character/personal qualities. *Important factors considered include:* recommendation(s), extracurricular activities, talent/ability, volunteer work. *Other factors considered include:* class rank, standardized test scores, interview, first generation, alumni/ae relation, geographical residence, state residency, racial/ethnic status, work experience, level of applicant's interest. **Freshman Admission Requirements:** High school diploma is required and GED is accepted *Academic units required: Academic units recommended:* 4 English, 3 math, 3 science, 3 foreign language, 3 social studies. **Freshman Admission Statistics:** 3,753 applied, 16.2% admitted, 43% enrolled. **Transfer Admission Requirements:** college transcript(s), essay or personal statement, statement of good standing from prior institution(s). Minimum college GPA of 2.0 required. Lowest grade transferable C-. **General Admission Information:** Application fee $70. Regular application deadline 1/1. Nonfall registration accepted. Admission may be deferred for a maximum of 1 year.

COSTS AND FINANCIAL AID

Required Forms and Deadlines: Business/Farm Supplement; CSS/Financial Aid PROFILE; FAFSA; Institution's own financial aid form; Noncustodial PROFILE; State aid form. **Notification of Awards:** Applicants will be notified of awards on or about 3/15. **Types of Aid:** *Need-based scholarships/grants:* College/university scholarship or grant aid from institutional funds; Federal Pell; Private scholarships; SEOG; State scholarships/grants. *Loans:* Direct PLUS loans; Direct Subsidized Stafford Loans; Direct Unsubsidized Stafford Loans. *Student Employment:* Federal Work-Study Program available. Institutional employment available. **Financial Aid Statistics:** 100% needy freshmen, 98% needy undergrads receive need-based scholarship or grant aid. 5% freshmen, 6% undergrads receive non-need-based scholarship or grant aid. 89% freshmen, 89% undergrads receive need-based self-help aid. 0% freshmen, 0% undergrads receive athletic scholarships. 34% freshmen, 40% undergrads receive any aid. 38% undergrads borrow to pay for school. Average cumulative indebtedness $21,569. **Criteria for awarding aid:** *Need-based:* Academics, Art, Leadership, Minority status, Music/drama *Non-need-based:* Academics, Leadership.

PLYMOUTH STATE UNIVERSITY

17 High Street, Plymouth, NH 03264
Phone: 603-535-2237 • **Financial Aid Phone:** 877-846-5755
E-mail: plymouthadmit@plymouth.edu • **CEEB Code:** 3690
Fax: 603-535-2714 • **Website:** www.plymouth.edu • **ACT Code:** 2518

This public school was founded in 1871. It has a 170 acre campus.

RATINGS

Admissions Selectivity Rating: 75   **Fire Safety Rating:** 91   **Green Rating:** 60*

STUDENTS AND FACULTY

Enrollment: 4,088. **Student Body:** 50% female, 50% male, 45% out-of-state, 1% international (19 countries represented). Asian 2%, African American 2%, Caucasian 83%, Hispanic 2%, Native American 1%, Pacific Islander <1%, Two or more races 2%, Race unknown 7%.
Retention and Graduation: 68% freshmen return for sophomore year. 44% freshmen graduate within 4 years. 57% freshmen graduate within 6 years.
Faculty: Student/faculty ratio 17:1. 192 full-time faculty, 72% hold PhDs, 10% are members of minority groups, 52% are women. 0% of classes are taught by teaching assistants.

ACADEMICS

Degrees: Bachelor's; Certificate; Doctoral/Research; Master's; Post-Bachelor's certificate; Post-Master's certificate **Classes:** Most classes have 20-29 students. **Most popular majors:** Education; Health And Physical Education/Fitness, General; Registered Nursing, Nursing Administration, Nursing Research And Clinical Nursing. **Special Study Options:** Cross-registration; Distance learning; Double major; Exchange student program (domestic); Honors program; Independent study; Internships; Student-designed major; Study abroad; Teacher certification program. Honors programs: University Honors Program, Business Honors, Psychology Honors. **Disability Services offered to physically disabled students:** Note-taking services; Reader services; Tape

recorders; Tutors. **Career services:** Alumni network; Alumni services; Career assessment; Career/job search classes; Internships; Regional alumni

FACILITIES

Housing: Apartments for married students; Apartments for single students; Coed dorms; Special housing for disabled student; Theme housing 80% of campus accessible to physically diasbled. **Special Academic Facilities/Equipment:** Karl Drerup Art gallery, Silver Cultural Arts Center, Sylvestre Planetarium, Child Development and Family Center (NAEYC accredited lab school for children 2-6 years old), meteorology lab, Geographic Information System lab, psychology lab, graphic design computer lab, Museum of the White Mountains, Indoor track, Outdoor center, Ice Arena, AllWell Center **Computers:** 75% of classrooms, 5% of dorms, 100% of libraries, 100% of dining areas, 100% of student union, 10% of common outdoor areas have wireless network access. Students can register for classes online. Administrative functions (other than registration) can be performed online.

CAMPUS LIFE

Environment: Village **Activities:** Campus Ministries; Choral groups; Concert band; Dance; Drama/theater; International Student Organization; Jazz band; Literary magazine; Model UN; Music ensembles; Musical theater; Pep band; Radio station; Student government; Student newspaper; Student-run film society; Yearbook 80 registered organizations, 13 honor societies, 4 religious organizations. 3 sororities. **Athletics (Intercollegiate):** *Men:* baseball, basketball, football, ice hockey, lacrosse, skiing (downhill/alpine), soccer, wrestling. *Women:* basketball, cheerleading, diving, field hockey, ice hockey, lacrosse, skiing (downhill/alpine), soccer, softball, swimming, tennis, volleyball. **On-Campus Highlights:** Hartman Union Building, Silver Center for the Arts, Ice Arena & Welcome Center, AllWell Center, Lamson Library—Information Commons **Environmental Initiatives:** New degree program.

ADMISSIONS

Freshman Academic Profile: Average high school GPA 3.0. 6% in top 10% of high school class, 18% in top 25% of high school class, 51% in top 50% of high school class. 83% from public high schools. **Test Scores:** SAT Math middle 50% range 450-570. SAT EBRW middle 50% range 440-560. ACT middle 50% range 19-25. Minimum internet-based TOEFL 71. Minimum paper TOEFL 530. **Basis for Candidate Selection:** *Very important factors considered include:* rigor of secondary school record. *Important factors considered include:* academic GPA, extracurricular activities. *Other factors considered include:* application essay, recommendation(s), talent/ability, character/personal qualities, volunteer work, work experience. **Freshman Admission Requirements:** High school diploma is required and GED is accepted *Academic units required:* 4 English, 3 math, 3 science, 1 science labs, 3 social studies, *Academic units recommended:* 2 foreign language. **Freshman Admission Statistics:** 6,715 applied, 78.8% admitted, 21% enrolled. **Transfer Admission Requirements:** High school transcript, college transcript(s), Minimum college GPA of 2.0 required. Lowest grade transferable C. **General Admission Information:** Application fee $50. Priority deadline 4/1. Nonfall registration accepted. Admission may be deferred for a maximum of 1 year.

COSTS AND FINANCIAL AID

Required Forms and Deadlines: FAFSA. **Notification of Awards:** Applicants will be notified of awards on a rolling basis beginning 11/30. **Types of Aid:** *Need-based scholarships/grants:* College/university scholarship or grant aid from institutional funds; Federal Pell; Private scholarships; SEOG; State scholarships/grants. *Loans:* Direct PLUS loans; Direct Subsidized Stafford Loans; Direct Unsubsidized Stafford Loans. *Student Employment:* Federal Work-Study Program available. Institutional employment available. **Financial Aid Statistics:** 60% needy freshmen, 61% needy undergrads receive need-based scholarship or grant aid. 74% freshmen, 49% undergrads receive non-need-based scholarship or grant aid. 96% freshmen, 97% undergrads receive need-based self-help aid. 0% freshmen, 0% undergrads receive athletic scholarships. 83% freshmen, 78% undergrads receive any aid. 87% undergrads borrow to pay for school. Average cumulative indebtedness $32,592. **Criteria for awarding aid:** *Non-need-based:* Academics, Alumni affiliation, Art, Leadership, Music/drama.

POINT LOMA NAZARENE UNIVERSITY

3900 Lomaland Drive, San Diego, CA 92106
Phone: 800-733-7779 • **Financial Aid Phone:** 619-849-2538
E-mail: admissions@pointloma.edu • **CEEB Code:** 4605
Fax: 619-849-2601 • **ACT Code:** 370

This private school, affiliated with the Nazarene Church, was founded in 1902. It has a 90 acre campus.

RATINGS

Admissions Selectivity Rating: 83 • **Fire Safety Rating:** 82 **Green Rating:** 78

STUDENTS AND FACULTY

Enrollment: 3,139. **Student Body:** 65% female, 35% male, 17% out-of-state, 1% international (24 countries represented). Asian 7%, African American 2%, Caucasian 53%, Hispanic 26%, Native American <1%, Pacific Islander 1%, Two or more races 8%, Race unknown 2%.
Retention and Graduation: 89% freshmen return for sophomore year. 64% freshmen graduate within 4 years. 77% freshmen graduate within 6 years. **Faculty:** Student/faculty ratio 14:1. 143 full-time faculty, 85% hold PhDs, 17% are members of minority groups, 41% are women. 0% of classes are taught by teaching assistants.

ACADEMICS

Degrees: Bachelor's; Certificate; Doctoral/Professional; Master's; Post-Master's certificate **Classes:** Most classes have 20-29 students. Most lab/discussion sessions have 10-19 students. **Most popular majors:** Pre-Medicine/Pre-Medical Studies; Registered Nursing, Nursing Administration, Nursing Research And Clinical Nursing; Business/Commerce, General. **Special Study Options:** Accelerated program; Distance learning; Double major; External degree program; Honors program; Independent study; Internships; Study abroad; Teacher certification program. Honors programs: Honors Scholars Program. **Disability Services offered to physically disabled students:** Note-taking services; Reader services; Tape recorders; Tutors. **Career services:** Alumni network; Alumni services; Career assessment; Career/job search classes; Internships; Regional alumni

FACILITIES

Housing: Apartments for single students; Men's dorms; Special housing for disabled student; Women's dorms 100% of campus accessible to physically diasbled. **Special Academic Facilities/Equipment:** Language lab, on-campus preschool, electron microscope. **Computers:** Students can register for classes online. Administrative functions (other than registration) can be performed online.

CAMPUS LIFE

Environment: Metropolis **Activities:** Campus Ministries; Choral groups; Concert band; Drama/theater; International Student Organization; Jazz band; Literary magazine; Music ensembles; Musical theater; Opera; Radio station; Student government; Student newspaper; Student-run film society; Symphony orchestra; Television station; Yearbook 30 registered organizations, 2 honor societies, 7 religious organizations. 3 fraternities, 3 sororities. **Athletics (Intercollegiate):** *Men:* baseball, basketball, cross-country, golf, soccer, tennis, track/field (outdoor). *Women:* basketball, cross-country, softball, tennis, track/field (outdoor), volleyball. **On-Campus Highlights:** ARC (student rec center), Bobby B's Coffee Shop, Sunset Deck, Greek Ampitheatre, Golden Gymnasium **Environmental Initiatives:** Over 80% renewable electricity

ADMISSIONS

Freshman Academic Profile: Average high school GPA 3.8. 31% in top 10% of high school class, 71% in top 25% of high school class, 92% in top 50% of high school class. **Test Scores:** SAT Math middle 50% range 540-640. SAT EBRW middle 50% range 560-650. ACT middle 50% range 23-28. Minimum internet-based TOEFL 80. Minimum paper TOEFL 550. **Basis for Candidate Selection:** *Very important factors considered include:* rigor of secondary school record, academic GPA, standardized test scores, character/personal qualities, religious affiliation/commitment. *Important factors considered include:* application essay, recommendation(s), interview. *Other factors considered include:* class rank, extracurricular activities, talent/ability, first generation, alumni/ae relation, geographical residence, state residency, level of applicant's interest. **Freshman Admission Requirements:** High school diploma is required and GED is accepted *Academic units recommended:* 4 English, 3 math, 3 science, 2 science labs, 2 foreign language, 2 social studies, 1 history. **Freshman Admission Statistics:** 3,007 applied, 76.3% admitted, 27% enrolled. **Transfer Admission Requirements:** college transcript(s), essay or personal statement, interview, Minimum college GPA of 2.0 required. Lowest grade transferable D. **General Admission Information:** Application fee $55. Priority deadline 2/15. Regular application deadline 2/15. Nonfall registration accepted.

COSTS AND FINANCIAL AID

Annual tuition $35,100. Room and board $10,450. Required fees $600. Average book expense $1,918. **Required Forms and Deadlines:** FAFSA. **Notification of Awards:** Applicants will be notified of awards on a rolling basis beginning 12/15. **Types of Aid:** *Need-based scholarships/grants:* College/university scholarship or grant aid from institutional funds; Federal Nursing Scholarships; Federal Pell; Private scholarships; SEOG; State scholarships/grants. *Loans:* Direct PLUS loans; Direct Subsidized Stafford Loans; Direct Unsubsidized Stafford Loans. **Financial Aid Statistics:** 94% needy freshmen, 93% needy undergrads receive need-based scholarship or grant aid. 10% freshmen, 8% undergrads receive non-need-based scholarship or grant aid. 90% freshmen, 92% undergrads receive need-based self-help aid. 2% freshmen, 3% undergrads receive athletic scholarships. 74% undergrads borrow to pay for school. Average cumulative indebtedness $32,649. **Criteria for awarding aid:** *Need-based:* Academics, Alumni affiliation, Leadership, Minority status, Religious affiliation *Non-need-based:* Academics, Art, Athletics, Job skills, Music/drama, Religious affiliation.

POINT PARK UNIVERSITY

201 Wood Street, Pittsburgh, PA 15222
Phone: 412-392-3430 • **Financial Aid Phone:** 412-392-3930
E-mail: enroll@pointpark.edu • **CEEB Code:** 2676
Fax: 412-391-1980 • **ACT Code:** 3530

This private school was founded in 1960.

RATINGS

Admissions Selectivity Rating: 76 **Fire Safety Rating:** 97 **Green Rating:** 60*

STUDENTS AND FACULTY

Enrollment: 3,167. **Student Body:** 58% female, 42% male, 21% out-of-state, 2% international (38 countries represented). Asian 1%, African American 17%, Caucasian 73%, Hispanic 3%, Native American <1%, Pacific Islander 0%, Two or more races 3%, Race unknown <1%.
Retention and Graduation: 74% freshmen return for sophomore year. **Faculty:** Student/faculty ratio 13:1. 133 full-time faculty, 74% hold PhDs, 10% are members of minority groups, 38% are women. 0% of classes are taught by teaching assistants.

ACADEMICS

Degrees: Associate; Bachelor's; Certificate; Master's; Post-Bachelor's certificate **Classes:** Most classes have 20-29 students. Most lab/discussion sessions have 20-29 students. **Most popular majors:** Teacher Education And Professional Development, Specific Subject Areas, Other; Dance, General; Drama And Dramatics/Theatre Arts, General. **Special Study Options:** Accelerated program; Cooperative education program; Cross-registration; Distance learning; Double major; Dual enrollment; English as a Second Language (ESL); Exchange student program (domestic); Honors program; Independent study; Internships; Liberal arts/career combination; Student-designed major; Study abroad; Teacher certification program; Weekend college. Honors programs: The Point Park Honors Program mission provides the foundation from which honors courses are developed. Honors courses will not be defined by more work but rather by a different kind of learning environment. Students will be introduced to the usual content and objectives of the course, but they will also develop in-depth understandings of topics. Students will be expected to develop appropriate and higher-level research, writing and critical thinking skills, which should result in major documented papers or projects. Students will be encouraged to become adventurous, independent thinkers. Students should experience a variety of learning activities that may include collaborative learning, field experience, debates, documented projects, interviews, and presentations. Evaluation will be based on performance, creativity, imagination, critical thinking, and risk taking rather than on more assignments and tests. Honors students will be expected to participate in the quest for knowledge by being prepared and willing to contribute to all class activities. To earn an honors certificate, students need to complete 18 credits of honors classes. An honors thesis or project is optional, depending on students' career and graduate study goals. Honors students also may join our Honors Student Organization and participate in a variety of leadership and community service efforts and projects inside and outside the Point Park community. Students annually are offered the chance to travel for an alternative spring break, and they can present papers and research at national and regional honors conferences. Every effort is made to encourage all of them to assume leadership positions and propose their own activities and endeavors to complement their work in the classroom. As benefits, students register for classes each semester before other students and new students move in ahead of other resident students. Students who complete program requirements will be recognized in the program at graduation and will receive a separate certificate and notation on their transcript. **Disability Services offered to physically disabled students:** Note-taking services; Reader services; Tape recorders; Tutors. **Career services:** Alumni network; Alumni services; Career assessment; Career/job search classes; Internships; Regional alumni

FACILITIES

Housing: Apartments for single students; Coed dorms; Special housing for disabled student; Theme housing; Women's dorms 95% of campus accessible to physically diasbled. **Special Academic Facilities/Equipment:** Theater, engineering technology labs, television and radio studios, digital film editing suites, dance studios **Computers:** 100% of classrooms, 100% of libraries, 100% of dining areas, 100% of student union, 100% of common outdoor areas have wireless network access. Students can register for classes online. Administrative functions (other than registration) can be performed online.

CAMPUS LIFE

Environment: Metropolis **Activities:** Campus Ministries; Choral groups; Dance; Drama/theater; International Student Organization; Literary magazine; Musical theater; Radio station; Student government; Student newspaper; Student-run film society; Television station 25 registered organizations, 3 honor societies, 2 religious organizations. **Athletics (Intercollegiate):** *Men:* baseball, basketball, cross-country, golf, soccer. *Women:* basketball, cross-country, golf, soccer, softball, volleyball. **On-Campus Highlights:** Point Cafe, Atrium Overlook, Recreation Center, Coffee Kiosk, Outdoor Patio **Environmental Initiatives:** Recycling

ADMISSIONS

Freshman Academic Profile: Average high school GPA 3.2. 10% in top 10% of high school class, 30% in top 25% of high school class, 66% in top 50% of high school class. **Test Scores:** SAT Math middle 50% range 450-560. SAT EBRW middle 50% range 460-580. ACT middle 50% range 20-26. Minimum paper TOEFL 500. **Basis for Candidate Selection:** *Very important factors considered include:* standardized test scores, talent/ability. *Important factors considered include:* rigor of secondary school record. *Other factors considered include:* academic GPA, recommendation(s). **Freshman Admission Requirements:** High school diploma is required and GED is accepted *Academic units recommended:* 4 English, 4 math, 3 science, 2 foreign language, 3 social studies, 3 history, 1 academic elective, 1 computer science, 1 visual/performing arts. **Freshman Admission Statistics:** 3,673 applied, 76.2% admitted, 19% enrolled. **Transfer Admission Requirements:** college transcript(s), Minimum college GPA of 2.0 required. Lowest grade transferable C. **General Admission Information:** Application fee $40. Nonfall registration accepted. Admission may be deferred for a maximum of 1 year.

COSTS AND FINANCIAL AID

Annual tuition $24,020. Room and board $9,920. Required fees $1,170. Average book expense $1,000. **Required Forms and Deadlines:** FAFSA. **Notification of Awards:** Applicants will be notified of awards on a rolling basis beginning 2/15. *Types of Aid: Need-based scholarships/grants:* College/university scholarship or grant aid from institutional funds; Federal Pell; Private scholarships; SEOG; State scholarships/grants. *Loans:* Direct PLUS loans; Direct Subsidized Stafford Loans; Direct Unsubsidized Stafford Loans. *Student Employment:* Federal Work-Study Program available. Institutional employment available. **Financial Aid Statistics:** 100% needy freshmen, 99% needy undergrads receive need-based scholarship or grant aid. 11% freshmen, 9% undergrads receive non-need-based scholarship or grant aid. 88% freshmen, 88% undergrads receive need-based self-help aid. 1% freshmen, 2% undergrads receive athletic scholarships. 100% freshmen, 93% undergrads receive any aid. **Criteria for awarding aid:** *Non-need-based:* Academics, Athletics, Music/drama.

POINT UNIVERSITY

507 West 10th Street, West Point, GA 31833
Phone: 706-385-1202 • **Financial Aid Phone:** 706-385-1045
E-mail: admissions@point.edu • **CEEB Code:** 5029
Fax: 706-645-9473 • **Website:** www.point.edu • **ACT Code:** 785

This private school, affiliated with the Christian (Nondenominational) Church, was founded in 1937.

RATINGS
Admissions Selectivity Rating: 85   **Fire Safety Rating:** 74   **Green Rating:** 60*

STUDENTS AND FACULTY
Enrollment: 1,358. **Student Body:** 50% female, 50% male, 37% out-of-state, 2% international (13 countries represented). Asian <1%, African American

34%, Caucasian 47%, Hispanic 6%, Native American <1%, Pacific Islander <1%, Two or more races 5%, Race unknown 5%. **Retention and Graduation:** 68% freshmen return for sophomore year. **Faculty:** Student/faculty ratio 18:1. 41 full-time faculty, 63% hold PhDs, 27% are members of minority groups, 59% are women. 0% of classes are taught by teaching assistants.

ACADEMICS

Degrees: Associate; Bachelor's; Certificate; **Master's Classes:** Most classes have 10-19 students. Most lab/discussion sessions have fewer than 10 students. **Most popular majors:** Kinesiology And Exercise Science; Bible/Biblical Studies; Business Administration And Management, General. **Special Study Options:** Accelerated program; Distance learning; Double major; Dual enrollment; Honors program; Independent study; Study abroad; Teacher certification program. Honors programs: Counseling Honor Program. **Disability Services offered to physically disabled students:** Note-taking services; Reader services; Tape recorders; Tutors. **Career services:** Alumni network; Alumni services; Career/job search classes; Internships

FACILITIES

Housing: Men's dorms; Theme housing; Women's dorms **Computers:** Students can register for classes online.

CAMPUS LIFE

Environment: Village **Activities:** Campus Ministries; Choral groups; Concert band; Marching band; Student government 2 fraternities, 2 sororities. **Athletics (Intercollegiate):** *Men:* baseball, basketball, golf, soccer. *Women:* basketball, soccer, volleyball. John Smith Lanier Academic Center, McKinney's Coffeehouse, Scott Fine Arts Center, Point Living Community, West Point Gym

ADMISSIONS

Freshman Academic Profile: Average high school GPA 3.2. **Test Scores:** SAT Math middle 50% range 410-520. SAT EBRW middle 50% range 400-490. ACT middle 50% range 17-22. Minimum internet-based TOEFL 80. Minimum paper TOEFL 550. **Basis for Candidate Selection:** *Very important factors considered include:* academic GPA, character/personal qualities, religious affiliation/commitment. *Important factors considered include:* rigor of secondary school record, class rank, standardized test scores, recommendation(s), extracurricular activities. *Other factors considered include:* application essay, interview, talent/ability, alumni/ae relation, volunteer work, work experience, level of applicant's interest. **Freshman Admission Requirements:** High school diploma is required and GED is accepted *Academic units recommended:* 4 English, 4 math, 4 science, 2 science labs, 2 foreign language, 3 social studies. **Freshman Admission Statistics:** 1,184 applied, 51.4% admitted, 53% enrolled. **Transfer Admission Requirements:** college transcript(s), statement of good standing from prior institution(s). Minimum college GPA of 2.0 required. Lowest grade transferable C. **General Admission Information:** Priority deadline 7/1. Regular application deadline 8/1. Nonfall registration accepted. Admission may be deferred for a maximum of 1 year.

COSTS AND FINANCIAL AID

Annual tuition $18,100. Room and board $7,700. Required fees $1,100. Average book expense $2,000. *Student Employment:* Federal Work-Study Program available. Institutional employment available. **Financial Aid Statistics:** 99% freshmen, 99% undergrads receive any aid.

POLYTECHNIC INSTITUTE OF NEW YORK UNIVERSITY—BROOKLYN

6 Metrotech Center, Brooklyn, NY 11201-2999
Phone: 718-260-5955 • **Financial Aid Phone:** 718-260-3025
E-mail: uadmit@poly.edu • **CEEB Code:** 2668
Fax: 718-260-3446 • **Website:** www.poly.edu • **ACT Code:** 2860

This private school was founded in 1854. It has a 3 acre campus.

RATINGS
Admissions Selectivity Rating: 86   **Fire Safety Rating:** 82   **Green Rating:** 60*

STUDENTS AND FACULTY
Enrollment: 2,000. **Student Body:** 20% female, 80% male, 19% out-of-state, 10% international (34 countries represented). Asian 35%, African American 6%, Caucasian 30%, Hispanic 10%, Native American <1%, Pacific Islander 0%, Two or more races 0%, Race unknown 9%. **Retention and Graduation:** 84% freshmen return for sophomore year. 15% grads go on to further study within 1 year. **Faculty:** Student/faculty ratio 14:1. 157 full-time faculty, 91% hold PhDs, 29% are members of minority groups, 17% are women. 0% of classes are taught by teaching assistants.

The Princeton Review's Complete Book of Colleges

ACADEMICS

Degrees: Bachelor's; Certificate; Doctoral; Doctoral/Research; Master's; Post-Bachelor's certificate **Classes:** Most classes have 20-29 students. **Most popular majors:** Civil Engineering, General; Electrical And Electronics Engineering; Mechanical Engineering. **Special Study Options:** Accelerated program; Cooperative education program; Distance learning; Double major; Dual enrollment; Honors program; Independent study; Internships; Study abroad. Honors programs: The Honors College serves as a magnet for attracting academically superior Undergraduates to the University. It accepts students of exceptional talent and promise from a variety of backgrounds. It offers outstanding Honors students the opportunity to earn a BS and possibly an MS degree in possibly as few as four years, including summers. Honors College students work one-on-one with faculty mentors, who, among other things, stress interdisciplinary research where appropriate, originality of thought, and active learning. Honors College students form a talented cadre of high-achievers who will become engineers, scientists, managers, and other professionals positioned for leadership roles in our emerging knowledge-based economy. They will also form a highly enthusiastic and supportive part of the University's alumni population and enhance the overall reputation of the University for delivering excellence in education. Combined degree programs: BA/MA; BA/MEng. **Disability Services offered to physically disabled students:** Note-taking services; Tape recorders; Tutors. **Career services:** Alumni network; Alumni services; Career assessment; Career/job search classes; Internships

FACILITIES

Housing: Coed dorms; Fraternity/sorority housing 100% of campus accessible to physically diasbled. **Special Academic Facilities/Equipment:** Electron microscope, supersonic wind tunnel. Art Displays in Student Center. **Computers:** 100% of classrooms, 100% of dorms, 100% of libraries, 100% of dining areas, 100% of student union, 100% of common outdoor areas have wireless network access. Students can register for classes online. Administrative functions (other than registration) can be performed online. Undergraduates are required to own a computer.

CAMPUS LIFE

Environment: Metropolis **Activities:** Campus Ministries; Drama/theater; Literary magazine; Radio station; Student government; Student newspaper; Student-run film society; Yearbook 36 registered organizations, 8 honor societies, 4 religious organizations. 3 fraternities, 1 sorority. **Athletics (Intercollegiate):** *Men:* baseball, basketball, cross-country, soccer, tennis, track/field (outdoor), volleyball; *Women:* basketball, cross-country, softball, tennis, track/field (outdoor), volleyball. **On-Campus Highlights:** Recreation Center—Wunsch Student Center, Fitness Center—Jacobs Building, Bern Dibner Library for Science and Technology, Jasper H. Kane Dining Hall—Rogers Hall, Gymnasium—Jacobs Building **Environmental Initiatives:** Enhanced/expanded recycling.

ADMISSIONS

Freshman Academic Profile: Average high school GPA 3.5. 46% in top 10% of high school class, 81% in top 25% of high school class, 95% in top 50% of high school class. 73% from public high schools. **Test Scores:** SAT Math middle 50% range 640-720. SAT EBRW middle 50% range 550-650. ACT middle 50% range 26-30. Minimum internet-based TOEFL 80. Minimum paper TOEFL 550. **Basis for Candidate Selection:** *Very important factors considered include:* rigor of secondary school record, standardized test scores. *Important factors considered include:* class rank. *Other factors considered include:* application essay, recommendation(s), interview. **Freshman Admission Requirements:** High school diploma is required and GED is accepted *Academic units required:* 4 English, 4 math, 4 science, 3 social studies, 2 academic electives, *Academic units recommended:* 2 foreign language. **Freshman Admission Statistics:** 3,284 applied, 74.7% admitted, 20% enrolled. **Transfer Admission Requirements:** college transcript(s), Minimum college GPA of 2.5 required. Lowest grade transferable c. **General Admission Information:** Application fee $65. Nonfall registration accepted. Admission may be deferred.

COSTS AND FINANCIAL AID

Annual tuition $40,060. Room and board $13,500. Required fees $1,268. Average book expense $1,500. **Required Forms and Deadlines:** CSS/Financial Aid PROFILE; FAFSA; Institution's own financial aid form; State aid form. **Notification of Awards:** Applicants will be notified of awards on a rolling basis beginning 3/15. **Types of Aid:** *Need-based scholarships/grants:* College/university scholarship or grant aid from institutional funds; Federal Pell; Private scholarships; SEOG; State scholarships/grants; United Negro College Fund. *Loans:* Direct PLUS loans; Direct Subsidized Stafford Loans; Direct Unsubsidized Stafford Loans. *Student Employment:* Federal Work-Study Program available. Institutional employment available. **Financial Aid Statistics:** 93% needy freshmen, 93% needy undergrads receive need-based scholarship or grant aid. 89% freshmen, 60% undergrads receive non-need-based scholarship or grant aid. 86% freshmen, 88% undergrads receive need-based self-help aid. 0% freshmen, 0% undergrads receive athletic scholarships. 97% freshmen, 92% undergrads receive any aid. **Criteria for awarding**

aid: *Need-based:* Academics, Leadership, Minority status *Non-need-based:* Academics, Minority status, State/district residency.

POLYTECHNIC UNIVERSITY OF PUERTO RICO

PO BOX 192017, San Juan, PR 00919-2017
Phone: 787.622.8000 • **Financial Aid Phone:** 787.622.8000 • **CEEB Code:** 614
Fax: 787.764.8712 • **Website:** www.pupr.edu

This private school was founded in 1966. It has a 8 acre campus.

RATINGS

Admissions Selectivity Rating: 70   **Fire Safety Rating:** 68   **Green Rating:** 61

STUDENTS AND FACULTY

Enrollment: 3,334. **Student Body:** 20% female, 80% male, international. Asian <1%, African American <1%, Caucasian <1%, Hispanic 100%, Race unknown <1%.
Retention and Graduation: 77% freshmen return for sophomore year. 73% grads go on to further study within 1 year. 2% grads pursue arts and sciences degrees. 2% grads pursue law degrees. 12% grads pursue business degrees. 1% grads pursue medical degrees. **Faculty:** Student/faculty ratio 11:1. 131 full-time faculty, 37% hold PhDs, 34% are women. 0% of classes are taught by teaching assistants.

ACADEMICS

Degrees: Associate; Bachelor's; Doctoral; **Master's Classes:** Most classes have 20-29 students. **Most popular majors:** Civil Engineering, General; Electrical And Electronics Engineering; Mechanical Engineering. **Special Study Options:** Cooperative education program; Distance learning; Honors program. Honors programs: In a continuing effort to provide educational opportunities consistent with the ability of the individual student, the University invites a select group of students with a GPA of 3.25 or higher to enroll in and benefit from the Honor Program and corresponding Scholarship. The mission is to provide a dynamic intellectual environment for honors students through counseling and multiple activities. The program is design to provide ample opportunities and high motivation to specially gifted students. This program consists of honors seminars, and special courses. The special courses enable students who excel to be challenged to their full intellectual capacity. The program is designed both to broaden and deepen the student's intellectual power. These specials courses are involve topics at the forefront of current scientific interest. General Requirements: New Students 1. General GPA more than 3.25. 2. 1,800 points or more in the academic achievement (evening section) of the College Board (Spanish, Mathematics and English). 3. Must approved 11 credits-hour or more per quarter. 4. Registration in honor courses. Regular Students 1. General GPA more than 3.25. 2. Must approved 11 credits-hour or more. 3. Must complete 33 credits-hour per academic year. 4. Registration in Honor courses. Transfer-in students 1. Must approved 11 credits-hour or more. 2. Must complete 33 credits-hour per academic year. 3. No more than 80 credits from other institutions. 4. Registration in Honor courses. **Disability Services offered to physically disabled students:** Note-taking services; Reader services; Tape recorders; Tutors. **Career services:** Career assessment; Career/job search classes; Internships

FACILITIES

Housing: Special housing for international students **Computers:** 100% of classrooms, 100% of libraries, 100% of dining areas, 100% of student union, 100% of common outdoor areas have wireless network access.

CAMPUS LIFE

Environment: Metropolis **Activities:** Choral groups; Dance; Student government 20 registered organizations, 1 honor society, 1 religious organization. **Athletics (Intercollegiate):** *Men:* basketball, cross-country, martial arts, table tennis, tennis, track/field (outdoor), volleyball, wrestling. *Women:* cross-country, martial arts, table tennis, tennis, track/field (outdoor), volleyball. Coffee Shop—Cafeteria Mi Casa, Gym Facility, Athletic Court—Sport Activities

ADMISSIONS

Freshman Academic Profile: Average high school GPA 3.2. 39% from public high schools. **Basis for Candidate Selection:** *Very important factors considered include:* academic GPA. *Other factors considered include:* standardized test scores. **Freshman Admission Requirements:** High school diploma is required and GED is accepted *Academic units required:* 3 English, 3 math, 3 science, 3 foreign language, 3 social studies. **Freshman Admission Statistics:** 611 applied, 85.3% admitted, 83% enrolled. **Transfer Admission Requirements:** college transcript(s). **General Admission Information:** Application fee $30. Nonfall registration accepted. Admission may be deferred for a maximum of 2 trimesters.

COSTS AND FINANCIAL AID

Annual tuition $7,488. Room and board $11,857. Required fees $840. Average book expense $2,342. **Required Forms and Deadlines:** FAFSA. *Student Employment:* Federal Work-Study Program available. **Financial Aid Statistics:** 97% needy freshmen, 97% needy undergrads receive need-based scholarship or grant aid. 53% freshmen, 33% undergrads receive non-need-based scholarship or grant aid. 12% freshmen, 20% undergrads receive need-based self-help aid. 66% freshmen, 41% undergrads receive athletic scholarships. 91% freshmen, 90% undergrads receive any aid.

POMONA COLLEGE

333 N. College Way, Claremont, CA 91711-6312
Phone: 909-621-8134 • **Financial Aid Phone:** 909-621-8205
E-mail: admissions@pomona.edu • **CEEB Code:** 4607
Fax: 909-621-8952 • **Website:** www.pomona.edu • **ACT Code:** 372

This private school was founded in 1887. It has a 140 acre campus.

RATINGS

Admissions Selectivity Rating: 98 **Fire Safety Rating:** 97 **Green Rating:** 98

STUDENTS AND FACULTY

Enrollment: 1,671. **Student Body:** 50% female, 50% male, 74% out-of-state, 11% international (41 countries represented). Asian 15%, African American 36%, Caucasian 36%, Hispanic 16%, Native American <1%, Pacific Islander <1%, Two or more races 7%, Race unknown 5%.
Retention and Graduation: 98% freshmen return for sophomore year. 92% freshmen graduate within 4 years. 97% freshmen graduate within 6 years. 20% grads go on to further study within 1 year. **Faculty:** Student/faculty ratio 8:1. 189 full-time faculty, 99% hold PhDs, 34% are members of minority groups, 42% are women. 0% of classes are taught by teaching assistants.

ACADEMICS

Degrees: Bachelor's **Classes:** Most classes have 10-19 students. Most lab/discussion sessions have 10-19 students. **Most popular majors:** Neuroscience; Mathematics; Economics. **Special Study Options:** Cross-registration; Double major; Exchange student program (domestic); Independent study; Internships; Student-designed major; Study abroad. **Disability Services offered to physically disabled students:** Note-taking services; Reader services; Tape recorders; Tutors. **Career services:** Alumni network; Alumni services; Career assessment; Career/job search classes; Internships; Regional alumni

FACILITIES

Housing: Coed dorms; Theme housing 85% of campus accessible to physically disabled. **Special Academic Facilities/Equipment:** Oldenborg Center for Foreign Languages, Museum of Art, Brackett Observatory **Computers:** 75% of classrooms, 50% of dorms, 100% of libraries, 100% of dining areas, 100% of student union, 100% of common outdoor areas have wireless network access. Administrative functions (other than registration) can be performed online.

CAMPUS LIFE

Environment: Town **Activities:** Campus Ministries; Choral groups; Concert band; Dance; Drama/theater; International Student Organization; Jazz band; Literary magazine; Model UN; Music ensembles; Musical theater; Pep band; Radio station; Student government; Student newspaper; Student-run film society; Symphony orchestra; Yearbook 280 registered organizations, 3 honor societies, 5 religious organizations. 3 fraternities. **Athletics (Intercollegiate):** *Men:* baseball, basketball, cross-country, diving, football, golf, soccer, swimming, tennis, track/field (outdoor), water polo. *Women:* basketball, cross-country, diving, golf, lacrosse, soccer, softball, swimming, tennis, track/field (outdoor), volleyball, water polo. **On-Campus Highlights:** Smith Campus Center, Sontag Greek Theater, Skyspace, The Coop, The Farm **Environmental Initiatives:** Pomona's Environmental Analysis Program incorporates sustainability across the curriculum in a variety of disciplines. The program offers 11 tracks within its major and minor, allowing students to focus on sustainability in a variety of natural science, social science, and humanities subjects. Sustainability is well incorporated across the curriculum.

ADMISSIONS

Freshman Academic Profile: 94% in top 10% of high school class, 100% in top 25% of high school class, 100% in top 50% of high school class. 68% from public high schools. **Test Scores:** SAT Math middle 50% range 660-

760. SAT EBRW middle 50% range 670-750. ACT middle 50% range 30-34. Minimum internet-based TOEFL 100. Minimum paper TOEFL 600. **Basis for Candidate Selection:** *Very important factors considered include:* rigor of secondary school record, class rank, academic GPA, application essay, standardized test scores, recommendation(s), extracurricular activities, talent/ability, character/personal qualities. *Important factors considered include:* interview. *Other factors considered include:* first generation, alumni/ae relation, racial/ethnic status, volunteer work, work experience. **Freshman Admission Requirements:** High school diploma or equivalent is not required *Academic units required:* 4 English, 3 math, 2 science, 2 science labs, 3 foreign language, 2 social studies, *Academic units recommended:* 4 English, 4 math, 4 science, 3 science labs, 4 foreign language, 4 social studies. **Freshman Admission Statistics:** 9,045 applied, 8.4% admitted, 58% enrolled. **Transfer Admission Requirements:** High school transcript, college transcript(s), essay or personal statement, standardized test scores, statement of good standing from prior institution(s). Lowest grade transferable C. **General Admission Information:** Application fee $70. Regular application deadline 1/1. Nonfall registration accepted. Admission may be deferred for a maximum of 1 year.

COSTS AND FINANCIAL AID

Annual tuition $50,720. Room and board $16,150. Required fees $355. Average book expense $900. **Required Forms and Deadlines:** Business/Farm Supplement; CSS/Financial Aid PROFILE; FAFSA; Noncustodial PROFILE; State aid form. **Notification of Awards:** Applicants will be notified of awards on or about 4/1. **Types of Aid:** *Need-based scholarships/grants:* College/university scholarship or grant aid from institutional funds; Federal Pell; Private scholarships; SEOG; State scholarships/grants. *Loans:* Direct PLUS loans; Direct Subsidized Stafford Loans; Direct Unsubsidized Stafford Loans. *Student Employment:* Federal Work-Study Program available. Institutional employment available. **Financial Aid Statistics:** 100% needy freshmen, 100% needy undergrads receive need-based scholarship or grant aid. 0% undergrads receive non-need-based scholarship or grant aid. 100% freshmen, 100% undergrads receive need-based self-help aid. 0% freshmen, 0% undergrads receive athletic scholarships. 58% freshmen, 54% undergrads receive any aid.

PONTIFICAL COLLEGE JOSEPHINUM

7625 North High Street, Columbus, OH 43235-1498
Phone: 614-885-5585 · **Financial Aid Phone:** 614-885-5585
E-mail: admissions@pcj.edu
Fax: 614-885-2307

This private school, affiliated with the Roman Catholic Church, was founded in 1888. It has a 100 acre campus.

RATINGS

Admissions Selectivity Rating: 85 **Fire Safety Rating:** 60* **Green Rating:** 60*

STUDENTS AND FACULTY

Enrollment: 78. **Student Body:** 0% female, 100% male, 64% out-of-state, 8% international (15 countries represented). Asian 1%, African American 0%, Caucasian 79%, Hispanic 10%, Native American 1%, Race unknown 0%.
Retention and Graduation: 92% freshmen return for sophomore year. 95% grads go on to further study within 1 year. 5% grads pursue arts and sciences degrees. **Faculty:** Student/faculty ratio 4:1. 17 full-time faculty, 76% hold PhDs, 0% are members of minority groups, 35% are women. 0% of classes are taught by teaching assistants.

ACADEMICS

Degrees: Bachelor's; Master's **Classes:** Most classes have fewer than 10 students. Most lab/discussion sessions have 10-19 students. **Special Study Options:** Cross-registration; Double major; Honors program; Independent study.

FACILITIES

Housing: Men's dorms

CAMPUS LIFE

Environment: Metropolis **Activities:** Choral groups 1 religious organizations.

ADMISSIONS

Freshman Academic Profile: 25% in top 10% of high school class, 35% in top 25% of high school class, 60% in top 50% of high school class. **Test Scores:** SAT Math middle 50% range 360-610. SAT EBRW middle 50% range 380-600. ACT middle 50% range 17-25. Minimum paper TOEFL 550. **Basis for Candidate Selection:** *Very important factors considered include:* rigor of secondary school record, standardized test scores, recommendation(s), religious affiliation/commitment. *Important factors considered include:*

academic GPA, application essay, interview. *Other factors considered include:* class rank, extracurricular activities, talent/ability, character/personal qualities, volunteer work. **Freshman Admission Requirements:** High school diploma is required and GED is accepted *Academic units required:* 4 English, 2 math, 1 science, 1 foreign language, 2 social studies, *Academic units recommended:* 4 math, 4 science, 2 foreign language, 4 social studies. **Freshman Admission Statistics:** 8 applied, 75.0% admitted, 100% enrolled. **Transfer Admission Requirements:** High school transcript, college transcript(s), essay or personal statement, interview, standardized test scores, Lowest grade transferable C. **General Admission Information:** Application fee $25. Priority deadline 7/31. Nonfall registration accepted.

COSTS AND FINANCIAL AID
Annual tuition $16,701. Room and board $7,908. Required fees $720. Average book expense $1,100. **Required Forms and Deadlines:** FAFSA; Institution's own financial aid form. **Types of Aid:** *Need-based scholarships/grants:* College/university scholarship or grant aid from institutional funds; Federal Pell; Private scholarships; SEOG; State scholarships/grants. *Student Employment:* Federal Work-Study Program available. **Financial Aid Statistics:** 83% needy undergrads receive need-based scholarship or grant aid. 0% undergrads receive non-need-based scholarship or grant aid. 100% freshmen, 33% undergrads receive need-based self-help aid. 0% freshmen, 0% undergrads receive athletic scholarships. **Criteria for awarding aid:** *Need-based:* Academics *Non-need-based:* Academics.

PORTLAND STATE UNIVERSITY

P.O. Box 751, Portland, OR 97207-0751
Phone: 503-725-3511 • **Financial Aid Phone:** 800-547-8887
E-mail: admissions@pdx.edu • **CEEB Code:** 4610
Fax: 503-725-5525 • **Website:** http://www.pdx.edu/ • **ACT Code:** 3492

This public school was founded in 1946. It has a 50 acre campus.

RATINGS
Admissions Selectivity Rating: 74   **Fire Safety Rating:** 85   **Green Rating:** 98

STUDENTS AND FACULTY
Enrollment: 18,631. **Student Body:** 54% female, 46% male, 15% out-of-state, 6% international (95 countries represented). Asian 9%, African American 4%, Caucasian 55%, Hispanic 14%, Native American 1%, Pacific Islander 1%, Two or more races 7%, Race unknown 4%.
Retention and Graduation: 71% freshmen return for sophomore year. 19% freshmen graduate within 4 years. 48% freshmen graduate within 6 years.
Faculty: Student/faculty ratio 18:1. 852 full-time faculty, 87% hold PhDs, 17% are members of minority groups, 49% are women. 5% of classes are taught by teaching assistants.

ACADEMICS
Degrees: Bachelor's; Certificate; Doctoral/Research; Master's; Post-Bachelor's certificate; Post-Master's certificate **Classes:** Most classes have fewer than 10 students. Most lab/discussion sessions have fewer than 10 students. **Most popular majors:** Psychology, General; Social Sciences, General; Business/Commerce, General. **Special Study Options:** Accelerated program; Cooperative education program; Distance learning; Double major; Dual enrollment; English as a Second Language (ESL); Exchange student program (domestic); Honors program; Independent study; Internships; Liberal arts/career combination; Study abroad; Teacher certification program. Honors programs: University Honors Program. **Disability Services offered to physically disabled students:** Note-taking services; Reader services; Tape recorders; Tutors. **Career services:** Alumni network; Alumni services; Career assessment; Career/job search classes; Internships.

FACILITIES
Housing: Apartments for married students; Apartments for single students; Coed dorms; Cooperative housing; Fraternity/sorority housing; Special housing for disabled student; Special housing for international students 95% of campus accessible to physically disabled. **Special Academic Facilities/Equipment:** Art galleries, audiovisual resources, classroom multimedia computer systems, learning lab, child development center, native american center. **Computers:** 50% of dorms, 100% of libraries, 100% of dining areas, 100% of student union, have wireless network access. Students can register for classes online. Administrative functions (other than registration) can be performed online.

CAMPUS LIFE
Environment: Metropolis **Activities:** Campus Ministries; Choral groups; Concert band; Dance; Drama/theater; International Student Organization; Jazz band; Literary magazine; Marching band; Model UN; Music ensembles; Musical theater; Opera; Radio station; Student government; Student newspaper; Student-run film society; Symphony orchestra; Television station 200 registered organizations, 10 honor societies, 14 religious organizations. 4 fraternities, 4 sororities. **Athletics (Intercollegiate):** *Men:* basketball, cross-country, football, tennis, track/field (outdoor), track/field (indoor). *Women:* basketball, cross-country, golf, soccer, softball, tennis, track/field (outdoor), track/field (indoor), volleyball. **On-Campus Highlights:** Park Blocks, Student Union Center, Simon Benson House, Peter Stott Center & Community Recreation Field **Environmental Initiatives:** Since 2002 PSU has focused on designing new buildings and retrofitting and renovating older campus buildings with sustainability in mind. Several PSU buildings serve as models of these kinds of innovative sustainable design and construction projects. These include the new Engineering Building, Broadway Housing Building, Stephen Epler Hall, and Native American Student and Community Center. In all but the latter, the US Green Building Council's LEED certification program was used as the measuring stick and standard for sustainable design and construction.

ADMISSIONS
Freshman Academic Profile: Average high school GPA 3.4. 15% in top 10% of high school class, 48% in top 25% of high school class, 85% in top 50% of high school class. 85% from public high schools. **Test Scores:** SAT Math middle 50% range 490-600. SAT EBRW middle 50% range 500-620. ACT middle 50% range 19-25. Minimum internet-based TOEFL 60. Minimum paper TOEFL 527. **Basis for Candidate Selection:** *Very important factors considered include:* rigor of secondary school record, academic GPA. *Other factors considered include:* application essay, standardized test scores. **Freshman Admission Requirements:** High school diploma is required and GED is accepted *Academic units required:* 4 English, 3 math, 3 science, 2 foreign language, 3 social studies, 1 history, *Academic units recommended:* 1 science labs. **Freshman Admission Statistics:** 6,815 applied, 92.4% admitted, 29% enrolled. **Transfer Admission Requirements:** college transcript(s), Minimum college GPA of 2.25 required. Lowest grade transferable D-. **General Admission Information:** Application fee $50. Priority deadline 6/1. Nonfall registration accepted. Admission may be deferred for a maximum of One year.

COSTS AND FINANCIAL AID
Annual in-state tuition $12,822. Annual out-of-state tuition $18,828. Room and board $12,822. Required fees $1,317. Average book expense $1,263. **Required Forms and Deadlines:** FAFSA. **Notification of Awards:** Applicants will be notified of awards on a rolling basis beginning 3/17. **Types of Aid:** *Need-based scholarships/grants:* College/university scholarship or grant aid from institutional funds; Federal Pell; Private scholarships; SEOG; State scholarships/grants. *Loans:* Direct PLUS loans; Direct Subsidized Stafford Loans; Direct Unsubsidized Stafford Loans. *Student Employment:* Federal Work-Study Program available. Institutional employment available. **Financial Aid Statistics:** 73% needy freshmen, 78% needy undergrads receive need-based scholarship or grant aid. 2% freshmen, 1% undergrads receive non-need-based scholarship or grant aid. 73% freshmen, 79% undergrads receive need-based self-help aid. 1% freshmen, 1% undergrads receive athletic scholarships. 75% freshmen, 56% undergrads receive any aid. Average cumulative indebtedness $32,018. **Criteria for awarding aid:** *Need-based:* Academics, Alumni affiliation, Art, Athletics, Leadership, Minority status, Music/drama *Non-need-based:* Academics, Alumni affiliation, Art, Athletics, Leadership, Minority status, Music/drama, State/district residency.

PRAIRIE VIEW A&M UNIVERSITY

P.O. Box 519, Prairie View, TX 77446
Phone: 936-261-3500 • **Financial Aid Phone:** 1-877-782-6830 • **CEEB Code:** 6580
Website: www.pvamu.edu • **ACT Code:** 4202

This public school was founded in 1876. It has a 1388 acre campus.

RATINGS
Admissions Selectivity Rating: 87   **Fire Safety Rating:** 82   **Green Rating:** 60*

STUDENTS AND FACULTY
Enrollment: 7,465. **Student Body:** 59% female, 41% male, 7% out-of-state, 2% international (40 countries represented). Asian 3%, African American 85%, Caucasian 2%, Hispanic 7%, Native American <1%, Pacific Islander <1%, Two or more races 1%, Race unknown <1%.

Retention and Graduation: 69% freshmen return for sophomore year. **Faculty:** Student/faculty ratio 17:1. 394 full-time faculty, 67% hold PhDs, 80% are members of minority groups, 39% are women.

ACADEMICS

Degrees: Bachelor's; Doctoral; **Master's Classes:** Most classes have fewer than 10 students. **Most popular majors:** Multi-/Interdisciplinary Studies, Other; Business Administration And Management, General. **Special Study Options:** Accelerated program; Cooperative education program; Distance learning; Double major; Dual enrollment; English as a Second Language (ESL); Exchange student program (domestic); Honors program; Independent study; Internships; Liberal arts/career combination; Study abroad; Teacher certification program; Weekend college. **Disability Services offered to physically disabled students:** Tape recorders; Tutors. **Career services:** Alumni network; Alumni services; Career assessment; Internships; Regional alumni

FACILITIES

Housing: Apartments for single students; Coed dorms; Special housing for disabled students 90% of campus accessible to physically disabled. **Computers:** 100% of classrooms, 100% of dorms, 100% of libraries, 75% of dining areas, 75% of student union, 50% of common outdoor areas have wireless network access. Students can register for classes online.

CAMPUS LIFE

Environment: Rural **Activities:** Campus Ministries; Choral groups; Concert band; Dance; Drama/theater; International Student Organization; Jazz band; Marching band; Music ensembles; Radio station; Student government; Student newspaper; Symphony orchestra; Television station; Yearbook 100 registered organizations, 15 honor societies, 6 religious organizations. 9 fraternities, 9 sororities. **Athletics (Intercollegiate):** *Men:* baseball, basketball, cross-country, football, golf, tennis, track/field (outdoor), track/field (indoor). *Women:* basketball, cheerleading, cross-country, golf, soccer, softball, tennis, track/field (outdoor), track/field (indoor), volleyball. **On-Campus Highlights:** Purple Zone Student Sports Bar, Memorial Student Center, Baby Dome, J.B. Coleman Library, Jazzman Coffee Cafe

ADMISSIONS

Freshman Academic Profile: Average high school GPA 2.9. 5% in top 10% of high school class, 21% in top 25% of high school class, 56% in top 50% of high school class. **Test Scores:** SAT Math middle 50% range 380-440. SAT EBRW middle 50% range 370-450. ACT middle 50% range 15-19. Minimum paper TOEFL 500. **Basis for Candidate Selection:** *Very important factors considered include:* academic GPA, standardized test scores. *Important factors considered include:* rigor of secondary school record. *Other factors considered include:* extracurricular activities, character/personal qualities, first generation, volunteer work, work experience. **Freshman Admission Requirements:** High school diploma is required and GED is accepted *Academic units required:* 4 English, 3 math, 2 science, 2.5 social studies, 1 computer science, 1 visual/ performing arts, and 0.5 unit from above areas or other academic areas. *Academic units recommended:* 4 English, 4 math, 4 science, 2 foreign language, 3.5 social studies, 1 computer science. **Freshman Admission Statistics:** 7,931 applied, 41.6% admitted, 52% enrolled. **Transfer Admission Requirements:** college transcript(s), statement of good standing from prior institution(s). Minimum college GPA of 2.0 required. Lowest grade transferable C. **General Admission Information:** Application fee $25. Priority deadline 6/1. Regular application deadline 6/1. Nonfall registration accepted. Admission may be deferred.

COSTS AND FINANCIAL AID

Annual in-state tuition $7,064. Annual out-of-state tuition $14,376. Room and board $7,064. Required fees $1,779. Average book expense $1,000. **Required Forms and Deadlines:** FAFSA; Institution's own financial aid form. **Notification of Awards:** Applicants will be notified of awards on or about 6/1. **Types of Aid:** *Need-based scholarships/grants:* College/university scholarship or grant aid from institutional funds; Federal Pell; Private scholarships; SEOG; State scholarships/grants; United Negro College Fund. *Loans:* Direct PLUS loans; Direct Subsidized Stafford Loans; Direct Unsubsidized Stafford Loans. *Student Employment:* Federal Work-Study Program available. Institutional employment available. **Financial Aid Statistics:** 69% needy freshmen, 63% needy undergrads receive need-based scholarship or grant aid. 35% freshmen, 18% undergrads receive non-need-based scholarship or grant aid. 94% freshmen, 90% undergrads receive need-based self-help aid. 1% freshmen, 4% undergrads receive athletic scholarships. 61% freshmen, 53% undergrads receive any aid. **Criteria for awarding aid:** *Need-based:* Academics, Athletics *Non-need-based:* Academics, Athletics, State/district residency.

PRATT INSTITUTE

200 Willoughby Avenue, Brooklyn, NY 11205
Phone: 718-636-3514 • **Financial Aid Phone:** 718-636-3599
E-mail: admissions@pratt.edu • **CEEB Code:** 2669
Fax: 718-636-3670 • **Website:** http://www.pratt.edu • **ACT Code:** 2862

This private school was founded in 1887. It has a 25 acre campus.

RATINGS

Admissions Selectivity Rating: 87   **Fire Safety Rating:** 84   **Green Rating:** 93

STUDENTS AND FACULTY

Enrollment: 3,396. **Student Body:** 69% female, 31% male, 72% out-of-state, 30% international (78 countries represented). Asian 13%, African American 4%, Caucasian 39%, Hispanic 10%, Native American <1%, Pacific Islander <1%, Two or more races 4%, Race unknown 1%.
Retention and Graduation: 88% freshmen return for sophomore year. 45% freshmen graduate within 4 years. 70% freshmen graduate within 6 years. **Faculty:** Student/faculty ratio 10:1. 157 full-time faculty, 79% hold PhDs, 20% are members of minority groups, 48% are women. 0% of classes are taught by teaching assistants.

ACADEMICS

Degrees: Associate; Bachelor's; Master's; Post-Master's certificate; Terminal Associate; Transfer Associate **Classes:** Most classes have 10-19 students. Most lab/discussion sessions have 10-19 students. **Most popular majors:** Architecture; Design And Visual Communications, General; Fine/Studio Arts, General. **Special Study Options:** English as a Second Language (ESL); Exchange student program (domestic); Independent study; Internships; Study abroad; Teacher certification program. Combined degree programs: BA/MA. **Disability Services offered to physically disabled students:** Note-taking services; Reader services; Tutors. **Career services:** Alumni network; Alumni services; Career assessment; Career/job search classes; Internships; Regional alumni

FACILITIES

Housing: Apartments for single students; Coed dorms; Special housing for disabled student; Theme housing; Wellness housing **Special Academic Facilities/Equipment:** Five art galleries, fine arts center, printmaking center, computer graphics lab. **Computers:** Undergraduates are required to own a computer.

CAMPUS LIFE

Environment: Metropolis **Activities:** Campus Ministries; International Student Organization; Literary magazine; Music ensembles; Radio station; Student government; Student newspaper; Student-run film society; Television station 50 registered organizations, 4 honor societies, 3 religious organizations. 3 fraternities, 1 sorority. **Athletics (Intercollegiate):** *Men:* basketball, cross-country, soccer, tennis, track/field (outdoor), track/field (indoor). *Women:* basketball, cross-country, soccer, tennis, track/field (outdoor), volleyball. **On-Campus Highlights:** studios, galleries, three cafeterias/coffee shops, athletic center, student union **Environmental Initiatives:** GIVETAKE (Launched 2016) Pratt's art supply recycling initiative, Givetake, opened its free store in the basement of Steuben Hall on the Brooklyn campus on August 22, 2016. The Pratt givetake materials re-use initiative collects (give) and offers (take) used art supplies, free of charge, to students. Since the initiate began in Aug 2016, we have college and given over 19,000 lbs of materials back to students!

ADMISSIONS

Freshman Academic Profile: Average high school GPA 3.8. **Test Scores:** SAT Math middle 50% range 560-680. SAT EBRW middle 50% range 530-630. ACT middle 50% range 25-29. Minimum internet-based TOEFL 79-80. Minimum paper TOEFL 550. **Basis for Candidate Selection:** *Very important factors considered include:* rigor of secondary school record, academic GPA, standardized test scores, talent/ability. *Important factors considered include:* application essay, character/personal qualities, alumni/ae relation, level of applicant's interest. *Other factors considered include:* interview, extracurricular activities, volunteer work, work experience. **Freshman Admission Requirements:** High school diploma is required and GED is accepted *Academic units recommended:* 4 English, 4 math, 2 science, 5 academic electives. **Freshman Admission Statistics:** 6,044 applied, 49.9% admitted, 23% enrolled. **Transfer Admission Requirements:** High school transcript, college transcript(s), essay or personal statement, statement of good standing from prior institution(s). Lowest grade transferable C. **General Admission Information:** Application fee $50. Regular application deadline 1/5. Nonfall registration accepted. Admission may be deferred for a maximum of 1 year.

COSTS AND FINANCIAL AID

Annual tuition $49,810. Room and board $12,622. Required fees $2,060. Average book expense $1,750. **Required Forms and Deadlines:** FAFSA; State aid form. **Notification of Awards:** Applicants will be notified of awards on a rolling basis beginning 3/1. **Types of Aid:** *Need-based scholarships/ grants:* College/university scholarship or grant aid from institutional funds; Federal Pell; SEOG; State scholarships/grants. *Loans:* Direct PLUS loans; Direct Subsidized Stafford Loans; Direct Unsubsidized Stafford Loans. *Student Employment:* Federal Work-Study Program available. Institutional employment available. **Financial Aid Statistics:** 54% needy undergrads receive need-based scholarship or grant aid. 99% freshmen, 86% undergrads receive non-need-based scholarship or grant aid. 100% freshmen, 60% undergrads receive need-based self-help aid. 0% freshmen, 0% undergrads receive athletic scholarships. 92% freshmen, 83% undergrads receive any aid. Average cumulative indebtedness $7,427. **Criteria for awarding aid:** *Need-based:* Academics *Non-need-based:* Academics.

PRESBYTERIAN COLLEGE

503 South Broad Street, Clinton, SC 29325
Phone: 864-833-8230 • **Financial Aid Phone:** 864-833-8287
E-mail: admissions@presby.edu • **CEEB Code:** 5540
Fax: 864-833-8195 • **Website:** www.presby.edu • **ACT Code:** 3874

This private school, affiliated with the Presbyterian Church, was founded in 1880. It has a 240 acre campus.

RATINGS

Admissions Selectivity Rating: 82   Fire Safety Rating: 97   Green Rating: 60*

STUDENTS AND FACULTY

Enrollment: 947. **Student Body:** 50% female, 50% male, 34% out-of-state, 5% international (23 countries represented). Asian 1%, African American 12%, Caucasian 75%, Hispanic 3%, Native American <1%, Pacific Islander 0%, Two or more races 3%, Race unknown 1%.
Retention and Graduation: 82% freshmen return for sophomore year. 62% freshmen graduate within 4 years. 68% freshmen graduate within 6 years. 28% grads go on to further study within 1 year. **Faculty:** Student/faculty ratio 13:1. 74 full-time faculty, 97% hold PhDs, 38% are women. 0% of classes are taught by teaching assistants.

ACADEMICS

Degrees: Bachelor's; Doctoral/Professional **Classes:** Most classes have 10-19 students. Most lab/discussion sessions have 10-19 students. **Most popular majors:** Biology/Biological Sciences, General; Psychology, General; Business Administration And Management, General. **Special Study Options:** Distance learning; Double major; Dual enrollment; English as a Second Language (ESL); Exchange student program (domestic); Honors program; Independent study; Internships; Study abroad; Teacher certification program. Honors programs: A variety of opportunities are available to highly motivated students with above average abilities through the normal programs of the College. These include research, internships, special projects, and directed studies. Presbyterian College also offers a special honors program for students who are chosen on the basis of their demonstrated ability. Students with a 3.20 GPA in all courses and a 3.40 GPA in all courses in the major field may, with the approval of departmental faculty, undertake an honors research program during the junior and/or senior years. Oral and written presentations of the results of the project will be required. Students who successfully complete the departmental honors research program will graduate with honors in the major field. **Disability Services offered to physically disabled students:** Tutors. **Career services:** Alumni network; Alumni services; Career assessment; Career/job search classes; Internships; Regional alumni

FACILITIES

Housing: Apartments for single students; Coed dorms; Fraternity/sorority housing; Men's dorms; Special housing for international students; Women's dorms 95% of campus accessible to physically disabled. **Special Academic Facilities/Equipment:** Art gallery, recital hall, media center, marine/ecological center, scanning and transmission electron microscopes, visible spectrophotometer. **Computers:** 95% of classrooms, 100% of dorms, 100% of libraries, 100% of dining areas, 100% of student union, 50% of common outdoor areas have wireless network access. Students can register for classes online. Administrative functions (other than registration) can be performed online.

CAMPUS LIFE

Environment: Village **Activities:** Campus Ministries; Choral groups; Concert band; Dance; Drama/theater; International Student Organization; Jazz band;

Literary magazine; Music ensembles; Pep band; Student government; Student newspaper; Symphony orchestra; Yearbook 85 registered organizations, 11 honor societies, 6 religious organizations. 6 fraternities, 3 sororities. **Athletics (Intercollegiate):** *Men:* baseball, basketball, cheerleading, cross-country, football, golf, lacrosse, soccer, tennis. *Women:* basketball, cheerleading, cross-country, golf, lacrosse, soccer, softball, tennis, volleyball. **On-Campus Highlights:** Neville Hall, Bailey Stadium, Springs Campus Center, Harrington Peachtree Academic Building, Thompson Library **Environmental Initiatives:** Energy conservation

ADMISSIONS

Freshman Academic Profile: Average high school GPA 3.3. 25% in top 10% of high school class, 62% in top 25% of high school class, 88% in top 50% of high school class. **Test Scores:** SAT Math middle 50% range 510-630. SAT EBRW middle 50% range 510-620. ACT middle 50% range 21-27. Minimum internet-based TOEFL 80. Minimum paper TOEFL 550. **Basis for Candidate Selection:** *Very important factors considered include:* rigor of secondary school record, class rank, academic GPA, application essay. *Important factors considered include:* recommendation(s), interview, extracurricular activities, talent/ability, character/personal qualities. *Other factors considered include:* standardized test scores, first generation, alumni/ae relation, volunteer work, work experience, level of applicant's interest. **Freshman Admission Requirements:** High school diploma is required and GED is accepted *Academic units required:* 4 English, 4 math, 2 science, 2 science labs, 2 foreign language, 2 social studies, 2 history, 2 academic electives, *Academic units recommended:* 4 science, 3 foreign language. **Freshman Admission Statistics:** 2,277 applied, 63.0% admitted, 19% enrolled. **Transfer Admission Requirements:** High school transcript, college transcript(s), essay or personal statement, standardized test scores, statement of good standing from prior institution(s). Lowest grade transferable C. **General Admission Information:** Priority deadline 12/1. Regular application deadline 6/30. Nonfall registration accepted. Admission may be deferred for a maximum of 1 year.

COSTS AND FINANCIAL AID

Annual tuition $34,982. Room and board $9,750. Required fees $2,860. Average book expense $1,200. **Required Forms and Deadlines:** FAFSA. **Notification of Awards:** Applicants will be notified of awards on a rolling basis beginning 3/1. **Types of Aid:** *Need-based scholarships/grants:* College/university scholarship or grant aid from institutional funds; Federal Pell; Private scholarships; SEOG; State scholarships/grants. *Loans:* Direct PLUS loans; Direct Subsidized Stafford Loans; Direct Unsubsidized Stafford Loans. *Student Employment:* Federal Work-Study Program available. **Financial Aid Statistics:** 100% needy freshmen, 100% needy undergrads receive need-based scholarship or grant aid. 52% freshmen, 36% undergrads receive non-need-based scholarship or grant aid. 63% freshmen, 100% undergrads receive need-based self-help aid. 7% freshmen, 8% undergrads receive athletic scholarships. 80% freshmen, 77% undergrads receive any aid. 61% undergrads borrow to pay for school. Average cumulative indebtedness $27,169. **Criteria for awarding aid:** *Need-based:* Alumni affiliation, Art, Job skills, Leadership, Minority status, Music/drama, Religious affiliation *Non-need-based:* Academics, Alumni affiliation, Athletics, Job skills, Leadership, Minority status, Music/drama, Religious affiliation, State/district residency.

PRESCOTT COLLEGE

220 Grove Avenue, Prescott, AZ 86301
Phone: 928-350-2100 • **Financial Aid Phone:** 928-350-1112
E-mail: admissions@prescott.edu • **CEEB Code:** 9295
Fax: 928-776-5242 • **Website:** www.prescott.edu • **ACT Code:** 5022

This private school was founded in 1966. It has a 13 acre campus.

RATINGS

Admissions Selectivity Rating: 74   Fire Safety Rating: 78   Green Rating: 60*

STUDENTS AND FACULTY

Enrollment: 351. **Student Body:** 60% female, 40% male, 60% out-of-state, 1% international (11 countries represented). Asian <1%, African American 2%, Caucasian 62%, Hispanic 7%, Native American 3%, Pacific Islander <1%, Two or more races 11%, Race unknown 13%.
Retention and Graduation: 73% freshmen return for sophomore year. 34% freshmen graduate within 4 years. 44% freshmen graduate within 6 years. **Faculty:** Student/faculty ratio 8:1. 33 full-time faculty, 39% hold PhDs, 3% are members of minority groups, 58% are women. 0% of classes are taught by teaching assistants.

ACADEMICS

Degrees: Bachelor's; Doctoral/Research; Master's; Post-Bachelor's certificate; Post-Master's certificate **Classes:** Most classes have 20-29 students. Most lab/discussion sessions have fewer than 10 students. **Most popular majors:** Environmental Studies; Elementary Education And Teaching; Education, Other. **Special Study Options:** Accelerated program; Cross-registration; Distance learning; Double major; Dual enrollment; Exchange student program (domestic); Independent study; Internships; Liberal arts/career combination; Student-designed major; Teacher certification program. **Disability Services offered to physically disabled students:** Note-taking services; Tape recorders; Tutors. **Career services:** Alumni network; Alumni services; Career assessment; Career/job search classes; Regional alumni

FACILITIES

Housing: Coed dorms; Special housing for disabled students 90% of campus accessible to physically diasbled. **Special Academic Facilities/Equipment:** Jenner Farm: An experimental agroecology farm. Centaur Leadership Services: Equine Assisted Learning and Equine Assisted Mental Health programs Kino Bay Center, MX: A field station on the Gulf of CA. Prescott College Art Gallery houses our visual arts center and Artist-in-Residence program. GIS Lab (Geographic Information Systems) Several Computer Labs Multi-Media Center **Computers:** 50% of classrooms, 100% of dorms, 100% of libraries, 100% of dining areas, 75% of common outdoor areas have wireless network access.

CAMPUS LIFE

Environment: Town **Activities:** Literary magazine; Student government 18 registered organizations. **On-Campus Highlights:** Crossroads Cafe, Crossroads Library, HUB (Helping Understand Bikes), Sam Hill Visual Arts Building, San Juan Gear Warehouse **Environmental Initiatives:** ACUPCC commitment and Climate Action Plan

ADMISSIONS

Freshman Academic Profile: 0% in top 10% of high school class, 0% in top 50% of high school class. 78% from public high schools. **Test Scores:** Minimum internet-based TOEFL 61. Minimum paper TOEFL 550. **Basis for Candidate Selection:** *Very important factors considered include:* rigor of secondary school record, academic GPA, application essay, recommendation(s). *Important factors considered include:* standardized test scores, extracurricular activities, character/personal qualities. *Other factors considered include:* interview, talent/ability, first generation, volunteer work, work experience. **Freshman Admission Requirements:** High school diploma is required and GED is accepted **Freshman Admission Statistics:** 394 applied, 94.2% admitted, 17% enrolled. **Transfer Admission Requirements:** college transcript(s), essay or personal statement, Lowest grade transferable C. **General Admission Information:** Priority deadline 3/1. Regular application deadline 8/15. Nonfall registration accepted. Admission may be deferred for a maximum of 1 year.

COSTS AND FINANCIAL AID

Annual tuition $29,880. Room and board $7,700. Required fees $530. Average book expense $982. **Required Forms and Deadlines:** FAFSA. **Notification of Awards:** Applicants will be notified of awards on a rolling basis beginning 1/15. **Types of Aid:** *Need-based scholarships/grants:* College/university scholarship or grant aid from institutional funds; Federal Pell; Private scholarships; SEOG; State scholarships/grants. *Loans:* Direct PLUS loans; Direct Subsidized Stafford Loans; Direct Unsubsidized Stafford Loans. *Student Employment:* Federal Work-Study Program available. Institutional employment available. **Financial Aid Statistics:** 100% needy freshmen, 100% needy undergrads receive need-based scholarship or grant aid. 4% freshmen, 5% undergrads receive non-need-based scholarship or grant aid. 96% freshmen, 95% undergrads receive need-based self-help aid. 0% freshmen, 0% undergrads receive athletic scholarships. 93% freshmen, 88% undergrads receive any aid. 72% undergrads borrow to pay for school. Average cumulative indebtedness $27,130. **Criteria for awarding aid:** *Non-need-based:* Academics, Leadership.

PRINCETON UNIVERSITY

PO Box 430, Princeton, NJ 08544-0430
Phone: 609-258-3060 • **Financial Aid Phone:** 609-258-3330
E-mail: uaoffice@princeton.edu • **CEEB Code:** 2672
Fax: 609-258-6743 • **Website:** www.princeton.edu • **ACT Code:** 2588

This private school was founded in 1746. It has a 500 acre campus.

RATINGS

Admissions Selectivity Rating: 99 **Fire Safety Rating:** 94 **Green Rating:** 86

STUDENTS AND FACULTY

Enrollment: 5,246. **Student Body:** 49% female, 51% male, 82% out-of-state, 12% international (99 countries represented). Asian 21%, African American 8%, Caucasian 43%, Hispanic 10%, Native American <1%, Pacific Islander <1%, Two or more races 4%, Race unknown 1%.
Retention and Graduation: 98% freshmen return for sophomore year. 89% freshmen graduate within 4 years. 97% freshmen graduate within 6 years. 19% grads go on to further study within 1 year. 0% grads pursue arts and sciences degrees. 1.8% grads pursue law degrees. 0% grads pursue business degrees. 1.9% grads pursue medical degrees. **Faculty:** Student/faculty ratio 5:1. 959 full-time faculty, 94% hold PhDs, 18% are members of minority groups, 32% are women. 0% of classes are taught by teaching assistants.

ACADEMICS

Degrees: Bachelor's; Doctoral/Research; **Master's Classes:** Most classes have 10-19 students. Most lab/discussion sessions have 10-19 students. **Most popular majors:** Computer Engineering, General; Public Administration; Economics, General. **Special Study Options:** Cross-registration; Exchange student program (domestic); Independent study; Student-designed major; Study abroad; Teacher certification program. **Disability Services offered to physically disabled students:** Note-taking services; Reader services; Tape recorders. **Career services:** Alumni network; Alumni services; Career assessment; Career/job search classes; Internships; Regional alumni

FACILITIES

Housing: Apartments for married students; Coed dorms; Cooperative housing; Special housing for disabled student; Wellness housing **Special Academic Facilities/Equipment:** Art Museum, Natural history museum, energy and environmental studies center, plasma physics lab, Center for Jewish Life, Center for Human Values, Woodrow WIlson School of Public and International Affairs, etc. **Computers:** 100% of classrooms, 100% of dorms, 70% of libraries, 100% of dining areas, 100% of student union, 20% of common outdoor areas have wireless network access. Students can register for classes online. Administrative functions (other than registration) can be performed online.

CAMPUS LIFE

Environment: Town **Activities:** Campus Ministries; Choral groups; Concert band; Dance; Drama/theater; International Student Organization; Jazz band; Literary magazine; Marching band; Model UN; Music ensembles; Musical theater; Opera; Pep band; Radio station; Student government; Student newspaper; Student-run film society; Symphony orchestra; Television station; Yearbook 250 registered organizations, 30 honor societies, 28 religious organizations. **Athletics (Intercollegiate):** *Men:* baseball, basketball, crew/rowing, cross-country, diving, fencing, football, golf, ice hockey, lacrosse, light weight football, soccer, squash, swimming, tennis, track/field (outdoor), track/field (indoor), volleyball, water polo, wrestling. *Women:* basketball, crew/rowing, cross-country, diving, fencing, field hockey, golf, ice hockey, lacrosse, soccer, softball, squash, swimming, tennis, track/field (outdoor), track/field (indoor), volleyball, water polo. **On-Campus Highlights:** Nassau Hall, Firestone Library, McCarter Theater, University Art Museum, University Chapel **Environmental Initiatives:** Greenhouse Gas reduction goal: 1990 levels by 2020 through local verifiable action, while adding more than 1 million gross square feet of built area, and without the purchase of offsets. 5.3 megawatt solar PV installation to be installed on campus properaty by 2012.

ADMISSIONS

Freshman Academic Profile: Average high school GPA 3.9. 94% in top 10% of high school class, 99% in top 25% of high school class, 100% in top 50% of high school class. 60% from public high schools. **Test Scores:** SAT Math middle 50% range 720-790. SAT EBRW middle 50% range 710-780. ACT middle 50% range 32-35. Minimum paper TOEFL 600. **Basis for Candidate Selection:** *Very important factors considered include:* rigor of secondary school record, class rank, academic GPA, application essay, standardized test scores, recommendation(s), extracurricular activities, talent/ability, character/personal qualities. *Other factors considered include:* interview, first generation, alumni/ae relation, geographical residence, racial/ethnic status, volunteer work, work experience. **Freshman Admission Requirements:** High school diploma or equivalent is not required *Academic units recommended:* 4 English, 4 math, 4 science, 2 science labs, 4 foreign language, 2 social studies, 2 history, 1 visual/performing arts. **Freshman Admission Statistics:** 31,056 applied, 6.4% admitted, 66% enrolled. **General Admission Information:** Application fee $65. Regular application deadline 1/1. Nonfall registration accepted. Admission may be deferred for a maximum of 1 year.

COSTS AND FINANCIAL AID
Annual tuition $47,140. Room and board $15,610. Average book expense $1,050. **Required Forms and Deadlines:** FAFSA; Institution's own financial aid form. **Notification of Awards:** Applicants will be notified of awards on or about 4/1. **Types of Aid:** *Need-based scholarships/grants:* College/university scholarship or grant aid from institutional funds; Federal Pell; Private scholarships; SEOG; State scholarships/grants. *Loans:* Direct PLUS loans; Direct Subsidized Stafford Loans; Direct Unsubsidized Stafford Loans. *Student Employment:* Federal Work-Study Program available. Institutional employment available. **Financial Aid Statistics:** 100% needy freshmen, 100% needy undergrads receive need-based scholarship or grant aid. 0% undergrads receive non-need-based scholarship or grant aid. 100% freshmen, 100% undergrads receive need-based self-help aid. 0% freshmen, 0% undergrads receive athletic scholarships. 59% freshmen, 59% undergrads receive any aid. 18% undergrads borrow to pay for school. Average cumulative indebtedness $8,908.

PRINCIPIA COLLEGE

1 Maybeck Place, Elsah, IL 62028
Phone: 618-374-5181 • **Financial Aid Phone:** 618-374-5628
E-mail: collegeadmissions@principia.edu • **CEEB Code:** 1630
Fax: 618-374-4000 • **Website:** www.principiacollege.edu • **ACT Code:** 1118

This private school, affiliated with the Christian Science Church, was founded in 1898. It has a 2600 acre campus.

RATINGS
Admissions Selectivity Rating: 83   **Fire Safety Rating:** 92   **Green Rating:** 93

STUDENTS AND FACULTY
Enrollment: 447. **Student Body:** 48% female, 52% male, 88% out-of-state, 18% international (28 countries represented). Asian <1%, African American 2%, Caucasian 73%, Hispanic 2%, Native American <1%, Pacific Islander 1%, Two or more races 1%, Race unknown 2%.
Retention and Graduation: 87% freshmen return for sophomore year. 71% freshmen graduate within 4 years. **Faculty:** Student/faculty ratio 6:1. 68 full-time faculty, 68% hold PhDs, 7% are members of minority groups, 44% are women. 0% of classes are taught by teaching assistants.

ACADEMICS
Degrees: Bachelor's **Classes:** Most classes have 20-29 students. Most lab/discussion sessions have 20-29 students. **Most popular majors:** Mass Communication/Media Studies; Education, General; Business Administration And Management, General. **Special Study Options:** Distance learning; Double major; Dual enrollment; Independent study; Internships; Liberal arts/career combination; Student-designed major; Study abroad; Teacher certification program. Honors programs: **Career services:** Alumni network; Career assessment; Career/job search classes; Internships; Regional alumni

FACILITIES
Housing: Apartments for married students; Coed dorms; Men's dorms; Theme housing; Women's dorms 80% of campus accessible to physically disabled. **Special Academic Facilities/Equipment:** Science Center with indoor aviary, research greenhouse, and extensive curated collections; School of Nations Museum and Classrooms; Voney Art Studio; School of Government; Merrick Wing for Performing Arts; Marshall Brooks Library

CAMPUS LIFE
Environment: Rural **Activities:** Choral groups; Dance; Drama/theater; International Student Organization; Jazz band; Literary magazine; Model UN; Music ensembles; Musical theater; Radio station; Student government; Student newspaper; Symphony orchestra; Television station; Yearbook 29 registered organizations, 1 honor society, 1 religious organization. **Athletics (Intercollegiate):** *Men:* baseball, basketball, cross-country, diving, football, soccer, swimming, tennis, track/field (outdoor), track/field (indoor). *Women:* basketball, cross-country, diving, soccer, swimming, tennis, track/field (outdoor),

track/field (indoor), volleyball. **On-Campus Highlights:** Piasa Pub, Hay Field House, Crafton Athletic Center, Science Center, Chapel **Environmental Initiatives:** 100% renewable energy (electricity)—recognized as a Gold Partner by the US Environmental Protection Agency's "Green Power Partnership"

ADMISSIONS
Freshman Academic Profile: Average high school GPA 3.3. 44% in top 10% of high school class, 50% in top 25% of high school class, 61% in top 50% of high school class. **Test Scores:** SAT Math middle 50% range 510-630. SAT EBRW middle 50% range 523-663. ACT middle 50% range 20-27. Minimum internet-based TOEFL 80. **Basis for Candidate Selection:** *Very important factors considered include:* academic GPA, application essay, standardized test scores, recommendation(s), character/personal qualities, religious affiliation/commitment. *Important factors considered include:* interview, extracurricular activities. *Other factors considered include:* rigor of secondary school record, class rank, talent/ability, level of applicant's interest. **Freshman Admission Requirements:** High school diploma is required and GED is accepted *Academic units required: Academic units recommended:* 4 English, 4 math, 3 science, 1 science labs, 2 foreign language, 1 social studies, 2 history, 2 academic electives. **Freshman Admission Statistics:** 134 applied, 91.0% admitted, 70% enrolled. **Transfer Admission Requirements:** High school transcript, college transcript(s), essay or personal statement, Minimum college GPA of 2.0 required. Lowest grade transferable C-. **General Admission Information:** Regular application deadline 7/1. Nonfall registration accepted. Admission may be deferred for a maximum of 1 year.

COSTS AND FINANCIAL AID
Annual tuition $28,770. Room and board $11,610. Required fees $700. Average book expense $1,000. **Required Forms and Deadlines:** CSS/Financial Aid PROFILE; Noncustodial PROFILE. **Notification of Awards:** Applicants will be notified of awards on a rolling basis beginning 1/1. **Types of Aid:** *Need-based scholarships/grants:* College/university scholarship or grant aid from institutional funds; Private scholarships. *Student Employment:* Institutional employment available. **Financial Aid Statistics:** 100% needy freshmen, 100% needy undergrads receive need-based scholarship or grant aid. 76% freshmen, 55% undergrads receive non-need-based scholarship or grant aid. 82% freshmen, 69% undergrads receive need-based self-help aid. 0% freshmen, 0% undergrads receive athletic scholarships. 96% freshmen, 96% undergrads receive any aid. 0% undergrads borrow to pay for school. **Criteria for awarding aid:** *Non-need-based:* Academics, Alumni affiliation, Leadership.

PROVIDENCE COLLEGE

1 Cunningham Square, Providence, RI 02918
Phone: 401-865-2535 • **Financial Aid Phone:** 401-865-2286
E-mail: pcadmiss@providence.edu • **CEEB Code:** 3693
Fax: 401-865-2826 • **Website:** www.providence.edu • **ACT Code:** 3806

This private school, affiliated with the Roman Catholic Church, was founded in 1917. It has a 105 acre campus.

RATINGS
Admissions Selectivity Rating: 88   **Fire Safety Rating:** 98   **Green Rating:** 60*

STUDENTS AND FACULTY
Enrollment: 4,233. **Student Body:** 55% female, 45% male, 91% out-of-state, 2% international (25 countries represented). Asian 1%, African American 4%, Caucasian 78%, Hispanic 9%, Native American <1%, Pacific Islander <1%, Two or more races 2%, Race unknown 4%.
Retention and Graduation: 92% freshmen return for sophomore year. 80% freshmen graduate within 4 years. 84% freshmen graduate within 6 years. 39% grads go on to further study within 1 year. 12% grads pursue arts and sciences degrees. 2% grads pursue law degrees. 8% grads pursue business degrees. 9% grads pursue medical degrees. **Faculty:** Student/faculty ratio 12:1. 298 full-time faculty, 88% hold PhDs, 13% are members of minority groups, 41% are women. 0% of classes are taught by teaching assistants.

ACADEMICS
Degrees: Associate; Bachelor's; Certificate; Master's; Post-Bachelor's certificate **Classes:** Most classes have 20-29 students. Most lab/discussion sessions have 20-29 students. **Most popular majors:** Biology/Biological Sciences, General; Finance, General; Marketing/Marketing Management, General. **Special Study Options:** Cross-registration; Distance learning; Double major; Dual enrollment; Exchange student program (domestic); Honors program; Independent study; Internships; Liberal arts/career combination; Student-

designed major; Study abroad; Teacher certification program. Honors programs: Liberal Arts Honors Program. **Disability Services offered to physically disabled students:** Note-taking services; Reader services; Tutors. **Career services:** Alumni network; Career assessment; Career/job search classes; Internships

FACILITIES

Housing: Coed dorms; Men's dorms; Special housing for disabled student; Theme housing; Wellness housing; Women's dorms 93% of campus accessible to physically diasbled. **Special Academic Facilities/Equipment:** Hunt-Cavanagh Art Gallery, Blackfriar Theatre, Science Center Complex, Computer and Language Labs, Smith Center for the Arts **Computers:** 100% of classrooms, 50% of dorms, 100% of libraries, 100% of dining areas, 100% of student union, 20% of common outdoor areas have wireless network access. Students can register for classes online. Administrative functions (other than registration) can be performed online.

CAMPUS LIFE

Environment: City **Activities:** Campus Ministries; Choral groups; Concert band; Dance; Drama/theater; International Student Organization; Jazz band; Literary magazine; Music ensembles; Musical theater; Pep band; Radio station; Student government; Student newspaper; Student-run film society; Television station; Yearbook 112 registered organizations, 18 honor societies, 2 religious organizations. **Athletics (Intercollegiate):** *Men:* basketball, cross-country, diving, ice hockey, lacrosse, soccer, swimming, track/field (outdoor), track/field (indoor). *Women:* basketball, cross-country, diving, field hockey, ice hockey, soccer, softball, swimming, tennis, track/field (outdoor), track/field (indoor), volleyball. **On-Campus Highlights:** Ryan Center for Business Studies, Ruane Center for the Humanities, McPhail's Entertainment Facility, Concannon Fitness Center, Slavin Center—Student Center **Environmental Initiatives:** Solar Energy—One of the primary energy efficient elements of the addition to Slavin Center is the 1,850 sq. ft. Building Integrated Photovoltaic (BIPV) array located on the roof about the Slavin Center lobby entrance. Photovoltaic cells capture the sun's energy and convert it directly into electricity.

ADMISSIONS

Freshman Academic Profile: Average high school GPA 3.4. 36% in top 10% of high school class, 65% in top 25% of high school class, 92% in top 50% of high school class. 57% from public high schools. **Test Scores:** SAT Math middle 50% range 580-670. SAT EBRW middle 50% range 580-660. ACT middle 50% range 26-30. Minimum internet-based TOEFL 90. Minimum paper TOEFL 577. **Basis for Candidate Selection:** *Very important factors considered include:* rigor of secondary school record, academic GPA, application essay. *Important factors considered include:* recommendation(s), extracurricular activities, character/personal qualities. *Other factors considered include:* class rank, standardized test scores, talent/ability, first generation, alumni/ae relation, geographical residence, racial/ethnic status, volunteer work, work experience, level of applicant's interest. **Freshman Admission Requirements:** High school diploma is required and GED is not accepted *Academic units required:* 4 English, 4 math, 3 science, 2 science labs, 3 foreign language, 2 social studies, 2 history, *Academic units recommended:* 4 English, 4 math, 4 science, 2 science labs, 4 foreign language, 2 social studies, 2 history. **Freshman Admission Statistics:** 11,251 applied, 51.5% admitted, 18% enrolled. **Transfer Admission Requirements:** High school transcript, college transcript(s), essay or personal statement, statement of good standing from prior institution(s). Minimum college GPA of 3.0 required. Lowest grade transferable c. **General Admission Information:** Application fee $65. Regular application deadline 1/15. Nonfall registration accepted. Admission may be deferred for a maximum of 1 year.

COSTS AND FINANCIAL AID

Required Forms and Deadlines: CSS/Financial Aid PROFILE; FAFSA. **Notification of Awards:** Applicants will be notified of awards on or about 3/15. **Types of Aid:** *Need-based scholarships/grants:* College/university scholarship or grant aid from institutional funds; Federal Pell; Private scholarships; SEOG; State scholarships/grants; United Negro College Fund. *Loans:* Direct PLUS loans; Direct Subsidized Stafford Loans; Direct Unsubsidized Stafford Loans. *Student Employment:* Federal Work-Study Program available. Institutional employment available. **Financial Aid Statistics:** 94% needy freshmen, 98% needy undergrads receive need-based scholarship or grant aid. 10% freshmen, 8% undergrads receive non-need-based scholarship or grant aid. 87% freshmen, 88% undergrads receive need-based self-help aid. 5% freshmen, 5% undergrads receive athletic scholarships. 84% freshmen, 81% undergrads receive any aid. 70% undergrads borrow to pay for school. Average cumulative indebtedness $39,775. **Criteria for awarding aid:** *Need-based:* Minority status, Music/drama *Non-need-based:* Academics, Athletics, Leadership, Minority status, Music/drama.

PURDUE UNIVERSITY—CALUMET

2200 169th St., Hammond, IN 46323-2094
Phone: 219-989-2213 • **Financial Aid Phone:** 219-989-2301
E-mail: adms@purduecal.edu • **CEEB Code:** 1638
Fax: 219-989-2775 • **Website:** http://www.purduecal.edu/ • **ACT Code:** 1233

This public school was founded in 1946. It has a 194 acre campus.

RATINGS

Admissions Selectivity Rating: 78   **Fire Safety Rating:** 95   **Green Rating:** 60*

STUDENTS AND FACULTY

Enrollment: 8,403. **Student Body:** 55% female, 45% male, 11% out-of-state, 3% international (39 countries represented). Asian 1%, African American 19%, Caucasian 61%, Hispanic 15%, Native American <1%, Race unknown 0%. **Retention and Graduation:** 69% freshmen return for sophomore year. **Faculty:** Student/faculty ratio 21:1. 268 full-time faculty, 69% hold PhDs, 21% are members of minority groups, 48% are women.

ACADEMICS

Degrees: Associate; Bachelor's; Certificate; Master's; Post-Bachelor's certificate **Classes:** Most classes have 20-29 students. Most lab/discussion sessions have 20-29 students. **Most popular majors:** Elementary Education And Teaching; Engineering, General; Marketing/Marketing Management, General. **Special Study Options:** Accelerated program; Cooperative education program; Distance learning; Double major; Dual enrollment; English as a Second Language (ESL); Honors program; Independent study; Internships; Study abroad; Teacher certification program; Weekend college. Honors programs: Purdue Calumet Honors Program. **Disability Services offered to physically disabled students:** Note-taking services; Reader services; Tape recorders; Tutors. **Career services:** Career assessment; Career/job search classes; Internships

FACILITIES

Housing: Apartments for single students 100% of campus accessible to physically diasbled. **Special Academic Facilities/Equipment:** Audio-visual services, urban development institute. **Computers:** Students can register for classes online. Administrative functions (other than registration) can be performed online.

CAMPUS LIFE

Environment: City **Activities:** Campus Ministries; Choral groups; Dance; Drama/theater; International Student Organization; Radio station; Student government; Student newspaper 56 registered organizations, 25 honor societies, 3 religious organizations. 2 fraternities, 3 sororities. **Athletics (Intercollegiate):** *Men:* basketball. *Women:* basketball. **On-Campus Highlights:** Physical Education and Recreation Building, Enrollment Services Center, Challenger Learning Center of Northwest Indiana **Environmental Initiatives:** Campus-wide Recycling

ADMISSIONS

Freshman Academic Profile: Average high school GPA 2.6. 10% in top 10% of high school class, 28% in top 25% of high school class, 58% in top 50% of high school class. **Test Scores:** SAT Math middle 50% range 410-520. SAT EBRW middle 50% range 410-510. ACT middle 50% range 17-23. Minimum paper TOEFL 550. **Basis for Candidate Selection:** *Important factors considered include:* rigor of secondary school record, class rank, academic GPA, standardized test scores. **Freshman Admission Requirements:** High school diploma is required and GED is accepted *Academic units required:* 4 English, 2 math, 1 science, 1 science labs, 2 foreign language, 1 social studies, 1 history, *Academic units recommended:* 4 English, 2 math, 2 science, 2 science labs, 2 foreign language, 2 social studies, 1 history. **Freshman Admission Statistics:** 5,884 applied, 69.4% admitted, 33% enrolled. **Transfer Admission Requirements:** High school transcript, Minimum college GPA of 2.0 required. Lowest grade transferable C. **General Admission Information:** Nonfall registration accepted. Admission may be deferred for a maximum of 1 semester.

COSTS AND FINANCIAL AID

Average book expense $1,125. **Required Forms and Deadlines:** FAFSA. **Notification of Awards:** Applicants will be notified of awards on a rolling basis beginning 4/15. **Types of Aid:** *Need-based scholarships/grants:* College/university scholarship or grant aid from institutional funds; Federal Pell; SEOG; State scholarships/grants. *Loans:* Direct PLUS loans; Direct Subsidized Stafford Loans; Direct Unsubsidized Stafford Loans. *Student Employment:* Federal Work-Study Program available. **Financial Aid Statistics:** 61% needy freshmen, 65% needy undergrads receive need-based scholarship or grant aid. 27% freshmen, 16% undergrads receive non-need-based scholarship or grant aid. 67% freshmen, 77% undergrads receive need-based self-help aid. 1% freshmen, 0% undergrads receive athletic scholarships. **Criteria for awarding aid:**

Need-based: Academics, Minority status *Non-need-based:* Academics, Athletics, Minority status, State/district residency.

PURDUE UNIVERSITY—WEST LAFAYETTE

475 Stadium Mall Drive, West Lafayette, IN 47907-2050
Phone: (765) 494-1776 • **Financial Aid Phone:** (765) 494-0998
E-mail: admissions@purdue.edu • **CEEB Code:** 1631
Fax: 765-494-0544 • **Website:** www.purdue.edu • **ACT Code:** 1230

This public school was founded in 1869. It has a 2602 acre campus.

RATINGS

Admissions Selectivity Rating: 89   **Fire Safety Rating:** 96   **Green Rating:** 96

STUDENTS AND FACULTY

Enrollment: 30,831. **Student Body:** 43% female, 57% male, 36% out-of-state, 16% international (123 countries represented). Asian 8%, African American 3%, Caucasian 63%, Hispanic 5%, Native American <1%, Pacific Islander <1%, Two or more races 3%, Race unknown 2%.
Retention and Graduation: 92% freshmen return for sophomore year. 51% freshmen graduate within 4 years. 79% freshmen graduate within 6 years. 21% grads go on to further study within 1 year. **Faculty:** Student/faculty ratio 13:1. 2,287 full-time faculty, 98% hold PhDs, 26% are members of minority groups, 35% are women. 24% of classes are taught by teaching assistants.

ACADEMICS

Degrees: Bachelor's; Certificate; Doctoral; Doctoral/Professional; Doctoral/ Research; Master's; Post-Bachelor's certificate; Post-Master's certificate; Terminal Associate **Classes:** Most classes have 10-19 students. Most lab/ discussion sessions have 20-29 students. **Most popular majors:** Computer Science; Mechanical Engineering; Mechanical Engineering/Mechanical Technology/Technician. **Special Study Options:** Accelerated program; Cooperative education program; Cross-registration; Distance learning; Double major; Dual enrollment; English as a Second Language (ESL); Honors program; Independent study; Internships; Liberal arts/career combination; Study abroad; Teacher certification program; Weekend college. Honors programs: University Honors Program. **Disability Services offered to physically disabled students:** Note-taking services; Reader services; Tape recorders; Tutors. **Career services:** Alumni network; Alumni services; Career assessment; Career/job search classes; Internships; Regional alumni

FACILITIES

Housing: Apartments for married students; Apartments for single students; Coed dorms; Cooperative housing; Fraternity/sorority housing; Men's dorms; Special housing for disabled student; Theme housing; Women's dorms 93.4% of campus accessible to physically diasbled. **Special Academic Facilities/ Equipment:** Hall of music, child development lab, speech and hearing clinic, small animal veterinary clinic, horticulture park, linear accelerator, tornado simulator, nuclear accelerator. **Computers:** 95% of classrooms, 5% of dorms, 95% of libraries, 90% of dining areas, 95% of student union, 5% of common outdoor areas have wireless network access. Students can register for classes online. Administrative functions (other than registration) can be performed online.

CAMPUS LIFE

Environment: Town **Activities:** Campus Ministries; Choral groups; Concert band; Dance; Drama/theater; International Student Organization; Jazz band; Literary magazine; Marching band; Model UN; Music ensembles; Pep band; Radio station; Student government; Student newspaper; Symphony orchestra; Television station 850 registered organizations, 25 honor societies, 66 religious organizations. 48 fraternities, 32 sororities. **Athletics (Intercollegiate):** *Men:* baseball, basketball, cross-country, diving, football, golf, swimming, tennis, track/field (outdoor), track/field (indoor), wrestling. *Women:* basketball, cross-country, diving, golf, soccer, softball, swimming, tennis, track/field (outdoor), track/field (indoor), volleyball. **On-Campus Highlights:** Pudue Memorial Union, Recreational Sports Center, Neil Armstrong Hall of Engineering, Marriott Hall (hospitality and tourism management program), Pao Hall for Visual and Performing Arts **Environmental Initiatives:** Friday Night Lights (FNL) was launched as a collaborative partnership between the Student Sustainability Council, Office of University Sustainability, Building Services, Building Deputies, Purdue Police Department, and numerous student

volunteers. Every Friday evening participants volunteer an hour of their time to turn off lights in classrooms of targeted academic buildings so they will not be left on over the weekend. Not only does this program reduce Purdue's energy use and carbon footprint, it also increases social capital among those on campus and, ultimately, trims Purdue's bottom line.

ADMISSIONS

Freshman Academic Profile: Average high school GPA 3.8. 44% in top 10% of high school class, 78% in top 25% of high school class, 97% in top 50% of high school class. **Test Scores:** SAT Math middle 50% range 580-710. SAT EBRW middle 50% range 570-670. ACT middle 50% range 25-31. Minimum internet-based TOEFL 80-88. **Basis for Candidate Selection:** *Very important factors considered include:* rigor of secondary school record, academic GPA, standardized test scores. *Important factors considered include:* application essay, recommendation(s), extracurricular activities, character/personal qualities, first generation. *Other factors considered include:* class rank, talent/ability, alumni/ae relation, geographical residence, state residency, racial/ethnic status, volunteer work, work experience, level of applicant's interest. **Freshman Admission Requirements:** High school diploma is required and GED is accepted *Academic units required:* 4 English, 3 math, 3 science, 2 science labs, 3 foreign language. **Freshman Admission Statistics:** 48,912 applied, 57.4% admitted, 27% enrolled. **Transfer Admission Requirements:** college transcript(s), essay or personal statement, statement of good standing from prior institution(s). Minimum college GPA of 2.5 required. Lowest grade transferable C. **General Admission Information:** Application fee $60. Priority deadline 2/1. Nonfall registration accepted.

COSTS AND FINANCIAL AID

Annual in-state tuition $10,030. Annual out-of-state tuition $28,010. Room and board $10,030. Required fees $784. Average book expense $1,160. **Required Forms and Deadlines:** FAFSA. **Notification of Awards:** Applicants will be notified of awards on or about 4/15. **Types of Aid:** *Need-based scholarships/ grants:* College/university scholarship or grant aid from institutional funds; Federal Pell; Private scholarships; SEOG; State scholarships/grants. *Loans:* Direct PLUS loans; Direct Subsidized Stafford Loans; Direct Unsubsidized Stafford Loans. *Student Employment:* Federal Work-Study Program available. Institutional employment available. **Financial Aid Statistics:** 62% needy freshmen, 64% needy undergrads receive need-based scholarship or grant aid. 49% freshmen, 43% undergrads receive non-need-based scholarship or grant aid. 73% freshmen, 79% undergrads receive need-based self-help aid. 1% freshmen, 1% undergrads receive athletic scholarships. 74% freshmen, 77% undergrads receive any aid. 46% undergrads borrow to pay for school. Average cumulative indebtedness $27,530. **Criteria for awarding aid:** *Non-need-based:* Academics, Athletics, Leadership, Music/drama, State/district residency.

QUEENS UNIVERSITY OF CHARLOTTE

1900 Selwyn Avenue, Charlotte, NC 28274
Phone: 704-337-2212 • **Financial Aid Phone:** 704-337-2225
E-mail: admissions@queens.edu • **CEEB Code:** 5560
Fax: 704-337-2403 • **Website:** www.queens.edu • **ACT Code:** 3148

This private school, affiliated with the Presbyterian Church, was founded in 1857. It has a 30 acre campus.

RATINGS

Admissions Selectivity Rating: 77   **Fire Safety Rating:** 70   **Green Rating:** 60*

STUDENTS AND FACULTY

Enrollment: 1,911. **Student Body:** 76% female, 24% male, 8% international. Asian 2%, African American 16%, Caucasian 55%, Hispanic 3%, Native American 1%, Two or more races 2%, Race unknown 13%. **Retention and Graduation:** 70% freshmen return for sophomore year. **Faculty:** Student/faculty ratio 12:1. 123 full-time faculty, 72% hold PhDs, 7% are members of minority groups, 68% are women. 0% of classes are taught by teaching assistants.

ACADEMICS

Degrees: Bachelor's; Master's; Post-Bachelor's certificate; Terminal Associate **Classes:** Most classes have 10-19 students. Most lab/discussion sessions have 10-19 students. **Special Study Options:** Accelerated program; Distance learning; Double major; Honors program; Independent study; Internships; Liberal arts/career combination; Study abroad; Teacher certification program; Weekend college. **Disability Services offered to physically disabled students:** Note-taking services; Reader services; Tape recorders; Tutors. **Career services:** Alumni network; Career/job search classes; Internships

FACILITIES

Housing: Coed dorms; Special housing for disabled students 63% of campus accessible to physically diasbled. **Special Academic Facilities/Equipment:** Three art galleries, rare books museum.

CAMPUS LIFE

Environment: Metropolis **Activities:** Campus Ministries; Choral groups; Concert band; Dance; Drama/theater; International Student Organization; Literary magazine; Model UN; Music ensembles; Musical theater; Student government; Student newspaper 38 registered organizations, 9 honor societies, 2 religious organizations. 2 fraternities, 4 sororities. **Athletics (Intercollegiate):** *Men:* basketball, cheerleading, cross-country, golf, lacrosse, soccer, tennis, track/field (outdoor). *Women:* basketball, cheerleading, cross-country, golf, lacrosse, soccer, softball, tennis, track/field (outdoor), volleyball. **On-Campus Highlights:** Levine.Center, The Lion's Den, Trexler Courtyard, Queens' Off-Campus Athletic Facility, Coffee Shop

ADMISSIONS

Freshman Academic Profile: Average high school GPA 3.5. 14% in top 10% of high school class, 39% in top 25% of high school class, 78% in top 50% of high school class. **Test Scores:** SAT Math middle 50% range 460-570. SAT EBRW middle 50% range 470-580. ACT middle 50% range 20-25. Minimum internet-based TOEFL 79. Minimum paper TOEFL 550. **Basis for Candidate Selection:** *Very important factors considered include:* rigor of secondary school record, academic GPA, standardized test scores, extracurricular activities, character/personal qualities. *Important factors considered include:* class rank, interview, volunteer work. *Other factors considered include:* application essay, recommendation(s), talent/ability, first generation, alumni/ae relation, work experience. **Freshman Admission Requirements:** High school diploma is required and GED is accepted *Academic units required:* 4 English, 3 math, 2 science, 1 science labs, 2 foreign language, 2 social studies. **Freshman Admission Statistics:** 2,199 applied, 73.6% admitted, 22% enrolled. **Transfer Admission Requirements:** High school transcript, college transcript(s), essay or personal statement, statement of good standing from prior institution(s). Minimum college GPA of 2.0 required. Lowest grade transferable C. **General Admission Information:** Application fee $40. Nonfall registration accepted. Admission may be deferred for a maximum of 1 year.

COSTS AND FINANCIAL AID

Required Forms and Deadlines: FAFSA; State aid form. **Notification of Awards:** Applicants will be notified of awards on a rolling basis beginning 3/15. **Types of Aid:** *Need-based scholarships/grants:* College/university scholarship or grant aid from institutional funds; Federal Pell; Private scholarships; SEOG; State scholarships/grants. *Loans:* Direct PLUS loans; Direct Subsidized Stafford Loans; Direct Unsubsidized Stafford Loans. *Student Employment:* Federal Work-Study Program available. Institutional employment available. **Financial Aid Statistics:** 100% needy freshmen, 99% needy undergrads receive need-based scholarship or grant aid. 18% freshmen, 15% undergrads receive non-need-based scholarship or grant aid. 79% freshmen, 83% undergrads receive need-based self-help aid. 11% freshmen, 10% undergrads receive athletic scholarships. **Criteria for awarding aid:** *Need-based:* Academics, Leadership, Minority status *Non-need-based:* Academics, Art, Athletics, Leadership, Minority status, Music/drama, Religious affiliation.

QUINCY UNIVERSITY

Registrars Office, Quincy, IL 62301-2699
Phone: 217-228-5210 • **Financial Aid Phone:** 217-228-5260
E-mail: admissions@quincy.edu • **CEEB Code:** 1645
Fax: 217-228-5479 • **Website:** www.quincy.edu • **ACT Code:** 1120

This private school, affiliated with the Roman Catholic Church, was founded in 1860. It has a 70 acre campus.

RATINGS

Admissions Selectivity Rating: 72   **Fire Safety Rating:** 97   **Green Rating:** 61

STUDENTS AND FACULTY

Enrollment: 1,075. **Student Body:** 56% female, 44% male, 28% out-of-state, (6 countries represented).
Retention and Graduation: 76% freshmen return for sophomore year. 22% grads go on to further study within 1 year. 11% grads pursue arts and sciences degrees. 2% grads pursue law degrees. 5% grads pursue business degrees. 2% grads pursue medical degrees. **Faculty:** Student/faculty ratio 14:1. 56 full-time faculty, 71% hold PhDs, 7% are members of minority groups, 39% are women. 0% of classes are taught by teaching assistants.

ACADEMICS

Degrees: Bachelor's; Master's; Transfer Associate **Classes:** Most classes have fewer than 10 students. Most lab/discussion sessions have 10-19 students. **Most popular majors:** Elementary Education And Teaching; Registered Nursing/Registered Nurse; Management Science. **Special Study Options:** Accelerated program; Distance learning; Double major; Dual enrollment; Honors program; Independent study; Internships; Student-designed major; Study abroad; Teacher certification program. Honors programs: The Honors Program provides an academically challenging course of study which adds an interdisciplinary dimension to a student's major field. The program promotes academic excellence through critical thinking, original research, exceptional writing, and public presentation of scholarship. **Disability Services offered to physically disabled students:** Note-taking services; Reader services; Tape recorders; Tutors. **Career services:** Alumni services; Career assessment; Career/job search classes; Internships

FACILITIES

Housing: Apartments for single students; Coed dorms; Fraternity/sorority housing; Special housing for disabled student; Special housing for international students; Theme housing 75% of campus accessible to physically diasbled. **Special Academic Facilities/Equipment:** Reading center for student teachers, multimedia and graphic design labs, TV broadcast studio, art gallery, 200-seat theater, environmental studies institute, hospital simulation lab, aviation facility with flight simulator. **Computers:** 100% of classrooms, 100% of dorms, 100% of libraries, 100% of dining areas, 100% of student union, 40% of common outdoor areas have wireless network access. Administrative functions (other than registration) can be performed online.

CAMPUS LIFE

Environment: Town **Activities:** Campus Ministries; Choral groups; Concert band; Dance; Drama/theater; Jazz band; Literary magazine; Marching band; Music ensembles; Musical theater; Pep band; Student government; Student newspaper; Student-run film society; Symphony orchestra 40 registered organizations, 8 honor societies, 2 religious organizations. 1 fraternity, 2 sororities. **Athletics (Intercollegiate):** *Men:* baseball, basketball, cross-country, football, golf, soccer, tennis, volleyball. *Women:* basketball, cross-country, golf, soccer, softball, tennis, volleyball. **On-Campus Highlights:** Health and Fitness Center, Student Success Center, QU Chapel, New Student Living Center, Brenner Library **Environmental Initiatives:** Residence hall renovation: Helein Hall renovations included use of recycled furniture and the installation of an energy-efficient VRV hvac system.

ADMISSIONS

Freshman Academic Profile: 76% from public high schools. **Test Scores:** SAT Math middle 50% range 410-490. SAT EBRW middle 50% range 460-490. ACT middle 50% range 19-25. Minimum internet-based TOEFL 61. Minimum paper TOEFL 500. **Basis for Candidate Selection:** *Very important factors considered include:* rigor of secondary school record, academic GPA. *Important factors considered include:* class rank, application essay, standardized test scores, recommendation(s), extracurricular activities, character/personal qualities, volunteer work, work experience, level of applicant's interest. *Other factors considered include:* interview, talent/ability. **Freshman Admission Requirements:** High school diploma is required and GED is accepted *Academic units recommended:* 4 English, 3 math, 3 science, 2 foreign language, 3 social studies. **Freshman Admission Statistics:** 903 applied, 88.9% admitted, 27% enrolled. **Transfer Admission Requirements:** college transcript(s), statement of good standing from prior institution(s). Minimum college GPA of 2.0 required. Lowest grade transferable D. **General Admission Information:** Application fee $25. Priority deadline 4/1. Nonfall registration accepted. Admission may be deferred.

COSTS AND FINANCIAL AID

Annual tuition $25,598. Room and board $11,336. Required fees $974. Average book expense $1,250. **Required Forms and Deadlines:** FAFSA. **Notification of Awards:** Applicants will be notified of awards on a rolling basis beginning 3/1. **Types of Aid:** *Need-based scholarships/grants:* College/university scholarship or grant aid from institutional funds; Federal Pell; Private scholarships; SEOG; State scholarships/grants. *Loans:* Direct PLUS loans; Direct Subsidized Stafford Loans; Direct Unsubsidized Stafford Loans. *Student Employment:* Federal Work-Study Program available. Institutional employment available. **Financial Aid Statistics:** 98% needy freshmen, 92% needy undergrads receive need-based scholarship or grant aid. 23% freshmen, 17% undergrads receive non-need-based scholarship or grant aid. 69% freshmen, 75% undergrads receive need-based self-help aid. 8% freshmen, 4% undergrads receive athletic scholarships. 100% freshmen, 93% undergrads receive any aid. **Criteria for awarding aid:** *Need-based:* Academics, Alumni affiliation, Art, Leadership, Minority status, Music/drama *Non-need-based:* Academics, Alumni affiliation, Art, Athletics, Leadership, Music/drama.

QUINNIPIAC UNIVERSITY

275 Mount Carmel Avenue, Hamden, CT 06518
Phone: 203-582-8600 • **Financial Aid Phone:** 203-582-8750
E-mail: admissions@qu.edu • **CEEB Code:** 3712
Fax: 203-582-8906 • **Website:** www.qu.edu • **ACT Code:** 582

This private school was founded in 1929. It has a 600 acre campus.

RATINGS

Admissions Selectivity Rating: 81   **Fire Safety Rating:** 98   **Green Rating:** 75

STUDENTS AND FACULTY

Enrollment: 7,249. **Student Body:** 61% female, 39% male, 71% out-of-state, 2% international (51 countries represented). Asian 3%, African American 4%, Caucasian 77%, Hispanic 9%, Native American <1%, Pacific Islander 0%, Two or more races 3%, Race unknown 2%.
Retention and Graduation: 86% freshmen return for sophomore year. 68% freshmen graduate within 4 years. 75% freshmen graduate within 6 years. 43% grads go on to further study within 1 year. 19% grads pursue arts and sciences degrees. 2% grads pursue law degrees. 14% grads pursue business degrees. 2% grads pursue medical degrees. **Faculty:** Student/faculty ratio 16:1. 378 full-time faculty, 89% hold PhDs, 18% are members of minority groups, 56% are women. 0% of classes are taught by teaching assistants.

ACADEMICS

Degrees: Bachelor's; Doctoral; Doctoral/Professional; Master's; Post-Bachelor's certificate; Post-Master's certificate **Classes:** Most classes have 20-29 students. Most lab/discussion sessions have 20-29 students. **Most popular majors:** Psychology, General; Registered Nursing/Registered Nurse; Business/Commerce, General. **Special Study Options:** Accelerated program; Distance learning; Double major; Honors program; Independent study; Internships; Liberal arts/career combination; Student-designed major; Study abroad; Teacher certification program. Honors programs: The University Honors Program, limited to 80-85 freshmen who are selected following their acceptance, provides challenging coursework and opportunities for learning and service. Combined degree programs: BA/JD; BA/MA. **Career services:** Alumni network; Alumni services; Career assessment; Career/job search classes; Internships; Regional alumni

FACILITIES

Housing: Apartments for single students; Coed dorms; Special housing for international students; Theme housing; Wellness housing 100% of campus accessible to physically diasbled. **Special Academic Facilities/Equipment:** Quinnipiac Polling Institute, Financial Technology Center, Motion Analysis Lab, Albert Schweitzer Institute, Critical Care Nursing Lab, Fully digital/high definition TV production studio,editing labs, news technology center. Irish Famine Museum "An Gorta Mor". **Computers:** 100% of classrooms, 100% of dorms, 100% of libraries, 100% of dining areas, 100% of student union, 100% of common outdoor areas have wireless network access. Students can register for classes online. Administrative functions (other than registration) can be performed online. Undergraduates are required to own a computer.

CAMPUS LIFE

Environment: Town **Activities:** Campus Ministries; Choral groups; Dance; Drama/theater; International Student Organization; Literary magazine; Model UN; Music ensembles; Pep band; Radio station; Student government; Student newspaper; Student-run film society; Television station; Yearbook 78 registered organizations, 8 honor societies, 3 religious organizations. 2 fraternities, 3 sororities. **Athletics (Intercollegiate):** *Men:* baseball, basketball, cross-country, ice hockey, lacrosse, soccer, tennis. *Women:* basketball, cheerleading, cross-country, field hockey, ice hockey, lacrosse, soccer, softball, tennis, track/field (outdoor), track/field (indoor), volleyball. **On-Campus Highlights:** Arnold Bernhard Library, Carl Hansen Student Center & Starbucks, Rocky Top student center with fitness facility, Mountainview Residence Hall, TD Bank Sport Center **Environmental Initiatives:** 100 percent of Quinnipiac electricity requirements on all three of its campuses have been purchased from renewable energy credits.

ADMISSIONS

Freshman Academic Profile: Average high school GPA 3.5. 22% in top 10% of high school class, 51% in top 25% of high school class, 91% in top 50% of high school class. 70% from public high schools. **Test Scores:** SAT Math middle 50% range 530-630. SAT EBRW middle 50% range 550-630. ACT middle 50% range 23-27. Minimum internet-based TOEFL 80. Minimum paper TOEFL 550. **Basis for Candidate Selection:** *Very important factors considered include:* rigor of secondary school record, academic GPA, level of applicant's interest. *Important factors considered include:* class rank, application essay, standardized test scores, recommendation(s), volunteer work. *Other factors considered include:* interview, extracurricular activities, talent/ability, character/personal qualities, first generation, alumni/ae relation, state residency, racial/ethnic status, work experience. **Freshman Admission Requirements:** High school diploma is required and GED is accepted *Academic units required:* 4 English, 3 math, 3 science, 2 science labs, 2 foreign language, 2 social studies, and 4 units from above areas or other academic areas. *Academic units recommended:* 4 English, 4 math, 4 science, 3 science labs, 2 foreign language, 3 social studies. **Freshman Admission Statistics:** 22,071 applied, 73.9% admitted, 12% enrolled. **Transfer Admission Requirements:** college transcript(s), essay or personal statement, Minimum college GPA of 2.5 required. Lowest grade transferable C. **General Admission Information:** Application fee $65. Priority deadline 2/1. Nonfall registration accepted. Admission may be deferred for a maximum of 1 year.

COSTS AND FINANCIAL AID

Annual tuition $45,540. Room and board $14,990. Required fees $2,440. Average book expense $800. **Required Forms and Deadlines:** FAFSA. **Notification of Awards:** Applicants will be notified of awards on a rolling basis beginning 1/20. **Types of Aid:** *Need-based scholarships/grants:* College/ university scholarship or grant aid from institutional funds; Federal Pell; Private scholarships; SEOG; State scholarships/grants. *Loans:* Direct PLUS loans; Direct Subsidized Stafford Loans; Direct Unsubsidized Stafford Loans. *Student Employment:* Federal Work-Study Program available. Institutional employment available. **Financial Aid Statistics:** 98% needy freshmen, 97% needy undergrads receive need-based scholarship or grant aid. 77% freshmen, 67% undergrads receive non-need-based scholarship or grant aid. 76% freshmen, 79% undergrads receive need-based self-help aid. 5% freshmen, 5% undergrads receive athletic scholarships. 88% freshmen, 83% undergrads receive any aid. 71% undergrads borrow to pay for school. Average cumulative indebtedness $47,217. **Criteria for awarding aid:** *Non-need-based:* Academics, Athletics.

See page 1002.

RADFORD UNIVERSITY

801 East Main Street, Radford, VA 24142
Phone: 540-831-5371 • **Financial Aid Phone:** 540-831-5408
E-mail: admissions@radford.edu • **CEEB Code:** 5565
Fax: 540-831-5038 • **Website:** www.radford.edu • **ACT Code:** 4422

This public school was founded in 1910. It has a 204 acre campus.

RATINGS

Admissions Selectivity Rating: 75   **Fire Safety Rating:** 98   **Green Rating:** 92

STUDENTS AND FACULTY

Enrollment: 8,376. **Student Body:** 57% female, 43% male, 6% out-of-state, 1% international (60 countries represented). Asian 1%, African American 17%, Caucasian 67%, Hispanic 7%, Native American <1%, Pacific Islander <1%, Two or more races 5%, Race unknown 2%.
Retention and Graduation: 76% freshmen return for sophomore year. 38% freshmen graduate within 4 years. 55% freshmen graduate within 6 years. 18% grads go on to further study within 1 year. **Faculty:** Student/faculty ratio 16:1. 460 full-time faculty, 83% hold PhDs, 12% are members of minority groups, 53% are women. 2% of classes are taught by teaching assistants.

ACADEMICS

Degrees: Bachelor's; Certificate; Doctoral Other; Master's; Post-Bachelor's certificate; Post-Master's certificate **Classes:** Most classes have 10-19 students. Most lab/discussion sessions have 10-19 students. **Most popular majors:** Physical Education Teaching And Coaching; Multi-/Interdisciplinary Studies, Other; Business Administration And Management, General. **Special Study Options:** Accelerated program; Cross-registration; Distance learning; Double major; Dual enrollment; English as a Second Language (ESL); Honors program; Independent study; Internships; Student-designed major; Study abroad; Teacher certification program. Honors programs: A hallmark of a Radford education is faculty-student collaboration and no where is that more evident than in the university's Honors Academy. Honors courses fulfill requirements in the Core Curriculum and are taught by faculty in a highly interactive and engaging environment. In addition, Honors Academy students enjoy early registration, may elect to live in a designated residence hall, are supported financially to present results of their work at professional and undergraduate conferences, and receive an honors scholarship. The honors curriculum leads students to achieve the status of "Highlander Scholar" during their careers at RU. To graduate with this distinction, a student must complete 27 credit hours of honors coursework, present an honors capstone project in a public forum, and have a cumulative GPA of 3.5 at the time of graduation. Status as a Highlander Scholar is noted on the student's diploma and transcript. **Disability Services offered to physically disabled students:** Note-taking services; Reader services; Tape recorders; Tutors. **Career services:** Alumni network; Alumni services; Career assessment; Career/job search classes; Internships; Regional alumni

FACILITIES

Housing: Apartments for single students; Coed dorms; Special housing for disabled student; Special housing for international students; Theme housing; Wellness housing 98% of campus accessible to physically diasbled. **Special Academic Facilities/Equipment:** College of Business and Economics; Covington Center for Visual and Performing Arts featuring international and national art exhibits; Museum of the Earth Sciences; 1,200-seat performance/lecture hall; also an observatory, planetarium, nature center, state-of-the-art motion analysis lab, clinical simulation center, cadaver lab, speech-language-hearing center and greenhouse **Computers:** 100% of classrooms, 100% of dorms, 100% of libraries, 100% of dining areas, 100% of student union, 100% of common outdoor areas have wireless network access. Students can register for classes online. Administrative functions (other than registration) can be performed online.

CAMPUS LIFE

Environment: Village **Activities:** Campus Ministries; Choral groups; Concert band; Dance; Drama/theater; International Student Organization; Jazz band; Literary magazine; Model UN; Music ensembles; Musical theater; Opera; Pep band; Radio station; Student government; Student newspaper; Student-run film society; Yearbook 237 registered organizations, 14 honor societies, 10 religious organizations. 15 fraternities, 10 sororities. **Athletics (Intercollegiate):** *Men:* baseball, basketball, cheerleading, cross-country, golf, soccer, tennis, track/field (outdoor), track/field (indoor). *Women:* basketball, cheerleading, cross-country, diving, field hockey, golf, soccer, softball, swimming, tennis, track/field (outdoor), track/field (indoor), volleyball. **On-Campus Highlights:** new Student Recreation & Wellness Center (opened fall 2014), College of Business & Economics building (Kyle Hall) (opened fall 2012), College of Humanities & Behaivoral Science building and Starbucks (2016), Hurlburt Student Center, including food court, game room and auditorium, Dedmon Center Complex, for cheering on Highlander Div 1 athletic events **Environmental Initiatives:** Buildings: Per University Policy, RU constructs and completes major renovations to LEED Silver or Gold standards. This year, Radford University earned its sixth LEED Gold designation on the College of Humanities and Behavioral Sciences (https://www.radford.edu/content/radfordcore/home/news/releases/2017/october/chbs-leed-gold.html). In addition, every building on campus is sub-metered, giving the university a clear and accurate way to monitor energy, water, and steam use, identify problem areas, and plan repairs or renovations.

ADMISSIONS

Freshman Academic Profile: Average high school GPA 3.2. 6% in top 10% of high school class, 21% in top 25% of high school class, 58% in top 50% of high school class. 93% from public high schools. **Test Scores:** SAT Math middle 50% range 460-540. SAT EBRW middle 50% range 480-580. ACT middle 50% range 17-23. Minimum internet-based TOEFL 68. Minimum paper TOEFL 520. **Basis for Candidate Selection:** *Very important factors considered include:* rigor of secondary school record. *Important factors considered include:* academic GPA. *Other factors considered include:* class rank, application essay, standardized test scores, recommendation(s), interview, extracurricular activities, talent/ability, character/personal qualities, first generation, alumni/ae relation, volunteer work, work experience, level of applicant's interest. **Freshman Admission Requirements:** High school diploma is required and GED is accepted *Academic units recommended:* 4 English, 4 math, 4 science, 4 science labs, 4 foreign language, 2 social studies, 2 history. **Freshman Admission Statistics:** 14,620 applied, 74.3% admitted, 17% enrolled. **Transfer Admission Requirements:** college transcript(s), Minimum college GPA of 2.0 required. Lowest grade transferable C. **General Admission Information:** Priority deadline 2/1. Nonfall registration accepted. Admission may be deferred for a maximum of 1 year.

COSTS AND FINANCIAL AID

Annual in-state tuition $9,131. Annual out-of-state tuition $19,042. Room and board $9,131. Required fees $3,220. Average book expense $1,200. **Required Forms and Deadlines:** FAFSA. **Notification of Awards:** Applicants will be notified of awards on a rolling basis beginning 4/15. **Types of Aid:** *Need-based scholarships/grants:* College/university scholarship or grant aid from institutional funds; Federal Pell; Private scholarships; SEOG; State scholarships/grants. *Loans:* Direct PLUS loans; Direct Subsidized Stafford Loans; Direct Unsubsidized Stafford Loans. *Student Employment:* Federal Work-Study Program available. Institutional employment available. **Financial Aid**

Statistics: 56% needy freshmen, 60% needy undergrads receive need-based scholarship or grant aid. 27% freshmen, 21% undergrads receive non-need-based scholarship or grant aid. 84% freshmen, 86% undergrads receive need-based self-help aid. 1% freshmen, 1% undergrads receive athletic scholarships. 79% freshmen, 77% undergrads receive any aid. 69% undergrads borrow to pay for school. Average cumulative indebtedness $29,103. **Criteria for awarding aid:** *Need-based:* Academics *Non-need-based:* Academics, Alumni affiliation, Art, Athletics, Leadership, Music/drama, State/district residency.

RAMAPO COLLEGE OF NEW JERSEY

505 Ramapo Valley Road, Mahwah, NJ 07430-1680
Phone: 201-684-7300 • **Financial Aid Phone:** 201-684-7550
E-mail: admissions@ramapo.edu • **CEEB Code:** 2884
Fax: 201-684-7964 • **Website:** www.ramapo.edu • **ACT Code:** 2591

This public school was founded in 1971. It has a 300 acre campus.

RATINGS

Admissions Selectivity Rating: 85   **Fire Safety Rating:** 97   **Green Rating:** 60*

STUDENTS AND FACULTY

Enrollment: 5,314. **Student Body:** 55% female, 45% male, 6% out-of-state, 2% international (27 countries represented). Asian 8%, African American 5%, Caucasian 64%, Hispanic 16%, Native American 1%, Pacific Islander <1%, Two or more races 1%, Race unknown 5%.
Retention and Graduation: 86% freshmen return for sophomore year. 60% freshmen graduate within 4 years. 74% freshmen graduate within 6 years. **Faculty:** Student/faculty ratio 18:1. 216 full-time faculty, 93% hold PhDs, 28% are members of minority groups, 51% are women. 0% of classes are taught by teaching assistants.

ACADEMICS

Degrees: Bachelor's; Certificate; Master's; Post-Master's certificate **Classes:** Most classes have 20-29 students. Most lab/discussion sessions have 20-29 students. **Most popular majors:** Speech Communication And Rhetoric; Psychology, General; Business Administration And Management, General. **Special Study Options:** Accelerated program; Cooperative education program; Cross-registration; Distance learning; Double major; Dual enrollment; Exchange student program (domestic); External degree program; Honors program; Independent study; Internships; Liberal arts/career combination; Student-designed major; Study abroad; Teacher certification program; Weekend college. Combined degree programs: BA/DDS; BA/MA; BA/MD. **Disability Services offered to physically disabled students:** Note-taking services; Reader services; Tape recorders; Tutors. **Career services:** Alumni network; Alumni services; Career assessment; Career/job search classes; Internships

FACILITIES

Housing: Coed dorms 100% of campus accessible to physically diasbled. **Special Academic Facilities/Equipment:** Art museum, media center, international telecommunications center, electron microscope, astronomical observatory, Holocaust Studies Center, new sports/fitness complex. A new Center for Science, Education and Technology was implemented, as well as a Sustainability Education Center, and a Spiritual Center. A new building for the Adler Center for Nursing Excellence will be started in 2012. **Computers:** 100% of classrooms, 100% of dorms, 100% of libraries, 100% of dining areas, 100% of student union, 60% of common outdoor areas have wireless network access. Students can register for classes online. Administrative functions (other than registration) can be performed online.

CAMPUS LIFE

Environment: Town **Activities:** Campus Ministries; Choral groups; Concert band; Dance; Drama/theater; International Student Organization; Jazz band; Literary magazine; Model UN; Music ensembles; Musical theater; Pep band; Radio station; Student government; Student newspaper; Television station; Yearbook 80 registered organizations, 19 honor societies, 7 religious organizations. 10 fraternities, 11 sororities. **Athletics (Intercollegiate):** *Men:* baseball, basketball, cross-country, soccer, swimming, tennis, track/field (outdoor), track/field (indoor), volleyball. *Women:* basketball, cross-country, field hockey, lacrosse, soccer, softball, swimming, tennis, track/field (outdoor), track/field (indoor), volleyball. **On-Campus Highlights:** Berrie Center for Performing and Visual Arts, The Pavilion, The Market Place at the Birch Tree Inn, J Lee's in the Student Center, The Bill Bradley Sports and Fitness center **Environmental Initiatives:**—Curriculum (and a new building for the Sustainability Education Center).

ADMISSIONS

Freshman Academic Profile: Average high school GPA 3.4. 16% in top

10% of high school class, 41% in top 25% of high school class, 79% in top 50% of high school class. **Test Scores:** SAT Math middle 50% range 520-610. SAT EBRW middle 50% range 530-620. ACT middle 50% range 21-26. Minimum internet-based TOEFL 90. Minimum paper TOEFL 550. **Basis for Candidate Selection:** *Very important factors considered include:* rigor of secondary school record, academic GPA. *Important factors considered include:* application essay, standardized test scores, recommendation(s), extracurricular activities, talent/ability. *Other factors considered include:* class rank, character/personal qualities, first generation, alumni/ae relation, geographical residence, state residency, racial/ethnic status, volunteer work, work experience, level of applicant's interest. **Freshman Admission Requirements:** High school diploma is required and GED is accepted *Academic units required:* 4 English, 3 math, 3 science, 2 science labs, 2 foreign language, 3 social studies, 3 academic electives. **Freshman Admission Statistics:** 6,695 applied, 57.4% admitted, 24% enrolled. **Transfer Admission Requirements:** college transcript(s), essay or personal statement, Minimum college GPA of 2.5 required. Lowest grade transferable C. **General Admission Information:** Application fee $65. Regular application deadline 3/1. Nonfall registration accepted. Admission may be deferred for a maximum of 1 year.

COSTS AND FINANCIAL AID

Annual in-state tuition $12,180. Annual out-of-state tuition $20,774. Room and board $12,180. Required fees $2,440. Average book expense $1,569. **Required Forms and Deadlines:** FAFSA; State aid form. **Notification of Awards:** Applicants will be notified of awards on a rolling basis beginning 4/1. **Types of Aid:** *Need-based scholarships/grants:* College/university scholarship or grant aid from institutional funds; Federal Nursing Scholarships; Federal Pell; Private scholarships; SEOG; State scholarships/grants. *Loans:* Direct PLUS loans; Direct Subsidized Stafford Loans; Direct Unsubsidized Stafford Loans. *Student Employment:* Federal Work-Study Program available. Institutional employment available. **Financial Aid Statistics:** 43% needy freshmen, 50% needy undergrads receive need-based scholarship or grant aid. 30% freshmen, 10% undergrads receive non-need-based scholarship or grant aid. 82% freshmen, 45% undergrads receive need-based self-help aid. 0% freshmen, 0% undergrads receive athletic scholarships. 80% freshmen, 74% undergrads receive any aid. 51% undergrads borrow to pay for school. Average cumulative indebtedness $10,715. **Criteria for awarding aid:** *Non-need-based:* Academics, Leadership, State/district residency.

See page 1004.

RANDOLPH COLLEGE

2500 Rivermont Avenue, Lynchburg, VA 24503-1555
Phone: 434-947-8100 • **Financial Aid Phone:** 434-947-8128
E-mail: admissions@randolphcollege.edu • **CEEB Code:** 5567
Fax: 434-947-8996 • **Website:** www.randolphcollege.com • **ACT Code:** 4388

This private school, affiliated with the Methodist Church, was founded in 1891. It has a 100 acre campus.

RATINGS

Admissions Selectivity Rating: 74   **Fire Safety Rating:** 95   **Green Rating:** 98

STUDENTS AND FACULTY

Enrollment: 651. **Student Body:** 63% female, 37% male, 29% out-of-state, 4% international (12 countries represented). Asian 3%, African American 15%, Caucasian 65%, Hispanic 6%, Pacific Islander <1%, Two or more races 6%, Race unknown <1%.
Retention and Graduation: 67% freshmen return for sophomore year. 54% freshmen graduate within 4 years. 59% freshmen graduate within 6 years.
Faculty: Student/faculty ratio 9:1. 71 full-time faculty, 94% hold PhDs, 15% are members of minority groups, 56% are women. 0% of classes are taught by teaching assistants.

ACADEMICS

Degrees: Bachelor's; **Master's Classes:** Most classes have 10-19 students.
Most popular majors: English Language And Literature, General; Biology/Biological Sciences, General; Psychology, General. **Special Study Options:** Accelerated program; Cross-registration; Double major; Dual enrollment; Exchange student program (domestic); Honors program; Independent study; Internships; Liberal arts/career combination; Student-designed major; Study abroad; Teacher certification program. Honors programs: Juniors and seniors

who have a cumulative 3.45 in all academic work and a 3.7 in the major are eligible to read for Honors in the Major. The Honors Program encourages students of exceptional ability to engage in independent and intensive study in their fields of interest. Combined degree programs: BA/MA; BA/MEng. **Disability Services offered to physically disabled students:** Note-taking services; Reader services; Tape recorders; Tutors. **Career services:** Alumni network; Alumni services; Career assessment; Internships; Regional alumni

FACILITIES

Housing: Apartments for single students; Coed dorms; Theme housing; Wellness housing 65% of campus accessible to physically diasbled. **Special Academic Facilities/Equipment:** The Rancolph College Art Collection (recognized as one of the most outstanding college collections in the nation), 100-acre equestrian center, language lab, science and math resource center, learning resources center, writing lab, nursery school, nature preserves, organic garden, observatory, electron microscope. **Computers:** 100% of classrooms, 100% of dorms, 100% of libraries, 100% of dining areas, 100% of student union, 100% of common outdoor areas have wireless network access. Students can register for classes online. Administrative functions (other than registration) can be performed online.

CAMPUS LIFE

Environment: City **Activities:** Campus Ministries; Choral groups; Dance; Drama/theater; International Student Organization; Literary magazine; Model UN; Music ensembles; Musical theater; Radio station; Student government; Student newspaper 40 registered organizations, 7 honor societies, 6 religious organizations. **Athletics (Intercollegiate):** *Men:* basketball, cross-country, equestrian sports, horseback riding, lacrosse, soccer, tennis. *Women:* basketball, cross-country, equestrian sports, horseback riding, lacrosse, soccer, softball, swimming, tennis, volleyball. **On-Campus Highlights:** The Maier Museum of Art, Randolph College Riding Center, The Greek Amphitheater, Organic Garden, New Student Center

ADMISSIONS

Freshman Academic Profile: Average high school GPA 3.4. 13% in top 10% of high school class, 35% in top 25% of high school class, 75% in top 50% of high school class. 80% from public high schools. **Test Scores:** SAT Math middle 50% range 460-580. SAT EBRW middle 50% range 492-610. ACT middle 50% range 19-25. **Basis for Candidate Selection:** *Very important factors considered include:* academic GPA. *Important factors considered include:* rigor of secondary school record, standardized test scores, extracurricular activities, alumni/ae relation, level of applicant's interest. *Other factors considered include:* class rank, application essay, recommendation(s), interview, talent/ability, character/personal qualities, first generation, volunteer work, work experience. **Freshman Admission Requirements:** High school diploma is required and GED is accepted *Academic units required:* 4 English, 3 math, 3 science, 2 science labs, 2 history, 1 academic elective, *Academic units recommended:* 4 math, 3 foreign language, 3 academic electives. **Freshman Admission Statistics:** 1,696 applied, 86.4% admitted, 14% enrolled. **Transfer Admission Requirements:** High school transcript, college transcript(s), essay or personal statement, Lowest grade transferable C-. **General Admission Information:** Priority deadline 11/15. Nonfall registration accepted. Admission may be deferred for a maximum of 2 years.

COSTS AND FINANCIAL AID

Annual tuition $39,000. Room and board $13,580. Required fees $695. Average book expense $1,230. **Notification of Awards:** Applicants will be notified of awards on a rolling basis beginning 10/1. **Types of Aid:** *Need-based scholarships/grants:* College/university scholarship or grant aid from institutional funds; Federal Pell; Private scholarships; SEOG; State scholarships/grants; United Negro College Fund. *Loans:* Direct PLUS loans; Direct Subsidized Stafford Loans; Direct Unsubsidized Stafford Loans. *Student Employment:* Federal Work-Study Program available. Institutional employment available. **Financial Aid Statistics:** 100% needy freshmen, 100% needy undergrads receive need-based scholarship or grant aid. 17% freshmen, 17% undergrads receive non-need-based scholarship or grant aid. 82% freshmen, 82% undergrads receive need-based self-help aid. 0% freshmen, 0% undergrads receive athletic scholarships. 99% freshmen, 99% undergrads receive any aid. 65% undergrads borrow to pay for school. Average cumulative indebtedness $35,199. **Criteria for awarding aid:** *Non-need-based:* Academics, Alumni affiliation, Art, Music/drama, Religious affiliation, State/district residency.

RANDOLPH-MACON COLLEGE

P. O. Box 5005, Ashland, VA 23005
Phone: 804-752-7305 • **Financial Aid Phone:** (804) 752-7259
E-mail: admissions@rmc.edu • **CEEB Code:** 5566
Fax: 804-752-4707 • **Website:** www.rmc.edu • **ACT Code:** 4386

This private school, affiliated with the Methodist Church, was founded in 1830. It has a 116 acre campus.

RATINGS
Admissions Selectivity Rating: 85   **Fire Safety Rating:** 93   **Green Rating:** 60*

STUDENTS AND FACULTY
Enrollment: 1,438. **Student Body:** 54% female, 46% male, 25% out-of-state, 1% international (20 countries represented). Asian 2%, African American 9%, Caucasian 77%, Hispanic 4%, Native American 1%, Pacific Islander <1%, Two or more races 4%, Race unknown 1%.
Retention and Graduation: 84% freshmen return for sophomore year. 60% freshmen graduate within 4 years. 66% freshmen graduate within 6 years. 20% grads go on to further study within 1 year. **Faculty:** Student/faculty ratio 11:1. 109 full-time faculty, 94% hold PhDs, 10% are members of minority groups, 50% are women. 0% of classes are taught by teaching assistants.

ACADEMICS
Degrees: Bachelor's **Classes:** Most classes have 20-29 students. Most lab/discussion sessions have 10-19 students. **Most popular majors:** Communication, General; Biology/Biological Sciences, General; Business/Commerce, General. **Special Study Options:** Accelerated program; Cross-registration; Double major; Dual enrollment; Exchange student program (domestic); Honors program; Independent study; Internships; Liberal arts/career combination; Study abroad; Teacher certification program. Honors programs: The Honors Program offers qualified students the opportunity to take special honors classes, participate in unique programs and events for honors students, and an Honors House for recreation and socializing. Combined degree programs: BA/MA; BA/MD; BA/MEng. **Disability Services offered to physically disabled students:** Note-taking services; Reader services; Tape recorders; Tutors. **Career services:** Alumni network; Alumni services; Career assessment; Career/job search classes; Internships; Regional alumni

FACILITIES
Housing: Apartments for single students; Coed dorms; Fraternity/sorority housing; Men's dorms; Special housing for disabled student; Special housing for international students; Theme housing; Wellness housing; Women's dorms 85% of campus accessible to physically diasbled. **Special Academic Facilities/Equipment:** Language lab, learning center, media center, greenhouse, observatory with telescope, electron microscopes, nuclear magnetic resonator, art gallery, fine arts center **Computers:** 20% of classrooms, 100% of dorms, 100% of libraries, 100% of dining areas, 100% of student union, 25% of common outdoor areas have wireless network access. Students can register for classes online. Administrative functions (other than registration) can be performed online.

CAMPUS LIFE
Environment: Village **Activities:** Campus Ministries; Choral groups; Concert band; Dance; Drama/theater; International Student Organization; Jazz band; Literary magazine; Music ensembles; Musical theater; Opera; Pep band; Radio station; Student government; Student newspaper; Student-run film society; Television station; Yearbook 102 registered organizations, 18 honor societies, 4 religious organizations. 6 fraternities, 4 sororities. **Athletics (Intercollegiate):** *Men:* baseball, basketball, football, golf, lacrosse, soccer, tennis. *Women:* basketball, field hockey, lacrosse, soccer, softball, swimming, tennis, volleyball.
On-Campus Highlights: Student Center at Brock Commons, Birdsong Residence Hall, Andrews Residence Hall, The Brock Sports and Recreation Center, Randolph-Macon Performing Arts Center **Environmental Initiatives:** Designing, Planning, Building and Operating a LEED-certified residence hall incorporating solar power, geothermal heat exchange, rainwater reclamation and other sustainable aspects

ADMISSIONS
Freshman Academic Profile: Average high school GPA 3.7. 19% in top 10% of high school class, 56% in top 25% of high school class, 84% in top 50% of high school class. 77% from public high schools. **Test Scores:** SAT Math middle 50% range 510-603. SAT EBRW middle 50% range 540-630. ACT middle 50% range 21-27. Minimum internet-based TOEFL 80. Minimum paper TOEFL 550. **Basis for Candidate Selection:** *Very important factors considered include:* rigor of secondary school record, academic GPA. *Important factors considered include:* class rank, application essay, standardized test scores,

recommendation(s). *Other factors considered include:* interview, extracurricular activities, talent/ability, character/personal qualities, first generation, alumni/ae relation, racial/ethnic status, volunteer work, work experience, level of applicant's interest. **Freshman Admission Requirements:** High school diploma is required and GED is accepted *Academic units required:* 4 English, 3 math, 2 science, 2 science labs, 2 foreign language, 2 social studies, 3 academic electives, *Academic units recommended:* 4 English, 4 math, 4 science, 4 science labs, 3 foreign language, 3 social studies, 4 academic electives. **Freshman Admission Statistics:** 2,820 applied, 62.2% admitted, 21% enrolled. **Transfer Admission Requirements:** High school transcript, college transcript(s), essay or personal statement, statement of good standing from prior institution(s). Minimum college GPA of 2.0 required. Lowest grade transferable C-. **General Admission Information:** Application fee $30. Priority deadline 2/1. Regular application deadline 3/1. Nonfall registration accepted. Admission may be deferred for a maximum of 1 year.

COSTS AND FINANCIAL AID
Annual tuition $40,000. Room and board $11,480. Required fees $1,300. Average book expense $1,200. **Required Forms and Deadlines:** FAFSA; State aid form. **Notification of Awards:** Applicants will be notified of awards on or about 3/1. **Types of Aid:** *Need-based scholarships/grants:* College/university scholarship or grant aid from institutional funds; Federal Pell; Private scholarships; SEOG; State scholarships/grants. *Loans:* Direct PLUS loans; Direct Subsidized Stafford Loans; Direct Unsubsidized Stafford Loans. *Student Employment:* Federal Work-Study Program available. Institutional employment available. **Financial Aid Statistics:** 100% needy freshmen, 100% needy undergrads receive need-based scholarship or grant aid. 30% freshmen, 27% undergrads receive non-need-based scholarship or grant aid. 69% freshmen, 72% undergrads receive need-based self-help aid. 0% freshmen, 0% undergrads receive athletic scholarships. 99% freshmen, 99% undergrads receive any aid. 70% undergrads borrow to pay for school. Average cumulative indebtedness $33,015. **Criteria for awarding aid:** *Need-based:* Academics, Religious affiliation *Non-need-based:* Academics, Alumni affiliation, Minority status, Religious affiliation, State/district residency.

REED COLLEGE

3203 SE Woodstock Boulevard, Portland, OR 97202-8199
Phone: 503-777-7511 • **Financial Aid Phone:** 503-777-7223
E-mail: admission@reed.edu • **CEEB Code:** 4654
Fax: 503-777-7553 • **Website:** www.reed.edu • **ACT Code:** 3494

This private school was founded in 1908. It has a 116 acre campus.

RATINGS
Admissions Selectivity Rating: 95   **Fire Safety Rating:** 96   **Green Rating:** 60*

STUDENTS AND FACULTY
Enrollment: 1,415. **Student Body:** 54% female, 46% male, 93% out-of-state, 10% international (46 countries represented). Asian 6%, African American 2%, Caucasian 60%, Hispanic 10%, Native American <1%, Pacific Islander <1%, Two or more races 8%, Race unknown 3%.
Retention and Graduation: 88% freshmen return for sophomore year. 65% freshmen graduate within 4 years. 80% freshmen graduate within 6 years. 65% grads go on to further study within 1 year. 48% grads pursue arts and sciences degrees. 5% grads pursue law degrees. 3% grads pursue business degrees. 4% grads pursue medical degrees. **Faculty:** Student/faculty ratio 10:1. 145 full-time faculty, 96% hold PhDs, 14% are members of minority groups, 42% are women. 0% of classes are taught by teaching assistants.

ACADEMICS
Degrees: Bachelor's; **Master's Classes:** Most classes have 20-29 students. **Most popular majors:** English Language And Literature, General; Psychology, General; Anthropology. **Special Study Options:** Cross-registration; Double major; Dual enrollment; Exchange student program (domestic); Independent study; Internships; Liberal arts/career combination; Student-designed major; Study abroad. **Disability Services offered to physically disabled students:** Note-taking services; Reader services; Tape recorders; Tutors. **Career services:** Alumni network; Alumni services; Career assessment; Career/job search classes; Internships; Regional alumni

FACILITIES

Housing: Apartments for single students; Coed dorms; Cooperative housing; Special housing for disabled student; Theme housing; Wellness housing; Women's dorms 85% of campus accessible to physically diasbled. **Special Academic Facilities/Equipment:** Art gallery, studio art building, language labs, computerized music listening lab, nuclear research reactor, 20 music practice rooms and midi lab, 760 seat auditorium, academic support center (quantitative skills, writing, math support), educational technology center **Computers:** 100% of classrooms, 100% of dorms, 100% of libraries, 100% of dining areas, 100% of student union, 50% of common outdoor areas have wireless network access. Students can register for classes online. Administrative functions (other than registration) can be performed online.

CAMPUS LIFE

Environment: Metropolis **Activities:** Campus Ministries; Choral groups; Dance; Drama/theater; International Student Organization; Jazz band; Literary magazine; Model UN; Music ensembles; Musical theater; Radio station; Student government; Student newspaper; Student-run film society; Symphony orchestra; Yearbook 130 registered organizations, 1 honor society, 5 religious organizations. **On-Campus Highlights:** Thesis Tower, Reed Research Reactor, Reed Canyon/watershed, Douglas F. Cooley Memorial Art Gallery **Environmental Initiatives:** LEED construction

ADMISSIONS

Freshman Academic Profile: Average high school GPA 3.9. 59% in top 10% of high school class, 85% in top 25% of high school class, 98% in top 50% of high school class. 59% from public high schools. **Test Scores:** SAT Math middle 50% range 640-760. SAT EBRW middle 50% range 670-740. ACT middle 50% range 30-33. Minimum internet-based TOEFL 100. Minimum paper TOEFL 600. **Basis for Candidate Selection:** *Very important factors considered include:* rigor of secondary school record, academic GPA, application essay. *Important factors considered include:* class rank, standardized test scores, recommendation(s), interview, level of applicant's interest. *Other factors considered include:* extracurricular activities, talent/ability, character/ personal qualities, first generation, alumni/ae relation, geographical residence, racial/ethnic status, volunteer work, work experience. **Freshman Admission Requirements:** High school diploma is required and GED is accepted *Academic units recommended:* 4 English, 3 math, 3 science, 3 foreign language, 3 social studies. **Freshman Admission Statistics:** 5,652 applied, 35.6% admitted, 21% enrolled. **Transfer Admission Requirements:** High school transcript, college transcript(s), essay or personal statement, standardized test scores, statement of good standing from prior institution(s). Lowest grade transferable C-. **General Admission Information:** Regular application deadline 1/15. Nonfall registration accepted. Admission may be deferred.

COSTS AND FINANCIAL AID

Annual tuition $51,850. Room and board $13,150. Required fees $300. Average book expense $1,050. **Required Forms and Deadlines:** Business/Farm Supplement; CSS/Financial Aid PROFILE; FAFSA; Noncustodial PROFILE. **Notification of Awards:** Applicants will be notified of awards on or about 4/1. **Types of Aid:** *Need-based scholarships/grants:* College/university scholarship or grant aid from institutional funds; Federal Pell; Private scholarships; SEOG; State scholarships/grants. *Loans:* Direct PLUS loans; Direct Subsidized Stafford Loans; Direct Unsubsidized Stafford Loans. *Student Employment:* Federal Work-Study Program available. Institutional employment available. **Financial Aid Statistics:** 98% needy freshmen, 98% needy undergrads receive need-based scholarship or grant aid. 0% undergrads receive non-need-based scholarship or grant aid. 100% freshmen, 100% undergrads receive need-based self-help aid. 0% freshmen, 0% undergrads receive athletic scholarships. 53% freshmen, 54% undergrads receive any aid. 44% undergrads borrow to pay for school. Average cumulative indebtedness $19,627.

See page 1006.

REGENT UNIVERSITY

1000 Regent University Drive, Virginia Beach, VA 23464
Phone: 800-373-5504 • **Financial Aid Phone:** 757-352-4125
E-mail: admissions@regent.edu • **CEEB Code:** 30913
Fax: 757-352-4381 • **Website:** www.regent.edu • **ACT Code:** 6738

This private school, affiliated with the Christian (Nondenominational) Church, was founded in 1978. It has a 70 acre campus.

RATINGS

Admissions Selectivity Rating: 76   **Fire Safety Rating:** 87   **Green Rating:** 61

STUDENTS AND FACULTY

Enrollment: 4,414. **Student Body:** 62% female, 38% male, 57% out-of-state, 1% international (19 countries represented). Asian 1%, African American 29%, Caucasian 52%, Hispanic 9%, Native American 1%, Pacific Islander <1%, Two or more races 5%, Race unknown 1%.
Retention and Graduation: 78% freshmen return for sophomore year. 24% freshmen graduate within 4 years. 46% freshmen graduate within 6 years. **Faculty:** Student/faculty ratio 21:1. 149 full-time faculty, 90% hold PhDs, 17% are members of minority groups, 32% are women. 0% of classes are taught by teaching assistants.

ACADEMICS

Degrees: Associate; Bachelor's; Certificate; Doctoral; Doctoral/Professional; Doctoral/Research; Master's; Post-Bachelor's certificate; Post-Master's certificate **Most popular majors:** Religion/Religious Studies; Psychology, General; Business/Commerce, General. **Special Study Options:** Distance learning; Double major; Dual enrollment; Honors program; Independent study; Internships; Liberal arts/career combination; Study abroad; Teacher certification program. Honors programs: The Honors Program serves as a foundation for a student's major courses over the span of four years. By offering a true core, all Honors students have a common educational experience that fosters the development of community and friendships. Combined degree programs: BA/MA. **Disability Services offered to physically disabled students:** Note-taking services; Reader services; Tape recorders; Tutors. **Career services:** Alumni network; Alumni services; Career assessment; Career/job search classes; Internships; Regional alumni

FACILITIES

Housing: Apartments for married students; Apartments for single students 100% of campus accessible to physically diasbled. **Special Academic Facilities/Equipment:** The 31,000-square-foot Student Center on Regent's Virginia Beach Campus, opened in 2003, offers a central location for campus and student services. The building houses the university gift shop, student organizations and meeting rooms, a cafe/coffee shop, computer lab, student lounge and offices for the Registrar, Admissions and Financial Aid. The 135,000-square-foot Communication & Performing Arts Center, opened in 2002, includes film and animation studios, a state-of-the-art main theatre, screening rooms and editing suites in one of the most technologically advanced communication buildings on the east coast. **Computers:** 80% of classrooms, 100% of dorms, 100% of libraries, 100% of student union, 50% of common outdoor areas have wireless network access. Students can register for classes online. Administrative functions (other than registration) can be performed online.

CAMPUS LIFE

Environment: City **Activities:** Campus Ministries; Choral groups; Concert band; Dance; Drama/theater; International Student Organization; Music ensembles; Musical theater; Student government; Student-run film society 47 registered organizations, 4 honor societies. **On-Campus Highlights:** The Student Center, Communication & Performing Arts, The Ordinary Cafe and Coffee Shop, Robertson Hall, University Library **Environmental Initiatives:** Our investments in "cool storage" systems since our beginning in 1978 allows us to shave peak demand when the power company desires. This helps reduce the size of the power plant needed to support this area. This results in a major decrease in greenhouse emissions for this area. This fact is recognized by VA Dominion Power —our supplier of electricity.

ADMISSIONS

Freshman Academic Profile: Average high school GPA 3.3. 13% in top 10% of high school class, 32% in top 25% of high school class, 58% in top 50% of high school class. **Test Scores:** SAT Math middle 50% range 460-580. SAT EBRW middle 50% range 500-600. ACT middle 50% range 19-26. Minimum internet-based TOEFL 90. Minimum paper TOEFL 577. **Basis for Candidate Selection:** *Very important factors considered include:* academic GPA, standardized test scores. *Important factors considered include:* application essay. *Other factors considered include:* rigor of secondary school record, recommendation(s), character/personal qualities. **Freshman Admission Requirements:** High school diploma is required and GED is accepted *Academic units recommended:* 4 English, 3 math, 3 science, 3 foreign language, 3 social studies. **Freshman Admission Statistics:** 1,887 applied, 81.1% admitted, 32% enrolled. **Transfer Admission Requirements:** college transcript(s), Lowest grade transferable c. **General Admission Information:** Application fee $50. Priority deadline 8/1. Regular application deadline 8/1. Nonfall registration accepted. Admission may be deferred for a maximum of One year.

COSTS AND FINANCIAL AID

Average book expense $1,000. **Required Forms and Deadlines:** FAFSA; State aid form. **Notification of Awards:** Applicants will be notified of awards on a rolling basis beginning 12/1. **Types of Aid:** *Need-based scholarships/ grants:* College/university scholarship or grant aid from institutional funds; Federal Pell; Private scholarships; State scholarships/grants. *Loans:* Direct

PLUS loans; Direct Subsidized Stafford Loans; Direct Unsubsidized Stafford Loans. *Student Employment:* Institutional employment available. **Financial Aid Statistics:** 97% needy freshmen, 91% needy undergrads receive need-based scholarship or grant aid. 16% freshmen, 7% undergrads receive non-need-based scholarship or grant aid. 90% freshmen, 95% undergrads receive need-based self-help aid. 0% freshmen, 0% undergrads receive athletic scholarships. 92% freshmen, 87% undergrads receive any aid. 71% undergrads borrow to pay for school. Average cumulative indebtedness $28,780. **Criteria for awarding aid:** *Non-need-based:* Academics, Alumni affiliation, Leadership.

REGIS COLLEGE

235 Wellesley Street, Weston, MA 02493-1571
Phone: 781-768-7100 • **Financial Aid Phone:** 781-768-7184
E-mail: admission@regiscollege.edu • **CEEB Code:** 3723
Fax: 781-768-7071 • **Website:** www.regiscollege.edu • **ACT Code:** 1886

This private school, affiliated with the Roman Catholic Church, was founded in 1927. It has a 131 acre campus.

RATINGS

Admissions Selectivity Rating: 72   **Fire Safety Rating:** 89   **Green Rating:** 60*

STUDENTS AND FACULTY

Enrollment: 1,235. **Student Body:** 79% female, 21% male, 19% out-of-state, 2% international (17 countries represented). Asian 4%, African American 19%, Caucasian 49%, Hispanic 11%, Native American <1%, Pacific Islander <1%, Two or more races 1%, Race unknown 12%.
Retention and Graduation: 82% freshmen return for sophomore year. 28% grads go on to further study within 1 year. 16% grads pursue arts and sciences degrees. 1% grads pursue law degrees. 2% grads pursue business degrees. 2% grads pursue medical degrees. **Faculty:** Student/faculty ratio 11:1. 96 full-time faculty, 70% hold PhDs, 9% are members of minority groups, 76% are women. 0% of classes are taught by teaching assistants.

ACADEMICS

Degrees: Associate; Bachelor's; Doctoral/Professional; Master's; Post-Master's certificate; Transfer Associate **Classes:** Most classes have 10-19 students. **Most popular majors:** Biology/Biological Sciences, General; Registered Nursing/Registered Nurse; Business/Commerce, General. **Special Study Options:** Accelerated program; Cross-registration; Double major; Dual enrollment; English as a Second Language (ESL); Exchange student program (domestic); Honors program; Independent study; Internships; Student-designed major; Study abroad; Teacher certification program. Honors programs: The Honors Program at Regis College offers qualified students a stimulating and challenging learning experience, and opportunities for distinguished scholarship. It prepares students to become leaders committed to the betterment of the human condition and our society, a goal that is central to the Regis College mission. **Disability Services offered to physically disabled students:** Note-taking services; Tape recorders; Tutors. **Career services:** Alumni network; Alumni services; Career assessment; Career/job search classes; Internships

FACILITIES

Housing: Coed dorms; Women's dorms 85% of campus accessible to physically diasbled. **Special Academic Facilities/Equipment:** Fine arts center, philatelic museum. **Computers:** 30% of classrooms, 100% of dorms, 100% of libraries, 100% of dining areas, 100% of student union, 15% of common outdoor areas have wireless network access. Students can register for classes online. Administrative functions (other than registration) can be performed online.

CAMPUS LIFE

Environment: Village **Activities:** Campus Ministries; Choral groups; Dance; Drama/theater; Literary magazine; Model UN; Music ensembles; Musical theater; Radio station; Student government; Yearbook 36 registered organizations, 10 honor societies, 2 religious organizations. **Athletics (Intercollegiate):** *Men:* basketball, diving, soccer, swimming. *Women:* basketball, diving, field hockey, lacrosse, soccer, softball, swimming, tennis, track/field (outdoor), track/field (indoor), volleyball. **On-Campus Highlights:** College Hall, Student Union, Tower, Athletic Complex, Fine Arts Center **Environmental Initiatives:** Replacement of steam boilers w/high efficiency designs

ADMISSIONS

Freshman Academic Profile: Average high school GPA 3.1. 10% in top 10% of high school class, 35% in top 25% of high school class, 66% in top 50% of high school class. 75% from public high schools. **Test Scores:** SAT Math middle 50% range 420-540. SAT EBRW middle 50% range 420-520. ACT

middle 50% range 19-23. Minimum internet-based TOEFL 79-80. Minimum paper TOEFL 550. **Basis for Candidate Selection:** *Very important factors considered include:* rigor of secondary school record, academic GPA, application essay, recommendation(s), character/personal qualities. *Important factors considered include:* class rank, interview, extracurricular activities, talent/ability, volunteer work, work experience. *Other factors considered include:* standardized test scores, first generation, alumni/ae relation, geographical residence, level of applicant's interest. **Freshman Admission Requirements:** High school diploma is required and GED is accepted *Academic units required:* 4 English, 3 math, 2 science, 1 science labs, 2 foreign language, 2 social studies, 3 academic electives, *Academic units recommended:* 4 math, 4 science, 3 foreign language, 4 social studies. **Freshman Admission Statistics:** 2,023 applied, 84.2% admitted, 16% enrolled. **Transfer Admission Requirements:** High school transcript, college transcript(s), essay or personal statement, Minimum college GPA of 2.0 required. Lowest grade transferable C. **General Admission Information:** Application fee $50. Priority deadline 2/15. Regular application deadline 6/1. Nonfall registration accepted. Admission may be deferred for a maximum of 1 year.

COSTS AND FINANCIAL AID

Annual tuition $37,540. Room and board $14,380. Average book expense $1,000. **Required Forms and Deadlines:** FAFSA. **Notification of Awards:** Applicants will be notified of awards on a rolling basis beginning 3/15. **Types of Aid:** *Need-based scholarships/grants:* College/university scholarship or grant aid from institutional funds; Federal Pell; Private scholarships; SEOG; State scholarships/grants. *Loans:* Direct PLUS loans; Direct Subsidized Stafford Loans; Direct Unsubsidized Stafford Loans. *Student Employment:* Federal Work-Study Program available. Institutional employment available. **Financial Aid Statistics:** 92% needy freshmen, 91% needy undergrads receive need-based scholarship or grant aid. 49% freshmen, 50% undergrads receive non-need-based scholarship or grant aid. 94% freshmen, 96% undergrads receive need-based self-help aid. 0% freshmen, 0% undergrads receive athletic scholarships. 91% freshmen, 84% undergrads receive any aid. 94% undergrads borrow to pay for school. Average cumulative indebtedness $49,217. **Criteria for awarding aid:** *Need-based:* Leadership, Minority status, Religious affiliation *Non-need-based:* Academics, Alumni affiliation, Religious affiliation.

See page 1008.

REGIS UNIVERSITY

3333 Regis Boulevard, Denver, CO 80221-1099
Phone: 303-458-4900 • **Financial Aid Phone:** 303-458-4126
E-mail: RUAdmissions@regis.edu • **CEEB Code:** 4656
Fax: 303-964-5534 • **Website:** www.regis.edu • **ACT Code:** 526

This private school, affiliated with the Roman Catholic Church, was founded in 1877. It has a 90 acre campus.

RATINGS

Admissions Selectivity Rating: 83   **Fire Safety Rating:** 65   **Green Rating:** 70

STUDENTS AND FACULTY

Enrollment: 3,972. **Student Body:** 61% female, 39% male, 38% out-of-state, 1% international (8 countries represented). Asian 5%, African American 5%, Caucasian 58%, Hispanic 20%, Native American <1%, Pacific Islander <1%, Two or more races 4%, Race unknown 7%.
Retention and Graduation: 80% freshmen return for sophomore year. **Faculty:** Student/faculty ratio 14:1. 280 full-time faculty, 84% hold PhDs, 13% are members of minority groups, 60% are women. 0% of classes are taught by teaching assistants.

ACADEMICS

Degrees: Bachelor's; Certificate; Doctoral/Professional; Master's; Post-Bachelor's certificate; Post-Master's certificate **Classes:** Most classes have 10-19 students. **Most popular majors:** Computer Science; Registered Nursing/Registered Nurse; Business Administration And Management, General. **Special Study Options:** Accelerated program; Distance learning; Double major; Dual enrollment; Honors program; Independent study; Internships; Liberal arts/career combination; Student-designed major; Study abroad; Teacher certification program; Weekend college. Honors programs: The Regis College Honors Program is available to self-motivated, conscientious Regis College students who wish to complete an alternate pathway through the core curriculum and be distinguished as an honors graduate Combined degree programs: BA/MA. **Disability Services offered to physically disabled students:** Note-taking services; Reader services; Tape recorders. **Career services:** Alumni services; Career assessment; Career/job search classes; Internships

FACILITIES

Housing: Apartments for single students; Coed dorms; Special housing for disabled student; Theme housing; Wellness housing 90% of campus accessible to physically diasbled. **Special Academic Facilities/Equipment:** Arboretum, O'Sullivan Art Gallery, Santos collection (Hispanic religious art; http://libguides.regis.edu/santo), Center for the study of war experience, Recorder Music Center (http://www.regis.edu/About-Regis-University/Centers-and-Institutes/Recorder-Music-Center.aspx) **Computers:** Administrative functions (other than registration) can be performed online.

CAMPUS LIFE

Environment: Metropolis **Activities:** Campus Ministries; Choral groups; Concert band; Dance; Drama/theater; International Student Organization; Jazz band; Literary magazine; Music ensembles; Musical theater; Radio station; Student government; Student newspaper; Yearbook 40 registered organizations, 1 honor society, 1 religious organization. **Athletics (Intercollegiate):** *Men:* baseball, basketball, cross-country, golf, soccer. *Women:* basketball, cross-country, lacrosse, soccer, softball, volleyball. Residence Halls, Student Center, Science Building, Chapel, Arboretum

ADMISSIONS

Freshman Academic Profile: Average high school GPA 3.6. 16% in top 10% of high school class, 39% in top 25% of high school class, 90% in top 50% of high school class. 58% from public high schools. **Test Scores:** SAT Math middle 50% range 470-570. SAT EBRW middle 50% range 480-600. ACT middle 50% range 22-26. Minimum internet-based TOEFL 82. Minimum paper TOEFL 550. **Basis for Candidate Selection:** *Very important factors considered include:* rigor of secondary school record, academic GPA, standardized test scores, character/personal qualities. *Other factors considered include:* class rank, application essay, recommendation(s), interview, extracurricular activities, talent/ability, first generation, alumni/ae relation, racial/ethnic status, work experience, level of applicant's interest. **Freshman Admission Requirements:** High school diploma is required and GED is accepted *Academic units recommended:* 4 English, 3 math, 2 science, 1 science labs, 2 foreign language, 2 social studies, 1 academic elective. **Freshman Admission Statistics:** 6,756 applied, 56.6% admitted, 13% enrolled. **Transfer Admission Requirements:** college transcript(s), essay or personal statement, Minimum college GPA of 2.0 required. **General Admission Information:** Priority deadline 4/15. Regular application deadline 8/1. Nonfall registration accepted. Admission may be deferred for a maximum of 1 year.

COSTS AND FINANCIAL AID

Annual tuition $34,100. Room and board $10,420. Required fees $350. Average book expense $1,800. **Required Forms and Deadlines:** FAFSA. **Notification of Awards:** Applicants will be notified of awards on a rolling basis beginning 3/15. **Types of Aid:** *Need-based scholarships/grants:* College/university scholarship or grant aid from institutional funds; Federal Pell; Private scholarships; SEOG; State scholarships/grants. *Loans:* Direct PLUS loans; Direct Subsidized Stafford Loans; Direct Unsubsidized Stafford Loans. *Student Employment:* Federal Work-Study Program available. Institutional employment available. **Financial Aid Statistics:** 100% needy freshmen, 86% needy undergrads receive need-based scholarship or grant aid. 14% freshmen, 10% undergrads receive non-need-based scholarship or grant aid. 71% freshmen, 79% undergrads receive need-based self-help aid. 7% freshmen, 5% undergrads receive athletic scholarships. 69% freshmen, 67% undergrads receive any aid. 61% undergrads borrow to pay for school. Average cumulative indebtedness $28,128. **Criteria for awarding aid:** *Need-based:* Academics, Athletics, Leadership, Music/drama, Religious affiliation *Non-need-based:* Academics, Athletics, Leadership, Music/drama, Religious affiliation, State/district residency.

REINHARDT COLLEGE

University Admissions Center, Waleska, GA 30183
Phone: 770-720-5526 • **Financial Aid Phone:** (770) 720-5667
E-mail: www.reinhardt.edu
Fax: 770-720-5899 • **Website:** www.reinhardt.edu • **ACT Code:** 856

This private school, affiliated with the Methodist Church, was founded in 1883. It has a 600 acre campus.

RATINGS

Admissions Selectivity Rating: 81   **Fire Safety Rating:** 97   **Green Rating:** 60*

STUDENTS AND FACULTY

Enrollment: 980. **Student Body:** 55% female, 45% male, 27% out-of-state, 0% international. Asian 1%, African American 13%, Caucasian 75%, Hispanic 4%, Native American 1%, Pacific Islander 0%, Two or more races 0%, Race unknown 6%.

Retention and Graduation: 56% freshmen return for sophomore year. 35% grads go on to further study within 1 year. 20% grads pursue arts and sciences degrees. 5% grads pursue law degrees. 45% grads pursue business degrees. 5% grads pursue medical degrees. **Faculty:** Student/faculty ratio 12:1. 62 full-time faculty, 74% hold PhDs, 11% are members of minority groups, 48% are women. 0% of classes are taught by teaching assistants.

ACADEMICS

Degrees: Associate; Bachelor's; Master's; Transfer Associate **Classes:** Most classes have 10-19 students. **Most popular majors:** Elementary Education And Teaching; Music; Business Administration And Management, General. **Special Study Options:** Accelerated program; Distance learning; Double major; Dual enrollment; External degree program; Honors program; Independent study; Student-designed major; Study abroad; Teacher certification program. Honors programs: The Honors Program is designed for students who are bright, curious and enjoy being challenged. Entering freshman with High Schjool GPA of at least 3.5 or a combined SAT of 1050 or higher, with verbal score of at least 580, will be invited to apply for admission to Reinhardt College's Honors Program. **Disability Services offered to physically disabled students:** Note-taking services; Reader services; Tape recorders; Tutors. **Career services:** Alumni services; Career assessment; Career/job search classes; Internships; Regional alumni

FACILITIES

Housing: Apartments for single students; Coed dorms; Men's dorms; Special housing for disabled student; Women's dorms 99% of campus accessible to physically diasbled. **Special Academic Facilities/Equipment:** Funk Heritage Center, Falany Performing Arts **Computers:** 100% of classrooms, 100% of dorms, 100% of libraries, 100% of student union, 5% of common outdoor areas have wireless network access. Students can register for classes online. Administrative functions (other than registration) can be performed online.

CAMPUS LIFE

Environment: Rural **Activities:** Campus Ministries; Choral groups; Concert band; Drama/theater; International Student Organization; Jazz band; Literary magazine; Music ensembles; Musical theater; Student government; Student newspaper; Student-run film society; Symphony orchestra; Television station; Yearbook 40 registered organizations, 6 honor societies, 5 religious organizations. **Athletics (Intercollegiate):** *Men:* baseball, basketball, cheerleading, cross-country, golf, soccer, tennis. *Women:* basketball, cheerleading, cross-country, golf, soccer, softball, tennis, volleyball. **On-Campus Highlights:** Falany Performing Arts Center, Funk Heritage Center, Gordy Center, Library, Class room building **Environmental Initiatives:** Recycle paper, RU Green

ADMISSIONS

Freshman Academic Profile: Average high school GPA 3.0. 63% in top 50% of high school class. 98% from public high schools. **Test Scores:** SAT Math middle 50% range 430-530. SAT EBRW middle 50% range 410-540. ACT middle 50% range 17-22. Minimum paper TOEFL 500. **Basis for Candidate Selection:** *Very important factors considered include:* academic GPA, standardized test scores. *Important factors considered include:* rigor of secondary school record, class rank. **Freshman Admission Requirements:** High school diploma is required and GED is accepted *Academic units required:* 4 English, 4 math, 3 science, 3 social studies, *Academic units recommended:* 2 foreign language. **Freshman Admission Statistics:** 1,310 applied, 58.7% admitted, 30% enrolled. **Transfer Admission Requirements:** college transcript(s), statement of good standing from prior institution(s). Minimum college GPA of 2.0 required. Lowest grade transferable C. **General Admission Information:** Application fee $25. Nonfall registration accepted. Admission may be deferred.

COSTS AND FINANCIAL AID

Required Forms and Deadlines: FAFSA; State aid form. **Notification of Awards:** Applicants will be notified of awards on a rolling basis beginning 1/1. **Types of Aid:** *Need-based scholarships/grants:* College/university scholarship or grant aid from institutional funds; Federal Pell; Private scholarships; SEOG; State scholarships/grants. *Loans:* Direct PLUS loans; Direct Subsidized Stafford Loans; Direct Unsubsidized Stafford Loans. *Student Employment:* Federal Work-Study Program available. **Financial Aid Statistics:** 99% needy freshmen, 98% needy undergrads receive need-based scholarship or grant aid. 7% freshmen, 7% undergrads receive non-need-based scholarship or grant aid. 76% freshmen, 75% undergrads receive need-based self-help aid. 9% freshmen, 7% undergrads receive athletic scholarships. **Criteria for awarding aid:** *Need-based:* Academics, Art, Athletics, Leadership, Music/drama, Religious affiliation *Non-need-based:* Academics, Art, Athletics, Leadership, Music/drama, Religious affiliation, State/district residency.

RENSSELAER POLYTECHNIC INSTITUTE

110 Eighth Street, Troy, NY 12180-3590
Phone: 518-276-6216 • **Financial Aid Phone:** 518-276-6813
E-mail: admissions@rpi.edu • **CEEB Code:** 2757
Fax: 518-276-4072 • **Website:** www.rpi.edu • **ACT Code:** 2866

This private school was founded in 1824. It has a 284 acre campus.

RATINGS
Admissions Selectivity Rating: 94   **Fire Safety Rating:** 94   **Green Rating:** 60*

STUDENTS AND FACULTY
Enrollment: 6,314. **Student Body:** 32% female, 68% male, 67% out-of-state, 14% international (44 countries represented). Asian 12%, African American 4%, Caucasian 53%, Hispanic 9%, Native American <1%, Pacific Islander <1%, Two or more races 7%, Race unknown 1%.
Retention and Graduation: 93% freshmen return for sophomore year. 61% freshmen graduate within 4 years. 83% freshmen graduate within 6 years. 24% grads go on to further study within 1 year. 5% grads pursue arts and sciences degrees. 2% grads pursue business degrees. 2% grads pursue medical degrees. **Faculty:** Student/faculty ratio 13:1. 467 full-time faculty, 94% hold PhDs, 29% are members of minority groups, 25% are women. 0% of classes are taught by teaching assistants.

ACADEMICS
Degrees: Bachelor's; Doctoral/Research; **Master's Classes:** Most classes have fewer than 10 students. **Most popular majors:** Computer Engineering, General; Electrical And Electronics Engineering; Business/Commerce, General. **Special Study Options:** Accelerated program; Cooperative education program; Cross-registration; Double major; Dual enrollment; Exchange student program (domestic); Honors program; Independent study; Internships; Liberal arts/career combination; Study abroad. Honors programs: The Rensselaer Medal Program, the Presidential Scholars Program Combined degree programs: BA/MEng. **Disability Services offered to physically disabled students:** Note-taking services; Reader services; Tape recorders; Tutors. **Career services:** Alumni network; Alumni services; Career assessment; Career/job search classes; Internships; Regional alumni

FACILITIES
Housing: Apartments for married students; Apartments for single students; Coed dorms; Fraternity/sorority housing; Special housing for disabled student; Theme housing 75% of campus accessible to physically disabled. **Special Academic Facilities/Equipment:** Shelnutt Art Gallery in the Student Union;The George M. Low Gallery (museum); Center for Terahertz Research; Nanoscale Science and Engineering Centers (NSEC); Center for Biotechnology and Interdisciplinary Studies; Gaerttner Linear Accelerator (LINAC) Laboratory; Hirsch Observatory; RPIdeaLab and Incubator Program (supports student business ventures); Rensselaer Technology Park; Darrin Fresh Water Institute at Lake George; Experimental Media and Performing Arts Center (EMPAC—under construction); Lighting Research Center; Social and Behavioral Research Laboratory; O.T. Swanson Multidisciplinary Laboratory; and other research centers and laboratories as described at www.rpi.edu/research/research_centers.html,Computational Center for Nanotechnology Innovations (CCNI); http://www.rpi.edu/dept/ess/greening/EECbooks.html Ecologic Environmental Library(EEC) **Computers:** 75% of classrooms, 75% of dorms, 100% of libraries, 75% of dining areas, 100% of student union, 75% of common outdoor areas have wireless network access. Students can register for classes online. Administrative functions (other than registration) can be performed online. Undergraduates are required to own a computer.

CAMPUS LIFE
Environment: City **Activities:** Campus Ministries; Choral groups; Concert band; Dance; Drama/theater; International Student Organization; Jazz band; Literary magazine; Music ensembles; Musical theater; Pep band; Radio station; Student government; Student newspaper; Student-run film society; Symphony orchestra; Television station; Yearbook 177 registered organizations, 40 honor societies, 11 religious organizations. 32 fraternities, 5 sororities. **Athletics (Intercollegiate):** *Men:* baseball, basketball, cross-country, diving, football, golf, ice hockey, lacrosse, soccer, swimming, tennis, track/field (outdoor), track/field (indoor). *Women:* basketball, cross-country, diving, field hockey, ice hockey, lacrosse, soccer, softball, swimming, tennis, track/field (outdoor), track/field (indoor). **On-Campus Highlights:** Rensselaer Union, Mueller Fitness Center, Experimental Media & Performing Arts Ctr, Houston Field House (hockey arena), ECAV **Environmental Initiatives:** Student Sustainability Task Force

ADMISSIONS
Freshman Academic Profile: Average high school GPA 3.8. 63% in top 10% of high school class, 91% in top 25% of high school class, 98% in top 50% of high school class. 70% from public high schools. **Test Scores:** SAT Math middle 50% range 680-770. SAT EBRW middle 50% range 640-730. ACT middle 50% range 28-32. Minimum internet-based TOEFL 88. Minimum paper TOEFL 570. **Basis for Candidate Selection:** *Very important factors considered include:* rigor of secondary school record, class rank, academic GPA, standardized test scores. *Important factors considered include:* application essay, recommendation(s), extracurricular activities, character/personal qualities, level of applicant's interest. *Other factors considered include:* talent/ability, first generation, alumni/ae relation, racial/ethnic status, volunteer work, work experience. **Freshman Admission Requirements:** High school diploma is required and GED is accepted *Academic units required:* 4 English, 4 math, 3 science, 3 social studies, *Academic units recommended:* 4 science, 3 social studies. **Freshman Admission Statistics:** 19,505 applied, 43.2% admitted, 20% enrolled. **Transfer Admission Requirements:** college transcript(s), statement of good standing from prior institution(s). Minimum college GPA of 3.0 required. Lowest grade transferable C. **General Admission Information:** Application fee $70. Nonfall registration accepted. Admission may be deferred for a maximum of 1 year.

COSTS AND FINANCIAL AID
Annual tuition $52,550. Room and board $15,260. Required fees $1,330. Average book expense $2,858. **Required Forms and Deadlines:** CSS/Financial Aid PROFILE; FAFSA. **Notification of Awards:** Applicants will be notified of awards on or about 3/15. **Types of Aid:** *Need-based scholarships/grants:* College/university scholarship or grant aid from institutional funds; Federal Pell; Private scholarships; SEOG; State scholarships/grants. *Loans:* Direct PLUS loans; Direct Subsidized Stafford Loans; Direct Unsubsidized Stafford Loans. *Student Employment:* Federal Work-Study Program available. Institutional employment available. **Financial Aid Statistics:** 100% needy freshmen, 100% needy undergrads receive need-based scholarship or grant aid. 18% freshmen, 13% undergrads receive non-need-based scholarship or grant aid. 99% freshmen, 97% undergrads receive need-based self-help aid. 1% freshmen, 1% undergrads receive athletic scholarships. 89% freshmen, 89% undergrads receive any aid. **Criteria for awarding aid:** *Need-based:* Academics, Alumni affiliation, Art, Leadership, Minority status, Music/drama *Non-need-based:* Academics, Alumni affiliation, Art, Athletics, Leadership, Minority status, Music/drama.

RHODE ISLAND COLLEGE

600 Mount Pleasant Avenue, Providence, RI 02908
Phone: 401-456-8234 • **Financial Aid Phone:** 401-456-8033
E-mail: admissions@ric.edu • **CEEB Code:** 3407
Fax: 401-456-8817 • **Website:** http://www.ric.edu • **ACT Code:** 3810

This public school was founded in 1854. It has a 180 acre campus.

RATINGS
Admissions Selectivity Rating: 76   **Fire Safety Rating:** 60*   **Green Rating:** 73

STUDENTS AND FACULTY
Enrollment: 6,903. **Student Body:** 69% female, 31% male, 14% out-of-state, <1% international. Asian 3%, African American 10%, Caucasian 58%, Hispanic 20%, Native American 1%, Pacific Islander <1%, Two or more races 2%, Race unknown 7%.
Retention and Graduation: 75% freshmen return for sophomore year. 20% freshmen graduate within 4 years. 46% freshmen graduate within 6 years. **Faculty:** Student/faculty ratio 14:1. 335 full-time faculty, 90% hold PhDs, 17% are members of minority groups, 61% are women.

ACADEMICS
Degrees: Bachelor's; Certificate; Doctoral/Professional; Doctoral/Research; Master's; Post-Bachelor's certificate; Post-Master's certificate **Special Study Options:** Double major; Dual enrollment; English as a Second Language (ESL); Exchange student program (domestic); Honors program; Independent study; Internships; Student-designed major; Study abroad; Teacher certification program.

FACILITIES
Housing: Coed dorms; Special housing for disabled students

CAMPUS LIFE
Environment: City **Activities:** Choral groups; Concert band; Dance; Drama/theater; International Student Organization; Jazz band; Literary magazine; Music ensembles; Musical theater; Radio station; Student government; Student

newspaper; Student-run film society; Symphony orchestra; Television station. **Environmental Initiatives:** 1. The Sustainable Communities Initiative at RIC is an innovative pilot project which works to further inform RIC students and the general public on the local and global issues of sustainability, while providing a vehicle through which to take action for positive change. SCI has already exposed RIC students and community members to some of the region's and nation's most recognized sustainability thought leaders, trained nearly twenty SCI Community Leaders from twelve Rhode Island communities, established a nine person leadership committee and has begun to collaboratively work on the development of a participatory research tool that will empower community residents to evaluate and improve the sustainability performance of their own town and cities.

ADMISSIONS

Freshman Academic Profile: 12% in top 10% of high school class, 36% in top 25% of high school class, 73% in top 50% of high school class. 75% from public high schools. **Test Scores:** SAT Math middle 50% range 430-530. SAT EBRW middle 50% range 450-560. ACT middle 50% range 15-22. Minimum internet-based TOEFL 80. Minimum paper TOEFL 550. **Basis for Candidate Selection:** *Very important factors considered include:* rigor of secondary school record, class rank, academic GPA. *Important factors considered include:* application essay, standardized test scores, recommendation(s). *Other factors considered include:* interview, extracurricular activities, talent/ability, alumni/ae relation, volunteer work, work experience. **Freshman Admission Requirements:** High school diploma is required and GED is accepted *Academic units required:* 4 English, 3 math, 2 science, 2 science labs, 2 foreign language, 2 social studies, 5 academic electives. **Freshman Admission Statistics:** 4,846 applied, 73.6% admitted, 29% enrolled. **General Admission Information:** Application fee $50. Regular application deadline 3/15. Nonfall registration accepted.

COSTS AND FINANCIAL AID

Annual in-state tuition $11,335. Annual out-of-state tuition $20,150. Room and board $11,335. Required fees $1,139. Average book expense $1,200. **Required Forms and Deadlines:** FAFSA; Institution's own financial aid form. **Notification of Awards:** Applicants will be notified of awards on a rolling basis beginning 2/15. **Types of Aid:** *Need-based scholarships/grants:* College/university scholarship or grant aid from institutional funds; Federal Pell; Private scholarships; SEOG; State scholarships/grants. *Loans:* Direct PLUS loans; Direct Subsidized Stafford Loans; Direct Unsubsidized Stafford Loans. *Student Employment:* Federal Work-Study Program available. Institutional employment available. **Financial Aid Statistics:** 81% needy freshmen, 81% needy undergrads receive need-based scholarship or grant aid. 3% freshmen, 2% undergrads receive non-need-based scholarship or grant aid. 85% freshmen, 83% undergrads receive need-based self-help aid. 0% freshmen, 0% undergrads receive athletic scholarships. 75% undergrads borrow to pay for school. Average cumulative indebtedness $26,624. **Criteria for awarding aid:** *Need-based:* Academics *Non-need-based:* Academics, Alumni affiliation, Art, Music/drama.

RHODE ISLAND SCHOOL OF DESIGN

2 College Street, Providence, RI 02903
Phone: 401-454-6300 • **Financial Aid Phone:** 401-454-6661
E-mail: admissions@risd.edu • **CEEB Code:** 3726
Fax: 401-454-6309 • **Website:** www.risd.edu • **ACT Code:** 3812

This private school was founded in 1877. It has a 19 acre campus.

RATINGS
Admissions Selectivity Rating: 94   **Fire Safety Rating:** 92   **Green Rating:** 60*

STUDENTS AND FACULTY
Enrollment: 506. **Student Body:** 66% female, 34% male, 95% out-of-state, 30% international (46 countries represented). Asian 19%, African American 3%, Caucasian 31%, Hispanic 8%, Native American <1%, Pacific Islander 0%, Two or more races 5%, Race unknown 4%.
Retention and Graduation: 95% freshmen return for sophomore year. 66% freshmen graduate within 4 years. 91% freshmen graduate within 6 years.
Faculty: Student/faculty ratio 10:1. 161 full-time faculty, 83% hold PhDs, 14% are members of minority groups, 44% are women.

ACADEMICS
Degrees: Bachelor's; Master's **Most popular majors:** Industrial And Product Design; Graphic Design; Illustration. **Special Study Options:** Cross-registration; Double major; Exchange student program (domestic); Independent study; Internships; Study abroad; Teacher certification program.

Honors programs: European Honors Program. See: http://www.risd.edu/Academics/International_Programs/European_Honors_Program/ Brown/RISD Dual Degree. See: http://www.risd.edu/Policies/Academic/Brown_RISD_Dual_Degree/. **Disability Services offered to physically disabled students:** Note-taking services; Reader services; Tape recorders; Tutors. **Career services:** Alumni network; Alumni services; Career assessment; Career/job search classes; Internships; Regional alumni

FACILITIES
Housing: Apartments for married students; Apartments for single students; Coed dorms; Special housing for disabled students 27% of campus accessible to physically diasbled. **Special Academic Facilities/Equipment:** Art museum with over 45 galleries, extensive facilities for glassblowing, metalsmithing, lithography, sculpture, painting, and other art disciplines, Nature Lab. Library with extensive photograph, print and materials collections. **Computers:** Administrative functions (other than registration) can be performed online.

CAMPUS LIFE
Environment: City **Activities:** Choral groups; Concert band; Dance; Drama/theater; International Student Organization; Literary magazine; Musical theater; Radio station; Student government; Student newspaper; Student-run film society; Yearbook 35 registered organizations, 5 religious organizations. **On-Campus Highlights:** The RISD Museum, The Edna Lawrence Nature Lab, RISD Fleet Library, Carr Haus

ADMISSIONS
Test Scores: SAT Math middle 50% range 560-710. SAT EBRW middle 50% range 570-660. ACT middle 50% range 25-31. Minimum internet-based TOEFL 93. Minimum paper TOEFL 580. **Basis for Candidate Selection:** *Very important factors considered include:* rigor of secondary school record, academic GPA, talent/ability. *Important factors considered include:* application essay, standardized test scores. *Other factors considered include:* recommendation(s), extracurricular activities, character/personal qualities, first generation, alumni/ae relation, geographical residence, racial/ethnic status, volunteer work, work experience. **Freshman Admission Requirements:** High school diploma is required and GED is accepted **Freshman Admission Statistics:** 3,420 applied, 28.8% admitted, 46% enrolled. **Transfer Admission Requirements:** college transcript(s), essay or personal statement, Lowest grade transferable C. **General Admission Information:** Application fee $60. Regular application deadline 2/1. Nonfall registration accepted. Admission may be deferred for a maximum of 1 year.

COSTS AND FINANCIAL AID
Annual tuition $48,210. Room and board $13,050. Required fees $260. Average book expense $2,700. **Required Forms and Deadlines:** CSS/Financial Aid PROFILE; FAFSA. **Notification of Awards:** Applicants will be notified of awards on or about 4/1. **Types of Aid:** *Need-based scholarships/grants:* College/university scholarship or grant aid from institutional funds; Federal Pell; Private scholarships; SEOG; State scholarships/grants. *Loans:* Direct PLUS loans; Direct Subsidized Stafford Loans; Direct Unsubsidized Stafford Loans. *Student Employment:* Federal Work-Study Program available. **Financial Aid Statistics:** 88% needy freshmen, 91% needy undergrads receive need-based scholarship or grant aid. 3% undergrads receive non-need-based scholarship or grant aid. 100% freshmen, 91% undergrads receive need-based self-help aid. 0% freshmen, 0% undergrads receive athletic scholarships. 42% freshmen, 41% undergrads receive any aid. 41% undergrads borrow to pay for school. Average cumulative indebtedness $31,037. **Criteria for awarding aid:** *Need-based:* Academics, Art *Non-need-based:* Academics, Art.

RHODES COLLEGE

2000 North Parkway, Memphis, TN 38112
Phone: 901-843-3700 • **Financial Aid Phone:** 901-843-3810
E-mail: adminfo@rhodes.edu • **CEEB Code:** 1730
Fax: 901-843-3631 • **Website:** http://www.rhodes.edu • **ACT Code:** 4008

This private school, affiliated with the Presbyterian Church, was founded in 1848. It has a 100 acre campus.

RATINGS
Admissions Selectivity Rating: 90   **Fire Safety Rating:** 87   **Green Rating:** 75

STUDENTS AND FACULTY

Enrollment: 1,975. **Student Body:** 56% female, 44% male, 72% out-of-state, 4% international (18 countries represented). Asian 6%, African American 8%, Caucasian 70%, Hispanic 6%, Native American <1%, Pacific Islander <1%, Two or more races 4%, Race unknown 2%.
Retention and Graduation: 91% freshmen return for sophomore year. 76% freshmen graduate within 4 years. 80% freshmen graduate within 6 years. 18% grads go on to further study within 1 year. **Faculty:** Student/faculty ratio 10:1. 180 full-time faculty, 98% hold PhDs, 15% are members of minority groups, 49% are women. 0% of classes are taught by teaching assistants.

ACADEMICS

Degrees: Bachelor's; **Master's Classes:** Most classes have 20-29 students. Most lab/discussion sessions have 20-29 students. **Most popular majors:** English Language And Literature, General; Biology/Biological Sciences, General; Business Administration And Management, General. **Special Study Options:** Cooperative education program; Cross-registration; Double major; Dual enrollment; Honors program; Independent study; Internships; Liberal arts/career combination; Student-designed major; Study abroad; Teacher certification program. Honors programs: The Honors program is a culminating experience in the major field, for seniors only. It is the principal means whereby a student may do more independent, intensive, and individual work than can be done in the regular degree programs. The Honors work offers an excellent introduction to graduate study as it employs the full resources of library and laboratory and encourages independent research and study. Honors is available in most majors. **Disability Services offered to physically disabled students:** Note-taking services; Reader services; Tape recorders; Tutors. **Career services:** Alumni network; Alumni services; Career assessment; Career/job search classes; Internships; Regional alumni

FACILITIES

Housing: Apartments for single students; Coed dorms; Men's dorms; Theme housing; Women's dorms 90% of campus accessible to physically diasbled. **Special Academic Facilities/Equipment:** 136,000 square foot library; Art gallery; archaeology lab; astronomy observation domes with 14 and 31.5 inch telescopes; machine and woodworking shops; scanning electron microscopes; cell culture lab; nuclear magnetic resonance instrument; gas chromatography systems; UV, X-ray, infrared, and atomic absorption spectrophotometers. **Computers:** 100% of classrooms, 100% of dorms, 100% of libraries, 100% of dining areas, 50% of common outdoor areas have wireless network access. Students can register for classes online. Administrative functions (other than registration) can be performed online.

CAMPUS LIFE

Environment: Metropolis **Activities:** Campus Ministries; Choral groups; Dance; Drama/theater; International Student Organization; Jazz band; Literary magazine; Model UN; Music ensembles; Musical theater; Pep band; Radio station; Student government; Student newspaper; Student-run film society; Symphony orchestra; Television station; Yearbook 115 registered organizations, 14 honor societies, 8 religious organizations. 7 fraternities, 6 sororities. **Athletics (Intercollegiate):** *Men:* baseball, basketball, cross-country, football, golf, soccer, swimming, tennis, track/field (outdoor). *Women:* basketball, cross-country, field hockey, golf, soccer, softball, swimming, tennis, track/field (outdoor), volleyball. **On-Campus Highlights:** Paul Barret, Jr. Library, The Middle Ground (coffee shop), Burrow Refectory (Cafeteria), Bryan Campus Life Center (athletic facility), Lynx Lair (Bar and Cafe) **Environmental Initiatives:** $500,000 Andrew W. Mellon Foundation grant to expand Environmental Studies initiatives through community partnerships

ADMISSIONS

Freshman Academic Profile: Average high school GPA 3.9. 35% in top 10% of high school class, 55% in top 25% of high school class, 67% in top 50% of high school class. 46% from public high schools. **Test Scores:** SAT Math middle 50% range 600-690. SAT EBRW middle 50% range 620-720. ACT middle 50% range 27-32. Minimum paper TOEFL 550. **Basis for Candidate Selection:** *Very important factors considered include:* rigor of secondary school record, class rank, academic GPA. *Important factors considered include:* application essay, standardized test scores, recommendation(s), character/personal qualities, alumni/ae relation, racial/ethnic status. *Other factors considered include:* interview, extracurricular activities, talent/ability, first generation, geographical residence, state residency, volunteer work, work experience, level of applicant's interest. **Freshman Admission Requirements:** High school diploma is required and GED is accepted *Academic units required:* 4 English, 3 math, 2 science, 2 science labs, 2 foreign language, 2 social studies, 3 academic electives. **Freshman Admission Statistics:** 4,733 applied, 51.0% admitted, 21% enrolled. **Transfer Admission Requirements:** High school transcript, college transcript(s), essay or personal statement, standardized test scores, statement of good standing from prior institution(s). Lowest grade transferable C-. **General Admission Information:** Priority deadline 1/15. Nonfall registration accepted. Admission may be deferred.

COSTS AND FINANCIAL AID

Annual tuition $46,194. Room and board $11,290. Required fees $310. Average book expense $1,125. **Required Forms and Deadlines:** FAFSA; Noncustodial PROFILE. **Types of Aid:** *Need-based scholarships/grants:* College/university scholarship or grant aid from institutional funds; Federal Pell; Private scholarships; SEOG; State scholarships/grants. *Loans:* Direct PLUS loans; Direct Subsidized Stafford Loans; Direct Unsubsidized Stafford Loans. *Student Employment:* Federal Work-Study Program available. Institutional employment available. **Financial Aid Statistics:** 99% needy freshmen, 100% needy undergrads receive need-based scholarship or grant aid. 48% freshmen, 32% undergrads receive non-need-based scholarship or grant aid. 55% freshmen, 65% undergrads receive need-based self-help aid. 0% freshmen, 0% undergrads receive athletic scholarships. 95% freshmen, 94% undergrads receive any aid. Average cumulative indebtedness $25,859. **Criteria for awarding aid:** *Need-based:* Minority status *Non-need-based:* Academics, Art, Minority status, Music/drama, Religious affiliation.

RICE UNIVERSITY

PO Box 1892, Houston, TX 77251-1892
Phone: 713-348-7423 • **Financial Aid Phone:** 713-348-4958
E-mail: admi@rice.edu • **CEEB Code:** 6609
Fax: 713-348-5952 • **Website:** www.rice.edu • **ACT Code:** 4152

This private school was founded in 1912. It has a 300 acre campus.

RATINGS

Admissions Selectivity Rating: 97   **Fire Safety Rating:** 95   **Green Rating:** 92

STUDENTS AND FACULTY

Enrollment: 3,970. **Student Body:** 47% female, 53% male, 52% out-of-state, 12% international (42 countries represented). Asian 26%, African American 7%, Caucasian 35%, Hispanic 15%, Native American <1%, Pacific Islander <1%, Two or more races 4%, Race unknown 2%.
Retention and Graduation: 97% freshmen return for sophomore year. 83% freshmen graduate within 4 years. 93% freshmen graduate within 6 years. **Faculty:** Student/faculty ratio 6:1. 680 full-time faculty, 99% hold PhDs, 21% are members of minority groups, 33% are women.

ACADEMICS

Degrees: Bachelor's; Doctoral; **Master's Classes:** Most classes have 20-29 students. Most lab/discussion sessions have 20-29 students. **Most popular majors:** Chemical Engineering; Biology/Biological Sciences, General; Economics, General. **Special Study Options:** Accelerated program; Cross-registration; Double major; Dual enrollment; Honors program; Independent study; Internships; Student-designed major; Study abroad; Teacher certification program. Honors programs: Honors programs through individual departments. Combined degree programs: BA/MD. **Disability Services offered to physically disabled students:** Note-taking services; Reader services; Tape recorders. **Career services:** Alumni network; Alumni services; Career assessment; Career/job search classes; Internships; Regional alumni

FACILITIES

Housing: Coed dorms; Special housing for disabled students 90% of campus accessible to physically diasbled. **Special Academic Facilities/Equipment:** Art gallery, museum, media center, language labs, computer labs, civil engineering lab, observatory and NASA equipment for students in space physics courses. **Computers:** 100% of classrooms, 100% of dorms, 1000% of libraries, 100% of dining areas, 100% of student union, 5% of common outdoor areas have wireless network access. Students can register for classes online. Administrative functions (other than registration) can be performed online.

CAMPUS LIFE

Environment: Metropolis **Activities:** Campus Ministries; Choral groups; Concert band; Dance; Drama/theater; International Student Organization; Jazz band; Literary magazine; Marching band; Music ensembles; Musical theater; Opera; Pep band; Radio station; Student government; Student newspaper; Student-run film society; Symphony orchestra; Television station; Yearbook 215 registered organizations, 11 honor societies, 14 religious organizations. **Athletics (Intercollegiate):** *Men:* baseball, basketball, cross-country, football, golf, tennis, track/field (outdoor), track/field (indoor). *Women:* basketball, cross-country, soccer, swimming, tennis, track/field (outdoor), track/field (indoor), volleyball. **On-Campus Highlights:** Rice Memorial Center, Baker Institute for

Public Policy, Brochstein Pavilion (cafe), Shepherd School of Music, Reckling Park—baseball stadium **Environmental Initiatives:** 1. Green Building. At present, we have roughly 1,000,000 square feet of facilities on campus that are under construction that will receive some level of LEED certification, including the student dormitory Duncan College which is targeted for LEED-Gold. In addition, an off-campus child care center is pursuing LEED certification. Also, an off-campus graduate student apartment complex has been designed to LEED standards although it will not be formally submitted for certification. With this complex, we anticipate savings in energy of about 30% and water savings of 20%. Further, the complex was constructed in an area with excellent pedestrian access, and it includes extensive bicycle storage along with shuttle bus service to campus and to major nearby grocery stores. Our campus standard for on-campus LEED certification for new buildings is LEED-Silver as a minimum. The University has also enjoyed significant successes with construction waste recycling, with many of our largest projects to date logging diversion rates of 85-90% to recycling.

ADMISSIONS

Freshman Academic Profile: 89% in top 10% of high school class, 97% in top 25% of high school class, 99% in top 50% of high school class. **Test Scores:** SAT Math middle 50% range 760-800. SAT EBRW middle 50% range 730-780. ACT middle 50% range 33-35. Minimum internet-based TOEFL 100. **Basis for Candidate Selection:** *Very important factors considered include:* rigor of secondary school record, class rank, academic GPA, application essay, standardized test scores, recommendation(s), extracurricular activities, talent/ability, character/personal qualities. *Other factors considered include:* interview, first generation, alumni/ae relation, geographical residence, state residency, racial/ethnic status, volunteer work, work experience, level of applicant's interest. **Freshman Admission Requirements:** High school diploma or equivalent is not required *Academic units required:* 4 English, 3 math, 2 science, 2 science labs, 2 foreign language, 2 social studies, 3 academic electives, *Academic units recommended:* 4 English, 4 math, 4 science, 3 science labs, 4 foreign language, 3 social studies, 3 academic electives. **Freshman Admission Statistics:** 18,063 applied, 15.9% admitted, 37% enrolled. **Transfer Admission Requirements:** High school transcript, college transcript(s), essay or personal statement, standardized test scores, statement of good standing from prior institution(s). Minimum college GPA of 3.2 required. Lowest grade transferable C-. **General Admission Information:** Application fee $75. Regular application deadline 1/1. Nonfall registration accepted. Admission may be deferred for a maximum of 2 years.

COSTS AND FINANCIAL AID

Annual tuition $44,900. Room and board $13,850. Required fees $708. Average book expense $1,200. **Required Forms and Deadlines:** Business/Farm Supplement; CSS/Financial Aid PROFILE; FAFSA; Noncustodial PROFILE. **Notification of Awards:** Applicants will be notified of awards on or about 4/1. **Types of Aid:** *Need-based scholarships/grants:* College/university scholarship or grant aid from institutional funds; Federal Pell; Private scholarships; SEOG; State scholarships/grants. *Loans:* Direct PLUS loans; Direct Subsidized Stafford Loans; Direct Unsubsidized Stafford Loans. *Student Employment:* Federal Work-Study Program available. Institutional employment available. **Financial Aid Statistics:** 97% needy freshmen, 98% needy undergrads receive need-based scholarship or grant aid. 7% freshmen, 4% undergrads receive non-need-based scholarship or grant aid. 61% freshmen, 72% undergrads receive need-based self-help aid. 6% freshmen, 7% undergrads receive athletic scholarships. 41% freshmen, 39% undergrads receive any aid. 27% undergrads borrow to pay for school. Average cumulative indebtedness $22,497. **Criteria for awarding aid:** *Non-need-based:* Academics, Art, Athletics, Leadership, Minority status, Music/drama, State/district residency.

RICHMOND, THE AMERICAN INTERNATIONAL UNIVERSITY IN LONDON

Queens Road, London, TW10 6JP
Phone: 617-450-5617 • **Financial Aid Phone:** 011-44-20-8332-8244
E-mail: us_admissions@richmond.ac.uk • **CEEB Code:** 823
Fax: 617-450-5601 • **Website:** http://www.richmond.ac.uk/ • **ACT Code:** 5244

This private school was founded in 1972. It has a 6 acre campus.

RATINGS
Admissions Selectivity Rating: 75   **Fire Safety Rating:** 72   **Green Rating:** 60*

STUDENTS AND FACULTY
Enrollment: 906. **Student Body:** 51% female, 49% male, international. Asian 0%,

---

Retention and Graduation: 72% freshmen return for sophomore year. 35% grads go on to further study within 1 year. **Faculty:** Student/faculty ratio 17:1. 41 full-time faculty, 85% hold PhDs, 39% are women. 0% of classes are taught by teaching assistants.

ACADEMICS

Degrees: Bachelor's; **Master's Classes:** Most classes have 20-29 students. Most lab/discussion sessions have 10-19 students. **Special Study Options:** English as a Second Language (ESL); Independent study; Internships; Liberal arts/career combination; Study abroad.

FACILITIES

Housing: Coed dorms; Men's dorms; Women's dorms **Computers:** Administrative functions (other than registration) can be performed online.

CAMPUS LIFE

Environment: Metropolis **Activities:** Choral groups; Dance; Drama/theater; Literary magazine; Music ensembles; Musical theater; Student government; Student newspaper; Yearbook 1 honor societies. **Athletics (Intercollegiate):** *Men:* rugby, soccer. *Women:* rugby. **On-Campus Highlights:** Caffe del Mondo Gourmet Coffee Shop, Wireless Computer Network, Student Common Room, Student Cafeteria

ADMISSIONS

Freshman Academic Profile: 29% in top 10% of high school class, 40% in top 25% of high school class, 94% in top 50% of high school class. 60% from public high schools. **Test Scores:** Minimum paper TOEFL 550. **Basis for Candidate Selection:** *Very important factors considered include:* rigor of secondary school record, academic GPA, application essay, recommendation(s). *Important factors considered include:* extracurricular activities. *Other factors considered include:* interview, talent/ability, character/personal qualities, alumni/ae relation. **Freshman Admission Requirements:** High school diploma is required and GED is accepted *Academic units required:* 4 English, 3 math, 3 science, **Transfer Admission Requirements:** college transcript(s), essay or personal statement, statement of good standing from prior institution(s). Minimum college GPA of 2.5 required. Lowest grade transferable C. **General Admission Information:** Application fee $50. Regular application deadline 3/1. Nonfall registration accepted. Admission may be deferred for a maximum of 1 year.

COSTS AND FINANCIAL AID

Annual tuition $38,000. Room and board $12,900. Average book expense $1,000. **Required Forms and Deadlines:** FAFSA. **Types of Aid:** *Need-based scholarships/grants:* College/university scholarship or grant aid from institutional funds; Private scholarships. **Financial Aid Statistics:** 80% freshmen, 70% undergrads receive any aid. **Criteria for awarding aid:** *Non-need-based:* Academics.

RIDER UNIVERSITY

2083 Lawrenceville Road, Lawrenceville, NJ 08648-3099
Phone: 609-896-5042 • **Financial Aid Phone:** 609-896-5360
E-mail: admissions@rider.edu • **CEEB Code:** 2758
Fax: 609-895-6645 • **Website:** www.rider.edu • **ACT Code:** 2590

This private school was founded in 1865. It has a 280 acre campus.

RATINGS
Admissions Selectivity Rating: 78   **Fire Safety Rating:** 83   **Green Rating:** 93

STUDENTS AND FACULTY
Enrollment: 3,978. **Student Body:** 58% female, 42% male, 23% out-of-state, 3% international (76 countries represented). Asian 5%, African American 12%, Caucasian 61%, Hispanic 14%, Native American <1%, Pacific Islander <1%, Two or more races 3%, Race unknown 2%. **Retention and Graduation:** 78% freshmen return for sophomore year. 8% grads go on to further study within 1 year. 4% grads pursue arts and sciences degrees. 2% grads pursue law degrees. 4% grads pursue business degrees. 2% grads pursue medical degrees. **Faculty:** Student/faculty ratio 11:1. 247 full-time faculty, 99% hold PhDs, 17% are members of minority groups, 49% are women. 0% of classes are taught by teaching assistants.

ACADEMICS
Degrees: Associate; Bachelor's; Master's; Post-Master's certificate **Classes:** Most classes have 10-19 students. Most lab/discussion sessions have 10-19 students. **Most popular majors:** Elementary Education And Teaching;

Business Administration, Management And Operations, Other; Accounting. **Special Study Options:** Cooperative education program; Cross-registration; Distance learning; Double major; English as a Second Language (ESL); Honors program; Independent study; Internships; Liberal arts/career combination; Study abroad; Teacher certification program; Weekend college. Honors programs: The Baccalaureate Honors Program is designed to enrich the educational opportunities for Rider students of proven intellectual capability who choose to become Baccalaureate Scholars. Through a series of team-taught seminars, small classes, personal contact with faculty, colloquia and symposia, as well as independent study opportunities, the scholars extend their ability to think critically, coherently, and systematically about the great themes, ideals and movements of their human heritage. Students may apply, or be invited, as entering freshmen, as currently enrolled freshmen or sophomores, or as transfer freshmen or sophomores. To be considered for the program incoming freshmen must be in the top 10 percent of their high school class. **Disability Services offered to physically disabled students:** Tape recorders; Tutors. **Career services:** Alumni network; Alumni services; Internships

FACILITIES

Housing: Apartments for single students; Coed dorms; Fraternity/sorority housing; Special housing for disabled student; Wellness housing; Women's dorms 73% of campus accessible to physically diasbled. **Special Academic Facilities/Equipment:** Art gallery, Holocaust/Genocide Resource Center **Computers:** Students can register for classes online. Administrative functions (other than registration) can be performed online.

CAMPUS LIFE

Environment: Village **Activities:** Campus Ministries; Choral groups; Concert band; Dance; Drama/theater; International Student Organization; Literary magazine; Model UN; Music ensembles; Musical theater; Opera; Pep band; Radio station; Student government; Student newspaper; Student-run film society; Television station; Yearbook 84 registered organizations, 24 honor societies, 6 religious organizations. 4 fraternities, 8 sororities. **Athletics (Intercollegiate):** *Men:* baseball, basketball, cheerleading, cross-country, diving, golf, soccer, swimming, tennis, track/field (outdoor), wrestling. *Women:* basketball, cheerleading, cross-country, diving, field hockey, soccer, softball, swimming, tennis, track/field (outdoor), volleyball. **On-Campus Highlights:** Residence Hall Quad, Alumni Gym, Student Recreation Center, Daly's Dining Hall/Cranberry Cafe, Academic Quad **Environmental Initiatives:** Signing the American College & University Presidents Climate Commitment and formation of the Energy and Sustainability Steering Committee in 2007 to implement strategic plan establishing sustainability initiatives for the university.

ADMISSIONS

Freshman Academic Profile: Average high school GPA 3.3. 15% in top 10% of high school class, 40% in top 25% of high school class, 75% in top 50% of high school class. **Test Scores:** SAT Math middle 50% range 460-560. SAT EBRW middle 50% range 456-550. ACT middle 50% range 19-24. Minimum internet-based TOEFL 80. Minimum paper TOEFL 550. **Basis for Candidate Selection:** *Very important factors considered include:* rigor of secondary school record, academic GPA, application essay, standardized test scores, recommendation(s). *Other factors considered include:* class rank, interview, extracurricular activities, talent/ability, character/personal qualities, alumni/ae relation, geographical residence, state residency, volunteer work, work experience, level of applicant's interest. **Freshman Admission Requirements:** High school diploma is required and GED is accepted *Academic units required:* 4 English, 3 math, *Academic units recommended:* 4 math, 4 science, 2 science labs, 2 foreign language, 2 social studies, 2 history. **Freshman Admission Statistics:** 9,172 applied, 69.4% admitted, 14% enrolled. **Transfer Admission Requirements:** college transcript(s), essay or personal statement, Minimum college GPA of 2.5 required. Lowest grade transferable C. **General Admission Information:** Application fee $50. Nonfall registration accepted. Admission may be deferred for a maximum of 1 year.

COSTS AND FINANCIAL AID

Annual tuition $39,080. Room and board $14,230. Required fees $740. Average book expense $1,500. **Required Forms and Deadlines:** FAFSA. **Notification of Awards:** Applicants will be notified of awards on a rolling basis beginning 2/1. **Types of Aid:** *Need-based scholarships/grants:* College/university scholarship or grant aid from institutional funds; Federal Pell; Private scholarships; SEOG; State scholarships/grants. *Loans:* Direct PLUS loans; Direct Subsidized Stafford Loans; Direct Unsubsidized Stafford Loans. *Student Employment:* Federal Work-Study Program available. Institutional employment available. **Financial Aid Statistics:** 99% needy freshmen, 98% needy undergrads receive need-based scholarship or grant aid. 14% freshmen, 15% undergrads receive non-need-based scholarship or grant aid. 73% freshmen, 78% undergrads receive need-based self-help aid. 6% freshmen, 6% undergrads receive athletic scholarships. Average cumulative indebtedness $36,032. **Criteria for awarding aid:** *Need-based:* Academics, Alumni affiliation, Athletics, Leadership, Music/drama *Non-need-based:* Academics, Leadership.

RINGLING SCHOOL OF ART & DESIGN

2700 North Tamiami Trail, Sarasota, FL 34234-5895
Phone: 941-351-5100 • **Financial Aid Phone:** 941-359-7532
E-mail: admissions@ringling.edu • **CEEB Code:** 5573
Fax: 941-359-7517 • **Website:** www.ringling.edu • **ACT Code:** 6724

This private school was founded in 1931. It has a 49 acre campus.

RATINGS

Admissions Selectivity Rating: 67   **Fire Safety Rating:** 86   **Green Rating:** 73

STUDENTS AND FACULTY

Enrollment: 1,331. **Student Body:** 65% female, 35% male, 46% out-of-state, 16% international (57 countries represented). Asian 8%, African American 3%, Caucasian 47%, Hispanic 16%, Native American 1%, Pacific Islander <1%, Two or more races 3%, Race unknown 6%.
Retention and Graduation: 87% freshmen return for sophomore year. 5% grads go on to further study within 1 year. **Faculty:** Student/faculty ratio 11:1. 102 full-time faculty, 61% hold PhDs, 5% are members of minority groups, 30% are women. 0% of classes are taught by teaching assistants.

ACADEMICS

Degrees: Bachelor's **Classes:** Most classes have 30-39 students. **Most popular majors:** Animation, Interactive Technology, Video Graphics And Special Effects; Illustration; Game And Interactive Media Design. **Special Study Options:** Cross-registration; Dual enrollment; English as a Second Language (ESL); Exchange student program (domestic); Independent study; Internships; Study abroad. **Disability Services offered to physically disabled students:** Note-taking services; Reader services; Tape recorders; Tutors. **Career services:** Alumni network; Alumni services; Career assessment; Career/job search classes; Internships; Regional alumni

FACILITIES

Housing: Apartments for married students; Apartments for single students; Coed dorms; Men's dorms; Special housing for disabled student; Theme housing; Wellness housing; Women's dorms 98% of campus accessible to physically diasbled. **Special Academic Facilities/Equipment:** Selby Gallery, Richard & Barbara Basch Gallery, Crossley Gallery, Goldstein Gallery, Englewood Art Center and Galleries, Hammon Commons Gallery, Longboat Key Art Center and Galleries, Willis A. Smith Construction, Inc. Galleries, Diane Roskamp Exhibition Halls, Verman Kimbrough Memorial Library, Academic Building, College book and supply store, College owned furnished apartments and residence halls, state-of-the-art studios, photography studios, Hammon Commons Dining Hall, The Brickman Cafe, Outtakes Cafe, Susan A. Palmer Recreation & Wellness Center, project rooms, labs, laundry facilities, mail room. **Computers:** 60% of classrooms, 100% of dorms, 100% of libraries, 100% of dining areas, 100% of student union, 60% of common outdoor areas have wireless network access. Students can register for classes online. Administrative functions (other than registration) can be performed online.

CAMPUS LIFE

Environment: City **Activities:** Campus Ministries; Choral groups; Dance; Drama/theater; International Student Organization; Student government; Television station 22 registered organizations, 2 religious organizations. **On-Campus Highlights:** Ulla Searing Student Center and deck, Selby Gallery, Crossley Gallery, Goldstein Library, Hammond Commons **Environmental Initiatives:** The College has an active sustainability committee comprised of staff, faculty and student members. the charge of the committee is to review current and proposed sustainability practices, provide oversight in the implementation of these practices and to raise awareness of sustainability practices.

ADMISSIONS

Freshman Academic Profile: Average high school GPA 3.3. **Test Scores:** Minimum internet-based TOEFL 61. Minimum paper TOEFL 500. **Basis for Candidate Selection:** *Very important factors considered include:* rigor of secondary school record, academic GPA, recommendation(s), talent/ability. *Important factors considered include:* application essay. *Other factors considered include:* interview, extracurricular activities, alumni/ae relation, geographical residence, volunteer work, work experience, level of applicant's interest. **Freshman Admission Requirements:** High school diploma is required and GED is accepted **Freshman Admission Statistics:** 1,752 applied, 78.1% admitted, 26% enrolled. **Transfer Admission Requirements:** High school transcript, college transcript(s), essay or personal statement, Minimum college GPA of 2.0 required. Lowest grade transferable C. **General Admission Information:** Application fee $70. Nonfall registration accepted. Admission may be deferred for a maximum of 2 years.

COSTS AND FINANCIAL AID

Required Forms and Deadlines: FAFSA. **Notification of Awards:** Applicants will be notified of awards on a rolling basis beginning 4/1. **Types of Aid:** *Need-based scholarships/grants:* College/university scholarship or grant aid from institutional funds; Federal Pell; Private scholarships; SEOG; State scholarships/grants. *Loans:* Direct PLUS loans; Direct Subsidized Stafford Loans; Direct Unsubsidized Stafford Loans. *Student Employment:* Federal Work-Study Program available. Institutional employment available. **Financial Aid Statistics:** 100% needy freshmen, 100% needy undergrads receive need-based scholarship or grant aid. 5% freshmen, 3% undergrads receive non-need-based scholarship or grant aid. 93% freshmen, 94% undergrads receive need-based self-help aid. 0% freshmen, 0% undergrads receive athletic scholarships. 96% freshmen, 76% undergrads receive any aid. 63% undergrads borrow to pay for school. Average cumulative indebtedness $44,384. **Criteria for awarding aid:** *Need-based:* Academics, Art *Non-need-based:* Academics, Art.

RIPON COLLEGE

Best Colleges

PO Box 248, Ripon, WI 54971
Phone: 920-748-8337 • **Financial Aid Phone:** 920-748-8301
E-mail: adminfo@ripon.edu • **CEEB Code:** 1664
Fax: 920-748-8335 • **Website:** www.ripon.edu • **ACT Code:** 4636

This private school was founded in 1851. It has a 250 acre campus.

RATINGS

Admissions Selectivity Rating: 81   **Fire Safety Rating:** 76   **Green Rating:** 65

STUDENTS AND FACULTY

Enrollment: 740. **Student Body:** 54% female, 46% male, 30% out-of-state, 4% international (12 countries represented). Asian 1%, African American 4%, Caucasian 80%, Hispanic 9%, Native American <1%, Pacific Islander 0%, Two or more races 3%, Race unknown <1%. **Retention and Graduation:** 71% freshmen return for sophomore year. 62% freshmen graduate within 4 years. 68% freshmen graduate within 6 years. 29% grads go on to further study within 1 year. 17% grads pursue arts and sciences degrees. 5% grads pursue law degrees. 1% grads pursue business degrees. 2% grads pursue medical degrees. **Faculty:** Student/faculty ratio 14:1. 61 full-time faculty, 98% hold PhDs, 10% are members of minority groups, 36% are women. 0% of classes are taught by teaching assistants.

ACADEMICS

Degrees: Bachelor's **Classes:** Most classes have 10-19 students. **Most popular majors:** Health And Physical Education/Fitness, General; Business/Commerce, General; History, General. **Special Study Options:** Double major; Exchange student program (domestic); Independent study; Internships; Student-designed major; Study abroad; Teacher certification program. **Disability Services offered to physically disabled students:** Tutors. **Career services:** Alumni network; Career assessment; Internships; Regional alumni

FACILITIES

Housing: Apartments for single students; Coed dorms; Fraternity/sorority housing; Men's dorms; Special housing for disabled student; Theme housing; Women's dorms **Special Academic Facilities/Equipment:** Caestecker Art Gallery, West Hall Museum, Farr Hall Greenhouse, Communicating Plus, Ceresco Prairie Conservancy, Lane Library Archives, language labs, WRPN college radio **Computers:** 2% of classrooms, 30% of libraries, 100% of dining areas, 60% of student union, have wireless network access.

CAMPUS LIFE

Environment: Village **Activities:** Campus Ministries; Choral groups; Concert band; Dance; Drama/theater; International Student Organization; Jazz band; Literary magazine; Music ensembles; Musical theater; Pep band; Radio station; Student government; Student newspaper; Student-run film society; Symphony orchestra; Television station; Yearbook 45 registered organizations, 13 honor societies, 2 religious organizations. 5 fraternities, 3 sororities. **Athletics (Intercollegiate):** *Men:* baseball, basketball, cross-country, cycling, football, golf, soccer, swimming, tennis, track/field (outdoor), track/field (indoor). *Women:* basketball, cross-country, cycling, golf, soccer, softball, swimming, tennis, track/field (outdoor), track/field (indoor), volleyball. **On-Campus Highlights:** Ceresco Prairie Conservancy, Caestecker Art Gallery, Great Hall, Willmore Center, Lounge and Starbucks Coffee

ADMISSIONS

Freshman Academic Profile: Average high school GPA 3.4. 16% in top 10% of high school class, 43% in top 25% of high school class, 79% in top 50% of high school class. 75% from public high schools. **Test Scores:** SAT Math middle 50% range 520-650. SAT EBRW middle 50% range 520-610. ACT middle 50% range 20-26. Minimum internet-based TOEFL 79. Minimum paper TOEFL 550. **Basis for Candidate Selection:** *Very important factors considered include:* rigor of secondary school record, interview. *Important factors considered include:* class rank, academic GPA, extracurricular activities, character/personal qualities. *Other factors considered include:* application essay, standardized test scores, recommendation(s), talent/ability, volunteer work. **Freshman Admission Requirements:** High school diploma is required and GED is accepted *Academic units required:* 4 English, 2 math, 2 science, 2 social studies, *Academic units recommended:* 4 math, 4 science, 2 foreign language, 4 social studies. **Freshman Admission Statistics:** 2,504 applied, 67.5% admitted, 14% enrolled. **Transfer Admission Requirements:** college transcript(s), essay or personal statement, statement of good standing from prior institution(s). Minimum college GPA of 2.0 required. Lowest grade transferable C. **General Admission Information:** Application fee $30. Priority deadline 3/15. Nonfall registration accepted. Admission may be deferred for a maximum of 1 year.

COSTS AND FINANCIAL AID

Annual tuition $43,508. Room and board $8,400. Required fees $300. Average book expense $750. **Required Forms and Deadlines:** FAFSA. **Notification of Awards:** Applicants will be notified of awards on a rolling basis beginning 3/1. **Types of Aid:** *Need-based scholarships/grants:* College/university scholarship or grant aid from institutional funds; Federal Pell; Private scholarships; SEOG; State scholarships/grants. *Loans:* Direct PLUS loans; Direct Subsidized Stafford Loans; Direct Unsubsidized Stafford Loans. *Student Employment:* Federal Work-Study Program available. Institutional employment available. **Financial Aid Statistics:** 100% needy freshmen, 100% needy undergrads receive need-based scholarship or grant aid. 22% freshmen, 16% undergrads receive non-need-based scholarship or grant aid. 74% freshmen, 81% undergrads receive need-based self-help aid. 0% freshmen, 0% undergrads receive athletic scholarships. 95% freshmen, 96% undergrads receive any aid. 80% undergrads borrow to pay for school. Average cumulative indebtedness $35,213. **Criteria for awarding aid:** *Non-need-based:* Academics, Alumni affiliation, Art, Leadership, Minority status, Music/drama, Religious affiliation, State/district residency.

See page 1010.

RIVIER COLLEGE

420 South Main Street, Nashua, NH 03060
Phone: 603-897-8219 • **Financial Aid Phone:** 603-897-8810
E-mail: rivadmit@rivier.edu • **CEEB Code:** 3728
Fax: 603-891-1799 • **Website:** www.rivier.edu • **ACT Code:** 2520

This private school, affiliated with the Roman Catholic Church, was founded in 1933. It has a 68 acre campus.

RATINGS

Admissions Selectivity Rating: 74   **Fire Safety Rating:** 89   **Green Rating:** 60*

STUDENTS AND FACULTY

Enrollment: 1,370. **Student Body:** 85% female, 15% male, 38% out-of-state, 0% international (12 countries represented). Asian 2%, African American 2%, Caucasian 75%, Hispanic 5%, Native American 1%, Pacific Islander 0%, Two or more races <1%, Race unknown 16%. **Retention and Graduation:** 78% freshmen return for sophomore year. **Faculty:** Student/faculty ratio 17:1. 68 full-time faculty, 75% hold PhDs, 65% are women. 0% of classes are taught by teaching assistants.

ACADEMICS

Degrees: Associate; Bachelor's; Certificate; Doctoral; Master's; Post-Bachelor's certificate; Post-Master's certificate **Classes:** Most classes have 20-29 students. Most lab/discussion sessions have 20-29 students. **Special Study Options:** Cross-registration; Distance learning; Double major; Dual enrollment; Independent study; Internships; Liberal arts/career combination; Student-designed major; Teacher certification program. **Disability Services offered to physically disabled students:** Note-taking services; Reader services; Tape recorders; Tutors. **Career services:** Alumni services; Career assessment; Career/job search classes; Internships

FACILITIES

Housing: Coed dorms; Wellness housing 75% of campus accessible to physically diasbled. **Special Academic Facilities/Equipment:** Art gallery, Early Childhood Center/Laboratory School, language lab, TV microscope, video/laser disk system, photospectrometer, high-performance liquid chromatograph, digital imaging lab, several art studios including a photography darkroom. **Computers:** 100% of classrooms, 100% of dorms, 100% of libraries, 100% of dining areas, 100% of student union, 100% of common outdoor areas have wireless network access. Administrative functions (other than registration) can be performed online.

CAMPUS LIFE

Environment: City **Activities:** Campus Ministries; Choral groups; Dance; Drama/theater; International Student Organization; Model UN; Music ensembles; Student government; Television station; Yearbook 30 registered organizations, 2 honor societies, 2 religious organizations. **Athletics (Intercollegiate):** *Men:* baseball, basketball, cross-country, soccer, volleyball. *Women:* basketball, cross-country, soccer, softball, volleyball. Regina Library, Muldoon Fitness Center, Dion Student Center

ADMISSIONS

Freshman Academic Profile: Average high school GPA 3.0. 6% in top 10% of high school class, 27% in top 25% of high school class, 71% in top 50% of high school class. **Test Scores:** SAT Math middle 50% range 410-510. SAT EBRW middle 50% range 410-510. ACT middle 50% range 17-21. Minimum paper TOEFL 500. **Basis for Candidate Selection:** *Very important factors considered include:* rigor of secondary school record, academic GPA. *Important factors considered include:* class rank, application essay, standardized test scores, extracurricular activities, talent/ability, volunteer work, work experience. *Other factors considered include:* recommendation(s), interview, character/personal qualities. **Freshman Admission Requirements:** High school diploma is required and GED is accepted *Academic units recommended:* 4 English, 3 math, 1 science, 1 science labs, 2 foreign language, 2 social studies, 1 history, 3 academic electives. **Freshman Admission Statistics:** 665 applied, 81.7% admitted, 36% enrolled. **Transfer Admission Requirements:** essay or personal statement, Minimum college GPA of 2.0 required. Lowest grade transferable C. **General Admission Information:** Application fee $25. Nonfall registration accepted. Admission may be deferred for a maximum of 1 year.

COSTS AND FINANCIAL AID

Annual tuition $25,410. Room and board $9,798. Required fees $600. Average book expense $1,200. **Required Forms and Deadlines:** FAFSA. **Notification of Awards:** Applicants will be notified of awards on a rolling basis beginning 3/1. **Types of Aid:** *Need-based scholarships/grants:* College/university scholarship or grant aid from institutional funds; Federal Pell; Private scholarships; SEOG; State scholarships/grants. *Loans:* Direct PLUS loans; Direct Subsidized Stafford Loans; Direct Unsubsidized Stafford Loans. *Student Employment:* Federal Work-Study Program available. Institutional employment available. **Financial Aid Statistics:** 100% needy freshmen, 91% needy undergrads receive need-based scholarship or grant aid. 4% freshmen, 4% undergrads receive non-need-based scholarship or grant aid. 91% freshmen, 93% undergrads receive need-based self-help aid. 0% freshmen, 0% undergrads receive athletic scholarships. 82% freshmen, 89% undergrads receive any aid. **Criteria for awarding aid:** *Need-based:* Academics *Non-need-based:* Academics, Alumni affiliation, Leadership.

ROANOKE BIBLE COLLEGE

The Emma Willard House, Elizabeth City, NC 27909-4054
Phone: 252-334-2028 · **Financial Aid Phone:** 252-334-2020
E-mail: admissions@roanokebible.edu
Fax: 252-334-2064 · **ACT Code:** 3153

This private school, affiliated with the Christian Church/Churches of Christ, was founded in 1948. It has a 20 acre campus.

RATINGS

Admissions Selectivity Rating: 86   **Fire Safety Rating:** 76   **Green Rating:** 60*

STUDENTS AND FACULTY

Retention and Graduation: 53% freshmen return for sophomore year. **Faculty:** Student/faculty ratio 10:1. 9 full-time faculty, 56% hold PhDs, 0% are members of minority groups, 33% are women. 0% of classes are taught by teaching assistants.

ACADEMICS

Degrees: Associate; Bachelor's; Certificate **Classes:** Most classes have 10-19 students. Most lab/discussion sessions have fewer than 10 students. **Most popular majors:** Bible/Biblical Studies. **Special Study Options:** Distance learning; Double major; Dual enrollment; Internships. **Disability Services offered to physically disabled students:** Tape recorders; Tutors.

FACILITIES

Housing: Apartments for married students; Apartments for single students; Men's dorms; Special housing for disabled student; Women's dorms 90% of campus accessible to physically diasbled. **Computers:** 80% of classrooms, 100% of libraries, have wireless network access.

CAMPUS LIFE

Environment: Village **Activities:** Choral groups; Drama/theater; Music ensembles; Musical theater; Student government; Yearbook 1 honor societies. **Athletics (Intercollegiate):** *Men:* basketball. *Women:* basketball, volleyball. **On-Campus Highlights:** On the Pasquotank River, New Married Housing apartments, New student life center **Environmental Initiatives:** Geothermal heating & cooling

ADMISSIONS

Freshman Academic Profile: Average high school GPA 2.8. 2% in top 10% of high school class, 14% in top 25% of high school class, 37% in top 50% of high school class. 87% from public high schools. **Test Scores:** SAT Math middle 50% range 420-590. SAT EBRW middle 50% range 410-565. Minimum internet-based TOEFL 80. Minimum paper TOEFL 500. **Basis for Candidate Selection:** *Very important factors considered include:* class rank, academic GPA, standardized test scores, recommendation(s), character/personal qualities, religious affiliation/commitment. *Important factors considered include:* rigor of secondary school record, application essay. *Other factors considered include:* interview, extracurricular activities, talent/ability, volunteer work, work experience, level of applicant's interest. **Freshman Admission Requirements:** High school diploma is required and GED is accepted *Academic units required:* 4 English, 3 math, 3 science, 2 science labs, 2 social studies, 2 history, 4 academic electives, *Academic units recommended:* 6 foreign language, 1 computer science. **Freshman Admission Statistics:** 127 applied, 55.9% admitted, 58% enrolled. **Transfer Admission Requirements:** college transcript(s), essay or personal statement, statement of good standing from prior institution(s). Minimum college GPA of 2.0 required. Lowest grade transferable C. **General Admission Information:** Application fee $50. Nonfall registration accepted. Admission may be deferred for a maximum of 1 semester.

COSTS AND FINANCIAL AID

Required Forms and Deadlines: FAFSA; Institution's own financial aid form. **Notification of Awards:** Applicants will be notified of awards on a rolling basis beginning 5/1. **Types of Aid:** *Need-based scholarships/grants:* College/university scholarship or grant aid from institutional funds; Federal Pell; Private scholarships; SEOG; State scholarships/grants. *Loans: Student Employment:* Federal Work-Study Program available. Institutional employment available. **Financial Aid Statistics:** 100% needy freshmen, 100% needy undergrads receive need-based scholarship or grant aid. 29% freshmen, 23% undergrads receive non-need-based scholarship or grant aid. 68% freshmen, 82% undergrads receive need-based self-help aid. 0% freshmen, 0% undergrads receive athletic scholarships. 88% freshmen, 90% undergrads receive any aid. **Criteria for awarding aid:** *Non-need-based:* Academics, Alumni affiliation, Art, Athletics, Leadership, Music/drama, Religious affiliation.

ROANOKE COLLEGE

221 College Lane, Salem, VA 24153-3794
Phone: 540-375-2270 · **Financial Aid Phone:** 540-375-2235
E-mail: admissions@roanoke.edu · **CEEB Code:** 5571
Fax: 540-375-2267 · **Website:** www.roanoke.edu · **ACT Code:** 4392

This private school, affiliated with the Lutheran Church, was founded in 1842. It has a 80 acre campus.

RATINGS

Admissions Selectivity Rating: 81   **Fire Safety Rating:** 89   **Green Rating:** 76

STUDENTS AND FACULTY

Enrollment: 1,990. **Student Body:** 58% female, 42% male, 48% out-of-state, 3% international (32 countries represented). Asian 1%, African American 6%,

Caucasian 80%, Hispanic 5%, Native American <1%, Pacific Islander <1%, Two or more races 5%, Race unknown 0%.
Retention and Graduation: 84% freshmen return for sophomore year. 62% freshmen graduate within 4 years. 67% freshmen graduate within 6 years. 21% grads go on to further study within 1 year. **Faculty:** Student/faculty ratio 11:1, 165 full-time faculty, 88% hold PhDs, 10% are members of minority groups, 52% are women. 0% of classes are taught by teaching assistants.

ACADEMICS

Degrees: Bachelor's **Classes:** Most classes have 10-19 students. Most lab/discussion sessions have 10-19 students. **Most popular majors:** Biology/Biological Sciences, General; Psychology, General; Business Administration And Management, General. **Special Study Options:** Accelerated program; Cross-registration; Distance learning; Double major; Dual enrollment; English as a Second Language (ESL); Honors program; Independent study; Internships; Liberal arts/career combination; Study abroad; Teacher certification program. Honors programs: The Honors Program is designed for students with excellent academic performance, broad extracurricular interests, and leadership abilities. The Honors Program has a unique core curriculum as well as an Honors Portfolio of supplemental activities and service involvements. A special Distinction Project provides a uniquely integrated experience, leading to a distinct recognition on the diploma and transcript. Honors housing and a strong honors community are also key parts of the program. Roanoke also offers the Fellows Program which gives students practical experience. Projects in research, entrepreneurship, service leadership and Information Technology are among the current offerings. **Disability Services offered to physically disabled students:** Note-taking services; Reader services; Tape recorders; Tutors. **Career services:** Alumni network; Alumni services; Career assessment; Career/job search classes; Internships; Regional alumni.

FACILITIES

Housing: Apartments for single students; Coed dorms; Fraternity/sorority housing; Special housing for disabled student; Special housing for international students; Theme housing; Women's dorms 80% of campus accessible to physically diasbled. **Special Academic Facilities/Equipment:** Fine arts center and gallery, community research center, language lab, church and society center. New athletic/health facility including indoor track and performance gymnasium. **Computers:** 100% of classrooms, 100% of libraries, 100% of dining areas, 100% of student union, 50% of common outdoor areas have wireless network access. Students can register for classes online. Administrative functions (other than registration) can be performed online.

CAMPUS LIFE

Environment: City **Activities:** Campus Ministries; Choral groups; Concert band; Dance; Drama/theater; International Student Organization; Jazz band; Literary magazine; Model UN; Music ensembles; Pep band; Radio station; Student government; Student newspaper; Student-run film society 85 registered organizations, 30 honor societies, 7 religious organizations. 4 fraternities, 4 sororities. **Athletics (Intercollegiate):** *Men:* baseball, basketball, cross-country, golf, lacrosse, soccer, tennis, track/field (outdoor), track/field (indoor). *Women:* basketball, cross-country, field hockey, lacrosse, soccer, softball, tennis, track/field (outdoor), track/field (indoor), volleyball. **On-Campus Highlights:** Cregger Center & Belk Fitness Center, Kerr Stadium, Fintel Library (& Little Green Hive coffee shop), Colket Center, New Hall (new residence hall) **Environmental Initiatives:** Lucas Hall was completely renovated and is LEED-Silver Certified. A new residence hall and a major new athletic center/campus community center were also built recently, to high efficiency environmental awareness standards, although the college is not seeking formal certification.

ADMISSIONS

Freshman Academic Profile: Average high school GPA 3.5. 16% in top 10% of high school class, 39% in top 25% of high school class, 77% in top 50% of high school class. 83% from public high schools. **Test Scores:** SAT Math middle 50% range 510-600. SAT EBRW middle 50% range 530-630. ACT middle 50% range 22-27. Minimum internet-based TOEFL 80. **Basis for Candidate Selection:** *Very important factors considered include:* rigor of secondary school record, academic GPA, character/personal qualities. *Important factors considered include:* class rank, standardized test scores, interview, extracurricular activities, level of applicant's interest. *Other factors considered include:* application essay, recommendation(s), talent/ability, alumni/ae relation, racial/ethnic status, volunteer work, work experience. **Freshman Admission Requirements:** High school diploma is required and GED is accepted *Academic units required:* 4 English, 3 math, 2 science, 2 science labs, 2 foreign language, 2 social studies, 5 academic electives, *Academic units recommended:* 2 foreign language. **Freshman Admission Statistics:** 5,117 applied, 67.2% admitted, 16% enrolled. **Transfer Admission Requirements:** High school transcript, college transcript(s), statement of good standing from prior institution(s). Minimum college GPA of 2.2 required. Lowest grade transferable C-. **General Admission Information:** Application fee $30. Regular application deadline 3/15. Nonfall registration accepted. Admission may be deferred for a maximum of 2 years.

COSTS AND FINANCIAL AID

Annual tuition $42,446. Room and board $13,690. Required fees $1,584. Average book expense $1,000. **Required Forms and Deadlines:** FAFSA; State aid form. **Notification of Awards:** Applicants will be notified of awards on a rolling basis beginning 12/15. **Types of Aid:** *Need-based scholarships/grants:* College/university scholarship or grant aid from institutional funds; Federal Pell; Private scholarships; SEOG; State scholarships/grants. *Loans:* Direct PLUS loans; Direct Subsidized Stafford Loans; Direct Unsubsidized Stafford Loans. *Student Employment:* Federal Work-Study Program available. Institutional employment available. **Financial Aid Statistics:** 99% needy freshmen, 98% needy undergrads receive need-based scholarship or grant aid. 100% freshmen, 97% undergrads receive non-need-based scholarship or grant aid. 75% freshmen, 77% undergrads receive need-based self-help aid. 0% freshmen, 0% undergrads receive athletic scholarships. 100% freshmen, 99% undergrads receive any aid. 77% undergrads borrow to pay for school. Average cumulative indebtedness $39,175. **Criteria for awarding aid:** *Need-based:* Academics, Minority status, Religious affiliation *Non-need-based:* Academics, Art, Minority status, Music/drama, Religious affiliation.

ROBERT MORRIS UNIVERSITY

6001 University Boulevard, Moon Township, PA 15108-1189
Phone: 412-397-5200 • **Financial Aid Phone:** (412) 397-6250
E-mail: admissionsoffice@rmu.edu • **CEEB Code:** 2769
Fax: 412-397-2425 • **Website:** www.rmu.edu • **ACT Code:** 3674

This private school was founded in 1921. It has a 230 acre campus.

RATINGS
Admissions Selectivity Rating: 71   **Fire Safety Rating:** 93   **Green Rating:** 60*

STUDENTS AND FACULTY
Enrollment: 4,213. **Student Body:** 43% female, 57% male, 13% out-of-state, 12% international (37 countries represented). Asian 1%, African American 6%, Caucasian 73%, Hispanic 2%, Native American <1%, Pacific Islander <1%, Two or more races 3%, Race unknown 2%.
Retention and Graduation: 81% freshmen return for sophomore year. 47% freshmen graduate within 4 years. 61% freshmen graduate within 6 years. 6% grads go on to further study within 1 year. **Faculty:** Student/faculty ratio 15:1. 202 full-time faculty, 91% hold PhDs, 21% are members of minority groups, 47% are women. 0% of classes are taught by teaching assistants.

ACADEMICS
Degrees: Bachelor's; Doctoral/Professional; Doctoral/Research; Master's; Post-Bachelor's certificate **Classes:** Most classes have fewer than 10 students. Most lab/discussion sessions have 10-19 students. **Most popular majors:** Engineering; Nursing; Registered Nursing/Registered Nurse. **Special Study Options:** Cooperative education program; Cross-registration; Distance learning; Double major; Honors program; Independent study; Internships; Study abroad; Teacher certification program. Honors programs: International Honors Program. **Disability Services offered to physically disabled students:** Note-taking services; Reader services; Tape recorders; Tutors. **Career services:** Alumni network; Alumni services; Career assessment; Career/job search classes; Internships; Regional alumni

FACILITIES
Housing: Apartments for single students; Coed dorms; Fraternity/sorority housing; Men's dorms; Special housing for disabled student; Theme housing 85% of campus accessible to physically diasbled. **Computers:** 50% of classrooms, 75% of libraries, 100% of dining areas, 100% of student union, 25% of common outdoor areas have wireless network access. Students can register for classes online. Administrative functions (other than registration) can be performed online.

CAMPUS LIFE
Environment: Metropolis **Activities:** Campus Ministries; Choral groups; Concert band; Dance; Drama/theater; International Student Organization; Jazz band; Literary magazine; Marching band; Music ensembles; Musical theater; Pep band; Radio station; Student government; Student newspaper; Student-run film society; Television station; Yearbook 97 registered organizations, 6 honor societies, 5 religious organizations. 4 fraternities, 3 sororities. **Athletics (Intercollegiate):** *Men:* basketball, football, golf, ice hockey, lacrosse, soccer, tennis, track/field (outdoor), track/field (indoor). *Women:* basketball, crew/rowing, field hockey, golf, ice hockey, lacrosse, soccer, softball, tennis, track/field (outdoor), track/field (indoor), volleyball. **On-Campus Highlights:** Student Center/PNC Cafe, Residence Halls, Walton Stadium, Arena, Health Club **Environmental Initiatives:** Recycling paper, cardboard, plastic, bottles and cans, and florescent bulbs

ADMISSIONS

Freshman Academic Profile: Average high school GPA 3.5. 14% in top 10% of high school class, 41% in top 25% of high school class, 75% in top 50% of high school class. 89% from public high schools. **Test Scores:** SAT Math middle 50% range 510-600. SAT EBRW middle 50% range 510-600. ACT middle 50% range 21-27. Minimum internet-based TOEFL 61. Minimum paper TOEFL 500. **Basis for Candidate Selection:** *Very important factors considered include:* academic GPA, standardized test scores. *Important factors considered include:* rigor of secondary school record, class rank, interview, extracurricular activities, talent/ability, character/personal qualities, level of applicant's interest. *Other factors considered include:* application essay, recommendation(s), alumni/ae relation, geographical residence, volunteer work, work experience. **Freshman Admission Requirements:** High school diploma is required and GED is accepted *Academic units required:* 4 English, 3 math, 2 science, 4 social studies, 3 academic electives, *Academic units recommended:* 2 foreign language. **Freshman Admission Statistics:** 2,459 applied, admitted, 15% enrolled. **Transfer Admission Requirements:** college transcript(s), statement of good standing from prior institution(s). Minimum college GPA of 2.0 required. Lowest grade transferable C. **General Admission Information:** Application fee $30. Nonfall registration accepted. Admission may be deferred for a maximum of 1 year.

COSTS AND FINANCIAL AID

Annual tuition $28,210. Room and board $11,180. Required fees $1,210. Average book expense $1,200. **Required Forms and Deadlines:** FAFSA. **Notification of Awards:** Applicants will be notified of awards on a rolling basis beginning 11/15. **Types of Aid:** *Need-based scholarships/grants:* College/university scholarship or grant aid from institutional funds; Federal Pell; Private scholarships; SEOG; State scholarships/grants. *Loans:* Direct PLUS loans; Direct Subsidized Stafford Loans; Direct Unsubsidized Stafford Loans. *Student Employment:* Federal Work-Study Program available. Institutional employment available. **Financial Aid Statistics:** 99% needy freshmen, 98% needy undergrads receive need-based scholarship or grant aid. 10% freshmen, 10% undergrads receive non-need-based scholarship or grant aid. 88% freshmen, 87% undergrads receive need-based self-help aid. 3% freshmen, 3% undergrads receive athletic scholarships. 80% freshmen, 71% undergrads receive any aid. 82% undergrads borrow to pay for school. Average cumulative indebtedness $39,431. **Criteria for awarding aid:** *Non-need-based:* Academics, Athletics.

ROBERT MORRIS UNIVERSITY (IL)

401 South State Street, Chicago, IL 60605
Phone: 800-762-5960 • **Financial Aid Phone:** 312-935-4077
E-mail: enroll@robertmorris.edu • **CEEB Code:** 1670
Fax: 312-935-4440 • **ACT Code:** 1121

This private school was founded in 1913.

RATINGS
Admissions Selectivity Rating: 84   **Fire Safety Rating:** 97   **Green Rating:** 72

STUDENTS AND FACULTY
Enrollment: 3,196. **Student Body:** 53% female, 47% male, 8% out-of-state, 1% international (27 countries represented). Asian 3%, African American 33%, Caucasian 38%, Hispanic 23%, Native American <1%, Pacific Islander <1%, Two or more races 1%, Race unknown 1%.
Retention and Graduation: 49% freshmen return for sophomore year. 16% grads go on to further study within 1 year. **Faculty:** Student/faculty ratio 20:1. 124 full-time faculty, 27% hold PhDs, 23% are members of minority groups, 48% are women.

ACADEMICS
Degrees: Associate; Bachelor's; **Master's Classes:** Most classes have 10-19 students. Most lab/discussion sessions have 20-29 students. **Most popular majors:** Information Technology; Graphic Design; Business Administration And Management, General. **Special Study Options:** Accelerated program; Double major; Honors program; Internships; Study abroad. **Disability Services offered to physically disabled students:** Note-taking services; Reader services; Tape recorders; Tutors. **Career services:** Alumni network; Alumni services; Career assessment; Career/job search classes; Internships

FACILITIES
Housing: Apartments for single students; Coed dorms 100% of campus accessible to physically diasbled.

CAMPUS LIFE
Environment: Metropolis **Activities:** Choral groups; Dance; International Student Organization; Jazz band; Literary magazine; Marching band; Pep

band; Student newspaper. Technology Library, Integration Center, Passport Chicago, Performing Arts Center, Art Gallery **Environmental Initiatives:** The establishment of the RMU Sustainability Council, which is represented on our Academic Council and was issued a Proclamation for its work.

ADMISSIONS

Freshman Academic Profile: Average high school GPA 2.7. 6% in top 10% of high school class, 19% in top 25% of high school class, 46% in top 50% of high school class. **Test Scores:** ACT middle 50% range 16-22. Minimum internet-based TOEFL 80. Minimum paper TOEFL 550. **Basis for Candidate Selection:** *Very important factors considered include:* rigor of secondary school record, class rank, academic GPA, interview. *Important factors considered include:* level of applicant's interest. *Other factors considered include:* standardized test scores, extracurricular activities, talent/ability, character/personal qualities, volunteer work, work experience. **Freshman Admission Requirements:** High school diploma is required and GED is accepted *Academic units recommended:* 4 English, 3 math, 2 science, 1 science labs, 2 foreign language, 2 social studies, 3 history. **Freshman Admission Statistics:** 2,786 applied, 34.0% admitted, enrolled. **General Admission Information:** Application fee $20. Nonfall registration accepted. Admission may be deferred for a maximum of 1 year.

COSTS AND FINANCIAL AID

Annual tuition $22,800. Room and board $11,754. **Required Forms and Deadlines:** FAFSA. **Types of Aid:** *Need-based scholarships/grants:* College/university scholarship or grant aid from institutional funds; Federal Pell; Private scholarships; SEOG; State scholarships/grants. *Loans: Student Employment:* Federal Work-Study Program available. **Financial Aid Statistics:** 83% needy freshmen, 80% needy undergrads receive need-based scholarship or grant aid. 43% freshmen, 73% undergrads receive non-need-based scholarship or grant aid. 89% freshmen, 81% undergrads receive need-based self-help aid. 16% freshmen, 17% undergrads receive athletic scholarships. 92% freshmen, 92% undergrads receive any aid. **Criteria for awarding aid:** *Need-based:* Academics, Art, Athletics, Leadership, Music/drama *Non-need-based:* Academics, Art, Athletics, Leadership, Music/drama, State/district residency.

ROBERTS WESLEYAN COLLEGE

2301 Westside Drive, Rochester, NY 14624-1997
Phone: 585-594-6400 • **Financial Aid Phone:** 585-594-6150
E-mail: admissions@roberts.edu • **CEEB Code:** 2805
Fax: 585-594-6371 • **Website:** www.roberts.edu • **ACT Code:** 2868

This private school, affiliated with the Free Methodist Church, was founded in 1866. It has a 188 acre campus.

RATINGS
Admissions Selectivity Rating: 86   **Fire Safety Rating:** 73   **Green Rating:** 60*

STUDENTS AND FACULTY
Enrollment: 1,288. **Student Body:** 69% female, 31% male, 7% out-of-state, 3% international (33 countries represented). Asian 1%, African American 12%, Caucasian 75%, Hispanic 5%, Native American <1%, Pacific Islander <1%, Two or more races 2%, Race unknown 2%.
Retention and Graduation: 80% freshmen return for sophomore year. 24% grads go on to further study within 1 year. **Faculty:** 92 full-time faculty, 72% hold PhDs, 7% are members of minority groups, 52% are women. 0% of classes are taught by teaching assistants.

ACADEMICS
Degrees: Bachelor's; **Master's Classes:** Most classes have 20-29 students. Most lab/discussion sessions have 10-19 students. **Most popular majors:** Elementary Education And Teaching; Music Teacher Education. **Special Study Options:** Accelerated program; Cross-registration; Distance learning; Double major; English as a Second Language (ESL); Honors program; Independent study; Internships; Liberal arts/career combination; Student-designed major; Study abroad; Teacher certification program. Combined degree programs: BA/MEng. **Disability Services offered to physically disabled students:** Note-taking services; Reader services; Tape recorders; Tutors. **Career services:** Alumni network; Alumni services; Career assessment; Internships; Regional alumni

FACILITIES
Housing: Apartments for married students; Apartments for single students; Coed dorms; Men's dorms; Special housing for disabled student; Women's dorms 71% of campus accessible to physically diasbled. **Special Academic Facilities/Equipment:** Davison Art Gallery **Computers:** 100% of classrooms,

100% of dorms, 100% of libraries, 100% of dining areas, 100% of student union, 70% of common outdoor areas have wireless network access. Students can register for classes online. Administrative functions (other than registration) can be performed online.

CAMPUS LIFE
Environment: City **Activities:** Campus Ministries; Choral groups; Concert band; Dance; Drama/theater; International Student Organization; Jazz band; Model UN; Music ensembles; Musical theater; Student government; Student newspaper; Symphony orchestra; Yearbook 28 registered organizations, 11 religious organizations. **Athletics (Intercollegiate):** *Men:* basketball, cross-country, golf, soccer, tennis, track/field (outdoor), track/field (indoor). *Women:* basketball, cross-country, soccer, tennis, track/field (outdoor), track/field (indoor), volleyball. **On-Campus Highlights:** Voller Athletic Center & Sports Complex, B. Thomas Golisano Library, Rinker Community Service Center, Crothers Clock Tower, Cultural Life Center

ADMISSIONS
Freshman Academic Profile: Average high school GPA 3.4. 24% in top 10% of high school class, 49% in top 25% of high school class, 85% in top 50% of high school class. **Test Scores:** SAT Math middle 50% range 470-590. SAT EBRW middle 50% range 470-600. ACT middle 50% range 20-27. Minimum internet-based TOEFL 75. Minimum paper TOEFL 540. **Basis for Candidate Selection:** *Very important factors considered include:* rigor of secondary school record, academic GPA, standardized test scores, interview, character/personal qualities, religious affiliation/commitment. *Important factors considered include:* application essay, recommendation(s), extracurricular activities. *Other factors considered include:* class rank, talent/ability, alumni/ae relation, volunteer work, level of applicant's interest. **Freshman Admission Requirements:** High school diploma is required and GED is accepted *Academic units required:* 4 English, 3 math, 3 science, 1 science labs, 3 social studies, *Academic units recommended:* 4 math, 4 science, 3 science labs, 3 foreign language. **Freshman Admission Statistics:** 1,928 applied, 46.5% admitted, 24% enrolled. **Transfer Admission Requirements:** college transcript(s), essay or personal statement, Minimum college GPA of 2.70 required. Lowest grade transferable C. **General Admission Information:** Application fee $35. Priority deadline 2/1. Nonfall registration accepted. Admission may be deferred for a maximum of 1 year.

COSTS AND FINANCIAL AID
Annual tuition $25,350. Room and board $9,264. Required fees $974. Average book expense $1,000. **Required Forms and Deadlines:** FAFSA; State aid form. **Notification of Awards:** Applicants will be notified of awards on a rolling basis beginning 3/1. **Types of Aid:** *Need-based scholarships/grants:* College/ university scholarship or grant aid from institutional funds; Federal Pell; Private scholarships; SEOG; State scholarships/grants. *Loans:* Direct PLUS loans; Direct Subsidized Stafford Loans; Direct Unsubsidized Stafford Loans. *Student Employment:* Federal Work-Study Program available. Institutional employment available. **Financial Aid Statistics:** 100% needy freshmen, 98% needy undergrads receive need-based scholarship or grant aid. 12% freshmen, 7% undergrads receive non-need-based scholarship or grant aid. 86% freshmen, 89% undergrads receive need-based self-help aid. 6% freshmen, 3% undergrads receive athletic scholarships. 98% freshmen, 97% undergrads receive any aid. **Criteria for awarding aid:** *Need-based:* Leadership *Non-need-based:* Academics, Alumni affiliation, Art, Athletics, Music/drama, Religious affiliation.

ROCHESTER COLLEGE

800 West Avon Road, Rochester Hills, MI 48307
Phone: 248-218-2031
E-mail: admissions@rc.edu • **CEEB Code:** 1516
Fax: 248-218-2035 • **Website:** www.rc.edu • **ACT Code:** 2072

This private school, affiliated with the Church of Christ, was founded in 1959. It has a 83 acre campus.

RATINGS
Admissions Selectivity Rating: 69   **Fire Safety Rating:** 60*   **Green Rating:** 60*

STUDENTS AND FACULTY
Student Body: 14% out-of-state, 3% international (10 countries represented). Asian 1%, African American 11%, Caucasian 83%, Hispanic 1%, Native American 1%, Race unknown 1%.
Retention and Graduation: 69% freshmen return for sophomore year.
Faculty: Student/faculty ratio 15:1. 32 full-time faculty, 28% hold PhDs, 34% are women. 0% of classes are taught by teaching assistants.

ACADEMICS
Degrees: Associate; Bachelor's; Master's; Transfer Associate **Classes:** Most classes have 10-19 students. Most lab/discussion sessions have 10-19 students. **Special Study Options:** Accelerated program; Cross-registration; Double major; Dual enrollment; Independent study; Internships; Liberal arts/career combination; Study abroad; Teacher certification program; Weekend college. **Disability Services offered to physically disabled students:** Note-taking services; Reader services. **Career services:** Alumni network; Alumni services; Career assessment; Career/job search classes; Internships

FACILITIES
Housing: Apartments for married students; Men's dorms; Special housing for disabled student; Women's dorms

CAMPUS LIFE
Environment: Village **Activities:** Choral groups; Drama/theater; Jazz band; Music ensembles; Student government; Student newspaper; Yearbook 19 registered organizations, 3 honor societies, 1 religious organization. **Athletics (Intercollegiate):** *Men:* baseball, basketball, cross-country, soccer, track/field (outdoor). *Women:* basketball, cross-country, softball, track/field (outdoor), volleyball.

ADMISSIONS
Test Scores: Minimum paper TOEFL 500. **Basis for Candidate Selection:** *Important factors considered include:* rigor of secondary school record, standardized test scores. *Other factors considered include:* interview. **Freshman Admission Requirements:** High school diploma is required and GED is accepted **Freshman Admission Statistics:** 277 applied, 83.4% admitted, 65% enrolled. **Transfer Admission Requirements:** High school transcript, college transcript(s), Minimum college GPA of 2.0 required. Lowest grade transferable C. **General Admission Information:** Application fee $25. Nonfall registration accepted. Admission may be deferred for a maximum of 2 years.

COSTS AND FINANCIAL AID
Annual tuition $9,462. Room and board $5,342. Required fees $600. Average book expense $600. **Required Forms and Deadlines:** FAFSA; Institution's own financial aid form. **Notification of Awards:** Applicants will be notified of awards on a rolling basis beginning 6/1. **Types of Aid:** *Need-based scholarships/ grants:* College/university scholarship or grant aid from institutional funds; Federal Pell; Private scholarships; SEOG; State scholarships/grants. *Loans:* Direct PLUS loans; Direct Subsidized Stafford Loans; Direct Unsubsidized Stafford Loans. *Student Employment:* Federal Work-Study Program available. Institutional employment available. **Financial Aid Statistics:** 87% needy freshmen receive need-based scholarship or grant aid. 79% freshmen, undergrads receive non-need-based scholarship or grant aid. 84% freshmen, undergrads receive need-based self-help aid. 29% freshmen receive athletic scholarships. **Criteria for awarding aid:** *Non-need-based:* Academics, Alumni affiliation, Athletics, Leadership, Music/drama.

ROCHESTER INSTITUTE OF TECHNOLOGY

One Lomb Memorial Drive, Rochester, NY 14623-5604
Phone: 585-475-6631 • **Financial Aid Phone:** 585-475-2186
E-mail: admissions@rit.edu • **CEEB Code:** 2760
Fax: 585-475-7424 • **Website:** www.rit.edu • **ACT Code:** 2870

This private school was founded in 1829. It has a 1300 acre campus.

RATINGS
Admissions Selectivity Rating: 88   **Fire Safety Rating:** 89   **Green Rating:** 96

STUDENTS AND FACULTY
Enrollment: 12,858. **Student Body:** 33% female, 67% male, 48% out-of-state, 7% international (71 countries represented). Asian 9%, African American 5%, Caucasian 66%, Hispanic 7%, Native American <1%, Pacific Islander <1%, Two or more races 4%, Race unknown 2%.
Retention and Graduation: 90% freshmen return for sophomore year. 28% freshmen graduate within 4 years. 70% freshmen graduate within 6 years. 14% grads go on to further study within 1 year. **Faculty:** Student/faculty ratio 13:1. 1,023 full-time faculty, 70% hold PhDs, 20% are members of minority groups, 36% are women. 1% of classes are taught by teaching assistants.

ACADEMICS

Degrees: Associate; Bachelor's; Certificate; Doctoral/Research; Master's; Post-Bachelor's certificate **Classes:** Most classes have 20-29 students. **Most popular majors:** Computer Science; Modeling, Virtual Environments And Simulation; Mechanical Engineering. **Special Study Options:** Accelerated program; Cooperative education program; Cross-registration; Distance learning; Double major; English as a Second Language (ESL); Exchange student program (domestic); Honors program; Independent study; Internships; Liberal arts/career combination; Student-designed major; Study abroad; Weekend college. Honors programs: The RIT Honors Program provides a variety of curricular and extracurricular options and special Honors housing Combined degree programs: BA/MEng. **Disability Services offered to physically disabled students:** Note-taking services; Reader services; Tape recorders; Tutors. **Career services:** Alumni network; Alumni services; Career assessment; Career/job search classes; Internships; Regional alumni

FACILITIES

Housing: Apartments for married students; Apartments for single students; Coed dorms; Fraternity/sorority housing; Special housing for disabled student; Special housing for international students; Theme housing; Wellness housing 100% of campus accessible to physically disabled. **Special Academic Facilities/Equipment:** Art galleries, microelectronic engineering center, RIT Inn and Conference Center, observatory, student-managed restaurant, packaging testing facility, media resource center, Sunday 2000 printing press, Center for manufacturing studies, two OC3 connections to Internet and Internet2, laser optics laboratory, an observatory, an animal care facility, more than 100 color and black-and-white photography darkrooms, electronic prepress and publishing equipment, ceramic kilns, glass furnaces, a blacksmithing area, and computer graphics and robotic labs **Computers:** 75% of classrooms, 25% of dorms, 100% of libraries, 100% of dining areas, 100% of student union, 100% of common outdoor areas have wireless network access. Students can register for classes online. Administrative functions (other than registration) can be performed online.

CAMPUS LIFE

Environment: City **Activities:** Campus Ministries; Choral groups; Concert band; Dance; Drama/theater; International Student Organization; Jazz band; Literary magazine; Music ensembles; Musical theater; Pep band; Radio station; Student government; Student newspaper; Student-run film society; Symphony orchestra; Yearbook 175 registered organizations, 9 honor societies, 5 religious organizations. 19 fraternities, 10 sororities. **Athletics (Intercollegiate):** *Men:* baseball, basketball, crew/rowing, cross-country, diving, ice hockey, lacrosse, soccer, swimming, tennis, track/field (outdoor), track/field (indoor), wrestling. *Women:* basketball, cheerleading, crew/rowing, cross-country, diving, ice hockey, lacrosse, soccer, softball, swimming, tennis, track/field (outdoor), track/field (indoor), volleyball. **On-Campus Highlights:** Java Wally's (Wallace Library coffee sho, Student Life Center/Field House/Ice Aren, ESPN Zone @ RIT Student Alumni Union, Ben and Jerry's (RIT Student Alumni Uni, The Cafe and Market at Crossroads **Environmental Initiatives:** RIT has signed of the American College & University Presidents Climate Commitment (ACUPCC) and established 2030 as the target date for neutrality.

ADMISSIONS

Freshman Academic Profile: Average high school GPA 3.6. 40% in top 10% of high school class, 74% in top 25% of high school class, 95% in top 50% of high school class. 85% from public high schools. **Test Scores:** SAT Math middle 50% range 600-700. SAT EBRW middle 50% range 590-680. ACT middle 50% range 26-32. Minimum internet-based TOEFL 79. Minimum paper TOEFL 550. **Basis for Candidate Selection:** *Very important factors considered include:* rigor of secondary school record, academic GPA. *Important factors considered include:* class rank, standardized test scores. *Other factors considered include:* application essay, recommendation(s), interview, extracurricular activities, talent/ability, character/personal qualities, first generation, alumni/ae relation, geographical residence, racial/ethnic status, volunteer work, work experience, level of applicant's interest. **Freshman Admission Requirements:** High school diploma is required and GED is accepted *Academic units required:* 4 English, 2 math, 2 science, 1 science labs, 4 social studies, 10 academic electives, *Academic units recommended:* 4 English, 3 math, 3 science, 2 science labs, 3 foreign language, 4 social studies, 5 academic electives. **Freshman Admission Statistics:** 20,451 applied, 56.7% admitted, 24% enrolled. **Transfer Admission Requirements:** college transcript(s), essay or personal statement, Minimum college GPA of 2.7 required. Lowest grade transferable C-. **General Admission Information:** Application fee $65. Priority deadline 1/15. Nonfall registration accepted. Admission may be deferred for a maximum of 1 year.

COSTS AND FINANCIAL AID

Annual tuition $39,506. Room and board $12,666. Required fees $562. Average book expense $1,066. **Required Forms and Deadlines:** FAFSA; State aid form. **Notification of Awards:** Applicants will be notified of awards on a rolling basis beginning 3/1. **Types of Aid:** *Need-based scholarships/grants:* College/university scholarship or grant aid from institutional funds; Federal Pell; Private scholarships; SEOG; State scholarships/grants. *Loans:* Direct PLUS loans;

Direct Subsidized Stafford Loans; Direct Unsubsidized Stafford Loans. *Student Employment:* Federal Work-Study Program available. Institutional employment available. **Financial Aid Statistics:** 95% needy freshmen, 95% needy undergrads receive need-based scholarship or grant aid. 30% freshmen, 34% undergrads receive non-need-based scholarship or grant aid. 90% freshmen, 90% undergrads receive need-based self-help aid. 0% freshmen, 0% undergrads receive athletic scholarships. 87% freshmen, 77% undergrads receive any aid. 76% undergrads borrow to pay for school. Average cumulative indebtedness $38,198. **Criteria for awarding aid:** *Need-based:* Academics *Non-need-based:* Academics, Art, Leadership.

See page 1012.

ROCKFORD UNIVERSITY

5050 E. State Street, Rockford, IL 61108-2393
Phone: 815-226-4050 • **Financial Aid Phone:** 815-226-4062
E-mail: RCAdmissions@rockford.edu • **CEEB Code:** 1665
Fax: 815-226-2822 • **Website:** www.rockford.edu • **ACT Code:** 1122

This private school was founded in 1847. It has a 130 acre campus.

RATINGS

Admissions Selectivity Rating: 86   **Fire Safety Rating:** 82   **Green Rating:** 60*

STUDENTS AND FACULTY

Enrollment: 857. **Student Body:** 61% female, 39% male, 10% out-of-state, <1% international. Asian 2%, African American 8%, Caucasian 69%, Hispanic 6%, Native American 0%, Race unknown 14%.
Faculty: Student/faculty ratio 9:1. 69 full-time faculty, 68% hold PhDs, 3% are members of minority groups, 42% are women. 0% of classes are taught by teaching assistants.

ACADEMICS

Degrees: Bachelor's; **Master's Classes:** Most classes have 10-19 students. **Most popular majors:** Education, General; Nursing/Registered Nurse (Rn, Asn, Bsn, Msn); Business/Commerce, General. **Special Study Options:** Accelerated program; Distance learning; Double major; English as a Second Language (ESL); Exchange student program (domestic); Honors program; Independent study; Internships; Study abroad; Teacher certification program. Honors programs: Honors program in Liberal Arts. **Disability Services offered to physically disabled students:** Note-taking services; Reader services; Tutors. **Career services:** Career assessment; Internships

FACILITIES

Housing: Coed dorms; Special housing for disabled student; Theme housing **Special Academic Facilities/Equipment:** Language lab. Art Gallery. Sculpture Garden. **Computers:** Students can register for classes online. Administrative functions (other than registration) can be performed online.

CAMPUS LIFE

Environment: City **Activities:** Campus Ministries; Choral groups; Dance; Drama/theater; International Student Organization; Literary magazine; Model UN; Music ensembles; Musical theater; Opera; Pep band; Student government 25 registered organizations, 6 honor societies, 1 religious organization. **Athletics (Intercollegiate):** *Men:* baseball, basketball, cross-country, football, golf, soccer, tennis, track/field (outdoor), track/field (indoor). *Women:* basketball, cross-country, golf, soccer, softball, tennis, track/field (outdoor), track/field (indoor), volleyball. **On-Campus Highlights:** Residence Halls, Seaver Gym, Lion's Den-student gathering place, Football/Soccer Stadium, Clark Arts Center **Environmental Initiatives:** Green Week

ADMISSIONS

Freshman Academic Profile: Average high school GPA 3.1. 18% in top 10% of high school class, 33% in top 25% of high school class, 65% in top 50% of high school class. **Test Scores:** ACT middle 50% range 19-24. Minimum internet-based TOEFL 79. Minimum paper TOEFL 550. **Basis for Candidate Selection:** *Very important factors considered include:* academic GPA. *Important factors considered include:* rigor of secondary school record, application essay, standardized test scores. *Other factors considered include:* class rank, recommendation(s). **Freshman Admission Requirements:** High school diploma is required and GED is accepted *Academic units required:* 4 English, 3 math, 3 science, 3 science labs, 3 social studies, 2 academic electives, *Academic units recommended:* 2 foreign language. **Freshman Admission Statistics:** 967 applied, 41.2% admitted, 23% enrolled. **Transfer Admission Requirements:** college transcript(s), statement of good standing from prior institution(s). Minimum college GPA of 2.3 required. Lowest grade transferable C. **General Admission Information:** Application fee $35. Nonfall registration accepted. Admission may be deferred for a maximum of 1 year.

COSTS AND FINANCIAL AID

Annual tuition $24,750. Room and board $6,950. Average book expense $1,200. **Required Forms and Deadlines:** FAFSA. **Notification of Awards:** Applicants will be notified of awards on a rolling basis beginning 3/1. **Types of Aid:** *Need-based scholarships/grants:* College/university scholarship or grant aid from institutional funds; Federal Pell; Private scholarships; SEOG; State scholarships/grants. *Loans:* Student Employment: Federal Work-Study Program available. Institutional employment available. **Financial Aid Statistics:** 98% needy freshmen, 95% needy undergrads receive need-based scholarship or grant aid. 12% freshmen, 16% undergrads receive non-need-based scholarship or grant aid. 95% freshmen, 98% undergrads receive need-based self-help aid. 0% freshmen, 0% undergrads receive athletic scholarships. 99% freshmen, 99% undergrads receive any aid. **Criteria for awarding aid:** *Need-based:* Academics *Non-need-based:* Academics, Alumni affiliation, Leadership, Minority status, Music/drama, State/district residency.

ROCKHURST UNIVERSITY

1100 Rockhurst Road, Kansas City, MO 64110
Phone: 816-501-4100 • **Financial Aid Phone:** 816-501-4600
E-mail: admission@rockhurst.edu • **CEEB Code:** 6611
Fax: 816-501-4241 • **Website:** www.rockhurst.edu • **ACT Code:** 2342

This private school, affiliated with the Roman Catholic Church, was founded in 1910. It has a 55 acre campus.

RATINGS

Admissions Selectivity Rating: 79   **Fire Safety Rating:** 80   **Green Rating:** 60*

STUDENTS AND FACULTY

Enrollment: 1,623. **Student Body:** 59% female, 41% male, 33% out-of-state, 1% international (17 countries represented). Asian 3%, African American 5%, Caucasian 72%, Hispanic 9%, Native American 1%, Pacific Islander 0%, Two or more races 3%, Race unknown 6%.
Retention and Graduation: 86% freshmen return for sophomore year. 65% freshmen graduate within 4 years. 75% freshmen graduate within 6 years. **Faculty:** Student/faculty ratio 13:1. 128 full-time faculty, 88% hold PhDs, 10% are members of minority groups, 55% are women. 0% of classes are taught by teaching assistants.

ACADEMICS

Degrees: Bachelor's; Certificate; Doctoral/Professional; Master's; Post-Bachelor's certificate **Classes:** Most classes have 20-29 students. Most lab/discussion sessions have 20-29 students. **Most popular majors:** Kinesiology And Exercise Science; Psychology, General; Business/Commerce, General. **Special Study Options:** Accelerated program; Cooperative education program; Cross-registration; Distance learning; Double major; Dual enrollment; Exchange student program (domestic); Honors program; Independent study; Internships; Liberal arts/career combination; Study abroad; Teacher certification program. Honors programs: The Rockhurst University Honors Program is for motivated and talented students, regardless of major, who want to be active participants in designing their education. Students find honors courses to be more innovative, personal, and challenging than other courses. The Benefits Beginning in the first year, honors students have specially designed core courses that are usually small in enrollment and are taught by some of the University's most creative faculty. During the sophomore through senior years, honors students may earn honors credit through "honors options"—individually designed projects that allow students to explore areas of their own interest under the mentorship of a professor. An honors option is typically an offshoot of a regular course, but an option can also be arranged as an independent study course. It is through the honors option that honors students shape their curriculum. **Disability Services offered to physically disabled students:** Note-taking services; Reader services; Tape recorders; Tutors. **Career services:** Alumni network; Alumni services; Career assessment; Career/job search classes; Internships; Regional alumni

FACILITIES

Housing: Apartments for single students; Coed dorms; Special housing for disabled student; Theme housing; Women's dorms **Special Academic Facilities/Equipment:** Greenlease Art Gallery, St. Ignatius Science Center. **Computers:** Students can register for classes online. Administrative functions (other than registration) can be performed online.

CAMPUS LIFE

Environment: Metropolis **Activities:** Campus Ministries; Choral groups; Dance; Drama/theater; International Student Organization; Literary magazine; Model UN; Music ensembles; Musical theater; Student government; Student newspaper 44 registered organizations, 4 honor societies, 6 religious

organizations. 3 fraternities, 3 sororities. **Athletics (Intercollegiate):** *Men:* baseball, basketball, golf, soccer, tennis. *Women:* basketball, golf, soccer, softball, tennis, volleyball. **On-Campus Highlights:** Rockhurst Bell Tower and Fountains, The Rock Room, Kinerk Commons, Learning Center, Einstein Brothers & Subway

ADMISSIONS

Freshman Academic Profile: Average high school GPA 3.6. 25% in top 10% of high school class, 56% in top 25% of high school class, 84% in top 50% of high school class. 51% from public high schools. **Test Scores:** SAT Math middle 50% range 540-640. SAT EBRW middle 50% range 510-590. ACT middle 50% range 22-27. Minimum internet-based TOEFL 79. Minimum paper TOEFL 550. **Basis for Candidate Selection:** *Very important factors considered include:* rigor of secondary school record, academic GPA. *Important factors considered include:* standardized test scores. *Other factors considered include:* recommendation(s), interview, extracurricular activities, talent/ability, character/personal qualities, alumni/ae relation, volunteer work. **Freshman Admission Requirements:** High school diploma is required and GED is accepted *Academic units recommended:* 4 English, 3 math, 3 science, 3 science labs, 2 foreign language, 3 social studies, 2 history, 4 academic electives. **Freshman Admission Statistics:** 3,115 applied, 72.5% admitted, 19% enrolled. **Transfer Admission Requirements:** college transcript(s), Minimum college GPA of 2.5 required. Lowest grade transferable C-. **General Admission Information:** Nonfall registration accepted. Admission may be deferred.

COSTS AND FINANCIAL AID

Annual tuition $35,800. Room and board $9,360. Required fees $790. Average book expense $1,530. **Required Forms and Deadlines:** FAFSA. **Notification of Awards:** Applicants will be notified of awards on a rolling basis beginning 1/1. **Types of Aid:** *Need-based scholarships/grants:* College/university scholarship or grant aid from institutional funds; Federal Pell; Private scholarships; SEOG; State scholarships/grants; United Negro College Fund. *Loans:* Direct PLUS loans; Direct Subsidized Stafford Loans; Direct Unsubsidized Stafford Loans. *Student Employment:* Federal Work-Study Program available. Institutional employment available. **Financial Aid Statistics:** 97% needy freshmen, 100% needy undergrads receive need-based scholarship or grant aid. 52% freshmen, 45% undergrads receive non-need-based scholarship or grant aid. 73% freshmen, 74% undergrads receive need-based self-help aid. 14% freshmen, 14% undergrads receive athletic scholarships. 100% freshmen, 98% undergrads receive any aid. 78% undergrads borrow to pay for school. Average cumulative indebtedness $23,753. **Criteria for awarding aid:** *Need-based:* Minority status, Religious affiliation *Non-need-based:* Academics, Alumni affiliation, Art, Athletics, Leadership, Music/drama.

ROCKY MOUNTAIN COLLEGE

1511 Poly Drive, Billings, MT 59102-1796
Phone: 406-657-1026 • **Financial Aid Phone:** 406-657-1031
E-mail: admissions@rocky.edu • **CEEB Code:** 4660
Fax: 406-657-1189 • **Website:** www.rocky.edu • **ACT Code:** 2426

This private school was founded in 1878. It has a 60 acre campus.

RATINGS

Admissions Selectivity Rating: 81   **Fire Safety Rating:** 87   • **Green Rating:** 63

STUDENTS AND FACULTY

Enrollment: 984. **Student Body:** 49% female, 51% male, 44% out-of-state, 4% international (16 countries represented). Asian 1%, African American 3%, Caucasian 82%, Hispanic 4%, Native American 2%, Pacific Islander 1%, Two or more races 2%, Race unknown 2%.
Retention and Graduation: 67% freshmen return for sophomore year. 18% grads go on to further study within 1 year. 16% grads pursue arts and sciences degrees. 1% grads pursue law degrees. 1% grads pursue business degrees. **Faculty:** Student/faculty ratio 12:1. 65 full-time faculty, 77% hold PhDs, 40% are women. 0% of classes are taught by teaching assistants.

ACADEMICS

Degrees: Associate; Bachelor's; **Master's Classes:** Most classes have 10-19 students. Most lab/discussion sessions have 10-19 students. **Most popular majors:** Biology/Biological Sciences, General; Airline/Commercial/Professional Pilot And Flight Crew; Business Administration And Management, General. **Special Study Options:** Accelerated program; Distance learning; Double major; Dual enrollment; English as a Second Language (ESL); Honors program; Independent study; Internships; Student-designed major; Study abroad; Teacher certification program. Honors programs: Successful honors students find that participation in this program not only brings them closer to professionals in their chosen fields, but also grants them a substantial credential in their applications to graduate schools or employment opportunities.

Disability Services offered to physically disabled students: Note-taking services; Reader services; Tape recorders; Tutors. **Career services:** Alumni network; Alumni services; Career assessment; Career/job search classes; Internships; Regional alumni

FACILITIES
Housing: Apartments for married students; Apartments for single students; Coed dorms; Special housing for disabled students 75% of campus accessible to physically diasbled. **Special Academic Facilities/Equipment:** Billings Studio Theater, museum, studio, flight simulator/flight school, equestrian facilities, geology collection. **Computers:** Students can register for classes online. Administrative functions (other than registration) can be performed online.

CAMPUS LIFE
Environment: City **Activities:** Campus Ministries; Choral groups; Concert band; Drama/theater; International Student Organization; Jazz band; Music ensembles; Musical theater; Pep band; Student government; Student newspaper; Yearbook 28 registered organizations, 1 honor society, 4 religious organizations. **Athletics (Intercollegiate):** *Men:* basketball, cheerleading, football, golf, skiing (downhill/alpine). *Women:* basketball, cheerleading, golf, skiing (downhill/alpine), soccer, volleyball. **On-Campus Highlights:** Prescott Hall, Morledge-Kimball Hall, Herb Klindt Field-Football Stadium, Fortin Athletic Center, Losekamp Hall-Music Theatre

ADMISSIONS
Freshman Academic Profile: Average high school GPA 3.4. 10% in top 10% of high school class, 36% in top 25% of high school class, 70% in top 50% of high school class. **Test Scores:** SAT Math middle 50% range 450-550. SAT EBRW middle 50% range 440-540. ACT middle 50% range 20-25. Minimum paper TOEFL 525. **Basis for Candidate Selection:** *Very important factors considered include:* academic GPA, standardized test scores, level of applicant's interest. *Important factors considered include:* rigor of secondary school record, application essay, recommendation(s). *Other factors considered include:* class rank, interview, extracurricular activities, talent/ability, character/personal qualities, first generation, alumni/ae relation, work experience. **Freshman Admission Requirements:** High school diploma is required and GED is accepted *Academic units required:* 4 English, 4 math, 3 science, 3 social studies, 2 history, 3 academic electives. **Freshman Admission Statistics:** 1,347 applied, 63.5% admitted, 31% enrolled. **Transfer Admission Requirements:** college transcript(s), Minimum college GPA of 2.0 required. Lowest grade transferable C-. **General Admission Information:** Application fee $35. Priority deadline 3/1. Nonfall registration accepted. Admission may be deferred for a maximum of 1 year.

COSTS AND FINANCIAL AID
Annual tuition $22,442. Room and board $7,160. Required fees $450. Average book expense $1,300. **Required Forms and Deadlines:** FAFSA. **Notification of Awards:** Applicants will be notified of awards on a rolling basis beginning 2/15. **Types of Aid:** *Need-based scholarships/grants:* College/university scholarship or grant aid from institutional funds; Federal Pell; Private scholarships; SEOG; State scholarships/grants. *Loans:* Direct PLUS loans; Direct Subsidized Stafford Loans; Direct Unsubsidized Stafford Loans. *Student Employment:* Federal Work-Study Program available. Institutional employment available. **Financial Aid Statistics:** 98% needy freshmen, 97% needy undergrads receive need-based scholarship or grant aid. 96% freshmen, 94% undergrads receive non-need-based scholarship or grant aid. 84% freshmen, 84% undergrads receive need-based self-help aid. 26% freshmen, 27% undergrads receive athletic scholarships. 90% freshmen, 90% undergrads receive any aid. **Criteria for awarding aid:** *Non-need-based:* Academics, Athletics.

ROCKY MOUNTAIN COLLEGE OF ART + DESIGN

1600 Pierce St, Denver, CO 80214
Phone: 303-753-6046 · **Financial Aid Phone:** 303-753-6046
E-mail: admissions@rmcad.edu
Fax: 303-567-7281 • **Website:** www.rmcad.edu • **ACT Code:** 5359

This proprietary school was founded in 1963. It has a 23 acre campus.

RATINGS
Admissions Selectivity Rating: 63   **Fire Safety Rating:** 60*   **Green Rating:** 60*

STUDENTS AND FACULTY
Enrollment: 1,074. **Student Body:** 65% female, 35% male, 53% out-of-state, <1% international. Asian 2%, African American 9%, Caucasian 60%, Hispanic 9%, Native American 4%, Pacific Islander 0%, Two or more races 1%, Race unknown 15%.

Retention and Graduation: 52% freshmen return for sophomore year. **Faculty:** Student/faculty ratio 9:1. 38 full-time faculty, 34% hold PhDs, 5% are members of minority groups, 55% are women.

ACADEMICS
Degrees: Bachelor's; Certificate; **Master's Classes:** Most classes have fewer than 10 students. Most lab/discussion sessions have 10-19 students. **Special Study Options:** Distance learning; Dual enrollment; Independent study; Internships. **Career services:** Alumni network; Alumni services; Career assessment; Career/job search classes; Internships

FACILITIES
Special Academic Facilities/Equipment: Philip Steele Gallery Fine Arts Exhibit Space Drive Up Gallery

CAMPUS LIFE
Environment: Metropolis **Activities:** Campus Ministries; Student government.

ADMISSIONS
Basis for Candidate Selection: *Important factors considered include:* academic GPA, interview, extracurricular activities. **Freshman Admission Requirements:** High school diploma is required and GED is accepted **Transfer Admission Requirements:** college transcript(s), Minimum college GPA of 2.0 required. **General Admission Information:** Application fee $50. Nonfall registration accepted. Admission may be deferred for a maximum of one semester.

COSTS AND FINANCIAL AID
Annual tuition $15,870. Room and board $8,640. Required fees $500. Average book expense $1,045. **Required Forms and Deadlines:** FAFSA; Institution's own financial aid form. **Types of Aid:** *Need-based scholarships/grants:* College/university scholarship or grant aid from institutional funds; Federal Pell; Private scholarships; SEOG; State scholarships/grants. *Loans:* Direct PLUS loans; Direct Subsidized Stafford Loans; Direct Unsubsidized Stafford Loans. *Student Employment:* Federal Work-Study Program available. **Criteria for awarding aid:** *Need-based:* Academics, Art *Non-need-based:* Academics, Art.

ROGER WILLIAMS UNIVERSITY

One Old Ferry Rd, Bristol, RI 02809-2921
Phone: 401-254-3500 • **Financial Aid Phone:** 401-254-3100
E-mail: admit@rwu.edu • **CEEB Code:** 3729
Website: www.rwu.edu • **ACT Code:** 3814

This private school was founded in 1956. It has a 140 acre campus.

RATINGS
Admissions Selectivity Rating: 75   **Fire Safety Rating:** 97   **Green Rating:** 77

STUDENTS AND FACULTY
Enrollment: 4,447. **Student Body:** 52% female, 48% male, 79% out-of-state, 3% international (56 countries represented). Asian 2%, African American 2%, Caucasian 77%, Hispanic 6%, Native American <1%, Pacific Islander <1%, Two or more races 2%, Race unknown 8%.
Retention and Graduation: 79% freshmen return for sophomore year. 55% freshmen graduate within 4 years. 65% freshmen graduate within 6 years. 20% grads go on to further study within 1 year. 3% grads pursue arts and sciences degrees. 3% grads pursue law degrees. 2% grads pursue business degrees. 0.2% grads pursue medical degrees. **Faculty:** Student/faculty ratio 14:1. 217 full-time faculty, 91% hold PhDs, 13% are members of minority groups, 42% are women. 0% of classes are taught by teaching assistants.

ACADEMICS
Degrees: Associate; Bachelor's; Certificate; Doctoral/Professional; Master's; Post-Bachelor's certificate **Classes:** Most classes have 10-19 students. Most lab/discussion sessions have 10-19 students. **Most popular majors:** Architecture; Psychology, General; Criminal Justice/Law Enforcement Administration. **Special Study Options:** Accelerated program; Cooperative education program; Distance learning; Double major; Dual enrollment; English as a Second Language (ESL); Exchange student program (domestic); Honors program; Independent study; Internships; Liberal arts/career combination; Student-designed major; Study abroad; Teacher certification program. Honors programs: 1. Alpha Chi Honors Society-University-wide association for Juniors and Seniors; 2. Four-year Honors Program-For full-time students in any major which includes special sections of general education classes, a unique group service project for juniors and a required senior thesis. The program includes a variety of cultural and co-curricular activities, as well as leadership opportunities; 3. Honors Society Associations-Department-level

honors associations within various disciplines Combined degree programs: BA/JD; BA/MA. **Disability Services offered to physically disabled students:** Note-taking services; Reader services; Tape recorders. Alumni network; Alumni services; Career assessment; Career/job search classes; Internships; Regional alumni

FACILITIES
Housing: Coed dorms; Theme housing; Wellness housing; Women's dorms **Special Academic Facilities/Equipment:** Marine and Natural Sciences Building with marine biology wetlab, School of Law and Law Library, Main Library, Architecture Building and Architecture Library, Performing Arts Center, Thomas J. Paolino Recreation Center, Global Heritage Hall, Sailing Center **Computers:** 100% of classrooms, 100% of dorms, 100% of libraries, 100% of dining areas, 100% of student union, 20% of common outdoor areas have wireless network access. Students can register for classes online. Administrative functions (other than registration) can be performed online.

CAMPUS LIFE
Environment: Village **Activities:** Campus Ministries; Choral groups; Dance; Drama/theater; Model UN; Music ensembles; Radio station; Student government; Student newspaper; Yearbook 93 registered organizations, 13 honor societies, 4 religious organizations. **Athletics (Intercollegiate):** *Men:* baseball, basketball, cross-country, diving, equestrian sports, lacrosse, sailing, soccer, swimming, tennis, track/field (outdoor), track/field (indoor), wrestling. *Women:* basketball, cross-country, diving, equestrian sports, lacrosse, sailing, soccer, softball, swimming, tennis, track/field (outdoor), track/field (indoor), volleyball. **On-Campus Highlights:** Recreation Center, Library, Dining Commons, Marine Science Wet Lab, Bookstore **Environmental Initiatives:** All renovation and new construction on campus meets LEED Silver standards

ADMISSIONS
Freshman Academic Profile: Average high school GPA 3.3. 85% from public high schools. **Test Scores:** SAT Math middle 50% range 500-600. SAT EBRW middle 50% range 550-630. ACT middle 50% range 24-18. **Basis for Candidate Selection:** *Very important factors considered include:* rigor of secondary school record, academic GPA, application essay, recommendation(s), character/personal qualities. *Important factors considered include:* extracurricular activities, volunteer work, work experience, level of applicant's interest. *Other factors considered include:* class rank, standardized test scores, interview, talent/ability, first generation, alumni/ae relation. **Freshman Admission Requirements:** High school diploma is required and GED is accepted *Academic units required:* 4 English, 3 math, 3 science, 2 science labs, 3 social studies, 2 history, 2 academic electives, *Academic units recommended:* 4 math, 4 science, 2 foreign language, 3 social studies, 3 history, 3 academic electives. **Freshman Admission Statistics:** 9,515 applied, 82.3% admitted, 14% enrolled. **Transfer Admission Requirements:** college transcript(s), essay or personal statement, Minimum college GPA of 2.5 required. Lowest grade transferable C. **General Admission Information:** Application fee $50. Priority deadline 2/1. Regular application deadline 2/1. Nonfall registration accepted. Admission may be deferred for a maximum of 1 year.

COSTS AND FINANCIAL AID
Annual tuition $30,326. Room and board $15,564. Required fees $2,184. Average book expense $900. **Required Forms and Deadlines:** FAFSA. **Types of Aid:** *Need-based scholarships/grants:* College/university scholarship or grant aid from institutional funds; Federal Pell; Private scholarships; SEOG; State scholarships/grants. *Loans:* Direct PLUS loans; Direct Subsidized Stafford Loans; Direct Unsubsidized Stafford Loans. *Student Employment:* Federal Work-Study Program available. Institutional employment available. **Financial Aid Statistics:** 87% needy freshmen, 69% needy undergrads receive need-based scholarship or grant aid. 97% freshmen, 86% undergrads receive non-need-based scholarship or grant aid. 85% freshmen, 70% undergrads receive need-based self-help aid. 0% freshmen, 0% undergrads receive athletic scholarships. 69% freshmen, 57% undergrads receive any aid. 58% undergrads borrow to pay for school. Average cumulative indebtedness $41,632. **Criteria for awarding aid:** *Non-need-based:* Academics, Leadership.

ROLLINS COLLEGE

1000 Holt Avenue, Winter Park, FL 32789-4499
Phone: 407-646-2161 • **Financial Aid Phone:** 407-646-2395
E-mail: admission@rollins.edu • **CEEB Code:** 5572
Fax: 407-646-1502 • **Website:** http://www.rollins.edu • **ACT Code:** 748

This private school was founded in 1885. It has a 80 acre campus.

RATINGS
Admissions Selectivity Rating: 86   **Fire Safety Rating:** 97   **Green Rating:** 86

STUDENTS AND FACULTY
Enrollment: 1,984. **Student Body:** 61% female, 39% male, 42% out-of-state, 10% international (57 countries represented). Asian 3%, African American 4%, Caucasian 60%, Hispanic 16%, Native American <1%, Pacific Islander 0%, Two or more races 4%, Race unknown 3%.
Retention and Graduation: 83% freshmen return for sophomore year. 68% freshmen graduate within 4 years. 75% freshmen graduate within 6 years. **Faculty:** Student/faculty ratio 10:1. 232 full-time faculty, 90% hold PhDs, 12% are members of minority groups, 50% are women. 0% of classes are taught by teaching assistants.

ACADEMICS
Degrees: Bachelor's; Doctoral/Research; **Master's Classes:** Most classes have 20-29 students. **Most popular majors:** Communication And Media Studies, Other; Economics, General; International Business/Trade/Commerce. **Special Study Options:** Accelerated program; Cross-registration; Double major; Dual enrollment; Exchange student program (domestic); Honors program; Independent study; Internships; Student-designed major; Study abroad; Teacher certification program. Honors programs: The academic excellence you will encounter at Rollins is reinforced every day through our acclaimed Honors Program. The Honors Program is designed for students who bring exceptional abilities and are looking for a heightened educational journey marked by a distinct core of interdisciplinary courses, team-taught honors seminars, significant independent research opportunities, and the chance to meet separately with distinguished visiting speakers and lecturers. The Honors Degree Program leads to a distinct and separate undergraduate degree Artium Baccalaureus Honoris, the Honors Bachelor of Arts Degree. **Disability Services offered to physically disabled students:** Note-taking services; Reader services; Tape recorders; Tutors. **Career services:** Alumni network; Alumni services; Career assessment; Career/job search classes; Internships

FACILITIES
Housing: Apartments for single students; Coed dorms; Fraternity/sorority housing; Special housing for disabled student; Theme housing 80% of campus accessible to physically diasbled. **Special Academic Facilities/Equipment:** Fine arts museum, 2 theatres, child development center, high-tech classrooms, outdoor classroom. **Computers:** 100% of classrooms, 100% of dorms, 100% of libraries, 100% of dining areas, 100% of student union, have wireless network access. Students can register for classes online. Administrative functions (other than registration) can be performed online.

CAMPUS LIFE
Environment: Town **Activities:** Campus Ministries; Choral groups; Concert band; Dance; Drama/theater; International Student Organization; Jazz band; Literary magazine; Marching band; Model UN; Music ensembles; Musical theater; Opera; Pep band; Radio station; Student government; Student newspaper; Student-run film society; Symphony orchestra; Television station 125 registered organizations, 5 honor societies, 5 religious organizations. 5 fraternities, 6 sororities. **Athletics (Intercollegiate):** *Men:* baseball, basketball, crew/rowing, cross-country, golf, lacrosse, sailing, soccer, swimming, tennis, water skiing. *Women:* basketball, crew/rowing, cross-country, golf, lacrosse, sailing, soccer, softball, swimming, tennis, volleyball, water skiing. **On-Campus Highlights:** Cornell Campus Center, Olin Library, Alfond Sports Center, Cornell Fine Arts Museum (Art Gallery), Rice Family Bookstore **Environmental Initiatives:** Reuse existing buildings, renovating and updating to conform to LEAD principles, but limited to and bound by LEAD criteria

ADMISSIONS
Freshman Academic Profile: Average high school GPA 3.3. 36% in top 10% of high school class, 67% in top 25% of high school class, 88% in top 50% of high school class. 51% from public high schools. **Test Scores:** SAT Math middle 50% range 590-670. SAT EBRW middle 50% range 605-680. ACT middle 50% range 25-30. Minimum internet-based TOEFL 80. Minimum paper TOEFL 550. **Basis for Candidate Selection:** *Very important factors*

considered include: rigor of secondary school record, academic GPA. *Important factors considered include:* application essay, standardized test scores, recommendation(s), extracurricular activities, talent/ability. *Other factors considered include:* class rank, character/personal qualities, first generation, alumni/ae relation, volunteer work, work experience, level of applicant's interest. **Freshman Admission Requirements:** High school diploma is required and GED is accepted *Academic units required:* 4 English, 3 math, 2 science, 2 foreign language, 2 social studies, 2 history, 2 academic electives, *Academic units recommended:* 4 English, 4 math, 4 science, 3 foreign language, 3 social studies, 3 history, 3 academic electives. **Freshman Admission Statistics:** 5,297 applied, 63.9% admitted, 16% enrolled. **Transfer Admission Requirements:** High school transcript, college transcript(s), essay or personal statement, statement of good standing from prior institution(s). Lowest grade transferable C-. **General Admission Information:** Application fee $50. Regular application deadline 2/1. Nonfall registration accepted. Admission may be deferred for a maximum of One year.

COSTS AND FINANCIAL AID

Annual tuition $49,760. Average book expense $742. **Required Forms and Deadlines:** FAFSA. **Notification of Awards:** Applicants will be notified of awards on a rolling basis beginning 3/1. **Types of Aid:** *Need-based scholarships/grants:* College/university scholarship or grant aid from institutional funds; Federal Pell; Private scholarships; SEOG; State scholarships/grants. *Loans:* Direct PLUS loans; Direct Subsidized Stafford Loans; Direct Unsubsidized Stafford Loans. *Student Employment:* Federal Work-Study Program available. Institutional employment available. **Financial Aid Statistics:** 99% needy freshmen, 100% needy undergrads receive need-based scholarship or grant aid. 15% freshmen, 15% undergrads receive non-need-based scholarship or grant aid. 75% freshmen, 81% undergrads receive need-based self-help aid. 5% freshmen, 6% undergrads receive athletic scholarships. 88% freshmen, 86% undergrads receive any aid. Average cumulative indebtedness $32,208. **Criteria for awarding aid:** *Non-need-based:* Academics, Art, Athletics, Leadership, Music/drama, State/district residency.

ROOSEVELT UNIVERSITY

430 South Michigan Avenue, Chicago, IL 60605
Phone: 877-277-5978 • **Financial Aid Phone:** (866) 421-0935
E-mail: admission@roosevelt.edu • **CEEB Code:** 1666
Fax: 847-619-4216 • **Website:** http://www.roosevelt.edu/Home.aspx • **ACT Code:** 1124

This private school was founded in 1945. It has a 34 acre campus.

RATINGS

Admissions Selectivity Rating: 74   **Fire Safety Rating:** 95   **Green Rating:** 84

STUDENTS AND FACULTY

Enrollment: 2,710. **Student Body:** 64% female, 36% male, 15% out-of-state, 4% international (42 countries represented). Asian 5%, African American 18%, Caucasian 45%, Hispanic 24%, Native American <1%, Pacific Islander <1%, Two or more races 3%, Race unknown 1%.
Retention and Graduation: 65% freshmen return for sophomore year. **Faculty:** Student/faculty ratio 11:1. 242 full-time faculty, 91% hold PhDs, 23% are members of minority groups, 43% are women. 0% of classes are taught by teaching assistants.

ACADEMICS

Degrees: Bachelor's; Doctoral/Professional; Doctoral/Research; Master's; Post-Bachelor's certificate **Classes:** Most classes have 20-29 students. Most lab/discussion sessions have 20-29 students. **Most popular majors:** Biology/Biological Sciences, General; Psychology, General; Musical Theatre. **Special Study Options:** Accelerated program; Distance learning; Double major; Dual enrollment; English as a Second Language (ESL); Exchange student program (domestic); Honors program; Independent study; Internships; Student-designed major; Study abroad; Teacher certification program. Honors programs: Roosevelt Honors program offers an enriched academic program combining the students' area of interest with an interdisciplinary approach that includes internships, and research opportunities. The Honors website is http://www.roosevelt.edu/honors Combined degree programs: BA/JD; BA/MA. **Disability Services offered to physically disabled students:** Note-taking services; Reader services; Tape recorders; Tutors. **Career services:** Alumni network; Alumni services; Career assessment; Career/job search classes; Internships; Regional alumni

FACILITIES

Housing: Apartments for single students; Coed dorms 90% of campus accessible to physically disabled. **Special Academic Facilities/Equipment:**

The university's Gage Gallery features the work of artists that aligns with the social justice mission of Roosevelt. Within one mile of the Chicago Campus is the Field Museum of Natural History, Shedd Aquarium, Adler Planetarium and Art Institute of Chicago. **Computers:** Students can register for classes online. Administrative functions (other than registration) can be performed online.

CAMPUS LIFE

Environment: Metropolis **Activities:** Choral groups; Concert band; Dance; Drama/theater; International Student Organization; Jazz band; Literary magazine; Music ensembles; Musical theater; Opera; Pep band; Radio station; Student government; Student newspaper; Symphony orchestra 48 registered organizations, 3 honor societies, 4 religious organizations. 1 fraternity, 2 sororities. Vertical Campus: 32-story building downtown Chicago, Auditorium Building: national historic landmark, University Center: largest multi-college residence hall in the US, Gage Building: historic classroom building overlooking Millennium Park, Schaumburg Campus: full service campus near Woodfield Mall **Environmental Initiatives:** Roosevelt has achieved LEED certification for both of its new campus buildings in the heart of downtown Chicago. LEED Gold for Wabash Building and LEED Silver for the Goodman Center. The university has also achieved SERF (Society of Environmentally Responsible Facilities) certification for the Wabash Building.

ADMISSIONS

Freshman Academic Profile: Average high school GPA 3.1. 8% in top 10% of high school class, 46% in top 25% of high school class, 62% in top 50% of high school class. 85% from public high schools. **Test Scores:** SAT Math middle 50% range 450-550. SAT EBRW middle 50% range 455-595. ACT middle 50% range 19-24. Minimum internet-based TOEFL 40. **Basis for Candidate Selection:** *Very important factors considered include:* academic GPA, standardized test scores. *Other factors considered include:* rigor of secondary school record, class rank, application essay, recommendation(s), interview, extracurricular activities, talent/ability, character/personal qualities, first generation, alumni/ae relation, level of applicant's interest. **Freshman Admission Requirements:** High school diploma is required and GED is accepted *Academic units required:* 4 English, 3 math, 2 science, 2 science labs, 2 social studies, *Academic units recommended:* 4 English, 4 math, 3 science, 3 science labs, 2 foreign language, 3 social studies, 2 history, 2 academic electives. **Freshman Admission Statistics:** 5,996 applied, 73.3% admitted, 8% enrolled. **Transfer Admission Requirements:** college transcript(s), statement of good standing from prior institution(s). Minimum college GPA of 2.0 required. Lowest grade transferable D. **General Admission Information:** Application fee $25. Priority deadline 8/15. Nonfall registration accepted. Admission may be deferred for a maximum of 1 year.

COSTS AND FINANCIAL AID

Annual tuition $28,963. Average book expense $1,200. **Required Forms and Deadlines:** FAFSA; Institution's own financial aid form. **Notification of Awards:** Applicants will be notified of awards on a rolling basis beginning 2/1. **Types of Aid:** *Need-based scholarships/grants:* College/university scholarship or grant aid from institutional funds; Federal Pell; Private scholarships; SEOG; State scholarships/grants. *Loans:* Direct PLUS loans; Direct Subsidized Stafford Loans; Direct Unsubsidized Stafford Loans. *Student Employment:* Federal Work-Study Program available. Institutional employment available. **Financial Aid Statistics:** 91% needy undergrads receive need-based scholarship or grant aid. 89% freshmen, 90% undergrads receive non-need-based scholarship or grant aid. 69% freshmen, 80% undergrads receive need-based self-help aid. 7% freshmen, 2% undergrads receive athletic scholarships. 94% freshmen, 90% undergrads receive any aid. **Criteria for awarding aid:** *Need-based:* Minority status *Non-need-based:* Academics, Alumni affiliation, Leadership, Minority status, Music/drama, State/district residency.

ROSE-HULMAN INSTITUTE OF TECHNOLOGY

5500 Wabash Avenue, Terre Haute, IN 47803-3999
Phone: 812-877-8213 • **Financial Aid Phone:** 812-877-8259
E-mail: admissions@rose-hulman.edu • **CEEB Code:** 1668
Fax: 812-877-8941 • **Website:** www.rose-hulman.edu • **ACT Code:** 1232

This private school was founded in 1874. It has a 200 acre campus.

RATINGS

Admissions Selectivity Rating: 92   **Fire Safety Rating:** 96   **Green Rating:** 79

STUDENTS AND FACULTY

Enrollment: 2,146. **Student Body:** 25% female, 75% male, 64% out-of-state, 15% international (11 countries represented). Asian 5%, African American 3%, Caucasian 68%, Hispanic 5%, Native American <1%, Pacific Islander <1%, Two or more races 5%, Race unknown 1%.

Retention and Graduation: 91% freshmen return for sophomore year. 67% freshmen graduate within 4 years. 81% freshmen graduate within 6 years. 18% grads go on to further study within 1 year. 16% grads pursue arts and sciences degrees. 0% grads pursue law degrees. 1% grads pursue business degrees. 1% grads pursue medical degrees. **Faculty:** Student/faculty ratio 11:1. 190 full-time faculty, 99% hold PhDs, 12% are members of minority groups, 24% are women. 0% of classes are taught by teaching assistants.

ACADEMICS

Degrees: Bachelor's; Master's **Most popular majors:** Computer Science; Chemical Engineering; Mechanical Engineering. **Special Study Options:** Accelerated program; Cooperative education program; Cross-registration; Double major; Dual enrollment; English as a Second Language (ESL); Exchange student program (domestic); Independent study; Study abroad. **Disability Services offered to physically disabled students:** Note-taking services; Reader services; Tape recorders; Tutors. **Career services:** Alumni network; Alumni services; Career assessment; Career/job search classes; Internships

FACILITIES

Housing: Apartments for single students; Coed dorms; Fraternity/sorority housing; Men's dorms; Theme housing 95% of campus accessible to physically diasbled. **Special Academic Facilities/Equipment:** Oakley Observatory **Computers:** 100% of classrooms, 5% of dorms, 100% of libraries, 100% of dining areas, 100% of student union, 25% of common outdoor areas have wireless network access. Students can register for classes online. Administrative functions (other than registration) can be performed online. Undergraduates are required to own a computer.

CAMPUS LIFE

Environment: Town **Activities:** Choral groups; Concert band; Dance; Drama/theater; International Student Organization; Jazz band; Music ensembles; Musical theater; Pep band; Radio station; Student government; Student newspaper; Symphony orchestra 105 registered organizations, 7 honor societies, 2 religious organizations. 8 fraternities, 3 sororities. **Athletics (Intercollegiate):** *Men:* baseball, basketball, cross-country, diving, football, golf, riflery, soccer, swimming, tennis, track/field (outdoor), track/field (indoor). *Women:* basketball, cross-country, diving, golf, riflery, soccer, softball, swimming, tennis, track/field (outdoor), track/field (indoor), volleyball. **On-Campus Highlights:** Sports and Recreation Center, Hatfield Hall, White Chapel, Branam Innovation Center **Environmental Initiatives:** Signing of the American College & University President's Climate Commitment

ADMISSIONS

Freshman Academic Profile: Average high school GPA 4.0. 64% in top 10% of high school class, 91% in top 25% of high school class, 100% in top 50% of high school class. 63% from public high schools. **Test Scores:** SAT Math middle 50% range 650-760. SAT EBRW middle 50% range 610-690. ACT middle 50% range 27-32. Minimum internet-based TOEFL 80. Minimum paper TOEFL 550. **Basis for Candidate Selection:** *Very important factors considered include:* rigor of secondary school record, class rank, academic GPA. *Important factors considered include:* standardized test scores, recommendation(s), extracurricular activities, character/personal qualities, volunteer work, work experience. *Other factors considered include:* application essay, talent/ability, alumni/ae relation, geographical residence, racial/ethnic status. **Freshman Admission Requirements:** High school diploma is required and GED is not accepted *Academic units required:* 4 English, 4 math, 3 science, 3 science labs, 2 social studies, 4 academic electives, *Academic units recommended:* 5 math, 4 science. **Freshman Admission Statistics:** 4,473 applied, 60.9% admitted, 20% enrolled. **Transfer Admission Requirements:** college transcript(s), essay or personal statement, statement of good standing from prior institution(s). Minimum college GPA of 3.0 required. Lowest grade transferable C. **General Admission Information:** Application fee $50. Priority deadline 11/1. Regular application deadline 2/1. Nonfall registration accepted. Admission may be deferred for a maximum of 1 year.

COSTS AND FINANCIAL AID

Annual tuition $44,847. Room and board $14,061. Required fees $915. Average book expense $1,500. **Required Forms and Deadlines:** FAFSA. **Notification of Awards:** Applicants will be notified of awards on or about 3/10. **Types of Aid:** *Need-based scholarships/grants:* College/university scholarship or grant aid from institutional funds; Federal Pell; SEOG; State scholarships/grants. *Loans:* Direct PLUS loans; Direct Subsidized Stafford Loans; Direct Unsubsidized Stafford Loans. *Student Employment:* Federal Work-Study Program available. Institutional employment available. **Financial Aid Statistics:** 83% needy freshmen, 85% needy undergrads receive need-based scholarship or grant aid.

100% freshmen, 99% undergrads receive non-need-based scholarship or grant aid. 89% freshmen, 87% undergrads receive need-based self-help aid. 0% freshmen, 0% undergrads receive athletic scholarships. 99% freshmen, 97% undergrads receive any aid. 65% undergrads borrow to pay for school. Average cumulative indebtedness $59,113. **Criteria for awarding aid:** *Need-based:* Academics, Minority status *Non-need-based:* Academics, Minority status.

ROSEMONT COLLEGE

1400 Montgomery Ave., Rosemont, PA 19010
Phone: 610-526-2966 • **Financial Aid Phone:** 610 527 0200
E-mail: admissions@rosemont.edu • **CEEB Code:** 2763
Fax: 610-520-4399 • **Website:** www.rosemont.edu • **ACT Code:** 3676

This private school, affiliated with the Roman Catholic Church, was founded in 1921. It has a 56 acre campus.

RATINGS

Admissions Selectivity Rating: 75   **Fire Safety Rating:** 83   **Green Rating:** 60*

STUDENTS AND FACULTY

Enrollment: 529. **Student Body:** 65% female, 35% male, 27% out-of-state, 2% international (11 countries represented). Asian 5%, African American 40%, Caucasian 38%, Hispanic 6%, Native American 0%, Pacific Islander 0%, Two or more races 4%, Race unknown 4%.

Retention and Graduation: 69% freshmen return for sophomore year. 36% grads go on to further study within 1 year. 35% grads pursue arts and sciences degrees. 2% grads pursue law degrees. 5% grads pursue business degrees. 9% grads pursue medical degrees. **Faculty:** Student/faculty ratio 10:1. 25 full-time faculty, 84% hold PhDs, 4% are members of minority groups, 48% are women. 0% of classes are taught by teaching assistants.

ACADEMICS

Degrees: Bachelor's; Master's; Post-Bachelor's certificate **Classes:** Most classes have 20-29 students. Most lab/discussion sessions have 20-29 students. **Most popular majors:** Biology/Biological Sciences, General; Art/Art Studies, General; Business/Commerce, General. **Special Study Options:** Accelerated program; Cross-registration; Distance learning; Double major; Honors program; Independent study; Internships; Liberal arts/career combination; Student-designed major; Study abroad; Teacher certification program. Honors programs: The Honors Program provides intellectually challenging and stimulating honors courses for students interested in a broad educational experience. Honors courses are either disciplinary or interdisciplinary, and are distinguished from regular offerings with respect to depth of study and work expectations. The classes are small and emphasize discussion, providing students with a more enhanced encounter with the material and encouraging interaction with faculty mentors and other motivated and talented students. Students in the honors program have the opportunity to attend lectures, visit museums, attend musical performances, and other intellectual and artistic events. An important goal of the honors program is to foster a discriminative awareness of social responsibility and to encourage service for the public good. Combined degree programs: BA/MA. **Disability Services offered to physically disabled students:** Note-taking services; Tape recorders; Tutors. **Career services:** Alumni services; Career assessment; Career/job search classes; Internships

FACILITIES

Housing: Coed dorms; Theme housing 45% of campus accessible to physically diasbled. **Special Academic Facilities/Equipment:** Rotwitt Performing Arts Center **Computers:** 25% of classrooms, 25% of dorms, 50% of libraries, 15% of dining areas, 15% of student union, 10% of common outdoor areas have wireless network access. Students can register for classes online. Administrative functions (other than registration) can be performed online.

CAMPUS LIFE

Environment: Village **Activities:** Campus Ministries; Choral groups; Concert band; Dance; Drama/theater; Jazz band; Literary magazine; Marching band; Music ensembles; Musical theater; Opera; Pep band; Radio station; Student government; Student newspaper; Yearbook 23 registered organizations, 6 honor societies, 3 religious organizations. **Athletics (Intercollegiate):** *Men:* basketball, softball, tennis. *Women:* basketball, field hockey, lacrosse, softball, tennis, volleyball. **On-Campus Highlights:** Campus Grill, The Grind Coffee Shop, Fitness Center **Environmental Initiatives:** Energy Star Procurement Policy.

ADMISSIONS

Freshman Academic Profile: Average high school GPA 3.3. 70% from public high schools. **Test Scores:** SAT Math middle 50% range 380-505. SAT EBRW middle 50% range 400-520. ACT middle 50% range 15-20. Minimum internet-based TOEFL 61. Minimum paper TOEFL 500. **Basis for Candidate Selection:** *Very important factors considered include:* rigor of secondary school record, academic GPA, standardized test scores, interview, level of applicant's interest. *Important factors considered include:* class rank, application essay, extracurricular activities, talent/ability, volunteer work. *Other factors considered include:* recommendation(s), character/personal qualities, alumni/ae relation, work experience. **Freshman Admission Requirements:** High school diploma is required and GED is accepted *Academic units required:* 4 English, 3 math, 3 science, 2 science labs, 1 social studies, 1 history, 7 academic electives, *Academic units recommended:* 4 English, 3 math, 3 science, 2 science labs, 2 foreign language, 2 social studies, 2 history, 4 academic electives. **Freshman Admission Statistics:** 875 applied, 70.6% admitted, 22% enrolled. **Transfer Admission Requirements:** college transcript(s), Minimum college GPA of 2.5 required. Lowest grade transferable C. **General Admission Information:** Priority deadline 8/1. Regular application deadline 8/1. Nonfall registration accepted. Admission may be deferred for a maximum of 1 year.

COSTS AND FINANCIAL AID

Annual tuition $18,500. Room and board $11,500. Required fees $980. Average book expense $1,500. **Required Forms and Deadlines:** FAFSA. **Notification of Awards:** Applicants will be notified of awards on a rolling basis beginning 3/1. **Types of Aid:** *Need-based scholarships/grants:* College/university scholarship or grant aid from institutional funds; Federal Pell; Private scholarships; SEOG; State scholarships/grants. *Loans: Student Employment:* Federal Work-Study Program available. Institutional employment available. **Financial Aid Statistics:** 99% needy freshmen, 99% needy undergrads receive need-based scholarship or grant aid. 10% freshmen, 12% undergrads receive non-need-based scholarship or grant aid. 95% freshmen, 99% undergrads receive need-based self-help aid. 0% freshmen, 0% undergrads receive athletic scholarships. 92% freshmen, 92% undergrads receive any aid. 90% undergrads borrow to pay for school. Average cumulative indebtedness $40,792. **Criteria for awarding aid:** *Need-based:* Academics, Art, Leadership *Non-need-based:* Academics, Alumni affiliation, Art, Leadership, Religious affiliation.

ROWAN UNIVERSITY

201 Mullica Hill Road, Glassboro, NJ 08028-1701
Phone: 856-256-4200 • **Financial Aid Phone:** 856-256-5186
E-mail: admissions@rowan.edu • **CEEB Code:** 2515
Fax: 856-256-4430 • **Website:** www.rowan.edu • **ACT Code:** 2560

This public school was founded in 1923. It has a 920 acre campus.

RATINGS

Admissions Selectivity Rating: 82   **Fire Safety Rating:** 97   **Green Rating:** 71

STUDENTS AND FACULTY

Enrollment: 11,819. **Student Body:** 47% female, 53% male, 5% out-of-state, 1% international (44 countries represented). Asian 6%, African American 9%, Caucasian 69%, Hispanic 9%, Native American <1%, Pacific Islander <1%, Two or more races 3%, Race unknown 3%.
Retention and Graduation: 86% freshmen return for sophomore year. **Faculty:** Student/faculty ratio 17:1. 95 full-time faculty, 33% hold PhDs, 11% are members of minority groups, 19% are women. 0% of classes are taught by teaching assistants.

ACADEMICS

Degrees: Bachelor's; Certificate; Doctoral; Doctoral Other; Doctoral/Professional; Doctoral/Research; Master's; Post-Bachelor's certificate; Post-Master's certificate **Classes:** Most classes have 10-19 students. Most lab/discussion sessions have 10-19 students. **Most popular majors:** Elementary Education And Teaching; Biology/Biological Sciences, General; Psychology, General. **Special Study Options:** Accelerated program; Cooperative education program; Cross-registration; Distance learning; Double major; Dual enrollment; English as a Second Language (ESL); Honors program; Independent study; Internships; Liberal arts/career combination; Study abroad; Teacher certification program; Weekend college. Honors programs: The Thomas N. Bantivoglio Honors Concentration offers qualified students access to a variety of academic, social, and cultural experiences including honors classes, the Honors Student Organization and events it sponsors, which include travel and cultural activities along the eastern seaboard. Students are guaranteed cluster housing and priority registration. Combined degree programs: BA/MA. **Disability Services offered to physically disabled students:** Note-taking services; Reader services; Tape recorders; Tutors. **Career services:** Alumni network; Alumni services; Career assessment; Career/job search classes; Internships; Regional alumni

FACILITIES

Housing: Apartments for single students; Coed dorms; Special housing for disabled student; Special housing for international students; Theme housing 95% of campus accessible to physically disabled. **Special Academic Facilities/Equipment:** Concert hall,Cave Automated Virtual Environment (CAVE),two production studios, Exercise Science Research Laboratory, Rowan University Assessment and Learning Center, 130-seat screening theater, Planetarium, Rowan Radio 89.7 WGLS-FM – main studio, production studio, news studio, record room, Cooper Medical School of Rowan University, Bantivoglio Honors Program and contains offices, a lounge and classroom space dedicated to honors students, glass collection, student recreation center, on-campus early childhood demonstration center, greenhouse for biological studies, observatory, art gallery, RCA museum in the library. **Computers:** 100% of classrooms, 100% of dorms, 100% of libraries, 100% of dining areas, 100% of student union, 100% of common outdoor areas have wireless network access. Students can register for classes online. Administrative functions (other than registration) can be performed online.

CAMPUS LIFE

Environment: Town **Activities:** Campus Ministries; Choral groups; Concert band; Dance; Drama/theater; Jazz band; Music ensembles; Musical theater; Opera; Pep band; Radio station; Student government; Student newspaper; Student-run film society; Symphony orchestra; Television station; Yearbook 135 registered organizations, 10 honor societies, 6 religious organizations. 10 fraternities, 10 sororities. **Athletics (Intercollegiate):** *Men:* baseball, basketball, cross-country, diving, football, soccer, swimming, track/field (outdoor), track/field (indoor). *Women:* basketball, cross-country, diving, field hockey, lacrosse, soccer, softball, swimming, track/field (outdoor), track/field (indoor), volleyball. **On-Campus Highlights:** Recreation Center, Student Center, Campbell Library, Savitz Hall (Student Services Building), Rowan Boulevard **Environmental Initiatives:** Energy use has decreased 25% from fiscal year 13 to base year 11 because of the operation of the central utility plant and the co-generation. Cut energy usage from 700000 mmbtu's to 510000 mmbtu's over 2 years. Generating electricity in the co-generation plant avoids our purchase of coal generated electricity.

ADMISSIONS

Freshman Academic Profile: Average high school GPA 3.5. **Test Scores:** SAT Math middle 50% range 520-630. SAT EBRW middle 50% range 490-590. Minimum internet-based TOEFL 79. Minimum paper TOEFL 550. **Basis for Candidate Selection:** *Very important factors considered include:* rigor of secondary school record. *Important factors considered include:* academic GPA, application essay, standardized test scores. *Other factors considered include:* class rank, recommendation(s), extracurricular activities, talent/ability, character/personal qualities, racial/ethnic status, volunteer work. **Freshman Admission Requirements:** High school diploma is required and GED is accepted *Academic units required:* 4 English, 3 math, 2 science, 2 science labs, 2 history, 5 academic electives, *Academic units recommended:* 4 math, 3 science, 3 science labs, 2 foreign language, 2 social studies, 1 visual/performing arts. **Freshman Admission Statistics:** 10,078 applied, 65.5% admitted, 29% enrolled. **Transfer Admission Requirements:** college transcript(s), Minimum college GPA of 2.0 required. Lowest grade transferable D. **General Admission Information:** Application fee $65. Regular application deadline 3/1. Nonfall registration accepted. Admission may be deferred for a maximum of 1 year.

COSTS AND FINANCIAL AID

Annual in-state tuition $11,406. Annual out-of-state tuition $17,030. Room and board $11,406. Required fees $3,540. Average book expense $1,500. **Required Forms and Deadlines:** FAFSA. **Notification of Awards:** Applicants will be notified of awards on a rolling basis beginning 3/16. **Types of Aid:** *Need-based scholarships/grants:* Federal Pell; Private scholarships; SEOG; State scholarships/grants. *Loans:* Direct PLUS loans; Direct Subsidized Stafford Loans; Direct Unsubsidized Stafford Loans. *Student Employment:* Federal Work-Study Program available. Institutional employment available. **Financial Aid Statistics:** 45% needy freshmen receive need-based scholarship or grant aid. 50% freshmen, 23% undergrads receive non-need-based scholarship or grant aid. 75% freshmen, 84% undergrads receive need-based self-help aid. 0% freshmen, 0% undergrads receive athletic scholarships. 83% freshmen, 73% undergrads receive any aid. **Criteria for awarding aid:** *Non-need-based:* Academics, Art, Music/drama.

RUSH UNIVERSITY

600 South Paulina, Chicago, IL 60612-3878
Phone: 312-942-7100 • **Financial Aid Phone:** 312-942-6256
E-mail: Rush_Admissions@rush.edu
Fax: 312-942-2219 • **Website:** www.rushu.rush.edu • **ACT Code:** 1617

This private school was founded in 1972. It has a 35 acre campus.

RATINGS
Admissions Selectivity Rating: 61   **Fire Safety Rating:** 79   **Green Rating:** 60*

STUDENTS AND FACULTY
Enrollment: 258. **Student Body:** 87% female, 13% male, 15% out-of-state, 2% international. Asian 18%, African American 7%, Caucasian 69%, Hispanic 3%, Native American <1%, Race unknown 2%.
Retention and Graduation: 25% grads go on to further study within 1 year. 5% grads pursue medical degrees. **Faculty:** Student/faculty ratio 8:1. 305 full-time faculty, 65% are women. 0% of classes are taught by teaching assistants.

ACADEMICS
Degrees: Bachelor's; Master's **Most popular majors:** Audiology/Audiologist And Speech-Language Pathology/Pathologist; Medicine; Nursing/Registered Nurse (Rn, Asn, Bsn, Msn). **Special Study Options:** Distance learning. **Disability Services offered to physically disabled students:** Tape recorders; Tutors. **Career services:** Alumni network; Alumni services; Career assessment; Career/job search classes; Internships; Regional alumni

FACILITIES
Housing: Apartments for married students; Apartments for single students 85% of campus accessible to physically diasbled.

CAMPUS LIFE
Environment: Metropolis **Activities:** Yearbook 15 registered organizations, 2 honor societies, 1 religious organization. **On-Campus Highlights:** Student Lounge, Computer lab (100+ stations), Library, Au Bon Pain **Environmental Initiatives:** Launched new recycling commitment and awareness campaign on Earth Day 2008.

ADMISSIONS
Freshman Academic Profile: 100% in top 50% of high school class. **Test Scores:** Minimum paper TOEFL 550. **Transfer Admission Requirements:** college transcript(s), essay or personal statement, Minimum college GPA of 2.7 required. Lowest grade transferable c. **General Admission Information:** Nonfall registration accepted.

COSTS AND FINANCIAL AID
Required Forms and Deadlines: Business/Farm Supplement; FAFSA; Institution's own financial aid form. **Types of Aid:** *Need-based scholarships/grants:* College/university scholarship or grant aid from institutional funds; Federal Pell; Private scholarships; SEOG; State scholarships/grants. *Loans: Student Employment:* Federal Work-Study Program available. Institutional employment available. **Financial Aid Statistics:** 74% needy undergrads receive need-based scholarship or grant aid. 13% undergrads receive non-need-based scholarship or grant aid. 88% undergrads receive need-based self-help aid. 0% undergrads receive athletic scholarships. 0% freshmen, 69% undergrads receive any aid. **Criteria for awarding aid:** *Non-need-based:* Academics, Leadership, Minority status.

RUST COLLEGE

150 Rust Avenue, Holly Springs, MS 38635
Phone: 662-252-8000 • **Financial Aid Phone:** 662-252-8000, x4062
E-mail: jb_mcdonald@rustcollege.edu
Fax: 662-252-8895 • **Website:** www.rustcollege.edu • **ACT Code:** 2240

This private school, affiliated with the Methodist Church, was founded in 1866. It has a 126 acre campus.

RATINGS
Admissions Selectivity Rating: 80   **Fire Safety Rating:** 60*   **Green Rating:** 60*

STUDENTS AND FACULTY
Enrollment: 922. **Student Body:** 63% female, 37% male, 5% international. Asian <1%, African American 93%, Caucasian 1%, Hispanic 0%, Native American 0%, Race unknown 1%.

Retention and Graduation: 53% freshmen return for sophomore year.
Faculty: Student/faculty ratio 17:1. 48 full-time faculty, 90% are members of minority groups, 40% are women. 0% of classes are taught by teaching assistants.

ACADEMICS
Degrees: Associate; Bachelor's **Classes:** Most classes have 20-29 students. Most lab/discussion sessions have 20-29 students. **Most popular majors:** Computer And Information Sciences, General; Biology/Biological Sciences, General; Business/Commerce, General. **Special Study Options:** Accelerated program; Distance learning; Double major; Dual enrollment; Honors program; Independent study; Internships; Liberal arts/career combination; Study abroad; Teacher certification program. **Disability Services offered to physically disabled students:** Tutors.

FACILITIES
Housing: Men's dorms; Women's dorms **Special Academic Facilities/ Equipment:** Dr. Ron Trojcak collection of African tribal art which includes fabrics, masks and statues used for religious ceremonies, weddings, ritual dance and funerals.

CAMPUS LIFE
Environment: Village **Activities:** Campus Ministries; Choral groups; Concert band; Drama/theater; International Student Organization; Marching band; Music ensembles; Pep band; Radio station; Student government; Student newspaper; Television station; Yearbook 35 registered organizations, 7 honor societies, 5 religious organizations. 3 fraternities, 4 sororities. **Athletics (Intercollegiate):** *Men:* baseball, basketball, cheerleading, cross-country, soccer, tennis, track/field (outdoor). *Women:* basketball, cheerleading, cross-country, softball, tennis, track/field (outdoor), volleyball. **On-Campus Highlights:** Leontyne Price Library Exhibits, James Elam Chapel, McDonald Science Building, David Beckley Conference Center, McMillan Multi-Purpose Center

ADMISSIONS
Freshman Academic Profile: 98% from public high schools. **Test Scores:** ACT middle 50% range 14-21. Minimum paper TOEFL 540. **Basis for Candidate Selection:** *Very important factors considered include:* first generation. *Important factors considered include:* rigor of secondary school record, class rank, academic GPA, application essay, standardized test scores, recommendation(s), character/personal qualities, alumni/ae relation, level of applicant's interest. *Other factors considered include:* talent/ability, volunteer work. **Freshman Admission Requirements:** High school diploma is required and GED is accepted *Academic units required:* 4 English, 3 math, 3 science, 3 social studies, 6 academic electives. **Freshman Admission Statistics:** 3,983 applied, 45.6% admitted, 16% enrolled. **Transfer Admission Requirements:** High school transcript, college transcript(s), statement of good standing from prior institution(s). Minimum college GPA of 2.0 required. Lowest grade transferable C. **General Admission Information:** Application fee $10. Priority deadline 7/15. Nonfall registration accepted. Admission may be deferred for a maximum of one year.

COSTS AND FINANCIAL AID
Annual tuition $8,100. Room and board $3,700. Average book expense $250. **Required Forms and Deadlines:** FAFSA; Institution's own financial aid form. **Notification of Awards:** Applicants will be notified of awards on a rolling basis beginning 4/1. **Types of Aid:** *Need-based scholarships/grants:* Federal Pell; Private scholarships; SEOG; United Negro College Fund. **Financial Aid Statistics:** 86% needy freshmen, 87% needy undergrads receive need-based scholarship or grant aid. 43% freshmen, 29% undergrads receive non-need-based scholarship or grant aid. 87% freshmen, 89% undergrads receive need-based self-help aid. 0% freshmen, 0% undergrads receive athletic scholarships. **Criteria for awarding aid:** *Non-need-based:* Academics, Leadership, Music/drama, Religious affiliation, State/district residency.

RUTGERS, THE STATE UNIVERSITY OF NEW JERSEY—CAMDEN

200 East Normal Street, Camden, NJ 08102
Phone: 856-225-6104 • **Financial Aid Phone:** 856-225-6039
E-mail: admissions@camden.rutgers.edu • **CEEB Code:** 2765
Fax: 856-225-6498 • **Website:** www.camden.rutgers.edu • **ACT Code:** 2592

This public school was founded in 1926. It has a 29 acre campus.

RATINGS
Admissions Selectivity Rating: 78   **Fire Safety Rating:** 79   **Green Rating:** 60*

STUDENTS AND FACULTY

Enrollment: 5,360. **Student Body:** 59% female, 41% male, 2% out-of-state, 2% international (24 countries represented). Asian 10%, African American 18%, Caucasian 49%, Hispanic 15%, Native American <1%, Pacific Islander <1%, Two or more races 4%, Race unknown 2%.
Retention and Graduation: 88% freshmen return for sophomore year. 25% freshmen graduate within 4 years. 58% freshmen graduate within 6 years.
Faculty: 315 full-time faculty, 99% hold PhDs, 17% are members of minority groups, 47% are women.

ACADEMICS

Degrees: Bachelor's; Doctoral/Professional; Doctoral/Research; Master's; Post-Bachelor's certificate; Post-Master's certificate **Classes:** Most classes have 10-19 students. **Most popular majors:** Psychology, General; Nursing/Registered Nurse (Rn, Asn, Bsn, Msn); Business Administration And Management, General. **Special Study Options:** Accelerated program; Cooperative education program; Cross-registration; Distance learning; Double major; Dual enrollment; English as a Second Language (ESL); Exchange student program (domestic); Honors program; Independent study; Internships; Liberal arts/career combination; Student-designed major; Study abroad; Teacher certification program; Weekend college. Combined degree programs: BA/JD; BA/MD. **Disability Services offered to physically disabled students:** Note-taking services; Reader services; Tape recorders; Tutors.

FACILITIES

Housing: Apartments for single students; Coed dorms; Special housing for disabled students **Computers:** Students can register for classes online. Administrative functions (other than registration) can be performed online.

CAMPUS LIFE

Environment: City **Activities:** Choral groups; Drama/theater; International Student Organization; Radio station; Student government; Student newspaper; Symphony orchestra; Yearbook 50 registered organizations, 11 honor societies, 4 fraternities, 4 sororities. **Athletics (Intercollegiate):** *Men:* baseball, basketball, cross-country, golf, soccer, track/field (outdoor). *Women:* basketball, cross-country, soccer, softball, track/field (outdoor), volleyball.

ADMISSIONS

Freshman Academic Profile: 12% in top 10% of high school class, 39% in top 25% of high school class, 76% in top 50% of high school class. **Test Scores:** SAT Math middle 50% range 500-590. SAT EBRW middle 50% range 500-590. Minimum internet-based TOEFL 79. Minimum paper TOEFL 550. **Basis for Candidate Selection:** *Very important factors considered include:* rigor of secondary school record, class rank, academic GPA, standardized test scores. *Other factors considered include:* application essay, recommendation(s), extracurricular activities, first generation, geographical residence, state residency, racial/ethnic status, volunteer work, work experience. **Freshman Admission Requirements:** High school diploma is required and GED is accepted *Academic units required:* 4 English, 3 math, 2 science, 2 foreign language, 5 academic electives. **Freshman Admission Statistics:** 11,338 applied, 69.3% admitted, 10% enrolled. **Transfer Admission Requirements:** High school transcript, college transcript(s), Minimum college GPA of NA required. **General Admission Information:** Application fee $70. Regular application deadline 12/1. Nonfall registration accepted. Admission may be deferred.

COSTS AND FINANCIAL AID

Student Employment: Federal Work-Study Program available. Institutional employment available. **Financial Aid Statistics:** 68% needy freshmen receive need-based scholarship or grant aid. 70% freshmen, 72% undergrads receive any aid. **Criteria for awarding aid:** *Need-based:* Academics, Alumni affiliation, Art, Leadership, Music/drama *Non-need-based:* Academics, Alumni affiliation, Art, Athletics, Leadership, Music/drama, State/district residency.

RUTGERS, THE STATE UNIVERSITY OF NEW JERSEY—NEW BRUNSWICK

200 University Hall, Piscataway, NJ 08854-8097
Phone: 732-932-4636 • **Financial Aid Phone:** 732-932-7305
E-mail: admissions@ugadm.rutgers.edu • **CEEB Code:** 2765
Website: www.newbrunswick.rutgers.edu • **ACT Code:** 2592

This public school was founded in 1766. It has a 2695 acre campus.

RATINGS

Admissions Selectivity Rating: 87   **Fire Safety Rating:** 89   **Green Rating:** 60*

STUDENTS AND FACULTY

Enrollment: 35,296. **Student Body:** 50% female, 50% male, 6% out-of-state, 9% international (117 countries represented). Asian 27%, African American 7%, Caucasian 39%, Hispanic 13%, Native American <1%, Pacific Islander <1%, Two or more races 3%, Race unknown 2%.
Retention and Graduation: 93% freshmen return for sophomore year. 60% freshmen graduate within 4 years. 80% freshmen graduate within 6 years.
Faculty: 2,092 full-time faculty, 99% hold PhDs, 19% are members of minority groups, 47% are women. 20% of classes are taught by teaching assistants.

ACADEMICS

Degrees: Associate; Bachelor's; Doctoral; Doctoral/Professional; Doctoral/Research; Master's; Post-Bachelor's certificate; Post-Master's certificate **Classes:** Most classes have 10-19 students. **Most popular majors:** Engineering, General; Biology/Biological Sciences, General. **Special Study Options:** Accelerated program; Cooperative education program; Cross-registration; Distance learning; Double major; Dual enrollment; English as a Second Language (ESL); Exchange student program (domestic); Honors program; Independent study; Internships; Liberal arts/career combination; Student-designed major; Study abroad; Teacher certification program; Weekend college. Combined degree programs: BA/MD. **Disability Services offered to physically disabled students:** Note-taking services; Reader services; Tape recorders; Tutors. **Career services:** Alumni network; Alumni services; Career assessment; Career/job search classes; Internships; Regional alumni

FACILITIES

Housing: Apartments for married students; Apartments for single students; Coed dorms; Cooperative housing; Fraternity/sorority housing; Men's dorms; Special housing for disabled student; Theme housing; Wellness housing; Women's dorms **Special Academic Facilities/Equipment:** Geology Museum, Zimmerli Museum, Mason Gross Performing Arts Center; NJ Museum of Agriculture; NJ Film Festival/RU Film Co-op; Rutgers Gardens **Computers:** Students can register for classes online. Administrative functions (other than registration) can be performed online.

CAMPUS LIFE

Environment: Town **Activities:** Campus Ministries; Choral groups; Concert band; Dance; Drama/theater; International Student Organization; Jazz band; Literary magazine; Marching band; Model UN; Music ensembles; Musical theater; Opera; Pep band; Radio station; Student government; Student newspaper; Student-run film society; Symphony orchestra; Television station; Yearbook 400 registered organizations, 24 honor societies, 29 fraternities, 15 sororities. **Athletics (Intercollegiate):** *Men:* baseball, basketball, cheerleading, cross-country, diving, football, golf, lacrosse, soccer, track/field (outdoor), track/field (indoor), wrestling. *Women:* basketball, cheerleading, crew/rowing, cross-country, diving, field hockey, golf, gymnastics, lacrosse, soccer, softball, swimming, tennis, track/field (outdoor), track/field (indoor), volleyball.
On-Campus Highlights: Geology Museum, Jane Voorhees Zimmereli Art Museum, Rutgers Display Gardens and Heylar Woods, Hutchenson Memorial Forest

ADMISSIONS

Freshman Academic Profile: 38% in top 10% of high school class, 76% in top 25% of high school class, 97% in top 50% of high school class. **Test Scores:** SAT Math middle 50% range 600-720. SAT EBRW middle 50% range 590-680. Minimum paper TOEFL 550. **Basis for Candidate Selection:** *Very important factors considered include:* rigor of secondary school record, academic GPA, standardized test scores. *Important factors considered include:* extracurricular activities. *Other factors considered include:* class rank, application essay, interview, talent/ability, character/personal qualities, first generation, geographical residence, state residency, racial/ethnic status, volunteer work, work experience. **Freshman Admission Requirements:** High school diploma is required and GED is accepted *Academic units required:* 4 English, 3 math, 2 science, 2 foreign language, 5 academic electives. **Freshman Admission Statistics:** 38,384 applied, 57.8% admitted, 28% enrolled. **Transfer Admission Requirements:** High school transcript, college transcript(s), Lowest grade transferable C. **General Admission Information:** Application fee $70. Priority deadline 12/1. Nonfall registration accepted. Admission may be deferred for a maximum of 1 year.

COSTS AND FINANCIAL AID
Types of Aid: Financial Aid Statistics: 67% needy freshmen receive need-based scholarship or grant aid. 67% freshmen, 69% undergrads receive any aid. **Criteria for awarding aid:** *Need-based:* Academics, Alumni affiliation, Art, Leadership, Music/drama *Non-need-based:* Academics, Alumni affiliation, Art, Athletics, Leadership, Music/drama, State/district residency.

RUTGERS, THE STATE UNIVERSITY OF NEW JERSEY—NEWARK CAMPUS

102 Warriner Hall, Newark, NJ 07102-1896
Phone: 973-353-5205 • **Financial Aid Phone:** 732-932-7305
E-mail: admissions@ugadm.rutgers.edu • **CEEB Code:** 2765
Fax: 973-353-1440 • **Website:** www.newark.rutgers.edu • **ACT Code:** 2592

This public school was founded in 1930. It has a 36 acre campus.

RATINGS
Admissions Selectivity Rating: 80   **Fire Safety Rating:** 83   **Green Rating:** 60*

STUDENTS AND FACULTY
Enrollment: 8,122. **Student Body:** 55% female, 45% male, 1% out-of-state, 5% international (84 countries represented). Asian 18%, African American 20%, Caucasian 23%, Hispanic 29%, Native American <1%, Pacific Islander <1%, Two or more races 3%, Race unknown 2%.
Retention and Graduation: 84% freshmen return for sophomore year. 37% freshmen graduate within 4 years. 68% freshmen graduate within 6 years. **Faculty:** 554 full-time faculty, 99% hold PhDs, 21% are members of minority groups, 36% are women. 9% of classes are taught by teaching assistants.

ACADEMICS
Degrees: Bachelor's; Doctoral/Professional; Doctoral/Research; Master's; Post-Bachelor's certificate; Post-Master's certificate **Classes:** Most classes have fewer than 10 students. **Most popular majors:** Biology/Biological Sciences, General; Nursing/Registered Nurse (Rn, Asn, Bsn, Msn); Business Administration And Management, General. **Special Study Options:** Accelerated program; Cooperative education program; Cross-registration; Distance learning; Double major; Dual enrollment; English as a Second Language (ESL); Exchange student program (domestic); Honors program; Independent study; Internships; Liberal arts/career combination; Student-designed major; Study abroad; Teacher certification program; Weekend college. Combined degree programs: BA/MA; BA/MD. **Disability Services offered to physically disabled students:** Note-taking services; Reader services; Tape recorders; Tutors.

FACILITIES
Housing: Apartments for married students; Apartments for single students; Coed dorms; Special housing for disabled student; Wellness housing **Special Academic Facilities/Equipment:** Institute of Jazz Studies, TV/Radio media center, Institute of Animal Behavior, Center for Crime Prevention Studies, Center for Negotiation and Conflict Resolution, Center for Molecular and Behaviorial Neuroscience, Center for Nursing Research **Computers:** Students can register for classes online. Administrative functions (other than registration) can be performed online.

CAMPUS LIFE
Activities: Campus Ministries; Choral groups; Concert band; Dance; Drama/theater; International Student Organization; Jazz band; Literary magazine; Marching band; Musical theater; Opera; Pep band; Radio station; Student government; Student newspaper; Symphony orchestra; Yearbook 80 registered organizations, 16 honor societies, 7 fraternities, 7 sororities. **Athletics (Intercollegiate):** *Men:* baseball, basketball, soccer, tennis, volleyball. *Women:* basketball, softball, tennis, volleyball. **On-Campus Highlights:** The Arts at Rutgers Newark, Robeson Campus Center, Athletic Center, Bradley Hall/Bookstore, Dana Library

ADMISSIONS
Freshman Academic Profile: 21% in top 10% of high school class, 53% in top 25% of high school class, 87% in top 50% of high school class. **Test Scores:** SAT Math middle 50% range 510-590. SAT EBRW middle 50% range 500-580. Minimum paper TOEFL 550. **Basis for Candidate Selection:** *Very*

important factors considered include: rigor of secondary school record, class rank, academic GPA, standardized test scores. *Other factors considered include:* application essay, recommendation(s), extracurricular activities, first generation, geographical residence, state residency, racial/ethnic status, volunteer work, work experience, level of applicant's interest. **Freshman Admission Requirements:** High school diploma is required and GED is accepted *Academic units required:* 4 English, 3 math, 2 science, 2 foreign language, 5 academic electives. **Freshman Admission Statistics:** 13,435 applied, 64.2% admitted, 15% enrolled. **Transfer Admission Requirements:** High school transcript, college transcript(s), Minimum college GPA of na required. **General Admission Information:** Application fee $70. Priority deadline 12/1. Nonfall registration accepted. Admission may be deferred for a maximum of 1 year.

COSTS AND FINANCIAL AID
Types of Aid: Financial Aid Statistics: 78% needy freshmen receive need-based scholarship or grant aid. 80% freshmen, 80% undergrads receive any aid. **Criteria for awarding aid:** *Need-based:* Academics, Alumni affiliation, Art, Leadership, Music/drama *Non-need-based:* Academics, Alumni affiliation, Art, Athletics, Leadership, Music/drama, State/district residency.

SACRED HEART UNIVERSITY

Best Colleges

5151 Park Avenue, Fairfield, CT 06825
Phone: 203-371-7880 • **Financial Aid Phone:** 203-371-7980
E-mail: enroll@sacredheart.edu • **CEEB Code:** 3780
Fax: 203-365-7607 • **Website:** www.sacredheart.edu • **ACT Code:** 589

This private school, affiliated with the Roman Catholic Church, was founded in 1963. It has a 350 acre campus.

RATINGS
Admissions Selectivity Rating: 85   **Fire Safety Rating:** 95   **Green Rating:** 61

STUDENTS AND FACULTY
Enrollment: 5,496. **Student Body:** 64% female, 36% male, 65% out-of-state, 1% international (26 countries represented). Asian 2%, African American 5%, Caucasian 74%, Hispanic 11%, Native American <1%, Pacific Islander <1%, Two or more races 2%, Race unknown 5%.
Retention and Graduation: 84% freshmen return for sophomore year. 67% freshmen graduate within 4 years. 72% freshmen graduate within 6 years. 21% grads go on to further study within 1 year. 31% grads pursue arts and sciences degrees. 10% grads pursue business degrees. **Faculty:** Student/faculty ratio 14:1. 296 full-time faculty, 81% hold PhDs, 10% are members of minority groups, 55% are women. 0% of classes are taught by teaching assistants.

ACADEMICS
Degrees: Associate; Bachelor's; Doctoral/Professional; Master's; Post-Master's certificate **Classes:** Most classes have fewer than 10 students. **Most popular majors:** Psychology, General; Registered Nursing/Registered Nurse; Business Administration And Management, General. **Special Study Options:** Accelerated program; Distance learning; Double major; Dual enrollment; English as a Second Language (ESL); Honors program; Independent study; Internships; Liberal arts/career combination; Student-designed major; Study abroad; Teacher certification program; Weekend college. Honors programs: Sacred Heart University offers a challenging curriculum of Honors-level courses. These studies will provide each student with the quest for the full meaning of our humanity exploring the following three components: (1) the cognitive, (2) the aesthetic and (3) the moral or ethical. The Program also includes advisement, cultural events, dinners with the University President and other events. Combined degree programs: BA/MA. **Disability Services offered to physically disabled students:** Note-taking services; Reader services; Tape recorders; Tutors. **Career services:** Alumni network; Alumni services; Career assessment; Career/job search classes; Internships; Regional alumni

FACILITIES
Housing: Apartments for single students; Coed dorms; Special housing for disabled student; Wellness housing **Special Academic Facilities/Equipment:** The Edgerton Center for the Performing Arts with top-of-the-line professional equipment. Frank and Marisa Martire Business & Communications Center with an active trading floor with 30 work stations, 13 Bloomberg terminals, wallboard ticker tapes and real time data from NASDAQ and NYSE; screening venues; smart classrooms with multi-media technology; interactive labs; a motion

capture lab; and two large television studios for TV, video and film production. Center for Healthcare Education with a medical gym, audiology suite, motion analysis and human performance labs, an immersive acute care simulation lab with video and data capture capability, a simulated outpatient suite, high-fidelity manikins, roles, a home-care suite, an expanded human anatomy lab, and many more learning resources featuring the latest technology. Computer Gaming Lab. Closed LAN laboratory. Motion capture lab. Fashion design studio. Art studios. 3D Printing Lab. Cadaver lab. **Computers:** 100% of classrooms, 100% of dorms, 100% of libraries, 100% of dining areas, 100% of student union, 100% of common outdoor areas have wireless network access. Students can register for classes online. Administrative functions (other than registration) can be performed online. Undergraduates are required to own a computer.

CAMPUS LIFE

Environment: Town **Activities:** Campus Ministries; Choral groups; Concert band; Dance; Drama/theater; International Student Organization; Jazz band; Literary magazine; Marching band; Model UN; Music ensembles; Musical theater; Pep band; Radio station; Student government; Student newspaper; Student-run film society; Television station; Yearbook 80 registered organizations, 14 honor societies, 4 religious organizations. 4 fraternities, 6 sororities. **Athletics (Intercollegiate):** *Men:* baseball, basketball, cross-country, fencing, football, golf, ice hockey, lacrosse, soccer, tennis, track/field (outdoor), track/field (indoor), volleyball, wrestling. *Women:* basketball, bowling, crew/rowing, cross-country, diving, equestrian sports, fencing, field hockey, golf, ice hockey, lacrosse, soccer, softball, swimming, tennis, track/field (outdoor), track/field (indoor), volleyball. **On-Campus Highlights:** Pitt Health and Recreation Center, Edgerton Center for Performing Arts, Linda E. McMahon Student Commons, Frank and Marisa Martire Business & Communications Center, Chapel of the Holy Spirit

ADMISSIONS

Freshman Academic Profile: Average high school GPA 3.5. 10% in top 10% of high school class, 29% in top 25% of high school class, 68% in top 50% of high school class. 75% from public high schools. **Test Scores:** SAT Math middle 50% range 530-600. SAT EBRW middle 50% range 530-600. ACT middle 50% range 23-27. Minimum internet-based TOEFL 80. Minimum paper TOEFL 550. **Basis for Candidate Selection:** *Very important factors considered include:* rigor of secondary school record, academic GPA, volunteer work, work experience. *Important factors considered include:* class rank, application essay, recommendation(s), interview, extracurricular activities, talent/ability, character/personal qualities, level of applicant's interest. *Other factors considered include:* standardized test scores, first generation, alumni/ae relation, geographical residence, state residency, religious affiliation/commitment, racial/ethnic status. **Freshman Admission Requirements:** High school diploma is required and GED is accepted *Academic units required:* 4 English, 3 math, 3 science, 1 science labs, 2 foreign language, 3 social studies, 3 history, 3 academic electives, *Academic units recommended:* 4 English, 4 math, 4 science, 2 science labs, 4 foreign language, 4 social studies, 4 history, 4 academic electives. **Freshman Admission Statistics:** 9,992 applied, 60.3% admitted, 23% enrolled. **Transfer Admission Requirements:** High school transcript, college transcript(s), essay or personal statement, Minimum college GPA of 2.5 required. Lowest grade transferable C-. **General Admission Information:** Application fee $50. Priority deadline 2/5. Nonfall registration accepted. Admission may be deferred for a maximum of 1 year.

COSTS AND FINANCIAL AID

Annual tuition $39,570. Room and board $14,770. Required fees $250. Average book expense $1,200. **Required Forms and Deadlines:** CSS/Financial Aid PROFILE; FAFSA; Noncustodial PROFILE. **Notification of Awards:** Applicants will be notified of awards on a rolling basis beginning 3/1. **Types of Aid:** *Need-based scholarships/grants:* College/university scholarship or grant aid from institutional funds; Federal Pell; Private scholarships; SEOG; State scholarships/grants. *Loans:* Direct PLUS loans; Direct Subsidized Stafford Loans; Direct Unsubsidized Stafford Loans. *Student Employment:* Federal Work-Study Program available. Institutional employment available. **Financial Aid Statistics:** 100% needy freshmen, 99% needy undergrads receive need-based scholarship or grant aid. 16% freshmen, 15% undergrads receive non-need-based scholarship or grant aid. 80% freshmen, 79% undergrads receive need-based self-help aid. 4% freshmen, 6% undergrads receive athletic scholarships. 70% freshmen, 63% undergrads receive any aid. 76% undergrads borrow to pay for school. Average cumulative indebtedness $40,240. **Criteria for awarding aid:** *Need-based:* Academics *Non-need-based:* Academics, Alumni affiliation, Art, Athletics, Leadership, Music/drama, Religious affiliation, State/district residency.

See page 1014.

SAGINAW VALLEY STATE UNIVERSITY

7400 Bay Road, University Center, MI 48710
Phone: 989-964-4200 • **Financial Aid Phone:** 989-964-4103
E-mail: admissions@svsu.edu • **CEEB Code:** 1766
Fax: 989-790-0180 • **Website:** www.svsu.edu • **ACT Code:** 2057

This public school was founded in 1963. It has a 782 acre campus.

RATINGS

Admissions Selectivity Rating: 79   **Fire Safety Rating:** 66   **Green Rating:** 60*

STUDENTS AND FACULTY

Enrollment: 7,498. **Student Body:** 59% female, 41% male, 2% out-of-state, 6% international (30 countries represented). Asian 1%, African American 8%, Caucasian 73%, Hispanic 4%, Native American <1%, Pacific Islander 0%, Two or more races 3%, Race unknown 4%.
Retention and Graduation: 74% freshmen return for sophomore year. 40% freshmen graduate within 6 years. 27% grads go on to further study within 1 year. **Faculty:** Student/faculty ratio 17:1. 291 full-time faculty, 88% hold PhDs, 46% are women. 0% of classes are taught by teaching assistants.

ACADEMICS

Degrees: Bachelor's; Doctoral/Professional; Master's; Post-Master's certificate **Classes:** Most classes have 10-19 students. Most lab/discussion sessions have 10-19 students. **Most popular majors:** Criminal Justice/Safety Studies; Social Work; Registered Nursing/Registered Nurse. **Special Study Options:** Accelerated program; Cooperative education program; Distance learning; Double major; Dual enrollment; English as a Second Language (ESL); Honors program; Independent study; Internships; Study abroad; Teacher certification program. Honors programs: The University Honors Program allows students to pursue their major and minor degree work, while providing enriched academic experiences in Honors courses, seminars, research projects, and social activities. The Honors experience enables students to work more intensively with active teacher/scholars and to participate in interdisciplinary courses. Honors students will have ample opportunity to develop as critical thinkers, active learners, and problem solvers. **Disability Services offered to physically disabled students:** Note-taking services; Reader services; Tutors. **Career services:** Alumni services; Career assessment; Internships

FACILITIES

Housing: Apartments for single students; Coed dorms; Special housing for disabled student; Theme housing 95% of campus accessible to physically disabled. **Special Academic Facilities/Equipment:** Sculpture gallery, fine arts center, center for health and physical education, independent testing lab, center for economic and business research, applied technology research center. **Computers:** Students can register for classes online. Administrative functions (other than registration) can be performed online.

CAMPUS LIFE

Environment: City **Activities:** Campus Ministries; Choral groups; Concert band; Dance; Drama/theater; International Student Organization; Jazz band; Literary magazine; Marching band; Model UN; Music ensembles; Musical theater; Pep band; Radio station; Student government; Student newspaper; Student-run film society 110 registered organizations, 8 honor societies, 9 religious organizations. 4 fraternities, 7 sororities. **Athletics (Intercollegiate):** *Men:* baseball, basketball, bowling, cheerleading, cross-country, football, golf, soccer, track/field (outdoor), track/field (indoor). *Women:* basketball, cheerleading, cross-country, soccer, softball, tennis, track/field (outdoor), track/field (indoor), volleyball. **On-Campus Highlights:** Student Center, Student Recreation Center (Ryder), Zahnow Library, Arbury Fine Arts Center, University Village **Environmental Initiatives:** Building buildings with energy savings in mind for many years.

ADMISSIONS

Freshman Academic Profile: Average high school GPA 3.4. 20% in top 10% of high school class, 45% in top 25% of high school class, 77% in top 50% of high school class. **Test Scores:** SAT Math middle 50% range 490-590. SAT EBRW middle 50% range 500-600. ACT middle 50% range 20-25. Minimum internet-based TOEFL 61. Minimum paper TOEFL 500. **Basis for Candidate Selection:** *Very important factors considered include:* academic GPA, standardized test scores, extracurricular activities. *Important factors considered include:* talent/ability. **Freshman Admission Requirements:** High school diploma is required and GED is accepted *Academic units recommended:* 4 English, 3 math, 3 science, 2 foreign language, 3 social studies. **Freshman Admission Statistics:** 6,457 applied, 73.8% admitted, 26% enrolled. **Transfer Admission Requirements:** college transcript(s), Minimum college GPA of 2.0 required. Lowest grade transferable C-. **General Admission Information:** Application fee $30. Nonfall registration accepted. Admission may be deferred for a maximum of 1 year.

COSTS AND FINANCIAL AID

Required Forms and Deadlines: CSS/Financial Aid PROFILE; FAFSA; Institution's own financial aid form. **Notification of Awards:** Applicants will be notified of awards on a rolling basis beginning 3/1. **Types of Aid:** *Need-based scholarships/grants:* College/university scholarship or grant aid from institutional funds; Federal Pell; Private scholarships; SEOG; State scholarships/grants. *Loans:* Direct PLUS loans; Direct Subsidized Stafford Loans; Direct Unsubsidized Stafford Loans. *Student Employment:* Federal Work-Study Program available. Institutional employment available. **Financial Aid Statistics:** 71% needy freshmen, 71% needy undergrads receive need-based scholarship or grant aid. 0% undergrads receive non-need-based scholarship or grant aid. 94% freshmen, 94% undergrads receive need-based self-help aid. 0% freshmen, 0% undergrads receive athletic scholarships. 94% freshmen, 95% undergrads receive any aid. **Criteria for awarding aid:** *Need-based:* Academics, Leadership, Minority status *Non-need-based:* Academics, Art, Athletics, Leadership, Minority status, Music/drama.

SAINT ANTHONY COLLEGE OF NURSING

995 Main St., Rockford, IL 61108-2468
Phone: 815-227-2141 · **Financial Aid Phone:** 815-395-5089
E-mail: admissions@sacn.edu
Fax: 815-227-2730 · **Website:** www.sacn.edu

This private school, affiliated with the Roman Catholic Church, was founded in 1915.

RATINGS

Admissions Selectivity Rating: 61   **Fire Safety Rating:** 60*   **Green Rating:** 60*

STUDENTS AND FACULTY

Enrollment: 230. **Student Body:** 89% female, 11% male, 10% out-of-state, 0% international (0 countries represented). Asian 5%, African American 2%, Caucasian 77%, Hispanic 13%, Native American 0%, Pacific Islander <1%, Two or more races 2%, Race unknown <1%.
Retention and Graduation: 100% freshmen return for sophomore year.
Faculty: Student/faculty ratio 7:1. 23 full-time faculty, 22% hold PhDs, 9% are members of minority groups, 91% are women. 0% of classes are taught by teaching assistants.

ACADEMICS

Degrees: Bachelor's; Doctoral Other; Master's; Post-Master's certificate **Classes:** Most classes have 10-19 students. Most lab/discussion sessions have 10-19 students. **Most popular majors:** Registered Nursing/Registered Nurse. **Special Study Options:** Independent study.

CAMPUS LIFE

Environment: City **Activities:** Student government 1 registered organization.

ADMISSIONS

Test Scores: Minimum paper TOEFL 550. **Basis for Candidate Selection:** *Very important factors considered include:* academic GPA. *Important factors considered include:* standardized test scores. *Other factors considered include:* level of applicant's interest. **Freshman Admission Requirements:** High school diploma is required and GED is accepted *Academic units required:* 2.5 science, **Transfer Admission Requirements:** college transcript(s), essay or personal statement, interview, Minimum college GPA of 2.5 required. Lowest grade transferable c. **General Admission Information:** Application fee $75. Priority deadline 9/15. Regular application deadline 2/15. Nonfall registration accepted.

COSTS AND FINANCIAL AID

Annual tuition $22,144. Required fees $481. **Types of Aid:** *Need-based scholarships/grants:* College/university scholarship or grant aid from institutional funds; Federal Pell; Private scholarships; State scholarships/grants. *Loans:* Direct PLUS loans; Direct Subsidized Stafford Loans; Direct Unsubsidized Stafford Loans. **Financial Aid Statistics:** 64% needy undergrads receive need-based scholarship or grant aid. 2% undergrads receive non-need-based scholarship or grant aid. 97% undergrads receive need-based self-help aid. 0% undergrads receive athletic scholarships. 0% freshmen, 86% undergrads receive any aid. **Criteria for awarding aid:** *Need-based:* Academics, Leadership *Non-need-based:* Academics.

SAINT FRANCIS MEDICAL CENTER COLLEGE OF NURSING

PO Box 208234, Peoria, IL 61603
Phone: 309-624-8980 · **Financial Aid Phone:** (309)655-4119
E-mail: janice.e.farquharson@osfhealthcare.org
Fax: 309-624-8973 · **Website:** http://www.sfmccon.edu/

This private school, affiliated with the Roman Catholic Church, was founded in 1905.

RATINGS

Admissions Selectivity Rating: 0   **Fire Safety Rating:** 98   **Green Rating:** 60*

STUDENTS AND FACULTY

Enrollment: 408. **Student Body:** 90% female, 10% male, 1% out-of-state, <1% international (2 countries represented). Asian 4%, African American 2%, Caucasian 91%, Hispanic 2%, Native American 0%, Pacific Islander 0%, Two or more races 0%, Race unknown 1%.
Faculty: Student/faculty ratio 10:1. 36 full-time faculty, 33% hold PhDs, 0% are members of minority groups, 97% are women. 0% of classes are taught by teaching assistants.

ACADEMICS

Degrees: Bachelor's; Doctoral; Master's; Post-Master's certificate **Special Study Options:** Accelerated program; Distance learning; Independent study; Study abroad. **Disability Services offered to physically disabled students:** Tutors.

FACILITIES

Housing: Coed dorms 1% of campus accessible to physically diasbled. **Computers:**

CAMPUS LIFE

Environment: City **Activities:** Student government.

ADMISSIONS

Freshman Admission Requirements: High school diploma is required and GED is accepted **Transfer Admission Requirements:** High school transcript, college transcript(s), essay or personal statement, statement of good standing from prior institution(s). Minimum college GPA of 2.50 required. Lowest grade transferable C. **General Admission Information:** Application fee $50. Priority deadline 9/15.

COSTS AND FINANCIAL AID

Annual tuition $19,140. Required fees $930. Average book expense $1,218. **Required Forms and Deadlines:** FAFSA; Institution's own financial aid form. **Notification of Awards:** Applicants will be notified of awards on a rolling basis beginning 5/15. **Types of Aid:** *Need-based scholarships/grants:* College/university scholarship or grant aid from institutional funds; Federal Pell; Private scholarships; State scholarships/grants. *Loans:* Direct PLUS loans; Direct Subsidized Stafford Loans; Direct Unsubsidized Stafford Loans. **Financial Aid Statistics:** 75% needy undergrads receive need-based scholarship or grant aid. 0% undergrads receive non-need-based scholarship or grant aid. 86% undergrads receive need-based self-help aid. 0% undergrads receive athletic scholarships. **Criteria for awarding aid:** *Non-need-based:* Academics, Alumni affiliation.

SAINT FRANCIS UNIVERSITY (PA)

PO Box 600, Loretto, PA 15940
Phone: 814-472-3000 · **Financial Aid Phone:** 814-472-3010
E-mail: admissions@francis.edu · **CEEB Code:** 2797
Fax: 814-472-3335 · **ACT Code:** 3682

This private school, affiliated with the Roman Catholic Church, was founded in 1847. It has a 600 acre campus.

RATINGS

Admissions Selectivity Rating: 79   **Fire Safety Rating:** 84   **Green Rating:** 60*

STUDENTS AND FACULTY

Enrollment: 1,703. **Student Body:** 63% female, 37% male, 20% out-of-state, 5% international (25 countries represented). Asian 1%, African American 6%,

Caucasian 79%, Hispanic 2%, Native American <1%, Pacific Islander <1%, Two or more races 1%, Race unknown 6%.
Retention and Graduation: 86% freshmen return for sophomore year. 29% grads go on to further study within 1 year. 5% grads pursue arts and sciences degrees. 3% grads pursue law degrees. 9% grads pursue business degrees. 3% grads pursue medical degrees. **Faculty:** Student/faculty ratio 14:1. 125 full-time faculty, 70% hold PhDs, 7% are members of minority groups, 56% are women. 0% of classes are taught by teaching assistants.

ACADEMICS
Degrees: Associate; Bachelor's; Doctoral/Professional; Master's; Post-Bachelor's certificate **Classes:** Most classes have 20-29 students. Most lab/discussion sessions have 20-29 students. **Most popular majors:** Physician Assistant; Health Professions And Related Clinical Sciences, Other; Business/Commerce, General. **Special Study Options:** Cooperative education program; Distance learning; Double major; English as a Second Language (ESL); Honors program; Independent study; Internships; Liberal arts/career combination; Student-designed major; Study abroad; Teacher certification program. Honors programs: The Saint Francis University (SFU) Honors Program is designed to challenge highly motivated students by making them part of a community of learners, while at the same time affording them the opportunity to devise a personal program of study. Students are introduced to the Honors Program through a year-long learning community experience consisting of a four-course sequence with intense critical thinking, writing and speaking components. Successful completion of this sequence waives the university speech requirement for the Honors student. Combined degree programs: BA/DDS; BA/MD. **Disability Services offered to physically disabled students:** Note-taking services; Tape recorders; Tutors. **Career services:** Alumni network; Career assessment; Career/job search classes; Internships

FACILITIES
Housing: Apartments for single students; Coed dorms; Fraternity/sorority housing; Men's dorms; Women's dorms 20% of campus accessible to physically diasbled. **Special Academic Facilities/Equipment:** Art museum, elementary-level library for education majors, physician assistant practice facilities, cadaver lab, physical therapy lab, Center of Excellence for Remote and Medically Underserved Areas. **Computers:** Administrative functions (other than registration) can be performed online. Undergraduates are required to own a computer.

CAMPUS LIFE
Environment: Rural **Activities:** Campus Ministries; Choral groups; Dance; Drama/theater; Jazz band; Marching band; Music ensembles; Pep band; Radio station; Student government; Student newspaper; Student-run film society; Television station; Yearbook 60 registered organizations, 9 honor societies, 10 religious organizations. 3 fraternities, 3 sororities. **Athletics (Intercollegiate):** *Men:* basketball, cross-country, football, golf, soccer, swimming, tennis, track/field (outdoor), track/field (indoor), volleyball. *Women:* basketball, cross-country, field hockey, golf, lacrosse, soccer, softball, swimming, tennis, track/field (outdoor), track/field (indoor), volleyball. **On-Campus Highlights:** DiSepio Institute, JFK Student Center, Immaculate Conception Chapel, Stokes Athletics Facility, Mt. Assisi Gardens

ADMISSIONS
Freshman Academic Profile: 30% in top 10% of high school class, 50% in top 25% of high school class, 83% in top 50% of high school class. 79% from public high schools. **Test Scores:** SAT Math middle 50% range 470-590. SAT EBRW middle 50% range 460-570. ACT middle 50% range 21-26. Minimum paper TOEFL 500. **Basis for Candidate Selection:** *Very important factors considered include:* rigor of secondary school record, class rank, academic GPA, standardized test scores, extracurricular activities. *Important factors considered include:* application essay, recommendation(s), interview, talent/ability, character/personal qualities, volunteer work.level of applicant's interest. *Other factors considered include:* alumni/ae relation, work experience. **Freshman Admission Requirements:** High school diploma is required and GED is accepted *Academic units required:* 4 English, 2 math, 1 science, 2 social studies, 7 academic electives, *Academic units recommended:* 4 English, 4 math, 2 science, 1 science labs, 2 foreign language, 2 social studies, 7 academic electives, 4 units from above areas or other academic areas. **Freshman Admission Statistics:** 2,045 applied, 70.0% admitted, 28% enrolled. **Transfer Admission Requirements:** High school transcript, college transcript(s), standardized test scores, statement of good standing from prior institution(s). Minimum college GPA of 2.0 required. Lowest grade transferable C. **General Admission Information:** Application fee $30. Priority deadline 4/1. Nonfall registration accepted. Admission may be deferred.

COSTS AND FINANCIAL AID
Annual tuition $30,028. Room and board $11,190. Required fees $1,100. Average book expense $2,000. **Required Forms and Deadlines:** FAFSA. **Notification of Awards:** Applicants will be notified of awards on a rolling basis beginning 3/1. **Types of Aid:** *Need-based scholarships/grants:* College/

university scholarship or grant aid from institutional funds; Federal Pell; Private scholarships; SEOG; State scholarships/grants. *Loans: Student Employment:* Federal Work-Study Program available. Institutional employment available. **Financial Aid Statistics:** 55% needy freshmen, 59% needy undergrads receive need-based scholarship or grant aid. 100% freshmen, 94% undergrads receive non-need-based scholarship or grant aid. 72% freshmen, 77% undergrads receive need-based self-help aid. 33% freshmen, 27% undergrads receive athletic scholarships. 98% freshmen receive any aid. **Criteria for awarding aid:** *Non-need-based:* Academics, Alumni affiliation, Athletics, Leadership, Music/drama, Religious affiliation.

See page 1018.

SAINT JOSEPH SEMINARY COLLEGE

75376 River Road, St. Benedict, LA 70457
Phone: 985-867-2273 • **Financial Aid Phone:** 985-867-2229
E-mail: registrar@sjasc.edu • **CEEB Code:** 6689
Fax: 985-327-1085 • **ACT Code:** 1604

This private school, affiliated with the Roman Catholic Church, was founded in 1891. It has a 1200 acre campus.

RATINGS
Admissions Selectivity Rating: 69 **Fire Safety Rating:** 60* **Green Rating:** 60*

STUDENTS AND FACULTY
Enrollment: 100. **Student Body:** 0% female, 100% male, 34% out-of-state, international. Asian 5%, Caucasian 69%, Hispanic 26%, Native American 0%, Race unknown 0%.
Faculty: Student/faculty ratio 7:1. 16 full-time faculty, 31% hold PhDs, 0% are members of minority groups, 44% are women. 0% of classes are taught by teaching assistants.

ACADEMICS
Degrees: Bachelor's **Special Study Options:** Distance learning; English as a Second Language (ESL); Independent study. **Disability Services offered to physically disabled students:** Tape recorders; Tutors.

FACILITIES
Housing: Men's dorms 100% of campus accessible to physically diasbled.

CAMPUS LIFE
Environment: Rural **Activities:** Choral groups; Drama/theater; Literary magazine; Student government; Student newspaper; Yearbook 1 religious organizations.

ADMISSIONS
Test Scores: Minimum paper TOEFL 520. **Basis for Candidate Selection:** *Very important factors considered include:* rigor of secondary school record, character/personal qualities, religious affiliation/commitment. *Important factors considered include:* standardized test scores, recommendation(s). *Other factors considered include:* class rank, interview, extracurricular activities, volunteer work. **Freshman Admission Requirements:** High school diploma is required and GED is accepted *Academic units required:* 3 English, 2 math, 2 science, 2 foreign language, 1 history, *Academic units recommended:* 3 English, 2 math, 2 science, 2 foreign language, 1 history. **Freshman Admission Statistics:** 11 applied, 100.0% admitted, 100% enrolled. **Transfer Admission Requirements:** High school transcript, college transcript(s), standardized test scores, Lowest grade transferable C. **General Admission Information:** Nonfall registration accepted.

COSTS AND FINANCIAL AID
Annual tuition $13,500. Room and board $13,040. Required fees $1,165. Average book expense $1,000. **Required Forms and Deadlines:** FAFSA; Institution's own financial aid form; State aid form. **Notification of Awards:** Applicants will be notified of awards on a rolling basis beginning 8/3. **Types of Aid:** *Need-based scholarships/grants:* College/university scholarship or grant aid from institutional funds; Federal Pell; Private scholarships; SEOG; State scholarships/grants. **Financial Aid Statistics:** 100% needy freshmen, 100% needy undergrads receive need-based scholarship or grant aid. 100% freshmen, 20% undergrads receive non-need-based scholarship or grant aid. 100% freshmen, 100% undergrads receive need-based self-help aid. 0% freshmen, 0% undergrads receive athletic scholarships.

SAINT JOSEPH'S COLLEGE (IN)

P.O. Box 890, Rensselaer, IN 47978
Phone: 219-866-6170 • **Financial Aid Phone:** 800.447.8781
E-mail: admissions@saintjoe.edu • **CEEB Code:** 1697
Fax: 219-866-6122 • **Website:** www.saintjoe.edu • **ACT Code:** 1240

This private school, affiliated with the Roman Catholic Church, was founded in 1889. It has a 180 acre campus.

RATINGS

Admissions Selectivity Rating: 74   **Fire Safety Rating:** 84   **Green Rating:** 60*

STUDENTS AND FACULTY

Enrollment: 948. **Student Body:** 52% female, 48% male, 24% out-of-state, 3% international (12 countries represented). Asian <1%, African American 10%, Caucasian 76%, Hispanic 6%, Native American <1%, Pacific Islander 0%, Two or more races 4%, Race unknown 1%.
Retention and Graduation: 68% freshmen return for sophomore year. 15% grads go on to further study within 1 year. 13% grads pursue arts and sciences degrees. 25% grads pursue law degrees. 33% grads pursue business degrees. 4% grads pursue medical degrees. **Faculty:** Student/faculty ratio 10:1. 80 full-time faculty, 69% hold PhDs, 9% are members of minority groups, 55% are women. 0% of classes are taught by teaching assistants.

ACADEMICS

Degrees: Bachelor's; Diploma; Master's; Post-Bachelor's certificate; Terminal Associate **Classes:** Most classes have 10-19 students. **Most popular majors:** Elementary Education And Teaching; Biology/Biological Sciences, General; Business/Commerce, General. **Special Study Options:** Accelerated program; Cross-registration; Double major; Dual enrollment; Honors program; Independent study; Internships; Liberal arts/career combination; Student-designed major; Study abroad; Teacher certification program. **Disability Services offered to physically disabled students:** Note-taking services; Reader services; Tape recorders; Tutors. **Career services:** Alumni network; Alumni services; Career assessment; Internships; Regional alumni

FACILITIES

Housing: Apartments for single students; Coed dorms; Men's dorms; Special housing for disabled student; Women's dorms 74% of campus accessible to physically diasbled. **Computers:** 100% of dorms, 100% of libraries, 100% of dining areas, have wireless network access.

CAMPUS LIFE

Environment: Village **Activities:** Campus Ministries; Choral groups; Concert band; Dance; Drama/theater; International Student Organization; Jazz band; Literary magazine; Marching band; Model UN; Music ensembles; Musical theater; Pep band; Radio station; Student government; Television station 41 registered organizations, 4 honor societies, 7 religious organizations. **Athletics (Intercollegiate):** *Men:* baseball, basketball, cross-country, football, golf, soccer, tennis, track/field (outdoor), track/field (indoor). *Women:* basketball, cross-country, golf, soccer, softball, tennis, track/field (outdoor), track/field (indoor), volleyball. **On-Campus Highlights:** Rev. Charles Banet, C.PP.S. Core Education Building, Saint Joseph's Chapel, Lourdes Grotto, Hanson Recreation Center/Fitness Center, Lake Banet

ADMISSIONS

Freshman Academic Profile: Average high school GPA 3.1. 8% in top 10% of high school class, 22% in top 25% of high school class, 61% in top 50% of high school class. 85% from public high schools. **Test Scores:** SAT Math middle 50% range 530-430. SAT EBRW middle 50% range 510-420. ACT middle 50% range 25-18. Minimum internet-based TOEFL 80. Minimum paper TOEFL 550. **Basis for Candidate Selection:** *Very important factors considered include:* academic GPA, standardized test scores. *Important factors considered include:* rigor of secondary school record. *Other factors considered include:* application essay, recommendation(s). **Freshman Admission Requirements:** High school diploma is required and GED is accepted **Freshman Admission Statistics:** 1,506 applied, 76.8% admitted, 20% enrolled. **Transfer Admission Requirements:** college transcript(s), Minimum college GPA of 2.0 required. Lowest grade transferable C-. **General Admission Information:** Application fee $25. Nonfall registration accepted. Admission may be deferred for a maximum of 1 academic year.

COSTS AND FINANCIAL AID

Annual tuition $28,252. Room and board $9,480. Required fees $430. Average book expense $900. **Required Forms and Deadlines:** FAFSA. **Notification of Awards:** Applicants will be notified of awards on a rolling basis beginning 3/1. **Types of Aid:** *Need-based scholarships/grants:* College/ university scholarship or grant aid from institutional funds; Federal Pell; Private scholarships; SEOG; State scholarships/grants. *Loans:* Direct PLUS loans;

Direct Subsidized Stafford Loans; Direct Unsubsidized Stafford Loans. *Student Employment:* Federal Work-Study Program available. Institutional employment available. **Financial Aid Statistics:** 99% needy freshmen, 97% needy undergrads receive need-based scholarship or grant aid. 22% freshmen, 30% undergrads receive non-need-based scholarship or grant aid. 71% freshmen, 67% undergrads receive need-based self-help aid. 9% freshmen, 7% undergrads receive athletic scholarships. 99% freshmen, 99% undergrads receive any aid. 83% undergrads borrow to pay for school. Average cumulative indebtedness $28,527. **Criteria for awarding aid:** *Non-need-based:* Academics, Alumni affiliation, Athletics, Music/drama, Religious affiliation.

SAINT JOSEPH'S UNIVERSITY (PA)

5600 City Avenue, Philadelphia, PA 19131
Phone: 888-BE-A-HAWK • **Financial Aid Phone:** 610-660-1556
E-mail: admit@sju.edu • **CEEB Code:** 2801
Fax: 610-660-1314 • **Website:** www.sju.edu • **ACT Code:** 3684

This private school, affiliated with the Roman Catholic-Jesuit Church, was founded in 1851. It has a 114 acre campus.

RATINGS

Admissions Selectivity Rating: 81   **Fire Safety Rating:** 90   **Green Rating:** 74

STUDENTS AND FACULTY

Enrollment: 5,004. **Student Body:** 55% female, 45% male, 53% out-of-state, 2% international (41 countries represented). Asian 2%, African American 6%, Caucasian 78%, Hispanic 7%, Native American <1%, Pacific Islander <1%, Two or more races 2%, Race unknown 2%.
Retention and Graduation: 91% freshmen return for sophomore year. 76% freshmen graduate within 4 years. 82% freshmen graduate within 6 years. 13% grads go on to further study within 1 year. 4% grads pursue arts and sciences degrees. 1.1% grads pursue law degrees. 2% grads pursue business degrees. 3.3% grads pursue medical degrees. **Faculty:** Student/faculty ratio 11:1. 308 full-time faculty, 91% hold PhDs, 18% are members of minority groups, 45% are women. 0% of classes are taught by teaching assistants.

ACADEMICS

Degrees: Associate; Bachelor's; Doctoral/Research; Master's; Post-Bachelor's certificate; Post-Master's certificate **Classes:** Most classes have 20-29 students. **Most popular majors:** Finance, General; Marketing/Marketing Management, General; Special Products Marketing Operations. **Special Study Options:** Accelerated program; Cooperative education program; Distance learning; Double major; Dual enrollment; English as a Second Language (ESL); Exchange student program (domestic); Honors program; Independent study; Internships; Student-designed major; Study abroad; Teacher certification program; Weekend college. Honors programs: There are distinctive benefits attached to belonging to the SJU Honors Program: Team-taught courses allow distinguished faculty members to share their knowledge and expertise with students in a challenging academic environment. Individual honors courses stress a detailed and thorough scholarly exploration of different fields of knowledge. Honors students register ahead of other students in their year. Honors suites in the residence halls allow like-minded students to live together, even as freshmen. Honors students are provided with free tickets and transportation to concerts and performances by world-renowned artists at some of Philadelphia's most revered centers of culture. Receptions, concerts and lectures are regularly sponsored by the Honors Program for Honors Students. Students have access to Claver House, a quiet retreat where honors students can study, work with personal computers and attend receptions. Students have opportunities to present research and creative work at national conferences and seminars; they are also kept informed about scholarship and funding opportunities for graduate and professional work. **Disability Services offered to physically disabled students:** Note-taking services; Reader services; Tape recorders; Tutors. **Career services:** Alumni network; Alumni services; Career assessment; Career/job search classes; Internships; Regional alumni

FACILITIES

Housing: Apartments for single students; Coed dorms; Men's dorms; Special housing for international students; Theme housing; Women's dorms 85% of campus accessible to physically diasbled. **Special Academic Facilities/ Equipment:** Post Learning Commons Claver House—Honors Program Mandeville Hall Merion Hall Moot Board Room University Gallery Wall Street Trading Room **Computers:** 100% of classrooms, 100% of dorms, 100%

of libraries, 100% of dining areas, 100% of student union, 10% of common outdoor areas have wireless network access. Students can register for classes online. Administrative functions (other than registration) can be performed online.

CAMPUS LIFE

Environment: Metropolis **Activities:** Campus Ministries; Choral groups; Dance; Drama/theater; International Student Organization; Jazz band; Literary magazine; Music ensembles; Musical theater; Pep band; Radio station; Student government; Student newspaper; Student-run film society; Yearbook 100 registered organizations, 20 honor societies, 4 fraternities, 4 sororities. **Athletics (Intercollegiate):** *Men:* baseball, basketball, crew/rowing, cross-country, golf, lacrosse, soccer, tennis, track/field (outdoor), track/field (indoor). *Women:* basketball, crew/rowing, cross-country, field hockey, lacrosse, soccer, softball, tennis, track/field (outdoor), track/field (indoor). **On-Campus Highlights:** Campion / The Perch, Post Learning Commons, Hagan Arena, Merion Hall, Hawks Landing **Environmental Initiatives:** We have a full-time office of Health, Safety and Environmental compliance.

ADMISSIONS

Freshman Academic Profile: Average high school GPA 3.6. 21% in top 10% of high school class, 51% in top 25% of high school class, 87% in top 50% of high school class. 50% from public high schools. **Test Scores:** SAT Math middle 50% range 550-650. SAT EBRW middle 50% range 560-640. ACT middle 50% range 23-28. Minimum internet-based TOEFL 79. Minimum paper TOEFL 550. **Basis for Candidate Selection:** *Very important factors considered include:* rigor of secondary school record, class rank, academic GPA. *Important factors considered include:* application essay, standardized test scores, recommendation(s). *Other factors considered include:* interview, extracurricular activities, talent/ability, character/personal qualities, first generation, alumni/ae relation, geographical residence, racial/ethnic status, volunteer work, work experience, level of applicant's interest. **Freshman Admission Requirements:** High school diploma is required and GED is accepted *Academic units required:* 4 English, 3 math, 3 science, 2 foreign language, 3 social studies, 5 academic electives. **Freshman Admission Statistics:** 8,972 applied, 77.2% admitted, 16% enrolled. **Transfer Admission Requirements:** High school transcript, college transcript(s), statement of good standing from prior institution(s). Minimum college GPA of 2.5 required. Lowest grade transferable C. **General Admission Information:** Application fee $50. Priority deadline 2/1. Nonfall registration accepted. Admission may be deferred.

COSTS AND FINANCIAL AID

Required Forms and Deadlines: FAFSA. **Notification of Awards:** Applicants will be notified of awards on a rolling basis beginning 3/31. **Types of Aid:** *Need-based scholarships/grants:* College/university scholarship or grant aid from institutional funds; Federal Pell; Private scholarships; SEOG; State scholarships/grants. *Loans:* Direct PLUS loans; Direct Subsidized Stafford Loans; Direct Unsubsidized Stafford Loans. *Student Employment:* Federal Work-Study Program available. Institutional employment available. **Financial Aid Statistics:** 97% needy freshmen, 95% needy undergrads receive need-based scholarship or grant aid. 66% freshmen, 69% undergrads receive non-need-based scholarship or grant aid. 72% freshmen, 70% undergrads receive need-based self-help aid. 3% freshmen, 5% undergrads receive athletic scholarships. 98% freshmen, 95% undergrads receive any aid. **Criteria for awarding aid:** *Need-based:* Academics, Athletics, Minority status, Music/drama *Non-need-based:* Academics, Alumni affiliation, Art, Athletics, Minority status, Music/drama.

SAINT LEO UNIVERSITY

P.O. Box 6665, Saint Leo, FL 33574-6665
Phone: (352)588-8283 • **Financial Aid Phone:** 800-240-7658
E-mail: admissions@saintleo.edu • **CEEB Code:** 5638
Fax: (352)588-8257 • **Website:** www.saintleo.edu • **ACT Code:** 755

This private school, affiliated with the Roman Catholic Church, was founded in 1889. It has a 297 acre campus.

RATINGS

Admissions Selectivity Rating: 75   **Fire Safety Rating:** 93   **Green Rating:** 60*

STUDENTS AND FACULTY

Enrollment: 2,367. **Student Body:** 54% female, 46% male, 29% out-of-state, 12% international (66 countries represented). Asian 2%, African American 13%, Caucasian 45%, Hispanic 19%, Native American <1%, Pacific Islander 0%, Two or more races 3%, Race unknown 6%.

Retention and Graduation: 71% freshmen return for sophomore year. **Faculty:** Student/faculty ratio 15:1. 125 full-time faculty, 82% hold PhDs, 10% are members of minority groups, 41% are women. 0% of classes are taught by teaching assistants.

ACADEMICS

Degrees: Associate; Bachelor's; Certificate; Doctoral/Professional; Master's; Post-Bachelor's certificate; Transfer Associate **Classes:** Most classes have 20-29 students. Most lab/discussion sessions have 20-29 students. **Most popular majors:** Psychology, General; Political Science And Government, General; Business Administration And Management, General. **Special Study Options:** Distance learning; Double major; Dual enrollment; English as a Second Language (ESL); Honors program; Independent study; Internships; Liberal arts/career combination; Study abroad; Teacher certification program; Weekend college. Honors programs: The Saint Leo University Honors Program consists of an integrated sequence of six interdisciplinary courses, spread over the first three years of college, and an extensive senior honors project carried out under the supervision of a distinguished faculty mentor. Combined degree programs: BA/DDS. **Disability Services offered to physically disabled students:** Note-taking services; Reader services; Tape recorders; Tutors. **Career services:** Alumni network; Alumni services; Career assessment; Career/job search classes; Internships

FACILITIES

Housing: Apartments for single students; Coed dorms; Men's dorms; Special housing for disabled student; Theme housing; Wellness housing; Women's dorms 95% of campus accessible to physically disabled. **Computers:** 95% of classrooms, 85% of dorms, 100% of libraries, 100% of dining areas, 100% of student union, 90% of common outdoor areas have wireless network access. Students can register for classes online. Administrative functions (other than registration) can be performed online.

CAMPUS LIFE

Environment: Rural **Activities:** Campus Ministries; Choral groups; Dance; Drama/theater; International Student Organization; Literary magazine; Music ensembles; Musical theater; Student government; Student newspaper; Yearbook 58 registered organizations, 12 honor societies, 7 religious organizations. 6 fraternities, 4 sororities. **Athletics (Intercollegiate):** *Men:* baseball, basketball, cross-country, golf, lacrosse, soccer, swimming, tennis. *Women:* basketball, cross-country, golf, soccer, softball, swimming, tennis, volleyball. **On-Campus Highlights:** School of Business, Kirk Hall, Student Community Center & Activities Building, Marion Bowman Activities Center, Swimming Pool

ADMISSIONS

Freshman Academic Profile: Average high school GPA 3.5. 10% in top 10% of high school class, 32% in top 25% of high school class, 69% in top 50% of high school class. 76% from public high schools. **Test Scores:** SAT Math middle 50% range 450-540. SAT EBRW middle 50% range 458-540. ACT middle 50% range 20-24. Minimum internet-based TOEFL 78. Minimum paper TOEFL 550. **Basis for Candidate Selection:** *Very important factors considered include:* rigor of secondary school record, academic GPA, standardized test scores, recommendation(s), character/personal qualities. *Important factors considered include:* interview, extracurricular activities, talent/ability, alumni/ae relation, volunteer work.level of applicant's interest. *Other factors considered include:* class rank, application essay, first generation, work experience. **Freshman Admission Requirements:** High school diploma is required and GED is accepted *Academic units recommended:* 4 English, 3 math, 2 science, 2 foreign language, 3 social studies, 2 academic electives. **Freshman Admission Statistics:** 3,865 applied, 72.5% admitted, 24% enrolled. **Transfer Admission Requirements:** college transcript(s), essay or personal statement, statement of good standing from prior institution(s). Minimum college GPA of 2.0 required. Lowest grade transferable D. **General Admission Information:** Application fee $40. Priority deadline 1/15. Nonfall registration accepted. Admission may be deferred for a maximum of 1 year.

COSTS AND FINANCIAL AID

Annual tuition $20,760. Room and board $10,210. Required fees $370. Average book expense $1,720. **Required Forms and Deadlines:** FAFSA; State aid form. **Notification of Awards:** Applicants will be notified of awards on a rolling basis beginning 1/1. **Types of Aid:** *Need-based scholarships/grants:* College/university scholarship or grant aid from institutional funds; Federal Pell; Private scholarships; SEOG; State scholarships/grants; United Negro College Fund. *Loans:* Direct PLUS loans; Direct Subsidized Stafford Loans; Direct Unsubsidized Stafford Loans. *Student Employment:* Federal Work-Study Program available. Institutional employment available. **Financial Aid Statistics:** 100% needy freshmen, 100% needy undergrads receive need-based scholarship or grant aid. 7% freshmen, 7% undergrads receive non-need-based scholarship or grant aid. 82% freshmen, 87% undergrads receive need-based self-help aid. 4% freshmen, 5% undergrads receive athletic scholarships. 99% freshmen, 89% undergrads receive any aid. 73% undergrads borrow to pay for school. Average cumulative indebtedness $28,456. **Criteria for awarding aid:** *Non-need-based:* Academics, Alumni affiliation, Athletics, Leadership, Minority status, Religious affiliation, State/district residency.

SAINT LOUIS UNIVERSITY

One North Grand Boulevard, Saint Louis, MO 63103
Phone: (314) 977-2500 • **Financial Aid Phone:** 314-977-2350
E-mail: admission@slu.edu • **CEEB Code:** 6629
Fax: (314) 977-7136 • **Website:** www.slu.edu • **ACT Code:** 2352

This private school, affiliated with the Roman Catholic-Jesuit Church, was founded in 1818. It has a 281 acre campus.

RATINGS

Admissions Selectivity Rating: 89   **Fire Safety Rating:** 93   **Green Rating:** 82

STUDENTS AND FACULTY

Enrollment: 7,209. **Student Body:** 60% female, 40% male, 59% out-of-state, 5% international (69 countries represented). Asian 10%, African American 6%, Caucasian 69%, Hispanic 6%, Native American <1%, Pacific Islander <1%, Two or more races 3%, Race unknown 1%.
Retention and Graduation: 90% freshmen return for sophomore year. 68% freshmen graduate within 4 years. 77% freshmen graduate within 6 years. 31% grads go on to further study within 1 year. **Faculty:** Student/faculty ratio 9:1. 701 full-time faculty, 90% hold PhDs, 16% are members of minority groups, 49% are women.

ACADEMICS

Degrees: Associate; Bachelor's; Certificate; Doctoral; Doctoral Other; Doctoral/Professional; Doctoral/Research; Master's; Post-Bachelor's certificate; Post-Master's certificate **Classes:** Most classes have 20-29 students. **Most popular majors:** Biology/Biological Sciences, General; Registered Nursing/Registered Nurse; Business Administration And Management, General.
Special Study Options: Accelerated program; Cooperative education program; Cross-registration; Distance learning; Double major; Dual enrollment; English as a Second Language (ESL); Exchange student program (domestic); Honors program; Independent study; Internships; Liberal arts/career combination; Student-designed major; Study abroad; Teacher certification program. Honors programs: The University Honors Program at Saint Louis University offers eligible students the opportunity to develop an individual course of study that complements their undergraduate major, leading to an Honors distinction on the transcript. Undergraduates from any of the schools and colleges at Saint Louis University can successfully pursue this distinction through the University Honors Program if they are admitted. The Saint Louis University Honors Program offers interdisciplinary programs and opportunities with reflective and expressive elements to students in the Honors Program. The University Honors Program offers seminar courses with integrated collaborative learning experiences including service learning, internships, and research. The University Honors Program offers Honors students the opportunity to earn university honors credit through reflective study abroad experiences. The University Honors Program offers Honors students a competitive grant ($1,200) to facilitate original research projects in their academic field of study. The University Honors Program offers Honors courses at the Saint Louis University Madrid Campus. The University Honors Program offers teaching assistant positions to undergraduate Honors students. The University Honors Program offers a residential learning community that is associated with core honors courses. The University Honors Program provides academic, cultural, and social opportunities. The University Honors Program provides peer mentorship programs. The University Honors Program provides individualized advising on post-baccalaureate scholarships and fellowships. Combined degree programs: BA/JD; BA/MA. **Disability Services offered to physically disabled students:** Note-taking services; Reader services; Tape recorders; Tutors. **Career services:** Alumni network; Alumni services; Career assessment; Career/job search classes; Internships; Regional alumni

FACILITIES

Housing: Apartments for single students; Coed dorms; Fraternity/sorority housing; Special housing for disabled student; Special housing for international students; Theme housing 95% of campus accessible to physically diasbled.
Special Academic Facilities/Equipment: Saint Louis University Museum of Art (SLUMA), Museum of Contemporary Religious Art (MOCRA), and The McNamee Gallery of Samuel Cupples House **Computers:** 100% of classrooms, 100% of dorms, 100% of libraries, 100% of dining areas, 100% of student union, 100% of common outdoor areas have wireless network access. Students can register for classes online. Administrative functions (other than registration) can be performed online.

CAMPUS LIFE

Environment: Metropolis **Activities:** Campus Ministries; Choral groups; Dance; Drama/theater; International Student Organization; Jazz band; Literary magazine; Model UN; Music ensembles; Musical theater; Pep band; Radio station; Student government; Student newspaper; Symphony orchestra; Television station 170 registered organizations, 25 honor societies, 36 religious organizations. 11 fraternities, 6 sororities. **Athletics (Intercollegiate):** *Men:* baseball, basketball, cross-country, diving, soccer, swimming, tennis, track/field (outdoor), track/field (indoor). *Women:* basketball, cross-country, diving, field hockey, soccer, softball, swimming, tennis, track/field (outdoor), track/field (indoor), volleyball. **On-Campus Highlights:** St. Francis Xavier Church, Busch Student Center, Pius Library, Simon Recreation Center, Chaifetz Arena

ADMISSIONS

Freshman Academic Profile: Average high school GPA 3.9. 50% in top 10% of high school class, 76% in top 25% of high school class, 94% in top 50% of high school class. **Test Scores:** SAT Math middle 50% range 580-700. SAT EBRW middle 50% range 590-690. ACT middle 50% range 25-31. Minimum internet-based TOEFL 80. Minimum paper TOEFL 550. **Basis for Candidate Selection:** *Very important factors considered include:* academic GPA, application essay, standardized test scores. *Important factors considered include:* rigor of secondary school record, interview, extracurricular activities, talent/ability, character/personal qualities, volunteer work. *Other factors considered include:* recommendation(s), first generation, alumni/ae relation, work experience, level of applicant's interest. **Freshman Admission Requirements:** High school diploma is required and GED is accepted *Academic units required:* 4 English, 4 math, 3 science, 3 foreign language, 3 social studies, 3 academic electives, *Academic units recommended:* 4 English, 4 math, 3 science, 3 foreign language, 3 social studies, 3 academic electives. **Freshman Admission Statistics:** 13,431 applied, 64.4% admitted, 19% enrolled. **Transfer Admission Requirements:** college transcript(s), Minimum college GPA of 2.0 required. Lowest grade transferable C. **General Admission Information:** Priority deadline 12/1. Regular application deadline 8/15. Nonfall registration accepted. Admission may be deferred for a maximum of 1 year.

COSTS AND FINANCIAL AID

Required Forms and Deadlines: FAFSA. **Notification of Awards:** Applicants will be notified of awards on a rolling basis beginning 2/1. **Types of Aid:** *Need-based scholarships/grants:* College/university scholarship or grant aid from institutional funds; Federal Nursing Scholarships; Federal Pell; Private scholarships; SEOG; State scholarships/grants. *Loans:* Direct PLUS loans; Direct Subsidized Stafford Loans; Direct Unsubsidized Stafford Loans. *Student Employment:* Federal Work-Study Program available. Institutional employment available. **Financial Aid Statistics:** 98% needy freshmen, 94% needy undergrads receive need-based scholarship or grant aid. 18% freshmen, 13% undergrads receive non-need-based scholarship or grant aid. 62% freshmen, 70% undergrads receive need-based self-help aid. 4% freshmen, 3% undergrads receive athletic scholarships. 97% freshmen, 89% undergrads receive any aid. 58% undergrads borrow to pay for school. Average cumulative indebtedness $33,299. **Criteria for awarding aid:** *Non-need-based:* Academics, Art, Athletics, Leadership, Music/drama, Religious affiliation.

See page 1020.

SAINT MARTIN'S UNIVERSITY

5000 Abbey Way SE, Lacey, WA 98503-7500
Phone: 360-438-4596 • **Financial Aid Phone:** (360) 438-4397
E-mail: admissions@stmartin.edu • **CEEB Code:** 4674
Fax: 360-412-6189 • **Website:** www.stmartin.edu • **ACT Code:** 4474

This private school, affiliated with the Roman Catholic Church, was founded in 1895. It has a 300 acre campus.

RATINGS

Admissions Selectivity Rating: 73   **Fire Safety Rating:** 60*   **Green Rating:** 60*

STUDENTS AND FACULTY

Enrollment: 1,203. **Student Body:** 50% female, 50% male, 28% out-of-state, 6% international (8 countries represented). Asian 7%, African American 7%, Caucasian 52%, Hispanic 14%, Native American 2%, Pacific Islander 4%, Two or more races 6%, Race unknown 3%.
Retention and Graduation: 76% freshmen return for sophomore year. 47% freshmen graduate within 4 years. 59% freshmen graduate within 6 years.
Faculty: Student/faculty ratio 11:1. 84 full-time faculty, 90% hold PhDs, 18% are members of minority groups, 45% are women. 0% of classes are taught by teaching assistants.

ACADEMICS

Degrees: Bachelor's; Certificate; Master's; Post-Bachelor's certificate; Post-Master's certificate **Classes:** Most classes have 10-19 students. **Most popular majors:** Mechanical Engineering; Biology/Biological Sciences, General; Business Administration And Management, General. **Special Study Options:** Distance learning; Double major; English as a Second Language (ESL); Exchange student program (domestic); Independent study; Internships; Study abroad; Teacher certification program. Combined degree programs: BA/MEng. **Disability Services offered to physically disabled students:** Note-taking services; Reader services; Tape recorders; Tutors. **Career services:** Alumni network; Alumni services; Career assessment; Career/job search classes; Regional alumni

FACILITIES

Housing: Apartments for single students; Coed dorms; Special housing for disabled students 85% of campus accessible to physically disabled. **Computers:** 80% of classrooms, 10% of dorms, 100% of libraries, 100% of dining areas, 100% of student union, have wireless network access. Students can register for classes online. Administrative functions (other than registration) can be performed online.

CAMPUS LIFE

Environment: Town **Activities:** Campus Ministries; Choral groups; Concert band; Dance; Drama/theater; International Student Organization; Jazz band; Model UN; Musical theater; Pep band; Student government; Student newspaper 23 registered organizations, 3 honor societies, 3 religious organizations. **Athletics (Intercollegiate):** *Men:* baseball, basketball, cross-country, golf, track/field (outdoor), track/field (indoor). *Women:* basketball, cross-country, golf, softball, track/field (outdoor), track/field (indoor), volleyball. **On-Campus Highlights:** O'Grady Library, Student Union Building, Recreation and Fitness Center, Baran/Burton/Spangler Halls, Abbey Church

ADMISSIONS

Freshman Academic Profile: Average high school GPA 3.4. 24% in top 10% of high school class, 52% in top 25% of high school class, 76% in top 50% of high school class. 50% from public high schools. **Test Scores:** SAT Math middle 50% range 490-590. SAT EBRW middle 50% range 490-600. ACT middle 50% range 18-24. Minimum internet-based TOEFL 54. Minimum paper TOEFL 480. **Basis for Candidate Selection:** *Very important factors considered include:* rigor of secondary school record, academic GPA. *Important factors considered include:* application essay, standardized test scores, recommendation(s), extracurricular activities, character/personal qualities, volunteer work. *Other factors considered include:* class rank, talent/ability, alumni/ae relation, work experience. **Freshman Admission Requirements:** High school diploma is required and GED is accepted *Academic units recommended:* 4 English, 3 math, 3 science, 1 science labs, 2 foreign language, 2 social studies, 3 academic electives. **Freshman Admission Statistics:** 1,367 applied, 97.5% admitted, 21% enrolled. **Transfer Admission Requirements:** college transcript(s), essay or personal statement, Minimum college GPA of 2.25 required. Lowest grade transferable C-. **General Admission Information:** Priority deadline 11/1. Regular application deadline 7/31. Nonfall registration accepted. Admission may be deferred for a maximum of One year.

COSTS AND FINANCIAL AID

Annual tuition $36,950. Room and board $11,445. Required fees $406. Average book expense $1,000. **Required Forms and Deadlines:** FAFSA. **Notification of Awards:** Applicants will be notified of awards on a rolling basis beginning 11/21. **Types of Aid:** *Need-based scholarships/grants:* College/ university scholarship or grant aid from institutional funds; Federal Pell; Private scholarships; SEOG; State scholarships/grants. *Loans:* Direct PLUS loans; Direct Subsidized Stafford Loans; Direct Unsubsidized Stafford Loans. *Student Employment:* Federal Work-Study Program available. Institutional employment available. **Financial Aid Statistics:** 99% needy freshmen, 99% needy undergrads receive need-based scholarship or grant aid. 26% freshmen, 19% undergrads receive non-need-based scholarship or grant aid. 58% freshmen, 69% undergrads receive need-based self-help aid. 17% freshmen, 9% undergrads receive athletic scholarships. 78% undergrads borrow to pay for school. Average cumulative indebtedness $27,807. **Criteria for awarding aid:** *Need-based:* Academics, Alumni affiliation, Art, Leadership, Minority status, Music/drama, Religious affiliation *Non-need-based:* Academics, Alumni affiliation, Art, Athletics, Leadership, Minority status, Music/drama, Religious affiliation, State/district residency.

SAINT MARY-OF-THE-WOODS COLLEGE

Guerin Hall, Saint Mary-of-the-Woods, IN 47876-0068
Phone: 812-535-5106 • **Financial Aid Phone:** 812-535-5100
E-mail: smwcadms@smwc.edu • **CEEB Code:** 1704
Fax: 812-535-5010 • **Website:** www.smwc.edu • **ACT Code:** 1242

This private school, affiliated with the Roman Catholic Church, was founded in 1840. It has a 67 acre campus.

RATINGS

Admissions Selectivity Rating: 76   **Fire Safety Rating:** 99   **Green Rating:** 60*

STUDENTS AND FACULTY

Enrollment: 1,176. **Student Body:** 97% female, 3% male, 30% out-of-state, (5 countries represented).
Retention and Graduation: 77% freshmen return for sophomore year. 18% grads go on to further study within 1 year. 15% grads pursue arts and sciences degrees. 1% grads pursue law degrees. 1% grads pursue business degrees. 1% grads pursue medical degrees. **Faculty:** Student/faculty ratio 8:1. 67 full-time faculty, 54% hold PhDs, 6% are members of minority groups, 66% are women. 0% of classes are taught by teaching assistants.

ACADEMICS

Degrees: Associate; Bachelor's; Certificate; Master's; Post-Bachelor's certificate; Post-Master's certificate; Transfer Associate **Classes:** Most classes have 20-29 students. Most lab/discussion sessions have 20-29 students. **Most popular majors:** Equestrian/Equine Studies; Elementary Education And Teaching; Biology/Biological Sciences, General. **Special Study Options:** Accelerated program; Cross-registration; Distance learning; Double major; External degree program; Honors program; Independent study; Internships; Student-designed major; Study abroad; Teacher certification program. **Disability Services offered to physically disabled students:** Tutors. **Career services:** Alumni network; Alumni services; Career assessment; Career/job search classes; Internships; Regional alumni

FACILITIES

Housing: Special housing for disabled student; Women's dorms 100% of campus accessible to physically disabled. **Special Academic Facilities/ Equipment:** Cecilian Auditorium and Conservatory of Music SMWC Art Gallery **Computers:** 100% of classrooms, 100% of dorms, 100% of libraries, 20% of dining areas, 15% of common outdoor areas have wireless network access. Students can register for classes online. Administrative functions (other than registration) can be performed online.

CAMPUS LIFE

Environment: Town **Activities:** Campus Ministries; Choral groups; Concert band; Dance; Drama/theater; International Student Organization; Jazz band; Literary magazine; Music ensembles; Musical theater; Student government; Student newspaper; Yearbook 30 registered organizations, 6 honor societies, 1 religious organization. **Athletics (Intercollegiate):** *Women:* basketball, equestrian sports, golf, soccer, softball, track/field (outdoor). **On-Campus Highlights:** Le Fer Hall (residence hall), Mari Hulman George School of Equine Studies, Softball/Soccer Fields, Cecilian Auditorium, Church of the Immaculate Conception **Environmental Initiatives:** recycling

ADMISSIONS

Freshman Academic Profile: Average high school GPA 3.3. 85% from public high schools. **Test Scores:** SAT Math middle 50% range 410-520. SAT EBRW middle 50% range 430-540. ACT middle 50% range 18-25. Minimum internet-based TOEFL 62. Minimum paper TOEFL 500. **Basis for Candidate Selection:** *Important factors considered include:* rigor of secondary school record, class rank, academic GPA, application essay, standardized test scores, recommendation(s). *Other factors considered include:* interview, talent/ability, character/personal qualities, level of applicant's interest. **Freshman Admission Requirements:** High school diploma is required and GED is accepted *Academic units required:* 8 English, 6 math, 6 science, 2 science labs, 4 foreign language, 4 social studies, 2 history, 10 academic electives, *Academic units recommended:* 8 English, 8 math, 8 science, 4 science labs, 6 foreign language, 6 social studies, 4 history, 7 academic electives. **Freshman Admission Statistics:** 268 applied, 77.6% admitted, 38% enrolled. **Transfer Admission Requirements:** college transcript(s), essay or personal statement, Minimum college GPA of 2.0 required. Lowest grade transferable C. **General Admission Information:** Application fee $30. Regular application deadline 8/8. Nonfall registration accepted. Admission may be deferred for a maximum of 1 year.

COSTS AND FINANCIAL AID

Annual tuition $20,900. Room and board $7,890. Required fees $650. Average book expense $900. **Required Forms and Deadlines:** FAFSA. **Notification of Awards:** Applicants will be notified of awards on a rolling basis beginning 12/1. **Types of Aid:** *Need-based scholarships/grants:* College/university scholarship or grant aid from institutional funds; Federal Pell; Private scholarships; SEOG; State scholarships/grants. *Student Employment:* Federal Work-Study Program available. Institutional employment available. **Financial Aid Statistics:** 77% needy freshmen, 92% needy undergrads receive need-based scholarship or grant aid. 76% freshmen, 12% undergrads receive non-need-based scholarship or grant aid. 49% freshmen, 83% undergrads receive need-based self-help aid. 10% freshmen, 4% undergrads receive athletic scholarships. 98% freshmen, 96% undergrads receive any aid. **Criteria for awarding aid:** *Need-based:* Academics, Alumni affiliation, Art, Athletics, Leadership, Music/drama *Non-need-based:* Academics, Alumni affiliation, Art, Athletics, Leadership, Music/drama.

SAINT MARY'S COLLEGE (CA)

1928 St. Mary's Road, PMB 4433, Moraga, CA 94575-4800
Phone: 925-631-4224 • **Financial Aid Phone:** 925-631-4370
E-mail: smcadmit@stmarys-ca.edu • **CEEB Code:** 4675
Fax: 925-376-7193 • **Website:** www.stmarys-ca.edu • **ACT Code:** 386

This private school, affiliated with the Roman Catholic Church, was founded in 1863. It has a 420 acre campus.

RATINGS
Admissions Selectivity Rating: 77   **Fire Safety Rating:** 93   **Green Rating:** 86

STUDENTS AND FACULTY
Enrollment: 2,762. **Student Body:** 59% female, 41% male, 11% out-of-state, 3% international (20 countries represented). Asian 11%, African American 4%, Caucasian 45%, Hispanic 26%, Native American <1%, Pacific Islander 1%, Two or more races 6%, Race unknown 3%.
Retention and Graduation: 65% freshmen graduate within 4 years. 76% freshmen graduate within 6 years. 27% grads go on to further study within 1 year. **Faculty:** Student/faculty ratio 11:1. 226 full-time faculty, 95% hold PhDs, 32% are members of minority groups, 55% are women. 0% of classes are taught by teaching assistants.

ACADEMICS
Degrees: Bachelor's; Doctoral/Research; **Master's Classes:** Most classes have fewer than 10 students. **Most popular majors:** Communication And Media Studies, Other; Psychology, Other; Business Administration, Management And Operations, Other. **Special Study Options:** Accelerated program; Cross-registration; Double major; Dual enrollment; Exchange student program (domestic); Honors program; Independent study; Internships; Liberal arts/career combination; Student-designed major; Study abroad; Teacher certification program. **Disability Services offered to physically disabled students:** Note-taking services; Reader services; Tape recorders; Tutors. **Career services:** Alumni network; Alumni services; Career assessment; Career/job search classes; Internships

FACILITIES
Housing: Apartments for single students; Coed dorms; Theme housing 90% of campus accessible to physically diasbled. **Special Academic Facilities/Equipment:** Hearst Art gallery Brousseau Hall, Science Building Geissberger Observatory **Computers:** 100% of classrooms, 100% of libraries, 100% of dining areas, 100% of student union, 70% of common outdoor areas have wireless network access. Students can register for classes online. Administrative functions (other than registration) can be performed online.

CAMPUS LIFE
Environment: Village **Activities:** Campus Ministries; Choral groups; Concert band; Dance; Drama/theater; International Student Organization; Jazz band; Literary magazine; Music ensembles; Musical theater; Pep band; Radio station; Student government; Student newspaper 56 registered organizations, 3 religious organizations. **Athletics (Intercollegiate):** *Men:* baseball, basketball, cheerleading, cross-country, golf, soccer, tennis. *Women:* basketball, cheerleading, crew/rowing, cross-country, lacrosse, soccer, softball, tennis, volleyball. **On-Campus Highlights:** Br. Alfred Brousseau Hall, Cassin Student Union and LeFevre Quad, College Chapel, Hearst Art Gallery, Oliver Dining Hall **Environmental Initiatives:** 2007 Summer reading program for incoming students focuses on global warming.

ADMISSIONS
Freshman Academic Profile: Average high school GPA 3.6. 61% from public high schools. **Test Scores:** SAT Math middle 50% range 520-610. SAT EBRW middle 50% range 540-630. ACT middle 50% range 22-27. Minimum internet-based TOEFL 79. Minimum paper TOEFL 550. **Basis for Candidate Selection:** *Very important factors considered include:* rigor of secondary school record, academic GPA. *Important factors considered include:* standardized test scores, first generation. *Other factors considered include:* class rank, application essay, recommendation(s), interview, extracurricular activities, talent/ability, character/personal qualities, alumni/ae relation, geographical residence, volunteer work, work experience, level of applicant's interest. **Freshman Admission Requirements:** High school diploma is required and GED is accepted *Academic units required:* 4 English, 3 math, 3 science, 1 science labs, 2 foreign language, 2 social studies, 1 history, *Academic units recommended:* 4 English, 4 math, 4 science, 1 science labs, 3 foreign language, 2 social studies, 1 history. **Freshman Admission Statistics:** 4,676 applied, 81.6% admitted, 18% enrolled. **Transfer Admission Requirements:** High school transcript, college transcript(s), essay or personal statement, Minimum college GPA of 2.3 required. Lowest grade transferable C-. **General Admission Information:** Application fee $60. Priority deadline 11/15. Regular application deadline 2/1. Nonfall registration accepted. Admission may be deferred for a maximum of 1 year.

COSTS AND FINANCIAL AID
Annual tuition $47,130. Room and board $15,370. Required fees $150. Average book expense $1,278. **Required Forms and Deadlines:** FAFSA. **Notification of Awards:** Applicants will be notified of awards on a rolling basis beginning 12/16. **Types of Aid:** *Need-based scholarships/grants:* College/university scholarship or grant aid from institutional funds; Federal Pell; Private scholarships; SEOG; State scholarships/grants. *Loans:* Direct PLUS loans; Direct Subsidized Stafford Loans; Direct Unsubsidized Stafford Loans. *Student Employment:* Federal Work-Study Program available. Institutional employment available. **Financial Aid Statistics:** 100% needy freshmen, 98% needy undergrads receive need-based scholarship or grant aid. 34% freshmen, 25% undergrads receive non-need-based scholarship or grant aid. 88% freshmen, 83% undergrads receive need-based self-help aid. 3% freshmen, 4% undergrads receive athletic scholarships. 77% freshmen, 74% undergrads receive any aid. 77% undergrads borrow to pay for school. Average cumulative indebtedness $31,203. **Criteria for awarding aid:** *Need-based:* Alumni affiliation, Minority status *Non-need-based:* Academics, Athletics, Leadership, Music/drama, Religious affiliation.

SAINT MARY'S COLLEGE (IN)

Admission office, Notre Dame, IN 46556
Phone: 574-284-4587 • **Financial Aid Phone:** 574-284-4557
E-mail: admission@saintmarys.edu • **CEEB Code:** 1702
Fax: 574-284-4841 • **Website:** www.saintmarys.edu • **ACT Code:** 1244

This private school, affiliated with the Roman Catholic Church, was founded in 1844. It has a 100 acre campus.

RATINGS
Admissions Selectivity Rating: 83   **Fire Safety Rating:** 90   **Green Rating:** 78

STUDENTS AND FACULTY
Enrollment: 1,489. **Student Body:** 100% female, 0% male, 70% out-of-state, 1% international (10 countries represented). Asian 2%, African American 2%, Caucasian 78%, Hispanic 11%, Native American <1%, Pacific Islander <1%, Two or more races 3%, Race unknown 2%.
Retention and Graduation: 84% freshmen return for sophomore year. 71% freshmen graduate within 4 years. 77% freshmen graduate within 6 years. 33% grads go on to further study within 1 year. 9% grads pursue arts and sciences degrees. 1% grads pursue law degrees. 2% grads pursue business degrees. 1% grads pursue medical degrees. **Faculty:** Student/faculty ratio 9:1. 144 full-time faculty, 92% hold PhDs, 15% are members of minority groups, 72% are women. 0% of classes are taught by teaching assistants.

ACADEMICS
Degrees: Bachelor's; Doctoral/Professional; Master's **Most popular majors:** Biology/Biological Sciences, General; Registered Nursing/Registered Nurse; Business Administration And Management, General. **Special Study Options:** Cross-registration; Distance learning; Double major; Exchange student program (domestic); Independent study; Internships; Liberal arts/career combination; Student-designed major; Study abroad; Teacher certification program. **Disability Services offered to physically disabled students:** Note-taking

services; Reader services; Tape recorders; Tutors. **Career services:** Alumni network; Alumni services; Career assessment; Career/job search classes; Internships; Regional alumni

FACILITIES

Housing: Apartments for single students; Special housing for disabled student; Women's dorms 100% of campus accessible to physically diasbled. **Special Academic Facilities/Equipment:** Greenhouse; animal facility; chemical instrumentation lab; incubators; cold room; assorted biological research equipment **Computers:** 80% of classrooms, 60% of dorms, 100% of libraries, 100% of dining areas, 100% of student union, have wireless network access. Students can register for classes online. Administrative functions (other than registration) can be performed online.

CAMPUS LIFE

Environment: City **Activities:** Campus Ministries; Choral groups; Concert band; Dance; Drama/theater; International Student Organization; Literary magazine; Marching band; Music ensembles; Musical theater; Opera; Pep band; Radio station; Student government; Student newspaper; Television station; Yearbook 78 registered organizations, 14 honor societies, 8 religious organizations. **Athletics (Intercollegiate):** *Women:* basketball, cross-country, diving, golf, soccer, softball, swimming, tennis, volleyball. **On-Campus Highlights:** Student Center/Noble Family Dining hall., Angela Athletic Facility, Spes Unica Academic Builidng, Moreau Center for the Arts / O'Laughlin, Madeleva Hall **Environmental Initiatives:** Campus Recycling Program

ADMISSIONS

Freshman Academic Profile: Average high school GPA 3.8. 28% in top 10% of high school class, 64% in top 25% of high school class, 93% in top 50% of high school class. 55% from public high schools. **Test Scores:** SAT Math middle 50% range 500-620. SAT EBRW middle 50% range 530-630. ACT middle 50% range 23-29. Minimum internet-based TOEFL 80. Minimum paper TOEFL 550. **Basis for Candidate Selection:** *Important factors considered include:* rigor of secondary school record, academic GPA, standardized test scores. *Other factors considered include:* class rank, application essay, recommendation(s), interview, extracurricular activities, talent/ability, character/personal qualities, first generation, alumni/ae relation, geographical residence, state residency, racial/ethnic status, volunteer work, work experience, level of applicant's interest. **Freshman Admission Requirements:** High school diploma is required and GED is accepted *Academic units required:* 4 English, 3 math, 2 science, 2 science labs, 2 foreign language, 3 history, *Academic units recommended:* 4 English, 4 math, 4 science, 2 science labs, 4 foreign language, 2 social studies. **Freshman Admission Statistics:** 1,830 applied, 78.3% admitted, 25% enrolled. **Transfer Admission Requirements:** High school transcript, college transcript(s), essay or personal statement, standardized test scores, statement of good standing from prior institution(s). Minimum college GPA of 3.0 required. Lowest grade transferable C. **General Admission Information:** Priority deadline 2/15. Nonfall registration accepted. Admission may be deferred.

COSTS AND FINANCIAL AID

Annual tuition $41,380. Room and board $12,580. Required fees $840. Average book expense $1,100. **Required Forms and Deadlines:** FAFSA. **Types of Aid:** *Need-based scholarships/grants:* College/university scholarship or grant aid from institutional funds; Federal Pell; Private scholarships; SEOG; State scholarships/grants. *Loans:* Direct PLUS loans; Direct Subsidized Stafford Loans; Direct Unsubsidized Stafford Loans. *Student Employment:* Federal Work-Study Program available. Institutional employment available. **Financial Aid Statistics:** 99% needy freshmen, 100% needy undergrads receive need-based scholarship or grant aid. 95% freshmen, 92% undergrads receive non-need-based scholarship or grant aid. 77% freshmen, 76% undergrads receive need-based self-help aid. 0% freshmen, 0% undergrads receive athletic scholarships. 99% freshmen, 98% undergrads receive any aid. 68% undergrads borrow to pay for school. Average cumulative indebtedness $31,036. **Criteria for awarding aid:** *Need-based:* Academics *Non-need-based:* Academics, Art, Music/drama.

SAINT MARY'S UNIVERSITY OF MINNESOTA

700 Terrace Heights, Winona, MN 55987-1399
Phone: 507-457-1700 • **Financial Aid Phone:** (612) 238-4552
E-mail: admission@smumn.edu • **CEEB Code:** 6632
Fax: 507-457-1722 • **Website:** www.smumn.edu • **ACT Code:** 2148

This private school, affiliated with the Roman Catholic Church, was founded in 1912. It has a 350 acre campus.

RATINGS

Admissions Selectivity Rating: 82 **Fire Safety Rating:** 94 **Green Rating:** 60*

STUDENTS AND FACULTY

Enrollment: 1,471. **Student Body:** 53% female, 47% male, 45% out-of-state, 3% international (16 countries represented). Asian 3%, African American 8%, Caucasian 66%, Hispanic 8%, Native American 1%, Pacific Islander <1%, Two or more races 1%, Race unknown 11%.
Retention and Graduation: 77% freshmen return for sophomore year. 54% freshmen graduate within 4 years. 58% freshmen graduate within 6 years. 12% grads go on to further study within 1 year. 9% grads pursue arts and sciences degrees. 1% grads pursue law degrees. 1% grads pursue business degrees. 1% grads pursue medical degrees. **Faculty:** Student/faculty ratio 18:1. 100 full-time faculty, 87% hold PhDs, 7% are members of minority groups, 40% are women. 0% of classes are taught by teaching assistants.

ACADEMICS

Degrees: Bachelor's; Certificate; Diploma; Doctoral; Doctoral/Professional; Doctoral/Research; Master's; Post-Bachelor's certificate; Post-Master's certificate **Classes:** Most classes have 10-19 students. Most lab/discussion sessions have 10-19 students. **Most popular majors:** Elementary Education And Teaching; Biology/Biological Sciences, General; Marketing/Marketing Management, General. **Special Study Options:** Cooperative education program; Cross-registration; Distance learning; Double major; Dual enrollment; English as a Second Language (ESL); Honors program; Independent study; Internships; Student-designed major; Study abroad; Teacher certification program. Honors programs: The Lasallian Honors Program is the general education core program for honors students. It is designed to provide an intellectually stimulating experience for bright and motivated students who wish to engage in "shared inquiry" in small, interdisciplinary classes. The hallmarks of the Honors Program are in-depth discussions of the Great Books and other notable texts of the Western and Eastern cultural traditions; service learning with organizations in the community; experiential learning in the fine arts; and participation in a community of learners who desire to grow intellectually, spiritually, and creatively. The program is grounded in the university mission and the Lasallian dispositions of faith, zeal, service, and community. The ultimate goal of the Lasallian Honors Program is to awaken and nurture the intellectual, spiritual, and personal development of learners in preparation for lives of servant leadership and appreciation of the world's intellectual and cultural heritages. **Disability Services offered to physically disabled students:** Note-taking services; Reader services; Tape recorders; Tutors. **Career services:** Alumni network; Alumni services; Career assessment; Career/job search classes; Internships

FACILITIES

Housing: Apartments for married students; Apartments for single students; Coed dorms; Men's dorms; Special housing for disabled student; Women's dorms 93% of campus accessible to physically diasbled. **Special Academic Facilities/Equipment:** Art gallery, performance center, laboratories, observatory. **Computers:** 100% of dorms, 100% of libraries, 100% of dining areas, 100% of student union, have wireless network access. Students can register for classes online. Administrative functions (other than registration) can be performed online.

CAMPUS LIFE

Environment: Town **Activities:** Campus Ministries; Choral groups; Concert band; Dance; Drama/theater; International Student Organization; Jazz band; Literary magazine; Music ensembles; Musical theater; Radio station; Student government; Student newspaper; Student-run film society; Symphony orchestra; Yearbook 80 registered organizations, 13 honor societies, 6 religious organizations. **Athletics (Intercollegiate):** *Men:* baseball, basketball, cross-country, diving, golf, ice hockey, skiing (nordic/cross-country), soccer, swimming, tennis, track/field (outdoor), track/field (indoor). *Women:* basketball, cross-country, diving, golf, ice hockey, skiing (nordic/cross-country), soccer, softball, swimming, tennis, track/field (outdoor), track/field (indoor), volleyball. **On-Campus Highlights:** Brother Leopold Hall, Gostomski Fieldhouse, Page Theatre, Toner Student Center, Outdoor Track and Field Complex **Environmental Initiatives:** ISO 14001 Certified Environmental Management System (EMS)

ADMISSIONS

Freshman Academic Profile: Average high school GPA 3.4. 65% from public high schools. **Test Scores:** SAT Math middle 50% range 460-610. SAT EBRW middle 50% range 500-600. ACT middle 50% range 20-25. Minimum internet-based TOEFL 79. Minimum paper TOEFL 520. **Basis for Candidate Selection:** *Very important factors considered include:* rigor of secondary school record, academic GPA. *Important factors considered include:* standardized test scores, talent/ability, character/personal qualities. *Other factors considered include:* class rank, application essay, recommendation(s), interview, extracurricular activities, alumni/ae relation, volunteer work, level of applicant's interest. **Freshman Admission Requirements:** High school diploma is required and GED is accepted *Academic units required:* 4 English, 3 math, 3 science, 2 science labs, 2 social studies, 6 academic electives, *Academic units recommended:* 2 foreign language. **Freshman Admission Statistics:** 2,417 applied, 64.4% admitted, 19% enrolled. **Transfer Admission Requirements:** High school transcript, college transcript(s), statement of good standing from prior institution(s). Minimum college GPA of 2.0 required. Lowest grade transferable C. **General Admission Information:** Application fee $25. Priority deadline 4/1. Regular application deadline 5/1. Nonfall registration accepted. Admission may be deferred for a maximum of 1 year.

COSTS AND FINANCIAL AID

Annual tuition $34,500. Room and board $9,080. Required fees $640. Average book expense $1,500. **Required Forms and Deadlines:** FAFSA. **Notification of Awards:** Applicants will be notified of awards on a rolling basis beginning 1/1. **Types of Aid:** *Need-based scholarships/grants:* College/university scholarship or grant aid from institutional funds; Federal Pell; Private scholarships; SEOG; State scholarships/grants. *Loans:* Direct PLUS loans; Direct Subsidized Stafford Loans; Direct Unsubsidized Stafford Loans. *Student Employment:* Federal Work-Study Program available. Institutional employment available. **Financial Aid Statistics:** 100% needy freshmen, 97% needy undergrads receive need-based scholarship or grant aid. 0% undergrads receive non-need-based scholarship or grant aid. 73% freshmen, 77% undergrads receive need-based self-help aid. 0% freshmen, 0% undergrads receive athletic scholarships. 98% freshmen, 96% undergrads receive any aid. 80% undergrads borrow to pay for school. Average cumulative indebtedness $39,196. **Criteria for awarding aid:** *Need-based:* Academics *Non-need-based:* Academics, Alumni affiliation, Art, Leadership, Music/drama.

SAINT MICHAEL'S COLLEGE

One Winooski Park, Colchester, VT 05439
Phone: 802-654-3000 • **Financial Aid Phone:** 802-654-3243
E-mail: admission@smcvt.edu • **CEEB Code:** 3757
Fax: 802-654-2906 • **Website:** www.smcvt.edu • **ACT Code:** 4312

This private school, affiliated with the Roman Catholic Church, was founded in 1904. It has a 440 acre campus.

RATINGS

Admissions Selectivity Rating: 79   **Fire Safety Rating:** 92   **Green Rating:** 91

STUDENTS AND FACULTY

Enrollment: 1,759. **Student Body:** 55% female, 45% male, 85% out-of-state, 4% international (19 countries represented). Asian 1%, African American 2%, Caucasian 83%, Hispanic 5%, Native American <1%, Pacific Islander <1%, Two or more races 2%, Race unknown 2%.
Retention and Graduation: 83% freshmen return for sophomore year. 71% freshmen graduate within 4 years. 78% freshmen graduate within 6 years. 12% grads go on to further study within 1 year. 6% grads pursue arts and sciences degrees. 1% grads pursue law degrees. 1% grads pursue business degrees. 2% grads pursue medical degrees. **Faculty:** Student/faculty ratio 13:1. 138 full-time faculty, 82% hold PhDs, 5% are members of minority groups, 43% are women. 0% of classes are taught by teaching assistants.

ACADEMICS

Degrees: Bachelor's; Master's; Post-Bachelor's certificate; Post-Master's certificate **Classes:** Most classes have 20-29 students. Most lab/discussion sessions have 10-19 students. **Most popular majors:** Biology/Biological Sciences, General; Psychology, General; Business/Commerce, General. **Special Study Options:** Accelerated program; Cross-registration; Distance learning; Double major; Dual enrollment; English as a Second Language (ESL); Exchange student program (domestic); Honors program; Independent study; Internships; Liberal arts/career combination; Student-designed major; Study abroad; Teacher certification program. Honors programs: The Honors Program at Saint Michael's provides additional challenges and opportunities to outstanding students through small group discussion, research and extra-curricular activities. Saint Michael's also has chapters of several national honors societies on campus including Phi Beta Kappa, and Delta Epsilon Sigma. Combined degree programs: BA/JD; BA/MA. **Disability Services offered to physically disabled students:** Note-taking services; Reader services; Tape recorders; Tutors. **Career services:** Alumni network; Alumni services; Career assessment; Career/job search classes; Internships; Regional alumni

FACILITIES

Housing: Apartments for single students; Coed dorms; Men's dorms; Special housing for disabled student; Special housing for international students; Theme housing; Wellness housing; Women's dorms 75% of campus accessible to physically diasbled. **Special Academic Facilities/Equipment:** Holcomb Observatory, McCarthy Arts Center Gallery, Maker Space. **Computers:** 90% of classrooms, 100% of dorms, 100% of libraries, 100% of dining areas, 100% of student union, have wireless network access. Students can register for classes online. Administrative functions (other than registration) can be performed online.

CAMPUS LIFE

Environment: City **Activities:** Campus Ministries; Choral groups; Concert band; Dance; Drama/theater; International Student Organization; Jazz band; Literary magazine; Music ensembles; Musical theater; Radio station; Student government; Student newspaper; Yearbook 50 registered organizations, 11 honor societies, 1 religious organization. **Athletics (Intercollegiate):** *Men:* baseball, basketball, cross-country, diving, golf, ice hockey, lacrosse, skiing (downhill/alpine), skiing (nordic/cross-country), soccer, swimming, tennis. *Women:* basketball, cross-country, diving, field hockey, ice hockey, lacrosse, skiing (downhill/alpine), skiing (nordic/cross-country), soccer, softball, swimming, tennis, volleyball. **On-Campus Highlights:** Dion Family Student Center, McCarthy Arts Center, Chapel of Saint Michael the Archangel, Vincent C. Ross Sports Center, Tarrant Student Recreational Center **Environmental Initiatives:** Energy Efficiency Programs: "Three Degree Challenge" to further reduce campus wide building temperatures by turning down thermostats to reduce energy consumption (in addition to reducing energy consumption, all new major appliances must be energy star certified; new building aims for LEED certification; all campus buildings on an Energy Management System to ensure efficient use of energy;

ADMISSIONS

Freshman Academic Profile: 25% in top 10% of high school class, 48% in top 25% of high school class, 76% in top 50% of high school class. 64% from public high schools. **Test Scores:** SAT Math middle 50% range 570-650. SAT EBRW middle 50% range 580-660. ACT middle 50% range 25-29. Minimum internet-based TOEFL 79-80. Minimum paper TOEFL 550. **Basis for Candidate Selection:** *Very important factors considered include:* rigor of secondary school record, class rank, academic GPA. *Important factors considered include:* application essay, standardized test scores, recommendation(s), talent/ability, character/personal qualities. *Other factors considered include:* interview, extracurricular activities, first generation, alumni/ae relation, geographical residence, state residency, racial/ethnic status, volunteer work, work experience, level of applicant's interest. **Freshman Admission Requirements:** High school diploma is required and GED is accepted *Academic units required:* 4 English, 4 math, 3 science, 2 science labs, 2 foreign language, 3 social studies, 3 history, *Academic units recommended:* 4 English, 4 math, 4 science, 3 science labs, 4 foreign language, 4 social studies, 4 history. **Freshman Admission Statistics:** 3,094 applied, 85.1% admitted, 16% enrolled. **Transfer Admission Requirements:** High school transcript, college transcript(s), essay or personal statement, standardized test scores, Minimum college GPA of 2.8 required. Lowest grade transferable C-. **General Admission Information:** Application fee $50. Priority deadline 11/1. Regular application deadline 2/1. Nonfall registration accepted. Admission may be deferred.

COSTS AND FINANCIAL AID

Annual tuition $45,050. Room and board $12,220. Required fees $325. Average book expense $1,200. **Required Forms and Deadlines:** FAFSA. **Notification of Awards:** Applicants will be notified of awards on a rolling basis beginning 1/30. **Types of Aid:** *Need-based scholarships/grants:* College/university scholarship or grant aid from institutional funds; Federal Pell; Private scholarships; SEOG; State scholarships/grants. *Loans:* Direct PLUS loans; Direct Subsidized Stafford Loans; Direct Unsubsidized Stafford Loans. *Student Employment:* Federal Work-Study Program available. Institutional employment available. **Financial Aid Statistics:** 100% needy freshmen, 99% needy undergrads receive need-based scholarship or grant aid. 26% freshmen, 20% undergrads receive non-need-based scholarship or grant aid. 70% freshmen, 77% undergrads receive need-based self-help aid. 1% freshmen, 1% undergrads receive athletic scholarships. 99% freshmen, 98% undergrads receive any aid.

72% undergrads borrow to pay for school. Average cumulative indebtedness $38,226. **Criteria for awarding aid:** *Non-need-based:* Academics, Art, Athletics, Music/drama.

See page 1022.

SAINT PETER'S UNIVERSITY

2641 Kennedy Boulevard, Jersey City, NJ 07306
Phone: 201-761-7100 • **Financial Aid Phone:** 201-761-6071
E-mail: admissions@saintpeters.edu • **CEEB Code:** 2806
Website: www.saintpeters.edu • **ACT Code:** 2604

This private school, affiliated with the Roman Catholic-Jesuit Church, was founded in 1872. It has a 10 acre campus.

RATINGS
Admissions Selectivity Rating: 74   **Fire Safety Rating:** 60*   **Green Rating:** 86

STUDENTS AND FACULTY
Enrollment: 2,589. **Student Body:** 64% female, 36% male, 10% out-of-state, 2% international (56 countries represented). Asian 7%, African American 23%, Caucasian 16%, Hispanic 41%, Native American <1%, Pacific Islander 1%, Two or more races 2%, Race unknown 9%.
Retention and Graduation: 81% freshmen return for sophomore year. 27% grads go on to further study within 1 year. 9% grads pursue arts and sciences degrees. 5% grads pursue law degrees. 6% grads pursue business degrees. 7% grads pursue medical degrees. **Faculty:** Student/faculty ratio 13:1. 118 full-time faculty, 85% hold PhDs, 18% are members of minority groups, 47% are women. 0% of classes are taught by teaching assistants.

ACADEMICS
Degrees: Associate; Bachelor's; Certificate; Doctoral/Professional; Master's; Post-Bachelor's certificate; Post-Master's certificate **Classes:** Most classes have 20-29 students. Most lab/discussion sessions have 20-29 students. **Most popular majors:** Biology/Biological Sciences, General; Registered Nursing/Registered Nurse; Business Administration And Management, General. **Special Study Options:** Accelerated program; Cooperative education program; Cross-registration; Distance learning; Double major; Dual enrollment; English as a Second Language (ESL); Exchange student program (domestic); Honors program; Independent study; Internships; Student-designed major; Study abroad; Teacher certification program; Weekend college. Honors programs: While Honors provides academic enrichment for highly motivated students, it is not a formal major or minor. Students enrolled in the program must complete a minimum of 30 credits designated as Honors courses, which include Honors core course seminars, Honors advanced electives, and 6 credits of Honors Thesis: research and independent study. Independent study projects must be approved by the Honors Program and the respective chairs of the student's major department. Independent study projects may carry departmental as well as Honors credit. Combined degree programs: BA/JD; BA/MD. **Disability Services offered to physically disabled students:** Note-taking services; Reader services; Tape recorders; Tutors. **Career services:** Career/job search classes; Internships

FACILITIES
Housing: Coed dorms; Special housing for disabled student; Wellness housing **Special Academic Facilities/Equipment:** TV production facilities, center for government affairs, radio station

CAMPUS LIFE
Environment: City **Activities:** Campus Ministries; Choral groups; Dance; Drama/theater; International Student Organization; Literary magazine; Model UN; Musical theater; Radio station; Student government; Student newspaper; Yearbook 45 registered organizations, 11 honor societies. **Athletics (Intercollegiate): Men:** baseball, basketball, cheerleading, cross-country, diving, football, golf, soccer, swimming, tennis, track/field (outdoor). *Women:* basketball, bowling, cheerleading, cross-country, diving, soccer, softball, swimming, tennis, track/field (outdoor), volleyball. MacMahon Student Center, Hudson Room—Dining Hall, Campus Ministry, Honors House, RLC Recreation Center **Environmental Initiatives:** Use of solar and wind energy

ADMISSIONS
Freshman Academic Profile: Average high school GPA 3.3. 18% in top 10% of high school class, 46% in top 25% of high school class, 75% in top 50% of high school class. **Test Scores:** SAT Math middle 50% range 420-520. SAT EBRW middle 50% range 410-510. ACT middle 50% range 16-23. Minimum internet-based TOEFL 79. Minimum paper TOEFL 550. **Basis for Candidate Selection:** *Very important factors considered:* rigor of secondary school

record, academic GPA. *Important factors considered include:* application essay, recommendation(s). *Other factors considered include:* class rank, standardized test scores, interview, extracurricular activities, character/personal qualities, first generation, alumni/ae relation, geographical residence, state residency, volunteer work, work experience, level of applicant's interest. **Freshman Admission Requirements:** High school diploma is required and GED is accepted *Academic units required:* 4 English, 3 math, 2 science, 1 science labs, 2 foreign language, 2 history. **Freshman Admission Statistics:** 4,611 applied, 74.3% admitted, 18% enrolled. **Transfer Admission Requirements:** college transcript(s), essay or personal statement, Minimum college GPA of 2.0 required. Lowest grade transferable C. **General Admission Information:** Priority deadline 12/15. Nonfall registration accepted. Admission may be deferred for a maximum of 1 year.

COSTS AND FINANCIAL AID
Required Forms and Deadlines: FAFSA; State aid form. **Notification of Awards:** Applicants will be notified of awards on a rolling basis beginning 1/1. **Types of Aid:** *Need-based scholarships/grants:* College/university scholarship or grant aid from institutional funds; Federal Pell; Private scholarships; SEOG; State scholarships/grants. *Loans:* Direct PLUS loans; Direct Subsidized Stafford Loans; Direct Unsubsidized Stafford Loans. *Student Employment:* Federal Work-Study Program available. Institutional employment available. **Financial Aid Statistics:** 99% needy freshmen, 97% needy undergrads receive need-based scholarship or grant aid. 7% freshmen, 5% undergrads receive non-need-based scholarship or grant aid. 72% freshmen, 79% undergrads receive need-based self-help aid. 3% freshmen, 3% undergrads receive athletic scholarships. 98% freshmen, 90% undergrads receive any aid. **Criteria for awarding aid:** *Need-based:* Academics, Athletics *Non-need-based:* Academics, Athletics.

SAINT VINCENT COLLEGE

300 Fraser Purchase Road, Latrobe, PA 15650-2690
Phone: 724-537-4540 • **Financial Aid Phone:** 800-782-5549
E-mail: admission@stvincent.edu • **CEEB Code:** 2808
Fax: 724-532-5069 • **Website:** www.stvincent.edu • **ACT Code:** 3686

This private school, affiliated with the Roman Catholic Church, was founded in 1846. It has a 200 acre campus.

RATINGS
Admissions Selectivity Rating: 85   **Fire Safety Rating:** 69   **Green Rating:** 60*

STUDENTS AND FACULTY
Enrollment: 1,617. **Student Body:** 50% female, 50% male, 12% out-of-state, 1% international (15 countries represented). Asian 1%, African American 3%, Caucasian 90%, Hispanic 2%, Native American <1%, Race unknown 3%.
Retention and Graduation: 84% freshmen return for sophomore year. 30% grads go on to further study within 1 year. **Faculty:** Student/faculty ratio 13:1. 91 full-time faculty, 84% hold PhDs, 2% are members of minority groups, 24% are women. 0% of classes are taught by teaching assistants.

ACADEMICS
Degrees: Bachelor's; Certificate; Master's; Post-Bachelor's certificate **Classes:** Most classes have 20-29 students. **Most popular majors:** Biology/Biological Sciences, General; Psychology, General; History, General. **Special Study Options:** Accelerated program; Cooperative education program; Cross-registration; Distance learning; Double major; Dual enrollment; External degree program; Honors program; Independent study; Internships; Liberal arts/career combination; Study abroad; Teacher certification program. Honors programs: Honors Classes Professors design Honors classes to challenge and reward students who seek substantial intellectual development in college. The quality, not the quantity of work, distinguishes Honors classes from other courses. Portfolio As part of their coursework in Honors classes, all students are required to submit a short reflective essay and sample of their work at the end of each Honors class. Honors Events Dinner and evening discussions based on a reading, or attendance of a play, a film, an art exhibit, etc., on campus provide a special, congenial setting for intellectual exchange as part of a course or an extracurricular event. Off-Campus Explorations All Honors students and faculty are regularly invited to attend a play, film, art exhibit, etc. Extended trips within the U.S. or abroad may be planned during breaks or the summer. Senior Capstone Projects Honors students in majors with a senior research or capstone project will be strongly encouraged to present their work in a special colloquium at Saint Vincent and at professional meetings in their research areas. Combined degree programs: BA/JD; BA/MEng. **Disability Services offered to physically disabled students:** Note-taking services; Tutors. **Career services:** Alumni network; Alumni services; Career assessment; Internships; Regional alumni

FACILITIES

Housing: Apartments for single students; Coed dorms 95% of campus accessible to physically diasbled. **Special Academic Facilities/Equipment:** Art gallery, life sciences research center, spectrophotometer, spectrometer, physiograph work stations, data acquisition work station, planetarium, observatory, radio telescope, instructional technology resource center. **Computers:** 75% of libraries, 100% of student union, 25% of common outdoor areas have wireless network access. Students can register for classes online. Administrative functions (other than registration) can be performed online.

CAMPUS LIFE

Environment: Village **Activities:** Campus Ministries; Choral groups; Dance; Drama/theater; International Student Organization; Literary magazine; Music ensembles; Musical theater; Pep band; Radio station; Student government; Student newspaper; Television station; Yearbook 43 registered organizations, 12 honor societies, 2 religious organizations. **Athletics (Intercollegiate):** *Men:* baseball, basketball, cross-country, football, golf, lacrosse, soccer, swimming, tennis, track/field (outdoor). *Women:* basketball, cross-country, field hockey, golf, lacrosse, soccer, softball, swimming, tennis, volleyball. **On-Campus Highlights:** Library, Carey Student Center, St. Benedict Hall, Basilica, Chuck Noll Field **Environmental Initiatives:** New construction on campus, including a current building project, will be green

ADMISSIONS

Freshman Academic Profile: Average high school GPA 3.6. 24% in top 10% of high school class, 54% in top 25% of high school class, 84% in top 50% of high school class. 67% from public high schools. **Test Scores:** SAT Math middle 50% range 490-600. SAT EBRW middle 50% range 480-590. ACT middle 50% range 20-26. Minimum paper TOEFL 550. **Basis for Candidate Selection:** *Very important factors considered include:* rigor of secondary school record, class rank, academic GPA. *Important factors considered include:* application essay, standardized test scores, character/personal qualities. *Other factors considered include:* recommendation(s), interview, extracurricular activities, talent/ability, first generation. **Freshman Admission Requirements:** High school diploma is required and GED is accepted *Academic units required:* 4 English, 3 math, 1 science, 1 science labs, 3 social studies, 5 academic electives, *Academic units recommended:* 4 English, 3 math, 3 science, 1 science labs, 2 foreign language, 3 social studies, 5 academic electives. **Freshman Admission Statistics:** 1,855 applied, 61.8% admitted, 37% enrolled. **Transfer Admission Requirements:** High school transcript, college transcript(s), essay or personal statement, statement of good standing from prior institution(s). Minimum college GPA of 2.5 required. Lowest grade transferable C-. **General Admission Information:** Application fee $25. Priority deadline 2/1. Regular application deadline 5/1. Nonfall registration accepted. Admission may be deferred for a maximum of 1 year.

COSTS AND FINANCIAL AID

Annual tuition $22,350. Room and board $7,242. Required fees $650. Average book expense $650. **Required Forms and Deadlines:** FAFSA; State aid form. **Notification of Awards:** Applicants will be notified of awards on a rolling basis beginning 3/1. **Types of Aid:** *Need-based scholarships/grants:* College/university scholarship or grant aid from institutional funds; Federal Pell; Private scholarships; SEOG; State scholarships/grants; United Negro College Fund. *Loans: Student Employment:* Federal Work-Study Program available. Institutional employment available. **Financial Aid Statistics:** 10% needy freshmen, 100% needy undergrads receive need-based scholarship or grant aid. 43% freshmen, 85% undergrads receive non-need-based scholarship or grant aid. 75% freshmen, 80% undergrads receive need-based self-help aid. 0% freshmen, 10% undergrads receive athletic scholarships. 99% freshmen, 96% undergrads receive any aid. **Criteria for awarding aid:** *Need-based:* Alumni affiliation *Non-need-based:* Academics, Alumni affiliation, Leadership, Minority status, Music/drama.

SAINT XAVIER UNIVERSITY

3700 West 103rd Street, Chicago, IL 60655
Phone: 773-298-3050
E-mail: admissions@sxu.edu • **CEEB Code:** 1708
Fax: 773-298-3076 • **Website:** www.sxu.edu • **ACT Code:** 1134

This private school, affiliated with the Roman Catholic Church, was founded in 1847. It has a 70 acre campus.

RATINGS

Admissions Selectivity Rating: 74   **Fire Safety Rating:** 60*   **Green Rating:** 60*

STUDENTS AND FACULTY

Enrollment: 2,897. **Student Body:** 67% female, 33% male, 5% out-of-state, <1% international. Asian 3%, African American 16%, Caucasian 50%, Hispanic 23%, Native American <1%, Pacific Islander 0%, Two or more races 2%, Race unknown 5%.
Retention and Graduation: 75% freshmen return for sophomore year. 10% grads go on to further study within 1 year. **Faculty:** Student/faculty ratio 13:1. 168 full-time faculty, 86% hold PhDs, 13% are members of minority groups, 57% are women. 0% of classes are taught by teaching assistants.

ACADEMICS

Degrees: Bachelor's; Certificate; Master's; Post-Bachelor's certificate; Post-Master's certificate **Classes:** Most classes have 10-19 students. Most lab/discussion sessions have 20-29 students. **Most popular majors:** Elementary Education And Teaching; Nursing/Registered Nurse (Rn, Asn, Bsn, Msn); Business/Commerce, General. **Special Study Options:** Accelerated program; Cooperative education program; Distance learning; Double major; Dual enrollment; English as a Second Language (ESL); External degree program; Honors program; Independent study; Internships; Liberal arts/career combination; Student-designed major; Study abroad; Teacher certification program; Weekend college. **Disability Services offered to physically disabled students:** Note-taking services; Reader services; Tape recorders; Tutors. **Career services:** Alumni services; Career assessment; Career/job search classes; Internships

FACILITIES

Housing: Apartments for single students; Coed dorms; Special housing for disabled students 98% of campus accessible to physically diasbled. **Computers:** Students can register for classes online. Administrative functions (other than registration) can be performed online.

CAMPUS LIFE

Environment: Metropolis **Activities:** Campus Ministries; Choral groups; Concert band; Dance; Drama/theater; International Student Organization; Jazz band; Literary magazine; Marching band; Music ensembles; Pep band; Radio station; Student government; Student newspaper; Student-run film society; Symphony orchestra; Yearbook 41 registered organizations, 2 honor societies, 2 religious organizations. **Athletics (Intercollegiate):** *Men:* baseball, basketball, football, soccer. *Women:* basketball, cross-country, soccer, softball, volleyball. **On-Campus Highlights:** Convocation and Athletic Center, McDonough Chapel and Mercy Ministry Center, McCarthy Hall, Speech language Pathology Clinic, Art Gallery

ADMISSIONS

Freshman Academic Profile: 25% in top 10% of high school class, 54% in top 25% of high school class, 84% in top 50% of high school class. 55% from public high schools. **Test Scores:** SAT Math middle 50% range 440-545. SAT EBRW middle 50% range 455-570. ACT middle 50% range 19-24. Minimum paper TOEFL 550. **Basis for Candidate Selection:** *Very important factors considered include:* academic GPA, application essay, standardized test scores. *Important factors considered include:* rigor of secondary school record. *Other factors considered include:* recommendation(s), interview, extracurricular activities, talent/ability, character/personal qualities, volunteer work, work experience, level of applicant's interest. **Freshman Admission Requirements:** High school diploma is required and GED is accepted *Academic units recommended:* 4 English, 3 math, 2 foreign language, 3 academic electives, 4 units from above areas or other academic areas. **Freshman Admission Statistics:** 6,693 applied, 79.3% admitted, 11% enrolled. **Transfer Admission Requirements:** college transcript(s), Minimum college GPA of 2.5 required. Lowest grade transferable C. **General Admission Information:** Application fee $25. Nonfall registration accepted. Admission may be deferred.

COSTS AND FINANCIAL AID

Annual tuition $29,990. Room and board $10,320. Required fees $820. Average book expense $1,200. **Required Forms and Deadlines:** FAFSA. **Notification of Awards:** Applicants will be notified of awards on a rolling basis beginning 2/15. **Types of Aid:** *Need-based scholarships/grants:* College/university scholarship or grant aid from institutional funds; Federal Pell; Private scholarships; SEOG; State scholarships/grants. *Student Employment:* Federal Work-Study Program available. Institutional employment available. **Financial Aid Statistics:** 100% needy freshmen, 99% needy undergrads receive need-based scholarship or grant aid. 98% freshmen, 92% undergrads receive non-need-based scholarship or grant aid. 84% freshmen, 87% undergrads receive need-based self-help aid. 12% freshmen, 9% undergrads receive athletic scholarships. **Criteria for awarding aid:** *Non-need-based:* Academics, Athletics, Music/drama.

SALEM COLLEGE

P.O. Box 10548, Winston-Salem, NC 27108
Phone: 336-721-2621 • **Financial Aid Phone:** 336-721-2808
E-mail: admissions@salem.edu • **CEEB Code:** 5607
Fax: 336-917-5572 • **Website:** www.salem.edu • **ACT Code:** 3156

This private school, affiliated with the Moravian Church, was founded in 1772. It has a 57 acre campus.

RATINGS
Admissions Selectivity Rating: 85   **Fire Safety Rating:** 86   **Green Rating:** 60*

STUDENTS AND FACULTY
Enrollment: 741. **Student Body:** 98% female, 2% male, 23% out-of-state, 13% international (22 countries represented). Asian 1%, African American 19%, Caucasian 60%, Hispanic 4%, Native American <1%, Race unknown 4%. **Retention and Graduation:** 78% freshmen return for sophomore year. 30% grads go on to further study within 1 year. 25% grads pursue arts and sciences degrees. 3% grads pursue law degrees. 5% grads pursue business degrees. **Faculty:** Student/faculty ratio 12:1. 57 full-time faculty, 86% hold PhDs, 9% are members of minority groups, 61% are women. 0% of classes are taught by teaching assistants.

ACADEMICS
Degrees: Bachelor's; **Master's Classes:** Most classes have 10-19 students. Most lab/discussion sessions have 20-29 students. **Most popular majors:** Sociology; Business/Commerce, General. **Special Study Options:** Cross-registration; Double major; Dual enrollment; Honors program; Independent study; Internships; Liberal arts/career combination; Student-designed major; Study abroad; Teacher certification program. **Career services:** Alumni network; Internships

FACILITIES
Housing: Apartments for single students; Women's dorms 75% of campus accessible to physically disabled. **Special Academic Facilities/Equipment:** Art gallery, fine arts center, Center for Women Writers, videoconferencing center **Computers:** Administrative functions (other than registration) can be performed online.

CAMPUS LIFE
Environment: City **Activities:** Choral groups; Dance; Drama/theater; Literary magazine; Marching band; Music ensembles; Musical theater; Student government; Student newspaper; Yearbook 26 registered organizations, 14 honor societies, 7 religious organizations. **Athletics (Intercollegiate):** *Women:* basketball, cross-country, field hockey, swimming, tennis, volleyball. **On-Campus Highlights:** back porch of Main Hall, Salem Grille/Java City, residence hall basement lounges **Environmental Initiatives:** Recylcle committment-all residence halls and academic buildings have paper, plastic and aluminum containers

ADMISSIONS
Freshman Academic Profile: Average high school GPA 3.7. 39% in top 10% of high school class, 67% in top 25% of high school class, 94% in top 50% of high school class. **Test Scores:** SAT Math middle 50% range 480-630. SAT EBRW middle 50% range 490-650. ACT middle 50% range 20-25. Minimum paper TOEFL 550. **Basis for Candidate Selection:** *Very important factors considered include:* rigor of secondary school record, academic GPA. *Important factors considered include:* class rank, application essay, standardized test scores, recommendation(s), extracurricular activities, talent/ability, character/personal qualities. *Other factors considered include:* interview, first generation, alumni/ae relation, volunteer work, level of applicant's interest. **Freshman Admission Requirements:** High school diploma is required and GED is accepted *Academic units required:* 4 English, 3 math, 3 science, 2 foreign language, 2 history. **Freshman Admission Statistics:** 435 applied, 69.4% admitted, 51% enrolled. **Transfer Admission Requirements:** High school transcript, college transcript(s), essay or personal statement, statement of good standing from prior institution(s). Minimum college GPA of 2.0 required. Lowest grade transferable C-. **General Admission Information:** Application fee $30. Priority deadline 3/1. Nonfall registration accepted. Admission may be deferred for a maximum of 1 year.

COSTS AND FINANCIAL AID
Annual tuition $18,850. Room and board $10,050. Required fees $340. Average book expense $900. **Required Forms and Deadlines:** FAFSA. **Notification of Awards:** Applicants will be notified of awards on a rolling basis beginning 3/1. **Types of Aid:** *Need-based scholarships/grants:* College/university scholarship or grant aid from institutional funds; Federal Pell; Private scholarships; SEOG; State scholarships/grants. **Financial Aid Statistics:** 80% needy freshmen, 71% needy undergrads receive need-based scholarship or grant aid. 96% freshmen, 95% undergrads receive non-need-based scholarship or grant aid. 88% freshmen, 83% undergrads receive need-based self-help aid. 0% freshmen, 0% undergrads receive athletic scholarships. **Criteria for awarding aid:** *Non-need-based:* Academics, Alumni affiliation, Leadership, Minority status, Music/drama, State/district residency.

SALEM STATE UNIVERSITY

352 Lafayette Street, Salem, MA 01970
Phone: 978-542-6210 • **Financial Aid Phone:** 978-542-6112
E-mail: admissions@salemstate.edu • **CEEB Code:** 3522
Fax: 978-542-6893 • **Website:** www.salemstate.edu

This public school was founded in 1854. It has a 108 acre campus.

RATINGS
Admissions Selectivity Rating: 82   **Fire Safety Rating:** 78   **Green Rating:** 60*

STUDENTS AND FACULTY
Enrollment: 7,296. **Student Body:** 61% female, 39% male, 3% out-of-state, 3% international. Asian 3%, African American 9%, Caucasian 76%, Hispanic 7%, Native American <1%, Pacific Islander 0%, Two or more races 0%, Race unknown 2%.
Faculty: Student/faculty ratio 14:1. 333 full-time faculty, 10% are members of minority groups, 54% are women. 0% of classes are taught by teaching assistants.

ACADEMICS
Degrees: Bachelor's; Certificate; Master's; Post-Bachelor's certificate; Post-Master's certificate **Classes:** Most classes have 10-19 students. **Most popular majors:** Education, General; Criminal Justice/Law Enforcement Administration; Business/Commerce, General. **Special Study Options:** Accelerated program; Cross-registration; Distance learning; Double major; Dual enrollment; English as a Second Language (ESL); Honors program; Independent study; Internships; Student-designed major; Study abroad; Teacher certification program. **Disability Services offered to physically disabled students:** Reader services; Tape recorders.

FACILITIES
Housing: Coed dorms; Other (please specify) 100% of campus accessible to physically diasbled. **Special Academic Facilities/Equipment:** Aquaculture center, On-campus elementary school, color TV studio, instructional media center.

CAMPUS LIFE
Environment: Village **Activities:** Choral groups; Concert band; Dance; Drama/theater; Jazz band; Literary magazine; Music ensembles; Musical theater; Radio station; Student government; Student newspaper 149 registered organizations, 13 honor societies, 3 religious organizations. **Athletics (Intercollegiate):** *Men:* baseball, basketball, cross-country, diving, golf, ice hockey, lacrosse, soccer, swimming, tennis, track/field (outdoor). *Women:* basketball, cross-country, diving, field hockey, lacrosse, soccer, softball, swimming, tennis, track/field (outdoor), volleyball.

ADMISSIONS
Test Scores: SAT Math middle 50% range 450-540. SAT EBRW middle 50% range 440-550. Minimum paper TOEFL 500. **Basis for Candidate Selection:** *Very important factors considered include:* rigor of secondary school record, academic GPA, standardized test scores. *Other factors considered include:* recommendation(s), interview, extracurricular activities, talent/ability, character/personal qualities, volunteer work, work experience, level of applicant's interest. **Freshman Admission Requirements:** High school diploma is required and GED is accepted *Academic units required:* 4 English, 3 math, 3 science, 2 science labs, 2 foreign language, 2 social studies, 1 history, 2 academic electives, 1 computer science, 1 visual/performing arts, *Academic units recommended:* 4 English, 3 math, 3 science, 2 science labs, 2 foreign language, 2 social studies, 3 history, 2 academic electives, 1 computer science, 1 visual/performing arts. **Freshman Admission Statistics:** 5,697 applied, 57.4% admitted, 31% enrolled. **Transfer Admission Requirements:** college transcript(s), Minimum college GPA of 2.0 required. Lowest grade transferable C-. **General Admission Information:** Application fee $75. Priority deadline 3/1. Regular application deadline 4/15. Nonfall registration accepted. Admission may be deferred for a maximum of 1 semester.

COSTS AND FINANCIAL AID

Required Forms and Deadlines: FAFSA. **Notification of Awards:** Applicants will be notified of awards on a rolling basis beginning 6/1. **Financial Aid Statistics:** 73% freshmen, 75% undergrads receive any aid.

SALISBURY UNIVERSITY

1101 Camden Avenue, Salisbury, MD 21801
Phone: 410-543-6161 • **Financial Aid Phone:** 410-543-6165
E-mail: www.salisbury.edu/admissions/ • **CEEB Code:** 2091
Fax: 410-546-6016 • **Website:** www.salisbury.edu • **ACT Code:** 1716

This public school was founded in 1925. It has a 184.8 acre campus.

RATINGS

Admissions Selectivity Rating: 84   **Fire Safety Rating:** 96   **Green Rating:** 93

STUDENTS AND FACULTY

Enrollment: 7,552. **Student Body:** 56% female, 44% male, 13% out-of-state, 1% international (33 countries represented). Asian 4%, African American 14%, Caucasian 71%, Hispanic 4%, Native American 1%, Pacific Islander <1%, Two or more races 3%, Race unknown 3%.
Retention and Graduation: 83% freshmen return for sophomore year. 48% freshmen graduate within 4 years. 70% freshmen graduate within 6 years.
Faculty: Student/faculty ratio 16:1. 435 full-time faculty, 87% hold PhDs, 15% are members of minority groups, 51% are women. 2% of classes are taught by teaching assistants.

ACADEMICS

Degrees: Bachelor's; Doctoral/Professional; Doctoral/Research; Master's; Post-Bachelor's certificate; Post-Master's certificate **Classes:** Most classes have 20-29 students. Most lab/discussion sessions have 10-19 students. **Most popular majors:** Biology/Biological Sciences, General; Kinesiology And Exercise Science; Registered Nursing/Registered Nurse. **Special Study Options:** Accelerated program; Cooperative education program; Cross-registration; Distance learning; Double major; Dual enrollment; English as a Second Language (ESL); Exchange student program (domestic); Honors program; Independent study; Internships; Student-designed major; Study abroad; Teacher certification program. Honors programs: The Thomas E. Bellavance Honors Program. **Disability Services offered to physically disabled students:** Note-taking services; Reader services; Tape recorders; Tutors. **Career services:** Alumni network; Alumni services; Career assessment; Career/job search classes; Internships; Regional alumni

FACILITIES

Housing: Apartments for single students; Coed dorms; Special housing for disabled student; Special housing for international students 95% of campus accessible to physically disabled. **Special Academic Facilities/Equipment:** Arboretum, Atrium Gallery, University Galleries, Delmarva History and Culture Research Center, Small Business Development Center, Ward Museum of Wildfowl Art, Blackbox Theatre, Perdue Museum of Business & Entrepreneurship, Guerrieri Academic Commons, Guerrieri University Center **Computers:** 100% of classrooms, 100% of dorms, 100% of libraries, 100% of dining areas, 100% of student union, have wireless network access. Students can register for classes online. Administrative functions (other than registration) can be performed online.

CAMPUS LIFE

Environment: Town **Activities:** Campus Ministries; Choral groups; Concert band; Dance; Drama/theater; International Student Organization; Jazz band; Literary magazine; Model UN; Music ensembles; Musical theater; Opera; Pep band; Radio station; Student government; Student newspaper; Student-run film society; Symphony orchestra; Television station 126 registered organizations, 23 honor societies, 8 religious organizations. 8 fraternities, 4 sororities. **Athletics (Intercollegiate):** *Men:* baseball, basketball, cross-country, football, lacrosse, soccer, swimming, tennis, track/field (outdoor). *Women:* basketball, cross-country, field hockey, lacrosse, soccer, softball, swimming, tennis, track/field (outdoor), volleyball. **On-Campus Highlights:** Guerrieri Academic Commons, The Commons (houses Bookstore and Dining Hall), Cool Beans Cyber Cafe, Maggs Gym / University Fitness Center, Red Square **Environmental Initiatives:** Construction of solar parking canopy that produces 765,000 Kwh annually

ADMISSIONS

Freshman Academic Profile: Average high school GPA 3.6. 16% in top 10% of high school class, 50% in top 25% of high school class, 84% in top 50% of high school class. 80% from public high schools. **Test Scores:** SAT Math middle 50% range 540-630. SAT EBRW middle 50% range 560-630. ACT middle 50% range 20-25. Minimum internet-based TOEFL 79. Minimum paper TOEFL 550. **Basis for Candidate Selection:** *Very important factors considered include:* rigor of secondary school record, academic GPA. *Important factors considered include:* class rank, standardized test scores. *Other factors considered include:* application essay, recommendation(s), extracurricular activities, talent/ability, character/personal qualities, first generation, alumni/ae relation, geographical residence, state residency, racial/ethnic status, volunteer work, work experience, level of applicant's interest. **Freshman Admission Requirements:** High school diploma is required and GED is accepted *Academic units required:* 4 English, 4 math, 3 science, 2 science labs, 2 foreign language, 3 social studies, *Academic units recommended:* 4 English, 4 math, 4 science, 3 science labs, 3 foreign language, 3 social studies, 3 academic electives. **Freshman Admission Statistics:** 8,171 applied, 65.0% admitted, 25% enrolled. **Transfer Admission Requirements:** college transcript(s), Minimum college GPA of 2.0 required. Lowest grade transferable C. **General Admission Information:** Application fee $50. Regular application deadline 1/15. Nonfall registration accepted. Admission may be deferred for a maximum of 1 year.

COSTS AND FINANCIAL AID

Annual in-state tuition $11,480. Annual out-of-state tuition $16,022. Room and board $11,480. Required fees $2,600. Average book expense $1,300. **Required Forms and Deadlines:** FAFSA. **Notification of Awards:** Applicants will be notified of awards on or about 3/15. **Types of Aid:** *Need-based scholarships/grants:* College/university scholarship or grant aid from institutional funds; Federal Pell; Private scholarships; SEOG; State scholarships/grants. *Loans:* Direct PLUS loans; Direct Subsidized Stafford Loans; Direct Unsubsidized Stafford Loans. *Student Employment:* Federal Work-Study Program available. Institutional employment available. **Financial Aid Statistics:** 83% needy freshmen, 78% needy undergrads receive need-based scholarship or grant aid. 0% undergrads receive non-need-based scholarship or grant aid. 78% freshmen, 82% undergrads receive need-based self-help aid. 0% freshmen, 0% undergrads receive athletic scholarships. 87% freshmen, 76% undergrads receive any aid. 59% undergrads borrow to pay for school. Average cumulative indebtedness $26,940. **Criteria for awarding aid:** *Need-based:* Academics, Job skills *Non-need-based:* Academics, Alumni affiliation, Art, Leadership, Music/drama, State/district residency.

SALVE REGINA UNIVERSITY

100 Ochre Point Avenue, Newport, RI 02840-4192
Phone: 401-341-2908 • **Financial Aid Phone:** 401-341-2140
E-mail: admissions@salve.edu • **CEEB Code:** 3759
Fax: 401-848-2823 • **Website:** www.salve.edu • **ACT Code:** 3816

This private school, affiliated with the Roman Catholic Church, was founded in 1947. It has a 80 acre campus.

RATINGS

Admissions Selectivity Rating: 79   **Fire Safety Rating:** 94   **Green Rating:** 64

STUDENTS AND FACULTY

Enrollment: 2,160. **Student Body:** 67% female, 33% male, 79% out-of-state, 2% international (21 countries represented). Asian 1%, African American 2%, Caucasian 81%, Hispanic 7%, Native American <1%, Pacific Islander <1%, Two or more races 3%, Race unknown 4%.
Retention and Graduation: 84% freshmen return for sophomore year. 70% freshmen graduate within 6 years. 29% grads go on to further study within 1 year. 22% grads pursue arts and sciences degrees. 8% grads pursue law degrees. 27% grads pursue business degrees. 2% grads pursue medical degrees.
Faculty: Student/faculty ratio 14:1. 127 full-time faculty, 79% hold PhDs, 6% are members of minority groups, 57% are women. 0% of classes are taught by teaching assistants.

ACADEMICS

Degrees: Associate; Bachelor's; Certificate; Doctoral/Professional; Doctoral/Research; Master's; Post-Bachelor's certificate; Post-Master's certificate **Classes:** Most classes have 20-29 students. Most lab/discussion sessions have fewer than 10 students. **Most popular majors:** Elementary Education And Teaching; Criminal Justice/Law Enforcement Administration; Registered Nursing/Registered Nurse. **Special Study Options:** Accelerated program; Distance learning; Double major; English as a Second Language (ESL); Honors program; Independent study; Internships; Liberal arts/career combination; Study abroad; Teacher certification program. Honors programs: The Pell Honors Program is open to students from all majors who receive the Dean's, Trustee's, or Presidential Scholarships, or who are nominated by Salve Regina faculty or the Admissions Office staff. The goal of the Pell Honors Program is to create a learning community of students from different disciplines. The honors education is an enhancement of the core curriculum with a focus in international relations and public policy emphasizing civic responsibility and action. Students are required to take classes together, participate in either an internship or study abroad experience, and write and publicly defend a senior thesis. Combined degree programs: BA/JD; BA/MA. **Disability Services offered to physically disabled students:** Note-taking services; Reader services; Tape recorders; Tutors. **Career services:** Alumni network; Alumni services; Career assessment; Career/job search classes; Internships; Regional alumni

FACILITIES

Housing: Apartments for single students; Coed dorms; Men's dorms; Special housing for disabled student; Special housing for international students; Theme housing; Women's dorms 85% of campus accessible to physically diasbled. **Special Academic Facilities/Equipment:** Hamilton Gallery, The Casino Theatre, Munroe Technology Center, Pell Center for International Relations and Public Policy, McKillop Library, Antone Academic Center, O'Hare Academic Center, Mercy Chapel & Spiritual Life Center **Computers:** 98% of classrooms, 10% of dorms, 100% of libraries, 100% of dining areas, 100% of student union, 25% of common outdoor areas have wireless network access. Students can register for classes online. Administrative functions (other than registration) can be performed online. Undergraduates are required to own a computer.

CAMPUS LIFE

Environment: Town **Activities:** Campus Ministries; Choral groups; Concert band; Dance; Drama/theater; International Student Organization; Jazz band; Literary magazine; Model UN; Music ensembles; Pep band; Radio station; Student government; Student newspaper; Student-run film society; Yearbook 42 registered organizations, 14 honor societies, 2 religious organizations. **Athletics (Intercollegiate):** *Men:* baseball, basketball, cross-country, football, ice hockey, lacrosse, soccer, tennis. *Women:* basketball, field hockey, ice hockey, lacrosse, soccer, softball, tennis, track/field (outdoor), volleyball. **On-Campus Highlights:** Miley Starbucks, Rodgers Recreation Athletic Center, O'Hare Academic & Antone Academic Cntrs, Library and Computer Labs, Our Lady of Mercy Chapel and Spiritual Center **Environmental Initiatives:** Recycling

ADMISSIONS

Freshman Academic Profile: Average high school GPA 3.4. 11% in top 10% of high school class, 42% in top 25% of high school class, 78% in top 50% of high school class. 69% from public high schools. **Test Scores:** SAT Math middle 50% range 530-610. SAT EBRW middle 50% range 550-620. ACT middle 50% range 23-27. Minimum internet-based TOEFL 80. Minimum paper TOEFL 500. **Basis for Candidate Selection:** *Very important factors considered include:* rigor of secondary school record, class rank, academic GPA. *Important factors considered include:* application essay, standardized test scores, recommendation(s). *Other factors considered include:* extracurricular activities, talent/ability, character/personal qualities, alumni/ae relation, racial/ethnic status, volunteer work, work experience, level of applicant's interest. **Freshman Admission Requirements:** High school diploma is required and GED is accepted *Academic units required:* 4 English, 3 math, 2 science, 2 science labs, 2 foreign language, 1 social studies, 4 academic electives. **Freshman Admission Statistics:** 4,991 applied, 71.9% admitted, 17% enrolled. **Transfer Admission Requirements:** High school transcript, college transcript(s), essay or personal statement, statement of good standing from prior institution(s). Minimum college GPA of 2.7 required. Lowest grade transferable C. **General Admission Information:** Application fee $50. Priority deadline 2/1. Nonfall registration accepted. Admission may be deferred for a maximum of 1 year.

COSTS AND FINANCIAL AID

Annual tuition $38,386. Room and board $14,060. Required fees $600. Average book expense $1,400. **Required Forms and Deadlines:** FAFSA. **Notification of Awards:** Applicants will be notified of awards on a rolling basis beginning 1/3. **Types of Aid:** *Need-based scholarships/grants:* College/ university scholarship or grant aid from institutional funds; Federal Pell; Private scholarships; SEOG; State scholarships/grants. *Loans:* Direct PLUS loans; Direct Subsidized Stafford Loans; Direct Unsubsidized Stafford Loans. *Student Employment:* Federal Work-Study Program available. Institutional employment available. **Financial Aid Statistics:** 98% needy freshmen, 100% needy undergrads receive need-based scholarship or grant aid. 8% freshmen, 9% undergrads receive non-need-based scholarship or grant aid. 97% freshmen, 89% undergrads receive need-based self-help aid. 0% freshmen, 0% undergrads receive athletic scholarships. 99% freshmen, 84% undergrads receive any aid. 69% undergrads borrow to pay for school. Average cumulative indebtedness $29,192. **Criteria for awarding aid:** *Non-need-based:* Academics, Alumni affiliation, Art.

SAM HOUSTON STATE UNIVERSITY

Box 2418, Huntsville, TX 77341-2418
Phone: 936-294-1828 • **Financial Aid Phone:** 936-294-1774
E-mail: admissions@shsu.edu • **CEEB Code:** 6643
Website: www.shsu.edu • **ACT Code:** 4162

This public school was founded in 1879. It has a 272 acre campus.

RATINGS

Admissions Selectivity Rating: 82   **Fire Safety Rating:** 92   **Green Rating:** 60*

STUDENTS AND FACULTY

Enrollment: 15,611. **Student Body:** 58% female, 42% male, 1% out-of-state, 1% international (59 countries represented). Asian 1%, African American 17%, Caucasian 58%, Hispanic 17%, Native American <1%, Pacific Islander <1%, Two or more races 2%, Race unknown 2%.
Faculty: Student/faculty ratio 25:1. 620 full-time faculty, 79% hold PhDs, 16% are members of minority groups, 45% are women. 5% of classes are taught by teaching assistants.

ACADEMICS

Degrees: Bachelor's; Diploma; Doctoral/Professional; Doctoral/Research; **Master's Classes:** Most classes have fewer than 10 students. **Most popular majors:** Multi-/Interdisciplinary Studies, Other; Criminal Justice/Safety Studies; Business/Commerce, General. **Special Study Options:** Accelerated program; Distance learning; Double major; Dual enrollment; English as a Second Language (ESL); Honors program; Independent study; Internships; Study abroad; Teacher certification program. Honors programs: The Honors student earns Honors credit in a variety of specially designated classes, and works toward the distinction of graduating 'With Honors' or 'With Highest Honors.' To qualify for graduation with honors, a student must have been a participant in the Honors Program and have completed 24 hours of Honors class credit, including participation in two interdisciplinary Honors seminars. To qualify for graduation 'With Highest Honors' a student must, in addition, complete a senior thesis in an approved discipline under the direction of a faculty member of his/her choice. The student will receive 6 credit hours of departmental course credit when completing the senior thesis. **Disability Services offered to physically disabled students:** Note-taking services; Reader services; Tape recorders. **Career services:** Alumni network; Alumni services; Career assessment; Career/job search classes; Internships; Regional alumni

FACILITIES

Housing: Apartments for single students; Coed dorms; Fraternity/sorority housing; Men's dorms; Special housing for disabled student; Theme housing; Women's dorms 85% of campus accessible to physically disabled. **Special Academic Facilities/Equipment:** Sam Houston Memorial Museum, on-campus elementary school, communications center for photography, radio, TV, and film, agricultural complex and university farm. **Computers:** Students can register for classes online. Administrative functions (other than registration) can be performed online.

CAMPUS LIFE

Environment: Town **Activities:** Campus Ministries; Choral groups; Concert band; Dance; Drama/theater; International Student Organization; Jazz band; Marching band; Music ensembles; Musical theater; Pep band; Radio station; Student government; Student newspaper; Symphony orchestra; Television station 185 registered organizations, 12 honor societies, 17 religious organizations. 16 fraternities, 10 sororities. **Athletics (Intercollegiate):** *Men:* baseball, basketball, cheerleading, cross-country, equestrian sports, football, golf, rodeo, soccer, softball, tennis, track/field (outdoor), track/field (indoor). *Women:* basketball, cheerleading, cross-country, equestrian sports, golf, rodeo, soccer, softball, tennis, track/field (outdoor), track/field (indoor), volleyball. **On-Campus Highlights:** Lowman Student Center, Health and Kinesiology Center, Bernard G. Johnson Coliseum, Mall Area, Old Main Pit **Environmental Initiatives:** Hired an Energy Manager.

ADMISSIONS

Freshman Academic Profile: 13% in top 10% of high school class, 42% in top 25% of high school class, 85% in top 50% of high school class. **Test Scores:** SAT Math middle 50% range 470-550. SAT EBRW middle 50% range 450-540. ACT middle 50% range 19-23. Minimum paper TOEFL 550. **Basis for Candidate Selection:** *Very important factors considered include:* class rank, standardized test scores. *Important factors considered include:* academic GPA. *Other factors considered include:* rigor of secondary school record, recommendation(s), extracurricular activities, talent/ability, character/personal qualities, volunteer work. **Freshman Admission Requirements:** High school diploma is required and GED is accepted *Academic units required:* 4 English,

4 math, 4 science, 2 foreign language, 2 social studies, 2 history, 6 academic electives, 1 computer science, 1 visual/performing arts, and 2 units from above areas or other academic areas. *Academic units recommended:* 4 English, 4 math, 4 science, 1 science labs, 2 foreign language, 2 social studies, 2 history, 6 academic electives, 1 computer science, 1 visual/performing arts, 2 units from above areas or other academic areas. **Freshman Admission Statistics:** 9,315 applied, 65.0% admitted, 40% enrolled. **Transfer Admission Requirements:** college transcript(s), statement of good standing from prior institution(s). Minimum college GPA of 2.0 required. Lowest grade transferable D. **General Admission Information:** Application fee $45. Priority deadline 6/15. Regular application deadline 8/1. Nonfall registration accepted.

COSTS AND FINANCIAL AID

Annual in-state tuition $8,324. Annual out-of-state tuition $16,470. Room and board $8,324. Required fees $2,744. Average book expense $1,124. **Required Forms and Deadlines:** FAFSA. **Notification of Awards:** Applicants will be notified of awards on a rolling basis beginning 3/15. **Types of Aid:** *Need-based scholarships/grants:* College/university scholarship or grant aid from institutional funds; Federal Pell; SEOG; State scholarships/grants. *Loans:* Direct PLUS loans; Direct Subsidized Stafford Loans; Direct Unsubsidized Stafford Loans. *Student Employment:* Federal Work-Study Program available. Institutional employment available. **Financial Aid Statistics:** 86% needy freshmen, 80% needy undergrads receive need-based scholarship or grant aid. 4% freshmen, 1% undergrads receive non-need-based scholarship or grant aid. 78% freshmen, 84% undergrads receive need-based self-help aid. 2% freshmen, 2% undergrads receive athletic scholarships. 79% freshmen, 71% undergrads receive any aid. **Criteria for awarding aid:** *Need-based:* Academics, Art, Music/drama *Non-need-based:* Academics, Alumni affiliation, Art, Athletics, Job skills, Leadership, Music/drama, Religious affiliation, State/district residency.

SAMFORD UNIVERSITY

800 Lakeshore Drive, Birmingham, AL 35229
Phone: 205-726-3673 • **Financial Aid Phone:** (205)726-2905
E-mail: admissions@samford.edu • **CEEB Code:** 1302
Fax: 205-726-2171 • **Website:** www.samford.edu • **ACT Code:** 16

This private school, affiliated with the Baptist Church, was founded in 1841. It has a 247.31 acre campus.

RATINGS

Admissions Selectivity Rating: 79   **Fire Safety Rating:** 96   **Green Rating:** 75

STUDENTS AND FACULTY

Enrollment: 3,324. **Student Body:** 65% female, 35% male, 67% out-of-state, 2% international (22 countries represented). Asian 1%, African American 7%, Caucasian 83%, Hispanic 4%, Native American <1%, Pacific Islander 0%, Two or more races 2%, Race unknown 1%.
Retention and Graduation: 89% freshmen return for sophomore year. 34% grads go on to further study within 1 year. **Faculty:** Student/faculty ratio 12:1. 352 full-time faculty, 87% hold PhDs, 11% are members of minority groups, 51% are women. 0% of classes are taught by teaching assistants.

ACADEMICS

Degrees: Bachelor's; Certificate; Doctoral/Professional; Doctoral/Research; Master's; Post-Bachelor's certificate; Post-Master's certificate **Classes:** Most classes have 10-19 students. **Most popular majors:** Journalism; Teacher Education, Multiple Levels; Registered Nursing/Registered Nurse. **Special Study Options:** Accelerated program; Cross-registration; Distance learning; Double major; Dual enrollment; English as a Second Language (ESL); Exchange student program (domestic); Honors program; Independent study; Internships; Liberal arts/career combination; Study abroad; Teacher certification program. Honors programs: University Fellows is Samford's honors college experience. The program offers an interdisciplinary great ideas core curriculum, international study in Italy, funding for academic enrichment and a four-year University Fellows scholarship. Admission to the program is highly competitive. Applicants should be intellectually curious, ambitious students who want to make connections across disciplines. The program is open to students from all Samford undergraduate majors, but students must be admitted as high school seniors. Micah Fellows is a four-year service-oriented, honors college experience grounded in the wisdom of Micah 6:8: "And what does the Lord require of you? To act justly, and to love mercy, and to walk humbly with your God." As part of an inspired community called to serve others, Micah Fellows devote their minds and talents to making Birmingham, and the world beyond, a better place. Through innovative course work, high-impact community development and service abroad, the Micah Fellows program will provide an intentional university experience connected to the world around you. **Disability Services offered to physically disabled students:** Note-taking services;

Reader services; Tape recorders; Tutors. **Career services:** Alumni network; Alumni services; Career assessment; Career/job search classes; Internships; Regional alumni

FACILITIES

Housing: Fraternity/sorority housing; Men's dorms; Women's dorms 100% of campus accessible to physically disabled. **Special Academic Facilities/Equipment:** Divinity school Global Center, Samford University Global Drug Information Center, Nursing school state-of-the-art human sumulation center, Medicinal Plant Conservatory, Business School Investment Trading Room, Sciencenter **Computers:** 100% of classrooms, 100% of libraries, 100% of dining areas, 100% of student union, have wireless network access. Students can register for classes online. Administrative functions (other than registration) can be performed online.

CAMPUS LIFE

Environment: Town **Activities:** Campus Ministries; Choral groups; Concert band; Dance; Drama/theater; International Student Organization; Jazz band; Literary magazine; Marching band; Model UN; Music ensembles; Musical theater; Opera; Pep band; Radio station; Student government; Student newspaper; Student-run film society; Symphony orchestra; Yearbook 119 registered organizations, 25 honor societies, 16 religious organizations. 6 fraternities, 6 sororities. **Athletics (Intercollegiate):** *Men:* baseball, basketball, cross-country, football, golf, tennis, track/field (outdoor). *Women:* basketball, cross-country, golf, soccer, softball, tennis, track/field (outdoor), volleyball. **On-Campus Highlights:** Andrew Gerow Hodges Chapel, Ralph W. Beeson University Center, Cooney Hall-Brock School of Buisness, Pete Hanna Center, Boyd E. Christenberry Planetarium **Environmental Initiatives:** The university strategic plan includes "conserve all resources" as one of the 16 goals.

ADMISSIONS

Freshman Academic Profile: Average high school GPA 3.6. 31% in top 10% of high school class, 57% in top 25% of high school class, 84% in top 50% of high school class. 48% from public high schools. **Test Scores:** SAT Math middle 50% range 500-618. SAT EBRW middle 50% range 520-620. ACT middle 50% range 23-29. Minimum internet-based TOEFL 90. Minimum paper TOEFL 575. **Basis for Candidate Selection:** *Very important factors considered include:* academic GPA, application essay, standardized test scores, recommendation(s), character/personal qualities. *Important factors considered include:* rigor of secondary school record, extracurricular activities, talent/ability, volunteer work.level of applicant's interest. *Other factors considered include:* alumni/ae relation, work experience. **Freshman Admission Requirements:** High school diploma is required and GED is accepted *Academic units required:* 4 English, 3 math, 2 science, 2 science labs, 2 foreign language, 2 history. **Freshman Admission Statistics:** 3,446 applied, 91.4% admitted, 29% enrolled. **Transfer Admission Requirements:** college transcript(s), essay or personal statement, statement of good standing from prior institution(s). Minimum college GPA of 2.5 required. Lowest grade transferable C-. **General Admission Information:** Application fee $40. Priority deadline 12/1. Nonfall registration accepted. Admission may be deferred for a maximum of 1 year.

COSTS AND FINANCIAL AID

Annual tuition $29,640. Room and board $10,280. Required fees $850. Average book expense $1,000. **Required Forms and Deadlines:** FAFSA; State aid form. **Notification of Awards:** Applicants will be notified of awards on a rolling basis beginning 3/1. **Types of Aid:** *Need-based scholarships/grants:* College/university scholarship or grant aid from institutional funds; Federal Nursing Scholarships; Federal Pell; Private scholarships; SEOG; State scholarships/grants; United Negro College Fund. *Loans:* Direct PLUS loans; Direct Subsidized Stafford Loans; Direct Unsubsidized Stafford Loans. *Student Employment:* Federal Work-Study Program available. Institutional employment available. **Financial Aid Statistics:** 100% needy freshmen, 96% needy undergrads receive need-based scholarship or grant aid. 24% freshmen, 20% undergrads receive non-need-based scholarship or grant aid. 68% freshmen, 75% undergrads receive need-based self-help aid. 3% freshmen, 4% undergrads receive athletic scholarships. 96% freshmen, 89% undergrads receive any aid. Average cumulative indebtedness $29,292. **Criteria for awarding aid:** *Non-need-based:* Academics, Alumni affiliation, Art, Athletics, Leadership, Minority status, Music/drama, Religious affiliation, State/district residency.

SAN DIEGO STATE UNIVERSITY

5500 Campanile Drive, San Diego, CA 92182-7455
Phone: 619-594-6336 • **Financial Aid Phone:** 619-594-6323 • **CEEB Code:** 4682
Website: www.sdsu.edu • **ACT Code:** 398

This public school was founded in 1897. It has a 288 acre campus.

RATINGS

Admissions Selectivity Rating: 90   **Fire Safety Rating:** 95   **Green Rating:** 83

STUDENTS AND FACULTY

Enrollment: 30,165. **Student Body:** 54% female, 46% male, 10% out-of-state, 7% international (114 countries represented). Asian 13%, African American 4%, Caucasian 33%, Hispanic 31%, Native American <1%, Pacific Islander <1%, Two or more races 7%, Race unknown 4%.
Retention and Graduation: 89% freshmen return for sophomore year. 36% freshmen graduate within 4 years. 75% freshmen graduate within 6 years.
Faculty: Student/faculty ratio 27:1. 876 full-time faculty, 88% hold PhDs, 29% are members of minority groups, 46% are women.

ACADEMICS

Degrees: Bachelor's; Doctoral Other; Doctoral/Professional; Doctoral/Research; Master's; Post-Bachelor's certificate **Classes:** Most classes have 10-19 students. Most lab/discussion sessions have fewer than 10 students.
Most popular majors: Health And Physical Education/Fitness, General; Psychology, General; Criminal Justice/Safety Studies. **Special Study Options:** Cross-registration; Distance learning; Double major; English as a Second Language (ESL); Exchange student program (domestic); External degree program; Honors program; Independent study; Internships; Liberal arts/career combination; Student-designed major; Study abroad; Teacher certification program. Honors programs: The Weber Honors College provides an academic environment in which students experience a dynamic, interactive, and engaged education. The objective of the Weber Honors College is to provide the richest possible intellectual experience by helping students become conversant in multiple disciplines, think flexibly, solve problems and pursue the creative expression of ideas. The Weber Honors College features a unique interdisciplinary curriculum made up of small, discussion-based seminars and innovative teaching techniques that promote active engagement in the subject area and prepare students for high-impact educational experiences beyond the classroom, including study abroad, research, leadership, service, and creative activity; and for future graduate work and successful careers regardless of their chosen field of study. **Disability Services offered to physically disabled students:** Note-taking services; Reader services; Tape recorders; Tutors.
Career services: Alumni network; Alumni services; Career assessment; Internships

FACILITIES

Housing: Apartments for single students; Coed dorms; Fraternity/sorority housing; Special housing for disabled student; Special housing for international students; Theme housing; Wellness housing 99% of campus accessible to physically diasbled. **Special Academic Facilities/Equipment:** Library, recital hall, performing arts theatres, health center, modern recreation center, 12,000-seat arena, top quality baseball stadium, aquaplex, observatories, PBS radio and television stations, seismology and weather stations. Recently completed projects include Aztec Student Union, renovated dining and residence halls at University Towers & Zura Hall and student recreation field. A retail / student housing development & Engineering & Sciences lab building, are currently under construction. **Computers:** Students can register for classes online. Administrative functions (other than registration) can be performed online.

CAMPUS LIFE

Environment: Metropolis **Activities:** Campus Ministries; Choral groups; Concert band; Dance; Drama/theater; International Student Organization; Jazz band; Literary magazine; Marching band; Music ensembles; Musical theater; Opera; Pep band; Radio station; Student government; Student newspaper; Student-run film society; Symphony orchestra; Television station 264 registered organizations, 6 honor societies, 14 religious organizations. 21 fraternities, 23 sororities. **Athletics (Intercollegiate):** *Men:* baseball, basketball, football, golf, soccer, tennis. *Women:* basketball, crew/rowing, cross-country, diving, golf, soccer, softball, swimming, tennis, track/field (outdoor), track/field (indoor), volleyball, water polo. Aztec Student Union, Aztec Recreation Center & Aquaplex, SDSU Library, Open Air Theatre and Viejas Arena, Starbucks

ADMISSIONS

Freshman Academic Profile: Average high school GPA 3.7. 31% in top 10% of high school class, 70% in top 25% of high school class, 95% in top 50% of high school class. 91% from public high schools. **Test Scores:** SAT Math middle 50% range 540-650. SAT EBRW middle 50% range 550-640. ACT middle 50% range 23-28. Minimum internet-based TOEFL 80. Minimum paper TOEFL 550. **Basis for Candidate Selection:** *Very important factors considered include:* rigor of secondary school record, academic GPA, standardized test scores. *Important factors considered include:* geographical residence, state residency. **Freshman Admission Requirements:** High school diploma is required and GED is accepted *Academic units required:* 4 English, 3 math, 2 science, 2 science labs, 2 foreign language, 1 social studies, 1 history, 1 academic elective, 1 visual/performing arts, *Academic units recommended:* 4 math. **Freshman Admission Statistics:** 60,697 applied, 35.2% admitted, 25% enrolled. **Transfer Admission Requirements:** college transcript(s), Lowest grade transferable D-. **General Admission Information:** Application fee $55. Regular application deadline 11/30. Nonfall registration accepted.

COSTS AND FINANCIAL AID

Annual in-state tuition $15,966. Annual out-of-state tuition $17,622. Room and board $15,966. Required fees $1,718. Average book expense $1,854. **Required Forms and Deadlines:** FAFSA; State aid form. **Notification of Awards:** Applicants will be notified of awards on a rolling basis beginning 3/15. **Types of Aid:** *Need-based scholarships/grants:* College/university scholarship or grant aid from institutional funds; Federal Pell; Private scholarships; SEOG; State scholarships/grants. *Loans:* Direct PLUS loans; Direct Subsidized Stafford Loans; Direct Unsubsidized Stafford Loans. *Student Employment:* Federal Work-Study Program available. Institutional employment available. **Financial Aid Statistics:** 62% needy freshmen, 80% needy undergrads receive need-based scholarship or grant aid. 54% freshmen, 41% undergrads receive non-need-based scholarship or grant aid. 100% freshmen, 98% undergrads receive need-based self-help aid. 2% freshmen, 1% undergrads receive athletic scholarships. 61% freshmen, 66% undergrads receive any aid. 49% undergrads borrow to pay for school. Average cumulative indebtedness $19,969. **Criteria for awarding aid:** *Need-based:* Academics, Alumni affiliation, Art, Leadership, Music/drama *Non-need-based:* Academics, Alumni affiliation, Art, Athletics, Leadership, Music/drama, State/district residency.

See page 1024.

SAN FRANCISCO STATE UNIVERSITY

1600 Holloway Avenue, San Francisco, CA 93132
Phone: 415-338-6486 • **Financial Aid Phone:** (415) 338-7000
E-mail: ugadmit@sfsu.edu • **CEEB Code:** 4684
Fax: 415-338-3880 • **Website:** www.sfsu.edu

This public school was founded in 1899. It has a 142 acre campus.

RATINGS

Admissions Selectivity Rating: 75   **Fire Safety Rating:** 88   **Green Rating:** 94

STUDENTS AND FACULTY

Enrollment: 25,903. **Student Body:** 56% female, 44% male, 1% out-of-state, 6% international (75 countries represented). Asian 26%, African American 5%, Caucasian 18%, Hispanic 33%, Native American <1%, Pacific Islander <1%, Two or more races 6%, Race unknown 4%.
Retention and Graduation: 79% freshmen return for sophomore year.
Faculty: Student/faculty ratio 23:1. 1,054 full-time faculty, 63% hold PhDs, 38% are members of minority groups, 56% are women.

ACADEMICS

Degrees: Bachelor's; Certificate; Doctoral; Doctoral Other; Doctoral/Professional; Doctoral/Research; Master's; Post-Bachelor's certificate; Post-Master's certificate **Classes:** Most classes have 10-19 students. Most lab/discussion sessions have 20-29 students. **Most popular majors:** Communication, General; Computer Science; Marketing/Marketing Management, General. **Special Study Options:** Accelerated program; Cooperative education program; Cross-registration; Distance learning; Double major; Dual enrollment; English as a Second Language (ESL); Exchange student program (domestic); Honors program; Independent study; Internships; Liberal arts/career combination; Student-designed major; Study abroad; Teacher certification program. **Disability Services offered to physically disabled students:** Note-taking services; Reader services; Tape recorders; Tutors. **Career services:** Alumni services; Career assessment; Career/job search classes; Internships

FACILITIES

Housing: Apartments for married students; Apartments for single students; Coed dorms; Special housing for disabled student; Special housing for international students; Theme housing; Wellness housing; Women's dorms **Special Academic Facilities/Equipment:** Treganza Anthropology Museum, Moss Landing Marine Laboratories, Romberg Tiburon Center for Environmental Studies, Sierra Nevada Field Campus, Sutro Egyptian Collection. **Computers:** 100% of classrooms, 100% of dorms, 100% of libraries, 100% of dining areas, 100% of student union, 100% of common outdoor areas have wireless network access. Students can register for classes online. Administrative functions (other than registration) can be performed online.

CAMPUS LIFE

Environment: Metropolis **Activities:** Choral groups; Concert band; Dance; Drama/theater; International Student Organization; Jazz band; Literary magazine; Marching band; Music ensembles; Musical theater; Opera; Radio station; Student government; Student newspaper; Student-run film society; Symphony orchestra; Television station 213 registered organizations, 6 honor societies, 13 religious organizations. 3 fraternities, 4 sororities. **Athletics (Intercollegiate):** *Men:* baseball, basketball, cross-country, soccer, wrestling. *Women:* basketball, cross-country, soccer, softball, track/field (outdoor), track/field (indoor), volleyball. **On-Campus Highlights:** J. Paul Leonard Library, Cesar Chavez Student Center, Cox Stadium, Residential Theme Communities, SFSU Fine Arts Gallery **Environmental Initiatives:** SF State is dedicated to reducing the campus' use of resources and its impact on climate change. Some of the projects that demonstrate that are: the Buy Recycled Campaign, purchasing 20% renewable energy, implementing a green cleaning program, hiring a Sustainability Programs Manager and a Sustainability Coordinator, offering alternative transportation incentives, pursuing LEED Gold for its new Rec and Wellness Center and diverting over 75% of the waste from the landfill.

ADMISSIONS

Freshman Academic Profile: Average high school GPA 3.2. 88% from public high schools. **Test Scores:** SAT Math middle 50% range 430-550. SAT EBRW middle 50% range 430-540. ACT middle 50% range 18-24. Minimum internet-based TOEFL 61. Minimum paper TOEFL 500. **Basis for Candidate Selection:** *Very important factors considered include:* rigor of secondary school record, academic GPA, standardized test scores. *Important factors considered include:* state residency. *Other factors considered include:* geographical residence. **Freshman Admission Requirements:** High school diploma is required and GED is accepted *Academic units required:* 4 English, 3 math, 2 science, 2 science labs, 2 foreign language, 1 social studies, 1 history, 1 academic elective, 1 visual/performing arts, *Academic units recommended:* 4 English, 4 math, 2 science, 2 science labs, 2 foreign language, 1 social studies, 1 history, 1 academic elective, 1 visual/performing arts. **Freshman Admission Statistics:** 34,524 applied, 70.5% admitted, 18% enrolled. **Transfer Admission Requirements:** college transcript(s), statement of good standing from prior institution(s). Minimum college GPA of 2.0 required. Lowest grade transferable D. **General Admission Information:** Application fee $55. Priority deadline 10/1. Regular application deadline 11/30. Nonfall registration accepted.

COSTS AND FINANCIAL AID

Annual in-state tuition $1,012. Annual out-of-state tuition $16,632. Required fees $1,012. Average book expense $1,900. **Required Forms and Deadlines:** FAFSA. **Notification of Awards:** Applicants will be notified of awards on a rolling basis beginning 4/15. **Types of Aid:** *Need-based scholarships/ grants:* College/university scholarship or grant aid from institutional funds; Federal Pell; Private scholarships; SEOG; State scholarships/grants. *Loans:* Direct PLUS loans; Direct Subsidized Stafford Loans; Direct Unsubsidized Stafford Loans. *Student Employment:* Federal Work-Study Program available. Institutional employment available. **Financial Aid Statistics:** 90% needy freshmen, 89% needy undergrads receive need-based scholarship or grant aid. 24% freshmen, 13% undergrads receive non-need-based scholarship or grant aid. 78% freshmen, 76% undergrads receive need-based self-help aid. 1% freshmen, 1% undergrads receive athletic scholarships. Average cumulative indebtedness $20,716. **Criteria for awarding aid:** *Need-based:* Academics, Athletics *Non-need-based:* Academics, Athletics.

SAN JOSE STATE UNIVERSITY

One Washington Square, San Jose, CA 95192-0016
Phone: 408-283-7500 • **Financial Aid Phone:** 408-283-7500
E-mail: admissions@sjsu.edu • **CEEB Code:** 4687
Fax: 408-924-2050 • **Website:** www.sjsu.edu

This public school was founded in 1857. It has a 154 acre campus.

RATINGS

Admissions Selectivity Rating: 82   **Fire Safety Rating:** 60*   **Green Rating:** 93

STUDENTS AND FACULTY

Enrollment: 27,778. **Student Body:** 48% female, 52% male, 1% out-of-state, 8% international (93 countries represented). Asian 36%, African American 3%, Caucasian 16%, Hispanic 28%, Native American <1%, Pacific Islander <1%, Two or more races 5%, Race unknown 4%.
Retention and Graduation: 87% freshmen return for sophomore year. 10% freshmen graduate within 4 years. 57% freshmen graduate within 6 years. **Faculty:** Student/faculty ratio 26:1. 726 full-time faculty, 10% are members of minority groups, 51% are women. 4% of classes are taught by teaching assistants.

ACADEMICS

Degrees: Bachelor's; Certificate; Doctoral/Professional; **Master's Classes:** Most classes have 10-19 students. Most lab/discussion sessions have 10-19 students. **Most popular majors:** Electrical And Electronics Engineering; Art/ Art Studies, General; Business Administration And Management, General. **Special Study Options:** Cooperative education program; Cross-registration; Distance learning; Double major; Dual enrollment; Honors program; Independent study; Internships; Liberal arts/career combination; Student-designed major; Study abroad; Teacher certification program; Weekend college. **Disability Services offered to physically disabled students:** Note-taking services; Reader services; Tutors. **Career services:** Alumni network; Alumni services; Career assessment; Career/job search classes; Internships

FACILITIES

Housing: Apartments for single students; Coed dorms; Fraternity/sorority housing; Men's dorms; Special housing for international students; Women's dorms 100% of campus accessible to physically disabled. **Special Academic Facilities/Equipment:** Martin Luther King, Jr. Library (Joint with City)Child development lab, Chicano resource center, Beethoven studies center, John Steinbeck research center, art metal foundry, natural history living museum (science education), science resource center, deep-sea research ship, electro-acoustical/recording studios, nuclear science and engineering labs. **Computers:** Students can register for classes online. Administrative functions (other than registration) can be performed online.

CAMPUS LIFE

Environment: Metropolis **Activities:** Campus Ministries; Choral groups; Concert band; Dance; Drama/theater; International Student Organization; Jazz band; Literary magazine; Marching band; Model UN; Music ensembles; Musical theater; Opera; Pep band; Radio station; Student government; Student newspaper; Student-run film society; Symphony orchestra 283 registered organizations, 13 honor societies, 20 religious organizations. 20 fraternities, 15 sororities. **Athletics (Intercollegiate):** *Men:* baseball, basketball, cheerleading, cross-country, diving, football, golf, soccer, softball, swimming, volleyball, water polo. *Women:* basketball, cheerleading, cross-country, diving, golf, gymnastics, soccer, softball, swimming, tennis, volleyball, water polo. **On-Campus Highlights:** Martin Luther King, Jr. Library, Student Union, Event Center, Tower Hall, Student Health Center

ADMISSIONS

Freshman Academic Profile: Average high school GPA 3.4. 89% from public high schools. **Test Scores:** SAT Math middle 50% range 520-620. SAT EBRW middle 50% range 510-610. ACT middle 50% range 19-26. Minimum internet-based TOEFL 80. Minimum paper TOEFL 550. **Basis for Candidate Selection:** *Very important factors considered include:* rigor of secondary school record, academic GPA, standardized test scores. *Important factors considered include:* geographical residence, state residency. **Freshman Admission Requirements:** High school diploma is required and GED is accepted *Academic units required:* 4 English, 3 math, 2 science, 2 science labs, 2 foreign language, 1 social studies, 1 history, 1 academic elective, 1 visual/performing arts, *Academic units recommended:* 4 math, 3 science, 3 science labs. **Freshman Admission Statistics:** 31,909 applied, 66.9% admitted, 21% enrolled. **Transfer Admission Requirements:** college transcript(s), statement of good standing from prior institution(s). Minimum college GPA of 2.0 required. Lowest grade transferable 2. **General Admission Information:** Application fee $55. Regular application deadline 11/30. Nonfall registration accepted.

COSTS AND FINANCIAL AID

Annual in-state tuition $16,250. Annual out-of-state tuition $14,976. Room and board $16,250. Required fees $1,979. Average book expense $1,948. **Required Forms and Deadlines:** FAFSA; State aid form. **Notification of Awards:** Applicants will be notified of awards on a rolling basis beginning 3/1. **Types of Aid:** *Need-based scholarships/grants:* College/university scholarship or grant aid from institutional funds; Federal Pell; Private scholarships; SEOG; State scholarships/grants. *Loans:* Direct PLUS loans; Direct Subsidized Stafford Loans; Direct Unsubsidized Stafford Loans. *Student Employment:* Federal Work-Study Program available. Institutional employment available. **Financial Aid Statistics:** 70% needy freshmen, 93% needy undergrads receive need-based scholarship or grant aid. 7% freshmen, 4% undergrads receive non-need-based scholarship or grant aid. 95% freshmen, 96% undergrads receive need-based self-help aid. 3% freshmen, 1% undergrads receive athletic scholarships. 40% freshmen, 39% undergrads receive any aid. 43% undergrads borrow to pay for school. Average cumulative indebtedness $19,797. **Criteria for awarding aid:** *Need-based:* Academics, Art, Athletics, Job skills, Leadership, Music/drama *Non-need-based:* Academics, Art, Athletics, Job skills, Leadership, Music/drama, State/district residency.

SANTA CLARA UNIVERSITY

500 El Camino Real, Santa Clara, CA 95053
Phone: 408-554-4700 • **Financial Aid Phone:** (408) 551-1000
E-mail: Admission@scu.edu • **CEEB Code:** 4851
Fax: 408-554-5255 • **Website:** www.scu.edu

This private school, affiliated with the Roman Catholic Church, was founded in 1851. It has a 106 acre campus.

RATINGS

Admissions Selectivity Rating: 91   Fire Safety Rating: 95   Green Rating: 98

STUDENTS AND FACULTY

Enrollment: 5,481. **Student Body:** 50% female, 50% male, 29% out-of-state, 4% international (37 countries represented). Asian 16%, African American 3%, Caucasian 50%, Hispanic 18%, Native American <1%, Pacific Islander <1%, Two or more races 7%, Race unknown 2%.
Retention and Graduation: 94% freshmen return for sophomore year. 85% freshmen graduate within 4 years. 90% freshmen graduate within 6 years. 24% grads go on to further study within 1 year. 15% grads pursue arts and sciences degrees. 3.2% grads pursue law degrees. 1% grads pursue business degrees. 3.2% grads pursue medical degrees. **Faculty:** Student/faculty ratio 11:1. 542 full-time faculty, 94% hold PhDs, 28% are members of minority groups, 44% are women. 0% of classes are taught by teaching assistants.

ACADEMICS

Degrees: Bachelor's; Doctoral; Doctoral/Professional; Doctoral/Research; Master's; Post-Bachelor's certificate **Classes:** Most classes have 10-19 students. Most lab/discussion sessions have 10-19 students. **Most popular majors:** Speech Communication And Rhetoric; Political Science And Government, General; Finance, General. **Special Study Options:** Cooperative education program; Double major; Honors program; Independent study; Internships; Liberal arts/career combination; Student-designed major; Study abroad. Honors programs: The University Honors Program provides Santa Clara's most able students with intellectual opportunities based in small, seminar-style classes. With 14 to 17 students each, seminars emphasize analytical rigor, effective expression, and interaction among professors and students. The course of study combines broadly based, liberal learning with depth of specialization in a major field. Honors Program classes are designed to fit within the curricula of the humanities, natural and social sciences, business, and engineering. Possible majors include every undergraduate field of study in the University. Combined degree programs: BA/MEng. **Disability Services offered to physically disabled students:** Note-taking services; Reader services; Tape recorders; Tutors. **Career services:** Alumni network; Alumni services; Career assessment; Career/job search classes; Internships; Regional alumni

FACILITIES

Housing: Apartments for single students; Coed dorms; Special housing for disabled student; Theme housing 95% of campus accessible to physically diasbled. **Special Academic Facilities/Equipment:** Art and history museum (de Saisset), mission church, theatre, media lab, retail management institute,

computer design center, engineering labs, Markkula Center for Applied Ethics, Center for Science, Technology, and Society, Ignatian Center for Jesuit Education **Computers:** 100% of classrooms, 100% of dorms, 100% of libraries, 100% of dining areas, 100% of student union, 90% of common outdoor areas have wireless network access. Students can register for classes online. Administrative functions (other than registration) can be performed online.

CAMPUS LIFE

Environment: City **Activities:** Campus Ministries; Choral groups; Dance; Drama/theater; International Student Organization; Jazz band; Literary magazine; Marching band; Model UN; Music ensembles; Musical theater; Opera; Pep band; Radio station; Student government; Student newspaper; Symphony orchestra; Yearbook 86 registered organizations, 25 honor societies, 5 religious organizations. **Athletics (Intercollegiate):** *Men:* baseball, basketball, crew/rowing, cross-country, golf, soccer, tennis, track/field (outdoor), water polo. *Women:* basketball, crew/rowing, cross-country, golf, soccer, softball, tennis, track/field (outdoor), volleyball, water polo. **On-Campus Highlights:** Historic Mission Church; Mission Gardens, Pat Malley Fitness Center, Harrington Learning Commons and Library, Benson Memorial Student Center, Patricia A. and Stephen C. Schott Admission & Enrollment Services Building

ADMISSIONS

Freshman Academic Profile: Average high school GPA 3.7. 57% in top 10% of high school class, 87% in top 25% of high school class, 99% in top 50% of high school class. 46% from public high schools. **Test Scores:** SAT Math middle 50% range 640-730. SAT EBRW middle 50% range 630-710. ACT middle 50% range 28-32. Minimum internet-based TOEFL 90. Minimum paper TOEFL 575. **Basis for Candidate Selection:** *Very important factors considered include:* rigor of secondary school record, academic GPA, application essay. *Important factors considered include:* class rank, standardized test scores, recommendation(s), extracurricular activities, talent/ability, character/personal qualities, first generation, alumni/ae relation, racial/ethnic status, volunteer work. *Other factors considered include:* geographical residence, state residency, religious affiliation/commitment, work experience, level of applicant's interest. **Freshman Admission Requirements:** High school diploma is required and GED is accepted *Academic units required:* 4 English, 3 math, 2 science, 2 science labs, 2 foreign language, 3 social studies, 1 academic elective, 1 visual/performing arts, *Academic units recommended:* 4 English, 4 math, 3 science, 3 science labs, 3 foreign language, 3 social studies, 2 academic electives, 2 visual/performing arts. **Freshman Admission Statistics:** 15,061 applied, 53.6% admitted, 17% enrolled. **Transfer Admission Requirements:** college transcript(s), essay or personal statement, Lowest grade transferable C. **General Admission Information:** Application fee $60. Regular application deadline 1/7. Nonfall registration accepted. Admission may be deferred for a maximum of One year, unless serving required military service or mission work.

COSTS AND FINANCIAL AID

Required Forms and Deadlines: CSS/Financial Aid PROFILE; FAFSA. **Notification of Awards:** Applicants will be notified of awards on or about 4/1. **Types of Aid:** *Need-based scholarships/grants:* College/university scholarship or grant aid from institutional funds; Federal Pell; Private scholarships; SEOG; State scholarships/grants. *Loans:* Direct PLUS loans; Direct Subsidized Stafford Loans; Direct Unsubsidized Stafford Loans. *Student Employment:* Federal Work-Study Program available. Institutional employment available. **Financial Aid Statistics:** 80% needy freshmen, 71% needy undergrads receive need-based scholarship or grant aid. 53% freshmen, 41% undergrads receive non-need-based scholarship or grant aid. 36% freshmen, 50% undergrads receive need-based self-help aid. 5% freshmen, 4% undergrads receive athletic scholarships. 70% freshmen, 77% undergrads receive any aid. 44% undergrads borrow to pay for school. Average cumulative indebtedness $27,385. **Criteria for awarding aid:** *Need-based:* Academics, Alumni affiliation *Non-need-based:* Academics, Athletics, Music/drama.

SANTA FE UNIVERSITY OF ART AND DESIGN

1600 St. Michaels Drive, Santa Fe, NM 87505-7634
Phone: 505-473-6937 • **Financial Aid Phone:** 505-473-6318
E-mail: admissions@santafeuniversity.edu
Fax: 505-473-6127 • **Website:** www.santafeuniversity.edu

This proprietary school was founded in 1874. It has a 65 acre campus.

RATINGS

Admissions Selectivity Rating: 65   Fire Safety Rating: 98   Green Rating: 65

STUDENTS AND FACULTY

Enrollment: 839. **Student Body:** 52% female, 48% male, 78% out-of-state, 5% international (21 countries represented). Asian 2%, African American 7%,

Caucasian 45%, Hispanic 28%, Native American 3%, Pacific Islander 2%, Two or more races 8%, Race unknown 1%.
Retention and Graduation: 64% freshmen return for sophomore year.
Faculty: Student/faculty ratio 15:1.

ACADEMICS

Degrees: Bachelor's; Certificate; **Master's Classes:** Most classes have 10-19 students. Most lab/discussion sessions have 10-19 students. **Most popular majors:** Graphic Design; Drama And Dramatics/Theatre Arts, General; Film/Cinema/Video Studies. **Special Study Options:** Distance learning; Double major; Dual enrollment; Exchange student program (domestic); Honors program; Independent study; Internships; Student-designed major; Study abroad. **Disability Services offered to physically disabled students:** Note-taking services; Reader services; Tape recorders; Tutors. **Career services:** Alumni services; Career assessment; Internships

FACILITIES

Housing: Apartments for single students; Coed dorms; Men's dorms; Special housing for disabled student; Women's dorms **Special Academic Facilities/Equipment:** Thaw Art History Library, Marion Center Photographic Library, Garson Studios, Visual Art Center, Greer Garson Theatre Centre **Computers:** Administrative functions (other than registration) can be performed online.

CAMPUS LIFE

Environment: Town **Activities:** Campus Ministries; Choral groups; Dance; Drama/theater; Jazz band; Literary magazine; Music ensembles; Musical theater; Student government; Student newspaper; Student-run film society 14 registered organizations, 1 honor societies. **Athletics (Intercollegiate):** *Men:* tennis. *Women:* tennis. **On-Campus Highlights:** Visual Arts Center, Garson Studios, Driscoll Fitness Center, Greer Garson Theatre Center, Fogelson Library

ADMISSIONS

Test Scores: Minimum internet-based TOEFL 79. Minimum paper TOEFL 550. **Basis for Candidate Selection:** *Very important factors considered include:* academic GPA, talent/ability. *Other factors considered include:* application essay, recommendation(s). **Freshman Admission Requirements:** High school diploma is required and GED is accepted *Academic units required:* 4 English, 2 math, 2 science, 2 science labs, 2 social studies, *Academic units recommended:* 4 English, 2 math, 2 science, 2 science labs, 2 foreign language, 2 social studies, 4 academic electives. **Freshman Admission Statistics:** 608 applied, 100.0% admitted, 41% enrolled. **Transfer Admission Requirements:** High school transcript, college transcript(s), essay or personal statement, Lowest grade transferable C-. **General Admission Information:** Application fee $50. Nonfall registration accepted. Admission may be deferred for a maximum of 1 year.

COSTS AND FINANCIAL AID

Annual tuition $28,836. Room and board $8,984. Required fees $1,300. Average book expense $1,400. **Required Forms and Deadlines:** FAFSA. **Notification of Awards:** Applicants will be notified of awards on a rolling basis beginning 3/1. **Types of Aid:** *Need-based scholarships/grants:* College/university scholarship or grant aid from institutional funds; Federal Pell; Private scholarships; SEOG. *Loans:* Direct PLUS loans; Direct Subsidized Stafford Loans; Direct Unsubsidized Stafford Loans. *Student Employment:* Federal Work-Study Program available. **Financial Aid Statistics:** 100% needy freshmen, 100% needy undergrads receive need-based scholarship or grant aid. 4% freshmen, 4% undergrads receive non-need-based scholarship or grant aid. 94% freshmen, 91% undergrads receive need-based self-help aid. 0% freshmen, 0% undergrads receive athletic scholarships. 99% freshmen receive any aid. **Criteria for awarding aid:** *Non-need-based:* Academics, Art, Music/drama.

SARAH LAWRENCE COLLEGE

Best Colleges

1 Mead Way, Bronxville, NY 10708-5999
Phone: 914-395-2510 • **Financial Aid Phone:** (914) 395 2570
E-mail: slcadmit@sarahlawrence.edu • **CEEB Code:** 2810
Fax: 914-395-2515 • **Website:** www.sarahlawrence.edu • **ACT Code:** 2904

This private school was founded in 1926. It has a 44 acre campus.

RATINGS

Admissions Selectivity Rating: 89   **Fire Safety Rating:** 96   **Green Rating:** 75

STUDENTS AND FACULTY

Enrollment: 1,355. **Student Body:** 72% female, 28% male, 78% out-of-state, 13% international (42 countries represented). Asian 5%, African American 4%, Caucasian 56%, Hispanic 9%, Native American <1%, Pacific Islander 0%, Two or more races 7%, Race unknown 6%.
Retention and Graduation: 82% freshmen return for sophomore year. 73% freshmen graduate within 4 years. 79% freshmen graduate within 6 years.
Faculty: Student/faculty ratio 9:1. 119 full-time faculty, 85% hold PhDs, 16% are members of minority groups, 48% are women. 0% of classes are taught by teaching assistants.

ACADEMICS

Degrees: Bachelor's; **Master's Classes:** Most classes have 20-29 students. Most lab/discussion sessions have 20-29 students. **Most popular majors:** Liberal Arts And Sciences/Liberal Studies. **Special Study Options:** Double major; Independent study; Internships; Student-designed major; Study abroad; Teacher certification program. Combined degree programs: BA/MA. **Disability Services offered to physically disabled students:** Note-taking services; Reader services; Tape recorders; Tutors. **Career services:** Alumni network; Alumni services; Career assessment; Career/job search classes; Internships

FACILITIES

Housing: Coed dorms; Men's dorms; Special housing for disabled student; Theme housing; Wellness housing; Women's dorms 60% of campus accessible to physically diasbled. **Special Academic Facilities/Equipment:** Performing arts center including a concert hall, dance studios,and theatres; visual arts center including studios, gallery, film theatre, sound stage, visual resources library; music building including music library; science center, early childhood center **Computers:** 100% of classrooms, 30% of dorms, 100% of libraries, 100% of dining areas, 100% of common outdoor areas have wireless network access. Administrative functions (other than registration) can be performed online.

CAMPUS LIFE

Environment: Metropolis **Activities:** Campus Ministries; Choral groups; Dance; Drama/theater; International Student Organization; Jazz band; Literary magazine; Model UN; Music ensembles; Musical theater; Radio station; Student government; Student newspaper; Student-run film society; Symphony orchestra; Yearbook 30 registered organizations, 3 religious organizations. **Athletics (Intercollegiate):** *Men:* basketball, crew/rowing, cross-country, equestrian sports, soccer, tennis. *Women:* crew/rowing, cross-country, equestrian sports, softball, swimming, tennis, volleyball. **On-Campus Highlights:** Campbell Sports Center, Tea Haus, The Pub at the Siegel Center, Library, Heimbold Visual Arts Center **Environmental Initiatives:** A sustainable living residence and a green roof on another dorm.

ADMISSIONS

Freshman Academic Profile: Average high school GPA 3.7. 25% in top 10% of high school class, 67% in top 25% of high school class, 89% in top 50% of high school class. 51% from public high schools. **Test Scores;** SAT Math middle 50% range 590-680. SAT EBRW middle 50% range 650-730. ACT middle 50% range 27-31. Minimum internet-based TOEFL 100. Minimum paper TOEFL 600. **Basis for Candidate Selection:** *Very important factors considered include:* rigor of secondary school record, application essay, recommendation(s). *Important factors considered include:* academic GPA, extracurricular activities, talent/ability, character/personal qualities. *Other factors considered include:* class rank, standardized test scores, interview, first generation, alumni/ae relation, geographical residence, racial/ethnic status, volunteer work, work experience, level of applicant's interest. **Freshman Admission Requirements:** High school diploma is required and GED is accepted *Academic units required:* 4 English, 2 math, 2 science, 2 foreign language, 2 history, *Academic units recommended:* 4 math, 4 science, 4 foreign language, 4 social studies, 4 history. **Freshman Admission Statistics:** 3,463 applied, 53.2% admitted, 21% enrolled. **Transfer Admission Requirements:** High school transcript, college transcript(s), essay or personal statement, statement of good standing from prior institution(s). Lowest grade transferable C. **General Admission Information:** Application fee $60. Regular application deadline 1/15. Nonfall registration accepted. Admission may be deferred for a maximum of 1 year.

COSTS AND FINANCIAL AID

Required Forms and Deadlines: CSS/Financial Aid PROFILE; FAFSA; Noncustodial PROFILE; State aid form. **Notification of Awards:** Applicants will be notified of awards on or about 4/1. **Types of Aid:** *Need-based scholarships/grants:* College/university scholarship or grant aid from institutional funds; Federal Pell; Private scholarships; SEOG; State scholarships/grants. *Loans:* Direct PLUS loans; Direct Subsidized Stafford Loans; Direct Unsubsidized Stafford Loans. *Student Employment:* Federal Work-Study Program available. Institutional employment available. **Financial Aid Statistics:** 98% needy freshmen, 97% needy undergrads receive need-based scholarship or grant aid. 16% freshmen, 14% undergrads receive non-need-based scholarship or grant aid. 80% freshmen, 75% undergrads receive need-based self-help aid. 0% freshmen, 0% undergrads receive athletic scholarships. 79% freshmen, 76% undergrads receive any aid. 35% undergrads borrow to pay for school. Average cumulative indebtedness $19,772. **Criteria for awarding aid:** *Need-based:* Academics, Leadership *Non-need-based:* Academics, Leadership.

SAVANNAH COLLEGE OF ART AND DESIGN

P.O. Box 3146, Savannah, GA 31402-3146
Phone: 912-525-5100 • **Financial Aid Phone:** 800-869-7223
E-mail: admission@scad.edu • **CEEB Code:** 5631
Fax: 912-525-5986 • **Website:** www.scad.edu • **ACT Code:** 855

This private school was founded in 1978.

RATINGS
Admissions Selectivity Rating: 80   **Fire Safety Rating:** 85   **Green Rating:** 61

STUDENTS AND FACULTY
Enrollment: 10,483. **Student Body:** 67% female, 33% male, 79% out-of-state, 21% international (115 countries represented). Asian 5%, African American 10%, Caucasian 52%, Hispanic 8%, Native American 1%, Pacific Islander <1%, Two or more races <1%, Race unknown 3%.
Retention and Graduation: 85% freshmen return for sophomore year. **Faculty:** Student/faculty ratio 19:1. 532 full-time faculty, 80% hold PhDs, 18% are members of minority groups, 40% are women. 0% of classes are taught by teaching assistants.

ACADEMICS
Degrees: Bachelor's; Certificate; Master's; Post-Master's certificate **Classes:** Most classes have 10-19 students. **Most popular majors:** Animation, Interactive Technology, Video Graphics And Special Effects; Fashion/Apparel Design; Graphic Design. **Special Study Options:** Accelerated program; Cooperative education program; Cross-registration; Distance learning; Double major; Dual enrollment; English as a Second Language (ESL); Independent study; Internships; Study abroad. **Disability Services offered to physically disabled students:** Note-taking services; Tape recorders; Tutors. **Career services:** Alumni network; Alumni services; Career assessment; Career/job search classes; Internships; Regional alumni

FACILITIES
Housing: Coed dorms; Special housing for disabled student; Women's dorms 82% of campus accessible to physically diasbled. **Special Academic Facilities/Equipment:** Art galleries; computer, video, photography, and design labs; SCAD Museum of Art **Computers:** 80% of classrooms, 100% of dorms, 100% of libraries, 100% of dining areas, 100% of student union, 50% of common outdoor areas have wireless network access. Students can register for classes online. Administrative functions (other than registration) can be performed online.

CAMPUS LIFE
Environment: City **Activities:** Campus Ministries; Choral groups; Dance; Drama/theater; International Student Organization; Literary magazine; Music ensembles; Musical theater; Radio station; Student newspaper; Television station 68 registered organizations, 2 honor societies, 3 religious organizations. **Athletics (Intercollegiate):** *Men:* baseball, basketball, cross-country, equestrian sports, golf, lacrosse, soccer, swimming, tennis. *Women:* basketball, cross-country, equestrian sports, golf, lacrosse, soccer, softball, swimming, tennis, volleyball. **On-Campus Highlights:** SCAD Museum of Art, Club SCAD, Jen Library, Cafe SCAD, Trustees Theatre

ADMISSIONS
Freshman Academic Profile: Average high school GPA 3.5. **Test Scores:** SAT Math middle 50% range 460-580. SAT EBRW middle 50% range 490-610. ACT middle 50% range 21-27. Minimum internet-based TOEFL 85. Minimum paper TOEFL 550. **Basis for Candidate Selection:** *Very important factors considered include:* academic GPA. *Important factors considered include:* rigor of secondary school record, standardized test scores, level of applicant's interest. *Other factors considered include:* class rank, application essay, recommendation(s), interview, extracurricular activities, talent/ability, character/personal qualities. **Freshman Admission Requirements:** High school diploma is required and GED is accepted **Freshman Admission Statistics:** 11,723 applied, 71.0% admitted, 28% enrolled. **Transfer Admission Requirements:** college transcript(s), Minimum college GPA of 2.0 required. Lowest grade transferable C. **General Admission Information:** Application fee $40. Nonfall registration accepted. Admission may be deferred for a maximum of 2 consec qtr.

COSTS AND FINANCIAL AID
Annual tuition $35,190. Room and board $13,905. Average book expense $2,025. **Required Forms and Deadlines:** FAFSA; State aid form. **Notification of Awards:** Applicants will be notified of awards on a rolling basis beginning 3/1. **Types of Aid:** *Need-based scholarships/grants:* College/university scholarship or grant aid from institutional funds; Federal Pell; Private scholarships; SEOG; State scholarships/grants; United Negro College Fund. *Loans:* Direct PLUS loans; Direct Subsidized Stafford Loans; Direct Unsubsidized Stafford Loans. *Student Employment:* Federal Work-Study Program available. Institutional employment available. **Financial Aid Statistics:** 61% needy freshmen, 63% needy undergrads receive need-based scholarship or grant aid. 98% freshmen, 91% undergrads receive non-need-based scholarship or grant aid. 88% freshmen, 92% undergrads receive need-based self-help aid. 1% freshmen, 1% undergrads receive athletic scholarships. 58% undergrads borrow to pay for school. Average cumulative indebtedness $40,718. **Criteria for awarding aid:** *Need-based:* Academics, Art, Music/drama *Non-need-based:* Academics, Alumni affiliation, Art, Athletics, Job skills, Leadership, Minority status, Music/drama.

SCHOOL OF THE ART INSTITUTE OF CHICAGO

36 South Wabash Avenue, Chicago, IL 60603
Phone: 312-629-6100 • **Financial Aid Phone:** 312-629-6600
E-mail: admiss@saic.edu • **CEEB Code:** 1713
Fax: 312-629-6101 • **Website:** www.saic.edu • **ACT Code:** 1136

This private school was founded in 1866.

RATINGS
Admissions Selectivity Rating: 82   **Fire Safety Rating:** 83   **Green Rating:** 61

STUDENTS AND FACULTY
Enrollment: 2,888. **Student Body:** 75% female, 25% male, 70% out-of-state, 25% international (68 countries represented). Asian 8%, African American 1%, Caucasian 42%, Hispanic 13%, Native American 0%, Pacific Islander 0%, Two or more races 4%, Race unknown 6%.
Retention and Graduation: 81% freshmen return for sophomore year. 0% grads pursue law degrees. 0% grads pursue business degrees. 0% grads pursue medical degrees. **Faculty:** 172 full-time faculty, 63% hold PhDs, 22% are members of minority groups, 46% are women.

ACADEMICS
Degrees: Bachelor's; Master's; Post-Bachelor's certificate **Special Study Options:** Cooperative education program; Cross-registration; Double major; English as a Second Language (ESL); Exchange student program (domestic); Independent study; Internships; Student-designed major; Study abroad; Teacher certification program. **Disability Services offered to physically disabled students:** Note-taking services; Reader services; Tape recorders; Tutors. **Career services:** Alumni network; Alumni services; Career assessment; Career/job search classes; Internships

FACILITIES
Housing: Coed dorms; Special housing for disabled students 99% of campus accessible to physically diasbled. **Special Academic Facilities/Equipment:** SAIC is directly affiliated with the Art Institute of Chicago. Other resources include: The Gene Siskel Film Center; Fashion Resource Center, John M. Flaxman Library and Screening Room Galleries (Betty Rymer, Sullivan Galleries, Student Union Galleries, project space and Gallery X), Joan Flasch Artists' Book Collection,Poetry Center, Roger Brown Resources, Video Data Bank, The Poetry Center, Visiting Artists' Program, Media Center **Computers:** Students can register for classes online. Administrative functions (other than registration) can be performed online. Undergraduates are required to own a computer.

CAMPUS LIFE
Environment: Metropolis **Activities:** Campus Ministries; Dance; Drama/theater; International Student Organization; Literary magazine; Radio station; Student government; Student newspaper; Student-run film society; Television station 43 registered organizations, 2 religious organizations. **On-Campus Highlights:** Leroy Neiman Student Center, Residence Halls, The Art Institute of Chicago, Gene Siskel Film Center, Studio Classrooms **Environmental Initiatives:** Incandescent light bulbs in dorm rooms have been replaced with CFLs and new low-flow restrictions have been installed in all dorm room showers and sinks. • Expected results are 206 Metric Tons of CO_2 not being release into the atmosphere and 1.7 Million Gallons of Water Saved annually

ADMISSIONS

Freshman Academic Profile: Average high school GPA 3.5. **Test Scores:** SAT Math middle 50% range 530-670. SAT EBRW middle 50% range 580-670. ACT middle 50% range 22-30. Minimum internet-based TOEFL 79. Minimum paper TOEFL 550. **Basis for Candidate Selection:** *Very important factors considered include:* rigor of secondary school record, application essay, standardized test scores, recommendation(s), talent/ability, character/personal qualities, level of applicant's interest. *Important factors considered include:* class rank, academic GPA, extracurricular activities, first generation, racial/ethnic status, volunteer work. *Other factors considered include:* interview, alumni/ae relation, geographical residence, state residency, work experience. **Freshman Admission Requirements:** High school diploma is required and GED is accepted **Freshman Admission Statistics:** 5,686 applied, 69.8% admitted, 16% enrolled. **Transfer Admission Requirements:** High school transcript, college transcript(s), essay or personal statement, Lowest grade transferable C. **General Admission Information:** Application fee $65. Priority deadline 11/15. Regular application deadline 6/1. Nonfall registration accepted. Admission may be deferred for a maximum of 1 year.

COSTS AND FINANCIAL AID

Annual tuition $44,910. Room and board $13,890. Required fees $860. Average book expense $1,770. **Required Forms and Deadlines:** FAFSA. **Notification of Awards:** Applicants will be notified of awards on a rolling basis beginning 3/1. **Types of Aid:** *Need-based scholarships/grants:* College/university scholarship or grant aid from institutional funds; Federal Pell; Private scholarships; SEOG; State scholarships/grants. *Loans: Student Employment:* Federal Work-Study Program available. Institutional employment available. **Financial Aid Statistics:** 99% needy freshmen receive need-based scholarship or grant aid. 98% freshmen, 99% undergrads receive any aid. **Criteria for awarding aid:** *Need-based:* Academics, Art *Non-need-based:* Academics, Art.

SCHOOL OF THE MUSEUM OF FINE ARTS

230 The Fenway, Boston, MA 02115
Phone: 617-369-3626 • **Financial Aid Phone:** 617-369-3684
E-mail: admissions@smfa.edu • **CEEB Code:** 3794
Fax: 617-369-4264 • **ACT Code:** 1895

This private school was founded in 1876. It has a 14 acre campus.

RATINGS

Admissions Selectivity Rating: 66   **Fire Safety Rating:** 90   **Green Rating:** 61

STUDENTS AND FACULTY

Enrollment: 278. **Student Body:** 73% female, 27% male, 53% out-of-state, 12% international (19 countries represented). Asian 3%, African American 2%, Caucasian 48%, Hispanic 12%, Native American 0%, Pacific Islander 0%, Two or more races 4%, Race unknown 18%.
Retention and Graduation: 78% freshmen return for sophomore year.
Faculty: Student/faculty ratio 8:1. 40 full-time faculty, 85% hold PhDs, 13% are members of minority groups, 68% are women. 5% of classes are taught by teaching assistants.

ACADEMICS

Degrees: Bachelor's; Certificate; Diploma; Master's; Post-Bachelor's certificate **Classes:** Most classes have fewer than 10 students. Most lab/discussion sessions have 10-19 students. **Most popular majors:** Fine/Studio Arts, General; Fine Arts And Art Studies, Other. **Special Study Options:** Cross-registration; Double major; Dual enrollment; Exchange student program (domestic); Independent study; Internships; Liberal arts/career combination; Student-designed major; Study abroad; Teacher certification program. **Career services:** Alumni network; Alumni services; Career/job search classes; Internships

FACILITIES

Housing: Coed dorms; Other (please specify) 100% of campus accessible to physically diasbled. **Special Academic Facilities/Equipment:** Museum of Fine Arts, Boston; Art galleries; welding equipment; darkrooms; digital equipment; kilns; and more! **Computers:** 100% of classrooms, 100% of dorms, 100% of libraries, 100% of dining areas, 100% of student union, have wireless network access. Students can register for classes online. Administrative functions (other than registration) can be performed online.

CAMPUS LIFE

Environment: Metropolis **Activities:** International Student Organization; Student government; Student-run film society 10 registered organizations. **On-Campus Highlights:** Classrooms and Studios, Museum of Fine Arts, Boston, Galleries and Exhibition Spaces, Museum and School Libraries, Art in

progress—everywhere you look **Environmental Initiatives:** Installed a new state of the art HVAC ventilation system, which includes interior vents and hoods customized for specific art making practices.

ADMISSIONS

Freshman Academic Profile: Average high school GPA 3.5. **Test Scores:** Minimum internet-based TOEFL 79. Minimum paper TOEFL 550. **Basis for Candidate Selection:** *Important factors considered include:* academic GPA, application essay, talent/ability, level of applicant's interest. *Other factors considered include:* rigor of secondary school record, class rank, recommendation(s), interview, extracurricular activities, character/personal qualities, volunteer work, work experience. **Freshman Admission Requirements:** High school diploma is required and GED is accepted *Academic units recommended:* 4 English, 3 math, 3 science, 2 science labs, 2 foreign language, 2 social studies, 2 history, 2 academic electives, 1 computer science, 2 visual/performing arts. **Freshman Admission Statistics:** 371 applied, 82.7% admitted, 12% enrolled. **Transfer Admission Requirements:** college transcript(s), essay or personal statement, Minimum college GPA of 1.75 required. Lowest grade transferable C-. **General Admission Information:** Application fee $65. Priority deadline 2/17. Nonfall registration accepted. Admission may be deferred for a maximum of 1 year.

COSTS AND FINANCIAL AID

Annual tuition $39,928. Required fees $1,300. Average book expense $1,600. **Required Forms and Deadlines:** FAFSA. **Notification of Awards:** Applicants will be notified of awards on a rolling basis beginning 4/1. **Types of Aid:** *Need-based scholarships/grants:* College/university scholarship or grant aid from institutional funds; Federal Pell; Private scholarships; SEOG; State scholarships/grants. *Loans:* Direct PLUS loans; Direct Subsidized Stafford Loans; Direct Unsubsidized Stafford Loans. *Student Employment:* Federal Work-Study Program available. Institutional employment available. **Financial Aid Statistics:** 95% needy freshmen, 94% needy undergrads receive need-based scholarship or grant aid. 100% freshmen, 99% undergrads receive non-need-based scholarship or grant aid. 95% freshmen, 89% undergrads receive need-based self-help aid. 0% freshmen, 0% undergrads receive athletic scholarships. 94% freshmen, 97% undergrads receive any aid. 69% undergrads borrow to pay for school. Average cumulative indebtedness $33,176. **Criteria for awarding aid:** *Non-need-based:* Art.

SCHOOL OF VISUAL ARTS

209 East 23rd Street, New York, NY 10010
Phone: 212-592-2100 • **Financial Aid Phone:** 212-592-2030
E-mail: admissions@sva.edu • **CEEB Code:** 2835
Fax: 212-592-2116 • **Website:** www.sva.edu • **ACT Code:** 2895

This proprietary school was founded in 1947.

RATINGS

Admissions Selectivity Rating: 81   **Fire Safety Rating:** 99   **Green Rating:** 60*

STUDENTS AND FACULTY

Enrollment: 3,332. **Student Body:** 55% female, 45% male, 57% out-of-state, 15% international (55 countries represented). Asian 13%, African American 3%, Caucasian 49%, Hispanic 10%, Native American 1%, Race unknown 9%.
Retention and Graduation: 86% freshmen return for sophomore year.
Faculty: Student/faculty ratio 9:1. 163 full-time faculty, 24% hold PhDs, 4% are members of minority groups, 31% are women.

ACADEMICS

Degrees: Bachelor's; **Master's Classes:** Most classes have 20-29 students. Most lab/discussion sessions have 10-19 students. **Most popular majors:** Graphic Design; Photography; Film/Video And Photographic Arts, Other. **Special Study Options:** English as a Second Language (ESL); Exchange student program (domestic); Honors program; Internships; Liberal arts/career combination; Study abroad; Teacher certification program. Honors programs: SVA offers an honors program for incoming freshmen; program involves a two year commitment, with an optional third year. **Disability Services offered to physically disabled students:** Note-taking services; Reader services; Tape recorders; Tutors. **Career services:** Alumni network; Alumni services; Internships

FACILITIES

Housing: Coed dorms; Women's dorms 100% of campus accessible to physically diasbled. **Special Academic Facilities/Equipment:** Visual Art Museum, Milton Glaser Design Study Center and Archives, 8 student galleries **Computers:** 100% of classrooms, 100% of libraries, 100% of student union, have wireless network access. Students can register for classes online. Administrative functions (other than registration) can be performed online.

CAMPUS LIFE

Environment: Metropolis **Activities:** Literary magazine; Radio station; Student government; Student-run film society; Yearbook 23 registered organizations, 3 religious organizations. **On-Campus Highlights:** Visual Arts Gallery, Westside Gallery, Visual Arts Museum, Visual Arts Student Association, Student Lounge **Environmental Initiatives:** Yes, we do recycle our trash, but we do it off site. Due to space limitations we don't have an area to collect and sort out recyclables from our trash, nor do we have the space to store the recyclables prior to shipment to an appropriate recycler. To accomplish this we rely on an outside contractor to collect our trash and sort it at their facilities. They ensure that anything that can be recycled from our trash finds its way to the recyclers.

ADMISSIONS

Freshman Academic Profile: Average high school GPA 3.1. 60% from public high schools. **Test Scores:** SAT Math middle 50% range 460-590. SAT EBRW middle 50% range 450-580. ACT middle 50% range 20-25. Minimum paper TOEFL 550. **Basis for Candidate Selection:** *Very important factors considered include:* rigor of secondary school record, academic GPA, application essay, interview, talent/ability, level of applicant's interest. *Other factors considered include:* standardized test scores, recommendation(s), extracurricular activities, alumni/ae relation, volunteer work, work experience. **Freshman Admission Requirements:** High school diploma is required and GED is accepted *Academic units recommended:* 4 English, 4 social studies, 4 history, 2 visual/performing arts. **Freshman Admission Statistics:** 2,530 applied, 69.0% admitted, 38% enrolled. **Transfer Admission Requirements:** college transcript(s), essay or personal statement, statement of good standing from prior institution(s). Minimum college GPA of 2.0 required. Lowest grade transferable C. **General Admission Information:** Application fee $50. Priority deadline 2/1. Nonfall registration accepted. Admission may be deferred for a maximum of 1 year.

COSTS AND FINANCIAL AID

Annual tuition $26,800. Average book expense $3,150. **Required Forms and Deadlines:** FAFSA; State aid form. **Notification of Awards:** Applicants will be notified of awards on a rolling basis beginning 2/15. **Types of Aid:** *Need-based scholarships/grants:* College/university scholarship or grant aid from institutional funds; Federal Pell; Private scholarships; SEOG; State scholarships/grants. *Loans: Student Employment:* Federal Work-Study Program available. **Financial Aid Statistics:** 68% needy freshmen, 68% needy undergrads receive need-based scholarship or grant aid. 19% freshmen, 19% undergrads receive non-need-based scholarship or grant aid. 96% freshmen, 97% undergrads receive need-based self-help aid. 0% freshmen, 0% undergrads receive athletic scholarships. 60% freshmen, 55% undergrads receive any aid. **Criteria for awarding aid:** *Non-need-based:* Art.

See page 1026.

SCHREINER UNIVERSITY

2100 Memorial Boulevard, Kerrville, TX 78028-5697
Phone: 830-792-7217 • **Financial Aid Phone:** 830-792-7217
E-mail: http://www.schreiner.edu/admission/index • **CEEB Code:** 6647
Fax: (830) 792-7226 • **Website:** www.schreiner.edu • **ACT Code:** 4168

This private school, affiliated with the Presbyterian Church, was founded in 1923. It has a 205 acre campus.

RATINGS

Admissions Selectivity Rating: 73   **Fire Safety Rating:** 62   **Green Rating:** 60*

STUDENTS AND FACULTY

Enrollment: 1,165. **Student Body:** 58% female, 42% male, 2% out-of-state, 1% international. Asian 1%, African American 4%, Caucasian 53%, Hispanic 40%, Native American <1%, Pacific Islander 0%, Two or more races 2%, Race unknown 0%.
Retention and Graduation: 71% freshmen return for sophomore year. 41% freshmen graduate within 4 years. 21% grads go on to further study within 1 year. **Faculty:** Student/faculty ratio 13:1. 67 full-time faculty, 78% hold PhDs, 13% are members of minority groups, 46% are women. 0% of classes are taught by teaching assistants.

ACADEMICS

Degrees: Associate; Bachelor's; Certificate; **Master's Classes:** Most classes have 10-19 students. Most lab/discussion sessions have 10-19 students. **Most popular majors:** Kinesiology And Exercise Science; Psychology, General; Registered Nursing/Registered Nurse. **Special Study Options:** Accelerated program; Cooperative education program; Distance learning; Double major;

Dual enrollment; Exchange student program (domestic); Honors program; Independent study; Internships; Liberal arts/career combination; Student-designed major; Study abroad; Teacher certification program. **Disability Services offered to physically disabled students:** Note-taking services; Reader services; Tape recorders; Tutors. **Career services:** Alumni network; Alumni services; Career assessment; Career/job search classes; Internships; Regional alumni

FACILITIES

Housing: Apartments for married students; Apartments for single students; Coed dorms; Special housing for disabled student; Theme housing; Wellness housing 97% of campus accessible to physically disabled. **Computers:** 100% of classrooms, 100% of dorms, 100% of libraries, 100% of dining areas, 100% of student union, 30% of common outdoor areas have wireless network access.

CAMPUS LIFE

Environment: Town **Activities:** Campus Ministries; Choral groups; Dance; Drama/theater; Literary magazine; Music ensembles; Musical theater; Pep band; Student government; Student newspaper; Symphony orchestra 35 registered organizations, 5 honor societies, 7 religious organizations. 2 fraternities, 2 sororities. **Athletics (Intercollegiate):** *Men:* baseball, basketball, golf, soccer, tennis. *Women:* basketball, cheerleading, golf, soccer, softball, tennis, volleyball. **On-Campus Highlights:** Caillioux Campus Activity Center, Logan Library, Griffin Welcome Center, Schriner Event Center, Mountaineer Fitness Center

ADMISSIONS

Freshman Academic Profile: Average high school GPA 3.6. 14% in top 10% of high school class, 37% in top 25% of high school class, 74% in top 50% of high school class. 98% from public high schools. **Test Scores:** SAT Math middle 50% range 480-560. SAT EBRW middle 50% range 480-580. ACT middle 50% range 19-24. Minimum internet-based TOEFL 79. Minimum paper TOEFL 550. **Basis for Candidate Selection:** *Very important factors considered include:* class rank, academic GPA, standardized test scores. *Important factors considered include:* rigor of secondary school record, application essay, character/personal qualities, volunteer work, work experience, level of applicant's interest. *Other factors considered include:* recommendation(s), interview, extracurricular activities, talent/ability. **Freshman Admission Requirements:** High school diploma is required and GED is accepted *Academic units recommended:* 4 English, 3 math, 3 science, 2 science labs, 2 foreign language, 2 social studies, 2 history, 3.5 academic electives, 1 computer science, 1 visual/performing arts, 2.5 units from above areas or other academic areas. **Freshman Admission Statistics:** 1,178 applied, 92.4% admitted, 31% enrolled. **Transfer Admission Requirements:** college transcript(s), Minimum college GPA of 2.0 required. Lowest grade transferable D. **General Admission Information:** Application fee $25. Priority deadline 5/1. Regular application deadline 8/1. Nonfall registration accepted. Admission may be deferred for a maximum of 1 semester.

COSTS AND FINANCIAL AID

Annual tuition $24,990. Room and board $10,152. Required fees $1,910. Average book expense $100. **Required Forms and Deadlines:** FAFSA. **Notification of Awards:** Applicants will be notified of awards on a rolling basis beginning 2/15. **Types of Aid:** *Need-based scholarships/grants:* College/university scholarship or grant aid from institutional funds; Federal Pell; Private scholarships; SEOG; State scholarships/grants. *Loans:* Direct PLUS loans; Direct Subsidized Stafford Loans; Direct Unsubsidized Stafford Loans. *Student Employment:* Federal Work-Study Program available. Institutional employment available. **Financial Aid Statistics:** 100% needy freshmen, 100% needy undergrads receive need-based scholarship or grant aid. 14% freshmen, 12% undergrads receive non-need-based scholarship or grant aid. 84% freshmen, 84% undergrads receive need-based self-help aid. 0% freshmen, 0% undergrads receive athletic scholarships. 99% freshmen, 97% undergrads receive any aid. **Criteria for awarding aid:** *Non-need-based:* Academics, Art, Leadership, Music/drama, Religious affiliation.

SCRIPPS COLLEGE

Best Colleges

1030 Columbia Avenue, Claremont, CA 91711
Phone: 909-621-8149 • **Financial Aid Phone:** 909-621-8275
E-mail: admission@scrippscollege.edu • **CEEB Code:** 4693
Fax: 909-607-7508 • **Website:** www.scrippscollege.edu • **ACT Code:** 426

This private school was founded in 1926. It has a 37 acre campus.

RATINGS

Admissions Selectivity Rating: 96   **Fire Safety Rating:** 79   **Green Rating:** 79

STUDENTS AND FACULTY

Enrollment: 1,059. **Student Body:** 100% female, 0% male, 50% out-of-state, 5% international. Asian 16%, African American 4%, Caucasian 53%, Hispanic 13%, Native American 0%, Pacific Islander <1%, Two or more races 4%, Race unknown 4%.
Retention and Graduation: 92% freshmen return for sophomore year. 83% freshmen graduate within 4 years. 88% freshmen graduate within 6 years. 19% grads go on to further study within 1 year. 8% grads pursue arts and sciences degrees. 1.3% grads pursue law degrees. 0% grads pursue business degrees. 1.3% grads pursue medical degrees. **Faculty:** Student/faculty ratio 10:1. 94 full-time faculty, 99% hold PhDs, 34% are members of minority groups, 57% are women. 0% of classes are taught by teaching assistants.

ACADEMICS

Degrees: Bachelor's; Post-Bachelor's certificate **Classes:** Most classes have 10-19 students. Most lab/discussion sessions have fewer than 10 students. **Most popular majors:** Biology/Biological Sciences, General; Psychology, General; Economics, General. **Special Study Options:** Accelerated program; Cross-registration; Double major; Independent study; Internships; Student-designed major; Study abroad. Combined degree programs: BA/MA; BA/MEng. **Disability Services offered to physically disabled students:** Note-taking services; Reader services; Tape recorders; Tutors. **Career services:** Alumni network; Alumni services; Career assessment; Career/job search classes; Internships; Regional alumni

FACILITIES

Housing: Apartments for single students; Special housing for disabled student; Women's dorms **Special Academic Facilities/Equipment:** Art center, music complex, dance studio, humanities museum and institute, science center, biological field station, and Tiernan Field House. The Tiernan Field House is a state-of-the art 24,000 square feet facility with an aerobics studio, cardio machine room, weight room, and other spaces for fitness and health education. **Computers:** 100% of classrooms, 100% of dorms, 100% of libraries, 100% of dining areas, 100% of common outdoor areas have wireless network access. Administrative functions (other than registration) can be performed online.

CAMPUS LIFE

Environment: Town **Activities:** Campus Ministries; Choral groups; Dance; Drama/theater; International Student Organization; Literary magazine; Model UN; Music ensembles; Radio station; Student government; Student newspaper; Symphony orchestra; Yearbook 200 registered organizations, 5 honor societies, 7 religious organizations. **Athletics (Intercollegiate):** *Women:* basketball, cross-country, diving, golf, lacrosse, soccer, softball, swimming, tennis, track/field (outdoor), volleyball, water polo. **On-Campus Highlights:** Williamson Gallery, Sallie Tiernan Field House, The Motley Coffeehouse, Malott Commons, Margaret Fowler Garden **Environmental Initiatives:** Establishment of a sustainability committee to serve as an advisory counsel to president regarding campus operations.

ADMISSIONS

Freshman Academic Profile: Average high school GPA 4.1. 73% in top 10% of high school class, 94% in top 25% of high school class, 98% in top 50% of high school class. **Test Scores:** SAT Math middle 50% range 630-730. SAT EBRW middle 50% range 660-730. ACT middle 50% range 29-33. Minimum internet-based TOEFL 100. Minimum paper TOEFL 600. **Basis for Candidate Selection:** *Very important factors considered include:* rigor of secondary school record, class rank, academic GPA, application essay, standardized test scores, recommendation(s), extracurricular activities, talent/ability, character/personal qualities. *Other factors considered include:* interview, first generation, alumni/ae relation, geographical residence, racial/ethnic status, volunteer work, work experience. **Freshman Admission Requirements:** High school diploma is required and GED is accepted *Academic units required:* 4 English, 3 math, 3 science, 3 foreign language, 3 social studies. **Freshman Admission Statistics:** 2,841 applied, 33.4% admitted, 34% enrolled. **Transfer**

Admission Requirements: High school transcript, college transcript(s), essay or personal statement, standardized test scores, statement of good standing from prior institution(s). Minimum college GPA of 3.0 required. Lowest grade transferable C. **General Admission Information:** Application fee $60. Regular application deadline 1/1. Nonfall registration accepted.

COSTS AND FINANCIAL AID

Annual tuition $52,748. Room and board $16,294. Required fees $218. Average book expense $800. **Required Forms and Deadlines:** Business/Farm Supplement; CSS/Financial Aid PROFILE; FAFSA; Noncustodial PROFILE; State aid form. **Notification of Awards:** Applicants will be notified of awards on or about 4/1. **Types of Aid:** *Need-based scholarships/grants:* College/university scholarship or grant aid from institutional funds; Federal Pell; Private scholarships; SEOG; State scholarships/grants. *Loans:* Direct PLUS loans; Direct Subsidized Stafford Loans; Direct Unsubsidized Stafford Loans. *Student Employment:* Federal Work-Study Program available. Institutional employment available. **Financial Aid Statistics:** 100% needy freshmen, 100% needy undergrads receive need-based scholarship or grant aid. 0% undergrads receive non-need-based scholarship or grant aid. 80% freshmen, 87% undergrads receive need-based self-help aid. 0% freshmen, 0% undergrads receive athletic scholarships. 39% undergrads borrow to pay for school. Average cumulative indebtedness $20,205. **Criteria for awarding aid:** *Non-need-based:* Academics, Leadership.

SEATTLE PACIFIC UNIVERSITY

3307 3rd Avenue West, Seattle, WA 98119-1997
Phone: 206-281-2021 • **Financial Aid Phone:** 206-281-2061
E-mail: admissions@spu.edu • **CEEB Code:** 4694
Fax: 206-281-2669 • **Website:** www.spu.edu • **ACT Code:** 4476

This private school, affiliated with the Free Methodist Church, was founded in 1891. It has a 40.77 acre campus.

RATINGS

Admissions Selectivity Rating: 73   **Fire Safety Rating:** 60*   **Green Rating:** 60*

STUDENTS AND FACULTY

Enrollment: 2,900. **Student Body:** 67% female, 33% male, 37% out-of-state, 5% international. Asian 12%, African American 4%, Caucasian 55%, Hispanic 12%, Native American <1%, Pacific Islander 1%, Two or more races 9%, Race unknown 2%.
Retention and Graduation: 79% freshmen return for sophomore year. 54% freshmen graduate within 4 years. 69% freshmen graduate within 6 years. **Faculty:** Student/faculty ratio 13:1. 209 full-time faculty, 80% hold PhDs, 16% are members of minority groups, 50% are women. 0% of classes are taught by teaching assistants.

ACADEMICS

Degrees: Bachelor's; Doctoral; Master's; Post-Master's certificate **Classes:** Most classes have fewer than 10 students. **Most popular majors:** Biology/Biological Sciences, General; Business/Commerce, General. **Special Study Options:** Distance learning; Double major; English as a Second Language (ESL); Exchange student program (domestic); External degree program; Honors program; Independent study; Internships; Liberal arts/career combination; Student-designed major; Study abroad; Teacher certification program. Honors programs: University Scholars. **Disability Services offered to physically disabled students:** Note-taking services; Reader services; Tape recorders. **Career services:** Alumni network; Alumni services; Career assessment; Career/job search classes; Internships

FACILITIES

Housing: Apartments for married students; Apartments for single students; Coed dorms; Special housing for disabled students **Special Academic Facilities/Equipment:** Art gallery, theatre facilities **Computers:** 100% of classrooms, 90% of dorms, 100% of libraries, 100% of dining areas, 100% of student union, 50% of common outdoor areas have wireless network access. Students can register for classes online. Administrative functions (other than registration) can be performed online.

CAMPUS LIFE

Environment: Metropolis **Activities:** Campus Ministries; Choral groups; Concert band; Dance; Drama/theater; International Student Organization; Jazz band; Literary magazine; Music ensembles; Musical theater; Pep band; Radio station; Student government; Student newspaper; Symphony orchestra; Yearbook 63 registered organizations, 1 honor society, 7 religious organizations. **Athletics (Intercollegiate):** *Men:* badminton, basketball, bowling, crew/rowing, cross-country, football, soccer, softball, table tennis, tennis, track/field (outdoor), track/field (indoor), volleyball, weight lifting. *Women:* badminton, basketball, bowling, crew/rowing, cross-country, football, gymnastics, soccer, softball, table tennis, tennis, track/field (outdoor), track/field (indoor), volleyball, weight lifting. **On-Campus Highlights:** Common Grounds, Royal Brougham Pavilion, Weter Lounge, Student Union Building, The Science Building **Environmental Initiatives:** 1. June 2010 completion of a solar photovoltaic installation atop our physics and engineering building. The installation was conceived as part of a senior honors project and returns to the grid the approximate amount of electricity consumed by our electric maintenance vehicles. A visible production meter in the second floor hallway allows students in the recently created Appropriate and Sustainable Engineering major to monitor its production.

ADMISSIONS

Freshman Academic Profile: Average high school GPA 3.5. **Test Scores:** SAT Math middle 50% range 490-610. SAT EBRW middle 50% range 500-620. ACT middle 50% range 21-27. Minimum internet-based TOEFL 79. Minimum paper TOEFL 550. **Basis for Candidate Selection:** *Very important factors considered include:* rigor of secondary school record, academic GPA, application essay, standardized test scores, recommendation(s). *Important factors considered include:* interview, extracurricular activities, talent/ability, character/personal qualities, first generation, state residency, religious affiliation/commitment, racial/ethnic status, volunteer work, work experience. *Other factors considered include:* class rank, alumni/ae relation, geographical residence, level of applicant's interest. **Freshman Admission Requirements:** High school diploma is required and GED is accepted *Academic units recommended:* 4 English, 3 math, 3 science, 3 foreign language, 2 history. **Freshman Admission Statistics:** 3,692 applied, 90.9% admitted, 19% enrolled. **Transfer Admission Requirements:** college transcript(s), essay or personal statement, Minimum college GPA of 2.5 required. Lowest grade transferable C. **General Admission Information:** Application fee $50. Regular application deadline 2/1. Nonfall registration accepted. Admission may be deferred.

COSTS AND FINANCIAL AID

Annual tuition $40,464. Room and board $11,232. Required fees $429. Average book expense $840. **Required Forms and Deadlines:** FAFSA. **Notification of Awards:** Applicants will be notified of awards on a rolling basis beginning 3/15. **Types of Aid:** *Need-based scholarships/grants:* College/university scholarship or grant aid from institutional funds; Federal Pell; Private scholarships; State scholarships/grants. *Loans:* Direct PLUS loans; Direct Subsidized Stafford Loans; Direct Unsubsidized Stafford Loans. *Student Employment:* Federal Work-Study Program available. Institutional employment available. **Financial Aid Statistics:** 100% needy freshmen, 99% needy undergrads receive need-based scholarship or grant aid. 0% undergrads receive non-need-based scholarship or grant aid. 92% freshmen, 93% undergrads receive need-based self-help aid. 1% freshmen, 2% undergrads receive athletic scholarships. 69% undergrads borrow to pay for school. Average cumulative indebtedness $28,880. **Criteria for awarding aid:** *Non-need-based:* Academics, Alumni affiliation, Art, Athletics, Leadership, Minority status, Music/drama, Religious affiliation.

SEATTLE UNIVERSITY

901 12th Ave, Seattle, WA 98122-1090
Phone: 206-296-2000 • **Financial Aid Phone:** 206-296-8020
E-mail: admissions@seattleu.edu • **CEEB Code:** 4695
Fax: 206-296-5656 • **Website:** www.seattleu.edu • **ACT Code:** 4478

This private school, affiliated with the Roman Catholic-Jesuit Church, was founded in 1891. It has a 50 acre campus.

RATINGS

Admissions Selectivity Rating: 85   Fire Safety Rating: 97   Green Rating: 99

STUDENTS AND FACULTY

Enrollment: 4,621. **Student Body:** 62% female, 38% male, 59% out-of-state, 10% international (80 countries represented). Asian 16%, African American 3%, Caucasian 44%, Hispanic 12%, Native American <1%, Pacific Islander 1%, Two or more races 8%, Race unknown 5%.
Retention and Graduation: 84% freshmen return for sophomore year. 64% freshmen graduate within 4 years. 74% freshmen graduate within 6 years. 14% grads go on to further study within 1 year. **Faculty:** Student/faculty ratio 11:1.

520 full-time faculty, 87% hold PhDs, 20% are members of minority groups, 50% are women. 0% of classes are taught by teaching assistants.

ACADEMICS

Degrees: Bachelor's; Doctoral/Professional; Master's; Post-Bachelor's certificate; Post-Master's certificate **Classes:** Most classes have fewer than 10 students. Most lab/discussion sessions have fewer than 10 students. **Most popular majors:** Liberal Arts And Sciences, General Studies And Humanities, Other; Registered Nursing/Registered Nurse; Business/Commerce, General. **Special Study Options:** Cross-registration; Distance learning; Double major; Honors program; Independent study; Internships; Liberal arts/career combination; Student-designed major; Study abroad; Teacher certification program. Honors programs: The university Honors program provides students of high ability and motivation the opportunity to join a small, select, two-year-long learning community. The program is taken in the freshman and sophomore years and fulfills most of the university's Core curriculum requirements. Students admitted to the program also receive a four-year Honors scholarship. Honors programs are also offered within majors such as History and English. The History Department offers a year-long, cohort model Honors program for qualified majors. It has the following distinctive features: • Highly selective • Students and faculty work together for full year • Thematic focus based on faculty expertise that changes annually • Students expected to present work at National History Honor Society's regional conference • Students required to present work to university community • At least three faculty review and approve final theses Students in the History Honors track complete an original research project that often, according to faculty reviews at the regional conference, "represents master's level work." Students' theses have won regional and national undergraduate History awards and several students have gone on to graduate work at well-known research institutions. The English Department's Honors program is a two-quarter opportunity for top seniors in literary studies and creative writing. As they pursue their original research and advanced creative work, qualified students receive one-on-one attention from faculty mentors who guide projects through all stages of development, including their presentation at Seattle University's Undergraduate Research Conference and other regional and national conferences. The curriculum of this program aims to deepen students' understanding of a topic of their choice, either for its own sake or in preparation for graduate school, to help them learn advanced research and composition methods. **Disability Services offered to physically disabled students:** Note-taking services; Reader services; Tape recorders; Tutors. **Career services:** Alumni network; Alumni services; Career assessment; Career/job search classes; Internships; Regional alumni

FACILITIES

Housing: Apartments for single students; Coed dorms; Special housing for disabled student; Theme housing; Wellness housing 95% of campus accessible to physically disabled. **Special Academic Facilities/Equipment:** a) Laser spectroscopy user facility in chemistry and mechanical engineering b) Award-winning Chapel of St. Ignatius, designed by architect Steven Holl; the spiritual center of campus c) SU is a pesticide-free campus, officially a Backyard Wildlife Sanctuary and features a Healing Garden, where plants have current or historical medicinal value, in front of the College of Nursing **Computers:** 100% of classrooms, 20% of dorms, 100% of libraries, 100% of dining areas, 100% of student union, 95% of common outdoor areas have wireless network access. Students can register for classes online. Administrative functions (other than registration) can be performed online.

CAMPUS LIFE

Environment: Metropolis **Activities:** Campus Ministries; Choral groups; Dance; Drama/theater; International Student Organization; Jazz band; Literary magazine; Model UN; Music ensembles; Pep band; Radio station; Student government; Student newspaper 130 registered organizations. **Athletics (Intercollegiate):** *Men:* baseball, basketball, cross-country, golf, soccer, swimming, tennis, track/field (outdoor), track/field (indoor). *Women:* basketball, cross-country, golf, soccer, softball, swimming, tennis, track/field (outdoor), track/field (indoor), volleyball. **On-Campus Highlights:** William F. Eisiminger Fitness Center, a modern fitness/wellness facility, Hawk's Nest Bistro in the Student Center, open late into the night, Lemieux Library and McGoldrick Learning Commons, Public artwork around campus, including a Dale Chihuly glass installation, Championship Field, the 2013 "Field of the Year" by Sports Turf Mngr Assctn **Environmental Initiatives:** Plastic bottled water is not sold anywhere on campus including: the bookstore, vending machines, athletics concession stands, restaurants, and catered events. Free, filtered water and bottle fillers are available at over 30 water fountains throughout campus. The Bookstore is selling a 27 ounce, steel water bottle at a discounted price to make owning a bottle affordable.

ADMISSIONS

Freshman Academic Profile: Average high school GPA 3.6. 33% in top 10% of high school class, 68% in top 25% of high school class, 94% in top 50% of high school class. 62% from public high schools. **Test Scores:** SAT Math middle 50% range 560-660. SAT EBRW middle 50% range 570-670. ACT middle 50%

range 24-29. Minimum internet-based TOEFL 68. Minimum paper TOEFL 520. **Basis for Candidate Selection:** *Very important factors considered include:* rigor of secondary school record, academic GPA, standardized test scores, character/personal qualities. *Important factors considered include:* application essay, recommendation(s), extracurricular activities, level of applicant's interest. *Other factors considered include:* class rank, interview, talent/ability, first generation, alumni/ae relation, geographical residence, state residency, religious affiliation/commitment, racial/ethnic status, volunteer work, work experience. **Freshman Admission Requirements:** High school diploma is required and GED is accepted *Academic units required:* 4 English, 3 math, 2 science, 2 science labs, 2 foreign language, 3 social studies, 1 history, 2 academic electives, *Academic units recommended:* 4 English, 3 math, 2 science, 2 science labs, 2 foreign language, 3 social studies, 1 history, 2 academic electives. **Freshman Admission Statistics:** 8,576 applied, 73.8% admitted, 15% enrolled. **Transfer Admission Requirements:** college transcript(s), essay or personal statement, statement of good standing from prior institution(s). Minimum college GPA of 2.25 required. Lowest grade transferable C-. **General Admission Information:** Application fee $55. Priority deadline 1/15. Nonfall registration accepted. Admission may be deferred for a maximum of 1 year.

COSTS AND FINANCIAL AID

Annual tuition $43,785. Room and board $13,288. Required fees $825. Average book expense $1,500. **Required Forms and Deadlines:** FAFSA. **Notification of Awards:** Applicants will be notified of awards on a rolling basis beginning 3/1. **Types of Aid:** *Need-based scholarships/grants:* College/university scholarship or grant aid from institutional funds; Federal Nursing Scholarships; Federal Pell; Private scholarships; SEOG; State scholarships/grants. *Loans:* Direct PLUS loans; Direct Subsidized Stafford Loans; Direct Unsubsidized Stafford Loans. *Student Employment:* Federal Work-Study Program available. Institutional employment available. **Financial Aid Statistics:** 84% needy freshmen, 91% needy undergrads receive need-based scholarship or grant aid. 58% freshmen, 45% undergrads receive non-need-based scholarship or grant aid. 71% freshmen, 74% undergrads receive need-based self-help aid. 5% freshmen, 5% undergrads receive athletic scholarships. 95% freshmen, 83% undergrads receive any aid. 67% undergrads borrow to pay for school. Average cumulative indebtedness $28,297. **Criteria for awarding aid:** *Need-based:* Academics, Athletics, Leadership, Minority status, Music/drama *Non-need-based:* Academics, Alumni affiliation, Athletics, Leadership, Minority status, Music/drama, State/district residency.

See page 1028.

SETON HALL UNIVERSITY

400 South Orange Avenue, South Orange, NJ 07079
Phone: (800) THE HALL • **Financial Aid Phone:** 973-761-9332
E-mail: thehall@shu.edu • **CEEB Code:** 2811
Fax: 973-275-2339 • **Website:** http://admissions.shu.edu/ • **ACT Code:** 2606

This private school, affiliated with the Roman Catholic Church, was founded in 1856. It has a 58 acre campus.

RATINGS
Admissions Selectivity Rating: 79   **Fire Safety Rating:** 92   **Green Rating:** 60*

STUDENTS AND FACULTY
Enrollment: 5,295. **Student Body:** 59% female, 41% male, 22% out-of-state, 2% international (71 countries represented). Asian 8%, African American 13%, Caucasian 51%, Hispanic 16%, Native American <1%, Pacific Islander <1%, Two or more races 2%, Race unknown 7%.
Retention and Graduation: 85% freshmen return for sophomore year. 30% grads go on to further study within 1 year. 9% grads pursue arts and sciences degrees. 7% grads pursue law degrees. 5% grads pursue business degrees. 9% grads pursue medical degrees. **Faculty:** 4% of classes are taught by teaching assistants.

ACADEMICS
Degrees: Bachelor's; Doctoral/Professional; Doctoral/Research; Master's; Post-Master's certificate **Most popular majors:** Speech Communication And Rhetoric; Communication, Journalism, And Related Programs, Other; Criminal Justice/Safety Studies. **Special Study Options:** Accelerated program; Cross-registration; Distance learning; Double major; Dual enrollment; English as a Second Language (ESL); Honors program; Independent study; Internships;

Liberal arts/career combination; Study abroad; Teacher certification program. Honors programs: University Honors Program fosters intellectual development through academic challenge. A structured sequence of colloquia and seminars helps to develop critical thinking abilities. Student study the great texts of the past and also have the opportunity to attend operas, theater, museums, concerts and other cultural events. Combined degree programs: BA/MA; BA/MEng. **Disability Services offered to physically disabled students:** Note-taking services; Reader services; Tape recorders; Tutors. **Career services:** Alumni network; Alumni services; Career assessment; Career/job search classes; Internships; Regional alumni

FACILITIES
Housing: 94% of campus accessible to physically diasbled. **Special Academic Facilities/Equipment:** Art studios, theatre-in-the-round, TV studio, radio station, Market Research Center, Trading Room, Sport Polling Center, Science and Technology Center, Nursing SIM laboratories (mock ER), art gallery, language labs, Academic Resource Center (tutoring center), Writing Center, Green House, organic garden, and observatory. **Computers:** 100% of classrooms, 100% of dorms, 100% of libraries, 100% of dining areas, 100% of student union, 100% of common outdoor areas have wireless network access. Students can register for classes online. Administrative functions (other than registration) can be performed online. Undergraduates are required to own a computer.

CAMPUS LIFE
Environment: Village **Activities:** 100 registered organizations, 13 honor societies, 3 religious organizations. **Athletics (Intercollegiate):** *Men:* baseball, basketball, cross-country, diving, golf, soccer, swimming, track/field (outdoor). *Women:* basketball, cross-country, diving, soccer, softball, swimming, tennis, track/field (outdoor). **On-Campus Highlights:** University Center, Recreation Center, Walsh Library, Dunkin Donuts, Chapel of the Immaculate Conception

ADMISSIONS
Freshman Academic Profile: Average high school GPA 3.5. 37% in top 10% of high school class, 61% in top 25% of high school class, 86% in top 50% of high school class. 70% from public high schools. **Test Scores:** SAT Math middle 50% range 510-610. SAT EBRW middle 50% range 490-590. ACT middle 50% range 22-27. Minimum paper TOEFL 550. **Freshman Admission Requirements:** High school diploma is required and GED is accepted *Academic units required:* 4 English, 3 math, 1 science, 1 science labs, 2 foreign language, 2 social studies, 4 academic electives. **Freshman Admission Statistics:** 10,180 applied, 84.4% admitted, 17% enrolled. **General Admission Information:** Application fee $55. Priority deadline 3/1. Nonfall registration accepted. Admission may be deferred for a maximum of 1 year.

COSTS AND FINANCIAL AID
Annual tuition $35,940. Room and board $11,522. Required fees $1,782. **Required Forms and Deadlines:** FAFSA. *Student Employment:* Federal Work-Study Program available. Institutional employment available. **Financial Aid Statistics:** 97% freshmen, 97% undergrads receive any aid. **Criteria for awarding aid:** *Non-need-based:* Academics, Alumni affiliation, Athletics, Leadership, Music/drama.

See page 1030.

SETON HILL UNIVERSITY

1 Seton Hill Drive, Greensburg, PA 15601
Phone: 724-838-4255 • **Financial Aid Phone:** 724-838-4293
E-mail: admit@setonhill.edu • **CEEB Code:** 2812
Fax: 724-830-1294 • **Website:** www.setonhill.edu • **ACT Code:** 3688

This private school, affiliated with the Roman Catholic Church, was founded in 1883. It has a 200 acre campus.

RATINGS
Admissions Selectivity Rating: 78   **Fire Safety Rating:** 88   **Green Rating:** 61

STUDENTS AND FACULTY
Enrollment: 1,650. **Student Body:** 65% female, 35% male, 23% out-of-state, 2% international (17 countries represented). Asian 1%, African American 8%, Caucasian 81%, Hispanic 4%, Native American <1%, Pacific Islander <1%, Two or more races 3%, Race unknown 1%.
Retention and Graduation: 84% freshmen return for sophomore year. 48% freshmen graduate within 4 years. 58% freshmen graduate within 6 years. 30% grads go on to further study within 1 year. 20% grads pursue arts and sciences degrees. 1% grads pursue law degrees. 3% grads pursue business degrees. 1% grads pursue medical degrees. **Faculty:** Student/faculty ratio 14:1. 100 full-time faculty, 82% hold PhDs, 5% are members of minority groups, 47% are women.

0% of classes are taught by teaching assistants.

ACADEMICS

Degrees: Bachelor's; Certificate; Master's; Post-Bachelor's certificate **Classes:** Most classes have 20-29 students. Most lab/discussion sessions have 10-19 students. **Most popular majors:** Psychology, General; Fine/Studio Arts, General; Business/Commerce, General. **Special Study Options:** Accelerated program; Cross-registration; Distance learning; Double major; Dual enrollment; English as a Second Language (ESL); External degree program; Honors program; Independent study; Internships; Liberal arts/career combination; Student-designed major; Study abroad; Teacher certification program; Weekend college. Honors programs: Honors Program has designated curriculum components. Combined degree programs: BA/JD. **Disability Services offered to physically disabled students:** Note-taking services; Reader services; Tape recorders; Tutors. **Career services:** Alumni network; Alumni services; Career assessment; Internships; Regional alumni

FACILITIES

Housing: Coed dorms; Other (please specify) 95% of campus accessible to physically disabled. **Special Academic Facilities/Equipment:** Art gallery, concert hall, theatre, Child Development Center, NEW- Performing Arts Center, Visual Arts Center, smart classrooms, Game System Center/MediaSphere, Recording Rooms. **Computers:** 100% of classrooms, 100% of dorms, 100% of libraries, 100% of dining areas, 100% of common outdoor areas have wireless network access. Students can register for classes online. Administrative functions (other than registration) can be performed online.

CAMPUS LIFE

Environment: Town **Activities:** Campus Ministries; Choral groups; Concert band; Dance; Drama/theater; International Student Organization; Jazz band; Literary magazine; Marching band; Music ensembles; Musical theater; Pep band; Student government; Student newspaper; Symphony orchestra 53 registered organizations, 4 honor societies, 7 religious organizations. **Athletics (Intercollegiate):** *Men:* baseball, basketball, cross-country, football, lacrosse, soccer, track/field (outdoor), track/field (indoor), wrestling. *Women:* basketball, cross-country, equestrian sports, field hockey, golf, lacrosse, soccer, softball, tennis, track/field (outdoor), track/field (indoor), volleyball. **On-Campus Highlights:** Griffin's Cove, McKenna Recreation Center, Sullivan Lounge, Residence Halls, Lowe Dining Hall **Environmental Initiatives:** Association of Independent Colleges and Universities of Pennsylvania self/peer assessment program

ADMISSIONS

Freshman Academic Profile: Average high school GPA 3.7. 20% in top 10% of high school class, 47% in top 25% of high school class, 81% in top 50% of high school class. **Test Scores:** SAT Math middle 50% range 510-610. SAT EBRW middle 50% range 510-610. ACT middle 50% range 20-27. Minimum internet-based TOEFL 79-80. Minimum paper TOEFL 550. **Basis for Candidate Selection:** *Very important factors considered include:* rigor of secondary school record, academic GPA, interview. *Important factors considered include:* class rank, standardized test scores, extracurricular activities, talent/ability, character/personal qualities. *Other factors considered include:* application essay, recommendation(s), alumni/ae relation, volunteer work, work experience, level of applicant's interest. **Freshman Admission Requirements:** High school diploma is required and GED is accepted *Academic units required:* 4 English, 2 math, 1 science, 1 science labs, 2 social studies, 4 academic electives, *Academic units recommended:* 4 English, 2 math, 1 science, 1 science labs, 2 foreign language, 2 social studies, 4 academic electives. **Freshman Admission Statistics:** 2,573 applied, 73.9% admitted, 14% enrolled. **Transfer Admission Requirements:** High school transcript, college transcript(s), statement of good standing from prior institution(s). Minimum college GPA of 2.0 required. Lowest grade transferable C-. **General Admission Information:** Application fee $35. Priority deadline 5/1. Regular application deadline 8/15. Nonfall registration accepted. Admission may be deferred for a maximum of 1 year.

COSTS AND FINANCIAL AID

Required Forms and Deadlines: FAFSA; Institution's own financial aid form; State aid form. **Notification of Awards:** Applicants will be notified of awards on a rolling basis beginning 11/30. **Types of Aid:** *Need-based scholarships/grants:* College/university scholarship or grant aid from institutional funds; Federal Pell; Private scholarships; SEOG; State scholarships/grants. *Loans:* Direct PLUS loans; Direct Subsidized Stafford Loans; Direct Unsubsidized Stafford Loans. *Student Employment:* Federal Work-Study Program available. Institutional employment available. **Financial Aid Statistics:** 100% needy freshmen, 100% needy undergrads receive need-based scholarship or grant aid. 18% freshmen, 12% undergrads receive non-need-based scholarship or grant aid. 76% freshmen, 82% undergrads receive need-based self-help aid. 10% freshmen, 10% undergrads receive athletic scholarships. 100% freshmen, 82% undergrads receive any aid. **Criteria for awarding aid:** *Need-based:* Job skills, Leadership, Minority status, Religious affiliation *Non-need-based:* Academics, Alumni affiliation, Art, Athletics, Music/drama.

SEWANEE—THE UNIVERSITY OF THE SOUTH

735 University Avenue, Sewanee, TN 37383-1000
Phone: 931-598-1238 • **Financial Aid Phone:** 931-598-1312
E-mail: admiss@sewanee.edu • **CEEB Code:** 1842
Fax: 931-538-3248 • **Website:** www.sewanee.edu • **ACT Code:** 4024

This private school, affiliated with the Episcopal Church, was founded in 1857. It has a 13000 acre campus.

RATINGS

Admissions Selectivity Rating: 90   **Fire Safety Rating:** 98   **Green Rating:** 83

STUDENTS AND FACULTY

Enrollment: 1,683. **Student Body:** 53% female, 47% male, 78% out-of-state, 3% international (26 countries represented). Asian 1%, African American 5%, Caucasian 82%, Hispanic 6%, Native American <1%, Pacific Islander 0%, Two or more races 3%, Race unknown 0%.
Retention and Graduation: 88% freshmen return for sophomore year. 72% freshmen graduate within 4 years. 77% freshmen graduate within 6 years.
Faculty: Student/faculty ratio 10:1. 164 full-time faculty, 96% hold PhDs, 15% are members of minority groups, 45% are women. 0% of classes are taught by teaching assistants.

ACADEMICS

Degrees: Bachelor's; Doctoral/Professional; Master's; Post-Bachelor's certificate; Post-Master's certificate **Classes:** Most classes have 10-19 students. Most lab/discussion sessions have 20-29 students. **Most popular majors:** English Language And Literature, General; Psychology, General; Economics, General. **Special Study Options:** Double major; Independent study; Internships; Student-designed major; Study abroad. Combined degree programs: BA/MEng. **Disability Services offered to physically disabled students:** Note-taking services; Reader services; Tape recorders; Tutors. **Career services:** Alumni network; Alumni services; Career assessment; Career/job search classes; Internships; Regional alumni

FACILITIES

Housing: Apartments for married students; Coed dorms; Fraternity/sorority housing; Men's dorms; Theme housing; Wellness housing; Women's dorms 90% of campus accessible to physically disabled. **Special Academic Facilities/Equipment:** Art gallery, observatory, keyboard collection, materials analysis lab with electron microscope, Landscape Analysis Lab, Ralston Music Listening Library. **Computers:** 80% of classrooms, 80% of dorms, 100% of libraries, 100% of dining areas, 100% of student union, 25% of common outdoor areas have wireless network access. Students can register for classes online. Administrative functions (other than registration) can be performed online.

CAMPUS LIFE

Environment: Village **Activities:** Campus Ministries; Choral groups; Dance; Drama/theater; International Student Organization; Jazz band; Literary magazine; Model UN; Music ensembles; Musical theater; Pep band; Radio station; Student government; Student newspaper; Student-run film society; Symphony orchestra; Yearbook 110 registered organizations, 9 honor societies, 11 religious organizations. 12 fraternities, 9 sororities. **Athletics (Intercollegiate):** *Men:* baseball, basketball, cross-country, diving, equestrian sports, football, golf, lacrosse, soccer, swimming, tennis, track/field (outdoor), track/field (indoor). *Women:* basketball, cheerleading, cross-country, diving, equestrian sports, field hockey, golf, lacrosse, soccer, softball, swimming, tennis, track/field (outdoor), track/field (indoor), volleyball. **On-Campus Highlights:** Outdoor recreation on Sewanee's 13,000 acre campus, McClurg Dining Hall, Abbo's Alley Ravine Garden, Fowler Sport and Fitness Center, Stirling's Coffee House **Environmental Initiatives:** In pursuit of a goal from our 2008 Strategic Planning Addendum, Sewanee's Sustainability Steering Committee developed a Sustainability Master Plan that has been formerly adopted. The plan, the first of its kind at Sewanee, is a blueprint for the institution's commitment to sustainability as we move forward, empowering Sewanee to teach and lead by example.

ADMISSIONS

Freshman Academic Profile: Average high school GPA 3.7. 36% in top 10% of high school class, 61% in top 25% of high school class, 88% in top 50% of high school class. 45% from public high schools. **Test Scores:** SAT Math middle 50% range 590-680. SAT EBRW middle 50% range 620-700. ACT middle 50% range 27-30. Minimum internet-based TOEFL 90. Minimum paper TOEFL 577. **Basis for Candidate Selection:** *Very important factors considered include:* rigor of secondary school record, academic GPA, recommendation(s). *Important factors considered include:* application essay, extracurricular activities, character/personal qualities, volunteer work, work experience. *Other factors considered include:* class rank, standardized test scores, interview, talent/ability, first generation, alumni/ae relation, geographical residence, level of applicant's interest. **Freshman Admission Requirements:** High school diploma is required and GED is not accepted *Academic units required:* 4 English, 3 math, 2 science, 2 science labs, 2 foreign language, 1 social studies, 1 history, *Academic units recommended:* 4 English, 4 math, 4 science, 3 science labs, 4 foreign language, 2 social studies, 2 history. **Freshman Admission Statistics:** 4,218 applied, 46.7% admitted, 23% enrolled. **Transfer Admission Requirements:** High school transcript, college transcript(s), essay or personal statement, standardized test scores, statement of good standing from prior institution(s). Minimum college GPA of 3.00 required. Lowest grade transferable C. **General Admission Information:** Regular application deadline 2/1. Nonfall registration accepted. Admission may be deferred for a maximum of one year.

COSTS AND FINANCIAL AID

Average book expense $1,200. **Required Forms and Deadlines:** CSS/Financial Aid PROFILE; FAFSA. **Notification of Awards:** Applicants will be notified of awards on a rolling basis beginning 2/1. **Types of Aid:** *Need-based scholarships/grants:* College/university scholarship or grant aid from institutional funds; Federal Pell; Private scholarships; SEOG; State scholarships/grants. *Loans:* Direct PLUS loans; Direct Subsidized Stafford Loans; Direct Unsubsidized Stafford Loans. *Student Employment:* Federal Work-Study Program available. Institutional employment available. **Financial Aid Statistics:** 98% needy freshmen, 98% needy undergrads receive need-based scholarship or grant aid. 22% freshmen, 25% undergrads receive non-need-based scholarship or grant aid. 75% freshmen, 74% undergrads receive need-based self-help aid. 0% freshmen, 0% undergrads receive athletic scholarships. 85% freshmen, 80% undergrads receive any aid. 43% undergrads borrow to pay for school. Average cumulative indebtedness $24,431. **Criteria for awarding aid:** *Need-based:* Academics, Religious affiliation *Non-need-based:* Academics, Art, Religious affiliation, State/district residency.

SHAW UNIVERSITY

118 East South Street, Raleigh, NC 27601
Phone: 919-546-8275 • **Financial Aid Phone:** 919-546-8565
E-mail: admissions@shawu.edu • **CEEB Code:** 5612
Fax: 919-546-8271 • **Website:** www.shawu.edu • **ACT Code:** 3158

This private school, affiliated with the Baptist Church, was founded in 1865. It has a 30 acre campus.

RATINGS
Admissions Selectivity Rating: 78   **Fire Safety Rating:** 60*   **Green Rating:** 60*

STUDENTS AND FACULTY
Enrollment: 1,545. **Student Body:** 58% female, 42% male, 37% out-of-state, 4% international (17 countries represented). Asian 1%, African American 74%, Caucasian 2%, Hispanic <1%, Native American <1%, Pacific Islander 1%, Two or more races 3%, Race unknown 15%.
Retention and Graduation: 43% freshmen return for sophomore year. **Faculty:** Student/faculty ratio 17:1. 76 full-time faculty, 71% are members of minority groups, 47% are women. 0% of classes are taught by teaching assistants.

ACADEMICS
Degrees: Bachelor's; Certificate; **Master's Classes:** Most classes have 10-19 students. **Most popular majors:** Social Work; Sociology; Business Administration And Management, General. **Special Study Options:** Accelerated program; Cross-registration; Distance learning; Double major; Dual enrollment; Honors program; Independent study; Internships; Liberal arts/career combination; Student-designed major; Study abroad; Teacher certification program; Weekend college. **Honors programs:** The Honors College of Shaw University nurtures excellence in select students who are highly motivated, talented and gifted, and who demonstrate a commitment to the learning process in reaching their potential to become scholars, leaders and role models. It is an innovative, multifaceted program designed to enhance the success of student scholars at Shaw University. Its initiative and activities concentrate on the growth and development of students' intellectual, ethical and leadership skills. **Disability Services offered to physically disabled students:** Note-taking services; Reader services; Tape recorders; Tutors.

FACILITIES
Housing: Men's dorms; Women's dorms **Special Academic Facilities/Equipment:** TV and film production facilities. Curriculum and Materials

Center. **Computers:** Students can register for classes online. Administrative functions (other than registration) can be performed online.

CAMPUS LIFE
Environment: City **Activities:** Campus Ministries; Choral groups; Concert band; Dance; Drama/theater; Jazz band; Marching band; Music ensembles; Musical theater; Pep band; Radio station; Student government; Student newspaper; Yearbook 4 honor societies, 4 fraternities, 4 sororities. **Athletics (Intercollegiate):** *Men:* baseball, basketball, cross-country, football, golf, tennis, track/field (outdoor), track/field (indoor). *Women:* basketball, bowling, cross-country, softball, tennis, track/field (outdoor), track/field (indoor), volleyball.

ADMISSIONS
Freshman Academic Profile: Average high school GPA 2.6. 2% in top 10% of high school class, 5% in top 25% of high school class, 30% in top 50% of high school class. 90% from public high schools. **Test Scores:** SAT Math middle 50% range 380-460. SAT EBRW middle 50% range 383-475. ACT middle 50% range 14-17. **Basis for Candidate Selection:** *Very important factors considered include:* rigor of secondary school record, academic GPA, recommendation(s), level of applicant's interest. *Important factors considered include:* class rank, application essay, standardized test scores, extracurricular activities, talent/ability, character/personal qualities, alumni/ae relation. *Other factors considered include:* geographical residence, state residency, volunteer work, work experience. **Freshman Admission Requirements:** High school diploma is required and GED is accepted *Academic units required:* 3 English, 2 math, 2 science, 2 social studies, 9 academic electives. **Freshman Admission Statistics:** 12,060 applied, 52.9% admitted, 8% enrolled. **Transfer Admission Requirements:** college transcript(s), Lowest grade transferable C. **General Admission Information:** Application fee $25. Priority deadline 7/30. Regular application deadline 7/30. Nonfall registration accepted. Admission may be deferred.

COSTS AND FINANCIAL AID
Annual tuition $11,808. Room and board $7,844. Required fees $4,672. Average book expense $1,300. **Required Forms and Deadlines:** FAFSA; Institution's own financial aid form; State aid form. **Notification of Awards:** Applicants will be notified of awards on a rolling basis beginning 2/1. **Types of Aid:** *Need-based scholarships/grants:* College/university scholarship or grant aid from institutional funds; Federal Pell; Private scholarships; SEOG; State scholarships/grants; United Negro College Fund. *Loans:* Direct PLUS loans; Direct Subsidized Stafford Loans; Direct Unsubsidized Stafford Loans. *Student Employment:* Federal Work-Study Program available. Institutional employment available. **Criteria for awarding aid:** *Need-based:* Alumni affiliation, Religious affiliation *Non-need-based:* Academics, Alumni affiliation, Art, Athletics, Music/drama, Religious affiliation.

SHAWNEE STATE UNIVERSITY

940 Second Street, Portsmouth, OH 45662
Phone: 740-351-4778 • **Financial Aid Phone:** 740-351-4357
E-mail: to_ssu@shawnee.edu • **CEEB Code:** 1790
Fax: 740-351-3111 • **Website:** www.shawnee.edu • **ACT Code:** 3336

This public school was founded in 1986. It has a 50 acre campus.

RATINGS
Admissions Selectivity Rating: 79   **Fire Safety Rating:** 95   **Green Rating:** 63

STUDENTS AND FACULTY
Enrollment: 3,756. **Student Body:** 56% female, 44% male, 11% out-of-state, 1% international (20 countries represented). Asian <1%, African American 6%, Caucasian 87%, Hispanic 1%, Native American 1%, Pacific Islander <1%, Two or more races 2%, Race unknown 3%.
Retention and Graduation: 57% freshmen return for sophomore year. **Faculty:** Student/faculty ratio 18:1. 145 full-time faculty, 59% hold PhDs, 10% are members of minority groups, 41% are women. 0% of classes are taught by teaching assistants.

ACADEMICS
Degrees: Associate; Bachelor's; Certificate; **Master's Classes:** Most classes have 10-19 students. **Most popular majors:** Biological And Biomedical Sciences, Other; Psychology, General; Business Administration And Management, General. **Special Study Options:** Accelerated program; Distance learning; Double major; Dual enrollment; English as a Second Language (ESL); Honors program; Independent study; Internships; Student-designed major; Study abroad; Teacher certification program. **Disability**

Services offered to physically disabled students: Note-taking services; Reader services; Tape recorders; Tutors. Career services: Alumni services; Career assessment; Career/job search classes; Internships

FACILITIES
Housing: Coed dorms; Theme housing 100% of campus accessible to physically diasbled. Special Academic Facilities/Equipment: Vern Riffe Center for the Arts; Clark Planetarium Computers: Students can register for classes online.

CAMPUS LIFE
Environment: Town Activities: Campus Ministries; Choral groups; Drama/theater; International Student Organization; Literary magazine; Music ensembles; Musical theater; Student government; Student newspaper 36 registered organizations, 2 honor societies, 3 religious organizations. 1 fraternity, 1 sorority. Athletics (Intercollegiate): Men: baseball, basketball, cross-country, golf, soccer. Women: basketball, cross-country, soccer, softball, tennis, volleyball. On-Campus Highlights: Vern Riffe Center for the Arts, University Center, Clark Planetarium Environmental Initiatives: geo-thermal chiller plant for new building

ADMISSIONS
Freshman Academic Profile: 12% in top 10% of high school class, 33% in top 25% of high school class, 63% in top 50% of high school class. Test Scores: SAT Math middle 50% range 433-628. SAT EBRW middle 50% range 440-588. ACT middle 50% range 18-24. Minimum internet-based TOEFL 60. Minimum paper TOEFL 500. Freshman Admission Requirements: High school diploma is required and GED is accepted Academic units recommended: 4 English, 3 math, 3 science, 2 foreign language, 3 social studies, 1 visual/performing arts. Freshman Admission Statistics: 3,686 applied, 74.1% admitted, 35% enrolled. Transfer Admission Requirements: High school transcript, college transcript(s), Minimum college GPA of 1.0 required. Lowest grade transferable D. General Admission Information: Nonfall registration accepted. Admission may be deferred.

COSTS AND FINANCIAL AID
Annual in-state tuition $9,552. Annual out-of-state tuition $11,504. Room and board $9,552. Required fees $1,113. Average book expense $1,440. Required Forms and Deadlines: FAFSA. Notification of Awards: Applicants will be notified of awards on a rolling basis beginning 3/15. Types of Aid: Need-based scholarships/grants: College/university scholarship or grant aid from institutional funds; Federal Pell; Private scholarships; SEOG; State scholarships/grants. Loans: Direct PLUS loans; Direct Subsidized Stafford Loans; Direct Unsubsidized Stafford Loans. Student Employment: Federal Work-Study Program available. Institutional employment available.

SHENANDOAH UNIVERSITY

1460 University Drive, Winchester, VA 22601-5195
Phone: 540.665.4581 • Financial Aid Phone: 540.665.4621
E-mail: admit@su.edu • CEEB Code: 5613
Fax: 540.665.4627 • Website: www.su.edu • ACT Code: 4396

This private school, affiliated with the Methodist Church, was founded in 1875. It has a 359 acre campus.

RATINGS
Admissions Selectivity Rating: 75   Fire Safety Rating: 92   Green Rating: 85

STUDENTS AND FACULTY
Enrollment: 2,055. Student Body: 60% female, 40% male, 40% out-of-state, 3% international (36 countries represented). Asian 3%, African American 11%, Caucasian 57%, Hispanic 7%, Native American 1%, Pacific Islander <1%, Two or more races 2%, Race unknown 16%.
Retention and Graduation: 80% freshmen return for sophomore year. 52% freshmen graduate within 4 years. 63% freshmen graduate within 6 years. 10% grads go on to further study within 1 year. 0% grads pursue arts and sciences degrees. 0% grads pursue law degrees. 0% grads pursue business degrees. 0% grads pursue medical degrees. Faculty: Student/faculty ratio 10:1. 251 full-time faculty, 78% hold PhDs, 14% are members of minority groups, 59% are women. 0% of classes are taught by teaching assistants.

ACADEMICS
Degrees: Bachelor's; Certificate; Doctoral/Professional; Doctoral/Research; Master's; Post-Bachelor's certificate; Post-Master's certificate Classes: Most classes have 20-29 students. Most popular majors: Physiology, Pathology And Related Sciences; Registered Nursing/Registered Nurse; Business Administration And Management, General. Special Study Options:

Accelerated program; Distance learning; Double major; Dual enrollment; English as a Second Language (ESL); Independent study; Internships; Study abroad; Teacher certification program; Weekend college. Disability Services offered to physically disabled students: Note-taking services; Reader services; Tape recorders; Tutors. Career services: Alumni network; Alumni services; Career assessment; Career/job search classes; Internships

FACILITIES
Housing: Apartments for married students; Apartments for single students; Coed dorms; Special housing for disabled students 91% of campus accessible to physically diasbled. Special Academic Facilities/Equipment: Pharmacy Apothecary Museum; Environmental Studies green rooftop garden; cadaver lab and nursing simulation suite in the Health & Life Sciences Building; Claude Moore Center for Literacy in the School of Education & Human Development (SEHD); a model computer classroom in SEHD, as well as the Academic Enrichment Center; Children's Literature Center and Media Center in the Alson H. Smith, Jr. Library. The library has two book scan stations, as well as a new online research tool, Discovery. Discovery is designed to provide a single, unified search interface for nearly all of the university's digital and print library content. The campus employs a WEPA (wireless everywhere, print anywhere) printing system. The Shenandoah River Campus at Cool Spring Battlefield is 195 acres of land along the Shenandoah River which serves as a field site where students learn by exploring history, environmental studies, and other disciplines in ways that supplement and reinforce classroom and laboratory learning. Shenandoah Conservatory has three academic observation rooms: a recording studio, a music therapy clinic, and the Collins Music Learning Suite, an innovative learning space for undergraduate and graduate music education students. The conservatory also provides a designated Mac Lab, which is a specialized music technology classroom; two classrooms designated for class piano; specialized rooms for film and acting; and specialized equipment for voice and a voice science lab. Shenandoah Conservatory became an All-Steinway School in June 2015, joining an elite group of schools and conservatories in the U.S. and abroad which bear this coveted status. James R. Wilkins, Jr., Athletics and Events Center. The center measures 77,000 square feet, 63,000 square feet of which is multipurpose field-house space designed for varsity competition and practice, with retractable seating for 1,600. Computers: 100% of classrooms, 100% of dorms, 100% of libraries, 100% of dining areas, 100% of student union, 25% of common outdoor areas have wireless network access. Students can register for classes online. Administrative functions (other than registration) can be performed online.

CAMPUS LIFE
Environment: Town Activities: Campus Ministries; Choral groups; Concert band; Dance; Drama/theater; International Student Organization; Jazz band; Literary magazine; Music ensembles; Musical theater; Pep band; Radio station; Student government; Student newspaper; Symphony orchestra 65 registered organizations, 2 honor societies, 2 religious organizations. 7 fraternities, 1 sorority. Athletics (Intercollegiate): Men: baseball, basketball, cross-country, football, golf, lacrosse, soccer, tennis. Women: basketball, cross-country, field hockey, lacrosse, soccer, softball, tennis, volleyball. On-Campus Highlights: Brandt Student Center, Ohrstrom-Bryant Theatre, James R. Aikens, Jr. Athletic & Events Center, Alson H. Smith, Jr. Library, Goodson Chapel / Recital Hall Environmental Initiatives: Continued refitting of lights, from incandescent to CF or LED.

ADMISSIONS
Freshman Academic Profile: Average high school GPA 3.5. Test Scores: SAT Math middle 50% range 500-590. SAT EBRW middle 50% range 510-610. ACT middle 50% range 20-26. Minimum internet-based TOEFL 79. Minimum paper TOEFL 550. Basis for Candidate Selection: Very important factors considered include: academic GPA. Important factors considered include: rigor of secondary school record, standardized test scores, extracurricular activities, talent/ability. Other factors considered include: application essay, recommendation(s), interview, character/personal qualities, first generation, volunteer work, work experience, level of applicant's interest. Freshman Admission Requirements: High school diploma is required and GED is accepted Academic units required: 4 English, 3 math, 2 science, 1 science labs, Academic units recommended: 2 foreign language. Freshman Admission Statistics: 1,737 applied, 83.2% admitted, 30% enrolled. Transfer Admission Requirements: college transcript(s), statement of good standing from prior institution(s). Minimum college GPA of 2.0 required. Lowest grade transferable C. General Admission Information: Application fee $30. Priority deadline 2/1. Nonfall registration accepted. Admission may be deferred for a maximum of 1 year.

COSTS AND FINANCIAL AID
Annual tuition $31,280. Room and board $10,370. Required fees $1,250. Average book expense $1,500. Required Forms and Deadlines: FAFSA; State aid form. Notification of Awards: Applicants will be notified of awards on a rolling basis beginning 1/15. Types of Aid: Need-based scholarships/grants: College/university scholarship or grant aid from institutional funds; Federal Pell; Private scholarships; SEOG; State scholarships/grants. Loans:

Direct PLUS loans; Direct Subsidized Stafford Loans; Direct Unsubsidized Stafford Loans. *Student Employment:* Federal Work-Study Program available. Institutional employment available. **Financial Aid Statistics:** 43% needy freshmen, 72% needy undergrads receive need-based scholarship or grant aid. 100% freshmen, 98% undergrads receive non-need-based scholarship or grant aid. 80% freshmen, 81% undergrads receive need-based self-help aid. 0% freshmen, 10% undergrads receive athletic scholarships. 99% freshmen, 98% undergrads receive any aid. 59% undergrads borrow to pay for school. Average cumulative indebtedness $22,392. **Criteria for awarding aid:** *Non-need-based:* Academics, Music/drama, Religious affiliation.

SHEPHERD UNIVERSITY

P.O. Box 5000, Shepherdstown, WV 25443-5000
Phone: 304-876-5212 • **Financial Aid Phone:** 304-876-5470
E-mail: admission@shepherd.edu • **CEEB Code:** 5615
Fax: 304-876-5165 • **Website:** www.shepherd.edu • **ACT Code:** 4532

This public school was founded in 1871. It has a 323 acre campus.

RATINGS

Admissions Selectivity Rating: 75   **Fire Safety Rating:** 88   **Green Rating:** 71

STUDENTS AND FACULTY

Enrollment: 1,846. **Student Body:** 34% female, 66% male, 33% out-of-state, 1% international (8 countries represented). Asian 2%, African American 9%, Caucasian 79%, Hispanic 4%, Native American <1%, Pacific Islander <1%, Two or more races 3%, Race unknown 1%.
Retention and Graduation: 65% freshmen return for sophomore year. 25% freshmen graduate within 4 years. 42% freshmen graduate within 6 years. 33% grads go on to further study within 1 year. 46% grads pursue arts and sciences degrees. 5% grads pursue law degrees. 20% grads pursue business degrees. 10% grads pursue medical degrees. **Faculty:** Student/faculty ratio 15:1. 136 full-time faculty, 91% hold PhDs, 11% are members of minority groups, 49% are women. 0% of classes are taught by teaching assistants.

ACADEMICS

Degrees: Bachelor's; Doctoral/Professional; **Master's Classes:** Most classes have 20-29 students. Most lab/discussion sessions have 10-19 students. **Most popular majors:** Teacher Education, Multiple Levels; Registered Nursing/Registered Nurse; Business Administration And Management, General. **Special Study Options:** Cooperative education program; Double major; Dual enrollment; English as a Second Language (ESL); Honors program; Independent study; Internships; Study abroad; Teacher certification program. Honors programs: See Honors Program on Web site www.shepherd.edu/honors. **Disability Services offered to physically disabled students:** Note-taking services; Reader services; Tape recorders; Tutors. **Career services:** Alumni network; Alumni services; Career assessment; Career/job search classes; Internships

FACILITIES

Housing: Apartments for single students; Coed dorms; Special housing for disabled student; Special housing for international students; Theme housing; Wellness housing 90% of campus accessible to physically disabled. **Special Academic Facilities/Equipment:** Nursery school, elementary education lab, art gallery, theaters, Steinway Concert Grand Piano, George Tyler Moore Center for the Study of the Civil War, Robert C. Byrd Center for Congressional History and Education, campus radio station, television production studio, veterans center, wellness center **Computers:** 90% of classrooms, 100% of libraries, 100% of dining areas, 100% of student union, 1% of common outdoor areas have wireless network access. Students can register for classes online. Administrative functions (other than registration) can be performed online.

CAMPUS LIFE

Environment: Village **Activities:** Campus Ministries; Choral groups; Concert band; Drama/theater; International Student Organization; Jazz band; Literary magazine; Marching band; Model UN; Music ensembles; Musical theater; Radio station; Student government; Student newspaper; Symphony orchestra 85 registered organizations, 9 honor societies, 4 religious organizations. 4 fraternities, 3 sororities. **Athletics (Intercollegiate):** *Men:* baseball, basketball, football, golf, soccer, tennis. *Women:* basketball, lacrosse, soccer, softball, tennis, volleyball. **On-Campus Highlights:** Butcher Athletic Center, Center for Contemporary Arts, Scarborough Library, Wellness Center, Student Center **Environmental Initiatives:** Recycling

ADMISSIONS

Freshman Academic Profile: Average high school GPA 3.4. 90% from public high schools. **Test Scores:** SAT Math middle 50% range 480-570. SAT EBRW middle 50% range 490-580. ACT middle 50% range 19-24.

Minimum internet-based TOEFL 79. Minimum paper TOEFL 550. **Basis for Candidate Selection:** *Very important factors considered include:* rigor of secondary school record, academic GPA, standardized test scores. *Important factors considered include:* talent/ability. *Other factors considered include:* class rank, application essay, recommendation(s), interview, extracurricular activities, character/personal qualities, alumni/ae relation, level of applicant's interest. **Freshman Admission Requirements:** High school diploma is required and GED is accepted *Academic units required:* 4 English, 4 math, 3 science, 3 science labs, 2 foreign language, 2 social studies, 1 history, 1 visual/performing arts. **Freshman Admission Statistics:** 1,573 applied, 89.1% admitted, 43% enrolled. **Transfer Admission Requirements:** college transcript(s), Minimum college GPA of 2.0 required. Lowest grade transferable D. **General Admission Information:** Application fee $45. Priority deadline 2/1. Regular application deadline 8/18. Nonfall registration accepted. Admission may be deferred for a maximum of 1 year.

COSTS AND FINANCIAL AID

Average book expense $1,000. **Required Forms and Deadlines:** FAFSA; State aid form. **Notification of Awards:** Applicants will be notified of awards on a rolling basis beginning 12/15. **Types of Aid:** *Need-based scholarships/grants:* College/university scholarship or grant aid from institutional funds; Federal Pell; Private scholarships; SEOG; State scholarships/grants. *Loans:* Direct PLUS loans; Direct Subsidized Stafford Loans; Direct Unsubsidized Stafford Loans. *Student Employment:* Federal Work-Study Program available. Institutional employment available. **Financial Aid Statistics:** 66% needy freshmen, 67% needy undergrads receive need-based scholarship or grant aid. 51% freshmen, 37% undergrads receive non-need-based scholarship or grant aid. 63% freshmen, 69% undergrads receive need-based self-help aid. 8% freshmen, 8% undergrads receive athletic scholarships. 91% freshmen, 82% undergrads receive any aid. 72% undergrads borrow to pay for school. Average cumulative indebtedness $30,526. **Criteria for awarding aid:** *Need-based:* Academics *Non-need-based:* Academics, Art, Athletics, Job skills, Leadership, Minority status, Music/drama, State/district residency.

SHIMER COLLEGE

Office of Admissions, Chicago, IL 60616
Phone: 312-235-3555 • **Financial Aid Phone:** 312-235-3507
E-mail: admission@shimer.edu • **CEEB Code:** 1717
Fax: 888-808-3133 • **Website:** http://www.shimer.edu/ • **ACT Code:** 1142

This private school was founded in 1853. It has a 140 acre campus.

RATINGS

Admissions Selectivity Rating: 82   **Fire Safety Rating:** 60*   **Green Rating:** 60*

STUDENTS AND FACULTY

Enrollment: 74. **Student Body:** 47% female, 53% male, 50% out-of-state, 0% international (4 countries represented). Asian 7%, African American 9%, Caucasian 68%, Hispanic 12%, Native American 0%, Pacific Islander 0%, Two or more races 0%, Race unknown 4%.
Retention and Graduation: 63% freshmen return for sophomore year. **Faculty:** Student/faculty ratio 7:1. 9 full-time faculty, 100% hold PhDs, 22% are members of minority groups, 33% are women. 0% of classes are taught by teaching assistants.

ACADEMICS

Degrees: Bachelor's **Classes:** Most classes have fewer than 10 students. Most lab/discussion sessions have fewer than 10 students. **Most popular majors:** Humanities/Humanistic Studies; Natural Sciences; Social Sciences, General. **Special Study Options:** Accelerated program; Cross-registration; Double major; Dual enrollment; Independent study; Liberal arts/career combination. Combined degree programs: BA/JD. **Career services:** Alumni network; Alumni services; Career/job search classes; Internships; Regional alumni

FACILITIES

Housing: Apartments for married students; Apartments for single students; Coed dorms; Special housing for disabled student; Theme housing 100% of campus accessible to physically disabled. **Special Academic Facilities/Equipment:** The Galvin Library has over one million volumes and 120 digital databases. The MTCC (student center) is an amazing place to eat, play and hang out. **Computers:** 100% of classrooms, 100% of dorms, 100% of libraries, 100% of dining areas, 100% of student union, 100% of common outdoor areas have wireless network access.

CAMPUS LIFE

Environment: Metropolis **Activities:** Campus Ministries; Choral groups; Concert band; Dance; Drama/theater; International Student Organization; Jazz band; Literary magazine; Music ensembles; Radio station; Student government; Student newspaper; Student-run film society; Symphony orchestra 10 religious organizations. **On-Campus Highlights:** The Shimer College space on the IIT Camp, The Galvin Library/Art Galery, McCormic Tribune Campus Center, Crown Hall, Keating Sports Center

ADMISSIONS

Freshman Academic Profile: Average high school GPA 3.0. 50% from public high schools. **Test Scores:** SAT Math middle 50% range 500-640. SAT EBRW middle 50% range 620-760. Minimum paper TOEFL 625. **Basis for Candidate Selection:** *Very important factors considered include:* application essay, recommendation(s), interview, level of applicant's interest. *Important factors considered include:* rigor of secondary school record, academic GPA, extracurricular activities, talent/ability, character/personal qualities. *Other factors considered include:* standardized test scores, first generation, alumni/ae relation, volunteer work, work experience. **Freshman Admission Requirements:** High school diploma is required and GED is accepted *Academic units recommended:* 4 English, 3 math, 3 science, 2 foreign language, 2 history, 1 visual/performing arts. **Freshman Admission Statistics:** 31 applied, 83.9% admitted, 46% enrolled. **Transfer Admission Requirements:** college transcript(s), essay or personal statement, interview, Lowest grade transferable C. **General Admission Information:** Application fee $25. Priority deadline 5/1. Nonfall registration accepted. Admission may be deferred for a maximum of 1 year.

COSTS AND FINANCIAL AID

Annual tuition $26,510. Room and board $10,626. Required fees $4,720. Average book expense $800. **Required Forms and Deadlines:** FAFSA. **Notification of Awards:** Applicants will be notified of awards on a rolling basis beginning 3/15. **Types of Aid:** *Need-based scholarships/grants:* College/university scholarship or grant aid from institutional funds; Federal Pell; Private scholarships; SEOG; State scholarships/grants. *Loans:* Direct PLUS loans; Direct Subsidized Stafford Loans; Direct Unsubsidized Stafford Loans. *Student Employment:* Federal Work-Study Program available. Institutional employment available. **Financial Aid Statistics:** 71% needy freshmen, 100% needy undergrads receive need-based scholarship or grant aid. 71% freshmen, 75% undergrads receive non-need-based scholarship or grant aid. 71% freshmen, 91% undergrads receive need-based self-help aid. 0% freshmen, 0% undergrads receive athletic scholarships. 74% freshmen, 84% undergrads receive any aid. **Criteria for awarding aid:** *Need-based:* Academics, Alumni affiliation *Non-need-based:* Academics, Alumni affiliation.

SHIPPENSBURG UNIVERSITY OF PENNSYLVANIA

1871 Old Main Drive, Shippensburg, PA 17257-2299
Phone: 717-477-1231 • **Financial Aid Phone:** 717-477-1131
E-mail: admiss@ship.edu • **CEEB Code:** 2657
Fax: 717-477-4016 • **Website:** www.ship.edu • **ACT Code:** 3714

This public school was founded in 1871. It has a 200 acre campus.

RATINGS
Admissions Selectivity Rating: 74   **Fire Safety Rating:** 98   **Green Rating:** 74

STUDENTS AND FACULTY
Enrollment: 5,475. **Student Body:** 50% female, 50% male, 7% out-of-state, 1% international (23 countries represented). Asian 2%, African American 10%, Caucasian 77%, Hispanic 6%, Native American <1%, Pacific Islander <1%, Two or more races 4%, Race unknown 1%.
Retention and Graduation: 71% freshmen return for sophomore year. 34% freshmen graduate within 4 years. 52% freshmen graduate within 6 years. **Faculty:** Student/faculty ratio 19:1. 299 full-time faculty, 90% hold PhDs, 18% are members of minority groups, 43% are women.

ACADEMICS
Degrees: Bachelor's; Certificate; Doctoral/Professional; Master's; Post-Bachelor's certificate; Post-Master's certificate **Classes:** Most classes have 10-19 students. Most lab/discussion sessions have fewer than 10 students. **Most popular majors:** Biology/Biological Sciences, General; Psychology, General; Criminal Justice/Safety Studies. **Special Study Options:** Accelerated program; Cooperative education program; Distance learning; Double major; Dual enrollment; Honors program; Independent study; Internships; Study abroad; Teacher certification program. Honors programs: Program in General Education and Psychology. **Disability Services offered to physically

disabled students:** Note-taking services; Reader services; Tutors. **Career services:** Alumni network; Alumni services; Career assessment; Career/job search classes; Internships; Regional alumni

FACILITIES
Housing: Apartments for single students; Coed dorms; Theme housing; Wellness housing 92% of campus accessible to physically disabled. **Special Academic Facilities/Equipment:** art gallery, vertebrate museum, on-campus elementary school, planetarium, electron microscope, NMR spectrometer, greenhouse, herbarium,Fashion Archives, Women's Center, Closed Circuit TV **Computers:** 95% of classrooms, 10% of dorms, 100% of libraries, 100% of dining areas, 95% of student union, 75% of common outdoor areas have wireless network access. Students can register for classes online. Administrative functions (other than registration) can be performed online.

CAMPUS LIFE
Environment: Village **Activities:** Campus Ministries; Choral groups; Concert band; Dance; Drama/theater; International Student Organization; Jazz band; Literary magazine; Marching band; Music ensembles; Musical theater; Radio station; Student government; Student newspaper; Television station; Yearbook 200 registered organizations, 23 honor societies, 8 religious organizations. 12 fraternities, 15 sororities. **Athletics (Intercollegiate):** *Men:* baseball, basketball, cross-country, football, soccer, swimming, track/field (outdoor), track/field (indoor), wrestling. *Women:* basketball, cross-country, field hockey, lacrosse, soccer, softball, swimming, tennis, track/field (outdoor), track/field (indoor), volleyball. **On-Campus Highlights:** Ceddia Union Building, Heiges Field House, Student Recreation Center, Learning Center, Lehman Library

ADMISSIONS
Freshman Academic Profile: Average high school GPA 3.2. 9% in top 10% of high school class, 25% in top 25% of high school class, 59% in top 50% of high school class. 87% from public high schools. **Test Scores:** SAT Math middle 50% range 480-570. SAT EBRW middle 50% range 480-570. ACT middle 50% range 18-23. Minimum internet-based TOEFL 66. Minimum paper TOEFL 550. **Basis for Candidate Selection:** *Very important factors considered include:* rigor of secondary school record, class rank, academic GPA, standardized test scores. *Other factors considered include:* application essay, recommendation(s), interview, extracurricular activities, talent/ability, character/personal qualities, volunteer work, work experience, level of applicant's interest. **Freshman Admission Requirements:** High school diploma is required and GED is accepted *Academic units recommended:* 4 English, 3 math, 3 science, 3 science labs, 3 foreign language, 3 units from above areas or other academic areas. **Freshman Admission Statistics:** 5,247 applied, 83.6% admitted, 28% enrolled. **Transfer Admission Requirements:** college transcript(s), statement of good standing from prior institution(s). Minimum college GPA of 2.2 required. Lowest grade transferable C. **General Admission Information:** Application fee $45. Nonfall registration accepted. Admission may be deferred for a maximum of 1 year.

COSTS AND FINANCIAL AID
Annual in-state tuition $12,010. Annual out-of-state tuition $16,858. Room and board $12,010. Required fees $3,086. Average book expense $1,200. **Required Forms and Deadlines:** FAFSA. **Types of Aid:** *Need-based scholarships/grants:* College/university scholarship or grant aid from institutional funds; Federal Pell; Private scholarships; SEOG; State scholarships/grants. *Loans:* Direct PLUS loans; Direct Subsidized Stafford Loans; Direct Unsubsidized Stafford Loans. *Student Employment:* Federal Work-Study Program available. Institutional employment available. **Financial Aid Statistics:** 74% needy freshmen, 74% needy undergrads receive need-based scholarship or grant aid. 3% freshmen, 4% undergrads receive non-need-based scholarship or grant aid. 95% freshmen, 94% undergrads receive need-based self-help aid. 6% freshmen, 6% undergrads receive athletic scholarships. 92% freshmen, 88% undergrads receive any aid. 80% undergrads borrow to pay for school. Average cumulative indebtedness $33,673. **Criteria for awarding aid:** *Need-based:* Academics *Non-need-based:* Academics, Athletics.

SHORTER COLLEGE

315 Shorter Avenue, Rome, GA 30165
Phone: 706-233-7319 • **Financial Aid Phone:** 706-233-7227
E-mail: admissions@shorter.edu • **CEEB Code:** 5616
Fax: 706-233-7224 • **Website:** www.shorter.edu • **ACT Code:** 860

This private school, affiliated with the Southern Baptist Church, was founded in 1873. It has a 150 acre campus.

RATINGS
Admissions Selectivity Rating: 79   **Fire Safety Rating:** 86   **Green Rating:** 60*

STUDENTS AND FACULTY

Enrollment: 1,581. **Student Body:** 55% female, 45% male, 12% out-of-state, 3% international (22 countries represented). Asian 1%, African American 17%, Caucasian 69%, Hispanic 4%, Native American <1%, Pacific Islander <1%, Two or more races 1%, Race unknown 4%.
Retention and Graduation: 68% freshmen return for sophomore year. 30% grads go on to further study within 1 year. **Faculty:** Student/faculty ratio 13:1. 92 full-time faculty, 70% hold PhDs, 9% are members of minority groups, 50% are women. 0% of classes are taught by teaching assistants.

ACADEMICS

Degrees: Associate; Bachelor's **Classes:** Most classes have 10-19 students. **Most popular majors:** Education, General; Visual And Performing Arts, General; Business Administration And Management, General. **Special Study Options:** Cross-registration; Double major; Dual enrollment; Honors program; Independent study; Internships; Student-designed major; Study abroad; Teacher certification program; Weekend college. Honors programs: Academy of Aristaeus: a four-year honors program featuring seminar discussions and a research project. **Disability Services offered to physically disabled students:** Note-taking services; Reader services; Tape recorders; Tutors. **Career services:** Career assessment; Career/job search classes; Internships

FACILITIES

Housing: Apartments for single students; Men's dorms; Women's dorms 70% of campus accessible to physically diasbled. **Special Academic Facilities/ Equipment:** Shorter History Museum **Computers:** Students can register for classes online. Administrative functions (other than registration) can be performed online.

CAMPUS LIFE

Environment: Town **Activities:** Campus Ministries; Choral groups; Concert band; Dance; Drama/theater; International Student Organization; Literary magazine; Marching band; Model UN; Music ensembles; Musical theater; Opera; Pep band; Radio station; Student government; Student newspaper; Student-run film society; Yearbook 34 registered organizations, 10 honor societies, 3 religious organizations. 3 fraternities, 3 sororities. **Athletics (Intercollegiate):** *Men:* baseball, basketball, cheerleading, cross-country, football, golf, soccer, tennis, track/field (outdoor). *Women:* basketball, cheerleading, cross-country, golf, lacrosse, soccer, softball, tennis, track/ field (outdoor), volleyball. **On-Campus Highlights:** Fitton Student Union, Winthrop-King Activities Center, Brookes Chapel, Ledbetter Baseball Complex, Ledbetter College of Business

ADMISSIONS

Freshman Academic Profile: Average high school GPA 3.3. 21% in top 10% of high school class, 47% in top 25% of high school class, 77% in top 50% of high school class. 95% from public high schools. **Test Scores:** SAT Math middle 50% range 430-550. SAT EBRW middle 50% range 420-550. ACT middle 50% range 18-24. Minimum paper TOEFL 500. **Basis for Candidate Selection:** *Very important factors considered include:* academic GPA, standardized test scores. *Important factors considered include:* rigor of secondary school record, class rank, application essay, talent/ability. *Other factors considered include:* recommendation(s), interview, extracurricular activities, character/personal qualities, first generation, alumni/ae relation, volunteer work, work experience, level of applicant's interest. **Freshman Admission Requirements:** High school diploma is required and GED is accepted *Academic units required:* 4 English, 4 math, 3 science, 2 foreign language, 3 history. **Freshman Admission Statistics:** 1,944 applied, 65.0% admitted, 32% enrolled. **Transfer Admission Requirements:** college transcript(s), statement of good standing from prior institution(s). Minimum college GPA of 2.0 required. Lowest grade transferable C. **General Admission Information:** Application fee $25. Nonfall registration accepted. Admission may be deferred for a maximum of 2 yearS.

COSTS AND FINANCIAL AID

Annual tuition $17,500. Room and board $8,600. Required fees $370. Average book expense $1,200. **Required Forms and Deadlines:** FAFSA; Institution's own financial aid form; State aid form. **Notification of Awards:** Applicants will be notified of awards on a rolling basis beginning 4/1. **Types of Aid:** *Need-based scholarships/grants:* College/university scholarship or grant aid from institutional funds; Federal Pell; Private scholarships; SEOG; State scholarships/grants. *Loans: Student Employment:* Federal Work-Study Program available. Institutional employment available. **Financial Aid Statistics:** 99% needy freshmen, 99% needy undergrads receive need-based scholarship or grant aid. 16% freshmen, 15% undergrads receive non-need-based scholarship or grant aid. 79% freshmen, 75% undergrads receive need-based self-help aid. 15% freshmen, 11% undergrads receive athletic scholarships. 99% freshmen, 99% undergrads receive any aid. **Criteria for awarding aid:** *Need-based:* Academics, Art, Athletics, Music/drama, Religious affiliation *Non-need-based:* Academics, Art, Athletics, Music/drama, Religious affiliation.

SIENA COLLEGE

515 Loudon Road, Loudonville, NY 12211
Phone: 518-783-2423 • **Financial Aid Phone:** 888-287-4362
E-mail: admissions@siena.edu • **CEEB Code:** 2814
Fax: 518-783-2436 • **Website:** www.siena.edu • **ACT Code:** 2878

This private school, affiliated with the Roman Catholic Church, was founded in 1937. It has a 175.3 acre campus.

RATINGS

Admissions Selectivity Rating: 80   **Fire Safety Rating:** 91   **Green Rating:** 63

STUDENTS AND FACULTY

Enrollment: 3,131. **Student Body:** 53% female, 47% male, 18% out-of-state, 2% international (16 countries represented). Asian 4%, African American 3%, Caucasian 79%, Hispanic 8%, Native American <1%, Pacific Islander <1%, Two or more races 2%, Race unknown 1%.
Retention and Graduation: 88% freshmen return for sophomore year. 74% freshmen graduate within 4 years. 78% freshmen graduate within 6 years. 32% grads go on to further study within 1 year. 14% grads pursue arts and sciences degrees. 2% grads pursue law degrees. 7% grads pursue business degrees. 4% grads pursue medical degrees. **Faculty:** Student/faculty ratio 12:1. 204 full-time faculty, 87% hold PhDs, 9% are members of minority groups, 43% are women. 0% of classes are taught by teaching assistants.

ACADEMICS

Degrees: Bachelor's; Certificate; **Master's Classes:** Most classes have fewer than 10 students. Most lab/discussion sessions have 10-19 students. **Most popular majors:** Biology, General; Psychology, General; Accounting. **Special Study Options:** Cooperative education program; Cross-registration; Double major; Dual enrollment; English as a Second Language (ESL); Honors program; Independent study; Internships; Liberal arts/career combination; Student-designed major; Study abroad; Teacher certification program. Honors programs: College-wide Honors program. Combined degree programs: BA/ DDS; BA/JD; BA/MA; BA/MD; BA/MEng. **Disability Services offered to physically disabled students:** Note-taking services; Reader services; Tape recorders; Tutors. **Career services:** Alumni network; Alumni services; Career assessment; Career/job search classes; Internships; Regional alumni

FACILITIES

Housing: Apartments for single students; Coed dorms; Special housing for disabled student; Special housing for international students 90% of campus accessible to physically diasbled. **Computers:** 20% of classrooms, 40% of dorms, 100% of libraries, 100% of dining areas, 100% of student union, have wireless network access. Students can register for classes online. Administrative functions (other than registration) can be performed online.

CAMPUS LIFE

Environment: Town **Activities:** Campus Ministries; Choral groups; Dance; Drama/theater; International Student Organization; Literary magazine; Model UN; Music ensembles; Musical theater; Opera; Pep band; Radio station; Student government; Student newspaper; Student-run film society; Symphony orchestra; Television station; Yearbook 70 registered organizations, 15 honor societies, 2 religious organizations. **Athletics (Intercollegiate):** *Men:* baseball, basketball, cross-country, golf, lacrosse, soccer, tennis. *Women:* basketball, cross-country, field hockey, golf, lacrosse, soccer, softball, swimming, tennis, volleyball, water polo. **On-Campus Highlights:** Sarazen Student Union, J. Spencer and Patricia Standish Library, MAC/ARC—Athletic Facilities, Siena Hall, Academic Quad

ADMISSIONS

Freshman Academic Profile: Average high school GPA 3.5. 22% in top 10% of high school class, 49% in top 25% of high school class, 85% in top 50% of high school class. 77% from public high schools. **Test Scores:** SAT Math middle 50% range 530-630. SAT EBRW middle 50% range 530-620. ACT middle 50% range 22-27. Minimum internet-based TOEFL 65. Minimum paper TOEFL 550. **Basis for Candidate Selection:** *Very important factors considered include:* rigor of secondary school record, academic GPA. *Important factors considered include:* recommendation(s), interview. *Other factors considered include:* class rank, application essay, standardized test scores, extracurricular activities, talent/ability, character/personal qualities, first generation, alumni/ ae relation, geographical residence, racial/ethnic status, volunteer work, work experience, level of applicant's interest. **Freshman Admission Requirements:** High school diploma is required and GED is accepted *Academic units required:* 4 English, 3 math, 3 science, 3 science labs, 2 foreign language, 3 social studies,

3 history, *Academic units recommended:* 4 English, 4 math, 4 science, 4 science labs, 3 foreign language, 4 social studies, 4 history. **Freshman Admission Statistics:** 7,626 applied, 77.9% admitted, 13% enrolled. **Transfer Admission Requirements:** college transcript(s), statement of good standing from prior institution(s). Minimum college GPA of 2.5 required. Lowest grade transferable C+. **General Admission Information:** Application fee $50. Priority deadline 2/15. Regular application deadline 2/15. Nonfall registration accepted. Admission may be deferred for a maximum of 1 year.

COSTS AND FINANCIAL AID

Annual tuition $36,675. Required fees $300. Average book expense $1,272. **Required Forms and Deadlines:** FAFSA; State aid form. **Notification of Awards:** Applicants will be notified of awards on or about 12/15. **Types of Aid:** *Need-based scholarships/grants:* College/university scholarship or grant aid from institutional funds; Federal Pell; Private scholarships; SEOG; State scholarships/ grants. *Loans:* Direct Subsidized Stafford Loans; Direct Unsubsidized Stafford Loans. *Student Employment:* Federal Work-Study Program available. Institutional employment available. **Financial Aid Statistics:** 100% needy freshmen, 100% needy undergrads receive need-based scholarship or grant aid. 95% freshmen, 93% undergrads receive non-need-based scholarship or grant aid. 77% freshmen, 79% undergrads receive need-based self-help aid. 10% freshmen, 8% undergrads receive athletic scholarships. 98% freshmen, 91% undergrads receive any aid. 77% undergrads borrow to pay for school. Average cumulative indebtedness $35,874. **Criteria for awarding aid:** *Need-based:* Academics, Alumni affiliation, Art, Athletics, Job skills, Leadership, Minority status, Music/drama *Non-need-based:* Academics, Athletics, Leadership, Minority status, State/district residency.

SIENA HEIGHTS UNIVERSITY

1247 E. Siena Heights Drive, Adrian, MI 49221
Phone: 517-264-7180 • **Financial Aid Phone:** 517-264-7110
E-mail: admissions@sienaheights.edu • **CEEB Code:** 2316
Fax: 517-264-7744 • **Website:** www.sienaheights.edu • **ACT Code:** 2052

This private school, affiliated with the Roman Catholic Church, was founded in 1919. It has a 55 acre campus.

RATINGS
Admissions Selectivity Rating: 78   **Fire Safety Rating:** 67   **Green Rating:** 60*

STUDENTS AND FACULTY
Enrollment: 2,307. **Student Body:** 57% female, 43% male, 12% out-of-state, <1% international (6 countries represented). Asian 1%, African American 13%, Caucasian 76%, Hispanic 5%, Native American 1%, Pacific Islander <1%, Two or more races 2%, Race unknown 2%.
Retention and Graduation: 59% freshmen return for sophomore year.
Faculty: 0% of classes are taught by teaching assistants.

ACADEMICS
Degrees: Associate; Bachelor's; Certificate; Master's; Post-Master's certificate **Classes:** Most classes have 10-19 students. Most lab/discussion sessions have 10-19 students. **Most popular majors:** Biology/Biological Sciences, General; Medical Radiologic Technology/Science, Radiation Therapist; Business Administration And Management, General. **Special Study Options:** Cooperative education program; Distance learning; Double major; Dual enrollment; English as a Second Language (ESL); Independent study; Internships; Student-designed major; Study abroad; Teacher certification program. **Disability Services offered to physically disabled students:** Note-taking services; Reader services; Tape recorders; Tutors. **Career services:** Alumni network; Alumni services; Career assessment; Career/job search classes; Internships; Regional alumni

FACILITIES
Housing: Apartments for married students; Coed dorms; Special housing for international students 90% of campus accessible to physically diasbled. **Special Academic Facilities/Equipment:** Klemm Gallery, Francoeur Theater, Stubnitz Lab Theater

CAMPUS LIFE
Environment: Village **Activities:** Campus Ministries; Choral groups; Concert band; Dance; Drama/theater; International Student Organization; Literary magazine; Marching band; Music ensembles; Musical theater; Pep band; Student government; Symphony orchestra. McLaughlin University Center, St. Dominic Chapel, The Mary & Sash Spencer Athletics Complex

ADMISSIONS
Freshman Academic Profile: Average high school GPA 3.2. 8% in top 10% of high school class, 22% in top 25% of high school class, 68% in top 50% of high

school class. **Test Scores:** ACT middle 50% range 19-23. **Basis for Candidate Selection:** *Very important factors considered include:* rigor of secondary school record, academic GPA, standardized test scores. *Important factors considered include:* class rank, application essay. **Freshman Admission Requirements:** High school diploma is required and GED is accepted **Freshman Admission Statistics:** 1,422 applied, 67.7% admitted, 31% enrolled. **General Admission Information:** Application fee $25. Nonfall registration accepted.

COSTS AND FINANCIAL AID
Annual tuition $21,250. Room and board $8,710. Required fees $640. **Types of Aid:** *Need-based scholarships/grants:* College/university scholarship or grant aid from institutional funds; Federal Pell; Private scholarships; SEOG; State scholarships/grants. *Loans:* Direct PLUS loans; Direct Subsidized Stafford Loans; Direct Unsubsidized Stafford Loans. *Student Employment:* Federal Work-Study Program available. **Financial Aid Statistics:** 99% freshmen receive any aid.

SIERRA NEVADA COLLEGE

999 Tahoe Blvd., Incline Village, NV 89451
Phone: 775-831-1314 • **Financial Aid Phone:** 775 8311314 x 7404
E-mail: admissions@sierraneveda.edu • **CEEB Code:** 9192
Fax: 775-831-6223 • **Website:** www.sierraneveda.edu • **ACT Code:** 2497

This private school was founded in 1969. It has a 25 acre campus.

RATINGS
Admissions Selectivity Rating: 72   **Fire Safety Rating:** 96   **Green Rating:** 77

STUDENTS AND FACULTY
Enrollment: 516. **Student Body:** 41% female, 59% male, 84% out-of-state, 7% international (14 countries represented). Asian 1%, African American 1%, Caucasian 72%, Hispanic 1%, Native American 3%, Pacific Islander 1%, Two or more races 0%, Race unknown 15%.
Retention and Graduation: 71% freshmen return for sophomore year.
Faculty: Student/faculty ratio 11:1. 36 full-time faculty, 61% hold PhDs, 14% are members of minority groups, 58% are women. 0% of classes are taught by teaching assistants.

ACADEMICS
Degrees: Bachelor's; Certificate; Diploma; **Master's Classes:** Most classes have 10-19 students. Most lab/discussion sessions have 10-19 students. **Most popular majors:** Multi/Interdisciplinary Studies, Other; Business, Management, Marketing, And Related Support Services, Other. **Special Study Options:** Accelerated program; Distance learning; Double major; English as a Second Language (ESL); Honors program; Independent study; Internships; Student-designed major; Study abroad. Honors programs: The Honors Program is designed to challenge and engage high-achieving students in study and co-curricular activities that foster their scholarship, initiative, and leadership. Combined degree programs: BA/MA. **Disability Services offered to physically disabled students:** Note-taking services; Tutors. **Career services:** Career assessment; Career/job search classes; Internships

FACILITIES
Housing: Coed dorms 99% of campus accessible to physically diasbled. **Special Academic Facilities/Equipment:** McLean Observatory

CAMPUS LIFE
Environment: Village **Activities:** Choral groups; International Student Organization; Literary magazine; Student government; Student newspaper 10 registered organizations, 1 honor society, 2 religious organizations. **Athletics (Intercollegiate):** *Men:* equestrian sports, skiing (downhill/alpine). *Women:* equestrian sports, skiing (downhill/alpine). Tahoe Center for Environmental Sciences, Prim Library, Patterson Dining Hall, Incline Village Recreation Center **Environmental Initiatives:** Sierra Nevada College's four Core Themes; " Sustainability, Professional Preparedness, Entrepreneurship, Liberal Art"

ADMISSIONS
Freshman Academic Profile: Average high school GPA 3.0. 0% in top 10% of high school class, 20% in top 25% of high school class, 50% in top 50% of high school class. 80% from public high schools. **Test Scores:** SAT Math middle 50% range 430-530. SAT EBRW middle 50% range 440-540. ACT middle 50% range 17-25. Minimum internet-based TOEFL 59. Minimum paper TOEFL 500. **Basis for Candidate Selection:** *Important factors considered include:* academic GPA, application essay, recommendation(s). *Other factors considered include:* rigor of secondary school record, class rank, standardized test scores, interview, extracurricular activities, talent/ability, character/personal qualities,

first generation, alumni/ae relation, geographical residence, state residency, religious affiliation/commitment, racial/ethnic status, volunteer work, work experience, level of applicant's interest. **Freshman Admission Requirements:** High school diploma is required and GED is accepted *Academic units recommended:* 4 English, 3 math, 2 science, 2 science labs, 2 social studies. **Freshman Admission Statistics:** 604 applied, 86.8% admitted, 17% enrolled. **Transfer Admission Requirements:** college transcript(s), essay or personal statement, Lowest grade transferable C. **General Admission Information:** Priority deadline 2/15. Regular application deadline 8/28. Nonfall registration accepted. Admission may be deferred for a maximum of 1 year.

COSTS AND FINANCIAL AID

Annual tuition $28,170. Room and board $12,066. Required fees $979. Average book expense $1,600. **Required Forms and Deadlines:** FAFSA. **Types of Aid:** *Need-based scholarships/grants:* College/university scholarship or grant aid from institutional funds; Federal Pell; Private scholarships; SEOG; State scholarships/grants. *Loans:* Direct PLUS loans; Direct Subsidized Stafford Loans; Direct Unsubsidized Stafford Loans. *Student Employment:* Federal Work-Study Program available. Institutional employment available. **Financial Aid Statistics:** 100% needy freshmen, 100% needy undergrads receive need-based scholarship or grant aid. 100% freshmen, 100% undergrads receive non-need-based scholarship or grant aid. 100% freshmen, 100% undergrads receive need-based self-help aid. 0% freshmen, 1% undergrads receive athletic scholarships. 62% freshmen, 65% undergrads receive any aid. **Criteria for awarding aid:** *Non-need-based:* Academics, Alumni affiliation, Athletics, State/district residency.

SIMMONS COLLEGE

300 The Fenway, Boston, MA 02115
Phone: 617-521-2051 • **Financial Aid Phone:** 617-521-2037
E-mail: ugadm@simmons.edu • **CEEB Code:** 3761
Fax: 617-521-3190 • **Website:** www.simmons.edu • **ACT Code:** 1892

This private school was founded in 1899. It has a 12 acre campus.

RATINGS
Admissions Selectivity Rating: 86   **Fire Safety Rating:** 85   **Green Rating:** 63

STUDENTS AND FACULTY
Enrollment: 1,731. **Student Body:** 100% female, 0% male, 40% out-of-state, 5% international (61 countries represented). Asian 10%, African American 6%, Caucasian 65%, Hispanic 6%, Native American <1%, Pacific Islander <1%, Two or more races 5%, Race unknown 2%.
Retention and Graduation: 84% freshmen return for sophomore year. 67% freshmen graduate within 4 years. 73% freshmen graduate within 6 years. 22% grads go on to further study within 1 year. 15% grads pursue arts and sciences degrees. 1% grads pursue law degrees. 2% grads pursue business degrees. 1% grads pursue medical degrees. **Faculty:** Student/faculty ratio 12:1. 245 full-time faculty, 75% hold PhDs, 23% are members of minority groups, 74% are women.

ACADEMICS
Degrees: Bachelor's; Doctoral; Doctoral/Professional; Doctoral/Research; Master's; Post-Master's certificate **Classes:** Most classes have 10-19 students. Most lab/discussion sessions have 10-19 students. **Most popular majors:** Nursing Practice. **Special Study Options:** Accelerated program; Cross-registration; Distance learning; Double major; Exchange student program (domestic); Honors program; Independent study; Internships; Liberal arts/career combination; Student-designed major; Study abroad; Teacher certification program. Honors programs: The Simmons College Honors Program is an interdisciplinary studies program that develops holistic thought leaders for the 21st century through rigorous curricular and experiential programming. The Honors Program engages motivated students, enhancing the undergraduate experience of students in all majors by guiding them through the complex intellectual tasks and problems. All Honors students are advised to seek depth in their major discipline and to enhance this knowledge through exploration of other departments and programs. Students in the Honors Program are part of a "community of scholars" and offered an enriched curriculum that is presented in small seminars and team-taught courses. This community includes professors who are teacher/scholars; bringing their own research and community engagement into the classroom and creating intellectual settings that challenge Honors students to push themselves beyond what they thought possible. Outside the classroom, the Honors Program gives

opportunities for students to expand their knowledge through study abroad opportunities, access to undergraduate research programs, connections to Honors alumnae/i, and engagement with the City of Boston. Combined degree programs: BA/MA. **Disability Services offered to physically disabled students:** Note-taking services; Reader services; Tape recorders; Tutors. **Career services:** Alumni network; Alumni services; Career assessment; Career/job search classes; Internships

FACILITIES
Housing: Special housing for disabled student; Theme housing; Wellness housing; Women's dorms 90% of campus accessible to physically diasbled. **Special Academic Facilities/Equipment:** Trustman Art Gallery, Nursing Simulation Lab, Rowing practice tanks in Sports Center, Comm Lab, Computer Labs **Computers:** 100% of classrooms, 5% of dorms, 100% of libraries, 100% of dining areas, 100% of student union, have wireless network access. Students can register for classes online. Administrative functions (other than registration) can be performed online.

CAMPUS LIFE
Environment: Metropolis **Activities:** Campus Ministries; Choral groups; Concert band; Dance; Drama/theater; International Student Organization; Jazz band; Literary magazine; Model UN; Music ensembles; Musical theater; Radio station; Student government; Student newspaper; Yearbook 91 registered organizations, 4 honor societies, 4 religious organizations. **Athletics (Intercollegiate):** *Women:* basketball, crew/rowing, diving, field hockey, lacrosse, soccer, softball, swimming, tennis, volleyball. **On-Campus Highlights:** Sports Center, Fens Cafe, Common Grounds, Bartol Hall, Lefavour Hall **Environmental Initiatives:** We are committed to maximizing recycling and composting opportunities to minimize landfill waste.

ADMISSIONS
Freshman Academic Profile: Average high school GPA 3.4. 36% in top 10% of high school class, 70% in top 25% of high school class, 94% in top 50% of high school class. 25% from public high schools. **Test Scores:** SAT Math middle 50% range 550-650. SAT EBRW middle 50% range 580-660. ACT middle 50% range 24-29. Minimum internet-based TOEFL 83. Minimum paper TOEFL 83. **Basis for Candidate Selection:** *Very important factors considered include:* academic GPA, standardized test scores. *Important factors considered include:* rigor of secondary school record, class rank, application essay, recommendation(s). *Other factors considered include:* interview, extracurricular activities. **Freshman Admission Requirements:** High school diploma is required and GED is accepted *Academic units required: Academic units recommended:* 4 English, 3 math, 3 science, 3 foreign language, 3 social studies, 3 history. **Freshman Admission Statistics:** 3,483 applied, 60.4% admitted, 19% enrolled. **Transfer Admission Requirements:** High school transcript, college transcript(s), essay or personal statement, statement of good standing from prior institution(s). Minimum college GPA of 2.8 required. Lowest grade transferable C+. **General Admission Information:** Application fee $55. Priority deadline 11/1. Regular application deadline 2/1. Nonfall registration accepted. Admission may be deferred for a maximum of 1 year.

COSTS AND FINANCIAL AID
Annual tuition $39,660. Room and board $15,200. Required fees $1,140. Average book expense $1,280. **Required Forms and Deadlines:** FAFSA; Institution's own financial aid form. **Notification of Awards:** Applicants will be notified of awards on a rolling basis beginning 3/15. **Types of Aid:** *Need-based scholarships/grants:* College/university scholarship or grant aid from institutional funds; Federal Pell; Private scholarships; SEOG; State scholarships/grants. *Loans:* Direct PLUS loans; Direct Subsidized Stafford Loans; Direct Unsubsidized Stafford Loans. *Student Employment:* Federal Work-Study Program available. **Financial Aid Statistics:** 100% needy freshmen, 100% needy undergrads receive need-based scholarship or grant aid. 11% freshmen, 6% undergrads receive non-need-based scholarship or grant aid. 84% freshmen, 89% undergrads receive need-based self-help aid. 0% freshmen, 0% undergrads receive athletic scholarships. 99% freshmen, 91% undergrads receive any aid. **Criteria for awarding aid:** *Non-need-based:* Academics, Alumni affiliation.

SKIDMORE COLLEGE

Best Colleges

815 North Broadway, Saratoga Springs, NY 12866-1632
Phone: 518-580-5570 • **Financial Aid Phone:** 518-580-5750
E-mail: admissions@skidmore.edu • **CEEB Code:** 2815
Fax: 518-580-5584 • **Website:** www.skidmore.edu • **ACT Code:** 2906

This private school was founded in 1903. It has a 890 acre campus.

RATINGS
Admissions Selectivity Rating: 94   **Fire Safety Rating:** 98   **Green Rating:** 94

STUDENTS AND FACULTY
Enrollment: 2,659. **Student Body:** 60% female, 40% male, 66% out-of-state, 11% international (61 countries represented). Asian 5%, African American 5%, Caucasian 63%, Hispanic 9%, Native American 0%, Pacific Islander 0%, Two or more races 4%, Race unknown 3%.
Retention and Graduation: 93% freshmen return for sophomore year. 84% freshmen graduate within 4 years. 87% freshmen graduate within 6 years. 16% grads go on to further study within 1 year. **Faculty:** Student/faculty ratio 8:1. 277 full-time faculty, 87% hold PhDs, 20% are members of minority groups, 53% are women. 0% of classes are taught by teaching assistants.

ACADEMICS
Degrees: Bachelor's **Classes:** Most classes have 10-19 students. Most lab/discussion sessions have 10-19 students. **Most popular majors:** Psychology, General; Social Sciences, Other; Business/Commerce, General. **Special Study Options:** Accelerated program; Cross-registration; Distance learning; Double major; Dual enrollment; Exchange student program (domestic); Honors program; Independent study; Internships; Liberal arts/career combination; Student-designed major; Study abroad; Teacher certification program. Honors programs: Honors Forum. **Disability Services offered to physically disabled students:** Note-taking services; Reader services; Tape recorders; Tutors. **Career services:** Alumni network; Alumni services; Career assessment; Career/job search classes; Internships; Regional alumni

FACILITIES
Housing: Apartments for single students; Coed dorms; Special housing for disabled students 75% of campus accessible to physically disabled. **Special Academic Facilities/Equipment:** Arthur Zankel Music Center Electronic Music Lab Frances Young Tang Museum and Art Gallery DocLab (audiovisual media and documentary storytelling tools) GIS Center for Interdisciplinary Research Lab Skidmore Community Garden Human-Performance Lab First Responder Health and Safety Lab Gene Expression Lab Microscopy Imaging Center Early Childhood Center (lab school affiliated with Education Department) Van Lennep Riding Center **Computers:** Students can register for classes online. Administrative functions (other than registration) can be performed online.

CAMPUS LIFE
Environment: Town **Activities:** Campus Ministries; Choral groups; Concert band; Dance; Drama/theater; International Student Organization; Jazz band; Literary magazine; Model UN; Music ensembles; Musical theater; Opera; Radio station; Student government; Student newspaper; Student-run film society; Symphony orchestra; Television station 80 registered organizations, 10 honor societies, 3 religious organizations. **Athletics (Intercollegiate):** *Men:* baseball, basketball, crew/rowing, diving, golf, ice hockey, lacrosse, soccer, swimming, tennis. *Women:* basketball, crew/rowing, diving, equestrian sports, field hockey, lacrosse, soccer, softball, swimming, tennis, volleyball.
On-Campus Highlights: Williamson Sports Center, Lucy Scribner Library, Case Student Center, Northwoods Village Apartments, Murray-Aikins Dining Hall **Environmental Initiatives:** Renewable energy projects: Skidmore has completed multiple small-scale and large-scale renewable energy projects. In 2014, the College completed the construction of a 2-megawatt solar array that provides about 12% of the College's electricity needs. In 2015, the College entered an agreement at a historical small-hydro facility. The facility was originally built in the early 1800's on an existing fault line, and was falling into disrepair before the agreement. We anticipate the facility will provide about 18% of the College's electricity needs once restoration work is complete. Skidmore is a leader in geothermal heating and cooling energy among higher education institutions. Currently, 40% of campus is heated and cooled using geothermal energy. An additional geothermal field is being installed in 2016, and this new system will increase this total to over 50% of campus. The College

has installed five solar thermal hot water arrays, and a sixth system will be installed in 2016. Our 2013 greenhouse gas (GHG) inventory shows a 48% decrease in scope one and scope two GHG emissions from 2000 levels. This inventory was completed before our most recent solar and small-hydro projects, and we anticipate significant reductions in our GHG emissions from these projects.

ADMISSIONS
Freshman Academic Profile: 29% in top 10% of high school class, 73% in top 25% of high school class, 92% in top 50% of high school class. 57% from public high schools. **Test Scores:** SAT Math middle 50% range 595-700. SAT EBRW middle 50% range 610-700. ACT middle 50% range 27-31. Minimum internet-based TOEFL 96-97. Minimum paper TOEFL 590. **Basis for Candidate Selection:** *Very important factors considered include:* rigor of secondary school record. *Important factors considered include:* class rank, academic GPA, application essay, recommendation(s), extracurricular activities, talent/ability, character/personal qualities, volunteer work, work experience, level of applicant's interest. *Other factors considered include:* standardized test scores, interview, first generation, alumni/ae relation, geographical residence, racial/ethnic status. **Freshman Admission Requirements:** High school diploma is required and GED is accepted *Academic units recommended:* 4 English, 4 math, 4 science, 3 science labs, 4 foreign language, 4 social studies. **Freshman Admission Statistics:** 10,053 applied, 24.5% admitted, 27% enrolled. **Transfer Admission Requirements:** High school transcript, college transcript(s), essay or personal statement, standardized test scores, statement of good standing from prior institution(s). Minimum college GPA of 2.7 required. Lowest grade transferable C. **General Admission Information:** Application fee $65. Regular application deadline 1/15. Nonfall registration accepted. Admission may be deferred for a maximum of 2 years.

COSTS AND FINANCIAL AID
Required Forms and Deadlines: CSS/Financial Aid PROFILE; Noncustodial PROFILE. **Notification of Awards:** Applicants will be notified of awards on or about 4/1. **Types of Aid:** *Need-based scholarships/grants:* College/university scholarship or grant aid from institutional funds; Federal Pell; Private scholarships; SEOG; State scholarships/grants. *Loans:* Direct PLUS loans; Direct Subsidized Stafford Loans; Direct Unsubsidized Stafford Loans. *Student Employment:* Federal Work-Study Program available. Institutional employment available. **Financial Aid Statistics:** 100% needy freshmen, 100% needy undergrads receive need-based scholarship or grant aid. 6% freshmen, 8% undergrads receive non-need-based scholarship or grant aid. 67% freshmen, 73% undergrads receive need-based self-help aid. 0% freshmen, 0% undergrads receive athletic scholarships. 49% freshmen, 51% undergrads receive any aid. 39% undergrads borrow to pay for school. Average cumulative indebtedness $25,001. **Criteria for awarding aid:** *Need-based:* Academics, Leadership *Non-need-based:* Music/drama.

See page 1032.

SLIPPERY ROCK UNIVERSITY OF PENNSYLVANIA

1 Morrow Way, Slippery Rock, PA 16057
Phone: 724-738-2015 • **Financial Aid Phone:** 724-738-2220
E-mail: asktherock@sru.edu • **CEEB Code:** 2658
Fax: 724-738-2913 • **Website:** http://www.sru.edu • **ACT Code:** 3716

This public school was founded in 1889. It has a 660 acre campus.

RATINGS
Admissions Selectivity Rating: 81   **Fire Safety Rating:** 98   **Green Rating:** 93

STUDENTS AND FACULTY
Enrollment: 7,567. **Student Body:** 57% female, 43% male, 10% out-of-state, 1% international (33 countries represented). Asian 1%, African American 5%, Caucasian 86%, Hispanic 2%, Native American <1%, Pacific Islander <1%, Two or more races 4%, Race unknown 1%.
Retention and Graduation: 81% freshmen return for sophomore year. 52% freshmen graduate within 4 years. 68% freshmen graduate within 6 years. 21% grads go on to further study within 1 year. **Faculty:** Student/faculty ratio 21:1. 349 full-time faculty, 88% hold PhDs, 18% are members of minority groups, 52% are women. 0% of classes are taught by teaching assistants.

ACADEMICS
Degrees: Bachelor's; Certificate; Doctoral/Professional; Doctoral/Research; Master's; Post-Bachelor's certificate **Classes:** Most classes have 20-29 students. Most lab/discussion sessions have fewer than 10 students. **Most popular**

majors: Special Education And Teaching, General; Occupational Safety And Health Technology/Technician; Health And Wellness, General. **Special Study Options:** Distance learning; Double major; Dual enrollment; English as a Second Language (ESL); Exchange student program (domestic); Honors program; Independent study; Internships; Liberal arts/career combination; Student-designed major; Study abroad; Teacher certification program. Honors programs: Undergraduate Honors Program. **Disability Services offered to physically disabled students:** Note-taking services; Reader services; Tape recorders; Tutors. **Career services:** Alumni services; Career assessment; Internships; Regional alumni

FACILITIES

Housing: Apartments for single students; Coed dorms; Special housing for disabled students 90% of campus accessible to physically diasbled. **Special Academic Facilities/Equipment:** Environmental education centers, planetarium, herbarium, artificial intelligence & robotics lab, 3-D printer, math emporium, SCALE-UP collaborative classroom, psychophysiology teaching system, sustainable enterprise accelerator, equestrian center, crime scene investigation room, counselor training & observation equipment, historic inn and museum of rural life, one-room schoolhouse museum. Residence halls offer Living Learning Communities (LLCs) with access to special facilities and equipment, formal and informal interaction with professors, opportunities for professional networking, and social & cultural activities. **Computers:** 80% of classrooms, 100% of dorms, 100% of libraries, 50% of dining areas, 100% of student union, 5% of common outdoor areas have wireless network access. Students can register for classes online. Administrative functions (other than registration) can be performed online.

CAMPUS LIFE

Environment: Rural **Activities:** Campus Ministries; Choral groups; Concert band; Dance; Drama/theater; International Student Organization; Jazz band; Literary magazine; Marching band; Model UN; Music ensembles; Musical theater; Radio station; Student government; Student newspaper; Student-run film society; Symphony orchestra; Television station 145 registered organizations, 37 honor societies, 4 religious organizations. 9 fraternities, 8 sororities. **Athletics (Intercollegiate):** *Men:* baseball, basketball, cheerleading, cross-country, football, soccer, track/field (outdoor), track/field (indoor). *Women:* basketball, cheerleading, cross-country, field hockey, lacrosse, soccer, softball, tennis, track/field (outdoor), track/field (indoor), volleyball. **On-Campus Highlights:** Aebersold Recreation Center, Residential Suite Complex and Living/Learning Communities, Robert M. Smith Student Center, Bailey Library, Advanced Science and Technology Building

ADMISSIONS

Freshman Academic Profile: Average high school GPA 3.4. 13% in top 10% of high school class, 36% in top 25% of high school class, 72% in top 50% of high school class. 95% from public high schools. **Test Scores:** SAT Math middle 50% range 500-580. SAT EBRW middle 50% range 500-580. ACT middle 50% range 19-24. Minimum internet-based TOEFL 61. Minimum paper TOEFL 500. **Basis for Candidate Selection:** *Important factors considered include:* rigor of secondary school record, class rank, academic GPA, standardized test scores. *Other factors considered include:* application essay, recommendation(s), talent/ability. **Freshman Admission Requirements:** High school diploma is required and GED is accepted *Academic units recommended:* 4 English, 3 math, 3 science, 1 science labs, 2 foreign language, 3 social studies, 3 history. **Freshman Admission Statistics:** 5,836 applied, 71.5% admitted, 38% enrolled. **Transfer Admission Requirements:** college transcript(s), Minimum college GPA of 2.0 required. Lowest grade transferable C. **General Admission Information:** Application fee $30. Nonfall registration accepted. Admission may be deferred for a maximum of 1 year.

COSTS AND FINANCIAL AID

Annual in-state tuition $10,312. Annual out-of-state tuition $11,238. Room and board $10,312. Required fees $2,713. Average book expense $1,550. **Required Forms and Deadlines:** FAFSA. **Notification of Awards:** Applicants will be notified of awards on a rolling basis beginning 12/16. **Types of Aid:** *Need-based scholarships/grants:* College/university scholarship or grant aid from institutional funds; Federal Pell; Private scholarships; SEOG; State scholarships/grants. *Loans:* Direct PLUS loans; Direct Subsidized Stafford Loans; Direct Unsubsidized Stafford Loans. *Student Employment:* Federal Work-Study Program available. Institutional employment available. **Financial Aid Statistics:** 60% needy freshmen, 65% needy undergrads receive need-based scholarship or grant aid. 50% freshmen, 28% undergrads receive non-need-based scholarship or grant aid. 90% undergrads receive need-based self-help aid. 4% freshmen, 3% undergrads receive athletic scholarships. 93% freshmen, 94% undergrads receive any aid. 87% undergrads borrow to pay for school. Average cumulative indebtedness $33,303. **Criteria for awarding aid:** *Need-based:* Academics, Minority status *Non-need-based:* Academics, Alumni affiliation, Art, Athletics, Job skills, Leadership, Minority status, Music/drama, State/district residency.

SMITH COLLEGE

Elm St., Northampton, MA 01063
Phone: 413-585-2500 • **Financial Aid Phone:** 413-585-2530
E-mail: admission@smith.edu • **CEEB Code:** 3762
Fax: 413-585-2527 • **Website:** www.smith.edu • **ACT Code:** 1894

This private school was founded in 1871. It has a 147 acre campus.

RATINGS
Admissions Selectivity Rating: 97   **Fire Safety Rating:** 84   **Green Rating:** 97

STUDENTS AND FACULTY
Enrollment: 2,519. **Student Body:** 100% female, 0% male, 79% out-of-state, 14% international (59 countries represented). Asian 11%, African American 7%, Caucasian 48%, Hispanic 10%, Native American <1%, Pacific Islander <1%, Two or more races 4%, Race unknown 6%.
Retention and Graduation: 93% freshmen return for sophomore year. 82% freshmen graduate within 4 years. 88% freshmen graduate within 6 years.
Faculty: 0% of classes are taught by teaching assistants.

ACADEMICS
Degrees: Bachelor's; Doctoral/Research; Master's; Post-Bachelor's certificate; Post-Master's certificate **Most popular majors:** Psychology, General; Economics, General; Political Science And Government, General. **Special Study Options:** Accelerated program; Cross-registration; Double major; Exchange student program (domestic); Honors program; Independent study; Internships; Student-designed major; Study abroad; Teacher certification program. **Disability Services offered to physically disabled students:** Note-taking services; Reader services; Tape recorders; Tutors. **Career services:** Alumni network; Alumni services; Career assessment; Career/job search classes; Internships; Regional alumni

FACILITIES
Housing: Cooperative housing; Wellness housing; Women's dorms 85% of campus accessible to physically diasbled. **Special Academic Facilities/Equipment:** Art museum, printing, darkroom, and sculpture facilities, dance, electronic music, television, and theatre studios, recital hall, rehearsal rooms, multimedia language lab, early childhood/elementary education campus school, two electronic classrooms, physiology and horticultural labs, animal care facilities, two electron microscopes, greenhouses, observatories. **Computers:** 85% of classrooms, 100% of dorms, 100% of libraries, 100% of dining areas, 100% of student union, 50% of common outdoor areas have wireless network access. Students can register for classes online. Administrative functions (other than registration) can be performed online.

CAMPUS LIFE
Environment: Town **Activities:** Campus Ministries; Choral groups; Concert band; Dance; Drama/theater; International Student Organization; Jazz band; Literary magazine; Model UN; Music ensembles; Musical theater; Radio station; Student government; Student newspaper; Television station; Yearbook 133 registered organizations, 3 honor societies, 9 religious organizations. **Athletics (Intercollegiate):** *Women:* basketball, crew/rowing, cross-country, diving, equestrian sports, field hockey, lacrosse, skiing (downhill/alpine), soccer, softball, squash, swimming, tennis, track/field (outdoor), track/field (indoor), volleyball. **On-Campus Highlights:** Smith Art Museum, The Botanical Gardens, Campus Center, Mendenhall Center for Performing Arts, Ford Hall (Engineering, science) **Environmental Initiatives:** A new natural gas fired cogeneration facility went online in October 2008, which generates most campus electric use and schieves 80% efficiency with new absorption chillers.

ADMISSIONS
Freshman Academic Profile: Average high school GPA 3.8. 72% in top 10% of high school class, 96% in top 25% of high school class, 100% in top 50% of high school class. 62% from public high schools. **Test Scores:** SAT Math middle 50% range 640-750. SAT EBRW middle 50% range 650-740. ACT middle 50% range 30-33. Minimum internet-based TOEFL 90. Minimum paper TOEFL 600. **Basis for Candidate Selection:** *Very important factors considered include:* rigor of secondary school record, academic GPA, application essay, recommendation(s), character/personal qualities. *Important factors considered include:* class rank, interview, extracurricular activities, talent/ability. *Other factors considered include:* standardized test scores, first generation, alumni/ae relation, racial/ethnic status, volunteer work, work experience. **Freshman Admission Requirements:** High school diploma or equivalent is not required *Academic units recommended:* 4 English, 3 math, 3 science, 3 science labs, 3 foreign language, 2 history, 1 academic elective. **Freshman Admission**

Statistics: 5,432 applied, 31.9% admitted, 37% enrolled. **Transfer Admission Requirements:** High school transcript, college transcript(s), essay or personal statement, statement of good standing from prior institution(s). Lowest grade transferable C. **General Admission Information:** Regular application deadline 1/15. Nonfall registration accepted. Admission may be deferred for a maximum of 1 year.

COSTS AND FINANCIAL AID

Annual tuition $49,760. Room and board $16,730. Required fees $284. Average book expense $800. **Required Forms and Deadlines:** CSS/Financial Aid PROFILE; FAFSA; Institution's own financial aid form; Noncustodial PROFILE. **Notification of Awards:** Applicants will be notified of awards on or about 4/1. **Types of Aid:** *Need-based scholarships/grants:* College/university scholarship or grant aid from institutional funds; Federal Pell; Private scholarships; SEOG; State scholarships/grants. *Loans:* Direct PLUS loans; Direct Subsidized Stafford Loans; Direct Unsubsidized Stafford Loans. *Student Employment:* Federal Work-Study Program available. Institutional employment available. **Financial Aid Statistics:** 97% needy freshmen, 98% needy undergrads receive need-based scholarship or grant aid. 2% freshmen, 1% undergrads receive non-need-based scholarship or grant aid. 94% freshmen, 94% undergrads receive need-based self-help aid. 0% freshmen, 0% undergrads receive athletic scholarships. 70% freshmen, 71% undergrads receive any aid. 62% undergrads borrow to pay for school. Average cumulative indebtedness $23,857. **Criteria for awarding aid:** *Non-need-based:* Academics, State/district residency.

SOKA UNIVERSITY OF AMERICA

1 University Drive, Aliso Viejo, CA 92656-8081
Phone: (949) 480-4150 • **Financial Aid Phone:** 949-480-4112
E-mail: admission@soka.edu • **CEEB Code:** 4066
Fax: (949) 480-4151 • **Website:** www.soka.edu • **ACT Code:** 467

This private school was founded in 1987. It has a 103 acre campus.

RATINGS

Admissions Selectivity Rating: 94   **Fire Safety Rating:** 96   **Green Rating:** 75

STUDENTS AND FACULTY

Enrollment: 411. **Student Body:** 62% female, 38% male, 46% out-of-state, 43% international (34 countries represented). Asian 13%, African American 4%, Caucasian 20%, Hispanic 10%, Native American 0%, Pacific Islander <1%, Two or more races 7%, Race unknown 2%.
Retention and Graduation: 94% freshmen return for sophomore year. 87% freshmen graduate within 4 years. 94% freshmen graduate within 6 years. 16% grads go on to further study within 1 year. 71% grads pursue arts and sciences degrees. 0% grads pursue law degrees. 0% grads pursue business degrees. 0% grads pursue medical degrees. **Faculty:** Student/faculty ratio 8:1. 44 full-time faculty, 98% hold PhDs, 43% are members of minority groups, 39% are women. 0% of classes are taught by teaching assistants.

ACADEMICS

Degrees: Bachelor's; Master's **Most popular majors:** Liberal Arts And Sciences/Liberal Studies. **Special Study Options:** Independent study; Internships; Study abroad. **Disability Services offered to physically disabled students:** Note-taking services; Reader services; Tape recorders; Tutors. **Career services:** Alumni network; Alumni services; Career assessment; Career/job search classes; Internships

FACILITIES

Housing: Coed dorms; Special housing for disabled student; Special housing for international students; Theme housing; Wellness housing 100% of campus accessible to physically diasbled. **Special Academic Facilities/Equipment:** Performing Arts Center, Black Box Theater, Art Gallery, Conference Center, Library, Information Technology Center **Computers:** Students can register for classes online. Administrative functions (other than registration) can be performed online. Undergraduates are required to own a computer.

CAMPUS LIFE

Environment: Town **Activities:** Choral groups; Concert band; Dance; Drama/theater; International Student Organization; Jazz band; Literary magazine; Model UN; Music ensembles; Musical theater; Student government; Student newspaper; Symphony orchestra 38 registered organizations, 1 religious organization. **Athletics (Intercollegiate):** *Men:* cross-country, diving, soccer, swimming, track/field (outdoor). *Women:* cross-country, diving, soccer, swimming, track/field (outdoor). **On-Campus Highlights:** Founders Hall Art Gallery, Student Center Dining Hall, Performing Arts Center, Recreation Center, Ikeda Library

ADMISSIONS

Freshman Academic Profile: Average high school GPA 4.0. 50% in top 10% of high school class, 90% in top 25% of high school class, 100% in top 50% of high school class. 97% from public high schools. **Test Scores:** SAT Math middle 50% range 610-720. SAT EBRW middle 50% range 590-670. ACT middle 50% range 27-31. **Basis for Candidate Selection:** *Very important factors considered include:* rigor of secondary school record, academic GPA, application essay, standardized test scores, recommendation(s), extracurricular activities, character/personal qualities. *Important factors considered include:* talent/ability, volunteer work.level of applicant's interest. *Other factors considered include:* class rank, interview, first generation, geographical residence, state residency, work experience. **Freshman Admission Requirements:** High school diploma is required and GED is accepted *Academic units recommended:* 4 English, 3 math, 2 science, 2 science labs, 2 foreign language, 1 social studies, 2 history. **Freshman Admission Statistics:** 489 applied, 37.2% admitted, 59% enrolled. **General Admission Information:** Application fee $45. Priority deadline 11/1. Regular application deadline 1/15. Nonfall registration accepted. Admission may be deferred for a maximum of 1 year.

COSTS AND FINANCIAL AID

Annual tuition $31,310. Room and board $12,530. Required fees $1,670. Average book expense $1,916. **Required Forms and Deadlines:** FAFSA; Institution's own financial aid form; State aid form. **Notification of Awards:** Applicants will be notified of awards on or about 3/15. **Types of Aid:** *Need-based scholarships/grants:* College/university scholarship or grant aid from institutional funds; Federal Pell; Private scholarships; SEOG; State scholarships/grants. *Loans:* Direct PLUS loans; Direct Subsidized Stafford Loans; Direct Unsubsidized Stafford Loans. *Student Employment:* Federal Work-Study Program available. Institutional employment available. **Financial Aid Statistics:** 100% needy freshmen, 100% needy undergrads receive need-based scholarship or grant aid. 100% freshmen, 100% undergrads receive non-need-based scholarship or grant aid. 53% freshmen, 49% undergrads receive need-based self-help aid. 3% freshmen, 3% undergrads receive athletic scholarships. 100% freshmen, 100% undergrads receive any aid. 57% undergrads borrow to pay for school. Average cumulative indebtedness $22,409. **Criteria for awarding aid:** *Need-based:* Academics *Non-need-based:* Academics, Athletics, Leadership, Minority status.

SONOMA STATE UNIVERSITY

Best Colleges

1801 East Cotati Avenue, Rohnert Park, CA 94928
Phone: 707-664-2778 • **Financial Aid Phone:** (707)664-2389
E-mail: student.outreach@sonoma.edu • **CEEB Code:** 4723
Fax: 707-664-2060 • **Website:** www.sonoma.edu • **ACT Code:** 431

This public school was founded in 1960. It has a 269 acre campus.

RATINGS

Admissions Selectivity Rating: 75   **Fire Safety Rating:** 92   **Green Rating:** 73

STUDENTS AND FACULTY

Enrollment: 8,517. **Student Body:** 62% female, 38% male, 2% international. Asian 5%, African American 2%, Caucasian 44%, Hispanic 33%, Native American <1%, Pacific Islander <1%, Two or more races 7%, Race unknown 6%.
Retention and Graduation: 77% freshmen return for sophomore year. 29% freshmen graduate within 4 years. 58% freshmen graduate within 6 years. **Faculty:** Student/faculty ratio 23:1. 250 full-time faculty, 99% hold PhDs, 20% are members of minority groups, 50% are women. 1% of classes are taught by teaching assistants.

ACADEMICS

Degrees: Bachelor's; **Master's Classes:** Most classes have 10-19 students. **Most popular majors:** Liberal Arts And Sciences, General Studies And Humanities, Other; Business/Commerce, General. **Special Study Options:** Accelerated program; Cross-registration; Distance learning; Double major; Dual enrollment; English as a Second Language (ESL); Exchange student program (domestic); External degree program; Honors program; Independent study; Internships; Liberal arts/career combination; Student-designed major; Study abroad; Teacher certification program. Combined degree programs: BA/MA. **Disability Services offered to physically disabled students:** Note-taking services; Reader services; Tape recorders; Tutors. **Career services:** Career/job search classes; Internships

FACILITIES

Housing: Apartments for single students; Coed dorms; Other (please specify) 99% of campus accessible to physically disabled. **Special Academic Facilities/ Equipment:** Performing arts center, observatory, electron microscope, seismograph, information technology center, environmental technology center, high technology high school,nature preserve **Computers:** 95% of classrooms, 90% of dorms, 100% of libraries, 85% of dining areas, 100% of student union, 20% of common outdoor areas have wireless network access. Students can register for classes online. Administrative functions (other than registration) can be performed online. Undergraduates are required to own a computer.

CAMPUS LIFE

Environment: Town **Activities:** Choral groups; Dance; Drama/theater; Jazz band; Literary magazine; Music ensembles; Musical theater; Opera; Pep band; Radio station; Student government; Student newspaper; Symphony orchestra 109 registered organizations, 2 honor societies, 4 religious organizations. 5 fraternities, 9 sororities. **Athletics (Intercollegiate):** *Men:* baseball, basketball, soccer, tennis. *Women:* basketball, cross-country, soccer, softball, tennis, track/ field (outdoor), volleyball. **On-Campus Highlights:** Schultz Information Center, Environmental Technology Center, Charlie Brown's (coffee shop), Observatory, University Recreation Center **Environmental Initiatives:** Energy efficiency

ADMISSIONS

Freshman Academic Profile: Average high school GPA 3.3. **Test Scores:** SAT Math middle 50% range 480-580. SAT EBRW middle 50% range 500-590. ACT middle 50% range 19-24. Minimum internet-based TOEFL 61. Minimum paper TOEFL 500. **Basis for Candidate Selection:** *Very important factors considered include:* academic GPA, standardized test scores. *Other factors considered include:* geographical residence. **Freshman Admission Requirements:** High school diploma is required and GED is accepted *Academic units required:* 4 English, 3 math, 2 science, 1 science labs, 2 foreign language, 2 history, 1 academic elective, 1 visual/performing arts, and 1 unit from above areas or other academic areas. **Freshman Admission Statistics:** 15,711 applied, 82.0% admitted, 14% enrolled. **Transfer Admission Requirements:** college transcript(s), Minimum college GPA of 2.0 required. Lowest grade transferable D. **General Admission Information:** Application fee $55. Priority deadline 3/1. Regular application deadline 11/30. Nonfall registration accepted.

COSTS AND FINANCIAL AID

Annual in-state tuition $13,554. Annual out-of-state tuition $17,622. Room and board $13,554. Required fees $1,982. Average book expense $1,854. **Required Forms and Deadlines:** FAFSA; State aid form. **Notification of Awards:** Applicants will be notified of awards on a rolling basis beginning 3/25. **Types of Aid:** *Need-based scholarships/grants:* College/university scholarship or grant aid from institutional funds; Federal Pell; Private scholarships; SEOG; State scholarships/grants. *Loans:* Direct PLUS loans; Direct Subsidized Stafford Loans; Direct Unsubsidized Stafford Loans. *Student Employment:* Federal Work-Study Program available. Institutional employment available. **Financial Aid Statistics:** 68% needy freshmen, 65% needy undergrads receive need-based scholarship or grant aid. 41% freshmen, 35% undergrads receive non-need-based scholarship or grant aid. 70% freshmen, 62% undergrads receive need-based self-help aid. 0% freshmen, 0% undergrads receive athletic scholarships. 59% freshmen, 51% undergrads receive any aid. **Criteria for awarding aid:** *Need-based:* Academics, Minority status *Non-need-based:* Academics, Alumni affiliation, Art, Athletics, Leadership, Minority status, Music/drama.

SOUTH DAKOTA SCHOOL
OF MINES & TECHNOLOGY

---

501 East St. Joseph Street, Rapid City, SD 57701-3995
Phone: 605-394-2414 • **Financial Aid Phone:** 605-394-2274
E-mail: admissions@sdsmt.edu • **CEEB Code:** 3470
Fax: 605-394-1979 • **Website:** www.sdsmt.edu • **ACT Code:** 3922

This public school was founded in 1885. It has a 120 acre campus.

RATINGS

Admissions Selectivity Rating: 80   **Fire Safety Rating:** 95   **Green Rating:** 76

STUDENTS AND FACULTY

Enrollment: 2,353. **Student Body:** 20% female, 80% male, 53% out-of-state, 3% international (25 countries represented). Asian 1%, African American 2%, Caucasian 84%, Hispanic 5%, Native American 2%, Pacific Islander <1%, Two

or more races 3%, Race unknown 1%.

Retention and Graduation: 78% freshmen return for sophomore year. 21% grads go on to further study within 1 year. 3% grads pursue arts and sciences degrees. 1% grads pursue law degrees. 1% grads pursue business degrees. 2% grads pursue medical degrees. **Faculty:** Student/faculty ratio 15:1. 151 full-time faculty, 85% hold PhDs, 15% are members of minority groups, 26% are women.

ACADEMICS

Degrees: Associate; Bachelor's; Certificate; Doctoral/Research; Master's; Post-Bachelor's certificate **Classes:** Most classes have 10-19 students. Most lab/discussion sessions have 10-19 students. **Most popular majors:** Chemical Engineering; Civil Engineering, General; Mechanical Engineering. **Special Study Options:** Cooperative education program; Cross-registration; Distance learning; Double major; Dual enrollment; English as a Second Language (ESL); Independent study; Internships; Study abroad. **Disability Services offered to physically disabled students:** Note-taking services; Reader services; Tape recorders; Tutors. **Career services:** Alumni network; Alumni services; Career assessment; Career/job search classes; Internships; Regional alumni

FACILITIES

Housing: Apartments for married students; Apartments for single students; Coed dorms; Fraternity/sorority housing; Special housing for disabled student; Wellness housing 81% of campus accessible to physically disabled. **Special Academic Facilities/Equipment:** Museum of geology and paleontology, electron microscope, engineering/mining experiment station, supersonic wind tunnel,3-D visualization lab, polymer processing lab, friction stir welding lab, high-frequency microwave lab, tech development lab, fluid computational dynamics lab, robotics lab, clean manufacturing lab, institute atmospheric science, paleontology research center and other research institutes. **Computers:** 100% of classrooms, 100% of dorms, 100% of libraries, 100% of dining areas, 100% of student union, 100% of common outdoor areas have wireless network access. Students can register for classes online. Administrative functions (other than registration) can be performed online.

CAMPUS LIFE

Environment: Town **Activities:** Campus Ministries; Choral groups; Concert band; Dance; Drama/theater; International Student Organization; Jazz band; Music ensembles; Pep band; Radio station; Student government; Student newspaper 67 registered organizations, 6 honor societies, 9 religious organizations. 4 fraternities, 2 sororities. **Athletics (Intercollegiate):** *Men:* basketball, cross-country, football, golf, track/field (outdoor), track/field (indoor). *Women:* basketball, cross-country, golf, track/field (outdoor), track/field (indoor), volleyball. **On-Campus Highlights:** Surbeck Student Center, King (Sports) Center, CAMP, Geology Museum, O'Harra Stadium (Dunham Field) **Environmental Initiatives:** A minimun of LEED Silver is required on all new construction or renovation

ADMISSIONS

Freshman Academic Profile: Average high school GPA 3.6. 24% in top 10% of high school class, 56% in top 25% of high school class, 86% in top 50% of high school class. **Test Scores:** SAT Math middle 50% range 550-660. SAT EBRW middle 50% range 490-630. ACT middle 50% range 24-29. Minimum internet-based TOEFL 68. Minimum paper TOEFL 520. **Basis for Candidate Selection:** *Very important factors considered include:* rigor of secondary school record, class rank, academic GPA, standardized test scores. *Other factors considered include:* extracurricular activities, talent/ability, character/personal qualities, volunteer work, work experience. **Freshman Admission Requirements:** High school diploma is required and GED is accepted *Academic units required:* 4 English, 4 math, 4 science, 3 science labs, 2 foreign language, 3 social studies, 0.5 computer science, 1 visual/performing arts, *Academic units recommended:* 4 English, 4 math, 4 science, 3 science labs, 2 foreign language, 3 social studies, 0.5 computer science, 1 visual/performing arts. **Freshman Admission Statistics:** 1,368 applied, 84.5% admitted, 43% enrolled. **Transfer Admission Requirements:** college transcript(s), statement of good standing from prior institution(s). Minimum college GPA of 2.0 required. Lowest grade transferable D. **General Admission Information:** Application fee $20. Nonfall registration accepted. Admission may be deferred for a maximum of 1 semester.

COSTS AND FINANCIAL AID

Annual in-state tuition $7,720. Annual out-of-state tuition $11,500. Room and board $7,720. Required fees $3,820. Average book expense $2,000. **Required Forms and Deadlines:** FAFSA. **Notification of Awards:** Applicants will be notified of awards on a rolling basis beginning 4/15. **Types of Aid:** *Need-based scholarships/grants:* College/university scholarship or grant aid from institutional funds; Federal Pell; Private scholarships; SEOG; State scholarships/ grants. *Loans:* Direct PLUS loans; Direct Subsidized Stafford Loans; Direct Unsubsidized Stafford Loans. *Student Employment:* Federal Work-Study Program available. Institutional employment available. **Financial Aid Statistics:** 77% needy freshmen, 65% needy undergrads receive need-based scholarship or grant aid. 60% freshmen, 38% undergrads receive non-need-based scholarship or grant aid. 79% freshmen, 84% undergrads receive need-based self-help aid. 4% freshmen, 4% undergrads receive athletic scholarships.

90% freshmen, 79% undergrads receive any aid. **Criteria for awarding aid:** *Non-need-based:* Academics, Athletics, Leadership, Minority status.

SOUTH DAKOTA STATE UNIVERSITY

1015 Campanile Ave., Brookings, SD 57007
Phone: 605-688-4121 • **Financial Aid Phone:** 605-688-4695
E-mail: sdsu.admissions@sdstate.edu • **CEEB Code:** 6653
Fax: 605-688-6891 • **Website:** www.sdstate.edu • **ACT Code:** 3924

This public school was founded in 1881. It has a 363 acre campus.

RATINGS

Admissions Selectivity Rating: 76   **Fire Safety Rating:** 64   **Green Rating:** 72

STUDENTS AND FACULTY

Enrollment: 9,725. **Student Body:** 51% female, 49% male, 4% international. Asian 1%, African American 2%, Caucasian 87%, Hispanic 2%, Native American 1%, Pacific Islander <1%, Two or more races 2%, Race unknown <1%.
Retention and Graduation: 77% freshmen return for sophomore year. 29% freshmen graduate within 4 years. 54% freshmen graduate within 6 years. **Faculty:** Student/faculty ratio 16:1. 570 full-time faculty, 74% hold PhDs, 21% are members of minority groups, 46% are women.

ACADEMICS

Degrees: Associate; Bachelor's; Certificate; Doctoral/Professional; Doctoral/Research; Master's; Post-Bachelor's certificate; Post-Master's certificate **Classes:** Most classes have 10-19 students. **Special Study Options:** Accelerated program; Cooperative education program; Cross-registration; Distance learning; Double major; Dual enrollment; English as a Second Language (ESL); Exchange student program (domestic); Honors program; Independent study; Internships; Study abroad; Teacher certification program. Honors programs: Van D. and Barbara B. Fishback Honors College See website http://www.sdstate.edu/Honors/index.cfm. **Disability Services offered to physically disabled students:** Note-taking services; Reader services; Tape recorders; Tutors. **Career services:** Career assessment; Career/job search classes; Internships

FACILITIES

Housing: Apartments for married students; Apartments for single students; Coed dorms; Fraternity/sorority housing; Special housing for disabled student; Wellness housing 99% of campus accessible to physically diasbled. **Special Academic Facilities/Equipment:** South Dakota Art Museum, South Dakota Agricultural Heritage Museum, Northern Plains Bio-stress Laboratory, Animal Disease Research and Diagnostic Lab, McCrory Gardens Education and Visitor Center **Computers:** 30% of classrooms, 100% of dorms, 100% of libraries, 100% of dining areas, 100% of student union, 20% of common outdoor areas have wireless network access. Students can register for classes online. Administrative functions (other than registration) can be performed online.

CAMPUS LIFE

Environment: Village **Activities:** Choral groups; Concert band; Dance; Drama/theater; International Student Organization; Jazz band; Literary magazine; Marching band; Model UN; Music ensembles; Musical theater; Pep band; Radio station; Student government; Student newspaper; Symphony orchestra; Yearbook 200 registered organizations, 32 honor societies, 14 religious organizations. 6 fraternities, 4 sororities. **Athletics (Intercollegiate):** *Men:* baseball, basketball, cross-country, diving, football, golf, swimming, tennis, track/field (outdoor), track/field (indoor), wrestling. *Women:* basketball, cross-country, diving, equestrian sports, golf, soccer, softball, swimming, tennis, track/field (outdoor), track/field (indoor), volleyball. **On-Campus Highlights:** Performing Arts Center, Dairy Bar, University Student Union, Frost Arena, South Dakota Art Museum **Environmental Initiatives:** Establishment of environmental stewardship and sustainability shared governance committee.

ADMISSIONS

Freshman Academic Profile: Average high school GPA 3.4. 14% in top 10% of high school class, 36% in top 25% of high school class, 68% in top 50% of high school class. **Test Scores:** SAT Math middle 50% range 500-630. SAT EBRW middle 50% range 480-630. ACT middle 50% range 20-26. Minimum internet-based TOEFL 61. Minimum paper TOEFL 500. **Basis for Candidate Selection:** *Very important factors considered include:* rigor of secondary school record, class rank, academic GPA, standardized test scores. *Other factors considered include:* application essay, recommendation(s). **Freshman Admission Requirements:** High school diploma is required and GED is accepted *Academic units required:* 4 English, 3 math, 3 science, 3

science labs, 3 social studies, 1 visual/performing arts. **Freshman Admission Statistics:** 5,551 applied, 91.4% admitted, 45% enrolled. **Transfer Admission Requirements:** High school transcript, college transcript(s), statement of good standing from prior institution(s). Minimum college GPA of 2.0 required. Lowest grade transferable D. **General Admission Information:** Application fee $20. Nonfall registration accepted.

COSTS AND FINANCIAL AID

Annual in-state tuition $7,744. Annual out-of-state tuition $10,439. Room and board $7,744. Required fees $1,250. Average book expense $1,500. **Required Forms and Deadlines:** FAFSA. **Notification of Awards:** Applicants will be notified of awards on a rolling basis beginning 4/1. *Student Employment:* Federal Work-Study Program available. Institutional employment available. **Financial Aid Statistics:** 50% needy freshmen, 50% needy undergrads receive need-based scholarship or grant aid. 20% freshmen, 14% undergrads receive non-need-based scholarship or grant aid. 89% freshmen, 92% undergrads receive need-based self-help aid. 4% freshmen, 5% undergrads receive athletic scholarships. 75% undergrads borrow to pay for school. Average cumulative indebtedness $28,796. **Criteria for awarding aid:** *Non-need-based:* Academics, Alumni affiliation, Art, Athletics, Leadership, Minority status, Music/drama, State/district residency.

SOUTHEAST MISSOURI STATE UNIVERSITY

One University Plaza, Cape Girardeau, MO 63701
Phone: 573-651-2590 • **Financial Aid Phone:** (573) 651-2253
E-mail: admissions@semo.edu • **CEEB Code:** 6655
Fax: 573-651-5936 • **Website:** www.semo.edu • **ACT Code:** 2366

This public school was founded in 1873. It has a 400 acre campus.

RATINGS

Admissions Selectivity Rating: 82   **Fire Safety Rating:** 93   **Green Rating:** 73

STUDENTS AND FACULTY

Enrollment: 8,988. **Student Body:** 57% female, 43% male, 20% out-of-state, 5% international (41 countries represented). Asian 1%, African American 10%, Caucasian 79%, Hispanic 2%, Native American <1%, Pacific Islander <1%, Two or more races 1%, Race unknown 1%.
Retention and Graduation: 74% freshmen return for sophomore year. 29% freshmen graduate within 4 years. 1% freshmen graduate within 6 years. **Faculty:** Student/faculty ratio 20:1. 409 full-time faculty, 75% hold PhDs, 16% are members of minority groups, 53% are women. 8% of classes are taught by teaching assistants.

ACADEMICS

Degrees: Associate; Bachelor's; Certificate; Master's; Post-Bachelor's certificate; Post-Master's certificate **Classes:** Most classes have 10-19 students. **Most popular majors:** General Studies; Registered Nursing/Registered Nurse; Business Administration And Management, General. **Special Study Options:** Accelerated program; Distance learning; Double major; Dual enrollment; English as a Second Language (ESL); Honors program; Independent study; Internships; Liberal arts/career combination; Student-designed major; Study abroad; Teacher certification program. Honors programs: The Jane Stephens Honors Program encourages intellectual perspective, addresses needs of outstanding students and contributes to the general advancement of learning. Honors students may choose from a variety of honors classes each semester and have the opportunity to work with an Honors Faculty mentor on a capstone, senior project. Honors students receive early registration in the Sophomore and Junior years. The Honors House on campus offers a computer lab, conference room, classroom, lounge, full kitchen and study areas for the use of honors students. Leadership opportunities in the program are available on the Student Honors Council, and our Honors Floor offers honors students suite-style housing in one of our newest residence halls. **Disability Services offered to physically disabled students:** Note-taking services; Reader services; Tape recorders; Tutors. **Career services:** Alumni services; Career assessment; Career/job search classes; Internships

FACILITIES

Housing: Coed dorms; Fraternity/sorority housing; Special housing for disabled student; Theme housing 100% of campus accessible to physically diasbled. **Special Academic Facilities/Equipment:** River Campus at Southeast; Crisp Museum;Bedell Performance Hall; Center for Faulkner Studies; Center for Scholarship in Teaching and Learning; Missouri Statewide Early Literacy Intervention Program (MSELIP); Writing Center; University Demonstration Farm; 4 corporate video studios, 2 radio stations; Southeast Explorer; SHOW (Southeast Health on Wheels); Linda Godwin Center for Science and Math Education **Computers:** 15% of dorms, 90% of libraries, 90% of dining areas,

90% of student union, 10% of common outdoor areas have wireless network access. Students can register for classes online. Administrative functions (other than registration) can be performed online.

CAMPUS LIFE

Environment: Town **Activities:** Campus Ministries; Choral groups; Concert band; Dance; Drama/theater; International Student Organization; Jazz band; Literary magazine; Marching band; Music ensembles; Musical theater; Opera; Pep band; Radio station; Student government; Student newspaper; Symphony orchestra 136 registered organizations, 8 honor societies, 14 religious organizations. 11 fraternities, 7 sororities. **Athletics (Intercollegiate):** *Men:* baseball, basketball, cheerleading, cross-country, football, track/field (outdoor), track/field (indoor). *Women:* basketball, cheerleading, cross-country, gymnastics, soccer, softball, tennis, track/field (outdoor), track/field (indoor), volleyball. **On-Campus Highlights:** River Campus (Visual/Performing Arts), Student Recreation Center & Aquatic Center, Kent Library Information Commons, The University Center, Academic Hall

ADMISSIONS

Freshman Academic Profile: Average high school GPA 3.4. 16% in top 10% of high school class, 42% in top 25% of high school class, 75% in top 50% of high school class. **Test Scores:** SAT Math middle 50% range 595-688. SAT EBRW middle 50% range 602.5-687.5. ACT middle 50% range 20-26. Minimum internet-based TOEFL 61. Minimum paper TOEFL 500. **Basis for Candidate Selection:** *Very important factors considered include:* rigor of secondary school record, academic GPA, standardized test scores. *Other factors considered include:* class rank. **Freshman Admission Requirements:** High school diploma is required and GED is accepted *Academic units required:* 4 English, 3 math, 3 science, 1 science labs, 2 social studies, 1 history, 3 academic electives, 1 visual/performing arts. **Freshman Admission Statistics:** 4,977 applied, 84.5% admitted, 43% enrolled. **Transfer Admission Requirements:** college transcript(s), Minimum college GPA of 2.0 required. Lowest grade transferable D. **General Admission Information:** Application fee $30. Priority deadline 12/1. Regular application deadline 7/1. Nonfall registration accepted.

COSTS AND FINANCIAL AID

Annual in-state tuition $8,963. Annual out-of-state tuition $11,718. Room and board $8,963. Required fees $1,002. Average book expense $514. **Required Forms and Deadlines:** FAFSA. **Notification of Awards:** Applicants will be notified of awards on a rolling basis beginning 2/1. **Types of Aid:** *Need-based scholarships/grants:* College/university scholarship or grant aid from institutional funds; Federal Pell; Private scholarships; SEOG; State scholarships/grants. *Loans:* Direct PLUS loans; Direct Subsidized Stafford Loans; Direct Unsubsidized Stafford Loans. *Student Employment:* Federal Work-Study Program available. Institutional employment available. **Financial Aid Statistics:** 94% needy freshmen, 88% needy undergrads receive need-based scholarship or grant aid. 13% freshmen, 7% undergrads receive non-need-based scholarship or grant aid. 59% freshmen, 72% undergrads receive need-based self-help aid. 2% freshmen, 2% undergrads receive athletic scholarships. 85% freshmen, 83% undergrads receive any aid. 64% undergrads borrow to pay for school. Average cumulative indebtedness $27,991. **Criteria for awarding aid:** *Need-based:* Academics, Minority status *Non-need-based:* Academics, Alumni affiliation, Art, Athletics, Job skills, Leadership, Minority status, Music/drama, State/district residency.

SOUTHEASTERN BIBLE COLLEGE

2545 Valleydale Road, Birmingham, AL 35244
Phone: (205) 970-9211
E-mail: info@sebc.edu
Fax: (205) 970-9207 • **Website:** www.sebc.edu

This private school was founded in 1935.

RATINGS

Admissions Selectivity Rating: 74   **Fire Safety Rating:** 60*   **Green Rating:** 60*

STUDENTS AND FACULTY

Student Body: 12% out-of-state, international.
Retention and Graduation: 67% freshmen return for sophomore year.
Faculty: Student/faculty ratio 8:1. 8 full-time faculty, 75% hold PhDs, 0% are members of minority groups, 25% are women. 0% of classes are taught by teaching assistants.

ACADEMICS

Degrees: Associate; Bachelor's; Diploma **Classes:** Most classes have fewer than 10 students. **Most popular majors:** Bible/Biblical Studies. **Special**

Study Options: Double major; Dual enrollment; Internships; Study abroad.
Disability Services offered to physically disabled students: Note-taking services; Tape recorders.

FACILITIES

Housing: Men's dorms; Special housing for disabled student; Women's dorms 100% of campus accessible to physically diasbled.

CAMPUS LIFE

Environment: Metropolis **Activities:** Campus Ministries; Music ensembles; Student government.

ADMISSIONS

Test Scores: ACT middle 50% range 18-23. **Basis for Candidate Selection:** *Very important factors considered include:* application essay, recommendation(s), interview, religious affiliation/commitment. *Important factors considered include:* character/personal qualities. *Other factors considered include:* academic GPA, standardized test scores. **Freshman Admission Requirements:** High school diploma is required and GED is accepted *Academic units recommended:* 4 English, 4 math, 4 science, 4 social studies, 8 academic electives. **Freshman Admission Statistics:** 18 applied, 100.0% admitted, 83% enrolled. **Transfer Admission Requirements:** High school transcript, college transcript(s), essay or personal statement, Minimum college GPA of 2.0 required. Lowest grade transferable C. **General Admission Information:** Application fee $30. Priority deadline 8/1. Nonfall registration accepted. Admission may be deferred for a maximum of 1 year.

COSTS AND FINANCIAL AID

Required Forms and Deadlines: FAFSA; Institution's own financial aid form. **Types of Aid:** *Need-based scholarships/grants:* College/university scholarship or grant aid from institutional funds; Federal Pell; SEOG. *Loans:* Direct PLUS loans; Direct Subsidized Stafford Loans; Direct Unsubsidized Stafford Loans. *Student Employment:* Federal Work-Study Program available. **Criteria for awarding aid:** *Need-based:* Academics, Leadership *Non-need-based:* Academics, Leadership.

SOUTHEASTERN LOUISIANA UNIVERSITY

548 Ned McGehee Dr, Hammond, LA 70402
Phone: 985-549-2066 • **Financial Aid Phone:** 985-549-2030
E-mail: admissions@southeastern.edu • **CEEB Code:** 6656
Fax: 985-549-5632 • **Website:** www.southeastern.edu • **ACT Code:** 1608

This public school was founded in 1925. It has a 365 acre campus.

RATINGS

Admissions Selectivity Rating: 77   **Fire Safety Rating:** 93   **Green Rating:** 79

STUDENTS AND FACULTY

Enrollment: 10,923. **Student Body:** 62% female, 38% male, 5% out-of-state, 2% international (55 countries represented). Asian 1%, African American 20%, Caucasian 62%, Hispanic 8%, Native American <1%, Pacific Islander <1%, Two or more races 5%, Race unknown 1%.
Retention and Graduation: 66% freshmen return for sophomore year. 40% freshmen graduate within 6 years. **Faculty:** Student/faculty ratio 19:1. 490 full-time faculty, 64% hold PhDs, 13% are members of minority groups, 58% are women. 0% of classes are taught by teaching assistants.

ACADEMICS

Degrees: Associate; Bachelor's; Doctoral/Professional; Doctoral/Research; Master's; Post-Bachelor's certificate; Post-Master's certificate **Classes:** Most classes have 10-19 students. **Most popular majors:** Biology/Biological Sciences, General; Registered Nursing/Registered Nurse; Business Administration And Management, General. **Special Study Options:** Accelerated program; Cross-registration; Distance learning; Double major; Dual enrollment; English as a Second Language (ESL); Honors program; Independent study; Internships; Study abroad; Teacher certification program. Honors programs: Reduced class size, scholarships, honors residence hall, achievement awards, and honor academic credit shown on the transcript. **Disability Services offered to physically disabled students:** Note-taking services; Reader services; Tutors. **Career services:** Alumni network; Alumni services; Career assessment; Internships

FACILITIES

Housing: Apartments for single students; Coed dorms; Fraternity/sorority housing; Women's dorms 95% of campus accessible to physically diasbled. **Special Academic Facilities/Equipment:** Contemporary Art Gallery, Radio Station, Television Station, Columbia Theatre, Maritime Museum **Computers:**

5% of classrooms, 100% of dorms, 100% of libraries, 50% of dining areas, 25% of student union, 25% of common outdoor areas have wireless network access. Students can register for classes online. Administrative functions (other than registration) can be performed online.

CAMPUS LIFE

Environment: Village **Activities:** Choral groups; Concert band; Dance; Drama/theater; International Student Organization; Literary magazine; Marching band; Music ensembles; Pep band; Radio station; Student government; Student newspaper; Television station; Yearbook 105 registered organizations, 11 honor societies, 12 religious organizations. 7 fraternities, 8 sororities. **Athletics (Intercollegiate):** *Men:* baseball, basketball, cross-country, football, golf, track/field (outdoor), track/field (indoor). *Women:* basketball, cross-country, soccer, softball, tennis, track/field (outdoor), track/field (indoor), volleyball. **On-Campus Highlights:** Student Union, Student Recreation Center, Library, Bookstore, Campus Dining Complex **Environmental Initiatives:** Renewable Energy – investment in solar power, on site waste oil biodiesel fuel production, proactive energy usage reduction management. The university has focused on these areas to reduce both waste and the need for grid power.

ADMISSIONS

Freshman Academic Profile: Average high school GPA 3.2. 14% in top 10% of high school class, 37% in top 25% of high school class, 69% in top 50% of high school class. **Test Scores:** ACT middle 50% range 20-24. Minimum internet-based TOEFL 61. Minimum paper TOEFL 500. **Basis for Candidate Selection:** *Very important factors considered include:* rigor of secondary school record, academic GPA, standardized test scores. **Freshman Admission Requirements:** High school diploma is required and GED is accepted *Academic units required:* 4 English, 4 math, 4 science, 2 foreign language, 4 social studies, 1 visual/performing arts. **Freshman Admission Statistics:** 4,402 applied, 88.4% admitted, 71% enrolled. **Transfer Admission Requirements:** college transcript(s), statement of good standing from prior institution(s). Minimum college GPA of 2.0 required. Lowest grade transferable D. **General Admission Information:** Application fee $20. Priority deadline 7/15. Regular application deadline 8/1. Nonfall registration accepted. Admission may be deferred for a maximum of 1 year.

COSTS AND FINANCIAL AID

Annual in-state tuition $8,340. Annual out-of-state tuition $18,255. Room and board $8,340. Required fees $2,376. Average book expense $1,300. **Required Forms and Deadlines:** FAFSA. **Notification of Awards:** Applicants will be notified of awards on a rolling basis beginning 4/1. **Types of Aid:** *Need-based scholarships/grants:* College/university scholarship or grant aid from institutional funds; Federal Pell; Private scholarships; SEOG; State scholarships/grants. *Loans:* Direct PLUS loans; Direct Subsidized Stafford Loans; Direct Unsubsidized Stafford Loans. *Student Employment:* Federal Work-Study Program available. Institutional employment available. **Financial Aid Statistics:** 65% needy freshmen, 66% needy undergrads receive need-based scholarship or grant aid. 68% freshmen, 52% undergrads receive non-need-based scholarship or grant aid. 56% freshmen, 62% undergrads receive need-based self-help aid. 3% freshmen, 3% undergrads receive athletic scholarships. 59% undergrads borrow to pay for school. Average cumulative indebtedness $21,517. **Criteria for awarding aid:** *Need-based:* Academics, Job skills, Leadership *Non-need-based:* Academics, Athletics, Job skills, Leadership, Music/drama, State/district residency.

SOUTHEASTERN OKLAHOMA STATE UNIVERSITY

1405 North 4th Avenue, Durant, OK 74701-0609
Phone: 580-745-2060 • **Financial Aid Phone:** 580-745-2186
E-mail: admissions@se.edu • **CEEB Code:** 6657
Fax: 580-745-4502 • **ACT Code:** 3438

This public school was founded in 1909. It has a 268 acre campus.

RATINGS

Admissions Selectivity Rating: 76   **Fire Safety Rating:** 88   **Green Rating:** 60*

STUDENTS AND FACULTY

Enrollment: 3,465. **Student Body:** 55% female, 45% male, 22% out-of-state, 1% international (28 countries represented). Asian 1%, African American 5%, Caucasian 59%, Hispanic 3%, Native American 31%, Race unknown 0%. **Retention and Graduation:** 58% freshmen return for sophomore year. **Faculty:** Student/faculty ratio 18:1. 143 full-time faculty, 74% hold PhDs, 17%

are members of minority groups, 41% are women. 0% of classes are taught by teaching assistants.

ACADEMICS

Degrees: Bachelor's; Master's; Post-Master's certificate **Classes:** Most classes have 10-19 students. Most lab/discussion sessions have 10-19 students. **Most popular majors:** Elementary Education And Teaching; Occupational Safety And Health Technology/Technician; Psychology, General. **Special Study Options:** Distance learning; Double major; Honors program; Independent study; Internships; Teacher certification program. Honors programs: Our Honors program offers six different scholarships ranging in value from $6,400 to $26,400 over four years. **Disability Services offered to physically disabled students:** Note-taking services; Reader services; Tape recorders; Tutors. **Career services:** Alumni network; Career assessment; Career/job search classes; Internships

FACILITIES

Housing: Apartments for single students; Coed dorms 100% of campus accessible to physically disabled. **Special Academic Facilities/Equipment:** Visual and Performing Arts Gallery **Computers:** 65% of classrooms, 50% of dorms, 100% of libraries, 100% of dining areas, 100% of student union, 50% of common outdoor areas have wireless network access. Students can register for classes online. Administrative functions (other than registration) can be performed online.

CAMPUS LIFE

Environment: Village **Activities:** Campus Ministries; Choral groups; Concert band; Dance; Drama/theater; International Student Organization; Jazz band; Literary magazine; Marching band; Music ensembles; Musical theater; Opera; Pep band; Radio station; Student government; Student newspaper; Yearbook 70 registered organizations, 12 honor societies, 8 religious organizations. 2 fraternities, 2 sororities. **Athletics (Intercollegiate):** *Men:* baseball, basketball, football, golf, tennis. *Women:* basketball, cross-country, softball, tennis, volleyball. **On-Campus Highlights:** Shearer Hall and Suites (New Apartments), New Student Union, Newly Renovated Football Stadium, New Basketball Arena, Campus of a Thousand Magnolias

ADMISSIONS

Freshman Academic Profile: Average high school GPA 3.3. 16% in top 10% of high school class, 40% in top 25% of high school class, 77% in top 50% of high school class. 99% from public high schools. **Test Scores:** ACT middle 50% range 18-23. Minimum paper TOEFL 500. **Basis for Candidate Selection:** *Very important factors considered include:* class rank, academic GPA, standardized test scores. *Other factors considered include:* rigor of secondary school record, recommendation(s), interview, talent/ability, character/personal qualities, state residency, level of applicant's interest. **Freshman Admission Requirements:** High school diploma is required and GED is accepted *Academic units required:* 4 English, 3 math, 2 science, 2 science labs, 3 history, 2 academic electives, *Academic units recommended:* 1 foreign language, 1 social studies, 1 computer science. **Freshman Admission Statistics:** 922 applied, 88.0% admitted, 76% enrolled. **Transfer Admission Requirements:** college transcript(s), Minimum college GPA of 2.0 required. Lowest grade transferable D. **General Admission Information:** Application fee $20. Nonfall registration accepted.

COSTS AND FINANCIAL AID

Annual in-state tuition $2,005. Annual out-of-state tuition $10,010. Room and board $2,005. Required fees $677. Average book expense $800. **Required Forms and Deadlines:** FAFSA; Institution's own financial aid form. **Notification of Awards:** Applicants will be notified of awards on a rolling basis beginning 4/15. **Types of Aid:** *Need-based scholarships/grants:* College/university scholarship or grant aid from institutional funds; Federal Pell; Private scholarships; SEOG; State scholarships/grants. *Loans: Student Employment:* Federal Work-Study Program available. Institutional employment available. **Financial Aid Statistics:** 71% needy freshmen, 81% needy undergrads receive need-based scholarship or grant aid. 45% freshmen, 33% undergrads receive non-need-based scholarship or grant aid. 37% freshmen, 59% undergrads receive need-based self-help aid. 10% freshmen, 7% undergrads receive athletic scholarships. 66% freshmen, 65% undergrads receive any aid. **Criteria for awarding aid:** *Non-need-based:* Academics, Alumni affiliation, Art, Athletics, Leadership, Minority status, Music/drama, State/district residency.

SOUTHEASTERN UNIVERSITY

1000 Longfellow Blvd., Lakeland, FL 33801
Phone: 863-667-5018 · **Financial Aid Phone:** 800-500-8760
E-mail: admission@seu.edu
Fax: 863-667-5200 • **Website:** http://www.seu.edu/

This private school, affiliated with the Assemblies of God Church, was founded in 1935. It has a 87 acre campus.

RATINGS
Admissions Selectivity Rating: 89   **Fire Safety Rating:** 99   **Green Rating:** 60*

STUDENTS AND FACULTY
Enrollment: 2,946. **Student Body:** 55% female, 45% male, 32% out-of-state, 2% international. Asian 1%, African American 15%, Caucasian 61%, Hispanic 17%, Native American <1%, Pacific Islander <1%, Two or more races 1%, Race unknown 4%.
Retention and Graduation: 66% freshmen return for sophomore year. **Faculty:** Student/faculty ratio 19:1. 118 full-time faculty, 72% hold PhDs, 16% are members of minority groups, 37% are women.

ACADEMICS
Degrees: Associate; Bachelor's; Certificate; Doctoral; Master's; Post-Bachelor's certificate **Classes:** Most classes have 20-29 students. Most lab/discussion sessions have 10-19 students. **Most popular majors:** Elementary Education And Teaching; Theology And Religious Vocations, Other; Psychology, General. **Special Study Options:** Distance learning; Double major; Dual enrollment; Honors program; Independent study; Internships; Study abroad; Teacher certification program. Honors programs: Honors Program. **Disability Services offered to physically disabled students:** Tutors. **Career services:** Career assessment; Internships

FACILITIES
Housing: Men's dorms; Women's dorms 100% of campus accessible to physically disabled.

CAMPUS LIFE
Environment: City **Activities:** Campus Ministries; Choral groups; Concert band; Dance; Drama/theater; International Student Organization; Jazz band; Music ensembles; Musical theater; Opera; Radio station; Student government; Student newspaper; Television station; Yearbook. Portico Coffeehouse, Chick-fil-A Express, Student Activity Center, Bolin Television Studio, Victory Field

ADMISSIONS
Freshman Academic Profile: 77% from public high schools. **Test Scores:** SAT Math middle 50% range 410-520. SAT EBRW middle 50% range 430-560. ACT middle 50% range 18-23. Minimum internet-based TOEFL 80. Minimum paper TOEFL 570. **Basis for Candidate Selection:** *Very important factors considered include:* character/personal qualities, religious affiliation/commitment. *Important factors considered include:* academic GPA, application essay, standardized test scores, recommendation(s), level of applicant's interest. *Other factors considered include:* rigor of secondary school record, class rank, interview, extracurricular activities, talent/ability, first generation, alumni/ae relation, volunteer work, work experience. **Freshman Admission Requirements:** High school diploma is required and GED is accepted *Academic units recommended:* 4 English, 4 math, 4 science, 1 science labs, 2 foreign language, 4 social studies. **Freshman Admission Statistics:** 3,402 applied, 43.9% admitted, 61% enrolled. **General Admission Information:** Application fee $40. Regular application deadline 5/1. Nonfall registration accepted. Admission may be deferred.

COSTS AND FINANCIAL AID
Required Forms and Deadlines: FAFSA; Institution's own financial aid form; State aid form. **Notification of Awards:** Applicants will be notified of awards on a rolling basis beginning 1/1. **Types of Aid:** *Need-based scholarships/grants:* College/university scholarship or grant aid from institutional funds; Federal Pell; Private scholarships; SEOG; State scholarships/grants. *Loans: Student Employment:* Federal Work-Study Program available. Institutional employment available. **Financial Aid Statistics:** 95% needy freshmen, 96% needy undergrads receive need-based scholarship or grant aid. 10% freshmen, 9% undergrads receive non-need-based scholarship or grant aid. 85% freshmen, 87% undergrads receive need-based self-help aid. 4% freshmen, 3% undergrads receive athletic scholarships. 90% freshmen receive any aid. **Criteria for awarding aid:** *Non-need-based:* Academics, Athletics, Leadership, Music/drama, State/district residency.

SOUTHERN ADVENTIST UNIVERSITY

P.O. Box 370, Collegedale, TN 37315
Phone: 423-236-2835 • **Financial Aid Phone:** 423-236-2894
E-mail: admissions@southern.edu • **CEEB Code:** 3518
Fax: 423-236-1835 • **ACT Code:** 4006

This private school, affiliated with the Seventh Day Adventist Church, was founded in 1892. It has a 1000 acre campus.

RATINGS
Admissions Selectivity Rating: 78   **Fire Safety Rating:** 94   **Green Rating:** 60*

STUDENTS AND FACULTY
Enrollment: 2,584. **Student Body:** 55% female, 45% male, 69% out-of-state, 5% international. Asian 6%, African American 12%, Caucasian 58%, Hispanic 19%, Native American <1%, Pacific Islander 1%, Two or more races <1%, Race unknown 0%.
Retention and Graduation: 72% freshmen return for sophomore year. 15% grads go on to further study within 1 year. 10% grads pursue arts and sciences degrees. 0% grads pursue law degrees. 1% grads pursue business degrees. 3% grads pursue medical degrees. **Faculty:** Student/faculty ratio 15:1. 146 full-time faculty, 64% hold PhDs, 12% are members of minority groups, 42% are women. 0% of classes are taught by teaching assistants.

ACADEMICS
Degrees: Associate; Bachelor's; Certificate; Master's; Post-Master's certificate **Classes:** Most classes have 20-29 students. Most lab/discussion sessions have 10-19 students. **Most popular majors:** Biology/Biological Sciences, General; Business/Commerce, General. **Special Study Options:** Double major; Dual enrollment; English as a Second Language (ESL); Honors program; Independent study; Internships; Study abroad; Teacher certification program. Honors programs: Southern Scholars program includes special projects, inter-disciplinary studies, and designated honors courses to provide a challenging and intellectually stimulating educational experience. Combined degree programs: BA/MA. **Disability Services offered to physically disabled students:** Note-taking services; Reader services; Tape recorders; Tutors.

FACILITIES
Housing: Apartments for married students; Apartments for single students; Men's dorms; Women's dorms 70% of campus accessible to physically disabled. **Special Academic Facilities/Equipment:** Near-Eastern archaeology teaching collection **Computers:** 100% of classrooms, 5% of dorms, 100% of libraries, 80% of dining areas, 10% of common outdoor areas have wireless network access. Students can register for classes online. Administrative functions (other than registration) can be performed online.

CAMPUS LIFE
Environment: Rural **Activities:** Campus Ministries; Choral groups; Concert band; Drama/theater; International Student Organization; Jazz band; Music ensembles; Radio station; Student government; Student newspaper; Student-run film society; Symphony orchestra; Television station; Yearbook 30 registered organizations, 8 honor societies, 3 religious organizations. **On-Campus Highlights:** Student Center, Wellness Center, The Village Market, KRs Place, Library **Environmental Initiatives:** Establishing environmental sustainability committee.

ADMISSIONS
Freshman Academic Profile: Average high school GPA 3.4. 18% from public high schools. **Test Scores:** SAT Math middle 50% range 430-560. SAT EBRW middle 50% range 460-580. ACT middle 50% range 19-25. Minimum paper TOEFL 550. **Basis for Candidate Selection:** *Very important factors considered include:* rigor of secondary school record, academic GPA, standardized test scores. **Freshman Admission Requirements:** High school diploma is required and GED is accepted *Academic units required:* 3 English, 2 math, 2 science, 1 social studies, 1 history, 9 academic electives, *Academic units recommended:* 4 English, 3 math, 3 science, 2 foreign language, 1 social studies, 2 history, 9 academic electives, 1 unit from above areas or other academic areas. **Freshman Admission Statistics:** 1,452 applied, 80.4% admitted, 54% enrolled. **Transfer Admission Requirements:** college transcript(s), Minimum college GPA of 2 required. Lowest grade transferable D. **General Admission Information:** Application fee $40. Regular application deadline 9/8. Nonfall registration accepted. Admission may be deferred for a maximum of 1 year.

COSTS AND FINANCIAL AID
Annual tuition $17,534. Room and board $5,786. Required fees $790. Average book expense $1,100. **Required Forms and Deadlines:** FAFSA. **Notification of Awards:** Applicants will be notified of awards on a rolling basis beginning 2/15. **Types of Aid:** *Need-based scholarships/grants:* College/university scholarship or grant aid from institutional funds; Federal Pell; Private

scholarships; SEOG; State scholarships/grants. *Loans: Student Employment:* Federal Work-Study Program available. Institutional employment available. **Financial Aid Statistics:** 99% needy freshmen, 98% needy undergrads receive need-based scholarship or grant aid. 82% freshmen, 55% undergrads receive non-need-based scholarship or grant aid. 83% freshmen, 86% undergrads receive need-based self-help aid. 0% freshmen, 0% undergrads receive athletic scholarships. 95% undergrads receive any aid. **Criteria for awarding aid:** *Need-based:* Academics, Art *Non-need-based:* Academics, Alumni affiliation, Art, Leadership, Music/drama.

SOUTHERN CALIFORNIA INSTITUTE OF ARCHITECTURE

960 East 3rd Street, Los Angeles, CA 90013-1822
Phone: 213.356.5320 · **Financial Aid Phone:** 213-356-5346
E-mail: admissions@sciarc.edu
Fax: 213-613-2260 • **Website:** www.sciarc.edu

This private school was founded in 1972.

RATINGS
Admissions Selectivity Rating: 70   **Fire Safety Rating:** 60*   **Green Rating:** 60*

STUDENTS AND FACULTY
Student Body: 40% out-of-state, 20% international (45 countries represented). Asian 24%, African American 1%, Caucasian 30%, Hispanic 18%, Race unknown 7%.
Retention and Graduation: 93% freshmen return for sophomore year.
Faculty: Student/faculty ratio 11:1. 33 full-time faculty, 33% are women.

ACADEMICS
Degrees: Bachelor's; Master's; Post-Master's certificate **Classes:** Most classes have 10-19 students. **Special Study Options:** Internships; Study abroad. **Career services:** Alumni network; Internships

FACILITIES
Special Academic Facilities/Equipment: SCI-Arc gallery, Wood/Metal Shop, Digital Fabrication shop **Computers:** Students can register for classes online.

CAMPUS LIFE
Environment: Metropolis **Activities:** Student government. **On-Campus Highlights:** SCI-Arc Gallery, Kappe Library, Wood/Metal Shop, Studios

ADMISSIONS
Test Scores: Minimum internet-based TOEFL 83. Minimum paper TOEFL 560. **Basis for Candidate Selection:** *Very important factors considered include:* academic GPA, character/personal qualities, level of applicant's interest. *Important factors considered include:* rigor of secondary school record, application essay, standardized test scores. *Other factors considered include:* recommendation(s), extracurricular activities, talent/ability, volunteer work, work experience. **Freshman Admission Requirements:** High school diploma is required and GED is accepted **Freshman Admission Statistics:** 276 applied, 54.7% admitted, 21% enrolled. **Transfer Admission Requirements:** college transcript(s), essay or personal statement, Lowest grade transferable C. **General Admission Information:** Application fee $85. Priority deadline 1/15. Regular application deadline 7/1. Nonfall registration accepted.

COSTS AND FINANCIAL AID
Annual tuition $27,500. Required fees $350. **Required Forms and Deadlines:** FAFSA; Institution's own financial aid form. **Types of Aid:** *Need-based scholarships/grants:* College/university scholarship or grant aid from institutional funds; Federal Pell; SEOG; State scholarships/grants. *Loans: Student Employment:* Federal Work-Study Program available. **Criteria for awarding aid:** *Need-based:* Academics *Non-need-based:* Academics, State/district residency.

SOUTHERN CONNECTICUT STATE UNIVERSITY

501 Crescent Street, New Haven, CT 06515-1202
Phone: 203-392-5644 • **CEEB Code:** 3662
Fax: 203-392-5727 • **Website:** www.southernct.edu

This public school was founded in 1893. It has a 168 acre campus.

RATINGS
Admissions Selectivity Rating: 75   **Fire Safety Rating:** 60*   **Green Rating:** 84

STUDENTS AND FACULTY
Enrollment: 8,525. **Student Body:** 60% female, 40% male, 4% out-of-state, <1% international (39 countries represented). Asian 3%, African American 16%, Caucasian 62%, Hispanic 10%, Native American <1%, Two or more races 2%, Race unknown 6%.
Retention and Graduation: 27% grads go on to further study within 1 year.
Faculty: Student/faculty ratio 17:1. 403 full-time faculty, 90% hold PhDs, 14% are members of minority groups, 45% are women.

ACADEMICS
Degrees: Bachelor's; Doctoral Other; Master's; Post-Master's certificate **Classes:** Most classes have 10-19 students. Most lab/discussion sessions have 10-19 students. **Special Study Options:** Accelerated program; Cooperative education program; Cross-registration; Distance learning; Double major; Dual enrollment; Exchange student program (domestic); External degree program; Honors program; Independent study; Internships; Liberal arts/career combination; Student-designed major; Study abroad; Teacher certification program. **Disability Services offered to physically disabled students:** Note-taking services; Reader services; Tape recorders; Tutors. **Career services:** Career/job search classes; Internships

FACILITIES
Housing: Apartments for single students; Coed dorms; Special housing for disabled student; Theme housing 95% of campus accessible to physically diasbled. **Special Academic Facilities/Equipment:** Art gallery, language lab, child development center, communication disorders center, planetarium and observatory, closed-circuit TV center.

CAMPUS LIFE
Environment: Village **Activities:** Campus Ministries; Choral groups; Dance; Drama/theater; International Student Organization; Literary magazine; Music ensembles; Musical theater; Pep band; Radio station; Student government; Student newspaper; Television station; Yearbook 63 registered organizations, 3 religious organizations. 2 fraternities, 4 sororities **Athletics (Intercollegiate):** *Men:* baseball, basketball, cross-country, football, golf, gymnastics, ice hockey, rugby, soccer, softball, swimming, track/field (outdoor), track/field (indoor), volleyball, wrestling. *Women:* basketball, cheerleading, cross-country, field hockey, golf, gymnastics, rugby, soccer, softball, swimming, track/field (outdoor), track/field (indoor), volleyball.

ADMISSIONS
Freshman Academic Profile: 5% in top 10% of high school class, 21% in top 25% of high school class, 60% in top 50% of high school class. 88% from public high schools. **Test Scores:** SAT Math middle 50% range 410-530. SAT EBRW middle 50% range 420-520. ACT middle 50% range 17-22. Minimum paper TOEFL 525. **Basis for Candidate Selection:** *Very important factors considered include:* rigor of secondary school record, academic GPA. *Important factors considered include:* class rank, application essay, standardized test scores, recommendation(s). *Other factors considered include:* extracurricular activities, talent/ability, character/personal qualities, first generation, volunteer work, work experience. **Freshman Admission Requirements:** High school diploma is required and GED is accepted *Academic units required:* 4 English, 3 math, 2 science, 1 science labs, 2 foreign language, 2 social studies, 2 history, *Academic units recommended:* 4 English, 4 math, 3 science, 4 foreign language, 3 social studies, 3 history. **Freshman Admission Statistics:** 4,978 applied, 75.5% admitted, 37% enrolled. **Transfer Admission Requirements:** college transcript(s), essay or personal statement, statement of good standing from prior institution(s). Minimum college GPA of 2.0 required. Lowest grade transferable C-. **General Admission Information:** Application fee $50. Regular application deadline 4/1. Nonfall registration accepted. Admission may be deferred for a maximum of 2 years.

COSTS AND FINANCIAL AID
Annual in-state tuition $10,687. Annual out-of-state tuition $15,137. Room and board $10,687. Required fees $4,256. Average book expense $1,400. **Required Forms and Deadlines:** FAFSA. **Types of Aid:** *Need-based scholarships/grants:* College/university scholarship or grant aid from institutional funds; Federal Pell; SEOG; State scholarships/grants. *Loans: Student Employment:*

Federal Work-Study Program available. Institutional employment available. **Financial Aid Statistics:** 75% needy freshmen, 76% needy undergrads receive need-based scholarship or grant aid. 25% freshmen, 15% undergrads receive non-need-based scholarship or grant aid. 79% freshmen, 88% undergrads receive need-based self-help aid. 1% freshmen, 2% undergrads receive athletic scholarships. **Criteria for awarding aid:** *Non-need-based:* Academics, Alumni affiliation, Athletics.

SOUTHERN ILLINOIS UNIVERSITY— CARBONDALE

Undergraduate Admissions, Mailcode 4710, Carbondale, IL 62901
Phone: 618-536-4405 • **Financial Aid Phone:** 618-453-4334
E-mail: admissions@siu.edu • **CEEB Code:** 1726
Fax: 618-453-4609 • **Website:** www.siu.edu • **ACT Code:** 1144

This public school was founded in 1869. It has a 1136 acre campus.

RATINGS
Admissions Selectivity Rating: 76   **Fire Safety Rating:** 93   **Green Rating:** 83

STUDENTS AND FACULTY
Enrollment: 10,896. **Student Body:** 46% female, 54% male, 17% out-of-state, 4% international (47 countries represented). Asian 2%, African American 16%, Caucasian 65%, Hispanic 9%, Native American <1%, Pacific Islander <1%, Two or more races 4%, Race unknown <1%.
Retention and Graduation: 68% freshmen return for sophomore year. 23% freshmen graduate within 4 years. 40% freshmen graduate within 6 years. **Faculty:** Student/faculty ratio 14:1. 833 full-time faculty, 71% hold PhDs, 22% are members of minority groups, 42% are women. 14% of classes are taught by teaching assistants.

ACADEMICS
Degrees: Associate; Bachelor's; Certificate; Doctoral/Professional; Doctoral/Research; Master's; Post-Bachelor's certificate **Classes:** Most classes have 10-19 students. Most lab/discussion sessions have 10-19 students. **Most popular majors:** Biology/Biological Sciences, General; Psychology, General; Accounting. **Special Study Options:** Accelerated program; Cooperative education program; Distance learning; Double major; Dual enrollment; English as a Second Language (ESL); Exchange student program (domestic); Honors program; Independent study; Internships; Student-designed major; Study abroad; Teacher certification program. Honors programs: University Honors Program—to reward its best undergraduates for their high academic achievement, intended to give the Honors Student a taste of the private-college experience at a state-university price. Classes are small, unique in character, and specially designed for University Honors Students by outstanding SIUC faculty. **Disability Services offered to physically disabled students:** Note-taking services; Reader services; Tape recorders; Tutors. **Career services:** Alumni services; Career assessment; Career/job search classes; Internships

FACILITIES
Housing: Apartments for married students; Apartments for single students; Coed dorms; Cooperative housing; Men's dorms; Special housing for disabled student; Theme housing; Wellness housing; Women's dorms 98% of campus accessible to physically disabled. **Special Academic Facilities/Equipment:** university press, coal research center, university museum, materials technology center, outdoor education laboratory, university farms, center for study of crime, electron microscopy center, cooperative wildlife research laboratory, cooperative fisheries research laboratory, vivarium, airport training facility, laboratory theater, center for archaeological investigations, small business incubator, public policy institute, dental and medical clinics, environmental center, media center **Computers:** 15% of classrooms, 100% of libraries, 95% of dining areas, 100% of student union, 70% of common outdoor areas have wireless network access. Students can register for classes online. Administrative functions (other than registration) can be performed online.

CAMPUS LIFE
Environment: Town **Activities:** Campus Ministries; Choral groups; Concert band; Dance; Drama/theater; International Student Organization; Jazz band; Literary magazine; Marching band; Model UN; Music ensembles; Musical theater; Opera; Pep band; Radio station; Student government; Student newspaper; Student-run film society; Symphony orchestra; Television station 408 registered organizations, 26 honor societies, 25 religious organizations. 20 fraternities, 8 sororities. **Athletics (Intercollegiate):** *Men:* baseball, basketball, cheerleading, cross-country, diving, football, golf, swimming, tennis, track/field (outdoor), track/field (indoor). *Women:* basketball, cheerleading, cross-country, diving, golf, softball, swimming, tennis, track/field (outdoor), track/field (indoor), volleyball. **On-Campus Highlights:** Morris Library, Student Center, Recreation Center, Saluki Stadium and SIU Arena, Campus Lake **Environmental Initiatives:** $4.0M campus-wide energy efficiency and conservation project to reduce purchased utilities.

ADMISSIONS
Freshman Academic Profile: Average high school GPA 3.1. 13% in top 10% of high school class, 38% in top 25% of high school class, 69% in top 50% of high school class. **Test Scores:** SAT Math middle 50% range 480-600. SAT EBRW middle 50% range 440-530. ACT middle 50% range 20-26. Minimum internet-based TOEFL 68. Minimum paper TOEFL 520. **Basis for Candidate Selection:** *Very important factors considered include:* rigor of secondary school record, class rank, academic GPA, standardized test scores. *Important factors considered include:* talent/ability. *Other factors considered include:* application essay, recommendation(s), interview, extracurricular activities, character/personal qualities, volunteer work, work experience. **Freshman Admission Requirements:** High school diploma is required and GED is accepted *Academic units required:* 4 English, 3 math, 3 science, 3 science labs, 3 social studies, 2 academic electives, *Academic units recommended:* 4 English, 4 math, 3 science, 3 science labs, 3 social studies, 2 academic electives. **Freshman Admission Statistics:** 7,941 applied, 76.2% admitted, 22% enrolled. **Transfer Admission Requirements:** college transcript(s), statement of good standing from prior institution(s). Minimum college GPA of 2.0 required. Lowest grade transferable D. **General Admission Information:** Application fee $40. Regular application deadline 5/1. Nonfall registration accepted. Admission may be deferred.

COSTS AND FINANCIAL AID
Required Forms and Deadlines: FAFSA. **Notification of Awards:** Applicants will be notified of awards on or about 3/15. **Types of Aid:** *Need-based scholarships/grants:* College/university scholarship or grant aid from institutional funds; Federal Pell; Private scholarships; SEOG; State scholarships/grants. *Loans:* Direct PLUS loans; Direct Subsidized Stafford Loans; Direct Unsubsidized Stafford Loans. *Student Employment:* Federal Work-Study Program available. Institutional employment available. **Financial Aid Statistics:** 68% needy freshmen, 66% needy undergrads receive need-based scholarship or grant aid. 34% freshmen, 28% undergrads receive non-need-based scholarship or grant aid. 89% freshmen, 88% undergrads receive need-based self-help aid. 2% freshmen, 2% undergrads receive athletic scholarships. 69% undergrads borrow to pay for school. Average cumulative indebtedness $33,288. **Criteria for awarding aid:** *Need-based:* Academics *Non-need-based:* Academics, Alumni affiliation, Art, Athletics, Leadership, Minority status, Music/drama, State/district residency.

See page 1034.

SOUTHERN ILLINOIS UNIVERSITY— EDWARDSVILLE

Box 1027, Edwardsville, IL 62026-1047
Phone: 618-650-3705 • **Financial Aid Phone:** 618-650-3880
E-mail: admissions@siue.edu • **CEEB Code:** 1759
Fax: 618-650-5013 • **Website:** www.siue.edu • **ACT Code:** 1147

This public school was founded in 1957. It has a 2660 acre campus.

RATINGS
Admissions Selectivity Rating: 74   **Fire Safety Rating:** 93   **Green Rating:** 89

STUDENTS AND FACULTY
Enrollment: 11,339. **Student Body:** 53% female, 47% male, 12% out-of-state, 1% international (39 countries represented). Asian 2%, African American 14%, Caucasian 74%, Hispanic 5%, Native American <1%, Pacific Islander <1%, Two or more races 3%, Race unknown 1%.
Retention and Graduation: 73% freshmen return for sophomore year. 27% freshmen graduate within 4 years. 48% freshmen graduate within 6 years. 31% grads go on to further study within 1 year. **Faculty:** Student/faculty ratio 20:1. 595 full-time faculty, 80% hold PhDs, 21% are members of minority groups, 48% are women. 4% of classes are taught by teaching assistants.

ACADEMICS
Degrees: Bachelor's; Doctoral; Doctoral Other; Doctoral/Professional; Doctoral/Research; Master's; Post-Bachelor's certificate; Post-Master's certificate **Classes:** Most classes have fewer than 10 students. Most lab/

discussion sessions have 20-29 students. **Most popular majors:** Psychology, General; Registered Nursing/Registered Nurse; Business Administration And Management, General. **Special Study Options:** Accelerated program; Cooperative education program; Distance learning; Double major; English as a Second Language (ESL); Honors program; Independent study; Internships; Student-designed major; Study abroad; Teacher certification program. Honors programs: URCA, Honors Program. **Disability Services offered to physically disabled students:** Note-taking services; Reader services; Tape recorders. **Career services:** Alumni network; Alumni services; Career assessment; Career/job search classes; Internships; Regional alumni

FACILITIES

Housing: Apartments for married students; Apartments for single students; Coed dorms; Special housing for disabled student; Wellness housing 100% of campus accessible to physically diasbled. **Special Academic Facilities/Equipment:** Art gallery, anthropology museum, language lab, center for advanced manufacturing and production, technology commercialization center, electron microscope, psychomotorskills lab, new engineering building and lab, observatory. **Computers:** Administrative functions (other than registration) can be performed online.

CAMPUS LIFE

Environment: Town **Activities:** Campus Ministries; Choral groups; Concert band; Dance; Drama/theater; International Student Organization; Jazz band; Literary magazine; Music ensembles; Musical theater; Opera; Pep band; Radio station; Student government; Student newspaper; Symphony orchestra 140 registered organizations, 15 honor societies, 9 religious organizations. 10 fraternities, 7 sororities. **Athletics (Intercollegiate):** *Men:* baseball, basketball, cross-country, golf, soccer, tennis, track/field (outdoor), track/field (indoor), wrestling. *Women:* basketball, cross-country, golf, soccer, softball, tennis, track/field (outdoor), track/field (indoor), volleyball. **On-Campus Highlights:** Morris University Center, Student Success Center, Starbucks/Kaldis Coffee, Residence Halls, Vadalebene Center—Student Fitness Center

ADMISSIONS

Freshman Academic Profile: Average high school GPA 3.4. 17% in top 10% of high school class, 43% in top 25% of high school class, 76% in top 50% of high school class. **Test Scores:** SAT Math middle 50% range 495-600. SAT EBRW middle 50% range 485-625. ACT middle 50% range 20-26. Minimum internet-based TOEFL 79. Minimum paper TOEFL 550. **Basis for Candidate Selection:** *Very important factors considered include:* academic GPA, standardized test scores. *Important factors considered include:* rigor of secondary school record, class rank. **Freshman Admission Requirements:** High school diploma is required and GED is accepted *Academic units required:* 4 English, 3 math, 3 science, 3 science labs, 3 social studies, 2 academic electives, *Academic units recommended:* 2 foreign language. **Freshman Admission Statistics:** 6,273 applied, 89.5% admitted, 32% enrolled. **Transfer Admission Requirements:** college transcript(s), Minimum college GPA of 2 required. Lowest grade transferable D. **General Admission Information:** Application fee $40. Priority deadline 12/1. Regular application deadline 7/19. Nonfall registration accepted. Admission may be deferred.

COSTS AND FINANCIAL AID

Annual in-state tuition $9,481. Annual out-of-state tuition $21,930. Room and board $9,481. Required fees $2,721. Average book expense $853. **Required Forms and Deadlines:** FAFSA. **Notification of Awards:** Applicants will be notified of awards on a rolling basis beginning 12/15. **Types of Aid:** *Need-based scholarships/grants:* College/university scholarship or grant aid from institutional funds; Federal Nursing Scholarships; Federal Pell; Private scholarships; SEOG; State scholarships/grants. *Loans:* Direct PLUS loans; Direct Subsidized Stafford Loans; Direct Unsubsidized Stafford Loans. *Student Employment:* Federal Work-Study Program available. Institutional employment available. **Financial Aid Statistics:** 80% needy freshmen, 75% needy undergrads receive need-based scholarship or grant aid. 71% freshmen, 34% undergrads receive non-need-based scholarship or grant aid. 78% freshmen, 82% undergrads receive need-based self-help aid. 1% freshmen, 1% undergrads receive athletic scholarships. 75% freshmen, 67% undergrads receive any aid. **Criteria for awarding aid:** *Non-need-based:* Academics, Art, Athletics, Leadership, Minority status, Music/drama.

SOUTHERN MAINE COMMUNITY COLLEGE

2 Fort Road, South Portland, ME 04106
Phone: (207) 741-5800
E-mail: admissions@smccme.edu
Fax: 207-741-5760 • **Website:** http://www.smccme.edu

This public school was founded in 1946. It has a 80 acre campus.

RATINGS

Admissions Selectivity Rating: 0   **Fire Safety Rating:** 60*   **Green Rating:** 60*

STUDENTS AND FACULTY

Enrollment: 4,962. **Student Body:** 54% female, 46% male, 1% international. Asian 2%, African American 8%, Caucasian 80%, Hispanic 3%, Native American 1%, Pacific Islander <1%, Two or more races 3%, Race unknown 3%. **Faculty:** Student/faculty ratio 18:1. 0% of classes are taught by teaching assistants.

ACADEMICS

Degrees: Associate; Certificate; Terminal Associate; Transfer Associate **Classes:** Most classes have 10-19 students. **Special Study Options:** Cross-registration; Distance learning; Double major; Dual enrollment; English as a Second Language (ESL); Honors program; Independent study; Internships; Liberal arts/career combination; Study abroad. **Disability Services offered to physically disabled students:** Note-taking services.

FACILITIES

Housing: Coed dorms; Men's dorms

CAMPUS LIFE

Environment: Town **Activities:** Choral groups; Drama/theater; Literary magazine; Student government; Student newspaper. Campus Center (offices, coffee shop, library, tutoring center)

ADMISSIONS

Test Scores: Minimum internet-based TOEFL 61. Minimum paper TOEFL 500. **Basis for Candidate Selection:** *Other factors considered include:* state residency. **Freshman Admission Requirements:** High school diploma is required and GED is accepted **General Admission Information:** Application fee $20. Nonfall registration accepted. Admission may be deferred.

COSTS AND FINANCIAL AID

Required Forms and Deadlines: FAFSA. **Types of Aid:** *Need-based scholarships/grants:* College/university scholarship or grant aid from institutional funds; Federal Pell; Private scholarships; State scholarships/grants. *Loans:* Direct PLUS loans; Direct Subsidized Stafford Loans; Direct Unsubsidized Stafford Loans.

SOUTHERN METHODIST UNIVERSITY

P.O. Box 750181, Dallas, TX 75275-0181
Phone: 214-768-2058 • **Financial Aid Phone:** 214-768-3417
E-mail: ugadmission@smu.edu • **CEEB Code:** 6660
Fax: 214-768-0103 • **Website:** www.smu.edu • **ACT Code:** 4171

This private school, affiliated with the Methodist Church, was founded in 1911. It has a 234 acre campus.

RATINGS

Admissions Selectivity Rating: 92   **Fire Safety Rating:** 97   **Green Rating:** 60*

STUDENTS AND FACULTY

Enrollment: 6,427. **Student Body:** 50% female, 50% male, 55% out-of-state, 9% international (62 countries represented). Asian 6%, African American 5%, Caucasian 65%, Hispanic 11%, Native American <1%, Pacific Islander <1%, Two or more races 4%, Race unknown <1%. **Retention and Graduation:** 91% freshmen return for sophomore year. 71% freshmen graduate within 4 years. 81% freshmen graduate within 6 years. **Faculty:** Student/faculty ratio 11:1. 758 full-time faculty, 82% hold PhDs, 18% are members of minority groups, 40% are women.

ACADEMICS

Degrees: Bachelor's; Doctoral; Doctoral/Professional; Doctoral/Research; Master's; Post-Bachelor's certificate; Post-Master's certificate **Classes:** Most classes have 20-29 students. Most lab/discussion sessions have 10-19 students. **Most popular majors:** Economics, General; Accounting; Finance, General. **Special Study Options:** Accelerated program; Cooperative education program; Distance learning; Double major; Dual enrollment; English as a Second Language (ESL); Exchange student program (domestic); Honors program; Independent study; Internships; Liberal arts/career combination; Student-designed major; Study abroad; Teacher certification program; Weekend college. Honors programs: The University Honors Program is designed to prepare Honors students for a new millennium to ensure that they can cope with the challenges of rapid change while taking advantage of the possibilities such a volatile and versatile world presents. The BBA Honors Program, which is separate from the University Honors Program, is composed of special sections of courses in accounting, finance, statistics, operations management, marketing, and management. Advertising Honors Program: A student may apply for the Temerlin Advertising Institute Honors program after completion of his or her first semester as a declared Advertising major. Combined degree programs: BA/MEng. **Disability Services offered to physically disabled students:** Note-taking services; Reader services; Tape recorders; Tutors. **Career services:** Alumni network; Alumni services; Career assessment; Career/job search classes; Internships; Regional alumni

FACILITIES

Housing: Apartments for married students; Apartments for single students; Coed dorms; Cooperative housing; Fraternity/sorority housing; Theme housing 95% of campus accessible to physically diasbled. **Special Academic Facilities/Equipment:** Art, natural history, and paleontology museums, southwest film/video archives, sculpture garden, performing arts theatres, pollen analysis and geothermal labs, electron microbe lab, microscopy lab, seismological observatory, institute of technology services, TV studio. **Computers:** 30% of classrooms, 100% of dorms, 100% of libraries, 100% of dining areas, 100% of student union, 10% of common outdoor areas have wireless network access. Students can register for classes online. Administrative functions (other than registration) can be performed online.

CAMPUS LIFE

Environment: Metropolis **Activities:** Campus Ministries; Choral groups; Concert band; Dance; Drama/theater; International Student Organization; Jazz band; Literary magazine; Marching band; Model UN; Music ensembles; Musical theater; Opera; Pep band; Radio station; Student government; Student newspaper; Student-run film society; Symphony orchestra; Television station; Yearbook 180 registered organizations, 15 honor societies, 27 religious organizations. 15 fraternities, 13 sororities. **Athletics (Intercollegiate):** *Men:* basketball, diving, football, golf, soccer, swimming, tennis, volleyball, water polo. *Women:* basketball, crew/rowing, cross-country, diving, equestrian sports, golf, soccer, swimming, tennis, track/field (outdoor), volleyball, water polo. **On-Campus Highlights:** Dallas Hall, Meadows Museum, Hughes Trigg Student Center, Gerald J Ford Stadium, Fondren Library **Environmental Initiatives:** Broad academic commitment: research from Geothermal Energy Lab has revealed widespread availability of green energy source. Geothermal Lab's partnership with Google.org has resulted in sophisticated mapping of geothermal resources across North America. Lab hosts annual geothermal conference attended by the international community. Undergraduate and Graduate environmental degrees available through three portals: the Environmental Studies and Environmental Science programs in Dedman College of Science and Humanities, and the Environmental and Civil Engineering Department of the Lyle School of Engineering.

ADMISSIONS

Freshman Academic Profile: Average high school GPA 3.6. 52% in top 10% of high school class, 79% in top 25% of high school class, 95% in top 50% of high school class. 44% from public high schools. **Test Scores:** SAT Math middle 50% range 640-730. SAT EBRW middle 50% range 630-710. ACT middle 50% range 28-32. Minimum internet-based TOEFL 80. Minimum paper TOEFL 550. **Basis for Candidate Selection:** *Very important factors considered include:* rigor of secondary school record, academic GPA, application essay, standard-ized test scores, recommendation(s). *Important factors considered include:* class rank, extracurricular activities, talent/ability, character/personal qualities. *Other factors considered include:* first generation, alumni/ae relation, racial/ethnic status, volunteer work, work experience, level of applicant's interest. **Freshman Admission Requirements:** High school diploma is required and GED is not accepted *Academic units required:* 4 English, 3 math, 3 science, 2 science labs, 2 foreign language, 3 social studies, *Academic units recommended:* 4 English, 4 math, 3 science, 2 science labs, 3 foreign language, 3 history, 3 academic electives. **Freshman Admission Statistics:** 13,128 applied, 48.8% admitted, 22% enrolled. **Transfer Admission Requirements:** college transcript(s), essay or personal statement, Minimum college GPA of 2.7 required. Lowest grade transferable C-. **General Admission Information:** Application fee $60. Priority deadline 1/15. Regular application deadline 1/15. Nonfall registration accepted. Admission may be deferred for a maximum of 1 year.

COSTS AND FINANCIAL AID

Annual tuition $48,365. Room and board $16,910. Required fees $6,128. Average book expense $800. **Required Forms and Deadlines:** CSS/Financial Aid PROFILE; FAFSA; Noncustodial PROFILE. **Notification of Awards:** Applicants will be notified of awards on or about 1/20. **Types of Aid:** *Need-based scholarships/grants:* College/university scholarship or grant aid from institutional funds; Federal Pell; Private scholarships; SEOG; State scholarships/grants. *Loans:* Direct PLUS loans; Direct Subsidized Stafford Loans; Direct Unsubsidized Stafford Loans. *Student Employment:* Federal Work-Study Program available. Institutional employment available. **Financial Aid Statistics:** 64% needy freshmen, 73% needy undergrads receive need-based scholarship or grant aid. 78% freshmen, 68% undergrads receive non-need-based scholarship or grant aid. 74% freshmen, 80% undergrads receive need-based self-help aid. 5% freshmen, 5% undergrads receive athletic scholarships. 73% freshmen, 70% undergrads receive any aid. Average cumulative indebtedness $29,601. **Criteria for awarding aid:** *Need-based:* Religious affiliation *Non-need-based:* Academics, Alumni affiliation, Art, Athletics, Leadership, Music/drama.

SOUTHERN NEW HAMPSHIRE UNIVERSITY

2500 North River Road, Manchester, NH 03106-1045
Phone: 603-645-9611 • **Financial Aid Phone:** 603-645-9645
E-mail: admission@snhu.edu • **CEEB Code:** 3649
Fax: 603-645-9693 • **Website:** www.snhu.edu • **ACT Code:** 2514

This private school was founded in 1932. It has a 300 acre campus.

RATINGS

Admissions Selectivity Rating: 73   **Fire Safety Rating:** 97   **Green Rating:** 60*

STUDENTS AND FACULTY

Enrollment: 1,929. **Student Body:** 52% female, 48% male, 55% out-of-state, 5% international (79 countries represented). Asian 1%, African American 1%, Caucasian 75%, Hispanic 2%, Native American <1%, Race unknown 15%. **Retention and Graduation:** 68% freshmen return for sophomore year. 12% grads go on to further study within 1 year. **Faculty:** Student/faculty ratio 16:1. 120 full-time faculty, 76% hold PhDs, 12% are members of minority groups, 38% are women. 0% of classes are taught by teaching assistants.

ACADEMICS

Degrees: Associate; Bachelor's; Certificate; Master's; Post-Bachelor's certificate; Post-Master's certificate **Classes:** Most classes have 10-19 students. Most lab/discussion sessions have 10-19 students. **Most popular majors:** Culinary Arts/Chef Training; Psychology, General; Business Administration And Management, General. **Special Study Options:** Accelerated program; Cooperative education program; Distance learning; Double major; Dual enrollment; English as a Second Language (ESL); Honors program; Independent study; Internships; Student-designed major; Study abroad; Teacher certification program; Weekend college. Honors programs: Three-Year Honors Program (B.S. in Business Administration) and our traditional four-year honors program (available in conjunction with most majors). **Disability Services offered to physically disabled students:** Note-taking services; Reader services; Tape recorders; Tutors. **Career services:** Alumni network; Alumni services; Career assessment; Career/job search classes; Internships

FACILITIES

Housing: Apartments for single students; Coed dorms; Special housing for disabled student; Theme housing; Wellness housing 85% of campus accessible to physically diasbled. **Special Academic Facilities/Equipment:** Art Gallery **Computers:** 100% of classrooms, 40% of dorms, 100% of libraries, 100% of dining areas, 100% of student union, have wireless network access. Students can register for classes online. Undergraduates are required to own a computer.

CAMPUS LIFE

Environment: City **Activities:** Campus Ministries; Choral groups; Concert band; Dance; Drama/theater; International Student Organization; Jazz band; Literary magazine; Model UN; Musical theater; Radio station; Student government; Student newspaper; Television station; Yearbook 58 registered organizations, 7 honor societies, 1 religious organization. 3 fraternities, 3 sororities. **Athletics (Intercollegiate):** *Men:* baseball, basketball, cheerleading, cross-country, golf, ice hockey, lacrosse, soccer, tennis. *Women:* basketball, cheerleading, cross-country, lacrosse, soccer, softball, tennis, volleyball. **On-Campus Highlights:** Center for Financial Studies, Fitness Center / Athletic Complex, Robert Frost Hall (Academic Building), McIninch Art Gallery, Last Chapter Pub **Environmental Initiatives:** Renewable Energy Hedge from 2007-2022 based on 17,500 megawatt hours of wind power output with PPM Energy Inc. By a financial swap, the hedge will flat line SNHU energy budget, and 100% offset energy green house gas use in the voluntary market with RECs, and provide the wind developer a consistent stream of income to facilitate more wind construction. This represents a new sustainable model of utility cost control based on long-term agreements between energy users and renewable developers.

ADMISSIONS

Freshman Academic Profile: Average high school GPA 3.0. 88% from public high schools. **Test Scores:** SAT Math middle 50% range 440-540. SAT EBRW middle 50% range 440-520. ACT middle 50% range 18-24. Minimum internet-based TOEFL 71. Minimum paper TOEFL 530. **Basis for Candidate Selection:** *Very important factors considered include:* rigor of secondary school record, academic GPA. *Important factors considered include:* application essay, recommendation(s), extracurricular activities, character/personal qualities, first generation, level of applicant's interest. *Other factors considered include:* class rank, standardized test scores, interview, talent/ability, alumni/ae relation, volunteer work, work experience. **Freshman Admission Requirements:** High school diploma is required and GED is accepted *Academic units required:* 4 English, 3 math, 3 science, 2 science labs, 2 foreign language, 2 social studies, 2 history. **Freshman Admission Statistics:** 3,124 applied, 84.2% admitted, 18% enrolled. **Transfer Admission Requirements:** High school transcript, college transcript(s), essay or personal statement, Minimum college GPA of 2.50 required. Lowest grade transferable C-. **General Admission Information:** Application fee $40. Priority deadline 3/15. Nonfall registration accepted. Admission may be deferred for a maximum of 1 year.

COSTS AND FINANCIAL AID

Required Forms and Deadlines: FAFSA. **Notification of Awards:** Applicants will be notified of awards on a rolling basis beginning 3/1. **Types of Aid:** *Need-based scholarships/grants:* College/university scholarship or grant aid from institutional funds; Federal Pell; Private scholarships; SEOG; State scholarships/grants. *Loans:* Direct PLUS loans; Direct Subsidized Stafford Loans; Direct Unsubsidized Stafford Loans. *Student Employment:* Federal Work-Study Program available. Institutional employment available. **Financial Aid Statistics:** 94% freshmen, 93% undergrads receive any aid. **Criteria for awarding aid:** *Need-based:* Academics *Non-need-based:* Academics, Alumni affiliation, Athletics, Leadership, State/district residency.

SOUTHERN OREGON UNIVERSITY

1250 Siskiyou Blvd., Ashland, OR 97520-5032
Phone: 541-552-6411 • **Financial Aid Phone:** (541)552-6600
E-mail: admissions@sou.edu • **CEEB Code:** 4702
Fax: 541-552-8403 • **Website:** www.sou.edu • **ACT Code:** 3496

This public school was founded in 1926. It has a 175 acre campus.

RATINGS

Admissions Selectivity Rating: 76   **Fire Safety Rating:** 88   **Green Rating:** 96

STUDENTS AND FACULTY

Enrollment: 4,064. **Student Body:** 59% female, 41% male, 40% out-of-state, 3% international (12 countries represented). Asian 2%, African American 2%, Caucasian 59%, Hispanic 12%, Native American 1%, Pacific Islander 1%, Two or more races 10%, Race unknown 10%.
Retention and Graduation: 68% freshmen return for sophomore year.
Faculty: Student/faculty ratio 21:1. 167 full-time faculty, 67% hold PhDs, 17% are members of minority groups, 44% are women. 0% of classes are taught by teaching assistants.

ACADEMICS

Degrees: Bachelor's; Certificate; Master's; Post-Bachelor's certificate **Classes:** Most classes have 20-29 students. Most lab/discussion sessions have 20-29 students. **Most popular majors:** Psychology, General; Visual And Performing Arts, General; Business Administration And Management, General. **Special Study Options:** Accelerated program; Cross-registration; Distance learning; Double major; Dual enrollment; English as a Second Language (ESL); Exchange student program (domestic); Honors program; Independent study; Internships; Student-designed major; Study abroad; Teacher certification program. Honors programs: SOU established an Honors College in Fall 13 with a mission & vision of combing real world projects with intellectual rigor, aiming to provide a challenging learning environment. Our creative curricula will take advantage of the university's unique location by drawing on the rich natural, cultural, and artistic resources that are Southern Oregon. Southern Oregon University seeks to create a community of learners prepared for a lifetime of intellectual curiosity, inquiry, scholarship, and service. The Honors College accepts students from every major and allows for a truly customizable academic plan. You are unique, so why stick with a generic course of study? If you think

one major just isn't enough for you, you can work with professors and advisors to create your own interdisciplinary major. Every Honors student will work with a community mentor: a local professional working in a field of your interest. With your mentor's guidance, you will conduct an applied research or a creative project and present it to a group composed of all those who helped you along the way. You can do corporate internships, write a groundbreaking sonnet cycle or one-act play, help a local business get on its feet, seek to disprove a popular theorem, and more. This is more than just networking; it's an exploration of the uncharted world some call "life after college." You will graduate with the necessary skills and experience to feel at home in your professional environment of choice. **Disability Services offered to physically disabled students:** Note-taking services; Reader services; Tape recorders; Tutors. **Career services:** Alumni network; Alumni services; Career assessment; Career/job search classes; Internships; Regional alumni

FACILITIES

Housing: Apartments for married students; Apartments for single students; Coed dorms; Special housing for disabled student; Special housing for international students; Theme housing; Wellness housing 80% of campus accessible to physically diasbled. **Special Academic Facilities/Equipment:** Art and history museums, art galleries, on-campus preschool and kindergarten, National Guard armory, United States Wildlife Forensics Lab. **Computers:** Students can register for classes online. Administrative functions (other than registration) can be performed online.

CAMPUS LIFE

Environment: Town **Activities:** Campus Ministries; Choral groups; Concert band; Dance; Drama/theater; International Student Organization; Jazz band; Literary magazine; Music ensembles; Musical theater; Pep band; Radio station; Student government; Student newspaper; Student-run film society; Symphony orchestra; Television station 52 registered organizations, 13 honor societies, 5 religious organizations. **Athletics (Intercollegiate):** *Men:* basketball, cross-country, football, track/field (outdoor), wrestling. *Women:* basketball, cross-country, soccer, softball, tennis, track/field (outdoor), volleyball. **On-Campus Highlights:** Hannon Library, Center for the Visual Arts, Student Union, Theatre Building, Residence Halls **Environmental Initiatives:** Through the student-initiated Green Energy Fee, SOU purchases Renewable Energy Certificates (RECs) to offset 100% of its electricity consumption and carbon offsets to offset 100% of its natural gas consumption. Among the 54 colleges and universities that are U. S. EPA Green Power Partners, SOU ranked #12 on the EPA's April 6, 2010 Top 20 College & University list.

ADMISSIONS

Freshman Academic Profile: Average high school GPA 3.3. 90% from public high schools. **Test Scores:** SAT Math middle 50% range 440-550. SAT EBRW middle 50% range 460-580. ACT middle 50% range 19-25. Minimum paper TOEFL 520. **Basis for Candidate Selection:** *Very important factors considered include:* academic GPA, standardized test scores. *Other factors considered include:* rigor of secondary school record, application essay, recommendation(s), interview, extracurricular activities, geographical residence, state residency, volunteer work. **Freshman Admission Requirements:** High school diploma is required and GED is accepted *Academic units required:* 4 English, 3 math, 2 science, 1 science labs, 2 foreign language, 3 social studies. **Freshman Admission Statistics:** 2,766 applied, 78.2% admitted, 31% enrolled. **Transfer Admission Requirements:** college transcript(s), Minimum college GPA of 2.2 required. Lowest grade transferable D-. **General Admission Information:** Application fee $60. Priority deadline 2/15. Nonfall registration accepted. Admission may be deferred for a maximum of 1 year.

COSTS AND FINANCIAL AID

Annual in-state tuition $11,610. Annual out-of-state tuition $21,460. Room and board $11,610. Required fees $1,710. Average book expense $999. **Required Forms and Deadlines:** FAFSA. **Notification of Awards:** Applicants will be notified of awards on a rolling basis beginning 3/2. **Types of Aid:** *Need-based scholarships/grants:* College/university scholarship or grant aid from institutional funds; Federal Pell; Private scholarships; SEOG; State scholarships/grants. *Loans:* Direct PLUS loans; Direct Subsidized Stafford Loans; Direct Unsubsidized Stafford Loans. *Student Employment:* Federal Work-Study Program available. Institutional employment available. **Financial Aid Statistics:** 77% needy freshmen, 43% needy undergrads receive need-based scholarship or grant aid. 59% freshmen, 45% undergrads receive non-need-based scholarship or grant aid. 73% freshmen, 41% undergrads receive need-based self-help aid. 7% freshmen, 5% undergrads receive athletic scholarships. 70% freshmen, 81% undergrads receive any aid. 89% undergrads borrow to pay for school. Average cumulative indebtedness $24,179. **Criteria for awarding aid:** *Need-based:* Academics *Non-need-based:* Academics, Athletics, State/district residency.

SOUTHERN UNIVERSITY AND A&M COLLEGE

Southern Branch Post Office, Baton Rouge, LA 70813
Phone: 225-771-2430 • **Financial Aid Phone:** 225-771-2790
E-mail: admit@subr.edu • **CEEB Code:** 6663
Fax: 225-771-2500 • **Website:** subr.edu • **ACT Code:** 1610

This public school was founded in 1880. It has a 884 acre campus.

RATINGS
Admissions Selectivity Rating: 83   **Fire Safety Rating:** 82   **Green Rating:** 60*

STUDENTS AND FACULTY
Enrollment: 6,830. **Student Body:** 61% female, 39% male, 19% out-of-state, 2% international (48 countries represented). Asian <1%, African American 95%, Caucasian 3%, Hispanic <1%, Native American <1%, Race unknown 0%. **Retention and Graduation:** 65% freshmen return for sophomore year. 16% grads go on to further study within 1 year. 15% grads pursue arts and sciences degrees. 1% grads pursue law degrees. 0% grads pursue business degrees. 0% grads pursue medical degrees. **Faculty:** Student/faculty ratio 16:1. 405 full-time faculty, 66% hold PhDs, 85% are members of minority groups, 47% are women. 0% of classes are taught by teaching assistants.

ACADEMICS
Degrees: Associate; Bachelor's; Master's; Post-Master's certificate **Classes:** Most classes have 10-19 students. Most lab/discussion sessions have 10-19 students. **Most popular majors:** Biology/Biological Sciences, General; Nursing/Registered Nurse (Rn, Asn, Bsn, Msn); Business Administration And Management, General. **Special Study Options:** Cooperative education program; Cross-registration; Distance learning; Double major; Dual enrollment; Exchange student program (domestic); Honors program; Independent study; Internships; Study abroad; Teacher certification program; Weekend college. Honors programs: The Honors College provides an enhances educational experience for students who have a history of strong academic achievement and who have demonstrated exceptional creativity or talent. The College also provides cultural and intellectual opportunities that are designed to motivae students to perform at the highest level of excellence that they are capable of and through which they may become knowledgeable and effective leaders. **Disability Services offered to physically disabled students:** Note-taking services; Tape recorders; Tutors. **Career services:** Career/job search classes; Internships

FACILITIES
Housing: Men's dorms; Special housing for disabled student; Women's dorms 100% of campus accessible to physically diasbled. **Special Academic Facilities/Equipment:** Jazz institute Southern Museum of Art **Computers:** 100% of classrooms, 20% of dorms, 100% of libraries, 50% of dining areas, 90% of student union, 25% of common outdoor areas have wireless network access. Students can register for classes online. Administrative functions (other than registration) can be performed online.

CAMPUS LIFE
Environment: Metropolis **Activities:** Choral groups; Concert band; Dance; Drama/theater; Jazz band; Literary magazine; Marching band; Music ensembles; Musical theater; Pep band; Student government; Student newspaper; Yearbook 88 registered organizations, 11 honor societies, 6 religious organizations. 4 fraternities, 4 sororities. **Athletics (Intercollegiate):** *Men:* baseball, basketball, cross-country, football, golf, tennis, track/field (outdoor). *Women:* basketball, cross-country, golf, softball, tennis, track/field (outdoor), volleyball. **On-Campus Highlights:** SUBR Museum of Art, Smith—Brown Student Union, Site of the original Red Stick for Baton, Bluff over the Mississippi River **Environmental Initiatives:** MS4-Stormwater Permit with the Parish of East Baton Rouge

ADMISSIONS
Freshman Academic Profile: Average high school GPA 2.8. 3% in top 10% of high school class, 13% in top 25% of high school class, 40% in top 50% of high school class. **Test Scores:** SAT Math middle 50% range 380-460. ACT middle 50% range 15-18. **Basis for Candidate Selection:** *Very important factors considered include:* rigor of secondary school record, class rank, academic GPA, standardized test scores. *Other factors considered include:* talent/ability. **Freshman Admission Requirements:** High school diploma is required and GED is accepted *Academic units required:* 4 English, 3 math, 3 science, 2 foreign language, 2 social studies, 1 history, and 1 unit from above areas or other academic areas. **Freshman Admission Statistics:** 4,703 applied, 52.7% admitted, 60% enrolled. **Transfer Admission Requirements:** High school transcript, college transcript(s), standardized test scores, statement of good standing from prior institution(s). Minimum college GPA of 2.0 required.

Lowest grade transferable C. **General Admission Information:** Application fee $20. Regular application deadline 7/1. Nonfall registration accepted. Admission may be deferred for a maximum of 2 semesters.

COSTS AND FINANCIAL AID
Annual in-state tuition $5,784. Annual out-of-state tuition $9,458. Room and board $5,784. Average book expense $1,200. **Required Forms and Deadlines:** FAFSA; Institution's own financial aid form. **Notification of Awards:** Applicants will be notified of awards on a rolling basis beginning 6/30. **Types of Aid:** *Need-based scholarships/grants:* College/university scholarship or grant aid from institutional funds; Federal Pell; Private scholarships; SEOG; State scholarships/grants. *Loans:* Direct PLUS loans; Direct Subsidized Stafford Loans; Direct Unsubsidized Stafford Loans. *Student Employment:* Federal Work-Study Program available. Institutional employment available. **Financial Aid Statistics:** 80% needy freshmen, 77% needy undergrads receive need-based scholarship or grant aid. 21% freshmen, 18% undergrads receive non-need-based scholarship or grant aid. 79% freshmen, 89% undergrads receive need-based self-help aid. 5% freshmen, 3% undergrads receive athletic scholarships. 89% freshmen, 85% undergrads receive any aid. **Criteria for awarding aid:** *Need-based:* Academics, Alumni affiliation, Athletics, Music/drama *Non-need-based:* Academics, Athletics.

SOUTHERN UTAH UNIVERSITY

351 W University Blvd, Cedar City, UT 84720
Phone: 435-586-7740 • **Financial Aid Phone:** 435-586-7735
E-mail: adminfo@suu.edu • **CEEB Code:** 4092
Fax: 435-865-8223 • **Website:** www.suu.edu • **ACT Code:** 4271

This public school was founded in 1897. It has a 113 acre campus.

RATINGS
Admissions Selectivity Rating: 77   **Fire Safety Rating:** 60*   **Green Rating:** 60*

STUDENTS AND FACULTY
Enrollment: 6,849. **Student Body:** 54% female, 46% male, 17% out-of-state, 6% international (46 countries represented). Asian 1%, African American 2%, Caucasian 75%, Hispanic 6%, Native American 1%, Pacific Islander 1%, Two or more races <1%, Race unknown 6%. **Retention and Graduation:** 71% freshmen return for sophomore year. 19% freshmen graduate within 4 years. 37% freshmen graduate within 6 years. **Faculty:** Student/faculty ratio 19:1. 303 full-time faculty, 60% hold PhDs, 7% are members of minority groups, 34% are women. 0% of classes are taught by teaching assistants.

ACADEMICS
Degrees: Associate; Bachelor's; Certificate; Diploma; Master's; Terminal Associate; Transfer Associate **Classes:** Most classes have 10-19 students. **Most popular majors:** General Studies; Biology/Biological Sciences, General; Psychology, General. **Special Study Options:** Cooperative education program; Distance learning; Double major; Dual enrollment; English as a Second Language (ESL); Exchange student program (domestic); Honors program; Independent study; Internships; Liberal arts/career combination; Student-designed major; Study abroad; Teacher certification program; Weekend college. **Disability Services offered to physically disabled students:** Note-taking services; Reader services; Tape recorders; Tutors. **Career services:** Alumni services; Career assessment; Career/job search classes; Internships

FACILITIES
Housing: Apartments for single students; Coed dorms; Special housing for disabled student; Special housing for international students; Theme housing **Special Academic Facilities/Equipment:** Art gallery, natural history museum, farm and ranch, TV studio.

CAMPUS LIFE
Environment: Village **Activities:** Campus Ministries; Choral groups; Concert band; Dance; Drama/theater; International Student Organization; Jazz band; Literary magazine; Marching band; Music ensembles; Musical theater; Opera; Pep band; Radio station; Student government; Student newspaper; Student-run film society; Symphony orchestra; Television station. **Athletics (Intercollegiate):** *Men:* baseball, basketball, cross-country, football, golf, track/field (outdoor). *Women:* basketball, cross-country, gymnastics, softball, tennis, track/field (outdoor). Shakespeare Festival, Carter Carillon, Student Center, Library

ADMISSIONS
Freshman Academic Profile: Average high school GPA 3.5. 18% in top 10% of high school class, 45% in top 25% of high school class, 73% in top 50% of high school class. **Test Scores:** SAT Math middle 50% range 500-

600. SAT EBRW middle 50% range 510-620. ACT middle 50% range 20-27. Minimum internet-based TOEFL 71. Minimum paper TOEFL 525. **Basis for Candidate Selection:** *Very important factors considered include:* academic GPA, standardized test scores. *Important factors considered include:* level of applicant's interest. **Freshman Admission Requirements:** High school diploma is required and GED is accepted *Academic units recommended:* 4 English, 3 math, 3 science, 1 science labs, 2 foreign language, 3 social studies. **Freshman Admission Statistics:** 11,693 applied, 75.8% admitted, 21% enrolled. **Transfer Admission Requirements:** college transcript(s), Minimum college GPA of 2.25 required. Lowest grade transferable D. **General Admission Information:** Application fee $50. Priority deadline 12/1. Regular application deadline 5/1. Nonfall registration accepted. Admission may be deferred for a maximum of 5 semesters.

COSTS AND FINANCIAL AID
Annual in-state tuition $7,067. Annual out-of-state tuition $19,530. Room and board $7,067. Required fees $758. Average book expense $1,600. **Required Forms and Deadlines:** FAFSA; Institution's own financial aid form. **Notification of Awards:** Applicants will be notified of awards on a rolling basis beginning 3/14. **Types of Aid:** *Need-based scholarships/grants:* College/university scholarship or grant aid from institutional funds; Federal Pell; Private scholarships; SEOG; State scholarships/grants. *Loans:* Direct PLUS loans; Direct Subsidized Stafford Loans; Direct Unsubsidized Stafford Loans. *Student Employment:* Federal Work-Study Program available. Institutional employment available. **Financial Aid Statistics:** 62% needy freshmen, 72% needy undergrads receive need-based scholarship or grant aid. 60% freshmen, 33% undergrads receive non-need-based scholarship or grant aid. 91% freshmen, 93% undergrads receive need-based self-help aid. 5% freshmen, 5% undergrads receive athletic scholarships. 51% undergrads borrow to pay for school. Average cumulative indebtedness $16,892. **Criteria for awarding aid:** *Non-need-based:* Academics, Alumni affiliation, Art, Athletics, Job skills, Leadership, Minority status, Music/drama, State/district residency.

SOUTHERN WESLEYAN UNIVERSITY

Wesleyan Drive, Central, SC 29630-1020
Phone: 864-644-5550 • **Financial Aid Phone:** 864-644-5500
E-mail: admissions@swu.edu • **CEEB Code:** 5896
Fax: 864-644-5972 • **Website:** www.swu.edu • **ACT Code:** 3837

This private school, affiliated with the Wesleyan Church, was founded in 1906. It has a 330 acre campus.

RATINGS
Admissions Selectivity Rating: 72   **Fire Safety Rating:** 77   **Green Rating:** 60*

STUDENTS AND FACULTY
Enrollment: 1,444. **Student Body:** 60% female, 40% male, 28% out-of-state, 1% international (9 countries represented). Asian <1%, African American 27%, Caucasian 61%, Hispanic 2%, Native American 1%, Pacific Islander 0%, Two or more races 0%, Race unknown 8%.
Retention and Graduation: 70% freshmen return for sophomore year.
Faculty: Student/faculty ratio 18:1. 58 full-time faculty, 72% hold PhDs, 12% are members of minority groups, 31% are women. 0% of classes are taught by teaching assistants.

ACADEMICS
Degrees: Associate; Bachelor's; **Master's Classes:** Most classes have 20-29 students. Most lab/discussion sessions have 10-19 students. **Most popular majors:** Elementary Education And Teaching; Religion/Religious Studies; Business/Commerce, General. **Special Study Options:** Cross-registration; Distance learning; Double major; Dual enrollment; English as a Second Language (ESL); Honors program; Independent study; Internships; Student-designed major; Study abroad; Teacher certification program. Honors programs: The honors program consists of specialized coursework, non-credit academic experiences, and service opportunities. Honors students must complete a research-based Honors Major Project in their Junior or Senior years. **Disability Services offered to physically disabled students:** Note-taking services; Reader services; Tape recorders; Tutors. **Career services:** Career assessment; Career/job search classes; Internships

FACILITIES
Housing: Apartments for single students; Coed dorms; Special housing for disabled student; Women's dorms 90% of campus accessible to physically disabled. **Special Academic Facilities/Equipment:** Freedom's Hill Historic Site, a restored abolitionist church founded in 1848 in Alamance County, NC. The church has many artifacts from its time as a site along the Underground Railroad including bullet holes in the door, evidence of the many attempts to frighten the congregation and impede their abolitionist activities. The Eleanor Gardner Collection: a collection of brass rubbings from medieval burial coverings, the earliest dating from the 12th century. The Faith Clayton Collection: extensive genealogical records from South Carolina and the southeast region of the U.S. The Wesleyana Collection: a compilation of classic theological works from the Wesleyan and Holiness denominational traditions. The Evatt Heritage Center, the university's historical museum and archive. **Computers:** 100% of classrooms, 50% of dorms, 100% of libraries, 100% of dining areas, 100% of student union, 25% of common outdoor areas have wireless network access. Students can register for classes online. Administrative functions (other than registration) can be performed online.

CAMPUS LIFE
Environment: Town **Activities:** Campus Ministries; Choral groups; Concert band; Drama/theater; Jazz band; Literary magazine; Music ensembles; Musical theater; Student government; Yearbook 12 registered organizations, 2 honor societies, 3 religious organizations. **Athletics (Intercollegiate):** *Men:* baseball, basketball, cross-country, golf, soccer. *Women:* basketball, cross-country, soccer, softball, volleyball. **On-Campus Highlights:** Jennings Campus Center, Java City Coffee Shop, Historic Tysinger Gymnasium, Student Apartment Complex **Environmental Initiatives:** Voluntary recycling of paper and plastic in residence halls and academic buildings. Materials are collected by the city.

ADMISSIONS
Freshman Academic Profile: Average high school GPA 3.5. 13% in top 10% of high school class, 34% in top 25% of high school class, 75% in top 50% of high school class. **Test Scores:** SAT Math middle 50% range 445-550. SAT EBRW middle 50% range 430-540. ACT middle 50% range 18-22. Minimum paper TOEFL 500. **Basis for Candidate Selection:** *Very important factors considered include:* academic GPA, standardized test scores. *Important factors considered include:* rigor of secondary school record, class rank, talent/ability, character/personal qualities. *Other factors considered include:* recommendation(s). **Freshman Admission Requirements:** High school diploma is required and GED is accepted *Academic units recommended:* 4 English, 2 math, 2 science, 2 social studies. **Freshman Admission Statistics:** 575 applied, 93.9% admitted, 31% enrolled. **Transfer Admission Requirements:** college transcript(s), Minimum college GPA of 2.0 required. Lowest grade transferable C. **General Admission Information:** Application fee $25. Regular application deadline 8/1. Nonfall registration accepted. Admission may be deferred for a maximum of 1 semester.

COSTS AND FINANCIAL AID
Annual tuition $19,950. Room and board $8,410. Required fees $600. Average book expense $1,020. **Required Forms and Deadlines:** FAFSA; Institution's own financial aid form. **Notification of Awards:** Applicants will be notified of awards on a rolling basis beginning 2/1. **Types of Aid:** *Need-based scholarships/grants:* College/university scholarship or grant aid from institutional funds; Federal Pell; Private scholarships; SEOG; State scholarships/grants. *Loans:* Direct PLUS loans; Direct Subsidized Stafford Loans; Direct Unsubsidized Stafford Loans. *Student Employment:* Federal Work-Study Program available. Institutional employment available. **Financial Aid Statistics:** 100% needy freshmen, 91% needy undergrads receive need-based scholarship or grant aid. 16% freshmen, 8% undergrads receive non-need-based scholarship or grant aid. 73% freshmen, 80% undergrads receive need-based self-help aid. 5% freshmen, 2% undergrads receive athletic scholarships. 100% freshmen, 99% undergrads receive any aid. **Criteria for awarding aid:** *Non-need-based:* Academics, Athletics, Music/drama, Religious affiliation.

SOUTHWEST BAPTIST UNIVERSITY

1600 University Ave, Bolivar, MO 65613-2597
Phone: 417-328-1810 • **Financial Aid Phone:** 417-328-1823
E-mail: admitme@sbuniv.edu • **CEEB Code:** 6664
Fax: 417-328-1808 • **ACT Code:** 2368

This private school, affiliated with the Southern Baptist Church, was founded in 1878. It has a 180 acre campus.

RATINGS
Admissions Selectivity Rating: 73   **Fire Safety Rating:** 77   **Green Rating:** 60*

STUDENTS AND FACULTY
Enrollment: 2,646. **Student Body:** 66% female, 34% male, 29% out-of-state, 1% international (16 countries represented). Asian 1%, African American 4%, Caucasian 86%, Hispanic 1%, Native American 1%, Race unknown 6%.
Retention and Graduation: 70% freshmen return for sophomore year.
Faculty: Student/faculty ratio 13:1. 116 full-time faculty, 59% hold PhDs, 2% are members of minority groups, 41% are women. 0% of classes are taught by

teaching assistants.

ACADEMICS

Degrees: Associate; Bachelor's; Certificate; Doctoral/Professional; Master's; Post-Master's certificate **Classes:** Most classes have 10-19 students. **Most popular majors:** Elementary Education And Teaching; Psychology, General; Business Administration And Management, General. **Special Study Options:** Cooperative education program; Distance learning; Double major; Dual enrollment; Exchange student program (domestic); Honors program; Independent study; Internships; Student-designed major; Study abroad; Teacher certification program. Honors programs: Our academic honors program consists of the following components: academics, servant leadership, intercultural experiences, spiritual growth, and enrichment opportunities. **Disability Services offered to physically disabled students:** Note-taking services; Reader services; Tutors. **Career services:** Career assessment; Career/job search classes

FACILITIES

Housing: Apartments for single students; Men's dorms; Special housing for disabled student; Women's dorms 95% of campus accessible to physically diasbled. **Special Academic Facilities/Equipment:** The Driskell Art Gallery Jester Learning and Performance Center Meyer Wellness and Sports Center **Computers:** 100% of classrooms, 100% of dorms, 100% of libraries, 100% of dining areas, 100% of student union, 40% of common outdoor areas have wireless network access. Administrative functions (other than registration) can be performed online.

CAMPUS LIFE

Environment: Village **Activities:** Campus Ministries; Choral groups; Concert band; Drama/theater; Jazz band; Music ensembles; Musical theater; Opera; Pep band; Student government; Student newspaper; Symphony orchestra; Yearbook 34 registered organizations, 8 honor societies, 10 religious organizations. **Athletics (Intercollegiate):** *Men:* baseball, basketball, cheerleading, cross-country, football, golf, tennis, track/field (outdoor), track/field (indoor). *Women:* basketball, cheerleading, cross-country, soccer, softball, tennis, track/field (outdoor), track/field (indoor), volleyball. **On-Campus Highlights:** Meyer Wellness and Sports Center, Jester Learning and Performance Center, Felix Goodson Student Union, Harriet K. Hutchens Library, Plaster Stadium

ADMISSIONS

Freshman Academic Profile: Average high school GPA 3.5. 22% in top 10% of high school class, 41% in top 25% of high school class, 67% in top 50% of high school class. **Test Scores:** SAT Math middle 50% range 450-600. SAT EBRW middle 50% range 410-560. ACT middle 50% range 20-26. Minimum paper TOEFL 550. **Basis for Candidate Selection:** *Very important factors considered include:* class rank, academic GPA, standardized test scores. *Important factors considered include:* rigor of secondary school record, application essay, recommendation(s). *Other factors considered include:* interview, talent/ability, character/personal qualities. **Freshman Admission Requirements:** High school diploma is required and GED is accepted *Academic units recommended:* 4 English, 3 math, 2 science, 2 social studies, 2 units from above areas or other academic areas. **Freshman Admission Statistics:** 1,617 applied, 92.3% admitted, 31% enrolled. **Transfer Admission Requirements:** High school transcript, college transcript(s), standardized test scores, Minimum college GPA of 2.0 required. Lowest grade transferable D. **General Admission Information:** Application fee $30. Nonfall registration accepted. Admission may be deferred for a maximum of 1 year.

COSTS AND FINANCIAL AID

Annual tuition $16,500. Room and board $5,720. Required fees $780. Average book expense $1,000. **Required Forms and Deadlines:** FAFSA; Institution's own financial aid form. **Notification of Awards:** Applicants will be notified of awards on a rolling basis beginning 3/1. **Types of Aid:** *Need-based scholarships/grants:* College/university scholarship or grant aid from institutional funds; Federal Pell; Private scholarships; SEOG; State scholarships/grants. *Loans: Student Employment:* Federal Work-Study Program available. Institutional employment available. **Financial Aid Statistics:** 66% needy freshmen, 68% needy undergrads receive need-based scholarship or grant aid. 93% freshmen, 80% undergrads receive non-need-based scholarship or grant aid. 80% freshmen, 84% undergrads receive need-based self-help aid. 16% freshmen, 12% undergrads receive athletic scholarships. 88% freshmen, 71% undergrads receive any aid. **Criteria for awarding aid:** *Non-need-based:* Academics, Alumni affiliation, Art, Athletics, Job skills, Leadership, Minority status, Music/drama, Religious affiliation, State/district residency.

SOUTHWESTERN COLLEGE (AZ)

Office of Undergraduate Admissions, Phoenix, AZ 85032
Phone: 602-386-4100 · **Financial Aid Phone:** (602) 386-4106
E-mail: admissions@arizonachristian.edu
Fax: 602-404-2159 • **Website:** www.arizonachristian.edu

This private school was founded in 1960. It has a 17 acre campus.

RATINGS

Admissions Selectivity Rating: 82   **Fire Safety Rating:** 85   **Green Rating:** 60*

STUDENTS AND FACULTY

Enrollment: 175. **Student Body:** 57% female, 43% male, 27% out-of-state, 2% international. Asian 2%, African American 8%, Caucasian 79%, Hispanic 8%, Native American 1%, Race unknown <1%.
Retention and Graduation: 56% freshmen return for sophomore year.
Faculty: Student/faculty ratio 16:1. 13 full-time faculty, 69% hold PhDs,

ACADEMICS

Degrees: Associate; Bachelor's **Classes:** Most classes have 10-19 students. **Special Study Options:** Dual enrollment; Independent study; Internships; Teacher certification program. **Disability Services offered to physically disabled students:** Tutors.

FACILITIES

Housing: Apartments for single students; Men's dorms; Women's dorms

CAMPUS LIFE

Environment: Metropolis **Activities:** Campus Ministries; Choral groups; Drama/theater; Jazz band; Music ensembles; Musical theater; Yearbook. **Athletics (Intercollegiate):** *Men:* basketball. *Women:* basketball, volleyball.

ADMISSIONS

Freshman Academic Profile: 72% from public high schools. **Test Scores:** SAT Math middle 50% range 450-560. SAT EBRW middle 50% range 460-570. ACT middle 50% range 19-24. Minimum internet-based TOEFL 61. Minimum paper TOEFL 500. **Basis for Candidate Selection:** *Very important factors considered include:* rigor of secondary school record, academic GPA, application essay, standardized test scores, recommendation(s), religious affiliation/commitment. *Important factors considered include:* class rank, character/personal qualities, level of applicant's interest. *Other factors considered include:* interview, extracurricular activities, talent/ability. **Freshman Admission Requirements:** High school diploma is required and GED is accepted **Freshman Admission Statistics:** 223 applied, 74.4% admitted, 60% enrolled. **Transfer Admission Requirements:** High school transcript, college transcript(s), essay or personal statement, statement of good standing from prior institution(s). Minimum college GPA of 2.0 required. Lowest grade transferable C. **General Admission Information:** Application fee $30. Priority deadline 3/1. Nonfall registration accepted. Admission may be deferred for a maximum of 1 semester.

COSTS AND FINANCIAL AID

Annual tuition $17,982. Room and board $7,374. Required fees $986. Average book expense $1,600. **Required Forms and Deadlines:** FAFSA; Institution's own financial aid form. **Notification of Awards:** Applicants will be notified of awards on a rolling basis beginning 5/1. **Types of Aid:** *Need-based scholarships/grants:* College/university scholarship or grant aid from institutional funds; Federal Pell; Private scholarships; SEOG; State scholarships/grants. *Loans:* Direct PLUS loans; Direct Subsidized Stafford Loans; Direct Unsubsidized Stafford Loans. *Student Employment:* Federal Work-Study Program available. Institutional employment available. **Financial Aid Statistics:** 0% freshmen, 0% undergrads receive athletic scholarships. **Criteria for awarding aid:** *Need-based:* Minority status *Non-need-based:* Academics, Alumni affiliation, Athletics, Leadership, Music/drama, Religious affiliation.

SOUTHWESTERN COLLEGE (KS)

100 College Street, Winfield, KS 67156
Phone: 620-229-6236 • **Financial Aid Phone:** (620)229-6215
E-mail: scadmit@sckans.edu • **CEEB Code:** 6670
Fax: 620-229-6344 • **Website:** www.sckans.edu • **ACT Code:** 1464

This private school, affiliated with the Methodist Church, was founded in 1885. It has a 85 acre campus.

RATINGS
Admissions Selectivity Rating: 73   **Fire Safety Rating:** 85   **Green Rating:** 60*

STUDENTS AND FACULTY
Enrollment: 1,471. **Student Body:** 48% female, 52% male, 34% out-of-state, 1% international (12 countries represented). Asian 2%, African American 8%, Caucasian 63%, Hispanic 6%, Native American 2%, Race unknown 18%.
Retention and Graduation: 70% freshmen return for sophomore year.
Faculty: Student/faculty ratio 12:1. 47 full-time faculty, 60% hold PhDs, 6% are members of minority groups, 38% are women. 0% of classes are taught by teaching assistants.

ACADEMICS
Degrees: Bachelor's; Master's; Post-Bachelor's certificate; Post-Master's certificate **Classes:** Most classes have 20-29 students. Most lab/discussion sessions have 10-19 students. **Most popular majors:** Elementary Education And Teaching; Nursing/Registered Nurse (Rn, Asn, Bsn, Msn); Business Administration And Management, General. **Special Study Options:** Accelerated program; Distance learning; Double major; Honors program; Independent study; Internships; Student-designed major; Teacher certification program. **Disability Services offered to physically disabled students:** Reader services; Tape recorders; Tutors.

FACILITIES
Housing: Apartments for married students; Apartments for single students; Coed dorms; Men's dorms; Women's dorms 90% of campus accessible to physically diasbled. **Special Academic Facilities/Equipment:** Ruth Warren Abbott Horticulture Lab Floyd and Ethel Moore Biological Field Station Norman E. Hege Education Center **Computers:** 100% of classrooms, 100% of dorms, 100% of libraries, 100% of dining areas, 100% of student union, 100% of common outdoor areas have wireless network access. Students can register for classes online. Administrative functions (other than registration) can be performed online.

CAMPUS LIFE
Environment: Village **Activities:** Campus Ministries; Choral groups; Concert band; Dance; Drama/theater; International Student Organization; Jazz band; Music ensembles; Musical theater; Pep band; Radio station; Student government; Student newspaper; Symphony orchestra; Television station; Yearbook 25 registered organizations, 2 honor societies, 7 religious organizations. 2 fraternities. **Athletics (Intercollegiate):** *Men:* basketball, cheerleading, cross-country, football, golf, soccer, tennis, track/field (outdoor), track/field (indoor). *Women:* basketball, cheerleading, cross-country, golf, soccer, softball, tennis, track/field (outdoor), track/field (indoor), volleyball.
On-Campus Highlights: Brand new Women's residence hall, Beech Science Center, Historic Stewart Field House, Christy Administration Building, Roy L. Smith Student Center (Newly re-modeled Cafeteria and bookstore) **Environmental Initiatives:** Kansas Envirothon

ADMISSIONS
Freshman Academic Profile: Average high school GPA 3.3. 16% in top 10% of high school class, 44% in top 25% of high school class, 73% in top 50% of high school class. 95% from public high schools. **Test Scores:** SAT Math middle 50% range 430-550. SAT EBRW middle 50% range 380-540. ACT middle 50% range 19-24. Minimum internet-based TOEFL 80. Minimum paper TOEFL 550. **Basis for Candidate Selection:** *Very important factors considered include:* rigor of secondary school record, academic GPA, standardized test scores. *Important factors considered include:* application essay. *Other factors considered include:* class rank, recommendation(s), interview, extracurricular activities, talent/ability, character/personal qualities, alumni/ae relation.
Freshman Admission Requirements: High school diploma is required and GED is accepted *Academic units required:* 4 English, 3 math, 2 science, 1 science labs, 2.5 social studies, 1 history. **Freshman Admission Statistics:** 293 applied, 90.1% admitted, 45% enrolled. **Transfer Admission Requirements:** college transcript(s), essay or personal statement, Minimum college GPA of 2.25 required. Lowest grade transferable C. **General Admission Information:** Application fee $25. Regular application deadline 8/25. Nonfall registration accepted.

COSTS AND FINANCIAL AID
Annual tuition $19,530. Room and board $5,750. Required fees $150. Average book expense $600. **Required Forms and Deadlines:** FAFSA. **Types of Aid:** *Need-based scholarships/grants:* College/university scholarship or grant aid from institutional funds; Federal Pell; SEOG; State scholarships/grants. *Loans:* Direct PLUS loans; Direct Subsidized Stafford Loans; Direct Unsubsidized Stafford Loans. *Student Employment:* Federal Work-Study Program available. Institutional employment available. **Financial Aid Statistics:** 100% needy freshmen, 98% needy undergrads receive need-based scholarship or grant aid. 9% freshmen, 7% undergrads receive non-need-based scholarship or grant aid. 82% freshmen, 85% undergrads receive need-based self-help aid. 25% freshmen, 25% undergrads receive athletic scholarships. 100% freshmen, 99% undergrads receive any aid. **Criteria for awarding aid:** *Non-need-based:* Academics, Athletics, Leadership, Minority status, Music/drama.

SOUTHWESTERN UNIVERSITY

PO Box 770, Georgetown, TX 78627-0770
Phone: 512-863-1200 • **Financial Aid Phone:** (512) 863–1259
E-mail: admission@southwestern.edu • **CEEB Code:** 6674
Fax: 512-863-9601 • **Website:** http://www.southwestern.edu/ • **ACT Code:** 4186

This private school, affiliated with the Methodist Church, was founded in 1840. It has a 703 acre campus.

RATINGS
Admissions Selectivity Rating: 89   **Fire Safety Rating:** 96   **Green Rating:** 88

STUDENTS AND FACULTY
Enrollment: 1,380. **Student Body:** 57% female, 43% male, 10% out-of-state, 1% international (12 countries represented). Asian 3%, African American 5%, Caucasian 61%, Hispanic 24%, Native American <1%, Pacific Islander <1%, Two or more races 5%, Race unknown 1%.
Retention and Graduation: 86% freshmen return for sophomore year. 67% freshmen graduate within 4 years. 74% freshmen graduate within 6 years. 25% grads go on to further study within 1 year. 5% grads pursue arts and sciences degrees. 3% grads pursue law degrees. 1% grads pursue business degrees. 4% grads pursue medical degrees. **Faculty:** Student/faculty ratio 11:1. 113 full-time faculty, 97% hold PhDs, 19% are members of minority groups, 51% are women. 0% of classes are taught by teaching assistants.

ACADEMICS
Degrees: Bachelor's **Classes:** Most classes have fewer than 10 students. Most lab/discussion sessions have 10-19 students. **Most popular majors:** Speech Communication And Rhetoric; Psychology, General; Business/Commerce, General. **Special Study Options:** Double major; Honors program; Independent study; Internships; Liberal arts/career combination; Student-designed major; Study abroad; Teacher certification program. Honors programs: Departmental honors, which are reflected on the diploma and transcript, are awarded after successful completion of a two semester honors course.
Disability Services offered to physically disabled students: Note-taking services; Reader services; Tape recorders; Tutors. **Career services:** Alumni network; Alumni services; Career assessment; Internships; Regional alumni

FACILITIES
Housing: Apartments for single students; Coed dorms; Fraternity/sorority housing; Men's dorms; Special housing for disabled student; Women's dorms 90% of campus accessible to physically diasbled. **Special Academic Facilities/Equipment:** Alma Thomas Fine Arts Center Red and Charline McCombs Campus Center Corbin J. Robertson Center for Fitness and Wellness Fountainwood Astronomical Observatory **Computers:** 100% of classrooms, 100% of dorms, 100% of libraries, 100% of dining areas, 100% of student union, 50% of common outdoor areas have wireless network access. Students can register for classes online. Administrative functions (other than registration) can be performed online.

CAMPUS LIFE
Environment: Town **Activities:** Campus Ministries; Choral groups; Concert band; Dance; Drama/theater; Jazz band; Literary magazine; Model UN; Music ensembles; Musical theater; Opera; Radio station; Student government; Student newspaper; Symphony orchestra 99 registered organizations, 14 honor societies, 10 religious organizations. 4 fraternities, 4 sororities. **Athletics (Intercollegiate):** *Men:* baseball, basketball, cross-country, diving, golf,

lacrosse, soccer, swimming, tennis, track/field (outdoor). *Women:* basketball, cross-country, diving, golf, soccer, softball, swimming, tennis, track/field (outdoor), volleyball. **On-Campus Highlights:** Robertson Center-indoor olympic size pool, McCombs Center-Student Center, Fountainwood Observatory, Academic Mall-grassy area in the middle of campus, Korouva Milkbar-student run coffee house **Environmental Initiatives:** 100% wind power. Formation of the Green Fund, specifically used to fund environmental and sustainable projects/initiatives on campus. Signing of the Talloires Declaration.

ADMISSIONS

Freshman Academic Profile: 37% in top 10% of high school class, 73% in top 25% of high school class, 96% in top 50% of high school class. 79% from public high schools. **Test Scores:** SAT Math middle 50% range 540-650. SAT EBRW middle 50% range 570-670. ACT middle 50% range 23-29. Minimum internet-based TOEFL 88. Minimum paper TOEFL 570. **Basis for Candidate Selection:** *Very important factors considered include:* rigor of secondary school record, class rank, academic GPA, application essay, standardized test scores, recommendation(s). *Important factors considered include:* interview, extracurricular activities, talent/ability, character/personal qualities, first generation, alumni/ae relation, geographical residence, state residency, racial/ethnic status, volunteer work. *Other factors considered include:* religious affiliation/commitment, work experience, level of applicant's interest. **Freshman Admission Requirements:** High school diploma is required and GED is accepted *Academic units required:* 4 English, 4 math, 3 science, 2 science labs, 2 foreign language, 2 social studies, 1 history, 1 academic elective, *Academic units recommended:* 4 English, 4 math, 4 science, 3 science labs, 3 foreign language, 3 social studies, 1 history, 1 academic elective. **Freshman Admission Statistics:** 4,133 applied, 43.1% admitted, 20% enrolled. **Transfer Admission Requirements:** High school transcript, college transcript(s), essay or personal statement, statement of good standing from prior institution(s). Minimum college GPA of 3.0 required. Lowest grade transferable C. **General Admission Information:** Regular application deadline 2/1. Nonfall registration accepted. Admission may be deferred for a maximum of 1 year.

COSTS AND FINANCIAL AID

Annual tuition $42,000. Room and board $12,000. Average book expense $1,300. **Required Forms and Deadlines:** FAFSA. **Notification of Awards:** Applicants will be notified of awards on a rolling basis beginning 12/15. **Types of Aid:** *Need-based scholarships/grants:* College/university scholarship or grant aid from institutional funds; Federal Pell; Private scholarships; SEOG; State scholarships/grants. *Loans:* Direct PLUS loans; Direct Subsidized Stafford Loans; Direct Unsubsidized Stafford Loans. *Student Employment:* Federal Work-Study Program available. Institutional employment available. **Financial Aid Statistics:** 100% needy freshmen, 99% needy undergrads receive need-based scholarship or grant aid. 96% freshmen, 96% undergrads receive non-need-based scholarship or grant aid. 75% freshmen, 80% undergrads receive need-based self-help aid. 0% freshmen, 0% undergrads receive athletic scholarships. 99% freshmen, 97% undergrads receive any aid. Average cumulative indebtedness $32,801. **Criteria for awarding aid:** *Need-based:* Academics *Non-need-based:* Academics, Alumni affiliation, Art, Leadership, Minority status, Music/drama, Religious affiliation.

See page 1036.

SPELMAN COLLEGE

350 Spelman Lane, Atlanta, GA 30314-4399
Phone: 404-270-5193 • **Financial Aid Phone:** 404-270-5212
E-mail: admiss@spelman.edu • **CEEB Code:** 5628
Fax: 404-270-5201 • **Website:** www.spelman.edu • **ACT Code:** 794

This private school was founded in 1881. It has a 39.1 acre campus.

RATINGS

Admissions Selectivity Rating: 89   **Fire Safety Rating:** 87   **Green Rating:** 61

STUDENTS AND FACULTY

Enrollment: 2,134. **Student Body:** 100% female, 0% male, 72% out-of-state, 1% international (10 countries represented). Asian 0%, African American 97%, Caucasian <1%, Hispanic <1%, Native American 2%, Pacific Islander 0%, Two or more races 1%, Race unknown 0%.
Retention and Graduation: 89% freshmen return for sophomore year. 69% freshmen graduate within 4 years. 75% freshmen graduate within 6 years.

Faculty: Student/faculty ratio 11:1. 173 full-time faculty, 92% hold PhDs, 86% are members of minority groups, 71% are women. 0% of classes are taught by teaching assistants.

ACADEMICS

Degrees: Bachelor's **Classes:** Most classes have 10-19 students. Most lab/discussion sessions have 20-29 students. **Most popular majors:** Biology, General; Psychology, General; Political Science And Government, General. **Special Study Options:** Cooperative education program; Cross-registration; Double major; Dual enrollment; Exchange student program (domestic); Honors program; Independent study; Internships; Student-designed major; Study abroad; Teacher certification program. Honors programs: Ethel Waddell Githii Honors Program: Founded in 1980, the Spelman College Honors Program, named for scholar-teacher Ethel Waddell Githii, is interdisciplinary in design recognizing the diversity of our faculty expertise and student creative scholarship. The Githii Honors Program creates original programming and targeted supports for our member students, and collaborates with academic departments and programs to provide a rich array of scholarly and creative venues. These include our annual reading and lecture series, special programs and workshops for the broader campus and the Atlanta community, and cultural engagements on and beyond the campus. The Program spotlights intellectual leadership as a habit of mind and a quality of the ethical citizen. **Disability Services offered to physically disabled students:** Note-taking services; Reader services; Tape recorders; Tutors. **Career services:** Career assessment; Career/job search classes; Internships

FACILITIES

Housing: Theme housing; Women's dorms 85% of campus accessible to physically diasbled. **Special Academic Facilities/Equipment:** Spelman College Museum of Fine Art, language lab, electron microscope. **Computers:** Students can register for classes online. Administrative functions (other than registration) can be performed online.

CAMPUS LIFE

Environment: Metropolis **Activities:** Campus Ministries; Choral groups; Concert band; Dance; Drama/theater; International Student Organization; Jazz band; Literary magazine; Music ensembles; Musical theater; Student government; Student newspaper; Symphony orchestra; Yearbook 17 registered organizations, 18 honor societies, 9 religious organizations. 4 sororities. **Athletics (Intercollegiate):** *Women:* basketball, cross-country, golf, soccer, softball, tennis, volleyball. **On-Campus Highlights:** Sister's Chapel, The Spelman College Museum of Fine Art, Camille Olivia Hanks-Cosby Academic Center, Albro, Falconer, Manley Science Center, The Oval and Alumni Arch

ADMISSIONS

Freshman Academic Profile: Average high school GPA 3.7. 21% in top 10% of high school class, 48% in top 25% of high school class, 69% in top 50% of high school class. **Test Scores:** SAT Math middle 50% range 520-590. SAT EBRW middle 50% range 550-625. ACT middle 50% range 22-26. Minimum internet-based TOEFL 120. Minimum paper TOEFL 550. **Basis for Candidate Selection:** *Very important factors considered include:* rigor of secondary school record, academic GPA, application essay, standardized test scores, recommendation(s), character/personal qualities. *Important factors considered include:* class rank, extracurricular activities, volunteer work. *Other factors considered include:* talent/ability, alumni/ae relation, geographical residence, work experience, level of applicant's interest. **Freshman Admission Requirements:** High school diploma is required and GED is accepted *Academic units required:* 4 English, 2 math, 2 science, 1 science labs, 2 foreign language, 2 social studies, 2 history, 1 academic elective, *Academic units recommended:* 4 English, 4 math, 4 science, 2 science labs, 2 foreign language, 3 social studies. **Freshman Admission Statistics:** 8,344 applied, 40.1% admitted, 16% enrolled. **Transfer Admission Requirements:** High school transcript, college transcript(s), Minimum college GPA of 2.0 required. Lowest grade transferable C. **General Admission Information:** Application fee $35. Regular application deadline 2/1. Nonfall registration accepted. Admission may be deferred for a maximum of one year.

COSTS AND FINANCIAL AID

Annual tuition $24,382. Room and board $13,461. Required fees $3,799. Average book expense $3,000. **Required Forms and Deadlines:** FAFSA; State aid form. **Notification of Awards:** Applicants will be notified of awards on a rolling basis beginning 2/15. **Types of Aid:** *Need-based scholarships/grants:* College/university scholarship or grant aid from institutional funds; Federal Pell; Private scholarships; SEOG; State scholarships/grants; United Negro College Fund. *Loans:* Direct PLUS loans; Direct Subsidized Stafford Loans; Direct Unsubsidized Stafford Loans. *Student Employment:* Federal Work-Study Program available. Institutional employment available. **Financial Aid Statistics:** 85% needy freshmen, 79% needy undergrads receive need-based scholarship or grant aid. 0% undergrads receive non-need-based scholarship or grant aid. 96% freshmen, 96% undergrads receive need-based self-help aid. 0% freshmen, 0% undergrads receive athletic scholarships. 84% freshmen, 90% undergrads receive any aid. 73% undergrads borrow to pay for school. Average cumulative indebtedness $38,430. **Criteria for awarding aid:** *Need-based:* Academics, Alumni affiliation, Leadership, Music/drama, Religious affiliation *Non-need-based:* Academics, Alumni affiliation, Music/drama, State/district residency.

SPRING ARBOR UNIVERSITY

106 East Main Street, Spring Arbor, MI 49283-9799
Phone: 517-750-6458 • **Financial Aid Phone:** 800-968-0011
E-mail: admissions@admin.arbor.edu • **CEEB Code:** 1732
Fax: 517-750-6620 • **Website:** www.arbor.edu • **ACT Code:** 2056

This private school, affiliated with the Free Methodist Church, was founded in 1873. It has a 100 acre campus.

RATINGS
Admissions Selectivity Rating: 80   **Fire Safety Rating:** 86   **Green Rating:** 60*

STUDENTS AND FACULTY
Enrollment: 2,603. **Student Body:** 69% female, 31% male, 12% out-of-state, (10 countries represented).
Retention and Graduation: 78% freshmen return for sophomore year. 22% grads go on to further study within 1 year. 8% grads pursue arts and sciences degrees. 0% grads pursue law degrees. 3% grads pursue business degrees. 8% grads pursue medical degrees. **Faculty:** Student/faculty ratio 15:1. 81 full-time faculty, 72% hold PhDs, 11% are members of minority groups, 32% are women. 0% of classes are taught by teaching assistants.

ACADEMICS
Degrees: Associate; Bachelor's; Master's; Post-Bachelor's certificate **Classes:** Most classes have 20-29 students. Most lab/discussion sessions have 20-29 students. **Most popular majors:** Elementary Education And Teaching; Secondary Education And Teaching; Psychology, General. **Special Study Options:** Accelerated program; Cross-registration; Distance learning; Double major; Dual enrollment; English as a Second Language (ESL); Honors program; Independent study; Internships; Student-designed major; Study abroad; Teacher certification program; Weekend college. Combined degree programs: BA/MEng. **Disability Services offered to physically disabled students:** Note-taking services; Reader services; Tape recorders; Tutors. **Career services:** Alumni network; Alumni services; Career assessment; Career/job search classes; Internships; Regional alumni

FACILITIES
Housing: Apartments for married students; Apartments for single students; Men's dorms; Special housing for disabled student; Special housing for international students; Women's dorms 80% of campus accessible to physically diasbled. **Special Academic Facilities/Equipment:** State-of-the-art academic building (Poling Center); the Poling Center features the CP Federal Credit Union Trading Center and is equipped with some of the same technology that is used daily on Wall Street including: An electronic wrap-around ticker, large light emitting diode (LED) financial data board, Bloomberg terminal, and continuous financial news feeds. Radio and TV studios, commercial writing/computer graphics lab, science center, art gallery. **Computers:** 90% of classrooms, 100% of dorms, 100% of libraries, 100% of dining areas, 75% of common outdoor areas have wireless network access. Students can register for classes online. Administrative functions (other than registration) can be performed online.

CAMPUS LIFE
Environment: Rural **Activities:** Campus Ministries; Choral groups; Concert band; Drama/theater; International Student Organization; Jazz band; Literary magazine; Model UN; Music ensembles; Musical theater; Opera; Pep band; Radio station; Student government; Student newspaper; Student-run film society; Symphony orchestra; Television station; Yearbook 50 registered organizations. **Athletics (Intercollegiate):** *Men:* baseball, basketball, cross-country, golf, soccer, tennis, track/field (outdoor), track/field (indoor). *Women:* basketball, cross-country, soccer, softball, tennis, track/field (outdoor), track/field (indoor), volleyball. **On-Campus Highlights:** Sacred Grounds (Starbucks), Ganton Art Gallery, Poling Center—CP Federal Trading Center, University Plaza, Student Life Center

ADMISSIONS
Freshman Academic Profile: Average high school GPA 3.4. 22% in top 10% of high school class, 48% in top 25% of high school class, 77% in top 50% of high school class. 80% from public high schools. **Test Scores:** SAT Math middle 50% range 460-580. SAT EBRW middle 50% range 480-585. ACT middle 50% range 20-26. Minimum paper TOEFL 525. **Basis for Candidate Selection:** *Very important factors considered include:* rigor of secondary

school record, standardized test scores, character/personal qualities. *Important factors considered include:* academic GPA. *Other factors considered include:* class rank, application essay, recommendation(s), interview, extracurricular activities, talent/ability, religious affiliation/commitment. **Freshman Admission Requirements:** High school diploma is required and GED is accepted *Academic units required:* 4 English, 3 math, 3 science, 3 science labs, 3 history, and 1 unit from above areas or other academic areas. *Academic units recommended:* 2 foreign language, 1 computer science. **Freshman Admission Statistics:** 2,698 applied, 65.0% admitted, 21% enrolled. **Transfer Admission Requirements:** High school transcript, college transcript(s), essay or personal statement, Minimum college GPA of 2.0 required. Lowest grade transferable C. **General Admission Information:** Application fee $30. Priority deadline 2/15. Regular application deadline 8/1. Nonfall registration accepted. Admission may be deferred.

COSTS AND FINANCIAL AID
Annual tuition $21,998. Room and board $7,900. Required fees $540. Average book expense $800. **Required Forms and Deadlines:** FAFSA. **Notification of Awards:** Applicants will be notified of awards on a rolling basis beginning 3/1. **Types of Aid:** *Need-based scholarships/grants:* College/university scholarship or grant aid from institutional funds; Federal Pell; Private scholarships; SEOG. *Loans:* Direct PLUS loans; Direct Subsidized Stafford Loans; Direct Unsubsidized Stafford Loans. *Student Employment:* Federal Work-Study Program available. Institutional employment available. **Financial Aid Statistics:** 100% needy freshmen, 99% needy undergrads receive need-based scholarship or grant aid. 10% freshmen, 10% undergrads receive non-need-based scholarship or grant aid. 83% freshmen, 84% undergrads receive need-based self-help aid. 22% freshmen, 19% undergrads receive athletic scholarships. 97% freshmen, 93% undergrads receive any aid. **Criteria for awarding aid:** *Non-need-based:* Academics, Art, Athletics, Minority status, Religious affiliation.

SPRING HILL COLLEGE

4000 Dauphin Street, Mobile, AL 36608
Phone: 251-380-3030 • **Financial Aid Phone:** (251) 380-2253
E-mail: admit@shc.edu • **CEEB Code:** 1733
Fax: 251-460-2186 • **Website:** www.shc.edu • **ACT Code:** 42

This private school, affiliated with the Roman Catholic-Jesuit Church, was founded in 1830. It has a 381 acre campus.

RATINGS
Admissions Selectivity Rating: 86   **Fire Safety Rating:** 84   **Green Rating:** 60*

STUDENTS AND FACULTY
Enrollment: 1,375. **Student Body:** 63% female, 37% male, 58% out-of-state, 4% international (23 countries represented). Asian 1%, African American 16%, Caucasian 68%, Hispanic 2%, Native American 1%, Pacific Islander <1%, Two or more races 5%, Race unknown 3%.
Retention and Graduation: 79% freshmen return for sophomore year. 44% freshmen graduate within 4 years. 53% freshmen graduate within 6 years. **Faculty:** Student/faculty ratio 14:1. 86 full-time faculty, 94% hold PhDs, 9% are members of minority groups, 49% are women. 0% of classes are taught by teaching assistants.

ACADEMICS
Degrees: Bachelor's; Certificate; Master's; Post-Bachelor's certificate; Post-Master's certificate **Classes:** Most classes have 10-19 students. **Most popular majors:** Speech Communication And Rhetoric; Psychology, General; Business Administration And Management, General. **Special Study Options:** Accelerated program; Distance learning; Double major; Dual enrollment; Honors program; Independent study; Internships; Student-designed major; Study abroad; Teacher certification program. Honors programs: SHC's 4-year Honors Program offers a challenging and rewarding course of study to academically gifted and motivated students. It is comprised of academic courses; seminar experiences; and additional opportunities for service, leadership, cultural exploration, and social interaction both on and off campus. Honors courses cover material in greater depth, use primary materials when possible, stress student participation and responsibility, and encourage high individual achievement. **Disability Services offered to physically disabled students:** Tutors. **Career services:** Alumni network; Alumni services; Career assessment; Career/job search classes; Internships; Regional alumni

FACILITIES
Housing: Apartments for single students; Coed dorms; Theme housing 90% of campus accessible to physically diasbled. **Special Academic Facilities/Equipment:** theater **Computers:** 50% of classrooms, 15% of dorms, 100%

of libraries, 100% of dining areas, 100% of student union, 25% of common outdoor areas have wireless network access. Students can register for classes online. Administrative functions (other than registration) can be performed online.

CAMPUS LIFE

Environment: Metropolis **Activities:** Campus Ministries; Choral groups; Dance; Drama/theater; Jazz band; Literary magazine; Student government; Student newspaper; Yearbook 66 registered organizations, 16 honor societies, 5 religious organizations. 3 fraternities, 5 sororities. **Athletics (Intercollegiate):** *Men:* baseball, basketball, cross-country, golf, soccer, tennis. *Women:* basketball, cross-country, golf, soccer, softball, tennis, volleyball. **On-Campus Highlights:** Student Center, Fairway Apartments, McKinney's at the Hill, Burke Library, Golf Course

ADMISSIONS

Freshman Academic Profile: Average high school GPA 3.6. 15% in top 10% of high school class, 50% in top 25% of high school class, 85% in top 50% of high school class. **Test Scores:** SAT Math middle 50% range 510-585. SAT EBRW middle 50% range 515-600. ACT middle 50% range 21-26. Minimum internet-based TOEFL 80. Minimum paper TOEFL 550. **Basis for Candidate Selection:** *Very important factors considered include:* rigor of secondary school record, academic GPA, standardized test scores. *Important factors considered include:* class rank, recommendation(s), interview. *Other factors considered include:* application essay, extracurricular activities, talent/ability, character/personal qualities, alumni/ae relation, volunteer work. **Freshman Admission Requirements:** High school diploma is required and GED is accepted *Academic units recommended:* 4 English, 3 math, 3 science, 1 science labs, 2 foreign language, 2 social studies, 1 history, 1 academic elective. **Freshman Admission Statistics:** 8,544 applied, 45.7% admitted, 10% enrolled. **Transfer Admission Requirements:** college transcript(s), statement of good standing from prior institution(s). Minimum college GPA of 2.5 required. Lowest grade transferable C-. **General Admission Information:** Application fee $25. Priority deadline 1/15. Regular application deadline 7/15. Nonfall registration accepted. Admission may be deferred for a maximum of 1 year.

COSTS AND FINANCIAL AID

Required Forms and Deadlines: FAFSA; State aid form. **Notification of Awards:** Applicants will be notified of awards on a rolling basis beginning 2/15. **Types of Aid:** *Need-based scholarships/grants:* College/university scholarship or grant aid from institutional funds; Federal Pell; Private scholarships; SEOG; State scholarships/grants. *Loans:* Direct PLUS loans; Direct Subsidized Stafford Loans; Direct Unsubsidized Stafford Loans. *Student Employment:* Federal Work-Study Program available. Institutional employment available. **Financial Aid Statistics:** 100% needy freshmen receive need-based scholarship or grant aid. **Criteria for awarding aid:** *Need-based:* Academics, Alumni affiliation, Athletics, Job skills, Leadership, Minority status *Non-need-based:* Academics, Alumni affiliation, Art, Athletics, Job skills, Leadership, Minority status, State/district residency.

ST. AMBROSE UNIVERSITY

518 W. Locust Street, Davenport, IA 52803-2898
Phone: 563-333-6300 • **Financial Aid Phone:** 563-333-5775
E-mail: admit@sau.edu • **CEEB Code:** 6617
Fax: 563-333-6038 • **Website:** www.sau.edu • **ACT Code:** 1352

This private school, affiliated with the Roman Catholic Church, was founded in 1882. It has a 118 acre campus.

RATINGS

Admissions Selectivity Rating: 79   **Fire Safety Rating:** 60*   **Green Rating:** 60*

STUDENTS AND FACULTY

Enrollment: 2,381. **Student Body:** 57% female, 43% male, 60% out-of-state, 3% international (14 countries represented). Asian 1%, African American 4%, Caucasian 78%, Hispanic 7%, Native American <1%, Pacific Islander <1%, Two or more races 2%, Race unknown 4%.
Retention and Graduation: 77% freshmen return for sophomore year. 19% grads go on to further study within 1 year. **Faculty:** Student/faculty ratio 12:1. 182 full-time faculty, 83% hold PhDs, 10% are members of minority groups, 37% are women. 0% of classes are taught by teaching assistants.

ACADEMICS

Degrees: Bachelor's; Certificate; Doctoral/Professional; Doctoral/Research; Master's; Post-Master's certificate **Classes:** Most classes have 20-29 students. Most lab/discussion sessions have 20-29 students. **Most popular majors:** Psychology, General; Nursing Science; Business/Commerce, General. **Special**

Study Options: Accelerated program; Cooperative education program; Distance learning; Double major; Honors program; Independent study; Internships; Liberal arts/career combination; Student-designed major; Study abroad; Teacher certification program. Honors programs: Honors Program study is open to students who have been accepted to St. Ambrose University pursuing any major, as per the requirements described below. Combined degree programs: BA/MA. **Disability Services offered to physically disabled students:** Note-taking services; Reader services; Tape recorders; Tutors. **Career services:** Alumni network; Alumni services; Career assessment; Career/job search classes; Internships; Regional alumni

FACILITIES

Housing: Apartments for single students; Coed dorms; Men's dorms; Special housing for disabled student; Theme housing; Women's dorms 95% of campus accessible to physically diasbled. **Special Academic Facilities/Equipment:** Art gallery, observatory, language lab, and distance learning classrooms, Gottlieb Conference, Rogo. **Computers:** 1% of classrooms, 27% of dorms, 100% of libraries, 100% of student union, have wireless network access. Students can register for classes online. Administrative functions (other than registration) can be performed online.

CAMPUS LIFE

Environment: City **Activities:** Campus Ministries; Choral groups; Concert band; Dance; Drama/theater; International Student Organization; Jazz band; Literary magazine; Marching band; Model UN; Music ensembles; Pep band; Radio station; Student government; Student newspaper; Symphony orchestra; Television station 26 registered organizations, 12 honor societies, 3 religious organizations. **Athletics (Intercollegiate):** *Men:* baseball, basketball, bowling, cheerleading, cross-country, football, golf, soccer, tennis, track/field (outdoor), track/field (indoor), volleyball. *Women:* basketball, bowling, cheerleading, cross-country, golf, soccer, softball, tennis, track/field (outdoor), track/field (indoor), volleyball. **On-Campus Highlights:** Rogalski Center (Student Union), Wellness Center, St. Vincent Fields, Chapel, Galvin Fine Arts Building

ADMISSIONS

Freshman Academic Profile: Average high school GPA 3.3. 71% from public high schools. **Test Scores:** ACT middle 50% range 20-25. Minimum internet-based TOEFL 79. Minimum paper TOEFL 550. **Basis for Candidate Selection:** *Very important factors considered include:* rigor of secondary school record, class rank, academic GPA, standardized test scores. *Other factors considered include:* application essay, recommendation(s), interview, extracurricular activities, talent/ability, character/personal qualities, first generation, alumni/ae relation, racial/ethnic status, volunteer work. **Freshman Admission Requirements:** High school diploma is required and GED is accepted *Academic units recommended:* 4 English, 3 math, 2 science, 2 science labs, 1 foreign language, 1 social studies, 1 history, 4 academic electives. **Freshman Admission Statistics:** 4,426 applied, 63.6% admitted, 16% enrolled. **Transfer Admission Requirements:** High school transcript, college transcript(s), standardized test scores, statement of good standing from prior institution(s). Minimum college GPA of 2.0 required. Lowest grade transferable D. **General Admission Information:** Nonfall registration accepted. Admission may be deferred.

COSTS AND FINANCIAL AID

Annual tuition $29,736. Room and board $10,164. Required fees $280. Average book expense $1,320. **Required Forms and Deadlines:** FAFSA. **Notification of Awards:** Applicants will be notified of awards on a rolling basis beginning 2/1. **Types of Aid:** *Need-based scholarships/grants:* College/university scholarship or grant aid from institutional funds; Federal Pell; Private scholarships; SEOG; State scholarships/grants. *Loans:* Direct PLUS loans; Direct Subsidized Stafford Loans; Direct Unsubsidized Stafford Loans. *Student Employment:* Federal Work-Study Program available. Institutional employment available. **Financial Aid Statistics:** 99% needy freshmen, 99% needy undergrads receive need-based scholarship or grant aid. 41% freshmen, 26% undergrads receive non-need-based scholarship or grant aid. 71% freshmen, 78% undergrads receive need-based self-help aid. 10% freshmen, 8% undergrads receive athletic scholarships. 99% freshmen, 88% undergrads receive any aid. **Criteria for awarding aid:** *Need-based:* Academics, Minority status *Non-need-based:* Academics, Alumni affiliation, Art, Athletics, Music/drama.

ST. ANDREWS PRESBYTERIAN COLLEGE

1700 Dogwood Mile, Laurinburg, NC 28352
Phone: 910-277-5555 • **Financial Aid Phone:** 910-277-5560
E-mail: admissions@sapc.edu • **CEEB Code:** 5214
Fax: 910-277-5020 • **Website:** sapc.edu • **ACT Code:** 3146

This private school, affiliated with the Presbyterian Church, was founded in 1958. It has a 600 acre campus.

RATINGS
Admissions Selectivity Rating: 73   **Fire Safety Rating:** 60*   **Green Rating:** 60*

STUDENTS AND FACULTY
Enrollment: 601. **Student Body:** 54% female, 46% male, 59% out-of-state, 12% international (8 countries represented). African American 12%, Caucasian 61%, Pacific Islander 0%, Two or more races 2%, Race unknown 14%. **Retention and Graduation:** 59% freshmen return for sophomore year. 40% grads go on to further study within 1 year. 0% grads pursue arts and sciences degrees. 0% grads pursue law degrees. 0% grads pursue business degrees. 0% grads pursue medical degrees. **Faculty:** Student/faculty ratio 15:1. 30 full-time faculty, 73% hold PhDs, 3% are members of minority groups, 47% are women. 0% of classes are taught by teaching assistants.

ACADEMICS
Degrees: Bachelor's; Diploma; Master's **Most popular majors:** Elementary Education And Teaching; English Language And Literature, General; Business/Commerce, General. **Special Study Options:** Double major; English as a Second Language (ESL); Honors program; Independent study; Internships; Student-designed major; Study abroad; Teacher certification program. **Disability Services offered to physically disabled students:** Note-taking services; Reader services; Tape recorders; Tutors. **Career services:** Alumni network; Alumni services; Career assessment; Career/job search classes; Internships; Regional alumni

FACILITIES
Housing: Coed dorms; Men's dorms; Women's dorms 90% of campus accessible to physically diasbled. **Special Academic Facilities/Equipment:** Art gallery, anthropology museum, science lab, electron microscopy center with three electron microscopes, psychology lab, artronics graphics computer, Scottish Heritage Foundation. **Computers:** 100% of libraries, 50% of dining areas, 100% of student union, have wireless network access. Administrative functions (other than registration) can be performed online.

CAMPUS LIFE
Environment: Rural **Activities:** 30 registered organizations, 3 honor societies, 1 religious organization. **Athletics (Intercollegiate):** *Men:* baseball, basketball, cross-country, equestrian sports, golf, horseback riding, lacrosse, soccer, track/field (outdoor), wrestling. *Women:* basketball, cross-country, equestrian sports, horseback riding, lacrosse, soccer, softball, track/field (outdoor), volleyball, wrestling. **On-Campus Highlights:** Equesterian Center, Morgan Jones Science Labs, Electronic and Fine Arts Center, Athletic Facilities, Art Studios

ADMISSIONS
Freshman Academic Profile: Average high school GPA 3.2. 7% in top 10% of high school class, 30% in top 25% of high school class, 66% in top 50% of high school class. **Test Scores:** SAT Math middle 50% range 355-605. Minimum paper TOEFL 550. **Basis for Candidate Selection:** *Important factors considered include:* academic GPA, standardized test scores, extracurricular activities, character/personal qualities. *Other factors considered include:* rigor of secondary school record, class rank, application essay, recommendation(s), interview, talent/ability, first generation, volunteer work, work experience. **Freshman Admission Requirements:** High school diploma is required and GED is accepted *Academic units required:* 3 English, 3 math, 3 science, 1 foreign language, 3 social studies. **Freshman Admission Statistics:** 926 applied, 57.1% admitted, 29% enrolled. **Transfer Admission Requirements:** High school transcript, college transcript(s), statement of good standing from prior institution(s). Minimum college GPA of 2.5 required. Lowest grade transferable C-. **General Admission Information:** Application fee $35. Nonfall registration accepted.

COSTS AND FINANCIAL AID
Annual tuition $23,682. Average book expense $1,800. **Types of Aid:** *Need-based scholarships/grants:* College/university scholarship or grant aid from institutional funds; Federal Pell; Private scholarships; SEOG; State scholarships/grants. *Loans:* Direct PLUS loans; Direct Subsidized Stafford Loans; Direct Unsubsidized Stafford Loans. *Student Employment:* Federal Work-Study Program available. Institutional employment available. **Financial Aid Statistics:** 99% needy freshmen, 98% needy undergrads receive need-based scholarship or grant aid. 9% freshmen, 8% undergrads receive non-need-based

scholarship or grant aid. 85% freshmen, 84% undergrads receive need-based self-help aid. 17% freshmen, 17% undergrads receive athletic scholarships. 99% freshmen, 98% undergrads receive any aid. **Criteria for awarding aid:** *Non-need-based:* Academics, Alumni affiliation, Art, Athletics, Job skills, Leadership, Music/drama, Religious affiliation.

ST. ANSELM COLLEGE

100 Saint Anselm Drive, Manchester, NH 03102-1310
Phone: 603-641-7500 • **Financial Aid Phone:** 603-641-7110
E-mail: admission@anselm.edu • **CEEB Code:** 3748
Fax: 603-641-7550 • **Website:** www.anselm.edu • **ACT Code:** 2522

This private school, affiliated with the Roman Catholic Church, was founded in 1889. It has a 380 acre campus.

RATINGS
Admissions Selectivity Rating: 81   **Fire Safety Rating:** 85   **Green Rating:** 60*

STUDENTS AND FACULTY
Enrollment: 1,956. **Student Body:** 61% female, 39% male, 78% out-of-state, 1% international (6 countries represented). Asian 1%, African American 2%, Caucasian 88%, Hispanic 4%, Native American <1%, Pacific Islander <1%, Two or more races 2%, Race unknown 3%. **Retention and Graduation:** 85% freshmen return for sophomore year. 78% freshmen graduate within 4 years. 80% freshmen graduate within 6 years. 16% grads go on to further study within 1 year. 11% grads pursue arts and sciences degrees. 3% grads pursue law degrees. 1% grads pursue business degrees. 2% grads pursue medical degrees. **Faculty:** Student/faculty ratio 11:1. 153 full-time faculty, 92% hold PhDs, 10% are members of minority groups, 54% are women. 0% of classes are taught by teaching assistants.

ACADEMICS
Degrees: Bachelor's **Classes:** Most classes have 10-19 students. Most lab/discussion sessions have 10-19 students. **Most popular majors:** Biology, General; Psychology, General; Registered Nursing/Registered Nurse. **Special Study Options:** Accelerated program; Cooperative education program; Cross-registration; Distance learning; Double major; Dual enrollment; Exchange student program (domestic); External degree program; Honors program; Independent study; Internships; Liberal arts/career combination; Study abroad; Teacher certification program. Honors programs: Honors Program for Chancellor Scholars. **Disability Services offered to physically disabled students:** Note-taking services; Reader services; Tape recorders; Tutors. **Career services:** Alumni network; Alumni services; Career assessment; Career/job search classes; Internships; Regional alumni

FACILITIES
Housing: Apartments for single students; Coed dorms; Men's dorms; Women's dorms **Special Academic Facilities/Equipment:** Alva de Mars Megan Chapel Art Center, New Hampshire Institute of Politics & Political Library, Izart Observatory, Koonz Theatre, Comiskey Studio (Fine Arts), Poisson Hall, Residential Living & Learning Community **Computers:** 100% of classrooms, 100% of dorms, 100% of libraries, 100% of dining areas, 100% of student union, have wireless network access. Students can register for classes online. Administrative functions (other than registration) can be performed online.

CAMPUS LIFE
Environment: City **Activities:** Campus Ministries; Choral groups; Dance; Drama/theater; International Student Organization; Jazz band; Literary magazine; Music ensembles; Musical theater; Student government; Student newspaper; Yearbook 120 registered organizations, 11 honor societies, 7 religious organizations. **Athletics (Intercollegiate):** *Men:* baseball, basketball, cross-country, football, golf, ice hockey, lacrosse, skiing (downhill/alpine), soccer, tennis. *Women:* basketball, cross-country, field hockey, golf, ice hockey, lacrosse, skiing (downhill/alpine), soccer, softball, tennis, volleyball. **On-Campus Highlights:** Residence Hall (Living and Learning Community), Geisel Library, Davison Dining Hall, New Hampshire Institute of Politics and Political Library, Abbey Church

ADMISSIONS
Freshman Academic Profile: Average high school GPA 3.3. 24% in top 10% of high school class, 55% in top 25% of high school class, 88% in top 50% of high school class. 65% from public high schools. **Test Scores:** SAT Math middle 50% range 560-650. SAT EBRW middle 50% range 580-650. ACT

middle 50% range 24-28. Minimum internet-based TOEFL 80. Minimum paper TOEFL 550. **Basis for Candidate Selection:** *Very important factors considered include:* rigor of secondary school record, academic GPA. *Important factors considered include:* recommendation(s), extracurricular activities, character/personal qualities, volunteer work, work experience. *Other factors considered include:* class rank, application essay, standardized test scores, talent/ability, first generation, alumni/ae relation, geographical residence, racial/ethnic status. **Freshman Admission Requirements:** High school diploma is required and GED is accepted *Academic units required:* 4 English, 3 math, 3 science, 2 science labs, 2 foreign language, 2 social studies, *Academic units recommended:* 4 English, 4 math, 4 science, 2 science labs, 4 foreign language, 4 social studies. **Freshman Admission Statistics:** 3,892 applied, 76.1% admitted, 18% enrolled. **Transfer Admission Requirements:** High school transcript, college transcript(s), essay or personal statement, standardized test scores, statement of good standing from prior institution(s). Minimum college GPA of 2.5 required. Lowest grade transferable C. **General Admission Information:** Application fee $50. Regular application deadline 2/1. Nonfall registration accepted. Admission may be deferred for a maximum of 1 year.

COSTS AND FINANCIAL AID

Annual tuition $38,960. Room and board $14,146. Required fees $1,030. Average book expense $1,000. **Required Forms and Deadlines:** CSS/Financial Aid PROFILE; FAFSA; Noncustodial PROFILE. **Notification of Awards:** Applicants will be notified of awards on a rolling basis beginning 2/1. **Types of Aid:** *Need-based scholarships/grants:* College/university scholarship or grant aid from institutional funds; Federal Pell; Private scholarships; SEOG; State scholarships/grants. *Loans:* Direct PLUS loans; Direct Subsidized Stafford Loans; Direct Unsubsidized Stafford Loans. *Student Employment:* Federal Work-Study Program available. Institutional employment available. **Financial Aid Statistics:** 99% needy freshmen, 100% needy undergrads receive need-based scholarship or grant aid. 25% freshmen, 21% undergrads receive non-need-based scholarship or grant aid. 80% freshmen, 82% undergrads receive need-based self-help aid. 0% freshmen, 5% undergrads receive athletic scholarships. 98% freshmen, 98% undergrads receive any aid. 81% undergrads borrow to pay for school. Average cumulative indebtedness $37,402. **Criteria for awarding aid:** *Need-based:* Academics, Alumni affiliation, Athletics, Leadership, Minority status, Music/drama, Religious affiliation *Non-need-based:* Academics, Alumni affiliation, Athletics, Leadership, Music/drama, State/district residency.

See page 1016.

ST. BONAVENTURE UNIVERSITY

Best Colleges

3261 West State Road, St. Bonaventure, NY 14778
Phone: 716-375-2434 • **Financial Aid Phone:** 716-375-2128
E-mail: admissions@sbu.edu • **CEEB Code:** 2793
Fax: 716-375-4005 • **Website:** www.sbu.edu • **ACT Code:** 2882

This private school, affiliated with the Roman Catholic Church, was founded in 1858. It has a 500 acre campus.

RATINGS

Admissions Selectivity Rating: 81   **Fire Safety Rating:** 87   **Green Rating:** 60*

STUDENTS AND FACULTY

Enrollment: 1,597. **Student Body:** 48% female, 52% male, 32% out-of-state, 3% international (17 countries represented). Asian 4%, African American 6%, Caucasian 70%, Hispanic 8%, Native American <1%, Pacific Islander <1%, Two or more races 2%, Race unknown 7%. **Retention and Graduation:** 84% freshmen return for sophomore year. 59% freshmen graduate within 4 years. 69% freshmen graduate within 6 years. 46% grads go on to further study within 1 year. **Faculty:** Student/faculty ratio 12:1. 127 full-time faculty, 78% hold PhDs, 8% are members of minority groups, 42% are women. 0% of classes are taught by teaching assistants.

ACADEMICS

Degrees: Bachelor's; Master's; Post-Bachelor's certificate; Post-Master's certificate **Classes:** Most classes have 20-29 students. Most lab/discussion sessions have 10-19 students. **Most popular majors:** Journalism; Biology/Biological Sciences, General; Business Administration And Management, General. **Special Study Options:** Accelerated program; Cross-registration; Double major; Exchange student program (domestic); Honors program;

Independent study; Internships; Liberal arts/career combination; Student-designed major; Study abroad; Teacher certification program. Honors programs: The Honors Program brings highly motivated and academically qualified students into novel, stimulating and productive interaction with faculty. **Disability Services offered to physically disabled students:** Note-taking services; Reader services; Tape recorders; Tutors. **Career services:** Alumni network; Alumni services; Career assessment; Career/job search classes; Internships; Regional alumni

FACILITIES

Housing: Apartments for single students; Coed dorms; Men's dorms; Special housing for disabled student; Theme housing; Wellness housing; Women's dorms 54% of campus accessible to physically diasbled. **Special Academic Facilities/Equipment:** Quick Center for the Arts, Digital Conferencing and Media Center, Franciscan Center for Social Concern, Franciscan Institute **Computers:** 100% of classrooms, have wireless network access. Students can register for classes online.

CAMPUS LIFE

Environment: Village **Activities:** Campus Ministries; Choral groups; Concert band; Dance; Drama/theater; International Student Organization; Jazz band; Literary magazine; Model UN; Music ensembles; Radio station; Student government; Student newspaper; Television station; Yearbook 47 registered organizations, 7 honor societies, 6 religious organizations. **Athletics (Intercollegiate):** *Men:* baseball, basketball, cross-country, diving, golf, soccer, swimming, tennis. *Women:* basketball, cross-country, diving, lacrosse, soccer, softball, swimming, tennis. **On-Campus Highlights:** Reilly Center, Richter Center, Quick Arts Center, Swan Business Center, Golf Course and Clubhouse **Environmental Initiatives:** New campus construction: St. Bonaventure's William F. Walsh Science Center and the Friedsam Memorial Library Rare Books addition use underground water for cooling systems, reducing the release of carbon dioxide.

ADMISSIONS

Freshman Academic Profile: Average high school GPA 3.4. 21% in top 10% of high school class, 47% in top 25% of high school class, 76% in top 50% of high school class. 78% from public high schools. **Test Scores:** SAT Math middle 50% range 510-610. SAT EBRW middle 50% range 510-610. ACT middle 50% range 21-27. Minimum internet-based TOEFL 79. Minimum paper TOEFL 550. **Basis for Candidate Selection:** *Very important factors considered include:* rigor of secondary school record, academic GPA, recommendation(s), character/personal qualities. *Important factors considered include:* application essay, standardized test scores, extracurricular activities, talent/ability, volunteer work. *Other factors considered include:* class rank, interview, first generation, alumni/ae relation, geographical residence, state residency, work experience, level of applicant's interest. **Freshman Admission Requirements:** High school diploma is required and GED is accepted *Academic units recommended:* 4 English, 3 math, 3 science, 3 science labs, 2 foreign language, 4 social studies. **Freshman Admission Statistics:** 2,986 applied, 70.5% admitted, 21% enrolled. **Transfer Admission Requirements:** High school transcript, college transcript(s), statement of good standing from prior institution(s). Minimum college GPA of 2.0 required. Lowest grade transferable C. **General Admission Information:** Priority deadline 2/15. Regular application deadline 7/30. Nonfall registration accepted. Admission may be deferred for a maximum of 1 year.

COSTS AND FINANCIAL AID

Annual tuition $32,336. Room and board $12,265. Required fees $965. Average book expense $800. **Required Forms and Deadlines:** FAFSA; State aid form. **Notification of Awards:** Applicants will be notified of awards on a rolling basis beginning 3/1. **Types of Aid:** *Need-based scholarships/grants:* College/university scholarship or grant aid from institutional funds; Federal Pell; Private scholarships; SEOG; State scholarships/grants. *Loans:* Direct PLUS loans; Direct Subsidized Stafford Loans; Direct Unsubsidized Stafford Loans. *Student Employment:* Federal Work-Study Program available. Institutional employment available. **Financial Aid Statistics:** 100% needy freshmen, 100% needy undergrads receive need-based scholarship or grant aid. 89% freshmen, 86% undergrads receive non-need-based scholarship or grant aid. 78% freshmen, 77% undergrads receive need-based self-help aid. 13% freshmen, 12% undergrads receive athletic scholarships. 99% freshmen, 97% undergrads receive any aid. **Criteria for awarding aid:** *Need-based:* Job skills *Non-need-based:* Academics, Athletics, Minority status, Music/drama, Religious affiliation, State/district residency.

ST. CATHERINE UNIVERSITY

2004 Randolph Avenue, Saint Paul, MN 55105
Financial Aid Phone: 651-690-6540
E-mail: admissions@stkate.edu • **CEEB Code:** 6105
Fax: 651-690-8868 • **Website:** www.stkate.edu • **ACT Code:** 2096

This private school, affiliated with the Roman Catholic Church, was founded in 1905. It has a 110 acre campus.

RATINGS

Admissions Selectivity Rating: 81   **Fire Safety Rating:** 88   **Green Rating:** 60*

STUDENTS AND FACULTY

Enrollment: 3,100. **Student Body:** 97% female, 3% male, 12% out-of-state, 1% international (34 countries represented). Asian 11%, African American 10%, Caucasian 61%, Hispanic 9%, Native American <1%, Pacific Islander <1%, Two or more races 4%, Race unknown 3%.
Retention and Graduation: 81% freshmen return for sophomore year. 37% freshmen graduate within 4 years. 58% freshmen graduate within 6 years. 28% grads go on to further study within 1 year. 2% grads pursue arts and sciences degrees. 4% grads pursue law degrees. 10% grads pursue business degrees. 2% grads pursue medical degrees. **Faculty:** Student/faculty ratio 10:1. 292 full-time faculty, 59% hold PhDs, 12% are members of minority groups, 81% are women. 0% of classes are taught by teaching assistants.

ACADEMICS

Degrees: Associate; Bachelor's; Certificate; Doctoral/Professional; Master's; Post-Bachelor's certificate; Terminal Associate **Classes:** Most classes have 20-29 students. **Most popular majors:** Elementary Education And Teaching; Social Work; Registered Nursing, Nursing Administration, Nursing Research And Clinical Nursing. **Special Study Options:** Cross-registration; Distance learning; Double major; Dual enrollment; Exchange student program (domestic); Honors program; Independent study; Internships; Student-designed major; Study abroad; Teacher certification program. Honors programs: Antonian Scholars are students who exhibit exceptional academic performance in the University and who show promise as learners, researchers, writers, performers, campus or community leaders, and/or creative thinkers. Scholars possess both creativity and love of learning. Scholars are inquisitive and hard working. They love challenges. Scholars are also students who want to take an active role in "tailoring" their college experiences to their needs, interests and passions. Scholars complete a five-component program that includes interdisciplinary seminars, as well as optional honors sections of TRW and/or GSJ, optional study abroad experiences, and a required Senior Honors Project. Scholars participate in at least two and up to four Honors seminars specifically designed for their learning needs and offered in an interdisciplinary format with two professors. All scholars as seniors are required to enroll in a four-credit independent study course in which they develop a senior project based on an interest, curiosity, or passion. Senior projects are completed with a faculty advisor and an interdisciplinary faculty committee who provide guidance and feedback on the project. Other privileges of membership in the Antonian Scholars Honors Program includes priority registration for courses each semester, special diplomas and commencement recognition, and leadership opportunities in the Honors Program Student Organization. Scholars also have opportunities on a regular basis to socialize, network, and converse with others in the Honors Program. Scholars have access to the Honor's Hub in Coeur de Catherine. The Hub is a quiet place to study when you need one and also a place where Scholars may gather for special activities or conversation. **Disability Services offered to physically disabled students:** Note-taking services; Reader services; Tape recorders; Tutors. **Career services:** Alumni network; Alumni services; Career assessment; Career/job search classes; Internships

FACILITIES

Housing: Apartments for single students; Theme housing; Wellness housing; Women's dorms 90% of campus accessible to physically diasbled. **Special Academic Facilities/Equipment:** Art gallery, theatre, recital hall, experimental psychology lab, language lab, observatory. **Computers:** Students can register for classes online. Administrative functions (other than registration) can be performed online.

CAMPUS LIFE

Environment: Metropolis **Activities:** Campus Ministries; Choral groups; Dance; Drama/theater; International Student Organization; Literary magazine; Music ensembles; Musical theater; Radio station; Student government; Student newspaper 40 registered organizations, 24 honor societies, 4 religious organizations. 1 sororities. **Athletics (Intercollegiate):** *Women:* basketball, cross-country, diving, ice hockey, soccer, softball, swimming, tennis, track/field (outdoor), track/field (indoor), volleyball. **On-Campus Highlights:** Coeur

de Catherine, English garden, Butler Center, Dew Drop Pond, Art Gallery **Environmental Initiatives:** Retrofitted older building with green roof

ADMISSIONS

Freshman Academic Profile: Average high school GPA 3.6. 24% in top 10% of high school class, 62% in top 25% of high school class, 94% in top 50% of high school class. 86% from public high schools. **Test Scores:** SAT Math middle 50% range 510-645. SAT EBRW middle 50% range 530-665. ACT middle 50% range 21-26. Minimum paper TOEFL 500. **Basis for Candidate Selection:** *Very important factors considered include:* rigor of secondary school record. *Important factors considered include:* class rank, academic GPA, application essay, standardized test scores, recommendation(s). *Other factors considered include:* interview, first generation, level of applicant's interest. **Freshman Admission Requirements:** High school diploma is required and GED is accepted *Academic units recommended:* 4 English, 3 math, 2 science, 4 foreign language, 2 social studies. **Freshman Admission Statistics:** 2,682 applied, 70.1% admitted, 21% enrolled. **Transfer Admission Requirements:** High school transcript, college transcript(s), statement of good standing from prior institution(s). Minimum college GPA of 2.0 required. Lowest grade transferable C-. **General Admission Information:** Priority deadline 4/15. Nonfall registration accepted. Admission may be deferred for a maximum of 1 year.

COSTS AND FINANCIAL AID

Required Forms and Deadlines: FAFSA; Institution's own financial aid form. **Types of Aid:** *Need-based scholarships/grants:* College/university scholarship or grant aid from institutional funds; Federal Nursing Scholarships; Federal Pell; Private scholarships; SEOG; State scholarships/grants. *Loans:* Direct PLUS loans; Direct Subsidized Stafford Loans; Direct Unsubsidized Stafford Loans. *Student Employment:* Federal Work-Study Program available. Institutional employment available. **Financial Aid Statistics:** 86% needy freshmen, 78% needy undergrads receive need-based scholarship or grant aid. 100% freshmen, 94% undergrads receive non-need-based scholarship or grant aid. 78% freshmen, 82% undergrads receive need-based self-help aid. 0% freshmen, 0% undergrads receive athletic scholarships. 94% freshmen, 93% undergrads receive any aid. 85% undergrads borrow to pay for school. Average cumulative indebtedness $39,150. **Criteria for awarding aid:** *Non-need-based:* Academics, Alumni affiliation, Leadership, State/district residency.

ST. CHARLES BORROMENO SEMINARY

100 East Wynnewood Road, Wynnewood, PA 19096
Phone: 610-785-6291 • **CEEB Code:**
Fax: 610-617-9267 • **Website:** www.scs.edu

This is a private school.

RATINGS

Admissions Selectivity Rating: 81   **Fire Safety Rating:** 60*   **Green Rating:** 60*

STUDENTS AND FACULTY

Enrollment: 47. **Student Body:** 0% female, 100% male, 25% out-of-state, international. Asian 2%, Caucasian 89%, Hispanic 9%,
Retention and Graduation: 77% freshmen return for sophomore year.
Faculty: Student/faculty ratio 6:1. 16 full-time faculty, 75% hold PhDs, 13% are women.

ACADEMICS

Degrees: Bachelor's; Certificate; Master's **Special Study Options:** Accelerated program; English as a Second Language (ESL); Independent study.

FACILITIES

Housing: Men's dorms; Wellness housing

CAMPUS LIFE

Activities: Choral groups; Drama/theater; Music ensembles; Student government; Student newspaper.

ADMISSIONS

Freshman Academic Profile: 33% in top 25% of high school class, 67% in top 50% of high school class. **Test Scores:** SAT Math middle 50% range 530-640. SAT EBRW middle 50% range 550-690. **Basis for Candidate Selection:** *Very important factors considered include:* application essay, recommendation(s), interview, religious affiliation/commitment, level of applicant's interest. *Important factors considered include:* character/personal qualities. *Other factors considered include:* talent/ability. **Freshman Admission Requirements:** High school diploma is required and GED is accepted *Academic units recommended:* 4 English, 3 math, 3 science, 3 foreign language, 3 social studies. **Freshman Admission Statistics:** 8 applied, 100.0% admitted, 88% enrolled. **General Admission Information:** Priority deadline 3/31. Regular application deadline

7/31. Nonfall registration accepted. Admission may be deferred.

COSTS AND FINANCIAL AID
Annual tuition $17,600. Room and board $11,820. Required fees $1,175. Average book expense $1,100. **Required Forms and Deadlines:** FAFSA; Institution's own financial aid form. **Notification of Awards:** Applicants will be notified of awards on a rolling basis beginning 3/1. **Types of Aid:** *Need-based scholarships/grants:* College/university scholarship or grant aid from institutional funds; Federal Pell; SEOG; State scholarships/grants. *Loans:* Direct PLUS loans; Direct Subsidized Stafford Loans; Direct Unsubsidized Stafford Loans. **Financial Aid Statistics:** 57% needy freshmen, 48% needy undergrads receive need-based scholarship or grant aid. 100% freshmen, 100% undergrads receive non-need-based scholarship or grant aid. 100% freshmen, 64% undergrads receive need-based self-help aid. 0% freshmen, 0% undergrads receive athletic scholarships.

ST. EDWARD'S UNIVERSITY

3001 South Congress Avenue, Austin, TX 78704-6489
Phone: 512-448-8500 • **Financial Aid Phone:** 512-448-8523
E-mail: seu.admit@stedwards.edu • **CEEB Code:** 6619
Fax: 512-464-8877 • **Website:** https://www.stedwards.edu • **ACT Code:** 4156

This private school, affiliated with the Roman Catholic Church, was founded in 1885. It has a 160 acre campus.

RATINGS
Admissions Selectivity Rating: 75   **Fire Safety Rating:** 92   **Green Rating:** 89

STUDENTS AND FACULTY
Enrollment: 3,930. **Student Body:** 61% female, 39% male, 13% out-of-state, 8% international (57 countries represented). Asian 3%, African American 4%, Caucasian 36%, Hispanic 43%, Native American 1%, Pacific Islander <1%, Two or more races 3%, Race unknown 2%.
Retention and Graduation: 80% freshmen return for sophomore year. 52% freshmen graduate within 4 years. 64% freshmen graduate within 6 years.
Faculty: Student/faculty ratio 13:1. 192 full-time faculty, 90% hold PhDs, 17% are members of minority groups, 54% are women. 0% of classes are taught by teaching assistants.

ACADEMICS
Degrees: Bachelor's; Master's; Post-Bachelor's certificate **Classes:** Most classes have 10-19 students. Most lab/discussion sessions have fewer than 10 students. **Most popular majors:** Communication, General; Biology/Biological Sciences, General; Psychology, General. **Special Study Options:** Double major; Honors program; Internships; Study abroad; Teacher certification program. Honors programs: The Honors Program is designed for students in the traditional undergraduate program who are academically talented and passionate about learning. Students in the program take a minimum of seven Honors seminars and complete an Honors Senior Thesis project. They must maintain a minimum GPA in Honors courses of 3.50. Many Honors seminars may be substituted for General Education requirements. The Honors Program offers students small classes with other highly motivated students and distinguished professors. Classes require a high level of student participation and emphasize writing and critical thinking. **Disability Services offered to physically disabled students:** Note-taking services; Reader services; Tape recorders; Tutors. **Career services:** Alumni network; Alumni services; Career assessment; Career/job search classes; Internships; Regional alumni

FACILITIES
Housing: Apartments for single students; Coed dorms; Theme housing 93% of campus accessible to physically diasbled. **Special Academic Facilities/Equipment:** St. Edwards University's historic Main Building is a registered Texas Historic Landmark, and it, along with Holy Cross Hall, earned St. Edwards the distinction of National Historic Site on March 16, 1973; The new Munday Library opened to students in fall 2013. **Computers:** 100% of classrooms, 100% of dorms, 100% of libraries, 100% of dining areas, 100% of student union, 100% of common outdoor areas have wireless network access. Students can register for classes online. Administrative functions (other than registration) can be performed online.

CAMPUS LIFE
Environment: Metropolis **Activities:** Campus Ministries; Choral groups; Concert band; Dance; Drama/theater; International Student Organization; Jazz band; Literary magazine; Model UN; Music ensembles; Pep band; Radio station; Student government; Student newspaper; Student-run film society; Television station 95 registered organizations, 10 honor societies, 3 religious organizations. **Athletics (Intercollegiate):** *Men:* baseball, basketball, golf,

soccer, tennis. *Women:* basketball, golf, soccer, softball, tennis, volleyball.
On-Campus Highlights: Historic Main Building (view of Austin), Meadows Coffee House, Munday Library, John Brooks Williams Natural Sciences Center, Meditation and Prayer Grotto/Sorin Oak

ADMISSIONS
Freshman Academic Profile: 24% in top 10% of high school class, 58% in top 25% of high school class, 88% in top 50% of high school class. 62% from public high schools. **Test Scores:** SAT Math middle 50% range 530-610. SAT EBRW middle 50% range 555-640. ACT middle 50% range 22-28. Minimum internet-based TOEFL 61. Minimum paper TOEFL 500. **Basis for Candidate Selection:** *Very important factors considered include:* rigor of secondary school record, academic GPA, application essay, standardized test scores. *Important factors considered include:* class rank, recommendation(s), extracurricular activities, volunteer work. *Other factors considered include:* interview, talent/ ability, character/personal qualities, first generation, alumni/ae relation, geographical residence, state residency, religious affiliation/commitment, racial/ethnic status, work experience, level of applicant's interest. **Freshman Admission Requirements:** High school diploma is required and GED is accepted *Academic units required:* 4 English, 3 math, 2 science, 2 science labs, 2 foreign language, 1 social studies, 2 history, *Academic units recommended:* 4 English, 4 math, 3 science, 3 science labs, 3 foreign language, 1 social studies, 3 history, 1 academic elective, 1 computer science. **Freshman Admission Statistics:** 5,519 applied, 84.2% admitted, 17% enrolled. **Transfer Admission Requirements:** High school transcript, college transcript(s), essay or personal statement, Minimum college GPA of 2.50 required. Lowest grade transferable C. **General Admission Information:** Application fee $50. Priority deadline 2/1. Regular application deadline 5/1. Nonfall registration accepted. Admission may be deferred for a maximum of 1 year.

COSTS AND FINANCIAL AID
Annual tuition $44,678. Room and board $13,650. Required fees $500. Average book expense $1,200. **Required Forms and Deadlines:** FAFSA. **Notification of Awards:** Applicants will be notified of awards on a rolling basis beginning 2/1. **Types of Aid:** *Need-based scholarships/grants:* College/ university scholarship or grant aid from institutional funds; Federal Pell; Private scholarships; SEOG; State scholarships/grants. *Loans:* Direct PLUS loans; Direct Subsidized Stafford Loans; Direct Unsubsidized Stafford Loans. *Student Employment:* Federal Work-Study Program available. Institutional employment available. **Financial Aid Statistics:** 92% needy freshmen, 90% needy undergrads receive need-based scholarship or grant aid. 72% freshmen, 69% undergrads receive non-need-based scholarship or grant aid. 73% freshmen, 74% undergrads receive need-based self-help aid. 6% freshmen, 5% undergrads receive athletic scholarships. 89% freshmen, 84% undergrads receive any aid. Average cumulative indebtedness $36,123. **Criteria for awarding aid:** *Need-based:* Academics *Non-need-based:* Academics, Athletics, Music/drama, State/ district residency.

ST. JOHN FISHER COLLEGE

3690 East Avenue, Rochester, NY 14618-3597
Phone: 585-385-8064 • **Financial Aid Phone:** 585-385-8042
E-mail: admissions@sjfc.edu • **CEEB Code:** 2798
Fax: 585-385-8386 • **Website:** http://www.sjfc.edu/ • **ACT Code:** 2798

This private school, affiliated with the Roman Catholic Church, was founded in 1948. It has a 154 acre campus.

RATINGS
Admissions Selectivity Rating: 83   **Fire Safety Rating:** 92   **Green Rating:** 63

STUDENTS AND FACULTY
Enrollment: 2,744. **Student Body:** 60% female, 40% male, 3% out-of-state, <1% international (2 countries represented). Asian 3%, African American 4%, Caucasian 84%, Hispanic 5%, Native American <1%, Pacific Islander <1%, Two or more races 2%, Race unknown 2%.
Retention and Graduation: 85% freshmen return for sophomore year. 63% freshmen graduate within 4 years. 71% freshmen graduate within 6 years. 4% grads pursue law degrees. 8% grads pursue business degrees. 2% grads pursue medical degrees. **Faculty:** Student/faculty ratio 12:1. 234 full-time faculty, 89% hold PhDs, 18% are members of minority groups, 54% are women. 0% of classes are taught by teaching assistants.

ACADEMICS
Degrees: Bachelor's; Certificate; Doctoral/Professional; Doctoral/Research; Master's; Post-Bachelor's certificate; Post-Master's certificate **Classes:** Most classes have fewer than 10 students. Most lab/discussion sessions have fewer

than 10 students. **Most popular majors:** Biology/Biological Sciences, General; Registered Nursing/Registered Nurse; Business Administration And Management, General. **Special Study Options:** Accelerated program; Cross-registration; Distance learning; Double major; Exchange student program (domestic); Honors program; Independent study; Internships; Liberal arts/career combination; Student-designed major; Study abroad; Teacher certification program; Weekend college. Honors programs: St John Fisher College Honors Program; Science Scholars Program. **Disability Services offered to physically disabled students:** Note-taking services; Reader services; Tape recorders; Tutors. **Career services:** Alumni network; Career assessment; Career/job search classes; Internships; Regional alumni

FACILITIES

Housing: Coed dorms; Special housing for disabled student; Women's dorms 100% of campus accessible to physically diasbled. **Special Academic Facilities/Equipment:** Student Campus Center, State-of-the-Art Laboratories, Two Electron Microscopes, Multimedia Computer Lab, TV Studio Childcare Center (for observation and development), Cyber Cafe, Skalny Welcome Center Art Gallery **Computers:** 25% of classrooms, 100% of libraries, 50% of dining areas, 100% of student union, 10% of common outdoor areas have wireless network access. Students can register for classes online. Administrative functions (other than registration) can be performed online.

CAMPUS LIFE

Environment: City **Activities:** Campus Ministries; Choral groups; Dance; Drama/theater; Literary magazine; Musical theater; Pep band; Student government; Student newspaper; Television station; Yearbook 70 registered organizations, 10 honor societies, 4 religious organizations. **Athletics (Intercollegiate):** *Men:* baseball, basketball, football, golf, lacrosse, soccer, tennis. *Women:* basketball, golf, lacrosse, soccer, softball, tennis, volleyball. **On-Campus Highlights:** Campus Center, Golisano Gateway- Cyber Cafe, Student Life Center, Growney Stadium, Lavery Library **Environmental Initiatives:** Commitment to buying local, fresh, organic produce and foods—http://www.sjfc.edu/student-life/dining/about/green.dot

ADMISSIONS

Freshman Academic Profile: Average high school GPA 3.5. 16% in top 10% of high school class, 52% in top 25% of high school class, 86% in top 50% of high school class. 92% from public high schools. **Test Scores:** SAT Math middle 50% range 530-620. SAT EBRW middle 50% range 530-610. ACT middle 50% range 22-26. Minimum internet-based TOEFL 80. Minimum paper TOEFL 550. **Basis for Candidate Selection:** *Very important factors considered include:* rigor of secondary school record, academic GPA, recommendation(s), character/personal qualities, alumni/ae relation. *Important factors considered include:* class rank, application essay, standardized test scores, interview, extracurricular activities, talent/ability, volunteer work, work experience, level of applicant's interest. *Other factors considered include:* first generation, geographical residence, state residency. **Freshman Admission Requirements:** High school diploma is required and GED is not accepted *Academic units recommended:* 4 English, 4 math, 4 science, 3 foreign language, 4 social studies. **Freshman Admission Statistics:** 4,432 applied, 64.5% admitted, 22% enrolled. **Transfer Admission Requirements:** college transcript(s), statement of good standing from prior institution(s). Minimum college GPA of 2.0 required. Lowest grade transferable C. **General Admission Information:** Priority deadline 1/15. Nonfall registration accepted. Admission may be deferred for a maximum of 2 semesters.

COSTS AND FINANCIAL AID

Annual tuition $32,540. Room and board $12,150. Required fees $580. Average book expense $1,100. **Required Forms and Deadlines:** FAFSA; State aid form. **Notification of Awards:** Applicants will be notified of awards on a rolling basis beginning 3/15. **Types of Aid:** *Need-based scholarships/grants:* College/university scholarship or grant aid from institutional funds; Federal Nursing Scholarships; Federal Pell; Private scholarships; SEOG; State scholarships/grants. *Loans:* Direct PLUS loans; Direct Subsidized Stafford Loans; Direct Unsubsidized Stafford Loans. *Student Employment:* Federal Work-Study Program available. Institutional employment available. **Financial Aid Statistics:** 100% needy freshmen, 99% needy undergrads receive need-based scholarship or grant aid. 74% freshmen, 72% undergrads receive non-need-based scholarship or grant aid. 92% freshmen, 93% undergrads receive need-based self-help aid. 0% freshmen, 0% undergrads receive athletic scholarships. 99% freshmen, 99% undergrads receive any aid. 85% undergrads borrow to pay for school. Average cumulative indebtedness $35,925. **Criteria for awarding aid:** *Need-based:* Academics *Non-need-based:* Academics, Leadership.

ST. JOHN'S COLLEGE (MD)

60 College Avenue, Annapolis, MD 21401
Phone: 410-626-2522 • **Financial Aid Phone:** 410-626-2502
E-mail: Annapolis.Admissions@sjc.edu • **CEEB Code:** 5598
Fax: 410-269-7916 • **Website:** www.sjc.edu • **ACT Code:** 1732

This private school was founded in 1696. It has a 36 acre campus.

RATINGS

Admissions Selectivity Rating: 90   **Fire Safety Rating:** 97   **Green Rating:** 60*

STUDENTS AND FACULTY

Enrollment: 458. **Student Body:** 47% female, 53% male, 62% out-of-state, 22% international (35 countries represented). Asian 4%, African American 2%, Caucasian 64%, Hispanic 6%, Native American 0%, Pacific Islander 0%, Two or more races 3%, Race unknown 0%.
Retention and Graduation: 87% freshmen return for sophomore year. 63% freshmen graduate within 4 years. 67% freshmen graduate within 6 years. 13% grads go on to further study within 1 year. 14% grads pursue arts and sciences degrees. 1% grads pursue law degrees. 0% grads pursue business degrees. 1% grads pursue medical degrees. **Faculty:** Student/faculty ratio 7:1. 65 full-time faculty, 88% hold PhDs, 9% are members of minority groups, 28% are women. 0% of classes are taught by teaching assistants.

ACADEMICS

Degrees: Bachelor's; Master's **Classes:** Most classes have 20-29 students. Most lab/discussion sessions have 10-19 students. **Most popular majors:** Liberal Arts And Sciences/Liberal Studies. **Special Study Options:** Exchange student program (domestic); Internships; Study abroad. **Disability Services offered to physically disabled students:** Reader services; Tape recorders; Tutors. **Career services:** Alumni network; Alumni services; Career assessment; Career/job search classes; Internships; Regional alumni

FACILITIES

Housing: Coed dorms; Wellness housing 80% of campus accessible to physically diasbled. **Special Academic Facilities/Equipment:** Art gallery, observatory, planetarium, pendulum, Ptolemy stone, Faraday cage, laboratories. **Computers:** 20% of dorms, 30% of common outdoor areas have wireless network access. Administrative functions (other than registration) can be performed online.

CAMPUS LIFE

Environment: Town **Activities:** Campus Ministries; Choral groups; Concert band; Dance; Drama/theater; International Student Organization; Jazz band; Literary magazine; Music ensembles; Student government; Student newspaper; Student-run film society; Symphony orchestra; Yearbook 64 registered organizations, 3 religious organizations. **On-Campus Highlights:** McDowell Hall (classrooms, Great Hall, and coffee shop), The Quad, Iglehart Hall (gymnasium), College Creek (boathouse and lawns), Greenfield Library **Environmental Initiatives:** purchasing renewable energy credits for 100% of our electric consumption

ADMISSIONS

Freshman Academic Profile: Average high school GPA 3.5. 36% in top 10% of high school class, 59% in top 25% of high school class, 87% in top 50% of high school class. 47% from public high schools. **Test Scores:** SAT Math middle 50% range 650-740. SAT EBRW middle 50% range 630-710. ACT middle 50% range 26-32. Minimum internet-based TOEFL 100. Minimum paper TOEFL 600. **Basis for Candidate Selection:** *Very important factors considered include:* application essay. *Important factors considered include:* rigor of secondary school record, recommendation(s), character/personal qualities, level of applicant's interest. *Other factors considered include:* class rank, academic GPA, standardized test scores, interview, extracurricular activities, talent/ability, first generation, alumni/ae relation, geographical residence, volunteer work, work experience. **Freshman Admission Requirements:** High school diploma is required and GED is accepted *Academic units required:* 3 math, 2 foreign language, *Academic units recommended:* 4 English, 4 math, 3 science, 3 science labs, 4 foreign language, 2 history. **Freshman Admission Statistics:** 753 applied, 54.6% admitted, 30% enrolled. **Transfer Admission Requirements:** High school transcript, college transcript(s), essay or personal statement. **General Admission Information:** Priority deadline 11/15. Nonfall registration accepted. Admission may be deferred for a maximum of 1 year.

COSTS AND FINANCIAL AID

Annual tuition $52,734. Room and board $12,602. Required fees $484. Average book expense $630. **Required Forms and Deadlines:** FAFSA; State aid form. **Notification of Awards:** Applicants will be notified of awards on a rolling basis beginning 12/15. **Types of Aid:** *Need-based scholarships/grants:* College/university scholarship or grant aid from institutional funds; Federal Pell; Private scholarships; SEOG; State scholarships/grants. *Loans:* Direct PLUS loans; Direct Subsidized Stafford Loans; Direct Unsubsidized Stafford Loans. *Student Employment:* Federal Work-Study Program available. Institutional employment available. **Financial Aid Statistics:** 99% needy freshmen, 98% needy undergrads receive need-based scholarship or grant aid. 27% freshmen, 19% undergrads receive non-need-based scholarship or grant aid. 96% freshmen, 97% undergrads receive need-based self-help aid. 0% freshmen, 0% undergrads receive athletic scholarships. 82% freshmen, 71% undergrads receive any aid. 83% undergrads borrow to pay for school. Average cumulative indebtedness $18,165. **Criteria for awarding aid:** *Non-need-based:* Academics.

ST. JOHN'S COLLEGE (NM)

1160 Camino Cruz Blanca, Santa Fe, NM 87505
Phone: 505-984-6060 • **Financial Aid Phone:** 505-984-6058
E-mail: SantaFe.Admissions@sjc.edu • **CEEB Code:** 4737
Website: www.sjc.edu • **ACT Code:** 2649

This private school was founded in 1696. It has a 250 acre campus.

RATINGS

Admissions Selectivity Rating: 86   **Fire Safety Rating:** 73   **Green Rating:** 73

STUDENTS AND FACULTY

Enrollment: 322. **Student Body:** 44% female, 56% male, 89% out-of-state, 26% international (28 countries represented). Asian 2%, African American 1%, Caucasian 55%, Hispanic 9%, Native American 0%, Pacific Islander 0%, Two or more races 6%, Race unknown 1%.
Retention and Graduation: 68% freshmen return for sophomore year. 53% freshmen graduate within 4 years. 65% freshmen graduate within 6 years. 14% grads go on to further study within 1 year. 0% grads pursue arts and sciences degrees. 0% grads pursue law degrees. 0% grads pursue business degrees. 0% grads pursue medical degrees. **Faculty:** Student/faculty ratio 8:1. 43 full-time faculty, 93% hold PhDs, 5% are members of minority groups, 26% are women. 0% of classes are taught by teaching assistants.

ACADEMICS

Degrees: Bachelor's; **Master's Classes:** Most classes have fewer than 10 students. Most lab/discussion sessions have 10-19 students. **Special Study Options:** Exchange student program (domestic); Internships; Study abroad. **Career services:** Alumni network; Alumni services; Career/job search classes; Internships; Regional alumni

FACILITIES

Housing: Apartments for married students; Apartments for single students; Coed dorms; Men's dorms; Special housing for disabled student; Special housing for international students; Wellness housing; Women's dorms 70% of campus accessible to physically diasbled. **Special Academic Facilities/Equipment:** Art gallery, wood working studio, pottery studio, science labs **Computers:** 75% of classrooms, 10% of dorms, 100% of dining areas, 100% of student union, 10% of common outdoor areas have wireless network access. Administrative functions (other than registration) can be performed online.

CAMPUS LIFE

Environment: Town **Activities:** Choral groups; Dance; Drama/theater; International Student Organization; Literary magazine; Music ensembles; Student government; Student newspaper 27 registered organizations. **On-Campus Highlights:** Student Activities Center, The Cave, Coffee Shop, Placita/Fish Pnd, Common rooms **Environmental Initiatives:** Paper, glass, plastic, cardboard recycling

ADMISSIONS

Freshman Academic Profile: Average high school GPA 3.5. 37% in top 10% of high school class, 48% in top 25% of high school class, 74% in top 50% of high school class. 50% from public high schools. **Test Scores:** SAT Math middle 50% range 560-680. SAT EBRW middle 50% range 630-670. ACT middle 50% range 23-32. Minimum internet-based TOEFL 79. Minimum paper TOEFL 550. **Basis for Candidate Selection:** *Very important factors considered*

include: application essay. *Important factors considered include:* rigor of secondary school record, recommendation(s), character/personal qualities, level of applicant's interest. *Other factors considered include:* class rank, academic GPA, standardized test scores, interview, extracurricular activities, talent/ability, first generation, alumni/ae relation, geographical residence, volunteer work, work experience. **Freshman Admission Requirements:** High school diploma is required and GED is accepted *Academic units required:* 3 math, 2 foreign language, *Academic units recommended:* 4 English, 4 math, 3 science, 3 science labs, 4 foreign language, 2 history. **Freshman Admission Statistics:** 342 applied, 63.2% admitted, 32% enrolled. **Transfer Admission Requirements:** High school transcript, college transcript(s), essay or personal statement. **General Admission Information:** Priority deadline 11/15. Nonfall registration accepted. Admission may be deferred for a maximum of 2 semesters.

COSTS AND FINANCIAL AID

Annual tuition $52,734. Room and board $12,148. Required fees $484. Average book expense $400. **Required Forms and Deadlines:** FAFSA. **Notification of Awards:** Applicants will be notified of awards on a rolling basis beginning 12/15. **Types of Aid:** *Need-based scholarships/grants:* College/university scholarship or grant aid from institutional funds; Federal Pell; Private scholarships; SEOG; State scholarships/grants. *Loans:* Direct PLUS loans; Direct Subsidized Stafford Loans; Direct Unsubsidized Stafford Loans. *Student Employment:* Federal Work-Study Program available. Institutional employment available. **Financial Aid Statistics:** 100% needy freshmen, 99% needy undergrads receive need-based scholarship or grant aid. 18% freshmen, 9% undergrads receive non-need-based scholarship or grant aid. 100% freshmen, 99% undergrads receive need-based self-help aid. 16% freshmen, 8% undergrads receive athletic scholarships. 100% freshmen, 81% undergrads receive any aid. 76% undergrads borrow to pay for school. Average cumulative indebtedness $26,195. **Criteria for awarding aid:** *Need-based:* Academics *Non-need-based:* Academics.

ST. JOHN'S UNIVERSITY (NY)

8000 Utopia Parkway, Queens, NY 11439
Phone: 718-990-2000 • **Financial Aid Phone:** 718-990-2000
E-mail: admhelp@stjohns.edu • **CEEB Code:** 2799
Fax: 718-990-2096 • **Website:** www.stjohns.edu • **ACT Code:** 2888

This private school, affiliated with the Roman Catholic Church, was founded in 1870. It has a 102 acre campus.

RATINGS

Admissions Selectivity Rating: 81   **Fire Safety Rating:** 94   **Green Rating:** 95

STUDENTS AND FACULTY

Enrollment: 11,758. **Student Body:** 57% female, 43% male, 25% out-of-state, 5% international (102 countries represented). Asian 16%, African American 17%, Caucasian 40%, Hispanic 8%, Native American 1%, Pacific Islander <1%, Two or more races 5%, Race unknown 8%.
Retention and Graduation: 84% freshmen return for sophomore year. 37% freshmen graduate within 4 years. 58% freshmen graduate within 6 years. 19% grads go on to further study within 1 year. 21% grads pursue arts and sciences degrees. 16.7% grads pursue law degrees. 29% grads pursue business degrees. 13.8% grads pursue medical degrees. **Faculty:** Student/faculty ratio 17:1. 638 full-time faculty, 93% hold PhDs, 27% are members of minority groups, 44% are women. 0% of classes are taught by teaching assistants.

ACADEMICS

Degrees: Associate; Bachelor's; Certificate; Doctoral/Professional; Doctoral/Research; Master's; Post-Bachelor's certificate; Post-Master's certificate **Classes:** Most classes have 10-19 students. Most lab/discussion sessions have 10-19 students. **Most popular majors:** Biology/Biological Sciences, General; Pharmacy. **Special Study Options:** Accelerated program; Cross-registration; Distance learning; Double major; Dual enrollment; English as a Second Language (ESL); Honors program; Independent study; Internships; Liberal arts/career combination; Study abroad; Teacher certification program. Honors programs: The University Honors Program is available to qualified incoming freshmen. The program primarily comprises honors versions of the courses which are part of the core curriculum and may be completed in any of the colleges and schools of the University. Honors Program students must complete 30 credits of honors-designated courses to complete the program. Additional options for obtaining honors credits are also available through high school advanced placement courses as well as in the University's study abroad programs. The Honors Program also features a range of special activities and events including theatre and music events as well as visits to the major New York City museums and walking tours of New York City. Combined degree programs: BA/JD; BA/MA. **Disability Services offered to physically disabled students:** Note-taking services; Reader services; Tape recorders; Tutors. **Career services:** Alumni network; Alumni services; Career assessment; Career/job search classes; Internships

FACILITIES

Housing: Apartments for single students; Coed dorms; Special housing for disabled student; Theme housing 90% of campus accessible to physically diasbled. **Special Academic Facilities/Equipment:** University Gallery; Instructional Media Center; Institute of Asian Studies; Health Education Resource Center; Center for Psychological Services; TV Center; Speech and Hearing Center and Reading and Writing Education Center. **Computers:** 100% of classrooms, 90% of dorms, 100% of libraries, 100% of dining areas, 100% of student union, 100% of common outdoor areas have wireless network access. Students can register for classes online. Administrative functions (other than registration) can be performed online. Undergraduates are required to own a computer.

CAMPUS LIFE

Environment: Metropolis **Activities:** Campus Ministries; Choral groups; Dance; Drama/theater; International Student Organization; Jazz band; Literary magazine; Music ensembles; Musical theater; Pep band; Radio station; Student government; Student newspaper; Student-run film society; Television station; Yearbook 180 registered organizations. **Athletics (Intercollegiate):** *Men:* baseball, basketball, fencing, golf, lacrosse, soccer, softball, table tennis, tennis, volleyball, weight lifting. *Women:* basketball, cross-country, fencing, soccer, softball, table tennis, tennis, track/field (outdoor), track/field (indoor), volleyball, weight lifting. **On-Campus Highlights:** The D'Angelo Center Living Room, The Great Lawn, Carnesecca Arena, The Peter J. Tobin College of Business, Homeland Security Lab **Environmental Initiatives:** Senior management signed the NYC Mayoral Challenge committing to 30% reduction in carbon emissions by the year 2017.

ADMISSIONS

Freshman Academic Profile: Average high school GPA 3.5. 31% in top 10% of high school class, 43% in top 25% of high school class, 77% in top 50% of high school class. 52% from public high schools. **Test Scores:** SAT Math middle 50% range 520-630. SAT EBRW middle 50% range 540-620. ACT middle 50% range 22-29. Minimum internet-based TOEFL 61. Minimum paper TOEFL 500. **Basis for Candidate Selection:** *Very important factors considered include:* rigor of secondary school record, academic GPA. *Important factors considered include:* standardized test scores. *Other factors considered include:* class rank, application essay, recommendation(s), extracurricular activities, talent/ability, character/personal qualities, alumni/ae relation, volunteer work, work experience, level of applicant's interest. **Freshman Admission Requirements:** High school diploma is required and GED is accepted *Academic units required:* 4 English, 2 math, 2 science, 1 history, *Academic units recommended:* 4 English, 3 math, 3 science, 2 foreign language, 2 social studies, 2 history. **Freshman Admission Statistics:** 27,179 applied, 67.7% admitted, 15% enrolled. **Transfer Admission Requirements:** college transcript(s), Lowest grade transferable C. **General Admission Information:** Priority deadline 2/1. Nonfall registration accepted. Admission may be deferred for a maximum of 1 year.

COSTS AND FINANCIAL AID

Annual tuition $39,690. Room and board $17,020. Required fees $830. Average book expense $626. **Required Forms and Deadlines:** FAFSA; State aid form. **Notification of Awards:** Applicants will be notified of awards on a rolling basis beginning 2/15. **Types of Aid:** *Need-based scholarships/grants:* College/university scholarship or grant aid from institutional funds; Federal Pell; Private scholarships; SEOG; State scholarships/grants. *Loans:* Direct PLUS loans; Direct Subsidized Stafford Loans; Direct Unsubsidized Stafford Loans. *Student Employment:* Federal Work-Study Program available. Institutional employment available. **Financial Aid Statistics:** 80% needy freshmen, 78% needy undergrads receive need-based scholarship or grant aid. 94% undergrads receive non-need-based scholarship or grant aid. 70% freshmen, 71% undergrads receive need-based self-help aid. 2% freshmen, 2% undergrads receive athletic scholarships. 98% freshmen, 96% undergrads receive any aid. 74% undergrads borrow to pay for school. Average cumulative indebtedness $34,234. **Criteria for awarding aid:** *Non-need-based:* Academics, Alumni affiliation, Art, Athletics, Leadership, Music/drama, Religious affiliation.

ST. JOSEPH'S COLLEGE

245 Clinton Avenue, Brooklyn, NY 11205
Phone: 718-940-5800 • **Financial Aid Phone:** (631) 687-2611
E-mail: brooklynas@sjcny.edu
Fax: 718-636-8303 • **Website:** www.sjcny.edu • **ACT Code:** 2890

This private school was founded in 1916. It has a 5 acre campus.

RATINGS
Admissions Selectivity Rating: 79   **Fire Safety Rating:** 60*   **Green Rating:** 60*

STUDENTS AND FACULTY
Enrollment: 953. **Student Body:** 67% female, 33% male, 4% out-of-state, 0% international (33 countries represented). Asian 7%, African American 24%, Caucasian 39%, Hispanic 20%, Native American <1%, Pacific Islander <1%, Two or more races 2%, Race unknown 9%.
Retention and Graduation: 81% freshmen return for sophomore year.
Faculty: Student/faculty ratio 11:1. 58 full-time faculty, 81% hold PhDs, 19% are members of minority groups, 41% are women. 0% of classes are taught by teaching assistants.

ACADEMICS
Degrees: Bachelor's; Certificate; Master's; Post-Bachelor's certificate **Classes:** Most classes have 20-29 students. Most lab/discussion sessions have 10-19 students. **Most popular majors:** Special Education And Teaching, General; Psychology, General; Business Administration And Management, General. **Special Study Options:** Accelerated program; Distance learning; Double major; English as a Second Language (ESL); Exchange student program (domestic); Honors program; Independent study; Internships; Liberal arts/career combination; Study abroad; Teacher certification program. Honors programs: **Disability Services offered to physically disabled students:** Note-taking services; Reader services; Tape recorders; Tutors. **Career services:** Alumni network; Alumni services; Career assessment; Internships

FACILITIES
Housing: Coed dorms 40% of campus accessible to physically diasbled. **Special Academic Facilities/Equipment:** Tuohy Student Lounge/Red Room; Student Life; The Hill Center; MCE Cafeteria; The Center for Student Involvement & Leadership; The Bear Cave **Computers:** Students can register for classes online.

CAMPUS LIFE
Environment: Metropolis **Activities:** Campus Ministries; Dance; Drama/theater; Musical theater; Student government; Student newspaper; Student-run film society 34 registered organizations, 8 honor societies, 2 religious organizations. 2 fraternities, 2 sororities. **On-Campus Highlights:** Tuohy Student Lounge/Red Room, Student Life, The Hill Center, MCE Cafeteria, The Center for Student Involvement & Leadership

ADMISSIONS
Freshman Academic Profile: Average high school GPA 3.3. 60% from public high schools. **Test Scores:** SAT Math middle 50% range 433-520. SAT EBRW middle 50% range 413-510. ACT middle 50% range 19-24. Minimum internet-based TOEFL 79. Minimum paper TOEFL 550. **Basis for Candidate Selection:** *Very important factors considered include:* academic GPA. *Important factors considered include:* rigor of secondary school record, class rank, application essay, standardized test scores, recommendation(s), character/personal qualities. *Other factors considered include:* interview, extracurricular activities, talent/ability, first generation, alumni/ae relation, volunteer work, work experience, level of applicant's interest. **Freshman Admission Requirements:** High school diploma is required and GED is accepted *Academic units required:* 4 English, 3 math, 3 science, 2 foreign language, 4 social studies, and 2 units from above areas or other academic areas. **Freshman Admission Statistics:** 1,903 applied, 62.1% admitted, 17% enrolled. **Transfer Admission Requirements:** college transcript(s), interview, statement of good standing from prior institution(s). Minimum college GPA of 2.0 required. **General Admission Information:** Application fee $25. Regular application deadline 8/31. Nonfall registration accepted. Admission may be deferred for a maximum of 1 year.

COSTS AND FINANCIAL AID
Annual tuition $25,930. Required fees $614. **Required Forms and Deadlines:** FAFSA; State aid form. **Notification of Awards:** Applicants will be notified of awards on a rolling basis beginning 3/30. **Types of Aid:** *Need-based scholarships/grants:* College/university scholarship or grant aid from institutional funds; Federal Pell; Private scholarships; SEOG; State scholarships/grants. *Loans:* Direct PLUS loans; Direct Subsidized Stafford Loans; Direct Unsubsidized Stafford Loans. *Student Employment:* Federal

Work-Study Program available. Institutional employment available. **Financial Aid Statistics:** 100% needy freshmen, 99% needy undergrads receive need-based scholarship or grant aid. 99% freshmen, 89% undergrads receive non-need-based scholarship or grant aid. 59% freshmen, 57% undergrads receive need-based self-help aid. 0% freshmen, 0% undergrads receive athletic scholarships. 62% freshmen, 63% undergrads receive any aid. 45% undergrads borrow to pay for school. Average cumulative indebtedness $23,124. **Criteria for awarding aid:** *Non-need-based:* Academics, Alumni affiliation.

ST. JOSEPH'S COLLEGE, NEW YORK (PATCHOGUE)

155 West Roe Blvd, Patchogue, NY 11772
Phone: 631-687-4500 • **Financial Aid Phone:** 631-687-2611
E-mail: longislandas@sjcny.edu • **CEEB Code:** 2802
Fax: 631-447-3601 • **Website:** www.sjcny.edu • **ACT Code:** 2923

This private school was founded in 1916. It has a 56 acre campus.

RATINGS
Admissions Selectivity Rating: 80   **Fire Safety Rating:** 60*   **Green Rating:** 63

STUDENTS AND FACULTY
Enrollment: 3,031. **Student Body:** 66% female, 34% male, 1% out-of-state, 0% international (8 countries represented). Asian 2%, African American 5%, Caucasian 68%, Hispanic 11%, Native American <1%, Pacific Islander <1%, Two or more races 2%, Race unknown 12%.
Retention and Graduation: 87% freshmen return for sophomore year.
Faculty: Student/faculty ratio 15:1. 107 full-time faculty, 79% hold PhDs, 5% are members of minority groups, 60% are women. 0% of classes are taught by teaching assistants.

ACADEMICS
Degrees: Bachelor's; Certificate; Master's; Post-Bachelor's certificate **Classes:** Most classes have fewer than 10 students. Most lab/discussion sessions have fewer than 10 students. **Most popular majors:** Special Education And Teaching, General; Business Administration And Management, General; Accounting. **Special Study Options:** Accelerated program; Distance learning; Double major; Honors program; Independent study; Internships; Liberal arts/career combination; Study abroad; Teacher certification program; Weekend college. Combined degree programs: BA/MA. **Disability Services offered to physically disabled students:** Note-taking services; Reader services; Tape recorders; Tutors. **Career services:** Alumni network; Alumni services; Career assessment; Career/job search classes; Internships

FACILITIES
Housing: 100% of campus accessible to physically disabled. **Special Academic Facilities/Equipment:** 3-D Printer, Technology Building, Computer Labs, Claire Rose Playhouse **Computers:** Students can register for classes online.

CAMPUS LIFE
Environment: Town **Activities:** Campus Ministries; Choral groups; Dance; Drama/theater; Literary magazine; Musical theater; Opera; Radio station; Student government; Student newspaper 34 registered organizations, 8 honor societies, 2 religious organizations. 2 fraternities, 2 sororities. **Athletics (Intercollegiate):** *Men:* baseball, basketball, cross-country, golf, soccer, tennis, track/field (outdoor). *Women:* basketball, cross-country, equestrian sports, soccer, softball, swimming, tennis, track/field (outdoor), volleyball. **On-Campus Highlights:** Cafeteria (Eagle's Nest) and Second Floor Lounge, John A. Danzi Athletic Center (Lobby), MVP Center for Performing Arts and Clare Rose Playhouse, Callahan Library, McGann Conference Center (for events)

ADMISSIONS
Freshman Academic Profile: Average high school GPA 3.6. 91% from public high schools. **Test Scores:** SAT Math middle 50% range 480-580. SAT EBRW middle 50% range 470-560. ACT middle 50% range 21-25. Minimum internet-based TOEFL 79. Minimum paper TOEFL 550. **Basis for Candidate Selection:** *Very important factors considered include:* rigor of secondary school record, class rank, academic GPA. *Important factors considered include:* application essay, standardized test scores, recommendation(s), interview, extracurricular activities, character/personal qualities. *Other factors considered include:* talent/ability, first generation, alumni/ae relation, volunteer work, work experience, level of applicant's interest. **Freshman Admission Requirements:** High school diploma is required and GED is accepted *Academic units required:* 4 English, 3 math, 3 science, 3 science labs, 2 foreign language, 4 social studies, 3 academic electives, 2 visual/performing arts, *Academic units recommended:* 4 English, 4 math, 4 science, 4 science labs, 3 foreign language, 4 social studies, 4 academic electives, 2 visual/performing arts. **Freshman Admission**

Statistics: 1,770 applied, 71.9% admitted, 34% enrolled. **Transfer Admission Requirements:** college transcript(s), Minimum college GPA of 2.0 required. **General Admission Information:** Application fee $25. Nonfall registration accepted. Admission may be deferred for a maximum of 1 year.

COSTS AND FINANCIAL AID
Annual tuition $25,930. Required fees $624. **Required Forms and Deadlines:** FAFSA; State aid form. **Notification of Awards:** Applicants will be notified of awards on a rolling basis beginning 3/30. **Types of Aid:** *Need-based scholarships/grants:* College/university scholarship or grant aid from institutional funds; Federal Pell; Private scholarships; SEOG; State scholarships/grants. *Loans:* Direct PLUS loans; Direct Subsidized Stafford Loans; Direct Unsubsidized Stafford Loans. *Student Employment:* Federal Work-Study Program available. Institutional employment available. **Financial Aid Statistics:** 78% needy freshmen, 96% needy undergrads receive need-based scholarship or grant aid. 98% freshmen, 87% undergrads receive non-need-based scholarship or grant aid. 63% freshmen, 67% undergrads receive need-based self-help aid. 0% freshmen, 0% undergrads receive athletic scholarships. 62% freshmen, 63% undergrads receive any aid. 66% undergrads borrow to pay for school. Average cumulative indebtedness $27,364. **Criteria for awarding aid:** *Non-need-based:* Academics, Alumni affiliation.

See page 1038.

ST. LAWRENCE UNIVERSITY

23 Romoda Drive, Canton, NY 13617
Phone: 315-229-5261 • **Financial Aid Phone:** 315-229-5265
E-mail: admissions@stlawu.edu • **CEEB Code:** 2805
Fax: 315-229-5818 • **Website:** www.stlawu.edu • **ACT Code:** 2896

This private school was founded in 1856. It has a 1000 acre campus.

RATINGS
Admissions Selectivity Rating: 90   **Fire Safety Rating:** 81   **Green Rating:** 87

STUDENTS AND FACULTY
Enrollment: 2,373. **Student Body:** 56% female, 44% male, 60% out-of-state, 9% international (62 countries represented). Asian 1%, African American 3%, Caucasian 78%, Hispanic 5%, Native American <1%, Pacific Islander 0%, Two or more races 2%, Race unknown 1%.
Retention and Graduation: 92% freshmen return for sophomore year. 82% freshmen graduate within 4 years. 85% freshmen graduate within 6 years. 18% grads go on to further study within 1 year. 6% grads pursue arts and sciences degrees. 1.9% grads pursue law degrees. 1% grads pursue business degrees. 2.3% grads pursue medical degrees. **Faculty:** Student/faculty ratio 11:1. 175 full-time faculty, 99% hold PhDs, 14% are members of minority groups, 50% are women. 0% of classes are taught by teaching assistants.

ACADEMICS
Degrees: Bachelor's; Master's; Post-Master's certificate **Classes:** Most classes have 10-19 students. Most lab/discussion sessions have 10-19 students. **Most popular majors:** Biology/Biological Sciences, General; Psychology, General; Economics, General. **Special Study Options:** Cross-registration; Double major; English as a Second Language (ESL); Exchange student program (domestic); Independent study; Internships; Student-designed major; Study abroad; Teacher certification program. Honors programs: The University Fellows program offers a stipend plus room for summer research on campus. This is a competitive program for students who wish to undertake a serious, independent academic project as their summer employment. **Disability Services offered to physically disabled students:** Note-taking services; Reader services; Tape recorders; Tutors. **Career services:** Alumni network; Alumni services; Career assessment; Career/job search classes; Internships

FACILITIES
Housing: Apartments for single students; Coed dorms; Fraternity/sorority housing; Special housing for disabled student; Special housing for international students; Theme housing; Wellness housing; Women's dorms 60% of campus accessible to physically disabled. **Special Academic Facilities/Equipment:** Art gallery, arts technology center, language lab, center for international education, environmental research facility, 76-acre forest preserve, two electron microscopes, microscopy and sleep labs, Neuroscience lab, sustainability lab, environmental field study center **Computers:** 100% of classrooms, 100% of dorms, 100% of libraries, 100% of dining areas, 100% of student union, 100%

of common outdoor areas have wireless network access. Students can register for classes online. Administrative functions (other than registration) can be performed online.

CAMPUS LIFE

Environment: Village **Activities:** Campus Ministries; Choral groups; Concert band; Dance; Drama/theater; International Student Organization; Jazz band; Literary magazine; Model UN; Music ensembles; Radio station; Student government; Student newspaper; Student-run film society; Yearbook 117 registered organizations, 22 honor societies, 4 religious organizations. 2 fraternities, 4 sororities. **Athletics (Intercollegiate):** *Men:* baseball, basketball, crew/rowing, cross-country, equestrian sports, football, golf, ice hockey, lacrosse, skiing (downhill/alpine), skiing (nordic/cross-country), soccer, squash, swimming, tennis, track/field (outdoor), track/field (indoor). *Women:* basketball, crew/rowing, cross-country, equestrian sports, field hockey, golf, ice hockey, lacrosse, skiing (downhill/alpine), skiing (nordic/cross-country), soccer, softball, squash, swimming, tennis, track/field (outdoor), track/field (indoor), volleyball. **On-Campus Highlights:** Newell Field House & Stafford Fitness Center, Brewer Bookstore, Johnson Hall of Science, Owen D. Young Library, Sullivan Student Center **Environmental Initiatives:** Pledge of climate neutrality

ADMISSIONS

Freshman Academic Profile: Average high school GPA 3.6. 46% in top 10% of high school class, 79% in top 25% of high school class, 95% in top 50% of high school class. 67% from public high schools. **Test Scores:** SAT Math middle 50% range 580-675. SAT EBRW middle 50% range 590-680. ACT middle 50% range 25-30. Minimum internet-based TOEFL 82. Minimum paper TOEFL 600. **Basis for Candidate Selection:** *Very important factors considered include:* rigor of secondary school record, academic GPA, application essay, recommendation(s), character/personal qualities. *Important factors considered include:* class rank, interview, extracurricular activities, racial/ethnic status. *Other factors considered include:* standardized test scores, talent/ability, first generation, alumni/ae relation, geographical residence, volunteer work, work experience, level of applicant's interest. **Freshman Admission Requirements:** High school diploma is required and GED is accepted *Academic units recommended:* 4 English, 4 math, 4 science, 4 foreign language, 2 social studies, 2 history. **Freshman Admission Statistics:** 5,866 applied, 48.3% admitted, 25% enrolled. **Transfer Admission Requirements:** High school transcript, college transcript(s), essay or personal statement, statement of good standing from prior institution(s). Lowest grade transferable C. **General Admission Information:** Application fee $60. Regular application deadline 2/1. Nonfall registration accepted. Admission may be deferred for a maximum of 1 year.

COSTS AND FINANCIAL AID

Annual tuition $50,830. Room and board $13,190. Required fees $370. Average book expense $750. **Required Forms and Deadlines:** FAFSA. **Types of Aid:** *Need-based scholarships/grants:* College/university scholarship or grant aid from institutional funds; Federal Pell; Private scholarships; SEOG; State scholarships/grants. *Loans:* Direct PLUS loans; Direct Subsidized Stafford Loans; Direct Unsubsidized Stafford Loans. *Student Employment:* Federal Work-Study Program available. Institutional employment available. **Financial Aid Statistics:** 100% needy freshmen, 100% needy undergrads receive need-based scholarship or grant aid. 74% freshmen, 70% undergrads receive non-need-based scholarship or grant aid. 70% freshmen, 74% undergrads receive need-based self-help aid. 2% freshmen, 2% undergrads receive athletic scholarships. 100% freshmen, 96% undergrads receive any aid. 58% undergrads borrow to pay for school. Average cumulative indebtedness $37,919. **Criteria for awarding aid:** *Need-based:* Academics, Minority status *Non-need-based:* Academics, Alumni affiliation, Leadership, Minority status.

See page 1040.

ST. LOUIS COLLEGE OF PHARMACY

4588 Parkview Place, Saint Louis, MO 63110
Phone: 314-367-8700
E-mail: connie.horrall@stlcop.edu • **CEEB Code:** 6626
Fax: 314-446-8310 • **Website:** www.stlcop.edu • **ACT Code:** 2346

This private school was founded in 1864. It has a 7 acre campus.

RATINGS

Admissions Selectivity Rating: 90   **Fire Safety Rating:** 77   **Green Rating:** 60*

STUDENTS AND FACULTY

Enrollment: 723. **Student Body:** 60% female, 40% male, 53% out-of-state, 1% international. Asian 22%, African American 5%, Caucasian 66%, Hispanic 1%, Native American <1%, Pacific Islander <1%, Two or more races 1%, Race unknown 4%.

Retention and Graduation: 92% freshmen return for sophomore year. **Faculty:** Student/faculty ratio 13:1. 91 full-time faculty, 100% hold PhDs, 9% are members of minority groups, 47% are women.

ACADEMICS

Degrees: Doctoral/Professional **Classes:** Most classes have 10-19 students. **Career services:** Alumni services; Internships

FACILITIES

Housing: Coed dorms

CAMPUS LIFE

Activities: Campus Ministries; Choral groups; Concert band; Drama/theater; International Student Organization; Literary magazine; Musical theater; Student government; Student newspaper; Yearbook 2 honor societies, 6 religious organizations. 5 fraternities. **Athletics (Intercollegiate):** *Men:* basketball, cheerleading, cross-country. *Women:* cheerleading, cross-country, volleyball.

ADMISSIONS

Freshman Academic Profile: Average high school GPA 3.7. 50% in top 10% of high school class, 33% in top 25% of high school class, 17% in top 50% of high school class. **Test Scores:** SAT Math middle 50% range 640-730. SAT EBRW middle 50% range 570-660. ACT middle 50% range 25-29. Minimum paper TOEFL 550. **Basis for Candidate Selection:** *Very important factors considered include:* rigor of secondary school record, academic GPA, application essay, standardized test scores, recommendation(s), level of applicant's interest. *Other factors considered include:* class rank, extracurricular activities, character/personal qualities, alumni/ae relation, volunteer work, work experience. **Freshman Admission Requirements:** High school diploma is required and GED is accepted *Academic units required:* 4 English, 4 math, 3 science, 2 science labs, *Academic units recommended:* 3 science. **Freshman Admission Statistics:** 555 applied, 62.7% admitted, 71% enrolled. **Transfer Admission Requirements:** college transcript(s), essay or personal statement, standardized test scores, Minimum college GPA of 3.0 required. Lowest grade transferable C. **General Admission Information:** Application fee $50. Priority deadline 12/15. Regular application deadline 2/1. Nonfall registration accepted.

COSTS AND FINANCIAL AID

Annual tuition $26,736. Room and board $9,555. Required fees $325. Average book expense $1,500. **Required Forms and Deadlines:** FAFSA. **Notification of Awards:** Applicants will be notified of awards on a rolling basis beginning 2/19. **Types of Aid:** *Need-based scholarships/grants:* College/university scholarship or grant aid from institutional funds; Federal Pell; Private scholarships; SEOG; State scholarships/grants. *Loans:* Direct PLUS loans; Direct Subsidized Stafford Loans; Direct Unsubsidized Stafford Loans. *Student Employment:* Federal Work-Study Program available. Institutional employment available. **Financial Aid Statistics:** 99% needy freshmen, 90% needy undergrads receive need-based scholarship or grant aid. 9% freshmen, 5% undergrads receive non-need-based scholarship or grant aid. 83% freshmen, 91% undergrads receive need-based self-help aid. 4% freshmen, 2% undergrads receive athletic scholarships. **Criteria for awarding aid:** *Need-based:* Academics, Athletics, Job skills, Minority status *Non-need-based:* Academics, Athletics, Job skills, State/district residency.

ST. MARY'S COLLEGE OF MARYLAND

47645 College Drive, St. Mary's City, MD 20686-3001
Phone: 240-895-5000 • **Financial Aid Phone:** 240-895-3000
E-mail: admissions@smcm.edu • **CEEB Code:** 5601
Fax: 240-895-5001 • **Website:** www.smcm.edu • **ACT Code:** 1736

This public school was founded in 1840. It has a 361 acre campus.

RATINGS

Admissions Selectivity Rating: 78   **Fire Safety Rating:** 88   **Green Rating:** 98

STUDENTS AND FACULTY

Enrollment: 1,544. **Student Body:** 58% female, 42% male, 7% out-of-state, <1% international (11 countries represented). Asian 4%, African American 9%, Caucasian 71%, Hispanic 8%, Native American <1%, Pacific Islander <1%, Two or more races 5%, Race unknown 2%.
Retention and Graduation: 87% freshmen return for sophomore year. 70% freshmen graduate within 4 years. 78% freshmen graduate within 6 years. **Faculty:** Student/faculty ratio 10:1. 139 full-time faculty, 99% hold PhDs, 16%

are members of minority groups, 50% are women. 0% of classes are taught by teaching assistants.

ACADEMICS

Degrees: Bachelor's; **Master's Classes:** Most classes have fewer than 10 students. **Most popular majors:** Biology/Biological Sciences, General; Psychology, General; Economics, General. **Special Study Options:** Cross-registration; Double major; Dual enrollment; Exchange student program (domestic); Independent study; Internships; Liberal arts/career combination; Student-designed major; Study abroad. **Disability Services offered to physically disabled students:** Note-taking services; Reader services; Tape recorders; Tutors. **Career services:** Alumni network; Alumni services; Career assessment; Career/job search classes; Internships; Regional alumni

FACILITIES

Housing: Apartments for single students; Coed dorms; Men's dorms; Special housing for disabled student; Special housing for international students; Theme housing; Wellness housing; Women's dorms 95% of campus accessible to physically diasbled. **Special Academic Facilities/Equipment:** Art gallery, archaeological sites, Historic St. Mary's City, historic state house of early Maryland settlers, electron microscope, freshwater and saltwater research facilities, research boat, campus farm **Computers:** 100% of classrooms, 20% of dorms, 100% of libraries, 100% of dining areas, 100% of student union, 100% of common outdoor areas have wireless network access. Students can register for classes online. Administrative functions (other than registration) can be performed online.

CAMPUS LIFE

Environment: Rural **Activities:** Campus Ministries; Choral groups; Dance; Drama/theater; Jazz band; Literary magazine; Model UN; Music ensembles; Radio station; Student government; Student newspaper; Symphony orchestra; Yearbook 117 registered organizations, 8 honor societies, 4 religious organizations. **Athletics (Intercollegiate):** *Men:* baseball, basketball, cross-country, lacrosse, sailing, soccer, swimming, tennis. *Women:* basketball, cross-country, field hockey, lacrosse, sailing, soccer, swimming, tennis, volleyball. **On-Campus Highlights:** Campus Center, Waterfront, Library, Athletics and Recreation Center, The Pub **Environmental Initiatives:** Purchasing approximately 80% of the school's total energy use in RECs to offset our carbon output.

ADMISSIONS

Freshman Academic Profile: Average high school GPA 3.3. 75% from public high schools. **Test Scores:** SAT Math middle 50% range 530-630. SAT EBRW middle 50% range 540-650. ACT middle 50% range 22-28. Minimum internet-based TOEFL 90. Minimum paper TOEFL 550. **Basis for Candidate Selection:** *Very important factors considered include:* rigor of secondary school record, academic GPA, application essay, standardized test scores, recommendation(s). *Important factors considered include:* class rank, extracurricular activities, talent/ability, character/personal qualities, volunteer work. *Other factors considered include:* interview, first generation, alumni/ae relation, geographical residence, state residency, racial/ethnic status, work experience, level of applicant's interest. **Freshman Admission Requirements:** High school diploma is required and GED is accepted *Academic units required:* 4 English, 3 math, 3 science, 2 science labs, 2 social studies, 1 history, *Academic units recommended:* 4 math, 4 foreign language, 3 social studies. **Freshman Admission Statistics:** 1,655 applied, 82.4% admitted, 25% enrolled. **Transfer Admission Requirements:** college transcript(s), essay or personal statement, Minimum college GPA of 3.0 required. Lowest grade transferable C-. **General Admission Information:** Application fee $50. Priority deadline 11/1. Regular application deadline 2/15. Nonfall registration accepted. Admission may be deferred for a maximum of 1.5 years.

COSTS AND FINANCIAL AID

Annual in-state tuition $12,816. Annual out-of-state tuition $27,097. Room and board $12,816. Required fees $2,850. Average book expense $800. **Required Forms and Deadlines:** FAFSA. **Notification of Awards:** Applicants will be notified of awards on a rolling basis beginning 12/15. **Types of Aid:** *Need-based scholarships/grants:* College/university scholarship or grant aid from institutional funds; Federal Pell; Private scholarships; SEOG; State scholarships/grants. *Loans:* Direct PLUS loans; Direct Subsidized Stafford Loans; Direct Unsubsidized Stafford Loans. *Student Employment:* Federal Work-Study Program available. Institutional employment available. **Financial Aid Statistics:** 89% needy freshmen, 73% needy undergrads receive need-based scholarship or grant aid. 55% freshmen, 61% undergrads receive non-need-based scholarship or grant aid. 67% freshmen, 68% undergrads receive need-based self-help aid. 0% freshmen, 0% undergrads receive athletic scholarships. 72% freshmen, 74% undergrads receive any aid. 53% undergrads borrow to pay for school. Average cumulative indebtedness $24,213. **Criteria for awarding aid:** *Non-need-based:* Academics, Leadership.

ST. MARY'S UNIVERSITY

One Camino Santa Maria, San Antonio, TX 78228-8503
Phone: 210.436.3126 • **Financial Aid Phone:** 210-436-3141
E-mail: uadm@stmarytx.edu • **CEEB Code:** 6637
Fax: 210.431.6742 • **Website:** http://www.stmarytx.edu/ • **ACT Code:** 4158

This private school, affiliated with the Roman Catholic Church, was founded in 1852. It has a 135 acre campus.

RATINGS

Admissions Selectivity Rating: 76   **Fire Safety Rating:** 87   **Green Rating:** 72

STUDENTS AND FACULTY

Enrollment: 2,268. **Student Body:** 53% female, 47% male, 9% out-of-state, 9% international (35 countries represented). Asian 2%, African American 3%, Caucasian 14%, Hispanic 68%, Native American <1%, Pacific Islander <1%, Two or more races 1%, Race unknown 3%.
Retention and Graduation: 76% freshmen return for sophomore year. 25% grads go on to further study within 1 year. 69% grads pursue arts and sciences degrees. 10% grads pursue law degrees. 8% grads pursue business degrees. 10% grads pursue medical degrees. **Faculty:** Student/faculty ratio 11:1. 210 full-time faculty, 93% hold PhDs, 24% are members of minority groups, 37% are women. 0% of classes are taught by teaching assistants.

ACADEMICS

Degrees: Bachelor's; Doctoral; Doctoral/Professional; Doctoral/Research; Master's; Post-Bachelor's certificate **Classes:** Most classes have 10-19 students. **Most popular majors:** Biology/Biological Sciences, General; Kinesiology And Exercise Science; Accounting. **Special Study Options:** Accelerated program; Cross-registration; Distance learning; Double major; Dual enrollment; Exchange student program (domestic); Honors program; Independent study; Internships; Study abroad; Teacher certification program. Honors programs: The Honors Program offers an academically challenging and personally enriching course of study designed to cultivate critical analysis, clear oral and written expression, aesthetic awareness and ethical judgment. In and out of the classroom we seek to prepare our future graduates for lives of leadership and service to their communities. Combined degree programs: BA/JD; BA/MA. **Disability Services offered to physically disabled students:** Note-taking services; Reader services; Tape recorders; Tutors. **Career services:** Alumni network; Alumni services; Career assessment; Career/job search classes; Internships; Regional alumni

FACILITIES

Housing: Coed dorms; Theme housing 80% of campus accessible to physically diasbled. **Special Academic Facilities/Equipment:** St. Mary's has many unique facilities available to our undergraduate students. Our Charles Cotrell Learning Commons includes extensive access to technology and on-site technological assistance, extended library hours and a Starbucks coffee shop. The space is popular with students who use the area for group and individual studying, socializing and breaks between classes. Students interested in fitness and recreation can visit our full-size gym, indoor track, rock-climbing wall, indoor swimming pool, racquetball courts, fitness studio, and multiple fields and basketball courts. Our science department houses Earth Science museum on the second floor which houses over 1300 samples of minerals, rocks, fossils, maps, and scientific instruments used for research purposes of undergraduates enrolled in the program. For our students interested in the arts, we offer art displays, a music and drama theatre, and an amphitheather. And in our Greehey School of Business, St. Mary's has a trading room that features a Trans-Lux LED jet ticker, a Trans-Lux data board, and a 57-inch LCD television for up-to-date financial information. **Computers:** 100% of classrooms, 100% of dorms, 100% of libraries, 100% of dining areas, 100% of student union, 80% of common outdoor areas have wireless network access. Students can register for classes online. Administrative functions (other than registration) can be performed online. Undergraduates are required to own a computer.

CAMPUS LIFE

Environment: Metropolis **Activities:** Campus Ministries; Choral groups; Concert band; Dance; Drama/theater; International Student Organization; Jazz band; Literary magazine; Model UN; Music ensembles; Musical theater; Opera; Pep band; Student government; Student newspaper 91 registered organizations, 1 religious organization. 4 fraternities, 4 sororities. **Athletics (Intercollegiate):** *Men:* baseball, basketball, cheerleading, golf, soccer, tennis. *Women:* basketball, cheerleading, cross-country, golf, soccer, softball, tennis, volleyball. **On-Campus Highlights:** Alumni Athletics and Convocation Center, University Center, Cottrell Learning Commons, Starbucks, Barrett Memorial Bell Tower **Environmental Initiatives:** Energy efficiency electric motors, chillers, lighting, Demand Energy Limiting

ADMISSIONS

Freshman Academic Profile: Average high school GPA 3.5. 27% in top 10% of high school class, 55% in top 25% of high school class, 81% in top 50% of high school class. 69% from public high schools. **Test Scores:** SAT Math middle 50% range 480-570. SAT EBRW middle 50% range 470-560. ACT middle 50% range 19-25. Minimum internet-based TOEFL 80. Minimum paper TOEFL 550. **Basis for Candidate Selection:** *Very important factors considered include:* rigor of secondary school record, academic GPA. *Important factors considered include:* standardized test scores. *Other factors considered include:* application essay, recommendation(s), interview, extracurricular activities, talent/ability, character/personal qualities, volunteer work, work experience, level of applicant's interest. **Freshman Admission Requirements:** High school diploma is required and GED is accepted *Academic units required:* 4 English, 3 math, 3 science, 2 foreign language, 3 social studies, 1 academic elective, *Academic units recommended:* 4 English, 4 math, 4 science, 3 foreign language, 4 social studies. **Freshman Admission Statistics:** 4,346 applied, 77.7% admitted, 17% enrolled. **Transfer Admission Requirements:** college transcript(s), Minimum college GPA of 2.5 required. Lowest grade transferable C-. **General Admission Information:** Priority deadline 1/15. Regular application deadline 8/31. Nonfall registration accepted. Admission may be deferred for a maximum of 1 year.

COSTS AND FINANCIAL AID

Annual tuition $27,520. Room and board $9,300. Required fees $680. Average book expense $1,300. **Required Forms and Deadlines:** FAFSA. **Notification of Awards:** Applicants will be notified of awards on a rolling basis beginning 10/1. **Types of Aid:** *Need-based scholarships/grants:* College/university scholarship or grant aid from institutional funds; Federal Pell; Private scholarships; SEOG; State scholarships/grants. *Loans:* Direct PLUS loans; Direct Subsidized Stafford Loans; Direct Unsubsidized Stafford Loans. *Student Employment:* Federal Work-Study Program available. Institutional employment available. **Financial Aid Statistics:** 100% needy freshmen, 98% needy undergrads receive need-based scholarship or grant aid. 9% freshmen, 7% undergrads receive non-need-based scholarship or grant aid. 80% freshmen, 84% undergrads receive need-based self-help aid. 4% freshmen, 6% undergrads receive athletic scholarships. 95% freshmen, 92% undergrads receive any aid. 77% undergrads borrow to pay for school. Average cumulative indebtedness $39,883. **Criteria for awarding aid:** *Need-based:* Academics *Non-need-based:* Academics, Alumni affiliation, Athletics, Music/drama, Religious affiliation, State/district residency.

ST. NORBERT COLLEGE

100 Grant Street, De Pere, WI 54115-2099
Phone: 920-403-3005 • **Financial Aid Phone:** 920-403-3071
E-mail: admit@snc.edu • **CEEB Code:** 1706
Fax: 920-403-4072 • **Website:** www.snc.edu • **ACT Code:** 4644

This private school, affiliated with the Roman Catholic Church, was founded in 1898. It has a 113 acre campus.

RATINGS
Admissions Selectivity Rating: 77   **Fire Safety Rating:** 90   **Green Rating:** 72

STUDENTS AND FACULTY
Enrollment: 2,041. **Student Body:** 57% female, 43% male, 22% out-of-state, 3% international (26 countries represented). Asian 2%, African American 1%, Caucasian 87%, Hispanic 4%, Native American 1%, Pacific Islander <1%, Two or more races 1%, Race unknown <1%.
Retention and Graduation: 83% freshmen return for sophomore year. 69% freshmen graduate within 4 years. 73% freshmen graduate within 6 years. 13% grads go on to further study within 1 year. **Faculty:** Student/faculty ratio 13:1. 142 full-time faculty, 92% hold PhDs, 11% are members of minority groups, 46% are women. 0% of classes are taught by teaching assistants.

ACADEMICS
Degrees: Bachelor's; **Master's Classes:** Most classes have 20-29 students. Most lab/discussion sessions have 20-29 students. **Most popular majors:** Speech Communication And Rhetoric; Elementary Education And Teaching; Business/Commerce, General. **Special Study Options:** Distance learning; Double major; English as a Second Language (ESL); Honors program; Independent study; Internships; Student-designed major; Study abroad; Teacher certification program. Honors programs: The Honors Program at St. Norbert College offers a sophisticated and demanding program of studies and readings to provide the most academically talented students with an enriched academic curriculum that is stimulating and challenging. **Disability Services offered to physically disabled students:** Note-taking services; Reader

services; Tape recorders; Tutors. **Career services:** Alumni network; Alumni services; Career assessment; Internships; Regional alumni

FACILITIES
Housing: Apartments for single students; Coed dorms; Special housing for disabled student; Theme housing; Women's dorms 82% of campus accessible to physically disabled. **Special Academic Facilities/Equipment:** Innovation studio; center for women's and gender studies; center for peace, justice and public understanding; marina; on-campus hotel and conference center; fine and performing arts centers; center for international education; center for leadership and service; children's center; Strategic Research Institute; center for Norbertine studies **Computers:** 100% of classrooms, 60% of dorms, 100% of libraries, 100% of dining areas, 100% of student union, have wireless network access. Students can register for classes online. Administrative functions (other than registration) can be performed online.

CAMPUS LIFE
Environment: Town **Activities:** Campus Ministries; Choral groups; Concert band; Dance; Drama/theater; International Student Organization; Jazz band; Literary magazine; Music ensembles; Musical theater; Opera; Pep band; Radio station; Student government; Student newspaper; Student-run film society; Television station; Yearbook 63 registered organizations, 10 honor societies, 3 religious organizations. 3 fraternities, 4 sororities. **Athletics (Intercollegiate):** *Men:* baseball, basketball, cross-country, football, golf, ice hockey, soccer, tennis, track/field (outdoor), track/field (indoor). *Women:* basketball, cross-country, golf, ice hockey, soccer, softball, tennis, track/field (outdoor), track/field (indoor), volleyball. **On-Campus Highlights:** The Ray Van Den Heuvel Campus Center, The Bush Fine Arts Center, The F.K. Bemis International Center, Mulva Family Fitness and Sports Center, New Mulva Library with Coffee Shop **Environmental Initiatives:** Designed new Mulva Library with solar water heating system.

ADMISSIONS
Freshman Academic Profile: Average high school GPA 3.5. 24% in top 10% of high school class, 54% in top 25% of high school class, 85% in top 50% of high school class. 72% from public high schools. **Test Scores:** ACT middle 50% range 22-27. Minimum internet-based TOEFL 80. Minimum paper TOEFL 550. **Basis for Candidate Selection:** *Very important factors considered include:* rigor of secondary school record, academic GPA, standardized test scores. *Other factors considered include:* class rank, application essay, recommendation(s), interview, extracurricular activities, talent/ability, character/personal qualities, first generation, alumni/ae relation, geographical residence, state residency, religious affiliation/commitment, racial/ethnic status, volunteer work, work experience, level of applicant's interest. **Freshman Admission Requirements:** High school diploma is required and GED is accepted *Academic units recommended:* 4 English, 3 math, 3 science, 3 science labs, 2 foreign language, 2 social studies, 2 history. **Freshman Admission Statistics:** 3,860 applied, 79.2% admitted, 17% enrolled. **Transfer Admission Requirements:** High school transcript, college transcript(s), essay or personal statement, standardized test scores, Minimum college GPA of 2.5 required. Lowest grade transferable C. **General Admission Information:** Priority deadline 4/1. Nonfall registration accepted. Admission may be deferred for a maximum of 2 years.

COSTS AND FINANCIAL AID
Annual tuition $37,314. Room and board $9,954. Required fees $815. Average book expense $950. **Required Forms and Deadlines:** FAFSA. **Notification of Awards:** Applicants will be notified of awards on a rolling basis beginning 1/1. **Types of Aid:** *Need-based scholarships/grants:* College/university scholarship or grant aid from institutional funds; Federal Pell; Private scholarships; SEOG; State scholarships/grants. *Loans:* Direct PLUS loans; Direct Subsidized Stafford Loans; Direct Unsubsidized Stafford Loans. *Student Employment:* Federal Work-Study Program available. Institutional employment available. **Financial Aid Statistics:** 99% needy freshmen, 97% needy undergrads receive need-based scholarship or grant aid. 2% freshmen, 3% undergrads receive non-need-based scholarship or grant aid. 77% freshmen, 79% undergrads receive need-based self-help aid. 0% freshmen, 0% undergrads receive athletic scholarships. 95% freshmen, 96% undergrads receive any aid. 74% undergrads borrow to pay for school. Average cumulative indebtedness $33,948. **Criteria for awarding aid:** *Need-based:* Academics, Art, Leadership, Minority status, Music/drama *Non-need-based:* Academics, Art, Leadership, Minority status, Music/drama, State/district residency.

See page 1042.

ST. OLAF COLLEGE

Best Colleges

1520 St. Olaf Avenue, Northfield, MN 55057
Phone: 507-786-3025 • **Financial Aid Phone:** 507-786-3019
E-mail: admissions@stolaf.edu • **CEEB Code:** 6638
Fax: 507-786-3832 • **Website:** http://wp.stolaf.edu • **ACT Code:** 2150

This private school, affiliated with the Lutheran Church, was founded in 1874. It has a 300 acre campus.

RATINGS
Admissions Selectivity Rating: 91   **Fire Safety Rating:** 82   **Green Rating:** 60*

STUDENTS AND FACULTY
Enrollment: 3,004. **Student Body:** 58% female, 42% male, 53% out-of-state, 10% international (80 countries represented). Asian 7%, African American 3%, Caucasian 71%, Hispanic 6%, Native American <1%, Pacific Islander <1%, Two or more races 3%, Race unknown 1%.
Retention and Graduation: 92% freshmen return for sophomore year. 85% freshmen graduate within 4 years. 88% freshmen graduate within 6 years. 19% grads go on to further study within 1 year. 13% grads pursue arts and sciences degrees. 3% grads pursue medical degrees. **Faculty:** Student/faculty ratio 12:1. 209 full-time faculty, 96% hold PhDs, 14% are members of minority groups, 45% are women. 0% of classes are taught by teaching assistants.

ACADEMICS
Degrees: Bachelor's **Classes:** Most classes have 10-19 students. Most lab/discussion sessions have 10-19 students. **Most popular majors:** Biology/Biological Sciences, General; Mathematics, General; Economics, General. **Special Study Options:** Cross-registration; Double major; Dual enrollment; Independent study; Internships; Student-designed major; Study abroad; Teacher certification program. **Disability Services offered to physically disabled students:** Note-taking services; Reader services; Tape recorders; Tutors. **Career services:** Alumni network; Alumni services; Career assessment; Career/job search classes; Internships; Regional alumni

FACILITIES
Housing: Coed dorms; Special housing for disabled student; Theme housing 80% of campus accessible to physically diasbled. **Special Academic Facilities/Equipment:** Kierkegaard Library, Flaten Art Museum, Norwegian American Historical Association archives **Computers:** 100% of classrooms, 100% of dorms, 100% of libraries, 100% of dining areas, 100% of student union, 100% of common outdoor areas have wireless network access. Students can register for classes online. Administrative functions (other than registration) can be performed online.

CAMPUS LIFE
Environment: Village **Activities:** Campus Ministries; Choral groups; Concert band; Dance; Drama/theater; International Student Organization; Jazz band; Literary magazine; Model UN; Music ensembles; Musical theater; Opera; Pep band; Radio station; Student government; Student newspaper; Student-run film society; Symphony orchestra 193 registered organizations, 18 honor societies, 16 religious organizations. **Athletics (Intercollegiate):** *Men:* baseball, basketball, cross-country, diving, football, golf, ice hockey, skiing (downhill/alpine), skiing (nordic/cross-country), soccer, swimming, tennis, track/field (outdoor), track/field (indoor), wrestling. *Women:* basketball, cross-country, diving, golf, ice hockey, skiing (downhill/alpine), skiing (nordic/cross-country), soccer, softball, swimming, tennis, track/field (outdoor), track/field (indoor), volleyball. **On-Campus Highlights:** Fireside Lounge, Buntrock Commons, The Lion's Pause (student-run nightclub), Tostrud Recreation Center

ADMISSIONS
Freshman Academic Profile: Average high school GPA 3.6. 44% in top 10% of high school class, 77% in top 25% of high school class, 94% in top 50% of high school class. 73% from public high schools. **Test Scores:** SAT Math middle 50% range 570-700. SAT EBRW middle 50% range 580-690. ACT middle 50% range 25-31. Minimum internet-based TOEFL 90. **Basis for Candidate Selection:** *Very important factors considered include:* rigor of secondary school record, academic GPA, application essay. *Important factors considered include:* class rank, standardized test scores, recommendation(s), interview, extracurricular activities, talent/ability, character/personal qualities. *Other factors considered include:* first generation, alumni/ae relation, geographical residence, state residency, religious affiliation/commitment, racial/ethnic status, volunteer work, work experience, level of applicant's interest. **Freshman Admission Requirements:** High school diploma is required and GED is accepted *Academic units recommended:* 4 English, 4 math, 4 science, 2 science labs, 4 foreign language, 4 social studies. **Freshman Admission Statistics:** 5,949 applied, 43.2% admitted, 31% enrolled. **Transfer Admission Requirements:** High school transcript, college transcript(s), essay or personal statement, standardized test scores, statement of good standing from prior institution(s). Minimum college GPA of 2.50 required. Lowest grade transferable C. **General Admission Information:** Regular application deadline 1/15. Nonfall registration accepted. Admission may be deferred for a maximum of 1 year.

COSTS AND FINANCIAL AID
Annual tuition $46,000. Room and board $10,430. Average book expense $1,000. **Required Forms and Deadlines:** CSS/Financial Aid PROFILE; FAFSA; Noncustodial PROFILE. **Notification of Awards:** Applicants will be notified of awards on or about 4/1. **Types of Aid:** *Need-based scholarships/grants:* College/university scholarship or grant aid from institutional funds; Federal Pell; Private scholarships; SEOG; State scholarships/grants. *Loans:* Direct PLUS loans; Direct Subsidized Stafford Loans; Direct Unsubsidized Stafford Loans. *Student Employment:* Federal Work-Study Program available. Institutional employment available. **Financial Aid Statistics:** 100% needy freshmen, 100% needy undergrads receive need-based scholarship or grant aid. 53% freshmen, 37% undergrads receive non-need-based scholarship or grant aid. 100% freshmen, 99% undergrads receive need-based self-help aid. 0% freshmen, 0% undergrads receive athletic scholarships. 92% freshmen, 93% undergrads receive any aid. Average cumulative indebtedness $27,945. **Criteria for awarding aid:** *Non-need-based:* Academics, Art, Leadership, Music/drama.

ST. THOMAS AQUINAS COLLEGE

125 Route 340, Sparkill, NY 10976
Phone: 845-398-4100 • **Financial Aid Phone:** 845-398-4106
E-mail: admissions@stac.edu • **CEEB Code:** 2807
Fax: 845-398-4372 • **Website:** www.stac.edu • **ACT Code:** 2897

This private school was founded in 1952. It has a 47 acre campus.

RATINGS
Admissions Selectivity Rating: 73   **Fire Safety Rating:** 97   **Green Rating:** 60*

STUDENTS AND FACULTY
Enrollment: 1,114. **Student Body:** 51% female, 49% male, 21% out-of-state, 5% international (16 countries represented). Asian 2%, African American 12%, Caucasian 51%, Hispanic 23%, Native American 0%, Pacific Islander <1%, Two or more races 1%, Race unknown 6%.
Retention and Graduation: 74% freshmen return for sophomore year. **Faculty:** Student/faculty ratio 12:1. 58 full-time faculty, 84% hold PhDs, 7% are members of minority groups, 59% are women. 0% of classes are taught by teaching assistants.

ACADEMICS
Degrees: Associate; Bachelor's; Master's; Post-Bachelor's certificate; Post-Master's certificate **Classes:** Most classes have 10-19 students. Most lab/discussion sessions have 10-19 students. **Most popular majors:** Education, General; Special Education And Teaching, General; Psychology, General. **Special Study Options:** Accelerated program; Cooperative education program; Cross-registration; Double major; Dual enrollment; English as a Second Language (ESL); Exchange student program (domestic); Honors program; Independent study; Internships; Liberal arts/career combination; Study abroad; Teacher certification program. Honors programs: Highly selective honors program with maximum 20 student each class. Honor students receive full scholarship. Combined degree programs: BA/MA. **Disability Services offered to physically disabled students:** Note-taking services; Tape recorders; Tutors. **Career services:** Alumni network; Alumni services; Career assessment; Career/job search classes; Internships; Regional alumni

FACILITIES
Housing: Apartments for single students; Men's dorms; Women's dorms 80% of campus accessible to physically diasbled. **Special Academic Facilities/Equipment:** Azarian-McCullough Art Gallery, Sullivan Theatre, Spellman Technology Corridor, Costello Hall Science and Technology Center **Computers:** Students can register for classes online.

CAMPUS LIFE
Environment: Village **Activities:** Campus Ministries; Choral groups; Concert band; Dance; Drama/theater; Literary magazine; Music ensembles; Musical theater; Radio station; Student government; Student newspaper; Yearbook 35 registered organizations, 8 honor societies, 1 religious organization. **Athletics (Intercollegiate):** *Men:* baseball, basketball, cross-country, golf, soccer, tennis, track/field (outdoor), track/field (indoor). *Women:* basketball, cross-country,

lacrosse, soccer, softball, tennis, track/field (outdoor). **On-Campus Highlights:** The College Commons, The Kraus Fitness Center, The Romano Alumni Center, The Art Gallery, The Techonology Corridor

ADMISSIONS

Freshman Academic Profile: Average high school GPA 3.0. 7% in top 10% of high school class, 23% in top 25% of high school class, 67% in top 50% of high school class. **Test Scores:** SAT Math middle 50% range 440-550. SAT EBRW middle 50% range 440-560. ACT middle 50% range 17-23. Minimum paper TOEFL 530. **Basis for Candidate Selection:** *Very important factors considered include:* rigor of secondary school record. *Important factors considered include:* standardized test scores, recommendation(s), interview, extracurricular activities, talent/ability. *Other factors considered include:* academic GPA, application essay, alumni/ae relation, volunteer work, work experience, level of applicant's interest. **Freshman Admission Requirements:** High school diploma is required and GED is accepted *Academic units required:* 4 English, 3 math, 3 science, 2 science labs, 3 foreign language, 4 social studies. **Freshman Admission Statistics:** 1,926 applied, 78.0% admitted, 16% enrolled. **Transfer Admission Requirements:** college transcript(s), statement of good standing from prior institution(s). Minimum college GPA of 2.0 required. Lowest grade transferable C. **General Admission Information:** Application fee $30. Nonfall registration accepted. Admission may be deferred for a maximum of one year.

COSTS AND FINANCIAL AID

Annual tuition $29,950. Room and board $12,750. Required fees $800. Average book expense $1,250. **Required Forms and Deadlines:** FAFSA. **Notification of Awards:** Applicants will be notified of awards on a rolling basis beginning 11/1. **Types of Aid:** *Need-based scholarships/grants:* College/university scholarship or grant aid from institutional funds; Federal Pell; Private scholarships; SEOG; State scholarships/grants. *Loans:* Direct PLUS loans; Direct Subsidized Stafford Loans; Direct Unsubsidized Stafford Loans. *Student Employment:* Federal Work-Study Program available. Institutional employment available. **Financial Aid Statistics:** 90% needy freshmen, 92% needy undergrads receive need-based scholarship or grant aid. 63% freshmen, 71% undergrads receive non-need-based scholarship or grant aid. 69% freshmen, 93% undergrads receive need-based self-help aid. 9% freshmen, 5% undergrads receive athletic scholarships. Average cumulative indebtedness $29,500. **Criteria for awarding aid:** *Need-based:* Academics, Athletics, Job skills, Minority status *Non-need-based:* Academics, Alumni affiliation, Art, Athletics, Leadership, Minority status, Music/drama, Religious affiliation.

ST. THOMAS UNIVERSITY

51 Dineen Drive, Fredericton, NB E3B 5G3
Phone: 506-452-0532
E-mail: admissions@stu.ca
Fax: 506-452-0617 • **Website:** http://www.stu.ca

This private school, affiliated with the Roman Catholic Church, was founded in 1910. It has a 21 acre campus.

RATINGS

Admissions Selectivity Rating: 87   **Fire Safety Rating:** 81   **Green Rating:** 60*

STUDENTS AND FACULTY

Enrollment: 2,475. **Student Body:** 66% female, 34% male, 27% out-of-state, 5% international (42 countries represented). Race unknown 95%. **Retention and Graduation:** 69% freshmen return for sophomore year. **Faculty:** Student/faculty ratio 19:1. 109 full-time faculty, 95% hold PhDs, 39% are women. 0% of classes are taught by teaching assistants.

ACADEMICS

Degrees: Bachelor's; Certificate; Post-Bachelor's certificate **Classes:** Most classes have 20-29 students. Most lab/discussion sessions have 20-29 students. **Most popular majors:** English Language And Literature, General; Psychology, General; Criminology. **Special Study Options:** Accelerated program; Cross-registration; Double major; English as a Second Language (ESL); Exchange student program (domestic); Honors program; Independent study; Student-designed major; Study abroad; Teacher certification program. **Disability Services offered to physically disabled students:** Note-taking services; Reader services; Tape recorders; Tutors. **Career services:** Career assessment; Career/job search classes; Internships

FACILITIES

Housing: Coed dorms; Women's dorms 80% of campus accessible to physically diasbled. **Computers:** 100% of dorms, 100% of libraries, 100% of dining areas, have wireless network access. Students can register for classes online. Administrative functions (other than registration) can be performed online.

CAMPUS LIFE

Environment: Town **Activities:** Campus Ministries; Choral groups; Drama/theater; International Student Organization; Jazz band; Model UN; Music ensembles; Musical theater; Radio station; Student government; Student newspaper; Student-run film society; Yearbook 5 religious organizations. **Athletics (Intercollegiate):** *Men:* basketball, cross-country, golf, ice hockey, rugby, soccer, volleyball. *Women:* basketball, cross-country, golf, ice hockey, rugby, soccer, volleyball. **On-Campus Highlights:** Margaret Norrie McCain Hall, Lower courtyard, J.B. O'Keefe Fitness Centre, Sir James Dunn Hall, The Black Box Theatre **Environmental Initiatives:** Recycle bins in all areas.

ADMISSIONS

Freshman Academic Profile: Average high school GPA 3.3. **Test Scores:** Minimum internet-based TOEFL 88. Minimum paper TOEFL 570. **Basis for Candidate Selection:** *Very important factors considered include:* academic GPA. *Other factors considered include:* application essay, standardized test scores, recommendation(s). **Freshman Admission Requirements:** High school diploma is required and GED is not accepted **Freshman Admission Statistics:** 1,345 applied, 80.7% admitted, 58% enrolled. **Transfer Admission Requirements:** college transcript(s), statement of good standing from prior institution(s). Lowest grade transferable D. **General Admission Information:** Application fee $35. Regular application deadline 8/31. Nonfall registration accepted. Admission may be deferred for a maximum of 1 year.

COSTS AND FINANCIAL AID

Average book expense $1,000.

ST. THOMAS UNIVERSITY

16401 Northwest 37th Avenue, Miami Gardens, FL 33054
Phone: 305-628-6546 • **Financial Aid Phone:** 305-628-6547
E-mail: signup@stu.edu • **CEEB Code:** 5076
Fax: 305-628-6591 • **Website:** www.stu.edu • **ACT Code:** 719

This private school, affiliated with the Roman Catholic Church, was founded in 1961. It has a 140 acre campus.

RATINGS

Admissions Selectivity Rating: 69   **Fire Safety Rating:** 95   **Green Rating:** 60*

STUDENTS AND FACULTY

Enrollment: 1,111. **Student Body:** 55% female, 45% male, 92% out-of-state, 15% international (57 countries represented). Asian 1%, African American 23%, Caucasian 12%, Hispanic 40%, Native American <1%, Pacific Islander 0%, Two or more races 1%, Race unknown 8%. **Retention and Graduation:** 70% freshmen return for sophomore year. **Faculty:** Student/faculty ratio 14:1. 105 full-time faculty, 89% hold PhDs, 30% are members of minority groups, 47% are women. 0% of classes are taught by teaching assistants.

ACADEMICS

Degrees: Bachelor's; Certificate; Doctoral/Professional; Doctoral/Research; Master's; Post-Bachelor's certificate; Post-Master's certificate **Most popular majors:** Psychology, General; Business Administration And Management, General; Organizational Behavior Studies. **Special Study Options:** Distance learning; Double major; Dual enrollment; English as a Second Language (ESL); Honors program; Independent study; Internships; Liberal arts/career combination; Teacher certification program. Honors programs: The St. Thomas University Honors Program is designed to provide an intensive and stimulating alternative for students who wish to enhance their college academic experience. Qualified students are offered the opportunity to take Honors courses in the subjects of their choice, and, if they desire, to work for an Honors degree. Combined degree programs: BA/JD. **Disability Services offered to physically disabled students:** Note-taking services; Reader services; Tape recorders; Tutors. **Career services:** Career assessment; Career/job search classes; Internships

FACILITIES

Housing: Men's dorms; Women's dorms 80% of campus accessible to physically diasbled. **Special Academic Facilities/Equipment:** Multimedia computer equipment, TV studio, Art Atrium Gallery. **Computers:** 100% of libraries, 100% of dining areas, have wireless network access. Students can register for classes online. Administrative functions (other than registration) can be performed online.

CAMPUS LIFE

Environment: Metropolis **Activities:** Campus Ministries; Choral groups; International Student Organization; Literary magazine; Radio station; Student government; Television station; Yearbook 26 registered organizations, 4 honor societies, 2 religious organizations. **Athletics (Intercollegiate):** *Men:* baseball, basketball, cross-country, golf, soccer, tennis. *Women:* basketball, cross-country, soccer, softball, tennis, volleyball. **On-Campus Highlights:** Campus Chapel, Library, Fernandez Family Center, Kennedy Hall

ADMISSIONS

Freshman Academic Profile: Average high school GPA 3.0. 6% in top 10% of high school class, 17% in top 25% of high school class, 53% in top 50% of high school class. **Test Scores:** SAT Math middle 50% range 408-500. SAT EBRW middle 50% range 410-510. ACT middle 50% range 16-21. Minimum paper TOEFL 525. **Basis for Candidate Selection:** *Very important factors considered include:* class rank, academic GPA, standardized test scores. *Important factors considered include:* rigor of secondary school record, application essay, recommendation(s), alumni/ae relation, level of applicant's interest. *Other factors considered include:* extracurricular activities, talent/ability, character/personal qualities, volunteer work, work experience. **Freshman Admission Requirements:** High school diploma is required and GED is accepted *Academic units required:* 4 English, 3 math, 2 science, 3 social studies, 6 academic electives. **Freshman Admission Statistics:** 727 applied, 45.7% admitted, 63% enrolled. **Transfer Admission Requirements:** college transcript(s), essay or personal statement, statement of good standing from prior institution(s). Minimum college GPA of 2.0 required. Lowest grade transferable C-. **General Admission Information:** Application fee $40. Nonfall registration accepted. Admission may be deferred for a maximum of One year.

COSTS AND FINANCIAL AID

Required Forms and Deadlines: FAFSA. **Notification of Awards:** Applicants will be notified of awards on a rolling basis beginning 3/1. **Types of Aid:** *Need-based scholarships/grants:* College/university scholarship or grant aid from institutional funds; Federal Pell; Private scholarships; SEOG; State scholarships/grants. *Loans:* Direct PLUS loans; Direct Subsidized Stafford Loans; Direct Unsubsidized Stafford Loans. *Student Employment:* Federal Work-Study Program available. Institutional employment available. **Financial Aid Statistics:** 77% needy freshmen, 76% needy undergrads receive need-based scholarship or grant aid. 100% freshmen, 99% undergrads receive non-need-based scholarship or grant aid. 56% freshmen, 55% undergrads receive need-based self-help aid. 12% freshmen, 15% undergrads receive athletic scholarships. **Criteria for awarding aid:** *Need-based:* Academics *Non-need-based:* Academics, Athletics, Leadership.

STANFORD UNIVERSITY

450 Serra Mall, Stanford, CA 94305-6106
Phone: 650-723-2091 • **Financial Aid Phone:** 650-723-3058
E-mail: admission@stanford.edu • **CEEB Code:** 4704
Fax: 650-723-6050 • **Website:** www.stanford.edu • **ACT Code:** 434

This private school was founded in 1885. It has a 8180 acre campus.

RATINGS

Admissions Selectivity Rating: 99   **Fire Safety Rating:** 89   **Green Rating:** 99

STUDENTS AND FACULTY

Enrollment: 7,056. **Student Body:** 50% female, 50% male, 59% out-of-state, 9% international (90 countries represented). Asian 22%, African American 7%, Caucasian 36%, Hispanic 16%, Native American 1%, Pacific Islander <1%, Two or more races 10%, Race unknown <1%.
Retention and Graduation: 98% freshmen return for sophomore year. 75% freshmen graduate within 4 years. 1% freshmen graduate within 6 years. 25% grads go on to further study within 1 year. **Faculty:** Student/faculty ratio 4:1. 1,630 full-time faculty, 99% hold PhDs, 23% are members of minority groups, 28% are women. 6% of classes are taught by teaching assistants.

ACADEMICS

Degrees: Bachelor's; Doctoral; Doctoral/Professional; Doctoral/Research; Master's; Post-Bachelor's certificate **Classes:** Most classes have 10-19 students. Most lab/discussion sessions have 10-19 students. **Most popular majors:** Computer Science; Engineering, General; Human Biology. **Special Study Options:** Distance learning; Double major; Exchange student program (domestic); Honors program; Independent study; Internships; Student-designed major; Study abroad. Honors programs: About 100 students annually participate in Bing Honors College. About 25 percent of each graduating class

earn departmental honors. Combined degree programs: BA/MA. **Disability Services offered to physically disabled students:** Note-taking services; Reader services; Tape recorders; Tutors. **Career services:** Alumni network; Alumni services; Career assessment; Career/job search classes; Internships; Regional alumni

FACILITIES

Housing: Apartments for married students; Apartments for single students; Coed dorms; Cooperative housing; Fraternity/sorority housing; Special housing for disabled student; Theme housing; Women's dorms 98% of campus accessible to physically disabled. **Special Academic Facilities/Equipment:** Three art museums, marine station, two observatories, biological preserve, linear accelerator, concert hall **Computers:** 100% of classrooms, 100% of dorms, 100% of libraries, 100% of dining areas, 100% of student union, 75% of common outdoor areas have wireless network access. Students can register for classes online. Administrative functions (other than registration) can be performed online.

CAMPUS LIFE

Environment: City **Activities:** Campus Ministries; Choral groups; Concert band; Dance; Drama/theater; International Student Organization; Jazz band; Literary magazine; Marching band; Model UN; Music ensembles; Musical theater; Opera; Pep band; Radio station; Student government; Student newspaper; Student-run film society; Symphony orchestra; Television station; Yearbook 600 registered organizations, 40 religious organizations. 17 fraternities, 11 sororities. **Athletics (Intercollegiate):** *Men:* baseball, basketball, crew/rowing, cross-country, diving, fencing, football, golf, gymnastics, sailing, soccer, swimming, tennis, track/field (outdoor), volleyball, water polo, wrestling. *Women:* basketball, crew/rowing, cross-country, diving, fencing, field hockey, golf, gymnastics, lacrosse, sailing, soccer, softball, squash, swimming, synchronized swimming, tennis, track/field (outdoor), volleyball, water polo. **On-Campus Highlights:** Cantor Center for the Visual Arts, The Anderson Collection at Stanford University, Memorial Church, Tresidder Memorial Union, Bing Concert Hall **Environmental Initiatives:** STANFORD ENERGY SYSTEM INNOVATIONS (SESI) Between 1987 and 2015, Stanford relied on a natural gas-fired combined heat and power (CHP) plant for virtually all its energy demand. Although efficient, its fossil-fuel based source caused the CHP to produce 90% of Stanford's GHG emissions and consume 25% of the campus' potable water supply. As a result, Stanford's GHG reduction strategy focused primarily on transforming the university's energy supply through a new CEF, which came online in April 2015, includes three large water tanks for thermal energy storage and a high voltage substation that receives electricity from the grid. A key feature of the CEF is an innovative heat recovery system that takes advantage of Stanford's overlap in heating and cooling needs. In addition to the CEF, the SESI project converted the heat supply of all buildings from steam to hot water. This new system is 70% more efficient than the CHP plant. The efficiencies gained from the new CEF and hot water conversion, along with the introduction of a 67 MW off-site solar plant and 4.5 MW of on-site solar, will reduce the university's overall GHG emissions by approximately 68% between 2011 and 2017.

ADMISSIONS

Freshman Academic Profile: Average high school GPA 4.0. 94% in top 10% of high school class, 99% in top 25% of high school class, 100% in top 50% of high school class. 59% from public high schools. SAT scores: SAT Math middle 50% range 700-780. SAT EBRW middle 50% range 690-760. ACT middle 50% range 32-35. **Basis for Candidate Selection:** *Very important factors considered include:* rigor of secondary school record, class rank, academic GPA, application essay, standardized test scores, recommendation(s), extracurricular activities, talent/ability, character/personal qualities. *Other factors considered include:* interview, first generation, alumni/ae relation, geographical residence, racial/ethnic status, volunteer work, work experience. **Freshman Admission Requirements:** High school diploma is required and GED is accepted *Academic units recommended:* 4 English, 4 math, 3 science, 3 science labs, 3 foreign language, 3 social studies. **Freshman Admission Statistics:** 44,073 applied, 4.7% admitted, 82% enrolled. **Transfer Admission Requirements:** High school transcript, college transcript(s), essay or personal statement, standardized test scores, statement of good standing from prior institution(s). Lowest grade transferable C-. **General Admission Information:** Application fee $90. Regular application deadline 1/2. Nonfall registration accepted. Admission may be deferred for a maximum of 2 years.

COSTS AND FINANCIAL AID

Annual tuition $48,987. Room and board $15,112. Required fees $630. Average book expense $1,455. **Required Forms and Deadlines: Notification of Awards:** CSS/Financial Aid PROFILE; FAFSA; Noncustodial PROFILE. **Types of Aid:** *Need-based scholarships/grants:* College/university scholarship or grant aid from institutional funds; Federal Pell; Private scholarships; SEOG; State scholarships/grants. *Loans:* Direct PLUS loans; Direct Subsidized Stafford Loans; Direct Unsubsidized Stafford Loans. *Student Employment:* Federal Work-Study Program available. Institutional employment available. **Financial Aid Statistics:** 95% needy freshmen, 99% needy undergrads receive need-based scholarship or grant aid. 3% freshmen, 3% undergrads receive non-need-based scholarship or grant aid. 59% freshmen, 76% undergrads receive need-based self-help aid. 7% freshmen, 7% undergrads receive athletic scholarships. 86% freshmen, 85% undergrads receive any aid. 22% undergrads borrow to pay for school. Average cumulative indebtedness $21,238. **Criteria for awarding aid:** *Non-need-based:* Athletics.

STATE UNIVERSITY OF NEW YORK AT BINGHAMTON

PO Box 6000, Binghamton, NY 13902-6001
Phone: 607-777-2171 • **Financial Aid Phone:** 607-777-2428
E-mail: admit@binghamton.edu • **CEEB Code:** 2535
Fax: 607-777-4445 • **Website:** www.binghamton.edu • **ACT Code:** 2956

This public school was founded in 1946. It has a 930 acre campus.

RATINGS

Admissions Selectivity Rating: 92   **Fire Safety Rating:** 95   **Green Rating:** 96

STUDENTS AND FACULTY

Enrollment: 13,693. **Student Body:** 49% female, 51% male, 7% out-of-state, 8% international (97 countries represented). Asian 14%, African American 5%, Caucasian 57%, Hispanic 11%, Native American <1%, Pacific Islander <1%, Two or more races 2%, Race unknown 2%.
Retention and Graduation: 91% freshmen return for sophomore year. 73% freshmen graduate within 4 years. 82% freshmen graduate within 6 years. 57% grads go on to further study within 1 year. 2.42% grads pursue law degrees. 9% grads pursue business degrees. 5.62% grads pursue medical degrees. **Faculty:** Student/faculty ratio 19:1. 754 full-time faculty, 92% hold PhDs, 30% are members of minority groups, 44% are women. 7% of classes are taught by teaching assistants.

ACADEMICS

Degrees: Bachelor's; Doctoral/Professional; Doctoral/Research; Master's; Post-Master's certificate **Classes:** Most classes have 10-19 students. Most lab/discussion sessions have 10-19 students. **Most popular majors:** Engineering, General; Psychology, General; Business Administration And Management, General. **Special Study Options:** Accelerated program; Cross-registration; Distance learning; Double major; Dual enrollment; English as a Second Language (ESL); Exchange student program (domestic); Honors program; Independent study; Internships; Liberal arts/career combination; Student-designed major; Study abroad; Teacher certification program. Honors programs: Binghamton University Scholars Program—See http://scholars.binghamton.edu Each academic department offers an honors program. Binghamton also has a PricewaterhouseCoopers Scholars program for students in the School of Management: Combined degree programs: BA/MA. **Disability Services offered to physically disabled students:** Note-taking services; Reader services; Tape recorders. **Career services:** Alumni network; Alumni services; Career assessment; Career/job search classes; Internships; Regional alumni

FACILITIES

Housing: Apartments for single students; Coed dorms; Special housing for disabled student; Theme housing; Wellness housing 95% of campus accessible to physically disabled. **Special Academic Facilities/Equipment:** Art museum & gallery, 10,000+ square foot fitness facility, performing arts center, indoor/outdoor theater, multi-climate and teaching greenhouse, sculpture foundry, 8,000-seat Events Center, Analytical and Diagnostics Laboratory, Electron Microscopy Facility, modular labs in Innovative Technologies Complex buildings, Public Archaeology Facility, 187-acre Nature Preserve, NYS Center of Excellence in Small Scale Systems Integration and Packaging. **Computers:** 95% of classrooms, 100% of dorms, 100% of libraries, 100% of dining areas, 100% of student union, 60% of common outdoor areas have wireless network access. Students can register for classes online. Administrative functions (other than registration) can be performed online.

CAMPUS LIFE

Environment: City **Activities:** Campus Ministries; Choral groups; Concert band; Dance; Drama/theater; International Student Organization; Jazz band; Literary magazine; Model UN; Music ensembles; Musical theater; Opera; Radio station; Student government; Student newspaper; Student-

run film society; Symphony orchestra; Television station; Yearbook 23 honor societies, 15 religious organizations. 23 fraternities, 23 sororities. **Athletics (Intercollegiate):** *Men:* baseball, basketball, cross-country, diving, golf, lacrosse, soccer, swimming, tennis, track/field (outdoor), track/field (indoor), wrestling. *Women:* basketball, cross-country, diving, lacrosse, soccer, softball, swimming, tennis, track/field (outdoor), track/field (indoor), volleyball. **On-Campus Highlights:** Union (The MarketPlace, Late Nite Binghamton, bookstore), FitSpace, Events Center (concerts, basketball, special events), Indoor/Outdoor Performing Arts Center, Nature Preserve **Environmental Initiatives:** Binghamton University designs, constructs, operates and maintains all new buildings following guidelines set forth by the U.S. Green Building Council's LEED rating system. Since 2004, Binghamton has obtained multiple LEED certifications under the New Construction program including 2 LEED, 3 LEED Silver, 7 LEED Gold, and 1 LEED Platinum for a total of 1,690,183 square feet of building space. This represents 27% of total building space owned by Binghamton University.

ADMISSIONS

Freshman Academic Profile: Average high school GPA 3.7. 90% from public high schools. **Test Scores:** SAT Math middle 50% range 650-720. SAT EBRW middle 50% range 640-711. ACT middle 50% range 28-31. Minimum internet-based TOEFL 83. Minimum paper TOEFL 560. **Basis for Candidate Selection:** *Very important factors considered include:* rigor of secondary school record, academic GPA, standardized test scores. *Important factors considered include:* class rank, application essay, recommendation(s), extracurricular activities. *Other factors considered include:* talent/ability, character/personal qualities, first generation, alumni/ae relation, geographical residence, state residency, racial/ethnic status, volunteer work, work experience, level of applicant's interest. **Freshman Admission Requirements:** High school diploma is required and GED is accepted *Academic units required:* 4 English, 3 math, 2 science, 3 foreign language, 2 social studies, *Academic units recommended:* 4 math, 4 science, 4 social studies, 4 history. **Freshman Admission Statistics:** 33,467 applied, 40.4% admitted, 20% enrolled. **Transfer Admission Requirements:** college transcript(s), Lowest grade transferable C-. **General Admission Information:** Application fee $50. Priority deadline 1/15. Nonfall registration accepted. Admission may be deferred for a maximum of 1 year.

COSTS AND FINANCIAL AID

Annual in-state tuition $14,577. Annual out-of-state tuition $21,550. Room and board $14,577. Required fees $2,853. Average book expense $1,000. **Required Forms and Deadlines:** FAFSA; State aid form. **Notification of Awards:** Applicants will be notified of awards on a rolling basis beginning 1/31. **Types of Aid:** *Need-based scholarships/grants:* College/university scholarship or grant aid from institutional funds; Federal Pell; Private scholarships; SEOG; State scholarships/grants. *Loans:* Direct PLUS loans; Direct Subsidized Stafford Loans; Direct Unsubsidized Stafford Loans. *Student Employment:* Federal Work-Study Program available. Institutional employment available. **Financial Aid Statistics:** 80% needy freshmen; 83% needy undergrads receive need-based scholarship or grant aid. 13% freshmen, 7% undergrads receive non-need-based scholarship or grant aid. 96% freshmen, 97% undergrads receive need-based self-help aid. 4% freshmen, 3% undergrads receive athletic scholarships. 81% freshmen, 70% undergrads receive any aid. 50% undergrads borrow to pay for school. Average cumulative indebtedness $25,718. **Criteria for awarding aid:** *Need-based:* Academics, Art, Athletics, Leadership, Minority status, Music/drama *Non-need-based:* Academics, Art, Athletics, Leadership, Minority status, Music/drama, State/district residency.

STATE UNIVERSITY OF NEW YORK AT GENESEO

1 College Circle, Geneseo, NY 14454
Phone: 585-245-5571 • **Financial Aid Phone:** 585-245-5731
E-mail: admissions@geneseo.edu • **CEEB Code:** 2540
Fax: 585-245-5550 • **Website:** www.geneseo.edu • **ACT Code:** 2936

This public school was founded in 1871. It has a 220 acre campus.

RATINGS

Admissions Selectivity Rating: 83   **Fire Safety Rating:** 91   **Green Rating:** 88

STUDENTS AND FACULTY

Enrollment: 5,465. **Student Body:** 60% female, 40% male, 2% out-of-state, 2% international (26 countries represented). Asian 6%, African American 3%,

Caucasian 76%, Hispanic 8%, Native American <1%, Pacific Islander <1%, Two or more races 3%, Race unknown 3%.
Retention and Graduation: 86% freshmen return for sophomore year. 68% freshmen graduate within 4 years. 1% freshmen graduate within 6 years. **Faculty:** Student/faculty ratio 19:1. 255 full-time faculty, 90% hold PhDs, 16% are members of minority groups, 45% are women. 0% of classes are taught by teaching assistants.

ACADEMICS

Degrees: Bachelor's; **Master's Classes:** Most classes have fewer than 10 students. **Most popular majors:** Biology, General; Psychology, General; Business Administration And Management, General. **Special Study Options:** Cross-registration; Distance learning; Double major; English as a Second Language (ESL); Honors program; Independent study; Internships; Study abroad; Teacher certification program. Honors programs: The Edgar Fellows Program is designed to enhance the academic experience of a small number of especially dedicated and accomplished students through specially designed seminar courses, research opportunities, close work with program advisors, and co-curricular activities. It is dedicated to its founder and longtime director, William J. Edgar. In the spirit of its founder, the Program values and fosters critical inquiry and the lively interchange of ideas between and among students and faculty. Combined degree programs: BA/DDS; BA/MA. **Disability Services offered to physically disabled students:** Note-taking services; Reader services. **Career services:** Alumni network; Alumni services; Career assessment; Career/job search classes; Internships

FACILITIES

Housing: Coed dorms; Special housing for disabled student; Special housing for international students; Theme housing 95% of campus accessible to physically disabled. **Special Academic Facilities/Equipment:** Four theatres, electron microscopes, Integrated Science Center, Wave tank, planetarium, particle accelerator, 3D printers, Trading Room, eGarden. **Computers:** 100% of classrooms, 60% of dorms, 100% of libraries, 100% of dining areas, 100% of student union, 10% of common outdoor areas have wireless network access. Students can register for classes online. Administrative functions (other than registration) can be performed online. Undergraduates are required to own a computer.

CAMPUS LIFE

Environment: Village **Activities:** Campus Ministries; Choral groups; Dance; Drama/theater; International Student Organization; Jazz band; Literary magazine; Model UN; Music ensembles; Musical theater; Pep band; Radio station; Student government; Student newspaper; Symphony orchestra 175 registered organizations, 12 honor societies, 7 religious organizations. 8 fraternities, 11 sororities. **Athletics (Intercollegiate):** *Men:* basketball, cross-country, diving, ice hockey, lacrosse, soccer, swimming, track/field (outdoor), track/field (indoor). *Women:* basketball, cross-country, diving, equestrian sports, field hockey, lacrosse, soccer, softball, swimming, tennis, track/field (outdoor), track/field (indoor), volleyball. **On-Campus Highlights:** MacVittie College Union, The Gazebo, Milne Library, Merritt Athletic Center, College Green **Environmental Initiatives:** Signing of the Presidents Climate Commitment. A final draft of the Climate Action Plan was released on July 2010.

ADMISSIONS

Freshman Academic Profile: Average high school GPA 3.6. 28% in top 10% of high school class, 64% in top 25% of high school class, 93% in top 50% of high school class. **Test Scores:** SAT Math middle 50% range 550-650. SAT EBRW middle 50% range 570-650. ACT middle 50% range 24-29. Minimum internet-based TOEFL 71. Minimum paper TOEFL 525. **Basis for Candidate Selection:** *Very important factors considered include:* rigor of secondary school record, standardized test scores. *Important factors considered include:* class rank, academic GPA, application essay, recommendation(s), extracurricular activities, talent/ability, racial/ethnic status. *Other factors considered include:* character/personal qualities, first generation, alumni/ae relation, state residency, volunteer work, work experience, level of applicant's interest. **Freshman Admission Requirements:** High school diploma is required and GED is accepted *Academic units recommended:* 4 English, 4 math, 4 science, 4 foreign language, 4 social studies. **Freshman Admission Statistics:** 8,789 applied, 72.4% admitted, 21% enrolled. **Transfer Admission Requirements:** High school transcript, college transcript(s), Minimum college GPA of 3.0 required. Lowest grade transferable D. **General Admission Information:** Application fee $50. Regular application deadline 1/1. Nonfall registration accepted. Admission may be deferred for a maximum of 1 year.

COSTS AND FINANCIAL AID

Annual in-state tuition $13,214. Annual out-of-state tuition $16,320. Room and board $13,214. Required fees $1,738. Average book expense $1,000. **Required Forms and Deadlines:** FAFSA; State aid form. **Notification of Awards:** Applicants will be notified of awards on a rolling basis beginning 3/15. **Types of Aid:** *Need-based scholarships/grants:* Federal Pell; SEOG; State scholarships/grants. *Loans:* Direct PLUS loans; Direct Subsidized Stafford Loans; Direct Unsubsidized Stafford Loans. *Student Employment:* Federal Work-Study

Program available. Institutional employment available. **Financial Aid Statistics:** 51% needy freshmen, 79% needy undergrads receive need-based scholarship or grant aid. 29% freshmen, 24% undergrads receive non-need-based scholarship or grant aid. 84% freshmen, 83% undergrads receive need-based self-help aid. 0% freshmen, 0% undergrads receive athletic scholarships. 71% freshmen, 66% undergrads receive any aid. 55% undergrads borrow to pay for school. Average cumulative indebtedness $24,784. **Criteria for awarding aid:** *Need-based:* Academics *Non-need-based:* Academics, Art, Leadership, Minority status, Music/drama, Religious affiliation, State/district residency.

STATE UNIVERSITY OF NEW YORK COLLEGE AT ONEONTA

108 Ravine Parkway, Oneonta, NY 13820
Phone: 607-436-2524 • **Financial Aid Phone:** 607-436-2532
E-mail: admissions@oneonta.edu • **CEEB Code:** 2542
Fax: 607-436-3074 • **Website:** www.oneonta.edu • **ACT Code:** 2940

This public school was founded in 1889. It has a 250 acre campus.

RATINGS

Admissions Selectivity Rating: 87   **Fire Safety Rating:** 91   **Green Rating:** 80

STUDENTS AND FACULTY

Enrollment: 5,804. **Student Body:** 60% female, 40% male, 1% out-of-state, 2% international (18 countries represented). Asian 1%, African American 3%, Caucasian 81%, Hispanic 4%, Native American <1%, Pacific Islander 0%, Two or more races 7%, Race unknown 2%.
Retention and Graduation: 84% freshmen return for sophomore year. **Faculty:** Student/faculty ratio 18:1. 259 full-time faculty, 86% hold PhDs, 17% are members of minority groups, 43% are women. 0% of classes are taught by teaching assistants.

ACADEMICS

Degrees: Bachelor's; Master's; Post-Bachelor's certificate; Post-Master's certificate **Classes:** Most classes have 20-29 students. **Most popular majors:** Elementary Education And Teaching; Secondary Education And Teaching; Family And Consumer Sciences/Home Economics Teacher Education. **Special Study Options:** Cross-registration; Distance learning; Double major; English as a Second Language (ESL); Independent study; Internships; Liberal arts/career combination; Study abroad; Teacher certification program. Combined degree programs: BA/MA; BA/MEng. **Disability Services offered to physically disabled students:** Note-taking services; Reader services; Tape recorders; Tutors. **Career services:** Alumni network; Alumni services; Career assessment; Career/job search classes; Internships; Regional alumni

FACILITIES

Housing: Coed dorms; Special housing for international students; Wellness housing **Special Academic Facilities/Equipment:** Science Discovery Center, digital planetarium, College Camp, Observatory, children's center, Biological Field Station at Cooperstown Campus **Computers:** 100% of classrooms, 100% of dorms, 100% of libraries, 100% of dining areas, 100% of student union, 100% of common outdoor areas have wireless network access. Students can register for classes online. Administrative functions (other than registration) can be performed online.

CAMPUS LIFE

Environment: Village **Activities:** Campus Ministries; Choral groups; Concert band; Dance; Drama/theater; International Student Organization; Jazz band; Literary magazine; Model UN; Music ensembles; Musical theater; Opera; Pep band; Radio station; Student government; Student newspaper; Student-run film society; Symphony orchestra; Television station; Yearbook 70 registered organizations, 14 honor societies, 4 religious organizations. 4 fraternities, 6 sororities. **Athletics (Intercollegiate):** *Men:* baseball, basketball, cross-country, diving, lacrosse, soccer, swimming, tennis, track/field (outdoor), track/field (indoor), wrestling. *Women:* basketball, cross-country, diving, field hockey, lacrosse, soccer, softball, swimming, tennis, track/field (outdoor), track/field (indoor), volleyball. **On-Campus Highlights:** Alumni Field House, Center for Multicultural Experiences, Hunt College Union, College Camp, Center for Social Responsibility and Community **Environmental Initiatives:** Recycling program

ADMISSIONS

Freshman Academic Profile: Average high school GPA 90.6. **Test Scores:** SAT Math middle 50% range 520-600. SAT EBRW middle 50% range 500-580. ACT middle 50% range 22-26. Minimum internet-based TOEFL 61. Minimum paper TOEFL 500. **Basis for Candidate Selection:** *Very important factors considered include:* rigor of secondary school record, academic GPA, standardized test scores. *Important factors considered include:* application essay, recommendation(s), talent/ability, character/personal qualities, volunteer work, work experience. *Other factors considered include:* class rank, interview, extracurricular activities, first generation, racial/ethnic status, level of applicant's interest. **Freshman Admission Requirements:** High school diploma is required and GED is accepted *Academic units required:* 4 English, 4 math, 4 science, 3 foreign language, 4 social studies, *Academic units recommended:* 4 foreign language. **Freshman Admission Statistics:** 12,031 applied, 43.1% admitted, 22% enrolled. **Transfer Admission Requirements:** college transcript(s), Minimum college GPA of 2.5 required. Lowest grade transferable C-. **General Admission Information:** Application fee $50. Nonfall registration accepted. Admission may be deferred for a maximum of 1 year.

COSTS AND FINANCIAL AID
Required Forms and Deadlines: FAFSA; Noncustodial PROFILE. **Notification of Awards:** Applicants will be notified of awards on a rolling basis beginning 3/1. **Types of Aid:** *Need-based scholarships/grants:* College/ university scholarship or grant aid from institutional funds; Federal Pell; Private scholarships; SEOG; State scholarships/grants. *Loans:* Direct PLUS loans; Direct Subsidized Stafford Loans; Direct Unsubsidized Stafford Loans. *Student Employment:* Federal Work-Study Program available. Institutional employment available. **Financial Aid Statistics:** 73% needy freshmen, 95% needy undergrads receive need-based scholarship or grant aid. 26% freshmen, 0% undergrads receive non-need-based scholarship or grant aid. 84% freshmen, 85% undergrads receive need-based self-help aid. 0% freshmen, 0% undergrads receive athletic scholarships. 83% freshmen, 66% undergrads receive any aid. **Criteria for awarding aid:** *Need-based:* Academics, Leadership, Minority status, Music/drama *Non-need-based:* Academics, Leadership, Minority status, Music/drama, State/district residency.

STATE UNIVERSITY OF NEW YORK— ALFRED STATE COLLEGE

10 Upper College Drive, Alfred, NY 14802
Phone: 607-587-4215 • **Financial Aid Phone:** 607-587-4253
E-mail: admissions@alfredstate.edu • **CEEB Code:** 2522
Fax: 607-587-4299 • **Website:** www.alfredstate.edu • **ACT Code:** 2910

This public school was founded in 1908. It has a 840 acre campus.

RATINGS
Admissions Selectivity Rating: 79   **Fire Safety Rating:** 92   **Green Rating:** 60*

STUDENTS AND FACULTY
Enrollment: 3,665. **Student Body:** 36% female, 64% male, 4% out-of-state, 1% international (10 countries represented). Asian 1%, African American 12%, Caucasian 72%, Hispanic 9%, Native American <1%, Pacific Islander <1%, Two or more races 3%, Race unknown 1%.
Retention and Graduation: 65% freshmen return for sophomore year. 37% freshmen graduate within 4 years. 51% freshmen graduate within 6 years. 38% grads go on to further study within 1 year. **Faculty:** Student/faculty ratio 18:1. 167 full-time faculty, 41% hold PhDs, 7% are members of minority groups, 34% are women. 0% of classes are taught by teaching assistants.

ACADEMICS
Degrees: Associate; Bachelor's; Certificate; Terminal Associate; Transfer Associate **Classes:** Most classes have fewer than 10 students. Most lab/ discussion sessions have 20-29 students. **Most popular majors:** Mechanical Engineering/Mechanical Technology/Technician; Construction Management; Business, Management, Marketing, And Related Support Services, Other. **Special Study Options:** Accelerated program; Cooperative education program; Cross-registration; Distance learning; Double major; English as a Second Language (ESL); Honors program; Independent study; Internships; Liberal arts/career combination; Student-designed major; Study abroad. Honors programs: Participants complete a series of seminars, as well as a substantial honors project and 10 hours of volunteer community service. **Disability Services offered to physically disabled students:** Note-taking services; Reader services; Tape recorders; Tutors. **Career services:** Alumni network; Career assessment; Career/job search classes

FACILITIES
Housing: Apartments for single students; Coed dorms; Fraternity/sorority housing; Special housing for disabled student; Special housing for international students; Theme housing; Wellness housing 100% of campus accessible to physically diasbled. **Computers:** 100% of classrooms, 100% of dorms, 100% of libraries, 100% of dining areas, 100% of common outdoor areas have

wireless network access. Students can register for classes online. Administrative functions (other than registration) can be performed online.

CAMPUS LIFE
Environment: Rural **Activities:** Campus Ministries; Choral groups; Concert band; Dance; Drama/theater; International Student Organization; Jazz band; Literary magazine; Music ensembles; Musical theater; Pep band; Radio station; Student government; Student newspaper; Symphony orchestra; Yearbook 60 registered organizations, 4 honor societies, 3 fraternities, 2 sororities. **Athletics (Intercollegiate):** *Men:* baseball, basketball, cheerleading, cross-country, football, lacrosse, soccer, swimming, track/field (outdoor), wrestling. *Women:* basketball, cheerleading, cross-country, soccer, softball, swimming, track/field (outdoor), volleyball. **On-Campus Highlights:** Student Leadership Center, Orvis (Athletic Center), Pioneer Center, Central Dining Hall, Upperclassmen Apartment Suite Complex **Environmental Initiatives:** Energy conservation, greenhouse gas inventory and shrinking our carbon footprint through renewable energy.

ADMISSIONS
Freshman Academic Profile: Average high school GPA 3.0. **Test Scores:** SAT Math middle 50% range 470-570. SAT EBRW middle 50% range 470-560. ACT middle 50% range 19-25. Minimum internet-based TOEFL 61. Minimum paper TOEFL 500. **Basis for Candidate Selection:** *Very important factors considered include:* rigor of secondary school record, academic GPA, standardized test scores. *Other factors considered include:* application essay, recommendation(s), interview, extracurricular activities, talent/ability, character/ personal qualities, volunteer work, work experience, level of applicant's interest. **Freshman Admission Requirements:** High school diploma is required and GED is accepted **Freshman Admission Statistics:** 5,395 applied, 67.7% admitted, 31% enrolled. **Transfer Admission Requirements:** High school transcript, college transcript(s), statement of good standing from prior institution(s). Minimum college GPA of 2.4 required. Lowest grade transferable C. **General Admission Information:** Application fee $50. Nonfall registration accepted. Admission may be deferred.

COSTS AND FINANCIAL AID
Annual in-state tuition $12,250. Annual out-of-state tuition $9,740. Room and board $12,250. Required fees $1,657. Average book expense $1,200. **Required Forms and Deadlines:** FAFSA; State aid form. **Types of Aid:** *Need-based scholarships/grants:* College/university scholarship or grant aid from institutional funds; Federal Pell; Private scholarships; SEOG; State scholarships/grants. *Loans:* Direct PLUS loans; Direct Subsidized Stafford Loans; Direct Unsubsidized Stafford Loans. *Student Employment:* Federal Work-Study Program available. Institutional employment available. **Financial Aid Statistics:** 83% needy freshmen, 79% needy undergrads receive need-based scholarship or grant aid. 34% freshmen, 29% undergrads receive non-need-based scholarship or grant aid. 87% freshmen, 86% undergrads receive need-based self-help aid. 0% freshmen, 0% undergrads receive athletic scholarships. 83% freshmen, 79% undergrads receive any aid. 88% undergrads borrow to pay for school. Average cumulative indebtedness $30,200. **Criteria for awarding aid:** *Non-need-based:* Academics, Alumni affiliation, Job skills, Music/drama, State/district residency.

STATE UNIVERSITY OF NEW YORK— BUFFALO STATE COLLEGE

1300 Elmwood Avenue, Buffalo, NY 14222
Phone: 716-878-4017 • **Financial Aid Phone:** 716-878-4902
E-mail: admissions@buffalostate.edu • **CEEB Code:** 2533
Fax: 716-878-6100 • **ACT Code:** 2930

This public school was founded in 1871. It has a 115 acre campus.

RATINGS
Admissions Selectivity Rating: 78   **Fire Safety Rating:** 81   **Green Rating:** 61

STUDENTS AND FACULTY
Enrollment: 8,360. **Student Body:** 57% female, 43% male, 1% out-of-state, 1% international (44 countries represented). Asian 3%, African American 31%, Caucasian 47%, Hispanic 13%, Native American 1%, Pacific Islander <1%, Two or more races 4%, Race unknown <1%.
Retention and Graduation: 68% freshmen return for sophomore year. 25% grads go on to further study within 1 year. 24% grads pursue arts and sciences degrees. 1% grads pursue law degrees. 3% grads pursue business degrees. 0% grads pursue medical degrees. **Faculty:** Student/faculty ratio 16:1. 382 full-time faculty, 86% hold PhDs, 21% are members of minority groups, 53% are women. 0% of classes are taught by teaching assistants.

ACADEMICS

Degrees: Bachelor's; Master's; Post-Master's certificate **Classes:** Most classes have 10-19 students. Most lab/discussion sessions have 10-19 students. **Most popular majors:** Communication, Journalism, And Related Programs, Other; Criminal Justice/Law Enforcement Administration; Business/Commerce, General. **Special Study Options:** Cooperative education program; Cross-registration; Distance learning; Double major; Dual enrollment; English as a Second Language (ESL); Exchange student program (domestic); Honors program; Independent study; Internships; Liberal arts/career combination; Study abroad; Teacher certification program. **Disability Services offered to physically disabled students:** Note-taking services; Reader services; Tape recorders; Tutors. **Career services:** Alumni network; Alumni services; Career assessment; Career/job search classes; Internships

FACILITIES

Housing: Coed dorms; Special housing for international students 100% of campus accessible to physically disabled. **Special Academic Facilities/ Equipment:** Burchfield Penney Art center, anthropology museum, concert hall with pipe organ, nature preserve. **Computers:** 10% of classrooms, 30% of libraries, 100% of dining areas, 50% of student union, 10% of common outdoor areas have wireless network access. Students can register for classes online. Administrative functions (other than registration) can be performed online.

CAMPUS LIFE

Environment: City **Activities:** Choral groups; Concert band; Dance; Drama/theater; International Student Organization; Jazz band; Literary magazine; Music ensembles; Radio station; Student government; Student newspaper; Student-run film society; Television station; Yearbook 75 registered organizations, 5 religious organizations. 10 fraternities, 10 sororities. **Athletics (Intercollegiate):** *Men:* basketball, cross-country, diving, football, ice hockey, soccer, swimming, track/field (outdoor), track/field (indoor). *Women:* basketball, cheerleading, cross-country, diving, ice hockey, lacrosse, soccer, softball, swimming, tennis, track/field (outdoor), track/field (indoor), volleyball. **On-Campus Highlights:** Burchfield Penny Art Center, Sports Arena, Houston Gymnasium/Fitness Center, Rockwell Hall/Performing Arts Center, Campus House **Environmental Initiatives:** 1) Creation of a campus wide recycling program for plastic, glass, metal, paper, cardboard, light bulbs, electronics, electronic media (printer cartridges, dvds, cds, VHS, cassettes, etc), batteries, shrink wrap, bubble wrap, and many other misc items! This was applied to every building on campus including the residential halls.

ADMISSIONS

Freshman Academic Profile: Average high school GPA 3.1. 3% in top 10% of high school class, 32% in top 25% of high school class, 74% in top 50% of high school class. **Test Scores:** SAT Math middle 50% range 380-490. SAT EBRW middle 50% range 390-490. ACT middle 50% range 19-22. Minimum paper TOEFL 500. **Basis for Candidate Selection:** *Very important factors considered include:* rigor of secondary school record, academic GPA, standardized test scores. *Important factors considered include:* class rank. *Other factors considered include:* application essay, recommendation(s), interview, extracurricular activities, talent/ability, character/personal qualities, first generation, volunteer work, work experience. **Freshman Admission Requirements:** High school diploma is required and GED is accepted *Academic units required:* 2 math, 2 science, *Academic units recommended:* 4 English, 3 math, 3 science, 3 foreign language, 4 history. **Freshman Admission Statistics:** 13,715 applied, 64.1% admitted, 19% enrolled. **Transfer Admission Requirements:** college transcript(s), statement of good standing from prior institution(s). Minimum college GPA of 2.0 required. Lowest grade transferable C. **General Admission Information:** Application fee $50. Nonfall registration accepted. Admission may be deferred for a maximum of 1 year.

COSTS AND FINANCIAL AID

Annual in-state tuition $12,614. Annual out-of-state tuition $16,320. Room and board $12,614. Required fees $1,199. Average book expense $1,037. **Required Forms and Deadlines:** FAFSA. **Notification of Awards:** Applicants will be notified of awards on a rolling basis beginning 5/1. **Types of Aid:** *Need-based scholarships/grants:* Federal Pell; SEOG; State scholarships/grants. **Financial Aid Statistics:** 81% needy freshmen, 76% needy undergrads receive need-based scholarship or grant aid. 19% freshmen, 13% undergrads receive non-need-based scholarship or grant aid. 72% freshmen, 69% undergrads receive need-based self-help aid. 0% freshmen, 0% undergrads receive athletic scholarships. 78% undergrads receive any aid. **Criteria for awarding aid:** *Non-need-based:* Academics, Minority status.

STATE UNIVERSITY OF NEW YORK— COBLESKILL

P.O. Box 30014, Cobleskill, NY 12043
Phone: 518-255-5525 • **Financial Aid Phone:** 518-255-5623
E-mail: admissions@cobleskill.edu • **CEEB Code:** 2524
Fax: 518-255-6769 • **Website:** www.cobleskill.edu • **ACT Code:** 2914

This public school was founded in 1916. It has a 750 acre campus.

RATINGS

Admissions Selectivity Rating: 76   **Fire Safety Rating:** 87   **Green Rating:** 72

STUDENTS AND FACULTY

Enrollment: 2,421. **Student Body:** 52% female, 48% male, 10% out-of-state, 1% international (11 countries represented). Asian 1%, African American 12%, Caucasian 74%, Hispanic 7%, Native American <1%, Pacific Islander 0%, Two or more races 0%, Race unknown 5%.
Retention and Graduation: 74% freshmen return for sophomore year. 63% grads go on to further study within 1 year. **Faculty:** Student/faculty ratio 18:1. 100 full-time faculty, 46% hold PhDs, 7% are members of minority groups, 33% are women. 0% of classes are taught by teaching assistants.

ACADEMICS

Degrees: Associate; Bachelor's; Certificate; Terminal Associate; Transfer Associate **Classes:** Most classes have fewer than 10 students. **Most popular majors:** Animal Sciences, General; Wildlife, Fish And Wildlands Science And Management; Business Administration And Management, General. **Special Study Options:** Accelerated program; Distance learning; English as a Second Language (ESL); Honors program; Independent study; Internships; Study abroad; Weekend college. **Disability Services offered to physically disabled students:** Note-taking services; Reader services; Tape recorders; Tutors. **Career services:** Alumni services; Career assessment; Career/job search classes; Internships

FACILITIES

Housing: Coed dorms; Special housing for disabled student; Special housing for international students **Special Academic Facilities/Equipment:** Art museum, 650 acre agricultural campus, distance learning classrooms, ski area, adult study center. **Computers:** Students can register for classes online. Administrative functions (other than registration) can be performed online.

CAMPUS LIFE

Environment: Village **Activities:** Campus Ministries; Choral groups; Drama/theater; International Student Organization; Jazz band; Student government 40 registered organizations, 1 honor society, 1 religious organization. **Athletics (Intercollegiate):** *Men:* baseball, basketball, cross-country, diving, equestrian sports, golf, lacrosse, soccer, swimming, tennis, track/field (outdoor), volleyball. *Women:* basketball, cross-country, diving, equestrian sports, golf, soccer, softball, swimming, tennis, track/field (outdoor), volleyball. **On-Campus Highlights:** Bouck Hall/Student Union, Brickyard Point, American Heritage, Foundation Equestrian Center, Grosvenor Art Gallery **Environmental Initiatives:** recycling—paper, plastics, metals, galss and cardboard box

ADMISSIONS

Freshman Academic Profile: Average high school GPA 82.0. 6% in top 10% of high school class, 22% in top 25% of high school class, 56% in top 50% of high school class. 98% from public high schools. **Test Scores:** SAT Math middle 50% range 380-500. SAT EBRW middle 50% range 380-500. ACT middle 50% range 17-22. Minimum paper TOEFL 500. **Basis for Candidate Selection:** *Very important factors considered include:* rigor of secondary school record, academic GPA, standardized test scores, level of applicant's interest. *Other factors considered include:* class rank, application essay, recommendation(s), interview, extracurricular activities, talent/ability, character/personal qualities, first generation, alumni/ae relation, geographical residence, state residency, volunteer work, work experience. **Freshman Admission Requirements:** High school diploma is required and GED is accepted *Academic units recommended:* 3 English, 3 math, 3 science, 3 science labs, 1 foreign language, 3 social studies, 3 history, 3 academic electives. **Freshman Admission Statistics:** 2,765 applied, 73.1% admitted, 39% enrolled. **Transfer Admission Requirements:** college transcript(s), Minimum college GPA of 2.25 required. Lowest grade transferable D. **General Admission Information:** Application fee $50. Nonfall registration accepted. Admission may be deferred for a maximum of 1 year.

COSTS AND FINANCIAL AID

Annual in-state tuition $11,720. Annual out-of-state tuition $15,320. Room and board $11,720. Required fees $1,279. Average book expense $1,200. **Required Forms and Deadlines:** FAFSA; State aid form. **Notification of Awards:**

Applicants will be notified of awards on a rolling basis beginning 3/15. **Types of Aid:** *Need-based scholarships/grants:* College/university scholarship or grant aid from institutional funds; Federal Pell; Private scholarships; SEOG; State scholarships/grants. *Loans:* Direct PLUS loans; Direct Subsidized Stafford Loans; Direct Unsubsidized Stafford Loans. *Student Employment:* Federal Work-Study Program available. Institutional employment available. **Financial Aid Statistics:** 100% needy freshmen, 99% needy undergrads receive need-based scholarship or grant aid. 33% freshmen, 22% undergrads receive non-need-based scholarship or grant aid. 84% freshmen, 80% undergrads receive need-based self-help aid. 0% freshmen, 0% undergrads receive athletic scholarships. 81% freshmen, 75% undergrads receive any aid. **Criteria for awarding aid:** *Non-need-based:* Academics, Alumni affiliation, Leadership, State/district residency.

STATE UNIVERSITY OF NEW YORK—THE COLLEGE AT BROCKPORT

350 New Campus Drive, Brockport, NY 14420
Phone: 585-395-2751 • **Financial Aid Phone:** (585)-395-2501
E-mail: admit@brockport.edu • **CEEB Code:** 2537
Fax: 585-395-5452 • **Website:** www.brockport.edu • **ACT Code:** 2928

This public school was founded in 1835. It has a 464 acre campus.

RATINGS
Admissions Selectivity Rating: 85   **Fire Safety Rating:** 86   **Green Rating:** 85

STUDENTS AND FACULTY
Enrollment: 7,132. **Student Body:** 57% female, 43% male, 2% out-of-state, 1% international (24 countries represented). Asian 2%, African American 11%, Caucasian 70%, Hispanic 7%, Native American <1%, Pacific Islander <1%, Two or more races 3%, Race unknown 5%.
Retention and Graduation: 79% freshmen return for sophomore year. 48% freshmen graduate within 4 years. 66% freshmen graduate within 6 years.
Faculty: Student/faculty ratio 17:1. 374 full-time faculty, 69% hold PhDs, 17% are members of minority groups, 54% are women.

ACADEMICS
Degrees: Bachelor's; Certificate; Master's; Post-Bachelor's certificate; Post-Master's certificate **Classes:** Most classes have 20-29 students. Most lab/discussion sessions have 10-19 students. **Most popular majors:** Kinesiology And Exercise Science; Registered Nursing/Registered Nurse; Business Administration And Management, General. **Special Study Options:** Accelerated program; Cross-registration; Distance learning; Double major; Dual enrollment; English as a Second Language (ESL); Honors program; Independent study; Internships; Student-designed major; Study abroad; Teacher certification program. Honors programs: 1)Honors College: Students in our Honors College Program enjoy the challenges and rewards of working with distinguished members of the faculty in small, interactive classes and in scholarly/creative projects, including the Honors Thesis capstone. 2)The Delta College Program is an alternative to the traditional College at Brockport General Education program, offering an interdisciplinary approach to the College's required undergraduate liberal arts and science courses. It is a time-variable degree program for highly-motivated students. Combined degree programs: BA/MA. **Disability Services offered to physically disabled students:** Note-taking services; Reader services; Tape recorders; Tutors. **Career services:** Alumni network; Alumni services; Career assessment; Career/job search classes; Internships; Regional alumni

FACILITIES
Housing: Apartments for single students; Coed dorms; Special housing for disabled students 95% of campus accessible to physically diasbled. **Special Academic Facilities/Equipment:** Special Events Recreation Center with state-of-the-art fitness center, indoor track and event space; Proscenium Theatre and Black Box performance space; modern dance facilities; art galleries; ceramic, painting, photography and sculpture studios; greenhouse; planetarium; electron microscope; nuclear magnetic resonance spectrometer; Faraday Cage; Geographic Information Systems (GIS) lab with Dopplar radar station; aquaculture ponds; environmental science deciduous woodlot; 25-foot research boat; 20 computer labs; "smart" classrooms; student learning center **Computers:** 100% of classrooms, 100% of dorms, 100% of libraries, 100% of dining areas, 100% of student union, 80% of common outdoor areas have wireless network access. Students can register for classes online. Administrative functions (other than registration) can be performed online.

CAMPUS LIFE
Environment: Village **Activities:** Choral groups; Dance; Drama/theater; International Student Organization; Jazz band; Literary magazine; Model UN; Music ensembles; Radio station; Student government; Student newspaper; Television station 71 registered organizations, 20 honor societies, 8 religious organizations. 6 fraternities, 3 sororities. **Athletics (Intercollegiate):** *Men:* baseball, basketball, cross-country, diving, football, ice hockey, lacrosse, soccer, swimming, track/field (outdoor), track/field (indoor), wrestling. *Women:* basketball, cross-country, diving, field hockey, gymnastics, lacrosse, soccer, softball, swimming, tennis, track/field (outdoor), track/field (indoor), volleyball. **On-Campus Highlights:** Seymour College Union, Drake Memorial Library, Hartwell Performance Center, Harrison Dining Hall, Special Events and Recreation Center **Environmental Initiatives:** We received the 2010 Pollution Prevention Award from the Rochester Business Journal for our comprehensive programs and continuing efforts to improve our sustainability performance.

ADMISSIONS
Freshman Academic Profile: Average high school GPA 2.9. 12% in top 10% of high school class, 34% in top 25% of high school class, 74% in top 50% of high school class. **Test Scores:** SAT Math middle 50% range 500-590. SAT EBRW middle 50% range 500-590. ACT middle 50% range 20-25. Minimum internet-based TOEFL 76. Minimum paper TOEFL 530. **Basis for Candidate Selection:** *Very important factors considered include:* rigor of secondary school record, academic GPA, standardized test scores. *Important factors considered include:* application essay, recommendation(s), character/personal qualities. *Other factors considered include:* class rank, extracurricular activities, talent/ability, volunteer work, work experience. **Freshman Admission Requirements:** High school diploma is required and GED is accepted *Academic units required:* 4 English, 3 math, 3 science, 1 science labs, 2 social studies, 2 history, 5 academic electives, 1 visual/performing arts, and 2.5 units from above areas or other academic areas. *Academic units recommended:* 4 English, 4 math, 3 science, 1 science labs, 3 foreign language, 2 social studies, 2 history, 5 academic electives, 1 visual/performing arts, 2.5 units from above areas or other academic areas. **Freshman Admission Statistics:** 9,628 applied, 53.2% admitted, 25% enrolled. **Transfer Admission Requirements:** college transcript(s), Minimum college GPA of 2.5 required. Lowest grade transferable D-. **General Admission Information:** Application fee $50. Regular application deadline 8/1. Nonfall registration accepted. Admission may be deferred for a maximum of 1 year.

COSTS AND FINANCIAL AID
Annual in-state tuition $12,904. Annual out-of-state tuition $16,320. Room and board $12,904. Required fees $1,484. Average book expense $1,330. **Required Forms and Deadlines:** FAFSA; State aid form. **Notification of Awards:** Applicants will be notified of awards on a rolling basis beginning 1/1. **Types of Aid:** *Need-based scholarships/grants:* College/university scholarship or grant aid from institutional funds; Federal Pell; Private scholarships; SEOG; State scholarships/grants. *Loans:* Direct PLUS loans; Direct Subsidized Stafford Loans; Direct Unsubsidized Stafford Loans. *Student Employment:* Federal Work-Study Program available. Institutional employment available. **Financial Aid Statistics:** 76% needy freshmen, 81% needy undergrads receive need-based scholarship or grant aid. 37% freshmen, 21% undergrads receive non-need-based scholarship or grant aid. 84% freshmen, 85% undergrads receive need-based self-help aid. 90% freshmen, 85% undergrads receive any aid. Average cumulative indebtedness $29,748. **Criteria for awarding aid:** *Non-need-based:* Academics, Alumni affiliation, Art, Leadership, Minority status, Music/drama.

STATE UNIVERSITY OF NEW YORK—THE COLLEGE AT OLD WESTBURY

PO Box 210, Old Westbury, NY 11568-0307
Phone: 516-876-3073 • **Financial Aid Phone:** 516-876-3247
E-mail: enroll@oldwestbury.edu • **CEEB Code:** 2866
Fax: 516-876-3307 • **Website:** www.oldwestbury.edu • **ACT Code:** 2939

This public school was founded in 1968. It has a 605 acre campus.

RATINGS
Admissions Selectivity Rating: 74   **Fire Safety Rating:** 88   **Green Rating:** 60*

STUDENTS AND FACULTY
Enrollment: 4,481. **Student Body:** 59% female, 41% male, 1% out-of-state, 1% international (58 countries represented). Asian 11%, African American 29%, Caucasian 29%, Hispanic 26%, Native American 1%, Pacific Islander <1%, Two or more races <1%, Race unknown 2%.

The Princeton Review's Complete Book of Colleges

Retention and Graduation: 81% freshmen return for sophomore year. 27% freshmen graduate within 4 years. 47% freshmen graduate within 6 years. **Faculty:** Student/faculty ratio 19:1. 164 full-time faculty, 91% hold PhDs, 38% are members of minority groups, 57% are women. 0% of classes are taught by teaching assistants.

ACADEMICS
Degrees: Bachelor's; Certificate; Master's; Post-Master's certificate **Classes:** Most classes have 10-19 students. **Most popular majors:** Biology/Biological Sciences, General; Psychology, General; Accounting. **Special Study Options:** Cross-registration; Distance learning; Double major; English as a Second Language (ESL); Exchange student program (domestic); Honors program; Independent study; Internships; Liberal arts/career combination; Study abroad; Teacher certification program. Honors programs: The Honors College teaches students to integrate learning methods by using in-depth primary source material and complex and intellectually challenging secondary sources. The program emphasizes critical thinking and experiential learning. **Disability Services offered to physically disabled students:** Note-taking services; Reader services; Tape recorders; Tutors. **Career services:** Alumni network; Alumni services; Career assessment; Career/job search classes; Internships; Regional alumni

FACILITIES
Housing: Coed dorms; Other (please specify) 90% of campus accessible to physically diasbled. **Special Academic Facilities/Equipment:** Art gallery, language lab, TV studio, radio station, recital hall, physical recreation center and Maguire Theatre. **Computers:** 100% of classrooms, 60% of dorms, 100% of libraries, 100% of dining areas, 100% of student union, 30% of common outdoor areas have wireless network access. Students can register for classes online. Administrative functions (other than registration) can be performed online.

CAMPUS LIFE
Environment: Village **Activities:** Campus Ministries; Choral groups; Dance; Drama/theater; International Student Organization; Music ensembles; Radio station; Student government; Student newspaper; Student-run film society; Yearbook 55 registered organizations, 5 honor societies, 2 religious organizations. 6 fraternities, 4 sororities. **Athletics (Intercollegiate):** *Men:* baseball, basketball, cross-country, golf, soccer, swimming, ultimate frisbee, volleyball. *Women:* basketball, cross-country, soccer, softball, swimming, ultimate frisbee, volleyball. **On-Campus Highlights:** Student Union, Clark Center (athletic facility), Library, Theatre, Art Gallery **Environmental Initiatives:** SEMPRA Energy Contract; One (1) solar installation; Gas consortium;

ADMISSIONS
Freshman Academic Profile: Average high school GPA 3.1. 85% from public high schools. **Test Scores:** SAT Math middle 50% range 470-550. SAT EBRW middle 50% range 480-550. ACT middle 50% range 19-21. Minimum internet-based TOEFL 65. Minimum paper TOEFL 513. **Basis for Candidate Selection:** *Very important factors considered include:* academic GPA, application essay, standardized test scores, recommendation(s). *Other factors considered include:* interview, character/personal qualities, alumni/ae relation. **Freshman Admission Requirements:** High school diploma is required and GED is accepted *Academic units required:* 4 English, 3 math, 3 science, 2 science labs, 1 foreign language, 3 social studies, 3.5 academic electives, 1 visual/performing arts, and 2.5 units from above areas or other academic areas. *Academic units recommended:* 4 English, 3 math, 3 science, 3 science labs, 3 foreign language, 4 social studies, 3 academic electives, 1 computer science. **Freshman Admission Statistics:** 3,752 applied, 78.2% admitted, 17% enrolled. **Transfer Admission Requirements:** college transcript(s), essay or personal statement, Minimum college GPA of 2.0 required. Lowest grade transferable C. **General Admission Information:** Application fee $50. Priority deadline 12/1. Nonfall registration accepted. Admission may be deferred for a maximum of one year.

COSTS AND FINANCIAL AID
Annual in-state tuition $11,020. Annual out-of-state tuition $16,320. Room and board $11,020. Required fees $1,213. Average book expense $2,500. **Required Forms and Deadlines:** FAFSA; Institution's own financial aid form; State aid form. **Notification of Awards:** Applicants will be notified of awards on or about 4/15. **Types of Aid:** *Need-based scholarships/grants:* College/university scholarship or grant aid from institutional funds; Federal Pell; Private scholarships; SEOG; State scholarships/grants. *Loans:* Direct PLUS loans; Direct Subsidized Stafford Loans; Direct Unsubsidized Stafford Loans. *Student Employment:* Federal Work-Study Program available. Institutional employment available. **Financial Aid Statistics:** 83% needy freshmen, 85% needy undergrads receive need-based scholarship or grant aid. 8% freshmen, 3% undergrads receive non-need-based scholarship or grant aid. 61% freshmen, 62% undergrads receive need-based self-help aid. 0% freshmen, 0% undergrads receive athletic scholarships. 72% freshmen, 67% undergrads receive any aid. 60% undergrads borrow to pay for school. Average cumulative indebtedness $19,141. **Criteria for awarding aid:** *Need-based:* Academics *Non-need-based:* Academics, State/district residency.

STATE UNIVERSITY OF NEW YORK—COLLEGE OF ENVIRONMENTAL SCIENCE AND FORESTRY

1 Forestry Drive, Syracuse, NY 13210
Phone: 315-470-6600 • **Financial Aid Phone:** 315-470-6706
E-mail: esfinfo@esf.edu • **CEEB Code:** 2530
Fax: 315-470-6933 • **Website:** www.esf.edu • **ACT Code:** 2948

This public school was founded in 1911. It has a 25000 acre campus.

RATINGS
Admissions Selectivity Rating: 88   **Fire Safety Rating:** 98   **Green Rating:** 99

STUDENTS AND FACULTY
Enrollment: 1,793. **Student Body:** 47% female, 53% male, 15% out-of-state, 2% international (8 countries represented). Asian 4%, African American 2%, Caucasian 80%, Hispanic 6%, Native American <1%, Two or more races 3%, Race unknown 4%.
Retention and Graduation: 83% freshmen return for sophomore year. 78% freshmen graduate within 6 years. 25% grads go on to further study within 1 year. **Faculty:** Student/faculty ratio 13:1. 121 full-time faculty, 17% are members of minority groups, 28% are women. 0% of classes are taught by teaching assistants.

ACADEMICS
Degrees: Associate; Bachelor's; Doctoral; Doctoral/Research; Master's; Post-Bachelor's certificate **Classes:** Most classes have 20-29 students. Most lab/discussion sessions have 10-19 students. **Most popular majors:** Environmental Science; Landscape Architecture; Environmental Biology. **Special Study Options:** Cooperative education program; Cross-registration; Distance learning; Double major; Honors program; Independent study; Internships; Study abroad. Honors programs: Lower Division Honors Program: freshmen & sophomores, all academic programs, highly selective, associated scholarship, mentoring, honors seminar, honors writing course. Upper Division Thesis Honors Program: juniors and seniors, 16 of 20 academic programs eligible, intensive research or creative projects guided by faculty mentors, thesis exploration seminar, related course work, Honors Thesis/Project course. Undergraduate research grants available. **Disability Services offered to physically disabled students:** Note-taking services; Reader services; Tape recorders; Tutors. **Career services:** Alumni network; Alumni services; Career assessment; Career/job search classes; Internships; Regional alumni

FACILITIES
Housing: Apartments for single students; Coed dorms; Fraternity/sorority housing; Special housing for disabled student; Wellness housing 95% of campus accessible to physically diasbled. **Special Academic Facilities/Equipment:** Plant and animal growth and environmental simulation chambers, wildlife collection, electron microscope, paper making facility, photogrammetric and geodetic facilities, hydrology flumes, weather measurement, biotechnology and bio-process engineering labs, landscape architecture computing lab and design studios, extensive green house facilities. **Computers:** 50% of classrooms, 100% of dorms, 100% of libraries, 100% of dining areas, 100% of student union, 10% of common outdoor areas have wireless network access. Students can register for classes online. Administrative functions (other than registration) can be performed online.

CAMPUS LIFE
Environment: City **Activities:** Campus Ministries; Choral groups; Concert band; Dance; Drama/theater; International Student Organization; Jazz band; Literary magazine; Marching band; Music ensembles; Musical theater; Pep band; Radio station; Student government; Student newspaper; Student-run film society; Symphony orchestra; Television station; Yearbook 300 registered organizations, 1 honor society, 13 religious organizations. 26 fraternities, 21 sororities. **Athletics (Intercollegiate):** *Men:* cross-country, golf, soccer. *Women:* cross-country, golf, soccer. **On-Campus Highlights:** Centennial Residence Hall, Gateway Center (Student Union), Green Houses and Wildlife Collection, College Quadrangle, Library **Environmental Initiatives:** (1) Biomass fueled power plant in Student Center provides up to 65% of campus heating and 20% of electricity (2) photovoltaic arrays/green roof (3) College owns and manages 25,000 acres of forest (providing carbon offsets).

ADMISSIONS

Freshman Academic Profile: Average high school GPA 3.8. 32% in top 10% of high school class, 62% in top 25% of high school class, 95% in top 50% of high school class. 90% from public high schools. **Test Scores:** SAT Math middle 50% range 570-650. SAT EBRW middle 50% range 580-650. ACT middle 50% range 24-28. Minimum internet-based TOEFL 79. Minimum paper TOEFL 550. **Basis for Candidate Selection:** *Very important factors considered include:* rigor of secondary school record, academic GPA, application essay, standardized test scores, level of applicant's interest. *Important factors considered include:* class rank, recommendation(s), extracurricular activities, talent/ability. *Other factors considered include:* interview, character/personal qualities, first generation, alumni/ae relation, geographical residence, state residency, racial/ethnic status, volunteer work, work experience. **Freshman Admission Requirements:** High school diploma is required and GED is accepted *Academic units required:* 4 English, 3 math, 3 science, 3 social studies, 1 history, *Academic units recommended:* 4 math, 4 science, 3 science labs, 3 foreign language. **Freshman Admission Statistics:** 1,815 applied, 52.2% admitted, 35% enrolled. **Transfer Admission Requirements:** High school transcript, college transcript(s), Minimum college GPA of 2.25 required. Lowest grade transferable C. **General Admission Information:** Application fee $50. Priority deadline 2/1. Nonfall registration accepted. Admission may be deferred for a maximum of 2 semesters.

COSTS AND FINANCIAL AID

Annual in-state tuition $15,160. Annual out-of-state tuition $16,320. Room and board $15,160. Required fees $1,898. Average book expense $1,200. **Required Forms and Deadlines:** FAFSA; State aid form. **Notification of Awards:** Applicants will be notified of awards on a rolling basis beginning 2/1. **Types of Aid:** *Need-based scholarships/grants:* College/university scholarship or grant aid from institutional funds; Federal Pell; Private scholarships; SEOG; State scholarships/grants. *Loans:* Direct PLUS loans; Direct Subsidized Stafford Loans; Direct Unsubsidized Stafford Loans. *Student Employment:* Federal Work-Study Program available. Institutional employment available. **Financial Aid Statistics:** 89% needy freshmen, 99% needy undergrads receive need-based scholarship or grant aid. 67% freshmen, 57% undergrads receive non-need-based scholarship or grant aid. 67% freshmen, 95% undergrads receive need-based self-help aid. 0% freshmen, 0% undergrads receive athletic scholarships. 91% freshmen, 93% undergrads receive any aid. 64% undergrads borrow to pay for school. Average cumulative indebtedness $24,269. **Criteria for awarding aid:** *Need-based:* Academics, Alumni affiliation, Leadership, Minority status *Non-need-based:* Academics, Alumni affiliation, Leadership, Minority status, State/district residency.

See page 1044.

STATE UNIVERSITY OF NEW YORK—CORTLAND

PO Box 2000, Cortland, NY 13045-0900
Phone: 607-753-4712 • **Financial Aid Phone:** 607-753-4717
E-mail: admissions@cortland.edu • **CEEB Code:** 2538
Fax: 607-753-5998 • **Website:** http://www2.cortland.edu/home/
ACT Code: 2932

This public school was founded in 1868. It has a 191 acre campus.

RATINGS

Admissions Selectivity Rating: 85   **Fire Safety Rating:** 65   **Green Rating:** 92

STUDENTS AND FACULTY

Enrollment: 6,276. **Student Body:** 57% female, 43% male, 4% out-of-state, 1% international (14 countries represented). Asian 1%, African American 6%, Caucasian 74%, Hispanic 11%, Native American <1%, Pacific Islander <1%, Two or more races 2%, Race unknown 5%.
Retention and Graduation: 78% freshmen return for sophomore year.
Faculty: Student/faculty ratio 17:1. 293 full-time faculty, 78% hold PhDs, 13% are members of minority groups, 53% are women. 0% of classes are taught by teaching assistants.

ACADEMICS

Degrees: Bachelor's; Master's; Post-Bachelor's certificate; Post-Master's certificate **Classes:** Most classes have 10-19 students. Most lab/discussion sessions have 10-19 students. **Special Study Options:** Cooperative education program; Cross-registration; Distance learning; Double major; Dual enrollment; Exchange student program (domestic); Honors program; Independent study; Internships; Liberal arts/career combination; Student-designed major; Study abroad; Teacher certification program. **Disability Services offered to physically disabled students:** Note-taking services; Reader services; Tape recorders; Tutors.

FACILITIES

Housing: Apartments for single students; Coed dorms; Cooperative housing; Special housing for disabled student; Special housing for international students; Wellness housing 75% of campus accessible to physically disabled. **Special Academic Facilities/Equipment:** Natural science museum, greenhouse, center for speech and hearing disorders, classrooms with integrated technologies, specialized labs to support various program offerings. **Computers:** Students can register for classes online. Administrative functions (other than registration) can be performed online.

CAMPUS LIFE

Environment: Village **Activities:** Campus Ministries; Choral groups; Dance; Drama/theater; International Student Organization; Literary magazine; Model UN; Music ensembles; Musical theater; Radio station; Student government; Student newspaper; Student-run film society; Symphony orchestra; Television station; Yearbook 100 registered organizations, 16 honor societies, 3 religious organizations. 2 fraternities, 5 sororities. **Athletics (Intercollegiate):** *Men:* baseball, basketball, cheerleading, cross-country, diving, football, gymnastics, ice hockey, lacrosse, soccer, swimming, track/field (outdoor), track/field (indoor), wrestling. *Women:* basketball, cheerleading, cross-country, diving, field hockey, golf, gymnastics, ice hockey, lacrosse, soccer, softball, swimming, tennis, track/field (outdoor), track/field (indoor), volleyball. **On-Campus Highlights:** Corey Union, Stadium Complex, Fitness Facilities, Dining Halls, Library

ADMISSIONS

Freshman Academic Profile: Average high school GPA 88.9. 10% in top 10% of high school class, 39% in top 25% of high school class, 50% in top 50% of high school class. 91% from public high schools. **Test Scores:** SAT Math middle 50% range 490-560. SAT EBRW middle 50% range 470-550. ACT middle 50% range 22-25. Minimum paper TOEFL 550. **Basis for Candidate Selection:** *Very important factors considered include:* rigor of secondary school record, academic GPA, standardized test scores. *Important factors considered include:* application essay, recommendation(s), extracurricular activities, talent/ability. *Other factors considered include:* class rank, interview, alumni/ae relation, geographical residence, state residency, racial/ethnic status, volunteer work, work experience. **Freshman Admission Requirements:** High school diploma is required and GED is accepted *Academic units required:* 4 English, 3 math, 3 science, 3 science labs, 3 foreign language, 4 social studies, *Academic units recommended:* 4 English, 4 math, 4 science, 4 science labs, 4 foreign language, 4 social studies. **Freshman Admission Statistics:** 11,060 applied, 50.8% admitted, 22% enrolled. **Transfer Admission Requirements:** High school transcript, college transcript(s), Minimum college GPA of 2.5 required. Lowest grade transferable C-. **General Admission Information:** Application fee $50. Priority deadline 12/1. Nonfall registration accepted. Admission may be deferred for a maximum of 1 year.

COSTS AND FINANCIAL AID

Annual in-state tuition $12,410. Annual out-of-state tuition $16,320. Room and board $12,410. Required fees $1,630. Average book expense $1,000. **Required Forms and Deadlines:** FAFSA; State aid form. **Notification of Awards:** Applicants will be notified of awards on a rolling basis beginning 3/15. **Types of Aid:** *Need-based scholarships/grants:* College/university scholarship or grant aid from institutional funds; Federal Pell; Private scholarships; SEOG; State scholarships/grants. *Loans:* Direct PLUS loans; Direct Subsidized Stafford Loans; Direct Unsubsidized Stafford Loans. **Financial Aid Statistics:** 71% needy freshmen, 72% needy undergrads receive need-based scholarship or grant aid. 37% freshmen, 24% undergrads receive non-need-based scholarship or grant aid. 87% freshmen, 87% undergrads receive need-based self-help aid. 0% freshmen, 0% undergrads receive athletic scholarships. 74% undergrads borrow to pay for school. Average cumulative indebtedness $28,070. **Criteria for awarding aid:** *Need-based:* Academics, Art, Leadership, Music/drama *Non-need-based:* Academics, Art, Leadership, Minority status, Music/drama, State/district residency.

STATE UNIVERSITY OF NEW YORK— EMPIRE STATE COLLEGE

Two Union Ave, Saratoga, NY 12866
Phone: 518-587-2100 • **Financial Aid Phone:** 518-587-2100
E-mail: admissions@esc.edu • **CEEB Code:** 2214
Fax: 518-587-9759 • **Website:** esc.edu • **ACT Code:** 2737

This public school was founded in 1971.

RATINGS
Admissions Selectivity Rating: 70   **Fire Safety Rating:** 60*   **Green Rating:** 60*

STUDENTS AND FACULTY
Enrollment: 10,128. **Student Body:** 62% female, 38% male, 8% out-of-state, 0% international. Asian 2%, African American 18%, Caucasian 66%, Hispanic 5%, Native American 1%, Pacific Islander 0%, Two or more races 1%, Race unknown 7%.
Faculty: Student/faculty ratio 9:1. 202 full-time faculty, 96% hold PhDs, 19% are members of minority groups, 64% are women. 0% of classes are taught by teaching assistants.

ACADEMICS
Degrees: Associate; Bachelor's; Certificate; Master's; Post-Bachelor's certificate **Classes:** Most classes have 10-19 students. Most lab/discussion sessions have fewer than 10 students. **Most popular majors:** Physical Sciences, Other; Community Organization And Advocacy; Business/Commerce, General. **Special Study Options:** Cross-registration; Distance learning; Double major; Dual enrollment; External degree program; Independent study; Internships; Student-designed major. Combined degree programs: BA/MA.

FACILITIES
Computers: Students can register for classes online. Administrative functions (other than registration) can be performed online.

CAMPUS LIFE
Environment: Village **Activities:** Literary magazine.

ADMISSIONS
Test Scores: Minimum paper TOEFL 550. **Basis for Candidate Selection:** *Very important factors considered include:* application essay, character/personal qualities. *Other factors considered include:* rigor of secondary school record, recommendation(s), talent/ability. **Freshman Admission Requirements:** High school diploma is required and GED is accepted **Freshman Admission Statistics:** 1,536 applied, 79.5% admitted, 72% enrolled. **Transfer Admission Requirements:** High school transcript, essay or personal statement, Lowest grade transferable C. **General Admission Information:** Priority deadline 6/1. Nonfall registration accepted. Admission may be deferred for a maximum of 3 years.

COSTS AND FINANCIAL AID
Annual out-of-state tuition $14,820. Required fees $395. **Required Forms and Deadlines:** FAFSA; State aid form. **Types of Aid:** *Need-based scholarships/grants:* College/university scholarship or grant aid from institutional funds; Federal Pell; Private scholarships; SEOG; State scholarships/grants. *Loans:* Direct PLUS loans; Direct Subsidized Stafford Loans; Direct Unsubsidized Stafford Loans. *Student Employment:* Federal Work-Study Program available. **Financial Aid Statistics:** 63% undergrads receive any aid. **Criteria for awarding aid:** *Need-based:* Academics, Minority status.

STATE UNIVERSITY OF NEW YORK— FASHION INSTITUTE OF TECHNOLOGY

Seventh Avenue at 27th Street, New York, NY 10001-5992
Phone: 212-217-3760 • **Financial Aid Phone:** 212-217-3560
E-mail: fitinfo@fitsuny.edu • **CEEB Code:** 2257
Fax: 212-217-3761 • **Website:** fitnyc.edu • **ACT Code:** 2744

This public school was founded in 1944.

RATINGS
Admissions Selectivity Rating: 0   **Fire Safety Rating:** 91   **Green Rating:** 60*

STUDENTS AND FACULTY
Enrollment: 8,229. **Student Body:** 86% female, 14% male, 14% international (70 countries represented). Asian 10%, African American 9%, Caucasian 47%, Hispanic 17%, Native American <1%, Pacific Islander <1%, Two or more races 4%, Race unknown <1%.
Faculty: Student/faculty ratio 17:1.

ACADEMICS
Degrees: Associate; Bachelor's; Certificate; **Master's Classes:** Most classes have 10-19 students. **Special Study Options:** Distance learning; English as a Second Language (ESL); Exchange student program (domestic); Honors program; Independent study; Internships; Liberal arts/career combination; Study abroad. **Disability Services offered to physically disabled students:** Note-taking services; Tutors. **Career services;** Alumni services; Career assessment; Career/job search classes; Internships

FACILITIES
Housing: Apartments for single students; Coed dorms; Special housing for disabled student; Wellness housing; Women's dorms **Special Academic Facilities/Equipment:** The Museum at FIT

CAMPUS LIFE
Environment: Metropolis **Activities:** Campus Ministries; Choral groups; Dance; Drama/theater; International Student Organization; Literary magazine; Musical theater; Radio station; Student government; Student newspaper; Television station; Yearbook 70 registered organizations, 7 honor societies, 1 religious organization. The Museum at FIT, David Dubinsky Student Center, Lari and Barbara Stanton Fitness Center, Gladys Marcus Library, Peter G. Scotese Computer-Aided Design and Communication Center

ADMISSIONS
Basis for Candidate Selection: *Very important factors considered include:* rigor of secondary school record, academic GPA, application essay, talent/ability. *Other factors considered include:* class rank, extracurricular activities, character/personal qualities, first generation, alumni/ae relation, volunteer work, work experience, level of applicant's interest. **Freshman Admission Requirements:** High school diploma is required and GED is accepted **General Admission Information:** Application fee $50. Regular application deadline 1/1. Nonfall registration accepted.

COSTS AND FINANCIAL AID
Required Forms and Deadlines: FAFSA; State aid form. **Notification of Awards:** Applicants will be notified of awards on a rolling basis beginning 4/1. **Types of Aid:** *Need-based scholarships/grants:* College/university scholarship or grant aid from institutional funds; Federal Pell; Private scholarships; SEOG; State scholarships/grants. *Loans:* Direct PLUS loans; Direct Subsidized Stafford Loans; Direct Unsubsidized Stafford Loans. *Student Employment:* Federal Work-Study Program available.

See page 934.

STATE UNIVERSITY OF NEW YORK—FREDONIA

280 Central Avenue, Fredonia, NY 14063
Phone: 716-673-3251 • **Financial Aid Phone:** 716-673-3253
E-mail: admissions@fredonia.edu • **CEEB Code:** 2539
Fax: 716-673-3249 • **Website:** www.fredonia.edu • **ACT Code:** 2934

This public school was founded in 1826. It has a 249 acre campus.

RATINGS
Admissions Selectivity Rating: 82   **Fire Safety Rating:** 87   **Green Rating:** 88

STUDENTS AND FACULTY
Enrollment: 4,366. **Student Body:** 57% female, 43% male, 4% out-of-state, 2% international (8 countries represented). Asian 2%, African American 8%, Caucasian 74%, Hispanic 9%, Native American 1%, Pacific Islander <1%, Two or more races 3%, Race unknown 2%.
Retention and Graduation: 79% freshmen return for sophomore year. 48% freshmen graduate within 4 years. 63% freshmen graduate within 6 years. 44% grads go on to further study within 1 year. **Faculty:** Student/faculty ratio 14:1. 252 full-time faculty, 87% hold PhDs, 8% are members of minority groups, 44% are women. 2% of classes are taught by teaching assistants.

ACADEMICS
Degrees: Bachelor's; Master's; Post-Master's certificate **Classes:** Most classes have 10-19 students. Most lab/discussion sessions have 10-19 students. **Most popular majors:** Elementary Education And Teaching; Music, Other;

Business/Commerce, General. **Special Study Options:** Accelerated program; Cooperative education program; Cross-registration; Distance learning; Double major; Dual enrollment; English as a Second Language (ESL); Exchange student program (domestic); Honors program; Independent study; Internships; Student-designed major; Study abroad; Teacher certification program. Honors programs: The honors program challenges and supports student learning through a series of specially designed seminars. Each seminar offers a unique educational experience, enabling students to work with some of the finest faculty members on campus in a small class setting. Honors students take four seminars, ideally within their freshman and sophomore years, which fulfill part of the university's general education requirements. We offer courses in the Arts, Humanities, Social Sciences and Natural Sciences. Students are also encouraged to participate in the honors colloquium and to take part in the many organized learning experiences outside of the classroom. Combined degree programs: BA/DDS. **Disability Services offered to physically disabled students:** Note-taking services; Reader services; Tape recorders; Tutors. **Career services:** Alumni network; Alumni services; Career assessment; Career/job search classes; Internships

FACILITIES

Housing: Apartments for single students; Coed dorms; Men's dorms; Special housing for international students; Theme housing; Wellness housing; Women's dorms 85% of campus accessible to physically disabled. **Special Academic Facilities/Equipment:** Art center, education and local history museums, teacher education research center, developmental reading center, Sheldon Communications Lab, SMART classrooms, greenhouse. **Computers:** 100% of classrooms, 100% of libraries, 100% of dining areas, 100% of student union, 85% of common outdoor areas have wireless network access. Students can register for classes online. Administrative functions (other than registration) can be performed online.

CAMPUS LIFE

Environment: Village **Activities:** Campus Ministries; Choral groups; Concert band; Dance; Drama/theater; International Student Organization; Jazz band; Literary magazine; Model UN; Music ensembles; Musical theater; Opera; Pep band; Radio station; Student government; Student newspaper; Student-run film society; Symphony orchestra; Television station 152 registered organizations, 22 honor societies, 5 religious organizations. 3 fraternities, 3 sororities. **Athletics (Intercollegiate):** *Men:* baseball, basketball, cross-country, diving, ice hockey, soccer, swimming, track/field (outdoor), track/field (indoor). *Women:* basketball, cheerleading, cross-country, diving, lacrosse, soccer, softball, swimming, tennis, track/field (outdoor), track/field (indoor), volleyball. **On-Campus Highlights:** University Commons, Michael C. Rockefeller Arts Center, Library, Natatorium-Swimming pool and diving area, Rosch Recital Hall **Environmental Initiatives:** Campus owned gas well

ADMISSIONS

Freshman Academic Profile: Average high school GPA 3.2. 15% in top 10% of high school class, 35% in top 25% of high school class, 68% in top 50% of high school class. 95% from public high schools. **Test Scores:** SAT Math middle 50% range 480-590. SAT EBRW middle 50% range 500-600. ACT middle 50% range 21-26. Minimum internet-based TOEFL 62. Minimum paper TOEFL 500. **Basis for Candidate Selection:** *Very important factors considered include:* rigor of secondary school record, academic GPA. *Important factors considered include:* class rank, application essay, standardized test scores, recommendation(s). *Other factors considered include:* extracurricular activities, talent/ability, character/personal qualities, alumni/ae relation, work experience. **Freshman Admission Requirements:** High school diploma is required and GED is accepted *Academic units required:* 4 English, 3 math, 3 science, 3 science labs, 3 foreign language, 4 social studies, *Academic units recommended:* 4 English, 4 math, 4 science, 4 science labs, 3 foreign language, 4 social studies, 1 academic elective. **Freshman Admission Statistics:** 5,474 applied, 64.9% admitted, 32% enrolled. **Transfer Admission Requirements:** college transcript(s), Minimum college GPA of 2.0 required. Lowest grade transferable D. **General Admission Information:** Application fee $50. Nonfall registration accepted. Admission may be deferred for a maximum of 1 year.

COSTS AND FINANCIAL AID

Annual in-state tuition $12,490. Annual out-of-state tuition $16,320. Room and board $12,490. Required fees $1,618. Average book expense $1,000. **Required Forms and Deadlines:** FAFSA; State aid form. **Notification of Awards:** Applicants will be notified of awards on a rolling basis beginning 12/1. **Types of Aid:** *Need-based scholarships/grants:* College/university scholarship or grant aid from institutional funds; Federal Pell; Private scholarships; SEOG; State scholarships/grants. *Loans:* Direct PLUS loans; Direct Subsidized Stafford Loans; Direct Unsubsidized Stafford Loans. *Student Employment:* Federal Work-Study Program available. **Financial Aid Statistics:** 76% needy freshmen, 74% needy undergrads receive need-based scholarship or grant aid. 63% freshmen, 33% undergrads receive non-need-based scholarship or grant aid. 84% freshmen, 82% undergrads receive need-based self-help aid. 0% freshmen, 0% undergrads receive athletic scholarships. 81% freshmen, 85% undergrads receive any aid. 82% undergrads borrow to pay for school. Average

cumulative indebtedness $32,083. **Criteria for awarding aid:** *Non-need-based:* Academics, Alumni affiliation, Art, Leadership, Minority status, Music/drama, State/district residency.

STATE UNIVERSITY OF NEW YORK—
INSTITUTE OF TECHNOLOGY AT UTICA/ROME

100 Seymour Rd, Utica, NY 13504
Phone: 315-792-7500 • **Financial Aid Phone:** 315-792-7210
E-mail: admissions@sunyit.edu • **CEEB Code:** 2896
Fax: 315-792-7837 • **Website:** www.sunyit.edu • **ACT Code:** 2953

This public school was founded in 1966. It has a 850 acre campus.

RATINGS

Admissions Selectivity Rating: 85   **Fire Safety Rating:** 60*   **Green Rating:** 60*

STUDENTS AND FACULTY

Enrollment: 1,893. **Student Body:** 38% female, 62% male, 1% out-of-state, 1% international (13 countries represented). Asian 3%, African American 8%, Caucasian 79%, Hispanic 7%, Native American <1%, Pacific Islander <1%, Two or more races 2%, Race unknown <1%.
Retention and Graduation: 84% freshmen return for sophomore year.
Faculty: Student/faculty ratio 18:1. 131 full-time faculty, 87% hold PhDs, 22% are members of minority groups, 32% are women.

ACADEMICS

Degrees: Bachelor's; Master's; Post-Bachelor's certificate; Post-Master's certificate **Classes:** Most classes have 10-19 students. Most lab/discussion sessions have fewer than 10 students. **Most popular majors:** Computer And Information Sciences, General; Mechanical Engineering/Mechanical Technology/Technician; Business Administration And Management, General. **Special Study Options:** Accelerated program; Cross-registration; Distance learning; Double major; Independent study; Internships; Study abroad. **Disability Services offered to physically disabled students:** Note-taking services; Reader services; Tape recorders; Tutors. **Career services:** Alumni network; Alumni services; Career assessment; Career/job search classes; Internships; Regional alumni

FACILITIES

Housing: Coed dorms; Special housing for disabled student; Special housing for international students 98% of campus accessible to physically disabled. **Special Academic Facilities/Equipment:** Gannett Gallery **Computers:** Students can register for classes online. Administrative functions (other than registration) can be performed online.

CAMPUS LIFE

Environment: Village **Activities:** Campus Ministries; Dance; Drama/theater; International Student Organization; Literary magazine; Radio station; Student government; Student newspaper; Television station; Yearbook 30 registered organizations, 4 honor societies, 1 religious organization. **Athletics (Intercollegiate):** *Men:* baseball, basketball, golf, lacrosse, soccer. *Women:* basketball, cross-country, golf, soccer, softball, volleyball. Student Center, Field House, Cayan Library

ADMISSIONS

Freshman Academic Profile: Average high school GPA 89.0. 17% in top 10% of high school class, 43% in top 25% of high school class, 83% in top 50% of high school class. 98% from public high schools. **Test Scores:** SAT Math middle 50% range 460-650. SAT EBRW middle 50% range 460-610. ACT middle 50% range 22-28. Minimum internet-based TOEFL 79. Minimum paper TOEFL 550. **Basis for Candidate Selection:** *Very important factors considered include:* rigor of secondary school record, academic GPA, standardized test scores, recommendation(s). *Important factors considered include:* class rank, application essay, interview, extracurricular activities. *Other factors considered include:* talent/ability, character/personal qualities, first generation, volunteer work, work experience. **Freshman Admission Requirements:** High school diploma is required and GED is accepted *Academic units required:* 4 English, 3 math, 3 science, 3 science labs, 2 social studies, 2 history, *Academic units recommended:* 4 math, 4 science, 4 science labs, 3 foreign language, 2 academic electives. **Freshman Admission Statistics:** 2,233 applied, 56.6% admitted, 27% enrolled. **Transfer Admission Requirements:** college transcript(s), statement of good standing from prior institution(s). Minimum college GPA of 2.5 required. Lowest grade transferable D. **General Admission Information:** Application fee $50. Priority deadline 3/1. Regular application deadline 7/15. Nonfall registration accepted. Admission may be deferred for a maximum of 1 year.

COSTS AND FINANCIAL AID

Annual in-state tuition $12,250. Annual out-of-state tuition $15,820. Room and board $12,250. Required fees $1,270. Average book expense $1,500. **Required Forms and Deadlines:** FAFSA; State aid form. **Notification of Awards:** Applicants will be notified of awards on a rolling basis beginning 3/15. **Types of Aid:** *Need-based scholarships/grants:* College/university scholarship or grant aid from institutional funds; Federal Pell; Private scholarships; SEOG; State scholarships/grants. *Loans:* Direct PLUS loans; Direct Subsidized Stafford Loans; Direct Unsubsidized Stafford Loans. *Student Employment:* Federal Work-Study Program available. Institutional employment available. **Financial Aid Statistics:** 90% needy freshmen, 87% needy undergrads receive need-based scholarship or grant aid. 63% freshmen, 30% undergrads receive non-need-based scholarship or grant aid. 98% freshmen, 99% undergrads receive need-based self-help aid. 0% freshmen, 0% undergrads receive athletic scholarships. **Criteria for awarding aid:** *Non-need-based:* Academics.

STATE UNIVERSITY OF NEW YORK— MARITIME COLLEGE

6 Pennyfield Ave, Throggs Neck, NY 10465
Phone: 718-409-7200 • **Financial Aid Phone:** 718-409-7227
E-mail: admissions@sunymaritime.edu
Fax: (718) 409-7465 • **Website:** www.sunymaritime.edu • **ACT Code:** 2954

This public school was founded in 1874. It has a 56 acre campus.

RATINGS

Admissions Selectivity Rating: 84   **Fire Safety Rating:** 89   **Green Rating:** 63

STUDENTS AND FACULTY

Enrollment: 1,633. **Student Body:** 12% female, 88% male, 24% out-of-state, 2% international (21 countries represented). Asian 5%, African American 4%, Caucasian 71%, Hispanic 13%, Native American <1%, Pacific Islander 0%, Two or more races 3%, Race unknown 3%.
Retention and Graduation: 85% freshmen return for sophomore year. 62% freshmen graduate within 6 years. 5% grads go on to further study within 1 year.
Faculty: Student/faculty ratio 15:1. 92 full-time faculty, 46% hold PhDs, 9% are members of minority groups, 21% are women. 0% of classes are taught by teaching assistants.

ACADEMICS

Degrees: Associate; Bachelor's; Certificate; Master's; Post-Bachelor's certificate **Classes:** Most classes have 20-29 students. Most lab/discussion sessions have 10-19 students. **Most popular majors:** Mechanical Engineering; Marine Science/Merchant Marine Officer; Business, Management, Marketing, And Related Support Services, Other. **Special Study Options:** Distance learning; Double major; Exchange student program (domestic); Independent study; Internships; Study abroad. Honors programs: **Disability Services offered to physically disabled students:** Note-taking services; Reader services; Tape recorders; Tutors. **Career services:** Alumni network; Alumni services; Career assessment; Career/job search classes; Internships; Regional alumni

FACILITIES

Housing: Coed dorms 81% of campus accessible to physically diasbled. **Special Academic Facilities/Equipment:** Maritime Industry Museum, Fort Schuyler(National Historic Landmark), Bridge Simulator, Liquid Cargo Simulator, 565 ft. Training Ship Empire State VI, Diesel Simulator, 2 Research Ships, State-of-the-Art Electrical Engineering Lab, NY State Strategic Center for Port and Maritime Security (224 ft USS Stalwart), Computerized Weather Station, Maritime College Waterfront Sailboat Fleet:20 Vanguard 420's, 6 Vanguard FJ's, 1 Laser, J-105, J-35, J-24, Colgate 26 **Computers:** 75% of classrooms, 30% of dorms, 100% of libraries, 50% of student union, have wireless network access. Students can register for classes online.

CAMPUS LIFE

Environment: Metropolis **Activities:** Campus Ministries; Choral groups; International Student Organization; Marching band; Music ensembles; Pep band; Student government; Yearbook 30 registered organizations, 4 religious organizations. **Athletics (Intercollegiate):** *Men:* baseball, basketball, cross-country, football, ice hockey, lacrosse, riflery, soccer, swimming. *Women:* basketball, crew/rowing, cross-country, lacrosse, riflery, soccer, softball, swimming, volleyball. **On-Campus Highlights:** Fort Schuyler, Empire State VI, The Maritime Industry Museum, Waterfront **Environmental Initiatives:** Energy Reduction Programs with NYPA

ADMISSIONS

Freshman Academic Profile: Average high school GPA 88.0. 33% in top 10% of high school class, 33% in top 25% of high school class, 67% in top 50% of high school class. **Test Scores:** SAT Math middle 50% range 550-630. SAT EBRW middle 50% range 550-623. ACT middle 50% range 22-26. Minimum internet-based TOEFL 79. Minimum paper TOEFL 550. **Basis for Candidate Selection:** *Very important factors considered include:* rigor of secondary school record, academic GPA. *Important factors considered include:* standardized test scores, recommendation(s). *Other factors considered include:* class rank, application essay, interview, extracurricular activities, talent/ability, character/personal qualities, first generation, alumni/ae relation, geographical residence, state residency, racial/ethnic status, volunteer work, work experience, level of applicant's interest. **Freshman Admission Requirements:** High school diploma is required and GED is accepted *Academic units required:* 3 English, 3 math, 3 science, 1 science labs, 1 foreign language, 3 social studies, 3 history, *Academic units recommended:* 4 English, 3 math, 4 science, 1 foreign language, 4 social studies. **Freshman Admission Statistics:** 1,272 applied, 69.5% admitted, 39% enrolled. **Transfer Admission Requirements:** High school transcript, college transcript(s), Minimum college GPA of 2.5 required. Lowest grade transferable 2. **General Admission Information:** Application fee $50. Regular application deadline 1/31. Nonfall registration accepted. Admission may be deferred.

COSTS AND FINANCIAL AID

Annual in-state tuition $12,134. Annual out-of-state tuition $16,320. Room and board $12,134. Required fees $1,404. Average book expense $1,500. **Required Forms and Deadlines:** FAFSA. **Notification of Awards:** Applicants will be notified of awards on a rolling basis beginning 3/15. **Types of Aid:** *Need-based scholarships/grants:* College/university scholarship or grant aid from institutional funds; Federal Pell; Private scholarships; SEOG; State scholarships/grants. *Loans:* Direct PLUS loans; Direct Subsidized Stafford Loans; Direct Unsubsidized Stafford Loans. *Student Employment:* Federal Work-Study Program available. Institutional employment available. **Financial Aid Statistics:** 54% needy freshmen, 65% needy undergrads receive need-based scholarship or grant aid. 42% freshmen, 33% undergrads receive non-need-based scholarship or grant aid. 80% freshmen, 82% undergrads receive need-based self-help aid. 0% freshmen, 0% undergrads receive athletic scholarships. 83% freshmen, 78% undergrads receive any aid. **Criteria for awarding aid:** *Need-based:* Academics, Leadership *Non-need-based:* Academics, Leadership, Minority status, State/district residency.

STATE UNIVERSITY OF NEW YORK—NEW PALTZ

1 Hawk Drive, New Paltz, NY 12561
Phone: 845-257-3200 • **Financial Aid Phone:** (845) 257-3250
E-mail: admissions@newpaltz.edu • **CEEB Code:** 2541
Fax: 845-257-3209 • **Website:** www.newpaltz.edu • **ACT Code:** 2938

This public school was founded in 1828. It has a 216 acre campus.

RATINGS

Admissions Selectivity Rating: 88   **Fire Safety Rating:** 94   **Green Rating:** 89

STUDENTS AND FACULTY

Enrollment: 6,582. **Student Body:** 62% female, 38% male, 3% out-of-state, 2% international (43 countries represented). Asian 6%, African American 6%, Caucasian 63%, Hispanic 18%, Native American <1%, Pacific Islander <1%, Two or more races 2%, Race unknown 3%.
Retention and Graduation: 87% freshmen return for sophomore year. 19% grads go on to further study within 1 year. **Faculty:** Student/faculty ratio 15:1. 372 full-time faculty, 83% hold PhDs, 19% are members of minority groups, 52% are women. 2% of classes are taught by teaching assistants.

ACADEMICS

Degrees: Bachelor's; Master's; Post-Bachelor's certificate; Post-Master's certificate **Classes:** Most classes have 10-19 students. Most lab/discussion sessions have 20-29 students. **Most popular majors:** Elementary Education And Teaching; Psychology, General; Sociology. **Special Study Options:** Accelerated program; Cross-registration; Distance learning; Double major; Dual enrollment; English as a Second Language (ESL); Honors program; Independent study; Internships; Student-designed major; Study abroad; Teacher certification program. Honors programs: The mission of the SUNY New Paltz Honors Program is to provide an enhanced intellectual experience in a climate conducive to interaction among highly motivated students and faculty. This experience will seek to develop and intensify skills from a conceptual point of view in a diverse multidisciplinary analytical environment that nurtures independent thinking, creativity, respect and social responsibility. **Disability**

Services offered to physically disabled students: Note-taking services; Reader services; Tape recorders; Tutors. **Career services:** Alumni services; Career assessment; Career/job search classes; Internships

FACILITIES

Housing: Coed dorms; Special housing for disabled student; Special housing for international students; Theme housing; Wellness housing 90% of campus accessible to physically diasbled. **Special Academic Facilities/Equipment:** Hudson Valley Advanced Manufacturing Center for 3D Printing, Samuel Dorsky Museum of Art, John Kirk Planetarium, Smolen Observatory, Resnick Engineering Hall, Coykendall Media Center, Communication Disorders Training Center and Clinic; Music Therapy Training Center and Clinic; Shepherd Recital Hall, Honors Center; Martin Luther King, Jr. Study Center. **Computers:** 70% of classrooms, 45% of dorms, 100% of libraries, 90% of dining areas, 90% of student union, 10% of common outdoor areas have wireless network access. Students can register for classes online. Administrative functions (other than registration) can be performed online.

CAMPUS LIFE

Environment: Village **Activities:** Campus Ministries; Choral groups; Concert band; Dance; Drama/theater; International Student Organization; Jazz band; Literary magazine; Model UN; Music ensembles; Musical theater; Opera; Radio station; Student government; Student newspaper; Symphony orchestra; Television station 196 registered organizations, 12 honor societies, 10 religious organizations. 11 fraternities, 17 sororities. **Athletics (Intercollegiate):** *Men:* baseball, basketball, cross-country, diving, soccer, swimming, tennis, volleyball. *Women:* basketball, cross-country, diving, field hockey, lacrosse, soccer, softball, swimming, tennis, volleyball. **On-Campus Highlights:** Samuel Dorsky Museum of Art, Student Union Building, Athletic and Wellness Center, Sojourner Truth Library, Hasbrouck Dining Hall **Environmental Initiatives:** Investing $2 million in a campus wide submetering system for electricity, natural gas, high temp hot water, and domestic water.

ADMISSIONS

Freshman Academic Profile: Average high school GPA 3.6. 20% in top 10% of high school class, 58% in top 25% of high school class, 91% in top 50% of high school class. 92% from public high schools. **Test Scores:** SAT Math middle 50% range 510-600. SAT EBRW middle 50% range 500-600. ACT middle 50% range 23-27. Minimum internet-based TOEFL 80. Minimum paper TOEFL 550. **Basis for Candidate Selection:** *Very important factors considered include:* rigor of secondary school record, academic GPA, standardized test scores. *Important factors considered include:* application essay, recommendation(s). *Other factors considered include:* extracurricular activities, talent/ability, volunteer work, work experience, level of applicant's interest. **Freshman Admission Requirements:** High school diploma is required and GED is accepted *Academic units required:* 4 English, 3 math, 3 science, 2 science labs, 2 foreign language, 4 social studies, 1 history, *Academic units recommended:* 4 English, 4 math, 4 science, 4 science labs, 4 foreign language, 4 social studies, 1 history. **Freshman Admission Statistics:** 14,042 applied, 42.9% admitted, 18% enrolled. **Transfer Admission Requirements:** college transcript(s), statement of good standing from prior institution(s). Minimum college GPA of 2.75 required. Lowest grade transferable C-. **General Admission Information:** Application fee $50. Regular application deadline 4/1. Nonfall registration accepted.

COSTS AND FINANCIAL AID

Average book expense $1,600. **Required Forms and Deadlines:** FAFSA; State aid form. **Notification of Awards:** Applicants will be notified of awards on a rolling basis beginning 4/1. **Types of Aid:** *Need-based scholarships/grants:* College/university scholarship or grant aid from institutional funds; Federal Pell; Private scholarships; SEOG; State scholarships/grants. *Loans:* Direct PLUS loans; Direct Subsidized Stafford Loans; Direct Unsubsidized Stafford Loans. *Student Employment:* Federal Work-Study Program available. Institutional employment available. **Financial Aid Statistics:** 54% needy freshmen, 59% needy undergrads receive need-based scholarship or grant aid. 10% freshmen, 8% undergrads receive non-need-based scholarship or grant aid. 87% freshmen, 89% undergrads receive need-based self-help aid. 0% freshmen, 0% undergrads receive athletic scholarships. Average cumulative indebtedness $26,283. **Criteria for awarding aid:** *Need-based:* Academics, Alumni affiliation, Art *Non-need-based:* Academics, Alumni affiliation, Art, Music/drama.

STATE UNIVERSITY OF NEW YORK—OSWEGO

7060 State Route 104, Oswego, NY 13126-3599
Phone: 315-312-2250 • **Financial Aid Phone:** 315-312-2248
E-mail: admiss@oswego.edu • **CEEB Code:** 2543
Fax: 315-312-3260 • **Website:** www.oswego.edu • **ACT Code:** 2942

This public school was founded in 1861. It has a 696 acre campus.

RATINGS

Admissions Selectivity Rating: 86   **Fire Safety Rating:** 86   **Green Rating:** 88

STUDENTS AND FACULTY

Enrollment: 7,089. **Student Body:** 49% female, 51% male, 3% out-of-state, 3% international (31 countries represented). Asian 3%, African American 9%, Caucasian 71%, Hispanic 12%, Native American <1%, Pacific Islander <1%, Two or more races 3%, Race unknown <1%. **Retention and Graduation:** 78% freshmen return for sophomore year. 66% freshmen graduate within 6 years. 19% grads go on to further study within 1 year. 22% grads pursue arts and sciences degrees. 4% grads pursue law degrees. 6% grads pursue business degrees. 5% grads pursue medical degrees. **Faculty:** Student/faculty ratio 17:1. 375 full-time faculty, 88% hold PhDs, 18% are members of minority groups, 48% are women. 0% of classes are taught by teaching assistants.

ACADEMICS

Degrees: Bachelor's; Master's; Post-Bachelor's certificate; Post-Master's certificate **Classes:** Most classes have 20-29 students. Most lab/discussion sessions have 20-29 students. **Most popular majors:** Mass Communication/Media Studies; Business Administration And Management, General; Accounting. **Special Study Options:** Accelerated program; Cooperative education program; Cross-registration; Distance learning; Double major; Dual enrollment; English as a Second Language (ESL); Exchange student program (domestic); External degree program; Honors program; Independent study; Internships; Liberal arts/career combination; Study abroad; Teacher certification program. Honors programs: Over 250 students participate in our campus wide Honors Program. Students will take smaller courses based on the program's core multidisciplinary courses in the social sciences, the natural sciences, the humanities, and philosophy, as well as several other courses in math, English, and a foreign language. The courses emphasize the interrelatedness of the disciplines, their historical and intellectual origins, their roles in modern society, and their impact on life in the future. Combined degree programs: BA/MA. **Disability Services offered to physically disabled students:** Note-taking services; Reader services; Tape recorders; Tutors. **Career services:** Alumni network; Alumni services; Career assessment; Career/job search classes; Internships; Regional alumni

FACILITIES

Housing: Coed dorms; Theme housing; Wellness housing 95% of campus accessible to physically diasbled. **Special Academic Facilities/Equipment:** Tyler Hall Art Galleries, Rice Creek Biological Field Station, curriculum materials center, electron microscopy lab, planetarium. **Computers:** 80% of classrooms, 10% of dorms, 100% of libraries, 100% of dining areas, 100% of student union, have wireless network access. Students can register for classes online. Administrative functions (other than registration) can be performed online.

CAMPUS LIFE

Environment: Village **Activities:** Choral groups; Concert band; Dance; Drama/theater; International Student Organization; Jazz band; Literary magazine; Music ensembles; Musical theater; Opera; Radio station; Student government; Student newspaper; Student-run film society; Symphony orchestra; Television station; Yearbook 148 registered organizations, 21 honor societies, 6 religious organizations. 13 fraternities, 10 sororities. **Athletics (Intercollegiate):** *Men:* baseball, basketball, cross-country, diving, golf, ice hockey, lacrosse, soccer, swimming, tennis, track/field (outdoor), track/field (indoor), wrestling. *Women:* basketball, cross-country, diving, field hockey, ice hockey, lacrosse, soccer, softball, swimming, tennis, track/field (outdoor), track/field (indoor), volleyball. **On-Campus Highlights:** Marano Campus Center, Penfield Library and Lake Effect Cafe, Richard S. Shineman Center of Science, Engineering & Innovation, The Village—Townhouses, Rich Hall, School of Business **Environmental Initiatives:** All major renovation and new construction to be LEED Gold certified.

ADMISSIONS

Freshman Academic Profile: Average high school GPA 3.5. 12% in top 10% of high school class, 52% in top 25% of high school class, 86% in top 50% of high school class. **Test Scores:** SAT Math middle 50% range 530-615. SAT

EBRW middle 50% range 545-610. ACT middle 50% range 22-27. Minimum internet-based TOEFL 79. **Basis for Candidate Selection:** *Very important factors considered include:* rigor of secondary school record, academic GPA. *Important factors considered include:* standardized test scores. *Other factors considered include:* class rank, application essay, recommendation(s), interview, extracurricular activities, talent/ability, character/personal qualities, first generation, alumni/ae relation, geographical residence, racial/ethnic status, volunteer work, work experience, level of applicant's interest. **Freshman Admission Requirements:** High school diploma is required and GED is accepted *Academic units required:* 4 English, 3 math, 3 science, 2 science labs, 2 foreign language, 4 social studies, *Academic units recommended:* 4 English, 4 math, 4 science, 3 science labs, 4 foreign language, 4 social studies. **Freshman Admission Statistics:** 11,727 applied, 53.7% admitted, 23% enrolled. **Transfer Admission Requirements:** college transcript(s), Minimum college GPA of 2.5 required. Lowest grade transferable D. **General Admission Information:** Application fee $50. Priority deadline 1/15. Nonfall registration accepted. Admission may be deferred for a maximum of 1 year.

COSTS AND FINANCIAL AID

Annual in-state tuition $13,740. Annual out-of-state tuition $16,320. Room and board $13,740. Required fees $1,521. Average book expense $800. **Required Forms and Deadlines:** FAFSA; State aid form. **Notification of Awards:** Applicants will be notified of awards on a rolling basis beginning 1/2. **Types of Aid:** *Need-based scholarships/grants:* College/university scholarship or grant aid from institutional funds; Federal Pell; Private scholarships; SEOG; State scholarships/grants. *Loans:* Direct PLUS loans; Direct Subsidized Stafford Loans; Direct Unsubsidized Stafford Loans. *Student Employment:* Federal Work-Study Program available. Institutional employment available. **Financial Aid Statistics:** 95% needy freshmen, 87% needy undergrads receive need-based scholarship or grant aid. 68% freshmen, 36% undergrads receive non-need-based scholarship or grant aid. 95% freshmen, 95% undergrads receive need-based self-help aid. 0% freshmen, 0% undergrads receive athletic scholarships. 93% freshmen, 85% undergrads receive any aid. 81% undergrads borrow to pay for school. Average cumulative indebtedness $28,810. **Criteria for awarding aid:** *Need-based:* Academics *Non-need-based:* Academics, State/district residency.

STATE UNIVERSITY OF NEW YORK—POTSDAM

44 Pierrepont Avenue, Potsdam, NY 13676
Phone: 315-267-2180 • **Financial Aid Phone:** 315-267-2162
E-mail: admissions@potsdam.edu • **CEEB Code:** 2545
Fax: 315-267-2163 • **Website:** www.potsdam.edu • **ACT Code:** 2946

This public school was founded in 1816. It has a 240 acre campus.

RATINGS

Admissions Selectivity Rating: 81   **Fire Safety Rating:** 89   **Green Rating:** 81

STUDENTS AND FACULTY

Enrollment: 3,296. **Student Body:** 58% female, 42% male, 4% out-of-state, 1% international (6 countries represented). Asian 2%, African American 13%, Caucasian 61%, Hispanic 15%, Native American 2%, Pacific Islander <1%, Two or more races 2%, Race unknown 4%.
Retention and Graduation: 75% freshmen return for sophomore year. 34% freshmen graduate within 4 years. 53% freshmen graduate within 6 years. 41% grads go on to further study within 1 year. 32% grads pursue arts and sciences degrees. 0% grads pursue law degrees. 0% grads pursue business degrees. 1% grads pursue medical degrees. **Faculty:** Student/faculty ratio 11:1. 261 full-time faculty, 84% hold PhDs, 16% are members of minority groups, 47% are women.

ACADEMICS

Degrees: Bachelor's; Master's; Post-Master's certificate **Classes:** Most classes have 20-29 students. **Most popular majors:** Elementary Education And Teaching; Psychology, General; Business Administration And Management, General. **Special Study Options:** Cross-registration; Distance learning; Double major; Dual enrollment; Exchange student program (domestic); Honors program; Independent study; Internships; Liberal arts/career combination; Student-designed major; Study abroad; Teacher certification program. Honors programs: The Honors Program offers special curricular, co-curricular, and extra curricular opportunities for our college's most academically talented students. Benefits include priority registration, honors courses, field trips,undergraduate research,housing, and select study abroad options. Combined degree programs: BA/MA. **Disability Services offered to physically disabled students:** Note-taking services; Reader services; Tape recorders; Tutors. **Career services:** Alumni network; Alumni services; Career assessment; Career/job search classes; Internships

FACILITIES

Housing: Apartments for single students; Coed dorms; Special housing for disabled student; Theme housing; Wellness housing 95% of campus accessible to physically diasbled. **Special Academic Facilities/Equipment:** Art gallery, anthropology museum, ecology museum, three performance halls, theatre, synthesizer music studios, planetarium, electron microscope, nuclear magnetic resonator, seismograph. **Computers:** 20% of classrooms, 100% of dorms, 100% of libraries, 100% of dining areas, 100% of student union, 40% of common outdoor areas have wireless network access. Students can register for classes online. Administrative functions (other than registration) can be performed online.

CAMPUS LIFE

Environment: Village **Activities:** Campus Ministries; Choral groups; Concert band; Dance; Drama/theater; International Student Organization; Jazz band; Literary magazine; Music ensembles; Musical theater; Opera; Pep band; Radio station; Student government; Student newspaper; Symphony orchestra 100 registered organizations, 17 honor societies, 3 religious organizations. 4 fraternities, 7 sororities. **Athletics (Intercollegiate):** *Men:* basketball, cross-country, diving, equestrian sports, golf, ice hockey, lacrosse, soccer, swimming. *Women:* basketball, cross-country, diving, equestrian sports, ice hockey, lacrosse, soccer, softball, swimming, tennis, volleyball. **On-Campus Highlights:** Performing Arts Center, Maxcy Hall Athletic Complex, Barrington Student Union, The Art Museum at SUNY Potsdam, The Crane School of Music **Environmental Initiatives:** Promote sustainability education through eco rep program

ADMISSIONS

Freshman Academic Profile: Average high school GPA 87.0. 6% in top 10% of high school class, 35% in top 25% of high school class, 59% in top 50% of high school class. 94% from public high schools. **Test Scores:** SAT Math middle 50% range 500-590. SAT EBRW middle 50% range 500-600. ACT middle 50% range 20-26. Minimum internet-based TOEFL 79. Minimum paper TOEFL 550. **Basis for Candidate Selection:** *Important factors considered include:* rigor of secondary school record, academic GPA, application essay, recommendation(s). *Other factors considered include:* standardized test scores, interview, extracurricular activities, talent/ability, character/personal qualities, volunteer work, work experience, level of applicant's interest. **Freshman Admission Requirements:** High school diploma is required and GED is accepted *Academic units required:* 4 English, 4 social studies, *Academic units recommended:* 4 English, 3 math, 3 science, 3 foreign language, 4 social studies, 1 visual/performing arts. **Freshman Admission Statistics:** 5,581 applied, 66.6% admitted, 21% enrolled. **Transfer Admission Requirements:** college transcript(s), Minimum college GPA of 2.0 required. Lowest grade transferable D. **General Admission Information:** Application fee $50. Nonfall registration accepted. Admission may be deferred for a maximum of 1 year.

COSTS AND FINANCIAL AID

Average book expense $1,340. **Required Forms and Deadlines:** FAFSA; State aid form. **Notification of Awards:** Applicants will be notified of awards on a rolling basis beginning 1/1. **Types of Aid:** *Need-based scholarships/grants:* College/university scholarship or grant aid from institutional funds; Federal Pell; Private scholarships; SEOG; State scholarships/grants. *Loans:* Direct PLUS loans; Direct Subsidized Stafford Loans; Direct Unsubsidized Stafford Loans. *Student Employment:* Federal Work-Study Program available. Institutional employment available. **Financial Aid Statistics:** 91% needy freshmen, 83% needy undergrads receive need-based scholarship or grant aid. 40% freshmen, 36% undergrads receive non-need-based scholarship or grant aid. 89% freshmen, 87% undergrads receive need-based self-help aid. 0% freshmen, 0% undergrads receive athletic scholarships. 97% freshmen, 81% undergrads receive any aid. 79% undergrads borrow to pay for school. Average cumulative indebtedness $28,582. **Criteria for awarding aid:** *Non-need-based:* Academics, Art, Leadership, Music/drama.

STATE UNIVERSITY OF NEW YORK— PURCHASE COLLEGE

735 Anderson Hill Road, Purchase, NY
Phone: 914-251-6300
E-mail: admissions@purchase.edu • **CEEB Code:** 2878
Fax: 914-251-6314 • **Website:** www.purchase.edu • **ACT Code:** 2931

This public school was founded in 1967. It has a 550 acre campus.

RATINGS

Admissions Selectivity Rating: 87   **Fire Safety Rating:** 60*   **Green Rating:** 60*

STUDENTS AND FACULTY

Enrollment: 2,498. **Student Body:** 32% female, 68% male, 15% out-of-state, 3% international (39 countries represented). Asian 4%, African American 12%, Caucasian 53%, Hispanic 22%, Native American <1%, Pacific Islander <1%, Two or more races 5%, Race unknown 1%.
Retention and Graduation: 83% freshmen return for sophomore year.
Faculty: Student/faculty ratio 14:1. 174 full-time faculty, 49% hold PhDs, 18% are members of minority groups, 52% are women. 1% of classes are taught by teaching assistants.

ACADEMICS

Degrees: Bachelor's; Certificate; Master's; Post-Bachelor's certificate; Post-Master's certificate **Classes:** Most classes have 20-29 students. **Most popular majors:** Liberal Arts And Sciences/Liberal Studies; Psychology; Arts, Entertainment,And Media Management. **Special Study Options:** Cross-registration; Distance learning; Double major; English as a Second Language (ESL); Independent study; Internships; Liberal arts/career combination; Student-designed major; Study abroad. **Disability Services offered to physically disabled students:** Note-taking services; Reader services; Tape recorders; Tutors. **Career services:** Alumni services; Career assessment; Career/job search classes; Internships

FACILITIES

Housing: Apartments for married students; Apartments for single students; Coed dorms; Special housing for disabled student; Special housing for international students; Theme housing; Wellness housing 100% of campus accessible to physically diasbled. **Special Academic Facilities/Equipment:** Museum, four-theatre performing arts center, visual arts facility, children's center, recording studio, electron microscopes. **Computers:** Students can register for classes online. Administrative functions (other than registration) can be performed online.

CAMPUS LIFE

Environment: Town **Activities:** Choral groups; Dance; Drama/theater; International Student Organization; Jazz band; Literary magazine; Music ensembles; Musical theater; Radio station; Student government; Student newspaper; Student-run film society; Television station 30 registered organizations. **Athletics (Intercollegiate):** *Men:* baseball, basketball, cross-country, golf, soccer, tennis, volleyball. *Women:* basketball, cross-country, soccer, softball, tennis, volleyball. **On-Campus Highlights:** The Performing Arts Center, The Neuberger Museum, State-of-the-Art Athletic Complex, Starbucks, Fort Awesome **Environmental Initiatives:** Commited to reduce GHG emissions by 80% by 2050 (Presidents Climate Commitment)

ADMISSIONS

Freshman Academic Profile: Average high school GPA 3.2. **Test Scores:** SAT Math middle 50% range 490-570. SAT EBRW middle 50% range 530-630. ACT middle 50% range 20-26. Minimum paper TOEFL 550. **Basis for Candidate Selection:** *Very important factors considered include:* academic GPA, application essay, talent/ability. *Important factors considered include:* rigor of secondary school record. *Other factors considered include:* class rank, standardized test scores, recommendation(s), interview, extracurricular activities, character/personal qualities. **Freshman Admission Requirements:** High school diploma is required and GED is accepted *Academic units recommended:* 4 English, 4 math, 3 science, 3 foreign language, 4 social studies, 2 academic electives. **Freshman Admission Statistics:** 5,841 applied, 51.9% admitted, 25% enrolled. **Transfer Admission Requirements:** college transcript(s), Minimum college GPA of 3.0 required. Lowest grade transferable D. **General Admission Information:** Application fee $50. Priority deadline 3/1. Regular application deadline 7/15. Nonfall registration accepted. Admission may be deferred.

COSTS AND FINANCIAL AID

Annual in-state tuition $13,334. Annual out-of-state tuition $16,320. Room and board $13,334. Required fees $1,828. Average book expense $1,250. **Required Forms and Deadlines:** FAFSA; State aid form. **Notification of Awards:** Applicants will be notified of awards on a rolling basis beginning 3/1. **Types of Aid:** *Need-based scholarships/grants:* College/university scholarship or grant aid from institutional funds; Federal Pell; Private scholarships; SEOG; State scholarships/grants. *Loans:* Direct PLUS loans; Direct Subsidized Stafford Loans; Direct Unsubsidized Stafford Loans. *Student Employment:* Federal Work-Study Program available. Institutional employment available. **Financial Aid Statistics:** 98% needy freshmen, 98% needy undergrads receive need-based scholarship or grant aid. 14% freshmen, 17% undergrads receive non-need-based scholarship or grant aid. 93% freshmen, 92% undergrads receive need-based self-help aid. 0% freshmen, 0% undergrads receive athletic scholarships. 68% undergrads borrow to pay for school. Average cumulative indebtedness $31,188. **Criteria for awarding aid:** *Need-based:* Academics, Art, Minority status, Music/drama *Non-need-based:* Academics, Art, Minority status, Music/drama.

STATE UNIVERSITY OF NEW YORK— STONY BROOK UNIVERSITY

Office of Admissions, Stony Brook, NY 11794-1901
Phone: 631-632-6868 • **Financial Aid Phone:** 631-632-6840
E-mail: enroll@stonybrook.edu • **CEEB Code:** 2548
Fax: 631-632-9898 • **Website:** www.stonybrook.edu/ • **ACT Code:** 2952

This public school was founded in 1957. It has a 1450 acre campus.

RATINGS

Admissions Selectivity Rating: 91   **Fire Safety Rating:** 91   **Green Rating:** 96

STUDENTS AND FACULTY

Enrollment: 17,215. **Student Body:** 47% female, 53% male, 6% out-of-state, 14% international (130 countries represented). Asian 24%, African American 7%, Caucasian 33%, Hispanic 12%, Native American <1%, Pacific Islander <1%, Two or more races 3%, Race unknown 6%.
Retention and Graduation: 90% freshmen return for sophomore year. 53% freshmen graduate within 4 years. 72% freshmen graduate within 6 years. 31% grads go on to further study within 1 year. **Faculty:** Student/faculty ratio 18:1. 1,075 full-time faculty, 91% hold PhDs, 21% are members of minority groups, 38% are women.

ACADEMICS

Degrees: Bachelor's; Doctoral; Doctoral/Professional; Doctoral/Research; Master's; Post-Bachelor's certificate; Post-Master's certificate **Classes:** Most classes have 20-29 students. Most lab/discussion sessions have 20-29 students. **Most popular majors:** Biology/Biological Sciences, General; Psychology; Health Services/Allied Health/Health Sciences, General. **Special Study Options:** Cooperative education program; Cross-registration; Distance learning; Double major; Dual enrollment; English as a Second Language (ESL); Exchange student program (domestic); Honors program; Independent study; Internships; Liberal arts/career combination; Student-designed major; Study abroad; Teacher certification program; Weekend college. Honors programs: BA/MD Combined degree programs: BA/MA. **Disability Services offered to physically disabled students:** Note-taking services; Reader services; Tape recorders; Tutors. **Career services:** Alumni network; Alumni services; Career assessment; Career/job search classes; Internships; Regional alumni

FACILITIES

Housing: Apartments for married students; Apartments for single students; Coed dorms; Wellness housing 75% of campus accessible to physically diasbled. **Special Academic Facilities/Equipment:** SAC Gallery, Staller Gallery, Wang Center, Tabler Center for the Arts **Computers:** 50% of classrooms, 50% of dorms, 50% of libraries, 50% of dining areas, 50% of student union, 50% of common outdoor areas have wireless network access. Students can register for classes online. Administrative functions (other than registration) can be performed online.

CAMPUS LIFE

Environment: Town **Activities:** Campus Ministries; Choral groups; Concert band; Dance; Drama/theater; International Student Organization; Jazz band;

Literary magazine; Marching band; Model UN; Music ensembles; Musical theater; Opera; Pep band; Radio station; Student government; Student newspaper; Student-run film society; Symphony orchestra; Television station 292 registered organizations, 6 honor societies, 25 religious organizations. 17 fraternities, 16 sororities. **Athletics (Intercollegiate):** *Men:* baseball, basketball, cross-country, diving, football, lacrosse, soccer, swimming, tennis, track/field (outdoor), track/field (indoor). *Women:* basketball, cross-country, diving, lacrosse, soccer, softball, swimming, tennis, track/field (outdoor), track/field (indoor), volleyball. **On-Campus Highlights:** Staller Center for the Arts, Sports Complex and Lavalle Stadium, Student Activities Center, Walter J. Hawrys Campus Recreation Center, The Charles B. Wang Center **Environmental Initiatives:** Commitment to obtain carbon neutrality by 2050.

ADMISSIONS

Freshman Academic Profile: Average high school GPA 3.8. 48% in top 10% of high school class, 81% in top 25% of high school class, 95% in top 50% of high school class. 90% from public high schools. **Test Scores:** SAT Math middle 50% range 620-730. SAT EBRW middle 50% range 590-680. ACT middle 50% range 26-31. Minimum internet-based TOEFL 80. Minimum paper TOEFL 550. **Basis for Candidate Selection:** *Very important factors considered include:* rigor of secondary school record, academic GPA, standardized test scores. *Important factors considered include:* application essay, recommendation(s). *Other factors considered include:* class rank, interview, extracurricular activities, talent/ability, character/personal qualities, first generation, alumni/ae relation, geographical residence, state residency, volunteer work, work experience, level of applicant's interest. **Freshman Admission Requirements:** High school diploma is required and GED is accepted *Academic units required:* 4 English, 4 math, 4 science, 4 social studies, *Academic units recommended:* 4 English, 4 math, 4 science, 3 foreign language, 4 social studies. **Freshman Admission Statistics:** 35,313 applied, 42.2% admitted, 21% enrolled. **Transfer Admission Requirements:** college transcript(s), Minimum college GPA of 3.0 required. Lowest grade transferable C. **General Admission Information:** Application fee $50. Priority deadline 1/15. Nonfall registration accepted. Admission may be deferred for a maximum of 2 semesters.

COSTS AND FINANCIAL AID

Annual in-state tuition $13,446. Annual out-of-state tuition $24,180. Room and board $13,446. Required fees $2,587. Average book expense $900. **Required Forms and Deadlines:** FAFSA; State aid form. **Notification of Awards:** Applicants will be notified of awards on a rolling basis beginning 4/1. **Types of Aid:** *Need-based scholarships/grants:* College/university scholarship or grant aid from institutional funds; Federal Pell; Private scholarships; SEOG; State scholarships/grants. *Loans:* Direct PLUS loans; Direct Subsidized Stafford Loans; Direct Unsubsidized Stafford Loans. *Student Employment:* Federal Work-Study Program available. Institutional employment available. **Financial Aid Statistics:** 89% needy freshmen, 84% needy undergrads receive need-based scholarship or grant aid. 12% freshmen, 5% undergrads receive non-need-based scholarship or grant aid. 89% freshmen, 91% undergrads receive need-based self-help aid. 2% freshmen, 1% undergrads receive athletic scholarships. 76% freshmen, 69% undergrads receive any aid. 55% undergrads borrow to pay for school. Average cumulative indebtedness $24,656. **Criteria for awarding aid:** *Need-based:* Academics, Leadership, Minority status *Non-need-based:* Academics, Alumni affiliation, Art, Athletics, Job skills, Leadership, Music/drama.

STATE UNIVERSITY OF NEW YORK— UNIVERSITY AT ALBANY

1400 Washington Avenue, Albany, NY 12222
Phone: 518-442-5435 • **Financial Aid Phone:** (518) 442-3202
E-mail: ugadmissions@albany.edu • **CEEB Code:** 2532
Fax: 518-442-5383 • **Website:** www.albany.edu • **ACT Code:** 2926

This public school was founded in 1844. It has a 795 acre campus.

RATINGS

Admissions Selectivity Rating: 85   **Fire Safety Rating:** 90   **Green Rating:** 94

STUDENTS AND FACULTY

Enrollment: 13,320. **Student Body:** 51% female, 49% male, 5% out-of-state, 5% international (84 countries represented). Asian 8%, African American 19%, Caucasian 45%, Hispanic 17%, Native American <1%, Pacific Islander <1%, Two or more races 3%, Race unknown 2%.
Retention and Graduation: 83% freshmen return for sophomore year. 56% freshmen graduate within 4 years. 65% freshmen graduate within 6 years.
Faculty: Student/faculty ratio 19:1. 676 full-time faculty, 95% hold PhDs, 22%

are members of minority groups, 41% are women. 10% of classes are taught by teaching assistants.

ACADEMICS

Degrees: Bachelor's; Doctoral/Research; Master's; Post-Bachelor's certificate; Post-Master's certificate **Classes:** Most classes have 20-29 students. Most lab/discussion sessions have 10-19 students. **Most popular majors:** English Language And Literature, General; Psychology, General; Business Administration And Management, General. **Special Study Options:** Accelerated program; Cross-registration; Distance learning; Double major; Dual enrollment; English as a Second Language (ESL); Honors program; Independent study; Internships; Liberal arts/career combination; Student-designed major; Study abroad. Honors programs: Our Presidential Scholars program combines merit scholarships, honors courses, priority registration, special housing, and faculty mentor opportunities. Combined degree programs: BA/JD; BA/MA; BA/MEng. **Disability Services offered to physically disabled students:** Tutors. **Career services:** Alumni network; Alumni services; Career assessment; Career/job search classes; Internships; Regional alumni

FACILITIES

Housing: Coed dorms; Special housing for international students; Theme housing; Wellness housing 99% of campus accessible to physically diasbled. **Special Academic Facilities/Equipment:** Performing Arts Center, Art Museum, art and dance studios, sculpture foundry, nuclear accelerator and advanced materials facilities, a peptide synthesis facility, recombinatnt DNA sequencing laboratories, and atmospheric science's Whiteface Mountain observational facility. **Computers:** 75% of classrooms, 100% of dorms, 100% of libraries, 75% of dining areas, 100% of student union, 75% of common outdoor areas have wireless network access. Students can register for classes online. Administrative functions (other than registration) can be performed online.

CAMPUS LIFE

Environment: City **Activities:** Campus Ministries; Choral groups; Concert band; Dance; Drama/theater; International Student Organization; Jazz band; Literary magazine; Model UN; Music ensembles; Musical theater; Pep band; Radio station; Student government; Student newspaper; Student-run film society; Symphony orchestra; Television station; Yearbook 200 registered organizations, 20 honor societies, 17 religious organizations. 11 fraternities, 18 sororities. **Athletics (Intercollegiate):** *Men:* baseball, basketball, cross-country, football, lacrosse, soccer, track/field (outdoor), track/field (indoor). *Women:* basketball, cross-country, field hockey, golf, lacrosse, soccer, softball, tennis, track/field (outdoor), track/field (indoor), volleyball. **On-Campus Highlights:** Campus Center with bookstore, cafes, and lounges, SEFCU Arena, Science Library /Main Library, Performing Arts Center, University Art Museum **Environmental Initiatives:** energy conservation

ADMISSIONS

Freshman Academic Profile: Average high school GPA 3.2. 16% in top 10% of high school class, 48% in top 25% of high school class, 82% in top 50% of high school class. **Test Scores:** SAT Math middle 50% range 500-590. SAT EBRW middle 50% range 500-600. ACT middle 50% range 22-26. Minimum internet-based TOEFL 79. Minimum paper TOEFL 550. **Basis for Candidate Selection:** *Very important factors considered include:* rigor of secondary school record, class rank, academic GPA, standardized test scores, recommendation(s), character/personal qualities. *Important factors considered include:* application essay. *Other factors considered include:* extracurricular activities, talent/ability, first generation, alumni/ae relation, geographical residence, volunteer work, work experience, level of applicant's interest. **Freshman Admission Requirements:** High school diploma is required and GED is accepted *Academic units required:* 4 English, 2 math, 2 science, 2 science labs, 1 foreign language, 3 social studies, 2 history, 4 academic electives, *Academic units recommended:* 4 math, 3 science, 3 science labs, 3 foreign language. **Freshman Admission Statistics:** 24,887 applied, 54.0% admitted, 21% enrolled. **Transfer Admission Requirements:** college transcript(s), essay or personal statement, statement of good standing from prior institution(s). Minimum college GPA of 2.5 required. Lowest grade transferable C. **General Admission Information:** Application fee $50. Priority deadline 3/1. Regular application deadline 3/1. Nonfall registration accepted. Admission may be deferred for a maximum of 1 year.

COSTS AND FINANCIAL AID

Annual in-state tuition $13,864. Annual out-of-state tuition $21,550. Room and board $13,864. Required fees $2,820. Average book expense $1,000. **Required Forms and Deadlines:** FAFSA. **Notification of Awards:** Applicants will be notified of awards on a rolling basis beginning 3/2. **Types of Aid:** *Need-based scholarships/grants:* College/university scholarship or grant aid from institutional funds; Federal Pell; Private scholarships; SEOG; State scholarships/grants. *Loans:* Direct PLUS loans; Direct Subsidized Stafford Loans; Direct Unsubsidized Stafford Loans. *Student Employment:* Federal Work-Study Program available. Institutional employment available. **Financial Aid Statistics:** 84% needy freshmen, 84% needy undergrads receive need-based scholarship or grant aid. 3% freshmen, 2% undergrads receive non-need-based scholarship or grant aid. 79% freshmen, 81% undergrads receive need-based self-help aid. 2% freshmen, 2% undergrads receive athletic scholarships. 64% freshmen, 57% undergrads receive any aid. **Criteria for awarding aid:** *Non-need-based:* Academics, Athletics, State/district residency.

STATE UNIVERSITY OF NEW YORK— UNIVERSITY AT BUFFALO

University at Buffalo, Buffalo, NY 14260-1660
Phone: 716-645-6900 • **Financial Aid Phone:** 716-645-2450
E-mail: ub-admissions@buffalo.edu • **CEEB Code:** 2925
Fax: 716-645-6411 • **Website:** www.buffalo.edu • **ACT Code:** 2978

This public school was founded in 1846. It has a 1346 acre campus.

RATINGS

Admissions Selectivity Rating: 86   **Fire Safety Rating:** 62   **Green Rating:** 98

STUDENTS AND FACULTY

Enrollment: 20,735. **Student Body:** 43% female, 57% male, 2% out-of-state, 16% international (87 countries represented). Asian 15%, African American 8%, Caucasian 48%, Hispanic 7%, Native American <1%, Pacific Islander <1%, Two or more races 2%, Race unknown 4%.
Retention and Graduation: 87% freshmen return for sophomore year. 57% freshmen graduate within 4 years. 75% freshmen graduate within 6 years.
Faculty: Student/faculty ratio 13:1. 1,283 full-time faculty, 98% hold PhDs, 28% are members of minority groups, 39% are women.

ACADEMICS

Degrees: Bachelor's; Certificate; Doctoral; Doctoral/Professional; Doctoral/Research; Master's; Post-Master's certificate Classes: Most classes have 10-19 students. Most lab/discussion sessions have 10-19 students. **Most popular majors:** Engineering, General; Social Sciences, General; Business Administration And Management, General. Special Study Options: Accelerated program; Cooperative education program; Cross-registration; Distance learning; Double major; Dual enrollment; English as a Second Language (ESL); Exchange student program (domestic); External degree program; Honors program; Independent study; Internships; Liberal arts/career combination; Student-designed major; Study abroad; Teacher certification program. **Honors programs:** There is a University Honors College as well as honors programs within the majors. Undergraduate research is an option in a variety of disciplines and often affords the student an opportunity to participate in cutting-edge research activities. See website: http://honors.buffalo.edu Combined degree programs: BA/MA. Disability Services offered to physically disabled students: Note-taking services; Reader services; Tape recorders; Tutors. Career services: Alumni network; Alumni services; Career/job search classes; Internships

FACILITIES

Housing: Apartments for married students; Apartments for single students; Coed dorms; Special housing for disabled student; Special housing for international students; Theme housing 90% of campus accessible to physically diasbled. **Special Academic Facilities/Equipment:** UB Art Gallery at the Center for the Arts, Slee Concert Hall, Marian E. White Anthropology Research Museum, The School of Pharmacy and Pharmaceutical Sciences Apothecary and Historical Exhibits, The Museum of Radiology and Medical Physics, The Museum of Neuroanatomy, Anderson Gallery, New York State Center of Excellence in Bioinformatics & Life Sciences (CBLS), Center for Computational Research (CCR), Center of Excellence for Document Analysis and Recognition (CEDAR), Center of Excellence in Materials Informatics, Buffalo Clinical and Translational Research Center (CTRC), New York State Center for Engineering Design and Industrial Innovation (NYSCEDII), Electronic Poetry Center, The Archaeological Survey, and numerous research centers. **Computers:** Students can register for classes online. Administrative functions (other than registration) can be performed online.

CAMPUS LIFE

Environment: City **Activities:** Campus Ministries; Choral groups; Concert band; Dance; Drama/theater; International Student Organization; Jazz band; Marching band; Model UN; Music ensembles; Musical theater; Opera; Pep band; Radio station; Student government; Student newspaper; Student-run film society; Symphony orchestra; Television station 215 registered organizations, 29 honor societies, 35 religious organizations. 22 fraternities, 17 sororities.
Athletics (Intercollegiate): *Men:* baseball, basketball, cross-country, football, soccer, swimming, tennis, track/field (outdoor), wrestling. *Women:* basketball, crew/rowing, cross-country, soccer, softball, swimming, tennis, track/field (outdoor), volleyball. **On-Campus Highlights:** Center for the Arts, Alumni

Arena and Athletic Stadium, Center for Computational Research, Apartment style student housing, The Commons (on-campus shopping)

ADMISSIONS

Freshman Academic Profile: Average high school GPA 3.6. 38% in top 10% of high school class, 73% in top 25% of high school class, 94% in top 50% of high school class. **Test Scores:** SAT Math middle 50% range 580-670. SAT EBRW middle 50% range 560-640. ACT middle 50% range 24-28. Minimum internet-based TOEFL 79. Minimum paper TOEFL 550. **Basis for Candidate Selection:** *Very important factors considered include:* rigor of secondary school record, academic GPA, standardized test scores. *Important factors considered include:* class rank, recommendation(s), interview. *Other factors considered include:* application essay, extracurricular activities, talent/ability, character/personal qualities, first generation, geographical residence, racial/ethnic status, volunteer work, work experience. **Freshman Admission Requirements:** High school diploma is required and GED is accepted *Academic units recommended:* 4 English, 3 math, 3 science, 3 foreign language, 4 social studies. **Freshman Admission Statistics:** 28,088 applied, 57.4% admitted, 26% enrolled. **Transfer Admission Requirements:** High school transcript, college transcript(s), essay or personal statement, Minimum college GPA of 2.5 required. Lowest grade transferable D. **General Admission Information:** Application fee $50. Priority deadline 11/15. Nonfall registration accepted.

COSTS AND FINANCIAL AID

Required Forms and Deadlines: FAFSA. **Notification of Awards:** Applicants will be notified of awards on a rolling basis beginning 2/1. **Types of Aid:** *Need-based scholarships/grants:* College/university scholarship or grant aid from institutional funds; Federal Nursing Scholarships; Federal Pell; Private scholarships; SEOG; State scholarships/grants. *Loans:* Direct PLUS loans; Direct Subsidized Stafford Loans; Direct Unsubsidized Stafford Loans. *Student Employment:* Federal Work-Study Program available. Institutional employment available. **Financial Aid Statistics:** 85% needy freshmen, 76% needy undergrads receive need-based scholarship or grant aid. 36% freshmen, 22% undergrads receive non-need-based scholarship or grant aid. 72% freshmen, 79% undergrads receive need-based self-help aid. 0% freshmen, 0% undergrads receive athletic scholarships. 65% freshmen, 64% undergrads receive any aid. **Criteria for awarding aid:** *Need-based:* Academics, Minority status, Music/drama *Non-need-based:* Academics, Art, Athletics, Minority status, Music/drama, State/district residency.

STATE UNIVERSITY OF NEW YORK—UPSTATE MEDICAL UNIVERSITY

766 Irving Avenue, Syracuse, NY 13210
Phone: 315-464-4570 • **Financial Aid Phone:** 315-464-4329
E-mail: admiss@upstate.edu • **CEEB Code:** 2547
Fax: 315-464-8867 • **ACT Code:** 2981

This public school was founded in 1850. It has a 25 acre campus.

RATINGS

Admissions Selectivity Rating: 61   **Fire Safety Rating:** 85   **Green Rating:** 60*

STUDENTS AND FACULTY

Enrollment: 328. **Student Body:** 75% female, 25% male, 9% out-of-state, international.
Faculty: 43 full-time faculty, 60% hold PhDs, 2% are members of minority groups, 70% are women. 0% of classes are taught by teaching assistants.

ACADEMICS

Degrees: Bachelor's; Doctoral; Doctoral Other; Doctoral/Professional; Doctoral/Research; Master's; Post-Master's certificate **Classes:** Most classes have fewer than 10 students. **Special Study Options:** Accelerated program; Distance learning; Independent study; Internships. **Disability Services offered to physically disabled students:** Note-taking services; Reader services; Tape recorders; Tutors. **Career services:** Alumni network; Regional alumni

FACILITIES

Housing: Apartments for married students; Apartments for single students; Coed dorms 100% of campus accessible to physically diasbled. **Special Academic Facilities/Equipment:** 350 bed Tertiary Care Hospital **Computers:** Administrative functions (other than registration) can be performed online.

CAMPUS LIFE

Environment: City **Activities:** Dance; International Student Organization; Student government 51 registered organizations, 3 religious organizations. **On-**

Campus Highlights: Weiskotten Hall, Silverman Hall, University Hospital, Institute for Human Performance, Campus Activities Building

ADMISSIONS

Test Scores: Minimum paper TOEFL 550. **Freshman Admission Requirements:** High school diploma is required and GED is accepted **Transfer Admission Requirements:** High school transcript, college transcript(s), essay or personal statement, interview, Minimum college GPA of 2.0 required. Lowest grade transferable C-. **General Admission Information:** Application fee $50. Nonfall registration accepted. Admission may be deferred for a maximum of 1 year.

COSTS AND FINANCIAL AID

Annual in-state tuition $10,422. Annual out-of-state tuition $13,380. Room and board $10,422. Required fees $575. Average book expense $1,070. **Required Forms and Deadlines:** FAFSA. *Types of Aid: Need-based scholarships/grants:* College/university scholarship or grant aid from institutional funds; Federal Pell; Private scholarships; SEOG; State scholarships/grants. *Loans:* Direct PLUS loans; Direct Subsidized Stafford Loans; Direct Unsubsidized Stafford Loans. *Student Employment:* Federal Work-Study Program available. Institutional employment available. **Financial Aid Statistics:** 18% needy undergrads receive need-based scholarship or grant aid. 27% undergrads receive non-need-based scholarship or grant aid. 13% undergrads receive need-based self-help aid. 78% freshmen receive any aid. **Criteria for awarding aid:** *Need-based:* Academics.

STEPHENS COLLEGE

Best Colleges

1200 East Broadway, Columbia, MO 65215
Phone: 573-876-7207 • **Financial Aid Phone:** 573-876-7106
E-mail: apply@stephens.edu • **CEEB Code:** 6683
Fax: 573-876-7237 • **Website:** http://www.stephens.edu/ • **ACT Code:** 2374

This private school was founded in 1833. It has a 47 acre campus.

RATINGS

Admissions Selectivity Rating: 83   **Fire Safety Rating:** 84   **Green Rating:** 61

STUDENTS AND FACULTY

Enrollment: 724. **Student Body:** 99% female, 1% male, 37% out-of-state, <1% international (1 countries represented). Asian 2%, African American 13%, Caucasian 69%, Hispanic 4%, Native American 1%, Pacific Islander <1%, Two or more races 6%, Race unknown 4%.
Retention and Graduation: 69% freshmen return for sophomore year.
Faculty: Student/faculty ratio 9:1. 54 full-time faculty, 57% hold PhDs, 9% are members of minority groups, 74% are women. 0% of classes are taught by teaching assistants.

ACADEMICS

Degrees: Associate; Bachelor's; Master's; Post-Bachelor's certificate; Post-Master's certificate **Classes:** Most classes have 20-29 students. Most lab/discussion sessions have 20-29 students. **Most popular majors:** Biology/Biological Sciences, General; Fashion/Apparel Design; Health Services/Allied Health/Health Sciences, General. **Special Study Options:** Accelerated program; Cross-registration; Distance learning; Double major; Dual enrollment; External degree program; Honors program; Independent study; Internships; Liberal arts/career combination; Student-designed major; Study abroad; Teacher certification program. Combined degree programs: BA/JD; BA/MA. **Disability Services offered to physically disabled students:** Note-taking services; Tutors. **Career services:** Alumni network; Alumni services; Career assessment; Career/job search classes; Internships; Regional alumni

FACILITIES

Housing: Apartments for single students; Fraternity/sorority housing; Special housing for disabled student; Theme housing; Women's dorms 80% of campus accessible to physically disabled. **Special Academic Facilities/Equipment:** Art gallery and historical costume collections, on-campus preschool, kindergarten, and elementary school, language lab. **Computers:** 100% of classrooms, 100% of dorms, 100% of libraries, 100% of dining areas, 100% of student union, have wireless network access. Students can register for classes online. Administrative functions (other than registration) can be performed online.

CAMPUS LIFE

Environment: City **Activities:** Campus Ministries; Choral groups; Dance; Drama/theater; Literary magazine; Music ensembles; Musical theater; Radio station; Student government; Student newspaper; Student-run film society; Television station; Yearbook 28 registered organizations, 11 honor societies, 3 religious organizations. 2 sororities. **Athletics (Intercollegiate):** *Women:* basketball, cross-country, softball, swimming, tennis, volleyball. **On-Campus Highlights:** Kaldi's @ Stars Cafe, Pet Central, Student Union, Equestrian Stables, Macklanburg Playhouse **Environmental Initiatives:** Recycling

ADMISSIONS

Freshman Academic Profile: Average high school GPA 3.3. 14% in top 10% of high school class, 44% in top 25% of high school class, 79% in top 50% of high school class. 80% from public high schools. **Test Scores:** SAT Math middle 50% range 440-570. SAT EBRW middle 50% range 450-620. ACT middle 50% range 20-25. Minimum paper TOEFL 550. **Basis for Candidate Selection:** *Very important factors considered include:* rigor of secondary school record, academic GPA, standardized test scores. *Important factors considered include:* recommendation(s), extracurricular activities, talent/ability, character/personal qualities. *Other factors considered include:* class rank, application essay, interview, volunteer work, work experience, level of applicant's interest. **Freshman Admission Requirements:** High school diploma is required and GED is accepted *Academic units recommended:* 4 English, 3 math, 2 science, 2 foreign language, 1 social studies. **Freshman Admission Statistics:** 1,168 applied, 61.0% admitted, 22% enrolled. **Transfer Admission Requirements:** High school transcript, college transcript(s), essay or personal statement, Minimum college GPA of 2.0 required. Lowest grade transferable C-. **General Admission Information:** Application fee $50. Priority deadline 1/18. Nonfall registration accepted. Admission may be deferred for a maximum of 1 year.

COSTS AND FINANCIAL AID

Annual tuition $30,144. Room and board $10,424. Required fees $200. Average book expense $1,000. **Required Forms and Deadlines:** FAFSA. **Notification of Awards:** Applicants will be notified of awards on a rolling basis beginning 10/1. **Types of Aid:** *Need-based scholarships/grants:* College/university scholarship or grant aid from institutional funds; Federal Pell; Private scholarships; SEOG; State scholarships/grants. *Loans:* Direct PLUS loans; Direct Subsidized Stafford Loans; Direct Unsubsidized Stafford Loans. *Student Employment:* Federal Work-Study Program available. Institutional employment available. **Financial Aid Statistics:** 100% needy freshmen, 100% needy undergrads receive need-based scholarship or grant aid. 84% freshmen, 93% undergrads receive non-need-based scholarship or grant aid. 100% freshmen, 100% undergrads receive need-based self-help aid. 1% freshmen, 2% undergrads receive athletic scholarships. 100% freshmen, 99% undergrads receive any aid. 93% undergrads borrow to pay for school. Average cumulative indebtedness $9,238. **Criteria for awarding aid:** *Non-need-based:* Academics, Alumni affiliation, Athletics, Leadership, Music/drama, State/district residency.

STERLING COLLEGE

125 W. Cooper, Sterling, KS 67579
Phone: 620-278-4275 • **Financial Aid Phone:** 620-278-4207
E-mail: admissions@sterling.edu • **CEEB Code:** 6684
Fax: 620-869-9021 • **Website:** www.sterling.edu • **ACT Code:** 1466

This private school, affiliated with the Presbyterian Church, was founded in 1887. It has a 42 acre campus.

RATINGS

Admissions Selectivity Rating: 87   **Fire Safety Rating:** 71   **Green Rating:** 60*

STUDENTS AND FACULTY

Enrollment: 657. **Student Body:** 47% female, 53% male, 63% out-of-state, (6 countries represented). Asian 2%, African American 12%, Caucasian 66%, Hispanic 15%, Native American 3%, Race unknown 3%.
Retention and Graduation: 62% freshmen return for sophomore year.
Faculty: Student/faculty ratio 12:1. 40 full-time faculty, 45% hold PhDs, 15% are members of minority groups, 35% are women. 0% of classes are taught by teaching assistants.

ACADEMICS

Degrees: Bachelor's **Classes:** Most classes have 10-19 students. Most lab/discussion sessions have 10-19 students. **Most popular majors:** Elementary Education And Teaching; Health And Physical Education/Fitness, General; Business/Commerce, General. **Special Study Options:** Distance learning; Double major; Dual enrollment; Honors program; Independent study; Internships; Student-designed major; Study abroad; Teacher certification program. Honors programs: Honors level general education classes are offered in interdisciplinary history, literature, religious. **Disability Services offered to physically disabled students:** Tutors. **Career services:** Alumni network; Alumni services; Career assessment; Internships

FACILITIES

Housing: Men's dorms; Women's dorms 80% of campus accessible to physically disabled. **Special Academic Facilities/Equipment:** History/cultural museum within Mabee Library **Computers:** Administrative functions (other than registration) can be performed online.

CAMPUS LIFE

Environment: Rural **Activities:** Campus Ministries; Choral groups; Concert band; Drama/theater; Jazz band; Literary magazine; Music ensembles; Musical theater; Radio station; Student government; Student newspaper; Television station; Yearbook 16 registered organizations, 4 honor societies, 2 religious organizations. **Athletics (Intercollegiate):** *Men:* baseball, basketball, cross-country, football, golf, soccer, track/field (outdoor). *Women:* basketball, cheerleading, cross-country, golf, soccer, softball, track/field (outdoor), volleyball. **On-Campus Highlights:** Gleason Phy. Educ. Center, Student Union, Cooper Hall, Residence Halls, Various outdoor spaces

ADMISSIONS

Freshman Academic Profile: Average high school GPA 3.3. 8% in top 10% of high school class, 17% in top 25% of high school class, 45% in top 50% of high school class. 80% from public high schools. **Test Scores:** SAT Math middle 50% range 420-510. SAT EBRW middle 50% range 400-520. ACT middle 50% range 19-24. Minimum internet-based TOEFL 70. Minimum paper TOEFL 525. **Basis for Candidate Selection:** *Very important factors considered include:* rigor of secondary school record, standardized test scores, character/personal qualities. *Important factors considered include:* academic GPA, application essay, recommendation(s), interview, extracurricular activities, religious affiliation/commitment, volunteer work.level of applicant's interest. *Other factors considered include:* class rank, talent/ability, first generation, alumni/ae relation, work experience. **Freshman Admission Requirements:** High school diploma is required and GED is accepted *Academic units recommended:* 4 English, 3 math, 3 science, 2 science labs, 2 foreign language, 1 social studies, 2 history, 1 academic elective, 1 computer science, 1 unit from above areas or other academic areas. **Freshman Admission Statistics:** 1,118 applied, 41.4% admitted, 30% enrolled. **Transfer Admission Requirements:** college transcript(s), essay or personal statement, Minimum college GPA of 2.2 required. Lowest grade transferable C-. **General Admission Information:** Application fee $25. Priority deadline 3/1. Nonfall registration accepted. Admission may be deferred for a maximum of 1 semester.

COSTS AND FINANCIAL AID

Annual tuition $23,400. Room and board $8,580. Average book expense $700. **Required Forms and Deadlines:** FAFSA. **Notification of Awards:** Applicants will be notified of awards on a rolling basis beginning 1/1. **Types of Aid:** *Need-based scholarships/grants:* College/university scholarship or grant aid from institutional funds; Federal Pell; Private scholarships; SEOG; State scholarships/grants. *Loans: Student Employment:* Federal Work-Study Program available. Institutional employment available. **Financial Aid Statistics:** 0% freshmen, 0% undergrads receive athletic scholarships. 100% freshmen, 96% undergrads receive any aid. **Criteria for awarding aid:** *Non-need-based:* Academics, Art, Athletics, Leadership, Music/drama.

STERLING COLLEGE (VT)

P.O. Box 72, Craftsbury Common, VT 05827
Phone: 802-586-7711 • **Financial Aid Phone:** 802-586-7711 x 103
E-mail: admission@sterlingcollege.edu • **CEEB Code:** 3752
Fax: 802-586-2596 • **Website:** www.sterlingcollege.edu • **ACT Code:** 6946

This private school was founded in 1958. It has a 430 acre campus.

RATINGS

Admissions Selectivity Rating: 70   **Fire Safety Rating:** 94   **Green Rating:** 97

STUDENTS AND FACULTY

Enrollment: 121. **Student Body:** 49% female, 51% male, 80% out-of-state, 3% international (4 countries represented). Asian 1%, African American 4%, Caucasian 83%, Hispanic 2%, Native American 0%, Pacific Islander 0%, Two or more races 2%, Race unknown 6%.
Retention and Graduation: 52% freshmen return for sophomore year. 3% grads go on to further study within 1 year. 0% grads pursue arts and sciences degrees. 0% grads pursue law degrees. 0% grads pursue business degrees. 0% grads pursue medical degrees. **Faculty:** Student/faculty ratio 6:1. 18 full-time

faculty, 22% hold PhDs, 0% are members of minority groups, 50% are women. 0% of classes are taught by teaching assistants.

ACADEMICS

Degrees: Bachelor's **Most popular majors:** Agroecology And Sustainable Agriculture. **Special Study Options:** Double major; Dual enrollment; Exchange student program (domestic); Independent study; Internships; Student-designed major; Study abroad. **Disability Services offered to physically disabled students:** Tutors. **Career services:** Alumni network; Alumni services; Career assessment; Career/job search classes; Internships; Regional alumni

FACILITIES

Housing: Apartments for married students; Coed dorms; Cooperative housing; Theme housing; Wellness housing **Special Academic Facilities/Equipment:** Library serves as art gallery. There is a 6—8 week rotation of Vermont artist displays. Campus also includes wind and solar-powered barns that serves as an instructional facility and lab, a greenhouse provides a working lab for plant and soil studies. Other facilities include: a woodshop, logging shop, sugarhouse, root cellar, darkroom, certified organic gardens, and a 32' tall climbing wall provides students with the ability to develop leadership and technical rock-climbing skills. **Computers:** 100% of classrooms, 100% of dorms, 100% of libraries, 100% of dining areas, 100% of student union, 100% of common outdoor areas have wireless network access. Administrative functions (other than registration) can be performed online.

CAMPUS LIFE

Environment: Rural **Activities:** Choral groups; Dance; Drama/theater; Literary magazine; Music ensembles; Student government; Student-run film society. **On-Campus Highlights:** Houston House Gardens, Sterling College Farm, Dunbar Dining Hall, Edible Forest Garden, Brown Library **Environmental Initiatives:** Curriculum is completely devoted to environmental stewardship.

ADMISSIONS

Freshman Academic Profile: Average high school GPA 3.2. 20% in top 10% of high school class, 33% in top 25% of high school class, 74% in top 50% of high school class. 64% from public high schools. **Test Scores:** Minimum internet-based TOEFL 61. Minimum paper TOEFL 500. **Basis for Candidate Selection:** *Very important factors considered include:* rigor of secondary school record, academic GPA, application essay, recommendation(s), interview, level of applicant's interest. *Important factors considered include:* class rank, extracurricular activities, talent/ability, character/personal qualities, volunteer work. *Other factors considered include:* alumni/ae relation, geographical residence, work experience. **Freshman Admission Requirements:** High school diploma is required and GED is accepted *Academic units required:* 4 English, 3 math, 2 science, 2 science labs, 2 social studies, 2 history, *Academic units recommended:* 4 English, 4 math, 3 science, 3 science labs, 2 foreign language, 2 social studies, 2 history. **Freshman Admission Statistics:** 101 applied, 72.3% admitted, 55% enrolled. **Transfer Admission Requirements:** High school transcript, college transcript(s), essay or personal statement, Minimum college GPA of 2.0 required. Lowest grade transferable C. **General Admission Information:** Application fee $35. Regular application deadline 4/1. Nonfall registration accepted. Admission may be deferred for a maximum of One year.

COSTS AND FINANCIAL AID

Annual tuition $32,592. Room and board $8,796. Required fees $3,700. Average book expense $900. **Required Forms and Deadlines:** FAFSA; Institution's own financial aid form; State aid form. **Notification of Awards:** Applicants will be notified of awards on a rolling basis beginning 2/1. **Types of Aid:** *Need-based scholarships/grants:* College/university scholarship or grant aid from institutional funds; Federal Pell; Private scholarships; SEOG; State scholarships/grants. *Loans:* Direct PLUS loans; Direct Subsidized Stafford Loans; Direct Unsubsidized Stafford Loans. *Student Employment:* Federal Work-Study Program available. Institutional employment available. **Financial Aid Statistics:** 100% needy freshmen, 100% needy undergrads receive need-based scholarship or grant aid. 22% undergrads receive non-need-based scholarship or grant aid. 100% freshmen, 100% undergrads receive need-based self-help aid. 0% freshmen, 0% undergrads receive athletic scholarships. 100% freshmen, 100% undergrads receive any aid. **Criteria for awarding aid:** *Need-based:* Academics, Leadership *Non-need-based:* Academics, Leadership, State/district residency.

STETSON UNIVERSITY

Best Colleges

421 North Woodland Boulevard, DeLand, FL 32723
Phone: 386-822-7100 • **Financial Aid Phone:** 800-688-7120
E-mail: admissions@stetson.edu • **CEEB Code:** 5630
Fax: 386-822-7112 • **Website:** stetson.edu • **ACT Code:** 756

This private school was founded in 1883. It has a 159 acre campus.

RATINGS

Admissions Selectivity Rating: 82   **Fire Safety Rating:** 81   **Green Rating:** 78

STUDENTS AND FACULTY

Enrollment: 3,047. **Student Body:** 57% female, 43% male, 27% out-of-state, 6% international (50 countries represented). Asian 2%, African American 8%, Caucasian 61%, Hispanic 16%, Native American <1%, Pacific Islander <1%, Two or more races 4%, Race unknown 2%.
Retention and Graduation: 78% freshmen return for sophomore year. 55% freshmen graduate within 4 years. 62% freshmen graduate within 6 years. 20% grads go on to further study within 1 year. 12% grads pursue arts and sciences degrees. 3% grads pursue law degrees. 3% grads pursue business degrees. 1% grads pursue medical degrees. **Faculty:** Student/faculty ratio 13:1. 268 full-time faculty, 94% hold PhDs, 17% are members of minority groups, 48% are women. 0% of classes are taught by teaching assistants.

ACADEMICS

Degrees: Bachelor's; Doctoral/Professional; Master's; Post-Master's certificate
Classes: Most classes have 10-19 students. Most lab/discussion sessions have 10-19 students. **Most popular majors:** Psychology, General; Health Services/Allied Health/Health Sciences, General. **Special Study Options:** Accelerated program; Distance learning; Double major; Honors program; Independent study; Internships; Liberal arts/career combination; Student-designed major; Study abroad; Teacher certification program: Honors programs: Stetson University Honors Program Combined degree programs: BA/JD. **Disability Services offered to physically disabled students:** Note-taking services; Reader services; Tape recorders; Tutors. **Career services:** Alumni network; Alumni services; Career assessment; Career/job search classes; Internships; Regional alumni

FACILITIES

Housing: Apartments for married students; Apartments for single students; Coed dorms; Fraternity/sorority housing; Men's dorms; Theme housing; Wellness housing; Women's dorms 77% of campus accessible to physically diasbled. **Special Academic Facilities/Equipment:** Language lab, art gallery, greenhouse with growth chambers, mineral museum, electron microscopes. **Computers:** 90% of classrooms, 100% of dorms, 100% of libraries, 95% of dining areas, 100% of student union, 30% of common outdoor areas have wireless network access. Students can register for classes online. Administrative functions (other than registration) can be performed online.

CAMPUS LIFE

Environment: Town **Activities:** Campus Ministries; Choral groups; Concert band; Dance; Drama/theater; International Student Organization; Jazz band; Literary magazine; Marching band; Music ensembles; Musical theater; Opera; Pep band; Radio station; Student government; Student newspaper; Student-run film society; Symphony orchestra 125 registered organizations, 24 honor societies, 8 religious organizations. 6 fraternities, 5 sororities. **Athletics (Intercollegiate):** Men: baseball, basketball, crew/rowing, cross-country, golf, soccer, tennis. Women: basketball, crew/rowing, cross-country, golf, soccer, softball, tennis, volleyball. **On-Campus Highlights:** Palm Court, Stetson Coffee Shop, Hollis Center, DuPont-Ball Library/Student Success Center, Lynn Business Center **Environmental Initiatives:** The Stetson College of Law is home to the Institute for Biodiversity Law and Policy. The Institute serves as an interdisciplinary focal point for education, research and service activities related to biodiversity issues, and is committed to environmental education and service from the local to the global scale. Each semester, the Institute sponsors several biodiversity lectures.

ADMISSIONS

Freshman Academic Profile: Average high school GPA 3.8. 22% in top 10% of high school class, 50% in top 25% of high school class, 84% in top 50% of high school class. **Test Scores:** SAT Math middle 50% range 540-640. SAT EBRW middle 50% range 570-650. ACT middle 50% range 23-29. Minimum internet-based TOEFL 79. Minimum paper TOEFL 550. **Basis for Candidate Selection:** *Very important factors considered:* rigor of

secondary school record, academic GPA. *Important factors considered include:* class rank, application essay, standardized test scores, recommendation(s), interview, extracurricular activities, talent/ability, character/personal qualities, volunteer work, work experience. *Other factors considered include:* alumni/ae relation, geographical residence, state residency, racial/ethnic status. **Freshman Admission Requirements:** High school diploma is required and GED is accepted *Academic units required:* 4 English, 3 math, 3 science, 2 foreign language, 2 social studies. **Freshman Admission Statistics:** 11,732 applied, 67.8% admitted, 11% enrolled. **Transfer Admission Requirements:** High school transcript, college transcript(s), essay or personal statement, standardized test scores, statement of good standing from prior institution(s). Minimum college GPA of 2.0 required. Lowest grade transferable C. **General Admission Information:** Application fee $50. Priority deadline 12/1. Nonfall registration accepted. Admission may be deferred.

COSTS AND FINANCIAL AID

Annual tuition $45,670. Room and board $13,052. Required fees $360. Average book expense $1,200. **Required Forms and Deadlines:** FAFSA. **Notification of Awards:** Applicants will be notified of awards on a rolling basis beginning 3/1. **Types of Aid:** *Need-based scholarships/grants:* College/university scholarship or grant aid from institutional funds; Federal Pell; Private scholarships; SEOG; State scholarships/grants. *Loans:* Direct PLUS loans; Direct Subsidized Stafford Loans; Direct Unsubsidized Stafford Loans. *Student Employment:* Federal Work-Study Program available. Institutional employment available. **Financial Aid Statistics:** 100% needy freshmen, 99% needy undergrads receive need-based scholarship or grant aid. 19% freshmen, 16% undergrads receive non-need-based scholarship or grant aid. 74% freshmen, 75% undergrads receive need-based self-help aid. 3% freshmen, 4% undergrads receive athletic scholarships. 100% freshmen, 99% undergrads receive any aid. 70% undergrads borrow to pay for school. Average cumulative indebtedness $31,457. **Criteria for awarding aid:** *Need-based:* Academics, Alumni affiliation, Art, Athletics, Leadership, Minority status, Music/drama, Religious affiliation *Non-need-based:* Academics, Alumni affiliation, Art, Athletics, Leadership, Minority status, Music/drama, Religious affiliation, State/district residency.

STEVENS INSTITUTE OF TECHNOLOGY

Best Colleges

Castle Point on Hudson, Hoboken, NJ 07030
Phone: 201-216-5194 • **Financial Aid Phone:** 201-216-8142
E-mail: admissions@stevens.edu • **CEEB Code:** 2819
Fax: 201-216-8348 • **Website:** http://www.stevens.edu/princetonreview • **ACT Code:** 2610

This private school was founded in 1870. It has a 55 acre campus.

RATINGS

Admissions Selectivity Rating: 95   **Fire Safety Rating:** 99   **Green Rating:** 77

STUDENTS AND FACULTY

Enrollment: 3,114. **Student Body:** 30% female, 70% male, 39% out-of-state, 4% international (29 countries represented). Asian 12%, African American 2%, Caucasian 67%, Hispanic 10%, Native American <1%, Race unknown 4%.
Retention and Graduation: 94% freshmen return for sophomore year. 42% freshmen graduate within 4 years. 83% freshmen graduate within 6 years. 24% grads go on to further study within 1 year. 5% grads pursue arts and sciences degrees. 2% grads pursue law degrees. 1% grads pursue business degrees. 4% grads pursue medical degrees. **Faculty:** Student/faculty ratio 10:1. 257 full-time faculty, 95% hold PhDs, 23% are members of minority groups, 26% are women. 0% of classes are taught by teaching assistants.

ACADEMICS

Degrees: Bachelor's; Doctoral; Master's; Post-Bachelor's certificate **Classes:** Most classes have 20-29 students. **Most popular majors:** Computer Science; Mechanical Engineering; Engineering, Other. **Special Study Options:** Accelerated program; Cooperative education program; Cross-registration; Distance learning; Double major; Dual enrollment; Honors program; Independent study; Internships; Study abroad. Honors programs: The Scholars Program allows high-achieving students to participate in research over the summer or take up to four tuition-free courses each summer. Scholars students may also complete their Bachelor's in three years or a combined bachelor's and Master's in four years at no extra cost. Combined degree programs: BA/DDS; BA/JD; BA/MD. **Disability Services offered to physically disabled**

students: Note-taking services; Tutors. **Career services:** Alumni network; Alumni services; Career assessment; Career/job search classes; Internships; Regional alumni

FACILITIES

Housing: Apartments for single students; Coed dorms; Fraternity/sorority housing; Theme housing; Women's dorms 100% of campus accessible to physically diasbled. **Special Academic Facilities/Equipment:** Art museum, electron microscope, ocean engineering lab, HDTV research facility, advanced telecommunications institute, environmental lab, design/manufacturing institute, wind tunnel, robotics lab, product management center, polymer processing institute. DeBaun Theater, a multi-media facility, wireless campus network **Computers:** 95% of classrooms, 100% of dorms, 100% of libraries, 100% of dining areas, 100% of student union, 99% of common outdoor areas have wireless network access. Students can register for classes online. Administrative functions (other than registration) can be performed online. Undergraduates are required to own a computer.

CAMPUS LIFE

Environment: Town **Activities:** Campus Ministries; Choral groups; Concert band; Dance; Drama/theater; International Student Organization; Jazz band; Music ensembles; Musical theater; Radio station; Student government; Student newspaper; Symphony orchestra; Television station; Yearbook 120 registered organizations, 12 honor societies, 6 religious organizations. 10 fraternities, 3 sororities. **Athletics (Intercollegiate):** *Men:* baseball, basketball, cross-country, fencing, lacrosse, soccer, swimming, tennis, track/field (outdoor), track/field (indoor), volleyball, wrestling. *Women:* basketball, cross-country, equestrian sports, fencing, field hockey, lacrosse, soccer, swimming, tennis, track/field (outdoor), track/field (indoor), volleyball. **On-Campus Highlights:** Schaefer Athletic Center, DeBaun Auditorium, Castle Point, overlooking Manhattan, Babbio Center, Pierce Dinning Hall with a NYC view **Environmental Initiatives:** Green minor

ADMISSIONS

Freshman Academic Profile: Average high school GPA 3.8. 72% in top 10% of high school class, 91% in top 25% of high school class, 99% in top 50% of high school class. **Test Scores:** SAT Math middle 50% range 680-760. SAT EBRW middle 50% range 640-710. ACT middle 50% range 29-33. Minimum internet-based TOEFL 80. **Basis for Candidate Selection:** *Very important factors considered include:* rigor of secondary school record, academic GPA, standardized test scores. *Important factors considered include:* talent/ability, character/personal qualities. *Other factors considered include:* class rank, application essay, recommendation(s), interview, extracurricular activities, first generation, alumni/ae relation, geographical residence, state residency, racial/ethnic status, volunteer work, work experience, level of applicant's interest. **Freshman Admission Requirements:** High school diploma is required and GED is accepted *Academic units required:* 4 English, 4 math, 3 science, 3 science labs, *Academic units recommended:* 4 science, 4 science labs, 2 foreign language, 2 social studies, 2 history, 4 academic electives. **Freshman Admission Statistics:** 8,335 applied, 43.9% admitted, 21% enrolled. **Transfer Admission Requirements:** High school transcript, college transcript(s), essay or personal statement, interview, Minimum college GPA of 3.0 required. Lowest grade transferable C. **General Admission Information:** Application fee $70. Regular application deadline 1/15. Nonfall registration accepted. Admission may be deferred for a maximum of 1 year.

COSTS AND FINANCIAL AID

Annual tuition $50,370. Room and board $15,244. Required fees $1,832. Average book expense $1,200. **Required Forms and Deadlines:** CSS/Financial Aid PROFILE; FAFSA. **Types of Aid:** *Need-based scholarships/grants:* College/university scholarship or grant aid from institutional funds; Federal Pell; Private scholarships; SEOG; State scholarships/grants; United Negro College Fund. *Loans:* Direct PLUS loans; Direct Subsidized Stafford Loans; Direct Unsubsidized Stafford Loans. *Student Employment:* Federal Work-Study Program available. Institutional employment available. **Financial Aid Statistics:** 43% needy freshmen, 61% needy undergrads receive need-based scholarship or grant aid. 97% freshmen, 94% undergrads receive non-need-based scholarship or grant aid. 62% freshmen, 73% undergrads receive need-based self-help aid. 0% freshmen, 0% undergrads receive athletic scholarships. 99% freshmen, 91% undergrads receive any aid. 75% undergrads borrow to pay for school. Average cumulative indebtedness $48,244. **Criteria for awarding aid:** *Non-need-based:* Academics, Leadership, Minority status, Music/drama.

STEVENSON UNIVERSITY

1525 Greenspring Valley Road, Stevenson, MD 21153-0641
Phone: 410-486-7001 • **Financial Aid Phone:** 443-352-4369
E-mail: admissions@stevenson.edu • **CEEB Code:** 2107
Fax: 443-352-4440 • **Website:** http://www.stevenson.edu • **ACT Code:** 1753

This private school was founded in 1947. It has a 168 acre campus.

RATINGS

Admissions Selectivity Rating: 81   **Fire Safety Rating:** 79   **Green Rating:** 60*

STUDENTS AND FACULTY

Enrollment: 3,826. **Student Body:** 65% female, 35% male, 21% out-of-state, (7 countries represented). Asian 3%, African American 29%, Caucasian 57%, Hispanic 4%, Native American <1%, Pacific Islander <1%, Two or more races 2%, Race unknown 4%.

Retention and Graduation: 75% freshmen return for sophomore year. 17% grads go on to further study within 1 year. **Faculty:** Student/faculty ratio 15:1. 130 full-time faculty, 74% hold PhDs, 15% are members of minority groups, 54% are women. 0% of classes are taught by teaching assistants.

ACADEMICS

Degrees: Bachelor's; Master's **Most popular majors:** Legal Assistant/Paralegal; Registered Nursing/Registered Nurse; Business Administration And Management, General. **Special Study Options:** Accelerated program; Cooperative education program; Cross-registration; Distance learning: Double major; Dual enrollment; Honors program; Independent study; Internships; Liberal arts/career combination; Student-designed major; Study abroad; Teacher certification program. Honors programs: Consistent with its mission, the Stevenson University Honors Program seeks to admit academically outstanding students who are interested in challenging themselves through a unique and stimulating curriculum that extends beyond traditional academic boundaries. **Disability Services offered to physically disabled students:** Note-taking services; Reader services; Tape recorders; Tutors. **Career services:** Alumni network; Alumni services; Career assessment; Internships; Regional alumni

FACILITIES

Housing: Apartments for single students; Theme housing; Wellness housing 100% of campus accessible to physically diasbled. **Special Academic Facilities/Equipment:** Art gallery and theatre. **Computers:** Students can register for classes online. Administrative functions (other than registration) can be performed online.

CAMPUS LIFE

Environment: Village **Activities:** Campus Ministries; Choral groups; Dance; Drama/theater; International Student Organization; Jazz band; Literary magazine; Marching band; Music ensembles; Pep band; Radio station; Student government; Student newspaper; Symphony orchestra 40 registered organizations, 10 honor societies, 4 religious organizations. 2 sororities. **Athletics (Intercollegiate):** *Men:* baseball, basketball, cheerleading, cross-country, golf, lacrosse, soccer, tennis, track/field (indoor), volleyball. *Women:* basketball, cheerleading, cross-country, field hockey, lacrosse, soccer, softball, tennis, track/field (indoor), volleyball. **On-Campus Highlights:** Rockland Center (Dining Hall/Student Ce), Community Center, The Wellness Center/Caves, New gym/stadium, Theater

ADMISSIONS

Freshman Academic Profile: Average high school GPA 3.2. 11% in top 10% of high school class, 31% in top 25% of high school class, 58% in top 50% of high school class. 70% from public high schools. **Test Scores:** SAT Math middle 50% range 450-560. SAT EBRW middle 50% range 440-540. ACT middle 50% range 18-23. Minimum paper TOEFL 550. **Basis for Candidate Selection:** *Very important factors considered include:* rigor of secondary school record, academic GPA. *Important factors considered include:* application essay, standardized test scores, recommendation(s), extracurricular activities, talent/ability, character/personal qualities. *Other factors considered include:* class rank, interview, first generation, alumni/ae relation, geographical residence, volunteer work, work experience, level of applicant's interest. **Freshman Admission Requirements:** High school diploma is required and GED is accepted *Academic units required:* 4 English, 3 math, 3 science, 2 science labs, 2 social studies, 1 history, 4 academic electives, *Academic units recommended:* 4 English, 3 math, 3 science, 2 science labs, 2 foreign language, 2 social studies, 1 history, 4 academic electives. **Freshman Admission Statistics:** 5,318 applied, 59.6% admitted, 24% enrolled. **Transfer Admission Requirements:** college transcript(s), statement of good standing from prior institution(s). Minimum college GPA of 2.5 required. Lowest grade transferable C. **General Admission Information:** Application fee $40. Priority deadline 3/1. Nonfall registration accepted. Admission may be deferred.

COSTS AND FINANCIAL AID

Annual tuition $25,210. Room and board $11,894. Required fees $1,872. Average book expense $1,250. **Required Forms and Deadlines:** FAFSA. **Notification of Awards:** Applicants will be notified of awards on a rolling basis beginning 3/15. **Types of Aid:** *Need-based scholarships/grants:* College/university scholarship or grant aid from institutional funds; Federal Pell; Private scholarships; SEOG; State scholarships/grants. *Loans:* Direct PLUS loans; Direct Subsidized Stafford Loans; Direct Unsubsidized Stafford Loans. *Student Employment:* Federal Work-Study Program available. Institutional employment available. **Financial Aid Statistics:** 99% needy freshmen, 96% needy undergrads receive need-based scholarship or grant aid. 9% freshmen, 8% undergrads receive non-need-based scholarship or grant aid. 79% freshmen, 79% undergrads receive need-based self-help aid. 0% freshmen, 0% undergrads receive athletic scholarships. **Criteria for awarding aid:** *Need-based:* Leadership, Minority status *Non-need-based:* Academics, Art, Leadership, Music/drama.

STOCKTON UNIVERSITY

101 Vera King Farris Drive, Galloway, NJ 08205
Phone: 609-652-4261 • **Financial Aid Phone:** 609-652-4203
E-mail: admissions@stockton.edu • **CEEB Code:** 2889
Fax: 609-748-5541 • **Website:** www.stockton.edu

This public school was founded in 1969. It has a 2000 acre campus.

RATINGS
Admissions Selectivity Rating: 77   **Fire Safety Rating:** 97   **Green Rating:** 90

STUDENTS AND FACULTY
Enrollment: 8,242. **Student Body:** 59% female, 41% male, 2% out-of-state, 1% international (6 countries represented). Asian 6%, African American 8%, Caucasian 68%, Hispanic 13%, Native American <1%, Pacific Islander <1%, Two or more races 2%, Race unknown 2%.
Retention and Graduation: 87% freshmen return for sophomore year. 54% freshmen graduate within 4 years. 73% freshmen graduate within 6 years. 33% grads go on to further study within 1 year. 71% grads pursue arts and sciences degrees. 5% grads pursue law degrees. 6% grads pursue business degrees. 4% grads pursue medical degrees. **Faculty:** Student/faculty ratio 17:1. 331 full-time faculty, 94% hold PhDs, 25% are members of minority groups, 54% are women. 0% of classes are taught by teaching assistants.

ACADEMICS
Degrees: Bachelor's; Doctoral/Professional; Doctoral/Research; Master's; Post-Bachelor's certificate; Post-Master's certificate **Classes:** Most classes have fewer than 10 students. Most lab/discussion sessions have 10-19 students. **Most popular majors:** Criminology; Health Services/Allied Health/Health Sciences, General. **Special Study Options:** Accelerated program; Cross-registration; Distance learning; Double major; Dual enrollment; English as a Second Language (ESL); Honors program; Independent study; Internships; Liberal arts/career combination; Student-designed major; Study abroad; Teacher certification program. Honors programs: Stockton Honors Program Combined degree programs: BA/MA. **Disability Services offered to physically disabled students:** Note-taking services; Reader services; Tape recorders; Tutors. **Career services:** Alumni network; Alumni services; Career assessment; Career/job search classes; Internships; Regional alumni

FACILITIES
Housing: Apartments for single students; Coed dorms; Special housing for disabled student; Theme housing; Wellness housing 100% of campus accessible to physically disabled. **Special Academic Facilities/Equipment:** Observatory, Nacote Creek field station, Holocaust Resource Center, Seaview Resort, The Sam Azeez Museum of Woodbine Heritage **Computers:** 100% of classrooms, 5% of dorms, 100% of libraries, 100% of dining areas, n/a% of student union, 10% of common outdoor areas have wireless network access. Students can register for classes online. Administrative functions (other than registration) can be performed online.

CAMPUS LIFE
Environment: Town **Activities:** Campus Ministries; Choral groups; Concert band; Dance; Drama/theater; International Student Organization; Jazz band; Literary magazine; Model UN; Music ensembles; Musical theater; Pep band; Radio station; Student government; Student newspaper; Television station; Yearbook 130 registered organizations, 6 honor societies, 5 religious organizations. 11 fraternities, 9 sororities. **Athletics (Intercollegiate):** *Men:* baseball, basketball, cheerleading, cross-country, lacrosse, soccer, track/field (outdoor), track/field (indoor). *Women:* basketball, cheerleading, crew/rowing, cross-country, field hockey, soccer, softball, tennis, track/field (outdoor), track/

field (indoor), volleyball. **On-Campus Highlights:** Campus Center, Performing Arts Center, Library, Housing options, Marine Field Station **Environmental Initiatives:** Alternative Energy: A. Solar electrical generation: 1200 KW capacity arrays operating on campus. This includes rooftop installations and shade canopies over parking lots. An additional 700 KW is under construction, expected to be operational in June of 2012. B. The GEOTHERMAL PROJECT provides up to 1650 tons of cooling capacity and allows portions of the building to be heated and cooled using the same equipment. C. Solar hot water heating has been installed on the roof of the newest residential facility, which accommodates 390 students.

ADMISSIONS
Freshman Academic Profile: 20% in top 10% of high school class, 47% in top 25% of high school class, 82% in top 50% of high school class. 88% from public high schools. **Test Scores:** SAT Math middle 50% range 500-590. SAT EBRW middle 50% range 510-610. ACT middle 50% range 19-25. Minimum internet-based TOEFL 80. Minimum paper TOEFL 550. **Basis for Candidate Selection:** *Very important factors considered include:* rigor of secondary school record, class rank, academic GPA. *Important factors considered include:* standardized test scores. *Other factors considered include:* application essay, recommendation(s), extracurricular activities, talent/ability, character/personal qualities, alumni/ae relation, volunteer work, work experience, level of applicant's interest. **Freshman Admission Requirements:** High school diploma is required and GED is accepted *Academic units required:* 4 English, 3 math, 2 science, 2 science labs, 2 social studies, 5 academic electives, *Academic units recommended:* 2 foreign language. **Freshman Admission Statistics:** 5,706 applied, 81.5% admitted, 34% enrolled. Minimum college GPA of 2.5 required. Lowest grade transferable C. **General Admission Information:** Application fee $50. Priority deadline 2/1. Regular application deadline 5/1. Nonfall registration accepted. Admission may be deferred for a maximum of 1 year.

COSTS AND FINANCIAL AID
Annual in-state tuition $12,120. Annual out-of-state tuition $15,599. Room and board $12,120. Required fees $4,758. Average book expense $1,597. **Required Forms and Deadlines:** FAFSA. **Notification of Awards:** Applicants will be notified of awards on a rolling basis beginning 4/1. **Types of Aid:** *Need-based scholarships/grants:* College/university scholarship or grant aid from institutional funds; Federal Pell; Private scholarships; SEOG; State scholarships/grants. *Loans:* Direct PLUS loans; Direct Subsidized Stafford Loans; Direct Unsubsidized Stafford Loans. *Student Employment:* Federal Work-Study Program available. Institutional employment available. **Financial Aid Statistics:** 68% needy freshmen, 59% needy undergrads receive need-based scholarship or grant aid. 36% freshmen, 27% undergrads receive non-need-based scholarship or grant aid. 79% undergrads receive need-based self-help aid. 0% freshmen, 0% undergrads receive athletic scholarships. 86% freshmen, 84% undergrads receive any aid. Average cumulative indebtedness $33,201. **Criteria for awarding aid:** *Non-need-based:* Academics, Art, Leadership, Minority status, Music/drama, State/district residency.

STONEHILL COLLEGE

320 Washington Street, Easton, MA 02357-5610
Phone: (508) 565-1373 • **Financial Aid Phone:** 508-565-1088
E-mail: admission@stonehill.edu • **CEEB Code:** 3770
Fax: (508) 565-1545 • **Website:** www.stonehill.edu • **ACT Code:** 1918

This private school, affiliated with the Roman Catholic Church, was founded in 1948. It has a 384 acre campus.

RATINGS
Admissions Selectivity Rating: 81   **Fire Safety Rating:** 98   **Green Rating:** 87

STUDENTS AND FACULTY
Enrollment: 2,494. **Student Body:** 59% female, 41% male, 40% out-of-state, 1% international (11 countries represented). Asian 2%, African American 4%, Caucasian 85%, Hispanic 4%, Native American <1%, Pacific Islander 0%, Two or more races 2%, Race unknown 2%.
Retention and Graduation: 85% freshmen return for sophomore year. 77% freshmen graduate within 4 years. 80% freshmen graduate within 6 years. 16% grads go on to further study within 1 year. 8% grads pursue arts and sciences degrees. 2% grads pursue law degrees. 1% grads pursue business degrees. 3% grads pursue medical degrees. **Faculty:** Student/faculty ratio 12:1. 169 full-time

faculty, 92% hold PhDs, 14% are members of minority groups, 46% are women. 0% of classes are taught by teaching assistants.

ACADEMICS

Degrees: Bachelor's **Classes:** Most classes have 10-19 students. **Most popular majors:** Biology/Biological Sciences, General; Psychology, General; Accounting. **Special Study Options:** Cross-registration; Double major; Dual enrollment; Exchange student program (domestic); Honors program; Independent study; Internships; Liberal arts/career combination; Student-designed major; Study abroad; Teacher certification program. Honors programs: The Moreau Honors Program requires 5 honors courses, a 1-credit service/leadership seminar, and a senior Honors Thesis in each student's academic major. **Disability Services offered to physically disabled students:** Note-taking services; Reader services; Tape recorders; Tutors. **Career services:** Alumni network; Alumni services; Career assessment; Career/job search classes; Internships

FACILITIES

Housing: Coed dorms; Special housing for disabled student; Theme housing; Wellness housing; Women's dorms 95% of campus accessible to physically diasbled. **Special Academic Facilities/Equipment:** Joseph W. Martin, Jr. Institute for Law and Society, Thomas and Mary Shields Science Center, Stonehill Industrial History Collection (a.k.a., shovel museum), Cushing-Martin Hall (art gallery and industrial history gallery), Center for Nonprofit Management, Hemingway Theatre, MacPhaidin Library, Sally Ames Blair Sports Complex, Thomas and Donna May Pavilion Ice Rink (seasonal) and observatory. **Computers:** 30% of classrooms, 80% of dorms, 100% of libraries, 100% of dining areas, 50% of student union, 20% of common outdoor areas have wireless network access. Students can register for classes online. Administrative functions (other than registration) can be performed online.

CAMPUS LIFE

Environment: Village **Activities:** Campus Ministries; Choral groups; Concert band; Dance; Drama/theater; International Student Organization; Jazz band; Literary magazine; Model UN; Music ensembles; Musical theater; Pep band; Radio station; Student government; Student newspaper; Student-run film society; Symphony orchestra; Yearbook 76 registered organizations, 19 honor societies, 3 religious organizations. **Athletics (Intercollegiate):** *Men:* baseball, basketball, cross-country, football, ice hockey, soccer, tennis, track/field (outdoor), track/field (indoor). *Women:* basketball, cross-country, equestrian sports, field hockey, lacrosse, soccer, softball, tennis, track/field (outdoor), track/field (indoor), volleyball. **On-Campus Highlights:** The Hill (entertainment/dining social space), The MacPhaidin Library, The Roche Dining Commons, The Shields Science Center, The Sally Blair Ames Sports Complex **Environmental Initiatives:** Joined AASHE (Association for the Advancement of Sustainability in Higher Education) and participated in the STARS survey earning a Silver rating in April 2016.

ADMISSIONS

Freshman Academic Profile: Average high school GPA 3.3. 22% in top 10% of high school class, 51% in top 25% of high school class, 88% in top 50% of high school class. 67% from public high schools. **Test Scores:** SAT Math middle 50% range 530-630. SAT EBRW middle 50% range 550-640. ACT middle 50% range 23-28. Minimum internet-based TOEFL 80. Minimum paper TOEFL 550. **Basis for Candidate Selection:** *Very important factors considered include:* rigor of secondary school record, class rank, academic GPA, talent/ability. *Important factors considered include:* application essay, recommendation(s), extracurricular activities. *Other factors considered include:* standardized test scores, interview, character/personal qualities, first generation, alumni/ae relation, geographical residence, religious affiliation/commitment, racial/ethnic status, volunteer work, work experience, level of applicant's interest. **Freshman Admission Requirements:** High school diploma is required and GED is accepted *Academic units required:* 4 English, 3 math, 3 science, 3 science labs, 3 foreign language, 3 history, *Academic units recommended:* 4 English, 4 math, 4 science, 3 science labs, 4 foreign language, 4 history. **Freshman Admission Statistics:** 6,260 applied, 72.1% admitted, 15% enrolled. **Transfer Admission Requirements:** High school transcript, college transcript(s), essay or personal statement, statement of good standing from prior institution(s). Minimum college GPA of 2.0 required. Lowest grade transferable C. **General Admission Information:** Application fee $60. Regular application deadline 1/15. Nonfall registration accepted. Admission may be deferred for a maximum of 1 year.

COSTS AND FINANCIAL AID

Annual tuition $41,300. Room and board $15,760. Average book expense $893. **Required Forms and Deadlines:** CSS/Financial Aid PROFILE; FAFSA; Noncustodial PROFILE. **Notification of Awards:** Applicants will be notified of awards on or about 4/1. **Types of Aid:** *Need-based scholarships/grants:* College/university scholarship or grant aid from institutional funds; Federal Pell; Private scholarships; SEOG; State scholarships/grants. *Loans:* Direct PLUS loans; Direct Subsidized Stafford Loans; Direct Unsubsidized Stafford Loans. *Student Employment:* Federal Work-Study Program available. Institutional employment available. **Financial Aid Statistics:** 99% needy freshmen, 97% needy undergrads receive need-based scholarship or grant aid. 28% freshmen, 21% undergrads receive non-need-based scholarship or grant aid. 70% freshmen, 77% undergrads receive need-based self-help aid. 3%

freshmen, 4% undergrads receive athletic scholarships. 99% freshmen, 95% undergrads receive any aid. Average cumulative indebtedness $35,462. **Criteria for awarding aid:** *Need-based:* Academics, Leadership *Non-need-based:* Academics, Athletics, Leadership.

SUFFOLK UNIVERSITY

8 Ashburton Place, Boston, MA 02108
Phone: (617) 573 8460 • **Financial Aid Phone:** 617-573-8470
E-mail: admission@suffolk.edu • **CEEB Code:** 3771
Fax: (617) 557 1574 • **Website:** www.suffolk.edu • **ACT Code:** 1920

This private school was founded in 1906.

RATINGS

Admissions Selectivity Rating: 75   **Fire Safety Rating:** 98   **Green Rating:** 73

STUDENTS AND FACULTY

Enrollment: 5,025. **Student Body:** 54% female, 46% male, 32% out-of-state, 22% international (114 countries represented). Asian 8%, African American 5%, Caucasian 47%, Hispanic 12%, Native American <1%, Pacific Islander <1%, Two or more races 2%, Race unknown 4%.
Retention and Graduation: 77% freshmen return for sophomore year. 45% freshmen graduate within 4 years. 60% freshmen graduate within 6 years. 10% grads go on to further study within 1 year. 3% grads pursue arts and sciences degrees. 1.5% grads pursue law degrees. 5% grads pursue business degrees. 0.4% grads pursue medical degrees. **Faculty:** Student/faculty ratio 13:1. 346 full-time faculty, 90% hold PhDs, 18% are members of minority groups, 49% are women.

ACADEMICS

Degrees: Associate; Bachelor's; Certificate; Diploma; Doctoral/Research; Master's; Post-Bachelor's certificate; Post-Master's certificate **Classes:** Most classes have 10-19 students. Most lab/discussion sessions have 20-29 students. **Special Study Options:** Accelerated program; Cooperative education program; Cross-registration; Distance learning; Double major; Dual enrollment; English as a Second Language (ESL); Exchange student program (domestic); Honors program; Independent study; Internships; Liberal arts/career combination; Study abroad. Honors programs: A Community of Scholars Suffolk University honors students work in collaboration with their school's program director and advisory committee to plan events that bring the honors community together on a regular basis outside of the classroom. Lectures by Suffolk University scholars or by noted intellectuals outside of the University, a variety of social events, visits to cultural and historical sites, and public service projects offer intellectual challenge, promote leadership, and develop networking skills with faculty, alumni, community, business, and government leaders. The program provides honors scholars with a broader context for their academic pursuits, while strengthening their sense of community. Special Benefits and Recognition for Honors Scholars: Honors scholars are eligible for a full tuition scholarship. In addition, honors scholars enjoy the following benefits and recognition: Guaranteed housing in University residence halls through the sophomore year; Priority course registration; Special honors program advisors; Application assistance, when applicable, for Fulbright, Marshall, Rhodes, and other post-graduate academic and scholarship programs; Honors Program designation on official academic transcript; and Special listing in commencement program. http://www.suffolk.edu/admission/gchonors.htm Combined degree programs: BA/JD; BA/MA. **Disability Services offered to physically disabled students:** Note-taking services; Reader services; Tape recorders; Tutors. **Career services:** Alumni network; Alumni services; Career assessment; Career/job search classes; Internships; Regional alumni

FACILITIES

Housing: Apartments for single students; Coed dorms **Special Academic Facilities/Equipment:** Marine biology field station in Maine, NESAD art gallery, Adams art gallery, C. Walsh Theatre and 10 West Street Theatre **Computers:** 100% of classrooms, 100% of dorms, 100% of libraries, 100% of dining areas, 100% of student union, 20% of common outdoor areas have wireless network access. Students can register for classes online. Administrative functions (other than registration) can be performed online.

CAMPUS LIFE

Environment: Metropolis **Activities:** Campus Ministries; Choral groups; Dance; Drama/theater; International Student Organization; Literary magazine; Model UN; Music ensembles; Musical theater; Radio station; Student government; Student newspaper; Television station; Yearbook 75 registered organizations, 11 honor societies, 3 religious organizations. 1 fraternity, 1 sorority. **Athletics (Intercollegiate): Men:** baseball, basketball, cross-country, golf, ice hockey, soccer, tennis. *Women:* basketball, cross-country, softball, tennis, volleyball. **On-Campus Highlights:** Sawyer Library, 73 Tremont Cafe, Sawyer Lounges, The Commons (5th floor Sargent), Sawyer Computer Lab

ADMISSIONS

Freshman Academic Profile: Average high school GPA 3.2. 12% in top 10% of high school class, 39% in top 25% of high school class, 69% in top 50% of high school class. 64% from public high schools. **Test Scores:** SAT Math middle 50% range 500-580. SAT EBRW middle 50% range 500-600. ACT middle 50% range 21-26. Minimum internet-based TOEFL 79. Minimum paper TOEFL 550. **Basis for Candidate Selection:** *Very important factors considered include:* rigor of secondary school record, academic GPA. *Important factors considered include:* class rank. *Other factors considered include:* application essay, standardized test scores, recommendation(s), interview, extracurricular activities, talent/ability, character/personal qualities, first generation, volunteer work, work experience, level of applicant's interest. **Freshman Admission Requirements:** High school diploma is required and GED is accepted *Academic units required:* 4 English, 3 math, 2 science, 1 science labs, 2 foreign language, 1 social studies, 1 history, 4 academic electives, *Academic units recommended:* 4 English, 4 math, 4 science, 3 science labs, 4 foreign language, 2 social studies, 3 history, 4 academic electives. **Freshman Admission Statistics:** 8,237 applied, 83.4% admitted, 16% enrolled. **Transfer Admission Requirements:** High school transcript, college transcript(s), essay or personal statement, Minimum college GPA of 2.5 required. Lowest grade transferable C. **General Admission Information:** Application fee $50. Regular application deadline 2/15. Nonfall registration accepted. Admission may be deferred for a maximum of 1 year.

COSTS AND FINANCIAL AID

Annual tuition $38,420. Room and board $17,846. Required fees $146. Average book expense $1,200. **Required Forms and Deadlines:** FAFSA. **Notification of Awards:** Applicants will be notified of awards on a rolling basis beginning 2/5. **Types of Aid:** *Need-based scholarships/grants:* College/university scholarship or grant aid from institutional funds; Federal Pell; Private scholarships; SEOG; State scholarships/grants. *Loans:* Direct PLUS loans; Direct Subsidized Stafford Loans; Direct Unsubsidized Stafford Loans. *Student Employment:* Federal Work-Study Program available. Institutional employment available. **Financial Aid Statistics:** 81% needy freshmen, 83% needy undergrads receive need-based scholarship or grant aid. 99% freshmen, 72% undergrads receive non-need-based scholarship or grant aid. 83% freshmen, 85% undergrads receive need-based self-help aid. 0% freshmen, 0% undergrads receive athletic scholarships. 94% freshmen, 73% undergrads receive any aid. 75% undergrads borrow to pay for school. Average cumulative indebtedness $42,584. **Criteria for awarding aid:** *Need-based:* Academics *Non-need-based:* Academics, Alumni affiliation.

SUSQUEHANNA UNIVERSITY

514 University Avenue, Selinsgrove, PA 17870
Phone: 570-372-4260 • **Financial Aid Phone:** 570-372-4450
E-mail: suadmiss@susqu.edu • **CEEB Code:** 2820
Fax: 570-372-2722 • **Website:** www.susqu.edu • **ACT Code:** 3720

This private school, affiliated with the Lutheran Church, was founded in 1858. It has a 325 acre campus.

RATINGS

Admissions Selectivity Rating: 82   **Fire Safety Rating:** 98   **Green Rating:** 82

STUDENTS AND FACULTY

Enrollment: 2,200. **Student Body:** 56% female, 44% male, 44% out-of-state, 2% international (21 countries represented). Asian 2%, African American 6%, Caucasian 80%, Hispanic 7%, Native American <1%, Pacific Islander <1%, Two or more races 3%, Race unknown 1%.
Retention and Graduation: 87% freshmen return for sophomore year. 66% freshmen graduate within 4 years. 71% freshmen graduate within 6 years.
Faculty: Student/faculty ratio 12:1. 139 full-time faculty, 90% hold PhDs, 18% are members of minority groups, 45% are women. 0% of classes are taught by teaching assistants.

ACADEMICS

Degrees: Bachelor's **Classes:** Most classes have 10-19 students. **Most popular majors:** Communication, General; Biology/Biological Sciences, General;

Business/Commerce, General. **Special Study Options:** Accelerated program; Cross-registration; Distance learning; Double major; Dual enrollment; English as a Second Language (ESL); Honors program; Independent study; Internships; Student-designed major; Study abroad; Teacher certification program. Honors programs: The Honors Program at Susquehanna offers a challenging curriculum to students interested in a more self-directed and interdisciplinary approach at the undergraduate level. The program is well suited to the intensely curious, active learner who values breadth of study and multiple perspectives. Discussion groups, lectures, off-campus visits and residential programs complement Honors Program courses. Combined degree programs: BA/DDS. **Disability Services offered to physically disabled students:** Note-taking services; Reader services; Tape recorders; Tutors. **Career services:** Alumni network; Alumni services; Career assessment; Career/job search classes; Internships; Regional alumni

FACILITIES

Housing: Apartments for single students; Coed dorms; Cooperative housing; Fraternity/sorority housing; Special housing for disabled student; Special housing for international students; Theme housing; Wellness housing 90% of campus accessible to physically disabled. **Computers:** 90% of classrooms, 10% of dorms, 100% of libraries, 100% of dining areas, 100% of student union, 30% of common outdoor areas have wireless network access. Students can register for classes online. Administrative functions (other than registration) can be performed online.

CAMPUS LIFE

Environment: Town **Activities:** Campus Ministries; Choral groups; Concert band; Dance; Drama/theater; International Student Organization; Jazz band; Literary magazine; Marching band; Model UN; Music ensembles; Musical theater; Opera; Pep band; Radio station; Student government; Student newspaper; Symphony orchestra; Television station; Yearbook 120 registered organizations, 24 honor societies, 12 religious organizations. 4 fraternities, 5 sororities. **Athletics (Intercollegiate): Men:** baseball, basketball, crew/rowing, cross-country, football, golf, lacrosse, soccer, swimming, tennis, track/field (outdoor), track/field (indoor). *Women:* basketball, crew/rowing, cross-country, field hockey, golf, lacrosse, soccer, softball, swimming, tennis, track/field (outdoor), track/field (indoor), volleyball. **On-Campus Highlights:** Sports and Fitness Complex, Blough-Weis Library, Charlie's, student-run coffee house, Trax, student-run entertainment venue, Starbucks **Environmental Initiatives:** New science facility and new student housing are LEED certified. This housing and two units built in 2010 utilize geo-thermal energy for heating and cooling.

ADMISSIONS

Freshman Academic Profile: Average high school GPA 3.5. 26% in top 10% of high school class, 57% in top 25% of high school class, 88% in top 50% of high school class. 86% from public high schools. **Test Scores:** SAT Math middle 50% range 530-610. SAT EBRW middle 50% range 540-630. ACT middle 50% range 22-28. Minimum internet-based TOEFL 81. Minimum paper TOEFL 550. **Basis for Candidate Selection:** *Very important factors considered include:* rigor of secondary school record, academic GPA. *Important factors considered include:* class rank, application essay, standardized test scores, recommendation(s), interview, extracurricular activities, talent/ability, character/personal qualities, alumni/ae relation, racial/ethnic status, volunteer work, work experience, level of applicant's interest. *Other factors considered include:* first generation, geographical residence, state residency. **Freshman Admission Requirements:** High school diploma is required and GED is accepted *Academic units required:* 4 English, 3 math, 2 science, 2 science labs, 2 foreign language, 2 social studies, 2 history, 2 academic electives, *Academic units recommended:* 4 English, 4 math, 3 science, 3 science labs, 4 foreign language, 4 social studies, 2 history, 3 academic electives. **Freshman Admission Statistics:** 6,033 applied, 68.3% admitted, 15% enrolled. **Transfer Admission Requirements:** High school transcript, college transcript(s), essay or personal statement, statement of good standing from prior institution(s). Minimum college GPA of 2.0 required. Lowest grade transferable C-. **General Admission Information:** Nonfall registration accepted. Admission may be deferred for a maximum of one year.

COSTS AND FINANCIAL AID

Required Forms and Deadlines: FAFSA; State aid form. **Notification of Awards:** Applicants will be notified of awards on a rolling basis beginning 11/15. **Types of Aid:** *Need-based scholarships/grants:* College/university scholarship or grant aid from institutional funds; Federal Pell; Private scholarships; SEOG; State scholarships/grants. *Loans:* Direct PLUS loans; Direct Subsidized Stafford Loans; Direct Unsubsidized Stafford Loans. *Student Employment:* Federal Work-Study Program available. Institutional employment available. **Financial Aid Statistics:** 100% needy freshmen, 100% needy undergrads receive need-based scholarship or grant aid. 19% freshmen, 15% undergrads receive non-need-based scholarship or grant aid. 79% freshmen, 83% undergrads receive need-based self-help aid. 0% freshmen, 0% undergrads receive athletic scholarships. 99% freshmen, 99% undergrads receive any aid. 81% undergrads borrow to pay for school. Average cumulative indebtedness $36,882. **Criteria**

for awarding aid: *Non-need-based:* Academics, Alumni affiliation, Leadership, Minority status, Music/drama.

SWARTHMORE COLLEGE

500 College Avenue, Swarthmore, PA 19081
Phone: 610-328-8300 • **Financial Aid Phone:** 610-328-8358
E-mail: admissions@swarthmore.edu • **CEEB Code:** 2821
Fax: 610-328-8580 • **Website:** www.swarthmore.edu • **ACT Code:** 3722

This private school was founded in 1864. It has a 425 acre campus.

RATINGS

Admissions Selectivity Rating: 98   **Fire Safety Rating:** 92   **Green Rating:** 85

STUDENTS AND FACULTY

Enrollment: 1,629. **Student Body:** 51% female, 49% male, 87% out-of-state, 13% international (70 countries represented). Asian 17%, African American 7%, Caucasian 41%, Hispanic 12%, Native American <1%, Pacific Islander <1%, Two or more races 7%, Race unknown 3%.
Retention and Graduation: 98% freshmen return for sophomore year. 89% freshmen graduate within 4 years. 94% freshmen graduate within 6 years. 26% grads go on to further study within 1 year. 10% grads pursue arts and sciences degrees. 2% grads pursue law degrees. 1% grads pursue business degrees. 2% grads pursue medical degrees. **Faculty:** Student/faculty ratio 8:1. 194 full-time faculty, 99% hold PhDs, 23% are members of minority groups, 47% are women. 0% of classes are taught by teaching assistants.

ACADEMICS

Degrees: Bachelor's **Classes:** Most classes have 10-19 students. Most lab/discussion sessions have 10-19 students. **Most popular majors:** Biology/Biological Sciences, General; Economics, General; Political Science And Government, General. **Special Study Options:** Accelerated program; Cross-registration; Double major; Exchange student program (domestic); Honors program; Independent study; Internships; Student-designed major; Study abroad; Teacher certification program. Honors programs: Modeled after the tutorial system at Oxford, the Swarthmore Honors Program brims with intellectual exploration. This engaging and dynamic program features small-group interaction with peers and faculty, a free and spirited exchange of ideas, independent research, and special projects. Students delve deeply into major and minor areas of study while being challenged to learn and lead discussions across disciplines. The program extolls independent evaluation, bringing more than 100 outside scholars to campus each year to assess students. This rare opportunity to go one-on-one with esteemed scholars, artists, and thinkers is a fitting capstone to the only undergraduate honors program of its kind in the United States. **Disability Services offered to physically disabled students:** Note-taking services; Reader services; Tape recorders; Tutors. **Career services:** Alumni network; Alumni services; Career assessment; Career/job search classes; Internships

FACILITIES

Housing: Apartments for single students; Coed dorms; Men's dorms; Special housing for disabled student; Theme housing; Women's dorms 90% of campus accessible to physically diasbled. **Special Academic Facilities/Equipment:** When you step onto the Swarthmore campus, you engage the world. A world of intellect and action, collaboration and connection. One where idyllic lawns and hills mark your journey to a class on robotics or international cinema. One with a dynamic array of arts spaces to enjoy — or stage — a performance. A place that crackles with diversity of culture and thought, whether it's chatting with a classmate from another continent in one of the campus coffee bars or listening to a Rhodes Scholar in the LEED-certified Science Center. A place replete with avenues of exploration, where you can immerse yourself in the Language Resource Center's many offerings, in the stars when at the College's observatory, or with any number of cultural experiences in center city Philadelphia, just a short train ride away. Whatever you make of your time at Swarthmore, you'll become equipped to excel in our rapidly changing world, attaining fulfillment as a person and citizen. Opportunity abounds. **Computers:** 100% of classrooms, 100% of dorms, 100% of libraries, 100% of dining areas, 100% of student union, 100% of common outdoor areas have wireless network access. Students can register for classes online. Administrative functions (other than registration) can be performed online.

CAMPUS LIFE

Environment: Village **Activities:** Campus Ministries; Choral groups; Dance; Drama/theater; International Student Organization; Jazz band; Literary magazine; Music ensembles; Musical theater; Radio station; Student government; Student newspaper; Student-run film society; Symphony orchestra; Yearbook 138 registered organizations, 3 honor societies, 12 religious organizations. 2 fraternities. **Athletics (Intercollegiate):** *Men:* baseball, basketball, cross-country, golf, lacrosse, soccer, swimming, tennis, track/field (outdoor), track/field (indoor). *Women:* badminton, basketball, cross-country, field hockey, lacrosse, soccer, softball, swimming, tennis, track/field (outdoor), track/field (indoor), volleyball. **On-Campus Highlights:** Kohlberg & Eldridge Commons Coffee Bars, Parrish Beach (the central campus lawn), Scott Outdoor Amphitheater, The Matchbox (wellness center), Paces (student-run cafe) **Environmental Initiatives:** 100% of the College's electrical demands are met by renewable energy credits and the College has made the decision to burn natural gas as it's primary fuel and convert the heat plant from #6 fuel oil to #2 fuel oil as it's back-up reserve.

ADMISSIONS

Freshman Academic Profile: 91% in top 10% of high school class, 99% in top 25% of high school class, 100% in top 50% of high school class. 59% from public high schools. **Test Scores:** SAT Math middle 50% range 690-780. SAT EBRW middle 50% range 690-760. ACT middle 50% range 31-34. **Basis for Candidate Selection:** *Very important factors considered include:* rigor of secondary school record, class rank, academic GPA, application essay, recommendation(s), character/personal qualities. *Important factors considered include:* standardized test scores, extracurricular activities. *Other factors considered include:* interview, talent/ability, first generation, alumni/ae relation, geographical residence, state residency, religious affiliation/commitment, racial/ethnic status, volunteer work, work experience, level of applicant's interest. **Freshman Admission Requirements:** High school diploma or equivalent is not required *Academic units recommended:* 4 English, 3 math, 3 science, 3 foreign language, 3 social studies, 3 history. **Freshman Admission Statistics:** 9,382 applied, 10.7% admitted, 39% enrolled. **Transfer Admission Requirements:** High school transcript, college transcript(s), essay or personal statement, standardized test scores, statement of good standing from prior institution(s). Lowest grade transferable C. **General Admission Information:** Application fee $60. Regular application deadline 1/1. Nonfall registration accepted. Admission may be deferred for a maximum of 1 year.

COSTS AND FINANCIAL AID

Annual tuition $50,424. Room and board $14,952. Required fees $398. Average book expense $1,336. **Required Forms and Deadlines:** CSS/Financial Aid PROFILE; FAFSA; Noncustodial PROFILE; State aid form. **Notification of Awards:** Applicants will be notified of awards on or about 4/1. **Types of Aid:** *Need-based scholarships/grants:* College/university scholarship or grant aid from institutional funds; Federal Pell; Private scholarships; SEOG; State scholarships/grants. *Loans:* Direct PLUS loans; Direct Subsidized Stafford Loans; Direct Unsubsidized Stafford Loans. *Student Employment:* Federal Work-Study Program available. Institutional employment available. **Financial Aid Statistics:** 100% needy freshmen, 100% needy undergrads receive need-based scholarship or grant aid. 0% undergrads receive non-need-based scholarship or grant aid. 99% freshmen, 98% undergrads receive need-based self-help aid. 0% freshmen, 0% undergrads receive athletic scholarships. 52% freshmen, 50% undergrads receive any aid. 31% undergrads borrow to pay for school. Average cumulative indebtedness $22,957. **Criteria for awarding aid:** *Non-need-based:* Academics, Leadership, State/district residency.

See page 1046.

SWEET BRIAR COLLEGE

P.O. Box 1053, Sweet Briar, VA 24595
Phone: 434-381-6142
E-mail: admissions@sbc.edu • **CEEB Code:** 5634
Fax: 434-381-6152 • **Website:** www.sbc.edu • **ACT Code:** 4406

This private school was founded in 1901. It has a 3250 acre campus.

RATINGS

Admissions Selectivity Rating: 73   **Fire Safety Rating:** 91   **Green Rating:** 60*

STUDENTS AND FACULTY

Enrollment: 281. **Student Body:** 100% female, 0% male, 47% out-of-state, <1% international (1 countries represented). Asian 2%, African American 9%, Caucasian 73%, Hispanic 10%, Native American 0%, Pacific Islander <1%, Two or more races 4%, Race unknown 1%.

Retention and Graduation: 72% freshmen return for sophomore year. 53% freshmen graduate within 4 years. 54% freshmen graduate within 6 years. **Faculty:** Student/faculty ratio 5:1. 59 full-time faculty, 93% hold PhDs, 8% are members of minority groups, 51% are women. 0% of classes are taught by teaching assistants.

ACADEMICS

Degrees: Bachelor's; **Master's Classes:** Most classes have 10-19 students. Most lab/discussion sessions have 10-19 students. **Most popular majors:** Biology/Biological Sciences, General; Psychology, General; Business/Commerce, General. **Special Study Options:** Accelerated program; Cross-registration; Double major; Dual enrollment; Exchange student program (domestic); Honors program; Independent study; Internships; Liberal arts/career combination; Student-designed major; Study abroad; Teacher certification program. Honors programs: The Honors Program at Sweet Briar is dedicated to enriching the intellectual life of the entire College community. The program is designed to engage all programs and academic disciplines and to provide opportunities for motivated students that emphasize both breadth and depth of study. The program offers recognition to those students who perform academically at an honors level, but also encourages the participation of all interested students in honors courses and co-curricular activities. **Career services:** Alumni network; Alumni services; Career assessment; Career/job search classes; Internships; Regional alumni

FACILITIES

Housing: Apartments for single students; Special housing for disabled student; Special housing for international students; Theme housing; Women's dorms **Special Academic Facilities/Equipment:** Art museum and galleries, college and local history museums, environmental education/nature center, equestrian center and trails, butterfly garden, community garden, 18 miles of hiking and biking trails, two lakes and boathouse, **Computers:** 60% of classrooms, 50% of dorms, 100% of libraries, 100% of dining areas, 100% of student union, 30% of common outdoor areas have wireless network access. Students can register for classes online. Administrative functions (other than registration) can be performed online.

CAMPUS LIFE

Environment: Rural **Activities:** Campus Ministries; Choral groups; Dance; Drama/theater; International Student Organization; Jazz band; Literary magazine; Music ensembles; Musical theater; Radio station; Student government; Student newspaper 61 registered organizations, 11 honor societies, 3 religious organizations. **Athletics (Intercollegiate):** *Women:* field hockey, horseback riding, lacrosse, soccer, softball, swimming, tennis, volleyball. **On-Campus Highlights: Environmental Initiatives:** Collegiate Clean Energy coalition: http://sbc.edu/news/uncategorized/virginia-private-colleges-announce-sustainability-initiative/

ADMISSIONS

Freshman Academic Profile: Average high school GPA 3.3. 17% in top 10% of high school class, 32% in top 25% of high school class, 68% in top 50% of high school class. **Test Scores:** SAT Math middle 50% range 463-550. SAT EBRW middle 50% range 530-630. ACT middle 50% range 20-28. **Basis for Candidate Selection:** *Very important factors considered include:* rigor of secondary school record, academic GPA. *Important factors considered include:* application essay, standardized test scores, recommendation(s). *Other factors considered include:* class rank, interview, extracurricular activities, talent/ability, character/personal qualities, first generation, alumni/ae relation, volunteer work, work experience. **Freshman Admission Requirements:** High school diploma is required and GED is accepted *Academic units required:* 4 English, 3 math, 3 science, 2 science labs, 2 foreign language, 3 social studies, *Academic units recommended:* 4 English, 4 math, 4 science, 3 science labs, 4 foreign language, 4 social studies. **Freshman Admission Statistics:** 361 applied, 92.8% admitted, 24% enrolled. **Transfer Admission Requirements:** High school transcript, college transcript(s), essay or personal statement, standardized test scores, statement of good standing from prior institution(s). Minimum college GPA of 2.5 required. Lowest grade transferable C-. **General Admission Information:** Nonfall registration accepted. Admission may be deferred for a maximum of 1 year.

COSTS AND FINANCIAL AID

Annual tuition $21,000. Room and board $13,000. Average book expense $1,250. **Required Forms and Deadlines:** FAFSA. **Types of Aid:** *Need-based scholarships/grants:* College/university scholarship or grant aid from institutional funds; Federal Pell; Private scholarships; SEOG; State scholarships/grants; United Negro College Fund. *Loans:* Direct PLUS loans; Direct Subsidized Stafford Loans; Direct Unsubsidized Stafford Loans. *Student Employment:* Federal Work-Study Program available. Institutional employment available. **Financial Aid Statistics:** 100% needy freshmen, 99% needy undergrads receive need-based scholarship or grant aid. 22% freshmen, 26% undergrads receive non-need-based scholarship or grant aid. 65% freshmen, 69% undergrads receive need-based self-help aid. 0% freshmen, 0% undergrads receive athletic scholarships. 100% freshmen, 99% undergrads receive any aid.

70% undergrads borrow to pay for school. Average cumulative indebtedness $33,026. **Criteria for awarding aid:** *Need-based:* Alumni affiliation *Non-need-based:* Academics, Art, Leadership, Music/drama, State/district residency.

SYRACUSE UNIVERSITY

900 South Crouse Ave., Syracuse, NY 13244-2130
Phone: 315-443-3611 • **Financial Aid Phone:** 315-443-1513
E-mail: orange@syr.edu • **CEEB Code:** 2823
Fax: 315-443-4226 • **Website:** https://www.syracuse.edu • **ACT Code:** 2968

This private school was founded in 1870. It has a 721 acre campus.

RATINGS

Admissions Selectivity Rating: 89   **Fire Safety Rating:** 96   **Green Rating:** 97

STUDENTS AND FACULTY

Enrollment: 14,788. **Student Body:** 54% female, 46% male, 60% out-of-state, 13% international (86 countries represented). Asian 7%, African American 7%, Caucasian 57%, Hispanic 10%, Native American 1%, Pacific Islander <1%, Two or more races 3%, Race unknown 3%.
Retention and Graduation: 91% freshmen return for sophomore year. 70% freshmen graduate within 4 years. 83% freshmen graduate within 6 years. **Faculty:** Student/faculty ratio 15:1. 1,129 full-time faculty, 90% hold PhDs, 21% are members of minority groups, 42% are women.

ACADEMICS

Degrees: Associate; Bachelor's; Certificate; Doctoral/Professional; Doctoral/Research; Master's; Post-Bachelor's certificate; Post-Master's certificate **Classes:** Most classes have 20-29 students. Most lab/discussion sessions have 10-19 students. **Most popular majors:** Architecture; Speech Communication And Rhetoric; Information Science/Studies. **Special Study Options:** Accelerated program; Cooperative education program; Cross-registration; Distance learning; Double major; Dual enrollment; English as a Second Language (ESL); Honors program; Independent study; Internships; Liberal arts/career combination; Student-designed major; Study abroad; Teacher certification program. Honors programs: The Renee Crown University Honors Program provides a compelling educational experience for accomplished students. Individuals who seek academic challenge and are prepared to invest the extra effort required to meet that challenge will flourish in this demanding and rewarding program. Syracuse University has had an Honors program since 1963. Our current program reflects the University's emphasis on enriched intellectual breadth and depth, command of language, collaborative capacity, global awareness, and civic engagement. While students pursue their chosen academic course of study in their individual departments, schools, and colleges, they immerse themselves in curricular enrichment and innovative scholarship offered by the program's seminars, cultural events, and close contact with faculty and other Honors students. The program is open to qualified students in all of the University's undergraduate schools and colleges. **Disability Services offered to physically disabled students:** Note-taking services; Reader services; Tape recorders; Tutors. **Career services:** Alumni network; Alumni services; Career assessment; Career/job search classes; Internships; Regional alumni

FACILITIES

Housing: Apartments for single students; Coed dorms; Fraternity/sorority housing; Special housing for disabled student; Theme housing; Wellness housing 95% of campus accessible to physically diasbled. **Special Academic Facilities/Equipment:** SUArt Galleries; The Warehouse Gallery; digital media convergence center; Syracuse Center of Excellence in Environmental and Energy Systems; Fidelity MOTUS 622i flight simulator for aerospace engineering; Ballentine Investment Institute; Community Darkrooms; Syracuse Stage professional equity theater; Bernice M. Wright Child Development Laboratory School; Belfer Audio Laboratory and Archive; Gebbie Speech, Language, and Hearing Clinic; Life Sciences Complex; SU Library Special Collections Research Center; UPSTATE: A Center for Design, Research and Real Estate at the SU Schoolof Architecture; Center on Human Policy; Center for Emerging Network Technologies and many other research centers. **Computers:** 75% of classrooms, 100% of dorms, 100% of libraries, 100% of dining areas, 100% of student union, 75% of common outdoor areas have wireless network access. Students can register for classes online. Administrative functions (other than registration) can be performed online.

CAMPUS LIFE

Environment: City **Activities:** Campus Ministries; Choral groups; Concert band; Dance; Drama/theater; International Student Organization; Jazz band; Literary magazine; Marching band; Model UN; Music ensembles; Musical theater; Opera; Pep band; Radio station; Student government; Student newspaper; Student-run film society; Symphony orchestra; Television station; Yearbook 347 registered organizations, 43 honor societies, 30 religious organizations. 29 fraternities, 19 sororities. **Athletics (Intercollegiate):** *Men:* basketball, cheerleading, crew/rowing, cross-country, diving, football, lacrosse, soccer, swimming, track/field (outdoor). *Women:* basketball, cheerleading, crew/rowing, cross-country, diving, field hockey, ice hockey, lacrosse, soccer, softball, swimming, tennis, track/field (outdoor), volleyball. **On-Campus Highlights:** Schine Student Center, Carrier Dome, Bird Library, Einhorn Family Walk, Archbold Gymnasium **Environmental Initiatives:** Through the Climate Action Plan SU is able to offer grant funding, up to $50,000, to faculty and students to who have projects that promote reductions in greenhouse gas emission and increase awareness about sustainability on campus. This grant program merges academic scholarship with the University's broad initiatives to meet energy efficiency goals, while having the campus become a test-bed for innovative ideas. These projects will help the University meets its goal of climate neutrality on or before Dec. 31, 2040.

ADMISSIONS

Freshman Academic Profile: Average high school GPA 3.6. 36% in top 10% of high school class, 69% in top 25% of high school class, 94% in top 50% of high school class. 65% from public high schools. **Test Scores:** SAT Math middle 50% range 580-680. SAT EBRW middle 50% range 580-670. ACT middle 50% range 25-30. **Basis for Candidate Selection:** *Very important factors considered include:* rigor of secondary school record, class rank, academic GPA, application essay, standardized test scores, recommendation(s), interview, extracurricular activities, talent/ability, character/personal qualities, volunteer work, level of applicant's interest. *Other factors considered include:* first generation, alumni/ae relation, geographical residence, state residency, racial/ethnic status, work experience. **Freshman Admission Requirements:** High school diploma is required and GED is accepted *Academic units recommended:* 4 English, 4 math, 4 science, 4 science labs, 3 foreign language, 4 social studies, 4 history. **Freshman Admission Statistics:** 33,099 applied, 46.9% admitted, 24% enrolled. **Transfer Admission Requirements:** college transcript(s), essay or personal statement, statement of good standing from prior institution(s). Lowest grade transferable C. **General Admission Information:** Application fee $75. Priority deadline 11/15. Regular application deadline 1/1. Nonfall registration accepted. Admission may be deferred for a maximum of 1 year.

COSTS AND FINANCIAL AID

Required Forms and Deadlines: CSS/Financial Aid PROFILE; FAFSA; Noncustodial PROFILE. **Notification of Awards:** Applicants will be notified of awards on or about 3/15. **Types of Aid:** *Need-based scholarships/grants:* College/university scholarship or grant aid from institutional funds; Federal Pell; Private scholarships; SEOG; State scholarships/grants. *Loans:* Direct PLUS loans; Direct Subsidized Stafford Loans; Direct Unsubsidized Stafford Loans. *Student Employment:* Federal Work-Study Program available. Institutional employment available. **Financial Aid Statistics:** 93% needy freshmen, 92% needy undergrads receive need-based scholarship or grant aid. 13% freshmen, 7% undergrads receive non-need-based scholarship or grant aid. 89% freshmen, 92% undergrads receive need-based self-help aid. 2% freshmen, 2% undergrads receive athletic scholarships. 71% freshmen, 73% undergrads receive any aid. Average cumulative indebtedness $37,753. **Criteria for awarding aid:** *Need-based:* Academics, Athletics *Non-need-based:* Academics, Art, Athletics, Music/drama.

TALLADEGA COLLEGE

627 West Battle Street, Talladega, AL 35160
Phone: 205-761-6235 • **Financial Aid Phone:** 256-761-6341
E-mail: admissions@talladega.edu
Fax: 205-362-0274 • **Website:** www.talladega.edu • **ACT Code:** 26

This private school, affiliated with the United Church of Christ, was founded in 1867. It has a 50 acre campus.

RATINGS

Admissions Selectivity Rating: 84   **Fire Safety Rating:** 91   **Green Rating:** 60*

STUDENTS AND FACULTY

Enrollment: 601. **Student Body:** 58% female, 42% male, 48% out-of-state, 0% international. Asian 0%, African American 95%, Caucasian 0%, Hispanic 4%, Native American 0%, Race unknown 0%.

Retention and Graduation: 43% freshmen return for sophomore year. 25% grads go on to further study within 1 year. 25% grads pursue arts and sciences degrees. 25% grads pursue law degrees. 25% grads pursue business degrees. 25% grads pursue medical degrees. **Faculty:** Student/faculty ratio 16:1. 29 full-time faculty, 62% hold PhDs, 66% are members of minority groups, 45% are women. 0% of classes are taught by teaching assistants.

ACADEMICS

Degrees: Bachelor's **Classes:** Most classes have 10-19 students. Most lab/discussion sessions have 10-19 students. **Most popular majors:** Biology/Biological Sciences, General; Psychology, General; Business/Commerce, General. **Special Study Options:** Double major; Dual enrollment; Independent study; Internships; Teacher certification program. **Disability Services offered to physically disabled students:** Note-taking services; Tape recorders; Tutors. **Career services:** Alumni network; Alumni services; Career assessment; Internships

FACILITIES

Housing: Men's dorms; Women's dorms 100% of campus accessible to physically disabled. **Special Academic Facilities/Equipment:** Savery Library, Home of the famous Amistad Murals, historic Swayne Hall, which is listed on the National Register; DeForest Chapel, which has the stained glass windows by famous artist, David Driskell; Goodnow Art Building **Computers:** 100% of libraries, 50% of common outdoor areas have wireless network access. Administrative functions (other than registration) can be performed online.

CAMPUS LIFE

Environment: Rural **Activities:** Choral groups; Concert band; Dance; Drama/theater; Jazz band; Student government; Student newspaper; Yearbook 40 registered organizations, 8 honor societies, 1 religious organization. 4 fraternities, 4 sororities. **Athletics (Intercollegiate):** *Men:* baseball, basketball, golf. *Women:* basketball, cheerleading, volleyball. **On-Campus Highlights:** Savery Library, DeForest Chapel, Swayne Hall, Callanan Hall, Fanning Hall

ADMISSIONS

Freshman Academic Profile: Average high school GPA 2.7. 90% from public high schools. **Test Scores:** SAT Math middle 50% range 340-410. SAT EBRW middle 50% range 320-460. ACT middle 50% range 16-19. Minimum paper TOEFL 500. **Basis for Candidate Selection:** *Very important factors considered include:* rigor of secondary school record, application essay, standardized test scores, recommendation(s), extracurricular activities, talent/ability, character/personal qualities, volunteer work, work experience. *Important factors considered include:* class rank. *Other factors considered include:* interview. **Freshman Admission Requirements:** High school diploma is required and GED is accepted *Academic units required:* 4 English, 2 math, 2 science, 3 social studies, and 2 units from above areas or other academic areas. **Freshman Admission Statistics:** 1,960 applied, 38.0% admitted, 24% enrolled. **Transfer Admission Requirements:** High school transcript, college transcript(s), essay or personal statement, standardized test scores, statement of good standing from prior institution(s). Minimum college GPA of 2.0 required. Lowest grade transferable C. **General Admission Information:** Application fee $25. Nonfall registration accepted. Admission may be deferred for a maximum of 2 years.

COSTS AND FINANCIAL AID

Annual tuition $6,720. Room and board $4,290. Required fees $408. Average book expense $1,000. **Required Forms and Deadlines:** CSS/Financial Aid PROFILE; FAFSA; Institution's own financial aid form; State aid form. **Notification of Awards:** Applicants will be notified of awards on or about 4/1. **Types of Aid:** *Need-based scholarships/grants:* College/university scholarship or grant aid from institutional funds; Federal Pell; Private scholarships; SEOG; State scholarships/grants; United Negro College Fund. **Financial Aid Statistics:** 45% needy freshmen, 26% needy undergrads receive need-based scholarship or grant aid. 45% freshmen, 26% undergrads receive non-need-based scholarship or grant aid. 0% freshmen, 0% undergrads receive need-based self-help aid. 0% freshmen, 0% undergrads receive athletic scholarships. 90% freshmen, 90% undergrads receive any aid. **Criteria for awarding aid:** *Need-based:* Leadership, Minority status, Religious affiliation *Non-need-based:* Academics, Alumni affiliation, Art, Athletics, Music/drama.

TARLETON STATE UNIVERSITY

Box T-0001 Tarleton Station, Stephenville, TX 76402
Phone: 254-968-9125 • **Financial Aid Phone:** 254-968-9070
E-mail: uadm@tarleton.edu • **CEEB Code:** 6817
Fax: 254-968-9951 • **ACT Code:** 4204

This public school was founded in 1899. It has a 125 acre campus.

RATINGS

Admissions Selectivity Rating: 78   **Fire Safety Rating:** 60*   **Green Rating:** 60*

STUDENTS AND FACULTY

Enrollment: 11,283. **Student Body:** 61% female, 39% male, 2% out-of-state, <1% international (33 countries represented). Asian 1%, African American 8%, Caucasian 66%, Hispanic 20%, Native American 1%, Pacific Islander <1%, Two or more races 3%, Race unknown 1%.
Retention and Graduation: 67% freshmen return for sophomore year. 26% freshmen graduate within 4 years. 46% freshmen graduate within 6 years.
Faculty: Student/faculty ratio 17:1. 393 full-time faculty, 19% are members of minority groups, 52% are women. 2% of classes are taught by teaching assistants.

ACADEMICS

Degrees: Associate; Bachelor's; Doctoral; **Master's Classes:** Most classes have 10-19 students. Most lab/discussion sessions have 10-19 students. **Most popular majors:** Multi-/Interdisciplinary Studies, Other; Kinesiology And Exercise Science; Psychology, General. **Special Study Options:** Accelerated program; Distance learning; Double major; Dual enrollment; Honors program; Internships; Study abroad; Teacher certification program. Honors programs: Offer honors classes in core curriculum subjects, including English, history, political science, chemistry, biology, geology, and speech. Courses offer intellectually challenging material, innovative approaches to the subject, increased opportunities for honing critical thinking and writing skills, and the opportunity to interact closely with similarly motivated students and with outstanding faculty. **Disability Services offered to physically disabled students:** Note-taking services; Reader services; Tape recorders; Tutors.
Career services: Alumni services; Career assessment; Career/job search classes; Internships

FACILITIES

Housing: Apartments for married students; Apartments for single students; Coed dorms; Men's dorms; Special housing for disabled student; Women's dorms 100% of campus accessible to physically diasbled. **Special Academic Facilities/Equipment:** Planetarium in Science Bldg. W.K. Gordon Center for Industrial History of Texas **Computers:** 100% of classrooms, 100% of dorms, 100% of libraries, 100% of student union, have wireless network access. Students can register for classes online. Administrative functions (other than registration) can be performed online.

CAMPUS LIFE

Environment: Village **Activities:** Campus Ministries; Choral groups; Concert band; Dance; Drama/theater; International Student Organization; Jazz band; Literary magazine; Marching band; Music ensembles; Musical theater; Pep band; Radio station; Student government; Student newspaper; Symphony orchestra; Yearbook 117 registered organizations, 13 honor societies, 13 religious organizations. 7 fraternities, 8 sororities. **Athletics (Intercollegiate):** *Men:* baseball, basketball, cheerleading, cross-country, football, rodeo, track/field (outdoor). *Women:* basketball, cheerleading, cross-country, golf, rodeo, softball, tennis, track/field (outdoor), volleyball. **On-Campus Highlights:** Barry B. Thompson Student Center, Recreational Sports Facility, Dick Smith Library, Wisdom Gym, Science Bldg with Planetarium **Environmental Initiatives:** 15% Electric from wind

ADMISSIONS

Freshman Academic Profile: 10% in top 10% of high school class, 29% in top 25% of high school class, 88% in top 50% of high school class. 97% from public high schools. **Test Scores:** SAT Math middle 50% range 480-560. SAT EBRW middle 50% range 480-570. ACT middle 50% range 18-23. Minimum internet-based TOEFL 190. Minimum paper TOEFL 520. **Basis for Candidate Selection:** *Very important factors considered include:* rigor of secondary school record, academic GPA, standardized test scores. *Important factors considered include:* class rank. **Freshman Admission Requirements:** High school diploma is required and GED is accepted *Academic units required:* 4 English, 3 math, 2 science, 2 social studies, 1 history, 2 academic electives, *Academic units recommended:* 3 science, 2 foreign language, 4 academic electives. **Freshman Admission Statistics:** 7,158 applied, 74.4% admitted, 33% enrolled. **Transfer Admission Requirements:** college transcript(s), Minimum college GPA of 2.0 required. Lowest grade transferable D. **General Admission Information:** Application fee $45. Priority deadline 12/1. Regular application deadline 6/1. Nonfall registration accepted.

COSTS AND FINANCIAL AID

Required Forms and Deadlines: FAFSA. **Notification of Awards:** Applicants will be notified of awards on a rolling basis beginning 5/1. **Types of Aid:** *Need-based scholarships/grants:* College/university scholarship or grant aid from institutional funds; Federal Pell; SEOG; State scholarships/grants. *Loans:* Direct PLUS loans; Direct Subsidized Stafford Loans; Direct Unsubsidized Stafford Loans. *Student Employment:* Federal Work-Study Program available. Institutional employment available. **Financial Aid Statistics:** 94% needy freshmen, 89% needy undergrads receive need-based scholarship or grant aid. 6% freshmen, 2% undergrads receive non-need-based scholarship or grant aid. 71% freshmen, 77% undergrads receive need-based self-help aid. 0% freshmen, 0% undergrads receive athletic scholarships. 57% freshmen, 37% undergrads receive any aid. 68% undergrads borrow to pay for school. Average cumulative indebtedness $26,507. **Criteria for awarding aid:** *Non-need-based:* Academics, Alumni affiliation, Athletics, Leadership, Music/drama.

TAYLOR UNIVERSITY

236 West Reade Avenue, Upland, IN 46989-1001
Phone: 765-998-5134 • **Financial Aid Phone:** 765-998-5358
E-mail: admissions@tayloru.edu • **CEEB Code:** 1802
Fax: 765-998-4925 • **Website:** www.taylor.edu • **ACT Code:** 1248

This private school, affiliated with the Evangelical Christian Interdenominational Church, was founded in 1846. It has a 952 acre campus.

RATINGS

Admissions Selectivity Rating: 82   **Fire Safety Rating:** 95   **Green Rating:** 64

STUDENTS AND FACULTY

Enrollment: 1,858. **Student Body:** 56% female, 44% male, 58% out-of-state, 5% international (36 countries represented). Asian 3%, African American 4%, Caucasian 83%, Hispanic 4%, Native American 1%, Pacific Islander <1%, Two or more races <1%, Race unknown 0%.
Retention and Graduation: 90% freshmen return for sophomore year. 71% freshmen graduate within 4 years. 79% freshmen graduate within 6 years. 22% grads go on to further study within 1 year. 27% grads pursue arts and sciences degrees. 2% grads pursue law degrees. 3% grads pursue business degrees. 2% grads pursue medical degrees. **Faculty:** Student/faculty ratio 13:1. 133 full-time faculty, 83% hold PhDs, 6% are members of minority groups, 30% are women. 0% of classes are taught by teaching assistants.

ACADEMICS

Degrees: Associate; Bachelor's; Diploma; **Master's Classes:** Most classes have 10-19 students. Most lab/discussion sessions have 10-19 students. **Most popular majors:** Elementary Education And Teaching; Biology/Biological Sciences, General; Kinesiology And Exercise Science. **Special Study Options:** Cooperative education program; Distance learning; Double major; Dual enrollment; English as a Second Language (ESL); Exchange student program (domestic); Honors program; Independent study; Internships; Student-designed major; Study abroad; Teacher certification program. Honors programs: Honors Program emphasizes to a greater extent than the general curriculum, integration of faith and learning, ideas and values in content and discussion and student initiative in format. Also offer Freshmen Irish Studies Program in Ireland. **Disability Services offered to physically disabled students:** Note-taking services; Reader services; Tape recorders; Tutors. **Career services:** Alumni network; Alumni services; Career assessment; Internships; Regional alumni

FACILITIES

Housing: Apartments for married students; Apartments for single students; Men's dorms; Wellness housing; Women's dorms 95% of campus accessible to physically diasbled. **Special Academic Facilities/Equipment:** Compton Art Gallery, Edwin W. Brown Collection/CS Lewis and Friends. Euler Science Complex provides 10kW Photo-Voltaic Solar Array. **Computers:** 100% of classrooms, 100% of dorms, 100% of libraries, 100% of dining areas, 100% of student union, 50% of common outdoor areas have wireless network access. Students can register for classes online. Administrative functions (other than registration) can be performed online.

CAMPUS LIFE

Environment: Rural **Activities:** Choral groups; Concert band; Drama/theater; International Student Organization; Jazz band; Literary magazine; Music ensembles; Musical theater; Opera; Pep band; Radio station; Student government; Student newspaper; Student-run film society; Symphony orchestra;

Television station; Yearbook 87 registered organizations, 7 honor societies, 23 religious organizations. **Athletics (Intercollegiate):** *Men:* baseball, basketball, cross-country, football, golf, soccer, tennis, track/field (outdoor), track/field (indoor). *Women:* basketball, cross-country, soccer, softball, tennis, track/field (outdoor), track/field (indoor), volleyball. **On-Campus Highlights:** LaRita R. Boren Campus Center, Kesler Student Activities Center, Rediger Chapel and Auditorium, Euler Science Complex, Zondervan Library **Environmental Initiatives:** The 127,000 sq. ft. Euler Science Complex, was completed in the summer of 2012, and subsequently obtained LEED status. This facility includes innovative sustainability features. This includes a 10kW photovoltaic system.

ADMISSIONS

Freshman Academic Profile: Average high school GPA 3.8. 35% in top 10% of high school class, 63% in top 25% of high school class, 88% in top 50% of high school class. 80% from public high schools. **Test Scores:** SAT Math middle 50% range 515-640. SAT EBRW middle 50% range 530-650. ACT middle 50% range 22-29. Minimum internet-based TOEFL 80. **Basis for Candidate Selection:** *Very important factors considered include:* rigor of secondary school record, academic GPA, application essay, standardized test scores, recommendation(s), character/personal qualities, religious affiliation/commitment. *Important factors considered include:* class rank, interview, extracurricular activities, volunteer work. *Other factors considered include:* talent/ability, first generation, alumni/ae relation, geographical residence, state residency, racial/ethnic status, work experience. **Freshman Admission Requirements:** High school diploma is required and GED is accepted *Academic units required:* 4 English, 3 math, 3 science, 3 science labs, 2 social studies, 3 academic electives, *Academic units recommended:* 4 math, 4 science, 4 science labs, 2 foreign language, 3 social studies, 1 computer science, 1 visual/performing arts. **Freshman Admission Statistics:** 1,673 applied, 86.8% admitted, 31% enrolled. **Transfer Admission Requirements:** High school transcript, college transcript(s), essay or personal statement, standardized test scores, statement of good standing from prior institution(s). Minimum college GPA of 2.5 required. Lowest grade transferable C+. **General Admission Information:** Application fee $15. Priority deadline 2/1. Regular application deadline 8/1. Nonfall registration accepted. Admission may be deferred for a maximum of 2 years.

COSTS AND FINANCIAL AID

Annual tuition $32,640. Required fees $245. Average book expense $1,200. **Required Forms and Deadlines:** FAFSA. **Notification of Awards:** Applicants will be notified of awards on a rolling basis beginning 3/1. **Types of Aid:** *Need-based scholarships/grants:* College/university scholarship or grant aid from institutional funds; Federal Pell; Private scholarships; SEOG; State scholarships/grants. *Loans:* Direct PLUS loans; Direct Subsidized Stafford Loans; Direct Unsubsidized Stafford Loans. *Student Employment:* Federal Work-Study Program available. Institutional employment available. **Financial Aid Statistics:** 100% needy freshmen, 100% needy undergrads receive need-based scholarship or grant aid. 19% freshmen, 18% undergrads receive non-need-based scholarship or grant aid. 81% freshmen, 82% undergrads receive need-based self-help aid. 6% freshmen, 7% undergrads receive athletic scholarships. 99% freshmen, 96% undergrads receive any aid. 62% undergrads borrow to pay for school. Average cumulative indebtedness $29,411. **Criteria for awarding aid:** *Need-based:* Art, Athletics, Leadership, Minority status, Music/drama, Religious affiliation *Non-need-based:* Academics, Alumni affiliation, Art, Athletics, Leadership, Minority status, Music/drama, Religious affiliation, State/district residency.

TECNOLÓGICO DE MONTERREY

Av. Eugenio Garza Sada, 2501 Sur, Col. T, Monterrey, Mexico
Phone: +52 (81) 8158-2269
E-mail: admisiones.mty@itesm.mx
Website: www.itesm.mx

This is a private school.

RATINGS
Admissions Selectivity Rating: 69   **Fire Safety Rating:** 60*   **Green Rating:** 60*

STUDENTS AND FACULTY
Enrollment: 55,015. **Student Body:** 43% female, 57% male, 22% out-of-state, international.
Retention and Graduation: 90% freshmen return for sophomore year.
Faculty: Student/faculty ratio 15:1. 1,609 full-time faculty, 57% hold PhDs, 38% are women.

ACADEMICS
Degrees: Bachelor's; Doctoral/Research; **Master's Classes:** Most classes have 20-29 students.

ADMISSIONS
Freshman Admission Statistics: 15,717 applied, 85.9% admitted, 74% enrolled.

TEMPLE UNIVERSITY

1801 North Broad Street, Philadelphia, PA 19122
Phone: 215-204-7200 • **Financial Aid Phone:** (215) 204-2244
E-mail: TUADM@TEMPLE.EDU • **CEEB Code:** 2906
Fax: 215-204-5694 • **Website:** www.temple.edu • **ACT Code:** 3724

This public school was founded in 1888. It has a 384 acre campus.

RATINGS
Admissions Selectivity Rating: 87   **Fire Safety Rating:** 98   **Green Rating:** 91

STUDENTS AND FACULTY
Enrollment: 29,007. **Student Body:** 53% female, 47% male, 21% out-of-state, 7% international (108 countries represented). Asian 12%, African American 13%, Caucasian 56%, Hispanic 7%, Native American <1%, Pacific Islander <1%, Two or more races 3%, Race unknown 3%.
Retention and Graduation: 90% freshmen return for sophomore year. 45% freshmen graduate within 4 years. 71% freshmen graduate within 6 years. 18% grads go on to further study within 1 year. **Faculty:** Student/faculty ratio 14:1. 1,483 full-time faculty, 89% hold PhDs, 21% are members of minority groups, 42% are women.

ACADEMICS
Degrees: Associate; Bachelor's; Certificate; Diploma; Doctoral; Doctoral/Professional; Doctoral/Research; Master's; Post-Bachelor's certificate; Post-Master's certificate; Terminal Associate; Transfer Associate **Classes:** Most classes have 10-19 students. Most lab/discussion sessions have 20-29 students. **Most popular majors:** Biology/Biological Sciences, General; Psychology, General; Business/Commerce, General. **Special Study Options:** Accelerated program; Cooperative education program; Distance learning; Double major; Dual enrollment; English as a Second Language (ESL); Exchange student program (domestic); Honors program; Independent study; Internships; Study abroad; Teacher certification program. Honors programs: The Honors Program at Temple University promotes intellectual curiosity and social courage, valuing academic excellence, integrity, and leadership. It is a community and network of scholars comprised of high-achieving undergraduate students, nationally recognized advisors and staff, faculty celebrated both for teaching and research, and impressive alumni at the top of their fields. Honors provides its students with enriching academic opportunities, guides them through co-curricular experiences, cultivates a dynamic and inclusive community, and offers strong encouragement and support. Combined degree programs: BA/DDS; BA/MA; BA/MD; BA/MEng. **Disability Services offered to physically disabled students:** Note-taking services; Reader services; Tape recorders; Tutors. **Career services:** Alumni services; Career assessment; Career/job search classes; Internships; Regional alumni

FACILITIES
Housing: Apartments for single students; Coed dorms; Special housing for disabled student; Theme housing 95% of campus accessible to physically diasbled. **Special Academic Facilities/Equipment:** Charles L. Blockson Afro-American Collection, Urban Archives, observatory, planetarium, Technology Center, Temple Gallery at Tyler School of Art **Computers:** 40% of classrooms, 30% of dorms, 80% of libraries, 90% of dining areas, 100% of student union, 40% of common outdoor areas have wireless network access. Students can register for classes online. Administrative functions (other than registration) can be performed online.

CAMPUS LIFE
Environment: Metropolis **Activities:** Choral groups; Concert band; Dance; Drama/theater; International Student Organization; Jazz band; Literary magazine; Marching band; Model UN; Music ensembles; Musical theater; Opera; Pep band; Radio station; Student government; Student newspaper; Student-run film society; Symphony orchestra; Television station; Yearbook 232 registered organizations, 12 honor societies, 24 religious organizations. 11 fraternities, 9 sororities. **Athletics (Intercollegiate):** *Men:* baseball,

basketball, cheerleading, crew/rowing, cross-country, football, golf, gymnastics, soccer, table tennis, tennis, track/field (outdoor), track/field (indoor). *Women:* basketball, cheerleading, crew/rowing, cross-country, fencing, field hockey, gymnastics, lacrosse, soccer, softball, table tennis, tennis, track/field (outdoor), track/field (indoor), volleyball. **On-Campus Highlights:** The TECH Center, Howard Gittis Student Center, The Liacouras Center, O'Connor Plaza and Founder's Garden, The Bell Tower

ADMISSIONS

Freshman Academic Profile: Average high school GPA 3.5. 21% in top 10% of high school class, 55% in top 25% of high school class, 90% in top 50% of high school class. **Test Scores:** SAT Math middle 50% range 560-650. SAT EBRW middle 50% range 570-660. ACT middle 50% range 24-29. Minimum internet-based TOEFL 79. **Basis for Candidate Selection:** *Very important factors considered include:* rigor of secondary school record, academic GPA. *Important factors considered include:* class rank. *Other factors considered include:* application essay, standardized test scores, recommendation(s), extracurricular activities, talent/ability, character/personal qualities, alumni/ae relation, geographical residence, state residency, volunteer work, work experience. **Freshman Admission Requirements:** High school diploma is required and GED is accepted *Academic units required:* 4 English, 3 math, 2 science, 1 science labs, 2 foreign language, 2 social studies, 1 history, 1 academic elective, 1 visual/performing arts, *Academic units recommended:* 4 English, 4 math, 3 science, 2 science labs, 2 foreign language, 2 social studies, 1 history, 3 academic electives, 1 visual/performing arts. **Freshman Admission Statistics:** 35,880 applied, 56.7% admitted, 25% enrolled. **Transfer Admission Requirements:** High school transcript, college transcript(s), essay or personal statement, Minimum college GPA of 2.50 required. Lowest grade transferable C. **General Admission Information:** Application fee $55. Priority deadline 11/1. Regular application deadline 2/1. Nonfall registration accepted. Admission may be deferred for a maximum of 1 year.

COSTS AND FINANCIAL AID

Annual in-state tuition $11,566. Annual out-of-state tuition $27,528. Room and board $11,566. Required fees $1,231. Average book expense $1,112. **Required Forms and Deadlines:** FAFSA. **Notification of Awards:** Applicants will be notified of awards on a rolling basis beginning 2/1. **Types of Aid:** *Need-based scholarships/grants:* College/university scholarship or grant aid from institutional funds; Federal Nursing Scholarships; Federal Pell; Private scholarships; SEOG; State scholarships/grants; United Negro College Fund. *Loans:* Direct PLUS loans; Direct Subsidized Stafford Loans; Direct Unsubsidized Stafford Loans. *Student Employment:* Federal Work-Study Program available. Institutional employment available. **Financial Aid Statistics:** 85% needy freshmen, 84% needy undergrads receive need-based scholarship or grant aid. 58% freshmen, 45% undergrads receive non-need-based scholarship or grant aid. 77% freshmen, 83% undergrads receive need-based self-help aid. 2% freshmen, 2% undergrads receive athletic scholarships. 90% freshmen, 83% undergrads receive any aid. 77% undergrads borrow to pay for school. Average cumulative indebtedness $37,708. **Criteria for awarding aid:** *Non-need-based:* Academics, Art, Athletics, Music/drama.

See page 1048.

TENNESSEE STATE UNIVERSITY

3500 John Merritt Boulevard, Nashville, TN 37209-1561
Phone: 615-963-3101
E-mail: jcade@tnstate.edu
Fax: 615-963-5108 • **Website:** www.tnstate.edu

This is a public school.

RATINGS

Admissions Selectivity Rating: 90   **Fire Safety Rating:** 60*   **Green Rating:** 60*

STUDENTS AND FACULTY

Enrollment: 7,000. **Student Body:** 63% female, 37% male, 49% out-of-state, 1% international. Asian 1%, African American 83%, Caucasian 15%, Hispanic 1%, Native American 0%, Race unknown 0%.
Retention and Graduation: 77% freshmen return for sophomore year. **Faculty:** Student/faculty ratio 22:1. 383 full-time faculty, 74% hold PhDs, 37% are members of minority groups, 42% are women.

ACADEMICS

Degrees: Associate; Bachelor's; **Master's Classes:** Most classes have 20-29 students. Most lab/discussion sessions have 10-19 students. **Special Study Options:** Cooperative education program; Cross-registration; Double major; Exchange student program (domestic); Honors program; Independent study; Internships; Liberal arts/career combination; Teacher certification program.

FACILITIES

Housing: Apartments for single students; Coed dorms; Men's dorms; Women's dorms

CAMPUS LIFE

Activities: Choral groups; Drama/theater; Jazz band; Marching band; Music ensembles; Radio station; Student government; Student newspaper; Yearbook.

ADMISSIONS

Freshman Academic Profile: Average high school GPA 3.0. 90% from public high schools. **Test Scores:** SAT Math middle 50% range 430-510. SAT EBRW middle 50% range 430-510. ACT middle 50% range 18-21. Minimum paper TOEFL 500. **Basis for Candidate Selection:** *Very important factors considered include:* standardized test scores, state residency. *Important factors considered include:* rigor of secondary school record, class rank, recommendation(s), geographical residence. *Other factors considered include:* extracurricular activities, talent/ability, character/personal qualities, alumni/ae relation. **Freshman Admission Requirements:** High school diploma is required and GED is accepted *Academic units required:* 4 English, 3 math, 2 science, 1 science labs, 2 foreign language, 1 social studies, 1 history, 1 academic elective. **Freshman Admission Statistics:** 6,344 applied, 34.7% admitted, 59% enrolled. **Transfer Admission Requirements:** college transcript(s), Minimum college GPA of 2.9 required. Lowest grade transferable C. **General Admission Information:** Application fee $15. Regular application deadline 8/1.

COSTS AND FINANCIAL AID

Annual in-state tuition $3,060. Annual out-of-state tuition $10,230. Room and board $3,060. Required fees $150. Average book expense $850. **Required Forms and Deadlines:** CSS/Financial Aid PROFILE; FAFSA; Noncustodial PROFILE. **Types of Aid:** *Need-based scholarships/grants:* Federal Pell; SEOG. *Loans:* Direct PLUS loans; Direct Subsidized Stafford Loans; Direct Unsubsidized Stafford Loans. **Financial Aid Statistics:** 66% needy freshmen, 64% needy undergrads receive need-based scholarship or grant aid. 25% freshmen, 24% undergrads receive non-need-based scholarship or grant aid. 77% freshmen, 76% undergrads receive need-based self-help aid. 1% freshmen receive athletic scholarships. **Criteria for awarding aid:** *Need-based:* Academics, Athletics.

TENNESSEE TECHNOLOGICAL UNIVERSITY

PO Box 5006, Cookeville, TN 38505
Phone: (931) 372-3888 • **Financial Aid Phone:** 931-372-3073
E-mail: admissions@tntech.edu • **CEEB Code:** 1804
Fax: (931) 372-6250 • **Website:** www.tntech.edu • **ACT Code:** 4012

This public school was founded in 1915. It has a 235 acre campus.

RATINGS

Admissions Selectivity Rating: 74   **Fire Safety Rating:** 80   **Green Rating:** 78

STUDENTS AND FACULTY

Enrollment: 9,647. **Student Body:** 45% female, 55% male, 3% out-of-state, 6% international. Asian 1%, African American 4%, Caucasian 84%, Hispanic 2%, Native American <1%, Pacific Islander <1%, Two or more races 2%, Race unknown <1%.
Retention and Graduation: 70% freshmen return for sophomore year. **Faculty:** Student/faculty ratio 21:1. 389 full-time faculty, 72% hold PhDs, 13% are members of minority groups, 40% are women. 1% of classes are taught by teaching assistants.

ACADEMICS

Degrees: Bachelor's; Doctoral; Master's; Post-Master's certificate **Classes:** Most classes have 10-19 students. Most lab/discussion sessions have 10-19 students. **Most popular majors:** Elementary Education And Teaching; Mechanical Engineering; Business/Commerce, General. **Special Study Options:** Cooperative education program; Distance learning; Double major; Dual enrollment; English as a Second Language (ESL); Honors program; Internships; Study abroad; Teacher certification program. **Disability Services offered to physically disabled students:** Note-taking services; Reader services; Tape recorders; Tutors. **Career services:** Alumni network; Alumni services; Career/job search classes; Internships; Regional alumni

FACILITIES

Housing: Apartments for married students; Apartments for single students; Coed dorms; Men's dorms; Special housing for disabled student; Special housing for international students; Theme housing; Women's dorms 99% of campus accessible to physically disabled. **Special Academic Facilities/Equipment:** 300-acre farm lab, electric power center, water resources center, manufacturing center. **Computers:** Students can register for classes online. Administrative functions (other than registration) can be performed online.

CAMPUS LIFE

Environment: Rural **Activities:** Campus Ministries; Choral groups; Concert band; Dance; Drama/theater; Jazz band; Literary magazine; Marching band; Music ensembles; Musical theater; Opera; Pep band; Radio station; Student government; Student newspaper; Symphony orchestra; Television station; Yearbook 182 registered organizations, 26 honor societies, 16 religious organizations. 12 fraternities, 8 sororities. **Athletics (Intercollegiate):** *Men:* baseball, basketball, cheerleading, cross-country, football, golf, riflery, tennis. *Women:* basketball, cheerleading, cross-country, golf, riflery, soccer, softball, tennis, track/field (outdoor), track/field (indoor), volleyball. **On-Campus Highlights:** Recreation/ Fitness Center, Barnes and Noble Bookstore, Joan Derryberry Art Gallery, New Residence Halls, Bryan Fine Arts Music Auditorium

ADMISSIONS

Freshman Academic Profile: Average high school GPA 3.4. 24% in top 10% of high school class, 50% in top 25% of high school class, 82% in top 50% of high school class. 80% from public high schools. **Test Scores:** SAT Math middle 50% range 490-640. SAT EBRW middle 50% range 480-600. ACT middle 50% range 20-26. Minimum paper TOEFL 500. **Basis for Candidate Selection:** *Very important factors considered include:* rigor of secondary school record, academic GPA, standardized test scores. *Other factors considered include:* application essay, recommendation(s), interview, extracurricular activities, character/personal qualities, alumni/ae relation. **Freshman Admission Requirements:** High school diploma is required and GED is accepted *Academic units required:* 4 English, 3 math, 2 science, 1 science labs, 2 foreign language, 1 social studies, 1 history, and 1 unit from above areas or other academic areas. **Freshman Admission Statistics:** 4,553 applied, 93.9% admitted, 45% enrolled. **Transfer Admission Requirements:** college transcript(s), Minimum college GPA of 2.0 required. Lowest grade transferable D. **General Admission Information:** Application fee $25. Priority deadline 12/15. Regular application deadline 8/1. Nonfall registration accepted. Admission may be deferred for a maximum of 1 semester.

COSTS AND FINANCIAL AID

Annual in-state tuition $7,382. Annual out-of-state tuition $18,000. Room and board $7,382. Required fees $1,034. Average book expense $1,500. **Required Forms and Deadlines:** FAFSA. **Notification of Awards:** Applicants will be notified of awards on a rolling basis beginning 3/15. **Types of Aid:** *Need-based scholarships/grants:* College/university scholarship or grant aid from institutional funds; Federal Pell; Private scholarships; SEOG; State scholarships/grants; United Negro College Fund. *Loans:* Direct PLUS loans; Direct Subsidized Stafford Loans; Direct Unsubsidized Stafford Loans. **Financial Aid Statistics:** 61% needy freshmen, 63% needy undergrads receive need-based scholarship or grant aid. 91% freshmen, 68% undergrads receive non-need-based scholarship or grant aid. 50% freshmen, 59% undergrads receive need-based self-help aid. 2% freshmen, 2% undergrads receive athletic scholarships. 91% freshmen, 89% undergrads receive any aid. **Criteria for awarding aid:** *Need-based:* Academics, Athletics *Non-need-based:* Academics, Alumni affiliation, Art, Athletics, Leadership, Minority status, Music/drama.

TEXAS A&M UNIVERSITY AT GALVESTON

P.O. Box 1675, Galveston, TX 77553
Phone: 409-740-4414 • **Financial Aid Phone:** 409-740-4418
E-mail: seaaggie@tamug.edu • **CEEB Code:** 6835
Fax: 409-740-4731 • **Website:** www.tamug.edu • **ACT Code:** 6592

This public school was founded in 1963. It has a 150 acre campus.

RATINGS

Admissions Selectivity Rating: 88   **Fire Safety Rating:** 92   **Green Rating:** 72

STUDENTS AND FACULTY

Enrollment: 50,392. **Student Body:** 49% female, 51% male, 13% out-of-state, 1% international (19 countries represented). Asian 6%, African American 3%, Caucasian 63%, Hispanic 23%, Native American <1%, Pacific Islander <1%, Two or more races 3%, Race unknown <1%.
Retention and Graduation: 91% freshmen return for sophomore year.
Faculty: Student/faculty ratio 15:1. 105 full-time faculty, 61% hold PhDs, 21% are members of minority groups, 33% are women. 3% of classes are taught by teaching assistants.

ACADEMICS

Degrees: Bachelor's; Doctoral; **Master's Classes:** Most classes have 10-19 students. **Most popular majors:** Naval Architecture And Marine Engineering; Marine Biology And Biological Oceanography. **Special Study Options:** Accelerated program; Cooperative education program; Double major; Dual enrollment; Independent study; Internships; Study abroad. **Disability Services offered to physically disabled students:** Note-taking services; Reader services; Tutors. **Career services:** Alumni network; Career assessment; Internships; Regional alumni

FACILITIES

Housing: Coed dorms; Special housing for disabled students 90% of campus accessible to physically diasbled. **Special Academic Facilities/Equipment:** USTS Texas Clipper II, Radar School/Ship Bridge Simulator, Engineering Laboratory Building, Sea Camp, Center for Bioacoustics, Center for Marine Training and Safety/TEEX, Laboratory for Oceanographic and Environmental Research, Galveston Bay Information Center, Center for Ports and Waterways, Coastal Zone Laboratory, GulfCet, Marine Mammal Research Program, Naval Science, Texas State Maritime Academy, Texas Institute of Oceanography, Texas Marine Mammal Stranding Network, Sea Turtle/Fisheries Ecology Lab. **Computers:** Students can register for classes online. Administrative functions (other than registration) can be performed online.

CAMPUS LIFE

Environment: Town **Activities:** Choral groups; Dance; Drama/theater; Literary magazine; Student government; Student newspaper; Yearbook 45 registered organizations, 16 honor societies, 4 religious organizations. **Athletics (Intercollegiate):** *Men:* crew/rowing, sailing. *Women:* crew/rowing, sailing. **On-Campus Highlights:** Mary Moody Northen Student Center, P.E. Facility, Small Boat Basin, Training Ship—General Rudder, Jack K. Williams Library

ADMISSIONS

Freshman Academic Profile: 66% in top 10% of high school class, 90% in top 25% of high school class, 99% in top 50% of high school class. 81% from public high schools. **Test Scores:** SAT Math middle 50% range 550-670. SAT EBRW middle 50% range 520-640. ACT middle 50% range 24-30. Minimum internet-based TOEFL 80. Minimum paper TOEFL 550. **Basis for Candidate Selection:** *Very important factors considered include:* rigor of secondary school record, class rank, academic GPA, standardized test scores, extracurricular activities, talent/ability. *Important factors considered include:* application essay, first generation, geographical residence, state residency, volunteer work, work experience. *Other factors considered include:* recommendation(s), character/personal qualities, level of applicant's interest. **Freshman Admission Requirements:** High school diploma is required and GED is accepted *Academic units required:* 4 English, 3 math, 3 science, 1 science labs, 2 foreign language, 3 social studies, 5 academic electives, 1 visual/performing arts, and 1 unit from above areas or other academic areas. *Academic units recommended:* 4 English, 4 math, 4 science, 2 science labs, 2 foreign language, 4 social studies, 7 academic electives, 1 visual/performing arts, 1 unit from above areas or other academic areas. **Freshman Admission Statistics:** 34,780 applied, 67.2% admitted, 43% enrolled. **Transfer Admission Requirements:** High school transcript, college transcript(s), essay or personal statement, Minimum college GPA of 2.5 required. Lowest grade transferable C. **General Admission Information:** Application fee $75. Priority deadline 12/1. Nonfall registration accepted.

COSTS AND FINANCIAL AID

Average book expense $1,246. **Required Forms and Deadlines:** FAFSA. **Notification of Awards:** Applicants will be notified of awards on or about 3/15. **Types of Aid:** *Need-based scholarships/grants:* College/university scholarship or grant aid from institutional funds; Federal Pell; Private scholarships; SEOG; State scholarships/grants. *Loans:* Direct PLUS loans; Direct Subsidized Stafford Loans; Direct Unsubsidized Stafford Loans. *Student Employment:* Federal Work-Study Program available. Institutional employment available. **Financial Aid Statistics:** 75% needy freshmen, 74% needy undergrads receive need-based scholarship or grant aid. 37% freshmen, 30% undergrads receive non-need-based scholarship or grant aid. 76% freshmen, 80% undergrads receive need-based self-help aid. 0% freshmen, 0% undergrads receive athletic scholarships. 45% freshmen, 56% undergrads receive any aid. **Criteria for awarding aid:** *Need-based:* Academics, Leadership *Non-need-based:* Academics, Leadership, State/district residency.

TEXAS A&M UNIVERSITY—COLLEGE STATION

P.O. Box 30014, College Station, TX 77843-3014
Phone: (979) 845-1060 • **Financial Aid Phone:** 979-845-3236
E-mail: admissions@tamu.edu • **CEEB Code:** 6003
Fax: (979) 458-1808 • **Website:** www.tamu.edu • **ACT Code:** 4198

This public school was founded in 1876. It has a 5200 acre campus.

RATINGS
Admissions Selectivity Rating: 88   **Fire Safety Rating:** 95   **Green Rating:** 91

STUDENTS AND FACULTY
Enrollment: 52,571. **Student Body:** 48% female, 52% male, 4% out-of-state, 1% international (77 countries represented). Asian 7%, African American 3%, Caucasian 62%, Hispanic 23%, Native American <1%, Pacific Islander <1%, Two or more races 3%, Race unknown <1%.
Retention and Graduation: 92% freshmen return for sophomore year. 54% freshmen graduate within 4 years. 82% freshmen graduate within 6 years. **Faculty:** Student/faculty ratio 21:1. 3,079 full-time faculty, 90% hold PhDs, 29% are members of minority groups, 36% are women. 10% of classes are taught by teaching assistants.

ACADEMICS
Degrees: Bachelor's; Doctoral/Professional; Doctoral/Research; Master's; Post-Bachelor's certificate; Post-Master's certificate **Classes:** Most classes have 10-19 students. Most lab/discussion sessions have fewer than 10 students. **Most popular majors:** Engineering, General; Biomedical Sciences, General; Business Administration And Management, General. **Special Study Options:** Accelerated program; Cooperative education program; Cross-registration; Distance learning; Double major; Dual enrollment; English as a Second Language (ESL); Honors program; Independent study; Internships; Liberal arts/career combination; Study abroad; Teacher certification program. **Disability Services offered to physically disabled students:** Note-taking services; Reader services; Tape recorders; Tutors. **Career services:** Alumni network; Alumni services; Career assessment; Career/job search classes; Internships; Regional alumni

FACILITIES
Housing: Apartments for married students; Apartments for single students; Coed dorms; Cooperative housing; Fraternity/sorority housing; Men's dorms; Special housing for international students; Theme housing; Women's dorms 85% of campus accessible to physically disabled. **Special Academic Facilities/Equipment:** Bush Library/Museum; Jordan International Collection; Corps of Cadets Center/Museum; Forsyth Center Gallary; MSC Visual Arts Gallary; J.Wayne Stark University Center Gallaries Oran W. Nicks Low Speed Wind Tunnel Astronomical Observatory Ocean Drilling Program Building **Computers:** 100% of classrooms, 10% of dorms, 100% of libraries, 100% of dining areas, 100% of student union, have wireless network access. Students can register for classes online. Administrative functions (other than registration) can be performed online.

CAMPUS LIFE
Environment: City **Activities:** Campus Ministries; Choral groups; Concert band; Dance; Drama/theater; International Student Organization; Jazz band; Literary magazine; Marching band; Music ensembles; Musical theater; Radio station; Student government; Student newspaper; Student-run film society; Symphony orchestra; Television station; Yearbook 725 registered organizations, 34 honor societies, 77 religious organizations. 33 fraternities, 23 sororities. **Athletics (Intercollegiate):** *Men:* baseball, basketball, cross-country, diving, football, golf, riflery, swimming, tennis, track/field (outdoor), track/field (indoor). *Women:* basketball, cross-country, diving, equestrian sports, golf, riflery, soccer, softball, swimming, tennis, track/field (outdoor), track/field (indoor), volleyball. **On-Campus Highlights:** Student Recreation Center, Kyle Field, Corps of Cadets, George Bush Presidential Library/Museum, Research Park **Environmental Initiatives:** Energy Stewardship Program

ADMISSIONS
Freshman Academic Profile: 60% in top 10% of high school class, 88% in top 25% of high school class, 98% in top 50% of high school class. **Test Scores:** SAT Math middle 50% range 570-690. SAT EBRW middle 50% range 570-670. ACT middle 50% range 25-30. Minimum internet-based TOEFL 80. Minimum paper TOEFL 550. **Basis for Candidate Selection:** *Very important factors considered include:* rigor of secondary school record, class rank, academic GPA,

standardized test scores, extracurricular activities, talent/ability. *Important factors considered include:* application essay, first generation, geographical residence, state residency, volunteer work, work experience. *Other factors considered include:* recommendation(s), character/personal qualities, level of applicant's interest. **Freshman Admission Requirements:** High school diploma is required and GED is accepted *Academic units required:* 4 English, 3 math, 3 science, 1 science labs, 2 foreign language, 3 social studies, 5 academic electives, 1 visual/performing arts, and 1 unit from above areas or other academic areas. *Academic units recommended:* 4 English, 4 math, 4 science, 2 science labs, 2 foreign language, 4 social studies, 7 academic electives, 1 visual/performing arts, 1 unit from above areas or other academic areas. **Freshman Admission Statistics:** 37,191 applied, 70.1% admitted, 45% enrolled. **Transfer Admission Requirements:** High school transcript, college transcript(s), Minimum college GPA of 2.5 required. Lowest grade transferable D. **General Admission Information:** Application fee $75. Regular application deadline 12/1. Nonfall registration accepted.

COSTS AND FINANCIAL AID
Annual in-state tuition $12,250. Annual out-of-state tuition $33,803. Room and board $12,250. Required fees $3,351. Average book expense $1,054. **Required Forms and Deadlines:** FAFSA. **Notification of Awards:** Applicants will be notified of awards on a rolling basis beginning 2/25. **Types of Aid:** *Need-based scholarships/grants:* College/university scholarship or grant aid from institutional funds; Federal Pell; Private scholarships; SEOG; State scholarships/grants. *Loans:* Direct PLUS loans; Direct Subsidized Stafford Loans; Direct Unsubsidized Stafford Loans. *Student Employment:* Federal Work-Study Program available. Institutional employment available. **Financial Aid Statistics:** 94% needy freshmen, 82% needy undergrads receive need-based scholarship or grant aid. 12% freshmen, 7% undergrads receive non-need-based scholarship or grant aid. 54% freshmen, 60% undergrads receive need-based self-help aid. 0% freshmen, 1% undergrads receive athletic scholarships. 75% freshmen, 70% undergrads receive any aid. Average cumulative indebtedness $24,072. **Criteria for awarding aid:** *Need-based:* Academics *Non-need-based:* Academics, Alumni affiliation, Art, Athletics, Job skills, Leadership, Music/drama, Religious affiliation, State/district residency.

TEXAS A&M UNIVERSITY—KINGSVILLE

MSC 105, Kingsville, TX 78363
Phone: 361-593-2315
E-mail: ksossrx@tamuk.edu
Fax: 361-593-2195 • **Website:** www.tamuk.edu

This is a public school.

RATINGS
Admissions Selectivity Rating: 65   **Fire Safety Rating:** 60*   **Green Rating:** 60*

STUDENTS AND FACULTY
Enrollment: 5,087. **Student Body:** 47% female, 53% male, 2% out-of-state, 1% international. Asian 1%, African American 5%, Caucasian 27%, Hispanic 66%, Native American <1%, Race unknown <1%.
Retention and Graduation: 59% freshmen return for sophomore year. **Faculty:** Student/faculty ratio 15:1. 276 full-time faculty, 70% hold PhDs, 24% are members of minority groups, 35% are women.

ACADEMICS
Degrees: Bachelor's; Master's; Post-Bachelor's certificate; Post-Master's certificate **Classes:** Most classes have 10-19 students. Most lab/discussion sessions have 10-19 students. **Special Study Options:** Accelerated program; Cooperative education program; Distance learning; Double major; English as a Second Language (ESL); Honors program; Internships; Study abroad; Teacher certification program.

FACILITIES
Housing: Apartments for married students; Coed dorms; Men's dorms; Women's dorms

CAMPUS LIFE
Activities: Choral groups; Concert band; Dance; Drama/theater; Jazz band; Marching band; Music ensembles; Musical theater; Pep band; Radio station; Student government; Student newspaper; Television station.

ADMISSIONS
Basis for Candidate Selection: *Important factors considered include:* rigor of secondary school record, class rank, standardized test scores. **Freshman Admission Requirements:** *Academic units recommended:* 4 English, 3 math, 3 science, 3 foreign language, 4 social studies, 3 history, 3 academic

electives. **Freshman Admission Statistics:** 2,105 applied, 99.4% admitted, 43% enrolled. Minimum college GPA of 2.0 required. **General Admission Information:** Application fee $15. Nonfall registration accepted. Admission may be deferred.

COSTS AND FINANCIAL AID

Annual in-state tuition $3,966. Annual out-of-state tuition $7,590. Room and board $3,966. Required fees $1,602. Average book expense $614. **Required Forms and Deadlines:** FAFSA. **Types of Aid: Financial Aid Statistics:** 92% needy freshmen, 100% needy undergrads receive need-based scholarship or grant aid. 31% freshmen, 71% undergrads receive non-need-based scholarship or grant aid. 87% freshmen, 82% undergrads receive need-based self-help aid. 0% freshmen, 0% undergrads receive athletic scholarships.

TEXAS A&M UNIVERSITY—SAN ANTONIO

One University Way, San Antonio, TX 78224
Phone: (210) 784-1300
E-mail: admissions.office@tamusa.edu or graduateadmissions@tamusa.edu
Fax: (210) 784-1492 • **Website:** www.tamusa.edu

This is a public school.

RATINGS

Admissions Selectivity Rating: 88   **Fire Safety Rating:** 60*   **Green Rating:** 60*

STUDENTS AND FACULTY

Enrollment: 5,455. **Student Body:** 60% female, 40% male, 1% out-of-state, 1% international. Asian 1%, African American 6%, Caucasian 18%, Hispanic 71%, Native American <1%, Pacific Islander <1%, Two or more races 2%, Race unknown <1%.
Retention and Graduation: 59% freshmen return for sophomore year.
Faculty: 163 full-time faculty, 33% are members of minority groups, 50% are women.

ACADEMICS

Degrees: Bachelor's; **Master's Classes:** Most classes have 20-29 students. Most lab/discussion sessions have 20-29 students. **Special Study Options:** Distance learning; Double major; Independent study; Internships; Teacher certification program; Weekend college.

FACILITIES

Housing: Coed dorms

CAMPUS LIFE

Activities: Choral groups; Student government; Student newspaper.

ADMISSIONS

Freshman Academic Profile: Average high school GPA 3.3. 6% in top 10% of high school class, 21% in top 25% of high school class, 55% in top 50% of high school class. **Test Scores:** SAT Math middle 50% range 450-530. SAT EBRW middle 50% range 460-530. ACT middle 50% range 17-20. **Basis for Candidate Selection:** *Very important factors considered include:* class rank, academic GPA, standardized test scores. *Other factors considered include:* rigor of secondary school record, application essay, recommendation(s), extracurricular activities, talent/ability, character/personal qualities, volunteer work, work experience. **Freshman Admission Requirements:** High school diploma is required and GED is accepted *Academic units required:* 4 English, 4 math, 4 science, 2 foreign language, 4 social studies. **Freshman Admission Statistics:** 6,912 applied, 34.5% admitted, 23% enrolled. **General Admission Information:** Application fee $15. Priority deadline 1/15. Regular application deadline 6/30. Nonfall registration accepted.

COSTS AND FINANCIAL AID

Annual out-of-state tuition $16,742. Room and board $10,326. Required fees $3,924. Average book expense $1,342. **Required Forms and Deadlines:** FAFSA; State aid form. **Types of Aid:** *Need-based scholarships/grants:* College/university scholarship or grant aid from institutional funds; Federal Pell; Private scholarships; SEOG; State scholarships/grants. *Loans:* Direct PLUS loans; Direct Subsidized Stafford Loans; Direct Unsubsidized Stafford Loans.

TEXAS A&M UNIVERSITY—TEXARKANA

P.O. Box 5518, Texarkana, TX 75505
Phone: (903) 223-3069
E-mail: admissions@tamut.edu
Fax: (903) 223-3140

This public school was founded in 1971. It has a 1 acre campus.

RATINGS

Admissions Selectivity Rating: 0   **Fire Safety Rating:** 60*   **Green Rating:** 60*

STUDENTS AND FACULTY

Enrollment: 1,030. **Student Body:** 71% female, 29% male, <1% international. Asian 1%, African American 15%, Caucasian 76%, Hispanic 6%, Native American 1%, Race unknown <1%.
Faculty: Student/faculty ratio 13:1. 59 full-time faculty, 15% are members of minority groups, 41% are women.

ACADEMICS

Degrees: Bachelor's; **Master's Classes:** Most classes have 10-19 students. **Most popular majors:** General Studies; Multi-/Interdisciplinary Studies, Other; Accounting. **Special Study Options:** Cross-registration; Distance learning; Independent study; Internships; Liberal arts/career combination; Study abroad; Teacher certification program. **Disability Services offered to physically disabled students:** Note-taking services; Tape recorders. **Career services:** Career/job search classes

FACILITIES

Housing: 100% of campus accessible to physically diasbled. **Computers:** Students can register for classes online. Administrative functions (other than registration) can be performed online.

CAMPUS LIFE

Environment: Village **Activities:** Student government; Student newspaper 20 registered organizations, 5 honor societies, 1 religious organization.

ADMISSIONS

Test Scores: Minimum paper TOEFL 550. **Transfer Admission Requirements:** college transcript(s), Minimum college GPA of 2.0 required. Lowest grade transferable D. **General Admission Information:** Nonfall registration accepted.

COSTS AND FINANCIAL AID

Required Forms and Deadlines: FAFSA; Institution's own financial aid form. **Notification of Awards:** Applicants will be notified of awards on or about 6/1. **Types of Aid:** *Need-based scholarships/grants:* College/university scholarship or grant aid from institutional funds; Federal Pell; Private scholarships; SEOG; State scholarships/grants. *Loans: Student Employment:* Federal Work-Study Program available. **Financial Aid Statistics:** 0% undergrads receive non-need-based scholarship or grant aid. 0% undergrads receive need-based self-help aid. 0% undergrads receive athletic scholarships. **Criteria for awarding aid:** *Need-based:* Academics *Non-need-based:* Academics, Alumni affiliation, Leadership, State/district residency.

TEXAS CHRISTIAN UNIVERSITY

2800 South University Drive, Fort Worth, TX 76129
Phone: 817-257-7490 • **Financial Aid Phone:** 817-257-7858
E-mail: frogmail@tcu.edu • **CEEB Code:** 6820
Fax: 817-257-7268 • **Website:** www.tcu.edu • **ACT Code:** 4206

This private school, affiliated with the Disciples of Christ Church, was founded in 1873. It has a 289.42 acre campus.

RATINGS

Admissions Selectivity Rating: 90   **Fire Safety Rating:** 98   **Green Rating:** 78

STUDENTS AND FACULTY

Enrollment: 8,983. **Student Body:** 59% female, 41% male, 46% out-of-state, 5% international (69 countries represented). Asian 3%, African American 5%,

Caucasian 71%, Hispanic 13%, Native American 1%, Pacific Islander <1%, Two or more races <1%, Race unknown 1%.
Retention and Graduation: 91% freshmen return for sophomore year. 69% freshmen graduate within 4 years. 83% freshmen graduate within 6 years. 31% grads go on to further study within 1 year. 35% grads pursue arts and sciences degrees. 6% grads pursue law degrees. 15% grads pursue business degrees. 7% grads pursue medical degrees. **Faculty:** Student/faculty ratio 13:1. 669 full-time faculty, 86% hold PhDs, 16% are members of minority groups, 48% are women. 2% of classes are taught by teaching assistants.

ACADEMICS

Degrees: Bachelor's; Certificate; Diploma; Doctoral/Professional; Doctoral/Research; Master's; Post-Bachelor's certificate; Post-Master's certificate **Classes:** Most classes have 20-29 students. Most lab/discussion sessions have 20-29 students. **Most popular majors:** Speech Communication And Rhetoric; Public Relations, Advertising, And Applied Communication; Registered Nursing/Registered Nurse. **Special Study Options:** Accelerated program; Distance learning; Double major; English as a Second Language (ESL); Honors program; Independent study; Internships; Liberal arts/career combination; Student-designed major; Study abroad; Teacher certification program. Honors programs: The John V. Roach Honors College offers academic programs for students of all majors. Students who complete all the Honors College requirements for both lower-division and upper-division Honors graduate as a John V. Roach Honors College Laureate and are recognized at a special ceremony prior to the University commencement. Students may also choose to complete only lower-division Honors (15 credit hours of specialized Honors courses linked to the core curriculum) or only upper-division Honors (either Departmental Honors earned through a thesis or creative project or University Honors achieved through successful work in four interdisciplinary colloquium courses.) **Disability Services offered to physically disabled students:** Note-taking services. **Career services:** Alumni network; Alumni services; Career assessment; Career/job search classes; Internships; Regional alumni

FACILITIES

Housing: Apartments for single students; Coed dorms; Fraternity/sorority housing; Men's dorms; Special housing for disabled student; Theme housing; Women's dorms 100% of campus accessible to physically diasbled. **Special Academic Facilities/Equipment:** geological center for remote sensing, nuclear magnetic resonance facility, observatory, film library, performance complex, behavioral research institute, meteorite collection, speech and hearing clinic, transmission electron microscope, Beowulf computing cluster, optical spectroscopy and microscopy laboratory, health professions learning center, new media writing center, multimedia editing suites, high-end computing lab, 3-D printing lab, radio station, cable TV studio, institute providing instruction for care and treatment of vulnerable children, Art exhibition hall,special collections, alumni and visitors center, Heritage Center,and a variety of athletic facilities. **Computers:** 100% of classrooms, 100% of dorms, 100% of libraries, 100% of dining areas, 100% of student union, 100% of common outdoor areas have wireless network access. Students can register for classes online. Administrative functions (other than registration) can be performed online.

CAMPUS LIFE

Environment: Metropolis **Activities:** Campus Ministries; Choral groups; Concert band; Dance; Drama/theater; International Student Organization; Jazz band; Literary magazine; Marching band; Model UN; Music ensembles; Musical theater; Opera; Pep band; Radio station; Student government; Student newspaper; Symphony orchestra; Yearbook 200 registered organizations, 29 honor societies, 17 religious organizations. 15 fraternities, 18 sororities. **Athletics (Intercollegiate):** *Men:* baseball, basketball, cross-country, diving, football, golf, swimming, tennis, track/field (outdoor), track/field (indoor). *Women:* basketball, cross-country, diving, equestrian sports, golf, riflery, soccer, swimming, tennis, track/field (outdoor), track/field (indoor), volleyball. **On-Campus Highlights:** Campus Commons & Frog Fountain, Amon G. Carter Stadium, University Recreation Center, Brown-Lupton University Union, Mary Couts Burnett Library

ADMISSIONS

Freshman Academic Profile: 57% from public high schools. **Test Scores:** SAT Math middle 50% range 560-670. SAT EBRW middle 50% range 570-660. ACT middle 50% range 25-30. Minimum internet-based TOEFL 80. Minimum paper TOEFL 550. **Basis for Candidate Selection:** *Very important factors considered include:* rigor of secondary school record, class rank, academic GPA. *Important factors considered include:* application essay, standardized test scores, recommendation(s), extracurricular activities, character/personal qualities, first generation, alumni/ae relation, racial/ethnic status, volunteer work, work experience. *Other factors considered include:* interview, talent/ability, geographical residence, state residency, religious affiliation/commitment, level of applicant's interest. **Freshman Admission Requirements:** High school diploma is required and GED is not accepted *Academic units required:* 4 English, 3 math, 3 science, 1 science labs, 2 foreign language, 3 social studies, 2 academic electives, *Academic units recommended:* 4 English, 4 math, 4 science,

1 science labs, 4 foreign language, 4 social studies. **Freshman Admission Statistics:** 19,740 applied, 41.1% admitted, 24% enrolled. **Transfer Admission Requirements:** college transcript(s), essay or personal statement, Minimum college GPA of 2.0 required. Lowest grade transferable C. **General Admission Information:** Application fee $50. Regular application deadline 2/1. Nonfall registration accepted. Admission may be deferred for a maximum of 1 year.

COSTS AND FINANCIAL AID

Required fees $90. Average book expense $970. **Required Forms and Deadlines:** CSS/Financial Aid PROFILE; FAFSA; Noncustodial PROFILE. **Notification of Awards:** Applicants will be notified of awards on a rolling basis beginning 12/15. *Types of Aid: Need-based scholarships/grants:* College/university scholarship or grant aid from institutional funds; Federal Pell; Private scholarships; SEOG; State scholarships/grants. *Loans:* Direct PLUS loans; Direct Subsidized Stafford Loans; Direct Unsubsidized Stafford Loans. *Student Employment:* Federal Work-Study Program available. Institutional employment available. **Financial Aid Statistics:** 94% needy freshmen, 93% needy undergrads receive need-based scholarship or grant aid. 68% freshmen, 62% undergrads receive non-need-based scholarship or grant aid. 72% freshmen, 76% undergrads receive need-based self-help aid. 4% freshmen, 4% undergrads receive athletic scholarships. 77% freshmen, 76% undergrads receive any aid. 37% undergrads borrow to pay for school. Average cumulative indebtedness $36,550. **Criteria for awarding aid:** *Non-need-based:* Academics, Alumni affiliation, Art, Minority status, Music/drama, Religious affiliation, State/district residency.

TEXAS LUTHERAN UNIVERSITY

1000 West Court, Seguin, TX 78155
Phone: 830-372-8050 · **Financial Aid Phone:** 830-372-8078
E-mail: admissions@tlu.edu
Fax: 830-372-8096 • **Website:** www.tlu.edu

This private school, affiliated with the Lutheran Church, was founded in 1891. It has a 184 acre campus.

RATINGS

Admissions Selectivity Rating: 87   **Fire Safety Rating:** 87   **Green Rating:** 60*

STUDENTS AND FACULTY

Enrollment: 1,341. **Student Body:** 52% female, 48% male, 1% out-of-state, <1% international (12 countries represented). Asian 1%, African American 11%, Caucasian 51%, Hispanic 34%, Native American <1%, Pacific Islander <1%, Two or more races 1%, Race unknown 3%.
Retention and Graduation: 72% freshmen return for sophomore year. 35% freshmen graduate within 4 years. 52% freshmen graduate within 6 years.
Faculty: Student/faculty ratio 14:1. 82 full-time faculty, 85% hold PhDs, 15% are members of minority groups, 52% are women. 0% of classes are taught by teaching assistants.

ACADEMICS

Degrees: Bachelor's; **Master's Classes:** Most classes have 10-19 students. Most lab/discussion sessions have 10-19 students. **Most popular majors:** Education, General; Kinesiology And Exercise Science; Business/Commerce, General. **Special Study Options:** Double major; Dual enrollment; Exchange student program (domestic); External degree program; Honors program; Independent study; Internships; Study abroad; Teacher certification program. **Disability Services offered to physically disabled students:** Note-taking services; Reader services; Tutors. **Career services:** Alumni network; Alumni services; Career/job search classes; Internships

FACILITIES

Housing: Apartments for married students; Apartments for single students; Coed dorms; Special housing for disabled students 95% of campus accessible to physically diasbled. **Special Academic Facilities/Equipment:** Mexican-American studies center, geological museum, Women's Studies Center **Computers:** 100% of classrooms, 100% of dorms, 100% of libraries, 100% of dining areas, 100% of student union, 100% of common outdoor areas have wireless network access. Students can register for classes online. Administrative functions (other than registration) can be performed online.

CAMPUS LIFE

Environment: Town **Activities:** Campus Ministries; Choral groups; Concert band; Drama/theater; International Student Organization; Jazz band; Literary magazine; Music ensembles; Musical theater; Pep band; Student government; Student newspaper; Symphony orchestra 53 registered organizations, 10 honor societies, 3 religious organizations. 5 fraternities, 4 sororities. **Athletics**

(Intercollegiate): *Men:* baseball, basketball, football, golf, soccer, tennis. *Women:* basketball, cross-country, golf, soccer, softball, tennis, track/field (outdoor), track/field (indoor), volleyball. **On-Campus Highlights:** Tschoepe Hall, Fitness Center, Alumni Student Center, Residence Halls, Hein Dining Hall **Environmental Initiatives:** Installation of more efficient HVAC system campus wide.

ADMISSIONS

Freshman Academic Profile: Average high school GPA 3.6. 17% in top 10% of high school class, 44% in top 25% of high school class, 78% in top 50% of high school class. **Test Scores:** SAT Math middle 50% range 488-570. SAT EBRW middle 50% range 480-580. ACT middle 50% range 19-24. Minimum internet-based TOEFL 80. Minimum paper TOEFL 550. **Basis for Candidate Selection:** *Very important factors considered include:* rigor of secondary school record, class rank, academic GPA, application essay, standardized test scores, recommendation(s). *Important factors considered include:* interview, talent/ability, character/personal qualities, volunteer work. *Other factors considered include:* extracurricular activities, work experience, level of applicant's interest. **Freshman Admission Requirements:** High school diploma is required and GED is accepted *Academic units required:* 4 English, 3 math, 3 science, 2 science labs, 2 foreign language, 3 social studies, 1 academic elective, *Academic units recommended:* 4 English, 4 math, 4 science, 2 science labs, 3 foreign language, 4 social studies, 1 computer science, 1 unit from above areas or other academic areas. **Freshman Admission Statistics:** 2,250 applied, 48.5% admitted, 38% enrolled. **Transfer Admission Requirements:** High school transcript, college transcript(s), essay or personal statement, statement of good standing from prior institution(s). Minimum college GPA of 2.25 required. Lowest grade transferable C. **General Admission Information:** Priority deadline 12/15. Regular application deadline 2/1. Nonfall registration accepted. Admission may be deferred for a maximum of 1 year.

COSTS AND FINANCIAL AID

Annual tuition $29,650. Room and board $9,720. Required fees $400. Average book expense $1,000. **Required Forms and Deadlines:** FAFSA; State aid form. **Notification of Awards:** Applicants will be notified of awards on a rolling basis beginning 3/1. **Types of Aid:** *Need-based scholarships/grants:* College/university scholarship or grant aid from institutional funds; Federal Pell; Private scholarships; SEOG; State scholarships/grants. *Loans:* Direct PLUS loans; Direct Subsidized Stafford Loans; Direct Unsubsidized Stafford Loans. *Student Employment:* Federal Work-Study Program available. Institutional employment available. **Financial Aid Statistics:** 100% needy freshmen, 99% needy undergrads receive need-based scholarship or grant aid. 5% freshmen, 2% undergrads receive non-need-based scholarship or grant aid. 80% freshmen, 79% undergrads receive need-based self-help aid. 0% freshmen, 0% undergrads receive athletic scholarships. 100% freshmen, 95% undergrads receive any aid. 73% undergrads borrow to pay for school. Average cumulative indebtedness $37,337. **Criteria for awarding aid:** *Non-need-based:* Academics, Alumni affiliation, Art, Leadership, Minority status, Music/drama, Religious affiliation.

TEXAS STATE UNIVERSITY

601 University Drive, San Marcos, TX 78666
Phone: 512-245-2364 • **Financial Aid Phone:** (512) 245 2315
E-mail: admissions@txstate.edu • **CEEB Code:** 6667
Fax: 512-245-8044 • **Website:** www.txstate.edu • **ACT Code:** 4178

This public school was founded in 1899. It has a 491 acre campus.

RATINGS

Admissions Selectivity Rating: 79   **Fire Safety Rating:** 95   **Green Rating:** 79

STUDENTS AND FACULTY

Enrollment: 34,180. **Student Body:** 57% female, 43% male, 2% out-of-state, 1% international (52 countries represented). Asian 2%, African American 10%, Caucasian 46%, Hispanic 37%, Native American <1%, Pacific Islander <1%, Two or more races 4%, Race unknown <1%. **Retention and Graduation:** 78% freshmen return for sophomore year. 27% freshmen graduate within 4 years. 54% freshmen graduate within 6 years. 12% grads go on to further study within 1 year. 7% grads pursue arts and sciences degrees. 1.6% grads pursue law degrees. 1% grads pursue business degrees. 1% grads pursue medical degrees. **Faculty:** Student/faculty ratio 21:1. 1,419 full-time faculty, 78% hold PhDs, 24% are members of minority groups, 50% are women. 4% of classes are taught by teaching assistants.

ACADEMICS

Degrees: Bachelor's; Doctoral; Doctoral/Professional; Master's; Post-Bachelor's certificate **Classes:** Most classes have 10-19 students. Most lab/discussion

sessions have 20-29 students. **Most popular majors:** Multi-/Interdisciplinary Studies, Other; Kinesiology And Exercise Science; Psychology, General. **Special Study Options:** Accelerated program; Distance learning; Double major; Dual enrollment; English as a Second Language (ESL); Exchange student program (domestic); Honors program; Independent study; Internships; Study abroad; Teacher certification program; Weekend college. Honors programs: To graduate in the University Honors Program, a student must complete at least five Honors Classes (which includes the Honors Thesis course) and maintain a minimum GPA of 3.25. Honors courses substitute for certain general education core curriculum and individual departmental requirements and thus become integral parts of the degree program. Combined degree programs: BA/DDS. **Disability Services offered to physically disabled students:** Note-taking services; Reader services; Tape recorders; Tutors. **Career services:** Alumni network; Alumni services; Career assessment; Career/job search classes; Internships

FACILITIES

Housing: Apartments for single students; Coed dorms; Fraternity/sorority housing; Men's dorms; Theme housing; Women's dorms 90% of campus accessible to physically disabled. **Special Academic Facilities/Equipment:** Child development center, aquifer research center, two demonstration farms, physical anthropology and archaeology laboratories. Southwestern Writer's Collection. Observatory with a 17 inch telescope. Anthropology forensics body farm. Clean room for microchip processing and development. **Computers:** 100% of classrooms, 100% of dorms, 100% of libraries, 100% of dining areas, 100% of student union, 100% of common outdoor areas have wireless network access. Students can register for classes online. Administrative functions (other than registration) can be performed online.

CAMPUS LIFE

Environment: Town **Activities:** Campus Ministries; Choral groups; Concert band; Dance; Drama/theater; International Student Organization; Jazz band; Literary magazine; Marching band; Model UN; Music ensembles; Musical theater; Opera; Pep band; Radio station; Student government; Student newspaper; Student-run film society; Symphony orchestra; Yearbook 254 registered organizations, 16 honor societies, 27 religious organizations. 18 fraternities, 14 sororities. **Athletics (Intercollegiate):** *Men:* baseball, basketball, cheerleading, cross-country, football, golf, track/field (outdoor). *Women:* basketball, cheerleading, cross-country, golf, soccer, softball, tennis, track/field (outdoor), volleyball. **On-Campus Highlights:** LBJ Student Center, Alkek Library, Student Recreation Center, The Quad, Sewell Park **Environmental Initiatives:** Established the Texas Rivers Systems Institute. Our programs and projects demonstrate our deep commitment to the careful stewardship of the world's freshwater resources. Through collaborative research, public advocacy, and education on river systems, the Institute affirms the unique role of water in our lives. As one of the earth's most remarkable resources, we are dedicated to preserving and protecting this irreplaceable gift—water.

ADMISSIONS

Freshman Academic Profile: 14% in top 10% of high school class, 51% in top 25% of high school class, 94% in top 50% of high school class. 98% from public high schools. **Test Scores:** SAT Math middle 50% range 510-590. SAT EBRW middle 50% range 510-610. ACT middle 50% range 20-26. Minimum internet-based TOEFL 78. Minimum paper TOEFL 550. **Basis for Candidate Selection:** *Very important factors considered include:* class rank, standardized test scores. *Other factors considered include:* rigor of secondary school record, application essay, extracurricular activities, talent/ability, first generation. **Freshman Admission Requirements:** High school diploma is required and GED is accepted *Academic units required:* 4 English, 4 math, 4 science, 2 science labs, 2 foreign language, 2 social studies, 2 history, 6 academic electives, 1 visual/performing arts, and 1 unit from above areas or other academic areas. *Academic units recommended:* 4 English, 4 math, 4 science, 2 science labs, 2 foreign language, 2 social studies, 2 history, 6 academic electives, 1 visual/performing arts, 1 unit from above areas or other academic areas. **Freshman Admission Statistics:** 24,277 applied, 73.0% admitted, 33% enrolled. **Transfer Admission Requirements:** college transcript(s), statement of good standing from prior institution(s). Minimum college GPA of 2.2 required. Lowest grade transferable D. **General Admission Information:** Application fee $75. Priority deadline 3/1. Regular application deadline 5/1. Nonfall registration accepted. Admission may be deferred.

COSTS AND FINANCIAL AID

Annual in-state tuition $9,132. Annual out-of-state tuition $19,990. Room and board $9,132. Required fees $2,468. Average book expense $780. **Required Forms and Deadlines:** FAFSA. **Notification of Awards:** Applicants will be notified of awards on a rolling basis beginning 5/1. **Types of Aid:** *Need-based scholarships/grants:* College/university scholarship or grant aid from institutional funds; Federal Pell; Private scholarships; SEOG; State scholarships/grants. *Loans:* Direct PLUS loans; Direct Subsidized Stafford Loans; Direct Unsubsidized Stafford Loans. *Student Employment:* Federal Work-Study Program available. Institutional employment available. **Financial Aid Statistics:** 80% needy freshmen, 80% needy undergrads receive need-based scholarship or grant aid. 13% freshmen, 7% undergrads receive non-need-based scholarship or grant aid. 76% freshmen, 78% undergrads receive need-based self-help aid. 0% freshmen, 1% undergrads receive athletic scholarships. 81% freshmen, 71% undergrads receive any aid. Average cumulative indebtedness $25,246. **Criteria for awarding aid:** *Need-based:* Academics, Art, Leadership, Minority status, Music/drama *Non-need-based:* Academics, Art, Athletics, Leadership, Minority status, Music/drama, State/district residency.

TEXAS TECH UNIVERSITY

Box 45005, Lubbock, TX 79409-5005
Phone: 806-742-1480 • **Financial Aid Phone:** 806-742-3681
E-mail: admissions@ttu.edu • **CEEB Code:** 6827
Fax: 806-742-0062 • **Website:** www.ttu.edu • **ACT Code:** 4220

This public school was founded in 1923. It has a 1839 acre campus.

RATINGS
Admissions Selectivity Rating: 83   **Fire Safety Rating:** 97   **Green Rating:** 76

STUDENTS AND FACULTY
Enrollment: 30,330. **Student Body:** 46% female, 54% male, 6% out-of-state, 5% international (90 countries represented). Asian 2%, African American 6%, Caucasian 56%, Hispanic 28%, Native American <1%, Pacific Islander <1%, Two or more races 2%, Race unknown <1%.
Retention and Graduation: 84% freshmen return for sophomore year. 35% freshmen graduate within 4 years. 59% freshmen graduate within 6 years.
Faculty: Student/faculty ratio 21:1. 1,534 full-time faculty, 22% are members of minority groups, 40% are women. 14% of classes are taught by teaching assistants.

ACADEMICS
Degrees: Bachelor's; Doctoral/Professional; Doctoral/Research; Master's; Post-Bachelor's certificate **Classes:** Most classes have 10-19 students. Most lab/discussion sessions have 10-19 students. **Most popular majors:** Kinesiology And Exercise Science; Psychology, General; Marketing/Marketing Management, General. **Special Study Options:** Accelerated program; Cooperative education program; Distance learning; Double major; Dual enrollment; English as a Second Language (ESL); External degree program; Honors program; Independent study; Internships; Student-designed major; Study abroad; Teacher certification program; Weekend college. Honors programs: Honors Studies is a special program under our Honors College for highly motivated and academically talented students who want to maximize their college education. Combined degree programs: BA/MA. **Disability Services offered to physically disabled students:** Note-taking services; Reader services; Tape recorders; Tutors. **Career services:** Alumni network; Alumni services; Career assessment; Career/job search classes; Internships; Regional alumni

FACILITIES
Housing: Apartments for single students; Coed dorms; Men's dorms; Special housing for disabled student; Women's dorms 100% of campus accessible to physically diasbled. **Special Academic Facilities/Equipment:** Museum, child development center, textile research center, agricultural research center, planetarium, ranching heritage center, semi-arid land studies center, seismological observatory. **Computers:** Students can register for classes online. Administrative functions (other than registration) can be performed online.

CAMPUS LIFE
Environment: City **Activities:** Campus Ministries; Choral groups; Concert band; Dance; Drama/theater; International Student Organization; Jazz band; Literary magazine; Marching band; Model UN; Music ensembles; Musical theater; Opera; Pep band; Radio station; Student government; Student newspaper; Student-run film society; Symphony orchestra; Television station; Yearbook 399 registered organizations, 33 honor societies, 35 religious organizations. 25 fraternities, 18 sororities. **Athletics (Intercollegiate):** *Men:* baseball, basketball, cross-country, football, golf, tennis, track/field (outdoor), track/field (indoor). *Women:* basketball, cross-country, golf, soccer, softball, tennis, track/field (outdoor), track/field (indoor), volleyball. **On-Campus Highlights:** Student Union Building, Student Recreation Center, Library, Classrooms, United Supermarkets Arena

ADMISSIONS
Freshman Academic Profile: Average high school GPA 3.8. 19% in top 10% of high school class, 50% in top 25% of high school class, 85% in top 50% of high school class. 88% from public high schools. **Test Scores:** SAT Math middle 50% range 530-620. SAT EBRW middle 50% range 540-620. ACT

middle 50% range 22-27. Minimum internet-based TOEFL 79. Minimum paper TOEFL 550. **Basis for Candidate Selection:** *Very important factors considered include:* rigor of secondary school record, class rank, academic GPA, standardized test scores. *Important factors considered include:* application essay, recommendation(s), extracurricular activities, talent/ability, character/personal qualities, volunteer work, work experience. *Other factors considered include:* first generation, geographical residence, level of applicant's interest. **Freshman Admission Requirements:** High school diploma is required and GED is accepted *Academic units required:* 4 English, 3 math, 3 science, 3 science labs, 2 foreign language, 5 academic electives, 1 visual/performing arts, and 4 units from above areas or other academic areas. *Academic units recommended:* 4 English, 4 math, 4 science, 4 science labs, 2 foreign language, 6 academic electives, 1 visual/performing arts, 5.5 units from above areas or other academic areas. **Freshman Admission Statistics:** 25,207 applied, 69.2% admitted, 34% enrolled. **Transfer Admission Requirements:** college transcript(s), statement of good standing from prior institution(s). Minimum college GPA of 2.25 required. Lowest grade transferable D-. **General Admission Information:** Application fee $75. Priority deadline 2/1. Regular application deadline 8/1. Nonfall registration accepted.

COSTS AND FINANCIAL AID
Required Forms and Deadlines: FAFSA. **Types of Aid:** *Need-based scholarships/grants:* College/university scholarship or grant aid from institutional funds; Federal Pell; Private scholarships; SEOG; State scholarships/grants. *Loans:* Direct PLUS loans; Direct Subsidized Stafford Loans; Direct Unsubsidized Stafford Loans. *Student Employment:* Federal Work-Study Program available. Institutional employment available. **Financial Aid Statistics:** 86% needy undergrads receive need-based scholarship or grant aid. 54% freshmen, 29% undergrads receive non-need-based scholarship or grant aid. 70% freshmen, 83% undergrads receive need-based self-help aid. 1% freshmen, 0% undergrads receive athletic scholarships. 47% freshmen, 61% undergrads receive any aid. **Criteria for awarding aid:** *Need-based:* Academics, Leadership, Music/drama *Non-need-based:* Academics, Art, Athletics, Job skills, Leadership, Music/drama.

TEXAS WOMAN'S UNIVERSITY

P O Box 425619, Denton, TX 76204-5589
Phone: 940-898-3188 • **Financial Aid Phone:** (940) 898-3050
E-mail: admissions@twu.edu • **CEEB Code:** 6826
Fax: 940-898-3081 • **Website:** www.twu.edu • **ACT Code:** 4224

This public school was founded in 1901. It has a 270 acre campus.

RATINGS
Admissions Selectivity Rating: 73   **Fire Safety Rating:** 99   **Green Rating:** 60*

STUDENTS AND FACULTY
Enrollment: 8,668. **Student Body:** 90% female, 10% male, 0% out-of-state, 1% international (62 countries represented). Asian 8%, African American 21%, Caucasian 40%, Hispanic 25%, Native American <1%, Pacific Islander <1%, Two or more races 4%, Race unknown 1%.
Retention and Graduation: 73% freshmen return for sophomore year. 4% grads go on to further study within 1 year. **Faculty:** Student/faculty ratio 14:1. 413 full-time faculty, 17% are members of minority groups, 76% are women.

ACADEMICS
Degrees: Bachelor's; Doctoral; Doctoral/Professional; Doctoral/Research; Master's; Post-Bachelor's certificate; Post-Master's certificate **Classes:** Most classes have 10-19 students. Most lab/discussion sessions have 10-19 students. **Special Study Options:** Accelerated program; Cooperative education program; Cross-registration; Distance learning; Double major; Dual enrollment; External degree program; Honors program; Independent study; Internships; Study abroad; Teacher certification program; Weekend college. Honors programs Honors Scholars Program www.twu.edu/honors/index. html Combined degree programs: BA/MEng. **Disability Services offered to physically disabled students:** Note-taking services; Reader services; Tape recorders; Tutors. **Career services:** Internships

FACILITIES
Housing: Apartments for married students; Apartments for single students; Coed dorms; Fraternity/sorority housing; Special housing for disabled student; Theme housing; Women's dorms 100% of campus accessible to physically diasbled. **Special Academic Facilities/Equipment:** Museum, radiation lab, language lab, Texas First Ladies Gown Collection Texas Women's Hall of Fame **Computers:** Students can register for classes online. Administrative functions (other than registration) can be performed online.

CAMPUS LIFE

Environment: City **Activities:** Campus Ministries; Choral groups; Dance; Drama/theater; International Student Organization; Jazz band; Music ensembles; Opera; Pep band; Student government; Student newspaper 94 registered organizations, 16 honor societies, 10 religious organizations. 9 sororities. **Athletics (Intercollegiate):** *Women:* basketball, gymnastics, soccer, softball, volleyball. **On-Campus Highlights:** Student Union, Pioneer Hall, Mega Computer Lab, Guinn/Stark High Rise Resident Halls, Little Chapel-in-the-Woods

ADMISSIONS

Freshman Academic Profile: Average high school GPA 3.1. 14% in top 10% of high school class, 29% in top 25% of high school class, 79% in top 50% of high school class. 93% from public high schools. **Test Scores:** SAT Math middle 50% range 430-530. SAT EBRW middle 50% range 410-530. ACT middle 50% range 17-17. Minimum paper TOEFL 550. **Basis for Candidate Selection:** *Very important factors considered include:* rigor of secondary school record, class rank, academic GPA. *Important factors considered include:* standardized test scores. *Other factors considered include:* recommendation(s), first generation. **Freshman Admission Requirements:** High school diploma is required and GED is accepted *Academic units required:* 4 English, 3 math, 3 science, 3 social studies, 1 academic elective, *Academic units recommended:* 4 English, 4 math, 4 science, 2 foreign language, 3.5 social studies, 5.5 academic electives, 1 computer science, 1 visual/performing arts, 1 unit from above areas or other academic areas. **Freshman Admission Statistics:** 4,582 applied, 85.3% admitted, 29% enrolled. **Transfer Admission Requirements:** college transcript(s), Minimum college GPA of 2.0 required. Lowest grade transferable D. **General Admission Information:** Application fee $50. Priority deadline 3/1. Regular application deadline 7/15. Nonfall registration accepted. Admission may be deferred for a maximum of 2 years.

COSTS AND FINANCIAL AID

Annual in-state tuition $6,780. Annual out-of-state tuition $16,510. Room and board $6,780. Required fees $2,345. Average book expense $1,050. **Required Forms and Deadlines:** FAFSA; Institution's own financial aid form. **Notification of Awards:** Applicants will be notified of awards on a rolling basis beginning 3/1. **Types of Aid:** *Need-based scholarships/grants:* College/university scholarship or grant aid from institutional funds; Federal Nursing Scholarships; Federal Pell; Private scholarships; SEOG; State scholarships/grants; United Negro College Fund. **Financial Aid Statistics:** 94% needy freshmen, 91% needy undergrads receive need-based scholarship or grant aid. 30% freshmen, 25% undergrads receive non-need-based scholarship or grant aid. 69% freshmen, 83% undergrads receive need-based self-help aid. 0% freshmen, 0% undergrads receive athletic scholarships. 77% freshmen, 85% undergrads receive any aid. **Criteria for awarding aid:** *Need-based:* Academics, Art, Athletics, Music/drama.

THIEL COLLEGE

75 College Avenue, Greenville, PA 16125
Phone: 724-589-2345 • **Financial Aid Phone:** 724-589-2178
E-mail: admissions@thiel.edu • **CEEB Code:** 2910
Fax: 724-589-2013 • **Website:** www.thiel.edu • **ACT Code:** 3730

This private school, affiliated with the Lutheran Church, was founded in 1866. It has a 135 acre campus.

RATINGS

Admissions Selectivity Rating: 77   **Fire Safety Rating:** 88   **Green Rating:** 60*

STUDENTS AND FACULTY

Enrollment: 1,019. **Student Body:** 43% female, 57% male, 37% out-of-state, 3% international (14 countries represented). Asian <1%, African American 6%, Caucasian 69%, Hispanic 2%, Native American <1%, Pacific Islander 0%, Two or more races 1%, Race unknown 18%.
Retention and Graduation: 67% freshmen return for sophomore year. 13% grads go on to further study within 1 year. 86% grads pursue arts and sciences degrees. 1% grads pursue law degrees. 12% grads pursue business degrees. 1% grads pursue medical degrees. **Faculty:** Student/faculty ratio 13:1. 64 full-time faculty, 73% hold PhDs, 8% are members of minority groups, 41% are women. 0% of classes are taught by teaching assistants.

ACADEMICS

Degrees: Associate; Bachelor's **Classes:** Most classes have 10-19 students. Most lab/discussion sessions have 10-19 students. **Most popular majors:** Elementary Education And Teaching; Biology/Biological Sciences, General; Business/Commerce, General. **Special Study Options:** Cooperative education

program; Distance learning; Double major; Dual enrollment; English as a Second Language (ESL); Honors program; Independent study; Internships; Liberal arts/career combination; Study abroad; Teacher certification program. Honors programs: Four year Honors Program with special courses for honors students. **Disability Services offered to physically disabled students:** Note-taking services; Reader services; Tape recorders; Tutors. **Career services:** Alumni network; Career assessment; Career/job search classes; Internships

FACILITIES

Housing: Apartments for single students; Coed dorms; Fraternity/sorority housing; Theme housing 90% of campus accessible to physically disabled. **Special Academic Facilities/Equipment:** Art Gallery, Blackbox Theater,Star Bucks Bistro **Computers:** Students can register for classes online. Undergraduates are required to own a computer.

CAMPUS LIFE

Environment: Rural **Activities:** Campus Ministries; Choral groups; Concert band; Dance; Drama/theater; International Student Organization; Jazz band; Literary magazine; Marching band; Music ensembles; Musical theater; Pep band; Radio station; Student government; Student newspaper; Symphony orchestra; Television station; Yearbook 40 registered organizations, 8 honor societies, 4 religious organizations. 3 fraternities, 4 sororities. **Athletics (Intercollegiate):** *Men:* baseball, basketball, cheerleading, cross-country, football, golf, soccer, track/field (outdoor), track/field (indoor), wrestling. *Women:* basketball, cheerleading, cross-country, soccer, softball, track/field (outdoor), track/field (indoor), volleyball. **On-Campus Highlights:** Howard Miller Student Center, Robinson Black Box Theater, New Student Appartments, Alumni Stadium, Paul Bush Memorial Fitness Center

ADMISSIONS

Freshman Academic Profile: Average high school GPA 3.0. 12% in top 10% of high school class, 25% in top 25% of high school class, 46% in top 50% of high school class. 88% from public high schools. **Test Scores:** SAT Math middle 50% range 420-520. SAT EBRW middle 50% range 410-510. ACT middle 50% range 18-23. Minimum paper TOEFL 450. **Basis for Candidate Selection:** *Very important factors considered include:* rigor of secondary school record, academic GPA, application essay, standardized test scores, recommendation(s), level of applicant's interest. *Important factors considered include:* class rank, character/personal qualities. *Other factors considered include:* interview, extracurricular activities, talent/ability, volunteer work, work experience. **Freshman Admission Requirements:** High school diploma is required and GED is accepted *Academic units recommended:* 4 English, 2 math, 2 science, 2 science labs, 2 foreign language, 3 social studies, 1 academic elective. **Freshman Admission Statistics:** 1,856 applied, 67.6% admitted, 28% enrolled. **Transfer Admission Requirements:** High school transcript, college transcript(s), essay or personal statement, interview, standardized test scores, statement of good standing from prior institution(s). Minimum college GPA of 2.0 required. Lowest grade transferable C. **General Admission Information:** Application fee $35. Priority deadline 4/1. Regular application deadline 7/1. Nonfall registration accepted. Admission may be deferred for a maximum of 1 year.

COSTS AND FINANCIAL AID

Required Forms and Deadlines: FAFSA; State aid form. **Notification of Awards:** Applicants will be notified of awards on a rolling basis beginning 2/15. **Types of Aid:** *Need-based scholarships/grants:* College/university scholarship or grant aid from institutional funds; Federal Pell; Private scholarships; SEOG; State scholarships/grants. *Loans:* Direct PLUS loans; Direct Subsidized Stafford Loans; Direct Unsubsidized Stafford Loans. *Student Employment:* Federal Work-Study Program available. Institutional employment available. **Financial Aid Statistics:** 100% needy undergrads receive need-based scholarship or grant aid. 0% undergrads receive non-need-based scholarship or grant aid. 100% undergrads receive need-based self-help aid. 0% freshmen, 0% undergrads receive athletic scholarships. **Criteria for awarding aid:** *Need-based:* Academics, Alumni affiliation, Leadership, Religious affiliation *Non-need-based:* Academics, Alumni affiliation, Leadership, Religious affiliation, State/district residency.

THOMAS AQUINAS COLLEGE

10,000 Ojai Road, Santa Paula, CA 93060
Phone: 805-525-4417 • **Financial Aid Phone:** 800-634-9797
E-mail: admissions@thomasaquinas.edu • **CEEB Code:** 4828
Fax: 805-421-5905 • **Website:** www.thomasaquinas.edu • **ACT Code:** 425

This private school, affiliated with the Roman Catholic Church, was founded in 1971. It has a 131 acre campus.

RATINGS
Admissions Selectivity Rating: 90   **Fire Safety Rating:** 94   **Green Rating:** 60*

STUDENTS AND FACULTY
Enrollment: 370. **Student Body:** 52% female, 48% male, 60% out-of-state, 2% international (9 countries represented). Asian 2%, African American 1%, Caucasian 72%, Hispanic 16%, Native American 1%, Pacific Islander <1%, Two or more races 5%, Race unknown 1%.
Retention and Graduation: 90% freshmen return for sophomore year. 73% freshmen graduate within 4 years. 79% freshmen graduate within 6 years. 12% grads go on to further study within 1 year. 7% grads pursue arts and sciences degrees. 1% grads pursue law degrees. 0% grads pursue business degrees. 0% grads pursue medical degrees. **Faculty:** Student/faculty ratio 11:1. 31 full-time faculty, 87% hold PhDs, 10% are women. 0% of classes are taught by teaching assistants.

ACADEMICS
Degrees: Bachelor's **Classes:** Most classes have 10-19 students. Most lab/discussion sessions have 10-19 students. **Most popular majors:** Liberal Arts And Sciences/Liberal Studies. **Career services:** Alumni network; Alumni services; Career assessment; Career/job search classes; Internships; Regional alumni

FACILITIES
Housing: Men's dorms; Women's dorms 100% of campus accessible to physically disabled. **Special Academic Facilities/Equipment:** St. Bernardine of Siena Library; Albertus Magnus Science Hall, St. Cecilia Performing Arts Hall

CAMPUS LIFE
Environment: Rural **Activities:** Campus Ministries; Choral groups; Dance; Drama/theater; Literary magazine; Music ensembles; Musical theater 2 registered organizations, 4 religious organizations. **On-Campus Highlights:** St. Joseph Commons, The Dumb Ox Coffee Shop, Dorm Commons, St. Bernardine Library, Student Lounge

ADMISSIONS
Freshman Academic Profile: Average high school GPA 3.8. 54% in top 10% of high school class, 72% in top 25% of high school class, 91% in top 50% of high school class. 6% from public high schools. **Test Scores:** SAT Math middle 50% range 570-670. SAT EBRW middle 50% range 630-710. ACT middle 50% range 25-30. Minimum internet-based TOEFL 80. Minimum paper TOEFL 570. **Basis for Candidate Selection:** *Very important factors considered include:* rigor of secondary school record, application essay, standardized test scores, recommendation(s), character/personal qualities, level of applicant's interest. *Important factors considered include:* academic GPA. *Other factors considered include:* class rank, interview, extracurricular activities, talent/ability, religious affiliation/commitment, volunteer work, work experience. **Freshman Admission Requirements:** High school diploma is required and GED is accepted *Academic units required:* 4 English, 3 math, 2 science, 2 foreign language, 2 history, *Academic units recommended:* 4 English, 4 math, 3 science, 2 science labs, 2 history, 3 academic electives. **Freshman Admission Statistics:** 192 applied, 71.9% admitted, 65% enrolled. **General Admission Information:** Nonfall registration accepted. Admission may be deferred for a maximum of 1 year.

COSTS AND FINANCIAL AID
Annual tuition $25,000. Room and board $8,400. Average book expense $50. **Required Forms and Deadlines:** FAFSA; Institution's own financial aid form; State aid form. **Notification of Awards:** Applicants will be notified of awards on a rolling basis beginning 2/1. **Types of Aid:** *Need-based scholarships/grants:* College/university scholarship or grant aid from institutional funds; Federal Pell; Private scholarships; State scholarships/grants. *Loans:* Direct PLUS loans; Direct Subsidized Stafford Loans; Direct Unsubsidized Stafford Loans. *Student Employment:* Institutional employment available. **Financial Aid Statistics:** 94% needy freshmen, 86% needy undergrads receive need-

based scholarship or grant aid. 0% undergrads receive non-need-based scholarship or grant aid. 100% freshmen, 100% undergrads receive need-based self-help aid. 0% freshmen, 0% undergrads receive athletic scholarships. 82% freshmen, 81% undergrads receive any aid. 85% undergrads borrow to pay for school. Average cumulative indebtedness $16,986.

THOMAS COLLEGE

180 West River Road, Waterville, ME 04901
Phone: 207-859-1101 • **Financial Aid Phone:** (207) 859-1105
E-mail: admiss@thomas.edu • **CEEB Code:** 2052
Fax: 207-859-1114 • **Website:** www.thomas.edu • **ACT Code:** 1663

This private school was founded in 1894. It has a 120 acre campus.

RATINGS
Admissions Selectivity Rating: 74   **Fire Safety Rating:** 96   **Green Rating:** 60*

STUDENTS AND FACULTY
Enrollment: 739. **Student Body:** 49% female, 51% male, 20% out-of-state, <1% international. Asian 1%, African American 2%, Caucasian 88%, Hispanic 1%, Native American <1%, Race unknown 9%.
Retention and Graduation: 63% freshmen return for sophomore year. 7% grads go on to further study within 1 year. 7% grads pursue business degrees. **Faculty:** Student/faculty ratio 18:1. 21 full-time faculty, 48% hold PhDs, 0% are members of minority groups, 38% are women. 0% of classes are taught by teaching assistants.

ACADEMICS
Degrees: Associate; Bachelor's; Master's; Terminal Associate; Transfer Associate **Classes:** Most classes have 10-19 students. Most lab/discussion sessions have 10-19 students. **Most popular majors:** Sport And Fitness Administration/Management; Accounting; Accounting And Business/Management. **Special Study Options:** Cross-registration; Distance learning; Double major; Internships; Study abroad; Teacher certification program. **Career services:** Career assessment; Internships

FACILITIES
Housing: Coed dorms 71% of campus accessible to physically disabled. **Computers:** Students can register for classes online. Administrative functions (other than registration) can be performed online.

CAMPUS LIFE
Environment: Rural **Activities:** Choral groups; Dance; Drama/theater; Student government; Student newspaper; Yearbook 26 registered organizations, 3 honor societies, 1 fraternities, 1 sorority. **Athletics (Intercollegiate):** *Men:* baseball, basketball, golf, lacrosse, soccer, tennis. *Women:* basketball, field hockey, lacrosse, soccer, softball, volleyball.

ADMISSIONS
Freshman Academic Profile: Average high school GPA 2.7. 7% in top 10% of high school class, 19% in top 25% of high school class, 54% in top 50% of high school class. **Test Scores:** SAT Math middle 50% range 390-510. SAT EBRW middle 50% range 400-500. ACT middle 50% range 13-22. Minimum paper TOEFL 530. **Basis for Candidate Selection:** *Very important factors considered include:* rigor of secondary school record, class rank, academic GPA, application essay, standardized test scores, recommendation(s). *Important factors considered include:* interview, extracurricular activities, character/personal qualities. *Other factors considered include:* talent/ability, first generation, alumni/ae relation, volunteer work, work experience, level of applicant's interest. **Freshman Admission Requirements:** High school diploma is required and GED is accepted *Academic units recommended:* 4 English, 3 math, 3 science, 2 foreign language, 2 social studies, 2 history. **Freshman Admission Statistics:** 483 applied, 82.8% admitted, 48% enrolled. **Transfer Admission Requirements:** High school transcript, college transcript(s), essay or personal statement, Minimum college GPA of 2.0 required. Lowest grade transferable C. **General Admission Information:** Application fee $50. Nonfall registration accepted. Admission may be deferred for a maximum of 2 years.

COSTS AND FINANCIAL AID
Annual tuition $17,280. Required fees $450. Average book expense $800. **Required Forms and Deadlines:** FAFSA. **Notification of Awards:** Applicants will be notified of awards on a rolling basis beginning 3/15. **Types of Aid:** *Need-based scholarships/grants:* College/university scholarship or grant aid from institutional funds; Federal Pell; Private scholarships; SEOG; State scholarships/grants. *Loans:* Direct PLUS loans; Direct Subsidized Stafford Loans; Direct Unsubsidized Stafford Loans. *Student Employment:* Federal Work-Study Program available. Institutional employment available. **Financial**

Aid Statistics: 100% needy freshmen, 98% needy undergrads receive need-based scholarship or grant aid. 31% freshmen, 19% undergrads receive non-need-based scholarship or grant aid. 90% freshmen, 90% undergrads receive need-based self-help aid. 0% freshmen, 0% undergrads receive athletic scholarships. 95% freshmen, 90% undergrads receive any aid. **Criteria for awarding aid:** *Need-based:* Academics *Non-need-based:* Academics.

THOMAS EDISON STATE COLLEGE

111 West State Street, Trenton, NJ 08608-1176
Phone: 888-442-8372 • **Financial Aid Phone:** 609-633-9658
E-mail: admissions@tesu.edu • **CEEB Code:** 2612
Fax: 609-984-8447 • **Website:** www.tesu.edu • **ACT Code:** 274872

This public school was founded in 1972. It has a 2 acre campus.

RATINGS
Admissions Selectivity Rating: 0   Fire Safety Rating: 60*   Green Rating: 61

STUDENTS AND FACULTY
Enrollment: 16,506. **Student Body:** 44% female, 56% male, 1% international (63 countries represented). Asian 4%, African American 15%, Caucasian 51%, Hispanic 9%, Native American 1%, Pacific Islander 1%, Two or more races 2%, Race unknown 16%.
Faculty:

ACADEMICS
Degrees: Associate; Bachelor's; Certificate; Doctoral; Master's; Post-Bachelor's certificate **Classes:** Most classes have 30-39 students. **Special Study Options:** Accelerated program; Distance learning; Dual enrollment; External degree program; Independent study; Student-designed major. **Career services:** Alumni network

FACILITIES
Computers: Students can register for classes online. Administrative functions (other than registration) can be performed online.

CAMPUS LIFE
Environment: City **Activities:** Student newspaper 3 honor societies.

ADMISSIONS
Test Scores: Minimum internet-based TOEFL 79. Minimum paper TOEFL 500. **Basis for Candidate Selection:** *Other factors considered include:* state residency. **Freshman Admission Requirements:** High school diploma is required and GED is accepted **Transfer Admission Requirements:** college transcript(s), Lowest grade transferable D. **General Admission Information:** Application fee $75. Admission may be deferred for a maximum of 6 months.

COSTS AND FINANCIAL AID
Annual out-of-state tuition $9,352. **Required Forms and Deadlines:** FAFSA; Institution's own financial aid form. **Notification of Awards:** Applicants will be notified of awards on a rolling basis beginning 3/1. **Types of Aid:** *Need-based scholarships/grants:* Federal Pell; Private scholarships; State scholarships/grants. **Financial Aid Statistics:** 17% undergrads receive any aid.

THOMAS JEFFERSON UNIVERSITY

130 South 9th Street, Philadelphia, PA 19107
Phone: 215-503-8890 • **Financial Aid Phone:** 215 9552867
E-mail: jchp@jefferson.edu • **CEEB Code:** 2903
Fax: 215-503-7241 • **Website:** www.jefferson.edu/jchp

This private school was founded in 1967.

RATINGS
Admissions Selectivity Rating: 61   Fire Safety Rating: 79   Green Rating: 60*

STUDENTS AND FACULTY
Enrollment: 827. **Student Body:** 83% female, 17% male, 27% out-of-state, 1% international. Asian 8%, African American 9%, Caucasian 71%, Hispanic 3%, Native American <1%, Race unknown 7%.
Faculty: Student/faculty ratio 14:1. 82 full-time faculty, 43% hold PhDs, 12% are members of minority groups, 85% are women.

ACADEMICS
Degrees: Associate; Bachelor's; Master's; Post-Bachelor's certificate; Post-Master's certificate; Transfer Associate **Classes:** Most classes have 10-19 students. Most lab/discussion sessions have 10-19 students. **Most popular majors:** Health Services/Allied Health/Health Sciences, General; Clinical Laboratory Science/Medical Technology/Technologist. **Special Study Options:** Accelerated program; Distance learning; Double major; Independent study; Internships; Study abroad. **Disability Services offered to physically disabled students:** Note-taking services; Reader services; Tutors. **Career services:** Alumni network; Alumni services; Career assessment; Career/job search classes; Regional alumni

FACILITIES
Housing: Apartments for married students; Apartments for single students; Coed dorms; Special housing for disabled students 80% of campus accessible to physically diasbled. **Special Academic Facilities/Equipment:** Copy of the famous Gross Clinic, New building with simulation labs. Located in the heart of Center City close to all historical sights as well as cultural events and museums. **Computers:** 100% of classrooms, 100% of dorms, 100% of libraries, have wireless network access. Students can register for classes online. Administrative functions (other than registration) can be performed online.

CAMPUS LIFE
Environment: Metropolis **Activities:** Choral groups; International Student Organization; Student government; Yearbook. **On-Campus Highlights:** New Education and Research Building, Famous painting called the Gross Clinic, Close to Historic Sites, Close to famous museums, Many fine restaurants and theaters

ADMISSIONS
Freshman Admission Requirements: High school diploma is required and GED is accepted **Transfer Admission Requirements:** college transcript(s), essay or personal statement, statement of good standing from prior institution(s). Minimum college GPA of 2.5 required. Lowest grade transferable C. **General Admission Information:** Application fee $50. Priority deadline 3/1. Nonfall registration accepted. Admission may be deferred.

COSTS AND FINANCIAL AID
Annual tuition $23,685. Required fees $400. Average book expense $1,495. **Required Forms and Deadlines:** FAFSA; Institution's own financial aid form. **Types of Aid:** *Need-based scholarships/grants:* College/university scholarship or grant aid from institutional funds; Federal Nursing Scholarships; Federal Pell; Private scholarships; SEOG; State scholarships/grants. *Loans:* Direct Subsidized Stafford Loans; Direct Unsubsidized Stafford Loans. *Student Employment:* Federal Work-Study Program available. Institutional employment available. **Criteria for awarding aid:** *Need-based:* Academics *Non-need-based:* Academics, Leadership, State/district residency.

THOMAS MORE COLLEGE

333 Thomas More Pkwy., Crestview Hills, KY 41017-3495
Phone: 859-344-3332 • **Financial Aid Phone:** 859-344-3319
E-mail: admissions@thomasmore.edu • **CEEB Code:** 3892
Fax: 859-344-3444 • **Website:** www.thomasmore.edu • **ACT Code:** 1560

This private school, affiliated with the Roman Catholic Church, was founded in 1921. It has a 100 acre campus.

RATINGS
Admissions Selectivity Rating: 71   Fire Safety Rating: 62   Green Rating: 60*

STUDENTS AND FACULTY
Enrollment: 1,399. **Student Body:** 49% female, 51% male, 47% out-of-state, 1% international. Asian 1%, African American 8%, Caucasian 76%, Hispanic 2%, Native American <1%, Pacific Islander <1%, Two or more races 5%, Race unknown 7%.
Retention and Graduation: 67% freshmen return for sophomore year. 17% grads go on to further study within 1 year. **Faculty:** Student/faculty ratio 16:1. 83 full-time faculty, 73% hold PhDs, 6% are members of minority groups, 49% are women. 0% of classes are taught by teaching assistants.

ACADEMICS
Degrees: Associate; Bachelor's; Certificate; **Master's Classes:** Most classes have 10-19 students. **Most popular majors:** Teacher Education And Professional Development, Specific Subject Areas, Other; Business/Commerce, General. **Special Study Options:** Accelerated program; Cooperative education program; Cross-registration; Distance learning; Double major; Dual enrollment; Honors program; Independent study; Internships; Liberal arts/career

combination; Student-designed major; Study abroad; Teacher certification program. Honors programs: Thomas More Honors Program. **Disability Services offered to physically disabled students:** Note-taking services; Reader services; Tape recorders; Tutors. Alumni services; Career assessment; Career/job search classes; Internships; Regional alumni

FACILITIES

Housing: Men's dorms; Women's dorms 99% of campus accessible to physically diasbled. **Special Academic Facilities/Equipment:** Observatory Biology Field Station

CAMPUS LIFE

Environment: Village **Activities:** Campus Ministries; Choral groups; Dance; Drama/theater; International Student Organization; Literary magazine; Marching band; Music ensembles; Student government.

ADMISSIONS

Test Scores: ACT middle 50% range 19-24. Minimum internet-based TOEFL 66. Minimum paper TOEFL 515. **Basis for Candidate Selection:** *Very important factors considered include:* academic GPA, standardized test scores. *Important factors considered include:* rigor of secondary school record. *Other factors considered include:* class rank, application essay, recommendation(s), interview, extracurricular activities, talent/ability, character/personal qualities, volunteer work. **Freshman Admission Requirements:** High school diploma is required and GED is accepted *Academic units required:* 4 English, 3 math, 3 science, 1 science labs, 2 foreign language, 3 social studies, *Academic units recommended:* 2 visual/performing arts. **Freshman Admission Statistics:** 2,416 applied, 91.2% admitted, 16% enrolled. **General Admission Information:** Priority deadline 3/15. Nonfall registration accepted.

COSTS AND FINANCIAL AID

Annual tuition $28,850. Room and board $7,592. Required fees $1,420. **Required Forms and Deadlines:** FAFSA; Institution's own financial aid form. **Notification of Awards:** Applicants will be notified of awards on a rolling basis beginning 3/1. **Types of Aid:** *Need-based scholarships/grants:* College/university scholarship or grant aid from institutional funds; Federal Pell; Private scholarships; SEOG; United Negro College Fund.

THOMAS MORE COLLEGE OF LIBERAL ARTS

6 Manchester Street, Merrimack, NH 03054-4818
Phone: 603-880-8308
E-mail: admissions@thomasmorecollege.edu
Fax: 603-880-9280 • **Website:** www.thomasmorecollege.edu • **ACT Code:** 3892

This private school, affiliated with the Roman Catholic Church, was founded in 1978. It has a 13 acre campus.

RATINGS

Admissions Selectivity Rating: 71   **Fire Safety Rating:** 60*   **Green Rating:** 60*

STUDENTS AND FACULTY

Enrollment: 92. **Student Body:** 48% female, 52% male, 84% out-of-state, 6% international. Asian 0%, African American 0%, Caucasian 72%, Hispanic 1%, Native American 0%, Race unknown 21%.
Retention and Graduation: 60% freshmen return for sophomore year. 52% grads go on to further study within 1 year. 48% grads pursue arts and sciences degrees. 8% grads pursue law degrees. 2% grads pursue business degrees. 2% grads pursue medical degrees. **Faculty:** Student/faculty ratio 12:1. 5 full-time faculty, 100% hold PhDs, 20% are women. 0% of classes are taught by teaching assistants.

ACADEMICS

Degrees: Bachelor's **Most popular majors:** Computer And Information Sciences, General; Business/Commerce, General. **Special Study Options:** Internships; Study abroad.

FACILITIES

Housing: Men's dorms; Women's dorms 70% of campus accessible to physically diasbled.

CAMPUS LIFE

Environment: Village **Activities:** Choral groups; Drama/theater.

ADMISSIONS

Freshman Academic Profile: 12% from public high schools. **Basis for Candidate Selection:** *Very important factors considered include:* application essay, recommendation(s), interview, character/personal qualities. *Important factors considered include:* talent/ability. *Other factors considered include:* rigor

of secondary school record, class rank, academic GPA, standardized test scores, extracurricular activities, religious affiliation/commitment, level of applicant's interest. **Freshman Admission Requirements:** High school diploma is required and GED is accepted *Academic units required:* 4 English, 3 math, 2 science, 2 science labs, 2 foreign language, 2 social studies, 2 history, *Academic units recommended:* 2 units from above areas or other academic areas. **Freshman Admission Statistics:** 75 applied, 54.7% admitted, 68% enrolled. **Transfer Admission Requirements:** college transcript(s), essay or personal statement, Lowest grade transferable C. **General Admission Information:** Nonfall registration accepted. Admission may be deferred.

COSTS AND FINANCIAL AID

Annual tuition $11,100. Room and board $8,000. Average book expense $525. **Required Forms and Deadlines:** FAFSA. **Notification of Awards:** Applicants will be notified of awards on a rolling basis beginning 3/15. **Types of Aid:** *Need-based scholarships/grants:* College/university scholarship or grant aid from institutional funds; Federal Pell; Private scholarships; SEOG; State scholarships/grants. **Financial Aid Statistics:** 100% needy freshmen, 100% needy undergrads receive need-based scholarship or grant aid. 70% freshmen, 62% undergrads receive need-based self-help aid. 0% freshmen, 0% undergrads receive athletic scholarships. **Criteria for awarding aid:** *Non-need-based:* Academics.

TIFFIN UNIVERSITY

155 Miami Street, Tiffin, OH 44883
Phone: 419-448-3423 • **Financial Aid Phone:** 419-448-3415
E-mail: admiss@tiffin.edu • **CEEB Code:** 1817
Fax: 419-443-5006 • **Website:** www.tiffin.edu/ • **ACT Code:** 3334

This private school was founded in 1888. It has a 110 acre campus.

RATINGS

Admissions Selectivity Rating: 81   **Fire Safety Rating:** 87   **Green Rating:** 60*

STUDENTS AND FACULTY

Enrollment: 2,595. **Student Body:** 53% female, 47% male, 34% out-of-state, 7% international (34 countries represented). Asian <1%, African American 17%, Caucasian 44%, Hispanic 3%, Native American <1%, Pacific Islander <1%, Two or more races 2%, Race unknown 26%.
Retention and Graduation: 62% freshmen return for sophomore year. 25% grads go on to further study within 1 year. **Faculty:** Student/faculty ratio 15:1. 72 full-time faculty, 61% hold PhDs, 4% are members of minority groups, 46% are women. 0% of classes are taught by teaching assistants.

ACADEMICS

Degrees: Associate; Bachelor's; Certificate; Master's; Post-Bachelor's certificate; Post-Master's certificate **Classes:** Most classes have 20-29 students. Most lab/discussion sessions have 10-19 students. **Most popular majors:** Forensic Science And Technology; Business Administration And Management, General; Marketing/Marketing Management, General. **Special Study Options:** Accelerated program; Cross-registration; Distance learning; Double major; Dual enrollment; English as a Second Language (ESL); Exchange student program (domestic); Honors program; Independent study; Internships; Student-designed major; Study abroad. Honors programs: We offer a Freshman Honors Program. **Disability Services offered to physically disabled students:** Reader services; Tape recorders; Tutors. **Career services:** Alumni network; Alumni services; Career assessment; Career/job search classes; Internships; Regional alumni

FACILITIES

Housing: Apartments for single students; Coed dorms; Fraternity/sorority housing; Men's dorms; Special housing for international students; Theme housing; Wellness housing; Women's dorms 85% of campus accessible to physically diasbled. **Special Academic Facilities/Equipment:** University Art Gallery Multi-Media Lab **Computers:** 100% of classrooms, 25% of dorms, 100% of libraries, 100% of dining areas, 100% of student union, have wireless network access. Students can register for classes online. Administrative functions (other than registration) can be performed online.

CAMPUS LIFE

Environment: Village **Activities:** Campus Ministries; Choral groups; Concert band; Dance; Drama/theater; International Student Organization; Jazz band; Literary magazine; Marching band; Model UN; Music ensembles; Musical theater; Pep band; Student government; Student newspaper; Symphony orchestra 32 registered organizations, 1 honor society, 2 religious organizations, 3 fraternities, 3 sororities. **Athletics (Intercollegiate):** *Men:* baseball, basketball, cheerleading, cross-country, equestrian sports, football, golf, soccer, tennis, track/field (outdoor), track/field (indoor). *Women:* basketball, cheerleading, cross-country, equestrian sports, golf, lacrosse, soccer, softball, tennis, track/field (outdoor), track/field (indoor), volleyball. **On-Campus Highlights:** Gillmor Student Center, Hayes Center for the Arts, Hertzer Technology Center, Main Classroom Building, Franks Hall **Environmental Initiatives:** Establishment of a Green Committee and formation of a Green Technologies Minor and Concentration

ADMISSIONS

Freshman Academic Profile: Average high school GPA 3.0. 75% from public high schools. **Test Scores:** SAT Math middle 50% range 400-500. SAT EBRW middle 50% range 420-500. ACT middle 50% range 17-22. Minimum internet-based TOEFL 61. Minimum paper TOEFL 500. **Basis for Candidate Selection:** *Very important factors considered include:* rigor of secondary school record, academic GPA, standardized test scores. *Other factors considered include:* application essay, recommendation(s), interview, extracurricular activities, talent/ability, character/personal qualities, alumni/ae relation, volunteer work, work experience, level of applicant's interest. **Freshman Admission Requirements:** High school diploma is required and GED is accepted *Academic units recommended:* 4 English, 4 math, 3 science, 1 science labs, 3 social studies, 0.5 history, 5 academic electives, 1 visual/performing arts, 0.5 unit from above areas or other academic areas. **Freshman Admission Statistics:** 4,384 applied, 54.0% admitted, 21% enrolled. **Transfer Admission Requirements:** High school transcript, college transcript(s), Minimum college GPA of 2.0 required. Lowest grade transferable C. **General Admission Information:** Application fee $20. Nonfall registration accepted. Admission may be deferred for a maximum of 1 year.

COSTS AND FINANCIAL AID

Annual tuition $21,510. Room and board $9,870. Average book expense $2,000. **Required Forms and Deadlines:** FAFSA. **Notification of Awards:** Applicants will be notified of awards on a rolling basis beginning 2/1. **Types of Aid:** *Need-based scholarships/grants:* College/university scholarship or grant aid from institutional funds; Federal Pell; Private scholarships; SEOG; State scholarships/grants. *Loans:* Direct PLUS loans; Direct Subsidized Stafford Loans; Direct Unsubsidized Stafford Loans. *Student Employment:* Federal Work-Study Program available. Institutional employment available. **Financial Aid Statistics:** 100% needy freshmen, 97% needy undergrads receive need-based scholarship or grant aid. 7% freshmen, 8% undergrads receive non-need-based scholarship or grant aid. 93% freshmen, 91% undergrads receive need-based self-help aid. 4% freshmen, 4% undergrads receive athletic scholarships. 95% freshmen, 95% undergrads receive any aid. **Criteria for awarding aid:** *Non-need-based:* Academics, Art, Athletics, Leadership, Music/drama, State/district residency.

TOCCOA FALLS COLLEGE

107 Kincaid Drive, Toccoa Falls, GA 30598
Phone: 888-785-5624 • **Financial Aid Phone:** 706-886-6831
E-mail: admissions@tfc.edu • **CEEB Code:** 5799
Fax: (706) 282-6012 • **Website:** www.tfc.edu • **ACT Code:** 868

This private school, affiliated with the Christian & Missionary Alliance Church, was founded in 1907. It has a 1100 acre campus.

RATINGS

Admissions Selectivity Rating: 85   Fire Safety Rating: 70   Green Rating: 60*

STUDENTS AND FACULTY

Enrollment: 796. **Student Body:** 53% female, 47% male, 23% out-of-state, 1% international. Asian 8%, African American 7%, Caucasian 72%, Hispanic 4%, Native American <1%, Pacific Islander <1%, Two or more races 2%, Race unknown 6%.
Retention and Graduation: 72% freshmen return for sophomore year. **Faculty:** Student/faculty ratio 14:1. 42 full-time faculty, 60% hold PhDs, 12% are members of minority groups, 31% are women. 0% of classes are taught by teaching assistants.

ACADEMICS

Degrees: Associate; Bachelor's; Certificate **Classes:** Most classes have 20-29 students. Most lab/discussion sessions have 10-19 students. **Most popular majors:** Elementary Education And Teaching; Missions/Missionary Studies And Missiology; Counseling Psychology. **Special Study Options:** Distance learning; Double major; Dual enrollment; Independent study; Internships; Study abroad; Teacher certification program. **Disability Services offered to physically disabled students:** Note-taking services; Reader services; Tutors. **Career services:** Career assessment

FACILITIES

Housing: Apartments for married students; Men's dorms; Special housing for international students; Wellness housing; Women's dorms 70% of campus accessible to physically diasbled. **Computers:** 40% of classrooms, 50% of dorms, 100% of libraries, 100% of dining areas, 50% of student union, 1% of common outdoor areas have wireless network access. Students can register for classes online. Administrative functions (other than registration) can be performed online.

CAMPUS LIFE

Environment: Village **Activities:** Campus Ministries; Choral groups; Concert band; Drama/theater; International Student Organization; Jazz band; Music ensembles; Radio station; Student government; Student newspaper; Yearbook. **Athletics (Intercollegiate):** *Men:* baseball, basketball, cross-country, golf, soccer, tennis. *Women:* basketball, cheerleading, cross-country, golf, soccer, tennis, volleyball. **On-Campus Highlights:** The Waterfall, Student Center, Gymnatorium, Eagle's Nest, Grace Chapel & Performing Arts Center

ADMISSIONS

Freshman Academic Profile: Average high school GPA 3.4. 10% in top 10% of high school class, 28% in top 25% of high school class, 63% in top 50% of high school class. 60% from public high schools. **Test Scores:** SAT Math middle 50% range 410-550. SAT EBRW middle 50% range 410-560. ACT middle 50% range 17-24. Minimum internet-based TOEFL 79. Minimum paper TOEFL 500. **Basis for Candidate Selection:** *Very important factors considered include:* rigor of secondary school record, academic GPA, application essay, standardized test scores, character/personal qualities, religious affiliation/commitment. *Other factors considered include:* recommendation(s), interview, extracurricular activities, talent/ability, volunteer work, work experience, level of applicant's interest. **Freshman Admission Requirements:** High school diploma is required and GED is accepted *Academic units recommended:* 4 English, 3 math, 3 science, 2 science labs, 3 social studies, 6 academic electives. **Freshman Admission Statistics:** 879 applied, 53.8% admitted, 42% enrolled. **Transfer Admission Requirements:** college transcript(s), essay or personal statement, Minimum college GPA of 2.0 required. Lowest grade transferable C-. **General Admission Information:** Application fee $25. Regular application deadline 8/1. Nonfall registration accepted. Admission may be deferred for a maximum of 2 years.

COSTS AND FINANCIAL AID

Annual tuition $21,334. Room and board $7,934. Required fees $770. Average book expense $1,000. **Required Forms and Deadlines:** FAFSA; Institution's own financial aid form; State aid form. **Notification of Awards:** Applicants will be notified of awards on a rolling basis beginning 11/1. **Types of Aid:** *Need-based scholarships/grants:* College/university scholarship or grant aid from institutional funds; Federal Pell; Private scholarships; SEOG; State scholarships/grants. *Loans:* Direct PLUS loans; Direct Subsidized Stafford Loans; Direct Unsubsidized Stafford Loans. **Financial Aid Statistics:** 44% needy freshmen, 100% needy undergrads receive need-based scholarship or grant aid. 9% freshmen, 8% undergrads receive non-need-based scholarship or grant aid. 83% freshmen, 82% undergrads receive need-based self-help aid. 0% freshmen, 0% undergrads receive athletic scholarships. 100% freshmen, 98% undergrads receive any aid. Average cumulative indebtedness $29,977. **Criteria for awarding aid:** *Need-based:* Academics, Leadership *Non-need-based:* Academics, Alumni affiliation, Leadership, Music/drama, Religious affiliation, State/district residency.

TOWSON UNIVERSITY

8000 York Road, Towson, MD 21252-0001
Phone: 410-704-2113 • **Financial Aid Phone:** 410-704-4236
E-mail: admissions@towson.edu • **CEEB Code:** 5404
Fax: 410-704-3030 • **Website:** www.towson.edu • **ACT Code:** 1718

This public school was founded in 1866. It has a 329 acre campus.

RATINGS

Admissions Selectivity Rating: 79   Fire Safety Rating: 92   Green Rating: 93

STUDENTS AND FACULTY

Enrollment: 19,367. **Student Body:** 60% female, 40% male, 14% out-of-state, 1% international (74 countries represented). Asian 6%, African American 21%, Caucasian 57%, Hispanic 8%, Native American <1%, Pacific Islander <1%, Two or more races 5%, Race unknown 2%.
Retention and Graduation: 85% freshmen return for sophomore year. 47% freshmen graduate within 4 years. 72% freshmen graduate within 6 years. 37%

grads go on to further study within 1 year. **Faculty:** Student/faculty ratio 17:1. 893 full-time faculty, 80% hold PhDs, 23% are members of minority groups, 58% are women. 0% of classes are taught by teaching assistants.

ACADEMICS

Degrees: Bachelor's; Doctoral/Professional; Doctoral/Research; Master's; Post-Bachelor's certificate; Post-Master's certificate **Classes:** Most classes have 20-29 students. Most lab/discussion sessions have 10-19 students. **Most popular majors:** Biology/Biological Sciences, General; Psychology, General; Business Administration And Management, General. **Special Study Options:** Cross-registration; Distance learning; Double major; Dual enrollment; English as a Second Language (ESL); Exchange student program (domestic); Honors program; Independent study; Internships; Liberal arts/career combination; Student-designed major; Study abroad; Teacher certification program. Honors programs: Honors College Combined degree programs: BA/MA. **Disability Services offered to physically disabled students:** Note-taking services; Reader services; Tape recorders. **Career services:** Alumni network; Alumni services; Career assessment; Career/job search classes; Internships; Regional alumni

FACILITIES

Housing: Apartments for single students; Coed dorms; Special housing for disabled student; Special housing for international students 80% of campus accessible to physically diasbled. **Special Academic Facilities/Equipment:** 3D printing lab Center for the Arts Galleries Asian Arts Gallery Media Center Watson-King Planetarium The TU Herbarium (BALT) Nursing Simulation Center Towson University Biodiversity Center (TUBC) T.Rowe Price Finance Lab Behavioral Lab Urban Environmental Biogeochemistry Laboratory Petrographic microscopes Laser ablation system Electron microscope Stream table **Computers:** 100% of classrooms, 100% of dorms, 100% of libraries, 100% of dining areas, 100% of student union, 100% of common outdoor areas have wireless network access. Students can register for classes online. Administrative functions (other than registration) can be performed online.

CAMPUS LIFE

Environment: Metropolis **Activities:** Campus Ministries; Choral groups; Concert band; Dance; Drama/theater; International Student Organization; Jazz band; Literary magazine; Marching band; Model UN; Music ensembles; Musical theater; Opera; Pep band; Radio station; Student government; Student newspaper; Student-run film society; Symphony orchestra; Television station 198 registered organizations, 15 honor societies, 12 religious organizations. 12 fraternities, 10 sororities. **Athletics (Intercollegiate):** *Men:* baseball, basketball, cheerleading, cross-country, diving, football, golf, lacrosse, soccer, swimming, tennis. *Women:* basketball, cheerleading, cross-country, diving, field hockey, gymnastics, lacrosse, soccer, softball, swimming, tennis, track/field (outdoor), volleyball. **On-Campus Highlights:** Johnny Unitas Stadium/SECU Arena, University Union, Burdick Hall-athletic facilities, West Village Commons, College of Liberal Arts Building **Environmental Initiatives:** Towson University is committed to creating changes, not just on campus, but in the larger Baltimore Metropolitan region. The Baltimore + Towson University (BTU) Partnership allows Towson University to work with over 300 organizations in Greater Baltimore and throughout Maryland to create positive impacts. BTU is about elevating the work that TU is already doing to better address the needs of the regions in areas such as high-quality and equitable education, lifelong health and well being, strong neighborhoods and sustainable communities, a thriving and competitive economy, and vibrant arts and cultural community.

ADMISSIONS

Freshman Academic Profile: Average high school GPA 3.6. 15% in top 10% of high school class, 41% in top 25% of high school class, 81% in top 50% of high school class. 87% from public high schools. **Test Scores:** SAT Math middle 50% range 520-600. SAT EBRW middle 50% range 535-610. ACT middle 50% range 21-25. Minimum internet-based TOEFL 70. **Basis for Candidate Selection:** *Very important factors considered include:* academic GPA. *Important factors considered include:* rigor of secondary school record, standardized test scores. *Other factors considered include:* class rank, application essay, recommendation(s), talent/ability, first generation. **Freshman Admission Requirements:** High school diploma is required and GED is accepted *Academic units required:* 4 English, 4 math, 3 science, 2 science labs, 2 foreign language, 3 social studies, 6 academic electives. **Freshman Admission Statistics:** 12,747 applied, 77.3% admitted, 28% enrolled. **Transfer Admission Requirements:** college transcript(s), Minimum college GPA of 2.0 required. Lowest grade transferable D. **General Admission Information:** Application fee $45. Priority deadline 12/1. Regular application deadline 1/17. Nonfall registration accepted. Admission may be deferred for a maximum of 1 year.

COSTS AND FINANCIAL AID

Annual in-state tuition $12,544. Annual out-of-state tuition $19,138. Room and board $12,544. Required fees $3,002. Average book expense $1,080. **Required Forms and Deadlines:** FAFSA; State aid form. **Notification of Awards:**

Applicants will be notified of awards on a rolling basis beginning 3/15. **Types of Aid:** *Need-based scholarships/grants:* College/university scholarship or grant aid from institutional funds; Federal Pell; Private scholarships; SEOG; State scholarships/grants. *Loans:* Direct PLUS loans; Direct Subsidized Stafford Loans; Direct Unsubsidized Stafford Loans. *Student Employment:* Federal Work-Study Program available. Institutional employment available. **Financial Aid Statistics:** 56% needy freshmen, 62% needy undergrads receive need-based scholarship or grant aid. 39% freshmen, 27% undergrads receive non-need-based scholarship or grant aid. 78% freshmen, 76% undergrads receive need-based self-help aid. 2% freshmen, 1% undergrads receive athletic scholarships. 75% freshmen, 73% undergrads receive any aid. 61% undergrads borrow to pay for school. Average cumulative indebtedness $25,483. **Criteria for awarding aid:** *Non-need-based:* Academics, Alumni affiliation, Art, Athletics, Leadership, Music/drama, State/district residency.

TRANSYLVANIA UNIVERSITY

300 North Broadway, Lexington, KY 40508-1797
Phone: 859-233-8242 • **Financial Aid Phone:** 859-233-8239
E-mail: admissions@transy.edu • **CEEB Code:** 1808
Fax: 859-281-3649 • **Website:** www.transy.edu • **ACT Code:** 1550

This private school, affiliated with the Disciples of Christ Church, was founded in 1780. It has a 36 acre campus.

RATINGS

Admissions Selectivity Rating: 80   **Fire Safety Rating:** 90   **Green Rating:** 72

STUDENTS AND FACULTY

Enrollment: 962. **Student Body:** 60% female, 40% male, 24% out-of-state, 3% international (7 countries represented). Asian 1%, African American 4%, Caucasian 80%, Hispanic 5%, Native American <1%, Pacific Islander 0%, Two or more races 4%, Race unknown 4%.
Retention and Graduation: 82% freshmen return for sophomore year. 69% freshmen graduate within 4 years. 75% freshmen graduate within 6 years. 41% grads go on to further study within 1 year. 55% grads pursue arts and sciences degrees. 23% grads pursue law degrees. 0% grads pursue business degrees. 7% grads pursue medical degrees. **Faculty:** Student/faculty ratio 11:1. 82 full-time faculty, 96% hold PhDs, 6% are members of minority groups, 46% are women. 0% of classes are taught by teaching assistants.

ACADEMICS

Degrees: Bachelor's **Classes:** Most classes have 20-29 students. Most lab/discussion sessions have 10-19 students. **Most popular majors:** Psychology, General; Business/Commerce, General; Accounting. **Special Study Options:** Double major; Independent study; Internships; Liberal arts/career combination; Student-designed major; Study abroad; Teacher certification program. **Disability Services offered to physically disabled students:** Note-taking services; Reader services; Tape recorders; Tutors. **Career services:** Alumni network; Alumni services; Career assessment; Career/job search classes; Internships; Regional alumni

FACILITIES

Housing: Apartments for single students; Coed dorms; Men's dorms; Women's dorms 90% of campus accessible to physically diasbled. **Special Academic Facilities/Equipment:** Art gallery, museum of early scientific apparatus, medical museum, language lab, transmission electron microscope. **Computers:** 20% of classrooms, 20% of dorms, 75% of libraries, 20% of dining areas, 100% of student union, 10% of common outdoor areas have wireless network access. Administrative functions (other than registration) can be performed online.

CAMPUS LIFE

Environment: Metropolis **Activities:** Campus Ministries; Choral groups; Concert band; Dance; Drama/theater; Jazz band; Literary magazine; Music ensembles; Musical theater; Opera; Radio station; Student government; Student newspaper 55 registered organizations, 10 honor societies, 7 religious organizations. 4 fraternities, 4 sororities. **Athletics (Intercollegiate):** *Men:* baseball, basketball, cheerleading, cross-country, diving, golf, soccer, swimming, tennis, track/field (outdoor). *Women:* basketball, cheerleading, cross-country, diving, field hockey, golf, soccer, softball, swimming, tennis, track/field (outdoor), volleyball. **On-Campus Highlights:** Cowgill Center, Beck Athletic and Recreation Center, Rafskeller, New Residence Halls, Jazzman's Cafe **Environmental Initiatives:** Developing a comprehensive sustainability master plan.

ADMISSIONS

Freshman Academic Profile: Average high school GPA 3.7, 34% in top 10% of high school class, 65% in top 25% of high school class, 87% in top 50% of high school class. 78% from public high schools. **Test Scores:** SAT Math middle 50% range 570-670. SAT EBRW middle 50% range 610-690. ACT middle 50% range 25-30. Minimum internet-based TOEFL 80. Minimum paper TOEFL 550. **Basis for Candidate Selection:** *Very important factors considered include:* rigor of secondary school record, academic GPA, application essay, standardized test scores. *Important factors considered include:* recommendation(s), extracurricular activities, talent/ability, character/personal qualities. *Other factors considered include:* class rank, interview, first generation, alumni/ae relation, geographical residence, racial/ethnic status, volunteer work, work experience. **Freshman Admission Requirements:** High school diploma is required and GED is accepted *Academic units required:* 4 English, 3 math, 3 science, 2 science labs, 2 foreign language, 2 social studies, 2 academic electives, *Academic units recommended:* 4 English, 4 math, 4 science, 3 science labs, 2 foreign language, 2 social studies, 1 history, 2 academic electives. **Freshman Admission Statistics:** 1,567 applied, 95.5% admitted, 19% enrolled. **Transfer Admission Requirements:** High school transcript, college transcript(s), essay or personal statement, Minimum college GPA of 2.75 required. Lowest grade transferable C-. **General Admission Information:** Priority deadline 11/1. Nonfall registration accepted. Admission may be deferred for a maximum of 1 year.

COSTS AND FINANCIAL AID

Annual tuition $37,170. Room and board $10,460. Required fees $1,580. Average book expense $1,000. **Required Forms and Deadlines:** FAFSA. **Notification of Awards:** Applicants will be notified of awards on or about 12/1. **Types of Aid:** *Need-based scholarships/grants:* College/university scholarship or grant aid from institutional funds; Federal Pell; Private scholarships; SEOG; State scholarships/grants. *Loans:* Direct PLUS loans; Direct Subsidized Stafford Loans; Direct Unsubsidized Stafford Loans. *Student Employment:* Federal Work-Study Program available. Institutional employment available. **Financial Aid Statistics:** 100% needy freshmen, 100% needy undergrads receive need-based scholarship or grant aid. 21% freshmen, 14% undergrads receive non-need-based scholarship or grant aid. 76% freshmen, 75% undergrads receive need-based self-help aid. 0% freshmen, 0% undergrads receive athletic scholarships. 99% freshmen, 98% undergrads receive any aid. 63% undergrads borrow to pay for school. Average cumulative indebtedness $30,514. **Criteria for awarding aid:** *Need-based:* Academics, Minority status, Religious affiliation *Non-need-based:* Academics, Art, Minority status, Music/drama, Religious affiliation, State/district residency.

TREVECCA NAZARENE UNIVERSITY

333 Murfreesboro Road, Nashville, TN 37210
Phone: 615-248-1320 · **Financial Aid Phone:** 615-248-1242
E-mail: admissions_und@trevecca.edu
Fax: 615-248-7406 • **Website:** www.trevecca.edu • **ACT Code:** 4016

This private school, affiliated with the Nazarene Church, was founded in 1901. It has a 80 acre campus.

RATINGS

Admissions Selectivity Rating: 82 **Fire Safety Rating:** 60* **Green Rating:** 60*

STUDENTS AND FACULTY

Enrollment: 2,112. **Student Body:** 62% female, 38% male, 33% out-of-state, 6% international (23 countries represented). Asian 1%, African American 12%, Caucasian 61%, Hispanic 9%, Native American <1%, Pacific Islander <1%, Two or more races 3%, Race unknown 7%.
Retention and Graduation: 76% freshmen return for sophomore year. 43% freshmen graduate within 4 years. 54% freshmen graduate within 6 years.
Faculty: Student/faculty ratio 18:1. 92 full-time faculty, 85% hold PhDs, 10% are members of minority groups, 40% are women.

ACADEMICS

Degrees: Associate; Bachelor's; Certificate; Doctoral/Research; Master's; Post-Master's certificate **Classes:** Most classes have 10-19 students. Most lab/discussion sessions have 10-19 students. **Most popular majors:** Psychology, General; Registered Nursing/Registered Nurse; Business Administration And Management, General. **Special Study Options:** Distance learning; Double major; Dual enrollment; Internships; Study abroad; Teacher certification program. **Disability Services offered to physically disabled students:** Note-taking services; Reader services; Tutors. **Career services:** Alumni services; Internships

FACILITIES

Housing: Men's dorms; Women's dorms **Computers:** 100% of classrooms, 100% of dorms, 100% of libraries, 100% of dining areas, 100% of student union, 100% of common outdoor areas have wireless network access. Administrative functions (other than registration) can be performed online.

CAMPUS LIFE

Environment: Metropolis **Activities:** Campus Ministries; Choral groups; Concert band; Drama/theater; International Student Organization; Jazz band; Literary magazine; Marching band; Music ensembles; Musical theater; Pep band; Student government; Student newspaper; Symphony orchestra; Yearbook. **Athletics (Intercollegiate):** *Men:* baseball, basketball, golf, soccer. *Women:* basketball, golf, soccer, softball, volleyball. **On-Campus Highlights:** Library, Student Center, Nineteen|01 (coffee shop), Moore gymnsium / wellness center

ADMISSIONS

Freshman Academic Profile: Average high school GPA 3.5. **Test Scores:** SAT Math middle 50% range 490-590. SAT EBRW middle 50% range 510-620. ACT middle 50% range 19-26. Minimum internet-based TOEFL 173. Minimum paper TOEFL 500. **Basis for Candidate Selection:** *Very important factors considered include:* academic GPA, standardized test scores, character/personal qualities. *Important factors considered include:* level of applicant's interest. *Other factors considered include:* rigor of secondary school record, class rank, application essay, recommendation(s), extracurricular activities, talent/ability. **Freshman Admission Requirements:** High school diploma is required and GED is accepted *Academic units recommended:* 4 English, 2 math, 1 science, 2 foreign language, 1 social studies, 1 history, 4 academic electives. **Freshman Admission Statistics:** 1,489 applied, 70.4% admitted, 40% enrolled. **Transfer Admission Requirements:** college transcript(s), Lowest grade transferable D. **General Admission Information:** Application fee $25. Priority deadline 4/1. Regular application deadline 8/1. Nonfall registration accepted. Admission may be deferred for a maximum of 1 year.

COSTS AND FINANCIAL AID

Annual tuition $24,698. Room and board $8,400. Required fees $900. **Notification of Awards:** Applicants will be notified of awards on a rolling basis beginning 12/1. **Types of Aid:** *Need-based scholarships/grants:* College/university scholarship or grant aid from institutional funds; Federal Pell; Private scholarships; SEOG; State scholarships/grants. *Loans:* Direct PLUS loans; Direct Subsidized Stafford Loans; Direct Unsubsidized Stafford Loans. *Student Employment:* Federal Work-Study Program available. Institutional employment available. **Financial Aid Statistics:** 96% undergrads receive any aid. 64% undergrads borrow to pay for school. Average cumulative indebtedness $30,667. **Criteria for awarding aid:** *Non-need-based:* Academics, Alumni affiliation, Athletics, Leadership, Minority status, Music/drama, Religious affiliation.

TRINE UNIVERSITY

1 University Avenue, Angola, IN 46703
Phone: 260-665-4100 • **Financial Aid Phone:** 260-664-4158
E-mail: admit@trine.edu • **CEEB Code:** 1811
Fax: 260-665-4578 • **Website:** www.trine.edu • **ACT Code:** 1250

This private school was founded in 1884. It has a 400 acre campus.

RATINGS

Admissions Selectivity Rating: 79 **Fire Safety Rating:** 87 **Green Rating:** 60*

STUDENTS AND FACULTY

Enrollment: 1,939. **Student Body:** 29% female, 71% male, 39% out-of-state, 6% international (14 countries represented). Asian 1%, African American 3%, Caucasian 81%, Hispanic 4%, Native American <1%, Pacific Islander <1%, Two or more races 3%, Race unknown 2%.
Retention and Graduation: 80% freshmen return for sophomore year.
Faculty: Student/faculty ratio 16:1. 113 full-time faculty, 63% hold PhDs, 12% are members of minority groups, 37% are women. 0% of classes are taught by teaching assistants.

ACADEMICS

Degrees: Associate; Bachelor's; Doctoral/Professional; **Master's Classes:** Most classes have 20-29 students. Most lab/discussion sessions have 20-29 students. **Most popular majors:** Civil Engineering, General; Mechanical Engineering; Criminal Justice/Safety Studies. **Special Study Options:** Accelerated program; Cooperative education program; Distance learning; Double major; Dual enrollment; English as a Second Language (ESL); Honors program; Independent study; Internships; Liberal arts/career combination; Student-designed major; Study abroad; Teacher certification program. Honors programs: Honors program began with Fall 2006 entering class of freshmen. Combined degree programs: BA/MA; BA/MEng. **Disability Services offered to physically disabled students:** Reader services; Tape recorders; Tutors. **Career services:** Alumni network; Alumni services; Career assessment; Internships; Regional alumni

FACILITIES

Housing: Coed dorms; Fraternity/sorority housing; Men's dorms; Special housing for disabled student; Theme housing; Women's dorms 95% of campus accessible to physically diasbled. **Special Academic Facilities/Equipment:** Lewis Hershey Museum; Wells Gallery of Engravings; Zollner Golf Course **Computers:** 100% of classrooms, 100% of dorms, 100% of libraries, 100% of dining areas, 100% of student union, have wireless network access. Students can register for classes online. Administrative functions (other than registration) can be performed online.

CAMPUS LIFE

Environment: Village **Activities:** Campus Ministries; Choral groups; Concert band; Dance; Drama/theater; International Student Organization; Jazz band; Literary magazine; Marching band; Music ensembles; Pep band; Radio station; Student government; Yearbook 35 registered organizations, 13 honor societies, 3 religious organizations. 8 fraternities, 6 sororities. **Athletics (Intercollegiate):** *Men:* baseball, basketball, cross-country, football, golf, lacrosse, soccer, tennis, track/field (outdoor), track/field (indoor), wrestling. *Women:* basketball, cross-country, golf, lacrosse, soccer, softball, tennis, track/field (outdoor), track/field (indoor), volleyball. **On-Campus Highlights:** University Center, Fawick Hall of Engineering featuring Innovation One, T Furth Center for Performing Arts, Zollner Golf Course (on campus), MTI Center (sports and gaming facility

ADMISSIONS

Freshman Academic Profile: Average high school GPA 3.5. 23% in top 10% of high school class, 51% in top 25% of high school class, 84% in top 50% of high school class. **Test Scores:** SAT Math middle 50% range 490-590. SAT EBRW middle 50% range 480-570. ACT middle 50% range 22-28. Minimum internet-based TOEFL 71. **Basis for Candidate Selection:** *Very important factors considered include:* rigor of secondary school record, class rank, academic GPA, standardized test scores. *Important factors considered include:* recommendation(s), extracurricular activities. *Other factors considered include:* talent/ability, character/personal qualities, alumni/ae relation, volunteer work, work experience. **Freshman Admission Requirements:** High school diploma is required and GED is accepted *Academic units required: Academic units recommended:* 4 English, 3 math, 3 science, 3 social studies. **Freshman Admission Statistics:** 3,502 applied, 70.1% admitted, 24% enrolled. **Transfer Admission Requirements:** High school transcript, college transcript(s), statement of good standing from prior institution(s). Minimum college GPA of 2.0 required. Lowest grade transferable C. **General Admission Information:** Priority deadline 6/1. Regular application deadline 8/1. Nonfall registration accepted. Admission may be deferred for a maximum of 1 year.

COSTS AND FINANCIAL AID

Annual tuition $31,700. Room and board $10,810. Required fees $475. Average book expense $1,200. **Required Forms and Deadlines:** FAFSA. **Notification of Awards:** Applicants will be notified of awards on a rolling basis beginning 3/10. **Types of Aid:** *Need-based scholarships/grants:* College/university scholarship or grant aid from institutional funds; Federal Pell; Private scholarships; SEOG; State scholarships/grants. *Loans:* Direct PLUS loans; Direct Subsidized Stafford Loans; Direct Unsubsidized Stafford Loans. *Student Employment:* Federal Work-Study Program available. Institutional employment available. **Financial Aid Statistics:** 100% needy freshmen, 99% needy undergrads receive need-based scholarship or grant aid. 100% freshmen, 100% undergrads receive non-need-based scholarship or grant aid. 94% freshmen, 90% undergrads receive need-based self-help aid. 0% freshmen, 0% undergrads receive athletic scholarships. 99% freshmen, 98% undergrads receive any aid. **Criteria for awarding aid:** *Non-need-based:* Academics, Alumni affiliation, Minority status, Music/drama.

TRINITY CHRISTIAN COLLEGE

6601 West College Drive, Palos Heights, IL 60463
Phone: (708) 239-4708 • **Financial Aid Phone:** (708) 239-4872
E-mail: admissions@trnty.edu • **CEEB Code:** 1820
Fax: (708) 239-4826 • **Website:** www.trnty.edu • **ACT Code:** 1165

This private school was founded in 1959. It has a 60 acre campus.

RATINGS

Admissions Selectivity Rating: 76   **Fire Safety Rating:** 88   **Green Rating:** 60*

STUDENTS AND FACULTY

Enrollment: 1,028. **Student Body:** 67% female, 33% male, 31% out-of-state, 10% international (12 countries represented). Asian 1%, African American 8%, Caucasian 64%, Hispanic 13%, Native American <1%, Pacific Islander <1%, Two or more races 1%, Race unknown 3%. **Retention and Graduation:** 86% freshmen return for sophomore year. 60% freshmen graduate within 4 years. 68% freshmen graduate within 6 years. 12% grads go on to further study within 1 year. 4% grads pursue arts and sciences degrees. 1% grads pursue law degrees. 1% grads pursue business degrees. 2% grads pursue medical degrees. **Faculty:** Student/faculty ratio 10:1. 70 full-time faculty, 66% hold PhDs, 9% are members of minority groups, 60% are women. 0% of classes are taught by teaching assistants.

ACADEMICS

Degrees: Bachelor's; Master's; Post-Master's certificate **Classes:** Most classes have fewer than 10 students. Most lab/discussion sessions have fewer than 10 students. **Most popular majors:** Elementary Education And Teaching; Registered Nursing/Registered Nurse; Business/Commerce, General. **Special Study Options:** Accelerated program; Distance learning; Double major; Dual enrollment; English as a Second Language (ESL); Honors program; Independent study; Internships; Liberal arts/career combination; Study abroad; Teacher certification program. Honors programs: The Trinity Honors Program challenges and academically supports gifted students through seminars, unique opportunities within the major program, and participation in co-curricular activities. **Disability Services offered to physically disabled students:** Reader services; Tape recorders; Tutors. **Career services:** Alumni network; Alumni services; Career assessment; Internships; Regional alumni

FACILITIES

Housing: Coed dorms 98% of campus accessible to physically diasbled. **Special Academic Facilities/Equipment:** Dutch Heritage Center. **Computers:** 100% of classrooms, 100% of dorms, 100% of libraries, 100% of dining areas, 100% of student union, 15% of common outdoor areas have wireless network access. Students can register for classes online. Administrative functions (other than registration) can be performed online.

CAMPUS LIFE

Environment: Metropolis **Activities:** Campus Ministries; Choral groups; Drama/theater; Jazz band; Literary magazine; Music ensembles; Musical theater; Student government; Student newspaper; Yearbook 15 registered organizations, 2 honor societies, 1 religious organization. **Athletics (Intercollegiate):** *Men:* baseball, basketball, cross-country, soccer, track/field (outdoor), track/field (indoor). *Women:* basketball, cross-country, soccer, softball, track/field (outdoor), track/field (indoor), volleyball. **On-Campus Highlights:** Bootsma Bookstore/Cafe, West Hall Rec, Chapel, South Hall Lobby, Cooper Center **Environmental Initiatives:** Recycling of paper, aluminum, and glass

ADMISSIONS

Freshman Academic Profile: Average high school GPA 3.4. 11% in top 10% of high school class, 24% in top 25% of high school class, 66% in top 50% of high school class. 54% from public high schools. **Test Scores:** SAT Math middle 50% range 510-600. SAT EBRW middle 50% range 545-595. ACT middle 50% range 19-26. Minimum internet-based TOEFL 79. Minimum paper TOEFL 550. **Basis for Candidate Selection:** *Very important factors considered include:* rigor of secondary school record, academic GPA, standardized test scores. *Important factors considered include:* application essay, recommendation(s), interview, extracurricular activities, talent/ability, character/personal qualities, religious affiliation/commitment. *Other factors considered include:* class rank, first generation, alumni/ae relation, geographical residence, volunteer work, work experience, level of applicant's interest. **Freshman Admission Requirements:** High school diploma is required and GED is accepted *Academic units required:* 6 English, 3 math, 2 science, 2 social studies, *Academic units recommended:* 4 English, 4 math, 3 science, 2 foreign language, 3 social studies, 2 history. **Freshman Admission Statistics:** 889 applied, 82.9% admitted, 26% enrolled. **Transfer Admission Requirements:** college transcript(s), essay or personal statement, interview, statement of good standing from prior institution(s). Minimum college GPA of 2.0 required. Lowest grade transferable C. **General Admission Information:** Application fee $30. Priority deadline 1/15. Nonfall registration accepted. Admission may be deferred for a maximum of 1 semester.

COSTS AND FINANCIAL AID

Annual tuition $29,700. Room and board $9,790. Required fees $250. Average book expense $1,100. **Required Forms and Deadlines:** FAFSA. **Notification of Awards:** Applicants will be notified of awards on a rolling basis beginning 12/15. **Types of Aid:** *Need-based scholarships/grants:* College/university scholarship or grant aid from institutional funds; Federal Nursing Scholarships; Federal Pell; Private scholarships; SEOG; State scholarships/grants. *Loans:* Direct PLUS loans; Direct Subsidized Stafford Loans; Direct Unsubsidized Stafford Loans. *Student Employment:* Federal Work-Study Program available. Institutional employment available. **Financial Aid Statistics:** 100% needy freshmen, 98% needy undergrads receive need-based scholarship or grant aid. 17% freshmen, 10% undergrads receive non-need-based scholarship or grant aid. 81% freshmen, 82% undergrads receive need-based self-help aid. 8% freshmen, 5% undergrads receive athletic scholarships. 100% freshmen, 98% undergrads receive any aid. 80% undergrads borrow to pay for school. Average cumulative indebtedness $31,321. **Criteria for awarding aid:** *Need-based:* Leadership *Non-need-based:* Academics, Alumni affiliation, Art, Athletics, Leadership, Minority status, Music/drama, Religious affiliation.

TRINITY COLLEGE (CT)

300 Summit Street, Hartford, CT 06016
Phone: 860-297-2180 • **Financial Aid Phone:** 860-297-2047
E-mail: admissions.office@trincoll.edu • **CEEB Code:** 3899
Fax: 860-297-2287 • **Website:** www.trincoll.edu • **ACT Code:** 598

This private school was founded in 1823. It has a 100 acre campus.

RATINGS
Admissions Selectivity Rating: 92 **Fire Safety Rating:** 95 **Green Rating:** 78

STUDENTS AND FACULTY
Enrollment: 2,225. **Student Body:** 48% female, 52% male, 80% out-of-state, 10% international (62 countries represented). Asian 4%, African American 6%, Caucasian 65%, Hispanic 7%, Native American <1%, Pacific Islander 0%, Two or more races 3%, Race unknown 5%.
Retention and Graduation: 90% freshmen return for sophomore year. 19% grads go on to further study within 1 year. 10% grads pursue arts and sciences degrees. 4% grads pursue law degrees. 1% grads pursue business degrees. 1% grads pursue medical degrees. **Faculty:** Student/faculty ratio 9:1. 207 full-time faculty, 92% hold PhDs, 18% are members of minority groups, 46% are women. 0% of classes are taught by teaching assistants.

ACADEMICS
Degrees: Bachelor's; **Master's Classes:** Most classes have 20-29 students. Most lab/discussion sessions have 10-19 students. **Most popular majors:** English Language And Literature, General; Economics, General; Political Science And Government, General. **Special Study Options:** Accelerated program; Cross-registration; Double major; Exchange student program (domestic); Honors program; Independent study; Internships; Student-designed major; Study abroad; Teacher certification program. Combined degree programs: BA/MEng. **Disability Services offered to physically disabled students:** Note-taking services; Reader services; Tape recorders; Tutors. **Career services:** Alumni network; Alumni services; Career assessment; Career/job search classes; Internships; Regional alumni

FACILITIES
Housing: Coed dorms; Fraternity/sorority housing; Special housing for disabled student; Theme housing; Wellness housing 60% of campus accessible to physically diasbled. **Special Academic Facilities/Equipment:** Watkinson Library; Austin Arts Center **Computers:** 95% of classrooms, 85% of dorms, 100% of libraries, 100% of dining areas, 100% of student union, 90% of common outdoor areas have wireless network access. Students can register for classes online. Administrative functions (other than registration) can be performed online.

CAMPUS LIFE
Environment: Metropolis **Activities:** Campus Ministries; Choral groups; Dance; Drama/theater; International Student Organization; Jazz band; Literary magazine; Model UN; Music ensembles; Musical theater; Radio station; Student government; Student newspaper; Student-run film society; Yearbook 105 registered organizations, 5 honor societies, 5 religious organizations. 7 fraternities, 3 sororities. **Athletics (Intercollegiate):** *Men:* baseball, basketball, crew/rowing, cross-country, diving, football, golf, ice hockey, lacrosse, soccer, squash, swimming, tennis, track/field (outdoor), track/field (indoor), wrestling. *Women:* basketball, crew/rowing, cross-country, diving, field hockey, ice hockey, lacrosse, soccer, softball, squash, swimming, tennis, track/field (outdoor), track/field (indoor), volleyball. **On-Campus Highlights:** The Learning Corridor, Library, The Science/Engineering Labs, Summit Suites (newest residence hall), The Chapel **Environmental Initiatives:** Reduced energy consumption in the dining halls through automated lighting and low-draw fume hoods as well as a new Building Automation System to increase control of temperatures on campus.

ADMISSIONS
Freshman Academic Profile: 50% in top 10% of high school class, 78% in top 25% of high school class, 96% in top 50% of high school class. 42% from public high schools. **Test Scores:** SAT Math middle 50% range 610-690. SAT EBRW middle 50% range 600-680. ACT middle 50% range 28-32. Minimum internet-based TOEFL 95. Minimum paper TOEFL 550. **Basis for Candidate Selection:** *Very important factors considered include:* rigor of secondary school record, character/personal qualities. *Important factors considered include:* academic GPA, application essay, recommendation(s), extracurricular activities, talent/ability, level of applicant's interest. *Other factors considered include:* class rank, standardized test scores, interview, first generation, alumni/ae relation, racial/ethnic status, volunteer work, work experience. **Freshman Admission Requirements:** High school diploma is required and GED is accepted *Academic units required:* 4 English, 3 math, 2 science, 2 science labs, 3 foreign language, 2 history. **Freshman Admission Statistics:** 6,073 applied, 34.0% admitted, 28% enrolled. **Transfer Admission Requirements:** High school transcript, college transcript(s), essay or personal statement, standardized test scores, statement of good standing from prior institution(s). Minimum college GPA of 3.0 required. Lowest grade transferable C-. **General Admission Information:** Application fee $65. Regular application deadline 1/1. Nonfall registration accepted. Admission may be deferred for a maximum of 1 year.

COSTS AND FINANCIAL AID
Annual tuition $52,280. Room and board $14,200. Required fees $2,490. Average book expense $1,000. **Required Forms and Deadlines:** CSS/Financial Aid PROFILE; FAFSA; Noncustodial PROFILE. **Notification of Awards:** Applicants will be notified of awards on or about 4/1. **Types of Aid:** *Need-based scholarships/grants:* College/university scholarship or grant aid from institutional funds; Federal Pell; Private scholarships; SEOG; State scholarships/grants. *Loans:* Direct PLUS loans; Direct Subsidized Stafford Loans; Direct Unsubsidized Stafford Loans. *Student Employment:* Federal Work-Study Program available. Institutional employment available. **Financial Aid Statistics:** 95% needy freshmen, 95% needy undergrads receive need-based scholarship or grant aid. 14% freshmen, 7% undergrads receive non-need-based scholarship or grant aid. 73% freshmen, 76% undergrads receive need-based self-help aid. 0% freshmen, 0% undergrads receive athletic scholarships. 49% freshmen, 45% undergrads receive any aid. **Criteria for awarding aid:** *Non-need-based:* Academics, Leadership.

TRINITY COLLEGE DUBLIN

The University of Dublin, Dublin, IR
Phone: (3531) 896-4500
E-mail: academic.registry@tcd.ie
Website: www.tcd.ie

This public school was founded in 1592. It has a 47 acre campus.

RATINGS
Admissions Selectivity Rating: 85 **Fire Safety Rating:** 90 **Green Rating:** 74

STUDENTS AND FACULTY
Enrollment: 11,839. **Student Body:** 60% female, 40% male, 15% out-of-state, (122 countries represented).
Retention and Graduation: 91% freshmen return for sophomore year. **Faculty:** Student/faculty ratio 17:1. 864 full-time faculty, 8% hold PhDs, 10% of classes are taught by teaching assistants.

ACADEMICS
Degrees: Bachelor's; Doctoral; Doctoral/Professional; Doctoral/Research; Master's; Post-Master's certificate **Special Study Options:** Cross-registration; Double major; English as a Second Language (ESL); Exchange student program (domestic); Honors program; Internships; Liberal arts/career combination; Study abroad; Teacher certification program. Honors programs: All degrees conferred by the University of Dublin are Honors Degrees. There are over 400 four-year full-time degree programmes on offer at the University for undergraduate students. **Disability Services offered to physically disabled students:** Note-taking services; Reader services; Tape recorders; Tutors. **Career services:** Alumni network; Alumni services; Career assessment; Career/job search classes; Internships; Regional alumni

FACILITIES
Housing: Apartments for married students; Apartments for single students; Coed dorms; Special housing for disabled student; Special housing for international students **Special Academic Facilities/Equipment:** Science Gallery. (www.sciencegallery.com) Zoology Museum. (http://www.tcd.ie/

Zoology/museum/) Geology Museum.(http://www.tcd.ie/Geology/museum/) Douglas Hyde Art Gallery. (www.douglashydegallery.com) Book of Kells Exhibition (http://www.tcd.ie/Library/bookofkells/)

CAMPUS LIFE

Environment: Metropolis **Activities:** Campus Ministries; Choral groups; Concert band; Dance; Drama/theater; International Student Organization; Jazz band; Literary magazine; Music ensembles; Musical theater; Radio station; Student government; Student newspaper; Student-run film society; Symphony orchestra; Television station. Science Gallery, Sports Centre, Dining Hall, Old Library, Pavillion

ADMISSIONS

Basis for Candidate Selection: *Very important factors considered include:* rigor of secondary school record, academic GPA, standardized test scores. *Important factors considered include:* application essay, recommendation(s). *Other factors considered include:* extracurricular activities, character/personal qualities, volunteer work, work experience, level of applicant's interest. **Freshman Admission Requirements:** High school diploma is required and GED is not accepted **Freshman Admission Statistics:** 18,995 applied, 15.8% admitted, 93% enrolled. **General Admission Information:** Application fee $35. Priority deadline 2/1. Regular application deadline 6/1. Nonfall registration accepted. Admission may be deferred for a maximum of 1 year.

COSTS AND FINANCIAL AID

Required Forms and Deadlines: FAFSA. **Types of Aid:** *Need-based scholarships/grants:* Private scholarships; State scholarships/grants. *Loans:* Direct PLUS loans; Direct Subsidized Stafford Loans; Direct Unsubsidized Stafford Loans. **Criteria for awarding aid:** *Non-need-based:* Academics, Leadership.

TRINITY COLLEGE OF FLORIDA

2430 Welbilt Boulevard, Trinity, FL 34655
Phone: 727-569-1411 · **Financial Aid Phone:** 727-569-1413
E-mail: admissions@trinitycollege.edu
Fax: 727-569-1410 • **Website:** www.trinitycollege.edu • **ACT Code:** 4876

This private school, affiliated with the Interdenominational, was founded in 1932. It has a 40 acre campus.

RATINGS

Admissions Selectivity Rating: 75   **Fire Safety Rating:** 86   **Green Rating:** 60*

STUDENTS AND FACULTY

Enrollment: 210. **Student Body:** 39% female, 61% male, 28% out-of-state, 1% international (2 countries represented). Asian <1%, African American 18%, Caucasian 64%, Hispanic 16%, Native American <1%, Race unknown 0%. **Retention and Graduation:** 67% freshmen return for sophomore year. 14% grads go on to further study within 1 year. **Faculty:** Student/faculty ratio 14:1. 6 full-time faculty, 83% hold PhDs, 0% are members of minority groups, 17% are women. 0% of classes are taught by teaching assistants.

ACADEMICS

Degrees: Associate; Bachelor's; Certificate; Terminal Associate **Most popular majors:** Pre-Theology/Pre-Ministerial Studies; Pastoral Studies/Counseling; Youth Ministry. **Special Study Options:** Accelerated program; Double major; Dual enrollment; Honors program; Independent study; Internships; Weekend college. Honors programs: Our honors program consists of 4 Great Books Seminars. **Disability Services offered to physically disabled students:** Tutors. **Career services:** Career assessment; Internships

FACILITIES

Housing: Men's dorms; Special housing for disabled student; Women's dorms 100% of campus accessible to physically diasbled. **Computers:** 100% of classrooms, 100% of dorms, 100% of libraries, 100% of dining areas, 100% of student union, have wireless network access.

CAMPUS LIFE

Environment: City **Activities:** Campus Ministries; Choral groups; Drama/theater; Student government; Yearbook 4 religious organizations. **Athletics (Intercollegiate):** *Men:* basketball. *Women:* volleyball. **On-Campus Highlights:** Epiphanies Coffee Shop, Library, Lounge Areas, Outdoor Gazebo, Horseshoe Pits

ADMISSIONS

Freshman Academic Profile: Average high school GPA 2.8. **Test Scores:** SAT Math middle 50% range 370-480. SAT EBRW middle 50% range 460-550. ACT middle 50% range 19-23. Minimum paper TOEFL 500. **Basis for**

Candidate Selection: *Very important factors considered include:* academic GPA, application essay, standardized test scores, recommendation(s), religious affiliation/commitment. *Important factors considered include:* character/personal qualities. *Other factors considered include:* extracurricular activities. **Freshman Admission Requirements:** High school diploma is required and GED is accepted *Academic units required:* 4 English, 4 math, 4 science, 2 foreign language, 2 social studies, 2 history. **Freshman Admission Statistics:** 79 applied, 84.8% admitted, 49% enrolled. **Transfer Admission Requirements:** High school transcript, college transcript(s), essay or personal statement, Minimum college GPA of 2.0 required. Lowest grade transferable C. **General Admission Information:** Application fee $25. Regular application deadline 8/2. Nonfall registration accepted. Admission may be deferred for a maximum of 1 year.

COSTS AND FINANCIAL AID

Annual tuition $11,024. Room and board $6,656. Required fees $800. Average book expense $1,185. **Required Forms and Deadlines:** FAFSA; Institution's own financial aid form. **Types of Aid:** *Need-based scholarships/grants:* College/university scholarship or grant aid from institutional funds; Federal Pell; Private scholarships; SEOG; State scholarships/grants. *Loans: Student Employment:* Federal Work-Study Program available. Institutional employment available. **Financial Aid Statistics:** 100% needy freshmen, 86% needy undergrads receive need-based scholarship or grant aid. 100% freshmen, 74% undergrads receive non-need-based scholarship or grant aid. 75% freshmen, 79% undergrads receive need-based self-help aid. 0% freshmen, 0% undergrads receive athletic scholarships. 99% freshmen, 99% undergrads receive any aid. **Criteria for awarding aid:** *Need-based:* Academics *Non-need-based:* Academics, Music/drama.

TRINITY INTERNATIONAL UNIVERSITY

2065 Half Day Road, Deerfield, IL 60015
Phone: 847-317-7000 • **Financial Aid Phone:** 847-317-7033
E-mail: tcadmissions@tiu.edu • **CEEB Code:** 1810
Fax: 847-317-8097 • **Website:** www.tiu.edu • **ACT Code:** 1150

This private school was founded in 1897. It has a 111 acre campus.

RATINGS

Admissions Selectivity Rating: 78   **Fire Safety Rating:** 82   **Green Rating:** 60*

STUDENTS AND FACULTY

Enrollment: 950. **Student Body:** 57% female, 43% male, 41% out-of-state, 1% international (38 countries represented). Asian 5%, African American 17%, Caucasian 63%, Hispanic 4%, Native American <1%, Race unknown 10%. **Retention and Graduation:** 66% freshmen return for sophomore year. 32% grads go on to further study within 1 year. **Faculty:** Student/faculty ratio 12:1. 43 full-time faculty, 84% hold PhDs, 14% are members of minority groups, 42% are women. 0% of classes are taught by teaching assistants.

ACADEMICS

Degrees: Bachelor's; Certificate; Master's; Post-Bachelor's certificate **Classes:** Most classes have 10-19 students. **Most popular majors:** Elementary Education And Teaching; Theology And Religious Vocations, Other; Business/Commerce, General. **Special Study Options:** Cross-registration; Double major; Dual enrollment; Honors program; Independent study; Internships; Study abroad; Teacher certification program. Honors programs: Trinity has adopted a model for an Honors Program that is intended to enhance the breadth and depth of your liberal-arts learning, but without the burden of many additional requirements. Hence, you will do honors work in the areas of your disciplinary major, general education, and special interdisciplinary classes, but virtually all of your honors work will also fulfill regular Trinity requirements. Combined degree programs: BA/MA. **Disability Services offered to physically disabled students:** Note-taking services; Reader services; Tape recorders; Tutors. **Career services:** Alumni services; Career assessment; Career/job search classes; Internships

FACILITIES

Housing: Apartments for married students; Apartments for single students; Men's dorms; Special housing for disabled student; Women's dorms 75% of campus accessible to physically diasbled. **Computers:** 100% of classrooms, 50% of dorms, 100% of libraries, 100% of student union, have wireless network access. Students can register for classes online. Administrative functions (other than registration) can be performed online.

CAMPUS LIFE

Environment: Village **Activities:** Campus Ministries; Choral groups; Concert band; Drama/theater; Jazz band; Music ensembles; Musical theater; Pep band;

Student government; Student newspaper; Symphony orchestra; Yearbook 33 registered organizations, 2 honor societies. **Athletics (Intercollegiate):** *Men:* baseball, basketball, football, soccer. *Women:* basketball, soccer, softball, volleyball. **On-Campus Highlights:** Lew Student Center, Trinity Hall, McLennan Academic Building, Rodine Global Ministry Building, Melton Dining Hall

ADMISSIONS

Freshman Academic Profile: Average high school GPA 3.3. 37% in top 10% of high school class, 43% in top 25% of high school class, 68% in top 50% of high school class. 69% from public high schools. **Test Scores:** SAT Math middle 50% range 440-600. SAT EBRW middle 50% range 445-610. ACT middle 50% range 19-26. Minimum paper TOEFL 530. **Basis for Candidate Selection:** *Very important factors considered include:* class rank, academic GPA, application essay, standardized test scores, recommendation(s), character/personal qualities, religious affiliation/commitment. *Other factors considered include:* rigor of secondary school record, extracurricular activities, talent/ability, first generation. **Freshman Admission Requirements:** High school diploma is required and GED is accepted *Academic units required:* 4 English, 2 math, 2 science, 1 science labs, 2 foreign language, 2 social studies, 2 history, 2 visual/performing arts. **Freshman Admission Statistics:** 466 applied, 80.5% admitted, 44% enrolled. **Transfer Admission Requirements:** High school transcript, college transcript(s), essay or personal statement, statement of good standing from prior institution(s). Minimum college GPA of 2.0 required. Lowest grade transferable C-. **General Admission Information:** Application fee $25. Nonfall registration accepted. Admission may be deferred for a maximum of 1 year.

COSTS AND FINANCIAL AID

Annual tuition $21,980. Room and board $7,430. Required fees $390. **Required Forms and Deadlines:** FAFSA. **Notification of Awards:** Applicants will be notified of awards on a rolling basis beginning 2/15. **Types of Aid:** *Need-based scholarships/grants:* College/university scholarship or grant aid from institutional funds; Federal Pell; Private scholarships; SEOG; State scholarships/grants. *Student Employment:* Federal Work-Study Program available. Institutional employment available. **Financial Aid Statistics:** 95% needy freshmen, 95% needy undergrads receive need-based scholarship or grant aid. 95% freshmen, 95% undergrads receive non-need-based scholarship or grant aid. 82% freshmen, 78% undergrads receive need-based self-help aid. 0% freshmen, 0% undergrads receive athletic scholarships. 90% freshmen, 86% undergrads receive any aid. **Criteria for awarding aid:** *Non-need-based:* Academics, Alumni affiliation, Athletics, Minority status, Music/drama, Religious affiliation.

TRINITY LUTHERAN COLLEGE

Office of Admission, Issaquah, WA 98029
Phone: 425-961-5510 • **Financial Aid Phone:** 425-961-5514
E-mail: admission@tlc.edu
Fax: 425-392-0404 • **Website:** www.tlc.edu

This private school, affiliated with the Lutheran Church, was founded in 1944.

RATINGS

Admissions Selectivity Rating: 71   **Fire Safety Rating:** 82   **Green Rating:** 60*

STUDENTS AND FACULTY

Enrollment: 91. **Student Body:** 53% female, 47% male, 35% out-of-state, 0% international. Asian 4%, African American 1%, Caucasian 89%, Hispanic 4%, Native American 1%, Race unknown 2%.
Retention and Graduation: 78% freshmen return for sophomore year.
Faculty: 13 full-time faculty,

ACADEMICS

Degrees: Associate; Bachelor's; Diploma; Post-Bachelor's certificate; Terminal Associate; Transfer Associate **Classes:** Most classes have 10-19 students. **Most popular majors:** Bible/Biblical Studies; Youth Ministry; Music; Other. **Special Study Options:** Double major; Independent study; Internships; Liberal arts/career combination; Student-designed major; Study abroad; Teacher certification program. **Disability Services offered to physically disabled students:** Note-taking services; Reader services; Tape recorders; Tutors. **Career services:** Alumni network; Alumni services; Career assessment; Internships; Regional alumni

FACILITIES

Housing: Apartments for married students; Apartments for single students; Coed dorms; Men's dorms; Special housing for disabled student; Women's

dorms **Computers:** Administrative functions (other than registration) can be performed online.

CAMPUS LIFE

Environment: Village **Activities:** Choral groups; Drama/theater; Music ensembles; Musical theater; Student government; Student newspaper; Yearbook. **Athletics (Intercollegiate):** *Men:* basketball, softball. *Women:* softball. **On-Campus Highlights:** Student Center, The Running Cup, Chapel, YMCA, Bookstore

ADMISSIONS

Freshman Academic Profile: 0% in top 10% of high school class, 33% in top 25% of high school class, 60% in top 50% of high school class. **Test Scores:** Minimum paper TOEFL 525. **Basis for Candidate Selection:** *Very important factors considered include:* recommendation(s), character/personal qualities. *Important factors considered include:* rigor of secondary school record, academic GPA, standardized test scores, religious affiliation/commitment, volunteer work. *Other factors considered include:* extracurricular activities, talent/ability, first generation, alumni/ae relation, work experience, level of applicant's interest. **Freshman Admission Requirements:** High school diploma is required and GED is accepted **Freshman Admission Statistics:** 113 applied, 59.3% admitted, 72% enrolled. **Transfer Admission Requirements:** college transcript(s), Minimum college GPA of 2.0 required. Lowest grade transferable C-. **General Admission Information:** Application fee $30. Priority deadline 6/15. Regular application deadline 8/15. Nonfall registration accepted. Admission may be deferred for a maximum of 2 years.

COSTS AND FINANCIAL AID

Annual tuition $13,714. Room and board $6,078. Required fees $450. Average book expense $500. **Required Forms and Deadlines:** FAFSA; Institution's own financial aid form. **Notification of Awards:** Applicants will be notified of awards on a rolling basis beginning 1/1. **Types of Aid:** *Need-based scholarships/grants:* College/university scholarship or grant aid from institutional funds; Federal Pell; Private scholarships; SEOG. *Loans:* Direct PLUS loans; Direct Subsidized Stafford Loans; Direct Unsubsidized Stafford Loans. *Student Employment:* Federal Work-Study Program available. Institutional employment available. **Criteria for awarding aid:** *Need-based:* Academics *Non-need-based:* Academics, Alumni affiliation, Art, Leadership, Music/drama, Religious affiliation.

TRINITY UNIVERSITY

One Trinity Place, San Antonio, TX 78212-7200
Phone: 210-999-7207 • **Financial Aid Phone:** (210) 999-8898
E-mail: admissions@trinity.edu • **CEEB Code:** 6831
Fax: 210-999-8164 • **Website:** www.trinity.edu • **ACT Code:** 4226

This private school, affiliated with the Presbyterian Church, was founded in 1869. It has a 117 acre campus.

RATINGS

Admissions Selectivity Rating: 92   **Fire Safety Rating:** 94   **Green Rating:** 74

STUDENTS AND FACULTY

Enrollment: 2,426. **Student Body:** 53% female, 47% male, 23% out-of-state, 6% international (60 countries represented). Asian 7%, African American 4%, Caucasian 56%, Hispanic 21%, Native American <1%, Pacific Islander 0%, Two or more races 5%, Race unknown 2%.
Retention and Graduation: 89% freshmen return for sophomore year. 72% freshmen graduate within 4 years. 80% freshmen graduate within 6 years. 33% grads go on to further study within 1 year. 2% grads pursue law degrees. 2% grads pursue medical degrees. **Faculty:** Student/faculty ratio 9:1. 236 full-time faculty, 99% hold PhDs, 21% are members of minority groups, 43% are women. 0% of classes are taught by teaching assistants.

ACADEMICS

Degrees: Bachelor's; **Master's Classes:** Most classes have 20-29 students. Most lab/discussion sessions have 10-19 students. **Most popular majors:** Communication, General; Engineering Science; Business Administration And Management, General. **Special Study Options:** Accelerated program; Double major; Honors program; Independent study; Internships; Liberal arts/career combination; Student-designed major; Study abroad; Teacher certification program. Honors programs: Honors Program Combined degree programs: BA/MA. **Disability Services offered to physically disabled students:** Note-taking services; Reader services; Tape recorders; Tutors. **Career services:** Alumni network; Alumni services; Career assessment; Career/job search classes; Internships; Regional alumni

FACILITIES

Housing: Coed dorms; Fraternity/sorority housing; Special housing for disabled student; Theme housing; Wellness housing 99% of campus accessible to physically diasbled. **Special Academic Facilities/Equipment:** Center for the Sciences & Innovation, Steiren Theatre, Richardson Communication Center, KRTU Radio Station, TigerTV Television Station, Ruth Taylor Arts Complex including art gallery, Laurie Auditorium **Computers:** 100% of classrooms, 100% of dorms, 100% of libraries, 100% of dining areas, 100% of student union, 100% of common outdoor areas have wireless network access. Students can register for classes online. Administrative functions (other than registration) can be performed online.

CAMPUS LIFE

Environment: Metropolis **Activities:** Campus Ministries; Choral groups; Concert band; Dance; Drama/theater; International Student Organization; Jazz band; Literary magazine; Model UN; Music ensembles; Musical theater; Opera; Pep band; Radio station; Student government; Student newspaper; Student-run film society; Symphony orchestra; Television station; Yearbook 130 registered organizations, 24 honor societies, 4 religious organizations. 7 fraternities, 6 sororities. **Athletics (Intercollegiate):** *Men:* baseball, basketball, cross-country, diving, football, golf, soccer, swimming, tennis, track/field (outdoor). *Women:* basketball, cross-country, diving, golf, soccer, softball, swimming, tennis, track/field (outdoor), volleyball. **On-Campus Highlights:** Center for the Sciences and Innovation, Stieren Theatre, Laurie Auditorium, Coates Library, Bell Athletic Center

ADMISSIONS

Freshman Academic Profile: Average high school GPA 3.6. 44% in top 10% of high school class, 76% in top 25% of high school class, 97% in top 50% of high school class. 66% from public high schools. **Test Scores:** SAT Math middle 50% range 610-700. SAT EBRW middle 50% range 610-710. ACT middle 50% range 27-32. **Basis for Candidate Selection:** *Very important factors considered include:* rigor of secondary school record, class rank, academic GPA, standardized test scores. *Important factors considered include:* application essay, recommendation(s), interview, extracurricular activities, talent/ability, character/personal qualities. *Other factors considered include:* first generation, alumni/ae relation, geographical residence, volunteer work, work experience, level of applicant's interest. **Freshman Admission Requirements:** High school diploma is required and GED is accepted *Academic units required:* 4 English, 3 math, 3 science, 2 science labs, 2 foreign language, 3 social studies, *Academic units recommended:* 4 English, 3 math, 3 science, 2 science labs, 2 foreign language, 3 social studies. **Freshman Admission Statistics:** 7,663 applied, 38.4% admitted, 22% enrolled. **Transfer Admission Requirements:** High school transcript, college transcript(s), essay or personal statement, statement of good standing from prior institution(s). Minimum college GPA of 3.0 required. Lowest grade transferable C-. **General Admission Information:** Regular application deadline 2/1. Nonfall registration accepted. Admission may be deferred.

COSTS AND FINANCIAL AID

Annual tuition $42,360. Room and board $13,464. Required fees $616. Average book expense $1,000. **Required Forms and Deadlines:** CSS/Financial Aid PROFILE; FAFSA. **Notification of Awards:** Applicants will be notified of awards on or about 3/15. **Types of Aid:** *Need-based scholarships/grants:* College/university scholarship or grant aid from institutional funds; Federal Pell; Private scholarships; SEOG; State scholarships/grants. *Loans:* Direct PLUS loans; Direct Subsidized Stafford Loans; Direct Unsubsidized Stafford Loans. *Student Employment:* Federal Work-Study Program available. Institutional employment available. **Financial Aid Statistics:** 100% needy freshmen, 98% needy undergrads receive need-based scholarship or grant aid. 39% freshmen, 24% undergrads receive non-need-based scholarship or grant aid. 53% freshmen, 62% undergrads receive need-based self-help aid. 0% freshmen, 0% undergrads receive athletic scholarships. 98% freshmen, 93% undergrads receive any aid. 45% undergrads borrow to pay for school. Average cumulative indebtedness $38,605. **Criteria for awarding aid:** *Need-based:* Academics *Non-need-based:* Academics, Art, Leadership, Music/drama.

TROY UNIVERSITY—TROY (FORMERLY TROY STATE UNIVERSITY)

University Avenue, Troy, AL 36082
Phone: 334-670-3179 • **Financial Aid Phone:** 334-670-3186
E-mail: admit@troy.edu • **CEEB Code:** 1738
Fax: 334-670-3733 • **Website:** www.troy.edu • **ACT Code:** 48

This public school was founded in 1887. It has a 906 acre campus.

RATINGS
Admissions Selectivity Rating: 74   **Fire Safety Rating:** 94   **Green Rating:** 60*

STUDENTS AND FACULTY
Enrollment: 13,634. **Student Body:** 60% female, 40% male, 31% out-of-state, 5% international. Asian 1%, African American 30%, Caucasian 53%, Hispanic 4%, Native American <1%, Pacific Islander <1%, Two or more races 3%, Race unknown 4%.
Retention and Graduation: 70% freshmen return for sophomore year. 20% freshmen graduate within 4 years. 41% freshmen graduate within 6 years.
Faculty: Student/faculty ratio 15:1. 531 full-time faculty, 26% hold PhDs, 17% are members of minority groups, 48% are women. 1% of classes are taught by teaching assistants.

ACADEMICS
Degrees: Associate; Bachelor's; Certificate; Doctoral/Professional; Master's; Post-Bachelor's certificate; Post-Master's certificate **Classes:** Most classes have 10-19 students. Most lab/discussion sessions have 10-19 students.
Most popular majors: Psychology, General; Business Administration And Management, General; Accounting. **Special Study Options:** Accelerated program; Cross-registration; Distance learning; Double major; Dual enrollment; English as a Second Language (ESL); External degree program; Honors program; Independent study; Internships; Study abroad; Teacher certification program; Weekend college. Honors programs: The University Honors Program, open to students in all undergraduate divisions of the university, is administered by the Honors Council and the director of university honors. The purpose of the University Honors Program is to offer the academically superior student a specially designed program, within a supportive community, that fosters critical thinking, intellectual development and social responsibility. This enhanced program is designed to provide a balance of common experience and flexibility addressed to individual achievement as well as a comprehensive framework on which to build disciplinary studies. The Honors Program also has an honors house on campus which houses both male and female students. Students should consult with the director of the University Honors Program and the director of University Housing for availabilities and stipulations. The house serves as a residence and a focal point for meetings and activities with the Honors Alliance, faculty and staff in the Honors Program. The official student voice within the program is the University Honors Alliance. Membership to the University Honors Alliance is offered to any student with a 3.3 grade point average or higher. There is an annual membership fee of $5. **Disability Services offered to physically disabled students:** Note-taking services; Reader services; Tape recorders; Tutors. Alumni network; Alumni services; Career assessment; Career/job search classes

FACILITIES
Housing: Apartments for married students; Apartments for single students; Coed dorms; Fraternity/sorority housing; Men's dorms; Special housing for international students; Women's dorms 95% of campus accessible to physically diasbled. **Special Academic Facilities/Equipment:** Art museum, recording studio. **Computers:** Students can register for classes online.

CAMPUS LIFE
Environment: Town **Activities:** Campus Ministries; Choral groups; Concert band; Dance; Drama/theater; International Student Organization; Jazz band; Literary magazine; Marching band; Music ensembles; Musical theater; Pep band; Radio station; Student government; Student newspaper; Student-run film society; Symphony orchestra; Television station; Yearbook 125 registered organizations, 22 honor societies, 7 religious organizations. 12 fraternities, 9 sororities. **Athletics (Intercollegiate):** *Men:* baseball, basketball, cheerleading, cross-country, football, golf, rodeo, tennis, track/field (outdoor). *Women:* basketball, cheerleading, cross-country, golf, rodeo, soccer, softball, tennis, track/field (outdoor), volleyball. **On-Campus Highlights:** Veterans Memorial Stadium, Malone Art Gallery, Hall of Honor/National Band Hall of Fame, Trojan Center, Rosa Parks Museum—Montgomery Campus **Environmental Initiatives:** recycling

ADMISSIONS
Freshman Academic Profile: Average high school GPA 3.4. **Test Scores:** SAT Math middle 50% range 465-605. SAT EBRW middle 50% range 480-600. ACT middle 50% range 18-25. Minimum internet-based TOEFL 80.

Minimum paper TOEFL 500. **Basis for Candidate Selection:** *Very important factors considered include:* rigor of secondary school record, academic GPA, standardized test scores. **Freshman Admission Requirements:** High school diploma is required and GED is accepted *Academic units required:* 3 English. **Freshman Admission Statistics:** 7,367 applied, 88.1% admitted, 33% enrolled. **Transfer Admission Requirements:** college transcript(s), Minimum college GPA of 2.0 required. Lowest grade transferable D. **General Admission Information:** Application fee $30. Nonfall registration accepted. Admission may be deferred for a maximum of 1 year.

COSTS AND FINANCIAL AID

Annual in-state tuition $7,946. Annual out-of-state tuition $20,224. Room and board $7,946. Required fees $2,043. Average book expense $1,138. **Required Forms and Deadlines:** FAFSA; Institution's own financial aid form. **Notification of Awards:** Applicants will be notified of awards on a rolling basis beginning 5/1. **Types of Aid:** *Need-based scholarships/grants:* College/ university scholarship or grant aid from institutional funds; Federal Pell; Private scholarships; SEOG; State scholarships/grants. *Loans: Student Employment:* Federal Work-Study Program available. **Financial Aid Statistics:** 54% needy freshmen, 62% needy undergrads receive need-based scholarship or grant aid. 58% freshmen, 47% undergrads receive non-need-based scholarship or grant aid. 100% freshmen, 99% undergrads receive need-based self-help aid. 2% freshmen, 33% undergrads receive athletic scholarships. **Criteria for awarding aid:** *Need-based:* Academics *Non-need-based:* Academics, Athletics, Leadership, Music/drama.

See page 1050.

TRUMAN STATE UNIVERSITY

100 E. Normal Ave., Kirksville, MO 63501
Phone: 660-785-4114 • **Financial Aid Phone:** 660-785-4130
E-mail: admissions@truman.edu • **CEEB Code:** 6483
Fax: 660-785-7456 • **Website:** http://www.truman.edu • **ACT Code:** 2336

This public school was founded in 1867. It has a 140 acre campus.

RATINGS

Admissions Selectivity Rating: 89   **Fire Safety Rating:** 98   **Green Rating:** 60*

STUDENTS AND FACULTY

Enrollment: 5,241. **Student Body:** 58% female, 42% male, 29% out-of-state, 7% international (45 countries represented). Asian 3%, African American 4%, Caucasian 79%, Hispanic 3%, Native American <1%, Pacific Islander <1%, Two or more races 3%, Race unknown 1%.
Retention and Graduation: 86% freshmen return for sophomore year. 59% freshmen graduate within 4 years. 75% freshmen graduate within 6 years. 35% grads go on to further study within 1 year. **Faculty:** Student/faculty ratio 16:1. 324 full-time faculty, 85% hold PhDs, 10% are members of minority groups, 44% are women. 1% of classes are taught by teaching assistants.

ACADEMICS

Degrees: Bachelor's; Master's; Post-Bachelor's certificate **Classes:** Most classes have 10-19 students. Most lab/discussion sessions have 10-19 students. **Most popular majors:** Biology/Biological Sciences, General; Psychology, General; Business Administration, Management And Operations. **Special Study Options:** Double major; Dual enrollment; English as a Second Language (ESL); Honors program; Independent study; Internships; Student-designed major; Study abroad; Teacher certification program. Honors programs: Honors Scholar Program: Students must complete five upper-level courses in math, social science, science and humanities with a 3.5 GPA in these 5 courses. Departmental honors are also available in some disciplines. **Disability Services offered to physically disabled students:** Note-taking services; Reader services; Tape recorders; Tutors. **Career services:** Alumni network; Alumni services; Career assessment; Career/job search classes; Internships; Regional alumni

FACILITIES

Housing: Apartments for married students; Apartments for single students; Coed dorms; Fraternity/sorority housing; Special housing for disabled student; Theme housing 99% of campus accessible to physically disabled. **Special Academic Facilities/Equipment:** Planetarium, art gallery, local history and artifacts museum, human performance lab, greenhouse, observatory,

and convergent media center (TV studio, newspaper, and radio station). **Computers:** 100% of classrooms, 100% of dorms, 100% of libraries, 75% of dining areas, 100% of student union, 90% of common outdoor areas have wireless network access. Students can register for classes online. Administrative functions (other than registration) can be performed online.

CAMPUS LIFE

Environment: Village **Activities:** Campus Ministries; Choral groups; Concert band; Dance; Drama/theater; International Student Organization; Jazz band; Literary magazine; Marching band; Model UN; Music ensembles; Musical theater; Opera; Pep band; Radio station; Student government; Student newspaper; Student-run film society; Symphony orchestra; Television station 282 registered organizations, 18 honor societies, 16 religious organizations. 16 fraternities, 11 sororities. **Athletics (Intercollegiate):** *Men:* baseball, basketball, cross-country, football, golf, soccer, swimming, tennis, track/field (outdoor), track/field (indoor), wrestling. *Women:* basketball, cross-country, golf, soccer, softball, swimming, tennis, track/field (outdoor), track/field (indoor), volleyball. **On-Campus Highlights:** Student Recreation Center, Pickler Memorial Library, Student Union Building, The Quadrangle, Starbucks

ADMISSIONS

Freshman Academic Profile: Average high school GPA 3.8. 51% in top 10% of high school class, 83% in top 25% of high school class, 98% in top 50% of high school class. 82% from public high schools. **Test Scores:** SAT Math middle 50% range 580-715. SAT EBRW middle 50% range 605-705. ACT middle 50% range 24-30. Minimum internet-based TOEFL 79. Minimum paper TOEFL 550. **Basis for Candidate Selection:** *Very important factors considered include:* rigor of secondary school record, class rank, academic GPA, standardized test scores. *Important factors considered include:* application essay. *Other factors considered include:* recommendation(s), extracurricular activities, talent/ability, character/personal qualities, first generation, alumni/ae relation, geographical residence, state residency, racial/ethnic status, volunteer work, work experience, level of applicant's interest. **Freshman Admission Requirements:** High school diploma is required and GED is accepted *Academic units required:* 4 English, 3 math, 3 science, 2 science labs, 2 foreign language, 2 social studies, 1 history, 5 academic electives, 1 visual/performing arts, and 3 units from above areas or other academic areas. *Academic units recommended:* 4 English, 4 math, 3 science, 2 science labs, 2 foreign language, 2 social studies, 1 history, 5 academic electives, 1 visual/performing arts, 3 units from above areas or other academic areas. **Freshman Admission Statistics:** 5,263 applied, 67.5% admitted, 37% enrolled. **Transfer Admission Requirements:** college transcript(s), essay or personal statement. **General Admission Information:** Priority deadline 12/1. Nonfall registration accepted. Admission may be deferred.

COSTS AND FINANCIAL AID

Annual in-state tuition $8,630. Annual out-of-state tuition $14,136. Room and board $8,630. Required fees $304. Average book expense $1,000. **Required Forms and Deadlines:** FAFSA. **Notification of Awards:** Applicants will be notified of awards on a rolling basis beginning 1/1. **Types of Aid:** *Need-based scholarships/grants:* College/university scholarship or grant aid from institutional funds; Federal Pell; Private scholarships; SEOG; State scholarships/grants. *Loans:* Direct PLUS loans; Direct Subsidized Stafford Loans; Direct Unsubsidized Stafford Loans. *Student Employment:* Federal Work-Study Program available. Institutional employment available. **Financial Aid Statistics:** 99% needy freshmen, 94% needy undergrads receive need-based scholarship or grant aid. 99% freshmen, 79% undergrads receive non-need-based scholarship or grant aid. 70% freshmen, 78% undergrads receive need-based self-help aid. 6% freshmen, 6% undergrads receive athletic scholarships. 99% freshmen, 86% undergrads receive any aid. 56% undergrads borrow to pay for school. Average cumulative indebtedness $24,811. **Criteria for awarding aid:** *Need-based:* Academics *Non-need-based:* Academics, Alumni affiliation, Art, Athletics, Leadership, Minority status, Music/drama, State/district residency.

See page 1052.

TUFTS UNIVERSITY

Best Colleges

2 The Green, Medford, MA 02155
Phone: 617-627-3170 • **Financial Aid Phone:** 617-627-2000
E-mail: undergraduate.admissions@tufts.edu • **CEEB Code:** 3901
Fax: 617-627-3860 • **Website:** www.tufts.edu • **ACT Code:** 1922

This private school was founded in 1852. It has a 150 acre campus.

RATINGS

Admissions Selectivity Rating: 97   **Fire Safety Rating:** 99   **Green Rating:** 92

STUDENTS AND FACULTY

Enrollment: 5,492. **Student Body:** 51% female, 49% male, 75% out-of-state, 10% international (74 countries represented). Asian 12%, African American 4%, Caucasian 57%, Hispanic 7%, Native American 0%, Pacific Islander 0%, Two or more races 5%, Race unknown 6%.
Retention and Graduation: 97% freshmen return for sophomore year. 87% freshmen graduate within 4 years. 93% freshmen graduate within 6 years. 14% grads go on to further study within 1 year. **Faculty:** Student/faculty ratio 9:1. 681 full-time faculty, 93% hold PhDs, 20% are members of minority groups, 45% are women. 1% of classes are taught by teaching assistants.

ACADEMICS

Degrees: Bachelor's; Certificate; Doctoral; Doctoral/Professional; Doctoral/Research; Master's; Post-Bachelor's certificate; Post-Master's certificate **Classes:** Most classes have fewer than 10 students. Most lab/discussion sessions have 20-29 students. **Most popular majors:** Computer Science; Economics; International Relations And Affairs. **Special Study Options:** Cross-registration; Double major; Dual enrollment; Exchange student program (domestic); Independent study; Internships; Student-designed major; Study abroad; Teacher certification program. Combined degree programs: BA/DDS; BA/MA; BA/MD; BA/MEng. **Disability Services offered to physically disabled students:** Note-taking services; Reader services; Tape recorders; Tutors. **Career services:** Alumni network; Alumni services; Career assessment; Career/job search classes; Internships; Regional alumni

FACILITIES

Housing: Apartments for single students; Coed dorms; Fraternity/sorority housing; Special housing for disabled student; Special housing for international students; Theme housing; Wellness housing; Women's dorms **Special Academic Facilities/Equipment:** Language lab, nutrition institute, research lab for physical electronics, bioelectrical and biochemical labs, computer-aided design (CAD) facility, electro-optics technology and environmental management centers. **Computers:** 50% of classrooms, 20% of dorms, 100% of libraries, 75% of dining areas, 100% of student union, 75% of common outdoor areas have wireless network access. Students can register for classes online. Administrative functions (other than registration) can be performed online.

CAMPUS LIFE

Environment: Metropolis **Activities:** Campus Ministries; Choral groups; Concert band; Dance; Drama/theater; International Student Organization; Jazz band; Literary magazine; Model UN; Music ensembles; Musical theater; Opera; Pep band; Radio station; Student government; Student newspaper; Student-run film society; Symphony orchestra; Television station; Yearbook 160 registered organizations, 4 honor societies, 6 religious organizations. 11 fraternities, 3 sororities. **Athletics (Intercollegiate):** *Men:* baseball, basketball, crew/rowing, cross-country, diving, football, golf, ice hockey, lacrosse, sailing, soccer, squash, swimming, tennis, track/field (outdoor), track/field (indoor). *Women:* basketball, cheerleading, crew/rowing, cross-country, diving, fencing, field hockey, golf, lacrosse, sailing, soccer, softball, squash, swimming, tennis, track/field (outdoor), track/field (indoor), volleyball. **On-Campus Highlights:** The Aidekman Arts Center, Tisch Library, Edwin Ginn Library, Gantcher Family Sports and Convocation Center and Tisch Sports and Fitness, Granoff Music Center, Mayer Campus Center **Environmental Initiatives:** Reduced green house gas emissions to below 1998 levels, working to further that with the creation of a new power plant that will decrease energy usage.

ADMISSIONS

Freshman Academic Profile: 59% from public high schools. **Test Scores:** SAT Math middle 50% range 710-780. SAT EBRW middle 50% range 700-760. ACT middle 50% range 31-34. Minimum internet-based TOEFL 100. Minimum paper TOEFL 600. **Basis for Candidate Selection:** *Very important factors considered include:* rigor of secondary school record, class rank, academic GPA, application essay, standardized test scores, recommendation(s), character/personal qualities. *Important factors considered include:*

extracurricular activities, talent/ability, volunteer work, work experience. *Other factors considered include:* interview, first generation, alumni/ae relation, geographical residence, racial/ethnic status, level of applicant's interest. **Freshman Admission Requirements:** High school diploma is required and GED is accepted *Academic units required:* 4 English, 4 math, 4 science, 3 foreign language, 4 social studies, *Academic units recommended:* 4 foreign language. **Freshman Admission Statistics:** 21,101 applied, 14.8% admitted, 45% enrolled. **Transfer Admission Requirements:** High school transcript, college transcript(s), essay or personal statement, standardized test scores, statement of good standing from prior institution(s). Lowest grade transferable C. **General Admission Information:** Application fee $75. Regular application deadline 1/1. Nonfall registration accepted. Admission may be deferred for a maximum of 1 year.

COSTS AND FINANCIAL AID

Required Forms and Deadlines: CSS/Financial Aid PROFILE; FAFSA; Noncustodial PROFILE. **Notification of Awards:** Applicants will be notified of awards on or about 4/1. **Types of Aid:** *Need-based scholarships/grants:* College/university scholarship or grant aid from institutional funds; Federal Pell; Private scholarships; SEOG; State scholarships/grants. *Loans:* Direct PLUS loans; Direct Subsidized Stafford Loans; Direct Unsubsidized Stafford Loans. *Student Employment:* Federal Work-Study Program available. Institutional employment available. **Financial Aid Statistics:** 92% needy freshmen, 93% needy undergrads receive need-based scholarship or grant aid. 5% freshmen, 4% undergrads receive non-need-based scholarship or grant aid. 90% freshmen, 91% undergrads receive need-based self-help aid. 0% freshmen, 0% undergrads receive athletic scholarships. 37% freshmen, 38% undergrads receive any aid. Average cumulative indebtedness $24,267. **Criteria for awarding aid:** *Non-need-based:* Academics.

TULANE UNIVERSITY

Best Colleges

6823 St. Charles Avenue, New Orleans, LA 70118
Phone: 504-865-5731 • **Financial Aid Phone:** 504-865-5723
E-mail: undergrad.admission@tulane.edu • **CEEB Code:** 6832
Fax: 504-862-8715 • **Website:** www.tulane.edu • **ACT Code:** 1614

This private school was founded in 1834. It has a 110 acre campus.

RATINGS

Admissions Selectivity Rating: 96   **Fire Safety Rating:** 95   **Green Rating:** 83

STUDENTS AND FACULTY

Enrollment: 6,571. **Student Body:** 59% female, 41% male, 77% out-of-state, 4% international (48 countries represented). Asian 5%, African American 4%, Caucasian 75%, Hispanic 7%, Native American <1%, Pacific Islander <1%, Two or more races 4%, Race unknown 1%.
Retention and Graduation: 93% freshmen return for sophomore year. 73% freshmen graduate within 4 years. 83% freshmen graduate within 6 years. **Faculty:** Student/faculty ratio 8:1. 767 full-time faculty, 95% hold PhDs, 18% are members of minority groups, 42% are women.

ACADEMICS

Degrees: Associate; Bachelor's; Certificate; Doctoral; Doctoral/Professional; Doctoral/Research; Master's; Post-Bachelor's certificate **Classes:** Most classes have 10-19 students. **Special Study Options:** Accelerated program; Cross-registration; Distance learning; Double major; English as a Second Language (ESL); Exchange student program (domestic); Honors program; Independent study; Internships; Liberal arts/career combination; Student-designed major; Study abroad; Teacher certification program. Honors programs: Tulane Honors Program Combined degree programs: BA/JD; BA/MA; BA/MD. **Disability Services offered to physically disabled students:** Note-taking services; Reader services; Tape recorders; Tutors. **Career services:** Alumni network; Alumni services; Career assessment; Career/job search classes; Internships; Regional alumni

FACILITIES

Housing: Apartments for married students; Apartments for single students; Coed dorms; Fraternity/sorority housing; Special housing for disabled student; Theme housing; Wellness housing; Women's dorms 60% of campus accessible to physically disabled. **Special Academic Facilities/Equipment:** Newcomb Art Gallery, Amistad Research Center, Latin American Library, Maxwell Music Library, Hogan Jazz Archives, Louisiana Special Collection, Manuscripts Department, Koch Herbarium, Tulane Museum of Natural History,

Government Documents, ByWater Institute **Computers:** 100% of classrooms, 100% of dorms, 100% of libraries, 100% of dining areas, 100% of student union, 100% of common outdoor areas have wireless network access. Students can register for classes online. Administrative functions (other than registration) can be performed online.

CAMPUS LIFE

Environment: Metropolis **Activities:** Campus Ministries; Choral groups; Concert band; Dance; Drama/theater; International Student Organization; Jazz band; Literary magazine; Marching band; Music ensembles; Musical theater; Pep band; Radio station; Student government; Student newspaper; Student-run film society; Symphony orchestra; Television station; Yearbook 250 registered organizations, 43 honor societies, 16 religious organizations. 15 fraternities, 11 sororities. **Athletics (Intercollegiate):** *Men:* baseball, basketball, cross-country, football, tennis, track/field (outdoor). *Women:* basketball, cross-country, diving, golf, swimming, tennis, track/field (outdoor), track/field (indoor), volleyball. **On-Campus Highlights:** Amistad Research Center, Newcomb Art Gallery, Reily Recreation Center, Howard Tilton Memorial Library, Yulman Stadium

ADMISSIONS

Freshman Academic Profile: Average high school GPA 3.6. 62% in top 10% of high school class, 88% in top 25% of high school class, 96% in top 50% of high school class. 57% from public high schools. **Test Scores:** SAT Math middle 50% range 660-750. SAT EBRW middle 50% range 670-740. ACT middle 50% range 30-33. Minimum paper TOEFL 550. **Basis for Candidate Selection:** *Very important factors considered include:* rigor of secondary school record, class rank, academic GPA, standardized test scores. *Important factors considered include:* application essay, recommendation(s), character/personal qualities. *Other factors considered include:* interview, extracurricular activities, talent/ability, first generation, alumni/ae relation, volunteer work, work experience, level of applicant's interest. **Freshman Admission Requirements:** High school diploma is required and GED is accepted *Academic units recommended:* 4 English, 3 math, 3 science, 3 science labs, 3 foreign language, 3 social studies. **Freshman Admission Statistics:** 35,622 applied, 21.5% admitted, 25% enrolled. **Transfer Admission Requirements:** High school transcript, college transcript(s), essay or personal statement, Minimum college GPA of 2.5 required. Lowest grade transferable C. **General Admission Information:** Priority deadline 11/1. Regular application deadline 11/15. Nonfall registration accepted. Admission may be deferred for a maximum of 1 year.

COSTS AND FINANCIAL AID

Annual tuition $48,920. Room and board $14,536. Required fees $4,040. Average book expense $1,200. **Required Forms and Deadlines:** Business/Farm Supplement; CSS/Financial Aid PROFILE; FAFSA; Noncustodial PROFILE. **Notification of Awards:** Applicants will be notified of awards on a rolling basis beginning 3/15. **Types of Aid:** *Need-based scholarships/grants:* College/university scholarship or grant aid from institutional funds; Federal Pell; Private scholarships; SEOG; State scholarships/grants. *Loans:* Direct PLUS loans; Direct Subsidized Stafford Loans; Direct Unsubsidized Stafford Loans. *Student Employment:* Federal Work-Study Program available. Institutional employment available. **Financial Aid Statistics:** 97% needy freshmen, 97% needy undergrads receive need-based scholarship or grant aid. 39% freshmen, 28% undergrads receive non-need-based scholarship or grant aid. 71% freshmen, 78% undergrads receive need-based self-help aid. 2% freshmen, 3% undergrads receive athletic scholarships. 38% undergrads borrow to pay for school. Average cumulative indebtedness $31,642. **Criteria for awarding aid:** *Non-need-based:* Academics, Athletics, Leadership, Music/drama, State/district residency.

TUSCULUM COLLEGE

P.O. Box 5051, Greeneville, TN 37743
Phone: 423-636-7300
E-mail: admissions@tusculum.edu • **CEEB Code:** 1812
Fax: 423-638-7166 • **ACT Code:** 4018

This private school, affiliated with the Presbyterian Church, was founded in 1794. It has a 142 acre campus.

RATINGS

Admissions Selectivity Rating: 72   **Fire Safety Rating:** 60*   **Green Rating:** 60*

STUDENTS AND FACULTY

Enrollment: 1,484. **Student Body:** 51% female, 49% male, 30% out-of-state, 5% international (8 countries represented). Asian <1%, African American 17%, Caucasian 70%, Hispanic 4%, Native American <1%, Pacific Islander <1%, Two or more races 2%, Race unknown 2%.

Retention and Graduation: 65% freshmen return for sophomore year. 33% freshmen graduate within 6 years. **Faculty:** Student/faculty ratio 17:1. 72 full-time faculty, 61% hold PhDs, 10% are members of minority groups, 49% are women.

ACADEMICS

Degrees: Associate; Bachelor's; **Master's Classes:** Most classes have 10-19 students. Most lab/discussion sessions have 10-19 students. **Most popular majors:** Elementary Education And Teaching; Biology/Biological Sciences, General; Business Administration And Management, General. **Special Study Options:** Cross-registration; Distance learning; Double major; Dual enrollment; Honors program; Independent study; Internships; Student-designed major; Study abroad; Teacher certification program.

FACILITIES

Housing: Coed dorms; Men's dorms; Special housing for disabled student; Theme housing; Women's dorms

CAMPUS LIFE

Environment: Village **Activities:** Campus Ministries; Choral groups; Concert band; Dance; Drama/theater; Jazz band; Literary magazine; Marching band; Music ensembles; Musical theater; Pep band; Radio station; Student government; Student newspaper; Yearbook.

ADMISSIONS

Test Scores: SAT Math middle 50% range 440-540. SAT EBRW middle 50% range 440-540. ACT middle 50% range 17-24. **Basis for Candidate Selection:** *Very important factors considered include:* rigor of secondary school record, application essay, standardized test scores. *Important factors considered include:* academic GPA, recommendation(s), character/personal qualities, volunteer work. level of applicant's interest. *Other factors considered include:* class rank, interview, extracurricular activities, talent/ability, first generation, alumni/ae relation, geographical residence, state residency, religious affiliation/commitment, racial/ethnic status, work experience. **Freshman Admission Requirements:** High school diploma is required and GED is accepted *Academic units recommended:* 4 English, 3 math, 2 science, 2 social studies, 2 history. **Freshman Admission Statistics:** 2,139 applied, 88.6% admitted, 17% enrolled. **General Admission Information:** Application fee $20. Nonfall registration accepted. Admission may be deferred.

TUSKEGEE UNIVERSITY

Kresge Center, Tuskegee, AL 36088
Phone: 334-727-8500 • **Financial Aid Phone:** 334-727-8088
E-mail: admissions@mytu.tuskegee.edu • **CEEB Code:** 1813
Fax: 334-727-5750 • **Website:** www.tuskegee.edu • **ACT Code:** 50

This private school was founded in 1881. It has a 5200 acre campus.

RATINGS

Admissions Selectivity Rating: 87   **Fire Safety Rating:** 97   **Green Rating:** 60*

STUDENTS AND FACULTY

Enrollment: 2,480. **Student Body:** 61% female, 39% male, 70% out-of-state, <1% international (19 countries represented). Asian <1%, African American 78%, Caucasian <1%, Hispanic <1%, Native American <1%, Pacific Islander 0%, Two or more races 0%, Race unknown 21%.
Retention and Graduation: 73% freshmen return for sophomore year. 23% grads go on to further study within 1 year. 11% grads pursue arts and sciences degrees. 2% grads pursue law degrees. 4% grads pursue business degrees. 3% grads pursue medical degrees. **Faculty:** Student/faculty ratio 14:1. 194 full-time faculty, 87% hold PhDs, 84% are members of minority groups, 32% are women. 0% of classes are taught by teaching assistants.

ACADEMICS

Degrees: Bachelor's; Doctoral/Professional; Doctoral/Research; Master's **Most popular majors:** Electrical And Electronics Engineering; Veterinary Medicine. **Special Study Options:** Cooperative education program; Distance learning; Double major; Dual enrollment; Honors program; Independent study; Internships; Study abroad; Teacher certification program. Honors programs: Co-Curricular Honors Program. **Disability Services offered to physically disabled students:** Note-taking services; Reader services; Tape recorders; Tutors. **Career services:** Alumni network; Career assessment; Career/job search classes; Internships; Regional alumni

FACILITIES

Housing: Apartments for married students; Apartments for single students; Coed dorms; Men's dorms 33% of campus accessible to physically diasbled. **Special Academic Facilities/Equipment:** Agricultural and natural history museum, electron microscopes, two nursery schools. **Computers:** 100% of classrooms, 100% of dorms, 100% of libraries, 100% of dining areas, 100% of student union, 100% of common outdoor areas have wireless network access. Students can register for classes online.

CAMPUS LIFE

Environment: Rural **Activities:** Campus Ministries; Choral groups; Concert band; Dance; Drama/theater; International Student Organization; Jazz band; Marching band; Pep band; Student government; Student newspaper; Symphony orchestra; Yearbook 36 registered organizations, 22 honor societies, 6 religious organizations. 5 fraternities, 6 sororities. **Athletics (Intercollegiate):** *Men:* baseball, basketball, cheerleading, cross-country, diving, fencing, football, golf, gymnastics, riflery, soccer, swimming, tennis, track/field (outdoor), track/field (indoor), volleyball. *Women:* basketball, cheerleading, cross-country, diving, fencing, golf, gymnastics, riflery, soccer, swimming, tennis, track/field (outdoor), track/field (indoor), volleyball. **On-Campus Highlights:** George Washington Carver Museum, Kellogg Conference Center, Tuskegee Chapel, The Tuskegee Cemetery, General Daniel Chappie James

ADMISSIONS

Freshman Academic Profile: Average high school GPA 3.2. 20% in top 10% of high school class, 60% in top 25% of high school class, 100% in top 50% of high school class. 88% from public high schools. **Test Scores:** SAT Math middle 50% range 420-520. SAT EBRW middle 50% range 440-510. ACT middle 50% range 18-23. Minimum internet-based TOEFL 62. Minimum paper TOEFL 500. **Basis for Candidate Selection:** *Very important factors considered include:* rigor of secondary school record, class rank, academic GPA, standardized test scores, recommendation(s), talent/ability. *Important factors considered include:* character/personal qualities, alumni/ae relation. *Other factors considered include:* application essay, interview, extracurricular activities, first generation, geographical residence, state residency, volunteer work, work experience. **Freshman Admission Requirements:** High school diploma is required and GED is accepted *Academic units required:* 4 English, 3 math, 2 science, 3 social studies, 4 academic electives. **Freshman Admission Statistics:** 9,582 applied, 35.7% admitted, 17% enrolled. **Transfer Admission Requirements:** college transcript(s), Minimum college GPA of 2.0 required. Lowest grade transferable C. **General Admission Information:** Application fee $25. Priority deadline 3/31. Regular application deadline 7/15. Nonfall registration accepted. Admission may be deferred for a maximum of 1 year.

COSTS AND FINANCIAL AID

Annual tuition $18,100. Room and board $8,510. Required fees $3,525. Average book expense $1,282. **Required Forms and Deadlines:** CSS/Financial Aid PROFILE; FAFSA; Institution's own financial aid form. **Types of Aid:** *Need-based scholarships/grants:* College/university scholarship or grant aid from institutional funds; Federal Nursing Scholarships; Federal Pell; Private scholarships; SEOG; State scholarships/grants; United Negro College Fund. *Loans:* Direct PLUS loans; Direct Subsidized Stafford Loans; Direct Unsubsidized Stafford Loans. *Student Employment:* Federal Work-Study Program available. Institutional employment available. **Financial Aid Statistics:** 100% needy freshmen, 100% needy undergrads receive need-based scholarship or grant aid. 17% freshmen, 22% undergrads receive non-need-based scholarship or grant aid. 100% freshmen, 68% undergrads receive need-based self-help aid. 7% freshmen, 9% undergrads receive athletic scholarships. 90% freshmen, 92% undergrads receive any aid. 49% undergrads borrow to pay for school. Average cumulative indebtedness $18,100. **Criteria for awarding aid:** *Need-based:* Academics, Athletics *Non-need-based:* Academics, Athletics, State/district residency.

UNION COLLEGE (KY)

310 College Street, Barbourville, KY 40906
Phone: 606-546-1229 · **Financial Aid Phone:** 606-546-1224
E-mail: enrollme@unionky.edu
Fax: 606-546-1667 • **Website:** www.unionky.edu • **ACT Code:** 15520

This private school, affiliated with the Methodist Church, was founded in 1879. It has a 100 acre campus.

RATINGS

Admissions Selectivity Rating: 77   **Fire Safety Rating:** 65   **Green Rating:** 60*

STUDENTS AND FACULTY

Enrollment: 794. **Student Body:** 47% female, 53% male, 26% out-of-state, 8% international (19 countries represented). Asian 1%, African American 12%, Caucasian 72%, Hispanic 2%, Native American <1%, Pacific Islander <1%, Two or more races 5%, Race unknown 1%. **Retention and Graduation:** 56% freshmen return for sophomore year. **Faculty:** Student/faculty ratio 12:1. 56 full-time faculty, 45% hold PhDs, 11% are members of minority groups, 45% are women. 0% of classes are taught by teaching assistants.

ACADEMICS

Degrees: Bachelor's; Master's; Post-Bachelor's certificate **Classes:** Most classes have 10-19 students. Most lab/discussion sessions have 10-19 students. **Most popular majors:** Special Education And Teaching, General; Psychology, General; Business Administration And Management, General. **Special Study Options:** Distance learning; Double major; Honors program; Independent study; Internships; Liberal arts/career combination; Student-designed major; Study abroad; Teacher certification program. Combined degree programs: BA/MA. **Disability Services offered to physically disabled students:** Reader services; Tape recorders; Tutors. **Career services:** Alumni network; Career assessment; Career/job search classes; Internships; Regional alumni

FACILITIES

Housing: Apartments for married students; Apartments for single students; Men's dorms; Women's dorms 50% of campus accessible to physically diasbled. **Computers:** 100% of classrooms, 100% of dorms, 100% of libraries, 100% of dining areas, 100% of student union, 50% of common outdoor areas have wireless network access. Students can register for classes online. Administrative functions (other than registration) can be performed online.

CAMPUS LIFE

Environment: Rural **Activities:** Choral groups; Drama/theater; Literary magazine; Pep band; Student government; Television station; Yearbook 23 registered organizations, 2 honor societies, 2 religious organizations. **Athletics (Intercollegiate):** *Men:* baseball, basketball, bowling, cheerleading, cross-country, cycling, football, golf, soccer, swimming, tennis, track/field (outdoor). *Women:* basketball, bowling, cheerleading, cross-country, cycling, golf, soccer, softball, swimming, tennis, track/field (outdoor), volleyball. **On-Campus Highlights:** Student Center, Sharp Center Coffee Shop, Fitness Center

ADMISSIONS

Test Scores: SAT Math middle 50% range 453-553. SAT EBRW middle 50% range 433-508. ACT middle 50% range 18-23. Minimum paper TOEFL 550. **Basis for Candidate Selection:** *Important factors considered include:* rigor of secondary school record, class rank, academic GPA, standardized test scores, level of applicant's interest. *Other factors considered include:* recommendation(s), extracurricular activities, talent/ability, character/personal qualities, first generation, alumni/ae relation, geographical residence, volunteer work. **Freshman Admission Requirements:** High school diploma is required and GED is accepted *Academic units recommended:* 4 English, 3 math, 2 science, 2 science labs, 1 foreign language, 2 social studies. **Freshman Admission Statistics:** 1,332 applied, 69.1% admitted, 23% enrolled. **Transfer Admission Requirements:** college transcript(s), Minimum college GPA of 2.0 required. Lowest grade transferable 2. **General Admission Information:** Application fee $10. Nonfall registration accepted. Admission may be deferred.

COSTS AND FINANCIAL AID

Annual tuition $22,720. Room and board $7,000. Required fees $640. **Required Forms and Deadlines:** FAFSA. **Notification of Awards:** Applicants will be notified of awards on a rolling basis beginning 3/1. **Types of Aid:** *Need-based scholarships/grants:* College/university scholarship or grant aid from institutional funds; Federal Pell; Private scholarships; SEOG; State scholarships/grants. *Loans:* Direct PLUS loans; Direct Subsidized Stafford Loans; Direct Unsubsidized Stafford Loans. *Student Employment:* Federal Work-Study Program available. Institutional employment available. **Financial Aid Statistics:** 98% needy freshmen, 95% needy undergrads receive need-based scholarship or grant aid. 7% freshmen, 11% undergrads receive non-need-based scholarship or grant aid. 89% freshmen, 82% undergrads receive need-based self-help aid. 0% freshmen, 0% undergrads receive athletic scholarships. 100% freshmen, 100% undergrads receive any aid. **Criteria for awarding aid:** *Need-based:* Academics, Alumni affiliation, Athletics, Job skills *Non-need-based:* Academics, Athletics, Job skills, Religious affiliation, State/district residency.

UNION COLLEGE (NY)

807 Union Street, Schenectady, NY 12308
Phone: 518-388-6112 • **Financial Aid Phone:** 518-388-6123
E-mail: admissions@union.edu • **CEEB Code:** 2920
Fax: 518-388-6986 • **Website:** www.union.edu • **ACT Code:** 2970

This private school was founded in 1795. It has a 100 acre campus.

RATINGS
Admissions Selectivity Rating: 93   **Fire Safety Rating:** 92   **Green Rating:** 93

STUDENTS AND FACULTY
Enrollment: 2,163. **Student Body:** 47% female, 53% male, 62% out-of-state, 7% international (37 countries represented). Asian 6%, African American 4%, Caucasian 72%, Hispanic 7%, Native American <1%, Pacific Islander 0%, Two or more races 3%, Race unknown <1%.
Retention and Graduation: 92% freshmen return for sophomore year. 79% freshmen graduate within 4 years. 85% freshmen graduate within 6 years. 20% grads go on to further study within 1 year. **Faculty:** Student/faculty ratio 10:1. 211 full-time faculty, 97% hold PhDs, 13% are members of minority groups, 44% are women. 0% of classes are taught by teaching assistants.

ACADEMICS
Degrees: Bachelor's **Classes:** Most classes have 10-19 students. **Most popular majors:** Mechanical Engineering; Psychology, General; Economics, General. **Special Study Options:** Accelerated program; Cross-registration; Double major; Dual enrollment; Honors program; Independent study; Internships; Liberal arts/career combination; Student-designed major; Study abroad; Teacher certification program. Honors programs: The Union Scholars program offers selected students the opportunity to take full advantage of the diverse intellectual experiences at Union. Specific features of the program are an enriched two-term version of First-Year Preceptorial; a sophomore independent study project with a professor of the student's choosing; the option to participate as a junior in a program in which students take a leadership role in the College's intellectual and social life; and a Scholars Colloquium run by students for presenting faculty and student research, in the senior year. Union Scholars use their extra courses to create an enriched program that meets their specific needs and interests. Combined degree programs: BA/JD. **Disability Services offered to physically disabled students:** Note-taking services; Reader services; Tape recorders. **Career services:** Alumni network; Alumni services; Career assessment; Career/job search classes; Internships; Regional alumni

FACILITIES
Housing: Apartments for single students; Coed dorms; Fraternity/sorority housing; Theme housing 80% of campus accessible to physically diasbled. **Special Academic Facilities/Equipment:** The Nott Memorial and its Mandeville Gallery; Yulman Theater; Burns Arts Atrium; Taylor Music Center and its Emerson Auditorium; Special Collections at Schaffer Library; Memorial Chapel; Jackson's Garden, an eight-acre formal garden and woodland. Academic facilities include the F.W. Olin Center, with high technology classrooms and laboratories, a multi-media auditorium, collaborative computer classrooms, and a 20-inch remote-controlled telescope. Science and engineering facilities include superconducting nuclear magnetic resonance spectrometer, two electron microscopes, tandem pelletron positive ion accelerator, a fully accessible machine lab, and Aerogel fabrication and analysis lab. **Computers:** 100% of classrooms, 75% of dorms, 100% of libraries, 100% of dining areas, 100% of student union, 100% of common outdoor areas have wireless network access. Students can register for classes online. Administrative functions (other than registration) can be performed online.

CAMPUS LIFE
Environment: Town **Activities:** Campus Ministries; Choral groups; Concert band; Dance; Drama/theater; International Student Organization; Jazz band; Literary magazine; Model UN; Music ensembles; Pep band; Radio station; Student government; Student newspaper; Student-run film society; Symphony orchestra; Television station; Yearbook 100 registered organizations, 13 honor societies, 7 religious organizations. 12 fraternities, 5 sororities. **Athletics (Intercollegiate):** *Men:* baseball, basketball, crew/rowing, cross-country, diving, football, ice hockey, lacrosse, soccer, swimming, tennis, track/field (outdoor), track/field (indoor). *Women:* basketball, crew/rowing, cross-country, diving, field hockey, ice hockey, lacrosse, soccer, softball, swimming, tennis, track/field (outdoor), track/field (indoor), volleyball. **On-Campus Highlights:** The Nott Memorial, Schaffer Library, Reamer Campus Center, Jackson's Garden, Wold Center for Science and Engineering **Environmental**

Initiatives: Incorporation of Sustainability into Union College's Mission, Presidential Priority & Strategic Plan.

ADMISSIONS
Freshman Academic Profile: Average high school GPA 3.4. 63% in top 10% of high school class, 88% in top 25% of high school class, 99% in top 50% of high school class. 65% from public high schools. **Test Scores:** SAT Math middle 50% range 640-730. SAT EBRW middle 50% range 630-700. ACT middle 50% range 29-32. Minimum internet-based TOEFL 90. Minimum paper TOEFL 600. **Basis for Candidate Selection:** *Very important factors considered include:* rigor of secondary school record, class rank, academic GPA. *Important factors considered include:* application essay, standardized test scores, recommendation(s), extracurricular activities, talent/ability, character/personal qualities, volunteer work, work experience. *Other factors considered include:* interview, first generation, alumni/ae relation, geographical residence, state residency, racial/ethnic status, level of applicant's interest. **Freshman Admission Requirements:** High school diploma is required and GED is not accepted *Academic units required:* 4 English, 3 math, 2 science, 2 science labs, 2 foreign language, 1 social studies, 1 history, *Academic units recommended:* 4 English, 4 math, 4 science, 4 science labs, 4 foreign language, 2 social studies, 2 history. **Freshman Admission Statistics:** 6,676 applied, 37.4% admitted, 23% enrolled. **Transfer Admission Requirements:** High school transcript, college transcript(s), essay or personal statement, statement of good standing from prior institution(s). Minimum college GPA of 3.0 required. Lowest grade transferable C. **General Admission Information:** Regular application deadline 1/15. Nonfall registration accepted. Admission may be deferred for a maximum of 2 years.

COSTS AND FINANCIAL AID
Annual tuition $53,019. Room and board $13,119. Required fees $471. Average book expense $1,500. **Required Forms and Deadlines:** CSS/Financial Aid PROFILE; FAFSA; Noncustodial PROFILE; State aid form. **Notification of Awards:** Applicants will be notified of awards on or about 3/25. **Types of Aid:** *Need-based scholarships/grants:* College/university scholarship or grant aid from institutional funds; Federal Pell; Private scholarships; SEOG; State scholarships/grants. *Loans:* Direct PLUS loans; Direct Subsidized Stafford Loans; Direct Unsubsidized Stafford Loans. *Student Employment:* Federal Work-Study Program available. Institutional employment available. **Financial Aid Statistics:** 98% needy freshmen, 94% needy undergrads receive need-based scholarship or grant aid. 9% freshmen, 11% undergrads receive non-need-based scholarship or grant aid. 93% freshmen, 94% undergrads receive need-based self-help aid. 0% freshmen, 0% undergrads receive athletic scholarships. 84% freshmen, 80% undergrads receive any aid. 54% undergrads borrow to pay for school. Average cumulative indebtedness $33,045. **Criteria for awarding aid:** *Need-based:* Academics *Non-need-based:* Academics.

See page 1054.

UNION INSTITUTE & UNIVERSITY

440 East McMillan Street, Cincinnati, OH 45206
Phone: 513-861-6400 • **Financial Aid Phone:** 800-486-3116
E-mail: admissions@myunion.edu
Fax: 513-861-3238 • **Website:** www.myunion.edu

This private school was founded in 1964.

RATINGS
Admissions Selectivity Rating: 61   **Fire Safety Rating:** 60*   **Green Rating:** 60*

STUDENTS AND FACULTY
Enrollment: 1,101. **Student Body:** 53% female, 47% male, 16% out-of-state, 0% international (24 countries represented). Asian 1%, African American 26%, Caucasian 33%, Hispanic 13%, Native American 1%, Pacific Islander <1%, Two or more races 2%, Race unknown 24%.
Retention and Graduation: 90% freshmen return for sophomore year. **Faculty:** Student/faculty ratio 9:1. 31 full-time faculty, 84% hold PhDs, 19% are members of minority groups, 52% are women. 0% of classes are taught by teaching assistants.

ACADEMICS
Degrees: Bachelor's; Doctoral; Doctoral/Research; **Master's Classes:** Most classes have 10-19 students. **Most popular majors:** Child Development; Liberal Arts And Sciences, General Studies And Humanities, Other; Criminal Justice/Law Enforcement Administration. **Special Study Options:** Cross-registration; Distance learning; Independent study; Internships; Teacher certification program. **Career services:** Alumni services; Career assessment

FACILITIES

Housing: 100% of campus accessible to physically diasbled. **Computers:** Students can register for classes online. Administrative functions (other than registration) can be performed online.

CAMPUS LIFE

Environment: Metropolis

ADMISSIONS

Basis for Candidate Selection: *Important factors considered include:* application essay, recommendation(s), interview, level of applicant's interest. *Other factors considered include:* extracurricular activities, talent/ability, character/personal qualities, volunteer work, work experience. **Freshman Admission Requirements:** High school diploma is required and GED is accepted **Transfer Admission Requirements:** college transcript(s), essay or personal statement, interview, Lowest grade transferable D. **General Admission Information:** Nonfall registration accepted. Admission may be deferred for a maximum of 1 year.

COSTS AND FINANCIAL AID

Required Forms and Deadlines: FAFSA; Institution's own financial aid form. **Notification of Awards:** Applicants will be notified of awards on a rolling basis beginning 5/1. **Types of Aid:** *Need-based scholarships/grants:* College/university scholarship or grant aid from institutional funds; Federal Pell; Private scholarships; SEOG; State scholarships/grants. *Student Employment:* Federal Work-Study Program available. **Criteria for awarding aid:** *Need-based:* Academics *Non-need-based:* Academics, State/district residency.

UNION UNIVERSITY

1050 Union University Drive, Jackson, TN 38305-3697
Phone: 731-661-5000 • **Financial Aid Phone:** 731-661-5015
E-mail: rgrimm@uu.edu • **CEEB Code:** 1826
Fax: 731-661-5017 • **ACT Code:** 4020

This private school, affiliated with the Southern Baptist Church, was founded in 1823. It has a 360 acre campus.

RATINGS

Admissions Selectivity Rating: 83   **Fire Safety Rating:** 86   **Green Rating:** 64

STUDENTS AND FACULTY

Enrollment: 2,567. **Student Body:** 62% female, 38% male, 31% out-of-state, 2% international (36 countries represented). Asian 1%, African American 14%, Caucasian 77%, Hispanic 2%, Native American <1%, Pacific Islander <1%, Two or more races 2%, Race unknown 2%.
Retention and Graduation: 93% freshmen return for sophomore year. 40% grads go on to further study within 1 year. **Faculty:** Student/faculty ratio 11:1. 229 full-time faculty, 83% hold PhDs, 10% are members of minority groups, 49% are women. 0% of classes are taught by teaching assistants.

ACADEMICS

Degrees: Associate; Bachelor's; Diploma; Doctoral; Doctoral Other; Doctoral/Professional; Doctoral/Research; Master's; Post-Master's certificate; Transfer Associate **Classes:** Most classes have fewer than 10 students. **Most popular majors:** Elementary Education And Teaching; Christian Studies; Nursing/Registered Nurse (Rn, Asn, Bsn, Msn). **Special Study Options:** Accelerated program; Cooperative education program; Cross-registration; Distance learning; Double major; Dual enrollment; English as a Second Language (ESL); Exchange student program (domestic); Honors program; Independent study; Internships; Study abroad; Teacher certification program. Honors programs: General Honors plus discipline-specific honors in Art, Biology, Business, Chemistry, Education, English, History, Math, Political Science, and Theology. **Disability Services offered to physically disabled students:** Note-taking services; Reader services; Tape recorders; Tutors. **Career services:** Alumni network; Alumni services; Career assessment; Career/job search classes; Internships; Regional alumni

FACILITIES

Housing: Apartments for married students; Men's dorms; Special housing for disabled student; Women's dorms 98% of campus accessible to physically diasbled. **Special Academic Facilities/Equipment:** Elementary education lab, 21st-century classroom, TV communications truck, nursing/health assessment labs, health and wellness center, art gallery. **Computers:** 75% of classrooms, 100% of dorms, 100% of libraries, 50% of dining areas, 100% of student union, have wireless network access. Administrative functions (other than registration) can be performed online.

CAMPUS LIFE

Environment: City **Activities:** Campus Ministries; Choral groups; Concert band; Drama/theater; International Student Organization; Jazz band; Literary magazine; Music ensembles; Pep band; Student government; Student newspaper; Student-run film society; Yearbook 67 registered organizations, 12 honor societies, 4 religious organizations. 3 fraternities, 3 sororities.
Athletics (Intercollegiate): *Men:* baseball, basketball, cheerleading, cross-country, golf, soccer. *Women:* basketball, cheerleading, cross-country, soccer, softball, volleyball. **On-Campus Highlights:** Bowld Commons, Residence Life Facilities, Providence Hall, White Hall, Jennings Hall **Environmental Initiatives:** Campus-wide recycling campaign for aluminum, plastics and paper. This includes pick up from all student residential areas as well as all buildings/offices.

ADMISSIONS

Freshman Academic Profile: Average high school GPA 3.7. 33% in top 10% of high school class, 62% in top 25% of high school class, 85% in top 50% of high school class. 57% from public high schools. **Test Scores:** SAT Math middle 50% range 520-670. SAT EBRW middle 50% range 500-680. ACT middle 50% range 22-29. Minimum internet-based TOEFL 80. Minimum paper TOEFL 550. **Basis for Candidate Selection:** *Very important factors considered include:* rigor of secondary school record, academic GPA, character/personal qualities, level of applicant's interest. *Important factors considered include:* class rank, standardized test scores, interview, extracurricular activities, talent/ability, religious affiliation/commitment. *Other factors considered include:* application essay, recommendation(s), first generation, alumni/ae relation, volunteer work, work experience. **Freshman Admission Requirements:** High school diploma is required and GED is accepted *Academic units required:* 4 English, 3 math, 3 science, 2 science labs, 1 foreign language, 2 social studies, 1 history, 1 academic elective, *Academic units recommended:* 4 English, 4 math, 4 science, 2 science labs, 2 foreign language, 2 social studies, 2 history, 4 academic electives, 1 computer science, 1 visual/performing arts. **Freshman Admission Statistics:** 1,930 applied, 74.2% admitted, 32% enrolled. **Transfer Admission Requirements:** college transcript(s), statement of good standing from prior institution(s). Minimum college GPA of 2.3 required. Lowest grade transferable C. **General Admission Information:** Application fee $35. Priority deadline 12/1. Regular application deadline 8/1. Nonfall registration accepted. Admission may be deferred for a maximum of 1 year.

COSTS AND FINANCIAL AID

Annual tuition $26,160. Room and board $8,430. Required fees $720. Average book expense $1,220. **Required Forms and Deadlines:** FAFSA; Institution's own financial aid form. **Notification of Awards:** Applicants will be notified of awards on a rolling basis beginning 12/1. **Types of Aid:** *Need-based scholarships/grants:* College/university scholarship or grant aid from institutional funds; Federal Nursing Scholarships; Federal Pell; Private scholarships; SEOG; State scholarships/grants. *Loans:* Direct PLUS loans; Direct Subsidized Stafford Loans; Direct Unsubsidized Stafford Loans. *Student Employment:* Federal Work-Study Program available. Institutional employment available. **Financial Aid Statistics:** 76% needy freshmen, 70% needy undergrads receive need-based scholarship or grant aid. 99% freshmen, 77% undergrads receive non-need-based scholarship or grant aid. 58% freshmen, 69% undergrads receive need-based self-help aid. 7% freshmen, 7% undergrads receive athletic scholarships. 99% freshmen, 99% undergrads receive any aid. **Criteria for awarding aid:** *Need-based:* Job skills, Minority status *Non-need-based:* Academics, Alumni affiliation, Art, Athletics, Job skills, Leadership, Minority status, Music/drama, Religious affiliation.

UNITED STATES AIR FORCE ACADEMY

2304 Cadet Drive, USAF Academy, CO 80840-5025
Phone: 719-333-2520
E-mail: rr_webmail@usafa.edu
Fax: 719-333-3012 • **Website:** www.academyadmissions.com • **ACT Code:** 530

This public school was founded in 1954. It has a 18000 acre campus.

RATINGS

Admissions Selectivity Rating: 99   **Fire Safety Rating:** 99   **Green Rating:** 74

STUDENTS AND FACULTY

Enrollment: 4,276. **Student Body:** 26% female, 74% male, 90% out-of-state, 1% international (22 countries represented). Asian 5%, African American 6%,

Caucasian 63%, Hispanic 11%, Native American <1%, Pacific Islander 1%, Two or more races 7%, Race unknown 5%.
Retention and Graduation: 94% freshmen return for sophomore year. 77% freshmen graduate within 4 years. 79% freshmen graduate within 6 years. 11% grads go on to further study within 1 year. 11% grads pursue arts and sciences degrees. 0.2% grads pursue law degrees. 0% grads pursue business degrees. 0.1% grads pursue medical degrees. **Faculty:** Student/faculty ratio 9:1. 504 full-time faculty, 59% hold PhDs, 10% are members of minority groups, 22% are women. 0% of classes are taught by teaching assistants.

ACADEMICS

Degrees: Bachelor's **Classes:** Most classes have 20-29 students. Most lab/discussion sessions have 20-29 students. **Most popular majors:** Aerospace, Aeronautical And Astronautical/Space Engineering; Systems Engineering; Business Administration And Management, General. **Special Study Options:** Double major; English as a Second Language (ESL); Exchange student program (domestic); Honors program; Independent study; Internships; Liberal arts/career combination; Study abroad. Honors programs: The Academy Scholars Program offers participating cadets a four-year experience featuring core substitute and upper-division courses. In addition to course offerings, the Academy Scholars Program also provides many opportunities beyond the curriculum, including participation in the National Collegiate Honors Council and the Aspen Institute: **Career services:** Alumni network; Alumni services; Career assessment; Internships; Regional alumni

FACILITIES

Housing: Coed dorms 0% of campus accessible to physically diasbled. **Special Academic Facilities/Equipment:** Polaris Hall, Center for Character and Leadership Development. CyberWorx, Innovation Center, teaching creative problem solving techniques to improve leadership and innovation-CTEF Building Human Performance Lab—Cadet Gym, Language learning center, laser and optics research center, Dept. of Engineering Mechanics Lab, US Air Force Academy visitor's center, consolidated educational training facility, Air Force Academy cadet chapel, American Legion Memorial Tower, Clune area athletic and speaking events (seats 6,000), Air Garden, Falcon Stadium, Holaday Athletic Center Aeronautics Lab, Meterology Lab, Arnold Hall Broadway Theater, ballroom and conference rooms, and historical displays. Visitors Center, Cadet Demographic Map as well as cadet life film **Computers:** 100% of classrooms, 100% of libraries, 100% of student union, have wireless network access. Students can register for classes online. Administrative functions (other than registration) can be performed online. Undergraduates are required to own a computer.

CAMPUS LIFE

Environment: Metropolis **Activities:** Campus Ministries; Choral groups; Concert band; Dance; Drama/theater; International Student Organization; Marching band; Model UN; Music ensembles; Musical theater; Pep band; Radio station; Student government; Symphony orchestra; Yearbook 77 registered organizations, 2 honor societies, 14 religious organizations. **Athletics (Intercollegiate):** *Men:* baseball, basketball, boxing, cheerleading, cross-country, diving, fencing, football, golf, gymnastics, ice hockey, lacrosse, riflery, soccer, swimming, tennis, track/field (outdoor), track/field (indoor), water polo, wrestling. *Women:* basketball, cheerleading, cross-country, diving, fencing, gymnastics, riflery, soccer, swimming, tennis, track/field (outdoor), track/field (indoor), volleyball. **On-Campus Highlights:** USAF Academy Chapel, Thunderbird Lookout and Air Field (Soaring, JUMP, etc), Falcon Stadium, Cadet Sports Complex, USAF Academy Visitor Center **Environmental Initiatives:** Solar

ADMISSIONS

Freshman Academic Profile: Average high school GPA 3.9. 54% in top 10% of high school class, 83% in top 25% of high school class, 96% in top 50% of high school class. 76% from public high schools. **Test Scores:** SAT Math middle 50% range 640-710. SAT EBRW middle 50% range 630-700. ACT middle 50% range 29-33. **Basis for Candidate Selection:** *Very important factors considered include:* rigor of secondary school record, class rank, academic GPA, application essay, standardized test scores, recommendation(s), interview, extracurricular activities, character/personal qualities, level of applicant's interest. *Important factors considered include:* talent/ability, volunteer work, work experience. *Other factors considered include:* first generation, alumni/ae relation, geographical residence, racial/ethnic status. **Freshman Admission Requirements:** High school diploma is required and GED is accepted *Academic units recommended:* 4 English, 4 math, 4 science, 4 science labs, 2 foreign language, 3 social studies, 3 history, 1 computer science. **Freshman Admission Statistics:** 10,202 applied, 11.7% admitted, 99% enrolled. **Transfer Admission Requirements:** High school transcript, college transcript(s), essay or personal statement, interview, standardized test scores, Minimum college GPA of 2.0 required. **General Admission Information:** Regular application deadline 12/31. Nonfall registration accepted.

COSTS AND FINANCIAL AID

Financial Aid Statistics: 0% undergrads borrow to pay for school.

UNITED STATES COAST GUARD ACADEMY

15 Mohegan Avenue, New London, CT 06320-8103
Phone: 860-444-8500
E-mail: USCGA.Admissions@uscga.edu • **CEEB Code:** 5807
Fax: 860-701-6700 • **Website:** www.uscga.edu • **ACT Code:** 600

This public school was founded in 1876. It has a 103 acre campus.

RATINGS
Admissions Selectivity Rating: 97   **Fire Safety Rating:** 91   **Green Rating:** 61

STUDENTS AND FACULTY
Enrollment: 898. **Student Body:** 35% female, 65% male, 95% out-of-state, 2% international (12 countries represented). Asian 7%, African American 4%, Caucasian 67%, Hispanic 10%, Native American <1%, Pacific Islander <1%, Two or more races 8%, Race unknown 2%.
Retention and Graduation: 90% freshmen return for sophomore year. **Faculty:** Student/faculty ratio 8:1. 115 full-time faculty, 56% hold PhDs, 12% are members of minority groups, 28% are women. 0% of classes are taught by teaching assistants.

ACADEMICS
Degrees: Bachelor's **Most popular majors:** Oceanography, Chemical And Physical; Political Science And Government, General; Business Administration And Management, General. **Special Study Options:** Cross-registration; Double major; English as a Second Language (ESL); Exchange student program (domestic); Honors program; Independent study; Internships. **Career services:** Alumni network; Career assessment; Regional alumni

FACILITIES
Housing: Coed dorms; Wellness housing 95% of campus accessible to physically diasbled. **Special Academic Facilities/Equipment:** CG Museum; Library; Visitors Center; Alumni Center **Computers:** 100% of classrooms, 65% of dorms, 100% of libraries, 50% of dining areas, 100% of student union, 50% of common outdoor areas have wireless network access. Students can register for classes online. Administrative functions (other than registration) can be performed online. Undergraduates are required to own a computer.

CAMPUS LIFE
Environment: City **Activities:** Campus Ministries; Choral groups; Concert band; Dance; Drama/theater; International Student Organization; Jazz band; Marching band; Model UN; Music ensembles; Musical theater; Pep band; Student government; Yearbook 2 honor societies, 7 religious organizations. **Athletics (Intercollegiate):** *Men:* baseball, basketball, crew/rowing, cross-country, diving, football, pistol, riflery, sailing, soccer, swimming, tennis, track/field (outdoor), track/field (indoor), wrestling. *Women:* basketball, cheerleading, crew/rowing, cross-country, diving, pistol, riflery, sailing, soccer, softball, swimming, track/field (outdoor), track/field (indoor), volleyball. **On-Campus Highlights:** Coast Guard Barque EAGLE, Coast Guard Museum, Sailing Center and Waterfront, Souvenier Shop (Military Exchange), Coast Guard Academy Chapel and Crown Park **Environmental Initiatives:** Federal Electronic Recycling Challenge Participant and winner 2008 and 2009.

ADMISSIONS
Freshman Academic Profile: Average high school GPA 3.8. 45% in top 10% of high school class, 79% in top 25% of high school class, 96% in top 50% of high school class. 76% from public high schools. **Test Scores:** SAT Math middle 50% range 610-690. SAT EBRW middle 50% range 570-660. ACT middle 50% range 26-31. Minimum internet-based TOEFL 90. Minimum paper TOEFL 560. **Basis for Candidate Selection:** *Very important factors considered include:* rigor of secondary school record, class rank, academic GPA, standardized test scores, extracurricular activities, character/personal qualities. *Important factors considered include:* application essay, recommendation(s), talent/ability. *Other factors considered include:* interview, first generation, alumni/ae relation, geographical residence, state residency, religious affiliation/commitment, racial/ethnic status, volunteer work, work experience, level of applicant's interest. **Freshman Admission Requirements:** High school diploma is required and GED is accepted *Academic units required:* 4 English, 4 math, 3 science, 3 science labs, *Academic units recommended:* 4 English, 4 math, 4 science, 3 science labs. **Freshman Admission Statistics:** 2,214 applied, 17.5% admitted, 75% enrolled. **Transfer Admission Requirements:** High school transcript, essay or personal statement, standardized test scores, statement of good standing from prior institution(s). **General Admission**

Information: Priority deadline 11/15. Regular application deadline 2/1. Nonfall registration accepted. Admission may be deferred for a maximum of 1 year.

COSTS AND FINANCIAL AID

Required fees $978. Average book expense $2,199. **Types of Aid: Financial Aid Statistics:** 0% freshmen, 0% undergrads receive athletic scholarships. 0% freshmen, 0% undergrads receive any aid.

UNITED STATES MERCHANT MARINE ACADEMY

300 Steamboat Road, Kings Point, NY 11024-1699
Phone: 516-726-5643 • **Financial Aid Phone:** 516-773-5295
E-mail: admissions@usmma.edu • **CEEB Code:** 2923
Fax: 516-773-5390 • **Website:** www.usmma.edu • **ACT Code:** 2974

This public school was founded in 1943. It has a 82 acre campus.

RATINGS

Admissions Selectivity Rating: 97   **Fire Safety Rating:** 98   **Green Rating:** 63

STUDENTS AND FACULTY

Enrollment: 952. **Student Body:** 17% female, 83% male, 87% out-of-state, 1% international (4 countries represented). Asian 8%, African American 3%, Caucasian 75%, Hispanic 10%, Native American 1%, Pacific Islander <1%, Two or more races 0%, Race unknown 3%.
Retention and Graduation: 89% freshmen return for sophomore year. 81% freshmen graduate within 4 years. 87% freshmen graduate within 6 years. **Faculty:** Student/faculty ratio 8:1. 113 full-time faculty, 9% are members of minority groups, 15% are women.

ACADEMICS

Degrees: Bachelor's; **Master's Classes:** Most classes have 20-29 students. Most lab/discussion sessions have 10-19 students. **Most popular majors:** Engineering, General; Naval Architecture And Marine Engineering; Transportation And Materials Moving, Other. **Special Study Options:** Honors program; Independent study; Internships; Study abroad. **Career services:** Alumni network; Alumni services; Career assessment; Career/job search classes; Internships

FACILITIES

Housing: Coed dorms **Special Academic Facilities/Equipment:** American Merchant Marine Museum **Computers:** Students can register for classes online. Administrative functions (other than registration) can be performed online. Undergraduates are required to own a computer.

CAMPUS LIFE

Environment: Town **Activities:** Campus Ministries; Choral groups; Concert band; Marching band; Pep band; Student government; Student newspaper; Yearbook 3 religious organizations. **Athletics (Intercollegiate):** *Men:* baseball, basketball, crew/rowing, cross-country, diving, football, golf, lacrosse, riflery, sailing, soccer, swimming, tennis, track/field (outdoor), volleyball, water polo, wrestling. *Women:* basketball, crew/rowing, cross-country, diving, golf, riflery, sailing, softball, swimming, tennis, track/field (outdoor), volleyball. American Merchant Marine Museum, Mariners' Chapel

ADMISSIONS

Freshman Academic Profile: 22% in top 10% of high school class, 64% in top 25% of high school class, 96% in top 50% of high school class. 75% from public high schools. **Test Scores:** SAT Math middle 50% range 630-660. SAT EBRW middle 50% range 570-660. Minimum internet-based TOEFL 83. Minimum paper TOEFL 540. **Basis for Candidate Selection:** *Very important factors considered include:* rigor of secondary school record, class rank, standardized test scores, extracurricular activities, character/personal qualities. *Important factors considered include:* academic GPA, application essay, recommendation(s), talent/ability, level of applicant's interest. *Other factors considered include:* interview, first generation, geographical residence, state residency, racial/ethnic status, volunteer work, work experience.
Freshman Admission Requirements: High school diploma is required and GED is accepted *Academic units required:* 3 English, 3 math, 1 science, 1 science labs, 8 academic electives, *Academic units recommended:* 4 English, 4 math, 3 science, 2 science labs, 2 foreign language. **Freshman Admission Statistics:** 1,855 applied, 22.2% admitted, 68% enrolled. **Transfer Admission Requirements:** High school transcript, college transcript(s), essay or personal statement, standardized test scores, statement of good standing from prior

institution(s). Minimum college GPA of 2.5 required. **General Admission Information:** Regular application deadline 3/1. Nonfall registration accepted.

COSTS AND FINANCIAL AID

Required fees $1,167. Average book expense $1,000. **Required Forms and Deadlines:** FAFSA; Institution's own financial aid form. **Notification of Awards:** Applicants will be notified of awards on a rolling basis beginning 5/1. **Types of Aid:** *Need-based scholarships/grants:* Federal Pell; Private scholarships; State scholarships/grants. *Loans:* Direct PLUS loans; Direct Subsidized Stafford Loans; Direct Unsubsidized Stafford Loans. **Financial Aid Statistics:** 100% needy freshmen, 100% needy undergrads receive need-based scholarship or grant aid. 100% freshmen, 100% undergrads receive non-need-based scholarship or grant aid. 100% freshmen, 100% undergrads receive need-based self-help aid. 0% freshmen, 0% undergrads receive athletic scholarships. 33% freshmen, 30% undergrads receive any aid. Average cumulative indebtedness $7,500.

UNITED STATES MILITARY ACADEMY

646 Swift Road, West Point, NY 10996-1905
Phone: 845-938-4041
E-mail: admissions@usma.edu • **CEEB Code:** 2924
Fax: 845-938-3021 • **Website:** www.westpoint.edu • **ACT Code:** 2976

This public school was founded in 1802. It has a 16080 acre campus.

RATINGS

Admissions Selectivity Rating: 99   **Fire Safety Rating:** 91   **Green Rating:** 60*

STUDENTS AND FACULTY

Enrollment: 4,491. **Student Body:** 22% female, 78% male, 94% out-of-state, 1% international (29 countries represented). Asian 8%, African American 12%, Caucasian 62%, Hispanic 10%, Native American 1%, Pacific Islander <1%, Two or more races 3%, Race unknown 1%.
Retention and Graduation: 98% freshmen return for sophomore year. 82% freshmen graduate within 4 years. 86% freshmen graduate within 6 years. 38% grads go on to further study within 1 year. 1% grads pursue arts and sciences degrees. 2% grads pursue medical degrees. **Faculty:** Student/faculty ratio 7:1. 611 full-time faculty, 52% hold PhDs, 10% are members of minority groups, 20% are women. 0% of classes are taught by teaching assistants.

ACADEMICS

Degrees: Bachelor's **Classes:** Most classes have 10-19 students. Most lab/discussion sessions have 10-19 students. **Most popular majors:** Engineering/Industrial Management; Economics, General; Business Administration And Management, General. **Special Study Options:** Double major; Exchange student program (domestic); Honors program; Independent study; Internships; Study abroad. Honors programs: Thayer Honors Program, offers a broad umbrella to provide comprehensive academic development for cadets with outstanding potential. The program offers systematic and sustained intellectual challenge, while affording and encouraging opportunities outside West Point's curricular path. The Thayer Honors Program is a powerful instrument to attract, retain, and develop young leaders of the highest caliber. Cadets in the program likewise serve as ambassadors for the military to their civilian counterparts, whether at academic conferences presenting their research, interning during summers, or for those who receive nationally-competitive scholarships, in graduate school following commissioning.

FACILITIES

Housing: Coed dorms 0% of campus accessible to physically diasbled.
Special Academic Facilities/Equipment: West Point Museum, American Revolutionary-era Fort Putnam, 4,500-seat Eisenhower Hall, 18-hole Golf Course, Victor Constant Ski Slope, Arvin Cadet Physical Development Center, Michie Stadium, Christi Arena, Gillis Field House, and Jefferson Hall Library. **Computers:** 100% of classrooms, 100% of libraries, 100% of student union, have wireless network access. Students can register for classes online. Administrative functions (other than registration) can be performed online. Undergraduates are required to own a computer.

CAMPUS LIFE

Environment: Village **Activities:** Campus Ministries; Choral groups; Drama/theater; International Student Organization; Literary magazine; Model UN; Music ensembles; Pep band; Radio station; Student government; Student-run film society; Television station; Yearbook 105 registered organizations,

7 honor societies, 13 religious organizations. **Athletics (Intercollegiate):** *Men:* baseball, basketball, cross-country, football, golf, gymnastics, ice hockey, lacrosse, riflery, soccer, swimming, tennis, track/field (outdoor), track/field (indoor), wrestling. *Women:* basketball, cross-country, riflery, soccer, softball, swimming, tennis, track/field (outdoor), track/field (indoor), volleyball. **On-Campus Highlights:** Cadet Chapel, Jefferson Hall Library, Eisenhower Hall, Michie Stadium, Trophy Point

ADMISSIONS

Freshman Academic Profile: 46% in top 10% of high school class, 74% in top 25% of high school class, 94% in top 50% of high school class. 80% from public high schools. **Test Scores:** SAT Math middle 50% range 600-710. SAT EBRW middle 50% range 585-690. ACT middle 50% range 23-28. Minimum internet-based TOEFL 75. Minimum paper TOEFL 500. **Basis for Candidate Selection:** *Very important factors considered include:* rigor of secondary school record, class rank, academic GPA, standardized test scores, extracurricular activities, character/personal qualities. *Important factors considered include:* application essay, recommendation(s), talent/ability, level of applicant's interest. *Other factors considered include:* interview, first generation, racial/ethnic status, volunteer work, work experience. **Freshman Admission Requirements:** High school diploma is required and GED is accepted *Academic units recommended:* 4 English, 4 math, 4 science, 2 science labs, 2 foreign language, 3 social studies, 1 history, 3 academic electives. **Freshman Admission Statistics:** 12,973 applied, 9.6% admitted, 98% enrolled. **General Admission Information:** Regular application deadline 2/28. Nonfall registration accepted.

COSTS AND FINANCIAL AID

Financial Aid Statistics: 0% freshmen, 0% undergrads receive any aid.

UNITED STATES NAVAL ACADEMY

121 Blake Road, Annapolis, MD 21402
Phone: 410-293-1858
E-mail: inquire@usna.edu • **CEEB Code:** 5809
Fax: 410-293-4348 • **Website:** www.usna.edu • **ACT Code:** 1742

This public school was founded in 1845. It has a 338 acre campus.

RATINGS

Admissions Selectivity Rating: 98   **Fire Safety Rating:** 77   **Green Rating:** 60*

STUDENTS AND FACULTY

Enrollment: 4,495. **Student Body:** 27% female, 73% male, 94% out-of-state, 1% international (29 countries represented). Asian 7%, African American 7%, Caucasian 63%, Hispanic 12%, Native American <1%, Pacific Islander 1%, Two or more races 9%, Race unknown 1%.
Retention and Graduation: 95% freshmen return for sophomore year. 90% freshmen graduate within 4 years. 91% freshmen graduate within 6 years. 15% grads go on to further study within 1 year. 14% grads pursue arts and sciences degrees. 0% grads pursue law degrees. 0% grads pursue business degrees. 1% grads pursue medical degrees. **Faculty:** Student/faculty ratio 8:1. 536 full-time faculty, 67% hold PhDs, 13% are members of minority groups, 31% are women. 0% of classes are taught by teaching assistants.

ACADEMICS

Degrees: Bachelor's; Diploma **Classes:** Most classes have 10-19 students. Most lab/discussion sessions have fewer than 10 students. **Most popular majors:** Mechanical Engineering; Economics, General; Political Science And Government, General. **Special Study Options:** Double major; Exchange student program (domestic); Honors program; Independent study; Study abroad. Honors programs: **Career services:** Alumni network; Alumni services

FACILITIES

Housing: Coed dorms **Special Academic Facilities/Equipment:** 34,000‐seat stadium, 5700‐seat basketball arena, Olympic pool with a diving well for 10‐meter diving boards, wrestling arena, hydraulically banked 200‐meter indoor track, 400‐meter outdoor track, indoor ice rink, 6 nautilus and weight rooms, facilities for gymnastics, boxing, volleyball, swimming, water polo, racquetball, basketball and personal conditioning, squash courts, climbing wall, baseball stadium, crew house, 18 hole golf course, soccer facility, a sailing center, indoor and outdoor tennis courts, and 2 athletic field houses. **Computers:** Students can register for classes online. Administrative functions (other than registration) can be performed online. Undergraduates are required to own a computer.

CAMPUS LIFE

Environment: Town **Activities:** Campus Ministries; Choral groups; Concert band; Dance; Drama/theater; International Student Organization; Jazz band; Literary magazine; Marching band; Model UN; Music ensembles; Musical theater; Pep band; Radio station; Student government; Student-run film society; Symphony orchestra; Yearbook 70 registered organizations, 10 honor societies, 8 religious organizations. **Athletics (Intercollegiate):** *Men:* baseball, basketball, crew/rowing, cross-country, diving, football, golf, gymnastics, lacrosse, light weight football, riflery, sailing, soccer, squash, swimming, tennis, track/field (outdoor), track/field (indoor), water polo, wrestling. *Women:* basketball, crew/rowing, cross-country, diving, lacrosse, riflery, sailing, soccer, swimming, tennis, track/field (outdoor), track/field (indoor), volleyball. **On-Campus Highlights:** Bancroft Hall, U.S. Naval Academy Museum, Armel-Leftwich Visitor Center, U.S. Naval Academy Chapel, Lejeune Hall

ADMISSIONS

Freshman Academic Profile: Average high school GPA 4.1. 57% in top 10% of high school class, 83% in top 25% of high school class, 97% in top 50% of high school class. 60% from public high schools. **Test Scores:** SAT Math middle 50% range 590-690. SAT EBRW middle 50% range 560-680. **Basis for Candidate Selection:** *Very important factors considered include:* rigor of secondary school record, class rank, academic GPA, application essay, recommendation(s), interview, extracurricular activities, character/personal qualities, level of applicant's interest. *Important factors considered include:* standardized test scores, talent/ability. *Other factors considered include:* first generation, alumni/ae relation, geographical residence, state residency, racial/ethnic status, volunteer work, work experience. **Freshman Admission Requirements:** High school diploma or equivalent is not required *Academic units recommended:* 4 English, 4 math, 2 science, 1 science labs, 2 foreign language, 2 history, 1 unit from above areas or other academic areas. **Freshman Admission Statistics:** 16,299 applied, 8.4% admitted, 87% enrolled. **General Admission Information:** Regular application deadline 1/31. Nonfall registration accepted.

COSTS AND FINANCIAL AID

Financial Aid Statistics: 0% freshmen, 0% undergrads receive athletic scholarships. 0% freshmen, 0% undergrads receive any aid. 0% undergrads borrow to pay for school.

UNITY COLLEGE

90 Quaker Hill Road, Unity, ME 04988
Phone: 800.624.1024 • **Financial Aid Phone:** 207-948-3131 ext 235
E-mail: admissions@unity.edu • **CEEB Code:** 3925
Fax: 207.948.9776 • **Website:** www.unity.edu • **ACT Code:** 3925

This private school was founded in 1965. It has a 225 acre campus.

RATINGS

Admissions Selectivity Rating: 84   **Fire Safety Rating:** 94   **Green Rating:** 95

STUDENTS AND FACULTY

Enrollment: 574. **Student Body:** 55% female, 45% male, 75% out-of-state, 0% international. Asian 1%, African American 1%, Caucasian 93%, Hispanic 2%, Native American 2%, Pacific Islander 0%, Two or more races 1%, Race unknown 0%.
Retention and Graduation: 83% freshmen return for sophomore year. 24% grads go on to further study within 1 year. 22% grads pursue arts and sciences degrees. 1% grads pursue law degrees. **Faculty:** Student/faculty ratio 12:1. 37 full-time faculty, 89% hold PhDs, 0% are members of minority groups, 54% are women. 0% of classes are taught by teaching assistants.

ACADEMICS

Degrees: Associate; Bachelor's **Most popular majors:** Natural Resources Law Enforcement And Protective Services; Wildlife, Fish And Wildlands Science And Management; Wildlife Biology. **Special Study Options:** Accelerated program; Double major; Independent study; Internships; Study abroad; Teacher certification program. Honors programs: Juniors and Seniors with a cumulative grade point average of 3.75 or higher may take one additional credit for no tuition charge. **Disability Services offered to physically disabled students:** Note-taking services; Reader services; Tape recorders; Tutors. **Career services:** Alumni network; Alumni services; Career assessment; Internships

FACILITIES

Housing: Coed dorms; Cooperative housing; Men's dorms; Special housing for disabled student; Theme housing; Women's dorms

CAMPUS LIFE

Environment: Rural **Activities:** Drama/theater; Literary magazine; Student government. Terra Haus, Student Center, Library, Wyman Commons, Unity Rocks **Environmental Initiatives:** We only offer environmental degree programs and every student studies sustainability through our Environmental Stewardship Core curriculum. Campus sustainability efforts are an outgrowth of our academic focus.

ADMISSIONS

Freshman Academic Profile: Average high school GPA 3.3. 14% in top 10% of high school class, 33% in top 25% of high school class, 55% in top 50% of high school class. 97% from public high schools. **Test Scores:** SAT Math middle 50% range 490-560. SAT EBRW middle 50% range 480-560. ACT middle 50% range 22-25. Minimum internet-based TOEFL 79-80. Minimum paper TOEFL 550. **Basis for Candidate Selection:** *Very important factors considered include:* rigor of secondary school record, academic GPA, application essay, level of applicant's interest. *Important factors considered include:* recommendation(s), extracurricular activities, talent/ability, character/personal qualities. *Other factors considered include:* class rank, standardized test scores, interview. **Freshman Admission Requirements:** High school diploma is required and GED is accepted *Academic units required:* 4 English, 3 math, 2 science, 2 science labs, 3 social studies, 3 history, *Academic units recommended:* 4 math, 3 science, 3 science labs, 2 foreign language. **Freshman Admission Statistics:** 737 applied, 61.5% admitted, 38% enrolled. **General Admission Information:** Application fee $25. Priority deadline 12/15. Regular application deadline 2/15. Nonfall registration accepted. Admission may be deferred for a maximum of 3 years.

COSTS AND FINANCIAL AID

Annual tuition $22,440. Room and board $8,380. Required fees $800. Average book expense $500. **Required Forms and Deadlines:** FAFSA. **Types of Aid:** *Need-based scholarships/grants:* College/university scholarship or grant aid from institutional funds; Federal Pell; Private scholarships; SEOG; State scholarships/grants. *Loans:* Direct PLUS loans; Direct Subsidized Stafford Loans; Direct Unsubsidized Stafford Loans. *Student Employment:* Federal Work-Study Program available. Institutional employment available. **Financial Aid Statistics:** 100% needy freshmen, 100% needy undergrads receive need-based scholarship or grant aid. 8% freshmen, 3% undergrads receive non-need-based scholarship or grant aid. 91% freshmen, 95% undergrads receive need-based self-help aid. 0% freshmen, 0% undergrads receive athletic scholarships. 98% freshmen, 98% undergrads receive any aid. **Criteria for awarding aid:** *Non-need-based:* Academics, Leadership, Minority status.

UNIVERSITÉ LAVAL—FACULTÉ DES SCIENCES DE L'ADMINISTRATION

2325 rue de la Terrasse, pavillon, Quebec, QC G1V 0A6
Phone: 418 656-3080 • **Financial Aid Phone:** 418 656-3332
E-mail: reg@reg.ulaval.ca • **CEEB Code:**
Fax: 1 418 656-5216 • **Website:** www.fsa.ulaval.ca • **ACT Code:**

This public school was founded in 1924. It has a 1.92 acre campus.

RATINGS

Admissions Selectivity Rating: 70   **Fire Safety Rating:** 60*   **Green Rating:** 60*

STUDENTS AND FACULTY

Enrollment: 2,009. **Student Body:** 43% female, 57% male, 3% international. Race unknown 97%.
Retention and Graduation: 75% freshmen return for sophomore year.

ACADEMICS

Degrees: Bachelor's; Certificate; Diploma; Master's; Post-Bachelor's certificate **Classes:** Most classes have 10-19 students. Most lab/discussion sessions have 10-19 students. **Special Study Options:** Cooperative education program; Exchange student program (domestic); Internships; Student-designed major; Study abroad. **Disability Services offered to physically disabled students:** Note-taking services; Reader services; Tape recorders. **Career services:** Alumni network; Alumni services; Career/job search classes; Internships

FACILITIES

Housing: Coed dorms; Men's dorms; Women's dorms 100% of campus accessible to physically disabled. **Computers:** 100% of classrooms, 100% of dorms, 100% of libraries, 100% of dining areas, 100% of student union, 100% of common outdoor areas have wireless network access. Students can register for classes online. Administrative functions (other than registration) can be performed online. Undergraduates are required to own a computer.

CAMPUS LIFE

Environment: Metropolis **Activities:** Choral groups; Concert band; Dance; Drama/theater; International Student Organization; Jazz band; Literary magazine; Model UN; Music ensembles; Radio station; Student government; Student newspaper 200 registered organizations. **Athletics (Intercollegiate):** *Men:* badminton, basketball, diving, golf, rugby, skiing (downhill/alpine), skiing (nordic/cross-country), soccer, swimming, track/field (outdoor), track/field (indoor), volleyball. *Women:* badminton, basketball, diving, golf, rugby, skiing (downhill/alpine), skiing (nordic/cross-country), soccer, swimming, track/field (outdoor), track/field (indoor), volleyball. **Environmental Initiatives:** See http://www.developpementdurable.ulaval.ca/agir/la_table_de_concertation_sur_le_developpement_durable/

ADMISSIONS

Basis for Candidate Selection: *Very important factors considered include:* rigor of secondary school record, academic GPA. *Other factors considered include:* standardized test scores, extracurricular activities, work experience. **Freshman Admission Requirements:** High school diploma is required and GED is not accepted **Freshman Admission Statistics:** 1,377 applied, 71.0% admitted, 57% enrolled. **General Admission Information:** Application fee $30. Priority deadline 3/1. Regular application deadline 8/1. Nonfall registration accepted.

COSTS AND FINANCIAL AID

Annual out-of-state tuition $5,956. Average book expense $2,000.

UNIVERSITY OF ADVANCING TECHNOLOGY (UAT)

2625 W. Baseline Rd, Tempe, AZ 85283-1056
Phone: 602-383-8228 • **Financial Aid Phone:** 602-383-8228
E-mail: admissions@uat.edu
Fax: 602-383-8222 • **Website:** www.uat.edu

This proprietary school was founded in 1983.

RATINGS

Admissions Selectivity Rating: 61   **Fire Safety Rating:** 60*   **Green Rating:** 60*

STUDENTS AND FACULTY

Enrollment: 1,090. **Student Body:** 10% female, 90% male, 6% out-of-state, <1% international. Asian 4%, African American 7%, Caucasian 61%, Hispanic 6%, Native American 1%, Race unknown 21%.
Faculty: Student/faculty ratio 12:1. 31 full-time faculty, 16% hold PhDs, 35% are women. 0% of classes are taught by teaching assistants.

ACADEMICS

Degrees: Associate; Bachelor's; **Master's Classes:** Most classes have 10-19 students. **Special Study Options:** Accelerated program; Cooperative education program; Distance learning; Double major; Independent study; Internships; Student-designed major. **Career services:** Alumni network; Alumni services; Career assessment; Career/job search classes; Internships; Regional alumni

FACILITIES

Housing: 100% of campus accessible to physically disabled. **Computers:** Administrative functions (other than registration) can be performed online.

CAMPUS LIFE

Environment: Metropolis **Activities:** Student government 1 religious organizations. **On-Campus Highlights:** The Cafe, UAT Library, Computer Commons, Robotics Lab, Founder's Hall

ADMISSIONS

Test Scores: Minimum paper TOEFL 550. **Basis for Candidate Selection:** *Very important factors considered include:* interview, talent/ability, character/personal qualities, level of applicant's interest. *Important factors considered include:* rigor of secondary school record. *Other factors considered include:* academic GPA, standardized test scores, volunteer work. **Freshman Admission Requirements:** High school diploma is required and GED is accepted **Transfer Admission Requirements:** High school transcript, college transcript(s), Minimum college GPA of 2.0 required. Lowest grade transferable C. **General Admission Information:** Nonfall registration accepted. Admission may be deferred for a maximum of 1 year.

COSTS AND FINANCIAL AID

Annual tuition $19,400. Average book expense $1,000. **Required Forms and Deadlines:** FAFSA. **Types of Aid:** *Need-based scholarships/grants:* College/university scholarship or grant aid from institutional funds; Federal Pell;

Private scholarships; SEOG. *Loans: Student Employment:* Federal Work-Study Program available.

THE UNIVERSITY OF AKRON

302 Buchtel Common, Akron, OH 44325-2001
Phone: 330-972-7100 • **Financial Aid Phone:** 800-621-3847
E-mail: admissions@uakron.edu • **CEEB Code:** 1829
Fax: 330-972-7022 • **Website:** www.uakron.edu • **ACT Code:** 3338

This public school was founded in 1870. It has a 223 acre campus.

RATINGS

Admissions Selectivity Rating: 74   **Fire Safety Rating:** 92   **Green Rating:** 60*

STUDENTS AND FACULTY

Enrollment: 18,137. **Student Body:** 47% female, 53% male, 4% out-of-state, 2% international (61 countries represented). Asian 2%, African American 13%, Caucasian 74%, Hispanic 2%, Native American <1%, Pacific Islander <1%, Two or more races 3%, Race unknown 3%.
Retention and Graduation: 74% freshmen return for sophomore year.
Faculty: Student/faculty ratio 19:1. 792 full-time faculty, 79% hold PhDs, 21% are members of minority groups, 42% are women. 4% of classes are taught by teaching assistants.

ACADEMICS

Degrees: Associate; Bachelor's; Certificate; Doctoral; Doctoral/Professional; Doctoral/Research; Master's; Post-Bachelor's certificate; Post-Master's certificate **Classes:** Most classes have 10-19 students. Most lab/discussion sessions have 10-19 students. **Most popular majors:** Mechanical Engineering; Biology/Biological Sciences, General; Marketing/Marketing Management, General. **Special Study Options:** Accelerated program; Cooperative education program; Distance learning; Double major; English as a Second Language (ESL); External degree program; Honors program; Independent study; Internships; Student-designed major; Study abroad; Teacher certification program; Weekend college. Honors programs: Honors Delegates, Engineering Program, Emerging Leaders Program Combined degree programs: BA/MD. **Disability Services offered to physically disabled students:** Note-taking services; Reader services; Tape recorders; Tutors. **Career services:** Alumni services; Career assessment; Career/job search classes; Internships

FACILITIES

Housing: Coed dorms; Fraternity/sorority housing; Men's dorms; Special housing for disabled student; Special housing for international students; Women's dorms 90% of campus accessible to physically diasbled. **Special Academic Facilities/Equipment:** Performing arts hall, nursery center, language lab, speech and hearing center, nursing learning resource labs, institute of polymer science and engineering, chemical lab, institute for health and social policy, Bliss Institute of Applied Politics, **Computers:** 100% of classrooms, 100% of dorms, 100% of libraries, 100% of dining areas, 100% of student union, 100% of common outdoor areas have wireless network access. Students can register for classes online. Administrative functions (other than registration) can be performed online.

CAMPUS LIFE

Environment: City **Activities:** Campus Ministries; Choral groups; Concert band; Dance; Drama/theater; International Student Organization; Jazz band; Marching band; Music ensembles; Musical theater; Pep band; Radio station; Student government; Student newspaper; Symphony orchestra; Television station; Yearbook 216 registered organizations, 30 honor societies, 12 religious organizations. 15 fraternities, 8 sororities. **Athletics (Intercollegiate):** *Men:* baseball, basketball, cheerleading, cross-country, football, golf, riflery, soccer, track/field (outdoor), track/field (indoor). *Women:* basketball, cheerleading, cross-country, diving, riflery, soccer, softball, swimming, tennis, track/field (outdoor), track/field (indoor), volleyball. **On-Campus Highlights:** Recreation Center, Student Union (includes food court, Starbucks), E.J. Thomas Performing Arts Hall, James A. Rhodes Arena, Robertson Cafe

ADMISSIONS

Freshman Academic Profile: Average high school GPA 3.2. 13% in top 10% of high school class, 38% in top 25% of high school class, 66% in top 50% of high school class. **Test Scores:** SAT Math middle 50% range 450-620. SAT EBRW middle 50% range 450-580. ACT middle 50% range 19-26. Minimum internet-based TOEFL 79. Minimum paper TOEFL 550. **Basis for Candidate Selection:** *Very important factors considered include:* rigor of secondary school record, class rank, academic GPA, standardized test scores. *Other factors considered include:* application essay, recommendation(s), extracurricular

activities, talent/ability, volunteer work, level of applicant's interest. **Freshman Admission Requirements:** High school diploma is required and GED is accepted *Academic units recommended:* 4 English, 3 math, 3 science, 2 foreign language, 3 social studies. **Freshman Admission Statistics:** 13,109 applied, 86.9% admitted, 32% enrolled. **Transfer Admission Requirements:** college transcript(s), statement of good standing from prior institution(s). Lowest grade transferable D-. **General Admission Information:** Application fee $45. Regular application deadline 7/1. Nonfall registration accepted. Admission may be deferred for a maximum of 2 semesters.

COSTS AND FINANCIAL AID

Annual in-state tuition $11,322. Annual out-of-state tuition $17,149. Room and board $11,322. Required fees $1,891. Average book expense $1,000. **Required Forms and Deadlines:** FAFSA; Institution's own financial aid form. **Notification of Awards:** Applicants will be notified of awards on a rolling basis beginning 4/1. **Types of Aid:** *Need-based scholarships/grants:* Federal Pell; SEOG. *Loans:* Direct PLUS loans; Direct Subsidized Stafford Loans; Direct Unsubsidized Stafford Loans. *Student Employment:* Federal Work-Study Program available. Institutional employment available. **Financial Aid Statistics:** 55% needy freshmen, 53% needy undergrads receive need-based scholarship or grant aid. 62% freshmen, 52% undergrads receive non-need-based scholarship or grant aid. 74% freshmen, 72% undergrads receive need-based self-help aid. 0% freshmen, 0% undergrads receive athletic scholarships. 78% freshmen, 81% undergrads receive any aid. **Criteria for awarding aid:** *Non-need-based:* Academics, Art, Athletics, Leadership, Music/drama, State/district residency.

THE UNIVERSITY OF ALABAMA AT BIRMINGHAM

1720 2nd Ave S, Birmingham, AL 35294-4412
Phone: 205-934-8221 • **Financial Aid Phone:** 205-934-8223
E-mail: chooseuab@uab.edu • **CEEB Code:** 1856
Fax: 205-975-7114 • **Website:** www.uab.edu • **ACT Code:** 56

This public school was founded in 1969. It has a 275 acre campus.

RATINGS

Admissions Selectivity Rating: 76   **Fire Safety Rating:** 95   **Green Rating:** 81

STUDENTS AND FACULTY

Enrollment: 12,811. **Student Body:** 60% female, 40% male, 11% out-of-state, 2% international (53 countries represented). Asian 6%, African American 26%, Caucasian 58%, Hispanic 3%, Native American <1%, Pacific Islander <1%, Two or more races 4%, Race unknown 1%.
Retention and Graduation: 82% freshmen return for sophomore year.
Faculty: Student/faculty ratio 18:1. 858 full-time faculty, 86% hold PhDs, 22% are members of minority groups, 47% are women. 3% of classes are taught by teaching assistants.

ACADEMICS

Degrees: Bachelor's; Certificate; Doctoral; Doctoral Other; Doctoral/Professional; Doctoral/Research; Master's; Post-Bachelor's certificate; Post-Master's certificate **Classes:** Most classes have fewer than 10 students. Most lab/discussion sessions have fewer than 10 students. **Most popular majors:** Speech Communication And Rhetoric; Biology/Biological Sciences, General; Psychology, General. **Special Study Options:** Accelerated program; Cooperative education program; Cross-registration; Distance learning; Double major; Dual enrollment; English as a Second Language (ESL); Exchange student program (domestic); Honors program; Independent study; Internships; Student-designed major; Study abroad; Teacher certification program. Honors programs: The University Honors Program is designed for students who want to satisfy their intellectual curiosity both inside and outside the classroom. The program is limited in size to 200 students who represent a wide variety of disciplines, backgrounds and interests. Without delaying progress toward a degree, the Honors College provides students an opportunity to participate in a community of committed scholars, to form close relationships with faculty, to explore new ideas, and to share their ideas, interests, and lives on a daily basis in the Honors House. Students have opportunities to work on independent projects, to travel, and to participate in special extracurricular activities. Those who complete the program are recognized with the designation "With

University Honors" on their transcripts and in the graduation program. Please visit our Univeristy Honors Program website for more information: http://main.uab.edu/Sites/undergraduate-programs/honors_college/ Combined degree programs: BA/MA; BA/MD. **Disability Services offered to physically disabled students:** Note-taking services; Reader services; Tape recorders. **Career services:** Alumni network; Alumni services; Career assessment; Career/job search classes; Internships; Regional alumni

FACILITIES

Housing: Apartments for married students; Apartments for single students; Coed dorms; Special housing for disabled student; Special housing for international students; Theme housing 100% of campus accessible to physically diasbled. **Special Academic Facilities/Equipment:** Museum of health sciences, Alys Stephens Center for the performing arts, Samuel Ullman Museum, Abroms-Engel Institute for the Visual Arts **Computers:** Students can register for classes online. Administrative functions (other than registration) can be performed online.

CAMPUS LIFE

Environment: Metropolis **Activities:** Campus Ministries; Choral groups; Concert band; Dance; Drama/theater; International Student Organization; Jazz band; Literary magazine; Marching band; Music ensembles; Musical theater; Opera; Pep band; Radio station; Student government; Student newspaper 150 registered organizations, 45 honor societies, 9 religious organizations. 9 fraternities, 8 sororities. **Athletics (Intercollegiate):** *Men:* baseball, basketball, football, golf, soccer, tennis. *Women:* basketball, cross-country, golf, riflery, soccer, softball, synchronized swimming, tennis, track/field (outdoor), track/field (indoor), volleyball. **On-Campus Highlights:** Student Recreation Center, Commons Dining Hall, Blazer Hall, Heritage Hall, Sterne Library **Environmental Initiatives:** Recycling

ADMISSIONS

Freshman Academic Profile: Average high school GPA 3.7. 28% in top 10% of high school class, 55% in top 25% of high school class, 83% in top 50% of high school class. **Test Scores:** ACT middle 50% range 21-28. Minimum internet-based TOEFL 77. **Basis for Candidate Selection:** *Very important factors considered include:* rigor of secondary school record, academic GPA, standardized test scores. **Freshman Admission Requirements:** High school diploma is required and GED is accepted *Academic units required:* 4 English, 3 math, 3 science, 2 science labs, 1 foreign language, 3 social studies, 3 academic electives. **Freshman Admission Statistics:** 7,555 applied, 91.8% admitted, 33% enrolled. **Transfer Admission Requirements:** college transcript(s), Minimum college GPA of 2.0 required. **General Admission Information:** Application fee $30. Priority deadline 6/1. Nonfall registration accepted. Admission may be deferred for a maximum of 1 year.

COSTS AND FINANCIAL AID

Annual out-of-state tuition $23,790. Room and board $11,682. Average book expense $1,200. **Required Forms and Deadlines:** FAFSA. **Notification of Awards:** Applicants will be notified of awards on a rolling basis beginning 3/15. **Types of Aid:** *Need-based scholarships/grants:* College/university scholarship or grant aid from institutional funds; Federal Pell; Private scholarships; SEOG; State scholarships/grants; United Negro College Fund. *Loans:* Direct PLUS loans; Direct Subsidized Stafford Loans; Direct Unsubsidized Stafford Loans. *Student Employment:* Federal Work-Study Program available. Institutional employment available. **Financial Aid Statistics:** 61% needy freshmen, 89% needy undergrads receive need-based scholarship or grant aid. 71% freshmen, 45% undergrads receive non-need-based scholarship or grant aid. 70% freshmen, 76% undergrads receive need-based self-help aid. 4% freshmen, 4% undergrads receive athletic scholarships. 63% undergrads borrow to pay for school. Average cumulative indebtedness $31,610. **Criteria for awarding aid:** *Need-based:* Academics, Alumni affiliation, Minority status *Non-need-based:* Academics, Alumni affiliation, Art, Athletics, Leadership, Minority status, Music/drama.

THE UNIVERSITY OF ALABAMA IN HUNTSVILLE

301 Sparkman Drive, Huntsville, AL 35899
Phone: 256-824-2773 • **Financial Aid Phone:** 256-824-2761
E-mail: uahadmissions@uah.edu • **CEEB Code:** 1854
Fax: 256-824-4539 • **Website:** www.uah.edu • **ACT Code:** 53

This public school was founded in 1950. It has a 400 acre campus.

RATINGS

Admissions Selectivity Rating: 82   **Fire Safety Rating:** 96   **Green Rating:** 73

STUDENTS AND FACULTY

Enrollment: 6,338. **Student Body:** 42% female, 58% male, 16% out-of-state, 3% international (75 countries represented). Asian 4%, African American 11%, Caucasian 72%, Hispanic 4%, Native American 1%, Pacific Islander 0%, Two or more races 2%, Race unknown 3%.
Retention and Graduation: 83% freshmen return for sophomore year. **Faculty:** Student/faculty ratio 17:1. 326 full-time faculty, 79% hold PhDs, 25% are members of minority groups, 43% are women. 3% of classes are taught by teaching assistants.

ACADEMICS

Degrees: Bachelor's; Certificate; Doctoral; Doctoral/Professional; Doctoral/Research; Master's; Post-Bachelor's certificate; Post-Master's certificate **Classes:** Most classes have 10-19 students. **Most popular majors:** Mechanical Engineering; Biology/Biological Sciences, General; Registered Nursing/Registered Nurse. **Special Study Options:** Cooperative education program; Cross-registration; Distance learning; Double major; Dual enrollment; English as a Second Language (ESL); Honors program; Independent study; Internships; Student-designed major; Study abroad; Teacher certification program. Honors programs: The Honors College at UAH provides academically talented undergraduate students with opportunities to develop their special talents and skills within an expanded and enriched version of the curriculum leading to an Honors Diploma. Honors coursework parallels regular offerings in all majors and programs. The courses include special interdisciplinary seminars, and opportunities for independent study and research/creative work, including the opportunity to work closely with faculty on special student projects. Students may participate in an Honors internship that offers active involvement in a business enterprise, professional organization, or government agency that has particular interest and relevance to the student's course of study. Participating students also benefit from the interaction the Honors College affords with other talented and highly motivated students. See http://honors.uah.edu for more information. Combined degree programs: BA/MA; BA/MEng. **Disability Services offered to physically disabled students:** Note-taking services; Reader services; Tutors. **Career services:** Alumni services; Career assessment; Career/job search classes; Internships

FACILITIES

Housing: Apartments for married students; Apartments for single students; Coed dorms; Cooperative housing; Fraternity/sorority housing; Special housing for disabled student; Theme housing 98% of campus accessible to physically diasbled. **Special Academic Facilities/Equipment:** UAH has an art museum and galleries, an optical observatory, a radio telescope, and a rooftop greenhouse used for research and lab experiences. The National Space and Technology Center located on our campus is shared between UAH, NASA and the National Weather Service. **Computers:** 25% of classrooms, 30% of dorms, 100% of libraries, 100% of dining areas, 100% of student union, 90% of common outdoor areas have wireless network access. Students can register for classes online. Administrative functions (other than registration) can be performed online.

CAMPUS LIFE

Environment: City **Activities:** Campus Ministries; Choral groups; Concert band; Dance; Drama/theater; International Student Organization; Jazz band; Model UN; Music ensembles; Musical theater; Opera; Pep band; Student government; Student newspaper 52 registered organizations, 24 honor societies, 5 religious organizations. 7 fraternities, 4 sororities. **Athletics (Intercollegiate):** *Men:* baseball, basketball, cheerleading, cross-country, ice hockey, soccer, tennis, track/field (outdoor), track/field (indoor). *Women:* basketball, cheerleading, cross-country, soccer, softball, tennis, track/field (outdoor), track/field (indoor), volleyball. **On-Campus Highlights:** Charger Union, University Fitness Center, Charger Village, Central Campus Residence Hall, Shelby Center **Environmental Initiatives:** A hazard chemical waste and waste minimization program has been in effect for over 15 years. Improved environmental awareness communications and training/learning opportunities will soon be available on the OEHS web site.

ADMISSIONS

Freshman Academic Profile: Average high school GPA 3.8. 29% in top 10% of high school class, 56% in top 25% of high school class, 85% in top 50% of high school class. 90% from public high schools. **Test Scores:** SAT Math middle 50% range 540-680. SAT EBRW middle 50% range 520-650. ACT middle 50% range 25-31. Minimum internet-based TOEFL 62. Minimum paper TOEFL 500. **Basis for Candidate Selection:** *Very important factors considered include:* academic GPA, standardized test scores. *Other factors considered include:* level of applicant's interest. **Freshman Admission Requirements:** High school diploma is required and GED is accepted *Academic units required:* 4 English, 3 math, 3 science, 4 social studies, 6 academic electives, *Academic units recommended:* 4 English, 4 math, 4 science, 2 science labs, 2 foreign language, 4 social studies, 6 academic electives. **Freshman Admission Statistics:** 4,545 applied, 76.3% admitted, 21% enrolled. **Transfer Admission Requirements:** college transcript(s), statement of good standing from prior institution(s). Minimum college GPA of 2.0 required. Lowest grade transferable D. **General Admission Information:** Application fee $30. Regular application deadline 8/20. Nonfall registration accepted. Admission may be deferred for a maximum of 1 year.

COSTS AND FINANCIAL AID

Annual in-state tuition $9,603. Annual out-of-state tuition $19,766. Room and board $9,603. Required fees $846. Average book expense $1,688. **Required Forms and Deadlines:** FAFSA. **Notification of Awards:** Applicants will be notified of awards on a rolling basis beginning 4/1. **Types of Aid:** *Need-based scholarships/grants:* College/university scholarship or grant aid from institutional funds; Federal Nursing Scholarships; Federal Pell; Private scholarships; SEOG; State scholarships/grants. *Loans:* Direct PLUS loans; Direct Subsidized Stafford Loans; Direct Unsubsidized Stafford Loans. *Student Employment:* Federal Work-Study Program available. Institutional employment available. **Financial Aid Statistics:** 87% needy freshmen, 84% needy undergrads receive need-based scholarship or grant aid. 26% freshmen, 10% undergrads receive non-need-based scholarship or grant aid. 67% freshmen, 80% undergrads receive need-based self-help aid. 6% freshmen, 4% undergrads receive athletic scholarships. 88% freshmen, 78% undergrads receive any aid. 54% undergrads borrow to pay for school. Average cumulative indebtedness $35,009. **Criteria for awarding aid:** *Non-need-based:* Academics, Art, Athletics, Leadership, Minority status, Music/drama.

THE UNIVERSITY OF ALABAMA—TUSCALOOSA

Box 870100, Tuscaloosa, AL 35487-0132
Phone: 205-348-5666 • **Financial Aid Phone:** 205-348-7949
E-mail: admissions@ua.edu • **CEEB Code:** 1830
Fax: 205-348-9046 • **Website:** www.ua.edu • **ACT Code:** 52

This public school was founded in 1831. It has a 1026 acre campus.

RATINGS

Admissions Selectivity Rating: 89   **Fire Safety Rating:** 81   **Green Rating:** 60*

STUDENTS AND FACULTY

Enrollment: 32,387. **Student Body:** 56% female, 44% male, 60% out-of-state, 2% international (60 countries represented). Asian 1%, African American 10%, Caucasian 78%, Hispanic 5%, Native American <1%, Pacific Islander <1%, Two or more races 3%, Race unknown <1%.
Retention and Graduation: 87% freshmen return for sophomore year. 44% freshmen graduate within 4 years. 68% freshmen graduate within 6 years. 28% grads go on to further study within 1 year. 5% grads pursue arts and sciences degrees. 3% grads pursue law degrees. 7% grads pursue business degrees. 3% grads pursue medical degrees. **Faculty:** Student/faculty ratio 23:1. 1,382 full-time faculty, 81% hold PhDs, 20% are members of minority groups, 45% are women. 29% of classes are taught by teaching assistants.

ACADEMICS

Degrees: Bachelor's; Doctoral/Professional; Doctoral/Research; Master's; Post-Master's certificate **Classes:** Most classes have 20-29 students. Most lab/discussion sessions have 20-29 students. **Most popular majors:** Mechanical Engineering; Registered Nursing/Registered Nurse; Finance, General. **Special Study Options:** Accelerated program; Cooperative education program; Cross-registration; Distance learning; Double major; Dual enrollment; English as a Second Language (ESL); Exchange student program (domestic); External degree program; Honors program; Independent study; Internships; Liberal arts/career combination; Student-designed major; Study abroad; Teacher certification program; Weekend college. Honors programs: The Honors College serves its students through the core Honors experience and other specialized programs, including the Randall Research Scholars Program and the University Fellows Experience. The Honors College also works collaboratively with other Colleges to create unique partnerships and departmental honors programs throughout the University, allowing Honors students to major in any discipline and adding to the diversity of the Honors experience. Students concentrating their studies in either a STEM discipline or in a traditionally creative discipline have the opportunity to complete coursework to earn an MBA from the Manderson Graduate School of Business in only one calendar year beyond the completion of an undergraduate degree. The STEM Path to the MBA and CREATE Path to the MBA programs are centered around innovative solutions to real-world problems and run in parallel to one another. The Accelerated Masters Program (AMP) allows Honors students to earn up to 15 dual-credit

hours towards a bachelors and masters degrees. Combined degree programs: BA/MA; BA/MEng. **Disability Services offered to physically disabled students:** Note-taking services; Reader services; Tape recorders; Tutors. **Career services:** Alumni network; Alumni services; Career assessment; Career/job search classes; Internships; Regional alumni

FACILITIES

Housing: Apartments for single students; Coed dorms; Fraternity/sorority housing; Men's dorms; Special housing for disabled student; Special housing for international students; Theme housing; Women's dorms 99% of campus accessible to physically disabled. **Special Academic Facilities/Equipment:** Art gallery, natural history museum, concert hall, archaeologic site and museum, arboretum, observatory, simulated coal mine, robotics lab, wind tunnel, artificial intelligence lab, jet propulsion engine mini-lab, special collections building. **Computers:** 55% of classrooms, 100% of dorms, 100% of libraries, 75% of dining areas, 100% of student union, 22% of common outdoor areas have wireless network access. Students can register for classes online. Administrative functions (other than registration) can be performed online.

CAMPUS LIFE

Environment: City **Activities:** Campus Ministries; Choral groups; Concert band; Dance; Drama/theater; International Student Organization; Jazz band; Literary magazine; Marching band; Model UN; Music ensembles; Musical theater; Opera; Pep band; Radio station; Student government; Student newspaper; Student-run film society; Symphony orchestra; Television station 294 registered organizations, 66 honor societies, 30 religious organizations. 31 fraternities, 23 sororities. **Athletics (Intercollegiate):** *Men:* baseball, basketball, cross-country, diving, football, golf, swimming, tennis, track/field (outdoor), track/field (indoor). *Women:* basketball, crew/rowing, cross-country, diving, golf, gymnastics, soccer, softball, swimming, tennis, track/field (outdoor), track/field (indoor), volleyball. **On-Campus Highlights:** Ferguson Center Student Union, Amelia Gayle Gorgas Library, Bryant-Denny Stadium, Malone-Hood Plaza/Foster Auditorium, Museum of Natural History **Environmental Initiatives:** Recycling has increased by 181% over fiscal year 2008. Currently we are recycling over 1,300 tons of recyclable material.

ADMISSIONS

Freshman Academic Profile: Average high school GPA 3.7. 39% in top 10% of high school class, 60% in top 25% of high school class, 83% in top 50% of high school class. **Test Scores:** SAT Math middle 50% range 520-640. SAT EBRW middle 50% range 530-640. ACT middle 50% range 23-32. Minimum internet-based TOEFL 79. Minimum paper TOEFL 550. **Basis for Candidate Selection:** *Very important factors considered include:* rigor of secondary school record, academic GPA, standardized test scores. *Important factors considered include:* class rank. *Other factors considered include:* application essay, recommendation(s), interview, extracurricular activities, talent/ability, character/personal qualities, first generation, alumni/ae relation, volunteer work, work experience. **Freshman Admission Requirements:** High school diploma is required and GED is accepted *Academic units required:* 4 English, 3 math, 3 science, 2 science labs, 1 foreign language, 4 social studies, 5 academic electives, *Academic units recommended:* 4 English, 3 math, 3 science, 2 science labs, 2 foreign language, 4 social studies, 5 academic electives. **Freshman Admission Statistics:** 38,129 applied, 53.3% admitted, 36% enrolled. **Transfer Admission Requirements:** college transcript(s), Minimum college GPA of 2.0 required. Lowest grade transferable D. **General Admission Information:** Application fee $40. Priority deadline 2/1. Nonfall registration accepted. Admission may be deferred for a maximum of one year.

COSTS AND FINANCIAL AID

Annual in-state tuition $9,974. Annual out-of-state tuition $28,100. Room and board $9,974. Average book expense $1,200. **Required Forms and Deadlines:** FAFSA. **Notification of Awards:** Applicants will be notified of awards on a rolling basis beginning 4/1. **Types of Aid:** *Need-based scholarships/grants:* College/university scholarship or grant aid from institutional funds; Federal Nursing Scholarships; Federal Pell; Private scholarships; SEOG; State scholarships/grants. *Loans:* Direct PLUS loans; Direct Subsidized Stafford Loans; Direct Unsubsidized Stafford Loans. *Student Employment:* Federal Work-Study Program available. Institutional employment available. **Financial Aid Statistics:** 79% needy freshmen, 75% needy undergrads receive need-based scholarship or grant aid. 66% freshmen, 51% undergrads receive non-need-based scholarship or grant aid. 68% freshmen, 78% undergrads receive need-based self-help aid. 2% freshmen, 2% undergrads receive athletic scholarships. 81% freshmen, 73% undergrads receive any aid. 47% undergrads borrow to pay for school. Average cumulative indebtedness $33,816. **Criteria for awarding aid:** *Need-based:* Academics *Non-need-based:* Academics, Alumni affiliation, Art, Athletics, Leadership, Minority status, Music/drama, State/district residency.

UNIVERSITY OF ALASKA ANCHORAGE

3211 Providence Drive, Anchorage, AK 99508-8046
Phone: 907-786-1480
E-mail: enroll@uaa.alaska.edu • **CEEB Code:** 4896
Fax: 907-786-4888 • **Website:** www.uaa.alaska.edu/ • **ACT Code:** 137

This public school was founded in 1954. It has a 384 acre campus.

RATINGS
Admissions Selectivity Rating: 73   **Fire Safety Rating:** 75   **Green Rating:** 60*

STUDENTS AND FACULTY
Enrollment: 13,390. **Student Body:** 58% female, 42% male, 10% out-of-state, <1% international (35 countries represented). Asian 7%, African American 4%, Caucasian 58%, Hispanic 7%, Native American 12%, Pacific Islander 1%, Two or more races 3%, Race unknown 6%.
Retention and Graduation: 73% freshmen return for sophomore year.
Faculty: Student/faculty ratio 12:1. 680 full-time faculty, 53% hold PhDs, 12% are members of minority groups, 52% are women. 0% of classes are taught by teaching assistants.

ACADEMICS
Degrees: Associate; Bachelor's; Certificate; Master's; Post-Bachelor's certificate; Post-Master's certificate **Classes:** Most classes have 10-19 students. Most lab/discussion sessions have 20-29 students. **Special Study Options:** Accelerated program; Cooperative education program; Cross-registration; Distance learning; Double major; Dual enrollment; English as a Second Language (ESL); Exchange student program (domestic); Honors program; Independent study; Internships; Liberal arts/career combination; Student-designed major; Study abroad; Teacher certification program. Honors programs: University Honors Program. **Disability Services offered to physically disabled students:** Note-taking services; Reader services; Tape recorders. **Career services:** Alumni services; Career assessment; Career/job search classes; Internships

FACILITIES
Housing: Apartments for single students; Coed dorms; Special housing for disabled student; Special housing for international students; Wellness housing 95% of campus accessible to physically diasbled. **Special Academic Facilities/Equipment:** Kimura and student Center Galleries. **Computers:** Students can register for classes online. Administrative functions (other than registration) can be performed online.

CAMPUS LIFE
Environment: City **Activities:** Campus Ministries; Choral groups; Dance; Drama/theater; International Student Organization; Jazz band; Literary magazine; Model UN; Music ensembles; Musical theater; Opera; Radio station; Student government; Student newspaper; Student-run film society 70 registered organizations, 5 honor societies, 5 religious organizations. 1 fraternity, 2 sororities. **Athletics (Intercollegiate):** *Men:* basketball, cross-country, ice hockey, skiing (downhill/alpine), skiing (nordic/cross-country). *Women:* basketball, cross-country, gymnastics, skiing (downhill/alpine), skiing (nordic/cross-country), volleyball. **On-Campus Highlights:** Campus Center, Wells Fargo Sports Center, Creekside Eatery, Cuddy Center, Student Health Center

ADMISSIONS
Freshman Academic Profile: 13% in top 10% of high school class, 32% in top 25% of high school class, 62% in top 50% of high school class. 95% from public high schools. **Test Scores:** SAT Math middle 50% range 440-570. SAT EBRW middle 50% range 430-580. Minimum paper TOEFL 450. **Basis for Candidate Selection:** *Very important factors considered include:* rigor of secondary school record. *Other factors considered include:* class rank, standardized test scores, talent/ability. **Freshman Admission Requirements:** High school diploma is required and GED is accepted **Freshman Admission Statistics:** 2,976 applied, 100.0% admitted, 61% enrolled. **Transfer Admission Requirements:** college transcript(s), statement of good standing from prior institution(s). Minimum college GPA of 2.0 required. Lowest grade transferable C. **General Admission Information:** Application fee $50. Regular application deadline 7/1. Nonfall registration accepted. Admission may be deferred for a maximum of 1 year.

COSTS AND FINANCIAL AID
Annual in-state tuition $9,827. Annual out-of-state tuition $17,400. Room and board $9,827. Required fees $832. Average book expense $1,575. **Required Forms and Deadlines:** FAFSA; Institution's own financial aid form. **Notification of Awards:** Applicants will be notified of awards on a rolling basis beginning 3/15. **Types of Aid:** *Need-based scholarships/grants:* College/university scholarship or grant aid from institutional funds; Federal Pell; Private scholarships; SEOG; State scholarships/grants. *Loans:* Student Employment:

Federal Work-Study Program available. Institutional employment available. **Financial Aid Statistics:** 84% needy freshmen, 74% needy undergrads receive need-based scholarship or grant aid. 11% freshmen, 3% undergrads receive non-need-based scholarship or grant aid. 66% freshmen, 75% undergrads receive need-based self-help aid. 2% freshmen, 1% undergrads receive athletic scholarships. **Criteria for awarding aid:** *Need-based:* Academics, Leadership, Minority status *Non-need-based:* Academics, Athletics.

UNIVERSITY OF ALASKA FAIRBANKS

PO Box 757500, Fairbanks, AK 99775-7480
Phone: 907-474-7500 • **Financial Aid Phone:** 888-474-7256
E-mail: admissions@uaf.edu • **CEEB Code:** 4866
Fax: 907-474-5379 • **Website:** www.uaf.edu • **ACT Code:** 64

This public school was founded in 1917. It has a 2250 acre campus.

RATINGS
Admissions Selectivity Rating: 85   **Fire Safety Rating:** 93   **Green Rating:** 60*

STUDENTS AND FACULTY
Enrollment: 5,445. **Student Body:** 55% female, 45% male, 14% out-of-state, 1% international (29 countries represented). Asian 1%, African American 2%, Caucasian 42%, Hispanic 6%, Native American 14%, Pacific Islander <1%, Two or more races 4%, Race unknown 29%.
Retention and Graduation: 75% freshmen return for sophomore year.
Faculty: Student/faculty ratio 11:1. 357 full-time faculty, 76% hold PhDs, 20% are members of minority groups, 43% are women.

ACADEMICS
Degrees: Associate; Bachelor's; Certificate; Doctoral/Research; Master's; Post-Bachelor's certificate; Terminal Associate; Transfer Associate **Classes:** Most classes have 10-19 students. **Most popular majors:** Mechanical Engineering; Biology/Biological Sciences, General; Business Administration And Management, General. **Special Study Options:** Accelerated program; Cooperative education program; Distance learning; Double major; Dual enrollment; English as a Second Language (ESL); Exchange student program (domestic); External degree program; Honors program; Independent study; Internships; Student-designed major; Study abroad; Teacher certification program. Honors programs: The Honors Program at UAF provides superior undergraduate students with intellectual opportunities greater than those generally found in university lecture halls. Honors students experience small classes, direct contact with top faculty members, a flexible curriculum and great encouragement to pursue their own intellectual interests. **Disability Services offered to physically disabled students:** Note-taking services; Reader services; Tape recorders; Tutors. **Career services:** Alumni network; Alumni services; Career assessment; Career/job search classes; Internships

FACILITIES
Housing: Apartments for married students; Apartments for single students; Coed dorms; Special housing for disabled student; Wellness housing 90% of campus accessible to physically diasbled. **Special Academic Facilities/Equipment:** Museum of natural/cultural history of Alaska and the North, Super Computer, extensive telecommunication network, Geophysical Institute, NASA earth station, Poker Flat Research Range, electron microscope, microprobe, International Arctic Research Center, Institute of Arctic Biology, Institute of Northern Engineering, Arctic Region Supercomputing Center, Institute of Marine Biology, Agriculture and Forestry Experiment Station, Office of Electronic Miniaturization, Alaska Native Language Center, Georgeson Botanical Gardens, Cold Climate Housing Research Center,Large Animal Research Station **Computers:** 100% of classrooms, 100% of dorms, 100% of libraries, 100% of dining areas, 100% of student union, 50% of common outdoor areas have wireless network access. Students can register for classes online. Administrative functions (other than registration) can be performed online.

CAMPUS LIFE
Environment: City **Activities:** Campus Ministries; Choral groups; Dance; Drama/theater; International Student Organization; Jazz band; Literary magazine; Model UN; Music ensembles; Radio station; Student government; Student newspaper; Symphony orchestra 122 registered organizations, 11 honor societies, 10 religious organizations. 1 fraternity, 1 sorority. **Athletics (Intercollegiate):** *Men:* basketball, cross-country, ice hockey, riflery, skiing (nordic/cross-country). *Women:* basketball, cross-country, riflery, skiing (nordic/cross-country), volleyball. **On-Campus Highlights:** Wood Center (includes food court), Student Recreation Center (SRC), Rasmuson Library, Groomed cross-country ski trails on campus, Hess Recreation Center

ADMISSIONS

Freshman Academic Profile: Average high school GPA 3.3. 18% in top 10% of high school class, 38% in top 25% of high school class, 69% in top 50% of high school class. **Test Scores:** SAT Math middle 50% range 480-610. SAT EBRW middle 50% range 480-610. ACT middle 50% range 18-26. Minimum internet-based TOEFL 79. **Basis for Candidate Selection:** *Very important factors considered include:* academic GPA, standardized test scores. **Freshman Admission Requirements:** High school diploma is required and GED is not accepted *Academic units required:* 4 English, 3 math, 3 science, 1 science labs, 3 social studies, *Academic units recommended:* 2 foreign language. **Freshman Admission Statistics:** 1,554 applied, 73.1% admitted, 70% enrolled. **Transfer Admission Requirements:** college transcript(s), Minimum college GPA of 2.0 required. Lowest grade transferable C. **General Admission Information:** Application fee $50. Priority deadline 2/15. Regular application deadline 6/15. Nonfall registration accepted. Admission may be deferred for a maximum of 1 year.

COSTS AND FINANCIAL AID

Annual in-state tuition $8,380. Annual out-of-state tuition $21,030. Room and board $8,380. Required fees $1,439. Average book expense $1,400. **Required Forms and Deadlines:** FAFSA; Institution's own financial aid form. **Notification of Awards:** Applicants will be notified of awards on a rolling basis beginning 3/1. **Types of Aid:** *Need-based scholarships/grants:* College/university scholarship or grant aid from institutional funds; Federal Pell; Private scholarships; SEOG; State scholarships/grants. *Loans:* Direct PLUS loans; Direct Subsidized Stafford Loans; Direct Unsubsidized Stafford Loans. *Student Employment:* Federal Work-Study Program available. Institutional employment available. **Financial Aid Statistics:** 89% needy freshmen, 87% needy undergrads receive need-based scholarship or grant aid. 14% freshmen, 9% undergrads receive non-need-based scholarship or grant aid. 44% freshmen, 59% undergrads receive need-based self-help aid. 2% freshmen, 3% undergrads receive athletic scholarships. 79% freshmen, 68% undergrads receive any aid. 48% undergrads borrow to pay for school. Average cumulative indebtedness $27,805. **Criteria for awarding aid:** *Need-based:* Academics *Non-need-based:* Academics, Art, Athletics, Music/drama, State/district residency.

UNIVERSITY OF ARIZONA

PO Box 210066, Tucson, AZ 85721-0073
Phone: 520-621-3237 • **Financial Aid Phone:** 520-621-1858
E-mail: admissions@arizona.edu • **CEEB Code:** 4832
Fax: 520-621-9799 • **Website:** http://www.arizona.edu • **ACT Code:** 96

This public school was founded in 1885. It has a 392 acre campus.

RATINGS

Admissions Selectivity Rating: 81   **Fire Safety Rating:** 91   **Green Rating:** 94

STUDENTS AND FACULTY

Enrollment: 34,049. **Student Body:** 52% female, 48% male, 31% out-of-state, 7% international (129 countries represented). Asian 5%, African American 4%, Caucasian 50%, Hispanic 27%, Native American 1%, Pacific Islander <1%, Two or more races 5%, Race unknown 1%.
Retention and Graduation: 83% freshmen return for sophomore year. 45% freshmen graduate within 4 years. 64% freshmen graduate within 6 years. 23% grads go on to further study within 1 year. 3% grads pursue arts and sciences degrees. 1% grads pursue law degrees. 1% grads pursue business degrees. 1% grads pursue medical degrees. **Faculty:** Student/faculty ratio 15:1. 1,985 full-time faculty, 96% hold PhDs, 22% are members of minority groups, 40% are women. 18% of classes are taught by teaching assistants.

ACADEMICS

Degrees: Bachelor's; Doctoral; Doctoral/Professional; Doctoral/Research; Master's; Post-Bachelor's certificate; Post-Master's certificate **Classes:** Most classes have 10-19 students. Most lab/discussion sessions have 10-19 students. **Most popular majors:** Cell/Cellular And Molecular Biology; Psychology, General; Political Science And Government, General. **Special Study Options:** Accelerated program; Cooperative education program; Cross-registration; Distance learning; Double major; Dual enrollment; English as a Second Language (ESL); Exchange student program (domestic); External degree program; Honors program; Independent study; Internships; Liberal arts/career combination; Student-designed major; Study abroad; Teacher certification program; Weekend college. Honors programs: For information on our Honors

College, visit: www.honors.arizona.edu Combined degree programs: BA/MA.
Disability Services offered to physically disabled students: Note-taking services; Reader services; Tape recorders; Tutors. **Career services:** Alumni network; Alumni services; Career assessment; Career/job search classes; Internships; Regional alumni

FACILITIES

Housing: Apartments for single students; Coed dorms; Fraternity/sorority housing; Special housing for disabled student; Special housing for international students; Theme housing; Wellness housing; Women's dorms 100% of campus accessible to physically diasbled. **Special Academic Facilities/Equipment:** Art, photography, and natural history museums, tree-ring lab, planetarium, optical sciences center, nuclear reactor. **Computers:** 100% of classrooms, 100% of dorms, 100% of libraries, 100% of dining areas, 100% of student union, 75% of common outdoor areas have wireless network access. Students can register for classes online. Administrative functions (other than registration) can be performed online.

CAMPUS LIFE

Environment: Metropolis **Activities:** Campus Ministries; Choral groups; Concert band; Dance; Drama/theater; International Student Organization; Jazz band; Literary magazine; Marching band; Model UN; Music ensembles; Musical theater; Opera; Pep band; Radio station; Student government; Student newspaper; Symphony orchestra; Television station; Yearbook 504 registered organizations, 13 honor societies, 13 religious organizations. 25 fraternities, 20 sororities. **Athletics (Intercollegiate):** *Men:* baseball, basketball, cross-country, diving, football, golf, swimming, tennis, track/field (outdoor). *Women:* basketball, cross-country, diving, golf, gymnastics, soccer, softball, swimming, tennis, track/field (outdoor), track/field (indoor), volleyball. **On-Campus Highlights:** Flandrau Science Center, Center for Creative Photography, UA Museum of Art, Athletics Events, Arizona State Museum **Environmental Initiatives:** The University of Arizona's top environmental commitments are conducting comprehensive research on environmental issues ranging from biodiversity, management, and global change.

ADMISSIONS

Freshman Academic Profile: Average high school GPA 3.3. 34% in top 10% of high school class, 61% in top 25% of high school class, 85% in top 50% of high school class. 86% from public high schools. **Test Scores:** SAT Math middle 50% range 560-690. SAT EBRW middle 50% range 540-650. ACT middle 50% range 21-28. Minimum internet-based TOEFL 70. **Basis for Candidate Selection:** *Very important factors considered include:* rigor of secondary school record, academic GPA. *Important factors considered include:* standardized test scores, extracurricular activities, talent/ability, character/personal qualities, level of applicant's interest. *Other factors considered include:* class rank, application essay, recommendation(s), first generation, volunteer work, work experience. **Freshman Admission Requirements:** High school diploma is required and GED is accepted *Academic units required:* 4 English, 4 math, 3 science, 3 science labs, 2 foreign language, 2 social studies, 1 visual/performing arts, *Academic units recommended:* 4 English, 4 math, 3 science, 3 science labs, 2 foreign language, 2 social studies, 1 visual/performing arts. **Freshman Admission Statistics:** 33,608 applied, 83.6% admitted, 26% enrolled. **Transfer Admission Requirements:** college transcript(s), Lowest grade transferable C. **General Admission Information:** Application fee $50. Priority deadline 5/1. Regular application deadline 5/1. Nonfall registration accepted.

COSTS AND FINANCIAL AID

Annual in-state tuition $11,300. Annual out-of-state tuition $31,067. Room and board $11,300. Required fees $1,382. Average book expense $800. **Required Forms and Deadlines:** FAFSA. **Notification of Awards:** Applicants will be notified of awards on a rolling basis beginning 2/1. **Types of Aid:** *Need-based scholarships/grants:* College/university scholarship or grant aid from institutional funds; Federal Pell; Private scholarships; SEOG; State scholarships/grants. *Loans:* Direct PLUS loans; Direct Subsidized Stafford Loans; Direct Unsubsidized Stafford Loans. *Student Employment:* Federal Work-Study Program available. Institutional employment available. **Financial Aid Statistics:** 94% needy freshmen, 89% needy undergrads receive need-based scholarship or grant aid. 12% freshmen, 9% undergrads receive non-need-based scholarship or grant aid. 58% freshmen, 66% undergrads receive need-based self-help aid. 1% freshmen, 1% undergrads receive athletic scholarships. 46% undergrads borrow to pay for school. Average cumulative indebtedness $23,273. **Criteria for awarding aid:** *Need-based:* Academics *Non-need-based:* Academics, Art, Athletics, Music/drama.

UNIVERSITY OF ARKANSAS AT PINE BLUFF

1200 N. University Drive, Pine Bluff, AR 71601
Phone: (870) 575-8492
E-mail: fultone@uapb.edu
Fax: (870) 575-4608 • **Website:** http://www.uapb.edu

This is a public school.

RATINGS

Admissions Selectivity Rating: 79   **Fire Safety Rating:** 60*   **Green Rating:** 60*

STUDENTS AND FACULTY

Enrollment: 3,048. **Student Body:** 58% female, 42% male, 33% out-of-state, <1% international. Asian <1%, African American 96%, Caucasian 3%, Hispanic <1%, Native American 0%, Race unknown <1%.
Retention and Graduation: 57% freshmen return for sophomore year. **Faculty:** Student/faculty ratio 18:1. 164 full-time faculty, 46% are members of minority groups, 54% are women.

ACADEMICS

Degrees: Associate; Bachelor's; Certificate; **Master's Classes:** Most classes have 10-19 students. Most lab/discussion sessions have 10-19 students. **Special Study Options:** Cooperative education program; Distance learning; Double major; Dual enrollment; Honors program; Internships; Study abroad; Teacher certification program.

FACILITIES

Housing: Men's dorms; Women's dorms

CAMPUS LIFE

Activities: Choral groups; Concert band; Drama/theater; Jazz band; Marching band; Radio station; Student government; Student newspaper; Television station; Yearbook.

ADMISSIONS

Freshman Academic Profile: 93% from public high schools. **Test Scores:** SAT Math middle 50% range 350-450. SAT EBRW middle 50% range 350-440. ACT middle 50% range 14-18. Minimum internet-based TOEFL 61. Minimum paper TOEFL 500. **Basis for Candidate Selection:** *Very important factors considered include:* rigor of secondary school record, standardized test scores. *Important factors considered include:* academic GPA. **Freshman Admission Requirements:** High school diploma is required and GED is accepted *Academic units required:* 4 English, 3 math, 3 science, 2 science labs, 2 foreign language, 1 social studies, 2 history, 4 academic electives. **Freshman Admission Statistics:** 2,169 applied, 64.3% admitted, 59% enrolled. **Transfer Admission Requirements:** High school transcript, college transcript(s). **General Admission Information:** Priority deadline 8/1. Nonfall registration accepted. Admission may be deferred.

COSTS AND FINANCIAL AID

Annual in-state tuition $6,070. Annual out-of-state tuition $7,710. Room and board $6,070. Required fees $1,199. Average book expense $1,000. **Required Forms and Deadlines:** FAFSA. **Types of Aid:** *Need-based scholarships/grants:* College/university scholarship or grant aid from institutional funds; Federal Pell; Private scholarships; SEOG; State scholarships/grants.

UNIVERSITY OF ARKANSAS—FAYETTEVILLE

125 ADMIN, Fayetteville, AR 72701
Phone: 479-575-5346 • **Financial Aid Phone:** (479) 575-3806
E-mail: uofa@uark.edu • **CEEB Code:** 6866
Fax: 479-575-7515 • **Website:** http://www.uark.edu • **ACT Code:** 144

This public school was founded in 1871. It has a 718 acre campus.

RATINGS

Admissions Selectivity Rating: 85   **Fire Safety Rating:** 92   **Green Rating:** 90

STUDENTS AND FACULTY

Enrollment: 22,756. **Student Body:** 53% female, 47% male, 45% out-of-state, 3% international (81 countries represented). Asian 3%, African American 5%, Caucasian 88%, Hispanic 10%, Native American 1%, Pacific Islander <1%, Two or more races 4%, Race unknown 1%.
Retention and Graduation: 82% freshmen return for sophomore year. 42% freshmen graduate within 4 years. 62% freshmen graduate within 6 years. 31% grads go on to further study within 1 year. 7% grads pursue arts and sciences degrees. 3% grads pursue law degrees. 3% grads pursue business degrees. 5% grads pursue medical degrees. **Faculty:** Student/faculty ratio 19:1. 1,185 full-time faculty, 84% hold PhDs, 17% are members of minority groups, 40% are women. 16% of classes are taught by teaching assistants.

ACADEMICS

Degrees: Bachelor's; Certificate; Doctoral; Doctoral/Professional; Doctoral/Research; Master's; Post-Bachelor's certificate; Post-Master's certificate **Classes:** Most classes have 10-19 students. **Most popular majors:** Registered Nursing/Registered Nurse; Finance, General; Marketing/Marketing Management, General. **Special Study Options:** Accelerated program; Cooperative education program; Cross-registration; Distance learning; Double major; Dual enrollment; English as a Second Language (ESL); Honors program; Independent study; Internships; Liberal arts/career combination; Student-designed major; Study abroad; Teacher certification program. Honors programs: The Honors College admitted 1,050 freshman in Fall 2016. Each year the Honors College awards up to 90 freshman fellowships that provide $70,000 over four years, and more than $1 million in study abroad and undergraduate research grants. The Honors College is nationally recognized for the high caliber of students it admits and graduates. Honors students enjoy small, in-depth classes, and programs are offered in all disciplines, tailored to students' academic interests, with interdisciplinary collaborations encouraged. One hundred percent of Honors College graduates have engaged in mentored research. Combined degree programs: BA/DDS; BA/JD; BA/MD. **Disability Services offered to physically disabled students:** Note-taking services; Reader services; Tape recorders; Tutors. **Career services:** Alumni network; Alumni services; Career assessment; Career/job search classes; Internships

FACILITIES

Housing: Apartments for single students; Coed dorms; Fraternity/sorority housing; Special housing for disabled student; Special housing for international students; Theme housing; Women's dorms 100% of campus accessible to physically disabled. **Special Academic Facilities/Equipment:** Entrepreneurial co-working space, McMillon Family Retail and Innovation Lab, Business Behavioral Research Lab, Faulkner Performing Arts center, Honors College networking area, equine pavilion, animal science center, optical network, high performance computing (supercomputing), nanoscale science and engineering building, center for space and planetary sciences, chamber for planetary and asteroid simulation, national center for reliable electric power, high density electronics research center, poultry research center, art galleries **Computers:** Students can register for classes online. Administrative functions (other than registration) can be performed online.

CAMPUS LIFE

Environment: City **Activities:** Campus Ministries; Choral groups; Concert band; Dance; Drama/theater; International Student Organization; Jazz band; Literary magazine; Marching band; Model UN; Music ensembles; Musical theater; Opera; Pep band; Radio station; Student government; Student newspaper; Symphony orchestra; Television station; Yearbook 340 registered organizations, 39 honor societies, 32 religious organizations. 16 fraternities, 11 sororities. **Athletics (Intercollegiate):** *Men:* baseball, basketball, cross-country, football, golf, tennis, track/field (outdoor), track/field (indoor). *Women:* basketball, cross-country, diving, golf, gymnastics, soccer, softball, swimming, tennis, track/field (outdoor), track/field (indoor), volleyball. **On-Campus Highlights:** Old Main: Iconic Image of Higher Education in the State of Arkansas., Steven L. Anderson Design Center: State-Of-The-Art Architectural Building, Senior Walk (every graduate's name engraved), The Nanoscale Material Science and Engineering Buidling, Reynolds Razorback Stadium **Environmental Initiatives:** ACUPCC Signatory, GHG inventory, climate action plan

ADMISSIONS

Freshman Academic Profile: Average high school GPA 3.7. 26% in top 10% of high school class, 54% in top 25% of high school class, 86% in top 50% of high school class. 82% from public high schools. **Test Scores:** SAT Math middle 50% range 550-640. SAT EBRW middle 50% range 560-640. ACT middle 50% range 23-29. Minimum internet-based TOEFL 79. Minimum paper TOEFL 550. **Basis for Candidate Selection:** *Very important factors considered include:* academic GPA, standardized test scores. *Other factors considered include:* rigor of secondary school record, class rank, application essay, recommendation(s), extracurricular activities, talent/ability, character/personal qualities, first generation, alumni/ae relation, geographical residence, state residency, volunteer work, work experience. **Freshman Admission**

Requirements: High school diploma is required and GED is accepted *Academic units required:* 4 English, 4 math, 3 science, 1 science labs, 1 social studies, 2 history, 2 academic electives, 0.5 visual/performing arts, *Academic units recommended:* 4 English, 4 math, 3 science, 1 science labs, 2 foreign language, 1 social studies, 2 history, 2 academic electives, 0.5 visual/performing arts. **Freshman Admission Statistics:** 21,715 applied, 66.0% admitted, 35% enrolled. **Transfer Admission Requirements:** college transcript(s), Minimum college GPA of 2.0 required. Lowest grade transferable C-. **General Admission Information:** Application fee $40. Priority deadline 11/1. Regular application deadline 8/1. Nonfall registration accepted.

COSTS AND FINANCIAL AID
Annual in-state tuition $10,332. Annual out-of-state tuition $21,552. Room and board $10,332. Required fees $1,616. Average book expense $1,046. **Required Forms and Deadlines:** FAFSA. **Notification of Awards:** Applicants will be notified of awards on or about 4/1. **Types of Aid:** *Need-based scholarships/grants:* College/university scholarship or grant aid from institutional funds; Federal Pell; Private scholarships; SEOG; State scholarships/grants. *Loans:* Direct PLUS loans; Direct Subsidized Stafford Loans; Direct Unsubsidized Stafford Loans. *Student Employment:* Federal Work-Study Program available. Institutional employment available. **Financial Aid Statistics:** 82% needy freshmen, 78% needy undergrads receive need-based scholarship or grant aid. 11% freshmen, 9% undergrads receive non-need-based scholarship or grant aid. 70% freshmen, 73% undergrads receive need-based self-help aid. 2% freshmen, 2% undergrads receive athletic scholarships. 79% freshmen, 72% undergrads receive any aid. 48% undergrads borrow to pay for school. Average cumulative indebtedness $24,768. **Criteria for awarding aid:** *Need-based:* Academics, Alumni affiliation, Leadership, Minority status *Non-need-based:* Academics, Alumni affiliation, Art, Athletics, Leadership, Minority status, Music/drama, State/district residency.

UNIVERSITY OF THE ARTS

320 South Broad Street, Philadelphia, PA 19102
Phone: 215-717-6049 • **Financial Aid Phone:** 215-717-6170
E-mail: admissions@uarts.edu • **CEEB Code:** 2664
Fax: 215-717-6045 • **Website:** www.uarts.edu • **ACT Code:** 3664

This private school was founded in 1876. It has a 18 acre campus.

RATINGS
Admissions Selectivity Rating: 78   **Fire Safety Rating:** 60*   **Green Rating:** 60*

STUDENTS AND FACULTY
Enrollment: 1,865. **Student Body:** 58% female, 42% male, 62% out-of-state, 5% international (19 countries represented). Asian 3%, African American 13%, Caucasian 62%, Hispanic 9%, Native American <1%, Pacific Islander 1%, Two or more races 4%, Race unknown 4%.
Retention and Graduation: 82% freshmen return for sophomore year.
Faculty: Student/faculty ratio 8:1. 113 full-time faculty, 0% of classes are taught by teaching assistants.

ACADEMICS
Degrees: Bachelor's; Diploma; Master's; Post-Bachelor's certificate **Classes:** Most classes have 50-99 students. Most lab/discussion sessions have 20-29 students. **Most popular majors:** Dance, General; Graphic Design; Illustration. **Special Study Options:** Cross-registration; Double major; Dual enrollment; English as a Second Language (ESL); Exchange student program (domestic); Honors program; Independent study; Internships; Liberal arts/career combination; Study abroad; Teacher certification program. Honors programs: The University Honors Program at the University of the Arts is an integrative model that asks scholars to seek out and understand the connections between all of their coursework, connecting what they discover in their studio, labor, rehearsal room with cultural and historical underpinnings they investigate in their liberal arts courses. **Disability Services offered to physically disabled students:** Note-taking services; Reader services; Tape recorders; Tutors. **Career services:** Alumni network; Alumni services; Career assessment; Career/job search classes; Internships

FACILITIES
Housing: Apartments for single students; Coed dorms 85% of campus accessible to physically diasbled. **Special Academic Facilities/Equipment:** Rosenwald-Wolf Gallery, Merriam Theater, Arts Bank, Borowsky Center for Publication arts, Gershman Y

CAMPUS LIFE
Environment: Metropolis **Activities:** Choral groups; Dance; Drama/theater; International Student Organization; Jazz band; Literary magazine; Music

ensembles; Musical theater; Student government; Student-run film society 5 registered organizations, 1 religious organization. Merriam Theater, Arts Bank, Caplan Studio Theater, Gallery One, Solmssen Court

ADMISSIONS
Test Scores: SAT Math middle 50% range 440-550. SAT EBRW middle 50% range 450-580. ACT middle 50% range 18-25. Minimum internet-based TOEFL 80. Minimum paper TOEFL 550. **Basis for Candidate Selection:** *Very important factors considered include:* rigor of secondary school record, interview, talent/ability. *Important factors considered include:* class rank, academic GPA, application essay, standardized test scores, extracurricular activities, level of applicant's interest. *Other factors considered include:* recommendation(s), alumni/ae relation, racial/ethnic status, volunteer work, work experience. **Freshman Admission Requirements:** High school diploma is required and GED is accepted *Academic units required:* 4 English, *Academic units recommended:* 3 math, 2 science, 2 foreign language, 2 social studies, 2 history, 2 units from above areas or other academic areas. **Freshman Admission Statistics:** 1,479 applied, 75.4% admitted, 41% enrolled. **Transfer Admission Requirements:** High school transcript, college transcript(s), essay or personal statement, standardized test scores, Minimum college GPA of 2.0 required. Lowest grade transferable C. **General Admission Information:** Application fee $60. Priority deadline 3/15. Nonfall registration accepted. Admission may be deferred for a maximum of 1 year.

COSTS AND FINANCIAL AID
Annual tuition $39,908. Room and board $14,552. **Required Forms and Deadlines:** FAFSA. **Notification of Awards:** Applicants will be notified of awards on a rolling basis beginning 3/15. **Types of Aid:** *Need-based scholarships/grants:* College/university scholarship or grant aid from institutional funds; Federal Pell; Private scholarships; SEOG; State scholarships/grants. *Loans:* Direct PLUS loans; Direct Subsidized Stafford Loans; Direct Unsubsidized Stafford Loans. *Student Employment:* Federal Work-Study Program available. Institutional employment available. **Financial Aid Statistics:** 95% needy freshmen, 94% needy undergrads receive need-based scholarship or grant aid. 10% freshmen, 5% undergrads receive non-need-based scholarship or grant aid. 99% freshmen, 98% undergrads receive need-based self-help aid. 0% freshmen, 0% undergrads receive athletic scholarships. 80% undergrads receive any aid. **Criteria for awarding aid:** *Non-need-based:* Academics, Art, Music/drama.

UNIVERSITY OF BALTIMORE

1420 North Charles Street, Baltimore, MD 21201
Phone: 410-837-4777 • **Financial Aid Phone:** (410)837-4763
E-mail: admissions@ubmall.ubalt.edu • **CEEB Code:** 5810
Fax: 410-837-4793 • **Website:** http://www.ubalt.edu/admission/

This public school was founded in 1925. It has a 11.3 acre campus.

RATINGS
Admissions Selectivity Rating: 83   **Fire Safety Rating:** 60*   **Green Rating:** 60*

STUDENTS AND FACULTY
Enrollment: 3,526. **Student Body:** 57% female, 43% male, 4% out-of-state, 3% international. Asian 4%, African American 38%, Caucasian 42%, Hispanic 4%, Native American <1%, Pacific Islander <1%, Two or more races 3%, Race unknown 5%.
Retention and Graduation: 18% grads go on to further study within 1 year. 10% grads pursue arts and sciences degrees. 2% grads pursue law degrees. 9% grads pursue business degrees. **Faculty:** Student/faculty ratio 16:1. 182 full-time faculty, 85% hold PhDs, 23% are members of minority groups, 45% are women. 0% of classes are taught by teaching assistants.

ACADEMICS
Degrees: Bachelor's; Certificate; Doctoral; Master's; Post-Bachelor's certificate; Post-Master's certificate **Classes:** Most classes have 10-19 students. Most lab/discussion sessions have 20-29 students. **Most popular majors:** Digital Communication And Media/Multimedia; Criminal Justice/Law Enforcement Administration; Business Administration And Management, General. **Special Study Options:** Accelerated program; Cooperative education program; Distance learning; Honors program; Independent study; Internships; Student-designed major; Study abroad. Combined degree programs: BA/JD; BA/MA. **Disability Services offered to physically disabled students:** Note-taking services; Reader services; Tape recorders; Tutors. **Career services:** Alumni network; Alumni services; Career assessment; Career/job search classes; Internships; Regional alumni

FACILITIES

Housing: 100% of campus accessible to physically diasbled. **Computers:** Students can register for classes online. Administrative functions (other than registration) can be performed online.

CAMPUS LIFE

Environment: Metropolis **Activities:** Drama/theater; International Student Organization; Literary magazine; Student government; Student newspaper 26 registered organizations, 11 honor societies, 2 religious organizations. **On-Campus Highlights:** Student Union **Environmental Initiatives:** 30% energy reduction contract with Energy Systems Group

ADMISSIONS

Freshman Academic Profile: Average high school GPA 3.0. **Test Scores:** SAT Math middle 50% range 410-540. SAT EBRW middle 50% range 420-560. ACT middle 50% range 17-21. Minimum paper TOEFL 550. **Basis for Candidate Selection:** *Important factors considered include:* rigor of secondary school record, class rank, academic GPA, standardized test scores. *Other factors considered include:* application essay, recommendation(s), extracurricular activities, talent/ability, character/personal qualities, first generation, alumni/ae relation, volunteer work, work experience. **Freshman Admission Requirements:** High school diploma is required and GED is accepted *Academic units required:* 4 English, 3 math, 3 science, 2 science labs, 3 social studies, 6 academic electives. **Freshman Admission Statistics:** 730 applied, 64.4% admitted, 51% enrolled. **Transfer Admission Requirements:** college transcript(s), Minimum college GPA of 2.0 required. Lowest grade transferable D. **General Admission Information:** Application fee $30. Priority deadline 2/15. Nonfall registration accepted. Admission may be deferred for a maximum of 1 year.

COSTS AND FINANCIAL AID

Annual in-state tuition $1,846. Annual out-of-state tuition $16,550. Required fees $1,846. **Required Forms and Deadlines:** FAFSA. **Types of Aid:** *Need-based scholarships/grants:* College/university scholarship or grant aid from institutional funds; Federal Pell; Private scholarships; SEOG; State scholarships/grants. *Loans:* Direct PLUS loans; Direct Subsidized Stafford Loans; Direct Unsubsidized Stafford Loans. *Student Employment:* Federal Work-Study Program available. Institutional employment available. **Financial Aid Statistics:** 90% needy freshmen, 91% needy undergrads receive need-based scholarship or grant aid. 0% undergrads receive non-need-based scholarship or grant aid. 65% freshmen, 72% undergrads receive need-based self-help aid. 0% freshmen, 0% undergrads receive athletic scholarships. 97% freshmen, 86% undergrads receive any aid. **Criteria for awarding aid:** *Need-based:* Academics *Non-need-based:* Academics, State/district residency.

UNIVERSITY OF BRIDGEPORT

126 Park Avenue, Bridgeport, CT 06604
Phone: 203-576-4552 • **Financial Aid Phone:** 203-576-4568
E-mail: admit@.bridgeport.edu • **CEEB Code:** 3914
Fax: 203-576-4941 • **ACT Code:** 602

This private school was founded in 1927. It has a 86 acre campus.

RATINGS

Admissions Selectivity Rating: 76   **Fire Safety Rating:** 91   **Green Rating:** 60*

STUDENTS AND FACULTY

Enrollment: 2,688. **Student Body:** 68% female, 32% male, 38% out-of-state, 11% international (74 countries represented). Asian 3%, African American 37%, Caucasian 27%, Hispanic 18%, Native American 1%, Pacific Islander <1%, Two or more races 3%,

Retention and Graduation: 62% freshmen return for sophomore year. 15% grads go on to further study within 1 year. 5% grads pursue arts and sciences degrees. 10% grads pursue law degrees. 10% grads pursue business degrees. 5% grads pursue medical degrees. **Faculty:** Student/faculty ratio 17:1. 121 full-time faculty, 79% hold PhDs, 19% are members of minority groups, 38% are women. 0% of classes are taught by teaching assistants.

ACADEMICS

Degrees: Associate; Bachelor's; Certificate; Doctoral/Professional; Doctoral/Research; Master's; Post-Bachelor's certificate; Post-Master's certificate **Classes:** Most classes have fewer than 10 students. Most lab/discussion sessions have fewer than 10 students. **Most popular majors:** Psychology, General; Dental Hygiene/Hygienist; Business/Commerce, General. **Special Study Options:** Accelerated program; Cooperative education program; Cross-

registration; Distance learning; Double major; English as a Second Language (ESL); Honors program; Independent study; Internships; Liberal arts/career combination; Student-designed major; Study abroad; Teacher certification program; Weekend college. **Disability Services offered to physically disabled students:** Note-taking services; Reader services; Tape recorders; Tutors. **Career services:** Alumni network; Alumni services; Career assessment; Career/job search classes; Internships; Regional alumni

FACILITIES

Housing: Coed dorms; Other (please specify) 80% of campus accessible to physically diasbled. **Computers:** 80% of classrooms, 100% of dorms, 100% of libraries, 30% of dining areas, 50% of student union, have wireless network access. Students can register for classes online. Administrative functions (other than registration) can be performed online.

CAMPUS LIFE

Environment: City **Activities:** Campus Ministries; Choral groups; Dance; International Student Organization; Literary magazine; Model UN; Music ensembles; Student government; Student newspaper; Yearbook 30 registered organizations, 11 honor societies, 6 religious organizations. 2 fraternities, 4 sororities. **Athletics (Intercollegiate):** *Men:* baseball, basketball, cross-country, soccer, swimming. *Women:* basketball, cross-country, gymnastics, lacrosse, soccer, softball, swimming, volleyball. **On-Campus Highlights:** Arnold Bernhard Center, Wheeler Recreation Center, John J. Cox Student Center, The University Gallery, Hubbell Gymnasium

ADMISSIONS

Freshman Academic Profile: Average high school GPA 3.0. 1% in top 10% of high school class, 32% in top 25% of high school class, 69% in top 50% of high school class. 90% from public high schools. **Test Scores:** SAT Math middle 50% range 410-500. SAT EBRW middle 50% range 410-490. ACT middle 50% range 18-21. Minimum internet-based TOEFL 61. Minimum paper TOEFL 500. **Basis for Candidate Selection:** *Very important factors considered include:* rigor of secondary school record, academic GPA, standardized test scores. *Important factors considered include:* class rank, application essay, recommendation(s), talent/ability, character/personal qualities, level of applicant's interest. *Other factors considered include:* interview, extracurricular activities, volunteer work, work experience. **Freshman Admission Requirements:** High school diploma is required and GED is accepted *Academic units required:* 4 English, 3 math, 2 science, 2 science labs, 2 social studies, 5 academic electives, *Academic units recommended:* 4 English, 3 math, 2 science, 2 science labs, 2 social studies, 5 academic electives. **Freshman Admission Statistics:** 5,736 applied, 63.5% admitted, 16% enrolled. **Transfer Admission Requirements:** college transcript(s), essay or personal statement, Minimum college GPA of 2.0 required. Lowest grade transferable C-. **General Admission Information:** Application fee $25. Priority deadline 4/1. Nonfall registration accepted. Admission may be deferred for a maximum of 1 year.

COSTS AND FINANCIAL AID

Annual tuition $25,950. Room and board $12,050. Required fees $2,190. Average book expense $1,500. **Required Forms and Deadlines:** FAFSA. **Notification of Awards:** Applicants will be notified of awards on a rolling basis beginning 3/1. **Types of Aid:** *Need-based scholarships/grants:* College/university scholarship or grant aid from institutional funds; Federal Pell; Private scholarships; SEOG; State scholarships/grants. *Loans:* Direct PLUS loans; Direct Subsidized Stafford Loans; Direct Unsubsidized Stafford Loans. *Student Employment:* Federal Work-Study Program available. Institutional employment available. **Financial Aid Statistics:** 85% needy freshmen, 87% needy undergrads receive need-based scholarship or grant aid. 96% freshmen, 89% undergrads receive non-need-based scholarship or grant aid. 86% freshmen, 88% undergrads receive need-based self-help aid. 3% freshmen, 8% undergrads receive athletic scholarships. 98% freshmen, 98% undergrads receive any aid. **Criteria for awarding aid:** *Non-need-based:* Academics, Art, Athletics, Leadership, Music/drama, State/district residency.

UNIVERSITY OF BRITISH COLUMBIA

1200–1874 East Mall, Brock Hall, Vancouver, BC V6T 1Z1
Phone: 1-604-822-3014 • **Financial Aid Phone:** 604-822-5111
E-mail: askme@interchange.ubc.ca
Fax: 604-822-3599 • **Website:** www.ubc.ca

This public school was founded in 1908. It has a 1000 acre campus.

RATINGS

Admissions Selectivity Rating: 71   **Fire Safety Rating:** 79   **Green Rating:** 97

STUDENTS AND FACULTY

Enrollment: 29,717. **Student Body:** 54% female, 46% male, (144 countries represented).
Retention and Graduation: 91% freshmen return for sophomore year. 50% grads go on to further study within 1 year. **Faculty:** Student/faculty ratio 15:1.

ACADEMICS

Degrees: Bachelor's; Certificate; Diploma; Doctoral; Doctoral/Professional; **Master's Classes:** Most classes have 10-19 students. **Most popular majors:** Computer And Information Sciences, General; Biological And Physical Sciences; Psychology, General. **Special Study Options:** Cooperative education program; Distance learning; Double major; Dual enrollment; English as a Second Language (ESL); Exchange student program (domestic); Honors program; Internships; Liberal arts/career combination; Student-designed major; Study abroad; Teacher certification program. Honors programs: UBC offers many honours programs for academically strong undergraduates. **Disability Services offered to physically disabled students:** Note-taking services; Reader services; Tape recorders; Tutors. **Career services:** Alumni network; Alumni services; Career assessment; Career/job search classes; Internships; Regional alumni

FACILITIES

Housing: Apartments for married students; Apartments for single students; Coed dorms; Fraternity/sorority housing; Men's dorms; Special housing for disabled student; Special housing for international students; Theme housing; Women's dorms 90% of campus accessible to physically diasbled. **Special Academic Facilities/Equipment:** Museum of Anthropology Barber Learning Centre Beaty Biodiversity Museum Geological Museum TRIUMF, sub-atomic particle research Botanical Gardens Nitobe Garden Old Auditorium Opera Theatre Belkin Art Gallery Chan Centre for Performing Arts Frederick Wood Theatre Irving K Barber Centre of Learning Liu International Studies Centre Green College (Graduate College) St.John's College (Graduate College) Centre for Intergrated Systems Research Wall Centre for Interdisciplinary Studies Model Crop Farm **Computers:** 100% of classrooms, 100% of dorms, 100% of libraries, 100% of dining areas, 100% of student union, 100% of common outdoor areas have wireless network access. Students can register for classes online. Administrative functions (other than registration) can be performed online.

CAMPUS LIFE

Environment: Metropolis **Activities:** Campus Ministries; Choral groups; Concert band; Dance; Drama/theater; International Student Organization; Literary magazine; Model UN; Music ensembles; Musical theater; Opera; Radio station; Student government; Student newspaper; Student-run film society; Symphony orchestra 250 registered organizations, 1 honor society, 7 religious organizations. 9 fraternities, 8 sororities. **Athletics (Intercollegiate):** *Men:* baseball, basketball, crew/rowing, cross-country, field hockey, football, golf, ice hockey, rugby, soccer, swimming, track/field (outdoor), volleyball. *Women:* basketball, crew/rowing, cross-country, field hockey, golf, ice hockey, rugby, soccer, swimming, track/field (outdoor), volleyball. **On-Campus Highlights:** Koerner Library, Museum of Anthropology, Chan Centre, Student Union Building, Barber Learning Centre **Environmental Initiatives:** UBC is a signatory to the Talloires Declaration. It has integrated sustainability into its vision statement and strategic plan and formed a President's Advisory Council on Sustainability. The UBC Sustainability Office opened in 1998 – the first of its kind in a Canadian university. UBC has created an advisory committee of faculty, staff, students and alumni on socially responsible investing. The committee advises the Board of Governors on issues of transparency, proxy votes, and socially responsible investment practices.

ADMISSIONS

Test Scores: Minimum internet-based TOEFL 90/120. **Basis for Candidate Selection:** *Very important factors considered include:* rigor of secondary school record, academic GPA. *Important factors considered include:* application essay. *Other factors considered include:* standardized test scores, recommendation(s), extracurricular activities, talent/ability, character/personal qualities, volunteer work, work experience, level of applicant's interest. **Freshman Admission Requirements:** High school diploma is required and GED is not accepted *Academic units required:* 4 English, 3 math, 12 academic electives. **Freshman Admission Statistics:** 27,134 applied, 48.5% admitted, 48% enrolled. **Transfer Admission Requirements:** college transcript(s), statement of good standing from prior institution(s). **General Admission Information:** Application fee $102. Priority deadline 1/31. Regular application deadline 1/31. Nonfall registration accepted. Admission may be deferred.

COSTS AND FINANCIAL AID

Required Forms and Deadlines: Institution's own financial aid form. **Types of Aid:** *Loans:* Direct PLUS loans; Direct Subsidized Stafford Loans; Direct Unsubsidized Stafford Loans. **Criteria for awarding aid:** *Need-based:* Academics, Athletics, Leadership *Non-need-based:* Academics, Athletics, Leadership.

UNIVERSITY OF CALIFORNIA—BERKELEY

110 Sproul Hall, Berkeley, CA 94720-5800
CEEB Code: 4833
Website: www.berkeley.edu • **ACT Code:** 444

This public school was founded in 1868. It has a 1232 acre campus.

RATINGS

Admissions Selectivity Rating: 98   **Fire Safety Rating:** 91   **Green Rating:** 97

STUDENTS AND FACULTY

Enrollment: 27,496. **Student Body:** 52% female, 48% male, 15% out-of-state, 14% international. Asian 35%, African American 2%, Caucasian 27%, Hispanic 14%, Native American <1%, Pacific Islander <1%, Two or more races 5%, Race unknown 3%.
Retention and Graduation: 97% freshmen return for sophomore year.
Faculty: Student/faculty ratio 17:1. 1,623 full-time faculty, 99% hold PhDs, 21% are members of minority groups, 35% are women. 0% of classes are taught by teaching assistants.

ACADEMICS

Degrees: Bachelor's; Doctoral/Professional; Doctoral/Research; Master's; Post-Bachelor's certificate **Classes:** Most classes have 20-29 students. Most lab/discussion sessions have 20-29 students. **Most popular majors:** Computer Engineering, General; English Language And Literature, General; Political Science And Government, General. **Special Study Options:** Accelerated program; Cross-registration; Double major; Dual enrollment; English as a Second Language (ESL); Exchange student program (domestic); Honors program; Independent study; Internships; Student-designed major; Study abroad. **Disability Services offered to physically disabled students:** Note-taking services; Reader services; Tape recorders; Tutors. **Career services:** Alumni services; Career assessment; Career/job search classes; Internships

FACILITIES

Housing: Apartments for married students; Apartments for single students; Coed dorms; Cooperative housing; Fraternity/sorority housing; Men's dorms; Special housing for disabled student; Special housing for international students; Theme housing; Women's dorms 95% of campus accessible to physically diasbled. **Special Academic Facilities/Equipment:** Lawrence Berkeley National Lab, Pacific Film Archive, Earthquake Data Center, Museums of art, anthropology, natural history, paleontology,Botanical Garden **Computers:** Students can register for classes online. Administrative functions (other than registration) can be performed online.

CAMPUS LIFE

Environment: City **Activities:** Campus Ministries; Choral groups; Concert band; Dance; Drama/theater; International Student Organization; Jazz band; Literary magazine; Marching band; Model UN; Music ensembles; Musical theater; Pep band; Radio station; Student government; Student newspaper; Student-run film society; Symphony orchestra; Television station; Yearbook 300 registered organizations, 6 honor societies, 28 religious organizations. 38 fraternities, 19 sororities. **Athletics (Intercollegiate):** *Men:* baseball, basketball, crew/rowing, cross-country, diving, football, golf, gymnastics, rugby, sailing, soccer, swimming, tennis, track/field (outdoor), water polo. *Women:* basketball, crew/rowing, cross-country, diving, field hockey, golf, gymnastics, lacrosse, sailing, soccer, softball, swimming, tennis, track/field (outdoor), volleyball, water polo. **On-Campus Highlights:** Botanical Gardens, Lawrence Hall of Science, Museum of Anthropology, Museum of Art **Environmental Initiatives:** Climate and Energy: Six years ago the campus set out to reduce its carbon footprint by one-third – to bring Berkeley's greenhouse gas emissions from campus operations back to the levels they were in 1990. Our most recent emissions inventory reveals that Berkeley has met this target, two years ahead of schedule. Ambitious at the outset, this voluntary target to reduce greenhouse gas emissions (GHG) to 1990 levels by 2014 puts Berkeley ahead of UC Policy and State of California guidelines which call for this level of reduction by the year 2020. We have reduced our emissions and met our first target by: Investing in energy efficiency and sustainable transportation practices. Since 2006, the campus has saved 20 million kWh of electricity through building retrofits and reduced fuel use by more than 1 million gallons by increasing the number of bicycle, pedestrian and mass-transit commuters. Buying Greener Power. The campus is using electricity that includes more solar and wind energy and less coal through purchases from Pacific Gas & Electric, a utility that is required by state law to provide power that by 2020 will include 33 percent renewable energy. Improving Data and Methods. UC Berkeley has improved the accuracy of its emissions inventory profile by using the best data available about campus energy use and by staying current with the best reporting methods.

ADMISSIONS

Freshman Academic Profile: Average high school GPA 3.9. 98% in top 10% of high school class, 100% in top 25% of high school class, 100% in top 50% of high school class. **Test Scores:** SAT Math middle 50% range 640-770. SAT EBRW middle 50% range 610-730. ACT middle 50% range 29-34. Minimum internet-based TOEFL 80. Minimum paper TOEFL 550. **Basis for Candidate Selection:** *Very important factors considered include:* rigor of secondary school record, academic GPA, application essay, standardized test scores. *Important factors considered include:* extracurricular activities, character/personal qualities, volunteer work, work experience. *Other factors considered include:* first generation, state residency. **Freshman Admission Requirements:** High school diploma is required and GED is accepted *Academic units required:* 4 English, 3 math, 2 science, 2 science labs, 2 foreign language, 2 history, 1 academic elective, 1 visual/performing arts, *Academic units recommended:* 4 English, 4 math, 3 science, 3 science labs, 3 foreign language, 2 history, 1 academic elective, 1 visual/performing arts. **Freshman Admission Statistics:** 78,924 applied, 15.3% admitted, 46% enrolled. **Transfer Admission Requirements:** essay or personal statement, Minimum college GPA of 2.4 required. Lowest grade transferable D. **General Admission Information:** Application fee $70. Regular application deadline 11/30. Nonfall registration accepted.

COSTS AND FINANCIAL AID

Annual in-state tuition $16,042. Annual out-of-state tuition $37,902. Room and board $16,042. Required fees $2,289. Average book expense $1,262. **Required Forms and Deadlines:** FAFSA; State aid form. **Notification of Awards:** Applicants will be notified of awards on or about 3/31. **Types of Aid:** *Need-based scholarships/grants:* College/university scholarship or grant aid from institutional funds; Federal Pell; Private scholarships; SEOG; State scholarships/grants. *Loans:* Direct PLUS loans; Direct Subsidized Stafford Loans; Direct Unsubsidized Stafford Loans. *Student Employment:* Federal Work-Study Program available. Institutional employment available. **Financial Aid Statistics:** 99% needy freshmen, 98% needy undergrads receive need-based scholarship or grant aid. 5% freshmen, 3% undergrads receive non-need-based scholarship or grant aid. 50% freshmen, 55% undergrads receive need-based self-help aid. 1% freshmen, 1% undergrads receive athletic scholarships. 38% undergrads borrow to pay for school. Average cumulative indebtedness $17,869. **Criteria for awarding aid:** *Need-based:* Academics *Non-need-based:* Academics, Athletics, Leadership.

UNIVERSITY OF CALIFORNIA—DAVIS

One Shields Ave, Davis, CA 95616
Phone: 530-752-2971 • **Financial Aid Phone:** 530-752-2396
E-mail: undergraduateadmissions@ucdavis.edu • **CEEB Code:** 4834
Fax: 530-752-1280 • **Website:** www.ucdavis.edu • **ACT Code:** 454

This public school was founded in 1908. It has a 5200 acre campus.

RATINGS

Admissions Selectivity Rating: 89   **Fire Safety Rating:** 95   **Green Rating:** 98

STUDENTS AND FACULTY

Enrollment: 29,982. **Student Body:** 59% female, 41% male, 5% out-of-state, 16% international (121 countries represented). Asian 28%, African American 2%, Caucasian 25%, Hispanic 21%, Native American <1%, Pacific Islander <1%, Two or more races 5%, Race unknown 2%. **Retention and Graduation:** 92% freshmen return for sophomore year. 40% grads go on to further study within 1 year. 23% grads pursue arts and sciences degrees. 4% grads pursue law degrees. 1% grads pursue business degrees. 12% grads pursue medical degrees. **Faculty:** Student/faculty ratio 19:1. 1,702 full-time faculty, 98% hold PhDs, 25% are members of minority groups, 39% are women.

ACADEMICS

Degrees: Bachelor's; Doctoral; Doctoral/Professional; Doctoral/Research; Master's; Post-Bachelor's certificate; Post-Master's certificate **Classes:** Most classes have fewer than 10 students. **Most popular majors:** Biology/Biological Sciences, General; Psychology, General; Economics, General. **Special Study Options:** Accelerated program; Cross-registration; Double

major; Dual enrollment; English as a Second Language (ESL); Honors program; Independent study; Internships; Student-designed major; Study abroad; Teacher certification program. Honors programs: The Davis Honors Challenge (DHC) is an innovative, open-application, campuswide honors program for highly motivated students. In addition to a mentor program and a residential living-learning option for first-year students, DHC offers students the opportunity to participate in an honors program for four years. Integrated Studies Honors Program (ISHP), the oldest continuous residential learning community in the UC system, is an invitational, residential honors program for first-year students. ISHP provides an academic residential community similar to those of the best small colleges and helps students integrate knowledge from the arts and humanities, natural sciences and engineering, and social sciences. **Disability Services offered to physically disabled students:** Note-taking services; Reader services; Tape recorders; Tutors.

FACILITIES

Housing: Apartments for married students; Apartments for single students; Coed dorms; Cooperative housing; Special housing for disabled student; Theme housing; Wellness housing; Women's dorms **Special Academic Facilities/Equipment:** Art galleries, 150-acre university arboretum, equestrian center, craft center, student experimental farm, nuclear lab, human performance lab, natural reserves, early childhood lab, raptor center, primate research center. **Computers:** Students can register for classes online. Administrative functions (other than registration) can be performed online.

CAMPUS LIFE

Environment: Town **Activities:** Campus Ministries; Choral groups; Concert band; Dance; Drama/theater; International Student Organization; Jazz band; Literary magazine; Marching band; Model UN; Music ensembles; Musical theater; Pep band; Radio station; Student government; Student newspaper; Student-run film society; Symphony orchestra; Television station; Yearbook 364 registered organizations, 1 honor society, 50 religious organizations. 28 fraternities, 21 sororities. **Athletics (Intercollegiate):** *Men:* baseball, basketball, cross-country, diving, football, golf, soccer, swimming, tennis, track/field (outdoor), track/field (indoor), water polo, wrestling. *Women:* basketball, crew/rowing, cross-country, diving, field hockey, golf, gymnastics, lacrosse, soccer, softball, swimming, tennis, track/field (outdoor), track/field (indoor), volleyball, water polo. **On-Campus Highlights:** Mondavi Center for the Performing Arts, Memorial Union/Coffee House, Activities and Recreation Center (The ARC), Manetti Shrem Museum of Art, The UC Davis Arboretum **Environmental Initiatives:** UC Davis is taking action to reduce greenhouse gas emissions and energy use on campus through programs like the Strategic Energy Partnership Program, which is improving energy conservation and energy efficiency on campus and has identified retrofit and recommissioning projects that will save more than 28 million kilowatt-hours and 2 million therms. The campus installed a 756kW solar photovoltaic system, which generates over 1 million kilowatt-hours a year. UC Davis has also embarked on an ambitious initiative to reduce lighting energy use by 60% in five years, which will reduce energy use and greenhouse gas emissions (www.sustainability.ucdavis.edu/news/2010/november/smart_lighting.html) and is pursuing a project to build an on-campus anaerobic biodigester that will generate about 2 million kilowatt-hours a year of clean, renewable electricity from campus organic wastes (news.ucdavis.edu/search/news_detail.lasso?id=10202). Work on climate issues at UC Davis includes everything from studying pollution in the Arctic atmosphere and building global climate models to the campus Climate Action Plan (CAP) and energy use reduction. UC Davis faculty and student research on climate change spans a wide range of investigation from basic inquiry to solution-based engineering work (climatechange.ucdavis.edu/). The CAP analyzes campus issues around greenhouse gas emissions reductions, energy use and energy sourcing (www.sustainability.ucdavis.edu/progress/climate/index.html).

ADMISSIONS

Freshman Academic Profile: Average high school GPA 4.0. 84% from public high schools. **Test Scores:** SAT Math middle 50% range 570-710. SAT EBRW middle 50% range 550-650. ACT middle 50% range 25-31. Minimum internet-based TOEFL 60. Minimum paper TOEFL 550. **Basis for Candidate Selection:** *Very important factors considered include:* rigor of secondary school record, academic GPA, application essay, standardized test scores. *Important factors considered include:* extracurricular activities, talent/ability, character/personal qualities, volunteer work. *Other factors considered include:* first generation, state residency, work experience. **Freshman Admission Requirements:** High school diploma is required and GED is accepted *Academic units required:* 4 English, 3 math, 2 science, 2 science labs, 2 foreign language, 2 history, 1 academic elective, 1 visual/performing arts, *Academic units recommended:* 4 English, 4 math, 3 science, 3 science labs, 3 foreign language, 2 history, 1 academic elective, 1 visual/performing arts. **Freshman Admission Statistics:** 70,214 applied, 43.5% admitted, 19% enrolled. **Transfer Admission Requirements:** High school transcript, college transcript(s), essay or personal statement, statement of good standing from prior institution(s). Lowest grade transferable D-. **General Admission Information:** Application fee $70. Regular application deadline 11/30. Nonfall registration accepted. Admission may be deferred for a maximum of 1 year.

COSTS AND FINANCIAL AID

Annual in-state tuition $14,838. Annual out-of-state tuition $37,902. Room and board $14,838. Required fees $2,826. Average book expense $1,601. **Required Forms and Deadlines:** FAFSA; State aid form. **Notification of Awards:** Applicants will be notified of awards on or about 3/14. **Types of Aid:** *Need-based scholarships/grants:* College/university scholarship or grant aid from institutional funds; Federal Pell; Private scholarships; SEOG; State scholarships/grants. *Loans:* Direct PLUS loans; Direct Subsidized Stafford Loans; Direct Unsubsidized Stafford Loans. **Financial Aid Statistics:** 97% needy freshmen, 96% needy undergrads receive need-based scholarship or grant aid. 2% freshmen, 1% undergrads receive non-need-based scholarship or grant aid. 62% freshmen, 57% undergrads receive need-based self-help aid. 1% freshmen, 1% undergrads receive athletic scholarships. 55% undergrads receive any aid. 56% undergrads borrow to pay for school. Average cumulative indebtedness $19,588. **Criteria for awarding aid:** *Need-based:* Academics, Athletics *Non-need-based:* Academics, Athletics.

UNIVERSITY OF CALIFORNIA—IRVINE

Office of Admissions and Relations with Schools, Irvine, CA 92697-1075
Phone: 949-824-6703 • **Financial Aid Phone:** 949-824-5337
E-mail: admissions@uci.edu • **CEEB Code:** 4859
Fax: 949-824-2951 • **Website:** www.uci.edu • **ACT Code:**

This public school was founded in 1965. It has a 1500 acre campus.

RATINGS

Admissions Selectivity Rating: 96   **Fire Safety Rating:** 88   **Green Rating:** 99

STUDENTS AND FACULTY

Enrollment: 29,307. **Student Body:** 53% female, 47% male, 3% out-of-state, 17% international (77 countries represented). Asian 36%, African American 2%, Caucasian 14%, Hispanic 26%, Native American <1%, Pacific Islander <1%, Two or more races 4%, Race unknown 1%.
Retention and Graduation: 94% freshmen return for sophomore year. 70% freshmen graduate within 4 years. 85% freshmen graduate within 6 years. **Faculty:** Student/faculty ratio 18:1. 1,290 full-time faculty, 98% hold PhDs, 29% are members of minority groups, 38% are women.

ACADEMICS

Degrees: Bachelor's; Doctoral/Professional; Doctoral/Research; Master's; Post-Bachelor's certificate **Classes:** Most classes have 20-29 students. Most lab/discussion sessions have 20-29 students. **Most popular majors:** Biology/Biological Sciences, General; Social Psychology; Public Health, Other. **Special Study Options:** Accelerated program; Cross-registration; Distance learning; Double major; Dual enrollment; English as a Second Language (ESL); Honors program; Independent study; Internships; Study abroad; Teacher certification program. Honors programs: Campuswide Honors Program (CHP). **Disability Services offered to physically disabled students:** Note-taking services; Reader services; Tape recorders; Tutors. **Career services:** Alumni network; Alumni services; Career assessment; Career/job search classes; Internships

FACILITIES

Housing: Apartments for married students; Apartments for single students; Coed dorms; Fraternity/sorority housing; Men's dorms; Special housing for disabled student; Special housing for international students; Theme housing; Women's dorms 95% of campus accessible to physically diasbled. **Special Academic Facilities/Equipment:** Museum of systemic biology, freshwater marsh reserve, electron microscope, nuclear reactor, laser institute, research facilities. **Computers:** 90% of classrooms, 100% of libraries, 100% of dining areas, 100% of student union, have wireless network access. Students can register for classes online. Administrative functions (other than registration) can be performed online.

CAMPUS LIFE

Environment: City **Activities:** Campus Ministries; Choral groups; Concert band; Dance; Drama/theater; International Student Organization; Jazz band; Literary magazine; Marching band; Model UN; Music ensembles; Musical theater; Opera; Pep band; Radio station; Student government; Student newspaper; Student-run film society; Symphony orchestra; Yearbook 484 registered organizations, 18 honor societies, 51 religious organizations. 21 fraternities, 23 sororities. **Athletics (Intercollegiate):** Men: baseball, basketball, cross-country, golf, sailing, soccer, tennis, track/field (outdoor), volleyball, water polo. Women: basketball, cross-country, golf, sailing, soccer, tennis, track/field (outdoor), volleyball, water polo. **On-Campus Highlights:** Anteater Recreation Center, Bren Events Center, UCI Student Center, Cross-Cultural Center, Arts Plaza **Environmental Initiatives:** The University of

California is a leader in water conservation and water efficiency. Every UC campus, including UCI, has committed to reducing per capita potable water consumption 20 percent by 2020 and 36 percent by 2025. The UCI Water Resources Working Group (WRWG) assembled the campus's first Water Action Plan in 2013, identifying strategies to achieve this goal. Since 2013 significant progress has been made in potable water reduction with more than 78 million gallons saved annually, largely due to plumbing fixture upgrades, landscape irrigation reduction, and replacement of once-through cooling equipment in labs. UCI is currently exceeding the 36 percent use reduction goal, achieving a current use reduction of 40 percent. In 2017, UCI set a stretch goal of reducing per capita water usage by 50 percent by 2025, with the 2017 Water Action Plan Update identifying strategies to reach this goal. A key strategy is a collaborative project with the Irvine Ranch Water District to replace potable water use in the central plant's cooling towers with recycled water. Currently under construction, this project will conserve approximately 80 million gallons of potable water annually and increase per capita water savings to a remarkable 54 percent. UCI's strong performance in water-wise operations is more than matched by the campus's academic expertise on this front. In addition to individual faculty research, a number of research centers are focused on water issues and/or host water-focused seminars throughout the year. These include: • The Center for Environmental Biology • The Center for Hydrometeorology and Remote Sensing • The Center for Land, Environment, and Natural Resources in UCI's School of Law • The Center for Unconventional Security Affairs • The Newkirk Center for Science and Society • The UCI Water Energy Nexus Center Additionally, examples of campuswide initiatives and community partnerships include: • Water UCI – This initiative coordinates collaboration across schools, departments, and existing research centers around questions of fundamental and applied water science, technology, management, and policy. • UC Stormwater Initiative – This multi-campus initiative led by UCI, is coordinating research between the southern UC campuses (Irvine, Los Angeles, Riverside, Santa Barbara, and San Diego) to develop innovations in how urban stormwater is collected and managed. • Salton Sea Initiative – This initiative mobilizes UCI's research, teaching, and service resources to address myriad sustainability challenges facing the Salton Sea region. The California Natural Resources Agency named UCI biologist Tim Bradley, director of the Salton Sea Initiative, to the science advisory committee for the state effort to preserve its largest inland body of water. • FloodRISE – This National Science Foundation (NSF)-funded project seeks to understand what factors and conditions allow parcel-level prediction of urban flooding to catalyze behavioral change in flood vulnerable communities. • UCI Water—Partnerships for International Research & Education – This NSF-funded project catalyzes, through research and education, the development and deployment of low-energy options for improving water productivity while protecting human and ecosystem health. • Borrego Springs Water Sustainability and Climate – This project evaluates the integrated water infrastructure of the arid, closed-basin Borrego Springs Aquifer System using a participatory science framework. • UCI/IRWD Steering Committee – Composed of UCI faculty and staff and Irvine Ranch Water District (IRWD) leadership, the committee promotes collaboration and coordination on water resource management, drought resilience, and university/water district collaboration on research and education opportunities.

ADMISSIONS

Freshman Academic Profile: Average high school GPA 4.0. 98% in top 10% of high school class, 100% in top 25% of high school class, 100% in top 50% of high school class. 75% from public high schools. **Test Scores:** SAT Math middle 50% range 590-730. SAT EBRW middle 50% range 580-680. Minimum internet-based TOEFL 80. Minimum paper TOEFL 550. **Basis for Candidate Selection:** *Very important factors considered include:* rigor of secondary school record, academic GPA, application essay, standardized test scores, extracurricular activities, talent/ability, volunteer work, work experience. *Important factors considered include:* character/personal qualities. *Other factors considered include:* first generation, geographical residence, state residency. **Freshman Admission Requirements:** High school diploma is required and GED is accepted *Academic units required:* 4 English, 3 math, 2 science, 2 science labs, 2 foreign language, 2 history, 1 academic elective, 1 visual/performing arts, *Academic units recommended:* 4 English, 4 math, 3 science, 3 science labs, 3 foreign language, 2 history, 1 academic elective, 1 visual/performing arts. **Freshman Admission Statistics:** 85,102 applied, 36.5% admitted, 21% enrolled. **Transfer Admission Requirements:** High school transcript, college transcript(s), essay or personal statement, Minimum college GPA of 2.0 required. Lowest grade transferable C. **General Admission Information:** Application fee $70. Regular application deadline 11/30. Nonfall registration accepted.

COSTS AND FINANCIAL AID

Student Employment: Federal Work-Study Program available. Institutional employment available. **Financial Aid Statistics:** 97% needy freshmen, 93% needy undergrads receive need-based scholarship or grant aid. 1% freshmen, 1% undergrads receive non-need-based scholarship or grant aid. 76% freshmen, 66% undergrads receive need-based self-help aid. 0% freshmen, 0% undergrads receive athletic scholarships. Average cumulative indebtedness $20,628.

UNIVERSITY OF CALIFORNIA—LOS ANGELES

405 Hilgard Avenue, Los Angeles, CA 90095-1436
Phone: 310-825-3101 • **Financial Aid Phone:** 310-206-0400 • **CEEB Code:** 4837
Fax: 310-206-1206 • **Website:** www.ucla.edu • **ACT Code:** 448

This public school was founded in 1919. It has a 419 acre campus.

RATINGS

Admissions Selectivity Rating: 98   **Fire Safety Rating:** 92   **Green Rating:** 90

STUDENTS AND FACULTY

Enrollment: 30,990. **Student Body:** 57% female, 43% male, 12% out-of-state, 12% international (116 countries represented). Asian 28%, African American 3%, Caucasian 27%, Hispanic 22%, Native American <1%, Pacific Islander <1%, Two or more races 5%, Race unknown 2%.
Retention and Graduation: 97% freshmen return for sophomore year. 75% freshmen graduate within 4 years. 91% freshmen graduate within 6 years. **Faculty:** Student/faculty ratio 17:1. 1,596 full-time faculty, 12% are members of minority groups, 35% are women. 0% of classes are taught by teaching assistants.

ACADEMICS

Degrees: Bachelor's; Doctoral/Professional; Doctoral/Research; **Master's Classes:** Most classes have 10-19 students. **Most popular majors:** Biology/Biological Sciences, General; Psychology, General; Business/Managerial Economics. **Special Study Options:** Accelerated program; Double major; Honors program; Independent study; Internships; Student-designed major; Study abroad. Honors programs: The College Honors Program. **Disability Services offered to physically disabled students:** Note-taking services; Reader services; Tape recorders; Tutors. **Career services:** Alumni network; Alumni services; Career assessment; Career/job search classes; Internships; Regional alumni

FACILITIES

Housing: Apartments for married students; Apartments for single students; Coed dorms; Cooperative housing; Fraternity/sorority housing; Special housing for disabled student; Theme housing; Wellness housing 100% of campus accessible to physically disabled. **Special Academic Facilities/Equipment:** Fowler Museum, Costen Institute of Archeology facility, Hammer Museum, Film and Television Archive, Embedded and Reconfigurable Systems Lab, Graphics & Vision Lab, Animation Lab, Ethnomusicology Archive, Jonsson Comprehensive Cancer Center labs, Basic Plasma Science facility, Planeterrella Aurora Simulator, Neuropsychiatric Institute labs, Brain Research Institute for Neuroscience and Genetics Research Labs, California NanoSystems Institute (CNSI) Labs, Broad Stem Cell Center Labs, Institute for Cell Mimetic Space Exploration facility, Particle Beam Physics lab, Southern California Particle Center, Simulation Center at the David Geffen School of Medicine, Ronald Regan Medical Center, Mattel Children's Hospital, Center for Population Research facility, California Census Research Data Center, LaKretz Center for California Conservation Science, Institute of Environmental and Sustainability facility, Stunt Ranch Reserve and Education Center, Luskin Conference Center, Lake Arrowhead Conference Center, Mildred E. Mathias Botanical Garden, Division of Laboratory Animal Medicine, Biological Collections, Grunwald Center for Graphic Arts, Franklin D. Murphy Sculpture Garden. Meteorite Collection and Gallery **Computers:** Students can register for classes online. Administrative functions (other than registration) can be performed online.

CAMPUS LIFE

Environment: Metropolis **Activities:** Campus Ministries; Choral groups; Concert band; Dance; Drama/theater; International Student Organization; Jazz band; Literary magazine; Marching band; Model UN; Music ensembles; Musical theater; Opera; Pep band; Radio station; Student government; Student newspaper; Student-run film society; Symphony orchestra; Television station; Yearbook 870 registered organizations, 21 honor societies, 38 religious organizations. 36 fraternities, 28 sororities. **Athletics (Intercollegiate):** *Men:* baseball, basketball, cross-country, football, golf, soccer, tennis, track/field (outdoor), track/field (indoor), volleyball, water polo. *Women:* basketball, crew/rowing, cross-country, diving, golf, gymnastics, soccer, softball, swimming, tennis, track/field (outdoor), track/field (indoor), volleyball, water polo. **On-Campus Highlights:** The UCLA Library, UCLA Fowler Museum of Cultural History, UCLA Book Store, DeNeve Plaza, Pauley Pavilion—Sports Hall of Fame **Environmental Initiatives:** The University of California and state legislation set a target of reducing greenhouse gas emissions to 1990 levels by 2020. UCLA's comprehensive Climate Action Plan lays out a plan for the university to achieve that goal by 2012, eight years ahead. The plan catalogues the steps the university has taken in the past and contains a detailed financial feasibility analysis for the initiatives that the university will undertake in energy and transportation to reduce greenhouse gas emissions. The initiatives outlined in the Climate Action Plan, in addition to addressing a critical environmental issue, will also conserve university resources and result in significant cost reductions. The energy initiatives have an average payback period of less than 5 years, with some lighting initiatives paying back through cost savings in less than a year. By demonstrating that it is possible to address climate change through concrete verifiable emissions reductions even in the toughest budget situation, UCLA is setting an example for the rest of California and the nation. The plan also catalogues academic and research initiatives at UCLA focused on climate change and sustainability. UCLA is a living laboratory for climate and sustainability research. Undergraduate and graduate students engage with staff and faculty to pilot new technologies and policies on the university campus. With over 25 research centers focused on climate and sustainability, UCLA is creating the technology and training the leaders of tomorrow, while leading by example in our own operations.

ADMISSIONS

Freshman Academic Profile: Average high school GPA 4.4. 97% in top 10% of high school class, 100% in top 25% of high school class, 100% in top 50% of high school class. 68% from public high schools. **Test Scores:** SAT Math middle 50% range 610-760. SAT EBRW middle 50% range 630-730. ACT middle 50% range 27-33. Minimum internet-based TOEFL 83. Minimum paper TOEFL 550. **Basis for Candidate Selection:** *Very important factors considered include:* rigor of secondary school record, academic GPA, application essay, standardized test scores. *Important factors considered include:* extracurricular activities, talent/ability, volunteer work, work experience. *Other factors considered include:* character/personal qualities, first generation, geographical residence. **Freshman Admission Requirements:** High school diploma is required and GED is accepted *Academic units required:* 4 English, 3 math, 2 science, 2 science labs, 2 foreign language, 2 history, 1 academic elective, 1 visual/performing arts, *Academic units recommended:* 4 English, 4 math, 3 science, 3 science labs, 3 foreign language, 2 history, 1 academic elective, 1 visual/performing arts. **Freshman Admission Statistics:** 102,242 applied, 16.1% admitted, 73% enrolled. **Transfer Admission Requirements:** college transcript(s), essay or personal statement, statement of good standing from prior institution(s). Minimum college GPA of 2.4 required. Lowest grade transferable D. **General Admission Information:** Application fee $70. Regular application deadline 11/30. Nonfall registration accepted.

COSTS AND FINANCIAL AID

Required Forms and Deadlines: FAFSA. **Notification of Awards:** Applicants will be notified of awards on a rolling basis beginning 3/15. **Types of Aid:** *Need-based scholarships/grants:* College/university scholarship or grant aid from institutional funds; Federal Nursing Scholarships; Federal Pell; Private scholarships; SEOG; State scholarships/grants; United Negro College Fund. *Loans:* Direct PLUS loans; Direct Subsidized Stafford Loans. *Student Employment:* Federal Work-Study Program available. Institutional employment available. **Financial Aid Statistics:** 97% needy freshmen, 96% needy undergrads receive need-based scholarship or grant aid. 2% freshmen, 1% undergrads receive non-need-based scholarship or grant aid. 57% freshmen, 62% undergrads receive need-based self-help aid. 1% freshmen, 1% undergrads receive athletic scholarships. 54% freshmen, 55% undergrads receive any aid. 46% undergrads borrow to pay for school. Average cumulative indebtedness $21,596. **Criteria for awarding aid:** *Non-need-based:* Academics, Art, Job skills.

UNIVERSITY OF CALIFORNIA—MERCED

5200 North Lake Raod, Merced, CA 95343
Phone: 209-228-7178 • **Financial Aid Phone:** 209 228-7178
E-mail: admissions@ucmerced.edu
Fax: 209-228-4244 • **Website:** http://www.ucmerced.edu • **ACT Code:** 450

This public school was founded in 2005. It has a 815 acre campus.

RATINGS

Admissions Selectivity Rating: 76   **Fire Safety Rating:** 96   **Green Rating:** 95

STUDENTS AND FACULTY

Enrollment: 5,092. **Student Body:** 50% female, 50% male, 0% out-of-state, 7% international (6 countries represented). Asian 21%, African American 5%, Caucasian 11%, Hispanic 51%, Native American <1%, Pacific Islander 1%, Two or more races 3%, Race unknown 1%.

Retention and Graduation: 81% freshmen return for sophomore year. 33% freshmen graduate within 4 years. 64% freshmen graduate within 6 years. **Faculty:** Student/faculty ratio 20:1. 348 full-time faculty, 88% hold PhDs, 32% are members of minority groups, 45% are women.

ACADEMICS
Degrees: Bachelor's; Doctoral/Research; **Master's Classes:** Most classes have 10-19 students. Most lab/discussion sessions have 10-19 students. **Special Study Options:** Accelerated program; Double major; Independent study; Internships; Study abroad. **Disability Services offered to physically disabled students:** Note-taking services. Alumni network; Alumni services; Career assessment; Internships; Regional alumni

FACILITIES
Housing: Coed dorms; Special housing for disabled students

CAMPUS LIFE
Environment: City **Activities:** Campus Ministries; Choral groups; Dance; Pep band; Radio station; Student government; Student newspaper; Student-run film society; Yearbook

ADMISSIONS
Freshman Academic Profile: Average high school GPA 3.6. **Test Scores:** SAT Math middle 50% range 440-550. SAT EBRW middle 50% range 420-520. ACT middle 50% range 18-23. Minimum internet-based TOEFL 80. Minimum paper TOEFL 550. **Basis for Candidate Selection:** *Very important factors considered include:* rigor of secondary school record, academic GPA, application essay, standardized test scores. *Important factors considered include:* class rank, extracurricular activities, talent/ability. *Other factors considered include:* recommendation(s), character/personal qualities, first generation, geographical residence, state residency, volunteer work, work experience, level of applicant's interest. **Freshman Admission Requirements:** High school diploma is required and GED is accepted *Academic units required:* 4 English, 3 math, 2 science, 2 science labs, 2 foreign language, 2 history, 1 academic elective, 1 visual/performing arts, *Academic units recommended:* 4 math, 3 science, 3 science labs, 3 foreign language. **Freshman Admission Statistics:** 22,574 applied, 69.2% admitted, 15% enrolled. **General Admission Information:** Application fee $70. Regular application deadline 11/30. Nonfall registration accepted. Admission may be deferred for a maximum of 1 year.

COSTS AND FINANCIAL AID
Annual out-of-state tuition $39,516. Room and board $15,923. Required fees $2,096. Average book expense $1,106. *Student Employment:* Federal Work-Study Program available. Institutional employment available.

UNIVERSITY OF CALIFORNIA—RIVERSIDE

900 University Ave., Riverside, CA 92521
Phone: 951-827-3411 • **Financial Aid Phone:** (951) 827-7249
E-mail: admissions@ucr.edu • **CEEB Code:** 4839
Fax: 951-827-6344 • **Website:** www.ucr.edu

This public school was founded in 1954. It has a 1200 acre campus.

RATINGS
Admissions Selectivity Rating: 92   **Fire Safety Rating:** 94   **Green Rating:** 98

STUDENTS AND FACULTY
Enrollment: 20,044. **Student Body:** 54% female, 46% male, 1% out-of-state, 3% international (100 countries represented). Asian 34%, African American 3%, Caucasian 11%, Hispanic 41%, Native American <1%, Pacific Islander <1%, Two or more races 6%, Race unknown 1%.
Retention and Graduation: 89% freshmen return for sophomore year. 53% freshmen graduate within 4 years. 75% freshmen graduate within 6 years. **Faculty:** Student/faculty ratio 22:1. 976 full-time faculty, 98% hold PhDs, 40% are members of minority groups, 35% are women. 0% of classes are taught by teaching assistants.

ACADEMICS
Degrees: Bachelor's; Doctoral; Doctoral Other; Doctoral/Professional; Doctoral/Research; **Master's Classes:** Most classes have 20-29 students. Most lab/discussion sessions have 20-29 students. **Most popular majors:** Biological And Biomedical Sciences, Other; Psychology, General; Business Administration And Management, General. **Special Study Options:** Accelerated program; Cooperative education program; Cross-registration; Distance learning; Double major; English as a Second Language (ESL); Honors program; Independent study; Internships; Study abroad; Teacher certification program. Honors programs: University Honors is designed for students who have shown through their own high achievement that they value intellectual challenges and want to be a part of an innovative, diverse, and demanding learning community. Students benefit from close interaction with Honors Faculty in small class settings, and with Professional Staff who provide developmental advising to help them optimize their educational experience at UCR. High impact, experiential learning opportunities available to Honors students include; undergraduate research, scholarly and creative work, internships, service learning, and faculty-led co-curricular activities. In addition Honors students are supported by a strong peer leader support system, faculty mentorship, Honors scholarship opportunities, and preparation for prestigious scholarships and awards. These experiences are designed to prepare students for participation in a senior thesis project that advances knowledge in their discipline, culminating in an Honors Thesis. Combined degree programs: BA/MA. **Disability Services offered to physically disabled students:** Note-taking services; Reader services; Tape recorders; Tutors. **Career services:** Alumni services; Career assessment; Career/job search classes; Internships

FACILITIES
Housing: Apartments for married students; Apartments for single students; Coed dorms; Special housing for disabled student; Special housing for international students; Theme housing **Special Academic Facilities/Equipment:** Art gallery, photography museum, botanical gardens, audio-visual resource center/studios, media resource center, statistical consulting center, citrus research center and agricultural experiment station, air pollution research center, center for environmental research and technology, water resources center, geophysics and planetary physics institute, center for bibliographical studies, center for family studies, center for crime and justice studies, natural reserve system, water resources center, salinity lab. **Computers:** 100% of classrooms, 15% of dorms, 100% of libraries, 100% of dining areas, 100% of student union, 100% of common outdoor areas have wireless network access. Students can register for classes online. Administrative functions (other than registration) can be performed online.

CAMPUS LIFE
Environment: City **Activities:** Campus Ministries; Choral groups; Concert band; Dance; Drama/theater; International Student Organization; Jazz band; Literary magazine; Model UN; Music ensembles; Pep band; Radio station; Student government; Student newspaper; Student-run film society; Symphony orchestra 264 registered organizations, 9 honor societies, 27 religious organizations. 20 fraternities, 20 sororities. **Athletics (Intercollegiate):** *Men:* baseball, basketball, cross-country, golf, soccer, tennis, track/field (outdoor), track/field (indoor). *Women:* basketball, cross-country, golf, soccer, softball, tennis, track/field (outdoor), track/field (indoor), volleyball. **On-Campus Highlights:** Basketball Games, Student Recreation Center and intramural sports, The Barn (music and comedy acts), Coffee Bean and Tea Leaf, The Highlander Union Building (HUB) **Environmental Initiatives:** UCR has a funded non-restrictive Office of Sustainability charged with coordinating sustainability initiatives throughout the campus supported by the Chancellor's Committee on Sustainability with the Chancellor serving as chair.

ADMISSIONS
Freshman Academic Profile: Average high school GPA 3.7. 94% in top 10% of high school class, 100% in top 25% of high school class, 100% in top 50% of high school class. 90% from public high schools. **Test Scores:** SAT Math middle 50% range 540-660. SAT EBRW middle 50% range 550-640. ACT middle 50% range 23-29. Minimum internet-based TOEFL 80. Minimum paper TOEFL 550. **Basis for Candidate Selection:** *Very important factors considered include:* rigor of secondary school record, academic GPA, application essay, standardized test scores. *Other factors considered include:* extracurricular activities, talent/ability, character/personal qualities, first generation, state residency, volunteer work, work experience. **Freshman Admission Requirements:** High school diploma is required and GED is accepted *Academic units required:* 4 English, 3 math, 2 science, 2 science labs, 2 foreign language, 2 history, 1 academic elective, 1 visual/performing arts, *Academic units recommended:* 4 English, 4 math, 3 science, 3 science labs, 3 foreign language, 2 history, 1 academic elective, 1 visual/performing arts. **Freshman Admission Statistics:** 43,682 applied, 57.2% admitted, 18% enrolled. **Transfer Admission Requirements:** college transcript(s), essay or personal statement, statement of good standing from prior institution(s). Minimum college GPA of 2.4 required. Lowest grade transferable D-. **General Admission Information:** Application fee $70. Regular application deadline 11/30. Nonfall registration accepted.

COSTS AND FINANCIAL AID
Annual out-of-state tuition $39,516. Room and board $17,000. Average book expense $1,300. **Required Forms and Deadlines:** FAFSA; State aid form. **Notification of Awards:** Applicants will be notified of awards on a rolling basis beginning 3/1. **Types of Aid:** *Need-based scholarships/grants:* College/

university scholarship or grant aid from institutional funds; Federal Pell; Private scholarships; SEOG; State scholarships/grants. *Loans:* Direct PLUS loans; Direct Subsidized Stafford Loans; Direct Unsubsidized Stafford Loans. *Student Employment:* Federal Work-Study Program available. Institutional employment available. **Financial Aid Statistics:** 97% needy freshmen, 96% needy undergrads receive need-based scholarship or grant aid. 1% freshmen, 1% undergrads receive non-need-based scholarship or grant aid. 78% freshmen, 68% undergrads receive need-based self-help aid. 0% freshmen, 0% undergrads receive athletic scholarships. 89% freshmen, 85% undergrads receive any aid. Average cumulative indebtedness $21,838. **Criteria for awarding aid:** *Need-based:* Academics *Non-need-based:* Academics, Alumni affiliation, Art, Athletics, Leadership.

UNIVERSITY OF CALIFORNIA—SAN DIEGO

9500 Gilman Drive, La Jolla, CA 92093-0021
Phone: 858-534-4831 • **Financial Aid Phone:** (858) 534-4480
E-mail: admissionsinfo@ucsd.edu • **CEEB Code:** 4836
Fax: 858-534-5723 • **Website:** www.ucsd.edu • **ACT Code:** 459

This public school was founded in 1960. It has a 1976 acre campus.

RATINGS
Admissions Selectivity Rating: 97   **Fire Safety Rating:** 92   **Green Rating:** 96

STUDENTS AND FACULTY
Enrollment: 9,892. **Student Body:** 97% female, 3% male, 6% out-of-state, 20% international (92 countries represented). Asian 38%, African American 2%, Caucasian 19%, Hispanic 18%, Native American <1%, Pacific Islander <1%, Two or more races 0%, Race unknown 3%.
Retention and Graduation: 94% freshmen return for sophomore year. 55% freshmen graduate within 4 years. 84% freshmen graduate within 6 years. 42% grads go on to further study within 1 year. 36% grads pursue arts and sciences degrees. 17% grads pursue law degrees. 9% grads pursue business degrees. 17% grads pursue medical degrees. **Faculty:** Student/faculty ratio 19:1. 1,123 full-time faculty, 98% hold PhDs, 28% are members of minority groups, 31% are women. 0% of classes are taught by teaching assistants.

ACADEMICS
Degrees: Bachelor's; Doctoral; Doctoral/Professional; Doctoral/Research; **Master's Classes:** Most classes have 10-19 students. Most lab/discussion sessions have 10-19 students. **Most popular majors:** Biological And Biomedical Sciences; Biology/Biological Sciences, General; Economics. **Special Study Options:** Accelerated program; Cooperative education program; Cross-registration; Double major; English as a Second Language (ESL); Exchange student program (domestic); Honors program; Independent study; Internships; Liberal arts/career combination; Student-designed major; Study abroad; Teacher certification program. Honors programs: Each of UCSDs six colleges offers an honors program. Honors programs differ from college to college and year to year. MUIR HONORS SEMINAR Honors programs at John Muir College have been established to provide outstanding students with enhanced educational experiences through close interaction with faculty and other honors students. The Muir 90 Honors Seminar is by invitation and focuses primarily on entering freshmen. Please consult the Muir Academic Advising Office for details on the honors program. During the fall quarter of their freshman year, entering freshmen with outstanding high school records are invited to enroll in the Muir 90 Honors Seminar, which is noted on the UC San Diego transcript for one unit and P/NP. Students meet with a variety of faculty members from different disciplines to learn more about their research and about academic enrichment opportunities at UC San Diego. The format consists of eight meetings for Fall Quarters. The program includes discussions about a particular current issue, with professors providing insight based upon their areas of expertise. ERC First Year Honors Seminar On the basis of outstanding high school grade point averages and College Board Scholastic Aptitude Test scores, a number of entering students are invited to participate in the ERC First-Year Honors Seminar. These weekly seminars are led by Provost Ann Craig, and she invites a variety of faculty colleagues and other knowledgeable individuals to discuss their own career development and research interests. The group also goes on field trips and takes advantage of additional educational opportunities on campus. ERC Second Year Honors Program Second-year honors students have the opportunity to select topics

from MMW courses and to pursue independent study with individual faculty members. Projects may extend for one to three quarters. Honors projects are often selected for presentation at the UCSD Undergraduate Research Conference held each spring. Cultural and social events such as lectures, plays, and visits to museums are also an important component of the honors programs. The Sixth College Honors Program: • Nurtures high-achieving students academically, intellectually, and socially • Increases students' awareness about opportunities of academic, social, and cultural engagement • Motivates students to become community leaders at Sixth College, at UCSD, and in communities outside the University The Sixth College provost and Sixth College associated faculty mentor and guide honors students through seminars, research, social, and cultural events, introducing students to the academic, cultural, artistic, and social richness of the campus. Participants in the Honors Program include: • New freshmen who have distinguished themselves academically in their high schools • New freshmen who complete at least 12 graded units with a 3.7 cumulative GPA during their first quarter at UCSD • Second-year honors students who maintain a minimum cumulative GPA of 3.5 Students must maintain a 3.5 cumulative GPA to remain in the Honors Program. Qualifications for Freshman Honors Sequence • o To be invited you must have accomplished the following: 1. High school grade point average of 3.8 or higher 2. College Board Scholastic Aptitude Test (SAT) scores of 700 or above in math, writing, and reading/ comprehension o If you have fulfilled these qualifications, you are invited to enroll in SXTH 20 Freshmen Honors Seminar (0 units) for the Fall Quarter. Qualifications for Sophomore Honors Sequence • o Second-year honors students who maintain a minimum cumulative GPA of 3.5 are invited to join the Sophomore Honors Sequence. o Options for sophomore honors students include: 1. Enrolling in SXTH 96 Sixth College Honors Apprentice Research Program/ Honors Project (2 units) AND/ OR 2. Enrolling in SXTH 60 Sophomore Honors Seminar (1 unit), covering issues pertaining to technology, society, and the arts. TMC Honors Program HONORS SEMINAR—TMC 20 The Honors Seminar is offered every quarter and is open to all class levels of honors students. The seminar meets for one hour a week during five to seven weeks of the quarter. This is a small group discussion section facilitated by faculty or visiting guest lecturers. Additionally this group of students meets informally and chats with the provost and guest lecturers about issues of interest to honors students. REVELLE HONORS SEMINAR / RESEARCH OPPORTUNITY To be eligible for the Revelle College Freshman Honors Program, incoming freshman must have a high school GPA of 3.8 or higher, achieved a Verbal SAT score of 700 or higher, as well as a Math SAT score of 700 or higher. Honors Program students are invited to register for Revelle 20, in an informal weekly seminar with a variety of faculty to learn about their research and about academic enrichment opportunities. This can be particularly valuable if you are not sure of your major and can lead to early research opportunities. The Honors Seminar is noted on the transcript, but earns zero units. If you are not invited for your incoming fall quarter as a freshman you may still be invited at the end of each quarter (once grades are posted) of your first academic year as long as you maintain a 3.7 GPA with 12 graded units in that quarter. This seminar gives you the opportunity to meet and mix with the other honor students. The program also offers the following perks: o Extra Advising: Take advantage of faculty advising either through your department or by the provost, if desired. Letters of recommendation for jobs or Internships are available directly from the provost. Learn about special summer opportunities. o Social Program: With other honor students, enjoy plays, concerts, seminars and special trips such as to the Super Computer facility, Scripps Institution of Oceanography, Balboa Park, and the Globe Theatre. All events are free! o Welcome Week Reception: Start the year right meeting faculty, staff, new honor students and returning students from this year's honors program. Make valuable connections. The Revelle Honors program is in addition to any scholarship you may have received, and it is meant to be only a small part of the excellent education you will receive at Revelle College and U.C. San Diego. There are three different ways by which you may learn more about the program, the college, and the University: o Admit Day: Attend Admit Day on Saturday, April 12, 2008 for a college session, a tour of the residence halls, and department presentations. o Contact: Revelle prides itself on individual attention to students; if you have questions please call the Revelle College Provost's Office at (858) 534-1571 or e-mail ehurreymayer@ucsd.edu. o Information Sessions: Information Sessions TBA through the Admissions Office. The Warren College Honors Program A Student's Perspective The Honors Program at Warren College is more than getting to state that we are college honors students. This program offers a vast expanse of cultural and educational opportunities that allow us to further develop our college experience. Tickets to theatre productions, admission to museum exhibits, and unique social gatherings are all common offers brought to us as both rewards for our hard work and encouragement to continue our commitment to excellence. We also offer the faculty lecture series, an activity exclusive to our program. While many students may think that this sounds like attending extra classes during free time for no credit, our lecture series includes some of the most-prestigious and most highly-recommended faculty members, speaking on subjects about which they are extremely passionate, not curriculums which they are assigned. These professors and lecturers are requested for this program because our students have attended their classes and lectures themselves, and feel that what these faculty members have to say is compelling and distinctive. In addition, for those of us who enjoy being active in our community, there is the Honors Council; a group of Honors students which meets every other week. The role of the council is to provide the student voice in the governing of the program. We get the chance to provide suggestions as to how our program is represented and run, and our main responsibility is to help create and organize the various events which are offered to the honors students. Along with programs I mentioned earlier, we are also active in facilitating scholars day and often get to speak with prospective honors students at various organization fairs. Combined degree programs: BA/MA; BA/MD; BA/MEng. **Disability Services offered to physically disabled students:** Note-taking services; Reader services; Tape recorders; Tutors. **Career services:** Alumni network; Alumni services; Career assessment; Career/job search classes; Internships; Regional alumni

FACILITIES

Housing: Apartments for married students; Apartments for single students; Coed dorms; Special housing for disabled student; Special housing for international students 100% of campus accessible to physically diasbled. **Special Academic Facilities/Equipment:** Art galleries, center for U.S.-Mexican studies, music recording studio, audiovisual center, center for music experimentation, aquarium, structural lab, San Diego supercomputer center,electron microscopes lab, the UC San Diego Medical Center, Scripps Institution of Oceanography, California Institute for Telecommunications and Information Technology (Calit2), Institute on Global Conflict and Cooperation; Institute of the Americas. **Computers:** 100% of classrooms, 100% of dorms, 100% of libraries, 100% of dining areas, 100% of student union, 30% of common outdoor areas have wireless network access. Students can register for classes online. Administrative functions (other than registration) can be performed online.

CAMPUS LIFE

Environment: Metropolis **Activities:** Campus Ministries; Choral groups; Concert band; Dance; Drama/theater; International Student Organization; Jazz band; Literary magazine; Marching band; Model UN; Music ensembles; Musical theater; Opera; Pep band; Radio station; Student government; Student newspaper; Student-run film society; Symphony orchestra; Television station; Yearbook 406 registered organizations, 5 honor societies, 46 religious organizations. 19 fraternities, 14 sororities. **Athletics (Intercollegiate):** *Men:* baseball, basketball, crew/rowing, cross-country, diving, fencing, golf, soccer, swimming, tennis, track/field (outdoor), volleyball, water polo. *Women:* basketball, crew/rowing, cross-country, diving, fencing, soccer, softball, swimming, tennis, track/field (outdoor), volleyball, water polo. **On-Campus Highlights:** Geisel Library, Stuart Art (sculpture) Gallery, Sun God Statue, Ocean Cliffs-Torrey Pines State Reserve, Stephen Birch Aquarium and Museum **Environmental Initiatives:** The LEED Gold Certified Sustainability Resource Center (SRC)

ADMISSIONS

Freshman Academic Profile: Average high school GPA 4.1. 100% in top 10% of high school class, 100% in top 25% of high school class, 100% in top 50% of high school class. **Test Scores:** SAT Math middle 50% range 590-720. SAT EBRW middle 50% range 550-660. ACT middle 50% range 26-32. Minimum paper TOEFL 550. **Basis for Candidate Selection:** *Very important factors considered include:* rigor of secondary school record, academic GPA, application essay, standardized test scores. *Important factors considered include:* extracurricular activities, talent/ability, character/personal qualities, state residency, volunteer work. *Other factors considered include:* first generation, geographical residence, work experience. **Freshman Admission Requirements:** High school diploma is required and GED is accepted *Academic units required:* 4 English, 3 math, 2 science, 2 science labs, 2 foreign language, 2 history, 1 academic elective, 1 visual/performing arts, *Academic units recommended:* 4 English, 4 math, 3 science, 3 science labs, 3 foreign language, 2 history, 1 academic elective, 1 visual/performing arts. **Freshman Admission Statistics:** 88,428 applied, 34.2% admitted, 19% enrolled. **Transfer Admission Requirements:** college transcript(s), essay or personal statement, statement of good standing from prior institution(s). Minimum college GPA of 2.4 required. Lowest grade transferable D. **General Admission Information:** Application fee $70. Regular application deadline 11/30.

COSTS AND FINANCIAL AID

Annual in-state tuition $13,254. Annual out-of-state tuition $40,644. Room and board $13,254. Required fees $3,553. Average book expense $1,198. **Required Forms and Deadlines:** FAFSA; State aid form. **Notification of Awards:** Applicants will be notified of awards on a rolling basis beginning 3/15. **Types of Aid:** *Need-based scholarships/grants:* College/university scholarship or grant aid from institutional funds; Federal Pell; Private scholarships; SEOG; State scholarships/grants. *Loans:* Direct PLUS loans; Direct Subsidized Stafford Loans; Direct Unsubsidized Stafford Loans. *Student Employment:* Federal Work-Study Program available. Institutional employment available. **Financial Aid Statistics:** 92% needy freshmen, 94% needy undergrads receive need-based scholarship or grant aid. 2% freshmen, 1% undergrads receive non-need-

based scholarship or grant aid. 78% freshmen, 76% undergrads receive need-based self-help aid. 0% freshmen, 0% undergrads receive athletic scholarships. 77% freshmen, 63% undergrads receive any aid. 60% undergrads borrow to pay for school. Average cumulative indebtedness $21,660. **Criteria for awarding aid:** *Need-based:* Academics, Art, Leadership, Minority status, Music/drama *Non-need-based:* Academics, Art, Athletics, Leadership, Minority status, Music/drama.

UNIVERSITY OF CALIFORNIA— SANTA BARBARA

552 University Road, Santa Barbara, CA 93106-2014
Phone: 805-893-2881 • **Financial Aid Phone:** (805) 893-2432
E-mail: admissions@sa.ucsb.edu • **CEEB Code:** 4835
Fax: 805-893-2676 • **Website:** www.ucsb.edu

This public school was founded in 1909. It has a 989 acre campus.

RATINGS

Admissions Selectivity Rating: 97   **Fire Safety Rating:** 95   **Green Rating:** 97

STUDENTS AND FACULTY

Enrollment: 22,186. **Student Body:** 54% female, 46% male, 4% out-of-state, 8% international (82 countries represented). Asian 21%, African American 2%, Caucasian 34%, Hispanic 26%, Native American <1%, Pacific Islander <1%, Two or more races 6%, Race unknown 1%.
Retention and Graduation: 92% freshmen return for sophomore year. 70% freshmen graduate within 4 years. 87% freshmen graduate within 6 years.
Faculty: Student/faculty ratio 17:1. 922 full-time faculty, 100% hold PhDs, 20% are members of minority groups, 38% are women.

ACADEMICS

Degrees: Bachelor's; Doctoral/Research; Master's; Post-Bachelor's certificate; Post-Master's certificate **Classes:** Most classes have 10-19 students. Most lab/discussion sessions have 10-19 students. **Most popular majors:** Biology/Biological Sciences, General; Psychology, General; Economics, General. **Special Study Options:** Accelerated program; Cross-registration; Double major; Dual enrollment; English as a Second Language (ESL); Exchange student program (domestic); Honors program; Independent study; Internships; Student-designed major; Study abroad; Teacher certification program. Honors programs: The Letters & Science Honors Program is designed to give students in the College of Letters and Science the opportunity to pursue their interests as part of a small community of scholars. The program connects such students to the resources of a large university, while providing an intimate collegiate atmosphere where students work closely with peers and professors in small classes, research laboratories, and special program and activities. Combined degree programs: BA/MA. **Disability Services offered to physically disabled students:** Note-taking services; Reader services; Tape recorders; Tutors. **Career services:** Career assessment; Career/job search classes; Internships

FACILITIES

Housing: Apartments for married students; Apartments for single students; Coed dorms; Cooperative housing; Fraternity/sorority housing; Special housing for international students; Theme housing; Wellness housing 100% of campus accessible to physically diasbled. **Special Academic Facilities/Equipment:** Art museum, centers for black studies, Chicano studies, and study of developing nations, institutes for applied behavioral sciences, community/organizational research, marine science, and theoretical physics, Channel Islands field station. **Computers:** 100% of dorms, 100% of dining areas, 100% of student union, have wireless network access. Students can register for classes online. Administrative functions (other than registration) can be performed online.

CAMPUS LIFE

Environment: City **Activities:** Campus Ministries; Choral groups; Concert band; Dance; Drama/theater; International Student Organization; Jazz band; Literary magazine; Model UN; Music ensembles; Musical theater; Opera; Pep band; Radio station; Student government; Student newspaper; Student-run film society; Symphony orchestra; Television station; Yearbook 508 registered organizations, 5 honor societies, 19 religious organizations. 17 fraternities, 18 sororities. **Athletics (Intercollegiate):** *Men:* baseball, basketball, cross-country, diving, golf, gymnastics, soccer, swimming, tennis, track/field (outdoor), volleyball, water polo. *Women:* basketball, cross-country, diving, gymnastics, soccer, softball, swimming, tennis, track/field (outdoor), volleyball, water polo. **On-Campus Highlights:** Storke Tower Plaza/University Center, University Art Museum, UCSB Davidson Library, Recreation Center, Career and Counseling Services Center **Environmental Initiatives:** 1) Green buildings: minimum silver and strive for gold LEED certification – six buildings are currently certified, including San Clemente Villages Graduate Housing – one of the largest Gold certified housing projects in the US – and Bren Hall – the first building in the US to receive two Platinum ratings for new construction and existing buildings. Plus, 24 additional existing buildings scheduled to be certified in the next couple years through the USGBC Portfolio Program. UCSB has the most LEED EB buildings in the UC System. We created Low Environmental Impact Cleaning Policy for the campus custodial services. All cleaning products and soaps used by the custodial staff are Green Seal certified. Plus toilet tissue, seat covers, and brown paper towels have 100% recycled content. Housing & Residential Services, supports solar water heating providing hot water for dorms, recycling used cooking oil from dining commons for biofuel, extensive recycling program including composting of food waste, purchasing local and/or organic foods for dining commons, using Green Seal cleaning products for custodial duties.

ADMISSIONS

Freshman Academic Profile: Average high school GPA 4.1. 100% in top 10% of high school class, 100% in top 25% of high school class, 100% in top 50% of high school class. 80% from public high schools. **Test Scores:** SAT Math middle 50% range 620-760. SAT EBRW middle 50% range 620-710. ACT middle 50% range 26-32. Minimum internet-based TOEFL 80. Minimum paper TOEFL 550. **Basis for Candidate Selection:** *Very important factors considered include:* academic GPA, application essay, standardized test scores. *Important factors considered include:* rigor of secondary school record. *Other factors considered include:* extracurricular activities, talent/ability, character/personal qualities, first generation, geographical residence, state residency, volunteer work, work experience. **Freshman Admission Requirements:** High school diploma is required and GED is accepted *Academic units required:* 4 English, 3 math, 2 science, 2 science labs, 2 foreign language, 2 history, 1 academic elective, 1 visual/performing arts, *Academic units recommended:* 4 English, 4 math, 3 science, 3 science labs, 3 foreign language, 2 history, 1 academic elective, 1 visual/performing arts. **Freshman Admission Statistics:** 80,319 applied, 32.7% admitted, 17% enrolled. **Transfer Admission Requirements:** High school transcript, college transcript(s), essay or personal statement, Minimum college GPA of 2.4 required. Lowest grade transferable D. **General Admission Information:** Application fee $70. Regular application deadline 11/30. Nonfall registration accepted.

COSTS AND FINANCIAL AID

Annual in-state tuition $14,778. Annual out-of-state tuition $40,644. Room and board $14,778. Required fees $1,779. Average book expense $1,143. **Required Forms and Deadlines:** FAFSA. **Types of Aid:** *Need-based scholarships/grants:* College/university scholarship or grant aid from institutional funds; Federal Pell; SEOG; State scholarships/grants. *Loans:* Direct PLUS loans; Direct Subsidized Stafford Loans; Direct Unsubsidized Stafford Loans. *Student Employment:* Federal Work-Study Program available. Institutional employment available. **Financial Aid Statistics:** 95% needy freshmen, 93% needy undergrads receive need-based scholarship or grant aid. 1% freshmen, 1% undergrads receive non-need-based scholarship or grant aid. 64% freshmen, 62% undergrads receive need-based self-help aid. 1% freshmen, 1% undergrads receive athletic scholarships. 60% undergrads receive any aid. 56% undergrads borrow to pay for school. Average cumulative indebtedness $20,978. **Criteria for awarding aid:** *Need-based:* Academics, Alumni affiliation, Art, Athletics, Music/drama *Non-need-based:* Academics, Alumni affiliation, Athletics.

UNIVERSITY OF CALIFORNIA—SANTA CRUZ

1156 High Street, Santa Cruz, CA 95064
Phone: 831-459-4008 • **Financial Aid Phone:** 831-459-2963
E-mail: admissions@ucsc.edu • **CEEB Code:** 4860
Fax: 831-459-4452 • **Website:** www.ucsc.edu

This public school was founded in 1965. It has a 2000 acre campus.

RATINGS

Admissions Selectivity Rating: 93   **Fire Safety Rating:** 80   **Green Rating:** 98

STUDENTS AND FACULTY

Enrollment: 17,577. **Student Body:** 50% female, 50% male, 4% out-of-state, 6% international (53 countries represented). Asian 22%, African American 2%, Caucasian 31%, Hispanic 28%, Native American <1%, Pacific Islander <1%, Two or more races 8%, Race unknown 2%.
Retention and Graduation: 90% freshmen return for sophomore year. 53% freshmen graduate within 4 years. 77% freshmen graduate within 6 years.
Faculty: Student/faculty ratio 18:1. 588 full-time faculty, 98% hold PhDs, 30% are members of minority groups, 40% are women. 0% of classes are taught by teaching assistants.

ACADEMICS

Degrees: Bachelor's; Doctoral; Doctoral/Research; Master's; Post-Bachelor's certificate Classes: Most classes have 10-19 students. Most lab/discussion sessions have 10-19 students. **Most popular majors:** Computer Science; Psychology, General; Business/Managerial Economics. Special Study Options: Cooperative education program; Distance learning; Double major; Exchange student program (domestic); Honors program; Independent study; Internships; Student-designed major; Study abroad; Teacher certification program. **Honors programs:** UCSC provides a variety of honors programs which are described on the following • Website: http://honors.ucsc.edu/honors-programs/index.html Combined degree programs: BA/MA. Disability Services offered to physically disabled students: Note-taking services; Reader services; Tape recorders; Tutors. **Career services:** Alumni network; Alumni services; Career assessment; Career/job search classes; Internships

FACILITIES

Housing: Apartments for married students; Apartments for single students; Coed dorms; Men's dorms; Special housing for international students; Theme housing; Wellness housing; Women's dorms 100% of campus accessible to physically disabled. **Special Academic Facilities/Equipment:** Eloise Pickard Smith Gallery Mary Porter Sesnon Gallery Center for Agroecology Wellness Center Long Marine Laboratory Arboretum **Computers:** 100% of classrooms, 100% of dorms, 100% of libraries, 100% of dining areas, 100% of student union, have wireless network access. Students can register for classes online. Administrative functions (other than registration) can be performed online.

CAMPUS LIFE

Environment: City **Activities:** Campus Ministries; Choral groups; Dance; Drama/theater; International Student Organization; Jazz band; Literary magazine; Model UN; Music ensembles; Musical theater; Opera; Radio station; Student government; Student newspaper; Student-run film society; Symphony orchestra; Television station 138 registered organizations, 3 honor societies, 19 religious organizations. 9 fraternities, 11 sororities. **Athletics (Intercollegiate):** *Men:* basketball, diving, soccer, swimming, tennis, volleyball. *Women:* basketball, cross-country, diving, golf, soccer, swimming, tennis, volleyball. **On-Campus Highlights:** Arboretum, Farm and Garden, East Field House, The Quarry, Pogonip Open Area Reserve **Environmental Initiatives:** Climate Action Plan: Achieve 2000 levels of emissions by 2014

ADMISSIONS

Freshman Academic Profile: Average high school GPA 3.5. 96% in top 10% of high school class, 100% in top 25% of high school class, 100% in top 50% of high school class. 85% from public high schools. **Test Scores:** SAT Math middle 50% range 580-690. SAT EBRW middle 50% range 580-680. ACT middle 50% range 24-30. Minimum internet-based TOEFL 80. Minimum paper TOEFL 550. **Basis for Candidate Selection:** *Very important factors considered include:* rigor of secondary school record, academic GPA, application essay, standardized test scores, state residency. *Important factors considered include:* extracurricular activities, talent/ability, character/personal qualities, first generation, geographical residence. *Other factors considered include:* volunteer work, work experience. **Freshman Admission Requirements:** High school diploma is required and GED is accepted *Academic units required:* 4 English, 3 math, 2 science, 2 science labs, 2 foreign language, 1 social studies, 1 history, 1 academic elective, 1 visual/performing arts, *Academic units recommended:* 4 English, 4 math, 3 science, 3 science labs, 3 foreign language, 1 social studies, 1 history, 1 academic elective, 1 visual/performing arts. **Freshman Admission Statistics:** 52,975 applied, 51.4% admitted, 15% enrolled. **Transfer Admission Requirements:** college transcript(s), essay or personal statement, statement of good standing from prior institution(s). Minimum college GPA of 2.4 required. Lowest grade transferable D. **General Admission Information:** Application fee $70. Regular application deadline 11/30. Nonfall registration accepted.

COSTS AND FINANCIAL AID

Annual out-of-state tuition $39,516. Room and board $16,071. Required fees $2,526. Average book expense $1,152. **Required Forms and Deadlines:** FAFSA; State aid form. **Notification of Awards:** Applicants will be notified of awards on a rolling basis beginning 4/1. **Types of Aid:** *Need-based scholarships/grants:* College/university scholarship or grant aid from institutional funds; Federal Pell; Private scholarships; SEOG; State scholarships/grants. *Loans:* Direct PLUS loans; Direct Subsidized Stafford Loans; Direct Unsubsidized Stafford Loans. *Student Employment:* Federal Work-Study Program available. Institutional employment available. **Financial Aid Statistics:** 95% needy freshmen, 95% needy undergrads receive need-based scholarship or grant aid. 1% freshmen, 1% undergrads receive non-need-based scholarship or grant aid. 78% freshmen, 76% undergrads receive need-based self-help aid. 0% freshmen, 0% undergrads receive athletic scholarships. 67% freshmen, 68% undergrads receive any aid. 64% undergrads borrow to pay for school. Average cumulative indebtedness $22,580. **Criteria for awarding aid:** *Need-based:* Academics, Alumni affiliation, Art, Leadership, Music/drama *Non-need-based:* Academics, Alumni affiliation, Art, Leadership, Music/drama.

UNIVERSITY OF CENTRAL ARKANSAS

201 Donaghey Avenue, Conway, AR 72035
Phone: 501-450-3128 • **Financial Aid Phone:** 501-450-3140
E-mail: admissions@uca.edu • **CEEB Code:** 6012
Fax: 501-450-5228 • **Website:** www.uca.edu/ • **ACT Code:** 118

This public school was founded in 1907. It has a 350 acre campus.

RATINGS

Admissions Selectivity Rating: 75   **Fire Safety Rating:** 62   **Green Rating:** 61

STUDENTS AND FACULTY

Enrollment: 9,034. **Student Body:** 59% female, 41% male, 9% out-of-state, 5% international (73 countries represented). Asian 2%, African American 17%, Caucasian 66%, Hispanic 5%, Native American 1%, Pacific Islander <1%, Two or more races 4%, Race unknown <1%.
Retention and Graduation: 72% freshmen return for sophomore year. 41% freshmen graduate within 6 years. **Faculty:** 0% of classes are taught by teaching assistants.

ACADEMICS

Degrees: Associate; Bachelor's; Certificate; Doctoral; Doctoral/Professional; Doctoral/Research; Master's; Post-Bachelor's certificate; Post-Master's certificate **Classes:** Most classes have 10-19 students. Most lab/discussion sessions have 20-29 students. **Special Study Options:** Accelerated program; Cooperative education program; Distance learning; Double major; Dual enrollment; English as a Second Language (ESL); Honors program; Independent study; Internships; Study abroad; Teacher certification program. **Disability Services offered to physically disabled students:** Note-taking services; Reader services; Tape recorders. **Career services:** Alumni network; Career/job search classes; Internships; Regional alumni

FACILITIES

Housing: Apartments for single students; Coed dorms; Fraternity/sorority housing; Special housing for disabled student; Special housing for international students; Women's dorms **Special Academic Facilities/Equipment:** Greenhouse, Baum Gellery, HPER Center, Planetarium, Technology Plaza, Smartboards, H.L. Minton Center for Geospatial Analysis and Research **Computers:** 100% of classrooms, 100% of dorms, 100% of libraries, 100% of dining areas, 100% of student union, 100% of common outdoor areas have wireless network access. Students can register for classes online. Administrative functions (other than registration) can be performed online.

CAMPUS LIFE

Environment: Town **Activities:** Campus Ministries; Choral groups; Concert band; Dance; Drama/theater; International Student Organization; Jazz band; Marching band; Model UN; Music ensembles; Musical theater; Pep band; Radio station; Student government; Student newspaper; Symphony orchestra; Television station; Yearbook 158 registered organizations, 11 honor societies, 16 religious organizations. 12 fraternities, 8 sororities. **Athletics (Intercollegiate):** *Men:* baseball, basketball, cheerleading, cross-country, football, golf, soccer, tennis, track/field (outdoor), track/field (indoor). *Women:* basketball, cheerleading, cross-country, golf, soccer, softball, tennis, track/field (outdoor), track/field (indoor), volleyball. **On-Campus Highlights:** Student Center, HPER Center, Baum Gallery, Estes Stadium, Farris Center

ADMISSIONS

Freshman Academic Profile: Average high school GPA 3.5. 21% in top 10% of high school class, 49% in top 25% of high school class, 79% in top 50% of high school class. **Test Scores:** SAT Math middle 50% range 500-580. SAT EBRW middle 50% range 470-555. ACT middle 50% range 21-27. Minimum internet-based TOEFL 61. Minimum paper TOEFL 500. **Basis for Candidate Selection:** *Very important factors considered include:* academic GPA, standardized test scores. **Freshman Admission Requirements:** High school diploma is required and GED is accepted *Academic units recommended:* 4 English, 4 math, 3 science, 3 social studies, 6 academic electives. **Freshman Admission Statistics:** 5,362 applied, 89.9% admitted, 40% enrolled. **Transfer Admission Requirements:** college transcript(s), statement of good standing

from prior institution(s). Minimum college GPA of 2.0 required. Lowest grade transferable C. **General Admission Information:** Application fee $25. Nonfall registration accepted. Admission may be deferred.

COSTS AND FINANCIAL AID

Student Employment: Federal Work-Study Program available. Institutional employment available.

UNIVERSITY OF CENTRAL FLORIDA

4000 Central Florida Blvd, Orlando, FL 32816-0111
Phone: 407-823-3000 • **Financial Aid Phone:** 407-823-2827
E-mail: admissions@ucf.edu • **CEEB Code:** 5233
Fax: 407-823-5625 • **Website:** www.ucf.edu • **ACT Code:** 735

This public school was founded in 1963. It has a 1415 acre campus.

RATINGS

Admissions Selectivity Rating: 89   **Fire Safety Rating:** 96   **Green Rating:** 92

STUDENTS AND FACULTY

Enrollment: 56,697. **Student Body:** 54% female, 46% male, 6% out-of-state, 2% international (147 countries represented). Asian 6%, African American 11%, Caucasian 49%, Hispanic 26%, Native American <1%, Pacific Islander <1%, Two or more races 4%, Race unknown 1%.
Retention and Graduation: 90% freshmen return for sophomore year. 40% freshmen graduate within 4 years. 70% freshmen graduate within 6 years. **Faculty:** Student/faculty ratio 30:1. 1,572 full-time faculty, 84% hold PhDs, 27% are members of minority groups, 43% are women. 5% of classes are taught by teaching assistants.

ACADEMICS

Degrees: Associate; Bachelor's; Certificate; Doctoral/Professional; Doctoral/Research; Master's; Post-Bachelor's certificate; Post-Master's certificate **Classes:** Most classes have 20-29 students. **Most popular majors:** Biomedical Sciences, General; Psychology, General; Health Services/Allied Health/Health Sciences, General. **Special Study Options:** Accelerated program; Cooperative education program; Distance learning; Double major; Dual enrollment; English as a Second Language (ESL); Honors program; Internships; Study abroad; Teacher certification program. Honors programs: The Burnett Honors College combines the intimacy of a small liberal arts college with the benefits of a large, research university located in a metropolitan environment. The mission of the College is to provide UCF's most academically talented and motivated students with a challenging and unique scholarly experience, creating a strong foundation for future achievements. The College strives to create a diverse learning community that fosters the pursuit of excellence, ethical, social, and civic responsibility, personal growth, and a passion for life-long learning. The Burnett Honors College offers two main tracks, University Honors and Honors in the Major. University Honors provides a special course of study to the most promising undergraduate students at the university. This program is geared toward incoming freshmen or students transferring from one of the five partner community colleges with an Honors A.A. degree. Primarily, the focus of Honors is to combine smaller classes with more engaged pedagogies. From the first day of class, students will participate in their learning experience instead of merely observing it. Honors students are encouraged to develop their intellects in ways that enhance their critical thinking, communication, team work, and creativity. University Honors curriculum comprises a special freshman symposium, General Education Program (GEP) courses, and specialized upper-division seminars and disciplinary core courses. Honors GEP courses are taught across the curriculum and are limited to enrollments of 20 students for all courses except English Composition, which is limited to 15 students. Upper division University Honors students take 9-15 hours of a combination of core courses in their fields and special interdisciplinary, team-taught, seminars. In addition, students participating in University Honors enroll in a well-respected and established first-year experience course, the Honors Symposium. Honors in the Major is a two-semester program designed where high-achieving junior and senior students undertake original and independent research in their major field under the supervision of a faculty committee. This research culminates in a thesis or creative project. Because of the diversity of student interests, academic departments oversee Honors in the Major course work. Combined degree programs: BA/JD; BA/MA; BA/MEng. **Disability Services offered to physically disabled students:** Note-taking services; Reader services; Tape recorders; Tutors. **Career services:** Alumni services; Career assessment; Career/job search classes

The Princeton Review's Complete Book of Colleges

FACILITIES

Housing: Apartments for single students; Coed dorms; Fraternity/sorority housing; Theme housing; Wellness housing 97% of campus accessible to physically diasbled. **Special Academic Facilities/Equipment:** Center for research and education in optics and lasers, arboretum, observatory, New student union, student recreation center. **Computers:** 100% of classrooms, 100% of dorms, 100% of libraries, 90% of dining areas, 100% of student union, 90% of common outdoor areas have wireless network access. Students can register for classes online. Administrative functions (other than registration) can be performed online.

CAMPUS LIFE

Environment: City **Activities:** Campus Ministries; Choral groups; Concert band; Drama/theater; International Student Organization; Jazz band; Literary magazine; Marching band; Model UN; Music ensembles; Musical theater; Pep band; Radio station; Student government; Student-run film society; Symphony orchestra; Television station 361 registered organizations, 36 honor societies, 29 religious organizations. 21 fraternities, 18 sororities. **Athletics (Intercollegiate):** *Men:* baseball, basketball, cheerleading, cross-country, football, golf, soccer, tennis. *Women:* basketball, cheerleading, crew/rowing, cross-country, golf, soccer, softball, tennis, track/field (outdoor), track/field (indoor), volleyball. **On-Campus Highlights:** Student Union, Recreation and Wellness Center, Bookstore (Starbucks cafe), Reflecting Pond, Spectrum Stadium & CFE Arena

ADMISSIONS

Freshman Academic Profile: Average high school GPA 3.9. 31% in top 10% of high school class, 70% in top 25% of high school class, 96% in top 50% of high school class. **Test Scores:** SAT Math middle 50% range 570-660. SAT EBRW middle 50% range 580-660. ACT middle 50% range 24-29. Minimum internet-based TOEFL 80. Minimum paper TOEFL 550. **Basis for Candidate Selection:** *Very important factors considered include:* rigor of secondary school record, academic GPA, standardized test scores. *Important factors considered include:* application essay. *Other factors considered include:* class rank, recommendation(s), extracurricular activities, talent/ability, character/personal qualities, first generation, alumni/ae relation, geographical residence, state residency, volunteer work, work experience, level of applicant's interest. **Freshman Admission Requirements:** High school diploma is required and GED is accepted *Academic units required:* 4 English, 4 math, 3 science, 2 science labs, 2 foreign language, 3 social studies, 2 academic electives. **Freshman Admission Statistics:** 37,693 applied, 49.9% admitted, 37% enrolled. **Transfer Admission Requirements:** college transcript(s). Minimum college GPA of 2.0 required. Lowest grade transferable D. **General Admission Information:** Application fee $30. Priority deadline 1/1. Regular application deadline 5/1. Nonfall registration accepted.

COSTS AND FINANCIAL AID

Annual in-state tuition $10,011. Annual out-of-state tuition $22,467. Room and board $10,011. Average book expense $1,152. **Required Forms and Deadlines:** FAFSA. **Notification of Awards:** Applicants will be notified of awards on a rolling basis beginning 3/15. **Types of Aid:** *Need-based scholarships/grants:* College/university scholarship or grant aid from institutional funds; Federal Pell; Private scholarships; SEOG; State scholarships/grants. *Loans:* Direct PLUS loans; Direct Subsidized Stafford Loans; Direct Unsubsidized Stafford Loans. *Student Employment:* Federal Work-Study Program available. Institutional employment available. **Financial Aid Statistics:** 66% needy freshmen, 71% needy undergrads receive need-based scholarship or grant aid. 65% freshmen, 45% undergrads receive non-need-based scholarship or grant aid. 54% freshmen, 62% undergrads receive need-based self-help aid. 1% freshmen, 1% undergrads receive athletic scholarships. 86% freshmen, 78% undergrads receive any aid. 52% undergrads borrow to pay for school. Average cumulative indebtedness $21,911. **Criteria for awarding aid:** *Need-based:* Academics, Athletics, Leadership, Minority status, Music/drama *Non-need-based:* Academics, Alumni affiliation, Athletics, Leadership, State/district residency.

See page 1056.

PO Box 800, Warrensburg, MO 64093
Phone: 660-543-4290 • **Financial Aid Phone:** 660-543-8266
E-mail: admit@ucmo.edu • **CEEB Code:** 6090
Fax: 660-543-8517 • **Website:** www.cmsu.edu • **ACT Code:** 2272

This public school was founded in 1871. It has a 1561 acre campus.

RATINGS

Admissions Selectivity Rating: 75 **Fire Safety Rating:** 62 **Green Rating:** 60*

STUDENTS AND FACULTY

Enrollment: 8,577. **Student Body:** 55% female, 45% male, 11% out-of-state, 2% international (60 countries represented). Asian 1%, African American 11%, Caucasian 75%, Hispanic 5%, Native American <1%, Pacific Islander <1%, Two or more races 5%, Race unknown 1%.
Retention and Graduation: 72% freshmen return for sophomore year. 25% freshmen graduate within 4 years. **Faculty:** Student/faculty ratio 18:1. 494 full-time faculty, 71% hold PhDs, 14% are members of minority groups, 49% are women.

ACADEMICS

Degrees: Bachelor's; Certificate; Master's; Post-Bachelor's certificate; Post-Master's certificate **Classes:** Most classes have 20-29 students. Most lab/discussion sessions have 10-19 students. **Most popular majors:** Education, General; Criminal Justice/Law Enforcement Administration; Marketing/Marketing Management, General. **Special Study Options:** Accelerated program; Cooperative education program; Cross-registration; Distance learning; Double major; Dual enrollment; English as a Second Language (ESL); Exchange student program (domestic); Honors program; Independent study; Internships; Liberal arts/career combination; Study abroad; Teacher certification program; Weekend college. **Disability Services offered to physically disabled students:** Note-taking services; Reader services; Tape recorders; Tutors.

FACILITIES

Housing: Apartments for married students; Apartments for single students; Coed dorms; Fraternity/sorority housing; Men's dorms; Special housing for disabled student; Women's dorms 95% of campus accessible to physically diasbled. **Special Academic Facilities/Equipment:** Art gallery,Nance Museum and Library of Antiquities, natural history museum, English language center, child development lab, speech and hearing lab, 260-acre farm, Missouri Safety center, National Police Institute, driving/safety range, center for technology and business research,airport for aviation program.Extended campus,Lee's Summit,MO.KCMW-FM,KMOS-TV, Public Broadcasting Stations **Computers:** Students can register for classes online. Administrative functions (other than registration) can be performed online.

CAMPUS LIFE

Environment: Village **Activities:** Campus Ministries; Choral groups; Concert band; Dance; Drama/theater; International Student Organization; Jazz band; Literary magazine; Marching band; Model UN; Music ensembles; Musical theater; Opera; Pep band; Radio station; Student government; Student newspaper; Student-run film society; Symphony orchestra; Television station 150 registered organizations, 24 honor societies, 14 religious organizations. 9 fraternities, 10 sororities. **Athletics (Intercollegiate):** *Men:* baseball, basketball, bowling, cross-country, football, golf, soccer, track/field (outdoor), wrestling. *Women:* basketball, bowling, cross-country, soccer, softball, track/field (outdoor), volleyball. **On-Campus Highlights:** Union Commons, Library, Recreation Center, Multi-purpose building

ADMISSIONS

Freshman Academic Profile: Average high school GPA 3.4. 10% in top 10% of high school class, 23% in top 25% of high school class, 29% in top 50% of high school class. 90% from public high schools. **Test Scores:** ACT middle 50% range 19-24. Minimum paper TOEFL 500. **Basis for Candidate Selection:** *Very important factors considered include:* class rank, academic GPA, standardized test scores. *Other factors considered include:* rigor of secondary school record, application essay. **Freshman Admission Requirements:** High school diploma is required and GED is accepted *Academic units required:* 4 English, 3 math, 2 science, 1 science labs, 3 social studies, 3 academic electives, 1 visual/performing arts. **Freshman Admission Statistics:** 4,748 applied, 83.9% admitted, 42% enrolled. **Transfer Admission Requirements:** college transcript(s), Minimum college GPA of 2.0 required. Lowest grade transferable C. **General Admission Information:** Application fee $30. Nonfall registration accepted. Admission may be deferred for a maximum of 3 semesters.

COSTS AND FINANCIAL AID

Annual in-state tuition $8,536. Annual out-of-state tuition $13,260. Room and board $8,536. Required fees $890. Average book expense $1,000. **Required Forms and Deadlines:** FAFSA; Institution's own financial aid form. **Notification of Awards:** Applicants will be notified of awards on or about 3/1. **Types of Aid:** *Need-based scholarships/grants:* College/university scholarship or grant aid from institutional funds; Federal Pell; Private scholarships; SEOG; State scholarships/grants. *Loans:* Direct PLUS loans; Direct Subsidized Stafford Loans; Direct Unsubsidized Stafford Loans. *Student Employment:* Federal Work-Study Program available. Institutional employment available. **Financial Aid Statistics:** 61% needy freshmen, 63% needy undergrads receive need-based scholarship or grant aid. 99% freshmen, 96% undergrads receive non-need-based scholarship or grant aid. 82% freshmen, 82% undergrads receive need-based self-help aid. 5% freshmen, 4% undergrads receive athletic scholarships. 51% freshmen, 61% undergrads receive any aid. **Criteria for awarding aid:** *Non-need-based:* Academics, Alumni affiliation, Art, Athletics, Leadership, Minority status, Music/drama, Religious affiliation, State/district residency.

UNIVERSITY OF CENTRAL OKLAHOMA

100 North University Drive, Edmond, OK 73034
Phone: 405-974-2727 • **Financial Aid Phone:** 405-974-2727
E-mail: onestop@uco.edu • **CEEB Code:** 6091
Fax: 405-974-3841 • **Website:** http://www.uco.edu • **ACT Code:** 3390

This public school was founded in 1890. It has a 200 acre campus.

RATINGS

Admissions Selectivity Rating: 78   Fire Safety Rating: 84   Green Rating: 60*

STUDENTS AND FACULTY

Enrollment: 14,788. **Student Body:** 58% female, 42% male, 3% out-of-state, 7% international (67 countries represented). Asian 3%, African American 9%, Caucasian 58%, Hispanic 9%, Native American 4%, Pacific Islander <1%, Two or more races 9%, Race unknown 1%.
Retention and Graduation: 62% freshmen return for sophomore year. **Faculty:** Student/faculty ratio 19:1. 513 full-time faculty, 78% hold PhDs, 13% are members of minority groups, 50% are women. 1% of classes are taught by teaching assistants.

ACADEMICS

Degrees: Associate; Bachelor's; Certificate; **Master's Classes:** Most classes have 20-29 students. **Most popular majors:** Psychology, General. **Special Study Options:** Accelerated program; Distance learning; Double major; Dual enrollment; English as a Second Language (ESL); Honors program; Independent study; Internships; Study abroad; Teacher certification program; Weekend college. **Disability Services offered to physically disabled students:** Note-taking services; Reader services; Tape recorders; Tutors. **Career services:** Alumni services; Career assessment; Career/job search classes; Internships

FACILITIES

Housing: Apartments for married students; Apartments for single students; Coed dorms; Fraternity/sorority housing; Men's dorms; Women's dorms 95% of campus accessible to physically disabled. **Special Academic Facilities/Equipment:** Melton Gallery, Donna Nigh Gallery, Design Gallery, Evan Hall Interior Design Gallery, African Art Collection, Archives Photography Collection, Bob Burke Collection, Thatcher Hall Gallery, Will Rogers Room Collection, Library Archives, Forensic Science Institute, Center for Transformative Learning, UCO Boathouse. **Computers:** 100% of classrooms, 100% of dorms, 100% of libraries, 100% of dining areas, 100% of student union, 50% of common outdoor areas have wireless network access. Students can register for classes online. Administrative functions (other than registration) can be performed online.

CAMPUS LIFE

Environment: Metropolis **Activities:** Campus Ministries; Choral groups; Concert band; Dance; Drama/theater; International Student Organization; Jazz band; Marching band; Model UN; Music ensembles; Musical theater; Pep band; Radio station; Student government; Student newspaper; Symphony orchestra; Television station; Yearbook 150 registered organizations, 27 honor societies, 16 religious organizations. 9 fraternities, 10 sororities. **Athletics (Intercollegiate):** *Men:* baseball, basketball, football, golf, wrestling. *Women:* basketball, cross-country, golf, soccer, softball, tennis, volleyball. **On-Campus Highlights:** Starbucks, Wellness Center, University Center, Chambers Library **Environmental Initiatives:** Use 100% wind power

ADMISSIONS

Freshman Academic Profile: Average high school GPA 3.3. 11% in top 10% of high school class, 35% in top 25% of high school class, 68% in top 50% of high school class. 91% from public high schools. **Test Scores:** ACT middle 50% range 19-24. Minimum internet-based TOEFL 83. Minimum paper TOEFL 560. **Basis for Candidate Selection:** *Very important factors considered include:* rigor of secondary school record, class rank, academic GPA, standardized test scores. *Other factors considered include:* extracurricular activities, talent/ability. **Freshman Admission Requirements:** High school diploma is required and GED is accepted *Academic units required:* 4 English, 3 math, 3 science, 3 science labs, 1 social studies, 2 history, *Academic units recommended:* 4 English, 4 math, 3 science, 3 science labs, 2 foreign language, 1 social studies, 3 history, 1 computer science. **Freshman Admission Statistics:** 5,122 applied, 69.9% admitted, 36% enrolled. **Transfer Admission Requirements:** college transcript(s), statement of good standing from prior institution(s). Minimum college GPA of 2.0 required. Lowest grade transferable D. **General Admission Information:** Application fee $90. Nonfall registration accepted. Admission may be deferred for a maximum of 1 semester.

COSTS AND FINANCIAL AID

Annual in-state tuition $7,130. Annual out-of-state tuition $14,033. Room and board $7,130. Required fees $939. Average book expense $1,200. **Required Forms and Deadlines:** FAFSA; Institution's own financial aid form. **Notification of Awards:** Applicants will be notified of awards on a rolling basis beginning 5/1. **Types of Aid:** *Need-based scholarships/grants:* College/university scholarship or grant aid from institutional funds; Federal Pell; Private scholarships; SEOG; State scholarships/grants. *Loans: Student Employment:* Federal Work-Study Program available. Institutional employment available. **Financial Aid Statistics:** 66% freshmen, 75% undergrads receive any aid. **Criteria for awarding aid:** *Need-based:* Academics, Alumni affiliation, Art, Athletics, Leadership, Minority status, Music/drama *Non-need-based:* Academics, Alumni affiliation, Art, Athletics, Leadership, Minority status, Music/drama, State/district residency.

UNIVERSITY OF CHARLESTON

2300 MacCorkle Ave SE, Charleston, WV 25304
Phone: 304-357-4750 • **Financial Aid Phone:** 304-357-4950
E-mail: admissions@ucwv.edu • **CEEB Code:** 5419
Fax: 304-357-4781 • **Website:** http://www.ucwv.edu/ • **ACT Code:** 4528

This private school was founded in 1888. It has a 24 acre campus.

RATINGS

Admissions Selectivity Rating: 78   Fire Safety Rating: 98   Green Rating: 61

STUDENTS AND FACULTY

Enrollment: 1,810. **Student Body:** 45% female, 55% male, 48% out-of-state, 7% international (40 countries represented). Asian 1%, African American 9%, Caucasian 48%, Hispanic 2%, Native American 1%, Pacific Islander <1%, Two or more races 0%, Race unknown 31%.
Retention and Graduation: 58% freshmen return for sophomore year. 49% freshmen graduate within 6 years. **Faculty:** Student/faculty ratio 15:1. 116 full-time faculty, 9% are members of minority groups, 67% are women.

ACADEMICS

Degrees: Associate; Bachelor's; Doctoral/Professional; **Master's Classes:** Most classes have 20-29 students. Most lab/discussion sessions have 10-19 students. **Most popular majors:** Biology/Biological Sciences, General; Registered Nursing/Registered Nurse; Business Administration And Management, General. **Special Study Options:** Accelerated program; Distance learning; Double major; Dual enrollment; English as a Second Language (ESL); Independent study; Internships; Liberal arts/career combination; Student-designed major; Study abroad; Teacher certification program. **Disability Services offered to physically disabled students:** Note-taking services; Reader services; Tape recorders; Tutors. **Career services:** Alumni network; Alumni services; Career assessment; Internships; Regional alumni

FACILITIES

Housing: Apartments for married students; Apartments for single students; Coed dorms; Special housing for disabled student; Theme housing **Special Academic Facilities/Equipment:** Erma Byrd Art Gallery **Computers:** 75% of classrooms, 100% of dorms, 100% of libraries, 100% of dining areas, 100% of student union, 50% of common outdoor areas have wireless network access. Students can register for classes online. Administrative functions (other than registration) can be performed online.

CAMPUS LIFE

Environment: City **Activities:** Campus Ministries; Choral groups; International Student Organization; Pep band; Student government; Student newspaper 39 registered organizations, 7 honor societies, 2 religious organizations. 2 fraternities, 3 sororities. **Athletics (Intercollegiate):** *Men:* baseball, basketball, football, golf, soccer, tennis. *Women:* basketball, crew/rowing, cross-country, golf, soccer, softball, tennis, track/field (outdoor), volleyball. **On-Campus Highlights:** Fitness Center, Innovation Center, Coffee Tavern and Student Union, University of Charleston Stadium, Pharmacy and Wellness Center **Environmental Initiatives:** Recycling on campus

ADMISSIONS

Freshman Academic Profile: Average high school GPA 3.3. **Test Scores:** SAT Math middle 50% range 420-510. SAT EBRW middle 50% range 440-520. ACT middle 50% range 18-22. Minimum internet-based TOEFL 61. Minimum paper TOEFL 500. **Basis for Candidate Selection:** *Very important factors considered include:* academic GPA. *Important factors considered include:* rigor of secondary school record. *Other factors considered include:* class rank, standardized test scores, recommendation(s), alumni/ae relation. **Freshman Admission Requirements:** High school diploma is required and GED is accepted *Academic units required:* 4 English, 4 math, 2 science, 2 science labs, 1 social studies, 1 history, 1 computer science, *Academic units recommended:* 1 foreign language, 1 visual/performing arts. **Freshman Admission Statistics:** 2,740 applied, 64.5% admitted, 19% enrolled. **Transfer Admission Requirements:** college transcript(s), Minimum college GPA of 2.25 required. Lowest grade transferable C. **General Admission Information:** Application fee $25. Priority deadline 5/1. Nonfall registration accepted. Admission may be deferred.

COSTS AND FINANCIAL AID

Annual tuition $29,400. Room and board $9,100. Required fees $1,200. Average book expense $1,800. **Required Forms and Deadlines:** FAFSA; Institution's own financial aid form; State aid form. **Notification of Awards:** Applicants will be notified of awards on a rolling basis beginning 3/1. **Types of Aid:** *Need-based scholarships/grants:* College/university scholarship or grant aid from institutional funds; Federal Pell; Private scholarships; SEOG; State scholarships/grants. *Loans:* Direct Subsidized Stafford Loans; Direct Unsubsidized Stafford Loans. *Student Employment:* Federal Work-Study Program available. Institutional employment available. **Financial Aid Statistics:** 81% needy undergrads receive need-based scholarship or grant aid. 100% freshmen, 100% undergrads receive non-need-based scholarship or grant aid. 100% freshmen, 81% undergrads receive need-based self-help aid. 49% freshmen, 34% undergrads receive athletic scholarships. 100% freshmen receive any aid. **Criteria for awarding aid:** *Need-based:* Minority status *Non-need-based:* Academics, Alumni affiliation, Art, Athletics, Leadership, Music/drama.

THE UNIVERSITY OF CHICAGO

Best Colleges

5801 S.Ellis Avenue, Chicago, IL 60637
Phone: 773-702-8650 • **Financial Aid Phone:** 773-702-8666
E-mail: collegeadmissions@uchicago.edu • **CEEB Code:** 1832
Fax: 773-702-4199 • **Website:** collegeadmissions@uchicago.edu
ACT Code: 1152

This private school was founded in 1890. It has a 217 acre campus.

RATINGS

Admissions Selectivity Rating: 99   **Fire Safety Rating:** 97   **Green Rating:** 95

STUDENTS AND FACULTY

Enrollment: 6,264. **Student Body:** 49% female, 51% male, 82% out-of-state, 13% international (77 countries represented). Asian 18%, African American 5%, Caucasian 42%, Hispanic 13%, Native American <1%, Pacific Islander 0%, Two or more races 6%, Race unknown 2%.
Retention and Graduation: 99% freshmen return for sophomore year. 88% freshmen graduate within 4 years. 93% freshmen graduate within 6 years.
Faculty: Student/faculty ratio 5:1. 1,403 full-time faculty, 100% hold PhDs, 21% are members of minority groups, 32% are women.

ACADEMICS

Degrees: Bachelor's; Doctoral; Doctoral/Professional; Doctoral/Research; **Master's Classes:** Most classes have 10-19 students. Most lab/discussion

sessions have fewer than 10 students. **Most popular majors:** Biology/Biological Sciences, General; Mathematics, General; Economics, General. **Special Study Options:** Accelerated program; Double major; English as a Second Language (ESL); Independent study; Internships; Student-designed major; Study abroad; Teacher certification program. Combined degree programs: BA/MA; BA/MD. **Disability Services offered to physically disabled students:** Note-taking services; Reader services; Tape recorders. **Career services:** Alumni network; Alumni services; Career assessment; Career/job search classes; Internships; Regional alumni

FACILITIES

Housing: Coed dorms; Special housing for disabled students **Special Academic Facilities/Equipment:** Smart Museum of Art, Renaissance Society, Oriental Institute Museum, D'Angelo Law Library, John Crerar Library, Joseph Regenstein Library, Social Services Administration Library, Yerkes Observatory, Laboratory Schools (PreK-12), Court Theater **Computers:** 100% of classrooms, 100% of dorms, 100% of libraries, 100% of dining areas, 100% of student union, 100% of common outdoor areas have wireless network access. Students can register for classes online.

CAMPUS LIFE

Environment: Metropolis **Activities:** Campus Ministries; Choral groups; Concert band; Dance; Drama/theater; International Student Organization; Jazz band; Literary magazine; Model UN; Music ensembles; Musical theater; Radio station; Student government; Student newspaper; Student-run film society; Symphony orchestra 400 registered organizations, 5 honor societies, 36 religious organizations. 10 fraternities, 3 sororities. **Athletics (Intercollegiate):** *Men:* baseball, basketball, cross-country, diving, football, soccer, swimming, tennis, track/field (outdoor), track/field (indoor), volleyball, wrestling. *Women:* basketball, cross-country, diving, soccer, softball, swimming, tennis, track/field (outdoor), track/field (indoor), volleyball. **On-Campus Highlights:** Logan Arts Center, Joseph Regenstein Library, Robie House, Gerald Ratner Athletics Center, Rockefeller Memorial Chapel

ADMISSIONS

Freshman Academic Profile: Average high school GPA 4.5. 99% in top 10% of high school class, 100% in top 25% of high school class, 100% in top 50% of high school class. **Test Scores:** SAT Math middle 50% range 750-800. SAT EBRW middle 50% range 730-780. ACT middle 50% range 32-35. Minimum internet-based TOEFL 100. Minimum paper TOEFL 600. **Basis for Candidate Selection:** *Very important factors considered include:* rigor of secondary school record, application essay, recommendation(s). *Important factors considered include:* standardized test scores, extracurricular activities, talent/ability, character/personal qualities. *Other factors considered include:* class rank, academic GPA, interview, first generation, alumni/ae relation, geographical residence, state residency, religious affiliation/commitment, racial/ethnic status, volunteer work, work experience. **Freshman Admission Requirements:** High school diploma is required and GED is accepted *Academic units recommended:* 4 English, 4 math, 4 science, 3 foreign language, 2 social studies, 2 history. **Freshman Admission Statistics:** 27,694 applied, 8.7% admitted, 72% enrolled. **Transfer Admission Requirements:** High school transcript, college transcript(s), essay or personal statement, standardized test scores, statement of good standing from prior institution(s). Minimum college GPA of 3.0 required. Lowest grade transferable 2. **General Admission Information:** Application fee $75. Regular application deadline 1/1. Nonfall registration accepted. Admission may be deferred for a maximum of 2 years.

COSTS AND FINANCIAL AID

Annual tuition $50,997. Room and board $15,093. Required fees $1,494. Average book expense $1,800. **Required Forms and Deadlines:** CSS/Financial Aid PROFILE; FAFSA; Institution's own financial aid form. **Notification of Awards:** Applicants will be notified of awards on or about 3/15. **Types of Aid:** *Need-based scholarships/grants:* College/university scholarship or grant aid from institutional funds; Federal Pell; Private scholarships; SEOG; State scholarships/grants. *Loans:* Direct PLUS loans; Direct Subsidized Stafford Loans; Direct Unsubsidized Stafford Loans. *Student Employment:* Federal Work-Study Program available. Institutional employment available. **Financial Aid Statistics:** 98% needy freshmen, 98% needy undergrads receive need-based scholarship or grant aid. 0% undergrads receive non-need-based scholarship or grant aid. 41% freshmen, 51% undergrads receive need-based self-help aid. 0% freshmen, 0% undergrads receive athletic scholarships. 64% freshmen, 62% undergrads receive any aid. 33% undergrads borrow to pay for school. Average cumulative indebtedness $23,852. **Criteria for awarding aid:** *Non-need-based:* Academics, Leadership.

UNIVERSITY OF CINCINNATI

P.O. Box 210063, Cincinnati, OH 45221-0091
Phone: 513-556-1100 • **Financial Aid Phone:** 513-556-1000
E-mail: admissions@uc.edu • **CEEB Code:** 1833
Fax: 513-556-1105 • **Website:** www.uc.edu • **ACT Code:** 3340

This public school was founded in 1819. It has a 473 acre campus.

RATINGS
Admissions Selectivity Rating: 81   **Fire Safety Rating:** 96   **Green Rating:** 99

STUDENTS AND FACULTY
Enrollment: 25,573. **Student Body:** 49% female, 51% male, 16% out-of-state, 4% international (110 countries represented). Asian 4%, African American 7%, Caucasian 74%, Hispanic 3%, Native American <1%, Pacific Islander <1%, Two or more races 4%, Race unknown 3%.
Retention and Graduation: 86% freshmen return for sophomore year. 34% freshmen graduate within 4 years. 69% freshmen graduate within 6 years.
Faculty: Student/faculty ratio 17:1. 2,212 full-time faculty, 21% are members of minority groups, 43% are women. 2% of classes are taught by teaching assistants.

ACADEMICS
Degrees: Associate; Bachelor's; Certificate; Doctoral; Doctoral/Professional; Doctoral/Research; Master's; Post-Bachelor's certificate; Post-Master's certificate; Terminal Associate; Transfer Associate **Classes:** Most classes have 20-29 students. Most lab/discussion sessions have fewer than 10 students. **Most popular majors:** Communication, General; Nursing/Registered Nurse (Rn, Asn, Bsn, Msn); Marketing/Marketing Management, General. **Special Study Options:** Accelerated program; Cooperative education program; Distance learning; Double major; Dual enrollment; English as a Second Language (ESL); Honors program; Independent study; Internships; Liberal arts/career combination; Student-designed major; Study abroad; Teacher certification program; Weekend college. Honors programs: The University Honors Program's (UHP) vision is to develop students into global citizen scholars who lead innovative efforts toward solving the world's complex problems. The UHP is built around an innovative pedagogical approach to honors education. It is focused on experiential, reflective and integrative learning as well as the following thematic areas: community engagement, creativity, global studies, leadership and research. The UHP is comprised of students in the top 5% of UC's undergraduate baccalaureate seeking population. The University Honors Program is committed to offering students an individualized, student-centered approach to a meaningful undergraduate experience. To that end, we are dedicated to: • Promoting activities that lead students to discover their passions and enhance their gifts and talents. • Coaching students to purposefully engage in experiential learning opportunities and reflection to maximize and integrate their learning. • Fostering a community that prioritizes transformational personal development, civic participation, and global responsibility. The college experience of these academically talented and motivated students is enriched through their honors experiences – honors seminars and honors experiential learning projects – and the compilation of a learning portfolio throughout their time in the UHP. http://www.uc.edu/honors honors@uc.edu 513-556-6254 Combined degree programs: BA/MA. **Disability Services offered to physically disabled students:** Note-taking services; Reader services; Tape recorders; Tutors. **Career services:** Alumni network; Alumni services; Career assessment; Career/job search classes; Internships; Regional alumni

FACILITIES
Housing: Apartments for married students; Apartments for single students; Coed dorms; Fraternity/sorority housing; Men's dorms; Theme housing; Women's dorms 100% of campus accessible to physically disabled. **Special Academic Facilities/Equipment:** Art museum, language lab, observatory. **Computers:** 50% of classrooms, 75% of libraries, 75% of dining areas, 55% of student union, 75% of common outdoor areas have wireless network access. Students can register for classes online. Administrative functions (other than registration) can be performed online.

CAMPUS LIFE
Environment: Metropolis **Activities:** Campus Ministries; Choral groups; Concert band; Dance; Drama/theater; International Student Organization; Jazz band; Marching band; Music ensembles; Musical theater; Opera; Pep band; Radio station; Student government; Student newspaper; Student-run film society; Symphony orchestra; Television station 250 registered organizations, 16 honor societies, 23 religious organizations. 23 fraternities, 10 sororities.

Athletics (Intercollegiate): *Men:* baseball, basketball, cheerleading, cross-country, diving, football, golf, soccer, swimming, track/field (outdoor). *Women:* basketball, cheerleading, cross-country, diving, golf, lacrosse, soccer, swimming, tennis, track/field (outdoor), track/field (indoor), volleyball. Tangeman University Center (TUC), Campus Recreation Center (CRC), Nippert Stadium, Main Street, Sheakley Lawn **Environmental Initiatives:** UC has commited to a policy that all new construction and major renovations on campus will be built to LEED standards, striving for at least Silver certification levels.

ADMISSIONS
Freshman Academic Profile: Average high school GPA 3.6. 22% in top 10% of high school class, 48% in top 25% of high school class, 81% in top 50% of high school class. **Test Scores:** SAT Math middle 50% range 560-680. SAT EBRW middle 50% range 560-660. ACT middle 50% range 23-28. Minimum internet-based TOEFL 66. **Basis for Candidate Selection:** *Very important factors considered include:* rigor of secondary school record, academic GPA, standardized test scores. *Important factors considered include:* application essay, recommendation(s), talent/ability. *Other factors considered include:* class rank, extracurricular activities, character/personal qualities, volunteer work, work experience. **Freshman Admission Requirements:** High school diploma is required and GED is accepted *Academic units required:* 4 English, 4 math, 3 science, 3 social studies, and 5 units from above areas or other academic areas. *Academic units recommended:* 2 foreign language. **Freshman Admission Statistics:** 21,161 applied, 78.1% admitted, 33% enrolled. **General Admission Information:** Application fee $50. Priority deadline 12/1. Regular application deadline 3/1. Nonfall registration accepted. Admission may be deferred for a maximum of 1 year.

COSTS AND FINANCIAL AID
Annual in-state tuition $11,118. Annual out-of-state tuition $24,656. Room and board $11,118. Required fees $1,678. Average book expense $1,500. **Required Forms and Deadlines:** FAFSA. **Notification of Awards:** Applicants will be notified of awards on a rolling basis beginning 3/1. **Types of Aid:** *Need-based scholarships/grants:* College/university scholarship or grant aid from institutional funds; Federal Pell; Private scholarships; SEOG; State scholarships/grants; United Negro College Fund. *Loans:* Direct PLUS loans; Direct Subsidized Stafford Loans; Direct Unsubsidized Stafford Loans. *Student Employment:* Federal Work-Study Program available. Institutional employment available. **Financial Aid Statistics:** 38% needy freshmen, 42% needy undergrads receive need-based scholarship or grant aid. 53% freshmen, 39% undergrads receive non-need-based scholarship or grant aid. 77% freshmen, 79% undergrads receive need-based self-help aid. 0% freshmen, 1% undergrads receive athletic scholarships. 84% freshmen, 77% undergrads receive any aid. 65% undergrads borrow to pay for school. Average cumulative indebtedness $28,970. **Criteria for awarding aid:** *Non-need-based:* Academics, Alumni affiliation, Art, Athletics, Leadership, Minority status, Music/drama, State/district residency.

UNIVERSITY OF COLORADO
AT COLORADO SPRINGS

1420 Austin Bluffs Parkway, Colorado Springs, CO 80918
Phone: 719-255-3084 • **Financial Aid Phone:** 719-262-3460
E-mail: go@uccs.edu • **CEEB Code:** 4874
Website: www.uccs.edu • **ACT Code:** 535

This public school was founded in 1965. It has a 550 acre campus.

RATINGS
Admissions Selectivity Rating: 73   **Fire Safety Rating:** 60*   **Green Rating:** 99

STUDENTS AND FACULTY
Enrollment: 8,868. **Student Body:** 53% female, 47% male, 11% out-of-state, 1% international (35 countries represented). Asian 3%, African American 4%, Caucasian 69%, Hispanic 14%, Native American 1%, Pacific Islander <1%, Two or more races 6%, Race unknown 3%.
Retention and Graduation: 71% freshmen return for sophomore year.
Faculty: Student/faculty ratio 17:1. 371 full-time faculty, 73% hold PhDs, 14% are members of minority groups, 51% are women.

ACADEMICS
Degrees: Bachelor's; Doctoral/Professional; Doctoral/Research; **Master's Classes:** Most classes have 10-19 students. Most lab/discussion sessions have 10-19 students. **Special Study Options:** Cross-registration; Distance learning; Double major; Dual enrollment; English as a Second Language (ESL); Exchange student program (domestic); Honors program; Independent study; Internships; Study abroad; Teacher certification program; Weekend college.

Honors programs: The University of Colorado-Colorado Springs (UCCS) Honors Program serves rigorously trained students who share a desire to become intentional learners. Honors at UCCS offers students a choice of two levels of participation: University Honors or Mountain Lion Honors. Read more at http://www.uccs.edu/~honors/. Combined degree programs: BA/MA. **Disability Services offered to physically disabled students:** Note-taking services; Reader services; Tape recorders; Tutors. **Career services:** Alumni network; Alumni services; Career assessment; Career/job search classes

FACILITIES

Housing: Apartments for single students; Coed dorms; Men's dorms; Special housing for disabled student; Theme housing; Women's dorms **Special Academic Facilities/Equipment:** Gallery of contemporary art. **Computers:** Students can register for classes online.

CAMPUS LIFE

Environment: Metropolis **Activities:** Choral groups; Dance; Drama/theater; International Student Organization; Literary magazine; Pep band; Radio station; Student government; Student newspaper; Television station 55 registered organizations, 7 religious organizations. 1 sororities. **Athletics (Intercollegiate):** *Men:* basketball, cross-country, golf, soccer, tennis, track/field (outdoor). *Women:* basketball, cross-country, softball, tennis, track/field (outdoor), volleyball. **On-Campus Highlights:** Kraemer Family Library, University Center, Recreation Center, Osborne Center for Science & Engineering, Columbine Hall

ADMISSIONS

Freshman Academic Profile: Average high school GPA 3.3. 13% in top 10% of high school class, 36% in top 25% of high school class, 70% in top 50% of high school class. **Test Scores:** SAT Math middle 50% range 472-600. SAT EBRW middle 50% range 470-590. ACT middle 50% range 21-25. Minimum paper TOEFL 550. **Basis for Candidate Selection:** *Very important factors considered include:* rigor of secondary school record, class rank, academic GPA, standardized test scores. *Other factors considered include:* application essay, recommendation(s). **Freshman Admission Requirements:** High school diploma is required and GED is accepted *Academic units required:* 4 English, 4 math, 3 science, 2 science labs, 1 foreign language, 3 social studies, 1 history, 2 academic electives, *Academic units recommended:* 4 English, 4 math, 3 science, 2 science labs, 1 foreign language, 3 social studies, 1 history, 2 academic electives. **Freshman Admission Statistics:** 7,352 applied, 89.1% admitted, 25% enrolled. **Transfer Admission Requirements:** High school transcript, college transcript(s), Minimum college GPA of 2.0 required. Lowest grade transferable C. **General Admission Information:** Application fee $50. Nonfall registration accepted. Admission may be deferred for a maximum of 3 terms.

COSTS AND FINANCIAL AID

Average book expense $1,800. **Required Forms and Deadlines:** FAFSA. **Notification of Awards:** Applicants will be notified of awards on a rolling basis beginning 4/15. **Types of Aid:** *Need-based scholarships/grants:* College/university scholarship or grant aid from institutional funds; Federal Pell; Private scholarships; SEOG; State scholarships/grants. *Loans:* Direct PLUS loans; Direct Subsidized Stafford Loans; Direct Unsubsidized Stafford Loans. **Financial Aid Statistics:** 58% needy freshmen, 65% needy undergrads receive need-based scholarship or grant aid. 39% freshmen, 24% undergrads receive non-need-based scholarship or grant aid. 79% freshmen, 84% undergrads receive need-based self-help aid. 2% freshmen, 2% undergrads receive athletic scholarships. **Criteria for awarding aid:** *Need-based:* Academics, Alumni affiliation, Athletics *Non-need-based:* Academics, Alumni affiliation, Athletics, Leadership, State/district residency.

UNIVERSITY OF COLORADO AT DENVER

P.O. Box 173364, Denver, CO 80217
Phone: 303-556-2704 • **Financial Aid Phone:** 303-556-2886
E-mail: admissions@cudenver.edu • **CEEB Code:** 4875
Fax: 303-556-4838 • **Website:** www.cudenver.edu • **ACT Code:** 533

This public school was founded in 1912. It has a 127 acre campus.

RATINGS

Admissions Selectivity Rating: 83   **Fire Safety Rating:** 60*   **Green Rating:** 60*

STUDENTS AND FACULTY

Enrollment: 8,327. **Student Body:** 55% female, 45% male, 4% out-of-state, 1% international (57 countries represented). Asian 10%, African American 5%, Caucasian 64%, Hispanic 12%, Native American 1%, Race unknown 8%. **Retention and Graduation:** 71% freshmen return for sophomore year. 7% grads go on to further study within 1 year. 19% grads pursue arts and sciences

degrees. 8% grads pursue business degrees. **Faculty:** Student/faculty ratio 15:1. 2,186 full-time faculty, 81% hold PhDs, 11% are members of minority groups, 47% are women.

ACADEMICS

Degrees: Bachelor's; Master's; Post-Master's certificate **Classes:** Most classes have 10-19 students. Most lab/discussion sessions have 10-19 students. **Most popular majors:** Biology/Biological Sciences, General; Psychology, General; Business/Commerce, General. **Special Study Options:** Accelerated program; Cooperative education program; Cross-registration; Distance learning; Double major; English as a Second Language (ESL); Honors program; Independent study; Internships; Student-designed major; Study abroad; Teacher certification program; Weekend college. **Disability Services offered to physically disabled students:** Note-taking services; Reader services; Tape recorders; Tutors. **Career services:** Alumni services; Career assessment; Internships

FACILITIES

Housing: Coed dorms 100% of campus accessible to physically diasbled. **Special Academic Facilities/Equipment:** Emmanual Gallery **Computers:** Students can register for classes online. Administrative functions (other than registration) can be performed online.

CAMPUS LIFE

Environment: Metropolis **Activities:** Choral groups; Dance; Drama/theater; Jazz band; Music ensembles; Musical theater; Student government; Student newspaper 77 registered organizations, 5 honor societies, 4 religious organizations. **On-Campus Highlights:** PE/Events Center and Emmanuel Gallery, The Auraria Library, Tivoli Student Union, St. Elizabeth's Church, King Academic and Performing Arts Center

ADMISSIONS

Freshman Academic Profile: Average high school GPA 3.3. 17% in top 10% of high school class, 43% in top 25% of high school class, 78% in top 50% of high school class. **Test Scores:** SAT Math middle 50% range 490-590. SAT EBRW middle 50% range 490-600. ACT middle 50% range 19-25. Minimum internet-based TOEFL 71. Minimum paper TOEFL 525. **Basis for Candidate Selection:** *Very important factors considered include:* rigor of secondary school record, class rank, academic GPA, standardized test scores. *Important factors considered include:* application essay, recommendation(s), level of applicant's interest. *Other factors considered include:* extracurricular activities, talent/ability, character/personal qualities. **Freshman Admission Requirements:** High school diploma is required and GED is accepted *Academic units required:* 4 English, 3 math, 3 science, 2 foreign language, 2 social studies, 1 academic elective, *Academic units recommended:* 4 English, 3 math, 3 science, 2 science labs, 2 foreign language, 2 social studies, 1 history, 1 academic elective. **Freshman Admission Statistics:** 2,968 applied, 68.9% admitted, 46% enrolled. **Transfer Admission Requirements:** college transcript(s), statement of good standing from prior institution(s). Minimum college GPA of 2.4 required. Lowest grade transferable C-. **General Admission Information:** Application fee $50. Priority deadline 7/22. Nonfall registration accepted. Admission may be deferred for a maximum of 1 year.

COSTS AND FINANCIAL AID

Annual in-state tuition $9,990. Annual out-of-state tuition $17,010. Room and board $9,990. Required fees $878. Average book expense $1,700. **Required Forms and Deadlines:** FAFSA; Institution's own financial aid form. **Notification of Awards:** Applicants will be notified of awards on a rolling basis beginning 5/1. **Types of Aid:** *Need-based scholarships/grants:* College/university scholarship or grant aid from institutional funds; Federal Nursing Scholarships; Federal Pell; Private scholarships; SEOG; State scholarships/grants. *Loans:* Direct PLUS loans; Direct Subsidized Stafford Loans; Direct Unsubsidized Stafford Loans. *Student Employment:* Federal Work-Study Program available. **Financial Aid Statistics:** 97% needy freshmen, 86% needy undergrads receive need-based scholarship or grant aid. 12% freshmen, 5% undergrads receive non-need-based scholarship or grant aid. 73% freshmen, 87% undergrads receive need-based self-help aid. 0% freshmen, 0% undergrads receive athletic scholarships. **Criteria for awarding aid:** *Need-based:* Academics, Minority status *Non-need-based:* Academics, Art, Leadership, Music/drama.

UNIVERSITY OF COLORADO—BOULDER

Best Colleges

Office of Admissions, Boulder, CO 80309-0552
Phone: 303-492-6301 • **Financial Aid Phone:** 303-492-5091 • **CEEB Code:** 4841
Fax: 303-735-2501 • **Website:** www.colorado.edu/ • **ACT Code:** 532

This public school was founded in 1876. It has a 600 acre campus.

RATINGS

Admissions Selectivity Rating: 83   **Fire Safety Rating:** 87   **Green Rating:** 95

STUDENTS AND FACULTY

Enrollment: 28,667. **Student Body:** 44% female, 56% male, 42% out-of-state, 7% international (82 countries represented). Asian 6%, African American 2%, Caucasian 68%, Hispanic 12%, Native American <1%, Pacific Islander <1%, Two or more races 5%, Race unknown 1%.
Retention and Graduation: 88% freshmen return for sophomore year. 45% freshmen graduate within 4 years. 69% freshmen graduate within 6 years.
Faculty: 12% of classes are taught by teaching assistants.

ACADEMICS

Degrees: Bachelor's; Doctoral/Professional; Doctoral/Research; Master's; Post-Master's certificate **Classes:** Most classes have 10-19 students. **Most popular majors:** Speech Communication And Rhetoric; Physiology, General; Psychology, General. **Special Study Options:** Accelerated program; Cooperative education program; Cross-registration; Distance learning; Double major; Dual enrollment; English as a Second Language (ESL); Exchange student program (domestic); Honors program; Independent study; Internships; Liberal arts/career combination; Student-designed major; Study abroad; Teacher certification program. Honors programs: The CU Honors Program offers a wide-ranging curriculum supported by thoughtful advising and close contact with faculty. The program aspires to provide the best education possible for the leaders of the future. The Honors Residential Academic Program (HRAP) is a co-educational living-learning community open to Honors-qualified freshmen and returning students in all majors in the College of Arts & Sciences. The Engineering Honors Residential Academic Program is open to qualified students in the college of Engineering and Applied Science. In these living and learning environments, students experience all of the advantages of a small college environment while also enjoying the diverse resources of a major university. The Norlin Scholars Program is a community of students with a broad, synthetic view of education that embraces active learning, creativity, and interdisciplinary scholarship. Norlin Scholars participate in small, specialized courses and other small-group experiences emphasizing critical thinking, collaboration, and written and oral communications skills. They also engage in research or creative work with faculty mentors. The Presidents Leadership Class (PLC) offers a unique opportunity to those students who want to make a difference for themselves and their community. The core of PLC is an academic program focusing on leadership development, personal development, and community service initiatives. PLC scholars receive a four-year scholarship. Combined degree programs: BA/MA. **Disability Services offered to physically disabled students:** Note-taking services; Reader services; Tape recorders; Tutors. **Career services:** Alumni network; Alumni services; Career assessment; Career/job search classes; Internships; Regional alumni

FACILITIES

Housing: Apartments for married students; Apartments for single students; Coed dorms; Fraternity/sorority housing; Special housing for disabled student; Theme housing 87% of campus accessible to physically diasbled. **Special Academic Facilities/Equipment:** Art museum and galleries, natural history museum, heritage center, observatory, planetarium and science center, electron microscopes, outdoor theater, video interactive foreign language laboratory, mountain research station, centrifuge laboratory, hands-on teaching and learning laboratory for engineering, production and performance studios with advanced technologies, multipurpose cultural/athletics/educational events and conference center, a premier concert hall, and an innovative multi-disciplinary Information Technology center. **Computers:** 100% of classrooms, 65% of dorms, 100% of libraries, 100% of dining areas, 100% of student union, 50% of common outdoor areas have wireless network access. Students can register for classes online. Administrative functions (other than registration) can be performed online.

CAMPUS LIFE

Environment: City **Activities:** Campus Ministries; Choral groups; Concert band; Dance; Drama/theater; International Student Organization; Jazz band; Literary magazine; Marching band; Model UN; Music ensembles; Musical theater; Opera; Pep band; Radio station; Student government; Student newspaper; Student-run film society; Symphony orchestra 300 registered organizations, 26 honor societies, 35 religious organizations. 20 fraternities, 19 sororities. **Athletics (Intercollegiate):** *Men:* basketball, cross-country, football, golf, skiing (downhill/alpine), skiing (nordic/cross-country), track/field (outdoor), track/field (indoor). *Women:* basketball, cross-country, golf, skiing (downhill/alpine), skiing (nordic/cross-country), soccer, tennis, track/field (outdoor), track/field (indoor), volleyball. **On-Campus Highlights:** Center for Community, University Memorial Center (UMC), Student Recreation Center, Norlin Library, Farrand Field **Environmental Initiatives:** EDUCATION AND RESEARCH: Campus commitment to environmental education and research has helped CU-Boulder become one of the nation's top environmental research universities. CU-Boulder's reputation and performance as a national leader in environmental issues and sustainability helps recruit and retain faculty with the recognized expertise to win leading-edge research awards, to contribute to the global sustainability knowledge base, and to enhance an already respected environmental studies department—one with integrated environmental content across the campus. Environmental Studies is an interdisciplinary program that draws from curricula in the earth and natural sciences as well as the social sciences. Undergraduate students have the opportunity to participate in three residential academic programs (RAPs) that emphasize environmental studies and sustainability. All offer smaller courses in the residences halls. The Baker RAP consists of a cohort of students with interest in the environment and in future careers in working on environmental problems, such as sustainable use of our resources. The Sustainable by Design RAP includes students with an interest in resource-efficient design, renewable energy, and environmental and social impacts of community development. The Sustainability and Social Innovation RAP guides students in developing innovative, self-sustaining solutions for addressing critical social and environmental issues around the globe.

ADMISSIONS

Freshman Academic Profile: Average high school GPA 3.7. 29% in top 10% of high school class, 59% in top 25% of high school class, 90% in top 50% of high school class. 88% from public high schools. **Test Scores:** SAT Math middle 50% range 570-680. SAT EBRW middle 50% range 580-665. ACT middle 50% range 25-30. Minimum internet-based TOEFL 75. Minimum paper TOEFL 537. **Basis for Candidate Selection:** *Very important factors considered include:* rigor of secondary school record, class rank, academic GPA, standardized test scores. *Important factors considered include:* application essay, recommendation(s), extracurricular activities, talent/ability, character/personal qualities, first generation. *Other factors considered include:* alumni/ae relation, geographical residence, state residency, racial/ethnic status, volunteer work, work experience, level of applicant's interest. **Freshman Admission Requirements:** High school diploma is required and GED is accepted *Academic units required:* 4 English, 4 math, 3 science, 2 science labs, 3 foreign language, 3 social studies, 1 history, and 1 unit from above areas or other academic areas. **Freshman Admission Statistics:** 36,149 applied, 79.8% admitted, 23% enrolled. **Transfer Admission Requirements:** High school transcript, college transcript(s), essay or personal statement, Lowest grade transferable C-. **General Admission Information:** Application fee $50. Priority deadline 11/15. Regular application deadline 1/15. Nonfall registration accepted. Admission may be deferred for a maximum of 1 year.

COSTS AND FINANCIAL AID

Annual in-state tuition $13,998. Annual out-of-state tuition $33,316. Room and board $13,998. Required fees $1,838. Average book expense $1,800. **Required Forms and Deadlines:** FAFSA. **Notification of Awards:** Applicants will be notified of awards on a rolling basis beginning 3/15. **Types of Aid:** *Need-based scholarships/grants:* College/university scholarship or grant aid from institutional funds; Federal Pell; Private scholarships; SEOG; State scholarships/grants. *Loans:* Direct PLUS loans; Direct Subsidized Stafford Loans; Direct Unsubsidized Stafford Loans. *Student Employment:* Federal Work-Study Program available. Institutional employment available. **Financial Aid Statistics:** 76% needy freshmen, 76% needy undergrads receive need-based scholarship or grant aid. 6% freshmen, 4% undergrads receive non-need-based scholarship or grant aid. 86% freshmen, 88% undergrads receive need-based self-help aid. 1% freshmen, 1% undergrads receive athletic scholarships. 43% undergrads borrow to pay for school. Average cumulative indebtedness $27,405. **Criteria for awarding aid:** *Need-based:* Academics, Alumni affiliation, Art, Athletics, Leadership, Music/drama *Non-need-based:* Academics, Alumni affiliation, Art, Athletics, Leadership, Music/drama, State/district residency.

UNIVERSITY OF CONNECTICUT

2131 Hillside Road, Storrs, CT 06268-3088
Phone: 860-486-3137 • **Financial Aid Phone:** 860-486-2819
E-mail: beahusky@uconn.edu • **CEEB Code:** 3915
Fax: 860-486-1476 • **Website:** www.uconn.edu • **ACT Code:** 604

This public school was founded in 1881. It has a 4109 acre campus.

RATINGS

Admissions Selectivity Rating: 84   **Fire Safety Rating:** 96   **Green Rating:** 99

STUDENTS AND FACULTY

Enrollment: 19,030. **Student Body:** 50% female, 50% male, 22% out-of-state, 6% international (71 countries represented). Asian 11%, African American 6%, Caucasian 60%, Hispanic 10%, Native American <1%, Pacific Islander <1%, Two or more races 3%, Race unknown 5%.
Retention and Graduation: 92% freshmen return for sophomore year. 70% freshmen graduate within 4 years. 82% freshmen graduate within 6 years. 28% grads go on to further study within 1 year. 13% grads pursue arts and sciences degrees. 1% grads pursue law degrees. 2% grads pursue business degrees. 5% grads pursue medical degrees. **Faculty:** Student/faculty ratio 16:1. 1,262 full-time faculty, 93% hold PhDs, 24% are members of minority groups, 40% are women. 19% of classes are taught by teaching assistants.

ACADEMICS

Degrees: Associate; Bachelor's; Diploma; Doctoral; Doctoral/Professional; Doctoral/Research; Master's; Post-Bachelor's certificate; Post-Master's certificate; Terminal Associate; Transfer Associate **Classes:** Most classes have 10-19 students. Most lab/discussion sessions have fewer than 10 students. **Most popular majors:** Communication And Media Studies; Psychology, General; Economics, General. **Special Study Options:** Accelerated program; Cooperative education program; Cross-registration; Distance learning; Double major; Dual enrollment; English as a Second Language (ESL); Exchange student program (domestic); External degree program; Honors program; Independent study; Internships; Liberal arts/career combination; Student-designed major; Study abroad; Teacher certification program. Honors programs: Honors Scholar Program for all Undergraduates Combined degree programs: BA/DDS; BA/JD; BA/MA; BA/MD. **Disability Services offered to physically disabled students:** Note-taking services; Tape recorders; Tutors. **Career services:** Alumni services; Career assessment; Internships

FACILITIES

Housing: Apartments for married students; Apartments for single students; Coed dorms; Fraternity/sorority housing; Men's dorms; Special housing for disabled student; Special housing for international students; Theme housing; Wellness housing; Women's dorms 90% of campus accessible to physically diasbled. **Special Academic Facilities/Equipment:** Art and natural history museums, child development labs, national undersea research center, arboretum, institute for social inquiry, institute of materials science, electron microscope labs. **Computers:** 90% of libraries, 5% of dining areas, 25% of student union, have wireless network access. Students can register for classes online. Administrative functions (other than registration) can be performed online.

CAMPUS LIFE

Environment: Town **Activities:** Campus Ministries; Choral groups; Concert band; Dance; Drama/theater; International Student Organization; Jazz band; Literary magazine; Marching band; Model UN; Music ensembles; Musical theater; Opera; Pep band; Radio station; Student government; Student newspaper; Student-run film society; Symphony orchestra; Television station; Yearbook 303 registered organizations, 29 honor societies, 17 religious organizations. 14 fraternities, 12 sororities. **Athletics (Intercollegiate):** *Men:* baseball, basketball, cross-country, diving, football, golf, ice hockey, soccer, swimming, tennis, track/field (outdoor), track/field (indoor). *Women:* basketball, crew/rowing, cross-country, diving, field hockey, ice hockey, lacrosse, soccer, softball, swimming, tennis, track/field (outdoor), track/field (indoor), volleyball. **On-Campus Highlights:** William Benton Museum of Art, UConn Dairy Bar, Puppetry Museum, J. Robert Donnelly Husky Heritage Sports Museum, Jorgensen Auditorium and Connecticut Repertory Theater **Environmental Initiatives:** 1. In January 2017, President Susan Herbst endorsed UConn's 2020 Vision Plan for Campus Sustainability and Climate Leadership, which outlines a number of specific environmental goals and strategies, including:—Increase the percentage of purchased power system-wide that consists of renewable energy from 40% to 100%—Increase the university's waste diversion rate from 47% to

60%—Increase the percentage of locally-grown food or community-based food from 35% to 40%—Reduce average daily potable water use by 30% Shortly after endorsing the 2020 Vision, President Herbst also joined more than 2,300 top executives and officials in the Grand Coalition's We Are Still In pledge, promising to continue pursuing ambitious climate action goals.

ADMISSIONS

Freshman Academic Profile: 51% in top 10% of high school class, 84% in top 25% of high school class, 98% in top 50% of high school class. 88% from public high schools. **Test Scores:** Minimum internet-based TOEFL 79. Minimum paper TOEFL 550. **Basis for Candidate Selection:** *Very important factors considered include:* rigor of secondary school record, class rank, academic GPA, standardized test scores. *Important factors considered include:* application essay, recommendation(s), extracurricular activities, talent/ability, character/personal qualities, first generation, volunteer work. *Other factors considered include:* alumni/ae relation, geographical residence, state residency, racial/ethnic status, work experience, level of applicant's interest. **Freshman Admission Requirements:** High school diploma is required and GED is accepted *Academic units required:* 4 English, 3 math, 2 science, 2 science labs, 2 foreign language, 2 social studies, 3 academic electives, *Academic units recommended:* 3 foreign language. **Freshman Admission Statistics:** 35,980 applied, 48.8% admitted, 22% enrolled. **Transfer Admission Requirements:** High school transcript, college transcript(s), essay or personal statement, Minimum college GPA of 2.7 required. Lowest grade transferable C. **General Admission Information:** Application fee $80. Regular application deadline 1/15. Nonfall registration accepted. Admission may be deferred for a maximum of 1 semester.

COSTS AND FINANCIAL AID

Annual in-state tuition $13,452. Annual out-of-state tuition $34,066. Room and board $13,452. Required fees $2,882. Average book expense $950.
Required Forms and Deadlines: FAFSA. **Notification of Awards:** Applicants will be notified of awards on a rolling basis beginning 3/1. **Types of Aid:** *Need-based scholarships/grants:* College/university scholarship or grant aid from institutional funds; Federal Pell; Private scholarships; SEOG; State scholarships/grants. *Loans:* Direct PLUS loans; Direct Subsidized Stafford Loans; Direct Unsubsidized Stafford Loans. *Student Employment:* Federal Work-Study Program available. Institutional employment available. **Financial Aid Statistics:** 68% needy freshmen, 72% needy undergrads receive need-based scholarship or grant aid. 44% freshmen, 30% undergrads receive non-need-based scholarship or grant aid. 68% freshmen, 73% undergrads receive need-based self-help aid. 3% freshmen, 2% undergrads receive athletic scholarships. 49% freshmen, 48% undergrads receive any aid. 64% undergrads borrow to pay for school. Average cumulative indebtedness $24,999. **Criteria for awarding aid:** *Non-need-based:* Academics, Art, Athletics, Leadership, Minority status, Music/drama.

UNIVERSITY OF DALLAS

1845 East Northgate Drive, Irving, TX 75062
Phone: 972-721-5266 • **Financial Aid Phone:** 972-721-5266
E-mail: crusader@udallas.edu • **CEEB Code:** 6868
Fax: 972-721-5017 • **Website:** www.udallas.edu • **ACT Code:** 4234

This private school, affiliated with the Roman Catholic Church, was founded in 1956. It has a 450 acre campus.

RATINGS

Admissions Selectivity Rating: 89   **Fire Safety Rating:** 88   **Green Rating:** 60*

STUDENTS AND FACULTY

Enrollment: 1,450. **Student Body:** 54% female, 46% male, 48% out-of-state, 4% international (19 countries represented). Asian 6%, African American 2%, Caucasian 61%, Hispanic 23%, Native American 1%, Pacific Islander <1%, Two or more races 3%, Race unknown 1%.
Retention and Graduation: 85% freshmen return for sophomore year. 65% freshmen graduate within 4 years. 68% freshmen graduate within 6 years. 28% grads go on to further study within 1 year. **Faculty:** Student/faculty ratio 11:1. 153 full-time faculty, 12% are members of minority groups, 39% are women. 0% of classes are taught by teaching assistants.

ACADEMICS

Degrees: Bachelor's; Doctoral; Doctoral/Professional; Doctoral/Research; Master's; Post-Bachelor's certificate **Classes:** Most classes have 20-29 students.

Most lab/discussion sessions have 30-39 students. **Most popular majors:** English Language And Literature, General; Biology/Biological Sciences, General; History, General. **Special Study Options:** Cooperative education program; Double major; Dual enrollment; Independent study; Internships; Liberal arts/career combination; Student-designed major; Study abroad; Teacher certification program. Honors programs: At UD, the academic rigor of our Core Curriculum is analogous to an Honors programs so we do not have a separate program or focus for that purpose. Combined degree programs: BA/MA. **Disability Services offered to physically disabled students:** Note-taking services; Reader services; Tape recorders; Tutors. **Career services:** Alumni network; Alumni services; Career assessment; Career/job search classes; Internships

FACILITIES

Housing: Apartments for single students; Coed dorms; Men's dorms; Women's dorms **Special Academic Facilities/Equipment:** Art gallery, theater, language science, and computer labs, observatory. **Computers:** 50% of classrooms, 100% of dorms, 100% of libraries, 20% of dining areas, 100% of student union, 50% of common outdoor areas have wireless network access. Students can register for classes online. Administrative functions (other than registration) can be performed online.

CAMPUS LIFE

Environment: City **Activities:** Campus Ministries; Choral groups; Dance; Drama/theater; International Student Organization; Literary magazine; Music ensembles; Musical theater; Student government; Student newspaper; Student-run film society; Yearbook 35 registered organizations, 4 honor societies, 5 religious organizations. **Athletics (Intercollegiate):** *Men:* baseball, basketball, cross-country, golf, lacrosse, soccer, track/field (outdoor). *Women:* basketball, cross-country, lacrosse, soccer, softball, track/field (outdoor), volleyball. **On-Campus Highlights:** Church of the Incarnation, Cappuccino Bar, The Mall, The Rathskeller, Art Village **Environmental Initiatives:** Student Government recycling committee and Environmental Alliance Club. SG provides recycling receptacles for cans and papers.

ADMISSIONS

Freshman Academic Profile: Average high school GPA 3.9. 37% in top 10% of high school class, 71% in top 25% of high school class, 95% in top 50% of high school class. 45% from public high schools. **Test Scores:** SAT Math middle 50% range 550-670. SAT EBRW middle 50% range 590-700. ACT middle 50% range 24-31. Minimum internet-based TOEFL 79. **Basis for Candidate Selection:** *Very important factors considered include:* rigor of secondary school record, academic GPA, application essay, standardized test scores, recommendation(s), character/personal qualities. *Important factors considered include:* talent/ability. *Other factors considered include:* class rank, interview, extracurricular activities, first generation, alumni/ae relation, volunteer work, work experience, level of applicant's interest. **Freshman Admission Requirements:** High school diploma is required and GED is accepted *Academic units required:* 4 English, 3 math, 3 science, 2 foreign language, 3 social studies, 3 history, 4 academic electives, 1 visual/performing arts, *Academic units recommended:* 4 English, 4 math, 3 science, 3 science labs, 3 foreign language, 4 social studies, 4 history, 4 academic electives, 2 visual/performing arts. **Freshman Admission Statistics:** 3,857 applied, 47.4% admitted, 23% enrolled. **Transfer Admission Requirements:** college transcript(s), essay or personal statement, statement of good standing from prior institution(s). Minimum college GPA of 2.5 required. Lowest grade transferable C-. **General Admission Information:** Application fee $50. Priority deadline 1/15. Regular application deadline 9/15. Nonfall registration accepted. Admission may be deferred for a maximum of 2 years.

COSTS AND FINANCIAL AID

Annual tuition $37,652. Room and board $12,400. Required fees $3,000. Average book expense $1,000. **Required Forms and Deadlines:** FAFSA. **Notification of Awards:** Applicants will be notified of awards on a rolling basis beginning 12/1. **Types of Aid:** *Need-based scholarships/grants:* College/university scholarship or grant aid from institutional funds; Federal Pell; Private scholarships; SEOG; State scholarships/grants. *Loans:* Direct PLUS loans; Direct Subsidized Stafford Loans; Direct Unsubsidized Stafford Loans. *Student Employment:* Federal Work-Study Program available. Institutional employment available. **Financial Aid Statistics:** 99% needy freshmen, 98% needy undergrads receive need-based scholarship or grant aid. 0% undergrads receive non-need-based scholarship or grant aid. 63% freshmen, 70% undergrads receive need-based self-help aid. 0% freshmen, 0% undergrads receive athletic scholarships. 96% freshmen, 94% undergrads receive any aid. Average cumulative indebtedness $32,921. **Criteria for awarding aid:** *Non-need-based:* Academics, Alumni affiliation, Art, Leadership, Minority status, Music/drama, Religious affiliation, State/district residency.

UNIVERSITY OF DAYTON

300 College Park, Dayton, OH 45469-1669
Phone: 937-229-4411 • **Financial Aid Phone:** 800-427-5029
E-mail: admission@udayton.edu • **CEEB Code:** 1834
Fax: 937-229-4729 • **Website:** www.udayton.edu • **ACT Code:** 3342

This private school, affiliated with the Roman Catholic Church, was founded in 1850. It has a 388 acre campus.

RATINGS

Admissions Selectivity Rating: 85   **Fire Safety Rating:** 81   **Green Rating:** 90

STUDENTS AND FACULTY

Enrollment: 8,422. **Student Body:** 48% female, 52% male, 52% out-of-state, 7% international (38 countries represented). Asian 1%, African American 3%, Caucasian 79%, Hispanic 5%, Native American <1%, Pacific Islander <1%, Two or more races 3%, Race unknown 1%.
Retention and Graduation: 90% freshmen return for sophomore year. 26% grads go on to further study within 1 year. **Faculty:** Student/faculty ratio 15:1. 563 full-time faculty, 88% hold PhDs, 19% are members of minority groups, 44% are women. 3% of classes are taught by teaching assistants.

ACADEMICS

Degrees: Bachelor's; Doctoral/Professional; Doctoral/Research; **Master's Classes:** Most classes have 20-29 students. Most lab/discussion sessions have 20-29 students. **Most popular majors:** Speech Communication And Rhetoric; Mechanical Engineering; Marketing/Marketing Management, General. **Special Study Options:** Accelerated program; Cooperative education program; Cross-registration; Distance learning; Double major; Dual enrollment; English as a Second Language (ESL); Exchange student program (domestic); Honors program; Independent study; Internships; Liberal arts/career combination; Student-designed major; Study abroad; Teacher certification program; Weekend college. Honors programs: The University Honors Program offers courses, programming, fellowship advising, funding, guidance and benefits to undergraduates who have superior academic records, culminating in an Honors-designated diploma. Through the Honors Program, students can develop their academic talents, explore the world, undertake extensive, self-directed research, and apply their knowledge for the benefit of others. Combined degree programs: BA/MA. **Disability Services offered to physically disabled students:** Note-taking services; Reader services; Tutors. **Career services:** Alumni network; Alumni services; Career assessment; Career/job search classes; Internships; Regional alumni

FACILITIES

Housing: Apartments for single students; Coed dorms; Cooperative housing; Fraternity/sorority housing; Special housing for disabled student; Special housing for international students; Theme housing; Wellness housing 95% of campus accessible to physically disabled. **Special Academic Facilities/Equipment:** UD Research Institute, Bombeck Family Learning Center, Learning Teaching Center, Davis Center for Portfolio Management, Marian Library, ArtStreet living-learning complex, RecPlex. **Computers:** 100% of classrooms, 100% of dorms, 100% of libraries, 100% of dining areas, 100% of student union, 100% of common outdoor areas have wireless network access. Students can register for classes online. Administrative functions (other than registration) can be performed online. Undergraduates are required to own a computer.

CAMPUS LIFE

Environment: City **Activities:** Campus Ministries; Choral groups; Concert band; Dance; Drama/theater; International Student Organization; Jazz band; Literary magazine; Marching band; Model UN; Music ensembles; Musical theater; Opera; Pep band; Radio station; Student government; Student newspaper; Symphony orchestra; Television station; Yearbook 200 registered organizations, 14 honor societies, 30 religious organizations. 13 fraternities, 9 sororities. **Athletics (Intercollegiate):** *Men:* baseball, basketball, cheerleading, cross-country, football, golf, soccer, tennis. *Women:* basketball, cheerleading, crew/rowing, cross-country, golf, soccer, softball, tennis, track/field (outdoor), track/field (indoor), volleyball. **On-Campus Highlights:** John F. Kennedy Memorial Union, Ryan C. Harris Learning-Teaching Center, University of Dayton Arena, University of Dayton Science Center, Kettering Laboratories; UDRI **Environmental Initiatives:** Composting program that has eliminated ~90% of waste from all campus dining halls complete with a total conversion to compostable disposable products for takeout and washable service ware for dine-in customers.

ADMISSIONS

Freshman Academic Profile: Average high school GPA 3.7. 29% in top 10% of high school class, 61% in top 25% of high school class, 87% in top 50% of high school class. 43% from public high schools. **Test Scores:** SAT Math middle 50% range 550-660. SAT EBRW middle 50% range 550-650. ACT middle 50% range 24-29. Minimum internet-based TOEFL 70. Minimum paper TOEFL 523. **Basis for Candidate Selection:** *Very important factors considered include:* rigor of secondary school record, class rank, academic GPA, application essay, standardized test scores. *Important factors considered include:* recommendation(s), extracurricular activities, character/personal qualities, alumni/ae relation, level of applicant's interest. *Other factors considered include:* talent/ability, first generation, racial/ethnic status, volunteer work, work experience. **Freshman Admission Requirements:** High school diploma is required and GED is accepted *Academic units recommended:* 4 English, 4 math, 4 science, 1 science labs, 2 foreign language, 4 social studies, 4 history, 4 computer science, 4 visual/performing arts. **Freshman Admission Statistics:** 15,942 applied, 71.7% admitted, 20% enrolled. **Transfer Admission Requirements:** High school transcript, college transcript(s), essay or personal statement, Minimum college GPA of 2.0 required. Lowest grade transferable C-. **General Admission Information:** Priority deadline 12/15. Regular application deadline 3/1. Nonfall registration accepted. Admission may be deferred.

COSTS AND FINANCIAL AID

Required Forms and Deadlines: FAFSA. **Notification of Awards:** Applicants will be notified of awards on a rolling basis beginning 2/17. **Types of Aid:** *Need-based scholarships/grants:* College/university scholarship or grant aid from institutional funds; Federal Pell; Private scholarships; SEOG; State scholarships/grants. *Loans:* Direct PLUS loans; Direct Subsidized Stafford Loans; Direct Unsubsidized Stafford Loans. *Student Employment:* Federal Work-Study Program available. Institutional employment available. **Financial Aid Statistics:** 100% needy freshmen, 99% needy undergrads receive need-based scholarship or grant aid. 19% freshmen, 22% undergrads receive non-need-based scholarship or grant aid. 70% freshmen, 81% undergrads receive need-based self-help aid. 2% freshmen, 2% undergrads receive athletic scholarships. 98% freshmen, 94% undergrads receive any aid. 62% undergrads borrow to pay for school. Average cumulative indebtedness $35,740. **Criteria for awarding aid:** *Need-based:* Academics, Alumni affiliation, Art, Athletics, Leadership, Minority status, Music/drama, Religious affiliation *Non-need-based:* Academics, Alumni affiliation, Art, Athletics, Leadership, Minority status, Music/drama, Religious affiliation, State/district residency.

UNIVERSITY OF DELAWARE

210 South College Ave., Newark, DE 19716
Phone: 302-831-8123 • **Financial Aid Phone:** 302-831-0520
E-mail: admissions@udel.edu • **CEEB Code:** 5811
Fax: 302-831-6905 • **Website:** http://www.udel.edu • **ACT Code:** 634

This public school was founded in 1743. It has a 1000 acre campus.

RATINGS

Admissions Selectivity Rating: 86   **Fire Safety Rating:** 98   **Green Rating:** 72

STUDENTS AND FACULTY

Enrollment: 17,669. **Student Body:** 58% female, 42% male, 62% out-of-state, 4% international (81 countries represented). Asian 5%, African American 5%, Caucasian 73%, Hispanic 8%, Native American <1%, Pacific Islander <1%, Two or more races 3%, Race unknown 1%.
Retention and Graduation: 92% freshmen return for sophomore year. 28% grads go on to further study within 1 year. 23% grads pursue arts and sciences degrees. 6% grads pursue law degrees. 9% grads pursue business degrees. 15% grads pursue medical degrees. **Faculty:** Student/faculty ratio 13:1. 1,198 full-time faculty, 91% hold PhDs, 21% are members of minority groups, 42% are women. 5% of classes are taught by teaching assistants.

ACADEMICS

Degrees: Associate; Bachelor's; Doctoral/Professional; Doctoral/Research; **Master's Classes:** Most classes have 10-19 students. Most lab/discussion sessions have 10-19 students. **Most popular majors:** Biology/Biological Sciences, General; Registered Nursing/Registered Nurse; Finance, General. **Special Study Options:** Accelerated program; Cooperative education

program; Distance learning; Double major; Dual enrollment; English as a Second Language (ESL); Honors program; Independent study; Internships; Liberal arts/career combination; Student-designed major; Study abroad; Teacher certification program. Honors programs: University Honors Program, http://honors.udel.edu/. **Disability Services offered to physically disabled students:** Note-taking services; Reader services; Tape recorders; Tutors. **Career services:** Alumni network; Alumni services; Career assessment; Career/job search classes; Internships; Regional alumni

FACILITIES

Housing: Apartments for married students; Apartments for single students; Coed dorms; Fraternity/sorority housing; Special housing for disabled student; Theme housing; Women's dorms 95% of campus accessible to physically diasbled. **Special Academic Facilities/Equipment:** University Museums, including the Old College Gallery, Mechanical Hall Gallery and Mineralogical Museum; the Historic Costume and Textile Collection; a variety of state-of-the-art research facilities serving several disciplines, including the Center for Composite Materials, Delaware Biotechnology Institute, Allen Biotechnology Laboratory, a coastal research vessel—the Hugh R. Sharp, art conservation laboratories at Winterthur Museum and Gardens and more than 40 research centers and institutes; a 350-acre Agricultural Teaching and Research Complex, including botanical gardens, livestock arena, working farm, botanical gardens and a 35-acre woodlot harboring numerous wild species of animals and birds; the University of Delaware Library, 6-acre research library containing over 2.8 million books and over 300 networked databases; 28 micro-computing sites; two student centers; athletic facilities, including the 23,000-seat Delaware Football Stadium, two ice arenas, the 5,000-seat Bob Carpenter Sports/Convocation Center, indoor and outdoor swimming pools, Fred Rullo Stadium and a variety of playing fields and training and recreational spaces; and a student-run restaurant, Vita Nova, and campus hotel that serves as a training site for students in the hotel, restaurant and institutional management department. Scheduled for completion in 2013 is a 194,000-square-foot Interdisciplinary Science and Engineering Laboratory. **Computers:** 100% of classrooms, 100% of dorms, 100% of libraries, 100% of dining areas, 100% of student union, 50% of common outdoor areas have wireless network access. Students can register for classes online. Administrative functions (other than registration) can be performed online.

CAMPUS LIFE

Environment: Town **Activities:** Campus Ministries; Choral groups; Concert band; Dance; Drama/theater; International Student Organization; Jazz band; Literary magazine; Marching band; Model UN; Music ensembles; Musical theater; Opera; Pep band; Radio station; Student government; Student newspaper; Student-run film society; Symphony orchestra; Television station 250 registered organizations, 23 honor societies, 24 religious organizations. 22 fraternities, 15 sororities. **Athletics (Intercollegiate):** *Men:* baseball, basketball, cross-country, diving, football, golf, lacrosse, soccer, swimming, tennis, track/field (outdoor). *Women:* basketball, crew/rowing, cross-country, diving, field hockey, lacrosse, soccer, softball, swimming, tennis, track/field (outdoor), track/field (indoor), volleyball. **On-Campus Highlights:** Interdisciplinary Science Engineering Lab, Trabant University Center, Memorial Hall, Carpenter Sports Building, Perkins Student Center **Environmental Initiatives:** The University of Delaware is launching a revolving energy loan fund dedicated to increase energy efficiency of campus buildings.

ADMISSIONS

Freshman Academic Profile: Average high school GPA 3.7. 31% in top 10% of high school class, 66% in top 25% of high school class, 92% in top 50% of high school class. 80% from public high schools. **Test Scores:** SAT Math middle 50% range 550-650. SAT EBRW middle 50% range 540-650. ACT middle 50% range 23-29. Minimum internet-based TOEFL 90. Minimum paper TOEFL 570. **Basis for Candidate Selection:** *Very important factors considered include:* rigor of secondary school record, academic GPA, state residency. *Important factors considered include:* application essay, standardized test scores, recommendation(s), extracurricular activities, talent/ability, character/personal qualities, volunteer work, work experience. *Other factors considered include:* class rank, interview, first generation, alumni/ae relation, geographical residence, racial/ethnic status, level of applicant's interest. **Freshman Admission Requirements:** High school diploma is required and GED is accepted *Academic units required:* 4 English, 3 math, 3 science, 2 science labs, 2 foreign language, 2 social studies, 2 history, 2 academic electives, *Academic units recommended:* 4 English, 4 math, 4 science, 3 science labs, 4 foreign language, 2 social studies, 2 history, 2 academic electives. **Freshman Admission Statistics:** 24,456 applied, 64.9% admitted, 25% enrolled. **Transfer Admission Requirements:** High school transcript, college transcript(s), essay or personal statement, statement of good standing from prior institution(s). Minimum college GPA of 2.5 required. Lowest grade transferable C. **General Admission Information:** Application fee $75. Regular application deadline 1/15. Nonfall registration accepted. Admission may be deferred for a maximum of 1 year.

COSTS AND FINANCIAL AID

Annual in-state tuition $12,332. Annual out-of-state tuition $31,860. Room and board $12,332. Required fees $1,290. Average book expense $800. **Required Forms and Deadlines:** FAFSA. **Notification of Awards:** Applicants will be notified of awards on a rolling basis beginning 3/15. **Types of Aid:** *Need-based scholarships/grants:* College/university scholarship or grant aid from institutional funds; Federal Pell; Private scholarships; SEOG; State scholarships/grants. *Loans:* Direct PLUS loans; Direct Subsidized Stafford Loans; Direct Unsubsidized Stafford Loans. *Student Employment:* Federal Work-Study Program available. Institutional employment available. **Financial Aid Statistics:** 92% needy freshmen, 81% needy undergrads receive need-based scholarship or grant aid. 9% freshmen, 7% undergrads receive non-need-based scholarship or grant aid. 75% freshmen, 82% undergrads receive need-based self-help aid. 2% freshmen, 2% undergrads receive athletic scholarships. 56% freshmen, 49% undergrads receive any aid. 61% undergrads borrow to pay for school. Average cumulative indebtedness $34,101. **Criteria for awarding aid:** *Need-based:* Academics, Art *Non-need-based:* Academics, Alumni affiliation, Art, Athletics, Leadership, Minority status, Music/drama, State/district residency.

See page 1058.

UNIVERSITY OF DENVER

2199 South University Boulevard, Denver, CO 80208
Phone: (303) 871-2036 • **Financial Aid Phone:** 303-871-4020
E-mail: admission@du.edu • **CEEB Code:** 4842
Fax: 303-871-3301 • **Website:** http://www.du.edu • **ACT Code:** 534

This private school was founded in 1864. It has a 125 acre campus.

RATINGS

Admissions Selectivity Rating: 89   **Fire Safety Rating:** 82   **Green Rating:** 86

STUDENTS AND FACULTY

Enrollment: 5,753. **Student Body:** 53% female, 47% male, 62% out-of-state, 7% international (51 countries represented). Asian 4%, African American 2%, Caucasian 69%, Hispanic 11%, Native American <1%, Pacific Islander <1%, Two or more races 4%, Race unknown 2%.
Retention and Graduation: 87% freshmen return for sophomore year. 65% freshmen graduate within 4 years. 75% freshmen graduate within 6 years. **Faculty:** Student/faculty ratio 11:1. 753 full-time faculty, 88% hold PhDs, 18% are members of minority groups, 44% are women. 3% of classes are taught by teaching assistants.

ACADEMICS

Degrees: Bachelor's; Certificate; Doctoral; Doctoral/Professional; Doctoral/Research; Master's; Post-Bachelor's certificate; Post-Master's certificate
Classes: Most classes have fewer than 10 students. Most lab/discussion sessions have 10-19 students. **Most popular majors:** Speech Communication And Rhetoric; Psychology, General; Finance, General. **Special Study Options:** Accelerated program; Cooperative education program; Distance learning; Double major; Dual enrollment; English as a Second Language (ESL); Honors program; Independent study; Internships; Student-designed major; Study abroad; Teacher certification program; Weekend college. Honors programs: The University of Denver offers a challenging Honors Program for talented students who seek an advanced liberal education, lively dialogue with their peers and faculty on important issues, study abroad in first-rate universities, and inspiring in-depth work in their majors. The aim of the program is to challenge students to cultivate strong habits of critical thinking, creativity, and scholarship and to offer close support for advanced work. Students in the Honors Program have the best of both worlds: the small classes and close community of a liberal arts college and the opportunities and resources of a research university. Combined degree programs: BA/JD; BA/MA. **Disability Services offered to physically disabled students:** Note-taking services; Reader services; Tape recorders; Tutors. **Career services:** Alumni network; Alumni services; Career assessment; Career/job search classes; Internships; Regional alumni

FACILITIES

Housing: Apartments for married students; Apartments for single students; Coed dorms; Fraternity/sorority housing; Theme housing; Wellness housing 85% of campus accessible to physically disabled. **Special Academic Facilities/Equipment:** Art gallery, performing arts center, centers for Judaic and Latin American studies, Anthropology Museum, center for child study, center for gifted and talented children, regional conservation center, high altitude research lab, law enforcement technology center, observatory. **Computers:** 75% of classrooms, 10% of dorms, 100% of libraries, 100% of dining areas, 100% of student union, 50% of common outdoor areas have wireless network access. Students can register for classes online. Administrative functions (other than registration) can be performed online. Undergraduates are required to own a computer.

CAMPUS LIFE

Environment: Metropolis **Activities:** Campus Ministries; Choral groups; Concert band; Dance; Drama/theater; International Student Organization; Jazz band; Literary magazine; Marching band; Model UN; Music ensembles; Musical theater; Opera; Pep band; Radio station; Student government; Student newspaper; Student-run film society; Symphony orchestra 160 registered organizations, 19 honor societies, 14 religious organizations. 9 fraternities, 6 sororities. **Athletics (Intercollegiate):** *Men:* basketball, diving, golf, ice hockey, lacrosse, skiing (downhill/alpine), skiing (nordic/cross-country), soccer, swimming, tennis. *Women:* basketball, diving, golf, gymnastics, lacrosse, skiing (downhill/alpine), skiing (nordic/cross-country), soccer, swimming, tennis, volleyball. **On-Campus Highlights:** Campus Green (Driscoll Lawn), Ritchie Center (athletic facility), Anderson Academic Commons (library), Newman Center (performing arts), Beans Cafe (inside Joy Burns Center) **Environmental Initiatives:** The University of Denver expanded from single stream recycling to outdoor bins and composting in two campus dining halls.

ADMISSIONS

Freshman Academic Profile: Average high school GPA 3.7. 42% in top 10% of high school class, 74% in top 25% of high school class, 96% in top 50% of high school class. **Test Scores:** SAT Math middle 50% range 570-670. SAT EBRW middle 50% range 590-680. ACT middle 50% range 25-30. Minimum internet-based TOEFL 80. Minimum paper TOEFL 550. **Basis for Candidate Selection:** *Very important factors considered include:* rigor of secondary school record, academic GPA, standardized test scores. *Important factors considered include:* application essay, recommendation(s), extracurricular activities, talent/ability, character/personal qualities. *Other factors considered include:* first generation, alumni/ae relation, geographical residence, racial/ethnic status, volunteer work, work experience, level of applicant's interest. **Freshman Admission Requirements:** High school diploma is required and GED is accepted *Academic units recommended:* 4 English, 3 math, 3 science, 2 science labs, 2 foreign language, 3 social studies. **Freshman Admission Statistics:** 19,904 applied, 58.0% admitted, 13% enrolled. **Transfer Admission Requirements:** college transcript(s), essay or personal statement, statement of good standing from prior institution(s). Lowest grade transferable C. **General Admission Information:** Application fee $65. Regular application deadline 1/15. Nonfall registration accepted. Admission may be deferred for a maximum of 1 year.

COSTS AND FINANCIAL AID

Annual tuition $49,392. Room and board $13,005. Required fees $1,164. Average book expense $1,200. **Required Forms and Deadlines:** CSS/Financial Aid PROFILE; FAFSA; Noncustodial PROFILE. **Notification of Awards:** Applicants will be notified of awards on or about 3/1. **Types of Aid:** *Need-based scholarships/grants:* College/university scholarship or grant aid from institutional funds; Federal Pell; Private scholarships; SEOG; State scholarships/grants. *Loans:* Direct PLUS loans; Direct Subsidized Stafford Loans; Direct Unsubsidized Stafford Loans. *Student Employment:* Federal Work-Study Program available. Institutional employment available. **Financial Aid Statistics:** 98% needy freshmen, 98% needy undergrads receive need-based scholarship or grant aid. 25% freshmen, 26% undergrads receive non-need-based scholarship or grant aid. 67% freshmen, 69% undergrads receive need-based self-help aid. 4% freshmen, 4% undergrads receive athletic scholarships. 85% freshmen, 83% undergrads receive any aid. 44% undergrads borrow to pay for school. Average cumulative indebtedness $31,077. **Criteria for awarding aid:** *Need-based:* Academics, Art, Athletics, Leadership, Music/drama *Non-need-based:* Academics, Art, Athletics, Leadership, Music/drama.

UNIVERSITY OF DUBUQUE

2000 University Avenue, Dubuque, IA 52001-5050
Phone: 319-589-3200 • **Financial Aid Phone:** 563-589-3396
E-mail: admssns@dbq.edu • **CEEB Code:** 6869
Fax: 319-589-3690 • **Website:** www.dbq.edu • **ACT Code:** 1358

This private school, affiliated with the Presbyterian Church, was founded in 1852. It has a 77 acre campus.

RATINGS
Admissions Selectivity Rating: 77   **Fire Safety Rating:** 96   **Green Rating:** 60*

STUDENTS AND FACULTY
Enrollment: 1,542. **Student Body:** 44% female, 56% male, 53% out-of-state, 1% international. Asian 2%, African American 12%, Caucasian 73%, Hispanic 3%, Native American 1%, Pacific Islander <1%, Two or more races 0%, Race unknown 8%.
Retention and Graduation: 68% freshmen return for sophomore year. 20% grads go on to further study within 1 year. 10% grads pursue arts and sciences degrees. 2% grads pursue law degrees. 3% grads pursue business degrees. 2% grads pursue medical degrees. **Faculty:** Student/faculty ratio 14:1. 87 full-time faculty, 56% hold PhDs, 6% are members of minority groups, 39% are women. 0% of classes are taught by teaching assistants.

ACADEMICS
Degrees: Bachelor's; Doctoral/Professional; Master's **Most popular majors:** Animation, Interactive Technology, Video Graphics And Special Effects; Airline/Commercial/Professional Pilot And Flight Crew; Business/Commerce, General. **Special Study Options:** Accelerated program; Cooperative education program; Cross-registration; Distance learning; Double major; Dual enrollment; Honors program; Independent study; Internships; Liberal arts/career combination; Student-designed major; Study abroad; Teacher certification program. Combined degree programs: BA/MA. **Disability Services offered to physically disabled students:** Note-taking services; Reader services; Tape recorders; Tutors. **Career services:** Alumni network; Alumni services; Career assessment; Career/job search classes; Internships; Regional alumni

FACILITIES
Housing: Apartments for married students; Apartments for single students; Coed dorms; Special housing for disabled students 50% of campus accessible to physically diasbled. **Special Academic Facilities/Equipment:** Art gallery, language labs, electron microscope, gas chromatograph/mass spectrometer, floating science lab on the Mississippi River, computer graphics/interactive media stduios, multimedia project production studio in the new Charles C. Myers Library **Computers:** 20% of classrooms, 100% of libraries, 100% of student union, have wireless network access. Students can register for classes online. Administrative functions (other than registration) can be performed online.

CAMPUS LIFE
Environment: Town **Activities:** Campus Ministries; Choral groups; Dance; Drama/theater; International Student Organization; Jazz band; Literary magazine; Music ensembles; Musical theater; Pep band; Student government; Student newspaper; Student-run film society; Yearbook 50 registered organizations, 2 honor societies, 3 religious organizations. 7 fraternities, 4 sororities. **Athletics (Intercollegiate):** *Men:* baseball, basketball, cross-country, football, golf, soccer, tennis, track/field (outdoor), track/field (indoor), wrestling. *Women:* basketball, cross-country, golf, soccer, softball, tennis, track/field (outdoor), track/field (indoor), volleyball. **On-Campus Highlights:** Coffee Shop, Stoltz Sports Center, Library, Student Union, Chlapaty Recreation & Wellness Center **Environmental Initiatives:** Campus-wide recycling

ADMISSIONS
Freshman Academic Profile: Average high school GPA 3.0. 7% in top 10% of high school class, 24% in top 25% of high school class, 54% in top 50% of high school class. 85% from public high schools. **Test Scores:** SAT Math middle 50% range 420-550. SAT EBRW middle 50% range 440-550. ACT middle 50% range 18-23. Minimum paper TOEFL 500. **Basis for Candidate Selection:** *Very important factors considered include:* rigor of secondary school record, class rank, application essay, standardized test scores, recommendation(s), character/personal qualities. *Other factors considered include:* interview, extracurricular activities, talent/ability, alumni/ae relation, volunteer work, work experience. **Freshman Admission Requirements:** High school diploma is required and GED is accepted *Academic units required:* 4 English, 3 math, 3 science, 3 social studies, 3 academic electives. *Academic units recommended:* 4 English, 3 math, 3 science, 3 social studies, 3 academic electives. **Freshman Admission Statistics:** 1,288 applied, 75.8% admitted, 42% enrolled. **Transfer Admission Requirements:** college transcript(s), Minimum college GPA of 2.0 required. Lowest grade transferable C. **General Admission Information:** Application fee $25. Nonfall registration accepted. Admission may be deferred for a maximum of 1 year.

COSTS AND FINANCIAL AID
Annual tuition $21,000. Room and board $7,370. Required fees $590. Average book expense $950. **Required Forms and Deadlines:** FAFSA. **Notification of Awards:** Applicants will be notified of awards on a rolling basis beginning 3/1. **Types of Aid:** *Need-based scholarships/grants:* College/university scholarship or grant aid from institutional funds; Federal Pell; Private scholarships; SEOG; State scholarships/grants. *Loans:* Direct PLUS loans; Direct Subsidized Stafford Loans; Direct Unsubsidized Stafford Loans. *Student Employment:* Federal Work-Study Program available. Institutional employment available. **Financial Aid Statistics:** 99% needy freshmen, 98% needy undergrads receive need-based scholarship or grant aid. 16% freshmen, 12% undergrads receive non-need-based scholarship or grant aid. 80% freshmen, 83% undergrads receive need-based self-help aid. 0% freshmen, 0% undergrads receive athletic scholarships. 85% freshmen, 85% undergrads receive any aid. **Criteria for awarding aid:** *Need-based:* Academics, Alumni affiliation, Minority status, Music/drama, Religious affiliation *Non-need-based:* Academics, Alumni affiliation, Leadership, Music/drama, State/district residency.

UNIVERSITY OF EVANSVILLE

1800 Lincoln Avenue, Evansville, IN 47722
Phone: 812-488-2468 • **Financial Aid Phone:** 812-488-2364
E-mail: admission@evansville.edu • **CEEB Code:** 1208
Fax: 812-488-4076 • **Website:** www.evansville.edu • **ACT Code:** 1188

This private school, affiliated with the Methodist Church, was founded in 1854. It has a 75 acre campus.

RATINGS
Admissions Selectivity Rating: 84   **Fire Safety Rating:** 64   **Green Rating:** 60*

STUDENTS AND FACULTY
Enrollment: 2,164. **Student Body:** 54% female, 46% male, 39% out-of-state, 15% international (55 countries represented). Asian 2%, African American 3%, Caucasian 71%, Hispanic 4%, Native American <1%, Pacific Islander 0%, Two or more races 2%, Race unknown 3%.
Retention and Graduation: 89% freshmen return for sophomore year. 18% grads go on to further study within 1 year. **Faculty:** Student/faculty ratio 12:1. 169 full-time faculty, 86% hold PhDs, 12% are members of minority groups, 41% are women. 0% of classes are taught by teaching assistants.

ACADEMICS
Degrees: Associate; Bachelor's; Doctoral/Professional; **Master's Classes:** Most classes have 10-19 students. Most lab/discussion sessions have 10-19 students. **Most popular majors:** Kinesiology And Exercise Science; Drama And Dramatics/Theatre Arts, General; Registered Nursing/Registered Nurse. **Special Study Options:** Cooperative education program; Double major; Dual enrollment; English as a Second Language (ESL); Honors program; Independent study; Internships; Study abroad; Teacher certification program. Honors programs: The Honors Program is designed to enhance one's academic and social experience at the University. Special honors courses are offered each semester, as is the opportunity to create an honors experience from virtually any non-honors course. An honors project serves as the program capstone and is expressed through research, publication, or performance. Special honors events include guest lectures, book and movie discussions, an annual philanthropic event, and off-campus trips. Honors students enjoy many benefits, such as priority class registration, honors campus housing, opportunity to apply for undergraduate research funds, and access to a 24-hour honors lounge equipped with computers and printers. The Honors Program is structured to allow students in each of the University's colleges and schools to participate. **Disability Services offered to physically disabled students:** Note-taking services; Tutors. **Career services:** Alumni network; Alumni services; Career assessment; Career/job search classes; Internships; Regional alumni

FACILITIES
Housing: Apartments for single students; Coed dorms; Fraternity/sorority housing; Men's dorms; Theme housing; Women's dorms 87% of campus accessible to physically diasbled. **Computers:** 100% of classrooms, 100% of dorms, 100% of libraries, 100% of dining areas, 100% of student union, 100% of common outdoor areas have wireless network access. Students can register for classes online. Administrative functions (other than registration) can be performed online.

CAMPUS LIFE

Environment: City **Activities:** Campus Ministries; Choral groups; Concert band; Dance; Drama/theater; International Student Organization; Jazz band; Literary magazine; Model UN; Music ensembles; Musical theater; Opera; Pep band; Radio station; Student government; Student newspaper; Student-run film society; Symphony orchestra; Yearbook 154 registered organizations, 11 honor societies, 10 religious organizations. 6 fraternities, 5 sororities. **Athletics (Intercollegiate):** *Men:* baseball, basketball, cross-country, diving, golf, soccer, swimming. *Women:* basketball, cross-country, diving, golf, soccer, softball, swimming, tennis, volleyball. **On-Campus Highlights:** Koch Center, Fitness Center, School of Business Administration, Ridgway University Center, Jazzman's Cafe

ADMISSIONS

Freshman Academic Profile: Average high school GPA 3.7. 34% in top 10% of high school class, 68% in top 25% of high school class, 90% in top 50% of high school class. **Test Scores:** SAT Math middle 50% range 500-620. SAT EBRW middle 50% range 490-600. ACT middle 50% range 23-29. Minimum internet-based TOEFL 61. Minimum paper TOEFL 500. **Basis for Candidate Selection:** *Very important factors considered include:* academic GPA, standardized test scores, talent/ability. *Important factors considered include:* rigor of secondary school record, alumni/ae relation, level of applicant's interest. *Other factors considered include:* class rank, application essay, recommendation(s), interview, extracurricular activities, character/personal qualities, first generation, geographical residence, state residency, religious affiliation/commitment, racial/ethnic status, volunteer work, work experience. **Freshman Admission Requirements:** High school diploma is required and GED is accepted *Academic units required:* 4 English, 3 math, 3 science, 2 social studies, 1 history, *Academic units recommended:* 4 math, 3 science labs, 2 foreign language. **Freshman Admission Statistics:** 4,033 applied, 70.9% admitted, 19% enrolled. **Transfer Admission Requirements:** High school transcript, college transcript(s), statement of good standing from prior institution(s). Minimum college GPA of 2.0 required. Lowest grade transferable C. **General Admission Information:** Nonfall registration accepted. Admission may be deferred for a maximum of 1 year.

COSTS AND FINANCIAL AID

Annual tuition $34,300. Room and board $12,160. Required fees $1,096. Average book expense $1,200. **Required Forms and Deadlines:** FAFSA. **Notification of Awards:** Applicants will be notified of awards on a rolling basis beginning 12/15. **Types of Aid:** *Need-based scholarships/grants:* College/university scholarship or grant aid from institutional funds; Federal Pell; Private scholarships; SEOG; State scholarships/grants. *Loans:* Direct PLUS loans; Direct Subsidized Stafford Loans; Direct Unsubsidized Stafford Loans. *Student Employment:* Federal Work-Study Program available. Institutional employment available. **Financial Aid Statistics:** 100% needy freshmen, 96% needy undergrads receive need-based scholarship or grant aid. 24% freshmen, 21% undergrads receive non-need-based scholarship or grant aid. 66% freshmen, 68% undergrads receive need-based self-help aid. 5% freshmen, 6% undergrads receive athletic scholarships. 95% freshmen, 94% undergrads receive any aid. 65% undergrads borrow to pay for school. Average cumulative indebtedness $35,346. **Criteria for awarding aid:** *Need-based:* Job skills *Non-need-based:* Academics, Alumni affiliation, Art, Athletics, Job skills, Music/drama, Religious affiliation.

THE UNIVERSITY OF FINDLAY

1000 North Main Street, Findlay, OH 45840
Phone: 419-434-4732 • **Financial Aid Phone:** 419-434-4791
E-mail: admissions@findlay.edu • **CEEB Code:** 1223
Fax: 419-434-4898 • **Website:** www.findlay.edu • **ACT Code:** 3272

This private school was founded in 1882. It has a 175 acre campus.

RATINGS

Admissions Selectivity Rating: 75 **Fire Safety Rating:** 82 **Green Rating:** 60*

STUDENTS AND FACULTY

Enrollment: 2,882. **Student Body:** 63% female, 37% male, 10% international (28 countries represented). Asian 1%, African American 4%, Caucasian 81%, Hispanic 2%, Native American <1%, Pacific Islander 0%, Two or more races 2%, Race unknown 1%.
Retention and Graduation: 78% freshmen return for sophomore year.
Faculty: Student/faculty ratio 16:1. 203 full-time faculty, 67% hold PhDs, 10% are members of minority groups, 48% are women. 10% of classes are taught by teaching assistants.

ACADEMICS

Degrees: Associate; Bachelor's; Doctoral; Doctoral/Professional; **Master's Classes:** Most classes have 20-29 students. Most lab/discussion sessions have 20-29 students. **Most popular majors:** Animal Sciences; Pre-Occupational Therapy Studies; Pre-Physical Therapy Studies. **Special Study Options:** Accelerated program; Cooperative education program; Distance learning; Double major; Dual enrollment; English as a Second Language (ESL); Exchange student program (domestic); External degree program; Honors program; Independent study; Internships; Liberal arts/career combination; Student-designed major; Study abroad; Teacher certification program; Weekend college. **Disability Services offered to physically disabled students:** Note-taking services; Tutors. **Career services:** Alumni services; Career assessment; Career/job search classes; Internships

FACILITIES

Housing: Apartments for single students; Coed dorms; Fraternity/sorority housing; Women's dorms 90% of campus accessible to physically disabled. **Special Academic Facilities/Equipment:** Fine arts pavilion, planetarium. Mazza Gallery (Children's Book Illustrations.)

CAMPUS LIFE

Environment: Village **Activities:** Campus Ministries; Choral groups; Concert band; Dance; Drama/theater; Literary magazine; Marching band; Music ensembles; Musical theater; Pep band; Radio station; Student government; Student newspaper; Television station. Center for Student Life and College of Business, Griffith Memorial Arch, Dr. C. Ricahrd Beckett Animal Science Building, Koehler Fitness and Recreation Complex, Mazza Museum

ADMISSIONS

Freshman Academic Profile: Average high school GPA 3.4. 26% in top 10% of high school class, 54% in top 25% of high school class, 80% in top 50% of high school class. 92% from public high schools. **Test Scores:** SAT Math middle 50% range 470-580. SAT EBRW middle 50% range 470-580. ACT middle 50% range 21-26. Minimum paper TOEFL 500. **Basis for Candidate Selection:** *Very important factors considered include:* rigor of secondary school record, academic GPA, standardized test scores. *Important factors considered include:* interview, extracurricular activities, talent/ability. *Other factors considered include:* class rank, application essay, recommendation(s), character/personal qualities, first generation, alnmni/ae relation, volunteer work. **Freshman Admission Requirements:** High school diploma is required and GED is accepted *Academic units required:* 4 English, 3 math, 3 science, 3 science labs, 2 social studies, 1 history, *Academic units recommended:* 4 English, 4 math, 4 science, 4 science labs, 2 foreign language, 3 social studies, 2 history, 1 academic elective. **Freshman Admission Statistics:** 3,081 applied, 83.8% admitted, 22% enrolled. **General Admission Information:** Regular application deadline 8/1. Nonfall registration accepted. Admission may be deferred for a maximum of 1 year.

COSTS AND FINANCIAL AID

Annual tuition $33,320. Room and board $9,720. Average book expense $1,000. **Required Forms and Deadlines:** FAFSA. **Notification of Awards:** Applicants will be notified of awards on a rolling basis beginning 11/1. **Types of Aid:** *Need-based scholarships/grants:* College/university scholarship or grant aid from institutional funds; Federal Pell; SEOG; State scholarships/grants. *Loans:* Direct PLUS loans; Direct Subsidized Stafford Loans; Direct Unsubsidized Stafford Loans. *Student Employment:* Federal Work-Study Program available. Institutional employment available. **Financial Aid Statistics:** 86% needy undergrads receive need-based scholarship or grant aid. 88% freshmen, 23% undergrads receive non-need-based scholarship or grant aid. 68% freshmen, 68% undergrads receive need-based self-help aid. 0% freshmen, 0% undergrads receive athletic scholarships. 75% undergrads borrow to pay for school. Average cumulative indebtedness $20,180.

UNIVERSITY OF FLORIDA

201 Criser Hall, Gainesville, FL 32611-4000
Phone: 352-392-1365 • **Financial Aid Phone:** (352) 392-1271
E-mail: webrequests@admissions.ufl.edu • **CEEB Code:** 5812
Fax: 352-392-2115 • **Website:** www.ufl.edu

This public school was founded in 1853. It has a 2000 acre campus.

RATINGS

Admissions Selectivity Rating: 93   **Fire Safety Rating:** 88   **Green Rating:** 94

STUDENTS AND FACULTY

Enrollment: 33,654. **Student Body:** 56% female, 44% male, 6% out-of-state, 2% international (152 countries represented). Asian 8%, African American 6%, Caucasian 55%, Hispanic 22%, Native American <1%, Pacific Islander 1%, Two or more races 3%, Race unknown 3%.
Retention and Graduation: 67% freshmen graduate within 4 years. 87% freshmen graduate within 6 years. **Faculty:** Student/faculty ratio 21:1. 3,543 full-time faculty, 85% hold PhDs, 26% are members of minority groups, 36% are women. 30% of classes are taught by teaching assistants.

ACADEMICS

Degrees: Associate; Bachelor's; Certificate; Doctoral Other; Doctoral/Professional; Doctoral/Research; Master's; Post-Bachelor's certificate; Post-Master's certificate; Transfer Associate **Classes:** Most classes have 10-19 students. Most lab/discussion sessions have 10-19 students. **Most popular majors:** Biology/Biological Sciences, General; Psychology, General; Finance, General. **Special Study Options:** Accelerated program; Cooperative education program; Cross-registration; Distance learning; Double major; Dual enrollment; English as a Second Language (ESL); Exchange student program (domestic); Honors program; Independent study; Internships; Liberal arts/career combination; Student-designed major; Study abroad; Teacher certification program. Honors programs: The University of Florida Honors Program blends the vast resources of a research university with the individualized attention often available only at small liberal arts colleges. With small classes taught by the top faculty at the university, the program offers students the opportunity to make the most of their educational experience. Close interaction with faculty often leads to undergraduate research projects, and students are encouraged to pursue such activities. Students in the Honors Program have the opportunity to live in the Honors Residential College at Hume Hall where they will be surrounded by like-minded individuals and engage in a unique living-learning community. **Disability Services offered to physically disabled students:** Note-taking services; Reader services; Tape recorders. **Career services:** Alumni services; Career assessment; Career/job search classes; Internships; Regional alumni

FACILITIES

Housing: Apartments for married students; Apartments for single students; Coed dorms; Fraternity/sorority housing; Special housing for disabled student; Special housing for international students; Theme housing; Wellness housing 90% of campus accessible to physically diasbled. **Special Academic Facilities/Equipment:** Natural history museum, art museum, art gallery, center for the performing arts, Aeolian Skinner organ, cast-bell carillon, citrus research center, coastal engineering wave tank, 100-kilowatt training and research reactor, academic computing center, microkelvin lab, self-contained intensive care hyperbaric chamber, Butterfly Rainforest **Computers:** 80% of classrooms, 100% of dorms, 100% of libraries, 100% of dining areas, 100% of student union, 100% of common outdoor areas have wireless network access. Students can register for classes online. Administrative functions (other than registration) can be performed online.

CAMPUS LIFE

Environment: City **Activities:** Campus Ministries; Choral groups; Concert band; Dance; Drama/theater; International Student Organization; Jazz band; Literary magazine; Marching band; Model UN; Music ensembles; Musical theater; Pep band; Radio station; Student government; Student newspaper; Student-run film society; Symphony orchestra; Television station; Yearbook 853 registered organizations. **Athletics (Intercollegiate):** *Men:* baseball, basketball, cross-country, diving, football, golf, swimming, tennis, track/field (outdoor), track/field (indoor). *Women:* basketball, cross-country, diving, golf, gymnastics, lacrosse, soccer, softball, swimming, tennis, track/field (outdoor), track/field (indoor), volleyball. **On-Campus Highlights:** Southwest Recreation Center, Plaza of Americas, Library West, Ben Hill Griffin Stadium, J. Wayne Reitz Student Union **Environmental Initiatives:** Zero Waste by 2015: As a

result of Dr. Machen's goal for Zero Waste by 2015, UF now recycles over 6,500 tons of material annually, approximately 43% of the waste stream. Additionally, UF strives to recycle at least 75% of its deconstruction debris and has instituted an Electronics Reuse/Recycling Policy and accompanying step-by-step guide for disposal and recycling. Indoor collection of paper, cans & bottles is institution-wide. UF initiated a Tail-gator recycling program for home game days in 2006 and the program has diverted more than 350,000 pounds of recyclables from the landfill since then. This program continues to grow through self-service stations and other outreach on campus and within the stadium. In 2013, UF began composting efforts on campus by taking the stadium "zero waste" through the football season- diverting an additional 50,000 pounds of organic waste from the landfill. UF researchers recycle Helium on campus and the Veterinary Medical Center repurposes animal waste through a composting partnership with the Forestry Service.

ADMISSIONS

Freshman Academic Profile: 70% from public high schools. **Test Scores:** SAT Math middle 50% range 620-710. SAT EBRW middle 50% range 620-700. ACT middle 50% range 28-32. **Basis for Candidate Selection:** *Very important factors considered include:* rigor of secondary school record, academic GPA, application essay, extracurricular activities, talent/ability, character/personal qualities, volunteer work. *Important factors considered include:* standardized test scores, first generation, geographical residence, work experience. *Other factors considered include:* class rank, alumni/ae relation, state residency, level of applicant's interest. **Freshman Admission Requirements:** High school diploma is required and GED is accepted *Academic units required:* 4 English, 4 math, 3 science, 2 science labs, 2 foreign language, 3 social studies. **Freshman Admission Statistics:** 32,747 applied, 42.0% admitted, 47% enrolled. **Transfer Admission Requirements:** High school transcript, college transcript(s), standardized test scores, Minimum college GPA of 2.0 required. **General Admission Information:** Application fee $30. Regular application deadline 11/1.

COSTS AND FINANCIAL AID

Annual in-state tuition $9,910. Annual out-of-state tuition $28,658. Room and board $9,910. Average book expense $1,210. **Required Forms and Deadlines:** FAFSA. **Notification of Awards:** Applicants will be notified of awards on a rolling basis beginning 4/2. **Types of Aid:** *Need-based scholarships/grants:* College/university scholarship or grant aid from institutional funds; Federal Pell; Private scholarships; SEOG; State scholarships/grants; United Negro College Fund. *Loans:* Direct PLUS loans; Direct Subsidized Stafford Loans; Direct Unsubsidized Stafford Loans. *Student Employment:* Federal Work-Study Program available. Institutional employment available. **Financial Aid Statistics:** 62% needy freshmen, 65% needy undergrads receive need-based scholarship or grant aid. 87% freshmen, 77% undergrads receive non-need-based scholarship or grant aid. 41% freshmen, 50% undergrads receive need-based self-help aid. 1% freshmen, 1% undergrads receive athletic scholarships. 94% freshmen, 91% undergrads receive any aid. 43% undergrads borrow to pay for school. Average cumulative indebtedness $21,028. **Criteria for awarding aid:** *Need-based:* Academics *Non-need-based:* Academics, Alumni affiliation, Art, Athletics, Leadership, Minority status, Music/drama, State/district residency.

UNIVERSITY OF GEORGIA

Administration Building, Athens, GA 30602-1633
Phone: 706-542-8776 • **Financial Aid Phone:** (706)542-6147
E-mail: adm-info@uga.edu • **CEEB Code:** 5813
Website: www.uga.edu • **ACT Code:** 872

This public school was founded in 1785. It has a 767 acre campus.

RATINGS

Admissions Selectivity Rating: 92   **Fire Safety Rating:** 88   **Green Rating:** 95

STUDENTS AND FACULTY

Enrollment: 22,919. **Student Body:** 56% female, 44% male, 11% out-of-state, 2% international (97 countries represented). Asian 10%, African American 8%, Caucasian 69%, Hispanic 6%, Native American <1%, Pacific Islander <1%, Two or more races 4%, Race unknown 1%.
Retention and Graduation: 96% freshmen return for sophomore year. 63% freshmen graduate within 4 years. 85% freshmen graduate within 6 years. **Faculty:** Student/faculty ratio 17:1. 2,028 full-time faculty, 94% hold PhDs,

19% are members of minority groups, 39% are women. 16% of classes are taught by teaching assistants.

ACADEMICS

Degrees: Bachelor's; Certificate; Doctoral; Doctoral/Professional; Doctoral/Research; Master's; Post-Bachelor's certificate; Post-Master's certificate **Classes:** Most classes have 10-19 students. Most lab/discussion sessions have fewer than 10 students. **Most popular majors:** Biology/Biological Sciences, General; Psychology, General; Finance, General. **Special Study Options:** Accelerated program; Cooperative education program; Cross-registration; Distance learning; Double major; Dual enrollment; Exchange student program (domestic); Honors program; Independent study; Internships; Liberal arts/career combination; Student-designed major; Study abroad; Teacher certification program. Honors programs: General Honors Program (university-wide), Foundation Fellows, Center for Undergraduate Research Summer Research Fellows, CURO Apprentice Program. **Disability Services offered to physically disabled students:** Note-taking services; Reader services; Tape recorders; Tutors. **Career services:** Alumni network; Alumni services; Career assessment; Career/job search classes; Internships; Regional alumni

FACILITIES

Housing: Apartments for married students; Apartments for single students; Coed dorms; Fraternity/sorority housing; Special housing for disabled student; Special housing for international students; Theme housing; Women's dorms 90% of campus accessible to physically diasbled. **Special Academic Facilities/Equipment:** Miller Learning Center, Georgia Museum of Art, Georgia Museum of Natural History, Ramsey Student Center for Physical Activities, Performing Arts Center, Tate Student Center, Richard B. Russell Building for Special Collections Libraries, Science Learning Center **Computers:** 90% of classrooms, 15% of dorms, 100% of libraries, 100% of dining areas, 100% of student union, 100% of common outdoor areas have wireless network access. Students can register for classes online. Administrative functions (other than registration) can be performed online.

CAMPUS LIFE

Environment: City **Activities:** Campus Ministries; Choral groups; Concert band; Dance; Drama/theater; International Student Organization; Jazz band; Literary magazine; Marching band; Model UN; Music ensembles; Musical theater; Opera; Pep band; Radio station; Student government; Student newspaper; Student-run film society; Symphony orchestra; Yearbook 597 registered organizations, 22 honor societies, 35 religious organizations. 34 fraternities, 25 sororities. **Athletics (Intercollegiate):** *Men:* baseball, basketball, cross-country, diving, football, golf, swimming, tennis, track/field (outdoor), track/field (indoor). *Women:* basketball, cross-country, diving, equestrian sports, golf, gymnastics, soccer, softball, swimming, tennis, track/field (outdoor), track/field (indoor), volleyball. **On-Campus Highlights:** Zell B. Miller Learning Center, Sanford Stadium, Ramsey Student Center for Physical Activ, Performing and Visual Arts Complex, Tate Student Center **Environmental Initiatives:** UGA's 2020 Strategic Plan (http://provost.uga.edu/documents/UGA_Strategic_Plan_2020_-_October_30_2012.pdf) Sustainability is a hallmark of the 2020 Strategic Plan. Campus sustainability is specifically included in Strategic Direction VII, and sustainability research and education to solve grand challenges is woven through all other strategic directions. Strategic Direction 7—Improving Stewardship of Natural Resources and Advancing Campus Sustainability Because the University of Georgia is committed by its land- and sea-grant mission to serve people living and working in Georgia along with our vision to be a leading university internationally, it is incumbent upon the University to provide leadership concerning unprecedented environmental challenges. It is equally important for the University to manage financial and human resources with the greatest of care and respect and to the maximum benefit of the state. A sustainable university is one that meets the needs of the present without compromising the ability of future generations to meet their needs. It also creates opportunities for students, faculty, and staff to enhance the quality of life throughout their communities (Working Group on Sustainability, 2009; World Commission on Environment and Development). A sustainable university acts as a living laboratory where sustainability is researched, taught, tested, and constantly refined. UGA must demonstrate and promote leadership in sustainable living and learning, contextualizing the local as part of the global in sustainability. Over the next decade, the University's campuses should be examples to others in reducing their environmental footprints to the greatest extent possible. This includes efforts to reduce energy use significantly, and intelligently, and carefully use and reuse scarce water resources, improve air and water quality, provide sustainable food and transportation options, purchase environmentally responsible products and equipment, increase recycling, and drastically reduce waste. Second, in the effort to prepare students for effective leadership on campus and beyond, sustainability should be infused into formal and informal educational opportunities throughout the University. Campus buildings and landscapes should be incorporated as teaching opportunities, which through design and functional interpretation will reveal innovative practices with the potential to enlighten and inform students and citizens about sound approaches to sustainable living. Third, research generated by UGA faculty and students as well as advances from the global community will be used to reduce dependency on fossil fuels, increase the reuse of materials, and continue the search for other methods that will reduce human impacts on the environment. A priority for the University at large is to design and construct buildings, plaza spaces, hardscapes, and other landscapes that embody the latest in environmental advances and to incorporate the increasing social nature of learning today by creating ample spaces for people to interact. To accomplish these goals, the University should establish a formal coordinating body to work with the UGA Office of Sustainability to develop and implement a comprehensive sustainability plan for the University. a. Strategic Priority: Annually evaluate and update the University's sustainability performance in instruction, research, public service, campus development, and operations activities. Benchmark: Stages for developing a systematic evaluation of the University's sustainability performance in instruction, research, public service, campus development, and operations activities. Goal: An annual report on the status of and progress in sustainability performance in instruction, research, public service, campus development, and operations activities by 2020. b. Strategic Priority: Demonstrate a commitment to reducing fossil fuel use, thereby reducing the University's carbon emissions. Pre-benchmark Activity: Calculate the University's carbon footprint. Benchmark: The University's carbon footprint when calculated. Goals: By 2020: Reduce carbon emissions by 20 percent. Reduce University consumption of energy by 25 percent. Increase purchase of energy from renewable sources by 10 percent. Increase generation of energy from renewable sources by 10 percent. c. Strategic Priority: Update UGA Guidelines for Design and Construction to incorporate, implement, and monitor current sustainable design strategies, including Leadership in Energy and Environmental Design (LEED) and Sustainable Sites Initiative standards when appropriate. Benchmark: Stages of completion of drafting, gaining support for, and implementing the guidelines. Goal: Updated Guidelines for Design and Construction by 2020. d. Strategic Priority: Integrate sustainability into the student experience through curricular and co-curricular activities both in the classroom and beyond. Pre-benchmark Activity: Develop a system for identifying and designating courses with a curricular sustainability component. Benchmark: The number of courses with curricular sustainability component when system is implemented. Goal: Increase number of courses with curricular sustainability component by 10 percent by 2020. Pre-benchmark Activity: Develop a system for identifying and designating co-curricular experiences with a sustainability component. Benchmark: The number of available co-curricular experiences with sustainability components when system is implemented. Goal: Increase number of available co-curricular experiences with sustainability components by 10 percent by 2020. e. Strategic Priority: Enhance the coordination, support, and awareness of the University's sustainability efforts by establishing a coordinating body to lead efforts, increasing endowments for sustainable activities and promoting campus sustainability efforts. Benchmark: Stages for establishing and charging a coordinating body to oversee sustainability efforts. Goal: A functioning coordinating body to oversee sustainability efforts by 2020. Benchmark: The level of endowment funds for sustainable activities in 2010-2011. Goal: Increase the endowment for sustainable activities by 25 percent by 2020. Benchmark: Stages of action to identify, develop, fund, and install interpretive signs for key campus sustainability efforts. Goal: Interpretive signs installed by 2020. f. Strategic Priority: Encourage the further development and use of mass transportation to and on campus. Benchmark: The number of campus bus passengers in 2010-2011. Goal: Increase the number of campus bus passengers by 2020. Benchmark: The number of faculty, staff, and students who commute to campus who use alternate modes of transportation such as mass transit, bicycles, or walking in 2010-2011. Goal: Increase by 20 percent the number of faculty, staff, and students who commute to campus using alternate modes of transportation such as mass transit, bicycles, or walking by 2020. Benchmark: The number of Alternative Transportation Permits in 2010-2011(2,100). Goal: Increase the number of Alternative Transportation Permits to 2,500 by 2020. Benchmark: The steps to develop and implement a carpool membership program. Goal: A carpool membership program with 1,000 users by 2020. g. Strategic Priority: Demonstrate a commitment to sustainability through reduced potable water usage, decreased waste, and increased use of sustainable and locally grown foods. Benchmark: The level of potable water usage in 2010-2011. Goal: Reduce potable water use by 40 percent by 2020. Benchmark: The level of waste stream to landfills in 2010-2011. Goal: Decrease waste stream to landfills by 65 percent by 2020. Benchmark: The level of sustainable and/or Georgia-grown foods in 2010-2011 (approximately 20 percent). Goal: Increase the use of sustainable and Georgia-grown foods to 35 percent by 2020. h. Strategic Priority: Develop and implement a process for evaluating opportunities for on-site renewable energy in capital projects. Benchmark: Stages of development and implementation of an evaluation process. Goal: Documented evaluations of opportunities for on-site renewable energy for each capital improvement project on campus by 2020.

ADMISSIONS

Freshman Academic Profile: Average high school GPA 4.0. 54% in top 10% of high school class, 90% in top 25% of high school class, 99% in top 50%

of high school class. 69% from public high schools. **Test Scores:** SAT Math middle 50% range 590-680. SAT EBRW middle 50% range 610-690. ACT middle 50% range 26-31. Minimum internet-based TOEFL 80. Minimum paper TOEFL 550. **Basis for Candidate Selection:** *Very important factors considered include:* rigor of secondary school record, academic GPA. *Important factors considered include:* standardized test scores. *Other factors considered include:* application essay, recommendation(s), extracurricular activities, talent/ability, character/personal qualities, first generation, volunteer work, work experience. **Freshman Admission Requirements:** High school diploma is required and GED is accepted *Academic units required:* 4 English, 4 math, 4 science, 2 science labs, 2 foreign language, 3 social studies, *Academic units recommended:* 4 English, 4 math, 4 science, 2 science labs, 3 foreign language, 3 social studies, 1 academic elective. **Freshman Admission Statistics:** 24,165 applied, 54.0% admitted, 45% enrolled. **Transfer Admission Requirements:** college transcript(s), Lowest grade transferable D. **General Admission Information:** Application fee $60. Priority deadline 10/15. Regular application deadline 1/1. Nonfall registration accepted. Admission may be deferred for a maximum of one academic year.

COSTS AND FINANCIAL AID

Required Forms and Deadlines: FAFSA. **Notification of Awards:** Applicants will be notified of awards on a rolling basis beginning 5/1. **Types of Aid:** *Need-based scholarships/grants:* College/university scholarship or grant aid from institutional funds; Federal Pell; Private scholarships; SEOG; State scholarships/grants. *Loans:* Direct PLUS loans; Direct Subsidized Stafford Loans; Direct Unsubsidized Stafford Loans. *Student Employment:* Federal Work-Study Program available. Institutional employment available. **Financial Aid Statistics:** 98% needy freshmen, 92% needy undergrads receive need-based scholarship or grant aid. 25% freshmen, 17% undergrads receive non-need-based scholarship or grant aid. 48% freshmen, 57% undergrads receive need-based self-help aid. 2% freshmen, 2% undergrads receive athletic scholarships. 47% freshmen, 48% undergrads receive any aid. 47% undergrads borrow to pay for school. Average cumulative indebtedness $21,730. **Criteria for awarding aid:** *Non-need-based:* Academics, Athletics, State/district residency.

UNIVERSITY OF GREAT FALLS

1301 20th Street South, Great Falls, MT 59405
Phone: 406-791-5200 • **Financial Aid Phone:** 406-791-5235
E-mail: enroll@ugf.edu • **CEEB Code:** 4058
Fax: 406-791-5209 • **Website:** www.ugf.edu • **ACT Code:** 2410

This private school, affiliated with the Roman Catholic Church, was founded in 1932. It has a 44 acre campus.

RATINGS
Admissions Selectivity Rating: 80   **Fire Safety Rating:** 60*   **Green Rating:** 60*

STUDENTS AND FACULTY
Enrollment: 612. **Student Body:** 63% female, 37% male, 20% out-of-state, international.
Retention and Graduation: 59% freshmen return for sophomore year. 20% grads pursue arts and sciences degrees. 100% grads pursue medical degrees. **Faculty:** Student/faculty ratio 12:1. 33 full-time faculty, 61% hold PhDs, 6% are members of minority groups, 33% are women. 0% of classes are taught by teaching assistants.

ACADEMICS
Degrees: Associate; Bachelor's; Master's; Terminal Associate; Transfer Associate **Classes:** Most classes have fewer than 10 students. **Most popular majors:** Elementary Education And Teaching; Psychology, General; Criminal Justice/Safety Studies. **Special Study Options:** Cooperative education program; Distance learning; Double major; Independent study; Internships; Liberal arts/career combination; Teacher certification program. **Disability Services offered to physically disabled students:** Note-taking services; Reader services; Tape recorders; Tutors. **Career services:** Alumni network; Alumni services; Career/job search classes; Internships

FACILITIES
Housing: Apartments for married students; Apartments for single students; Coed dorms 85% of campus accessible to physically diasbled. **Special Academic Facilities/Equipment:** Art museum; Dr. Hong Herbarium. **Computers:** 70% of classrooms, 100% of dorms, 100% of libraries, 100% of student union, have wireless network access. Students can register for classes online.

CAMPUS LIFE
Environment: Town **Activities:** Campus Ministries; Choral groups; Concert band; Dance; Drama/theater; Jazz band; Music ensembles; Musical theater; Pep band; Radio station; Student government; Student newspaper; Symphony orchestra 10 registered organizations, 2 honor societies, 1 religious organization. **Athletics (Intercollegiate):** *Men:* basketball, cheerleading, cross-country, golf, track/field (outdoor), wrestling. *Women:* basketball, cheerleading, cross-country, golf, soccer, softball, track/field (outdoor), volleyball. **On-Campus Highlights:** Student Center, Wellness Center, Athletic Facility, Art Gallery

ADMISSIONS
Freshman Academic Profile: Average high school GPA 3.4. 87% from public high schools. **Test Scores:** SAT Math middle 50% range 360-490. SAT EBRW middle 50% range 330-430. ACT middle 50% range 18-24. Minimum paper TOEFL 500. **Basis for Candidate Selection:** *Important factors considered include:* rigor of secondary school record, academic GPA, application essay, standardized test scores, interview, character/personal qualities, religious affiliation/commitment, level of applicant's interest. *Other factors considered include:* class rank, recommendation(s), extracurricular activities, talent/ability, first generation, racial/ethnic status, volunteer work, work experience. **Freshman Admission Requirements:** High school diploma is required and GED is accepted *Academic units required:* 4 English, 3 math, 3 science, 1 science labs, 1 social studies, 3 history, 5 academic electives, *Academic units recommended:* 4 English, 3 math, 3 science, 1 science labs, 2 foreign language, 2 social studies, 3 history, 3 academic electives. **Freshman Admission Statistics:** 278 applied, 73.4% admitted, 59% enrolled. **Transfer Admission Requirements:** college transcript(s), essay or personal statement, Minimum college GPA of 2.0 required. Lowest grade transferable C. **General Admission Information:** Application fee $35. Priority deadline 6/1. Regular application deadline 8/30. Nonfall registration accepted. Admission may be deferred for a maximum of 2 semesters.

COSTS AND FINANCIAL AID
Annual tuition $15,500. Room and board $6,490. Required fees $900. Average book expense $500. **Required Forms and Deadlines:** FAFSA. **Notification of Awards:** Applicants will be notified of awards on a rolling basis beginning 3/1. **Types of Aid:** *Need-based scholarships/grants:* College/university scholarship or grant aid from institutional funds; Federal Pell; Private scholarships; SEOG; State scholarships/grants. *Loans: Student Employment:* Federal Work-Study Program available. Institutional employment available. **Financial Aid Statistics:** 69% needy freshmen, 73% needy undergrads receive need-based scholarship or grant aid. 92% freshmen, 92% undergrads receive non-need-based scholarship or grant aid. 90% freshmen, 93% undergrads receive need-based self-help aid. 47% freshmen, 38% undergrads receive athletic scholarships. 46% freshmen, 50% undergrads receive any aid. **Criteria for awarding aid:** *Need-based:* Job skills, Minority status, Religious affiliation *Non-need-based:* Academics, Alumni affiliation, Art, Athletics, Job skills, Leadership, Minority status, Music/drama, Religious affiliation, State/district residency.

UNIVERSITY OF HARTFORD

200 Bloomfield Avenue, West Hartford, CT 06117
Phone: 860-768-4296 • **Financial Aid Phone:** 800-947-4303
E-mail: admissions@mail.hartford.edu • **CEEB Code:** 3436
Fax: 860-768-4961 • **Website:** www.hartford.edu • **ACT Code:** 606

This private school was founded in 1877. It has a 320 acre campus.

RATINGS
Admissions Selectivity Rating: 76   **Fire Safety Rating:** 78   **Green Rating:** 60*

STUDENTS AND FACULTY
Enrollment: 4,924. **Student Body:** 51% female, 49% male, 51% out-of-state, 6% international (50 countries represented). Asian 3%, African American 16%, Caucasian 56%, Hispanic 12%, Native American <1%, Pacific Islander <1%, Two or more races 3%, Race unknown 4%.
Retention and Graduation: 75% freshmen return for sophomore year. 22% grads go on to further study within 1 year. 39% grads pursue arts and sciences degrees. 2% grads pursue law degrees. 14% grads pursue business degrees. 2% grads pursue medical degrees. **Faculty:** Student/faculty ratio 9:1. 366 full-time faculty, 71% hold PhDs, 14% are members of minority groups, 42% are women. 0% of classes are taught by teaching assistants.

ACADEMICS
Degrees: Associate; Bachelor's; Certificate; Diploma; Doctoral; Doctoral/Professional; Doctoral/Research; Master's; Post-Bachelor's certificate; Post-

Master's certificate **Classes:** Most classes have 20-29 students. Most lab/discussion sessions have 10-19 students. **Most popular majors:** Architectural Engineering Technology/Technician; Psychology, General. **Special Study Options:** Accelerated program; Cross-registration; Distance learning; Double major; Dual enrollment; English as a Second Language (ESL); Exchange student program (domestic); Honors program; Independent study; Internships; Liberal arts/career combination; Student-designed major; Study abroad; Teacher certification program; Weekend college. **Disability Services offered to physically disabled students:** Note-taking services; Reader services; Tutors.

FACILITIES

Housing: Apartments for single students; Coed dorms; Special housing for disabled student; Theme housing; Wellness housing; Women's dorms **Special Academic Facilities/Equipment:** Museum of presidential memorabilia, Art Gallery, off-campus child care center for student teaching, learning skills and language lab, audio-visual aids center, 8,000-acre environmental center. **Computers:** Students can register for classes online. Administrative functions (other than registration) can be performed online.

CAMPUS LIFE

Environment: Metropolis **Activities:** Campus Ministries; Choral groups; Concert band; Dance; Drama/theater; International Student Organization; Jazz band; Literary magazine; Music ensembles; Musical theater; Opera; Pep band; Radio station; Student government; Student newspaper; Student-run film society; Symphony orchestra; Television station; Yearbook 93 registered organizations, 22 honor societies, 7 religious organizations. 16 fraternities, 14 sororities. **Athletics (Intercollegiate):** *Men:* baseball, basketball, cross-country, golf, lacrosse, soccer, tennis, track/field (outdoor), track/field (indoor). *Women:* basketball, cross-country, golf, soccer, softball, tennis, track/field (outdoor), track/field (indoor), volleyball. **On-Campus Highlights:** Museum of American Political Life, Art Gallery, Sports Center, Java City Coffee House, Hawk's Nest

ADMISSIONS

Freshman Academic Profile: 76% from public high schools. **Test Scores:** SAT Math middle 50% range 460-580. SAT EBRW middle 50% range 460-580. ACT middle 50% range 20-26. Minimum paper TOEFL 550. **Basis for Candidate Selection:** *Very important factors considered include:* rigor of secondary school record. *Important factors considered include:* class rank, academic GPA, standardized test scores. *Other factors considered include:* application essay, recommendation(s), interview, extracurricular activities, talent/ability, character/personal qualities. **Freshman Admission Requirements:** High school diploma is required and GED is accepted *Academic units required:* 4 English, 2 math, 2 science, 2 social studies, 2 history, 4 academic electives, *Academic units recommended:* 3 math, 3 science, 2 foreign language. **Freshman Admission Statistics:** 15,526 applied, 71.9% admitted, 12% enrolled. **Transfer Admission Requirements:** college transcript(s), Minimum college GPA of 2.2 required. Lowest grade transferable C-. **General Admission Information:** Application fee $35. Nonfall registration accepted. Admission may be deferred for a maximum of 1 year.

COSTS AND FINANCIAL AID

Annual tuition $36,088. Room and board $12,346. Required fees $2,822. Average book expense $1,020. **Required Forms and Deadlines:** FAFSA. **Notification of Awards:** Applicants will be notified of awards on a rolling basis beginning 3/1. **Types of Aid:** *Need-based scholarships/grants:* College/university scholarship or grant aid from institutional funds; Federal Pell; Private scholarships; SEOG; State scholarships/grants. *Loans:* Direct PLUS loans; Direct Subsidized Stafford Loans; Direct Unsubsidized Stafford Loans. **Financial Aid Statistics:** 97% freshmen, 95% undergrads receive any aid. **Criteria for awarding aid:** *Non-need-based:* Academics, Art, Athletics, Music/drama, State/district residency.

UNIVERSITY OF HAWAII AT HILO

200 West Kawili Street, Hilo, HI 96720-4091
Phone: 808-974-7414 · **Financial Aid Phone:** 808-974-7323
E-mail: uhhadm@hawaii.edu
Fax: 808-933-0861 · **ACT Code:** 904

This public school was founded in 1970. It has a 225 acre campus.

RATINGS

Admissions Selectivity Rating: 80   **Fire Safety Rating:** 60*   **Green Rating:** 60*

STUDENTS AND FACULTY

Enrollment: 3,385. **Student Body:** 59% female, 41% male, 35% out-of-state, 5% international. Asian 19%, African American 1%, Caucasian 24%, Hispanic

10%, Native American 1%, Pacific Islander 12%, Two or more races 27%, Race unknown <1%.
Retention and Graduation: 69% freshmen return for sophomore year.
Faculty: Student/faculty ratio 14:1. 227 full-time faculty, 44% are women. 0% of classes are taught by teaching assistants.

ACADEMICS

Degrees: Bachelor's; Certificate; Master's; Post-Bachelor's certificate **Classes:** Most classes have fewer than 10 students. Most lab/discussion sessions have fewer than 10 students. **Most popular majors:** Psychology, General; Business, Management, Marketing, And Related Support Services, Other. **Special Study Options:** Cross-registration; Distance learning; Double major; Dual enrollment; English as a Second Language (ESL); Exchange student program (domestic); Honors program; Independent study; Internships; Student-designed major; Study abroad; Teacher certification program. **Disability Services offered to physically disabled students:** Note-taking services; Reader services; Tape recorders; Tutors. **Career services:** Alumni network; Alumni services; Career assessment; Internships

FACILITIES

Housing: Apartments for married students; Apartments for single students; Coed dorms; Special housing for disabled students 90% of campus accessible to physically diasbled. **Computers:** Students can register for classes online. Administrative functions (other than registration) can be performed online.

CAMPUS LIFE

Environment: Town **Activities:** Choral groups; Dance; Drama/theater; Jazz band; Literary magazine; Music ensembles; Radio station; Student government; Student newspaper 43 registered organizations, 4 religious organizations. **Athletics (Intercollegiate):** *Men:* baseball, basketball, cross-country, golf, tennis. *Women:* cross-country, softball, tennis, volleyball. **On-Campus Highlights:** University Classroom Building (opened Fall '02), University Campus Center Plaza (opening Sp '04), University Lava Landing (Student Cyber Lounge), University Mo`okini Library, University Theatre

ADMISSIONS

Freshman Academic Profile: Average high school GPA 3.3. 17% in top 10% of high school class, 47% in top 25% of high school class, 82% in top 50% of high school class. **Test Scores:** SAT Math middle 50% range 440-600. SAT EBRW middle 50% range 440-560. ACT middle 50% range 17-24. Minimum paper TOEFL 500. **Basis for Candidate Selection:** *Very important factors considered include:* rigor of secondary school record. *Important factors considered include:* class rank, academic GPA, standardized test scores. *Other factors considered include:* application essay, recommendation(s), extracurricular activities, talent/ability. **Freshman Admission Requirements:** High school diploma is required and GED is accepted *Academic units required:* 4 English, 3 math, 3 science, 3 science labs, 7 academic electives, *Academic units recommended:* 4 English, 4 math, 4 science, 3 science labs, 2 foreign language, 2 social studies, 2 history. **Freshman Admission Statistics:** 1,500 applied, 72.3% admitted, 44% enrolled. **Transfer Admission Requirements:** college transcript(s), Minimum college GPA of 2.0 required. Lowest grade transferable C. **General Admission Information:** Application fee $50. Priority deadline 3/1. Regular application deadline 7/1. Nonfall registration accepted. Admission may be deferred for a maximum of 1 semester.

COSTS AND FINANCIAL AID

Annual in-state tuition $7,134. Annual out-of-state tuition $17,112. Room and board $7,134. Required fees $304. Average book expense $1,017. **Required Forms and Deadlines:** FAFSA. **Notification of Awards:** Applicants will be notified of awards on a rolling basis beginning 4/12. **Types of Aid:** *Need-based scholarships/grants:* College/university scholarship or grant aid from institutional funds; Federal Pell; Private scholarships; SEOG; State scholarships/grants. *Loans: Student Employment:* Federal Work-Study Program available. Institutional employment available. **Financial Aid Statistics:** 78% needy freshmen, 79% needy undergrads receive need-based scholarship or grant aid. 15% freshmen, 17% undergrads receive non-need-based scholarship or grant aid. 56% freshmen, 65% undergrads receive need-based self-help aid. 3% freshmen, 3% undergrads receive athletic scholarships. **Criteria for awarding aid:** *Need-based:* Academics *Non-need-based:* Academics, Art, Athletics, Leadership, Minority status, Music/drama.

UNIVERSITY OF HAWAII—MANOA

2500 Campus Road, Honolulu, HI 96822
Phone: 808-956-8975 • **Financial Aid Phone:** 808-956-7251
E-mail: manoa.admissions@hawaii.edu • **CEEB Code:** 4867
Fax: 808-956-4148 • **Website:** http://manoa.hawaii.edu • **ACT Code:** 902

This public school was founded in 1907. It has a 320 acre campus.

RATINGS

Admissions Selectivity Rating: 77   **Fire Safety Rating:** 89   **Green Rating:** 60*

STUDENTS AND FACULTY

Enrollment: 22,020. **Student Body:** 31% female, 69% male, 26% out-of-state, 8% international (67 countries represented). Asian 26%, African American 1%, Caucasian 29%, Hispanic 1%, Native American <1%, Pacific Islander 16%, Two or more races 12%, Race unknown 1%.
Retention and Graduation: 79% freshmen return for sophomore year. 90% freshmen graduate within 4 years. 60% freshmen graduate within 6 years. **Faculty:** Student/faculty ratio 10:1. 1,153 full-time faculty, 89% hold PhDs, 46% are members of minority groups, 46% are women.

ACADEMICS

Degrees: Bachelor's; Doctoral/Professional; Doctoral/Research; Master's; Post-Bachelor's certificate **Classes:** Most classes have 10-19 students. Most lab/discussion sessions have 10-19 students. **Most popular majors:** Biology/ Biological Sciences, General; Psychology, General; Registered Nursing/ Registered Nurse. **Special Study Options:** Cooperative education program; Distance learning; Double major; English as a Second Language (ESL); Exchange student program (domestic); Honors program; Independent study; Internships; Student-designed major; Study abroad; Teacher certification program. Honors programs: Selected Studies Program. **Disability Services offered to physically disabled students:** Note-taking services; Reader services; Tape recorders. **Career services:** Alumni services; Career assessment; Career/job search classes; Internships

FACILITIES

Housing: Apartments for married students; Apartments for single students; Coed dorms; Special housing for disabled student; Theme housing 40% of campus accessible to physically diasbled. **Special Academic Facilities/ Equipment:** UH Art and Commons Galleries, John Young Museum, John F. Kennedy Theatre, Lyon Arboretum, Waikiki Aquarium, Sunset (travel industry) Library, Chuck Gee Technology Learning Center, Advanced Computing Research Laboratory, Environmental Engineering Lab, Hawaii Center for Advanced Communications, Coral Reef Science Laboratory, traditionally designed Korean Studies Building, Coconut Island marine biology labs, Wong Audio-Visual Center, language lab, speech and hearing and dental hygiene clinics, law library, Hawaiian lo'i(garden), electron microscope and laser laboratories, ship and submersible research fleet, and Maui Super Computer,Jakuan Tea House. **Computers:** Students can register for classes online. Administrative functions (other than registration) can be performed online.

CAMPUS LIFE

Environment: Metropolis **Activities:** Campus Ministries; Choral groups; Concert band; Dance; Drama/theater; International Student Organization; Jazz band; Literary magazine; Marching band; Music ensembles; Musical theater; Pep band; Radio station; Student government; Student newspaper; Student-run film society; Symphony orchestra 161 registered organizations, 7 honor societies, 24 religious organizations. 3 fraternities, 2 sororities. **Athletics (Intercollegiate):** *Men:* baseball, basketball, cheerleading, diving, football, golf, sailing, swimming, tennis, volleyball. *Women:* basketball, cheerleading, cross-country, diving, golf, sailing, soccer, softball, swimming, tennis, track/field (outdoor), track/field (indoor), volleyball, water polo. **On-Campus Highlights:** Campus Center, Queen Lili'uokalani Ctr for Student Svcs, Quad Courtyard, Sinclair Library, Hamilton Library **Environmental Initiatives:** Creation & convening of Manoa Sustainability Corps

ADMISSIONS

Freshman Academic Profile: Average high school GPA 3.5. 26% in top 10% of high school class, 55% in top 25% of high school class, 87% in top 50% of high school class. **Test Scores:** SAT Math middle 50% range 490-610. SAT EBRW middle 50% range 480-580. ACT middle 50% range 21-26. Minimum internet-based TOEFL 61. Minimum paper TOEFL 500. **Basis for Candidate Selection:** *Very important factors considered include: rigor of secondary school*

record, academic GPA, standardized test scores. *Important factors considered include:* class rank, state residency. *Other factors considered include:* application essay, recommendation(s), interview, extracurricular activities, talent/ability, geographical residence. **Freshman Admission Requirements:** High school diploma is required and GED is accepted *Academic units required:* 4 English, 3 math, 3 science, 3 social studies, 5 academic electives. **Freshman Admission Statistics:** 8,523 applied, 82.9% admitted, 28% enrolled. **Transfer Admission Requirements:** college transcript(s), Minimum college GPA of 2.5 required. Lowest grade transferable D. **General Admission Information:** Application fee $70. Priority deadline 1/5. Regular application deadline 3/1. Nonfall registration accepted.

COSTS AND FINANCIAL AID

Annual out-of-state tuition $32,904. Room and board $13,673. Required fees $860. Average book expense $1,012. **Required Forms and Deadlines:** FAFSA. **Notification of Awards:** Applicants will be notified of awards on a rolling basis beginning 4/1. **Types of Aid:** *Need-based scholarships/ grants:* College/university scholarship or grant aid from institutional funds; Federal Pell; Private scholarships; SEOG; State scholarships/grants. *Loans:* Direct PLUS loans; Direct Subsidized Stafford Loans; Direct Unsubsidized Stafford Loans. *Student Employment:* Federal Work-Study Program available. Institutional employment available. **Financial Aid Statistics:** 98% needy freshmen, 93% needy undergrads receive need-based scholarship or grant aid. 25% freshmen, 23% undergrads receive non-need-based scholarship or grant aid. 53% freshmen, 63% undergrads receive need-based self-help aid. 2% freshmen, 2% undergrads receive athletic scholarships. 62% freshmen, 59% undergrads receive any aid. Average cumulative indebtedness $24,225. **Criteria for awarding aid:** *Need-based:* Academics *Non-need-based:* Academics, Alumni affiliation, Art, Athletics, Leadership, Music/drama, State/district residency.

UNIVERSITY OF HAWAII—WEST OAHU

91-1001 Farrington Hwy, Kapolei, HI 96707
Phone: 808-689-2900 • **Financial Aid Phone:** 808-454-4700
E-mail: uhwo.admissions@hawaii.edu • **CEEB Code:** 1042
Fax: 808-689-2901 • **Website:** www.uhwo.hawaii.edu • **ACT Code:** 6465

This public school was founded in 1976.

RATINGS

Admissions Selectivity Rating: 71   **Fire Safety Rating:** 60*   **Green Rating:** 60*

STUDENTS AND FACULTY

Enrollment: 1,950. **Student Body:** 67% female, 33% male, 2% out-of-state, <1% international (16 countries represented). Asian 41%, African American 1%, Caucasian 14%, Hispanic 1%, Native American <1%, Pacific Islander 27%, Two or more races 14%, Race unknown <1%.
Retention and Graduation: 67% freshmen return for sophomore year. **Faculty:** Student/faculty ratio 18:1. 51 full-time faculty, 92% hold PhDs, 51% are members of minority groups, 41% are women. 0% of classes are taught by teaching assistants.

ACADEMICS

Degrees: Bachelor's; Certificate **Classes:** Most classes have 10-19 students. Most lab/discussion sessions have 10-19 students. **Most popular majors:** Elementary Education And Teaching; Psychology, General; Business/ Commerce, General. **Special Study Options:** Distance learning; Double major; Teacher certification program. **Disability Services offered to physically disabled students:** Note-taking services; Reader services; Tape recorders.

FACILITIES

Housing: 100% of campus accessible to physically diasbled. **Computers:** 10% of classrooms, 30% of common outdoor areas have wireless network access. Students can register for classes online.

CAMPUS LIFE

Environment: Town **Activities:** Student government 12 registered organizations, 1 honor societies. **Environmental Initiatives:** All buildings being constructed at new campus are LEED Silver Certified or above.

ADMISSIONS

Freshman Academic Profile: 74% from public high schools. **Test Scores:** Minimum internet-based TOEFL 79. Minimum paper TOEFL 550. **Basis for Candidate Selection:** *Very important factors considered include:* academic GPA. *Important factors considered include:* rigor of secondary school record. *Other factors considered include:* application essay, standardized test scores, recommendation(s), interview, extracurricular activities, first generation, geographical residence, state residency. **Freshman Admission Requirements:** High school diploma is required and GED is accepted *Academic units required:* 4 English, 3 math, 3 science, 3 social studies, 5 academic electives, and 4 units from above areas or other academic areas. **Freshman Admission Statistics:** 908 applied, 51.4% admitted, 64% enrolled. Minimum college GPA of 2.0 required. Lowest grade transferable D. **General Admission Information:** Application fee $50. Priority deadline 3/1. Regular application deadline 8/1. Nonfall registration accepted. Admission may be deferred for a maximum of 1 semester.

COSTS AND FINANCIAL AID
Annual out-of-state tuition $16,656. **Required Forms and Deadlines:** FAFSA. **Notification of Awards:** Applicants will be notified of awards on a rolling basis beginning 4/15. *Types of Aid: Need-based scholarships/grants:* Federal Pell; Private scholarships; SEOG; State scholarships/grants. *Loans:* Direct PLUS loans; Direct Subsidized Stafford Loans; Direct Unsubsidized Stafford Loans. *Student Employment:* Federal Work-Study Program available. Institutional employment available. **Financial Aid Statistics:** 40% needy freshmen, 69% needy undergrads receive need-based scholarship or grant aid. 70% freshmen, 10% undergrads receive non-need-based scholarship or grant aid. 20% freshmen, 62% undergrads receive need-based self-help aid. 0% freshmen, 0% undergrads receive athletic scholarships. **Criteria for awarding aid:** *Need-based:* Academics *Non-need-based:* Academics.

UNIVERSITY OF HOUSTON

4800 Calhoun Road, Houston, TX 77204-2023
Phone: 713-743-1010 • **Financial Aid Phone:** 713-743-1010
E-mail: admissions@uh.edu • **CEEB Code:** 6870
Fax: 713-743-7542 • **Website:** www.uh.edu • **ACT Code:** 4236

This public school was founded in 1927. It has a 594 acre campus.

RATINGS
Admissions Selectivity Rating: 87   **Fire Safety Rating:** 98   **Green Rating:** 87

STUDENTS AND FACULTY
Enrollment: 36,088. **Student Body:** 49% female, 51% male, 1% out-of-state, 4% international (107 countries represented). Asian 22%, African American 10%, Caucasian 24%, Hispanic 35%, Native American <1%, Pacific Islander <1%, Two or more races 3%, Race unknown 2%. **Retention and Graduation:** 85% freshmen return for sophomore year. 25% freshmen graduate within 4 years. 54% freshmen graduate within 6 years. **Faculty:** Student/faculty ratio 22:1. 1,560 full-time faculty, 86% hold PhDs, 29% are members of minority groups, 41% are women. 1% of classes are taught by teaching assistants.

ACADEMICS
Degrees: Bachelor's; Doctoral/Professional; Doctoral/Research; **Master's Classes:** Most classes have 10-19 students. Most lab/discussion sessions have 10-19 students. **Most popular majors:** Biology/Biological Sciences, General; Psychology, General; Business Administration And Management, General. **Special Study Options:** Accelerated program; Cooperative education program; Cross-registration; Distance learning; Double major; Dual enrollment; English as a Second Language (ESL); Exchange student program (domestic); Honors program; Independent study; Internships; Student-designed major; Study abroad; Teacher certification program; Weekend college. Honors programs: The Honors College at the University of Houston is a nationally recognized, intellectually stimulating learning community. As a vibrant, leading presence within the University, the Honors College attracts highly talented and motivated students and educators to a collegial environment where tradition is honored and possibilities are both created and realized. **Disability Services offered to physically disabled students:** Note-taking services; Reader services; Tape recorders. **Career services:** Alumni network; Alumni services; Career assessment; Career/job search classes; Internships

FACILITIES
Housing: Apartments for married students; Apartments for single students; Coed dorms; Fraternity/sorority housing; Special housing for disabled student; Theme housing; Wellness housing 98% of campus accessible to physically diasbled. **Special Academic Facilities/Equipment:** Blaffer Art gallery language lab University Hilton (the coffee shop and cafe staffed by students in College of Hotel and Restaurant Management) Moores School of Music Opera

House Alley Theatre (temporary location) **Computers:** 100% of classrooms, 25% of dorms, 100% of libraries, 25% of dining areas, 100% of student union, 25% of common outdoor areas have wireless network access. Students can register for classes online. Administrative functions (other than registration) can be performed online.

CAMPUS LIFE
Environment: Metropolis **Activities:** Campus Ministries; Choral groups; Concert band; Dance; Drama/theater; International Student Organization; Jazz band; Literary magazine; Marching band; Music ensembles; Musical theater; Opera; Pep band; Radio station; Student government; Student newspaper; Student-run film society; Symphony orchestra; Television station; Yearbook 350 registered organizations, 25 honor societies, 39 religious organizations. 21 fraternities, 19 sororities. **Athletics (Intercollegiate):** *Men:* baseball, basketball, cross-country, football, golf, track/field (outdoor), track/field (indoor). *Women:* basketball, cross-country, diving, soccer, softball, swimming, tennis, track/field (outdoor), track/field (indoor), volleyball. **On-Campus Highlights:** Student Center, Campus Recreation and Wellness Center, Student Center Satellite, Blaffer Gallery, Center for Student Involvement **Environmental Initiatives:** Education of the campus community through communications, events, and campus as a living laboratory: One of the main goals of our sustainability program is to create a culture of sustainability on campus. The Office of Sustainability hosts numerous events throughout the year to show members of the campus community what resources and behaviors they can utilize to become more sustainable in their everyday lives. These include theme speakers, documentary screenings, workshops, competitions and Sustainability Fest, our largest annual event that features over 30 sustainability-themed community and campus organizations and departments. The festival attracts hundreds of attendees, who get to explore all the resources and opportunities offered by a wide range of exhibitors. Additionally, the Office of Sustainability works with the Auxiliary Services marketing team to publish university press releases and share various articles and events via social media, as well as through a monthly newsletter that is sent to over 2,000 subscribers. Lastly, several parts of the campus serve as a living laboratory for students and researchers. Our pocket prairie, known as Shasta's Prairie, was established in May 2016. It serves as a habitat for pollinators and native grass species, as well as a study site for students in the biology and ecology programs at The University.

ADMISSIONS
Freshman Academic Profile: 32% in top 10% of high school class, 65% in top 25% of high school class, 88% in top 50% of high school class. 93% from public high schools. **Test Scores:** SAT Math middle 50% range 550-640. SAT EBRW middle 50% range 560-640. ACT middle 50% range 23-27. Minimum internet-based TOEFL 79. Minimum paper TOEFL 550. **Basis for Candidate Selection:** *Very important factors considered include:* rigor of secondary school record, class rank, academic GPA, standardized test scores. *Other factors considered include:* application essay, recommendation(s), extracurricular activities, talent/ability, first generation, volunteer work, work experience. **Freshman Admission Requirements:** High school diploma is required and GED is accepted *Academic units required:* 4 English, 3 math, 3 science, 2 science labs, 3 social studies, *Academic units recommended:* 4 math, 4 science, 2 foreign language, 1 history, 1 visual/performing arts. **Freshman Admission Statistics:** 20,768 applied, 61.1% admitted, 39% enrolled. **Transfer Admission Requirements:** college transcript(s), Minimum college GPA of 2.0 required. Lowest grade transferable C-. **General Admission Information:** Application fee $75. Priority deadline 11/15. Regular application deadline 6/15. Nonfall registration accepted.

COSTS AND FINANCIAL AID
Annual in-state tuition $9,984. Annual out-of-state tuition $26,355. Room and board $9,984. Required fees $982. Average book expense $1,300. **Required Forms and Deadlines:** FAFSA. **Notification of Awards:** Applicants will be notified of awards on a rolling basis beginning 3/1. **Types of Aid:** *Need-based scholarships/grants:* College/university scholarship or grant aid from institutional funds; Federal Pell; Private scholarships; SEOG; State scholarships/grants. *Loans:* Direct PLUS loans; Direct Subsidized Stafford Loans; Direct Unsubsidized Stafford Loans. *Student Employment:* Federal Work-Study Program available. Institutional employment available. **Financial Aid Statistics:** 90% needy freshmen, 78% needy undergrads receive need-based scholarship or grant aid. 7% freshmen, 4% undergrads receive non-need-based scholarship or grant aid. 52% freshmen, 64% undergrads receive need-based self-help aid. 1% freshmen, 1% undergrads receive athletic scholarships. 87% freshmen, 77% undergrads receive any aid. 51% undergrads borrow to pay for school. Average cumulative indebtedness $23,665. **Criteria for awarding aid:** *Need-based:* Academics, Leadership *Non-need-based:* Academics, Alumni affiliation, Art, Athletics, Job skills, Leadership, Music/drama, State/district residency.

UNIVERSITY OF HOUSTON—CLEAR LAKE

2700 Bay Area Boulevard, Houston, TX 77058-1098
Phone: 281-283-2500 • **Financial Aid Phone:** 281-283-2480
E-mail: admissions@uhcl.edu • **CEEB Code:** 6916
Fax: 281-283-2522

This public school was founded in 1974. It has a 524 acre campus.

RATINGS
Admissions Selectivity Rating: 0   **Fire Safety Rating:** 60*   **Green Rating:** 60*

STUDENTS AND FACULTY
Enrollment: 4,689. **Student Body:** 68% female, 32% male, 0% out-of-state, 2% international (45 countries represented). Asian 6%, African American 9%, Caucasian 49%, Hispanic 32%, Native American <1%, Pacific Islander <1%, Two or more races <1%, Race unknown 1%.
Faculty: Student/faculty ratio 17:1. 247 full-time faculty, 86% hold PhDs, 27% are members of minority groups, 46% are women.

ACADEMICS
Degrees: Bachelor's; Certificate; Doctoral; Master's; Post-Bachelor's certificate; Post-Master's certificate **Classes:** Most classes have 10-19 students. **Most popular majors:** Multi-/Interdisciplinary Studies, Other; Psychology, General; Accounting. **Special Study Options:** Cooperative education program; Distance learning; Double major; Dual enrollment; English as a Second Language (ESL); Independent study; Internships; Study abroad; Teacher certification program; Weekend college. **Disability Services offered to physically disabled students:** Note-taking services; Reader services; Tape recorders; Tutors. **Career services:** Alumni network; Alumni services; Career assessment; Career/job search classes; Internships

FACILITIES
Housing: 100% of campus accessible to physically diasbled. **Special Academic Facilities/Equipment:** Student Art Gallery Fitness Center/Fitness Zone **Computers:** 100% of classrooms, 100% of libraries, 100% of dining areas, 100% of student union, 100% of common outdoor areas have wireless network access. Students can register for classes online. Administrative functions (other than registration) can be performed online.

CAMPUS LIFE
Environment: Metropolis **Activities:** International Student Organization; Literary magazine; Student government; Student newspaper; Student-run film society 70 registered organizations, 16 honor societies, 5 religious organizations. **On-Campus Highlights:** Student Serivce Building, Bayou Building, Library, Delta Building, Computer Labs

ADMISSIONS
Test Scores: Minimum internet-based TOEFL 79. Minimum paper TOEFL 550. **Freshman Admission Requirements:** High school diploma is required and GED is accepted **Transfer Admission Requirements:** college transcript(s), standardized test scores, statement of good standing from prior institution(s). Minimum college GPA of 2.0 required. Lowest grade transferable D-. **General Admission Information:** Application fee $45. Regular application deadline 6/1. Nonfall registration accepted. Admission may be deferred for a maximum of 1 year.

COSTS AND FINANCIAL AID
Annual in-state tuition $1,372. Annual out-of-state tuition $16,992. Required fees $1,372. **Types of Aid:** *Need-based scholarships/grants:* College/university scholarship or grant aid from institutional funds; Federal Pell; SEOG; State scholarships/grants. *Loans:* Direct PLUS loans; Direct Subsidized Stafford Loans; Direct Unsubsidized Stafford Loans. *Student Employment:* Federal Work-Study Program available. Institutional employment available. **Financial Aid Statistics:** 41% undergrads receive any aid. **Criteria for awarding aid:** *Need-based:* Academics, Art, Leadership, Minority status.

UNIVERSITY OF HOUSTON—DOWNTOWN

One Main Street, Houston, TX 77002-1001
Phone: 713-221-8522 • **Financial Aid Phone:** 713-221-8041
E-mail: uhdadmit@uhd.edu
Fax: 713-221-8522 • **Website:** www.uhd.edu

This public school was founded in 1974. It has a 24 acre campus.

RATINGS
Admissions Selectivity Rating: 73   **Fire Safety Rating:** 60*   **Green Rating:** 61

STUDENTS AND FACULTY
Enrollment: 12,313. **Student Body:** 61% female, 39% male, 1% out-of-state, 5% international (65 countries represented). Asian 9%, African American 20%, Caucasian 16%, Hispanic 48%, Native American <1%, Pacific Islander <1%, Two or more races 1%, Race unknown 1%.
Retention and Graduation: 72% freshmen return for sophomore year. 3% freshmen graduate within 4 years. 21% freshmen graduate within 6 years.
Faculty: Student/faculty ratio 19:1. 376 full-time faculty, 84% hold PhDs, 39% are members of minority groups, 47% are women. 0% of classes are taught by teaching assistants.

ACADEMICS
Degrees: Bachelor's; Master's; Post-Bachelor's certificate **Classes:** Most classes have 20-29 students. Most lab/discussion sessions have 10-19 students. **Most popular majors:** Multi-/Interdisciplinary Studies, Other; Psychology, General; Accounting. **Special Study Options:** Distance learning; Double major; Dual enrollment; English as a Second Language (ESL); Honors program; Independent study; Internships; Study abroad; Teacher certification program; Weekend college. Honors programs: The UHD Scholars Academy promotes scholarship and student success for students in the Science, Technology, Engineering and Mathematics (STEM) fields. The Academy supports 160 students annually through scholarships, mentoring, and broadening experiences student success components. The program addresses UHD's commitment to increase the number of underrepresented graduating with STEM degrees and increasing advancement qualifications and preparation into graduate/professional degrees and the STEM workforce. About 39% of the 500+ alumni from the Academy have pursued advanced degrees. 91% remain in STEM after graduation in roles involving graduate/professional schools/programs or in the workforce. **Disability Services offered to physically disabled students:** Note-taking services; Tape recorders; Tutors. **Career services:** Alumni services; Career assessment; Career/job search classes; Internships

FACILITIES
Housing: 95% of campus accessible to physically diasbled. **Special Academic Facilities/Equipment:** O'Kane Gallery **Computers:** Students can register for classes online. Administrative functions (other than registration) can be performed online.

CAMPUS LIFE
Environment: Metropolis **Activities:** Campus Ministries; Drama/theater; International Student Organization; Jazz band; Literary magazine; Model UN; Student government; Student newspaper 52 registered organizations, 3 honor societies, 2 religious organizations. 4 fraternities, 4 sororities. **Athletics (Intercollegiate):** *Men:* badminton, basketball, bowling, football, soccer, softball, tennis, volleyball, weight lifting. *Women:* badminton, basketball, bowling, soccer, softball, tennis, volleyball, weight lifting. **On-Campus Highlights:** 40,000 Windows Cafe, O' Kane Gallery, Food court and adjoining Coffee House, Jesse H. Jones Student Life Center, O' Kane Theatre

ADMISSIONS
Freshman Academic Profile: 6% in top 10% of high school class, 32% in top 25% of high school class, 76% in top 50% of high school class. 86% from public high schools. **Test Scores:** SAT Math middle 50% range 460-540. SAT EBRW middle 50% range 460-538. ACT middle 50% range 17-21. Minimum internet-based TOEFL 80. Minimum paper TOEFL 550. **Basis for Candidate Selection:** *Very important factors considered include:* class rank, academic GPA, standardized test scores. *Important factors considered include:* rigor of secondary school record. **Freshman Admission Requirements:** High school diploma is required and GED is accepted *Academic units required:* 4 English, 4 math, 4 science, 2 foreign language, 2 social studies, 2 history, 5.5 academic electives, 1 visual/performing arts, and 1.5 units from above areas or other academic areas. **Freshman Admission Statistics:** 3,931 applied, 84.1% admitted, 29% enrolled. **Transfer Admission Requirements:** college transcript(s), Lowest grade transferable C. **General Admission Information:** Application fee $50. Regular application deadline 7/1. Nonfall registration accepted. Admission may be deferred.

COSTS AND FINANCIAL AID

Annual in-state tuition $1,166. Annual out-of-state tuition $18,315. Required fees $1,166. **Required Forms and Deadlines:** FAFSA. **Types of Aid:** *Need-based scholarships/grants:* College/university scholarship or grant aid from institutional funds; Federal Pell; Private scholarships; SEOG; State scholarships/grants. *Loans:* Direct PLUS loans; Direct Subsidized Stafford Loans; Direct Unsubsidized Stafford Loans. *Student Employment:* Federal Work-Study Program available. Institutional employment available. **Financial Aid Statistics:** 85% needy freshmen, 75% needy undergrads receive need-based scholarship or grant aid. 0% freshmen, 5% undergrads receive non-need-based scholarship or grant aid. 2% freshmen, 3% undergrads receive need-based self-help aid. 0% freshmen, 0% undergrads receive athletic scholarships. 81% freshmen, 78% undergrads receive any aid. 52% undergrads borrow to pay for school. Average cumulative indebtedness $22,812. **Criteria for awarding aid:** *Need-based:* Academics, Leadership *Non-need-based:* Leadership.

UNIVERSITY OF HOUSTON—VICTORIA

3007 N. Ben Wilson St., Victoria, TX 77901-4450
Phone: 361-570-4110 · **Financial Aid Phone:** 316-570-4131
E-mail: admissions@uhv.edu
Fax: 361-580-5500 • **Website:** www.uhv.edu

This public school was founded in 1973.

RATINGS

Admissions Selectivity Rating: 78   **Fire Safety Rating:** 60*   **Green Rating:** 60*

STUDENTS AND FACULTY

Enrollment: 2,991. **Student Body:** 66% female, 34% male, 2% international (39 countries represented). Asian 8%, African American 16%, Caucasian 37%, Hispanic 34%, Native American <1%, Pacific Islander <1%, Two or more races 2%, Race unknown 1%.
Retention and Graduation: 55% freshmen return for sophomore year. **Faculty:** Student/faculty ratio 18:1. 136 full-time faculty, 87% hold PhDs, 32% are members of minority groups, 49% are women. 0% of classes are taught by teaching assistants.

ACADEMICS

Degrees: Bachelor's; Master's; Post-Bachelor's certificate; Post-Master's certificate **Classes:** Most classes have 10-19 students. Most lab/discussion sessions have 10-19 students. **Most popular majors:** Education, General; Multi-/Interdisciplinary Studies, Other; Business/Commerce, General. **Special Study Options:** Accelerated program; Distance learning; Double major; Dual enrollment; Independent study; Internships; Study abroad; Teacher certification program. **Disability Services offered to physically disabled students:** Note-taking services; Tutors. **Career services:** Alumni services; Career assessment; Career/job search classes; Internships

FACILITIES

Housing: Coed dorms 100% of campus accessible to physically diasbled. **Computers:** Students can register for classes online. Administrative functions (other than registration) can be performed online.

CAMPUS LIFE

Environment: City **Activities:** International Student Organization; Literary magazine; Student government. **Athletics (Intercollegiate):** *Men:* baseball. *Women:* softball. Jaguar Village, Library, Student Center, University North, Athletics Office

ADMISSIONS

Test Scores: SAT Math middle 50% range 390-480. SAT EBRW middle 50% range 380-460. ACT middle 50% range 15-19. Minimum paper TOEFL 79. **Basis for Candidate Selection:** *Very important factors considered include:* rigor of secondary school record. *Important factors considered include:* class rank, academic GPA, standardized test scores. *Other factors considered include:* application essay, recommendation(s), interview, extracurricular activities, talent/ability, character/personal qualities, first generation, alumni/ae relation, geographical residence, state residency, level of applicant's interest. **Freshman Admission Requirements:** High school diploma is required and GED is accepted **Freshman Admission Statistics:** 3,950 applied, 55.6% admitted, 16% enrolled. **Transfer Admission Requirements:** college transcript(s), standardized test scores, Minimum college GPA of 2.0 required. Lowest grade transferable C. **General Admission Information:** Nonfall registration accepted. Admission may be deferred.

COSTS AND FINANCIAL AID

Annual in-state tuition $7,853. Annual out-of-state tuition $19,264. Room and board $7,853. Required fees $1,567. Average book expense $1,129. **Required Forms and Deadlines:** FAFSA; Institution's own financial aid form. **Notification of Awards:** Applicants will be notified of awards on a rolling basis beginning 3/30. **Types of Aid:** *Need-based scholarships/grants:* College/university scholarship or grant aid from institutional funds; Federal Pell; Private scholarships; SEOG; State scholarships/grants. *Loans:* Direct PLUS loans; Direct Subsidized Stafford Loans; Direct Unsubsidized Stafford Loans. *Student Employment:* Federal Work-Study Program available. Institutional employment available. **Financial Aid Statistics:** 73% undergrads receive any aid. **Criteria for awarding aid:** *Need-based:* Academics *Non-need-based:* Academics, Athletics, Leadership, State/district residency.

UNIVERSITY OF IDAHO

875 Perimeter Drive MS 2282, Moscow, ID 83844-4264
Phone: (208) 885-6326 • **Financial Aid Phone:** 208-885-6312
E-mail: admappl@uidaho.edu • **CEEB Code:** 4843
Fax: (208) 885-9119 • **Website:** http://www.uidaho.edu/ • **ACT Code:** 928

This public school was founded in 1889. It has a 810 acre campus.

RATINGS

Admissions Selectivity Rating: 81   •   **Fire Safety Rating:** 89   **Green Rating:** 76

STUDENTS AND FACULTY

Enrollment: 7,685. **Student Body:** 48% female, 52% male, 21% out-of-state, 5% international (57 countries represented). Asian 1%, African American 1%, Caucasian 74%, Hispanic 11%, Native American 1%, Pacific Islander <1%, Two or more races 4%, Race unknown 2%.
Retention and Graduation: 82% freshmen return for sophomore year. 30% freshmen graduate within 4 years. 55% freshmen graduate within 6 years. 12% grads go on to further study within 1 year. **Faculty:** Student/faculty ratio 14:1. 679 full-time faculty, 87% hold PhDs, 14% are members of minority groups, 35% are women. 6% of classes are taught by teaching assistants.

ACADEMICS

Degrees: Bachelor's; Certificate; Doctoral/Professional; Doctoral/Research; Master's; Post-Bachelor's certificate; Post-Master's certificate **Classes:** Most classes have 10-19 students. Most lab/discussion sessions have 10-19 students. **Most popular majors:** Mechanical Engineering; General Studies; Psychology, General. **Special Study Options:** Accelerated program; Cooperative education program; Cross-registration; Distance learning; Double major; Dual enrollment; English as a Second Language (ESL); Exchange student program (domestic); Honors program; Independent study; Internships; Study abroad; Teacher certification program. Honors programs: Established in 1983, the University Honors Program offers a stimulating course of study and the advantages of an enriched learning community for over 500 students from all colleges and majors. The UHP's diverse curriculum, including special topic courses and innovative seminars, serves a variety of needs and interests. Beyond the classroom, the program's extracurricular opportunities include concerts, plays, films, lectures and other off-campus excursions that foster cultural enrichment, friendship, and learning. Honors classes offer opportunities to explore subjects and methods in significant depth— students find that their education and their academic performance are enhanced by strong mentoring relationships with faculty devoted to enabling each student to fulfill his or her potential, and by the lively, participation-based modes of learning in small classes. Lower-division honors core courses enable students to learn with their peers in small classes taught by honors faculty. Moreover, each year the program offers innovative upper-division seminars, with each class limited to fifteen students. Honors students are frequently interested in and encouraged to apply for exchanges to other American universities or to universities abroad. As part of a dynamic, broad-based education, members are also encouraged to participate in domestic or international exchange programs, and to take advantage of opportunities to engage in laboratory or field-based research programs as well as internships and other forms of cooperative education. Combined degree programs: BA/MA. **Disability Services offered to physically disabled students:** Note-taking services; Reader services; Tape recorders; Tutors. **Career services:** Alumni network; Alumni services; Career assessment; Career/job search classes; Internships; Regional alumni

FACILITIES

Housing: Apartments for married students; Apartments for single students; Coed dorms; Cooperative housing; Fraternity/sorority housing; Men's dorms; Special housing for disabled student; Special housing for international students; Theme housing; Women's dorms 87% of campus accessible to physically diasbled. **Special Academic Facilities/Equipment:** Arboretum & Botanical Garden, Integrated Research and Innovation Center (IRIC), Lionel Hampton International Jazz Collection, experimental forest, Optical Imaging Center, electron microscope, 3D Modeling (CAVE) Technology, Anechoic chamber, on-campus preschool. **Computers:** 100% of classrooms, 100% of dorms, 100% of libraries, 100% of dining areas, 100% of student union, have wireless network access. Students can register for classes online. Administrative functions (other than registration) can be performed online.

CAMPUS LIFE

Environment: Town **Activities:** Campus Ministries; Choral groups; Concert band; Dance; Drama/theater; International Student Organization; Jazz band; Literary magazine; Marching band; Model UN; Music ensembles; Musical theater; Opera; Pep band; Radio station; Student government; Student newspaper; Student-run film society; Symphony orchestra; Television station 190 registered organizations, 13 honor societies, 20 religious organizations. 18 fraternities, 9 sororities. **Athletics (Intercollegiate):** *Men:* basketball, cross-country, football, golf, track/field (outdoor), track/field (indoor). *Women:* basketball, cross-country, golf, soccer, swimming, track/field (outdoor), track/field (indoor), volleyball. **On-Campus Highlights:** Idaho Commons -common areas, food and meeting rooms, Student Recreation Center, Bruce M. Pitman Center, Kibbie Dome—athletics, Integrated Research and Innovation Center **Environmental Initiatives:** $35 mil ESCO for energy conservation projects currently underway

ADMISSIONS

Freshman Academic Profile: Average high school GPA 3.4. 20% in top 10% of high school class, 42% in top 25% of high school class, 74% in top 50% of high school class. 90% from public high schools. **Test Scores:** SAT Math middle 50% range 500-610. SAT EBRW middle 50% range 510-620. ACT middle 50% range 20-26. Minimum internet-based TOEFL 70. Minimum paper TOEFL 525. **Basis for Candidate Selection:** *Very important factors considered include:* academic GPA, standardized test scores. **Freshman Admission Requirements:** High school diploma is required and GED is accepted *Academic units required:* 4 English, 3 math, 3 science, 1 science labs, 2.5 social studies, 1.5 academic electives, and 1 unit from above areas or other academic areas. **Freshman Admission Statistics:** 7,087 applied, 73.1% admitted, 30% enrolled. **Transfer Admission Requirements:** college transcript(s), Minimum college GPA of 2.0 required. Lowest grade transferable D. **General Admission Information:** Application fee $60. Priority deadline 2/15. Regular application deadline 8/1. Nonfall registration accepted. Admission may be deferred.

COSTS AND FINANCIAL AID

Annual in-state tuition $8,670. Annual out-of-state tuition $21,670. Room and board $8,670. Required fees $2,142. Average book expense $1,292. **Required Forms and Deadlines:** FAFSA. **Notification of Awards:** Applicants will be notified of awards on a rolling basis beginning 12/20. **Types of Aid:** *Need-based scholarships/grants:* College/university scholarship or grant aid from institutional funds; Federal Pell; Private scholarships; SEOG; State scholarships/grants. *Loans:* Direct PLUS loans; Direct Subsidized Stafford Loans; Direct Unsubsidized Stafford Loans. *Student Employment:* Federal Work-Study Program available. Institutional employment available. **Financial Aid Statistics:** 73% needy freshmen, 73% needy undergrads receive need-based scholarship or grant aid. 86% freshmen, 59% undergrads receive non-need-based scholarship or grant aid. 74% freshmen, 78% undergrads receive need-based self-help aid. 4% freshmen, 3% undergrads receive athletic scholarships. 90% freshmen, 80% undergrads receive any aid. 64% undergrads borrow to pay for school. Average cumulative indebtedness $26,539. **Criteria for awarding aid:** *Need-based:* Academics *Non-need-based:* Academics, Alumni affiliation, Art, Athletics, Leadership, Minority status, Music/drama, State/district residency.

UNIVERSITY OF ILLINOIS AT CHICAGO

601 S. Morgan Ave., Chicago, IL 60607-7161
Phone: 312-996-4350 • **Financial Aid Phone:** 312-996-5563
E-mail: uicadmit@uic.edu • **CEEB Code:** 1851
Fax: 312-413-7628 • **Website:** http://www.uic.edu • **ACT Code:** 1155

This public school was founded in 1982. It has a 240 acre campus.

RATINGS

Admissions Selectivity Rating: 80   **Fire Safety Rating:** 98   **Green Rating:** 93

STUDENTS AND FACULTY

Enrollment: 19,204. **Student Body:** 51% female, 49% male, 3% out-of-state, 4% international (65 countries represented). Asian 24%, Caucasian 33%, Hispanic 36%, Native American <1%, Pacific Islander <1%, Two or more races 3%, Race unknown 1%.
Retention and Graduation: 80% freshmen return for sophomore year. 31% freshmen graduate within 4 years. 1% freshmen graduate within 6 years.
Faculty: Student/faculty ratio 17:1. 1,200 full-time faculty, 88% hold PhDs, 25% are members of minority groups, 48% are women.

ACADEMICS

Degrees: Bachelor's; Doctoral; Doctoral/Professional; Doctoral/Research; Master's; Post-Bachelor's certificate; Post-Master's certificate **Classes:** Most classes have 20-29 students. **Most popular majors:** Biology/Biological Sciences, General; Psychology, General; Registered Nursing/Registered Nurse. **Special Study Options:** Accelerated program; Cooperative education program; Cross-registration; Distance learning; Double major; Dual enrollment; Honors program; Independent study; Internships; Student-designed major; Study abroad; Teacher certification program. Honors programs: Guaranteed Preferred Program Admission Honors College. President Award Program "PAP" and President Award Program Honors. Combined degree programs: BA/DDS; BA/MD. **Disability Services offered to physically disabled students:** Note-taking services; Tutors. **Career services:** Alumni network; Alumni services; Career assessment; Career/job search classes; Internships; Regional alumni

FACILITIES

Housing: Apartments for married students; Apartments for single students; Coed dorms; Special housing for disabled student; Special housing for international students; Theme housing 80% of campus accessible to physically diasbled. **Special Academic Facilities/Equipment:** Jane Addams Hull House Museum Richard J. Daley Library **Computers:** 95% of classrooms, 100% of dorms, 100% of libraries, 100% of dining areas, 100% of student union, have wireless network access. Students can register for classes online. Administrative functions (other than registration) can be performed online.

CAMPUS LIFE

Environment: Metropolis **Activities:** Campus Ministries; Choral groups; Concert band; Dance; Drama/theater; International Student Organization; Jazz band; Literary magazine; Music ensembles; Musical theater; Pep band; Radio station; Student government; Student newspaper 370 registered organizations, 10 honor societies, 33 religious organizations. 13 fraternities, 15 sororities. **Athletics (Intercollegiate):** *Men:* baseball, basketball, cross-country, diving, gymnastics, soccer, swimming, tennis, track/field (outdoor). *Women:* basketball, cross-country, diving, gymnastics, softball, swimming, tennis, track/field (outdoor), volleyball. **On-Campus Highlights:** Student Center East, Student Center West, UIC Pavilion, Student Services Building, Student Recreation Facility **Environmental Initiatives:** establishment of Office of Sustainability

ADMISSIONS

Freshman Academic Profile: Average high school GPA 3.3. 25% in top 10% of high school class, 58% in top 25% of high school class, 89% in top 50% of high school class. 76% from public high schools. **Test Scores:** SAT Math middle 50% range 550-680. SAT EBRW middle 50% range 530-650. ACT middle 50% range 20-26. Minimum internet-based TOEFL 80. Minimum paper TOEFL 550. **Basis for Candidate Selection:** *Very important factors considered include:* rigor of secondary school record, class rank, academic GPA, standardized test scores. *Important factors considered include:* application essay. *Other factors considered include:* recommendation(s), extracurricular activities, level of applicant's interest. **Freshman Admission Requirements:** High school diploma is required and GED is accepted *Academic units required:* 4 English, 3 math, 3 science, 2 foreign language, 3 social studies, *Academic units recommended:* 4 math. **Freshman Admission Statistics:** 18,768 applied, 77.1% admitted, 28% enrolled. **Transfer Admission Requirements:** college transcript(s), Minimum college GPA of 2.5 required. **General Admission Information:** Application fee $50. Regular application deadline 1/15. Nonfall registration accepted.

COSTS AND FINANCIAL AID

Annual in-state tuition $10,960. Annual out-of-state tuition $23,440. Room and board $10,960. Required fees $3,120. Average book expense $1,400. **Required Forms and Deadlines:** FAFSA. **Notification of Awards:** Applicants will be notified of awards on a rolling basis beginning 3/15. **Types of Aid:** *Need-based scholarships/grants:* College/university scholarship or grant aid from institutional funds; Federal Pell; Private scholarships; SEOG; State scholarships/grants. *Loans:* Direct PLUS loans; Direct Subsidized Stafford Loans; Direct Unsubsidized Stafford Loans. *Student Employment:* Federal Work-Study Program available. Institutional employment available. **Financial Aid Statistics:** 84% needy freshmen, 81% needy undergrads receive need-based scholarship or grant aid. 5% freshmen, 3% undergrads receive non-need-based scholarship or grant aid. 70% freshmen, 77% undergrads receive need-based self-help aid. 1% freshmen, 1% undergrads receive athletic scholarships. 62% freshmen, 60% undergrads receive any aid. Average cumulative indebtedness $23,669. **Criteria for awarding aid:** *Need-based:* Music/drama *Non-need-based:* Academics, Art, Athletics.

UNIVERSITY OF ILLINOIS AT SPRINGFIELD

One University Plaza, Springfield, IL 62703-5407
Phone: 217-206-4847 • **Financial Aid Phone:** 217-206-6724
E-mail: admissions@uis.edu • **CEEB Code:** 834
Fax: 217-206-6620 • **Website:** www.uis.edu • **ACT Code:** 1137

This public school was founded in 1969. It has a 746 acre campus.

RATINGS
Admissions Selectivity Rating: 85   **Fire Safety Rating:** 89   **Green Rating:** 93

STUDENTS AND FACULTY
Enrollment: 2,833. **Student Body:** 49% female, 51% male, 14% out-of-state, 4% international (18 countries represented). Asian 3%, African American 14%, Caucasian 66%, Hispanic 9%, Native American <1%, Pacific Islander <1%, Two or more races 3%, Race unknown 1%.
Retention and Graduation: 78% freshmen return for sophomore year. 36% freshmen graduate within 4 years. 50% freshmen graduate within 6 years.
Faculty: Student/faculty ratio 13:1. 215 full-time faculty, 88% hold PhDs, 15% are members of minority groups, 46% are women.

ACADEMICS
Degrees: Bachelor's; Doctoral/Research; Master's; Post-Bachelor's certificate; Post-Master's certificate **Classes:** Most classes have fewer than 10 students. Most lab/discussion sessions have 10-19 students. **Most popular majors:** Computer Science; Psychology, General; Business Administration And Management, General. **Special Study Options:** Distance learning; English as a Second Language (ESL); Honors program; Independent study; Internships; Study abroad; Teacher certification program. Honors programs: Interdisciplinary four-year baccalaureate experience for highly qualified freshman. **Disability Services offered to physically disabled students:** Note-taking services; Reader services; Tape recorders. **Career services:** Alumni network; Alumni services; Career assessment; Career/job search classes; Internships; Regional alumni

FACILITIES
Housing: Apartments for married students; Apartments for single students; Coed dorms; Special housing for disabled student; Special housing for international students; Theme housing; Wellness housing 99% of campus accessible to physically disabled. **Special Academic Facilities/Equipment:** Norris L. Brookens Library, Sangamon Auditorium, Observatory **Computers:** 100% of classrooms, 100% of dorms, 100% of libraries, 100% of dining areas, 100% of student union, 100% of common outdoor areas have wireless network access. Students can register for classes online. Administrative functions (other than registration) can be performed online.

CAMPUS LIFE
Environment: City **Activities:** Campus Ministries; Choral groups; Concert band; Dance; Drama/theater; International Student Organization; Jazz band; Model UN; Music ensembles; Pep band; Radio station; Student government; Student newspaper; Student-run film society 76 registered organizations. **Athletics (Intercollegiate):** *Men:* basketball, golf, soccer, tennis. *Women:* basketball, cheerleading, golf, soccer, softball, tennis, volleyball. **On-Campus Highlights:** Student Union, University Hall, Recreation and Athletic Center, Public Affairs Center **Environmental Initiatives:** New student union is being designed to LEED Gold standards

---

ADMISSIONS

Freshman Academic Profile: Average high school GPA 3.6. 24% in top 10% of high school class, 54% in top 25% of high school class, 84% in top 50% of high school class. 90% from public high schools. **Test Scores:** ACT middle 50% range 20-27. Minimum internet-based TOEFL 61. Minimum paper TOEFL 500. **Basis for Candidate Selection:** *Very important factors considered include:* academic GPA, standardized test scores. *Important factors considered include:* rigor of secondary school record, class rank. *Other factors considered include:* application essay, recommendation(s). **Freshman Admission Requirements:** High school diploma is required and GED is accepted *Academic units required:* 4 English, 3 math, 3 science, 2 science labs, 2 foreign language, 3 social studies. **Freshman Admission Statistics:** 1,746 applied, 52.4% admitted, 30% enrolled. **Transfer Admission Requirements:** college transcript(s), Minimum college GPA of 2.0 required. Lowest grade transferable D. **General Admission Information:** Application fee $50. Nonfall registration accepted. Admission may be deferred for a maximum of 1 term.

COSTS AND FINANCIAL AID

Average book expense $1,200. **Required Forms and Deadlines:** FAFSA. **Notification of Awards:** Applicants will be notified of awards on a rolling basis beginning 1/1. **Types of Aid:** *Need-based scholarships/grants:* College/university scholarship or grant aid from institutional funds; Federal Pell; Private scholarships; SEOG; State scholarships/grants. *Loans:* Direct PLUS loans; Direct Subsidized Stafford Loans; Direct Unsubsidized Stafford Loans. *Student Employment:* Federal Work-Study Program available. Institutional employment available. **Financial Aid Statistics:** 98% needy freshmen, 89% needy undergrads receive need-based scholarship or grant aid. 19% freshmen, 15% undergrads receive non-need-based scholarship or grant aid. 72% freshmen, 81% undergrads receive need-based self-help aid. 8% freshmen, 3% undergrads receive athletic scholarships. 80% freshmen, 71% undergrads receive any aid. 69% undergrads borrow to pay for school. Average cumulative indebtedness $24,652. **Criteria for awarding aid:** *Need-based:* Academics, Alumni affiliation, Art, Athletics, Job skills, Leadership, Minority status, Music/drama *Non-need-based:* Academics, Alumni affiliation, Art, Athletics, Job skills, Leadership, Minority status, Music/drama, State/district residency.

UNIVERSITY OF ILLINOIS AT URBANA-CHAMPAIGN

601 E. John St., Champaign, IL 61801-3028
Phone: 217-333-0302 • **Financial Aid Phone:** 217-333-0100
E-mail: http://admissions.illinois.edu/contact_u • **CEEB Code:** 4607
Fax: 217-244-4614 • **Website:** illinois.edu • **ACT Code:** 1154

This public school was founded in 1867. It has a 1783 acre campus.

RATINGS
Admissions Selectivity Rating: 89   **Fire Safety Rating:** 60*   **Green Rating:** 98

STUDENTS AND FACULTY
Enrollment: 32,752. **Student Body:** 45% female, 55% male, 14% out-of-state, 16% international (90 countries represented). Asian 18%, African American 6%, Caucasian 47%, Hispanic 10%, Native American <1%, Pacific Islander <1%, Two or more races 3%, Race unknown <1%.
Retention and Graduation: 94% freshmen return for sophomore year.
Faculty: 1,930 full-time faculty, 93% hold PhDs, 27% are members of minority groups, 35% are women.

ACADEMICS
Degrees: Bachelor's; Certificate; Doctoral/Professional; Doctoral/Research; Master's; Post-Bachelor's certificate; Post-Master's certificate **Classes:** Most classes have 10-19 students. Most lab/discussion sessions have 10-19 students. **Special Study Options:** Cooperative education program; Cross-registration; Distance learning; Double major; English as a Second Language (ESL); Honors program; Independent study; Internships; Student-designed major; Study abroad; Teacher certification program. **Disability Services offered to physically disabled students:** Note-taking services; Reader services; Tape recorders; Tutors. **Career services:** Alumni network; Alumni services; Career assessment; Career/job search classes; Internships; Regional alumni

FACILITIES

Housing: Apartments for married students; Coed dorms; Cooperative housing; Fraternity/sorority housing; Special housing for disabled student; Theme housing; Women's dorms 100% of campus accessible to physically disabled. **Special Academic Facilities/Equipment:** Art, cultural and natural history museums, performing arts center, National Center for Supercomputing Applications, Beckman Institute, Siebel Computer Science Center, University Library (37 separate libraries and centers on campus), Japan House and Gardens, State Farm Center for large concerts, Allerton Park and Conference Center, Arboretum, and the Illini Student Union **Computers:** 85% of classrooms, 100% of dorms, 100% of libraries, 100% of dining areas, 100% of student union, 1% of common outdoor areas have wireless network access. Students can register for classes online. Administrative functions (other than registration) can be performed online.

CAMPUS LIFE

Environment: City **Activities:** Choral groups; Concert band; Dance; Drama/theater; International Student Organization; Jazz band; Literary magazine; Marching band; Music ensembles; Musical theater; Opera; Pep band; Radio station; Student government; Student newspaper; Student-run film society; Symphony orchestra; Television station; Yearbook 1000 registered organizations, 30 honor societies, 95 religious organizations. 60 fraternities, 36 sororities. **Athletics (Intercollegiate): Men:** baseball, basketball, cheerleading, cross-country, football, golf, gymnastics, tennis, track/field (outdoor), wrestling. *Women:* basketball, cheerleading, cross-country, diving, golf, gymnastics, soccer, softball, swimming, tennis, track/field (outdoor), volleyball. **On-Campus Highlights: Environmental Initiatives:** The state-of-the-art Business Instructional Facility at the University of Illinois has earned the world's highest honor for sustainable, environmentally friendly construction and design. The building is the first business facility at a public university anywhere in the world to earn platinum certification.

ADMISSIONS

Freshman Academic Profile: 49% in top 10% of high school class, 82% in top 25% of high school class, 99% in top 50% of high school class. **Test Scores:** SAT Math middle 50% range 700-790. SAT EBRW middle 50% range 580-690. ACT middle 50% range 26-32. **Basis for Candidate Selection:** *Very important factors considered include:* rigor of secondary school record, academic GPA. *Important factors considered include:* application essay, standardized test scores, extracurricular activities, talent/ability. *Other factors considered include:* class rank, character/personal qualities, first generation, geographical residence, state residency, racial/ethnic status, volunteer work, work experience. **Freshman Admission Requirements:** High school diploma is required and GED is accepted *Academic units required:* 4 English, 3 math, 2 science, 2 science labs, 2 foreign language, 2 social studies, 2 academic electives, *Academic units recommended:* 4 English, 4 math, 4 science, 4 science labs, 4 foreign language, 4 social studies, 4 academic electives. **Freshman Admission Statistics:** 38,093 applied, 60.1% admitted, 33% enrolled. **Transfer Admission Requirements:** college transcript(s), essay or personal statement, Lowest grade transferable D. **General Admission Information:** Application fee $50. Priority deadline 11/1. Regular application deadline 12/1. Nonfall registration accepted. Admission may be deferred for a maximum of 1 year.

COSTS AND FINANCIAL AID

Annual in-state tuition $11,308. Annual out-of-state tuition $27,658. Room and board $11,308. Required fees $3,832. Average book expense $1,200. **Required Forms and Deadlines:** FAFSA. **Notification of Awards:** Applicants will be notified of awards on a rolling basis beginning 3/10. **Types of Aid:** *Need-based scholarships/grants:* College/university scholarship or grant aid from institutional funds; Federal Pell; Private scholarships; SEOG; State scholarships/grants; United Negro College Fund. *Loans:* Direct PLUS loans; Direct Subsidized Stafford Loans; Direct Unsubsidized Stafford Loans. *Student Employment:* Federal Work-Study Program available. Institutional employment available. **Financial Aid Statistics:** 80% needy freshmen, 83% needy undergrads receive need-based scholarship or grant aid. 20% freshmen, 11% undergrads receive non-need-based scholarship or grant aid. 80% freshmen, 82% undergrads receive need-based self-help aid. 1% freshmen, 1% undergrads receive athletic scholarships. 50% undergrads borrow to pay for school. Average cumulative indebtedness $25,448. **Criteria for awarding aid:** *Need-based:* Academics, Art, Athletics, Leadership, Minority status, Music/drama *Non-need-based:* Academics, Alumni affiliation, Art, Athletics, Leadership, Minority status, Music/drama, State/district residency.

UNIVERSITY OF THE INCARNATE WORD

4301 Broadway, San Antonio, TX 78209-6397
Phone: 210-829-6005 • **Financial Aid Phone:** 210-829-6008
E-mail: admis@uiwtx.edu • **CEEB Code:** 6303
Fax: 210-829-3921 • **Website:** www.uiw.edu • **ACT Code:** 4106

This private school, affiliated with the Roman Catholic Church, was founded in 1881. It has a 154 acre campus.

RATINGS

Admissions Selectivity Rating: 72   **Fire Safety Rating:** 93   **Green Rating:** 64

STUDENTS AND FACULTY

Enrollment: 5,807. **Student Body:** 60% female, 40% male, 8% out-of-state, 5% international (34 countries represented). Asian 2%, African American 7%, Caucasian 19%, Hispanic 56%, Native American <1%, Pacific Islander <1%, Two or more races 2%, Race unknown 7%. **Retention and Graduation:** 76% freshmen return for sophomore year. **Faculty:** Student/faculty ratio 15:1. 334 full-time faculty, 49% hold PhDs, 36% are members of minority groups, 53% are women.

ACADEMICS

Degrees: Associate; Bachelor's; Certificate; Doctoral/Professional; Doctoral/Research; **Master's Classes:** Most classes have 10-19 students. Most lab/discussion sessions have 10-19 students. **Most popular majors:** Psychology, General; Health Services/Allied Health/Health Sciences, General; Business Administration And Management, General. **Special Study Options:** Accelerated program; Distance learning; Double major; Dual enrollment; English as a Second Language (ESL); Honors program; Independent study; Internships; Study abroad; Teacher certification program. Honors programs: The UIW Honors Program. Participation in the unique opportunities of the Honors Program exposes the student to new ideas and academic challenges, develops your critical thinking, and enhances their professional development. Combined degree programs: BA/MA. **Disability Services offered to physically disabled students:** Note-taking services; Reader services; Tape recorders; Tutors. **Career services:** Alumni services; Career assessment; Career/job search classes; Internships

FACILITIES

Housing: Apartments for single students; Coed dorms; Men's dorms; Special housing for disabled student; Special housing for international students; Women's dorms **Computers:** 100% of classrooms, 100% of dorms, 100% of libraries, 100% of dining areas, 100% of student union, 100% of common outdoor areas have wireless network access. Students can register for classes online. Administrative functions (other than registration) can be performed online. Undergraduates are required to own a computer.

CAMPUS LIFE

Environment: Metropolis **Activities:** Campus Ministries; Choral groups; Concert band; Dance; Drama/theater; International Student Organization; Jazz band; Literary magazine; Marching band; Music ensembles; Musical theater; Pep band; Radio station; Student government; Student newspaper; Symphony orchestra; Television station 58 registered organizations, 8 honor societies, 2 religious organizations. 2 fraternities, 4 sororities. **Athletics (Intercollegiate): Men:** baseball, basketball, cross-country, football, golf, soccer, swimming, tennis, track/field (outdoor). *Women:* basketball, cross-country, golf, soccer, softball, swimming, synchronized swimming, tennis, track/field (outdoor), volleyball. **On-Campus Highlights:** Student Engagement Center, Chick-Fil-A, Library, Wellness Center, Dubuis Lawn

ADMISSIONS

Freshman Academic Profile: Average high school GPA 3.5. 16% in top 10% of high school class, 40% in top 25% of high school class, 70% in top 50% of high school class. **Test Scores:** SAT Math middle 50% range 460-550. SAT EBRW middle 50% range 480-570. ACT middle 50% range 17-23. Minimum internet-based TOEFL 79. Minimum paper TOEFL 650. **Basis for Candidate Selection:** *Very important factors considered include:* rigor of secondary school record, academic GPA, standardized test scores. *Important factors considered include:* class rank. *Other factors considered include:* application essay, recommendation(s), interview, extracurricular activities, talent/ability, character/personal qualities, alumni/ae relation, geographical residence, volunteer work, work experience, level of applicant's interest. **Freshman Admission Requirements:** High school diploma is required and GED is accepted *Academic units required:* 4 English, 3 math, 3 science, 2 foreign language, 3 social studies, 1 visual/performing arts, *Academic units recommended:* 4 English, 4 math, 3 science, 2 foreign language, 4 social studies, 1 visual/performing arts. **Freshman Admission Statistics:** 4,149 applied, 93.9% admitted, 21% enrolled. **Transfer Admission Requirements:**

college transcript(s), Minimum college GPA of 2.50 required. Lowest grade transferable C. **General Admission Information:** Application fee $20. Priority deadline 2/1. Nonfall registration accepted. Admission may be deferred for a maximum of 1 term.

COSTS AND FINANCIAL AID

Annual tuition $27,000. Room and board $11,880. Required fees $1,898. Average book expense $1,200. **Required Forms and Deadlines:** FAFSA. **Notification of Awards:** Applicants will be notified of awards on a rolling basis beginning 2/15. **Types of Aid:** *Need-based scholarships/grants:* College/university scholarship or grant aid from institutional funds; Federal Nursing Scholarships; Federal Pell; Private scholarships; SEOG; State scholarships/grants. *Loans:* Direct PLUS loans; Direct Subsidized Stafford Loans; Direct Unsubsidized Stafford Loans. *Student Employment:* Federal Work-Study Program available. Institutional employment available. **Financial Aid Statistics:** 96% needy freshmen, 99% needy undergrads receive need-based scholarship or grant aid. 0% freshmen, 0% undergrads receive non-need-based scholarship or grant aid. 74% freshmen, 80% undergrads receive need-based self-help aid. 4% freshmen, 4% undergrads receive athletic scholarships. 99% freshmen receive any aid. 76% undergrads borrow to pay for school. Average cumulative indebtedness $43,998. **Criteria for awarding aid:** *Non-need-based:* Academics, Alumni affiliation, Art, Athletics, Leadership, Music/drama, Religious affiliation, State/district residency.

UNIVERSITY OF INDIANAPOLIS

1400 East Hanna Avenue, Indianapolis, IN 46227-3697
Phone: 317-788-3216 • **Financial Aid Phone:** 317-788-3217
E-mail: admissions@uindy.edu • **CEEB Code:** 1321
Fax: 317-788-3300 • **Website:** www.uindy.edu • **ACT Code:** 1204

This private school, affiliated with the Methodist Church, was founded in 1902. It has a 65 acre campus.

RATINGS
Admissions Selectivity Rating: 75   **Fire Safety Rating:** 72   **Green Rating:** 60*

STUDENTS AND FACULTY

Enrollment: 4,138. **Student Body:** 68% female, 32% male, 9% out-of-state, 5% international (47 countries represented). Asian 1%, African American 13%, Caucasian 73%, Hispanic 2%, Native American <1%, Pacific Islander <1%, Two or more races 2%, Race unknown 4%.
Retention and Graduation: 74% freshmen return for sophomore year.
Faculty: Student/faculty ratio 15:1. 218 full-time faculty, 76% hold PhDs, 6% are members of minority groups, 57% are women. 0% of classes are taught by teaching assistants.

ACADEMICS

Degrees: Associate; Bachelor's; Doctoral/Professional; Doctoral/Research; **Master's Classes:** Most classes have 10-19 students. Most lab/discussion sessions have 10-19 students. **Most popular majors:** Psychology, General; Registered Nursing/Registered Nurse; Business/Commerce, General. **Special Study Options:** Accelerated program; Cross-registration; Distance learning; Double major; Dual enrollment; English as a Second Language (ESL); Honors program; Independent study; Internships; Liberal arts/career combination; Student-designed major; Study abroad; Teacher certification program. **Disability Services offered to physically disabled students:** Note-taking services; Reader services; Tape recorders; Tutors. **Career services:** Internships; Regional alumni

FACILITIES

Housing: Apartments for married students; Apartments for single students; Coed dorms; Women's dorms 90% of campus accessible to physically diasbled. **Special Academic Facilities/Equipment:** Developmental preschool, art gallery, observatory. **Computers:** 100% of classrooms, 100% of dorms, 100% of libraries, 100% of dining areas, 100% of student union, 100% of common outdoor areas have wireless network access.

CAMPUS LIFE

Environment: Metropolis **Activities:** Campus Ministries; Choral groups; Concert band; Dance; Drama/theater; International Student Organization; Jazz band; Literary magazine; Music ensembles; Musical theater; Opera; Pep band; Radio station; Student government; Student newspaper; Television station; Yearbook 53 registered organizations, 14 honor societies, 4 religious organizations. **Athletics (Intercollegiate):** *Men:* baseball, basketball, cross-country, diving, football, golf, soccer, swimming, tennis, track/field (outdoor), wrestling. *Women:* basketball, cross-country, diving, golf, soccer, softball, swimming, tennis, track/field (outdoor), volleyball. **On-Campus Highlights:**

Ruth Lilly Fitness Center, Schwitzer Center, Krannert Memorial Library, Christel Dehaan Fine Arts Center, Martin Hall

ADMISSIONS

Freshman Academic Profile: Average high school GPA 3.4. 27% in top 10% of high school class, 56% in top 25% of high school class, 88% in top 50% of high school class. **Test Scores:** SAT Math middle 50% range 460-570. SAT EBRW middle 50% range 450-560. ACT middle 50% range 19-25. Minimum paper TOEFL 500. **Basis for Candidate Selection:** *Very important factors considered include:* rigor of secondary school record, academic GPA. *Important factors considered include:* standardized test scores. *Other factors considered include:* class rank, recommendation(s), interview, talent/ability. **Freshman Admission Requirements:** High school diploma is required and GED is accepted *Academic units required:* 4 English, 3 math, 2 science, 1 science labs, 2 foreign language, 2 social studies, 1 history, 3 academic electives, 1 computer science, 2 visual/performing arts, *Academic units recommended:* 4 English, 3 math, 3 science, 2 science labs, 3 foreign language, 2 social studies, 1 history, 3 academic electives, 1 computer science, 2 visual/performing arts. **Freshman Admission Statistics:** 5,396 applied, 78.7% admitted, 19% enrolled. **Transfer Admission Requirements:** High school transcript, college transcript(s), standardized test scores, statement of good standing from prior institution(s). Minimum college GPA of 2.0 required. Lowest grade transferable C-. **General Admission Information:** Application fee $25. Regular application deadline 8/20. Nonfall registration accepted. Admission may be deferred.

COSTS AND FINANCIAL AID

Annual tuition $23,590. Room and board $9,090. Required fees $240. Average book expense $1,076. **Required Forms and Deadlines:** FAFSA; Institution's own financial aid form. **Notification of Awards:** Applicants will be notified of awards on a rolling basis beginning 3/1. **Types of Aid:** *Need-based scholarships/grants:* College/university scholarship or grant aid from institutional funds; Federal Pell; Private scholarships; SEOG; State scholarships/grants. *Loans:* Direct PLUS loans; Direct Subsidized Stafford Loans; Direct Unsubsidized Stafford Loans. *Student Employment:* Federal Work-Study Program available. Institutional employment available. **Financial Aid Statistics:** 57% needy freshmen, 68% needy undergrads receive need-based scholarship or grant aid. 99% freshmen, 70% undergrads receive non-need-based scholarship or grant aid. 78% freshmen, 79% undergrads receive need-based self-help aid. 8% freshmen, 8% undergrads receive athletic scholarships. 99% freshmen, 98% undergrads receive any aid. **Criteria for awarding aid:** *Non-need-based:* Academics, Alumni affiliation, Art, Athletics, Job skills, Music/drama, Religious affiliation, State/district residency.

UNIVERSITY OF IOWA

101 Jessup Hall, Iowa City, IA 52242
Phone: 319-335-3847 • **Financial Aid Phone:** 319-335-1450
E-mail: admissions@uiowa.edu • **CEEB Code:** 6681
Fax: 319-333-1535 • **Website:** www.uiowa.edu • **ACT Code:** 1356

This public school was founded in 1847. It has a 1700 acre campus.

RATINGS
Admissions Selectivity Rating: 81   **Fire Safety Rating:** 92   **Green Rating:** 60*

STUDENTS AND FACULTY

Enrollment: 23,349. **Student Body:** 53% female, 47% male, 37% out-of-state, 9% international (64 countries represented). Asian 4%, African American 3%, Caucasian 71%, Hispanic 8%, Native American <1%, Pacific Islander <1%, Two or more races 3%, Race unknown 2%.
Retention and Graduation: 87% freshmen return for sophomore year. 54% freshmen graduate within 4 years. 1% freshmen graduate within 6 years. **Faculty:** Student/faculty ratio 16:1. 1,377 full-time faculty, 99% hold PhDs, 20% are members of minority groups, 33% are women. 10% of classes are taught by teaching assistants.

ACADEMICS

Degrees: Bachelor's; Doctoral/Professional; Doctoral/Research; Master's; Post-Bachelor's certificate; Post-Master's certificate **Classes:** Most classes have fewer than 10 students. Most lab/discussion sessions have 10-19 students. **Most popular majors:** Engineering, General; Pre-Medicine/Pre-Medical Studies; Business/Commerce, General. **Special Study Options:** Accelerated program; Cooperative education program; Distance learning; Double major; Dual enrollment; English as a Second Language (ESL); Exchange student program (domestic); External degree program; Honors program; Independent study; Internships; Liberal arts/career combination; Student-designed major; Study abroad; Teacher certification program. Honors programs: Honors Students enjoy ample opportunities for original research, cultural exploration, artistic invention, political action, community service, and more. Students can design their own programs of study, choose from a rich array of Iowa innovations, or learn almost any discipline in the world. To feed sparks from its students, Honors adds superb advisers, events, facilities, grants, and projects. Combined degree programs: BA/DDS; BA/MA; BA/MEng. **Disability Services offered to physically disabled students:** Note-taking services; Reader services; Tape recorders; Tutors. **Career services:** Career assessment; Career/job search classes; Internships; Regional alumni

FACILITIES

Housing: Apartments for married students; Apartments for single students; Coed dorms; Fraternity/sorority housing; Theme housing; Wellness housing 99% of campus accessible to physically diasbled. **Special Academic Facilities/ Equipment:** National Advanced Driving Simulator, electron microscope, laser facility, Oakdale Research park, UI Hygienic Lab, UI Center for Biocatalysis & Bioprocessing, UI Research Foundation, survey research facilities, natural history museum, Medical Museum, Old Capitol Museum, Main Library and 7 departmental libraries, information arcade, newspaper production lab, TV lab, UI Technology Innovation Center, Project Art, Fraternal Order of Eagles Diabetes Research Center, and Center for the Book. **Computers:** 100% of classrooms, 25% of dorms, 100% of libraries, 25% of dining areas, 90% of student union, 15% of common outdoor areas have wireless network access. Students can register for classes online. Administrative functions (other than registration) can be performed online.

CAMPUS LIFE

Environment: City **Activities:** Campus Ministries; Choral groups; Concert band; Dance; Drama/theater; International Student Organization; Jazz band; Literary magazine; Marching band; Model UN; Music ensembles; Musical theater; Opera; Pep band; Radio station; Student government; Student newspaper; Student-run film society; Symphony orchestra; Television station 488 registered organizations, 21 honor societies, 24 religious organizations. 18 fraternities, 18 sororities. **Athletics (Intercollegiate):** *Men:* baseball, basketball, cheerleading, cross-country, diving, football, golf, gymnastics, swimming, tennis, track/field (outdoor), track/field (indoor), wrestling. *Women:* basketball, cheerleading, crew/rowing, cross-country, diving, field hockey, golf, gymnastics, soccer, softball, swimming, tennis, track/field (outdoor), track/ field (indoor), volleyball. **On-Campus Highlights:** Kinnick Stadium/Carver Hawkeye Arena, Campus Recreation and Wellness Center, Finkbine Golf Course, Pentacrest/Old Capitol, UI Main Library **Environmental Initiatives:** The University of Iowa has established seven 2020 Sustainability Targets that include goals for energy conservation, renewable energy, waste diversion, reduced carbon impact of transportation, increasing student opportunities to learn and practice sustainability principles, support sustainability research and develop partnerships to advance collaborative initiatives. The UI was the first certified Tree Campus in Iowa.The number of LEED-Accredited Professionals on staff in Facilities Management tripled to total 17.

ADMISSIONS

Freshman Academic Profile: Average high school GPA 3.7. 30% in top 10% of high school class, 61% in top 25% of high school class, 91% in top 50% of high school class. 90% from public high schools. **Test Scores:** SAT Math middle 50% range 570-690. SAT EBRW middle 50% range 570-680. ACT middle 50% range 23-28. Minimum internet-based TOEFL 80. Minimum paper TOEFL 530. **Basis for Candidate Selection:** *Very important factors considered include:* rigor of secondary school record, class rank, academic GPA, standardized test scores. *Other factors considered include:* recommendation(s), talent/ability, character/personal qualities, state residency. **Freshman Admission Requirements:** High school diploma is required and GED is accepted *Academic units required:* 4 English, 3 math, 3 science, 2 foreign language, 3 social studies, *Academic units recommended:* 4 math. **Freshman Admission Statistics:** 27,734 applied, 86.0% admitted, 21% enrolled. **Transfer Admission Requirements:** High school transcript, college transcript(s), Minimum college GPA of 2.5 required. Lowest grade transferable D. **General Admission Information:** Application fee $40. Regular application deadline 5/1. Nonfall registration accepted. Admission may be deferred.

COSTS AND FINANCIAL AID

Annual in-state tuition $10,450. Annual out-of-state tuition $29,130. Room and board $10,450. Required fees $1,479. Average book expense $950. **Required Forms and Deadlines:** FAFSA. **Notification of Awards:** Applicants will be notified of awards on a rolling basis beginning 11/15. **Types of Aid:** *Need-based scholarships/grants:* College/university scholarship or grant aid from institutional funds; Federal Pell; Private scholarships; SEOG; State scholarships/grants. *Loans:* Direct PLUS loans; Direct Subsidized Stafford Loans; Direct Unsubsidized Stafford Loans. *Student Employment:* Federal Work-Study Program available. Institutional employment available. **Financial Aid Statistics:** 77% needy freshmen, 73% needy undergrads receive need-based

scholarship or grant aid. 75% freshmen, 52% undergrads receive non-need-based scholarship or grant aid. 85% freshmen, 90% undergrads receive need-based self-help aid. 2% freshmen, 2% undergrads receive athletic scholarships. 79% freshmen, 72% undergrads receive any aid. 53% undergrads borrow to pay for school. Average cumulative indebtedness $27,715. **Criteria for awarding aid:** *Need-based:* Academics *Non-need-based:* Academics, Alumni affiliation, Art, Athletics, Leadership, Music/drama, State/district residency.

UNIVERSITY OF JAMESTOWN

6000 College Lane, Jamestown, ND 58405-0001
Phone: 701-252-3467 · **Financial Aid Phone:** 701-252-3467
E-mail: admissions@uj.edu
Fax: 701-253-4318 • **Website:** www.uj.edu • **ACT Code:** 3200

This private school, affiliated with the Presbyterian Church, was founded in 1883. It has a 110 acre campus.

RATINGS

Admissions Selectivity Rating: 79 **Fire Safety Rating:** 80 **Green Rating:** 60*

STUDENTS AND FACULTY

Enrollment: 892. **Student Body:** 49% female, 51% male, 49% out-of-state, 10% international (20 countries represented). Asian 1%, African American 4%, Caucasian 75%, Hispanic 7%, Native American 1%, Pacific Islander 1%, Two or more races 0%, Race unknown 1%.
Retention and Graduation: 72% freshmen return for sophomore year. 40% freshmen graduate within 4 years. 52% freshmen graduate within 6 years. 13% grads go on to further study within 1 year. 9% grads pursue arts and sciences degrees. 1% grads pursue law degrees. 1% grads pursue business degrees. 6% grads pursue medical degrees. **Faculty:** Student/faculty ratio 12:1. 71 full-time faculty, 62% hold PhDs, 4% are members of minority groups, 58% are women. 0% of classes are taught by teaching assistants.

ACADEMICS

Degrees: Bachelor's; Doctoral/Professional; **Master's Classes:** Most classes have 10-19 students. Most lab/discussion sessions have 10-19 students. **Most popular majors:** Elementary Education And Teaching; Registered Nursing/ Registered Nurse; Business/Commerce, General. **Special Study Options:** Cooperative education program; Double major; Dual enrollment; English as a Second Language (ESL); Exchange student program (domestic); Honors program; Independent study; Internships; Liberal arts/career combination; Student-designed major; Study abroad; Teacher certification program. Honors programs: Character and Leadership Program. The heart of the Character in Leadership program is its academic core. Each student who participates will receive a minor in leadership. University of Jamestown values its reputation for quality education and therefore is committed through its Character in Leadership Program to providing a broad and sound intellectual foundation that will enable its students to provide ethical leadership in an ever-changing world. **Disability Services offered to physically disabled students:** Note-taking services; Reader services; Tape recorders; Tutors. **Career services:** Alumni network; Alumni services; Career assessment; Career/job search classes; Internships

FACILITIES

Housing: Apartments for married students; Apartments for single students; Coed dorms; Special housing for disabled students 80% of campus accessible to physically diasbled. **Computers:** 95% of classrooms, 100% of dorms, 100% of libraries, 100% of dining areas, 100% of student union, 50% of common outdoor areas have wireless network access. Students can register for classes online. Administrative functions (other than registration) can be performed online.

CAMPUS LIFE

Environment: Village **Activities:** Campus Ministries; Choral groups; Concert band; Dance; Drama/theater; International Student Organization; Jazz band; Literary magazine; Music ensembles; Musical theater; Pep band; Student government; Student newspaper 35 registered organizations, 6 honor societies, 5 religious organizations. **Athletics (Intercollegiate):** *Men:* baseball, basketball, cross-country, football, golf, track/field (outdoor), track/ field (indoor), wrestling. *Women:* basketball, cross-country, golf, soccer, softball, track/field (outdoor), track/field (indoor), volleyball, wrestling. **On-Campus Highlights:** Nafus Student Center—Java Hut, Jimmie Connection, Newman Center, Residence Hall lounges, Reiland Fine Arts Center

ADMISSIONS

Freshman Academic Profile: Average high school GPA 3.4. 15% in top 10% of high school class, 37% in top 25% of high school class, 73% in top 50% of high school class. **Test Scores:** SAT Math middle 50% range 480-530. SAT EBRW middle 50% range 460-520. ACT middle 50% range 19-24. Minimum internet-based TOEFL 70. Minimum paper TOEFL 525. **Basis for Candidate Selection:** *Very important factors considered include:* academic GPA, standardized test scores. *Other factors considered include:* rigor of secondary school record, application essay, recommendation(s), interview, extracurricular activities, talent/ability, character/personal qualities, alumni/ae relation, level of applicant's interest. **Freshman Admission Requirements:** High school diploma is required and GED is accepted *Academic units recommended:* 4 English, 3 math, 4 science, 2 foreign language, 3 social studies. **Freshman Admission Statistics:** 1,154 applied, 65.3% admitted, 31% enrolled. **Transfer Admission Requirements:** High school transcript, college transcript(s), statement of good standing from prior institution(s). Minimum college GPA of 2.5 required. Lowest grade transferable c. **General Admission Information:** Priority deadline 5/1. Nonfall registration accepted. Admission may be deferred.

COSTS AND FINANCIAL AID

Annual tuition $21,196. Room and board $7,886. Required fees $780. Average book expense $1,300. **Required Forms and Deadlines:** FAFSA. **Notification of Awards:** Applicants will be notified of awards on a rolling basis beginning 10/15. **Types of Aid:** *Need-based scholarships/grants:* Federal Pell; Private scholarships; SEOG; State scholarships/grants. *Loans:* Direct PLUS loans; Direct Subsidized Stafford Loans; Direct Unsubsidized Stafford Loans. *Student Employment:* Federal Work-Study Program available. Institutional employment available. **Financial Aid Statistics:** 100% needy freshmen, 100% needy undergrads receive need-based scholarship or grant aid. 22% freshmen, 19% undergrads receive non-need-based scholarship or grant aid. 74% freshmen, 75% undergrads receive need-based self-help aid. 32% freshmen, 27% undergrads receive athletic scholarships. 100% freshmen, 98% undergrads receive any aid. 70% undergrads borrow to pay for school. Average cumulative indebtedness $25,368. **Criteria for awarding aid:** *Non-need-based:* Academics, Alumni affiliation, Art, Athletics, Job skills, Leadership, Music/drama, Religious affiliation.

UNIVERSITY OF KANSAS

Office of Admissions, Lawrence, KS 66045-7576
Phone: 785-864-3911 • **Financial Aid Phone:** 785-864-4700
E-mail: adm@ku.edu • **CEEB Code:** 6871
Fax: 785-864-5017 • **Website:** https://www.ku.edu/ • **ACT Code:** 1470

This public school was founded in 1865. It has a 1000 acre campus.

RATINGS

Admissions Selectivity Rating: 77   Fire Safety Rating: 97   Green Rating: 83

STUDENTS AND FACULTY

Enrollment: 18,903. **Student Body:** 51% female, 49% male, 28% out-of-state, 6% international (76 countries represented). Asian 5%, African American 4%, Caucasian 71%, Hispanic 8%, Native American <1%, Pacific Islander <1%, Two or more races 5%, Race unknown 1%.
Retention and Graduation: 83% freshmen return for sophomore year. 42% freshmen graduate within 4 years. 63% freshmen graduate within 6 years. 31% grads go on to further study within 1 year. **Faculty:** Student/faculty ratio 17:1. 1,359 full-time faculty, 90% hold PhDs, 21% are members of minority groups, 41% are women. 15% of classes are taught by teaching assistants.

ACADEMICS

Degrees: Bachelor's; Certificate; Doctoral/Professional; Doctoral/Research; Master's; Post-Bachelor's certificate; Post-Master's certificate **Classes:** Most classes have fewer than 10 students. Most lab/discussion sessions have 10-19 students. **Most popular majors:** Journalism; Biology/Biological Sciences, General; Business/Commerce, General. **Special Study Options:** Accelerated program; Cooperative education program; Distance learning; Double major; Dual enrollment; English as a Second Language (ESL); Honors program; Independent study; Internships; Liberal arts/career combination; Study abroad; Teacher certification program. Honors programs: The University Honors Program is one of the oldest and best Honors programs in the country. It provides enriched educational opportunities to academically talented, promising, and motivated undergraduate students. These opportunities include

priority enrollment, small honors courses with top faculty, specialized advising, experiential learning (research, internships, study abroad, cultural and social activities and community service) and special programs. web site at http://www.honors.ku.edu/. **Disability Services offered to physically disabled students:** Note-taking services; Reader services; Tape recorders; Tutors. **Career services:** Career assessment; Career/job search classes; Internships

FACILITIES

Housing: Apartments for single students; Coed dorms; Cooperative housing; Fraternity/sorority housing; Theme housing; Women's dorms 95% of campus accessible to physically diasbled. **Special Academic Facilities/Equipment:** 12 libraries (including art and architecture, engineering, law, medical, music and dance, rare research materials, special collections, and science), performing arts center, organ recital hall, museums (art, anthropology, classical, entomology, invertebrate paleontology, and natural history), film studio, student operated radio and television stations, public radio station, herbarium, space technology center, observatory, Robert J. Dole Institute for Politics, Hall Center for the Humanities, Center for International Business Education and Research, ecological reserves, Biological Survey, Geological Survey, Information and Telecommunication Technology Center, energy research center, flight research lab, Transportation Research Center, 400+ bed hospital for clinical learning, Hoglund Brain Imaging Center, Center on Aging.

CAMPUS LIFE

Environment: City **Activities:** Choral groups; Concert band; Dance; Drama/theater; International Student Organization; Jazz band; Literary magazine; Marching band; Model UN; Music ensembles; Musical theater; Opera; Pep band; Radio station; Student government; Student newspaper; Symphony orchestra; Television station 476 registered organizations, 14 honor societies, 39 religious organizations. 27 fraternities, 16 sororities. **Athletics (Intercollegiate): Men:** baseball, basketball, cross-country, football, golf, track/field (outdoor), track/field (indoor). *Women:* basketball, crew/rowing, cross-country, diving, golf, soccer, softball, swimming, tennis, track/field (outdoor), track/field (indoor), volleyball. **On-Campus Highlights:** Spencer Museum of Art, Kansas Union and Bookstore, Natural History Museum, Booth Hall of Athletics, DeBruce Center, and Allen Fieldhouse, Robert J. Dole Institute of Politics **Environmental Initiatives:** In fall 2011, the University of Kansas released its campus sustainability plan, Building Sustainable Traditions, which establishes a vision for a more sustainable campus and outlines specific strategies for achieving the goals of the plan. Action steps are focused in 9 key areas: administration, research & curriculum, student life, energy, built environment, campus grounds, procurement, waste, and transportation. (http://www.sustainability.ku.edu/Plan/)

ADMISSIONS

Freshman Academic Profile: Average high school GPA 3.6. 26% in top 10% of high school class, 58% in top 25% of high school class, 88% in top 50% of high school class. **Test Scores:** ACT middle 50% range 23-28. **Basis for Candidate Selection:** *Very important factors considered include:* academic GPA, standardized test scores. **Freshman Admission Requirements:** High school diploma is required and GED is accepted *Academic units required:* 4 English, 3 math, 3 science, 1 science labs, 3 social studies, 3 academic electives, *Academic units recommended:* 4 English, 4 math, 3 science, 3 social studies, 3 academic electives. **Freshman Admission Statistics:** 14,538 applied, 93.4% admitted, 31% enrolled. **Transfer Admission Requirements:** college transcript(s), Minimum college GPA of 2.5 required. Lowest grade transferable C. **General Admission Information:** Application fee $40. Priority deadline 11/1. Nonfall registration accepted.

COSTS AND FINANCIAL AID

Annual in-state tuition $10,060. Annual out-of-state tuition $25,586. Room and board $10,060. Required fees $1,006. Average book expense $1,080. **Required Forms and Deadlines:** FAFSA. **Notification of Awards:** Applicants will be notified of awards on a rolling basis beginning 4/1. **Types of Aid:** *Need-based scholarships/grants:* College/university scholarship or grant aid from institutional funds; Federal Pell; Private scholarships; SEOG; State scholarships/grants. *Loans:* Direct PLUS loans; Direct Subsidized Stafford Loans; Direct Unsubsidized Stafford Loans. *Student Employment:* Federal Work-Study Program available. Institutional employment available. **Financial Aid Statistics:** 84% needy freshmen, 76% needy undergrads receive need-based scholarship or grant aid. 10% freshmen, 7% undergrads receive non-need-based scholarship or grant aid. 69% freshmen, 76% undergrads receive need-based self-help aid. 2% freshmen, 2% undergrads receive athletic scholarships. 77% freshmen, 65% undergrads receive any aid. 52% undergrads borrow to pay for school. Average cumulative indebtedness $27,479. **Criteria for awarding aid:** *Need-based:* Academics, Alumni affiliation, Art, Job skills, Leadership, Minority status, Music/drama *Non-need-based:* Academics, Alumni affiliation, Art, Athletics, Leadership, Minority status, Music/drama, State/district residency.

UNIVERSITY OF KENTUCKY

101 Main Building, Lexington, KY 40506
Phone: 859-257-2000 • **Financial Aid Phone:** (859) 257-3172
E-mail: admissions@uky.edu • **CEEB Code:** 1837
Fax: (859) 257-3823 • **Website:** www.uky.edu • **ACT Code:** 1554

This public school was founded in 1865. It has a 687 acre campus.

RATINGS

Admissions Selectivity Rating: 80   **Fire Safety Rating:** 91   **Green Rating:** 60*

STUDENTS AND FACULTY

Enrollment: 22,078. **Student Body:** 55% female, 45% male, 31% out-of-state, 2% international (117 countries represented). Asian 3%, African American 8%, Caucasian 76%, Hispanic 5%, Native American <1%, Pacific Islander <1%, Two or more races 4%, Race unknown 3%.
Retention and Graduation: 83% freshmen return for sophomore year. 40% freshmen graduate within 4 years. 61% freshmen graduate within 6 years.
Faculty: Student/faculty ratio 17:1. 1,397 full-time faculty, 92% hold PhDs, 19% are members of minority groups, 39% are women. 20% of classes are taught by teaching assistants.

ACADEMICS

Degrees: Bachelor's; Certificate; Doctoral/Professional; Doctoral/Research; Master's; Post-Bachelor's certificate; Post-Master's certificate **Classes:** Most classes have 10-19 students. Most lab/discussion sessions have 20-29 students. **Special Study Options:** Accelerated program; Cooperative education program; Distance learning; Double major; Dual enrollment; English as a Second Language (ESL); Exchange student program (domestic); Honors program; Independent study; Internships; Student-designed major; Study abroad; Teacher certification program; Weekend college. Combined degree programs: BA/MA. **Disability Services offered to physically disabled students:** Note-taking services; Reader services.

FACILITIES

Housing: Apartments for single students; Coed dorms; Fraternity/sorority housing; Men's dorms 95% of campus accessible to physically disabled. **Special Academic Facilities/Equipment:** Anthropology and art museums, center for the humanities, centers for equine research, cancer research, and robotics, pharmacy manufacturing lab. **Computers:** 30% of classrooms, 10% of dorms, 100% of libraries, 80% of dining areas, 70% of student union, 50% of common outdoor areas have wireless network access. Students can register for classes online. Administrative functions (other than registration) can be performed online.

CAMPUS LIFE

Environment: City **Activities:** Campus Ministries; Choral groups; Concert band; Dance; Drama/theater; International Student Organization; Jazz band; Literary magazine; Marching band; Model UN; Music ensembles; Musical theater; Opera; Pep band; Radio station; Student government; Student newspaper; Symphony orchestra; Television station; Yearbook 348 registered organizations, 28 honor societies, 20 religious organizations. 19 fraternities, 16 sororities. **Athletics (Intercollegiate):** *Men:* baseball, basketball, cheerleading, cross-country, diving, football, golf, riflery, soccer, swimming, tennis, track/field (outdoor), track/field (indoor). *Women:* basketball, cheerleading, cross-country, diving, golf, gymnastics, riflery, soccer, softball, swimming, tennis, track/field (outdoor), track/field (indoor), volleyball. **On-Campus Highlights:** W.T. Young Library, Johnson Fitness Center, Memorial Coliseum, Arboretum, Memorial Hall

ADMISSIONS

Freshman Academic Profile: Average high school GPA 3.7. 29% in top 10% of high school class, 58% in top 25% of high school class, 86% in top 50% of high school class. **Test Scores:** SAT Math middle 50% range 490-630. SAT EBRW middle 50% range 550-660. ACT middle 50% range 22-28. Minimum paper TOEFL 527. **Basis for Candidate Selection:** *Very important factors considered include:* rigor of secondary school record, academic GPA, standardized test scores. *Important factors considered include:* application essay, recommendation(s). *Other factors considered include:* class rank, interview, extracurricular activities, talent/ability, character/personal qualities, alumni/ae relation, geographical residence, state residency, volunteer work. **Freshman Admission Requirements:** High school diploma is required and GED is accepted *Academic units required:* 4 English, 3 math, 3 science, 1 science labs, 3 foreign language, 3 social studies, 7 academic electives, 1

visual/performing arts, and 1 unit from above areas or other academic areas. **Freshman Admission Statistics:** 22,653 applied, 80.1% admitted, 27% enrolled. **Transfer Admission Requirements:** college transcript(s), Minimum college GPA of 2.0 required. Lowest grade transferable D. **General Admission Information:** Application fee $50. Priority deadline 2/15. Regular application deadline 2/15. Nonfall registration accepted. Admission may be deferred for a maximum of 1 year.

COSTS AND FINANCIAL AID

Annual in-state tuition $12,184. Annual out-of-state tuition $24,845. Room and board $12,184. Required fees $1,311. Average book expense $1,000. **Required Forms and Deadlines:** FAFSA. **Notification of Awards:** Applicants will be notified of awards on a rolling basis beginning 3/15. **Types of Aid:** *Need-based scholarships/grants:* College/university scholarship or grant aid from institutional funds; Federal Pell; Private scholarships; SEOG; State scholarships/grants. *Loans:* Direct PLUS loans; Direct Subsidized Stafford Loans; Direct Unsubsidized Stafford Loans. *Student Employment:* Federal Work-Study Program available. **Financial Aid Statistics:** 46% needy freshmen, 49% needy undergrads receive need-based scholarship or grant aid. 90% freshmen, 73% undergrads receive non-need-based scholarship or grant aid. 60% freshmen, 70% undergrads receive need-based self-help aid. 3% freshmen, 3% undergrads receive athletic scholarships. 40% freshmen, 38% undergrads receive any aid. **Criteria for awarding aid:** *Need-based:* Academics, Alumni affiliation, Minority status *Non-need-based:* Academics, Alumni affiliation, Art, Athletics, Job skills, Leadership, Minority status, Music/drama, State/district residency.

UNIVERSITY OF KING'S COLLEGE

Registrars Office, Halifax, NS B3H 2A1
Phone: 902-422-1271
E-mail: admissions@ukings.ns.ca
Fax: 902-423-3357 • **Website:** www.ukings.ca

This public school was founded in 1789. It has a 3 acre campus.

RATINGS

Admissions Selectivity Rating: 73   **Fire Safety Rating:** 60*   **Green Rating:** 60*

STUDENTS AND FACULTY

Enrollment: 1,137. **Student Body:** 57% female, 43% male, 53% out-of-state, (6 countries represented).
Faculty: Student/faculty ratio 25:1. 51 full-time faculty, 71% hold PhDs, 31% are women. 0% of classes are taught by teaching assistants.

ACADEMICS

Degrees: Bachelor's **Classes:** Most classes have 20-29 students. Most lab/discussion sessions have 10-19 students. **Most popular majors:** English Language And Literature, General; Psychology, General; Sociology. **Special Study Options:** Cooperative education program; Double major; Honors program; Internships; Study abroad. **Career services:** Career assessment; Career/job search classes

FACILITIES

Housing: Coed dorms; Men's dorms; Women's dorms **Computers:** Students can register for classes online. Administrative functions (other than registration) can be performed online.

CAMPUS LIFE

Environment: Metropolis **Activities:** Choral groups; Dance; Drama/theater; Literary magazine; Radio station; Student government; Student newspaper; Student-run film society; Yearbook. **Athletics (Intercollegiate):** *Men:* badminton, basketball, soccer, volleyball. *Women:* badminton, basketball, soccer, volleyball. **On-Campus Highlights:** The Pit, The Wardroom, The Manning Room, The Library, The Quad

ADMISSIONS

Test Scores: Minimum paper TOEFL 580. **Basis for Candidate Selection:** *Very important factors considered include:* rigor of secondary school record, standardized test scores. **Freshman Admission Requirements:** High school diploma is required and GED is not accepted **Freshman Admission Statistics:** 904 applied, 46.7% admitted, 73% enrolled. **Transfer Admission Requirements:** college transcript(s), Lowest grade transferable C. **General Admission Information:** Application fee $45. Priority deadline 3/1. Regular application deadline 6/1. Nonfall registration accepted. Admission may be deferred for a maximum of One year.

COSTS AND FINANCIAL AID

Average book expense $1,000.

UNIVERSITY OF LA VERNE

1950 Third Street, La Verne, CA 91750
Phone: (800) 876-4858 • **Financial Aid Phone:** 1-800-649-0160
E-mail: admission@laverne.edu • **CEEB Code:** 4381
Fax: (909) 392-2714 • **Website:** www.laverne.edu • **ACT Code:** 295

This private school was founded in 1891. It has a 66 acre campus.

RATINGS

Admissions Selectivity Rating: 85   **Fire Safety Rating:** 93   **Green Rating:** 98

STUDENTS AND FACULTY

Enrollment: 2,859. **Student Body:** 59% female, 41% male, 4% out-of-state, 5% international (24 countries represented). Asian 6%, African American 5%, Caucasian 25%, Hispanic 51%, Native American <1%, Pacific Islander 1%, Two or more races 5%, Race unknown 2%.
Retention and Graduation: 85% freshmen return for sophomore year.
Faculty: Student/faculty ratio 13:1. 233 full-time faculty, 0% of classes are taught by teaching assistants.

ACADEMICS

Degrees: Bachelor's; Certificate; Doctoral/Professional; Doctoral/Research; Master's; Post-Bachelor's certificate **Classes:** Most classes have 10-19 students. Most lab/discussion sessions have fewer than 10 students. **Most popular majors:** Biology/Biological Sciences, General; Psychology, General; Business Administration And Management, General. **Special Study Options:** Distance learning; Double major; English as a Second Language (ESL); Exchange student program (domestic); Honors program; Independent study; Internships; Liberal arts/career combination; Student-designed major; Study abroad; Teacher certification program; Weekend college. Honors programs: La Verne Global Ideas Honors Program The La Verne Honors Program offers a challenging intellectual experience that complements any major at the university. Open to students with proven academic success in high school, the rigorous curriculum is taught by passionate and knowledgeable professors, and allows students an opportunity to complete most general education requirements in accelerated fashion. **Disability Services offered to physically disabled students:** Note-taking services; Reader services; Tape recorders; Tutors. **Career services:** Alumni services; Career assessment; Career/job search classes; Internships; Regional alumni

FACILITIES

Housing: Coed dorms; Men's dorms; Special housing for disabled student; Special housing for international students; Women's dorms **Special Academic Facilities/Equipment:** Greenhouse and Animal Care Facility; Montana Field Station—Magpie Ranch; Photography and Art galleries; The Microscopy and Imaging Center; Jeagar science specimen Museum **Computers:** 100% of classrooms, 100% of dorms, 100% of libraries, 100% of dining areas, 100% of student union, 100% of common outdoor areas have wireless network access. Students can register for classes online. Administrative functions (other than registration) can be performed online.

CAMPUS LIFE

Environment: Town **Activities:** Campus Ministries; Choral groups; Dance; Drama/theater; International Student Organization; Literary magazine; Model UN; Music ensembles; Musical theater; Radio station; Student government; Student newspaper; Student-run film society; Television station 40 registered organizations, 2 honor societies, 1 religious organization. 3 fraternities, 6 sororities. **Athletics (Intercollegiate):** *Men:* baseball, basketball, cross-country, diving, football, golf, soccer, swimming, tennis, track/field (outdoor), water polo. *Women:* basketball, cross-country, diving, soccer, softball, swimming, tennis, track/field (outdoor), volleyball, water polo. **On-Campus Highlights:** Campus Center, Sneaky Park (outdoor events), Barbara's Place Bistro, South Quad, The Rock **Environmental Initiatives:** Total Recycling Program

ADMISSIONS

Freshman Academic Profile: Average high school GPA 3.5. 18% in top 10% of high school class, 54% in top 25% of high school class, 86% in top 50% of high school class. **Test Scores:** SAT Math middle 50% range 470-570. SAT EBRW middle 50% range 470-560. ACT middle 50% range 20-24. Minimum internet-based TOEFL 80. Minimum paper TOEFL 550. **Basis for Candidate Selection:** *Very important factors considered include:* rigor of secondary school record, academic GPA, application essay, standardized test scores, recommendation(s), extracurricular activities, character/personal qualities. *Important factors considered include:* class rank. *Other factors considered include:* interview, talent/ability, first generation, alumni/ae relation, geographical residence, volunteer work, work experience, level of applicant's interest. **Freshman Admission Requirements:** High school diploma is required and GED is accepted *Academic units required:* 4 English, 3 math, 2

science, 1 science labs, 2 social studies, 3 history, *Academic units recommended:* 4 English, 4 math, 2 science, 2 science labs, 2 foreign language, 2 social studies, 3 history, 2 academic electives. **Freshman Admission Statistics:** 8,179 applied, 47.2% admitted, 19% enrolled. **Transfer Admission Requirements:** college transcript(s), essay or personal statement, Minimum college GPA of 2.7 required. Lowest grade transferable C-. **General Admission Information:** Application fee $50. Priority deadline 2/1. Nonfall registration accepted. Admission may be deferred for a maximum of 1 year.

COSTS AND FINANCIAL AID

Annual tuition $37,100. Room and board $12,510. Required fees $1,460. Average book expense $1,746. **Required Forms and Deadlines:** FAFSA; State aid form. **Types of Aid:** *Need-based scholarships/grants:* College/university scholarship or grant aid from institutional funds; Federal Pell; Private scholarships; SEOG; State scholarships/grants. *Loans:* Direct PLUS loans; Direct Subsidized Stafford Loans; Direct Unsubsidized Stafford Loans. *Student Employment:* Federal Work-Study Program available. Institutional employment available. **Financial Aid Statistics:** 70% needy freshmen, 67% needy undergrads receive need-based scholarship or grant aid. 99% freshmen, 99% undergrads receive non-need-based scholarship or grant aid. 93% freshmen, 93% undergrads receive need-based self-help aid. 0% freshmen, 0% undergrads receive athletic scholarships. 87% freshmen, 83% undergrads receive any aid. 82% undergrads borrow to pay for school. Average cumulative indebtedness $30,844. **Criteria for awarding aid:** *Need-based:* Academics *Non-need-based:* Academics, Alumni affiliation, Art, Leadership, Minority status, Music/drama, Religious affiliation.

THE UNIVERSITY OF LETHBRIDGE

4401 University Drive, Lethbridge, AB T1K 3M4
Phone: 403-382-7134 • **Financial Aid Phone:** 403-329-2585
E-mail: admissions@uleth.ca
Fax: 403-329-5159 • **Website:** www.uleth.ca • **ACT Code:** 5202

This public school was founded in 1967. It has a 576 acre campus.

RATINGS

Admissions Selectivity Rating: 68   **Fire Safety Rating:** 60*   **Green Rating:** 60*

STUDENTS AND FACULTY

Student Body: 10% out-of-state, (56 countries represented). Asian 0%, **Retention and Graduation:** 81% freshmen return for sophomore year.

ACADEMICS

Degrees: Bachelor's; Certificate; Diploma; Doctoral; Master's; Post-Bachelor's certificate; Post-Master's certificate **Classes:** Most classes have fewer than 10 students. Most lab/discussion sessions have fewer than 10 students. **Most popular majors:** Registered Nursing/Registered Nurse; Business Administration And Management, General; Accounting. **Special Study Options:** Accelerated program; Cooperative education program; Double major; Dual enrollment; English as a Second Language (ESL); Exchange student program (domestic); Independent study; Internships; Student-designed major; Study abroad; Teacher certification program. **Disability Services offered to physically disabled students:** Note-taking services; Reader services; Tape recorders; Tutors. **Career services:** Alumni services; Career assessment; Career/job search classes; Internships

FACILITIES

Housing: Apartments for married students; Apartments for single students; Coed dorms; Special housing for disabled students 100% of campus accessible to physically diasbled. **Special Academic Facilities/Equipment:** Art Gallery, Theatres. **Computers:** 100% of classrooms, 100% of libraries, 100% of dining areas, 100% of student union, have wireless network access. Students can register for classes online. Administrative functions (other than registration) can be performed online.

CAMPUS LIFE

Environment: City **Activities:** Choral groups; Concert band; Dance; Drama/theater; International Student Organization; Jazz band; Literary magazine; Music ensembles; Musical theater; Opera; Radio station; Student government; Student newspaper; Student-run film society; Symphony orchestra 1 fraternities, 1 sorority. **Athletics (Intercollegiate):** *Men:* basketball, ice hockey, soccer, swimming, track/field (outdoor). *Women:* basketball, ice hockey, rugby, soccer, swimming, track/field (outdoor).

ADMISSIONS

Test Scores: Minimum internet-based TOEFL 80. Minimum paper TOEFL 550. **Basis for Candidate Selection:** *Very important factors considered*

include: rigor of secondary school record. *Other factors considered include:* class rank, standardized test scores. **Freshman Admission Requirements:** High school diploma is required and GED is not accepted **Freshman Admission Statistics:** 2,997 applied, 84.3% admitted, 49% enrolled. **Transfer Admission Requirements:** college transcript(s). **General Admission Information:** Application fee $100. Priority deadline 3/1. Regular application deadline 6/30. Nonfall registration accepted. Admission may be deferred for a maximum of 1 semester.

COSTS AND FINANCIAL AID

Annual in-state tuition $6,268. Annual out-of-state tuition $4,974. Room and board $6,268. Required fees $1,015. **Required Forms and Deadlines:** Institution's own financial aid form. **Types of Aid:** *Need-based scholarships/grants:* Other (please specify). *Student Employment:* Institutional employment available. **Criteria for awarding aid:** *Non-need-based:* Academics, Athletics, Leadership.

UNIVERSITY OF LOUISIANA AT LAFAYETTE

P.O. Drawer 41008, Lafayette, LA 70504
Phone: 337-482-6553 • **Financial Aid Phone:** 337-482-6506
E-mail: enroll@louisiana.edu • **CEEB Code:** 6672
Fax: 337-482-1112 • **Website:** www.louisiana.edu • **ACT Code:** 1612

This public school was founded in 1898. It has a 1375 acre campus.

RATINGS

Admissions Selectivity Rating: 87   **Fire Safety Rating:** 94   **Green Rating:** 60*

STUDENTS AND FACULTY

Enrollment: 14,667. **Student Body:** 56% female, 44% male, 8% out-of-state, 2% international (101 countries represented). Asian 2%, African American 21%, Caucasian 68%, Hispanic 3%, Native American <1%, Pacific Islander <1%, Two or more races 2%, Race unknown 1%.
Retention and Graduation: 76% freshmen return for sophomore year.
Faculty: Student/faculty ratio 23:1. 598 full-time faculty, 62% hold PhDs, 20% are members of minority groups, 45% are women.

ACADEMICS

Degrees: Bachelor's; Doctoral; Master's; Post-Bachelor's certificate; Post-Master's certificate **Classes:** Most classes have 10-19 students. Most lab/discussion sessions have 10-19 students. **Most popular majors:** Biology/Biological Sciences, General; Nursing/Registered Nurse (Rn, Asn, Bsn, Msn); Business Administration And Management, General. **Special Study Options:** Accelerated program; Cooperative education program; Cross-registration; Distance learning; Double major; Dual enrollment; Exchange student program (domestic); Honors program; Independent study; Internships; Student-designed major; Study abroad; Teacher certification program. Honors programs: Honors Baccalaureate degree is available. **Disability Services offered to physically disabled students:** Note-taking services; Reader services; Tape recorders; Tutors. **Career services:** Career assessment; Career/job search classes

FACILITIES

Housing: Apartments for married students; Apartments for single students; Fraternity/sorority housing; Men's dorms; Women's dorms 85% of campus accessible to physically diasbled. **Special Academic Facilities/Equipment:** Art museum, experimental farm, primate center, CAD/CAM laboratory, marine research facility, on campus restaurant and hotel with instructional facilities, 2 nuclear accelerators, 2 electron microscopes, radio station and television production studio, nursery school laboratory, Louisiana Emersive Technologies Enterprise **Computers:** Students can register for classes online. Administrative functions (other than registration) can be performed online.

CAMPUS LIFE

Environment: City **Activities:** Campus Ministries; Choral groups; Concert band; Dance; Drama/theater; International Student Organization; Jazz band; Literary magazine; Marching band; Music ensembles; Musical theater; Opera; Radio station; Student government; Student newspaper; Symphony orchestra; Yearbook 155 registered organizations, 14 honor societies, 8 religious organizations. 11 fraternities, 9 sororities. **Athletics (Intercollegiate):** *Men:* baseball, basketball, cheerleading, cross-country, football, golf, tennis, track/field (outdoor), track/field (indoor). *Women:* basketball, cheerleading, cross-country, soccer, softball, tennis, track/field (outdoor), track/field (indoor),

volleyball. **On-Campus Highlights:** University Museum, Student Center, Cajun Field, Cajundome, Dupre Library

ADMISSIONS

Freshman Academic Profile: Average high school GPA 3.3. 19% in top 10% of high school class, 43% in top 25% of high school class, 74% in top 50% of high school class. **Test Scores:** SAT Math middle 50% range 490-590. SAT EBRW middle 50% range 470-590. ACT middle 50% range 21-25. Minimum paper TOEFL 525. **Basis for Candidate Selection:** *Very important factors considered include:* rigor of secondary school record, class rank, academic GPA, standardized test scores. *Other factors considered include:* state residency. **Freshman Admission Requirements:** High school diploma is required and GED is accepted *Academic units required:* 4 English, 4 math, 3 science, 2 foreign language, 1 social studies, 2 history, 1 visual/performing arts, and 1 unit from above areas or other academic areas. **Freshman Admission Statistics:** 9,386 applied, 55.8% admitted, 56% enrolled. **Transfer Admission Requirements:** college transcript(s), Lowest grade transferable D. **General Admission Information:** Application fee $25. Priority deadline 7/20. Nonfall registration accepted. Admission may be deferred for a maximum of 1 semester.

COSTS AND FINANCIAL AID

Annual in-state tuition $8,566. Annual out-of-state tuition $17,316. Room and board $8,566. Required fees $2,033. Average book expense $1,200. **Required Forms and Deadlines:** FAFSA. **Notification of Awards:** Applicants will be notified of awards on a rolling basis beginning 4/1. **Types of Aid:** *Need-based scholarships/grants:* College/university scholarship or grant aid from institutional funds; Federal Nursing Scholarships; Federal Pell; Private scholarships; SEOG; State scholarships/grants. *Student Employment:* Federal Work-Study Program available. Institutional employment available. **Financial Aid Statistics:** 96% needy freshmen, 88% needy undergrads receive need-based scholarship or grant aid. 15% freshmen, 9% undergrads receive non-need-based scholarship or grant aid. 49% freshmen, 60% undergrads receive need-based self-help aid. 2% freshmen, 3% undergrads receive athletic scholarships. 87% freshmen, 72% undergrads receive any aid. **Criteria for awarding aid:** *Need-based:* Job skills.

UNIVERSITY OF LOUISVILLE

2301 South Third Street, Louisville, KY 40292
Phone: 502-852-6531 • **Financial Aid Phone:** (502) 852-5511
E-mail: admitme@louisville.edu
Fax: 502-852-4776 • **Website:** www.louisville.edu • **ACT Code:** 1556

This public school was founded in 1798. It has a 640.12 acre campus.

RATINGS

Admissions Selectivity Rating: 81   **Fire Safety Rating:** 90   **Green Rating:** 88

STUDENTS AND FACULTY

Enrollment: 14,550. **Student Body:** 51% female, 49% male, 17% out-of-state, 1% international (58 countries represented). Asian 4%, African American 11%, Caucasian 73%, Hispanic 5%, Native American <1%, Pacific Islander <1%, Two or more races 5%, Race unknown <1%.
Retention and Graduation: 81% freshmen return for sophomore year. 31% freshmen graduate within 4 years. 54% freshmen graduate within 6 years.
Faculty: Student/faculty ratio 15:1. 936 full-time faculty, 88% hold PhDs, 23% are members of minority groups, 43% are women. 3% of classes are taught by teaching assistants.

ACADEMICS

Degrees: Associate; Bachelor's; Certificate; Doctoral/Professional; Doctoral/Research; Master's; Post-Bachelor's certificate; Post-Master's certificate **Classes:** Most classes have 20-29 students. Most lab/discussion sessions have 10-19 students. **Most popular majors:** Speech Communication And Rhetoric; Biology/Biological Sciences, General; Registered Nursing/Registered Nurse. **Special Study Options:** Accelerated program; Cooperative education program; Cross-registration; Distance learning; Double major; English as a Second Language (ESL); Exchange student program (domestic); Honors program; Independent study; Internships; Study abroad; Teacher certification program. Combined degree programs: BA/MA. **Disability Services offered to physically disabled students:** Note-taking services; Reader services; Tape recorders; Tutors. **Career services:** Alumni services; Career assessment; Career/job search classes; Internships

FACILITIES

Housing: Apartments for married students; Apartments for single students; Coed dorms; Fraternity/sorority housing; Men's dorms; Special housing for disabled student; Theme housing; Women's dorms 95% of campus accessible to physically diasbled. **Computers:** Administrative functions (other than registration) can be performed online.

CAMPUS LIFE

Environment: Metropolis **Activities:** Campus Ministries; Choral groups; Concert band; Dance; Drama/theater; International Student Organization; Jazz band; Literary magazine; Marching band; Music ensembles; Musical theater; Opera; Pep band; Student government; Student newspaper; Student-run film society; Symphony orchestra 237 registered organizations, 7 honor societies, 18 religious organizations. 13 fraternities, 10 sororities. **Athletics (Intercollegiate):** *Men:* baseball, basketball, cheerleading, cross-country, diving, football, golf, soccer, swimming, tennis, track/field (outdoor). *Women:* basketball, cheerleading, crew/rowing, cross-country, diving, field hockey, golf, lacrosse, soccer, softball, swimming, tennis, track/field (outdoor), volleyball.

ADMISSIONS

Freshman Academic Profile: Average high school GPA 3.6. 85% from public high schools. **Test Scores:** SAT Math middle 50% range 490-600. SAT EBRW middle 50% range 470-605. ACT middle 50% range 22-29. Minimum internet-based TOEFL 79-80. Minimum paper TOEFL 550. **Basis for Candidate Selection:** *Very important factors considered include:* rigor of secondary school record, academic GPA, standardized test scores. *Other factors considered include:* class rank, recommendation(s), extracurricular activities, talent/ability, state residency, racial/ethnic status, volunteer work, work experience. **Freshman Admission Requirements:** High school diploma is required and GED is accepted *Academic units required:* 4 English, 3 math, 3 science, 1 science labs, 2 foreign language, 3 social studies, 5 academic electives, 1 visual/performing arts, and 5 units from above areas or other academic areas. *Academic units recommended:* 4 math, 4 science, 3 foreign language. **Freshman Admission Statistics:** 10,767 applied, 75.6% admitted, 34% enrolled. **Transfer Admission Requirements:** college transcript(s), Minimum college GPA of 2.0 required. Lowest grade transferable D. **General Admission Information:** Application fee $25. Priority deadline 2/15. Regular application deadline 8/1. Nonfall registration accepted. Admission may be deferred.

COSTS AND FINANCIAL AID

Annual in-state tuition $8,374. Annual out-of-state tuition $26,090. Room and board $8,374. Required fees $196. Average book expense $1,200. **Required Forms and Deadlines:** FAFSA. **Types of Aid:** *Need-based scholarships/grants:* College/university scholarship or grant aid from institutional funds; Federal Pell; Private scholarships; SEOG; State scholarships/grants. *Loans:* Direct PLUS loans; Direct Subsidized Stafford Loans; Direct Unsubsidized Stafford Loans. *Student Employment:* Federal Work-Study Program available. Institutional employment available. **Financial Aid Statistics:** 96% needy freshmen, 89% needy undergrads receive need-based scholarship or grant aid. 20% freshmen, 13% undergrads receive non-need-based scholarship or grant aid. 54% freshmen, 63% undergrads receive need-based self-help aid. 4% freshmen, 3% undergrads receive athletic scholarships. 97% freshmen, 79% undergrads receive any aid. **Criteria for awarding aid:** *Non-need-based:* Academics, Art, Athletics, Leadership, Minority status, Music/drama, State/district residency.

UNIVERSITY OF LYNCHBURG

1501 Lakeside Drive, Lynchburg, VA 24501
Phone: 434-544-8300 • **Financial Aid Phone:** (434) 544-8230
E-mail: admissions@lynchburg.edu • **CEEB Code:** 5372
Fax: 434-544-8653 • **Website:** www.lynchburg.edu • **ACT Code:** 4368

This private school, affiliated with the Disciples of Christ Church, was founded in 1903. It has a 264 acre campus.

RATINGS

Admissions Selectivity Rating: 79   **Fire Safety Rating:** 80   **Green Rating:** 61

STUDENTS AND FACULTY

Enrollment: 1,978. **Student Body:** 60% female, 40% male, 49% out-of-state, 2% international (15 countries represented). Asian 1%, African American 10%, Caucasian 76%, Hispanic 4%, Native American <1%, Pacific Islander 0%, Two or more races 4%, Race unknown 2%.

Retention and Graduation: 75% freshmen return for sophomore year. 51% freshmen graduate within 4 years. 1% freshmen graduate within 6 years. 18% grads go on to further study within 1 year. 21% grads pursue arts and sciences degrees. 12% grads pursue business degrees. **Faculty:** Student/faculty ratio 11:1. 162 full-time faculty, 89% hold PhDs, 6% are members of minority groups, 54% are women. 0% of classes are taught by teaching assistants.

ACADEMICS

Degrees: Bachelor's; Doctoral Other; Doctoral/Professional; Doctoral/Research; Master's; Post-Bachelor's certificate; Post-Master's certificate **Classes:** Most classes have 10-19 students. Most lab/discussion sessions have 10-19 students. **Most popular majors:** Speech Communication And Rhetoric; Teacher Education And Professional Development, Specific Levels And Methods, Other; Registered Nursing, Nursing Administration, Nursing Research And Clinical Nursing. **Special Study Options:** Cross-registration; Distance learning; Double major; English as a Second Language (ESL); Honors program; Independent study; Internships; Study abroad; Teacher certification program. **Honors programs:** Westover Honors Program. **Disability Services offered to physically disabled students:** Note-taking services; Reader services; Tape recorders; Tutors. **Career services:** Alumni network; Alumni services; Career assessment; Career/job search classes; Internships; Regional alumni

FACILITIES

Housing: Apartments for single students; Coed dorms; Fraternity/sorority housing; Men's dorms; Special housing for disabled student; Special housing for international students; Theme housing; Wellness housing; Women's dorms 90% of campus accessible to physically diasbled. **Special Academic Facilities/Equipment:** Daura Art Gallery, Claytor Nature Study Center, Ramsey-Freer Herbarium, cadaver lab; Schewel Hall audio-visual and television studios, Dillard Fine Arts Center, Belk Observatory **Computers:** 20% of dorms, 100% of libraries, 100% of dining areas, 100% of student union, have wireless network access. Students can register for classes online. Administrative functions (other than registration) can be performed online.

CAMPUS LIFE

Environment: City **Activities:** Campus Ministries; Choral groups; Concert band; Dance; Drama/theater; International Student Organization; Jazz band; Literary magazine; Model UN; Music ensembles; Musical theater; Pep band; Student government; Student newspaper; Symphony orchestra 90 registered organizations, 14 honor societies, 10 religious organizations. 4 fraternities, 6 sororities. **Athletics (Intercollegiate):** *Men:* baseball, basketball, cheerleading, cross-country, golf, lacrosse, soccer, tennis, track/field (outdoor), track/field (indoor). *Women:* basketball, cheerleading, cross-country, equestrian sports, field hockey, lacrosse, soccer, softball, tennis, track/field (outdoor), track/field (indoor), volleyball. **On-Campus Highlights:** Shellenberger Field, Drysdale Student Center, Claytor Nature Study Center, Knight-Capron Library, Westover Room **Environmental Initiatives:** Recovery of College Lake. Working with the Army Corp of Engineers, and the state of Virginia, Lynchburg College is attempting to restore College Lake.

ADMISSIONS

Freshman Academic Profile: Average high school GPA 3.4. 80% from public high schools. **Test Scores:** SAT Math middle 50% range 490-580. SAT EBRW middle 50% range 510-600. ACT middle 50% range 19-24. Minimum internet-based TOEFL 78. Minimum paper TOEFL 550. **Basis for Candidate Selection:** *Very important factors considered include:* rigor of secondary school record, academic GPA, standardized test scores. *Important factors considered include:* interview. *Other factors considered include:* application essay, recommendation(s), extracurricular activities, talent/ability, character/personal qualities, volunteer work, work experience, level of applicant's interest. **Freshman Admission Requirements:** High school diploma is required and GED is accepted *Academic units required:* 4 English, 3 math, 3 science, 2 science labs, 2 foreign language, 2 social studies, 2 history, *Academic units recommended:* 4 English, 4 math, 4 science, 2 science labs, 3 foreign language, 2 social studies, 2 history, 1 academic elective. **Freshman Admission Statistics:** 4,880 applied, 74.5% admitted, 14% enrolled. **Transfer Admission Requirements:** college transcript(s), Minimum college GPA of 2.0 required. Lowest grade transferable C. **General Admission Information:** Application fee $30. Nonfall registration accepted. Admission may be deferred.

COSTS AND FINANCIAL AID

Annual tuition $36,720. Room and board $10,680. Required fees $970. Average book expense $1,200. **Required Forms and Deadlines:** FAFSA; State aid form. **Notification of Awards:** Applicants will be notified of awards on a rolling basis beginning 12/1. **Types of Aid:** *Need-based scholarships/grants:* College/university scholarship or grant aid from institutional funds; Federal Pell; SEOG. *Loans:* Direct PLUS loans; Direct Subsidized Stafford Loans; Direct Unsubsidized Stafford Loans. *Student Employment:* Federal Work-Study Program available. Institutional employment available. **Financial Aid Statistics:** 100% needy freshmen, 99% needy undergrads receive need-based scholarship or grant aid. 19% freshmen, 14% undergrads receive non-need-based scholarship or grant aid. 80% freshmen, 85% undergrads receive need-based self-help aid. 0% freshmen, 0% undergrads receive athletic scholarships. 80% freshmen, 74% undergrads receive any aid. 77% undergrads borrow to pay for school. Average cumulative indebtedness $35,614. **Criteria for awarding aid:** *Need-based:* Minority status, Religious affiliation *Non-need-based:* Academics, Art, Leadership, Music/drama, Religious affiliation, State/district residency.

UNIVERSITY OF MAINE

Best Colleges

168 College Ave, Orono, ME 04469-5713
Phone: 207-581-1561 • **Financial Aid Phone:** 207-581-1324
E-mail: umaineadmissions@maine.edu • **CEEB Code:** 3916
Fax: 207-581-1213 • **Website:** www.umaine.edu • **ACT Code:** 1664

This public school was founded in 1865. It has a 660 acre campus.

RATINGS
Admissions Selectivity Rating: 74   **Fire Safety Rating:** 98   **Green Rating:** 96

STUDENTS AND FACULTY
Enrollment: 8,836. **Student Body:** 47% female, 53% male, 35% out-of-state, 2% international (35 countries represented). Asian 2%, African American 2%, Caucasian 84%, Hispanic 4%, Native American 1%, Pacific Islander 0%, Two or more races 3%, Race unknown 2%.
Retention and Graduation: 75% freshmen return for sophomore year. 38% freshmen graduate within 4 years. 58% freshmen graduate within 6 years.
Faculty: Student/faculty ratio 16:1. 512 full-time faculty, 88% hold PhDs, 9% are members of minority groups, 39% are women. 8% of classes are taught by teaching assistants.

ACADEMICS
Degrees: Bachelor's; Doctoral; Doctoral/Research; Master's; Post-Bachelor's certificate; Post-Master's certificate **Classes:** Most classes have fewer than 10 students. Most lab/discussion sessions have 10-19 students. **Most popular majors:** Psychology, General; Registered Nursing/Registered Nurse; Business Administration And Management, General. **Special Study Options:** Accelerated program; Cooperative education program; Distance learning; Double major; Dual enrollment; English as a Second Language (ESL); Exchange student program (domestic); Honors program; Independent study; Internships; Liberal arts/career combination; Study abroad; Teacher certification program. Honors programs: UMaine's Honors College is a dynamic program offering students from Maine and beyond the advantages of both a great research university and a rigorous liberal arts education within a tight-knit community. Named a UMaine Signature Program "for strengths in research and education," the Honors College provides exemplary student-centered and community-engaged learning experiences for undergraduates as it prepares them for the 21st century workplace and society. One of the oldest and most respected Honors programs in the country, the tradition of personalized teaching of legendary Maine professors like Vincent Hartgen and Robert Thomson has been adapted to meet the needs of a growing number of in-state and out-of state students. The intellectual breadth and scholarly depth of the highly interdisciplinary faculty provide unique opportunities for our students. Small classes combined with the living-learning communities of Colvin and Balentine Halls provide Honors students with opportunities for engaged, interdisciplinary learning. The College continues to innovate, build capacity, create partnerships and enhance the lives of future leaders in business, science, education, and the arts. **Disability Services offered to physically disabled students:** Note-taking services; Reader services; Tape recorders; Tutors. **Career services:** Alumni network; Alumni services; Career assessment; Career/job search classes; Internships; Regional alumni

FACILITIES
Housing: Apartments for married students; Apartments for single students; Coed dorms; Fraternity/sorority housing; Special housing for disabled student; Special housing for international students; Theme housing; Wellness housing 90% of campus accessible to physically diasbled. **Special Academic Facilities/Equipment:** Emera Astronomy Center; Hudson Museum; Lord Hall Gallery; Innovative Media, Research and Commercialization Center; Wyeth Family Studio Art Center; Collins Center for the Arts; Minsky Recital Hall; Cyrus Pavilion; Fay Hyland Arboretum; Lyle E. Littlefield Ornamentals Trial Garden; Page Farm and Home Museum; Demeritt Forest; Alfond Arena and Stadium;

New Balance Student Recreation Center; Advanced Manufacturing Center; Franco-American Center; Foster Center for Student Innovation; Laboratory for Surface Science and Technology; and the Advanced Structures and Composites Center. **Computers:** 100% of classrooms, 10% of dorms, 100% of libraries, 100% of dining areas, 100% of student union, 50% of common outdoor areas have wireless network access. Students can register for classes online. Administrative functions (other than registration) can be performed online.

CAMPUS LIFE
Environment: Village **Activities:** Campus Ministries; Choral groups; Concert band; Dance; Drama/theater; International Student Organization; Jazz band; Literary magazine; Marching band; Music ensembles; Musical theater; Opera; Pep band; Radio station; Student government; Student newspaper; Student-run film society; Symphony orchestra 224 registered organizations, 42 honor societies, 7 religious organizations. 13 fraternities, 6 sororities. **Athletics (Intercollegiate):** *Men:* baseball, basketball, cross-country, diving, football, ice hockey, soccer, swimming, track/field (outdoor), track/field (indoor). *Women:* basketball, cross-country, diving, field hockey, ice hockey, soccer, softball, swimming, track/field (outdoor), track/field (indoor), volleyball. **On-Campus Highlights:** New Balance Student Recreation Center, Alfond Arena, Bear's Den, Collins Center for the Arts, The Mall (grass quad central to campus) **Environmental Initiatives:** UMaine has developed a master plan centered on sustainability, restoring habitat, avoiding sprawl, maximizing solar orientation, and reducing carbon emissions.

ADMISSIONS
Freshman Academic Profile: Average high school GPA 3.3. 18% in top 10% of high school class, 44% in top 25% of high school class, 76% in top 50% of high school class. **Test Scores:** SAT Math middle 50% range 520-620. SAT EBRW middle 50% range 530-630. ACT middle 50% range 22-27. Minimum internet-based TOEFL 79. Minimum paper TOEFL 550. **Basis for Candidate Selection:** *Very important factors considered include:* rigor of secondary school record, class rank, academic GPA, standardized test scores. *Important factors considered include:* application essay, recommendation(s). *Other factors considered include:* interview, extracurricular activities, talent/ability, character/personal qualities, volunteer work, work experience. **Freshman Admission Requirements:** High school diploma is required and GED is accepted *Academic units required:* 4 English, 3 math, 2 science, 2 science labs, 2 social studies, 4 academic electives, *Academic units recommended:* 4 English, 4 math, 4 science, 3 science labs, 2 foreign language, 2 social studies, 1 history, 4 academic electives. **Freshman Admission Statistics:** 13,231 applied, 92.3% admitted, 19% enrolled. **Transfer Admission Requirements:** High school transcript, college transcript(s), essay or personal statement, Minimum college GPA of 2.0 required. Lowest grade transferable C-. **General Admission Information:** Application fee $40. Priority deadline 2/1. Regular application deadline 2/1. Nonfall registration accepted. Admission may be deferred for a maximum of 2 semesters.

COSTS AND FINANCIAL AID
Annual in-state tuition $10,136. Annual out-of-state tuition $27,960. Room and board $10,136. Required fees $2,322. Average book expense $1,000. **Required Forms and Deadlines:** FAFSA. **Notification of Awards:** Applicants will be notified of awards on a rolling basis beginning 1/1. **Types of Aid:** *Need-based scholarships/grants:* College/university scholarship or grant aid from institutional funds; Federal Pell; Private scholarships; SEOG; State scholarships/grants. *Loans:* Direct PLUS loans; Direct Subsidized Stafford Loans; Direct Unsubsidized Stafford Loans. *Student Employment:* Federal Work-Study Program available. Institutional employment available. **Financial Aid Statistics:** 94% needy freshmen, 87% needy undergrads receive need-based scholarship or grant aid. 12% freshmen, 7% undergrads receive non-need-based scholarship or grant aid. 79% freshmen, 84% undergrads receive need-based self-help aid. 2% freshmen, 2% undergrads receive athletic scholarships. 93% freshmen, 83% undergrads receive any aid. Average cumulative indebtedness $34,923. **Criteria for awarding aid:** *Need-based:* Academics, Alumni affiliation, Art, Athletics, Job skills, Leadership, Minority status, Music/drama, Religious affiliation *Non-need-based:* Academics, Alumni affiliation, Art, Athletics, Job skills, Leadership, Minority status, Music/drama, Religious affiliation, State/district residency.

UNIVERSITY OF MAINE AT FARMINGTON

111 South Street, Farmington, ME 04938
Phone: 207-778-7050 • **Financial Aid Phone:** 207-778-7100
E-mail: umfadmit@maine.edu • **CEEB Code:** 3506
Fax: 207-778-8182 • **Website:** www.umf.maine.edu • **ACT Code:** 1640

This public school was founded in 1863. It has a 55 acre campus.

RATINGS

Admissions Selectivity Rating: 75   **Fire Safety Rating:** 91   **Green Rating:** 93

STUDENTS AND FACULTY

Enrollment: 1,741. **Student Body:** 66% female, 34% male, 16% out-of-state, <1% international (9 countries represented). Asian 1%, African American 2%, Caucasian 89%, Hispanic 2%, Native American <1%, Pacific Islander <1%, Two or more races 2%, Race unknown 3%.
Retention and Graduation: 72% freshmen return for sophomore year. 35% freshmen graduate within 4 years. 51% freshmen graduate within 6 years.
Faculty: Student/faculty ratio 13:1. 114 full-time faculty, 86% hold PhDs, 5% are members of minority groups, 61% are women. 0% of classes are taught by teaching assistants.

ACADEMICS

Degrees: Bachelor's; Certificate; Master's; Post-Bachelor's certificate **Classes:** Most classes have 20-29 students. Most lab/discussion sessions have 20-29 students. **Most popular majors:** Elementary Education And Teaching; Secondary Education And Teaching; Psychology, General. **Special Study Options:** Accelerated program; Cross-registration; Distance learning; Double major; Dual enrollment; Exchange student program (domestic); Honors program; Independent study; Internships; Liberal arts/career combination; Student-designed major; Study abroad; Teacher certification program. Honors programs: UMF Honors Program. **Disability Services offered to physically disabled students:** Note-taking services; Reader services; Tape recorders; Tutors. **Career services:** Alumni network; Alumni services; Career assessment; Career/job search classes; Internships; Regional alumni

FACILITIES

Housing: Coed dorms; Cooperative housing; Special housing for disabled student; Theme housing; Wellness housing; Women's dorms 95% of campus accessible to physically diasbled. **Special Academic Facilities/Equipment:** Astronomy Observatory, Alice James Books poetry journal, assistive learning center, and on-site nursery school and day care as a teaching environment **Computers:** 100% of classrooms, 100% of dorms, 100% of libraries, 100% of dining areas, 100% of student union, 100% of common outdoor areas have wireless network access. Students can register for classes online. Administrative functions (other than registration) can be performed online.

CAMPUS LIFE

Environment: Village **Activities:** Campus Ministries; Choral groups; Dance; Drama/theater; International Student Organization; Literary magazine; Music ensembles; Musical theater; Radio station; Student government; Student newspaper; Symphony orchestra; Television station; Yearbook 52 registered organizations, 3 honor societies, 3 religious organizations. **Athletics (Intercollegiate):** *Men:* baseball, basketball, cross-country, golf, soccer. *Women:* basketball, cross-country, field hockey, soccer, softball, volleyball. **On-Campus Highlights:** Recreation and Fitness Center, Emery Community Arts Center, Mantor Cafe/Mantor Library, Kalikow Education Center, Student Center & Beaver Lodge **Environmental Initiatives:** Completion of two LEED-certified buildings and a third building which meets most qualifications for LEED standard.

ADMISSIONS

Freshman Academic Profile: Average high school GPA 3.1. 14% in top 10% of high school class, 42% in top 25% of high school class, 84% in top 50% of high school class. 89% from public high schools. **Test Scores:** SAT Math middle 50% range 470-575. SAT EBRW middle 50% range 500-600. ACT middle 50% range 22-26. Minimum internet-based TOEFL 79. Minimum paper TOEFL 550. **Basis for Candidate Selection:** *Very important factors considered include:* rigor of secondary school record, academic GPA. *Important factors considered include:* class rank, application essay, recommendation(s). *Other factors considered include:* standardized test scores, interview, extracurricular activities, talent/ability, character/personal qualities, first generation, alumni/ae relation, geographical residence, state residency, volunteer work, work experience, level of applicant's interest. **Freshman Admission Requirements:** High school diploma is required and GED is accepted *Academic units required:* 4 English, 3 math, 3 science, 2 science labs, 3 social studies, *Academic units recommended:* 2 foreign language. **Freshman Admission Statistics:** 1,939 applied, 82.6% admitted, 27% enrolled. **Transfer Admission Requirements:**

High school transcript, college transcript(s), essay or personal statement, Minimum college GPA of 2.5 required. Lowest grade transferable c. **General Admission Information:** Nonfall registration accepted. Admission may be deferred for a maximum of one year.

COSTS AND FINANCIAL AID

Required Forms and Deadlines: FAFSA. **Notification of Awards:** Applicants will be notified of awards on a rolling basis beginning 2/1. **Types of Aid:** *Need-based scholarships/grants:* College/university scholarship or grant aid from institutional funds; Federal Pell; Private scholarships; SEOG; State scholarships/grants. *Loans:* Direct PLUS loans; Direct Subsidized Stafford Loans; Direct Unsubsidized Stafford Loans. *Student Employment:* Federal Work-Study Program available. Institutional employment available. **Financial Aid Statistics:** 96% needy freshmen, 93% needy undergrads receive need-based scholarship or grant aid. 7% freshmen, 4% undergrads receive non-need-based scholarship or grant aid. 86% freshmen, 90% undergrads receive need-based self-help aid. 0% freshmen, 0% undergrads receive athletic scholarships. 98% freshmen, 93% undergrads receive any aid. 89% undergrads borrow to pay for school. Average cumulative indebtedness $30,648. **Criteria for awarding aid:** *Non-need-based:* Academics, Leadership, Minority status, Music/drama, State/district residency.

UNIVERSITY OF MAINE AT MACHIAS

9 O Brien Avenue, Machias, ME 04654
Phone: 207-255-1318 • **Financial Aid Phone:** 207-255-1203
E-mail: ummadmissions@maine.edu • **CEEB Code:** 3956
Fax: 207-255-1363 • **Website:** www.umm.maine.edu • **ACT Code:** 1666

This public school was founded in 1909. It has a 42 acre campus.

RATINGS

Admissions Selectivity Rating: 72   **Fire Safety Rating:** 76   **Green Rating:** 60*

STUDENTS AND FACULTY

Enrollment: 554. **Student Body:** 65% female, 35% male, 24% out-of-state, 4% international (18 countries represented). Asian 1%, African American 1%, Caucasian 88%, Hispanic 2%, Native American 4%, Race unknown 0%.
Retention and Graduation: 73% freshmen return for sophomore year.
Faculty: Student/faculty ratio 15:1. 30 full-time faculty, 73% hold PhDs, 3% are members of minority groups, 33% are women. 0% of classes are taught by teaching assistants.

ACADEMICS

Degrees: Bachelor's **Classes:** Most classes have 10-19 students. Most lab/discussion sessions have 10-19 students. **Most popular majors:** Elementary Education And Teaching; Marine Biology And Biological Oceanography; Parks, Recreation And Leisure Facilities Management, General. **Special Study Options:** Cooperative education program; Distance learning; Double major; Dual enrollment; Honors program; Independent study; Internships; Student-designed major; Study abroad; Teacher certification program. **Disability Services offered to physically disabled students:** Reader services; Tape recorders; Tutors. **Career services:** Career assessment; Internships

FACILITIES

Housing: Coed dorms 85% of campus accessible to physically diasbled. **Special Academic Facilities/Equipment:** Art Gallery Book Arts Print Shop Geographic Information Systems Laboratory and Service Center **Computers:** 100% of classrooms, 100% of dorms, 100% of libraries, 100% of dining areas, 100% of student union, 100% of common outdoor areas have wireless network access. Students can register for classes online. Administrative functions (other than registration) can be performed online.

CAMPUS LIFE

Environment: Rural **Activities:** Campus Ministries; Choral groups; Dance; Drama/theater; Literary magazine; Music ensembles; Musical theater; Pep band; Radio station; Student government 38 registered organizations, 2 religious organizations. 5 fraternities, 4 sororities. **Athletics (Intercollegiate):** *Men:* basketball, soccer. *Women:* basketball, soccer, volleyball. **On-Campus Highlights:** Aquatics/Fitness Center/Gymnasium, Residence Halls, Wireless Computer Lab/Classroom, Performing Arts Center, Early Care and Education Center **Environmental Initiatives:** Green Council

ADMISSIONS

Freshman Academic Profile: 13% in top 10% of high school class, 24% in top 25% of high school class, 63% in top 50% of high school class. **Test Scores:** SAT Math middle 50% range 400-530. SAT EBRW middle 50% range

440-530. ACT middle 50% range 15-25. Minimum paper TOEFL 500. **Basis for Candidate Selection:** *Very important factors considered include:* rigor of secondary school record, application essay, recommendation(s), interview. *Important factors considered include:* class rank, standardized test scores, extracurricular activities. *Other factors considered include:* talent/ability, character/personal qualities, volunteer work, work experience. **Freshman Admission Requirements:** High school diploma is required and GED is accepted *Academic units required:* 4 English, 3 math, 2 science, 2 science labs, 2 social studies, *Academic units recommended:* 2 foreign language, 3 academic electives. **Freshman Admission Statistics:** 381 applied, 91.6% admitted, 32% enrolled. **Transfer Admission Requirements:** High school transcript, college transcript(s), statement of good standing from prior institution(s). Minimum college GPA of 2.0 required. Lowest grade transferable C-. **General Admission Information:** Application fee $40. Regular application deadline 8/15. Nonfall registration accepted. Admission may be deferred for a maximum of 1 year.

COSTS AND FINANCIAL AID

Annual in-state tuition $6,574. Annual out-of-state tuition $16,550. Room and board $6,574. Average book expense $650. **Required Forms and Deadlines:** FAFSA. **Notification of Awards:** Applicants will be notified of awards on a rolling basis beginning 3/1. **Types of Aid:** *Need-based scholarships/grants:* College/university scholarship or grant aid from institutional funds; Federal Pell; Private scholarships; SEOG; State scholarships/grants. *Loans: Student Employment:* Federal Work-Study Program available. Institutional employment available. **Financial Aid Statistics:** 97% needy freshmen, 87% needy undergrads receive need-based scholarship or grant aid. 9% freshmen, 6% undergrads receive non-need-based scholarship or grant aid. 81% freshmen, 81% undergrads receive need-based self-help aid. 0% freshmen, 0% undergrads receive athletic scholarships. 82% freshmen, 74% undergrads receive any aid. **Criteria for awarding aid:** *Need-based:* Academics, Art, Leadership *Non-need-based:* Academics, Alumni affiliation, Art, Leadership, Minority status, Music/drama, State/district residency.

UNIVERSITY OF MAINE—AUGUSTA

46 University Drive, Augusta, ME 04330
Phone: 207-621-3465 • **Financial Aid Phone:** 207-621-3455
E-mail: umaadm@maine.edu • **CEEB Code:** 3929
Fax: 207-621-3333 • **Website:** www.uma.edu • **ACT Code:** 1641

This public school was founded in 1965. It has a 159 acre campus.

RATINGS

Admissions Selectivity Rating: 67   **Fire Safety Rating:** 60*   **Green Rating:** 60*

STUDENTS AND FACULTY

Enrollment: 4,523. **Student Body:** 73% female, 27% male, 3% out-of-state, <1% international (5 countries represented). Asian 1%, African American 1%, Caucasian 85%, Hispanic 1%, Native American 2%, Pacific Islander <1%, Two or more races 2%, Race unknown 8%.
Retention and Graduation: 53% freshmen return for sophomore year. 40% grads go on to further study within 1 year. **Faculty:** Student/faculty ratio 18:1. 103 full-time faculty, 56% hold PhDs, 0% are members of minority groups, 58% are women. 0% of classes are taught by teaching assistants.

ACADEMICS

Degrees: Associate; Bachelor's; Certificate; Terminal Associate; Transfer Associate **Classes:** Most classes have 20-29 students. Most lab/discussion sessions have 10-19 students. **Most popular majors:** Social Sciences, General; Health Services/Allied Health/Health Sciences, General. **Special Study Options:** Cross-registration; Distance learning; Double major; Dual enrollment; Honors program; Independent study; Internships; Liberal arts/career combination; Student-designed major; Study abroad; Teacher certification program. Honors programs: UMA Honors Program—augments a student's academic and co-curricular experience. **Disability Services offered to physically disabled students:** Note-taking services. **Career services:** Career assessment; Career/job search classes

FACILITIES

Housing: 99% of campus accessible to physically diasbled. **Special Academic Facilities/Equipment:** Jewett Gallery, Katz Library, Student Center **Computers:** 100% of classrooms, 100% of libraries, 100% of dining areas, 100% of student union, 100% of common outdoor areas have wireless network access. Students can register for classes online. Administrative functions (other than registration) can be performed online.

CAMPUS LIFE

Environment: Village **Activities:** Drama/theater; International Student Organization; Jazz band; Literary magazine; Music ensembles; Pep band; Student government; Student newspaper 23 registered organizations, 1 honor society, 1 religious organization. **Athletics (Intercollegiate):** *Men:* basketball, golf. *Women:* basketball, golf, soccer. **On-Campus Highlights:** Katz Library, Student Center, Michael Klahr Holocaust Education Resource Center, Campus Center at UCB, Huskins Lounge at UCB **Environmental Initiatives:** Reduce—Reuse—Recycle program in place since 1990.

ADMISSIONS

Freshman Academic Profile: 95% from public high schools. **Test Scores:** Minimum paper TOEFL 500. **Basis for Candidate Selection:** *Important factors considered include:* rigor of secondary school record, academic GPA. *Other factors considered include:* class rank, application essay, standardized test scores, recommendation(s), interview, extracurricular activities, talent/ability, character/personal qualities, first generation. **Freshman Admission Requirements:** High school diploma is required and GED is accepted *Academic units required:* 4 English, 2 math, 2 science, 2 science labs, 2 social studies, 2 history, *Academic units recommended:* 3 math, 3 science. **Freshman Admission Statistics:** 875 applied, 93.4% admitted, 63% enrolled. **Transfer Admission Requirements:** college transcript(s), Minimum college GPA of 2.0 required. Lowest grade transferable C. **General Admission Information:** Application fee $40. Priority deadline 6/15. Regular application deadline 8/15. Nonfall registration accepted. Admission may be deferred for a maximum of 1 year.

COSTS AND FINANCIAL AID

Annual out-of-state tuition $15,750. Required fees $938. **Required Forms and Deadlines:** FAFSA. **Notification of Awards:** Applicants will be notified of awards on a rolling basis beginning 3/15. **Types of Aid:** *Need-based scholarships/grants:* College/university scholarship or grant aid from institutional funds; Federal Pell; Private scholarships; SEOG; State scholarships/grants. *Loans:* Direct PLUS loans; Direct Subsidized Stafford Loans; Direct Unsubsidized Stafford Loans. *Student Employment:* Federal Work-Study Program available. Institutional employment available. **Financial Aid Statistics:** 87% needy freshmen, 86% needy undergrads receive need-based scholarship or grant aid. 0% freshmen, 1% undergrads receive non-need-based scholarship or grant aid. 81% freshmen, 90% undergrads receive need-based self-help aid. 0% freshmen, 0% undergrads receive athletic scholarships. 64% freshmen, 72% undergrads receive any aid. **Criteria for awarding aid:** *Non-need-based:* Academics, Athletics, Leadership, Music/drama, State/district residency.

UNIVERSITY OF MAINE—FORT KENT

23 University Drive, Fort Kent, ME 04743
Phone: 888-879-8635 • **Financial Aid Phone:** 207-834-7607
E-mail: umfkadm@maine.maine.edu • **CEEB Code:** 3393
Fax: 207-834-7609 • **Website:** www.umfk.maine.edu • **ACT Code:** 1642

This public school was founded in 1878. It has a 52 acre campus.

RATINGS

Admissions Selectivity Rating: 71   **Fire Safety Rating:** 99   **Green Rating:** 63

STUDENTS AND FACULTY

Enrollment: 1,036. **Student Body:** 73% female, 27% male, 14% out-of-state, 7% international. Asian 1%, African American 3%, Caucasian 79%, Hispanic 3%, Native American 1%, Pacific Islander <1%, Two or more races 3%, Race unknown 3%.
Retention and Graduation: 61% freshmen return for sophomore year. 19% freshmen graduate within 4 years. 33% freshmen graduate within 6 years. 5% grads go on to further study within 1 year. 3% grads pursue arts and sciences degrees. **Faculty:** Student/faculty ratio 14:1. 34 full-time faculty, 44% hold PhDs, 3% are members of minority groups, 41% are women. 0% of classes are taught by teaching assistants.

ACADEMICS

Degrees: Associate; Bachelor's; Certificate **Classes:** Most classes have 20-29 students. Most lab/discussion sessions have 10-19 students. **Most popular majors:** Behavioral Sciences; Registered Nursing, Nursing Administration, Nursing Research And Clinical Nursing; Business/Commerce, General. **Special Study Options:** Cross-registration; Distance learning; Double major; Independent study; Internships; Student-designed major; Study abroad; Teacher certification program. **Disability Services offered to physically disabled students:** Note-taking services; Reader services; Tape recorders;

Tutors. **Career services:** Alumni services; Career assessment; Career/job search classes; Internships

FACILITIES

Housing: Coed dorms 90% of campus accessible to physically diasbled. **Computers:** 100% of classrooms, 100% of dorms, 100% of libraries, 100% of dining areas, 100% of student union, 100% of common outdoor areas have wireless network access. Students can register for classes online. Administrative functions (other than registration) can be performed online.

CAMPUS LIFE

Environment: Rural **Activities:** Campus Ministries; Drama/theater; Student government 25 registered organizations, 1 honor society, 1 religious organization. 1 sororities. **Athletics (Intercollegiate):** *Men:* basketball, cross-country, golf, skiing (downhill/alpine), skiing (nordic/cross-country), soccer. *Women:* basketball, cross-country, golf, skiing (downhill/alpine), skiing (nordic/cross-country), soccer, volleyball. **On-Campus Highlights:** Bengal's Lair, The Lodge (res hall), Library, Learning Center

ADMISSIONS

Freshman Academic Profile: Average high school GPA 3.0. 9% in top 10% of high school class, 24% in top 25% of high school class, 68% in top 50% of high school class. 96% from public high schools. **Test Scores:** SAT Math middle 50% range 410-560. SAT EBRW middle 50% range 450-550. ACT middle 50% range 17-22. Minimum paper TOEFL 500. **Basis for Candidate Selection:** *Very important factors considered include:* level of applicant's interest. *Important factors considered include:* rigor of secondary school record, class rank, academic GPA, application essay, recommendation(s), talent/ability, character/personal qualities, first generation, geographical residence, state residency, volunteer work. *Other factors considered include:* standardized test scores, interview, extracurricular activities, alumni/ae relation, work experience. **Freshman Admission Requirements:** High school diploma is required and GED is accepted *Academic units required:* 4 English, 2 math, 2 science, 2 science labs, *Academic units recommended:* 2 foreign language. **Freshman Admission Statistics:** 572 applied, 97.2% admitted, 24% enrolled. **Transfer Admission Requirements:** High school transcript, college transcript(s), essay or personal statement, Lowest grade transferable C-. **General Admission Information:** Application fee $40. Regular application deadline 8/15. Nonfall registration accepted. Admission may be deferred.

COSTS AND FINANCIAL AID

Annual in-state tuition $7,910. Annual out-of-state tuition $11,190. Room and board $7,910. Required fees $1,125. Average book expense $500. **Required Forms and Deadlines:** CSS/Financial Aid PROFILE; FAFSA; Institution's own financial aid form; State aid form. **Notification of Awards:** Applicants will be notified of awards on a rolling basis beginning 3/15. **Types of Aid:** *Need-based scholarships/grants:* College/university scholarship or grant aid from institutional funds; Federal Nursing Scholarships; Federal Pell; Private scholarships; SEOG; State scholarships/grants. *Loans:* Direct PLUS loans; Direct Subsidized Stafford Loans; Direct Unsubsidized Stafford Loans. *Student Employment:* Federal Work-Study Program available. Institutional employment available. **Financial Aid Statistics:** 100% needy freshmen, 94% needy undergrads receive need-based scholarship or grant aid. 4% freshmen, 4% undergrads receive non-need-based scholarship or grant aid. 77% freshmen, 84% undergrads receive need-based self-help aid. 0% freshmen, 0% undergrads receive athletic scholarships. 78% freshmen, 58% undergrads receive any aid. 66% undergrads borrow to pay for school. Average cumulative indebtedness $29,910. **Criteria for awarding aid:** *Need-based:* Academics, Leadership *Non-need-based:* Academics, Alumni affiliation, Job skills, Leadership, State/district residency.

UNIVERSITY OF MAINE—PRESQUE ISLE

181 Main Street, Presque Isle, ME 04769
Phone: 207-768-9532 • **Financial Aid Phone:** 207-768-9510
E-mail: admissions@umpi.edu • **CEEB Code:** 3008
Fax: 207-768-9777 • **Website:** www.umpi.edu

This public school was founded in 1903. It has a 150 acre campus.

RATINGS

Admissions Selectivity Rating: 73   **Fire Safety Rating:** 84   **Green Rating:** 63

STUDENTS AND FACULTY

Enrollment: 833. **Student Body:** 62% female, 38% male, 4% out-of-state, 8% international (3 countries represented). Asian <1%, African American 3%, Caucasian 79%, Hispanic 2%, Native American 3%, Pacific Islander 0%, Two or more races 3%, Race unknown 4%.

Retention and Graduation: 65% freshmen return for sophomore year. **Faculty:** Student/faculty ratio 15:1. 42 full-time faculty, 64% hold PhDs, 5% are members of minority groups, 48% are women. 0% of classes are taught by teaching assistants.

ACADEMICS

Degrees: Associate; Bachelor's; Certificate **Classes:** Most classes have 10-19 students. **Most popular majors:** Elementary Education And Teaching; Liberal Arts And Sciences/Liberal Studies; Business/Commerce, General. **Special Study Options:** Accelerated program; Distance learning; Double major; Dual enrollment; Exchange student program (domestic); Honors program; Independent study; Internships; Study abroad; Teacher certification program. Honors programs: **Disability Services offered to physically disabled students:** Note-taking services; Reader services; Tape recorders; Tutors. **Career services:** Alumni services; Career assessment; Career/job search classes; Internships

FACILITIES

Housing: Apartments for married students; Coed dorms; Special housing for disabled students 100% of campus accessible to physically diasbled. **Special Academic Facilities/Equipment:** Art Gallery and Gentile Hall **Computers:** Students can register for classes online. Administrative functions (other than registration) can be performed online.

CAMPUS LIFE

Environment: Village **Activities:** Campus Ministries; Dance; International Student Organization; Radio station; Student government; Student newspaper 27 registered organizations, 1 honor society, 1 religious organization. 1 fraternity, 1 sorority. **Athletics (Intercollegiate):** *Men:* baseball, basketball, cross-country, golf, skiing (nordic/cross-country), soccer. *Women:* basketball, cross-country, skiing (nordic/cross-country), soccer, softball, volleyball. **On-Campus Highlights:** Caroline D. Gentile Hall, Campus Center, Center for Innovative Learning, Fitness Center, Owl's Nest

ADMISSIONS

Freshman Academic Profile: Average high school GPA 3.0. 3% in top 10% of high school class, 15% in top 25% of high school class, 45% in top 50% of high school class. **Test Scores:** SAT Math middle 50% range 397-532. SAT EBRW middle 50% range 394-528. ACT middle 50% range 18-23. Minimum internet-based TOEFL 71. Minimum paper TOEFL 530. **Basis for Candidate Selection:** *Very important factors considered include:* rigor of secondary school record. *Important factors considered include:* academic GPA, application essay, recommendation(s). *Other factors considered include:* class rank, standardized test scores, interview, extracurricular activities, talent/ability, character/personal qualities, first generation, alumni/ae relation, volunteer work, work experience, level of applicant's interest. **Freshman Admission Requirements:** High school diploma is required and GED is accepted *Academic units recommended:* 4 English, 3 math, 2 science, 2 science labs, 2 foreign language, 3 social studies, 2 academic electives. **Freshman Admission Statistics:** 1,442 applied, 77.1% admitted, 7% enrolled. **Transfer Admission Requirements:** High school transcript, college transcript(s), essay or personal statement, statement of good standing from prior institution(s). Minimum college GPA of 2.0 required. Lowest grade transferable c-. **General Admission Information:** Application fee $40. Nonfall registration accepted. Admission may be deferred.

COSTS AND FINANCIAL AID

Annual in-state tuition $8,044. Annual out-of-state tuition $9,900. Room and board $8,044. Required fees $700. Average book expense $900. **Required Forms and Deadlines:** FAFSA. **Notification of Awards:** Applicants will be notified of awards on a rolling basis beginning 3/1. **Types of Aid:** *Need-based scholarships/grants:* College/university scholarship or grant aid from institutional funds; Federal Pell; Private scholarships; SEOG; State scholarships/grants. *Loans:* Direct PLUS loans; Direct Subsidized Stafford Loans; Direct Unsubsidized Stafford Loans. *Student Employment:* Federal Work-Study Program available. Institutional employment available. **Financial Aid Statistics:** 99% needy freshmen, 98% needy undergrads receive need-based scholarship or grant aid. 7% freshmen, 5% undergrads receive non-need-based scholarship or grant aid. 74% freshmen, 77% undergrads receive need-based self-help aid. 0% freshmen, 0% undergrads receive athletic scholarships. 83% freshmen, 76% undergrads receive any aid. 84% undergrads borrow to pay for school. Average cumulative indebtedness $25,713. **Criteria for awarding aid:** *Non-need-based:* Academics.

UNIVERSITY OF MARY HARDIN-BAYLOR

900 College St, Belton, TX 76513
Phone: 254-295-4520 • **Financial Aid Phone:** 254-295-4517
E-mail: admissions@umhb.edu • **CEEB Code:** 3588
Fax: 254-295-5049 • **Website:** www.umhb.edu • **ACT Code:** 4128

This private school, affiliated with the Baptist Church, was founded in 1845. It has a 125 acre campus.

RATINGS

Admissions Selectivity Rating: 74   **Fire Safety Rating:** 79   **Green Rating:** 60*

STUDENTS AND FACULTY

Enrollment: 3,173. **Student Body:** 63% female, 37% male, 2% out-of-state, 2% international (12 countries represented). Asian 2%, African American 15%, Caucasian 57%, Hispanic 20%, Native American 1%, Pacific Islander <1%, Two or more races 3%, Race unknown 1%.
Retention and Graduation: 69% freshmen return for sophomore year.
Faculty: Student/faculty ratio 19:1. 167 full-time faculty, 74% hold PhDs, 14% are members of minority groups, 55% are women. 0% of classes are taught by teaching assistants.

ACADEMICS

Degrees: Bachelor's; Doctoral/Professional; Doctoral/Research; Master's; Post-Master's certificate **Classes:** Most classes have 10-19 students. Most lab/discussion sessions have 10-19 students. **Most popular majors:** Elementary Education And Teaching; Registered Nursing/Registered Nurse. **Special Study Options:** Distance learning; Double major; Dual enrollment; English as a Second Language (ESL); Honors program; Independent study; Internships; Study abroad; Teacher certification program. Honors programs: Lower Level Honors Program—approximately the top 10% of UMHB's entering freshman class. Freshman year offerings include English and religion, and sophomore year offerings are interdisciplinary courses in the humanities and social sciences. Upper Level Honors Program—Minimum requirements for completion of this program is the completion of three upper level courses designated as honors level and the completion of HNRS 3110 "Great Books and Ideas" and HNRS 3120 "living Issues". Successful completion of these requirements will allow the student to graduate with the cum laude designation. To receive the higher designations of magna cum laude or summa cum laude, the student must also successfully complete an Honors Research Project. This project must include original research and both written and oral presentations of that research to the Honors Committee. **Disability Services offered to physically disabled students:** Note-taking services; Reader services; Tape recorders; Tutors.
Career services: Alumni network; Alumni services; Career assessment; Career/job search classes; Internships; Regional alumni

FACILITIES

Housing: Apartments for single students; Men's dorms; Special housing for disabled student; Women's dorms 85% of campus accessible to physically disabled. **Special Academic Facilities/Equipment:** Language lab **Computers:** 100% of classrooms, 100% of dorms, 100% of libraries, 100% of dining areas, 100% of student union, 80% of common outdoor areas have wireless network access. Students can register for classes online. Administrative functions (other than registration) can be performed online.

CAMPUS LIFE

Environment: Town **Activities:** Campus Ministries; Choral groups; Concert band; Drama/theater; International Student Organization; Jazz band; Literary magazine; Model UN; Music ensembles; Musical theater; Opera; Pep band; Student government; Student newspaper; Student-run film society; Yearbook .51 registered organizations, 5 honor societies, 7 religious organizations. **Athletics (Intercollegiate):** *Men:* baseball, basketball, football, golf, soccer, tennis. *Women:* basketball, golf, soccer, softball, tennis, volleyball. **On-Campus Highlights:** Isabelle Rutherford Meyer Nursing Education Center, Baugh Center for the Visual Arts, Crusader Stadium, Bawcom Student Union Building, Mayborn Campus Center (exercise/fitness facilities)

ADMISSIONS

Freshman Academic Profile: Average high school GPA 3.6. 20% in top 10% of high school class, 50% in top 25% of high school class, 84% in top 50% of high school class. **Test Scores:** SAT Math middle 50% range 470-570. SAT EBRW middle 50% range 460-560. ACT middle 50% range 20-26. **Basis for Candidate Selection:** *Very important factors considered include:* class rank, standardized test scores. *Important factors considered include:* academic GPA. *Other factors considered include:* rigor of secondary school record, application essay, recommendation(s), interview, extracurricular activities, talent/ability, character/personal qualities, first generation, alumni/ae relation, geographical

residence, state residency, religious affiliation/commitment, racial/ethnic status, volunteer work, work experience, level of applicant's interest. **Freshman Admission Requirements:** High school diploma is required and GED is accepted *Academic units required:* 4 English, 3 math, 3 science, 2 foreign language, 3.5 social studies. **Freshman Admission Statistics:** 7,504 applied, 80.4% admitted, 12% enrolled. **Transfer Admission Requirements:** college transcript(s), Minimum college GPA of 2.0 required. Lowest grade transferable C. **General Admission Information:** Application fee $35. Nonfall registration accepted. Admission may be deferred for a maximum of 1 semester.

COSTS AND FINANCIAL AID

Required Forms and Deadlines: FAFSA. **Notification of Awards:** Applicants will be notified of awards on a rolling basis beginning 2/15. **Types of Aid:** *Need-based scholarships/grants:* College/university scholarship or grant aid from institutional funds; Federal Nursing Scholarships; Federal Pell; Private scholarships; SEOG; State scholarships/grants. *Loans:* Direct PLUS loans; Direct Subsidized Stafford Loans; Direct Unsubsidized Stafford Loans. *Student Employment:* Federal Work-Study Program available. Institutional employment available. **Financial Aid Statistics:** 100% needy freshmen, 99% needy undergrads receive need-based scholarship or grant aid. 7% freshmen, 5% undergrads receive non-need-based scholarship or grant aid. 83% freshmen, 84% undergrads receive need-based self-help aid. 0% freshmen, 0% undergrads receive athletic scholarships. 84% freshmen, 87% undergrads receive any aid. 78% undergrads borrow to pay for school. Average cumulative indebtedness $35,011. **Criteria for awarding aid:** *Need-based:* Academics, Alumni affiliation, Art, Job skills, Leadership, Music/drama, Religious affiliation.

UNIVERSITY OF MARY WASHINGTON

1301 College Avenue, Fredericksburg, VA 22401
Phone: 540-654-2000 • **Financial Aid Phone:** 540-654-2468
E-mail: admit@umw.edu • **CEEB Code:** 5398
Fax: 540-654-1857 • **Website:** www.umw.edu • **ACT Code:** 4414

This public school was founded in 1908. It has a 234 acre campus.

RATINGS

Admissions Selectivity Rating: 81   **Fire Safety Rating:** 93   **Green Rating:** 82

STUDENTS AND FACULTY

Enrollment: 4,366. **Student Body:** 64% female, 36% male, 8% out-of-state, 1% international (50 countries represented). Asian 4%, African American 8%, Caucasian 69%, Hispanic 9%, Native American <1%, Pacific Islander <1%, Two or more races 6%, Race unknown 3%.
Retention and Graduation: 84% freshmen return for sophomore year. 60% freshmen graduate within 4 years. 71% freshmen graduate within 6 years. 15% grads go on to further study within 1 year. 10% grads pursue arts and sciences degrees, 1% grads pursue law degrees. 1% grads pursue business degrees. 1% grads pursue medical degrees. **Faculty:** Student/faculty ratio 14:1. 251 full-time faculty, 86% hold PhDs, 19% are members of minority groups, 49% are women. 0% of classes are taught by teaching assistants.

ACADEMICS

Degrees: Bachelor's; Certificate; Master's; Post-Bachelor's certificate **Classes:** Most classes have fewer than 10 students. **Most popular majors:** Biology/Biological Sciences, General; Psychology, General; Business Administration And Management, General. **Special Study Options:** Accelerated program; Distance learning; Double major; Honors program; Independent study; Internships; Student-designed major; Study abroad; Teacher certification program. Honors programs: UMW's honors program offers highly motivated and advanced undergraduates the opportunity to enhance their intellectual growth through rigorous honors-designated coursework, interdisciplinary seminars, strong internship experiences, extended research and creative projects, and intriguing community service endeavors. **Career services:** Alumni network; Alumni services; Career assessment; Career/job search classes; Internships; Regional alumni

FACILITIES

Housing: Apartments for single students; Coed dorms; Men's dorms; Special housing for disabled student; Special housing for international students; Theme housing; Wellness housing; Women's dorms 75% of campus accessible to physically disabled. **Special Academic Facilities/Equipment:** Two art galleries, Center for Historic Preservation, language labs, Leidecker Center for Asian Studies, cartography lab, greenhouse. **Computers:** 100% of classrooms, 100% of dorms, 100% of libraries, 100% of dining areas, 100% of student union, 5% of common outdoor areas have wireless network access. Students can register for classes online. Administrative functions (other than registration) can be performed online.

CAMPUS LIFE

Environment: City **Activities:** Campus Ministries; Choral groups; Concert band; Dance; Drama/theater; International Student Organization; Jazz band; Literary magazine; Model UN; Music ensembles; Musical theater; Radio station; Student government; Student newspaper; Student-run film society; Symphony orchestra; Yearbook 120 registered organizations, 23 honor societies, 10 religious organizations. **Athletics (Intercollegiate):** *Men:* baseball, basketball, crew/rowing, cross-country, equestrian sports, lacrosse, soccer, swimming, tennis, track/field (outdoor), track/field (indoor). *Women:* basketball, crew/rowing, cross-country, equestrian sports, field hockey, lacrosse, soccer, softball, swimming, tennis, track/field (outdoor), track/field (indoor), volleyball. **On-Campus Highlights:** Ball Circle, University Center, Hurley Convergence Center, Palmieri Plaza Fountain, Lee Hall **Environmental Initiatives:** In July 2010, UMW adopted sustainability policies and practices committing to reducing solid waste, conserving energy and water, encouraging the purchasing of products to promote sustainability and promote alternative methods of transportation.

ADMISSIONS

Freshman Academic Profile: Average high school GPA 3.6. 16% in top 10% of high school class, 46% in top 25% of high school class, 85% in top 50% of high school class. 77% from public high schools. **Test Scores:** SAT Math middle 50% range 530-610. SAT EBRW middle 50% range 550-654. ACT middle 50% range 22-27. Minimum internet-based TOEFL 80. Minimum paper TOEFL 570. **Basis for Candidate Selection:** *Very important factors considered include:* rigor of secondary school record, academic GPA. *Important factors considered include:* class rank, application essay, standardized test scores, recommendation(s). *Other factors considered include:* interview, extracurricular activities, talent/ability, character/personal qualities, first generation, alumni/ae relation, geographical residence, state residency, racial/ethnic status, volunteer work, work experience, level of applicant's interest. **Freshman Admission Requirements:** High school diploma is required and GED is accepted *Academic units required:* 4 English, 3 math, 3 science, 3 science labs, 3 foreign language, 3 social studies, 3 history, *Academic units recommended:* 4 English, 4 math, 4 science, 4 science labs, 4 foreign language, 2 social studies, 2 history. **Freshman Admission Statistics:** 5,977 applied, 73.5% admitted, 22% enrolled. **Transfer Admission Requirements:** High school transcript, college transcript(s), essay or personal statement, statement of good standing from prior institution(s). Minimum college GPA of 2.0 required. Lowest grade transferable C. **General Admission Information:** Application fee $50. Priority deadline 2/1. Regular application deadline 2/1. Nonfall registration accepted. Admission may be deferred for a maximum of one year.

COSTS AND FINANCIAL AID

Annual in-state tuition $11,118. Annual out-of-state tuition $20,362. Room and board $11,118. Required fees $5,858. Average book expense $1,200. **Required Forms and Deadlines:** FAFSA. **Notification of Awards:** Applicants will be notified of awards on a rolling basis beginning 12/1. **Types of Aid:** *Need-based scholarships/grants:* College/university scholarship or grant aid from institutional funds; Federal Pell; Private scholarships; SEOG; State scholarships/grants. *Loans:* Direct PLUS loans; Direct Subsidized Stafford Loans; Direct Unsubsidized Stafford Loans. *Student Employment:* Federal Work-Study Program available. Institutional employment available. **Financial Aid Statistics:** 66% needy freshmen, 64% needy undergrads receive need-based scholarship or grant aid. 70% freshmen, 41% undergrads receive non-need-based scholarship or grant aid. 74% freshmen, 81% undergrads receive need-based self-help aid. 0% freshmen, 0% undergrads receive athletic scholarships. 67% freshmen, 63% undergrads receive any aid. 51% undergrads borrow to pay for school. Average cumulative indebtedness $19,444. **Criteria for awarding aid:** *Need-based:* Academics, Art, Music/drama *Non-need-based:* Academics, Alumni affiliation, Art, Leadership, Music/drama, State/district residency.

UNIVERSITY OF MARYLAND, BALTIMORE COUNTY

1000 Hilltop Circle, Baltimore, MD 21250
Phone: 410-455-2292 • **Financial Aid Phone:** 410-455-2387
E-mail: admissions@umbc.edu • **CEEB Code:** 5835
Fax: 410-455-1094 • **Website:** www.umbc.edu • **ACT Code:** 1751

This public school was founded in 1966. It has a 530 acre campus.

RATINGS

Admissions Selectivity Rating: 87   **Fire Safety Rating:** 98   **Green Rating:** 74

STUDENTS AND FACULTY

Enrollment: 11,129. **Student Body:** 45% female, 55% male, 5% out-of-state, 4% international (96 countries represented). Asian 22%, African American 18%, Caucasian 41%, Hispanic 7%, Native American <1%, Pacific Islander <1%, Two or more races 4%, Race unknown 3%.
Retention and Graduation: 88% freshmen return for sophomore year. 38% freshmen graduate within 4 years. 64% freshmen graduate within 6 years. 49% grads go on to further study within 1 year. 30% grads pursue arts and sciences degrees. 1.4% grads pursue law degrees. 2% grads pursue business degrees. 4.7% grads pursue medical degrees. **Faculty:** Student/faculty ratio 18:1. 546 full-time faculty, 85% hold PhDs, 26% are members of minority groups, 48% are women. 2% of classes are taught by teaching assistants.

ACADEMICS

Degrees: Bachelor's; Certificate; Doctoral; Doctoral/Research; Master's; Post-Bachelor's certificate **Classes:** Most classes have 10-19 students. Most lab/discussion sessions have 10-19 students. **Most popular majors:** Computer And Information Sciences, General; Biology/Biological Sciences, General; Psychology, Other. **Special Study Options:** Accelerated program; Cooperative education program; Cross-registration; Double major; Dual enrollment; English as a Second Language (ESL); Honors program; Independent study; Internships; Liberal arts/career combination; Student-designed major; Study abroad; Teacher certification program. Honors programs: UMBC Honors College, Meyerhoff (Science, Technology, Engineering, and Mathematics), Scholars Program, Sherman Teacher Education Scholars Program, Sondheim Scholars Programs, Center for Women and Information Technology (CWIT) Scholars Program, Humanities Scholars Program, Linehan Scholars Program, Cyber Scholars Progam Combined degree programs: BA/MA; BA/MEng. **Disability Services offered to physically disabled students:** Note-taking services; Reader services; Tape recorders; Tutors. **Career services:** Alumni network; Alumni services; Career assessment; Career/job search classes; Internships; Regional alumni

FACILITIES

Housing: Coed dorms; Special housing for disabled student; Special housing for international students; Theme housing 95% of campus accessible to physically diasbled. **Special Academic Facilities/Equipment:** Albin O. Kuhn Library and Gallery, Center for Art and Visual Culture, Women's Center, Center for Environmental Science, Center for Photonics Technology, Center for Women and Information Technology, Center on Research and Teaching in Social Work, Howard Hughes Medical Institute at UMBC, Imaging Research Center, Institute for Global Electronic Commerce, Joint Center for Earth Systems Technology, Laboratory for Healthcare Informatics, Maryland Center for Telecommunications Research, Maryland Institute for Policy Analysis and Research, bwtech@umbc Research and Technology Park and Incubator and Accelerator, Shriver Center, UMBC Technology Center, Goddard Earth Science and Technology Center. **Computers:** 100% of classrooms, 80% of dorms, 100% of libraries, 100% of dining areas, 100% of student union, 40% of common outdoor areas have wireless network access. Students can register for classes online. Administrative functions (other than registration) can be performed online.

CAMPUS LIFE

Environment: Metropolis **Activities:** Campus Ministries; Choral groups; Concert band; Dance; Drama/theater; International Student Organization; Jazz band; Literary magazine; Marching band; Model UN; Music ensembles; Musical theater; Opera; Pep band; Radio station; Student government; Student newspaper; Student-run film society; Symphony orchestra 230 registered organizations, 8 honor societies, 20 religious organizations. 11 fraternities, 12 sororities. **Athletics (Intercollegiate):** *Men:* baseball, basketball, cheerleading, cross-country, diving, lacrosse, soccer, swimming, tennis, track/field (outdoor), track/field (indoor). *Women:* basketball, cheerleading, cross-country, diving, lacrosse, soccer, softball, swimming, tennis, track/field (outdoor), track/field (indoor), volleyball. **On-Campus Highlights:** Albin O. Kuhn Library and Gallery, The Commons (Student Center), Perfoming Arts and Humanities Building, Howard Hughes Medical Institute Lab, Retriever Activities Center **Environmental Initiatives:** Climate Commitment Task Force (students, faculty, staff) will commence implementation of its Climate Action Plan and reduce our carbon footprint.

ADMISSIONS

Freshman Academic Profile: Average high school GPA 3.8. 25% in top 10% of high school class, 56% in top 25% of high school class, 85% in top 50% of high school class. **Test Scores:** SAT Math middle 50% range 590-690. SAT EBRW middle 50% range 550-670. ACT middle 50% range 24-29. Minimum internet-based TOEFL 48. Minimum paper TOEFL 460. **Basis for Candidate Selection:** *Very important factors considered include:* rigor of secondary school record, academic GPA, application essay, standardized test scores, recommendation(s). *Important factors considered include:* class rank, talent/ability. *Other factors considered include:* extracurricular activities, character/personal qualities, volunteer work, work experience. **Freshman Admission Requirements:** High school diploma is required and GED is accepted *Academic units required:* 4 English, 4 math, 3 science, 2 foreign language, 3 social studies, 3 history, and 3 units from above areas or other academic areas. *Academic units recommended:* 4 English, 4 math, 3 science, 2 foreign language, 3 units from above areas or other academic areas. **Freshman Admission Statistics:** 11,201 applied, 60.2% admitted, 23% enrolled. **Transfer Admission Requirements:** college transcript(s), statement of good standing from prior institution(s). Minimum college GPA of 2.5 required. Lowest grade transferable D. **General Admission Information:** Application fee $50. Priority deadline 11/1. Regular application deadline 2/1. Nonfall registration accepted. Admission may be deferred for a maximum of 1 year.

COSTS AND FINANCIAL AID

Annual in-state tuition $11,568. Annual out-of-state tuition $24,492. Room and board $11,568. Required fees $1,530. Average book expense $1,200. **Required Forms and Deadlines:** FAFSA. **Notification of Awards:** Applicants will be notified of awards on a rolling basis beginning 3/25. **Types of Aid:** *Need-based scholarships/grants:* College/university scholarship or grant aid from institutional funds; Federal Pell; Private scholarships; SEOG; State scholarships/grants; United Negro College Fund. *Loans:* Direct PLUS loans; Direct Subsidized Stafford Loans; Direct Unsubsidized Stafford Loans. *Student Employment:* Federal Work-Study Program available. Institutional employment available. **Financial Aid Statistics:** 76% needy freshmen, 77% needy undergrads receive need-based scholarship or grant aid. 30% freshmen, 11% undergrads receive non-need-based scholarship or grant aid. 60% freshmen, 70% undergrads receive need-based self-help aid. 3% freshmen, 2% undergrads receive athletic scholarships. 74% freshmen, 70% undergrads receive any aid. 51% undergrads borrow to pay for school. Average cumulative indebtedness $26,391. **Criteria for awarding aid:** *Non-need-based:* Academics, Alumni affiliation, Art, Athletics, Music/drama.

See page 1060.

UNIVERSITY OF MARYLAND, COLLEGE PARK

Mitchell Building, College Park, MD 20742-5235
Phone: 301-314-8385 • **Financial Aid Phone:** 301-314-9000
E-mail: um-admit@umd.edu • **CEEB Code:** 5814
Fax: 301-314-9693 • **Website:** http://www.umd.edu • **ACT Code:** 1746

This public school was founded in 1856. It has a 1335 acre campus.

RATINGS

Admissions Selectivity Rating: 94   **Fire Safety Rating:** 90   **Green Rating:** 93

STUDENTS AND FACULTY

Enrollment: 29,273. **Student Body:** 47% female, 53% male, 22% out-of-state, 5% international (63 countries represented). Asian 17%, African American 12%, Caucasian 50%, Hispanic 10%, Native American <1%, Pacific Islander <1%, Two or more races 4%, Race unknown 1%.
Retention and Graduation: 96% freshmen return for sophomore year. 67% freshmen graduate within 4 years. 85% freshmen graduate within 6 years. 21%

grads go on to further study within 1 year. 1.6% grads pursue law degrees. 11% grads pursue business degrees. 3.7% grads pursue medical degrees. **Faculty:** Student/faculty ratio 18:1. 1,830 full-time faculty, 92% hold PhDs, 24% are members of minority groups, 38% are women. 12% of classes are taught by teaching assistants.

ACADEMICS

Degrees: Bachelor's; Certificate; Doctoral/Professional; Doctoral/Research; Master's; Post-Bachelor's certificate; Post-Master's certificate **Classes:** Most classes have 20-29 students. **Most popular majors:** Biology/Biological Sciences, General; Criminology; Economics, General. **Special Study Options:** Accelerated program; Cooperative education program; Cross-registration; Distance learning; Double major; Dual enrollment; English as a Second Language (ESL); Exchange student program (domestic); External degree program; Honors program; Independent study; Internships; Liberal arts/career combination; Student-designed major; Study abroad; Teacher certification program. Honors programs: Gemstone, Honors, Honors Humanities Combined degree programs: BA/JD; BA/MA; BA/MEng. **Disability Services offered to physically disabled students:** Note-taking services; Reader services; Tape recorders; Tutors. **Career services:** Alumni network; Alumni services; Career assessment; Career/job search classes; Internships; Regional alumni

FACILITIES

Housing: Apartments for single students; Coed dorms; Cooperative housing; Fraternity/sorority housing; Special housing for disabled student; Special housing for international students; Theme housing; Wellness housing; Women's dorms **Special Academic Facilities/Equipment:** Aerospace buoyancy lab, art gallery, international piano archives, center for architectural design and research, model nuclear reactor, wind tunnel. **Computers:** 100% of classrooms, 100% of dorms, 100% of libraries, 100% of dining areas, 100% of student union, 100% of common outdoor areas have wireless network access. Students can register for classes online. Administrative functions (other than registration) can be performed online.

CAMPUS LIFE

Environment: Metropolis **Activities:** Campus Ministries; Choral groups; Concert band; Dance; Drama/theater; International Student Organization; Jazz band; Literary magazine; Marching band; Model UN; Music ensembles; Musical theater; Opera; Pep band; Radio station; Student government; Student newspaper; Student-run film society; Symphony orchestra; Television station; Yearbook 574 registered organizations, 53 honor societies, 55 religious organizations. 36 fraternities, 27 sororities. **Athletics (Intercollegiate):** *Men:* baseball, basketball, cross-country, football, golf, lacrosse, soccer, swimming, tennis, track/field (outdoor), track/field (indoor), wrestling. *Women:* basketball, cheerleading, cross-country, field hockey, golf, gymnastics, lacrosse, soccer, softball, swimming, tennis, track/field (outdoor), track/field (indoor), volleyball, water polo. **On-Campus Highlights:** Clarice Smith Performing Arts Center, Adele H. Stamp Student Union, Eppley Recreation Center, Chevy Chase Bank Field at Byrd Stadium, Comcast Center **Environmental Initiatives:** The Green Office Program engages staff, faculty and students in a voluntary, self-guided initiative that promotes best environmental practices at the University of Maryland. The program supports and promotes offices that are taking steps toward reducing their environmental footprint. Learn more at http://www. sustainability.umd.edu/content/culture/green_offices.php

ADMISSIONS

Freshman Academic Profile: Average high school GPA 4.3. 72% in top 10% of high school class, 90% in top 25% of high school class, 99% in top 50% of high school class. **Test Scores:** SAT Math middle 50% range 650-750. SAT EBRW middle 50% range 640-720. ACT middle 50% range 29-33. Minimum internet-based TOEFL 100. **Basis for Candidate Selection:** *Very important factors considered include:* rigor of secondary school record, academic GPA, standardized test scores. *Important factors considered include:* class rank, application essay, recommendation(s), talent/ability, first generation, state residency. *Other factors considered include:* extracurricular activities, character/personal qualities, alumni/ae relation, geographical residence, racial/ethnic status, volunteer work, work experience. **Freshman Admission Requirements:** High school diploma is required and GED is accepted *Academic units required:* 4 English, 4 math, 3 science, 2 science labs, 2 foreign language, 3 social studies, *Academic units recommended:* 4 English, 4 math, 3 science, 2 science labs, 2 foreign language, 3 social studies. **Freshman Admission Statistics:** 33,907 applied, 44.5% admitted, 27% enrolled. **Transfer Admission Requirements:** college transcript(s), essay or personal statement, statement of good standing from prior institution(s). Lowest grade transferable C. **General Admission Information:** Application fee $75. Priority deadline 11/1. Regular application deadline 1/20. Nonfall registration accepted. Admission may be deferred for a maximum of 1 year.

COSTS AND FINANCIAL AID

Annual in-state tuition $12,004. Annual out-of-state tuition $31,688. Room and board $12,004. Required fees $1,918. Average book expense $1,250. **Required**

Forms and Deadlines: FAFSA. **Notification of Awards:** Applicants will be notified of awards on a rolling basis beginning 4/1. **Types of Aid:** *Need-based scholarships/grants:* College/university scholarship or grant aid from institutional funds; Federal Pell; Private scholarships; SEOG; State scholarships/grants. *Loans:* Direct PLUS loans; Direct Subsidized Stafford Loans; Direct Unsubsidized Stafford Loans. *Student Employment:* Federal Work-Study Program available. Institutional employment available. **Financial Aid Statistics:** 85% needy freshmen, 80% needy undergrads receive need-based scholarship or grant aid. 12% freshmen, 6% undergrads receive non-need-based scholarship or grant aid. 84% freshmen, 92% undergrads receive need-based self-help aid. 1% freshmen, 1% undergrads receive athletic scholarships. 86% freshmen, 72% undergrads receive any aid. Average cumulative indebtedness $26,818. **Criteria for awarding aid:** *Need-based:* Academics *Non-need-based:* Academics, Art, Athletics, Leadership, Music/drama, State/district residency.

UNIVERSITY OF MASSACHUSETTS—AMHERST

University Admissions Center, Amherst, MA 01003
Phone: 413-545-0222 • **Financial Aid Phone:** 413-545-0801
E-mail: mail@admissions.umass.edu • **CEEB Code:** 3917
Fax: 413-545-4312 • **Website:** www.umass.edu • **ACT Code:** 1924

This public school was founded in 1863. It has a 1463 acre campus.

RATINGS
Admissions Selectivity Rating: 87   **Fire Safety Rating:** 93   **Green Rating:** 98

STUDENTS AND FACULTY
Enrollment: 23,010. **Student Body:** 50% female, 50% male, 18% out-of-state, 6% international (78 countries represented). Asian 10%, African American 4%, Caucasian 64%, Hispanic 6%, Native American <1%, Pacific Islander <1%, Two or more races 3%, Race unknown 6%.
Retention and Graduation: 91% freshmen return for sophomore year. 67% freshmen graduate within 4 years. 77% freshmen graduate within 6 years. 18% grads go on to further study within 1 year. 0.6% grads pursue law degrees. 1% grads pursue business degrees. 1.3% grads pursue medical degrees. **Faculty:** Student/faculty ratio 17:1. 1,352 full-time faculty, 95% hold PhDs, 21% are members of minority groups, 44% are women.

ACADEMICS
Degrees: Associate; Bachelor's; Certificate; Doctoral/Professional; Doctoral/Research; Master's; Post-Bachelor's certificate **Classes:** Most classes have 10-19 students. Most lab/discussion sessions have 10-19 students. **Most popular majors:** Biology, General; Biology/Biological Sciences, General; Psychology, General. **Special Study Options:** Accelerated program; Cooperative education program; Cross-registration; Distance learning; Double major; Dual enrollment; English as a Second Language (ESL); Exchange student program (domestic); Honors program; Independent study; Internships; Liberal arts/career combination; Student-designed major; Study abroad; Teacher certification program. Honors programs: Commonwealth Honors College provides a diverse community of academically talented students at the University of Massachusetts Amherst with extensive opportunities for analysis, research, leadership development and international experience. Small honors classes foster intellectual exchange and close interaction with faculty, offering the advantages of a small college alongside all the resources of a nationally recognized research university. The honors curriculum promotes education that is both broad and deep. Through honors general education courses, students reach beyond the boundaries of their academic major, while advanced scholarship tracks afford students opportunities to delve deeply into topics of interest and contribute new and original knowledge to their fields of study. In addition, the honors college offers an array of leadership development opportunities, community-engaged research, entrepreneurial initiatives, and international programs—all designed to foster global perspectives, diverse viewpoints, dialogue on social justice, and responsible research skills. Combined degree programs: BA/MA. **Disability Services offered to physically disabled students:** Note-taking services; Reader services; Tape recorders. **Career services:** Alumni network; Alumni services; Career assessment; Career/job search classes; Internships

FACILITIES
Housing: Apartments for married students; Apartments for single students; Coed dorms; Fraternity/sorority housing; Men's dorms; Special housing for disabled student; Special housing for international students; Theme housing; Wellness housing; Women's dorms **Special Academic Facilities/Equipment:** Computer Science Complex, Polymer Research Institute, Herter (Art) Gallery, University Museum of Contemporary Art, Natural History Museum, Fine Arts Center, Mullins Center (sports and entertainment arena), Learning Commons, Botanical Gardens, Astronomical Observatory **Computers:** 97% of classrooms, 10% of dorms, 100% of libraries, 100% of dining areas, 100% of student union, 20% of common outdoor areas have wireless network access. Students can register for classes online. Administrative functions (other than registration) can be performed online.

CAMPUS LIFE
Environment: Town **Activities:** Campus Ministries; Choral groups; Concert band; Dance; Drama/theater; International Student Organization; Jazz band; Literary magazine; Marching band; Model UN; Music ensembles; Musical theater; Opera; Pep band; Radio station; Student government; Student newspaper; Student-run film society; Symphony orchestra; Television station; Yearbook 291 registered organizations, 30 honor societies, 14 religious organizations. 21 fraternities, 15 sororities. **Athletics (Intercollegiate):** *Men:* baseball, basketball, cross-country, diving, football, ice hockey, lacrosse, soccer, swimming, track/field (outdoor), track/field (indoor). *Women:* basketball, crew/rowing, cross-country, diving, field hockey, lacrosse, soccer, softball, swimming, tennis, track/field (outdoor), track/field (indoor). **On-Campus Highlights:** The Campus Center & Student Union, The Learning Commons, The Recreation Center, The Mullins Center, The Fine Arts Center **Environmental Initiatives:** 1. In Spring 2016, UMass Amherst established the School of Earth & Sustainability (SES), a cross-disciplinary partnership between the Departments of Environmental Conservation, Geosciences, Landscape Architecture & Regional Planning and Stockbridge School of Agriculture as well as the Environmental Microbiology group from the Department of Microbiology. SES joins diverse academic programs, research, and outreach that share a common focus on earth, sustainability, and environmental sciences. Together, our community includes over 100 world-class faculty, 1300 undergraduate students, 320 graduate students as well as many research scientists, technicians and support staff. The SES provides UMass with a learning community dedicated to training the next generation of scholars and environmental leaders who will increase our understanding of how the planet works and solve the global challenges of sustainability. www.umass.edu/ses

ADMISSIONS
Freshman Academic Profile: Average high school GPA 3.9. 34% in top 10% of high school class, 73% in top 25% of high school class, 97% in top 50% of high school class. **Test Scores:** SAT Math middle 50% range 590-690. SAT EBRW middle 50% range 590-670. ACT middle 50% range 26-31. Minimum internet-based TOEFL 80. **Basis for Candidate Selection:** *Very important factors considered include:* rigor of secondary school record, academic GPA, standardized test scores. *Important factors considered include:* class rank, application essay, recommendation(s), extracurricular activities, talent/ability, character/personal qualities, first generation, work experience, level of applicant's interest. *Other factors considered include:* alumni/ae relation, geographical residence, state residency, racial/ethnic status, volunteer work. **Freshman Admission Requirements:** High school diploma is required and GED is accepted *Academic units required:* 4 English, 4 math, 3 science, 2 science labs, 2 foreign language, 2 social studies, 2 academic electives. **Freshman Admission Statistics:** 41,922 applied, 57.5% admitted, 20% enrolled. **Transfer Admission Requirements:** college transcript(s), essay or personal statement. Minimum college GPA of 2.5 required. Lowest grade transferable C-. **General Admission Information:** Application fee $80. Regular application deadline 1/15. Nonfall registration accepted. Admission may be deferred.

COSTS AND FINANCIAL AID
Required Forms and Deadlines: FAFSA. **Notification of Awards:** Applicants will be notified of awards on a rolling basis beginning 12/15. **Types of Aid:** *Need-based scholarships/grants:* College/university scholarship or grant aid from institutional funds; Federal Pell; Private scholarships; SEOG; State scholarships/grants. *Loans:* Direct PLUS loans; Direct Subsidized Stafford Loans; Direct Unsubsidized Stafford Loans. *Student Employment:* Federal Work-Study Program available. Institutional employment available. **Financial Aid Statistics:** 91% needy freshmen, 87% needy undergrads receive need-based scholarship or grant aid. 11% freshmen, 7% undergrads receive non-need-based scholarship or grant aid. 85% freshmen, 90% undergrads receive need-based self-help aid. 1% freshmen, 1% undergrads receive athletic scholarships. 90% freshmen, 85% undergrads receive any aid. 68% undergrads borrow to pay for school. Average cumulative indebtedness $31,397. **Criteria for awarding aid:** *Non-need-based:* Academics, Art, Athletics, Music/drama, State/district residency.

UNIVERSITY OF MASSACHUSETTS—BOSTON

100 Morrissey Boulevard, Boston, MA 02125-3393
Phone: 617-287-6100 • **Financial Aid Phone:** 617-287-6300
E-mail: undergrad.admissions@umb.edu • **CEEB Code:** 3924
Fax: 617-287-5999 • **Website:** www.umb.edu

This public school was founded in 1964. It has a 120 acre campus.

RATINGS
Admissions Selectivity Rating: 77   **Fire Safety Rating:** 60*   **Green Rating:** 96

STUDENTS AND FACULTY
Enrollment: 12,159. **Student Body:** 53% female, 47% male, 5% out-of-state, 12% international (150 countries represented). Asian 13%, African American 17%, Caucasian 34%, Hispanic 16%, Native American <1%, Pacific Islander <1%, Two or more races 3%, Race unknown 6%.
Retention and Graduation: 77% freshmen return for sophomore year. 21% freshmen graduate within 4 years. 48% freshmen graduate within 6 years.
Faculty: Student/faculty ratio 17:1. 700 full-time faculty, 98% hold PhDs, 24% are members of minority groups, 50% are women. 0% of classes are taught by teaching assistants.

ACADEMICS
Degrees: Bachelor's; Certificate; Doctoral/Professional; Doctoral/Research; Master's; Post-Bachelor's certificate; Post-Master's certificate **Classes:** Most classes have 20-29 students. Most lab/discussion sessions have 10-19 students.
Most popular majors: Management Science. **Special Study Options:** Cooperative education program; Cross-registration; Distance learning; Double major; Dual enrollment; English as a Second Language (ESL); Exchange student program (domestic); Honors program; Independent study; Internships; Liberal arts/career combination; Student-designed major; Study abroad; Teacher certification program. Honors programs: The University Honors Program seeks to meet the needs of students who thrive on intellectual challenge by offering special interdisciplinary academic opportunities outside the major. Combined degree programs: BA/MA. **Disability Services offered to physically disabled students:** Note-taking services; Reader services; Tape recorders; Tutors. **Career services:** Alumni network; Alumni services; Career assessment; Career/job search classes; Internships; Regional alumni

FACILITIES
Housing: 100% of campus accessible to physically diasbled. **Special Academic Facilities/Equipment:** Campus 1st LEED Gold Academic Bldg (ISC, 2015), Campus' Second LEED Gold bldg. (Univ Hall, 2016), UMass Harbor Walk, Harbor Art gallery, Art installation and sculpture inside buildings and outdoors, Greenhouse, Solar photo-voltaic installation on top of Wheatley Hall, adaptive computer lab, Healey library gallery space and special collections displays, Nantucket Field Station for immersive environmental studies, Marine sailing vessels at UMB Fox Point Pavilion for faculty,student and community marine education opportunities. **Computers:** 100% of classrooms, 100% of libraries, 100% of dining areas, 100% of student union, have wireless network access. Students can register for classes online. Administrative functions (other than registration) can be performed online.

CAMPUS LIFE
Environment: Metropolis **Activities:** Campus Ministries; Choral groups; Concert band; Dance; Drama/theater; International Student Organization; Jazz band; Literary magazine; Model UN; Music ensembles; Radio station; Student government; Student newspaper; Student-run film society; Symphony orchestra 75 registered organizations, 1 honor societies. **Athletics (Intercollegiate):** *Men:* baseball, basketball, cross-country, ice hockey, lacrosse, soccer, tennis, track/field (outdoor), track/field (indoor). *Women:* basketball, cross-country, ice hockey, soccer, softball, tennis, track/field (outdoor), track/field (indoor), volleyball. **On-Campus Highlights:** New Campus Center, Clark Athletic Center, Waterfront area and weekly boat tours, Greenhouse, Healey Library **Environmental Initiatives:** New first ever UMass System Sustainability Policy of 2016: Annual reporting and bench marking sustainability metrics in 10 priority areas: 1) sustainability strategic planning 2) clean energy 3) climate resilience and preparedness 4) green building design and sustainable campus operations 5) sustainable transportation 6) waste reduction and recycling 7) environmentally preferable purchasing 8) sustainable food services 9) sustainable water systems 10) academic programming, research, community engagement. Link: https://www.umassp.edu/sites/umassp.edu/files/content/T16-055-Sustainability%20Policy_12.9.16.pdf

ADMISSIONS
Freshman Academic Profile: Average high school GPA 3.3. **Test Scores:** SAT Math middle 50% range 510-600. SAT EBRW middle 50% range 490-600.

ACT middle 50% range 21-26. Minimum internet-based TOEFL 79. **Basis for Candidate Selection:** *Very important factors considered include:* rigor of secondary school record, academic GPA, standardized test scores. *Important factors considered include:* application essay, recommendation(s), character/personal qualities. *Other factors considered include:* extracurricular activities, talent/ability, first generation, volunteer work, work experience. **Freshman Admission Requirements:** High school diploma is required and GED is accepted *Academic units required:* 4 English, 4 math, 3 science, 3 science labs, 2 foreign language, 1 social studies, 1 history, 2 academic electives. **Freshman Admission Statistics:** 10,507 applied, 75.1% admitted, 24% enrolled. **Transfer Admission Requirements:** college transcript(s), essay or personal statement, statement of good standing from prior institution(s). Minimum college GPA of 2.5 required. Lowest grade transferable C-. **General Admission Information:** Application fee $60. Priority deadline 11/1. Regular application deadline 3/1. Nonfall registration accepted. Admission may be deferred for a maximum of 1 year.

COSTS AND FINANCIAL AID
Annual out-of-state tuition $32,660. Required fees $325. **Types of Aid: Financial Aid Statistics:** 93% needy freshmen, 91% needy undergrads receive need-based scholarship or grant aid. 5% freshmen, 2% undergrads receive non-need-based scholarship or grant aid. 92% freshmen, 96% undergrads receive need-based self-help aid. 0% freshmen, 0% undergrads receive athletic scholarships. **Criteria for awarding aid:** *Need-based:* Academics *Non-need-based:* Academics, Leadership, State/district residency.

UNIVERSITY OF MASSACHUSETTS—DARTMOUTH

285 Old Westport Road, North Dartmouth, MA 02747-2300
Phone: (508) 999-8605 • **Financial Aid Phone:** 508-999-8643
E-mail: admissions@umassd.edu • **CEEB Code:** 3786
Fax: (508) 999-8755 • **Website:** http://www.umassd.edu/ • **ACT Code:** 1906

This public school was founded in 1895. It has a 710 acre campus.

RATINGS
Admissions Selectivity Rating: 74   **Fire Safety Rating:** 91   **Green Rating:** 90

STUDENTS AND FACULTY
Enrollment: 6,559. **Student Body:** 48% female, 52% male, 7% out-of-state, 2% international (41 countries represented). Asian 4%, African American 16%, Caucasian 61%, Hispanic 10%, Native American <1%, Pacific Islander 0%, Two or more races 4%, Race unknown 4%.
Retention and Graduation: 74% freshmen return for sophomore year. 30% freshmen graduate within 4 years. 49% freshmen graduate within 6 years.
Faculty: Student/faculty ratio 16:1. 401 full-time faculty, 84% hold PhDs, 21% are members of minority groups, 47% are women. 3% of classes are taught by teaching assistants.

ACADEMICS
Degrees: Bachelor's; Certificate; Doctoral/Professional; Doctoral/Research; Master's; Post-Bachelor's certificate; Post-Master's certificate **Classes:** Most classes have 20-29 students. **Most popular majors:** Mechanical Engineering; Psychology, General; Registered Nursing, Nursing Administration, Nursing Research And Clinical Nursing, Other. **Special Study Options:** Accelerated program; Cooperative education program; Cross-registration; Distance learning; Double major; Dual enrollment; English as a Second Language (ESL); Exchange student program (domestic); Honors program; Independent study; Internships; Student-designed major; Study abroad; Teacher certification program. Honors programs: Honors Program Combined degree programs: BA/JD; BA/MA. **Disability Services offered to physically disabled students:** Note-taking services; Reader services; Tape recorders; Tutors. **Career services:** Alumni network; Career/job search classes; Internships

FACILITIES
Housing: Apartments for single students; Coed dorms; Special housing for disabled student; Theme housing; Wellness housing 97% of campus accessible to physically diasbled. **Special Academic Facilities/Equipment:** Art gallery, language center, center for Jewish culture, Robert F. Kennedy assassination archives, electron microscope, observatory, marine research vessels, Business Innovation Research Center, School of Marine Science and Technology **Computers:** 100% of classrooms, 100% of dorms, 100% of libraries, 100% of dining areas, 100% of student union, 100% of common outdoor areas have wireless network access. Students can register for classes online. Administrative functions (other than registration) can be performed online.

CAMPUS LIFE

Environment: Town **Activities:** Campus Ministries; Choral groups; Concert band; Dance; Drama/theater; International Student Organization; Jazz band; Literary magazine; Model UN; Music ensembles; Radio station; Student government; Student newspaper; Symphony orchestra; Yearbook 103 registered organizations, 5 honor societies, 6 religious organizations. 5 fraternities, 3 sororities. **Athletics (Intercollegiate):** *Men:* baseball, basketball, cross-country, diving, football, golf, ice hockey, lacrosse, soccer, swimming, tennis, track/field (outdoor), track/field (indoor). *Women:* basketball, cheerleading, cross-country, diving, equestrian sports, field hockey, golf, lacrosse, soccer, softball, swimming, tennis, track/field (outdoor), track/field (indoor), volleyball. **On-Campus Highlights:** Tripp Athletic Center, Claire T. Carney Library, Woodlawn Commons, MacLean Campus Center, Corsair Cafe **Environmental Initiatives:** Large scale energy performance. Lighting, heating, AC, water, sewer

ADMISSIONS

Freshman Academic Profile: Average high school GPA 3.2. 88% from public high schools. **Test Scores:** SAT Math middle 50% range 500-590. SAT EBRW middle 50% range 500-600. ACT middle 50% range 19-26. Minimum internet-based TOEFL 79. Minimum paper TOEFL 550. **Basis for Candidate Selection:** *Very important factors considered include:* rigor of secondary school record, academic GPA, standardized test scores. *Other factors considered include:* application essay, recommendation(s), extracurricular activities, talent/ability, character/personal qualities, first generation, alumni/ae relation, volunteer work, work experience. **Freshman Admission Requirements:** High school diploma is required and GED is accepted *Academic units required:* 4 English, 4 math, 3 science, 3 science labs, 2 foreign language, 1 social studies, 1 history, 2 academic electives. **Freshman Admission Statistics:** 7,959 applied, 84.3% admitted, 20% enrolled. **Transfer Admission Requirements:** college transcript(s), essay or personal statement, Minimum college GPA of 2.5 required. Lowest grade transferable C-. **General Admission Information:** Application fee $60. Priority deadline 3/1. Nonfall registration accepted. Admission may be deferred for a maximum of 2 semesters.

COSTS AND FINANCIAL AID

Required Forms and Deadlines: FAFSA. **Notification of Awards:** Applicants will be notified of awards on a rolling basis beginning 2/1. **Types of Aid:** *Need-based scholarships/grants:* College/university scholarship or grant aid from institutional funds; Federal Pell; Private scholarships; SEOG; State scholarships/grants. *Loans:* Direct PLUS loans; Direct Subsidized Stafford Loans; Direct Unsubsidized Stafford Loans. *Student Employment:* Federal Work-Study Program available. Institutional employment available. **Financial Aid Statistics:** 77% freshmen, 73% undergrads receive any aid. **Criteria for awarding aid:** *Non-need-based:* Academics, Minority status, State/district residency.

UNIVERSITY OF MASSACHUSETTS—LOWELL

One University Avenue, Lowell, MA 01854-2874
Phone: 978-934-3931 • **Financial Aid Phone:** 978-934-4220
E-mail: admissions@uml.edu • **CEEB Code:** 3911
Fax: 978-934-3086 • **Website:** www.uml.edu • **ACT Code:** 1854

This public school was founded in 1894. It has a 150 acre campus.

RATINGS

Admissions Selectivity Rating: 83   **Fire Safety Rating:** 97   **Green Rating:** 92

STUDENTS AND FACULTY

Enrollment: 13,284. **Student Body:** 38% female, 62% male, 9% out-of-state, 4% international (66 countries represented). Asian 10%, African American 6%, Caucasian 62%, Hispanic 11%, Native American <1%, Pacific Islander <1%, Two or more races 3%, Race unknown 4%. **Retention and Graduation:** 86% freshmen return for sophomore year. 39% freshmen graduate within 4 years. 60% freshmen graduate within 6 years. **Faculty:** Student/faculty ratio 17:1. 616 full-time faculty, 90% hold PhDs, 25% are members of minority groups, 44% are women. 2% of classes are taught by teaching assistants.

ACADEMICS

Degrees: Associate; Bachelor's; Certificate; Doctoral/Professional; Doctoral/Research; Master's; Post-Bachelor's certificate; Post-Master's certificate; Terminal Associate; Transfer Associate **Classes:** Most classes have 20-29 students. Most lab/discussion sessions have 10-19 students. **Most popular majors:** Information Science/Studies; Criminal Justice/Law Enforcement

Administration; Business Administration And Management, General. **Special Study Options:** Accelerated program; Cooperative education program; Cross-registration; Distance learning; Double major; Dual enrollment; Honors program; Independent study; Internships; Study abroad; Teacher certification program. Honors programs: The Honors College at UMass Lowell offers high-achieving students individualized instruction in small groups, often in seminar format; opportunities for undergraduate research; special "Commonwealth Honors Program Scholar" designation on transcripts and diplomas—upon completion of program requirements; opportunity to live on one of the Honors floors in the residence halls; and Honors Program social events. Combined degree programs: BA/MA; BA/MEng. **Disability Services offered to physically disabled students:** Note-taking services; Reader services; Tape recorders; Tutors. **Career services:** Alumni network; Alumni services; Career assessment; Career/job search classes; Internships; Regional alumni

FACILITIES

Housing: Apartments for single students; Coed dorms; Theme housing; Wellness housing 90% of campus accessible to physically disabled. **Special Academic Facilities/Equipment:** Language lab, media center, audio-visual department, Centers for Learning, Center for field studies, Center for Performing and Visual Arts, Center for Health Promotion, Research Nuclear Reactor. New $19.5 million recreation center which includes multi court gymnasium, 1/8 mile indoor elevated track, aerobics room, game rooms, locker rooms, and a sauna. Also included are meeting rooms and an indoor/outdoor food court. **Computers:** 50% of classrooms, 90% of dorms, 100% of libraries, 100% of dining areas, 100% of student union, 75% of common outdoor areas have wireless network access. Students can register for classes online. Administrative functions (other than registration) can be performed online.

CAMPUS LIFE

Environment: City **Activities:** Campus Ministries; Choral groups; Concert band; Dance; Drama/theater; International Student Organization; Jazz band; Literary magazine; Marching band; Model UN; Music ensembles; Pep band; Radio station; Student government; Student newspaper; Student-run film society; Symphony orchestra; Yearbook 100 registered organizations, 16 honor societies, 4 religious organizations. **Athletics (Intercollegiate):** *Men:* baseball, basketball, crew/rowing, cross-country, golf, ice hockey, soccer, track/field (outdoor), track/field (indoor). *Women:* basketball, crew/rowing, cross-country, field hockey, soccer, softball, track/field (outdoor), track/field (indoor), volleyball. **On-Campus Highlights:** University Crossing, Campus Recreation Center, O'Leary Library Learning Commons, Saab Emerging Technologies and Innovation Center, Health and Social Science Building

ADMISSIONS

Freshman Academic Profile: Average high school GPA 3.6. 21% in top 10% of high school class, 52% in top 25% of high school class, 87% in top 50% of high school class. 88% from public high schools. **Test Scores:** SAT Math middle 50% range 570-660. SAT EBRW middle 50% range 560-650. ACT middle 50% range 24-29. Minimum internet-based TOEFL 79. Minimum paper TOEFL 550. **Basis for Candidate Selection:** *Very important factors considered include:* rigor of secondary school record, academic GPA. *Important factors considered include:* application essay, standardized test scores, recommendation(s), character/personal qualities. *Other factors considered include:* class rank, extracurricular activities, talent/ability, first generation, alumni/ae relation, geographical residence, state residency, racial/ethnic status, volunteer work, work experience, level of applicant's interest. **Freshman Admission Requirements:** High school diploma is required and GED is accepted *Academic units required:* 4 English, 4 math, 3 science, 3 science labs, 2 foreign language, 1 social studies, 1 history, 2 academic electives, *Academic units recommended:* 4 English, 4 math, 4 science, 3 science labs, 2 foreign language, 1 social studies, 1 history, 2 academic electives. **Freshman Admission Statistics:** 11,113 applied, 68.7% admitted, 26% enrolled. **Transfer Admission Requirements:** college transcript(s), Minimum college GPA of 2.0 required. Lowest grade transferable c-. **General Admission Information:** Application fee $60. Priority deadline 11/1. Regular application deadline 2/1. Nonfall registration accepted. Admission may be deferred for a maximum of 1 year.

COSTS AND FINANCIAL AID

Required Forms and Deadlines: FAFSA. **Notification of Awards:** Applicants will be notified of awards on a rolling basis beginning 1/1. **Types of Aid:** *Need-based scholarships/grants:* College/university scholarship or grant aid from institutional funds; Federal Pell; Private scholarships; SEOG; State scholarships/grants. *Loans:* Direct PLUS loans; Direct Subsidized Stafford Loans; Direct Unsubsidized Stafford Loans. **Financial Aid Statistics:** 93% needy freshmen, 87% needy undergrads receive need-based scholarship or grant aid. 7% freshmen, 4% undergrads receive non-need-based scholarship or grant aid. 90% freshmen, 93% undergrads receive need-based self-help aid. 4% freshmen, 3% undergrads receive athletic scholarships. 89% freshmen, 82% undergrads receive any aid. 81% undergrads borrow to pay for school. Average cumulative indebtedness $30,915. **Criteria for awarding aid:** *Need-based:*

Academics *Non-need-based:* Academics, Alumni affiliation, Art, Athletics, Leadership, Minority status, Music/drama, State/district residency.

UNIVERSITY OF MEMPHIS

101 Wilder Tower, Memphis, TN 38152
Phone: 901-678-2111 • **Financial Aid Phone:** 901-678-4825
E-mail: recruitment@memphis.edu • **CEEB Code:** 1459
Fax: 901-678-3053 • **Website:** www.memphis.edu • **ACT Code:** 3992

This public school was founded in 1912. It has a 1160 acre campus.

RATINGS
Admissions Selectivity Rating: 84   **Fire Safety Rating:** 92   **Green Rating:** 60*

STUDENTS AND FACULTY
Enrollment: 16,741. **Student Body:** 61% female, 39% male, 10% out-of-state, 1% international (53 countries represented). Asian 3%, African American 40%, Caucasian 49%, Hispanic 3%, Native American <1%, Pacific Islander <1%, Two or more races 3%, Race unknown 1%.
Retention and Graduation: 76% freshmen return for sophomore year.
Faculty: Student/faculty ratio 14:1. 136 full-time faculty, 59% hold PhDs, 14% are members of minority groups, 57% are women.

ACADEMICS
Degrees: Bachelor's; Doctoral/Professional; Doctoral/Research; Master's; Post-Bachelor's certificate; Post-Master's certificate **Classes:** Most classes have 20-29 students. Most lab/discussion sessions have 10-19 students. **Most popular majors:** General Studies; Biology/Biological Sciences, General; Psychology, General. **Special Study Options:** Accelerated program; Cooperative education program; Cross-registration; Distance learning; Double major; Dual enrollment; English as a Second Language (ESL); Exchange student program (domestic); External degree program; Honors program; Independent study; Internships; Liberal arts/career combination; Student-designed major; Study abroad; Teacher certification program. Honors programs: The Honors Program offers students the opportunity to take small classes and interdisciplinary seminars with the University's most outstanding faculty. The program also includes many wonderful opportunities beyond the classroom such as study abroad, independent research, and co-curricular activities. Honors students also have the chance to participate in nationally recognized undergraduate research conferences and extend their learning through internships and public service.
Disability Services offered to physically disabled students: Note-taking services; Reader services; Tape recorders. **Career services:** Alumni network; Alumni services; Career assessment; Career/job search classes; Internships; Regional alumni

FACILITIES
Housing: Apartments for married students; Apartments for single students; Coed dorms; Cooperative housing; Fraternity/sorority housing; Men's dorms; Special housing for disabled student; Women's dorms 95% of campus accessible to physically diasbled. **Special Academic Facilities/Equipment:** Center for Earthquake Research & Information Institute of Egyptian Art & Archaeology Bureau of Business and Economic Research **Computers:** 100% of classrooms, 55% of dorms, 100% of libraries, 100% of dining areas, 100% of student union, 10% of common outdoor areas have wireless network access. Students can register for classes online. Administrative functions (other than registration) can be performed online.

CAMPUS LIFE
Environment: Metropolis **Activities:** Campus Ministries; Choral groups; Concert band; Dance; Drama/theater; International Student Organization; Jazz band; Literary magazine; Marching band; Music ensembles; Musical theater; Opera; Pep band; Radio station; Student government; Student newspaper; Symphony orchestra 140 registered organizations, 20 honor societies, 12 religious organizations. 14 fraternities, 11 sororities. **Athletics (Intercollegiate): Men:** baseball, basketball, cross-country, football, golf, riflery, soccer, tennis, track/field (outdoor). *Women:* basketball, cross-country, golf, riflery, soccer, softball, tennis, track/field (outdoor), volleyball. **On-Campus Highlights:** Rose Theater Lecture Hall, FedEx Institute of Technology, Finch Recreation Facility, Harris Concert Hall, Newly opened University Center **Environmental Initiatives:** Energy Conservation

ADMISSIONS
Freshman Academic Profile: Average high school GPA 3.3. 1% in top 10% of high school class, 42% in top 25% of high school class, 79% in top 50% of high school class. **Test Scores:** SAT Math middle 50% range 440-590. SAT EBRW middle 50% range 440-570. ACT middle 50% range 20-25. Minimum

paper TOEFL 550. **Basis for Candidate Selection:** *Very important factors considered include:* rigor of secondary school record, academic GPA, standardized test scores. *Other factors considered include:* application essay, recommendation(s), talent/ability, character/personal qualities, first generation, work experience. **Freshman Admission Requirements:** High school diploma is required and GED is accepted *Academic units required:* 4 English, 3 math, 2 science, 1 science labs, 2 foreign language, 1 social studies, 1 history, 1 visual/performing arts. **Freshman Admission Statistics:** 6,798 applied, 62.4% admitted, 53% enrolled. **Transfer Admission Requirements:** college transcript(s), standardized test scores, Lowest grade transferable C. **General Admission Information:** Application fee $25. Regular application deadline 7/1. Nonfall registration accepted.

COSTS AND FINANCIAL AID
Required Forms and Deadlines: FAFSA. **Notification of Awards:** Applicants will be notified of awards on a rolling basis beginning 3/15. **Types of Aid:** *Need-based scholarships/grants:* College/university scholarship or grant aid from institutional funds; Federal Pell; Private scholarships; SEOG; State scholarships/grants. *Loans:* Direct PLUS loans; Direct Subsidized Stafford Loans; Direct Unsubsidized Stafford Loans. *Student Employment:* Federal Work-Study Program available. Institutional employment available. **Financial Aid Statistics:** 67% needy freshmen, 71% needy undergrads receive need-based scholarship or grant aid. 49% freshmen, 62% undergrads receive non-need-based scholarship or grant aid. 59% freshmen, 81% undergrads receive need-based self-help aid. 3% freshmen, 2% undergrads receive athletic scholarships. 95% freshmen, 91% undergrads receive any aid. **Criteria for awarding aid:** *Need-based:* Academics, Leadership, Minority status *Non-need-based:* Academics, Alumni affiliation, Art, Athletics, Leadership, Music/drama, State/district residency.

UNIVERSITY OF MIAMI

P.O. Box 248025, Coral Gables, FL 33124-4616
Phone: 305-284-4323 • **Financial Aid Phone:** 305-284-2270
E-mail: admission@miami.edu • **CEEB Code:** 5815
Fax: 305-284-2507 • **Website:** www.miami.edu • **ACT Code:** 760

This private school was founded in 1925. It has a 239 acre campus.

RATINGS
Admissions Selectivity Rating: 92   **Fire Safety Rating:** 91   **Green Rating:** 91

STUDENTS AND FACULTY
Enrollment: 10,608. **Student Body:** 52% female, 48% male, 55% out-of-state, 15% international (118 countries represented). Asian 5%, African American 8%, Caucasian 42%, Hispanic 23%, Native American <1%, Pacific Islander <1%, Two or more races 3%, Race unknown 4%.
Retention and Graduation: 91% freshmen return for sophomore year. 72% freshmen graduate within 4 years. 84% freshmen graduate within 6 years. 33% grads go on to further study within 1 year. 10% grads pursue arts and sciences degrees. 6% grads pursue law degrees. 1% grads pursue business degrees. 6% grads pursue medical degrees. **Faculty:** Student/faculty ratio 12:1. 1,115 full-time faculty, 88% hold PhDs, 35% are members of minority groups, 41% are women. 7% of classes are taught by teaching assistants.

ACADEMICS
Degrees: Bachelor's; Certificate; Doctoral/Professional; Doctoral/Research; Master's; Post-Bachelor's certificate; Post-Master's certificate **Classes:** Most classes have 20-29 students. Most lab/discussion sessions have 10-19 students. **Most popular majors:** Biology/Biological Sciences, General; Psychology, General; Finance, General. **Special Study Options:** Accelerated program; Cooperative education program; Distance learning; Double major; Dual enrollment; English as a Second Language (ESL); Honors program; Independent study; Internships; Liberal arts/career combination; Student-designed major; Study abroad; Teacher certification program; Weekend college. Honors programs: The Foote Fellows Honors Program allows students to pursue their interests and explore the topics they are most passionate about by exempting them from general education requirements. Invitation to the program is offered only to the highest achieving admitted students in each school and college. There are also Dual-Degree Programs in Medicine, Law, Latin American Studies, Marine Geology, Biology, Biochemistry & Molecular Biology, Exercise Physiology and Computer Science. Combined degree

programs: BA/JD; BA/MD. **Disability Services offered to physically disabled students:** Note-taking services; Reader services; Tape recorders; Tutors. **Career services:** Alumni services; Career assessment; Career/job search classes; Internships

FACILITIES

Housing: Apartments for single students; Coed dorms; Fraternity/sorority housing; Special housing for disabled student; Theme housing **Special Academic Facilities/Equipment:** Lowe Art Museum, Gusman Concert Hall, Clarke Recital Hall, Jerry Herman Ring Theatre, Bill Cosford Cinema, Sheldon and Myrna Palley Pavillion for Contemporary Glass and Studio Arts, BankUnited Center, Martha and Austin Weeks Music Library and Technology Center, Wellness Center, state-of-the-art computer labs, digital television studios, film sound stage, a radio station, a new Student Activities Center, a new seawater research facility and new North and South studio wings at our Frost School of Music. **Computers:** 100% of classrooms, 100% of dorms, 100% of libraries, 100% of dining areas, 100% of student union, 100% of common outdoor areas have wireless network access. Students can register for classes online. Administrative functions (other than registration) can be performed online.

CAMPUS LIFE

Environment: Town **Activities:** Campus Ministries; Choral groups; Concert band; Dance; Drama/theater; International Student Organization; Jazz band; Literary magazine; Marching band; Model UN; Music ensembles; Musical theater; Opera; Pep band; Radio station; Student government; Student newspaper; Student-run film society; Symphony orchestra; Television station; Yearbook. **Athletics (Intercollegiate):** *Men:* baseball, basketball, cheerleading, cross-country, football, tennis, track/field (outdoor), track/field (indoor). *Women:* basketball, cheerleading, crew/rowing, cross-country, diving, golf, soccer, swimming, tennis, track/field (outdoor), track/field (indoor), volleyball. **On-Campus Highlights:** Student Center Complex (student union), Herbert Wellness Center, Lakeside Patio Stage, Foote Green at Richter Library, Intramural fields outside Hecht/Stanford Residential Colleges **Environmental Initiatives:** The President signed the ACUPCC. The University also hired a sustainability coordinator.

ADMISSIONS

Freshman Academic Profile: Average high school GPA 35.0. 46% in top 10% of high school class, 77% in top 25% of high school class, 94% in top 50% of high school class. 62% from public high schools. **Test Scores:** SAT Math middle 50% range 610-720. SAT EBRW middle 50% range 610-690. ACT middle 50% range 28-32. Minimum internet-based TOEFL 80. Minimum paper TOEFL 550. **Basis for Candidate Selection:** *Very important factors considered include:* rigor of secondary school record, class rank, academic GPA, application essay, standardized test scores, recommendation(s), extracurricular activities, character/personal qualities. *Important factors considered include:* talent/ability, volunteer work, work experience. *Other factors considered include:* first generation, alumni/ae relation, geographical residence, racial/ethnic status, level of applicant's interest. **Freshman Admission Requirements:** High school diploma is required and GED is accepted *Academic units recommended:* 4 English, 4 math, 3 science, 2 science labs, 2 foreign language, 3 social studies, 2 history, 1 computer science, 1 visual/performing arts. **Freshman Admission Statistics:** 30,634 applied, 36.7% admitted, 20% enrolled. **Transfer Admission Requirements:** college transcript(s), statement of good standing from prior institution(s). Lowest grade transferable C. **General Admission Information:** Application fee $70. Regular application deadline 1/1. Nonfall registration accepted. Admission may be deferred for a maximum of 1 year.

COSTS AND FINANCIAL AID

Annual tuition $47,040. Room and board $13,666. Required fees $1,444. Average book expense $1,000. **Required Forms and Deadlines:** Business/Farm Supplement; CSS/Financial Aid PROFILE; FAFSA; Noncustodial PROFILE. **Notification of Awards:** Applicants will be notified of awards on a rolling basis beginning 1/20. **Types of Aid:** *Need-based scholarships/grants:* College/university scholarship or grant aid from institutional funds; Federal Pell; Private scholarships; SEOG; State scholarships/grants. *Loans:* Direct PLUS loans; Direct Subsidized Stafford Loans; Direct Unsubsidized Stafford Loans. **Student Employment:** Federal Work-Study Program available. Institutional employment available. **Financial Aid Statistics:** 30% needy freshmen, 51% needy undergrads receive need-based scholarship or grant aid. 96% freshmen, 92% undergrads receive non-need-based scholarship or grant aid. 63% freshmen, 66% undergrads receive need-based self-help aid. 0% freshmen, 0% undergrads receive athletic scholarships. 85% freshmen, 74% undergrads receive any aid. 37% undergrads borrow to pay for school. Average cumulative indebtedness $21,500. **Criteria for awarding aid:** *Need-based:* Alumni affiliation, Art, Job skills, Leadership, Minority status *Non-need-based:* Academics, Athletics, Music/drama, State/district residency.

UNIVERSITY OF MICHIGAN—ANN ARBOR

500 S. State St., Ann Arbor, MI 48109-1316
Phone: 734-764-7433 • **Financial Aid Phone:** 734-763-6600 • **CEEB Code:** 1839
Fax: 734-936-0740 • **Website:** umich.edu • **ACT Code:** 2062

This public school was founded in 1817. It has a 3207 acre campus.

RATINGS
Admissions Selectivity Rating: 96   **Fire Safety Rating:** 88   **Green Rating:** 90

STUDENTS AND FACULTY
Enrollment: 29,550. **Student Body:** 50% female, 50% male, 41% out-of-state, 7% international (92 countries represented). Asian 14%, African American 4%, Caucasian 61%, Hispanic 6%, Native American <1%, Pacific Islander <1%, Two or more races 4%, Race unknown 4%.
Retention and Graduation: 97% freshmen return for sophomore year. 77% freshmen graduate within 4 years. 92% freshmen graduate within 6 years.
Faculty: Student/faculty ratio 15:1. 2,852 full-time faculty, 89% hold PhDs, 26% are members of minority groups, 42% are women. 36% of classes are taught by teaching assistants.

ACADEMICS
Degrees: Bachelor's; Doctoral; Doctoral/Professional; Doctoral/Research; Master's; Post-Bachelor's certificate; Post-Master's certificate **Classes:** Most classes have 10-19 students. Most lab/discussion sessions have 10-19 students. **Most popular majors:** Experimental Psychology; Economics, General; Business Administration And Management, General. **Special Study Options:** Accelerated program; Cooperative education program; Cross-registration; Distance learning; Double major; Dual enrollment; English as a Second Language (ESL); Exchange student program (domestic); External degree program; Honors program; Independent study; Internships; Liberal arts/career combination; Student-designed major; Study abroad; Teacher certification program; Weekend college. Honors programs: LSA Honors Program; departmental honors programs Combined degree programs: BA/MA; BA/MEng. **Disability Services offered to physically disabled students:** Note-taking services; Reader services; Tape recorders; Tutors. **Career services:** Alumni network; Alumni services; Career assessment; Career/job search classes; Internships

FACILITIES
Housing: Apartments for married students; Apartments for single students; Coed dorms; Cooperative housing; Fraternity/sorority housing; Special housing for disabled student; Theme housing; Wellness housing; Women's dorms 95% of campus accessible to physically diasbled. **Special Academic Facilities/Equipment:** Anthropology, archaeology, art, dentistry, natural science, musical instruments, paleontology, and zoology museums; planetarium, electron microscope, athletic campus, medical center, nuclear lab, botanical garden, herbarium, arboretum. **Computers:** 85% of classrooms, 40% of dorms, 80% of libraries, 95% of dining areas, 80% of student union, 10% of common outdoor areas have wireless network access. Students can register for classes online. Administrative functions (other than registration) can be performed online.

CAMPUS LIFE
Environment: City **Activities:** Campus Ministries; Choral groups; Concert band; Dance; Drama/theater; International Student Organization; Jazz band; Literary magazine; Marching band; Model UN; Music ensembles; Musical theater; Opera; Pep band; Radio station; Student government; Student newspaper; Student-run film society; Symphony orchestra; Television station; Yearbook 1000 registered organizations, 13 honor societies, 67 religious organizations. 39 fraternities, 27 sororities. **Athletics (Intercollegiate):** *Men:* baseball, basketball, cheerleading, cross-country, diving, football, golf, gymnastics, ice hockey, swimming, tennis, track/field (outdoor), track/field (indoor), wrestling. *Women:* basketball, cheerleading, crew/rowing, cross-country, diving, field hockey, golf, gymnastics, soccer, softball, swimming, tennis, track/field (outdoor), track/field (indoor), volleyball, water polo. **On-Campus Highlights:** Michigan Stadium, Michigan Union, Diag, Campus Recreation Buildings, Wave Field **Environmental Initiatives:** Formal announcement of Campus Sustainability goals. http://sustainability.umich.edu/news/leadership-voice-president-colemans-speech-about-going-green-staying-blue-sustainability-michig

ADMISSIONS
Freshman Academic Profile: Average high school GPA 3.9. **Test Scores:** SAT Math middle 50% range 670-770. SAT EBRW middle 50% range 660-

730. ACT middle 50% range 30-33. Minimum internet-based TOEFL 100. Minimum paper TOEFL 600. **Basis for Candidate Selection:** *Very important factors considered include:* rigor of secondary school record, academic GPA. *Important factors considered include:* application essay, standardized test scores, recommendation(s), character/personal qualities, first generation. *Other factors considered include:* extracurricular activities, talent/ability, alumni/ae relation, geographical residence, state residency, volunteer work, work experience, level of applicant's interest. **Freshman Admission Requirements:** High school diploma is required and GED is accepted *Academic units required:* 4 English, 3 math, 3 science, 1 science labs, 2 foreign language, 1 social studies, 3 history, *Academic units recommended:* 4 English, 4 math, 4 science, 1 science labs, 4 foreign language, 1 social studies, 3 history, 1 computer science, 2 visual/performing arts. **Freshman Admission Statistics:** 59,886 applied, 26.5% admitted, 43% enrolled. **Transfer Admission Requirements:** High school transcript, college transcript(s), essay or personal statement, statement of good standing from prior institution(s). Minimum college GPA of 3.0 required. Lowest grade transferable C. **General Admission Information:** Application fee $75. Priority deadline 11/1. Regular application deadline 2/1. Nonfall registration accepted. Admission may be deferred for a maximum of 1 year.

COSTS AND FINANCIAL AID

Annual in-state tuition $11,198. Annual out-of-state tuition $48,814. Room and board $11,198. Required fees $328. Average book expense $1,048. **Required Forms and Deadlines:** CSS/Financial Aid PROFILE; FAFSA. **Notification of Awards:** Applicants will be notified of awards on a rolling basis beginning 3/15. **Types of Aid:** *Need-based scholarships/grants:* College/university scholarship or grant aid from institutional funds; Federal Pell; Private scholarships; SEOG; State scholarships/grants. *Loans:* Direct PLUS loans; Direct Subsidized Stafford Loans; Direct Unsubsidized Stafford Loans. *Student Employment:* Federal Work-Study Program available. Institutional employment available. **Financial Aid Statistics:** 83% needy freshmen, 82% needy undergrads receive need-based scholarship or grant aid. 71% freshmen, 63% undergrads receive non-need-based scholarship or grant aid. 70% freshmen, 78% undergrads receive need-based self-help aid. 2% freshmen, 3% undergrads receive athletic scholarships. 68% freshmen, 61% undergrads receive any aid. 44% undergrads borrow to pay for school. Average cumulative indebtedness $25,712. **Criteria for awarding aid:** *Need-based:* Academics *Non-need-based:* Academics, Alumni affiliation, Art, Athletics, Leadership, Music/drama, Religious affiliation, State/district residency.

UNIVERSITY OF MICHIGAN—DEARBORN

4901 Evergreen Road, Dearborn, MI 48128-1491
Phone: 313-593-5100 • **Financial Aid Phone:** 734-763-6600
E-mail: admissions@umd.umich.edu • **CEEB Code:** 1861
Fax: 313-436-9167 • **Website:** umdearborn.edu • **ACT Code:** 2074

This public school was founded in 1959. It has a 230 acre campus.

RATINGS
Admissions Selectivity Rating: 83   **Fire Safety Rating:** 60*   **Green Rating:** 60*

STUDENTS AND FACULTY
Enrollment: 6,843. **Student Body:** 48% female, 52% male, 4% out-of-state, 2% international (27 countries represented). Asian 7%, African American 10%, Caucasian 69%, Hispanic 6%, Native American <1%, Pacific Islander <1%, Two or more races 3%, Race unknown 3%.
Retention and Graduation: 81% freshmen return for sophomore year. 27% grads go on to further study within 1 year. 10% grads pursue arts and sciences degrees. 2.6% grads pursue law degrees. 4% grads pursue business degrees. 1.3% grads pursue medical degrees. **Faculty:** Student/faculty ratio 15:1. 322 full-time faculty, 87% hold PhDs, 34% are members of minority groups, 41% are women. 0% of classes are taught by teaching assistants.

ACADEMICS
Degrees: Bachelor's; Doctoral/Professional; Master's; Post-Bachelor's certificate **Classes:** Most classes have 10-19 students. **Most popular majors:** Mechanical Engineering; Biology/Biological Sciences, General; Psychology, General. **Special Study Options:** Cooperative education program; Cross-registration; Distance learning; Double major; Dual enrollment; Honors program; Independent study; Internships; Liberal arts/career combination; Student-designed major; Study abroad; Teacher certification program. Honors programs: Honors Transfers Innovators. **Disability Services offered to physically disabled students:** Note-taking services; Reader services; Tutors.

FACILITIES
Housing: 100% of campus accessible to physically diasbled.

CAMPUS LIFE
Environment: City **Activities:** Campus Ministries; Choral groups; International Student Organization; Literary magazine; Radio station; Student government; Student newspaper. McKinley Cafe/University Center, The Fieldhouse, Berkowitz Art Gallery, Henry Ford Estate and Trails

ADMISSIONS
Freshman Academic Profile: Average high school GPA 4.0. 28% in top 10% of high school class, 59% in top 25% of high school class, 90% in top 50% of high school class. **Test Scores:** ACT middle 50% range 21-27. Minimum internet-based TOEFL 80. Minimum paper TOEFL 550. **Basis for Candidate Selection:** *Very important factors considered include:* academic GPA, standardized test scores. *Other factors considered include:* application essay, interview, alumni/ae relation. **Freshman Admission Requirements:** High school diploma is required and GED is accepted *Academic units recommended:* 4 English, 4 math, 2 science, 1 science labs, 2 foreign language, 4 social studies, 4 history. **Freshman Admission Statistics:** 5,312 applied, 62.5% admitted, 29% enrolled. **Transfer Admission Requirements:** High school transcript, college transcript(s), Lowest grade transferable C. **General Admission Information:** Application fee $30. Regular application deadline 5/1. Nonfall registration accepted. Admission may be deferred for a maximum of 1 year.

COSTS AND FINANCIAL AID
Annual in-state tuition $10,872. Annual out-of-state tuition $46,676. Room and board $10,872. Required fees $328. Average book expense $1,048. **Required Forms and Deadlines:** FAFSA. **Notification of Awards:** Applicants will be notified of awards on a rolling basis beginning 3/15. **Types of Aid:** *Need-based scholarships/grants:* College/university scholarship or grant aid from institutional funds; Federal Pell; Private scholarships; SEOG; State scholarships/grants. *Loans:* Direct PLUS loans; Direct Subsidized Stafford Loans; Direct Unsubsidized Stafford Loans. *Student Employment:* Federal Work-Study Program available. Institutional employment available. **Financial Aid Statistics:** 90% needy freshmen, 84% needy undergrads receive need-based scholarship or grant aid. 50% freshmen, 34% undergrads receive non-need-based scholarship or grant aid. 86% freshmen, 92% undergrads receive need-based self-help aid. 2% freshmen, 2% undergrads receive athletic scholarships. 68% freshmen, 61% undergrads receive any aid. 65% undergrads borrow to pay for school. Average cumulative indebtedness $27,346. **Criteria for awarding aid:** *Need-based:* Leadership *Non-need-based:* Academics, Alumni affiliation, Art, Athletics, Job skills, Leadership, Minority status, Music/drama, State/district residency.

UNIVERSITY OF MICHIGAN—FLINT

303 E. Kearsley St., Flint, MI 48502
Phone: 810-762-3300 • **Financial Aid Phone:** 810-762-3444
E-mail: admissions@umflint.edu • **CEEB Code:** 1853
Fax: 810-762-3272 • **Website:** www.umflint.edu • **ACT Code:** 2063

This public school was founded in 1956. It has a 76 acre campus.

RATINGS
Admissions Selectivity Rating: 80   **Fire Safety Rating:** 96   **Green Rating:** 73

STUDENTS AND FACULTY
Enrollment: 5,669. **Student Body:** 61% female, 39% male, 2% out-of-state, 4% international (29 countries represented). Asian 2%, African American 13%, Caucasian 70%, Hispanic 4%, Native American 1%, Pacific Islander <1%, Two or more races 3%, Race unknown 2%.
Retention and Graduation: 77% freshmen return for sophomore year. 15% freshmen graduate within 4 years. 44% freshmen graduate within 6 years. **Faculty:** Student/faculty ratio 13:1. 326 full-time faculty, 77% hold PhDs, 19% are members of minority groups, 52% are women. 0% of classes are taught by teaching assistants.

ACADEMICS
Degrees: Bachelor's; Doctoral/Professional; Doctoral/Research; Master's; Post-Bachelor's certificate; Post-Master's certificate **Classes:** Most classes have 20-29 students. Most lab/discussion sessions have 20-29 students. **Most popular majors:** Psychology; Health Professions And Related Programs; Business, Management, Marketing, And Related Support Services. **Special Study Options:** Accelerated program; Cooperative education program; Distance learning; Double major; Dual enrollment; English as a Second

Language (ESL); Honors program; Independent study; Internships; Student-designed major; Study abroad; Teacher certification program. Honors programs: 4-yr University Honors Scholar Program 2-yr Phase I Freshman/Sophmore Honors Scholar Program 2-yr Phase II Junior/Senior Honors Scholar Program. **Disability Services offered to physically disabled students:** Note-taking services; Reader services; Tape recorders; Tutors. **Career services:** Alumni services; Career assessment; Career/job search classes; Internships

FACILITIES

Housing: Coed dorms 97% of campus accessible to physically diasbled. **Special Academic Facilities/Equipment:** Frances Wilson Thompson Library **Computers:** 100% of classrooms, 100% of dorms, 100% of libraries, 100% of dining areas, 100% of student union, have wireless network access. Students can register for classes online. Administrative functions (other than registration) can be performed online.

CAMPUS LIFE

Environment: City **Activities:** Choral groups; Concert band; Dance; Drama/theater; International Student Organization; Jazz band; Literary magazine; Music ensembles; Musical theater; Student government; Student newspaper 99 registered organizations, 7 honor societies, 6 religious organizations. 4 fraternities, 5 sororities. **On-Campus Highlights:** Recreation Center, University Center/Student Union, University Pavilion/Food Court/Bookstore, Resident's Hall and Riverfront, Frances Willson Thompson Library **Environmental Initiatives:** Recycling and Waste Minimization

ADMISSIONS

Freshman Academic Profile: Average high school GPA 3.4. 18% in top 10% of high school class, 43% in top 25% of high school class, 80% in top 50% of high school class. 92% from public high schools. **Test Scores:** SAT Math middle 50% range 460-590: SAT EBRW middle 50% range 490-610. ACT middle 50% range 20-26. Minimum internet-based TOEFL 61. Minimum paper TOEFL 500. **Basis for Candidate Selection:** *Very important factors considered include:* academic GPA, standardized test scores. *Important factors considered include:* extracurricular activities. *Other factors considered include:* class rank, application essay, recommendation(s), interview, talent/ability, first generation. **Freshman Admission Requirements:** High school diploma is required and GED is accepted *Academic units recommended:* 4 English, 4 math, 3 science, 3 foreign language, 3 history. **Freshman Admission Statistics:** 4,558 applied, 65.1% admitted, 23% enrolled. **Transfer Admission Requirements:** High school transcript, college transcript(s), Minimum college GPA of 2.0 required. Lowest grade transferable 2. **General Admission Information:** Application fee $30. Priority deadline 5/1. Regular application deadline 8/22. Nonfall registration accepted. Admission may be deferred for a maximum of 1 year.

COSTS AND FINANCIAL AID

Annual in-state tuition $8,437. Annual out-of-state tuition $21,222. Room and board $8,437. Required fees $432. Average book expense $1,000. **Required Forms and Deadlines:** FAFSA. **Notification of Awards:** Applicants will be notified of awards on a rolling basis beginning 12/15. **Types of Aid:** *Need-based scholarships/grants:* College/university scholarship or grant aid from institutional funds; Federal Pell; Private scholarships; SEOG; State scholarships/grants. *Loans:* Direct PLUS loans; Direct Subsidized Stafford Loans; Direct Unsubsidized Stafford Loans. *Student Employment:* Federal Work-Study Program available. Institutional employment available. **Financial Aid Statistics:** 74% needy freshmen, 75% needy undergrads receive need-based scholarship or grant aid. 33% freshmen, 22% undergrads receive non-need-based scholarship or grant aid. 80% freshmen, 83% undergrads receive need-based self-help aid. 0% freshmen, 0% undergrads receive athletic scholarships. 72% freshmen, 70% undergrads receive any aid. 64% undergrads borrow to pay for school. Average cumulative indebtedness $27,358. **Criteria for awarding aid:** *Need-based:* Academics, Art *Non-need-based:* Academics, Art, Leadership, Music/drama.

UNIVERSITY OF MINNESOTA, CROOKSTON

Eastern Michigan University, Crookston, MN 56716-5001
Phone: 218-281-8569 • **Financial Aid Phone:** 218-281-8563
E-mail: UMCinfo@umn.edu • **CEEB Code:** 6893
Fax: 218-281-8575 • **Website:** http://www1.crk.umn.edu/ • **ACT Code:** 2129

This public school was founded in 1966. It has a 37 acre campus.

RATINGS

Admissions Selectivity Rating: 79   **Fire Safety Rating:** 99   **Green Rating:** 75

STUDENTS AND FACULTY

Enrollment: 1,876. **Student Body:** 50% female, 50% male, 28% out-of-state, 4% international (35 countries represented). Asian 2%, African American 7%, Caucasian 80%, Hispanic 3%, Native American <1%, Pacific Islander <1%, Two or more races 1%, Race unknown 2%.
Retention and Graduation: 66% freshmen return for sophomore year. 12% grads go on to further study within 1 year. **Faculty:** Student/faculty ratio 20:1. 66 full-time faculty, 53% hold PhDs, 6% are members of minority groups, 41% are women. 0% of classes are taught by teaching assistants.

ACADEMICS

Degrees: Bachelor's; Certificate **Classes:** Most classes have fewer than 10 students. **Most popular majors:** Animal Sciences, General; Natural Resources/Conservation, General; Business Administration And Management, General. **Special Study Options:** Cooperative education program; Cross-registration; Distance learning; Double major; Dual enrollment; English as a Second Language (ESL); Honors program; Independent study; Internships; Student-designed major; Study abroad; Teacher certification program. Honors programs: The UMC Honors Program was developed to inspire and transform students' writing, discussion, and critical thinking skills in such a way that reflects high expectations for academically successful students. The program nurtures and challenges students to explore ideas, assess values, and develop leadership skills. Honors coursework addresses the diverse and global atmosphere in which we live. In addition, students in the Honors Program will have the opportunity for various social outings outside of the normal campus experience. Key features of the program consist of a required course that introduces the student to the rigors of the Honors Program; final requirements which include an honors proposal course that culminates in an honors essay; and a research or creative project that requires a public defense. The Honors Program includes the following components: 1. Honors courses (courses developed or to be developed include leadership, orientation courses, global perspective courses, composi¬tion courses) 2. Honors options (faculty-mentored, student-organized discussion groups) 3. Honors contracts (honors activities incorporated into "regular" courses) 4. Honors colloquia, leadership development, and cultural enrichment 5. Honors national or international experience 6. Honors essay, research or creative project (capstone experience). **Disability Services offered to physically disabled students:** Note-taking services; Reader services; Tape recorders; Tutors. **Career services:** Alumni services; Career assessment; Career/job search classes; Internships

FACILITIES

Housing: Apartments for single students; Coed dorms; Special housing for disabled students 90% of campus accessible to physically diasbled. **Special Academic Facilities/Equipment:** The new Immersive Visualization and Informatics Lab, one of only two in the Upper Midwest, allows faculty members and software engineering students to develop 3-D computer models and simulations; the Equine Arena and Stables feature a 90 x 120 ft. heated indoor riding arena, 45-stall horse stables, training pen, round pen, breeding phantom and stocks, and tack room; the Alseth NWSA Business Board Room is a classroom featuring state-of-the-art technology for business and marketing students; the Early Childhood Development Center provides students the opportunity to observe and participate in a teacher-training laboratory at a fully operational child care facility; the Production Horticulture Building and Greenhouse Complex is a production horticulture lab where horticulture students gain direct experience with the culture, care, and growth of commercial horticulture crops; the Bergland Laboratory is center for teaching, applied student lab experiences, and research in the agronomic, botanical, and horticultural sciences; located adjacent to campus, the 85-acre Red River Valley Natural History Area contains prairie, marshland, and forest ecosystems and is used extensively for practice in conservation techniques and nature observation. **Computers:** 20% of classrooms, 100% of dorms, 100% of libraries, 75% of dining areas, 100% of student union, 25% of common outdoor areas have wireless network access. Students can register for classes online. Administrative functions (other than registration) can be performed online.

CAMPUS LIFE

Environment: Village **Activities:** Campus Ministries; Choral groups; Drama/theater; International Student Organization; Jazz band; Musical theater; Pep band; Student government 38 registered organizations, 1 honor society, 2 religious organizations. 1 fraternity, 1 sorority. **Athletics (Intercollegiate):** *Men:* baseball, basketball, football, golf, ice hockey. *Women:* basketball, equestrian sports, golf, soccer, softball, tennis, volleyball. **On-Campus Highlights:** Sargeant Student Center, University Teaching and Outreach Center, Sports Center, Bergland Laboratory, Centennial Hall Student Apartments **Environmental Initiatives:** 1. Evaluate the reduction of coal as a primary feedstock for the campus energy and supplement with renewable fuels.

ADMISSIONS

Freshman Academic Profile: Average high school GPA 3.2. 12% in top 10% of high school class, 31% in top 25% of high school class, 65% in top 50% of high school class. **Test Scores:** SAT Math middle 50% range 470-510. SAT

EBRW middle 50% range 430-480. ACT middle 50% range 19-24. Minimum internet-based TOEFL 68. Minimum paper TOEFL 520. **Basis for Candidate Selection:** *Very important factors considered include:* rigor of secondary school record, class rank, academic GPA, standardized test scores. *Other factors considered include:* application essay, recommendation(s). **Freshman Admission Requirements:** High school diploma is required and GED is accepted *Academic units required:* 4 English, 3 math, 3 science, 2 science labs, 3 social studies, *Academic units recommended:* 2 foreign language. **Freshman Admission Statistics:** 927 applied, 71.4% admitted, 41% enrolled. **Transfer Admission Requirements:** college transcript(s), Minimum college GPA of 2.0 required. Lowest grade transferable D. **General Admission Information:** Application fee $30. Nonfall registration accepted. Admission may be deferred for a maximum of 1 semester.

COSTS AND FINANCIAL AID
Annual in-state tuition $8,418. Annual out-of-state tuition $10,180. Room and board $8,418. Required fees $1,520. Average book expense $1,200. **Required Forms and Deadlines:** FAFSA. **Notification of Awards:** Applicants will be notified of awards on a rolling basis beginning 3/1. **Types of Aid:** *Need-based scholarships/grants:* College/university scholarship or grant aid from institutional funds; Federal Pell; Private scholarships; SEOG; State scholarships/grants. *Loans:* Direct PLUS loans; Direct Subsidized Stafford Loans; Direct Unsubsidized Stafford Loans. *Student Employment:* Federal Work-Study Program available. Institutional employment available. **Financial Aid Statistics:** 96% needy freshmen, 90% needy undergrads receive need-based scholarship or grant aid. 11% freshmen, 8% undergrads receive non-need-based scholarship or grant aid. 74% freshmen, 78% undergrads receive need-based self-help aid. 9% freshmen, 4% undergrads receive athletic scholarships. 88% freshmen, 48% undergrads receive any aid. 80% undergrads borrow to pay for school. Average cumulative indebtedness $28,309. **Criteria for awarding aid:** *Non-need-based:* Academics, Alumni affiliation, Athletics, Leadership, Minority status, Music/drama, State/district residency.

UNIVERSITY OF MINNESOTA—DULUTH

1049 University Drive, Duluth, MN 55812-3000
Phone: 218-726-7171 • **Financial Aid Phone:** (218) 726-8000
E-mail: umdadmis@d.umn.edu • **CEEB Code:** 6873
Fax: 218-726-7040 • **Website:** www.d.umn.edu • **ACT Code:** 2157

This public school was founded in 1947. It has a 247 acre campus.

RATINGS
Admissions Selectivity Rating: 79   **Fire Safety Rating:** 93   **Green Rating:** 95

STUDENTS AND FACULTY
Enrollment: 9,051. **Student Body:** 45% female, 55% male, 12% out-of-state, 2% international (42 countries represented). Asian 3%, African American 2%, Caucasian 85%, Hispanic 3%, Native American 1%, Pacific Islander <1%, Two or more races 3%, Race unknown 1%.
Retention and Graduation: 78% freshmen return for sophomore year. 16% grads go on to further study within 1 year. **Faculty:** Student/faculty ratio 18:1. 508 full-time faculty, 74% hold PhDs, 18% are members of minority groups, 45% are women.

ACADEMICS
Degrees: Bachelor's; Certificate; Doctoral/Professional; Master's; Post-Bachelor's certificate **Classes:** Most classes have 10-19 students. Most lab/discussion sessions have 10-19 students. **Most popular majors:** Elementary Education And Teaching; Biology/Biological Sciences, General; Business Administration And Management, General. **Special Study Options:** Accelerated program; Cooperative education program; Cross-registration; Distance learning; Double major; Dual enrollment; English as a Second Language (ESL); Exchange student program (domestic); Honors program; Independent study; Internships; Liberal arts/career combination; Student-designed major; Study abroad; Teacher certification program; Weekend college. Honors programs: The Honors Program offers motivated students who are serious about their intellectual and personal growth a variety of special classes enhanced by cultural events and activities, as well as leadership and research opportunities. **Disability Services offered to physically disabled students:** Note-taking services; Reader services; Tape recorders; Tutors. **Career services:** Alumni services; Career assessment; Career/job search classes; Internships

FACILITIES
Housing: Apartments for single students; Coed dorms; Men's dorms; Special housing for disabled student; Theme housing; Women's dorms 100% of campus

accessible to physically diasbled. **Special Academic Facilities/Equipment:** Art museum, planetarium, music performance hall, theatre. **Computers:** 100% of classrooms, 100% of libraries, 100% of dining areas, 100% of student union, have wireless network access. Students can register for classes online. Administrative functions (other than registration) can be performed online.

CAMPUS LIFE
Environment: Village **Activities:** Campus Ministries; Choral groups; Concert band; Dance; Drama/theater; International Student Organization; Jazz band; Marching band; Music ensembles; Musical theater; Opera; Pep band; Radio station; Student government; Student newspaper; Student-run film society; Symphony orchestra 150 registered organizations, 10 honor societies, 7 religious organizations. 2 fraternities, 2 sororities. **Athletics (Intercollegiate):** *Men:* baseball, basketball, cross-country, football, ice hockey, track/field (outdoor), track/field (indoor). *Women:* basketball, cross-country, ice hockey, soccer, softball, tennis, track/field (outdoor), track/field (indoor), volleyball. **On-Campus Highlights:** Solon Campus Center, Library, Residence Halls, Kirby Student Center Food Court, Sports and Health Center **Environmental Initiatives:** LEED

ADMISSIONS
Freshman Academic Profile: Average high school GPA 3.5. 17% in top 10% of high school class, 42% in top 25% of high school class, 85% in top 50% of high school class. 94% from public high schools. **Test Scores:** SAT Math middle 50% range 500-610. SAT EBRW middle 50% range 450-590. ACT middle 50% range 22-26. Minimum internet-based TOEFL 80. Minimum paper TOEFL 550. **Basis for Candidate Selection:** *Very important factors considered include:* academic GPA, standardized test scores. *Important factors considered include:* rigor of secondary school record. *Other factors considered include:* class rank, application essay, recommendation(s), extracurricular activities, talent/ability, character/personal qualities, first generation, alumni/ae relation, geographical residence, state residency, racial/ethnic status, volunteer work, work experience. **Freshman Admission Requirements:** High school diploma is required and GED is accepted *Academic units required:* 4 English, 4 math, 3 science, 2 foreign language, 3 social studies, 1 visual/performing arts. **Freshman Admission Statistics:** 7,973 applied, 76.6% admitted, 35% enrolled. **Transfer Admission Requirements:** High school transcript, college transcript(s), Minimum college GPA of 2.0 required. Lowest grade transferable D. **General Admission Information:** Application fee $40. Priority deadline 12/1. Regular application deadline 6/15. Nonfall registration accepted.

COSTS AND FINANCIAL AID
Required Forms and Deadlines: FAFSA. **Notification of Awards:** Applicants will be notified of awards on a rolling basis beginning 2/1. **Types of Aid:** *Need-based scholarships/grants:* College/university scholarship or grant aid from institutional funds; Federal Pell; Private scholarships; SEOG; State scholarships/grants. *Loans:* Direct PLUS loans; Direct Subsidized Stafford Loans; Direct Unsubsidized Stafford Loans. *Student Employment:* Federal Work-Study Program available. Institutional employment available. **Financial Aid Statistics:** 100% needy freshmen, 97% needy undergrads receive need-based scholarship or grant aid. 25% freshmen, 27% undergrads receive non-need-based scholarship or grant aid. 84% freshmen, 87% undergrads receive need-based self-help aid. 0% freshmen, 0% undergrads receive athletic scholarships. 85% freshmen, 81% undergrads receive any aid. **Criteria for awarding aid:** *Need-based:* Alumni affiliation, Athletics, Minority status *Non-need-based:* Academics, Alumni affiliation, Art, Athletics, Leadership, Minority status, Music/drama, State/district residency.

UNIVERSITY OF MINNESOTA, MORRIS

600 E 4th St, Morris, MN 56267
Phone: 320-589-6035 • **Financial Aid Phone:** 800-992-8863 / 320-589-6046
E-mail: http://admissions.morris.umn.edu/contact • **CEEB Code:** 6890
Fax: 320-589-6051 • **Website:** www.morris.umn.edu • **ACT Code:** 2155

This public school was founded in 1959. It has a 130 acre campus.

RATINGS
Admissions Selectivity Rating: 85   **Fire Safety Rating:** 98   **Green Rating:** 97

STUDENTS AND FACULTY
Enrollment: 1,552. **Student Body:** 56% female, 44% male, 17% out-of-state, 11% international (21 countries represented). Asian 3%, African American 2%, Caucasian 58%, Hispanic 5%, Native American 8%, Pacific Islander 0%, Two or more races 13%, Race unknown <1%.
Retention and Graduation: 80% freshmen return for sophomore year. 50% freshmen graduate within 4 years. 59% freshmen graduate within 6 years. 20%

grads go on to further study within 1 year. 81% grads pursue arts and sciences degrees. 0% grads pursue law degrees. 2% grads pursue business degrees. 5% grads pursue medical degrees. **Faculty:** Student/faculty ratio 11:1. 125 full-time faculty, 93% hold PhDs, 12% are members of minority groups, 44% are women. 0% of classes are taught by teaching assistants.

ACADEMICS

Degrees: Bachelor's **Classes:** Most classes have 10-19 students. Most lab/discussion sessions have 10-19 students. **Most popular majors:** Biology/Biological Sciences, General; Psychology, General; Economics, General. **Special Study Options:** Cross-registration; Distance learning; Double major; Dual enrollment; English as a Second Language (ESL); Exchange student program (domestic); Honors program; Independent study; Internships; Student-designed major; Study abroad; Teacher certification program. Honors programs: The University of Minnesota, Morris Honors Program provides motivated, high-achieving students a distinctive, academically challenging intellectual experience amplifying and complementing the Morris liberal arts education. Successful completion of the Honors Program, an interdisciplinary curriculum team-taught by faculty from across the campus, provides the student a Morris degree "with Honors" in recognition of their achievement. **Disability Services offered to physically disabled students:** Note-taking services; Reader services; Tape recorders; Tutors. **Career services:** Alumni network; Alumni services; Career assessment; Career/job search classes; Internships

FACILITIES

Housing: Apartments for single students; Coed dorms; Special housing for disabled student; Theme housing 70% of campus accessible to physically diasbled. **Special Academic Facilities/Equipment:** Morrison Art Gallery, conservatory, observatory **Computers:** Students can register for classes online. Administrative functions (other than registration) can be performed online.

CAMPUS LIFE

Environment: Rural **Activities:** Campus Ministries; Choral groups; Concert band; Dance; Drama/theater; International Student Organization; Jazz band; Literary magazine; Music ensembles; Musical theater; Radio station; Student government; Student newspaper; Symphony orchestra 90 registered organizations, 5 honor societies, 12 religious organizations. **Athletics (Intercollegiate):** *Men:* baseball, basketball, football, golf, tennis, track/field (outdoor), track/field (indoor). *Women:* basketball, cross-country, diving, golf, soccer, softball, swimming, tennis, track/field (outdoor), track/field (indoor), volleyball. **On-Campus Highlights:** Student Center — KUMM, Turtle Mountain café, Regional Fitness Center — Indoor/Outdoor Center, pools, Science Center, Humanities Fine Arts Center — gallery, concerts, recitals, The Mall — outdoor grass/recreation area **Environmental Initiatives:** 1. Morris is actively working to become a sustainable and low-carbon community, and renewable energy research and demonstration is a big part of that effort. Morris receives power from two 1.65 MW University of Minnesota wind turbines. We receive 60% of our annual electricity from wind. We have an on-campus biomass gasification research and demonstration platform. We have solar thermal and solar PV projects on campus. And we have completed a multi-million dollar energy service contract to retrofit the campus for conservation.

ADMISSIONS

Freshman Academic Profile: Average high school GPA 3.6. 24% in top 10% of high school class, 49% in top 25% of high school class, 84% in top 50% of high school class. 95% from public high schools. **Test Scores:** SAT Math middle 50% range 590-710. SAT EBRW middle 50% range 560-680. ACT middle 50% range 22-28. Minimum internet-based TOEFL 79. Minimum paper TOEFL 550. **Basis for Candidate Selection:** *Very important factors considered include:* rigor of secondary school record, class rank, academic GPA, standardized test scores. *Important factors considered include:* extracurricular activities, talent/ability, character/personal qualities, volunteer work, work experience. *Other factors considered include:* application essay, recommendation(s), interview, first generation. **Freshman Admission Requirements:** High school diploma is required and GED is accepted *Academic units required:* 4 English, 4 math, 3 science, 2 foreign language, 3 social studies. **Freshman Admission Statistics:** 3,211 applied, 63.8% admitted, 17% enrolled. **Transfer Admission Requirements:** college transcript(s), essay or personal statement, statement of good standing from prior institution(s). Minimum college GPA of 2.5 required. Lowest grade transferable D. **General Admission Information:** Application fee $35. Priority deadline 12/15. Regular application deadline 3/15. Nonfall registration accepted. Admission may be deferred for a maximum of 1 year.

COSTS AND FINANCIAL AID

Required Forms and Deadlines: FAFSA. **Notification of Awards:** Applicants will be notified of awards on a rolling basis beginning 4/1. **Types of Aid:** *Need-based scholarships/grants:* College/university scholarship or grant aid from institutional funds; Federal Pell; Private scholarships; SEOG; State scholarships/grants. *Loans:* Direct PLUS loans; Direct Subsidized Stafford Loans; Direct Unsubsidized Stafford Loans. *Student Employment:*

Federal Work-Study Program available. Institutional employment available. **Financial Aid Statistics:** 97% needy freshmen, 96% needy undergrads receive need-based scholarship or grant aid. 9% freshmen, 9% undergrads receive non-need-based scholarship or grant aid. 63% freshmen, 63% undergrads receive need-based self-help aid. 0% freshmen, 0% undergrads receive athletic scholarships. 93% freshmen, 89% undergrads receive any aid. Average cumulative indebtedness $25,732. **Criteria for awarding aid:** *Non-need-based:* Academics.

UNIVERSITY OF MINNESOTA—TWIN CITIES

100 Church St. S.E., Minneapolis, MN 55455-0213
Phone: 612-625-2008 • **Financial Aid Phone:** 612-624-1111 or 1-800-400-8636 • **CEEB Code:** 6874
Fax: 612-626-1693 • **Website:** https://twin-cities.umn.edu/ • **ACT Code:** 2156

This public school was founded in 1851. It has a 2000 acre campus.

RATINGS

Admissions Selectivity Rating: 90   **Fire Safety Rating:** 88   **Green Rating:** 94

STUDENTS AND FACULTY

Enrollment: 31,535. **Student Body:** 52% female, 48% male, 27% out-of-state, 9% international (139 countries represented). Asian 10%, African American 5%, Caucasian 68%, Hispanic 4%, Native American <1%, Pacific Islander <1%, Two or more races 4%, Race unknown 1%.
Retention and Graduation: 93% freshmen return for sophomore year. 64% freshmen graduate within 4 years. 80% freshmen graduate within 6 years. **Faculty:** Student/faculty ratio 17:1. 2,599 full-time faculty, 80% hold PhDs, 18% are members of minority groups, 43% are women.

ACADEMICS

Degrees: Bachelor's; Certificate; Diploma; Doctoral; Doctoral/Professional; Doctoral/Research; Master's; Post-Bachelor's certificate; Post-Master's certificate **Classes:** Most classes have 10-19 students. Most lab/discussion sessions have fewer than 10 students. **Most popular majors:** Journalism; Rhetoric And Composition; Psychology, General. **Special Study Options:** Accelerated program; Cooperative education program; Cross-registration; Distance learning; Double major; Dual enrollment; English as a Second Language (ESL); Exchange student program (domestic); External degree program; Honors program; Independent study; Internships; Liberal arts/career combination; Student-designed major; Study abroad; Teacher certification program. Honors programs: Honors, Undergraduate Research Opportunities Program Combined degree programs: BA/MA; BA/MD. **Disability Services offered to physically disabled students:** Note-taking services; Reader services; Tape recorders; Tutors. **Career services:** Alumni network; Alumni services; Career assessment; Career/job search classes; Internships; Regional alumni

FACILITIES

Housing: Apartments for married students; Apartments for single students; Coed dorms; Cooperative housing; Fraternity/sorority housing; Special housing for disabled student; Special housing for international students **Special Academic Facilities/Equipment:** Frederick R. Weisman Art Museum, Bell Museum of Natural History, Ted Mann Concert Hall, Recreational Sports Center, Civil Engineering Building, Basic Sciences/Biomedical Engineering Building, Coffman Memorial Union, West Bank Arts Quarter, Goldstein Gallery, Arboretum **Computers:** Students can register for classes online. Administrative functions (other than registration) can be performed online.

CAMPUS LIFE

Environment: Metropolis **Activities:** Choral groups; Concert band; Dance; Drama/theater; International Student Organization; Jazz band; Literary magazine; Marching band; Model UN; Music ensembles; Musical theater; Opera; Pep band; Radio station; Student government; Student newspaper; Student-run film society; Symphony orchestra; Television station 600 registered organizations, 10 religious organizations. 22 fraternities, 12 sororities. **Athletics (Intercollegiate):** *Men:* baseball, basketball, cross-country, diving, football, golf, gymnastics, ice hockey, swimming, tennis, track/field (outdoor), track/field (indoor), wrestling. *Women:* basketball, cheerleading, cross-country, diving, golf, gymnastics, ice hockey, soccer, softball, swimming, tennis, track/field (outdoor), track/field (indoor), volleyball. **On-Campus Highlights:** Weisman Art

Museum, McNamara Alumni Center, TCF Bank Stadium, Goldstein Gallery, Northrup Memorial Auditorium **Environmental Initiatives:** The University of Minnesota adopted a systemwide sustainability and energy efficiency policy in 2004 founded on earlier waste abatement and energy policies. The University established goals to implement the policy, including one of the most important undertakings as a systemwide signatory of the American College and University Presidents' Climate Commitment (2008). The commitment and Climate Action Plan (CAP) include reducing our carbon footprint but also integrating climate science into the fiber of the university—curriculum, research, outreach and engagement. The University of Minnesota engages its students and faculty in various ways. The It All Adds Up campaign strives to raise awareness within the campus community about energy use and to encourage the community to use energy more efficiently. It All Adds Up has resulted in over 14,000 individual pledges campus wide to conserve energy. When combined with other energy conservation efforts, they helped the University avoid more than $6.8 million (cumulatively about $15 Million) in energy costs, and resulted in the release of nearly 112,000 fewer tons of CO2 into the atmosphere annually. Greenhouse gas emissions from energy sources dropped by 22% compared to the 2008 baseline. The University also received the Xcel Energy's Platinum award in 2013 for its long term commitment to energy conservation. In collaboration between It All Adds Up and Housing and Residential Life, the Live Green Games Program was created with the ultimate goal of encouraging students to participate in energy conservation to help the University meet it's goals. In 2013, a new gaming feature was piloted in order to make sustainability fun and effortless. A list of green acts was promoted among students, showing how they could help create a more sustainable campus, community and world. The pilot resulted in over 7000 acts of green – saving 125 tons of carbon, over 97,000 gallons of water and 252,000kWh electricity. The University Services Sustainability Office collaborates with faculty to raise awareness of the campus CAP. For example, the Sustainability Director presented on the CAP, which was featured in Architecture 5750—Planning and Design of the University, a course offered through College of Design. The Sustainability Office participated on the steering committee and work teams to update the City of Minneapolis Climate Action Plan, which provides a roadmap to guide Minneapolis towards greenhouse gas emissions reduction targets. The Twin Cities and Morris campuses, Twin Cities Sustainability Education program and Institute on the Environmental provided space and some support for the Next Generation Congress – a group of students who developed long term environmental policy recommendations and delivered them to the Governor's Environmental Congress. The recommendations included addressing climate impacts by supporting renewable energy and sustainable energy and building practices. Some of these students connected through programs and education the University offered to raised awareness about energy and climate, such as It All Adds Up and the Sustainability Minor. The student leaders who helped organize the efforts received the Assn. for the Advancement of Sustainability in Higher Education (AASHE) Student Leadership Award. Links: http://italladdsup.umn.edu/news/platinum.award_03132013.php http://ow.ly/tDUAt http://ow.ly/tDUWF

ADMISSIONS

Freshman Academic Profile: 50% in top 10% of high school class, 84% in top 25% of high school class, 99% in top 50% of high school class. **Test Scores:** SAT Math middle 50% range 650-760. SAT EBRW middle 50% range 620-720. ACT middle 50% range 26-31. Minimum internet-based TOEFL 79. **Basis for Candidate Selection:** *Very important factors considered include:* rigor of secondary school record, class rank, academic GPA, standardized test scores. *Other factors considered include:* extracurricular activities, talent/ability, character/personal qualities, first generation, alumni/ae relation, geographical residence, racial/ethnic status, volunteer work, work experience. **Freshman Admission Requirements:** High school diploma is required and GED is accepted *Academic units required:* 4 English, 4 math, 3 science, 1 science labs, 2 foreign language, 3 social studies, 1 visual/performing arts, *Academic units recommended:* 4 English, 4 math, 4 science, 1 science labs, 2 foreign language, 3 social studies, 1 visual/performing arts. **Freshman Admission Statistics:** 43,720 applied, 49.6% admitted, 29% enrolled. **Transfer Admission Requirements:** college transcript(s), Minimum college GPA of 2.0 required. Lowest grade transferable D. **General Admission Information:** Application fee $55. Priority deadline 11/1. Nonfall registration accepted. Admission may be deferred.

COSTS AND FINANCIAL AID

Required Forms and Deadlines: FAFSA; Institution's own financial aid form. **Notification of Awards:** Applicants will be notified of awards on a rolling basis beginning 2/15. **Types of Aid:** *Need-based scholarships/grants:* College/university scholarship or grant aid from institutional funds; Federal Nursing Scholarships; Federal Pell; Private scholarships; SEOG; State scholarships/grants. *Loans:* Direct PLUS loans; Direct Subsidized Stafford Loans; Direct Unsubsidized Stafford Loans. *Student Employment:* Federal Work-Study Program available. Institutional employment available. **Financial Aid Statistics:** 84% needy freshmen, 83% needy undergrads receive need-based

scholarship or grant aid. 10% freshmen, 7% undergrads receive non-need-based scholarship or grant aid. 81% freshmen, 82% undergrads receive need-based self-help aid. 1% freshmen, 0% undergrads receive athletic scholarships. 59% undergrads borrow to pay for school. Average cumulative indebtedness $26,006. **Criteria for awarding aid:** *Non-need-based:* Academics, Art, Athletics, Job skills, Leadership, Minority status, Music/drama, State/district residency.

UNIVERSITY OF MISSISSIPPI

PO Box 1848, University, MS 38677
Phone: 662-915-7226 • **Financial Aid Phone:** 800-891-4596
E-mail: admissions@olemiss.edu • **CEEB Code:** 1840
Fax: 662-915-5869 • **Website:** www.olemiss.edu • **ACT Code:** 2250

This public school was founded in 1844. It has a 3391 acre campus.

RATINGS

Admissions Selectivity Rating: 79   **Fire Safety Rating:** 90   **Green Rating:** 60*

STUDENTS AND FACULTY

Enrollment: 18,975. **Student Body:** 56% female, 44% male, 44% out-of-state, 1% international. Asian 2%, African American 13%, Caucasian 78%, Hispanic 3%, Native American <1%, Pacific Islander <1%, Two or more races 2%, Race unknown <1%.
Retention and Graduation: 85% freshmen return for sophomore year.
Faculty: Student/faculty ratio 18:1. 1,045 full-time faculty, 76% hold PhDs, 21% are members of minority groups, 49% are women.

ACADEMICS

Degrees: Bachelor's; Doctoral; Doctoral/Professional; Doctoral/Research; Master's; Post-Bachelor's certificate; Post-Master's certificate **Classes:** Most classes have 10-19 students. Most lab/discussion sessions have 10-19 students. **Most popular majors:** Elementary Education And Teaching; Accounting; Marketing/Marketing Management, General. **Special Study Options:** Accelerated program; Cooperative education program; Distance learning; Double major; Dual enrollment; English as a Second Language (ESL); Exchange student program (domestic); Honors program; Independent study; Internships; Study abroad; Teacher certification program. Honors programs: Sally McDonnell-Barksdale Honors College. **Disability Services offered to physically disabled students:** Note-taking services; Reader services; Tape recorders.

FACILITIES

Housing: Apartments for married students; Apartments for single students; Fraternity/sorority housing; Men's dorms; Special housing for international students; Theme housing; Wellness housing; Women's dorms **Special Academic Facilities/Equipment:** Sally McDonnell-Barksdale Honors College, Croft Institute for International Studies, National Food Service Management Institute, Mississippi Center for Supercomputing Research,Art and archaeology museums, Sarah Isom Center for Women & Gender Studies, Center for Study of Southern Culture,William Faulkner home, Marine Minerals Research Institute, National Center for Physical Acoustics, National Center for Natural Products Research, Biological Field Station, Barksdale Reading Institute, Ford Center for the Performing Arts, William Winter Institutue for Racial Reconciliation, Paris-Yates Chapel, Trent Lott Leadership Institute, Living Blues Archive, Student Media Center, Center for Inclusion and Cross-Cultural Engagement,Mary Buie Museum, Luckyday Residential College **Computers:** 30% of classrooms, 100% of dorms, 100% of libraries, 80% of dining areas, 100% of student union, 30% of common outdoor areas have wireless network access. Students can register for classes online. Administrative functions (other than registration) can be performed online.

CAMPUS LIFE

Environment: Village **Activities:** Campus Ministries; Choral groups; Concert band; Dance; Drama/theater; International Student Organization; Jazz band; Marching band; Music ensembles; Musical theater; Opera; Pep band; Radio station; Student government; Student newspaper; Symphony orchestra; Television station; Yearbook 250 registered organizations, 25 honor societies, 21 religious organizations, 18 fraternities, 13 sororities. **Athletics (Intercollegiate):** *Men:* baseball, basketball, cheerleading, cross-country, football, golf, tennis, track/field (outdoor), track/field (indoor). *Women:* basketball, cheerleading, cross-country, golf, riflery, soccer, softball, tennis, track/field (outdoor), track/field (indoor), volleyball. **On-Campus Highlights:** The Grove, Gertrude C. Ford Center for the Performing Arts, Vaught-Hemingway Football Stadium, The Pavillion Basketball Arena, Starbucks Coffee Shop **Environmental Initiatives:** UM is installing SmartMeters on the majority of campus buildings.

ADMISSIONS

Freshman Academic Profile: Average high school GPA 3.6. 25% in top 10% of high school class, 50% in top 25% of high school class, 80% in top 50% of high school class. **Test Scores:** SAT Math middle 50% range 500-620. SAT EBRW middle 50% range 500-610. ACT middle 50% range 22-29. Minimum paper TOEFL 550. **Basis for Candidate Selection:** *Important factors considered include:* academic GPA, standardized test scores. *Other factors considered include:* rigor of secondary school record, class rank. **Freshman Admission Requirements:** High school diploma is required and GED is accepted *Academic units required:* 4 English, 3 math, 3 science, 2 science labs, 2 foreign language, 3 social studies, 0.5 computer science, 1 visual/performing arts, *Academic units recommended:* 4 English, 4 math, 4 science, 2 science labs, 2 foreign language, 4 social studies, 0.5 computer science, 1 visual/performing arts, 2 units from above areas or other academic areas. **Freshman Admission Statistics:** 17,918 applied, 78.3% admitted, 28% enrolled. **Transfer Admission Requirements:** college transcript(s), Minimum college GPA of 2.0 required. Lowest grade transferable D. **General Admission Information:** Application fee $40. Priority deadline 4/1. Nonfall registration accepted. Admission may be deferred.

COSTS AND FINANCIAL AID

Annual out-of-state tuition $23,454. Required fees $100. Average book expense $1,200. **Required Forms and Deadlines:** FAFSA. **Notification of Awards:** Applicants will be notified of awards on a rolling basis beginning 4/1. **Types of Aid:** *Need-based scholarships/grants:* College/university scholarship or grant aid from institutional funds; Federal Pell; Private scholarships; SEOG; State scholarships/grants. *Loans:* Direct PLUS loans; Direct Subsidized Stafford Loans; Direct Unsubsidized Stafford Loans. *Student Employment:* Federal Work-Study Program available. Institutional employment available. **Financial Aid Statistics:** 88% needy freshmen, 84% needy undergrads receive need-based scholarship or grant aid. 16% freshmen, 10% undergrads receive non-need-based scholarship or grant aid. 70% freshmen, 75% undergrads receive need-based self-help aid. 1% freshmen, 1% undergrads receive athletic scholarships. 87% freshmen, 81% undergrads receive any aid. 50% undergrads borrow to pay for school. Average cumulative indebtedness $27,535. **Criteria for awarding aid:** *Need-based:* Academics, Leadership *Non-need-based:* Academics, Alumni affiliation, Art, Athletics, Leadership, Music/drama, State/district residency.

UNIVERSITY OF MISSOURI

230 Jesse Hall, Columbia, MO 65211
Phone: 573-882-7786 • **Financial Aid Phone:** 573-882-7506
E-mail: MU4U@missouri.edu • **CEEB Code:** 260735
Fax: 573-882-7887 • **Website:** www.missouri.edu • **ACT Code:** 2382

This public school was founded in 1839. It has a 1262 acre campus.

RATINGS

Admissions Selectivity Rating: 81   **Fire Safety Rating:** 95   **Green Rating:** 91

STUDENTS AND FACULTY

Enrollment: 23,455. **Student Body:** 52% female, 48% male, 21% out-of-state, 4% international (120 countries represented). Asian 3%, African American 7%, Caucasian 78%, Hispanic 4%, Native American <1%, Pacific Islander <1%, Two or more races 3%, Race unknown 1%.
Retention and Graduation: 87% freshmen return for sophomore year. 68% freshmen graduate within 6 years. **Faculty:** Student/faculty ratio 18:1. 1,246 full-time faculty, 91% hold PhDs, 23% are members of minority groups, 41% are women.

ACADEMICS

Degrees: Bachelor's; Doctoral; Doctoral/Professional; Doctoral/Research; Master's; Post-Master's certificate **Classes:** Most classes have 20-29 students. Most lab/discussion sessions have 20-29 students. **Most popular majors:** Journalism; Biological And Biomedical Sciences, Other; Business/Commerce,

General. **Special Study Options:** Accelerated program; Cooperative education program; Cross-registration; Distance learning; Double major; English as a Second Language (ESL); Exchange student program (domestic); External degree program; Honors program; Independent study; Internships; Liberal arts/career combination; Student-designed major; Study abroad; Teacher certification program. Honors programs: Honors College Combined degree programs: BA/MA. **Disability Services offered to physically disabled students:** Note-taking services; Reader services; Tape recorders; Tutors. **Career services:** Alumni network; Alumni services; Career assessment; Career/job search classes; Internships; Regional alumni

FACILITIES

Housing: Apartments for married students; Coed dorms; Fraternity/sorority housing; Men's dorms; Women's dorms 100% of campus accessible to physically disabled. **Special Academic Facilities/Equipment:** Life Sciences Center for Research Tiger Place, a licensed care facility Department of Nursing James B Nutter Family Information Ellis Library Museum of Anthropology Museum of Art and Archeology World's most powerful university research reactor for Nuclear Medicine one of 15 European Union Centers on college campuses MU Botanic Garden **Computers:** 100% of classrooms, 10% of dorms, 100% of libraries, 100% of dining areas, 100% of student union, 10% of common outdoor areas have wireless network access. Students can register for classes online. Administrative functions (other than registration) can be performed online.

CAMPUS LIFE

Environment: City **Activities:** Campus Ministries; Choral groups; Concert band; Dance; Drama/theater; International Student Organization; Jazz band; Literary magazine; Marching band; Model UN; Music ensembles; Musical theater; Opera; Pep band; Radio station; Student government; Student newspaper; Student-run film society; Symphony orchestra; Television station; Yearbook 598 registered organizations, 25 honor societies, 47 religious organizations. 32 fraternities, 19 sororities. **Athletics (Intercollegiate):** *Men:* baseball, basketball, cross-country, diving, football, golf, swimming, track/field (outdoor), track/field (indoor), wrestling. *Women:* basketball, cheerleading, cross-country, diving, golf, gymnastics, soccer, softball, swimming, tennis, track/field (outdoor), track/field (indoor), volleyball. **On-Campus Highlights:** Student Recreation Center—expanded & renovated in 2005, Mizzou Arena—home of Tiger Basketball, Memorial Stadium—home of Tiger Football, Jesse Hall—administration; concert hall, Life Sciences Center—interdisciplinary research facility **Environmental Initiatives:** Signatory to ACUPCC climate change commitment.

ADMISSIONS

Freshman Academic Profile: 30% in top 10% of high school class, 59% in top 25% of high school class, 89% in top 50% of high school class. **Test Scores:** SAT Math middle 50% range 550-670. SAT EBRW middle 50% range 570-680. ACT middle 50% range 23-29. Minimum internet-based TOEFL 61. Minimum paper TOEFL 500. **Basis for Candidate Selection:** *Very important factors considered include:* academic GPA, standardized test scores. *Important factors considered include:* rigor of secondary school record, class rank. *Other factors considered include:* application essay, recommendation(s), talent/ability, first generation, racial/ethnic status, volunteer work, work experience, level of applicant's interest. **Freshman Admission Requirements:** High school diploma is required and GED is accepted *Academic units required:* 4 English, 4 math, 3 science, 1 science labs, 2 foreign language, 3 social studies, and 1 unit from above areas or other academic areas. **Freshman Admission Statistics:** 16,373 applied, 78.1% admitted, 32% enrolled. **Transfer Admission Requirements:** college transcript(s), Minimum college GPA of 2.5 required. **General Admission Information:** Application fee $60. Priority deadline 5/1. Nonfall registration accepted. Admission may be deferred.

COSTS AND FINANCIAL AID

Annual in-state tuition $10,676. Annual out-of-state tuition $25,179. Room and board $10,676. Required fees $1,327. Average book expense $1,372. **Required Forms and Deadlines:** FAFSA. **Notification of Awards:** Applicants will be notified of awards on a rolling basis beginning 12/15. **Types of Aid:** *Need-based scholarships/grants:* College/university scholarship or grant aid from institutional funds; Federal Nursing Scholarships; Federal Pell; Private scholarships; SEOG; State scholarships/grants. *Loans:* Direct PLUS loans; Direct Subsidized Stafford Loans; Direct Unsubsidized Stafford Loans. *Student Employment:* Federal Work-Study Program available. Institutional employment available. **Financial Aid Statistics:** 84% needy freshmen, 80% needy undergrads receive need-based scholarship or grant aid. 8% freshmen, 5% undergrads receive non-need-based scholarship or grant aid. 72% freshmen, 76% undergrads receive need-based self-help aid. 1% freshmen, 1% undergrads receive athletic scholarships. **Criteria for awarding aid:** *Need-based:* Academics, Alumni affiliation, Art, Athletics, Leadership, Minority status, Music/drama *Non-need-based:* Academics, Alumni affiliation, Art, Athletics, Leadership, Minority status, Music/drama, State/district residency.

UNIVERSITY OF MISSOURI—KANSAS CITY

5100 Rockhill Road, Kansas City, MO 64114
Phone: 816-235-1111 • **Financial Aid Phone:** 816-235-1154
E-mail: admit@umkc.edu • **CEEB Code:** 6872
Fax: 816-235-5544 • **Website:** www.umkc.edu • **ACT Code:** 2380

This public school was founded in 1929. It has a 191 acre campus.

RATINGS
Admissions Selectivity Rating: 84   **Fire Safety Rating:** 82   **Green Rating:** 97

STUDENTS AND FACULTY
Enrollment: 7,872. **Student Body:** 57% female, 43% male, 20% out-of-state, 5% international (53 countries represented). Asian 8%, African American 14%, Caucasian 57%, Hispanic 12%, Native American <1%, Pacific Islander <1%, Two or more races 4%, Race unknown 3%.
Retention and Graduation: 74% freshmen return for sophomore year. 26% freshmen graduate within 4 years. 48% freshmen graduate within 6 years. **Faculty:** Student/faculty ratio 14:1. 732 full-time faculty, 83% hold PhDs, 22% are members of minority groups, 48% are women. 0% of classes are taught by teaching assistants.

ACADEMICS
Degrees: Bachelor's; Doctoral; Doctoral/Professional; Doctoral/Research; Master's; Post-Bachelor's certificate; Post-Master's certificate **Classes:** Most classes have fewer than 10 students. Most lab/discussion sessions have 10-19 students. **Most popular majors:** Liberal Arts And Sciences/Liberal Studies; Health Services/Allied Health/Health Sciences, General. **Special Study Options:** Accelerated program; Distance learning; Double major; Dual enrollment; English as a Second Language (ESL); Honors program; Independent study; Internships; Liberal arts/career combination; Student-designed major; Study abroad; Teacher certification program; Weekend college. Honors programs: UMKC Honors Program Combined degree programs: BA/JD; BA/MD. **Disability Services offered to physically disabled students:** Note-taking services; Reader services; Tape recorders; Tutors. **Career services:** Alumni network; Alumni services; Career assessment; Career/job search classes; Internships

FACILITIES
Housing: Apartments for married students; Apartments for single students; Coed dorms; Fraternity/sorority housing; Special housing for disabled student; Special housing for international students 98% of campus accessible to physically diasbled. **Special Academic Facilities/Equipment:** Art gallery, professional theater, geosciences museums, language lab, observatory. **Computers:** 90% of classrooms, 100% of dorms, 100% of libraries, 100% of dining areas, 100% of student union, have wireless network access. Students can register for classes online. Administrative functions (other than registration) can be performed online.

CAMPUS LIFE
Environment: Metropolis **Activities:** Campus Ministries; Choral groups; Concert band; Dance; Drama/theater; International Student Organization; Jazz band; Literary magazine; Model UN; Music ensembles; Musical theater; Opera; Pep band; Radio station; Student government; Student newspaper; Student-run film society; Symphony orchestra 200 registered organizations, 32 honor societies, 13 religious organizations. 6 fraternities, 7 sororities. **Athletics (Intercollegiate):** *Men:* basketball, cheerleading, cross-country, golf, riflery, soccer, tennis, track/field (outdoor). *Women:* basketball, cheerleading, cross-country, golf, riflery, softball, tennis, track/field (outdoor), volleyball. **On-Campus Highlights:** UMKC Student Union, Swinney Recreation Center, Robot Cafe at Miller-Nichols Library, Warkoczewski Public Observatory, Minsky's Pizza **Environmental Initiatives:** Recycling

ADMISSIONS
Freshman Academic Profile: Average high school GPA 3.4. 31% in top 10% of high school class, 60% in top 25% of high school class, 88% in top 50% of high school class. **Test Scores:** ACT middle 50% range 21-28. Minimum internet-based TOEFL 61. Minimum paper TOEFL 500. **Basis for Candidate Selection:** *Very important factors considered include:* rigor of secondary school record, class rank, academic GPA, standardized test scores. *Other factors considered include:* application essay, recommendation(s), interview, extracurricular activities, talent/ability, character/personal qualities, first generation, volunteer work, work experience. **Freshman Admission Requirements:** High school diploma is required and GED is accepted *Academic units required:* 4 English, 4 math, 3 science, 1 science labs, 2 foreign language, 3 social studies, 1 visual/performing arts. **Freshman Admission Statistics:** 5,065 applied, 64.1% admitted, 38% enrolled. **Transfer Admission**

Requirements: college transcript(s), Minimum college GPA of 2.0 required. Lowest grade transferable D. **General Admission Information:** Application fee $45. Priority deadline 4/1. Nonfall registration accepted. Admission may be deferred for a maximum of 2 semesters.

COSTS AND FINANCIAL AID
Annual in-state tuition $10,150. Annual out-of-state tuition $24,605. Room and board $10,150. Required fees $1,384. Average book expense $1,002.
Required Forms and Deadlines: FAFSA. **Notification of Awards:** Applicants will be notified of awards on a rolling basis beginning 4/15. **Types of Aid:** *Need-based scholarships/grants:* College/university scholarship or grant aid from institutional funds; Federal Nursing Scholarships; Federal Pell; Private scholarships; SEOG; State scholarships/grants; United Negro College Fund. *Loans:* Direct PLUS loans; Direct Subsidized Stafford Loans; Direct Unsubsidized Stafford Loans. *Student Employment:* Federal Work-Study Program available. Institutional employment available. **Financial Aid Statistics:** 92% needy freshmen, 80% needy undergrads receive need-based scholarship or grant aid. 5% freshmen, 2% undergrads receive non-need-based scholarship or grant aid. 69% freshmen, 76% undergrads receive need-based self-help aid. 2% freshmen, 2% undergrads receive athletic scholarships. 92% freshmen, 79% undergrads receive any aid. 61% undergrads borrow to pay for school. Average cumulative indebtedness $25,912. **Criteria for awarding aid:** *Need-based:* Academics, Alumni affiliation, Art, Athletics, Leadership, Minority status, Music/drama *Non-need-based:* Academics, Alumni affiliation, Art, Athletics, Leadership, Minority status, Music/drama, State/district residency.

UNIVERSITY OF MISSOURI—SAINT LOUIS

One University Boulevard, St. Louis, MO 63121-4400
Phone: 314-516-5451 • **Financial Aid Phone:** 314-516-5526
E-mail: admissions@umsl.edu • **CEEB Code:** 6889
Fax: 314-516-5310 • **Website:** www.umsl.edu • **ACT Code:** 2383

This public school was founded in 1963. It has a 350 acre campus.

RATINGS
Admissions Selectivity Rating: 79   **Fire Safety Rating:** 85   **Green Rating:** 60*

STUDENTS AND FACULTY
Enrollment: 7,322. **Student Body:** 55% female, 45% male, 11% out-of-state, 3% international (46 countries represented). Asian 5%, African American 17%, Caucasian 64%, Hispanic 3%, Native American <1%, Pacific Islander <1%, Two or more races 3%, Race unknown 4%.
Retention and Graduation: 74% freshmen return for sophomore year. 14% grads go on to further study within 1 year. 36% grads pursue arts and sciences degrees. 4% grads pursue law degrees. 28% grads pursue business degrees. 1% grads pursue medical degrees. **Faculty:** Student/faculty ratio 18:1. 432 full-time faculty, 75% hold PhDs, 20% are members of minority groups, 54% are women. 35% of classes are taught by teaching assistants.

ACADEMICS
Degrees: Bachelor's; Certificate; Doctoral; Doctoral/Professional; Doctoral/Research; Master's; Post-Bachelor's certificate; Post-Master's certificate **Classes:** Most classes have 10-19 students. Most lab/discussion sessions have 10-19 students. **Most popular majors:** Psychology, General; Registered Nursing/Registered Nurse; Business/Commerce, General. **Special Study Options:** Accelerated program; Cooperative education program; Cross-registration; Distance learning; Double major; Dual enrollment; English as a Second Language (ESL); Exchange student program (domestic); External degree program; Honors program; Independent study; Internships; Student-designed major; Study abroad; Teacher certification program. Honors programs: Pierre Laclede Honors College offers a four-year (for freshmen) and a two-year (for internal and external transfers) honors program through which students can meet their General Education and some other graduation requirements (e.g., advanced composition, global awareness, cultural diversity). Most instruction is in small seminars (average enrollment is 15). There is a six-hour independent study requirement, and a writing program engages all students and includes a capstone which aids students in job and graduate school applications. Combined degree programs: BA/MA. **Disability Services offered to physically disabled students:** Note-taking services; Reader services; Tape recorders. **Career services:** Alumni services; Career assessment; Internships

FACILITIES
Housing: Apartments for married students; Apartments for single students; Coed dorms; Fraternity/sorority housing; Special housing for disabled student; Special housing for international students; Theme housing;

Wellness housing 100% of campus accessible to physically diasbled. **Special Academic Facilities/Equipment:** Art galleries, language, writing labs, math labs Mercantile Library, and observatory, radio station **Computers:** 68% of classrooms, 90% of dorms, 90% of libraries, 100% of dining areas, 90% of student union, 60% of common outdoor areas have wireless network access. Students can register for classes online. Administrative functions (other than registration) can be performed online.

CAMPUS LIFE

Environment: Metropolis **Activities:** Campus Ministries; Choral groups; Concert band; Dance; Drama/theater; International Student Organization; Jazz band; Literary magazine; Model UN; Music ensembles; Musical theater; Opera; Pep band; Radio station; Student government; Student newspaper; Student-run film society 125 registered organizations, 24 honor societies, 9 religious organizations. 3 fraternities, 3 sororities. **Athletics (Intercollegiate):** *Men:* baseball, basketball, golf, soccer, tennis. *Women:* basketball, golf, soccer, softball, tennis, volleyball. **On-Campus Highlights:** Millennium Student Center, Touhill Performing Arts Center, Recreation & Wellness Center, Gallery 210, Science Learning Building **Environmental Initiatives:** Energy Conservation

ADMISSIONS

Freshman Academic Profile: Average high school GPA 3.5. 27% in top 10% of high school class, 58% in top 25% of high school class, 88% in top 50% of high school class. 81% from public high schools. **Test Scores:** SAT Math middle 50% range 535-625. SAT EBRW middle 50% range 530-600. ACT middle 50% range 22-27. Minimum internet-based TOEFL 61. Minimum paper TOEFL 500. **Basis for Candidate Selection:** *Very important factors considered include:* rigor of secondary school record, class rank, academic GPA, standardized test scores. *Other factors considered include:* application essay, recommendation(s). **Freshman Admission Requirements:** High school diploma is required and GED is accepted *Academic units required:* 4 English, 4 math, 3 science, 1 science labs, 2 foreign language, 3 social studies, and 1 unit from above areas or other academic areas. **Freshman Admission Statistics:** 1,970 applied, 75.9% admitted, 32% enrolled. **Transfer Admission Requirements:** college transcript(s), Minimum college GPA of 2.0 required. Lowest grade transferable D. **General Admission Information:** Application fee $35. Regular application deadline 9/7. Nonfall registration accepted. Admission may be deferred for a maximum of 1 academic year.

COSTS AND FINANCIAL AID

Required Forms and Deadlines: FAFSA. **Notification of Awards:** Applicants will be notified of awards on a rolling basis beginning 12/1. **Types of Aid:** *Need-based scholarships/grants:* College/university scholarship or grant aid from institutional funds; Federal Nursing Scholarships; Federal Pell; Private scholarships; SEOG; State scholarships/grants; United Negro College Fund. *Loans:* Direct PLUS loans; Direct Subsidized Stafford Loans; Direct Unsubsidized Stafford Loans. *Student Employment:* Federal Work-Study Program available. Institutional employment available. **Financial Aid Statistics:** 90% needy freshmen, 82% needy undergrads receive need-based scholarship or grant aid. 19% freshmen, 11% undergrads receive non-need-based scholarship or grant aid. 66% freshmen, 83% undergrads receive need-based self-help aid. 4% freshmen, 2% undergrads receive athletic scholarships. 91% freshmen, 78% undergrads receive any aid. 61% undergrads borrow to pay for school. Average cumulative indebtedness $24,186. **Criteria for awarding aid:** *Need-based:* Academics, Alumni affiliation, Art, Leadership, Minority status, Music/drama *Non-need-based:* Academics, Alumni affiliation, Art, Athletics, Music/drama, State/district residency.

UNIVERSITY OF MOBILE

5735 College Parkway, Mobile, AL 36613-2842
Phone: 251-442-2222 • **Financial Aid Phone:** 251-442-2222
E-mail: enrollmentservices@umobile.edu • **CEEB Code:** 1515
Website: www.umobile.edu • **ACT Code:** 29

This private school, affiliated with the Southern Baptist Church, was founded in 1961. It has a 880 acre campus.

RATINGS

Admissions Selectivity Rating: 86   **Fire Safety Rating:** 90   **Green Rating:** 61

STUDENTS AND FACULTY

Enrollment: 1,276. **Student Body:** 63% female, 37% male, 23% out-of-state, 3% international (28 countries represented). Asian 1%, African American 19%, Caucasian 57%, Hispanic 2%, Native American 1%, Pacific Islander <1%, Two or more races 3%, Race unknown 13%.

Retention and Graduation: 69% freshmen return for sophomore year. 25% freshmen graduate within 4 years. 45% freshmen graduate within 6 years. 17% grads go on to further study within 1 year. 5% grads pursue arts and sciences degrees. 2% grads pursue law degrees. 5% grads pursue business degrees. 1% grads pursue medical degrees. **Faculty:** Student/faculty ratio 14:1. 73 full-time faculty, 59% hold PhDs, 7% are members of minority groups, 58% are women. 0% of classes are taught by teaching assistants.

ACADEMICS

Degrees: Associate; Bachelor's; **Master's Classes:** Most classes have 10-19 students. Most lab/discussion sessions have fewer than 10 students. **Most popular majors:** Elementary Education And Teaching; Registered Nursing/Registered Nurse; Business Administration And Management, General. **Special Study Options:** Accelerated program; Distance learning; Double major; Dual enrollment; Honors program; Independent study; Internships; Study abroad; Teacher certification program. Honors programs: Exploring the great books and the enduring questions; join a community of enthusiastic students like yourself; take courses designed not to make you do more work, but do the kind of work that will help you become a thinking leader; earn the "Honors Scholar" designation and seal on your diploma and transcript; participate in special events, such as an annual honor dinner hosted by President Foley; have frequent access to honors faculty; benefit from honors roundtable designed to help students prepare for and apply to graduate school, seek grants and scholarships, and pursue post-graduate career opportunities. Combined degree programs: BA/MA. **Disability Services offered to physically disabled students:** Tutors. **Career services:** Alumni services; Career assessment; Career/job search classes; Internships

FACILITIES

Housing: Apartments for single students; Men's dorms; Women's dorms 100% of campus accessible to physically diasbled. **Special Academic Facilities/Equipment:** Donald Art Gallery and Recording Studio **Computers:** 10% of classrooms, 100% of dorms, 100% of libraries, 50% of dining areas, 100% of student union, 20% of common outdoor areas have wireless network access. Students can register for classes online. Administrative functions (other than registration) can be performed online.

CAMPUS LIFE

Environment: City **Activities:** Campus Ministries; Choral groups; Concert band; Drama/theater; International Student Organization; Jazz band; Music ensembles; Musical theater; Opera; Pep band; Student government; Symphony orchestra 52 registered organizations, 12 honor societies, 3 religious organizations. **Athletics (Intercollegiate):** *Men:* baseball, basketball, cross-country, golf, soccer, tennis. *Women:* basketball, cheerleading, cross-country, golf, soccer, softball, tennis, volleyball. **On-Campus Highlights:** Newly renovated School of Nursing & science labs, Library/Commons, Recording Studio, Dorms—Faulkner and Samford Halls, Baseball Field/Swimming Pool **Environmental Initiatives:** Recycling

ADMISSIONS

Freshman Academic Profile: Average high school GPA 3.5. 23% in top 10% of high school class, 53% in top 25% of high school class, 80% in top 50% of high school class. **Test Scores:** SAT Math middle 50% range 450-540. SAT EBRW middle 50% range 460-560. ACT middle 50% range 20-25. Minimum internet-based TOEFL 61. Minimum paper TOEFL 500. **Basis for Candidate Selection:** *Very important factors considered include:* academic GPA, standardized test scores. **Freshman Admission Requirements:** High school diploma is required and GED is accepted *Academic units recommended:* 4 English, 3 math, 3 science, 2 foreign language, 3 social studies, 3 history. **Freshman Admission Statistics:** 1,493 applied, 47.0% admitted, 32% enrolled. **Transfer Admission Requirements:** college transcript(s), Minimum college GPA of 2.75 required. Lowest grade transferable C. **General Admission Information:** Application fee $25. Nonfall registration accepted. Admission may be deferred for a maximum of 1 year.

COSTS AND FINANCIAL AID

Required Forms and Deadlines: FAFSA; Institution's own financial aid form; State aid form. **Notification of Awards:** Applicants will be notified of awards on a rolling basis beginning 12/1. **Types of Aid:** *Need-based scholarships/grants:* College/university scholarship or grant aid from institutional funds; Federal Nursing Scholarships; Federal Pell; Private scholarships; SEOG; State scholarships/grants. *Loans:* Direct PLUS loans; Direct Subsidized Stafford Loans; Direct Unsubsidized Stafford Loans. *Student Employment:* Federal Work-Study Program available. Institutional employment available. **Financial Aid Statistics:** 77% needy freshmen, 63% needy undergrads receive need-based scholarship or grant aid. 100% freshmen, 88% undergrads receive non-need-based scholarship or grant aid. 44% freshmen, 6% undergrads receive need-based self-help aid. 3% freshmen, 2% undergrads receive athletic scholarships. 73% undergrads borrow to pay for school. Average cumulative indebtedness $31,266. **Criteria for awarding aid:** *Non-need-based:* Academics, Alumni affiliation, Athletics, Music/drama, Religious affiliation.

UNIVERSITY OF MONTANA

32 Campus Drive, Missoula, MT 59812
Phone: 243-6266 • **Financial Aid Phone:** 406-243-5373
E-mail: admiss@umontana.edu • **CEEB Code:** 4489
Fax: 406-243-5711 • **Website:** www.umt.edu • **ACT Code:** 2422

This public school was founded in 1893. It has a 220 acre campus.

RATINGS

Admissions Selectivity Rating: 75   **Fire Safety Rating:** 90   **Green Rating:** 81

STUDENTS AND FACULTY

Enrollment: 8,958. **Student Body:** 55% female, 45% male, 28% out-of-state, 1% international (68 countries represented). Asian 1%, African American 1%, Caucasian 79%, Hispanic 5%, Native American 3%, Pacific Islander <1%, Two or more races 4%, Race unknown 5%.
Retention and Graduation: 69% freshmen return for sophomore year. 25% freshmen graduate within 4 years. 49% freshmen graduate within 6 years. 26% grads go on to further study within 1 year. **Faculty:** Student/faculty ratio 17:1. 521 full-time faculty, 79% hold PhDs, 10% are members of minority groups, 40% are women. 9% of classes are taught by teaching assistants.

ACADEMICS

Degrees: Associate; Bachelor's; Certificate; Doctoral/Professional; Doctoral/Research; Master's; Post-Bachelor's certificate; Post-Master's certificate; Terminal Associate; Transfer Associate **Classes:** Most classes have 20-29 students. Most lab/discussion sessions have 20-29 students. **Most popular majors:** Forest Management/Forest Resources Management; Psychology, General; Business Administration And Management, General. **Special Study Options:** Cooperative education program; Cross-registration; Distance learning; Double major; Dual enrollment; English as a Second Language (ESL); Exchange student program (domestic); External degree program; Honors program; Independent study; Internships; Study abroad; Teacher certification program. **Honors programs:** The Davidson Honors College offers talented and motivated students an academic and social community as an important part of their undergraduate experience at The University of Montana, regardless of their major disciplines. Honors courses are taught by many of the best scholars on campus and are generally limited to twenty students. The Honors College encourages its students to participate in community service activities, international educational experiences and undergraduate research. Combined degree programs: BA/JD. **Disability Services offered to physically disabled students:** Note-taking services; Reader services; Tape recorders; Tutors.
Career services: Alumni network; Alumni services; Career assessment; Career/job search classes; Internships; Regional alumni

FACILITIES

Housing: Apartments for married students; Apartments for single students; Coed dorms; Fraternity/sorority housing; Men's dorms; Special housing for disabled student; Special housing for international students; Theme housing; Women's dorms 87% of campus accessible to physically diasbled. **Special Academic Facilities/Equipment:** On main campus: clinical psychology center; environmental studies lab; geology field camp; several biological, biomedical, kinesiology, physiology, forestry-related, and other research labs or centers; art galleries; broadcast media center (public radio and television) and performing arts-radio-television building; practical ethics center; extensive presentation technology equipment and services, and others. Other locations: biological station, experimental forest, two-year college of technology (two locations), Fort Missoula field research center, and others. **Computers:** 20% of classrooms, 100% of libraries, 60% of dining areas, 100% of student union, 5% of common outdoor areas have wireless network access. Students can register for classes online. Administrative functions (other than registration) can be performed online.

CAMPUS LIFE

Environment: City **Activities:** Campus Ministries; Choral groups; Concert band; Dance; Drama/theater; International Student Organization; Jazz band; Literary magazine; Marching band; Model UN; Music ensembles; Musical theater; Opera; Pep band; Radio station; Student government; Student newspaper; Symphony orchestra; Television station 150 registered organizations, 5 fraternities, 4 sororities. **Athletics (Intercollegiate):** *Men:* basketball, cheerleading, cross-country, football, tennis, track/field (outdoor), track/field (indoor). *Women:* basketball, cheerleading, cross-country, golf, soccer, tennis, track/field (outdoor), track/field (indoor), volleyball. **On-Campus**

Highlights: Adams Event Center (sports, entertainment, etc.), Washington-Grizzly Stadium (football, other), Campus Recreation Center (student recreation), University Center (student center, movie theater), Performing Arts-RadioTV Center (public radio-TV) **Environmental Initiatives:** Climate Action Plan to reach carbon neutrality by 2020 and biannual Greenhouse Gas Inventories are completed by a full-time Sustainability Coordinator and the Sustainable Campus Committee.

ADMISSIONS

Freshman Academic Profile: Average high school GPA 3.6. 17% in top 10% of high school class, 42% in top 25% of high school class, 73% in top 50% of high school class. **Test Scores:** SAT Math middle 50% range 520-620. SAT EBRW middle 50% range 540-650. ACT middle 50% range 21-26. Minimum internet-based TOEFL 70. Minimum paper TOEFL 525. **Basis for Candidate Selection:** *Very important factors considered include:* rigor of secondary school record, class rank, academic GPA, standardized test scores. *Important factors considered include:* extracurricular activities, talent/ability. *Other factors considered include:* application essay, recommendation(s). **Freshman Admission Requirements:** High school diploma is required and GED is accepted *Academic units required:* 4 English, 3 math, 2 science, 2 science labs, 3 social studies, 2 history, *Academic units recommended:* 2 foreign language, 2 computer science, 2 visual/performing arts, 2 units from above areas or other academic areas. **Freshman Admission Statistics:** 6,182 applied, 92.6% admitted, 29% enrolled. **Transfer Admission Requirements:** college transcript(s), Minimum college GPA of 2.0 required. Lowest grade transferable D. **General Admission Information:** Application fee $30. Priority deadline 3/1. Nonfall registration accepted. Admission may be deferred for a maximum of 1 year.

COSTS AND FINANCIAL AID

Annual in-state tuition $9,178. Annual out-of-state tuition $23,062. Room and board $9,178. Required fees $1,881. Average book expense $1,400. **Required Forms and Deadlines:** FAFSA. **Notification of Awards:** Applicants will be notified of awards on a rolling basis beginning 3/16. **Types of Aid:** *Need-based scholarships/grants:* College/university scholarship or grant aid from institutional funds; Federal Pell; Private scholarships; SEOG; State scholarships/grants. *Loans:* Direct PLUS loans; Direct Subsidized Stafford Loans; Direct Unsubsidized Stafford Loans. *Student Employment:* Federal Work-Study Program available. Institutional employment available. **Financial Aid Statistics:** 68% needy freshmen, 65% needy undergrads receive need-based scholarship or grant aid. 84% freshmen, 56% undergrads receive non-need-based scholarship or grant aid. 79% freshmen, 82% undergrads receive need-based self-help aid. 1% freshmen, 1% undergrads receive athletic scholarships. 62% freshmen, 56% undergrads receive any aid. 57% undergrads borrow to pay for school. Average cumulative indebtedness $23,927. **Criteria for awarding aid:** *Need-based:* Academics, Minority status *Non-need-based:* Academics, Athletics, Leadership, Music/drama, State/district residency.

THE UNIVERSITY OF MONTANA—WESTERN

710 South Atlantic, Dillon, MT 59725
Phone: 406-683-7331
E-mail: admissions@umwestern.edu • **CEEB Code:** 4945
Fax: 406-683-7493 • **Website:** https://w.umwestern.edu/ • **ACT Code:** 2428

This public school was founded in 1893. It has a 34 acre campus.

RATINGS

Admissions Selectivity Rating: 83   **Fire Safety Rating:** 60*   **Green Rating:** 60*

STUDENTS AND FACULTY

Enrollment: 1,467. **Student Body:** 61% female, 39% male, 24% out-of-state, 0% international (1 countries represented). Asian 1%, African American 1%, Caucasian 86%, Hispanic 4%, Native American 3%, Pacific Islander <1%, Two or more races 2%, Race unknown 3%.
Retention and Graduation: 68% freshmen return for sophomore year. 50% grads go on to further study within 1 year. **Faculty:** Student/faculty ratio 19:1. 62 full-time faculty, 87% hold PhDs, 0% are members of minority groups, 48% are women. 0% of classes are taught by teaching assistants.

ACADEMICS

Degrees: Associate; Bachelor's; Certificate **Classes:** Most classes have fewer than 10 students. **Most popular majors:** Elementary Education And Teaching; Business/Commerce, General. **Special Study Options:** Cooperative education program; Distance learning; Double major; Dual enrollment; Honors program; Independent study; Internships; Study abroad; Teacher certification program.

Disability Services offered to physically disabled students: Note-taking services; Reader services; Tape recorders; Tutors. Career services: Alumni services; Career assessment; Career/job search classes; Internships

FACILITIES

Housing: Apartments for married students; Apartments for single students; Coed dorms; Men's dorms; Special housing for disabled student; Special housing for international students; Women's dorms 90% of campus accessible to physically disabled. Special Academic Facilities/Equipment: Art gallery, outdoor education center, learning center. Computers: Students can register for classes online. Administrative functions (other than registration) can be performed online.

CAMPUS LIFE

Environment: Rural Activities: Campus Ministries; Choral groups; Drama/theater; Music ensembles; Musical theater; Radio station; Student government 25 registered organizations, 2 honor societies, 2 religious organizations. Athletics (Intercollegiate): Men: basketball, cheerleading, football, golf, rodeo. Women: basketball, cheerleading, golf, rodeo, volleyball. On-Campus Highlights: SUB (Sudent Union Building), Straugh Arena, The Cup, STC Tech Building, Bark'n Bite

ADMISSIONS

Freshman Academic Profile: Average high school GPA 3.1. 7% in top 10% of high school class, 23% in top 25% of high school class, 51% in top 50% of high school class. 96% from public high schools. Test Scores: SAT Math middle 50% range 420-530. SAT EBRW middle 50% range 430-540. ACT middle 50% range 17-22. Minimum paper TOEFL 500. Basis for Candidate Selection: Very important factors considered include: rigor of secondary school record, class rank, academic GPA, standardized test scores. Freshman Admission Requirements: High school diploma is required and GED is accepted Academic units required: 4 English, 3 math, 2 science, 2 science labs, 2 social studies, 1 history, 2 academic electives, Academic units recommended: 4 English, 4 math, 3 science, 2 science labs, 2 social studies, 1 history, 3 academic electives. Freshman Admission Statistics: 785 applied, 67.8% admitted, 63% enrolled. Transfer Admission Requirements: college transcript(s), Minimum college GPA of 2.0 required. Lowest grade transferable c. General Admission Information: Application fee $30. Priority deadline 7/1. Nonfall registration accepted. Admission may be deferred for a maximum of 1 year.

COSTS AND FINANCIAL AID

Required Forms and Deadlines: FAFSA. Notification of Awards: Applicants will be notified of awards on a rolling basis beginning 3/1. Types of Aid: Need-based scholarships/grants: College/university scholarship or grant aid from institutional funds; Federal Pell; Private scholarships; SEOG; State scholarships/grants. Loans: Direct PLUS loans; Direct Subsidized Stafford Loans; Direct Unsubsidized Stafford Loans. Student Employment: Federal Work-Study Program available. Institutional employment available. Financial Aid Statistics: 93% needy freshmen, 78% needy undergrads receive need-based scholarship or grant aid. 34% freshmen, 26% undergrads receive non-need-based scholarship or grant aid. 82% freshmen, 72% undergrads receive need-based self-help aid. 10% freshmen, 3% undergrads receive athletic scholarships. 67% undergrads borrow to pay for school. Average cumulative indebtedness $20,669. Criteria for awarding aid: Need-based: Academics, Alumni affiliation, Art, Leadership, Minority status Non-need-based: Academics, Alumni affiliation, Art, Athletics, Leadership, State/district residency.

UNIVERSITY OF MONTEVALLO

Station 6001, Montevallo, AL 35115
Phone: 205-665-6030 • Financial Aid Phone: 205-665-6050
E-mail: admissions@montevallo.edu • CEEB Code: 1004
Fax: 205-665-6032 • Website: http://www.montevallo.edu/ • ACT Code: 4

This public school was founded in 1896. It has a 160 acre campus.

RATINGS

Admissions Selectivity Rating: 70   Fire Safety Rating: 82   Green Rating: 60*

STUDENTS AND FACULTY

Enrollment: 2,329. Student Body: 68% female, 32% male, 2% international (23 countries represented). Asian 1%, African American 16%, Caucasian 69%, Hispanic 5%, Native American <1%, Pacific Islander <1%, Two or more races 3%, Race unknown 3%.
Retention and Graduation: 78% freshmen return for sophomore year. 26% freshmen graduate within 4 years. 50% freshmen graduate within 6 years.
Faculty: Student/faculty ratio 16:1. 141 full-time faculty, 96% hold PhDs, 8%

are members of minority groups, 50% are women. 0% of classes are taught by teaching assistants.

ACADEMICS

Degrees: Bachelor's; Master's; Post-Master's certificate Classes: Most classes have 10-19 students. Most lab/discussion sessions have 10-19 students. Most popular majors: Elementary Education And Teaching; Health And Physical Education/Fitness, General; Business Administration And Management, General. Special Study Options: Accelerated program; Cross-registration; Distance learning; Double major; Dual enrollment; Honors program; Independent study; Internships; Study abroad; Teacher certification program. Honors programs: The Mission of the University of Montevallo's Honors Program is to provide intellectually talented students with specially designed academic offerings, co-curricular activities, and recognition. The Honors Program provides students with three special features in their college experience: (1) classes, with limited enrollment, specially designed and taught by demanding and supportive faculty to elicit the students' powers, (2) time spent in one another's company, and (3) encouragement, public and private, to persevere. The Honors Program provides these features through a spectrum of academic offerings, opportunities for recognition, and extracurricular activities. The Honors Program is designed to enhance a students' University experience. Students pursue a major and minor in their area of interest, while taking honors courses at specific times during their academic career. Disability Services offered to physically disabled students: Note-taking services; Reader services; Tape recorders; Tutors. Career services: Alumni services; Career assessment

FACILITIES

Housing: Apartments for married students; Coed dorms; Fraternity/sorority housing; Men's dorms; Special housing for disabled student; Women's dorms Special Academic Facilities/Equipment: Art gallery, child development, speech and hearing, traffic safety, and undergraduate liberal studies centers, mass communications center with cable TV broadcasting capabilities. Computers: 98% of classrooms, 85% of dorms, 100% of libraries, 100% of dining areas, 100% of student union, 75% of common outdoor areas have wireless network access. Students can register for classes online. Administrative functions (other than registration) can be performed online.

CAMPUS LIFE

Environment: Rural Activities: Campus Ministries; Choral groups; Concert band; Dance; Drama/theater; International Student Organization; Jazz band; Model UN; Music ensembles; Musical theater; Student government; Student newspaper; Television station; Yearbook 93 registered organizations, 26 honor societies, 8 religious organizations. 7 fraternities, 8 sororities. Athletics (Intercollegiate): Men: baseball, basketball, golf, soccer. Women: basketball, cross-country, golf, soccer, tennis, volleyball. On-Campus Highlights: Cafeteria, Student Activity Center, Main Quad, University of Montevallo Student Lake, Intramural Fields Environmental Initiatives: Campus lighting retrofit to energy saving bulbs.

ADMISSIONS

Freshman Academic Profile: 90% from public high schools. Test Scores: Minimum internet-based TOEFL 71. Minimum paper TOEFL 525. Basis for Candidate Selection: Very important factors considered include: rigor of secondary school record. Other factors considered include: class rank, academic GPA, interview, extracurricular activities, talent/ability. Freshman Admission Requirements: High school diploma is required and GED is accepted Academic units required: 4 English, 2 math, 2 science, 4 social studies, 4 academic electives. Freshman Admission Statistics: 1,868 applied, 66.6% admitted, 39% enrolled. Transfer Admission Requirements: college transcript(s), Minimum college GPA of 2.0 required. Lowest grade transferable D. General Admission Information: Application fee $30. Regular application deadline 8/1. Nonfall registration accepted. Admission may be deferred.

COSTS AND FINANCIAL AID

Annual in-state tuition $6,400. Annual out-of-state tuition $20,550. Room and board $6,400. Required fees $670. Average book expense $2,050. Required Forms and Deadlines: FAFSA. Notification of Awards: Applicants will be notified of awards on a rolling basis beginning 3/25. Types of Aid: Need-based scholarships/grants: College/university scholarship or grant aid from institutional funds; Federal Pell; Private scholarships; SEOG; State scholarships/grants. Loans: Direct PLUS loans; Direct Subsidized Stafford Loans; Direct Unsubsidized Stafford Loans. Student Employment: Federal Work-Study Program available. Institutional employment available. Financial Aid Statistics: 85% needy freshmen, 84% needy undergrads receive need-based scholarship or grant aid. 18% freshmen, 10% undergrads receive non-need-based scholarship or grant aid. 79% freshmen, 85% undergrads receive need-based self-help aid. 4% freshmen, 4% undergrads receive athletic scholarships. 87% freshmen, 77% undergrads receive any aid. Criteria for awarding aid: Need-based: Academics Non-need-based: Academics, Alumni affiliation, Art, Athletics, Leadership, Minority status, Music/drama.

UNIVERSITY OF MOUNT UNION

1972 Clark Ave, Alliance, OH 44601-3993
Phone: 330-823-2590 • **Financial Aid Phone:** 877-543-9185
E-mail: admission@mountunion.edu • **CEEB Code:** 1492
Fax: 330-823-5097 • **Website:** www.mountunion.edu • **ACT Code:** 3298

This private school, affiliated with the Methodist Church, was founded in 1846. It has a 123 acre campus.

RATINGS

Admissions Selectivity Rating: 77   **Fire Safety Rating:** 90   **Green Rating:** 85

STUDENTS AND FACULTY

Enrollment: 2,049. **Student Body:** 48% female, 52% male, 17% out-of-state, <1% international (12 countries represented). Asian 1%, African American 6%, Caucasian 81%, Hispanic 3%, Native American 1%, Pacific Islander <1%, Two or more races 4%, Race unknown 5%.
Retention and Graduation: 75% freshmen return for sophomore year. 62% freshmen graduate within 6 years. 15% grads go on to further study within 1 year. 10% grads pursue arts and sciences degrees. 1% grads pursue law degrees. 1% grads pursue business degrees. **Faculty:** Student/faculty ratio 13:1. 139 full-time faculty, 89% hold PhDs, 12% are members of minority groups, 47% are women. 0% of classes are taught by teaching assistants.

ACADEMICS

Degrees: Bachelor's; Doctoral Other; **Master's Classes:** Most classes have 10-19 students. Most lab/discussion sessions have 10-19 students. **Most popular majors:** Early Childhood Education And Teaching; Sport And Fitness Administration/Management; Business Administration And Management, General. **Special Study Options:** Accelerated program; Cooperative education program; Double major; Dual enrollment; English as a Second Language (ESL); Honors program; Independent study; Internships; Liberal arts/career combination; Student-designed major; Study abroad; Teacher certification program. Honors programs: The Honors Program at the University of Mount Union offers integrated learning opportunities and challenges for motivated students with exceptional academic potential. The program is designed to foster intellectual curiosity, leadership, initiative, creativity, civic-mindedness and a high standard of performance. Two honors tracks are available: University Honors and Honors in the Major. A qualified student may participate in either or both tracks. The first, University Honors, fulfills a student's Integrative Core requirements and includes a First Year Seminar, three Honors Foundations courses plus an elective in the fourth Foundations area, an Honors Theme, which comprises one Honors theme course plus a Theme project to be completed in conjunction with an upper-level course of the student's choosing, and an Honors Capstone. The Honors in the Major Program offers the opportunity for intensive, individual study in a major. Honors in the Major is earned by completing honors projects in regular courses. Although the nature of honors work will vary, it should involve intellectual creativity and may take such forms as research, investigation, or artistic effort. The student initiates and plans the honors project and works closely with one or more faculty members in carrying it out. The University of Mount Union Honors Program offers eligible students an exceptional educational opportunity and a supportive community of students focused on academic achievement and social responsibility. **Disability Services offered to physically disabled students:** Note-taking services; Reader services; Tutors. **Career services:** Alumni network; Alumni services; Career assessment; Career/job search classes; Internships; Regional alumni

FACILITIES

Housing: Apartments for single students; Coed dorms; Fraternity/sorority housing; Men's dorms; Special housing for disabled student; Special housing for international students; Theme housing; Women's dorms 95% of campus accessible to physically disabled. **Special Academic Facilities/Equipment:** Art gallery, ecological center, observatory, educational media center. **Computers:** 100% of classrooms, 90% of dorms, 100% of libraries, 100% of dining areas, 100% of student union, 50% of common outdoor areas have wireless network access. Students can register for classes online. Administrative functions (other than registration) can be performed online.

CAMPUS LIFE

Environment: Town **Activities:** Campus Ministries; Choral groups; Concert band; Dance; Drama/theater; International Student Organization; Jazz band; Literary magazine; Marching band; Model UN; Music ensembles; Musical theater; Pep band; Radio station; Student government; Student newspaper; Symphony orchestra; Television station; Yearbook 80 registered organizations, 16 honor societies, 10 religious organizations. 4 fraternities, 4 sororities. **Athletics (Intercollegiate):** *Men:* baseball, basketball, cross-country, diving, football, golf, soccer, swimming, tennis, track/field (outdoor), track/field (indoor), wrestling. *Women:* basketball, cheerleading, cross-country, diving, golf, soccer, softball, swimming, tennis, track/field (outdoor), track/field (indoor), volleyball. **On-Campus Highlights:** Hoover Price Campus Center, Kolenbrander Harter Information Center, McPherson Athletic Building, Dewald Chapel, Bracy Hall Science Building **Environmental Initiatives:** Sustainability (Climate Action) Plan

ADMISSIONS

Freshman Academic Profile: Average high school GPA 3.4. 18% in top 10% of high school class, 45% in top 25% of high school class, 78% in top 50% of high school class. 88% from public high schools. **Test Scores:** SAT Math middle 50% range 490-590. SAT EBRW middle 50% range 490-610. ACT middle 50% range 20-25. Minimum internet-based TOEFL 80. Minimum paper TOEFL 550. **Basis for Candidate Selection:** *Very important factors considered include:* rigor of secondary school record, class rank, academic GPA, standardized test scores. *Important factors considered include:* recommendation(s). *Other factors considered include:* application essay, extracurricular activities, talent/ability, character/personal qualities, alumni/ae relation, racial/ethnic status, volunteer work, work experience. **Freshman Admission Requirements:** High school diploma is required and GED is accepted *Academic units recommended:* 4 English, 3 math, 3 science, 2 science labs, 2 foreign language, 3 social studies. **Freshman Admission Statistics:** 2,020 applied, 81.1% admitted, 33% enrolled. **Transfer Admission Requirements:** High school transcript, college transcript(s), essay or personal statement, statement of good standing from prior institution(s). Minimum college GPA of 2.0 required. Lowest grade transferable C. **General Admission Information:** Priority deadline 3/1. Nonfall registration accepted. Admission may be deferred for a maximum of one semester.

COSTS AND FINANCIAL AID

Annual tuition $29,560. Required fees $330. Average book expense $1,100. **Required Forms and Deadlines:** FAFSA. **Notification of Awards:** Applicants will be notified of awards on a rolling basis beginning 12/1. **Types of Aid:** *Need-based scholarships/grants:* College/university scholarship or grant aid from institutional funds; Federal Pell; SEOG; State scholarships/grants. *Loans:* Direct PLUS loans; Direct Subsidized Stafford Loans; Direct Unsubsidized Stafford Loans. *Student Employment:* Federal Work-Study Program available. Institutional employment available. **Financial Aid Statistics:** 100% needy freshmen, 100% needy undergrads receive need-based scholarship or grant aid. 10% freshmen, 11% undergrads receive non-need-based scholarship or grant aid. 90% freshmen, 88% undergrads receive need-based self-help aid. 0% freshmen, 0% undergrads receive athletic scholarships. 88% freshmen, 90% undergrads receive any aid. 68% undergrads borrow to pay for school. Average cumulative indebtedness $37,800. **Criteria for awarding aid:** *Need-based:* Religious affiliation *Non-need-based:* Academics, Alumni affiliation, Art, Job skills, Leadership, Minority status, Music/drama, Religious affiliation, State/district residency.

UNIVERSITY OF NEBRASKA AT OMAHA

6001 Dodge Street, Omaha, NE 68182
Phone: 402-554-2393 • **Financial Aid Phone:** 402-554-2327
E-mail: unoadmissions@unomaha.edu • **CEEB Code:** 6420
Fax: 402-554-3472 • **Website:** www.unomaha.edu • **ACT Code:** 2464

This public school was founded in 1908. It has a 577 acre campus.

RATINGS

Admissions Selectivity Rating: 83   **Fire Safety Rating:** 97   **Green Rating:** 90

STUDENTS AND FACULTY

Enrollment: 12,153. **Student Body:** 52% female, 48% male, 7% out-of-state, 3% international (62 countries represented). Asian 3%, African American 7%, Caucasian 72%, Hispanic 9%, Native American <1%, Pacific Islander <1%, Two or more races 3%, Race unknown 3%.
Retention and Graduation: 75% freshmen return for sophomore year. 21% grads go on to further study within 1 year. **Faculty:** Student/faculty ratio 17:1. 520 full-time faculty, 83% hold PhDs, 18% are members of minority groups, 44% are women. 4% of classes are taught by teaching assistants.

ACADEMICS

Degrees: Bachelor's; Doctoral Other; Master's; Post-Bachelor's certificate; Post-Master's certificate **Classes:** Most classes have 10-19 students. Most lab/discussion sessions have 10-19 students. **Most popular majors:** Criminal Justice/Safety Studies; Business Administration And Management, General. **Special Study Options:** Cooperative education program; Cross-registration;

Distance learning; Double major; Dual enrollment; English as a Second Language (ESL); Exchange student program (domestic); Honors program; Independent study; Internships; Student-designed major; Study abroad; Teacher certification program. Honors programs: UNO Honors Program includes many opportunities such as Early Registration, Honors-only courses, Honors-priority Housing, Honors domestic and international semesters, Honors internships, and a Washington Center affiliation. **Disability Services offered to physically disabled students:** Note-taking services; Reader services; Tape recorders; Tutors. **Career services:** Career assessment; Career/job search classes; Internships

FACILITIES

Housing: Coed dorms 99% of campus accessible to physically diasbled. **Special Academic Facilities/Equipment:** Center for Afghanistan studies, physical education facility, Strauss Performing Arts Center, Speech Center, Writing Center, Math/Science Center, Peter Kiewit Information Technology Building, and Career Center. **Computers:** 100% of classrooms, 100% of dorms, 100% of libraries, 100% of dining areas, 100% of student union, 85% of common outdoor areas have wireless network access. Students can register for classes online. Administrative functions (other than registration) can be performed online.

CAMPUS LIFE

Environment: Metropolis **Activities:** Campus Ministries; Choral groups; Concert band; Dance; Drama/theater; International Student Organization; Jazz band; Literary magazine; Marching band; Model UN; Music ensembles; Musical theater; Opera; Pep band; Radio station; Student government; Student newspaper; Student-run film society; Symphony orchestra; Television station 127 registered organizations, 23 honor societies, 14 religious organizations. 6 fraternities, 8 sororities. **Athletics (Intercollegiate):** *Men:* baseball, basketball, football, ice hockey, wrestling. *Women:* basketball, cross-country, diving, golf, soccer, softball, swimming, tennis, track/field (outdoor), track/field (indoor), volleyball. **On-Campus Highlights:** University Library, The Health, Physical Education & Rec. Building, Milo Bail Student Center, Durham Science Center, The Peter Kiewit Institute **Environmental Initiatives:** To identify sustainability opportunities and to develop a recommended action plan for each

ADMISSIONS

Freshman Academic Profile: Average high school GPA 3.4. 15% in top 10% of high school class, 40% in top 25% of high school class, 75% in top 50% of high school class. 90% from public high schools. **Test Scores:** ACT middle 50% range 20-26. Minimum internet-based TOEFL 61. Minimum paper TOEFL 500. **Basis for Candidate Selection:** *Very important factors considered include:* rigor of secondary school record, class rank, standardized test scores. *Other factors considered include:* character/personal qualities. **Freshman Admission Requirements:** High school diploma is required and GED is accepted *Academic units required:* 4 English, 3 math, 3 science, 1 science labs, 2 foreign language, 1 social studies, 2 history, 1 academic elective. **Freshman Admission Statistics:** 4,955 applied, 70.8% admitted, 54% enrolled. **Transfer Admission Requirements:** college transcript(s), statement of good standing from prior institution(s). Minimum college GPA of 2.0 required. Lowest grade transferable C-. **General Admission Information:** Application fee $45. Regular application deadline 8/1. Nonfall registration accepted.

COSTS AND FINANCIAL AID

Annual in-state tuition $8,090. Annual out-of-state tuition $15,520. Room and board $8,090. Required fees $1,370. Average book expense $1,000. **Required Forms and Deadlines:** FAFSA. **Notification of Awards:** Applicants will be notified of awards on a rolling basis beginning 4/15. **Types of Aid:** *Need-based scholarships/grants:* College/university scholarship or grant aid from institutional funds; Federal Pell; Private scholarships; SEOG; State scholarships/grants. *Loans:* Direct PLUS loans; Direct Subsidized Stafford Loans; Direct Unsubsidized Stafford Loans. *Student Employment:* Federal Work-Study Program available. Institutional employment available. **Financial Aid Statistics:** 60% needy freshmen, 64% needy undergrads receive need-based scholarship or grant aid. 13% freshmen, 14% undergrads receive non-need-based scholarship or grant aid. 54% freshmen, 68% undergrads receive need-based self-help aid. 3% freshmen, 2% undergrads receive athletic scholarships. 80% freshmen, 81% undergrads receive any aid. **Criteria for awarding aid:** *Need-based:* Academics, Leadership *Non-need-based:* Academics, Alumni affiliation, Art, Athletics, Leadership, Music/drama, State/district residency.

UNIVERSITY OF NEBRASKA—LINCOLN

1400 R St, Lincoln, NE 68588-0417
Phone: 402-472-2023 • **Financial Aid Phone:** 402-472-2030
E-mail: admissions@unl.edu • **CEEB Code:** 6877
Fax: 402-472-0670 • **Website:** http://www.unl.edu • **ACT Code:** 2482

This public school was founded in 1869. It has a 623 acre campus.

RATINGS

Admissions Selectivity Rating: 87   **Fire Safety Rating:** 85   **Green Rating:** 90

STUDENTS AND FACULTY

Enrollment: 20,954. **Student Body:** 48% female, 52% male, 23% out-of-state, 9% international (107 countries represented). Asian 3%, African American 3%, Caucasian 75%, Hispanic 6%, Native American <1%, Pacific Islander <1%, Two or more races 3%, Race unknown 1%.
Retention and Graduation: 83% freshmen return for sophomore year. 39% freshmen graduate within 4 years. 68% freshmen graduate within 6 years. 23% grads go on to further study within 1 year. **Faculty:** Student/faculty ratio 21:1. 1,117 full-time faculty, 90% hold PhDs, 21% are members of minority groups, 32% are women.

ACADEMICS

Degrees: Bachelor's; Doctoral/Professional; Doctoral/Research; Master's; Post-Bachelor's certificate; Post-Master's certificate **Classes:** Most classes have fewer than 10 students. Most lab/discussion sessions have fewer than 10 students. **Most popular majors:** Public Relations, Advertising, And Applied Communication; Psychology, General; Business Administration And Management, General. **Special Study Options:** Accelerated program; Cooperative education program; Cross-registration; Distance learning; Double major; English as a Second Language (ESL); Exchange student program (domestic); Honors program; Independent study; Internships; Liberal arts/career combination; Student-designed major; Study abroad; Teacher certification program. Honors programs: The University Honors Program offers top students in all majors opportunities to enhance their educational experience and distinguish themselves. University Honors students enjoy small classes, work closely with faculty on coursework and undergraduate research projects, belong to a community of high-achieving student leaders on campus, receive mentorship from upperclass Honors students, have opportunities to live in Honors housing, and are eligible for Honors-specific scholarships. This customizable program offers students the advantages of a leading research university with the benefits of a small, liberal arts environment. The Jeffrey S. Raikes School of Computer Science and Management is a leader in interdisciplinary education and innovation. Each year the Raikes School selects a cohort of 30-35 high achieving students with demonstrated interest in technology and business. Driven by a project-oriented curriculum and real-world application and alongside industry and community partners, students leverage design and model thinking to develop human-centered solutions to wicked problems. The College of Business Administration Honors Academy is a four-year, cohort-based, enhanced business leadership program for high-ability students who have the potential and desire to become the next generation of business leaders. Each year the Academy selects 40-45 students who complete most of their foundation and core business courses together as a cohort using an action-based learning style focused on the development of critical thinking, technical and communication skills. Students learn to develop solutions for real-world business problems and create social and intellectual bonds. Combined degree programs: BA/DDS; BA/JD; BA/MD; BA/MEng. **Disability Services offered to physically disabled students:** Note-taking services; Reader services; Tape recorders; Tutors. **Career services:** Alumni network; Alumni services; Career assessment; Career/job search classes; Internships

FACILITIES

Housing: Apartments for married students; Apartments for single students; Coed dorms; Cooperative housing; Fraternity/sorority housing; Special housing for disabled student; Special housing for international students; Women's dorms 95% of campus accessible to physically diasbled. **Special Academic Facilities/Equipment:** art museum; state natural history museum; planetarium; observatory; center for performing arts; arboretum; Center for Great Plains Studies; center for biomaterials and genetic research; international quilt study center and museum; diocles laser/extreme light lab; midwest roadside safety facility; food industries complex; center for mass spectrometry; animal science complex; veterinary animal research/diagnosis center; center for brain, biology and behavior; Nebraska Innovation Campus; Adele Coryell Hall Learning Commons

CAMPUS LIFE

Environment: City **Activities:** Campus Ministries; Choral groups; Concert band; Dance; Drama/theater; International Student Organization; Jazz band;

Literary magazine; Marching band; Model UN; Music ensembles; Musical theater; Opera; Pep band; Radio station; Student government; Student newspaper; Student-run film society; Symphony orchestra; Television station 335 registered organizations, 57 honor societies, 25 religious organizations. 27 fraternities, 18 sororities. **Athletics (Intercollegiate):** *Men:* baseball, basketball, cross-country, football, golf, gymnastics, rodeo, tennis, track/field (outdoor), track/field (indoor), wrestling. *Women:* basketball, bowling, cross-country, diving, golf, gymnastics, riflery, rodeo, soccer, softball, swimming, tennis, track/field (outdoor), track/field (indoor), volleyball. **On-Campus Highlights:** Student Union, Campus Recreation Center, Arboretum and Sculpture Garden, Memorial Stadium and Hewitt Center, Adele Coryell Hall Learning Commons **Environmental Initiatives:** Recycling of paper, plastic, aluminum and many other materials A student government initiative has resulted in UNL eliminating the use of polystyrene, also known as Styrofoam, for food packaging in 2016.

ADMISSIONS
Freshman Academic Profile: Average high school GPA 3.6. 26% in top 10% of high school class, 53% in top 25% of high school class, 85% in top 50% of high school class. **Test Scores:** SAT Math middle 50% range 550-700. SAT EBRW middle 50% range 550-680. ACT middle 50% range 22-29. Minimum internet-based TOEFL 70. Minimum paper TOEFL 523. **Basis for Candidate Selection:** *Very important factors considered include:* class rank, standardized test scores. *Important factors considered include:* rigor of secondary school record. *Other factors considered include:* academic GPA. **Freshman Admission Requirements:** High school diploma is required and GED is accepted *Academic units required:* 4 English, 4 math, 3 science, 1 science labs, 2 foreign language, 1 social studies, 2 history. **Freshman Admission Statistics:** 14,947 applied, 64.4% admitted, 51% enrolled. **Transfer Admission Requirements:** High school transcript, college transcript(s), Minimum college GPA of 2.0 required. Lowest grade transferable D. **General Admission Information:** Application fee $45. Priority deadline 3/1. Regular application deadline 5/1. Nonfall registration accepted.

COSTS AND FINANCIAL AID
Annual in-state tuition $10,670. Annual out-of-state tuition $22,425. Room and board $10,670. Required fees $1,762. Average book expense $1,024. **Required Forms and Deadlines:** FAFSA. **Notification of Awards:** Applicants will be notified of awards on a rolling basis beginning 4/1. **Types of Aid:** *Need-based scholarships/grants:* College/university scholarship or grant aid from institutional funds; Federal Pell; Private scholarships; SEOG; State scholarships/grants. *Loans:* Direct PLUS loans; Direct Subsidized Stafford Loans; Direct Unsubsidized Stafford Loans. *Student Employment:* Federal Work-Study Program available. Institutional employment available. **Financial Aid Statistics:** 81% needy freshmen, 76% needy undergrads receive need-based scholarship or grant aid. 9% freshmen, 7% undergrads receive non-need-based scholarship or grant aid. 71% freshmen, 71% undergrads receive need-based self-help aid. 3% freshmen, 3% undergrads receive athletic scholarships. 90% freshmen, 78% undergrads receive any aid. 55% undergrads borrow to pay for school. Average cumulative indebtedness $23,231. **Criteria for awarding aid:** *Need-based:* Music/drama *Non-need-based:* Academics, Alumni affiliation, Art, Athletics, Leadership, Music/drama, State/district residency.

UNIVERSITY OF NEBRASKA MEDICAL CENTER

987815 Nebr Med Ctr, Omaha, NE 68198-4230
Phone: 402-559-6864 · **Financial Aid Phone:** 402-559-4109
E-mail: ttonjes@unmc.edu
Fax: 402-559-6796 • **Website:** http://www.unmc.edu/

This public school was founded in 1902.

RATINGS
Admissions Selectivity Rating: 61   **Fire Safety Rating:** 60*   **Green Rating:** 60*

STUDENTS AND FACULTY
Enrollment: 812. **Student Body:** 88% female, 12% male, 12% out-of-state, 1% international. Asian 1%, African American 1%, Caucasian 93%, Hispanic 3%, Native American 1%,
Faculty: 768 full-time faculty, 90% hold PhDs, 14% are members of minority groups, 39% are women.

ACADEMICS
Degrees: Bachelor's; Master's; Post-Bachelor's certificate; Post-Master's certificate **Classes:** Most classes have 10-19 students. Most lab/discussion sessions have fewer than 10 students. **Most popular majors:** Medicine; Nursing/Registered Nurse (Rn, Asn, Bsn, Msn); Pharmacy. **Special Study Options:** Accelerated program; Distance learning; Honors program;

Independent study. **Disability Services offered to physically disabled students:** Note-taking services; Tutors.

CAMPUS LIFE
Environment: Metropolis **Activities:** Student government; Student newspaper.

ADMISSIONS
Test Scores: Minimum paper TOEFL 551. **Transfer Admission Requirements:** college transcript(s), Lowest grade transferable c. **General Admission Information:** Nonfall registration accepted.

COSTS AND FINANCIAL AID
Annual out-of-state tuition $18,900. Required fees $310. Average book expense $950. **Required Forms and Deadlines:** FAFSA; Institution's own financial aid form. **Notification of Awards:** Applicants will be notified of awards on or about 4/1. **Types of Aid:** *Need-based scholarships/grants:* College/university scholarship or grant aid from institutional funds; Federal Pell; Private scholarships; SEOG; State scholarships/grants. *Student Employment:* Federal Work-Study Program available. Institutional employment available. **Financial Aid Statistics:** 79% needy undergrads receive need-based scholarship or grant aid. 4% undergrads receive non-need-based scholarship or grant aid. 90% undergrads receive need-based self-help aid. 0% undergrads receive athletic scholarships. **Criteria for awarding aid:** *Non-need-based:* Academics, Leadership, Minority status.

UNIVERSITY OF NEVADA, LAS VEGAS

4505 S. Maryland Parkway, Las Vegas, NV 89154-1021
Phone: 702-774-8658
E-mail: admissions@unlv.edu • **CEEB Code:** 4861
Fax: 702-774-8008 • **Website:** www.unlv.edu • **ACT Code:** 2496

This public school was founded in 1957. It has a 337 acre campus.

RATINGS
Admissions Selectivity Rating: 75   **Fire Safety Rating:** 60*   **Green Rating:** 60*

STUDENTS AND FACULTY
Enrollment: 23,329. **Student Body:** 56% female, 44% male, 11% out-of-state, 4% international (84 countries represented). Asian 15%, African American 8%, Caucasian 35%, Hispanic 26%, Native American <1%, Pacific Islander 1%, Two or more races 9%, Race unknown 1%.
Retention and Graduation: 74% freshmen return for sophomore year. **Faculty:** Student/faculty ratio 20:1. 776 full-time faculty, 90% hold PhDs, 18% are members of minority groups, 33% are women. 11% of classes are taught by teaching assistants.

ACADEMICS
Degrees: Bachelor's; Certificate; Doctoral/Professional; Doctoral/Research; Master's; Post-Bachelor's certificate; Post-Master's certificate **Classes:** Most classes have 20-29 students. Most lab/discussion sessions have 20-29 students. **Most popular majors:** Elementary Education And Teaching; Psychology, General; Hospitality Administration/Management, General. **Special Study Options:** Accelerated program; Cooperative education program; Double major; Dual enrollment; English as a Second Language (ESL); Exchange student program (domestic); Honors program; Independent study; Internships; Student-designed major; Study abroad; Teacher certification program. **Disability Services offered to physically disabled students:** Note-taking services; Reader services; Tape recorders; Tutors. **Career services:** Alumni network; Alumni services; Career assessment; Career/job search classes; Internships; Regional alumni

FACILITIES
Housing: Coed dorms; Special housing for disabled student; Special housing for international students **Special Academic Facilities/Equipment:** Art galleries, national supercomputing center for energy and environment, natural history museum, arboretum, 3 theaters, concert hall, law school, dental school, international gaming institute, professional practice school for teachers. **Computers:** Students can register for classes online. Administrative functions (other than registration) can be performed online.

CAMPUS LIFE
Environment: Metropolis **Activities:** Campus Ministries; Choral groups; Concert band; Dance; Drama/theater; International Student Organization; Jazz band; Literary magazine; Marching band; Model UN; Music ensembles; Musical theater; Opera; Pep band; Radio station; Student government; Student newspaper; Student-run film society; Symphony orchestra; Television station; Yearbook 24 honor societies, 14 religious organizations. 8 fraternities,

6 sororities. **Athletics (Intercollegiate):** *Men:* baseball, basketball, football, golf, soccer, swimming, tennis. *Women:* basketball, cross-country, equestrian sports, golf, soccer, softball, swimming, tennis, track/field (outdoor), volleyball. **On-Campus Highlights:** Lied Library, Artemus W. Ham Concert Hall, Moyer Student Union, Judy Bailey Theatre, Student Services Complex

ADMISSIONS

Freshman Academic Profile: Average high school GPA 3.3. 23% in top 10% of high school class, 52% in top 25% of high school class, 82% in top 50% of high school class. **Test Scores:** SAT Math middle 50% range 450-560. SAT EBRW middle 50% range 440-560. ACT middle 50% range 18-25. Minimum paper TOEFL 500. **Basis for Candidate Selection:** *Very important factors considered include:* rigor of secondary school record, academic GPA. *Important factors considered include:* standardized test scores. **Freshman Admission Requirements:** High school diploma is required and GED is not accepted *Academic units required:* 4 English, 3 math, 3 science, 2 science labs, 3 social studies. **Freshman Admission Statistics:** 7,666 applied, 88.5% admitted, 56% enrolled. **Transfer Admission Requirements:** college transcript(s), Minimum college GPA of 2.0 required. Lowest grade transferable D-. **General Admission Information:** Application fee $60. Priority deadline 2/1. Regular application deadline 7/1. Nonfall registration accepted. Admission may be deferred for a maximum of 1 year.

COSTS AND FINANCIAL AID

Average book expense $1,224. **Required Forms and Deadlines:** FAFSA. **Types of Aid:** *Need-based scholarships/grants:* College/university scholarship or grant aid from institutional funds; Federal Pell; Private scholarships; SEOG; State scholarships/grants. *Loans:* Direct PLUS loans; Direct Subsidized Stafford Loans; Direct Unsubsidized Stafford Loans. *Student Employment:* Federal Work-Study Program available. Institutional employment available. **Financial Aid Statistics:** 64% needy freshmen, 67% needy undergrads receive need-based scholarship or grant aid. 77% freshmen, 48% undergrads receive non-need-based scholarship or grant aid. 84% freshmen, 90% undergrads receive need-based self-help aid. 2% freshmen, 2% undergrads receive athletic scholarships. 41% undergrads borrow to pay for school. Average cumulative indebtedness $24,891. **Criteria for awarding aid:** *Need-based:* Academics, Alumni affiliation *Non-need-based:* Academics, Alumni affiliation, Athletics, Music/drama.

UNIVERSITY OF NEW ENGLAND

11 Hills Beach Road, Biddeford, ME 04005-9599
Phone: 207-602-2297 • **Financial Aid Phone:** 207-602-2342
E-mail: admissions@une.edu • **CEEB Code:** 3751
Fax: 207-602-5900 • **Website:** www.une.edu • **ACT Code:** 3751

This private school was founded in 1831. It has a 550 acre campus.

RATINGS

Admissions Selectivity Rating: 73   **Fire Safety Rating:** 99   **Green Rating:** 93

STUDENTS AND FACULTY

Enrollment: 2,360. **Student Body:** 70% female, 30% male, 70% out-of-state, <1% international (6 countries represented). Asian 3%, African American 1%, Caucasian 88%, Hispanic <1%, Native American <1%, Two or more races 2%, Race unknown 5%.
Retention and Graduation: 78% freshmen return for sophomore year. 54% freshmen graduate within 4 years. 60% freshmen graduate within 6 years. 31% grads go on to further study within 1 year. **Faculty:** Student/faculty ratio 13:1. 285 full-time faculty, 72% hold PhDs, 9% are members of minority groups, 56% are women. 0% of classes are taught by teaching assistants.

ACADEMICS

Degrees: Bachelor's; Doctoral/Professional; Doctoral/Research; Master's; Post-Bachelor's certificate; Post-Master's certificate **Classes:** Most classes have 10-19 students. **Most popular majors:** Biomedical Sciences, General; Kinesiology And Exercise Science; Registered Nursing/Registered Nurse. **Special Study Options:** Accelerated program; Double major; Independent study; Internships; Liberal arts/career combination; Study abroad; Teacher certification program. Honors programs: The College of Arts and Sciences offers an honors program to qualified applicants. **Disability Services offered to physically disabled students:** Note-taking services; Tape recorders. **Career services:** Alumni services; Career assessment; Career/job search classes

FACILITIES

Housing: Coed dorms; Theme housing; Wellness housing **Special Academic Facilities/Equipment:** Payson Art Gallery; Maine Women Writers Collection; Marine Science Center; Performance Enhancement and Evaluation Center for health sciences (PEEC); Center for Health Ethics, Law and Policy; Center for Transcultural Health; and New England Institute of Cognitive Science and Evolutionary Psychology. **Computers:** Students can register for classes online.

CAMPUS LIFE

Environment: Town **Activities:** Choral groups; Dance; Drama/theater; International Student Organization; Jazz band; Literary magazine; Model UN; Music ensembles; Musical theater; Pep band; Radio station; Student government; Student newspaper; Yearbook 36 registered organizations, 3 honor societies, 1 religious organization. **Athletics (Intercollegiate):** *Men:* basketball, cross-country, golf, lacrosse, soccer. *Women:* basketball, cross-country, field hockey, golf, lacrosse, soccer, softball, swimming, volleyball. **On-Campus Highlights:** Marine Science Center, Alfond Health Science Center, UNE Beach (on Atlantic Ocean and Saco River), Danielle N. Ripich Commons, Harold Alfond Forum (Athletics) **Environmental Initiatives:** UNE joined as an institutional member of the Planetary Health Alliance in April 2017. Interested faculty and staff from UNE have formed a University Planetary Health Steering Committee to explore how UNE can contribute to the field of Planetary Health and how Planetary Health concepts can be more fully integrated into our curriculum and student learning experience. UNE is uniquely positioned to contribute to the field of planetary health due to the wide breadth of expertise in the College of Arts and Sciences and the more human-health focused colleges of Pharmacy, Osteopathic Medicine and the Westbrook College of Health Professions. The Planetary Health Alliance was founded on the premise that we are entrenched in a new era, the Anthropocene, where our industrial society has firmly implanted itself into the deep ranks of time. In this era, problems occurring in our environment are problems impacting human health – and they must be looked at as a singular issue with a unified solution.

ADMISSIONS

Freshman Academic Profile: Average high school GPA 3.4. **Test Scores:** Minimum internet-based TOEFL 79. Minimum paper TOEFL 550. **Basis for Candidate Selection:** *Very important factors considered include:* rigor of secondary school record, academic GPA. *Important factors considered include:* class rank. *Other factors considered include:* application essay, standardized test scores, recommendation(s), extracurricular activities, talent/ability, character/personal qualities, alumni/ae relation, geographical residence, volunteer work, work experience, level of applicant's interest. **Freshman Admission Requirements:** High school diploma is required and GED is accepted *Academic units required:* 4 English, 3 math, 3 science, 2 science labs, 2 social studies, 2 history, *Academic units recommended:* 4 math, 4 science, 3 science labs, 2 foreign language, 4 social studies, 4 history, 4 academic electives. **Freshman Admission Statistics:** 5,087 applied, 80.7% admitted, 16% enrolled. **Transfer Admission Requirements:** college transcript(s), Minimum college GPA of 2.0 required. Lowest grade transferable C-. **General Admission Information:** Application fee $40. Priority deadline 12/1. Nonfall registration accepted. Admission may be deferred for a maximum of 1 year.

COSTS AND FINANCIAL AID

Annual tuition $35,240. Room and board $13,580. Required fees $1,290. **Types of Aid:** *Student Employment:* Federal Work-Study Program available. Institutional employment available. **Financial Aid Statistics:** 98% freshmen, 98% undergrads receive any aid.

See page 1062.

UNIVERSITY OF NEW HAMPSHIRE

105 Main Street, Durham, NH 03824
Phone: 603-862-1360 • **Financial Aid Phone:** 603-862-3600
E-mail: admissions@unh.edu • **CEEB Code:** 3918
Fax: 603-862-0077 • **Website:** www.unh.edu • **ACT Code:** 2524

This public school was founded in 1866. It has a 2600 acre campus.

RATINGS

Admissions Selectivity Rating: 79   **Fire Safety Rating:** 98   **Green Rating:** 99

STUDENTS AND FACULTY

Enrollment: 12,847. **Student Body:** 55% female, 45% male, 53% out-of-state, 4% international (41 countries represented). Asian 3%, African American 1%, Caucasian 83%, Hispanic 3%, Native American <1%, Pacific Islander <1%, Two or more races 2%, Race unknown 4%.

Retention and Graduation: 86% freshmen return for sophomore year. 68% freshmen graduate within 4 years. 77% freshmen graduate within 6 years. 21% grads go on to further study within 1 year. 10% grads pursue arts and sciences degrees. 0.6% grads pursue law degrees. 2% grads pursue business degrees. 1% grads pursue medical degrees. **Faculty:** Student/faculty ratio 18:1. 654 full-time faculty, 88% hold PhDs, 16% are members of minority groups, 46% are women. 2% of classes are taught by teaching assistants.

ACADEMICS

Degrees: Associate; Bachelor's; Doctoral; Doctoral/Professional; Doctoral/Research; Master's; Post-Bachelor's certificate; Post-Master's certificate; Terminal Associate **Classes:** Most classes have 10-19 students. **Most popular majors:** Biomedical Sciences, General; Psychology, General; Business Administration And Management, General. **Special Study Options:** Accelerated program; Cross-registration; Distance learning; Double major; Dual enrollment; English as a Second Language (ESL); Exchange student program (domestic); Honors program; Independent study; Internships; Student-designed major; Study abroad; Teacher certification program; Weekend college. Honors programs: The UNH honors program offers small and dynamic classes, opportunities for research and study overseas, individualized advising and a close and supportive community. Combined degree programs: BA/MA; BA/MD. **Disability Services offered to physically disabled students:** Note-taking services; Reader services; Tape recorders; Tutors. **Career services:** Alumni network; Alumni services; Career assessment; Career/job search classes; Internships; Regional alumni

FACILITIES

Housing: Apartments for married students; Apartments for single students; Coed dorms; Special housing for disabled student; Special housing for international students; Theme housing 88% of campus accessible to physically diasbled. **Special Academic Facilities/Equipment:** Art gallery, radio station, optical observatory, marine research labs (coastal, estuarine, island), interoperability lab, experiential learning center with challenge course, electron microscope, child development center, journalism lab, writing center, experimental wind tunnel, agricultural and equine facilities including an organic research dairy farm and sustainable agriculture facilities, advanced manufacturing center, nursing simulation lab, instructional and recreational climbing wall, exercise physiology lab, sawmill, language labs, performing arts center, survey center, nature preserve and university museum. **Computers:** 5% of classrooms, 100% of dorms, 100% of libraries, 100% of student union, 2% of common outdoor areas have wireless network access. Students can register for classes online. Administrative functions (other than registration) can be performed online.

CAMPUS LIFE

Environment: Village **Activities:** Campus Ministries; Choral groups; Concert band; Dance; Drama/theater; International Student Organization; Jazz band; Literary magazine; Marching band; Model UN; Music ensembles; Musical theater; Opera; Pep band; Radio station; Student government; Student newspaper; Student-run film society; Symphony orchestra; Yearbook 187 registered organizations, 18 honor societies, 10 religious organizations. 10 fraternities, 7 sororities. **Athletics (Intercollegiate):** *Men:* basketball, cross-country, football, ice hockey, skiing (downhill/alpine), skiing (nordic/cross-country), soccer, track/field (outdoor), track/field (indoor). *Women:* basketball, cross-country, diving, field hockey, gymnastics, ice hockey, lacrosse, skiing (downhill/alpine), skiing (nordic/cross-country), soccer, swimming, track/field (outdoor), track/field (indoor), volleyball. **On-Campus Highlights:** Dimond Library, Whittemore Center, Hamel Recreation Center, Student Union/Holloway Commons, College Woods **Environmental Initiatives:** 1. The UNH USustainability Academy (UNHSA) is the oldest endowed sustainability program in higher education in the U.S. and has worked with the larger campus community over nearly 15 years to develop UNH's unique sustainable learning community model and to foster sustainability locally, statewide, and regionally. www.sustainableunh.unh.edu

ADMISSIONS

Freshman Academic Profile: Average high school GPA 3.5. 20% in top 10% of high school class, 49% in top 25% of high school class, 86% in top 50% of high school class. 80% from public high schools. **Test Scores:** SAT Math middle 50% range 530-630. SAT EBRW middle 50% range 550-630. ACT middle 50% range 23-28. Minimum internet-based TOEFL 80. Minimum paper TOEFL 550. **Basis for Candidate Selection:** *Very important factors considered include:* rigor of secondary school record, class rank, academic GPA. *Important factors considered include:* recommendation(s). *Other factors considered include:* application essay, standardized test scores, extracurricular activities, talent/ability, character/personal qualities, first generation, alumni/ae

relation, geographical residence, state residency, racial/ethnic status, volunteer work, work experience. **Freshman Admission Requirements:** High school diploma is required and GED is accepted *Academic units required:* 4 English, 3 math, 3 science, 2 science labs, 2 foreign language, 3 social studies, *Academic units recommended:* 4 English, 4 math, 4 science, 3 science labs, 3 foreign language, 3 social studies, 1 visual/performing arts. **Freshman Admission Statistics:** 19,964 applied, 76.5% admitted, 20% enrolled. **Transfer Admission Requirements:** High school transcript, college transcript(s), essay or personal statement, interview, standardized test scores, Minimum college GPA of 2.8 required. Lowest grade transferable C. **General Admission Information:** Application fee $50. Regular application deadline 2/1. Nonfall registration accepted. Admission may be deferred for a maximum of 1 year.

COSTS AND FINANCIAL AID

Annual in-state tuition $11,266. Annual out-of-state tuition $29,340. Room and board $11,266. Required fees $3,297. Average book expense $1,200. **Required Forms and Deadlines:** FAFSA. **Notification of Awards:** Applicants will be notified of awards on a rolling basis beginning 12/1. **Types of Aid:** *Need-based scholarships/grants:* College/university scholarship or grant aid from institutional funds; Federal Pell; Private scholarships; SEOG; State scholarships/grants. *Loans:* Direct PLUS loans; Direct Subsidized Stafford Loans; Direct Unsubsidized Stafford Loans. *Student Employment:* Federal Work-Study Program available. Institutional employment available. **Financial Aid Statistics:** 75% needy freshmen, 71% needy undergrads receive need-based scholarship or grant aid. 8% freshmen, 6% undergrads receive non-need-based scholarship or grant aid. 95% freshmen, 96% undergrads receive need-based self-help aid. 1% freshmen, 2% undergrads receive athletic scholarships. 88% freshmen, 80% undergrads receive any aid. 79% undergrads borrow to pay for school. Average cumulative indebtedness $38,799. **Criteria for awarding aid:** *Need-based:* Academics, Alumni affiliation, Art, Athletics, Minority status *Non-need-based:* Academics, Art, Athletics, Leadership, Music/drama.

UNIVERSITY OF NEW HAVEN

300 Boston Post Road, West Haven, CT 06516
Financial Aid Phone: 203-932-7315
E-mail: admissions@newhaven.edu • **CEEB Code:** 3663
Fax: 203-931-6093 • **Website:** www.newhaven.edu • **ACT Code:** 576

This private school was founded in 1920. It has a 82 acre campus.

RATINGS

Admissions Selectivity Rating: 74 • **Fire Safety Rating:** 60* • **Green Rating:** 60*

STUDENTS AND FACULTY

Enrollment: 5,147. **Student Body:** 53% female, 47% male, 56% out-of-state, 6% international (35 countries represented). Asian 3%, African American 12%, Caucasian 61%, Hispanic 12%, Native American <1%, Pacific Islander <1%, Two or more races 1%, Race unknown 5%.

Retention and Graduation: 79% freshmen return for sophomore year. 52% freshmen graduate within 4 years. 60% freshmen graduate within 6 years. **Faculty:** Student/faculty ratio 16:1. 263 full-time faculty, 81% hold PhDs, 22% are members of minority groups, 34% are women.

ACADEMICS

Degrees: Associate; Bachelor's; Certificate; Doctoral/Research; Master's; Post-Bachelor's certificate; Post-Master's certificate **Classes:** Most classes have 20-29 students. Most lab/discussion sessions have fewer than 10 students. **Most popular majors:** Psychology, General; Criminal Justice/Law Enforcement Administration; Forensic Science And Technology. **Special Study Options:** Accelerated program; Cooperative education program; Cross-registration; Distance learning; Double major; Dual enrollment; English as a Second Language (ESL); Exchange student program (domestic); Honors program; Independent study; Internships; Liberal arts/career combination; Study abroad. **Disability Services offered to physically disabled students:** Note-taking services; Reader services; Tape recorders; Tutors. **Career services:** Alumni network; Alumni services; Career assessment; Career/job search classes; Internships

FACILITIES

Housing: Apartments for single students; Coed dorms; Special housing for disabled student; Theme housing; Wellness housing **Special Academic**

Facilities/Equipment: Institute of Forensic Science; Fire Science Laboratories; Dental Hygiene Center; Bergami Learning Center for Finance & Technology **Computers:**

CAMPUS LIFE
Environment: Town **Activities:** Campus Ministries; Dance; Drama/theater; International Student Organization; Marching band; Model UN; Music ensembles; Pep band; Radio station; Student government; Student newspaper; Yearbook 50 registered organizations, 5 honor societies, 1 religious organization. 2 fraternities, 3 sororities. **Athletics (Intercollegiate):** *Men:* baseball, basketball, cross-country, golf, lacrosse, soccer, track/field (outdoor), track/field (indoor), volleyball. *Women:* basketball, cheerleading, cross-country, lacrosse, soccer, softball, tennis, volleyball.

ADMISSIONS
Freshman Academic Profile: Average high school GPA 3.4. 15% in top 10% of high school class, 39% in top 25% of high school class, 75% in top 50% of high school class. **Test Scores:** SAT Math middle 50% range 500-600. SAT EBRW middle 50% range 510-610. ACT middle 50% range 21-27. Minimum internet-based TOEFL 80. **Basis for Candidate Selection:** *Very important factors considered include:* academic GPA, standardized test scores. *Important factors considered include:* application essay, recommendation(s). *Other factors considered include:* rigor of secondary school record, interview, extracurricular activities, character/personal qualities, volunteer work, work experience, level of applicant's interest. **Freshman Admission Requirements:** High school diploma is required and GED is accepted *Academic units recommended:* 4 English, 3 math, 3 science, 2 science labs, 2 foreign language, 3 social studies. **Freshman Admission Statistics:** 9,953 applied, 87.8% admitted, 17% enrolled. **Transfer Admission Requirements:** High school transcript, college transcript(s), Minimum college GPA of 2.5 required. Lowest grade transferable C. **General Admission Information:** Application fee $50. Priority deadline 3/1. Nonfall registration accepted.

COSTS AND FINANCIAL AID
Required Forms and Deadlines: FAFSA. **Notification of Awards:** Applicants will be notified of awards on a rolling basis beginning 1/15. **Types of Aid:** *Need-based scholarships/grants:* College/university scholarship or grant aid from institutional funds; Federal Pell; Private scholarships; SEOG; State scholarships/grants. *Loans:* Direct PLUS loans; Direct Subsidized Stafford Loans; Direct Unsubsidized Stafford Loans. *Student Employment:* Federal Work-Study Program available. Institutional employment available. **Financial Aid Statistics:** 100% needy freshmen, 100% needy undergrads receive need-based scholarship or grant aid. 12% freshmen, 12% undergrads receive non-need-based scholarship or grant aid. 82% freshmen, 81% undergrads receive need-based self-help aid. 1% freshmen, 1% undergrads receive athletic scholarships. 80% undergrads borrow to pay for school. Average cumulative indebtedness $46,449. **Criteria for awarding aid:** *Non-need-based:* Academics, Art, Athletics.

See page 1064.

UNIVERSITY OF NEW MEXICO

1 University of New Mexico, Albuquerque, NM 86131
Phone: 505-277-2446 • **Financial Aid Phone:** 505-277-8900
E-mail: apply@unm.edu • **CEEB Code:** 4845
Fax: 505-277-6686 • **Website:** www.unm.edu • **ACT Code:** 2650

This public school was founded in 1889. It has a 769 acre campus.

RATINGS
Admissions Selectivity Rating: 89 **Fire Safety Rating:** 80 **Green Rating:** 60*

STUDENTS AND FACULTY
Enrollment: 18,913. **Student Body:** 56% female, 44% male, 13% out-of-state, 2% international (92 countries represented). Asian 4%, African American 2%, Caucasian 32%, Hispanic 49%, Native American 6%, Pacific Islander <1%, Two or more races 4%, Race unknown 1%.
Retention and Graduation: 19% freshmen graduate within 4 years. 48% freshmen graduate within 6 years. **Faculty:** Student/faculty ratio 16:1. 1,103 full-time faculty, 78% hold PhDs, 23% are members of minority groups, 49% are women.

ACADEMICS
Degrees: Associate; Bachelor's; Certificate; Doctoral/Professional; Doctoral/Research; Master's; Post-Bachelor's certificate; Post-Master's certificate **Classes:** Most classes have 20-29 students. **Most popular majors:** Biology/Biological Sciences, General; Psychology, General; Business Administration And Management, General. **Special Study Options:** Accelerated program; Cooperative education program; Distance learning; Double major; Dual enrollment; English as a Second Language (ESL); Exchange student program (domestic); Honors program; Independent study; Internships; Student-designed major; Study abroad; Teacher certification program; Weekend college. Honors programs: The University Honors Program offers the chance to explore major contemporary ideas and values in small interdisciplinary seminars with the additional benefits of personal interaction with outstanding UNM faculty, opportunities for upper-division independent research, social and cultural events, lecture series, and opportunities to participate in regional and national honors conferences. UHP students do not major in University Honors. They graduate with a degree from one of UNM's degree-granting colleges or schools. Combined degree programs: BA/MD; BA/MEng. **Disability Services offered to physically disabled students:** Note-taking services; Reader services; Tape recorders; Tutors. **Career services:** Alumni network; Alumni services; Career assessment; Career/job search classes; Internships; Regional alumni

FACILITIES
Housing: Apartments for married students; Apartments for single students; Coed dorms; Fraternity/sorority housing; Special housing for disabled student; Special housing for international students; Theme housing 100% of campus accessible to physically diasbled. **Special Academic Facilities/Equipment:** Museums of art, anthropology, geology, and Southwestern biology, lithography institute, meteoritics institute, electron and electron scanning microscopes, nuclear reactor, robotics lab, observatory, planetarium, Science and Technology Park. **Computers:** 100% of classrooms, 100% of dorms, 100% of libraries, 100% of dining areas, 100% of student union, 85% of common outdoor areas have wireless network access. Students can register for classes online. Administrative functions (other than registration) can be performed online.

CAMPUS LIFE
Environment: Metropolis **Activities:** Campus Ministries; Choral groups; Concert band; Dance; Drama/theater; International Student Organization; Jazz band; Literary magazine; Marching band; Model UN; Music ensembles; Musical theater; Opera; Pep band; Radio station; Student government; Student newspaper; Student-run film society; Symphony orchestra; Television station 375 registered organizations, 20 honor societies, 23 religious organizations. 9 fraternities, 10 sororities. **Athletics (Intercollegiate):** *Men:* baseball, basketball, cross-country, football, golf, skiing (downhill/alpine), skiing (nordic/cross-country), soccer, tennis, track/field (outdoor), track/field (indoor). *Women:* basketball, cross-country, diving, golf, skiing (downhill/alpine), skiing (nordic/cross-country), soccer, softball, swimming, tennis, track/field (outdoor), track/field (indoor), volleyball. **On-Campus Highlights:** SUB (Student Union Building), Duck Pond, Zimmerman Library, Popejoy Hall—Performing Arts Center, Residency Halls **Environmental Initiatives:** In November 2009 UNM submitted its first Climate Action Plan to the American College and University Presidents Climate Commitment website and set a climate neutrality target date of year 2050. UNM will use a multi-tiered approach to reducing our greenhouse gas emissions. The tiers are behavior- based energy conservation, technological improvements in utilities production and consumption, renewable energy, and alternative transportation.

ADMISSIONS
Freshman Academic Profile: Average high school GPA 3.4. **Test Scores:** SAT Math middle 50% range 470-580. SAT EBRW middle 50% range 460-590. ACT middle 50% range 19-25. Minimum internet-based TOEFL 68. Minimum paper TOEFL 520. **Basis for Candidate Selection:** *Very important factors considered include:* rigor of secondary school record, academic GPA. *Important factors considered include:* standardized test scores. *Other factors considered include:* application essay, interview, extracurricular activities, talent/ability, volunteer work, work experience. **Freshman Admission Requirements:** High school diploma is required and GED is accepted *Academic units required:* 4 English, 4 math, 3 science, 2 foreign language, 2 science labs, 2 social studies, 1 history. **Freshman Admission Statistics:** 11,347 applied, 49.4% admitted, 57% enrolled. **Transfer Admission Requirements:** college transcript(s), Minimum college GPA of 2.0 required. Lowest grade transferable C. **General Admission Information:** Application fee $25. Priority deadline 5/1. Nonfall registration accepted. Admission may be deferred.

COSTS AND FINANCIAL AID
Room and board $8,690. **Required Forms and Deadlines:** FAFSA. **Notification of Awards:** Applicants will be notified of awards on a rolling basis beginning 4/15. **Types of Aid:** *Need-based scholarships/grants:* College/university scholarship or grant aid from institutional funds; Federal Nursing Scholarships; Federal Pell; Private scholarships; SEOG; State scholarships/grants; United Negro College Fund. *Loans:* Direct PLUS loans; Direct

Subsidized Stafford Loans; Direct Unsubsidized Stafford Loans. *Student Employment:* Federal Work-Study Program available. **Criteria for awarding aid:** *Need-based:* Minority status *Non-need-based:* Academics, Alumni affiliation, Art, Athletics, Job skills, Leadership, Minority status, Music/drama, Religious affiliation, State/district residency.

UNIVERSITY OF NEW ORLEANS

2000 Lakeshore Dr., New Orleans, LA 70148
Phone: 504-280-6595 • **Financial Aid Phone:** 504-280-6603
E-mail: admissions@uno.edu • **CEEB Code:** 6379
Fax: 504-280-3973 • **Website:** www.uno.edu • **ACT Code:** 1591

This public school was founded in 1958. It has a 195 acre campus.

RATINGS
Admissions Selectivity Rating: 87   **Fire Safety Rating:** 89   **Green Rating:** 60*

STUDENTS AND FACULTY
Enrollment: 5,917. **Student Body:** 49% female, 51% male, 4% international (61 countries represented). Asian 9%, African American 15%, Caucasian 52%, Hispanic 13%, Native American <1%, Pacific Islander <1%, Two or more races 4%, Race unknown 3%.
Retention and Graduation: 62% freshmen return for sophomore year. 14% freshmen graduate within 4 years. 32% freshmen graduate within 6 years. **Faculty:** Student/faculty ratio 22:1. 243 full-time faculty, 82% hold PhDs, 21% are members of minority groups, 35% are women.

ACADEMICS
Degrees: Bachelor's; Doctoral/Research; Master's; Post-Bachelor's certificate **Most popular majors:** Biology/Biological Sciences, General; Multi-/Interdisciplinary Studies, Other; Business Administration And Management, General. **Special Study Options:** Accelerated program; Cooperative education program; Cross-registration; Distance learning; Double major; Dual enrollment; English as a Second Language (ESL); Exchange student program (domestic); Honors program; Independent study; Internships; Study abroad; Teacher certification program. **Disability Services offered to physically disabled students:** Note-taking services; Reader services; Tape recorders; Tutors. **Career services:** Alumni network; Alumni services; Career assessment; Career/job search classes; Internships; Regional alumni

FACILITIES
Housing: Apartments for married students; Coed dorms; Theme housing 100% of campus accessible to physically diasbled. **Special Academic Facilities/Equipment:** Performing Arts Center, Nims Center Studios (motion picture and television production facility), Eisenhower leadership studies center, Louisiana and Special Collections, The Cove (a student dining and entertainment center that is home to Jazz at the Sandbar, a unique performance series in which students are paired with professional jazz musicians) **Computers:** 100% of libraries, 100% of student union, have wireless network access. Students can register for classes online. Administrative functions (other than registration) can be performed online.

CAMPUS LIFE
Environment: Metropolis **Activities:** Campus Ministries; Choral groups; Concert band; Dance; Drama/theater; International Student Organization; Jazz band; Literary magazine; Model UN; Music ensembles; Musical theater; Pep band; Radio station; Student government; Student newspaper; Student-run film society 120 registered organizations, 7 religious organizations. 9 fraternities, 8 sororities. **Athletics (Intercollegiate):** *Men:* baseball, basketball, diving, golf, swimming, tennis. *Women:* basketball, diving, swimming, tennis, volleyball. **On-Campus Highlights:** Recreation and Fitness Center, The University Center, Ponchartrain Hall, Earl K. Long Library, The Cove

ADMISSIONS
Freshman Academic Profile: Average high school GPA 3.2. 15% in top 10% of high school class, 34% in top 25% of high school class, 64% in top 50% of high school class. **Test Scores:** SAT Math middle 50% range 510-610. SAT EBRW middle 50% range 520-640. ACT middle 50% range 20-25. **Basis for Candidate Selection:** *Very important factors considered include:* academic GPA, standardized test scores. **Freshman Admission Requirements:** High school diploma is required and GED is accepted *Academic units required:* 4 English, 4 math, 4 science, 2 foreign language, 4 social studies,

1 visual/performing arts. **Freshman Admission Statistics:** 3,736 applied, 56.6% admitted, 45% enrolled. **Transfer Admission Requirements:** college transcript(s), Minimum college GPA of 2.25 required. Lowest grade transferable D. **General Admission Information:** Application fee $25. Priority deadline 12/15. Regular application deadline 7/15. Nonfall registration accepted.

COSTS AND FINANCIAL AID
Annual in-state tuition $10,575. Annual out-of-state tuition $10,926. Room and board $10,575. Required fees $2,394. Average book expense $1,300. **Required Forms and Deadlines:** FAFSA; Institution's own financial aid form. **Notification of Awards:** Applicants will be notified of awards on or about 1/15. **Types of Aid:** *Need-based scholarships/grants:* College/university scholarship or grant aid from institutional funds; Federal Pell; Private scholarships; SEOG; State scholarships/grants. *Loans:* Direct PLUS loans; Direct Subsidized Stafford Loans; Direct Unsubsidized Stafford Loans. *Student Employment:* Federal Work-Study Program available. Institutional employment available. **Financial Aid Statistics:** 76% needy freshmen, 61% needy undergrads receive need-based scholarship or grant aid. 72% freshmen, 50% undergrads receive non-need-based scholarship or grant aid. 43% freshmen, 46% undergrads receive need-based self-help aid. 2% freshmen, 2% undergrads receive athletic scholarships. 68% freshmen, 64% undergrads receive any aid. 55% undergrads borrow to pay for school. Average cumulative indebtedness $19,861. **Criteria for awarding aid:** *Need-based:* Academics, Alumni affiliation, Art, Athletics, Job skills, Leadership, Minority status, Music/drama *Non-need-based:* Academics, Athletics, Music/drama.

THE UNIVERSITY OF NORTH CAROLINA AT ASHEVILLE

One University Heights, Asheville, NC 28804-8502
Phone: 828-251-6481 • **Financial Aid Phone:** 828-251-6535
E-mail: admissions@unca.edu • **CEEB Code:** 5013
Fax: 828-251-6482 • **Website:** www.unca.edu • **ACT Code:** 3064

This public school was founded in 1927. It has a 365 acre campus.

RATINGS
Admissions Selectivity Rating: 80   **Fire Safety Rating:** 97   **Green Rating:** 90

STUDENTS AND FACULTY
Enrollment: 3,497. **Student Body:** 57% female, 43% male, 11% out-of-state, 1% international (13 countries represented). Asian 2%, African American 5%, Caucasian 78%, Hispanic 6%, Native American 1%, Pacific Islander <1%, Two or more races 4%, Race unknown 3%.
Retention and Graduation: 75% freshmen return for sophomore year. 42% freshmen graduate within 4 years. 62% freshmen graduate within 6 years. 15% grads go on to further study within 1 year. 68% grads pursue arts and sciences degrees. 2% grads pursue law degrees. 12% grads pursue business degrees. 2% grads pursue medical degrees. **Faculty:** Student/faculty ratio 13:1. 224 full-time faculty, 88% hold PhDs, 17% are members of minority groups, 46% are women. 0% of classes are taught by teaching assistants.

ACADEMICS
Degrees: Bachelor's; Master's; Post-Bachelor's certificate **Classes:** Most classes have 10-19 students. **Most popular majors:** Biology/Biological Sciences, General; Psychology, General; Business Administration And Management, General. **Special Study Options:** Cooperative education program; Cross-registration; Distance learning; Double major; Dual enrollment; Honors program; Independent study; Internships; Student-designed major; Study abroad; Teacher certification program. Honors programs: University Honors Program. Designed for talented and motivated students, the Honors curriculum complements the core general education curriculum and major curricula. Successful completion of the Honors Program enables the student to graduate with Distinction as a University Scholar. (See http://honors.unca.edu for further information.) Undergraduate Research Program. The Undergraduate Research Program at UNCA seeks to encourage the establishment of faculty/student research pairs who work together on a project of mutual interest. Research may be performed in any discipline on campus. Students who have made oral presentations at symposia and have had their work reviewed and published can receive recognition as University Research Scholars. (See http://www.unca.

edu/urp/ for more information.) **Disability Services offered to physically disabled students:** Note-taking services; Reader services; Tape recorders; Tutors. **Career services:** Alumni network; Alumni services; Career assessment; Career/job search classes; Internships; Regional alumni

FACILITIES

Housing: Coed dorms; Special housing for disabled student; Special housing for international students; Theme housing; Wellness housing 95% of campus accessible to physically diasbled. **Special Academic Facilities/Equipment:** •STEAM Studio at The RAMP for science, technology, engineering, art and math (STEAM) •Bob Moog Electric Music Studio (Dr. Moog, inventor of the Moog Synthesizer, was Research Professor of Music at UNC Asheville) •N.C. Center for Health & Wellness, including BodPod, Balance Lab, Biofeedback Lab, Meditation Space •Lookout Observatory, optical telescope for astronomical research •Botanical Gardens **Computers:** 1% of classrooms, 100% of libraries, 100% of dining areas, 90% of student union, have wireless network access. Students can register for classes online. Administrative functions (other than registration) can be performed online.

CAMPUS LIFE

Environment: Town **Activities:** Campus Ministries; Choral groups; Concert band; Dance; Drama/theater; International Student Organization; Jazz band; Literary magazine; Model UN; Music ensembles; Musical theater; Pep band; Radio station; Student government; Student newspaper; Student-run film society 82 registered organizations, 14 honor societies, 10 religious organizations. 1 fraternity, 2 sororities. **Athletics (Intercollegiate):** *Men:* baseball, basketball, cheerleading, cross-country, soccer, tennis, track/field (outdoor). *Women:* basketball, cheerleading, cross-country, soccer, tennis, track/field (outdoor), volleyball. **On-Campus Highlights:** Sherrill Center for Health and Wellness, Main Campus Quadrangle, Highsmith Union, Asheville Botanical Gardens, Argo Tea in Ramsey Library **Environmental Initiatives:** Sustainability has been enshrined in our current strategic plan as one of the 3 core values of the institution: "We must continue our commitment to sustainability and support of the natural environment, human communities, and the financial health of the institution. Our commitment to sustainability includes building and strengthening alliances on campus and beyond by encouraging active participation with community organizations and partners, promoting enduring alumni engagement, and facilitating inclusive discussions about a sustainable future. We must sustain affordable higher education and continue to identify new sources of support while also operating effectively and efficiently. We educate students about all dimensions of sustainability by integrating environmental literacy throughout the curriculum and by modeling sustainable campus practices. We will continue to build our students' capacities to strengthen the health and resilience of our community and environment, at the local and global levels, by providing high quality instructional expertise and by supporting sustainability-related learning opportunities."

ADMISSIONS

Freshman Academic Profile: Average high school GPA 3.4. 15% in top 10% of high school class, 44% in top 25% of high school class, 88% in top 50% of high school class. 88% from public high schools. **Test Scores:** SAT Math middle 50% range 530-610. SAT EBRW middle 50% range 550-650. ACT middle 50% range 22-27. Minimum internet-based TOEFL 79. Minimum paper TOEFL 550. **Basis for Candidate Selection:** *Very important factors considered include:* rigor of secondary school record, class rank, academic GPA. *Important factors considered include:* application essay, standardized test scores, recommendation(s), talent/ability, character/personal qualities, level of applicant's interest. *Other factors considered include:* interview, extracurricular activities, first generation, alumni/ae relation, geographical residence, state residency, racial/ethnic status, volunteer work, work experience. **Freshman Admission Requirements:** High school diploma is required and GED is not accepted *Academic units required:* 4 English, 4 math, 3 science, 1 science labs, 2 foreign language, 1 social studies, 1 history, *Academic units recommended:* 4 academic electives. **Freshman Admission Statistics:** 3,358 applied, 81.3% admitted, 24% enrolled. **Transfer Admission Requirements:** college transcript(s), Minimum college GPA of 2.50 required. Lowest grade transferable C. **General Admission Information:** Application fee $75. Priority deadline 11/15. Regular application deadline 2/15. Nonfall registration accepted. Admission may be deferred for a maximum of One year.

COSTS AND FINANCIAL AID

Annual in-state tuition $9,106. Annual out-of-state tuition $20,845. Room and board $9,106. Required fees $3,023. Average book expense $1,200. **Required Forms and Deadlines:** FAFSA. **Notification of Awards:** Applicants will be notified of awards on a rolling basis beginning 3/15. **Types of Aid:** *Need-based scholarships/grants:* College/university scholarship or grant aid from institutional funds; Federal Pell; Private scholarships; SEOG; State scholarships/grants. *Loans:* Direct PLUS loans; Direct Subsidized Stafford Loans; Direct Unsubsidized Stafford Loans. *Student Employment:* Federal Work-Study Program available. Institutional employment available. **Financial Aid Statistics:** 92% needy freshmen, 94% needy undergrads receive

need-based scholarship or grant aid. 11% freshmen, 12% undergrads receive non-need-based scholarship or grant aid. 68% freshmen, 72% undergrads receive need-based self-help aid. 3% freshmen, 3% undergrads receive athletic scholarships. 71% freshmen, 71% undergrads receive any aid. 53% undergrads borrow to pay for school. Average cumulative indebtedness $22,026. **Criteria for awarding aid:** *Need-based:* Academics, Job skills, Leadership, Music/drama *Non-need-based:* Academics, Alumni affiliation, Art, Athletics, Job skills, Leadership, Music/drama, State/district residency.

THE UNIVERSITY OF NORTH CAROLINA AT CHAPEL HILL

103 South Building, Chapel Hill, NC 27599-2200
Phone: 919-966-3621 • **Financial Aid Phone:** 919-962-8396
E-mail: unchelp@admissions.unc.edu • **CEEB Code:** 5816
Fax: 919-962-3045 • **Website:** www.unc.edu • **ACT Code:** 3162

This public school was founded in 1789. It has a 729 acre campus.

RATINGS

Admissions Selectivity Rating: 97   **Fire Safety Rating:** 97   **Green Rating:** 95

STUDENTS AND FACULTY

Enrollment: 18,683. **Student Body:** 59% female, 41% male, 16% out-of-state, 3% international (93 countries represented). Asian 11%, African American 8%, Caucasian 62%, Hispanic 8%, Native American <1%, Pacific Islander <1%, Two or more races 4%, Race unknown 4%.
Retention and Graduation: 97% freshmen return for sophomore year. 84% freshmen graduate within 4 years. 91% freshmen graduate within 6 years. 24% grads go on to further study within 1 year. 12% grads pursue arts and sciences degrees. 1.9% grads pursue law degrees. 2% grads pursue business degrees. 5.2% grads pursue medical degrees. **Faculty:** Student/faculty ratio 13:1. 1,667 full-time faculty, 85% hold PhDs, 20% are members of minority groups, 45% are women. 22% of classes are taught by teaching assistants.

ACADEMICS

Degrees: Bachelor's; Certificate; Doctoral/Professional; Doctoral/Research; **Master's Classes:** Most classes have 10-19 students. Most lab/discussion sessions have 20-29 students. **Most popular majors:** Biology/Biological Sciences, General; Psychology, General; Economics, General. **Special Study Options:** Cross-registration; Distance learning; Double major; Dual enrollment; Honors program; Independent study; Internships; Student-designed major; Study abroad; Teacher certification program. Honors programs: see http://www.honors.unc.edu/ Combined degree programs: BA/MA. **Disability Services offered to physically disabled students:** Note-taking services; Reader services; Tape recorders; Tutors. **Career services:** Alumni network; Alumni services; Career assessment; Career/job search classes; Internships; Regional alumni

FACILITIES

Housing: Apartments for married students; Apartments for single students; Coed dorms; Fraternity/sorority housing; Men's dorms; Special housing for disabled student; Special housing for international students; Theme housing; Wellness housing; Women's dorms 97% of campus accessible to physically diasbled. **Special Academic Facilities/Equipment:** Ackland Art Museum, Folklore council, Institute of Folk Music, Ba A Maker Space, Kenan-Flagler Business Capital Markets Lab, Basketball Museum, Institute of Latin American Studies, Center for Innovation and Sustainability in Local Media, Institute of Marine Sciences, Sitterson Hall Computer Museum, Center for the Study of the American South, Institute of Natural Science, Research Laboratory of Anthropology, Morehead Planetarium, Paul Green Theatre, 1789 Venture Lab for entrepreneurship, Playmakers Theater, Southern Historical Collection, Memorial Hall. **Computers:** 75% of classrooms, 15% of dorms, 100% of libraries, 100% of dining areas, 100% of student union, 50% of common outdoor areas have wireless network access. Students can register for classes online. Administrative functions (other than registration) can be performed online. Undergraduates are required to own a computer.

CAMPUS LIFE

Environment: Town **Activities:** Campus Ministries; Choral groups; Concert band; Dance; Drama/theater; International Student Organization; Jazz band;

Literary magazine; Marching band; Model UN; Music ensembles; Musical theater; Opera; Pep band; Radio station; Student government; Student newspaper; Student-run film society; Symphony orchestra; Television station; Yearbook 635 registered organizations, 19 honor societies, 42 religious organizations. 35 fraternities, 23 sororities. **Athletics (Intercollegiate):** *Men:* baseball, basketball, cross-country, diving, fencing, football, golf, lacrosse, soccer, swimming, tennis, track/field (outdoor), track/field (indoor), wrestling. *Women:* basketball, crew/rowing, cross-country, diving, fencing, field hockey, golf, gymnastics, lacrosse, soccer, softball, swimming, tennis, track/field (outdoor), track/field (indoor), volleyball. **On-Campus Highlights:** The Pit, McCorkle Place, Polk Place, Dean Smith Center, Student Union **Environmental Initiatives:** Partnered with Orange (County) Water and Sewer Authority (OWASA) to install a water reclamation and reuse system that replaced 218 million gallons of potable water in FY 2016. Started in summer 2009, the system provides makeup water at campus cooling towers, irrigates athletic fields and grounds, and flushes toilets in new buildings adjacent to the distribution network.

ADMISSIONS

Freshman Academic Profile: Average high school GPA 4.7. 78% in top 10% of high school class, 96% in top 25% of high school class, 100% in top 50% of high school class. 82% from public high schools. **Test Scores:** SAT Math middle 50% range 620-720. SAT EBRW middle 50% range 640-720. ACT middle 50% range 27-32. Minimum internet-based TOEFL 100. Minimum paper TOEFL 600. **Basis for Candidate Selection:** *Very important factors considered include:* rigor of secondary school record, application essay, standardized test scores, recommendation(s), extracurricular activities, talent/ability, character/personal qualities, state residency. *Important factors considered include:* class rank, academic GPA, volunteer work, work experience. *Other factors considered include:* first generation, alumni/ae relation, racial/ethnic status. **Freshman Admission Requirements:** High school diploma is required and GED is not accepted *Academic units required:* 4 English, 4 math, 3 science, 1 science labs, 2 foreign language, 1 social studies, 1 history, 1 academic elective. **Freshman Admission Statistics:** 40,919 applied, 23.7% admitted, 45% enrolled. **Transfer Admission Requirements:** High school transcript, college transcript(s), essay or personal statement, statement of good standing from prior institution(s). Minimum college GPA of 2.0 required. Lowest grade transferable C. **General Admission Information:** Application fee $80. Regular application deadline 10/15. Nonfall registration accepted. Admission may be deferred for a maximum of 1 year.

COSTS AND FINANCIAL AID

Annual in-state tuition $11,556. Annual out-of-state tuition $32,602. Room and board $11,556. Required fees $1,986. Average book expense $1,604. **Required Forms and Deadlines:** CSS/Financial Aid PROFILE; FAFSA. **Notification of Awards:** Applicants will be notified of awards on a rolling basis beginning 3/15. **Types of Aid:** *Need-based scholarships/grants:* College/university scholarship or grant aid from institutional funds; Federal Pell; Private scholarships; SEOG; State scholarships/grants. *Loans:* Direct PLUS loans; Direct Subsidized Stafford Loans; Direct Unsubsidized Stafford Loans. *Student Employment:* Federal Work-Study Program available. Institutional employment available. **Financial Aid Statistics:** 93% needy freshmen, 91% needy undergrads receive need-based scholarship or grant aid. 6% freshmen, 4% undergrads receive non-need-based scholarship or grant aid. 66% freshmen, 73% undergrads receive need-based self-help aid. 2% freshmen, 2% undergrads receive athletic scholarships. 67% freshmen, 63% undergrads receive any aid. Average cumulative indebtedness $20,127. **Criteria for awarding aid:** *Need-based:* Academics, Leadership *Non-need-based:* Academics, Alumni affiliation, Art, Athletics, Leadership, Music/drama, Religious affiliation, State/district residency.

THE UNIVERSITY OF NORTH CAROLINA
AT CHARLOTTE

9201 University City Boulevard, Charlotte, NC 28223-0001
Phone: 704-687-5507 • **Financial Aid Phone:** 704-687-5504
E-mail: admissions@uncc.edu • **CEEB Code:** 5105
Fax: 704-687-6483 • **Website:** www.uncc.edu • **ACT Code:** 3163

This public school was founded in 1946. It has a 1000 acre campus.

RATINGS

Admissions Selectivity Rating: 84   **Fire Safety Rating:** 96   **Green Rating:** 87

STUDENTS AND FACULTY

Enrollment: 23,622. **Student Body:** 47% female, 53% male, 4% out-of-state, 3% international (92 countries represented). Asian 7%, African American 16%, Caucasian 58%, Hispanic 10%, Native American <1%, Pacific Islander <1%, Two or more races 5%, Race unknown 2%.
Retention and Graduation: 83% freshmen return for sophomore year. 29% freshmen graduate within 4 years. 54% freshmen graduate within 6 years. **Faculty:** Student/faculty ratio 19:1. 1,160 full-time faculty, 84% hold PhDs, 21% are members of minority groups, 47% are women. 5% of classes are taught by teaching assistants.

ACADEMICS

Degrees: Bachelor's; Doctoral; Doctoral/Professional; Doctoral/Research; Master's; Post-Bachelor's certificate; Post-Master's certificate **Classes:** Most classes have 10-19 students. Most lab/discussion sessions have 10-19 students. **Most popular majors:** Speech Communication And Rhetoric; Psychology, General; Business Administration And Management, General. **Special Study Options:** Accelerated program; Cooperative education program; Cross-registration; Distance learning; Double major; Dual enrollment; English as a Second Language (ESL); Exchange student program (domestic); External degree program; Honors program; Independent study; Internships; Study abroad; Teacher certification program. Honors programs: A variety of honors programs are available in the College of Arts and Architecture, Belk College of Business, College of Computing and Informatics, College of Education, and the College of Engineering. Honors programs are also available in the following departments: Anthropology, Art History, Biological Sciences, Chemistry, Communication Studies, Criminal Justice, English, Geography & Earth Science, History, Kinesiology, Languages & Culture Studies, Latin American Studies, Mathematics, Philosophy, Physics & Optical Science, Political Science, Psychology, Religious Studies, and Sociology. There is also a University Honors Program in the Honors College. The University Honors Program is a four year program that welcomes students from any major. **Disability Services offered to physically disabled students:** Note-taking services; Reader services; Tape recorders; Tutors. **Career services:** Alumni network; Alumni services; Career assessment; Career/job search classes; Internships; Regional alumni

FACILITIES

Housing: Apartments for single students; Coed dorms; Fraternity/sorority housing; Special housing for disabled student; Special housing for international students; Theme housing; Wellness housing 90% of campus accessible to physically diasbled. **Special Academic Facilities/Equipment:** Largest research library in the Southern Piedmont region with more than three million volumes; NC's Urban Research University; Energy Production and Infrastructure Center; renovated fitness gymnasium; two botanical gardens that span 10 acres; McMillan greenhouse with a tropical conservatory; PORTAL which stands for Partnership, Outreach and Research to Accelerate Learning, is a business incubator and corporate innovation center that offers a unique and flexible environment for emerging enterprises, Center City building, Engineering Early College High School, Charlotte Research Institute **Computers:** 10% of classrooms, 10% of dorms, 30% of libraries, 70% of dining areas, 30% of student union, 10% of common outdoor areas have wireless network access. Students can register for classes online. Administrative functions (other than registration) can be performed online.

CAMPUS LIFE

Environment: Metropolis **Activities:** Campus Ministries; Choral groups; Concert band; Dance; Drama/theater; International Student Organization; Jazz band; Literary magazine; Marching band; Model UN; Music ensembles; Musical theater; Opera; Pep band; Radio station; Student government; Student newspaper; Student-run film society; Symphony orchestra; Television station 222 registered organizations, 25 honor societies, 22 religious organizations. 14 fraternities, 10 sororities. **Athletics (Intercollegiate):** *Men:* baseball, basketball, cross-country, golf, soccer, tennis, track/field (outdoor). *Women:* basketball, cross-country, soccer, softball, tennis, track/field (outdoor), volleyball. **On-Campus Highlights:** Popp Martin Student Union, SoVi (South Village Dining Hall), Belk Gym, The Prospector, J Murrey Atkins Library **Environmental Initiatives:** Energy and Water Conservation initiatives led by a full-time Energy Manager.

ADMISSIONS

Freshman Academic Profile: Average high school GPA 4.0. 17% in top 10% of high school class, 50% in top 25% of high school class, 83% in top 50% of high school class. 86% from public high schools. **Test Scores:** SAT Math middle 50% range 550-630. SAT EBRW middle 50% range 560-630. ACT middle 50% range 22-26. Minimum internet-based TOEFL 70. Minimum paper TOEFL 523. **Basis for Candidate Selection:** *Very important factors considered include:* rigor of secondary school record, academic GPA, standardized test scores. *Other factors considered include:* extracurricular activities, talent/ability, character/personal qualities, geographical residence, state residency, work experience, level of applicant's interest. **Freshman Admission Requirements:** High school diploma is required and GED is accepted *Academic units required:*

4 English, 4 math, 3 science, 1 science labs, 2 foreign language, 1 social studies, 1 history, *Academic units recommended:* 3 foreign language. **Freshman Admission Statistics:** 16,743 applied, 66.1% admitted, 30% enrolled. **Transfer Admission Requirements:** High school transcript, college transcript(s), statement of good standing from prior institution(s). Minimum college GPA of 2.0 required. Lowest grade transferable C. **General Admission Information:** Application fee $60. Regular application deadline 6/1. Nonfall registration accepted.

COSTS AND FINANCIAL AID

Annual in-state tuition $10,780. Annual out-of-state tuition $17,246. Room and board $10,780. Required fees $3,211. Average book expense $1,200. **Required Forms and Deadlines:** FAFSA. **Notification of Awards:** Applicants will be notified of awards on or about 3/1. **Types of Aid:** *Need-based scholarships/ grants:* College/university scholarship or grant aid from institutional funds; Federal Pell; Private scholarships; SEOG; State scholarships/grants; United Negro College Fund. *Loans:* Direct PLUS loans; Direct Subsidized Stafford Loans; Direct Unsubsidized Stafford Loans. *Student Employment:* Federal Work-Study Program available. Institutional employment available. **Financial Aid Statistics:** 72% needy freshmen, 77% needy undergrads receive need-based scholarship or grant aid. 23% freshmen, 14% undergrads receive non-need-based scholarship or grant aid. 80% freshmen, 79% undergrads receive need-based self-help aid. 0% freshmen, 0% undergrads receive athletic scholarships. 73% freshmen, 79% undergrads receive any aid. 67% undergrads borrow to pay for school. Average cumulative indebtedness $27,397. **Criteria for awarding aid:** *Non-need-based:* Academics, Alumni affiliation, Art, Athletics, Job skills, Leadership, Minority status, Music/drama, Religious affiliation, State/district residency.

THE UNIVERSITY OF NORTH CAROLINA AT GREENSBORO

PO Box 26170, Greensboro, NC 27402-6170
Phone: 336-334-5243 • **Financial Aid Phone:** 336-334-5702
E-mail: admissions@uncg.edu • **CEEB Code:** 5913
Fax: 336-334-4180 • **Website:** www.uncg.edu • **ACT Code:** 3166

This public school was founded in 1891. It has a 357 acre campus.

RATINGS

Admissions Selectivity Rating: 80   **Fire Safety Rating:** 99   **Green Rating:** 81

STUDENTS AND FACULTY

Enrollment: 15,988. **Student Body:** 66% female, 34% male, 5% out-of-state, 2% international (38 countries represented). Asian 5%, African American 29%, Caucasian 49%, Hispanic 9%, Native American <1%, Pacific Islander <1%, Two or more races 5%, Race unknown <1%.
Retention and Graduation: 76% freshmen return for sophomore year. 29% freshmen graduate within 4 years. 53% freshmen graduate within 6 years.
Faculty: Student/faculty ratio 18:1. 801 full-time faculty, 79% hold PhDs, 24% are members of minority groups, 55% are women. 20% of classes are taught by teaching assistants.

ACADEMICS

Degrees: Bachelor's; Doctoral/Professional; Doctoral/Research; Master's; Post-Bachelor's certificate; Post-Master's certificate **Classes:** Most classes have 10-19 students. Most lab/discussion sessions have 10-19 students. **Most popular majors:** Biology/Biological Sciences, General; Psychology, General; Business Administration And Management, General. **Special Study Options:** Accelerated program; Cross-registration; Distance learning; Double major; Dual enrollment; English as a Second Language (ESL); Honors program; Independent study; Internships; Student-designed major; Study abroad; Teacher certification program. Honors programs: The International Honors Program is geared towards motivated, high-achieving incoming first-year students and current UNCG students who have completed fewer than 30 hours, pursuing all majors. New first-year students take a 1-credit Honors Colloquium, which introduces them to the Honors experience and to UNCG, and a 3-credit 100-level Honors First-Year Seminar. (Current students substitute a 200-level seminar for the 100-level seminar.) In order to complete the requirements of the program, by graduation, students need to complete three additional 200-level International Honors seminars, achieve proficiency (the 204 level) of

a second language, and study abroad, typically for a semester at one of UNCG's 100+ exchange partner institutions. Honors students in good standing receive a travel scholarship, currently $1,300, which helps offset the cost of plane fare. The International Honors Program is very flexible, and teaches students to think and read critically, to craft clear arguments, and to find their place in an increasingly interdependent world. Once you begin taking courses in your major field, you can enroll in the Disciplinary Honors Program. Program requirements vary by academic department, but in general, you complete special coursework in your major field of study and have the option of studying overseas. You also undertake a Senior Honors Project – typically a major research paper, project, or performance. To be eligible to enroll in this program you must have a UNCG GPA of at least 3.30. Students who successfully complete the requirements of both the International Honors Program and Disciplinary Honors Programs are awarded Full University Honors upon graduation. This award constitutes the University's highest academic honor. Combined degree programs: BA/MA. **Disability Services offered to physically disabled students:** Note-taking services; Reader services; Tape recorders; Tutors. **Career services:** Alumni network; Alumni services; Career assessment; Career/job search classes; Internships

FACILITIES

Housing: Apartments for single students; Coed dorms; Special housing for disabled student; Special housing for international students; Theme housing; Women's dorms 95% of campus accessible to physically disabled. **Special Academic Facilities/Equipment:** Weatherspoon Art Gallery, 45,000 sq.ft. Student Center, Music Building, Sullivan Building, 216,000 sq.ft. recreation facility, recreation field, outdoor courts, track, tennis courts, golf greens, Piney Lake park, Gatewood Gallery, UNCG Auditorium, Taylor Theater **Computers:** 90% of dorms, 35% of libraries, have wireless network access. Students can register for classes online. Administrative functions (other than registration) can be performed online.

CAMPUS LIFE

Environment: City **Activities:** Campus Ministries; Choral groups; Concert band; Dance; Drama/theater; International Student Organization; Jazz band; Literary magazine; Marching band; Model UN; Music ensembles; Musical theater; Opera; Pep band; Radio station; Student government; Student newspaper; Student-run film society; Symphony orchestra 200 registered organizations, 23 honor societies, 13 religious organizations. 11 fraternities, 11 sororities. **Athletics (Intercollegiate):** *Men:* baseball, basketball, cross-country, golf, soccer, tennis, wrestling. *Women:* basketball, cross-country, golf, soccer, softball, tennis, volleyball. **On-Campus Highlights:** Kaplan Center for Wellness, Elliott University Center, Weatherspoon Art Museum, Peabody Park, UNCG Theatre **Environmental Initiatives:** Commitment to become carbon neutral by 2050

ADMISSIONS

Freshman Academic Profile: Average high school GPA 3.7. 13% in top 10% of high school class, 39% in top 25% of high school class, 77% in top 50% of high school class. 95% from public high schools. **Test Scores:** SAT Math middle 50% range 510-580. SAT EBRW middle 50% range 520-600. ACT middle 50% range 20-25. Minimum internet-based TOEFL 79. Minimum paper TOEFL 550. **Basis for Candidate Selection:** *Very important factors considered include:* rigor of secondary school record, academic GPA. *Important factors considered include:* standardized test scores. *Other factors considered include:* class rank, application essay, recommendation(s), extracurricular activities, volunteer work. **Freshman Admission Requirements:** High school diploma is required and GED is accepted *Academic units required:* 4 English, 4 math, 3 science, 1 science labs, 2 foreign language, 2 social studies. **Freshman Admission Statistics:** 8,524 applied, 78.0% admitted, 42% enrolled. **Transfer Admission Requirements:** High school transcript, college transcript(s), standardized test scores, statement of good standing from prior institution(s). Minimum college GPA of 2.0 required. Lowest grade transferable 2. **General Admission Information:** Application fee $65. Priority deadline 11/1. Regular application deadline 3/1. Nonfall registration accepted.

COSTS AND FINANCIAL AID

Annual in-state tuition $2,828. Annual out-of-state tuition $19,582. Required fees $2,828. Average book expense $1,000. **Required Forms and Deadlines:** FAFSA. **Notification of Awards:** Applicants will be notified of awards on a rolling basis beginning 3/15. **Types of Aid:** *Need-based scholarships/ grants:* College/university scholarship or grant aid from institutional funds; Federal Pell; Private scholarships; SEOG; State scholarships/grants. *Loans:* Direct PLUS loans; Direct Subsidized Stafford Loans; Direct Unsubsidized Stafford Loans. *Student Employment:* Federal Work-Study Program available. Institutional employment available. **Financial Aid Statistics:** 75% needy freshmen, 67% needy undergrads receive need-based scholarship or grant aid. 71% freshmen, 65% undergrads receive non-need-based scholarship or grant aid. 63% freshmen, 69% undergrads receive need-based self-help aid. 1% freshmen, 1% undergrads receive athletic scholarships. 87% freshmen, 81% undergrads receive any aid. 89% undergrads borrow to pay for school. Average cumulative indebtedness $27,073. **Criteria for awarding aid:** *Need-based:* Academics *Non-need-based:* Academics, Athletics, Music/drama, Religious affiliation, State/district residency.

THE UNIVERSITY OF NORTH CAROLINA AT PEMBROKE

P.O Box 1510, Pembroke, NC 28372
Phone: 910-521-6262 • **Financial Aid Phone:** 910-521-6255
E-mail: admissions@uncp.edu • **CEEB Code:** 5534
Fax: 910-521-6497 • **Website:** www.uncp.edu • **ACT Code:** 3138

This public school was founded in 1887. It has a 264 acre campus.

RATINGS

Admissions Selectivity Rating: 75　　**Fire Safety Rating:** 97　　**Green Rating:** 90

STUDENTS AND FACULTY

Enrollment: 5,508. **Student Body:** 60% female, 40% male, 2% out-of-state, 1% international (20 countries represented). Asian 2%, African American 36%, Caucasian 37%, Hispanic 6%, Native American 15%, Pacific Islander <1%, Two or more races 2%, Race unknown 2%.
Retention and Graduation: 67% freshmen return for sophomore year. **Faculty:** Student/faculty ratio 16:1. 295 full-time faculty, 79% hold PhDs, 25% are members of minority groups, 51% are women. 0% of classes are taught by teaching assistants.

ACADEMICS

Degrees: Bachelor's; **Master's Classes:** Most classes have 10-19 students. Most lab/discussion sessions have 20-29 students. **Most popular majors:** Criminal Justice/Safety Studies; Sociology; Business Administration And Management, General. **Special Study Options:** Accelerated program; Cross-registration; Distance learning; Double major; Dual enrollment; English as a Second Language (ESL); Exchange student program (domestic); Honors program; Independent study; Internships; Study abroad; Teacher certification program. Honors programs: The Esther G. Maynor Honors College began in 2001 to attract top scholars to UNCP, and provide an environment that stimulates academic and personal growth. Combined degree programs: BA/MA. **Disability Services offered to physically disabled students:** Note-taking services; Reader services; Tape recorders; Tutors. **Career services:** Alumni network; Alumni services; Career assessment; Career/job search classes; Internships

FACILITIES

Housing: Apartments for single students; Coed dorms; Men's dorms; Women's dorms 99% of campus accessible to physically diasbled. **Special Academic Facilities/Equipment:** Native American Resources Center and Museum; Nursing's Clinical Learning Center **Computers:** 100% of classrooms, 50% of dorms, 100% of libraries, 100% of dining areas, 100% of student union, 30% of common outdoor areas have wireless network access. Students can register for classes online. Administrative functions (other than registration) can be performed online. Undergraduates are required to own a computer.

CAMPUS LIFE

Environment: Rural **Activities:** Campus Ministries; Choral groups; Concert band; Dance; Drama/theater; International Student Organization; Jazz band; Marching band; Music ensembles; Musical theater; Radio station; Student government; Student newspaper; Television station; Yearbook 70 registered organizations, 11 honor societies, 5 religious organizations. 10 fraternities, 11 sororities. **Athletics (Intercollegiate):** *Men:* baseball, basketball, cheerleading, cross-country, football, golf, soccer, track/field (outdoor), wrestling. *Women:* basketball, cheerleading, cross-country, golf, soccer, softball, tennis, track/field (outdoor), volleyball. **On-Campus Highlights:** English E.Jones Health and Physical Education Center, Native American Resource Center/Museum, Givens Performing Arts Center, UNCP Bookstore/ University Center, Higher Ground Ropes Course **Environmental Initiatives:** Planning & Construction Dept. mandates all new facilities to be LEED certified.

ADMISSIONS

Freshman Academic Profile: Average high school GPA 3.4. 11% in top 10% of high school class, 34% in top 25% of high school class, 73% in top 50% of high school class. 95% from public high schools. **Test Scores:** SAT Math middle 50% range 420-500. SAT EBRW middle 50% range 410-490. ACT middle 50% range 18-22. Minimum internet-based TOEFL 68. Minimum paper TOEFL 520. **Basis for Candidate Selection:** *Very important factors considered include:* rigor of secondary school record, academic GPA, standardized test

scores. *Other factors considered include:* class rank, geographical residence, state residency. **Freshman Admission Requirements:** High school diploma is required and GED is accepted *Academic units required:* 4 English, 4 math, 3 science, 1 science labs, 2 foreign language, 1 social studies, 1 history. **Freshman Admission Statistics:** 4,596 applied, 74.4% admitted, 36% enrolled. **Transfer Admission Requirements:** High school transcript, college transcript(s), statement of good standing from prior institution(s). Minimum college GPA of 2.0 required. Lowest grade transferable C. **General Admission Information:** Application fee $45. Priority deadline 7/15. Regular application deadline 7/31. Nonfall registration accepted. Admission may be deferred for a maximum of 1 year.

COSTS AND FINANCIAL AID

Annual in-state tuition $8,572. Annual out-of-state tuition $14,475. Room and board $8,572. Required fees $2,285. Average book expense $1,505. **Required Forms and Deadlines:** FAFSA. **Notification of Awards:** Applicants will be notified of awards on a rolling basis beginning 4/15. **Types of Aid:** *Need-based scholarships/grants:* College/university scholarship or grant aid from institutional funds; Federal Pell; SEOG; State scholarships/grants. *Loans:* Direct PLUS loans; Direct Subsidized Stafford Loans; Direct Unsubsidized Stafford Loans. *Student Employment:* Federal Work-Study Program available. **Financial Aid Statistics:** 86% needy freshmen, 84% needy undergrads receive need-based scholarship or grant aid. 15% freshmen, 13% undergrads receive non-need-based scholarship or grant aid. 87% freshmen, 86% undergrads receive need-based self-help aid. 1% freshmen, 1% undergrads receive athletic scholarships. 79% freshmen, 75% undergrads receive any aid. Average cumulative indebtedness $24,169. **Criteria for awarding aid:** *Need-based:* Academics, Alumni affiliation, Art, Athletics, Music/drama *Non-need-based:* Academics, Alumni affiliation, Art, Athletics, Minority status, Music/drama.

THE UNIVERSITY OF NORTH CAROLINA AT WILMINGTON

601 South College Rd, Wilmington, NC 28403-5904
Phone: 910-962-3243 • **Financial Aid Phone:** 910-962-3177
E-mail: admissions@uncw.edu • **CEEB Code:** 5907
Fax: 910-962-3038 • **Website:** www.uncw.edu • **ACT Code:** 3174

This public school was founded in 1947. It has a 661 acre campus.

RATINGS

Admissions Selectivity Rating: 85　　**Fire Safety Rating:** 97　　**Green Rating:** 89

STUDENTS AND FACULTY

Enrollment: 14,183. **Student Body:** 62% female, 38% male, 12% out-of-state, 1% international (53 countries represented). Asian 2%, African American 4%, Caucasian 78%, Hispanic 7%, Native American <1%, Pacific Islander <1%, Two or more races 4%, Race unknown 3%.
Retention and Graduation: 87% freshmen return for sophomore year. 54% freshmen graduate within 4 years. 72% freshmen graduate within 6 years. 17% grads go on to further study within 1 year. **Faculty:** Student/faculty ratio 18:1. 647 full-time faculty, 84% hold PhDs, 17% are members of minority groups, 51% are women. 1% of classes are taught by teaching assistants.

ACADEMICS

Degrees: Bachelor's; Doctoral/Professional; Doctoral/Research; Master's; Post-Bachelor's certificate; Post-Master's certificate **Most popular majors:** Psychology, General; Registered Nursing/Registered Nurse; Business Administration And Management, General. **Special Study Options:** Accelerated program; Distance learning; Double major; Dual enrollment; English as a Second Language (ESL); Honors program; Independent study; Internships; Study abroad; Teacher certification program. Honors programs: The HONORS SCHOLARS COLLEGE at UNCW is designed to offer academically talented students challenging and exciting experiences both in and out of the classroom. A student may begin with general honors in the first two years, and then go on to departmental honors in their major. In their freshman and sophomore years, students take special interdisciplinary honors seminars and honors sections of university studies courses. Honors classes are small—generally not over 20 students—to encourage discussion and faculty-student interaction. In any given semester, an honors scholar will enroll in both honors and other university classes, enhancing his or her experiences in many academic areas with a wide variety of students. In their junior and senior years, honors students will propose and carry out an honors "capstone" experience—a scholarly project in the student's major. This involves independent work and close interaction with a faculty sponsor. Many of these have led to publication and presentations at professional conferences. Overall, the program encourages curiosity, critical thinking, and independent work skills by offering exciting academic and cultural activities as well as the opportunity for close working and social relationships with the faculty. **Disability Services offered to physically disabled students:** Note-taking services; Reader services; Tape recorders; Tutors. **Career services:** Alumni network; Alumni services; Career assessment; Career/job search classes; Internships; Regional alumni

FACILITIES

Housing: Apartments for single students; Coed dorms; Fraternity/sorority housing; Special housing for disabled student; Special housing for international students; Theme housing; Wellness housing 90% of campus accessible to physically diasbled. **Special Academic Facilities/Equipment:** Largest research library in the Southern Piedmont region with more than three million volumes; NC's Urban Research University; Energy Production and Infrastructure Center; renovated fitness gymnasium; two botanical gardens that span 10 acres; McMillan greenhouse with a tropical conservatory; PORTAL which stands for Partnership, Outreach and Research to Accelerate Learning, is a business incubator and corporate innovation center that offers a unique and flexible environment for emerging enterprises, Center City building, Engineering Early College High School, Charlotte Research Institute **Computers:** 10% of classrooms, 10% of dorms, 30% of libraries, 70% of dining areas, 30% of student union, 10% of common outdoor areas have wireless network access. Students can register for classes online. Administrative functions (other than registration) can be performed online.

CAMPUS LIFE

Environment: Metropolis **Activities:** Campus Ministries; Choral groups; Concert band; Dance; Drama/theater; International Student Organization; Jazz band; Literary magazine; Marching band; Model UN; Music ensembles; Musical theater; Opera; Pep band; Radio station; Student government; Student newspaper; Student-run film society; Symphony orchestra; Television station 222 registered organizations, 25 honor societies, 22 religious organizations. 14 fraternities, 10 sororities. **Athletics (Intercollegiate):** *Men:* baseball, basketball, cross-country, golf, soccer, tennis, track/field (outdoor). *Women:* basketball, cross-country, soccer, softball, tennis, track/field (outdoor), volleyball. **On-Campus Highlights:** Popp Martin Student Union, SoVi (South Village Dining Hall), Belk Gym, The Prospector, J Murrey Atkins Library **Environmental Initiatives:** Energy and Water Conservation initiatives led by a full-time Energy Manager.

ADMISSIONS

Freshman Academic Profile: Average high school GPA 4.2. 25% in top 10% of high school class, 62% in top 25% of high school class, 93% in top 50% of high school class. 86% from public high schools. **Test Scores:** SAT Math middle 50% range 580-650. SAT EBRW middle 50% range 600-660. ACT middle 50% range 23-27. Minimum internet-based TOEFL 70. Minimum paper TOEFL 523. **Basis for Candidate Selection:** *Very important factors considered include:* rigor of secondary school record, academic GPA, standardized test scores. *Other factors considered include:* extracurricular activities, talent/ability, character/personal qualities, geographical residence, state residency, work experience, level of applicant's interest. **Freshman Admission Requirements:** High school diploma is required and GED is accepted *Academic units required:* 4 English, 4 math, 3 science, 1 science labs, 2 foreign language, 1 social studies, 1 history, *Academic units recommended:* 3 foreign language. **Freshman Admission Statistics:** 11,677 applied, 66.5% admitted, 28% enrolled. **Transfer Admission Requirements:** High school transcript, college transcript(s), statement of good standing from prior institution(s). Minimum college GPA of 2.0 required. Lowest grade transferable C. **General Admission Information:** Application fee $60. Regular application deadline 6/1. Nonfall registration accepted.

COSTS AND FINANCIAL AID

Annual in-state tuition $10,780. Annual out-of-state tuition $17,246. Room and board $10,780. Required fees $3,211. Average book expense $1,200. **Required Forms and Deadlines:** FAFSA. **Notification of Awards:** Applicants will be notified of awards on or about 3/1. **Types of Aid:** *Need-based scholarships/grants:* College/university scholarship or grant aid from institutional funds; Federal Pell; Private scholarships; SEOG; State scholarships/grants; United Negro College Fund. *Loans:* Direct PLUS loans; Direct Subsidized Stafford Loans; Direct Unsubsidized Stafford Loans. *Student Employment:* Federal Work-Study Program available. Institutional employment available. **Financial Aid Statistics:** 72% needy freshmen, 77% needy undergrads receive need-based scholarship or grant aid. 23% freshmen, 14% undergrads receive non-need-based scholarship or grant aid. 80% freshmen, 79% undergrads receive need-based self-help aid. 0% freshmen, 0% undergrads receive athletic scholarships. 73% freshmen, 79% undergrads receive any aid. 67% undergrads borrow to pay for school. Average cumulative indebtedness $27,397. **Criteria for awarding aid:** *Non-need-based:* Academics, Alumni affiliation, Art, Athletics, Job skills, Leadership, Minority status, Music/drama, Religious affiliation, State/district residency.

UNIVERSITY OF NORTH DAKOTA

3501 University Avenue Stop 8357, Grand Forks, ND 58202
Phone: 701-777-3000 • **Financial Aid Phone:** 701-777-3121
E-mail: admissions@UND.edu • **CEEB Code:** 6878
Fax: 701-777-2721 • **Website:** http://und.edu • **ACT Code:** 3218

This public school was founded in 1883. It has a 521 acre campus.

RATINGS

Admissions Selectivity Rating: 80   **Fire Safety Rating:** 87   **Green Rating:** 81

STUDENTS AND FACULTY

Enrollment: 10,351. **Student Body:** 44% female, 56% male, 61% out-of-state, 5% international (72 countries represented). Asian 2%, African American 2%, Caucasian 81%, Hispanic 3%, Native American 1%, Pacific Islander <1%; Two or more races 3%, Race unknown 1%.
Retention and Graduation: 81% freshmen return for sophomore year. 25% freshmen graduate within 4 years. 21% grads go on to further study within 1 year. 6% grads pursue arts and sciences degrees. 2% grads pursue law degrees. 2% grads pursue business degrees. 1.3% grads pursue medical degrees. **Faculty:** Student/faculty ratio 21:1. 677 full-time faculty, 73% hold PhDs, 10% are members of minority groups, 44% are women.

ACADEMICS

Degrees: Bachelor's; Certificate; Doctoral/Professional; Doctoral/Research; Master's; Post-Bachelor's certificate; Post-Master's certificate **Classes:** Most classes have fewer than 10 students. Most lab/discussion sessions have 20-29 students. **Most popular majors:** Engineering; Health Professions And Related Programs; Business, Management, Marketing, And Related Support Services. **Special Study Options:** Accelerated program; Cooperative education program; Cross-registration; Distance learning; Double major; Dual enrollment; English as a Second Language (ESL); Exchange student program (domestic); External degree program; Honors program; Independent study; Internships; Liberal arts/career combination; Student-designed major; Study abroad; Teacher certification program; Weekend college. Honors programs: Students may participate in the Honors Program throughout their undergraduate career. Students in any college of the University may enroll in the Honors Program. Most students graduate from the Program as "Scholars in the Honors Program" while also fulfilling a major in the Colleges, but the Honors Program also offers the option of creating an individually designed program of study through Honors.This option may result in either a B.A. or a B.S. degree earned through the College of Arts and Sciences. **Disability Services offered to physically disabled students:** Note-taking services; Reader services; Tape recorders. **Career services:** Alumni network; Alumni services; Career assessment; Career/job search classes; Internships; Regional alumni

FACILITIES

Housing: Apartments for married students; Apartments for single students; Coed dorms; Fraternity/sorority housing; Men's dorms; Special housing for disabled student; Theme housing; Wellness housing; Women's dorms 99% of campus accessible to physically diasbled. **Special Academic Facilities/Equipment:** Hughes Fine Arts Center, Burtness Theatre, North Dakota Museum of Art, Chester Fritz Auditorium, mining/mineral resources research institute/energy research center, remote sensing institute, aviation facilities, meteorology data center,Ralph Engelstad Arena. **Computers:** 70% of classrooms, 100% of dorms, 100% of libraries, 50% of dining areas, 100% of student union, have wireless network access. Students can register for classes online. Administrative functions (other than registration) can be performed online.

CAMPUS LIFE

Environment: Town **Activities:** Campus Ministries; Choral groups; Concert band; Dance; Drama/theater; International Student Organization; Jazz band; Marching band; Music ensembles; Musical theater; Pep band; Student government; Student newspaper; Symphony orchestra 230 registered organizations, 42 honor societies, 3 religious organizations. 13 fraternities, 7 sororities. **Athletics (Intercollegiate):** *Men:* baseball, basketball, cross-country, diving, football, golf, ice hockey, swimming, track/field (outdoor), track/field (indoor). *Women:* basketball, cross-country, diving, golf, ice hockey, soccer, softball, swimming, tennis, track/field (outdoor), track/field (indoor), volleyball. **On-Campus Highlights:** Ralph Engelstad Arena, Wellness Center, Wilkerson Commons, Memorial Union, School of Medicine and Health Sciences **Environmental Initiatives:** Recycling

ADMISSIONS

Freshman Academic Profile: Average high school GPA 3.5. 17% in top 10% of high school class, 43% in top 25% of high school class, 75% in top 50% of high school class. 92% from public high schools. **Test Scores:** SAT Math middle 50% range 520-640. SAT EBRW middle 50% range 530-630. ACT middle 50% range 21-26. Minimum internet-based TOEFL 71. Minimum paper TOEFL 525. **Basis for Candidate Selection:** *Very important factors considered include:* rigor of secondary school record, academic GPA, standardized test scores. *Important factors considered include:* class rank. *Other factors considered include:* recommendation(s). **Freshman Admission Requirements:** High school diploma is required and GED is accepted *Academic units required:* 4 English, 3 math, 3 science, 3 science labs, 3 social studies, 1 visual/performing arts. **Freshman Admission Statistics:** 5,230 applied, 83.5% admitted, 44% enrolled. **Transfer Admission Requirements:** college transcript(s), Minimum college GPA of 2.0 required. **General Admission Information:** Application fee $35. Priority deadline 5/1. Nonfall registration accepted. Admission may be deferred.

COSTS AND FINANCIAL AID

Annual in-state tuition $8,226. Annual out-of-state tuition $18,546. Room and board $8,226. Required fees $1,501. Average book expense $1,000. **Required Forms and Deadlines:** FAFSA. **Notification of Awards:** Applicants will be notified of awards on a rolling basis beginning 2/15. **Types of Aid:** *Need-based scholarships/grants:* College/university scholarship or grant aid from institutional funds; Federal Pell; Private scholarships; SEOG; State scholarships/grants. *Loans:* Direct PLUS loans; Direct Subsidized Stafford Loans; Direct Unsubsidized Stafford Loans. *Student Employment:* Federal Work-Study Program available. Institutional employment available.

UNIVERSITY OF NORTH FLORIDA

1 UNF Drive, Jacksonville, FL 32224-7699
Phone: 904-620-5555 • **Financial Aid Phone:** 904-620-2698
E-mail: admissions@unf.edu • **CEEB Code:** 9841
Fax: 904-620-2414 • **Website:** www.unf.edu • **ACT Code:** 5490

This public school was founded in 1965. It has a 1300 acre campus.

RATINGS

Admissions Selectivity Rating: 85   **Fire Safety Rating:** 80   **Green Rating:** 60*

STUDENTS AND FACULTY

Enrollment: 13,962. **Student Body:** 56% female, 44% male, 4% out-of-state, 1% international (112 countries represented). Asian 5%, African American 9%, Caucasian 67%, Hispanic 12%, Native American <1%, Pacific Islander <1%, Two or more races 5%, Race unknown <1%.
Retention and Graduation: 81% freshmen return for sophomore year. 26% freshmen graduate within 4 years. 54% freshmen graduate within 6 years.
Faculty: Student/faculty ratio 18:1. 568 full-time faculty, 83% hold PhDs, 19% are members of minority groups, 47% are women. 0% of classes are taught by teaching assistants.

ACADEMICS

Degrees: Associate; Bachelor's; Doctoral/Professional; Doctoral/Research; Master's; Post-Bachelor's certificate; Post-Master's certificate **Most popular majors:** Mass Communication/Media Studies; Psychology, General; Registered Nursing/Registered Nurse. **Special Study Options:** Accelerated program; Cooperative education program; Distance learning; Double major; Dual enrollment; English as a Second Language (ESL); Exchange student program (domestic); Honors program; Independent study; Internships; Study abroad; Teacher certification program; Weekend college. Honors programs: The Honors Program at the University of North Florida offers talented students a unique approach to higher education. Averaging only 20 students, Honors seminars apply active learning in interdisciplinary settings. The goal is to build a community of learners who have the power to take their learning outside the classroom, enabling them to take what they read in their text and apply it to the outside world. In addition, Honors students are offered special funding opportunities to enable them to learn through travel, internships, and research. The Honors Program provides students with a personalized education that is usually only available at small liberal arts colleges but at the price of a state university tuition. **Disability Services offered to physically disabled students:** Note-taking services; Reader services; Tape recorders. **Career services:** Alumni network; Alumni services; Career assessment; Career/job search classes; Internships

FACILITIES

Housing: Apartments for single students; Coed dorms; Special housing for disabled students **Special Academic Facilities/Equipment:** Art gallery, bird sanctuary, Fine Arts Center, **Computers:** 100% of classrooms, 50% of dorms, 100% of libraries, 50% of dining areas, 100% of student union, 100% of common outdoor areas have wireless network access. Students can register for classes online. Administrative functions (other than registration) can be performed online.

CAMPUS LIFE

Environment: Metropolis **Activities:** Campus Ministries; Choral groups; Concert band; Drama/theater; International Student Organization; Jazz band; Literary magazine; Music ensembles; Radio station; Student government; Student newspaper; Television station 140 registered organizations, 8 honor societies, 29 religious organizations. 14 fraternities, 10 sororities **Athletics (Intercollegiate):** *Men:* baseball, basketball, cheerleading, cross-country, golf, soccer, tennis, track/field (outdoor), track/field (indoor). *Women:* basketball, cheerleading, cross-country, diving, soccer, softball, swimming, tennis, track/field (outdoor), track/field (indoor), volleyball. **On-Campus Highlights:** Student Union, Bookstore, Art Gallery, Nature Trails, Osprey Challenge Course (includes Zip Line) **Environmental Initiatives:** Requiring LEED Silver or comparable compliance

ADMISSIONS

Freshman Academic Profile: Average high school GPA 3.9. 15% in top 10% of high school class, 43% in top 25% of high school class, 79% in top 50% of high school class. 81% from public high schools. **Test Scores:** SAT Math middle 50% range 530-630. SAT EBRW middle 50% range 560-650. ACT middle 50% range 21-26. Minimum internet-based TOEFL 61. Minimum paper TOEFL 500. **Basis for Candidate Selection:** *Very important factors considered include:* rigor of secondary school record, academic GPA, standardized test scores. *Other factors considered include:* class rank, application essay, recommendation(s), extracurricular activities, talent/ability, volunteer work, work experience, level of applicant's interest. **Freshman Admission Requirements:** High school diploma is required and GED is accepted *Academic units required:* 4 English, 4 math, 3 science, 1 science labs, 2 foreign language, 3 social studies, 2 academic electives. **Freshman Admission Statistics:** 14,305 applied, 58.7% admitted, 27% enrolled. **Transfer Admission Requirements:** college transcript(s), Minimum college GPA of 2.0 required. Lowest grade transferable D. **General Admission Information:** Application fee $30. Priority deadline 11/16. Nonfall registration accepted. Admission may be deferred for a maximum of 2 semesters.

COSTS AND FINANCIAL AID

Annual out-of-state tuition $17,999. Room and board $9,772. Required fees $2,113. Average book expense $1,200. **Required Forms and Deadlines:** FAFSA. **Notification of Awards:** Applicants will be notified of awards on a rolling basis beginning 3/15. **Types of Aid:** *Need-based scholarships/grants:* College/university scholarship or grant aid from institutional funds; Federal Pell; Private scholarships; SEOG; State scholarships/grants. *Loans:* Direct PLUS loans; Direct Subsidized Stafford Loans; Direct Unsubsidized Stafford Loans. *Student Employment:* Federal Work-Study Program available. Institutional employment available. **Financial Aid Statistics:** 68% needy freshmen, 64% needy undergrads receive need-based scholarship or grant aid. 55% freshmen, 35% undergrads receive non-need-based scholarship or grant aid. 62% freshmen, 60% undergrads receive need-based self-help aid. 2% freshmen, 2% undergrads receive athletic scholarships. 76% freshmen, 71% undergrads receive any aid. 50% undergrads borrow to pay for school. Average cumulative indebtedness $18,685. **Criteria for awarding aid:** *Need-based:* Academics *Non-need-based:* Academics, Athletics, Leadership, Minority status, Music/drama, State/district residency.

UNIVERSITY OF NORTH TEXAS

1155 Union Circle #311425, Denton, TX 76203-5017
Phone: 940-565-2681 • **Financial Aid Phone:** 940-565-3901
E-mail: undergrad@unt.edu • **CEEB Code:** 6481
Fax: 940-565-2408 • **Website:** www.unt.edu • **ACT Code:** 4136

This public school was founded in 1890. It has a 875 acre campus.

RATINGS

Admissions Selectivity Rating: 85   **Fire Safety Rating:** 93   **Green Rating:** 95

STUDENTS AND FACULTY

Enrollment: 29,481. **Student Body:** 52% female, 48% male, 4% out-of-state, 3% international (164 countries represented). Asian 6%, African American 13%, Caucasian 53%, Hispanic 20%, Native American 1%, Pacific Islander <1%, Two or more races 3%, Race unknown 1%.

Retention and Graduation: 76% freshmen return for sophomore year. **Faculty:** Student/faculty ratio 23:1. 963 full-time faculty, 81% hold PhDs, 30% are members of minority groups, 40% are women. 11% of classes are taught by teaching assistants.

ACADEMICS

Degrees: Bachelor's; Doctoral; Doctoral/Professional; Doctoral/Research; Master's; Post-Bachelor's certificate **Classes:** Most classes have 10-19 students. Most lab/discussion sessions have 10-19 students. **Most popular majors:** Biology/Biological Sciences, General; Multi-/Interdisciplinary Studies, Other; Business/Commerce, General. **Special Study Options:** Distance learning; Double major; Dual enrollment; English as a Second Language (ESL); Exchange student program (domestic); Honors program; Independent study; Internships; Student-designed major; Study abroad; Teacher certification program. Honors programs: University of North Texas Honors College Combined degree programs: BA/MA. **Disability Services offered to physically disabled students:** Note-taking services; Reader services; Tape recorders; Tutors. **Career services:** Alumni network; Alumni services; Career assessment; Career/job search classes; Internships; Regional alumni

FACILITIES

Housing: Apartments for single students; Coed dorms; Fraternity/sorority housing; Men's dorms; Special housing for disabled student; Special housing for international students; Theme housing; Wellness housing; Women's dorms 90% of campus accessible to physically disabled. **Special Academic Facilities/Equipment:** laser, observatory, accelerators, recreational facility, music facilities, environmental sciences building, planetarium, art galleries **Computers:** 75% of classrooms, 30% of dorms, 100% of libraries, 100% of dining areas, 100% of student union, 10% of common outdoor areas have wireless network access. Students can register for classes online. Administrative functions (other than registration) can be performed online.

CAMPUS LIFE

Environment: City **Activities:** Campus Ministries; Choral groups; Concert band; Dance; Drama/theater; International Student Organization; Jazz band; Literary magazine; Marching band; Model UN; Music ensembles; Musical theater; Opera; Pep band; Radio station; Student government; Student newspaper; Student-run film society; Symphony orchestra; Television station 330 registered organizations, 40 honor societies, 34 religious organizations. 23 fraternities, 16 sororities. **Athletics (Intercollegiate):** *Men:* basketball, cross-country, football, golf, softball, track/field (indoor). *Women:* basketball, cross-country, diving, golf, soccer, softball, swimming, tennis, track/field (indoor), volleyball. **On-Campus Highlights:** UNT Housing, Student Recreation Center, Apogee Stadium, Murchison Performing Arts Center, Eagle Student Services Center **Environmental Initiatives:** In 2011 UNT completed construction on three community sized wind turbine's located at the university's Eagle Point. The project was funded through a 2.2 million dollar grant awarded by the State Energy Conservation Office. Since their completion the wind turbines have generated 284,182 kWh of energy.

ADMISSIONS

Freshman Academic Profile: 20% in top 10% of high school class, 52% in top 25% of high school class, 90% in top 50% of high school class. 95% from public high schools. **Test Scores:** SAT Math middle 50% range 510-610. SAT EBRW middle 50% range 490-600. ACT middle 50% range 20-26. Minimum internet-based TOEFL 79. Minimum paper TOEFL 550. **Basis for Candidate Selection:** *Very important factors considered include:* rigor of secondary school record, class rank, academic GPA, standardized test scores. *Important factors considered include:* application essay, recommendation(s). *Other factors considered include:* extracurricular activities, talent/ability, character/personal qualities, first generation, geographical residence, volunteer work, work experience, level of applicant's interest. **Freshman Admission Requirements:** High school diploma is required and GED is accepted *Academic units required:* 4 English, 4 math, 4 science, 4 science labs, 2 foreign language, 2 social studies, 2 history, 3.5 academic electives, 1 computer science, 1 visual/performing arts. **Freshman Admission Statistics:** 16,326 applied, 61.5% admitted, 44% enrolled. **Transfer Admission Requirements:** college transcript(s), statement of good standing from prior institution(s). Minimum college GPA of 2.5 required. Lowest grade transferable D. **General Admission Information:** Application fee $60. Priority deadline 3/1. Regular application deadline 8/1. Nonfall registration accepted. Admission may be deferred.

COSTS AND FINANCIAL AID

Annual in-state tuition $7,356. Annual out-of-state tuition $17,364. Room and board $7,356. Required fees $2,590. Average book expense $1,000. **Required Forms and Deadlines:** FAFSA. **Notification of Awards:** Applicants will be notified of awards on a rolling basis beginning 4/1. **Types of Aid:** *Need-based scholarships/grants:* College/university scholarship or grant aid from institutional funds; Federal Pell; Private scholarships; SEOG; State scholarships/grants. *Loans:* Direct PLUS loans; Direct Subsidized Stafford Loans; Direct Unsubsidized Stafford Loans. *Student Employment:*

Federal Work-Study Program available. Institutional employment available. **Financial Aid Statistics:** 82% needy freshmen, 74% needy undergrads receive need-based scholarship or grant aid. 50% freshmen, 27% undergrads receive non-need-based scholarship or grant aid. 80% freshmen, 84% undergrads receive need-based self-help aid. 0% freshmen, 1% undergrads receive athletic scholarships. 88% freshmen, 71% undergrads receive any aid.

UNIVERSITY OF NORTHERN COLORADO

501 20th Street, Greeley, CO 80639
Phone: 970-351-2881 • **Financial Aid Phone:** 970-351-2502
E-mail: admissions@unco.edu • **CEEB Code:** 4074
Fax: 970-351-2984 • **Website:** www.unco.edu • **ACT Code:** 502

This public school was founded in 1890. It has a 243 acre campus.

RATINGS

Admissions Selectivity Rating: 74   **Fire Safety Rating:** 96   **Green Rating:** 63

STUDENTS AND FACULTY

Enrollment: 9,100. **Student Body:** 65% female, 35% male, 16% out-of-state, 1% international (35 countries represented). Asian 2%, African American 5%, Caucasian 61%, Hispanic 21%, Native American <1%, Pacific Islander <1%, Two or more races 5%, Race unknown 5%. **Retention and Graduation:** 71% freshmen return for sophomore year. 28% freshmen graduate within 4 years. 48% freshmen graduate within 6 years. 26% grads go on to further study within 1 year. 57% grads pursue arts and sciences degrees. 4.5% grads pursue law degrees. 4% grads pursue business degrees. 8.1% grads pursue medical degrees. **Faculty:** Student/faculty ratio 18:1. 502 full-time faculty, 76% hold PhDs, 12% are members of minority groups, 53% are women. 18% of classes are taught by teaching assistants.

ACADEMICS

Degrees: Bachelor's; Doctoral/Professional; Doctoral/Research; **Master's Classes:** Most classes have 10-19 students. Most lab/discussion sessions have 10-19 students. **Most popular majors:** Kinesiology And Exercise Science; Registered Nursing/Registered Nurse; Business Administration And Management, General. **Special Study Options:** Cooperative education program; Cross-registration; Distance learning; Double major; Dual enrollment; English as a Second Language (ESL); Exchange student program (domestic); External degree program; Honors program; Independent study; Internships; Student-designed major; Study abroad; Teacher certification program. Honors programs: The University Honors Program, Life of the Mind, McNair Scholars Program, President's Leadership Program, Reisher Family Scholarship Program and Stryker Institute for Leadership Development each has its own eligibility requirements and distinctive program characteristics. The Schulze Endowment fosters a university-wide interest in interdisciplinary studies with various activities. Collectively, the seven programs provide a broad spectrum of academic enrichment opportunities for students on the university campus. Combined degree programs: BA/MA. **Disability Services offered to physically disabled students:** Note-taking services; Reader services; Tape recorders; Tutors. **Career services:** Alumni network; Alumni services; Career assessment; Career/job search classes; Internships; Regional alumni

FACILITIES

Housing: Apartments for married students; Apartments for single students; Coed dorms; Fraternity/sorority housing; Special housing for disabled student; Special housing for international students; Theme housing; Women's dorms 100% of campus accessible to physically disabled. **Special Academic Facilities/Equipment:** Art Museum, Music Library, James A. Michener Collection **Computers:** 100% of classrooms, 100% of dorms, 100% of libraries, 100% of dining areas, 100% of student union, 5% of common outdoor areas have wireless network access. Students can register for classes online. Administrative functions (other than registration) can be performed online.

CAMPUS LIFE

Environment: City **Activities:** Campus Ministries; Choral groups; Concert band; Dance; Drama/theater; International Student Organization; Jazz band; Literary magazine; Marching band; Music ensembles; Musical theater; Opera; Student government; Student newspaper; Student-run film society; Symphony orchestra; Television station 137 registered organizations, 9 honor societies, 18 religious organizations. 9 fraternities, 8 sororities. **Athletics (Intercollegiate):** *Men:* baseball, basketball, football, golf, tennis, track/field (outdoor), wrestling. *Women:* basketball, cross-country, diving, golf, soccer, softball, swimming, tennis, track/field (outdoor), volleyball. **On-Campus Highlights:** University Center, James Michener Library, Recreation Center, Cultural & Resource Centers

ADMISSIONS

Freshman Academic Profile: Average high school GPA 3.4. 13% in top 10% of high school class, 36% in top 25% of high school class, 74% in top 50% of high school class. **Test Scores:** SAT Math middle 50% range 490-610. SAT EBRW middle 50% range 510-620. ACT middle 50% range 19-25. Minimum internet-based TOEFL 70. Minimum paper TOEFL 520. **Basis for Candidate Selection:** *Very important factors considered include:* class rank, academic GPA, standardized test scores. *Other factors considered include:* rigor of secondary school record, application essay, recommendation(s), interview, extracurricular activities, talent/ability, character/personal qualities, first generation, alumni/ae relation, geographical residence, state residency, volunteer work, work experience, level of applicant's interest. **Freshman Admission Requirements:** High school diploma is required and GED is accepted *Academic units recommended:* 4 English, 4 math, 3 science, 2 science labs, 1 foreign language, 2 social studies, 1 history, 2 academic electives. **Freshman Admission Statistics:** 7,481 applied, 89.1% admitted, 32% enrolled. **Transfer Admission Requirements:** college transcript(s), statement of good standing from prior institution(s). Minimum college GPA of 2.4 required. Lowest grade transferable C. **General Admission Information:** Application fee $45. Priority deadline 3/1. Regular application deadline 8/1. Nonfall registration accepted. Admission may be deferred for a maximum of 1 year.

COSTS AND FINANCIAL AID

Annual in-state tuition $10,982. Annual out-of-state tuition $18,960. Room and board $10,982. Required fees $2,171. Average book expense $1,350. **Required Forms and Deadlines:** FAFSA. **Notification of Awards:** Applicants will be notified of awards on a rolling basis beginning 3/1. **Types of Aid:** *Need-based scholarships/grants:* College/university scholarship or grant aid from institutional funds; Federal Pell; Private scholarships; SEOG; State scholarships/grants. *Loans:* Direct PLUS loans; Direct Subsidized Stafford Loans; Direct Unsubsidized Stafford Loans. *Student Employment:* Federal Work-Study Program available. Institutional employment available. **Financial Aid Statistics:** 88% needy freshmen, 83% needy undergrads receive need-based scholarship or grant aid. 71% freshmen, 55% undergrads receive non-need-based scholarship or grant aid. 78% freshmen, 81% undergrads receive need-based self-help aid. 3% freshmen, 3% undergrads receive athletic scholarships. 67% freshmen, 68% undergrads receive any aid. 60% undergrads borrow to pay for school. Average cumulative indebtedness $27,393. **Criteria for awarding aid:** *Need-based:* Academics *Non-need-based:* Academics, Athletics, Music/drama.

UNIVERSITY OF NORTHERN IOWA

1227 West 27th Street, Cedar Falls, IA 50614-0018
Phone: 319-273-2281 • **Financial Aid Phone:** 319-273-2701
E-mail: admissions@uni.edu • **CEEB Code:** 6307
Fax: 319-273-2885 • **Website:** www.uni.edu • **ACT Code:** 1322

This public school was founded in 1876. It has a 910 acre campus.

RATINGS

Admissions Selectivity Rating: 76   **Fire Safety Rating:** 89   **Green Rating:** 96

STUDENTS AND FACULTY

Enrollment: 9,836. **Student Body:** 57% female, 43% male, 6% out-of-state, 3% international (47 countries represented). Asian 1%, African American 3%, Caucasian 82%, Hispanic 4%, Native American <1%, Pacific Islander <1%, Two or more races 2%, Race unknown 4%.
Retention and Graduation: 81% freshmen return for sophomore year. 40% freshmen graduate within 4 years. 67% freshmen graduate within 6 years. 17% grads go on to further study within 1 year. 7% grads pursue arts and sciences degrees. 1% grads pursue law degrees. 1% grads pursue business degrees. 4% grads pursue medical degrees. **Faculty:** Student/faculty ratio 18:1. 508 full-time faculty, 79% hold PhDs, 15% are members of minority groups, 48% are women. 5% of classes are taught by teaching assistants.

ACADEMICS

Degrees: Bachelor's; Certificate; Doctoral Other; Master's; Post-Master's certificate **Classes:** Most classes have 20-29 students. Most lab/discussion sessions have 10-19 students. **Most popular majors:** Elementary Education And Teaching; Psychology, General; Accounting. **Special Study Options:** Accelerated program; Cooperative education program; Distance learning; Double major; Dual enrollment; English as a Second Language (ESL); Exchange student program (domestic); External degree program; Honors program; Independent study; Internships; Liberal arts/career combination;

Student-designed major; Study abroad; Teacher certification program; Weekend college. Honors programs: University Honors Program—includes all 4 colleges and is open to all majors. www.uni.edu/honors. **Disability Services offered to physically disabled students:** Note-taking services; Reader services; Tape recorders; Tutors. **Career services:** Alumni network; Alumni services; Career assessment; Career/job search classes; Internships

FACILITIES

Housing: Apartments for married students; Apartments for single students; Coed dorms; Fraternity/sorority housing; Men's dorms; Theme housing; Wellness housing; Women's dorms 95% of campus accessible to physically diasbled. **Special Academic Facilities/Equipment:** Natural history museum, art gallery, greenhouse and biological preserves, Lakeside biology lab and field lab for conservation problems, Tallgrass Prairie Center,Arctic Social and Environmental Systems (ARCSES) Research Lab, speech and hearing clinic, Small Business Development Center, Iowa Waste Reduction Center, Center for Applied Research in Metal Casting, Performing Arts Center, Center for Energy and Environmental Education, Center for Social and Behavioral Research. **Computers:** 80% of classrooms, 75% of libraries, 100% of dining areas, 100% of student union, have wireless network access. Students can register for classes online. Administrative functions (other than registration) can be performed online.

CAMPUS LIFE

Environment: Town **Activities:** Campus Ministries; Choral groups; Concert band; Dance; Drama/theater; International Student Organization; Jazz band; Literary magazine; Marching band; Model UN; Music ensembles; Musical theater; Opera; Pep band; Radio station; Student government; Student newspaper; Symphony orchestra; Yearbook 278 registered organizations, 18 honor societies, 21 religious organizations. 5 fraternities, 4 sororities. **Athletics (Intercollegiate):** *Men:* basketball, cross-country, football, golf, track/field (outdoor), track/field (indoor), wrestling. *Women:* basketball, cross-country, diving, golf, soccer, softball, swimming, tennis, track/field (outdoor), track/field (indoor), volleyball. **On-Campus Highlights:** Wellness Recreation Center, Gallagher-Bluedorn Performing Arts Center, Piazza and Rialto Dining Centers, Maucker Student Union, UNI-DOME and McLeod Center **Environmental Initiatives:** Provost's Fellow for Sustainability The University of Northern Iowa (UNI) has a long history of incorporating sustainability-related topics across the academy. In the past, this has occurred through a combination of individual and group efforts. The most recent step undertaken to strategically advance and elevate these efforts was the creation of the inaugural Provost's Fellow for Sustainability, designed to help shepherd these faculty initiatives. This past academic year, UNI named Dr. Michael Childers as the first Fellow to serve in this role. The Fellow was a vital investment by the university into the faculty's ownership of UNI Strategic Plan's call to create a vibrant and sustainable campus community. An assistant professor in the history department, Dr. Childers spent the year facilitating campus-wide sustainability initiatives within the academy and providing leadership in furthering sustainability-related curriculum. Childers began the fellowship by holding a series of one-on-one conversations with facility and staff to gather their visions of what direction UNI should take on issues of sustainability. He quickly discovered that while sustainability enjoys broad support from across campus, there was a lack of awareness and cohesion which hindered efforts in sustainability education and other initiatives. Building upon his conversations, Childers implemented a plan to bridge those communication gaps and build greater faculty leadership. After reaching out to other universities which had addressed similar issues, he worked with individuals throughout campus to establish a faculty sustainability board. Comprised of eleven faculty from nine different departments, the new board will work to expand UNI's Sustainability Certificate and provide leadership in the university's implementing a fundamental awareness of need for environmental, economic, and cultural sustainability for all UNI graduates. Childers is looking forward to his second year as sustainability fellow in working with the advisory board to further sustainability education across UNI's curriculum.

ADMISSIONS

Freshman Academic Profile: Average high school GPA 3.5. 17% in top 10% of high school class, 46% in top 25% of high school class, 82% in top 50% of high school class. 92% from public high schools. **Test Scores:** ACT middle 50% range 24-21. Minimum internet-based TOEFL 79. Minimum paper TOEFL 550. **Basis for Candidate Selection:** *Very important factors considered include:* rigor of secondary school record, class rank, academic GPA, standardized test scores. *Other factors considered include:* application essay, recommendation(s), interview, talent/ability, first generation. **Freshman Admission Requirements:** High school diploma is required and GED is accepted *Academic units required:* 4 English, 3 math, 3 science, 3 social studies, 2 academic electives, *Academic units recommended:* 1 science labs, 2 foreign language. **Freshman Admission Statistics:** 5,494 applied, 80.8% admitted, 41% enrolled. **Transfer Admission Requirements:** college transcript(s), Lowest grade transferable D. **General Admission Information:** Application fee $40. Nonfall registration accepted. Admission may be deferred.

COSTS AND FINANCIAL AID

Annual in-state tuition $8,781. Annual out-of-state tuition $17,998. Room and board $8,781. Required fees $1,243. Average book expense $900. **Required Forms and Deadlines:** FAFSA. **Notification of Awards:** Applicants will be notified of awards on a rolling basis beginning 1/15. **Types of Aid:** *Need-based scholarships/grants:* College/university scholarship or grant aid from institutional funds; Federal Pell; Private scholarships; SEOG; State scholarships/grants. *Loans:* Direct PLUS loans; Direct Subsidized Stafford Loans; Direct Unsubsidized Stafford Loans. *Student Employment:* Federal Work-Study Program available. Institutional employment available. **Financial Aid Statistics:** 60% needy freshmen, 58% needy undergrads receive need-based scholarship or grant aid. 75% freshmen, 47% undergrads receive non-need-based scholarship or grant aid. 72% freshmen, 76% undergrads receive need-based self-help aid. 2% freshmen, 2% undergrads receive athletic scholarships. 95% freshmen, 91% undergrads receive any aid. 72% undergrads borrow to pay for school. Average cumulative indebtedness $23,391. **Criteria for awarding aid:** *Need-based:* Academics, Minority status *Non-need-based:* Academics, Alumni affiliation, Art, Athletics, Leadership, Minority status, Music/drama, State/district residency.

UNIVERSITY OF NOTRE DAME

220 Main Building, Notre Dame, IN 46556
Phone: 574-631-7505 • **Financial Aid Phone:** 574-631-6436
E-mail: admissions@nd.edu • **CEEB Code:** 1841
Fax: 574-631-8865 • **Website:** www.nd.edu • **ACT Code:** 1252

This private school, affiliated with the Roman Catholic Church, was founded in 1842. It has a 1250 acre campus.

RATINGS

Admissions Selectivity Rating: 98 **Fire Safety Rating:** 98 **Green Rating:** 92

STUDENTS AND FACULTY

Enrollment: 8,527. **Student Body:** 47% female, 53% male, 92% out-of-state, 6% international (68 countries represented). Asian 5%, African American 4%, Caucasian 69%, Hispanic 11%, Native American <1%, Pacific Islander <1%, Two or more races 5%, Race unknown 1%.
Retention and Graduation: 98% freshmen return for sophomore year. 92% freshmen graduate within 4 years. 95% freshmen graduate within 6 years. 22% grads go on to further study within 1 year. 0% grads pursue arts and sciences degrees. 0% grads pursue law degrees. 0% grads pursue business degrees. 0% grads pursue medical degrees. **Faculty:** Student/faculty ratio 10:1. 1,188 full-time faculty, 90% hold PhDs, 22% are members of minority groups, 30% are women. 9% of classes are taught by teaching assistants.

ACADEMICS

Degrees: Bachelor's; Doctoral/Professional; Doctoral/Research; **Master's Classes:** Most classes have 10-19 students. **Most popular majors:** Psychology, General; Political Science And Government, General; Finance, General. **Special Study Options:** Cross-registration; Double major; Dual enrollment; Exchange student program (domestic); Honors program; Independent study; Internships; Liberal arts/career combination; Student-designed major; Study abroad. **Disability Services offered to physically disabled students:** Note-taking services; Reader services; Tape recorders; Tutors. **Career services:** Alumni network; Alumni services; Career assessment; Career/job search classes; Internships

FACILITIES

Housing: Apartments for married students; Men's dorms; Women's dorms 95% of campus accessible to physically disabled. **Special Academic Facilities/Equipment:** Snite Museum of Art DeBartolo Performing Arts Center Stinson-Remick engineering clean room LOBUND Laboratory for germ-free research Radiation Laboratory **Computers:** Students can register for classes online. Administrative functions (other than registration) can be performed online.

CAMPUS LIFE

Environment: City **Activities:** Campus Ministries; Choral groups; Concert band; Dance; Drama/theater; Jazz band; Literary magazine; Marching band; Model UN; Music ensembles; Musical theater; Opera; Pep band; Radio station; Student government; Student newspaper; Student-run film society; Symphony orchestra; Television station; Yearbook 299 registered organizations, 10 honor

societies, 11 religious organizations. **Athletics (Intercollegiate):** *Men:* baseball, basketball, cross-country, diving, fencing, football, golf, ice hockey, lacrosse, soccer, swimming, tennis, track/field (outdoor). *Women:* basketball, crew/rowing, cross-country, diving, fencing, golf, lacrosse, soccer, softball, swimming, tennis, track/field (outdoor), volleyball. **On-Campus Highlights:** Grotto, The Golden Dome (Main Building), Basilica of the Sacred Heart, Notre Dame Stadium, Eck Center **Environmental Initiatives:** Expansion of Office of Sustainability to include 3 full time staff and 7 interns; development of metrics and quantitative goals in 7 key sustainability areas

ADMISSIONS

Freshman Academic Profile: 91% in top 10% of high school class, 98% in top 25% of high school class, 100% in top 50% of high school class. 42% from public high schools. **Test Scores:** SAT Math middle 50% range 690-770. SAT EBRW middle 50% range 680-750. ACT middle 50% range 32-34. Minimum internet-based TOEFL 110.2. **Basis for Candidate Selection:** *Very important factors considered include:* rigor of secondary school record. *Important factors considered include:* class rank, academic GPA, application essay, standardized test scores, recommendation(s), extracurricular activities, talent/ability, character/personal qualities, alumni/ae relation, volunteer work. *Other factors considered include:* first generation, religious affiliation/commitment, racial/ethnic status, work experience, level of applicant's interest. **Freshman Admission Requirements:** High school diploma is required and GED is not accepted *Academic units required:* 4 English, 3 math, 2 science, 2 science labs, 2 foreign language, 2 history, 3 academic electives, *Academic units recommended:* 4 English, 4 math, 4 science, 2 science labs, 4 foreign language, 4 history. **Freshman Admission Statistics:** 19,564 applied, 18.9% admitted, 55% enrolled. **Transfer Admission Requirements:** High school transcript, college transcript(s), essay or personal statement, standardized test scores, statement of good standing from prior institution(s). Minimum college GPA of 3.0 required. Lowest grade transferable C. **General Admission Information:** Application fee $75. Regular application deadline 1/1. Nonfall registration accepted. Admission may be deferred for a maximum of 1 year.

COSTS AND FINANCIAL AID

Annual tuition $52,884. Room and board $15,410. Required fees $507. Average book expense $1,050. **Required Forms and Deadlines:** Business/Farm Supplement; CSS/Financial Aid PROFILE; FAFSA. **Notification of Awards:** Applicants will be notified of awards on a rolling basis beginning 2/15. **Types of Aid:** *Need-based scholarships/grants:* College/university scholarship or grant aid from institutional funds; Federal Pell; Private scholarships; SEOG; State scholarships/grants. *Loans:* Direct PLUS loans; Direct Subsidized Stafford Loans; Direct Unsubsidized Stafford Loans. *Student Employment:* Federal Work-Study Program available. Institutional employment available. **Financial Aid Statistics:** 93% needy freshmen, 97% needy undergrads receive need-based scholarship or grant aid. 18% freshmen, 16% undergrads receive non-need-based scholarship or grant aid. 81% freshmen, 83% undergrads receive need-based self-help aid. 5% freshmen, 5% undergrads receive athletic scholarships. 66% freshmen, 77% undergrads receive any aid. 47% undergrads borrow to pay for school. Average cumulative indebtedness $28,406. **Criteria for awarding aid:** *Need-based:* Academics *Non-need-based:* Academics, Athletics.

UNIVERSITY OF OKLAHOMA

660 Parrington Oval, Norman, OK 73019
Phone: 405-325-2252 • **Financial Aid Phone:** (405) 325-5505
E-mail: admrec@ou.edu • **CEEB Code:** 6879
Fax: 405-325-7124 • **Website:** www.ou.edu • **ACT Code:** 3442

This public school was founded in 1890. It has a 4138.39 acre campus.

RATINGS

Admissions Selectivity Rating: 86 **Fire Safety Rating:** 97 **Green Rating:** 90

STUDENTS AND FACULTY

Enrollment: 22,324. **Student Body:** 51% female, 49% male, 33% out-of-state, 4% international (120 countries represented). Asian 6%, African American 5%, Caucasian 61%, Hispanic 10%, Native American 4%, Pacific Islander <1%, Two or more races 8%, Race unknown 2%.
Retention and Graduation: 92% freshmen return for sophomore year. 40% freshmen graduate within 4 years. 68% freshmen graduate within 6 years.

Faculty: Student/faculty ratio 18:1. 1,484 full-time faculty, 84% hold PhDs, 21% are members of minority groups, 44% are women. 5% of classes are taught by teaching assistants.

ACADEMICS

Degrees: Bachelor's; Doctoral; Doctoral/Professional; Doctoral/Research; Master's; Post-Bachelor's certificate; Post-Master's certificate **Classes:** Most classes have 20-29 students. Most lab/discussion sessions have 20-29 students. **Most popular majors:** Registered Nursing/Registered Nurse; Accounting; Finance, General. **Special Study Options:** Accelerated program; Cooperative education program; Distance learning; Double major; Dual enrollment; English as a Second Language (ESL); External degree program; Honors program; Independent study; Internships; Liberal arts/career combination; Student-designed major; Study abroad; Teacher certification program; Weekend college. Honors programs: Honors at Oxford: This summer program enables students to study at Oxford (while living at Brasenose College). While there, students work in private tutorials with distinguished Oxford dons. Students can earn up to 6 hours of honors credit in one of our four classes that are offered. Honors in Germany: Honors student travel to Leipzig, Germany in June, live at the University of Leipzig, study German, and take a course on German-American literary relations. Students also focus on experiencing and exploring major sites for the history and memory of WWII in Germany by taking day trips from Leipzig to major WWII-related sites and Germany. Students earn up to six hours of Honors credit. Honors Undergraduate Research Assistant Program: Honors Undergraduate Research Assistant Program provides undergraduates the opportunity to work with professors as research assistants on specific projects. Student assistants are expected to work 10 hours a week for 10 weeks for $6 an hour. Honors College students with at least 15 hours of college credit and a 3.4+ GPA are eligible to apply. Medical Humanities Scholars Program: The Honors College and the University of Oklahoma College of Medicine have created a special pathway (through a bachelor of arts degree leading to a medical doctorate) for up to five high school students each year who wish to study the humanistic aspects of medicine as undergraduates. Through a special admissions process, the Medical Humanities Scholars are accepted at the medical school as part of their application to OU's undergraduate honors program. The Honors College has also created a Medical Humanities Minor open to all honors students wishing to study medicine from the perspectives of history, sociology, anthropology, bioethics, literature, and economics. BP INSPIRE: To encourage students to study in energy-related fields, BP-one of the world's largest energy companies-offers a scholarship program through the Honors College. The BP INSPIRE Scholarship program recruits students from the Mewbourne College of Earth & Energy, the College of Engineering, and the Price College of Business. The program is designed to help students gain a global perspective and an understanding of a variety of topics in the national interest. Honors Undergraduate Writing Assistant Program: The Honors Undergraduate Writing Assistant Program includes assistants who receive a stipend to work as writing assistants for the required freshman American Perspectives courses. Students who wish to be writing assistants apply to the program and, if they are selected, participate in a required upper-division preparatory course that focuses on composition pedagogy, research and writing skills, and strategies for commenting and conferencing on students writing. Honors Undergraduate Research Opportunities Program: The Undergraduate Research Opportunities Program is open to all undergraduates at OU. Each semester the Honors College awards more than $12,500 to undergraduate students and their faculty mentors for research and creative activity. Undergraduate Research Day: Each spring the college hosts an Undergraduate Research Day, in which scholars, Honors students or not, share their research with the peers. The Honors College, Phi Beta Kappa and Phi Kappa Phi give cash awards to the best presentations in various categories. Conversations with the Dean: Each week the Dean of the Honors College has in a distinguished professor, author, diplomat, politician, or some other important community or intellectual figure to discuss world events. With the Dean as moderator, students are encouraged to participate in vibrant discussion with the week's important guest. Honors College Reading Groups: The Dean and Honors College faculty assign a book of their individual choosing to students who voluntarily join an Honors College Reading Group. Limited to 15 students per group, the books are provided free of charge to participants who then meet as a group, one hour a week, to discuss the assigned pages with the professor. There is no charge for this activity, there are no grades, and students may come and go as they please. The aim is to encourage students to read, think, and discuss with other Honors College students important topics of mutual interest, whether fiction or non-fiction. A newly established Reading Group links a current OU course with course taught at Gymnase d'Yverdon in Switzerland. The two will progress through a specified text and visit via Skype once a month to discuss the text's place in literature, history, it's message, accuracy, etc. The Honors Undergraduate Research Journal: The Honors Undergraduate Research Journal is a forum in which Honors students of all majors have the opportunity to have their work published. A panel of Honors College professors who annually appoint an editorial board of about eight Honors students advises THURJ. The board accepts research papers, poetry, and short stories of which the top submissions are published every spring. Freshman Summer Reading Series: Each summer all incoming freshmen receive a free, theme-based book chosen by the faculty. The students are encouraged to actively engage the material (the book arrives at the student's home in late June), which provides the incoming class with a common intellectual experience that the faculty and students can build on during their first semester in order to develop and nurture a collective intellectual community. Combined degree programs: BA/MA; BA/MEng. **Disability Services offered to physically disabled students:** Note-taking services; Reader services; Tutors. **Career services:** Alumni services; Career assessment; Career/job search classes; Internships; Regional alumni

FACILITIES

Housing: Apartments for married students; Apartments for single students; Coed dorms; Fraternity/sorority housing; Men's dorms; Special housing for disabled student; Special housing for international students; Women's dorms 95% of campus accessible to physically disabled. **Special Academic Facilities/Equipment:** The Fred Jones Jr. Museum of Art, Sam Noble Museum of Natural History, National Weather Center, National Severe Storms Laboratory, Radar Innovations Laboratory, Collaborative Learning Center, Biological Station, History of Science Collection, Western History Collection, Oklahoma Geological Survey, Stephenson Research and Technology Center, Innovation Hub **Computers:** 60% of classrooms, 80% of dorms, 100% of libraries, 75% of dining areas, 100% of student union, 80% of common outdoor areas have wireless network access. Students can register for classes online. Administrative functions (other than registration) can be performed online.

CAMPUS LIFE

Environment: City **Activities:** Campus Ministries; Choral groups; Concert band; Dance; Drama/theater; International Student Organization; Literary magazine; Marching band; Model UN; Music ensembles; Musical theater; Opera; Pep band; Radio station; Student government; Student newspaper; Student-run film society; Symphony orchestra; Television station; Yearbook 388 registered organizations, 17 honor societies, 39 religious organizations. 30 fraternities, 20 sororities. **Athletics (Intercollegiate):** *Men:* baseball, basketball, cross-country, football, golf, gymnastics, tennis, track/field (outdoor), track/field (indoor), wrestling. *Women:* basketball, crew/rowing, cross-country, golf, gymnastics, soccer, softball, tennis, track/field (outdoor), track/field (indoor), volleyball. **On-Campus Highlights:** Fred Jones Jr. Museum of Art, The Gaylord Family Oklahoma Memorial Stadium, Sam Noble Ok. Museum of Natural History, Oklahoma Memorial Union, Bizzell Memorial Library **Environmental Initiatives:** 1. American College and University Presidents Climate Commitment (ACUPCC) – In April of 2007, the University became a charter signatory to the American College and University Presidents Climate Commitment. As part of our commitment to create tangible actions to assist in decreasing our greenhouse gas emissions, OU has offered free access to the Cleveland Area Rapid Transit's (CART) Norman routes to all students, faculty, and staff; committed to purchasing 100% of our electricity from renewable energy; implemented green building standards for new construction; and formed an energy management team. To date, the University has decreased our emissions greater than 60%. In 2016, the American College and University Presidents' Climate Commitment transitioned to Second Nature's Carbon commitment.

ADMISSIONS

Freshman Academic Profile: Average high school GPA 3.6. 36% in top 10% of high school class, 65% in top 25% of high school class, 92% in top 50% of high school class. **Test Scores:** SAT Math middle 50% range 570-690. SAT EBRW middle 50% range 580-690. ACT middle 50% range 23-29. Minimum internet-based TOEFL 79. Minimum paper TOEFL 550. **Basis for Candidate Selection:** *Very important factors considered include:* rigor of secondary school record, class rank, academic GPA, standardized test scores. *Important factors considered include:* application essay, recommendation(s). *Other factors considered include:* interview, extracurricular activities, talent/ability, character/personal qualities, alumni/ae relation, volunteer work, work experience, level of applicant's interest. **Freshman Admission Requirements:** High school diploma is required and GED is accepted *Academic units required:* 4 English, 3 math, 3 science, 3 science labs, 1 social studies, 2 history, 2 academic electives, *Academic units recommended:* 4 math, 4 science, 2 foreign language, 1 computer science. **Freshman Admission Statistics:** 16,777 applied, 68.9% admitted, 39% enrolled. **Transfer Admission Requirements:** college transcript(s), Lowest grade transferable D. **General Admission Information:** Application fee $40. Priority deadline 12/15. Regular application deadline 2/1. Nonfall registration accepted. Admission may be deferred for a maximum of 1 academic year.

COSTS AND FINANCIAL AID

Required Forms and Deadlines: FAFSA. **Notification of Awards:** Applicants will be notified of awards on a rolling basis beginning 1/15. **Types of Aid:** *Need-based scholarships/grants:* College/university scholarship or grant aid from institutional funds; Federal Pell; Private scholarships; SEOG; State scholarships/grants; United Negro College Fund. *Loans:* Direct PLUS loans;

Direct Subsidized Stafford Loans; Direct Unsubsidized Stafford Loans. *Student Employment:* Federal Work-Study Program available. Institutional employment available. **Financial Aid Statistics:** 48% needy freshmen, 57% needy undergrads receive need-based scholarship or grant aid. 70% freshmen, 52% undergrads receive non-need-based scholarship or grant aid. 65% freshmen, 71% undergrads receive need-based self-help aid. 1% freshmen, 1% undergrads receive athletic scholarships. 88% freshmen, 86% undergrads receive any aid. 44% undergrads borrow to pay for school. Average cumulative indebtedness $28,444. **Criteria for awarding aid:** *Need-based:* Academics *Non-need-based:* Academics, Alumni affiliation, Art, Athletics, Leadership, Music/drama, Religious affiliation.

UNIVERSITY OF OREGON

1226 University of Oregon, Eugene, OR 97403-1217
Phone: 541-346-3201 • **Financial Aid Phone:** 800-760-6953
E-mail: uoadmit@uoregon.edu • **CEEB Code:** 4846
Fax: 541-346-5815 • **Website:** www.uoregon.edu • **ACT Code:** 3498

This public school was founded in 1876. It has a 295 acre campus.

RATINGS

Admissions Selectivity Rating: 78   **Fire Safety Rating:** 86   **Green Rating:** 99

STUDENTS AND FACULTY

Enrollment: 19,163. **Student Body:** 54% female, 46% male, 43% out-of-state, 12% international (80 countries represented). Asian 6%, African American 2%, Caucasian 58%, Hispanic 12%, Native American 1%, Pacific Islander <1%, Two or more races 8%, Race unknown 1%.
Retention and Graduation: 86% freshmen return for sophomore year. 52% freshmen graduate within 4 years. 72% freshmen graduate within 6 years.
Faculty: Student/faculty ratio 17:1. 1,131 full-time faculty, 98% hold PhDs, 16% are members of minority groups, 45% are women. 17% of classes are taught by teaching assistants.

ACADEMICS

Degrees: Bachelor's; Doctoral/Professional; Doctoral/Research; Master's; Post-Bachelor's certificate; Post-Master's certificate **Classes:** Most classes have fewer than 10 students. Most lab/discussion sessions have fewer than 10 students. **Most popular majors:** Social Sciences, General; Economics, General; Business/Commerce, General. **Special Study Options:** Distance learning; Double major; Dual enrollment; English as a Second Language (ESL); Exchange student program (domestic); Honors program; Independent study; Internships; Liberal arts/career combination; Student-designed major; Study abroad; Teacher certification program. Honors programs: Robert D. Clark Honors College, College of Arts and Sciences Society of College Scholars, Professional Distinctions program, Dean's List, Junior Scholars, and 21 honor societies based on scholarship, leadership, and service. **Disability Services offered to physically disabled students:** Note-taking services; Reader services; Tape recorders; Tutors. **Career services:** Alumni network; Alumni services; Career assessment; Career/job search classes; Internships; Regional alumni

FACILITIES

Housing: Apartments for married students; Apartments for single students; Coed dorms; Cooperative housing; Fraternity/sorority housing; Theme housing; Wellness housing 95% of campus accessible to physically disabled. **Special Academic Facilities/Equipment:** Jordan Schnitzer Museum of Art; Museum of Natural and Cultural History; James Warsaw Sports Marketing Center; Lundquist Center for Entrepreneurship; University of Oregon Many Nations Longhouse; Green Chemistry Laboratory and Alice C. Tyler Instrumentation Center; Future Music Oregon, a computer music center in the School of Music; Pine Mountain Observatory (Bend, Oregon); Oregon Institute of Marine Biology (Oregon Coast); Central Oregon programs affiliated with the Oregon University System Cascades Campus (Bend, Oregon); Urban Architecture program and BetterBricks Daylighting Laboratory at the University of Oregon Portland Center (Portland, Oregon). **Computers:** 95% of classrooms, 35% of dorms, 100% of libraries, 100% of dining areas, 100% of student union, 30% of common outdoor areas have wireless network access. Students can register for classes online. Administrative functions (other than registration) can be performed online.

CAMPUS LIFE

Environment: City **Activities:** Campus Ministries; Choral groups; Concert band; Dance; Drama/theater; International Student Organization; Jazz band; Literary magazine; Marching band; Music ensembles; Musical theater; Opera; Pep band; Radio station; Student government; Student newspaper; Student-run film society; Symphony orchestra; Television station 250 registered organizations, 22 honor societies, 20 religious organizations. 12 fraternities, 10 sororities. **Athletics (Intercollegiate):** *Men:* baseball, basketball, cross-country, football, golf, tennis, track/field (outdoor). *Women:* basketball, cross-country, golf, gymnastics, lacrosse, soccer, softball, tennis, track/field (outdoor), volleyball. **On-Campus Highlights:** University of Oregon Duck Store, Knight Library, Erb Memorial Union, Laverne Krauss Gallery in Lawrence Hall, Watch sports at Autzen, Hayward, or Matt Knight Arena **Environmental Initiatives:** Created the Oregon Model for Sustainable Development which puts a cap on building energy consumption.

ADMISSIONS

Freshman Academic Profile: Average high school GPA 3.6. 20% in top 10% of high school class, 56% in top 25% of high school class, 88% in top 50% of high school class. **Test Scores:** SAT Math middle 50% range 530-630. SAT EBRW middle 50% range 550-640. ACT middle 50% range 22-28. Minimum internet-based TOEFL 61. Minimum paper TOEFL 500. **Basis for Candidate Selection:** *Very important factors considered include:* rigor of secondary school record, academic GPA. *Important factors considered include:* application essay, standardized test scores. *Other factors considered include:* class rank, extracurricular activities, talent/ability, character/personal qualities, first generation, geographical residence, state residency, racial/ethnic status, volunteer work, work experience. **Freshman Admission Requirements:** High school diploma is required and GED is accepted *Academic units required:* 4 English, 3 math, 3 science, 2 foreign language, 3 social studies, *Academic units recommended:* 1 science labs. **Freshman Admission Statistics:** 20,317 applied, 82.8% admitted, 23% enrolled. **Transfer Admission Requirements:** college transcript(s), Minimum college GPA of 2.25 required. Lowest grade transferable D-. **General Admission Information:** Application fee $65. Regular application deadline 1/15. Nonfall registration accepted. Admission may be deferred for a maximum of 1 year.

COSTS AND FINANCIAL AID

Annual in-state tuition $12,450. Annual out-of-state tuition $32,535. Room and board $12,450. Required fees $2,076. Average book expense $1,125. **Required Forms and Deadlines:** FAFSA. **Notification of Awards:** Applicants will be notified of awards on a rolling basis beginning 4/15. **Types of Aid:** *Need-based scholarships/grants:* College/university scholarship or grant aid from institutional funds; Federal Pell; Private scholarships; SEOG; State scholarships/grants. *Loans:* Direct PLUS loans; Direct Subsidized Stafford Loans; Direct Unsubsidized Stafford Loans. *Student Employment:* Federal Work-Study Program available. Institutional employment available. **Financial Aid Statistics:** 72% needy freshmen, 73% needy undergrads receive need-based scholarship or grant aid. 6% freshmen, 3% undergrads receive non-need-based scholarship or grant aid. 76% freshmen, 80% undergrads receive need-based self-help aid. 2% freshmen, 2% undergrads receive athletic scholarships. 85% freshmen, 91% undergrads receive any aid. 47% undergrads borrow to pay for school. Average cumulative indebtedness $25,542. **Criteria for awarding aid:** *Need-based:* Academics, Athletics, Leadership, Minority status, Music/drama *Non-need-based:* Academics, Athletics, Leadership, Minority status, Music/drama, State/district residency.

UNIVERSITY OF THE OZARKS

415 N. College Avenue, Clarksville, AR 72830
Phone: 479-979-1227 • **Financial Aid Phone:** 479-979-1221
E-mail: admiss@ozarks.edu • **CEEB Code:** 6111
Fax: 479-979-1417 • **Website:** www.ozarks.edu • **ACT Code:** 120

This private school, affiliated with the Presbyterian Church, was founded in 1834. It has a 50 acre campus.

RATINGS

Admissions Selectivity Rating: 82   **Fire Safety Rating:** 93   **Green Rating:** 60*

STUDENTS AND FACULTY

Enrollment: 615. **Student Body:** 55% female, 45% male, 29% out-of-state, 14% international (13 countries represented). Asian 1%, African American 4%, Caucasian 71%, Hispanic 6%, Native American 2%, Pacific Islander 0%, Two or more races 1%, Race unknown 1%.
Retention and Graduation: 64% freshmen return for sophomore year.
Faculty: Student/faculty ratio 11:1. 49 full-time faculty, 69% hold PhDs, 8%

are members of minority groups, 37% are women. 0% of classes are taught by teaching assistants.

ACADEMICS
Degrees: Bachelor's **Classes:** Most classes have 20-29 students. **Most popular majors:** Physical Education Teaching And Coaching; Biology/Biological Sciences, General; Business Administration And Management, General. **Special Study Options:** Cooperative education program; Double major; Dual enrollment; Independent study; Internships; Liberal arts/career combination; Study abroad; Teacher certification program. **Disability Services offered to physically disabled students:** Note-taking services; Reader services; Tape recorders; Tutors. **Career services:** Alumni network; Alumni services; Career assessment; Career/job search classes; Internships; Regional alumni

FACILITIES
Housing: Apartments for married students; Apartments for single students; Coed dorms; Men's dorms; Women's dorms 100% of campus accessible to physically diasbled. **Special Academic Facilities/Equipment:** Walton Fine Arts Center; Stephens Gallery; Smith-Broyles Science Center; Walker Hall Teacher Education and Communications Center; Rogers Conference Center **Computers:** 100% of libraries, have wireless network access.

CAMPUS LIFE
Environment: Village **Activities:** Campus Ministries; Choral groups; Drama/theater; International Student Organization; Literary magazine; Music ensembles; Radio station; Student government; Student-run film society; Television station; Yearbook 40 registered organizations, 5 honor societies, 6 religious organizations. **Athletics (Intercollegiate):** *Men:* baseball, basketball, cheerleading, cross-country, soccer, tennis. *Women:* basketball, cheerleading, cross-country, soccer, softball, tennis. **On-Campus Highlights:** Seay Student Center, Walton Fine Arts Center, Walker Education and Communications Buil, Robson Library, Rogers Conference Center

ADMISSIONS
Freshman Academic Profile: Average high school GPA 3.3. 18% in top 10% of high school class, 44% in top 25% of high school class, 76% in top 50% of high school class. 92% from public high schools. **Test Scores:** SAT Math middle 50% range 443-560. SAT EBRW middle 50% range 450-570. ACT middle 50% range 19-25. Minimum paper TOEFL 500. **Basis for Candidate Selection:** *Important factors considered include:* standardized test scores. *Other factors considered include:* rigor of secondary school record, academic GPA, application essay, recommendation(s), interview, extracurricular activities, talent/ability, character/personal qualities, alumni/ae relation, volunteer work, work experience, level of applicant's interest. **Freshman Admission Requirements:** High school diploma is required and GED is accepted *Academic units recommended:* 4 English, 4 math, 3 science, 2 science labs, 2 foreign language, 1 social studies, 2 history. **Freshman Admission Statistics:** 1,372 applied, 59.3% admitted, 25% enrolled. **Transfer Admission Requirements:** college transcript(s), Minimum college GPA of 2.0 required. Lowest grade transferable C. **General Admission Information:** Application fee $30. Priority deadline 4/1. Nonfall registration accepted. Admission may be deferred.

COSTS AND FINANCIAL AID
Annual tuition $21,450. Room and board $6,500. Required fees $600. Average book expense $800. **Required Forms and Deadlines:** FAFSA. **Notification of Awards:** Applicants will be notified of awards on a rolling basis beginning 3/1. **Types of Aid:** *Need-based scholarships/grants:* College/university scholarship or grant aid from institutional funds; Federal Nursing Scholarships; Federal Pell; Private scholarships; SEOG; State scholarships/grants; United Negro College Fund. *Loans: Student Employment:* Federal Work-Study Program available. Institutional employment available. **Financial Aid Statistics:** 97% needy freshmen, 97% needy undergrads receive need-based scholarship or grant aid. 0% undergrads receive non-need-based scholarship or grant aid. 82% freshmen, 85% undergrads receive need-based self-help aid. 0% freshmen, 0% undergrads receive athletic scholarships. 100% freshmen, 98% undergrads receive any aid. **Criteria for awarding aid:** *Need-based:* Academics, Alumni affiliation, Art, Leadership, Minority status, Music/drama, Religious affiliation *Non-need-based:* Academics, Alumni affiliation, Art, Leadership, Minority status, Music/drama, Religious affiliation, State/district residency.

UNIVERSITY OF THE PACIFIC

Best Colleges

3601 Pacific Avenue, Stockton, CA 95211
Phone: 209-946-2211 • **Financial Aid Phone:** 209-946-2421
E-mail: admissions@pacific.edu • **CEEB Code:** 4065
Fax: 209-946-4213 • **Website:** www.pacific.edu • **ACT Code:** 240

This private school was founded in 1851. It has a 175 acre campus.

RATINGS
Admissions Selectivity Rating: 82   **Fire Safety Rating:** 93   **Green Rating:** 95

STUDENTS AND FACULTY
Enrollment: 3,474. **Student Body:** 53% female, 47% male, 7% out-of-state, 6% international (66 countries represented). Asian 37%, African American 3%, Caucasian 25%, Hispanic 19%, Native American <1%, Pacific Islander <1%, Two or more races 5%, Race unknown 4%.
Retention and Graduation: 82% freshmen return for sophomore year. **Faculty:** Student/faculty ratio 12:1. 443 full-time faculty, 91% hold PhDs, 22% are members of minority groups, 43% are women.

ACADEMICS
Degrees: Bachelor's; Doctoral/Professional; Doctoral/Research; **Master's Classes:** Most classes have 10-19 students. Most lab/discussion sessions have 10-19 students. **Most popular majors:** Engineering, General; Biology/Biological Sciences, General; Business/Commerce, General. **Special Study Options:** Accelerated program; Cooperative education program; Distance learning; Double major; Dual enrollment; English as a Second Language (ESL); Exchange student program (domestic); Honors program; Independent study; Internships; Liberal arts/career combination; Student-designed major; Study abroad; Teacher certification program. Honors programs: Freshman Honors Program, Powell Scholars, Pacific Legal Scholars, Humanities Scholars Combined degree programs: BA/DDS. **Disability Services offered to physically disabled students:** Note-taking services; Reader services; Tape recorders; Tutors.

FACILITIES
Housing: Apartments for married students; Apartments for single students; Coed dorms; Cooperative housing; Fraternity/sorority housing; Special housing for international students; Theme housing 90% of campus accessible to physically diasbled. **Special Academic Facilities/Equipment:** John Muir Collection, Dave and Iola Brubeck Collection, Brubeck Institute for Jazz Studies, Reynolds Art Gallery **Computers:** 100% of classrooms, 90% of dorms, 100% of libraries, 100% of dining areas, 100% of student union, 30% of common outdoor areas have wireless network access. Students can register for classes online. Administrative functions (other than registration) can be performed online.

CAMPUS LIFE
Environment: City **Activities:** Campus Ministries; Choral groups; Concert band; Dance; Drama/theater; International Student Organization; Jazz band; Literary magazine; Model UN; Music ensembles; Musical theater; Opera; Pep band; Radio station; Student government; Student newspaper; Student-run film society; Yearbook 100 registered organizations, 14 honor societies, 10 religious organizations. 8 fraternities, 7 sororities. **Athletics (Intercollegiate):** *Men:* baseball, basketball, golf, swimming, tennis, volleyball, water polo. *Women:* basketball, cross-country, field hockey, soccer, softball, swimming, tennis, volleyball, water polo. **On-Campus Highlights:** Brubeck Istitute for Jazz Studies, John Muir Collection and Center, Alex Spanos Center, Reynolds Art Gallery, Pharmacy and Health Sciences Bldg **Environmental Initiatives:** Natural Resource Institute

ADMISSIONS
Freshman Academic Profile: Average high school GPA 3.5. 37% in top 10% of high school class, 40% in top 25% of high school class, 92% in top 50% of high school class. 82% from public high schools. **Test Scores:** SAT Math middle 50% range 530-670. SAT EBRW middle 50% range 500-630. ACT middle 50% range 23-30. Minimum internet-based TOEFL 52. Minimum paper TOEFL 475. **Basis for Candidate Selection:** *Very important factors considered include:* rigor of secondary school record. *Important factors considered include:* academic GPA, standardized test scores, extracurricular activities, first generation. *Other factors considered include:* class rank, application essay, recommendation(s), talent/ability, character/personal qualities, alumni/ae relation, geographical residence, racial/ethnic status, volunteer work, work

experience. **Freshman Admission Requirements:** High school diploma is required and GED is accepted *Academic units recommended:* 4 English, 4 math, 3 science labs, 2 foreign language, 2 social studies, 1 history, 1 academic elective, 1 visual/performing arts. **Freshman Admission Statistics:** 8,870 applied, 66.0% admitted, 12% enrolled. **Transfer Admission Requirements:** college transcript(s), statement of good standing from prior institution(s). Minimum college GPA of 3.0 required. Lowest grade transferable C. **General Admission Information:** Application fee $35. Priority deadline 11/15. Regular application deadline 8/15. Nonfall registration accepted. Admission may be deferred for a maximum of 1 year.

COSTS AND FINANCIAL AID
Annual tuition $45,786. Room and board $13,356. Required fees $560. Average book expense $1,854. **Required Forms and Deadlines:** FAFSA. **Notification of Awards:** Applicants will be notified of awards on a rolling basis beginning 3/1. **Types of Aid:** *Need-based scholarships/grants:* College/ university scholarship or grant aid from institutional funds; Federal Pell; Private scholarships; SEOG; State scholarships/grants. *Loans:* Direct PLUS loans; Direct Subsidized Stafford Loans; Direct Unsubsidized Stafford Loans. **Financial Aid Statistics:** 99% needy freshmen, 97% needy undergrads receive need-based scholarship or grant aid. 0% undergrads receive non-need-based scholarship or grant aid. 89% freshmen, 95% undergrads receive need-based self-help aid. 4% freshmen, 4% undergrads receive athletic scholarships. 91% freshmen, 83% undergrads receive any aid. 67% undergrads borrow to pay for school. Average cumulative indebtedness $28,810. **Criteria for awarding aid:** *Need-based:* Academics *Non-need-based:* Academics, Athletics, Leadership, Music/drama, Religious affiliation.

UNIVERSITY OF PENNSYLVANIA

1 College Hall, Room 100, Philadelphia, PA 19104
Phone: 215-898-7507 • **Financial Aid Phone:** 215-898-1988
E-mail: info@admissions.upenn.edu • **CEEB Code:** 2926
Fax: 215-898-7507 • **Website:** www.upenn.edu • **ACT Code:** 3732

This private school was founded in 1740. It has a 279 acre campus.

RATINGS
Admissions Selectivity Rating: 99   **Fire Safety Rating:** 84   **Green Rating:** 94

STUDENTS AND FACULTY
Enrollment: 10,033. **Student Body:** 51% female, 49% male, 81% out-of-state, 13% international (126 countries represented). Asian 21%, African American 7%, Caucasian 43%, Hispanic 10%, Native American <1%, Pacific Islander <1%, Two or more races 5%, Race unknown 2%.
Retention and Graduation: 98% freshmen return for sophomore year. 86% freshmen graduate within 4 years. 96% freshmen graduate within 6 years. 20% grads go on to further study within 1 year. 5% grads pursue arts and sciences degrees. 4% grads pursue law degrees. 1% grads pursue business degrees. 5% grads pursue medical degrees. **Faculty:** Student/faculty ratio 6:1. 1,519 full-time faculty, 100% hold PhDs, 22% are members of minority groups, 39% are women. 5% of classes are taught by teaching assistants.

ACADEMICS
Degrees: Associate; Bachelor's; Certificate; Doctoral; Doctoral Other; Doctoral/Professional; Doctoral/Research; Master's; Post-Bachelor's certificate; Post-Master's certificate; Terminal Associate **Classes:** Most classes have fewer than 10 students. Most lab/discussion sessions have fewer than 10 students. **Most popular majors:** Economics, General; Registered Nursing/Registered Nurse; Finance, General. **Special Study Options:** Accelerated program; Cross-registration; Distance learning; Double major; Dual enrollment; English as a Second Language (ESL); Exchange student program (domestic); Honors program; Independent study; Internships; Liberal arts/career combination; Student-designed major; Study abroad; Teacher certification program. Honors programs: Penn's general honors program is called the Benjamin Franklin Scholars program, although the honors program for students in business is called Joseph Wharton Scholars. There are specialized honors programs including Fisher Program in Management and Technology, the Huntsman Program in International Studies and Business, the Vagelos Scholars Program in Molecular Life Sciences, and the Civic Scholars Program which offers opportunities to integrate community service and academics. The University Scholars Program is open to already matriculated students who are interested

in engaging in high-level research. Combined degree programs: BA/DDS; BA/ JD; BA/MA; BA/MEng. **Disability Services offered to physically disabled students:** Note-taking services; Reader services; Tape recorders; Tutors. **Career services:** Alumni network; Alumni services; Career assessment; Internships; Regional alumni

FACILITIES
Housing: Apartments for married students; Apartments for single students; Coed dorms; Fraternity/sorority housing; Special housing for disabled student; Theme housing; Wellness housing 92% of campus accessible to physically disabled. **Special Academic Facilities/Equipment:** Art gallery, anthropology museum, institute for contemporary art, language lab, large animal research center, primate research center, arboretum, observatory, wind tunnel, electron microscope. **Computers:** 85% of classrooms, 100% of dorms, 100% of libraries, 85% of dining areas, 100% of student union, 25% of common outdoor areas have wireless network access. Students can register for classes online. Administrative functions (other than registration) can be performed online.

CAMPUS LIFE
Environment: Metropolis **Activities:** Campus Ministries; Choral groups; Concert band; Dance; Drama/theater; International Student Organization; Jazz band; Literary magazine; Marching band; Model UN; Music ensembles; Musical theater; Opera; Pep band; Radio station; Student government; Student newspaper; Student-run film society; Symphony orchestra; Television station; Yearbook 350 registered organizations, 9 honor societies, 29 religious organizations. 35 fraternities, 13 sororities. **Athletics (Intercollegiate):** *Men:* baseball, basketball, crew/rowing, cross-country, diving, fencing, football, golf, lacrosse, light weight football, soccer, squash, swimming, tennis, track/field (outdoor), track/field (indoor), wrestling. *Women:* basketball, crew/rowing, cross-country, diving, fencing, field hockey, golf, gymnastics, lacrosse, soccer, softball, squash, swimming, tennis, track/field (outdoor), track/field (indoor), volleyball. **On-Campus Highlights:** University of Pennsylvania Museum, Institute of Contemporary Art, Walnut Street shops and restuarants, Annenberg Center, Franklin Field **Environmental Initiatives:** Building optimization implementation, a program to optimize building systems in high-energy-use buildings to reduce their utility use and carbon footprint. This effort is enhanced by Penn's comprehensive building metering program.

ADMISSIONS
Freshman Academic Profile: Average high school GPA 3.9. 96% in top 10% of high school class, 100% in top 25% of high school class, 100% in top 50% of high school class. 60% from public high schools. **Test Scores:** SAT Math middle 50% range 720-790. SAT EBRW middle 50% range 700-770. ACT middle 50% range 32-35. **Basis for Candidate Selection:** *Very important factors considered include:* rigor of secondary school record, academic GPA, application essay, standardized test scores, recommendation(s), character/ personal qualities. *Important factors considered include:* class rank, interview, extracurricular activities, talent/ability. *Other factors considered include:* first generation, alumni/ae relation, geographical residence, state residency, racial/ ethnic status, volunteer work, work experience, level of applicant's interest. **Freshman Admission Requirements:** High school diploma or equivalent is not required *Academic units recommended:* 4 English, 4 math, 3 science, 3 science labs, 4 foreign language, 2 social studies, 3 history. **Freshman Admission Statistics:** 40,413 applied, 9.3% admitted, 65% enrolled. **Transfer Admission Requirements:** High school transcript, college transcript(s), essay or personal statement, standardized test scores, statement of good standing from prior institution(s). Lowest grade transferable C. **General Admission Information:** Application fee $75. Regular application deadline 1/5. Nonfall registration accepted. Admission may be deferred for a maximum of 1 year.

COSTS AND FINANCIAL AID
Annual tuition $49,220. Room and board $15,616. Required fees $6,364. **Required Forms and Deadlines:** Business/Farm Supplement; CSS/Financial Aid PROFILE; FAFSA; Institution's own financial aid form; Noncustodial PROFILE. **Notification of Awards:** Applicants will be notified of awards on or about 4/1. **Types of Aid:** *Need-based scholarships/grants:* College/ university scholarship or grant aid from institutional funds; Federal Pell; Private scholarships; SEOG; State scholarships/grants. *Loans:* Direct PLUS loans; Direct Subsidized Stafford Loans; Direct Unsubsidized Stafford Loans. *Student Employment:* Federal Work-Study Program available. Institutional employment available. **Financial Aid Statistics:** 99% needy freshmen, 99% needy undergrads receive need-based scholarship or grant aid. 0% undergrads receive non-need-based scholarship or grant aid. 100% freshmen, 100% undergrads receive need-based self-help aid. 0% freshmen, 0% undergrads receive athletic scholarships. 47% freshmen, 45% undergrads receive any aid. 28% undergrads borrow to pay for school. Average cumulative indebtedness $26,157.

UNIVERSITY OF PHOENIX

4035 E. Elwood Street, Phoenix, AZ 85040
Phone: 480-446-4600 · **Financial Aid Phone:** 1-800-921-1904
Website: www.phoenix.edu

This proprietary school was founded in 1976.

RATINGS
Admissions Selectivity Rating: 0   **Fire Safety Rating:** 60*   **Green Rating:** 60*

STUDENTS AND FACULTY
Enrollment: 332,377. **Student Body:** 69% female, 31% male, 3% international. Asian 2%, African American 18%, Caucasian 39%, Hispanic 9%, Native American 1%, Race unknown 28%.
Retention and Graduation: 39% freshmen return for sophomore year.
Faculty: Student/faculty ratio 43:1. 1,410 full-time faculty, 23% hold PhDs, 19% are members of minority groups, 46% are women. 0% of classes are taught by teaching assistants.

ACADEMICS
Degrees: Associate; Bachelor's; Certificate; Doctoral; Master's; Post-Bachelor's certificate; Post-Master's certificate; Transfer Associate **Classes:** Most classes have 10-19 students. Most lab/discussion sessions have 10-19 students.
Most popular majors: Health/Health Care Administration/Management; Business Administration And Management, General; Accounting. **Special Study Options:** Accelerated program; Distance learning; Independent study. **Disability Services offered to physically disabled students:** Tape recorders. **Career services:** Alumni network

FACILITIES
Housing: 100% of campus accessible to physically disabled. **Computers:** Students can register for classes online. Administrative functions (other than registration) can be performed online.

CAMPUS LIFE
Environment: Metropolis **Activities:** 2 honor societies.

ADMISSIONS
Test Scores: Minimum paper TOEFL 550. **Basis for Candidate Selection:** *Very important factors considered include:* work experience. *Other factors considered include:* recommendation(s). **Freshman Admission Requirements:** High school diploma is required and GED is accepted **Transfer Admission Requirements:** college transcript(s). **General Admission Information:** Nonfall registration accepted.

UNIVERSITY OF PIKEVILLE

147 Sycamore Street, Pikeville, KY 41501
Phone: 606-218-5251 · **Financial Aid Phone:** 606-218-5247
E-mail: wewantyou@upike.edu · **CEEB Code:** 1980
Fax: 606-218-5255 · **Website:** http://www.upike.edu/ · **ACT Code:** 1540

This private school, affiliated with the Presbyterian Church, was founded in 1889. It has a 25 acre campus.

RATINGS
Admissions Selectivity Rating: 71   **Fire Safety Rating:** 87   **Green Rating:** 60*

STUDENTS AND FACULTY
Enrollment: 1,244. **Student Body:** 51% female, 49% male, 20% out-of-state, 4% international (22 countries represented). Asian 1%, African American 12%, Caucasian 81%, Hispanic 2%, Native American <1%, Pacific Islander <1%, Two or more races 0%, Race unknown 0%.
Retention and Graduation: 58% freshmen return for sophomore year. 32% grads go on to further study within 1 year. 0% grads pursue arts and sciences degrees. 0% grads pursue law degrees. 75% grads pursue business degrees. 0% grads pursue medical degrees. **Faculty:** Student/faculty ratio 15:1. 69 full-time faculty, 59% hold PhDs, 4% are members of minority groups, 57% are women. 0% of classes are taught by teaching assistants.

ACADEMICS
Degrees: Associate; Bachelor's; Doctoral/Professional; Master's; Terminal Associate **Classes:** Most classes have 10-19 students. Most lab/discussion

---

sessions have 10-19 students. **Most popular majors:** Biology, General; Criminal Justice/Safety Studies; Business/Commerce, General. **Special Study Options:** Double major; Dual enrollment; English as a Second Language (ESL); Internships; Liberal arts/career combination; Student-designed major; Study abroad; Teacher certification program. **Disability Services offered to physically disabled students:** Reader services; Tape recorders; Tutors.
Career services: Career/job search classes

FACILITIES
Housing: Coed dorms; Men's dorms; Theme housing; Women's dorms 97% of campus accessible to physically disabled.

CAMPUS LIFE
Environment: Village **Activities:** Campus Ministries; Choral groups; Dance; Pep band; Student government; Student newspaper; Television station 40 registered organizations, 6 honor societies, 2 religious organizations. **Athletics (Intercollegiate): Men:** baseball, basketball, bowling, cheerleading, cross-country, football, golf, soccer, tennis. *Women:* basketball, bowling, cheerleading, cross-country, golf, soccer, softball, tennis, volleyball. **On-Campus Highlights:** Coal Building, Armington Science Building, Allara Library, Record Memorial Building, Administration Building

ADMISSIONS
Freshman Academic Profile: Average high school GPA 3.1. 14% in top 10% of high school class, 27% in top 25% of high school class, 61% in top 50% of high school class. 99% from public high schools. **Test Scores:** SAT Math middle 50% range 400-470. SAT EBRW middle 50% range 410-460. ACT middle 50% range 18-23. Minimum internet-based TOEFL 78. **Freshman Admission Requirements:** High school diploma is required and GED is accepted *Academic units recommended:* 4 English, 3 math, 3 science, 2 social studies, 1 history. **Freshman Admission Statistics:** 2,408 applied, 100.0% admitted, 13% enrolled. **Transfer Admission Requirements:** High school transcript, college transcript(s), standardized test scores, statement of good standing from prior institution(s). Lowest grade transferable C. **General Admission Information:** Regular application deadline 8/15. Nonfall registration accepted. Admission may be deferred.

COSTS AND FINANCIAL AID
Annual tuition $19,600. Room and board $8,376. Average book expense $2,500. **Required Forms and Deadlines:** FAFSA. **Notification of Awards:** Applicants will be notified of awards on a rolling basis beginning 2/1. **Types of Aid:** *Need-based scholarships/grants:* College/university scholarship or grant aid from institutional funds; Federal Pell; Private scholarships; SEOG; State scholarships/grants. *Loans:* Direct PLUS loans; Direct Subsidized Stafford Loans; Direct Unsubsidized Stafford Loans. *Student Employment:* Federal Work-Study Program available. **Financial Aid Statistics:** 100% needy freshmen, 100% needy undergrads receive need-based scholarship or grant aid. 58% freshmen, 48% undergrads receive non-need-based scholarship or grant aid. 86% freshmen, 84% undergrads receive need-based self-help aid. 0% freshmen, 0% undergrads receive athletic scholarships. 100% freshmen, 97% undergrads receive any aid. 76% undergrads borrow to pay for school. Average cumulative indebtedness $27,645. **Criteria for awarding aid:** *Need-based:* Academics, Alumni affiliation, Athletics, Music/drama.

UNIVERSITY OF PITTSBURGH AT BRADFORD

300 Campus Drive, Bradford, PA 16701
Phone: 814-362-7555 · **Financial Aid Phone:** 814-362-7550
E-mail: Admissions@upb.pitt.edu · **CEEB Code:** 2935
Fax: 814-362-5150 · **Website:** www.upb.pitt.edu · **ACT Code:** 3731

This public school was founded in 1963. It has a 317 acre campus.

RATINGS
Admissions Selectivity Rating: 86   **Fire Safety Rating:** 94   **Green Rating:** 77

STUDENTS AND FACULTY
Enrollment: 1,304. **Student Body:** 55% female, 45% male, 23% out-of-state, 3% international (16 countries represented). Asian 2%, African American 13%, Caucasian 68%, Hispanic 5%, Native American <1%, Pacific Islander <1%, Two or more races 3%, Race unknown 5%.
Retention and Graduation: 69% freshmen return for sophomore year. 35% freshmen graduate within 4 years. 46% freshmen graduate within 6 years. 20% grads go on to further study within 1 year. 21% grads pursue arts and sciences degrees. 3% grads pursue law degrees. 2% grads pursue business degrees. 3% grads pursue medical degrees. **Faculty:** Student/faculty ratio 16:1. 75 full-time faculty, 71% hold PhDs, 17% are members of minority groups, 40% are women. 0% of classes are taught by teaching assistants.

ACADEMICS

Degrees: Associate; Bachelor's; Terminal Associate; Transfer Associate **Classes:** Most classes have 10-19 students. Most lab/discussion sessions have fewer than 10 students. **Most popular majors:** Biology/Biological Sciences, General; Criminal Justice/Law Enforcement Administration; Business/Commerce, General. **Special Study Options:** Cross-registration; Distance learning; Double major; Dual enrollment; External degree program; Independent study; Internships; Study abroad; Teacher certification program. Honors programs: The University of Pittsburgh at Bradford offers the Scholars Program which is designed to create a learning community for outstanding students at Pitt-Bradford. **Disability Services offered to physically disabled students:** Note-taking services; Reader services; Tape recorders; Tutors. **Career services:** Alumni network; Alumni services; Career assessment; Internships; Regional alumni

FACILITIES

Housing: Apartments for single students; Coed dorms; Special housing for disabled students 99% of campus accessible to physically diasbled. **Special Academic Facilities/Equipment:** Ceramics Studio, Biodiesal Lab, Television and Radio Broadcast Labs, Marilyn Horne Museum **Computers:** 100% of classrooms, 100% of dorms, 90% of libraries, 90% of dining areas, 100% of student union, 50% of common outdoor areas have wireless network access. Students can register for classes online. Administrative functions (other than registration) can be performed online.

CAMPUS LIFE

Environment: Village **Activities:** Campus Ministries; Choral groups; Dance; Drama/theater; International Student Organization; Literary magazine; Music ensembles; Pep band; Radio station; Student government 54 registered organizations, 8 honor societies, 1 religious organization. 3 fraternities, 3 sororities. **Athletics (Intercollegiate):** *Men:* baseball, basketball, cross-country, golf, soccer, swimming, tennis. *Women:* basketball, cross-country, golf, soccer, softball, swimming, tennis, volleyball. **On-Campus Highlights:** Sport and Fitness Center, The Commons, Student apartments, Blaisdell Hall (Fine Arts Building), Smart classrooms **Environmental Initiatives:** Installation of a 2.6 kW solar array to power a sustainability information center in the student commons which connects to energy monitors that were installed on every building on campus.

ADMISSIONS

Freshman Academic Profile: Average high school GPA 3.3. 13% in top 10% of high school class, 35% in top 25% of high school class, 73% in top 50% of high school class. 91% from public high schools. **Test Scores:** SAT Math middle 50% range 480-570. SAT EBRW middle 50% range 490-590. ACT middle 50% range 20-24. Minimum internet-based TOEFL 79-80. Minimum paper TOEFL 550. **Basis for Candidate Selection:** *Very important factors considered include:* level of applicant's interest. *Important factors considered include:* rigor of secondary school record, academic GPA, standardized test scores, interview. *Other factors considered include:* class rank, application essay, recommendation(s), extracurricular activities, talent/ability, character/personal qualities, volunteer work, work experience. **Freshman Admission Requirements:** High school diploma is required and GED is accepted *Academic units required:* 4 English, 2 math, 1 science, 1 science labs, 2 foreign language, 1 history, 5 academic electives, *Academic units recommended:* 4 English, 2.5 math, 2 science, 2 science labs, 2 foreign language, 1 history, 5 academic electives. **Freshman Admission Statistics:** 2,852 applied, 48.7% admitted, 25% enrolled. **Transfer Admission Requirements:** college transcript(s), statement of good standing from prior institution(s). Minimum college GPA of 2.0 required. Lowest grade transferable C-. **General Admission Information:** Priority deadline 5/1. Nonfall registration accepted. Admission may be deferred for a maximum of 1 year.

COSTS AND FINANCIAL AID

Annual in-state tuition $9,058. Annual out-of-state tuition $24,184. Room and board $9,058. Required fees $960. Average book expense $1,000. **Required Forms and Deadlines:** FAFSA. **Notification of Awards:** Applicants will be notified of awards on a rolling basis beginning 4/1. **Types of Aid:** *Need-based scholarships/grants:* College/university scholarship or grant aid from institutional funds; Federal Pell; Private scholarships; SEOG; State scholarships/grants. *Loans:* Direct PLUS loans; Direct Subsidized Stafford Loans; Direct Unsubsidized Stafford Loans. *Student Employment:* Federal Work-Study Program available. Institutional employment available. **Financial Aid Statistics:** 94% needy freshmen, 98% needy undergrads receive need-based scholarship or grant aid. 8% freshmen, 7% undergrads receive non-need-based scholarship or grant aid. 91% freshmen, 91% undergrads receive need-based self-help aid. 0% freshmen, 0% undergrads receive athletic scholarships. 83% freshmen, 85% undergrads receive any aid. Average cumulative indebtedness $34,020. **Criteria for awarding aid:** *Need-based:* Minority status *Non-need-based:* Academics, Alumni affiliation, State/district residency.

See page 1066.

UNIVERSITY OF PITTSBURGH AT GREENSBURG

150 Finoli Drive, Greensburg, PA 15601
Phone: 724-836-9880 • **Financial Aid Phone:** 724-836-9881
E-mail: upgadmit@pitt.edu • **CEEB Code:** 2936
Fax: 724-836-7471 • **Website:** www.greensburg.pitt.edu • **ACT Code:** 3733

This public school was founded in 1963. It has a 217 acre campus.

RATINGS

Admissions Selectivity Rating: 75 **Fire Safety Rating:** 60* **Green Rating:** 60*

STUDENTS AND FACULTY

Enrollment: 1,578. **Student Body:** 52% female, 48% male, 2% out-of-state, 1% international. Asian 4%, African American 6%, Caucasian 79%, Hispanic 4%, Native American <1%, Pacific Islander <1%, Two or more races 3%, Race unknown 3%.
Retention and Graduation: 76% freshmen return for sophomore year. 26% grads go on to further study within 1 year. 11% grads pursue arts and sciences degrees. 1% grads pursue law degrees. 2% grads pursue business degrees. 1% grads pursue medical degrees. **Faculty:** Student/faculty ratio 20:1. 76 full-time faculty, 83% hold PhDs, 13% are members of minority groups, 57% are women. 0% of classes are taught by teaching assistants.

ACADEMICS

Degrees: Bachelor's; Certificate **Classes:** Most classes have 10-19 students. Most lab/discussion sessions have fewer than 10 students. **Most popular majors:** Biology/Biological Sciences, General; Psychology, General; Management Information Systems, General. **Special Study Options:** Cross-registration; Double major; Dual enrollment; Exchange student program (domestic); Independent study; Internships; Liberal arts/career combination; Student-designed major; Study abroad; Teacher certification program. **Disability Services offered to physically disabled students:** Note-taking services; Reader services; Tape recorders; Tutors. **Career services:** Alumni network; Alumni services; Career assessment; Career/job search classes; Internships; Regional alumni

FACILITIES

Housing: Coed dorms; Theme housing 95% of campus accessible to physically diasbled. **Computers:** 100% of libraries, 100% of dining areas, 100% of student union, have wireless network access. Students can register for classes online. Administrative functions (other than registration) can be performed online.

CAMPUS LIFE

Environment: Village **Activities:** Campus Ministries; Choral groups; Dance; Drama/theater; International Student Organization; Literary magazine; Musical theater; Student government; Student newspaper 25 registered organizations, 8 honor societies, 3 religious organizations. **Athletics (Intercollegiate):** *Men:* baseball, basketball, cross-country, golf, soccer, tennis. *Women:* basketball, cross-country, golf, soccer, softball, volleyball. **On-Campus Highlights:** Academic Village, Coffee House, Fireside Lounge, Wagner Dining Hall, Ferguson Theater

ADMISSIONS

Freshman Academic Profile: Average high school GPA 3.5. 15% in top 10% of high school class, 47% in top 25% of high school class, 84% in top 50% of high school class. 95% from public high schools. **Test Scores:** SAT Math middle 50% range 460-560. SAT EBRW middle 50% range 460-550. ACT middle 50% range 18-24. Minimum internet-based TOEFL 80. Minimum paper TOEFL 550. **Basis for Candidate Selection:** *Very important factors considered include:* rigor of secondary school record, class rank, academic GPA, standardized test scores. *Other factors considered include:* application essay, recommendation(s), interview, extracurricular activities, talent/ability, character/personal qualities, volunteer work, level of applicant's interest. **Freshman Admission Requirements:** High school diploma is required and GED is accepted *Academic units required:* 4 English, 2 math, 1 science, 1 science labs, 4 foreign language, 2 social studies, 2 history, 1 academic elective, *Academic units recommended:* 4 English, 4 math, 2 science, 4 foreign language, 2 social studies, 2 history, 3 academic electives, 1 computer science. **Freshman Admission Statistics:** 1,538 applied, 80.7% admitted, 35% enrolled. **Transfer Admission Requirements:** High school transcript, college transcript(s), statement of good standing from prior institution(s). Minimum college GPA of 2.0 required. Lowest grade transferable C. **General Admission Information:** Application fee $45. Nonfall registration accepted. Admission may be deferred for a maximum of 1 year.

COSTS AND FINANCIAL AID

Annual in-state tuition $9,490. Annual out-of-state tuition $23,268. Room and board $9,490. Required fees $920. **Required Forms and Deadlines:** FAFSA;

State aid form. **Notification of Awards:** Applicants will be notified of awards on a rolling basis beginning 3/15. **Types of Aid:** *Need-based scholarships/grants:* College/university scholarship or grant aid from institutional funds; Federal Pell; Private scholarships; SEOG; State scholarships/grants; United Negro College Fund. *Loans:* Direct PLUS loans; Direct Subsidized Stafford Loans; Direct Unsubsidized Stafford Loans. *Student Employment:* Federal Work-Study Program available. Institutional employment available. **Financial Aid Statistics:** 83% needy freshmen, 79% needy undergrads receive need-based scholarship or grant aid. 8% freshmen, 4% undergrads receive non-need-based scholarship or grant aid. 83% freshmen, 87% undergrads receive need-based self-help aid. 0% freshmen, 0% undergrads receive athletic scholarships. **Criteria for awarding aid:** *Non-need-based:* Academics, Leadership, Minority status.

UNIVERSITY OF PITTSBURGH AT JOHNSTOWN

450 Schoolhouse Road, Johnstown, PA 15904
Phone: 814-269-7050 • **Financial Aid Phone:** 814-269-7045
E-mail: upjadmit@pitt.edu • **CEEB Code:** 2934
Fax: 814-269-7044 • **Website:** www.upj.pitt.edu • **ACT Code:**

This public school was founded in 1927. It has a 655 acre campus.

RATINGS
Admissions Selectivity Rating: 74   **Fire Safety Rating:** 88   **Green Rating:** 60*

STUDENTS AND FACULTY
Enrollment: 2,814. **Student Body:** 45% female, 55% male, 2% out-of-state, 2% international (20 countries represented). Asian 1%, African American 3%, Caucasian 87%, Hispanic 1%, Native American <1%, Pacific Islander <1%, Two or more races 2%, Race unknown 3%.
Retention and Graduation: 82% freshmen return for sophomore year. 8% grads pursue arts and sciences degrees. 1% grads pursue law degrees. 1% grads pursue business degrees. 2% grads pursue medical degrees. **Faculty:** 0% of classes are taught by teaching assistants.

ACADEMICS
Degrees: Associate; Bachelor's; Certificate **Classes:** Most classes have 10-19 students. **Most popular majors:** Computer Engineering, General; Civil Engineering Technology/Technician; Electrical, Electronic And Communications Engineering Technology/Technician. **Special Study Options:** Accelerated program; Cross-registration; Double major; Dual enrollment; Independent study; Internships; Liberal arts/career combination; Student-designed major; Study abroad; Teacher certification program. Honors programs: **Disability Services offered to physically disabled students:** Note-taking services; Reader services; Tutors. **Career services:** Alumni network; Alumni services; Career/job search classes; Internships; Regional alumni

FACILITIES
Housing: Coed dorms; Fraternity/sorority housing; Special housing for disabled student; Theme housing 100% of campus accessible to physically diasbled. **Special Academic Facilities/Equipment:** Art museum, performing arts center, language lab, Idea Lab, Mountain Cat Mission Control—The Region's First Social Media Training Center **Computers:** 75% of classrooms, 100% of libraries, 50% of dining areas, 100% of student union, 50% of common outdoor areas have wireless network access. Administrative functions (other than registration) can be performed online.

CAMPUS LIFE
Environment: City **Activities:** Campus Ministries; Choral groups; Concert band; Dance; Drama/theater; Literary magazine; Model UN; Music ensembles; Musical theater; Radio station; Student government; Student newspaper; Television station 70 registered organizations, 11 honor societies, 3 religious organizations. 5 fraternities, 3 sororities. **Athletics (Intercollegiate):** *Men:* baseball, basketball, golf, soccer, wrestling. *Women:* basketball, cheerleading, cross-country, golf, soccer, track/field (outdoor), volleyball. **On-Campus Highlights:** Student Union Building, Sports & Wellness Center, Nursing and Health Sciences Building, Living/Learning Center, Performing Arts Center

ADMISSIONS
Freshman Academic Profile: Average high school GPA 3.5. 14% in top 10% of high school class, 40% in top 25% of high school class, 72% in top 50% of high school class. **Test Scores:** SAT Math middle 50% range 460-570. SAT EBRW middle 50% range 450-550. ACT middle 50% range 20-25. Minimum internet-based TOEFL 80. Minimum paper TOEFL 550. **Basis for Candidate Selection:** *Very important factors considered include:* rigor of secondary school record, class rank, academic GPA. *Important factors considered include:*

standardized test scores, interview, extracurricular activities, talent/ability, volunteer work.level of applicant's interest. *Other factors considered include:* application essay, recommendation(s), character/personal qualities, racial/ethnic status, work experience. **Freshman Admission Requirements:** High school diploma is required and GED is accepted *Academic units required:* 4 English, 2 math, 2 science, 1 science labs, 2 foreign language, 4 social studies. **Freshman Admission Statistics:** 3,456 applied, 81.0% admitted, 26% enrolled. **Transfer Admission Requirements:** High school transcript, college transcript(s), Minimum college GPA of 2.0 required. Lowest grade transferable C. **General Admission Information:** Regular application deadline 5/1. Nonfall registration accepted. Admission may be deferred for a maximum of 1 year.

COSTS AND FINANCIAL AID
Required Forms and Deadlines: FAFSA. **Notification of Awards:** Applicants will be notified of awards on a rolling basis beginning 3/1. **Types of Aid:** *Need-based scholarships/grants:* College/university scholarship or grant aid from institutional funds; Federal Pell; Private scholarships; SEOG; State scholarships/grants. *Loans:* Direct PLUS loans; Direct Subsidized Stafford Loans; Direct Unsubsidized Stafford Loans. *Student Employment:* Federal Work-Study Program available. Institutional employment available. **Financial Aid Statistics:** 85% needy freshmen, 77% needy undergrads receive need-based scholarship or grant aid. 6% freshmen, 4% undergrads receive non-need-based scholarship or grant aid. 84% freshmen, 87% undergrads receive need-based self-help aid. 3% freshmen, 2% undergrads receive athletic scholarships. 80% freshmen, 80% undergrads receive any aid. 85% undergrads borrow to pay for school. Average cumulative indebtedness $34,127. **Criteria for awarding aid:** *Need-based:* Academics, Athletics, Minority status, Music/drama *Non-need-based:* Academics, Alumni affiliation, Athletics, Leadership, State/district residency.

UNIVERSITY OF PITTSBURGH— PITTSBURGH CAMPUS

4200 Fifth Avenue, Pittsburgh, PA 15260
Phone: 412-624-7488 • **Financial Aid Phone:** 412-624-7488
E-mail: oafa@pitt.edu • **CEEB Code:** 2927
Fax: 412-648-8815 • **Website:** www.pitt.edu • **ACT Code:** 3734

This public school was founded in 1787. It has a 145 acre campus.

RATINGS
Admissions Selectivity Rating: 90   **Fire Safety Rating:** 91   **Green Rating:** 92

STUDENTS AND FACULTY
Enrollment: 19,134. **Student Body:** 51% female, 49% male, 28% out-of-state, 4% international (55 countries represented). Asian 10%, African American 5%, Caucasian 72%, Hispanic 4%, Native American <1%, Pacific Islander <1%, Two or more races 4%, Race unknown 1%.
Retention and Graduation: 93% freshmen return for sophomore year. 65% freshmen graduate within 4 years. 81% freshmen graduate within 6 years. 31% grads go on to further study within 1 year. 37% grads pursue arts and sciences degrees. 8% grads pursue law degrees. 3% grads pursue business degrees. 10% grads pursue medical degrees. **Faculty:** Student/faculty ratio 15:1. 1,762 full-time faculty, 94% hold PhDs, 19% are members of minority groups, 45% are women.

ACADEMICS
Degrees: Associate; Bachelor's; Certificate; Doctoral; Doctoral/Professional; Doctoral/Research; Master's; Post-Bachelor's certificate; Post-Master's certificate **Classes:** Most classes have 10-19 students. Most lab/discussion sessions have 20-29 students. Most popular majors: Psychology, General; Registered Nursing/Registered Nurse; Finance, General. **Special Study Options:** Accelerated program; Cooperative education program; Cross-registration; Distance learning; Double major; Dual enrollment; English as a Second Language (ESL); Exchange student program (domestic); External degree program; Honors program; Independent study; Internships; Liberal arts/career combination; Student-designed major; Study abroad; Teacher certification program. Honors programs: University Honors College—see http://www.honorscollege.pitt.edu/ Combined degree programs: BA/DDS; BA/JD; BA/MD. **Disability Services offered to physically disabled students:** Note-taking services. **Career services:** Alumni network; Alumni services; Career assessment; Career/job search classes; Internships; Regional alumni

FACILITIES

Housing: Apartments for single students; Coed dorms; Fraternity/sorority housing; Special housing for disabled student; Special housing for international students; Theme housing; Wellness housing 90% of campus accessible to physically diasbled. **Special Academic Facilities/Equipment:** Stephen Foster Memorial, Allegheny Observatory, Jazz Hall of Fame **Computers:** 100% of classrooms, 25% of dorms, 100% of libraries, 100% of dining areas, 100% of student union, 50% of common outdoor areas have wireless network access. Students can register for classes online. Administrative functions (other than registration) can be performed online.

CAMPUS LIFE

Environment: City **Activities:** Campus Ministries; Choral groups; Concert band; Dance; Drama/theater; International Student Organization; Jazz band; Literary magazine; Marching band; Model UN; Music ensembles; Musical theater; Pep band; Radio station; Student government; Student newspaper; Student-run film society; Symphony orchestra; Television station 395 registered organizations, 17 honor societies, 20 fraternities, 16 sororities. **Athletics (Intercollegiate):** *Men:* baseball, basketball, cross-country, diving, football, soccer, swimming, track/field (outdoor), wrestling. *Women:* basketball, cross-country, diving, gymnastics, soccer, softball, swimming, tennis, track/field (outdoor), volleyball. **On-Campus Highlights:** Cathedral of Learning, William Pitt Union, Heinz Chapel, Petersen Event Center, Sennott Square **Environmental Initiatives:** ENERGY CENTER: The Facilities Management Division recently consolidated all energy-related operations to a single location. The newly constructed Energy Center space is designed to increase collaboration among energy managers, engineers, utility analysts, and energy management system personnel. These personnel will use new and existing controls and diagnostic tools to place an even greater focus on ensuring optimal building operations and incorporating new technologies into building system designs to further energy conservation on campus. A new command center provides technicians and managers with consolidated access to the building automation system and other diagnostic tools.

ADMISSIONS

Freshman Academic Profile: Average high school GPA 4.1. 52% in top 10% of high school class, 86% in top 25% of high school class, 99% in top 50% of high school class. **Test Scores:** SAT Math middle 50% range 620-718. SAT EBRW middle 50% range 620-700. ACT middle 50% range 27-32. Minimum internet-based TOEFL 100. Minimum paper TOEFL 600. **Basis for Candidate Selection:** *Very important factors considered include:* rigor of secondary school record, academic GPA, standardized test scores. *Important factors considered include:* application essay. *Other factors considered include:* class rank, recommendation(s), extracurricular activities, talent/ability, character/personal qualities, first generation, alumni/ae relation, geographical residence, state residency, racial/ethnic status, volunteer work, work experience, level of applicant's interest. **Freshman Admission Requirements:** High school diploma is required and GED is not accepted *Academic units required:* 4 English, 3 math, 3 science, 3 science labs, 2 foreign language, 2 social studies, 3 academic electives, *Academic units recommended:* 4 English, 4 math, 4 science, 4 science labs, 3 foreign language, 3 social studies, 5 academic electives. **Freshman Admission Statistics:** 27,679 applied, 59.7% admitted, 24% enrolled. **Transfer Admission Requirements:** High school transcript, college transcript(s), essay or personal statement, Lowest grade transferable C. **General Admission Information:** Application fee $45. Nonfall registration accepted. Admission may be deferred for a maximum of 1 year.

COSTS AND FINANCIAL AID

Annual in-state tuition $10,950. Annual out-of-state tuition $29,692. Room and board $10,950. Required fees $950. Average book expense $773. **Required Forms and Deadlines:** FAFSA; State aid form. **Notification of Awards:** Applicants will be notified of awards on a rolling basis beginning 2/1. **Types of Aid:** *Need-based scholarships/grants:* College/university scholarship or grant aid from institutional funds; Federal Nursing Scholarships; Federal Pell; Private scholarships; SEOG; State scholarships/grants. *Loans:* Direct PLUS loans; Direct Subsidized Stafford Loans; Direct Unsubsidized Stafford Loans. *Student Employment:* Federal Work-Study Program available. Institutional employment available. **Financial Aid Statistics:** 80% needy freshmen, 70% needy undergrads receive need-based scholarship or grant aid. 8% freshmen, 5% undergrads receive non-need-based scholarship or grant aid. 83% freshmen, 88% undergrads receive need-based self-help aid. 3% freshmen, 2% undergrads receive athletic scholarships. 63% freshmen, 58% undergrads receive any aid. 63% undergrads borrow to pay for school. Average cumulative indebtedness $38,045. **Criteria for awarding aid:** *Non-need-based:* Academics, Athletics, Minority status.

UNIVERSITY OF PORTLAND

5000 N. Willamette Boulevard, Portland, OR 97203-5798
Phone: 503-943-7147 • **Financial Aid Phone:** 503-943-7311
E-mail: admissions@up.edu • **CEEB Code:** 4847
Fax: 503-943-7315 • **Website:** www.up.edu • **ACT Code:** 3500

This private school, affiliated with the Roman Catholic Church, was founded in 1901. It has a 130 acre campus.

RATINGS

Admissions Selectivity Rating: 88   **Fire Safety Rating:** 92   **Green Rating:** 60*

STUDENTS AND FACULTY

Enrollment: 3,762. **Student Body:** 60% female, 40% male, 73% out-of-state, 3% international (38 countries represented). Asian 12%, African American 1%, Caucasian 58%, Hispanic 12%, Native American <1%, Pacific Islander 2%, Two or more races 9%, Race unknown 3%.
Retention and Graduation: 91% freshmen return for sophomore year. 15% grads go on to further study within 1 year. **Faculty:** Student/faculty ratio 13:1. 240 full-time faculty, 64% hold PhDs, 8% are members of minority groups, 52% are women. 0% of classes are taught by teaching assistants.

ACADEMICS

Degrees: Bachelor's; Doctoral/Professional; Master's; Post-Master's certificate **Classes:** Most classes have fewer than 10 students. Most lab/discussion sessions have fewer than 10 students. **Most popular majors:** Mechanical Engineering; Biology/Biological Sciences, General; Registered Nursing, Nursing Administration, Nursing Research And Clinical Nursing. **Special Study Options:** Cross-registration; Double major; Honors program; Independent study; Internships; Liberal arts/career combination; Study abroad; Teacher certification program. Honors programs: The honors program provides an exciting intellectual challenge for highly motivated students whit above average high school records. The program is designed to facilitate learning through special small classes which permit a high level of student-faculty interaction. Honors students may be enrolled in any major. **Disability Services offered to physically disabled students:** Note-taking services; Reader services; Tutors. **Career services:** Alumni network; Alumni services; Career assessment; Career/job search classes; Internships

FACILITIES

Housing: Coed dorms; Men's dorms; Theme housing; Women's dorms 80% of campus accessible to physically diasbled. **Special Academic Facilities/Equipment:** Art gallery, observatory. **Computers:** 100% of classrooms, 100% of dorms, 100% of libraries, 100% of dining areas, 100% of student union, 100% of common outdoor areas have wireless network access. Students can register for classes online. Administrative functions (other than registration) can be performed online.

CAMPUS LIFE

Environment: Metropolis **Activities:** Campus Ministries; Choral groups; Concert band; Dance; Drama/theater; International Student Organization; Jazz band; Literary magazine; Music ensembles; Musical theater; Pep band; Radio station; Student government; Student newspaper; Student-run film society; Symphony orchestra; Yearbook 40 registered organizations, 15 honor societies, 9 religious organizations. **Athletics (Intercollegiate):** *Men:* baseball, basketball, cross-country, golf, soccer, tennis, track/field (outdoor). *Women:* basketball, cross-country, golf, soccer, tennis, track/field (outdoor), volleyball. **On-Campus Highlights:** Commons, St. Mary's Lounge, Beauchamp Recreation Center, The Cove, The Anchor **Environmental Initiatives:** Food for Thought (with Michael Pollan), April 2011; Confluences, Water and Justice (with Maude Barlow), May 2010;Portland host and active participant of Focus the Nation, January 30, 2008

ADMISSIONS

Freshman Academic Profile: Average high school GPA 3.7. 44% in top 10% of high school class, 75% in top 25% of high school class, 97% in top 50% of high school class. 60% from public high schools. **Test Scores:** SAT Math middle 50% range 540-640. SAT EBRW middle 50% range 540-660. Minimum internet-based TOEFL 71. Minimum paper TOEFL 525. **Basis for Candidate Selection:** *Very important factors considered include:* rigor of secondary school record, academic GPA, standardized test scores. *Important factors considered include:* class rank, application essay, recommendation(s), extracurricular activities, talent/ability, work experience. *Other factors considered include:* interview, character/personal qualities, first generation, alumni/ae relation, geographical residence, religious affiliation/commitment, racial/ethnic status, level of applicant's interest. **Freshman Admission Requirements:** High school diploma is required and GED is accepted *Academic units required:*

4 English, 3 math, 3 science, 2 foreign language, 3 social studies, 2 history, 7 academic electives, *Academic units recommended:* 4 English, 4 math, 4 science, 3 foreign language, 4 social studies, 4 history, 7 academic electives. **Freshman Admission Statistics:** 11,911 applied, 61.0% admitted, 13% enrolled. **Transfer Admission Requirements:** college transcript(s), essay or personal statement, Minimum college GPA of 2.5 required. Lowest grade transferable C. **General Admission Information:** Application fee $50. Priority deadline 2/1. Regular application deadline 2/1. Nonfall registration accepted. Admission may be deferred for a maximum of 1 year.

COSTS AND FINANCIAL AID
Annual tuition $41,844. Room and board $12,394. Required fees $170. Average book expense $864. **Required Forms and Deadlines:** FAFSA. **Notification of Awards:** Applicants will be notified of awards on a rolling basis beginning 3/1. **Types of Aid:** *Need-based scholarships/grants:* College/university scholarship or grant aid from institutional funds; Federal Nursing Scholarships; Federal Pell; Private scholarships; SEOG; State scholarships/grants. *Loans:* Direct PLUS loans; Direct Subsidized Stafford Loans; Direct Unsubsidized Stafford Loans. *Student Employment:* Federal Work-Study Program available. **Financial Aid Statistics:** 76% needy freshmen, 78% needy undergrads receive need-based scholarship or grant aid. 96% freshmen, 93% undergrads receive non-need-based scholarship or grant aid. 71% freshmen, 75% undergrads receive need-based self-help aid. 1% freshmen, 3% undergrads receive athletic scholarships. 98% freshmen, 95% undergrads receive any aid. Average cumulative indebtedness $28,249. **Criteria for awarding aid:** *Need-based:* Academics, Minority status *Non-need-based:* Academics, Athletics, Leadership, Minority status, Music/drama.

UNIVERSITY OF PUGET SOUND

1500 North Warner Street, Tacoma, WA 98416-1062
Phone: 253-879-3211 • **Financial Aid Phone:** 253-879-3214
E-mail: admission@pugetsound.edu • **CEEB Code:** 4067
Fax: 253-879-3993 • **Website:** www.pugetsound.edu • **ACT Code:** 4450

This private school was founded in 1888. It has a 97 acre campus.

RATINGS
Admissions Selectivity Rating: 84   **Fire Safety Rating:** 65   **Green Rating:** 79

STUDENTS AND FACULTY
Enrollment: 2,413. **Student Body:** 60% female, 40% male, 78% out-of-state, 1% international (10 countries represented). Asian 6%, African American 1%, Caucasian 71%, Hispanic 8%, Native American <1%, Pacific Islander <1%, Two or more races 9%, Race unknown 4%.
Retention and Graduation: 86% freshmen return for sophomore year. 72% freshmen graduate within 4 years. 78% freshmen graduate within 6 years.
Faculty: Student/faculty ratio 11:1. 233 full-time faculty, 93% hold PhDs, 13% are members of minority groups, 50% are women. 0% of classes are taught by teaching assistants.

ACADEMICS
Degrees: Bachelor's; Doctoral/Professional; **Master's Classes:** Most classes have 10-19 students. Most lab/discussion sessions have 10-19 students.
Most popular majors: Biology/Biological Sciences, General; Psychology, General; Business/Commerce, General. **Special Study Options:** Cooperative education program; Double major; Honors program; Independent study; Internships; Liberal arts/career combination; Student-designed major; Study abroad; Teacher certification program. Honors programs: Business Leadership Program; Honors Program. **Disability Services offered to physically disabled students:** Note-taking services; Reader services; Tape recorders; Tutors. **Career services:** Alumni network; Alumni services; Career assessment; Career/job search classes; Internships; Regional alumni

FACILITIES
Housing: Apartments for single students; Coed dorms; Fraternity/sorority housing; Special housing for disabled student; Theme housing; Wellness housing **Special Academic Facilities/Equipment:** Art gallery, natural history museum, concert hall, transmission and scanning electron microscopes, spectrometers, exercise science lab, observatory, paleomagnetic and X-ray lab, physiology labs, and DNA Sequencer **Computers:** 30% of classrooms, 30% of dorms, 95% of libraries, 95% of dining areas, 85% of student union, 10%

of common outdoor areas have wireless network access. Students can register for classes online. Administrative functions (other than registration) can be performed online.

CAMPUS LIFE
Environment: City **Activities:** Campus Ministries; Choral groups; Concert band; Dance; Drama/theater; International Student Organization; Jazz band; Literary magazine; Model UN; Music ensembles; Musical theater; Opera; Pep band; Radio station; Student government; Student newspaper; Student-run film society; Symphony orchestra; Yearbook 77 registered organizations, 2 honor societies, 12 religious organizations. 4 fraternities, 4 sororities. **Athletics (Intercollegiate):** *Men:* baseball, basketball, crew/rowing, cross-country, football, golf, soccer, swimming, tennis, track/field (outdoor), track/field (indoor). *Women:* basketball, crew/rowing, cross-country, golf, lacrosse, soccer, softball, swimming, tennis, track/field (outdoor), track/field (indoor), volleyball. **On-Campus Highlights:** Diversions Cafe, Glass gazebo Oppenheimer Cafe, Collins Memorial Library rocking chairs, Science Center atrium, Theme House Row **Environmental Initiatives:** In 2005, President Thomas established the Sustainability Advisory Committee (SAC), which reports to the president through the Vice President of Student Affairs and the Vice President for Finance and Administration. The president empowered the committee to advise on and implement sustainability policies and programs on campus and collaboratively with our regional community. The committee addresses sustainability across the institution and in partnership with external organizations. It also uniquely engages students, faculty, and staff in comprehensive, collaborative, and strategic sustainability endeavors.

ADMISSIONS
Freshman Academic Profile: Average high school GPA 3.5. 34% in top 10% of high school class, 66% in top 25% of high school class, 91% in top 50% of high school class. 70% from public high schools. **Test Scores:** SAT Math middle 50% range 570-680. SAT EBRW middle 50% range 580-690. ACT middle 50% range 25-31. Minimum internet-based TOEFL 85. **Basis for Candidate Selection:** *Very important factors considered include:* rigor of secondary school record, academic GPA, application essay, character/personal qualities. *Important factors considered include:* recommendation(s), extracurricular activities, talent/ability, alumni/ae relation, volunteer work, work experience. *Other factors considered include:* class rank, standardized test scores, interview, first generation, racial/ethnic status, level of applicant's interest. **Freshman Admission Requirements:** High school diploma is required and GED is accepted *Academic units recommended:* 4 English, 3 math, 3 science, 3 science labs, 2 foreign language, 3 social studies, 3 history, 1 visual/performing arts. **Freshman Admission Statistics:** 5,958 applied, 83.9% admitted, 12% enrolled. **Transfer Admission Requirements:** college transcript(s), essay or personal statement, statement of good standing from prior institution(s). Minimum college GPA of 2.0 required. Lowest grade transferable D. **General Admission Information:** Application fee $60. Priority deadline 1/15. Regular application deadline 1/15. Nonfall registration accepted. Admission may be deferred for a maximum of 1 year.

COSTS AND FINANCIAL AID
Annual tuition $49,510. Room and board $12,540. Required fees $266. Average book expense $1,000. **Required Forms and Deadlines:** FAFSA. **Notification of Awards:** Applicants will be notified of awards on or about 3/15. **Types of Aid:** *Need-based scholarships/grants:* College/university scholarship or grant aid from institutional funds; Federal Pell; Private scholarships; SEOG; State scholarships/grants. *Loans:* Direct PLUS loans; Direct Subsidized Stafford Loans; Direct Unsubsidized Stafford Loans. *Student Employment:* Federal Work-Study Program available. Institutional employment available. **Financial Aid Statistics:** 98% needy freshmen, 96% needy undergrads receive need-based scholarship or grant aid. 16% freshmen, 13% undergrads receive non-need-based scholarship or grant aid. 76% freshmen, 78% undergrads receive need-based self-help aid. 0% freshmen, 0% undergrads receive athletic scholarships. 96% freshmen, 94% undergrads receive any aid. 58% undergrads borrow to pay for school. Average cumulative indebtedness $33,130. **Criteria for awarding aid:** *Need-based:* Academics, Minority status, Religious affiliation *Non-need-based:* Academics, Alumni affiliation, Art, Leadership, Music/drama, Religious affiliation.

UNIVERSITY OF REDLANDS

PO Box 3080, Redlands, Redlands, CA 92373
Phone: 909-748-8074 • **Financial Aid Phone:** 909-748-8047
E-mail: admissions@redlands.edu • **CEEB Code:** 4848
Fax: 909-335-4089 • **Website:** www.redlands.edu • **ACT Code:** 464

This private school was founded in 1907. It has a 160 acre campus.

RATINGS
Admissions Selectivity Rating: 81   **Fire Safety Rating:** 86   **Green Rating:** 60*

STUDENTS AND FACULTY
Enrollment: 2,402. **Student Body:** 58% female, 42% male, 30% out-of-state, 2% international (17 countries represented). Asian 6%, African American 3%, Caucasian 52%, Hispanic 25%, Native American 1%, Pacific Islander 1%, Two or more races 6%, Race unknown 4%.
Retention and Graduation: 87% freshmen return for sophomore year. 19% grads go on to further study within 1 year. 5% grads pursue law degrees. 20% grads pursue business degrees. 2% grads pursue medical degrees. **Faculty:** Student/faculty ratio 12:1. 169 full-time faculty, 0% of classes are taught by teaching assistants.

ACADEMICS
Degrees: Bachelor's; Certificate; Diploma; Doctoral; Doctoral/Research; Master's; Post-Bachelor's certificate; Post-Master's certificate **Classes:** Most classes have 10-19 students. Most lab/discussion sessions have 10-19 students. **Most popular majors:** Liberal Arts And Sciences/Liberal Studies; Psychology, General; Business/Commerce, General. **Special Study Options:** Accelerated program; Cross-registration; Distance learning; Double major; Exchange student program (domestic); Honors program; Independent study; Internships; Liberal arts/career combination; Student-designed major; Study abroad; Teacher certification program. Honors programs: The Johnston Center for Integrative Studies allows students to design their own majors in consultation with faculty advisors. Students write contracts for their courses and receive narrative evaluations in lieu of traditional grades. The center has received national acclaim for its innovative approaches to education. **Disability Services offered to physically disabled students:** Note-taking services; Reader services; Tutors. **Career services:** Alumni services; Career/job search classes; Regional alumni

FACILITIES
Housing: Apartments for married students; Apartments for single students; Coed dorms; Fraternity/sorority housing; Special housing for disabled student; Special housing for international students; Theme housing; Women's dorms 75% of campus accessible to physically diasbled. **Special Academic Facilities/Equipment:** Art gallery, Far East art collection, Southwest collection, center for communicative disorders, language lab, Helen and Vernon Farquar Anthropology Lab, Physics Laser Photonics Lab, Irvine Map Library, Geographic Information System lab. **Computers:** 100% of classrooms, 100% of dorms, 100% of libraries, 100% of dining areas, 100% of student union, 100% of common outdoor areas have wireless network access. Students can register for classes online. Administrative functions (other than registration) can be performed online.

CAMPUS LIFE
Environment: Town **Activities:** Campus Ministries; Choral groups; Concert band; Dance; Drama/theater; International Student Organization; Jazz band; Literary magazine; Music ensembles; Musical theater; Opera; Radio station; Student government; Student newspaper; Symphony orchestra; Yearbook 105 registered organizations, 8 honor societies, 8 religious organizations. 5 fraternities, 5 sororities. **Athletics (Intercollegiate):** *Men:* baseball, basketball, cross-country, diving, football, golf, soccer, swimming, tennis, track/field (outdoor), water polo. *Women:* basketball, cross-country, diving, golf, lacrosse, soccer, softball, swimming, tennis, track/field (outdoor), volleyball, water polo. **On-Campus Highlights:** Armacost Library, Peppers Art Center, Currier Gymnasium/Fitness Center, Chapel, Post Office **Environmental Initiatives:** Co-Generation facility to provide power to much of the campus

ADMISSIONS
Freshman Academic Profile: Average high school GPA 3.5. 22% in top 10% of high school class, 55% in top 25% of high school class, 88% in top 50% of high school class. **Test Scores:** SAT Math middle 50% range 490-600. SAT EBRW middle 50% range 490-590. ACT middle 50% range 22-27. Minimum

paper TOEFL 550. **Basis for Candidate Selection:** *Very important factors considered include:* academic GPA. *Important factors considered include:* rigor of secondary school record, application essay, standardized test scores, recommendation(s). *Other factors considered include:* class rank, interview, extracurricular activities, talent/ability, character/personal qualities, first generation, alumni/ae relation, geographical residence, racial/ethnic status, volunteer work, work experience. **Freshman Admission Requirements:** High school diploma is required and GED is accepted *Academic units required:* 4 English, 3 math, 2 science, 2 science labs, 2 foreign language, 2 social studies, *Academic units recommended:* 3 science, 3 foreign language, 3 social studies. **Freshman Admission Statistics:** 4,562 applied, 74.7% admitted, 17% enrolled. **Transfer Admission Requirements:** High school transcript, college transcript(s), essay or personal statement, Minimum college GPA of 2.5 required. Lowest grade transferable C. **General Admission Information:** Application fee $30. Priority deadline 11/15. Regular application deadline 1/15. Nonfall registration accepted. Admission may be deferred for a maximum of 2 semesters.

COSTS AND FINANCIAL AID
Annual tuition $47,722. Room and board $13,862. Required fees $350. Average book expense $1,850. **Required Forms and Deadlines:** FAFSA. **Notification of Awards:** Applicants will be notified of awards on a rolling basis beginning 2/17. **Types of Aid:** *Need-based scholarships/grants:* College/university scholarship or grant aid from institutional funds; Federal Pell; Private scholarships; SEOG; State scholarships/grants. *Loans:* Direct PLUS loans; Direct Subsidized Stafford Loans; Direct Unsubsidized Stafford Loans. *Student Employment:* Federal Work-Study Program available. **Financial Aid Statistics:** 100% needy freshmen, 99% needy undergrads receive need-based scholarship or grant aid. 74% freshmen, 57% undergrads receive non-need-based scholarship or grant aid. 84% freshmen, 91% undergrads receive need-based self-help aid. 0% freshmen, 0% undergrads receive athletic scholarships. 94% freshmen, 94% undergrads receive any aid. **Criteria for awarding aid:** *Non-need-based:* Academics, Art, Music/drama.

UNIVERSITY OF RHODE ISLAND

Newman Hall, Kingston, RI 02881
Phone: 401-874-7100 • **Financial Aid Phone:** 401-874-7530
E-mail: admission@uri.edu • **CEEB Code:** 3919
Fax: 401-874-5523 • **Website:** www.uri.edu • **ACT Code:** 3818

This public school was founded in 1892. It has a 1300 acre campus.

RATINGS
Admissions Selectivity Rating: 82   **Fire Safety Rating:** 89   **Green Rating:** 95

STUDENTS AND FACULTY
Enrollment: 13,993. **Student Body:** 57% female, 43% male, 46% out-of-state, 1% international (38 countries represented). Asian 3%, African American 5%, Caucasian 73%, Hispanic 10%, Native American <1%, Pacific Islander <1%, Two or more races 3%, Race unknown 5%.
Retention and Graduation: 85% freshmen return for sophomore year. 47% freshmen graduate within 4 years. 66% freshmen graduate within 6 years. **Faculty:** Student/faculty ratio 17:1. 757 full-time faculty, 87% hold PhDs, 20% are members of minority groups, 50% are women.

ACADEMICS
Degrees: Bachelor's; Certificate; Doctoral Other; Doctoral/Professional; Doctoral/Research; Master's; Post-Bachelor's certificate **Classes:** Most classes have 20-29 students. Most lab/discussion sessions have 20-29 students. **Most popular majors:** Kinesiology And Exercise Science; Psychology, General; Registered Nursing/Registered Nurse. **Special Study Options:** Cross-registration; Distance learning; Double major; Dual enrollment; Exchange student program (domestic); Honors program; Independent study; Internships; Liberal arts/career combination; Study abroad; Teacher certification program; Weekend college. Honors programs: The Honors Program at URI features small classes, a nationally renowned Honors Colloquium, National Scholarship for upper class students, advising and honors housing for upper class students. Combined degree programs: BA/MA; BA/MEng. **Disability Services offered to physically disabled students:** Note-taking services; Reader services; Tape recorders. **Career services:** Alumni network; Alumni services; Career assessment; Internships; Regional alumni

FACILITIES

Housing: Apartments for married students; Apartments for single students; Coed dorms; Fraternity/sorority housing; Special housing for disabled student; Special housing for international students; Theme housing; Wellness housing 90% of campus accessible to physically diasbled. **Special Academic Facilities/ Equipment:** Center for robotic research, animal science farm, planetarium, Watson House Museum, Narragansett Bay Campus for Marine Sciences, American historic textiles museum, aquaculture center, fisheries and marine technology laboratory, center for biotechnology and life sciences, human performance laboratory. **Computers:** 50% of classrooms, 100% of dorms, 100% of libraries, 75% of dining areas, 100% of student union, 25% of common outdoor areas have wireless network access. Students can register for classes online. Administrative functions (other than registration) can be performed online.

CAMPUS LIFE

Environment: Village **Activities:** Campus Ministries; Choral groups; Concert band; Dance; Drama/theater; International Student Organization; Jazz band; Literary magazine; Marching band; Music ensembles; Musical theater; Opera; Pep band; Radio station; Student government; Student newspaper; Student-run film society; Television station; Yearbook 100 registered organizations, 40 honor societies, 5 religious organizations. 11 fraternities, 9 sororities. **Athletics (Intercollegiate):** *Men:* baseball, basketball, cheerleading, cross-country, football, golf, soccer, track/field (outdoor), track/field (indoor). *Women:* basketball, cheerleading, crew/rowing, cross-country, diving, soccer, softball, swimming, tennis, track/field (outdoor), track/field (indoor), volleyball. **On-Campus Highlights:** Ryan Center and Boss Ice Arena, Fascitelli Wellness & Fitness Center, Memorial Student Union, Multicultural Center, Hope Dining Commons **Environmental Initiatives:** Development of a sustainability component to the general education requirements for all undergraduate students

ADMISSIONS

Freshman Academic Profile: Average high school GPA 3.5. 17% in top 10% of high school class, 48% in top 25% of high school class, 85% in top 50% of high school class. **Test Scores:** SAT Math middle 50% range 530-620. SAT EBRW middle 50% range 550-630. ACT middle 50% range 23-27. Minimum internet-based TOEFL 79. **Basis for Candidate Selection:** *Very important factors considered include:* rigor of secondary school record, academic GPA. *Important factors considered include:* class rank, standardized test scores. *Other factors considered include:* application essay, recommendation(s), extracurricular activities, talent/ability, character/personal qualities, first generation, alumni/ae relation, geographical residence, state residency, racial/ethnic status, volunteer work, work experience, level of applicant's interest. **Freshman Admission Requirements:** High school diploma is required and GED is accepted *Academic units required:* 4 English, 3 math, 2 science, 1 science labs, 2 foreign language, 2 social studies, 5 academic electives. **Freshman Admission Statistics:** 22,667 applied, 68.9% admitted, 22% enrolled. **Transfer Admission Requirements:** college transcript(s), essay or personal statement, statement of good standing from prior institution(s). Minimum college GPA of 2.5 required. Lowest grade transferable C. **General Admission Information:** Application fee $65. Regular application deadline 2/1. Nonfall registration accepted. Admission may be deferred for a maximum of 1 year.

COSTS AND FINANCIAL AID

Annual in-state tuition $12,274. Annual out-of-state tuition $28,252. Room and board $12,274. Required fees $1,790. Average book expense $1,200. **Required Forms and Deadlines:** FAFSA. **Notification of Awards:** Applicants will be notified of awards on a rolling basis beginning 3/15. **Types of Aid:** *Need-based scholarships/grants:* College/university scholarship or grant aid from institutional funds; Federal Pell; Private scholarships; SEOG; State scholarships/grants. *Loans:* Direct PLUS loans; Direct Subsidized Stafford Loans; Direct Unsubsidized Stafford Loans. *Student Employment:* Federal Work-Study Program available. Institutional employment available. **Financial Aid Statistics:** 83% needy freshmen, 86% needy undergrads receive need-based scholarship or grant aid. 20% freshmen, 12% undergrads receive non-need-based scholarship or grant aid. 82% freshmen, 77% undergrads receive need-based self-help aid. 0% freshmen, 0% undergrads receive athletic scholarships. 89% freshmen, 85% undergrads receive any aid. 77% undergrads borrow to pay for school. Average cumulative indebtedness $32,750. **Criteria for awarding aid:** *Need-based:* Alumni affiliation, Art, Minority status, Music/drama *Non-need-based:* Academics, Alumni affiliation, Art, Athletics, Music/drama.

UNIVERSITY OF RICHMOND

28 Westhampton Way, Richmond, VA 23173
Phone: 804-289-8640 • **Financial Aid Phone:** 804-289-8438
E-mail: admission@richmond.edu • **CEEB Code:** 5569
Fax: 804-287-6003 • **Website:** www.richmond.edu • **ACT Code:** 4410

This private school was founded in 1830. It has a 350 acre campus.

RATINGS

Admissions Selectivity Rating: 94   **Fire Safety Rating:** 94   **Green Rating:** 93

STUDENTS AND FACULTY

Enrollment: 2,907. **Student Body:** 52% female, 48% male, 80% out-of-state, 9% international (60 countries represented). Asian 9%, African American 7%, Caucasian 57%, Hispanic 9%, Native American <1%, Pacific Islander 0%, Two or more races 4%, Race unknown 4%.
Retention and Graduation: 93% freshmen return for sophomore year. 83% freshmen graduate within 4 years. 88% freshmen graduate within 6 years. 22% grads go on to further study within 1 year. 5% grads pursue arts and sciences degrees. 2% grads pursue law degrees. 1% grads pursue business degrees. 5% grads pursue medical degrees. **Faculty:** Student/faculty ratio 8:1. 343 full-time faculty, 94% hold PhDs, 15% are members of minority groups, 45% are women. 0% of classes are taught by teaching assistants.

ACADEMICS

Degrees: Bachelor's; Doctoral/Professional; **Master's Classes:** Most classes have 10-19 students. **Most popular majors:** Biology/Biological Sciences, General; Business Administration And Management, General; Organizational Behavior Studies. **Special Study Options:** Cross-registration; Double major; English as a Second Language (ESL); Exchange student program (domestic); Honors program; Independent study; Internships; Student-designed major; Study abroad; Teacher certification program. **Disability Services offered to physically disabled students:** Note-taking services; Reader services; Tape recorders; Tutors. **Career services:** Alumni network; Alumni services; Career assessment; Career/job search classes; Internships; Regional alumni

FACILITIES

Housing: Apartments for single students; Coed dorms; Men's dorms; Special housing for disabled student; Theme housing; Women's dorms 93% of campus accessible to physically diasbled. **Special Academic Facilities/Equipment:** Museum of art and print study center, greenhouse, electron microscope, radionuclide complex, neuroscience research lab, music technology lab, art technology lab, spatial analysis lab, herbarium, high field nuclear magnetic resonance spectrometer, gallery of design from nature, ancient world gallery, real-time stock trading floor, digital scholarship lab, center for pro bono law clinic, Virginia Baptist Historical Society museum, Speech Center, Jepson School of Leadership, Center for Civic Engagement **Computers:** 100% of classrooms, 100% of dorms, 100% of libraries, 100% of dining areas, 100% of student union, 100% of common outdoor areas have wireless network access. Students can register for classes online. Administrative functions (other than registration) can be performed online.

CAMPUS LIFE

Environment: City **Activities:** Campus Ministries; Choral groups; Concert band; Dance; Drama/theater; International Student Organization; Jazz band; Literary magazine; Model UN; Music ensembles; Musical theater; Pep band; Radio station; Student government; Student newspaper; Student-run film society; Symphony orchestra 208 registered organizations, 28 honor societies, 17 religious organizations. 6 fraternities, 8 sororities. **Athletics (Intercollegiate):** *Men:* baseball, basketball, cross-country, football, golf, soccer, tennis, track/field (outdoor), track/field (indoor). *Women:* basketball, cross-country, diving, field hockey, golf, lacrosse, soccer, swimming, tennis, track/field (outdoor), track/field (indoor). **On-Campus Highlights:** Boatwright Memorial Library and 8:15 Coffee Shop, Weinstein Fitness Center, Tyler Haynes Commons, Carole Weinstein International Center, Heilman Dining Center ("D-Hall") **Environmental Initiatives:** The University of Richmond has a committed to being carbon neutral by 2050 with interim goals of 30% below 2008 levels by 2020 and 65% below 2008 levels by 2035. As of our last GHG accounting in 2017, we have reduced our greenhouse gas emissions 24% below 2008 levels. We accomplished this by installing a 205 kW rooftop solar array, transitioning from coal to natural gas for heating, completing dozens of energy efficiency upgrades, and setting a LEED Silver minimum requirement on all new construction.

ADMISSIONS

Freshman Academic Profile: 62% in top 10% of high school class, 92% in top 25% of high school class, 98% in top 50% of high school class. 61% from public high schools. **Test Scores:** SAT Math middle 50% range 640-750. SAT EBRW middle 50% range 630-710. ACT middle 50% range 29-32. Minimum internet-based TOEFL 80. Minimum paper TOEFL 550. **Basis for Candidate Selection:** *Very important factors considered include:* rigor of secondary school record, academic GPA. *Important factors considered include:* class rank, application essay, standardized test scores, recommendation(s), extracurricular activities, talent/ability, character/personal qualities. *Other factors considered include:* first generation, alumni/ae relation, geographical residence, state residency, racial/ethnic status, volunteer work, work experience, level of applicant's interest. **Freshman Admission Requirements:** High school diploma is required and GED is accepted *Academic units required:* 4 English, 3 math, 2 science, 2 science labs, 2 foreign language, 2 history, *Academic units recommended:* 4 English, 4 math, 4 science, 4 science labs, 4 foreign language, 4 history. **Freshman Admission Statistics:** 10,013 applied, 33.0% admitted, 24% enrolled. **Transfer Admission Requirements:** High school transcript, college transcript(s), essay or personal statement, statement of good standing from prior institution(s). Minimum college GPA of 2.0 required. Lowest grade transferable C. **General Admission Information:** Application fee $50. Regular application deadline 1/15. Nonfall registration accepted. Admission may be deferred for a maximum of 1 year.

COSTS AND FINANCIAL AID

Annual tuition $52,610. Room and board $12,250. Average book expense $1,100. **Required Forms and Deadlines:** CSS/Financial Aid PROFILE; FAFSA; Noncustodial PROFILE. **Notification of Awards:** Applicants will be notified of awards on or about 4/1. **Types of Aid:** *Need-based scholarships/grants:* College/university scholarship or grant aid from institutional funds; Federal Pell; Private scholarships; SEOG; State scholarships/grants. *Loans:* Direct PLUS loans; Direct Subsidized Stafford Loans; Direct Unsubsidized Stafford Loans. *Student Employment:* Federal Work-Study Program available. Institutional employment available. **Financial Aid Statistics:** 99% needy freshmen, 98% needy undergrads receive need-based scholarship or grant aid. 27% freshmen, 18% undergrads receive non-need-based scholarship or grant aid. 72% freshmen, 80% undergrads receive need-based self-help aid. 8% freshmen, 8% undergrads receive athletic scholarships. 59% freshmen, 67% undergrads receive any aid. 40% undergrads borrow to pay for school. Average cumulative indebtedness $27,670. **Criteria for awarding aid:** *Non-need-based:* Academics, Art, Athletics, Leadership, Music/drama.

UNIVERSITY OF RIO GRANDE

P O Box 500, Rio Grande, OH 45774
Phone: 740-245-7206 • **Financial Aid Phone:** 740-245-7219
E-mail: admissions@rio.edu • **CEEB Code:** 1663
Fax: 740-245-7260 • **Website:** rio.edu • **ACT Code:** 3324

This private school was founded in 1876. It has a 190 acre campus.

RATINGS

Admissions Selectivity Rating: 78   **Fire Safety Rating:** 87   **Green Rating:** 60*

STUDENTS AND FACULTY

Enrollment: 1,165. **Student Body:** 65% female, 35% male, 4% out-of-state, 2% international. Asian <1%, African American 5%, Caucasian 81%, Hispanic 1%, Native American <1%, Pacific Islander <1%, Two or more races <1%, Race unknown 10%.
Retention and Graduation: 50% freshmen return for sophomore year. 0% grads go on to further study within 1 year. 0% grads pursue arts and sciences degrees. 0% grads pursue law degrees. 0% grads pursue business degrees. 0% grads pursue medical degrees. **Faculty:** Student/faculty ratio 20:1. 77 full-time faculty, 45% hold PhDs, 4% are members of minority groups, 44% are women. 0% of classes are taught by teaching assistants.

ACADEMICS

Degrees: Associate; Bachelor's; Certificate; **Master's Classes:** Most classes have fewer than 10 students. Most lab/discussion sessions have 20-29 students. **Most popular majors:** Elementary Education And Teaching; Business/Office Automation/Technology/Data Entry. **Special Study Options:** Accelerated program; Cooperative education program; Distance learning; Double major; Dual enrollment; English as a Second Language (ESL); Honors program; Independent study; Internships; Liberal arts/career combination; Student-designed major; Study abroad; Teacher certification program. **Disability Services offered to physically disabled students:** Note-taking services;

Reader services; Tape recorders; Tutors. **Career services:** Alumni services; Career assessment; Internships

FACILITIES

Housing: Coed dorms; Men's dorms; Special housing for disabled student; Wellness housing; Women's dorms 75% of campus accessible to physically diasbled. **Special Academic Facilities/Equipment:** Archives of local and college history, art museum, fine woodworking, theater, art annex, Greer Museum for history and art. **Computers:** 75% of classrooms, 100% of dorms, 100% of libraries, 100% of dining areas, 100% of student union, 25% of common outdoor areas have wireless network access. Students can register for classes online. Administrative functions (other than registration) can be performed online.

CAMPUS LIFE

Environment: Rural **Activities:** Campus Ministries; Choral groups; Concert band; Dance; Drama/theater; Jazz band; Literary magazine; Music ensembles; Musical theater; Pep band; Radio station; Student government; Student newspaper; Television station 34 registered organizations, 4 honor societies, 3 religious organizations. 4 fraternities, 5 sororities. **Athletics (Intercollegiate):** *Men:* baseball, basketball, cross-country, soccer, track/field (outdoor), track/field (indoor). *Women:* basketball, cheerleading, cross-country, soccer, softball, track/field (outdoor), track/field (indoor), volleyball. **On-Campus Highlights:** Food Court, Red Zone, Lyne Center, Library, Food Court **Environmental Initiatives:** Recycling program, some solar powered equipment, energy usage reduction program, trayless Tuesdays in the cafeteria

ADMISSIONS

Freshman Academic Profile: Average high school GPA 2.9. 5% in top 10% of high school class, 20% in top 25% of high school class, 49% in top 50% of high school class. 95% from public high schools. **Test Scores:** ACT middle 50% range 17-22. Minimum paper TOEFL 400. **Basis for Candidate Selection:** *Other factors considered include:* class rank, academic GPA, standardized test scores. **Freshman Admission Requirements:** High school diploma is required and GED is accepted *Academic units required:* 4 English, 3 math, 3 science, 1 science labs, 3 social studies, 7 academic electives, *Academic units recommended:* 2 science labs, 2 foreign language, 2 history, 9 academic electives. **Freshman Admission Statistics:** 1,909 applied, 69.4% admitted, 44% enrolled. **Transfer Admission Requirements:** High school transcript, college transcript(s), statement of good standing from prior institution(s). Minimum college GPA of 0 required. Lowest grade transferable D. **General Admission Information:** Application fee $25. Nonfall registration accepted. Admission may be deferred.

COSTS AND FINANCIAL AID

Annual tuition $23,260. Room and board $9,920. Required fees $600. Average book expense $1,200. **Required Forms and Deadlines:** FAFSA; Institution's own financial aid form. **Notification of Awards:** Applicants will be notified of awards on a rolling basis beginning 1/15. **Types of Aid:** *Need-based scholarships/grants:* College/university scholarship or grant aid from institutional funds; Federal Pell; Private scholarships; SEOG; State scholarships/grants. *Loans:* Direct PLUS loans; Direct Subsidized Stafford Loans; Direct Unsubsidized Stafford Loans. *Student Employment:* Federal Work-Study Program available. Institutional employment available. **Financial Aid Statistics:** 69% needy freshmen, 68% needy undergrads receive need-based scholarship or grant aid. 72% freshmen, 71% undergrads receive non-need-based scholarship or grant aid. 59% freshmen, 61% undergrads receive need-based self-help aid. 79% freshmen, 28% undergrads receive athletic scholarships. 78% freshmen, 77% undergrads receive any aid. 74% undergrads borrow to pay for school. Average cumulative indebtedness $32,722. **Criteria for awarding aid:** *Need-based:* Academics *Non-need-based:* Academics, Alumni affiliation, Athletics, Leadership, Music/drama, State/district residency.

UNIVERSITY OF ROCHESTER

Best Colleges

300 Wilson Blvd., Rochester, NY 14627
Phone: 585-275-3221 • **Financial Aid Phone:** 585-275-3226
E-mail: admit@admissions.rochester.edu • **CEEB Code:** 2928
Fax: 585-461-4595 • **Website:** www.rochester.edu • **ACT Code:** 2980

This private school was founded in 1850. It has a 655 acre campus.

RATINGS
Admissions Selectivity Rating: 93   **Fire Safety Rating:** 95   **Green Rating:** 79

STUDENTS AND FACULTY
Enrollment: 5,570. **Student Body:** 48% female, 52% male, 26% international (114 countries represented). Asian 11%, African American 5%, Caucasian 42%, Hispanic 7%, Native American <1%, Pacific Islander <1%, Two or more races 3%, Race unknown 6%.
Retention and Graduation: 97% freshmen return for sophomore year. 34% grads go on to further study within 1 year. **Faculty:** Student/faculty ratio 10:1.

ACADEMICS
Degrees: Bachelor's; Doctoral; Doctoral/Professional; Doctoral/Research; Master's; Post-Bachelor's certificate; Post-Master's certificate **Classes:** Most classes have 10-19 students. Most lab/discussion sessions have 10-19 students. **Most popular majors:** Biology/Biological Sciences, General; Psychology, General; Economics, General. **Special Study Options:** Accelerated program; Cooperative education program; Cross-registration; Double major; Dual enrollment; English as a Second Language (ESL); Honors program; Independent study; Internships; Liberal arts/career combination; Student-designed major; Study abroad; Teacher certification program. Honors programs: Exceptional undergraduates interested in studying medicine, engineering, or education may pursue one of the following Combined-Admission Programs (CAP), which guarantee admission to professional or graduate school upon successful completion of undergraduate study: • Rochester Early Medical Scholars (REMS), an eight-year BA/BS–MD program. Admitted students enter the University with a guarantee of admission to the School of Medicine and Dentistry. • Graduate Engineering at Rochester (GEAR), a five-year BS-MS program. Admitted students enter the University with assurance of admission into one of seven engineering master's programs at the Hajim School of Engineering. • Guaranteed Rochester Accelerated Degree in Education (GRADE), a five-year BA/BS–MS program. Admitted students enter the University with a guarantee of admission to the Margaret Warner Graduate School of Education. Combined degree programs: BA/MA; BA/MD. **Disability Services offered to physically disabled students:** Note-taking services; Reader services; Tape recorders; Tutors. **Career services:** Alumni network; Alumni services; Career assessment; Internships

FACILITIES
Housing: Apartments for married students; Apartments for single students; Coed dorms; Fraternity/sorority housing; Men's dorms; Special housing for disabled student; Special housing for international students; Theme housing; Wellness housing; Women's dorms 90% of campus accessible to physically disabled. **Special Academic Facilities/Equipment:** Anthony Center for Women's Leadership, Arthur Kornberg Medical Research Building, C.E.K. Mees Observatory, Center for Biomedical Ultrasound, Center for Electronic Imaging Systems, Center for Future Health, Center for Visual Science, Clinical and Translational Sciences Building, Eastman Theatre, Frederick Douglas Institute for African and African-American, Institute for Popular Music, Institute of Optics, Laboratory for Laser Energetics, Medical Center, Memorial Art Gallery, Omega Laser Facility, Sign Language Research Center, Skalny Center for Polish and Central European Studies, W. Allen Wallis Institute of Political Economy **Computers:** 100% of classrooms, 30% of dorms, 100% of libraries, 100% of dining areas, 100% of student union, have wireless network access. Students can register for classes online. Administrative functions (other than registration) can be performed online.

CAMPUS LIFE
Environment: City **Activities:** Campus Ministries; Choral groups; Concert band; Dance; Drama/theater; International Student Organization; Jazz band; Literary magazine; Marching band; Model UN; Music ensembles; Musical theater; Opera; Pep band; Radio station; Student government; Student newspaper; Student-run film society; Symphony orchestra; Television station; Yearbook 224 registered organizations, 6 honor societies, 14 religious organizations. 17 fraternities, 13 sororities. **Athletics (Intercollegiate):**

Men: baseball, basketball, cross-country, diving, football, golf, soccer, squash, swimming, tennis, track/field (outdoor), track/field (indoor). *Women:* basketball, crew/rowing, cross-country, diving, field hockey, golf, lacrosse, soccer, softball, swimming, tennis, track/field (outdoor), track/field (indoor), volleyball. **On-Campus Highlights:** Eastman Theater, Memorial Art Gallery, Rush Rhees Library, Interfaith Chapel, Robert B. Goergen Athletic Center **Environmental Initiatives:** For the fourth year in a row, the University of Rochester has been recognized as a Tree Campus USA by the Arbor Day Foundation. The program recognizes college campuses that have made a commitment to effective urban forest management by planting, preserving, and protecting tree resources and that engage staff, students, and the community in conservation goals. To become a Tree Campus, the University must maintain five standards – have a campus tree advisory committee, a campus tree care plan, dedicated annual expenditures, Arbor Day observance, and a service learning project. This past year, Dan Schied, manager of Horticulture and Grounds, gave several "tree tours" around campus, as well as lead two new tree planting ceremonies with students on campus in celebration of Earth Day and Arbor Day.

ADMISSIONS
Freshman Academic Profile: Average high school GPA 3.8. 74% from public high schools. **Test Scores:** SAT Math middle 50% range 650-770. SAT EBRW middle 50% range 600-720. ACT middle 50% range 29-33. Minimum internet-based TOEFL 100. Minimum paper TOEFL 600. **Basis for Candidate Selection:** *Very important factors considered include:* rigor of secondary school record, recommendation(s), character/personal qualities. *Important factors considered include:* academic GPA, application essay, standardized test scores, interview, extracurricular activities, talent/ability. *Other factors considered include:* class rank, first generation, alumni/ae relation, geographical residence, racial/ethnic status, volunteer work, work experience, level of applicant's interest. **Freshman Admission Requirements:** High school diploma is required and GED is accepted **Freshman Admission Statistics:** 17,069 applied, 35.1% admitted, 24% enrolled. **Transfer Admission Requirements:** college transcript(s), essay or personal statement, Lowest grade transferable C. **General Admission Information:** Application fee $50. Regular application deadline 1/5. Nonfall registration accepted. Admission may be deferred.

COSTS AND FINANCIAL AID
Annual tuition $52,867. Room and board $15,860. Required fees $958. Average book expense $1,310. **Required Forms and Deadlines:** CSS/Financial Aid PROFILE; FAFSA; Noncustodial PROFILE; State aid form. **Notification of Awards:** Applicants will be notified of awards on or about 4/1. **Types of Aid:** *Need-based scholarships/grants:* College/university scholarship or grant aid from institutional funds; Federal Pell; Private scholarships; SEOG; State scholarships/grants. *Loans:* Direct PLUS loans; Direct Subsidized Stafford Loans; Direct Unsubsidized Stafford Loans. *Student Employment:* Federal Work-Study Program available. Institutional employment available. **Financial Aid Statistics:** 100% needy freshmen, 99% needy undergrads receive need-based scholarship or grant aid. 15% freshmen, 14% undergrads receive non-need-based scholarship or grant aid. 81% freshmen, 83% undergrads receive need-based self-help aid. 0% freshmen, 0% undergrads receive athletic scholarships. 85% freshmen receive any aid. 58% undergrads borrow to pay for school. Average cumulative indebtedness $30,873. **Criteria for awarding aid:** *Need-based:* Academics, Music/drama *Non-need-based:* Academics, Alumni affiliation, Art, Leadership, Music/drama.

THE UNIVERSITY OF SAINT FRANCIS (IN)

2701 Spring Street, Fort Wayne, IN 46808
Phone: 260-399-8000 • **Financial Aid Phone:** 260-399-8003
E-mail: admis@sf.edu • **CEEB Code:** 1693
Fax: 260-399-8152 • **Website:** www.sf.edu • **ACT Code:** 1238

This private school, affiliated with the Roman Catholic Church, was founded in 1890. It has a 100 acre campus.

RATINGS
Admissions Selectivity Rating: 72   **Fire Safety Rating:** 97   **Green Rating:** 60*

STUDENTS AND FACULTY
Enrollment: 1,840. **Student Body:** 71% female, 29% male, 10% out-of-state, 1% international (7 countries represented). Asian 2%, African American 7%, Caucasian 79%, Hispanic 7%, Native American <1%, Pacific Islander <1%, Two or more races 3%, Race unknown 2%.
Retention and Graduation: 72% freshmen return for sophomore year. 39% freshmen graduate within 4 years. 56% freshmen graduate within 6 years. 13% grads go on to further study within 1 year. 2% grads pursue arts and sciences

degrees. 0.58% grads pursue law degrees. 2% grads pursue business degrees. 1.16% grads pursue medical degrees. **Faculty:** Student/faculty ratio 10:1. 135 full-time faculty, 44% hold PhDs, 5% are members of minority groups, 64% are women. 0% of classes are taught by teaching assistants.

ACADEMICS

Degrees: Associate; Bachelor's; Certificate; Master's; Post-Master's certificate **Classes:** Most classes have 10-19 students. **Most popular majors:** Health And Wellness, General; Registered Nursing/Registered Nurse; Business Administration And Management, General. **Special Study Options:** Cooperative education program; Cross-registration; Distance learning; Double major; Dual enrollment; Honors program; Independent study; Internships; Student-designed major; Teacher certification program. Honors programs: John Duns Scotus Honors Program. **Disability Services offered to physically disabled students:** Note-taking services; Reader services; Tape recorders; Tutors. **Career services:** Alumni services; Career assessment; Internships

FACILITIES

Housing: Apartments for single students; Coed dorms; Special housing for disabled students **Special Academic Facilities/Equipment:** Five art galleries (John P. Weatherhead Gallery, The Goldfish Gallery, The Artist Spotlight Gallery, Lupke Gallery, Rolland Gallery); Robert Goldstine Performing Arts Center; Health Sciences Simulation Lab; North Campus Auditorium; music technology digital recording studio; School of Creative Arts specialized facilities and studios; nature preserve

CAMPUS LIFE

Environment: City **Activities:** Campus Ministries; Choral groups; Dance; Drama/theater; Jazz band; Literary magazine; Marching band; Music ensembles; Musical theater; Pep band; Student government; Student newspaper; Student-run film society. Pope John Paul II Center—Library, Collaboratory, Campus Shoppe, Lounges, Cyber Fresh Cafe, Hutzell Fitness Center, Business Center – Cougar Cafe and Study Spaces, Residence Hall Lounges

ADMISSIONS

Freshman Academic Profile: Average high school GPA 3.4. 14% in top 10% of high school class, 40% in top 25% of high school class, 80% in top 50% of high school class. 84% from public high schools. **Test Scores:** SAT Math middle 50% range 480-560. SAT EBRW middle 50% range 480-580. ACT middle 50% range 19-24. Minimum internet-based TOEFL 80. Minimum paper TOEFL 550. **Basis for Candidate Selection:** *Very important factors considered include:* rigor of secondary school record, academic GPA, standardized test scores. *Important factors considered include:* class rank. *Other factors considered include:* application essay, recommendation(s), interview, extracurricular activities, volunteer work, work experience, level of applicant's interest. **Freshman Admission Requirements:** High school diploma is required and GED is accepted *Academic units required:* 4 English, 3 math, 2 science, 2 social studies, 1 history, 1 academic elective, *Academic units recommended:* 4 English, 4 math, 3 science, 3 social studies, 1 history, 4 academic electives. **Freshman Admission Statistics:** 1,249 applied, 98.7% admitted, 37% enrolled. **General Admission Information:** Nonfall registration accepted. Admission may be deferred for a maximum of one semester.

COSTS AND FINANCIAL AID

Annual tuition $29,360. Room and board $9,840. Required fees $1,070. Average book expense $1,200. **Required Forms and Deadlines:** FAFSA. **Notification of Awards:** Applicants will be notified of awards on a rolling basis beginning 12/1. **Types of Aid:** *Need-based scholarships/grants:* College/university scholarship or grant aid from institutional funds; Federal Pell; Private scholarships; SEOG; State scholarships/grants. *Loans:* Direct PLUS loans; Direct Subsidized Stafford Loans; Direct Unsubsidized Stafford Loans. *Student Employment:* Federal Work-Study Program available. Institutional employment available. **Financial Aid Statistics:** 100% needy freshmen, 99% needy undergrads receive need-based scholarship or grant aid. 14% freshmen, 11% undergrads receive non-need-based scholarship or grant aid. 85% freshmen, 88% undergrads receive need-based self-help aid. 12% freshmen, 9% undergrads receive athletic scholarships. 100% freshmen, 98% undergrads receive any aid. 87% undergrads borrow to pay for school. Average cumulative indebtedness $37,167. **Criteria for awarding aid:** *Need-based:* Academics, Art, Athletics, Music/drama *Non-need-based:* Academics, Art, Athletics, Music/drama, State/district residency.

UNIVERSITY OF SAINT JOSEPH

1678 Asylum Avenue, West Hartford, CT 06117
Phone: 860-231-5216 • **Financial Aid Phone:** 860-231-5223
E-mail: admissions@usj.edu • **CEEB Code:**
Fax: 860-231-5744 • **Website:** www.usj.edu • **ACT Code:**

This private school, affiliated with the Roman Catholic Church, was founded in 1932. It has a 90 acre campus.

RATINGS

Admissions Selectivity Rating: 74   **Fire Safety Rating:** 99   **Green Rating:** 60*

STUDENTS AND FACULTY

Enrollment: 759. **Student Body:** 98% female, 2% male, 5% out-of-state, 1% international. Asian 5%, African American 15%, Caucasian 55%, Hispanic 16%, Native American <1%, Pacific Islander 0%, Two or more races 1%, Race unknown 7%.
Retention and Graduation: 75% freshmen return for sophomore year. 61% freshmen graduate within 4 years. 68% freshmen graduate within 6 years. **Faculty:** Student/faculty ratio 9:1. 134 full-time faculty, 84% hold PhDs, 22% are members of minority groups, 69% are women. 0% of classes are taught by teaching assistants.

ACADEMICS

Degrees: Bachelor's; Certificate; Doctoral/Professional; Master's; Post-Bachelor's certificate; Post-Master's certificate **Classes:** Most classes have 10-19 students. **Most popular majors:** Psychology, General; Social Work; Registered Nursing/Registered Nurse. **Special Study Options:** Accelerated program; Distance learning; Double major; Honors program; Independent study; Internships; Liberal arts/career combination; Student-designed major; Study abroad; Teacher certification program; Weekend college. Combined degree programs: BA/MA. **Career services:** Alumni services; Career assessment; Career/job search classes; Internships; Regional alumni

FACILITIES

Housing: Apartments for single students; Coed dorms; Special housing for disabled student; Theme housing; Women's dorms **Special Academic Facilities/Equipment:** Art Museum 2 Lab Schools **Computers:** Students can register for classes online.

CAMPUS LIFE

Environment: Town **Activities:** Campus Ministries; Choral groups; Dance; Drama/theater; International Student Organization; Literary magazine; Student government. **Athletics (Intercollegiate):** *Women:* basketball, cross-country, diving, lacrosse, soccer, softball, swimming, tennis, volleyball. Hoffman Auditorium, O'Connell Athletic Center, The Art Museum, The Jay's Nest, Lourdes Hall: Renovated home of the Physician Assistant Program

ADMISSIONS

Freshman Academic Profile: Average high school GPA 3.4. 31% in top 10% of high school class, 54% in top 25% of high school class, 84% in top 50% of high school class. **Test Scores:** SAT Math middle 50% range 470-570. SAT EBRW middle 50% range 500-590. ACT middle 50% range 19-22. Minimum paper TOEFL 550. **Basis for Candidate Selection:** *Very important factors considered include:* academic GPA. *Important factors considered include:* rigor of secondary school record, class rank, recommendation(s), character/personal qualities, volunteer work, work experience, level of applicant's interest. *Other factors considered include:* application essay, standardized test scores, interview, extracurricular activities, talent/ability, first generation, alumni/ae relation. **Freshman Admission Requirements:** High school diploma is required and GED is accepted *Academic units required:* **Freshman Admission Statistics:** 649 applied, 90.3% admitted, 23% enrolled. **Transfer Admission Requirements:** High school transcript, college transcript(s), Lowest grade transferable C. **General Admission Information:** Application fee $50. Nonfall registration accepted. Admission may be deferred for a maximum of 2 semesters.

COSTS AND FINANCIAL AID

Annual tuition $37,360. Room and board $10,548. Required fees $1,812. Average book expense $1,000. **Required Forms and Deadlines:** FAFSA. **Notification of Awards:** Applicants will be notified of awards on a rolling basis beginning 11/15. **Types of Aid:** *Need-based scholarships/grants:* College/university scholarship or grant aid from institutional funds; Federal Nursing Scholarships; Federal Pell; Private scholarships; SEOG; State scholarships/grants. *Loans:* Direct PLUS loans; Direct Subsidized Stafford Loans; Direct Unsubsidized Stafford Loans. *Student Employment:* Federal Work-Study Program available. Institutional employment available. **Financial Aid Statistics:** 99% needy freshmen, 96% needy undergrads receive need-based scholarship or grant aid. 7% freshmen, 6% undergrads receive non-need-based scholarship or grant aid. 92% freshmen, 95% undergrads receive need-based self-help aid. 0% freshmen, 0% undergrads receive athletic scholarships. 76% undergrads borrow to pay for school. Average cumulative indebtedness $35,144. **Criteria for awarding aid:** *Non-need-based:* Academics, Leadership, Minority status.

See page 1068.

UNIVERSITY OF SAINT MARY (KS)

4100 South Fourth Street Trafficway, Leavenworth, KS 66048
Phone: 913-682-5151 • **Financial Aid Phone:** 913-758-4303
E-mail: admissions@stmary.edu • **CEEB Code:** 6630
Fax: 913-758-6140 • **Website:** www.stmary.edu • **ACT Code:** 1458

This private school, affiliated with the Roman Catholic Church, was founded in 1923. It has a 240 acre campus.

RATINGS
Admissions Selectivity Rating: 86   **Fire Safety Rating:** 60*   **Green Rating:** 60*

STUDENTS AND FACULTY
Enrollment: 745. **Student Body:** 48% female, 52% male, 50% out-of-state, 1% international (2 countries represented). Asian 2%, African American 12%, Caucasian 55%, Hispanic 14%, Native American 1%, Pacific Islander 1%, Two or more races 1%, Race unknown 14%.
Retention and Graduation: 66% freshmen return for sophomore year. 33% freshmen graduate within 4 years. 44% freshmen graduate within 6 years.
Faculty: Student/faculty ratio 9:1. 64 full-time faculty, 77% hold PhDs, 16% are members of minority groups, 56% are women. 0% of classes are taught by teaching assistants.

ACADEMICS
Degrees: Associate; Bachelor's; Doctoral/Professional; **Master's Classes:** Most classes have 10-19 students. Most lab/discussion sessions have 10-19 students. **Most popular majors:** Biology/Biological Sciences, General; Sport And Fitness Administration/Management; Registered Nursing/Registered Nurse. **Special Study Options:** Accelerated program; Distance learning; Double major; Honors program; Independent study; Internships; Study abroad; Teacher certification program. Honors programs: USM Honors Program. **Disability Services offered to physically disabled students:** Note-taking services; Tutors.

FACILITIES
Housing: Coed dorms **Special Academic Facilities/Equipment:** Lincoln Library Collection, Art Gallery, Craig Scripture Collection, Civil War Collection **Computers:** Students can register for classes online. Administrative functions (other than registration) can be performed online.

CAMPUS LIFE
Environment: Town **Activities:** Campus Ministries; Choral groups; Concert band; Drama/theater; International Student Organization; Student government 22 registered organizations, 2 honor societies, 2 religious organizations. **Athletics (Intercollegiate):** *Men:* baseball, basketball, football, soccer. *Women:* basketball, soccer, softball, volleyball. De Paul Library and the Active Learning Center, Student Life and Campus Ministry, Berkel Stadium, Saint Joseph Dining Hall, Front Circle

ADMISSIONS
Freshman Academic Profile: Average high school GPA 3.2. 1% in top 10% of high school class, 8% in top 25% of high school class, 36% in top 50% of high school class. 80% from public high schools. **Test Scores:** SAT Math middle 50% range 490-580. SAT EBRW middle 50% range 470-575. ACT middle 50% range 19-24. Minimum internet-based TOEFL 80. Minimum paper TOEFL 550. **Basis for Candidate Selection:** *Very important factors considered include:* academic GPA, standardized test scores. *Other factors considered include:* rigor of secondary school record, class rank, recommendation(s). **Freshman Admission Requirements:** High school diploma is required and GED is accepted *Academic units required:* 4 English, 2 math, 2 science, *Academic units recommended:* 4 English, 4 math, 4 science, 2 science labs, 2 foreign language, 2 social studies, 2 history, 4 academic electives. **Freshman Admission Statistics:** 1,001 applied, 49.2% admitted, 29% enrolled. **Transfer Admission Requirements:** college transcript(s), Minimum college GPA of 2.0 required. Lowest grade transferable C. **General Admission Information:** Application fee $25. Nonfall registration accepted.

COSTS AND FINANCIAL AID
Annual tuition $27,880. Room and board $8,140. Required fees $810. Average book expense $2,550. **Required Forms and Deadlines:** FAFSA; State aid form. **Notification of Awards:** Applicants will be notified of awards on a rolling basis beginning 2/15. **Types of Aid:** *Need-based scholarships/grants:* College/university scholarship or grant aid from institutional funds; Federal Pell; Private scholarships; SEOG; State scholarships/grants. *Loans:* Direct PLUS loans; Direct Subsidized Stafford Loans; Direct Unsubsidized Stafford Loans. *Student Employment:* Federal Work-Study Program available. **Financial Aid Statistics:** 78% needy freshmen, 81% needy undergrads receive need-based scholarship or grant aid. 100% freshmen, 91% undergrads receive non-need-based scholarship or grant aid. 81% freshmen, 83% undergrads receive need-based self-help aid. 74% freshmen, 44% undergrads receive athletic scholarships. 84% undergrads borrow to pay for school. Average cumulative indebtedness $28,460. **Criteria for awarding aid:** *Non-need-based:* Academics, Alumni affiliation, Art, Athletics, Leadership, Music/drama, Religious affiliation.

UNIVERSITY OF SAINT THOMAS (MN)

2115 Summit Avenue, Saint Paul, MN 55105
Phone: (651) 962-6150 • **Financial Aid Phone:** 651-962-6550
E-mail: admissions@stthomas.edu • **CEEB Code:** 6110
Fax: (651) 962-6160 • **Website:** www.stthomas.edu • **ACT Code:** 2102

This private school, affiliated with the Roman Catholic Church, was founded in 1885. It has a 78 acre campus.

RATINGS
Admissions Selectivity Rating: 78   **Fire Safety Rating:** 96   **Green Rating:** 85

STUDENTS AND FACULTY
Enrollment: 6,085. **Student Body:** 46% female, 54% male, 19% out-of-state, 3% international (79 countries represented). Asian 4%, African American 3%, Caucasian 81%, Hispanic 5%, Native American <1%, Pacific Islander <1%, Two or more races 3%, Race unknown 1%.
Retention and Graduation: 88% freshmen return for sophomore year. 65% freshmen graduate within 4 years. 77% freshmen graduate within 6 years. 24% grads go on to further study within 1 year. **Faculty:** Student/faculty ratio 14:1. 447 full-time faculty, 91% hold PhDs, 16% are members of minority groups, 41% are women. 0% of classes are taught by teaching assistants.

ACADEMICS
Degrees: Bachelor's; Certificate; Doctoral Other; Doctoral/Professional; Doctoral/Research; Master's; Post-Bachelor's certificate; Post-Master's certificate; Transfer Associate **Classes:** Most classes have 10-19 students. **Special Study Options:** Cross-registration; Distance learning; Double major; English as a Second Language (ESL); Honors program; Independent study; Internships; Student-designed major; Study abroad; Teacher certification program. Honors programs: The Aquinas Scholars Program is the undergraduate honors program. Its purpose is to provide opportunities for motivated and curious students to deepen and enrich their undergraduate education. Combined degree programs: BA/MEng. **Disability Services offered to physically disabled students:** Note-taking services; Reader services; Tape recorders; Tutors. **Career services:** Alumni network; Alumni services; Career assessment; Career/job search classes; Internships; Regional alumni

FACILITIES
Housing: Apartments for single students; Coed dorms; Fraternity/sorority housing; Men's dorms; Special housing for disabled student; Special housing for international students; Theme housing; Wellness housing; Women's dorms 5% of campus accessible to physically diasbled. **Special Academic Facilities/Equipment:** Seminary; a Gallery **Computers:** 100% of classrooms, 100% of dorms, 100% of libraries, 100% of dining areas, 100% of student union, 100% of common outdoor areas have wireless network access. Students can register for classes online. Administrative functions (other than registration) can be performed online.

CAMPUS LIFE
Environment: Metropolis **Activities:** Campus Ministries; Choral groups; Concert band; Dance; Drama/theater; International Student Organization; Jazz band; Literary magazine; Music ensembles; Musical theater; Pep band; Radio station; Student government; Student newspaper; Student-run film society; Television station; Yearbook 114 registered organizations, 7 religious organizations. 1 fraternity. **Athletics (Intercollegiate):** *Men:* baseball, basketball, cross-country, diving, football, golf, ice hockey, soccer, swimming,

tennis, track/field (outdoor), track/field (indoor). *Women:* basketball, cross-country, diving, golf, ice hockey, soccer, softball, swimming, tennis, track/field (outdoor), track/field (indoor), volleyball. **On-Campus Highlights:** Anderson Student Center, Anderson Athletic and Rec Center, Scooters non-alcoholic pub and restaurant, Frey Science and Engineering Center, Chapel of St. Thomas Aquinas **Environmental Initiatives:** The University of St. Thomas recently received a three-year foundation grant of $575,000 to support an integrated university-wide system and culture of sustainability. The grant enabled the university to hire a full time staff member to coordinate campus sustainability initiatives.

ADMISSIONS

Freshman Academic Profile: Average high school GPA 3.6. 24% in top 10% of high school class, 56% in top 25% of high school class, 89% in top 50% of high school class. 75% from public high schools. **Test Scores:** SAT Math middle 50% range 550-670. SAT EBRW middle 50% range 560-660. ACT middle 50% range 24-29. Minimum internet-based TOEFL 80. Minimum paper TOEFL 550. **Basis for Candidate Selection:** *Very important factors considered include:* rigor of secondary school record, academic GPA, standardized test scores. *Important factors considered include:* class rank, application essay. *Other factors considered include:* recommendation(s), extracurricular activities, talent/ability, character/personal qualities, alumni/ae relation, geographical residence, racial/ethnic status, volunteer work. **Freshman Admission Requirements:** High school diploma is required and GED is accepted *Academic units required:* 3 math, *Academic units recommended:* 4 English, 4 math, 2 science, 4 foreign language. **Freshman Admission Statistics:** 6,255 applied, 84.7% admitted, 26% enrolled. **Transfer Admission Requirements:** High school transcript, college transcript(s), essay or personal statement, statement of good standing from prior institution(s). Minimum college GPA of 2.3 required. Lowest grade transferable C-. **General Admission Information:** Nonfall registration accepted. Admission may be deferred for a maximum of 1 year.

COSTS AND FINANCIAL AID

Annual tuition $40,224. Room and board $10,054. Required fees $909. Average book expense $1,000. **Required Forms and Deadlines:** FAFSA. **Notification of Awards:** Applicants will be notified of awards on a rolling basis beginning 1/15. **Types of Aid:** *Need-based scholarships/grants:* College/university scholarship or grant aid from institutional funds; Federal Pell; Private scholarships; SEOG; State scholarships/grants. *Loans:* Direct PLUS loans; Direct Subsidized Stafford Loans; Direct Unsubsidized Stafford Loans. *Student Employment:* Federal Work-Study Program available. Institutional employment available. **Financial Aid Statistics:** 98% needy freshmen, 98% needy undergrads receive need-based scholarship or grant aid. 19% freshmen, 15% undergrads receive non-need-based scholarship or grant aid. 76% freshmen, 80% undergrads receive need-based self-help aid. 0% freshmen, 0% undergrads receive athletic scholarships. 99% freshmen, 94% undergrads receive any aid. 65% undergrads borrow to pay for school. Average cumulative indebtedness $40,403. **Criteria for awarding aid:** *Non-need-based:* Academics, Music/drama.

UNIVERSITY OF SAN DIEGO

5998 Alcala Park, San Diego, CA 92110-2492
Phone: 619-260-4506 • **Financial Aid Phone:** 619-260-4514
E-mail: admissions@sandiego.edu • **CEEB Code:** 4849
Fax: 619-260-6836 • **Website:** www.sandiego.edu • **ACT Code:** 394

This private school, affiliated with the Roman Catholic Church, was founded in 1949. It has a 180 acre campus.

RATINGS

Admissions Selectivity Rating: 89   Fire Safety Rating: 91   Green Rating: 98

STUDENTS AND FACULTY

Enrollment: 5,677. **Student Body:** 54% female, 46% male, 38% out-of-state, 8% international (57 countries represented). Asian 8%, African American 4%, Caucasian 52%, Hispanic 20%, Native American <1%, Pacific Islander <1%, Two or more races 6%, Race unknown 2%.
Retention and Graduation: 90% freshmen return for sophomore year. 66% freshmen graduate within 4 years. 78% freshmen graduate within 6 years. 15% grads go on to further study within 1 year. 36% grads pursue arts and sciences degrees. 12% grads pursue law degrees. 10% grads pursue business degrees.

16% grads pursue medical degrees. **Faculty:** Student/faculty ratio 14:1. 458 full-time faculty, 95% hold PhDs, 24% are members of minority groups, 47% are women. 0% of classes are taught by teaching assistants.

ACADEMICS

Degrees: Bachelor's; Doctoral Other; Doctoral/Professional; Doctoral/Research; Master's; Post-Bachelor's certificate **Classes:** Most classes have 10-19 students. Most lab/discussion sessions have 20-29 students. **Most popular majors:** Communication And Media Studies; Business Administration And Management, General; Finance, General. **Special Study Options:** Double major; English as a Second Language (ESL); Honors program; Independent study; Internships; Liberal arts/career combination; Study abroad; Teacher certification program. Honors programs: Phi Beta Kappa, Honors Program. **Disability Services offered to physically disabled students:** Note-taking services; Reader services; Tape recorders. **Career services:** Alumni network; Alumni services; Career assessment; Career/job search classes; Internships; Regional alumni

FACILITIES

Housing: Apartments for single students; Coed dorms; Men's dorms; Special housing for disabled student; Theme housing; Women's dorms 85% of campus accessible to physically diasbled. **Special Academic Facilities/Equipment:** Art gallery, peace and justice institute, child development center, language labs. **Computers:** 100% of classrooms, 100% of dorms, 100% of libraries, 100% of dining areas, 100% of student union, 100% of common outdoor areas have wireless network access. Students can register for classes online. Administrative functions (other than registration) can be performed online.

CAMPUS LIFE

Environment: Metropolis **Activities:** Campus Ministries; Choral groups; Concert band; Dance; Drama/theater; International Student Organization; Jazz band; Marching band; Model UN; Music ensembles; Musical theater; Opera; Pep band; Radio station; Student government; Student newspaper; Television station 129 registered organizations, 20 honor societies, 2 religious organizations. 5 fraternities, 6 sororities. **Athletics (Intercollegiate):** *Men:* baseball, basketball, crew/rowing, cross-country, football, golf, soccer, tennis. *Women:* basketball, cheerleading, crew/rowing, cross-country, diving, soccer, softball, swimming, tennis, track/field (outdoor), volleyball. **On-Campus Highlights:** Aromas Coffee House, Donald P. Shiley Center for Science and Technology, Jenny Craig Pavilion (Sporting/concert venue), Joan B. Kroc Institute for Peace and Justice, Student Life Pavilion **Environmental Initiatives:** The University of San Diego's E-waste center helps reduce the greenhouse gases, and landfill waste generated by the community as well as recycling E-waste produced by students, staff and the institution. The E-waste Center collects unwanted electronics from the community and recycles them. The usable components in these electronics are separated and sold, and the rest is processed and sent for recycling. This reduces landfill waste, hazardous waste, and greenhouse gas emissions of the community. As the ownership of these material is transferred to the E-waste center, the emissions reductions once they are recycled safely is 'owned' by USD. The E-waste center is managed as a non-profit and employs students, who can use the opportunity to earn and income while learning about recycling electronic waste.

ADMISSIONS

Freshman Academic Profile: Average high school GPA 3.9. 40% in top 10% of high school class, 75% in top 25% of high school class, 96% in top 50% of high school class. 55% from public high schools. **Test Scores:** SAT Math middle 50% range 590-680. SAT EBRW middle 50% range 590-670. ACT middle 50% range 26-30. Minimum internet-based TOEFL 80. Minimum paper TOEFL 550. **Basis for Candidate Selection:** *Very important factors considered include:* rigor of secondary school record, academic GPA, standardized test scores. *Important factors considered include:* class rank, application essay, recommendation(s), extracurricular activities, talent/ability, character/personal qualities, alumni/ae relation, religious affiliation/commitment, volunteer work. *Other factors considered include:* interview, first generation, geographical residence, racial/ethnic status, work experience, level of applicant's interest. **Freshman Admission Requirements:** High school diploma is required and GED is accepted *Academic units required:* 4 English, 3 math, 3 science, 2 science labs, 3 foreign language, 2 social studies, *Academic units recommended:* 4 English, 4 math, 4 science, 3 science labs, 4 foreign language, 3 social studies. **Freshman Admission Statistics:** 14,739 applied, 49.8% admitted, 16% enrolled. **Transfer Admission Requirements:** High school transcript, college transcript(s), essay or personal statement, Minimum college GPA of 3.0 required. Lowest grade transferable C. **General Admission Information:** Application fee $55. Regular application deadline 12/15. Nonfall registration accepted. Admission may be deferred for a maximum of one year.

COSTS AND FINANCIAL AID

Annual tuition $48,750. Room and board $12,980. Required fees $608. Average book expense $1,920. **Required Forms and Deadlines:** FAFSA. **Notification of Awards:** Applicants will be notified of awards on a rolling basis beginning

3/1. **Types of Aid:** *Need-based scholarships/grants:* College/university scholarship or grant aid from institutional funds; Federal Nursing Scholarships; Federal Pell; Private scholarships; SEOG; State scholarships/grants. *Loans:* Direct PLUS loans; Direct Subsidized Stafford Loans; Direct Unsubsidized Stafford Loans. *Student Employment:* Federal Work-Study Program available. Institutional employment available. **Financial Aid Statistics:** 96% needy freshmen, 95% needy undergrads receive need-based scholarship or grant aid. 71% freshmen, 51% undergrads receive non-need-based scholarship or grant aid. 70% freshmen, 77% undergrads receive need-based self-help aid. 2% freshmen, 2% undergrads receive athletic scholarships. 84% freshmen, 73% undergrads receive any aid. 53% undergrads borrow to pay for school. Average cumulative indebtedness $29,646. **Criteria for awarding aid:** *Need-based:* Academics, Leadership, Religious affiliation *Non-need-based:* Academics, Athletics, Leadership, Music/drama, Religious affiliation.

UNIVERSITY OF SAN FRANCISCO

2130 Fulton Street, San Francisco, CA 94117
Phone: 415-422-6563 • **Financial Aid Phone:** 415-422-2020
E-mail: admission@usfca.edu • **CEEB Code:** 1325
Fax: 415-422-2217 • **Website:** www.usfca.edu • **ACT Code:** 466

This private school, affiliated with the Roman Catholic Church, was founded in 1855. It has a 55 acre campus.

RATINGS
Admissions Selectivity Rating: 80   **Fire Safety Rating:** 60*   **Green Rating:** 75

STUDENTS AND FACULTY
Enrollment: 6,664. **Student Body:** 62% female, 38% male, 23% out-of-state, 18% international (63 countries represented). Asian 22%, African American 3%, Caucasian 26%, Hispanic 21%, Native American <1%, Pacific Islander 1%, Two or more races 7%, Race unknown 7%.
Retention and Graduation: 86% freshmen return for sophomore year.
Faculty: 0% of classes are taught by teaching assistants.

ACADEMICS
Degrees: Bachelor's; Doctoral/Professional; Doctoral/Research; Master's; Post-Bachelor's certificate; Post-Master's certificate **Classes:** Most classes have 10-19 students. Most lab/discussion sessions have fewer than 10 students. **Most popular majors:** Psychology, General; Nursing/Registered Nurse (Rn, Asn, Bsn, Msn); Business/Commerce, General. **Special Study Options:** Accelerated program; Cooperative education program; Cross-registration; Distance learning; Double major; English as a Second Language (ESL); Exchange student program (domestic); External degree program; Honors program; Independent study; Internships; Liberal arts/career combination; Study abroad; Teacher certification program. Honors programs: The Honors Program in the Humanities offered through in the College of Arts and Sciences, but open to students in all majors, provides high-achieving students the intellectual challenge and opportunity to develop analytical and critical thinking skills through an integrated program of seminars. The Louise M. Davies Forum at the University of San Francisco is a challenging intellectual program that focuses on "The Search for Values in Contemporary America." The Davies Forum examines the turbulent state of American society in the last half of the 20th century and the present and fosters an analysis of the country's current struggle to define its purpose and direction. The St. Ignatius Institute is a great books program in the Jesuit, Catholic intellectual tradition that offers an alternative to the USF Core Curriculum. The curriculum focuses on foundational texts in the Western intellectual tradition through reading classic thinkers and writers such as Homer, Dante, Austen, and Nietzsche. Courses, such as Ancient Greek and Roman Literature, Medieval Thought, Modern Philosophy, and Music and Art are taught in seminar-sized classes. The Martín-Baró Scholars Program invites selected freshmen to participate in an opportunity to live, learn, and build community in the multicultural city of San Francisco. This two-semester program explores issues of social justice and diversity through a blend of academic study and real-world application. Students selected for the Martín-Baró Scholars Program will attend classes together and live as a community in a designated residence hall to form a comprehensive and engaging learning environment. The above programs are across majors and disciplines. There are honors programs in each of the colleges. Refer to URL: http://www.usfca.edu/admission/undergraduate/honors/

Combined degree programs: BA/JD; BA/MA; BA/MEng. **Disability Services offered to physically disabled students:** Note-taking services; Reader services; Tape recorders; Tutors. **Career services:** Career assessment; Career/job search classes; Internships

FACILITIES
Housing: Apartments for single students; Coed dorms; Special housing for disabled student; Special housing for international students; Theme housing; Wellness housing; Women's dorms 100% of campus accessible to physically diasbled. **Special Academic Facilities/Equipment:** Rare Book Room, Ricci Institute for Chinese-Western Cultural History **Computers:** 25% of classrooms, 25% of dorms, 25% of dining areas, 75% of student union, 25% of common outdoor areas have wireless network access. Students can register for classes online. Administrative functions (other than registration) can be performed online.

CAMPUS LIFE
Environment: Metropolis **Activities:** Campus Ministries; Choral groups; Dance; Drama/theater; International Student Organization; Jazz band; Literary magazine; Marching band; Music ensembles; Musical theater; Pep band; Radio station; Student government; Student newspaper; Television station; Yearbook 90 registered organizations, 14 honor societies, 4 fraternities, 4 sororities. **Athletics (Intercollegiate):** *Men:* baseball, basketball, cross-country, golf, riflery, soccer, tennis, track/field (outdoor). *Women:* basketball, cross-country, golf, riflery, soccer, tennis, track/field (outdoor), volleyball. **On-Campus Highlights:** Koret Health and Recreation Center, War Memorial Gym, St. Ignatius Church, Harney Science Center, Lone Mountain Campus **Environmental Initiatives:** Sustainability. Placed 5th in National competition in Recyclemania. Currently, USF's co-generation plant produces about half of lower campus' peak energy needs. Located in the basement of Gleeson Library, the plant converts natural gas into electricity. Although the conversion of natural gas to energy does produce some emissions, natural gas is considered the cleanest of the fossil fuels. The plant gets its co-generation designation because it also captures heat lost during the conversion process and uses that to provide some of the heat lower campus uses. The plant provides about 38 percent of lower campus' heating needs. Additionally, the university uses thermal panels on top of Phelan, Gillson, and Hayes-Healy halls. The panels differ from solar panels in that they heat water directly rather than producing electricity, providing some of the hot water needed in those halls.

ADMISSIONS
Freshman Academic Profile: Average high school GPA 3.5. 31% from public high schools. **Test Scores:** SAT Math middle 50% range 520-630. SAT EBRW middle 50% range 510-620. ACT middle 50% range 23-28. Minimum internet-based TOEFL 65. **Basis for Candidate Selection:** *Very important factors considered include:* rigor of secondary school record, academic GPA, application essay, standardized test scores. *Important factors considered include:* class rank, recommendation(s), extracurricular activities, character/personal qualities, volunteer work. *Other factors considered include:* interview, talent/ability, first generation, alumni/ae relation, racial/ethnic status, work experience. **Freshman Admission Requirements:** High school diploma is required and GED is accepted *Academic units required:* 4 English, 3 math, 2 science, 2 foreign language, 3 social studies, 6 academic electives, and 2 units from above areas or other academic areas. **Freshman Admission Statistics:** 15,441 applied, 70.6% admitted, 15% enrolled. **Transfer Admission Requirements:** college transcript(s), essay or personal statement, Minimum college GPA of 2.5 required. Lowest grade transferable C. **General Admission Information:** Application fee $65. Regular application deadline 1/15. Nonfall registration accepted. Admission may be deferred for a maximum of 1 semester.

COSTS AND FINANCIAL AID
Annual tuition $45,760. Room and board $14,330. Required fees $490. Average book expense $1,600. **Required Forms and Deadlines:** CSS/Financial Aid PROFILE; FAFSA. **Notification of Awards:** Applicants will be notified of awards on a rolling basis beginning 4/1. **Types of Aid:** *Need-based scholarships/grants:* College/university scholarship or grant aid from institutional funds; Federal Nursing Scholarships; Federal Pell; Private scholarships; SEOG; State scholarships/grants. *Loans:* Direct PLUS loans; Direct Subsidized Stafford Loans; Direct Unsubsidized Stafford Loans. *Student Employment:* Federal Work-Study Program available. Institutional employment available. **Financial Aid Statistics:** 76% needy freshmen, 84% needy undergrads receive need-based scholarship or grant aid. 76% freshmen, 62% undergrads receive non-need-based scholarship or grant aid. 98% freshmen, 98% undergrads receive need-based self-help aid. 1% freshmen, 2% undergrads receive athletic scholarships. 87% freshmen, 81% undergrads receive any aid. 55% undergrads borrow to pay for school. Average cumulative indebtedness $34,114. **Criteria for awarding aid:** *Need-based:* Academics, Alumni affiliation, Athletics, Minority status *Non-need-based:* Academics, Athletics, Minority status.

See page 1070.

UNIVERSITY OF SCIENCE & ARTS OF OKLAHOMA

1727 West Alabama, Chickasha, OK 73018
Phone: 405-574-1357 • **Financial Aid Phone:** 405-574-1240
E-mail: usao-admissions@usao.edu • **CEEB Code:** 6544
Fax: 405-574-1220 • **Website:** www.usao.edu • **ACT Code:** 3418

This public school was founded in 1908. It has a 75 acre campus.

RATINGS
Admissions Selectivity Rating: 82   **Fire Safety Rating:** 96   **Green Rating:** 60*

STUDENTS AND FACULTY
Enrollment: 847. **Student Body:** 66% female, 34% male, 14% out-of-state, 8% international (22 countries represented). Asian 1%, African American 5%, Caucasian 63%, Hispanic 7%, Native American 14%, Pacific Islander 0%, Two or more races 0%, Race unknown 2%.
Retention and Graduation: 78% freshmen return for sophomore year.
Faculty: Student/faculty ratio 12:1. 54 full-time faculty, 87% hold PhDs, 11% are members of minority groups, 52% are women. 0% of classes are taught by teaching assistants.

ACADEMICS
Degrees: Bachelor's **Classes:** Most classes have 10-19 students. Most lab/discussion sessions have 20-29 students. **Most popular majors:** Elementary Education And Teaching; Psychology, General; Business Administration And Management, General. **Special Study Options:** Accelerated program; Double major; Independent study; Internships; Liberal arts/career combination; Student-designed major; Study abroad; Teacher certification program.
Disability Services offered to physically disabled students: Note-taking services; Tutors. **Career services:** Career assessment; Career/job search classes; Internships

FACILITIES
Housing: Apartments for single students; Coed dorms; Special housing for disabled students 100% of campus accessible to physically diasbled. **Special Academic Facilities/Equipment:** Language labs, speech and hearing clinic, multiple computer labs, herbarium **Computers:** 100% of classrooms, 85% of dorms, 100% of libraries, 100% of dining areas, 100% of student union, 100% of common outdoor areas have wireless network access.

CAMPUS LIFE
Environment: Village **Activities:** Campus Ministries; Choral groups; Concert band; Dance; Drama/theater; International Student Organization; Jazz band; Literary magazine; Music ensembles; Musical theater; Pep band; Student government; Student newspaper 24 registered organizations, 7 honor societies, 4 religious organizations. 1 fraternity, 1 sorority. **Athletics (Intercollegiate):** *Men:* baseball, basketball, cheerleading, soccer. *Women:* basketball, cheerleading, soccer, softball. **On-Campus Highlights:** Lawson Court, Nash Library, Student Center, Bill Smith Ballpark, The Grill

ADMISSIONS
Freshman Academic Profile: Average high school GPA 3.4. 25% in top 10% of high school class, 47% in top 25% of high school class, 78% in top 50% of high school class. 90% from public high schools. **Test Scores:** SAT Math middle 50% range 410-510. SAT EBRW middle 50% range 390-490. ACT middle 50% range 19-24. Minimum internet-based TOEFL 61. Minimum paper TOEFL 500. **Basis for Candidate Selection:** *Very important factors considered include:* class rank, academic GPA, standardized test scores. *Other factors considered include:* recommendation(s), talent/ability. **Freshman Admission Requirements:** High school diploma is required and GED is accepted *Academic units required:* 4 English, 3 math, 3 science, 3 science labs, 2 social studies, 1 history, 2 academic electives, *Academic units recommended:* 4 English, 4 math, 4 science, 4 science labs, 2 foreign language, 2 social studies, 1 history, 2 academic electives, 1 computer science, 2 visual/performing arts.
Freshman Admission Statistics: 706 applied, 66.0% admitted, 48% enrolled.
Transfer Admission Requirements: college transcript(s), Minimum college GPA of 2.0 required. Lowest grade transferable D. **General Admission Information:** Application fee $40. Regular application deadline 9/2. Nonfall registration accepted. Admission may be deferred for a maximum of 1 year.

COSTS AND FINANCIAL AID
Required Forms and Deadlines: FAFSA. **Notification of Awards:** Applicants will be notified of awards on a rolling basis beginning 3/1. **Types of Aid:** *Need-based scholarships/grants:* College/university scholarship or grant aid from institutional funds; Federal Pell; Private scholarships; SEOG; State scholarships/grants. *Loans:* Direct PLUS loans; Direct Subsidized Stafford Loans; Direct Unsubsidized Stafford Loans. *Student Employment:* Federal Work-Study Program available. Institutional employment available. **Financial Aid Statistics:** 93% needy freshmen, 92% needy undergrads receive need-based scholarship or grant aid. 13% freshmen, 11% undergrads receive non-need-based scholarship or grant aid. 63% freshmen, 69% undergrads receive need-based self-help aid. 12% freshmen, 11% undergrads receive athletic scholarships. 93% freshmen, 89% undergrads receive any aid. 52% undergrads borrow to pay for school. Average cumulative indebtedness $24,460. **Criteria for awarding aid:** *Need-based:* Academics, Art, Athletics, Leadership, Music/drama *Non-need-based:* Academics, Art, Athletics, Leadership, Music/drama, State/district residency.

UNIVERSITY OF THE SCIENCES IN PHILADELPHIA

600 South 43rd Street, Philadelphia, PA 19104-4495
Phone: 215-596-8810 • **Financial Aid Phone:** (215)596-8894
E-mail: admit@usciences.edu • **CEEB Code:** 2663
Fax: 215-596-8821 • **ACT Code:** 3671

This private school was founded in 1821. It has a 35 acre campus.

RATINGS
Admissions Selectivity Rating: 87   **Fire Safety Rating:** 80   **Green Rating:** 61

STUDENTS AND FACULTY
Enrollment: 2,427. **Student Body:** 61% female, 39% male, 59% out-of-state, 2% international (20 countries represented). Asian 36%, African American 5%, Caucasian 46%, Hispanic 2%, Native American <1%, Pacific Islander <1%, Two or more races 2%, Race unknown 7%.
Retention and Graduation: 88% freshmen return for sophomore year.
Faculty: Student/faculty ratio 10:1. 191 full-time faculty, 82% hold PhDs, 20% are members of minority groups, 52% are women. 0% of classes are taught by teaching assistants.

ACADEMICS
Degrees: Bachelor's; Certificate; Doctoral; Doctoral/Professional; Doctoral/Research; **Master's Classes:** Most classes have 20-29 students. Most lab/discussion sessions have 20-29 students. **Most popular majors:** Biology/Biological Sciences, General; Pharmacy; Physical Therapy/Therapist.
Special Study Options: Cross-registration; Double major; Honors program; Independent study; Internships; Study abroad. Honors programs: The Honors Program at University of the Sciences offers exceptional students the opportunity for specialized, intensive learning experiences both inside and outside the classroom. As an honors student, you will take part in special honors classes and recitations. The workload for these classes is not harder than others at University of the Sciences, but different. For example you may do smaller, more advanced experiments in a lab course. You may tour historic sites for a history class, or meet with a visiting author in your writing class. You will work in smaller classes and have more independent and group projects. **Disability Services offered to physically disabled students:** Note-taking services; Reader services; Tape recorders; Tutors. **Career services:** Alumni services; Career assessment; Career/job search classes; Internships

FACILITIES
Housing: Apartments for single students; Coed dorms; Fraternity/sorority housing; Wellness housing 90% of campus accessible to physically diasbled. **Special Academic Facilities/Equipment:** Pharmacy museum, electron microscope. **Computers:** 80% of classrooms, 100% of dorms, 100% of libraries, 100% of dining areas, 40% of common outdoor areas have wireless network access. Students can register for classes online. Administrative functions (other than registration) can be performed online.

CAMPUS LIFE
Environment: Metropolis **Activities:** Choral groups; Concert band; Dance; Drama/theater; Literary magazine; Musical theater; Student government; Student newspaper; Yearbook 66 registered organizations, 6 honor societies, 6 religious organizations. 2 fraternities, 2 sororities. **Athletics (Intercollegiate):** *Men:* baseball, basketball, cross-country, golf, riflery, tennis. *Women:* basketball, cross-country, golf, riflery, softball, tennis, volleyball. **On-Campus Highlights:** McNeil Science and Technology Center, Athletic Recreation Center, Wilson Hall, Marvin Sampson Museum, Griffith Hall **Environmental Initiatives:** All "On the Go" containers are fully recyclable.

ADMISSIONS
Freshman Academic Profile: Average high school GPA 3.6. 45% in top 10% of high school class, 80% in top 25% of high school class, 98% in top 50% of

high school class. **Test Scores:** SAT Math middle 50% range 550-650. SAT EBRW middle 50% range 520-590. ACT middle 50% range 22-27. Minimum paper TOEFL 550. **Basis for Candidate Selection:** *Very important factors considered include:* rigor of secondary school record, class rank, academic GPA, standardized test scores. *Other factors considered include:* application essay, recommendation(s), interview, extracurricular activities, character/ personal qualities, alumni/ae relation, volunteer work, work experience, level of applicant's interest. **Freshman Admission Requirements:** High school diploma is required and GED is accepted *Academic units required:* 4 English, 3 math, 3 science, 2 science labs, 1 social studies, 1 history, 4 academic electives, *Academic units recommended:* 4 English, 4 math, 3 science, 3 science labs, 1 social studies, 1 history, 4 academic electives. **Freshman Admission Statistics:** 4,099 applied, 61.3% admitted, 18% enrolled. **Transfer Admission Requirements:** college transcript(s), standardized test scores, Minimum college GPA of 3.0 required. Lowest grade transferable C. **General Admission Information:** Application fee $45. Nonfall registration accepted. Admission may be deferred for a maximum of 1 year.

COSTS AND FINANCIAL AID

Annual tuition $34,336. Required fees $1,760. Average book expense $1,050. **Required Forms and Deadlines:** FAFSA. **Notification of Awards:** Applicants will be notified of awards on a rolling basis beginning 2/15. **Types of Aid:** *Need-based scholarships/grants:* College/university scholarship or grant aid from institutional funds; Federal Pell; Private scholarships; SEOG; State scholarships/grants. *Loans:* Direct PLUS loans; Direct Subsidized Stafford Loans; Direct Unsubsidized Stafford Loans. *Student Employment:* Federal Work-Study Program available. Institutional employment available. **Financial Aid Statistics:** 81% needy freshmen, 82% needy undergrads receive need-based scholarship or grant aid. 97% freshmen, 88% undergrads receive non-need-based scholarship or grant aid. 77% freshmen, 84% undergrads receive need-based self-help aid. 1% freshmen, 7% undergrads receive athletic scholarships. 100% freshmen, 89% undergrads receive any aid. **Criteria for awarding aid:** *Need-based:* Academics, Athletics *Non-need-based:* Academics, Athletics.

UNIVERSITY OF SCRANTON

800 Linden Street, Scranton, PA 18510
Phone: 570-941-7540 • **Financial Aid Phone:** 570-941-7701
E-mail: admissions@scranton.edu • **CEEB Code:** 2929
Fax: 570-941-5928 • **Website:** www.scranton.edu • **ACT Code:** 3736

This private school, affiliated with the Roman Catholic-Jesuit Church, was founded in 1888. It has a 58 acre campus.

RATINGS

Admissions Selectivity Rating: 84   **Fire Safety Rating:** 94   **Green Rating:** 81

STUDENTS AND FACULTY

Enrollment: 3,695. **Student Body:** 58% female, 42% male, 61% out-of-state, 1% international (40 countries represented). Asian 2%, African American 2%, Caucasian 80%, Hispanic 9%, Native American <1%, Pacific Islander <1%, Two or more races 2%, Race unknown 2%.
Retention and Graduation: 87% freshmen return for sophomore year. 72% freshmen graduate within 4 years. 77% freshmen graduate within 6 years. 38% grads go on to further study within 1 year. 72% grads pursue arts and sciences degrees. 4% grads pursue law degrees. 10% grads pursue business degrees. 10% grads pursue medical degrees. **Faculty:** Student/faculty ratio 12:1. 281 full-time faculty, 89% hold PhDs, 9% are members of minority groups, 41% are women. 2% of classes are taught by teaching assistants.

ACADEMICS

Degrees: Associate; Bachelor's; Certificate; Doctoral/Professional; Doctoral/ Research; Master's; Post-Bachelor's certificate; Post-Master's certificate
Classes: Most classes have 10-19 students. Most lab/discussion sessions have 10-19 students. **Most popular majors:** Biology/Biological Sciences, General; Kinesiology And Exercise Science; Registered Nursing/Registered Nurse. **Special Study Options:** Accelerated program; Cross-registration; Distance learning; Double major; Dual enrollment; Exchange student program (domestic); Honors program; Independent study; Internships; Student-designed major; Study abroad; Teacher certification program. Honors programs: Special Jesuit Liberal Arts Honors Program (SJLA) provides an

alternative approach to satisfying general education requirements by pairing selected students with designated faculty in a curriculum that is deeply rooted in philosophy and dedicated to serving the common good. Honors Program students take seminars together and work one-on-one with professors in tutorials. The program culminates with a senior creative or research project. Business Leadership Honors Program is a highly selective program in which students explore concepts of leadership through special seminars and courses in management, ethics, strategy and analysis. Combined degree programs: BA/ MA. **Disability Services offered to physically disabled students:** Note-taking services; Reader services; Tape recorders; Tutors. **Career services:** Alumni network; Alumni services; Career assessment; Career/job search classes; Internships; Regional alumni

FACILITIES

Housing: Apartments for single students; Coed dorms; Men's dorms; Special housing for disabled student; Theme housing; Women's dorms 100% of campus accessible to physically diasbled. **Special Academic Facilities/Equipment:** Hope Horn Gallery in Hyland Hall; Scranton Heritage Room, Weinberg Memorial Library; The Estate; Houlihan-McLean Center **Computers:** 40% of classrooms, 100% of dorms, 100% of libraries, 100% of dining areas, 100% of student union, 90% of common outdoor areas have wireless network access. Students can register for classes online. Administrative functions (other than registration) can be performed online.

CAMPUS LIFE

Environment: City **Activities:** Campus Ministries; Choral groups; Concert band; Dance; Drama/theater; International Student Organization; Jazz band; Literary magazine; Music ensembles; Musical theater; Radio station; Student government; Student newspaper; Symphony orchestra; Television station; Yearbook 50 registered organizations, 32 honor societies, 14 religious organizations. **Athletics (Intercollegiate):** *Men:* baseball, basketball, cross-country, golf, ice hockey, lacrosse, soccer, swimming, tennis, wrestling. *Women:* basketball, cross-country, field hockey, lacrosse, soccer, softball, swimming, tennis, volleyball. **On-Campus Highlights:** Loyola Science Center, state-of-the-art facility for the natural sciences, DeNaples Center—the hub and heart of our social life on campus, The Harry and Jeanette Weinberg Memorial Library, Brennan Hall—home of the Kania School of Management, Leahy Hall—new, $47.5 million home for the health sciences **Environmental Initiatives:** 1. We have incorporated energy efficient technology in our new construction and renovations over the past 20 years. We had one LEED Silver building, one LEED Gold building, and then recently opened 117,421 GSF Leahy Hall which is LEED silver. All of our campus is using green cleaning supplies and practices.

ADMISSIONS

Freshman Academic Profile: Average high school GPA 3.5. 32% in top 10% of high school class, 63% in top 25% of high school class, 89% in top 50% of high school class. **Test Scores:** SAT Math middle 50% range 530-640. SAT EBRW middle 50% range 550-640. ACT middle 50% range 23-28. Minimum internet-based TOEFL 80. **Basis for Candidate Selection:** *Very important factors considered include:* rigor of secondary school record, class rank, academic GPA, standardized test scores. *Important factors considered include:* extracurricular activities. *Other factors considered include:* application essay, recommendation(s), interview, talent/ability, character/personal qualities, alumni/ae relation, volunteer work, work experience, level of applicant's interest. **Freshman Admission Requirements:** High school diploma is required and GED is accepted *Academic units required:* 4 English, 3 math, 1 science, 2 foreign language, 2 history, and 4 units from above areas or other academic areas. *Academic units recommended:* 4 English, 4 math, 2 science, 2 foreign language, 3 history, 4 units from above areas or other academic areas. **Freshman Admission Statistics:** 10,002 applied, 74.8% admitted, 12% enrolled. **Transfer Admission Requirements:** High school transcript, college transcript(s), Minimum college GPA of 2.75 required. Lowest grade transferable C. **General Admission Information:** Priority deadline 11/15. Regular application deadline 3/1. Nonfall registration accepted. Admission may be deferred for a maximum of 1 year.

COSTS AND FINANCIAL AID

Required Forms and Deadlines: FAFSA. **Notification of Awards:** Applicants will be notified of awards on a rolling basis beginning 1/15. **Types of Aid:** *Need-based scholarships/grants:* College/university scholarship or grant aid from institutional funds; Federal Pell; Private scholarships; SEOG; State scholarships/grants: *Loans:* Direct PLUS loans; Direct Subsidized Stafford Loans; Direct Unsubsidized Stafford Loans. *Student Employment:* Federal Work-Study Program available. Institutional employment available. **Financial Aid Statistics:** 96% needy freshmen, 96% needy undergrads receive need-based scholarship or grant aid. 11% freshmen, 8% undergrads receive non-need-based scholarship or grant aid. 81% freshmen, 85% undergrads receive need-based self-help aid. 0% freshmen, 0% undergrads receive athletic scholarships. 96% freshmen, 96% undergrads receive any aid. 73% undergrads borrow to pay for school. Average cumulative indebtedness $42,423. **Criteria**

for awarding aid: *Need-based:* Minority status *Non-need-based:* Academics, Minority status.

UNIVERSITY OF SOUTH ALABAMA

307 N. University Boulevard, Mobile, AL 36688-0002
Phone: 251-460-6141 • **Financial Aid Phone:** (251) 460-6231
E-mail: recruitment@southalabama.edu • **CEEB Code:** 1880
Fax: 251-460-7876 • **Website:** www.southalabama.edu • **ACT Code:** 59

This public school was founded in 1963. It has a 1225 acre campus.

RATINGS

Admissions Selectivity Rating: 77   **Fire Safety Rating:** 65   **Green Rating:** 65

STUDENTS AND FACULTY

Enrollment: 10,712. **Student Body:** 56% female, 44% male, 18% out-of-state, 6% international (69 countries represented). Asian 3%, African American 23%, Caucasian 59%, Hispanic 3%, Native American 1%, Pacific Islander <1%, Two or more races 3%, Race unknown 2%.
Retention and Graduation: 78% freshmen return for sophomore year. 19% freshmen graduate within 4 years. 40% freshmen graduate within 6 years.
Faculty: Student/faculty ratio 18:1. 601 full-time faculty, 78% hold PhDs, 16% are members of minority groups, 51% are women.

ACADEMICS

Degrees: Bachelor's; Certificate; Doctoral/Professional; Doctoral/Research; Master's; Post-Bachelor's certificate; Post-Master's certificate **Classes:** Most classes have fewer than 10 students. **Most popular majors:** Elementary Education And Teaching; Health/Medical Preparatory Programs, Other; Registered Nursing/Registered Nurse. **Special Study Options:** Accelerated program; Cooperative education program; Cross-registration; Distance learning; Double major; Dual enrollment; English as a Second Language (ESL); Exchange student program (domestic); Honors program; Independent study; Internships; Student-designed major; Study abroad; Teacher certification program; Weekend college. Honors programs: Honors College. **Disability Services offered to physically disabled students:** Note-taking services; Reader services; Tape recorders. **Career services:** Alumni services; Career assessment; Career/job search classes; Internships

FACILITIES

Housing: Apartments for single students; Coed dorms; Fraternity/sorority housing; Special housing for disabled student; Theme housing; Wellness housing **Special Academic Facilities/Equipment:** Museum/gallery complex, three hospitals, center for clinical education in health programs, engineering labs. **Computers:** Students can register for classes online. Administrative functions (other than registration) can be performed online. Undergraduates are required to own a computer.

CAMPUS LIFE

Environment: City **Activities:** Campus Ministries; Choral groups; Concert band; Dance; Drama/theater; International Student Organization; Jazz band; Literary magazine; Marching band; Music ensembles; Musical theater; Opera; Pep band; Radio station; Student government; Student newspaper; Student-run film society; Symphony orchestra; Television station 185 registered organizations, 2 honor societies, 1 religious organization. 8 fraternities, 8 sororities. **Athletics (Intercollegiate):** *Men:* baseball, basketball, cross-country, football, golf, tennis, track/field (outdoor). *Women:* basketball, cross-country, golf, soccer, softball, tennis, track/field (outdoor), volleyball. **On-Campus Highlights:** Mitchell Center (arena), Stanky Field, John W. Laidlaw Performing Arts Center, Intramural Field Complex, Moulton Bell Tower

ADMISSIONS

Freshman Academic Profile: Average high school GPA 3.6. 84% from public high schools. **Test Scores:** SAT Math middle 50% range 500-590. SAT EBRW middle 50% range 510-610. ACT middle 50% range 20-26. Minimum internet-based TOEFL 61. Minimum paper TOEFL 500. **Basis for Candidate Selection:** *Very important factors considered include:* academic GPA, standardized test scores. **Freshman Admission Requirements:** High school diploma is required and GED is accepted *Academic units required:* 4 English, 3 math, 3 science, 2 science labs, 3 social studies, 3 academic electives. **Freshman Admission Statistics:** 6,035 applied, 81.4% admitted, 38% enrolled. **Transfer Admission Requirements:** college transcript(s), Minimum college GPA of 2.0 required. Lowest grade transferable D. **General Admission Information:** Application fee $45. Regular application deadline 7/15. Nonfall registration accepted. Admission may be deferred for a maximum of 2 years.

COSTS AND FINANCIAL AID

Annual in-state tuition $7,490. Annual out-of-state tuition $18,780. Room and board $7,490. Average book expense $1,300. **Required Forms and Deadlines:** FAFSA. **Types of Aid:** *Need-based scholarships/grants:* College/university scholarship or grant aid from institutional funds; Federal Pell; Private scholarships; SEOG; State scholarships/grants. *Loans:* Direct PLUS loans; Direct Subsidized Stafford Loans; Direct Unsubsidized Stafford Loans. *Student Employment:* Federal Work-Study Program available. Institutional employment available. **Financial Aid Statistics:** 91% needy freshmen, 84% needy undergrads receive need-based scholarship or grant aid. 92% freshmen, 84% undergrads receive non-need-based scholarship or grant aid. 93% freshmen, 93% undergrads receive need-based self-help aid. 3% freshmen, 3% undergrads receive athletic scholarships. 83% freshmen, 61% undergrads receive any aid. **Criteria for awarding aid:** *Non-need-based:* Academics, Alumni affiliation, Art, Athletics, Job skills, Leadership, Minority status, Music/drama, State/district residency.

UNIVERSITY OF SOUTH CAROLINA—AIKEN

471 University Parkway, Aiken, SC 29801
Phone: 803-641-3366 • **Financial Aid Phone:** 803-641-3476
E-mail: admit@usca.edu • **CEEB Code:** 5840
Fax: 803-641-3727 • **Website:** www.usca.edu • **ACT Code:** 3879

This public school was founded in 1961. It has a 453 acre campus.

RATINGS

Admissions Selectivity Rating: 83   **Fire Safety Rating:** 95   **Green Rating:** 76

STUDENTS AND FACULTY

Enrollment: 3,131. **Student Body:** 64% female, 36% male, 11% out-of-state, 4% international (30 countries represented). Asian 1%, African American 27%, Caucasian 58%, Hispanic 4%, Native American 1%, Pacific Islander <1%, Two or more races 4%, Race unknown 1%.
Retention and Graduation: 72% freshmen return for sophomore year.
Faculty: Student/faculty ratio 15:1. 152 full-time faculty, 79% hold PhDs, 16% are members of minority groups, 48% are women. 0% of classes are taught by teaching assistants.

ACADEMICS

Degrees: Bachelor's; Master's **Classes:** Most classes have 10-19 students. Most lab/discussion sessions have 10-19 students. **Most popular majors:** Kinesiology And Exercise Science; Registered Nursing/Registered Nurse; Business Administration And Management, General. **Special Study Options:** Cooperative education program; Distance learning; Double major; Dual enrollment; English as a Second Language (ESL); Honors program; Independent study; Internships; Student-designed major; Study abroad; Teacher certification program. Honors programs: The USCA Honors Program is designed to increase the educational opportunities for the academically well qualified and highly motivated student. Designed in accordance with the principles of the National Collegiate Honors Council, the USC Aiken Honors Program provides an enriched academic experience, both in and out of the classroom, for outstanding students committed to reaching their highest potential as scholars and creative thinkers. For details on our Honors Program or the other high quality academic opportunities awaiting you at USC Aiken, please call on our Office of Admissions toll free at 888.WOW.USCA or locally at 803.641.3366. The Honors Director may be reached at 803.641.3291. **Disability Services offered to physically disabled students:** Note-taking services; Reader services; Tape recorders. **Career services:** Alumni network; Alumni services; Career assessment; Career/job search classes; Internships; Regional alumni

FACILITIES

Housing: Apartments for single students; Coed dorms; Special housing for disabled student; Theme housing 100% of campus accessible to physically diasbled. **Special Academic Facilities/Equipment:** Ruth Patrick Science Education Center Etherredge Center (Fine Arts Center) Wellness Center Planetarium Natatorium **Computers:** 100% of classrooms, 100% of dorms, 100% of libraries, 100% of dining areas, 100% of student union, 100% of common outdoor areas have wireless network access. Students can register for classes online. Administrative functions (other than registration) can be performed online.

CAMPUS LIFE

Environment: Town **Activities:** Campus Ministries; Choral groups; Concert band; Dance; Drama/theater; International Student Organization; Jazz band;

Literary magazine; Music ensembles; Musical theater; Pep band; Student government; Student newspaper; Yearbook 89 registered organizations, 12 honor societies, 7 religious organizations. 5 fraternities, 7 sororities. **Athletics (Intercollegiate):** *Men:* baseball, basketball, cheerleading, golf, soccer, tennis. *Women:* basketball, cheerleading, cross-country, soccer, softball, tennis, volleyball. **On-Campus Highlights:** DuPont Planetarium in the Ruth Patrick Science Education Center, The Etherredge Center for Visual and Performing Arts, The Wellness Center and Natatorium, Student Activities Center, Pacer Commons Student Housing **Environmental Initiatives:** Obtain State Energy Department stimulus funding approval to 'jump start' significant energy conservation actions. The energy conservation projects will reduce each building's energy use (kWh) by 18%—reducing the carbon footprint from purchased electricity by at least 20%.

ADMISSIONS

Freshman Academic Profile: Average high school GPA 3.8. 15% in top 10% of high school class, 40% in top 25% of high school class, 80% in top 50% of high school class. 92% from public high schools. **Test Scores:** SAT Math middle 50% range 420-530. SAT EBRW middle 50% range 430-530. ACT middle 50% range 18-23. Minimum internet-based TOEFL 80. Minimum paper TOEFL 550. **Basis for Candidate Selection:** *Very important factors considered include:* rigor of secondary school record, class rank, academic GPA, standardized test scores. **Freshman Admission Requirements:** High school diploma is required and GED is accepted *Academic units required:* 4 English, 4 math, 3 science, 3 science labs, 2 foreign language, 2 social studies, 1 history, 4 academic electives, *Academic units recommended:* 1 computer science, 1 visual/performing arts. **Freshman Admission Statistics:** 2,177 applied, 60.5% admitted, 47% enrolled. **Transfer Admission Requirements:** college transcript(s), statement of good standing from prior institution(s). Minimum college GPA of 2.0 required. Lowest grade transferable C. **General Admission Information:** Application fee $45. Priority deadline 6/1. Regular application deadline 8/1. Nonfall registration accepted. Admission may be deferred for a maximum of 1 year.

COSTS AND FINANCIAL AID

Annual in-state tuition $7,466. Annual out-of-state tuition $19,788. Room and board $7,466. Required fees $314. Average book expense $1,656. **Required Forms and Deadlines:** FAFSA. **Notification of Awards:** Applicants will be notified of awards on a rolling basis beginning 4/20. **Types of Aid:** *Need-based scholarships/grants:* College/university scholarship or grant aid from institutional funds; Federal Pell; Private scholarships; SEOG; State scholarships/grants. *Loans:* Direct PLUS loans; Direct Subsidized Stafford Loans; Direct Unsubsidized Stafford Loans. *Student Employment:* Federal Work-Study Program available. Institutional employment available. **Financial Aid Statistics:** 95% needy freshmen, 83% needy undergrads receive need-based scholarship or grant aid. 10% freshmen, 9% undergrads receive non-need-based scholarship or grant aid. 70% freshmen, 78% undergrads receive need-based self-help aid. 4% freshmen, 4% undergrads receive athletic scholarships. 72% freshmen, 69% undergrads receive any aid. 75% undergrads borrow to pay for school. Average cumulative indebtedness $31,289. **Criteria for awarding aid:** *Need-based:* Leadership *Non-need-based:* Academics, Alumni affiliation, Art, Athletics, Leadership, Minority status, Music/drama, State/district residency.

UNIVERSITY OF SOUTH CAROLINA—BEAUFORT

1 University Blvd, Bluffton, SC 29909
Phone: 843-208-8000 • **Financial Aid Phone:** 843-521-3104
E-mail: admissions@uscb.edu • **CEEB Code:** 5845
Fax: 843-208-8290 • **Website:** www.uscb.edu • **ACT Code:** 3835

This public school was founded in 1959. It has a 213 acre campus.

RATINGS

Admissions Selectivity Rating: 69 **Fire Safety Rating:** 60* **Green Rating:** 60*

STUDENTS AND FACULTY

Enrollment: 1,773. **Student Body:** 63% female, 37% male, 22% out-of-state, (14 countries represented).
Retention and Graduation: 54% freshmen return for sophomore year.
Faculty: Student/faculty ratio 18:1. 59 full-time faculty, 76% hold PhDs, 15% are members of minority groups, 47% are women.

ACADEMICS

Degrees: Associate; Bachelor's **Classes:** Most classes have 10-19 students. Most lab/discussion sessions have 10-19 students. **Most popular majors:** Registered Nursing, Nursing Administration, Nursing Research And Clinical

Nursing; Business Administration And Management, General; Hospitality Administration/Management, General. **Special Study Options:** Cooperative education program; Cross-registration; Distance learning; Dual enrollment; Independent study; Internships; Study abroad; Teacher certification program; Weekend college. **Disability Services offered to physically disabled students:** Note-taking services; Reader services; Tape recorders; Tutors. **Career services:** Career/job search classes; Internships

FACILITIES

Housing: Apartments for single students; Coed dorms; Special housing for disabled students **Special Academic Facilities/Equipment:** Science and Technology building Center for the Arts **Computers:** Students can register for classes online. Administrative functions (other than registration) can be performed online.

CAMPUS LIFE

Environment: Village **Activities:** Choral groups; Drama/theater; Literary magazine; Music ensembles; Musical theater; Student government; Student newspaper 11 registered organizations. **Athletics (Intercollegiate):** *Men:* baseball, cross-country, golf, track/field (outdoor). **On-Campus Highlights:** Sandbar Cafe, Campus Center Gym, Library, Center for the Arts

ADMISSIONS

Test Scores: Minimum paper TOEFL 550. **Basis for Candidate Selection:** *Very important factors considered include:* rigor of secondary school record, academic GPA, standardized test scores. *Important factors considered include:* class rank. **Freshman Admission Requirements:** High school diploma is required and GED is accepted *Academic units required:* 4 English, 4 math, 3 science, 3 science labs, 2 foreign language, 2 social studies, 1 history, 1 academic elective, 1 visual/performing arts, and 1 unit from above areas or other academic areas. *Academic units recommended:* 1 computer science. **Freshman Admission Statistics:** 1,434 applied, 74.6% admitted, 40% enrolled. **Transfer Admission Requirements:** college transcript(s), Minimum college GPA of 2.0 required. Lowest grade transferable C-. **General Admission Information:** Application fee $40. Nonfall registration accepted.

COSTS AND FINANCIAL AID

Required Forms and Deadlines: FAFSA. **Notification of Awards:** Applicants will be notified of awards on a rolling basis beginning 5/31. **Types of Aid:** *Need-based scholarships/grants:* College/university scholarship or grant aid from institutional funds; Federal Pell; Private scholarships; SEOG; State scholarships/grants. *Loans: Student Employment:* Federal Work-Study Program available. **Financial Aid Statistics:** 35% freshmen, 65% undergrads receive any aid. **Criteria for awarding aid:** *Need-based:* Academics *Non-need-based:* Academics, State/district residency.

UNIVERSITY OF SOUTH CAROLINA—COLUMBIA

Best Colleges

Office of Undergraduate Admissions, Columbia, SC 29208
Phone: 803-777-7700 • **Financial Aid Phone:** (803) 777-8134
E-mail: admissions-ugrad@sc.edu • **CEEB Code:** 5818
Fax: 803-777-0101 • **Website:** www.sc.edu • **ACT Code:** 3880

This public school was founded in 1801. It has a 444 acre campus.

RATINGS

Admissions Selectivity Rating: 86 **Fire Safety Rating:** 96 **Green Rating:** 85

STUDENTS AND FACULTY

Enrollment: 25,950. **Student Body:** 54% female, 46% male, 40% out-of-state, 3% international (115 countries represented). Asian 3%, African American 10%, Caucasian 75%, Hispanic 5%, Native American <1%, Pacific Islander <1%, Two or more races 4%, Race unknown 1%.
Retention and Graduation: 89% freshmen return for sophomore year. 59% freshmen graduate within 4 years. 75% freshmen graduate within 6 years.
Faculty: Student/faculty ratio 17:1. 1,527 full-time faculty, 89% hold PhDs, 21% are members of minority groups, 44% are women.

ACADEMICS

Degrees: Associate; Bachelor's; Doctoral; Doctoral/Professional; Doctoral/Research; Master's; Post-Bachelor's certificate; Post-Master's certificate **Classes:** Most classes have 20-29 students. Most lab/discussion sessions have 20-29 students. **Most popular majors:** Experimental Psychology; Criminal Justice/

Law Enforcement Administration; Registered Nursing, Nursing Administration, Nursing Research And Clinical Nursing. **Special Study Options:** Accelerated program; Cooperative education program; Cross-registration; Distance learning; Double major; Dual enrollment; English as a Second Language (ESL); Exchange student program (domestic); External degree program; Honors program; Independent study; Internships; Student-designed major; Study abroad; Teacher certification program; Weekend college. Honors programs: The Honors College is a small college of about 1,000 students, all of whom excel in academics. What makes the Honors College different is its ability to weave engaging, exciting course offerings into any undergraduate major. You choose your major and set up your course schedule just like any other student at the University. But your choices include classes especially for Honors College students over 100 courses each semester. **Disability Services offered to physically disabled students:** Note-taking services; Reader services; Tape recorders. **Career services:** Alumni services; Career assessment; Career/job search classes; Internships

FACILITIES

Housing: Apartments for married students; Apartments for single students; Coed dorms; Fraternity/sorority housing; Men's dorms; Special housing for disabled student; Special housing for international students; Wellness housing; Women's dorms 85% of campus accessible to physically disabled. **Special Academic Facilities/Equipment:** Art gallery, movie theater, McKissick Museum, South Caroliniana Library, Melton Observatory, Gibbes Planetarium, Melton Observatory, Filtration Research Engineering Demonstration Unit, Belser Arboretum, A.C. Moore Gardens. **Computers:** Students can register for classes online. Administrative functions (other than registration) can be performed online.

CAMPUS LIFE

Environment: City **Activities:** Campus Ministries; Choral groups; Concert band; Dance; Drama/theater; International Student Organization; Jazz band; Literary magazine; Marching band; Music ensembles; Musical theater; Opera; Pep band; Radio station; Student government; Student newspaper; Student-run film society; Symphony orchestra; Television station 300 registered organizations, 25 honor societies, 32 religious organizations. 20 fraternities, 14 sororities. **Athletics (Intercollegiate):** *Men:* baseball, basketball, diving, football, golf, racquetball, soccer, softball, swimming, tennis, track/field (outdoor). *Women:* basketball, cross-country, diving, equestrian sports, golf, racquetball, soccer, softball, swimming, tennis, track/field (outdoor), volleyball. **On-Campus Highlights:** Strom Thurmond Wellness & Fitness Center, Russell House University Union, Greek Village, Williams-Brice Stadium—Home of the 2012 Outback Bowl Champs, Historic Horseshoe **Environmental Initiatives:** Sustainable Carolina represents all the sustainability efforts on campus and utilizes over 40 student interns to implement the campus sustainability plan. The program is based on leadership development and allows students to apply sustainability practices on campus. Last year students put in nearly 20,000 hours working, learning and training on sustainability issues.

ADMISSIONS

Freshman Academic Profile: Average high school GPA 4.1. 28% in top 10% of high school class, 61% in top 25% of high school class, 91% in top 50% of high school class. **Test Scores:** SAT Math middle 50% range 580-670. SAT EBRW middle 50% range 590-660. ACT middle 50% range 25-30. Minimum internet-based TOEFL 77. Minimum paper TOEFL 550. **Basis for Candidate Selection:** *Very important factors considered include:* rigor of secondary school record, academic GPA, standardized test scores. *Other factors considered include:* class rank, application essay, recommendation(s), extracurricular activities, talent/ability, character/personal qualities, first generation, state residency, racial/ethnic status, volunteer work, work experience. **Freshman Admission Requirements:** High school diploma is required and GED is accepted *Academic units required:* 4 English, 4 math, 3 science, 3 science labs, 2 foreign language, 2 social studies, 1 history, 1 academic elective, 1 visual/performing arts, and 1 unit from above areas or other academic areas. **Freshman Admission Statistics:** 26,019 applied, 72.3% admitted, 31% enrolled. **Transfer Admission Requirements:** college transcript(s), Minimum college GPA of 2.25 required. Lowest grade transferable C-. **General Admission Information:** Application fee $65. Priority deadline 12/1. Regular application deadline 12/1. Nonfall registration accepted. Admission may be deferred for a maximum of 1 year.

COSTS AND FINANCIAL AID

Annual in-state tuition $10,008. Annual out-of-state tuition $31,962. Room and board $10,008. Required fees $400. Average book expense $1,023. **Required Forms and Deadlines:** FAFSA. **Notification of Awards:** Applicants will be notified of awards on a rolling basis beginning 4/1. **Types of Aid:** *Need-based scholarships/grants:* College/university scholarship or grant aid from institutional funds; Federal Nursing Scholarships; Federal Pell; Private scholarships; SEOG; State scholarships/grants; United Negro College Fund. *Loans:* Direct PLUS loans; Direct Subsidized Stafford Loans; Direct Unsubsidized Stafford Loans. *Student Employment:* Federal Work-

Study Program available. Institutional employment available. **Financial Aid Statistics:** 42% needy freshmen, 55% needy undergrads receive need-based scholarship or grant aid. 90% freshmen, 63% undergrads receive non-need-based scholarship or grant aid. 71% freshmen, 80% undergrads receive need-based self-help aid. 2% freshmen, 2% undergrads receive athletic scholarships. 96% freshmen, 87% undergrads receive any aid. Average cumulative indebtedness $28,518. **Criteria for awarding aid:** *Non-need-based:* Academics, Alumni affiliation, Art, Athletics, Job skills, Leadership, Minority status, Music/drama, Religious affiliation, State/district residency.

THE UNIVERSITY OF SOUTH DAKOTA

414 East Clark St, Vermillion, SD 57069
Phone: 605-677-5434 • **Financial Aid Phone:** 605-677-5446
E-mail: admissions@usd.edu • **CEEB Code:** 6881
Fax: 605-677-6323 • **Website:** www.usd.edu • **ACT Code:** 3928

This public school was founded in 1862. It has a 273 acre campus.

RATINGS

Admissions Selectivity Rating: 79   **Fire Safety Rating:** 98   **Green Rating:** 64

STUDENTS AND FACULTY

Enrollment: 6,166. **Student Body:** 62% female, 38% male, 35% out-of-state, 2% international (46 countries represented). Asian 1%, African American 3%, Caucasian 84%, Hispanic 4%, Native American 2%, Pacific Islander <1%, Two or more races 3%, Race unknown <1%.
Retention and Graduation: 72% freshmen return for sophomore year. 39% freshmen graduate within 4 years. 57% freshmen graduate within 6 years. 48% grads go on to further study within 1 year. 26% grads pursue arts and sciences degrees. 9% grads pursue law degrees. 9% grads pursue business degrees. 9% grads pursue medical degrees. **Faculty:** Student/faculty ratio 17:1. 432 full-time faculty, 64% hold PhDs, 17% are members of minority groups, 48% are women. 8% of classes are taught by teaching assistants.

ACADEMICS

Degrees: Associate; Bachelor's; Certificate; Doctoral/Professional; Doctoral/Research; Master's; Post-Bachelor's certificate **Classes:** Most classes have 10-19 students. Most lab/discussion sessions have 10-19 students. **Most popular majors:** Education, General; Psychology, General; Business/Commerce, General. **Special Study Options:** Accelerated program; Cross-registration; Distance learning; Double major; Dual enrollment; English as a Second Language (ESL); Exchange student program (domestic); External degree program; Honors program; Independent study; Internships; Liberal arts/career combination; Student-designed major; Study abroad; Teacher certification program. Honors programs: University Honors Program. The program has its own core curriculum that replaces the University's general education requirements. Thesis Scholars Program, Alumni Student Scholars Program, Law Honors Scholars Program Combined degree programs: BA/MA. **Disability Services offered to physically disabled students:** Note-taking services; Reader services; Tape recorders; Tutors. **Career services:** Alumni network; Alumni services; Career assessment; Career/job search classes; Internships

FACILITIES

Housing: Apartments for married students; Apartments for single students; Coed dorms; Fraternity/sorority housing; Special housing for disabled student; Theme housing 96% of campus accessible to physically disabled. **Special Academic Facilities/Equipment:** W.H. Over Museum, The National Music Museum, Oscar Howe Art Gallery, Center for Instructional Design and Delivery, Institute of American Indian Studies, Native American Cultural Center, Disaster Mental Health Institute, Neuharth Center for Excellence in Journalism, Missouri Rive Institute. **Computers:** 60% of classrooms, 100% of libraries, 100% of dining areas, 100% of student union, have wireless network access. Students can register for classes online. Administrative functions (other than registration) can be performed online.

CAMPUS LIFE

Environment: Village **Activities:** Campus Ministries; Choral groups; Concert band; Dance; Drama/theater; International Student Organization; Jazz band; Marching band; Music ensembles; Musical theater; Opera; Pep band; Radio station; Student government; Student newspaper; Student-run film society;

Symphony orchestra; Television station 120 registered organizations, 6 honor societies, 6 religious organizations. 8 fraternities, 3 sororities. **Athletics (Intercollegiate):** *Men:* basketball, cross-country, diving, football, golf, swimming, track/field (outdoor), track/field (indoor). *Women:* basketball, cross-country, diving, golf, soccer, softball, swimming, tennis, track/field (outdoor), track/field (indoor), volleyball. **On-Campus Highlights:** Al Neuharth Media Center, The National Music Museum, The Dakota Dome, Belbas Student Service Center, Muenster University Center **Environmental Initiatives:** Creation of the Sustainability Task Force for evaluation, monitoring and policy creation.

ADMISSIONS

Freshman Academic Profile: Average high school GPA 3.3. 14% in top 10% of high school class, 36% in top 25% of high school class, 69% in top 50% of high school class. 75% from public high schools. **Test Scores:** SAT Math middle 50% range 500-630. SAT EBRW middle 50% range 510-590. ACT middle 50% range 20-25. Minimum internet-based TOEFL 81. Minimum paper TOEFL 550. **Basis for Candidate Selection:** *Very important factors considered include:* rigor of secondary school record, class rank, academic GPA, standardized test scores. *Other factors considered include:* application essay, recommendation(s), extracurricular activities, talent/ability, character/personal qualities, geographical residence, state residency, racial/ethnic status, volunteer work, work experience. **Freshman Admission Requirements:** High school diploma is required and GED is accepted *Academic units required:* 4 English, 3 math, 3 science labs, 3 social studies, *Academic units recommended:* 4 math, 4 science, 2 foreign language, 1 unit from above areas or other academic areas. **Freshman Admission Statistics:** 3,865 applied, 86.9% admitted, 40% enrolled. **Transfer Admission Requirements:** High school transcript, college transcript(s), Minimum college GPA of 2.0 required. Lowest grade transferable D. **General Admission Information:** Application fee $20. Nonfall registration accepted.

COSTS AND FINANCIAL AID

Annual in-state tuition $8,030. Annual out-of-state tuition $10,438. Room and board $4,113. Required fees $8,030. Average book expense $1,200. **Required Forms and Deadlines:** FAFSA. **Types of Aid:** *Need-based scholarships/grants:* College/university scholarship or grant aid from institutional funds; Federal Pell; Private scholarships; SEOG; State scholarships/grants; United Negro College Fund. *Loans:* Direct PLUS loans; Direct Subsidized Stafford Loans; Direct Unsubsidized Stafford Loans. *Student Employment:* Federal Work-Study Program available. Institutional employment available. **Financial Aid Statistics:** 47% needy freshmen receive need-based scholarship or grant aid. 94% freshmen, 81% undergrads receive any aid. **Criteria for awarding aid:** *Non-need-based:* Academics, Art, Athletics, Leadership, Minority status, Music/drama.

UNIVERSITY OF SOUTH FLORIDA

4202 East Fowler Avenue, Tampa, FL 33620-9951
Phone: 813-974-3350 • **Financial Aid Phone:** 813-974-4700
E-mail: admissions@usf.edu • **CEEB Code:** 5828
Fax: 813-974-9689 • **Website:** www.usf.edu • **ACT Code:** 761

This public school was founded in 1956. It has a 1562 acre campus.

RATINGS

Admissions Selectivity Rating: 89   **Fire Safety Rating:** 96   **Green Rating:** 94

STUDENTS AND FACULTY

Enrollment: 30,918. **Student Body:** 54% female, 46% male, 6% out-of-state, 6% international (145 countries represented). Asian 7%, African American 10%, Caucasian 48%, Hispanic 21%, Native American <1%, Pacific Islander <1%, Two or more races 4%, Race unknown 3%.
Retention and Graduation: 17% grads go on to further study within 1 year. 10% grads pursue business degrees. **Faculty:** Student/faculty ratio 22:1. 1,278 full-time faculty, 81% hold PhDs, 28% are members of minority groups, 45% are women. 24% of classes are taught by teaching assistants.

ACADEMICS

Degrees: Associate; Bachelor's; Doctoral/Professional; Doctoral/Research; **Master's Classes:** Most classes have 20-29 students. Most lab/discussion sessions have 20-29 students. **Most popular majors:** Biomedical Sciences,

General; Psychology, General; Health Services/Allied Health/Health Sciences, General. **Special Study Options:** Accelerated program; Distance learning; Double major; Dual enrollment; English as a Second Language (ESL); Exchange student program (domestic); Honors program; Independent study; Internships; Study abroad; Teacher certification program. Honors programs: Honors College: http://honors.usf.edu/ Combined degree programs: BA/MA; BA/MD; BA/MEng. **Disability Services offered to physically disabled students:** Note-taking services; Reader services; Tape recorders. **Career services:** Alumni services; Career assessment; Career/job search classes; Internships

FACILITIES

Housing: Apartments for married students; Apartments for single students; Fraternity/sorority housing; Special housing for disabled students 100% of campus accessible to physically disabled. **Special Academic Facilities/Equipment:** Art museum and galleries, contemporary art museum, graphic studio, anthropology museum, fitness center, par course. **Computers:** 80% of classrooms, 35% of dorms, 100% of libraries, 50% of dining areas, 100% of student union, 50% of common outdoor areas have wireless network access. Students can register for classes online. Administrative functions (other than registration) can be performed online.

CAMPUS LIFE

Environment: Metropolis **Activities:** Campus Ministries; Choral groups; Concert band; Dance; Drama/theater; International Student Organization; Jazz band; Literary magazine; Marching band; Model UN; Music ensembles; Musical theater; Opera; Pep band; Radio station; Student government; Student newspaper; Student-run film society; Symphony orchestra 507 registered organizations, 33 honor societies, 42 religious organizations. 16 fraternities, 22 sororities. **Athletics (Intercollegiate):** *Men:* baseball, basketball, cheerleading, cross-country, football, golf, sailing, soccer, tennis, track/field (outdoor), track/field (indoor). *Women:* basketball, cheerleading, cross-country, golf, sailing, soccer, softball, tennis, track/field (outdoor), track/field (indoor), volleyball. **On-Campus Highlights:** Marshall Center, The Tampa Campus Library, Contemporary Art Museum, Botanical Gardens, Sun Dome **Environmental Initiatives:** USF's 2008 Going Green Tampa Bay sustainability EXPO which drew over 3,000 visitors

ADMISSIONS

Freshman Academic Profile: Average high school GPA 3.9. 37% in top 10% of high school class, 71% in top 25% of high school class, 93% in top 50% of high school class. **Test Scores:** SAT Math middle 50% range 570-660. SAT EBRW middle 50% range 580-650. ACT middle 50% range 24-29. Minimum internet-based TOEFL 79. Minimum paper TOEFL 550. **Basis for Candidate Selection:** *Very important factors considered include:* academic GPA, standardized test scores. *Other factors considered include:* rigor of secondary school record, class rank, talent/ability, first generation, geographical residence. **Freshman Admission Requirements:** High school diploma is required and GED is accepted *Academic units required:* 4 English, 4 math, 3 science, 2 science labs, 2 foreign language, 3 social studies, 2 academic electives. **Freshman Admission Statistics:** 36,861 applied, 43.6% admitted, 26% enrolled. **Transfer Admission Requirements:** college transcript(s), statement of good standing from prior institution(s). Minimum college GPA of 2.3 required. Lowest grade transferable D. **General Admission Information:** Application fee $30. Priority deadline 11/1. Regular application deadline 3/15. Nonfall registration accepted. Admission may be deferred for a maximum of 3 terms.

COSTS AND FINANCIAL AID

Annual in-state tuition $9,700. Annual out-of-state tuition $17,250. Room and board $9,700. Required fees $74. Average book expense $1,200. **Required Forms and Deadlines:** FAFSA. **Notification of Awards:** Applicants will be notified of awards on a rolling basis beginning 3/1. **Types of Aid:** *Need-based scholarships/grants:* College/university scholarship or grant aid from institutional funds; Federal Pell; Private scholarships; SEOG; State scholarships/grants. *Loans:* Direct PLUS loans; Direct Subsidized Stafford Loans; Direct Unsubsidized Stafford Loans. *Student Employment:* Federal Work-Study Program available. Institutional employment available. **Financial Aid Statistics:** 88% needy freshmen, 84% needy undergrads receive need-based scholarship or grant aid. 7% freshmen, 4% undergrads receive non-need-based scholarship or grant aid. 56% freshmen, 66% undergrads receive need-based self-help aid. 1% freshmen, 1% undergrads receive athletic scholarships. 70% freshmen, 66% undergrads receive any aid. 57% undergrads borrow to pay for school. Average cumulative indebtedness $22,337. **Criteria for awarding aid:** *Need-based:* Academics *Non-need-based:* Academics, Art, Athletics, Leadership, Music/drama, State/district residency.

UNIVERSITY OF SOUTH FLORIDA— ST. PETERSBURG

140 Seventh St. South, St. Petersburg, FL 33701-5016
Phone: 727-873-4142 • **Financial Aid Phone:** (727) 873-4128
E-mail: admissions@usfsp.edu
Fax: 813-873-4525 • **Website:** http://www.usfsp.edu • **ACT Code:** 761

This public school was founded in 1965. It has a 48 acre campus.

RATINGS
Admissions Selectivity Rating: 89 **Fire Safety Rating:** 99 **Green Rating:** 94

STUDENTS AND FACULTY
Enrollment: 4,162. **Student Body:** 63% female, 37% male, 4% out-of-state, 1% international. Asian 4%, African American 8%, Caucasian 63%, Hispanic 17%, Native American <1%, Pacific Islander <1%, Two or more races 4%, Race unknown 3%.
Retention and Graduation: 19% grads go on to further study within 1 year.
Faculty: Student/faculty ratio 16:1. 158 full-time faculty, 80% hold PhDs, 23% are members of minority groups, 49% are women. 0% of classes are taught by teaching assistants.

ACADEMICS
Degrees: Associate; Bachelor's; Certificate; **Master's Classes:** Most classes have 20-29 students. Most lab/discussion sessions have 20-29 students. **Most popular majors:** Teacher Education, Multiple Levels; Biology/Biological Sciences, General; Psychology, General. **Special Study Options:** Distance learning; Double major; Dual enrollment; Honors program; Independent study; Internships; Study abroad; Teacher certification program. **Disability Services offered to physically disabled students:** Note-taking services; Reader services; Tape recorders. Alumni services; Career assessment; Internships

FACILITIES
Housing: Coed dorms; Special housing for disabled student; Theme housing

CAMPUS LIFE
Environment: City **Activities:** Campus Ministries; Choral groups; Dance; Radio station; Student government; Student newspaper. Waterfront, Pool, Butterfly Garden, Fish tank in University Student Center, Bullseye

ADMISSIONS
Freshman Academic Profile: Average high school GPA 3.7. 17% in top 10% of high school class, 46% in top 25% of high school class, 84% in top 50% of high school class. 87% from public high schools. **Test Scores:** SAT Math middle 50% range 530-600. SAT EBRW middle 50% range 550-630. ACT middle 50% range 22-26. Minimum internet-based TOEFL 79. Minimum paper TOEFL 550. **Basis for Candidate Selection:** *Other factors considered include:* rigor of secondary school record, academic GPA, standardized test scores, volunteer work. **Freshman Admission Requirements:** High school diploma is required and GED is accepted *Academic units required:* 4 English, 4 math, 3 science, 2 science labs, 2 foreign language, 3 social studies, 2 academic electives. **Freshman Admission Statistics:** 5,575 applied, 39.9% admitted, 29% enrolled. **General Admission Information:** Application fee $30. Priority deadline 1/15. Regular application deadline 5/1. Nonfall registration accepted.

COSTS AND FINANCIAL AID
Annual out-of-state tuition $15,120. Room and board $10,808. Required fees $1,615. Average book expense $1,200. **Required Forms and Deadlines:** FAFSA. **Notification of Awards:** Applicants will be notified of awards on a rolling basis beginning 3/1. **Types of Aid:** *Need-based scholarships/grants:* College/university scholarship or grant aid from institutional funds; Federal Pell; Private scholarships; SEOG; State scholarships/grants. *Loans:* Direct PLUS loans; Direct Subsidized Stafford Loans; Direct Unsubsidized Stafford Loans. *Student Employment:* Federal Work-Study Program available. Institutional employment available. **Financial Aid Statistics:** 70% freshmen, 62% undergrads receive any aid.

UNIVERSITY OF SOUTHERN CALIFORNIA

University Park, Los Angeles, CA 90089-0911
Phone: 213-740-1111 • **Financial Aid Phone:** 213-740-4444
E-mail: admitusc@usc.edu • **CEEB Code:** 4852
Fax: 213-821-0200 • **Website:** www.usc.edu • **ACT Code:** 470

This private school was founded in 1880. It has a 229 acre campus.

RATINGS
Admissions Selectivity Rating: 98 **Fire Safety Rating:** 97 **Green Rating:** 84

STUDENTS AND FACULTY
Enrollment: 19,059. **Student Body:** 51% female, 49% male, 35% out-of-state, 13% international (114 countries represented). Asian 21%, African American 5%, Caucasian 40%, Hispanic 14%, Native American <1%, Pacific Islander <1%, Two or more races 6%, Race unknown 1%.
Retention and Graduation: 96% freshmen return for sophomore year. 77% freshmen graduate within 4 years. 92% freshmen graduate within 6 years.
Faculty: Student/faculty ratio 8:1. 2,133 full-time faculty, 91% hold PhDs, 30% are members of minority groups, 40% are women.

ACADEMICS
Degrees: Bachelor's; Doctoral; Doctoral Other; Doctoral/Professional; Doctoral/Research; Master's; Post-Bachelor's certificate; Post-Master's certificate **Classes:** Most classes have 10-19 students. Most lab/discussion sessions have 10-19 students. **Most popular majors:** Social Sciences, General; Visual And Performing Arts, General; Business Administration And Management, General. **Special Study Options:** Cooperative education program; Distance learning; Double major; English as a Second Language (ESL); Exchange student program (domestic); Honors program; Independent study; Internships; Liberal arts/career combination; Student-designed major; Study abroad. Honors programs: Thematic Option Program Multimedia Scholarship Combined degree programs: BA/MA; BA/MEng. **Disability Services offered to physically disabled students:** Note-taking services; Reader services; Tape recorders; Tutors. **Career services:** Alumni network; Alumni services; Career assessment; Internships; Regional alumni

FACILITIES
Housing: Apartments for married students; Apartments for single students; Coed dorms; Cooperative housing; Fraternity/sorority housing; Special housing for disabled student; Special housing for international students; Theme housing; Wellness housing 97% of campus accessible to physically diasbled. **Special Academic Facilities/Equipment:** USC Fisher Museum of Art; Hancock Memorial Museum; specialized architecture and fine arts galleries, studios, and labs; media labs; cinema scoring sound stage; recording studios; theatres and recital halls; exercise physiology lab; specialized engineering laboratories; biomedical imaging labs; Center for Electron Microscopy and Microanalysis; genomic research facilities; GIS research lab; USC Shoah Foundation Institute visual history archive; Archival Research Center; High-Performance Computing Center; public computing centers and labs; extensive wireless access to the USC network; classrooms outfitted with multiple webcams and microphones **Computers:** 15% of classrooms, 10% of dorms, 100% of libraries, 100% of dining areas, 100% of student union, 90% of common outdoor areas have wireless network access. Students can register for classes online. Administrative functions (other than registration) can be performed online.

CAMPUS LIFE
Environment: Metropolis **Activities:** Campus Ministries; Choral groups; Concert band; Dance; Drama/theater; International Student Organization; Jazz band; Literary magazine; Marching band; Model UN; Music ensembles; Musical theater; Opera; Pep band; Radio station; Student government; Student newspaper; Student-run film society; Symphony orchestra; Television station; Yearbook 676 registered organizations, 49 honor societies, 74 religious organizations. 41 fraternities, 23 sororities. **Athletics (Intercollegiate):** *Men:* baseball, basketball, diving, football, golf, swimming, tennis, track/field (outdoor), volleyball, water polo. *Women:* basketball, crew/rowing, cross-country, diving, golf, soccer, swimming, tennis, track/field (outdoor), volleyball, water polo. **On-Campus Highlights:** Tutor Campus Center, Galen Center (event & training pavilion), Leavey Library (open 24 hours), Heritage Hall (athletic awards), Fisher Museum of Art **Environmental Initiatives:** Energy Efficiency & Innovation: USC employs a full time Director of Energy Services to manage energy programs including lighting retrofits, equipment upgrades, and a recent retrofit of chillers, cooling towers, and pumps throughout the

University, including a three million gallon centralized thermal energy storage tank installed below ground. The 3 million-gallon thermal energy water storage (TES) system was built 40 feet below ground. It is estimated that the new system conserves about 4,500 megawatt-hours of electricity a year by circulating chilled water to air conditioning systems throughout the University Park Campus, significantly expanding the capacity of the campus' existing chilled-water system while reducing utility use. The warmer water coming back through pipes has a chance to chill overnight before it is recirculated which allows USC to shift much of the kilowatt-hour usage to off-peak hours when electricity is more available. The entire system was conceived in 2001 and completed in 2005.

ADMISSIONS

Freshman Academic Profile: Average high school GPA 3.8. 88% in top 10% of high school class, 96% in top 25% of high school class, 100% in top 50% of high school class. 54% from public high schools. **Test Scores:** SAT Math middle 50% range 650-770. SAT EBRW middle 50% range 650-730. ACT middle 50% range 30-34. **Basis for Candidate Selection:** *Very important factors considered include:* rigor of secondary school record, academic GPA, application essay, standardized test scores, recommendation(s). *Important factors considered include:* extracurricular activities, talent/ability, character/personal qualities. *Other factors considered include:* class rank, interview, first generation, alumni/ae relation, racial/ethnic status, volunteer work, work experience. **Freshman Admission Requirements:** High school diploma is required and GED is not accepted *Academic units required:* 4 English, 3 math, 2 science, 2 science labs, 2 foreign language, 2 social studies, 3 academic electives, *Academic units recommended:* 4 English, 4 math, 3 science, 3 science labs, 3 foreign language, 3 social studies, 3 academic electives. **Freshman Admission Statistics:** 55,676 applied, 16.2% admitted, 37% enrolled. **Transfer Admission Requirements:** High school transcript, college transcript(s), essay or personal statement, Lowest grade transferable C-. **General Admission Information:** Application fee $85. Priority deadline 12/1. Regular application deadline 1/15. Nonfall registration accepted. Admission may be deferred for a maximum of one year.

COSTS AND FINANCIAL AID

Annual tuition $53,448. Room and board $14,885. Required fees $1,225. Average book expense $1,200. **Required Forms and Deadlines:** Business/Farm Supplement; CSS/Financial Aid PROFILE; FAFSA; Noncustodial PROFILE. **Notification of Awards:** Applicants will be notified of awards on or about 4/1. **Types of Aid:** *Need-based scholarships/grants:* College/university scholarship or grant aid from institutional funds; Federal Pell; Private scholarships; SEOG; State scholarships/grants. *Loans:* Direct PLUS loans; Direct Subsidized Stafford Loans; Direct Unsubsidized Stafford Loans. *Student Employment:* Federal Work-Study Program available. Institutional employment available. **Financial Aid Statistics:** 86% needy freshmen, 91% needy undergrads receive need-based scholarship or grant aid. 66% freshmen, 47% undergrads receive non-need-based scholarship or grant aid. 89% freshmen, 94% undergrads receive need-based self-help aid. 3% freshmen, 2% undergrads receive athletic scholarships. 68% freshmen, 65% undergrads receive any aid. 41% undergrads borrow to pay for school. Average cumulative indebtedness $27,882. **Criteria for awarding aid:** *Non-need-based:* Academics, Alumni affiliation, Art, Athletics, Leadership, Music/drama.

UNIVERSITY OF SOUTHERN INDIANA

8600 University Boulevard, Evansville, IN 47712
Phone: 812-464-1765 • **Financial Aid Phone:** 812-464-1767
E-mail: enroll@usi.edu • **CEEB Code:** 1335
Fax: 812-465-7154 • **Website:** www.usi.edu • **ACT Code:** 1207

This public school was founded in 1965. It has a 1400 acre campus.

RATINGS

Admissions Selectivity Rating: 73   **Fire Safety Rating:** 80   **Green Rating:** 77

STUDENTS AND FACULTY

Enrollment: 7,662. **Student Body:** 62% female, 38% male, 13% out-of-state, 2% international (60 countries represented). Asian 1%, African American 4%, Caucasian 86%, Hispanic 3%, Native American <1%, Pacific Islander <1%, Two or more races 2%, Race unknown <1%.
Retention and Graduation: 71% freshmen return for sophomore year. 21% freshmen graduate within 4 years. 40% freshmen graduate within 6 years. 25% grads go on to further study within 1 year. **Faculty:** Student/faculty ratio 17:1. 352 full-time faculty, 71% hold PhDs, 11% are members of minority groups, 53% are women. 0% of classes are taught by teaching assistants.

ACADEMICS

Degrees: Associate; Bachelor's; Certificate; Doctoral/Professional; Master's; Post-Bachelor's certificate; Post-Master's certificate; Transfer Associate **Classes:** Most classes have 20-29 students. Most lab/discussion sessions have 20-29 students. **Most popular majors:** Psychology, General; Registered Nursing/Registered Nurse; Business Administration And Management, General. **Special Study Options:** Accelerated program; Cooperative education program; Distance learning; Double major; Dual enrollment; English as a Second Language (ESL); Honors program; Independent study; Internships; Study abroad; Teacher certification program. Honors programs: The Honors Program at the University of Southern Indiana offers a selective, demanding, and rewarding program for students who are searching for an intellectual challenge and are prepared to invest extra effort to meet that challenge. Honors students benefit from smaller classes, close contact with faculty, grants to study abroad, research opportunities, exciting extracurricular activities, and the Honors living learning community. The Honors Program provides students with a supportive community of fellow Honors students who are academically motivated and talented. The USI Honors Program offers a broad range of opportunities for personal and academic growth. The most outstanding feature of the program is the students themselves. Their motivation and creativity stimulate the entire University campus. **Disability Services offered to physically disabled students:** Note-taking services; Reader services; Tape recorders; Tutors. **Career services:** Alumni network; Alumni services; Career assessment; Career/job search classes; Internships

FACILITIES

Housing: Apartments for single students; Coed dorms; Fraternity/sorority housing; Special housing for disabled student; Special housing for international students; Theme housing 95% of campus accessible to physically diasbled. **Special Academic Facilities/Equipment:** The McCutchan Art Center, Pace Galleries, Griffin Center, Bent Twig Outdoor Education Center **Computers:** 100% of classrooms, 100% of dorms, 100% of libraries, 100% of dining areas, 100% of student union, 100% of common outdoor areas have wireless network access. Students can register for classes online. Administrative functions (other than registration) can be performed online.

CAMPUS LIFE

Environment: City **Activities:** Campus Ministries; Choral groups; Dance; Drama/theater; International Student Organization; Jazz band; Literary magazine; Pep band; Radio station; Student government; Student newspaper; Television station 102 registered organizations, 6 honor societies, 7 religious organizations. 7 fraternities, 4 sororities. **Athletics (Intercollegiate):** *Men:* baseball, basketball, cross-country, golf, soccer, tennis, track/field (outdoor), track/field (indoor). *Women:* basketball, cross-country, golf, soccer, softball, tennis, track/field (outdoor), track/field (indoor), volleyball. **On-Campus Highlights:** University Center, Recreation, Fitness, and Wellness Center, Rice Library, USI Performance Center (Teaching Theatre), USI-Burdette Trail **Environmental Initiatives:** Established environmental stewardship committee

ADMISSIONS

Freshman Academic Profile: Average high school GPA 3.4. 13% in top 10% of high school class, 37% in top 25% of high school class, 71% in top 50% of high school class. 86% from public high schools. **Test Scores:** SAT Math middle 50% range 480-580. SAT EBRW middle 50% range 490-590. ACT middle 50% range 19-25. Minimum internet-based TOEFL 71. Minimum paper TOEFL 55. **Basis for Candidate Selection:** *Very important factors considered include:* academic GPA, standardized test scores. *Important factors considered include:* class rank. *Other factors considered include:* rigor of secondary school record, application essay, recommendation(s), interview, extracurricular activities, talent/ability, character/personal qualities, volunteer work. **Freshman Admission Requirements:** High school diploma is required and GED is accepted *Academic units recommended:* 4 English, 4 math, 2 science, 2 foreign language, 2 social studies, 2 history, 2 academic electives. **Freshman Admission Statistics:** 4,569 applied, 93.6% admitted, 40% enrolled. **Transfer Admission Requirements:** High school transcript, college transcript(s), Minimum college GPA of 2.0 required. Lowest grade transferable C-. **General Admission Information:** Application fee $40. Regular application deadline 8/15. Nonfall registration accepted. Admission may be deferred for a maximum of 1 semester.

COSTS AND FINANCIAL AID

Annual in-state tuition $8,838. Annual out-of-state tuition $18,116. Room and board $8,838. Required fees $510. Average book expense $1,140. **Required Forms and Deadlines:** FAFSA. **Notification of Awards:** Applicants will be notified of awards on a rolling basis beginning 4/1. **Types of Aid:** *Need-based scholarships/grants:* College/university scholarship or grant aid from institutional funds; Federal Nursing Scholarships; Federal Pell; Private scholarships; SEOG; State scholarships/grants; United Negro College Fund. *Loans:* Direct PLUS loans; Direct Subsidized Stafford Loans; Direct Unsubsidized Stafford Loans. *Student Employment:* Federal Work-

Study Program available. Institutional employment available. **Financial Aid Statistics:** 65% needy freshmen, 81% needy undergrads receive need-based scholarship or grant aid. 44% freshmen, 45% undergrads receive non-need-based scholarship or grant aid. 84% freshmen, 85% undergrads receive need-based self-help aid. 2% freshmen, 4% undergrads receive athletic scholarships. 91% undergrads receive any aid. 69% undergrads borrow to pay for school. Average cumulative indebtedness $24,762. **Criteria for awarding aid:** *Need-based:* Academics *Non-need-based:* Academics, Art, Athletics, Leadership, Music/drama, State/district residency.

UNIVERSITY OF SOUTHERN MAINE

PO Box 9300, Portland, ME 04104
Phone: 207-780-5670 • **Financial Aid Phone:** 207-780-5250
E-mail: usmadm@usm.maine.edu • **CEEB Code:** 9762
Fax: 207-780-5640 • **Website:** www.usm.maine.edu • **ACT Code:** 1644

This public school was founded in 1878. It has a 144 acre campus.

RATINGS

Admissions Selectivity Rating: 72   Fire Safety Rating: 85   Green Rating: 60*

STUDENTS AND FACULTY

Enrollment: 5,359. **Student Body:** 57% female, 43% male, 11% out-of-state, 1% international (19 countries represented). Asian 2%, African American 4%, Caucasian 82%, Hispanic 2%, Native American 1%, Pacific Islander <1%, Two or more races 3%, Race unknown 5%.
Retention and Graduation: 63% freshmen return for sophomore year.
Faculty: Student/faculty ratio 16:1. 248 full-time faculty, 84% hold PhDs, 7% are members of minority groups, 48% are women. 0% of classes are taught by teaching assistants.

ACADEMICS

Degrees: Bachelor's; Certificate; Doctoral; Doctoral/Professional; Doctoral/Research; Master's; Post-Bachelor's certificate; Post-Master's certificate
Classes: Most classes have 10-19 students. **Most popular majors:** Biology/Biological Sciences, General; Registered Nursing/Registered Nurse; Business Administration And Management, General. **Special Study Options:** Cooperative education program; Cross-registration; Distance learning; Double major; Dual enrollment; English as a Second Language (ESL); Exchange student program (domestic); Honors program; Independent study; Internships; Liberal arts/career combination; Student-designed major; Study abroad; Teacher certification program; Weekend college. Honors programs: Russell Scholars—living/learning community, USM honors program, Pioneers program. **Disability Services offered to physically disabled students:** Note-taking services; Reader services; Tape recorders; Tutors. **Career services:** Alumni network; Alumni services; Career/job search classes; Internships

FACILITIES

Housing: Apartments for married students; Apartments for single students; Coed dorms; Fraternity/sorority housing; Special housing for disabled student; Special housing for international students; Theme housing; Wellness housing 90% of campus accessible to physically diasbled. **Special Academic Facilities/Equipment:** Southworth Planetarium, Osher Map Collection and Smith Center for Cartographic Education, WMPG (radio station), Free Press (campus newspaper), various art galleries on all three campuses, and **Computers:** Students can register for classes online. Administrative functions (other than registration) can be performed online.

CAMPUS LIFE

Environment: City **Activities:** Campus Ministries; Choral groups; Concert band; Dance; Drama/theater; International Student Organization; Jazz band; Literary magazine; Model UN; Music ensembles; Musical theater; Opera; Radio station; Student government; Student newspaper; Symphony orchestra 100 registered organizations, 2 honor societies, 3 religious organizations. 4 fraternities, 4 sororities. **Athletics (Intercollegiate):** *Men:* baseball, basketball, cheerleading, cross-country, golf, ice hockey, lacrosse, soccer, tennis, track/field (outdoor), track/field (indoor), wrestling. *Women:* basketball, cheerleading, cross-country, field hockey, golf, ice hockey, lacrosse, soccer, softball, tennis, track/field (outdoor), track/field (indoor), volleyball. **On-Campus Highlights:** Art Gallery, Costello Sports Complex, Russell Theater and Concert Hall, Southworth Planetarium, WMPG Radio Station

ADMISSIONS

Freshman Academic Profile: Average high school GPA 3.0. 5% in top 10% of high school class, 26% in top 25% of high school class, 61% in top 50% of high school class. **Test Scores:** SAT Math middle 50% range 440-550. SAT EBRW

middle 50% range 420-550. ACT middle 50% range 19-25. Minimum internet-based TOEFL 80. **Basis for Candidate Selection:** *Very important factors considered include:* rigor of secondary school record, class rank, academic GPA. *Important factors considered include:* application essay, standardized test scores. *Other factors considered include:* recommendation(s), interview, extracurricular activities, talent/ability, character/personal qualities, first generation, alumni/ae relation, geographical residence, state residency, racial/ethnic status, volunteer work, work experience, level of applicant's interest. **Freshman Admission Requirements:** High school diploma is required and GED is accepted *Academic units required:* 4 English, 3 math, 2 science, 2 science labs, 2 social studies, 1 history, *Academic units recommended:* 3 science, 3 science labs, 3 social studies, 1 history. **Freshman Admission Statistics:** 3,402 applied, 87.8% admitted, 24% enrolled. **Transfer Admission Requirements:** High school transcript, college transcript(s), essay or personal statement, Minimum college GPA of 2.0 required. Lowest grade transferable C-. **General Admission Information:** Application fee $40. Nonfall registration accepted. Admission may be deferred.

COSTS AND FINANCIAL AID

Annual in-state tuition $9,400. Annual out-of-state tuition $19,950. Room and board $9,400. Required fees $1,330. Average book expense $1,220. **Required Forms and Deadlines:** FAFSA. **Notification of Awards:** Applicants will be notified of awards on a rolling basis beginning 3/15. **Types of Aid:** *Need-based scholarships/grants:* College/university scholarship or grant aid from institutional funds; Federal Pell; Private scholarships; SEOG; State scholarships/grants. *Loans:* Direct PLUS loans; Direct Subsidized Stafford Loans; Direct Unsubsidized Stafford Loans. *Student Employment:* Federal Work-Study Program available. Institutional employment available. **Financial Aid Statistics:** 75% needy freshmen, 84% needy undergrads receive need-based scholarship or grant aid. 5% freshmen, 3% undergrads receive non-need-based scholarship or grant aid. 79% freshmen, 87% undergrads receive need-based self-help aid. 0% freshmen, 0% undergrads receive athletic scholarships. **Criteria for awarding aid:** *Need-based:* Academics, Music/drama *Non-need-based:* Academics, Music/drama, State/district residency.

UNIVERSITY OF SOUTHERN MISSISSIPPI

118 College Drive #5001, Hattiesburg, MS 39406
Phone: 601-266-5000 • **Financial Aid Phone:** (601) 266-4774
E-mail: admissions@usm.edu • **CEEB Code:** 1479
Fax: 601-266-5148 • **Website:** www.usm.edu • **ACT Code:** 2218

This public school was founded in 1910. It has a 1090 acre campus.

RATINGS

Admissions Selectivity Rating: 89   Fire Safety Rating: 90   Green Rating: 60*

STUDENTS AND FACULTY

Enrollment: 11,689. **Student Body:** 63% female, 37% male, 16% out-of-state, 2% international. Asian 1%, African American 29%, Caucasian 61%, Hispanic 3%, Native American <1%, Pacific Islander <1%, Two or more races 2%, Race unknown 1%.
Retention and Graduation: 74% freshmen return for sophomore year.
Faculty: Student/faculty ratio 17:1. 687 full-time faculty, 79% hold PhDs, 16% are members of minority groups, 48% are women.

ACADEMICS

Degrees: Bachelor's; Certificate; Doctoral; Master's; Post-Bachelor's certificate; Post-Master's certificate **Classes:** Most classes have 10-19 students. **Most popular majors:** Elementary Education And Teaching; Psychology, General; Nursing/Registered Nurse (Rn, Asn, Bsn, Msn). **Special Study Options:** Distance learning; Double major; Dual enrollment; English as a Second Language (ESL); Exchange student program (domestic); Honors program; Internships; Study abroad; Teacher certification program. **Disability Services offered to physically disabled students:** Note-taking services; Reader services; Tape recorders; Tutors. **Career services:** Alumni services; Career assessment; Career/job search classes; Internships

FACILITIES

Housing: Fraternity/sorority housing; Men's dorms; Special housing for disabled student; Theme housing; Women's dorms **Special Academic Facilities/Equipment:** Museum of Art **Computers:** 100% of classrooms, 100% of dorms, 100% of libraries, 100% of dining areas, 100% of student union, 30% of common outdoor areas have wireless network access. Students can register for classes online. Administrative functions (other than registration) can be performed online.

CAMPUS LIFE

Environment: City **Activities:** Campus Ministries; Choral groups; Concert band; Dance; Drama/theater; International Student Organization; Jazz band; Literary magazine; Marching band; Music ensembles; Musical theater; Opera; Pep band; Radio station; Student government; Student newspaper; Student-run film society; Symphony orchestra; Yearbook 8 honor societies, 20 religious organizations. 15 fraternities, 11 sororities. **Athletics (Intercollegiate):** *Men:* baseball, basketball, football, golf, tennis, track/field (outdoor), track/field (indoor). *Women:* basketball, cross-country, golf, soccer, softball, tennis, track/field (outdoor), track/field (indoor), volleyball. **On-Campus Highlights:** Starbucks, Thad Cochran Center, Barnes & Nobles Bookstore **Environmental Initiatives:** Recycling (12+ years)

ADMISSIONS

Freshman Academic Profile: Average high school GPA 3.3. 88% from public high schools. **Test Scores:** SAT Math middle 50% range 510-650. SAT EBRW middle 50% range 430-540. ACT middle 50% range 20-26. Minimum internet-based TOEFL 71. Minimum paper TOEFL 525. **Basis for Candidate Selection:** *Very important factors considered include:* academic GPA, standardized test scores. *Important factors considered include:* class rank. **Freshman Admission Requirements:** High school diploma is required and GED is accepted *Academic units required:* 4 English, 3 math, 3 science, 3 science labs, 1 foreign language, 3 social studies, 2 academic electives, 0.5 computer science, *Academic units recommended:* 4 English, 4 math, 4 science, 3 science labs, 1 foreign language, 4 social studies, 2 academic electives, 0.5 computer science, 1 visual/performing arts. **Freshman Admission Statistics:** 6,607 applied, 45.7% admitted, 52% enrolled. **Transfer Admission Requirements:** college transcript(s), statement of good standing from prior institution(s). Minimum college GPA of 2.0 required. Lowest grade transferable D. **General Admission Information:** Application fee $40. Nonfall registration accepted.

COSTS AND FINANCIAL AID

Annual in-state tuition $9,012. Annual out-of-state tuition $9,854. Room and board $9,012. Average book expense $1,200. **Required Forms and Deadlines:** FAFSA. **Notification of Awards:** Applicants will be notified of awards on a rolling basis beginning 12/15. **Types of Aid:** *Need-based scholarships/grants:* College/university scholarship or grant aid from institutional funds; Federal Pell; Private scholarships; SEOG; State scholarships/grants. *Loans:* Direct PLUS loans; Direct Subsidized Stafford Loans; Direct Unsubsidized Stafford Loans. *Student Employment:* Federal Work-Study Program available. Institutional employment available. **Financial Aid Statistics:** 69% needy freshmen, 68% needy undergrads receive need-based scholarship or grant aid. 69% freshmen, 57% undergrads receive non-need-based scholarship or grant aid. 69% freshmen, 75% undergrads receive need-based self-help aid. 6% freshmen, 4% undergrads receive athletic scholarships. 62% freshmen, 63% undergrads receive any aid. 68% undergrads borrow to pay for school. Average cumulative indebtedness $28,700. **Criteria for awarding aid:** *Need-based:* Academics *Non-need-based:* Academics, Alumni affiliation, Art, Athletics, Leadership, Music/drama, State/district residency.

UNIVERSITY OF ST. FRANCIS

500 Wilcox Street, Joliet, IL 60435
Phone: 815-740-2270 • **Financial Aid Phone:** 866-890-8331
E-mail: admissions@stfrancis.edu • **CEEB Code:** 1130
Fax: 815-740-5078 • **Website:** www.stfrancis.edu • **ACT Code:** 1000

This private school, affiliated with the Roman Catholic Church, was founded in 1920. It has a 18 acre campus.

RATINGS

Admissions Selectivity Rating: 87   **Fire Safety Rating:** 99   **Green Rating:** 77

STUDENTS AND FACULTY

Enrollment: 1,329. **Student Body:** 63% female, 37% male, 5% out-of-state, 4% international (13 countries represented). Asian 2%, African American 8%, Caucasian 60%, Hispanic 22%, Native American <1%, Pacific Islander <1%, Two or more races 4%, Race unknown <1%.
Retention and Graduation: 80% freshmen return for sophomore year. 41% freshmen graduate within 4 years. 63% freshmen graduate within 6 years. 19% grads go on to further study within 1 year. **Faculty:** Student/faculty ratio 12:1. 95 full-time faculty, 76% hold PhDs, 17% are members of minority groups, 64% are women. 0% of classes are taught by teaching assistants.

ACADEMICS

Degrees: Bachelor's; Certificate; Doctoral; Doctoral Other; Doctoral/Research; Master's; Post-Bachelor's certificate; Post-Master's certificate **Classes:** Most classes have 20-29 students. Most lab/discussion sessions have fewer than 10 students. **Most popular majors:** Education; Registered Nursing/Registered Nurse; Business/Commerce, General. **Special Study Options:** Distance learning; Double major; Dual enrollment; English as a Second Language (ESL); Honors program; Independent study; Internships; Student-designed major; Study abroad; Teacher certification program. Honors programs: Duns Scotus Fellow/Scholars Program is designed to create a learning community of motivated students who are challenged to excel academically. **Disability Services offered to physically disabled students:** Note-taking services; Reader services; Tape recorders; Tutors. **Career services:** Alumni network; Alumni services; Career assessment; Career/job search classes; Internships; Regional alumni

FACILITIES

Housing: Apartments for single students; Coed dorms; Special housing for disabled student; Theme housing; Wellness housing 100% of campus accessible to physically diasbled. **Special Academic Facilities/Equipment:** Wireless and multimedia classrooms, numerous science laboratories, testing centers, private music practice and instruction rooms, digital audio and recording arts studio, 2D/3D design labs and equipment, medical and skills simulation labs, a cadaver lab, a mock trial courtroom, a business incubator, an art & design complex with studio spaces for senior students, an international student center, golf studio, a greenhouse, numerous multi-purpose spaces, on-campus beehives, and an outdoor challenge course. **Computers:** 100% of classrooms, 100% of dorms, 100% of libraries, 100% of dining areas, 100% of student union, 100% of common outdoor areas have wireless network access. Students can register for classes online. Administrative functions (other than registration) can be performed online.

CAMPUS LIFE

Environment: City **Activities:** Campus Ministries; Choral groups; Dance; Drama/theater; International Student Organization; Music ensembles; Musical theater; Opera; Radio station; Student government; Student newspaper; Symphony orchestra; Television station 29 registered organizations, 13 honor societies, 1 religious organization. **Athletics (Intercollegiate):** *Men:* baseball, basketball, cross-country, football, golf, soccer, tennis, track/field (outdoor), track/field (indoor). *Women:* basketball, cheerleading, cross-country, golf, soccer, softball, tennis, track/field (outdoor), track/field (indoor), volleyball. **On-Campus Highlights:** Bistro, Fireside Lounge in Motherhouse, The Abbey, Bernie's Pub, The Quad **Environmental Initiatives:** Campus wide recycling

ADMISSIONS

Freshman Academic Profile: Average high school GPA 3.5. 12% in top 10% of high school class, 41% in top 25% of high school class, 74% in top 50% of high school class. 88% from public high schools. **Test Scores:** SAT Math middle 50% range 540-610. SAT EBRW middle 50% range 490-630. ACT middle 50% range 20-25. Minimum internet-based TOEFL 79. Minimum paper TOEFL 550. **Basis for Candidate Selection:** *Very important factors considered include:* rigor of secondary school record, class rank, academic GPA, standardized test scores. *Other factors considered include:* application essay, recommendation(s), interview. **Freshman Admission Requirements:** High school diploma is required and GED is accepted *Academic units required:* 4 English, 3 math, 2 science, 1 science labs, 2 social studies, 3 academic electives, and 3 units from above areas or other academic areas. **Freshman Admission Statistics:** 1,560 applied, 51.7% admitted, 29% enrolled. **Transfer Admission Requirements:** college transcript(s), statement of good standing from prior institution(s). Minimum college GPA of 2.5 required. **General Admission Information:** Application fee $30. Regular application deadline 8/1. Nonfall registration accepted. Admission may be deferred for a maximum of 1 year.

COSTS AND FINANCIAL AID

Annual tuition $32,000. Required fees $320. **Required Forms and Deadlines:** FAFSA; Institution's own financial aid form. **Notification of Awards:** Applicants will be notified of awards on a rolling basis beginning 10/15. **Types of Aid:** *Need-based scholarships/grants:* College/university scholarship or grant aid from institutional funds; Federal Pell; Private scholarships; SEOG; State scholarships/grants. *Loans:* Direct PLUS loans; Direct Subsidized Stafford Loans; Direct Unsubsidized Stafford Loans. *Student Employment:* Federal Work-Study Program available. Institutional employment available. **Financial Aid Statistics:** 63% needy freshmen, 99% needy undergrads receive need-based scholarship or grant aid. 24% freshmen, 15% undergrads receive non-need-based scholarship or grant aid. 71% freshmen, 77% undergrads receive need-based self-help aid. 5% freshmen, 6% undergrads receive athletic scholarships. 100% freshmen, 93% undergrads receive any aid. 79% undergrads borrow to pay for school. Average cumulative indebtedness $31,506. **Criteria for awarding aid:** *Need-based:* Academics, Art, Athletics, Leadership, Minority status, Music/drama, Religious affiliation *Non-need-based:* Academics, Alumni affiliation, Art, Athletics, Leadership, Minority status, Music/drama, Religious affiliation, State/district residency.

UNIVERSITY OF ST. THOMAS

3800 Montrose Boulevard, Houston, TX 77006-4696
Phone: 713-525-3500 • **Financial Aid Phone:** 713-525-2151
E-mail: admissions@stthom.edu • **CEEB Code:** 6880
Fax: 713-525-3558 • **Website:** www.stthom.edu • **ACT Code:** 4238

This private school, affiliated with the Roman Catholic Church, was founded in 1947. It has a 23 acre campus.

RATINGS
Admissions Selectivity Rating: 78   **Fire Safety Rating:** 95   **Green Rating:** 60*

STUDENTS AND FACULTY
Enrollment: 1,782. **Student Body:** 62% female, 38% male, 3% out-of-state, 9% international (38 countries represented). Asian 11%, African American 6%, Caucasian 23%, Hispanic 45%, Native American <1%, Pacific Islander <1%, Two or more races 3%, Race unknown 2%.
Retention and Graduation: 31% freshmen graduate within 4 years. 57% freshmen graduate within 6 years. **Faculty:** Student/faculty ratio 11:1. 153 full-time faculty, 94% hold PhDs, 31% are members of minority groups, 45% are women. 0% of classes are taught by teaching assistants.

ACADEMICS
Degrees: Diploma; Doctoral/Research; Master's; Post-Bachelor's certificate; Post-Master's certificate **Classes:** Most classes have 10-19 students. Most lab/discussion sessions have 10-19 students. **Most popular majors:** Biology/Biological Sciences, General; Psychology, General; Registered Nursing/Registered Nurse. **Special Study Options:** Accelerated program; Distance learning; Double major; Dual enrollment; Honors program; Independent study; Internships; Liberal arts/career combination; Student-designed major; Study abroad; Teacher certification program; Weekend college. Honors programs: The Honors Program at the University of St. Thomas is a four-year interdisciplinary program for students of exceptional intellectual ability, motivation, and curiosity. It is designed not simply to provoke students to master specific disciplines such as philosophy, history, mathematics, and natural science but to offer an experience which integrates, on the deepest and most profound level, the intellectual, cultural and spiritual foundations of a liberal arts education. Combined degree programs: BA/MA. **Disability Services offered to physically disabled students:** Note-taking services; Reader services; Tape recorders; Tutors. **Career services:** Alumni network; Alumni services; Career assessment; Internships

FACILITIES
Housing: Apartments for single students; Coed dorms; Men's dorms; Special housing for disabled student; Women's dorms 90% of campus accessible to physically diasbled. **Special Academic Facilities/Equipment:** Tutorial Services Center, Chapel of St. Basil, Doherty Library, Link-Lee Mansion, Little Archaeology Gallery **Computers:** 100% of classrooms, 100% of libraries, 100% of dining areas, 100% of common outdoor areas have wireless network access. Students can register for classes online. Administrative functions (other than registration) can be performed online.

CAMPUS LIFE
Environment: Metropolis **Activities:** Campus Ministries; Choral groups; Drama/theater; International Student Organization; Jazz band; Literary magazine; Music ensembles; Musical theater; Opera; Student government; Student newspaper 69 registered organizations, 22 honor societies, 5 religious organizations. **Athletics (Intercollegiate):** *Men:* basketball, soccer. *Women:* volleyball. **On-Campus Highlights:** Jerabeck Activity and Athletic Center, Crooker Student Center, Chapel of St. Basil, Guinan, Academic Mall **Environmental Initiatives:** Campus Recycling of glass, aluminum, plastic & paper

ADMISSIONS
Freshman Academic Profile: Average high school GPA 3.7. 23% in top 10% of high school class, 29% in top 25% of high school class, 84% in top 50% of high school class. 70% from public high schools. **Test Scores:** SAT Math middle 50% range 530-615. SAT EBRW middle 50% range 540-620. ACT middle 50% range 21-27. Minimum internet-based TOEFL 79. Minimum paper TOEFL 550. **Basis for Candidate Selection:** *Very important factors considered include:* academic GPA, standardized test scores. *Important factors considered include:* rigor of secondary school record, application essay. *Other factors considered include:* recommendation(s), interview, extracurricular activities, talent/ability, character/personal qualities, first generation, alumni/ae relation, volunteer work, work experience, level of applicant's interest.
Freshman Admission Requirements: High school diploma is required and GED is accepted *Academic units required:* 4 English, 3 math, 3 science,

2 science labs, 2 foreign language, 2 social studies, 1 history, and 3 units from above areas or other academic areas. *Academic units recommended:* 4 English, 3 math, 3 science, 2 science labs, 2 foreign language, 2 social studies, 1 history. **Freshman Admission Statistics:** 1,060 applied, 80.9% admitted, 34% enrolled. **Transfer Admission Requirements:** college transcript(s), Minimum college GPA of 2.50 required. Lowest grade transferable C. **General Admission Information:** Priority deadline 12/1. Regular application deadline 5/1. Nonfall registration accepted. Admission may be deferred for a maximum of 1 year.

COSTS AND FINANCIAL AID
Required Forms and Deadlines: FAFSA. **Notification of Awards:** Applicants will be notified of awards on a rolling basis beginning 2/15. **Types of Aid:** *Need-based scholarships/grants:* College/university scholarship or grant aid from institutional funds; Federal Pell; Private scholarships; SEOG; State scholarships/grants. *Loans:* Direct PLUS loans; Direct Subsidized Stafford Loans; Direct Unsubsidized Stafford Loans. *Student Employment:* Federal Work-Study Program available. Institutional employment available. **Financial Aid Statistics:** 97% needy freshmen, 98% needy undergrads receive need-based scholarship or grant aid. 8% freshmen, 6% undergrads receive non-need-based scholarship or grant aid. 51% freshmen, 61% undergrads receive need-based self-help aid. 1% freshmen, 3% undergrads receive athletic scholarships. 90% freshmen, 74% undergrads receive any aid. 50% undergrads borrow to pay for school. Average cumulative indebtedness $26,455. **Criteria for awarding aid:** *Non-need-based:* Academics, Athletics, Music/drama, Religious affiliation.

UNIVERSITY OF TAMPA

401 West Kennedy Boulevard, Tampa, FL 33606-1490
Phone: 813-253-6211 • **Financial Aid Phone:** (813) 253-6219
E-mail: admissions@ut.edu • **CEEB Code:** 5819
Fax: 813-258-7398 • **Website:** www.ut.edu • **ACT Code:** 762

This private school was founded in 1931. It has a 110 acre campus.

RATINGS
Admissions Selectivity Rating: 86   **Fire Safety Rating:** 98   **Green Rating:** 62

STUDENTS AND FACULTY
Enrollment: 7,956. **Student Body:** 58% female, 42% male, 70% out-of-state, 10% international (116 countries represented). Asian 2%, African American 5%, Caucasian 61%, Hispanic 13%, Native American <1%, Pacific Islander <1%, Two or more races 3%, Race unknown 6%.
Retention and Graduation: 78% freshmen return for sophomore year. 48% freshmen graduate within 4 years. 59% freshmen graduate within 6 years. 14% grads go on to further study within 1 year. 4% grads pursue arts and sciences degrees. 1.4% grads pursue law degrees. 4% grads pursue business degrees. 2.5% grads pursue medical degrees. **Faculty:** Student/faculty ratio 17:1. 338 full-time faculty, 90% hold PhDs, 14% are members of minority groups, 45% are women. 0% of classes are taught by teaching assistants.

ACADEMICS
Degrees: Bachelor's; Certificate; Master's; Post-Bachelor's certificate; Post-Master's certificate **Classes:** Most classes have 10-19 students. Most lab/discussion sessions have 20-29 students. **Most popular majors:** Criminology; Finance, General; Marketing/Marketing Management, General. **Special Study Options:** Double major; Honors program; Independent study; Internships; Study abroad; Teacher certification program. Honors programs: UT's Honors Program offers special classes that are developed to enhance creative thinking processes while meeting general distribution requirements. **Disability Services offered to physically disabled students:** Note-taking services; Reader services; Tutors. **Career services:** Alumni network; Alumni services; Career assessment; Career/job search classes; Internships

FACILITIES
Housing: Apartments for single students; Coed dorms; Special housing for disabled student; Theme housing 100% of campus accessible to physically diasbled. **Special Academic Facilities/Equipment:** Victorian art and furniture museum, theatres, studios, music center, language lab, H.B.Plant Museum, marine science research center on Tampa Bay, an entrepreneurship center, a fully equipped research vessel for marine science studies, a music facility, writing and language labs, an academic center for excellence, a graphic

design studio, a marine science lab, and art studios. **Computers:** 50% of classrooms, 25% of dorms, 100% of libraries, 80% of dining areas, 100% of student union, 80% of common outdoor areas have wireless network access. Students can register for classes online. Administrative functions (other than registration) can be performed online.

CAMPUS LIFE

Environment: Metropolis **Activities:** Campus Ministries; Choral groups; Concert band; Dance; Drama/theater; International Student Organization; Jazz band; Literary magazine; Model UN; Music ensembles; Musical theater; Pep band; Radio station; Student government; Student newspaper; Student-run film society; Symphony orchestra; Television station; Yearbook 145 registered organizations, 13 honor societies, 8 religious organizations. 9 fraternities, 10 sororities. **Athletics (Intercollegiate):** *Men:* baseball, basketball, cross-country, golf, soccer, swimming. *Women:* basketball, crew/rowing, cross-country, soccer, softball, swimming, tennis, volleyball. **On-Campus Highlights:** Vaughn Student Center, Plant Hall, Stadium Center, Vaughn Center Courtyard, Martinez Sports Center

ADMISSIONS

Freshman Academic Profile: Average high school GPA 3.4. 18% in top 10% of high school class, 46% in top 25% of high school class, 81% in top 50% of high school class. 78% from public high schools. **Test Scores:** SAT Math middle 50% range 530-610. SAT EBRW middle 50% range 540-620. ACT middle 50% range 22-27. Minimum internet-based TOEFL 79. Minimum paper TOEFL 550. **Basis for Candidate Selection:** *Very important factors considered include:* rigor of secondary school record, academic GPA, standardized test scores. *Important factors considered include:* application essay, recommendation(s), talent/ability. *Other factors considered include:* class rank, interview, extracurricular activities, character/personal qualities, first generation, alumni/ae relation, volunteer work, work experience, level of applicant's interest. **Freshman Admission Requirements:** High school diploma is required and GED is accepted *Academic units required:* 4 English, 3 math, 3 science, 2 science labs, 2 foreign language, 3 social studies, 3 academic electives. **Freshman Admission Statistics:** 20,495 applied, 53.3% admitted, 20% enrolled. **Transfer Admission Requirements:** college transcript(s), Minimum college GPA of 2.2 required. Lowest grade transferable C. **General Admission Information:** Application fee $40. Priority deadline 11/15. Nonfall registration accepted. Admission may be deferred for a maximum of 1 term.

COSTS AND FINANCIAL AID

Required Forms and Deadlines: FAFSA. **Notification of Awards:** Applicants will be notified of awards on a rolling basis beginning 3/1. **Types of Aid:** *Need-based scholarships/grants:* College/university scholarship or grant aid from institutional funds; Federal Nursing Scholarships; Federal Pell; Private scholarships; SEOG; State scholarships/grants. *Loans:* Direct PLUS loans; Direct Subsidized Stafford Loans; Direct Unsubsidized Stafford Loans. *Student Employment:* Federal Work-Study Program available. Institutional employment available. **Financial Aid Statistics:** 100% needy freshmen, 98% needy undergrads receive need-based scholarship or grant aid. 95% freshmen, 96% undergrads receive non-need-based scholarship or grant aid. 84% freshmen, 85% undergrads receive need-based self-help aid. 3% freshmen, 4% undergrads receive athletic scholarships. 93% freshmen, 89% undergrads receive any aid. 60% undergrads borrow to pay for school. Average cumulative indebtedness $31,464. **Criteria for awarding aid:** *Non-need-based:* Academics, Art, Athletics, Leadership, Music/drama.

See page 1072.

UNIVERSITY OF TENNESSEE AT CHATTANOOGA

615 McCallie Avenue, Chattanooga, TN 37403
Phone: 423-425-4662 • **Financial Aid Phone:** 423-425-4677
E-mail: utcmocs@utc.edu • **CEEB Code:** 1831
Fax: 423-425-4157 • **Website:** www.utc.edu • **ACT Code:** 4022

This public school was founded in 1886. It has a 134 acre campus.

RATINGS

Admissions Selectivity Rating: 77   **Fire Safety Rating:** 96   **Green Rating:** 78

STUDENTS AND FACULTY

Enrollment: 10,097. **Student Body:** 56% female, 44% male, 6% out-of-state, 1% international (26 countries represented). Asian 2%, African American 10%, Caucasian 76%, Hispanic 4%, Native American <1%, Pacific Islander <1%, Two or more races 4%, Race unknown 2%.
Retention and Graduation: 73% freshmen return for sophomore year. 22% freshmen graduate within 4 years. 45% freshmen graduate within 6 years.

Faculty: Student/faculty ratio 14:1. 469 full-time faculty, 81% hold PhDs, 17% are members of minority groups, 49% are women.

ACADEMICS

Degrees: Bachelor's; Doctoral/Professional; Doctoral/Research; Master's; Post-Bachelor's certificate; Post-Master's certificate **Classes:** Most classes have 10-19 students. Most lab/discussion sessions have 10-19 students. **Most popular majors:** Biology/Biological Sciences, General; Health And Physical Education/Fitness; Business Administration And Management, General. **Special Study Options:** Accelerated program; Cooperative education program; Cross-registration; Distance learning; Double major; Dual enrollment; English as a Second Language (ESL); Exchange student program (domestic); Honors program; Independent study; Internships; Liberal arts/career combination; Student-designed major; Study abroad; Teacher certification program. Honors programs: The University Honors College offers two honors programs. The first is the Brock Scholars Program, a four-year program that delivers a classical liberal arts education with a curriculum based on fulfilling most general education categories with honors seminars. The second is the Departmental Honors Program, a program in which eligible students from any UTC department can complete an honors thesis project in their major area of study. http://www.utc.edu/Academic/UniversityHonors/. **Disability Services offered to physically disabled students:** Note-taking services; Reader services; Tape recorders; Tutors. **Career services:** Alumni services; Career/job search classes; Internships

FACILITIES

Housing: Apartments for single students; Coed dorms; Special housing for disabled student; Special housing for international students; Theme housing 95% of campus accessible to physically diasbled. **Special Academic Facilities/Equipment:** Walker Teaching Resource Center; Jones Observatory; Institute of Archaeology; Odor Research Center; SIM Center; Challenger Center; Center for Applied Social Research; The Ochs Center for Metropolitan Studies. **Computers:** 90% of classrooms, 100% of libraries, 100% of dining areas, 100% of student union, 60% of common outdoor areas have wireless network access. Students can register for classes online. Administrative functions (other than registration) can be performed online.

CAMPUS LIFE

Environment: City **Activities:** Campus Ministries; Choral groups; Concert band; Dance; Drama/theater; International Student Organization; Jazz band; Literary magazine; Marching band; Model UN; Music ensembles; Musical theater; Opera; Pep band; Radio station; Student government; Student newspaper; Student-run film society; Symphony orchestra; Television station 130 registered organizations, 34 honor societies, 8 religious organizations. 7 fraternities, 7 sororities. **Athletics (Intercollegiate):** *Men:* basketball, cross-country, football, golf, tennis, track/field (outdoor), wrestling. *Women:* basketball, cross-country, golf, soccer, softball, tennis, track/field (outdoor), volleyball. **On-Campus Highlights:** Aquatic and Recreation Center, New UTC Library, The Crossroads, Challenger Center **Environmental Initiatives:** Central Plan Improvements

ADMISSIONS

Freshman Academic Profile: Average high school GPA 3.5. 75% from public high schools. **Test Scores:** SAT Math middle 50% range 510-610. SAT EBRW middle 50% range 530-630. ACT middle 50% range 21-26. Minimum internet-based TOEFL 61. Minimum paper TOEFL 500. **Basis for Candidate Selection:** *Very important factors considered include:* rigor of secondary school record, academic GPA, standardized test scores. *Important factors considered include:* character/personal qualities. *Other factors considered include:* application essay, recommendation(s), extracurricular activities, talent/ability, volunteer work, work experience. **Freshman Admission Requirements:** High school diploma is required and GED is accepted *Academic units required:* 4 English, 4 math, 3 science, 3 science labs, 2 foreign language, 2 history, 1 visual/performing arts. **Freshman Admission Statistics:** 7,235 applied, 82.8% admitted, 36% enrolled. **Transfer Admission Requirements:** college transcript(s), Minimum college GPA of 2.0 required. Lowest grade transferable D. **General Admission Information:** Application fee $30. Regular application deadline 5/1. Nonfall registration accepted. Admission may be deferred for a maximum of 1 semester.

COSTS AND FINANCIAL AID

Annual in-state tuition $8,786. Annual out-of-state tuition $23,006. Room and board $8,786. Required fees $1,776. Average book expense $1,400. **Required Forms and Deadlines:** FAFSA. **Notification of Awards:** Applicants will be notified of awards on a rolling basis beginning 1/20. **Types of Aid:** *Need-based scholarships/grants:* College/university scholarship or grant aid from institutional funds; Federal Pell; Private scholarships; SEOG; State scholarships/grants. *Loans:* Direct PLUS loans; Direct Subsidized Stafford Loans; Direct Unsubsidized Stafford Loans. *Student Employment:* Federal Work-Study Program available. Institutional employment available. **Financial Aid Statistics:** 96% needy freshmen, 85% needy undergrads receive need-based scholarship or grant aid. 4% freshmen, 3% undergrads receive non-need-based scholarship or grant aid. 74% freshmen, 77% undergrads receive need-based self-help aid. 2% freshmen, 2% undergrads receive athletic scholarships. 65% freshmen, 63% undergrads receive any aid. 58% undergrads borrow to pay for school. Average cumulative indebtedness $22,917. **Criteria for awarding aid:** *Need-based:* Academics *Non-need-based:* Academics, Alumni affiliation, Art, Athletics, Leadership, Music/drama, State/district residency.

UNIVERSITY OF TENNESSEE AT KNOXVILLE

527 Andy Holt Tower, Knoxville, TN 37996-0230
Phone: 865-974-1111 • **Financial Aid Phone:** (865) 974-1111
E-mail: admissions@utk.edu • **CEEB Code:** 1843
Website: http://www.utk.edu • **ACT Code:** 4026

This public school was founded in 1794. It has a 600 acre campus.

RATINGS

Admissions Selectivity Rating: 83   **Fire Safety Rating:** 96   **Green Rating:** 94

STUDENTS AND FACULTY

Enrollment: 22,151. **Student Body:** 50% female, 50% male, 13% out-of-state, 1% international (42 countries represented). Asian 4%, African American 7%, Caucasian 78%, Hispanic 4%, Native American <1%, Pacific Islander 0%, Two or more races 3%, Race unknown 3%.
Retention and Graduation: 86% freshmen return for sophomore year. 46% freshmen graduate within 4 years. 70% freshmen graduate within 6 years.
Faculty: Student/faculty ratio 17:1. 1,567 full-time faculty, 87% hold PhDs, 19% are members of minority groups, 44% are women.

ACADEMICS

Degrees: Bachelor's; Doctoral; Doctoral/Professional; Doctoral/Research; Master's; Post-Bachelor's certificate **Classes:** Most classes have 20-29 students. Most lab/discussion sessions have 20-29 students. **Most popular majors:** Biology/Biological Sciences, General; Kinesiology And Exercise Science; Logistics, Materials, And Supply Chain Management. **Special Study Options:** Accelerated program; Cooperative education program; Distance learning; Double major; Dual enrollment; English as a Second Language (ESL); Exchange student program (domestic); External degree program; Honors program; Independent study; Internships; Liberal arts/career combination; Student-designed major; Study abroad; Teacher certification program. Honors programs: a. Chancellor's Honors Program b. Haslam Scholars Program c. Leadership Honors Program d. 1794 Scholars Program e. College Scholars Program f. Global Leadership Scholars Program g. College of Engineering Honors Program h. College of Agricultural and Natural Resources Honors Program i. College of Social Work Honors Program j. Howard H. Baker Jr. Center for Public Policy's Baker Scholars Program k. The Math Honors Program l. Additional departmental honors programs. **Disability Services offered to physically disabled students:** Note-taking services; Reader services; Tape recorders; Tutors. **Career services:** Alumni network; Alumni services; Career assessment; Career/job search classes; Internships; Regional alumni

FACILITIES

Housing: Apartments for single students; Coed dorms; Fraternity/sorority housing; Men's dorms; Special housing for disabled student; Theme housing; Wellness housing; Women's dorms 95% of campus accessible to physically diasbled. **Special Academic Facilities/Equipment:** McClung Museum of Natural History and Culture has collections in anthropology, archaeology, decorative arts, local history, and natural history. Exhibits showcase the geologic, historical, and artistic past of Tennessee as well as cultures from around the globe. Ewing Gallery of Art – on campus and UT Downtown Gallery in nearby downtown Knoxville exhibit a wide range of art, media, graphic design, architectural drawings and photographs. The new Natalie L. Haslam Music Center and the Cox Auditorium in the Alumni Memorial Building host hundreds of shows every year ranging from UT Opera and choral groups to string, wind, and jazz ensembles and a wide variety of bands. Clarence Brown Theatre—is home to the Clarence Brown Theatre Professional Company, the University Company, and the undergraduate performance group. The theatre produces plays and musicals that often feature nationally renowned guest artists. UT is one of only 27 professional theaters based at a university. The International House is a multi-cultural gathering and programming facility

where individuals from all over the globe come together to share experiences. Howard H. Baker Jr. Center for Public Policy is a nonpartisan institute devoted to education and scholarship and civic engagement. Through classes, public lectures, research, and outreach programs, the center provides policy makers, citizens, scholars, and students with the information and skills needed to work effectively within our political system. **Computers:** 100% of classrooms, 100% of dorms, 100% of libraries, 100% of dining areas, 100% of student union, 25% of common outdoor areas have wireless network access. Students can register for classes online.

CAMPUS LIFE

Environment: City **Activities:** Campus Ministries; Choral groups; Concert band; Dance; Drama/theater; International Student Organization; Jazz band; Literary magazine; Marching band; Model UN; Music ensembles; Musical theater; Opera; Pep band; Radio station; Student government; Student newspaper; Student-run film society; Symphony orchestra; Television station; Yearbook 450 registered organizations, 90 honor societies, 30 religious organizations. 23 fraternities, 18 sororities. **Athletics (Intercollegiate):** *Men:* baseball, basketball, cheerleading, cross-country, diving, football, golf, swimming, tennis, track/field (outdoor), track/field (indoor). *Women:* basketball, cheerleading, crew/rowing, cross-country, diving, golf, soccer, softball, swimming, tennis, track/field (outdoor), track/field (indoor), volleyball. **On-Campus Highlights:** Neyland Stadium, Student Union, Ayres Hall and the Hill, Johnson-Ward Pedestrian Mall and Walkway, T-Recs (Student Recreation Center) **Environmental Initiatives:** Climate Action Plan

ADMISSIONS

Freshman Academic Profile: Average high school GPA 3.9. **Test Scores:** SAT Math middle 50% range 560-650. SAT EBRW middle 50% range 580-660. ACT middle 50% range 24-30. Minimum internet-based TOEFL 70. Minimum paper TOEFL 523. **Basis for Candidate Selection:** *Very important factors considered include:* rigor of secondary school record, academic GPA, standardized test scores. *Important factors considered include:* application essay, recommendation(s), extracurricular activities, talent/ability, character/personal qualities, first generation, alumni/ae relation, volunteer work, work experience. *Other factors considered include:* class rank, level of applicant's interest. **Freshman Admission Requirements:** High school diploma is required and GED is accepted *Academic units required: Academic units recommended:* 4 English, 4 math, 3 science, 3 science labs, 2 foreign language, 1 social studies, 1 history, 1 visual/performing arts. **Freshman Admission Statistics:** 18,872 applied, 77.0% admitted, 34% enrolled. **Transfer Admission Requirements:** High school transcript, college transcript(s), statement of good standing from prior institution(s). Minimum college GPA of 2.0 required. Lowest grade transferable C. **General Admission Information:** Application fee $50. Priority deadline 11/11. Nonfall registration accepted.

COSTS AND FINANCIAL AID

Annual in-state tuition $10,696. Annual out-of-state tuition $29,300. Room and board $10,696. Required fees $1,860. Average book expense $1,598. **Required Forms and Deadlines:** FAFSA. **Notification of Awards:** Applicants will be notified of awards on a rolling basis beginning 3/15. **Types of Aid:** *Need-based scholarships/grants:* College/university scholarship or grant aid from institutional funds; Federal Pell; Private scholarships; SEOG; State scholarships/grants. *Loans:* Direct PLUS loans; Direct Subsidized Stafford Loans; Direct Unsubsidized Stafford Loans. *Student Employment:* Federal Work-Study Program available. **Financial Aid Statistics:** 95% needy freshmen, 88% needy undergrads receive need-based scholarship or grant aid. 0% undergrads receive non-need-based scholarship or grant aid. 100% freshmen, 99% undergrads receive need-based self-help aid. 2% freshmen, 2% undergrads receive athletic scholarships. 89% freshmen, 93% undergrads receive any aid. 51% undergrads borrow to pay for school. Average cumulative indebtedness $24,420. **Criteria for awarding aid:** *Need-based:* Academics, Minority status *Non-need-based:* Academics, Art, Athletics, Leadership, Minority status, Music/drama, State/district residency.

UNIVERSITY OF TENNESSEE AT MARTIN

554 University Street, Martin, TN 38238
Phone: 731-881-7020 · **Financial Aid Phone:** 731-881-7031
E-mail: admitme@utm.edu
Fax: 731-881-7029 • **Website:** www.utm.edu • **ACT Code:** 4032

This public school was founded in 1900. It has a 930 acre campus.

RATINGS

Admissions Selectivity Rating: 83   **Fire Safety Rating:** 91   **Green Rating:** 63

STUDENTS AND FACULTY

Enrollment: 5,525. **Student Body:** 58% female, 42% male, 8% out-of-state, 2% international (20 countries represented). Asian 1%, African American 14%, Caucasian 78%, Hispanic 3%, Native American <1%, Pacific Islander 0%, Two or more races 2%, Race unknown 0%.

Retention and Graduation: 76% freshmen return for sophomore year. 23% freshmen graduate within 4 years. 50% freshmen graduate within 6 years. 19% grads go on to further study within 1 year. **Faculty:** Student/faculty ratio 15:1. 286 full-time faculty, 71% hold PhDs, 11% are members of minority groups, 46% are women. 0% of classes are taught by teaching assistants.

ACADEMICS

Degrees: Bachelor's; **Master's Classes:** Most classes have 10-19 students. Most lab/discussion sessions have fewer than 10 students. **Most popular majors:** Agricultural Business And Management, General; Registered Nursing/Registered Nurse; Management Information Systems, General. **Special Study Options:** Accelerated program; Cooperative education program; Cross-registration; Distance learning; Double major; Dual enrollment; English as a Second Language (ESL); Exchange student program (domestic); Honors program; Independent study; Internships; Student-designed major; Study abroad; Teacher certification program. Honors programs: University Scholars Honors Seminar. **Disability Services offered to physically disabled students:** Note-taking services; Reader services; Tape recorders; Tutors. **Career services:** Alumni network; Alumni services; Career assessment; Career/job search classes; Internships; Regional alumni

FACILITIES

Housing: Apartments for married students; Apartments for single students; Coed dorms; Men's dorms; Special housing for disabled student; Women's dorms 100% of campus accessible to physically diasbled. **Special Academic Facilities/Equipment:** Paul Meek Library contains Houston Gordon University Museum **Computers:** 100% of classrooms, 50% of dorms, 100% of libraries, 100% of dining areas, 100% of student union, 100% of common outdoor areas have wireless network access. Students can register for classes online. Administrative functions (other than registration) can be performed online.

CAMPUS LIFE

Environment: Village **Activities:** Campus Ministries; Choral groups; Concert band; Dance; Drama/theater; International Student Organization; Jazz band; Literary magazine; Marching band; Model UN; Music ensembles; Musical theater; Pep band; Radio station; Student government; Student newspaper; Student-run film society; Television station; Yearbook 100 registered organizations, 27 honor societies, 11 religious organizations. 12 fraternities, 8 sororities. **Athletics (Intercollegiate):** *Men:* baseball, basketball, cross-country, football, golf, riflery, rodeo. *Women:* basketball, cheerleading, cross-country, equestrian sports, riflery, rodeo, soccer, softball, tennis, volleyball. **On-Campus Highlights:** Boling University Center, Paul Meek Library, Student Recreation Center, Elam Center and Intramural facilities, Quad **Environmental Initiatives:** Establishing a Recycling Facility to collect campus and community recyclables. The campus recycles its paper, cardboard, cans and plastic bottles.

ADMISSIONS

Freshman Academic Profile: Average high school GPA 3.5. 16% in top 10% of high school class, 44% in top 25% of high school class, 78% in top 50% of high school class. 92% from public high schools. **Test Scores:** ACT middle 50% range 20-25. Minimum internet-based TOEFL 61. Minimum paper TOEFL 500. **Basis for Candidate Selection:** *Very important factors considered include:* rigor of secondary school record, academic GPA, standardized test scores. **Freshman Admission Requirements:** High school diploma is required and GED is accepted *Academic units required:* 4 English, 4 math, 3 science, 1 science labs, 2 foreign language, 1 social studies, 1 history, 1 visual/performing arts. **Freshman Admission Statistics:** 4,884 applied, 61.5% admitted, 35% enrolled. **Transfer Admission Requirements:** High school transcript, college transcript(s), Minimum college GPA of 2.0 required. Lowest grade transferable D. **General Admission Information:** Application fee $30. Priority deadline 8/1. Nonfall registration accepted. Admission may be deferred for a maximum of 1 year.

COSTS AND FINANCIAL AID

Annual in-state tuition $5,976. Annual out-of-state tuition $12,960. Room and board $5,976. Required fees $1,418. Average book expense $1,250. **Required Forms and Deadlines:** FAFSA. **Notification of Awards:** Applicants will be notified of awards on a rolling basis beginning 3/15. **Types of Aid:** *Need-based scholarships/grants:* College/university scholarship or grant aid from institutional funds; Federal Pell; Private scholarships; SEOG; State scholarships/grants. *Loans:* Direct PLUS loans; Direct Subsidized Stafford Loans; Direct Unsubsidized Stafford Loans. *Student Employment:* Federal Work-Study Program available. Institutional employment available. **Financial Aid Statistics:** 68% needy freshmen, 68% needy undergrads receive need-based scholarship or grant aid. 100% freshmen, 100% undergrads receive

non-need-based scholarship or grant aid. 54% freshmen, 66% undergrads receive need-based self-help aid. 8% freshmen, 6% undergrads receive athletic scholarships. 72% freshmen, 72% undergrads receive any aid. 66% undergrads borrow to pay for school. Average cumulative indebtedness $28,077. **Criteria for awarding aid:** *Need-based:* Academics *Non-need-based:* Academics, Alumni affiliation, Art, Athletics, Leadership, Minority status, Music/drama, State/district residency.

THE UNIVERSITY OF TEXAS AT ARLINGTON

Box 19088, Arlington, TX 76019-0111
Phone: 817-272-6287 • **Financial Aid Phone:** 817-272-3561
E-mail: admissions@uta.edu • **CEEB Code:** 6013
Fax: 817-272-3435 • **Website:** www.uta.edu • **ACT Code:** 4200

This public school was founded in 1895. It has a 420 acre campus.

RATINGS

Admissions Selectivity Rating: 85   **Fire Safety Rating:** 96   **Green Rating:** 79

STUDENTS AND FACULTY

Enrollment: 25,414. **Student Body:** 56% female, 44% male, 3% out-of-state, 4% international (123 countries represented). Asian 12%, African American 15%, Caucasian 40%, Hispanic 26%, Native American <1%, Pacific Islander <1%, Two or more races 3%, Race unknown 1%.

Retention and Graduation: 74% freshmen return for sophomore year. **Faculty:** Student/faculty ratio 22:1. 941 full-time faculty, 28% are members of minority groups, 42% are women. 16% of classes are taught by teaching assistants.

ACADEMICS

Degrees: Bachelor's; Doctoral; Doctoral/Professional; Doctoral/Research; Master's; Post-Bachelor's certificate; Post-Master's certificate **Classes:** Most classes have 10-19 students. Most lab/discussion sessions have 10-19 students. **Most popular majors:** Registered Nursing/Registered Nurse; Business Administration And Management, General. **Special Study Options:** Cross-registration; Distance learning; Double major; Dual enrollment; English as a Second Language (ESL); Honors program; Independent study; Internships; Student-designed major; Study abroad; Teacher certification program. Honors programs: We have the only Honors College in N. Texas. Freshmen interest groups, honors study abroad. Combined degree programs: BA/MD. **Disability Services offered to physically disabled students:** Note-taking services; Reader services; Tape recorders; Tutors. **Career services:** Alumni services; Career assessment; Career/job search classes; Internships

FACILITIES

Housing: Apartments for married students; Apartments for single students; Coed dorms; Fraternity/sorority housing; Men's dorms; Women's dorms 95% of campus accessible to physically diasbled. **Special Academic Facilities/Equipment:** Cartographic history library, maps collection, minority cultures collection, library of Texana and Mexican war. Continuing Education Work Force Development Center. material, planetarium, Automation and Robotics Research institute, Wave Scattering Research Center **Computers:** Students can register for classes online. Administrative functions (other than registration) can be performed online.

CAMPUS LIFE

Environment: Metropolis **Activities:** Campus Ministries; Choral groups; Concert band; Dance; Drama/theater; International Student Organization; Jazz band; Literary magazine; Marching band; Music ensembles; Opera; Radio station; Student government; Student newspaper; Student-run film society; Symphony orchestra 459 registered organizations, 30 honor societies, 27 religious organizations. 12 fraternities, 13 sororities. **Athletics (Intercollegiate):** *Men:* baseball, basketball, cross-country, golf, tennis, track/field (outdoor). *Women:* basketball, cross-country, softball, tennis, track/field (outdoor), volleyball. **On-Campus Highlights:** Click Cafe in Library, E. H. Hereford University Center, Maverick Activities Center, Library Mall, College Park Center **Environmental Initiatives:** Transportation programs like car sharing, ride share, bike program

ADMISSIONS

Freshman Academic Profile: 28% in top 10% of high school class, 75% in top 25% of high school class, 98% in top 50% of high school class. **Test Scores:** SAT Math middle 50% range 500-620. SAT EBRW middle 50% range 460-580. ACT middle 50% range 20-26. Minimum internet-based TOEFL 79. Minimum paper TOEFL 550. **Basis for Candidate Selection:** *Very important factors considered include:* class rank, academic GPA, standardized test scores. *Important factors considered include:* rigor of secondary school record. *Other factors considered include:* application essay, recommendation(s), extracurricular activities, talent/ability, character/personal qualities, first generation, volunteer work, work experience, level of applicant's interest. **Freshman Admission Requirements:** High school diploma is required and GED is not accepted *Academic units required:* 4 English, 3 math, 3 science, 2 foreign language, 3 social studies, 5 academic electives, and 5 units from above areas or other academic areas. *Academic units recommended:* 4 English, 4 math, 3 science, 3 foreign language, 4 social studies, 5 academic electives. **Freshman Admission Statistics:** 10,679 applied, 60.0% admitted, 42% enrolled. **Transfer Admission Requirements:** High school transcript, college transcript(s), Minimum college GPA of 2.25 required. Lowest grade transferable C. **General Admission Information:** Application fee $50. Priority deadline 6/1. Nonfall registration accepted. Admission may be deferred for a maximum of 1 year.

COSTS AND FINANCIAL AID

Annual in-state tuition $7,864. Annual out-of-state tuition $19,497. Room and board $7,864. Average book expense $1,160. **Required Forms and Deadlines:** FAFSA. **Notification of Awards:** Applicants will be notified of awards on a rolling basis beginning 4/1. **Types of Aid:** *Need-based scholarships/grants:* College/university scholarship or grant aid from institutional funds; Federal Pell; Private scholarships; SEOG; State scholarships/grants; United Negro College Fund. *Loans:* Direct PLUS loans; Direct Subsidized Stafford Loans; Direct Unsubsidized Stafford Loans. *Student Employment:* Federal Work-Study Program available. Institutional employment available. **Financial Aid Statistics:** 74% needy freshmen, 80% needy undergrads receive need-based scholarship or grant aid. 50% freshmen, 31% undergrads receive non-need-based scholarship or grant aid. 94% freshmen, 95% undergrads receive need-based self-help aid. 0% freshmen, 0% undergrads receive athletic scholarships. 65% freshmen, 68% undergrads receive any aid. **Criteria for awarding aid:** *Need-based:* Academics, Athletics *Non-need-based:* Academics, Art, Athletics, Leadership, Music/drama.

THE UNIVERSITY OF TEXAS AT AUSTIN

P.O. Box 8058, Austin, TX 78713-8058
Phone: 512-475-7399 • **Financial Aid Phone:** (512) 475-6203 • **CEEB Code:** 6882
Fax: 512-471-8102 • **Website:** http://www.utexas.edu • **ACT Code:** 4240

This public school was founded in 1883. It has a 436 acre campus.

RATINGS

Admissions Selectivity Rating: 93   Fire Safety Rating: 84   Green Rating: 90

STUDENTS AND FACULTY

Enrollment: 39,965. **Student Body:** 53% female, 47% male, 6% out-of-state, 5% international (96 countries represented). Asian 21%, African American 4%, Caucasian 41%, Hispanic 23%, Native American <1%, Pacific Islander <1%, Two or more races 4%, Race unknown 1%.
Retention and Graduation: 95% freshmen return for sophomore year. 58% freshmen graduate within 4 years. 83% freshmen graduate within 6 years.
Faculty: Student/faculty ratio 18:1. 2,637 full-time faculty, 89% hold PhDs, 22% are members of minority groups, 41% are women.

ACADEMICS

Degrees: Bachelor's; Certificate; Doctoral/Professional; Doctoral/Research; Master's; Post-Bachelor's certificate **Classes:** Most classes have 10-19 students. Most lab/discussion sessions have 10-19 students. **Most popular majors:** Computer And Information Sciences, General; Biology/Biological Sciences, General; Economics, General. **Special Study Options:** Accelerated program; Cooperative education program; Cross-registration; Distance learning; Double major; Dual enrollment; English as a Second Language (ESL); Exchange student program (domestic); Honors program; Independent study; Internships; Liberal arts/career combination; Student-designed major; Study abroad; Teacher certification program. Honors programs: Business Honors Program, Engineering Honors Programs, Liberal Arts Honors Program, Plan II Honors Program, Natural Sciences Honors Programs: Turing Scholars Program in Computer Science, Human Ecology Honors, Dean's Scholars, Health Science Scholars, Polymathic Scholars, Moody College Honors Program. **Disability Services offered to physically disabled students:** Note-taking services; Reader services; Tape recorders; Tutors. **Career services:** Alumni network; Alumni services; Career assessment; Internships; Regional alumni

FACILITIES

Housing: Apartments for married students; Apartments for single students; Coed dorms; Men's dorms; Special housing for disabled student; Special housing for international students; Women's dorms **Special Academic Facilities/Equipment:** Blanton Museum of Art, Lyndon Baines Johnson Presidential Library/Museum, Performing Arts Center, Texas Memorial Museum, Harry Ransom Humanities Research Center. **Computers:** Students can register for classes online. Administrative functions (other than registration) can be performed online.

CAMPUS LIFE

Environment: Metropolis **Activities:** Campus Ministries; Choral groups; Concert band; Dance; Drama/theater; International Student Organization; Jazz band; Literary magazine; Marching band; Model UN; Music ensembles; Musical theater; Radio station; Student government; Student newspaper; Student-run film society; Symphony orchestra; Television station; Yearbook 900 registered organizations, 15 honor societies, 95 religious organizations. 26 fraternities, 22 sororities. **Athletics (Intercollegiate):** *Men:* baseball, basketball, cross-country, diving, football, golf, swimming, tennis, track/field (outdoor). *Women:* basketball, crew/rowing, cross-country, diving, golf, soccer, softball, swimming, tennis, track/field (outdoor), volleyball. **On-Campus Highlights:** The Tower, Darrell K Royal-Texas Memorial Stadium, LBJ Presidential Library, Blanton Museum of Art, Student Activities Center **Environmental Initiatives:** Incorporation of sustainability principles throughout the institution's approved Campus Master Plan (May 2013).

ADMISSIONS

Freshman Academic Profile: 74% in top 10% of high school class, 17% in top 25% of high school class, 99% in top 50% of high school class. **Test Scores:** SAT Math middle 50% range 610-740. SAT EBRW middle 50% range 620-720. ACT middle 50% range 26-33. Minimum internet-based TOEFL 79. Minimum paper TOEFL 550. **Basis for Candidate Selection:** *Very important factors considered include:* rigor of secondary school record, class rank. *Important factors considered include:* application essay, standardized test scores, extracurricular activities, talent/ability, volunteer work, work experience. *Other factors considered include:* recommendation(s), character/personal qualities, first generation, state residency, racial/ethnic status, level of applicant's interest. **Freshman Admission Requirements:** High school diploma is required and GED is accepted *Academic units required:* 4 English, 4 math, 4 science, 2 foreign language, 4 social studies, 6 academic electives. **Freshman Admission Statistics:** 51,033 applied, 36.5% admitted, 45% enrolled. **Transfer Admission Requirements:** college transcript(s), essay or personal statement, Minimum college GPA of 3.0 required. Lowest grade transferable C. **General Admission Information:** Application fee $75. Regular application deadline 12/1. Nonfall registration accepted.

COSTS AND FINANCIAL AID

Annual in-state tuition $10,070. Annual out-of-state tuition $36,744. Room and board $10,070. Average book expense $662. **Required Forms and Deadlines:** FAFSA; Institution's own financial aid form. **Notification of Awards:** Applicants will be notified of awards on a rolling basis beginning 3/15. **Types of Aid:** *Need-based scholarships/grants:* College/university scholarship or grant aid from institutional funds; Federal Pell; Private scholarships; SEOG; State scholarships/grants. *Loans:* Direct PLUS loans; Direct Subsidized Stafford Loans; Direct Unsubsidized Stafford Loans. *Student Employment:* Federal Work-Study Program available. Institutional employment available. **Financial Aid Statistics:** 75% needy freshmen, 80% needy undergrads receive need-based scholarship or grant aid. 39% freshmen, 23% undergrads receive non-need-based scholarship or grant aid. 71% freshmen, 69% undergrads receive need-based self-help aid. 2% freshmen, 4% undergrads receive athletic scholarships. 42% undergrads receive any aid. 45% undergrads borrow to pay for school. Average cumulative indebtedness $25,338. **Criteria for awarding aid:** *Need-based:* Academics, Art, Leadership, Music/drama *Non-need-based:* Academics, Art, Athletics, Leadership, Music/drama, State/district residency.

THE UNIVERSITY OF TEXAS AT BROWNSVILLE

901 Eden Rd, Brownsville, TX 78520
Phone: 956-882-8295 • **Financial Aid Phone:** 956-882-8814
E-mail: admissions@utb.edu • **CEEB Code:** 6825
Fax: 956-882-7810 • **Website:** www.utb.edu

This public school was founded in 1926.

RATINGS

Admissions Selectivity Rating: 65   Fire Safety Rating: 60*   Green Rating: 60*

STUDENTS AND FACULTY

Enrollment: 10,145. **Student Body:** 60% female, 40% male, 4% out-of-state, 4% international (21 countries represented). Asian <1%, African American <1%, Caucasian 5%, Hispanic 90%, Native American <1%, Race unknown 1%. **Faculty:** 366 full-time faculty, 59% hold PhDs, 46% are members of minority groups, 43% are women. 0% of classes are taught by teaching assistants.

ACADEMICS

Degrees: Associate; Bachelor's; Certificate; Master's; Terminal Associate; Transfer Associate **Classes:** Most classes have fewer than 10 students. **Most popular majors:** Multi-/Interdisciplinary Studies, Other; Psychology, General; Business/Commerce, General. **Special Study Options:** Cooperative education program; Distance learning; Double major; Dual enrollment; English as a Second Language (ESL); Independent study; Internships; Teacher certification program. **Disability Services offered to physically disabled students:** Note-taking services; Reader services; Tape recorders; Tutors.

FACILITIES

Housing: Apartments for single students; Coed dorms; Men's dorms; Special housing for disabled student; Women's dorms **Computers:** Students can register for classes online. Administrative functions (other than registration) can be performed online.

CAMPUS LIFE

Environment: City **Activities:** Choral groups; Concert band; Dance; Drama/theater; Jazz band; Music ensembles; Opera; Radio station; Student government; Student newspaper 56 registered organizations, 6 honor societies. **Athletics (Intercollegiate):** *Men:* baseball, golf. *Women:* golf, volleyball.

ADMISSIONS

Freshman Academic Profile: Average high school GPA 2.6. 10% in top 10% of high school class, 27% in top 25% of high school class, 57% in top 50% of high school class. 95% from public high schools. **Freshman Admission Requirements:** High school diploma or equivalent is not required *Academic units required:* 4 English, 2 math, 2 science, 2 science labs, 2 foreign language, 4 social studies, 2 history, 1 academic elective, and 3 units from above areas or other academic areas. *Academic units recommended:* 4 English, 4 math, 3 science, 3 science labs, 3 foreign language, 4 social studies, 2 history, 4 academic electives, 3 units from above areas or other academic areas. **Freshman Admission Statistics:** 3,594 applied, 100.0% admitted, 48% enrolled. **Transfer Admission Requirements:** High school transcript, college transcript(s), Minimum college GPA of 2.0 required. Lowest grade transferable C. **General Admission Information:** Priority deadline 4/1. Regular application deadline 7/1. Nonfall registration accepted. Admission may be deferred for a maximum of 1 year.

COSTS AND FINANCIAL AID

Average book expense $615. **Required Forms and Deadlines:** FAFSA. **Notification of Awards:** Applicants will be notified of awards on or about 5/1. **Types of Aid:** *Need-based scholarships/grants:* College/university scholarship or grant aid from institutional funds; Federal Pell; Private scholarships; SEOG; State scholarships/grants. *Loans:* **Criteria for awarding aid:** *Need-based:* Academics *Non-need-based:* Academics, Art, Athletics, Leadership, Music/drama.

THE UNIVERSITY OF TEXAS AT DALLAS

800 West Campbell Road, Richardson, TX 75080-3021
Phone: 972-883-2270 • **Financial Aid Phone:** 972-883-2941
E-mail: interest@utdallas.edu • **CEEB Code:** 6897
Fax: 972-883-2599 • **Website:** www.utdallas.edu • **ACT Code:** 4243

This public school was founded in 1969. It has a 500 acre campus.

RATINGS

Admissions Selectivity Rating: 85   **Fire Safety Rating:** 94   **Green Rating:** 77

STUDENTS AND FACULTY

Enrollment: 18,091. **Student Body:** 43% female, 57% male, 4% out-of-state, 4% international (78 countries represented). Asian 31%, African American 6%, Caucasian 34%, Hispanic 18%, Native American <1%, Pacific Islander <1%, Two or more races 4%, Race unknown 2%. **Retention and Graduation:** 87% freshmen return for sophomore year. 52%

freshmen graduate within 4 years. 69% freshmen graduate within 6 years. **Faculty:** Student/faculty ratio 23:1. 895 full-time faculty, 86% hold PhDs, 28% are members of minority groups, 31% are women. 5% of classes are taught by teaching assistants.

ACADEMICS

Degrees: Bachelor's; Doctoral/Professional; Doctoral/Research; Master's; Post-Bachelor's certificate **Classes:** Most classes have 10-19 students. **Most popular majors:** Computer And Information Sciences, General; Mechanical Engineering; Biology/Biological Sciences, General. **Special Study Options:** Accelerated program; Cooperative education program; Cross-registration; Distance learning; Double major; Dual enrollment; English as a Second Language (ESL); Honors program; Independent study; Internships; Liberal arts/career combination; Student-designed major; Study abroad; Teacher certification program. Honors programs: UTD's Honors College offers small classes, innovative instruction, world class faculty, bright and inquisitive colleagues, and an array of extracurricular events to provide special opportunities for professional and personal growth. Combined degree programs: BA/MA. **Disability Services offered to physically disabled students:** Note-taking services; Reader services; Tape recorders; Tutors. **Career services:** Alumni network; Alumni services; Career assessment; Career/job search classes; Internships

FACILITIES

Housing: Apartments for married students; Apartments for single students; Coed dorms; Other (please specify) 100% of campus accessible to physically diasbled. **Special Academic Facilities/Equipment:** McDermott Library Special Collections which includes History of Aviation Collection, Wineburgh Philatelic Research Library and Louise B. Belsterling Botanical Library. **Computers:** 80% of classrooms, 100% of dorms, 100% of libraries, 100% of student union, 5% of common outdoor areas have wireless network access. Students can register for classes online.

CAMPUS LIFE

Environment: Metropolis **Activities:** Choral groups; Concert band; Dance; Drama/theater; International Student Organization; Jazz band; Literary magazine; Model UN; Music ensembles; Musical theater; Pep band; Radio station; Student government; Student newspaper; Student-run film society; Symphony orchestra; Television station 142 registered organizations, 8 honor societies, 9 religious organizations. 9 fraternities, 6 sororities. **Athletics (Intercollegiate):** *Men:* baseball, basketball, cross-country, golf, soccer, tennis. *Women:* basketball, cross-country, golf, soccer, softball, tennis, volleyball. **On-Campus Highlights:** The Pub (coffeehouse), Comet Cafe, Student Union / Plinth, Activity Center, University Village clubhouses **Environmental Initiatives:** Campus recycling program

ADMISSIONS

Freshman Academic Profile: 36% in top 10% of high school class, 64% in top 25% of high school class, 89% in top 50% of high school class. 92% from public high schools. **Test Scores:** SAT Math middle 50% range 620-730. SAT EBRW middle 50% range 600-700. ACT middle 50% range 26-32. Minimum internet-based TOEFL 80. Minimum paper TOEFL 550. **Basis for Candidate Selection:** *Very important factors considered include:* rigor of secondary school record, class rank, academic GPA, standardized test scores. *Important factors considered include:* application essay. *Other factors considered include:* recommendation(s), extracurricular activities, state residency, volunteer work, work experience, level of applicant's interest. **Freshman Admission Requirements:** High school diploma is required and GED is accepted *Academic units required:* 4 English, 4 math, 3 science, 3 science labs, 2 foreign language, 3 social studies, 1.5 academic electives, 0.5 visual/performing arts, *Academic units recommended:* 4 English, 4 math, 3 science, 3 science labs, 3 foreign language, 4 social studies, 2.5 academic electives, 1 computer science, 1 visual/performing arts, 2 units from above areas or other academic areas. **Freshman Admission Statistics:** 11,791 applied, 76.0% admitted, 35% enrolled. **Transfer Admission Requirements:** college transcript(s), Minimum college GPA of 2.5 required. Lowest grade transferable C. **General Admission Information:** Application fee $50. Regular application deadline 7/1. Nonfall registration accepted. Admission may be deferred for a maximum of One year.

COSTS AND FINANCIAL AID

Annual in-state tuition $11,112. Annual out-of-state tuition $34,644. Room and board $11,112. Average book expense $1,200. **Required Forms and Deadlines:** FAFSA. **Notification of Awards:** Applicants will be notified of awards on a rolling basis beginning 3/1. **Types of Aid:** *Need-based scholarships/grants:* College/university scholarship or grant aid from institutional funds; Federal Pell; Private scholarships; SEOG; State scholarships/grants. *Loans:* Direct PLUS loans; Direct Subsidized Stafford Loans; Direct Unsubsidized Stafford Loans. *Student Employment:* Federal Work-Study Program available. Institutional employment available. **Financial Aid Statistics:** 91% needy freshmen, 89% needy undergrads receive need-based scholarship or grant aid. 13% freshmen, 7% undergrads receive non-need-based scholarship or grant aid.

85% freshmen, 90% undergrads receive need-based self-help aid. 0% freshmen, 0% undergrads receive athletic scholarships. 78% freshmen, 71% undergrads receive any aid. 35% undergrads borrow to pay for school. Average cumulative indebtedness $20,432. **Criteria for awarding aid:** *Need-based:* Academics *Non-need-based:* Academics.

THE UNIVERSITY OF TEXAS AT EL PASO

500 W. University Ave., El Paso, TX 79968-0510
Phone: 915-747-5890
E-mail: www.academics.utep.edu • **CEEB Code:** 6829
Fax: 915-747-8893 • **Website:** http://www.utep.edu/ • **ACT Code:** 4223

This public school was founded in 1913. It has a 330 acre campus.

RATINGS

Admissions Selectivity Rating: 71   **Fire Safety Rating:** 75   **Green Rating:** 60*

STUDENTS AND FACULTY

Enrollment: 19,078. **Student Body:** 54% female, 46% male, 3% out-of-state, 5% international (65 countries represented). Asian 1%, African American 3%, Caucasian 8%, Hispanic 81%, Native American <1%, Pacific Islander <1%, Two or more races <1%, Race unknown 2%.
Retention and Graduation: 72% freshmen return for sophomore year.
Faculty: Student/faculty ratio 21:1. 2% of classes are taught by teaching assistants.

ACADEMICS

Degrees: Bachelor's; Doctoral/Professional; Doctoral/Research; Master's; Post-Bachelor's certificate; Post-Master's certificate **Classes:** Most classes have 20-29 students. Most lab/discussion sessions have 20-29 students. **Most popular majors:** Multi-/Interdisciplinary Studies, Other; Psychology, General; Criminal Justice/Safety Studies. **Special Study Options:** Accelerated program; Cooperative education program; Distance learning; Double major; English as a Second Language (ESL); Exchange student program (domestic); Honors program; Independent study; Internships; Student-designed major; Study abroad; Teacher certification program. Combined degree programs: BA/MA. **Disability Services offered to physically disabled students:** Note-taking services; Reader services; Tape recorders. **Career services:** Alumni services; Career assessment; Internships

FACILITIES

Housing: 90% of campus accessible to physically diasbled. **Special Academic Facilities/Equipment:** Cross-cultural ethnic study center, natural history and cultural museum, solar pond and solar house, electron microscope, atmospheric and acoustic research lab, seismic observatory. **Computers:** Students can register for classes online. Administrative functions (other than registration) can be performed online.

CAMPUS LIFE

Environment: Metropolis **Activities:** Choral groups; Concert band; Dance; Drama/theater; International Student Organization; Jazz band; Marching band; Music ensembles; Musical theater; Radio station; Student government; Student newspaper 1 honor societies, 1 religious organization. 6 fraternities, 4 sororities. **Athletics (Intercollegiate):** *Men:* basketball, cross-country, football, golf, track/field (outdoor), track/field (indoor). *Women:* basketball, cross-country, golf, riflery, soccer, softball, tennis, track/field (outdoor), track/field (indoor), volleyball.

ADMISSIONS

Freshman Academic Profile: Average high school GPA 3.2. 17% in top 10% of high school class, 40% in top 25% of high school class, 69% in top 50% of high school class. 94% from public high schools. **Test Scores:** SAT Math middle 50% range 420-530. SAT EBRW middle 50% range 390-500. ACT middle 50% range 17-22. **Basis for Candidate Selection:** *Important factors considered include:* rigor of secondary school record, class rank, academic GPA, standardized test scores. **Freshman Admission Requirements:** High school diploma is required and GED is accepted *Academic units required:* 4 English, 4 math, 4 science, 4 science labs, 2 social studies, 4 history, 6 computer science, 1 visual/performing arts, and 1.5 units from above areas or other academic areas. **Freshman Admission Statistics:** 6,240 applied, 99.8% admitted, 27% enrolled. **Transfer Admission Requirements:** college transcript(s), Minimum college GPA of 2.0 required. Lowest grade transferable D. **General Admission Information:** Nonfall registration accepted. Admission may be deferred for a maximum of 1 semester.

COSTS AND FINANCIAL AID

Annual in-state tuition $8,924. Annual out-of-state tuition $16,095. Room and board $8,924. Required fees $1,649. Average book expense $1,160. *Student Employment:* Federal Work-Study Program available. Institutional employment available. **Financial Aid Statistics:** 88% needy freshmen, 88% needy undergrads receive need-based scholarship or grant aid. 26% freshmen, 14% undergrads receive non-need-based scholarship or grant aid. 82% freshmen, 86% undergrads receive need-based self-help aid. 1% freshmen, 1% undergrads receive athletic scholarships. 77% freshmen, 65% undergrads receive any aid.

THE UNIVERSITY OF TEXAS AT TYLER

3900 University Blvd., Tyler, TX 75799
Phone: 903-566-7203 · **Financial Aid Phone:** 903-566-7180
E-mail: admrequest@uttyler.edu
Fax: 903-566-7068 • **Website:** www.uttyler.edu

This public school was founded in 1971. It has a 204 acre campus.

RATINGS

Admissions Selectivity Rating: 85   **Fire Safety Rating:** 93   **Green Rating:** 60*

STUDENTS AND FACULTY

Enrollment: 6,059. **Student Body:** 57% female, 43% male, 1% out-of-state, 2% international (45 countries represented). Asian 3%, African American 9%, Caucasian 58%, Hispanic 16%, Native American <1%, Pacific Islander <1%, Two or more races 8%, Race unknown 3%.
Retention and Graduation: 62% freshmen return for sophomore year. 14% grads go on to further study within 1 year.

ACADEMICS

Degrees: Bachelor's; Doctoral/Professional; Doctoral/Research; Master's; Post-Master's certificate **Classes:** Most classes have 10-19 students. Most lab/discussion sessions have 10-19 students. **Most popular majors:** Multi-/Interdisciplinary Studies, Other; Nursing/Registered Nurse (Rn, Asn, Bsn, Msn); Business/Managerial Economics. **Special Study Options:** Cooperative education program; Distance learning; Double major; Dual enrollment; Honors program; Independent study; Internships; Student-designed major; Study abroad; Teacher certification program. **Disability Services offered to physically disabled students:** Note-taking services; Reader services. **Career services:** Career assessment; Career/job search classes

FACILITIES

Housing: Coed dorms **Computers:** Students can register for classes online. Administrative functions (other than registration) can be performed online.

CAMPUS LIFE

Environment: City **Activities:** Choral groups; International Student Organization; Jazz band; Model UN; Music ensembles; Pep band; Student government; Student newspaper 73 registered organizations, 6 honor societies, 4 fraternities, 4 sororities. **Athletics (Intercollegiate):** *Men:* baseball, basketball, cheerleading, cross-country, golf, soccer, tennis. *Women:* basketball, cheerleading, cross-country, golf, soccer, tennis, volleyball. **On-Campus Highlights:** Herrington Patriot Center, Riter Tower and Plaza, Cowan Fine and Performing Art Center, Bill Ratliff Engineering and Science Complex, University Center

ADMISSIONS

Freshman Academic Profile: Average high school GPA 3.4. 10% in top 10% of high school class, 35% in top 25% of high school class, 64% in top 50% of high school class. **Test Scores:** SAT Math middle 50% range 490-590. SAT EBRW middle 50% range 480-570. ACT middle 50% range 20-25. Minimum paper TOEFL 550. **Basis for Candidate Selection:** *Very important factors considered include:* rigor of secondary school record, class rank, academic GPA, standardized test scores, level of applicant's interest. *Important factors considered include:* extracurricular activities, talent/ability, character/personal qualities, first generation, volunteer work. *Other factors considered include:* work experience. **Freshman Admission Requirements:** High school diploma is required and GED is accepted *Academic units required:* 4 English, 3 math, 3 science, 2 foreign language, 3 social studies, *Academic units recommended:* 4 math, 4 science, 3 science labs, 4 social studies, 4 history. **Freshman Admission Statistics:** 2,468 applied, 64.5% admitted, 49% enrolled. **Transfer Admission Requirements:** college transcript(s), Minimum college GPA of 2.0 required. Lowest grade transferable C. **General Admission Information:** Application fee $40. Regular application deadline 8/24. Nonfall registration accepted. Admission may be deferred for a maximum of 1 year.

COSTS AND FINANCIAL AID

Required Forms and Deadlines: FAFSA; Institution's own financial aid form. **Types of Aid:** *Need-based scholarships/grants:* College/university scholarship or grant aid from institutional funds; Federal Pell; Private scholarships; SEOG; State scholarships/grants. *Loans:* **Criteria for awarding aid:** *Non-need-based:* Academics, Art, Music/drama.

THE UNIVERSITY OF TEXAS MEDICAL BRANCH

301 University Boulevard, Galveston, TX 77555-1305
Phone: 409-772-1215 • **Financial Aid Phone:** 409-772-1215
E-mail: enrollment.services@utmb.edu • **CEEB Code:** 6887
Fax: 409-772-4466 • **Website:** www.utmb.edu

This public school was founded in 1891. It has a 85 acre campus.

RATINGS
Admissions Selectivity Rating: 0   **Fire Safety Rating:** 60*   **Green Rating:** 60*

STUDENTS AND FACULTY
Enrollment: 492. **Student Body:** 80% female, 20% male, 1% out-of-state, 2% international (34 countries represented). Asian 18%, African American 18%, Caucasian 42%, Hispanic 14%, Native American 1%, Race unknown 5%.
Faculty:

ACADEMICS
Degrees: Bachelor's; Doctoral/Professional; Doctoral/Research; Master's; Post-Master's certificate **Classes:** Most classes have 20-29 students. Most lab/discussion sessions have 20-29 students. **Most popular majors:** Respiratory Care Therapy/Therapist; Clinical Laboratory Science/Medical Technology/Technologist; Nursing/Registered Nurse (Rn, Asn, Bsn, Msn). **Special Study Options:** Distance learning; Independent study; Internships. **Disability Services offered to physically disabled students:** Note-taking services; Reader services; Tape recorders; Tutors. **Career services:** Alumni network; Alumni services; Internships

FACILITIES
Housing: Apartments for married students; Apartments for single students; Coed dorms; Fraternity/sorority housing 100% of campus accessible to physically disabled. **Special Academic Facilities/Equipment:** Moody Medical Library **Computers:** Students can register for classes online. Administrative functions (other than registration) can be performed online.

CAMPUS LIFE
Environment: Town **Activities:** Student government; Student newspaper; Yearbook 94 registered organizations, 4 honor societies, 7 religious organizations. 5 fraternities. **On-Campus Highlights:** Joe Jamail Student Center, Rosenberg House, Ashbel Smith Building, Alumni Field House, Moody Medical Library

ADMISSIONS
Test Scores: Minimum paper TOEFL 550. **Transfer Admission Requirements:** college transcript(s), Minimum college GPA of 2.0 required. Lowest grade transferable C. **General Admission Information:**

COSTS AND FINANCIAL AID
Required Forms and Deadlines: FAFSA. **Types of Aid:** *Need-based scholarships/grants:* College/university scholarship or grant aid from institutional funds; Federal Pell; Private scholarships; SEOG; State scholarships/grants. *Loans:* Direct PLUS loans; Direct Subsidized Stafford Loans; Direct Unsubsidized Stafford Loans. *Student Employment:* Federal Work-Study Program available. Institutional employment available. **Criteria for awarding aid:** *Need-based:* Academics, Minority status *Non-need-based:* Academics, Minority status, State/district residency.

THE UNIVERSITY OF TEXAS—PAN AMERICAN

1201 West University Drive, Edinburg, TX 78539-2999
Phone: (956) 665-2999 • **Financial Aid Phone:** 956-665-2501
E-mail: admissions@utrgv.edu • **CEEB Code:** 6570
Fax: (956) 665-2687 • **Website:** www.utrgv.edu • **ACT Code:** 4142

This public school was founded in 1927. It has a 331 acre campus.

RATINGS
Admissions Selectivity Rating: 77   **Fire Safety Rating:** 79   **Green Rating:** 84

STUDENTS AND FACULTY
Enrollment: 24,677. **Student Body:** 56% female, 44% male, 0% out-of-state, 0% international (25 countries represented). Asian 1%, African American 2%, Caucasian 13%, Hispanic 67%, Native American <1%, Pacific Islander 0%, Two or more races 0%, Race unknown 16%.
Retention and Graduation: 76% freshmen return for sophomore year.
Faculty: 1,041 full-time faculty, 54% are members of minority groups, 41% are women.

ACADEMICS
Degrees: Bachelor's; Doctoral/Research; Master's; Post-Bachelor's certificate **Classes:** Most classes have 10-19 students. **Most popular majors:** Biology/Biological Sciences, General; Multi-/Interdisciplinary Studies, Other; Business Administration And Management, General. **Special Study Options:** Accelerated program; Distance learning; Double major; Dual enrollment; English as a Second Language (ESL); Exchange student program (domestic); Honors program; Independent study; Internships; Study abroad; Teacher certification program. Honors programs: PRE-MEDICAL HONORS COLLEGE with Baylor College of Medicine. Combined degree programs: BA/MA. **Disability Services offered to physically disabled students:** Note-taking services; Reader services; Tape recorders; Tutors. **Career services:** Alumni services; Career assessment; Internships

FACILITIES
Housing: Apartments for married students; Apartments for single students; Men's dorms; Special housing for disabled student; Women's dorms 95% of campus accessible to physically disabled. **Computers:** Students can register for classes online. Administrative functions (other than registration) can be performed online.

CAMPUS LIFE
Environment: Town **Activities:** Campus Ministries; Choral groups; Concert band; Dance; Drama/theater; International Student Organization; Jazz band; Literary magazine; Music ensembles; Musical theater; Opera; Pep band; Radio station; Student government; Student newspaper; Student-run film society; Symphony orchestra; Television station; Yearbook 80 registered organizations, 9 honor societies, 7 religious organizations. 4 fraternities, 1 sorority. **Athletics (Intercollegiate):** *Men:* baseball, basketball, cross-country, golf, tennis, track/field (outdoor). *Women:* basketball, cross-country, golf, tennis, track/field (outdoor), volleyball. **On-Campus Highlights:** Visitors Center, Science Courtyard, Residence Halls, Student Union **Environmental Initiatives:** The direction of disposal of hazardous waste streams toward recycling or reuse.

ADMISSIONS
Freshman Academic Profile: 17% in top 10% of high school class, 47% in top 25% of high school class, 80% in top 50% of high school class. 99% from public high schools. **Test Scores:** SAT Math middle 50% range 430-530. SAT EBRW middle 50% range 410-520. ACT middle 50% range 17-21. Minimum internet-based TOEFL 63. Minimum paper TOEFL 500. **Basis for Candidate Selection:** *Very important factors considered include:* class rank, standardized test scores. *Important factors considered include:* rigor of secondary school record, academic GPA, application essay, level of applicant's interest. *Other factors considered include:* extracurricular activities, talent/ability, character/personal qualities, volunteer work, work experience. **Freshman Admission Requirements:** High school diploma is required and GED is accepted *Academic units required:* 4 English, 3 math, 2 science, 3 social studies, 7.5 academic electives, 1 visual/performing arts, and 1.5 units from above areas or other academic areas. *Academic units recommended:* 4 English, 4 math, 4 science, 2 foreign language, 4 social studies, 5.5 academic electives, 1 visual/performing arts, 1.5 units from above areas or other academic areas. **Freshman Admission Statistics:** 9,055 applied, 82.2% admitted, 56% enrolled. **Transfer Admission Requirements:** college transcript(s), Minimum college GPA of 2.0 required. Lowest grade transferable D. **General Admission Information:** Priority deadline 2/1. Regular application deadline 7/1. Nonfall registration accepted.

COSTS AND FINANCIAL AID

Average book expense $1,194. **Required Forms and Deadlines:** FAFSA. **Notification of Awards:** Applicants will be notified of awards on or about 3/15. **Types of Aid:** *Need-based scholarships/grants:* College/university scholarship or grant aid from institutional funds; Federal Pell; Private scholarships; SEOG; State scholarships/grants. *Loans:* Direct PLUS loans; Direct Subsidized Stafford Loans; Direct Unsubsidized Stafford Loans. *Student Employment:* Federal Work-Study Program available. Institutional employment available. **Financial Aid Statistics:** 98% needy freshmen, 96% needy undergrads receive need-based scholarship or grant aid. 2% freshmen, 11% undergrads receive non-need-based scholarship or grant aid. 29% freshmen, 46% undergrads receive need-based self-help aid. 1% freshmen, 1% undergrads receive athletic scholarships. 62% undergrads borrow to pay for school. Average cumulative indebtedness $16,178. **Criteria for awarding aid:** *Need-based:* Academics, Athletics *Non-need-based:* Academics, Alumni affiliation, Art, Athletics.

THE UNIVERSITY OF TEXAS—SAN ANTONIO

One UTSA Circle, San Antonio, TX 78249-0617
Phone: (210) 458-8000 • **Financial Aid Phone:** 210-458-8000
E-mail: prospects@utsa.edu • **CEEB Code:** 6919
Fax: 210-458-7857 • **Website:** http://www.utsa.edu/ • **ACT Code:** 4239

This public school was founded in 1969. It has a 725 acre campus.

RATINGS

Admissions Selectivity Rating: 80   **Fire Safety Rating:** 84   **Green Rating:** 60*

STUDENTS AND FACULTY

Enrollment: 25,709. **Student Body:** 50% female, 50% male, 2% out-of-state, 2% international (74 countries represented). Asian 6%, African American 9%, Caucasian 23%, Hispanic 55%, Native American <1%, Pacific Islander <1%, Two or more races 3%, Race unknown 1%.
Retention and Graduation: 74% freshmen return for sophomore year. 15% freshmen graduate within 4 years. 37% freshmen graduate within 6 years.
Faculty: Student/faculty ratio 25:1. 885 full-time faculty, 86% hold PhDs, 35% are members of minority groups, 38% are women.

ACADEMICS

Degrees: Bachelor's; Certificate; Doctoral/Research; Master's; Post-Bachelor's certificate **Classes:** Most classes have 20-29 students. Most lab/discussion sessions have 10-19 students. **Most popular majors:** Kinesiology And Exercise Science; Psychology, General; Criminal Justice/Safety Studies. **Special Study Options:** Distance learning; Double major; Dual enrollment; English as a Second Language (ESL); Honors program; Independent study; Internships; Student-designed major; Study abroad; Teacher certification program.
Disability Services offered to physically disabled students: Note-taking services; Reader services; Tape recorders; Tutors. **Career services:** Alumni network; Alumni services; Career assessment; Career/job search classes; Internships; Regional alumni

FACILITIES

Housing: Apartments for single students; Coed dorms; Theme housing 85% of campus accessible to physically disabled. **Special Academic Facilities/Equipment:** The Institute of Texan Cultures **Computers:** Students can register for classes online. Administrative functions (other than registration) can be performed online.

CAMPUS LIFE

Environment: Metropolis **Activities:** Campus Ministries; Choral groups; Concert band; Dance; International Student Organization; Jazz band; Literary magazine; Marching band; Model UN; Music ensembles; Musical theater; Opera; Pep band; Student government; Student newspaper; Television station 140 registered organizations, 40 honor societies, 9 religious organizations. 10 fraternities, 9 sororities. **Athletics (Intercollegiate):** *Men:* baseball, basketball, cross-country, golf, tennis, track/field (outdoor), track/field (indoor). *Women:* basketball, cross-country, soccer, softball, tennis, track/field (outdoor), track/field (indoor), volleyball. Sombrilla, University Center, Library, Campus Rec, The Paseo

ADMISSIONS

Freshman Academic Profile: 17% in top 10% of high school class, 58% in top 25% of high school class, 90% in top 50% of high school class. **Test Scores:** SAT Math middle 50% range 510-600. SAT EBRW middle 50% range 520-610. ACT middle 50% range 20-25. Minimum internet-based TOEFL 79. Minimum paper TOEFL 550. **Basis for Candidate Selection:** *Very*

important factors considered include: rigor of secondary school record, class rank, academic GPA, standardized test scores. *Important factors considered include:* application essay, recommendation(s), extracurricular activities, talent/ability. *Other factors considered include:* first generation, volunteer work, work experience. **Freshman Admission Requirements:** High school diploma is required and GED is accepted *Academic units required:* 4 English, 3 math, 3 science, 2 foreign language, 3 social studies, 3 history, 2 computer science, 1 visual/performing arts, and 1 unit from above areas or other academic areas. **Freshman Admission Statistics:** 15,973 applied, 79.5% admitted, 40% enrolled. **Transfer Admission Requirements:** college transcript(s), Minimum college GPA of 2.0 required. Lowest grade transferable D. **General Admission Information:** Application fee $60. Priority deadline 3/1. Regular application deadline 6/1. Nonfall registration accepted.

COSTS AND FINANCIAL AID

Annual in-state tuition $7,190. Annual out-of-state tuition $20,634. Room and board $7,190. Required fees $2,745. Average book expense $1,500. **Required Forms and Deadlines:** FAFSA. **Notification of Awards:** Applicants will be notified of awards on a rolling basis beginning 3/1. **Types of Aid:** *Need-based scholarships/grants:* College/university scholarship or grant aid from institutional funds; Federal Pell; Private scholarships; SEOG; State scholarships/grants. *Loans:* Direct PLUS loans; Direct Subsidized Stafford Loans; Direct Unsubsidized Stafford Loans. *Student Employment:* Federal Work-Study Program available. Institutional employment available. **Financial Aid Statistics:** 86% needy freshmen, 84% needy undergrads receive need-based scholarship or grant aid. 2% freshmen, 2% undergrads receive non-need-based scholarship or grant aid. 67% freshmen, 71% undergrads receive need-based self-help aid. 1% freshmen, 1% undergrads receive athletic scholarships. 63% undergrads borrow to pay for school. Average cumulative indebtedness $26,763. **Criteria for awarding aid:** *Non-need-based:* Academics, Alumni affiliation, Art, Athletics, Job skills, Leadership, Music/drama, State/district residency.

UNIVERSITY OF TORONTO

172 St. George Street, Toronto, ON M5R 0A3
Phone: 416-978-2190
E-mail: admissions.help@utoronto.ca • **CEEB Code:** 982
Fax: 416-978-7022 • **Website:** www.utoronto.ca

This public school was founded in 1827. It has a 1767 acre campus.

RATINGS

Admissions Selectivity Rating: 61   **Fire Safety Rating:** 79   **Green Rating:** 60*

STUDENTS AND FACULTY

Enrollment: 69,761. **Student Body:** 55% female, 45% male, 8% out-of-state, (166 countries represented).
Faculty: 5,854 full-time faculty,

ACADEMICS

Degrees: Bachelor's; Certificate; Diploma; Doctoral; Doctoral Other; Doctoral/Professional; Doctoral/Research; Master's; Post-Bachelor's certificate; Post-Master's certificate **Special Study Options:** Cooperative education program; Double major; English as a Second Language (ESL); Exchange student program (domestic); Honors program; Internships; Study abroad; Teacher certification program. **Disability Services offered to physically disabled students:** Note-taking services; Reader services; Tape recorders; Tutors. **Career services:** Career/job search classes

FACILITIES

Housing: Apartments for married students; Coed dorms; Cooperative housing; Men's dorms; Women's dorms **Computers:** Students can register for classes online. Administrative functions (other than registration) can be performed online.

CAMPUS LIFE

Environment: Metropolis **Activities:** Choral groups; Concert band; Dance; Drama/theater; Jazz band; Literary magazine; Music ensembles; Opera; Radio station; Student government; Student newspaper; Student-run film society; Symphony orchestra 200 registered organizations, 49 religious organizations. **Athletics (Intercollegiate):** *Men:* badminton, baseball, basketball, crew/rowing, cross-country, curling, fencing, football, golf, ice hockey, lacrosse, mountain biking, rugby, skiing (nordic/cross-country), soccer, squash, swimming, tennis, track/field (outdoor), track/field (indoor), volleyball, water polo, wrestling. *Women:* badminton, basketball, crew/rowing, cross-country, curling, fencing, field hockey, ice hockey, lacrosse, mountain biking, rugby, skiing (nordic/cross-country), soccer, squash, swimming, tennis, track/field (outdoor), track/field (indoor), volleyball, water polo, wrestling. **On-Campus Highlights:** Hart House, The Athletic Centre, Justine Barnike Gallery, Thomas Fisher Rare Book Library, Convocation Hall

ADMISSIONS

Test Scores: Minimum paper TOEFL 600. **Basis for Candidate Selection:** *Very important factors considered include:* academic GPA, standardized test scores. **Freshman Admission Requirements:** High school diploma is required and GED is accepted **Transfer Admission Requirements:** High school transcript, college transcript(s), standardized test scores. **General Admission Information:** Application fee $225. Regular application deadline 3/1. Nonfall registration accepted.

COSTS AND FINANCIAL AID

Annual out-of-state tuition $6,220. Room and board $12,528. Average book expense $1,000.

UNIVERSITY OF TULSA

800 South Tucker Drive, Tulsa, OK 74104
Phone: 918-631-2307 • **Financial Aid Phone:** 918-631-2526
E-mail: admission@utulsa.edu • **CEEB Code:** 6883
Fax: 918-631-5003 • **Website:** utulsa.edu • **ACT Code:** 3444

This private school, affiliated with the Presbyterian Church, was founded in 1894. It has a 209 acre campus.

RATINGS

Admissions Selectivity Rating: 94   **Fire Safety Rating:** 97   **Green Rating:** 83

STUDENTS AND FACULTY

Enrollment: 3,316. **Student Body:** 44% female, 56% male, 41% out-of-state, 19% international (53 countries represented). Asian 5%, African American 5%, Caucasian 57%, Hispanic 6%, Native American 3%, Pacific Islander <1%, Two or more races 3%, Race unknown 2%. **Retention and Graduation:** 88% freshmen return for sophomore year. 50% freshmen graduate within 4 years. 69% freshmen graduate within 6 years. 34% grads go on to further study within 1 year. 15% grads pursue arts and sciences degrees. 2% grads pursue law degrees. 9% grads pursue business degrees. 5% grads pursue medical degrees. **Faculty:** Student/faculty ratio 11:1. 350 full-time faculty, 95% hold PhDs, 18% are members of minority groups, 34% are women. 4% of classes are taught by teaching assistants.

ACADEMICS

Degrees: Bachelor's; Doctoral; Doctoral/Professional; Doctoral/Research; Master's; Post-Bachelor's certificate **Classes:** Most classes have 10-19 students. Most lab/discussion sessions have 20-29 students. **Most popular majors:** Computer Science; Psychology, General; Finance, General. **Special Study Options:** Accelerated program; Distance learning; Double major; English as a Second Language (ESL); Honors program; Independent study; Internships; Liberal arts/career combination; Student-designed major; Study abroad; Teacher certification program. Honors programs: The Honors Program is a four-year course of study consisting of 18 hours of academic credit. In small classes and individual tutorials, students pursue a critical examination of the moral and political commitments, scientific achievments, and artistic sensibilities that have shaped the modern world. The program culminates in the senior year with students designing and executing individual research projects. The Tulsa Undergraduate Research Challenge (TURC) is an innovative program that enables undergraduates to take challenging courses and conduct advanced research with the guidance of top professors. Its aim is to create leaders in scholarship, research, and public life. The centerpiece of the program is research; the goal of such research may be to deliver papers at academic conferences, to produce publishable articles, or to initiate meaningful community projects. Combined degree programs: BA/JD; BA/MA; BA/MEng. **Disability Services offered to physically disabled students:** Note-taking services; Reader services; Tape recorders; Tutors. **Career services:** Alumni network; Alumni services; Career assessment; Career/job search classes; Internships; Regional alumni

FACILITIES

Housing: Apartments for married students; Apartments for single students; Coed dorms; Fraternity/sorority housing; Men's dorms; Special housing for disabled student; Theme housing; Women's dorms 97% of campus accessible to physically diasbled. **Special Academic Facilities/Equipment:** Alexandre Hogue Art Gallery, Biotechnology Institute, Center for Communicative Disorders, Gilcrease Art Museum Charge-Coupled Camera Microscope, Donald W. Reynolds Center (site of a state-of-the-art athletic training program), Education Technology Lab, Electron Microscopes, Kendall Theatre, McFarlin Library Special Collections (focus on American, British, and Irish Literature of the late 19th and early 20th centuries, and on Native American History and Law), Multimedia "board-room" style classrooms (3), ONEOK Multimedia Auditorium, Sadie Adwan Communication Lab, Sidney Born Technical Library (contains an outstanding collection concerning energy, most notably petroleum), Sun Computer Work Stations, World's largest research flow-loop in Petroleum Engr. North Campus Research Lab (dedicated to petroleum engineering research with specialized areas for undergraduate and graduate research studies), Boulder Building for Oxley College of Health Sciences (newly funded area for research in the area of health and behavioral sciences located in the downtown Tulsa OK area around other businesses, the labs in this building are fully fitted with state of the art lab and medical testing equipment). **Computers:** 100% of classrooms, 100% of dorms, 100% of libraries, 100% of dining areas, 100% of student union, 100% of common outdoor areas have wireless network access. Students can register for classes online. Administrative functions (other than registration) can be performed online.

CAMPUS LIFE

Environment: Metropolis **Activities:** Campus Ministries; Choral groups; Concert band; Dance; Drama/theater; International Student Organization; Jazz band; Literary magazine; Marching band; Music ensembles; Musical theater; Opera; Pep band; Radio station; Student government; Student newspaper; Student-run film society; Symphony orchestra; Television station 245 registered organizations, 40 honor societies, 21 religious organizations. 7 fraternities, 9 sororities. **Athletics (Intercollegiate):** *Men:* basketball, cheerleading, cross-country, football, golf, soccer, tennis, track/field (outdoor), track/field (indoor). *Women:* basketball, cheerleading, crew/rowing, cross-country, golf, soccer, softball, tennis, track/field (outdoor), track/field (indoor), volleyball. **On-Campus Highlights:** Collins Fitness Center, Reynolds Center, McFarlin Library, Allen Chapman Student Union, Lorton Performance Center **Environmental Initiatives:** The School of Engineering and Natural Sciences partnered with the local utility company to develop and install a 300kW Solar Panel array on top of our Tennis facility. The project was completed in September of 2016. It produces enough energy to cover the usage of the tennis sporting complex. Overall, students were able to analyze real world data and work with he installing contractor. This project was our first step in establishing a greener footprint. Over the past 5 years we have decreased energy consumption by more than 10% while growing more than 450,000 new square feet of academic and living areas. We continue to invest and install new green technologies. In Aug 2016, we installed our first dual-port hybrid vehicle charging station on campus and made it free for the community to use.

ADMISSIONS

Freshman Academic Profile: Average high school GPA 3.9. 70% in top 10% of high school class, 85% in top 25% of high school class, 97% in top 50% of high school class. 72% from public high schools. **Test Scores:** SAT Math middle 50% range 560-720. SAT EBRW middle 50% range 590-720. ACT middle 50% range 25-32. Minimum internet-based TOEFL 70. Minimum paper TOEFL 525. **Basis for Candidate Selection:** *Very important factors considered include:* rigor of secondary school record, academic GPA, standardized test scores. *Important factors considered include:* class rank, application essay, recommendation(s), interview, level of applicant's interest. *Other factors considered include:* extracurricular activities, talent/ability, character/personal qualities, first generation, alumni/ae relation, racial/ethnic status, volunteer work, work experience. **Freshman Admission Requirements:** High school diploma is required and GED is accepted *Academic units recommended:* 4 English, 4 math, 3 science, 3 science labs, 2 foreign language, 3 social studies, 1 computer science, 1 visual/performing arts. **Freshman Admission Statistics:** 7,869 applied, 39.0% admitted, 24% enrolled. **Transfer Admission Requirements:** college transcript(s), essay or personal statement, statement of good standing from prior institution(s). Minimum college GPA of 2.5 required. Lowest grade transferable c. **General Admission Information:** Application fee $50. Priority deadline 1/15. Nonfall registration accepted. Admission may be deferred for a maximum of 1 year.

COSTS AND FINANCIAL AID

Annual tuition $39,012. Room and board $11,116. Required fees $540. Average book expense $1,200. **Required Forms and Deadlines:** FAFSA. **Notification of Awards:** Applicants will be notified of awards on a rolling basis beginning 2/1. **Types of Aid:** *Need-based scholarships/grants:* College/university scholarship or grant aid from institutional funds; Federal Pell; Private scholarships; SEOG; State scholarships/grants. *Loans:* Direct PLUS loans; Direct Subsidized Stafford Loans; Direct Unsubsidized Stafford Loans. *Student Employment:* Federal Work-Study Program available. Institutional employment available. **Financial Aid Statistics:** 33% needy freshmen, 36%

needy undergrads receive need-based scholarship or grant aid. 96% freshmen, 94% undergrads receive non-need-based scholarship or grant aid. 50% freshmen, 54% undergrads receive need-based self-help aid. 12% freshmen, 10% undergrads receive athletic scholarships. 91% freshmen, 86% undergrads receive any aid. 48% undergrads borrow to pay for school. Average cumulative indebtedness $34,136. **Criteria for awarding aid:** *Need-based:* Minority status *Non-need-based:* Academics, Alumni affiliation, Art, Athletics, Leadership, Minority status, Music/drama, Religious affiliation.

See page 1074.

UNIVERSITY OF UTAH

201 S. Presidents Circle, Salt Lake City, UT 84112
Phone: 801-581-8761 • **Financial Aid Phone:** 801-581-6211
E-mail: admissions@utah.edu • **CEEB Code:** 4853
Fax: 801-585-7864 • **Website:** www.utah.edu • **ACT Code:** 4274

This public school was founded in 1850. It has a 1535 acre campus.

RATINGS

Admissions Selectivity Rating: 84   **Fire Safety Rating:** 89   **Green Rating:** 94

STUDENTS AND FACULTY

Enrollment: 23,402. **Student Body:** 46% female, 54% male, 19% out-of-state, 5% international (87 countries represented). Asian 6%, African American 1%, Caucasian 69%, Hispanic 13%, Native American <1%, Pacific Islander <1%, Two or more races 5%, Race unknown 1%.
Retention and Graduation: 91% freshmen return for sophomore year. 31% freshmen graduate within 4 years. 67% freshmen graduate within 6 years. 26% grads go on to further study within 1 year. **Faculty:** Student/faculty ratio 16:1. 1,508 full-time faculty, 83% hold PhDs, 15% are members of minority groups, 39% are women. 22% of classes are taught by teaching assistants.

ACADEMICS

Degrees: Bachelor's; Doctoral; Doctoral/Professional; Doctoral/Research; Master's; Post-Bachelor's certificate; Post-Master's certificate **Classes:** Most classes have 10-19 students. Most lab/discussion sessions have 10-19 students. **Most popular majors:** Communication, General; Psychology, General; Economics, General. **Special Study Options:** Accelerated program; Distance learning; Double major; Dual enrollment; English as a Second Language (ESL); Exchange student program (domestic); Honors program; Independent study; Internships; Student-designed major; Study abroad; Teacher certification program. Honors programs: The Honors College is recognized for its Engaged Learning Opportunities—signature experiences that bring students and community partners together in collaboration, resulting in real-world applications.By addressing some of today's most important and relevant issues, students engage directly with the world around them and learn how they can make a difference in their own communities. Honors students regularly go on to some of the nation's best graduate programs. Combined degree programs: BA/MEng. **Disability Services offered to physically disabled students:** Note-taking services; Reader services; Tape recorders; Tutors. **Career services:** Alumni network; Alumni services; Career assessment; Career/job search classes; Internships

FACILITIES

Housing: Apartments for married students; Apartments for single students; Coed dorms; Men's dorms; Special housing for disabled student; Theme housing; Women's dorms 90% of campus accessible to physically disabled. **Special Academic Facilities/Equipment:** Museum of natural history, museum of fine arts, observatory, arboretum, environmental biological research facilities, human genetics lab. **Computers:** 100% of classrooms, 100% of dorms, 100% of libraries, 100% of dining areas, 100% of student union, 60% of common outdoor areas have wireless network access. Students can register for classes online. Administrative functions (other than registration) can be performed online.

CAMPUS LIFE

Environment: Metropolis **Activities:** Campus Ministries; Choral groups; Concert band; Dance; Drama/theater; International Student Organization; Jazz band; Literary magazine; Marching band; Music ensembles; Musical theater; Opera; Pep band; Radio station; Student government; Student newspaper; Student-run film society; Symphony orchestra; Television station 238 registered

organizations, 41 honor societies, 9 religious organizations. 7 fraternities, 6 sororities. **Athletics (Intercollegiate):** *Men:* baseball, basketball, cheerleading, diving, football, golf, skiing (downhill/alpine), skiing (nordic/cross-country), swimming, tennis. *Women:* basketball, cheerleading, cross-country, diving, gymnastics, skiing (downhill/alpine), skiing (nordic/cross-country), soccer, softball, swimming, tennis, track/field (outdoor), track/field (indoor), volleyball. **On-Campus Highlights:** Rice Eccles Stadium, Jon M. Huntsman Center, University Union, Marriott Library, Student Life Center **Environmental Initiatives:** Transportation: Free public transportation (Ed-Pass) for all students, staff and faculty; gas-electric hybrid, biodiesel, and natural gas-powered campus vehicles.

ADMISSIONS

Freshman Academic Profile: Average high school GPA 3.6. 91% from public high schools. **Test Scores:** SAT Math middle 50% range 550-680. SAT EBRW middle 50% range 560-670. ACT middle 50% range 22-29. Minimum internet-based TOEFL 80. Minimum paper TOEFL 550. **Basis for Candidate Selection:** *Very important factors considered include:* rigor of secondary school record, academic GPA. *Important factors considered include:* standardized test scores. *Other factors considered include:* class rank, extracurricular activities, talent/ability, character/personal qualities, first generation, alumni/ae relation, geographical residence, state residency, racial/ethnic status, volunteer work, work experience. **Freshman Admission Requirements:** High school diploma is required and GED is accepted *Academic units required:* 4 English, 2 math, 3 science, 1 science labs, 2 foreign language, 1 history, 4 academic electives. **Freshman Admission Statistics:** 22,400 applied, 66.2% admitted, 28% enrolled. **Transfer Admission Requirements:** college transcript(s), statement of good standing from prior institution(s). Minimum college GPA of 2.6 required. Lowest grade transferable D-. **General Admission Information:** Application fee $55. Priority deadline 12/1. Regular application deadline 4/1. Nonfall registration accepted. Admission may be deferred for a maximum of 7 semesters.

COSTS AND FINANCIAL AID

Required Forms and Deadlines: FAFSA. **Notification of Awards:** Applicants will be notified of awards on a rolling basis beginning 3/1. **Types of Aid:** *Need-based scholarships/grants:* College/university scholarship or grant aid from institutional funds; Federal Nursing Scholarships; Federal Pell; Private scholarships; SEOG; State scholarships/grants. *Loans:* Direct PLUS loans; Direct Subsidized Stafford Loans; Direct Unsubsidized Stafford Loans. *Student Employment:* Federal Work-Study Program available. Institutional employment available. **Financial Aid Statistics:** 88% needy freshmen, 82% needy undergrads receive need-based scholarship or grant aid. 16% freshmen, 7% undergrads receive non-need-based scholarship or grant aid. 79% freshmen, 90% undergrads receive need-based self-help aid. 2% freshmen, 2% undergrads receive athletic scholarships. 75% freshmen, 64% undergrads receive any aid. 39% undergrads borrow to pay for school. Average cumulative indebtedness $21,081. **Criteria for awarding aid:** *Non-need-based:* Academics, Alumni affiliation, Art, Athletics, Leadership, Minority status, Music/drama, State/district residency.

UNIVERSITY OF VERMONT

South Prospect Street, Burlington, VT 05401-3596
Phone: 802-656-3370 • **Financial Aid Phone:** (802) 656-5700
E-mail: admissions@uvm.edu • **CEEB Code:** 3920
Fax: 802-656-8611 • **Website:** www.uvm.edu • **ACT Code:** 4322

This public school was founded in 1791. It has a 460 acre campus.

RATINGS

Admissions Selectivity Rating: 87   **Fire Safety Rating:** 98   **Green Rating:** 99

STUDENTS AND FACULTY

Enrollment: 10,513. **Student Body:** 58% female, 42% male, 71% out-of-state, 6% international (51 countries represented). Asian 3%, African American 1%, Caucasian 81%, Hispanic 4%, Native American <1%, Pacific Islander <1%, Two or more races 3%, Race unknown 2%.
Retention and Graduation: 86% freshmen return for sophomore year. 62% freshmen graduate within 4 years. 75% freshmen graduate within 6 years. 18% grads go on to further study within 1 year. 9% grads pursue arts and sciences degrees. 1% grads pursue law degrees. 0% grads pursue business degrees. 0.4%

grads pursue medical degrees. **Faculty:** Student/faculty ratio 17:1. 629 full-time faculty, 84% hold PhDs, 15% are members of minority groups, 47% are women. 2% of classes are taught by teaching assistants.

ACADEMICS

Degrees: Bachelor's; Doctoral/Professional; Doctoral/Research; Master's; Post-Bachelor's certificate; Post-Master's certificate **Classes:** Most classes have 10-19 students. Most lab/discussion sessions have 10-19 students. **Most popular majors:** Environmental Studies; Mechanical Engineering; Business Administration And Management, General. **Special Study Options:** Cooperative education program; Cross-registration; Distance learning; Double major; Dual enrollment; English as a Second Language (ESL); Exchange student program (domestic); Honors program; Independent study; Internships; Liberal arts/career combination; Student-designed major; Study abroad; Teacher certification program. Honors programs: The Honors College is a residential learning community where students live together and take classes in one of UVM's newest residence halls. Honors College students are simultaneously enrolled in one of seven other UVM undergraduate colleges or schools. Honors College courses comprise approximately 20% of a students overall coursework and include a year-long common first year seminar, a choice of a variety of sophomore seminars, a junior year thesis prep course, and a senior year thesis, creative project or practicum. Upon graduation, program completers are designated as Honors College Scholars. Combined degree programs: BA/JD. **Disability Services offered to physically disabled students:** Note-taking services; Reader services; Tape recorders; Tutors. **Career services:** Alumni network; Alumni services; Career assessment; Career/job search classes; Internships; Regional alumni

FACILITIES

Housing: Apartments for married students; Apartments for single students; Coed dorms; Fraternity/sorority housing; Theme housing; Wellness housing 90% of campus accessible to physically disabled. **Special Academic Facilities/Equipment:** Art/ethnography museum, chemistry/physics library, medical library, on-campus preschool, government research and world affairs centers, agricultural experiment station, horse farm, multinuclear magnetic resonance spectrometers, mass spectrometer. **Computers:** 10% of classrooms, 15% of dorms, 100% of libraries, 100% of dining areas, 100% of student union, 5% of common outdoor areas have wireless network access. Students can register for classes online. Administrative functions (other than registration) can be performed online.

CAMPUS LIFE

Environment: Town **Activities:** Campus Ministries; Choral groups; Concert band; Dance; Drama/theater; International Student Organization; Jazz band; Literary magazine; Music ensembles; Musical theater; Pep band; Radio station; Student government; Student newspaper; Student-run film society; Symphony orchestra; Television station 140 registered organizations, 30 honor societies, 10 religious organizations. 9 fraternities, 6 sororities. **Athletics (Intercollegiate):** *Men:* basketball, cross-country, ice hockey, lacrosse, skiing (downhill/alpine), skiing (nordic/cross-country), soccer, track/field (outdoor), track/field (indoor). *Women:* basketball, cross-country, diving, field hockey, ice hockey, lacrosse, skiing (downhill/alpine), skiing (nordic/cross-country), soccer, swimming, track/field (outdoor), track/field (indoor). **On-Campus Highlights:** Davis Student Center, Bailey-Howe Library, Henderson's Cafe, Athletic Complex/Fitness Center, Campus Green **Environmental Initiatives:** Reporting jointly to the Associate Vice Provost for Teaching & Learning and the VP for Finances, the Office of Sustainability supports the infusion of sustainability into operations, student life, curriculum, and communications, managing University commitments for energy, food, and sustainability education

ADMISSIONS

Freshman Academic Profile: Average high school GPA 3.7. 38% in top 10% of high school class, 76% in top 25% of high school class, 98% in top 50% of high school class. 70% from public high schools. **Test Scores:** SAT Math middle 50% range 580-670. SAT EBRW middle 50% range 600-680. ACT middle 50% range 25-30. Minimum internet-based TOEFL 90. Minimum paper TOEFL 577. **Basis for Candidate Selection:** *Very important factors considered include:* rigor of secondary school record. *Important factors considered include:* class rank, academic GPA, application essay, standardized test scores, character/personal qualities, state residency. *Other factors considered include:* recommendation(s), extracurricular activities, talent/ability, first generation, alumni/ae relation, geographical residence, racial/ethnic status, volunteer work, work experience, level of applicant's interest. **Freshman Admission Requirements:** High school diploma is required and GED is accepted *Academic units required:* 4 English, 3 math, 2 science, 1 science labs, 2 foreign language, 3 social studies. **Freshman Admission Statistics:** 21,991 applied, 67.2% admitted, 18% enrolled. **Transfer Admission Requirements:** High school transcript, college transcript(s), essay or personal statement, Minimum college GPA of 2.5 required. Lowest grade transferable C. **General Admission Information:** Application fee $55. Regular application deadline 1/15. Nonfall registration accepted. Admission may be deferred for a maximum of 1 year.

COSTS AND FINANCIAL AID

Annual in-state tuition $12,022. Annual out-of-state tuition $39,120. Room and board $12,022. Required fees $2,236. Average book expense $1,200. **Required Forms and Deadlines:** FAFSA. **Notification of Awards:** Applicants will be notified of awards on a rolling basis beginning 3/15. **Types of Aid:** *Need-based scholarships/grants:* College/university scholarship or grant aid from institutional funds; Federal Pell; Private scholarships; SEOG; State scholarships/grants. *Loans:* Direct PLUS loans; Direct Subsidized Stafford Loans; Direct Unsubsidized Stafford Loans. *Student Employment:* Federal Work-Study Program available. Institutional employment available. **Financial Aid Statistics:** 99% needy freshmen, 97% needy undergrads receive need-based scholarship or grant aid. 12% freshmen, 8% undergrads receive non-need-based scholarship or grant aid. 69% freshmen, 74% undergrads receive need-based self-help aid. 2% freshmen, 2% undergrads receive athletic scholarships. 93% freshmen, 83% undergrads receive any aid. 61% undergrads borrow to pay for school. Average cumulative indebtedness $27,006. **Criteria for awarding aid:** *Need-based:* Academics, Athletics, Leadership, Minority status, Music/drama *Non-need-based:* Academics, Alumni affiliation, Athletics, Leadership, Minority status, Music/drama, State/district residency.

See page 1076.

UNIVERSITY OF VIRGINIA

Office of Admission, Charlottesville, VA 22906
Phone: 434-982-3200 • **Financial Aid Phone:** 434-982-4757
E-mail: undergradadmission@virginia.edu • **CEEB Code:** 5820
Fax: 434-924-3587 • **Website:** www.virginia.edu • **ACT Code:** 4412

This public school was founded in 1819. It has a 1167 acre campus.

RATINGS

Admissions Selectivity Rating: 97   **Fire Safety Rating:** 90   **Green Rating:** 96

STUDENTS AND FACULTY

Enrollment: 16,089. **Student Body:** 54% female, 46% male, 27% out-of-state, 4% international (122 countries represented). Asian 14%, African American 7%, Caucasian 58%, Hispanic 7%, Native American <1%, Pacific Islander <1%, Two or more races 4%, Race unknown 6%.
Retention and Graduation: 97% freshmen return for sophomore year. 88% freshmen graduate within 4 years. 95% freshmen graduate within 6 years. **Faculty:** Student/faculty ratio 15:1. 1,482 full-time faculty, 91% hold PhDs, 18% are members of minority groups, 39% are women. 36% of classes are taught by teaching assistants.

ACADEMICS

Degrees: Bachelor's; Certificate; Doctoral/Professional; Doctoral/Research; Master's; Post-Bachelor's certificate; Post-Master's certificate **Classes:** Most classes have 20-29 students. Most lab/discussion sessions have 20-29 students. **Most popular majors:** Biology/Biological Sciences, General; Economics, General; Business/Commerce, General. **Special Study Options:** Accelerated program; Cooperative education program; Distance learning; Double major; English as a Second Language (ESL); Exchange student program (domestic); Honors program; Independent study; Internships; Liberal arts/career combination; Student-designed major; Study abroad; Teacher certification program. Honors programs: Jefferson Scholars: Full scholarship given to approximately 30 students per year. Special lectures and discussions with distinguished University faculty; all first year Jefferson Scholars take part in an outdoor leadership experience; all rising-second year Jefferson Scholars, prior to the beginning of school, participate in a two-week Institute for Leadership and Citizenship designed to foster a deeper understanding of the art of leadership and the importance of citizenship. Additionally, all Jefferson Scholars are granted an opportunity to travel and study abroad between their second and third year. Scholars may elect to spend three weeks of study at either Regent's College in England or the Erasmus Institute in Tuscany, Italy. Following the structured tutorial, each Scholar designs and completes two weeks of travel and independent inquiry. Echols Scholars-School of Arts and Sciences. Separate dormitory, with Rodman Scholars, for first-year students. Flexible degree requirements; exemption from some requirements; preference for courses. Rodman Scholars-School of Engineering and Applied Sciences. Separate dormitory, with Echols Scholars, for first-year students. Special courses designed only for Rodman Scholars in first two years. **Disability Services**

offered to physically disabled students: Note-taking services; Reader services; Tape recorders; Tutors. **Career services:** Alumni network; Alumni services; Career assessment; Career/job search classes; Internships; Regional alumni

FACILITIES

Housing: Apartments for married students; Apartments for single students; Coed dorms; Fraternity/sorority housing; Special housing for international students; Theme housing 100% of campus accessible to physically diasbled. **Special Academic Facilities/Equipment:** 15 libraries, art museum, experimental farm, biological station, observatory/planetarium, nuclear information center, media center (multimedia editing). **Computers:** 100% of classrooms, 100% of dorms, 100% of libraries, 100% of dining areas, 100% of student union, 26-50% of common outdoor areas have wireless network access. Students can register for classes online. Administrative functions (other than registration) can be performed online.

CAMPUS LIFE

Environment: City **Activities:** Campus Ministries; Choral groups; Concert band; Dance; Drama/theater; International Student Organization; Jazz band; Literary magazine; Marching band; Model UN; Music ensembles; Musical theater; Opera; Pep band; Radio station; Student government; Student newspaper; Student-run film society; Symphony orchestra; Television station; Yearbook 7 honor societies, 44 religious organizations. 28 fraternities, 15 sororities. **Athletics (Intercollegiate):** *Men:* baseball, basketball, cross-country, diving, football, golf, lacrosse, soccer, swimming, tennis, track/field (outdoor), track/field (indoor), wrestling. *Women:* basketball, crew/rowing, cross-country, diving, field hockey, golf, lacrosse, soccer, softball, swimming, tennis, track/field (outdoor), track/field (indoor), volleyball. **On-Campus Highlights:** Rotunda/Academical Village (orig campus), Alderman and Clemons Libraries, John Paul Jones Arena, Football, Baseball, and Soccer Stadiums, Aquatic and Fitness Center **Environmental Initiatives:** Academics: The University of Virginia offers 70+ courses in 8 different schools with significant focus on sustainability, including a global sustainability course, a new course model cross listed and taught jointly by faculty from Engineering, Architecture, and Commerce. In Spring 2011, the University created the interdisciplinary Global Sustainability minor.

ADMISSIONS

Freshman Academic Profile: Average high school GPA 4.3. 88% in top 10% of high school class, 98% in top 25% of high school class, 100% in top 50% of high school class. 72% from public high schools. **Test Scores:** SAT Math middle 50% range 640-740. SAT EBRW middle 50% range 650-730. ACT middle 50% range 29-33. **Basis for Candidate Selection:** *Very important factors considered include:* rigor of secondary school record, class rank, academic GPA, recommendation(s), character/personal qualities, state residency. *Important factors considered include:* application essay, standardized test scores, extracurricular activities, talent/ability. *Other factors considered include:* first generation, alumni/ae relation, geographical residence, racial/ethnic status, volunteer work, work experience. **Freshman Admission Requirements:** High school diploma is required and GED is accepted *Academic units required:* 4 English, 4 math, 2 science, 2 foreign language, 1 social studies, *Academic units recommended:* 5 math, 4 science, 5 foreign language, 4 social studies. **Freshman Admission Statistics:** 36,779 applied, 27.3% admitted, 38% enrolled. **Transfer Admission Requirements:** High school transcript, college transcript(s), essay or personal statement, standardized test scores, statement of good standing from prior institution(s). Minimum college GPA of 2.0 required. Lowest grade transferable C. **General Admission Information:** Application fee $60. Regular application deadline 1/1. Nonfall registration accepted. Admission may be deferred for a maximum of 1 year.

COSTS AND FINANCIAL AID

Annual in-state tuition $10,726. Annual out-of-state tuition $44,241. Room and board $10,726. Required fees $2,734. Average book expense $1,320. **Required Forms and Deadlines:** CSS/Financial Aid PROFILE; FAFSA. **Notification of Awards:** Applicants will be notified of awards on or about 4/5. **Types of Aid:** *Need-based scholarships/grants:* College/university scholarship or grant aid from institutional funds; Federal Nursing Scholarships; Federal Pell; Private scholarships; SEOG; State scholarships/grants. *Loans:* Direct PLUS loans; Direct Subsidized Stafford Loans; Direct Unsubsidized Stafford Loans. *Student Employment:* Federal Work-Study Program available. Institutional employment available. **Financial Aid Statistics:** 85% needy freshmen, 84% needy undergrads receive need-based scholarship or grant aid. 7% freshmen, 7% undergrads receive non-need-based scholarship or grant aid. 62% freshmen, 64% undergrads receive need-based self-help aid. 3% freshmen, 3% undergrads receive athletic scholarships. 55% freshmen, 50% undergrads receive any aid. 33% undergrads borrow to pay for school. Average cumulative indebtedness $24,598. **Criteria for awarding aid:** *Need-based:* Academics, Leadership, Minority status *Non-need-based:* Academics, Athletics, Leadership, Minority status, Music/drama, State/district residency.

UNIVERSITY OF VIRGINIA'S COLLEGE AT WISE

1 College Avenue, Wise, VA 24293
Phone: 276-328-0102
E-mail: admissions@uvawise.edu • **CEEB Code:** 5124
Fax: 276-328-0251 • **Website:** www.uvawise.edu • **ACT Code:** 4343

This public school was founded in 1954. It has a 367 acre campus.

RATINGS

Admissions Selectivity Rating: 76   **Fire Safety Rating:** 60*   **Green Rating:** 60*

STUDENTS AND FACULTY

Enrollment: 1,629. **Student Body:** 52% female, 48% male, 5% out-of-state, <1% international. Asian 1%, African American 7%, Caucasian 90%, Hispanic 2%, Native American <1%, Race unknown 0%.
Retention and Graduation: 73% freshmen return for sophomore year. 14% grads go on to further study within 1 year. 7% grads pursue arts and sciences degrees. 6% grads pursue law degrees. 4% grads pursue business degrees. 1% grads pursue medical degrees. **Faculty:** Student/faculty ratio 16:1. 91 full-time faculty, 29% hold PhDs, 13% are members of minority groups, 41% are women. 0% of classes are taught by teaching assistants.

ACADEMICS

Degrees: Bachelor's **Classes:** Most classes have 10-19 students. Most lab/discussion sessions have 10-19 students. **Special Study Options:** Accelerated program; Cooperative education program; Distance learning; Double major; Dual enrollment; Honors program; Independent study; Internships; Student-designed major; Study abroad; Teacher certification program. **Disability Services offered to physically disabled students:** Note-taking services; Reader services; Tape recorders; Tutors. **Career services:** Alumni services; Career assessment; Career/job search classes; Internships

FACILITIES

Housing: Apartments for single students; Coed dorms; Men's dorms; Special housing for disabled student; Women's dorms 95% of campus accessible to physically diasbled. **Computers:** Administrative functions (other than registration) can be performed online.

CAMPUS LIFE

Environment: Rural **Activities:** Choral groups; Concert band; Dance; Drama/theater; Literary magazine; Music ensembles; Musical theater; Pep band; Radio station; Student government; Student newspaper; Television station; Yearbook 40 registered organizations, 3 honor societies, 3 religious organizations. 3 fraternities, 2 sororities. **Athletics (Intercollegiate):** *Men:* baseball, basketball, cross-country, football, golf, tennis, track/field (outdoor). *Women:* basketball, cross-country, softball, tennis, track/field (outdoor), volleyball.

ADMISSIONS

Freshman Academic Profile: Average high school GPA 3.3. 18% in top 10% of high school class, 40% in top 25% of high school class, 78% in top 50% of high school class. 99% from public high schools. **Test Scores:** SAT Math middle 50% range 430-530. SAT EBRW middle 50% range 420-530. ACT middle 50% range 16-21. Minimum paper TOEFL 550. **Basis for Candidate Selection:** *Very important factors considered include:* rigor of secondary school record, class rank. *Important factors considered include:* standardized test scores, talent/ability. *Other factors considered include:* application essay, recommendation(s), interview, extracurricular activities, character/personal qualities, racial/ethnic status, volunteer work, work experience. **Freshman Admission Requirements:** High school diploma is required and GED is accepted *Academic units required:* 4 English, 3 math, 2 science, 2 science labs, 2 foreign language, 1 social studies, 1 history, 5 academic electives. **Freshman Admission Statistics:** 987 applied, 77.6% admitted, 46% enrolled. **Transfer Admission Requirements:** college transcript(s), Minimum college GPA of 2.3 required. Lowest grade transferable C-. **General Admission Information:** Application fee $25. Priority deadline 4/1. Regular application deadline 8/1. Nonfall registration accepted. Admission may be deferred for a maximum of 1 year.

COSTS AND FINANCIAL AID

Required Forms and Deadlines: FAFSA. **Notification of Awards:** Applicants will be notified of awards on a rolling basis beginning 4/1. **Types of Aid:** *Need-based scholarships/grants:* College/university scholarship or grant aid from institutional funds; Federal Pell; Private scholarships; SEOG; State scholarships/grants. *Loans: Student Employment:* Federal Work-Study Program available. Institutional employment available. **Criteria for awarding aid:** *Need-based:* Academics, Alumni affiliation, Athletics, Leadership, Minority status *Non-need-based:* Academics, Alumni affiliation, Art, Athletics, Job skills, Leadership, Music/drama, State/district residency.

UNIVERSITY OF WASHINGTON

Box 355852, Seattle, WA 98195-5852
Phone: 206-543-9686 • **Financial Aid Phone:** 206-543-6101 • **CEEB Code:** 4854
Fax: 206-685-3655 • **Website:** www.washington.edu • **ACT Code:** 4484

This public school was founded in 1861. It has a 634 acre campus.

RATINGS
Admissions Selectivity Rating: 91   **Fire Safety Rating:** 95   **Green Rating:** 99

STUDENTS AND FACULTY
Enrollment: 30,475. **Student Body:** 53% female, 47% male, 18% out-of-state, 15% international (84 countries represented). Asian 24%, African American 3%, Caucasian 40%, Hispanic 8%, Native American <1%, Pacific Islander <1%, Two or more races 7%, Race unknown 1%.
Retention and Graduation: 94% freshmen return for sophomore year. 65% freshmen graduate within 4 years. 84% freshmen graduate within 6 years.
Faculty: Student/faculty ratio 19:1. 2,055 full-time faculty, 83% hold PhDs, 22% are members of minority groups, 44% are women.

ACADEMICS
Degrees: Bachelor's; Doctoral; Doctoral/Professional; Doctoral/Research; Master's; Post-Master's certificate **Classes:** Most classes have fewer than 10 students. **Most popular majors:** Computer Science; Engineering, General; Business Administration And Management, General. **Special Study Options:** Cooperative education program; Cross-registration; Distance learning; Double major; Dual enrollment; English as a Second Language (ESL); Exchange student program (domestic); Honors program; Independent study; Internships; Student-designed major; Study abroad; Teacher certification program. Honors programs: We have a University Honors Program, as well as departmental honors options. **Disability Services offered to physically disabled students:** Note-taking services; Reader services; Tape recorders; Tutors. **Career services:** Alumni network; Alumni services; Career assessment; Career/job search classes; Internships; Regional alumni

FACILITIES
Housing: Apartments for married students; Apartments for single students; Coed dorms; Fraternity/sorority housing; Special housing for disabled student; Theme housing 100% of campus accessible to physically disabled. **Special Academic Facilities/Equipment:** Multiple art galleries, an anthropology and natural history museum, arboretum, closed-circuit TV studio. **Computers:** 100% of dorms, 100% of libraries, 100% of student union, have wireless network access. Students can register for classes online. Administrative functions (other than registration) can be performed online.

CAMPUS LIFE
Environment: Metropolis **Activities:** Choral groups; Concert band; Dance; Drama/theater; International Student Organization; Jazz band; Literary magazine; Marching band; Model UN; Music ensembles; Musical theater; Opera; Pep band; Radio station; Student government; Student newspaper; Student-run film society; Symphony orchestra; Television station 711 registered organizations, 13 honor societies, 52 religious organizations. 31 fraternities, 16 sororities. **Athletics (Intercollegiate):** *Men:* baseball, basketball, crew/rowing, cross-country, football, golf, soccer, tennis, track/field (outdoor). *Women:* basketball, crew/rowing, cross-country, golf, gymnastics, soccer, softball, tennis, track/field (outdoor), volleyball. **On-Campus Highlights:** Henry Art Gallery, Burke Museum, Meany Hall for Performing Arts, Football games at Husky Stadium, Waterfront Activities Center (WAC) **Environmental Initiatives:** College of the Environment http://coenv.washington.edu/

ADMISSIONS
Freshman Academic Profile: Average high school GPA 3.8. **Test Scores:** SAT Math middle 50% range 600-730. SAT EBRW middle 50% range 590-690. ACT middle 50% range 27-32. Minimum internet-based TOEFL 76. Minimum paper TOEFL 540. **Basis for Candidate Selection:** *Very important factors considered include:* rigor of secondary school record, academic GPA, application essay. *Important factors considered include:* standardized test scores, extracurricular activities, talent/ability, first generation, volunteer work, work experience. *Other factors considered include:* character/personal qualities, state residency. **Freshman Admission Requirements:** High school diploma or equivalent is not required *Academic units required:* 4 English, 3 math, 2 science, 2 science labs, 2 foreign language, 3 social studies, 0.5 academic electives, 1 visual/performing arts, *Academic units recommended:* 4

English, 4 math, 4 science, 3 science labs, 3 foreign language, 4 social studies, 1 history, 1 computer science, 1 visual/performing arts. **Freshman Admission Statistics:** 44,877 applied, 46.4% admitted, 33% enrolled. **Transfer Admission Requirements:** High school transcript, college transcript(s), essay or personal statement, Minimum college GPA of 2.5 required. Lowest grade transferable.7. **General Admission Information:** Application fee $70. Regular application deadline 11/15. Nonfall registration accepted.

COSTS AND FINANCIAL AID
Average book expense $825. **Required Forms and Deadlines:** FAFSA. **Notification of Awards:** Applicants will be notified of awards on or about 4/1. **Types of Aid:** *Need-based scholarships/grants:* College/university scholarship or grant aid from institutional funds; Federal Pell; Private scholarships; SEOG; State scholarships/grants. *Loans:* Direct PLUS loans; Direct Subsidized Stafford Loans; Direct Unsubsidized Stafford Loans. *Student Employment:* Federal Work-Study Program available. Institutional employment available. **Financial Aid Statistics:** 74% needy freshmen, 77% needy undergrads receive need-based scholarship or grant aid. 15% freshmen, 6% undergrads receive non-need-based scholarship or grant aid. 79% freshmen, 81% undergrads receive need-based self-help aid. 1% freshmen, 1% undergrads receive athletic scholarships. 60% freshmen, 60% undergrads receive any aid. 40% undergrads borrow to pay for school. Average cumulative indebtedness $21,900. **Criteria for awarding aid:** *Need-based:* Academics, Art, Leadership, Music/drama *Non-need-based:* Academics, Alumni affiliation, Art, Athletics, Leadership, Music/drama, State/district residency.

UNIVERSITY OF WASHINGTON—BOTHELL

Box 358500, Bothell, WA 98011
Phone: 425-352-5000 • **Financial Aid Phone:** 425-352-5240
E-mail: uwbinfo@uw.edu • **CEEB Code:** 4467
Fax: 425-352-5455 • **Website:** www.uwb.edu • **ACT Code:** 4497

This public school was founded in 1990. It has a 128 acre campus.

RATINGS
Admissions Selectivity Rating: 78   **Fire Safety Rating:** 60*   **Green Rating:** 61

STUDENTS AND FACULTY
Enrollment: 5,329. **Student Body:** 49% female, 51% male, 2% out-of-state, 9% international. Asian 27%, African American 6%, Caucasian 39%, Hispanic 10%, Native American <1%, Pacific Islander 1%, Two or more races 6%, Race unknown 2%.
Retention and Graduation: 88% freshmen return for sophomore year. 43% freshmen graduate within 4 years. 64% freshmen graduate within 6 years.
Faculty: Student/faculty ratio 20:1. 218 full-time faculty, 83% hold PhDs, 31% are members of minority groups, 53% are women.

ACADEMICS
Degrees: Bachelor's; **Master's Classes:** Most classes have 20-29 students. Most lab/discussion sessions have 20-29 students. **Special Study Options:** Cross-registration; Double major; English as a Second Language (ESL); Independent study; Internships; Student-designed major; Study abroad; Teacher certification program. **Career services:** Alumni network; Alumni services; Career assessment; Career/job search classes; Internships; Regional alumni

FACILITIES
Housing: Coed dorms; Special housing for disabled student; Theme housing **Special Academic Facilities/Equipment:** The Sarah Simonds Green Conservatory was completed in the summer of 2013. This 2,800 square foot complex on the western edge of the wetlands houses a 1,600 square foot greenhouse, classroom, and support space for education, research, and public outreach.

CAMPUS LIFE
Environment: City **Activities:** Campus Ministries; Dance; International Student Organization; Literary magazine; Radio station; Student government; Student newspaper; Student-run film society. STEM buildings, library, ARC, Conservatory, book store

ADMISSIONS
Freshman Academic Profile: Average high school GPA 3.4. **Test Scores:** SAT Math middle 50% range 520-620. SAT EBRW middle 50% range 510-610. ACT middle 50% range 19-26. Minimum internet-based TOEFL 76. Minimum paper TOEFL 540. **Basis for Candidate Selection:** *Very important factors considered include:* rigor of secondary school record, academic GPA,

application essay, standardized test scores, character/personal qualities. *Important factors considered include:* extracurricular activities, volunteer work, work experience, level of applicant's interest. *Other factors considered include:* recommendation(s), talent/ability. **Freshman Admission Requirements:** High school diploma is required and GED is accepted *Academic units required:* 4 English, 3 math, 2 science, 2 science labs, 2 foreign language, 3 social studies, 0.5 academic electives, 0.5 visual/performing arts, *Academic units recommended:* 4 English, 4 math, 4 science, 3 science labs, 2 foreign language, 4 social studies, 1 visual/performing arts. **Freshman Admission Statistics:** 3,148 applied, 80.1% admitted, 32% enrolled. **General Admission Information:** Application fee $60. Priority deadline 1/15. Nonfall registration accepted. Admission may be deferred.

COSTS AND FINANCIAL AID

Required Forms and Deadlines: FAFSA. **Notification of Awards:** Applicants will be notified of awards on or about 4/1. **Types of Aid:** *Need-based scholarships/grants:* College/university scholarship or grant aid from institutional funds; Federal Pell; Private scholarships; SEOG; State scholarships/grants. *Loans:* Direct PLUS loans; Direct Subsidized Stafford Loans; Direct Unsubsidized Stafford Loans. *Student Employment:* Federal Work-Study Program available. Institutional employment available. **Financial Aid Statistics:** 87% needy freshmen, 96% needy undergrads receive need-based scholarship or grant aid. 3% freshmen, 1% undergrads receive non-need-based scholarship or grant aid. 61% freshmen, 68% undergrads receive need-based self-help aid. 0% freshmen, 0% undergrads receive athletic scholarships. 52% undergrads borrow to pay for school. Average cumulative indebtedness $19,900. **Criteria for awarding aid:** *Need-based:* Academics, Art, Leadership, Music/drama *Non-need-based:* Academics, Alumni affiliation, Art, Athletics, Leadership, Music/drama, State/district residency.

UNIVERSITY OF WASHINGTON—TACOMA

1900 Commerce Campus, Tacoma, WA 98402-3100
Phone: 253.692.4742
E-mail: uwtinfo@uw.edu
Fax: 253.692.4414 • **Website:** http://www.tacoma.uw.edu/

This is a public school.

RATINGS

Admissions Selectivity Rating: 76   **Fire Safety Rating:** 60*   **Green Rating:** 60*

STUDENTS AND FACULTY

Enrollment: 4,412. **Student Body:** 52% female, 48% male, 1% out-of-state, 4% international. Asian 19%, African American 8%, Caucasian 41%, Hispanic 15%, Native American 1%, Pacific Islander 1%, Two or more races 9%, Race unknown 2%.
Retention and Graduation: 76% freshmen return for sophomore year. 40% freshmen graduate within 4 years. 60% freshmen graduate within 6 years.
Faculty: Student/faculty ratio 16:1. 257 full-time faculty, 76% hold PhDs, 23% are members of minority groups, 53% are women.

ACADEMICS

Degrees: Bachelor's; Doctoral/Research; Master's; Post-Bachelor's certificate **Classes:** Most classes have 30-39 students. Most lab/discussion sessions have 10-19 students. **Special Study Options:** Cross-registration; Distance learning; Double major; Dual enrollment; Honors program; Independent study; Internships; Student-designed major; Study abroad; Teacher certification program.

FACILITIES

Housing: Apartments for single students

CAMPUS LIFE

Activities: Campus Ministries; Drama/theater; International Student Organization; Literary magazine; Student government; Student newspaper.

ADMISSIONS

Freshman Academic Profile: Average high school GPA 3.3. **Test Scores:** SAT Math middle 50% range 490-590. SAT EBRW middle 50% range 490-600. ACT middle 50% range 18-24. **Basis for Candidate Selection:** *Very important factors considered include:* rigor of secondary school record, academic GPA. *Important factors considered include:* application essay, standardized test scores. *Other factors considered include:* extracurricular activities, talent/ability, character/personal qualities, first generation, volunteer work, work experience, level of applicant's interest. **Freshman Admission Requirements:** High school diploma or equivalent is not required *Academic*

units required: 4 English, 3 math, 2 science, 2 science labs, 2 foreign language, 3 social studies, 0.5 academic electives, 0.5 visual/performing arts, and 1 unit from above areas or other academic areas. **Freshman Admission Statistics:** 1,982 applied, 83.9% admitted, 35% enrolled. **General Admission Information:** Application fee $60. Priority deadline 1/15. Regular application deadline 6/30. Nonfall registration accepted. Admission may be deferred for a maximum of 4 quarters.

COSTS AND FINANCIAL AID

Average book expense $825. **Required Forms and Deadlines:** FAFSA. **Notification of Awards:** Applicants will be notified of awards on or about 4/1. **Types of Aid:** *Need-based scholarships/grants:* College/university scholarship or grant aid from institutional funds; Federal Pell; Private scholarships; SEOG; State scholarships/grants. *Loans:* Direct PLUS loans; Direct Subsidized Stafford Loans; Direct Unsubsidized Stafford Loans. **Financial Aid Statistics:** 87% needy freshmen receive need-based scholarship or grant aid. **Criteria for awarding aid:** *Need-based:* Academics, Art, Leadership, Music/drama *Non-need-based:* Academics, Alumni affiliation, Art, Athletics, Leadership, Music/drama, State/district residency.

UNIVERSITY OF WEST ALABAMA

Station 4, Livingston, AL 35470
Phone: 205-652-3578 • **Financial Aid Phone:** 205-652-3576
E-mail: admissions@uwa.edu
Fax: 205-652-3522 • **Website:** http://www.uwa.edu/ • **ACT Code:** 24

This public school was founded in 1835. It has a 514 acre campus.

RATINGS

Admissions Selectivity Rating: 88   **Fire Safety Rating:** 87   **Green Rating:** 70

STUDENTS AND FACULTY

Enrollment: 2,106. **Student Body:** 55% female, 45% male, 20% out-of-state, 5% international (28 countries represented). Asian <1%, African American 44%, Caucasian 42%, Hispanic 2%, Native American <1%, Pacific Islander <1%, Two or more races 3%, Race unknown 3%.
Retention and Graduation: 67% freshmen return for sophomore year. 13% freshmen graduate within 4 years. 32% freshmen graduate within 6 years.
Faculty: Student/faculty ratio 13:1. 130 full-time faculty, 70% hold PhDs, 15% are members of minority groups, 59% are women. 0% of classes are taught by teaching assistants.

ACADEMICS

Degrees: Associate; Bachelor's; Certificate; Master's; Post-Master's certificate **Classes:** Most classes have 20-29 students. Most lab/discussion sessions have 20-29 students. **Most popular majors:** Physical Education Teaching And Coaching; Registered Nursing/Registered Nurse; Business Administration And Management, General. **Special Study Options:** Accelerated program; Cooperative education program; Distance learning; Double major; Dual enrollment; English as a Second Language (ESL); Honors program; Independent study; Internships; Student-designed major; Study abroad; Teacher certification program. Combined degree programs: BA/MEng. **Disability Services offered to physically disabled students:** Note-taking services; Tutors. **Career services:** Alumni services; Career assessment

FACILITIES

Housing: Apartments for single students; Coed dorms; Theme housing; Wellness housing 90% of campus accessible to physically disabled. **Computers:** Administrative functions (other than registration) can be performed online.

CAMPUS LIFE

Environment: Rural **Activities:** Campus Ministries; Choral groups; Concert band; Dance; Drama/theater; International Student Organization; Jazz band; Marching band; Music ensembles; Pep band; Student government; Student newspaper; Television station; Yearbook 30 registered organizations, 8 honor societies, 5 religious organizations. 7 fraternities, 6 sororities. **Athletics (Intercollegiate):** *Men:* baseball, basketball, cheerleading, cross-country, football, rodeo. *Women:* basketball, cheerleading, cross-country, rodeo, softball, volleyball. Student Union Building (SUB), Student Recreation Center, Tiger Stadium, Lake LU/Nature Trails, Young Hall Cafeteria

ADMISSIONS

Freshman Academic Profile: 88% from public high schools. **Test Scores:** ACT middle 50% range 18-23. Minimum internet-based TOEFL 90. Minimum paper TOEFL 580. **Basis for Candidate Selection:** *Very important factors considered include:* rigor of secondary school record, academic GPA, standardized test scores. **Freshman Admission Requirements:** High school diploma is required and GED is accepted *Academic units required:* 3 English, 3 math, 3 science, 3 social studies, 3 academic electives. **Freshman Admission Statistics:** 7,388 applied, 28.2% admitted, 22% enrolled. **Transfer Admission Requirements:** college transcript(s), statement of good standing from prior institution(s). Minimum college GPA of 2.0 required. Lowest grade transferable C. **General Admission Information:** Application fee $40. Priority deadline 6/1. Regular application deadline 8/18. Nonfall registration accepted. Admission may be deferred for a maximum of 1 year.

COSTS AND FINANCIAL AID

Annual in-state tuition $7,080. Annual out-of-state tuition $15,228. Room and board $7,080. Required fees $1,590. Average book expense $1,216. **Required Forms and Deadlines:** FAFSA. **Notification of Awards:** Applicants will be notified of awards on a rolling basis beginning 4/15. **Types of Aid:** *Need-based scholarships/grants:* College/university scholarship or grant aid from institutional funds; Federal Pell; Private scholarships; SEOG; State scholarships/grants; United Negro College Fund. *Loans:* Direct PLUS loans; Direct Subsidized Stafford Loans; Direct Unsubsidized Stafford Loans. *Student Employment:* Federal Work-Study Program available. Institutional employment available. **Financial Aid Statistics:** 64% needy freshmen, 75% needy undergrads receive need-based scholarship or grant aid. 65% freshmen, 40% undergrads receive non-need-based scholarship or grant aid. 12% freshmen, 15% undergrads receive need-based self-help aid. 13% freshmen, 15% undergrads receive athletic scholarships. 87% freshmen, 73% undergrads receive any aid. 70% undergrads borrow to pay for school. Average cumulative indebtedness $19,843. **Criteria for awarding aid:** *Non-need-based:* Academics, Alumni affiliation, Art, Athletics, Leadership, Music/drama, State/district residency.

UNIVERSITY OF WEST FLORIDA

11000 University Parkway, Pensacola, FL 32514-5750
Phone: 850-474-2230 • **Financial Aid Phone:** 850-474-2400
E-mail: admissions@uwf.edu • **CEEB Code:** 5833
Fax: 850-474-3360 • **Website:** http://uwf.edu • **ACT Code:** 771

This public school was founded in 1963. It has a 1600 acre campus.

RATINGS

Admissions Selectivity Rating: 89 **Fire Safety Rating:** 89 **Green Rating:** 60*

STUDENTS AND FACULTY

Enrollment: 9,786. **Student Body:** 57% female, 43% male, 9% out-of-state, 2% international (71 countries represented). Asian 3%, African American 13%, Caucasian 65%, Hispanic 9%, Native American <1%, Pacific Islander <1%, Two or more races 5%, Race unknown 2%.
Retention and Graduation: 72% freshmen return for sophomore year.
Faculty: Student/faculty ratio 22:1. 338 full-time faculty, 17% are members of minority groups, 44% are women.

ACADEMICS

Degrees: Associate; Bachelor's; Certificate; Doctoral; Master's; Post-Master's certificate **Classes:** Most classes have 10-19 students. Most lab/discussion sessions have 10-19 students. **Most popular majors:** Biology/Biological Sciences, General; Psychology, General; Accounting. **Special Study Options:** Cooperative education program; Distance learning; Dual enrollment; English as a Second Language (ESL); Exchange student program (domestic); Honors program; Independent study; Internships; Study abroad; Teacher certification program. **Disability Services offered to physically disabled students:** Note-taking services; Reader services; Tape recorders; Tutors. **Career services:** Alumni services; Career assessment; Career/job search classes; Internships

FACILITIES

Housing: Apartments for married students; Apartments for single students; Coed dorms; Fraternity/sorority housing; Special housing for disabled students 80% of campus accessible to physically diasbled. **Special Academic Facilities/Equipment:** Archeology museum,instructional media center, biology, chemistry, physics, and psychology labs, property on the Gulf of Mexico for marine and ecology research. **Computers:** 100% of classrooms, 100% of libraries, 100% of dining areas, 100% of student union, 100% of common outdoor areas have wireless network access. Students can register for classes online. Administrative functions (other than registration) can be performed online.

CAMPUS LIFE

Environment: City **Activities:** Campus Ministries; Choral groups; Concert band; Dance; Drama/theater; International Student Organization; Jazz band; Music ensembles; Musical theater; Pep band; Radio station; Student government; Student newspaper; Symphony orchestra; Television station 157 registered organizations, 15 honor societies, 17 religious organizations. 10 fraternities, 7 sororities. **Athletics (Intercollegiate):** *Men:* baseball, basketball, cross-country, golf, soccer, tennis. *Women:* basketball, cross-country, golf, soccer, softball, tennis, volleyball. **On-Campus Highlights:** The Commons (has cafeteria and bookstore), Fitness Facilities, Center for Fine and Performing Arts, Nature Trails, Library **Environmental Initiatives:** All new buildings must be at least L.E.E.D Silver Certified

ADMISSIONS

Freshman Academic Profile: Average high school GPA 3.6. 14% in top 10% of high school class, 38% in top 25% of high school class, 74% in top 50% of high school class. **Test Scores:** SAT Math middle 50% range 460-550. SAT EBRW middle 50% range 470-570. ACT middle 50% range 20-26. Minimum internet-based TOEFL 78/80. Minimum paper TOEFL 550. **Basis for Candidate Selection:** *Very important factors considered include:* rigor of secondary school record, academic GPA, standardized test scores. *Other factors considered include:* application essay, recommendation(s), extracurricular activities, talent/ability, character/personal qualities, first generation, alumni/ae relation, geographical residence, state residency, volunteer work, work experience. **Freshman Admission Requirements:** High school diploma is required and GED is accepted *Academic units required:* 4 English, 3 math, 3 science, 2 science labs, 2 foreign language, 3 social studies, 4 academic electives. **Freshman Admission Statistics:** 7,104 applied, 41.5% admitted, 44% enrolled. **Transfer Admission Requirements:** college transcript(s), Minimum college GPA of 2.0 required. Lowest grade transferable D. **General Admission Information:** Application fee $30. Regular application deadline 6/30. Nonfall registration accepted. Admission may be deferred for a maximum of one year.

COSTS AND FINANCIAL AID

Annual in-state tuition $9,912. Annual out-of-state tuition $19,241. Room and board $9,912. Average book expense $1,200. **Required Forms and Deadlines:** FAFSA. **Notification of Awards:** Applicants will be notified of awards on a rolling basis beginning 3/1. **Types of Aid:** *Need-based scholarships/grants:* College/university scholarship or grant aid from institutional funds; Federal Pell; Private scholarships; SEOG; State scholarships/grants. *Loans:* Direct PLUS loans; Direct Subsidized Stafford Loans; Direct Unsubsidized Stafford Loans. *Student Employment:* Federal Work-Study Program available. Institutional employment available. **Financial Aid Statistics:** 92% needy freshmen, 85% needy undergrads receive need-based scholarship or grant aid. 3% freshmen, 3% undergrads receive non-need-based scholarship or grant aid. 63% freshmen, 68% undergrads receive need-based self-help aid. 2% freshmen, 2% undergrads receive athletic scholarships. **Criteria for awarding aid:** *Need-based:* Academics, Leadership *Non-need-based:* Academics, Alumni affiliation, Art, Athletics, Leadership, Minority status, Music/drama.

UNIVERSITY OF WEST GEORGIA

1601 Maple Street, Carrollton, GA 30118
Phone: 678-839-5600 • **Financial Aid Phone:** 678-839-6421
E-mail: admiss@westga.edu • **CEEB Code:** 5900
Fax: 678-839-4747 • **Website:** www.westga.edu • **ACT Code:** 878

This public school was founded in 1906. It has a 645 acre campus.

RATINGS

Admissions Selectivity Rating: 83 **Fire Safety Rating:** 96 **Green Rating:** 63

STUDENTS AND FACULTY

Enrollment: 11,229. **Student Body:** 63% female, 37% male, 6% out-of-state, 1% international (65 countries represented). Asian 1%, African American 38%, Caucasian 48%, Hispanic 6%, Native American <1%, Pacific Islander <1%, Two or more races 4%, Race unknown 2%.
Retention and Graduation: 72% freshmen return for sophomore year. 17% freshmen graduate within 4 years. 45% freshmen graduate within 6 years.
Faculty: Student/faculty ratio 20:1. 451 full-time faculty, 74% hold PhDs, 21% are members of minority groups, 57% are women. 0% of classes are taught by teaching assistants.

ACADEMICS

Degrees: Bachelor's; Doctoral/Research; Master's; Post-Bachelor's certificate; Post-Master's certificate **Classes:** Most classes have 10-19 students. Most lab/

discussion sessions have 10-19 students. **Most popular majors:** Biological And Biomedical Sciences; Psychology; Business, Management, Marketing, And Related Support Services. **Special Study Options:** Accelerated program; Cooperative education program; Cross-registration; Distance learning; Double major; Dual enrollment; External degree program; Honors program; Independent study; Internships; Study abroad; Teacher certification program. **Disability Services offered to physically disabled students:** Note-taking services; Reader services; Tape recorders; Tutors. Alumni services; Career assessment; Internships

FACILITIES

Housing: Apartments for married students; Apartments for single students; Coed dorms; Fraternity/sorority housing; Special housing for disabled student; Special housing for international students; Theme housing; Wellness housing 80% of campus accessible to physically diasbled. **Special Academic Facilities/Equipment:** Archaeology Lab, West Georgia Observatory, Bruce Bobick Art Gallery, Townsend Center for the Performing Arts, Kathy Cashen Recital Hall, TV studio. **Computers:** 20% of classrooms, 10% of dorms, 100% of libraries, 100% of dining areas, 100% of student union, 80% of common outdoor areas have wireless network access. Students can register for classes online. Administrative functions (other than registration) can be performed online.

CAMPUS LIFE

Environment: City **Activities:** Campus Ministries; Choral groups; Concert band; Dance; Drama/theater; International Student Organization; Jazz band; Literary magazine; Marching band; Music ensembles; Musical theater; Pep band; Radio station; Student government; Student newspaper; Television station 131 registered organizations, 32 honor societies, 17 religious organizations. 14 fraternities, 8 sororities. **Athletics (Intercollegiate):** *Men:* baseball, basketball, cheerleading, cross-country, football, golf. *Women:* basketball, cheerleading, cross-country, golf, soccer, softball, volleyball. **On-Campus Highlights:** Technology Enhanced Learning Center (TLC), Bookstore, Ingram Library, Football Stadium, Campus Center

ADMISSIONS

Freshman Academic Profile: Average high school GPA 3.2. 95% from public high schools. **Test Scores:** SAT Math middle 50% range 430-510. ACT middle 50% range 18-22. Minimum internet-based TOEFL 69. Minimum paper TOEFL 523. **Basis for Candidate Selection:** *Very important factors considered include:* academic GPA, standardized test scores. **Freshman Admission Requirements:** High school diploma is required and GED is accepted *Academic units required:* 4 English, 4 math, 4 science, 2 science labs, 2 foreign language, 1 social studies, 2 history. **Freshman Admission Statistics:** 7,912 applied, 58.6% admitted, 47% enrolled. **Transfer Admission Requirements:** college transcript(s), Minimum college GPA of 2.0 required. Lowest grade transferable D. **General Admission Information:** Application fee $40. Priority deadline 2/1. Regular application deadline 6/1. Nonfall registration accepted. Admission may be deferred for a maximum of 1 year.

COSTS AND FINANCIAL AID

Annual in-state tuition $10,218. Annual out-of-state tuition $18,812. Room and board $10,218. Required fees $1,962. Average book expense $1,500. **Required Forms and Deadlines:** FAFSA. **Notification of Awards:** Applicants will be notified of awards on a rolling basis beginning 5/1. **Types of Aid:** *Need-based scholarships/grants:* College/university scholarship or grant aid from institutional funds; Federal Nursing Scholarships; Federal Pell; Private scholarships; SEOG; State scholarships/grants; United Negro College Fund. *Loans:* Direct PLUS loans; Direct Subsidized Stafford Loans; Direct Unsubsidized Stafford Loans. *Student Employment:* Federal Work-Study Program available. Institutional employment available. **Financial Aid Statistics:** 64% needy freshmen, 67% needy undergrads receive need-based scholarship or grant aid. 18% freshmen, 13% undergrads receive non-need-based scholarship or grant aid. 90% freshmen, 90% undergrads receive need-based self-help aid. 2% freshmen, 2% undergrads receive athletic scholarships. 76% undergrads borrow to pay for school. Average cumulative indebtedness $26,874. **Criteria for awarding aid:** *Need-based:* Academics, Alumni affiliation, Art, Job skills, Leadership, Minority status, Music/drama, Religious affiliation *Non-need-based:* Academics, Alumni affiliation, Art, Athletics, Job skills, Leadership, Minority status, Music/drama, Religious affiliation.

UNIVERSITY OF WINDSOR

401 Sunset Ave, Windsor, ON N9B3P4
Phone: 519-253-3000 • **Financial Aid Phone:** 519-253-3000
E-mail: registrar@uwindsor.ca
Fax: 519-971-3653 • **Website:** www.uwindsor.ca

This public school was founded in 1857. It has a 125 acre campus.

RATINGS
Admissions Selectivity Rating: 68   **Fire Safety Rating:** 88   **Green Rating:** 83

STUDENTS AND FACULTY
Enrollment: 12,180. **Student Body:** 52% female, 48% male, (83 countries represented).
Faculty: Student/faculty ratio 23:1. 573 full-time faculty, 84% hold PhDs, 39% are women.

ACADEMICS
Degrees: Bachelor's; Certificate; Doctoral; **Master's Classes:** Most classes have 10-19 students. Most lab/discussion sessions have 10-19 students. **Most popular majors:** Engineering, General; Social Sciences, Other; Registered Nursing, Nursing Administration, Nursing Research And Clinical Nursing, Other. **Special Study Options:** Cooperative education program; Distance learning; Double major; English as a Second Language (ESL); Exchange student program (domestic); Honors program; Independent study; Internships; Study abroad; Teacher certification program. Honors programs: As a comprehensive university we have distinguished ourselves at many levels, with program offerings across a broad array of academic and professional programs. Our Outstanding Scholars Program, entrance and in-course awards, Deans' Honour Rolls, and President's Medal are among the many opportunities that exist to motivate you to fulfill your academic potential. **Disability Services offered to physically disabled students:** Note-taking services; Reader services; Tape recorders; Tutors. **Career services:** Alumni network; Alumni services; Career assessment; Career/job search classes; Internships

FACILITIES
Housing: Apartments for married students; Apartments for single students; Coed dorms; Cooperative housing; Fraternity/sorority housing; Special housing for disabled student; Special housing for international students 85% of campus accessible to physically diasbled. **Special Academic Facilities/Equipment:** Ed Lumley Centre for Engineering Innovation(CEI) C.A.R.E. (Centre for Automotive Research and Education) GLIER (Great Lakes Institute for Environemntal Research) Jackman Dramatic Art Centre (Theatrical space) Bio-Learning Centre (BLC) Biotechnology Laboratory Odette School of Business Financial Markets lab and Entrepreneurship Practice & Innovation Centre (EPICentre) **Computers:** 100% of classrooms, 100% of dorms, 100% of libraries, 100% of dining areas, 100% of student union, 100% of common outdoor areas have wireless network access. Students can register for classes online. Administrative functions (other than registration) can be performed online.

CAMPUS LIFE
Environment: City **Activities:** Campus Ministries; Choral groups; Dance; Drama/theater; International Student Organization; Jazz band; Literary magazine; Model UN; Music ensembles; Musical theater; Radio station; Student government; Student newspaper; Student-run film society; Television station 116 registered organizations, 1 honor society, 13 religious organizations. 3 fraternities, 3 sororities. **Athletics (Intercollegiate):** *Men:* basketball, cross-country, football, ice hockey, soccer, track/field (outdoor), track/field (indoor), volleyball. *Women:* basketball, cross-country, ice hockey, soccer, track/field (outdoor), track/field (indoor), volleyball. **On-Campus Highlights:** CAW Student Centre, Centre for Engineering Innovation (CEI), St. Denis Athletic Centre/Stadium, Forge Fitness facility, Leddy Library/Tim Hortons **Environmental Initiatives:** In January 2013, the Environmental Advocate was appointed, the University of Windsor Joined AASHE, and the sustainability website was created. The Environmental Advocate is also a member of the Ontario College and University Sustainability Professionals.

ADMISSIONS
Test Scores: Minimum internet-based TOEFL 83, essay 21. **Basis for Candidate Selection:** *Very important factors considered include:* rigor of secondary school record, academic GPA. *Other factors considered include:* standardized test scores, recommendation(s), interview, extracurricular activities, geographical residence. **Freshman Admission Requirements:** High school diploma is required and GED is not accepted **Freshman Admission Statistics:** 9,470 applied, 74.1% admitted, 33% enrolled. **Transfer Admission Requirements:** college transcript(s). **General Admission Information:** Application fee $120. Nonfall registration accepted.

COSTS AND FINANCIAL AID

Annual in-state tuition $10,604. Room and board $10,604. **Required Forms and Deadlines:** FAFSA; Institution's own financial aid form. **Notification of Awards:** Applicants will be notified of awards on a rolling basis beginning 8/1. **Types of Aid:** *Loans:* Direct PLUS loans; Direct Subsidized Stafford Loans; Direct Unsubsidized Stafford Loans. **Criteria for awarding aid:** *Need-based:* Academics, Athletics, Leadership *Non-need-based:* Academics, Athletics, Leadership.

UNIVERSITY OF WISCONSIN—EAU CLAIRE

105 Garfield Avenue, Eau Claire, WI 54701
Phone: 715-836-5415 • **Financial Aid Phone:** 715-836-5606
E-mail: admissions@uwec.edu • **CEEB Code:** 1913
Fax: 715-831-4799 • **Website:** www.uwec.edu • **ACT Code:** 4670

This public school was founded in 1916. It has a 337 acre campus.

RATINGS

Admissions Selectivity Rating: 78   **Fire Safety Rating:** 91   **Green Rating:** 74

STUDENTS AND FACULTY

Enrollment: 9,905. **Student Body:** 61% female, 39% male, 30% out-of-state, 2% international (23 countries represented). Asian 3%, African American 1%, Caucasian 88%, Hispanic 3%, Native American <1%, Pacific Islander <1%, Two or more races 2%, Race unknown <1%.
Retention and Graduation: 82% freshmen return for sophomore year. 34% freshmen graduate within 4 years. 67% freshmen graduate within 6 years. 15% grads go on to further study within 1 year. 22% grads pursue arts and sciences degrees. 5% grads pursue law degrees. 5% grads pursue business degrees. 4% grads pursue medical degrees. **Faculty:** Student/faculty ratio 22:1. 389 full-time faculty, 76% hold PhDs, 19% are members of minority groups, 50% are women. 0% of classes are taught by teaching assistants.

ACADEMICS

Degrees: Associate; Bachelor's; Certificate; Doctoral/Professional; Master's; Post-Bachelor's certificate; Post-Master's certificate; Transfer Associate **Classes:** Most classes have 20-29 students. Most lab/discussion sessions have 20-29 students. **Most popular majors:** Biology/Biological Sciences, General; Psychology, General; Registered Nursing/Registered Nurse. **Special Study Options:** Accelerated program; Distance learning; Double major; Dual enrollment; English as a Second Language (ESL); Exchange student program (domestic); External degree program; Honors program; Independent study; Internships; Student-designed major; Study abroad; Teacher certification program. **Disability Services offered to physically disabled students:** Note-taking services; Reader services; Tape recorders; Tutors. **Career services:** Alumni network; Alumni services; Career assessment; Career/job search classes; Internships; Regional alumni

FACILITIES

Housing: Apartments for single students; Coed dorms; Theme housing; Wellness housing 90% of campus accessible to physically disabled. **Special Academic Facilities/Equipment:** Art Gallery, Greenhouses, Bird Museum, Communication and Journalism Center, Human Development Center, Materials Science Center (wide array of instrumentation for materials imaging, elemental/chemical analysis, physical/mechanical properties analysis and sample preparation), Natural Preserve, Nursing Clinical Simulation/Skills Lab, Planetarium, Ropes Course, Special Collections (including John L. Buchholz Jazz Library and the Frederick G. and Joan Christopherson Schmidt Robert Frost Collection) **Computers:** 50% of classrooms, 10% of dorms, 100% of libraries, 100% of dining areas, 100% of student union, 100% of common outdoor areas have wireless network access. Students can register for classes online. Administrative functions (other than registration) can be performed online.

CAMPUS LIFE

Environment: City **Activities:** Campus Ministries; Choral groups; Concert band; Dance; Drama/theater; International Student Organization; Jazz band; Literary magazine; Marching band; Model UN; Music ensembles; Musical theater; Opera; Pep band; Radio station; Student government; Student newspaper; Student-run film society; Symphony orchestra; Television station 240 registered organizations, 30 honor societies, 16 religious organizations. 2 fraternities, 3 sororities. **Athletics (Intercollegiate):** *Men:* basketball, cross-country, diving, football, golf, ice hockey, swimming, tennis, track/field (outdoor), track/field (indoor), wrestling. *Women:* basketball, cross-country, diving, golf, gymnastics, ice hockey, soccer, softball, swimming, tennis, track/

field (outdoor), track/field (indoor), volleyball. **On-Campus Highlights:** Chippewa River Footbridge, Davies Center (Student Center/Union), McPhee Center (Athletic Facility), Hass Fine Arts Center, Higher Ground (Recreational Facility) **Environmental Initiatives:** Creation of an energy performance contract to provide $3.4 million in energy conservation measures across campus, including heating and ventilation, lighting, water conservation, etc.

ADMISSIONS

Freshman Academic Profile: 16% in top 10% of high school class, 48% in top 25% of high school class, 91% in top 50% of high school class. **Test Scores:** SAT Math middle 50% range 530-650. SAT EBRW middle 50% range 510-640. ACT middle 50% range 21-26. Minimum internet-based TOEFL 79. Minimum paper TOEFL 550. **Basis for Candidate Selection:** *Very important factors considered include:* rigor of secondary school record, class rank, academic GPA. *Important factors considered include:* application essay, standardized test scores. *Other factors considered include:* recommendation(s), interview, extracurricular activities, talent/ability, character/personal qualities, first generation, geographical residence, state residency, racial/ethnic status, volunteer work, work experience, level of applicant's interest. **Freshman Admission Requirements:** High school diploma is required and GED is accepted *Academic units required:* 4 English, 3 math, 3 science, 3 social studies, 4 academic electives. **Freshman Admission Statistics:** 5,990 applied, 85.7% admitted, 46% enrolled. **Transfer Admission Requirements:** High school transcript, college transcript(s), statement of good standing from prior institution(s). Minimum college GPA of 2.0 required. Lowest grade transferable D-. **General Admission Information:** Application fee $50. Priority deadline 12/1. Regular application deadline 8/20. Nonfall registration accepted.

COSTS AND FINANCIAL AID

Annual in-state tuition $7,538. Annual out-of-state tuition $15,281. Room and board $7,538. Required fees $1,455. Average book expense $400. **Required Forms and Deadlines:** FAFSA. **Notification of Awards:** Applicants will be notified of awards on a rolling basis beginning 4/15. **Types of Aid:** *Need-based scholarships/grants:* College/university scholarship or grant aid from institutional funds; Federal Nursing Scholarships; Federal Pell; Private scholarships; SEOG; State scholarships/grants. *Loans:* Direct PLUS loans; Direct Subsidized Stafford Loans; Direct Unsubsidized Stafford Loans. *Student Employment:* Federal Work-Study Program available. Institutional employment available. **Financial Aid Statistics:** 83% needy freshmen, 82% needy undergrads receive need-based scholarship or grant aid. 4% freshmen, 3% undergrads receive non-need-based scholarship or grant aid. 94% freshmen, 94% undergrads receive need-based self-help aid. 0% freshmen, 0% undergrads receive athletic scholarships. 84% freshmen, 74% undergrads receive any aid. 72% undergrads borrow to pay for school. Average cumulative indebtedness $26,295. **Criteria for awarding aid:** *Need-based:* Academics, Minority status *Non-need-based:* Academics, Art, Leadership, Minority status, Music/drama, State/district residency.

UNIVERSITY OF WISCONSIN—GREEN BAY

2420 Nicolet Drive, Green Bay, WI 53411-7001
Phone: 920-465-2111 • **Financial Aid Phone:** (920)465-2075
E-mail: admissions@uwgb.edu • **CEEB Code:** 1859
Fax: 920-465-5754 • **Website:** http://www.uwgb.edu/ • **ACT Code:** 4688

This public school was founded in 1965. It has a 700 acre campus.

RATINGS

Admissions Selectivity Rating: 73   **Fire Safety Rating:** 88   **Green Rating:** 77

STUDENTS AND FACULTY

Enrollment: 5,492. **Student Body:** 66% female, 34% male, 9% out-of-state, 1% international (27 countries represented). Asian 3%, African American 2%, Caucasian 84%, Hispanic 5%, Native American 1%, Pacific Islander <1%, Two or more races 3%, Race unknown <1%.
Retention and Graduation: 73% freshmen return for sophomore year. 30% freshmen graduate within 4 years. 51% freshmen graduate within 6 years. 15% grads go on to further study within 1 year. 7% grads pursue arts and sciences degrees. 1% grads pursue law degrees. 3% grads pursue business degrees. 1% grads pursue medical degrees. **Faculty:** Student/faculty ratio 23:1. 182 full-time faculty, 87% hold PhDs, 22% are members of minority groups, 49% are women. 0% of classes are taught by teaching assistants.

ACADEMICS

Degrees: Associate; Bachelor's; Doctoral/Professional; **Master's Classes:** Most classes have 10-19 students. Most lab/discussion sessions have fewer than

10 students. **Most popular majors:** Multi-/Interdisciplinary Studies, Other; Psychology, General; Business Administration And Management, General. **Special Study Options:** Cross-registration; Distance learning; Double major; Exchange student program (domestic); External degree program; Independent study; Internships; Liberal arts/career combination; Student-designed major; Study abroad; Teacher certification program. **Disability Services offered to physically disabled students:** Note-taking services; Reader services; Tape recorders. **Career services:** Alumni network; Alumni services; Career/job search classes; Internships

FACILITIES

Housing: Apartments for single students; Coed dorms; Other (please specify) 99% of campus accessible to physically diasbled. **Special Academic Facilities/Equipment:** 290-acre arboretum, Herbarium, regional Performing Arts Center **Computers:** 75% of classrooms, 100% of dorms, 100% of libraries, 100% of dining areas, 100% of student union, 10% of common outdoor areas have wireless network access. Students can register for classes online. Administrative functions (other than registration) can be performed online.

CAMPUS LIFE

Environment: City **Activities:** Campus Ministries; Choral groups; Concert band; Dance; Drama/theater; International Student Organization; Jazz band; Literary magazine; Music ensembles; Musical theater; Pep band; Radio station; Student government; Student newspaper; Student-run film society; Television station 100 registered organizations, 7 honor societies, 5 religious organizations. 2 fraternities, 2 sororities. **Athletics (Intercollegiate):** *Men:* basketball, cheerleading, cross-country, diving, golf, skiing (nordic/cross-country), soccer, swimming, tennis. *Women:* basketball, cheerleading, cross-country, diving, golf, skiing (nordic/cross-country), soccer, softball, swimming, tennis, volleyball. **On-Campus Highlights:** Weidner Center for Performing Arts, Kress Event Center, Common Grounds Coffee Shop, Lambeau Cottage on the shores of Green B, Shorewood Golf Course/Clubhouse **Environmental Initiatives:** Building integrated photovoltaics in Mary Ann Cofrin Hall (http://www.buildingsolar.com/index.html)

ADMISSIONS

Freshman Academic Profile: Average high school GPA 3.3. 95% from public high schools. **Test Scores:** SAT Math middle 50% range 465-555. SAT EBRW middle 50% range 450-595. ACT middle 50% range 20-25. Minimum internet-based TOEFL 61. Minimum paper TOEFL 500. **Basis for Candidate Selection:** *Very important factors considered include:* rigor of secondary school record, academic GPA, level of applicant's interest. *Important factors considered include:* application essay, standardized test scores, extracurricular activities, volunteer work, work experience. *Other factors considered include:* recommendation(s), interview, talent/ability, character/personal qualities, geographical residence, state residency, racial/ethnic status. **Freshman Admission Requirements:** High school diploma is required and GED is accepted *Academic units required:* 4 English, 3 math, 3 science, 1 science labs, 3 social studies, 4 academic electives, *Academic units recommended:* 4 English, 3 math, 3 science, 1 science labs, 2 foreign language, 3 social studies, 4 academic electives. **Freshman Admission Statistics:** 2,151 applied, 94.7% admitted, 48% enrolled. **Transfer Admission Requirements:** college transcript(s), Minimum college GPA of 2.0 required. Lowest grade transferable D. **General Admission Information:** Application fee $50. Priority deadline 4/15. Nonfall registration accepted. Admission may be deferred for a maximum of 1 year.

COSTS AND FINANCIAL AID

Annual in-state tuition $7,306. Annual out-of-state tuition $14,148. Room and board $7,306. Required fees $1,580. Average book expense $800. **Required Forms and Deadlines:** FAFSA. **Notification of Awards:** Applicants will be notified of awards on a rolling basis beginning 1/1. **Types of Aid:** *Need-based scholarships/grants:* College/university scholarship or grant aid from institutional funds; Federal Pell; Private scholarships; SEOG; State scholarships/grants. *Loans:* Direct PLUS loans; Direct Subsidized Stafford Loans; Direct Unsubsidized Stafford Loans. *Student Employment:* Federal Work-Study Program available. Institutional employment available. **Financial Aid Statistics:** 73% needy freshmen, 75% needy undergrads receive need-based scholarship or grant aid. 4% freshmen, 3% undergrads receive non-need-based scholarship or grant aid. 74% freshmen, 74% undergrads receive need-based self-help aid. 1% freshmen, 1% undergrads receive athletic scholarships. 88% freshmen, 80% undergrads receive any aid. 77% undergrads borrow to pay for school. Average cumulative indebtedness $28,940. **Criteria for awarding aid:** *Non-need-based:* Academics, Art, Athletics, Leadership, Minority status, Music/drama.

UNIVERSITY OF WISCONSIN—LA CROSSE

1725 State Street, La Crosse, WI 54601-3742
Phone: 608-785-8939 • **Financial Aid Phone:** 608-785-8604
E-mail: admissions@uwlax.edu • **CEEB Code:** 1914
Fax: 608-785-8940 • **Website:** www.uwlax.edu • **ACT Code:** 4672

This public school was founded in 1909. It has a 120 acre campus.

RATINGS

Admissions Selectivity Rating: 82 **Fire Safety Rating:** 62 **Green Rating:** 60*

STUDENTS AND FACULTY

Enrollment: 9,397. **Student Body:** 56% female, 44% male, 18% out-of-state, 1% international (20 countries represented). Asian 2%, African American 1%, Caucasian 90%, Hispanic 3%, Native American <1%, Pacific Islander <1%, Two or more races 3%, Race unknown <1%.
Retention and Graduation: 83% freshmen return for sophomore year. 42% freshmen graduate within 4 years. 71% freshmen graduate within 6 years.
Faculty: Student/faculty ratio 19:1. 468 full-time faculty, 83% hold PhDs, 12% are members of minority groups, 50% are women. 0% of classes are taught by teaching assistants.

ACADEMICS

Degrees: Associate; Bachelor's; Certificate; Doctoral/Professional; Doctoral/Research; Master's; Post-Bachelor's certificate; Post-Master's certificate **Classes:** Most classes have 20-29 students. **Most popular majors:** Biology/Biological Sciences, General; Kinesiology And Exercise Science; Psychology, General. **Special Study Options:** Distance learning; Double major; Dual enrollment; English as a Second Language (ESL); Exchange student program (domestic); Honors program; Independent study; Internships; Study abroad; Teacher certification program. **Disability Services offered to physically disabled students:** Note-taking services; Reader services; Tape recorders; Tutors. **Career services:** Alumni services; Career assessment; Career/job search classes; Internships

FACILITIES

Housing: Apartments for single students; Coed dorms; Special housing for disabled student; Special housing for international students; Theme housing 98% of campus accessible to physically diasbled. **Special Academic Facilities/Equipment:** Planetarium, Health Science Center, Mississippi Valley Archaeology Center, River Studies Center, Small Business Development Center **Computers:** Students can register for classes online. Administrative functions (other than registration) can be performed online.

CAMPUS LIFE

Environment: City **Activities:** Campus Ministries; Choral groups; Concert band; Dance; Drama/theater; International Student Organization; Jazz band; Literary magazine; Marching band; Music ensembles; Musical theater; Radio station; Student government; Student newspaper; Symphony orchestra; Television station 180 registered organizations, 13 honor societies, 10 religious organizations. 4 fraternities, 2 sororities. **Athletics (Intercollegiate):** *Men:* baseball, basketball, cross-country, diving, football, swimming, tennis, track/field (outdoor), track/field (indoor), wrestling. *Women:* basketball, cross-country, diving, gymnastics, soccer, softball, swimming, tennis, track/field (outdoor), track/field (indoor), volleyball. **On-Campus Highlights:** Murphy Library, The Student Union, Centennial Hall, The Recreational Eagle Center, Whitney Center

ADMISSIONS

Freshman Academic Profile: 21% in top 10% of high school class, 58% in top 25% of high school class, 95% in top 50% of high school class. **Test Scores:** SAT Math middle 50% range 560-660. SAT EBRW middle 50% range 560-670. ACT middle 50% range 22-26. Minimum internet-based TOEFL 73. Minimum paper TOEFL 550. **Basis for Candidate Selection:** *Very important factors considered include:* rigor of secondary school record, class rank, academic GPA, standardized test scores. *Important factors considered include:* application essay, extracurricular activities, volunteer work.level of applicant's interest. *Other factors considered include:* recommendation(s), interview, talent/ability, character/personal qualities, first generation, alumni/ae relation, geographical residence, state residency, racial/ethnic status, work experience. **Freshman Admission Requirements:** High school diploma is required and GED is accepted *Academic units required:* 4 English, 3 math, 3 science, 2 science labs, 3 social studies, 4 academic electives, *Academic units recommended:* 4 English, 4 math, 4 science, 3 science labs, 3 foreign language, 4 social studies. **Freshman Admission Statistics:** 5,880 applied, 81.3% admitted, 44% enrolled. **Transfer Admission Requirements:** college transcript(s), statement of good standing from prior institution(s). Minimum college GPA of

3.0 required. Lowest grade transferable D-. **General Admission Information:** Application fee $50. Priority deadline 2/1. Nonfall registration accepted.

COSTS AND FINANCIAL AID
Required Forms and Deadlines: FAFSA. **Types of Aid:** *Need-based scholarships/grants:* College/university scholarship or grant aid from institutional funds; Federal Pell; Private scholarships; SEOG; State scholarships/grants. *Loans:* Direct PLUS loans; Direct Subsidized Stafford Loans; Direct Unsubsidized Stafford Loans. *Student Employment:* Federal Work-Study Program available. Institutional employment available. **Financial Aid Statistics:** 41% needy freshmen, 63% needy undergrads receive need-based scholarship or grant aid. 57% freshmen, 32% undergrads receive non-need-based scholarship or grant aid. 77% freshmen, 83% undergrads receive need-based self-help aid. 0% freshmen, 0% undergrads receive athletic scholarships. 88% freshmen, 77% undergrads receive any aid. 69% undergrads borrow to pay for school. Average cumulative indebtedness $26,487. **Criteria for awarding aid:** *Non-need-based:* Academics, Alumni affiliation, Art, Leadership, Minority status, Music/drama.

UNIVERSITY OF WISCONSIN—MADISON

161 Bascom Hall, Madison, WI 53715–1007
Phone: 608-262-3961 • **Financial Aid Phone:** 608-262-3060
E-mail: onwisconsin@admissions.wisc.edu • **CEEB Code:** 1846
Fax: 608-262-7706 • **Website:** www.wisc.edu • **ACT Code:** 4656

This public school was founded in 1848. It has a 936 acre campus.

RATINGS
Admissions Selectivity Rating: 92   **Fire Safety Rating:** 83   **Green Rating:** 60*

STUDENTS AND FACULTY
Enrollment: 29,931. **Student Body:** 51% female, 49% male, 34% out-of-state, 9% international (102 countries represented). Asian 6%, African American 2%, Caucasian 73%, Hispanic 5%, Native American <1%, Pacific Islander <1%, Two or more races 3%, Race unknown 1%.
Retention and Graduation: 95% freshmen return for sophomore year. 61% freshmen graduate within 4 years. 87% freshmen graduate within 6 years.
Faculty: Student/faculty ratio 18:1. 2,392 full-time faculty, 90% hold PhDs, 20% are members of minority groups, 40% are women.

ACADEMICS
Degrees: Bachelor's; Doctoral; Doctoral/Professional; Doctoral/Research; Master's; Post-Bachelor's certificate **Classes:** Most classes have 10-19 students. Most lab/discussion sessions have 10-19 students. **Most popular majors:** Biology/Biological Sciences, General; Economics, General; Political Science And Government, General. **Special Study Options:** Accelerated program; Cooperative education program; Distance learning; Double major; Dual enrollment; English as a Second Language (ESL); Exchange student program (domestic); Honors program; Independent study; Internships; Liberal arts/career combination; Student-designed major; Study abroad; Teacher certification program. **Disability Services offered to physically disabled students:** Note-taking services; Reader services; Tape recorders; Tutors. **Career services:** Alumni network; Career assessment; Career/job search classes; Internships

FACILITIES
Housing: Coed dorms; Cooperative housing; Fraternity/sorority housing; Men's dorms; Theme housing; Wellness housing; Women's dorms 90% of campus accessible to physically disabled. **Special Academic Facilities/Equipment:** Art, physics, and geology museums, nuclear reactor, arboretum, botanical gardens, observatory, campus dairy store (campus-made ice cream and cheese), american indian burial mounds **Computers:** 100% of classrooms, 25% of dorms, 100% of libraries, 100% of dining areas, 100% of student union, 100% of common outdoor areas have wireless network access. Students can register for classes online. Administrative functions (other than registration) can be performed online.

CAMPUS LIFE
Environment: City **Activities:** Choral groups; Concert band; Dance; Drama/theater; International Student Organization; Jazz band; Literary magazine; Marching band; Music ensembles; Musical theater; Opera; Pep band; Radio station; Student government; Student newspaper; Student-run film society;

Symphony orchestra; Television station; Yearbook 685 registered organizations, 27 honor societies, 26 fraternities, 11 sororities. **Athletics (Intercollegiate):** *Men:* basketball, cheerleading, crew/rowing, cross-country, football, golf, ice hockey, soccer, swimming, tennis, track/field (outdoor), wrestling. *Women:* basketball, cheerleading, crew/rowing, cross-country, golf, ice hockey, soccer, softball, swimming, tennis, track/field (outdoor), volleyball. **On-Campus Highlights:** Allen Centennial Gardens, Kohl Center, Memorial Union Terrace, Chazen Museum of Art, Babcock Hall Dairy Plant and Store **Environmental Initiatives:** Our conservation efforts in the last four years have reduced campus energy consumption by over 1 trillion BTUs and water consumption by 178,000,000 gallons annually.

ADMISSIONS
Freshman Academic Profile: Average high school GPA 3.8. 52% in top 10% of high school class, 89% in top 25% of high school class, 99% in top 50% of high school class. **Test Scores:** SAT Math middle 50% range 660-760. SAT EBRW middle 50% range 620-690. ACT middle 50% range 27-31. **Basis for Candidate Selection:** *Very important factors considered include:* rigor of secondary school record, class rank, academic GPA. *Important factors considered include:* application essay, standardized test scores, state residency. *Other factors considered include:* recommendation(s), extracurricular activities, talent/ability, character/personal qualities, first generation, alumni/ae relation, racial/ethnic status, volunteer work, work experience, level of applicant's interest. **Freshman Admission Requirements:** High school diploma is required and GED is accepted *Academic units required:* 4 English, 4 math, 3 science, 4 foreign language, 3 social studies, and 2 units from above areas or other academic areas. *Academic units recommended:* 4 English, 4 math, 4 science, 4 foreign language, 4 social studies, 2 units from above areas or other academic areas. **Freshman Admission Statistics:** 35,615 applied, 53.8% admitted, 35% enrolled. **Transfer Admission Requirements:** High school transcript, college transcript(s), essay or personal statement, Lowest grade transferable D. **General Admission Information:** Application fee $60. Regular application deadline 2/1. Nonfall registration accepted. Admission may be deferred for a maximum of 1 year.

COSTS AND FINANCIAL AID
Annual in-state tuition $1,260. Annual out-of-state tuition $33,523. Required fees $1,260. Average book expense $1,200. **Required Forms and Deadlines:** FAFSA. **Notification of Awards:** Applicants will be notified of awards on a rolling basis beginning 3/1. **Types of Aid:** *Need-based scholarships/grants:* College/university scholarship or grant aid from institutional funds; Federal Pell; Private scholarships; SEOG; State scholarships/grants. *Loans:* Direct PLUS loans; Direct Subsidized Stafford Loans; Direct Unsubsidized Stafford Loans. *Student Employment:* Federal Work-Study Program available. Institutional employment available. **Financial Aid Statistics:** 94% needy freshmen, 77% needy undergrads receive need-based scholarship or grant aid. 11% freshmen, 9% undergrads receive non-need-based scholarship or grant aid. 80% freshmen, 82% undergrads receive need-based self-help aid. 1% freshmen, 1% undergrads receive athletic scholarships. 46% undergrads borrow to pay for school. Average cumulative indebtedness $27,831. **Criteria for awarding aid:** *Need-based:* Academics, Alumni affiliation, Minority status *Non-need-based:* Academics, Alumni affiliation, Art, Athletics, Leadership, Minority status, Music/drama, State/district residency.

UNIVERSITY OF WISCONSIN—MILWAUKEE

P.O. Box 413, Milwaukee, WI 53211
Phone: 414-229-2222 • **Financial Aid Phone:** 414-229-4541
E-mail: uwmlook@uwm.edu • **CEEB Code:** 1473
Fax: 414-229-6940 • **Website:** www4.uwm.edu • **ACT Code:** 4658

This public school was founded in 1956. It has a 93 acre campus.

RATINGS
Admissions Selectivity Rating: 69   **Fire Safety Rating:** 97   **Green Rating:** 96

STUDENTS AND FACULTY
Enrollment: 20,000. **Student Body:** 51% female, 49% male, 11% out-of-state, 4% international (88 countries represented). Asian 7%, African American 8%, Caucasian 67%, Hispanic 10%, Native American <1%, Pacific Islander <1%, Two or more races 4%, Race unknown <1%.
Retention and Graduation: 72% freshmen return for sophomore year.
Faculty: Student/faculty ratio 19:1. 1,010 full-time faculty, 73% hold PhDs, 22% are members of minority groups, 46% are women.

ACADEMICS

Degrees: Bachelor's; Certificate; Doctoral; Doctoral/Professional; Doctoral/Research; Master's; Post-Bachelor's certificate; Post-Master's certificate **Classes:** Most classes have 10-19 students. Most lab/discussion sessions have 10-19 students. **Most popular majors:** Education, General; Psychology, General; Marketing/Marketing Management, General. **Special Study Options:** Accelerated program; Cooperative education program; Cross-registration; Distance learning; Double major; Dual enrollment; English as a Second Language (ESL); External degree program; Honors program; Independent study; Internships; Liberal arts/career combination; Student-designed major; Study abroad; Teacher certification program; Weekend college. Honors programs: UWM Honors College Combined degree programs: BA/MA; BA/MEng. **Disability Services offered to physically disabled students:** Note-taking services; Reader services; Tape recorders; Tutors. **Career services:** Alumni network; Alumni services; Career assessment; Career/job search classes; Internships

FACILITIES

Housing: Apartments for single students; Coed dorms; Special housing for disabled students **Special Academic Facilities/Equipment:** Art and geology museums, childhood education center, foreign language resource center, Great Lakes research facility and environmental studies field station, planetarium.

CAMPUS LIFE

Environment: Metropolis **Activities:** Campus Ministries; Choral groups; Concert band; Dance; Drama/theater; International Student Organization; Jazz band; Literary magazine; Model UN; Music ensembles; Musical theater; Opera; Pep band; Radio station; Student government; Student newspaper; Student-run film society; Symphony orchestra 250 registered organizations, 1 honor society, 4 religious organizations. 8 fraternities, 4 sororities. **Athletics (Intercollegiate):** *Men:* baseball, basketball, cross-country, diving, soccer, swimming, track/field (outdoor). *Women:* basketball, cross-country, soccer, swimming, tennis, track/field (outdoor), volleyball. The Grind Coffee Shop, Student Union, Klotche Recreation Center, Golda Meier Library, Sandburg Residence Hall **Environmental Initiatives:** Performance Contracting—Energy Matters is UWM's energy efficiency project with a goal to achieve an energy reduction of 25% by 2013, reduce campus use of fossil fuels, and provide comfortable study and work space. With more than 50% of the project complete, results are showing an even faster rate of return with a 42% savings.

ADMISSIONS

Freshman Academic Profile: Average high school GPA 3.1. 9% in top 10% of high school class, 19% in top 25% of high school class, 67% in top 50% of high school class. **Test Scores:** Minimum internet-based TOEFL 68. Minimum paper TOEFL 520. **Basis for Candidate Selection:** *Very important factors considered include:* rigor of secondary school record, academic GPA, standardized test scores. *Important factors considered include:* application essay. *Other factors considered include:* class rank, recommendation(s), interview, extracurricular activities, talent/ability, character/personal qualities, first generation, racial/ethnic status, volunteer work, work experience. **Freshman Admission Requirements:** High school diploma is required and GED is accepted *Academic units required:* 4 English, 3 math, 3 science, 1 science labs, 3 social studies, 4 academic electives, *Academic units recommended:* 4 English, 4 math, 4 science, 1 science labs, 2 foreign language, 4 social studies, 4 academic electives. **Freshman Admission Statistics:** 9,834 applied, 72.4% admitted, 44% enrolled. **Transfer Admission Requirements:** High school transcript, college transcript(s), Minimum college GPA of 2.0 required. Lowest grade transferable D-. **General Admission Information:** Application fee $50. Priority deadline 3/1. Regular application deadline 8/11. Nonfall registration accepted. Admission may be deferred for a maximum of 1 year.

COSTS AND FINANCIAL AID

Annual in-state tuition $10,560. Annual out-of-state tuition $9,685. Room and board $10,560. Required fees $1,444. Average book expense $800. **Required Forms and Deadlines:** FAFSA. **Notification of Awards:** Applicants will be notified of awards on a rolling basis beginning 3/15. **Types of Aid:** *Need-based scholarships/grants:* College/university scholarship or grant aid from institutional funds; Federal Pell; Private scholarships; SEOG; State scholarships/grants. *Loans:* Direct PLUS loans; Direct Subsidized Stafford Loans; Direct Unsubsidized Stafford Loans. *Student Employment:* Federal Work-Study Program available. Institutional employment available. **Financial Aid Statistics:** 59% needy freshmen, 57% needy undergrads receive need-based scholarship or grant aid. 29% freshmen, 20% undergrads receive non-need-based scholarship or grant aid. 79% freshmen, 78% undergrads receive need-based self-help aid. 1% freshmen, <1% undergrads receive athletic scholarships. 76% undergrads borrow to pay for school. Average cumulative indebtedness $36,945. **Criteria for awarding aid:** *Need-based:* Academics, Music/drama *Non-need-based:* Academics, Art, Athletics, Leadership.

UNIVERSITY OF WISCONSIN—OSHKOSH

800 Algoma Boulevard, Oshkosh, WI 54901
Phone: 920-424-0202 • **Financial Aid Phone:** 920-424-4025
E-mail: oshadmuw@uwosh.edu • **CEEB Code:** 1916
Fax: 920-424-1098 • **Website:** http://www.uwosh.edu/home • **ACT Code:** 4674

This public school was founded in 1871. It has a 192 acre campus.

RATINGS
Admissions Selectivity Rating: 80   **Fire Safety Rating:** 60*   **Green Rating:** 99

STUDENTS AND FACULTY
Enrollment: 10,771. **Student Body:** 57% female, 43% male, 3% out-of-state, 1% international (32 countries represented). Asian 4%, African American 2%, Caucasian 88%, Hispanic 3%, Native American 1%, Pacific Islander <1%, Two or more races 1%, Race unknown <1%.
Retention and Graduation: 75% freshmen return for sophomore year. **Faculty:** Student/faculty ratio 22:1. 416 full-time faculty, 84% hold PhDs, 12% are members of minority groups, 47% are women. 0% of classes are taught by teaching assistants.

ACADEMICS
Degrees: Associate; Bachelor's; Certificate; Master's **Most popular majors:** Elementary Education And Teaching; Registered Nursing, Nursing Administration, Nursing Research And Clinical Nursing, Other; Business/Commerce, General. **Special Study Options:** Accelerated program; Cooperative education program; Distance learning; Double major; Dual enrollment; English as a Second Language (ESL); Exchange student program (domestic); Honors program; Independent study; Internships; Liberal arts/career combination; Student-designed major; Study abroad; Teacher certification program; Weekend college. **Disability Services offered to physically disabled students:** Note-taking services; Reader services; Tape recorders; Tutors. **Career services:** Alumni network; Career assessment; Career/job search classes; Internships

FACILITIES
Housing: Coed dorms; Fraternity/sorority housing; Men's dorms; Special housing for disabled student; Theme housing; Women's dorms **Special Academic Facilities/Equipment:** Art gallery, ceramics lab, aquatic research laboratory, electron microscope. **Computers:** Students can register for classes online.

CAMPUS LIFE
Environment: City **Activities:** Campus Ministries; Choral groups; Concert band; Dance; Drama/theater; International Student Organization; Jazz band; Literary magazine; Model UN; Music ensembles; Musical theater; Pep band; Radio station; Student government; Student newspaper; Student-run film society; Television station 175 registered organizations; 15 honor societies, 6 religious organizations. 8 fraternities, 5 sororities. **Athletics (Intercollegiate):** *Men:* baseball, basketball, cross-country, diving, football, soccer, swimming, tennis, track/field (outdoor), track/field (indoor), wrestling. *Women:* basketball, cross-country, diving, golf, gymnastics, soccer, softball, swimming, tennis, track/field (outdoor), track/field (indoor), volleyball. Sage Hall—LEEDS certification, Horizon Village—State of Art res hall **Environmental Initiatives:** Leadership in adopting renewable energy, from 2003 as the largest purchaser of renewable electricity in the State of Wisconsin to the recent construction of the first commercial-scale dry anerobic biodigester in the Western Hemisphere.

ADMISSIONS
Freshman Academic Profile: Average high school GPA 3.3. 10% in top 10% of high school class, 37% in top 25% of high school class, 84% in top 50% of high school class. 90% from public high schools. **Test Scores:** ACT middle 50% range 20-24. Minimum internet-based TOEFL 70. Minimum paper TOEFL 525. **Basis for Candidate Selection:** *Very important factors considered include:* rigor of secondary school record, class rank, academic GPA, standardized test scores. *Important factors considered include:* application essay, recommendation(s), first generation. *Other factors considered include:* interview, extracurricular activities, talent/ability, character/personal qualities, alumni/ae relation, volunteer work, work experience. **Freshman Admission Requirements:** High school diploma is required and GED is accepted *Academic units required:* 4 English, 3 math, 3 science, 3 science labs, 3 social studies, 2 history, 4 academic electives, *Academic units recommended:* 4 math, 4 science, 4 science labs, 2 foreign language, 4 social studies, 1 history, 1 visual/performing arts. **Freshman Admission Statistics:** 6,052 applied, 68.5% admitted, 44% enrolled. **Transfer Admission Requirements:** college transcript(s), Minimum college GPA of 2.50 required. Lowest grade transferable D. **General Admission Information:** Application fee $44. Nonfall registration accepted. Admission may be deferred.

COSTS AND FINANCIAL AID

Annual in-state tuition $6,926. Annual out-of-state tuition $14,934. Room and board $6,926. Average book expense $1,000. **Required Forms and Deadlines:** FAFSA. **Notification of Awards:** Applicants will be notified of awards on or about 4/15. **Types of Aid:** *Need-based scholarships/grants:* College/university scholarship or grant aid from institutional funds; Federal Nursing Scholarships; Federal Pell; Private scholarships; SEOG; State scholarships/grants; United Negro College Fund. *Loans:* Direct PLUS loans; Direct Subsidized Stafford Loans; Direct Unsubsidized Stafford Loans. *Student Employment:* Federal Work-Study Program available. Institutional employment available. **Financial Aid Statistics:** 53% needy freshmen, 55% needy undergrads receive need-based scholarship or grant aid. 35% freshmen, 20% undergrads receive non-need-based scholarship or grant aid. 29% freshmen, 20% undergrads receive need-based self-help aid. 0% freshmen, 0% undergrads receive athletic scholarships. **Criteria for awarding aid:** *Need-based:* Academics, Art, Job skills, Leadership, Minority status, Music/drama *Non-need-based:* Academics, Art, Job skills, Leadership, Minority status, Music/drama, State/district residency.

UNIVERSITY OF WISCONSIN—PLATTEVILLE

1 University Plaza, Platteville, WI 53818
Phone: (608)342-1125 • **Financial Aid Phone:** 608-342-6188
E-mail: admit@uwplatt.edu • **CEEB Code:** 1917
Fax: (608)342-1122 • **Website:** www.uwplatt.edu • **ACT Code:** 4676

This public school was founded in 1866. It has a 820 acre campus.

RATINGS
Admissions Selectivity Rating: 84   **Fire Safety Rating:** 78   **Green Rating:** 90

STUDENTS AND FACULTY
Enrollment: 7,427. **Student Body:** 33% female, 67% male, 24% out-of-state, 1% international (10 countries represented). Asian 1%, African American 1%, Caucasian 89%, Hispanic 3%, Native American <1%, Pacific Islander <1%, Two or more races 3%, Race unknown 1%.
Retention and Graduation: 79% freshmen return for sophomore year. 19% freshmen graduate within 4 years. 51% freshmen graduate within 6 years. **Faculty:** Student/faculty ratio 21:1. 316 full-time faculty, 75% hold PhDs, 22% are members of minority groups, 37% are women. 0% of classes are taught by teaching assistants.

ACADEMICS
Degrees: Associate; Bachelor's; Certificate; Master's; Post-Bachelor's certificate **Classes:** Most classes have 10-19 students. Most lab/discussion sessions have 10-19 students. **Most popular majors:** Mechanical Engineering; Criminal Justice/Safety Studies; Business Administration And Management, General. **Special Study Options:** Cooperative education program; Distance learning; Double major; Dual enrollment; Exchange student program (domestic); External degree program; Honors program; Independent study; Internships; Study abroad; Teacher certification program. **Disability Services offered to physically disabled students:** Note-taking services; Reader services; Tape recorders; Tutors. Alumni services

FACILITIES
Housing: Apartments for single students; Coed dorms; Men's dorms; Special housing for disabled student; Wellness housing; Women's dorms 95% of campus accessible to physically diasbled. **Special Academic Facilities/Equipment:** Electron microscope Nohr Art Gallery Southwest Wisconsin Room/Archives North American Manx Museum Forensic Investigation Crime Scene House Pioneer Farm **Computers:**

CAMPUS LIFE
Environment: Village **Activities:** Campus Ministries; Choral groups; Concert band; Dance; Drama/theater; International Student Organization; Jazz band; Literary magazine; Marching band; Music ensembles; Musical theater; Pep band; Radio station; Student government; Student newspaper; Symphony orchestra; Television station. Markee Pioneer Student Center, Bridgeway Commons, Williams Fieldhouse, Pioneer Farm, Karrmann Library

ADMISSIONS
Freshman Academic Profile: 13% in top 10% of high school class, 37% in top 25% of high school class, 76% in top 50% of high school class. 94% from public high schools. **Test Scores:** SAT Math middle 50% range 605-655. SAT EBRW middle 50% range 542-688. ACT middle 50% range 20-25. Minimum paper TOEFL 550. **Basis for Candidate Selection:** *Very important factors considered include:* rigor of secondary school record, class rank, academic GPA, application essay, standardized test scores, talent/ability, character/personal qualities, level of applicant's interest. *Important factors considered include:* extracurricular activities, first generation, alumni/ae relation, volunteer work, work experience. *Other factors considered include:* recommendation(s), geographical residence, racial/ethnic status. **Freshman Admission Requirements:** High school diploma is required and GED is accepted *Academic units required:* 4 English, 3 math, 3 science, 2 science labs, 3 social studies, 4 academic electives. **Freshman Admission Statistics:** 3,711 applied, 79.1% admitted, 48% enrolled. **General Admission Information:** Application fee $50. Nonfall registration accepted. Admission may be deferred.

COSTS AND FINANCIAL AID
Annual out-of-state tuition $14,148. Room and board $7,160. Required fees $1,245. Average book expense $550. **Required Forms and Deadlines:** FAFSA. **Types of Aid:** *Need-based scholarships/grants:* State scholarships/grants.

UNIVERSITY OF WISCONSIN—RIVER FALLS

410 South Third Street, River Falls, WI 54022
Phone: 715-425-3500 • **Financial Aid Phone:** 715-425-3141
E-mail: admissions@uwrf.edu • **CEEB Code:** 3923
Website: www.uwrf.edu • **ACT Code:** 1918

This public school was founded in 1874. It has a 226 acre campus.

RATINGS
Admissions Selectivity Rating: 80   **Fire Safety Rating:** 60*   **Green Rating:** 90

STUDENTS AND FACULTY
Enrollment: 5,501. **Student Body:** 61% female, 39% male, 49% out-of-state, 1% international (20 countries represented). Asian 3%, African American 2%, Caucasian 88%, Hispanic 4%, Native American <1%, Pacific Islander <1%, Two or more races 2%, Race unknown <1%.
Retention and Graduation: 73% freshmen return for sophomore year. 28% freshmen graduate within 4 years. 53% freshmen graduate within 6 years. **Faculty:** Student/faculty ratio 18:1. 263 full-time faculty, 13% are members of minority groups, 46% are women. 0% of classes are taught by teaching assistants.

ACADEMICS
Degrees: Associate; Bachelor's; Master's; Post-Bachelor's certificate; Post-Master's certificate **Classes:** Most classes have 10-19 students. Most lab/discussion sessions have fewer than 10 students. **Most popular majors:** Animal Sciences, General; Elementary Education And Teaching; Business Administration And Management, General. **Special Study Options:** Cooperative education program; Cross-registration; Distance learning; Double major; Dual enrollment; English as a Second Language (ESL); Exchange student program (domestic); External degree program; Honors program; Independent study; Internships; Liberal arts/career combination; Study abroad; Teacher certification program. Honors programs: The UW-River Falls Honors Program is designed to meet the educational needs of students who have an outstanding record of academic achievement and a true sense of intellectual adventure. It allows students to experience a variety of course types and educationally related experiences while gaining academic credit. Students enrolled in the program may choose Honors sections of many general education classes, take introductory and advanced Honors seminars, participate in Honors colloquia, complete an Honors thesis/project, enroll in a service-learning experience for credit and receive credits for participation in the intellectual and creative life of the UW-River Falls community and elsewhere. All of these experiences are gained while still keeping within the major and minor requirements of an Honors student's academic program. **Disability Services offered to physically disabled students:** Note-taking services; Reader services; Tape recorders; Tutors. **Career services:** Alumni network; Alumni services; Career assessment; Career/job search classes; Internships; Regional alumni

FACILITIES
Housing: Coed dorms; Special housing for disabled student; Theme housing; Women's dorms 100% of campus accessible to physically diasbled. **Special Academic Facilities/Equipment:** Local history museum, 20-inch reflecting telescope, observatory, electron microscope, greenhouse, lab farms, educational technology center. **Computers:** Students can register for classes online. Administrative functions (other than registration) can be performed online.

CAMPUS LIFE

Environment: Village **Activities:** Campus Ministries; Choral groups; Concert band; Dance; Drama/theater; International Student Organization; Jazz band; Literary magazine; Model UN; Music ensembles; Musical theater; Pep band; Radio station; Student government; Student newspaper; Symphony orchestra; Television station 120 registered organizations, 9 honor societies, 12 religious organizations. 5 fraternities, 4 sororities. **Athletics (Intercollegiate):** *Men:* basketball, cross-country, football, ice hockey, swimming, track/field (outdoor), track/field (indoor). *Women:* basketball, cross-country, golf, ice hockey, soccer, softball, swimming, tennis, track/field (outdoor), track/field (indoor), volleyball. **On-Campus Highlights:** University Student Center, Leadership Center, Knowles/Hunt Recreation Complex, Chalmer Davee Library, Educational Technology Center

ADMISSIONS

Freshman Academic Profile: Average high school GPA 3.4. 11% in top 10% of high school class, 34% in top 25% of high school class, 73% in top 50% of high school class. **Test Scores:** ACT middle 50% range 20-25. Minimum paper TOEFL 500. **Basis for Candidate Selection:** *Very important factors considered include:* rigor of secondary school record, class rank, standardized test scores. *Important factors considered include:* academic GPA, application essay. *Other factors considered include:* recommendation(s), extracurricular activities, talent/ability, character/personal qualities, first generation, racial/ethnic status, volunteer work, work experience. **Freshman Admission Requirements:** High school diploma is required and GED is accepted *Academic units required:* 4 English, 3 math, 3 science, 3 social studies, 4 academic electives, *Academic units recommended:* 4 English, 4 math, 4 science, 1 science labs, 2 foreign language, 4 social studies, 4 academic electives. **Freshman Admission Statistics:** 3,450 applied, 74.5% admitted, 52% enrolled. **Transfer Admission Requirements:** college transcript(s), statement of good standing from prior institution(s). Minimum college GPA of 2.6 required. Lowest grade transferable D. **General Admission Information:** Application fee $44. Priority deadline 2/1. Nonfall registration accepted. Admission may be deferred for a maximum of 1 year.

COSTS AND FINANCIAL AID

Annual in-state tuition $6,576. Annual out-of-state tuition $14,001. Room and board $6,576. Required fees $1,592. Average book expense $370. **Required Forms and Deadlines:** FAFSA. **Notification of Awards:** Applicants will be notified of awards on a rolling basis beginning 3/25. **Types of Aid:** *Need-based scholarships/grants:* College/university scholarship or grant aid from institutional funds; Federal Pell; Private scholarships; SEOG; State scholarships/grants. *Loans:* Direct PLUS loans; Direct Subsidized Stafford Loans; Direct Unsubsidized Stafford Loans. *Student Employment:* Federal Work-Study Program available. Institutional employment available. **Financial Aid Statistics:** 55% needy freshmen, 57% needy undergrads receive need-based scholarship or grant aid. 18% freshmen, 24% undergrads receive non-need-based scholarship or grant aid. 85% freshmen, 82% undergrads receive need-based self-help aid. 0% freshmen, 0% undergrads receive athletic scholarships. 77% freshmen, 68% undergrads receive any aid. 77% undergrads borrow to pay for school. Average cumulative indebtedness $27,232. **Criteria for awarding aid:** *Need-based:* Academics, Art, Leadership, Minority status, Music/drama *Non-need-based:* Academics, Art, Leadership, Minority status, Music/drama, State/district residency.

UNIVERSITY OF WISCONSIN—STEVENS POINT

2100 Main Street, Stevens Point, WI 54481
Phone: 715-346-2441 • **Financial Aid Phone:** 715-346-4771
E-mail: admiss@uwsp.edu • **CEEB Code:** 1919
Fax: 715-346-3296 • **Website:** www.uwsp.edu • **ACT Code:** 4680

This public school was founded in 1894. It has a 335 acre campus.

RATINGS

Admissions Selectivity Rating: 80   **Fire Safety Rating:** 79   **Green Rating:** 97

STUDENTS AND FACULTY

Enrollment: 8,684. **Student Body:** 52% female, 48% male, 11% out-of-state, 2% international (37 countries represented). Asian 3%, African American 2%, Caucasian 87%, Hispanic 4%, Native American 1%, Pacific Islander 0%, Two or more races 2%, Race unknown <1%.
Retention and Graduation: 14% grads go on to further study within 1 year. 20% grads pursue arts and sciences degrees. 0.2% grads pursue law degrees. 1% grads pursue business degrees. 0.2% grads pursue medical degrees.
Faculty: Student/faculty ratio 21:1. 369 full-time faculty, 89% hold PhDs, 10%

are members of minority groups, 43% are women. 0% of classes are taught by teaching assistants.

ACADEMICS

Degrees: Associate; Bachelor's; Doctoral/Professional; **Master's Classes:** Most classes have 20-29 students. Most lab/discussion sessions have 10-19 students. **Most popular majors:** Natural Resources/Conservation, General; Biological And Physical Sciences; Business/Commerce, General. **Special Study Options:** Accelerated program; Distance learning; Double major; Dual enrollment; English as a Second Language (ESL); Honors program; Independent study; Internships; Student-designed major; Study abroad; Teacher certification program. **Disability Services offered to physically disabled students:** Note-taking services; Reader services; Tape recorders; Tutors. **Career services:** Alumni network; Alumni services; Career assessment; Career/job search classes; Internships; Regional alumni

FACILITIES

Housing: Coed dorms; Men's dorms; Special housing for international students; Theme housing; Wellness housing; Women's dorms 100% of campus accessible to physically disabled. **Special Academic Facilities/Equipment:** Art galleries, costume and goblet collections, museum of natural history, early childhood study institute, communicative disorders center, map center, observatory, planetarium, Foucault pendulum, nature preserve, environmental station, groundwater center, herbarium, aviary, wellness institute. **Computers:** 100% of classrooms, 10% of dorms, 100% of libraries, 100% of dining areas, 100% of student union, have wireless network access. Students can register for classes online. Administrative functions (other than registration) can be performed online.

CAMPUS LIFE

Environment: Town **Activities:** Campus Ministries; Choral groups; Dance; Drama/theater; International Student Organization; Jazz band; Model UN; Music ensembles; Musical theater; Opera; Pep band; Radio station; Student government; Student newspaper; Student-run film society; Symphony orchestra; Television station 185 registered organizations, 12 honor societies, 9 religious organizations. 4 fraternities, 3 sororities. **Athletics (Intercollegiate):** *Men:* baseball, basketball, cross-country, diving, football, ice hockey, swimming, track/field (outdoor), wrestling. *Women:* basketball, cross-country, diving, golf, ice hockey, soccer, softball, swimming, tennis, track/field (outdoor), volleyball. **On-Campus Highlights:** University Center/Brewhouse, Schmeeckle Reserve/ Wisconsin Conservation Hall of, Health Enhancement Center, Allen Recreation Center, Fine Arts Building **Environmental Initiatives:** In December 2012, UWSP hired an energy service company (ESCO) through the WI Performance Contracting Program. Work was completed in 2016 so we are currently evaluating results. In 2012, we received LEED-NC Gold for a residence hall. We are in the final construction stages of a science building that was built to LEED-Gold equivalency.

ADMISSIONS

Freshman Academic Profile: Average high school GPA 3.1. 11% in top 10% of high school class, 33% in top 25% of high school class, 73% in top 50% of high school class. **Test Scores:** SAT Math middle 50% range 410-523. SAT EBRW middle 50% range 405-565. ACT middle 50% range 20-25. Minimum internet-based TOEFL 70. **Basis for Candidate Selection:** *Very important factors considered include:* rigor of secondary school record, class rank, academic GPA, standardized test scores. *Important factors considered include:* application essay, recommendation(s), talent/ability, first generation. *Other factors considered include:* interview, extracurricular activities, character/personal qualities, alumni/ae relation, geographical residence, state residency, racial/ethnic status, volunteer work, work experience. **Freshman Admission Requirements:** High school diploma is required and GED is accepted *Academic units required:* 4 English, 3 math, 3 science, 3 social studies, 4 academic electives, *Academic units recommended:* 4 English, 4 math, 4 science, 4 social studies, 4 academic electives. **Freshman Admission Statistics:** 4,901 applied, 74.5% admitted, 49% enrolled. **Transfer Admission Requirements:** High school transcript, college transcript(s), statement of good standing from prior institution(s). Minimum college GPA of 2.25 required. Lowest grade transferable D. **General Admission Information:** Nonfall registration accepted.

COSTS AND FINANCIAL AID

Annual in-state tuition $3,414. Annual out-of-state tuition $15,940. Room and board $3,414. Required fees $1,374. Average book expense $500. **Required Forms and Deadlines:** FAFSA. **Notification of Awards:** Applicants will be notified of awards on a rolling basis beginning 3/1. **Types of Aid:** *Need-based scholarships/grants:* College/university scholarship or grant aid from institutional funds; Federal Pell; Private scholarships; SEOG; State scholarships/grants. *Loans:* Direct PLUS loans; Direct Subsidized Stafford Loans; Direct Unsubsidized Stafford Loans. *Student Employment:* Federal Work-Study Program available. Institutional employment available. **Financial Aid Statistics:** 71% needy freshmen, 71% needy undergrads receive need-based scholarship or grant aid. 61% freshmen, 62% undergrads receive non-need-based scholarship or grant aid. 90% freshmen, 90% undergrads receive need-based self-help aid. 0% freshmen, 0% undergrads receive athletic scholarships. 65% freshmen, 68% undergrads receive any aid. Average cumulative indebtedness $25,030. **Criteria for awarding aid:** *Non-need-based:* Academics, Alumni affiliation, Art, Music/drama.

UNIVERSITY OF WISCONSIN—STOUT

712 South Broadway, Menomonie, WI 54751
Phone: 715-232-1232 • **Financial Aid Phone:** 715-232-1363
E-mail: admissions@uwstout.edu • **CEEB Code:** 1740
Fax: 715-232-1667 • **Website:** www.uwstout.edu • **ACT Code:** 4652

This public school was founded in 1891. It has a 110 acre campus.

RATINGS
Admissions Selectivity Rating: 75   **Fire Safety Rating:** 62   **Green Rating:** 87

STUDENTS AND FACULTY
Enrollment: 7,935. **Student Body:** 43% female, 57% male, 33% out-of-state, 2% international (28 countries represented). Asian 3%, African American 2%, Caucasian 87%, Hispanic 1%, Native American <1%, Pacific Islander <1%, Two or more races 4%, Race unknown <1%.
Retention and Graduation: 69% freshmen return for sophomore year. 24% freshmen graduate within 4 years. 54% freshmen graduate within 6 years. 9% grads go on to further study within 1 year. **Faculty:** Student/faculty ratio 20:1. 391 full-time faculty, 76% hold PhDs, 13% are members of minority groups, 45% are women. 0% of classes are taught by teaching assistants.

ACADEMICS
Degrees: Bachelor's; Certificate; Doctoral/Professional; Master's; Post-Bachelor's certificate; Post-Master's certificate **Classes:** Most classes have fewer than 10 students. Most lab/discussion sessions have fewer than 10 students. **Most popular majors:** Design And Applied Arts, Other; Business/Commerce, General; Hospitality Administration/Management, General. **Special Study Options:** Accelerated program; Cooperative education program; Cross-registration; Distance learning; Double major; Dual enrollment; English as a Second Language (ESL); Exchange student program (domestic); External degree program; Honors program; Independent study; Internships; Study abroad; Teacher certification program. Honors programs: The University Honors Program (UHP) is designed to enhance the education of students challenging them to think in more depth and detail and to provide the opportunity to meet other students while doing so. **Disability Services offered to physically disabled students:** Note-taking services; Reader services; Tutors. **Career services:** Alumni services; Career/job search classes; Internships

FACILITIES
Housing: Apartments for single students; Coed dorms; Special housing for disabled student; Wellness housing 100% of campus accessible to physically diasbled. **Special Academic Facilities/Equipment:** Specialized labs support degree programs throughout the campus. Furlong Art Gallery in Micheal's Hall. **Computers:** Students can register for classes online. Administrative functions (other than registration) can be performed online. Undergraduates are required to own a computer.

CAMPUS LIFE
Environment: Village **Activities:** Campus Ministries; Choral groups; Concert band; Dance; Drama/theater; International Student Organization; Jazz band; Literary magazine; Marching band; Model UN; Music ensembles; Musical theater; Pep band; Radio station; Student government; Student newspaper; Student-run film society 120 registered organizations, 1 honor society, 12 religious organizations. 5 fraternities, 3 sororities. **Athletics (Intercollegiate):** *Men:* baseball, basketball, cross-country, football, ice hockey, track/field (outdoor). *Women:* basketball, cross-country, gymnastics, soccer, softball, tennis, track/field (outdoor), volleyball. **On-Campus Highlights:** Millenium Hall, Athletic Complex, Ropes Course- Climbing Wall- In-line Skating, Student Center, Micheels Hall

ADMISSIONS
Freshman Academic Profile: Average high school GPA 3.2. 9% in top 10% of high school class, 31% in top 25% of high school class, 64% in top 50% of high school class. **Test Scores:** ACT middle 50% range 19-25. Minimum paper TOEFL 500. **Basis for Candidate Selection:** *Very important factors considered include:* class rank, academic GPA, standardized test scores. *Important factors considered include:* rigor of secondary school record,

application essay. *Other factors considered include:* recommendation(s), interview, extracurricular activities, talent/ability, character/personal qualities, first generation, alumni/ae relation, racial/ethnic status, volunteer work, work experience, level of applicant's interest. **Freshman Admission Requirements:** *Academic units required:* 4 English, 3 math, 3 science, 3 social studies, 4 academic electives, *Academic units recommended:* 4 math. **Freshman Admission Statistics:** 3,267 applied, 86.0% admitted, 54% enrolled. **Transfer Admission Requirements:** college transcript(s), statement of good standing from prior institution(s). Minimum college GPA of 2.5 required. Lowest grade transferable D-. **General Admission Information:** Application fee $50. Priority deadline 1/1.

COSTS AND FINANCIAL AID
Room and board $6,744. Required fees $2,442. Average book expense $408. **Notification of Awards:** Applicants will be notified of awards on a rolling basis beginning 1/27. **Types of Aid:** *Need-based scholarships/grants:* Other (please specify). *Loans:* Direct Subsidized Stafford Loans. *Student Employment:* Federal Work-Study Program available. Institutional employment available. **Financial Aid Statistics:** 49% needy freshmen, 72% needy undergrads receive need-based scholarship or grant aid. 36% freshmen, 27% undergrads receive non-need-based scholarship or grant aid. 92% freshmen, 92% undergrads receive need-based self-help aid. 0% freshmen, 0% undergrads receive athletic scholarships. 71% freshmen, 74% undergrads receive any aid. 79% undergrads borrow to pay for school. Average cumulative indebtedness $30,563. **Criteria for awarding aid:** *Non-need-based:* Academics.

UNIVERSITY OF WISCONSIN—SUPERIOR

Belknap and Catlin, Superior, WI 54880-4500
Phone: 715-394-8230 • **Financial Aid Phone:** 715-394-8200
E-mail: admissions@uwsuper.edu • **CEEB Code:** 1920
Fax: 715-394-8407 • **Website:** www.uwsuper.edu • **ACT Code:** 4682

This public school was founded in 1893. It has a 230 acre campus.

RATINGS
Admissions Selectivity Rating: 83   **Fire Safety Rating:** 84   **Green Rating:** 60*

STUDENTS AND FACULTY
Enrollment: 2,234. **Student Body:** 62% female, 38% male, 49% out-of-state, 9% international (50 countries represented). Asian 1%, African American 2%, Caucasian 80%, Hispanic 3%, Native American 2%, Pacific Islander <1%, Two or more races 3%, Race unknown <1%.
Retention and Graduation: 72% freshmen return for sophomore year. 24% freshmen graduate within 4 years. 44% freshmen graduate within 6 years. **Faculty:** Student/faculty ratio 14:1. 114 full-time faculty, 68% hold PhDs, 12% are members of minority groups, 54% are women. 0% of classes are taught by teaching assistants.

ACADEMICS
Degrees: Associate; Bachelor's; Certificate; Master's; Post-Bachelor's certificate; Post-Master's certificate **Classes:** Most classes have 10-19 students. Most lab/discussion sessions have fewer than 10 students. **Most popular majors:** Communication, General; Business Administration And Management, General; Elementary Education And Teaching. **Special Study Options:** Accelerated program; Cooperative education program; Cross-registration; Distance learning; Double major; Dual enrollment; English as a Second Language (ESL); Exchange student program (domestic); External degree program; Independent study; Internships; Liberal arts/career combination; Student-designed major; Study abroad; Teacher certification program. **Disability Services offered to physically disabled students:** Note-taking services; Reader services; Tape recorders; Tutors. **Career services:** Alumni network; Alumni services; Career assessment; Career/job search classes; Internships; Regional alumni

FACILITIES
Housing: Apartments for married students; Coed dorms; Special housing for disabled student; Special housing for international students **Special Academic Facilities/Equipment:** TV, radio, and film facilities,observatory, greenhouse,two art galleries, recital hall, four theaters, modern health and wellness center and student union. **Computers:** 40% of classrooms, 100% of libraries, 100% of dining areas, 100% of student union, 20% of common outdoor areas have wireless network access. Students can register for classes online. Administrative functions (other than registration) can be performed online.

CAMPUS LIFE

Environment: City **Activities:** Campus Ministries; Choral groups; Concert band; Dance; Drama/theater; International Student Organization; Jazz band; Literary magazine; Music ensembles; Musical theater; Opera; Pep band; Radio station; Student government; Student newspaper; Symphony orchestra 70 registered organizations, 1 honor society, 5 religious organizations. 1 sororities. **Athletics (Intercollegiate):** *Men:* baseball, basketball, cross-country, ice hockey, soccer, track/field (outdoor), track/field (indoor). *Women:* basketball, cross-country, golf, ice hockey, soccer, softball, track/field (outdoor), track/field (indoor), volleyball. **On-Campus Highlights:** Health and Wellness Center, Jim Dan Hill Library (newly renovated including fireplaces and snack area), Swenson Hall, Yellowjacket Union (newly opened Jan 2010), Multicultural Center **Environmental Initiatives:** LEED certification for new buildings

ADMISSIONS

Freshman Academic Profile: Average high school GPA 3.2. 6% in top 10% of high school class, 26% in top 25% of high school class, 57% in top 50% of high school class. **Test Scores:** SAT Math middle 50% range 515-595. SAT EBRW middle 50% range 505-580. ACT middle 50% range 19-23. Minimum internet-based TOEFL 61. Minimum paper TOEFL 500. **Basis for Candidate Selection:** *Very important factors considered include:* rigor of secondary school record. *Important factors considered include:* class rank, academic GPA, standardized test scores. *Other factors considered include:* application essay, recommendation(s), interview, extracurricular activities, talent/ability, character/personal qualities, first generation, racial/ethnic status, volunteer work, work experience. **Freshman Admission Requirements:** High school diploma is required and GED is accepted *Academic units required:* 4 English, 3 math, 3 science, 3 social studies, 4 academic electives, *Academic units recommended:* 4 math, 4 science, 2 foreign language, 4 social studies. **Freshman Admission Statistics:** 1,002 applied, 71.7% admitted, 48% enrolled. **Transfer Admission Requirements:** college transcript(s), Minimum college GPA of 2.0 required. Lowest grade transferable D. **General Admission Information:** Application fee $44. Priority deadline 4/1. Regular application deadline 8/1. Nonfall registration accepted. Admission may be deferred.

COSTS AND FINANCIAL AID

Annual in-state tuition $6,730. Annual out-of-state tuition $14,108. Room and board $6,730. Required fees $1,574. Average book expense $1,000. **Required Forms and Deadlines:** FAFSA. **Notification of Awards:** Applicants will be notified of awards on a rolling basis beginning 12/21. **Types of Aid:** *Need-based scholarships/grants:* College/university scholarship or grant aid from institutional funds; Federal Pell; Private scholarships; SEOG; State scholarships/grants. *Loans:* Direct PLUS loans; Direct Subsidized Stafford Loans; Direct Unsubsidized Stafford Loans. *Student Employment:* Federal Work-Study Program available. Institutional employment available. **Financial Aid Statistics:** 58% needy freshmen, 67% needy undergrads receive need-based scholarship or grant aid. 51% freshmen, 28% undergrads receive non-need-based scholarship or grant aid. 81% freshmen, 87% undergrads receive need-based self-help aid. 0% freshmen, 0% undergrads receive athletic scholarships. 54% freshmen, 64% undergrads receive any aid. 76% undergrads borrow to pay for school. Average cumulative indebtedness $29,139. **Criteria for awarding aid:** *Need-based:* Academics, Art, Minority status, Music/drama *Non-need-based:* Academics, Alumni affiliation, Art, Leadership, Minority status, Music/drama, State/district residency.

UNIVERSITY OF WISCONSIN—WHITEWATER

800 West Main Street, Whitewater, WI 53190-1791
Phone: 262-472-1440 • **Financial Aid Phone:** 262-472-1130
E-mail: uwwadmit@uww.edu • **CEEB Code:** 1921
Fax: 262-472-1515 • **Website:** http://www.uww.edu/ • **ACT Code:** 4684

This public school was founded in 1868. It has a 385 acre campus.

RATINGS

Admissions Selectivity Rating: 77   **Fire Safety Rating:** 84   **Green Rating:** 89

STUDENTS AND FACULTY

Enrollment: 8,999. **Student Body:** 50% female, 50% male, 4% out-of-state, <1% international (69 countries represented). Asian 2%, African American 4%, Caucasian 90%, Hispanic 2%, Native American <1%, Race unknown <1%. **Retention and Graduation:** 74% freshmen return for sophomore year. **Faculty:** Student/faculty ratio 22:1. 392 full-time faculty, 85% hold PhDs, 18% are members of minority groups, 44% are women. 0% of classes are taught by teaching assistants.

ACADEMICS

Degrees: Associate; Bachelor's; **Master's Classes:** Most classes have 10-19 students. **Most popular majors:** Elementary Education And Teaching; Physical Education Teaching And Coaching. **Special Study Options:** Accelerated program; Cooperative education program; Cross-registration; Distance learning; Double major; Dual enrollment; English as a Second Language (ESL); Exchange student program (domestic); External degree program; Honors program; Independent study; Internships; Liberal arts/career combination; Student-designed major; Study abroad; Teacher certification program; Weekend college. Honors programs: General academic honors program. **Disability Services offered to physically disabled students:** Note-taking services; Reader services; Tape recorders; Tutors. **Career services:** Career assessment; Career/job search classes; Internships

FACILITIES

Housing: Coed dorms; Special housing for disabled student; Special housing for international students; Women's dorms 100% of campus accessible to physically diasbled. **Special Academic Facilities/Equipment:** Two electron microscopes, State of the Art Theater/Auditorium. **Computers:** Students can register for classes online. Administrative functions (other than registration) can be performed online.

CAMPUS LIFE

Environment: Village **Activities:** Choral groups; Concert band; Dance; Drama/theater; Jazz band; Literary magazine; Marching band; Music ensembles; Musical theater; Opera; Radio station; Student government; Student newspaper; Symphony orchestra; Television station 130 registered organizations, 4 honor societies, 8 religious organizations. 9 fraternities, 8 sororities. **Athletics (Intercollegiate):** *Men:* baseball, basketball, cross-country, diving, football, soccer, swimming, tennis, track/field (outdoor), track/field (indoor), wrestling. *Women:* basketball, bowling, cross-country, diving, golf, gymnastics, soccer, softball, swimming, tennis, track/field (outdoor), track/field (indoor), volleyball. **On-Campus Highlights:** New Kachel Field House, University Center, Underground Dance Club, Ritazza Coffee Shop, Warhawk Room

ADMISSIONS

Freshman Academic Profile: 9% in top 10% of high school class, 32% in top 25% of high school class, 77% in top 50% of high school class. 90% from public high schools. **Test Scores:** SAT Math middle 50% range 480-600. ACT middle 50% range 20-24. Minimum paper TOEFL 500. **Basis for Candidate Selection:** *Very important factors considered include:* rigor of secondary school record, class rank, standardized test scores. *Other factors considered include:* academic GPA, application essay, recommendation(s), interview, extracurricular activities, talent/ability, character/personal qualities, first generation, geographical residence, state residency, racial/ethnic status, volunteer work, work experience, level of applicant's interest. **Freshman Admission Requirements:** High school diploma is required and GED is accepted *Academic units required:* 4 English, 3 math, 3 science, 1 science labs, 3 social studies, 4 academic electives, *Academic units recommended:* 4 math, 4 science, 2 foreign language, 4 social studies. **Freshman Admission Statistics:** 5,570 applied, 75.6% admitted, 43% enrolled. **Transfer Admission Requirements:** High school transcript, college transcript(s), Minimum college GPA of 2.0 required. Lowest grade transferable D-. **General Admission Information:** Application fee $35. Priority deadline 1/1. Nonfall registration accepted. Admission may be deferred for a maximum of 3 terms.

COSTS AND FINANCIAL AID

Annual in-state tuition $4,322. Annual out-of-state tuition $13,042. Room and board $4,322. Required fees $710. Average book expense $170. **Required Forms and Deadlines:** FAFSA. **Notification of Awards:** Applicants will be notified of awards on a rolling basis beginning 4/1. **Types of Aid:** *Need-based scholarships/grants:* College/university scholarship or grant aid from institutional funds; Federal Pell; Private scholarships; SEOG; State scholarships/grants. *Loans:* Direct PLUS loans; Direct Subsidized Stafford Loans; Direct Unsubsidized Stafford Loans. **Financial Aid Statistics:** 38% needy freshmen, 44% needy undergrads receive need-based scholarship or grant aid. 28% freshmen, 14% undergrads receive non-need-based scholarship or grant aid. 90% freshmen, 89% undergrads receive need-based self-help aid. 0% freshmen, 0% undergrads receive athletic scholarships. 52% freshmen, 42% undergrads receive any aid. **Criteria for awarding aid:** *Need-based:* Academics, Leadership, Minority status *Non-need-based:* Academics, Alumni affiliation, Art, Leadership, Minority status, Music/drama, State/district residency.

UNIVERSITY OF WYOMING

Best Colleges

1000 E. University Ave, Laramie, WY 82071
Phone: 307-766-5160 • **Financial Aid Phone:** 307-766-2116
E-mail: admissions@uwyo.edu • **CEEB Code:** 4855
Fax: 307-766-4042 • **Website:** www.uwyo.edu • **ACT Code:** 5006

This public school was founded in 1886. It has a 785 acre campus.

RATINGS
Admissions Selectivity Rating: 76   **Fire Safety Rating:** 91   **Green Rating:** 76

STUDENTS AND FACULTY
Enrollment: 9,623. **Student Body:** 50% female, 50% male, 33% out-of-state, 4% international (67 countries represented). Asian 1%, African American 1%, Caucasian 71%, Hispanic 7%, Native American <1%, Pacific Islander <1%, Two or more races 4%, Race unknown 10%.
Retention and Graduation: 78% freshmen return for sophomore year. 27% freshmen graduate within 4 years. 55% freshmen graduate within 6 years. **Faculty:** Student/faculty ratio 15:1. 723 full-time faculty, 78% hold PhDs, 9% are members of minority groups, 39% are women. 10% of classes are taught by teaching assistants.

ACADEMICS
Degrees: Bachelor's; Certificate; Doctoral/Professional; Doctoral/Research; Master's; Post-Bachelor's certificate **Classes:** Most classes have 10-19 students. Most lab/discussion sessions have fewer than 10 students. **Most popular majors:** Mechanical Engineering; Psychology, General; Registered Nursing/Registered Nurse. **Special Study Options:** Accelerated program; Distance learning; Double major; English as a Second Language (ESL); Exchange student program (domestic); External degree program; Honors program; Independent study; Internships; Student-designed major; Study abroad. Honors programs: The University Honors Program provides highly motivated students a series of curricular and extracurricular opportunities. Most students are selected for the program prior to their freshman year, although the program welcomes UW and transfer students up to the beginning of the junior year. Each year the Honors Program awards scholarships to qualifying students who are beginning their undergraduate education or who are entering the University as transfer students. The honors students organize extracurricular activities, have a student lounge and computers for their use, and have the option of living on one of the honors floors in the residence halls or in the Honors House. Courses offered in the honors program are restricted to honors program students; exceptions must be approved by the Honors program office. Combined degree programs: BA/MEng. **Disability Services offered to physically disabled students:** Note-taking services; Reader services; Tape recorders; Tutors. **Career services:** Alumni network; Alumni services; Career assessment; Career/job search classes; Internships; Regional alumni

FACILITIES
Housing: Apartments for married students; Apartments for single students; Coed dorms; Fraternity/sorority housing; Men's dorms; Special housing for disabled student; Theme housing; Women's dorms 95% of campus accessible to physically diasbled. **Special Academic Facilities/Equipment:** Art gallery, Geology museum, American Heritage Center, Rocky Mountain Herbarium, Solheim Mycology Herbarium, art museum, planetarium, environmental biology lab, anthropology museum, on-site elementary school, state veterinary lab, infrared telescope observatory, lysimeter lab, insect museum and gallery room, Wyoming Geographic Information Science Center, Writing Center, Wyoming Cooperative Fishery and Wildlife Research Unit **Computers:** 75% of classrooms, 20% of dorms, 100% of libraries, 5% of dining areas, 100% of student union, 10% of common outdoor areas have wireless network access. Students can register for classes online. Administrative functions (other than registration) can be performed online.

CAMPUS LIFE
Environment: Town **Activities:** Campus Ministries; Choral groups; Concert band; Dance; Drama/theater; International Student Organization; Jazz band; Literary magazine; Marching band; Model UN; Music ensembles; Musical theater; Opera; Pep band; Radio station; Student government; Student newspaper; Student-run film society; Symphony orchestra; Television station 223 registered organizations, 41 honor societies, 17 religious organizations. 8 fraternities, 6 sororities. **Athletics (Intercollegiate):** *Men:* basketball, cheerleading, cross-country, diving, football, golf, swimming, track/field (outdoor), track/field (indoor), wrestling. *Women:* basketball, cheerleading, cross-country, diving, golf, soccer, swimming, tennis, track/field (outdoor), track/field (indoor), volleyball. **On-Campus Highlights:** Wyoming Student Union, Half Acre Gym, Geology Museum, Buchanan Center for the Performing Arts, American Heritage Center and Art Museum **Environmental Initiatives:** Campus Sustainability Committee

ADMISSIONS
Freshman Academic Profile: Average high school GPA 3.5. 24% in top 10% of high school class, 51% in top 25% of high school class, 82% in top 50% of high school class. **Test Scores:** SAT Math middle 50% range 520-640. SAT EBRW middle 50% range 520-650. ACT middle 50% range 22-27. Minimum internet-based TOEFL 76. Minimum paper TOEFL 540. **Basis for Candidate Selection:** *Very important factors considered include:* rigor of secondary school record, academic GPA, standardized test scores. *Other factors considered include:* application essay. **Freshman Admission Requirements:** High school diploma is required and GED is accepted *Academic units required:* 4 English, 4 math, 4 science, 3 science labs, 2 foreign language, 3 social studies, 2 academic electives, and 2 units from above areas or other academic areas. *Academic units recommended:* 4 English, 4 math, 4 science, 3 science labs, 2 foreign language, 3 social studies, 2 academic electives, 2 units from above areas or other academic areas. **Freshman Admission Statistics:** 4,306 applied, 96.8% admitted, 41% enrolled. **Transfer Admission Requirements:** college transcript(s), Minimum college GPA of 2.0 required. Lowest grade transferable D. **General Admission Information:** Application fee $40. Regular application deadline 8/10. Nonfall registration accepted. Admission may be deferred for a maximum of 1 year.

COSTS AND FINANCIAL AID
Annual in-state tuition $10,320. Annual out-of-state tuition $15,480. Room and board $10,320. Required fees $1,347. Average book expense $1,200. **Required Forms and Deadlines:** FAFSA. **Notification of Awards:** Applicants will be notified of awards on a rolling basis beginning 3/16. **Types of Aid:** *Need-based scholarships/grants:* College/university scholarship or grant aid from institutional funds; Federal Pell; Private scholarships; SEOG; State scholarships/grants. *Loans:* Direct PLUS loans; Direct Subsidized Stafford Loans; Direct Unsubsidized Stafford Loans. *Student Employment:* Federal Work-Study Program available. Institutional employment available. **Financial Aid Statistics:** 60% needy freshmen, 66% needy undergrads receive need-based scholarship or grant aid. 90% freshmen, 70% undergrads receive non-need-based scholarship or grant aid. 51% freshmen, 61% undergrads receive need-based self-help aid. 6% freshmen, 4% undergrads receive athletic scholarships. 45% undergrads borrow to pay for school. Average cumulative indebtedness $25,378. **Criteria for awarding aid:** *Need-based:* Academics, Athletics, Job skills, Minority status *Non-need-based:* Academics, Alumni affiliation, Art, Athletics, Leadership, Minority status, Music/drama, State/district residency.

UPPER IOWA UNIVERSITY

605 Washington St, Fayette, IA 52142-1859
Phone: 800-553-4150 • **Financial Aid Phone:** 800-553-4150
E-mail: admission@uiu.edu
Fax: 563-425-5277 • **ACT Code:** 1360

This private school was founded in 1857. It has a 80 acre campus.

RATINGS
Admissions Selectivity Rating: 71   **Fire Safety Rating:** 84   **Green Rating:** 70

STUDENTS AND FACULTY
Enrollment: 3,859. **Student Body:** 62% female, 38% male, 55% out-of-state, 2% international (30 countries represented). Asian 1%, African American 20%, Caucasian 66%, Hispanic 6%, Native American <1%, Pacific Islander <1%, Two or more races 2%, Race unknown 3%.
Retention and Graduation: 63% freshmen return for sophomore year. 25% grads go on to further study within 1 year. 29% grads pursue arts and sciences degrees. 1% grads pursue law degrees. 17% grads pursue business degrees. 5% grads pursue medical degrees. **Faculty:** Student/faculty ratio 17:1. 78 full-time faculty, 59% hold PhDs, 3% are members of minority groups, 55% are women. 0% of classes are taught by teaching assistants.

ACADEMICS
Degrees: Associate; Bachelor's; Certificate; Master's; Terminal Associate; Transfer Associate **Classes:** Most classes have fewer than 10 students. Most lab/discussion sessions have 30-39 students. **Most popular majors:** Psychology, General; Public Administration And Social Service Professions; Human Services, General. **Special Study Options:** Accelerated program; Distance learning; Double major; Dual enrollment; English as a Second

Language (ESL); External degree program; Honors program; Independent study; Internships; Liberal arts/career combination; Student-designed major; Study abroad; Teacher certification program. **Disability Services offered to physically disabled students:** Note-taking services; Reader services; Tape recorders; Tutors. **Career services:** Alumni services; Career assessment; Career/job search classes; Internships; Regional alumni

FACILITIES

Housing: Coed dorms; Men's dorms; Special housing for disabled student; Women's dorms 70% of campus accessible to physically diasbled. **Special Academic Facilities/Equipment:** Bing Art Gallery, Library archives **Computers:** 100% of classrooms, 100% of dorms, 100% of libraries, 100% of dining areas, 100% of student union, 33% of common outdoor areas have wireless network access. Students can register for classes online. Administrative functions (other than registration) can be performed online.

CAMPUS LIFE

Environment: Rural **Activities:** Campus Ministries; Choral groups; Dance; Drama/theater; International Student Organization; Literary magazine; Radio station; Student government; Student newspaper; Yearbook 40 registered organizations, 1 honor society, 1 religious organization. 4 fraternities, 5 sororities. **Athletics (Intercollegiate):** *Men:* baseball, basketball, cross-country, football, golf, soccer, wrestling. *Women:* basketball, cross-country, golf, soccer, softball, tennis, volleyball. **On-Campus Highlights:** Student Center, Liberal Arts Center, Dorman Gym, Andres Center for Business and Education, Suite style housing **Environmental Initiatives:** Geothermal Heating/Cooling

ADMISSIONS

Freshman Academic Profile: Average high school GPA 3.1. 22% in top 10% of high school class, 27% in top 25% of high school class, 57% in top 50% of high school class. **Test Scores:** SAT Math middle 50% range 430-890. ACT middle 50% range 17-24. Minimum internet-based TOEFL 61. Minimum paper TOEFL 500. **Basis for Candidate Selection:** *Very important factors considered include:* academic GPA, standardized test scores. *Other factors considered include:* rigor of secondary school record, class rank, recommendation(s). **Freshman Admission Requirements:** High school diploma is required and GED is accepted **Freshman Admission Statistics:** 1,121 applied, 94.2% admitted, 20% enrolled. **Transfer Admission Requirements:** High school transcript, college transcript(s), Lowest grade transferable D-. **General Admission Information:** Nonfall registration accepted. Admission may be deferred for a maximum of 2 years.

COSTS AND FINANCIAL AID

Annual tuition $28,850. Room and board $8,370. Required fees $750. Average book expense $1,500. **Required Forms and Deadlines:** FAFSA. **Notification of Awards:** Applicants will be notified of awards on a rolling basis beginning 3/1. **Types of Aid:** *Need-based scholarships/grants:* College/university scholarship or grant aid from institutional funds; Federal Pell; Private scholarships; SEOG; State scholarships/grants. *Loans:* Direct PLUS loans; Direct Subsidized Stafford Loans; Direct Unsubsidized Stafford Loans. *Student Employment:* Federal Work-Study Program available. **Financial Aid Statistics:** 45% needy freshmen, 85% needy undergrads receive need-based scholarship or grant aid. 3% freshmen, 7% undergrads receive non-need-based scholarship or grant aid. 97% freshmen, 95% undergrads receive need-based self-help aid. 0% freshmen, 0% undergrads receive athletic scholarships. 100% freshmen, 90% undergrads receive any aid. 96% undergrads borrow to pay for school. Average cumulative indebtedness $18,863. **Criteria for awarding aid:** *Need-based:* Academics, Alumni affiliation *Non-need-based:* Academics, Alumni affiliation, Athletics.

URSINUS COLLEGE

601 East Main St, Collegeville, PA 19426
Phone: 610-409-3200 • **Financial Aid Phone:** 610-409-3600
E-mail: admission@ursinus.edu • **CEEB Code:** 2931
Fax: 610-409-3197 • **Website:** www.ursinus.edu • **ACT Code:** 3738

This private school was founded in 1869. It has a 170 acre campus.

RATINGS

Admissions Selectivity Rating: 79 **Fire Safety Rating:** 97 **Green Rating:** 85

STUDENTS AND FACULTY

Enrollment: 1,485. **Student Body:** 53% female, 47% male, 40% out-of-state, 2% international (20 countries represented). Asian 4%, African American 7%, Caucasian 74%, Hispanic 7%, Native American <1%, Pacific Islander <1%, Two or more races 3%, Race unknown 2%.
Retention and Graduation: 85% freshmen return for sophomore year. 75% freshmen graduate within 4 years. 77% freshmen graduate within 6 years. 23% grads go on to further study within 1 year. 56% grads pursue arts and sciences degrees. 4.1% grads pursue law degrees. 1% grads pursue business degrees. 26% grads pursue medical degrees. **Faculty:** Student/faculty ratio 11:1. 121 full-time faculty, 93% hold PhDs, 19% are members of minority groups, 57% are women. 0% of classes are taught by teaching assistants.

ACADEMICS

Degrees: Bachelor's **Classes:** Most classes have 10-19 students. Most lab/discussion sessions have 10-19 students. **Most popular majors:** Biology/Biological Sciences, General; Psychology, General; Economics, General. **Special Study Options:** Double major; Dual enrollment; Exchange student program (domestic); Honors program; Independent study; Internships; Student-designed major; Study abroad; Teacher certification program. Honors programs: Students can participate in Summer Fellows, a unique program where students from any subject get paid to do independent work on a subject they come up with. That work often leads to an Honors Project: a year-long, in-depth project that is the ultimate conclusion to a student's career. **Disability Services offered to physically disabled students:** Note-taking services; Reader services; Tape recorders; Tutors. **Career services:** Alumni network; Alumni services; Career assessment; Career/job search classes; Internships; Regional alumni

FACILITIES

Housing: Coed dorms; Men's dorms; Special housing for disabled student; Special housing for international students; Theme housing; Women's dorms **Special Academic Facilities/Equipment:** The Philip and Muriel Berman Museum of Art; The Kaleidoscope Performing Arts Center; F.W. Olin Hall for Humanities; Bomberger Hall; Pfahler Hall of Science; Thomas Hall; Floy Lewis Bakes Field House; Mossbauer Spectrometer. **Computers:** 100% of classrooms, 100% of libraries, 100% of dining areas, 100% of student union, 50% of common outdoor areas have wireless network access. Students can register for classes online. Administrative functions (other than registration) can be performed online. Undergraduates are required to own a computer.

CAMPUS LIFE

Environment: Town **Activities:** Campus Ministries; Choral groups; Concert band; Dance; Drama/theater; International Student Organization; Jazz band; Literary magazine; Model UN; Music ensembles; Musical theater; Pep band; Radio station; Student government; Student newspaper; Student-run film society; Television station; Yearbook 88 registered organizations, 27 honor societies, 4 religious organizations. 7 fraternities, 7 sororities. **Athletics (Intercollegiate):** *Men:* baseball, basketball, cross-country, football, golf, lacrosse, soccer, swimming, tennis, track/field (outdoor), track/field (indoor), wrestling. *Women:* basketball, cross-country, field hockey, golf, gymnastics, lacrosse, soccer, softball, swimming, tennis, track/field (outdoor), track/field (indoor), volleyball. **On-Campus Highlights:** The Kaleidoscope Performing Arts Centerl, Philip and Muriel Berman Museum of Art, Pfahler Hall of Science, Ursinus Organic Garden, Floy Lewis Bakes Athletics Center **Environmental Initiatives:** Environmental education, both academic and co-curricular, through our ENV department and our Office of Sustainability

ADMISSIONS

Freshman Academic Profile: Average high school GPA 3.3. 25% in top 10% of high school class, 53% in top 25% of high school class, 81% in top 50% of high school class. **Test Scores:** SAT Math middle 50% range 550-650. SAT EBRW middle 50% range 560-660. ACT middle 50% range 24-30. Minimum internet-based TOEFL 80. **Basis for Candidate Selection:** *Very important factors considered include:* rigor of secondary school record, academic GPA, character/personal qualities. *Important factors considered include:* class rank, application essay, recommendation(s), interview, extracurricular activities, talent/ability. *Other factors considered include:* standardized test scores, first generation, alumni/ae relation, geographical residence, state residency, racial/ethnic status, volunteer work, work experience, level of applicant's interest. **Freshman Admission Requirements:** High school diploma is required and GED is accepted *Academic units required:* 4 English, 3 math, 1 science, 1 science labs, 2 foreign language, 1 social studies, 5 academic electives, *Academic units recommended:* 4 English, 4 math, 4 science, 3 science labs, 3 foreign language, 4 social studies. **Freshman Admission Statistics:** 3,488 applied, 78.2% admitted, 15% enrolled. **Transfer Admission Requirements:** High school transcript, college transcript(s), essay or personal statement, standardized test scores, Minimum college GPA of 3.0 required. Lowest grade transferable C. **General Admission Information:** Priority deadline 2/1. Nonfall registration accepted. Admission may be deferred for a maximum of 1 year.

COSTS AND FINANCIAL AID

Annual tuition $52,050. Room and board $12,750. Average book expense $1,000. **Required Forms and Deadlines:** FAFSA; State aid form. **Notification of Awards:** Applicants will be notified of awards on or about 3/15. **Types of Aid:** *Need-based scholarships/grants:* College/university scholarship or grant aid from institutional funds; Federal Pell; Private scholarships; SEOG; State scholarships/grants. *Loans:* Direct PLUS loans; Direct Subsidized Stafford Loans; Direct Unsubsidized Stafford Loans. *Student Employment:* Federal Work-Study Program available. Institutional employment available. **Financial Aid Statistics:** 100% needy freshmen, 100% needy undergrads receive need-based scholarship or grant aid. 25% freshmen, 20% undergrads receive non-need-based scholarship or grant aid. 78% freshmen, 74% undergrads receive need-based self-help aid. 0% freshmen, 0% undergrads receive athletic scholarships. 99% freshmen, 97% undergrads receive any aid. 74% undergrads borrow to pay for school. Average cumulative indebtedness $38,537. **Criteria for awarding aid:** *Need-based:* Academics *Non-need-based:* Academics, Alumni affiliation, Leadership, Minority status, Music/drama, State/district residency.

URSULINE COLLEGE

2550 Lander Road, Pepper Pike, OH 44124-4398
Phone: 440-449-4203 • **Financial Aid Phone:** 440-646-8309
E-mail: admission@ursuline.edu • **CEEB Code:** 1848
Fax: 440-684-6138 • **Website:** www.ursuline.edu

This private school, affiliated with the Roman Catholic Church, was founded in 1871. It has a 110 acre campus.

RATINGS

Admissions Selectivity Rating: 72   **Fire Safety Rating:** 88   **Green Rating:** 60*

STUDENTS AND FACULTY

Enrollment: 641. **Student Body:** 93% female, 7% male, 8% out-of-state, 2% international (6 countries represented). Asian 1%, African American 26%, Caucasian 62%, Hispanic 3%, Native American 0%, Pacific Islander 0%, Two or more races 3%, Race unknown 4%.
Retention and Graduation: 59% freshmen return for sophomore year. 5% grads go on to further study within 1 year. **Faculty:** Student/faculty ratio 7:1. 66 full-time faculty, 68% hold PhDs, 9% are members of minority groups, 85% are women. 0% of classes are taught by teaching assistants.

ACADEMICS

Degrees: Bachelor's; Certificate; Doctoral/Professional; Master's; Post-Bachelor's certificate; Post-Master's certificate **Classes:** Most classes have 10-19 students. Most lab/discussion sessions have fewer than 10 students. **Most popular majors:** Psychology, General; Health Services/Allied Health/Health Sciences, General. **Special Study Options:** Accelerated program; Cross-registration; Double major; Dual enrollment; Independent study; Internships; Teacher certification program. **Disability Services offered to physically disabled students:** Note-taking services; Reader services; Tape recorders; Tutors. **Career services:** Career assessment; Internships

FACILITIES

Housing: Coed dorms; Theme housing; Women's dorms 98% of campus accessible to physically disabled. **Special Academic Facilities/Equipment:** Fritsche Gallery (Art) New Athletic Center **Computers:** 100% of classrooms, 100% of libraries, 100% of dining areas, have wireless network access.

CAMPUS LIFE

Environment: City **Activities:** Campus Ministries; Drama/theater; Literary magazine; Student government 21 registered organizations, 4 honor societies. **Athletics (Intercollegiate):** *Women:* basketball, bowling, cross-country, golf, soccer, softball, swimming, tennis, track/field (outdoor), volleyball. **On-Campus Highlights:** Bishop Anthony M. Pilla Student Learning Center, Florence O'Donnell Wasmer Gallery, Joseph J. Mullen Academic Center, Ralph M. Besse Library **Environmental Initiatives:** Increased Recycling Energy Conservation Renewable Energy

ADMISSIONS

Freshman Academic Profile: Average high school GPA 3.3. 16% in top 10% of high school class, 45% in top 25% of high school class, 74% in top 50% of high school class. 94% from public high schools. **Test Scores:** SAT Math middle 50% range 440-535. SAT EBRW middle 50% range 425-590. ACT middle 50% range 19-24. Minimum internet-based TOEFL 60. Minimum paper TOEFL 500. **Basis for Candidate Selection:** *Very important factors considered include:* academic GPA, standardized test scores. *Other factors considered include:* rigor of secondary school record, class rank, application essay, recommendation(s), interview, alumni/ae relation. **Freshman Admission Requirements:** High school diploma is required and GED is accepted *Academic units recommended:* 4 English, 3 math, 3 science, 2 science labs, 2 foreign language, 3 social studies, 1 visual/performing arts, 1 unit from above areas or other academic areas. **Freshman Admission Statistics:** 723 applied, 88.0% admitted, 18% enrolled. **Transfer Admission Requirements:** college transcript(s), essay or personal statement, Minimum college GPA of 2.5 required. Lowest grade transferable c. **General Admission Information:** Regular application deadline 2/1. Nonfall registration accepted. Admission may be deferred for a maximum of 1 year.

COSTS AND FINANCIAL AID

Required Forms and Deadlines: FAFSA. **Notification of Awards:** Applicants will be notified of awards on a rolling basis beginning 2/15. **Types of Aid:** *Need-based scholarships/grants:* College/university scholarship or grant aid from institutional funds; Federal Nursing Scholarships; Federal Pell; Private scholarships; SEOG; State scholarships/grants. *Loans:* Direct PLUS loans; Direct Subsidized Stafford Loans; Direct Unsubsidized Stafford Loans. *Student Employment:* Federal Work-Study Program available. **Financial Aid Statistics:** 100% needy freshmen, 96% needy undergrads receive need-based scholarship or grant aid. 20% freshmen, 13% undergrads receive non-need-based scholarship or grant aid. 84% freshmen, 88% undergrads receive need-based self-help aid. 17% freshmen, 12% undergrads receive athletic scholarships. 100% freshmen, 80% undergrads receive any aid. 98% undergrads borrow to pay for school. Average cumulative indebtedness $37,900. **Criteria for awarding aid:** *Need-based:* Athletics, Minority status *Non-need-based:* Academics, Alumni affiliation, Art, Athletics, Job skills, Minority status.

UTAH STATE UNIVERSITY

Old Main Hill, Logan, UT 84322-0160
Phone: 435-797-1079 • **Financial Aid Phone:** 435-797-0173
E-mail: admit@usu.edu
Fax: 435-797-3708 • **Website:** www.usu.edu • **ACT Code:** 4276

This public school was founded in 1888. It has a 400 acre campus.

RATINGS

Admissions Selectivity Rating: 74   **Fire Safety Rating:** 82   **Green Rating:** 92

STUDENTS AND FACULTY

Enrollment: 21,473. **Student Body:** 52% female, 48% male, 27% out-of-state, 1% international (59 countries represented). Asian 1%, African American 1%, Caucasian 82%, Hispanic 6%, Native American 2%, Pacific Islander <1%, Two or more races 2%, Race unknown 5%.
Retention and Graduation: 69% freshmen return for sophomore year. 32% grads go on to further study within 1 year. **Faculty:** 972 full-time faculty, 80% hold PhDs, 11% are members of minority groups, 38% are women. 7% of classes are taught by teaching assistants.

ACADEMICS

Degrees: Associate; Bachelor's; Certificate; Doctoral/Professional; Doctoral/Research; Master's; Post-Bachelor's certificate; Terminal Associate; Transfer Associate **Classes:** Most classes have 10-19 students. Most lab/discussion sessions have 10-19 students. **Most popular majors:** Economics, General; Communication Sciences And Disorders, General; Business Administration And Management, General. **Special Study Options:** Accelerated program; Cooperative education program; Cross-registration; Distance learning; Double major; Dual enrollment; English as a Second Language (ESL); Exchange student program (domestic); Honors program; Independent study; Internships; Liberal arts/career combination; Student-designed major; Study abroad; Teacher certification program; Weekend college. Honors programs: The Honors Program is a community of scholars whose curiosity, creativity, and enthusiasm for learning foster educational achievement and personal growth. Our students are going places—graduate school, professional school, terrific jobs. Honors offers undergraduate students intensive seminars, experimental and interdisciplinary courses, writing projects, leadership opportunities, artistic and social activities. Our classes are smaller, allowing students to get to know professors and encouraging classroom interaction and discussion. We allow students to define their own interests and pursue them through "contracts" with professors, fostering close contact with professors. Other advantages include priority registration, an Honors-only computer lab, the Honors lounge and study areas. Starting in Fall 2005, Honors expects to offer housing. **Disability Services offered to physically disabled students:** Note-taking services;

Reader services; Tape recorders. **Career services:** Alumni network; Alumni services; Career assessment; Career/job search classes; Internships; Regional alumni

FACILITIES

Housing: Apartments for married students; Apartments for single students; Coed dorms; Fraternity/sorority housing; Men's dorms; Special housing for disabled student; Special housing for international students; Theme housing; Women's dorms 97% of campus accessible to physically diasbled. **Special Academic Facilities/Equipment:** Art gallery, agricultural and engineering experiment station, water research lab, wildlife and fishery research unit, on-campus school, intermountain herbarium, electron microscope, space dynamics lab. **Computers:** 99% of classrooms, 95% of dorms, 99% of libraries, 99% of dining areas, 99% of student union, 50% of common outdoor areas have wireless network access. Students can register for classes online. Administrative functions (other than registration) can be performed online.

CAMPUS LIFE

Environment: Town **Activities:** Campus Ministries; Choral groups; Concert band; Dance; Drama/theater; International Student Organization; Jazz band; Marching band; Music ensembles; Musical theater; Opera; Pep band; Radio station; Student government; Student newspaper; Student-run film society; Symphony orchestra; Television station 194 registered organizations, 32 honor societies, 8 religious organizations. 5 fraternities, 3 sororities. **Athletics (Intercollegiate)** *Men:* basketball, cross-country, football, golf, tennis, track/field (outdoor), track/field (indoor). *Women:* basketball, cross-country, gymnastics, soccer, softball, tennis, track/field (outdoor), track/field (indoor), volleyball. **On-Campus Highlights:** Aggie Recreation Center, Dee Glen Smith Spectrum, Merrill-Cazier Library, Taggart Student Center, The Quad **Environmental Initiatives:** Increased efficiency All the new buildings on campus on USU campus are LEED Silver or higher, and projects must achieve EA Credit 3, enhanced commissioning. According to LEED, this can result in 5%–10% improvements in energy efficiency, ensure personnel know how to operate key building systems, and catch mistakes like incorrectly installed equipment. Many buildings have been retro-commisioned to ensure existing buildings are operating efficiently. Non-potable water is used for irrigation. Irrigation systems use central computer controls to maximize efficiency, and water lines are regularly inspected for leaks. Campus housing has installed 6500 LEDs and water efficienct shower heads.

ADMISSIONS

Freshman Academic Profile: Average high school GPA 3.5. 20% in top 10% of high school class, 44% in top 25% of high school class, 74% in top 50% of high school class. **Test Scores:** SAT Math middle 50% range 510-620. SAT EBRW middle 50% range 490-600. ACT middle 50% range 21-27. Minimum internet-based TOEFL 71. **Basis for Candidate Selection:** *Very important factors considered include:* academic GPA, standardized test scores. *Other factors considered include:* rigor of secondary school record, class rank, recommendation(s). **Freshman Admission Requirements:** High school diploma is required and GED is accepted *Academic units required: Academic units recommended:* 4 English, 4 math, 3 science, 3 science labs, 2 foreign language, 3.5 social studies. **Freshman Admission Statistics:** 15,555 applied, 89.1% admitted, 31% enrolled. **Transfer Admission Requirements:** college transcript(s), Minimum college GPA of 2.2 required. Lowest grade transferable D. **General Admission Information:** Application fee $50. Nonfall registration accepted. Admission may be deferred for a maximum of 2 years.

COSTS AND FINANCIAL AID

Annual in-state tuition $6,060. Annual out-of-state tuition $19,657. Room and board $6,060. Required fees $1,070. Average book expense $824. **Required Forms and Deadlines:** FAFSA. **Notification of Awards:** Applicants will be notified of awards on a rolling basis beginning 4/1. **Types of Aid:** *Need-based scholarships/grants:* College/university scholarship or grant aid from institutional funds; Federal Pell; Private scholarships; SEOG; State scholarships/grants. *Loans:* Direct PLUS loans; Direct Subsidized Stafford Loans; Direct Unsubsidized Stafford Loans. *Student Employment:* Federal Work-Study Program available. Institutional employment available. **Financial Aid Statistics:** 74% needy undergrads receive need-based scholarship or grant aid. 64% freshmen, 43% undergrads receive non-need-based scholarship or grant aid. 49% freshmen, 54% undergrads receive need-based self-help aid. 2% freshmen, 1% undergrads receive athletic scholarships. 81% freshmen, 80% undergrads receive any aid. 47% undergrads borrow to pay for school. Average cumulative indebtedness $19,172. **Criteria for awarding aid:** *Non-need-based:* Academics, Alumni affiliation, Art, Athletics, Leadership, Minority status, Music/drama, Religious affiliation, State/district residency.

UTICA COLLEGE

1600 Burrstone Road, Utica, NY 13502-4892
Phone: 315-792-3006 • **Financial Aid Phone:** 315-792-3179
E-mail: admiss@utica.edu • **CEEB Code:** 2932
Fax: 315-792-3003 • **Website:** www.utica.edu • **ACT Code:** 2932

This private school was founded in 1946. It has a 128 acre campus.

RATINGS

Admissions Selectivity Rating: 73   **Fire Safety Rating:** 88   **Green Rating:** 71

STUDENTS AND FACULTY

Enrollment: 3,637. **Student Body:** 60% female, 40% male, 19% out-of-state, 1% international (40 countries represented). Asian 3%, African American 12%, Caucasian 67%, Hispanic 9%, Native American <1%, Pacific Islander <1%, Two or more races 3%, Race unknown 4%.
Retention and Graduation: 76% freshmen return for sophomore year. 35% freshmen graduate within 4 years. 49% freshmen graduate within 6 years. 46% grads go on to further study within 1 year. 1% grads pursue medical degrees.
Faculty: Student/faculty ratio 13:1. 150 full-time faculty, 78% hold PhDs, 11% are members of minority groups, 47% are women. 0% of classes are taught by teaching assistants.

ACADEMICS

Degrees: Bachelor's; Certificate; Doctoral/Professional; Master's; Post-Bachelor's certificate **Classes:** Most classes have 10-19 students. Most lab/discussion sessions have fewer than 10 students. **Most popular majors:** Corrections And Criminal Justice, Other; Health Services/Allied Health/Health Sciences, General. **Special Study Options:** Accelerated program; Distance learning; Double major; English as a Second Language (ESL); Honors program; Independent study; Internships; Study abroad; Teacher certification program; Weekend college. **Disability Services offered to physically disabled students:** Note-taking services; Reader services; Tape recorders; Tutors. **Career services:** Alumni network; Alumni services; Career assessment; Career/job search classes; Internships

FACILITIES

Housing: Apartments for single students; Coed dorms; Special housing for disabled student; Special housing for international students; Theme housing 85% of campus accessible to physically diasbled. **Special Academic Facilities/Equipment:** Edith Langley Barrett Art Gallery **Computers:** 95% of classrooms, 10% of dorms, 100% of libraries, 100% of dining areas, 100% of student union, have wireless network access. Students can register for classes online. Administrative functions (other than registration) can be performed online.

CAMPUS LIFE

Environment: City **Activities:** Campus Ministries; Choral groups; Concert band; Dance; Drama/theater; International Student Organization; Jazz band; Literary magazine; Music ensembles; Radio station; Student government; Student newspaper; Television station; Yearbook 80 registered organizations, 8 honor societies, 4 religious organizations. 5 fraternities, 4 sororities. **Athletics (Intercollegiate):** *Men:* baseball, basketball, cross-country, diving, football, golf, ice hockey, lacrosse, soccer, swimming, tennis, track/field (outdoor). *Women:* basketball, cross-country, diving, field hockey, ice hockey, lacrosse, soccer, softball, swimming, tennis, track/field (outdoor), volleyball, water polo. **On-Campus Highlights:** Strebel Student Center and Lounge, Pioneer Cafe, Clark Athletic Center, Romano Hall Lounge, Library Cafe **Environmental Initiatives:** Committee on sustainability formed in 2007.

ADMISSIONS

Freshman Academic Profile: Average high school GPA 3.1. 10% in top 10% of high school class, 33% in top 25% of high school class, 65% in top 50% of high school class. **Test Scores:** SAT Math middle 50% range 480-590. SAT EBRW middle 50% range 500-590. ACT middle 50% range 20-26. Minimum paper TOEFL 525. **Basis for Candidate Selection:** *Very important factors considered include:* rigor of secondary school record, academic GPA. *Important factors considered include:* application essay, standardized test scores, level of applicant's interest. *Other factors considered include:* class rank, recommendation(s), interview, extracurricular activities, talent/ability, character/personal qualities, first generation, alumni/ae relation, volunteer work, work experience. **Freshman Admission Requirements:** High school diploma is required and GED is accepted *Academic units required:* 4 English, 3 math, 3 science, 1 foreign language, 4 social studies, 3.5 academic electives, 1 visual/performing arts, and 2.5 units from above areas or other academic areas. **Freshman Admission Statistics:** 5,656 applied, 83.7% admitted, 12% enrolled. **Transfer Admission Requirements:** college transcript(s), essay or personal statement, Minimum college GPA of 2.50 required. Lowest grade transferable C. **General Admission Information:** Application fee $40. Priority deadline 3/1. Nonfall registration accepted. Admission may be deferred for a maximum of one year.

COSTS AND FINANCIAL AID
Annual tuition $20,127. Room and board $10,828. Required fees $550. Average book expense $1,400. **Required Forms and Deadlines:** FAFSA; State aid form. **Notification of Awards:** Applicants will be notified of awards on a rolling basis beginning 2/1. **Types of Aid:** *Need-based scholarships/grants:* College/university scholarship or grant aid from institutional funds; Federal Pell; Private scholarships; SEOG; State scholarships/grants. *Loans:* Direct PLUS loans; Direct Subsidized Stafford Loans; Direct Unsubsidized Stafford Loans. *Student Employment:* Federal Work-Study Program available. Institutional employment available. **Financial Aid Statistics:** 100% needy freshmen, 87% needy undergrads receive need-based scholarship or grant aid. 10% freshmen, 8% undergrads receive non-need-based scholarship or grant aid. 97% freshmen, 94% undergrads receive need-based self-help aid. 0% freshmen, 0% undergrads receive athletic scholarships. 96% freshmen, 95% undergrads receive any aid. 85% undergrads borrow to pay for school. Average cumulative indebtedness $33,336. **Criteria for awarding aid:** *Non-need-based:* Academics, Alumni affiliation, Minority status.

VALDOSTA STATE UNIVERSITY

1500 North Patterson Street, Valdosta, GA 31698
Phone: 229-333-5791 • **Financial Aid Phone:** 229-333-5935
E-mail: admissions@valdosta.edu • **CEEB Code:** 5855
Fax: 229-333-5482 • **Website:** http://www.valdosta.edu/ • **ACT Code:** 874

This public school was founded in 1906. It has a 180 acre campus.

RATINGS
Admissions Selectivity Rating: 85   **Fire Safety Rating:** 63   **Green Rating:** 60*

STUDENTS AND FACULTY
Enrollment: 10,638. **Student Body:** 60% female, 40% male, 4% out-of-state, 1% international (73 countries represented). Asian 1%, African American 34%, Caucasian 54%, Hispanic 4%, Native American <1%, Pacific Islander <1%, Two or more races 3%, Race unknown 2%.
Retention and Graduation: 67% freshmen return for sophomore year.
Faculty: Student/faculty ratio 23:1. 489 full-time faculty, 77% hold PhDs, 15% are members of minority groups, 48% are women. 2% of classes are taught by teaching assistants.

ACADEMICS
Degrees: Associate; Bachelor's; Doctoral; Master's; Post-Master's certificate **Classes:** Most classes have 10-19 students. Most lab/discussion sessions have 10-19 students. **Most popular majors:** Biology/Biological Sciences, General; Psychology, General; Registered Nursing/Registered Nurse. **Special Study Options:** Accelerated program; Cooperative education program; Distance learning; Double major; Dual enrollment; English as a Second Language (ESL); External degree program; Honors program; Independent study; Internships; Study abroad; Teacher certification program; Weekend college. Honors programs: Valdosta State University Honors College. **Disability Services offered to physically disabled students:** Note-taking services; Reader services; Tape recorders; Tutors. **Career services:** Alumni services; Career assessment; Career/job search classes; Internships

FACILITIES
Housing: Apartments for single students; Coed dorms; Special housing for disabled student; Special housing for international students; Theme housing 100% of campus accessible to physically diasbled. **Special Academic Facilities/Equipment:** Planetarium; Herbarium; Art Gallery; VSU Archives **Computers:** Students can register for classes online. Administrative functions (other than registration) can be performed online.

CAMPUS LIFE
Environment: City **Activities:** Campus Ministries; Choral groups; Concert band; Dance; Drama/theater; International Student Organization; Jazz band; Literary magazine; Marching band; Model UN; Music ensembles; Opera; Pep band; Radio station; Student government; Student newspaper; Symphony orchestra; Television station; Yearbook 140 registered organizations, 22 honor societies, 11 religious organizations. 12 fraternities, 10 sororities. **Athletics (Intercollegiate):** *Men:* baseball, basketball, cross-country, football, golf, tennis. *Women:* basketball, cheerleading, cross-country, softball, tennis, volleyball. **On-Campus Highlights:** Student Recreation Center, Student

Union, Odum Library, Front Lawn, Palms Dining Center **Environmental Initiatives:** Recycling

ADMISSIONS
Freshman Academic Profile: Average high school GPA 3.1. **Test Scores:** SAT Math middle 50% range 460-540. SAT EBRW middle 50% range 470-540. ACT middle 50% range 20-23. Minimum paper TOEFL 523. **Basis for Candidate Selection:** *Very important factors considered include:* academic GPA, standardized test scores. *Important factors considered include:* rigor of secondary school record, class rank, extracurricular activities, talent/ability, character/personal qualities. **Freshman Admission Requirements:** High school diploma is required and GED is not accepted *Academic units required:* 4 English, 4 math, 3 science, 2 science labs, 2 foreign language, 3 social studies. **Freshman Admission Statistics:** 7,950 applied, 58.5% admitted, 48% enrolled. **Transfer Admission Requirements:** college transcript(s), Minimum college GPA of 2.0 required. Lowest grade transferable D. **General Admission Information:** Application fee $40. Regular application deadline 6/1. Nonfall registration accepted. Admission may be deferred for a maximum of 1 year.

COSTS AND FINANCIAL AID
Annual in-state tuition $6,850. Annual out-of-state tuition $13,224. Room and board $6,850. Required fees $1,910. Average book expense $1,200. **Required Forms and Deadlines:** FAFSA. **Notification of Awards:** Applicants will be notified of awards on a rolling basis beginning 4/15. **Types of Aid:** *Need-based scholarships/grants:* College/university scholarship or grant aid from institutional funds; Federal Nursing Scholarships; Federal Pell; Private scholarships; SEOG; State scholarships/grants. *Loans:* Direct PLUS loans; Direct Subsidized Stafford Loans; Direct Unsubsidized Stafford Loans. *Student Employment:* Federal Work-Study Program available. Institutional employment available. **Financial Aid Statistics:** 89% needy freshmen, 82% needy undergrads receive need-based scholarship or grant aid. 6% freshmen, 5% undergrads receive non-need-based scholarship or grant aid. 87% freshmen, 77% undergrads receive need-based self-help aid. 1% freshmen, 0% undergrads receive athletic scholarships. 76% freshmen, 70% undergrads receive any aid. **Criteria for awarding aid:** *Need-based:* Art, Athletics, Minority status, Music/drama *Non-need-based:* Academics, Art, Athletics, Minority status, Music/drama, State/district residency.

VALPARAISO UNIVERSITY

Kretzmann Hall, Valparaiso, IN 46383
Phone: 219-464-5011 • **Financial Aid Phone:** 219-464-5015
E-mail: undergrad.admission@valpo.edu • **CEEB Code:** 1874
Fax: 219-464-6898 • **Website:** http://www.valpo.edu • **ACT Code:** 1256

This private school, affiliated with the Lutheran Church, was founded in 1859. It has a 350 acre campus.

RATINGS
Admissions Selectivity Rating: 80   **Fire Safety Rating:** 84   **Green Rating:** 84

STUDENTS AND FACULTY
Enrollment: 3,213. **Student Body:** 55% female, 45% male, 55% out-of-state, 4% international (27 countries represented). Asian 2%, African American 6%, Caucasian 71%, Hispanic 10%, Native American <1%, Pacific Islander <1%, Two or more races 3%, Race unknown 3%.
Retention and Graduation: 83% freshmen return for sophomore year. 62% freshmen graduate within 4 years. 72% freshmen graduate within 6 years. 18% grads go on to further study within 1 year. 12% grads pursue arts and sciences degrees. 0.49% grads pursue law degrees. 9% grads pursue business degrees. 0.65% grads pursue medical degrees. **Faculty:** Student/faculty ratio 11:1. 310 full-time faculty, 88% hold PhDs, 13% are members of minority groups, 44% are women. 0% of classes are taught by teaching assistants.

ACADEMICS
Degrees: Associate; Bachelor's; Certificate; Doctoral/Professional; Master's; Post-Bachelor's certificate; Post-Master's certificate; Terminal Associate **Most popular majors:** Mechanical Engineering; Biology/Biological Sciences, General; Registered Nursing/Registered Nurse. **Special Study Options:** Accelerated program; Cooperative education program; Cross-registration; Distance learning; Double major; English as a Second Language (ESL); Exchange student program (domestic); Honors program; Independent study; Internships; Liberal arts/career combination; Student-designed major; Study abroad; Teacher certification program. Honors programs: Christ College, VU's honors college, provides an honors-level liberal arts curriculum dedicated to the study and practice of the basic arts of inquiry and committed to

educational processes that enable students to achieve a measure of intellectual independence. Combined degree programs: BA/JD; BA/MA. **Disability Services offered to physically disabled students:** Note-taking services; Reader services; Tape recorders; Tutors. **Career services:** Alumni network; Alumni services; Career assessment; Career/job search classes; Internships; Regional alumni

FACILITIES

Housing: Apartments for single students; Coed dorms; Fraternity/sorority housing; Theme housing; Women's dorms 60% of campus accessible to physically diasbled. **Special Academic Facilities/Equipment:** Art museum, galleries, language lab, planetarium, electron microscope, observatory, TV Studio, weather station, Virtual Nursing Learning Center, VisBox, non-linear video editing, Christopher Center for Learning and Information Resources, Doppler Radar facility **Computers:** 60% of classrooms, 100% of dorms, 100% of libraries, 100% of dining areas, 100% of student union, 15% of common outdoor areas have wireless network access. Students can register for classes online. Administrative functions (other than registration) can be performed online.

CAMPUS LIFE

Environment: Town **Activities:** Campus Ministries; Choral groups; Concert band; Dance; Drama/theater; International Student Organization; Jazz band; Literary magazine; Music ensembles; Musical theater; Pep band; Radio station; Student government; Student newspaper; Symphony orchestra; Television station; Yearbook 94 registered organizations, 33 honor societies, 7 religious organizations. 9 fraternities, 7 sororities. **Athletics (Intercollegiate):** *Men:* baseball, basketball, cross-country, diving, football, golf, soccer, swimming, tennis, track/field (outdoor), track/field (indoor). *Women:* basketball, bowling, cross-country, diving, golf, soccer, softball, swimming, tennis, track/field (outdoor), track/field (indoor), volleyball. **On-Campus Highlights:** Harre Union, Christopher Center for Library & Information Resources, VU Center for the Arts, Chapel of the Resurrection, Athletics-Recreation Center

ADMISSIONS

Freshman Academic Profile: Average high school GPA 3.7. 32% in top 10% of high school class, 63% in top 25% of high school class, 94% in top 50% of high school class. **Test Scores:** SAT Math middle 50% range 530-640. SAT EBRW middle 50% range 530-630. ACT middle 50% range 23-29. Minimum internet-based TOEFL 80. Minimum paper TOEFL 550. **Basis for Candidate Selection:** *Very important factors considered include:* rigor of secondary school record, academic GPA, standardized test scores. *Important factors considered include:* class rank, extracurricular activities, talent/ability, character/personal qualities, alumni/ae relation. *Other factors considered include:* application essay, recommendation(s), interview, first generation, religious affiliation/commitment, racial/ethnic status, volunteer work, level of applicant's interest. **Freshman Admission Requirements:** High school diploma is required and GED is accepted *Academic units required:* 4 English, 3 math, 2 science, 2 science labs, 2 foreign language, 2 history, 3 academic electives, *Academic units recommended:* 4 English, 4 math, 3 science, 3 science labs, 2 foreign language, 1 social studies, 2 history, 3 academic electives. **Freshman Admission Statistics:** 7,954 applied, 84.3% admitted, 12% enrolled. **Transfer Admission Requirements:** college transcript(s), essay or personal statement, statement of good standing from prior institution(s). Minimum college GPA of 2.0 required. Lowest grade transferable C-. **General Admission Information:** Priority deadline 12/1. Nonfall registration accepted. Admission may be deferred for a maximum of 1 year.

COSTS AND FINANCIAL AID

Annual tuition $39,000. Required fees $1,260. Average book expense $1,200. **Required Forms and Deadlines:** FAFSA. **Notification of Awards:** Applicants will be notified of awards on a rolling basis beginning 12/15. **Types of Aid:** *Need-based scholarships/grants:* College/university scholarship or grant aid from institutional funds; Federal Pell; Private scholarships; SEOG; State scholarships/grants. *Loans:* Direct PLUS loans; Direct Subsidized Stafford Loans; Direct Unsubsidized Stafford Loans. *Student Employment:* Federal Work-Study Program available. Institutional employment available. **Financial Aid Statistics:** 99% needy freshmen, 100% needy undergrads receive need-based scholarship or grant aid. 21% freshmen, 17% undergrads receive non-need-based scholarship or grant aid. 58% freshmen, 70% undergrads receive need-based self-help aid. 2% freshmen, 3% undergrads receive athletic scholarships. 94% freshmen, 92% undergrads receive any aid. Average cumulative indebtedness $37,294. **Criteria for awarding aid:** *Need-based:* Religious affiliation *Non-need-based:* Academics, Alumni affiliation, Art, Athletics, Leadership, Music/drama, Religious affiliation, State/district residency.

VANDERBILT UNIVERSITY

2305 West End Ave., Nashville, TN 37203
Phone: 615-322-2561 • **Financial Aid Phone:** 800-288-0204
E-mail: admissions@vanderbilt.edu • **CEEB Code:** 1871
Fax: 615-343-7765 • **Website:** www.vanderbilt.edu • **ACT Code:** 4036

This private school was founded in 1873. It has a 323 acre campus.

RATINGS

Admissions Selectivity Rating: 99   **Fire Safety Rating:** 91   **Green Rating:** 98

STUDENTS AND FACULTY

Enrollment: 6,856. **Student Body:** 51% female, 49% male, 90% out-of-state, 8% international (50 countries represented). Asian 13%, African American 10%, Caucasian 48%, Hispanic 10%, Native American 1%, Pacific Islander <1%, Two or more races 5%, Race unknown 5%.
Retention and Graduation: 97% freshmen return for sophomore year. 86% freshmen graduate within 4 years. 92% freshmen graduate within 6 years. 33% grads go on to further study within 1 year. 22% grads pursue arts and sciences degrees. 12.6% grads pursue law degrees. 7% grads pursue business degrees. 23.7% grads pursue medical degrees. **Faculty:** Student/faculty ratio 7:1. 975 full-time faculty, 94% hold PhDs, 17% are members of minority groups, 40% are women.

ACADEMICS

Degrees: Bachelor's; Doctoral; Doctoral/Professional; Doctoral/Research; Master's; Post-Master's certificate **Classes:** Most classes have 10-19 students. Most lab/discussion sessions have 20-29 students. **Most popular majors:** Engineering Science; Multi-/Interdisciplinary Studies, Other; Social Sciences, General. **Special Study Options:** Accelerated program; Double major; Dual enrollment; English as a Second Language (ESL); Honors program; Independent study; Internships; Liberal arts/career combination; Student-designed major; Study abroad; Teacher certification program. Honors programs: Alpha Lambda Delta, Phi Eta Sigma, Lotus Eaters Sophomore Honor Society, Athenian Honorary, Omicron Delta Kappa, Mortar Board Combined degree programs: BA/MA. **Disability Services offered to physically disabled students:** Note-taking services; Reader services; Tape recorders; Tutors. **Career services:** Alumni network; Career assessment; Career/job search classes; Internships

FACILITIES

Housing: Apartments for single students; Coed dorms; Fraternity/sorority housing; Men's dorms; Special housing for disabled student; Theme housing; Women's dorms 95% of campus accessible to physically diasbled. **Special Academic Facilities/Equipment:** Freedom Forum First Amendment Center, Biological Sciences/Medical Research Building III, Dyer Observatory, Kennedy Center, Martha Rivers Ingram Center for the Performing Arts, E. Bronson Ingram Studio Arts Center, Student Life Center **Computers:** 100% of classrooms, 100% of dorms, 100% of libraries, 100% of dining areas, 100% of student union, 100% of common outdoor areas have wireless network access. Students can register for classes online. Administrative functions (other than registration) can be performed online.

CAMPUS LIFE

Environment: Metropolis **Activities:** Campus Ministries; Choral groups; Concert band; Dance; Drama/theater; International Student Organization; Jazz band; Literary magazine; Marching band; Model UN; Music ensembles; Musical theater; Opera; Pep band; Radio station; Student government; Student newspaper; Student-run film society; Symphony orchestra; Television station; Yearbook 329 registered organizations, 20 honor societies, 18 religious organizations. 19 fraternities, 12 sororities. **Athletics (Intercollegiate):** *Men:* baseball, basketball, cross-country, football, golf, tennis. *Women:* basketball, cross-country, golf, lacrosse, soccer, tennis, track/field (outdoor). **On-Campus Highlights:** The Commons, The Wond'ry, Student Recreation Center, Student Life Center, Sarratt Student Center **Environmental Initiatives:** 1. Greenhouse gas emissions reduction—Overall greenhouse gas emissions from Vanderbilt's campus and medical center decreased by 12 percent from an all-time high reached in 2008—and by 7 percent from 2005 to 2011—even though Vanderbilt has seen significant growth in square footage, staff, students and research dollars over the last four years. GHG emissions per square foot have gone down 21 percent over the past seven years, which reflects a lot of hard work to improve the energy efficiency of existing buildings, some that are very old, as well as new construction and renovation projects that have incorporated excellent energy efficiency. GHG emissions per person, per student, per research dollar, per inpatient day and per ambulatory visit also have trended significantly in a positive direction since 2005. Most university greenhouse gas inventory reports do not include research and/or patient care activity, making Vanderbilt's report more comprehensive than most and also more comprehensive than what is now required by the Environmental Protection Agency.

ADMISSIONS

Freshman Academic Profile: Average high school GPA 3.8. 90% in top 10% of high school class, 96% in top 25% of high school class, 98% in top 50% of high school class. 65% from public high schools. **Test Scores:** SAT Math middle 50% range 700-790. SAT EBRW middle 50% range 700-760. ACT middle 50% range 32-35. Minimum internet-based TOEFL 100. **Basis for Candidate Selection:** *Very important factors considered include:* rigor of secondary school record, class rank, academic GPA, application essay, standardized test scores, extracurricular activities, character/personal qualities. *Important factors considered include:* recommendation(s), talent/ability. *Other factors considered include:* interview, first generation, alumni/ae relation, geographical residence, state residency, racial/ethnic status, volunteer work, work experience. **Freshman Admission Requirements:** High school diploma is required and GED is accepted *Academic units required:* 4 English, 3 math, 3 science, 2 science labs, 2 foreign language, 2 social studies, 1 history, 3 academic electives, *Academic units recommended:* 4 English, 4 math, 4 science, 3 science labs, 2 foreign language, 3 social studies, 1 history, 3 academic electives. **Freshman Admission Statistics:** 31,462 applied, 10.9% admitted, 47% enrolled. **Transfer Admission Requirements:** college transcript(s), essay or personal statement, statement of good standing from prior institution(s). Lowest grade transferable C. **General Admission Information:** Application fee $50. Priority deadline 1/1. Regular application deadline 1/1. Nonfall registration accepted. Admission may be deferred for a maximum of 1 year.

COSTS AND FINANCIAL AID

Annual tuition $46,500. Room and board $15,584. Required fees $1,164. Average book expense $1,294. **Required Forms and Deadlines:** CSS/ Financial Aid PROFILE; FAFSA. **Notification of Awards:** Applicants will be notified of awards on or about 4/1. **Types of Aid:** *Need-based scholarships/ grants:* College/university scholarship or grant aid from institutional funds; Federal Pell; Private scholarships; SEOG; State scholarships/grants; United Negro College Fund. *Loans:* Direct PLUS loans; Direct Subsidized Stafford Loans; Direct Unsubsidized Stafford Loans. *Student Employment:* Federal Work-Study Program available. Institutional employment available. **Financial Aid Statistics:** 89% needy freshmen, 92% needy undergrads receive need-based scholarship or grant aid. 51% freshmen, 42% undergrads receive non-need-based scholarship or grant aid. 40% freshmen, 49% undergrads receive need-based self-help aid. 4% freshmen, 3% undergrads receive athletic scholarships. 69% freshmen, 65% undergrads receive any aid. Average cumulative indebtedness $24,122. **Criteria for awarding aid:** *Need-based:* Academics, Leadership, Music/drama *Non-need-based:* Academics, Athletics, Leadership, Music/drama, State/district residency.

See page 1080.

VANDERCOOK COLLEGE OF MUSIC

3140 South Federal Street, Chicago, IL 60616-3731
Phone: 312-788-1120 • **Financial Aid Phone:** 312-788-1146
E-mail: admissions@vandercook.edu • **CEEB Code:** 1872
Fax: 312-225-5211 • **Website:** www.vandercook.edu • **ACT Code:** 1156

This private school was founded in 1909. It has a 1 acre campus.

RATINGS

Admissions Selectivity Rating: 73   **Fire Safety Rating:** 62   **Green Rating:** 60*

STUDENTS AND FACULTY

Enrollment: 90. **Student Body:** 47% female, 53% male, 23% out-of-state, 2% international (2 countries represented). African American 3%, Caucasian 59%, Hispanic 24%, Native American 0%, Pacific Islander 1%, Two or more races 3%, Race unknown 7%.
Retention and Graduation: 73% freshmen return for sophomore year. 57% freshmen graduate within 4 years. 76% freshmen graduate within 6 years.
Faculty: Student/faculty ratio 3:1. 13 full-time faculty, 54% hold PhDs, 23% are members of minority groups, 62% are women. 0% of classes are taught by teaching assistants.

ACADEMICS

Degrees: Bachelor's; **Master's Classes:** Most classes have 10-19 students. Most lab/discussion sessions have 10-19 students. **Special Study Options:** Teacher certification program. Honors programs: VanderCook does not offer teaching assistantships. All courses are taught by faculty members only. **Career services:** Alumni services; Career/job search classes

FACILITIES

Housing: Apartments for married students; Apartments for single students; Coed dorms; Fraternity/sorority housing; Other (please specify) 0% of campus accessible to physically diasbled.

CAMPUS LIFE

Environment: Metropolis **Activities:** Choral groups; Concert band; Jazz band; Music ensembles; Musical theater; Radio station; Symphony orchestra 5 registered organizations, 1 fraternities.

ADMISSIONS

Freshman Academic Profile: Average high school GPA 3.0. 100% in top 50% of high school class. 80% from public high schools. **Test Scores:** SAT Math middle 50% range 450-540. SAT EBRW middle 50% range 430-530. ACT middle 50% range 21-29. Minimum internet-based TOEFL 70. Minimum paper TOEFL 500. **Basis for Candidate Selection:** *Very important factors considered include:* academic GPA, application essay, standardized test scores, recommendation(s), interview, talent/ability, character/personal qualities. *Important factors considered include:* extracurricular activities, alumni/ae relation, level of applicant's interest. *Other factors considered include:* rigor of secondary school record, class rank, first generation. **Freshman Admission Requirements:** High school diploma is required and GED is accepted *Academic units recommended:* 3 English, 2 math, 2 science, 2 foreign language, 3 social studies, 3 units from above areas or other academic areas. **Freshman Admission Statistics:** 38 applied, 100.0% admitted, 39% enrolled. **Transfer Admission Requirements:** High school transcript, college transcript(s), essay or personal statement, interview, standardized test scores, Minimum college GPA of 2.5 required. Lowest grade transferable C. **General Admission Information:** Application fee $35. Priority deadline 4/1. Nonfall registration accepted. Admission may be deferred for a maximum of 1 year.

COSTS AND FINANCIAL AID

Annual tuition $26,458. Room and board $12,074. Required fees $1,886. Average book expense $1,900. **Required Forms and Deadlines:** FAFSA. **Notification of Awards:** Applicants will be notified of awards on a rolling basis beginning 3/1. **Types of Aid:** *Need-based scholarships/grants:* College/ university scholarship or grant aid from institutional funds; Federal Pell; Private scholarships; SEOG; State scholarships/grants; United Negro College Fund. *Loans:* Direct PLUS loans; Direct Subsidized Stafford Loans; Direct Unsubsidized Stafford Loans. *Student Employment:* Federal Work-Study Program available. Institutional employment available. **Financial Aid Statistics:** 100% needy freshmen, 56% needy undergrads receive need-based scholarship or grant aid. 100% freshmen, 99% undergrads receive need-based self-help aid. 0% freshmen, 0% undergrads receive athletic scholarships. 100% freshmen, 95% undergrads receive any aid. 77% undergrads borrow to pay for school. Average cumulative indebtedness $47,042. **Criteria for awarding aid:** *Non-need-based:* Academics, Alumni affiliation, Music/drama.

VASSAR COLLEGE

124 Raymond Avenue, Poughkeepsie, NY 12604
Phone: 845-437-7300 • **Financial Aid Phone:** 845-437-5320
E-mail: admissions@vassar.edu • **CEEB Code:** 2956
Website: www.vassar.edu • **ACT Code:** 2982

This private school was founded in 1861. It has a 1000 acre campus.

RATINGS

Admissions Selectivity Rating: 96   **Fire Safety Rating:** 87   **Green Rating:** 88

STUDENTS AND FACULTY

Enrollment: 2,323. **Student Body:** 59% female, 41% male, 75% out-of-state, 7% international (54 countries represented). Asian 13%, African American 4%, Caucasian 57%, Hispanic 11%, Native American <1%, Pacific Islander 0%, Two or more races 7%, Race unknown <1%.

Retention and Graduation: 96% freshmen return for sophomore year. 85% freshmen graduate within 4 years. 90% freshmen graduate within 6 years. 19% grads go on to further study within 1 year. 49% grads pursue arts and sciences degrees. 16% grads pursue law degrees. 10% grads pursue business degrees. 9% grads pursue medical degrees. **Faculty:** Student/faculty ratio 8:1. 281 full-time faculty, 89% hold PhDs, 27% are members of minority groups, 45% are women. 0% of classes are taught by teaching assistants.

ACADEMICS

Degrees: Bachelor's; **Master's Classes:** Most classes have 10-19 students. Most lab/discussion sessions have 20-29 students. **Most popular majors:** Psychology, General; Economics, General; Political Science And Government, General. **Special Study Options:** Cooperative education program; Cross-registration; Double major; Exchange student program (domestic); Independent study; Internships; Liberal arts/career combination; Student-designed major; Study abroad; Teacher certification program. Combined degree programs: BA/MA. **Disability Services offered to physically disabled students:** Note-taking services; Reader services; Tape recorders. **Career services:** Alumni network; Alumni services; Career assessment; Career/job search classes; Internships; Regional alumni

FACILITIES

Housing: Apartments for single students; Coed dorms; Cooperative housing; Special housing for disabled student; Special housing for international students; Wellness housing; Women's dorms 75% of campus accessible to physically disabled. **Special Academic Facilities/Equipment:** Art center, theatres, nursery school, environmental field station, geology museum, electron microscope, observatory, Skinner Music Hall, Fitness Center **Computers:** 100% of classrooms, 100% of dorms, 100% of libraries, 100% of dining areas, 100% of student union, 80% of common outdoor areas have wireless network access. Students can register for classes online. Administrative functions (other than registration) can be performed online.

CAMPUS LIFE

Environment: Town **Activities:** Campus Ministries; Choral groups; Concert band; Dance; Drama/theater; International Student Organization; Jazz band; Literary magazine; Model UN; Music ensembles; Musical theater; Opera; Radio station; Student government; Student newspaper; Student-run film society; Symphony orchestra; Yearbook 105 registered organizations, 2 honor societies, 11 religious organizations. **Athletics (Intercollegiate):** *Men:* baseball, basketball, crew/rowing, cross-country, diving, fencing, lacrosse, soccer, squash, swimming, tennis, track/field (outdoor), volleyball. *Women:* basketball, crew/rowing, cross-country, diving, fencing, field hockey, golf, lacrosse, soccer, squash, swimming, tennis, track/field (outdoor), volleyball. **On-Campus Highlights:** Library, Bridge for Laboratory Sciences, Class of 1951 Observatory, Frances Lehman Loeb Art Center, Center for Drama and Film **Environmental Initiatives:** Tree Campus USA & Landscaping choices – in 2012/13 CCS and B&G worked together to phase out the use of harmful pesticides on campus to more environmentally friendly products. Concurrently, we have just been certified by Tree Campus USA, approved a formal tree care plan and seek to transition 3+ acres of lawn to naturalized habitat areas in spring 2013. During Winter 12/13 we have switched to a salt water brine solution, that has cut our total usage of salt on campus by 50%.

ADMISSIONS

Freshman Academic Profile: 65% in top 10% of high school class, 93% in top 25% of high school class, 99% in top 50% of high school class. 66% from public high schools. **Test Scores:** SAT Math middle 50% range 680-760. SAT EBRW middle 50% range 690-750. ACT middle 50% range 31-33. Minimum internet-based TOEFL 100. Minimum paper TOEFL 600. **Basis for Candidate Selection:** *Very important factors considered include:* rigor of secondary school record, academic GPA. *Important factors considered include:* class rank, application essay, standardized test scores, recommendation(s), extracurricular activities, talent/ability, character/personal qualities. *Other factors considered include:* interview, first generation, alumni/ae relation, geographical residence, racial/ethnic status, volunteer work, work experience. **Freshman Admission Requirements:** High school diploma is required and GED is accepted *Academic units recommended:* 4 English, 4 math, 4 science, 3 science labs, 4 foreign language, 2 social studies, 2 history. **Freshman Admission Statistics:** 7,746 applied, 23.8% admitted, 34% enrolled. **Transfer Admission Requirements:** High school transcript, college transcript(s), essay or personal statement, standardized test scores, statement of good standing from prior institution(s). Minimum college GPA of 3.0 required. Lowest grade transferable C. **General Admission Information:** Application fee $70. Regular application deadline 1/1. Nonfall registration accepted. Admission may be deferred for a maximum of 1 year.

COSTS AND FINANCIAL AID

Annual tuition $54,410. Room and board $12,900. Required fees $800. Average book expense $900. **Required Forms and Deadlines:** CSS/Financial Aid PROFILE; FAFSA; Noncustodial PROFILE. **Notification of Awards:**

Applicants will be notified of awards on or about 3/30. **Types of Aid:** *Need-based scholarships/grants:* College/university scholarship or grant aid from institutional funds; Federal Pell; Private scholarships; SEOG; State scholarships/grants. *Loans:* Direct PLUS loans; Direct Subsidized Stafford Loans; Direct Unsubsidized Stafford Loans. *Student Employment:* Federal Work-Study Program available. Institutional employment available. **Financial Aid Statistics:** 98% needy freshmen, 100% needy undergrads receive need-based scholarship or grant aid. 0% undergrads receive non-need-based scholarship or grant aid. 100% freshmen, 100% undergrads receive need-based self-help aid. 0% freshmen, 0% undergrads receive athletic scholarships. 61% freshmen, 58% undergrads receive any aid. 47% undergrads borrow to pay for school. Average cumulative indebtedness $17,847.

VAUGHN COLLEGE OF AERONAUTICS AND TECHNOLOGY

86-01 23rd Avenue, Flushing, NY 11369
Phone: 718-429-6600 • **Financial Aid Phone:** 718-429-6600
E-mail: admitme@vaughn.edu • **CEEB Code:** 2001
Fax: 718-779-2231 • **Website:** www.vaughn.edu

This private school was founded in 1932. It has a 6 acre campus.

RATINGS

Admissions Selectivity Rating: 80   **Fire Safety Rating:** 96   **Green Rating:** 60*

STUDENTS AND FACULTY

Enrollment: 1,605. **Student Body:** 13% female, 87% male, 11% out-of-state, 2% international. Asian 12%, African American 22%, Caucasian 13%, Hispanic 38%, Native American <1%, Pacific Islander 3%, Two or more races 5%, Race unknown 5%.
Retention and Graduation: 66% freshmen return for sophomore year. 0% grads pursue business degrees. **Faculty:** Student/faculty ratio 15:1. 41 full-time faculty, 49% hold PhDs, 37% are members of minority groups, 20% are women. 0% of classes are taught by teaching assistants.

ACADEMICS

Degrees: Associate; Bachelor's; Certificate; **Master's Classes:** Most classes have 20-29 students. Most lab/discussion sessions have 20-29 students. **Most popular majors:** Airframe Mechanics And Aircraft Maintenance Technology/Technician; Aeronautics/Aviation/Aerospace Science And Technology, General; Airline/Commercial/Professional Pilot And Flight Crew. **Special Study Options:** Accelerated program; Distance learning; Independent study; Internships; Liberal arts/career combination. **Disability Services offered to physically disabled students:** Tutors. **Career services:** Alumni network; Alumni services; Career assessment; Career/job search classes; Internships

FACILITIES

Housing: Coed dorms; Special housing for disabled student; Theme housing; Wellness housing 100% of campus accessible to physically disabled. **Computers:** 100% of classrooms, 100% of dorms, 100% of libraries, 100% of dining areas, 100% of common outdoor areas have wireless network access. Administrative functions (other than registration) can be performed online.

CAMPUS LIFE

Environment: Metropolis **Activities:** Dance; International Student Organization; Student government 21 registered organizations, 1 honor societies. **Athletics (Intercollegiate):** *Men:* basketball, soccer. *Women:* tennis. **On-Campus Highlights:** Flight Simulator Complex, Engineering Laboratories, Air Traffic Control Simulator Laboratory, Observation Tower, Library

ADMISSIONS

Freshman Academic Profile: Average high school GPA 86.0. **Test Scores:** SAT Math middle 50% range 459-560. SAT EBRW middle 50% range 432-533. ACT middle 50% range 19-24. Minimum internet-based TOEFL 80. Minimum paper TOEFL 580. **Basis for Candidate Selection:** *Very important factors considered include:* rigor of secondary school record, academic GPA. *Important factors considered include:* standardized test scores, extracurricular activities, volunteer work.level of applicant's interest. *Other factors considered include:* application essay, recommendation(s), interview, talent/ability, character/personal qualities, work experience. **Freshman Admission Requirements:** High school diploma is required and GED is accepted *Academic units required:* 4 English, 3 math, 2 science, 2 science labs, 1 social studies, *Academic units recommended:* 4 English, 4 math, 3 science, 3 science labs, 4 social studies. **Freshman Admission Statistics:** 813 applied, 74.8% admitted, 51% enrolled.

Transfer Admission Requirements: college transcript(s), Minimum college GPA of 2.0 required. Lowest grade transferable C. **General Admission Information:** Application fee $40. Priority deadline 3/1. Nonfall registration accepted. Admission may be deferred for a maximum of 1 year.

COSTS AND FINANCIAL AID

Annual tuition $20,840. Room and board $12,365. Required fees $800. Average book expense $2,160. **Required Forms and Deadlines:** FAFSA; State aid form. **Notification of Awards:** Applicants will be notified of awards on a rolling basis beginning 4/15. **Types of Aid:** *Need-based scholarships/grants:* College/university scholarship or grant aid from institutional funds; Federal Pell; Private scholarships; SEOG; State scholarships/grants. *Loans:* Direct PLUS loans; Direct Subsidized Stafford Loans; Direct Unsubsidized Stafford Loans. *Student Employment:* Federal Work-Study Program available. Institutional employment available. **Financial Aid Statistics:** 99% needy freshmen, 91% needy undergrads receive need-based scholarship or grant aid. 29% freshmen, 24% undergrads receive non-need-based scholarship or grant aid. 96% freshmen, 79% undergrads receive need-based self-help aid. 0% freshmen, 0% undergrads receive athletic scholarships. 94% freshmen, 95% undergrads receive any aid. **Criteria for awarding aid:** *Need-based:* Academics, Leadership *Non-need-based:* Academics, Alumni affiliation, Leadership.

VERMONT TECHNICAL COLLEGE

PO Box 500, Randolph Ctr, VT 05061
Phone: (802) 728-1444
E-mail: admissions@vtc.edu
Fax: (802) 728-1321 • **Website:** http://www.vtc.edu/

This is a public school.

RATINGS
Admissions Selectivity Rating: 84   **Fire Safety Rating:** 60*   **Green Rating:** 60*

STUDENTS AND FACULTY
Enrollment: 1,399. **Student Body:** 49% female, 51% male, 14% out-of-state, 2% international. Asian 2%, African American 2%, Caucasian 85%, Hispanic 3%, Native American 1%, Pacific Islander 0%, Two or more races 4%, Race unknown 2%.
Retention and Graduation: 70% freshmen return for sophomore year. 25% freshmen graduate within 4 years. 43% freshmen graduate within 6 years.
Faculty: Student/faculty ratio 12:1. 80 full-time faculty, 24% hold PhDs, 49% are women.

ACADEMICS
Degrees: Associate; Bachelor's; Certificate; **Master's Classes:** Most classes have fewer than 10 students. Most lab/discussion sessions have fewer than 10 students. **Special Study Options:** Distance learning; Double major; Dual enrollment; English as a Second Language (ESL); Honors program; Independent study; Internships.

FACILITIES
Housing: Coed dorms; Special housing for disabled student; Wellness housing

CAMPUS LIFE
Activities: International Student Organization; Model UN; Radio station; Student government.

ADMISSIONS
Freshman Academic Profile: Average high school GPA 85.0. 7% in top 10% of high school class, 25% in top 25% of high school class, 59% in top 50% of high school class. **Test Scores:** SAT Math middle 50% range 430-620. SAT EBRW middle 50% range 470-570. ACT middle 50% range 20-23. **Basis for Candidate Selection:** *Very important factors considered include:* rigor of secondary school record. *Important factors considered include:* academic GPA, standardized test scores. *Other factors considered include:* class rank, application essay, recommendation(s). **Freshman Admission Requirements:** High school diploma is required and GED is accepted *Academic units required:* 4 English, 3 math, 2 science, 1 science labs, 2 social studies, *Academic units recommended:* 4 math, 4 science, 1 history. **Freshman Admission Statistics:** 684 applied, 63.3% admitted, 46% enrolled. **General Admission Information:** Application fee $47. Nonfall registration accepted.

COSTS AND FINANCIAL AID
Annual out-of-state tuition $26,568. Room and board $10,598. Required fees $1,212. Average book expense $1,000. **Required Forms and Deadlines:** FAFSA; State aid form. **Types of Aid:** *Need-based scholarships/grants:* College/

university scholarship or grant aid from institutional funds; Federal Nursing Scholarships; Federal Pell; Private scholarships; SEOG; State scholarships/grants. *Loans:* Direct PLUS loans; Direct Subsidized Stafford Loans; Direct Unsubsidized Stafford Loans.

VILLA MARIA COLLEGE OF BUFFALO

240 Pine Ridge Road, Buffalo, NY 14225
Phone: 716-961-1805 • **Financial Aid Phone:** 716-961-1850
E-mail: admissions@villa.edu
Fax: 716-896-0705 • **ACT Code:** 2983

This private school, affiliated with the Roman Catholic Church, was founded in 1960. It has a 9 acre campus.

RATINGS
Admissions Selectivity Rating: 69   **Fire Safety Rating:** 60*   **Green Rating:** 60*

STUDENTS AND FACULTY
Enrollment: 469. **Student Body:** 68% female, 32% male, 3% out-of-state, 0% international (0 countries represented). Asian 1%, African American 26%, Caucasian 61%, Hispanic 6%, Native American <1%, Pacific Islander <1%, Two or more races 5%, Race unknown <1%.
Retention and Graduation: 59% freshmen return for sophomore year.
Faculty: Student/faculty ratio 8:1. 29 full-time faculty, 52% hold PhDs, 59% are women. 0% of classes are taught by teaching assistants.

ACADEMICS
Degrees: Associate; Bachelor's; Certificate **Classes:** Most classes have 20-29 students. Most lab/discussion sessions have 10-19 students. **Most popular majors:** Visual And Performing Arts, General; Physical Therapy Technician/Assistant. **Special Study Options:** Cross-registration; Double major; Dual enrollment; Internships; Liberal arts/career combination. **Disability Services offered to physically disabled students:** Tutors. **Career services:** Alumni services; Career assessment; Career/job search classes; Internships

FACILITIES
Housing: 80% of campus accessible to physically diasbled. **Special Academic Facilities/Equipment:** Art Gallery, Music Building, Recording Studio, Student Center, Athletic Center, Art Shop **Computers:** 100% of libraries, 100% of dining areas, have wireless network access. Students can register for classes online. Administrative functions (other than registration) can be performed online.

CAMPUS LIFE
Environment: City **Activities:** Campus Ministries; Choral groups; Jazz band; Literary magazine; Music ensembles; Student government 1 honor societies. **On-Campus Highlights:** Athletic/Student Center, Recording Studio, Art Gallery, Felician Hall

ADMISSIONS
Freshman Academic Profile: Average high school GPA 3.0. 28% in top 25% of high school class, 52% in top 50% of high school class. 93% from public high schools. **Test Scores:** Minimum internet-based TOEFL 133. Minimum paper TOEFL 450. **Basis for Candidate Selection:** *Very important factors considered include:* academic GPA, application essay, interview, talent/ability. *Important factors considered include:* level of applicant's interest. *Other factors considered include:* rigor of secondary school record, standardized test scores, recommendation(s), volunteer work, work experience. **Freshman Admission Requirements:** High school diploma is required and GED is accepted *Academic units recommended:* 4 English, 3 math, 3 science, 4 social studies, 4 history. **Freshman Admission Statistics:** 248 applied, 79.8% admitted, 55% enrolled. **Transfer Admission Requirements:** college transcript(s), interview, Lowest grade transferable C. **General Admission Information:** Nonfall registration accepted. Admission may be deferred for a maximum of 2 semesters.

COSTS AND FINANCIAL AID
Annual tuition $18,520. Required fees $650. **Required Forms and Deadlines:** FAFSA. **Notification of Awards:** Applicants will be notified of awards on a rolling basis beginning 2/15. **Types of Aid:** *Need-based scholarships/grants:* College/university scholarship or grant aid from institutional funds; Federal Pell; Private scholarships; SEOG; State scholarships/grants. *Loans: Student Employment:* Federal Work-Study Program available. **Financial Aid Statistics:** 98% needy freshmen, 99% needy undergrads receive need-based scholarship or grant aid. 49% freshmen, 78% undergrads receive

non-need-based scholarship or grant aid. 19% freshmen, 15% undergrads receive need-based self-help aid. 0% freshmen, 0% undergrads receive athletic scholarships. 99% freshmen, 92% undergrads receive any aid. **Criteria for awarding aid:** *Need-based:* Academics, Alumni affiliation, Art, Leadership *Non-need-based:* Academics, Alumni affiliation, Art, Leadership.

VILLANOVA UNIVERSITY

800 Lancaster Avenue, Villanova, PA 19085
Phone: 610-519-4000 • **Financial Aid Phone:** 610-519-4010
E-mail: gotovu@villanova.edu • **CEEB Code:** 2959
Fax: 610-519-6450 • **Website:** www.villanova.edu • **ACT Code:** 3744

This private school, affiliated with the Roman Catholic Church, was founded in 1842. It has a 254 acre campus.

RATINGS

Admissions Selectivity Rating: 96 **Fire Safety Rating:** 97 **Green Rating:** 92

STUDENTS AND FACULTY

Enrollment: 6,857. **Student Body:** 53% female, 47% male, 79% out-of-state, 2% international (49 countries represented). Asian 6%, African American 5%, Caucasian 74%, Hispanic 8%, Native American <1%, Pacific Islander 0%, Two or more races 3%, Race unknown 2%.
Retention and Graduation: 95% freshmen return for sophomore year. 87% freshmen graduate within 4 years. 90% freshmen graduate within 6 years. 23% grads go on to further study within 1 year. 7% grads pursue arts and sciences degrees. 5% grads pursue law degrees. 1% grads pursue business degrees. 2% grads pursue medical degrees. **Faculty:** Student/faculty ratio 11:1. 618 full-time faculty, 16% are members of minority groups, 40% are women. 1% of classes are taught by teaching assistants.

ACADEMICS

Degrees: Associate; Bachelor's; Doctoral/Professional; Doctoral/Research; Master's; Post-Bachelor's certificate; Post-Master's certificate **Classes:** Most classes have 10–19 students. Most lab/discussion sessions have fewer than 10 students. **Most popular majors:** Mass Communication/Media Studies; Registered Nursing/Registered Nurse; Finance, General. **Special Study Options:** Accelerated program; Cooperative education program; Cross-registration; Distance learning; Double major; Dual enrollment; English as a Second Language (ESL); External degree program; Honors program; Independent study; Internships; Liberal arts/career combination; Student-designed major; Study abroad; Teacher certification program. Honors programs: The Honors Program at Villanova stands at the forefront of Villanova's long commitment to excellence. Our outstanding faculty educates our gifted students to be the transformative leaders the world needs. We prepare our students for distinguished careers in law, politics, education, business, medicine, and many other fields. We encourage our Honors students to actively engage in the creation of culture, at Villanova, and beyond. We inspire them to connect their rich talents with a strong sense of their responsibility to lives of service. We are a community of learners who delight in the life of the mind and in each other. Honors students across all colleges at Villanova are challenged by a rigorous four-year comprehensive program of studies. They attend small, discussion-based seminars, undertake original research projects, and are mentored by nationally-renowned scholars. Our community values diverse backgrounds and perspectives, as well as international study. In short, Villanova is one of the nation's premier Catholic universities, and Honors students enjoy the best Villanova has to offer. The Honors Program seeks leaders who display sharp, critical intelligence; a passion for service; and a broad range of intellectual interests. Visit www.honorsprogram.villanova.edu to learn more about the opportunities an Honors education at Villanova affords. Combined degree programs: BA/MA. **Disability Services offered to physically disabled students:** Note-taking services; Reader services; Tape recorders; Tutors. **Career services:** Alumni network; Alumni services; Career assessment; Career/job search classes; Internships; Regional alumni

FACILITIES

Housing: Apartments for single students; Coed dorms; Special housing for disabled students 95% of campus accessible to physically disabled. **Special Academic Facilities/Equipment:** Driscoll Hall, home of the Villanova College of Nursing; the Villanova School of Business Applied Finance Lab; the Structural Engineering Teaching and Research Laboratory; the Augustinian

Historical Museum, and the Villanova Observatory. **Computers:** 90% of classrooms, 90% of dorms, 100% of libraries, 100% of dining areas, 100% of student union, 10% of common outdoor areas have wireless network access. Students can register for classes online. Administrative functions (other than registration) can be performed online. Undergraduates are required to own a computer.

CAMPUS LIFE

Environment: Village **Activities:** Campus Ministries; Choral groups; Concert band; Dance; Drama/theater; International Student Organization; Jazz band; Literary magazine; Marching band; Model UN; Music ensembles; Musical theater; Pep band; Radio station; Student government; Student newspaper; Student-run film society; Symphony orchestra; Television station; Yearbook 250 registered organizations, 34 honor societies, 15 religious organizations. 9 fraternities, 9 sororities. **Athletics (Intercollegiate):** *Men:* baseball, basketball, cheerleading, cross-country, diving, football, golf, lacrosse, soccer, swimming, tennis, track/field (outdoor), track/field (indoor). *Women:* basketball, cheerleading, crew/rowing, cross-country, diving, field hockey, lacrosse, soccer, softball, swimming, tennis, track/field (outdoor), track/field (indoor), volleyball, water polo. **On-Campus Highlights:** St. Thomas of Villanova Church, Davis Center for Athletics and Fitness, Villanova University Shop, Connelly Center and Cinema, Bartley Hall Exchange **Environmental Initiatives:** Academic programs: The master's degree in sustainable engineering; the first-year environmental leadership learning community; bachelor's degrees in environmental science and environmental studies; an undergraduate minor in sustainability; a biology master's degree, graduate certificate, and advanced graduate certificate with a concentration in ecology, evolution, and organismal biology; a master's degree in water resources and environmental engineering, and a graduate certificate in urban water resources design.

ADMISSIONS

Freshman Academic Profile: Average high school GPA 4.1. 65% in top 10% of high school class, 95% in top 25% of high school class, 98% in top 50% of high school class. 53% from public high schools. **Test Scores:** SAT Math middle 50% range 630–730. SAT EBRW middle 50% range 620–710. ACT middle 50% range 30–33. Minimum internet-based TOEFL 85 (IETLS 7). Minimum paper TOEFL 550. **Basis for Candidate Selection:** *Very important factors considered include:* rigor of secondary school record, class rank, academic GPA, standardized test scores. *Important factors considered include:* application essay, recommendation(s), extracurricular activities, talent/ability, character/personal qualities, volunteer work, work experience. *Other factors considered include:* first generation, alumni/ae relation, geographical residence, state residency, racial/ethnic status, level of applicant's interest. **Freshman Admission Requirements:** High school diploma is required and GED is accepted *Academic units required:* 4 English, 4 math, 4 science, 2 science labs, 2 foreign language, 2 academic electives, and 4 units from above areas or other academic areas. *Academic units recommended:* 4 English, 4 math, 4 science, 3 science labs, 4 foreign language, 2 academic electives, 4 units from above areas or other academic areas. **Freshman Admission Statistics:** 21,112 applied, 36.0% admitted, 23% enrolled. **Transfer Admission Requirements:** High school transcript, college transcript(s), essay or personal statement, standardized test scores, statement of good standing from prior institution(s). Lowest grade transferable C. **General Admission Information:** Application fee $80. Priority deadline 12/15. Regular application deadline 1/15. Admission may be deferred for a maximum of 1 year.

COSTS AND FINANCIAL AID

Annual tuition $50,554. Room and board $13,548. Required fees $670. Average book expense $1,100. **Required Forms and Deadlines:** CSS/Financial Aid PROFILE. **Notification of Awards:** Applicants will be notified of awards on or about 4/1. **Types of Aid:** *Need-based scholarships/grants:* College/university scholarship or grant aid from institutional funds; Federal Pell; Private scholarships; SEOG; State scholarships/grants. *Loans:* Direct PLUS loans; Direct Subsidized Stafford Loans; Direct Unsubsidized Stafford Loans. *Student Employment:* Federal Work-Study Program available. Institutional employment available. **Financial Aid Statistics:** 91% needy freshmen, 91% needy undergrads receive need-based scholarship or grant aid. 24% freshmen, 27% undergrads receive non-need-based scholarship or grant aid. 86% freshmen, 87% undergrads receive need-based self-help aid. 3% freshmen, 3% undergrads receive athletic scholarships. 67% freshmen, 68% undergrads receive any aid. 55% undergrads borrow to pay for school. Average cumulative indebtedness $33,588. **Criteria for awarding aid:** *Need-based:* Religious affiliation *Non-need-based:* Academics, Alumni affiliation, Athletics, Leadership, Minority status, Religious affiliation.

VIRGINIA COMMONWEALTH UNIVERSITY

Box 842527, Richmond, VA 23284
Phone: 804-828-1222 • **Financial Aid Phone:** 804-828-6669
E-mail: upgrad@vcu.edu • **CEEB Code:** 5570
Fax: 804-828-1899 • **Website:** www.vcu.edu

This public school was founded in 1838. It has a 150.2 acre campus.

RATINGS
Admissions Selectivity Rating: 80   **Fire Safety Rating:** 94   **Green Rating:** 98

STUDENTS AND FACULTY
Enrollment: 22,563. **Student Body:** 60% female, 40% male, 7% out-of-state, 3% international (77 countries represented). Asian 13%, African American 19%, Caucasian 46%, Hispanic 9%, Native American <1%, Pacific Islander <1%, Two or more races 6%, Race unknown 3%.
Retention and Graduation: 83% freshmen return for sophomore year. 40% freshmen graduate within 4 years. 63% freshmen graduate within 6 years. **Faculty:** Student/faculty ratio 18:1. 1,242 full-time faculty, 22% are members of minority groups, 49% are women.

ACADEMICS
Degrees: Bachelor's; Certificate; Doctoral/Professional; Doctoral/Research; Master's; Post-Bachelor's certificate; Post-Master's certificate **Classes:** Most classes have 10-19 students. Most lab/discussion sessions have 10-19 students. **Most popular majors:** Biology/Biological Sciences, General; Health And Physical Education/Fitness, General; Psychology, General. **Special Study Options:** Accelerated program; Cooperative education program; Distance learning; Double major; Dual enrollment; English as a Second Language (ESL); Honors program; Independent study; Internships; Student-designed major; Study abroad; Teacher certification program. Honors programs: VCU Honors College—students gain a small, liberal arts college experience while being fully engaged in a large, urban university. The students will be part of a diverse and supportive community of students, faculty, and staff who will ease your transition from high school to college. Take small, discussion-based classes in place of larger, more lecture-oriented classes, giving you the opportunity to engage more closely with your classmates and more meaningfully with our outstanding faculty. Engage in local community service and have unique study-abroad options. Have an Honors advisor in addition to the advisor in your major. Gain access to special housing and scholarships. Receive early registration privileges. enjoy unique professional development opportunities. students come from all majors and participate in a wide variety of activities and organizations on and off campus, typically in leadership positions. Combined degree programs: BA/DDS; BA/MD. **Disability Services offered to physically disabled students:** Note-taking services; Reader services; Tape recorders; Tutors. **Career services:** Alumni network; Alumni services; Career assessment; Career/job search classes; Internships; Regional alumni

FACILITIES
Housing: Apartments for single students; Coed dorms; Special housing for disabled student; Special housing for international students; Theme housing; Wellness housing 90% of campus accessible to physically diasbled. **Special Academic Facilities/Equipment:** Anderson Gallery, Student Art Gallery, Larrick Student Center, Shafer Ct. Dining Facilities, Student Commons, Siegel Center, Cabell Library, Biotech Research Bldgs., Tompkins McCaw Library,VCU Bookstores and the Rice Center **Computers:** 75% of classrooms, 100% of dorms, 100% of libraries, 100% of dining areas, 100% of student union, 25% of common outdoor areas have wireless network access. Students can register for classes online. Administrative functions (other than registration) can be performed online. Undergraduates are required to own a computer.

CAMPUS LIFE
Environment: Metropolis **Activities:** Campus Ministries; Choral groups; Concert band; Dance; Drama/theater; International Student Organization; Jazz band; Literary magazine; Model UN; Music ensembles; Musical theater; Opera; Pep band; Radio station; Student government; Student newspaper; Student-run film society; Symphony orchestra 377 registered organizations, 30 religious organizations. 22 fraternities, 13 sororities. **Athletics (Intercollegiate):** *Men:* baseball, basketball, cross-country, golf, soccer, tennis, track/field (outdoor). *Women:* basketball, cross-country, field hockey, soccer, tennis, track/field (outdoor), volleyball. **On-Campus Highlights:** Student Commons, Cabell Library, Siegel Center, Anderson Gallery, Shafer Court

ADMISSIONS
Freshman Academic Profile: Average high school GPA 3.6. 17% in top 10% of high school class, 29% in top 25% of high school class, 46% in top 50% of high school class. **Test Scores:** SAT Math middle 50% range 520-620. SAT

EBRW middle 50% range 556-672. ACT middle 50% range 21-28. Minimum internet-based TOEFL 80. Minimum paper TOEFL 550. **Basis for Candidate Selection:** *Very important factors considered include:* rigor of secondary school record, academic GPA. *Important factors considered include:* application essay. *Other factors considered include:* class rank, standardized test scores, recommendation(s), extracurricular activities, talent/ability, character/personal qualities, first generation, geographical residence, volunteer work. **Freshman Admission Requirements:** High school diploma is required and GED is accepted *Academic units required:* 4 English, 3 math, 3 science, 1 science labs, 2 foreign language, 1 social studies, 2 history, *Academic units recommended:* 4 English, 4 math, 4 science, 1 science labs, 3 foreign language, 1 social studies, 3 history, 1 visual/performing arts. **Freshman Admission Statistics:** 16,847 applied, 76.6% admitted, 33% enrolled. **Transfer Admission Requirements:** college transcript(s), Minimum college GPA of 2.25 required. Lowest grade transferable C. **General Admission Information:** Application fee $65. Nonfall registration accepted. Admission may be deferred.

COSTS AND FINANCIAL AID
Required Forms and Deadlines: FAFSA. **Notification of Awards:** Applicants will be notified of awards on a rolling basis beginning 4/1. **Types of Aid:** *Need-based scholarships/grants:* College/university scholarship or grant aid from institutional funds; Federal Nursing Scholarships; Federal Pell; Private scholarships; SEOG; State scholarships/grants; United Negro College Fund. *Loans:* Direct PLUS loans; Direct Subsidized Stafford Loans; Direct Unsubsidized Stafford Loans. *Student Employment:* Federal Work-Study Program available. Institutional employment available. **Financial Aid Statistics:** 68% needy freshmen, 68% needy undergrads receive need-based scholarship or grant aid. 28% freshmen, 19% undergrads receive non-need-based scholarship or grant aid. 77% freshmen, 84% undergrads receive need-based self-help aid. 2% freshmen, 1% undergrads receive athletic scholarships. 77% freshmen, 65% undergrads receive any aid. 63% undergrads borrow to pay for school. Average cumulative indebtedness $31,512. **Criteria for awarding aid:** *Need-based:* Academics *Non-need-based:* Academics, Alumni affiliation, Art, Athletics, Leadership, Music/drama.

VIRGINIA MILITARY INSTITUTE

VMI Office of Admissions, Lexington, VA 24450-0304
Phone: 540-464-7211 • **Financial Aid Phone:** 540-464-7208
E-mail: admissions@vmi.edu • **CEEB Code:** 5858
Fax: 540-464-7746 • **Website:** www.vmi.edu • **ACT Code:** 4418

This public school was founded in 1839. It has a 140 acre campus.

RATINGS
Admissions Selectivity Rating: 89   **Fire Safety Rating:** 79   **Green Rating:** 60*

STUDENTS AND FACULTY
Enrollment: 1,722. **Student Body:** 12% female, 88% male, 36% out-of-state, 2% international (9 countries represented). Asian 4%, African American 6%, Caucasian 79%, Hispanic 7%, Native American 1%, Pacific Islander <1%, Two or more races 1%, Race unknown <1%.
Retention and Graduation: 87% freshmen return for sophomore year. 63% freshmen graduate within 4 years. 77% freshmen graduate within 6 years. 8% grads go on to further study within 1 year. 3% grads pursue arts and sciences degrees. 2% grads pursue law degrees. 1% grads pursue business degrees. 1% grads pursue medical degrees. **Faculty:** Student/faculty ratio 11:1. 136 full-time faculty, 97% hold PhDs, 14% are members of minority groups, 35% are women. 0% of classes are taught by teaching assistants.

ACADEMICS
Degrees: Bachelor's **Classes:** Most classes have 10-19 students. Most lab/discussion sessions have 10-19 students. **Most popular majors:** Mechanical Engineering; Business/Managerial Economics; History, General. **Special Study Options:** Cross-registration; Double major; Honors program; Independent study; Internships; Study abroad. Honors programs: Institute Honors Program, departmental honors programs. **Career services:** Alumni network; Career assessment; Career/job search classes; Internships

FACILITIES
Housing: 50% of campus accessible to physically diasbled. **Special Academic Facilities/Equipment:** VMI Museum George C. Marshall Museum **Computers:** Students can register for classes online. Administrative functions (other than registration) can be performed online.

CAMPUS LIFE
Environment: Village **Activities:** Campus Ministries; Choral groups; Concert band; Dance; Drama/theater; International Student Organization;

Jazz band; Literary magazine; Marching band; Music ensembles; Musical theater; Pep band; Student government; Student newspaper; Yearbook 50 registered organizations, 11 honor societies, 3 religious organizations. **Athletics (Intercollegiate):** *Men:* baseball, basketball, cross-country, football, golf, lacrosse, riflery, soccer, swimming, track/field (outdoor), track/field (indoor), wrestling. *Women:* cross-country, riflery, soccer, swimming, track/field (outdoor), track/field (indoor). **On-Campus Highlights:** VMI Museum, George C. Marshall Museum

ADMISSIONS

Freshman Academic Profile: Average high school GPA 3.7. 15% in top 10% of high school class, 45% in top 25% of high school class, 81% in top 50% of high school class. 84% from public high schools. **Test Scores:** SAT Math middle 50% range 540-640. SAT EBRW middle 50% range 560-640. ACT middle 50% range 23-28. Minimum paper TOEFL 500. **Basis for Candidate Selection:** *Very important factors considered include:* rigor of secondary school record, class rank, standardized test scores, character/personal qualities. *Important factors considered include:* interview, extracurricular activities, state residency, racial/ethnic status, volunteer work. *Other factors considered include:* application essay, recommendation(s), talent/ability, alumni/ae relation, geographical residence, work experience, level of applicant's interest. **Freshman Admission Requirements:** High school diploma is required and GED is not accepted *Academic units required:* 4 English, 3 math, 3 science, 3 science labs, 3 foreign language, 2 social studies, 1 history, *Academic units recommended:* 4 English, 4 math, 4 science, 4 science labs, 4 foreign language, 2 social studies, 1 history. **Freshman Admission Statistics:** 1,718 applied, 53.1% admitted, 49% enrolled. **Transfer Admission Requirements:** High school transcript, college transcript(s), standardized test scores, Minimum college GPA of 2.0 required. Lowest grade transferable C. **General Admission Information:** Application fee $40. Regular application deadline 2/1. Nonfall registration accepted.

COSTS AND FINANCIAL AID

Average book expense $1,000. **Required Forms and Deadlines:** FAFSA; Institution's own financial aid form. **Notification of Awards:** Applicants will be notified of awards on or about 3/15. **Types of Aid:** *Need-based scholarships/grants:* College/university scholarship or grant aid from institutional funds; Federal Pell; Private scholarships; SEOG; State scholarships/grants. *Loans:* Direct PLUS loans; Direct Subsidized Stafford Loans; Direct Unsubsidized Stafford Loans. **Financial Aid Statistics:** 75% needy freshmen, 75% needy undergrads receive need-based scholarship or grant aid. 27% freshmen, 28% undergrads receive non-need-based scholarship or grant aid. 43% freshmen, 48% undergrads receive need-based self-help aid. 11% freshmen, 7% undergrads receive athletic scholarships. 85% freshmen, 82% undergrads receive any aid. **Criteria for awarding aid:** *Need-based:* Academics *Non-need-based:* Academics, Alumni affiliation, Athletics, Leadership, Music/drama.

VIRGINIA STATE UNIVERSITY

One Hayden Drive, Petersburg, VA 23806
Phone: 804-524-5902 • **Financial Aid Phone:** (804) 524-5990
E-mail: admiss@vsu.edu • **CEEB Code:** 5860
Fax: 804-524-5055 • **Website:** www.vsu.edu • **ACT Code:** 4424

This public school was founded in 1882. It has a 246 acre campus.

RATINGS

Admissions Selectivity Rating: 72   **Fire Safety Rating:** 60*   **Green Rating:** 60*

STUDENTS AND FACULTY

Enrollment: 4,481. **Student Body:** 60% female, 40% male, 32% out-of-state, <1% international (29 countries represented). Asian <1%, African American 85%, Caucasian 3%, Hispanic 2%, Native American <1%, Pacific Islander 0%, Two or more races 0%, Race unknown 9%.
Retention and Graduation: 61% freshmen return for sophomore year. **Faculty:** Student/faculty ratio 13:1. 296 full-time faculty, 42% are women. 0% of classes are taught by teaching assistants.

ACADEMICS

Degrees: Associate; Bachelor's; Doctoral/Research; Master's; Post-Bachelor's certificate **Classes:** Most classes have 10-19 students. Most lab/discussion sessions have 10-19 students. **Most popular majors:** Physical Education Teaching And Coaching; Liberal Arts And Sciences/Liberal Studies; Sociology. **Special Study Options:** Cooperative education program; Double major; Dual enrollment; Honors program; Independent study; Internships; Study abroad; Teacher certification program. **Disability Services offered to physically**

disabled students: Note-taking services; Reader services; Tutors. **Career services:** Alumni network; Internships

FACILITIES

Housing: Apartments for single students; Coed dorms; Men's dorms; Women's dorms 90% of campus accessible to physically diasbled. **Computers:** Administrative functions (other than registration) can be performed online.

CAMPUS LIFE

Environment: Town **Activities:** Campus Ministries; Choral groups; Concert band; Dance; Drama/theater; Jazz band; Literary magazine; Marching band; Music ensembles; Pep band; Radio station; Student government; Student newspaper; Television station; Yearbook 70 registered organizations, 6 honor societies, 4 religious organizations. 5 fraternities, 4 sororities. **Athletics (Intercollegiate):** *Men:* baseball, basketball, cheerleading, cross-country, football, golf, tennis, track/field (outdoor), track/field (indoor). *Women:* basketball, bowling, cheerleading, cross-country, golf, softball, tennis, track/field (outdoor), track/field (indoor), volleyball.

ADMISSIONS

Freshman Academic Profile: Average high school GPA 2.9. 3% in top 10% of high school class, 17% in top 25% of high school class, 53% in top 50% of high school class. **Test Scores:** SAT Math middle 50% range 380-460. SAT EBRW middle 50% range 380-460. ACT middle 50% range 15-19. Minimum paper TOEFL 500. **Basis for Candidate Selection:** *Very important factors considered include:* rigor of secondary school record, academic GPA, standardized test scores. *Important factors considered include:* application essay, recommendation(s). *Other factors considered include:* extracurricular activities, talent/ability, character/personal qualities, first generation, alumni/ae relation, geographical residence, state residency, volunteer work, work experience. **Freshman Admission Requirements:** High school diploma is required and GED is accepted *Academic units required:* 4 English, 3 math, 2 science, 1 science labs, 2 history, *Academic units recommended:* 2 foreign language, 2 social studies. **Freshman Admission Statistics:** 5,923 applied, 80.1% admitted, 19% enrolled. **Transfer Admission Requirements:** college transcript(s), essay or personal statement, statement of good standing from prior institution(s). Minimum college GPA of 2.0 required. Lowest grade transferable C. **General Admission Information:** Application fee $25. Priority deadline 3/31. Regular application deadline 5/1. Nonfall registration accepted.

COSTS AND FINANCIAL AID

Annual in-state tuition $10,128. Annual out-of-state tuition $14,132. Room and board $10,128. Required fees $3,126. Average book expense $1,300. **Required Forms and Deadlines:** FAFSA; Institution's own financial aid form. **Notification of Awards:** Applicants will be notified of awards on a rolling basis beginning 3/1. **Types of Aid:** *Need-based scholarships/grants:* College/university scholarship or grant aid from institutional funds; Federal Pell; Private scholarships; SEOG; State scholarships/grants. *Loans:* Direct PLUS loans; Direct Subsidized Stafford Loans; Direct Unsubsidized Stafford Loans. *Student Employment:* Federal Work-Study Program available. Institutional employment available. **Financial Aid Statistics:** 80% needy freshmen, 80% needy undergrads receive need-based scholarship or grant aid. 22% freshmen, 22% undergrads receive non-need-based scholarship or grant aid. 72% freshmen, 72% undergrads receive need-based self-help aid. 3% freshmen, 3% undergrads receive athletic scholarships. **Criteria for awarding aid:** *Need-based:* Academics, Alumni affiliation, Art, Athletics, Leadership, Minority status *Non-need-based:* Academics, Alumni affiliation, Art, Athletics, Job skills, Leadership, Minority status, Music/drama, Religious affiliation.

VIRGINIA TECH

800 Drillfield Drive, Blacksburg, VA 24061
Phone: 540-231-6267 • **Financial Aid Phone:** 540-231-5179
E-mail: admissions@vt.edu • **CEEB Code:** 5859
Fax: 540-231-3242 • **Website:** www.vt.edu • **ACT Code:** 4420

This public school was founded in 1872. It has a 2600 acre campus.

RATINGS

Admissions Selectivity Rating: 87   **Fire Safety Rating:** 87   **Green Rating:** 96

STUDENTS AND FACULTY

Enrollment: 27,120. **Student Body:** 43% female, 57% male, 24% out-of-state, 6% international (116 countries represented). Asian 10%, African American 4%,

Caucasian 66%, Hispanic 6%, Native American <1%, Pacific Islander <1%, Two or more races 4%, Race unknown 3%.
Retention and Graduation: 93% freshmen return for sophomore year. 63% freshmen graduate within 4 years. 84% freshmen graduate within 6 years. 31% grads go on to further study within 1 year. **Faculty:** Student/faculty ratio 14:1. 1,806 full-time faculty, 91% hold PhDs, 19% are members of minority groups, 34% are women.

ACADEMICS
Degrees: Associate; Bachelor's; Doctoral/Professional; Doctoral/Research; Master's; Post-Bachelor's certificate; Post-Master's certificate **Classes:** Most classes have fewer than 10 students. Most lab/discussion sessions have 10-19 students. **Most popular majors:** Engineering, General; Biology/Biological Sciences, General; Business Administration And Management, General. **Special Study Options:** Accelerated program; Cooperative education program; Distance learning; Double major; English as a Second Language (ESL); Honors program; Independent study; Internships; Liberal arts/career combination; Study abroad; Teacher certification program. Combined degree programs: BA/MA. **Disability Services offered to physically disabled students:** Note-taking services; Reader services; Tape recorders; Tutors. **Career services:** Alumni network; Alumni services; Career assessment; Career/job search classes; Internships

FACILITIES
Housing: Coed dorms; Fraternity/sorority housing; Men's dorms; Special housing for disabled student; Theme housing; Wellness housing; Women's dorms 60% of campus accessible to physically diasbled. **Special Academic Facilities/Equipment:** Art gallery, digital music facilities, multimedia labs, Black Cultural Center, television studio, anaerobic lab, CAD-CAM labs, observatory, wind tunnel, farms, Math Emporium, the CAVE (virtual reality learning facility), Virtual Reality Cave, New Center for the Arts **Computers:** Students can register for classes online. Administrative functions (other than registration) can be performed online. Undergraduates are required to own a computer.

CAMPUS LIFE
Environment: Town **Activities:** Campus Ministries; Choral groups; Concert band; Dance; Drama/theater; International Student Organization; Jazz band; Literary magazine; Marching band; Model UN; Music ensembles; Musical theater; Opera; Pep band; Radio station; Student government; Student newspaper; Student-run film society; Television station; Yearbook 600 registered organizations, 32 honor societies, 53 religious organizations. 31 fraternities, 12 sororities. **Athletics (Intercollegiate):** *Men:* baseball, basketball, cheerleading, cross-country, diving, football, golf, soccer, swimming, tennis, track/field (outdoor), track/field (indoor), ultimate frisbee, water polo. *Women:* basketball, cheerleading, cross-country, diving, lacrosse, soccer, softball, swimming, tennis, track/field (outdoor), track/field (indoor), ultimate frisbee, volleyball, water polo. The Pylons, Drillfield, Goodwin Hall, Squires Student Center, Newman Library **Environmental Initiatives:** The "Virginia Tech Climate Action Commitment" and Sustainability Plan Implementation" Virginia Tech is committed to being a Leader in Campus Sustainability. In April 2008 former Virginia Tech President Charles W. Steger charged the Energy and Sustainability Committee to develop a climate commitment and accompanying sustainability plan that was unique to our university. The "Virginia Tech Climate Action Commitment & Sustainability Plan (VTCAC&SP)" was developed as a comprehensive working document that addressed specific actions to be implemented in six broad sustainability categories to include: administrative structure and governance, facilities infrastructure, facilities operations, transportation, behavior and campus life, and academic programs. On June 1, 2009 the Virginia Tech Board of Visitors unanimously approved "The Virginia Tech Climate Action Commitment" and it became university policy (Presidential Policy Memorandum No. 262). The VTCAC contained 14 specific points and included the establishment of greenhouse gas emission reduction targets, the pursuit of USGBC LEED Silver ratings or higher for all future new construction and major renovations projects, and the creation of a sustainability office to oversee the implementation of our sustainability plan and to coordinate programs for campus sustainability and outreach. The Office of Energy and Sustainability established and maintained a comprehensive system to track our sustainability progress in over 100 specific areas of interest. During academic year 2012-13 the Energy and Sustainability Committee revised the VTCAC to take advantage of the many successes achieved and lessons learned in the initial three years of implementation. On May 6, 2013 University Council approved the "Update to the Virginia Tech Climate Action Commitment" (Presidential Policy Memorandum No. 262, Rev 1). See: http://www.it.vpas.vt.edu/docs/sust/op18/PPM262rev1.pdf Virginia Tech is a charter member of the AASHE's "Sustainability, Tracking, Assessment, and Rating System (STARS)." STARS is nationally recognized in higher education as the best management and reporting tool available to evaluate the effectiveness of your sustainability program. During academic year 2014-15, the Energy and Sustainability Committee reviewed and updated the VTCAC&SP. In the "2014 Update and Supplement to the 2009 VTCAC&SP" the university has decided to have the AASHE STARS Program serve as our primary "Sustainability Plan" with additions based on initiatives that are unique to Virginia Tech. See: http://www.it.vpas.vt.edu/docs/sust/PA2/2014_SP_SupplementWithAppendices.pdf On October 15, 2014 Virginia Tech received a STARS "Gold Rating" (version 1.2). Our overall score of 71.02 points placed the university in the top 10% of the nearly 300 colleges and universities having received a STARS rating as of that point in time. See: https://stars.aashe.org/institutions/virginia-tech-va/report/2014-10-15/ In addition to receiving recognition at the national level, Virginia Tech is the recipient of six Governor's Environment Excellence Awards during the period 2008 through 2015 (two Gold and four Bronze), and this represents the most of any college or university in the Commonwealth of Virginia.

ADMISSIONS
Freshman Academic Profile: Average high school GPA 4.0. 38% in top 10% of high school class, 77% in top 25% of high school class, 98% in top 50% of high school class. **Test Scores:** SAT Math middle 50% range 590-690. SAT EBRW middle 50% range 590-670. ACT middle 50% range 25-30. Minimum paper TOEFL 550. **Basis for Candidate Selection:** *Very important factors considered include:* rigor of secondary school record, academic GPA, standardized test scores. *Other factors considered include:* application essay, recommendation(s), extracurricular activities, talent/ability, character/personal qualities, first generation, alumni/ae relation, geographical residence, state residency, racial/ethnic status, volunteer work, work experience, level of applicant's interest. **Freshman Admission Requirements:** High school diploma is required and GED is accepted *Academic units required:* 4 English, 3 math, 2 science, 2 science labs, 1 social studies, 1 history, 4 academic electives, *Academic units recommended:* 4 math, 3 science, 3 foreign language. **Freshman Admission Statistics:** 27,423 applied, 70.1% admitted, 36% enrolled. **Transfer Admission Requirements:** High school transcript, college transcript(s), Minimum college GPA of 3.0 required. Lowest grade transferable C. **General Admission Information:** Application fee $60. Regular application deadline 1/15. Nonfall registration accepted. Admission may be deferred for a maximum of 1 year.

COSTS AND FINANCIAL AID
Annual in-state tuition $8,690. Annual out-of-state tuition $28,273. Room and board $8,690. Required fees $2,137. Average book expense $1,150. **Required Forms and Deadlines:** FAFSA. **Notification of Awards:** Applicants will be notified of awards on or about 4/1. **Types of Aid:** *Need-based scholarships/grants:* College/university scholarship or grant aid from institutional funds; Federal Nursing Scholarships; Federal Pell; Private scholarships; SEOG; State scholarships/grants; United Negro College Fund. *Loans:* Direct PLUS loans; Direct Subsidized Stafford Loans; Direct Unsubsidized Stafford Loans. *Student Employment:* Federal Work-Study Program available. Institutional employment available. **Financial Aid Statistics:** 65% needy freshmen, 71% needy undergrads receive need-based scholarship or grant aid. 50% freshmen, 37% undergrads receive non-need-based scholarship or grant aid. 82% freshmen, 83% undergrads receive need-based self-help aid. 2% freshmen, 2% undergrads receive athletic scholarships. 75% undergrads receive any aid. 53% undergrads borrow to pay for school. Average cumulative indebtedness $28,873. **Criteria for awarding aid:** *Need-based:* Academics, Art, Leadership, Minority status, Music/drama *Non-need-based:* Academics, Art, Athletics, Leadership, Minority status, Music/drama, State/district residency.

VIRGINIA WESLEYAN COLLEGE

5817 Wesleyan Drive, Virginia Beach, VA 23455
Phone: 757-455-3208 • **Financial Aid Phone:** 757-455-3345
E-mail: admissions@vwu.edu • **CEEB Code:** 5867
Fax: 757-461-5238 • **Website:** www.vwu.edu • **ACT Code:** 4429

This private school, affiliated with the Methodist Church, was founded in 1961. It has a 300 acre campus.

RATINGS
Admissions Selectivity Rating: 79   **Fire Safety Rating:** 79   **Green Rating:** 86

STUDENTS AND FACULTY
Enrollment: 1,369. **Student Body:** 60% female, 40% male, 26% out-of-state, 1% international (9 countries represented). Asian 1%, African American 27%, Caucasian 49%, Hispanic 9%, Native American 1%, Pacific Islander <1%, Two or more races 7%, Race unknown 5%.

Retention and Graduation: 63% freshmen return for sophomore year. 46% freshmen graduate within 4 years. 52% freshmen graduate within 6 years. 32% grads go on to further study within 1 year. 1% grads pursue law degrees. 1% grads pursue business degrees. **Faculty:** Student/faculty ratio 12:1. 91 full-time faculty, 92% hold PhDs, 11% are members of minority groups, 46% are women. 0% of classes are taught by teaching assistants.

ACADEMICS

Degrees: Bachelor's; Certificate; **Master's Classes:** Most classes have 10-19 students. Most lab/discussion sessions have fewer than 10 students. **Most popular majors:** Criminal Justice/Safety Studies; Social Sciences, General; Business Administration And Management, General. **Special Study Options:** Cross-registration; Double major; Honors program; Independent study; Internships; Liberal arts/career combination; Student-designed major; Study abroad; Teacher certification program. Honors programs: Wesleyan Scholars is an honors program which is designed for applicants with superior high school achievement records. The Honors and Scholars program, including Wesleyan Scholars, offers academically challenging honors courses and stimulating co-curricular experiences. Program enhancement is also offered through PORTfolio, a selective program designed to integrate the liberal arts with experiential learning opportunities available in Hampton Roads. **Disability Services offered to physically disabled students:** Note-taking services; Reader services; Tape recorders; Tutors. **Career services:** Alumni network; Career/job search classes; Internships; Regional alumni

FACILITIES

Housing: Apartments for single students; Coed dorms; Fraternity/sorority housing; Special housing for disabled student; Theme housing; Wellness housing; Women's dorms 90% of campus accessible to physically disabled. **Special Academic Facilities/Equipment:** Greenhouse, language lab, teleconferencing facility, social science teach. and learn. lab, radio station, TV studio, Barclay Sheaks Art Gallery, computerized classrooms, Internet access all classrooms, 24-hr. computer lab, Lambuth M. Clarke Hall with state-of-the-art teaching technologies, three academic villages combining residences and campus offices and services. **Computers:** 20% of classrooms, 100% of libraries, 100% of student union, have wireless network access. Students can register for classes online. Administrative functions (other than registration) can be performed online.

CAMPUS LIFE

Environment: Metropolis **Activities:** Campus Ministries; Choral groups; Dance; Drama/theater; International Student Organization; Literary magazine; Marching band; Model UN; Music ensembles; Musical theater; Radio station; Student government; Student newspaper; Yearbook 60 registered organizations, 19 honor societies, 4 religious organizations. 3 fraternities, 4 sororities. **Athletics (Intercollegiate):** *Men:* baseball, basketball, cross-country, golf, lacrosse, soccer, tennis, track/field (outdoor), track/field (indoor). *Women:* basketball, cheerleading, cross-country, field hockey, lacrosse, soccer, softball, tennis, track/field (outdoor), track/field (indoor), volleyball. **On-Campus Highlights:** Jane P. Batten Student Center, Trinder Athletic Center, The Marlin Restaurant, Alpine Tower, Lake Taylor **Environmental Initiatives:** Green Roof

ADMISSIONS

Freshman Academic Profile: Average high school GPA 3.2. 15% in top 10% of high school class, 33% in top 25% of high school class, 63% in top 50% of high school class. 86% from public high schools. **Test Scores:** SAT Math middle 50% range 463-570. SAT EBRW middle 50% range 490-590. ACT middle 50% range 19-25. **Basis for Candidate Selection:** *Very important factors considered include:* rigor of secondary school record, academic GPA, standardized test scores, level of applicant's interest. *Important factors considered include:* extracurricular activities. *Other factors considered include:* recommendation(s), interview, talent/ability, character/personal qualities, first generation, alumni/ae relation, volunteer work, work experience. **Freshman Admission Requirements:** High school diploma is required and GED is accepted *Academic units required:* 4 English, 3 math, 2 science, 2 science labs, 2 foreign language, 1 history, 1 computer science, *Academic units recommended:* 4 English, 3 math, 2 science, 2 science labs, 2 foreign language, 1 history, 4 academic electives, 1 computer science. **Freshman Admission Statistics:** 2,200 applied, 70.9% admitted, 27% enrolled. **Transfer Admission Requirements:** High school transcript, college transcript(s), essay or personal statement, statement of good standing from prior institution(s). Minimum college GPA of 2.5 required. Lowest grade transferable C. **General Admission Information:** Priority deadline 3/1. Nonfall registration accepted. Admission may be deferred for a maximum of 1 term.

COSTS AND FINANCIAL AID

Annual tuition $36,010. Room and board $9,256. Required fees $650. Average book expense $1,500. **Required Forms and Deadlines:** FAFSA; State aid form. **Notification of Awards:** Applicants will be notified of awards on a rolling basis beginning 10/15. **Types of Aid:** *Need-based scholarships/grants:* College/

university scholarship or grant aid from institutional funds; Federal Pell; Private scholarships; SEOG; State scholarships/grants; Direct Subsidized Stafford Loans; Direct Unsubsidized Stafford Loans. *Student Employment:* Federal Work-Study Program available. Institutional employment available. **Financial Aid Statistics:** 100% needy freshmen, 100% needy undergrads receive need-based scholarship or grant aid. 19% freshmen, 17% undergrads receive non-need-based scholarship or grant aid. 78% freshmen, 78% undergrads receive need-based self-help aid. 0% freshmen, 0% undergrads receive athletic scholarships. 99% freshmen, 98% undergrads receive any aid. **Criteria for awarding aid:** *Need-based:* Art, Job skills, Music/drama *Non-need-based:* Academics, Alumni affiliation, Leadership, Religious affiliation, State/district residency.

VITERBO UNIVERSITY

900 Viterbo Drive, La Crosse, WI 54601
Phone: 608-796-3010 • **Financial Aid Phone:** 608-496-3900
E-mail: admission@viterbo.edu • **CEEB Code:** 1878
Fax: 608-796-3020 • **ACT Code:** 4662

This private school, affiliated with the Roman Catholic Church, was founded in 1890. It has a 25 acre campus.

RATINGS

Admissions Selectivity Rating: 73   **Fire Safety Rating:** 73   **Green Rating:** 60*

STUDENTS AND FACULTY

Enrollment: 1,922. **Student Body:** 71% female, 29% male, 19% out-of-state, 1% international (15 countries represented). Asian 1%, African American 1%, Caucasian 93%, Hispanic 1%, Native American 1%, Race unknown 2%. **Retention and Graduation:** 74% freshmen return for sophomore year. 7% grads go on to further study within 1 year. 4% grads pursue arts and sciences degrees. 1% grads pursue law degrees. 0% grads pursue business degrees. 2% grads pursue medical degrees. **Faculty:** Student/faculty ratio 13:1. 110 full-time faculty, 56% hold PhDs, 4% are members of minority groups, 56% are women. 0% of classes are taught by teaching assistants.

ACADEMICS

Degrees: Associate; Bachelor's; Master's; Post-Bachelor's certificate; Terminal Associate; Transfer Associate **Classes:** Most classes have 10-19 students. **Most popular majors:** Elementary Education And Teaching; Nursing/Registered Nurse (Rn, Asn, Bsn, Msn); Business Administration And Management, General. **Special Study Options:** Accelerated program; Cross-registration; Distance learning; Double major; Dual enrollment; Honors program; Independent study; Internships; Liberal arts/career combination; Student-designed major; Study abroad; Teacher certification program; Weekend college. Honors programs: The mission of the Viterbo University Honors Program is to provide a supportive, enriched learning environment responsive to the educational needs of highly able and exceptionally motivated undergraduate students who are committed to achieving academic excellence. The program provides honors sections of regular, general education courses, honors credit within regular sections, interdisciplinary Honors Capstone courses, oversight of senior honors projects, and increased opportunity for undergraduate research and creative activity. The program complements and enhances the Liberal Arts mission of the university. Together, honors students and faculty constitute a community of scholars. **Disability Services offered to physically disabled students:** Note-taking services; Reader services; Tape recorders; Tutors. **Career services:** Alumni network; Alumni services; Career assessment; Career/job search classes; Internships; Regional alumni

FACILITIES

Housing: Apartments for single students; Coed dorms; Other (please specify) 90% of campus accessible to physically disabled. **Special Academic Facilities/Equipment:** Fine Arts Center; Center for Ethics, Science and Technology with distance education labs and video conferencing; Nursing center with labs and simulated equipment; new recreation and education center co-sponsored by Viterbo University and the Boys and Girls Club **Computers:** Students can register for classes online. Administrative functions (other than registration) can be performed online.

CAMPUS LIFE

Environment: Town **Activities:** Choral groups; Dance; Drama/theater; Literary magazine; Music ensembles; Musical theater; Opera; Pep band; Student government; Student newspaper 22 registered organizations, 2 honor societies, 2 religious organizations. **Athletics (Intercollegiate):** *Men:* baseball, basketball, golf, soccer. *Women:* basketball, golf, soccer, softball, volleyball.

On-Campus Highlights: Reinhart Center for Ethics, Science and Technology, Fine Arts Center, Amie Mathy Center for Recreation and Education, Student Activity Center, Dancing Francis

ADMISSIONS

Freshman Academic Profile: Average high school GPA 3.3. 13% in top 10% of high school class, 39% in top 25% of high school class, 73% in top 50% of high school class. 97% from public high schools. **Test Scores:** ACT middle 50% range 20-24. Minimum paper TOEFL 550. **Basis for Candidate Selection:** *Very important factors considered include:* rigor of secondary school record, academic GPA, standardized test scores, character/personal qualities, level of applicant's interest. *Important factors considered include:* class rank, interview, talent/ability. *Other factors considered include:* application essay, recommendation(s), extracurricular activities, first generation, alumni/ae relation, volunteer work. **Freshman Admission Requirements:** High school diploma is required and GED is accepted *Academic units required:* 3 English, 2 math, 2 science, 2 social studies, 5 academic electives, *Academic units recommended:* 4 English, 2 math, 2 science, 2 science labs, 2 foreign language, 2 social studies, 5 academic electives. **Freshman Admission Statistics:** 1,107 applied, 88.7% admitted, 32% enrolled. **Transfer Admission Requirements:** High school transcript, college transcript(s), statement of good standing from prior institution(s). Minimum college GPA of 2.0 required. Lowest grade transferable C-. **General Admission Information:** Application fee $25. Priority deadline 8/1. Nonfall registration accepted. Admission may be deferred for a maximum of 2 years.

COSTS AND FINANCIAL AID

Annual tuition $18,170. Room and board $6,140. Required fees $420. Average book expense $800. **Required Forms and Deadlines:** FAFSA; Institution's own financial aid form. **Notification of Awards:** Applicants will be notified of awards on a rolling basis beginning 4/1. **Types of Aid:** *Need-based scholarships/grants:* College/university scholarship or grant aid from institutional funds; Federal Pell; Private scholarships; SEOG; State scholarships/grants. *Loans: Student Employment:* Federal Work-Study Program available. Institutional employment available. **Financial Aid Statistics:** 98% needy freshmen, 97% needy undergrads receive need-based scholarship or grant aid. 6% freshmen, 6% undergrads receive non-need-based scholarship or grant aid. 94% freshmen, 93% undergrads receive need-based self-help aid. 0% freshmen, 1% undergrads receive athletic scholarships. 98% freshmen, 89% undergrads receive any aid. **Criteria for awarding aid:** *Need-based:* Academics, Alumni affiliation *Non-need-based:* Academics, Alumni affiliation, Art, Athletics, Leadership, Minority status, Music/drama.

WABASH COLLEGE

P.O. Box 352, Crawfordsville, IN 47933
Phone: 765-361-6225 • **Financial Aid Phone:** 765-361-6370
E-mail: admissions@wabash.edu • **CEEB Code:** 1895
Fax: 765-361-6437 • **Website:** www.wabash.edu • **ACT Code:** 1260

This private school was founded in 1832. It has a 60 acre campus.

RATINGS

Admissions Selectivity Rating: 86   **Fire Safety Rating:** 92   **Green Rating:** 65

STUDENTS AND FACULTY

Enrollment: 861. **Student Body:** 0% female, 100% male, 22% out-of-state, 7% international (16 countries represented). Asian 1%, African American 6%, Caucasian 73%, Hispanic 8%, Native American <1%, Pacific Islander 0%, Two or more races 3%, Race unknown 2%.
Retention and Graduation: 87% freshmen return for sophomore year. 72% freshmen graduate within 4 years. 77% freshmen graduate within 6 years. 25% grads go on to further study within 1 year. 6% grads pursue arts and sciences degrees. 6% grads pursue law degrees. 1% grads pursue business degrees. 5% grads pursue medical degrees. **Faculty:** Student/faculty ratio 10:1. 82 full-time faculty, 100% hold PhDs, 9% are members of minority groups, 39% are women. 0% of classes are taught by teaching assistants.

ACADEMICS

Degrees: Bachelor's **Classes:** Most classes have 10-19 students. Most lab/discussion sessions have 10-19 students. **Most popular majors:** Economics, General; Political Science And Government, General; History, General. **Special**

Study Options: Double major; Independent study; Internships; Student-designed major; Study abroad; Teacher certification program. Combined degree programs: BA/MEng. **Disability Services offered to physically disabled students:** Note-taking services; Reader services; Tape recorders; Tutors. **Career services:** Alumni network; Alumni services; Career assessment; Career/job search classes; Internships; Regional alumni

FACILITIES

Housing: Fraternity/sorority housing; Men's dorms; Other (please specify) 70% of campus accessible to physically diasbled. **Special Academic Facilities/Equipment:** Malcolm X Institute of Black Studies, two art galleries, language lab, electron microscope, atomic absorption, nuclear and infrared spectrometers, Beowulf Supercomputer, Center of Inquiry in the Liberal Arts, Wabash Center for Teaching and Learning in Theology and Religion, Ramsey Archival Center **Computers:** 100% of classrooms, 100% of dorms, 100% of libraries, 100% of dining areas, 100% of student union, 100% of common outdoor areas have wireless network access. Administrative functions (other than registration) can be performed online.

CAMPUS LIFE

Environment: Village **Activities:** Campus Ministries; Choral groups; Concert band; Dance; Drama/theater; International Student Organization; Jazz band; Literary magazine; Music ensembles; Musical theater; Pep band; Radio station; Student government; Student newspaper; Student-run film society; Symphony orchestra; Yearbook 65 registered organizations, 7 honor societies, 5 religious organizations. 9 fraternities. **Athletics (Intercollegiate):** *Men:* baseball, basketball, cross-country, diving, football, golf, soccer, swimming, tennis, track/field (outdoor), track/field (indoor), wrestling. **On-Campus Highlights:** Allen Athletics and Recreation Center, Wabash Chapel, Fine Arts Center, Sparks Student Center, 1832 Brew Coffee Shop **Environmental Initiatives:** Printing Quota that saved 240,000 sheets of paper in the first semester (among 900 students)

ADMISSIONS

Freshman Academic Profile: Average high school GPA 3.7. 27% in top 10% of high school class, 57% in top 25% of high school class, 95% in top 50% of high school class. 83% from public high schools. **Test Scores:** SAT Math middle 50% range 540-650. SAT EBRW middle 50% range 530-630. ACT middle 50% range 23-28. Minimum internet-based TOEFL 80. Minimum paper TOEFL 550. **Basis for Candidate Selection:** *Very important factors considered include:* rigor of secondary school record, class rank, academic GPA, level of applicant's interest. *Important factors considered include:* standardized test scores, interview, extracurricular activities, talent/ability. *Other factors considered include:* application essay, recommendation(s), character/personal qualities, first generation, alumni/ae relation, geographical residence, racial/ethnic status, volunteer work, work experience. **Freshman Admission Requirements:** High school diploma is required and GED is accepted *Academic units recommended:* 4 English, 4 math, 2 science, 2 science labs, 2 foreign language, 2 social studies, 2 history, 2 academic electives. **Freshman Admission Statistics:** 1,304 applied, 63.0% admitted, 28% enrolled. **Transfer Admission Requirements:** High school transcript, college transcript(s), essay or personal statement, standardized test scores, statement of good standing from prior institution(s). Lowest grade transferable C. **General Admission Information:** Application fee $50. Priority deadline 10/15. Regular application deadline 1/15. Nonfall registration accepted. Admission may be deferred for a maximum of 1 year.

COSTS AND FINANCIAL AID

Annual tuition $42,800. Room and board $9,850. Required fees $850. Average book expense $1,000. **Required Forms and Deadlines:** FAFSA. **Notification of Awards:** Applicants will be notified of awards on a rolling basis beginning 12/15. **Types of Aid:** *Need-based scholarships/grants:* College/university scholarship or grant aid from institutional funds; Federal Pell; Private scholarships; SEOG; State scholarships/grants; United Negro College Fund. *Loans:* Direct PLUS loans; Direct Subsidized Stafford Loans; Direct Unsubsidized Stafford Loans. *Student Employment:* Federal Work-Study Program available. Institutional employment available. **Financial Aid Statistics:** 99% needy freshmen, 98% needy undergrads receive need-based scholarship or grant aid. 20% freshmen, 15% undergrads receive non-need-based scholarship or grant aid. 79% freshmen, 83% undergrads receive need-based self-help aid. 0% freshmen, 0% undergrads receive athletic scholarships. 99% freshmen, 95% undergrads receive any aid. 91% undergrads borrow to pay for school. Average cumulative indebtedness $32,916. **Criteria for awarding aid:** *Need-based:* Academics *Non-need-based:* Academics, Art, Leadership, Music/drama.

WAGNER COLLEGE

One Campus Road, Staten Island, NY 10301
Phone: 718-390-3411 • **Financial Aid Phone:** 718-390-3183
E-mail: adm@wagner.edu • **CEEB Code:** 2966
Fax: 718-390-3105 • **Website:** www.wagner.edu • **ACT Code:** 2984

This private school was founded in 1883. It has a 110 acre campus.

RATINGS
Admissions Selectivity Rating: 82   **Fire Safety Rating:** 98   **Green Rating:** 61

STUDENTS AND FACULTY
Enrollment: 1,793. **Student Body:** 63% female, 37% male, 54% out-of-state, 4% international. Asian 3%, African American 8%, Caucasian 66%, Hispanic 11%, Native American <1%, Pacific Islander <1%, Two or more races 3%, Race unknown 5%.
Retention and Graduation: 81% freshmen return for sophomore year. 63% freshmen graduate within 4 years. 70% freshmen graduate within 6 years. 42% grads go on to further study within 1 year. 23% grads pursue arts and sciences degrees. 4% grads pursue law degrees. 26% grads pursue business degrees. 6% grads pursue medical degrees. **Faculty:** Student/faculty ratio 13:1. 110 full-time faculty, 87% hold PhDs, 10% are members of minority groups, 50% are women. 0% of classes are taught by teaching assistants.

ACADEMICS
Degrees: Bachelor's; Doctoral/Professional; Master's; Post-Master's certificate **Classes:** Most classes have 10-19 students. **Most popular majors:** Visual And Performing Arts, General; Nursing Science; Business/Commerce, General. **Special Study Options:** Accelerated program; Double major; Exchange student program (domestic); Honors program; Independent study; Internships; Liberal arts/career combination; Student-designed major; Study abroad; Teacher certification program; Weekend college. **Disability Services offered to physically disabled students:** Note-taking services; Reader services; Tape recorders; Tutors. **Career services:** Alumni network; Alumni services; Internships

FACILITIES
Housing: Coed dorms; Fraternity/sorority housing; Theme housing; Wellness housing 50% of campus accessible to physically diasbled. **Special Academic Facilities/Equipment:** Art gallery, early childhood center, nursing resource center, planetarium, two electron microscopes, solar energy project, theater. **Computers:** 90% of classrooms, 100% of dorms, 100% of libraries, 100% of dining areas, 100% of student union, 50% of common outdoor areas have wireless network access. Students can register for classes online. Administrative functions (other than registration) can be performed online.

CAMPUS LIFE
Environment: Metropolis **Activities:** Campus Ministries; Choral groups; Concert band; Dance; Drama/theater; International Student Organization; Jazz band; Marching band; Model UN; Music ensembles; Musical theater; Radio station; Student government; Student newspaper; Yearbook 66 registered organizations, 11 honor societies, 4 religious organizations. 5 fraternities, 4 sororities. **Athletics (Intercollegiate):** *Men:* baseball, basketball, cross-country, football, golf, lacrosse, tennis, track/field (outdoor), track/field (indoor). *Women:* basketball, cross-country, golf, lacrosse, soccer, softball, swimming, tennis, track/field (outdoor), track/field (indoor), water polo. **On-Campus Highlights:** Wagner Student Union, Spiro Sports Center, Horrmann Library, Main Hall Theatre, Foundation Hall **Environmental Initiatives:** competing in Recylemania, Spring 2009

ADMISSIONS
Freshman Academic Profile: Average high school GPA 3.6. 25% in top 10% of high school class, 50% in top 25% of high school class, 88% in top 50% of high school class. 67% from public high schools. **Test Scores:** SAT Math middle 50% range 530-630. SAT EBRW middle 50% range 540-620. ACT middle 50% range 23-30. Minimum internet-based TOEFL 79. Minimum paper TOEFL 550. **Basis for Candidate Selection:** *Very important factors considered include:* rigor of secondary school record, class rank, academic GPA. *Important factors considered include:* application essay, recommendation(s), interview, extracurricular activities, talent/ability, character/personal qualities. *Other factors considered include:* standardized test scores, volunteer work, work experience, level of applicant's interest. **Freshman Admission Requirements:** High school diploma is required and GED is accepted *Academic units required:*

4 English, 3 math, 2 science, 1 science labs, 2 foreign language, 3 history, 7 academic electives. **Freshman Admission Statistics:** 2,834 applied, 69.7% admitted, 22% enrolled. **Transfer Admission Requirements:** college transcript(s), essay or personal statement, statement of good standing from prior institution(s). Minimum college GPA of 3.0 required. Lowest grade transferable C. **General Admission Information:** Application fee $60. Priority deadline 12/1. Regular application deadline 2/15. Nonfall registration accepted. Admission may be deferred for a maximum of 1 year.

COSTS AND FINANCIAL AID
Annual tuition $44,800. Room and board $13,650. Required fees $580. Average book expense $832. **Required Forms and Deadlines:** FAFSA; State aid form. **Notification of Awards:** Applicants will be notified of awards on a rolling basis beginning 1/31. **Types of Aid:** *Need-based scholarships/grants:* College/university scholarship or grant aid from institutional funds; Federal Pell; Private scholarships; SEOG; State scholarships/grants. *Loans:* Direct PLUS loans; Direct Subsidized Stafford Loans; Direct Unsubsidized Stafford Loans. *Student Employment:* Federal Work-Study Program available. Institutional employment available. **Financial Aid Statistics:** 100% needy freshmen, 99% needy undergrads receive need-based scholarship or grant aid. 0% undergrads receive non-need-based scholarship or grant aid. 77% freshmen, 78% undergrads receive need-based self-help aid. 8% freshmen, 7% undergrads receive athletic scholarships. 98% freshmen, 93% undergrads receive any aid. **Criteria for awarding aid:** *Non-need-based:* Academics, Athletics, Leadership, Music/drama.

WAKE FOREST UNIVERSITY

P.O. Box 7373 Reynolda Station, Winston Salem, NC 27109
Phone: 336-758-5201 • **Financial Aid Phone:** (336)758-5154
E-mail: admissions@wfu.edu • **CEEB Code:** 5885
Fax: 336-758-4324 • **Website:** www.wfu.edu • **ACT Code:** 3168

This private school was founded in 1834. It has a 340 acre campus.

RATINGS
Admissions Selectivity Rating: 95   **Fire Safety Rating:** 96   **Green Rating:** 85

STUDENTS AND FACULTY
Enrollment: 5,101. **Student Body:** 54% female, 46% male, 78% out-of-state, 10% international (27 countries represented). Asian 4%, African American 7%, Caucasian 70%, Hispanic 7%, Native American <1%, Pacific Islander <1%, Two or more races 3%, Race unknown <1%.
Retention and Graduation: 94% freshmen return for sophomore year. 84% freshmen graduate within 4 years. 88% freshmen graduate within 6 years. 32% grads go on to further study within 1 year. 28% grads pursue arts and sciences degrees. 15.8% grads pursue law degrees. 36% grads pursue business degrees. 16.8% grads pursue medical degrees. **Faculty:** Student/faculty ratio 11:1. 579 full-time faculty, 93% hold PhDs, 17% are members of minority groups, 43% are women. 0% of classes are taught by teaching assistants.

ACADEMICS
Degrees: Bachelor's; Doctoral/Professional; Doctoral/Research; Master's; Post-Bachelor's certificate **Classes:** Most classes have 30-39 students. Most lab/discussion sessions have 30-39 students. **Most popular majors:** Psychology, General; Political Science And Government, General; Business/Commerce, General. **Special Study Options:** Cross-registration; Distance learning; Double major; Dual enrollment; Honors program; Independent study; Internships; Study abroad; Teacher certification program. Honors programs: For highly qualified students, a series of interdisciplinary honors courses are offered. Additionally, for students especially talented in individual areas of study, most departments in the College offer special studies leading to graduation with honors in a particular discipline. **Disability Services offered to physically disabled students:** Note-taking services; Reader services; Tape recorders; Tutors. **Career services:** Alumni network; Alumni services; Career assessment; Career/job search classes; Internships; Regional alumni

FACILITIES
Housing: Apartments for single students; Coed dorms; Fraternity/sorority housing; Theme housing; Wellness housing **Special Academic Facilities/Equipment:** Museum of Anthropology; Charlotte and Philip Hanes Art Gallery; Scales Fine Arts Center; Reynolda House, Museum of American Art;

Laser and Electron Microscope Labs. **Computers:** 100% of classrooms, 100% of dorms, 100% of libraries, 100% of dining areas, 100% of student union, 5% of common outdoor areas have wireless network access. Students can register for classes online. Administrative functions (other than registration) can be performed online. Undergraduates are required to own a computer.

CAMPUS LIFE

Environment: City **Activities:** Campus Ministries; Choral groups; Concert band; Dance; Drama/theater; International Student Organization; Jazz band; Literary magazine; Marching band; Model UN; Music ensembles; Musical theater; Pep band; Radio station; Student government; Student newspaper; Student-run film society; Symphony orchestra; Television station; Yearbook 168 registered organizations, 16 honor societies, 16 religious organizations. 14 fraternities, 9 sororities. **Athletics (Intercollegiate):** *Men:* baseball, basketball, cheerleading, cross-country, football, golf, soccer, tennis, track/field (outdoor), track/field (indoor). *Women:* basketball, cheerleading, cross-country, field hockey, golf, soccer, tennis, track/field (outdoor), track/field (indoor), volleyball. **On-Campus Highlights:** Charlotte and Philip Hanes Art Gallery, Museum of Anthropology, The Z. Smith Reynolds Library, Wait Chapel, Benson University Center **Environmental Initiatives:** Campus Master Plan: Wake Forest has completed a new campus master plan that will guide development over the next 50 years. Heavily integrated into that plan are tenents for sustainable design (e.g. LEED) as well as stormwater management and biohabitat protection. This new master plan will guide the campus in integrating sustainability within the built and natural environments for the years ahead.

ADMISSIONS

Freshman Academic Profile: 77% in top 10% of high school class, 93% in top 25% of high school class, 98% in top 50% of high school class. 65% from public high schools. **Test Scores:** SAT Math middle 50% range 630-730. SAT EBRW middle 50% range 630-710. ACT middle 50% range 28-32. Minimum paper TOEFL 600. **Basis for Candidate Selection:** *Very important factors considered include:* rigor of secondary school record, class rank, academic GPA, application essay, character/personal qualities. *Important factors considered include:* recommendation(s), interview, extracurricular activities, talent/ability. *Other factors considered include:* standardized test scores, first generation, alumni/ae relation, geographical residence, state residency, religious affiliation/commitment, racial/ethnic status, volunteer work, level of applicant's interest. **Freshman Admission Requirements:** High school diploma is required and GED is accepted *Academic units required:* 4 English, 3 math, 1 science, 2 foreign language, 2 social studies, *Academic units recommended:* 4 English, 4 math, 4 science, 4 foreign language, 4 social studies. **Freshman Admission Statistics:** 13,071 applied, 27.6% admitted, 37% enrolled. **Transfer Admission Requirements:** High school transcript, college transcript(s), essay or personal statement, statement of good standing from prior institution(s). Minimum college GPA of 2.0 required. Lowest grade transferable C. **General Admission Information:** Application fee $65. Regular application deadline 1/1. Nonfall registration accepted.

COSTS AND FINANCIAL AID

Annual tuition $52,348. Room and board $16,032. Required fees $974. Average book expense $1,500. **Required Forms and Deadlines:** CSS/Financial Aid PROFILE; FAFSA; Noncustodial PROFILE; State aid form. **Notification of Awards:** Applicants will be notified of awards on a rolling basis beginning 4/1. **Types of Aid:** *Need-based scholarships/grants:* College/university scholarship or grant aid from institutional funds; Federal Pell; Private scholarships; SEOG; State scholarships/grants; United Negro College Fund. *Loans:* Direct PLUS loans; Direct Subsidized Stafford Loans; Direct Unsubsidized Stafford Loans. *Student Employment:* Federal Work-Study Program available. Institutional employment available. **Financial Aid Statistics:** 93% needy freshmen, 95% needy undergrads receive need-based scholarship or grant aid. 55% freshmen, 54% undergrads receive non-need-based scholarship or grant aid. 90% freshmen, 93% undergrads receive need-based self-help aid. 3% freshmen, 3% undergrads receive athletic scholarships. 39% freshmen, 34% undergrads receive any aid. 39% undergrads borrow to pay for school. Average cumulative indebtedness $36,546. **Criteria for awarding aid:** *Non-need-based:* Academics, Alumni affiliation, Art, Athletics, Leadership, Music/drama, Religious affiliation, State/district residency.

WALLA WALLA UNIVERSITY

204 South College Avenue, College Place, WA 99324-1198
Phone: (509) 527-2615 • **Financial Aid Phone:** (509) 527-2815
E-mail: info@wallawalla.edu • **CEEB Code:** 4940
Fax: (509) 527-2253 • **Website:** www.wallawalla.edu • **ACT Code:** 4486

This private school, affiliated with the Seventh Day Adventist Church, was founded in 1892. It has a 77 acre campus.

RATINGS

Admissions Selectivity Rating: 67   **Fire Safety Rating:** 62   **Green Rating:** 60*

STUDENTS AND FACULTY

Enrollment: 1,549. **Student Body:** 50% female, 50% male, 59% out-of-state, 3% international (30 countries represented). African American 3%, Caucasian 74%, Hispanic 10%, Native American 1%, Pacific Islander 7%, Race unknown 1%.
Retention and Graduation: 78% freshmen return for sophomore year.
Faculty: 112 full-time faculty, 69% hold PhDs, 6% are members of minority groups, 39% are women. 0% of classes are taught by teaching assistants.

ACADEMICS

Degrees: Associate; Bachelor's; Diploma; **Master's Classes:** Most classes have 10-19 students. **Most popular majors:** Engineering, General; Social Work; Business/Commerce, General. **Special Study Options:** Cooperative education program; Distance learning; Double major; Honors program; Independent study; Internships; Liberal arts/career combination; Study abroad; Teacher certification program. **Disability Services offered to physically disabled students:** Note-taking services; Reader services; Tape recorders; Tutors. **Career services:** Alumni network; Career assessment; Career/job search classes; Internships

FACILITIES

Housing: Apartments for married students; Apartments for single students; Men's dorms; Special housing for international students; Wellness housing; Women's dorms 75% of campus accessible to physically diasbled. **Special Academic Facilities/Equipment:** Marine station on the Rosario Strait of the Puget Sound in Washington state. **Computers:** Students can register for classes online.

CAMPUS LIFE

Environment: Town **Activities:** Campus Ministries; Choral groups; Concert band; Drama/theater; International Student Organization; Jazz band; Literary magazine; Music ensembles; Radio station; Student government; Student newspaper; Symphony orchestra; Television station; Yearbook 33 registered organizations, 7 honor societies, 6 religious organizations. **Athletics (Intercollegiate):** *Men:* basketball, golf, soccer, volleyball. *Women:* basketball, softball, volleyball. **On-Campus Highlights:** The Dairy Express, Peterson Memorial Library, The Student Association Center, Winter Educational Complex: gym/climbing wall/pool, The College Store

ADMISSIONS

Freshman Academic Profile: 9% from public high schools. **Test Scores:** Minimum paper TOEFL 550. **Basis for Candidate Selection:** *Very important factors considered include:* rigor of secondary school record, academic GPA, recommendation(s). *Important factors considered include:* character/personal qualities, level of applicant's interest. *Other factors considered include:* class rank, standardized test scores, extracurricular activities, talent/ability. **Freshman Admission Requirements:** High school diploma is required and GED is accepted *Academic units required:* 4 English, 3 math, 2 science, 2 science labs, 2 history, *Academic units recommended:* 4 English, 4 math, 3 science, 2 science labs, 2 foreign language, 1 social studies, 2 history. **Freshman Admission Statistics:** 626 applied, 89.0% admitted, 54% enrolled. **Transfer Admission Requirements:** college transcript(s), Minimum college GPA of 2.0 required. Lowest grade transferable D-. **General Admission Information:** Application fee $40. Nonfall registration accepted. Admission may be deferred.

COSTS AND FINANCIAL AID

Annual tuition $23,670. Room and board $5,655. Required fees $528. Average book expense $1,068. **Required Forms and Deadlines:** FAFSA; Institution's own financial aid form. **Notification of Awards:** Applicants will be notified of awards on a rolling basis beginning 3/1. **Types of Aid:** *Need-based scholarships/grants:* College/university scholarship or grant aid from institutional funds; Federal Nursing Scholarships; Federal Pell; Private scholarships; SEOG; State scholarships/grants. *Loans:* Direct PLUS loans; Direct Subsidized Stafford Loans; Direct Unsubsidized Stafford Loans. *Student Employment:* Federal Work-Study Program available. Institutional employment available. **Financial Aid Statistics:** 79% needy freshmen, 79% needy undergrads receive need-based scholarship or grant aid. 99% freshmen, 80% undergrads receive non-need-based scholarship or grant aid. 89% freshmen, 93% undergrads receive need-based self-help aid. 0% freshmen, 0% undergrads receive athletic scholarships. 84% freshmen, 83% undergrads receive any aid. **Criteria for awarding aid:** *Need-based:* Academics, Alumni affiliation *Non-need-based:* Academics, Leadership, Music/drama.

WALSH COLLEGE

PO Box 7006, Troy, MI 48007-7006
Phone: 248-823-1610 · **Financial Aid Phone:** 248-823-1285
E-mail: admissions@walshcollege.edu
Fax: 248-823-1611 • **Website:** www.walshcollege.edu

This private school was founded in 1922. It has a 20 acre campus.

RATINGS
Admissions Selectivity Rating: 0   **Fire Safety Rating:** 60*   **Green Rating:** 60*

STUDENTS AND FACULTY
Enrollment: 929. **Student Body:** 47% female, 53% male, 0% out-of-state, 2% international (46 countries represented). Asian 4%, African American 6%, Caucasian 84%, Hispanic 2%, Native American <1%, Pacific Islander <1%, Two or more races 1%, Race unknown 1%.
Faculty: Student/faculty ratio 13:1. 23 full-time faculty, 78% hold PhDs, 4% are members of minority groups, 52% are women. 0% of classes are taught by teaching assistants.

ACADEMICS
Degrees: Bachelor's; Master's; Post-Bachelor's certificate; Post-Master's certificate **Most popular majors:** Biology/Biological Sciences, General; Pharmacy. **Special Study Options:** Distance learning; Double major; Independent study; Internships. **Disability Services offered to physically disabled students:** Note-taking services; Reader services; Tape recorders; Tutors. **Career services:** Alumni network; Alumni services; Career assessment; Career/job search classes; Internships

FACILITIES
Housing: 100% of campus accessible to physically diasbled. **Computers:** 100% of classrooms, 100% of libraries, 100% of dining areas, have wireless network access. Students can register for classes online. Administrative functions (other than registration) can be performed online.

CAMPUS LIFE
Environment: City **Activities:** International Student Organization 6 registered organizations, 1 honor societies. **On-Campus Highlights:** Barry Center

ADMISSIONS
Test Scores: Minimum internet-based TOEFL 79. Minimum paper TOEFL 550. **Transfer Admission Requirements:** college transcript(s), Minimum college GPA of 2.0 required. Lowest grade transferable C. **General Admission Information:** Application fee $25.

COSTS AND FINANCIAL AID
Annual tuition $9,850. **Required Forms and Deadlines:** FAFSA. **Types of Aid:** *Need-based scholarships/grants:* College/university scholarship or grant aid from institutional funds; Federal Pell; SEOG; State scholarships/grants. *Student Employment:* Federal Work-Study Program available. **Financial Aid Statistics:** 64% needy undergrads receive need-based scholarship or grant aid. 18% undergrads receive non-need-based scholarship or grant aid. 100% undergrads receive need-based self-help aid. 0% undergrads receive athletic scholarships. **Criteria for awarding aid:** *Need-based:* Academics, Minority status *Non-need-based:* Academics.

WALSH UNIVERSITY

2020 East Maple St., North Canton, OH 44720-3396
Phone: 330-490-7172 • **Financial Aid Phone:** 330-490-7367
E-mail: admissions@walsh.edu • **CEEB Code:** 1926
Fax: 330-490-7165 • **Website:** www.walsh.edu • **ACT Code:** 3349

This private school, affiliated with the Roman Catholic Church, was founded in 1958. It has a 140 acre campus.

RATINGS
Admissions Selectivity Rating: 76   **Fire Safety Rating:** 92   **Green Rating:** 61

STUDENTS AND FACULTY
Enrollment: 2,157. **Student Body:** 61% female, 39% male, 7% out-of-state, 4% international (30 countries represented). Asian 1%, African American 6%, Caucasian 75%, Hispanic 3%, Native American <1%, Pacific Islander <1%, Two or more races 2%, Race unknown 9%.
Retention and Graduation: 80% freshmen return for sophomore year. 16% grads go on to further study within 1 year. 9% grads pursue arts and sciences degrees. 1% grads pursue law degrees. 3% grads pursue business degrees. 2% grads pursue medical degrees. **Faculty:** Student/faculty ratio 13:1. 132 full-time faculty, 67% hold PhDs, 7% are members of minority groups, 55% are women. 0% of classes are taught by teaching assistants.

ACADEMICS
Degrees: Associate; Bachelor's; Certificate; Doctoral/Professional; **Master's Classes:** Most classes have 10-19 students. Most lab/discussion sessions have 10-19 students. **Most popular majors:** Biology/Biological Sciences, General; Registered Nursing/Registered Nurse; Business Administration And Management, General. **Special Study Options:** Accelerated program; Distance learning; Double major; Dual enrollment; English as a Second Language (ESL); Exchange student program (domestic); External degree program; Honors program; Independent study; Internships; Liberal arts/career combination; Study abroad; Teacher certification program. Honors programs: Honors Program students may pursue any major and have opportunity annually to attend the national honors conference, where Walsh students frequently present their research. The Blouin Scholars Program in Global Studies at Walsh University provides students with a unique opportunity to become part of a community of students and faculty dedicated to using scholarship and service to address major global issues. As a Blouin Scholar, you will live and take classes with a cohort of students who are similarly dedicated to become leaders in service to the global community. All classes are built into the Walsh University core curriculum—you still choose your own majors and minors—and center on a common global theme. You will be supported with opportunities such as global learning in Africa and Europe, special lectures and co-curricular activities, and priority registration and advising procedures. Combined degree programs: BA/MA. **Disability Services offered to physically disabled students:** Reader services; Tape recorders; Tutors. **Career services:** Alumni network; Alumni services; Career assessment; Internships; Regional alumni

FACILITIES
Housing: Apartments for single students; Coed dorms; Special housing for disabled student; Special housing for international students; Wellness housing 100% of campus accessible to physically diasbled. **Special Academic Facilities/Equipment:** bioinformatics lab, Hoover Historical Center (corporate and local history), human cadaver lab (prosection for undergrad), Gathering Garden for Education activities with schoolchildren, Religious Education Center, two Anatomage virtual dissection tables that display 3D images of human anatomy with stunning detail in a multitude of layers, views and perspectives. **Computers:** 10% of classrooms, 12% of dorms, 100% of libraries, 100% of dining areas, 100% of student union, 5% of common outdoor areas have wireless network access. Students can register for classes online. Administrative functions (other than registration) can be performed online.

CAMPUS LIFE
Environment: City **Activities:** Campus Ministries; Choral groups; Dance; Drama/theater; International Student Organization; Literary magazine; Marching band; Music ensembles; Pep band; Radio station; Student government; Student newspaper; Yearbook 30 registered organizations, 10 honor societies, 3 religious organizations. **Athletics (Intercollegiate):** *Men:* baseball, basketball, cheerleading, cross-country, football, golf, soccer, tennis, track/field (outdoor), track/field (indoor). *Women:* basketball, cheerleading, cross-country, golf, soccer, softball, tennis, track/field (outdoor), track/field (indoor), volleyball. **On-Campus Highlights:** David Campus Center, Alumni Arena, Birk Center for the Arts, Barrette Business and Community Center, Drouin Library **Environmental Initiatives:** HVAC & electrical managament system

ADMISSIONS

Freshman Academic Profile: Average high school GPA 3.4. 17% in top 10% of high school class, 43% in top 25% of high school class, 76% in top 50% of high school class. 71% from public high schools. **Test Scores:** SAT Math middle 50% range 430-620. SAT EBRW middle 50% range 450-630. ACT middle 50% range 18-27. Minimum internet-based TOEFL 61. Minimum paper TOEFL 500. **Basis for Candidate Selection:** *Very important factors considered include:* rigor of secondary school record, academic GPA. *Important factors considered include:* recommendation(s). *Other factors considered include:* class rank, application essay, standardized test scores, interview, extracurricular activities, character/personal qualities, volunteer work, work experience. **Freshman Admission Requirements:** High school diploma is required and GED is accepted *Academic units recommended:* 4 English, 3 math, 3 science, 2 foreign language, 3 social studies, 1 academic elective. **Freshman Admission Statistics:** 1,480 applied, 80.7% admitted, 37% enrolled. **Transfer Admission Requirements:** High school transcript, college transcript(s), Minimum college GPA of 2.0 required. Lowest grade transferable C. **General Admission Information:** Application fee $25. Regular application deadline 8/15. Nonfall registration accepted. Admission may be deferred for a maximum of 1 year.

COSTS AND FINANCIAL AID

Annual tuition $26,300. Room and board $9,920. Required fees $1,410. Average book expense $1,104. **Required Forms and Deadlines:** FAFSA. **Notification of Awards:** Applicants will be notified of awards on a rolling basis beginning 2/15. **Types of Aid:** *Need-based scholarships/grants:* College/university scholarship or grant aid from institutional funds; Federal Pell; Private scholarships; SEOG; State scholarships/grants. *Loans:* Direct PLUS loans; Direct Subsidized Stafford Loans; Direct Unsubsidized Stafford Loans. *Student Employment:* Federal Work-Study Program available. Institutional employment available. **Financial Aid Statistics:** 80% needy freshmen, 79% needy undergrads receive need-based scholarship or grant aid. 100% freshmen, 87% undergrads receive non-need-based scholarship or grant aid. 81% freshmen, 78% undergrads receive need-based self-help aid. 18% freshmen, 19% undergrads receive athletic scholarships. 99% freshmen, 93% undergrads receive any aid. 85% undergrads borrow to pay for school. Average cumulative indebtedness $29,702. **Criteria for awarding aid:** *Non-need-based:* Academics, Alumni affiliation, Athletics, Music/drama, Religious affiliation, State/district residency.

WARNER PACIFIC COLLEGE

2219 SE 68th Avenue, Portland, OR 97215
Phone: 503-517-1020 • **Financial Aid Phone:** 503-517-1091
E-mail: admissions@warnerpacific.edu • **CEEB Code:** 4595
Fax: 503-517-1540 • **Website:** http://www.warnerpacific.edu/

This private school, affiliated with the Church of God, was founded in 1937. It has a 15 acre campus.

RATINGS

Admissions Selectivity Rating: 82   **Fire Safety Rating:** 73   **Green Rating:** 60*

STUDENTS AND FACULTY

Enrollment: 501. **Student Body:** 56% female, 44% male, 35% out-of-state, (12 countries represented). Asian 4%, African American 7%, Caucasian 66%, Hispanic 9%, Native American <1%, Pacific Islander 2%, Two or more races 6%, Race unknown 5%.
Retention and Graduation: 32% freshmen return for sophomore year. 7% grads go on to further study within 1 year. 2% grads pursue arts and sciences degrees. 2% grads pursue business degrees. 1% grads pursue medical degrees. **Faculty:** Student/faculty ratio 11:1. 31 full-time faculty, 68% hold PhDs, 10% are members of minority groups, 35% are women. 0% of classes are taught by teaching assistants.

ACADEMICS

Degrees: Associate; Bachelor's; Certificate; **Master's Classes:** Most classes have 20-29 students. **Most popular majors:** Human Development And Family Studies, General; Biology/Biological Sciences, General; Business Administration, Management And Operations, Other. **Special Study Options:** Double major; Exchange student program (domestic); Independent study; Internships; Liberal arts/career combination; Student-designed major; Study abroad; Teacher certification program. **Disability Services offered to physically disabled students:** Note-taking services; Reader services; Tape recorders; Tutors. **Career services:** Alumni network; Alumni services; Career assessment; Internships

FACILITIES

Housing: Apartments for married students; Apartments for single students; Men's dorms; Special housing for disabled student; Women's dorms 50% of campus accessible to physically disabled. **Special Academic Facilities/Equipment:** Early learning center **Computers:** 100% of classrooms, 10% of dorms, 100% of libraries, 100% of dining areas, 100% of student union, 50% of common outdoor areas have wireless network access.

CAMPUS LIFE

Environment: Metropolis **Activities:** Campus Ministries; Choral groups; Concert band; Drama/theater; International Student Organization; Jazz band; Literary magazine; Music ensembles; Student government; Student newspaper; Yearbook 20 registered organizations, 2 religious organizations. **Athletics (Intercollegiate):** *Men:* basketball, cross-country, golf, soccer, track/field (outdoor), track/field (indoor). *Women:* basketball, cross-country, golf, soccer, track/field (outdoor), track/field (indoor), volleyball. **On-Campus Highlights:** Tabor Grind Coffee Shop, Dining Hall, Student Union Building, Otto F. Linn Library, A.F. Gray lawn

ADMISSIONS

Freshman Academic Profile: Average high school GPA 3.2. 8% in top 10% of high school class, 25% in top 25% of high school class, 77% in top 50% of high school class. **Test Scores:** SAT Math middle 50% range 410-550. SAT EBRW middle 50% range 420-550. ACT middle 50% range 16-22. Minimum internet-based TOEFL 71. Minimum paper TOEFL 525. **Basis for Candidate Selection:** *Very important factors considered include:* academic GPA, standardized test scores. *Other factors considered include:* application essay, recommendation(s), religious affiliation/commitment. **Freshman Admission Requirements:** High school diploma is required and GED is accepted *Academic units recommended:* 4 English, 2 math, 2 science, 1 science labs, 3 social studies. **Freshman Admission Statistics:** 948 applied, 52.7% admitted, 15% enrolled. **Transfer Admission Requirements:** college transcript(s), essay or personal statement, Minimum college GPA of 2.5 required. Lowest grade transferable d. **General Admission Information:** Nonfall registration accepted. Admission may be deferred for a maximum of 3 years.

COSTS AND FINANCIAL AID

Annual tuition $18,370. Room and board $7,690. Required fees $660. Average book expense $1,300. **Required Forms and Deadlines:** FAFSA. **Notification of Awards:** Applicants will be notified of awards on a rolling basis beginning 3/1. **Types of Aid:** *Need-based scholarships/grants:* College/university scholarship or grant aid from institutional funds; Federal Pell; Private scholarships; SEOG; State scholarships/grants. *Loans:* Direct PLUS loans; Direct Subsidized Stafford Loans; Direct Unsubsidized Stafford Loans. *Student Employment:* Federal Work-Study Program available. Institutional employment available. **Financial Aid Statistics:** 97% needy freshmen, 93% needy undergrads receive need-based scholarship or grant aid. 95% freshmen, 89% undergrads receive non-need-based scholarship or grant aid. 94% freshmen, 91% undergrads receive need-based self-help aid. 9% freshmen, 5% undergrads receive athletic scholarships. 99% freshmen, 99% undergrads receive any aid. **Criteria for awarding aid:** *Non-need-based:* Academics, Alumni affiliation, Athletics, Leadership, Music/drama, Religious affiliation, State/district residency.

WARREN WILSON COLLEGE

P.O. Box 9000, Asheville, NC 28815-9000
Phone: 828-771-2073 • **Financial Aid Phone:** 828-771-2082
E-mail: admit@warren-wilson.edu • **CEEB Code:** 5886
Fax: 828-298-1440 • **Website:** www.warren-wilson.edu • **ACT Code:** 3170

This private school was founded in 1894. It has a 1100 acre campus.

RATINGS

Admissions Selectivity Rating: 79   **Fire Safety Rating:** 69   **Green Rating:** 88

STUDENTS AND FACULTY

Enrollment: 582. **Student Body:** 62% female, 38% male, 74% out-of-state, (14 countries represented).
Retention and Graduation: 62% freshmen return for sophomore year. 53% freshmen graduate within 6 years. **Faculty:** Student/faculty ratio 9:1. 64 full-time faculty, 13% are members of minority groups, 0% of classes are taught by teaching assistants.

ACADEMICS

Degrees: Bachelor's; **Master's Classes:** Most classes have 10-19 students. Most lab/discussion sessions have 10-19 students. **Most popular majors:** Environmental Studies; Biology/Biological Sciences, General; Psychology, General. **Special Study Options:** Cross-registration; Double major; English as a Second Language (ESL); Honors program; Independent study; Internships; Liberal arts/career combination; Student-designed major; Study abroad. Honors programs: Natural Sciences Honors Program English Honors Program. **Disability Services offered to physically disabled students:** Tutors. **Career services:** Alumni network; Alumni services; Career assessment; Career/job search classes; Internships; Regional alumni

FACILITIES

Housing: Coed dorms; Cooperative housing; Men's dorms; Special housing for disabled student; Theme housing; Wellness housing; Women's dorms 90% of campus accessible to physically disabled. **Special Academic Facilities/Equipment:** Bannerman Technology Center, WWC Tech Lab, Geographic Information Systems Lab, Warren Wilson Archaeological Site, Environmental Leadership Center, Holden Visual Arts Center & Gallery, Kittredge Theatre and Community Arts Center, Amphitheatre, Gossman/Cannon Climbing Tower, Blacksmithing Shop, Fine Woodworking Shop, Fiber Arts Studio, 3D Studio (ceramics, sculpture, kiln and foundry), and the Lucy Fletcher Studios (painting, drawing, senior studio spaces, photography darkrooms).

CAMPUS LIFE

Environment: City **Activities:** Campus Ministries; Choral groups; Dance; Drama/theater; International Student Organization; Jazz band; Literary magazine; Music ensembles; Musical theater; Student government; Student newspaper 25 registered organizations, 5 religious organizations. **Athletics (Intercollegiate):** *Men:* basketball, cross-country, diving, kayaking, mountain biking, soccer, swimming, ultimate frisbee. *Women:* basketball, cross-country, diving, kayaking, mountain biking, soccer, swimming, ultimate frisbee. **On-Campus Highlights:** Sage Cafe, Holden Arts Center, Witherspoon/Morse Science Center, Dogwood-a short hike to this great view, Cow Pie Cafe (Vegetarian/Vegan) **Environmental Initiatives:** Climate Action Plan to achieve 80% reduction in emissions campus wide by 2020 includes our formal climate change partnership with city of Asheville;quarterly emissions reports to support changes;college solar array KW's sold to NC Green Power for sustainability outreach to community to influence reduction in GHG's; 100% renewable energy wind credits purchased each year equal to total campus electric use; INSULATE! weatherization program in region for people in poverty where faculty/students and staff to do a house a weekend to provide assistance and reduce regional GHG emissions.

ADMISSIONS

Freshman Academic Profile: 80% from public high schools. **Test Scores:** SAT Math middle 50% range 530-615. SAT EBRW middle 50% range 610-670. ACT middle 50% range 25-29. Minimum internet-based TOEFL 75. Minimum paper TOEFL 550. **Basis for Candidate Selection:** *Very important factors considered include:* rigor of secondary school record, recommendation(s). *Important factors considered include:* academic GPA, interview, volunteer work, work experience. *Other factors considered include:* class rank, application essay, standardized test scores, extracurricular activities, talent/ability, character/personal qualities, first generation. **Freshman Admission Requirements:** High school diploma is required and GED is accepted *Academic units required: Academic units recommended:* 4 English, 3 math, 2 science, 2 science labs, 2 foreign language, 3 social studies. **Freshman Admission Statistics:** 1,003 applied, 79.4% admitted, 18% enrolled. **Transfer Admission Requirements:** High school transcript, college transcript(s), standardized test scores, Minimum college GPA of 3.0 required. Lowest grade transferable C. **General Admission Information:** Priority deadline 2/1. Nonfall registration accepted. Admission may be deferred for a maximum of 1 year.

COSTS AND FINANCIAL AID

Annual tuition $35,536. Room and board $10,980. Required fees $744. Average book expense $850. **Required Forms and Deadlines:** FAFSA; State aid form. **Notification of Awards:** Applicants will be notified of awards on a rolling basis beginning 3/1. **Types of Aid:** *Need-based scholarships/grants:* College/university scholarship or grant aid from institutional funds; Federal Pell; Private scholarships; SEOG; State scholarships/grants. *Loans:* Direct PLUS loans; Direct Subsidized Stafford Loans; Direct Unsubsidized Stafford Loans. *Student Employment:* Federal Work-Study Program available. Institutional employment available. **Financial Aid Statistics:** 100% needy freshmen, 100% needy undergrads receive need-based scholarship or grant aid. 28% freshmen, 27% undergrads receive non-need-based scholarship or grant aid. 100% freshmen, 100% undergrads receive need-based self-help aid. 0% freshmen, 0% undergrads receive athletic scholarships. 90% freshmen, 80% undergrads receive any aid. 71% undergrads borrow to pay for school. Average cumulative indebtedness $20,768. **Criteria for awarding aid:** *Need-based:* Academics *Non-need-based:* Academics, Art, Leadership.

WARTBURG COLLEGE

100 Wartburg Blvd., Waverly, IA 50677-0903
Phone: 319-352-8264 • **Financial Aid Phone:** 319-352-8262
E-mail: admissions@wartburg.edu • **CEEB Code:** 6926
Fax: 319-352-8579 • **Website:** www.wartburg.edu • **ACT Code:** 1364

This private school, affiliated with the Lutheran Church, was founded in 1852. It has a 118 acre campus.

RATINGS

Admissions Selectivity Rating: 78   **Fire Safety Rating:** 82   **Green Rating:** 97

STUDENTS AND FACULTY

Enrollment: 1,493. **Student Body:** 53% female, 47% male, 33% out-of-state, 8% international (55 countries represented). Asian 1%, African American 5%, Caucasian 75%, Hispanic 5%, Native American 0%, Pacific Islander <1%, Two or more races 3%, Race unknown 3%.
Retention and Graduation: 79% freshmen return for sophomore year. 60% freshmen graduate within 4 years. 66% freshmen graduate within 6 years. 24% grads go on to further study within 1 year. 6% grads pursue arts and sciences degrees. 1% grads pursue law degrees. 1% grads pursue business degrees. 6% grads pursue medical degrees. **Faculty:** Student/faculty ratio 11:1. 94 full-time faculty, 88% hold PhDs, 6% are members of minority groups, 47% are women. 0% of classes are taught by teaching assistants.

ACADEMICS

Degrees: Bachelor's **Classes:** Most classes have 10-19 students. Most lab/discussion sessions have fewer than 10 students. **Most popular majors:** Mass Communication/Media Studies; Biology/Biological Sciences, General; Business Administration, Management And Operations. **Special Study Options:** Accelerated program; Double major; Dual enrollment; Honors program; Independent study; Internships; Student-designed major; Study abroad; Teacher certification program. Honors programs: Scholars Program—features small seminar classes, distinguished speaker series, sophomore-year program of lectures, concerts, and performances, student involvement in designing courses and activities, variety of social and travel opportunities, student-designed senior project Combined degree programs: BA/JD; BA/MA; BA/MEng. **Disability Services offered to physically disabled students:** Note-taking services; Reader services; Tutors. **Career services:** Alumni network; Alumni services; Career assessment; Career/job search classes; Internships; Regional alumni

FACILITIES

Housing: Apartments for single students; Coed dorms; Men's dorms; Theme housing; Women's dorms 85% of campus accessible to physically disabled. **Special Academic Facilities/Equipment:** Waldemar A. Schmidt Art Gallery, Bachman Fine Arts Center, Institute for Leadership Education, Platte Observatory, prairie preserve learning space, state-of-the-art library study spaces, Center for Community Engagement, Wartburg-Waverly Sports & Wellness Center **Computers:** 30% of classrooms, 10% of dorms, 100% of libraries, 100% of dining areas, 100% of student union, 10% of common outdoor areas have wireless network access. Students can register for classes online. Administrative functions (other than registration) can be performed online.

CAMPUS LIFE

Environment: Village **Activities:** Campus Ministries; Choral groups; Concert band; Dance; Drama/theater; International Student Organization; Jazz band; Literary magazine; Model UN; Music ensembles; Musical theater; Opera; Pep band; Radio station; Student government; Student newspaper; Student-run film society; Symphony orchestra; Television station; Yearbook 90 registered organizations, 12 honor societies, 9 religious organizations. **Athletics (Intercollegiate):** *Men:* baseball, basketball, cross-country, football, golf, soccer, tennis, track/field (outdoor), track/field (indoor), wrestling. *Women:* basketball, cross-country, golf, soccer, softball, tennis, track/field (outdoor), track/field (indoor), volleyball. **On-Campus Highlights:** Konditorei Coffee Shop/Vogel Library, Wartburg-Waverly Sports & Wellness Center, Saemann Student Center, Walston-Hoover Stadium, Old Main (on National Historic Registry) **Environmental Initiatives:** LEED requirements for new Sports and Wellness Center

ADMISSIONS

Freshman Academic Profile: Average high school GPA 3.6. 27% in top 10% of high school class, 53% in top 25% of high school class, 82% in top 50% of high school class. **Test Scores:** SAT Math middle 50% range 478-603. ACT middle 50% range 21-27. Minimum internet-based TOEFL 55. Minimum paper TOEFL 480. **Basis for Candidate Selection:** *Very important factors considered include:* rigor of secondary school record, class rank, academic

GPA, standardized test scores, recommendation(s). *Important factors considered include:* interview, character/personal qualities. *Other factors considered include:* extracurricular activities, talent/ability, volunteer work, work experience, level of applicant's interest. **Freshman Admission Requirements:** High school diploma is required and GED is accepted *Academic units required:* 4 English, 3 math, 3 science, 2 foreign language, 2 social studies, *Academic units recommended:* 1 computer science. **Freshman Admission Statistics:** 4,342 applied, 76.9% admitted, 14% enrolled. **Transfer Admission Requirements:** High school transcript, college transcript(s), standardized test scores, statement of good standing from prior institution(s). Minimum college GPA of 2.0 required. Lowest grade transferable C-. **General Admission Information:** Priority deadline 12/1. Nonfall registration accepted. Admission may be deferred.

COSTS AND FINANCIAL AID

Annual tuition $40,220. Room and board $9,995. Required fees $1,060. Average book expense $1,100. **Required Forms and Deadlines:** FAFSA. **Notification of Awards:** Applicants will be notified of awards on a rolling basis beginning 3/1. *Types of Aid: Need-based scholarships/grants:* College/university scholarship or grant aid from institutional funds; Federal Pell; Private scholarships; SEOG; State scholarships/grants. *Loans:* Direct PLUS loans; Direct Subsidized Stafford Loans; Direct Unsubsidized Stafford Loans. *Student Employment:* Federal Work-Study Program available. Institutional employment available. **Financial Aid Statistics:** 100% needy freshmen, 100% needy undergrads receive need-based scholarship or grant aid. 21% freshmen, 19% undergrads receive non-need-based scholarship or grant aid. 100% freshmen, 80% undergrads receive need-based self-help aid. 0% freshmen, 0% undergrads receive athletic scholarships. 100% freshmen, 99% undergrads receive any aid. 75% undergrads borrow to pay for school. Average cumulative indebtedness $39,794. **Criteria for awarding aid:** *Need-based:* Minority status *Non-need-based:* Academics, Alumni affiliation, Leadership, Music/drama, Religious affiliation.

WASHBURN UNIVERSITY

1700 SW College Ave, Topeka, KS 66621
Phone: 785-670-1030
E-mail: admissions@washburn.edu
Fax: 785-670-1113 • **Website:** www.washburn.edu

This is a public school.

RATINGS

Admissions Selectivity Rating: 73   **Fire Safety Rating:** 60*   **Green Rating:** 60*

STUDENTS AND FACULTY

Enrollment: 4,900. **Student Body:** 59% female, 41% male, 7% out-of-state, international.
Retention and Graduation: 68% freshmen return for sophomore year.
Faculty: Student/faculty ratio 13:1. 286 full-time faculty, 84% hold PhDs, 14% are members of minority groups, 55% are women.

ACADEMICS

Degrees: Associate; Bachelor's; Certificate; Doctoral/Professional; Master's; Post-Bachelor's certificate; Post-Master's certificate **Classes:** Most classes have fewer than 10 students. Most lab/discussion sessions have fewer than 10 students. **Special Study Options:** Cooperative education program; Cross-registration; Distance learning; Double major; Dual enrollment; English as a Second Language (ESL); Honors program; Independent study; Internships; Liberal arts/career combination; Student-designed major; Study abroad; Teacher certification program.

FACILITIES

Housing: Apartments for single students; Coed dorms; Fraternity/sorority housing; Wellness housing

CAMPUS LIFE

Activities: Campus Ministries; Choral groups; Concert band; Dance; Drama/theater; International Student Organization; Jazz band; Literary magazine; Marching band; Model UN; Music ensembles; Musical theater; Pep band; Student government; Student newspaper; Student-run film society; Symphony orchestra; Television station; Yearbook.

ADMISSIONS

Freshman Academic Profile: Average high school GPA 3.4. 13% in top 10% of high school class, 34% in top 25% of high school class, 67% in top 50% of high school class. 96% from public high schools. **Test Scores:**

ACT middle 50% range 19-25. Minimum paper TOEFL 450. **Basis for Candidate Selection:** *Very important factors considered include:* rigor of secondary school record, academic GPA, standardized test scores. **Freshman Admission Requirements:** High school diploma is required and GED is accepted *Academic units recommended:* 4 English, 3 math, 3 science, 2 foreign language, 3 social studies, 1 history, 1 computer science. **Freshman Admission Statistics:** 1,458 applied, 98.8% admitted, 56% enrolled. **Transfer Admission Requirements:** college transcript(s), statement of good standing from prior institution(s). Minimum college GPA of 2.0 required. Lowest grade transferable 1. **General Admission Information:** Application fee $20. Regular application deadline 8/1. Nonfall registration accepted.

COSTS AND FINANCIAL AID

Annual in-state tuition $6,830. Annual out-of-state tuition $17,640. Room and board $6,830. Required fees $110. Average book expense $1,000. **Required Forms and Deadlines:** FAFSA. **Notification of Awards:** Applicants will be notified of awards on a rolling basis beginning 4/1. *Types of Aid: Need-based scholarships/grants:* College/university scholarship or grant aid from institutional funds; Federal Pell; Private scholarships; SEOG; State scholarships/grants. *Loans:* Direct PLUS loans; Direct Subsidized Stafford Loans; Direct Unsubsidized Stafford Loans. **Financial Aid Statistics:** 60% needy freshmen, 63% needy undergrads receive need-based scholarship or grant aid. 68% freshmen, 50% undergrads receive non-need-based scholarship or grant aid. 70% freshmen, 73% undergrads receive need-based self-help aid. 5% freshmen, 4% undergrads receive athletic scholarships. 68% undergrads borrow to pay for school. Average cumulative indebtedness $24,665. **Criteria for awarding aid:** *Non-need-based:* Academics, Alumni affiliation, Art, Athletics, Job skills, Leadership, Minority status, Music/drama, Religious affiliation, State/district residency.

WASHINGTON & JEFFERSON COLLEGE

60 South Lincoln Street, Washington, PA 15301
Phone: 724-223-6025 • **Financial Aid Phone:** 724-223-6019
E-mail: admission@washjeff.edu • **CEEB Code:** 2967
Fax: 724-223-6534 • **Website:** www.washjeff.edu • **ACT Code:** 3746

This private school was founded in 1781. It has a 60 acre campus.

RATINGS

Admissions Selectivity Rating: 88   **Fire Safety Rating:** 95   **Green Rating:** 87

STUDENTS AND FACULTY

Enrollment: 1,378. **Student Body:** 47% female, 53% male, 23% out-of-state, 4% international (20 countries represented). Asian 2%, African American 5%, Caucasian 75%, Hispanic 5%, Native American <1%, Pacific Islander <1%, Two or more races 4%, Race unknown 5%.
Retention and Graduation: 87% freshmen return for sophomore year. 67% freshmen graduate within 4 years. 70% freshmen graduate within 6 years. 33% grads go on to further study within 1 year. 45% grads pursue arts and sciences degrees. 14% grads pursue law degrees. 3% grads pursue business degrees. 10% grads pursue medical degrees. **Faculty:** Student/faculty ratio 11:1. 111 full-time faculty, 93% hold PhDs, 16% are members of minority groups, 48% are women. 0% of classes are taught by teaching assistants.

ACADEMICS

Degrees: Bachelor's; Master's; Post-Bachelor's certificate **Classes:** Most classes have 10-19 students. **Most popular majors:** Psychology, General; Business/Commerce, General; Accounting. **Special Study Options:** Accelerated program; Double major; Dual enrollment; English as a Second Language (ESL); Honors program; Independent study; Internships; Liberal arts/career combination; Student-designed major; Study abroad; Teacher certification program. Honors programs: The Washington Fellows is an honors program designed for exceptional students who are interested in challenging themselves in their years at W&J and desire a deep engagement in the liberal arts and sciences. All majors offer honors programs for students who wish to complete advanced research in their senior year. Research is presented orally, in writing, and often at national conferences. In addition, the Magellan program allows outstanding students to pursue independent research during the summer that is funded by the College. Combined degree programs: BA/JD; BA/MD; BA/MEng. **Disability Services offered to physically disabled students:** Note-taking services; Reader services; Tape recorders; Tutors. **Career services:**

Alumni network; Alumni services; Career assessment; Career/job search classes; Internships; Regional alumni

FACILITIES

Housing: Apartments for single students; Coed dorms; Fraternity/sorority housing; Men's dorms; Special housing for disabled student; Special housing for international students; Theme housing; Wellness housing; Women's dorms 90% of campus accessible to physically diasbled. **Special Academic Facilities/Equipment:** Abernathy Field Station, Olin Fine Arts Center, laser scanning confocal microscope facility, atomic force microscope, 3-D printers, mass spectrometer/gas chromatograph, microplate reader, cell culture labs, isolator lab, X-ray diffraction unit, neuropsychology lab, atomic absorption unit, nuclear magnetic resonance (NMR) lab, refrigerated centrifuge, global learning unit, language lab, spectrometers. **Computers:** 100% of classrooms, 100% of dorms, 100% of libraries, 100% of dining areas, 100% of student union, 95% of common outdoor areas have wireless network access. Students can register for classes online. Administrative functions (other than registration) can be performed online.

CAMPUS LIFE

Environment: Village **Activities:** Campus Ministries; Choral groups; Concert band; Dance; Drama/theater; International Student Organization; Jazz band; Literary magazine; Model UN; Music ensembles; Musical theater; Pep band; Radio station; Student government; Student newspaper; Student-run film society; Yearbook 94 registered organizations, 21 honor societies, 4 religious organizations. 6 fraternities, 4 sororities. **Athletics (Intercollegiate):** *Men:* baseball, basketball, cheerleading, cross-country, diving, football, golf, lacrosse, soccer, swimming, tennis, track/field (outdoor), track/field (indoor), water polo, wrestling. *Women:* basketball, cheerleading, cross-country, diving, field hockey, golf, lacrosse, soccer, softball, swimming, tennis, track/field (outdoor), track/field (indoor), volleyball, water polo. **On-Campus Highlights:** The Hub (Student Center), Swanson Wellness Center, Technology Center, Rossin Campus Center/George & Tom's, The Ski Lodge/Barista **Environmental Initiatives:** Signed the ACUPCC, created the Sustainability Committee and a Climate Action Plan, which outlines many past accomplishments and current initiatives.

ADMISSIONS

Freshman Academic Profile: Average high school GPA 3.7. 34% in top 10% of high school class, 62% in top 25% of high school class, 88% in top 50% of high school class. 82% from public high schools. **Test Scores:** SAT Math middle 50% range 550-640. SAT EBRW middle 50% range 570-650. ACT middle 50% range 23-28. Minimum internet-based TOEFL 85. Minimum paper TOEFL 563. **Basis for Candidate Selection:** *Very important factors considered include:* rigor of secondary school record, class rank, academic GPA, application essay, recommendation(s), interview, character/personal qualities. *Important factors considered include:* extracurricular activities. *Other factors considered include:* standardized test scores, talent/ability, alumni/ae relation, geographical residence, state residency, racial/ethnic status, volunteer work, work experience, level of applicant's interest. **Freshman Admission Requirements:** High school diploma is required and GED is accepted *Academic units required:* 3 English, 3 math, 1 science, 1 science labs, 2 foreign language, 6 academic electives, *Academic units recommended:* 4 English, 4 math, 2 science, 2 science labs, 3 foreign language, 6 academic electives. **Freshman Admission Statistics:** 5,358 applied, 47.9% admitted, 13% enrolled. **Transfer Admission Requirements:** High school transcript, college transcript(s), essay or personal statement, standardized test scores, statement of good standing from prior institution(s). Minimum college GPA of 2.50 required. Lowest grade transferable C. **General Admission Information:** Application fee $25. Priority deadline 1/15. Regular application deadline 3/1. Nonfall registration accepted. Admission may be deferred for a maximum of 1 year.

COSTS AND FINANCIAL AID

Average book expense $800. **Required Forms and Deadlines:** FAFSA. **Notification of Awards:** Applicants will be notified of awards on a rolling basis beginning 12/15. **Types of Aid:** *Need-based scholarships/grants:* College/university scholarship or grant aid from institutional funds; Federal Pell; Private scholarships; SEOG; State scholarships/grants. *Loans:* Direct PLUS loans; Direct Subsidized Stafford Loans; Direct Unsubsidized Stafford Loans. *Student Employment:* Federal Work-Study Program available. Institutional employment available. **Financial Aid Statistics:** 88% needy freshmen, 85% needy undergrads receive need-based scholarship or grant aid. 99% freshmen, 92% undergrads receive non-need-based scholarship or grant aid. 85% freshmen, 85% undergrads receive need-based self-help aid. 0% freshmen, 0% undergrads receive athletic scholarships. 100% freshmen, 99% undergrads receive any aid. **Criteria for awarding aid:** *Need-based:* Academics *Non-need-based:* Academics, Alumni affiliation, Leadership.

WASHINGTON AND LEE UNIVERSITY

204 W. Washington Street, Lexington, VA 24450-0303
Phone: 540-458-8710 • **Financial Aid Phone:** 540-458-8720
E-mail: admissions@wlu.edu • **CEEB Code:** 5887
Fax: 540-458-8062 • **Website:** www.wlu.edu • **ACT Code:** 4430

This private school was founded in 1749. It has a 430 acre campus.

RATINGS

Admissions Selectivity Rating: 97　　**Fire Safety Rating:** 60*　　**Green Rating:** 86

STUDENTS AND FACULTY

Enrollment: 1,819. **Student Body:** 48% female, 52% male, 84% out-of-state, 4% international (30 countries represented). Asian 3%, African American 2%, Caucasian 83%, Hispanic 5%, Native American 0%, Pacific Islander 0%, Two or more races 3%, Race unknown 1%.
Retention and Graduation: 96% freshmen return for sophomore year. 89% freshmen graduate within 4 years. 92% freshmen graduate within 6 years. 17% grads go on to further study within 1 year. 9% grads pursue arts and sciences degrees. 3.5% grads pursue law degrees. 2% grads pursue business degrees. 2.4% grads pursue medical degrees. **Faculty:** Student/faculty ratio 8:1. 204 full-time faculty, 94% hold PhDs, 11% are members of minority groups, 37% are women. 0% of classes are taught by teaching assistants.

ACADEMICS

Degrees: Bachelor's; Doctoral/Professional **Classes:** Most classes have 20-29 students. Most lab/discussion sessions have 10-19 students. **Most popular majors:** Economics, General; Business/Commerce, General; Accounting And Business/Management. **Special Study Options:** Double major; Exchange student program (domestic); Honors program; Independent study; Internships; Liberal arts/career combination; Student-designed major; Study abroad; Teacher certification program. Honors programs: University Scholars, Bonner Scholars, Johnson Scholars. **Disability Services offered to physically disabled students:** Note-taking services; Reader services; Tape recorders; Tutors. **Career services:** Alumni network; Career assessment; Career/job search classes; Internships; Regional alumni

FACILITIES

Housing: Apartments for single students; Coed dorms; Fraternity/sorority housing; Special housing for disabled student; Special housing for international students; Theme housing 80% of campus accessible to physically diasbled. **Special Academic Facilities/Equipment:** Center for International Education IQ Center, Collaborative Teaching and Learning Space History and porcelain museums Lenfest Performing Arts Center Communications labs Nuclear science lab Scanning electron microscope **Computers:** Students can register for classes online. Administrative functions (other than registration) can be performed online.

CAMPUS LIFE

Environment: Village **Activities:** Campus Ministries; Choral groups; Concert band; Dance; Drama/theater; International Student Organization; Jazz band; Literary magazine; Music ensembles; Musical theater; Pep band; Radio station; Student government; Student newspaper; Student-run film society; Symphony orchestra; Television station; Yearbook 90 registered organizations, 5 honor societies, 11 religious organizations. 14 fraternities, 5 sororities. **Athletics (Intercollegiate):** *Men:* baseball, basketball, cross-country, equestrian sports, football, golf, lacrosse, soccer, swimming, tennis, track/field (outdoor), track/field (indoor), wrestling. *Women:* basketball, cheerleading, cross-country, equestrian sports, field hockey, lacrosse, soccer, swimming, tennis, track/field (outdoor), track/field (indoor), volleyball. **On-Campus Highlights:** The Village, Elrod University Commons, Lenfest Center for the Arts, Lee Museum and Chapel, Tea Room at International Learning Center

ADMISSIONS

Freshman Academic Profile: 85% in top 10% of high school class, 99% in top 25% of high school class, 100% in top 50% of high school class. 52% from public high schools. **Test Scores:** SAT Math middle 50% range 670-750. SAT EBRW middle 50% range 680-740. ACT middle 50% range 31-33. **Basis for Candidate Selection:** *Very important factors considered include:* rigor of secondary school record, class rank, extracurricular activities, character/personal qualities. *Important factors considered include:* academic GPA, standardized test scores, recommendation(s). *Other factors considered include:* application essay, interview, talent/ability, first generation, alumni/ae relation, geographical residence, state residency, racial/ethnic status, volunteer work, work experience, level of applicant's interest. **Freshman Admission Requirements:** High school diploma is required and GED is accepted *Academic units required:* 4 English, 3 math, 1 science, 1 science labs, 3 foreign language, 1 social studies, 1 history, 4 academic electives, *Academic units recommended:* 4 English, 4 math, 4 science, 4 foreign language, 2 social studies, 2 history, 4 academic electives. **Freshman Admission Statistics:** 5,455 applied, 22.0% admitted, 39% enrolled. **Transfer Admission Requirements:** High school transcript, college transcript(s), essay or personal statement, standardized test scores, statement of good standing from prior institution(s). Minimum college GPA of 2.0 required. Lowest grade transferable C. **General Admission Information:** Application fee $60. Regular application deadline 1/1. Nonfall registration accepted. Admission may be deferred for a maximum of 1 year.

COSTS AND FINANCIAL AID

Annual tuition $49,170. Required fees $1,000. Average book expense $1,800. **Required Forms and Deadlines:** CSS/Financial Aid PROFILE; FAFSA; Noncustodial PROFILE. **Notification of Awards:** Applicants will be notified of awards on or about 4/1. *Types of Aid: Need-based scholarships/ grants:* College/university scholarship or grant aid from institutional funds; Federal Pell; Private scholarships; SEOG; State scholarships/grants. *Loans:* Direct PLUS loans; Direct Subsidized Stafford Loans; Direct Unsubsidized Stafford Loans. *Student Employment:* Federal Work-Study Program available. Institutional employment available. **Financial Aid Statistics:** 100% needy freshmen, 100% needy undergrads receive need-based scholarship or grant aid. 30% freshmen, 25% undergrads receive non-need-based scholarship or grant aid. 63% freshmen, 63% undergrads receive need-based self-help aid. 0% freshmen, 0% undergrads receive athletic scholarships. 49% undergrads receive any aid. Average cumulative indebtedness $21,683. **Criteria for awarding aid:** *Need-based:* Academics *Non-need-based:* Academics.

WASHINGTON COLLEGE

300 Washington Avenue, Chestertown, MD 21620
Phone: 410-778-7700 • **Financial Aid Phone:** 410-778-7214
E-mail: wc_admissions@washcoll.edu • **CEEB Code:** 5888
Fax: 410-778-7287 • **Website:** www.washcoll.edu • **ACT Code:** 1754

This private school was founded in 1782. It has a 144 acre campus.

RATINGS

Admissions Selectivity Rating: 88   **Fire Safety Rating:** 97   **Green Rating:** 63

STUDENTS AND FACULTY

Enrollment: 1,449. **Student Body:** 58% female, 42% male, 55% out-of-state, 9% international (32 countries represented). Asian 3%, African American 8%, Caucasian 69%, Hispanic 6%, Native American 1%, Pacific Islander <1%, Two or more races 1%, Race unknown 3%.
Retention and Graduation: 85% freshmen return for sophomore year. 73% freshmen graduate within 4 years. 76% freshmen graduate within 6 years. 50% grads go on to further study within 1 year. 12% grads pursue arts and sciences degrees. 4% grads pursue law degrees. 8% grads pursue business degrees. 3% grads pursue medical degrees. **Faculty:** Student/faculty ratio 11:1. 116 full-time faculty, 98% hold PhDs, 10% are members of minority groups, 49% are women. 0% of classes are taught by teaching assistants.

ACADEMICS

Degrees: Bachelor's **Classes:** Most classes have 20-29 students. Most lab/ discussion sessions have 10-19 students. **Most popular majors:** Biology/ Biological Sciences, General; Psychology, General; Business Administration And Management, General. **Special Study Options:** Cross-registration; Double major; Dual enrollment; Exchange student program (domestic); Honors program; Independent study; Internships; Liberal arts/career combination; Student-designed major; Study abroad; Teacher certification program. Honors programs: The Douglass Cater Society of Junior Fellows is the College's flagship academic enrichment program—one that rewards creativity, initiative and intellectual curiosity with competitive grants to support self-directed undergraduate research and scholarship anywhere in the world. The intent is to bring together the best and brightest in what founder Douglass Cater called "a companionship of learning." **Career services:** Alumni network; Alumni services; Career assessment; Career/job search classes; Internships; Regional alumni

FACILITIES

Housing: Apartments for single students; Coed dorms; Fraternity/sorority housing; Men's dorms; Theme housing; Wellness housing; Women's dorms 90%

of campus accessible to physically diasbled. **Special Academic Facilities/ Equipment:** Language lab, computer classroom, C.V. Starr Center for the Study of the American Experience, The Center for the Environment and Society, O'Neill Literary House **Computers:** Administrative functions (other than registration) can be performed online.

CAMPUS LIFE

Environment: Rural **Activities:** Campus Ministries; Choral groups; Concert band; Dance; Drama/theater; International Student Organization; Jazz band; Literary magazine; Model UN; Music ensembles; Musical theater; Student government; Student newspaper; Yearbook 50 registered organizations, 13 honor societies, 4 religious organizations. 4 fraternities, 3 sororities. **Athletics (Intercollegiate):** *Men:* baseball, basketball, crew/rowing, lacrosse, sailing, soccer, swimming, tennis. *Women:* basketball, crew/rowing, field hockey, lacrosse, sailing, soccer, softball, swimming, tennis, volleyball. **On-Campus Highlights:** Miller Library, Johnson Lifetime Fitness Center, Gibson Center for the Arts, O'Neill Literary House, Hodson Commons Student Center **Environmental Initiatives:** George Goes Green (G3) is Washington College's initiative for stewardship and sustainability. Situated on Maryland's Eastern Shore, the College is surrounded by the coastal and inland waters of the Chesapeake Bay, which informs our sense of history, our sense of self, and our sense of place. Our benefactor George Washington promoted sustainable economic cycles by advocating compost as a method to amend damaged soils. Today, Washington College is nationally renowned for promoting sustainability. Green at a Glance: Chesapeake Semester composting recycling environmentally-friendly products local foods native plant landscaping green facilities

ADMISSIONS

Freshman Academic Profile: Average high school GPA 3.7. 38% in top 10% of high school class, 70% in top 25% of high school class, 91% in top 50% of high school class. **Test Scores:** SAT Math middle 50% range 540-630. SAT EBRW middle 50% range 550-670. ACT middle 50% range 23-29. **Basis for Candidate Selection:** *Very important factors considered include:* rigor of secondary school record, academic GPA, interview, level of applicant's interest. *Important factors considered include:* class rank, application essay, standardized test scores. *Other factors considered include:* recommendation(s), extracurricular activities, talent/ability, character/personal qualities, first generation, alumni/ae relation, geographical residence, state residency, racial/ ethnic status, volunteer work, work experience. **Freshman Admission Requirements:** High school diploma is required and GED is accepted *Academic units required:* 4 English, 3 math, 3 science, 2 science labs, 2 foreign language, 2 social studies, 2 history, *Academic units recommended:* 4 English, 4 math, 4 science, 3 science labs, 4 foreign language, 2 social studies, 2 history. **Freshman Admission Statistics:** 5,515 applied, 47.6% admitted, 14% enrolled. **Transfer Admission Requirements:** High school transcript, college transcript(s), essay or personal statement, statement of good standing from prior institution(s). **General Admission Information:** Regular application deadline 2/15. Nonfall registration accepted. Admission may be deferred.

COSTS AND FINANCIAL AID

Average book expense $1,400. **Required Forms and Deadlines:** FAFSA. **Notification of Awards:** Applicants will be notified of awards on a rolling basis beginning 2/1. *Types of Aid: Need-based scholarships/grants:* College/ university scholarship or grant aid from institutional funds; Federal Pell; Private scholarships; SEOG; State scholarships/grants. *Loans:* Direct PLUS loans; Direct Subsidized Stafford Loans; Direct Unsubsidized Stafford Loans. *Student Employment:* Federal Work-Study Program available. Institutional employment available. **Financial Aid Statistics:** 100% needy freshmen, 100% needy undergrads receive need-based scholarship or grant aid. 22% freshmen, 21% undergrads receive non-need-based scholarship or grant aid. 76% freshmen, 82% undergrads receive need-based self-help aid. 0% freshmen, 0% undergrads receive athletic scholarships. 95% freshmen, 92% undergrads receive any aid. 64% undergrads borrow to pay for school. Average cumulative indebtedness $36,991. **Criteria for awarding aid:** *Non-need-based:* Academics, Art, Music/ drama.

See page 1082.

WASHINGTON STATE UNIVERSITY

PO Box 645910, Pullman, WA 99164-1067
Phone: 509-335-5586 • **Financial Aid Phone:** 509-335-9711
E-mail: admissions@wsu.edu • **CEEB Code:** 3800
Fax: 509-335-4902 • **Website:** www.wsu.edu • **ACT Code:** 4482

This public school was founded in 1890. It has a 1745 acre campus.

RATINGS
Admissions Selectivity Rating: 81   **Fire Safety Rating:** 92   **Green Rating:** 96

STUDENTS AND FACULTY
Enrollment: 24,797. **Student Body:** 52% female, 48% male, 13% out-of-state, 5% international (78 countries represented). Asian 6%, African American 3%, Caucasian 61%, Hispanic 15%, Native American 1%, Pacific Islander <1%, Two or more races 7%, Race unknown 2%.
Retention and Graduation: 81% freshmen return for sophomore year. 38% freshmen graduate within 4 years. 62% freshmen graduate within 6 years. **Faculty:** Student/faculty ratio 15:1. 1,368 full-time faculty, 86% hold PhDs, 15% are members of minority groups, 44% are women. 17% of classes are taught by teaching assistants.

ACADEMICS
Degrees: Bachelor's; Certificate; Doctoral; Doctoral/Professional; Doctoral/Research; Master's; Post-Bachelor's certificate; Post-Master's certificate
Classes: Most classes have 10-19 students. Most lab/discussion sessions have 20-29 students. **Most popular majors:** Engineering; Social Sciences; Business, Management, Marketing, And Related Support Services. **Special Study Options:** Accelerated program; Cooperative education program; Cross-registration; Distance learning; Double major; Dual enrollment; English as a Second Language (ESL); Exchange student program (domestic); External degree program; Honors program; Independent study; Internships; Liberal arts/career combination; Student-designed major; Study abroad; Teacher certification program. Honors programs: The Washington State University Honors College is one of the oldest and most highly regarded public university honors colleges in the country. It attracts top students in all majors from throughout the United States and around the world. The Honors College curriculum emphasizes global awareness and international impact. It immerses students in the study of international issues, builds their proficiency in a second language, and encourages them to study abroad. Instead of lecturing, professors teach courses interactively, inspiring discussions among students. Honors students conduct research as undergraduates, exploring an academic question of importance to them, documenting their analysis and conclusions, and orally presenting their work to faculty. The Honors College deepens students' intellectual curiosity and builds a lifelong love of learning, as well as skills in critical thinking, writing, public presentation, and information literacy. Graduates emerge with the tools required to become leaders in their fields.
Disability Services offered to physically disabled students: Note-taking services; Reader services; Tape recorders; Tutors. **Career services:** Alumni network; Alumni services; Career assessment; Career/job search classes; Internships

FACILITIES
Housing: Apartments for married students; Apartments for single students; Coed dorms; Cooperative housing; Fraternity/sorority housing; Men's dorms; Special housing for disabled student; Special housing for international students; Theme housing; Wellness housing; Women's dorms 95% of campus accessible to physically diasbled. **Special Academic Facilities/Equipment:** Museums, displays and collections, including a natural history museum, museum of art, museum of anthropology, an entomological collection, a veterinary anatomy teaching museum, and geology museums. Livestock centers, labs, and barns, including beef and dairy centers, a cattle feeding lab, a meats lab, and feed plant. Radio and TV stations. Digital recording studio. Music listening library. Fine arts studio facilities with specialized equipment. International center for exchanging cultural knowledge. Child development lab. Financial markets lab (trading room). Food sensory evaluation lab. Culinary lab and teaching kitchen. social and economic sciences research center. Planetarium and astronomical observatory. Specialized teaching and research labs for science and engineering, including a bio-molecular x-ray crystallography center, a genomics and gene sequencing lab, a virtual reality computer-integrated manufacturing lab, a hydraulics lab, laboratory for atmospheric research, and more. Wildlife center. Ecological reserves. Greenhouses, vivaria, and herbaria. Agronomic research farms, a horticultural orchard, and an organic teaching farm. On-campus market for locally grown, alumni-grown, and organic produce. Veterinary teaching hospital. Human anatomy lab. Water research center. Nuclear radiation center. **Computers:** 100% of classrooms, 100% of dorms, 100% of libraries, 100% of dining areas, 100% of student union, 25% of common outdoor areas have wireless network access. Students can register for classes online. Administrative functions (other than registration) can be performed online.

CAMPUS LIFE
Environment: Town **Activities:** Campus Ministries; Choral groups; Concert band; Dance; Drama/theater; International Student Organization; Jazz band; Literary magazine; Marching band; Model UN; Music ensembles; Musical theater; Opera; Pep band; Radio station; Student government; Student newspaper; Student-run film society; Symphony orchestra; Television station; Yearbook 300 registered organizations, 36 honor societies, 19 religious organizations. 26 fraternities, 13 sororities. **Athletics (Intercollegiate):** *Men:* baseball, basketball, cross-country, football, golf, track/field (outdoor). *Women:* basketball, crew/rowing, cross-country, golf, soccer, swimming, tennis, track/field (outdoor), volleyball. **On-Campus Highlights:** Compton Union Building (CUB), Terrell Friendship Mall, Student Recreation Center, Beasley Performing Arts Coliseum, Martin Stadium **Environmental Initiatives:** Sustainability & Environment Committee, established by the President of WSU. Meets monthly and has campus-wide representation.

ADMISSIONS
Freshman Academic Profile: Average high school GPA 3.4. **Test Scores:** SAT Math middle 50% range 510-610. SAT EBRW middle 50% range 510-610. ACT middle 50% range 20-26. Minimum internet-based TOEFL 79. Minimum paper TOEFL 550. **Basis for Candidate Selection:** *Very important factors considered include:* academic GPA, standardized test scores. *Important factors considered include:* rigor of secondary school record, class rank. *Other factors considered include:* application essay, recommendation(s), extracurricular activities, talent/ability, character/personal qualities, volunteer work, work experience. **Freshman Admission Requirements:** High school diploma is required and GED is accepted *Academic units required:* 4 English, 3 math, 2 science, 2 foreign language, 3 social studies, 1 visual/performing arts, and 1 unit from above areas or other academic areas. *Academic units recommended:* 4 English, 4 math, 2 science, 2 foreign language, 3 social studies, 1 visual/performing arts, 1 unit from above areas or other academic areas. **Freshman Admission Statistics:** 22,565 applied, 73.1% admitted, 28% enrolled. **Transfer Admission Requirements:** college transcript(s), Minimum college GPA of 2.5 required. Lowest grade transferable D. **General Admission Information:** Application fee $50. Priority deadline 1/31. Nonfall registration accepted.

COSTS AND FINANCIAL AID
Annual out-of-state tuition $23,956. Room and board $11,356. Required fees $1,861. Average book expense $960. **Required Forms and Deadlines:** FAFSA; State aid form. **Notification of Awards:** Applicants will be notified of awards on a rolling basis beginning 4/15. **Types of Aid:** *Need-based scholarships/grants:* College/university scholarship or grant aid from institutional funds; Federal Nursing Scholarships; Federal Pell; Private scholarships; SEOG; State scholarships/grants. *Loans:* Direct PLUS loans; Direct Subsidized Stafford Loans; Direct Unsubsidized Stafford Loans. *Student Employment:* Federal Work-Study Program available. Institutional employment available. **Financial Aid Statistics:** 87% needy freshmen, 86% needy undergrads receive need-based scholarship or grant aid. 72% freshmen, 46% undergrads receive non-need-based scholarship or grant aid. 63% freshmen, 69% undergrads receive need-based self-help aid. 2% freshmen, 1% undergrads receive athletic scholarships. 86% freshmen, 73% undergrads receive any aid. 58% undergrads borrow to pay for school. Average cumulative indebtedness $25,874. **Criteria for awarding aid:** *Need-based:* Academics *Non-need-based:* Academics, Alumni affiliation, Art, Athletics, Job skills, Leadership, Minority status, Music/drama, Religious affiliation, State/district residency.

WASHINGTON UNIVERSITY IN ST. LOUIS

Campus Box 1089, St. Louis, MO 63130-4899
Phone: 314-935-6000 • **Financial Aid Phone:** 888-547-6670
E-mail: admissions@wustl.edu • **CEEB Code:** 6929
Fax: 314-935-4290 • **Website:** wustl.edu • **ACT Code:** 2386

This private school was founded in 1853. It has a 169 acre campus.

RATINGS
Admissions Selectivity Rating: 98   **Fire Safety Rating:** 97   **Green Rating:** 95

STUDENTS AND FACULTY
Enrollment: 7,253. **Student Body:** 53% female, 47% male, 91% out-of-state, 7% international (50 countries represented). Asian 17%, African American 8%, Caucasian 52%, Hispanic 9%, Native American <1%, Pacific Islander <1%, Two or more races 5%, Race unknown 2%.
Retention and Graduation: 97% freshmen return for sophomore year. 88% freshmen graduate within 4 years. 94% freshmen graduate within 6 years. 23% grads go on to further study within 1 year. 4% grads pursue arts and sciences degrees. 1% grads pursue law degrees. 2% grads pursue business degrees. 6% grads pursue medical degrees. **Faculty:** Student/faculty ratio 8:1. 948 full-time faculty, 94% hold PhDs, 23% are members of minority groups, 38% are women.

ACADEMICS
Degrees: Associate; Bachelor's; Certificate; Doctoral; Doctoral/Professional; Doctoral/Research; Master's; Post-Bachelor's certificate; Post-Master's certificate **Classes:** Most classes have 10-19 students. Most lab/discussion sessions have 20-29 students. **Most popular majors:** Engineering, General; Social Sciences, General; Business Administration And Management, General. **Special Study Options:** Accelerated program; Cooperative education program; Cross-registration; Double major; Dual enrollment; English as a Second Language (ESL); Independent study; Internships; Liberal arts/career combination; Student-designed major; Study abroad; Teacher certification program. Combined degree programs: BA/MA; BA/MEng. **Disability Services offered to physically disabled students:** Note-taking services; Reader services; Tape recorders; Tutors. **Career services:** Alumni network; Alumni services; Career assessment; Career/job search classes; Internships; Regional alumni

FACILITIES
Housing: Apartments for married students; Apartments for single students; Coed dorms; Cooperative housing; Fraternity/sorority housing; Wellness housing 95% of campus accessible to physically disabled. **Special Academic Facilities/Equipment:** 12 university-wide and 56 school-based research centers and institutes, 59-acre medical campus, observatory, plant growth facility, international writer's center, laboratory science building, theater, art museum, maker space, state-of-the-art recreation facility, center for entrepreneurship and innovation, career centers, and state-of-the-art architecture and art studios **Computers:** Students can register for classes online. Administrative functions (other than registration) can be performed online.

CAMPUS LIFE
Environment: City **Activities:** Campus Ministries; Choral groups; Concert band; Dance; Drama/theater; International Student Organization; Jazz band; Literary magazine; Model UN; Music ensembles; Musical theater; Opera; Pep band; Radio station; Student government; Student newspaper; Student-run film society; Symphony orchestra; Television station 200 registered organizations, 18 honor societies, 19 religious organizations. 12 fraternities, 6 sororities. **Athletics (Intercollegiate):** *Men:* baseball, basketball, cross-country, diving, football, soccer, swimming, tennis, track/field (outdoor), track/field (indoor). *Women:* basketball, cross-country, diving, golf, soccer, softball, swimming, tennis, track/field (outdoor), track/field (indoor), volleyball. **On-Campus Highlights:** Art Museum, Whispers Cafe in Olin Library, Danforth University Center, Brookings Quadrangle, South 40 Residential Area

ADMISSIONS
Freshman Academic Profile: 87% in top 10% of high school class, 98% in top 25% of high school class, 100% in top 50% of high school class. 56% from public high schools. **Test Scores:** SAT Math middle 50% range 750-800. SAT EBRW middle 50% range 720-770. ACT middle 50% range 32-34. **Basis for Candidate Selection:** *Very important factors considered include:* rigor of secondary school record, class rank, academic GPA, application

essay, standardized test scores, recommendation(s), extracurricular activities, talent/ability, character/personal qualities, volunteer work, work experience. *Important factors considered include:* level of applicant's interest. *Other factors considered include:* interview, first generation, alumni/ae relation, geographical residence, racial/ethnic status. **Freshman Admission Requirements:** High school diploma is required and GED is accepted *Academic units required:* 4 English, 3 math, 3 science, 2 science labs, 2 foreign language, 2 social studies, 2 history, *Academic units recommended:* 4 English, 4 math, 4 science, 4 science labs, 4 foreign language, 4 social studies, 4 history. **Freshman Admission Statistics:** 30,463 applied, 16.0% admitted, 37% enrolled. **Transfer Admission Requirements:** college transcript(s), essay or personal statement, statement of good standing from prior institution(s). Lowest grade transferable C. **General Admission Information:** Application fee $75. Regular application deadline 1/2. Nonfall registration accepted. Admission may be deferred for a maximum of 2 years.

COSTS AND FINANCIAL AID
Annual tuition $52,400. Room and board $16,440. Required fees $999. Average book expense $1,010. **Required Forms and Deadlines:** CSS/Financial Aid PROFILE; FAFSA; Noncustodial PROFILE. **Notification of Awards:** Applicants will be notified of awards on or about 4/1. **Types of Aid:** *Need-based scholarships/grants:* College/university scholarship or grant aid from institutional funds; Federal Pell; Private scholarships; SEOG; State scholarships/grants; United Negro College Fund. *Loans:* Direct PLUS loans; Direct Subsidized Stafford Loans; Direct Unsubsidized Stafford Loans. *Student Employment:* Federal Work-Study Program available. Institutional employment available. **Financial Aid Statistics:** 95% needy freshmen, 97% needy undergrads receive need-based scholarship or grant aid. 11% freshmen, 6% undergrads receive non-need-based scholarship or grant aid. 75% freshmen, 67% undergrads receive need-based self-help aid. 0% freshmen, 0% undergrads receive athletic scholarships. 50% freshmen, 53% undergrads receive any aid. 30% undergrads borrow to pay for school. Average cumulative indebtedness $23,577. **Criteria for awarding aid:** *Need-based:* Academics *Non-need-based:* Academics, Art, Leadership.

WATKINS COLLEGE OF ART, DESIGN & FILM

2298 Rosa L Parks Blvd, Nashville, TN 37228
Phone: 615-277-7418 • **Financial Aid Phone:** 615-277-7421
E-mail: admissions@watkins.edu
Fax: 615-383-4849 • **Website:** www.watkins.edu • **ACT Code:** 4027

This private school was founded in 1895. It has a 13 acre campus.

RATINGS
Admissions Selectivity Rating: 78   **Fire Safety Rating:** 96   **Green Rating:** 60*

STUDENTS AND FACULTY
Student Body: 30% out-of-state, (4 countries represented).
Retention and Graduation: 53% freshmen return for sophomore year. 10% grads go on to further study within 1 year. 10% grads pursue arts and sciences degrees. **Faculty:** Student/faculty ratio 7:1. 20 full-time faculty, 60% hold PhDs, 0% are members of minority groups, 50% are women. 0% of classes are taught by teaching assistants.

ACADEMICS
Degrees: Bachelor's; Post-Bachelor's certificate **Classes:** Most classes have 20-29 students. Most lab/discussion sessions have 10-19 students. **Most popular majors:** Graphic Design; Film/Cinema/Video Studies; Fine/Studio Arts, General. **Special Study Options:** Cooperative education program; Dual enrollment; Independent study; Internships; Study abroad. **Disability Services offered to physically disabled students:** Note-taking services; Reader services; Tape recorders; Tutors. **Career services:** Alumni network; Alumni services; Career assessment; Career/job search classes; Internships

FACILITIES
Housing: Apartments for single students; Coed dorms; Special housing for disabled student; Women's dorms 100% of campus accessible to physically disabled. **Special Academic Facilities/Equipment:** Brownlee O. Currey Gallery **Computers:** 100% of classrooms, 100% of dorms, 100% of libraries, 100% of dining areas, 100% of student union, 50% of common outdoor areas have wireless network access. Administrative functions (other than registration) can be performed online.

CAMPUS LIFE
Environment: Metropolis **Activities:** Student-run film society.
Environmental Initiatives: Recycling Program

ADMISSIONS

Freshman Academic Profile: 60% from public high schools. **Test Scores:** ACT middle 50% range 20-25. Minimum internet-based TOEFL 60. Minimum paper TOEFL 340. **Basis for Candidate Selection:** *Very important factors considered include:* application essay, talent/ability, level of applicant's interest. *Important factors considered include:* academic GPA, standardized test scores, recommendation(s), character/personal qualities. *Other factors considered include:* rigor of secondary school record, class rank, interview, extracurricular activities, volunteer work. **Freshman Admission Requirements:** High school diploma is required and GED is accepted *Academic units recommended:* 3 English, 2 math, 2 science, 1 foreign language, 3 social studies, 3 history, 3 computer science, 4 visual/performing arts. **Freshman Admission Statistics:** 113 applied, 83.2% admitted, 61% enrolled. **Transfer Admission Requirements:** college transcript(s), essay or personal statement, Minimum college GPA of 3.0 required. Lowest grade transferable C. **General Admission Information:** Application fee $50. Priority deadline 5/1. Regular application deadline 7/15. Nonfall registration accepted. Admission may be deferred for a maximum of 1 semester.

COSTS AND FINANCIAL AID

Annual tuition $18,900. Required fees $1,560. Average book expense $1,500. **Required Forms and Deadlines:** FAFSA; Institution's own financial aid form. **Notification of Awards:** Applicants will be notified of awards on a rolling basis beginning 5/1. **Types of Aid:** *Need-based scholarships/grants:* College/ university scholarship or grant aid from institutional funds; Federal Pell; Private scholarships; SEOG; State scholarships/grants. *Student Employment:* Federal Work-Study Program available. Institutional employment available. **Financial Aid Statistics:** 68% needy freshmen, 83% needy undergrads receive need-based scholarship or grant aid. 37% freshmen, 10% undergrads receive non-need-based scholarship or grant aid. 100% freshmen, 83% undergrads receive need-based self-help aid. 0% freshmen, 0% undergrads receive athletic scholarships. 50% freshmen, 40% undergrads receive any aid. **Criteria for awarding aid:** *Non-need-based:* Academics, Art.

WAYLAND BAPTIST UNIVERSITY

1900 West 7th street, Plainview, TX 79072
Phone: 806-291-3500 • **Financial Aid Phone:** 806-291-3520
E-mail: admityou@wbu.edu
Fax: 806-291-1963 • **ACT Code:** 4246

This private school, affiliated with the Southern Baptist Church, was founded in 1908. It has a 80 acre campus.

RATINGS

Admissions Selectivity Rating: 73   **Fire Safety Rating:** 88   **Green Rating:** 60*

STUDENTS AND FACULTY

Enrollment: 3,715. **Student Body:** 48% female, 52% male, 31% out-of-state, 1% international (20 countries represented). Asian 2%, African American 16%, Caucasian 43%, Hispanic 28%, Native American 1%, Pacific Islander 1%, Two or more races 4%, Race unknown 4%.
Retention and Graduation: 45% freshmen return for sophomore year. **Faculty:** Student/faculty ratio 8:1. 174 full-time faculty, 78% hold PhDs, 14% are members of minority groups, 34% are women. 0% of classes are taught by teaching assistants.

ACADEMICS

Degrees: Associate; Bachelor's; Certificate; Doctoral/Research; Master's; Transfer Associate **Classes:** Most classes have 10-19 students. Most lab/ discussion sessions have 10-19 students. **Most popular majors:** Liberal Arts And Sciences, General Studies And Humanities, Other; Criminal Justice/Law Enforcement Administration; Business Administration And Management, General. **Special Study Options:** Accelerated program; Distance learning; Double major; External degree program; Honors program; Internships; Study abroad; Teacher certification program. Honors programs: The Honors Program offered by Wayland is designed to challenge the academically superior student to develop initiative and abilities beyond what is expected in a normal course of study. Electing an Honors program offers breadth and depth of content through independent study and research, aiding the student in preparation for entering a career upon graduation or attending graduate school in a field of choice. Honors work represents the highest level of academic work available at Wayland on the undergraduate level. **Disability Services offered to physically disabled students:** Note-taking services; Reader services; Tutors. **Career services:** Career assessment

FACILITIES

Housing: Apartments for married students; Apartments for single students; Men's dorms; Women's dorms 100% of campus accessible to physically disabled. **Special Academic Facilities/Equipment:** Llano Estacado Museum. **Computers:** 80% of classrooms, 80% of dorms, 100% of libraries, 100% of dining areas, have wireless network access. Students can register for classes online. Administrative functions (other than registration) can be performed online.

CAMPUS LIFE

Environment: Town **Activities:** Campus Ministries; Choral groups; Concert band; Dance; Drama/theater; International Student Organization; Marching band; Music ensembles; Musical theater; Pep band; Radio station; Student government; Student newspaper; Television station; Yearbook 34 registered organizations, 4 honor societies, 7 religious organizations. **Athletics (Intercollegiate):** *Men:* baseball, basketball, cheerleading, cross-country, golf, soccer, track/field (outdoor), track/field (indoor). *Women:* basketball, cheerleading, cross-country, golf, soccer, track/field (outdoor), track/field (indoor), volleyball. **On-Campus Highlights:** McClung University Center, Mabee Learning Resource Center, Gates Hall, Hutcherson Gymnasium, Harral Auditorium **Environmental Initiatives:** Installed energy efficient lighting campuswide.

ADMISSIONS

Freshman Academic Profile: Average high school GPA 3.3. 9% in top 10% of high school class, 29% in top 25% of high school class, 60% in top 50% of high school class. 86% from public high schools. **Test Scores:** SAT Math middle 50% range 420-530. SAT EBRW middle 50% range 390-520. ACT middle 50% range 18-23. Minimum internet-based TOEFL 61. Minimum paper TOEFL 500. **Basis for Candidate Selection:** *Very important factors considered include:* class rank, standardized test scores. *Important factors considered include:* rigor of secondary school record. **Freshman Admission Requirements:** High school diploma is required and GED is accepted *Academic units required:* 3 English, 2 math, 2 science, 2 history, *Academic units recommended:* 3 math, 3 science. **Freshman Admission Statistics:** 548 applied, 97.3% admitted, 59% enrolled. **Transfer Admission Requirements:** college transcript(s), statement of good standing from prior institution(s). Minimum college GPA of 2.0 required. Lowest grade transferable D. **General Admission Information:** Application fee $35. Priority deadline 8/1. Nonfall registration accepted.

COSTS AND FINANCIAL AID

Annual tuition $14,850. Room and board $6,072. Required fees $1,080. Average book expense $1,650. **Required Forms and Deadlines:** FAFSA; Institution's own financial aid form; State aid form. **Notification of Awards:** Applicants will be notified of awards on a rolling basis beginning 2/1. **Types of Aid:** *Need-based scholarships/grants:* College/university scholarship or grant aid from institutional funds; Federal Pell; Private scholarships; SEOG; State scholarships/ grants. *Loans:* Direct PLUS loans; Direct Subsidized Stafford Loans; Direct Unsubsidized Stafford Loans. *Student Employment:* Federal Work-Study Program available. Institutional employment available. **Financial Aid Statistics:** 99% needy freshmen, 97% needy undergrads receive need-based scholarship or grant aid. 11% freshmen, 9% undergrads receive non-need-based scholarship or grant aid. 68% freshmen, 77% undergrads receive need-based self-help aid. 13% freshmen, 8% undergrads receive athletic scholarships. 66% freshmen, 65% undergrads receive any aid. **Criteria for awarding aid:** *Need-based:* Academics *Non-need-based:* Academics, Alumni affiliation, Art, Athletics, Leadership, Music/drama, Religious affiliation.

WAYNE STATE COLLEGE

1111 Main Street, Wayne, NE 68787
Phone: 402-375-7234 • **Financial Aid Phone:** 402-375-7230
E-mail: admit1@wsc.edu • **CEEB Code:** 6469
Fax: 402-375-7204 • **Website:** www.wsc.edu • **ACT Code:** 2472

This public school was founded in 1909. It has a 128 acre campus.

RATINGS

Admissions Selectivity Rating: 71   **Fire Safety Rating:** 60*   **Green Rating:** 60*

STUDENTS AND FACULTY

Enrollment: 2,610. **Student Body:** 57% female, 43% male, 15% out-of-state, 1% international (25 countries represented). Asian 1%, African American 3%, Caucasian 81%, Hispanic 9%, Native American 1%, Pacific Islander <1%, Two or more races 3%, Race unknown 2%.

Retention and Graduation: 69% freshmen return for sophomore year. 25% freshmen graduate within 4 years. 48% freshmen graduate within 6 years. **Faculty:** Student/faculty ratio 19:1. 118 full-time faculty, 86% hold PhDs, 6% are members of minority groups, 48% are women. 5% of classes are taught by teaching assistants.

ACADEMICS

Degrees: Bachelor's; Master's; Post-Master's certificate **Classes:** Most classes have 10-19 students. Most lab/discussion sessions have 10-19 students. **Special Study Options:** Cooperative education program; Distance learning; Double major; Dual enrollment; English as a Second Language (ESL); Honors program; Independent study; Internships; Study abroad; Teacher certification program. **Disability Services offered to physically disabled students:** Note-taking services; Reader services; Tape recorders; Tutors. **Career services:** Alumni network; Alumni services; Career assessment; Career/job search classes; Internships

FACILITIES

Housing: Coed dorms **Special Academic Facilities/Equipment:** Art gallery, fine arts center, planetarium, recreation center, telecommunications network. **Computers:** 100% of classrooms, 100% of dorms, 100% of libraries, 100% of dining areas, 100% of student union, 40% of common outdoor areas have wireless network access. Students can register for classes online. Administrative functions (other than registration) can be performed online.

CAMPUS LIFE

Environment: Rural **Activities:** Campus Ministries; Choral groups; Concert band; Dance; Drama/theater; International Student Organization; Jazz band; Literary magazine; Marching band; Music ensembles; Musical theater; Pep band; Radio station; Student government; Student newspaper; Television station 96 registered organizations, 18 honor societies, 7 religious organizations. 2 fraternities, 3 sororities. **Athletics (Intercollegiate):** *Men:* baseball, basketball, cross-country, football, golf, track/field (outdoor), track/field (indoor). *Women:* basketball, cross-country, golf, soccer, softball, track/field (outdoor), track/field (indoor), volleyball.

ADMISSIONS

Freshman Academic Profile: Average high school GPA 3.3. 12% in top 10% of high school class, 30% in top 25% of high school class, 59% in top 50% of high school class. **Test Scores:** ACT middle 50% range 18-25. Minimum paper TOEFL 550. **Freshman Admission Requirements:** High school diploma is required and GED is accepted *Academic units recommended:* 4 English, 3 math, 2 science, 2 foreign language, 3 social studies, 2 computer science, 2 visual/performing arts. **Freshman Admission Statistics:** 1,706 applied, 100.0% admitted, 36% enrolled. **Transfer Admission Requirements:** college transcript(s), Minimum college GPA of 2.0 required. Lowest grade transferable C-. **General Admission Information:** Priority deadline 12/1. Regular application deadline 8/21. Nonfall registration accepted. Admission may be deferred.

COSTS AND FINANCIAL AID

Required Forms and Deadlines: FAFSA. **Notification of Awards:** Applicants will be notified of awards on a rolling basis beginning 4/1. **Types of Aid:** *Need-based scholarships/grants:* College/university scholarship or grant aid from institutional funds; Federal Pell; Private scholarships; SEOG; State scholarships/grants. *Loans:* Direct PLUS loans; Direct Subsidized Stafford Loans; Direct Unsubsidized Stafford Loans. *Student Employment:* Federal Work-Study Program available. Institutional employment available. **Financial Aid Statistics:** 78% needy freshmen, 69% needy undergrads receive need-based scholarship or grant aid. 75% freshmen, 72% undergrads receive non-need-based scholarship or grant aid. 78% freshmen, 75% undergrads receive need-based self-help aid. 8% freshmen, 8% undergrads receive athletic scholarships. **Criteria for awarding aid:** *Non-need-based:* Academics, Art, Athletics, Leadership, Minority status, Music/drama, Religious affiliation, State/district residency.

WAYNE STATE UNIVERSITY

42 W. Warren Ave., Detroit, MI 48202
Phone: 313-577-2100 • **Financial Aid Phone:** 313-577-2100
E-mail: studentservice@wayne.edu • **CEEB Code:** 1898
Website: www.wayne.edu • **ACT Code:** 2064

This public school was founded in 1868. It has a 200 acre campus.

RATINGS

Admissions Selectivity Rating: 80   **Fire Safety Rating:** 84   **Green Rating:** 63

STUDENTS AND FACULTY

Enrollment: 16,768. **Student Body:** 55% female, 45% male, 2% out-of-state, 2% international (40 countries represented). Asian 10%, African American 17%, Caucasian 59%, Hispanic 5%, Native American <1%, Pacific Islander <1%, Two or more races 4%, Race unknown 3%. **Retention and Graduation:** 81% freshmen return for sophomore year. 19% freshmen graduate within 4 years. 47% freshmen graduate within 6 years. **Faculty:** Student/faculty ratio 16:1. 1,034 full-time faculty, 27% are members of minority groups, 46% are women.

ACADEMICS

Degrees: Bachelor's; Certificate; Doctoral/Professional; Doctoral/Research; Master's; Post-Bachelor's certificate; Post-Master's certificate **Classes:** Most classes have 10-19 students. Most lab/discussion sessions have 10-19 students. **Most popular majors:** Biology/Biological Sciences, General; Psychology, General; Health Professions And Related Clinical Sciences, Other. **Special Study Options:** Accelerated program; Cooperative education program; Distance learning; Double major; Dual enrollment; English as a Second Language (ESL); Honors program; Independent study; Internships; Study abroad; Teacher certification program. Honors programs: The Irvin D. Reid Honors College is city-based and service-oriented; we promote excellence and challenge our students to engage the world around them as problem-solvers and leaders. Our curriculum requires that students inform themselves about what it means to be citizens, of this city, this country, the world; we give our students tools, tools to be catalysts for innovation and improvement, and the skills necessary to create powerful solutions. Honors also offers a number of pre-professional programs such as MedStart, HealthPro Start and BStart, designed to prepare and transition students into graduate and professional programs in medicine, health sciences and business. Combined degree programs: BA/MA; BA/MD; BA/MEng. **Disability Services offered to physically disabled students:** Note-taking services; Reader services; Tape recorders; Tutors. **Career services:** Career assessment; Career/job search classes; Internships

FACILITIES

Housing: Apartments for married students; Apartments for single students; Coed dorms; Special housing for disabled student; Theme housing 100% of campus accessible to physically disabled. **Special Academic Facilities/Equipment:** Detroit Institute of Arts; Detroit Historical Museum; Detroit Science Museum; Charles H Wright Museum of African American History; Planetarium **Computers:** Students can register for classes online. Administrative functions (other than registration) can be performed online.

CAMPUS LIFE

Environment: Metropolis **Activities:** Campus Ministries; Choral groups; Concert band; Dance; Drama/theater; International Student Organization; Jazz band; Marching band; Model UN; Music ensembles; Musical theater; Pep band; Radio station; Student government; Student newspaper; Student-run film society; Symphony orchestra 166 registered organizations, 4 honor societies, 12 religious organizations. 7 fraternities, 8 sororities. **Athletics (Intercollegiate):** *Men:* baseball, basketball, cross-country, diving, fencing, football, golf, ice hockey, swimming, tennis. *Women:* basketball, cross-country, diving, fencing, ice hockey, softball, swimming, tennis, volleyball. **On-Campus Highlights:** Recreation and Fitness Center, Student Center Building, Starbucks, Jimmy Johns, Residence Halls **Environmental Initiatives:** Past and ongoing LEED certified buildings being constructed.

ADMISSIONS

Freshman Academic Profile: Average high school GPA 3.4. 19% in top 10% of high school class, 47% in top 25% of high school class, 79% in top 50% of high school class. **Test Scores:** SAT Math middle 50% range 500-600. SAT EBRW middle 50% range 510-260. ACT middle 50% range 21-27. Minimum internet-based TOEFL 79. Minimum paper TOEFL 550. **Basis for Candidate Selection:** *Very important factors considered include:* academic GPA, standardized test scores. *Other factors considered include:* rigor of secondary school record, application essay, recommendation(s). **Freshman Admission Requirements:** High school diploma is required and GED is accepted *Academic units recommended:* 4 English, 4 math, 3 science, 2 foreign language, 3 social studies, 2 visual/performing arts. **Freshman Admission Statistics:** 15,331 applied, 67.4% admitted, 26% enrolled. **Transfer Admission Requirements:** college transcript(s), Minimum college GPA of 2.0 required. Lowest grade transferable C. **General Admission Information:** Application fee $25. Regular application deadline 8/1. Nonfall registration accepted. Admission may be deferred for a maximum of 1 year.

COSTS AND FINANCIAL AID

Annual in-state tuition $10,106. Annual out-of-state tuition $28,151. Room and board $10,106. Required fees $1,457. Average book expense $1,196. **Required Forms and Deadlines:** FAFSA. **Notification of Awards:** Applicants will be notified of awards on a rolling basis beginning 3/31. **Types of Aid:** *Need-based scholarships/grants:* College/university scholarship or grant aid from institutional funds; Federal Pell; Private scholarships; SEOG; State scholarships/grants; United Negro College Fund. *Loans:* Direct PLUS loans; Direct Subsidized Stafford Loans; Direct Unsubsidized Stafford Loans. *Student Employment:* Federal Work-Study Program available. Institutional employment available. **Financial Aid Statistics:** 79% needy freshmen, 75% needy undergrads receive need-based scholarship or grant aid. 71% freshmen, 54% undergrads receive non-need-based scholarship or grant aid. 63% freshmen, 73% undergrads receive need-based self-help aid. 2% freshmen, 1% undergrads receive athletic scholarships. 93% freshmen, 85% undergrads receive any aid. 73% undergrads borrow to pay for school. Average cumulative indebtedness $24,516. **Criteria for awarding aid:** *Need-based:* Academics, Art, Leadership *Non-need-based:* Academics, Art, Athletics, Leadership, Music/drama.

WAYNESBURG UNIVERSITY

51 West College Street, Waynesburg, PA 15370
Phone: 724-852-3248 • **Financial Aid Phone:** 724-852-3208
E-mail: admissions@waynesburg.edu • **CEEB Code:** 2969
Fax: 724-627-8124 • **Website:** www.waynesburg.edu • **ACT Code:** 3748

This private school, affiliated with the Presbyterian Church, was founded in 1849. It has a 30 acre campus.

RATINGS
Admissions Selectivity Rating: 72   **Fire Safety Rating:** 96   **Green Rating:** 60*

STUDENTS AND FACULTY
Enrollment: 1,371. **Student Body:** 59% female, 41% male, 21% out-of-state, <1% international (4 countries represented). Asian 1%, African American 4%, Caucasian 86%, Hispanic 2%, Native American <1%, Pacific Islander 0%, Two or more races 3%, Race unknown 4%.
Retention and Graduation: 76% freshmen return for sophomore year. 58% freshmen graduate within 4 years. 66% freshmen graduate within 6 years. 94% grads go on to further study within 1 year. 33% grads pursue arts and sciences degrees. 2% grads pursue law degrees. 2% grads pursue business degrees. 27% grads pursue medical degrees. **Faculty:** Student/faculty ratio 13:1. 78 full-time faculty, 67% hold PhDs, 51% are women. 0% of classes are taught by teaching assistants.

ACADEMICS
Degrees: Bachelor's; Doctoral/Professional; Doctoral/Research; **Master's Classes:** Most classes have 20-29 students. Most lab/discussion sessions have 10-19 students. **Most popular majors:** Criminal Justice/Law Enforcement Administration; Registered Nursing/Registered Nurse; Business Administration And Management, General. **Special Study Options:** Accelerated program; Distance learning; Double major; Dual enrollment; Honors program; Independent study; Internships; Student-designed major; Study abroad; Teacher certification program. Honors programs: The Waynesburg University Honors Program exists to foster the further development of students who have demonstrated a commitment to academic excellence. Through enhanced learning opportunities both in and out of the classroom, the Honors Program seeks to develop the intellect of such students by emphasizing the pursuit of intellectual curiosity, reflective and meditative engagement with significant texts, and critical thinking across the disciplines. The goal of the program is the intellectual development of engaged and thoughtful Christian leaders through the pursuit of a challenging liberal arts experience. Through a course of study emphasizing rigorous academic and experiential inquiry, Honors Students may complete the program through a combination of traditional coursework and opportunities outside the classroom. These include interdisciplinary projects, Honors Colloquia, campus leadership, and independent research, among many others. These opportunities are designed to foster the curiosity and critical thinking skills of Honors Students, and to build a community of scholars. The Honors Program at Waynesburg University serves as a model of and laboratory for excellence in interdisciplinary learning, service to the community, intercultural awareness, and leadership development. Combined degree programs: BA/MA. **Disability Services offered to physically disabled students:** Note-taking services; Reader services; Tape recorders; Tutors. **Career services:** Alumni network; Alumni services; Career assessment; Career/job search classes; Internships; Regional alumni

FACILITIES
Housing: Men's dorms; Special housing for disabled student; Women's dorms 98% of campus accessible to physically diasbled. **Special Academic Facilities/Equipment:** Geology, biology, archaeology, and ceramics museum, arboretum, 174-acre farm, Center for Research and Economic Development. **Computers:** 95% of classrooms, 95% of libraries, 100% of dining areas, 100% of student union, 20% of common outdoor areas have wireless network access. Students

can register for classes online. Administrative functions (other than registration) can be performed online.

CAMPUS LIFE
Environment: Village **Activities:** Campus Ministries; Choral groups; Concert band; Drama/theater; Jazz band; Literary magazine; Music ensembles; Musical theater; Pep band; Radio station; Student government; Student newspaper; Television station; Yearbook 40 registered organizations, 16 honor societies, 7 religious organizations. **Athletics (Intercollegiate):** *Men:* baseball, basketball, cross-country, football, golf, soccer, tennis, track/field (outdoor), wrestling. *Women:* basketball, cross-country, golf, lacrosse, soccer, softball, tennis, track/field (outdoor), volleyball. **On-Campus Highlights:** Roberts Chapel, Simulation Lab-Nursing Department, Communication Department, Stover Campus Center, New Residence Halls

ADMISSIONS
Freshman Academic Profile: Average high school GPA 3.6. 15% in top 10% of high school class, 36% in top 25% of high school class, 74% in top 50% of high school class. 85% from public high schools. **Test Scores:** SAT Math middle 50% range 480-580. SAT EBRW middle 50% range 500-580. ACT middle 50% range 18-24. Minimum internet-based TOEFL 80. **Basis for Candidate Selection:** *Very important factors considered include:* rigor of secondary school record, class rank, academic GPA, standardized test scores, interview. *Important factors considered include:* extracurricular activities. *Other factors considered include:* application essay, recommendation(s), character/personal qualities, alumni/ae relation, volunteer work, work experience, level of applicant's interest. **Freshman Admission Requirements:** High school diploma is required and GED is accepted *Academic units required:* 4 English, 3 math, 2 science, 2 science labs, 2 social studies, 5 academic electives, *Academic units recommended:* 3 science, 2 foreign language. **Freshman Admission Statistics:** 1,608 applied, 95.3% admitted, 26% enrolled. **Transfer Admission Requirements:** High school transcript, college transcript(s), statement of good standing from prior institution(s). Minimum college GPA of 2.5 required. Lowest grade transferable C. **General Admission Information:** Application fee $20. Nonfall registration accepted.

COSTS AND FINANCIAL AID
Annual tuition $23,970. Room and board $10,164. Required fees $850. Average book expense $1,400. **Required Forms and Deadlines:** FAFSA. **Notification of Awards:** Applicants will be notified of awards on a rolling basis beginning 2/15. **Types of Aid:** *Need-based scholarships/grants:* College/university scholarship or grant aid from institutional funds; Federal Pell; Private scholarships; SEOG; State scholarships/grants. *Loans:* Direct PLUS loans; Direct Subsidized Stafford Loans; Direct Unsubsidized Stafford Loans. *Student Employment:* Federal Work-Study Program available. Institutional employment available. **Financial Aid Statistics:** 98% needy freshmen, 98% needy undergrads receive need-based scholarship or grant aid. 13% freshmen, 12% undergrads receive non-need-based scholarship or grant aid. 83% freshmen, 85% undergrads receive need-based self-help aid. 0% freshmen, 0% undergrads receive athletic scholarships. 94% freshmen, 87% undergrads receive any aid. 42% undergrads borrow to pay for school. Average cumulative indebtedness $25,615. **Criteria for awarding aid:** *Need-based:* Academics, Job skills, Leadership, Religious affiliation *Non-need-based:* Academics, Alumni affiliation, Job skills, Leadership, Religious affiliation, State/district residency.

WEBB INSTITUTE

298 Crescent Beach Road, Glen Cove, NY 11542
Phone: 516-671-8355 • **Financial Aid Phone:** 516-403-5928
E-mail: admissions@webb.edu • **CEEB Code:** 2970
Fax: 516-674-9838 • **Website:** www.webb.edu • **ACT Code:** 2987

This private school was founded in 1889. It has a 26 acre campus.

RATINGS
Admissions Selectivity Rating: 97   **Fire Safety Rating:** 98   **Green Rating:** 61

STUDENTS AND FACULTY
Enrollment: 98. **Student Body:** 20% female, 80% male, 78% out-of-state, 0% international (2 countries represented). Asian 11%, African American 0%, Caucasian 81%, Hispanic 1%, Native American 0%, Pacific Islander 0%, Two or more races 5%, Race unknown 2%.

Retention and Graduation: 93% freshmen return for sophomore year. 68% freshmen graduate within 4 years. 77% freshmen graduate within 6 years. 10% grads go on to further study within 1 year. **Faculty:** Student/faculty ratio 9:1. 10 full-time faculty, 60% hold PhDs, 0% are members of minority groups, 10% are women. 0% of classes are taught by teaching assistants.

ACADEMICS

Degrees: Bachelor's **Classes:** Most classes have 30-39 students. **Special Study Options:** Double major; Independent study; Internships; Study abroad. **Career services:** Alumni network; Alumni services; Career/job search classes; Internships; Regional alumni

FACILITIES

Housing: Coed dorms; Men's dorms; Women's dorms 70% of campus accessible to physically diasbled. **Special Academic Facilities/Equipment:** Towing tank for model testing, marine engineering lab, other state-of-the-art laboratories **Computers:** 100% of classrooms, 100% of dorms, 100% of libraries, 100% of dining areas, 100% of student union, 100% of common outdoor areas have wireless network access.

CAMPUS LIFE

Environment: Village **Activities:** Choral groups; Jazz band; Music ensembles; Student government; Yearbook 2 registered organizations. **Athletics (Intercollegiate):** *Men:* basketball, cross-country, sailing, soccer, tennis, volleyball. *Women:* basketball, cross-country, sailing, soccer, tennis, volleyball. **On-Campus Highlights:** Stevenson Taylor Hall, Brockett Pub, Waterfront Facility, Robinson Model Tank, Haeberle Lab

ADMISSIONS

Freshman Academic Profile: Average high school GPA 4.0. 44% in top 10% of high school class, 56% in top 25% of high school class, 0% in top 50% of high school class. 81% from public high schools. **Test Scores:** SAT Math middle 50% range 760-790. SAT EBRW middle 50% range 680-750. ACT middle 50% range 30-34. **Basis for Candidate Selection:** *Very important factors considered include:* rigor of secondary school record, class rank, academic GPA, application essay, standardized test scores, recommendation(s), interview, character/personal qualities, level of applicant's interest. *Important factors considered include:* extracurricular activities, talent/ability. *Other factors considered include:* volunteer work, work experience. **Freshman Admission Requirements:** High school diploma is required and GED is not accepted *Academic units required:* 4 English, 4 math, 2 science, 2 science labs, 2 social studies, 4 academic electives. **Freshman Admission Statistics:** 106 applied, 34.9% admitted, 76% enrolled. **Transfer Admission Requirements:** High school transcript, college transcript(s), interview, standardized test scores, Minimum college GPA of 3.5 required. **General Admission Information:** Application fee $60. Priority deadline 10/15. Regular application deadline 2/1. Nonfall registration accepted. Admission may be deferred for a maximum of 1 year.

COSTS AND FINANCIAL AID

Annual tuition $49,750. Room and board $14,750. Required fees $425. Average book expense $700. **Required Forms and Deadlines:** Business/Farm Supplement; FAFSA; Institution's own financial aid form. **Notification of Awards:** Applicants will be notified of awards on or about 6/1. **Types of Aid:** *Need-based scholarships/grants:* College/university scholarship or grant aid from institutional funds; Federal Pell; Private scholarships; State scholarships/grants. *Loans:* Direct PLUS loans; Direct Subsidized Stafford Loans; Direct Unsubsidized Stafford Loans. **Financial Aid Statistics:** 100% needy freshmen, 100% needy undergrads receive need-based scholarship or grant aid. 33% freshmen, 53% undergrads receive non-need-based scholarship or grant aid. 100% freshmen, 100% undergrads receive need-based self-help aid. 0% freshmen, 0% undergrads receive athletic scholarships. 23% freshmen, 18% undergrads receive any aid. **Criteria for awarding aid:** *Non-need-based:* Academics.

WEBBER INTERNATIONAL UNIVERSITY

P.O. Box 96, Babson Park, FL 33827
Phone: 863-628-2910 • **Financial Aid Phone:** 863-638-2930
E-mail: admissions@webber.edu • **CEEB Code:** 5893
Fax: 863-638-1591 • **Website:** www.webber.edu • **ACT Code:** 773

This private school was founded in 1927. It has a 110 acre campus.

RATINGS

Admissions Selectivity Rating: 89   **Fire Safety Rating:** 91   **Green Rating:** 60*

STUDENTS AND FACULTY

Enrollment: 681. **Student Body:** 31% female, 69% male, 13% out-of-state, 24% international (45 countries represented). Asian 1%, African American 22%, Caucasian 39%, Hispanic 11%, Native American <1%, Pacific Islander 0%, Two or more races 2%, Race unknown 1%.
Retention and Graduation: 7% grads go on to further study within 1 year. 0% grads pursue arts and sciences degrees. 2% grads pursue law degrees. 5% grads pursue business degrees. 0% grads pursue medical degrees. **Faculty:** Student/faculty ratio 23:1. 21 full-time faculty, 71% hold PhDs, 10% are members of minority groups, 33% are women. 0% of classes are taught by teaching assistants.

ACADEMICS

Degrees: Associate; Bachelor's; **Master's Classes:** Most classes have 20-29 students. Most lab/discussion sessions have 10-19 students. **Most popular majors:** Parks, Recreation And Leisure Facilities Management, General; Business/Commerce, General; Business Administration And Management, General. **Special Study Options:** Cooperative education program; Cross-registration; Distance learning; Double major; Dual enrollment; English as a Second Language (ESL); Exchange student program (domestic); External degree program; Independent study; Internships; Weekend college. **Disability Services offered to physically disabled students:** Tutors. **Career services:** Career assessment; Career/job search classes; Internships

FACILITIES

Housing: Men's dorms; Women's dorms 90% of campus accessible to physically diasbled. **Computers:** Administrative functions (other than registration) can be performed online.

CAMPUS LIFE

Environment: Rural **Activities:** International Student Organization; Marching band; Student government; Student newspaper 6 registered organizations. **Athletics (Intercollegiate):** *Men:* baseball, basketball, bowling, cheerleading, cross-country, football, golf, soccer, tennis, track/field (outdoor). *Women:* basketball, bowling, cheerleading, cross-country, golf, soccer, softball, tennis, track/field (outdoor), volleyball. **On-Campus Highlights:** Student Union, Fitness Center, Computer Lab, Career Center

ADMISSIONS

Freshman Academic Profile: Average high school GPA 3.1. 72% in top 10% of high school class, 100% in top 25% of high school class, 0% in top 50% of high school class. 75% from public high schools. **Test Scores:** SAT Math middle 50% range 430-530. SAT EBRW middle 50% range 430-510. ACT middle 50% range 17-23. Minimum paper TOEFL 500. **Basis for Candidate Selection:** *Very important factors considered include:* academic GPA, standardized test scores. *Important factors considered include:* rigor of secondary school record. *Other factors considered include:* class rank, application essay, recommendation(s), interview, character/personal qualities, alumni/ae relation. **Freshman Admission Requirements:** High school diploma is required and GED is accepted *Academic units required:* 4 English, 2 math, 1 science, 2 social studies, and 2 units from above areas or other academic areas. *Academic units recommended:* 3 math, 3 science, 1 foreign language, 2 history, 4 academic electives. **Freshman Admission Statistics:** 710 applied, 50.6% admitted, 42% enrolled. **Transfer Admission Requirements:** college transcript(s), statement of good standing from prior institution(s). Minimum college GPA of 2.0 required. Lowest grade transferable C. **General Admission Information:** Application fee $35.

COSTS AND FINANCIAL AID

Annual tuition $21,686. Average book expense $1,148. **Required Forms and Deadlines:** FAFSA; Institution's own financial aid form. **Types of Aid:** *Need-based scholarships/grants:* College/university scholarship or grant aid from institutional funds; Federal Pell; Private scholarships; SEOG; State scholarships/grants. *Loans:* Direct PLUS loans; Direct Subsidized Stafford Loans; Direct Unsubsidized Stafford Loans. *Student Employment:* Federal Work-Study Program available. Institutional employment available. **Financial Aid Statistics:** 98% needy freshmen, 97% needy undergrads receive need-based scholarship or grant aid. 5% freshmen, 6% undergrads receive non-need-based scholarship or grant aid. 83% freshmen, 81% undergrads receive need-based self-help aid. 10% freshmen, 16% undergrads receive athletic scholarships. 97% freshmen, 96% undergrads receive any aid. **Criteria for awarding aid:** *Need-based:* Academics, Athletics, Leadership *Non-need-based:* Academics, Athletics, Leadership.

WEBER STATE UNIVERSITY

1103 University Circle, Ogden, UT 84408-1137
Phone: 801-626-6743 • **Financial Aid Phone:** 801-626-7569
E-mail: admissions@weber.edu • **CEEB Code:** 4941
Fax: 801-626-6747 • **Website:** weber.edu/ • **ACT Code:** 4282

This public school was founded in 1889. It has a 508.9 acre campus.

RATINGS
Admissions Selectivity Rating: 72   **Fire Safety Rating:** 94   **Green Rating:** 91

STUDENTS AND FACULTY
Enrollment: 16,473. **Student Body:** 58% female, 42% male, 10% out-of-state, 2% international (61 countries represented). Asian 2%, African American 2%, Caucasian 74%, Hispanic 12%, Native American 1%, Pacific Islander 1%, Two or more races 3%, Race unknown 4%.
Retention and Graduation: 62% freshmen return for sophomore year. 14% freshmen graduate within 4 years. 35% freshmen graduate within 6 years. 22% grads go on to further study within 1 year. **Faculty:** Student/faculty ratio 21:1. 521 full-time faculty, 82% hold PhDs, 12% are members of minority groups, 46% are women. 0% of classes are taught by teaching assistants.

ACADEMICS
Degrees: Associate; Bachelor's; Certificate; Master's; Post-Bachelor's certificate; Post-Master's certificate; Terminal Associate; Transfer Associate **Classes:** Most classes have 10-19 students. Most lab/discussion sessions have 10-19 students. **Most popular majors:** Computer Science; Registered Nursing/Registered Nurse; Business Administration And Management, General. **Special Study Options:** Accelerated program; Cooperative education program; Distance learning; Double major; Dual enrollment; English as a Second Language (ESL); Exchange student program (domestic); External degree program; Honors program; Independent study; Internships; Student-designed major; Study abroad; Teacher certification program. Honors programs: Weber State University's Honors Program offers you small, challenging and creative courses, as well as opportunities for leadership and social interaction. An "Honors" designation on your transcript and diploma makes you more attractive to employers, graduate schools and professional programs. Combined degree programs: BA/MA. **Disability Services offered to physically disabled students:** Note-taking services; Reader services; Tape recorders; Tutors. **Career services:** Alumni network; Alumni services; Career assessment; Career/job search classes; Internships; Regional alumni

FACILITIES
Housing: Apartments for single students; Coed dorms; Men's dorms; Special housing for disabled student; Wellness housing; Women's dorms 99% of campus accessible to physically disabled. **Special Academic Facilities/Equipment:** Art gallery, language lab, TV studio, communication arts/technologies facilities, natural science museum, herbarium, planetarium, aerospace technology equipment for developing satellite projects, dental hygiene clinic. **Computers:** 50% of classrooms, 50% of dorms, 100% of libraries, 100% of dining areas, 100% of student union, 100% of common outdoor areas have wireless network access. Students can register for classes online. Administrative functions (other than registration) can be performed online.

CAMPUS LIFE
Environment: City **Activities:** Campus Ministries; Choral groups; Concert band; Dance; Drama/theater; International Student Organization; Jazz band; Literary magazine; Marching band; Model UN; Music ensembles; Musical theater; Opera; Pep band; Radio station; Student government; Student newspaper; Student-run film society; Symphony orchestra; Television station 100 registered organizations, 1 honor society, 4 religious organizations. 2 fraternities, 3 sororities. **Athletics (Intercollegiate):** *Men:* basketball, cheerleading, cross-country, football, golf, tennis, track/field (outdoor), track/field (indoor). *Women:* basketball, cheerleading, cross-country, golf, soccer, tennis, track/field (outdoor), track/field (indoor), volleyball. **On-Campus Highlights:** Health and Physical Education Center, J. Farrell Shepherd Union Building, Ethel Wattis Kimball Visual Arts Center, Elizabeth Dee Shaw Stewart Stadium, Val A. Browning Center for the Performing Arts **Environmental Initiatives:** Weber State University is in the process of upgrading all interior and exterior campus lighting to high-efficiency flourescents, CLFs and LEDs in some applications. This project began last year and will continue for another 3 years.

ADMISSIONS
Freshman Academic Profile: Average high school GPA 3.3. 99% from public high schools. **Test Scores:** ACT middle 50% range 18-24. **Basis for Candidate Selection:** *Other factors considered include:* standardized test scores. **Freshman Admission Requirements:** High school diploma is required and GED is accepted *Academic units recommended:* 4 English, 2 math, 2 science, 2 foreign language, 1 history, 4 academic electives. **Freshman Admission Statistics:** 6,255 applied, 100.0% admitted, 50% enrolled. **Transfer Admission Requirements:** college transcript(s), Minimum college GPA of 2.0 required. Lowest grade transferable C. **General Admission Information:** Application fee $30. Priority deadline 3/15. Regular application deadline 8/31. Nonfall registration accepted. Admission may be deferred for a maximum of 1 year.

COSTS AND FINANCIAL AID
Annual in-state tuition $8,400. Annual out-of-state tuition $14,321. Room and board $8,400. Required fees $939. Average book expense $1,200. **Required Forms and Deadlines:** FAFSA; Institution's own financial aid form. **Notification of Awards:** Applicants will be notified of awards on a rolling basis beginning 3/15. **Types of Aid:** *Need-based scholarships/grants:* College/university scholarship or grant aid from institutional funds; Federal Pell; Private scholarships; SEOG; State scholarships/grants. *Loans:* Direct PLUS loans; Direct Subsidized Stafford Loans; Direct Unsubsidized Stafford Loans. *Student Employment:* Federal Work-Study Program available. Institutional employment available. **Financial Aid Statistics:** 60% needy freshmen, 68% needy undergrads receive need-based scholarship or grant aid. 15% freshmen, 34% undergrads receive non-need-based scholarship or grant aid. 51% freshmen, 56% undergrads receive need-based self-help aid. 4% freshmen, 3% undergrads receive athletic scholarships. 82% freshmen, 63% undergrads receive any aid. 21% undergrads borrow to pay for school. Average cumulative indebtedness $22,029. **Criteria for awarding aid:** *Need-based:* Academics, Alumni affiliation, Art, Job skills, Minority status, Music/drama *Non-need-based:* Academics, Alumni affiliation, Art, Athletics, Job skills, Leadership, Minority status, Music/drama, State/district residency.

WEBSTER UNIVERSITY

470 East Lockwood Avenue, Saint Louis, MO 63119-3194
Phone: 314-246-7800 • **Financial Aid Phone:** 314-968-6992
E-mail: admit@webster.edu • **CEEB Code:** 6933
Fax: 314-246-7116 • **Website:** www.webster.edu • **ACT Code:** 2388

This private school was founded in 1915. It has a 47 acre campus.

RATINGS
Admissions Selectivity Rating: 86   **Fire Safety Rating:** 89   **Green Rating:** 60*

STUDENTS AND FACULTY
Enrollment: 2,721. **Student Body:** 55% female, 45% male, 27% out-of-state, 5% international (56 countries represented). Asian 2%, African American 13%, Caucasian 64%, Hispanic 5%, Native American <1%, Pacific Islander <1%, Two or more races 3%, Race unknown 8%.
Retention and Graduation: 78% freshmen return for sophomore year. 14% grads go on to further study within 1 year. **Faculty:** Student/faculty ratio 9:1. 200 full-time faculty, 85% hold PhDs, 16% are members of minority groups, 48% are women. 0% of classes are taught by teaching assistants.

ACADEMICS
Degrees: Bachelor's; Certificate; Doctoral Other; Doctoral/Research; Master's; Post-Bachelor's certificate; Post-Master's certificate **Most popular majors:** Psychology, General; Registered Nursing/Registered Nurse; Business Administration And Management, General. **Special Study Options:** Cooperative education program; Cross-registration; Distance learning; Double major; English as a Second Language (ESL); Independent study; Internships; Liberal arts/career combination; Student-designed major; Study abroad; Teacher certification program. Combined degree programs: BA/MA. **Disability Services offered to physically disabled students:** Note-taking services; Reader services; Tape recorders; Tutors. **Career services:** Alumni network; Alumni services; Career assessment; Internships

FACILITIES
Housing: Apartments for single students; Coed dorms; Special housing for disabled student; Special housing for international students 85% of campus accessible to physically disabled. **Computers:** 10% of classrooms, 12% of dorms, 50% of libraries, 100% of dining areas, 100% of student union, 60% of common outdoor areas have wireless network access. Students can register for classes online. Administrative functions (other than registration) can be performed online.

CAMPUS LIFE
Environment: Metropolis **Activities:** Campus Ministries; Choral groups; Dance; Drama/theater; International Student Organization; Jazz band;

Literary magazine; Music ensembles; Musical theater; Opera; Radio station; Student government; Student newspaper; Student-run film society; Symphony orchestra; Television station 62 registered organizations, 1 honor society, 1 religious organization. 1 fraternity. **Athletics (Intercollegiate):** *Men:* baseball, basketball, cross-country, golf, soccer, tennis, track/field (outdoor). *Women:* basketball, cross-country, soccer, softball, tennis, track/field (outdoor), volleyball. **On-Campus Highlights:**

ADMISSIONS

Freshman Academic Profile: Average high school GPA 3.5. 20% in top 10% of high school class, 47% in top 25% of high school class, 76% in top 50% of high school class. **Test Scores:** ACT middle 50% range 21-27. Minimum internet-based TOEFL 80. **Basis for Candidate Selection:** *Very important factors considered include:* academic GPA, standardized test scores. *Important factors considered include:* rigor of secondary school record, class rank, talent/ability. *Other factors considered include:* application essay, recommendation(s), interview, extracurricular activities, character/personal qualities, first generation, alumni/ae relation, geographical residence, volunteer work, work experience, level of applicant's interest. **Freshman Admission Requirements:** High school diploma is required and GED is accepted *Academic units recommended:* 4 English, 3 math, 3 science, 2 science labs, 2 foreign language, 3 social studies, 3 academic electives, 1 visual/performing arts. **Freshman Admission Statistics:** 1,994 applied, 56.1% admitted, 37% enrolled. **Transfer Admission Requirements:** college transcript(s), essay or personal statement, Minimum college GPA of 2.5 required. Lowest grade transferable C. **General Admission Information:** Application fee $35. Priority deadline 3/1. Regular application deadline 8/1. Nonfall registration accepted. Admission may be deferred for a maximum of 1 year.

COSTS AND FINANCIAL AID

Annual tuition $25,300. Room and board $10,860. Required fees $200. Average book expense $1,000. **Required Forms and Deadlines:** FAFSA; Institution's own financial aid form. **Notification of Awards:** Applicants will be notified of awards on a rolling basis beginning 2/1. **Types of Aid:** *Need-based scholarships/ grants:* College/university scholarship or grant aid from institutional funds; Federal Pell; Private scholarships; SEOG; State scholarships/grants. *Loans:* Direct PLUS loans; Direct Subsidized Stafford Loans; Direct Unsubsidized Stafford Loans. *Student Employment:* Federal Work-Study Program available. Institutional employment available. **Financial Aid Statistics:** 98% needy freshmen, 90% needy undergrads receive need-based scholarship or grant aid. 95% freshmen, 87% undergrads receive non-need-based scholarship or grant aid. 97% freshmen, 90% undergrads receive need-based self-help aid. 0% freshmen, 0% undergrads receive athletic scholarships. 78% undergrads borrow to pay for school. Average cumulative indebtedness $31,548. **Criteria for awarding aid:** *Need-based:* Minority status *Non-need-based:* Academics, Art, Leadership, Music/drama.

WELLESLEY COLLEGE

106 Central Street, Wellesley, MA 02481-8203
Phone: 781-283-2270 • **Financial Aid Phone:** 781-283-2360
E-mail: admission@wellesley.edu • **CEEB Code:** 3957
Fax: 781-283-3678 • **Website:** www.wellesley.edu • **ACT Code:** 1926

This private school was founded in 1870. It has a 500 acre campus.

RATINGS

Admissions Selectivity Rating: 97   **Fire Safety Rating:** 98   **Green Rating:** 89

STUDENTS AND FACULTY

Enrollment: 2,375. **Student Body:** 100% female, 0% male, 87% out-of-state, 13% international (88 countries represented). Asian 23%, African American 6%, Caucasian 39%, Hispanic 12%, Native American <1%, Pacific Islander 0%, Two or more races 6%, Race unknown <1%.
Retention and Graduation: 95% freshmen return for sophomore year. 78% freshmen graduate within 4 years. 90% freshmen graduate within 6 years. 18% grads go on to further study within 1 year. 24% grads pursue arts and sciences degrees. 13% grads pursue law degrees. 3% grads pursue business degrees. 10% grads pursue medical degrees. **Faculty:** Student/faculty ratio 7:1. 309 full-time faculty, 93% hold PhDs, 25% are members of minority groups, 60% are women. 0% of classes are taught by teaching assistants.

ACADEMICS

Degrees: Bachelor's **Classes:** Most classes have fewer than 10 students. **Most popular majors:** Computer Science; Psychology, General; Economics, General. **Special Study Options:** Cooperative education program; Cross-registration; Double major; Exchange student program (domestic); Honors program; Independent study; Internships; Student-designed major; Study abroad; Teacher certification program. Combined degree programs: BA/MA. **Disability Services offered to physically disabled students:** Note-taking services; Reader services; Tape recorders; Tutors. **Career services:** Alumni network; Alumni services; Career assessment; Career/job-search classes; Internships; Regional alumni

FACILITIES

Housing: Apartments for single students; Cooperative housing; Theme housing; Women's dorms 85% of campus accessible to physically diasbled. **Special Academic Facilities/Equipment:** Clapp Library Davis Museum and Cultural Center Harambee House Houghton Memorial Chapel Hunnewell Arboretum, Alexandra Botanic Gardens, and Ferguson Greenhouses Jewett Art Museum Keohane Sports Center Knapp Media and Technology Center Knapp Social Science Center Lake Waban Pforzheimer Learning and Teaching Center Ruth Nagel Jones Theatre Science Center, Slater International Center Wang Campus Center Wellesley Centers for Women Whitin Observatory, including 3 telescopes **Computers:** 100% of classrooms, 100% of dorms, 100% of libraries, 100% of dining areas, 100% of student union, 5% of common outdoor areas have wireless network access. Students can register for classes online. Administrative functions (other than registration) can be performed online.

CAMPUS LIFE

Environment: Town **Activities:** Campus Ministries; Choral groups; Concert band; Dance; Drama/theater; International Student Organization; Jazz band; Literary magazine; Model UN; Music ensembles; Radio station; Student government; Student newspaper; Student-run film society; Symphony orchestra; Television station; Yearbook 160 registered organizations, 7 honor societies, 30 religious organizations. **Athletics (Intercollegiate):** *Women:* basketball, crew/rowing, cross-country, diving, fencing, field hockey, golf, lacrosse, soccer, softball, squash, swimming, tennis, track/field (outdoor), track/field (indoor), volleyball. **On-Campus Highlights:** Wang Campus Center, Davis Museum and Cultural Center, Clapp Library and Knapp Media Center, Science Center, Lake Waban

ADMISSIONS

Freshman Academic Profile: 81% in top 10% of high school class, 96% in top 25% of high school class, 99% in top 50% of high school class. 62% from public high schools. **Test Scores:** SAT Math middle 50% range 670-770. SAT EBRW middle 50% range 690-760. ACT middle 50% range 30-33. **Basis for Candidate Selection:** *Very important factors considered include:* rigor of secondary school record, academic GPA, recommendation(s), character/personal qualities. *Important factors considered include:* class rank, application essay, standardized test scores, extracurricular activities, talent/ability. *Other factors considered include:* interview, first generation, alumni/ae relation, geographical residence, state residency, racial/ethnic status, volunteer work, work experience, level of applicant's interest. **Freshman Admission Requirements:** High school diploma or equivalent is not required *Academic units recommended:* 4 English, 4 math, 3 science, 2 science labs, 4 foreign language, 4 social studies, 4 history. **Freshman Admission Statistics:** 5,666 applied, 22.1% admitted, 48% enrolled. **Transfer Admission Requirements:** High school transcript, college transcript(s), essay or personal statement, interview, standardized test scores, statement of good standing from prior institution(s). Lowest grade transferable C. **General Admission Information:** Application fee $50. Regular application deadline 1/15. Nonfall registration accepted. Admission may be deferred for a maximum of 1 year.

COSTS AND FINANCIAL AID

Required Forms and Deadlines: CSS/Financial Aid PROFILE; FAFSA; Noncustodial PROFILE. **Notification of Awards:** Applicants will be notified of awards on or about 4/1. **Types of Aid:** *Need-based scholarships/grants:* College/university scholarship or grant aid from institutional funds; Federal Pell; Private scholarships; SEOG; State scholarships/grants; United Negro College Fund. *Loans:* Direct PLUS loans; Direct Subsidized Stafford Loans; Direct Unsubsidized Stafford Loans. *Student Employment:* Federal Work-Study Program available. Institutional employment available. **Financial Aid Statistics:** 96% needy freshmen, 100% needy undergrads receive need-based scholarship or grant aid. 0% undergrads receive non-need-based scholarship or grant aid. 89% freshmen, 91% undergrads receive need-based self-help aid. 0% freshmen, 0% undergrads receive athletic scholarships. 61% freshmen, 61% undergrads receive any aid. 49% undergrads borrow to pay for school. Average cumulative indebtedness $12,455.

WELLS COLLEGE

170 Main Street, Aurora, NY 13026
Phone: 315-364-3264 • **Financial Aid Phone:** 315-364-3289
E-mail: admissions@wells.edu • **CEEB Code:** 2971
Fax: 315-364-3227 • **Website:** www.wells.edu • **ACT Code:** 2971

This private school was founded in 1868. It has a 365 acre campus.

RATINGS
Admissions Selectivity Rating: 82   **Fire Safety Rating:** 90   **Green Rating:** 92

STUDENTS AND FACULTY
Enrollment: 552. **Student Body:** 71% female, 29% male, 32% out-of-state, 2% international (13 countries represented). Asian 2%, African American 6%, Caucasian 67%, Hispanic 4%, Native American 1%, Race unknown 18%. **Retention and Graduation:** 76% freshmen return for sophomore year. 25% grads go on to further study within 1 year. 18% grads pursue arts and sciences degrees. 4% grads pursue law degrees. 1% grads pursue business degrees. 2% grads pursue medical degrees. **Faculty:** Student/faculty ratio 10:1. 39 full-time faculty, 95% hold PhDs, 18% are members of minority groups, 54% are women. 0% of classes are taught by teaching assistants.

ACADEMICS
Degrees: Bachelor's **Classes:** Most classes have 10-19 students. Most lab/discussion sessions have 10-19 students. **Most popular majors:** English Language And Literature, General; Molecular Biology; Psychology, General. **Special Study Options:** Accelerated program; Cross-registration; Double major; English as a Second Language (ESL); Independent study; Internships; Student-designed major; Study abroad; Teacher certification program. **Disability Services offered to physically disabled students:** Tutors. **Career services:** Alumni network; Alumni services; Career assessment; Internships; Regional alumni

FACILITIES
Housing: Coed dorms; Women's dorms 58% of campus accessible to physically diasbled. **Special Academic Facilities/Equipment:** Two greenhouses, environmentally regulated animal room, the college theatre (Phillips Auditorium), recital hall, electronic music studio, 15 pianos, a Dowd harpsichord, an early instrument collection, a sculpture and ceramics studio, dark rooms, painting and drawing studio, a Book Arts Center, lithography presses, an extensive art library, art gallery, general and specialized clusters for the social sciences, foreign languages, and natural and mathematical sciences. **Computers:** 10% of classrooms, 90% of dorms, 100% of libraries, 100% of student union, have wireless network access. Students can register for classes online. Administrative functions (other than registration) can be performed online.

CAMPUS LIFE
Environment: Rural **Activities:** Choral groups; Dance; Drama/theater; Literary magazine; Model UN; Music ensembles; Student government; Student newspaper; Yearbook 35 registered organizations, 2 honor societies, 2 religious organizations. **Athletics (Intercollegiate):** *Men:* basketball, cross-country, golf, lacrosse, soccer, swimming. *Women:* basketball, cross-country, field hockey, golf, lacrosse, soccer, softball, swimming, tennis. **On-Campus Highlights:** Sommer Center, Boat House, Schwartz Student Union, Macmillan Hall, Main Building

ADMISSIONS
Freshman Academic Profile: Average high school GPA 3.5. 31% in top 10% of high school class, 65% in top 25% of high school class, 91% in top 50% of high school class. 88% from public high schools. **Test Scores:** SAT Math middle 50% range 480-600. SAT EBRW middle 50% range 500-630. ACT middle 50% range 22-27. Minimum paper TOEFL 550. **Basis for Candidate Selection:** *Very important factors considered include:* rigor of secondary school record, academic GPA, standardized test scores, recommendation(s), extracurricular activities. *Important factors considered include:* application essay, interview. *Other factors considered include:* class rank, talent/ability, character/personal qualities, alumni/ae relation, volunteer work, work experience, level of applicant's interest. **Freshman Admission Requirements:** High school diploma is required and GED is accepted *Academic units required:* 4 English, 3 math, 2 science, 2 science labs, 1 social studies, 3 history, 2 academic electives, *Academic units recommended:* 4 math, 3 science, 3 science labs, 2 foreign language, 2 social studies, 2 history, 3 academic electives, 2 units from above areas or other academic areas. **Freshman Admission Statistics:** 1,673 applied, 67.2% admitted, 13% enrolled. **Transfer Admission Requirements:** High school transcript, college transcript(s), essay or personal statement, standardized test scores, statement of good standing from prior institution(s). Minimum college GPA of 2.0 required. Lowest grade transferable C-. **General**

Admission Information: Application fee $40. Priority deadline 12/15. Regular application deadline 3/1. Nonfall registration accepted. Admission may be deferred for a maximum of 1 year.

COSTS AND FINANCIAL AID
Annual tuition $33,200. Room and board $11,900. Required fees $1,500. Average book expense $800. **Required Forms and Deadlines:** FAFSA. **Notification of Awards:** Applicants will be notified of awards on a rolling basis beginning 3/1. **Types of Aid:** *Need-based scholarships/grants:* College/university scholarship or grant aid from institutional funds; Federal Pell; Private scholarships; SEOG; State scholarships/grants. *Loans: Student Employment:* Federal Work-Study Program available. Institutional employment available. **Financial Aid Statistics:** 93% needy freshmen, 93% needy undergrads receive need-based scholarship or grant aid. 13% freshmen, 15% undergrads receive non-need-based scholarship or grant aid. 75% freshmen, 70% undergrads receive need-based self-help aid. 0% freshmen, 0% undergrads receive athletic scholarships. 96% freshmen, 95% undergrads receive any aid. **Criteria for awarding aid:** *Non-need-based:* Academics, Alumni affiliation, Leadership.

See page 1084.

WENTWORTH INSTITUTE OF TECHNOLOGY

550 Huntington Avenue, Boston, MA 02115-5998
Phone: 617-989-4000 • **Financial Aid Phone:** 617-989-4174
E-mail: admissions@wit.edu • **CEEB Code:** 3958
Fax: 617-989-4010 • **Website:** www.wit.edu

This private school was founded in 1904. It has a 31 acre campus.

RATINGS
Admissions Selectivity Rating: 73   **Fire Safety Rating:** 97   **Green Rating:** 82

STUDENTS AND FACULTY
Enrollment: 4,204. **Student Body:** 20% female, 80% male, 34% out-of-state, 8% international (53 countries represented). Asian 7%, African American 4%, Caucasian 62%, Hispanic 10%, Native American <1%, Pacific Islander <1%, Two or more races 2%, Race unknown 6%. **Retention and Graduation:** 84% freshmen return for sophomore year. 47% freshmen graduate within 4 years. 65% freshmen graduate within 6 years. 17% grads go on to further study within 1 year. 11% grads pursue arts and sciences degrees. 2% grads pursue business degrees. **Faculty:** Student/faculty ratio 17:1. 158 full-time faculty, 56% hold PhDs, 20% are members of minority groups, 31% are women. 0% of classes are taught by teaching assistants.

ACADEMICS
Degrees: Associate; Bachelor's; Certificate; **Master's Classes:** Most classes have 20-29 students. **Most popular majors:** Architecture; Mechanical Engineering; Construction Management. **Special Study Options:** Accelerated program; Cooperative education program; Distance learning; Double major; Dual enrollment; English as a Second Language (ESL); Study abroad; Weekend college. **Disability Services offered to physically disabled students:** Note-taking services; Reader services; Tape recorders; Tutors. **Career services:** Alumni network; Alumni services; Career assessment; Career/job search classes; Internships

FACILITIES
Housing: Coed dorms; Special housing for international students 75% of campus accessible to physically diasbled. **Computers:** 100% of classrooms, 100% of dorms, 100% of libraries, 100% of dining areas, have wireless network access. Students can register for classes online. Administrative functions (other than registration) can be performed online.

CAMPUS LIFE
Environment: Metropolis **Activities:** Campus Ministries; Choral groups; Dance; Drama/theater; International Student Organization; Jazz band; Marching band; Model UN; Music ensembles; Musical theater; Radio station; Student government; Symphony orchestra 50 registered organizations, 3 honor societies, 1 religious organization. **Athletics (Intercollegiate):** *Men:* baseball, basketball, golf, ice hockey, lacrosse, riflery, soccer, tennis, volleyball. *Women:* basketball, golf, riflery, soccer, softball, tennis, volleyball. **On-Campus Highlights:** 525 Huntington Avenue (newest residence hall), Flanagan Campus Center (cafe, library, student activities), Computer Info Systems Networking Lab, Design Studios, Center for Science and Biomedical Engineering

ADMISSIONS
Freshman Academic Profile: Average high school GPA 3.1. **Test Scores:** SAT Math middle 50% range 550-650. SAT EBRW middle 50% range 530-620. ACT middle 50% range 21-28. Minimum internet-based TOEFL 79. Minimum

paper TOEFL 550. **Basis for Candidate Selection:** *Important factors considered include:* rigor of secondary school record, academic GPA, application essay, standardized test scores, recommendation(s). *Other factors considered include:* extracurricular activities, talent/ability, character/personal qualities, first generation, alumni/ae relation, geographical residence, racial/ethnic status, volunteer work, work experience, level of applicant's interest. **Freshman Admission Requirements:** High school diploma is required and GED is accepted *Academic units required:* 4 English, 3 math, 2 science, 1 science labs, *Academic units recommended:* 4 math. **Freshman Admission Statistics:** 6,172 applied, 91.9% admitted, 17% enrolled. **Transfer Admission Requirements:** High school transcript, college transcript(s), essay or personal statement, Lowest grade transferable C. **General Admission Information:** Application fee $50. Priority deadline 2/15. Nonfall registration accepted. Admission may be deferred for a maximum of 1 academic year.

COSTS AND FINANCIAL AID

Annual tuition $32,954. Required fees $2,023. Average book expense $1,500. **Required Forms and Deadlines:** FAFSA. **Types of Aid:** *Need-based scholarships/grants:* College/university scholarship or grant aid from institutional funds; Federal Pell; Private scholarships; SEOG; State scholarships/grants. *Loans:* Direct PLUS loans; Direct Subsidized Stafford Loans; Direct Unsubsidized Stafford Loans. *Student Employment:* Federal Work-Study Program available. Institutional employment available. **Financial Aid Statistics:** 87% needy freshmen, 77% needy undergrads receive need-based scholarship or grant aid. 99% freshmen, 89% undergrads receive non-need-based scholarship or grant aid. 90% freshmen, 86% undergrads receive need-based self-help aid. 0% freshmen, 0% undergrads receive athletic scholarships. 91% freshmen, 78% undergrads receive any aid. 81% undergrads borrow to pay for school. Average cumulative indebtedness $23,017. **Criteria for awarding aid:** *Non-need-based:* Academics, Leadership, State/district residency.

See page 1086.

WESLEYAN COLLEGE

4760 Forsyth Road, Macon, GA 31210-4462
Phone: 478-477-1110 • **Financial Aid Phone:** 478-757-5167
E-mail: admissions@wesleyancollege.edu • **CEEB Code:** 5895
Fax: 478-757-4030 • **Website:** www.wesleyancollege.edu • **ACT Code:** 876

This private school, affiliated with the Methodist Church, was founded in 1836. It has a 200 acre campus.

RATINGS

Admissions Selectivity Rating: 89   **Fire Safety Rating:** 96   **Green Rating:** 82

STUDENTS AND FACULTY

Enrollment: 501. **Student Body:** 100% female, 0% male, 10% out-of-state, 15% international (20 countries represented). Asian 2%, African American 29%, Caucasian 42%, Hispanic 5%, Native American <1%, Pacific Islander <1%, Two or more races 5%, Race unknown 2%.
Retention and Graduation: 56% freshmen graduate within 6 years. 30% grads go on to further study within 1 year. 10% grads pursue arts and sciences degrees. 1% grads pursue law degrees. 15% grads pursue business degrees. 4% grads pursue medical degrees. **Faculty:** Student/faculty ratio 7:1. 56 full-time faculty, 80% hold PhDs, 9% are members of minority groups, 68% are women. 0% of classes are taught by teaching assistants.

ACADEMICS

Degrees: Bachelor's; **Master's Classes:** Most classes have 10-19 students. **Most popular majors:** Registered Nursing/Registered Nurse; Business Administration, Management And Operations, Other; Accounting. **Special Study Options:** Accelerated program; Cross-registration; Double major; Dual enrollment; Honors program; Independent study; Internships; Student-designed major; Study abroad; Teacher certification program. Honors programs: Honors Thesis. **Disability Services offered to physically disabled students:** Note-taking services; Reader services; Tape recorders; Tutors. **Career services:** Alumni network; Career assessment; Career/job search classes; Internships; Regional alumni

FACILITIES

Housing: Apartments for single students; Special housing for disabled student; Women's dorms 89% of campus accessible to physically diasbled. **Special Academic Facilities/Equipment:** Art and history museums, special collection of Georgiana and Americana, Confucius Institute, equestrian center. **Computers:** 80% of classrooms, 100% of libraries, 100% of dining areas, 100% of student union, 50% of common outdoor areas have wireless network access.

Students can register for classes online. Administrative functions (other than registration) can be performed online.

CAMPUS LIFE

Environment: City **Activities:** Campus Ministries; Choral groups; Dance; Drama/theater; International Student Organization; Literary magazine; Model UN; Music ensembles; Student government 40 registered organizations, 10 honor societies, 5 religious organizations. **Athletics (Intercollegiate):** *Women:* basketball, cross-country, equestrian sports, soccer, softball, tennis, volleyball. **On-Campus Highlights:** Library with 24 hour access, Matthews Athletic Center, Equestrian Center, Arboretum, Lake **Environmental Initiatives:** Plastic Bottle Policy

ADMISSIONS

Freshman Academic Profile: Average high school GPA 3.5. 28% in top 10% of high school class, 58% in top 25% of high school class, 88% in top 50% of high school class. 80% from public high schools. **Test Scores:** SAT Math middle 50% range 490-580. SAT EBRW middle 50% range 530-610. ACT middle 50% range 21-24. Minimum internet-based TOEFL 80. Minimum paper TOEFL 550. **Basis for Candidate Selection:** *Very important factors considered include:* academic GPA. *Important factors considered include:* rigor of secondary school record, class rank, standardized test scores, level of applicant's interest. *Other factors considered include:* application essay, recommendation(s), interview, extracurricular activities, talent/ability, character/personal qualities, first generation, alumni/ae relation, volunteer work, work experience. **Freshman Admission Requirements:** High school diploma is required and GED is accepted *Academic units required: Academic units recommended:* 4 English, 3 math, 3 science, 3 science labs, 2 foreign language, 4 social studies, 4 academic electives, 2 visual/performing arts. **Freshman Admission Statistics:** 309 applied, 46.6% admitted, 51% enrolled. **Transfer Admission Requirements:** college transcript(s), essay or personal statement, statement of good standing from prior institution(s). Minimum college GPA of 2.5 required. Lowest grade transferable C. **General Admission Information:** Application fee $30. Nonfall registration accepted. Admission may be deferred for a maximum of 1 year.

COSTS AND FINANCIAL AID

Annual tuition $22,000. Room and board $9,860. Required fees $1,000. **Required Forms and Deadlines:** FAFSA; Institution's own financial aid form. **Notification of Awards:** Applicants will be notified of awards on a rolling basis beginning 10/1. **Types of Aid:** *Need-based scholarships/grants:* College/university scholarship or grant aid from institutional funds; Federal Pell; Private scholarships; SEOG; State scholarships/grants. *Loans:* Direct PLUS loans; Direct Subsidized Stafford Loans; Direct Unsubsidized Stafford Loans. *Student Employment:* Federal Work-Study Program available. Institutional employment available. **Financial Aid Statistics:** 100% needy freshmen, 99% needy undergrads receive need-based scholarship or grant aid. 18% freshmen, 17% undergrads receive non-need-based scholarship or grant aid. 69% freshmen, 76% undergrads receive need-based self-help aid. 0% freshmen, 0% undergrads receive athletic scholarships. 95% freshmen, 85% undergrads receive any aid. 57% undergrads borrow to pay for school. Average cumulative indebtedness $35,392. **Criteria for awarding aid:** *Need-based:* Academics, Alumni affiliation, Job skills, Religious affiliation *Non-need-based:* Academics, Alumni affiliation, Art, Job skills, Leadership, Music/drama, Religious affiliation, State/district residency.

WESLEYAN UNIVERSITY

70 Wyllys Avenue, Middletown, CT 06459
Phone: 860-685-3000 • **Financial Aid Phone:** 860-685-2800
E-mail: admission@wesleyan.edu • **CEEB Code:** 3959
Fax: 860-685-3001 • **Website:** www.wesleyan.edu • **ACT Code:** 614

This private school was founded in 1831. It has a 316 acre campus.

RATINGS

Admissions Selectivity Rating: 97   **Fire Safety Rating:** 93   **Green Rating:** 96

STUDENTS AND FACULTY

Enrollment: 2,887. **Student Body:** 54% female, 46% male, 92% out-of-state, 12% international (53 countries represented). Asian 8%, African American 6%, Caucasian 54%, Hispanic 11%, Native American <1%, Pacific Islander <1%, Two or more races 5%, Race unknown 3%.

Retention and Graduation: 95% freshmen return for sophomore year. 85% freshmen graduate within 4 years. 1% freshmen graduate within 6 years. 13% grads go on to further study within 1 year. 9% grads pursue arts and sciences degrees. 1.4% grads pursue law degrees. 0% grads pursue business degrees. 0.8% grads pursue medical degrees. **Faculty:** Student/faculty ratio 8:1. 369 full-time faculty, 93% hold PhDs, 21% are members of minority groups, 44% are women. 0% of classes are taught by teaching assistants.

ACADEMICS

Degrees: Bachelor's; Doctoral/Research; Master's; Post-Master's certificate **Classes:** Most classes have 20-29 students. Most lab/discussion sessions have 10-19 students. **Most popular majors:** Psychology, General; Economics, General. **Special Study Options:** Accelerated program; Cross-registration; Double major; Dual enrollment; Exchange student program (domestic); Honors program; Independent study; Internships; Student-designed major; Study abroad. Combined degree programs: BA/MA. **Disability Services offered to physically disabled students:** Note-taking services; Reader services; Tape recorders; Tutors. **Career services:** Alumni network; Alumni services; Career assessment; Internships; Regional alumni

FACILITIES

Housing: Apartments for single students; Coed dorms; Fraternity/sorority housing; Men's dorms; Special housing for disabled student; Theme housing; Wellness housing; Women's dorms 54% of campus accessible to physically disabled. **Special Academic Facilities/Equipment:** Art center, art galleries, Center for Afro-American studies, East Asian Studies Center, Cinema Archives, concert hall, public affairs center, language lab, electron microscope, observatory, nuclear magnetic resonance spectrometers. **Computers:** 90% of classrooms, 100% of dorms, 90% of libraries, 90% of dining areas, 100% of student union, 90% of common outdoor areas have wireless network access. Students can register for classes online. Administrative functions (other than registration) can be performed online.

CAMPUS LIFE

Environment: Town **Activities:** Campus Ministries; Choral groups; Concert band; Dance; Drama/theater; International Student Organization; Jazz band; Literary magazine; Model UN; Music ensembles; Musical theater; Pep band; Radio station; Student government; Student newspaper; Student-run film society; Symphony orchestra; Yearbook 220 registered organizations, 2 honor societies, 10 religious organizations. 9 fraternities, 4 sororities. **Athletics (Intercollegiate):** *Men:* baseball, basketball, crew/rowing, cross-country, diving, football, golf, ice hockey, lacrosse, soccer, squash, swimming, tennis, track/field (outdoor), track/field (indoor), wrestling. *Women:* basketball, crew/rowing, cross-country, diving, field hockey, ice hockey, lacrosse, soccer, softball, squash, swimming, tennis, track/field (outdoor), track/field (indoor), volleyball. **On-Campus Highlights:** Center for the Arts, Freeman Athletic Center, Center for Film Studies, Olin Memorial Library, Van Vleck Observatory **Environmental Initiatives:** Energy conservation activities resulting in a 28% reduction of energy consumption campus wide and the construction of 3 PV solar system with a combined output of 215 kW.

ADMISSIONS

Freshman Academic Profile: 60% in top 10% of high school class, 92% in top 25% of high school class, 98% in top 50% of high school class. 52% from public high schools. **Test Scores:** SAT Math middle 50% range 640-760. SAT EBRW middle 50% range 660-740. ACT middle 50% range 29-33. Minimum internet-based TOEFL 100. Minimum paper TOEFL 600. **Basis for Candidate Selection:** *Very important factors considered include:* rigor of secondary school record. *Important factors considered include:* class rank, academic GPA, application essay, recommendation(s), talent/ability, character/personal qualities, first generation, racial/ethnic status. *Other factors considered include:* standardized test scores, interview, extracurricular activities, alumni/ae relation, geographical residence, volunteer work, work experience. **Freshman Admission Requirements:** High school diploma is required and GED is accepted *Academic units recommended:* 4 English, 4 math, 4 science, 3 science labs, 4 foreign language, 4 social studies, 4 history. **Freshman Admission Statistics:** 12,360 applied, 16.3% admitted, 38% enrolled. **Transfer Admission Requirements:** High school transcript, college transcript(s), essay or personal statement, standardized test scores, statement of good standing from prior institution(s). Lowest grade transferable C-. **General Admission Information:** Application fee $55. Regular application deadline 1/1. Nonfall registration accepted. Admission may be deferred.

COSTS AND FINANCIAL AID

Required fees $300. Average book expense $1,200. **Required Forms and Deadlines:** CSS/Financial Aid PROFILE; FAFSA; Noncustodial PROFILE. **Notification of Awards:** Applicants will be notified of awards on or about 4/1. **Types of Aid:** *Need-based scholarships/grants:* College/university scholarship or grant aid from institutional funds; Federal Pell; Private scholarships; SEOG; State scholarships/grants. *Loans:* Direct PLUS loans; Direct Subsidized Stafford Loans; Direct Unsubsidized Stafford Loans. *Student Employment:* Federal

Work-Study Program available. Institutional employment available. **Financial Aid Statistics:** 92% needy freshmen, 93% needy undergrads receive need-based scholarship or grant aid. 4% freshmen, 3% undergrads receive non-need-based scholarship or grant aid. 88% freshmen, 91% undergrads receive need-based self-help aid. 0% freshmen, 0% undergrads receive athletic scholarships. 53% freshmen, 48% undergrads receive any aid. 43% undergrads borrow to pay for school. Average cumulative indebtedness $22,495.

WEST CHESTER UNIVERSITY OF PENNSYLVANIA

Messikomer Hall, West Chester, PA 19383
Phone: 610-436-3411 • **Financial Aid Phone:** 610-436-2627
E-mail: www.wcupa.edu/admissions • **CEEB Code:** 3328
Fax: 610-436-2907 • **Website:** www.wcupa.edu • **ACT Code:** 3750

This public school was founded in 1871. It has a 409.05 acre campus.

RATINGS

Admissions Selectivity Rating: 82   **Fire Safety Rating:** 98   **Green Rating:** 88

STUDENTS AND FACULTY

Enrollment: 14,435. **Student Body:** 59% female, 41% male, 11% out-of-state, <1% international (70 countries represented). Asian 2%, African American 11%, Caucasian 75%, Hispanic 6%, Native American <1%, Pacific Islander <1%, Two or more races 3%, Race unknown 1%.
Retention and Graduation: 85% freshmen return for sophomore year. 49% freshmen graduate within 4 years. 73% freshmen graduate within 6 years. **Faculty:** Student/faculty ratio 19:1. 694 full-time faculty, 84% hold PhDs, 14% are members of minority groups, 55% are women. 0% of classes are taught by teaching assistants.

ACADEMICS

Degrees: Bachelor's; Doctoral/Professional; Doctoral/Research; Master's; Post-Bachelor's certificate **Classes:** Most classes have 20-29 students. Most lab/discussion sessions have 20-29 students. **Most popular majors:** Early Childhood Education And Teaching; Psychology, General; Business Administration And Management, General. **Special Study Options:** Accelerated program; Cross-registration; Distance learning; Double major; Dual enrollment; English as a Second Language (ESL); Exchange student program (domestic); Honors program; Independent study; Internships; Liberal arts/career combination; Student-designed major; Study abroad; Teacher certification program. Honors programs: The Honors College has two distinct academic programs. The Honors Core Program for incoming First Year Students with a maximum of 80 seats offered each fall and the Honors Seminar Program geared toward transfer students and WCU students with a minimum of 30 earned credits. **Disability Services offered to physically disabled students:** Note-taking services; Reader services; Tape recorders; Tutors. **Career services:** Alumni network; Alumni services; Career assessment; Internships; Regional alumni

FACILITIES

Housing: Apartments for single students; Coed dorms; Special housing for disabled student; Special housing for international students; Theme housing 95% of campus accessible to physically disabled. **Special Academic Facilities/Equipment:** HEAT (Heat Illness Evaluation Avoidance and Treatment) Institute, Geology Museum, Planetarium, Observatory, Darlington Herbarium, Robert B. Gordon Natural Area for Environmental Studies, Emilie K. Asplundh Concert Hall, The John Baker Gallery at The E.O. Bull Center for the Arts, E. O. Bull Main Stage Theatre, J. Peter Adler Studio Theatre, Madeleine Wing Adler Theatre, Knauer Gallery, Gates Family Recital Hall, Outdoor Classroom & Native Plant & Ornithology Lab, Presser Music Library, Harvey Green Library, Speech and Hearing Clinic, Sturzebecker Health Science Center, Swope Music Building and the Performing Arts Center, The Poetry Center, Southeastern Pennsylvania Autism Resource Center and D-CAP (DubC Autism Program) **Computers:** 100% of classrooms, 20% of dorms, 100% of libraries, 100% of dining areas, 100% of student union, 100% of common outdoor areas have wireless network access. Students can register for classes online. Administrative functions (other than registration) can be performed online.

CAMPUS LIFE

Environment: Town **Activities:** Campus Ministries; Choral groups; Concert band; Dance; Drama/theater; International Student Organization; Jazz band; Literary magazine; Marching band; Model UN; Music ensembles; Musical theater; Opera; Pep band; Radio station; Student government; Student newspaper; Student-run film society; Symphony orchestra; Television station; Yearbook 233 registered organizations, 26 honor societies, 12 religious organizations. 12 fraternities, 13 sororities. **Athletics (Intercollegiate):** *Men:* baseball, basketball, cross-country, diving, football, golf, soccer, swimming, tennis, track/field (outdoor). *Women:* basketball, cheerleading, cross-country, diving, field hockey, golf, gymnastics, lacrosse, rugby, soccer, softball, swimming, tennis, track/field (outdoor), volleyball. **On-Campus Highlights:** Student Recreation Center, Lawrence Center, Library and Starbuck's Cafe by Academic Quad, Sykes Student Union Building, Swope Music Building and Performing Arts Center **Environmental Initiatives:** More than half of all buildings on campus (55%) are heated and cooled using geothermal exchange systems. Most of the remaining buildings are heated and cooled with high-efficiency natural gas boilers. These investments have significantly decreased WCU's use of fossil fuels and its per-square-foot and per-person carbon emissions, and allowed the university to decommission its coal-fired boiler plant.

ADMISSIONS

Freshman Academic Profile: Average high school GPA 3.4. 10% in top 10% of high school class, 32% in top 25% of high school class, 69% in top 50% of high school class. 85% from public high schools. **Test Scores:** SAT Math middle 50% range 510-600. SAT EBRW middle 50% range 530-610. ACT middle 50% range 21-26. Minimum internet-based TOEFL 80. Minimum paper TOEFL 550. **Basis for Candidate Selection:** *Very important factors considered include:* rigor of secondary school record, class rank, academic GPA. *Important factors considered include:* standardized test scores. *Other factors considered include:* application essay, extracurricular activities, talent/ability, character/personal qualities, state residency, racial/ethnic status, volunteer work, work experience. **Freshman Admission Requirements:** High school diploma is required and GED is accepted *Academic units required:* 4 English, 3 math, 3 science, 2 science labs, 2 social studies, 2 history, 2 academic electives, *Academic units recommended:* 4 English, 4 math, 3 science, 2 foreign language, 2 social studies, 2 history, 2 academic electives, 1 visual/performing arts. **Freshman Admission Statistics:** 12,667 applied, 68.5% admitted, 30% enrolled. **Transfer Admission Requirements:** college transcript(s), essay or personal statement, Minimum college GPA of 2.0 required. Lowest grade transferable C. **General Admission Information:** Application fee $45. Priority deadline 2/1. Nonfall registration accepted.

COSTS AND FINANCIAL AID

Average book expense $1,200. **Required Forms and Deadlines:** FAFSA. **Notification of Awards:** Applicants will be notified of awards on a rolling basis beginning 3/1. **Types of Aid:** *Need-based scholarships/grants:* College/university scholarship or grant aid from institutional funds; Federal Pell; Private scholarships; SEOG; State scholarships/grants. *Loans:* Direct PLUS loans; Direct Subsidized Stafford Loans; Direct Unsubsidized Stafford Loans. *Student Employment:* Federal Work-Study Program available. Institutional employment available. **Financial Aid Statistics:** 49% needy freshmen, 58% needy undergrads receive need-based scholarship or grant aid. 25% freshmen, 16% undergrads receive non-need-based scholarship or grant aid. 88% freshmen, 88% undergrads receive need-based self-help aid. 1% freshmen, 1% undergrads receive athletic scholarships. 79% freshmen, 73% undergrads receive any aid. 74% undergrads borrow to pay for school. Average cumulative indebtedness $33,814. **Criteria for awarding aid:** *Need-based:* Academics, Minority status *Non-need-based:* Academics, Art, Athletics, Leadership, Music/drama.

WEST SUBURBAN COLLEGE OF NURSING

PO Box 430, Oak Park, IL 60302
Phone: 708-763-6530 · **Financial Aid Phone:** (708) 763-1426
E-mail: admission@wscn.edu
Fax: 708-763-1531 • **Website:** www.wscn.edu

This private school, affiliated with the Roman Catholic Church, was founded in 1914.

RATINGS
Admissions Selectivity Rating: 0   **Fire Safety Rating:** 60*   **Green Rating:** 60*

STUDENTS AND FACULTY
Enrollment: 236. **Student Body:** 86% female, 14% male, 0% international. Asian 24%, African American 10%, Caucasian 40%, Hispanic 13%, Native American 0%, Race unknown 13%.
Retention and Graduation: 0% grads go on to further study within 1 year. 0% grads pursue arts and sciences degrees. 0% grads pursue law degrees. 0% grads pursue business degrees. 0% grads pursue medical degrees. **Faculty:** Student/faculty ratio 10:1. 23 full-time faculty, 17% hold PhDs, 17% are members of minority groups, 100% are women. 0% of classes are taught by teaching assistants.

ACADEMICS
Degrees: Bachelor's; **Master's Classes:** Most classes have 20-29 students. Most lab/discussion sessions have 10-19 students. **Special Study Options:** Accelerated program. **Career services:** Alumni services; Career assessment

FACILITIES
Housing: 0% of campus accessible to physically diasbled. **Computers:** 100% of classrooms, 100% of libraries, 100% of dining areas, have wireless network access. Students can register for classes online. Administrative functions (other than registration) can be performed online. Undergraduates are required to own a computer.

CAMPUS LIFE
Environment: Metropolis **Activities:** Student government 2 registered organizations.

ADMISSIONS
Freshman Admission Requirements: High school diploma is required and GED is accepted **Transfer Admission Requirements:** college transcript(s), essay or personal statement, standardized test scores, Minimum college GPA of 2.75 required. Lowest grade transferable C. **General Admission Information:** Application fee $30. Regular application deadline 4/1. Admission may be deferred for a maximum of 1 semester.

COSTS AND FINANCIAL AID
Types of Aid: *Need-based scholarships/grants:* College/university scholarship or grant aid from institutional funds; Federal Nursing Scholarships; Federal Pell; Private scholarships; SEOG; State scholarships/grants. *Student Employment:* Federal Work-Study Program available. Institutional employment available. **Financial Aid Statistics:** 100% needy undergrads receive need-based scholarship or grant aid. 18% undergrads receive non-need-based scholarship or grant aid. 79% undergrads receive need-based self-help aid. 0% undergrads receive athletic scholarships. 86% undergrads receive any aid. **Criteria for awarding aid:** *Need-based:* Academics *Non-need-based:* Academics.

WEST TEXAS A&M UNIVERSITY

PO Box 60999, Canyon, TX 79016-0001
Phone: 806-651-2020 • **Financial Aid Phone:** 806-651-2055
E-mail: admissions@mail.wtamu.edu • **CEEB Code:** 3665
Fax: 806-651-5268 • **Website:** www.wtamu.edu • **ACT Code:** 4250

This public school was founded in 1910. It has a 135 acre campus.

RATINGS
Admissions Selectivity Rating: 90   **Fire Safety Rating:** 91   **Green Rating:** 61

STUDENTS AND FACULTY
Enrollment: 7,383. **Student Body:** 57% female, 43% male, 14% out-of-state, 2% international (37 countries represented). Asian 2%, African American 5%, Caucasian 58%, Hispanic 28%, Native American <1%, Pacific Islander <1%, Two or more races 3%, Race unknown 3%.
Retention and Graduation: 64% freshmen return for sophomore year. 25% freshmen graduate within 4 years. 41% freshmen graduate within 6 years. 22% grads go on to further study within 1 year. **Faculty:** Student/faculty ratio 20:1. 342 full-time faculty, 63% hold PhDs, 14% are members of minority groups, 46% are women. 4% of classes are taught by teaching assistants.

ACADEMICS
Degrees: Bachelor's; Doctoral/Research; **Master's Classes:** Most classes have 10-19 students. **Most popular majors:** Multi-/Interdisciplinary Studies, Other; Registered Nursing/Registered Nurse; Business/Commerce, General. **Special Study Options:** Accelerated program; Cooperative education program; Distance learning; Double major; English as a Second Language (ESL); Honors program; Independent study; Internships; Liberal arts/career combination; Study abroad; Teacher certification program. Honors programs: The Honors Program at West Texas A&M University is committed to providing exceptional students with challenging academic studies, innovative approaches to instruction; increased opportunities for improving skills in critical thinking, research, developing creative works and writing; expanded cultural knowledge; and the opportunity to interact closely with faculty and similarly motivated students. **Disability Services offered to physically disabled students:** Note-taking services; Reader services; Tape recorders; Tutors. **Career services:** Alumni network; Alumni services; Career assessment; Career/job search classes; Internships; Regional alumni

FACILITIES

Housing: Coed dorms; Fraternity/sorority housing; Men's dorms; Special housing for disabled student; Women's dorms 100% of campus accessible to physically diasbled. **Special Academic Facilities/Equipment:** Regional History Museum, Research Center, Panhandle Plains Historical Museum, Killgore Research Center. **Computers:** Students can register for classes online. Administrative functions (other than registration) can be performed online.

CAMPUS LIFE

Environment: Village **Activities:** Campus Ministries; Choral groups; Concert band; Dance; Drama/theater; International Student Organization; Jazz band; Literary magazine; Marching band; Music ensembles; Musical theater; Opera; Pep band; Radio station; Student government; Student newspaper; Symphony orchestra; Television station; Yearbook 110 registered organizations, 15 honor societies, 13 religious organizations. 5 fraternities, 5 sororities. **Athletics (Intercollegiate):** *Men:* baseball, basketball, cross-country, football, golf, soccer. *Women:* basketball, cheerleading, cross-country, equestrian sports, golf, soccer, softball, volleyball. **On-Campus Highlights:** Panhandle-Plains Historical Museum, Jack B. Kelley Student Center, Virgil Henson Activities Center, Old Main (first building built on campus), WTAMU Horse Center

ADMISSIONS

Freshman Academic Profile: 15% in top 10% of high school class, 43% in top 25% of high school class, 80% in top 50% of high school class. 97% from public high schools. **Test Scores:** SAT Math middle 50% range 490-580. SAT EBRW middle 50% range 490-590. ACT middle 50% range 19-23. Minimum internet-based TOEFL 190. Minimum paper TOEFL 520. **Basis for Candidate Selection:** *Very important factors considered include:* class rank, academic GPA, standardized test scores. *Important factors considered include:* rigor of secondary school record. **Freshman Admission Requirements:** High school diploma is required and GED is accepted *Academic units required:* 4 English, 4 math, 4 science, 2 foreign language, 3.5 social studies, 6 academic electives, 1 visual/performing arts, and 1.5 units from above areas or other academic areas. **Freshman Admission Statistics:** 6,116 applied, 38.4% admitted, 53% enrolled. **Transfer Admission Requirements:** college transcript(s), Minimum college GPA of 2.0 required. Lowest grade transferable C. **General Admission Information:** Application fee $40. Priority deadline 8/1. Regular application deadline 8/1. Nonfall registration accepted. Admission may be deferred for a maximum of 1 semester.

COSTS AND FINANCIAL AID

Annual in-state tuition $7,196. Annual out-of-state tuition $6,279. Room and board $7,196. Required fees $2,392. Average book expense $1,000. **Required Forms and Deadlines:** FAFSA. **Notification of Awards:** Applicants will be notified of awards on a rolling basis beginning 3/1. **Types of Aid:** *Need-based scholarships/grants:* College/university scholarship or grant aid from institutional funds; Federal Pell; Private scholarships; SEOG; State scholarships/grants. *Loans:* Direct PLUS loans; Direct Subsidized Stafford Loans; Direct Unsubsidized Stafford Loans. **Financial Aid Statistics:** 80% needy freshmen, 78% needy undergrads receive need-based scholarship or grant aid. 49% freshmen, 36% undergrads receive non-need-based scholarship or grant aid. 75% freshmen, 80% undergrads receive need-based self-help aid. 2% freshmen, 3% undergrads receive athletic scholarships. 52% freshmen, 53% undergrads receive any aid. 62% undergrads borrow to pay for school. Average cumulative indebtedness $24,525. **Criteria for awarding aid:** *Need-based:* Academics *Non-need-based:* Academics, Art, Athletics, Leadership, Music/drama.

WEST VIRGINIA STATE UNIVERSITY

P.O. Box 1000, Institute, WV 25112
Phone: 304-766-3033 • **Financial Aid Phone:** 304-766-3131
E-mail: admissions@wvstateu.edu • **CEEB Code:** 5903
Fax: 304-766-5182 • **Website:** www.wvstateu.edu • **ACT Code:** 4538

This public school was founded in 1891. It has a 95 acre campus.

RATINGS

Admissions Selectivity Rating: 71   **Fire Safety Rating:** 60*   **Green Rating:** 60*

STUDENTS AND FACULTY

Enrollment: 2,033. **Student Body:** 54% female, 46% male, 8% out-of-state, 1% international (8 countries represented). Asian <1%, African American 14%, Caucasian 65%, Hispanic 1%, Native American <1%, Pacific Islander 0%, Two or more races 10%, Race unknown 9%.
Retention and Graduation: 59% freshmen return for sophomore year. 6% grads go on to further study within 1 year. 3% grads pursue arts and sciences

degrees. 1% grads pursue law degrees. 1% grads pursue business degrees. 1% grads pursue medical degrees.

ACADEMICS

Degrees: Bachelor's; **Master's Classes:** Most classes have 10-19 students. Most lab/discussion sessions have fewer than 10 students. **Most popular majors:** Elementary Education And Teaching; General Studies; Business Administration And Management, General. **Special Study Options:** Cooperative education program; Distance learning; Dual enrollment; English as a Second Language (ESL). **Disability Services offered to physically disabled students:** Tutors.

FACILITIES

Housing: Apartments for married students; Coed dorms; Men's dorms; Women's dorms **Special Academic Facilities/Equipment:** On-campus day-care center, art gallery, ROTC Hall of Fame, Sports Hall of Fame.

CAMPUS LIFE

Environment: Village **Activities:** Choral groups; Concert band; Jazz band; Literary magazine; Marching band; Music ensembles; Radio station; Student government; Student newspaper; Television station; Yearbook 4 honor societies, 2 religious organizations. 6 fraternities, 3 sororities. **Athletics (Intercollegiate):** *Men:* baseball, basketball, cross-country, football, softball, tennis, track/field (outdoor), volleyball. *Women:* basketball, cross-country, softball, tennis, track/field (outdoor), volleyball.

ADMISSIONS

Freshman Academic Profile: 99% from public high schools. **Test Scores:** SAT Math middle 50% range 400-500. SAT EBRW middle 50% range 390-510. ACT middle 50% range 17-22. **Freshman Admission Requirements:** High school diploma is required and GED is accepted; High school diploma is required and GED is not accepted *Academic units required:* 4 English, 2 math, 2 science, 2 foreign language, 3 social studies, 1 history. **Freshman Admission Statistics:** 1,439 applied, 94.1% admitted, 27% enrolled. **Transfer Admission Requirements:** college transcript(s), Minimum college GPA of 2.0 required. Lowest grade transferable D. **General Admission Information:** Application fee $20. Regular application deadline 8/22. Nonfall registration accepted.

COSTS AND FINANCIAL AID

Annual in-state tuition $3,550. Annual out-of-state tuition $5,150. Room and board $3,550. Required fees $125. Average book expense $500. **Required Forms and Deadlines:** FAFSA; Institution's own financial aid form.

WEST VIRGINIA UNIVERSITY

Presidents Office, Morgantown, WV 26506-6009
Phone: 304-293-2121 • **Financial Aid Phone:** 304-293-5242
E-mail: go2wvu@mail.wvu.edu • **CEEB Code:** 5904
Fax: 304-293-3080 • **Website:** www.wvu.edu • **ACT Code:** 4540

This public school was founded in 1867. It has a 2800 acre campus.

RATINGS

Admissions Selectivity Rating: 81   **Fire Safety Rating:** 98   **Green Rating:** 81

STUDENTS AND FACULTY

Enrollment: 21,705. **Student Body:** 47% female, 53% male, 43% out-of-state, 7% international (75 countries represented). Asian 1%, African American 4%, Caucasian 79%, Hispanic 4%, Native American <1%, Pacific Islander <1%, Two or more races 4%, Race unknown <1%.
Retention and Graduation: 80% freshmen return for sophomore year. 32% freshmen graduate within 4 years. 57% freshmen graduate within 6 years.
Faculty: 1,142 full-time faculty, 78% hold PhDs, 15% are members of minority groups, 44% are women.

ACADEMICS

Degrees: Bachelor's; Doctoral; Doctoral/Professional; Doctoral/Research; **Master's Classes:** Most classes have 20-29 students. Most lab/discussion sessions have 20-29 students. **Most popular majors:** Journalism; Engineering, General; Business Administration And Management, General. **Special Study Options:** Accelerated program; Cooperative education program; Distance learning; Double major; English as a Second Language (ESL); Exchange student program (domestic); External degree program; Honors program;

Independent study; Internships; Student-designed major; Study abroad; Teacher certification program. Honors programs: Honors Leadership Academy Combined degree programs: BA/MA. **Disability Services offered to physically disabled students:** Note-taking services; Reader services; Tape recorders; Tutors. **Career services:** Alumni network; Alumni services; Career assessment; Career/job search classes; Internships

FACILITIES

Housing: Apartments for married students; Apartments for single students; Coed dorms; Fraternity/sorority housing; Men's dorms; Special housing for disabled student; Special housing for international students; Theme housing; Wellness housing; Women's dorms 99% of campus accessible to physically diasbled. **Special Academic Facilities/Equipment:** Art galleries, creative arts center, arboretum, herbarium, planetarium, concurrent engineering research center, discovery lab (for inventors), Appalachian hardwood center, small business development center, pharmacy museum, coal and energy museum, center for economic research, fluidization center, center for software development. **Computers:** 80% of classrooms, 75% of dorms, 100% of libraries, 40% of dining areas, 100% of student union, 10% of common outdoor areas have wireless network access. Students can register for classes online. Administrative functions (other than registration) can be performed online.

CAMPUS LIFE

Environment: Town **Activities:** Campus Ministries; Choral groups; Concert band; Dance; Drama/theater; International Student Organization; Jazz band; Literary magazine; Marching band; Model UN; Music ensembles; Musical theater; Pep band; Radio station; Student government; Student newspaper; Symphony orchestra 370 registered organizations, 31 honor societies, 28 religious organizations. 14 fraternities, 9 sororities. **Athletics (Intercollegiate):** *Men:* baseball, basketball, diving, football, riflery, soccer, swimming, wrestling. *Women:* basketball, crew/rowing, cross-country, diving, gymnastics, riflery, soccer, swimming, tennis, track/field (outdoor), track/field (indoor), volleyball. **On-Campus Highlights:** Student Recreation Center, Mountainlair (Student Union), Personal Rapid Transit (PRT), Mountaineer Field, Historic Woodburn Circle **Environmental Initiatives:** 1. Energy performance management and emissions reduction through a performance contract (approx. $30 million) between WVU and Siemens Inc. Behavior-based energy management program is currently being implemented to educate and empower faculty, staff, and students to be better stewards of energy resources.

ADMISSIONS

Freshman Academic Profile: Average high school GPA 3.5. 18% in top 10% of high school class, 44% in top 25% of high school class, 77% in top 50% of high school class. **Test Scores:** ACT middle 50% range 21-27. Minimum internet-based TOEFL 61. Minimum paper TOEFL 550. **Basis for Candidate Selection:** *Very important factors considered include:* academic GPA, standardized test scores. *Important factors considered include:* rigor of secondary school record, state residency. *Other factors considered include:* extracurricular activities, talent/ability. **Freshman Admission Requirements:** High school diploma is required and GED is accepted *Academic units required:* 4 English, 4 math, 3 science, 3 science labs, 2 foreign language, 3 social studies, 1 visual/performing arts. **Freshman Admission Statistics:** 20,594 applied, 71.9% admitted, 35% enrolled. **Transfer Admission Requirements:** college transcript(s), Minimum college GPA of 2.0 required. Lowest grade transferable D. **General Admission Information:** Application fee $45. Priority deadline 3/1. Regular application deadline 8/1. Nonfall registration accepted. Admission may be deferred for a maximum of 1 year.

COSTS AND FINANCIAL AID

Annual out-of-state tuition $23,616. Average book expense $900. **Required Forms and Deadlines:** FAFSA. **Notification of Awards:** Applicants will be notified of awards on a rolling basis beginning 3/15. **Types of Aid:** *Need-based scholarships/grants:* College/university scholarship or grant aid from institutional funds; Federal Nursing Scholarships; Federal Pell; Private scholarships; SEOG; State scholarships/grants. *Loans:* Direct PLUS loans; Direct Subsidized Stafford Loans; Direct Unsubsidized Stafford Loans. *Student Employment:* Federal Work-Study Program available. Institutional employment available. **Financial Aid Statistics:** 70% needy freshmen, 70% needy undergrads receive need-based scholarship or grant aid. 94% freshmen, 86% undergrads receive non-need-based scholarship or grant aid. 92% freshmen, 92% undergrads receive need-based self-help aid. 1% freshmen, 2% undergrads receive athletic scholarships. 72% freshmen, 75% undergrads receive any aid. 64% undergrads borrow to pay for school. Average cumulative indebtedness $34,105. **Criteria for awarding aid:** *Need-based:* Academics *Non-need-based:* Academics, Alumni affiliation, Art, Athletics, Job skills, Leadership, Minority status, Music/drama, Religious affiliation, State/district residency.

WEST VIRGINIA UNIVERSITY INSTITUTE OF TECHNOLOGY

405 Fayette Pike, Montgomery, WV 25136
Phone: 304-442-3167
E-mail: admissions@wvutech.edu
Fax: 304-442-3097 • **Website:** www.wvutech.edu

This is a public school.

RATINGS

Admissions Selectivity Rating: 78   **Fire Safety Rating:** 60*   **Green Rating:** 60*

STUDENTS AND FACULTY

Enrollment: 2,001. **Student Body:** 39% female, 61% male, 6% out-of-state, 4% international. Asian 1%, African American 8%, Caucasian 87%, Hispanic 1%, Native American <1%, Race unknown 0%.
Retention and Graduation: 62% freshmen return for sophomore year.
Faculty: Student/faculty ratio 16:1. 119 full-time faculty, 47% hold PhDs, 18% are members of minority groups, 28% are women.

ACADEMICS

Degrees: Associate; Bachelor's; Certificate; **Master's Classes:** Most classes have 10-19 students. Most lab/discussion sessions have 10-19 students. **Special Study Options:** Cooperative education program; Distance learning; Double major; Dual enrollment; Internships; Student-designed major.

FACILITIES

Housing: Coed dorms; Fraternity/sorority housing; Men's dorms; Women's dorms

CAMPUS LIFE

Activities: Choral groups; Concert band; Drama/theater; Jazz band; Marching band; Music ensembles; Pep band; Student government; Student newspaper.

ADMISSIONS

Freshman Academic Profile: Average high school GPA 3.2. 20% in top 10% of high school class, 21% in top 25% of high school class, 43% in top 50% of high school class. 88% from public high schools. **Test Scores:** SAT Math middle 50% range 400-580. SAT EBRW middle 50% range 380-530. ACT middle 50% range 17-23. Minimum paper TOEFL 500. **Basis for Candidate Selection:** *Very important factors considered include:* rigor of secondary school record, standardized test scores. *Other factors considered include:* class rank, recommendation(s), interview, extracurricular activities, talent/ability, character/personal qualities, alumni/ae relation, state residency, volunteer work. **Freshman Admission Requirements:** High school diploma is required and GED is accepted *Academic units required:* 4 English, 2 math, 2 science, 2 science labs, 3 social studies, *Academic units recommended:* 4 English, 3 math, 2 science, 2 science labs, 2 foreign language, 3 social studies. **Freshman Admission Statistics:** 1,191 applied, 74.1% admitted, 47% enrolled. **Transfer Admission Requirements:** college transcript(s), Minimum college GPA of 1.7 required. Lowest grade transferable D. **General Admission Information:** Priority deadline 8/3. Nonfall registration accepted. Admission may be deferred for a maximum of 1 semester.

COSTS AND FINANCIAL AID

Annual in-state tuition $4,896. Annual out-of-state tuition $8,400. Room and board $4,896. Average book expense $800. **Required Forms and Deadlines:** FAFSA; Institution's own financial aid form. **Notification of Awards:** Applicants will be notified of awards on a rolling basis beginning 3/3. **Types of Aid:** *Need-based scholarships/grants:* College/university scholarship or grant aid from institutional funds; Federal Pell; Private scholarships; SEOG; State scholarships/grants. *Loans:* Direct PLUS loans; Direct Subsidized Stafford Loans; Direct Unsubsidized Stafford Loans. **Financial Aid Statistics:** 78% needy freshmen, 78% needy undergrads receive need-based scholarship or grant aid. 70% freshmen, 48% undergrads receive non-need-based scholarship or grant aid. 59% freshmen, 70% undergrads receive need-based self-help aid. 2% freshmen, 6% undergrads receive athletic scholarships. **Criteria for awarding aid:** *Need-based:* Academics, Athletics, Music/drama *Non-need-based:* Academics, Alumni affiliation, Art, Athletics, Music/drama.

WEST VIRGINIA WESLEYAN COLLEGE

59 College Avenue, Buckhannon, WV 26201
Phone: 304-473-8510 • **Financial Aid Phone:** 304-473-8080
E-mail: admission@wvwc.edu • **CEEB Code:** 5905
Fax: 304-473-8108 • **Website:** www.wvwc.edu • **ACT Code:** 4544

This private school, affiliated with the Methodist Church, was founded in 1890. It has a 180 acre campus.

RATINGS
Admissions Selectivity Rating: 78   **Fire Safety Rating:** 60*   **Green Rating:** 60*

STUDENTS AND FACULTY
Enrollment: 1,304. **Student Body:** 56% female, 44% male, 38% out-of-state, 6% international (22 countries represented). Asian <1%, African American 9%, Caucasian 78%, Hispanic 3%, Native American <1%, Pacific Islander <1%, Two or more races 4%, Race unknown <1%.
Retention and Graduation: 74% freshmen return for sophomore year. 38% freshmen graduate within 4 years. 50% freshmen graduate within 6 years. 35% grads go on to further study within 1 year. 57% grads pursue arts and sciences degrees. 11% grads pursue law degrees. 16% grads pursue business degrees. 6% grads pursue medical degrees. **Faculty:** Student/faculty ratio 13:1. 83 full-time faculty, 69% hold PhDs, 7% are members of minority groups, 53% are women. 0% of classes are taught by teaching assistants.

ACADEMICS
Degrees: Bachelor's; Master's; Post-Bachelor's certificate; Post-Master's certificate **Classes:** Most classes have 10-19 students. Most lab/discussion sessions have 10-19 students. **Most popular majors:** Elementary Education And Teaching; Kinesiology And Exercise Science; Business Administration And Management, General. **Special Study Options:** Distance learning; Double major; English as a Second Language (ESL); Exchange student program (domestic); Honors program; Independent study; Internships; Liberal arts/career combination; Student-designed major; Study abroad; Teacher certification program. Honors programs: The Honors Program is offered to recognize and challenge the College's most academically talented students. Participation is voluntary for all qualified students. Combined degree programs: BA/MA. **Disability Services offered to physically disabled students:** Note-taking services; Reader services; Tape recorders; Tutors. **Career services:** Alumni network; Alumni services; Career/job search classes; Internships

FACILITIES
Housing: Coed dorms; Fraternity/sorority housing; Men's dorms; Special housing for disabled student; Women's dorms **Computers:** Students can register for classes online. Undergraduates are required to own a computer.

CAMPUS LIFE
Environment: Village **Activities:** Campus Ministries; Choral groups; Concert band; Dance; Drama/theater; International Student Organization; Jazz band; Literary magazine; Marching band; Music ensembles; Musical theater; Opera; Pep band; Radio station; Student government; Student newspaper; Yearbook 75 registered organizations, 31 honor societies, 6 religious organizations. 6 fraternities, 5 sororities. **Athletics (Intercollegiate):** *Men:* baseball, basketball, cross-country, football, golf, soccer, softball, swimming, tennis, track/field (outdoor), track/field (indoor). *Women:* basketball, cross-country, golf, lacrosse, soccer, swimming, tennis, track/field (outdoor), track/field (indoor), volleyball. **On-Campus Highlights:** David E. Reemsnyder Research Center, Sunny Bucks (Convienence Store), Wesley Chapel, Sleeth Art Gallery, Virginia Thomas Law Center for the Performing Arts

ADMISSIONS
Freshman Academic Profile: Average high school GPA 3.5. 20% in top 10% of high school class, 49% in top 25% of high school class, 83% in top 50% of high school class. 88% from public high schools. **Test Scores:** SAT Math middle 50% range 485-580. SAT EBRW middle 50% range 470-590. ACT middle 50% range 19-25. Minimum paper TOEFL 500. **Basis for Candidate Selection:** *Very important factors considered include:* rigor of secondary school record, academic GPA, talent/ability. *Important factors considered include:* class rank, standardized test scores, extracurricular activities, character/personal qualities, volunteer work, work experience, level of applicant's interest. *Other factors considered include:* application essay, recommendation(s), interview. **Freshman Admission Requirements:** High school diploma is required and GED is accepted *Academic units required:* 4 English, 3 math, 3 science, 1 science labs, 3 social studies, *Academic units recommended:* 2 foreign language. **Freshman Admission Statistics:** 2,272 applied, 70.6% admitted, 23% enrolled. **Transfer Admission Requirements:** High school transcript, college transcript(s), statement of good standing from prior institution(s). Minimum college

GPA of 2.50 required. Lowest grade transferable C-. **General Admission Information:** Application fee $35. Priority deadline 2/1. Regular application deadline 8/15. Nonfall registration accepted. Admission may be deferred for a maximum of 1 year.

COSTS AND FINANCIAL AID
Annual tuition $28,574. Room and board $8,248. Required fees $1,178. Average book expense $2,500. **Required Forms and Deadlines:** FAFSA. **Notification of Awards:** Applicants will be notified of awards on a rolling basis beginning 3/1. **Types of Aid:** *Need-based scholarships/grants:* College/university scholarship or grant aid from institutional funds; Federal Nursing Scholarships; Federal Pell; Private scholarships; SEOG; State scholarships/grants. *Loans:* Direct PLUS loans; Direct Subsidized Stafford Loans; Direct Unsubsidized Stafford Loans. *Student Employment:* Federal Work-Study Program available. Institutional employment available. **Financial Aid Statistics:** 100% needy freshmen, 100% needy undergrads receive need-based scholarship or grant aid. 22% freshmen, 17% undergrads receive non-need-based scholarship or grant aid. 80% freshmen, 85% undergrads receive need-based self-help aid. 4% freshmen, 7% undergrads receive athletic scholarships. 99% freshmen, 98% undergrads receive any aid. 71% undergrads borrow to pay for school. Average cumulative indebtedness $29,296. **Criteria for awarding aid:** *Need-based:* Art, Leadership, Music/drama *Non-need-based:* Academics, Alumni affiliation, Art, Athletics, Leadership, Music/drama, Religious affiliation.

See page 1088.

WESTERN CAROLINA UNIVERSITY

102 Camp Building, Cullowhee, NC 28723
Phone: 828-227-7317 • **Financial Aid Phone:** 828-227-7290
E-mail: admiss@email.wcu.edu • **CEEB Code:** 5897
Fax: 828-227-7319 • **Website:** www.wcu.edu • **ACT Code:** 3172

This public school was founded in 1889. It has a 682 acre campus.

RATINGS
Admissions Selectivity Rating: 87   **Fire Safety Rating:** 94   **Green Rating:** 82

STUDENTS AND FACULTY
Enrollment: 9,234. **Student Body:** 55% female, 45% male, 7% out-of-state, 1% international (28 countries represented). Asian 1%, African American 6%, Caucasian 79%, Hispanic 7%, Native American 1%, Pacific Islander <1%, Two or more races 4%, Race unknown 1%.
Retention and Graduation: 79% freshmen return for sophomore year. 40% freshmen graduate within 4 years. 59% freshmen graduate within 6 years. **Faculty:** Student/faculty ratio 17:1. 511 full-time faculty, 77% hold PhDs, 8% are members of minority groups, 50% are women. 1% of classes are taught by teaching assistants.

ACADEMICS
Degrees: Bachelor's; Doctoral/Professional; Doctoral/Research; Master's; Post-Bachelor's certificate; Post-Master's certificate **Classes:** Most classes have 20-29 students. Most lab/discussion sessions have fewer than 10 students. **Most popular majors:** Junior High/Intermediate/Middle School Education And Teaching; Criminal Justice/Safety Studies; Registered Nursing/Registered Nurse. **Special Study Options:** Cooperative education program; Distance learning; Double major; Dual enrollment; English as a Second Language (ESL); Exchange student program (domestic); Honors program; Independent study; Internships; Student-designed major; Study abroad; Teacher certification program. Honors programs: Western has a residential Honors College designed to enhance the academic and social university experience for high-achieving students. The college consists of honors courses throughout liberal studies with an emphasis on special projects and undergraduate research in the major. Also, special housing, academic, leadership and social programs are available for honors students. **Disability Services offered to physically disabled students:** Note-taking services; Reader services; Tape recorders; Tutors. **Career services:** Alumni network; Alumni services; Career assessment; Internships

FACILITIES
Housing: Apartments for married students; Coed dorms; Fraternity/sorority housing; Men's dorms; Special housing for disabled student; Theme housing; Wellness housing; Women's dorms 91% of campus accessible to physically disabled. **Special Academic Facilities/Equipment:** Fine Arts Gallery, Mountain Heritage Center, Reading Center, North Carolina Center for the Advancement of Teaching, Speech/Hearing Center, Center for Applied Technology, CATA Lab (high technology computer lab), Fine and Performing

Arts Center, Institute for the Economy and the Future, Public Policy Institute **Computers:** 90% of classrooms, 10% of dorms, 100% of libraries, 70% of dining areas, 100% of student union, 50% of common outdoor areas have wireless network access. Students can register for classes online. Administrative functions (other than registration) can be performed online. Undergraduates are required to own a computer.

CAMPUS LIFE

Environment: Rural **Activities:** Campus Ministries; Choral groups; Concert band; Dance; Drama/theater; International Student Organization; Jazz band; Literary magazine; Marching band; Model UN; Music ensembles; Musical theater; Pep band; Radio station; Student government; Student newspaper; Student-run film society; Television station 103 registered organizations, 7 honor societies, 12 religious organizations. 11 fraternities, 8 sororities **Athletics (Intercollegiate):** *Men:* baseball, basketball, cheerleading, cross-country, football, golf, track/field (outdoor), track/field (indoor). *Women:* basketball, cheerleading, cross-country, golf, soccer, softball, tennis, track/field (outdoor), track/field (indoor), volleyball. **On-Campus Highlights:** University Center, Campus Recreation Center, Hunter Library, Courtyard Dining Hall, Ramsey Regional Activity Center **Environmental Initiatives:** Currently have one building under construction that will meet LEED certification standards (completed summer 2017) and another academic building in design phase.

ADMISSIONS

Freshman Academic Profile: Average high school GPA 3.8. 13% in top 10% of high school class, 38% in top 25% of high school class, 78% in top 50% of high school class. **Test Scores:** SAT Math middle 50% range 440-550. ACT middle 50% range 19-24. Minimum internet-based TOEFL 79. Minimum paper TOEFL 550. **Basis for Candidate Selection:** *Very important factors considered include:* rigor of secondary school record, class rank, academic GPA, standardized test scores, level of applicant's interest. *Important factors considered include:* application essay, recommendation(s), extracurricular activities, talent/ability, character/personal qualities, work experience. *Other factors considered include:* interview, first generation, geographical residence, state residency. **Freshman Admission Requirements:** High school diploma is required and GED is accepted *Academic units required:* 4 English, 4 math, 3 science, 3 science labs, 2 foreign language, 2 social studies, 1 history, 4 academic electives, *Academic units recommended:* 4 English, 4 math, 3 science, 3 science labs, 2 foreign language, 2 social studies, 1 history, 8 academic electives. **Freshman Admission Statistics:** 19,476 applied, 38.8% admitted, 26% enrolled. **Transfer Admission Requirements:** college transcript(s), statement of good standing from prior institution(s). Minimum college GPA of 2.0 required. Lowest grade transferable C. **General Admission Information:** Application fee $65. Priority deadline 11/15. Regular application deadline 3/1. Nonfall registration accepted.

COSTS AND FINANCIAL AID

Annual in-state tuition $3,220. Annual out-of-state tuition $14,364. Required fees $3,220. Average book expense $932. **Required Forms and Deadlines:** FAFSA; Institution's own financial aid form. **Notification of Awards:** Applicants will be notified of awards on a rolling basis beginning 4/1. **Types of Aid:** *Need-based scholarships/grants:* College/university scholarship or grant aid from institutional funds; Federal Pell; Private scholarships; SEOG; State scholarships/grants. *Loans:* Direct PLUS loans; Direct Subsidized Stafford Loans; Direct Unsubsidized Stafford Loans. *Student Employment:* Federal Work-Study Program available. Institutional employment available. **Financial Aid Statistics:** 96% needy freshmen, 94% needy undergrads receive need-based scholarship or grant aid. 3% freshmen, 3% undergrads receive non-need-based scholarship or grant aid. 75% freshmen, 78% undergrads receive need-based self-help aid. 4% freshmen, 4% undergrads receive athletic scholarships. **Criteria for awarding aid:** *Need-based:* Academics, Minority status *Non-need-based:* Academics, Art, Athletics, Leadership, Music/drama, State/district residency.

WESTERN CONNECTICUT STATE UNIVERSITY

181 White Street, Danbury, CT 06810-6855
Phone: 203-837-9000 • **Financial Aid Phone:** 203-837-8588
E-mail: admissions@wcsu.edu • **CEEB Code:** 3350
Fax: 203-837-8338 • **Website:** www.wcsu.edu • **ACT Code:** 558

This public school was founded in 1903. It has a 364 acre campus.

RATINGS

Admissions Selectivity Rating: 79   **Fire Safety Rating:** 91   **Green Rating:** 60*

STUDENTS AND FACULTY

Enrollment: 4,890. **Student Body:** 52% female, 48% male, 9% out-of-state, <1% international (10 countries represented). Asian 4%, African American 11%, Caucasian 61%, Hispanic 18%, Native American <1%, Pacific Islander <1%, Two or more races 3%, Race unknown 3%.
Retention and Graduation: 74% freshmen return for sophomore year. 20% freshmen graduate within 4 years. 44% freshmen graduate within 6 years.
Faculty: Student/faculty ratio 13:1. 220 full-time faculty, 90% hold PhDs, 20% are members of minority groups, 52% are women. 0% of classes are taught by teaching assistants.

ACADEMICS

Degrees: Associate; Bachelor's; Doctoral/Professional; Master's; Post-Master's certificate **Classes:** Most classes have 10-19 students. Most lab/discussion sessions have 10-19 students. **Most popular majors:** Elementary Education And Teaching; Philosophy And Religious Studies; Criminal Justice/Police Science. **Special Study Options:** Cooperative education program; Cross-registration; Distance learning; Dual enrollment; Honors program; Independent study; Internships; Student-designed major; Study abroad; Teacher certification program. Honors programs: University Scholars Program. **Disability Services offered to physically disabled students:** Note-taking services; Reader services; Tape recorders; Tutors. **Career services:** Career assessment; Career/job search classes; Internships

FACILITIES

Housing: Apartments for single students; Coed dorms; Other (please specify) 100% of campus accessible to physically diasbled. **Special Academic Facilities/Equipment:** Language lab, observatory, electron microscope, nature preserve, computer-enhanced classrooms, business library, Jane Goodall Institute. **Computers:** 50% of classrooms, 80% of dorms, 100% of libraries, 100% of dining areas, 100% of student union, have wireless network access. Students can register for classes online. Administrative functions (other than registration) can be performed online.

CAMPUS LIFE

Environment: City **Activities:** Campus Ministries; Choral groups; Concert band; Dance; Drama/theater; International Student Organization; Jazz band; Literary magazine; Music ensembles; Musical theater; Opera; Pep band; Radio station; Student government; Student newspaper; Symphony orchestra 40 registered organizations, 8 honor societies, 3 religious organizations. 3 fraternities, 4 sororities. **Athletics (Intercollegiate):** *Men:* baseball, basketball, football, lacrosse, soccer, tennis. *Women:* basketball, field hockey, lacrosse, soccer, softball, swimming, tennis, volleyball. **On-Campus Highlights:** Student Centers (Midtown and Westside), O'Neill Center, Science Building, White Hall, Ancell Classroom Building **Environmental Initiatives:** Think Green: Go Blue recycling efforts (with distribution campus wide of an instruction brochure).

ADMISSIONS

Freshman Academic Profile: Average high school GPA 85.0. 6% in top 10% of high school class, 24% in top 25% of high school class, 66% in top 50% of high school class. 90% from public high schools. **Test Scores:** SAT Math middle 50% range 490-590. SAT EBRW middle 50% range 500-590. Minimum internet-based TOEFL 79. Minimum paper TOEFL 550. **Basis for Candidate Selection:** *Very important factors considered include:* rigor of secondary school record, standardized test scores, talent/ability. *Important factors considered include:* class rank, academic GPA, extracurricular activities, level of applicant's interest. *Other factors considered include:* application essay, recommendation(s), interview, character/personal qualities, alumni/ae relation, state residency, racial/ethnic status, volunteer work, work experience. **Freshman Admission Requirements:** High school diploma is required and GED is accepted *Academic units required:* 4 English, 3 math, 2 science, 2 science labs, 2 foreign language, 1 social studies, 1 history. **Freshman Admission Statistics:** 5,671 applied, 70.8% admitted, 21% enrolled. **Transfer Admission Requirements:** college transcript(s), Minimum college GPA of 2.0 required. Lowest grade transferable C-. **General Admission Information:** Application fee $50. Nonfall registration accepted. Admission may be deferred for a maximum of 1 year.

COSTS AND FINANCIAL AID

Annual in-state tuition $12,622. Annual out-of-state tuition $16,882. Room and board $12,622. Required fees $4,994. Average book expense $1,300. **Required Forms and Deadlines:** FAFSA; Institution's own financial aid form. **Notification of Awards:** Applicants will be notified of awards on a rolling basis beginning 4/15. **Types of Aid:** *Need-based scholarships/grants:* College/university scholarship or grant aid from institutional funds; Federal Pell; Private scholarships; SEOG; State scholarships/grants. *Loans:* Direct PLUS loans; Direct Subsidized Stafford Loans; Direct Unsubsidized Stafford Loans. *Student Employment:* Federal Work-Study Program available. Institutional employment available. **Financial Aid Statistics:** 95% needy freshmen, 83% needy undergrads receive need-based scholarship or grant aid. 2% freshmen, 1% undergrads receive non-need-based scholarship or grant aid. 75% freshmen,

81% undergrads receive need-based self-help aid. 0% freshmen, 0% undergrads receive athletic scholarships. 63% freshmen, 61% undergrads receive any aid. Average cumulative indebtedness $31,229. **Criteria for awarding aid:** *Need-based:* Academics, Art, Minority status, Music/drama *Non-need-based:* Academics, Art, Minority status, Music/drama.

WESTERN ILLINOIS UNIVERSITY

1 University Circle, Macomb, IL 61455-1390
Phone: 309-298-3157 • **Financial Aid Phone:** 309-298-2446
E-mail: admissions@wiu.edu • **CEEB Code:** 1900
Fax: 309-298-3111 • **Website:** http://www.wiu.edu • **ACT Code:** 1158

This public school was founded in 1899. It has a 1050 acre campus.

RATINGS

Admissions Selectivity Rating: 79   **Fire Safety Rating:** 89   **Green Rating:** 65

STUDENTS AND FACULTY

Enrollment: 7,599. **Student Body:** 51% female, 49% male, 10% out-of-state, 1% international (61 countries represented). Asian 1%, African American 22%, Caucasian 59%, Hispanic 12%, Native American <1%, Pacific Islander <1%, Two or more races 3%, Race unknown 2%.
Retention and Graduation: 68% freshmen return for sophomore year. 30% freshmen graduate within 4 years. 50% freshmen graduate within 6 years. 37% grads go on to further study within 1 year. 1.3% grads pursue law degrees. 2.6% grads pursue medical degrees. **Faculty:** Student/faculty ratio 14:1. 556 full-time faculty, 73% hold PhDs, 20% are members of minority groups, 45% are women. 3% of classes are taught by teaching assistants.

ACADEMICS

Degrees: Bachelor's; Doctoral/Research; Master's; Post-Bachelor's certificate; Post-Master's certificate **Classes:** Most classes have 10-19 students. Most lab/discussion sessions have 20-29 students. **Most popular majors:** Biology/Biological Sciences, General; Psychology; Criminal Justice/Law Enforcement Administration. **Special Study Options:** Distance learning; Double major; Dual enrollment; English as a Second Language (ESL); External degree program; Honors program; Independent study; Internships; Student-designed major; Study abroad; Teacher certification program; Weekend college. Honors programs: Illinois Centennial Honors College http://www.wiu.edu/centennial_honors_college/ Combined degree programs: BA/MA. **Disability Services offered to physically disabled students:** Note-taking services; Reader services; Tape recorders; Tutors. **Career services:** Alumni network; Alumni services; Career assessment; Career/job search classes; Internships

FACILITIES

Housing: Apartments for married students; Apartments for single students; Coed dorms; Cooperative housing; Fraternity/sorority housing; Special housing for disabled student; Special housing for international students; Theme housing; Wellness housing 95% of campus accessible to physically disabled. **Special Academic Facilities/Equipment:** Art gallery, Geology museum, electron microscope, multicultural center **Computers:** 100% of classrooms, 100% of dorms, 100% of libraries, 100% of dining areas, 100% of student union, 100% of common outdoor areas have wireless network access. Students can register for classes online. Administrative functions (other than registration) can be performed online.

CAMPUS LIFE

Environment: Village **Activities:** Campus Ministries; Choral groups; Concert band; Dance; Drama/theater; International Student Organization; Jazz band; Literary magazine; Marching band; Model UN; Music ensembles; Musical theater; Opera; Pep band; Radio station; Student government; Student newspaper; Student-run film society; Symphony orchestra; Television station 200 registered organizations, 25 honor societies, 12 religious organizations. 14 fraternities, 11 sororities. **Athletics (Intercollegiate):** *Men:* baseball, basketball, cross-country, diving, football, golf, soccer, swimming, tennis, track/field (outdoor), track/field (indoor). *Women:* basketball, cheerleading, cross-country, diving, golf, soccer, softball, swimming, tennis, track/field (outdoor), track/field (indoor), volleyball. **On-Campus Highlights:** University Union, Student Recreation Center, Leslie Malpass Library, Hanson Field, Multicultural Center **Environmental Initiatives:** WIU has received numerous energy efficiency grants from the Illinois Department of Commerce and Economic Opportunity, which total over $2,400,000 in the last six years.

ADMISSIONS

Freshman Academic Profile: Average high school GPA 3.2. 10% in top 10% of high school class, 30% in top 25% of high school class, 69% in top

50% of high school class. 91% from public high schools. **Test Scores:** ACT middle 50% range 18-23. Minimum internet-based TOEFL 73. Minimum paper TOEFL 533. **Basis for Candidate Selection:** *Very important factors considered include:* academic GPA, standardized test scores. *Other factors considered include:* rigor of secondary school record. **Freshman Admission Requirements:** High school diploma is required and GED is accepted *Academic units required:* 4 English, 3 math, 3 science, 3 social studies, 2 academic electives. **Freshman Admission Statistics:** 9,767 applied, 60.0% admitted, 21% enrolled. **Transfer Admission Requirements:** college transcript(s), Minimum college GPA of 2.0 required. Lowest grade transferable D. **General Admission Information:** Application fee $30. Nonfall registration accepted. Admission may be deferred.

COSTS AND FINANCIAL AID

Average book expense $1,200. **Required Forms and Deadlines:** FAFSA. **Notification of Awards:** Applicants will be notified of awards on a rolling basis beginning 1/15. **Types of Aid:** *Need-based scholarships/grants:* College/university scholarship or grant aid from institutional funds; Federal Pell; Private scholarships; SEOG; State scholarships/grants. *Loans:* Direct PLUS loans; Direct Subsidized Stafford Loans; Direct Unsubsidized Stafford Loans. *Student Employment:* Federal Work-Study Program available. Institutional employment available. **Financial Aid Statistics:** 74% needy freshmen, 68% needy undergrads receive need-based scholarship or grant aid. 57% freshmen, 45% undergrads receive non-need-based scholarship or grant aid. 91% freshmen, 92% undergrads receive need-based self-help aid. 3% freshmen, 4% undergrads receive athletic scholarships. 91% freshmen, 89% undergrads receive any aid. 83% undergrads borrow to pay for school. Average cumulative indebtedness $30,721. **Criteria for awarding aid:** *Non-need-based:* Academics, Alumni affiliation, Art, Athletics, Leadership, Minority status, Music/drama.

WESTERN KENTUCKY UNIVERSITY

1906 College Heights Blvd., Bowling Green, KY 42101-1020
Phone: 270-745-2551 • **Financial Aid Phone:** 270-745-2755
E-mail: admission@wku.edu • **CEEB Code:** 1901
Fax: 270-745-6133 • **Website:** www.wku.edu • **ACT Code:** 1562

This public school was founded in 1906. It has a 235 acre campus.

RATINGS

Admissions Selectivity Rating: 73   **Fire Safety Rating:** 98   **Green Rating:** 87

STUDENTS AND FACULTY

Enrollment: 14,529. **Student Body:** 57% female, 43% male, 21% out-of-state, 4% international (53 countries represented). Asian 1%, African American 10%, Caucasian 77%, Hispanic 3%, Native American <1%, Pacific Islander <1%, Two or more races 3%, Race unknown <1%.
Retention and Graduation: 70% freshmen return for sophomore year. 28% freshmen graduate within 4 years. 51% freshmen graduate within 6 years. **Faculty:** Student/faculty ratio 18:1. 754 full-time faculty, 77% hold PhDs, 18% are members of minority groups, 51% are women. 1% of classes are taught by teaching assistants.

ACADEMICS

Degrees: Associate; Bachelor's; Certificate; Doctoral/Professional; Master's; Post-Bachelor's certificate; Post-Master's certificate **Classes:** Most classes have fewer than 10 students. Most lab/discussion sessions have greater than 100 students. **Most popular majors:** Biology/Biological Sciences, General; Registered Nursing/Registered Nurse; Business Administration And Management, General. **Special Study Options:** Accelerated program; Cooperative education program; Distance learning; Double major; Dual enrollment; English as a Second Language (ESL); Honors program; Independent study; Internships; Student-designed major; Study abroad; Teacher certification program; Weekend college. Honors programs: Mahurin Honors College at WKU and Gatton Academy of Mathematics and Science Combined degree programs: BA/MA. **Disability Services offered to physically disabled students:** Note-taking services; Reader services; Tape recorders; Tutors. **Career services:** Alumni network; Alumni services; Career assessment; Career/job search classes; Internships; Regional alumni

FACILITIES

Housing: Apartments for married students; Apartments for single students; Coed dorms; Fraternity/sorority housing; Men's dorms; Special housing for international students; Theme housing; Wellness housing; Women's dorms **Special Academic Facilities/Equipment:** Hardin Planetarium, Bell Observatory and Weather Station, Kentucky Museum, Baker Arboretum,

Downing Museum, WKU Farm, Mass Media and Technology Hall **Computers:** 100% of classrooms, 68% of dorms, 100% of libraries, 100% of dining areas, 100% of student union, have wireless network access. Students can register for classes online. Administrative functions (other than registration) can be performed online.

CAMPUS LIFE

Environment: Town **Activities:** Campus Ministries; Choral groups; Concert band; Dance; Drama/theater; International Student Organization; Jazz band; Literary magazine; Marching band; Model UN; Music ensembles; Musical theater; Opera; Pep band; Radio station; Student government; Student newspaper; Student-run film society; Symphony orchestra; Television station; Yearbook 360 registered organizations, 28 honor societies, 23 religious organizations. 18 fraternities, 13 sororities. **Athletics (Intercollegiate):** *Men:* baseball, basketball, cross-country, diving, football, golf, riflery, swimming, tennis, track/field (outdoor), track/field (indoor). *Women:* basketball, cross-country, diving, golf, riflery, soccer, swimming, tennis, track/field (outdoor), track/field (indoor), volleyball. **On-Campus Highlights:** Downing Student Union, Preston Health and Activities Center, E.A. Diddle Arena, Houchens Industries-L.T. Smith Stadium, Jody Richards Hall (Mass Media and Technology) **Environmental Initiatives:** Sustainability-oriented staff positions and Sustainability Committee, Education for Sustainability resolution adopted 2010, Sustainability in operations, services, and academics included in 2010-2012 University Strategic Plan.

ADMISSIONS

Freshman Academic Profile: Average high school GPA 3.3. 22% in top 10% of high school class, 46% in top 25% of high school class, 72% in top 50% of high school class. **Test Scores:** SAT Math middle 50% range 470-580. SAT EBRW middle 50% range 500-600. ACT middle 50% range 19-27. Minimum internet-based TOEFL 71. Minimum paper TOEFL 525. **Basis for Candidate Selection:** *Very important factors considered include:* academic GPA, standardized test scores. **Freshman Admission Requirements:** High school diploma is required and GED is accepted *Academic units required:* 4 English, 3 math, 3 science, 1 science labs, 2 foreign language, 3 social studies, 1 history, 5 academic electives, and 1 unit from above areas or other academic areas. **Freshman Admission Statistics:** 9,804 applied, 95.5% admitted, 33% enrolled. **Transfer Admission Requirements:** college transcript(s), statement of good standing from prior institution(s). Minimum college GPA of 2.0 required. Lowest grade transferable D°. **General Admission Information:** Application fee $45. Regular application deadline 8/1. Nonfall registration accepted. Admission may be deferred.

COSTS AND FINANCIAL AID

Annual in-state tuition $8,350. Annual out-of-state tuition $25,512. Room and board $8,350. Average book expense $1,000. **Required Forms and Deadlines:** FAFSA. **Notification of Awards:** Applicants will be notified of awards on a rolling basis beginning 3/1. **Types of Aid:** *Need-based scholarships/ grants:* College/university scholarship or grant aid from institutional funds; Federal Pell; Private scholarships; SEOG; State scholarships/grants; United Negro College Fund. *Loans:* Direct PLUS loans; Direct Subsidized Stafford Loans; Direct Unsubsidized Stafford Loans. *Student Employment:* Federal Work-Study Program available. Institutional employment available. **Financial Aid Statistics:** 64% needy freshmen, 63% needy undergrads receive need-based scholarship or grant aid. 89% freshmen, 69% undergrads receive non-need-based scholarship or grant aid. 63% freshmen, 70% undergrads receive need-based self-help aid. 2% freshmen, 3% undergrads receive athletic scholarships. 93% freshmen, 87% undergrads receive any aid. 61% undergrads borrow to pay for school. Average cumulative indebtedness $28,081. **Criteria for awarding aid:** *Non-need-based:* Academics, Alumni affiliation, Art, Athletics, Job skills, Leadership, Minority status, Music/drama, Religious affiliation, State/district residency.

WESTERN MICHIGAN UNIVERSITY

1903 W Michigan Ave, Kalamazoo, MI 49008-5211
Phone: 269-387-2000 • **Financial Aid Phone:** 269-387-6000
E-mail: ask-wmu@wmich.edu • **CEEB Code:** 1902
Fax: 269-387-2096 • **Website:** https://wmich.edu/ • **ACT Code:** 2066

This public school was founded in 1903. It has a 1289 acre campus.

RATINGS

Admissions Selectivity Rating: 75   **Fire Safety Rating:** 88   **Green Rating:** 86

STUDENTS AND FACULTY

Enrollment: 17,704. **Student Body:** 49% female, 51% male, 10% out-of-state, 4% international (57 countries represented). Asian 2%, African American 12%, Caucasian 71%, Hispanic 6%, Native American <1%, Pacific Islander <1%, Two or more races 4%, Race unknown 1%.
Retention and Graduation: 78% freshmen return for sophomore year. 22% freshmen graduate within 4 years. 51% freshmen graduate within 6 years. **Faculty:** Student/faculty ratio 17:1. 926 full-time faculty, 77% hold PhDs, 20% are members of minority groups, 46% are women. 12% of classes are taught by teaching assistants.

ACADEMICS

Degrees: Bachelor's; Certificate; Doctoral/Professional; Doctoral/Research; Master's; Post-Bachelor's certificate; Post-Master's certificate **Classes:** Most classes have 10-19 students. **Most popular majors:** Psychology, General; Health And Medical Administrative Services, Other; Business Administration And Management, General. **Special Study Options:** Accelerated program; Cooperative education program; Cross-registration; Distance learning; Double major; Dual enrollment; English as a Second Language (ESL); Honors program; Independent study; Internships; Student-designed major; Study abroad; Teacher certification program. Honors programs: The Lee Honors College The mission of the Carl and Winifred Lee Honors College is to provide an exceptional undergraduate experience for high achieving students, to inspire in our graduates a thirst for the lifelong pursuit of creative inquiry and discovery, to provide our students with the skill and passion to address critical challenges, and to foster personal responsibility informed by a global perspective. Combined degree programs: BA/MA; BA/MEng. **Disability Services offered to physically disabled students:** Reader services; Tutors. **Career services:** Alumni network; Career assessment; Career/job search classes; Internships

FACILITIES

Housing: Apartments for married students; Apartments for single students; Coed dorms; Fraternity/sorority housing; Men's dorms; Special housing for disabled student; Theme housing; Women's dorms 85% of campus accessible to physically disabled. **Special Academic Facilities/Equipment:** Archives & Regional History Library; Aviation flight simulators; Behavioral research and development center; Business incubator for student entrepreneurs and inventors; Business technology and research park; Center for electron microscopy; Historic farm sustainability living/learning community with permaculture landscape; Nuclear accelerator; Particle accelerator; Pilot plant for manufacturing and printing of paper and fiber recovery; Stock trading room with electronic ticker and terminals **Computers:** 100% of classrooms, 25% of dorms, 100% of libraries, 100% of dining areas, 100% of student union, 100% of common outdoor areas have wireless network access. Students can register for classes online. Administrative functions (other than registration) can be performed online.

CAMPUS LIFE

Environment: City **Activities:** Campus Ministries; Choral groups; Concert band; Dance; Drama/theater; International Student Organization; Jazz band; Literary magazine; Marching band; Model UN; Music ensembles; Musical theater; Opera; Pep band; Radio station; Student government; Student newspaper; Student-run film society; Symphony orchestra 300 registered organizations, 7 honor societies, 21 religious organizations. 16 fraternities, 11 sororities. **Athletics (Intercollegiate):** *Men:* baseball, basketball, football, ice hockey, soccer, tennis. *Women:* basketball, cross-country, golf, gymnastics, soccer, softball, tennis, track/field (outdoor), track/field (indoor), volleyball. **On-Campus Highlights:** Bernhard Center, Waldo Library, Student Recreation Center, Miller Auditorium, Valley Dining Center **Environmental Initiatives:** Strategic Planning for Sustainability—Climate Action Plan (2012); University Strategic Plan Implementation utilizing the Sustainability Tracking, Assessment, and Rating System program as an overarching framework for evaluation; Sustainability Across Research & Teaching Survey, Luncheon Series, and Faculty Learning Community; Humanities Center Climate Change Study Group and lecture series; creation of a 7000 square foot Office for Sustainability building hosting several 2012 events; Office for Sustainability website upgrade www.wmich.edu/sustainability and http://www.youtube.com/user/WMUSustainability.

ADMISSIONS

Freshman Academic Profile: Average high school GPA 3.4. 11% in top 10% of high school class, 33% in top 25% of high school class, 70% in top 50% of high school class. **Test Scores:** SAT Math middle 50% range 470-590. SAT EBRW middle 50% range 490-600. ACT middle 50% range 20-26. Minimum internet-based TOEFL 61. Minimum paper TOEFL 500. **Basis for Candidate Selection:** *Very important factors considered include:* academic GPA, standardized test scores. *Important factors considered include:* rigor of secondary school record. *Other factors considered include:* application essay, recommendation(s), extracurricular activities. **Freshman Admission Requirements:** High school diploma is required and GED is accepted

Academic units recommended: 4 English, 3 math, 3 science, 2 foreign language, 3 social studies. **Freshman Admission Statistics:** 14,263 applied, 82.3% admitted, 27% enrolled. **Transfer Admission Requirements:** college transcript(s), Minimum college GPA of 2.0 required. Lowest grade transferable C. **General Admission Information:** Application fee $40. Nonfall registration accepted.

COSTS AND FINANCIAL AID

Annual in-state tuition $9,848. Annual out-of-state tuition $13,776. Room and board $9,848. Required fees $923. Average book expense $958. **Required Forms and Deadlines:** FAFSA. **Notification of Awards:** Applicants will be notified of awards on a rolling basis beginning 12/10. **Types of Aid:** *Need-based scholarships/grants:* College/university scholarship or grant aid from institutional funds; Federal Pell; Private scholarships; SEOG; State scholarships/grants. *Loans:* Direct PLUS loans; Direct Subsidized Stafford Loans; Direct Unsubsidized Stafford Loans. *Student Employment:* Federal Work-Study Program available. Institutional employment available. **Financial Aid Statistics:** 63% needy freshmen, 70% needy undergrads receive need-based scholarship or grant aid. 53% freshmen, 31% undergrads receive non-need-based scholarship or grant aid. 79% freshmen, 84% undergrads receive need-based self-help aid. 1% freshmen, 1% undergrads receive athletic scholarships. 83% freshmen, 83% undergrads receive any aid. 75% undergrads borrow to pay for school. Average cumulative indebtedness $35,454. **Criteria for awarding aid:** *Need-based:* Academics *Non-need-based:* Academics, Alumni affiliation, Art, Athletics, Music/drama, State/district residency.

WESTERN NEW ENGLAND UNIVERSITY

1215 Wilbraham Road, Springfield, MA 01119
Phone: 413-782-1321 • **Financial Aid Phone:** 413-796-2080
E-mail: learn@wne.edu • **CEEB Code:** 3962
Fax: 413-782-1777 • **ACT Code:** 1930

This private school was founded in 1919. It has a 215 acre campus.

RATINGS

Admissions Selectivity Rating: 75   Fire Safety Rating: 71   Green Rating: 61

STUDENTS AND FACULTY

Enrollment: 2,717. **Student Body:** 38% female, 62% male, 48% out-of-state, 3% international (19 countries represented). Asian 3%, African American 6%, Caucasian 73%, Hispanic 8%, Native American <1%, Pacific Islander <1%, Two or more races 2%, Race unknown 4%.
Retention and Graduation: 76% freshmen return for sophomore year. 22% grads go on to further study within 1 year. 8% grads pursue arts and sciences degrees. 1.5% grads pursue law degrees. 7% grads pursue business degrees. 1.2% grads pursue medical degrees. **Faculty:** Student/faculty ratio 12:1. 237 full-time faculty, 86% hold PhDs, 10% are members of minority groups, 41% are women. 1% of classes are taught by teaching assistants.

ACADEMICS

Degrees: Associate; Bachelor's; Certificate; Doctoral/Professional; Doctoral/Research; Master's; Post-Bachelor's certificate **Classes:** Most classes have 10-19 students. Most lab/discussion sessions have 10-19 students. **Most popular majors:** Mechanical Engineering; Psychology, General; Accounting. **Special Study Options:** Accelerated program; Cross-registration; Distance learning; Double major; Dual enrollment; English as a Second Language (ESL); Exchange student program (domestic); Honors program; Independent study; Internships; Liberal arts/career combination; Student-designed major; Study abroad; Teacher certification program. Honors programs: The Honors Program at Western New England University gives academically qualified and motivated students the opportunity to join a community of like students and participate in challenging courses taught by some of the University's best faculty. Honors students generally take one honors course per semester for their first three years and work on a senior honors project during their final year. Combined degree programs: BA/JD; BA/MEng. **Disability Services offered to physically disabled students:** Note-taking services; Reader services; Tape recorders. **Career services:** Alumni network; Career assessment; Internships

FACILITIES

Housing: Apartments for married students; Apartments for single students; Coed dorms; Special housing for disabled student; Theme housing **Special Academic Facilities/Equipment:** Art Gallery; Math, Writing and Science Centers **Computers:** Students can register for classes online. Administrative functions (other than registration) can be performed online.

CAMPUS LIFE

Environment: City **Activities:** Campus Ministries; Choral groups; Concert band; Dance; Drama/theater; International Student Organization; Jazz band; Literary magazine; Model UN; Music ensembles; Musical theater; Pep band; Radio station; Student government; Student newspaper; Student-run film society; Television station; Yearbook 60 registered organizations, 8 honor societies. **Athletics (Intercollegiate):** *Men:* baseball, basketball, cross-country, football, golf, ice hockey, lacrosse, soccer, tennis, wrestling. *Women:* basketball, cross-country, field hockey, lacrosse, soccer, softball, swimming, tennis, volleyball. **On-Campus Highlights:** Alumni Healthful Living Center, St Germain Campus Center, D'Amour Library, Computer Labs, Rock Cafe

ADMISSIONS

Freshman Academic Profile: Average high school GPA 3.4. 11% in top 10% of high school class, 39% in top 25% of high school class, 74% in top 50% of high school class. **Test Scores:** SAT Math middle 50% range 510-610. SAT EBRW middle 50% range 480-580. ACT middle 50% range 22-27. Minimum internet-based TOEFL 79. Minimum paper TOEFL 550. **Basis for Candidate Selection:** *Very important factors considered include:* academic GPA, standardized test scores. *Important factors considered include:* rigor of secondary school record. *Other factors considered include:* class rank, application essay, recommendation(s), interview, extracurricular activities, talent/ability, character/personal qualities, alumni/ae relation, volunteer work, work experience. **Freshman Admission Requirements:** High school diploma is required and GED is accepted *Academic units required:* 4 English, 2 math, 1 science, 1 science labs, 1 social studies, 1 history, *Academic units recommended:* 4 English, 4 math, 2 science, 2 science labs, 2 foreign language, 2 social studies, 2 history. **Freshman Admission Statistics:** 6,399 applied, 79.6% admitted, 14% enrolled. **Transfer Admission Requirements:** High school transcript, college transcript(s), Minimum college GPA of 2.3 required. Lowest grade transferable C-. **General Admission Information:** Application fee $40. Priority deadline 2/15. Nonfall registration accepted. Admission may be deferred for a maximum of 1 year.

COSTS AND FINANCIAL AID

Annual tuition $32,524. Room and board $13,214. Required fees $2,350. Average book expense $1,240. **Required Forms and Deadlines:** FAFSA. **Notification of Awards:** Applicants will be notified of awards on a rolling basis beginning 3/1. **Types of Aid:** *Need-based scholarships/grants:* College/university scholarship or grant aid from institutional funds; Federal Pell; Private scholarships; SEOG; State scholarships/grants. *Loans:* Direct PLUS loans; Direct Subsidized Stafford Loans; Direct Unsubsidized Stafford Loans. *Student Employment:* Federal Work-Study Program available. Institutional employment available. **Financial Aid Statistics:** 100% needy freshmen, 100% needy undergrads receive need-based scholarship or grant aid. 11% freshmen, 9% undergrads receive non-need-based scholarship or grant aid. 87% freshmen, 87% undergrads receive need-based self-help aid. 0% freshmen, 0% undergrads receive athletic scholarships. 96% freshmen, 93% undergrads receive any aid. 84% undergrads borrow to pay for school. Average cumulative indebtedness $44,013. **Criteria for awarding aid:** *Need-based:* Academics, Alumni affiliation, Leadership, Minority status *Non-need-based:* Academics, Music/drama.

WESTERN OREGON UNIVERSITY

345 N Monmouth Avenue, Monmouth, OR 97361
Phone: 503-838-8211 • **Financial Aid Phone:** 877-877-1593
E-mail: wolfgram@wou.edu • **CEEB Code:** 4585
Fax: 503-838-8067 • **Website:** www.wou.edu • **ACT Code:** 3480

This public school was founded in 1856. It has a 157 acre campus.

RATINGS

Admissions Selectivity Rating: 67   Fire Safety Rating: 95   Green Rating: 60*

STUDENTS AND FACULTY

Enrollment: 4,696. **Student Body:** 62% female, 38% male, 23% out-of-state, 6% international (19 countries represented). Asian 5%, African American 4%, Caucasian 61%, Hispanic 16%, Native American 2%, Pacific Islander 3%, Two or more races <1%, Race unknown 4%.
Retention and Graduation: 72% freshmen return for sophomore year. 22% freshmen graduate within 4 years. 44% freshmen graduate within 6 years. **Faculty:** Student/faculty ratio 15:1. 287 full-time faculty, 71% hold PhDs, 14% are members of minority groups, 54% are women. 0% of classes are taught by teaching assistants.

The Princeton Review's Complete Book of Colleges

ACADEMICS

Degrees: Associate; Bachelor's; Certificate; Master's; Post-Bachelor's certificate **Classes:** Most classes have 10-19 students. Most lab/discussion sessions have 10-19 students. **Most popular majors:** Teacher Education, Multiple Levels; Social Sciences, General; Business/Commerce, General. **Special Study Options:** Cross-registration; Distance learning; Double major; Dual enrollment; Exchange student program (domestic); Honors program; Independent study; Internships; Student-designed major; Study abroad; Teacher certification program. Honors programs: WOU Honors Program. **Disability Services offered to physically disabled students:** Note-taking services; Reader services; Tape recorders; Tutors. **Career services:** Career/job search classes; Internships

FACILITIES

Housing: Apartments for married students; Apartments for single students; Coed dorms; Men's dorms; Special housing for disabled student; Special housing for international students; Theme housing; Wellness housing; Women's dorms 95% of campus accessible to physically diasbled. **Computers:** 70% of classrooms, 90% of dorms, 100% of libraries, 90% of dining areas, 90% of student union, 20% of common outdoor areas have wireless network access. Students can register for classes online. Administrative functions (other than registration) can be performed online.

CAMPUS LIFE

Environment: Village **Activities:** Campus Ministries; Choral groups; Concert band; Dance; Drama/theater; International Student Organization; Jazz band; Literary magazine; Marching band; Model UN; Music ensembles; Musical theater; Pep band; Radio station; Student government; Student newspaper 50 registered organizations, 4 honor societies, 6 religious organizations. **Athletics (Intercollegiate):** *Men:* baseball, basketball, cheerleading, cross-country, football, track/field (outdoor). *Women:* basketball, cheerleading, cross-country, soccer, softball, track/field (outdoor), volleyball. **On-Campus Highlights:** Wayne and Lynn Hamersly Library, Neal Werner University Center, Paul Jensen Arctic Museum, Campbell Hall Art Gallery, Arbor Park Apartments **Environmental Initiatives:** paper recyling

ADMISSIONS

Freshman Academic Profile: Average high school GPA 3.3. 95% from public high schools. **Test Scores:** Minimum paper TOEFL 500. **Basis for Candidate Selection:** *Very important factors considered include:* rigor of secondary school record, class rank, academic GPA. *Important factors considered include:* recommendation(s), talent/ability. *Other factors considered include:* application essay, standardized test scores, character/personal qualities, first generation. **Freshman Admission Requirements:** High school diploma is required and GED is accepted *Academic units required:* 4 English, 3 math, 2 foreign language, 3 social studies, *Academic units recommended:* 4 English, 3 math, 2 foreign language, 3 social studies. **Freshman Admission Statistics:** 2,942 applied, 80.6% admitted, 34% enrolled. **Transfer Admission Requirements:** college transcript(s), Minimum college GPA of 2.0 required. Lowest grade transferable D-. **General Admission Information:** Application fee $60. Nonfall registration accepted.

COSTS AND FINANCIAL AID

Annual in-state tuition $10,203. Annual out-of-state tuition $23,895. Room and board $10,203. Required fees $1,758. Average book expense $1,299. **Required Forms and Deadlines:** FAFSA. **Notification of Awards:** Applicants will be notified of awards on a rolling basis beginning 3/15. **Types of Aid:** *Need-based scholarships/grants:* College/university scholarship or grant aid from institutional funds; Federal Pell; Private scholarships; SEOG; State scholarships/grants; United Negro College Fund. *Loans:* Direct PLUS loans; Direct Subsidized Stafford Loans; Direct Unsubsidized Stafford Loans. *Student Employment:* Federal Work-Study Program available. **Financial Aid Statistics:** 88% needy freshmen, 91% needy undergrads receive need-based scholarship or grant aid. 4% freshmen, 3% undergrads receive non-need-based scholarship or grant aid. 84% freshmen, 86% undergrads receive need-based self-help aid. 3% freshmen, 2% undergrads receive athletic scholarships. 65% freshmen, 58% undergrads receive any aid. 67% undergrads borrow to pay for school. Average cumulative indebtedness $30,586. **Criteria for awarding aid:** *Need-based:* Academics *Non-need-based:* Academics, Athletics, Leadership, Music/drama.

WESTERN STATE COLORADO UNIVERSITY

600 N. Adams St., Gunnison, CO 81231
Financial Aid Phone: (970) 943-3085
E-mail: discover@western.edu • **CEEB Code:** 4946
Fax: (970) 943-2363 • **Website:** www.western.edu • **ACT Code:** 536

This public school was founded in 1911. It has a 228 acre campus.

RATINGS

Admissions Selectivity Rating: 74   **Fire Safety Rating:** 96   **Green Rating:** 83

STUDENTS AND FACULTY

Enrollment: 1,899. **Student Body:** 41% female, 59% male, 70% out-of-state, <1% international (7 countries represented). Asian 1%, African American 3%, Caucasian 71%, Hispanic 11%, Native American 1%, Pacific Islander <1%, Two or more races 5%, Race unknown 8%.
Retention and Graduation: 64% freshmen return for sophomore year. 21% freshmen graduate within 4 years. 41% freshmen graduate within 6 years. 15% grads go on to further study within 1 year. **Faculty:** Student/faculty ratio 18:1. 122 full-time faculty, 84% hold PhDs, 4% are members of minority groups, 43% are women. 0% of classes are taught by teaching assistants.

ACADEMICS

Degrees: Bachelor's; Master's; Post-Bachelor's certificate **Classes:** Most classes have 10-19 students. Most lab/discussion sessions have 10-19 students. **Most popular majors:** Biology/Biological Sciences, General; Parks, Recreation And Leisure Studies; Business Administration And Management, General. **Special Study Options:** Accelerated program; Distance learning; Double major; Dual enrollment; Exchange student program (domestic); Honors program; Independent study; Internships; Liberal arts/career combination; Study abroad; Teacher certification program. Honors programs: Honors Program—based on the National Collegiate Honors Council-modeled City of Text explores urban environments, while the Partners in the Parks: Black Canyon of the Gunnison course immerses students in the ecosystems of one of America's most amazing national parks. **Disability Services offered to physically disabled students:** Note-taking services; Reader services; Tape recorders; Tutors. **Career services:** Alumni network; Alumni services; Career assessment; Career/job search classes; Internships; Regional alumni

FACILITIES

Housing: Apartments for married students; Apartments for single students; Coed dorms; Special housing for disabled student; Theme housing 80% of campus accessible to physically diasbled. **Computers:** 100% of classrooms, 50% of dorms, 100% of libraries, 100% of dining areas, 100% of student union, have wireless network access. Students can register for classes online. Administrative functions (other than registration) can be performed online.

CAMPUS LIFE

Environment: Rural **Activities:** Campus Ministries; Choral groups; Concert band; Dance; Drama/theater; International Student Organization; Jazz band; Literary magazine; Music ensembles; Pep band; Radio station; Student government; Student newspaper; Symphony orchestra; Television station 60 registered organizations, 8 honor societies, 5 religious organizations. **Athletics (Intercollegiate):** *Men:* basketball, cross-country, football, track/field (outdoor), track/field (indoor), wrestling. *Women:* basketball, cross-country, track/field (outdoor), track/field (indoor), volleyball. **On-Campus Highlights:** Unviersity Center—new student center, Hurst Hall —renovated science building, Kelley Hall—renovated social sciences, Mountaineer Field House — Highest Elevation NCAA basketball Court, Borick Business—new business building **Environmental Initiatives:** President's Climate Committment—which is a significant challenge for one of the coldest locations in the nation and the isolated nature of Gunnison

ADMISSIONS

Freshman Academic Profile: Average high school GPA 3.1. 8% in top 10% of high school class, 25% in top 25% of high school class, 49% in top 50% of high school class. **Test Scores:** SAT Math middle 50% range 500-590. SAT EBRW middle 50% range 500-590. ACT middle 50% range 20-25. Minimum paper TOEFL 550. **Basis for Candidate Selection:** *Very important factors considered include:* rigor of secondary school record, class rank, academic GPA, standardized test scores. *Important factors considered include:* application essay, recommendation(s). *Other factors considered include:* interview, extracurricular activities, talent/ability, character/personal qualities, first generation, alumni/ae relation, volunteer work, work experience. **Freshman Admission Requirements:** High school diploma is required and GED is accepted *Academic units required:* **Freshman Admission Statistics:** 1,955 applied, 86.0% admitted, 27% enrolled. **Transfer Admission Requirements:** college transcript(s), Minimum college GPA of 2.0 required. Lowest grade transferable C. **General Admission Information:** Application fee $30. Priority deadline 6/1. Nonfall registration accepted.

COSTS AND FINANCIAL AID
Required Forms and Deadlines: FAFSA. **Notification of Awards:** Applicants will be notified of awards on a rolling basis beginning 3/15. **Types of Aid:** *Need-based scholarships/grants:* College/university scholarship or grant aid from institutional funds; Federal Pell; Private scholarships; SEOG; State scholarships/grants. *Loans:* Direct PLUS loans; Direct Subsidized Stafford Loans; Direct Unsubsidized Stafford Loans. *Student Employment:* Federal Work-Study Program available. Institutional employment available. **Financial Aid Statistics:** 92% needy freshmen, 90% needy undergrads receive need-based scholarship or grant aid. 90% freshmen, 47% undergrads receive non-need-based scholarship or grant aid. 72% freshmen, 75% undergrads receive need-based self-help aid. 5% freshmen, 6% undergrads receive athletic scholarships. 85% freshmen, 75% undergrads receive any aid. 66% undergrads borrow to pay for school. Average cumulative indebtedness $25,589. **Criteria for awarding aid:** *Non-need-based:* Academics, Art, Athletics, Leadership, Music/drama.

See page 1090.

WESTERN UNIVERSITY

1151 Richmond St., London, ON N6A 3K7
Phone: 519-661-2100 • **Financial Aid Phone:** 519-661-2100
E-mail: reg-admissions@uwo.ca
Fax: 519-661-3710 • **Website:** www.westernu.ca • **ACT Code:** 4837

This public school was founded in 1878. It has a 1200 acre campus.

RATINGS
Admissions Selectivity Rating: 70   **Fire Safety Rating:** 80   **Green Rating:** 87

STUDENTS AND FACULTY
Student Body: international (76 countries represented).
Retention and Graduation: 93% freshmen return for sophomore year.
Faculty: 1,391 full-time faculty, 34% are women.

ACADEMICS
Degrees: Bachelor's; Certificate; Diploma; Doctoral; Doctoral/Research; Master's; Post-Bachelor's certificate **Classes:** Most classes have 10-19 students. Most lab/discussion sessions have 10-19 students. **Most popular majors:** Biology/Biological Sciences, General; Health Services/Allied Health/Health Sciences, General. **Special Study Options:** Accelerated program; Cooperative education program; Cross-registration; Distance learning; Double major; Dual enrollment; English as a Second Language (ESL); Exchange student program (domestic); Honors program; Independent study; Internships; Liberal arts/career combination; Student-designed major; Study abroad; Teacher certification program. Honors programs: Scholar's Electives—http://success. uwo.ca/index.cfm/scholars/scholars-electives/ Combined degree programs: BA/JD. **Disability Services offered to physically disabled students:** Note-taking services; Reader services; Tape recorders. **Career services:** Alumni services; Career assessment; Career/job search classes; Internships

FACILITIES
Housing: Apartments for married students; Apartments for single students; Coed dorms; Men's dorms; Special housing for disabled student; Special housing for international students; Theme housing; Wellness housing; Women's dorms 93.5% of campus accessible to physically disabled. **Special Academic Facilities/Equipment:** McIntosh Gallery http://mcintoshgallery. ca/ Hume Cronyn Memorial Observatory http://cronyn.uwo.ca Western Student Recreation Centre http://www.campusrec.uwo.ca/ University Hospital—on-campus teaching hospital The Wind, Engineering and Environment Institute—World's first hexagonal wind tunnel http://www.eng.uwo.ca/windeee/ Map and Data Centre https://www.lib.uwo.ca/madgic The Sherwood Fox Arboretum http://www.uwo.ca/biology/research/biology_facilities/arboretum.html LEED Gold Certified Claudette Mackay-Lassonde Pavilion http://www.eng.uwo.ca/cmlp/ Propel—Entrepreneurship centre and student business incubator http://propel.uwo.ca/ Wellness Education Centre—central hub for students to ask questions and learn about the many health and wellness resources available on and off campus (includes Nutritionist and Sexual Violence Prevention Education)—http://se.uwo.ca/student_experience/wellness_initiatives/wellness_education_centre.html **Computers:** 100% of libraries, 100% of student union, have wireless network access. Students can register for classes online. Administrative functions (other than registration) can be performed online.

CAMPUS LIFE
Environment: Metropolis **Activities:** Campus Ministries; Choral groups; Concert band; Dance; Drama/theater; International Student Organization; Jazz band; Literary magazine; Marching band; Model UN; Music ensembles; Musical theater; Opera; Radio station; Student government; Student newspaper; Student-run film society; Symphony orchestra; Television station 189 registered organizations, 14 fraternities, 5 sororities. **Athletics (Intercollegiate):** *Men:* badminton, baseball, basketball, crew/rowing, cross-country, curling, fencing, football, golf, ice hockey, rugby, soccer, squash, swimming, tennis, track/field (outdoor), track/field (indoor), volleyball, water polo, wrestling. *Women:* badminton, basketball, crew/rowing, cross-country, curling, fencing, field hockey, golf, ice hockey, lacrosse, rugby, soccer, squash, swimming, tennis, track/field (outdoor), track/field (indoor), volleyball, wrestling. **On-Campus Highlights:** University Community Centre, Western Student Recreation Centre, TD Stadium, Paul Davenport Theatre, Western Student Services Building **Environmental Initiatives:** Hiring an employee dedicated to sustainability initiatives on campus.

ADMISSIONS
Freshman Academic Profile: Average high school GPA 89.3. **Test Scores:** Minimum internet-based TOEFL 83. Minimum paper TOEFL 550. **Basis for Candidate Selection:** *Very important factors considered include:* rigor of secondary school record, academic GPA, standardized test scores. *Other factors considered include:* recommendation(s), extracurricular activities, talent/ability, first generation, volunteer work, work experience. **Freshman Admission Requirements:** High school diploma is required and GED is not accepted **Freshman Admission Statistics:** 33,924 applied, 57.6% admitted, 27% enrolled. **Transfer Admission Requirements:** High school transcript, college transcript(s), Lowest grade transferable C. **General Admission Information:** Application fee $155. Priority deadline 3/1. Regular application deadline 6/1. Nonfall registration accepted. Admission may be deferred for a maximum of 1 year.

COSTS AND FINANCIAL AID
Annual in-state tuition $1,373. Required fees $1,373. Average book expense $1,500. **Required Forms and Deadlines:** FAFSA; Institution's own financial aid form; State aid form. **Types of Aid:** *Need-based scholarships/grants:* College/university scholarship or grant aid from institutional funds; Private scholarships; State scholarships/grants. *Loans: Student Employment:* Institutional employment available. **Criteria for awarding aid:** *Need-based:* Academics, Alumni affiliation, Art, Athletics, Leadership, Minority status, Music/drama *Non-need-based:* Academics, Alumni affiliation, Art, Athletics, Leadership, Minority status, Music/drama, State/district residency.

WESTERN WASHINGTON UNIVERSITY

516 High St., Bellingham, WA 98225-9009
Phone: 360-650-3440 • **Financial Aid Phone:** 360.650.2422
E-mail: admit@wwu.edu • **CEEB Code:** 4947
Fax: 360-650-7369 • **Website:** http://www.wwu.edu/ • **ACT Code:** 4490

This public school was founded in 1893. It has a 223 acre campus.

RATINGS
Admissions Selectivity Rating: 78   **Fire Safety Rating:** 86   **Green Rating:** 92

STUDENTS AND FACULTY
Enrollment: 14,876. **Student Body:** 56% female, 44% male, 11% out-of-state, 1% international (41 countries represented). Asian 6%, African American 2%, Caucasian 72%, Hispanic 9%, Native American <1%, Pacific Islander <1%, Two or more races 9%, Race unknown 1%.
Retention and Graduation: 81% freshmen return for sophomore year. 38% freshmen graduate within 4 years. 69% freshmen graduate within 6 years.
Faculty: Student/faculty ratio 18:1. 643 full-time faculty, 88% hold PhDs, 16% are members of minority groups, 45% are women. 2% of classes are taught by teaching assistants.

ACADEMICS
Degrees: Bachelor's; Certificate; Master's; Post-Master's certificate **Classes:** Most classes have fewer than 10 students. **Most popular majors:** English Language And Literature, General; Social Sciences, Other; Business Administration, Management And Operations, Other. **Special Study Options:** Accelerated program; Cooperative education program; Cross-registration; Distance learning; Double major; Dual enrollment; English as a Second Language (ESL); Exchange student program (domestic); External degree program; Honors program; Independent study; Internships; Liberal arts/career

combination; Student-designed major; Study abroad; Teacher certification program. Honors programs: Honors Program features small classes and interaction between students and faculty. It is an exciting opportunity for accomplished students who would like a more intimate college experience within the setting of a larger institution. Honors students are welcome to pursue any academic major, and all students complete a self-designed capstone senior project. **Disability Services offered to physically disabled students:** Note-taking services; Reader services; Tape recorders; Tutors. **Career services:** Alumni network; Alumni services; Career assessment; Career/job search classes; Internships; Regional alumni

FACILITIES

Housing: Apartments for married students; Apartments for single students; Coed dorms; Special housing for disabled student; Special housing for international students; Theme housing; Wellness housing 100% of campus accessible to physically diasbled. **Special Academic Facilities/Equipment:** Outdoor art museum, planetarium, electronic music studio, air pollution lab, motor vehicle research lab, marine lab, wind tunnel, electron microscope, neutron generator lab. **Computers:** 100% of classrooms, 100% of dorms, 100% of libraries, 100% of dining areas, 100% of student union, 100% of common outdoor areas have wireless network access. Students can register for classes online. Administrative functions (other than registration) can be performed online.

CAMPUS LIFE

Environment: City **Activities:** Campus Ministries; Choral groups; Concert band; Dance; Drama/theater; International Student Organization; Jazz band; Literary magazine; Model UN; Music ensembles; Musical theater; Opera; Pep band; Radio station; Student government; Student newspaper; Student-run film society; Symphony orchestra 200 registered organizations, 4 honor societies, 18 religious organizations. **Athletics (Intercollegiate):** *Men:* basketball, cheerleading, crew/rowing, cross-country, golf, soccer, track/field (outdoor), track/field (indoor). *Women:* basketball, cheerleading, crew/rowing, cross-country, golf, soccer, softball, track/field (outdoor), track/field (indoor), volleyball. **On-Campus Highlights:** Viking Union Student Center, Red Square, Performing Arts Center, Sehome Arboretum, Student Recreation Center **Environmental Initiatives:** WWU Green Energy Fee The GEF pays for purchase of Renewable Energy Credits to offset 100% of WWU's CO2 emissions from electrical energy consumption, and pays for approximately $260,000 per year of on-campus sustainability projects. Due to our purchase of Renewable Energy Credits, WWU is ranked 17th by the EPA for largest higher ed. purchase of renewable energy in the US. This year's projects include a $167,000 solar array, high-speed hand driers, conversion of parking lot lights to high-efficiency LEDs, a paper towel composting system, and water bottle refilling stations.

ADMISSIONS

Freshman Academic Profile: Average high school GPA 3.4. 22% in top 10% of high school class, 53% in top 25% of high school class, 88% in top 50% of high school class. 91% from public high schools. **Test Scores:** SAT Math middle 50% range 530-630. SAT EBRW middle 50% range 550-650. ACT middle 50% range 22-28. Minimum internet-based TOEFL 80. Minimum paper TOEFL 550. **Basis for Candidate Selection:** *Very important factors considered include:* rigor of secondary school record. *Important factors considered include:* academic GPA, application essay, standardized test scores, level of applicant's interest. *Other factors considered include:* class rank, recommendation(s), extracurricular activities, talent/ability, character/personal qualities, first generation, alumni/ae relation, geographical residence, state residency, volunteer work, work experience. **Freshman Admission Requirements:** High school diploma is required and GED is accepted *Academic units required:* 4 English, 3 math, 2 science, 1 science labs, 2 foreign language, 3 social studies, 0.5 visual/performing arts. **Freshman Admission Statistics:** 11,244 applied, 84.8% admitted, 33% enrolled. **Transfer Admission Requirements:** college transcript(s), statement of good standing from prior institution(s). Minimum college GPA of 2.0 required. Lowest grade transferable D-. **General Admission Information:** Application fee $60. Regular application deadline 1/31. Nonfall registration accepted. Admission may be deferred for a maximum of 1 year.

COSTS AND FINANCIAL AID

Required Forms and Deadlines: Institution's own financial aid form. **Notification of Awards:** Applicants will be notified of awards on a rolling basis beginning 3/20. **Types of Aid:** *Need-based scholarships/grants:* College/university scholarship or grant aid from institutional funds; Federal Pell; Private scholarships; SEOG; State scholarships/grants. *Loans:* Direct PLUS loans; Direct Subsidized Stafford Loans; Direct Unsubsidized Stafford Loans. *Student Employment:* Federal Work-Study Program available. Institutional employment available. **Financial Aid Statistics:** 85% needy freshmen, 77% needy undergrads receive need-based scholarship or grant aid. 9% freshmen, 4% undergrads receive non-need-based scholarship or grant aid. 74% freshmen, 81% undergrads receive need-based self-help aid. 0% freshmen, 1% undergrads

receive athletic scholarships. 54% freshmen, 49% undergrads receive any aid. 55% undergrads borrow to pay for school. Average cumulative indebtedness $19,727. **Criteria for awarding aid:** *Need-based:* Academics, Leadership *Non-need-based:* Academics, Alumni affiliation, Art, Athletics, Job skills, Leadership, Minority status, Music/drama, State/district residency.

WESTFIELD STATE UNIVERSITY

577 Western Avenue, Westfield, MA 01086
Phone: 413-572-5218 • **Financial Aid Phone:** 413-572-5218
E-mail: admissions@westfield.ma.edu • **CEEB Code:** 3523
Fax: 413-572-0520 • **Website:** www.westfield.ma.edu • **ACT Code:** 1912

This public school was founded in 1839. It has a 227 acre campus.

RATINGS

Admissions Selectivity Rating: 74   **Fire Safety Rating:** 87   **Green Rating:** 74

STUDENTS AND FACULTY

Enrollment: 5,332. **Student Body:** 54% female, 46% male, 7% out-of-state, <1% international (18 countries represented). Asian 2%, African American 5%, Caucasian 75%, Hispanic 10%, Native American <1%, Pacific Islander <1%, Two or more races 5%, Race unknown 4%.
Retention and Graduation: 79% freshmen return for sophomore year. 53% freshmen graduate within 4 years. 65% freshmen graduate within 6 years. **Faculty:** Student/faculty ratio 16:1. 229 full-time faculty, 89% hold PhDs, 18% are members of minority groups, 50% are women. 0% of classes are taught by teaching assistants.

ACADEMICS

Degrees: Bachelor's; Master's; Post-Bachelor's certificate **Classes:** Most classes have 20-29 students. Most lab/discussion sessions have 10-19 students. **Most popular majors:** Liberal Arts And Sciences/Liberal Studies; Criminal Justice/Safety Studies; Business/Commerce, General. **Special Study Options:** Cross-registration; Distance learning; Double major; Dual enrollment; Exchange student program (domestic); Honors program; Independent study; Internships; Student-designed major; Study abroad; Teacher certification program. **Disability Services offered to physically disabled students:** Note-taking services; Reader services; Tutors. **Career services:** Alumni network; Alumni services; Career assessment; Career/job search classes; Internships

FACILITIES

Housing: Apartments for single students; Coed dorms; Special housing for disabled student; Theme housing; Wellness housing 75% of campus accessible to physically diasbled. **Special Academic Facilities/Equipment:** Art gallery, language lab, electron microscope, television studio, GIS laboratory

CAMPUS LIFE

Environment: Town **Activities:** Campus Ministries; Choral groups; Concert band; Dance; Drama/theater; International Student Organization; Jazz band; Literary magazine; Music ensembles; Musical theater; Pep band; Radio station; Student government; Student newspaper; Symphony orchestra; Television station; Yearbook. **Athletics (Intercollegiate):** *Men:* baseball, basketball, cross-country, football, golf, soccer, track/field (outdoor). *Women:* basketball, cheerleading, cross-country, field hockey, soccer, softball, swimming, volleyball. Ely Library, Woodward Athletic Center, Dining Commons, Dower Center for the Arts, Horace Mann Center **Environmental Initiatives:** RecycleMania: participated in the targeted paper competition in 2015

ADMISSIONS

Freshman Academic Profile: Average high school GPA 3.1. 5% in top 10% of high school class, 20% in top 25% of high school class, 55% in top 50% of high school class. **Test Scores:** SAT Math middle 50% range 480-570. SAT EBRW middle 50% range 490-580. ACT middle 50% range 20-25. Minimum internet-based TOEFL 79. Minimum paper TOEFL 550. **Basis for Candidate Selection:** *Very important factors considered include:* rigor of secondary school record, academic GPA, standardized test scores. *Other factors considered include:* application essay, recommendation(s), extracurricular activities, talent/ability, character/personal qualities, volunteer work, work experience, level of applicant's interest. **Freshman Admission Requirements:** High school diploma is required and GED is accepted *Academic units required:* 4 English, 4 math, 3 science, 2 science labs, 2 foreign language, 1 social studies, 1 history, 2 academic electives. **Freshman Admission Statistics:** 4,356 applied, 85.5% admitted, 27% enrolled. **Transfer Admission Requirements:** college transcript(s), Minimum college GPA of 2.0 required. Lowest grade transferable C-. **General Admission Information:** Application fee $50. Regular application deadline 3/1. Nonfall registration accepted. Admission may be deferred for a maximum of 1 semester.

COSTS AND FINANCIAL AID

Annual in-state tuition $10,689. Annual out-of-state tuition $7,050. Room and board $10,689. Required fees $8,745. Average book expense $1,050. **Required Forms and Deadlines:** FAFSA. **Notification of Awards:** Applicants will be notified of awards on a rolling basis beginning 2/1. **Types of Aid:** *Need-based scholarships/grants:* College/university scholarship or grant aid from institutional funds; Federal Pell; Private scholarships; SEOG; State scholarships/grants. *Loans:* Direct PLUS loans; Direct Subsidized Stafford Loans; Direct Unsubsidized Stafford Loans. *Student Employment:* Federal Work-Study Program available. Institutional employment available. **Financial Aid Statistics:** 70% needy freshmen, 69% needy undergrads receive need-based scholarship or grant aid. 33% freshmen, 25% undergrads receive non-need-based scholarship or grant aid. 87% freshmen, 97% undergrads receive need-based self-help aid. 0% freshmen, 0% undergrads receive athletic scholarships. 62% freshmen, 57% undergrads receive any aid. Average cumulative indebtedness $29,602. **Criteria for awarding aid:** *Non-need-based:* Academics.

WESTMINSTER COLLEGE (MO)

501 Westminster Avenue, Fulton, MO 65251
Phone: 573-592-5251 • **Financial Aid Phone:** (800) 475-3361
E-mail: admissions@westminster-mo.edu • **CEEB Code:** 6937
Fax: 573-592-5255 • **Website:** http://www.westminster-mo.edu/ • **ACT Code:** 2392

This private school, affiliated with the Presbyterian Church, was founded in 1851. It has a 86 acre campus.

RATINGS

Admissions Selectivity Rating: 73   **Fire Safety Rating:** 87   **Green Rating:** 61

STUDENTS AND FACULTY

Enrollment: 764. **Student Body:** 44% female, 56% male, 19% out-of-state, 6% international (69 countries represented). Asian 2%, African American 7%, Caucasian 70%, Hispanic 4%, Native American 2%, Pacific Islander 0%, Two or more races 0%, Race unknown 10%.
Retention and Graduation: 73% freshmen return for sophomore year. 30% grads go on to further study within 1 year. 10% grads pursue arts and sciences degrees. 4% grads pursue law degrees. 6% grads pursue business degrees. 3% grads pursue medical degrees. **Faculty:** Student/faculty ratio 11:1. 46 full-time faculty, 96% hold PhDs, 4% are members of minority groups, 41% are women. 0% of classes are taught by teaching assistants.

ACADEMICS

Degrees: Bachelor's **Most popular majors:** Biology/Biological Sciences, General; Political Science And Government, General; Business/Commerce, General. **Special Study Options:** Cooperative education program; Cross-registration; Distance learning; Double major; Dual enrollment; English as a Second Language (ESL); Exchange student program (domestic); Honors program; Independent study; Internships; Liberal arts/career combination; Student-designed major; Study abroad; Teacher certification program. Honors programs: The new Westminster College Honors Program is exciting for high achieving students, providing high impact, deep learning opportunities. Designed for a limited number of qualified students, the Honors Program includes a highly specialized, dynamic honors curriculum. The program includes an array of experiences that develop academic skills, leadership skills, and global perspectives. Combined degree programs: BA/MEng. **Disability Services offered to physically disabled students:** Note-taking services; Reader services; Tape recorders; Tutors. **Career services:** Alumni services; Career assessment; Career/job search classes; Internships; Regional alumni

FACILITIES

Housing: Apartments for single students; Coed dorms; Fraternity/sorority housing; Men's dorms; Special housing for disabled student; Theme housing; Women's dorms 70% of campus accessible to physically diasbled. **Special Academic Facilities/Equipment:** Winston Churchill Memorial Museum, Coulter Science Center, language lab, NMR spectrometer, laser equipment. **Computers:** 100% of classrooms, 100% of libraries, 100% of dining areas, 100% of student union, 40% of common outdoor areas have wireless network access. Students can register for classes online. Administrative functions (other than registration) can be performed online.

CAMPUS LIFE

Environment: Village **Activities:** Campus Ministries; Choral groups; Dance; Drama/theater; International Student Organization; Jazz band; Literary magazine; Model UN; Music ensembles; Pep band; Student government; Student newspaper 49 registered organizations, 15 honor societies, 2 religious organizations. 6 fraternities, 3 sororities. **Athletics (Intercollegiate):** *Men:* baseball, basketball, cheerleading, cross-country, football, golf, soccer, tennis, track/field (outdoor). *Women:* basketball, cheerleading, cross-country, golf, soccer, softball, tennis, track/field (outdoor), volleyball. **On-Campus Highlights:** Coulter Science Center, Johnson College Inn (student center), Hunter Activity Center, Library, Wetterau Athletic Facility

ADMISSIONS

Freshman Academic Profile: Average high school GPA 3.4. 13% in top 10% of high school class, 26% in top 25% of high school class, 70% in top 50% of high school class. 70% from public high schools. **Test Scores:** SAT Math middle 50% range 515-575. SAT EBRW middle 50% range 500-600. ACT middle 50% range 21-26. Minimum paper TOEFL 550. **Basis for Candidate Selection:** *Very important factors considered include:* rigor of secondary school record, standardized test scores, character/personal qualities. *Important factors considered include:* class rank, academic GPA, recommendation(s), extracurricular activities, volunteer work. *Other factors considered include:* application essay, interview, talent/ability, alumni/ae relation, work experience. **Freshman Admission Requirements:** High school diploma is required and GED is accepted *Academic units required:* 4 English, 3 math, 2 science, 2 science labs, *Academic units recommended:* 2 foreign language, 2 social studies, 2 academic electives. **Freshman Admission Statistics:** 1,035 applied, 90.1% admitted, 19% enrolled. **Transfer Admission Requirements:** college transcript(s), Lowest grade transferable C. **General Admission Information:** Nonfall registration accepted. Admission may be deferred for a maximum of 1 year.

COSTS AND FINANCIAL AID

Annual tuition $25,700. Room and board $10,140. Required fees $1,900. Average book expense $1,100. **Required Forms and Deadlines:** FAFSA. **Notification of Awards:** Applicants will be notified of awards on a rolling basis beginning 3/15. **Types of Aid:** *Need-based scholarships/grants:* College/university scholarship or grant aid from institutional funds; Federal Pell; Private scholarships; SEOG; State scholarships/grants. *Loans:* Direct PLUS loans; Direct Subsidized Stafford Loans; Direct Unsubsidized Stafford Loans. *Student Employment:* Federal Work-Study Program available. Institutional employment available. **Financial Aid Statistics:** 100% needy freshmen, 100% needy undergrads receive need-based scholarship or grant aid. 0% undergrads receive non-need-based scholarship or grant aid. 88% freshmen, 88% undergrads receive need-based self-help aid. 0% freshmen, 0% undergrads receive athletic scholarships. 100% freshmen, 98% undergrads receive any aid. 17% undergrads borrow to pay for school. Average cumulative indebtedness $29,573. **Criteria for awarding aid:** *Non-need-based:* Academics, Alumni affiliation, Leadership, Minority status, Music/drama, Religious affiliation.

WESTMINSTER COLLEGE (PA)

319 South Market Street, New Wilmington, PA 16172
Phone: 724-946-7100 • **Financial Aid Phone:** (724) 946-6171
E-mail: admis@westminster.edu • **CEEB Code:** 2975
Fax: 724-946-7171 • **Website:** www.westminster.edu • **ACT Code:** 2975

This private school, affiliated with the Presbyterian Church, was founded in 1852. It has a 350 acre campus.

RATINGS

Admissions Selectivity Rating: 73   **Fire Safety Rating:** 97   **Green Rating:** 60*

STUDENTS AND FACULTY

Enrollment: 1,168. **Student Body:** 54% female, 46% male, 1% international (1 countries represented). Asian 1%, African American 5%, Caucasian 71%, Hispanic 1%, Native American <1%, Pacific Islander 0%, Two or more races 2%, Race unknown 18%.
Retention and Graduation: 83% freshmen return for sophomore year. 21% grads go on to further study within 1 year. 3% grads pursue law degrees. 2% grads pursue business degrees. 3% grads pursue medical degrees. **Faculty:** Student/faculty ratio 11:1. 90 full-time faculty, 93% hold PhDs, 3% are members of minority groups, 48% are women. 0% of classes are taught by teaching assistants.

ACADEMICS

Degrees: Bachelor's; **Master's Classes:** Most classes have 10-19 students. Most lab/discussion sessions have 10-19 students. **Most popular majors:** Education, General; Biology/Biological Sciences, General; Business Administration And Management, General. **Special Study Options:** Distance learning; Double major; Dual enrollment; Exchange student program (domestic); Honors program; Independent study; Internships; Liberal arts/career combination; Student-designed major; Study abroad; Teacher certification program. Honors programs; The College broadly supports the All-College Honors Program, which is a four-year curriculum. Students enter the program in their first-year, and students from all majors are eligible to participate. Combined degree programs: BA/MA. **Disability Services offered to physically disabled students:** Note-taking services; Reader services; Tape recorders; Tutors. **Career services:** Alumni network; Alumni services; Career assessment; Career/job search classes; Internships; Regional alumni

FACILITIES

Housing: Coed dorms; Fraternity/sorority housing; Men's dorms; Special housing for disabled student; Theme housing; Women's dorms 90% of campus accessible to physically disabled. **Special Academic Facilities/Equipment:** On-campus preschool, Moeller pipe organs, planetarium, observatory, electron microscopes, X-ray diffractor, spectrometer. **Computers:** Administrative functions (other than registration) can be performed online.

CAMPUS LIFE

Environment: Village **Activities:** Campus Ministries; Choral groups; Concert band; Dance; Drama/theater; Jazz band; Literary magazine; Marching band; Model UN; Music ensembles; Musical theater; Opera; Pep band; Radio station; Student government; Student newspaper; Symphony orchestra; Television station; Yearbook 60 registered organizations, 21 honor societies, 3 religious organizations. 5 fraternities, 5 sororities. **Athletics (Intercollegiate):** *Men:* baseball, basketball, cheerleading, cross-country, football, golf, soccer, swimming, tennis, track/field (outdoor), track/field (indoor). *Women:* basketball, cheerleading, cross-country, golf, soccer, softball, swimming, tennis, track/field (outdoor), track/field (indoor), volleyball. McKelvey Campus Center, The HUB (McGill Library), Memorial Field House, Brittain Lake, Orr Auditorium

ADMISSIONS

Freshman Academic Profile: Average high school GPA 3.5. 22% in top 10% of high school class, 42% in top 25% of high school class, 75% in top 50% of high school class. 90% from public high schools. **Test Scores:** SAT Math middle 50% range 460-570. SAT EBRW middle 50% range 460-570. ACT middle 50% range 20-26. Minimum internet-based TOEFL 79. Minimum paper TOEFL 550. **Basis for Candidate Selection:** *Very important factors considered include:* rigor of secondary school record, academic GPA. *Important factors considered include:* class rank, standardized test scores. *Other factors considered include:* application essay, recommendation(s), extracurricular activities, talent/ability, character/personal qualities, alumni/ae relation, volunteer work, level of applicant's interest. **Freshman Admission Requirements:** High school diploma is required and GED is accepted *Academic units required:* 4 English, 3 math, 2 science, 2 science labs, 2 foreign language, 2 social studies, 1 academic elective. **Freshman Admission Statistics:** 2,125 applied, 91.2% admitted, 19% enrolled. **Transfer Admission Requirements:** High school transcript, college transcript(s), essay or personal statement, interview, standardized test scores, Minimum college GPA of 2.5 required. Lowest grade transferable c. **General Admission Information:** Application fee $35. Regular application deadline 5/1. Nonfall registration accepted. Admission may be deferred for a maximum of 1 year.

COSTS AND FINANCIAL AID

Annual tuition $34,830. Room and board $11,020. Required fees $1,400. Average book expense $1,700. **Required Forms and Deadlines:** FAFSA; Institution's own financial aid form. **Notification of Awards:** Applicants will be notified of awards on a rolling basis beginning 12/15. **Types of Aid:** *Need-based scholarships/grants:* College/university scholarship or grant aid from institutional funds; Federal Pell; Private scholarships; SEOG; State scholarships/grants. *Loans:* Direct PLUS loans; Direct Subsidized Stafford Loans; Direct Unsubsidized Stafford Loans. *Student Employment:* Federal Work-Study Program available. **Financial Aid Statistics:** 100% needy freshmen, 99% needy undergrads receive need-based scholarship or grant aid. 99% freshmen, 97% undergrads receive non-need-based scholarship or grant aid. 79% freshmen, 81% undergrads receive need-based self-help aid. 0% freshmen, 0% undergrads receive athletic scholarships. **Criteria for awarding aid:** *Need-based:* Academics *Non-need-based:* Academics, Alumni affiliation, Leadership, Minority status, Music/drama, Religious affiliation, State/district residency.

WESTMINSTER COLLEGE OF SALT LAKE CITY

1840 South 1300 East, Salt Lake City, UT 54105
Phone: 801-832-2200 • **Financial Aid Phone:** 801-832-2502
E-mail: admission@westminstercollege.edu • **CEEB Code:** 4948
Fax: 801-832-3101 • **Website:** www.westminstercollege.edu • **ACT Code:** 4284

This private school was founded in 1875. It has a 27 acre campus.

RATINGS

Admissions Selectivity Rating: 77   **Fire Safety Rating:** 95   **Green Rating:** 92

STUDENTS AND FACULTY

Enrollment: 2,002. **Student Body:** 59% female, 41% male, 39% out-of-state, 5% international (43 countries represented). Asian 3%, African American 2%, Caucasian 71%, Hispanic 11%, Native American 1%, Pacific Islander <1%, Two or more races 5%, Race unknown 3%.
Retention and Graduation: 80% freshmen return for sophomore year. 10% grads go on to further study within 1 year. 5% grads pursue arts and sciences degrees. 0.38% grads pursue law degrees. 2% grads pursue business degrees. 1.3% grads pursue medical degrees. **Faculty:** Student/faculty ratio 9:1. 152 full-time faculty, 91% hold PhDs, 12% are members of minority groups, 47% are women. 0% of classes are taught by teaching assistants.

ACADEMICS

Degrees: Bachelor's; Master's; Post-Bachelor's certificate **Classes:** Most classes have 10-19 students. Most lab/discussion sessions have 20-29 students. **Most popular majors:** Social Sciences, General; Health Services/Allied Health/Health Sciences, General. **Special Study Options:** Accelerated program; Cooperative education program; Cross-registration; Distance learning; Double major; Dual enrollment; English as a Second Language (ESL); Honors program; Independent study; Internships; Liberal arts/career combination; Student-designed major; Study abroad; Teacher certification program; Weekend college. **Disability Services offered to physically disabled students:** Note-taking services; Reader services; Tape recorders; Tutors. **Career services:** Alumni network; Alumni services; Career assessment; Career/job search classes; Internships; Regional alumni

FACILITIES

Housing: Apartments for single students; Coed dorms; Special housing for disabled students 98% of campus accessible to physically disabled. **Special Academic Facilities/Equipment:** Emma Ecceles Jones Conservatory, Gore School of Business, Giovale Library, Meldrum Science Center, Climbing Wall, Converse Hall, Dolores Dore Eccles Health, Wellness, and Athletic Center **Computers:** 100% of classrooms, 100% of dorms, 100% of libraries, 100% of dining areas, 100% of student union, 25% of common outdoor areas have wireless network access. Students can register for classes online. Administrative functions (other than registration) can be performed online.

CAMPUS LIFE

Environment: Metropolis **Activities:** Campus Ministries; Choral groups; Dance; Drama/theater; International Student Organization; Jazz band; Literary magazine; Music ensembles; Musical theater; Opera; Student government; Student newspaper; Student-run film society; Symphony orchestra 55 registered organizations, 4 honor societies, 4 religious organizations. **Athletics (Intercollegiate):** *Men:* basketball, cross-country, golf, lacrosse, skiing (downhill/alpine), snowboarding, soccer, track/field (outdoor), track/field (indoor). *Women:* basketball, cross-country, golf, lacrosse, skiing (downhill/alpine), snowboarding, soccer, track/field (outdoor), track/field (indoor), volleyball. **On-Campus Highlights:** Shaw Student Center, Meldrum Science Center, Bassis Center for Student Learning, Dolores Dore Eccles Health, Wellness, and Athletic, Emma Eccles Jones Conservatory **Environmental Initiatives:** With guidance from the Environmental Center, students completed the STARS assessment in 2010, achieving a Silver rating. Westminster scored particularly well in co-curricular and curricular sustainability efforts.

ADMISSIONS

Freshman Academic Profile: Average high school GPA 3.6. 28% in top 10% of high school class, 53% in top 25% of high school class, 88% in top 50% of high school class. **Test Scores:** SAT Math middle 50% range 530-628. SAT EBRW middle 50% range 530-640. ACT middle 50% range 21-28. Minimum internet-based TOEFL 45. **Basis for Candidate Selection:** *Very important factors considered include:* rigor of secondary school record, academic GPA, application essay, standardized test scores, recommendation(s). *Important factors considered include:* class rank, interview, extracurricular activities, talent/ability, character/personal qualities. *Other factors considered include:* first generation, alumni/ae relation, volunteer work, work experience. **Freshman Admission Requirements:** High school diploma is required and GED is accepted *Academic units required:* 4 English, 2 math, 3 science, 2 foreign language, 2 social studies, 1 history, 2 academic electives, *Academic units recommended:* 4 English, 3 math, 3 science, 3 foreign language, 2 social studies, 1 history, 3 academic electives. **Freshman Admission Statistics:** 1,702 applied, 92.7% admitted, 23% enrolled. **Transfer Admission Requirements:** High school transcript, college transcript(s), essay or personal statement, Minimum college GPA of 2.5 required. Lowest grade transferable C-. **General Admission Information:** Application fee $50. Nonfall registration accepted. Admission may be deferred for a maximum of 2 years.

COSTS AND FINANCIAL AID
Annual tuition $33,040. Room and board $9,244. Required fees $520. **Required Forms and Deadlines:** FAFSA. **Notification of Awards:** Applicants will be notified of awards on a rolling basis beginning 2/1. **Types of Aid:** *Need-based scholarships/grants:* College/university scholarship or grant aid from institutional funds; Federal Pell; Private scholarships; SEOG; State scholarships/grants. *Loans:* Direct PLUS loans; Direct Subsidized Stafford Loans; Direct Unsubsidized Stafford Loans. *Student Employment:* Federal Work-Study Program available. Institutional employment available. **Financial Aid Statistics:** 100% needy freshmen, 99% needy undergrads receive need-based scholarship or grant aid. 15% freshmen, 13% undergrads receive non-need-based scholarship or grant aid. 86% freshmen, 86% undergrads receive need-based self-help aid. 3% freshmen, 4% undergrads receive athletic scholarships. 99% freshmen, 93% undergrads receive any aid. 59% undergrads borrow to pay for school. Average cumulative indebtedness $30,442. **Criteria for awarding aid:** *Need-based:* Academics, Alumni affiliation, Art, Leadership, Religious affiliation *Non-need-based:* Academics, Alumni affiliation, Art, Athletics, Leadership, Minority status, Music/drama.

WESTMONT COLLEGE

955 La Paz Road, Santa Barbara, CA 93108
Phone: 805-565-6200 • **Financial Aid Phone:** 888-963-4624
E-mail: admissions@westmont.edu • **CEEB Code:** 4950
Fax: 805-565-6234 • **Website:** www.westmont.edu • **ACT Code:** 478

This private school, affiliated with the Christian (Nondenominational) Church, was founded in 1937. It has a 133 acre campus.

RATINGS
Admissions Selectivity Rating: 82   **Fire Safety Rating:** 60*   **Green Rating:** 60*

STUDENTS AND FACULTY
Enrollment: 1,289. **Student Body:** 61% female, 39% male, 25% out-of-state, 1% international (8 countries represented). Asian 6%, African American 1%, Caucasian 67%, Hispanic 12%, Native American <1%, Pacific Islander 1%, Two or more races 8%, Race unknown 4%.
Retention and Graduation: 85% freshmen return for sophomore year.
Faculty: Student/faculty ratio 11:1. 96 full-time faculty, 90% hold PhDs, 13% are members of minority groups, 39% are women. 0% of classes are taught by teaching assistants.

ACADEMICS
Degrees: Bachelor's; Post-Bachelor's certificate **Classes:** Most classes have 20-29 students. Most lab/discussion sessions have 20-29 students. **Most popular majors:** English/Language Arts Teacher Education; Cell/Cellular And Molecular Biology. **Special Study Options:** Accelerated program; Cross-registration; Double major; Exchange student program (domestic); Honors program; Independent study; Internships; Liberal arts/career combination; Student-designed major; Study abroad; Teacher certification program. Honors programs: Some general education courses are designated as honors courses. **Disability Services offered to physically disabled students:** Note-taking services; Reader services; Tape recorders; Tutors. **Career services:** Career assessment; Career/job search classes; Internships

FACILITIES
Housing: Apartments for single students; Coed dorms 65% of campus accessible to physically diasbled. **Special Academic Facilities/Equipment:** Reynolds Art Gallery features the gallery, art studios and classrooms; Carroll Observatory houses a 24-inch reflector telescope; Mericos Whittier Science facility includes state of the art technical equipment such as ultracentrifuge, Fouriertransform NMR spectrometer, etc., as well as the pre-med center; Voskuyl Library holds over 150,000 bound volumes; the physics department is developing advanced experiments for the lab; Ellen Porter Hall of Fine Arts showcases ten to twenty live musical and theatrical performances each

year; Physiology Lab and Fithess Center for Kinesiology studies. **Computers:** Administrative functions (other than registration) can be performed online.

CAMPUS LIFE
Environment: City **Activities:** Campus Ministries; Choral groups; Concert band; Dance; Drama/theater; International Student Organization; Jazz band; Literary magazine; Model UN; Music ensembles; Musical theater; Student government; Student newspaper; Symphony orchestra; Yearbook 50 registered organizations, 7 honor societies, 40 religious organizations. **Athletics (Intercollegiate):** *Men:* baseball, basketball, cross-country, soccer, tennis, track/field (outdoor). *Women:* basketball, cross-country, soccer, tennis, track/field (outdoor), volleyball.

ADMISSIONS
Freshman Academic Profile: Average high school GPA 3.8. 29% in top 10% of high school class, 66% in top 25% of high school class, 94% in top 50% of high school class. 70% from public high schools. **Test Scores:** SAT Math middle 50% range 540-660. SAT EBRW middle 50% range 520-650. ACT middle 50% range 24-29. Minimum paper TOEFL 560. **Basis for Candidate Selection:** *Very important factors considered include:* academic GPA, standardized test scores, character/personal qualities. *Important factors considered include:* rigor of secondary school record, application essay, recommendation(s), interview, extracurricular activities, talent/ability, religious affiliation/commitment, level of applicant's interest. *Other factors considered include:* class rank, first generation, alumni/ae relation, geographical residence, racial/ethnic status, volunteer work, work experience. **Freshman Admission Requirements:** High school diploma is required and GED is accepted *Academic units required:* 4 English, 3 math, 3 science, 2 science labs, 2 foreign language, 1 social studies, 1 history, 2 academic electives, *Academic units recommended:* 3 foreign language, 4 academic electives. **Freshman Admission Statistics:** 2,145 applied, 70.2% admitted, 20% enrolled. **Transfer Admission Requirements:** High school transcript, college transcript(s), essay or personal statement, statement of good standing from prior institution(s). Lowest grade transferable C-. **General Admission Information:** Application fee $40. Priority deadline 2/15. Regular application deadline 8/15. Nonfall registration accepted.

COSTS AND FINANCIAL AID
Annual tuition $38,960. Room and board $12,580. Required fees $1,030. Average book expense $1,600. **Required Forms and Deadlines:** FAFSA; Institution's own financial aid form. **Notification of Awards:** Applicants will be notified of awards on a rolling basis beginning 4/1. **Types of Aid:** *Need-based scholarships/grants:* College/university scholarship or grant aid from institutional funds; Federal Pell; Private scholarships; SEOG; State scholarships/grants. *Loans:* Direct PLUS loans; Direct Subsidized Stafford Loans; Direct Unsubsidized Stafford Loans. *Student Employment:* Federal Work-Study Program available. Institutional employment available. **Financial Aid Statistics:** 99% needy freshmen, 99% needy undergrads receive need-based scholarship or grant aid. 11% freshmen, 12% undergrads receive non-need-based scholarship or grant aid. 98% freshmen, 88% undergrads receive need-based self-help aid. 6% undergrads receive athletic scholarships. 85% undergrads receive any aid. **Criteria for awarding aid:** *Non-need-based:* Academics, Art, Athletics, Music/drama.

WHEATON COLLEGE (IL)

501 College Avenue, Wheaton, IL 60187
Phone: 630-752-5011 • **Financial Aid Phone:** 630-752-5021
E-mail: admissions@wheaton.edu • **CEEB Code:** 1905
Fax: 630-752-5285 • **Website:** www.wheaton.edu • **ACT Code:** 1160

This private school, affiliated with the Christian non-denominational Church, was founded in 1860. It has a 80 acre campus.

RATINGS
Admissions Selectivity Rating: 88   **Fire Safety Rating:** 94   **Green Rating:** 70

STUDENTS AND FACULTY
Enrollment: 2,356. **Student Body:** 55% female, 45% male, 72% out-of-state, 3% international (40 countries represented). Asian 9%, African American 3%, Caucasian 75%, Hispanic 6%, Native American <1%, Pacific Islander 0%, Two or more races 4%, Race unknown <1%.
Retention and Graduation: 93% freshmen return for sophomore year. 80%

freshmen graduate within 4 years. 89% freshmen graduate within 6 years. 21% grads go on to further study within 1 year. 12% grads pursue arts and sciences degrees. 1.1% grads pursue law degrees. 0% grads pursue business degrees. 6.3% grads pursue medical degrees. **Faculty:** Student/faculty ratio 11:1. 222 full-time faculty, 95% hold PhDs, 16% are members of minority groups, 35% are women. 0% of classes are taught by teaching assistants.

ACADEMICS

Degrees: Bachelor's; Doctoral/Professional; Doctoral/Research; Master's; Post-Bachelor's certificate **Classes:** Most classes have 20-29 students. Most lab/discussion sessions have fewer than 10 students. **Most popular majors:** English Language And Literature, General; Biology/Biological Sciences, General; Business/Managerial Economics. **Special Study Options:** Cross-registration; Double major; Exchange student program (domestic); Independent study; Internships; Liberal arts/career combination; Student-designed major; Study abroad; Teacher certification program. Honors programs: Some departments offer qualified students to submit an honors project. **Disability Services offered to physically disabled students:** Note-taking services; Reader services; Tape recorders; Tutors. **Career services:** Alumni network; Alumni services; Career assessment; Career/job search classes; Internships; Regional alumni

FACILITIES

Housing: Apartments for married students; Apartments for single students; Coed dorms; Cooperative housing; Men's dorms; Women's dorms 97% of campus accessible to physically disabled. **Special Academic Facilities/Equipment:** The Billy Graham Center Museum, The Black Hills Science Station, the Center for Applied Christian Ethics (CACE) HoneyRock is the year-round Northwoods Camp and Campus of Wheaton College. The Wheaton Center for Faith, Politics, and Economics The Marion E. Wade Center The Meyer Science Center contains a unique, interactive atrium museum featuring the Perry Mastodon, a geology exhibit, a natural history exhibit, a Foucault pendulum, and additional exhibits. **Computers:** 10% of classrooms, 100% of dorms, 100% of libraries, 100% of dining areas, 100% of student union, 75% of common outdoor areas have wireless network access. Students can register for classes online. Administrative functions (other than registration) can be performed online.

CAMPUS LIFE

Environment: Town **Activities:** Campus Ministries; Choral groups; Concert band; Dance; Drama/theater; International Student Organization; Jazz band; Literary magazine; Model UN; Music ensembles; Musical theater; Opera; Pep band; Student government; Student newspaper; Student-run film society; Symphony orchestra 85 registered organizations, 13 honor societies, 12 religious organizations. **Athletics (Intercollegiate):** *Men:* baseball, basketball, cross-country, football, golf, soccer, swimming, tennis, track/field (outdoor), track/field (indoor), wrestling. *Women:* basketball, cross-country, golf, soccer, softball, swimming, tennis, track/field (outdoor), track/field (indoor), volleyball, water polo. **On-Campus Highlights:** "The Stupe" grill in the Beamer Student Center, C.S. Lewis reading room in the Wade Center, Rock climbing wall in the Student Recreation Complex, Perry Mastodon exhibit in the Meyer Science Center, Billy Graham Center museum **Environmental Initiatives:** Environmental Science Major

ADMISSIONS

Freshman Academic Profile: Average high school GPA 3.7. 47% in top 10% of high school class, 73% in top 25% of high school class, 93% in top 50% of high school class. 48% from public high schools. **Test Scores:** SAT Math middle 50% range 600-690. SAT EBRW middle 50% range 630-720. ACT middle 50% range 27-32. Minimum internet-based TOEFL 95. Minimum paper TOEFL 587. **Basis for Candidate Selection:** *Very important factors considered include:* rigor of secondary school record, academic GPA, application essay, standardized test scores, recommendation(s), character/personal qualities, religious affiliation/commitment. *Important factors considered include:* interview, extracurricular activities, talent/ability, volunteer work. *Other factors considered include:* class rank, first generation, alumni/ae relation, geographical residence, state residency, racial/ethnic status, work experience, level of applicant's interest. **Freshman Admission Requirements:** High school diploma is required and GED is accepted *Academic units required:* 4 English, 3 math, 3 science, 2 foreign language, 3 social studies, *Academic units recommended:* 4 English, 4 math, 4 science, 3 foreign language, 4 social studies. **Freshman Admission Statistics:** 1,693 applied, 85.0% admitted, 40% enrolled. **Transfer Admission Requirements:** High school transcript, college transcript(s), essay or personal statement, Minimum college GPA of 3.0 required. Lowest grade transferable C-. **General Admission Information:** Application fee $50. Regular application deadline 1/10. Nonfall registration accepted. Admission may be deferred for a maximum of 1 year.

COSTS AND FINANCIAL AID

Annual tuition $36,420. Room and board $10,180. Average book expense $800. **Required Forms and Deadlines:** FAFSA. **Notification of Awards:**

Applicants will be notified of awards on a rolling basis beginning 12/31. **Types of Aid:** *Need-based scholarships/grants:* College/university scholarship or grant aid from institutional funds; Federal Pell; Private scholarships; SEOG; State scholarships/grants. *Loans:* Direct PLUS loans; Direct Subsidized Stafford Loans; Direct Unsubsidized Stafford Loans. *Student Employment:* Federal Work-Study Program available. Institutional employment available. **Financial Aid Statistics:** 100% needy freshmen, 99% needy undergrads receive need-based scholarship or grant aid. 29% freshmen, 28% undergrads receive non-need-based scholarship or grant aid. 77% freshmen, 77% undergrads receive need-based self-help aid. 0% freshmen, 0% undergrads receive athletic scholarships. 86% freshmen, 79% undergrads receive any aid. 54% undergrads borrow to pay for school. Average cumulative indebtedness $27,354. **Criteria for awarding aid:** *Non-need-based:* Academics, Alumni affiliation, Art, Minority status, Music/drama.

WHEATON COLLEGE (MA)

26 East Main Street, Norton, MA 02766
Phone: 508-286-8251 • **Financial Aid Phone:** 508-286-8232
E-mail: admission@wheatoncollege.edu • **CEEB Code:** 3963
Fax: 508-286-8271 • **Website:** www.wheatoncollege.edu • **ACT Code:** 1932

This private school was founded in 1834. It has a 478 acre campus.

RATINGS

| Admissions Selectivity Rating: 88 | Fire Safety Rating: 99 | Green Rating: 74 |

STUDENTS AND FACULTY

Enrollment: 1,677. **Student Body:** 61% female, 39% male, 63% out-of-state, 10% international (71 countries represented). Asian 5%, African American 6%, Caucasian 65%, Hispanic 8%, Native American <1%, Pacific Islander <1%, Two or more races 3%, Race unknown 1%.
Retention and Graduation: 88% freshmen return for sophomore year. 74% freshmen graduate within 4 years. 78% freshmen graduate within 6 years. **Faculty:** Student/faculty ratio 10:1. 137 full-time faculty, 93% hold PhDs, 20% are members of minority groups, 55% are women. 0% of classes are taught by teaching assistants.

ACADEMICS

Degrees: Bachelor's **Classes:** Most classes have 20-29 students. Most lab/discussion sessions have 20-29 students. **Most popular majors:** Psychology, General; Economics, General; Business Administration And Management, General. **Special Study Options:** Accelerated program; Cross-registration; Double major; Dual enrollment; Exchange student program (domestic); Honors program; Independent study; Internships; Student-designed major; Study abroad; Teacher certification program. Combined degree programs: BA/MA. **Disability Services offered to physically disabled students:** Note-taking services; Reader services; Tape recorders; Tutors. **Career services:** Alumni network; Alumni services; Career assessment; Career/job search classes; Internships; Regional alumni

FACILITIES

Housing: Apartments for single students; Coed dorms; Men's dorms; Special housing for disabled student; Special housing for international students; Theme housing; Wellness housing; Women's dorms **Special Academic Facilities/Equipment:** Art gallery, radio station, planetarium, observatory, language lab, photography darkrooms, dance studio, media center, greenhouse, GIS lab, Imaging Center for Undergraduate Collaboration (ICUC), Graphics Design lab, Wheaton Autonomous Learning Lab (WHALE), on-campus nursery school, early childhood lab. **Computers:** 100% of classrooms, 100% of dorms, 100% of libraries, 100% of dining areas, 100% of student union, have wireless network access. Students can register for classes online. Administrative functions (other than registration) can be performed online.

CAMPUS LIFE

Environment: Village **Activities:** Campus Ministries; Choral groups; Dance; Drama/theater; International Student Organization; Jazz band; Literary magazine; Model UN; Music ensembles; Musical theater; Radio station; Student government; Student newspaper; Student-run film society; Symphony orchestra; Yearbook 60 registered organizations, 8 honor societies, 4 religious organizations. **Athletics (Intercollegiate):** *Men:* baseball, basketball, cross-country, diving, lacrosse, soccer, swimming, tennis, track/field (outdoor), track/field (indoor). *Women:* basketball, cross-country, diving, field hockey, lacrosse, soccer, softball, swimming, synchronized swimming, tennis, track/field (outdoor), track/field (indoor), volleyball. **On-Campus Highlights:** Mars Center for Science and Technology, Mars Arts and Humanities Arts facility, Haas Athletic Center, Mary Lyon Hall (Wheaton's oldest building), Balfour-Hood Campus Center **Environmental Initiatives:** 1.3 MW solar field

ADMISSIONS

Freshman Academic Profile: Average high school GPA 3.4. 26% in top 10% of high school class, 55% in top 25% of high school class, 85% in top 50% of high school class. 78% from public high schools. **Test Scores:** SAT Math middle 50% range 560-670. SAT EBRW middle 50% range 590-680. ACT middle 50% range 26-30. Minimum internet-based TOEFL 90. Minimum paper TOEFL 580. **Basis for Candidate Selection:** *Very important factors considered include:* rigor of secondary school record, academic GPA, application essay, recommendation(s), character/personal qualities. *Important factors considered include:* extracurricular activities, talent/ability, alumni/ae relation, level of applicant's interest. *Other factors considered include:* class rank, standardized test scores, interview, first generation, geographical residence, state residency, racial/ethnic status, volunteer work, work experience. **Freshman Admission Requirements:** High school diploma is required and GED is accepted *Academic units required:* 4 English, *Academic units recommended:* 4 math, 4 science. 4 foreign language, 4 social studies, 4 history. **Freshman Admission Statistics:** 6,089 applied, 47.9% admitted, 17% enrolled. **Transfer Admission Requirements:** High school transcript, college transcript(s), essay or personal statement, statement of good standing from prior institution(s). Minimum college GPA of 3.0 required. Lowest grade transferable C. **General Admission Information:** Application fee $60. Regular application deadline 1/1. Nonfall registration accepted. Admission may be deferred for a maximum of 1 year.

COSTS AND FINANCIAL AID

Annual tuition $50,520. Room and board $12,968. Required fees $330. Average book expense $940. **Required Forms and Deadlines:** Business/Farm Supplement; CSS/Financial Aid PROFILE; FAFSA; Noncustodial PROFILE. **Notification of Awards:** Applicants will be notified of awards on or about 3/15. **Types of Aid:** *Need-based scholarships/grants:* College/university scholarship or grant aid from institutional funds; Federal Pell; Private scholarships; SEOG; State scholarships/grants. *Loans:* Direct PLUS loans; Direct Subsidized Stafford Loans; Direct Unsubsidized Stafford Loans. *Student Employment:* Federal Work-Study Program available. Institutional employment available. **Financial Aid Statistics:** 100% needy freshmen, 99% needy undergrads receive need-based scholarship or grant aid. 20% freshmen, 10% undergrads receive non-need-based scholarship or grant aid. 94% freshmen, 97% undergrads receive need-based self-help aid. 0% freshmen, 0% undergrads receive athletic scholarships. 92% freshmen, 85% undergrads receive any aid. Average cumulative indebtedness $33,040. **Criteria for awarding aid:** *Need-based:* Academics *Non-need-based:* Academics.

WHEELING JESUIT UNIVERSITY

316 Washington Avenue, Wheeling, WV 26003
Phone: 304-243-2359 • **Financial Aid Phone:** (304) 243–2304
E-mail: admiss@wju.edu • **CEEB Code:** 5906
Fax: 304-243-2397 • **Website:** www.wju.edu • **ACT Code:** 4546

This private school, affiliated with the Roman Catholic-Jesuit Church, was founded in 1954. It has a 65 acre campus.

RATINGS

Admissions Selectivity Rating: 72   **Fire Safety Rating:** 98   **Green Rating:** 76

STUDENTS AND FACULTY

Enrollment: 929. **Student Body:** 51% female, 49% male, 68% out-of-state, 5% international (27 countries represented). Asian 1%, African American 8%, Caucasian 75%, Hispanic 3%, Native American 1%, Pacific Islander 1%, Two or more races 2%, Race unknown 5%.
Retention and Graduation: 71% freshmen return for sophomore year. 22% grads go on to further study within 1 year. **Faculty:** Student/faculty ratio 10:1. 77 full-time faculty, 81% hold PhDs, 3% are members of minority groups, 51% are women. 0% of classes are taught by teaching assistants.

ACADEMICS

Degrees: Bachelor's; Doctoral/Professional; Master's; Post-Bachelor's certificate; Post-Master's certificate **Classes:** Most classes have 20-29 students. Most lab/discussion sessions have 10-19 students. **Most popular majors:** Psychology, General; Registered Nursing/Registered Nurse; Business

Administration And Management, General. **Special Study Options:** Distance learning; Double major; Dual enrollment; English as a Second Language (ESL); Exchange student program (domestic); Honors program; Independent study; Internships; Liberal arts/career combination; Student-designed major; Study abroad; Teacher certification program. Honors programs: The Laut Honors program, which is designed to introduce students to aspects of the arts and sciences that are not available in the regular curriculum in order to inspire and awaken curiosity through a variety of enriching experiences offered. **Disability Services offered to physically disabled students:** Note-taking services; Reader services; Tutors. **Career services:** Alumni network; Alumni services; Career/job search classes; Internships; Regional alumni

FACILITIES

Housing: Apartments for married students; Apartments for single students; Coed dorms; Special housing for disabled student; Special housing for international students; Theme housing; Women's dorms 85% of campus accessible to physically disabled. **Special Academic Facilities/Equipment:** Mount de Chantal Conservatory of Music, Challenger Learning Center, Lantz Farm **Computers:** 10% of classrooms, 100% of libraries, 100% of dining areas, 100% of student union, 10% of common outdoor areas have wireless network access. Students can register for classes online. Administrative functions (other than registration) can be performed online.

CAMPUS LIFE

Environment: City **Activities:** Campus Ministries; Choral groups; Drama/theater; International Student Organization; Literary magazine; Musical theater; Student government; Student newspaper 30 registered organizations, 9 honor societies, 6 religious organizations. **Athletics (Intercollegiate):** *Men:* baseball, basketball, cross-country, golf, lacrosse, soccer, swimming, track/field (outdoor), track/field (indoor). *Women:* basketball, cross-country, golf, soccer, softball, swimming, track/field (outdoor), track/field (indoor), volleyball. **On-Campus Highlights:** McDonough Center Athletic Complex, Cardinal Commons Coffee shop, Rathskeller, Mount deChantal Recital Hall, Chapel of Mary & Joseph **Environmental Initiatives:** Faculty/student research related to environmental topics.

ADMISSIONS

Freshman Academic Profile: Average high school GPA 3.3. 17% in top 10% of high school class, 36% in top 25% of high school class, 69% in top 50% of high school class. 62% from public high schools. **Test Scores:** SAT Math middle 50% range 450-540. SAT EBRW middle 50% range 440-520. ACT middle 50% range 18-23. Minimum internet-based TOEFL 80. Minimum paper TOEFL 550. **Basis for Candidate Selection:** *Very important factors considered include:* academic GPA, standardized test scores. *Important factors considered include:* rigor of secondary school record. *Other factors considered include:* class rank, application essay, recommendation(s), interview, extracurricular activities, talent/ability, character/personal qualities, first generation, alumni/ae relation, volunteer work, work experience, level of applicant's interest. **Freshman Admission Requirements:** High school diploma is required and GED is accepted *Academic units required:* 4 English, 3 math, 2 science, 2 science labs, 2 social studies, 1 history, 4 academic electives, *Academic units recommended:* 4 English, 3 math, 3 science, 3 science labs, 2 foreign language, 2 social studies, 1 history, 4 academic electives. **Freshman Admission Statistics:** 1,020 applied, 93.2% admitted, 23% enrolled. **Transfer Admission Requirements:** college transcript(s), Minimum college GPA of 2.3 required. Lowest grade transferable C. **General Admission Information:** Application fee $25. Nonfall registration accepted. Admission may be deferred for a maximum of one semester.

COSTS AND FINANCIAL AID

Annual tuition $27,000. Room and board $7,796. Required fees $1,110. Average book expense $1,300. **Required Forms and Deadlines:** FAFSA. **Notification of Awards:** Applicants will be notified of awards on a rolling basis beginning 11/1. **Types of Aid:** *Need-based scholarships/grants:* College/university scholarship or grant aid from institutional funds; Federal Pell; Private scholarships; SEOG; State scholarships/grants. *Loans:* Direct PLUS loans; Direct Subsidized Stafford Loans; Direct Unsubsidized Stafford Loans. *Student Employment:* Federal Work-Study Program available. Institutional employment available. **Financial Aid Statistics:** 88% needy freshmen, 69% needy undergrads receive need-based scholarship or grant aid. 100% freshmen, 96% undergrads receive non-need-based scholarship or grant aid. 78% freshmen, 74% undergrads receive need-based self-help aid. 8% freshmen, 10% undergrads receive athletic scholarships. 100% freshmen, 99% undergrads receive any aid. 71% undergrads borrow to pay for school. Average cumulative indebtedness $37,762. **Criteria for awarding aid:** *Non-need-based:* Academics, Alumni affiliation, Athletics, Music/drama, Religious affiliation.

WHEELOCK COLLEGE

200 Riverway, Boston, MA 02215
Phone: 617-879-2206 • **Financial Aid Phone:** 617-879-2443
E-mail: undergrad@wheelock.edu • **CEEB Code:** 3964
Fax: 617-879-2449 • **Website:** www.wheelock.edu • **ACT Code:** 1934

This private school was founded in 1888. It has a 6 acre campus.

RATINGS
Admissions Selectivity Rating: 71   **Fire Safety Rating:** 92   **Green Rating:** 61

STUDENTS AND FACULTY
Enrollment: 809. **Student Body:** 84% female, 16% male, 39% out-of-state, 2% international (15 countries represented). Asian 4%, African American 13%, Caucasian 60%, Hispanic 11%, Pacific Islander <1%, Two or more races 3%, Race unknown 7%.
Retention and Graduation: 68% freshmen return for sophomore year. 25% grads go on to further study within 1 year. 0% grads pursue arts and sciences degrees. 0% grads pursue law degrees. 0% grads pursue business degrees. 0% grads pursue medical degrees. **Faculty:** Student/faculty ratio 10:1. 75 full-time faculty, 85% hold PhDs, 25% are members of minority groups, 73% are women. 0% of classes are taught by teaching assistants.

ACADEMICS
Degrees: Bachelor's; Master's; Post-Bachelor's certificate **Classes:** Most classes have 20-29 students. Most lab/discussion sessions have 20-29 students. **Most popular majors:** Developmental And Child Psychology; Counseling Psychology; Social Work. **Special Study Options:** Cross-registration; Distance learning; Double major; Honors program; Independent study; Internships; Liberal arts/career combination; Study abroad; Teacher certification program. Combined degree programs: BA/MA. **Disability Services offered to physically disabled students:** Note-taking services; Reader services; Tape recorders; Tutors. **Career services:** Alumni network; Career assessment; Career/job search classes; Internships

FACILITIES
Housing: Coed dorms; Women's dorms 85% of campus accessible to physically diasbled.

CAMPUS LIFE
Environment: Metropolis **Activities:** Dance; Drama/theater; Literary magazine; Musical theater; Student government 20 registered organizations, 1 honor society, 1 religious organization. **Athletics (Intercollegiate):** *Men:* basketball, tennis. *Women:* basketball, diving, field hockey, soccer, softball, swimming. **On-Campus Highlights:** Wheelock Family Theater

ADMISSIONS
Freshman Academic Profile: Average high school GPA 2.9. 11% in top 10% of high school class, 33% in top 25% of high school class, 57% in top 50% of high school class. 76% from public high schools. **Test Scores:** SAT Math middle 50% range 400-520. SAT EBRW middle 50% range 410-542. ACT middle 50% range 18-24. Minimum internet-based TOEFL 80. Minimum paper TOEFL 550. **Basis for Candidate Selection:** *Very important factors considered include:* rigor of secondary school record, academic GPA, application essay. *Important factors considered include:* standardized test scores, recommendation(s), extracurricular activities, volunteer work, work experience, level of applicant's interest. *Other factors considered include:* class rank, interview, talent/ability, character/personal qualities. **Freshman Admission Requirements:** High school diploma is required and GED is accepted *Academic units required:* 4 English, 3 math, 2 science, 1 science labs, 1 social studies, 2 history, 3 academic electives, *Academic units recommended:* 4 English, 3 math, 2 science, 1 science labs, 1 social studies, 2 history, 3 academic electives. **Freshman Admission Statistics:** 1,331 applied, 95.4% admitted, 17% enrolled. **Transfer Admission Requirements:** High school transcript, college transcript(s), essay or personal statement, Minimum college GPA of 2.0 required. Lowest grade transferable C. **General Admission Information:** Priority deadline 3/1. Regular application deadline 5/1. Nonfall registration accepted. Admission may be deferred for a maximum of 1 year.

COSTS AND FINANCIAL AID
Annual tuition $33,600. Room and board $14,400. Required fees $1,125. **Required Forms and Deadlines:** FAFSA. **Notification of Awards:** Applicants will be notified of awards on a rolling basis beginning 3/1. **Types of Aid:** *Need-based scholarships/grants:* College/university scholarship or grant aid from institutional funds; Federal Pell; SEOG; State scholarships/grants. *Loans:* Direct PLUS loans; Direct Subsidized Stafford Loans; Direct Unsubsidized Stafford Loans. *Student Employment:* Federal Work-Study Program available. Institutional employment available. **Financial Aid Statistics:** 0% freshmen,

0% undergrads receive athletic scholarships. **Criteria for awarding aid:** *Need-based:* Academics, Leadership *Non-need-based:* Academics, Leadership, State/district residency.

WHITMAN COLLEGE

345 Boyer Avenue, Walla Walla, WA 99362
Phone: 509-527-5176 • **Financial Aid Phone:** 509-527-5178
E-mail: admission@whitman.edu • **CEEB Code:** 4951
Fax: 509-527-4967 • **Website:** https://www.whitman.edu • **ACT Code:** 4492

This private school was founded in 1883. It has a 117 acre campus.

RATINGS
Admissions Selectivity Rating: 92   **Fire Safety Rating:** 90   **Green Rating:** 89

STUDENTS AND FACULTY
Enrollment: 1,468. **Student Body:** 57% female, 43% male, 66% out-of-state, 7% international (26 countries represented). Asian 5%, African American 2%, Caucasian 69%, Hispanic 7%, Native American 1%, Pacific Islander <1%, Two or more races 7%, Race unknown 2%.
Retention and Graduation: 94% freshmen return for sophomore year. 79% freshmen graduate within 4 years. 88% freshmen graduate within 6 years. **Faculty:** Student/faculty ratio 9:1. 165 full-time faculty, 93% hold PhDs, 12% are members of minority groups, 50% are women. 0% of classes are taught by teaching assistants.

ACADEMICS
Degrees: Bachelor's **Classes:** Most classes have 10-19 students. Most lab/discussion sessions have 10-19 students. **Most popular majors:** Biology, General; Biochemistry, Biophysics And Molecular Biology, Other; Psychology, General. **Special Study Options:** Accelerated program; Cooperative education program; Cross-registration; Double major; Dual enrollment; Exchange student program (domestic); Honors program; Independent study; Internships; Liberal arts/career combination; Student-designed major; Study abroad. Combined degree programs: BA/JD; BA/MA. **Disability Services offered to physically disabled students:** Note-taking services; Reader services; Tape recorders; Tutors. **Career services:** Alumni network; Alumni services; Career assessment; Internships; Regional alumni

FACILITIES
Housing: Coed dorms; Fraternity/sorority housing; Theme housing; Women's dorms 96% of campus accessible to physically diasbled. **Special Academic Facilities/Equipment:** Art gallery, Asian art collection, anthropology museum, planetarium, outdoor observatory, two electron microscopes, outdoor sculpture walk, technology/video-conferencing center, rock-climbing walls, organic garden. **Computers:** 100% of classrooms, 100% of dorms, 100% of libraries, 100% of dining areas, 100% of student union, 40% of common outdoor areas have wireless network access. Students can register for classes online. Administrative functions (other than registration) can be performed online.

CAMPUS LIFE
Environment: Town **Activities:** Campus Ministries; Choral groups; Concert band; Dance; Drama/theater; International Student Organization; Jazz band; Literary magazine; Model UN; Music ensembles; Musical theater; Radio station; Student government; Student newspaper; Student-run film society; Symphony orchestra; Yearbook 80 registered organizations, 3 honor societies, 7 religious organizations. 4 fraternities, 3 sororities. **Athletics (Intercollegiate):** *Men:* baseball, basketball, cross-country, golf, soccer, swimming, tennis. *Women:* basketball, cross-country, golf, soccer, swimming, tennis, volleyball. **On-Campus Highlights:** Reid Campus Center, Ankeny Field (Main Quad), Baker Ferguson Fitness Center, Penrose Library, Harper Joy Theatre

ADMISSIONS
Freshman Academic Profile: Average high school GPA 3.8. 59% in top 10% of high school class, 88% in top 25% of high school class, 98% in top 50% of high school class. 62% from public high schools. **Test Scores:** SAT Math middle 50% range 510-680. SAT EBRW middle 50% range 510-690. ACT middle 50% range 26-31. Minimum internet-based TOEFL 85. Minimum paper TOEFL 560. **Basis for Candidate Selection:** *Very important factors considered include:* rigor of secondary school record, academic GPA, application essay. *Important factors considered include:* recommendation(s), extracurricular activities, talent/ability, character/personal qualities. *Other factors considered*

include: class rank, standardized test scores, interview, first generation, alumni/ae relation, geographical residence, state residency, religious affiliation/commitment, racial/ethnic status, volunteer work, work experience, level of applicant's interest. **Freshman Admission Requirements:** High school diploma is required and GED is accepted *Academic units recommended:* 4 English, 4 math, 3 science, 3 science labs, 2 foreign language, 2 social studies, 2 history. **Freshman Admission Statistics:** 4,081 applied, 51.7% admitted, 18% enrolled. **Transfer Admission Requirements:** High school transcript, college transcript(s), essay or personal statement, statement of good standing from prior institution(s). Lowest grade transferable C-. **General Admission Information:** Application fee $50. Priority deadline 11/15. Regular application deadline 1/15. Nonfall registration accepted. Admission may be deferred for a maximum of 1 year.

COSTS AND FINANCIAL AID

Average book expense $1,400. **Required Forms and Deadlines:** CSS/Financial Aid PROFILE; FAFSA; Noncustodial PROFILE. **Notification of Awards:** Applicants will be notified of awards on or about 4/1. **Types of Aid:** *Need-based scholarships/grants:* College/university scholarship or grant aid from institutional funds; Federal Pell; Private scholarships; SEOG; State scholarships/grants. *Loans:* Direct PLUS loans; Direct Subsidized Stafford Loans; Direct Unsubsidized Stafford Loans. *Student Employment:* Federal Work-Study Program available. Institutional employment available. **Financial Aid Statistics:** 100% needy freshmen, 100% needy undergrads receive need-based scholarship or grant aid. 32% freshmen, 37% undergrads receive non-need-based scholarship or grant aid. 73% freshmen, 81% undergrads receive need-based self-help aid. 0% freshmen, 0% undergrads receive athletic scholarships. 80% freshmen, 77% undergrads receive any aid. 38% undergrads borrow to pay for school. Average cumulative indebtedness $18,089. **Criteria for awarding aid:** *Need-based:* Academics, Art, Minority status, Music/drama *Non-need-based:* Academics, Art, Minority status, Music/drama.

WHITTIER COLLEGE

13406 Philadelphia Street, Whittier, CA 90608
Phone: 562-907-4238 • **Financial Aid Phone:** 562-907-4285
E-mail: admissions@whittier.edu • **CEEB Code:** 4952
Fax: 562-907-4870 • **Website:** www.whittier.edu • **ACT Code:** 480

This private school was founded in 1887. It has a 75 acre campus.

RATINGS

Admissions Selectivity Rating: 79   Fire Safety Rating: 95   Green Rating: 60*

STUDENTS AND FACULTY

Enrollment: 1,664. **Student Body:** 56% female, 44% male, 16% out-of-state, 3% international (24 countries represented). Asian 7%, African American 5%, Caucasian 27%, Hispanic 50%, Native American <1%, Pacific Islander <1%, Two or more races 7%, Race unknown 1%.
Retention and Graduation: 78% freshmen return for sophomore year. 62% freshmen graduate within 4 years. 69% freshmen graduate within 6 years. 18% grads go on to further study within 1 year. 7% grads pursue arts and sciences degrees. 2% grads pursue law degrees. 3% grads pursue business degrees. 1% grads pursue medical degrees. **Faculty:** Student/faculty ratio 12:1. 119 full-time faculty, 95% hold PhDs, 30% are members of minority groups, 51% are women. 0% of classes are taught by teaching assistants.

ACADEMICS

Degrees: Bachelor's; Doctoral/Professional; **Master's Classes:** Most classes have 10-19 students. Most lab/discussion sessions have 10-19 students. **Most popular majors:** Psychology, General; Political Science And Government, General; Business Administration And Management, General. **Special Study Options:** Double major; Independent study; Internships; Liberal arts/career combination; Student-designed major; Study abroad; Teacher certification program. Combined degree programs: BA/JD. **Disability Services offered to physically disabled students:** Note-taking services; Reader services; Tape recorders. **Career services:** Alumni network; Alumni services; Career assessment; Career/job search classes; Internships; Regional alumni

FACILITIES

Housing: Apartments for single students; Coed dorms; Special housing for disabled student; Theme housing 60% of campus accessible to physically

diasbled. **Special Academic Facilities/Equipment:** Performing arts center, on-campus pre-school/ elementary school, image processing lab, state-of-the-art nightclub, on-air radio studio and production room, video production room **Computers:** 100% of classrooms, 100% of dorms, 100% of libraries, 100% of dining areas, 100% of student union, have wireless network access. Students can register for classes online. Administrative functions (other than registration) can be performed online.

CAMPUS LIFE

Environment: City **Activities:** Campus Ministries; Choral groups; Dance; Drama/theater; International Student Organization; Jazz band; Literary magazine; Model UN; Music ensembles; Radio station; Student government; Student newspaper; Student-run film society; Television station; Yearbook 60 registered organizations, 17 honor societies, 6 religious organizations. 4 fraternities, 5 sororities. **Athletics (Intercollegiate):** *Men:* baseball, basketball, cross-country, diving, football, golf, lacrosse, soccer, swimming, tennis, track/field (outdoor), water polo. *Women:* basketball, cross-country, diving, lacrosse, soccer, softball, swimming, tennis, track/field (outdoor), volleyball, water polo. **On-Campus Highlights:** The Campus Center, Bonnie Bell Wardman Library, Donald Graham Athletics Center, Ruth B. Shannon Center for the Performing Arts, the Rock (campus icon) **Environmental Initiatives:** Climate Commitment signatory

ADMISSIONS

Freshman Academic Profile: Average high school GPA 3.5. 21% in top 10% of high school class, 63% in top 25% of high school class, 92% in top 50% of high school class. **Test Scores:** SAT Math middle 50% range 500-600. SAT EBRW middle 50% range 510-620. ACT middle 50% range 21-27. Minimum paper TOEFL 550. **Basis for Candidate Selection:** *Very important factors considered include:* rigor of secondary school record, academic GPA, application essay, recommendation(s), character/personal qualities. *Important factors considered include:* interview, extracurricular activities, talent/ability, volunteer work. *Other factors considered include:* class rank, standardized test scores, first generation, alumni/ae relation, geographical residence, state residency, racial/ethnic status, work experience. **Freshman Admission Requirements:** High school diploma is required and GED is accepted *Academic units required:* 3 English, 2 math, 1 science, 1 science labs, 2 foreign language, 1 social studies, *Academic units recommended:* 4 English, 3 math, 2 science, 3 foreign language, 2 social studies. **Freshman Admission Statistics:** 4,585 applied, 99.4% admitted, 11% enrolled. **Transfer Admission Requirements:** High school transcript, college transcript(s), essay or personal statement, Lowest grade transferable C-. **General Admission Information:** Application fee $50. Priority deadline 2/1. Nonfall registration accepted. Admission may be deferred for a maximum of 1 year.

COSTS AND FINANCIAL AID

Annual tuition $45,730. Room and board $13,310. Required fees $390. Average book expense $800. **Required Forms and Deadlines:** FAFSA. **Notification of Awards:** Applicants will be notified of awards on a rolling basis beginning 2/15. **Types of Aid:** *Need-based scholarships/grants:* College/university scholarship or grant aid from institutional funds; Federal Pell; Private scholarships; SEOG; State scholarships/grants. *Loans:* Direct PLUS loans; Direct Subsidized Stafford Loans; Direct Unsubsidized Stafford Loans. *Student Employment:* Federal Work-Study Program available. **Financial Aid Statistics:** 83% needy freshmen, 88% needy undergrads receive need-based scholarship or grant aid. 17% freshmen, 11% undergrads receive non-need-based scholarship or grant aid. 80% freshmen, 83% undergrads receive need-based self-help aid. 0% freshmen, 0% undergrads receive athletic scholarships. 92% freshmen, 89% undergrads receive any aid. 79% undergrads borrow to pay for school. Average cumulative indebtedness $33,323. **Criteria for awarding aid:** *Need-based:* Job skills, Leadership, Religious affiliation *Non-need-based:* Academics, Alumni affiliation, Art, Minority status, Music/drama.

WHITWORTH UNIVERSITY

300 West Hawthorne Road, Spokane, WA 99251
Phone: 509-777-4786 • **Financial Aid Phone:** 509-777-4335
E-mail: admissions@whitworth.edu • **CEEB Code:** 4953
Fax: 509-777-3758 • **Website:** www.whitworth.edu • **ACT Code:** 4494

This private school, affiliated with the Presbyterian Church, was founded in 1890. It has a 200 acre campus.

RATINGS

Admissions Selectivity Rating: 82   Fire Safety Rating: 87   Green Rating: 60*

STUDENTS AND FACULTY

Enrollment: 2,227. **Student Body:** 60% female, 40% male, 33% out-of-state, 4% international (42 countries represented). Asian 5%, African American 2%, Caucasian 70%, Hispanic 9%, Native American 1%, Pacific Islander 1%, Two or more races 7%, Race unknown 1%.
Retention and Graduation: 85% freshmen return for sophomore year. 65% freshmen graduate within 4 years. 75% freshmen graduate within 6 years. 16% grads go on to further study within 1 year. **Faculty:** Student/faculty ratio 11:1. 184 full-time faculty, 75% hold PhDs, 9% are members of minority groups, 45% are women. 0% of classes are taught by teaching assistants.

ACADEMICS

Degrees: Bachelor's; Master's; Post-Bachelor's certificate; Post-Master's certificate **Classes:** Most classes have fewer than 10 students. **Most popular majors:** Multi-/Interdisciplinary Studies, Other; Social Sciences, General; Business Administration And Management, General. **Special Study Options:** Accelerated program; Cross-registration; Distance learning; Double major; Dual enrollment; English as a Second Language (ESL); Exchange student program (domestic); Honors program; Independent study; Internships; Liberal arts/career combination; Student-designed major; Study abroad; Teacher certification program. Honors programs: The George F Whitworth Honors Program allows high-achieving, motivated students who are admitted with honors to be eligible for a menu of challenging academic-enrichment experiences over their four years at Whitworth. The strength of the program is that the student directs himself/herself through a diverse set of learning experiences across multiple disciplines. These experiences may include honors general education or interdisciplinary courses, honors courses within a major, advanced seminars, honors creative projects, honors research, honors off-campus programs, and honors internships. **Disability Services offered to physically disabled students:** Note-taking services; Reader services; Tape recorders. **Career services:** Alumni network; Alumni services; Career assessment; Career/job search classes; Internships; Regional alumni

FACILITIES

Housing: Coed dorms; Men's dorms; Special housing for disabled student; Theme housing; Women's dorms 80% of campus accessible to physically diasbled. **Special Academic Facilities/Equipment:** Language laboratory, art gallery, computer labs, acoustically superb recital hall, music technology lab, music-composition lab, state-of-the-art chemistry laboratories and instrumentation, two green houses, computer-graphics laboratory and student gallery in the Lied Center for the Visual Arts, **Computers:** Students can register for classes online. Administrative functions (other than registration) can be performed online.

CAMPUS LIFE

Environment: City **Activities:** Campus Ministries; Choral groups; Concert band; Dance; Drama/theater; International Student Organization; Jazz band; Literary magazine; Music ensembles; Musical theater; Radio station; Student government; Student newspaper; Symphony orchestra; Yearbook 50 registered organizations, 5 honor societies. **Athletics (Intercollegiate):** *Men:* baseball, basketball, cheerleading, cross-country, football, golf, soccer, swimming, tennis, track/field (outdoor). *Women:* basketball, cheerleading, cross-country, golf, soccer, softball, swimming, tennis, track/field (outdoor), volleyball. **On-Campus Highlights:** Hixson Student Union Building Mind & Hearth Coffee Shop, University Rec Center, Robinson Science Center, Cowles Music Center, Fieldhouse

ADMISSIONS

Freshman Academic Profile: Average high school GPA 3.8. 36% in top 10% of high school class, 70% in top 25% of high school class, 94% in top 50% of high school class. 79% from public high schools. **Test Scores:** SAT Math middle 50% range 540-650. SAT EBRW middle 50% range 550-660. ACT middle 50% range 23-29. Minimum internet-based TOEFL 79. Minimum paper TOEFL 550. **Basis for Candidate Selection:** *Very important factors considered include:* academic GPA, application essay, recommendation(s). *Important factors considered include:* rigor of secondary school record, standardized test scores, interview, extracurricular activities, character/personal qualities. *Other factors considered include:* talent/ability, first generation, alumni/ae relation, geographical residence, state residency, racial/ethnic status, volunteer work, work experience, level of applicant's interest. **Freshman Admission Requirements:** High school diploma is required and GED is accepted *Academic units recommended:* 4 English, 3 math, 3 science, 2 science labs, 2 foreign language, 2 social studies, 2 history. **Freshman Admission Statistics:** 3,166 applied, 89.0% admitted, 18% enrolled. **Transfer Admission Requirements:** High school transcript, college transcript(s), essay or personal statement, standardized test scores, statement of good standing from prior institution(s). Minimum college GPA of 2.5 required. Lowest grade transferable C-. **General Admission Information:** Priority deadline 3/1. Regular application deadline 8/1. Nonfall registration accepted. Admission may be deferred for a maximum of 1 year.

COSTS AND FINANCIAL AID

Annual tuition $41,086. Room and board $11,496. Required fees $1,100. Average book expense $840. **Required Forms and Deadlines:** FAFSA. **Notification of Awards:** Applicants will be notified of awards on a rolling basis beginning 1/17. **Types of Aid:** *Need-based scholarships/grants:* College/university scholarship or grant aid from institutional funds; Federal Pell; Private scholarships; SEOG; State scholarships/grants. *Loans:* Direct PLUS loans; Direct Subsidized Stafford Loans; Direct Unsubsidized Stafford Loans. *Student Employment:* Federal Work-Study Program available. Institutional employment available. **Financial Aid Statistics:** 99% needy freshmen, 99% needy undergrads receive need-based scholarship or grant aid. 12% freshmen, 10% undergrads receive non-need-based scholarship or grant aid. 86% freshmen, 84% undergrads receive need-based self-help aid. 0% freshmen, 0% undergrads receive athletic scholarships. 100% freshmen, 98% undergrads receive any aid. 61% undergrads borrow to pay for school. Average cumulative indebtedness $28,294. **Criteria for awarding aid:** *Need-based:* Academics, Music/drama *Non-need-based:* Academics, Alumni affiliation, Art, Minority status, Music/drama.

WICHITA STATE UNIVERSITY

1845 Fairmount, Wichita, KS 67260
Phone: 316-978-3085 • **Financial Aid Phone:** 1-855-978-1787
E-mail: admissions@wichita.edu • **CEEB Code:** 6884
Fax: 316-978-3174 • **Website:** www.wichita.edu • **ACT Code:** 1472

This public school was founded in 1895. It has a 330 acre campus.

RATINGS

Admissions Selectivity Rating: 73　　**Fire Safety Rating:** 84　　**Green Rating:** 62

STUDENTS AND FACULTY

Enrollment: 10,970. **Student Body:** 53% female, 47% male, 9% out-of-state, 7% international (75 countries represented). Asian 7%, African American 6%, Caucasian 60%, Hispanic 12%, Native American 1%, Pacific Islander <1%, Two or more races 5%, Race unknown 2%.
Retention and Graduation: 73% freshmen return for sophomore year. 22% freshmen graduate within 4 years. 47% freshmen graduate within 6 years. **Faculty:** Student/faculty ratio 20:1. 505 full-time faculty, 71% hold PhDs, 20% are members of minority groups, 45% are women. 22% of classes are taught by teaching assistants.

ACADEMICS

Degrees: Associate; Bachelor's; Certificate; Doctoral; Doctoral/Professional; Doctoral/Research; Master's; Post-Bachelor's certificate; Post-Master's certificate; Terminal Associate; Transfer Associate **Classes:** Most classes have 10-19 students. Most lab/discussion sessions have 10-19 students. **Most popular majors:** Mechanical Engineering; Liberal Arts And Sciences, General Studies And Humanities, Other; Accounting. **Special Study Options:** Accelerated program; Cooperative education program; Cross-registration; Distance learning; Double major; Dual enrollment; English as a Second Language (ESL); Exchange student program (domestic); Honors program; Independent study; Internships; Liberal arts/career combination; Study abroad; Teacher certification program. Honors programs: The Dorothy and Bill Cohen Honors College at WSU aims to prepare students for innovative intellectual, creative and professional work in a complex society. We sit at the heart of an urban university with high research activity and a commitment to benefit the region and beyond. Honors students reflect these characteristics, while seeking to enrich their lives and the lives of others. **Disability Services offered to physically disabled students:** Note-taking services; Reader services; Tape recorders; Tutors. **Career services:** Alumni network; Alumni services; Career assessment; Career/job search classes; Internships; Regional alumni

FACILITIES

Housing: Apartments for married students; Apartments for single students; Coed dorms; Fraternity/sorority housing; Other (please specify) 98% of campus accessible to physically diasbled. **Special Academic Facilities/Equipment:** Art museum, performance hall, media resource center, observatory, national institute of aviation research, supersonic wind tunnels,24-hour study room in library, outdoor sculpture collection, new dorm opened on campus in fall 2014. The Innovation Campus has various laboratories, a community maker-space, and a mixed-use area, along with partnerships with companies to give students hands-on experience. **Computers:** Students can register for classes online. Administrative functions (other than registration) can be performed online.

CAMPUS LIFE

Environment: Metropolis **Activities:** Campus Ministries; Choral groups; Concert band; Dance; Drama/theater; International Student Organization; Jazz band; Literary magazine; Model UN; Music ensembles; Musical theater; Opera; Pep band; Radio station; Student government; Student newspaper; Student-run film society; Symphony orchestra 140 registered organizations, 11 honor societies, 10 religious organizations. 11 fraternities, 10 sororities. **Athletics (Intercollegiate):** *Men:* baseball, basketball, bowling, cheerleading, cross-country, golf, rugby, swimming, tennis, track/field (outdoor). *Women:* basketball, bowling, cheerleading, cross-country, golf, softball, swimming, tennis, track/field (outdoor), volleyball. **On-Campus Highlights:** Rhatigan Student Center, Ulrich Museum of Art, Heskett Center, Shocker Hall, Food Truck Plaza **Environmental Initiatives:** Recycle Program

ADMISSIONS

Freshman Academic Profile: Average high school GPA 3.4. 20% in top 10% of high school class, 44% in top 25% of high school class, 80% in top 50% of high school class. **Test Scores:** SAT Math middle 50% range 500-657. SAT EBRW middle 50% range 500-622. ACT middle 50% range 20-27. Minimum internet-based TOEFL 72. Minimum paper TOEFL 530. **Basis for Candidate Selection:** *Very important factors considered include:* rigor of secondary school record, academic GPA, standardized test scores. *Important factors considered include:* class rank. *Other factors considered include:* extracurricular activities, talent/ability, volunteer work. **Freshman Admission Requirements:** High school diploma is required and GED is accepted *Academic units required:* 4 English, 3 math, 3 science, 1 science labs, 3 social studies, 3 history, 3 academic electives, *Academic units recommended:* 4 English, 3 math, 3 science, 1 science labs, 3 foreign language, 3 social studies, 3 history, 3 academic electives, 3 computer science. **Freshman Admission Statistics:** 5,469 applied, 97.1% admitted, 28% enrolled. **Transfer Admission Requirements:** college transcript(s), Minimum college GPA of 2.0 required. Lowest grade transferable C. **General Admission Information:** Application fee $30. Nonfall registration accepted. Admission may be deferred for a maximum of 2 years.

COSTS AND FINANCIAL AID

Annual out-of-state tuition $15,503. Room and board $10,000. Required fees $1,887. Average book expense $1,000. **Required Forms and Deadlines:** FAFSA. **Notification of Awards:** Applicants will be notified of awards on a rolling basis beginning 8/1. **Types of Aid:** *Need-based scholarships/grants:* College/university scholarship or grant aid from institutional funds; Federal Pell; Private scholarships; SEOG; State scholarships/grants; United Negro College Fund. *Loans:* Direct PLUS loans; Direct Subsidized Stafford Loans; Direct Unsubsidized Stafford Loans. *Student Employment:* Federal Work-Study Program available. Institutional employment available. **Financial Aid Statistics:** 65% needy freshmen, 74% needy undergrads receive need-based scholarship or grant aid. 64% freshmen, 32% undergrads receive non-need-based scholarship or grant aid. 70% freshmen, 78% undergrads receive need-based self-help aid. 5% freshmen, 3% undergrads receive athletic scholarships. 67% freshmen, 88% undergrads receive any aid. 61% undergrads borrow to pay for school. Average cumulative indebtedness $39,122. **Criteria for awarding aid:** *Need-based:* Leadership, Music/drama *Non-need-based:* Academics, Alumni affiliation, Art, Athletics, Job skills.

WIDENER UNIVERSITY

One University Place, Chester, PA 19013
Phone: 610-499-4126 • **Financial Aid Phone:** 610-499-4161
E-mail: admissions.office@widener.edu • **CEEB Code:** 2642
Fax: 610-499-4676 • **Website:** www.widener.edu • **ACT Code:** 3652

This private school was founded in 1821. It has a 110 acre campus.

RATINGS

Admissions Selectivity Rating: 80   **Fire Safety Rating:** 60*   **Green Rating:** 60*

STUDENTS AND FACULTY

Enrollment: 3,200. **Student Body:** 56% female, 44% male, 40% out-of-state, 2% international (38 countries represented). Asian 4%, African American 13%, Caucasian 71%, Hispanic 5%, Native American <1%, Pacific Islander <1%, Two or more races 3%, Race unknown 1%.
Retention and Graduation: 80% freshmen return for sophomore year. 44% freshmen graduate within 4 years. 57% freshmen graduate within 6 years. 20% grads go on to further study within 1 year. **Faculty:** Student/faculty ratio 14:1. 273 full-time faculty, 89% hold PhDs, 15% are members of minority groups, 56% are women. 0% of classes are taught by teaching assistants.

ACADEMICS

Degrees: Associate; Bachelor's; Certificate; Doctoral/Professional; Doctoral/Research; **Master's Classes:** Most classes have 10-19 students. Most lab/discussion sessions have 20-29 students. **Most popular majors:** Psychology, General; Registered Nursing/Registered Nurse; Business/Commerce, General. **Special Study Options:** Accelerated program; Cooperative education program; Distance learning; Double major; Dual enrollment; Honors program; Independent study; Internships; Liberal arts/career combination; Student-designed major; Study abroad; Teacher certification program; Weekend college. Honors programs: Honors Program in General Education Combined degree programs: BA/MA; BA/MD; BA/MEng. **Disability Services offered to physically disabled students:** Note-taking services; Reader services; Tape recorders; Tutors. **Career services:** Alumni network; Alumni services; Career assessment; Career/job search classes; Regional alumni

FACILITIES

Housing: Coed dorms; Cooperative housing; Fraternity/sorority housing; Men's dorms; Theme housing; Wellness housing; Women's dorms **Special Academic Facilities/Equipment:** Art gallery, restaurant lab, child development center education lab, recording studio, commercial graphics lab, physical therapy lab, science labs, engineering labs, nursing labs, multimedia classrooms, Media Center **Computers:** Students can register for classes online. Administrative functions (other than registration) can be performed online.

CAMPUS LIFE

Environment: Town **Activities:** Campus Ministries; Choral groups; Concert band; Dance; Drama/theater; International Student Organization; Jazz band; Literary magazine; Marching band; Music ensembles; Pep band; Radio station; Student government; Student-run film society; Television station; Yearbook 80 registered organizations, 29 honor societies, 3 religious organizations. 7 fraternities, 3 sororities. **Athletics (Intercollegiate):** *Men:* baseball, basketball, cross-country, football, golf, lacrosse, soccer, swimming, tennis, track/field (outdoor), track/field (indoor). *Women:* basketball, cheerleading, cross-country, field hockey, lacrosse, soccer, softball, swimming, tennis, track/field (outdoor), track/field (indoor), volleyball. **On-Campus Highlights:** University Center, Java City and Residential Restaurant, Schwartz Athletic Center, Observatory, Art Gallery

ADMISSIONS

Freshman Academic Profile: Average high school GPA 3.5. 12% in top 10% of high school class, 41% in top 25% of high school class, 81% in top 50% of high school class. **Test Scores:** SAT Math middle 50% range 510-590. SAT EBRW middle 50% range 510-590. ACT middle 50% range 20-25. Minimum paper TOEFL 500. **Basis for Candidate Selection:** *Very important factors considered include:* rigor of secondary school record, class rank, academic GPA, standardized test scores. *Other factors considered include:* application essay, recommendation(s), interview, extracurricular activities, talent/ability, character/personal qualities, alumni/ae relation, volunteer work, level of applicant's interest. **Freshman Admission Requirements:** High school diploma is required and GED is accepted *Academic units required:* 4 English, 3 math, 3 science, 2 foreign language, 3 social studies, 3 academic electives, *Academic units recommended:* 4 English, 4 math, 4 science, 2 science labs, 2 foreign language, 4 social studies, 3 academic electives. **Freshman Admission Statistics:** 6,045 applied, 65.4% admitted, 20% enrolled. **Transfer Admission Requirements:** college transcript(s), Minimum college GPA of 2.0 required. Lowest grade transferable C. **General Admission Information:** Priority deadline 2/15. Nonfall registration accepted. Admission may be deferred for a maximum of 1 academic year.

COSTS AND FINANCIAL AID

Annual tuition $43,296. Room and board $14,024. Required fees $870. Average book expense $1,300. **Required Forms and Deadlines:** FAFSA. **Notification of Awards:** Applicants will be notified of awards on a rolling basis beginning 1/30. **Types of Aid:** *Need-based scholarships/grants:* College/university scholarship or grant aid from institutional funds; Federal Pell; Private scholarships; SEOG; State scholarships/grants. *Loans:* Direct PLUS loans; Direct Subsidized Stafford Loans; Direct Unsubsidized Stafford Loans. *Student Employment:* Federal Work-Study Program available. Institutional employment available. **Financial Aid Statistics:** 98% needy freshmen, 97% needy undergrads receive need-based scholarship or grant aid. 96% freshmen, 91% undergrads receive non-need-based scholarship or grant aid. 93% freshmen, 93% undergrads receive need-based self-help aid. 0% freshmen, 0% undergrads receive athletic scholarships. 99% freshmen, 90% undergrads receive any aid. **Criteria for awarding aid:** *Need-based:* Academics *Non-need-based:* Academics, Leadership, Music/drama.

WILKES UNIVERSITY

84 W South St, Wilkes-Barre, PA 18766
Phone: 570-408-4400 • **Financial Aid Phone:** 570-408-2000
E-mail: admissions@wilkes.edu • **CEEB Code:** 2977
Fax: 570-408-4904 • **Website:** www.wilkes.edu • **ACT Code:** 3756

This private school was founded in 1933. It has a 27 acre campus.

RATINGS
Admissions Selectivity Rating: 78   **Fire Safety Rating:** 87   **Green Rating:** 60*

STUDENTS AND FACULTY
Enrollment: 2,379. **Student Body:** 46% female, 54% male, 19% out-of-state, 9% international (12 countries represented). Asian 2%, African American 5%, Caucasian 71%, Hispanic 6%, Native American <1%, Pacific Islander <1%, Two or more races 3%, Race unknown 3%.
Retention and Graduation: 76% freshmen return for sophomore year. 47% freshmen graduate within 4 years. 60% freshmen graduate within 6 years.
Faculty: Student/faculty ratio 14:1. 180 full-time faculty, 91% hold PhDs, 12% are members of minority groups, 46% are women. 0% of classes are taught by teaching assistants.

ACADEMICS
Degrees: Bachelor's; Doctoral/Professional; Doctoral/Research; **Master's Classes:** Most classes have 10-19 students. Most lab/discussion sessions have 10-19 students. **Most popular majors:** Mechanical Engineering; Psychology, General; Registered Nursing/Registered Nurse. **Special Study Options:** Accelerated program; Cooperative education program; Cross-registration; Distance learning; Double major; Dual enrollment; English as a Second Language (ESL); External degree program; Honors program; Independent study; Internships; Student-designed major; Study abroad; Teacher certification program; Weekend college. **Disability Services offered to physically disabled students:** Note-taking services; Reader services; Tape recorders; Tutors. **Career services:** Alumni network; Alumni services; Career assessment; Career/job search classes; Internships; Regional alumni

FACILITIES
Housing: Apartments for single students; Coed dorms; Men's dorms; Women's dorms **Special Academic Facilities/Equipment:** Art gallery, performing arts center, electron microscope, television studio. **Computers:** Students can register for classes online. Administrative functions (other than registration) can be performed online.

CAMPUS LIFE
Environment: City **Activities:** Campus Ministries; Choral groups; Dance; Drama/theater; International Student Organization; Jazz band; Literary magazine; Marching band; Music ensembles; Musical theater; Pep band; Radio station; Student government; Student newspaper; Television station; Yearbook 65 registered organizations, 19 honor societies. **Athletics (Intercollegiate):** *Men:* baseball, basketball, cross-country, football, golf, soccer, tennis, wrestling. *Women:* basketball, cross-country, field hockey, lacrosse, soccer, softball, tennis, volleyball.

ADMISSIONS
Freshman Academic Profile: Average high school GPA 3.5. 23% in top 10% of high school class, 51% in top 25% of high school class, 84% in top 50% of high school class. **Test Scores:** SAT Math middle 50% range 520-610. SAT EBRW middle 50% range 520-610. ACT middle 50% range 21-26. Minimum internet-based TOEFL 61. Minimum paper TOEFL 500. **Basis for Candidate Selection:** *Very important factors considered include:* rigor of secondary school record, class rank. *Important factors considered include:* academic GPA, standardized test scores, extracurricular activities, character/personal qualities. *Other factors considered include:* recommendation(s), interview, talent/ability, alumni/ae relation, volunteer work, work experience. **Freshman Admission Requirements:** High school diploma is required and GED is accepted *Academic units recommended:* 4 English, 3 math, 3 science, 2 science labs, 2 foreign language, 3 social studies, 1 computer science. **Freshman Admission Statistics:** 4,067 applied, 75.3% admitted, 20% enrolled. **Transfer Admission Requirements:** college transcript(s), statement of good standing from prior institution(s). Minimum college GPA of 2.0 required. Lowest grade transferable C. **General Admission Information:** Application fee $40. Nonfall registration accepted. Admission may be deferred for a maximum of 1 year.

COSTS AND FINANCIAL AID
Annual tuition $31,946. Room and board $13,746. Required fees $1,622. Average book expense $1,500. **Required Forms and Deadlines:** FAFSA. **Notification of Awards:** Applicants will be notified of awards on a rolling basis beginning 3/1. **Types of Aid:** *Need-based scholarships/grants:* College/

university scholarship or grant aid from institutional funds; Federal Pell; Private scholarships; SEOG; State scholarships/grants. *Loans:* Direct PLUS loans; Direct Subsidized Stafford Loans; Direct Unsubsidized Stafford Loans. *Student Employment:* Federal Work-Study Program available. Institutional employment available. **Financial Aid Statistics:** 99% needy freshmen, 98% needy undergrads receive need-based scholarship or grant aid. 77% freshmen, 78% undergrads receive non-need-based scholarship or grant aid. 90% freshmen, 89% undergrads receive need-based self-help aid. 0% freshmen, 0% undergrads receive athletic scholarships. 97% freshmen, 90% undergrads receive any aid. 82% undergrads borrow to pay for school. Average cumulative indebtedness $43,241. **Criteria for awarding aid:** *Non-need-based:* Academics, Leadership, Minority status, Music/drama.

WILLAMETTE UNIVERSITY

900 State Street, Salem, OR 97301
Phone: 503-370-6303 • **Financial Aid Phone:** 503-370-6273
E-mail: bearcat@willamette.edu • **CEEB Code:** 4954
Fax: 503-375-5363 • **Website:** http://www.willamette.edu • **ACT Code:** 3504

This private school, affiliated with the Methodist Church, was founded in 1842. It has a 72 acre campus.

RATINGS
Admissions Selectivity Rating: 86   **Fire Safety Rating:** 98   **Green Rating:** 87

STUDENTS AND FACULTY
Enrollment: 1,772. **Student Body:** 58% female, 42% male, 77% out-of-state, 1% international (30 countries represented). Asian 9%, African American 2%, Caucasian 61%, Hispanic 13%, Native American 1%, Pacific Islander <1%, Two or more races 9%, Race unknown 3%.
Retention and Graduation: 86% freshmen return for sophomore year. 66% freshmen graduate within 4 years. 73% freshmen graduate within 6 years. 23% grads go on to further study within 1 year. 8% grads pursue arts and sciences degrees. 1% grads pursue law degrees. 4% grads pursue business degrees. 2% grads pursue medical degrees. **Faculty:** Student/faculty ratio 11:1. 199 full-time faculty, 95% hold PhDs, 19% are members of minority groups, 46% are women. 0% of classes are taught by teaching assistants.

ACADEMICS
Degrees: Bachelor's; Doctoral/Professional; Master's **Most popular majors:** Biology/Biological Sciences, General; Psychology, General; Economics, General. **Special Study Options:** Accelerated program; Cross-registration; Double major; Dual enrollment; Exchange student program (domestic); Independent study; Internships; Student-designed major; Study abroad; Teacher certification program. Honors programs: Our challenging curriculum includes a variety of opportunities for individualized honors study, for example: Presidential Scholars (senior year), Carson Undergraduate Research Program, Science Collaborative Research Program, various departmental honors programs. Combined degree programs: BA/JD. **Disability Services offered to physically disabled students:** Note-taking services; Reader services; Tape recorders; Tutors. **Career services:** Alumni network; Career assessment; Career/job search classes; Internships

FACILITIES
Housing: Apartments for single students; Coed dorms; Fraternity/sorority housing; Other (please specify) 95% of campus accessible to physically diasbled. **Special Academic Facilities/Equipment:** Student Art purchased annually,and displayed in all public access buildings, Hallie Ford Museum of Art,Collections and papers of Congressional leaders from Oregon,Electron Microscope Lab (scanning and transmission), Herbarium, Japanese and Botanical Gardens, Carnegie Library(fully restored) **Computers:** 100% of classrooms, 100% of dorms, 100% of libraries, 100% of dining areas, 100% of student union, 50% of common outdoor areas have wireless network access. Students can register for classes online. Administrative functions (other than registration) can be performed online.

CAMPUS LIFE
Environment: City **Activities:** Campus Ministries; Choral groups; Concert band; Dance; Drama/theater; International Student Organization; Jazz band; Literary magazine; Model UN; Music ensembles; Musical theater; Opera; Student government; Student newspaper; Student-run film society; Symphony

orchestra; Yearbook 107 registered organizations, 7 honor societies, 5 religious organizations. 4 fraternities, 3 sororities. **Athletics (Intercollegiate):** *Men:* baseball, basketball, crew/rowing, cross-country, football, golf, soccer, swimming, tennis, track/field (outdoor), track/field (indoor). *Women:* basketball, crew/rowing, cross-country, golf, soccer, softball, swimming, tennis, track/field (outdoor), track/field (indoor), volleyball. **On-Campus Highlights:** Hallie Ford Museum of Art, Montag Student Center, Sparks Sports and Recreation Center, Willamette Bistro, Mill Stream on campus **Environmental Initiatives:** Kaneko Commons Residential Hall Ford Hall-Academic Building Purchased Zena Forest-nearby 308 Acre Sustainable forest for research and teaching New Construction Achieved LEED Gold status in 2007. Photo Voltaic panels, solar hot water heating, rainwater reclamation for flushing toilets, FSC wood products, Indoor Air Quality measures, low/no VOC materials and products, sustainability educational signage, high recycled content materials, energy efficient boilers, lighting control system, Energy Management System controls, 50% reduction in irrigation, low flow plumbing fixtures, use of plate to plate heat exchangers, sun shades, 95% recycle of construction waste, reflective roof coatings, use of local materials & labor, FSC cert furnishings, Fat Spaniel PV panel monitoring, electrical use monitoring, FLEX CAR program initiated, purchase of Green Power, energy star appliances, and more.

ADMISSIONS

Freshman Academic Profile: Average high school GPA 3.8. 47% in top 10% of high school class, 75% in top 25% of high school class, 93% in top 50% of high school class. 75% from public high schools. **Test Scores:** SAT Math middle 50% range 550-660. SAT EBRW middle 50% range 570-680. ACT middle 50% range 26-31. Minimum internet-based TOEFL 85. Minimum paper TOEFL 560. **Basis for Candidate Selection:** *Very important factors considered include:* rigor of secondary school record, class rank, academic GPA, application essay, standardized test scores. *Important factors considered include:* recommendation(s), interview. *Other factors considered include:* extracurricular activities, talent/ability, character/personal qualities, first generation, alumni/ae relation, geographical residence, racial/ethnic status. **Freshman Admission Requirements:** High school diploma is required and GED is accepted *Academic units recommended:* 4 English, 4 math, 4 science, 4 foreign language, 4 social studies, 4 academic electives, 4 visual/performing arts. **Freshman Admission Statistics:** 4,484 applied, 89.1% admitted, 11% enrolled. **Transfer Admission Requirements:** High school transcript, college transcript(s), essay or personal statement, statement of good standing from prior institution(s). Lowest grade transferable C. **General Admission Information:** Application fee $50. Priority deadline 1/15. Regular application deadline 1/15. Nonfall registration accepted. Admission may be deferred for a maximum of 1 year.

COSTS AND FINANCIAL AID

Annual tuition $49,750. Room and board $12,440. Required fees $324. Average book expense $950. **Required Forms and Deadlines:** FAFSA. **Notification of Awards:** Applicants will be notified of awards on a rolling basis beginning 4/1. **Types of Aid:** *Need-based scholarships/grants:* College/university scholarship or grant aid from institutional funds; Federal Pell; Private scholarships; SEOG; State scholarships/grants. *Loans:* Direct PLUS loans; Direct Subsidized Stafford Loans; Direct Unsubsidized Stafford Loans. *Student Employment:* Federal Work-Study Program available. Institutional employment available. **Financial Aid Statistics:** 99% needy freshmen, 99% needy undergrads receive need-based scholarship or grant aid. 30% freshmen, 17% undergrads receive non-need-based scholarship or grant aid. 79% freshmen, 78% undergrads receive need-based self-help aid. 0% freshmen, 0% undergrads receive athletic scholarships. 100% freshmen, 92% undergrads receive any aid. Average cumulative indebtedness $29,766. **Criteria for awarding aid:** *Need-based:* Academics, Alumni affiliation, Leadership, Minority status, Music/drama, Religious affiliation *Non-need-based:* Academics, Alumni affiliation, Leadership, Minority status, Music/drama, Religious affiliation.

WILLIAM JEWELL COLLEGE

500 College Hill, Liberty, MO 64068
Phone: 816-415-7511 • **Financial Aid Phone:** 816-415-5974
E-mail: admission@william.jewell.edu • **CEEB Code:** 6941
Fax: 816-415-5040 • **Website:** www.jewell.edu • **ACT Code:** 2394

This private school was founded in 1849. It has a 200 acre campus.

RATINGS

Admissions Selectivity Rating: 87   **Fire Safety Rating:** 88   **Green Rating:** 60*

STUDENTS AND FACULTY

Enrollment: 928. **Student Body:** 59% female, 41% male, 42% out-of-state, 4% international (19 countries represented). Asian 1%, African American 5%, Caucasian 79%, Hispanic 4%, Native American <1%, Pacific Islander <1%, Two or more races 5%, Race unknown 2%.
Retention and Graduation: 77% freshmen return for sophomore year. 54% freshmen graduate within 4 years. 59% freshmen graduate within 6 years. 28% grads go on to further study within 1 year. 12% grads pursue arts and sciences degrees. 1% grads pursue law degrees. 9% grads pursue business degrees. 3% grads pursue medical degrees. **Faculty:** Student/faculty ratio 9:1. 82 full-time faculty, 85% hold PhDs, 2% are members of minority groups, 46% are women. 0% of classes are taught by teaching assistants.

ACADEMICS

Degrees: Bachelor's; Master's; Post-Bachelor's certificate **Classes:** Most classes have 20-29 students. Most lab/discussion sessions have 10-19 students. **Most popular majors:** Biology/Biological Sciences, General; Registered Nursing/Registered Nurse; Business Administration And Management, General. **Special Study Options:** Accelerated program; Distance learning; Double major; Honors program; Independent study; Internships; Liberal arts/career combination; Student-designed major; Study abroad; Teacher certification program. Honors programs: The Oxbridge Honors Program combines British tutorial methods of instruction with opportunities for a year of study in Oxford, England. **Disability Services offered to physically disabled students:** Note-taking services; Reader services; Tape recorders. **Career services:** Alumni network; Alumni services; Career assessment; Career/job search classes; Internships; Regional alumni

FACILITIES

Housing: Coed dorms; Fraternity/sorority housing; Men's dorms; Special housing for disabled student; Wellness housing; Women's dorms 80% of campus accessible to physically disabled. **Special Academic Facilities/Equipment:** Art gallery, observatory, language and computer labs, high-ropes course, greenhouse **Computers:** 80% of classrooms, 20% of dorms, 25% of libraries, 80% of dining areas, 90% of student union, have wireless network access. Students can register for classes online. Administrative functions (other than registration) can be performed online.

CAMPUS LIFE

Environment: Town **Activities:** Campus Ministries; Choral groups; Concert band; Dance; Drama/theater; International Student Organization; Jazz band; Literary magazine; Music ensembles; Musical theater; Opera; Pep band; Student government; Student newspaper; Symphony orchestra 70 registered organizations, 13 honor societies, 7 religious organizations. 4 fraternities, 4 sororities. **Athletics (Intercollegiate):** *Men:* baseball, basketball, cheerleading, cross-country, football, golf, soccer, tennis, track/field (outdoor), track/field (indoor). *Women:* basketball, cheerleading, cross-country, golf, soccer, softball, tennis, track/field (outdoor), track/field (indoor), volleyball. **On-Campus Highlights:** Pryor Learning Commons—intellectual and innovative technology center, Mabee Center—athletic facility, The Quad—central campus quadrangle, Yates-Gill College Union—student union, First-year residence hall commons **Environmental Initiatives:** Campus recycling program

ADMISSIONS

Freshman Academic Profile: Average high school GPA 3.7. 26% in top 10% of high school class, 57% in top 25% of high school class, 88% in top 50% of high school class. 90% from public high schools. **Test Scores:** SAT Math middle 50% range 550-610. SAT EBRW middle 50% range 440-630. ACT middle 50% range 23-28. Minimum internet-based TOEFL 79. Minimum paper TOEFL 550. **Basis for Candidate Selection:** *Very important factors considered include:* rigor of secondary school record, academic GPA. *Important factors considered include:* class rank, standardized test scores, recommendation(s), extracurricular activities, talent/ability, character/personal qualities, level of applicant's interest. *Other factors considered include:* application essay, interview, first generation, alumni/ae relation, volunteer work, work experience. **Freshman Admission Requirements:** High school diploma is required and GED is accepted *Academic units required:* 4 English, 3 math, 3 science, 1 science labs, 2 foreign language, 3 social studies, *Academic units recommended:* 4 math, 3 foreign language, 2 academic electives. **Freshman Admission Statistics:** 1,608 applied, 48.7% admitted, 25% enrolled. **Transfer Admission Requirements:** college transcript(s), statement of good standing from prior institution(s). Minimum college GPA of 2.5 required. Lowest grade transferable C-. **General Admission Information:** Priority deadline 10/15. Nonfall registration accepted. Admission may be deferred for a maximum of 1 year.

COSTS AND FINANCIAL AID

Annual tuition $33,500. Room and board $9,930. Required fees $900. Average book expense $800. **Required Forms and Deadlines:** FAFSA. **Notification of Awards:** Applicants will be notified of awards on a rolling basis beginning 11/1. **Types of Aid:** *Need-based scholarships/grants:* College/university scholarship or grant aid from institutional funds; Federal Pell; Private scholarships; SEOG; State scholarships/grants; United Negro College Fund. *Loans:* Direct PLUS loans; Direct Subsidized Stafford Loans; Direct Unsubsidized Stafford Loans. *Student Employment:* Federal Work-Study Program available. Institutional employment available. **Financial Aid Statistics:** 100% needy freshmen, 91% needy undergrads receive need-based scholarship or grant aid. 100% freshmen, 94% undergrads receive non-need-based scholarship or grant aid. 72% freshmen, 74% undergrads receive need-based self-help aid. 7% freshmen, 14% undergrads receive athletic scholarships. 100% freshmen, 99% undergrads receive any aid. 69% undergrads borrow to pay for school. Average cumulative indebtedness $31,183. **Criteria for awarding aid:** *Need-based:* Leadership *Non-need-based:* Academics, Alumni affiliation, Athletics, Music/drama.

WILLIAM PATERSON UNIVERSITY

300 Pompton Road, Wayne, NJ 07470
Phone: 973-720-2125 • **Financial Aid Phone:** 973-720-3945
E-mail: admissions@wpunj.edu • **CEEB Code:** 2518
Fax: 973-720-2910 • **Website:** www.wpunj.edu • **ACT Code:** 2584

This public school was founded in 1855. It has a 370 acre campus.

RATINGS
Admissions Selectivity Rating: 72   **Fire Safety Rating:** 98   **Green Rating:** 84

STUDENTS AND FACULTY

Enrollment: 8,705. **Student Body:** 54% female, 46% male, 2% out-of-state, 1% international (37 countries represented). Asian 7%, African American 17%, Caucasian 39%, Hispanic 32%, Native American <1%, Pacific Islander 0%, Two or more races 3%, Race unknown 2%.
Retention and Graduation: 77% freshmen return for sophomore year. 27% freshmen graduate within 4 years. 55% freshmen graduate within 6 years. 22% grads go on to further study within 1 year. **Faculty:** Student/faculty ratio 14:1. 410 full-time faculty, 91% hold PhDs, 35% are members of minority groups, 50% are women. 0% of classes are taught by teaching assistants.

ACADEMICS

Degrees: Bachelor's; Doctoral/Professional; Master's; Post-Bachelor's certificate; Post-Master's certificate **Classes:** Most classes have 20-29 students. Most lab/discussion sessions have 10-19 students. **Most popular majors:** Speech Communication And Rhetoric; Psychology, General; Criminal Justice/Safety Studies. **Special Study Options:** Accelerated program; Cross-registration; Distance learning; Double major; Dual enrollment; English as a Second Language (ESL); Exchange student program (domestic); Honors program; Independent study; Internships; Liberal arts/career combination; Study abroad; Teacher certification program. Honors programs: University Honors College offers honors research tracks as well as honors general education courses. For more information please visit our Honors College http://www.wpunj.edu/honors-program Combined degree programs: BA/MA. **Disability Services offered to physically disabled students:** Note-taking services; Reader services; Tape recorders; Tutors. **Career services:** Alumni network; Alumni services; Career assessment; Career/job search classes; Internships

FACILITIES

Housing: Apartments for single students; Coed dorms; Special housing for disabled students 88% of campus accessible to physically disabled. **Special**

Academic Facilities/Equipment: Art galleries; Collection of NJ State Documents; Collection of William Paterson's private papers; Interactive television classroom; Neurobiology facility; E-Trading Campus Network with ATM technology; Center for Computer Art and Animation; State-of-the-art electron microscopy facility; Teleconference Center with uplink and downlink capabilities; 44,000 square foot, state-of-the-art studio art facility; Center for Electro-Acoustic Music (CEM); E-Trade Financial Learning Center, a real-time simulated trading and financial educational facility; Russ Berrie Institute for Professional Sales including real-time Sales Laboratory **Computers:** Students can register for classes online. Administrative functions (other than registration) can be performed online.

CAMPUS LIFE

Environment: Town **Activities:** Campus Ministries; Choral groups; Dance; Drama/theater; Literary magazine; Model UN; Music ensembles; Musical theater; Opera; Pep band; Radio station; Student government; Student newspaper; Student-run film society; Symphony orchestra; Television station; Yearbook 61 registered organizations, 21 honor societies, 4 religious organizations. 11 fraternities, 10 sororities. **Athletics (Intercollegiate):** *Men:* baseball, basketball, football, soccer, swimming. *Women:* basketball, cheerleading, field hockey, soccer, softball, swimming, volleyball. **On-Campus Highlights:** Student Center: Coffee Cafe (Starbucks), College of Business E-Trading Center, Power Art Gallery, Science Complex, Library **Environmental Initiatives:** ACUPCC

ADMISSIONS

Freshman Academic Profile: Average high school GPA 3.1. **Test Scores:** SAT Math middle 50% range 460-550. SAT EBRW middle 50% range 470-570. ACT middle 50% range 18-24. Minimum internet-based TOEFL 79-80. Minimum paper TOEFL 550. **Basis for Candidate Selection:** *Very important factors considered include:* rigor of secondary school record, academic GPA. *Important factors considered include:* standardized test scores. *Other factors considered include:* application essay, recommendation(s), interview, extracurricular activities, talent/ability, character/personal qualities, alumni/ae relation, volunteer work, level of applicant's interest. **Freshman Admission Requirements:** High school diploma is required and GED is accepted *Academic units required:* 4 English, 3 math, 2 science, 2 science labs, 2 social studies, 5 academic electives. **Freshman Admission Statistics:** 7,933 applied, 92.4% admitted, 18% enrolled. **Transfer Admission Requirements:** college transcript(s), Minimum college GPA of 2.00 required. Lowest grade transferable C. **General Admission Information:** Application fee $50. Priority deadline 12/1. Regular application deadline 6/1. Nonfall registration accepted. Admission may be deferred for a maximum of 1 year.

COSTS AND FINANCIAL AID

Annual in-state tuition $9,540. Annual out-of-state tuition $14,131. Room and board $9,540. Required fees $8,832. Average book expense $1,600. **Required Forms and Deadlines:** FAFSA. **Notification of Awards:** Applicants will be notified of awards on a rolling basis beginning 2/1. **Types of Aid:** *Need-based scholarships/grants:* College/university scholarship or grant aid from institutional funds; Federal Pell; SEOG; State scholarships/grants. *Loans:* Direct PLUS loans; Direct Subsidized Stafford Loans; Direct Unsubsidized Stafford Loans. *Student Employment:* Federal Work-Study Program available. Institutional employment available. **Financial Aid Statistics:** 69% needy freshmen, 68% needy undergrads receive need-based scholarship or grant aid. 33% freshmen, 25% undergrads receive non-need-based scholarship or grant aid. 77% freshmen, 80% undergrads receive need-based self-help aid. 0% freshmen, 0% undergrads receive athletic scholarships. 89% freshmen, 78% undergrads receive any aid. 76% undergrads borrow to pay for school. Average cumulative indebtedness $33,068. **Criteria for awarding aid:** *Need-based:* Academics *Non-need-based:* Academics, Art, Music/drama.

WILLIAM PEACE UNIVERSITY

Admission office, Raleigh, NC 27604
Phone: 919.508.2214 • **Financial Aid Phone:** 919.508.2214
E-mail: admissions@peace.edu
Fax: 919.508.2306 • **Website:** www.peace.edu • **ACT Code:** 3136

This private school, affiliated with the Presbyterian Church, was founded in 1857. It has a 21 acre campus.

RATINGS
Admissions Selectivity Rating: 72   **Fire Safety Rating:** 60*   **Green Rating:** 61

STUDENTS AND FACULTY

Enrollment: 1,076. **Student Body:** 72% female, 28% male, 6% out-of-state, <1% international. Asian 2%, African American 34%, Caucasian 43%, Hispanic 4%, Native American 1%, Pacific Islander 0%, Two or more races 5%, Race unknown 11%.
Retention and Graduation: 63% freshmen return for sophomore year. **Faculty:** Student/faculty ratio 15:1. 24 full-time faculty, 79% hold PhDs, 4% are members of minority groups, 58% are women. 0% of classes are taught by teaching assistants.

ACADEMICS

Degrees: Bachelor's **Special Study Options:** Cross-registration; Distance learning; Double major; Honors program; Independent study; Internships; Liberal arts/career combination; Study abroad; Teacher certification program; Weekend college. **Career services:** Alumni network; Career assessment; Career/job search classes; Internships

FACILITIES

Housing: Apartments for single students; Coed dorms; Women's dorms

CAMPUS LIFE

Environment: Metropolis **Activities:** Campus Ministries; Choral groups; Dance; Drama/theater; Literary magazine; Music ensembles; Musical theater; Student government; Student newspaper. Hermann Athletic Center, Peace Perk (coffee shop), Bookstore, Sand Volleyball Court, Campus Green

ADMISSIONS

Freshman Academic Profile: Average high school GPA 3.1. 6% in top 10% of high school class, 26% in top 25% of high school class, 57% in top 50% of high school class. **Test Scores:** SAT Math middle 50% range 400-510. SAT EBRW middle 50% range 410-520. ACT middle 50% range 16-21. Minimum internet-based TOEFL 80. Minimum paper TOEFL 550. **Basis for Candidate Selection:** *Very important factors considered include:* rigor of secondary school record, academic GPA, standardized test scores. *Important factors considered include:* application essay, recommendation(s), interview, extracurricular activities, volunteer work.level of applicant's interest. *Other factors considered include:* class rank, talent/ability, character/personal qualities, alumni/ae relation, geographical residence, work experience. **Freshman Admission Requirements:** High school diploma is required and GED is accepted *Academic units required:* 4 English, 3 math, 3 science, 2 science labs, 2 social studies, *Academic units recommended:* 4 math, 2 foreign language. **Freshman Admission Statistics:** 1,083 applied, 90.9% admitted, 33% enrolled. **General Admission Information:** Application fee $35. Nonfall registration accepted. Admission may be deferred for a maximum of 1 year.

COSTS AND FINANCIAL AID

Annual tuition $24,450. Room and board $9,450. Required fees $200. **Required Forms and Deadlines:** FAFSA. **Notification of Awards:** Applicants will be notified of awards on a rolling basis beginning 3/15. **Types of Aid:** *Need-based scholarships/grants:* College/university scholarship or grant aid from institutional funds; Federal Pell; Private scholarships; SEOG; State scholarships/grants. *Loans:* Direct PLUS loans; Direct Subsidized Stafford Loans; Direct Unsubsidized Stafford Loans. *Student Employment:* Federal Work-Study Program available. **Financial Aid Statistics:** 84% needy freshmen, 85% needy undergrads receive need-based scholarship or grant aid. 76% freshmen, 88% undergrads receive non-need-based scholarship or grant aid. 94% freshmen, undergrads receive need-based self-help aid. 0% freshmen, 0% undergrads receive athletic scholarships. 91% freshmen, 91% undergrads receive any aid. **Criteria for awarding aid:** *Non-need-based:* Academics, Leadership, Music/drama.

WILLIAM PENN UNIVERSITY

201 Trueblood Avenue, Oskaloosa, IA 52577
Phone: 641-673-1012
E-mail: admissions@wmpenn.edu • **CEEB Code:** 6943
Fax: 641-673-2113 • **Website:** www.wmpenn.edu • **ACT Code:** 1372

This private school, affiliated with the Quaker Church, was founded in 1873. It has a 53 acre campus.

RATINGS

Admissions Selectivity Rating: 71   **Fire Safety Rating:** 60*   **Green Rating:** 60*

STUDENTS AND FACULTY

Enrollment: 1,586. **Student Body:** 48% female, 52% male, 28% out-of-state, 2% international. Asian 1%, African American 15%, Caucasian 68%, Hispanic

---

7%, Native American 1%, Pacific Islander <1%, Two or more races 1%, Race unknown 5%.
Faculty: Student/faculty ratio 14:1. 35 full-time faculty, 49% hold PhDs, 3% are members of minority groups, 29% are women. 0% of classes are taught by teaching assistants.

ACADEMICS

Degrees: Associate; Bachelor's; Master's; Transfer Associate **Classes:** Most classes have 10-19 students. Most lab/discussion sessions have 20-29 students. **Most popular majors:** Education, General; Psychology, General; Business/Commerce, General. **Special Study Options:** Cooperative education program; Distance learning; Double major; Independent study; Internships; Study abroad; Teacher certification program. **Disability Services offered to physically disabled students:** Tape recorders; Tutors. **Career services:** Alumni services; Career/job search classes; Internships

FACILITIES

Housing: Apartments for married students; Apartments for single students; Coed dorms; Men's dorms; Special housing for international students; Women's dorms 75% of campus accessible to physically disabled. **Special Academic Facilities/Equipment:** Foyer Gallery, Mid-East art and artifact collection.

CAMPUS LIFE

Environment: Village **Activities:** Campus Ministries; Choral groups; Concert band; Dance; Drama/theater; International Student Organization; Jazz band; Literary magazine; Marching band; Music ensembles; Musical theater; Pep band; Radio station; Student government; Student newspaper; Student-run film society; Yearbook 34 registered organizations, 3 honor societies, 4 religious organizations, 3 fraternities, 3 sororities. **Athletics (Intercollegiate):** *Men:* baseball, basketball, cheerleading, cross-country, football, golf, soccer, track/field (outdoor), wrestling. *Women:* basketball, cheerleading, cross-country, soccer, softball, track/field (outdoor), volleyball. Penn Activity Center (PAC), Market St Hall (new residence hall), Musco Technology Center (MTC), Penn Hall, Library

ADMISSIONS

Freshman Academic Profile: 14% in top 25% of high school class, 47% in top 50% of high school class. 97% from public high schools. **Test Scores:** Minimum internet-based TOEFL 61. Minimum paper TOEFL 500. **Basis for Candidate Selection:** *Very important factors considered include:* rigor of secondary school record, academic GPA. *Important factors considered include:* class rank, standardized test scores, character/personal qualities. *Other factors considered include:* application essay, recommendation(s), interview, extracurricular activities, talent/ability, alumni/ae relation, volunteer work, work experience. **Freshman Admission Requirements:** High school diploma is required and GED is accepted *Academic units recommended:* 4 English, 3 math, 3 science, 2 foreign language, 2 social studies, 2 history, 2 academic electives. **Freshman Admission Statistics:** 841 applied, 53.5% admitted, 53% enrolled. **Transfer Admission Requirements:** college transcript(s), Minimum college GPA of 2.0 required. Lowest grade transferable D. **General Admission Information:** Application fee $20. Priority deadline 7/1. Nonfall registration accepted.

COSTS AND FINANCIAL AID

Annual tuition $22,840. Room and board $5,472. Required fees $370. Average book expense $1,150. **Required Forms and Deadlines:** FAFSA. **Notification of Awards:** Applicants will be notified of awards on a rolling basis beginning 1/1. **Types of Aid:** *Need-based scholarships/grants:* College/university scholarship or grant aid from institutional funds; Federal Pell; Private scholarships; SEOG; State scholarships/grants. *Loans: Student Employment:* Federal Work-Study Program available. Institutional employment available. **Criteria for awarding aid:** *Need-based:* Academics, Alumni affiliation, Athletics, Leadership, Music/drama, Religious affiliation *Non-need-based:* Academics, Alumni affiliation, Athletics, Leadership, Music/drama, Religious affiliation.

WILLIAMS COLLEGE

995 Main St., Williamstown, MA 01267
Phone: 413-597-2211 • **Financial Aid Phone:** (413) 597-4181
E-mail: admission@williams.edu • **CEEB Code:** 3965
Fax: 413-597-4052 • **Website:** www.williams.edu • **ACT Code:** 1936

This private school was founded in 1793. It has a 450 acre campus.

RATINGS

Admissions Selectivity Rating: 98   **Fire Safety Rating:** 60*   **Green Rating:** 91

STUDENTS AND FACULTY

Enrollment: 2,030. **Student Body:** 47% female, 53% male, 86% out-of-state, 8% international (57 countries represented). Asian 13%, African American 8%, Caucasian 51%, Hispanic 13%, Native American <1%, Pacific Islander 0%, Two or more races 6%, Race unknown 1%.
Retention and Graduation: 98% freshmen return for sophomore year. 86% freshmen graduate within 4 years. 94% freshmen graduate within 6 years. **Faculty:** Student/faculty ratio 7:1. 292 full-time faculty, 97% hold PhDs, 25% are members of minority groups, 45% are women. 0% of classes are taught by teaching assistants.

ACADEMICS

Degrees: Bachelor's; **Master's Classes:** Most classes have 10-19 students. Most lab/discussion sessions have 10-19 students. **Most popular majors:** English Language And Literature, General; Mathematics, General; Economics, General. **Special Study Options:** Cross-registration; Double major; Independent study; Student-designed major; Study abroad. **Disability Services offered to physically disabled students:** Note-taking services; Reader services; Tape recorders; Tutors. **Career services:** Alumni network; Alumni services; Career/job search classes; Internships; Regional alumni

FACILITIES

Housing: Apartments for married students; Coed dorms; Cooperative housing; Special housing for disabled students **Special Academic Facilities/Equipment:** Hopkins Observatory; Williams College Museum of Art; Adams Memorial Theatre; Chapin Rare Books Library; Spencer Studio Art Building, '62 Center for Theatre and Dance, Hopkins Experimental Forest **Computers:** 100% of classrooms, 100% of dorms, 100% of libraries, 100% of dining areas, 100% of student union, 100% of common outdoor areas have wireless network access. Students can register for classes online. Administrative functions (other than registration) can be performed online.

CAMPUS LIFE

Environment: Village **Activities:** Campus Ministries; Choral groups; Concert band; Dance; Drama/theater; International Student Organization; Jazz band; Literary magazine; Marching band; Music ensembles; Musical theater; Opera; Pep band; Radio station; Student government; Student newspaper; Student-run film society; Symphony orchestra; Yearbook 110 registered organizations, 3 honor societies, 8 religious organizations. **Athletics (Intercollegiate):** *Men:* baseball, basketball, crew/rowing, cross-country, diving, football, golf, ice hockey, lacrosse, skiing (downhill/alpine), skiing (nordic/cross-country), soccer, squash, swimming, tennis, track/field (outdoor), track/field (indoor), wrestling. *Women:* basketball, crew/rowing, cross-country, diving, field hockey, golf, ice hockey, lacrosse, skiing (downhill/alpine), skiing (nordic/cross-country), soccer, softball, squash, swimming, tennis, track/field (outdoor), track/field (indoor), volleyball. **On-Campus Highlights:** Paresky Student Center, Sawyer Library, Williams College Museum of Art, '62 Center for Theatre and Dance, Williams Bookstore

ADMISSIONS

Freshman Academic Profile: 88% in top 10% of high school class, 98% in top 25% of high school class, 99% in top 50% of high school class. 49% from public high schools. **Test Scores:** SAT Math middle 50% range 690-790. SAT EBRW middle 50% range 710-780. ACT middle 50% range 31-35. **Basis for Candidate Selection:** *Very important factors considered include:* rigor of secondary school record, class rank, academic GPA, standardized test scores, recommendation(s), character/personal qualities. *Important factors considered include:* application essay, extracurricular activities, talent/ability, first generation, alumni/ae relation, racial/ethnic status, volunteer work, work experience. *Other factors considered include:* geographical residence, religious affiliation/commitment. **Freshman Admission Requirements:** High school diploma or equivalent is not required *Academic units recommended:* 4

English, 4 math, 4 science, 3 science labs, 4 foreign language, 4 social studies. **Freshman Admission Statistics:** 8,593 applied, 14.6% admitted, 44% enrolled. **Transfer Admission Requirements:** High school transcript, college transcript(s), essay or personal statement, standardized test scores, statement of good standing from prior institution(s). Minimum college GPA of 3.5 required. Lowest grade transferable C-. **General Admission Information:** Application fee $65. Regular application deadline 1/1. Nonfall registration accepted. Admission may be deferred.

COSTS AND FINANCIAL AID

Required Forms and Deadlines: CSS/Financial Aid PROFILE; FAFSA; Noncustodial PROFILE. **Notification of Awards:** Applicants will be notified of awards on or about 4/1. *Types of Aid: Need-based scholarships/grants:* College/university scholarship or grant aid from institutional funds; Federal Pell; SEOG; State scholarships/grants. *Loans:* Direct PLUS loans; Direct Subsidized Stafford Loans; Direct Unsubsidized Stafford Loans. *Student Employment:* Federal Work-Study Program available. Institutional employment available. **Financial Aid Statistics:** 99% needy freshmen, 99% needy undergrads receive need-based scholarship or grant aid. 0% undergrads receive non-need-based scholarship or grant aid. 100% freshmen, 100% undergrads receive need-based self-help aid. 0% freshmen, 0% undergrads receive athletic scholarships. 50% freshmen, 49% undergrads receive any aid. 43% undergrads borrow to pay for school. Average cumulative indebtedness $15,687.

WILMINGTON COLLEGE (DE)

320 DuPont Highway, New Castle, DE 19720
Phone: 302-328-9401
E-mail: mlee@wilmcoll.edu • **CEEB Code:** 5925
Fax: 302-328-5902 • **Website:** www.wilmcoll.edu • **ACT Code:** 635

This private school was founded in 1967. It has a 15 acre campus.

RATINGS

Admissions Selectivity Rating: 61   **Fire Safety Rating:** 60*   **Green Rating:** 60*

STUDENTS AND FACULTY

Enrollment: 4,399. **Student Body:** 53% female, 47% male, 3% out-of-state, 0% international. Asian 1%, African American 14%, Caucasian 64%, Hispanic 2%, Native American <1%, Race unknown 19%.
Retention and Graduation: 87% freshmen return for sophomore year. 50% grads go on to further study within 1 year. 9% grads pursue arts and sciences degrees. 10% grads pursue law degrees. 80% grads pursue business degrees. 1% grads pursue medical degrees. **Faculty:** Student/faculty ratio 18:1. 0% of classes are taught by teaching assistants.

ACADEMICS

Degrees: Associate; Bachelor's; Certificate; Master's; Post-Master's certificate **Classes:** Most classes have 20-29 students. **Most popular majors:** Education, General; Business/Commerce, General. **Special Study Options:** Accelerated program; Cooperative education program; Distance learning; Double major; Independent study; Internships; Teacher certification program; Weekend college. **Disability Services offered to physically disabled students:** Tutors. **Career services:** Alumni services; Career assessment; Career/job search classes; Internships

CAMPUS LIFE

Environment: Village **Activities:** Student government 1 honor societies. **Athletics (Intercollegiate):** *Men:* baseball, basketball, cross-country, soccer. *Women:* basketball, softball.

ADMISSIONS

Test Scores: Minimum paper TOEFL 500. **Basis for Candidate Selection:** *Important factors considered include:* rigor of secondary school record, recommendation(s).* **Freshman Admission Requirements:** High school diploma is required and GED is accepted; High school diploma is required and GED is not accepted **Transfer Admission Requirements:** college transcript(s), Minimum college GPA of 2.0 required. Lowest grade transferable C. **General Admission Information:** Application fee $25. Nonfall registration accepted. Admission may be deferred for a maximum of 1 year.

COSTS AND FINANCIAL AID

Annual tuition $6,060. Required fees $50. Average book expense $500. **Required Forms and Deadlines:** FAFSA. *Student Employment:* Federal Work-Study Program available.

WILMINGTON COLLEGE (OH)

1870 Quaker Way, Wilmington, OH
Phone: 937-382-6661 • **CEEB Code:** 1909
Website: www.wilmington.edu • **ACT Code:** 3362

This private school, affiliated with the Quaker Church, was founded in 1870. It has a 65 acre campus.

RATINGS
Admissions Selectivity Rating: 91   **Fire Safety Rating:** 60*   **Green Rating:** 60*

STUDENTS AND FACULTY
Enrollment: 1,274. **Student Body:** 56% female, 44% male, 6% out-of-state, 1% international. Asian <1%, African American 11%, Caucasian 72%, Hispanic 1%, Native American 1%, Pacific Islander 0%, Two or more races 3%, Race unknown 11%.
Retention and Graduation: 67% freshmen return for sophomore year.
Faculty: Student/faculty ratio 14:1. 66 full-time faculty, 0% of classes are taught by teaching assistants.

ACADEMICS
Degrees: Bachelor's; **Master's Classes:** Most classes have 10-19 students. Most lab/discussion sessions have 10-19 students. **Most popular majors:** Bible/Biblical Studies; Psychology, General; Business Administration And Management, General. **Special Study Options:** Cross-registration; Double major; Dual enrollment; Honors program; Independent study; Internships; Liberal arts/career combination; Student-designed major; Study abroad; Teacher certification program; Weekend college. **Disability Services offered to physically disabled students:** Note-taking services; Reader services; Tape recorders; Tutors. **Career services:** Alumni services; Internships

FACILITIES
Housing: Apartments for single students; Coed dorms; Fraternity/sorority housing; Men's dorms; Women's dorms 100% of campus accessible to physically diasbled. **Special Academic Facilities/Equipment:** Hiroshima-Nagasaki memorial collection and peace resource center, education lab, language lab, three farms, observatory, electron microscope.

CAMPUS LIFE
Environment: Rural **Activities:** Campus Ministries; Choral groups; Drama/theater; Music ensembles; Musical theater; Pep band; Student government; Student newspaper; Yearbook 48 registered organizations, 3 honor societies, 3 religious organizations. 6 fraternities, 5 sororities. **Athletics (Intercollegiate):** *Men:* baseball, basketball, cheerleading, cross-country, football, golf, soccer, swimming, tennis, track/field (outdoor), wrestling. *Women:* basketball, cheerleading, cross-country, golf, soccer, softball, swimming, tennis, track/field (outdoor), volleyball. **On-Campus Highlights:** Residence Hall room, Athletic Center, Student Center/Dining Hall, Computer labs, Class room

ADMISSIONS
Freshman Academic Profile: Average high school GPA 3.2. 11% in top 10% of high school class, 36% in top 25% of high school class, 70% in top 50% of high school class. **Test Scores:** SAT Math middle 50% range 420-550. SAT EBRW middle 50% range 440-560. ACT middle 50% range 18-23. Minimum paper TOEFL 500. **Basis for Candidate Selection:** *Very important factors considered include:* academic GPA. *Important factors considered include:* rigor of secondary school record, class rank, standardized test scores, talent/ability, character/personal qualities, alumni/ae relation. *Other factors considered include:* recommendation(s), interview, extracurricular activities, volunteer work, level of applicant's interest. **Freshman Admission Requirements:** High school diploma is required and GED is accepted *Academic units required:* 4 English, 2 math, 2 science, 2 science labs, *Academic units recommended:* 2 foreign language, 2 social studies. **Freshman Admission Statistics:** 1,651 applied, 28.3% admitted, 45% enrolled. **Transfer Admission Requirements:** college transcript(s), statement of good standing from prior institution(s). Minimum college GPA of 2.0 required. Lowest grade transferable C-. **General Admission Information:** Regular application deadline 8/1. Nonfall registration accepted.

COSTS AND FINANCIAL AID
Annual tuition $25,214. Room and board $8,520. Required fees $500. *Student Employment:* Federal Work-Study Program available. Institutional employment available.

WILSON COLLEGE

1015 Philadelphia Avenue, Chambersburg, PA 17201
Phone: 717-262-2002 • **Financial Aid Phone:** 717-262-2016
E-mail: admissions@wilson.edu • **CEEB Code:** 2979
Fax: 717-262-2546 • **ACT Code:** 3758

This private school, affiliated with the Presbyterian Church, was founded in 1869. It has a 300 acre campus.

RATINGS
Admissions Selectivity Rating: 85   **Fire Safety Rating:** 87   **Green Rating:** 60*

STUDENTS AND FACULTY
Enrollment: 515. **Student Body:** 92% female, 8% male, 24% out-of-state, 4% international (10 countries represented). Asian <1%, African American 5%, Caucasian 76%, Hispanic 3%, Native American 0%, Pacific Islander 0%, Two or more races 2%, Race unknown 10%.
Retention and Graduation: 57% freshmen return for sophomore year. 30% grads go on to further study within 1 year. 6% grads pursue arts and sciences degrees. 9% grads pursue law degrees. 8% grads pursue business degrees. 8% grads pursue medical degrees. **Faculty:** Student/faculty ratio 10:1. 45 full-time faculty, 82% hold PhDs, 7% are members of minority groups, 56% are women. 0% of classes are taught by teaching assistants.

ACADEMICS
Degrees: Associate; Bachelor's; **Master's Classes:** Most classes have 10-19 students. Most lab/discussion sessions have 10-19 students. **Most popular majors:** Equestrian/Equine Studies; Elementary Education And Teaching; Veterinary/Animal Health Technology/Technician And Veterinary Assistant. **Special Study Options:** Cooperative education program; Cross-registration; Double major; English as a Second Language (ESL); Honors program; Independent study; Internships; Liberal arts/career combination; Student-designed major; Study abroad; Teacher certification program. Honors programs: Wilson Scholars Program. **Disability Services offered to physically disabled students:** Note-taking services; Reader services; Tape recorders; Tutors. **Career services:** Alumni network; Alumni services; Career assessment; Career/job search classes; Internships

FACILITIES
Housing: Women's dorms 49% of campus accessible to physically diasbled. **Special Academic Facilities/Equipment:** Archives, Bogigian Art gallery, Dance Studio, Helen M. Beach '24 Veterinary Medical Center, Penn Hall Equestrian Center, Natural History Museum, electron microscope, NMR spectrometer. **Computers:** 50% of classrooms, 100% of dining areas, 100% of student union, 15% of common outdoor areas have wireless network access. Students can register for classes online. Administrative functions (other than registration) can be performed online.

CAMPUS LIFE
Environment: Village **Activities:** Campus Ministries; Choral groups; Dance; Drama/theater; International Student Organization; Literary magazine; Music ensembles; Radio station; Student government; Student newspaper; Yearbook 35 registered organizations, 1 honor society, 4 religious organizations. **Athletics (Intercollegiate):** *Women:* basketball, field hockey, gymnastics, lacrosse, soccer, softball, tennis. **On-Campus Highlights:** Penn Hall Equestrian Center, Helen M. Beach '24 Veterinary Medical Center, Complex for Science, Math & Technology, Prentis Hall Women with Children Residence, Lenfest Commons with Fitness Center and Coffee House **Environmental Initiatives:** Organic farm

ADMISSIONS
Freshman Academic Profile: Average high school GPA 3.4. 22% in top 10% of high school class, 50% in top 25% of high school class, 82% in top 50% of high school class. 84% from public high schools. **Test Scores:** SAT Math middle 50% range 430-550. SAT EBRW middle 50% range 450-570. ACT middle 50% range 21-23. Minimum internet-based TOEFL 61. Minimum paper TOEFL 500. **Basis for Candidate Selection:** *Very important factors considered include:* rigor of secondary school record. *Important factors considered include:* class rank, academic GPA, recommendation(s). *Other factors considered include:* application essay, standardized test scores, interview, extracurricular activities, talent/ability, character/personal qualities, alumni/ae relation, volunteer work, work experience. **Freshman Admission Requirements:** High school diploma is required and GED is accepted *Academic units required:* 4 English, 3 math, 2 science, 2 science labs, 2 foreign language, 4 social studies. **Freshman Admission Statistics:** 563 applied, 50.3% admitted, 33% enrolled. **Transfer Admission Requirements:** High school transcript, college transcript(s), essay or personal statement, Minimum

college GPA of 2.0 required. Lowest grade transferable C. **General Admission Information:** Priority deadline 4/30. Nonfall registration accepted. Admission may be deferred for a maximum of 1 year.

COSTS AND FINANCIAL AID

Annual tuition $28,745. Room and board $9,710. Required fees $595. Average book expense $1,000. **Required Forms and Deadlines:** FAFSA; Institution's own financial aid form; State aid form. **Notification of Awards:** Applicants will be notified of awards on a rolling basis beginning 2/15. **Types of Aid:** *Need-based scholarships/grants:* College/university scholarship or grant aid from institutional funds; Federal Pell; Private scholarships; SEOG; State scholarships/grants. *Loans: Student Employment:* Federal Work-Study Program available. Institutional employment available. **Financial Aid Statistics:** 100% needy freshmen, 99% needy undergrads receive need-based scholarship or grant aid. 11% freshmen, 9% undergrads receive non-need-based scholarship or grant aid. 83% freshmen, 81% undergrads receive need-based self-help aid. 0% freshmen, 0% undergrads receive athletic scholarships. 99% freshmen, 97% undergrads receive any aid. **Criteria for awarding aid:** *Need-based:* Academics, Art, Leadership, Music/drama, Religious affiliation *Non-need-based:* Academics, Alumni affiliation, Religious affiliation, State/district residency.

WINGATE UNIVERSITY

P.O. Box 159, Wingate, NC 28174
Phone: 704-233-8200 • **Financial Aid Phone:** 704-233-8209
E-mail: admit@wingate.edu • **CEEB Code:** 5908
Fax: 704-233-8110 • **Website:** www.wingate.edu • **ACT Code:** 3176

This private school was founded in 1896. It has a 390 acre campus.

RATINGS

Admissions Selectivity Rating: 72   **Fire Safety Rating:** 87   **Green Rating:** 60*

STUDENTS AND FACULTY

Enrollment: 2,586. **Student Body:** 61% female, 39% male, 27% out-of-state, 4% international (21 countries represented). Asian 2%, African American 17%, Caucasian 58%, Hispanic 4%, Native American <1%, Pacific Islander <1%, Two or more races 9%, Race unknown 4%.
Retention and Graduation: 73% freshmen return for sophomore year. 41% freshmen graduate within 4 years. 53% freshmen graduate within 6 years. 20% grads go on to further study within 1 year. 9% grads pursue arts and sciences degrees. 2% grads pursue law degrees. 8% grads pursue business degrees. 1% grads pursue medical degrees. **Faculty:** Student/faculty ratio 16:1. 195 full-time faculty, 86% hold PhDs, 10% are members of minority groups, 56% are women. 0% of classes are taught by teaching assistants.

ACADEMICS

Degrees: Bachelor's; Doctoral/Professional; Doctoral/Research; Master's; Post-Bachelor's certificate; Post-Master's certificate **Classes:** Most classes have 20-29 students. Most lab/discussion sessions have 10-19 students. **Most popular majors:** Biology/Biological Sciences, General; Psychology, General; Business Administration And Management, General. **Special Study Options:** Cross-registration; Double major; Dual enrollment; Honors program; Independent study; Internships; Study abroad; Teacher certification program. **Honors programs:** Our University Honors program offers students 18 hours of honors courses covering a spectrum of disciplines. Students may travel to New York City as part of the program. **Disability Services offered to physically disabled students:** Note-taking services; Tape recorders; Tutors. **Career services:** Alumni network; Career assessment; Career/job search classes; Internships

FACILITIES

Housing: Apartments for single students; Coed dorms; Fraternity/sorority housing; Men's dorms; Special housing for disabled student; Women's dorms 95% of campus accessible to physically diasbled. **Special Academic Facilities/Equipment:** Batte Fine Arts Center **Computers:** Administrative functions (other than registration) can be performed online.

CAMPUS LIFE

Environment: Town **Activities:** Campus Ministries; Choral groups; Drama/theater; International Student Organization; Literary magazine; Model UN; Music ensembles; Opera; Pep band; Student government; Student newspaper; Yearbook 45 registered organizations, 10 honor societies, 8 religious organizations. 4 fraternities, 4 sororities. **Athletics (Intercollegiate):** *Men:* baseball, basketball, cheerleading, cross-country, football, golf, lacrosse, soccer, swimming, tennis. *Women:* basketball, cheerleading, cross-country, golf, soccer, softball, swimming, tennis, volleyball. **On-Campus Highlights:** George A.

Batte Jr. Fine Arts Center, Kondike Grill, Irwin Belk Football Stadium, Ethel's Cafe (in the Ethel K. Smith Library), Jefferson Clubhouse

ADMISSIONS

Freshman Academic Profile: Average high school GPA 3.3. 18% in top 10% of high school class, 50% in top 25% of high school class, 72% in top 50% of high school class. 85% from public high schools. **Test Scores:** SAT Math middle 50% range 480-570. SAT EBRW middle 50% range 470-570. ACT middle 50% range 18-23. Minimum paper TOEFL 550. **Basis for Candidate Selection:** *Very important factors considered include:* academic GPA, standardized test scores. *Important factors considered include:* rigor of secondary school record, class rank. *Other factors considered include:* recommendation(s), extracurricular activities, talent/ability, character/personal qualities. **Freshman Admission Requirements:** High school diploma is required and GED is accepted *Academic units recommended:* 4 English, 3 math, 2 science, 1 science labs, 2 foreign language, 2 social studies. **Freshman Admission Statistics:** 15,198 applied, 93.2% admitted, 8% enrolled. **Transfer Admission Requirements:** High school transcript, college transcript(s), statement of good standing from prior institution(s). Minimum college GPA of 2.0 required. Lowest grade transferable C. **General Admission Information:** Priority deadline 4/1. Nonfall registration accepted. Admission may be deferred for a maximum of 1 year.

COSTS AND FINANCIAL AID

Annual tuition $33,166. Room and board $10,780. Average book expense $2,000. **Required Forms and Deadlines:** FAFSA; State aid form. **Notification of Awards:** Applicants will be notified of awards on a rolling basis beginning 3/1. **Types of Aid:** *Need-based scholarships/grants:* College/university scholarship or grant aid from institutional funds; Federal Pell; Private scholarships; SEOG; State scholarships/grants. *Loans:* Direct PLUS loans; Direct Subsidized Stafford Loans; Direct Unsubsidized Stafford Loans. *Student Employment:* Federal Work-Study Program available. Institutional employment available. **Financial Aid Statistics:** 100% needy freshmen, 99% needy undergrads receive need-based scholarship or grant aid. 17% freshmen, 16% undergrads receive non-need-based scholarship or grant aid. 82% freshmen, 84% undergrads receive need-based self-help aid. 11% freshmen, 11% undergrads receive athletic scholarships. 97% freshmen, 96% undergrads receive any aid. **Criteria for awarding aid:** *Need-based:* Athletics *Non-need-based:* Academics, Alumni affiliation, Art, Athletics, Leadership, Music/drama, Religious affiliation.

WINONA STATE UNIVERSITY

P.O. Box 5838, Winona, MN 55987
Phone: 507-457-5100 • **Financial Aid Phone:** 507-457-5090
E-mail: admissions@winona.edu • **CEEB Code:** 6680
Fax: 507-457-5620 • **Website:** www.winona.edu • **ACT Code:** 2162

This public school was founded in 1858. It has a 125 acre campus.

RATINGS

Admissions Selectivity Rating: 80   **Fire Safety Rating:** 93   **Green Rating:** 81

STUDENTS AND FACULTY

Enrollment: 7,280. **Student Body:** 64% female, 36% male, 28% out-of-state, 2% international (45 countries represented). Asian 2%, African American 3%, Caucasian 85%, Hispanic 3%, Native American <1%, Pacific Islander <1%, Two or more races 3%, Race unknown 1%.
Retention and Graduation: 78% freshmen return for sophomore year. 38% freshmen graduate within 4 years. 61% freshmen graduate within 6 years. 11% grads go on to further study within 1 year. **Faculty:** Student/faculty ratio 18:1. 338 full-time faculty, 83% hold PhDs, 15% are members of minority groups, 53% are women. 1% of classes are taught by teaching assistants.

ACADEMICS

Degrees: Associate; Bachelor's; Doctoral/Research; Master's; Post-Bachelor's certificate; Post-Master's certificate **Classes:** Most classes have 10-19 students. **Most popular majors:** Elementary Education And Teaching; Biology/Biological Sciences, General; Registered Nursing/Registered Nurse. **Special Study Options:** Distance learning; Double major; Dual enrollment; English as a Second Language (ESL); Independent study; Internships; Student-designed major; Study abroad; Teacher certification program. **Disability Services offered to physically disabled students:** Note-taking services; Reader services; Tape recorders. **Career services:** Alumni network; Alumni services; Career assessment; Internships; Regional alumni

FACILITIES

Housing: Apartments for single students; Coed dorms; Men's dorms; Special housing for disabled student; Theme housing; Women's dorms 100% of campus accessible to physically diasbled. **Special Academic Facilities/Equipment:** Paul Watkins Art Gallery, KQAL Radio Station, Performing Arts Center **Computers:** 100% of classrooms, 50% of dorms, 100% of libraries, 100% of dining areas, 100% of student union, 85% of common outdoor areas have wireless network access. Students can register for classes online. Administrative functions (other than registration) can be performed online. Undergraduates are required to own a computer.

CAMPUS LIFE

Environment: Town **Activities:** Campus Ministries; Choral groups; Concert band; Dance; Drama/theater; International Student Organization; Jazz band; Literary magazine; Model UN; Music ensembles; Musical theater; Pep band; Radio station; Student government; Student newspaper; Symphony orchestra 208 registered organizations, 14 honor societies, 10 religious organizations. 2 fraternities, 3 sororities. **Athletics (Intercollegiate):** *Men:* baseball, basketball, cross-country, football, golf. *Women:* basketball, cross-country, golf, gymnastics, soccer, softball, tennis, track/field (outdoor), track/field (indoor), volleyball. **On-Campus Highlights:** The Library, Lourdes Hall—Residential College, Central Courtyard/Clock Tower/Gazebo, The Smaug—Kryzsko Commons, Integrated Wellness Complex **Environmental Initiatives:** Recycling / Post Consumer Waste Reduction

ADMISSIONS

Freshman Academic Profile: Average high school GPA 3.4. 10% in top 10% of high school class, 31% in top 25% of high school class, 70% in top 50% of high school class. **Test Scores:** ACT middle 50% range 20-25. Minimum internet-based TOEFL 68. Minimum paper TOEFL 520. **Basis for Candidate Selection:** *Very important factors considered include:* rigor of secondary school record, class rank, academic GPA, standardized test scores. **Freshman Admission Requirements:** High school diploma is required and GED is accepted *Academic units required:* 4 English, 3 math, 3 science, 3 science labs, 2 foreign language, 2 social studies, 1 history, 1 academic elective. **Freshman Admission Statistics:** 7,468 applied, 66.5% admitted, 32% enrolled. **Transfer Admission Requirements:** college transcript(s), Minimum college GPA of 2.4 required. Lowest grade transferable D. **General Admission Information:** Application fee $20. Regular application deadline 7/1. Nonfall registration accepted. Admission may be deferred for a maximum of 1 year.

COSTS AND FINANCIAL AID

Annual in-state tuition $8,066. Annual out-of-state tuition $13,298. Room and board $8,066. Required fees $2,004. Average book expense $900. **Required Forms and Deadlines:** FAFSA. **Notification of Awards:** Applicants will be notified of awards on a rolling basis beginning 12/1. **Types of Aid:** *Need-based scholarships/grants:* College/university scholarship or grant aid from institutional funds; Federal Pell; Private scholarships; SEOG; State scholarships/grants. *Loans:* Direct PLUS loans; Direct Subsidized Stafford Loans; Direct Unsubsidized Stafford Loans. *Student Employment:* Federal Work-Study Program available. Institutional employment available. **Financial Aid Statistics:** 74% needy freshmen, 69% needy undergrads receive need-based scholarship or grant aid. 18% freshmen, 10% undergrads receive non-need-based scholarship or grant aid. 84% freshmen, 88% undergrads receive need-based self-help aid. 33% freshmen, 19% undergrads receive athletic scholarships. 61% freshmen, 58% undergrads receive any aid. 76% undergrads borrow to pay for school. Average cumulative indebtedness $35,221. **Criteria for awarding aid:** *Non-need-based:* Academics, Alumni affiliation, Art, Athletics, Minority status, Music/drama.

WINTHROP UNIVERSITY

701 Oakland Avenue, Rock Hill, SC 29733
Phone: 803-323-2191 • **Financial Aid Phone:** 803-323-2189
E-mail: admissions@winthrop.edu • **CEEB Code:** 5910
Fax: 803-323-2137 • **Website:** www.winthrop.edu • **ACT Code:** 3884

This public school was founded in 1886. It has a 445 acre campus.

RATINGS

Admissions Selectivity Rating: 82   Fire Safety Rating: 92   Green Rating: 80

STUDENTS AND FACULTY

Enrollment: 4,786. **Student Body:** 68% female, 32% male, 8% out-of-state, 2% international (39 countries represented). Asian 1%, African American 30%, Caucasian 58%, Hispanic 4%, Native American <1%, Pacific Islander <1%, Two or more races 4%, Race unknown <1%.

Retention and Graduation: 77% freshmen return for sophomore year. 25% grads go on to further study within 1 year. 6% grads pursue arts and sciences degrees. 0% grads pursue law degrees. 4% grads pursue business degrees. 1% grads pursue medical degrees. **Faculty:** Student/faculty ratio 14:1. 282 full-time faculty, 89% hold PhDs, 14% are members of minority groups, 54% are women. 0% of classes are taught by teaching assistants.

ACADEMICS

Degrees: Bachelor's; Certificate; Master's; Post-Bachelor's certificate; Post-Master's certificate **Classes:** Most classes have fewer than 10 students. Most lab/discussion sessions have 10-19 students. **Most popular majors:** Biology/Biological Sciences, General; Design And Visual Communications, General; Business/Commerce, General. **Special Study Options:** Cooperative education program; Cross-registration; Distance learning; Double major; Dual enrollment; English as a Second Language (ESL); Exchange student program (domestic); Honors program; Independent study; Internships; Liberal arts/career combination; Student-designed major; Study abroad; Teacher certification program. Honors programs: The Winthrop University Honors Program is designed to enrich the college experience for highly talented and motivated students. Through interactions with outstanding faculty and peers, a vital community of scholars is created that embraces the pursuit of knowledge for the enhancement of intellectual and personal growth. **Disability Services offered to physically disabled students:** Note-taking services; Reader services; Tape recorders. **Career services:** Alumni network; Alumni services; Career assessment; Career/job search classes; Internships; Regional alumni

FACILITIES

Housing: Apartments for single students; Coed dorms; Theme housing; Women's dorms 90% of campus accessible to physically diasbled. **Special Academic Facilities/Equipment:** Art gallery, Early Childhood Laboratory School, Music Conservatory, Academic Success Center and Trading Center in the business college. **Computers:** 25% of classrooms, 10% of dorms, 100% of libraries, 100% of dining areas, 100% of student union, 10% of common outdoor areas have wireless network access. Students can register for classes online. Administrative functions (other than registration) can be performed online.

CAMPUS LIFE

Environment: Town **Activities:** Campus Ministries; Choral groups; Concert band; Dance; Drama/theater; International Student Organization; Jazz band; Literary magazine; Marching band; Model UN; Music ensembles; Musical theater; Opera; Pep band; Radio station; Student government; Student newspaper; Television station; Yearbook 184 registered organizations, 23 honor societies, 10 religious organizations. 8 fraternities, 9 sororities. **Athletics (Intercollegiate):** *Men:* baseball, basketball, cross-country, golf, soccer, tennis, track/field (outdoor). *Women:* basketball, cross-country, golf, soccer, softball, tennis, track/field (outdoor), volleyball. **On-Campus Highlights:** DiGiorgio Campus Center, Winthrop University Recreational and Research Complex, Winthrop Art Galleries, Starbucks, West Recreation Center **Environmental Initiatives:** Very strong recycling program.

ADMISSIONS

Freshman Academic Profile: Average high school GPA 3.9. 22% in top 10% of high school class, 51% in top 25% of high school class, 87% in top 50% of high school class. **Test Scores:** SAT Math middle 50% range 450-560. SAT EBRW middle 50% range 460-570. ACT middle 50% range 20-26. Minimum internet-based TOEFL 68. Minimum paper TOEFL 520. **Basis for Candidate Selection:** *Very important factors considered include:* rigor of secondary school record, academic GPA, standardized test scores. *Other factors considered include:* application essay, recommendation(s), interview, extracurricular activities, talent/ability, volunteer work. **Freshman Admission Requirements:** High school diploma is required and GED is accepted *Academic units required:* 4 English, 4 math, 3 science, 3 science labs, 2 foreign language, 2 social studies, 1 history, 1 academic elective, 1 visual/performing arts, and 1 unit from above areas or other academic areas. **Freshman Admission Statistics:** 4,876 applied, 67.1% admitted, 33% enrolled. **Transfer Admission Requirements:** college transcript(s), statement of good standing from prior institution(s). Minimum college GPA of 2.0 required. Lowest grade transferable C. **General Admission Information:** Application fee $40. Regular application deadline 5/1. Nonfall registration accepted. Admission may be deferred.

COSTS AND FINANCIAL AID

Annual in-state tuition $8,572. Annual out-of-state tuition $28,090. Room and board $8,572. Average book expense $1,000. **Required Forms and Deadlines:** FAFSA. **Notification of Awards:** Applicants will be notified of awards on a rolling basis beginning 3/1. **Types of Aid:** *Need-based scholarships/grants:* College/university scholarship or grant aid from institutional funds; Federal Pell; Private scholarships; SEOG; State scholarships/grants. *Loans:* Direct PLUS loans; Direct Subsidized Stafford Loans; Direct Unsubsidized Stafford Loans. *Student Employment:* Federal Work-Study Program available. Institutional employment available. **Financial Aid Statistics:** 99% needy freshmen, 90% needy undergrads receive need-based scholarship or grant aid. 18% freshmen, 12% undergrads receive non-need-based scholarship or grant aid. 72% freshmen, 81% undergrads receive need-based athletic scholarships. 2% freshmen, 3% undergrads receive need-based self-help aid. 70% freshmen, 83% undergrads receive any aid. **Criteria for awarding aid:** *Non-need-based:* Academics, Art, Athletics, Leadership, Music/drama.

WISCONSIN LUTHERAN COLLEGE

8800 West Bluemound Road, Milwaukee, WI 53226
Phone: 414-443-8811 • **Financial Aid Phone:** 414-443-8856
E-mail: admissions@wlc.edu • **CEEB Code:** 1513
Fax: 414-443-8514 • **Website:** www.wlc.edu • **ACT Code:** 4699

This private school, affiliated with the Lutheran Church, was founded in 1973. It has a 21 acre campus.

RATINGS
Admissions Selectivity Rating: 79   **Fire Safety Rating:** 75   **Green Rating:** 60*

STUDENTS AND FACULTY
Enrollment: 707. **Student Body:** 56% female, 44% male, 23% out-of-state, 2% international (9 countries represented). Asian 2%, African American 4%, Caucasian 89%, Hispanic 2%, Native American <1%, Race unknown 1%. **Retention and Graduation:** 76% freshmen return for sophomore year. **Faculty:** Student/faculty ratio 10:1. 60 full-time faculty, 67% hold PhDs, 33% are women. 0% of classes are taught by teaching assistants.

ACADEMICS
Degrees: Bachelor's; **Master's Classes:** Most classes have fewer than 10 students. Most lab/discussion sessions have 10-19 students. **Most popular majors:** Speech Communication And Rhetoric; Biology/Biological Sciences, General; Psychology, General. **Special Study Options:** Double major; Dual enrollment; English as a Second Language (ESL); Independent study; Internships; Student-designed major; Study abroad; Teacher certification program. **Disability Services offered to physically disabled students:** Note-taking services; Reader services; Tape recorders; Tutors. **Career services:** Alumni network; Career assessment; Internships

FACILITIES
Housing: Apartments for single students; Men's dorms; Women's dorms 90% of campus accessible to physically diasbled. **Special Academic Facilities/ Equipment:** Center for Arts and Performance, Science Hall **Computers:** Students can register for classes online.

CAMPUS LIFE
Environment: Metropolis **Activities:** Campus Ministries; Choral groups; Concert band; Dance; International Student Organization; Jazz band; Music ensembles; Pep band; Student government; Student newspaper 31 registered organizations. **Athletics (Intercollegiate):** *Men:* baseball, basketball, cross-country, football, golf, soccer, tennis, track/field (outdoor), track/field (indoor). *Women:* basketball, cross-country, golf, soccer, softball, tennis, track/field (outdoor), track/field (indoor), volleyball. **On-Campus Highlights:** Residence Halls, Center for Arts and Performance, Chapel, The Warrior Underground, The Recreation Complex

ADMISSIONS
Freshman Academic Profile: Average high school GPA 3.3. 18% in top 10% of high school class, 43% in top 25% of high school class, 77% in top 50% of high school class. **Test Scores:** ACT middle 50% range 21-26. Minimum paper TOEFL 550. **Basis for Candidate Selection:** *Important factors considered include:* rigor of secondary school record, academic GPA, standardized test scores, recommendation(s), character/personal qualities, religious affiliation/ commitment, level of applicant's interest. *Other factors considered include:* class rank, application essay, interview, extracurricular activities, talent/ability, first generation, alumni/ae relation, racial/ethnic status, volunteer work, work experience. **Freshman Admission Requirements:** High school diploma is required and GED is accepted *Academic units required:* 4 English, 3 math, 2 science, 1 science labs, 2 foreign language, 2 history, 3 academic electives, *Academic units recommended:* 4 English, 4 math, 3 science, 2 science labs, 4 foreign language, 2 history, 3 academic electives. **Freshman Admission Statistics:** 646 applied, 76.3% admitted, 46% enrolled. **Transfer Admission Requirements:** college transcript(s), statement of good standing from prior institution(s). Minimum college GPA of 2.5 required. Lowest grade transferable CD. **General Admission Information:** Application fee $20. Priority deadline 3/1. Nonfall registration accepted. Admission may be deferred for a maximum of 1 semester.

COSTS AND FINANCIAL AID
Annual tuition $21,040. Room and board $7,700. Required fees $140. Average book expense $700. **Required Forms and Deadlines:** Business/Farm Supplement; FAFSA; Institution's own financial aid form. **Notification of Awards:** Applicants will be notified of awards on a rolling basis beginning 3/15. **Types of Aid:** *Need-based scholarships/grants:* College/university scholarship or grant aid from institutional funds; Federal Pell; Private scholarships; SEOG; State scholarships/grants. *Loans: Student Employment:* Federal Work-Study Program available. Institutional employment available. **Financial Aid Statistics:** 100% needy freshmen, 99% needy undergrads receive need-based scholarship or grant aid. 11% freshmen, 10% undergrads receive non-need-based scholarship or grant aid. 91% freshmen, 91% undergrads receive need-based self-help aid. 0% freshmen, 0% undergrads receive athletic scholarships. 100% freshmen, 98% undergrads receive any aid. **Criteria for awarding aid:** *Need-based:* Academics, Leadership, Minority status *Non-need-based:* Academics, Art, Leadership, Music/drama.

WITTENBERG UNIVERSITY

P.O. Box 720, Springfield, OH 45501
Phone: 937-327-6314 • **Financial Aid Phone:** 937-327-7321
E-mail: admission@wittenberg.edu • **CEEB Code:** 1922
Fax: 937-327-6379 • **Website:** www.wittenberg.edu • **ACT Code:** 3364

This private school, affiliated with the Lutheran Church, was founded in 1845. It has a 114 acre campus.

RATINGS
Admissions Selectivity Rating: 79   **Fire Safety Rating:** 98   **Green Rating:** 60*

STUDENTS AND FACULTY
Enrollment: 1,786. **Student Body:** 53% female, 47% male, 24% out-of-state, 1% international (12 countries represented). Asian 1%, African American 10%, Caucasian 76%, Hispanic 4%, Native American <1%, Pacific Islander <1%, Two or more races 6%, Race unknown 1%. **Retention and Graduation:** 72% freshmen return for sophomore year. 61% freshmen graduate within 4 years. 67% freshmen graduate within 6 years. 28% grads go on to further study within 1 year. 10% grads pursue arts and sciences degrees. 3% grads pursue law degrees. 2% grads pursue business degrees. 2% grads pursue medical degrees. **Faculty:** Student/faculty ratio 13:1. 115 full-time faculty, 94% hold PhDs, 14% are members of minority groups, 45% are women. 0% of classes are taught by teaching assistants.

ACADEMICS
Degrees: Bachelor's; **Master's Classes:** Most classes have 20-29 students. Most lab/discussion sessions have 20-29 students. **Most popular majors:** Biology/Biological Sciences, General; Business/Commerce, General. **Special Study Options:** Cross-registration; Distance learning; Double major; Dual enrollment; Honors program; Independent study; Internships; Liberal arts/career combination; Student-designed major; Study abroad; Teacher certification program. Honors programs: Honors Program, 3-2 Engineering Program, Pre-Health Programs. **Disability Services offered to physically disabled students:** Note-taking services; Reader services; Tape recorders; Tutors. **Career services:** Alumni network; Alumni services; Career assessment; Career/job search classes; Internships; Regional alumni

FACILITIES
Housing: Apartments for married students; Apartments for single students; Coed dorms; Fraternity/sorority housing; Special housing for disabled student; Special housing for international students; Women's dorms 81% of campus accessible to physically diasbled. **Special Academic Facilities/Equipment:** Language lab, electron microscope, observatory. **Computers:** 50% of classrooms, 100% of libraries, 100% of dining areas, 100% of student union, 100% of common outdoor areas have wireless network access. Students can register for classes online. Administrative functions (other than registration) can be performed online.

CAMPUS LIFE
Environment: Town **Activities:** Campus Ministries; Choral groups; Concert band; Dance; Drama/theater; International Student Organization; Jazz band; Literary magazine; Model UN; Music ensembles; Musical theater; Opera; Pep band; Radio station; Student government; Student newspaper; Student-run

film society; Symphony orchestra; Yearbook 126 registered organizations, 24 honor societies, 10 religious organizations. 6 fraternities, 5 sororities. **Athletics (Intercollegiate):** *Men:* baseball, basketball, cross-country, diving, football, golf, lacrosse, soccer, swimming, tennis, track/field (outdoor), track/field (indoor). *Women:* basketball, cheerleading, cross-country, diving, field hockey, golf, lacrosse, soccer, softball, swimming, tennis, track/field (outdoor), track/field (indoor), volleyball. **On-Campus Highlights:** HPERC Athletic Center, Benham Pence Student Center, Hollenbeck Hall, Weaver Observatory, Thomas Library

ADMISSIONS

Freshman Academic Profile: Average high school GPA 3.4. 14% in top 10% of high school class, 39% in top 25% of high school class, 72% in top 50% of high school class. 80% from public high schools. **Test Scores:** SAT Math middle 50% range 510-575. SAT EBRW middle 50% range 540-650. ACT middle 50% range 22-28. Minimum paper TOEFL 550. **Basis for Candidate Selection:** *Very important factors considered include:* rigor of secondary school record, class rank, academic GPA. *Important factors considered include:* application essay, recommendation(s), extracurricular activities, talent/ability, character/personal qualities, volunteer work. *Other factors considered include:* standardized test scores, interview, first generation, alumni/ae relation, work experience. **Freshman Admission Requirements:** High school diploma is required and GED is accepted *Academic units required:* 4 English, 3 math, 3 science, 2 science labs, 2 foreign language, 2 history, *Academic units recommended:* 4 English, 4 math, 5 science, 2 science labs, 3 foreign language, 3 history. **Freshman Admission Statistics:** 7,249 applied, 72.2% admitted, 10% enrolled. **Transfer Admission Requirements:** college transcript(s), Minimum college GPA of 2.0 required. Lowest grade transferable C. **General Admission Information:** Application fee $40. Priority deadline 3/15. Nonfall registration accepted. Admission may be deferred for a maximum of 1 year.

COSTS AND FINANCIAL AID

Annual tuition $38,680. Room and board $10,356. Required fees $800. Average book expense $1,000. **Required Forms and Deadlines:** FAFSA. **Notification of Awards:** Applicants will be notified of awards on a rolling basis beginning 3/1. **Types of Aid:** *Need-based scholarships/grants:* College/university scholarship or grant aid from institutional funds; Federal Pell; Private scholarships; SEOG; State scholarships/grants; United Negro College Fund. *Loans:* Direct PLUS loans; Direct Subsidized Stafford Loans; Direct Unsubsidized Stafford Loans. *Student Employment:* Federal Work-Study Program available. Institutional employment available. **Financial Aid Statistics:** 100% needy freshmen, 100% needy undergrads receive need-based scholarship or grant aid. 0% undergrads receive non-need-based scholarship or grant aid. 82% freshmen, 80% undergrads receive need-based self-help aid. 0% freshmen, 0% undergrads receive athletic scholarships. 100% freshmen, 95% undergrads receive any aid. 73% undergrads borrow to pay for school. Average cumulative indebtedness $34,178. **Criteria for awarding aid:** *Need-based:* Academics, Alumni affiliation, Art, Leadership, Minority status, Music/drama, Religious affiliation *Non-need-based:* Academics, Alumni affiliation, Art, Minority status, Music/drama, Religious affiliation, State/district residency.

WOFFORD COLLEGE

429 North Church Street, Spartanburg, SC 29303-3663
Phone: 864-597-4130 • **Financial Aid Phone:** (864) 597-4160
E-mail: admission@wofford.edu • **CEEB Code:** 5912
Fax: 864-597-4147 • **Website:** www.wofford.edu • **ACT Code:** 3886

This private school, affiliated with the Methodist Church, was founded in 1854. It has a 175 acre campus.

RATINGS

Admissions Selectivity Rating: 86   **Fire Safety Rating:** 94   **Green Rating:** 60*

STUDENTS AND FACULTY

Enrollment: 1,582. **Student Body:** 53% female, 47% male, 46% out-of-state, 2% international (24 countries represented). Asian 2%, African American 8%, Caucasian 79%, Hispanic 4%, Native American <1%, Pacific Islander <1%, Two or more races 4%, Race unknown <1%.
Retention and Graduation: 90% freshmen return for sophomore year. 77% freshmen graduate within 4 years. 81% freshmen graduate within 6 years.
Faculty: Student/faculty ratio 10:1. 146 full-time faculty, 89% hold PhDs, 11%

are members of minority groups, 42% are women. 0% of classes are taught by teaching assistants.

ACADEMICS

Degrees: Bachelor's **Classes:** Most classes have 10-19 students. **Most popular majors:** Biology/Biological Sciences, General; Business/Managerial Economics; Finance, General. **Special Study Options:** Accelerated program; Cross-registration; Double major; Dual enrollment; Independent study; Internships; Student-designed major; Study abroad; Teacher certification program. Combined degree programs: BA/MEng. **Disability Services offered to physically disabled students:** Note-taking services; Reader services; Tape recorders; Tutors. **Career services:** Alumni network; Alumni services; Career assessment; Career/job search classes; Internships; Regional alumni

FACILITIES

Housing: Apartments for single students; Coed dorms; Special housing for disabled student; Wellness housing 85% of campus accessible to physically disabled. **Special Academic Facilities/Equipment:** In 2017 the Rosalind Sallenger Richardson Center for the Arts opened as the home of academic programs in art history, film and digital media, studio art and theatre. The building includes several gallery spaces and a 300-seat theatre as well as practice and workshop spaces. Other gallery spaces on campus include the Sandor Teszler Library Gallery and the Martha Cloud Chapman Gallery. The Michael S. Brown Village Center is the home to high-impact programs that blend the curricular with the co-curricular so learning at Wofford happens around the clock and around the globe. The MSBVC includes The Space in the Mungo Center (professional development, internship and entrepreneurship assistance), the Center for Community-Based Learning (a program focused on civic engagement and social impact) and International Programs (the home of Wofford's nationally ranked study abroad program and support for international students and faculty). The college also offers the Goodall Environmental Studies Center located in Glendale Shoals as a laboratory and classroom space where students interact with the local community and environment. **Computers:** 100% of classrooms, 10% of dorms, 100% of libraries, 100% of dining areas, 100% of student union, 40% of common outdoor areas have wireless network access. Students can register for classes online. Administrative functions (other than registration) can be performed online.

CAMPUS LIFE

Environment: City **Activities:** Campus Ministries; Choral groups; Concert band; Dance; Drama/theater; International Student Organization; Jazz band; Literary magazine; Music ensembles; Pep band; Radio station; Student government; Student newspaper; Yearbook 105 registered organizations, 10 honor societies, 8 religious organizations. 8 fraternities, 4 sororities. **Athletics (Intercollegiate):** *Men:* baseball, basketball, cross-country, football, golf, riflery, soccer, tennis, track/field (outdoor), track/field (indoor). *Women:* basketball, cross-country, golf, riflery, soccer, tennis, track/field (outdoor), track/field (indoor), volleyball. **On-Campus Highlights:** The Wofford Village, The Rosalind Sallenger Richardson Center for the Arts, Historic Main Building/Leonard Auditorium, The Stuart H. Johnson Greek Village, Jerry Richardson Indoor Stadium **Environmental Initiatives:** The Milliken Sustainability Initiative at Wofford College is an innovative program that connects the college with both the Northside and Glendale neighborhoods near Wofford's campus through exploration of community and sustainability. The initiative includes a new energy metering and monitoring system at the college with savings fueling student social entrepreneurs and their sustainable ideas.

ADMISSIONS

Freshman Academic Profile: Average high school GPA 3.7. 43% in top 10% of high school class, 76% in top 25% of high school class, 95% in top 50% of high school class. 63% from public high schools. **Test Scores:** SAT Math middle 50% range 550-650. SAT EBRW middle 50% range 570-660. ACT middle 50% range 24-30. Minimum internet-based TOEFL 80. Minimum paper TOEFL 550. **Basis for Candidate Selection:** *Very important factors considered include:* rigor of secondary school record, academic GPA. *Important factors considered include:* class rank, application essay, extracurricular activities, talent/ability, character/personal qualities. *Other factors considered include:* standardized test scores, recommendation(s), interview, first generation, alumni/ae relation, geographical residence, state residency, religious affiliation/commitment, racial/ethnic status, volunteer work, work experience, level of applicant's interest. **Freshman Admission Requirements:** High school diploma is required and GED is accepted *Academic units required:* 4 English, 4 math, 3 science, 3 science labs, 3 foreign language, 3 social studies, *Academic units recommended:* 4 English, 4 math, 3 science, 3 science labs, 3 foreign language, 3 social studies, 1 history, 1 academic elective, 1 computer science, 1 visual/performing arts. **Freshman Admission Statistics:** 3,092 applied, 69.3% admitted, 21% enrolled. **Transfer Admission Requirements:** High school transcript, college transcript(s), essay or personal statement, standardized test scores, statement of good standing from prior institution(s). Minimum college GPA of 2.5 required. Lowest grade transferable C. **General Admission Information:** Application fee $35. Regular application deadline 1/15. Nonfall registration accepted. Admission may be deferred for a maximum of 1 year.

COSTS AND FINANCIAL AID

Annual tuition $42,335. Room and board $12,685. Required fees $1,510. Average book expense $1,200. **Required Forms and Deadlines:** FAFSA. **Notification of Awards:** Applicants will be notified of awards on or about 3/15. **Types of Aid:** *Need-based scholarships/grants:* College/university scholarship or grant aid from institutional funds; Federal Pell; Private scholarships; SEOG; State scholarships/grants. *Loans:* Direct PLUS loans; Direct Subsidized Stafford Loans; Direct Unsubsidized Stafford Loans. *Student Employment:* Federal Work-Study Program available. Institutional employment available. **Financial Aid Statistics:** 100% needy freshmen, 100% needy undergrads receive need-based scholarship or grant aid. 36% freshmen, 31% undergrads receive non-need-based scholarship or grant aid. 49% freshmen, 54% undergrads receive need-based self-help aid. 9% freshmen, 12% undergrads receive athletic scholarships. 96% freshmen, 94% undergrads receive any aid. Average cumulative indebtedness $31,102. **Criteria for awarding aid:** *Need-based:* Job skills *Non-need-based:* Academics, Alumni affiliation, Art, Athletics, Job skills, Leadership, Minority status, Music/drama, Religious affiliation, State/district residency.

WOODBURY UNIVERSITY

7500 N Glenoaks Boulevard, Burbank, CA 91504-1052
Phone: 818-252-5221 • **Financial Aid Phone:** 818-252-5273
E-mail: info@woodbury.edu • **CEEB Code:** 4955
Website: https://woodbury.edu/ • **ACT Code:** 481

This private school was founded in 1884. It has a 22 acre campus.

RATINGS

Admissions Selectivity Rating: 80   **Fire Safety Rating:** 95   **Green Rating:** 60*

STUDENTS AND FACULTY

Enrollment: 1,023. **Student Body:** 51% female, 49% male, 15% out-of-state, 21% international. Asian 9%, African American 3%, Caucasian 32%, Hispanic 31%, Native American <1%, Pacific Islander <1%, Two or more races 3%, Race unknown 1%.
Retention and Graduation: 73% freshmen return for sophomore year. 26% freshmen graduate within 4 years. 52% freshmen graduate within 6 years. **Faculty:** Student/faculty ratio 9:1. 71 full-time faculty, 77% hold PhDs, 20% are members of minority groups, 39% are women. 0% of classes are taught by teaching assistants.

ACADEMICS

Degrees: Bachelor's; **Master's Classes:** Most classes have 10-19 students. Most lab/discussion sessions have 10-19 students. **Special Study Options:** Double major; Independent study; Internships; Student-designed major; Study abroad. **Disability Services offered to physically disabled students:** Note-taking services; Reader services; Tutors. **Career services:** Alumni services; Career assessment; Internships

FACILITIES

Housing: Coed dorms 90% of campus accessible to physically diasbled. **Special Academic Facilities/Equipment:** Art Gallery; Architecture Gallery; **Computers:** 100% of classrooms, 100% of libraries, 100% of dining areas, have wireless network access. Students can register for classes online. Administrative functions (other than registration) can be performed online. Undergraduates are required to own a computer.

CAMPUS LIFE

Environment: City **Activities:** International Student Organization; Student government; Student-run film society 20 registered organizations, 3 honor societies, 2 fraternities, 2 sororities.

ADMISSIONS

Freshman Academic Profile: Average high school GPA 3.3. **Test Scores:** SAT Math middle 50% range 455-588. SAT EBRW middle 50% range 500-600. ACT middle 50% range 19-24. Minimum internet-based TOEFL 61. **Basis for Candidate Selection:** *Very important factors considered include:* academic GPA. *Important factors considered include:* rigor of secondary school record. *Other factors considered include:* application essay, standardized test scores, recommendation(s), volunteer work, work experience, level of applicant's interest. **Freshman Admission Requirements:** High school diploma is required and GED is accepted *Academic units recommended:* 4 English, 4 math, 4 science, 1 science labs, 2 foreign language, 2 social studies, 2 history, 2 academic electives, 1 computer science, 1 visual/performing arts, 1 unit from above areas or other academic areas. **Freshman Admission Statistics:** 1,327

applied, 61.6% admitted, 14% enrolled. **Transfer Admission Requirements:** college transcript(s), Minimum college GPA of 2.5 required. Lowest grade transferable C. **General Admission Information:** Application fee $75. Priority deadline 3/1. Nonfall registration accepted. Admission may be deferred for a maximum of 1 year.

COSTS AND FINANCIAL AID

Annual tuition $38,370. Room and board $11,920. Required fees $1,410. Average book expense $1,917. **Required Forms and Deadlines:** CSS/Financial Aid PROFILE; FAFSA; Noncustodial PROFILE. **Notification of Awards:** Applicants will be notified of awards on a rolling basis beginning 12/1. **Types of Aid:** *Need-based scholarships/grants:* College/university scholarship or grant aid from institutional funds; Federal Pell; Private scholarships; SEOG; State scholarships/grants. *Loans:* Direct PLUS loans; Direct Subsidized Stafford Loans; Direct Unsubsidized Stafford Loans. *Student Employment:* Federal Work-Study Program available. Institutional employment available. **Financial Aid Statistics:** 98% needy freshmen, 99% needy undergrads receive need-based scholarship or grant aid. 6% freshmen, 2% undergrads receive non-need-based scholarship or grant aid. 86% freshmen, 89% undergrads receive need-based self-help aid. 0% freshmen, 0% undergrads receive athletic scholarships. 79% freshmen, 86% undergrads receive any aid. 87% undergrads borrow to pay for school. Average cumulative indebtedness $40,626. **Criteria for awarding aid:** *Non-need-based:* Academics.

WORCESTER POLYTECHNIC INSTITUTE

Best Colleges

100 Institute Road, Worcester, MA 01609
Phone: 508-831-5286 • **Financial Aid Phone:** 508-831-5469
E-mail: admissions@wpi.edu • **CEEB Code:** 3969
Fax: 508-831-5875 • **Website:** https://www.wpi.edu/ • **ACT Code:** 1942

This private school was founded in 1865. It has a 95 acre campus.

RATINGS

Admissions Selectivity Rating: 94   **Fire Safety Rating:** 91   **Green Rating:** 91

STUDENTS AND FACULTY

Enrollment: 4,337. **Student Body:** 36% female, 64% male, 57% out-of-state, 11% international (69 countries represented). Asian 3%, African American 3%, Caucasian 64%, Hispanic 9%, Native American <1%, Pacific Islander 0%, Two or more races 2%, Race unknown 8%.
Retention and Graduation: 95% freshmen return for sophomore year. 82% freshmen graduate within 4 years. 89% freshmen graduate within 6 years. 26% grads go on to further study within 1 year. 95% grads pursue arts and sciences degrees. 1% grads pursue law degrees. 2% grads pursue business degrees. 1% grads pursue medical degrees. **Faculty:** Student/faculty ratio 13:1. 389 full-time faculty, 93% hold PhDs, 17% are members of minority groups, 31% are women. 0% of classes are taught by teaching assistants.

ACADEMICS

Degrees: Bachelor's; Doctoral/Research; Master's; Post-Master's certificate **Most popular majors:** Computer Science; Electrical And Electronics Engineering; Mechanical Engineering. **Special Study Options:** Accelerated program; Cooperative education program; Cross-registration; Distance learning; Double major; English as a Second Language (ESL); Independent study; Internships; Liberal arts/career combination; Student-designed major; Study abroad; Teacher certification program. Honors programs: **Disability Services offered to physically disabled students:** Note-taking services; Reader services; Tape recorders; Tutors. **Career services:** Alumni network; Alumni services; Career assessment; Career/job search classes; Internships; Regional alumni

FACILITIES

Housing: Apartments for single students; Coed dorms; Fraternity/sorority housing; Special housing for disabled student; Wellness housing 88% of campus accessible to physically diasbled. **Special Academic Facilities/Equipment:** State-of-the-art specialized laboratories in all science and engineering research departments, including: two atomic-force microscopes, medical imaging lab, fire science lab, laser holography lab, computer music lab; Life Sciences and Bioengineering Center at Gateway Park **Computers:** 100% of classrooms, 100% of dorms, 100% of libraries, 100% of dining areas, 100% of student union, 100% of common outdoor areas have wireless network access. Students can register for classes online. Administrative functions (other than registration) can be performed online.

CAMPUS LIFE

Environment: City **Activities:** Campus Ministries; Choral groups; Concert band; Dance; Drama/theater; International Student Organization; Jazz band; Literary magazine; Model UN; Music ensembles; Musical theater; Pep band; Radio station; Student government; Student newspaper; Symphony orchestra; Yearbook 200 registered organizations, 20 honor societies, 4 religious organizations. 13 fraternities, 3 sororities. **Athletics (Intercollegiate):** *Men:* baseball, basketball, crew/rowing, cross-country, diving, football, soccer, swimming, track/field (outdoor), track/field (indoor), wrestling. *Women:* basketball, crew/rowing, cross-country, diving, field hockey, soccer, softball, swimming, track/field (outdoor), track/field (indoor), volleyball. **On-Campus Highlights:** Quadrangle, Campus Center, The Goat's Head Restaurant, Gordon Library, Sports & Recreation Center

ADMISSIONS

Freshman Academic Profile: Average high school GPA 3.9. 68% in top 10% of high school class, 92% in top 25% of high school class, 100% in top 50% of high school class. **Test Scores:** SAT Math middle 50% range 660-730. SAT EBRW middle 50% range 620-710. ACT middle 50% range 28-32. Minimum internet-based TOEFL 80. Minimum paper TOEFL 550. **Basis for Candidate Selection:** *Very important factors considered include:* rigor of secondary school record, academic GPA. *Important factors considered include:* class rank, standardized test scores, recommendation(s), extracurricular activities, character/personal qualities. *Other factors considered include:* application essay, interview, talent/ability, first generation, alumni/ae relation, geographical residence, racial/ethnic status, volunteer work, work experience, level of applicant's interest. **Freshman Admission Requirements:** High school diploma is required and GED is accepted *Academic units required:* 4 English, 4 math, 2 science, 2 science labs, *Academic units recommended:* 4 science, 2 foreign language, 2 social studies, 1 history, 1 computer science. **Freshman Admission Statistics:** 10,331 applied, 48.5% admitted, 22% enrolled. **Transfer Admission Requirements:** college transcript(s), essay or personal statement, statement of good standing from prior institution(s). Minimum college GPA of 3.0 required. Lowest grade transferable C. **General Admission Information:** Application fee $65. Regular application deadline 2/1. Nonfall registration accepted. Admission may be deferred for a maximum of 1 year.

COSTS AND FINANCIAL AID

Annual tuition $47,988. Room and board $14,218. Required fees $640. Average book expense $1,000. **Required Forms and Deadlines:** CSS/Financial Aid PROFILE; FAFSA; Noncustodial PROFILE. **Notification of Awards:** Applicants will be notified of awards on or about 4/1. **Types of Aid:** *Need-based scholarships/grants:* College/university scholarship or grant aid from institutional funds; Federal Pell; Private scholarships; SEOG; State scholarships/grants. *Loans:* Direct PLUS loans; Direct Subsidized Stafford Loans; Direct Unsubsidized Stafford Loans. *Student Employment:* Federal Work-Study Program available. Institutional employment available. **Financial Aid Statistics:** 100% needy freshmen, 96% needy undergrads receive need-based scholarship or grant aid. 32% freshmen, 34% undergrads receive non-need-based scholarship or grant aid. 53% freshmen, 54% undergrads receive need-based self-help aid. 0% freshmen, 0% undergrads receive athletic scholarships. 98% freshmen, 95% undergrads receive any aid. **Criteria for awarding aid:** *Need-based:* Academics, Minority status *Non-need-based:* Academics, Leadership, Minority status.

See page 1092.

WORCESTER STATE UNIVERSITY

486 Chandler Street, Worcester, MA 01602-2597
Phone: 508-929-8040 • **Financial Aid Phone:** 508-929-8058
E-mail: admissions@worcester.edu • **CEEB Code:** 3524
Fax: 508-929-8183 • **Website:** www.worcester.edu • **ACT Code:** 1914

This public school was founded in 1874. It has a 58 acre campus.

RATINGS

Admissions Selectivity Rating: 79   Fire Safety Rating: 99   Green Rating: 95

STUDENTS AND FACULTY

Enrollment: 4,891. **Student Body:** 59% female, 41% male, 4% out-of-state, 1% international (27 countries represented). Asian 4%, African American 8%, Caucasian 68%, Hispanic 11%, Native American <1%, Pacific Islander <1%, Two or more races 3%, Race unknown 4%.

Retention and Graduation: 80% freshmen return for sophomore year. **Faculty:** Student/faculty ratio 18:1. 204 full-time faculty, 80% hold PhDs, 13% are members of minority groups, 56% are women. 0% of classes are taught by teaching assistants.

ACADEMICS

Degrees: Bachelor's; Master's; Post-Bachelor's certificate; Post-Master's certificate **Classes:** Most classes have 10-19 students. Most lab/discussion sessions have fewer than 10 students. **Most popular majors:** Psychology, General; Criminal Justice/Safety Studies; Business Administration And Management, General. **Special Study Options:** Accelerated program; Cross-registration; Distance learning; Double major; Dual enrollment; English as a Second Language (ESL); Exchange student program (domestic); Honors program; Independent study; Internships; Liberal arts/career combination; Study abroad; Teacher certification program. Honors programs: Commonwealth Honors Program: The mission of the honors program at Worcester State University is to offer all qualified students an outstanding undergraduate experience through courses that emphasize innovative pedagogy and the values of liberal learning. Honors classes are small (often fewer than 20 students) and are designed to encourage active and lifelong learning. Small classes and extracurricular programs provide honors students with greater interaction between their peers and a select core of dedicated faculty members. In addition to stimulating classes, honors students also enjoy campus speakers, field trips to cultural centers, occasional luncheons with faculty members, and an annual dinner with the college president. Founded in 1996, the program currently enrolls 340 students and recently earned accreditation as a Commonwealth Honors Program from the Massachusetts Board of Higher Education. Combined degree programs: BA/MA. **Disability Services offered to physically disabled students:** Note-taking services; Reader services; Tape recorders; Tutors. **Career services:** Alumni network; Alumni services; Career assessment; Career/job search classes; Internships; Regional alumni

FACILITIES

Housing: Coed dorms; Men's dorms; Special housing for disabled student; Special housing for international students; Theme housing; Women's dorms 100% of campus accessible to physically diasbled. **Special Academic Facilities/Equipment:** Art Studio **Computers:** 100% of classrooms, 100% of dorms, 100% of libraries, 100% of dining areas, 100% of student union, 100% of common outdoor areas have wireless network access. Students can register for classes online. Administrative functions (other than registration) can be performed online. Undergraduates are required to own a computer.

CAMPUS LIFE

Environment: City **Activities:** Campus Ministries; Choral groups; Concert band; Dance; Drama/theater; Jazz band; Literary magazine; Music ensembles; Radio station; Student government; Student newspaper; Student-run film society; Television station; Yearbook 39 registered organizations, 17 honor societies, 1 religious organization. **Athletics (Intercollegiate):** *Men:* baseball, basketball, cheerleading, cross-country, football, golf, ice hockey, soccer, track/field (outdoor), track/field (indoor). *Women:* basketball, cheerleading, cross-country, field hockey, lacrosse, soccer, softball, tennis, track/field (outdoor), track/field (indoor), volleyball. **On-Campus Highlights:** Wellness Center, Student Center, Science and Technology Building, Food Court, Sullivan Commons Woo Cafe **Environmental Initiatives:** Last year I reported that we had installed our first (dual head) charging station. It was installed in July of 2015 and saw limited activity for the rest of 2015. This year I am happy to report that 2016 saw more than a half dozed EV's purchased by members of our campus community. We are now getting ready to install our second charging station because the first is full every day. This office ran two more "EV Test Drive Days" which were both successful.

ADMISSIONS

Freshman Academic Profile: Average high school GPA 3.2. 91% from public high schools. **Test Scores:** SAT Math middle 50% range 460-560. SAT EBRW middle 50% range 430-540. ACT middle 50% range 20-26. Minimum internet-based TOEFL 79. Minimum paper TOEFL 550. **Basis for Candidate Selection:** *Very important factors considered include:* rigor of secondary school record, academic GPA, standardized test scores. *Important factors considered include:* class rank, character/personal qualities. *Other factors considered include:* application essay, recommendation(s), extracurricular activities, talent/ability, first generation, alumni/ae relation, geographical residence, state residency, racial/ethnic status, volunteer work. **Freshman Admission Requirements:** High school diploma is required and GED is accepted *Academic units required:* 4 English, 4 math, 3 science, 2 science labs, 2 foreign language, 1 social studies, 1 history, 2 academic electives, *Academic units recommended:* 3 science labs. **Freshman Admission Statistics:** 3,876 applied, 70.6% admitted, 29% enrolled. **Transfer Admission Requirements:** High school transcript, college transcript(s), statement of good standing from prior institution(s). Minimum college GPA of 2.5 required. Lowest grade transferable C-. **General Admission Information:** Application fee $50. Priority deadline 3/1. Regular application deadline 5/1. Nonfall registration accepted. Admission may be deferred for a maximum of 1 year.

COSTS AND FINANCIAL AID

Annual in-state tuition $12,006. Annual out-of-state tuition $7,050. Room and board $12,006. Required fees $8,562. Average book expense $1,368. **Required Forms and Deadlines:** FAFSA. **Notification of Awards:** Applicants will be notified of awards on a rolling basis beginning 3/1. **Types of Aid:** *Need-based scholarships/grants:* College/university scholarship or grant aid from institutional funds; Federal Pell; Private scholarships; SEOG; State scholarships/grants. *Loans:* Direct PLUS loans; Direct Subsidized Stafford Loans; Direct Unsubsidized Stafford Loans. *Student Employment:* Federal Work-Study Program available. Institutional employment available. **Financial Aid Statistics:** 86% needy freshmen, 81% needy undergrads receive need-based scholarship or grant aid. 52% freshmen, 36% undergrads receive non-need-based scholarship or grant aid. 98% freshmen, 94% undergrads receive need-based self-help aid. 0% freshmen, 0% undergrads receive athletic scholarships, 65% freshmen, 61% undergrads receive any aid. 78% undergrads borrow to pay for school. Average cumulative indebtedness $28,940. **Criteria for awarding aid:** *Non-need-based:* Academics.

WRIGHT STATE UNIVERSITY

3640 Colonel Glenn Highway, Dayton, OH 45435
Phone: 937-775-5700 • **Financial Aid Phone:** 937-775-5405
E-mail: admissions@wright.edu • **CEEB Code:** 1179
Fax: 937-775-4410 • **Website:** www.wright.edu • **ACT Code:** 3295

This public school was founded in 1967. It has a 557 acre campus.

RATINGS
Admissions Selectivity Rating: 74   **Fire Safety Rating:** 93   **Green Rating:** 75

STUDENTS AND FACULTY

Enrollment: 11,251. **Student Body:** 52% female, 48% male, 5% out-of-state, 3% international. Asian 3%, African American 11%, Caucasian 75%, Hispanic 4%, Native American <1%, Pacific Islander <1%, Two or more races 4%, Race unknown 1%.
Retention and Graduation: 63% freshmen return for sophomore year. 19% freshmen graduate within 4 years. 36% freshmen graduate within 6 years.
Faculty: 1% of classes are taught by teaching assistants.

ACADEMICS

Degrees: Bachelor's; Certificate; Doctoral Other; Doctoral/Professional; Doctoral/Research; Master's; Post-Bachelor's certificate; Post-Master's certificate **Classes:** Most classes have 10-19 students. Most lab/discussion sessions have 10-19 students. **Most popular majors:** Mechanical Engineering; Biology/Biological Sciences, General; Registered Nursing/Registered Nurse. **Special Study Options:** Cooperative education program; Cross-registration; Distance learning; Double major; Dual enrollment; English as a Second Language (ESL); Honors program; Independent study; Internships; Student-designed major; Study abroad; Teacher certification program; Weekend college. Honors programs: The University Honors Program was created in 1972 to meet the needs of the university's brightest, most ambitious students. Approximately 7% of Wright State undergraduates are enrolled in the University Honors Program. It is open to students of all majors and provides a varied, dedicated curriculum, including interdisciplinary courses, service learning, study abroad, and independent research. **Disability Services offered to physically disabled students:** Note-taking services; Reader services; Tape recorders; Tutors. **Career services:** Alumni network; Alumni services; Career assessment; Career/job search classes; Internships

FACILITIES

Housing: Apartments for married students; Apartments for single students; Coed dorms; Special housing for disabled student; Theme housing 100% of campus accessible to physically diasbled. **Special Academic Facilities/ Equipment:** Art gallery located in the Creative Arts Center; Tom Hanks Center for Motion Pictures; Student Success Center; Garden of the Senses; Robert and Elaine Stein Galleries; Neuroscience Engineering Collaboration Building **Computers:** 100% of classrooms, 100% of dorms, 100% of libraries, 100% of dining areas, 100% of student union, have wireless network access. Students can register for classes online. Administrative functions (other than registration) can be performed online.

CAMPUS LIFE

Environment: City **Activities:** Campus Ministries; Choral groups; Concert band; Dance; Drama/theater; International Student Organization; Jazz band; Literary magazine; Model UN; Music ensembles; Musical theater; Opera; Pep band; Radio station; Student government; Student newspaper; Symphony

orchestra; Television station 145 registered organizations, 22 honor societies, 9 religious organizations. 8 fraternities, 8 sororities. **Athletics (Intercollegiate):** *Men:* baseball, basketball, cheerleading, cross-country, diving, golf, soccer, swimming, tennis. *Women:* basketball, cheerleading, cross-country, diving, soccer, softball, swimming, tennis, track/field (outdoor), volleyball. **On-Campus Highlights:** Student Union, Creative Arts Center, Rec Center, Paul Laurence Dunbar Library, Nutter Center **Environmental Initiatives:** Matthew O. Diggs III Laboratory for Life Sciences Research achieved LEED Gold status, the first laboratory in Ohio to achieve LEED-NC Gold status.

ADMISSIONS

Freshman Academic Profile: Average high school GPA 3.3. 18% in top 10% of high school class, 40% in top 25% of high school class, 68% in top 50% of high school class. **Test Scores:** SAT Math middle 50% range 490-630. SAT EBRW middle 50% range 490-640. ACT middle 50% range 19-25. Minimum internet-based TOEFL 61. **Basis for Candidate Selection:** *Very important factors considered include:* rigor of secondary school record, academic GPA, standardized test scores. *Important factors considered include:* class rank. *Other factors considered include:* recommendation(s), state residency. **Freshman Admission Requirements:** High school diploma is required and GED is accepted *Academic units required:* 4 English, 4 math, 3 science, 3 science labs, 3 social studies, *Academic units recommended:* 2 foreign language, 1 visual/performing arts. **Freshman Admission Statistics:** 5,826 applied, 96.8% admitted, 40% enrolled. **Transfer Admission Requirements:** college transcript(s), Minimum college GPA of 2.0 required. Lowest grade transferable D. **General Admission Information:** Application fee $30. Regular application deadline 8/20. Nonfall registration accepted. Admission may be deferred for a maximum of One year.

COSTS AND FINANCIAL AID

Required Forms and Deadlines: FAFSA. **Notification of Awards:** Applicants will be notified of awards on or about 12/15. **Types of Aid:** *Need-based scholarships/grants:* College/university scholarship or grant aid from institutional funds; Federal Nursing Scholarships; Federal Pell; Private scholarships; SEOG; State scholarships/grants; United Negro College Fund. *Loans:* Direct PLUS loans; Direct Subsidized Stafford Loans; Direct Unsubsidized Stafford Loans. *Student Employment:* Federal Work-Study Program available. Institutional employment available. **Financial Aid Statistics:** 87% needy freshmen, 80% needy undergrads receive need-based scholarship or grant aid. 12% freshmen, 8% undergrads receive non-need-based scholarship or grant aid. 91% freshmen, 93% undergrads receive need-based self-help aid. 2% freshmen, 2% undergrads receive athletic scholarships. 87% freshmen, 75% undergrads receive any aid. **Criteria for awarding aid:** *Need-based:* Academics, Art, Minority status, Music/drama *Non-need-based:* Academics, Alumni affiliation, Art, Athletics, Leadership, Minority status, Music/drama, State/district residency.

XAVIER UNIVERSITY OF LOUISIANA

One Drexel Drive, New Orleans, LA 70125
Phone: 504-520-7388 • **Financial Aid Phone:** 504-520-7835
E-mail: apply@xula.edu • **CEEB Code:** 6975
Fax: 504-520-7941 • **Website:** www.xula.edu • **ACT Code:** 1618

This private school, affiliated with the Roman Catholic Church, was founded in 1915. It has a 29 acre campus.

RATINGS
Admissions Selectivity Rating: 82   **Fire Safety Rating:** 99   **Green Rating:** 60*

STUDENTS AND FACULTY

Enrollment: 2,266. **Student Body:** 73% female, 27% male, 46% out-of-state, 2% international (8 countries represented). Asian 7%, African American 78%, Caucasian 3%, Hispanic 3%, Native American <1%, Pacific Islander <1%, Two or more races 4%, Race unknown 4%.
Retention and Graduation: 70% freshmen return for sophomore year. 30% freshmen graduate within 4 years. 44% freshmen graduate within 6 years. 31% grads go on to further study within 1 year. **Faculty:** Student/faculty ratio 14:1. 219 full-time faculty, 95% hold PhDs, 43% are members of minority groups, 46% are women. 0% of classes are taught by teaching assistants.

ACADEMICS

Degrees: Bachelor's; Doctoral/Professional; Doctoral/Research; **Master's Classes:** Most classes have 10-19 students. Most lab/discussion sessions have 10-19 students. **Most popular majors:** Pre-Medicine/Pre-Medical Studies; Pre-Pharmacy Studies. **Special Study Options:** Accelerated program; Cooperative education program; Cross-registration; Distance learning; Double major; Dual enrollment; Exchange student program (domestic); Honors program; Independent study; Internships; Study abroad; Teacher certification program. Combined degree programs: BA/MEng. **Disability Services offered to physically disabled students:** Note-taking services; Reader services; Tape recorders; Tutors. **Career services:** Career assessment; Career/job search classes; Internships

FACILITIES

Housing: Coed dorms; Men's dorms; Special housing for disabled student; Wellness housing; Women's dorms 100% of campus accessible to physically diasbled. **Special Academic Facilities/Equipment:** University Library Archives **Computers:** 100% of classrooms, 100% of dorms, 100% of libraries, 100% of dining areas, 100% of student union, 100% of common outdoor areas have wireless network access. Students can register for classes online. Administrative functions (other than registration) can be performed online.

CAMPUS LIFE

Environment: Metropolis **Activities:** Campus Ministries; Choral groups; Concert band; Dance; Drama/theater; International Student Organization; Jazz band; Literary magazine; Musical theater; Opera; Pep band; Radio station; Student government; Student newspaper; Symphony orchestra; Television station; Yearbook 88 registered organizations, 8 honor societies, 1 religious organization. 4 fraternities, 4 sororities. **Athletics (Intercollegiate):** *Men:* basketball, cross-country, tennis, track/field (outdoor), track/field (indoor), *Women:* basketball, cross-country, tennis, track/field (outdoor), track/field (indoor), volleyball. **On-Campus Highlights:** University Center, Convocation Center, Library, The Science Quad, St. Joseph's Resource Center

ADMISSIONS

Freshman Academic Profile: Average high school GPA 3.4. 28% in top 10% of high school class, 54% in top 25% of high school class, 78% in top 50% of high school class. **Test Scores:** SAT Math middle 50% range 470-590. SAT EBRW middle 50% range 493-590. ACT middle 50% range 20-25. Minimum paper TOEFL 550. **Basis for Candidate Selection:** *Very important factors considered include:* rigor of secondary school record, academic GPA, standardized test scores, recommendation(s). *Important factors considered include:* class rank, application essay. *Other factors considered include:* interview, extracurricular activities, talent/ability, character/personal qualities, alumni/ae relation, racial/ethnic status, volunteer work. **Freshman Admission Requirements:** High school diploma is required and GED is accepted *Academic units required:* 4 English, 2 math, 2 science, 1 social studies, 7 academic electives, *Academic units recommended:* 4 math, 3 science, 1 foreign language, 1 history. **Freshman Admission Statistics:** 7,164 applied, 64.1% admitted, 16% enrolled. **Transfer Admission Requirements:** college transcript(s), Minimum college GPA of 2.00 required. Lowest grade transferable C. **General Admission Information:** Priority deadline 3/1. Regular application deadline 7/1. Admission may be deferred.

COSTS AND FINANCIAL AID

Annual tuition $21,212. Room and board $9,534. Required fees $2,394. Average book expense $1,300. **Required Forms and Deadlines:** FAFSA. **Types of Aid:** *Need-based scholarships/grants:* College/university scholarship or grant aid from institutional funds; Federal Pell; SEOG; State scholarships/grants; United Negro College Fund. *Loans:* Direct PLUS loans; Direct Subsidized Stafford Loans; Direct Unsubsidized Stafford Loans. *Student Employment:* Federal Work-Study Program available. Institutional employment available. **Financial Aid Statistics:** 65% needy freshmen, 65% needy undergrads receive need-based scholarship or grant aid. 91% freshmen, 79% undergrads receive non-need-based scholarship or grant aid. 93% freshmen, 95% undergrads receive need-based self-help aid. 3% freshmen, 4% undergrads receive athletic scholarships. 94% freshmen, 24% undergrads receive any aid. **Criteria for awarding aid:** *Need-based:* Academics, Art, Athletics, Music/drama.

XAVIER UNIVERSITY (OH)

3800 Victory Parkway, Cincinnati, OH 45207-5311
Phone: 513-745-3301 • **Financial Aid Phone:** 513-745-3142
E-mail: xuadmit@xavier.edu • **CEEB Code:** 1965
Fax: 513-745-4319 • **Website:** www.xavier.edu • **ACT Code:** 3366

This private school, affiliated with the Roman Catholic-Jesuit Church, was founded in 1831. It has a 189 acre campus.

RATINGS

Admissions Selectivity Rating: 80   **Fire Safety Rating:** 88   **Green Rating:** 78

STUDENTS AND FACULTY

Enrollment: 4,572. **Student Body:** 54% female, 46% male, 53% out-of-state, 2% international (45 countries represented). Asian 3%, African American 9%, Caucasian 75%, Hispanic 6%, Native American <1%, Pacific Islander <1%, Two or more races 4%, Race unknown 1%.
Retention and Graduation: 84% freshmen return for sophomore year. 61% freshmen graduate within 4 years. 69% freshmen graduate within 6 years. 21% grads go on to further study within 1 year. 5% grads pursue arts and sciences degrees. 0.5% grads pursue law degrees. 2% grads pursue business degrees. 0.4% grads pursue medical degrees. **Faculty:** Student/faculty ratio 12:1. 352 full-time faculty, 79% hold PhDs, 15% are members of minority groups, 55% are women. 0% of classes are taught by teaching assistants.

ACADEMICS

Degrees: Associate; Bachelor's; Certificate; Doctoral/Professional; Master's; Post-Bachelor's certificate; Post-Master's certificate; Terminal Associate **Classes:** Most classes have 20-29 students. Most lab/discussion sessions have 20-29 students. **Most popular majors:** Liberal Arts And Sciences/Liberal Studies; Biology/Biological Sciences, General; Registered Nursing/Registered Nurse. **Special Study Options:** Cooperative education program; Cross-registration; Distance learning; Double major; Dual enrollment; English as a Second Language (ESL); Exchange student program (domestic); Honors program; Independent study; Internships; Study abroad; Teacher certification program; Weekend college. Honors programs: University Scholars Progam; Philosophy, Politics and the Public; Honors Bachelors of Arts. **Disability Services offered to physically disabled students:** Note-taking services; Reader services; Tape recorders; Tutors. **Career services:** Alumni network; Alumni services; Career assessment; Career/job search classes; Internships; Regional alumni

FACILITIES

Housing: Apartments for single students; Coed dorms; Special housing for disabled student; Theme housing 99% of campus accessible to physically diasbled. **Special Academic Facilities/Equipment:** Student-run art gallery, Montessori lab school, The Fifth Third Trading Room, and an observatory. **Computers:** 100% of classrooms, 100% of dorms, 100% of libraries, 100% of dining areas, 100% of student union, 100% of common outdoor areas have wireless network access. Students can register for classes online. Administrative functions (other than registration) can be performed online.

CAMPUS LIFE

Environment: Metropolis **Activities:** Campus Ministries; Choral groups; Concert band; Dance; Drama/theater; International Student Organization; Literary magazine; Model UN; Music ensembles; Musical theater; Pep band; Student government; Student newspaper; Television station 124 registered organizations, 10 honor societies, 11 religious organizations. **Athletics (Intercollegiate):** *Men:* baseball, basketball, cheerleading, cross-country, golf, soccer, swimming, tennis, track/field (outdoor), track/field (indoor). *Women:* basketball, cheerleading, cross-country, golf, soccer, swimming, tennis, track/field (outdoor), track/field (indoor), volleyball. **On-Campus Highlights:** Cintas Center basketball arena, Conaton Learning Commons, The Gallagher Student Center, Smith Hall, home to William's College of Business, Fenwick Place, residence hall and home to the Hoff Dining Commons **Environmental Initiatives:** Growth and investment 'All-In': Linking the growth of new undergraduate and Masters programs- with more students, regular field trips, social events, and lecture series—with the leadership team's investment of time and talent participating on and leading local boards: Watershed Council, Economics of Compassion Board, Southwest Ohio sustainable farming board, and Green Business Council.

ADMISSIONS

Freshman Academic Profile: Average high school GPA 3.6. 16% in top 10% of high school class, 45% in top 25% of high school class, 80% in top 50% of high school class. 52% from public high schools. **Test Scores:** SAT Math middle 50% range 520-620. SAT EBRW middle 50% range 540-620. ACT middle 50% range 22-28. Minimum internet-based TOEFL 79. Minimum paper TOEFL 550. **Basis for Candidate Selection:** *Very important factors considered include:* rigor of secondary school record, academic GPA, standardized test scores. *Important factors considered include:* application essay, recommendation(s), extracurricular activities, character/personal qualities, volunteer work. *Other factors considered include:* class rank, talent/ability, first generation, alumni/ae relation, work experience, level of applicant's interest. **Freshman Admission Requirements:** High school diploma is required and GED is accepted *Academic units recommended:* 4 English, 3 math, 3 science, 2 foreign language, 3 social studies, 5 academic electives, 1 unit from above areas or other academic areas. **Freshman Admission Statistics:** 13,006 applied, 73.9% admitted, 13% enrolled. **Transfer Admission Requirements:** High school transcript, college transcript(s), statement of good standing from prior institution(s). Minimum college GPA of 2.0 required. Lowest grade transferable C-. **General Admission Information:** Application fee $35. Priority deadline 2/1. Nonfall registration accepted. Admission may be deferred for a maximum of 1 year.

COSTS AND FINANCIAL AID

Annual tuition $38,300. Room and board $12,780. Required fees $230. Average book expense $1,000. **Required Forms and Deadlines:** FAFSA. **Notification of Awards:** Applicants will be notified of awards on a rolling basis beginning 12/15. **Types of Aid:** *Need-based scholarships/grants:* College/university scholarship or grant aid from institutional funds; Federal Pell; Private scholarships; SEOG; State scholarships/grants; United Negro College Fund. *Loans:* Direct PLUS loans; Direct Subsidized Stafford Loans; Direct Unsubsidized Stafford Loans. *Student Employment:* Federal Work-Study Program available. Institutional employment available. **Financial Aid Statistics:** 97% needy freshmen, 67% needy undergrads receive need-based scholarship or grant aid. 32% freshmen, 30% undergrads receive non-need-based scholarship or grant aid. 61% freshmen, 62% undergrads receive need-based self-help aid. 3% freshmen, 3% undergrads receive athletic scholarships. 99% freshmen, 92% undergrads receive any aid. Average cumulative indebtedness $32,108. **Criteria for awarding aid:** *Need-based:* Job skills *Non-need-based:* Academics, Alumni affiliation, Art, Athletics, Leadership, Music/drama, Religious affiliation.

YALE UNIVERSITY

PO Box 208234, New Haven, CT 06520-8234
Phone: 203-432-9300 • **Financial Aid Phone:** 203-432-2700
E-mail: student.questions@yale.edu • **CEEB Code:** 3987
Fax: 203-432-9392 • **Website:** www.yale.edu • **ACT Code:** 618

This private school was founded in 1701. It has a 342 acre campus.

RATINGS

Admissions Selectivity Rating: 99   **Fire Safety Rating:** 62   **Green Rating:** 92

STUDENTS AND FACULTY

Enrollment: 5,532. **Student Body:** 49% female, 51% male, 93% out-of-state, 11% international (118 countries represented). Asian 17%, African American 7%, Caucasian 47%, Hispanic 11%, Native American 1%, Pacific Islander <1%, Two or more races 6%, Race unknown 1%.
Retention and Graduation: 99% freshmen return for sophomore year. 21% grads go on to further study within 1 year. 7% grads pursue arts and sciences degrees. 4% grads pursue law degrees. 4% grads pursue medical degrees.
Faculty: Student/faculty ratio 6:1. 1,159 full-time faculty, 93% hold PhDs, 28% are members of minority groups, 36% are women.

ACADEMICS

Degrees: Bachelor's; Doctoral/Professional; Doctoral/Research; Master's; Post-Master's certificate **Classes:** Most classes have 20-29 students. Most lab/discussion sessions have 20-29 students. **Most popular majors:** Economics, General; Political Science And Government, General; History, General. **Special Study Options:** Accelerated program; Double major; English as a Second Language (ESL); Honors program; Independent study; Internships; Liberal arts/career combination; Student-designed major; Study abroad. Combined degree programs: BA/MA. **Disability Services offered to physically disabled students:** Note-taking services; Reader services; Tape recorders; Tutors. **Career services:** Alumni network; Alumni services; Career/job search classes; Internships; Regional alumni

FACILITIES

Housing: Coed dorms; Special housing for disabled students **Special Academic Facilities/Equipment:** Yale British Art Museum, Yale Art Gallery, Peabody Museum of Natural History, Jackson Institute for Global Affairs, Center for Engineering Innovation and Design, clean room, wind tunnel, engine testing facility, graphic workstations, robotics labs, nuclear accelerators, nuclear magnetic resonance spectrometers, optical spectroscopy instruments, high-resolution mass spectrometer, x-ray diffraction instruments, scanning electron microscopes, observatories, biospheric studies institute **Computers:** 100% of classrooms, 100% of dorms, 100% of libraries, 100% of dining areas, 100% of student union, 100% of common outdoor areas have wireless network access. Students can register for classes online. Administrative functions (other than registration) can be performed online.

CAMPUS LIFE

Environment: City **Activities:** Choral groups; Concert band; Dance; Drama/theater; Jazz band; Literary magazine; Marching band; Music ensembles; Musical theater; Opera; Pep band; Radio station; Student government; Student newspaper; Student-run film society; Symphony orchestra; Television station; Yearbook 350 registered organizations. **Athletics (Intercollegiate):** *Men:* baseball, basketball, crew/rowing, cross-country, diving, fencing, football, golf, ice hockey, lacrosse, sailing, soccer, squash, swimming, tennis, track/field (outdoor), track/field (indoor). *Women:* basketball, crew/rowing, cross-country, diving, fencing, field hockey, golf, gymnastics, ice hockey, lacrosse, sailing, soccer, softball, squash, swimming, tennis, track/field (outdoor), track/field (indoor), volleyball. **On-Campus Highlights:** Old Campus, Sterling Memorial Library, Yale Art Gallery, Beinecke Rare Book and Manuscript Library, Payne-Whitney Gymnasium **Environmental Initiatives:** The university pledged to a greenhouse gas commitment of 43% below 2005 levels by 2020.

ADMISSIONS

Freshman Academic Profile: 97% in top 10% of high school class, 99% in top 25% of high school class, 100% in top 50% of high school class. 57% from public high schools. **Test Scores:** SAT Math middle 50% range 710-800. SAT EBRW middle 50% range 720-800. ACT middle 50% range 31-35. Minimum internet-based TOEFL 100. Minimum paper TOEFL 600. **Basis for Candidate Selection:** *Very important factors considered include:* rigor of secondary school record, class rank, academic GPA, application essay, standardized test scores, recommendation(s), extracurricular activities, talent/ability, character/personal qualities. *Other factors considered include:* interview, first generation, alumni/ae relation, geographical residence, state residency, racial/ethnic status, volunteer work, work experience. **Freshman Admission Requirements:** High school diploma is required and GED is accepted **Freshman Admission Statistics:** 30,236 applied, 6.7% admitted, 67% enrolled. **Transfer Admission Requirements:** High school transcript, college transcript(s), essay or personal statement, standardized test scores, statement of good standing from prior institution(s). Lowest grade transferable C. **General Admission Information:** Application fee $80. Regular application deadline 1/1. Nonfall registration accepted. Admission may be deferred for a maximum of one year.

COSTS AND FINANCIAL AID

Annual tuition $49,480. Room and board $15,170. Average book expense $3,580. **Required Forms and Deadlines:** CSS/Financial Aid PROFILE; FAFSA; Institution's own financial aid form; Noncustodial PROFILE. **Notification of Awards:** Applicants will be notified of awards on or about 4/1. **Types of Aid:** *Need-based scholarships/grants:* College/university scholarship or grant aid from institutional funds; Federal Pell; Private scholarships; SEOG; State scholarships/grants; United Negro College Fund. *Loans:* Direct PLUS loans; Direct Subsidized Stafford Loans; Direct Unsubsidized Stafford Loans. **Financial Aid Statistics:** 100% needy freshmen, 100% needy undergrads receive need-based scholarship or grant aid. 0% undergrads receive non-need-based scholarship or grant aid. 73% freshmen, 85% undergrads receive need-based self-help aid. 0% freshmen, 0% undergrads receive athletic scholarships. 51% freshmen, 52% undergrads receive any aid. 17% undergrads borrow to pay for school. Average cumulative indebtedness $15,521.

YESHIVA UNIVERSITY

500 West 185th Street, New York, NY 10033-3299
Phone: 212-960-5277
E-mail: yuadmit@yu.edu • **CEEB Code:** 2990
Fax: 212-960-0086 • **Website:** www.yu.edu • **ACT Code:** 2992

This private school was founded in 1886. It has a 12 acre campus.

RATINGS
Admissions Selectivity Rating: 88   **Fire Safety Rating:** 60*   **Green Rating:** 60*

STUDENTS AND FACULTY
Enrollment: 2,866. **Student Body:** 46% female, 54% male, 35% out-of-state, 12% international (53 countries represented). Asian <1%, African American <1%, Caucasian 82%, Hispanic 2%, Native American <1%, Race unknown 4%. **Retention and Graduation:** 90% freshmen return for sophomore year. **Faculty:** Student/faculty ratio 7:1. 0% of classes are taught by teaching assistants.

ACADEMICS
Degrees: Bachelor's; **Master's Classes:** Most classes have fewer than 10 students. Most lab/discussion sessions have fewer than 10 students. **Most popular majors:** Jewish/Judaic Studies; Psychology, General; Political Science And Government, General. **Special Study Options:** Double major; Honors program; Independent study; Internships; Student-designed major; Study abroad; Teacher certification program. Combined degree programs: BA/MA. **Career services:** Career assessment; Career/job search classes; Internships

FACILITIES
Housing: Apartments for married students; Apartments for single students; Men's dorms; Women's dorms **Special Academic Facilities/Equipment:** Archives and rare book collection, museum of Jewish art, architecture, history, and culture.

CAMPUS LIFE
Activities: Choral groups; Concert band; Drama/theater; Jazz band; Literary magazine; Music ensembles; Musical theater; Radio station; Student government; Student newspaper; Yearbook. **Athletics (Intercollegiate):** *Men:* basketball, tennis, volleyball. *Women:* basketball, tennis.

ADMISSIONS
Freshman Academic Profile: Average high school GPA 3.5. 48% in top 10% of high school class, 77% in top 25% of high school class, 95% in top 50% of high school class. **Test Scores:** SAT Math middle 50% range 550-680. SAT EBRW middle 50% range 550-690. ACT middle 50% range 22-28. Minimum paper TOEFL 500. **Basis for Candidate Selection:** *Important factors considered include:* rigor of secondary school record, academic GPA, application essay, standardized test scores, interview, extracurricular activities, talent/ability. *Other factors considered include:* volunteer work, work experience. **Freshman Admission Requirements:** High school diploma is required and GED is accepted *Academic units recommended:* 4 English, 2 math, 2 science, 2 foreign language, 2 social studies. **Freshman Admission Statistics:** 2,027 applied, 62.6% admitted, 65% enrolled. **Transfer Admission Requirements:** High school transcript, college transcript(s), essay or personal statement, interview, standardized test scores, Lowest grade transferable 75. **General Admission Information:** Application fee $40. Regular application deadline 2/15. Nonfall registration accepted. Admission may be deferred.

COSTS AND FINANCIAL AID
Annual tuition $31,594. Required fees $500. Average book expense $1,224. **Required Forms and Deadlines:** Business/Farm Supplement; CSS/Financial Aid PROFILE; FAFSA; Institution's own financial aid form; Noncustodial PROFILE; State aid form. **Types of Aid:** *Need-based scholarships/grants:* College/university scholarship or grant aid from institutional funds; Federal Pell; Private scholarships; SEOG; State scholarships/grants. *Loans: Student Employment:* Federal Work-Study Program available. Institutional employment available. **Financial Aid Statistics:** 89% needy freshmen, 85% needy undergrads receive need-based scholarship or grant aid. 14% freshmen, 10% undergrads receive non-need-based scholarship or grant aid. 80% freshmen, 77% undergrads receive need-based self-help aid. 0% freshmen, 0% undergrads receive athletic scholarships. **Criteria for awarding aid:** *Non-need-based:* Academics.

YORK COLLEGE

PO Box 3062400, York, NE 68467
Phone: 402-363-5627 • **Financial Aid Phone:** 402-363-5625
E-mail: enroll@york.edu
Fax: 402-363-5623 • **Website:** www.york.edu • **ACT Code:** 2484

This private school, affiliated with the Church of Christ, was founded in 1890. It has a 200 acre campus.

RATINGS
Admissions Selectivity Rating: 84   **Fire Safety Rating:** 97   **Green Rating:** 60*

STUDENTS AND FACULTY
Enrollment: 385. **Student Body:** 51% female, 49% male, 69% out-of-state, 1% international (6 countries represented). Asian 2%, African American 5%, Caucasian 73%, Hispanic 4%, Native American 0%, Race unknown 15%. **Retention and Graduation:** 55% freshmen return for sophomore year. **Faculty:** Student/faculty ratio 7:1. 33 full-time faculty, 36% hold PhDs, 3% are members of minority groups, 27% are women. 0% of classes are taught by teaching assistants.

ACADEMICS
Degrees: Associate; Bachelor's; Transfer Associate **Classes:** Most classes have 20-29 students. Most lab/discussion sessions have 20-29 students. **Most popular majors:** Education, General; Psychology, General; Business Administration And Management, General. **Special Study Options:** Double major; Dual enrollment; Internships; Student-designed major; Teacher certification program. **Career services:** Alumni network; Career assessment

FACILITIES
Housing: Apartments for married students; Men's dorms; Special housing for disabled student; Women's dorms 60% of campus accessible to physically diasbled. **Computers:** 100% of libraries, 100% of student union, have wireless network access.

CAMPUS LIFE
Environment: Village **Activities:** Campus Ministries; Choral groups; Drama/theater; Literary magazine; Music ensembles; Musical theater; Student government; Student newspaper; Yearbook 12 registered organizations, 2 honor societies, 1 religious organization. 4 fraternities, 4 sororities. **Athletics (Intercollegiate):** *Men:* baseball, basketball, soccer, wrestling. *Women:* basketball, soccer, softball, volleyball. **On-Campus Highlights:** Mackey Center, Prayer Chapel, Spiritual Life Center/Coffee Shop, Gurganus Hall, Freeman Center

ADMISSIONS
Freshman Academic Profile: Average high school GPA 3.4. 13% in top 10% of high school class, 25% in top 25% of high school class, 60% in top 50% of high school class. **Test Scores:** SAT Math middle 50% range 440-560. SAT EBRW middle 50% range 450-590. ACT middle 50% range 18-26. Minimum paper TOEFL 500. **Basis for Candidate Selection:** *Very important factors considered include:* rigor of secondary school record, class rank, academic GPA, standardized test scores. *Other factors considered include:* application essay, recommendation(s), extracurricular activities, talent/ability, character/personal qualities, first generation, alumni/ae relation, religious affiliation/commitment, volunteer work, level of applicant's interest. **Freshman Admission Requirements:** High school diploma is required and GED is accepted *Academic units required:* 3 English, 2 math, 2 science, 1 social studies, 1 history, *Academic units recommended:* 4 English, 4 math, 4 science, 3 foreign language, 4 social studies, 4 history. **Freshman Admission Statistics:** 531 applied, 56.9% admitted, 30% enrolled. **Transfer Admission Requirements:** High school transcript, college transcript(s), Minimum college GPA of 2 required. Lowest grade transferable 1. **General Admission Information:** Application fee $20. Priority deadline 3/31. Regular application deadline 8/31. Nonfall registration accepted. Admission may be deferred.

COSTS AND FINANCIAL AID
Annual tuition $12,500. Room and board $4,500. Required fees $1,500. Average book expense $1,500. **Required Forms and Deadlines:** FAFSA. **Notification of Awards:** Applicants will be notified of awards on a rolling basis beginning 3/1. **Types of Aid:** *Need-based scholarships/grants:* College/university scholarship or grant aid from institutional funds; Federal Pell; Private scholarships; SEOG; State scholarships/grants. *Loans:* Direct PLUS loans; Direct Subsidized Stafford Loans; Direct Unsubsidized Stafford Loans. *Student Employment:* Federal Work-Study Program available. **Financial Aid Statistics:** 0% freshmen, 0% undergrads receive athletic scholarships. 89% freshmen, 89% undergrads receive any aid. **Criteria for awarding aid:** *Non-need-based:* Academics, Athletics, Leadership, Music/drama.

YORK COLLEGE OF PENNSYLVANIA

441 Country Club Road, York, PA 17403-3651
Phone: 717-849-1600 • **Financial Aid Phone:** 717-849-1682
E-mail: admissions@ycp.edu • **CEEB Code:** 2991
Fax: 717-849-1607 • **Website:** www.ycp.edu • **ACT Code:** 3762

This private school was founded in 1787. It has a 190 acre campus.

RATINGS
Admissions Selectivity Rating: 77   **Fire Safety Rating:** 97   **Green Rating:** 63

STUDENTS AND FACULTY
Enrollment: 4,847. **Student Body:** 55% female, 45% male, 42% out-of-state, <1% international (32 countries represented). Asian 1%, African American 5%, Caucasian 83%, Hispanic 5%, Native American <1%, Pacific Islander <1%, Two or more races 3%, Race unknown 2%.
Retention and Graduation: 75% freshmen return for sophomore year. **Faculty:** Student/faculty ratio 16:1. 189 full-time faculty, 81% hold PhDs, 4% are members of minority groups, 43% are women. 0% of classes are taught by teaching assistants.

ACADEMICS
Degrees: Associate; Bachelor's; Doctoral/Professional; Master's; Post-Master's certificate **Classes:** Most classes have 20-29 students. **Most popular majors:** Biology/Biological Sciences, General; Registered Nursing/Registered Nurse; Business Administration And Management, General. **Special Study Options:** Cooperative education program; Double major; Dual enrollment; Independent study; Internships; Liberal arts/career combination; Student-designed major; Study abroad; Teacher certification program. Honors programs: **Disability Services offered to physically disabled students:** Note-taking services; Reader services; Tutors. **Career services:** Alumni network; Alumni services; Career assessment; Career/job search classes; Internships; Regional alumni

FACILITIES
Housing: Apartments for single students; Coed dorms; Fraternity/sorority housing; Special housing for disabled student; Theme housing; Wellness housing 98% of campus accessible to physically diasbled. **Special Academic Facilities/Equipment:** Music, arts, and communication center, nursing education center, humanities center **Computers:** 50% of classrooms, 35% of dorms, 100% of libraries, 100% of dining areas, 80% of student union, 65% of common outdoor areas have wireless network access. Students can register for classes online. Administrative functions (other than registration) can be performed online.

CAMPUS LIFE
Environment: Town **Activities:** Campus Ministries; Choral groups; Concert band; Dance; Drama/theater; International Student Organization; Jazz band; Literary magazine; Model UN; Music ensembles; Musical theater; Radio station; Student government; Student newspaper; Symphony orchestra; Television station 80 registered organizations, 7 honor societies, 4 religious organizations. 9 fraternities, 7 sororities. **Athletics (Intercollegiate):** *Men:* baseball, basketball, cheerleading, cross-country, golf, lacrosse, soccer, swimming, tennis, track/field (outdoor), wrestling. *Women:* basketball, cheerleading, cross-country, field hockey, lacrosse, soccer, softball, swimming, tennis, track/field (outdoor), volleyball. **On-Campus Highlights:** Collegiate Performing Arts Center, Grumbacher Sports & Fitness Center, West Campus Community Center, York College Art Galleries, Student Union Spart's Den

ADMISSIONS
Freshman Academic Profile: Average high school GPA 3.5. 12% in top 10% of high school class, 40% in top 25% of high school class, 77% in top 50% of high school class. **Test Scores:** SAT Math middle 50% range 480-578. SAT EBRW middle 50% range 470-560. ACT middle 50% range 20-25. Minimum internet-based TOEFL 72. Minimum paper TOEFL 530. **Basis for Candidate Selection:** *Very important factors considered include:* rigor of secondary school record, academic GPA. *Important factors considered include:* class rank, standardized test scores, character/personal qualities. *Other factors considered include:* application essay, recommendation(s), interview, extracurricular activities, talent/ability, alumni/ae relation, volunteer work, work experience, level of applicant's interest. **Freshman Admission Requirements:** High school diploma is required and GED is accepted *Academic units required:* 4 English, 3 math, 3 science, 2 foreign language, 3 social studies, *Academic units recommended:* 4 English, 4 math, 4 science, 2 foreign language, 3 social studies. **Freshman Admission Statistics:** 9,934 applied, 73.5% admitted, 22% enrolled. **Transfer Admission Requirements:** college transcript(s), Minimum college GPA of 2.0 required. Lowest grade transferable C. **General Admission Information:** Nonfall registration accepted. Admission may be deferred for a maximum of 1 year.

COSTS AND FINANCIAL AID
Annual tuition $15,350. Room and board $9,580. Required fees $1,660. Average book expense $1,200. **Required Forms and Deadlines:** FAFSA. **Notification of Awards:** Applicants will be notified of awards on a rolling basis beginning 3/1. **Types of Aid:** *Need-based scholarships/grants:* College/university scholarship or grant aid from institutional funds; Federal Pell; Private scholarships; SEOG; State scholarships/grants. *Loans:* Direct PLUS loans; Direct Subsidized Stafford Loans; Direct Unsubsidized Stafford Loans. *Student Employment:* Federal Work-Study Program available. Institutional employment available. **Financial Aid Statistics:** 61% needy freshmen, 67% needy undergrads receive need-based scholarship or grant aid. 99% freshmen, 78% undergrads receive non-need-based scholarship or grant aid. 85% freshmen, 89% undergrads receive need-based self-help aid. 0% freshmen, 0% undergrads receive athletic scholarships. 99% freshmen, 89% undergrads receive any aid. **Criteria for awarding aid:** *Need-based:* Minority status *Non-need-based:* Academics, Alumni affiliation, Minority status, Music/drama.

YORK UNIVERSITY

4700 Keele Street, Toronto, ON M3J 1P3
Phone: 416-736-5000 • **Financial Aid Phone:** 416-872-9675
E-mail: intlenq@yorku.ca • **CEEB Code:** 894
Fax: 416-736-5536 • **Website:** www.yorku.ca • **ACT Code:**

This public school was founded in 1959. It has a 550 acre campus.

RATINGS
Admissions Selectivity Rating: 0   **Fire Safety Rating:** 62   **Green Rating:** 95

STUDENTS AND FACULTY
Enrollment: 48,631. **Student Body:** 59% female, 41% male, (170 countries represented). Asian 0%,
Faculty: Student/faculty ratio 17:1. 1,480 full-time faculty, 46% are women.

ACADEMICS
Degrees: Bachelor's; Certificate; Diploma; Doctoral; Doctoral/Research; Master's; Post-Bachelor's certificate **Classes:** Most classes have 40-49 students. Most lab/discussion sessions have 20-29 students. **Most popular majors:** Psychology, General. **Special Study Options:** Accelerated program; Distance learning; Double major; English as a Second Language (ESL); Exchange student program (domestic); Honors program; Independent study; Internships; Student-designed major; Study abroad; Teacher certification program. **Disability Services offered to physically disabled students:** Note-taking services; Reader services; Tape recorders; Tutors. **Career services:** Career assessment; Career/job search classes; Internships

FACILITIES
Housing: Apartments for married students; Apartments for single students; Coed dorms; Men's dorms; Special housing for disabled student; Special housing for international students; Theme housing; Women's dorms **Special Academic Facilities/Equipment:** 5 museums with more than 4.4 million items. Observatory with 2 telescopes. Robotics laboratory. 2 professionally staffed art galleries. 6 student-run art exhibition spaces. 3 theatres. 2 cinemas. 1 screening room. Wide-variety professional standard film and video production facilities. **Computers:** Students can register for classes online. Administrative functions (other than registration) can be performed online.

CAMPUS LIFE
Environment: Metropolis **Activities:** Choral groups; Concert band; Dance; Drama/theater; International Student Organization; Jazz band; Model UN; Music ensembles; Pep band; Radio station; Student government; Student newspaper; Symphony orchestra; Yearbook 259 registered organizations, 35 religious organizations. **Athletics (Intercollegiate):** *Men:* badminton, basketball, cross-country, fencing, football, ice hockey, soccer, swimming, tennis, track/field (outdoor), volleyball, water polo. *Women:* badminton, basketball, cross-country, fencing, field hockey, ice hockey, rugby, soccer, swimming, tennis, track/field (outdoor), volleyball, water polo. **On-Campus Highlights:** York Lanes: on-campus mall, Tait McKenzie Centre: sports complex, Student Centre: food court/lounge/club, Accolade East: theatre, art gallery, Central Square: Scott library, food court

ADMISSIONS
Test Scores: Minimum internet-based TOEFL 83. Minimum paper TOEFL 560. **Basis for Candidate Selection:** *Very important factors considered include:* rigor of secondary school record, academic GPA. *Important factors considered include:* standardized test scores. *Other factors considered*

include: class rank, interview. **Freshman Admission Requirements:** High school diploma is required and GED is not accepted **Transfer Admission Requirements:** college transcript(s), Minimum college GPA of 2.5 required. Lowest grade transferable C. **General Admission Information:** Application fee $100. Nonfall registration accepted. Admission may be deferred for a maximum of 1 year.

COSTS AND FINANCIAL AID
Annual in-state tuition $7,702. Annual out-of-state tuition $6,712. Room and board $7,702. Average book expense $1,000. **Required Forms and Deadlines:** FAFSA. *Student Employment:* Institutional employment available. **Financial Aid Statistics:** 0% undergrads receive athletic scholarships. **Criteria for awarding aid:** *Need-based:* Leadership *Non-need-based:* Academics, Art, Music/drama.

YOUNGSTOWN STATE UNIVERSITY

One University Plaza, Youngstown, OH 44555
Phone: 330-941-2000 • **Financial Aid Phone:** 330-941-3505
E-mail: enroll@ysu.edu • **CEEB Code:** 1975
Fax: 330-941-3674 • **Website:** www.ysu.edu • **ACT Code:** 3368

This public school was founded in 1908. It has a 160 acre campus.

RATINGS
Admissions Selectivity Rating: 83   **Fire Safety Rating:** 96   **Green Rating:** 60*

STUDENTS AND FACULTY
Enrollment: 10,117. **Student Body:** 51% female, 49% male, 15% out-of-state, 4% international (70 countries represented). Asian 1%, African American 9%, Caucasian 75%, Hispanic 4%, Native American <1%, Pacific Islander <1%, Two or more races 3%, Race unknown 4%.
Retention and Graduation: 76% freshmen return for sophomore year. 14% freshmen graduate within 4 years. 36% freshmen graduate within 6 years. **Faculty:** Student/faculty ratio 17:1. 399 full-time faculty, 87% hold PhDs, 17% are members of minority groups, 44% are women.

ACADEMICS
Degrees: Associate; Bachelor's; Certificate; Diploma; Doctoral; Doctoral/Professional; Doctoral/Research; Master's; Post-Bachelor's certificate; Post-Master's certificate; Terminal Associate; Transfer Associate **Classes:** Most classes have 10-19 students. Most lab/discussion sessions have 10-19 students. **Most popular majors:** General Studies; Criminal Justice/Safety Studies; Registered Nursing/Registered Nurse. **Special Study Options:** Accelerated program; Cooperative education program; Cross-registration; Distance learning; Double major; Dual enrollment; English as a Second Language (ESL); Exchange student program (domestic); Honors program; Independent study; Internships; Student-designed major; Study abroad; Teacher certification program. Honors programs: The Honors Program at Youngstown State University, which began in 1977, creates a community of intellectual excellence with students of all majors able to participate. More than 700 YSU students are part of the Honors Program. Students engage in coursework, volunteerism, leadership, and involvement in student organizations. A residential option is also available for students seeking a robust living-learning honors community. Whether the student commutes or resides on campus, an abundance of opportunities exist to connect students to other honors students, faculty, staff, and alumni. When exceptional students are brought together from diverse disciplines and challenged with extraordinary courses and learning experiences outside the classroom, the overall collegiate experience is enhanced. Honors students may further benefit by securing national scholarships; gaining acceptance into graduate programs, receiving assistantships, and landing their dream job. The completion of the program requirements results in recognition at graduation, on the Honors Diploma and a special notation on the student's transcript. **Disability Services offered to physically disabled students:** Note-taking services; Reader services; Tape recorders; Tutors. **Career services:** Alumni services; Career assessment; Career/job search classes; Internships; Regional alumni

FACILITIES
Housing: Apartments for married students; Apartments for single students; Coed dorms; Fraternity/sorority housing; Women's dorms 98% of campus accessible to physically diasbled. **Special Academic Facilities/Equipment:** Art museum, human services development center, engineering services center, planetarium, center for urban studies, industrial development center.

CAMPUS LIFE
Environment: City **Activities:** Campus Ministries; Choral groups; Concert band; Dance; Drama/theater; International Student Organization; Jazz band; Marching band; Model UN; Music ensembles; Musical theater; Opera; Pep band; Radio station; Student government; Student newspaper; Student-run film society; Symphony orchestra; Yearbook. Stambaugh Stadium, Beeghly Center, Andrews Wellness Center, Watts Center, Kilcawley Center

ADMISSIONS
Freshman Academic Profile: Average high school GPA 3.3. 13% in top 10% of high school class, 34% in top 25% of high school class, 67% in top 50% of high school class. **Test Scores:** SAT Math middle 50% range 490-620. SAT EBRW middle 50% range 490-600. ACT middle 50% range 19-25. Minimum internet-based TOEFL 61. Minimum paper TOEFL 500. **Basis for Candidate Selection:** *Very important factors considered include:* rigor of secondary school record, academic GPA, standardized test scores. *Important factors considered include:* class rank. **Freshman Admission Requirements:** High school diploma is required and GED is accepted *Academic units recommended:* 4 English, 4 math, 3 science, 1 science labs, 2 foreign language, 3 social studies, 1 visual/performing arts. **Freshman Admission Statistics:** 9,765 applied, 65.3% admitted, 35% enrolled. **General Admission Information:** Application fee $45. Regular application deadline 8/1. Nonfall registration accepted. Admission may be deferred for a maximum of 1 year.

COSTS AND FINANCIAL AID
Annual out-of-state tuition $14,088. Room and board $9,090. Required fees $115. **Required Forms and Deadlines:** FAFSA; Institution's own financial aid form. **Notification of Awards:** Applicants will be notified of awards on a rolling basis beginning 12/15. **Types of Aid:** *Need-based scholarships/grants:* College/university scholarship or grant aid from institutional funds; Federal Pell; Private scholarships; SEOG; State scholarships/grants. *Loans:* Direct PLUS loans; Direct Subsidized Stafford Loans; Direct Unsubsidized Stafford Loans. *Student Employment:* Federal Work-Study Program available. Institutional employment available. **Financial Aid Statistics:** 79% needy freshmen, 76% needy undergrads receive need-based scholarship or grant aid. 55% freshmen, 43% undergrads receive non-need-based scholarship or grant aid. 83% freshmen, 87% undergrads receive need-based self-help aid. 6% freshmen, 5% undergrads receive athletic scholarships. 94% freshmen, 90% undergrads receive any aid. **Criteria for awarding aid:** *Need-based:* Academics, Art, Athletics, Leadership, Minority status, Music/drama *Non-need-based:* Academics, Alumni affiliation, Athletics, State/district residency.

SCHOOL SAYS . . .

In this section you'll find hundreds of colleges with extended listings describing admissions, curriculum, internships, and much more. This is your chance to get in-depth information on colleges that interest you. The Princeton Review charges each school a small fee to be listed, and the editorial responsibility is solely that of the college.

ALLEGHENY COLLEGE

Allegheny College is one of the country's oldest and most dynamic private liberal arts institutions. Allegheny is the nation's premier college for students with "Unusual Combinations" of interests, skills, and talents.

AT A GLANCE

Recognized as one of Loren Pope's 40 Colleges That Change Lives, Allegheny College is one of the nation's oldest and most dynamic private liberal arts institutions. Allegheny is a leader in higher education innovation, having been recognized as Number 1 in Undergraduate Research among four-year colleges by the Council on Undergraduate Research (2016) and as the country's sixth most innovative national liberal arts college by U.S. News and World Report (2018).

Allegheny is the nation's premier college for students with "Unusual Combinations" of interests, skills, and talents. At Allegheny, when members of the college community talk about unusual combinations, they mean it as a tremendous compliment—a compliment that recognizes the unique character of each student.

When you look around, you'll see a college president who studies decision-making by modern American presidents and then rolls up his sleeves for grassroots community service; an aspiring diplomat singing in the choir and building a bike path; a future physician who edits the college newspaper and pole vaults on an international stage. Unusual combinations, yes, but at Allegheny they are everyday examples of students exploring all of their talents, all of their passions.

Central to the college's focus on experiential learning is the Allegheny Gateway, which helps students connect classroom learning with real-world experience. Since its introduction in 2015, the Gateway has received national attention. It is a central location for collaboration and study in which students can access résumé and career services, pre-professional and graduate school advising, research funding and fellowships, internship opportunities, and more.

LOCATION AND ENVIRONMENT

Allegheny's beautiful 79-acre central campus includes historic architecture and cobblestone streets interspersed with advanced facilities bristling with the latest communications and research technology. Located on a hill overlooking the City of Meadville, Pa., the campus is a short walk to downtown and all the amenities you'll need to enjoy the Allegheny experience. Outdoor opportunities also abound on our 203-acre recreation area near campus and in the local community.

CAMPUS HIGHLIGHTS

- The Allegheny Gateway, which brings together nine offices that help students connect classroom learning with real-world experience
- Nationally acclaimed science complex
- Newly renovated psychology and neuroscience facility
- Multimillion-dollar center for communication arts and theatre
- Center for Business and Economics
- Environmental science center
- The Carrden, a hands-on learning and teaching garden
- GIS Learning Laboratory
- Observatory and planetarium
- David V. Wise Sport & Fitness Center
- Olympic-style track and turf field
- 203-acre recreation area and 283-acre nature preserve
- North Village I and II offer townhouse-style student apartments and suite-style residences
- Tippie Alumni Center in historic Cochran Hall
- WARC radio and ACTV television stations
- Bowman, Penelec & Megahan art galleries
- Special-interest houses (past houses include an international theme and a jazz theme)
- Dance studios and performance spaces

MAJORS AND DEGREES OFFERED

Allegheny is one of the few liberal arts colleges in the country that will ask you to choose both a major and a minor. Allegheny encourages unusual combinations of majors and minors, helping to cultivate the creative, big-picture thinking most desired by employers and graduate schools.

Allegheny offers more than 40 majors and programs spanning the humanities, social sciences, and natural sciences, as well as interdisciplinary majors, leading to Bachelor of Arts and Bachelor of Science degrees. The College also offers pre-professional programs (including pre-medicine and pre-law), and students have opportunities to design their own majors and minors.

Every Allegheny student conducts significant research with faculty mentors, culminating in our distinctive undergraduate thesis—the Senior Comp. Students often engage in research prior to the senior project, including in classroom/lab opportunities, independent study, and summer research opportunities.

TUITION, ROOM, BOARD, FEES

Tuition and Fees: $47,540

Room and Board: $12,140

FINANCIAL AID

The Princeton Review features Allegheny in their "Colleges That Pay You Back" rating, which measures 40 weighted data points including academics, cost, financial aid, student debt, graduation rates, alumni salaries and job satisfaction.

Aid totaling $45 million was awarded to Allegheny students in 2017–18. Through generous support from our alumni, Allegheny is able to provide and Need-Based Grant Assistance to supplement over $21 million in aid awarded to students from federal, state, and private sources. Consequently, Allegheny's financial assistance allows many students the opportunity to make a college choice based on value and fit, rather than financial constraints.

Allegheny's Trustee Scholarship is a merit-based award, from $10,000 to $30,000 per year, that any student who submits an admissions application will be evaluated to receive. The award is based on the same criteria that we value in the admission process: strength and rigor of academics, test scores (optional), essays and recommendations, and a student's contributions and achievements outside of the classroom. Based on those factors, students can receive up to $30,000 per year.

Because Allegheny encourages students to challenge themselves in the classroom, the Trustee Scholarship is guaranteed for eight semesters of full-time enrollment at Allegheny or for Allegheny-sponsored programs.

STUDENT ORGANIZATIONS AND ACTIVITIES

Our Student Population

2,100 students

45 states represented

56 countries represented

It is our students who make Allegheny the vibrant, creative, and innovative place that it is.

We invite students to explore all of their interests and talents. At Allegheny, opportunities to pursue one's passions are limited only by the imagination.

Allegheny has more than 120 clubs and organizations that are run and led by students spanning areas like activism and politics, performing arts and media, and spiritual and religious life, and recreation and club sports. We are also home to 10 nationally affiliated social Greek organizations and were founding members of both the NCAA and North Coast Athletic Conference (NCAC).

These activities help develop students' leadership skills and make a lasting impact on Allegheny's campus culture. That's because Allegheny is all about active learning and fun-not just learning about foreign policy in class, but arguing for change. Not just writing papers on social activism, but working to educate others. Our students create, laugh, dance, play, explore and serve together every day.

FACULTY

Our faculty members are people who pride themselves on being teachers first-they will advise and support you to move beyond what you can even imagine now. They will provide you with opportunities and challenges that will lead you from hard work and dedication to extraordinary outcomes.

Allegheny students don't have to wait behind graduate students for research positions on faculty-led projects but instead are actively engaged as research collaborators. Students follow the guidance of faculty mentors through research, conference presentations, co-authored articles, and faculty-led study tours.

ADMISSIONS PROCESS

Allegheny's Admissions Committee values the hard work you do on a daily basis, and they give the greatest weight to the rigor of your high school courses and your performance. Also considered are your school/community activities, recommendations, personal character and qualities, essay, demonstrated interest, and special talents.

Allegheny embraces the concept that standardized test scores do not exclusively reflect a student's full range of abilities or potential to succeed in college. As a result, Allegheny is now test optional. SAT I or ACT scores are optional for U.S. citizens and permanent residents.

Apply today at (https://sites.allegheny.edu/admissions/apply/) allegheny.edu/apply. Allegheny is also a member of The Common Application.

ARKANSAS STATE UNIVERSITY

AT A GLANCE

Arkansas State's mission is to educate leaders, enhance intellectual growth and enrich lives. Founded in 1909, A-State is the second-largest university in the state and a leader within the Delta and Mid-South region. It hosts the first osteopathic medical school in the state of Arkansas, NYIT's College of Osteopathic Medicine, and opened the first U.S.-style residential campus in Mexico in fall 2017.

Dedicated to teaching, research, and service, the university provides students with the broad educational foundations that help them develop critical thinking, decision-making, analytical, and communication skills. The university is the state's leading provider of nursing graduates, early childhood educators, and agricultural business graduates. In addition, A-State has top-ranked programs in creative media and speech communication. Degree programs in the nursing and health professions are in great demand nationwide, and A-State boasts clinical affiliations with more than 500 health care facilities, where both physical therapy and occupational therapy doctoral programs are emphasized, alongside a doctoral nurse practitioner program. A-State offers management education that includes international business, technology, entrepreneurship, and economic development through action-based learning. Arkansas State is also home to the state-of-the-art Arkansas Biosciences Institute, where graduate and undergraduate students conduct cutting-edge research.

The campus has seen more than $150 million in renovations and new facilities in the past six years, including the expansion of on-campus housing by 500 residents for fall 2017.

LOCATION AND ENVIRONMENT

Located in Jonesboro, Ark., and situated in the northeast corner of Arkansas, A-State is connected by interstate to Memphis on the east and St. Louis to the north; less than two hours by four-lane highway to Little Rock.

CAMPUS FACILITIES & EQUIPMENT

Home to the Arkansas Biosciences Institute, A-State is the location of the first osteopathic medical school in Arkansas with New York Institute of Technology's College of Osteopathic Medicine in historic Wilson Hall. One of the largest instructional buildings in higher education in Arkansas opened in 2015 at A-State: the 130,000 square foot Humanities and Social Sciences.

A pedestrian campus, A-State is also the first Bicycle Friendly University in Arkansas. A 2016 national survey ranked Arkansas State as one of the safest residential campuses, and another placed A-State's security in the top 10.

Campus life is currently at an all-time peak with record participation in on-campus activities and groups during the past five years. With residence hall occupancy at historic highs, space for 500 more graduate and undergraduate students were added for fall 2017.

A-State is the cultural hub of the region with the largest concert venue, the Convocation Center, as well as the largest concert hall and theatre located at Fowler Center. The Bradbury Art Museum is the region's leading facility. Arkansas State's Heritage Sites program operate four nationally or internationally known museum locations including the Johnny Cash Boyhood Home and the Hemingway-Pfeiffer Museum.

Annual events include the Agribusiness Conference hosted by the College of Agriculture, Engineering and Technology; the Delta Symposium hosted by the College of Liberal Arts and Communication; and the Women's Business Leadership Forum hosted by the College of Business. Among the major cultural events spanning multiple disciplines are the Delta Symposium and the Johnny Cash Heritage Festival.

Located in Jonesboro, Ark., and situated in the northeast corner of Arkansas, A-State is connected by interstate highways 55/555 to Memphis on the east and St. Louis to the north; and is less than two hours by the recently designated Future I-57 four-lane highway to Little Rock.

Jonesboro is one of the fastest growing cities in Arkansas, and has seen remarkable growth in the medical sector with over $1 billion of new facilities completed or under construction related to health care. The town has one of the lowest unemployment rates in the state. As the commercial hub of the region, Jonesboro's business activity is considered one of the fastest expanding in the state and in the Delta region. The city serves an 18-county retail trade area of a half-million residents.

ACADEMIC PROGRAMS

Arkansas State University has been selected as one of the top-70 institutions of higher education in the Southern region by the editors of U.S. News & World Report magazine in the 2016 edition of "America's Best Colleges." Arkansas State is also ranked in the top Southern universities by Princeton Review. Among our individual academic programs, A-State has notable achievements, including the following:

- One of the nation's top-20 nursing programs according to NurseJournal.org;

- Back-to-back No. 10 rankings (2016 and 2017) in U.S. News & World Report's best online MBA programs;

- A large international students enrollment;

- The largest online enrollment in the state of Arkansas with 34 programs delivered 100 percent online;

- A vibrant on-campus community with a residence hall capacity of 3,700;

- An incoming freshman class with an average ACT score of 23.6;

- Home to an Honors College with an enrollment of almost 1,000 students in the program;

- A veteran-friendly campus, recognized repeatedly by Military Times magazine, sponsors one of America's oldest ROTC units, and home to the Beck PRIDE Center for America's wounded veterans.

- Most A-State faculty members hold the highest possible degrees and are recognized leaders in their fields.

In addition, Arkansas State's First-Year Experience received the Apple Distinguished Program award. A-State offers "Degree in 3" for accelerated undergraduate completion, as well as articulation agreements to facilitate transfer students from two-year colleges. Study Abroad is a major component of student experience at A-State. Students outside Arkansas should inquire about Beyond Boundaries scholarship opportunities.

MAJORS AND DEGREES OFFERED

As of fall 2017, Arkansas State had 45 degree programs with 161 major fields of study offered at the doctoral, specialist, master, bachelor, and associate degree levels. Master's degree programs were initiated in 1955, and A-State began offering its first doctoral degree program, educational leadership, in the fall of 1992. Arkansas State has seen continued growth in doctoral programs, adding Environmental Science in 1998, Heritage Studies in 2001, Molecular Biosciences in 2006, Physical Therapy in 2008, Nursing Practice in 2012, and Occupational Therapy in 2016.

A-State is a leader in meeting Arkansas's need for educators and health care professionals. The College of Education and Behavioral Science graduates more teachers, counselors, and administrators than any other Arkansas institution, while the College of Nursing and Health Professions is among the state's leaders in graduating nurses with bachelor's degrees.

Arkansas State's commitment to excellence in higher education is demonstrated through its accreditation by The Higher Learning Commission of the North Central Association of Colleges and Schools, as well as more than 20 specialized accrediting organizations. A-State also holds membership in national and international organizations that support the highest educational standards.

TUITION, ROOM, BOARD, FEES

Based on a 15-hour schedule, resident students at Arkansas State University pay approximately $8,478 for tuition and fees for an academic year and an average of $8,762 in room and board costs. Non-resident students pay $14,778 in tuition and fees. Federal Title Four Programs are available to all eligible students through the FAFSA application process. A-State's awarding practices promote equity to all students keeping in mind the neediest populations.

FINANCIAL AID

Based on 17–18 reporting of finance data, 92 percent of the First-Time Full-Time students receive some financial aid. Approximately 40 percent receive PELL and 69 percent receive State / local governmental support to pursue education at Arkansas State University. A significantly higher number of students (80 percent of the FTFT degree seeking undergraduates) pay in-state tuition.

STUDENT ORGANIZATIONS AND ACTIVITIES

Arkansas State's student body comes from all 50 states and over 60 countries. On-campus life is at record participation levels with new housing opening in the Fall 2017 for both upper-division undergraduate students and for graduate student housing.

Incoming students will find more than 200 campus organizations, more than 20 men's and women's intramural sports, 17 national Greek organizations, and NCAA Football Bowl Subdivision intercollegiate athletic programs to enhance their university experience. Today, the institution has more than 80,000 alumni and meets the needs of individuals and communities at all points along the educational continuum.

ADMISSIONS PROCESS

Unconditional undergraduate admission is based on high school grade point average, official ACT score or comparable SAT, ASSET or Compass score taken within five years prior to the application date. The minimum grade point average accepted for unconditional admission is 2.75 and the minimum ACT or comparable score is 21.

ASSUMPTION COLLEGE

AT A GLANCE

Established in 1904 by the Augustinians of the Assumption, Assumption College is a Catholic coeducational institution known for its classic liberal arts curriculum and strong academic programs.

Assumption College is a place of big ideas and generous hearts, people who inspire you to grow as a student and as a human being. The educational experience is grounded in the rich Catholic intellectual tradition, which cultivates both the intellect and the personal values that students need to meet the demands of a constantly changing world. Undergraduates and graduate students closely interact with faculty members and staff in a thriving community that forms graduates known for critical intelligence, thoughtful citizenship and compassionate service.

At Assumption, 90 percent of our 2,000 undergraduates live on campus and housing is guaranteed for all four years. The campus is lively seven days a week with academic programming, activities sponsored by student clubs and organizations, community service opportunities, campus ministry programs and intercollegiate, intramural and club sports.

LOCATION AND ENVIRONMENT

Assumption College is located on a 185-acre private campus, nestled in a beautiful, residential neighborhood. When you step onto the campus you will feel the immediate sense of community.

The campus is just minutes from downtown Worcester, a bustling metropolitan mecca for the more than 35,000 students attending area colleges and universities. Businesses, government offices and nonprofit organizations provide our students with numerous internships and job opportunities. Assumption students also enjoy access to first-class restaurants and shops, museums, local sports teams and entertainment venues. Students enjoy the best of both worlds—a secure suburban setting with easy access to urban advantages.

Assumption offers a unique study abroad opportunity at its own campus in Rome, Italy. Staffed by full-time Assumption faculty, this semester-long experience lets students explore the country as a "living classroom."

CAMPUS FACILITIES & EQUIPMENT

Assumption is dedicated to providing enhanced, or new, learning and student life facilities.

The new Tsotsis Family Academic Center, a 60,000-square-foot state-of-the-art academic building, contains 13 high-tech, flexible classrooms, seminar rooms, common study spaces, a 400-seat performance hall, a rehearsal room, a multi-purpose space, faculty offices for the Assumption Core Texts and Enduring Questions Program, the Business Studies Department, the Honors Program, the Center for Teaching Excellence, and a new Center for the Study of Ethics.

More than half a million dollars in renovations were completed in Taylor Dining Hall, the primary dining facility on campus that offers students an array of meal options for breakfast, lunch and dinner.

The 8,800-square-foot Tinsley Campus Ministry Center expands and enriches programs that contribute to the spiritual formation of students.

The campus of the College's top-ten ranked study abroad program in Rome, Italy, underwent a $1 million renovation, creating a modern living and learning environment for students spending a semester studying in Rome.

OFF-CAMPUS OPPORTUNITIES

Assumption encourages students to expand their horizons. In addition to the Rome campus, undergraduates can spend a semester or a year studying abroad—from France and England, to Japan, the Czech Republic and Australia, to name a few locations. Many students also augment their education and hone professional skills through local, regional, national and international internships. Assumption students have worked at diverse organizations around the globe, from the Department of Commerce, Central America Bureau and the Department of State (NAFTA Agreement), to Smith Barney, Fidelity, Morgan Stanley, ABC News, and the Alliance Francaise in Paris.

ACADEMIC PROGRAMS

With majors and minors in business, sciences and professional programs, you are sure to find an academic area of interest to you—whether you enter college knowing what that is, or if you figure it out once you get here. And with a dedicated faculty that will guide you each step of the way, your path to success will be clearly lit.

Assumption offers various areas of study—from diverse major and minor combinations to unique partnership programs, pre-professional to accelerated master's degrees.

Accounting; Accounting—Fraud Examination & Forensic; Actuarial Science; Applied Behavior Analysis; Art History; Biology; Biotechnology & Molecular Biology; Business; Chemistry; Clinical Health Professions; Communications; Communication Sciences and Disorders; Community Service Learning; Comparative Literature; Computer Science; Criminology; Data Analytics; Economics; Education (elementary, middle school, secondary); English; Environmental Science; Finance; French; German Studies; Global Studies; Graphic Design; Health Sciences; History; Human Services and Rehabilitation Studies; Information Technology; International Business; Italian Studies; Law, Ethics and Constitutional Studies; Management; Marketing; Mathematics; Medieval and Early Modern Studies; Modern and Classical Languages and Cultures; Molecular Biology; Music; Neuroscience; Occupational Therapy; Organizational Communication; Peace and Conflict Studies; Philosophy; Physical Therapy; Physics; Political Science; Psychology; Sociology; Spanish; Sport Management; Studio Art; Theology; Women's Studies

MAJORS AND DEGREES OFFERED

Area, Ethnic, Cultural, and Gender Studies

- Italian Studies
- Latin American Studies
- Women's Studies

Biological and Biomedical Sciences

- Biology/Biological Sciences, General
- Biotechnology
- Molecular Biology

Business, Management, Marketing, and Related Support Services

- Accounting
- Actuarial Science
- Business Administration and Management, General
- International Business/Trade/Commerce
- Marketing/Marketing Management, General

Communication, Journalism, and Related Programs

- Organizational Communication, General

Computer and Information Sciences and Support Services

- Computer Science

Education

- Teacher Education, Multiple Levels

English Language and Literature/Letters

- English Language and Literature, General

Health Professions and Related Clinical Sciences

- Rehabilitation and Therapeutic Professions

History

- History, General

Mathematics and Statistics

- Mathematics, General

Multi/Interdisciplinary Studies
- International/Global Studies

Natural Resources and Conservation
- Environmental Science

Philosophy and Religious Studies
- Philosophy

Physical Sciences
- Chemistry, General

Psychology
- Psychology, General

Social Sciences
- Criminology
- Economics, General
- International Economics
- Political Science and Government, General
- Sociology

Theology and Religious Vocations
- Theology/Theological Studies

Visual and Performing Arts
- Art History
- Graphic Design
- Music, General

TUITION, ROOM, BOARD, FEES

Tuition $38,850

Room and Board $12,195

Fees $750

FINANCIAL AID

More than 90 percent of Assumption students receive some form of financial assistance, and we're committed to providing you with a consistent level of institutional grants and scholarships all four years. Assumption College will pair you with a personal financial aid advisor who will work with you and your family throughout your four years to pursue federal, state and private funding. You'll also have access to a variety of payment options, including a 10-month, interest-free payment plan.

The Assumption College Merit Scholarship Program is based on academic and cocurricular merit, not financial need. It reflects the College's commitment to promoting a culture of academic excellence and leadership. All students who are accepted for admission to Assumption College are considered for scholarship awards, which range from $12,000–$21,000.

In line with our mission, Assumption's $25,000 Light the Way Scholarship is awarded to up to 50 students who utilize their abilities to Light the Way for others. Whether it's community service to help people in need, innovation to improve society, or volunteering to heal our planet, this scholarship recognizes and supports students who positively impact the world in their own meaningful way.

To apply for financial aid, families must complete the Free Application for Federal Student Aid (FAFSA) by February 15.

STUDENT ORGANIZATIONS AND ACTIVITIES

Our campus buzzes with activity. There is an abundance of events and campus traditions to celebrate as a Greyhound. From attending lectures by renowned speakers, to cheering on the Greyhounds, to grabbing a cup of coffee with friends at the Dunkin' Donuts in Hagan Campus Center, Pup Cup to Spring Concert, Homecoming to Midnight Madness. There's always something happening on the Assumption campus.

Students are encouraged to get involved, you can participate in more than 60 student-run clubs and organizations; whether academic clubs or service groups, theatrical productions or the incredibly popular intramural sports teams.

Accounting Club; ACTV; AC Allies; ADAPT; Advocates for Life; African Dance Club; ALANA Network; Assumption Against Cancer; Best Buddies; Campus Activities Board; Cheerleading; Chinese Students and Friends Association; Chorale; Dance Team; Equestrian Team; Esports Club; Figure Skating Club; Food Recovery Network; GAME; Graphic Design Club; Greenhounds; Heights Yearbook; Hound Sound; Human Services Club; Latin Dance; Le Provocateur; Love Your Melon; Martial Arts Club; Medlife; Men's Club Basketball; Men's Club Volleyball; Moot Court; NSSLHA; Outdoors Club; PAWS; Phi Sigma Tau; Psychology Club; Social Justice Ambassadors; Student Philanthropy; Ultimate Frisbee; Women's Club Basketball; Women's Club Volleyball; Womens' Studies Club; Young Conservative's Club; Running Club

ADMISSIONS PROCESS

The Admissions Committee understands that grading standards vary from school to school, or from one course to another. Class rank provides some context in which to place the grades of students applying from a given school. Some schools also provide grade distribution charts. Finally, the Admissions Committee also considers whether the applicant's grade-point average or rank-in-class is weighted or unweighted.

The number of solid academic courses, including the number of honors or Advanced Placement-level courses, are considered during the application review process. Submission of standardized test scores (SAT-1 or ACT) is optional and applicants who choose not to submit SAT or ACT test scores will not be penalized in the review for admission.

Application Requirements:
- A completed Common Application
- An official high school transcript including senior grades
- A letter of recommendation from a counselor or teacher
- Standardized test scores (optional). Should you want your test scores included in your application review, the school code for the SAT is 3009 and the ACT code is 1782. Test scores must be submitted from the testing center.
- A $50 non-refundable application fee
- ZeeMee video to showcase your personality. Add your ZeeMee link to your Common Application (optional)

Application Deadlines:

Early Decision Deadline is November 1

Early Action Deadline is November 1

Early Action II Deadline is December 15

Regular Decision Deadline is February 15

BABSON COLLEGE

AT A GLANCE

Babson College is a small, private business college located just outside of Boston, MA, founded in 1919 by Roger Babson most well known as the No. 1 undergraduate school for entrepreneurship for the 21st consecutive time and as the No. 1 college for international students . There are many ways to make an impact in the world—the people of Babson prove it every day. Our community—composed of students, staff, alumni, faculty, and friends of the college—is committed to embodying the spirit of Entrepreneurial Thought & Action® in a wide variety of roles, companies, and industries.

LOCATION AND ENVIRONMENT

Residential campus located in Wellesley, MA, just 10 miles west of Boston.

CAMPUS FACILITIES & EQUIPMENT

Innovation Center, Arthur M. Blank Center for Entrepreneurship, Center for Women's Entrepreneurial Leadership, Stephen D. Culter Center for Investments & Finance, The Lewis Institute, Babson Recreation and Athletics Center (completion scheduled for fall 2019).

OFF-CAMPUS OPPORTUNITIES

Weekday shuttle between Babson, Olin and Wellesley College, Thursday-Saturday shuttle to the Woodland MBTA Station and Copley Square, Boston (drop off only), Sunday shuttle to local food store, mall, Woodland MBTA Station.

ACADEMICS

Students can customize their business degree with optional concentrations. We currently offer 27 concentrations.

MAJORS AND DEGREES OFFERED

Babson offers a Bachelor of Science degree to future leaders looking to create social and economic value around the world. The academic experience at Babson is uniquely designed for students who want to study business while developing an entrepreneurial mindset and gaining real-world experience. Our focus on Entrepreneurial Thought and Action® enables you to discover your strengths, pursue your passions, and create your path to success.

At Babson, you learn to:

- Think entrepreneurially, turning ideas into action
- Communicate effectively when writing and speaking
- Understand global and multicultural perspectives
- Lead teams effectively to tackle challenges
- Analyze data to gain insights and develop strategies
- Create socially responsible and ethical business solutions

TUITION, ROOM, BOARD, FEES

2017–2018 total estimated cost: $68,482 Tuition: $49,664

Room: $10,222

Meal Plan: $5,616

FINANCIAL AID

Babson awards $43 million in undergraduate aid; $36 million comes directly from Babson in grants and scholarships. Approximately 50 percent of Babson's undergraduates receive financial assistance. Babson meets approximately 97 percent of students' demonstrated need. Babson commits to each student's level of Babson Grant for four years, provided there are no major changes to the family's financial circumstances or a change in the number of the student's siblings in college.

We require the FAFSA and the CSS Profile in order to be considered for Financial Aid. In addition to Financial Aid, we award many scholarships based on merit and other criteria.

STUDENT ORGANIZATIONS AND ACTIVITIES

115+ student clubs and organizations. Highlights include the Babson Dance Ensemble, Improv Troupe, Babson Fashion Group, Babson's Community of Developers & Entrepreneurs (CODE), and Investment Club. NCAA Division III Varsity Athletic Programs, 22 varsity sports—11 for men, 11 for women—club sports, and recreational programming. 21 percent of the student population participate in Greek Life. We have 3 Sororities, 4 Fraternities, and 2 co-ed Business Fraternities.

ADMISSIONS PROCESS

Babson College bases its acceptance of students on both academic and nonacademic factors. The academic factors include high school record, recommendations, standardized test scores, and essays. The nonacademic factors include extracurricular activities, demonstrated leadership, character/personal qualities, volunteer work, work experience, creativity and enthusiasm and a willingness to contribute to the Babson community in meaningful ways. Graduation from secondary school is required for admission. The most competitive students have taken approximately 5 solid academic courses per year at the highest available level (Honors, Advanced Placement or International Baccalaureate). The SAT I or ACT is required for admission. The TOEFL or IELTS is required for students who are nonnative English speakers. Babson offers several application programs. Students may apply Early Decision (binding process), Early Action or Regular Decision. The deadline for Early Decision and Early Action is November 1. The Regular Decision Deadline is early January. Transfer students may apply for September entrance by March 15 and for January entrance by October 15.

BARNARD COLLEGE

AT A GLANCE

Barnard is the most sought-after liberal arts college for women in the US. Barnard provides a cosmopolitan setting, dynamic academic programs, access to internships and a unique partnership with Columbia University.

Barnard is a small, highly selective liberal arts college for women located in New York City. The student body of just over 2,500 are part of a diverse and close-knit community and study with leading scholars who serve as dedicated, accessible mentors and teachers in intimate classes. Founded in 1889, Barnard also engages in a unique partnership with Columbia University, situated directly across the street. Students have access to additional course offerings, extracurricular activities, NCAA Division I Ivy League athletics and a fully coed social life. The location in New York City grants students access to thousands of internship opportunities in addition to unparalleled cultural, intellectual and social resources. Barnard's diverse student body includes residents from nearly every state and more than 50 countries worldwide. About 40 percent of the student body identify as students of color, and 8 percent are non-US citizens or permanent residents.

LOCATION AND ENVIRONMENT

Barnard is located north of Central Park on the upper west side of Manhattan, in the safe and student-friendly Morningside Heights neighborhood, directly across the street from Columbia University. The campus occupies 4 acres of urban property along Broadway between 116th and 120th streets and serves as an oasis from the hustle and bustle of New York City. The south end of the campus, referred to as the Quad, contains 4 interconnected residence halls; 11 Additional residence halls provide those entering as first-years guaranteed housing for four years. Some housing is provided for transfers but is not guaranteed. The Diana Center, a 70,000-square-foot student center, is the hub of campus life. The College is completing a new center for teaching and learning, The Milstein Center, scheduled to open in August 2018. It will house a dynamic library that incorporates state-of-the art technologies and learning spaces in an interactive setting. It will act also as an academic core for the campus, linking departments and disciplines, both physically and philosophically.

CAMPUS FACILITIES & EQUIPMENT

The Quad is located at the south end of campus and includes four residence hall buildings: Brooks, Hewitt, Reid and Sulzberger. The Arthur Ross Courtyard is located in the Quad. The Jan R. and Marley Blue Lewis '05 Parlor is located on the 1st floor of Brooks Hall and is a reading room for quiet study.

The Diana Center, the hub for campus life, is located in the center of campus. Housed within are Liz's Place cafe and the Millicent Carey McIntosh Student Dining Room. The Louise Heublein McCagg '59 Gallery, located on the 4th floor. The gallery hosts student exhibitions coordinated by the Art History and Architecture Departments. The Green Roof, located on the 6th floor of The Diana Center, is used both as a classroom, research area and as an event space. It also has terrific birds eye views of campus and the surrounding neighborhood.

Lehman Lawn is located in the center of the campus, adjacent to The Diana Center and in front the soon-to-be-opened Milstein Center.

Under construction: The Milstein Center, a 128,000 square foot Teaching a learning Center. The new building will house:

- A library with a core collection of books, journals, special collections and archives that support a strong liberal arts education.

- A digital commons with five innovative teaching labs (movement lab, empirical reasoning center, digital humanities lab, creativity lab, and multimedia lab) and a range of flexible learning spaces that utilize new media and digital technologies.

- A computational science center equipped to support students and faculty in pioneering scientific, mathematical, and computational methods research, which physically connects to science classrooms and labs in neighboring Altschul Hall.

- Inviting student spaces that include a variety of active and quiet study areas for individuals and groups.

- Flexible, technologically current classrooms for seminars and large group instruction.

- Conferencing facilities connected to meeting and event spaces in The Diana Center.

- Departmental offices for economics, history, political science and urban studies.

- Homes for two signature programs: the Barnard Center for Research on Women and the Athena Center for Leadership Studies.

- A small café, serving coffee and grab-and-go items.

- Accessible outdoor terraces.

OFF-CAMPUS OPPORTUNITIES

Barnard's location offers its students a variety of work experiences through more than 3,000 internships. More than two thirds of Barnard students participate in internships throughout the academic year and/or summer. Furthermore, Barnard has a rich history and tradition of study abroad dating back to the 1930s. Qualified students are eligible to study in nearly 100 programs in more than fifty countries worldwide. Students may also participate in a domestic exchange with Spelman College in Atlanta or Howard University in Washington, D.C.

ACADEMICS

First-Year Experience: The First-Year Experience includes two required seminar classes: First-Year Writing, focusing on reading literary texts critically and writing effectively, and First-Year Seminar, emphasizing disciplinary and interdisciplinary content that challenges students to write and speak persuasively. First-year students are also required to take one course in Physical Education.

Foundations

The Distributional Requirements, called Foundations, are designed to expose students to a variety of disciplines, approaches, and skills that, together, form the whole of a liberal arts education. The requirements are designed to be flexible; students choose from a wide spectrum of courses and take two courses each in languages, arts and humanities, social sciences, and sciences (one of which includes a lab). Furthermore, students follow Modes of Thinking that include one course each in of the following. Courses taken to satisfy the Distributional Requirements can also be used to satisfy the Modes of Thinking requirement:

- Thinking Locally–New York City—where students examine the community and environment in which they find themselves as residents of New York City to better understand the significance of local context.

- Thinking through Global Inquiry—where students consider communities, places, and experiences beyond their immediate location, expanding their perspectives on the world and their place in it.

- Thinking about Social Difference—where students examine how difference is defined, lived, and challenged, and the disparities of power and resources in all their manifestations.

- Thinking with Historical Perspective—where students examine the ways in which historical context shapes and conditions the world, challenging them to see the past with fresh eyes.

- Thinking Quantitatively and Empirically—where students are exposed to numbers, data, graphs, and mathematical methods, in order to better understand quantitative and empirical approaches to thinking and problem solving.

- Thinking Technologically and Digitally—where students discover new ways of learning that open up innovative fields of study, including computational science and coding, digital arts and humanities, geographic information systems, and digital design.

MAJORS AND DEGREES OFFERED

American Studies; Ancient Studies; Anthropology; Architecture; Art History; Asian and Middle Eastern Cultures; Biochemistry; Biological Sciences; Biopsychology; Chemistry; Comparative Literature; Computer Science; Dance; Economic History; Economics; Economics and Mathematics; English; Environmental Biology; Environmental Science; Foreign Area Studies; French; German; Greek (Classics); Greek and Latin; History; Italian; Jewish Studies; Latin (Classics); Mathematics; Medieval and Renaissance Studies; Music; Philosophy; Physics & Astronomy; Political Science; Psychology; Religion; Russian (Slavic); Sociology; Spanish & Latin American Cultures; Statistics; Theatre; Urban Studies; Women's Studies

The College provides a unique education program, leading to teaching certification with a specific urban studies track, and prepares students for programs in health and medicine, law, and business, as well as further study in a variety of graduate programs. Barnard College also offers double-and joint-degree programs in cooperation with other schools within the Columbia community. These include a five-year M.P.A./M.I.A. (3-2) program offered in conjunction with the School of International and Public Affairs. Through the School of Engineering and Applied Science, Barnard students can pursue a five-year (3-2) program in all branches of engineering, leading to both a B.A. and a B.S. degree. Through an agreement with List College of the Jewish Theological Seminary, students can simultaneously earn a B.A. degree from Barnard and a B.A. at JTS.

For a select group of scholars who meet specific eligibility requirements, the Arthur O. Eve Higher Education Opportunity Program (HEOP) and Barnard Opportunity Program (BOP) offer an additional pathway to admission to Barnard. A lending library, laptop computers, free tutoring, mentoring, study skills workshops, and graduate school preparation and career guidance are available to all BOP and HEOP Scholars, in addition to the resources and support they receive as Barnard students. To be considered for HEOP, students must be residents of New York State.

TUITION, ROOM, BOARD, FEES

Total Basic Budget

Tuition and Fees: $53,062

Room and Board°: $16,100

Books/Supplies: $1,150

Miscellaneous: $1,370

Total Basic Budget: $71,682

FINANCIAL AID

Barnard College is 100 percent need-blind in our review of US citizens and permanent residents applying as first-year students. We are need-aware for transfer students. We meet 100 percent of demonstrated need with need-based financial aid for US Citizens and Permanent Residents. We offer a limited amount of aid to international citizens and do not offer merit or athletic scholarships. Our policies reflect our commitment to making Barnard a realistic option for families, regardless of finances, and to ensuring qualified applicants are able to afford to attend.

Average Institutional grant: $38,265

% of First year students receiving financial aid: 39%

Pell Grant Recipients (total Population): 16%

Class of 2017 financial aid indebtedness: $17,848

STUDENT ORGANIZATIONS AND ACTIVITIES

Barnard women have access to more than eighty clubs and organizations on the Barnard campus. Add to this list hundreds of additional dually recognized clubs with members from both Barnard and Columbia, provided for through Barnard's partnership with the University. Student groups include performance groups, academic and pre-professional, ethnic and cultural, language, community service, and publications. Social interaction and cooperation between Barnard and Columbia groups is virtually seamless, with Barnard women regularly joining and leading many Columbia organizations.

RECOGNIZED BARNARD STUDENT ORGANIZATIONS AND ACTIVITIES:
PRE-PROFESSIONAL

The Athena Pre-Law Society; Barnard Psychology Society; Barnard Chemical Society; Barnard Quantitative Society; CU Pre-Veterinary Society; Network for Pre-Medical Students; Pre-Health Students Organization; Smart Women Lead; Smart Women Securities

CULTURAL

Asian American Alliance; African Students Association; Barnard Organization of Soul Sisters (BOSS); Caribbean Students Association; Chinese Students Club; Club Bangla; Club Q; Club Zamana; Columbia Japan Society; CU SAFA (South-Asian Feminist Alliance); Haitian Students' Association; Korean Students Association; Liga Filipina; Mujeres; Organization of Pakistani Students; Sounds of China; Taiwanese American Students Association; Turath, The Arab Students Association

PERFORMANCE

Bacchantae; Bach Society; Barnard Columbia Ancient Drama Group; Barnard Flute Choir; Columbia Musical Theatre Society; CoLab Performing Arts Collective; Columbia Raas; CUPAL; Control Top; CUBE (CU Ballet Ensemble); CU Dhoom; CU Players; King's Crown Shakespeare Troupe; Latenite Theatre; New Opera Workshop; NOMADS; Orchesis; Philolexian Society; Raw Elementz; Roya Persian Dance Group; Sabor; Taal; Third Wheel Improv; VDay; XMAS!

SPECIAL INTEREST

Barnard Movement Exchange; Barnard Outdoor Adventure Team; Barnard EcoReps; Barnard Writing Collective; Columbia University Sign Language Club; Nightline Peer-Listening Hotline; She's the First; Sprout Up; Take Back the Night; WBAR

PUBLICATIONS

Barnard Bite; Barnard Bulletin; Echoes; Hoot Magazine; HerCampus

ADMISSIONS PROCESS

The Committee on Admissions selects young women of proven academic strength who exhibit the potential for further intellectual growth. Careful consideration is given to candidates' high school records, recommendations, writing skills, standardized test scores, special abilities and interests, and personal and educational context.

Admission to Barnard is highly selective and candidates for admission to the first-year class are expected to have taken a highly rigorous college-preparatory program. Barnard also requires first-year candidates to submit scores from the SAT Reasoning Test or the ACT. Students educated in a non-English-speaking setting or who have studied in English for less than four years must also take the TOEFL or IELTS exam. An interview is recommended for first-year students, but it is not required. Early decision applications must be submitted by November 1. Regular applications must be received by January 1. There is a non-refundable application fee of $75. Transfer applications must be submitted by November 1 for consideration for January enrollment and by March 15 for consideration for September enrollment.

BECKER COLLEGE

AT A GLANCE

Future-focused Becker College has an average placement rate of over 90 percent for employment or further study. Becker prepares over 1,800 students from across the globe to be creative, innovative, and adaptive to the ever-changing world.

Becker College is an undergraduate and graduate, career-focused college; it is a private, independent, co-educational institution with undergraduate (associate and bachelor) degrees; graduate degrees; and adult education degrees (associate and bachelor). The College is dedicated to providing a supportive and inclusive learning community that prepares graduates for their first to last careers.

The College prepares students across all majors to navigate what experts have described as the greatest velocity of change in human history through a foundation in learning agility known as The Agile Mindset. Becker believes The Agile Mindset is essential for success in the increasingly complex, automated, and hyper-connected world of the 21st century. It forms the foundation of the College's core curricula.

The Agile Mindset merges learning agility and value-creation orientation with a focus on four uniquely human skillsets: empathy to understand the needs of others and inspire innovation; divergent thinking to explore possibilities and discover opportunities where they may not appear to exist; an entrepreneurial outlook to create new value regardless of job position; and social and emotional intelligence to collaborate effectively with others in interdisciplinary teams.

Becker College traces its history to 1784-one of the nation's top-25 oldest institutions of higher learning-with a founding charter signed by American Revolutionaries John Hancock and Samuel Adams.

LOCATION AND ENVIRONMENT

Becker's Worcester campus is situated in the Elm Park section of Worcester, MA; a quiet area of tree-lined streets and historic homes, including 15 residence halls. The campus is a short walk from the downtown business district, which is also home to two additional apartment-style residence halls. An academic building, library, and health science center are located on the Worcester campus quad, and a number of other college properties dot the neighborhood. The city of Worcester (pop. 182,544) is New England's second largest urban center.

On the Leicester campus, former homes dating from the 19th century, now student housing and faculty offices, surround a lush town common. There are eight residence halls, and additional facilities include a campus center and fitness facility, academic buildings, an auditorium, library, gymnasium, athletic field, the Lenfest Animal Health Center-a teaching facility which includes a veterinary clinic that is open to the public, and a public mental health counseling clinic for training students in the Master in Mental Health Counseling Program. The Becker College Equestrian Center is just a few scenic miles away, in Paxton, Mass.

Becker College maintains a shuttle schedule, from morning to evening, and on weekends, between the Worcester and Leicester campuses, and from the Worcester campus to Bancroft Hall and Houghton Hall, located in downtown Worcester.

CAMPUS FACILITIES & EQUIPMENT

In 2018, Becker opened the Colleen C. Barrett Center for Global Innovation and Entrepreneurship—a 10,000 sq. ft. state-of-the-art academic building that includes an AR/VR lab, game studio lab, esports club, Yunus Social Business Centre, the Massachusetts Digital Games Institute, faculty offices and meeting rooms, and facilities dedicated to new enterprise incubation.

The Lenfest Animal Health Center, a unique experience in higher education, is a teaching facility which includes a veterinary clinic open to the public, which sees about 1,000 clients a year for wellness care and non-urgent medical and surgical care for dogs, cats, other small mammals, and birds. Students in the Master in Mental Health Counseling program gain experience through a public, on-campus clinic.

Becker is home to the first Yunus Social Business Centre in the U.S. This Centre empowers individuals to identify real-world problems and create self-sustaining business solutions that have social impact while generating jobs and entrepreneurial opportunities that drive economic development regionally and around the world.

On Becker's Worcester campus, the Massachusetts Digital Games Institute (MassDiGI) operates as the statewide center for economic development, entrepreneurship, and academic cooperation in the Commonwealth's interactive media and game development ecosystem.

The Becker College Equestrian Center is situated on 30 acres of land and includes expansive turn-out pastures for the horses, an indoor riding arena, and a large outdoor ring. The center offers full board for horses and lessons to both Becker College students and the public.

The John J. Dorsey, Sr., Crime Scene Lab gives students the opportunity to assess a crime scene, understand the nature of physical evidence, learn the proper actions of the initial responding officer, perform evidence recognition and preservation tasks, and ultimately solve the crime.

OFF-CAMPUS OPPORTUNITIES

Worcester offers a wide array of social, cultural, and recreational opportunities, including entertainment and sports arenas, first-class museums, the Hanover Theatre, outdoor recreation areas, and a wide range of shopping and dining options.

Worcester features world-renowned museums and concert halls, theatres, and galleries, as well as a wealth of performing groups, ethnic festivals, artists of every discipline, restaurants, specialty shops, and hotels. Becker students also have access to facilities, events, courses, and activities at the 10 other colleges in the Worcester area, and provides regular trips to shopping malls and fun exploration of the New England area.

Just an hour away from Boston and Springfield, Mass., Providence, R.I., and Hartford, Conn., Worcester is at the crossroads of several major routes, including the Massachusetts Turnpike (I-90), Interstates 290 and 395, and Routes 146 and 20. Worcester also offers a regional airport, with service to New York. Becker College offers internship programs through Semester in the City, study abroad options through its partnerships with the Center for International Studies (CIS), CIEE, and Semester at Sea, and a wide range of service trips to such locations as Haiti, Jamaica, Boston, and more.

ACADEMIC PROGRAMS

At Becker, preparing students appropriately for the future of work means cultivating adaptive learners with Agile Mindsets who can leverage the uniquely human skills of empathy, divergent thinking, an entrepreneurial outlook, and social and emotional intelligence to adapt and thrive in a world that is increasingly volatile, uncertain, complex, and ambiguous. The Agile Mindset is the academic foundation that equips students to navigate change and create new value in the hyper-connected, automated world of the 21st century. Students are encouraged to develop creative and divergent thinking, both in and out of the classroom, which engages and empowers them to approach the future with the ability to adapt to a world in which change is a constant.

MAJORS AND DEGREES OFFERED
SCHOOL OF ANIMAL STUDIES & NATURAL SCIENCES

- Biology
- Equine Studies
- Veterinary Science
  - o Veterinary Technology
  - o Pre-Veterinary
  - o Laboratory Animal Sciences
- Animal Care (AS)
- Veterinary Technology (AS)

SCHOOL OF DESIGN & TECHNOLOGY

- Applied Computer Science
- Business Administration (AS, BS)
  - o Computer Information Systems
  - o Data Science
  - o Management
  - o Marketing
  - o Sport Management
- Design/Graphic Design
- Interactive Media Design
  - o Game Arts
  - o Game Design
  - o Game Development & Programming
  - o Game Production & Management
- Interactive Media Design: BA and MFA (4+1)

SCHOOL OF NURSING & BEHAVIORAL SCIENCES

- Exercise Science
  - o Health and Fitness
  - o Pre-Physical Therapy / Health Science
- Nursing (AS)
- Nursing

SCHOOL OF HUMANITIES & SOCIAL SCIENCES

- Criminal Justice (AS, BS)
  - o Forensic Science/Criminalistics
  - o Forensic Psychology
  - o Homeland Security
- Global Citizenship
- Early Childhood and Youth Education (BA)
- Early Childhood Education (AS)
- Legal Studies
- Liberal Arts (AA, BA)
- Psychology (AA, BA)
  - o Addictions Counseling
  - o Applied Behavior Analysis
  - o Mental Health Counseling
  - o Pre-Med / Health Studies
  - o Mental Health Counseling (MA)
- Undecided/Exploratory First Year

TUITION, ROOM, BOARD, FEES

Full Time Tuition (12–18 credits per semester) $35,600

On Campus Room Board $13,800

Required Fees $3,600

FINANCIAL AID

Financial aid is available for all eligible students through federal, state, and Becker College programs.

STUDENT ORGANIZATIONS AND ACTIVITIES

Becker College students participate in an active community through a variety of social, educational, and cultural programs. The Becker College experience provides students with numerous opportunities to get involved, to follow their passion, to take initiative, and to be a leader.

Becker College is home to more than 25 student organizations-from music to cosplay, pre-veterinary clubs to business, P.R.I.D.E. esports, and more. Students are welcome to develop their interests and apply to establish new clubs. Campus events and programs for Becker College students are planned by Becker College students. The Campus Activities Board (CAB) is a student organization that works in conjunction with the Office of Campus Activities and Student Leadership.CAB provides weekly student-led social, cultural, and educational events for Becker College students that align with the College's goals and mission. Any Becker College student can join CAB. Other opportunities include Becker's 17 Division III Varsity Sports.

ADMISSIONS PROCESS

To learn more about Becker College call 877.523.2537, email admissions@becker. edu, or visit www.becker.edu.

Complete applications must include:

- A completed application for admission, www.becker.edu/apply. Students may also submit an application through The Common Application.
- An official copy of the secondary school transcript. Students who have received a General Equivalency Diploma (GED) must forward an official score report.
- SAT I or ACT scores. The Becker College CEEB code is 3079.
- Optional letter of recommendation. Becker College recognizes that all students are individuals and will consider each applicant's personal strengths and achievements. Any other supporting materials that are submitted will be considered.
- Optional essay on any topic, 250-500 words in length.

BELMONT UNIVERSITY

AT A GLANCE

Belmont University sits on 75 historic acres in the heart of Nashville, Tennessee, a thriving metropolis known worldwide as Music City. Belmont University is among the fastest growing Christian universities in the nation with approximately 8,000 students hailing from every state and 36 countries. Belmont University is accredited by the Commission on Colleges of the Southern Association of Colleges and Schools to award baccalaureate, master's, and doctoral degrees. Belmont offers over 90 areas of undergraduate study, more than 25 master's programs and five doctoral degrees through its nine colleges: Jack C. Massey College of Business, Liberal Arts & Social Sciences, Mike Curb College of Entertainment and Music Business, Gordon E. Inman College of Health Sciences & Nursing, Law, Pharmacy, Theology & Christian Ministry, Science & Mathematics, and Visual & Performing Arts.

LOCATION AND ENVIRONMENT

Belmont University occupies a 75-acre campus in Nashville, Tennessee, just two miles from downtown and adjacent to the world-famous Music Row. With more than 1.7 million residents, the metropolitan Nashville area is a cultural, educational, health-care, commercial, and financial center in the mid-South. Practical educational opportunities, offered through diverse curriculums, provide students with the hands-on experience they need in preparation for a meaningful career. The city's location, halfway between the northern and southern boundaries of the United States, with three intersecting interstate highways and an international airport, makes it accessible to students from across the country.

CAMPUS FACILITIES & EQUIPMENT

Significant growth extends to our facilities as well, with Belmont adding more than half-a-billion dollars in new construction, renovation and property acquisition in the past 17 years. In fact, the past seven years alone have seen the opening of 14 new or renovated buildings on campus. In 2010, the Pharmacy and Physical Therapy programs moved into the new McWhorter Hall. The Randall and Sadie Baskin Center was completed in 2012, home to the College of Law—the first new law school in Middle Tennessee in nearly a century.

That same year also brought the opening of McAfee Concert Hall, providing a stunning new large venue for music performances with world-class acoustics. In 2014, Belmont opened the Janet Ayers Academic Center—the largest building on campus and home to the Colleges of Liberal Arts and Social Sciences, Theology and Christian Ministry, and Sciences and Mathematics, along with Belmont's first intentionally-designed chapel.

In 2015, Belmont cut the ribbon on the technology-laden R. Milton and Denice Johnson Center, providing a new home for the Curb College of Entertainment and Music Business and the media studies program, as well as a vibrant new 950-seat cafeteria.

A renovated Massey Business Center, home of the Jack C. Massey College of Business, was completed in January 2016 featuring new state-of-the-art classroom and learning spaces for Belmont's nationally ranked business programs.

In early 2017, Belmont celebrated the grand-reopening of the renovated Gabhart Student Center, a new home for student meeting space and support services. Months later, Belmont celebrated the opening of The Belmont Store, a new campus retail outlet and spirit shop, as well as, the Gallery of Iconic Guitars, known as the GIG, Music City's premier venue designed to celebrate some of the most rare guitars and stringed instruments ever known.

Belmont open the renovated Hitch Building, in fall 2017, with new practice, rehearsal, office and classroom spaces for the School of Music and Department of Sport Science. And in that same span, Belmont has also completed 5 new residence halls, bringing the number of on-campus resident spaces to nearly 3,500. Currently under construction is Belmont's largest residence hall to date, which will accommodate more than 600 students when completed.

OFF-CAMPUS OPPORTUNITIES

A Christian Community of Learning and Service

Belmont is a student-focused, Christian community of learning and service where students hear from their first visit to campus until the day they graduate that they are created for a purpose in life. The Belmont faculty and staff dedicate themselves to preparing and empowering students to find their passion and use it to change the world. The university seeks to show every student how the love of Christ can compel them to lead lives of disciplined intelligence, compassion, courage and faith.

In fact, Belmont students, faculty and staff are consistently challenged to look at the hardest circumstances and ask, "What can we do?" Students are encouraged to engage and transform the world, locally and globally, by participation in disaster relief trips to everywhere from the tsunami-stricken areas of Southeast Asia to the Gulf Coast after Hurricane Katrina. Students serve locally at various relief and community organizations in Nashville throughout the year, and student-athletes take part annually in sports evangelism mission trips to South Africa, Ukraine and Brazil. Others have taken advantage of what they're learning at Belmont, incorporating their major studies into various service projects around the world, including working with orphans in India and assisting with physical therapy needs in Guatemala.

ACADEMIC PROGRAMS

Intent on being a leader among teaching universities, Belmont brings together the best of liberal arts and professional education in a Christian community of learning and service. Belmont was ranked fifth on the U.S. News & World Report listing of "Best Universities" in the South and named a "Most Innovative" university for the 2018 edition of America's Best Colleges, making Belmont the highest ranked university in Tennessee in this category. Both Rolling Stone and Time magazines have hailed Belmont's Mike Curb College of Entertainment & Music Business as one of the best music business programs in the country. The Jack C. Massey Graduate School of Business has been named the best MBA program in the region, while Belmont's business administration and accounting programs have been accredited by AACSB International, the premier accrediting agency in that arena, placing Belmont amongst less than 1 percent of the world's business schools. Moreover, Belmont University's undergraduate School of Business consistently achieves a Top 100 national ranking in BusinessWeek's annual report on "The Best Undergrad B-Schools" in the U.S. Belmont's Enactus team has won multiple national championships and a World Cup.

Located in the heart of Music City, one of Belmont's consistent success stories is its world-renowned music and music business programs, including songwriting. Several big names in the music industry started their careers at Belmont including, Christian recording artists Ginny Owens and Steven Curtis Chapman, and country stars Trisha Yearwood, Lee Ann Womack, Brad Paisley, Josh Turner and Florida Georgia Line, plus alternative rock band Judah and the Lion. The annual "Christmas at Belmont" concert showcases performing ensembles from many different genres and has been broadcast nationwide on PBS for several years.

Students who have passions outside of the music industry also have a home at Belmont. From international business and accounting to education, theology, nursing, journalism and the humanities, Belmont provides avenues of learning for almost any interest. Recent program additions include an undergraduate degree in public health, global leadership studies, legal studies, sport administration, °fashion design, °fashion merchandising, °interior design (° pending SACSCOC approval), in addition to, a four-year dual PharmD/MBA degree, a Master of Arts in Mental Health Counseling and a Doctor of Nursing Practice program.

Belmont faculty members display a consistent commitment to excellence as well. Multiple professors have been awarded Fulbright awards, including a nursing professor who spent a year in Uganda as a guest lecturer while conducting research on how standards of nursing are adapted to austere conditions. Also, five Belmont professors (Finance, Psychology, Spanish, Philosophy and Mathematics) have been chosen as Tennessee Professor of the Year by CASE/Carnegie Foundation since 2000.

Belmont's boundaries extend beyond the Nashville campus through its Cool Springs campus and organized programs such as the Washington Center program and Belmont West in Los Angeles and Belmont East in New York City and Washington D.C. Study-abroad programs place students in China, Costa Rica, Great Britain, France, Germany, Italy, Russia, South Africa and Spain, among other foreign nations.

MAJORS AND DEGREES OFFERED

Belmont University is accredited by the Commission on Colleges of the Southern Association of Colleges and Schools to award baccalaureate, master's, and doctoral degrees. Belmont grants seven undergraduate degrees: the Bachelor of Arts, the Bachelor of Business Administration, the Bachelor of Fine Arts, the Bachelor of Music, the Bachelor of Science, the Bachelor of Science in Nursing, and the Bachelor of Social Work.

Undergraduate majors or concentrations are offered in:

Jack C. Massey College of Business

Accounting; Economics; Entrepreneurship; Finance; General Business; International Business; International Economics; Management; Management Information Systems; Marketing; Social Entrepreneurship

Mike Curb College of Entertainment & Music Business

Audio & Video Production; Audio Engineering Technology; Entertainment Industry Studies; Journalism; Mass Communication; Motion Pictures; Multimedia Production; Music Business; Publishing; Songwriting ; Video Production

Gordon E. Inman College of Health Sciences & Nursing

Nursing ; Public Health; Social Work ;

College of Liberal Arts & Social Sciences

School of Education

Early Childhood Education; Elementary Education; Exercise Science; Secondary Education; Sport Administration

School of Humanities

Asian Studies; English; French; German ; Philosophy; Spanish

School of Social Sciences

Communication Studies; Corporate Communication; History; International Politics; Political Science; Politics & Public Law; Public Relations; Sociology

College of Sciences & Mathematics

Applied Mathematics; Biochemistry & Molecular Biology; Biology; Chemistry; Computer Science; Engineering Physics; Environmental Science; Mathematics; Neuroscience; Pharmaceutical Studies; Physics; Physics—Pre Health; Psychology; Web Programming & Development

College of Theology & Christian Ministry

Biblical Languages; Biblical Studies; Christian Leadership; Church Leadership & Administration; Faith & Social Justice; Philosophy of Religion; Religion & the Arts; Religious Studies; Worship Leadership

College of Visual & Performing Arts

Department of Art

Art; Art Education; Art History; Design Communications; Studio Art

Department of Theatre & Dance

Theatre & Drama; Theatre Directing; Theatre Education; Theatre Performance; Theatre Production Design

O'More School of Design

°Fashion Design; °Fashion Merchandising; °Interior Design (°pending SACSCOC approval)

School of Music

Church Music; Commercial Music; Music (Bachelor of Arts); Music Composition; Music Education; Music Performance; Music Theory; Music Therapy; Music with an Outside Minor; Musical Theatre; Piano Pedagogy

Interdisciplinary Programs

Global Leadership Studies ; Legal Studies

Pre-Professional Programs Available In:

Pre-Allied Health; Pre-Dental; Pre-Law; Pre-Medical; Pre-Occupational Therapy; Pre-Optometry; Pre-Pharmacy; Pre-Physical Therapy; Pre-Veterinary

School Says . . .

TUITION, ROOM, BOARD, FEES

The total cost of attending Belmont is only 80 percent of the national average for a private college. For a full-time undergraduate student living on campus, the total cost for the 2018–19 academic year is approximately $46,430 which includes tuition, fees, room, and board.

FINANCIAL AID

The financial aid program at Belmont combines merit-based assistance with need-based assistance to make the university education affordable. Institutional merit awards range from highly selective full-tuition Presidential Scholarships to various levels of partial merit awards. Athletic and artistic scholarships are also available. Belmont also administers traditional state and federal financial aid programs. Campus employment is available. Parents may arrange monthly tuition payments through an outside vendor. To apply for need-based financial assistance, the student must complete the Free Application for Federal Student Aid (FAFSA). FAFSA Code: 003479

STUDENT ORGANIZATIONS AND ACTIVITIES

Belmont's campus life offers 180+ clubs and organizations. The popular intramurals program includes everything from flag football and basketball to wiffleball and dodgeball. With more than half of Belmont's undergrads living on campus there's always something going on from socials, movie nights and concerts to the annual Fall Follies and Curb College Showcase Series.

And in terms of student activities, there's a club or group for nearly every interest. Belmont is home to six nationally recognized sororities and three nationally recognized fraternities representing NPC, IFC and NPHC. The Bruins are big on giving back, too, logging more than 200,000 hours of community service annually.

ATHLETICS

In addition to celebrating academic excellence and phenomenal growth, Belmont boasts 17 intercollegiate sports teams. The Belmont Bruins men's basketball team won the Ohio Valley Conference regular season championship in 2013, 2014, and 2015 and made its seventh appearance in the NCAA National Tournament in 2015 and competed in the NIT in 2014, 2016, and 2017. The Belmont Bruins women's basketball team made its first appearance in the NCAA National Tournament in 2016, 2017, and 2018. Baseball, both cross country teams, and the volleyball team have earned recent conference titles. Belmont student-athletes excel in the classroom, too, as Belmont has won the conference's All-Academic Trophy multiple times. The award is given annually to the conference school with the greatest percentage of student-athletes who earned a GPA of 3.0 or higher.

ADMISSIONS PROCESS

Belmont's Admissions Committee considers applications based on the total picture that a student's credentials present. High school students will be considered competitive for admission if they present a rigorous course of college-preparatory, academic studies. Students should have an above-average academic and cumulative grade point average and rank in the top half of their graduating class. Any college-level work is also expected to be at the above-average level. A strong correlation between high school grades and entrance examination scores is expected. The essays, list of activities, and recommendations are also strongly considered as indicators of success at Belmont. Additional requirements such as portfolios or auditions are considered in conjunction with the academic credentials for those programs that require them. Each application is considered on an individual basis. No two applicants will present the same credentials or the same "fit" with the university. Our desire is to work with each student to determine the likelihood of that student to enroll in, graduate from, and use the benefits of the Belmont educational experience.

For more information, contact:
Office of Admissions
Belmont University
1900 Belmont Boulevard
Nashville, TN 37212
615-460-6785
800-56ENROLL
Fax: 615-460-5434
admissions@belmont.edu
www.belmont.edu
CEEB Code: 1058
ACT Code: 3946

895

BELOIT COLLEGE

AT A GLANCE

Beloit College is a four-year, independent, national college of liberal arts and sciences in southern Wisconsin. Students can expect to receive a premium education from scholars who put teaching first and involve students as much as possible in hands-on research. Small class sizes often result in professors becoming influential mentors, who empower their students to discover what they love to do and put into practice their newfound skills and knowledge to make a remarkable difference in the world. The result is that by the time Beloiters graduate, they haven't just accrued a transcript; they've compiled a strong résumé that demonstrates an ability to think critically and creatively, communicate clearly, and collaborate effectively with diverse groups of people.

Beloit's 1,350 students come from nearly every state and more than 40 countries. With an incredible breadth of opportunities, a historic campus with modern facilities, a nationally recognized faculty, and creative, motivated students, Beloit is truly a "college that changes lives." Founded in 1846 on the Midwestern frontier, Beloit is Wisconsin's first college.

LOCATION AND ENVIRONMENT

Beloit's 40-acre campus is just across the Wisconsin-Illinois state line and is conveniently located just a short drive from three major cities: Chicago (90 miles northwest), Madison (50 miles south), and Milwaukee (70 miles southwest). Beloit's academic buildings are clustered around lawns dotted with trees and twenty ancient North American Indian mounds. Most students live on campus, as Beloit is a residential college that requires students to live in college-operated residence facilities for at least six semesters of full-time enrollment. Beloiters have a variety of housing options to choose from, including traditional residence halls, fraternities (3) and sororities (3), apartments, and special interest houses. All residences halls are within easy walking distance of classrooms, studio locations, and the college's athletic facilities.

Banks, restaurants, and shops can be found within a short walking distance, in downtown Beloit just two blocks from campus. On Saturdays from May through October, students like to attend the region's most popular farmers' market. For ten days each winter, students, local residents, and visitors flock to the Beloit Film Festival (BIFF), where more than 100 films are screened in downtown venues. Year-round, active students venture to one of several nearby parks to exercise, or when it's warm, to listen to outdoor concerts.

CAMPUS FACILITIES & EQUIPMENT

Beloit's academic buildings are both historic and cutting edge and are located toward the southern half of campus. Particularly noteworthy are Beloit's two on-campus teaching museums. The Logan Museum of Anthropology houses approximately 15,000 ethnographic—and over 200,000 archaeological objects—from 129 countries and more than 600 cultural groups. The Wright Museum holds approximately 6,000 works of art in its permanent collection. Significant collections include American Impressionism, Modernist paintings, a collection of 19th century plaster casts, German Expressionism, and Japanese Modern prints. Both museums offer students professional opportunities to conduct real museum work in collaboration with faculty and staff.

The Laura Aldrich Neese Performing Arts theatre complex features a large thrust stage theater built to Equity standards, a black box theater with flexible staging, a scenic design studio, costume shop, makeup rooms, dressing rooms, and a greenroom.

The recently named Marjorie and James Sanger Center for the Sciences is a platinum LEED-certified green building that houses the Biology, Chemistry, Geology, Math and Computer Science, Physics, and Psychology departments. Besides its spectacular four-story open foyer, roof garden, and rain garden, the Center features student offices and space for studio format and inquiry-based courses that integrate class, laboratory, and collaborative group work. Special facilities include a visualization lab, a 1,900 square-foot greenhouse with three climate zones, a herbarium, and a rooftop small-telescope astronomy area. Off-campus facilities include Chamberlin Springs, 50 acres of oak and hickory woods and wildlife northwest of the city; the Smith Limnology Lab, a small boat launch and aquatic station on the Rock River; and Newark Road Prairie State Natural Area, a 32.5-acre virgin prairie with more than 300 species of flowering plants.

Several campus buildings are within walking distance downtown: the Hendricks Center for the Arts, a performing arts center; Turtle Creek, the Beloit College bookstore; and The Center for Entrepreneurship in Liberal Education (CELEB), a newly renovated laboratory for entrepreneurship education. Six blocks east of campus, sports fans can head to Strong Stadium Complex and watch the competition from the 3,000-seat stands; the stadium is home to the football, baseball, tennis, softball, and soccer teams. Back on campus, the entire student body can exercise in the Sports Center, which features two racquetball courts, a weight and training room, three full-sized basketball courts, and a six-lane, 25-yard pool.

Currently, the college is in the process of converting a decommissioned powerhouse, located next to campus along the nearby Rock River, into a new student union and recreation center. This one-of-a-kind reimagining of an industrial building will feature student life spaces, conference rooms, fitness and training facilities, an indoor track, a competition pool, and a wellness center. Funded entirely by donations and grant money (no student tuition dollars), the Powerhouse will officially open for campus and community use in fall 2019.

OFF-CAMPUS OPPORTUNITIES

Each year, roughly 140-160 Beloiters choose to study abroad for one or two semesters and travel to more than 40 countries to do so. Students study worldwide through a combination of college programs, offerings by other institutions and partners, and direct enrollment in universities. Domestic off-campus study programs are also robust. Current North American programs open to Beloit College students are: a semester in environmental science at the Marine Biological Laboratory in Woods Hole, MA; public affairs programs at American University in Washington, D.C.; an arts, entrepreneurship, and urban studies program in Chicago, IL; the Newberry Seminar in Chicago, IL; and the Oak Ridge Science Semester at the Oak Ridge National Laboratory near Knoxville, TN.

The college also offers Cities in Transitions courses, which provide opportunities for students to strengthen their language skills and pursue independent study projects in China, Ecuador, Germany, Japan, Russia, and Senegal. Beloit's Liberal Arts in Practice Center is a great resource for students, providing them with as much as $400,000 in student project funding annually.

ACADEMIC PROGRAMS

Beloit offers a variety of programs that supplement and complement its curriculum. The Initiatives program is designed to support students through their first four semesters of college. The program kicks off during New Student Days, a weeklong orientation that introduces students both to the Beloit College campus and community and to Beloit's distinctive approach to the liberal arts. First-year students participate in their first course: an interdisciplinary seminar called an "FYI," and then, the student's professor also becomes their advisor for the next three semesters. Through the Initiatives program, students also become eligible to apply for Venture Grants at the end of their sophomore year. These grants allow students to pursue intellectually challenging activities that are self-testing or will benefit others and the campus community.

Advising Practicum, a full-day series of workshops and discussions held every semester before advising week, is designed to help students reflect on Beloit's educational opportunities and develop an academic plan tailored to individual interests and goals.

In the summer, the Center for Language Studies offers intensive summer language instruction in Chinese, Japanese, and Russian. The anthropology field training program has taken students to excavation sites from Colorado to Chile, and geology field expeditions include trips to Iceland, New Zealand, and Scotland. Each spring, students present their research at a conference-style Student Symposium event, and in the fall, International Symposium Day is a forum set aside for students to present research and projects they have conducted abroad. Beloit students serve on the editorial board of the Beloit Fiction Journal. Each year, the college brings as many as six groundbreaking scholars and artists to campus, who join the community for an extended stay as part of a distinguished residency program.

MAJORS AND DEGREES OFFERED

Beloit offers undergraduate degree programs exclusively and confers Bachelor of Arts and Bachelor of Science degrees. There are more than 50 fields of study in 31 departments.

Fields of study (and possible major concentrations) include: anthropology, art and art history (art history; studio art), biochemistry, biology (ecology, evolution, and behavioral; environmental; molecular, cellular, and integrative), chemistry (applied; biological; environmental), classics (classical civilization; classical philology), cognitive science, comparative literature, computer science, critical identity studies, economics (international political economy; business economics), education and youth studies (Children and schools; Adolescents and schools; Youth and society), English (literary studies; creative writing), engineering program, environmental studies (environmental communication and arts; environmental justice and citizenship), geology (environmental), health and society, history, interdisciplinary studies (self-designed), international relations, mathematics, modern languages and literatures (Chinese language and culture; French; Japanese language and culture; modern languages; Russian; Spanish), music, philosophy, physics and astronomy, political science, psychology, religious studies, sociology, and theatre, dance and media studies (dance; media studies; performance; production).

Teacher Certification (BA, BS): Children and schools (middle childhood/early adolescence, grades 1–8); Adolescents and schools (early adolescence/adolescence, grades 6–12); Art education (early childhood-adolescence, ages birth–21).

Minors: African studies, anthropology, art and art history (art history; studio art), Asian studies, biology, chemistry, classical civilization, cognitive science, computer science, critical identity studies, English, environmental studies, European studies, geology, health & society, history, interdisciplinary studies, journalism, Latin American and Caribbean studies, Law and Justice , mathematics, medieval studies, modern languages (Chinese; French; German studies; Japanese; Russian; Spanish), museum studies, music, philosophy, physics, political science, religious studies, Russian studies, and theatre, dance and media studies (dance, theatre performance; theatre production).

Pre-professional programs: Engineering programs (3-2 and 4-2); environmental management and forestry program; pre-law preparation; and pre-health professions preparation.

TUITION, ROOM, BOARD, FEES

$49,564 tuition

$280 Activities fee

$196 Health/Wellness fee

$8,830 for room and board

Total: $58,870

FINANCIAL AID

Overview

Beloit College is committed to making the Beloit experience affordable for all admitted students. During the 2016–2017 academic year, 98 percent of enrolling first-year students received Beloit gift aid. The average financial aid award (including federal loans and work study) was $36,857.

Bottom line

Full tuition at Beloit costs $49,564 for the academic year. Housing costs an additional $5,030, and a full meal plan runs $3,800 (this plan is required for all first-year students). In addition, there's also a $280 student activity fee, and a $196 health and wellness charge. Families can expect to pay another $1,502 in estimated health insurance costs. Books and supplies often run around $1,000. Finally, it is recommended that students set aside another $1,300 for personal expenses.

STUDENT ORGANIZATIONS AND ACTIVITIES

Beloit students are remarkably unique, passionate, and involved. They do what needs doing, change what needs changing, and create what needs creating. Students serve on college governance and search committees, establish their own organizations, orchestrate events such as the annual Folk 'n' Blues music festival, and host their own radio and cable TV shows. The college has more than 60 active student clubs ranging in focus from ballroom dance to ultimate frisbee to yoga.

An NCAA Division III school, Beloit competes in the Midwest Conference and has 19 varsity teams. Men's varsity teams include: baseball, basketball, cross country, football, lacrosse, soccer, swimming and diving, and track and field. Women's varsity teams include: basketball, cross country, lacrosse, soccer, softball, swimming and diving, tennis, track and field, and volleyball.

ADMISSIONS PROCESS

Beloit offers two binding early decision plans. Early Decision I deadline is November 1 with notification by December 1; Early Decision II deadline is January 15 with notification by February 15. In addition, there are two non-binding early action plans with deadlines of either November 1 or December 1; notification is December 1 and January 1, respectively. The regular decision priority application deadline is January 15, with notification rolling by mid-March. Applications received after January 15 will be given full consideration as space remains available. Admitted students have until May 1 to reply to Beloit.

Review of transfer applications for the fall term begins March 15 and continues through the spring; the deadline for the spring term is October 15. Notification for transfer applications is rolling.

Deadline

Early Decision I	November 1
Early Action I	November 1
Early Action II	December 1
Early Decision II	January 15
Regular Decision	January 15

BENTLEY UNIVERSITY

AT A GLANCE

Business is Everywhere...Prepare Here

Bentley University is preparing students for career and life success, because business is everywhere. Businesses today are creating sustainable energy, developing life-saving drugs and inventing new technologies each day that change the way we live. A Bentley education prepares students to succeed in any field through a distinctive fusion of business and the arts and sciences. Students look at the world through a broader lens that embraces fusion and innovation, technological mastery and cultural literacy, practical expertise and the ability to effectively communicate with others. Bentley graduates know how the world works, and how it thinks. Because that's what it means to prepare at Bentley—and to leave Bentley prepared for anything.

When you come to Bentley, you will join a group of global and talented individuals who understand and apply information to decision-making, use the latest technology, know how to connect people and ideas, and operate comfortably with ambiguity and risk.

LOCATION AND ENVIRONMENT

Bentley's location in Waltham, Massachusetts-just minutes west of Boston—puts the city within easy reach. As the country's ultimate university town, Boston's options range from theater to art exhibits, dance clubs to concerts, and championship sports to world-class shopping. Bentley's free shuttle makes regular trips to Harvard Square in Cambridge, just a subway ride from Boston. Boston also offers many opportunities for internships and jobs after graduation.

CAMPUS FACILITIES & EQUIPMENT

Concepts taught in the classroom are put to use in several high-tech learning laboratories.

Bentley's financial Trading Room combines state-of-the-art technology and real-time data to offer first-hand exposure to financial concepts in simulated trading sessions. Resources include Bloomberg, Capital IQ, Datastream, FactSet, Thomson One Analytics, Portfolio Analysis, MATLAB, S&P Compustat, and Worldscope.

The Center for Marketing Technology plays an integral role in marketing programs. Students gain a full grasp of software options, familiarity with research tools and techniques, and knowledge of new digital marketing frameworks.

The Accounting Center for Electronic Learning and Business Management (ACELAB) introduces cutting-edge technologies that are reshaping the accounting profession. Students have access to auditing and tax preparation software as well as other professional applications from industry leaders such as SAP and Oracle.

The Computer Information Systems (CIS) Sandbox is Bentley's technology social learning space where students gather to collaborate on projects, work one-on-one with tutors, participate in IT workshops, build mobile apps, create video games, and explore new technology trends and devices.

The Center for Languages and International Collaboration (CLIC) is a key resource for language courses, international studies majors, and students with an interest in global issues. The center promotes collaboration among Bentley students and their counterparts overseas.

The Media and Culture Labs and Studio feature resources for video production and editing as well as digital photography. The lab provides students with industry-standard software programs for screenwriting, sound mixing, graphic design, and DVD authoring.

The Bentley Library is outfitted with computer workstations, group study rooms, and wireless network access. It also has an exceptional number of online database resources. In 2010, Bentley was ranked 14th on the Princeton Review's list of best college libraries.

OFF-CAMPUS OPPORTUNITIES

Hands-on experience is emphasized across the curriculum. Internships, study abroad, service-learning, and other opportunities allow students to apply classroom theory in the community. More than 90 percent of seniors complete one internship and over 70 percent complete two or more, building valuable work experience and networking connections. Some of the top internship employers include Fidelity Investments, the TJX Companies, Liberty Mutual, Bain & Company, and all of the Big Four accounting firms.

Bentley students can gain insight into different cultures by studying abroad. Programs take place in more than 25 countries and vary in length from one week to a full academic year. Through Bentley's Service-Learning Center, students build skills in business, communication, and teamwork while assisting nonprofit and community-based organizations both locally and internationally.

ACADEMIC PROGRAMS

The Bentley curriculum is a unique fusion of business and the liberal arts. The university's 4,200 undergraduates benefit from a breadth of programs and the ability to combine subjects to best fit their interests. A Bentley education also focuses on gaining hands-on experience in the classroom. Students benefit from classes where they partner with outside companies to solve current business problems and present their solutions directly to company executives. Bentley also offers top applicants a chance to enroll in the Honors Program. Participants select honors-level courses each semester that offer extra intellectual challenge in a seminar atmosphere.

MAJORS AND DEGREES OFFERED

The Bentley curriculum is a groundbreaking integration of business and the arts and sciences that has been featured in the Wall Street Journal. "It's not about pitting lifelong learning skills against professional skills," President Gloria Larson told the paper. "A college degree should reflect both."

To that end, Bachelor of Science (B.S.) degree programs enable our students to gain in-depth knowledge and skills in specific business disciplines: accountancy, actuarial science, computer information systems, corporate finance and accounting, creative industries, economics–finance, finance, information design and corporate communication, information systems audit and control, management, managerial economics, marketing, mathematical sciences and professional sales.

Bentley also offers Bachelor of Arts (B.A.) degree programs with majors in global studies, health studies, history, liberal arts, media and culture, philosophy, public policy, Spanish studies, and sustainable science. All Bachelor of Arts students gain business experience through either the Business Studies Major (BSM) or minor. All students can also choose from minors such as entrepreneurial studies, law, and sports management. The Liberal Studies Major (LSM), an optional double major, can be combined with any business program. It provides students with a competitive edge by building meaningful connections across and within disciplines. To complete the LSM, students do not need to take any extra courses beyond those normally required. It allows students to add another credential to their degree, helping them stand out to employers. LSM concentrations include American studies; diversity and society; earth, environment, and global sustainability; ethics and social responsibility; global perspectives; health and industry; media arts and society; and quantitative perspectives.

FINANCIAL AID

Bentley's financial aid program includes both scholarships based on academic achievement, which are awarded through the admission process, as well as grants based on financial need. Bentley administered over $95 million in aid to undergraduate students last year. More than 75 percent of aid came as Bentley-funded grants and scholarships. Significant institutional resources are committed each year so that all academically qualified students have access to a Bentley education regardless of their financial resources. Currently, more than 70 percent of undergraduates receive some type of financial assistance-including grants, scholarships, loans and/or work study.

STUDENT ORGANIZATIONS AND ACTIVITIES

Approximately 98 percent of freshmen live on campus. Twenty-three residence halls provide a range of housing options: dorms, suites, and apartments. Housing is provided for all four years; all residence halls are air-conditioned and typically include study lounges, exercise facilities, TV lounges, and game rooms.

Students live and learn in a multicultural environment that prepares them to thrive in today's diverse world. International students representing nearly 100 countries make up about 25 percent of the student body and bring valuable perspectives to the Bentley community.

Supporting Bentley's commitment to diversity are offices such as the Multicultural Center, Spiritual Life Center, Center for International Students and Scholars, Equity Center, Center for Women in Business, and the Women's Center.

The Student Center is the hub of campus activity and is home to 921 Dining Room and more than 100 student organizations. These groups represent academics, the arts, media, fraternity and sorority life, and cultural interests.

Athletic programs are a Bentley hallmark and include intramurals, recreational sports, and more than 20 varsity teams in NCAA Divisions I and II. The Dana Athletic Center houses a weight and fitness complex, food court, locker rooms, a gym, a basketball court, volleyball and racquetball courts, a competition-size pool with a diving tank, and saunas. Outdoor facilities include soccer and baseball fields, a track, and tennis courts. In 2018, Bentley opened our new, state-of-the-art multipurpose arena which hosts our NCAA Division I hockey team and prominent university events such as career fairs, high-profile speakers, alumni events and concerts. The 76,000 square foot facility marks Bentley's continued rise as a modern, nationally-recognized business university and is a prime example of sustainable design and energy efficiency.

ADMISSIONS PROCESS

Bentley University accepts the Common Application. Candidates for the fall semester are notified by the end of March; spring semester candidates and transfers are notified on a rolling basis.

Prospective students can visit bentley.edu/undergraduate/applying for application information and deadlines. For more information, students should contact:

Office of Undergraduate Admission

Bentley University

175 Forest Street

Waltham, Massachusetts 02452-4705

Phone: 781.891.2244

800.523.2354 (toll-free)

Fax: 781.891.3414

E-mail: ugadmission@bentley.edu

BERRY COLLEGE

AT A GLANCE

A quick 90-minute drive north of Atlanta and nestled in the rolling mountains of northwest Georgia, Berry offers you an education nationally recognized for its quality and value. U.S. News & World Report has previously ranked Berry as the nation's #1 "Up-and-Coming" liberal arts college, as well as the #3 best value school in the South.

Berry has delivered much more than exceptional rankings since our founding in 1902. Berry seeks to educate the entire you: through an education of your mind, the practical experience of hands-on work and fostering of your commitment to service. Berry prepares you to embrace the world. Students who strive to improve the places where they work and live, every day, will find a welcoming home here.

LOCATION AND ENVIRONMENT

It's impossible to replicate this experience elsewhere. Berry College offers you the world's largest campus conveniently located between Atlanta and Chattanooga… and though we prefer to not be so boastful, it is a pretty cool fact that our campus is so large we have our own zip code! It's a challenge to describe 27,000 acres of inspiration: you need to be here to grasp the distinctive residential college that is Berry.

This is a place of inspiration, often recognized as one of the most beautiful campuses in the world. In fact, there's a certain feeling students get the exact moment they realized they belong here. Often, it's the first time they set foot on campus, a feeling described simply as "awe." Not merely a place to study for four years, our campus distinctively offers you more than 40 miles of biking trails, 15 miles for horseback riding, and another 40 miles of hiking and running trails… all here at home on your campus!

ACADEMIC PROGRAMS

Every day, we are exposed to differences–differences of style, opinions, language, upbringing and more, and expected to engage with the ever-changing world around us. Increasingly, graduates are expected to work with others on complex problems or issues that require the integration of knowledge, skills and ideas from multiple disciplines. Our Foundations Curriculum will allow you to explore your interests and to expand your thinking by asking you to step outside of your comfort zone. Grounded in the tradition of a liberal arts education and designed for the professional environment of the 21st century, our curriculum will provide you with knowledge, effective communication skills, problem-solving skills and rich cultural experiences.

Choose from over 55 majors and 35 minors and work with students, faculty and staff, forming teams that encourage many voices. Through asking yourself and those around you the challenging questions our society faces, you will learn to adapt and to approach problems from a different point of view. Berry students are proud to think with their hearts and to work with their hands.

Berry offers you an academic opportunity to learn without barriers while pursuing your passions. Berry's academic programs translate to successful career preparation for life after college. Take full advantage of the student work program, and put yourself above other job candidates with your hands-on experience. This is where you realize the payoff to your Berry education. The Work Experience Program, recognized as one of the premier opportunities in the nation, provides meaningful on-campus work experience, fosters entrepreneurship, reduces the costs of your education and prepares you for a fulfilling career.

TUITION, ROOM, BOARD, FEES

At Berry, we work with you to make sure you are aware of all of the scholarship opportunities available and we award more than $38 million in institutional aid each year. That translates into 98 percent of our undergraduate students receiving financial aid.

FINANCIAL AID

Our application is available on August 1. The Free Application for Federal Student Aid (FAFSA) is available on October 1. Send your application and your FAFSA to us early so that we can partner with you in making a sound financial plan for your college education. The financial aid process can be scary, but it doesn't have to be. Simply contact us or schedule a campus visit, and we'll talk through your options with you. More information can be found at http://www.berry.edu/aid/.

STUDENT ORGANIZATIONS AND ACTIVITIES

When you enroll at Berry, you join a community more than 100 years in the making. Each year we celebrate our own version of homecoming known as Mountain Day, and your participation joins you to decades of Berry students. Don't miss the campus-wide talent show, Mountain Day Olympics with your residence hall, the Grand March and fall carnival (lovingly known as "Marthapalooza" on campus in honor of our founder, Martha Berry.)

Find your friends in the Berry community close at hand, where on-campus living for all four years is an expectation. Choose from traditional residential halls or join a Living Learning Community in your first year, and then select from a variety of suite-style and apartment-style housing in future years. Be a part of this community through the shared experiences of living, learning, working and exploring together.

Pursue your athletic passions as a Berry Viking in the Southern Athletic Association of NCAA Division III. Foster your competitive side in our stadium, Valhalla, and take advantage of The Rome Tennis Center at Berry College, the nation's largest hard court tennis facility. Compete as a member of one of our 21 intercollegiate sports including football, lacrosse, outdoor track, basketball, soccer, tennis, cross country, swimming & diving, golf, baseball, volleyball, softball and equestrian.

A wide array of student organizations, clubs, programs and activities offer you a constant social schedule. Whether you're interested in Ultimate Frisbee or rowing, honing your media experience with the student newspaper or literary magazine, celebrating and advancing multicultural awareness or serving the Berry community, you'll find it difficult to fit everything in.

Perhaps the real beauty of Berry resides in the fact that you can have the best of both worlds: a sprawling campus that's a quick drive from bustling city life in Atlanta, Birmingham and Chattanooga. Of course, downtown Rome is right around the corner from campus. Spend an evening at one of the city's numerous restaurants before catching a movie or a Rome Braves baseball game, and discover this hidden gem of a college town in the scenic mountains that define northwest Georgia.

ADMISSIONS PROCESS

We want you to be prepared to succeed in any program you choose at Berry from day one. Show us you're ready by taking challenging courses when you can (AP, IB, Dual-Enrollment, etc.). You can best prepare for opportunities at Berry by taking:

- 4 years of English
- 4 years of science-including biology, chemistry and physics
- Mathematics through precalculus
- 3 years of social studies
- 2 years of a foreign language

You are more than a number here. We will ask you for additional information like an SAT or an ACT, and want to know more about you through 1-1 conversations and essays. If you have questions about the admissions process we're here to help.

For more information about admissions recommendations, visit www.berry.edu/admission/ or call us at 1-800-BERRY-GA today.

BETHANY COLLEGE (WV)

AT A GLANCE

There was never a more glorious place to go to college. The rolling hillsides in the foothills of the Allegheny Mountains never lose their beauty throughout the seasons. For more than 175 years, Bethany has been a highly contemporary institution based in the tradition of the liberal arts. Once you visit our campus, you're ours, history is all around you.

LOCATION AND ENVIRONMENT

The campus includes beautiful historic landmarks, modern well-equipped classrooms, spacious sports/recreational areas, indoor and outdoor theaters, art galleries, an equestrian center, a teaching greenhouse and more.

CAMPUS FACILITIES & EQUIPMENT

The campus features a wide array of studies, in addition to beautiful architecture with a green academic mall. Facilities include beautiful historic landmarks, a newly renovated dining facility, modern well-equipped classrooms, spacious sports/recreational areas, indoor and outdoor theaters, art galleries, a teaching greenhouse and more.

More than 90 percent of students live in spacious on-campus apartments, residential halls or fraternity/sorority houses, which include Internet, cable TV and more. Computer labs with Internet and library access, e-mail, digital media labs, rehearsal halls, research and language labs, The McCann Learning Center for academic support, and other amenities are provided.

The Thomas Phillips Johnson Health and Recreation Center includes Hummel Fieldhouse (Nutting Gymnasium), three-court multi-use gymnasium (Sandwen Arena), Knight Natatorium (Olympic-size pool), two racquetball courts, a free-weight exercise fitness center with cardiovascular equipment, and an indoor jogging track. The Cummins Community Center is a state-of-the-art, 24-hour fitness center.

Outdoor Facilities: A multi-purpose stadium (Bison Stadium) with artificial turf and lights primarily serves football, lacrosse, and track and field. Hoag Soccer Field, John Cunningham Soccer Complex, equestrian center, 6 tennis courts, baseball and softball fields, football practice fields, and additional playing fields for intramural and club sports are at your convenience.

OFF-CAMPUS OPPORTUNITIES

When you want to venture beyond our 1,300-acre campus, America's Most Livable City, Pittsburgh is only a 50-minute drive from campus and Wheeling, West Virginia; Washington, Pennsylvania; and Steubenville, Ohio are less than a half-hour away.

ACADEMICS

The College offers a wide array of studies, awarding Bachelor of Science, Bachelor of Arts, and Master of Arts in Teaching degrees. Students may choose from more than 25 departmental and 6 interdisciplinary majors, many with options for emphasis. Students also have the option of including one or more of 35 optional minors as part of their programs.

- Accounting
- Biology (options for emphasis on Biology, Biochemistry, and Biology Education)
- Chemistry (options for emphasis on Professional Chemistry, Forensic Chemistry, Biochemistry, and Chemistry Education)
- Communications and Media Arts (options for emphasis on Digital Media and Production, Graphics, Integrated Media and Marketing, and Sports Communication)
- Computer Science
- Computer Science and Accounting (Dual Major)
- Cybersecurity
- Cybersecurity—Information Assurance
- Economics (options for emphasis on Managerial Economics and International Economics)
- Economics and Mathematics (Dual Major)
- Education (Elementary Education; Middle Childhood Education through individual department programs in the areas of English, General Science, Mathematics, Physical Education, Social Studies, and Spanish; Secondary Education through individual department programs in the areas of Art, Biology, Chemistry, English, Mathematics, Physical Education, Psychology, Social Studies, and Spanish)
- English (options for emphasis on Creative Writing, Education, Literature, and Writing and Language)
- Environmental Science (Interdisciplinary)
- Finance
- German Studies (Interdisciplinary)
- History
- International Business
- International Economics with study abroad (Interdisciplinary)
- International Relations (Interdisciplinary)
- Management
- Marketing
- Mathematics (options for emphasis on Mathematics, Mathematics-Economics, Mathematics-Physics, Mathematics-Computer Science, Mathematics-Actuarial Science, and Mathematics Education)

- Music
- Music Technology (Interdisciplinary)
- Physical Education and Sports Studies (options for emphasis on Sports Management, Recreational and Athletic Programming, and Teaching Physical Education)
- Pre-Engineering/Physical Science
- Political Science
- Psychology (options for emphasis on Scientific Psychology, Human Services, Pre-Physical Therapy, and Pre-Occupational Therapy)
- Psychology and Education (Interdisciplinary)
- Psychology, Religion, and Culture (Interdisciplinary)
- Psychology and Social Work (Dual Major)
- Religious Studies
- Social Work
- Spanish
- Theatre (options for emphasis on Performance and Technical Theatre)
- Visual Art

Pre-Professional Studies

- Pre-Dentistry
- Pre-Engineering
- Pre-Law
- Pre-Medical
- Pre-Ministry
- Pre-Occupational Therapy
- Pre-Physical Therapy
- Pre-Veterinary

MAJORS AND DEGREES OFFERED

The College offers a wide array of studies, awarding Bachelor of Science, Bachelor of Arts, and Master of Arts in Teaching degrees. Students may choose from more than 25 departmental and 6 interdisciplinary majors, many with options for emphasis. Students also have the option of including one or more of 35 optional minors as part of their programs.

TUITION, ROOM, BOARD, FEES

The 2016–17 costs for resident students enrolled in the Fall 2016 semester or later are:

Tuition	$27,292
Fees	$1,209
Housing	$4,800 to $5,200 (depending on option)
Meals	$5,268
Books	$1,200
Transportation	$1,000
Total	$40,769 (Total cost may vary depending on housing option)

FINANCIAL AID

We are dedicated to making a financial commitment to our students. If your desire is to receive a Bethany education, our financial aid office will do everything we can to make it affordable for you and your family.

The College also awards scholarships based on academic performance, leadership capability and other academic factors. Additionally, need-based aid is awarded to all eligible students in accordance with FAFSA results. Financial aid packages generally consist of loans, grants, scholarships and student employment.

STUDENT ORGANIZATIONS AND ACTIVITIES

Bethany offers more than 50 student organizations: scholastic and honorary, government, special interest and departmental.

Greek organizations include Phi Kappa Tau, Delta Tau Delta, Phi Mu, Alpha Xi Delta, Alpha Sigma Phi, Zeta Tau Alpha and Beta Theta Pi.

Bethany's 22 varsity athletic teams (11 women's and 11 men's) compete in the NCAA Division III Presidents Athletic Conference (PAC) and the Eastern College Athletic Association (ECAC). Bethany affords you the opportunity to become involved and find a home away from home. Whether it's the fraternity or sorority you join, the roommate you have, the team you play on, or the classes you take—you will have friends for life. You're in an historic college town, and you can study abroad. Earn yourself some bragging rights and become part of a long lineage of successful alumni, a big extended family—in all fields of work, and in all parts of the world.

ADMISSIONS PROCESS

Throughout our history, Bethany's alumni have achieved great success—become part of Bethany's tradition of academic excellence. You will learn, live and grow in an environment that encourages you to become involved in your education and your future.

Bethany College specializes in a personalized admission process for each student. At Bethany, our enrollment counselors evaluate each applicant individually and because of this, we are not limited by designated 'cut-offs.'

- Application Deadline: Rolling
- Apply Online: http://www.bethanywv.edu/admissions-aid/apply/
- Interview Required: No, but strongly recommended
- Enrollment Toll Free Number: (304) 829-7611
- Enrollment E-mail: enrollment@bethanywv.edu

BOSTON UNIVERSITY

AT A GLANCE

Is Boston University the right place for you? With an average class size of 27 students and a student-to-faculty ratio of 10:1, you'll find yourself in classes taught by Pulitzer Prize winners, Nobel Laureates, Fulbright scholars, or a MacArthur fellow. If hands-on research is what interests you, the Undergraduate Research Opportunities Program (UROP) offers hundreds of research opportunities across all areas of study. You'll have the rare opportunity to participate in research across the humanities, arts, and sciences as early as your freshman year. And if you're not sure what academic pathway you'd like to pursue, BU offers more than 250 programs of study to choose from. So you can take classes in subjects as varied as biology, broadcast journalism, business, computer engineering, elementary education, film, international relations, physical therapy, psychology, and theatre, just to name a few. Add hundreds of extracurricular activities and the exciting city of Boston, and you'll never experience a dull moment as a BU student.

LOCATION AND ENVIRONMENT

Located in the heart of Boston, students experience the city as an extension of the campus. No other city can compete with Boston's remarkable concentration of higher education institutions, world-renowned medical centers, and historic and cultural attractions. The city provides many opportunities for impressive internship and research positions and is home to world-class attractions including the Museum of Fine Arts, Fenway Park, and the Boston Symphony Orchestra. With four years of guaranteed campus housing, and 75 percent of undergraduates living on campus all four years, the campus feels like a true residential community in the heart of Boston.

Types of Transportation Available to Campus

By the MBTA (The "T"): Take the Green Line train (Boston College, "B" line) to BU East. Exit and cross Commonwealth Avenue to Granby Street. Turn left on Bay State Road. The Admissions Reception Center is located on the right side, at 233 Bay State Road. For route and fare information, visit the "T" online at www.mbta.com. By Air: Taxis to Boston University from Boston's Logan International Airport may take approximately 30 minutes (fare: approximately $30). From the airport, the "T" may take an hour and requires a transfer from the Blue Line to the Green Line at Government Center Station. For more information visit Logan International Airport online at www.massport.com. By Bus or Train: Amtrak service and major bus companies arrive at Boston's South Station. Taxis to Boston University take approximately 20 minutes (fare: approximately $20). The "T" may take 40 minutes and requires a transfer from the Red Line to the Green Line at Park Street Station.

Driving Instructions to Campus

From West of Boston: Take Interstate 90 (Massachusetts Turnpike) to Exit 18 (Brighton/Cambridge). Follow signs for Cambridge down the ramp to the second set of lights. Turn right at the lights (do not cross over the bridge/Charles River) and travel on Soldiers Field Road/Storrow Drive to the second Boston University exit. Follow the Local Directions below. From North of Boston: Take Route 93 South to the Storrow Drive exit (Exit 26). Continue on Storrow Drive to the Kenmore Square exit (left exit). Follow signs for Kenmore Square. Follow the Local Directions below. From South of Boston: Take Interstate 93 North/Route 3 North to Storrow Drive exit (Exit 26). Go west on Storrow Drive to Kenmore Square exit (left exit). Follow signs for Kenmore Square. Follow the local directions below. Local Directions: Turn right off the exit ramp at the traffic light (Beacon Street). Stay to the right to enter Bay State Road. The Admissions Reception Center will be on the right, 233 Bay State Road. Parking: Metered parking is available in front of the Reception Center on Bay State Road.

CAMPUS FACILITIES & EQUIPMENT

Boston University's academic and athletic facilities are some of the best in the country. The Engineering Product Innovation Center (EPIC) is home to a full carpentry and machine shop, 3D printers, a metals foundry, and laboratories. The BUild Lab: IDG Capital Student Innovation Center fosters innovation and entrepreneurship across the campus. Students can connect with advisers, collaborate with other students, and get help with matters from design and prototyping to legal advice and marketing. The new Joan & Edgar Booth Theatre and College of Fine Arts Production Center, studio space for visual arts students, practice rooms for music, and a 575-seat music performance center, are indicative of BU's support for the arts. The Student Village provides first-rate recreation and athletics with the Fitness & Recreation Center and Agganis Arena, as well as high-rise apartments and dining. The University also offers the Yawkey Center for Student Services, which houses the Center for Career Development, Educational Resource Center, Pre-Professional Advising Offices, and two stories of dining in Marciano Commons.

OFF-CAMPUS OPPORTUNITIES

The opportunities to learn outside the classroom are limitless thanks to BU's location in the heart of the city. In fact, 91 percent of undergraduates participate in at least one internship before graduating. Students can intern with top-tier financial services, biomedical, or engineering companies. The city is also home to world-class museums and art galleries, top-ranked hospitals and health services facilities, and more. BU's Center for Career Development works to provide students with the resources to secure internships in any number of fields.

Boston University has one of the world's most extensive study abroad programs. Among the University's 100+ programs are language and liberal arts programs; programs that combine studies with internships; fieldwork programs for students wishing to pursue academic or scientific research; and summer programs. Programs are available in Argentina, Australia, Belgium, China, Denmark, Ecuador, England, France, Germany, Ghana, India, Ireland, Israel, Italy, Japan, Mexico, Morocco, New Zealand, Singapore, South Korea, Spain, Switzerland, Tanzania, and Turkey. There are also programs available in Los Angeles, New York, Silicon Valley, and Washington, D.C.

ACADEMIC PROGRAMS

What does it mean to study at a world-class research university? You don't have to be science-minded to thrive in BU's culture of inquiry. As a university receiving more than $400 million in research funding annually and a member of the prestigious Association of American Universities (AAU), we expect students to formulate bold questions and seek out the answers.

The academic flexibility offered by BU can maximize the value of your degree. Choose from more than 250 programs of study, Dual Degree programs, combined BA/MA programs, and chances to take coursework across schools and colleges. Think psychology and economics, or business and international relations.

Students complete general education requirements through the BU Hub, an innovative new general education program that is integrated with majors and minors. Students take courses of interest while exploring areas ranging from global citizenship to scientific and social inquiry to ethical reasoning or digital communication. The Hub is robust in its options for experiential learning and co-curriculars, and its signature feature, the BU Cross-College Challenge, offers an opportunity to work with a team of students from across BU's schools and colleges.

TUITION, ROOM, BOARD, FEES

Tuition for the 2018–19 academic year is $52,816; standard room and board is $15,720. Additional mandatory fees are $1,132. Allowances for the cost of books, supplies, travel, and other incidental expenses brings the total cost of attendance for a student to $72,816.

FINANCIAL AID

Boston University Financial Assistance offers a wide variety of financial assistance programs and provides resources to help inform students and their families about payment strategies and financing options. Merit awards, need-based scholarships, loans, student employment, and a payment plan are all offered.

University need-based scholarships are offered based on several factors, including calculated financial eligibility, academic achievement, and the availability of funds for a student's program of study. While every effort is made to assist students with limited resources, the university does not have sufficient funds to offer a grant award to every admitted student who has calculated financial eligibility. If need-based scholarship aid is offered in your first year, the same amount is guaranteed for each of your undergraduate years through The BU Scholarship Assurance.

STUDENT ORGANIZATIONS AND ACTIVITIES

Boston University students are extremely engaged, participating in academic clubs, cultural or religious organizations, and community service groups. There are more than 450 student organizations and more than 40 intramural and club sports that students can participate in. You can get involved with organizations such as Alianza Latina, BU Habitat for Humanity, the Debate Society, or the Alpine Ski Team. A separate student government exists at each school and college to manage student affairs, and the Student Union includes members who represent all schools and colleges within the university.

ADMISSIONS PROCESS

The Board of Admissions evaluates each prospective student holistically. The Board's main focus centers on the rigor of a student's high school record, but required standardized test scores (SAT and ACT), personal qualities and integrity, interests, teacher and counselor references, and other relevant attributes are also considered carefully. All candidates must have graduated from high school or earned an equivalency diploma to be considered. For admission to the College of Fine Arts, most students are not required to submit the SAT or ACT but must either audition or submit a portfolio (some programs also require pre-screening). A few select programs require interviews for admission.

Students should visit www.bu.edu/admissions for additional information. Boston University also considers students with transferable credit from other institutions for admission. Boston University considers transfer applicants for September or January admission, depending on the program of interest.

Boston University offers early decision and early decision 2 (which are binding agreements), and regular decision programs. All applications for early decision must be submitted by November 1, applications for early decision 2 and regular decision must be submitted by January 2. Accelerated program applications must be submitted by November 15. Applications for admission to qualify for the Presidential or Trustee Scholarships must be submitted by December 1.

Transfer students seeking January admission must submit their application forms by November 1. Those seeking September admission must submit their application forms by March 1.

Transfer students cannot be admitted to the Accelerated Liberal Arts Medical or Dental Programs; or the nutrition or six-year, combined AT/DPT and DPT programs in the College of Health & Rehabilitation Sciences: Sargent College. Transfer students may not apply for January admission to the School of Theatre in the College of Fine Arts. They also cannot apply as "undeclared" to any school or college.

Boston University accepts qualified applicants regardless of age, color, disability, national origin, race, religion, sexual orientation, or gender to all of its activities and programs.

BRYANT UNIVERSITY

AT A GLANCE

Inspiring a new generation of innovative leaders, Bryant today is the culmination of more than 150 years of continuous growth and evolution. Throughout our history, we've embraced new ways of thinking to deliver academic programs that anticipate the future in a changing world.

At Bryant, innovative teaching and learning create agile, globally-minded leaders and problem-solvers who are prepared with the knowledge, skills, and qualities of character for success. Our curriculum offers an integrated liberal arts and business education renowned as path-breaking. Forward-thinking pedagogies and our culture of innovation will help you form the types of intangible skills that will prepare you to succeed, today and far beyond.

World-class faculty integrate theoretical and applied concepts in a broad range of majors. Academic life is enhanced by rich co-curricular opportunities, service learning programs, and internships for engaged, real-world learning. Combined with our student-centered community, you'll find we create an experience that integrates living and learning for an immersive student life.

We know the Bryant experience prepares world-ready graduates. Our impressive outcomes, and the return on investment our students receive, highlight the success that's possible with a Bryant degree: 99 percent of our graduates are employed or enrolled in graduate school within six months of graduation. The median starting salary for Bryant's Class of 2017 is $59,000.

LOCATION AND ENVIRONMENT

Our stunning, 428-acre campus in Smithfield, Rhode Island, has a small-town feel with access to major cities. Bryant is just 15 minutes from downtown Providence, an hour from Boston, and three hours from New York City.

Our strategic location provides you with exciting internship and employment opportunities within driving distance, including the headquarters of multinational corporations such as CVS and Hasbro, small businesses, and tech startups.

CAMPUS FACILITIES & EQUIPMENT

SImce 1996, Bryant has invested $250 million in its contemporary facilities, which are purpose-built for student success. In the fall of 2016, we unveiled our groundbreaking Academic Innovation Center, where innovative learning is fostered in a creative environment designed for a new generation of pedagogy in both Bryant's College of Business and College of Arts and Sciences. The building's flexible, interactive environment is a living example of Bryant's entrepreneurial spirit and enthusiasm for real-world learning. The University also is a leader among academic institutions in its use of technology to provide more effective support and learning. All students receive a fully loaded laptop upon arrival.

Bryant University recently completed its largest and most transformative facilities initiative since moving from Providence to Smithfield 45 years ago. The projects added more than 250,000 square feet of new facilities, including the award-winning Academic Innovation Center, the Bulldog Strength & Conditioning Center, a new Master of Science in Physician Assistant Studies facility, and the Conaty Indoor Practice Center.

OFF-CAMPUS OPPORTUNITIES

Bryant's progressive international partnerships prepare visionary citizens of the world and enable you to apply your energy, knowledge, and skills in ways that transcend borders, with opportunities that span academics, business and culture.

With the University's first-of-its-kind campus in China, you'll have the chance to learn and exchange ideas with this area of the world. Study-abroad opportunities range from the traditional semester abroad to our distinctive Sophomore International Experience, a three-credit course with a 10- to 12-day faculty-led travel component. Costa Rica, England, Malaysia, and Singapore are among the destinations where you can deepen your understanding of diverse cultures and the interconnected global economy.

ACADEMIC PROGRAMS

At Bryant University, you'll study both business and the arts and sciences—meaning you'll major in one and minor in the other. You'll learn how to innovate—and collaborate—to solve problems, and gain real-world experience from the very first semester. You'll form a globally-minded approach to industry and culture, and learn through opportunities that advance positive societal change.

Many courses include strategic affiliations with Fortune 500 companies. The exposure you gain through these classroom partnerships is unparalleled. You'll graduate with real experiences that give you a competitive edge. Beyond the classroom, co-curricular opportunities and internships sharpen your learning.

Most of all, you'll be inspired to excel. Our globally recognized professors will spark your learning in every class you take. About 84 percent hold Ph.D.s or have a terminal degree in their field. On our campus, where we have no large lecture halls and no teaching assistants, faculty truly become mentors and coaches.

MAJORS AND DEGREES OFFERED

At Bryant your academic path will foster creativity and integrative thinking while you study across traditional academic lines. Our students graduate with a major in business and a complementary minor in the liberal arts or with a liberal arts major and a business minor. Bryant offers more than 100 courses of study ranging from Applied Analytics and Supply Chain Management to Environmental Science and Literary and Cultural Studies.

We offer the following degrees:

Undergraduate: Bachelor of Arts, Bachelor of Science, Bachelor of Science in Business Administration, Bachelor of Science in Data Science, and Bachelor of Science in International Business.

Graduate: Master of Business Administration, Master of Science in Taxation, Master of Professional Accountancy, Master of Science in Physician Assistant Studies, and Master of Arts in Communication.

TUITION, ROOM, BOARD, FEES

Tuition°, 2018–2019: $43,076 (includes a new laptop)

°Room and board: $15,702 (double occupancy; 19 meals per week)

Student activity fee: $422

Technology fee: $475

FINANCIAL AID

THE VALUE of a Bryant education is measured in the academic, professional, cultural, and personal growth opportunities available to help students achieve success.

However, the University understands that financing a student's education is a vital part of the decision about which college to attend. To help ease that financial burden, Bryant awarded roughly $16 million in grants and scholarships to incoming students in the fall of 2017.

STUDENT ORGANIZATIONS AND ACTIVITIES

More than 100 student organizations including academic clubs, community service groups, and cultural clubs offer you a wide variety of activities where you can develop leadership, collaboration, and other skills. And through our first-year program and close-knit community, we'll purposefully help you build meaningful connections with organizations and student groups across campus as part of your student experience.

With 22 Division I athletic teams, the Bulldogs' team spirit inspires not only Bryant students and faculty but also the local community to turn out for football, basketball, and lacrosse games, among others.

Bryant University students come from 22 states and territories and from 22 countries. Currently, about 60 percent students are male and 40 percent students are female.

ADMISSIONS PROCESS

Bryant offers several options to apply for admission. Early applications are accepted under Early Decision 1, Early Action, and Early Decision 2 programs.

To contact the Office of Admission, call 1-800-622-7001 or email admission@bryant.edu.

Contact:

Bryant University

(800) 622-7002

admission@bryant.edu

admission.bryant.edu

BUCKNELL UNIVERSITY

AT A GLANCE

- 9:1 student-faculty ratio
- All classes are taught by faculty
- 94 percent of first-year students return as sophomores
- 86 percent of our students graduate within four years—well above the national average

Established in 1846, Bucknell University is highly selective, private, nonsectarian, coeducational, residential and undergraduate, with a small graduate program. Bucknell offers more than 50 majors and 65 minors in the arts, engineering, humanities, management, and natural and social sciences.

LOCATION AND ENVIRONMENT

With its green spaces and striking vistas, Bucknell's 450-acre campus is a quintessential college environment in the heart of scenic central Pennsylvania. The restaurants and shops of downtown Lewisburg–including the historic Campus Theatre–lie within walking distance of campus. The surrounding Susquehanna Valley provides plentiful options for year-round outdoor adventures, including kayaking, hiking and cross-country skiing. The University is located within three to four hours' driving distance of Baltimore, New York City, Philadelphia, Pittsburgh and Washington, D.C.

For more information about Bucknell's location, see bucknell.edu/visit.

CAMPUS FACILITIES & EQUIPMENT

Bucknell's campus features state-of-the-art facilities for performing arts, poetry, science, engineering, athletics and more, all accessible to undergraduates.

Bertrand Library holds nearly 709,000 volumes, providing access to books, maps, journals (both electronic and print) and 221 databases, and offers a video-editing lab, thousands of audiovisual materials and multimedia equipment. Computer labs are available across campus, and there are more than 1150 wireless access points to ensure almost complete wireless coverage no matter where you go.

Resources include a film/media production clinic, GIS lab, performing arts center, poetry center and more. Science and engineering programs offer sophisticated instrumentation available for student use, including a structural testing lab, an atomic force microscope and a nuclear magnetic resonance spectrometer.

CAREER DEVELOPMENT

At Bucknell, you'll take advantage of career services such as advising, networking, mock interviews, internship support and employer fairs. You can explore your career options and network with alumni through summer internships with corporations, government organizations and nonprofits locally, nationally and internationally. An externship program provides job-shadowing opportunities for sophomores. Graduates join a well-connected alumni network and are prepared with the skills and experience to succeed in the workplace or continued education.

The career placement rate for recent Bucknell graduates is consistently high: 97 percent of the Class of 2016 was employed, in graduate school, both employed and in graduate school, preparing for graduate school or volunteering within nine months of graduation.

OFF-CAMPUS OPPORTUNITIES

Bucknell is a residential university, so most students live on campus, but learning, service, research and recreation extend off campus. You will have the opportunity to volunteer as close as the local nursing home, community center and sustainable farm and as far away as New Orleans and Nicaragua. Every year, students travel off campus to conduct research with faculty mentors. Destinations have included Alaska, Australia and Suriname.

More than 49 percent of students spend a summer, semester or year studying off campus through one of the University's own "Bucknell in" programs or more than 400 other approved programs in Africa, Asia, Europe, Oceania, and North and South America.

ACADEMIC PROGRAMS

Bucknell's faculty includes 361 full-time, tenure-line members. Our 9:1 student-faculty ratio means you will get to know your professors personally and they will provide help and advice—and not just in class. There are many opportunities to become involved in scholarly research and creative projects.

At Bucknell, your professors will challenge you to think critically, develop your ideas thoughtfully and apply what you learn. These skills will enrich your life and career whether you're working in business, education, research, medicine, law, the arts, service—or wherever your path takes you.

Learn more at bucknell.edu/facultystories.

- Global & Off-campus Education—Gain global perspective as you take part in semester or summer off-campus experiences in University-approved programs around the world, plus our own "Bucknell in" off-campus study programs in locations including Athens, Barbados, Denmark, France, Ghana, London, New Orleans, South Africa and Spain.

- Undergraduate research—Work side-by-side with faculty on intensive research projects during the semester or over the summer.

- Geisinger-Bucknell Autism & Developmental Medicine Center—Pursue clinical care, research and education in partnership with Geisinger Health System.

- Griot Institute for Africana Studies—Focus on intellectual and creative interdisciplinary investigation of the cultures, histories, narratives, peoples, geographies and arts of Africa and the African diaspora.

- Bucknell Institute for Public Policy—Investigate issues such as aging, labor, migration, health care, education, political polling and taxation.

- Institute for Leadership in Technology & Management—Participate in an intensive summer program that focuses on globalization, ethics, communication skills, critical thinking, teamwork and leadership.

- Bucknell Center for Sustainability & the Environment—Get involved in environmental and nature-related research or service.

- Bucknell Public Interest Program—Secure a stipend to cover your living expenses while you intern at a nonprofit organization.

- Residential Colleges–Theme-based living and learning program. Participating first-year students take a class together and join in programs and social activities that complement classroom learning. View your choices at bucknell.edu/ResColleges

- Civic Engagement—Participate in academically based service-learning and co-curricular community service locally, nationally and internationally.

MAJORS AND DEGREES OFFERED

You can choose from more than 50 majors and 65 minors at Bucknell. Students build robots, write and perform in their own plays, and debate solutions to global issues. Engineers can make art, artists can analyze DNA, and philosophers can write business plans. You will choose your own path, but what unites everyone is a shared enthusiasm for learning and a desire to achieve deeper levels of understanding about life and the world.

The College of Arts & Sciences offers bachelor's degrees in arts, humanities, natural sciences and social sciences. Master's degrees are available in select disciplines.

The Freeman College of Management, accredited by the Association to Advance Collegiate Schools of Business (AACSB), offers Bachelor of Science degrees in business administration with four majors: accounting & financial management; global management; managing for sustainability; and markets, innovation & design.

The College of Engineering offers a Bachelor of Science degree in eight majors, a five-year dual degree in engineering and management, a five-year dual degree in engineering and the liberal arts, and a five-year combined bachelor's and master's degree.

Learn more about academic programs at bucknell.edu/majors.

TUITION, ROOM, BOARD, FEES

For the 2017–18 academic year, tuition and fees are set at:

Tuition and fees: $53,986

Room and Board: $13,150

FINANCIAL AID

Bucknell's Office of Financial Aid is here to help you with advice and information about the financial aid process. We offer a range of financial aid options, including need-based grants and scholarships, limited academic and arts merit scholarships, loans and student employment. We consider each family's financial circumstances on an individual basis. If your circumstances remain relatively constant from year to year, you apply by the deadline and you maintain satisfactory academic progress, we will award you need-based aid at about the same level each year.

- The average total need-based financial aid package for a student in the Class of 2021 is $37,500, including need-based grants and scholarships, loans and work-study.

- About 52 percent of students receive financial aid from Bucknell, and 62 percent receive financial aid of some form.

- The average federal student loan debt upon graduation for those who graduated in the Class of 2017 and borrowed is about $22,600.

Bucknell offers an education that provides lifelong personal and career benefits, and is ranked #3 among best-value liberal arts colleges for mid-career salary by PayScale 2017.

Important note: If you are applying for Bucknell University financial aid, you must submit your CSS PROFILE by November 15 for Early Decision I and January 15 for Early Decision II and Regular Decision applications. To apply for federal financial aid, complete the Free Application for Federal Student Aid (FAFSA).

STUDENT ORGANIZATIONS AND ACTIVITIES

Bucknell's undergraduate student body includes 3,600 students from most states and 45 countries. You'll join active students whose voices are valued in the classroom, lab and creative spaces, in student government and throughout the University community.

Take advantage of speaker series, arts performances and scholarly lectures on campus. Become a member or leader of a student-run organization. From participating in undergraduate research, the arts, honor societies, and cultural, political or religious organizations, to exploring the outdoors, you'll find your niche. You can compete in and support Division I athletics as well as intramural and club sports, and stay active with our state-of-the-art fitness center. About half of sophomores, juniors and seniors participate in fraternity and sorority life, and students frequently volunteer in the local community or through one of our many national and international service opportunities.

Learn more at bucknell.edu/studentstories.

ADMISSIONS PROCESS

Bucknell is looking for students with high academic achievement and leadership or creative skills, a sense of commitment to community and a desire to achieve broad learning throughout life. Grades, test scores and recommendations are extremely important, but we also look for students who are daring, who show us they'll cultivate their interests inside and outside the classroom, and who contribute to the world in thoughtful, bold and compassionate ways.

Apply for admission through the Common Application at www.commonapp.org. Early Decision students should also complete an Early Decision Form.

Deadlines

- Regular Decision applications should be filed by January 15 for notification by April 1.

- Early Decision candidates may apply for Early Decision I consideration by November 15 or Early Decision II consideration by January 15.

- Transfer student information is available at bucknell.edu/transfer. Applications for transfer students should be submitted by November 1 for spring enrollment and March 15 for fall enrollment.

For detailed information about admissions at Bucknell and to sign up for our mailing list, go to bucknell.edu/admissions.

We invite you to visit our beautiful campus to learn more about our academic and co-curricular opportunities, meet faculty and students, and see for yourself how you will discover your path to success—by way of Bucknell.

View visit options at bucknell.edu/visit

Take a virtual tour at bucknell.edu/virtualtour

Get in touch with us at admissions@bucknell.edu

CABRINI UNIVERSITY

AT A GLANCE

Cabrini University offers a supportive community that helps students discover who they are and what they can accomplish in their lives, in their careers, and in society. Students can choose from 35+ majors and enhance their experience with minors, dual degrees, advanced coursework for graduate school, and honors research.

With a 16:1 student:faculty ratio, students receive personalized attention from professors and staff who care about their success. And their success continues after graduation, with 92 percent of graduates employed or pursuing graduate work within six months of earning their degree.

We are a Catholic institution, founded in 1957 by the Missionary Sisters of the Sacred Heart of Jesus, with a mission to provide academic excellence, leadership development, and a commitment to social justice. Through international partnerships, community engagement, and hands-on experiences, students find their voice and how they can work for universal human rights and dignity.

Cabrini enrolls about 1,650 undergraduates and 800 students in graduate and doctoral programs.

LOCATION AND ENVIRONMENT

Cabrini is a coeducational residential university located 12 miles from Philadelphia in Radnor, PA. Our campus is tucked onto 112-acres of peaceful woods, surrounded by a suburban setting with nearby shopping, restaurants, and recreation.

CAMPUS FACILITIES & EQUIPMENT

Cabrini has 12 residence halls comprised of single rooms, doubles, suites, and apartments. The remodeled Dixon House houses 75 upper-class students, and the renovated Woodcrest Hall provides a great central location for first-year students.

In 2016, the addition of the Thomas P. Nerney Athletic and Recreation Pavilion added 38,000+ square feet to Cabrini's existing sports and recreation complex, including a state-of-the-art workout room, modern aerobic studios, lounge space, and a cafe. This addition complements our state-of-the-art science building, which includes facilities for our exercise-science laboratory.

OFF-CAMPUS OPPORTUNITIES

Cabrini is a short train ride to Philadelphia, and only two hours away from New York City and Washington, DC. The campus is also located 10 minutes from the King of Prussia Mall, the second largest mall in the country. A campus shuttle takes students to nearby locations, including the mall and train station.

ACADEMIC PROGRAMS

A core part of Cabrini University's mission is to provide an excellent academic experience that will help students grow as individuals and as leaders. This experience starts with Cabrini's award-winning First Year Experience Program, which helps students transition to college and creates a supportive community where they can learn who they are and how they can succeed.

In the first year, students have the opportunity to live and/or study with classmates who share a common interest through Learning Communities and can begin to build strong connections with their faculty. Through the Engagements with the Common Good courses, students explore societal issues and consider possible solutions to inequity around the world. If students need additional support, Cabrini's Center for Student Success offers free peer tutoring, writing and math support, academic advising guidance, and counseling services.

Our Honors Program is dedicated to honing students' critical-thinking skills, developing creative and imaginative impulses, and pushing them to expand their intellectual horizons. The program strives to model lifelong learning, giving students the tools they need to succeed inside and outside the academic setting.

As early as the second semester of a student's first year, he or she has the opportunity to study abroad in semester, summer-, or year-long programs or to enroll in one of the short-term study abroad courses offered each spring semester. Students have studied science in Switzerland, the Spanish language and culture in Madrid, the European Union in Amsterdam, and theater in London.

MAJORS AND DEGREES OFFERED

Cabrini offers more than 35 undergraduate programs, including biology, criminology, communication, education (with teacher certification), English, finance, health science, psychology, and social work; and 10 pre-professional programs, including pre-dentistry, pre-pharmacy, pre-law, and pre-physician assistant studies. Students also can create their own major, minor, or concentration.

After graduating with a bachelor's degree, students can continue their academic careers at Cabrini by pursuing graduate work in one of our six master's programs and our two doctoral programs.

TUITION, ROOM, BOARD, FEES

Full-time (12–18 credits) tuition and fees for the 2018–19 year is $31,920, which is below the national average for private institutions. Room and board, on average, cost $12,266 per year.

FINANCIAL AID

Cabrini is committed to providing an affordable, quality education, which is why 98 percent of our students receive financial aid and the average Cabrini financial award is $16,500. In addition, students may be eligible for PHEAA Grants (PA residents only), Pell Grants, and federal financial aid.

STUDENT ORGANIZATIONS AND ACTIVITIES

Whether it's Cabrini Day or EPIC Week, Homecoming, or trips to Broadway, Cabrini's student-driven Center for Student Engagement and Leadership makes sure campus never slows down. With more than 300 student events each year and more than 50 student clubs and organizations—from intramural sports to honors societies to professional organizations—students have many opportunities to engage and get involved. Students can also experience the outdoors through Cabrini Recreation trips like rock climbing and paddle boarding.

Cabrini has 19 Division III sports teams that compete in the Eastern Collegiate Athletic Conference and the Colonial States Athletic Conference and have won 106 CSAC Championships.

Our Nerney Leadership Institute offers leadership training and mentoring. Plus, students can make a difference with the Wolfington Center, which organizes service and social advocacy projects in the local community and around the world.

ADMISSIONS PROCESS

Cabrini University is test-optional and does not require students to submit their SAT or ACT scores. However, students may still choose to submit their scores; use SAT code 2071 and ACT code 3532.

To apply to Cabrini (undergraduate):

1. Complete the online application form at cabrini.edu/apply or commonapp.org.

2. Request that your high school send an official transcript to the Cabrini Admissions Office.

3. Submit a personal statement (250+ words, topic of your choice) in a Word document or PDF to essays@cabrini.edu.

4. Submit an application fee or fee waiver.

Recommended Materials (optional):

1. Activity résumé

2. Letter(s) of recommendation

3. ZeeMee link

To apply to Cabrini (transfer):

1. Complete the online application form at cabrini.edu/apply

2. Send transcripts from your college or university (if you've already earned 24+ credits).

3. Submit a schedule of additional classes you'll finish before attending Cabrini (if applicable).

4. Provide a brief personal statement (250+ words, topic of your choice) in a Word document or PDF to essays@cabrini.edu.

5. Submit an application fee or fee waiver.

For more information about visiting or applying to Cabrini, email admit@cabrini.edu.

CENTRAL CONNECTICUT STATE UNIVERSITY

AT A GLANCE

With the lowest tuition and fees among the comprehensive public universities in the state, Central Connecticut State University is considered the best value.

Dedicated to learning in the liberal arts and sciences, the University comprises five schools: Carol Ammon College of Liberal Arts & Social Sciences; and the schools of Business; Education & Professional Studies; Engineering, Science & Technology; and Graduate Studies. CCSU offers full- and part-time undergraduate programs in more than 100 areas of study.

LOCATION AND ENVIRONMENT

CCSU is located in suburban New Britain, in the center of Connecticut. It's approximately two hours from Boston or New York. The campus has been extensively renovated and continues to expand and upgrade academic and student facilities. The University is surrounded by a pleasant, residential neighborhood, with shopping and dining facilities nearby.

CAMPUS FACILITIES & EQUIPMENT

With new and renovated buildings CCSU's campus offers the classic collegiate style of architecture. Academic buildings are equipped with "smart classrooms" and seminar rooms. The Student Center provides lounges, dining services, conference and game rooms, information services, and a range of other support services. Three theatres provide space for plays, concerts, and guest lectures. The S.T. Chen Art Gallery hosts shows by student, faculty, and visiting artists. The Student Technology Center features 250 computers plus printers and scanners for student use. Campus-based TV and radio stations provide exciting entertainment as well as opportunities to learn about the professions. The Elihu Burritt Library provides access to over 2 million books through an online catalog, a wide array of electronic databases and online resources, and special collections ranging from the unparalleled collection of Polish American materials to the Equity Archive. The University also offers many athletic facilities, including an Olympic-sized swimming pool, modern exercise equipment, a state-of-the-art fitness center, a weight-training room, and an athletic training center. Approximately 26 percent of the students live on campus in eight residence halls.

OFF-CAMPUS OPPORTUNITIES

The School of Education has many connections to area schools, including several Professional Development Schools, which provide CCSU students opportunities to perfect their teaching skills in a full range of elementary and secondary classrooms.

The School of Engineering, Science & Technology offers a wide array of internship opportunities in area engineering, manufacturing, and technology businesses.

The Center for International Education, nationally recognized for the quality of its Study Abroad programs, offers students a rich variety of study-abroad opportunities at more than 40 locations throughout the world and provides academic and cultural programs that promote a better understanding of peoples and cultures.

The University and the New Britain Museum of American Art (an internationally acclaimed museum) have a partnership allowing students and faculty to visit the museum for free.

ACADEMICS

CCSU also offers a number of interdisciplinary programs as well as independently designed majors. The Honors Program, a challenging interdisciplinary program of study for academically qualified students, offers half and full-tuition merit scholarships and a variety of other benefits and resources, including a new Honors Lab.

MAJORS AND DEGREES OFFERED

CCSU is accredited by the New England Association of Schools and Colleges (NEASC). The University operates on a two-semester calendar and offers four summer sessions plus one winter session.

Undergraduate programs include: Accounting; Anthropology; Art (Art History); Athletic Training; Biochemistry; Biology (Ecology; Biodiversity; Evolutionary; Environmental Science; General); Biomolecular Sciences; Chemistry; Civil Engineering; Civil Engineering Technology; Communication (Media Studies; Strategic Communications); Computer Engineering Technology; Computer Science; Construction Management; Criminology; Dance Education; Design (Graphic/Information); Digital Printing Graphics Technology; Early Childhood Studies & Infant/Toddler Mental Health; Earth Sciences; Economics (General Operations Research); Education (Elementary; K-12; Secondary; Special Education); Electronics Technology; Engineering &Technology Education; Engineering Technology; English; Entrepreneurship; Exercise Science; Finance; French; Geography (Environmental; General Regional; Planning; Geographic Information Science; Tourism); German; History; Hospitality & Tourism; Industrial Technology (Electro-Mechanical Technology; Environmental & Occupational Safety; Graphics Technology; Manufacturing; Networking Technology; Technology Management); Interdisciplinary Science (Environmental Interpretation; Physical Sciences); International Business; International Studies; Italian; Journalism; Management (Entrepreneurship; Human Resource); Management Information Systems; Manufacturing Engineering Technology; Marketing; Mathematics (Actuarial; Statistics); Mechanical Engineering; Mechanical Engineering Technology; Media Studies; Music; Nursing (BSN & RN to BSN); Philosophy; Physical Education (Exercise Science & Health Promotion); Physics; Political Science (General; Public Administration); Psychology; Robotics & Mechatronics; Social Sciences; Social Work; Sociology; Spanish; Special Studies; Theatre.

Degrees: BA, BFA (Theatre); BS; BSN; BS-RN, Teacher Certification (elementary; secondary; k–12)

TUITION, ROOM, BOARD, FEES

TUITION & FEES (per year)

CT Resident

Tuition & fees $10,225

Housing (double occupancy) $6,820

Food (cost varies per meal plan) $4,996

Total $22,041

Out-of-State Resident

Tuition & fees $22,914

Housing (double occupancy) $6,820

Food (cost varies per meal plan) $4,996

Total $34,730

Annual costs for books, travel and personal expenses will vary and be about $2,500

FINANCIAL AID

Approximately 75 percent of CCSU full-time students receive some form of financial aid. CCSU's office of Financial Aid works with students to help them meet educational expenses from their first year until graduation. To apply for financial aid students must complete the FAFSA form. For more information, call 860.832.2200, e-mail FinancialAid3@ccsu.edu, or on the Web at www.ccsu.edu/finaid.

STUDENT ORGANIZATIONS AND ACTIVITIES

CCSU serves approximately 12,000 students—9,550 undergraduate and 2,450 graduate. Our distinguished alumni include successful business men and women, the first Latina state supreme court justice, CEOs in a wide range of industries and corporations, leading academics at national universities, award-winning educators and educational leaders, trainers and coaches at high schools and colleges as well as top NFL and MLB teams, journalists, novelists, and artists—each and all demonstrating that success begins with CCSU.

There are 130 student clubs and organizations, which cover a broad range of interests: academic—such as the Anthropology or the Investment clubs; athletics—such as the crew or flying clubs; cultural—for example, the art club, the jazz band, and other musical organizations; ethnic—such as the Black Student Union, Latin American Students Organization, and the Muslim Student Association; religious—such as Hillel and the Newman Club; and such honors organizations as Delta Mu Delta, Lambda Delta, and Kappa Delta Pi. On-campus entertainment is wide and varied, including, most recently, "Devils Den@ 10"—student-run entertainment on Thursday evenings.

ADMISSIONS PROCESS

CCSU is a learning community of students with a broad range of abilities, interests, and backgrounds. We value excellence and achievement in academic scholarship, community involvement, and extracurricular activities. Our admissions process evaluates the readiness of applicants to succeed based on past demonstrations of academic and personal successes.

CCSU has a "rolling" admissions policy, not a set admissions deadline, which gives students greater flexibility in applying. The University urges prospective students to apply as early as possible in their senior year. The University begins accepting students for the fall semester in mid-October and will continue to review applications until the class is filled.

First-year applicants are considered on the basis of performance in college preparatory classes, rank in class, SAT or ACT test scores, recommendations, and community and extracurricular involvement and leadership. A personal essay is required. For some applicants an interview with a representative of the Office of Recruitment & Admissions may be necessary. If the applicant ranks in the top 20 percent of his/her class, is an A-B student, and has SAT scores of 1100 or higher, the student should consider CCSU's Honors Program; call 860-832-2938 for details. CCSU accepts most Advanced Placement (AP) courses for college credit, provided the minimum CCSU required score is achieved. Check with Admissions for the required scores.

Admission criteria include graduation from a regionally accredited secondary school. High school work should include college preparatory courses in: English (four years); Mathematics (covering algebra I, geometry, and algebra II); Science (two years including one-year lab science); Social sciences (two to three years including U.S. history). Coursework in foreign language is recommended (at least three consecutive years of the same foreign language up through the third level will satisfy the foreign language proficiency required of all CCSU-enrolled students). Students whose preparation does not follow this pattern may still qualify for admission if, in the judgment of the Director of Recruitment and Admissions, there is strong evidence that they have the potential to complete a degree program or if they meet other established criteria as authorized by the University President under authority delegated by the Board of Regents of the Connecticut State College & University System. Applicants who are not graduates of a secondary school should submit their secondary school transcript up to the time of withdrawal and a copy of their high school equivalency diploma and scores.

The most important thing for the applicant to remember is to provide as much information as possible achievements, awards, and examples of leadership when applying.

HOW TO APPLY

Students are encouraged to apply online at www.ccsu.edu/apply. For paper applications, please provide the Office of Recruitment & Admissions with 1) completed application for undergraduate admission 2) official high school transcript, SAT or ACT test scores, recommendations, and essay and 3) a non-refundable application fee of $50. All correspondence should be sent to the Office of Recruitment and Admissions, CCSU, P.O. Box 4010, 1615 Stanley Street, New Britain, CT 06050-4010. Tours and information sessions may be arranged by calling 860.832.2289 or via e-mail at: admissions@ccsu.edu.

CHRISTOPHER NEWPORT UNIVERSITY

AT A GLANCE

Christopher Newport University provides a liberal arts and sciences education that stimulates intellectual inquiry and fosters civic engagement. CNU students acquire qualities of mind and spirit that prepare them to lead lives of significance.

A four-year public university in Newport News, Virginia, Christopher Newport enrolls 5,000 students in rigorous academic programs through the College of Arts and Humanities, the College of Natural and Behavioral Sciences, the College of Social Sciences, and the Luter School of Business. CNU offers great teaching and small class sizes with an emphasis on leadership, civic engagement and honor.

At Christopher Newport, we want you to be successful in your studies. Even more importantly, we want you to lead a life of significance. With that in mind, we have designed an undergraduate experience to instruct and inspire great leaders for the 21st century. We want students who will make the world a better place—young women and men with a passion for engagement and a strong sense of civic responsibility.

CNU's outstanding curriculum shapes hearts and minds for a lifetime of service. From the moment you arrive on campus, you will discover countless opportunities to develop strong leadership traits. Your journey begins in the classroom, where you will study with distinguished faculty—accomplished scholars of outstanding quality. Outside the classroom—from athletics to clubs and student organizations—you will enhance your leadership skills by collaborating with your peers. Together, you will work on projects and initiatives that make a lasting impact on our campus, community and world.

LOCATION AND ENVIRONMENT

Located in Southeastern Virginia, CNU's picturesque, 260-acre campus is in the heart of one of the most historic—and beautiful—areas of the United States and conveniently located amid popular Virginia attractions including Williamsburg and Virginia Beach. When you venture off campus, you'll find unlimited activities for all interests as well as cultural and historical treasures within a short walk or drive.

CAMPUS FACILITIES

Christopher Newport is committed to providing extraordinary buildings that support great learning and activities. We've completed nearly $1 billion in capital construction in recent years and have built a beautiful campus with world-class facilities that include dazzling and wildly popular residence halls. You'll enjoy our Freeman Sports and Convocation Center, Ferguson Center for the Arts, David Student Union, Trible Library—the intellectual heart of campus, Forbes Hall—an integrated science center with cutting-edge labs and technology, Luter Hall—home to the College of Social Sciences and the Luter School of Business, McMurran Hall—which includes our liberal arts and humanities programs, and Christopher Newport Hall—our Student Success Center.

ACADEMICS

Learning Communities

All freshmen are placed into a Learning Community based on their interests, which facilitates a successful transition from high school to college. Living together, sharing multiple classes with a small group of students and collaborating with faculty enable learning beyond the classroom while providing extra support.

President's Leadership Program

Make an impact through the President's Leadership Program (PLP). Selected freshman applicants have excelled in their academic studies and have demonstrated a passion for engagement. Through challenging courses, public service, foreign study and other targeted opportunities, PLP empowers leadership students to become caring, knowledgeable and effective leaders for America and the world. The President's Leadership Program offers priority registration, annual scholarships and study abroad awards.

Honors Program

This unique program offers students more freedom to customize their academic experience for their personal and professional aspirations. The Honors Program allows more time for interdisciplinary seminar-style courses and challenges students by means of study abroad, independent research, internships, jobs and volunteer experience relevant to their passions. Each student receives an annual residential scholarship (including a study abroad stipend), as well as priority housing in an Honors Learning Community and priority course registration.

Undergraduate Research and Creative Activity

CNU undergraduates engage in cutting-edge research and creative activities. In all fields of study, students collaborate with faculty mentors on key research, make conference presentations, and publish books and scholarly journal articles with faculty. Each spring the Paideia conference showcases outstanding student research, and the Summer Scholars Program offers paid research assistantships.

Pre-Law Program

Interested in pursuing a career in law? The nation's top law schools seek applicants who have received a well-rounded undergraduate education—one like the liberal arts and sciences curriculum Christopher Newport offers. Many of our pre-law students pursue a philosophy of law minor or an American studies major with a constitutional studies concentration. Regardless of your undergraduate field of study, our Pre-Law Program is designed to help you gain admission to one of the nation's top 25 law schools.

Pre-Med and Pre-Health Program

Medical schools and other graduate programs seek applicants with a well-rounded undergraduate education. The Pre-Med and Pre-Health Program at Christopher Newport assists students pursuing any academic major to prepare for post-graduate study. In addition to the necessary prerequisite coursework, we offer several resources to help you gain admission to your professional school of choice—from academic and career advising to mentoring, clinical internships, workshops and seminars.

Study Abroad

We encourage you to study abroad, either accompanied by CNU faculty or independently. Learn about different cultures while falling in love with America. You may choose to study for an entire semester, a year or more briefly between academic terms. These rich cultural experiences are as unique as the destinations. With scholarship opportunities available, the world is your classroom! CNU students have recently spent semesters or full academic years in Australia, Costa Rica, England, France, Germany, Greece, India, Italy, Japan, Mexico, Russia, Scotland, Spain and many other locales.

Bachelor's to Master's Five-Year Program

Students can obtain a bachelor's and master's degree in the following five-year programs:

- Master of Arts in Teaching
- Master of Science in Applied Physics and Computer Science
- Master of Science in Environmental Science

Center for Academic Success

Throughout the CNU experience, the Center for Academic Success offers tutoring, workshops, seminars and one-on-one assistance to help students improve their academic performance with effective study strategies. Peer writing consultants available in the Writing Center offer specialized help with all stages of the writing process.

Center for Career Planning

The Center for Career Planning directly assists students with academic major exploration, landing a first job or gaining admission to a top graduate school. Workshops, seminars, job fairs, on-campus interviews and career counseling—a full range of services—are available to students and alumni.

Service

Christopher Newport students make a positive difference in the life of our campus, community and world. We offer countless opportunities—from service-learning initiatives and projects like Habitat for Humanity to the philanthropic work of our Greek organizations and student-athletes, among others. Through a partnership with the prestigious Bonner Foundation, CNU joins a national network of more than 75 colleges and universities who support four-year, service scholarships.

MAJORS AND DEGREES OFFERED

We offer more than 90 areas of study in the liberal arts and sciences, providing a breadth and depth of knowledge that will prepare you to take advantage of any opportunity that presents itself in today's global marketplace. Through Christopher Newport's rigorous curriculum you will learn to think critically and communicate effectively while developing the tools and skills that will serve you for a lifetime.

Areas of Study

Accounting; African-American Studies; American Studies (Constitutional Studies; Humanities; Social Science); Applied Physics; Asian Studies; Biochemistry; Biology; Biology—Cellular, Molecular and Physiological; Biology—Environmental; Biology—Integrative; Biology—Organismal; Business Administration; Chemistry; Childhood Studies; Civic Engagement and Social Entrepreneurship; Classical Studies (Classical Languages; Classical Studies); Communication Studies; Computer Engineering; Computer Science; Dance; Digital Humanities; Economics (Mathematical Economics); Electrical Engineering; English (Literature; Writing); Environmental Studies; Film Studies; Finance; Fine Arts (Art History; Studio Art); French; German; Greek Studies; History; Human Rights and Conflict Resolution; Information Science; Information Systems; Interdisciplinary Studies; International Culture and Business; Judeo-Christian Studies; Latin; Latin American Studies; Leadership Studies; Linguistics; Management; Marketing; Mathematics; Mathematics—Computational and Applied (Biology and Life Sciences; Computational Chemistry; Economics; Physics, Dynamics and Engineering); Medieval and Renaissance Studies; Middle East and North Africa Studies; Military Science (ROTC); Museum Studies; Music (Choral Music Education; Composition; Instrumental Music Education; Performance); Neuroscience; Philosophy (Pre-Seminary Studies; Studies in Religion); Philosophy and Religion; Philosophy of Law; Photography and Video Art; Political Science; Psychology; Social Work; Sociology (Anthropology; Criminology); Spanish; Theater (Acting; Arts Administration; Design/Technical Theater; Directing/Dramatic Literature; Music Theater/Dance; Theater Studies); U.S. National Security Studies; Women's and Gender Studies

Advising Tracks

Biotechnology and Management

Pre-Health

Pre-Law

Pre-Med

Bachelor's to Master's Five-Year Program

Applied Physics and Computer Science

Environmental Science

Teaching (MAT)

TUITION, ROOM, BOARD, FEES

Christopher Newport offers exceptional academics, stunning facilities and a vibrant campus life. Yet we recognize paying for college can be a challenge. That's why we distribute nearly $50 million in aid to students each year. Most assistance comes in the form of federal and state grants, scholarships to reward merit and help students with financial need, educational loans, and college work-study programs.

2017–18 Costs per Year

In-State Tuition: $13,654

In-State Room and Board: $11,544

Total: $25,198

Out-of-State Tuition: $25,850

Out-of-State Room and Board: $11,544

Total: $37,394

FINANCIAL AID

Important New FAFSA Deadline:

To apply for financial aid or scholarships, submit your FAFSA by the December 15 preferred filing deadline or the March 1 priority filing deadline.

ADMISSION PROCESS

We encourage students to apply to Christopher Newport as early as possible due to our selective admission standards. We anticipate receiving 8,000 applications for only 1,200 spaces in the fall freshman class. Students applying for Early Decision or Early Action will receive priority consideration for admission as well as academic scholarships.

Application Plan	Deadline to Apply	Notification Date
Early Decision	November 15	December 15
Early Action	December 1	January 15
Regular Decision	February 1	March 15

We're a Common App School! Apply online at freshman.cnu.edu.

Application Review

When reviewing applications we consider each student's academic grades and curriculum, with special attention given to honors, Advanced Placement, International Baccalaureate or dual-enrollment courses. We also look for students who demonstrate leadership ability, a commitment to service and community involvement, exemplary talents, and diverse experiences. As part of the application review, CNU requires a personal statement or essay of no fewer than 250 words to learn more about you, your goals and ideas.

Admission Interviews

Any high school senior planning to apply is strongly encouraged to interview at Christopher Newport. This personal interaction is an important part of the application process. It is a great way to enhance your admission application and receive a personalized introduction to CNU. We want to meet you one-on-one to learn about you—your qualities, experiences and goals we can't discern from your test scores or GPA. An interview is required for Honors and PLP applicants.

CLEMSON UNIVERSITY

AT A GLANCE

Set in a college town with a beautiful backdrop of lakeshore and mountains, Clemson University attracts students,looking for a rigorous academic experience, world-class research opportunities, strong sense of community and vibrant school spirit. We invite you to pursue greatness here.

One of the country's most selective public research universities, Clemson was founded in 1889 with a mission to be a "high seminary of learning" dedicated to teaching, research and service. Today, these three concepts remain at the heart of the University and provide the framework for an exceptional educational experience.

At Clemson professors take the time to get to know students and explore innovative ways of teaching. Exceptional teaching is one reason our retention and graduation rates rank among the highest in the country for public universities.

Exceptional teaching is also why Clemson continues to attract an increasingly talented student body. In 2017 more than half of the entering freshmen were ranked in the top 10 percent of their high school classes, and the freshman class averaged 1302 on the critical reading and math sections of the SAT.

The University is committed to the success of its students. For the fall 2016 class, Clemson's student retention rate was 93 percent. Much of this is due to the Academic Success Center (ASC), which is recognized nationally and internationally for its programs in collegiate learning. The ASC is housed in a 35,000-square-foot facility where it offers free one-on-one tutoring services for more than 80 courses as well as for additional courses as the need arises. Peer-Assisted Learning, academic skills workshops and academic coaching are also available—free to all Clemson students

Clemson has also received national recognition for its innovative Communication Across the Curriculum (CAC) program, which makes writing across all curriculums a priority. At Clemson, CAC has become a standard teaching method used in nearly every department to provide real-life challenges that require students to think and communicate effectively.

From cheering on the Tigers at a football game to socializing at the Hendrix Student Center, Clemson students can participate in a wide variety of activities outside the classroom. The more than 400 campus clubs and organizations include fraternities and sororities, as well as honorary, international, military, performing arts, political, professional, religious, service, social interest, special interest, sports and fitness, and student media.

With 19 intercollegiate sports, Clemson offers exciting spectator sports year-round. Clemson is a charter member of the Atlantic Coast Conference and is an NCAA Division I school. Admission to regular-season home events is included in University fees for full-time students.

Admissions:

864-656-2287

clemson.edu/admissions/undergraduate

Campus Tours:

864-656-4789

clemson.edu/visitors

LOCATION AND ENVIRONMENT

Clemson University is located in Clemson, S.C., a town of about 14,000 located in the middle of the I-85 corridor between Atlanta, Ga., and Charlotte, N.C. The 1,400-acre campus is next door to the S.C. Botanical Garden and borders the shores of Hartwell Lake and the foothills of the Blue Ridge Mountains.

CAMPUS FACILITIES & EQUIPMENT

Fike Recreation Center

Fike is a 200,000-square-foot recreation center that features a fitness atrium complete with a suspended running track that overlooks the indoor courts. It's also equipped with indoor swimming facilities, fitness studios, racquetball courts, state-of-the-art cardio equipment, weights, locker rooms and a climbing wall.

Health Center

Redfern Health Center provides medical services, counseling and psychological services, and health-related programs like alcohol and drug education. It's one of the nation's few on-campus accredited health centers.

Hendrix Student Center

The Hendrix Student Center is the hub of campus activity and is located a step away from most housing. Here you can find people taking a yoga class or enjoying a meal at the food court. It's home to the University bookstore and offers plenty of quiet places to stop and study. It also has a movie theater, ice cream parlor and much more.

Housing

Located within a 10- to 15-minute walk to class, Clemson's 23 residence halls and four apartment communities offer a vast selection of living arrangements.

Information Technology

The University's wireless networking capability lets students communicate with professors and classmates, read online course materials, check email and conduct research—all from their own laptops.

Watt Family Innovation Center

The Watt Family Innovation Center offers a collaborative environment where students can engage with faculty and industry leaders to generate ideas and solve problems. Engineering and technology feature prominently in the 70,000-square-foot space for teaching and research, from the two-story media grid and moveable electronic walls to the lights that automatically sense when someone is in a room.

OFF-CAMPUS OPPORTUNITIES

Study Abroad

Clemson students are strongly encouraged to incorporate a study-abroad experience in their overall Clemson journey. Programs are available on six continents for all disciplines and interests. These include faculty-led programs, exchange programs and programs available through Clemson's partnerships with study-abroad providers and institutions. Students in a variety of majors also have opportunities at Clemson campuses in South Carolina and around the world, including the Archbold Center in Dominica; the Daniel Center in Genoa, Italy; and the Brussels Center in Belgium.

Cooperative Education

The Cooperative Education program provides an opportunity for students to alternate periods of academic study with semesters of paid, career-related, engaged-learning experiences to bridge the gap between academic study and its application in professional practice. Clemson's career center pairs about 2,200 students annually with companies seeking interns or co-op students. Internships are also available on campus where students can work part or full-time, with many in full-time positions having the option of earning credit. The Princeton Review ranks Clemson's career services program as the No. 5 career office in the nation.

Community Service

An important aspect of Clemson is its dedication to improving the world through public service. In a typical year, Clemson students contribute over 100,000 service hours, earning the University national recognition on the President's Higher Education Community Service Honor Roll. Opportunities to make a difference are available through student service organizations, ongoing service projects and one-time service events—on campus, in the community, across the nation or around the world. The 2015 National Survey on Student Engagement reports that 61 percent of first-year Clemson students and 94 percent of seniors said "at least some" of their courses included high-impact practices such as service-learning.

MAJORS AND DEGREES OFFERED

Students can select from more than 80 undergraduate and 119 graduate degree programs offered by seven colleges: Agriculture, Forestry and Life Sciences; Architecture, Arts and Humanities; Behavioral, Social and Health Sciences; Business; Education; Engineering, Computing and Applied Sciences; and Science. To find out what majors are available go to: clemson.edu/degrees.

Clemson University is accredited by the Commission on Colleges of the Southern Association of Colleges and Schools to award bachelor's, master's, specialist and doctoral degrees. Questions about the accreditation of Clemson University can be directed to the Commission on Colleges at 1866 Southern Lane, Decatur, Georgia 30033-4097; phone: 404-679-4500.

Honors College

Calhoun Honors College is a University wide program that combines the strengths of a public, land-grant university with those of a highly selective small college. Calhoun Scholars may choose to pursue departmental honors within their specific academic discipline. In addition, EUREKA! (Experiences in Undergraduate Research, Exploration and Knowledge Advancement) is a unique and exciting program that enables honors students to pursue research and scholarly activities with faculty members across all disciplines. The advantages of membership in the Honors College include priority registration, extended library loan privileges, honors research grants and a special living-learning community.

The National Scholars Program is a highly selective program for exceptional students who strive to meet their highest intellectual potential. One of its goals is to develop the interests and talents students need to compete for Rhodes, Marshall and Truman scholarships; Fulbright Grants; National Science Foundation Graduate Fellowships; and other prestigious international fellowships. In 2016, seven Clemson students received National Science Foundation Graduate Fellowships. Two recent Clemson graduates received Fulbright grants to conduct research or teach abroad, and one student was named a Goldwater Scholar.

Undergraduate Research

Clemson's Creative Inquiry (CI) program allows undergraduate students to engage in research about problems that spring from their own curiosity, from a professor's challenge or from the pressing needs of the world around them. Team-based investigations are led by a faculty mentor and typically span two to four semesters. Students take ownership of their projects and take the risks necessary to solve problems and get answers. This invaluable experience produces exceptional graduates, capable of thinking critically, solving problems as a team, and communicating and presenting their ideas to others. In 2015–16, 4,917 students participated in 421 CI teams.

Programs for Educational Enrichment and Retention

Clemson's nationally recognized Programs for Educational Enrichment and Retention (PEER) is committed to improving the academic performance of underrepresented students in engineering and science. According to a 2016 survey by the magazine Diverse: Issues In Higher Education, Clemson is the nation's 20th highest producer of African-American undergraduates receiving baccalaureate degrees.

Living-Learning Communities

Living-learning communities offer the chance for students to live and work with others who have similar interests and goals. There are living options for students interested in business, engineering and science, civics and service, honors courses, professional golf management and much more. Recognized as a national model, the communities are designed to help students be more successful by offering on-site advising and academic support, common course assignments, guest speakers, service opportunities and a variety of social activities.

TUITION, ROOM, BOARD, FEES

Estimated Costs for 2016–17 Academic Year

S.C. Resident Full Time

Tuition and Fees° $14,708

Room and Board (approximate) $9,144

Books and Supplies (approximate) $1,308

Total $25,160

Nonresident Full Time

Tuition and Fees° $34,590

Room and Board (approximate) $9,144

Books and Supplies (approximate) $1,308

Total $45,042

Other Expenses

Estimated Personal and Transportation Expenses $3,502

One-time computer cost°° $1,800

°Assumes health and other mandatory fees (required for all full-time students) and average lab and loan fees.

°°All students are required to own a laptop computer. For details, go to clemson.edu/laptop.

FINANCIAL AID

Each year Clemson awards financial aid in the form of grants, scholarships, loans and part-time employment to more than 18,000 students. Overall, 84 percent of Clemson students receive awards ranging from $500 to all-inclusive cost coverage. Ninety-nine percent of first-time in-state students receive state scholarships. All financial aid is awarded annually, and FAFSA applications for the next year are available in January. Entering freshmen are evaluated on a competitive basis for scholarships using the admission application.

STUDENT ORGANIZATIONS AND ACTIVITIES

At Clemson, school spirit is a color Solid Orange and it's hard to miss on fall Saturdays in Death Valley when more than 80,000 fans cheer on the Clemson Tigers. Take a walk through campus on any night, and you'll see the campus alive with students playing intramural sports, going to concerts, attending Greek mixers or gathering to meet with any of Clemson's 400+ student organizations.

ADMISSIONS PROCESS

In 2016, the University received about 23,506 applications for a fall freshman class of 3,685.

For freshman applicants, the following factors are considered: class standing, standardized test scores (SAT or ACT), high school curriculum, grades and choice of major. All entering freshmen must have completed 4 credits of English, 3 credits of mathematics, 3 credits of laboratory science, 3 credits of a foreign language (in the same language), 3 credits of social sciences, 1 credit of U.S. history, 1 credit of physical education or ROTC, and 1 credit of fine arts.

To be considered for transfer admission, candidates must have completed a full year of college study (a minimum of 30 semester hours or 45 quarter hours of transferable work), earned a cumulative GPA of at least 2.5 on a 4.0 scale (3.0 preferred) and completed freshman-level courses in English, science and mathematics for their intended major at Clemson.

Application deadlines for freshman admission are December 1 (priority date for fall semester), May 1 (fall semester), and December 15 (spring semester). For transfer admissions, the application deadlines are July 1 (fall semester) and December 15 (spring semester).

CLEVELAND INSTITUTE OF ART

AT A GLANCE

Cleveland Institute of Art is one of the nation's leading accredited independent colleges of art and design.

Offering 15 majors in fine art, design, craft and digital arts, the college has been an educational cornerstone in Cleveland, Ohio since 1882, producing graduates who enter the workforce as studio artists, designers, photographers, contemporary craftsmen, entrepreneurs, and educators.

LOCATION AND ENVIRONMENT

Our location in University Circle, Cleveland's cultural hub, gives our students access to some of the finest museums, schools, performing arts venues, parks, and galleries in one of the most culturally dense square miles anywhere in the U.S. University Circle was named by Forbes Magazine as one of the most beautiful communities in the country. The neighborhood is home to world-renowned cultural, educational, and healthcare institutions and more than 11,000 students.

CAMPUS FACILITIES & EQUIPMENT

The state-of-the-art facilities at the Cleveland Institute of Art provide students with space designed specifically for studying, living, and exhibiting art and design.

CIA's campus is home to the Reinberger Gallery, a gallery that presents exhibitions, events, and lectures; the Peter B. Lewis Theater, home of CIA's nationally acclaimed Cinematheque film program; the Jessica R. Gund Memorial Library, which has collections specifically developed for the visual artist, designer, and craftsperson; and individual studio spaces for all students once they enter their major in their sophomore year.

First and second-year students live on campus in CIA-owned housing. First-year students live in our Uptown Residence Hall, which opened in 2014. Designed in consultation with students, these two-bedroom suites house two students per bedroom, each with their own bath. Bedrooms are connected by a common work area and kitchenette. Second-year students reside in our new upperclass residence hall, which feature four-person suites with individual bedrooms. Both residence halls offer workout spaces, on-site printing, and free laundry.

Our campus is a creative, friendly environment that allows students to pursue their dreams. Visit our campus and see for yourself.

OFF-CAMPUS OPPORTUNITIES

Cleveland Institute of Art's campus is less than five miles from downtown Cleveland, where you can sample the city's hottest restaurants, take in a music or comedy show, tour independent galleries, take art walks, and visit community festivals. If you're a sports fan, plan on cheering on the Cleveland Indians, Cavaliers, or Browns at their downtown venues.

ACADEMICS

At CIA, we've made an academic commitment to helping students build better futures by engaging them in community-based learning, real-world projects, and social practices. Through a selection of field-based courses, focusing on real-world projects and engagement with external partners, our students graduate with experience engaging the community through their work. From our early relationships with the auto industry, to relationships today with NASA, students from across disciplines are learning the skills necessary to be successful in the 21st century.

MAJORS AND DEGREES OFFERED

Cleveland Institute of Art offers 15 majors in art, design, craft, and digital media. You enter your major as a sophomore and spend three intense years building skills and mastering techniques. CIA faculty will encourage you to develop a wider perspective by experimenting with media outside your major through interdisciplinary study.

TUITION, ROOM, BOARD, FEES

Estimated full-time tuition is US$38,980. Estimated fees are $2,750. Housing for incoming first-year students is $8,400 for our apartment-style residence halls, and $2,700 for meal plan.

FINANCIAL AID

Cleveland Institute of Art offers merit and need-based financial aid, as well as federal and state financial aid. 90 percent of incoming first-year students enrolling for 2016–17 received scholarships. Average financial aid package for 2015–16 was $37,868.

CIA's Office of Financial Aid is committed to helping students find ways to fund their education. Financial aid officers work with students to craft a personalized financial aid package that combines merit and need-based scholarships, federal loans and grants, scholarships, loans, and work study programs.

STUDENT ORGANIZATIONS AND ACTIVITIES

With approximately 625 students from around the country and the world, CIA offers a personal educational experience with the benefits of a larger institution. Surrounded by creative-minded friends and mentors, CIA students find inspiration inside and outside of the studio. Students also experience a community full of cultural energy, ethnic neighborhoods, and a vibrant downtown, all accessible by public transportation.

When not in the studio, CIA students can enjoy organized activities, annual campus traditions, and various student groups that specialize in topics from academics to religion. Some favorite traditions include late-night breakfasts during finals, the wildly creative Halloween costume party, and the year-end school-wide picnic.

ADMISSIONS PROCESS

To be considered for admission, you must follow the application procedures and criteria below.

1. Complete the application online at cia.edu/apply

2. Submit the $40 application fee. Make checks payable to the Cleveland Institute of Art.

3. Complete a personal statement, in which you describe your purpose for attending a college of art and design, what led you to this decision, and why you have chosen to apply at CIA.

4. Arrange to have your high school transcripts sent to the Office of Admissions. If you have successfully completed 24 college credits and attended a regionally accredited college or university full time for a year or more, have your college transcripts sent instead.

5. Have one letter of recommendation completed on your behalf. We suggest this be from an art teacher. We also will accept this letter from a counselor or someone who understands your desire to pursue an arts education.

6. Optional: Request SAT or ACT test results be sent to CIA. Our identification numbers are SAT-1152 and ACT-3243. International students whose first language is not English must submit the TOEFL with a minimum score of 550 PBT (paper-based test) or equivalent 213 CBT (computer-based test) or 79 IBT (Internet-based test). We also accept a band score of at least 6.0 on the IELTS or completion of Level 112 of ESL coursework.

7. Submit your portfolio of artwork. All work can be submitted via our online application (go.cia.edu) or through slideroom.com. Your portfolio should consist of no fewer than 12 and no more than 20 pieces of work. Please carefully follow all our portfolio guidelines.

Application materials should be submitted online. Our mailing address, if paper-based materials need to be forwarded is: Cleveland Institute of Art, Office of Admissions, 11610 Euclid Avenue, Cleveland, OH 44106.

Applications can be submitted at any time before the first day of classes and will be considered as long as space is available. However, candidates are encouraged to follow application deadlines to ensure eligibility for merit scholarships and institutional financial aid. Dates and deadlines can be viewed online.

Applications are welcome from all qualified students. The admissions committee bases its decisions on a careful review of all credentials submitted by the applicant. Acceptance decisions are made without regard to race, color, sex, sexual orientation, gender expression, marital status, age, ethnic or national origin, religion, creed, veteran status, or physical or mental disability in accordance with federal, state, and local laws.

Visit cia.edu/admissions for more info.

THE COLLEGE OF NEW JERSEY

AT A GLANCE

The College of New Jersey (TCNJ) has created a culture of constant questioning. In small classes, students and faculty members collaborate in a rewarding process. They seek to understand fundamental principles, apply key concepts, reveal new problems and pursue lines of inquiry to gain a fluency of thought in their disciplines. This transformative process is at the core of the educational experience at The College.

In order to enhance student development and empowerment, TCNJ's curriculum is built around five key experiences which permeate every major across seven academic schools. Small classes prioritizing discussion and inquiry create a Personalized, Rigorous, and Collaborative Learning Environment where students and faculty work side by side in developing skills and applying concepts. Undergraduate Research, Mentored Internships, and Field Experiences give TCNJ students opportunities to get out of the classroom, develop their professional skill sets, and discover exciting career paths and academic endeavors. Passion for civic responsibility and a commitment to Community-Engaged Learning ensures that TCNJ graduates enter the professional world as top-notch scholars and citizens. Opportunities for Global Engagement found on campus and facilitated through internationally recognized study-abroad programs allow students to expand their internal scope and frame their academic goals and achievements in a truly global context. Finally, academic and extracurricular programs designed to foster Leadership Development help students build confidence and decision-making skills that they will need to solve the problems of tomorrow and build a brighter future.

TCNJ admits a diverse class each year full of ambitious students, eager to build on their educational foundations and dive into new topics. These students will ultimately find a home away from home on campus, and 95 percent of first-year students will return for their second year. The most successful admits are prepared to steer their own academic pursuits toward post-graduation goals of graduate school, professional training, or satisfying careers.

Prestigious graduate schools, including the University of Pennsylvania, Georgetown Law School, Maxwell School at Syracuse University, NYU Law School, and Harvard, Yale, and Northwestern Universities, routinely welcome TCNJ alumni into their ranks. TCNJ graduates boast a 64 percent acceptance rate into Medical School and an 88 percent acceptance rate into Law School.

Many top corporations recruit TCNJ graduates, providing avenues into rewarding jobs directly after graduation. Other barometers of student success include the 100 percent pass rate of education majors taking the state teacher preparation test and the 94 percent three-year pass rate for nursing students obtaining their license. The numerous learning opportunities at The College prepare students to prosper in any arena after the completion of their undergraduate career.

LOCATION AND ENVIRONMENT

Neoclassical Georgian Colonial architecture, meticulous landscaping and intentional design merge to meet the evolving needs of the TCNJ community. Students enjoy a campus with 289 acres of trees, lakes, and open spaces within the suburban setting of Ewing Township, New Jersey. Two out of three undergraduate students take part in the on-campus residence hall experience. The residence halls vary in configuration from the first-year towers to suites and townhouse arrangements for upper class students. The College ensures that on-campus housing is available to all students in their first two years, with out-of-state students guaranteed to receive housing for all four years of study.

Nearby cities, such as Princeton, Trenton, Philadelphia, and New York, allow for abundant entertainment, employment, and social options. Many courses incorporate field trips to New York City or Washington DC.

In 2015, TCNJ completed the first phase of the Campus Town project. Adding an attractive downtown component to an already appealing campus, Campus Town offers students brand new residential opportunities, a pristine Barnes and Noble bookstore and café, and a comprehensive fitness center. Retail and dining establishments such as Panera Bread and Yummy Sushi have been incorporated as well, with additional businesses scheduled to open throughout 2018.

CAMPUS FACILITIES & EQUIPMENT

Learning, like everything else, is contextual. The surroundings in which students learn and the tools they use influence their experience. Not surprisingly, the College supports its educational aspirations with careful attention to the quality of its facilities. In the first quarter of the 21st century, more than $250 million in ongoing and new facilities construction is ensuring that TCNJ students continue to thrive in an environment that not only meets their academic, athletic, social and living needs, but extends their reach resulting in higher scholarship, better health and fitness, closer community, and greater comfort.

Recent additions to campus include the Campus Town project, a newly renovated student center, and a state-of-the-art STEM Complex.

OFF-CAMPUS OPPORTUNITIES

TCNJ fosters global engagement with a robust offering of programs that build students' intercultural competence. For education abroad, TCNJ offers an extensive portfolio of short-term and long-term opportunities through study abroad partnerships, faculty-led programs, global student teaching, and internships. TCNJ welcomes global students and provides support services such as personalized language support and academic advising.

Mentored internships, both on and off campus, expose students to career options as they gain professional skills. With the College's location providing easy access to New York, Philadelphia, and other corporate centers, numerous internships are available either for pay or college credit.

Faculty mentors lend their advice and help students locate and procure appropriate opportunities including fellowships, research positions and internships. Students may also use resources at the Career Center to find positions in New York, Philadelphia, or with one of TCNJ's many corporate, government, or research partners located closer to campus.

ACADEMICS

A Liberal Learning Curriculum ensures that all students are grounded in the values of civic responsibility, intellectual and scholarly growth, and that they receive a well-rounded education in the liberal arts.

In 2004, the College completed a transformation of its curriculum requiring students to complete fewer courses, while adding depth to each course pursued. All courses have been transformed and contain significant out-of-class requirements that provide for student and faculty interaction.

These small classes enable dialog between students and TCNJ's accomplished teaching staff. This staff is composed of professors with terminal degrees in exclusivity; no courses are taught by graduate students or Teacher's Assistants. The College shapes its curricula and educational experiences around the concept of Personalized, Collaborative, and Rigorous Intellectual Development.

The required First-Year Seminar, the cornerstone of the Liberal Learning program, introduces students to the habits of mind and the methodologies of research; The seminar format of no more than 15 students reinforces the message that students are not passive recipients of knowledge but rather active contributors in their own learning. Liberal Learning requirements are grouped by diversity and community engagement goals that can be self-designed or designated as interdisciplinary concentrations.

Top students may enroll in TCNJ's Honors Program, designed to provide a core curriculum with additional challenges and opportunities for individualized work. Most honors classes take an interdisciplinary approach and encourage collaboration between faculty and students from multiple academic departments and disciplines. Independent study arrangements fall easily within the parameters of the Honors Program, as well.

MAJORS AND DEGREES OFFERED

The College of New Jersey hosts seven schools: Arts and Communication; Business; Education; Engineering; Humanities and Social Sciences; Nursing, Health & Exercise Science; and Science. The College offers programs leading to the Bachelor of Arts, Bachelor of Fine Arts, Bachelor of Music, Bachelor of Science, and Bachelor of Science in Nursing degrees.

TCNJ grants degrees in the following majors: Accountancy, African American Studies, Art Education (K–12), Art History, Biology°, Biomedical Engineering, Business Administration (specializations in Finance, Interdisciplinary Business, Management, and Marketing), Chemistry°, Civil Engineering, Communication Studies, Computer Engineering, Computer Science, Criminology, Early Childhood Education; Economics°, Education of the Deaf and Hard of Hearing, Electrical Engineering, Elementary Education, Engineering Science (specializations in Engineering Management or Policy and Society), English°, Global Business, Health and Exercise Science, Health and Physical Education (K–12), History°, Interactive Multimedia, International Studies, i-STEM Education, Journalism and Professional Writing, Mathematics°, Mechanical Engineering, Music (options in Education and Performance), Nursing, Philosophy, Physics°, Political Science, Psychology, Public Health, Sociology, Spanish°, Special Education, Speech Pathology, Technology Education /Pre-Engineering (K–12), Urban Education, Visual Arts (options in Fine Arts, Graphic Design, and Lens-Based Art), and Women's, Gender, and Sexuality Studies.

°Programs in which students may prepare for teacher certification

The College also offers a unique Self-Designed major option, catering to students who wish to forge their own academic path.

In addition to full degree programs, students may also choose to complete a minor, in one of the previously mentioned fields or another subject area, such as, Classical Studies, Comparative Literature, Religion, Public Administration, and Communication Disorders.

Specialized Programs

TCNJ offers a number of 5-year combined Master of Arts in Teaching degrees with dual certification in Elementary Education, and either Special Education, Urban Education, or Deaf and Hard-of-Hearing Education. Students may also enroll in a 7-year BS/MD degree program with the New Jersey Medical School (Newark) or a 7-year BS/OD degree program with the State University of New York College of Optometry. The College offers a Medical Careers Advisory Committee for premed students and a Pre-Law Advisement Committee for students planning a career in law. 64 percent of TCNJ undergraduates seeking Admission into Medical School and 88 percent of TCNJ undergraduates seeking Admission into Law School are accepted into their top choice programs. Both of these figures significantly exceed national averages.

TUITION, ROOM, BOARD, FEES

Because TCNJ is a public institution, costs are lower than most comparable private institutions. The tuition and fees for undergraduates in the 2017–2018 academic year are as follow:

In-state tuition and fees: $16,148

Out-of-state tuition and fees: $27,577

Room and board (all students): $13,200

FINANCIAL AID

Close to 50 percent of full-time undergraduates benefit from financial aid, whether from merit-based scholarships, work-study programs, loans, or government/institutional grants. All students seeking financial aid at the state or federal level must submit the Free Application for Federal Student Aid (FAFSA) form or renewal FAFSA to apply. The Title IV FAFSA Code for The College is 002642.

TCNJ also offers institutional need-based scholarships. Institutional need-based aid considerations are made based on information from the FAFSA.

Students may compete for the College's merit scholarships. These awards are offered to those applicants with top SAT/ACT scores and class rankings. Over the last six years, TCNJ has given scholarships totaling more than $30 million.

School Says . . .

STUDENT ORGANIZATIONS AND ACTIVITIES

Classroom learning at TCNJ is complemented by an extensive and acclaimed Leadership Development Program. Life outside the classroom is not something students do on the side. It is an extension of the learning experience. At every turn from the first year on, students blur the boundary between living and learning, closing the gap between "scholar" and "citizen."

More than 250 student organizations flourish at The College. Right off the bat, students are encouraged to discover their passion through the various clubs and activities offered. Anyone can find an intramural sports team, Greek organization, cultural club, or academic group to suit their interests. Many students build friendships as well as personal networks and optimize their leisure time participating in these groups. In addition, the College Union Board-administered by TCNJ students-organizes large-scale events including concerts, performances, and comedy shows.

The College's highly successful Division III athletic programs also provide an opportunity to socialize and cheer on fellow classmates. TCNJ fields ten sports for men and ten for women. With more than 40 national titles, The College holds the record for the highest number of championship and runner-up titles since Division III was implemented in 1979. For those looking for something a little less competitive, intramural and club sports, including flag football, volleyball, softball, floor hockey, and basketball, have thriving coed leagues of their own. Intramural and club teams play in state, regional, and national tournaments.

ADMISSIONS PROCESS

The admissions committee at TCNJ accepts a class of motivated, ambitious, and highly talented students. Most successful applicants have taken 16 college-preparatory units in high school, demonstrating mastery of the core academic areas of Science, Math, Language Arts, Social Sciences, and Foreign Languages. They also show impressive class ranks and SAT/ACT scores. Most students admitted fall within the top 10 percent of their graduating class. The committee also considers extracurricular involvement, individual pursuits, and community participation. Standardized test scores are not required for students applying into the Art or Music disciplines.

The College of New Jersey is Common Application exclusive. The application deadline for Spring enrollment is November 1. The Regular Decision application deadline for Fall enrollment is February 1. There is a $75 application fee. Candidates who apply only to The College of New Jersey under the Early Decision agreement may apply before November 1 and will be notified on or before December 1. Early Decision applicants unable to complete and submit their application prior to November 1 may also choose to apply before January 1 and receive notification on or before February 1. Students applying to the seven-year Accelerated Medical program must apply by December 1. For Fall enrollment, the College requires incoming students to pay an enrollment deposit of $600 no later than May 1.

For more information, students should contact:

The College of New Jersey

P.O. Box 7718

Ewing, New Jersey 08628-0718

United States

Phone: 609-771-2131

Website: https://tcnj.pages.tcnj.edu/

DAEMEN COLLEGE

AT A GLANCE

Daemen College is a private, nonsectarian, co-educational, comprehensive college located in Amherst, NY. Our suburban location offers convenient access to metropolitan Buffalo. Daemen is committed to an academic atmosphere that leads to open inquiry and debate. With over 50 majors, Daemen offers students a creative balance between programs providing career preparation and education in the liberal arts. Programs in the major and the competency-based core curriculum encourage students to expand their horizons beyond the classroom through internships, service learning, clinical and field experiences, collaborative research with faculty, and study abroad. Daemen is distinguished by a low student/faculty ratio and consistently small class sizes, which encourage students to interact with professors and grow as individuals. Daemen has approximately 1,700 undergraduate and 800 graduate students.

LOCATION AND ENVIRONMENT

Daemen's beautiful 46-acre campus is located in Amherst, New York, a peaceful suburb of Buffalo. Daemen's campus is close to many major rail, plane, and motor routes. While the campus setting is tranquil and residential, Buffalo is a vibrant cultural city, bustling with world-class entertainment, such as the Philharmonic Orchestra, the Albright-Knox Art Gallery, and Shea's Theater. The greater Buffalo area is rich with sports and recreational activities all year round, whether it be skiing and swimming, or watching our professional sports teams. Niagara Falls is only 30 minutes away and Toronto is just two hours by car. On campus, the numerous trees and open green spaces create a lovely environment to work and study.

CAMPUS FACILITIES & EQUIPMENT

Modern apartment-style residence halls provide separate housing for male and female students, in addition to our existing five-story residence hall. All residence halls have kitchens, laundry facilities, lounges, and free Wi-Fi. Full-service meals are served in the main dining hall, with an a la carte selection in The Den. The recreation room and The Den are popular spots for socializing and relaxing during the day or evening.

The Research and Information Commons is a technological showcase that has become the hub of academic research, as well as the academic and social heart of the campus.

The Haberman Gacioch Center for Visual & Performing Arts is a dramatic space which features The Peter and Elizabeth C. Tower Gallery, studios for animation, illustration, figure drawing and painting, graphic design production area, computer labs, faculty offices and the Sr. Jeanne File Art History Resource Center. The building was designed with green technology and uses geothermal heating to contain energy costs.

Patricia E. Curtis Hall houses Physician Assistant, Psychology, and Social Work offices.

The Academic and Wellness Center, a multi-use building, is located across from Daemen's Main Street campus, providing 25,000 square feet of educational classrooms and lab areas primarily for the physical therapy, athletic training, and health promotion programs, as well as student lounges, office space, and indoor recreational and fitness space for the Daemen community.

OFF-CAMPUS OPPORTUNITIES

Daemen empowers students to engage in co-curricular activities in the real world to connect their education outside of the classroom.

The Career Services team offers a variety of services to assist students across all academic disciplines, as well as a lifetime resource to alumni in all phases of their career decision-making and job search. Career Services helps students find an internship so that they can gain real-world experience in their area of interest. Students often express how prepared they feel to have had the chance to experience what careers in their fields are really like. As an added bonus, internship employers sometimes offer Daemen interns full-time positions after graduation. The opportunities are local, national, or international, including opportunities with the Washington Internship Institute. Each year Career Services brings employers to campus for career and internship fairs.

Global Programs coordinates distinctive study abroad opportunities designed to facilitate students' professional aspirations. International study is a staple of the Daemen experience. In today's global economy, it makes sense to learn all you can about different cultures, political systems, and histories. An international experience is beneficial whether it's a week, semester, or even a year. Students have studied in Australia, China, Costa Rica, England, France, Greece, Italy, Mexico, and many other countries.

Daemen believes in "learning through service." Each academic year, nearly 400 Daemen students contribute over 14,000 volunteer hours to make a difference in the lives of youth, families, and communities. In the process, students serve, learn, and gain the leadership, cross-cultural, and communication skills necessary to become civic-minded individuals prepared to participate in a democratic society. Students can choose from a variety of service-learning courses and site placements in settings that include Boys & Girls Clubs, community centers, soup kitchens, housing rehabilitation and refugee resettlement agencies, shelters for the homeless, nursing homes, and many other health and human service agencies.

ACADEMICS

Daemen College offers BA, BFA, BS, MS, MPH, MSW and DPT programs.

Majors offered at Daemen include: Accounting BS/MS, Animation, Art (Applied Theater, Drawing, Graphic Design, Illustration, Painting, Sculpture, Visual Arts Education K–12), Arts Administration BS/MS, Athletic Training BS/MS, Biology (Adolescence Education Biology 7–12), Biology/Cytotechnology BS/MS, Biochemistry, Business Administration (Human Resource Management, International Business, Marketing, Sport Management), Business Administration/International Business BS/MS, Education (Adolescence Special Education 7–12, Childhood Education 1–6, Childhood Education/Special Education1–6, Early Childhood Education/Special Education B–2), English (Adolescence Education English 7–12, Professional Writing and Rhetoric), French (Adolescence Education French 7–12), Health Promotion (Community Health, Complementary and Alternative Health Care Practices, Health and Fitness), Health Promotion/Public Health BS/MS, History, History and Political Science (Adolescence Education History and Political Science 7–12), Mathematics, (Adolescence Education Mathematics 7–12), Natural Sciences (Environmental Studies, Forensic Science, Health Science), Nursing (1+2+1 Partner Curriculum Program, RN-BS), Paralegal, Physical Therapy BS,NS/DPT, Physician Assistant BS/MS, Political Science, Psychology, Religious Studies, Social Work, Spanish (Adolescence Education Spanish 7–12), Sustainability—Global and Local, Pre-Professional Programs (Pre-Medicine, Pre-Dentistry, Pre-Pharmacy and Pre-Veterinary).

Graduate programs include Athletic Training, Applied Behavior Analysis, Arts Administration, Dietetic Internship, Education: Special Education Childhood Education 1-6), Executive Leadership and Innovation, International Business, Nursing, Physical Therapy DPT, Physician Assistant, Public Health MPH, and Social Work MSW.

MAJORS AND DEGREES OFFERED

Daemen College is committed to complementing the depth of study in a major field with a well-rounded academic understanding in the liberal arts. The College's core curriculum ensures that every student graduates with the following seven core competencies: critical thinking and creative problem solving; communication skills; information and literacy; civic responsibility; contextual competency; affective awareness; and moral and ethical discernment. This innovative core curriculum competes with those of Ivy League Institutions and prepares the student in a holistic manner which not only makes them more marketable upon graduation but instructs them on alternative ways of approaching education and learning.

Daemen provides students with small classes and a caring and committed faculty, allowing for a personalized educational experience. Academics at Daemen will challenge you to test your knowledge, raise your expectations, and think critically and creatively. Daemen's core competencies, honors program, academic exchanges, global programs, and undergraduate research are just a few examples of what makes the College challenging and distinctive.

Daemen students are well-prepared for professional success. The vast majority obtain a professional position or admission to graduate study in less than a year after graduation. They are leaders in their communities, with a strong dedication to the improvement of the communities in which they live.

TUITION, ROOM, BOARD, FEES

Tuition for the 2017–2018 academic year is $27,450, with additional fees of $540. Room and board are approximately $12,346. (Cost varies according to meal plan and residence facility.)

FINANCIAL AID

Daemen strives to create individualized financial aid packages for you and your family that will meet your needs and enable you to get the most out of your college education. Daemen offers merit-based scholarships and need-based financial assistance. Approximately 96 percent of current students receive some form of financial assistance. Daemen participates in all federal and state programs.

Learning to navigate the financial aid system can be a daunting task. That's why Daemen has trained professionals on hand to assist you every step of the way. The Admissions staff and Financial Aid counselors will assist you and your family with the process and will ensure you understand the necessary paperwork and deadlines required in order for you to receive the best financial aid package available.

STUDENT ORGANIZATIONS AND ACTIVITIES

Student activities provide for the development of the whole person outside of the classroom. The Director of Student Activities on campus helps students participate in recognized organizations, form new ones, and plan events. With over 60 student organizations the possibilities for involvement at Daemen are limitless. Whether your interests are in art or skiing, there is bound to be something that grabs your interest and introduces you to students who share similar passions. Daemen believes that now is the time to discover exactly who you are; cultivating your hidden talents, taking new risks and challenging yourself to grow are all part of the Daemen experience. Daemen encourages all students to become actively engaged in the campus community.

Athletics

Daemen Athletics is an NCAA Division II member of the East Coast Conference. Wildcat Athletics sponsors 17 teams, including men's and women's basketball, volleyball, soccer, tennis, cross country, track and field, men's golf, women's bowling, and women's triathlon. Students have the opportunity to participate in recreation and intramural programs, and competitive club sports.

ADMISSIONS PROCESS

The average student score on the SAT is 1145 and the average GPA is 91. Daemen has a rolling admissions policy.

The admissions staff helps guide students through the process from start to finish. Prospective students can apply for free online at daemen.edu/apply or commonapp.org.

Visit us on the web at daemen.edu or take a virtual tour at daemen.edu/virtualtour.

The best way to get to know Daemen is in person. On your visit, we'll take you on a campus tour, arrange for you to meet professors and current students, and plan a one-on-one meeting with an admissions counselor. To schedule your appointment, contact the Office of Admissions at 800-462-7652 or 716-839-8225. You may make an individual visit Mon-Sat, attend our Fall and Spring Open Houses, or join us for many of our other special admissions events. We hope to see you on campus soon! For more information, email us at admissions@daemen.edu.

DESALES UNIVERSITY

AT A GLANCE

DeSales University is a medium-sized, Catholic liberal arts university for men and women administered by the Oblates of St. Francis de Sales.

Founded in 1964, DeSales University is a Catholic liberal arts university that offers courses in a wide range of disciplines. DeSales provides personal attention, small class size, and a feeling of community. The University uses a holistic approach to help students develop a "sense of self," enabling all students to reach their personal and academic potential. This student-centered philosophy is conveyed by an enthusiastic, accessible faculty.

LOCATION AND ENVIRONMENT

DeSales University's suburban campus is located 15 minutes south of Bethlehem and Allentown, Pa., and only 1 hour from Philadelphia, 90 minutes from Scranton and Wilkes-Barre, Pa., less than 2 hours from New York City, and 3 hours from Baltimore. The campus is 500 acres with more than 16 major buildings.

CAMPUS FACILITIES & EQUIPMENT

The Priscilla Payne Hurd Science Center, a 37,500-square-foot facility, is equipped with up-to-date computers, labs, and medical equipment. The Hurd Science Center also features a sterile molecular/cell biology suite, complete with a freezer room, bench room, support room, dark room, and instrument room. An ecology/environmental lab with a growing chamber, an analytical/physical chemistry/inorganic laboratory, and a bioinformatics/physics lab also inhabit the two-story building.

The Labuda Center for the Performing Arts houses the theatre, dance, and TV/Film majors and features a 473-seat main stage theatre, the 187-seat black box theatre, and a TV/film studio with a control room. Dance rehearsal space as well as costume and scene shops are also featured.

The Gambet Center for Business and Health Care Education is a 77,000-square-foot academic building that houses the school's business division and health care majors. It features a simulated trading room for business and finance majors, standardized patient areas, and a gross anatomy lab.

The DeSales University Center features many menu choices—especially for healthy eaters—in a food-court setting. There are three other food venues on campus located in the academic buildings as well as the McShea Student Union.

Trexler Library has a collection of more than 500,000 items and there are electronic databases of newspapers, journal articles, and the Oxford Dictionary of National Biography. There are computer and multimedia labs and a staff who will help with any research topic. Trexler Library has wireless access both with personal laptops or laptops that can be borrowed to use in the building. The Library's resources can be accessed from anywhere on campus. There is online access to databases and full-text journal articles. Students can also instant message a librarian with a question.

OFF-CAMPUS OPPORTUNITIES

Allentown and Bethlehem are a short 15-minute drive from campus and offer many dining, shopping, and outdoor activities, including the Promenade Shops at Saucon Valley, just minutes from campus. The Lehigh Valley, aka 'College Valley,' boasts beautiful hiking and biking trails, historic sites, museums, cultural festivals, and Dorney Park and Wildwater Kingdom. Skiing at nearby Blue Mountain and other Pocono resorts is just a short drive away. The Poconos also offer white water rafting trips down the Lehigh and Delaware Rivers.

ACADEMIC PROGRAMS

DeSales University defines "global competence" as using an open, inquisitive mind to understand the norms and expectations of other cultures, and using this acquired knowledge to communicate and to work effectively outside of one's usual environment in the promotion of human solidarity. DeSales University presents opportunities for students to enlarge their world view, from activities and concerts to short and long-term study abroad programs.

Study abroad programs through DeSales present the opportunity for our students to live and work in this vibrantly interdependent world, and range from semester-long study to short-stay travel of 10 days. Our students can spend semesters in England, Greece, Italy, Ireland, Switzerland, France, Australia, Tokyo, and Monte Carlo. More importantly, DeSales uses a model of intense hands-on engagement through short-stay co-curricular trips of students, faculty, and staff. Trips to Ireland, Germany, India, Istanbul, South Africa, and Austria for short-stay intensive travel have been combined with academic courses, the activities of student organizations, or out-of-season competition for our athletic teams.

Freshman students are asked to participate in the Character U program, a self-assessment program based on the Golden Counsels of St. Francis de Sales. Each month, University programming addresses one of these Golden Counsels or traits including patience, trust and cooperation, and perseverance. The DeSales Experience offers opportunities to learn and lead outside the classroom. The University's Academic Resource Center can offer assistance in reading comprehension, study skills, time management, and effective writing techniques. Additionally, they can help find a tutor if you need it or provide you with the opportunity to become a peer tutor.

CAREER SERVICES AND PLACEMENT

The Career Development Center can help students strategically showcase skills and stand out from a sea of competitors. The Center starts early by helping students define goals and make the right major and career choices. Job shadowing, learning to network, practice for interviews, and preparing resumes are all part of the process.

MAJORS AND DEGREES OFFERED

DeSales University offers more than 35 bachelor's degrees including 8 pre-professional programs, and 8 graduate programs through the divisions of business, liberal arts and social sciences, performing arts, natural sciences, and health care. Our more popular majors include criminal justice, theatre, medical studies, and business administration.

The newest majors are economics, health communication, healthcare administration, homeland security, and supply chain management. A new track within the business department is financial planning.

Special Programs

At DeSales, qualified business, nursing, criminal justice, and computer science majors have an option to earn both a bachelor's degree and a master's degree in five years. Qualified health science or medical studies majors are guaranteed an interview into the doctor of physical therapy program or the graduate physician assistant program respectively.

DeSales also has an Exploratory Studies Program, a structured program that helps students determine his or her major. This program includes a 3-credit course called Major Decision Making that will introduce different majors while fulfilling an elective requirement for graduation. Another exploratory course—Career Development and Planning—is available in the spring semester.

TUITION, ROOM, BOARD, FEES

Tuition and Fees (2017–18): $34,500

Room and Board: $12,800

Student & Technology Fee: $1,600

Total: $48,900

FINANCIAL AID

Nine out of 10 DeSales University students receive financial aid in the form of grants, scholarships, work study, and loans. About 85 percent of the students receive grants directly from DeSales University, and funds are also available from federal and state programs to those who qualify. The amount of aid received and the composition of an aid package will depend on financial need and on academic achievement and potential.

Academic scholarships are also available through DeSales University. All applicants for admission are automatically considered for each of the scholarships offered by the University.

Students can also compete for one of six full-tuition Leadership Scholarships by writing an essay about leadership and service experience and, if selected, participating in an interview.

STUDENT ORGANIZATIONS AND ACTIVITIES

There are more than 1,600 full-time undergraduate students and about 64 percent live on campus. The male to female ratio is 43 percent to 57 percent. More than 11 percent of our undergraduate students are Hispanic and 8.9 percent are American minorities. Our students come to DeSales from 25 states and 7 other countries with many coming from Pennsylvania.

DeSales University has more than 30 campus organizations, including the Student Activities crew, which helps plan student events, bus trips, and on-campus performances. The McShea Student Union includes a student activities lounge open to students for entertainment and socializing and a café that offers another dining option in the form of a Sandella's Cafe. The McShea Student Union has been renovated to accommodate increased special events such as independent movie nights, comedians, music acts, and expanded space for programs sponsored by various student organizations.

DeSales University has 19 intercollegiate varsity sports teams and all are members of the NCAA Division III, Middle Atlantic States Collegiate Athletic Corporation (MAC) Freedom Conference, and the Eastern College Athletic Conference (ECAC).

The University's men's sports are baseball, basketball, cross-country, golf, lacrosse, soccer, tennis, and indoor and outdoor track and field. Women's sports are basketball, cross-country, field hockey, lacrosse, soccer, softball, indoor and outdoor track and field, tennis, and volleyball. The University also has club sports, including cheerleading, cycling, disc golf, equestrian, ice hockey, and men's volleyball.

There are intramural sports for all seasons, or students can visit the Billera Hall fitness center, which offers aerobic, Nautilus, and free-weight training.

ADMISSIONS PROCESS

To Apply for Admission you need to:

Complete a DeSales University application and submit it to our Admissions Office.

Have your high school guidance department send your official high school transcript to our Admissions Office.

Have your standardized test scores (SAT or ACT) sent to our Admissions Office. Our code number for SAT scores is 2021. Submitting SAT or ACT test scores is strongly encouraged but not required for the following majors: dance, early childhood education, exploratory studies (undeclared), marriage & family studies, philosophy, psychology, Spanish, sport and exercise physiology, sport management, and theology. Students who don't submit test scores will need to have a personal interview with the admissions office.

Have a guidance counselor and teacher complete the recommendation forms and send to our Admissions Office.

DIGIPEN INSTITUTE OF TECHNOLOGY

AT A GLANCE

DigiPen Institute of Technology is an educational leader in the teaching and advancement of the arts and computer sciences as applied to the world of game and software development. As the first school in the world to offer a bachelor's degree in game simulation technology, DigiPen has advanced the digital entertainment industry by preparing students to become skilled artists, designers, and engineers.

Through a combined academic focus on both theory and application, students graduate with a deep foundational knowledge of their chosen field and a portfolio of work that is demonstrative of their practical and creative capabilities. DigiPen alumni have proven to be among the most sought-after employees in the games industry and beyond. In addition to being credited on well over 1,000 popular game titles over the last 20 years, they continue to advance the boundaries of what technology can accomplish.

LOCATION AND ENVIRONMENT

DigiPen's campus is located in Redmond, Washington, a global hub for game and software development. The region is home to more than 400 interactive media companies, including tech industry giants like Microsoft, Nintendo, Amazon, and several more.

Situated about 15 miles east of Seattle, the Redmond area is home to much more than a wide range of successful economic enterprises. It's a renowned center of artistic excellence, cultural diversity, and beautiful outdoor surroundings.

DigiPen also operates at two international campuses in Singapore and Bilbao, Spain.

CAMPUS FACILITIES & EQUIPMENT

Students at DigiPen go beyond the textbook—putting knowledge and theory into daily practice through extensive project coursework that brings together multiple areas of study including art, music, design, and computer science. As such, the DigiPen campus features several dedicated lab spaces, including:

- Two large-scale production labs dedicated to game project teams.
- Two music and sound labs, complete with recording studio, instrument practice rooms, and digital audio workstations.
- A Nintendo console development lab with special access to licensed software development kits.
- A computer engineering lab.
- An MFA computer lab.
- Numerous game lab spaces for prototyping and play testing projects, from board games to video games.

As a testing ground for new ideas, DigiPen students regularly work and experiment with emerging technologies, such as virtual and augmented reality devices. Thanks to industry connections with local technology companies, DigiPen students have been among the first to get their hands on software development kits for products like the HTC Vive, Microsoft HoloLens, and more. Compared to most institutions, DigiPen provides its students with an unparalleled depth of hands-on experience that—combined with their solid knowledge base—gives them a competitive edge when beginning their careers.

In addition to DigiPen's lab and classroom spaces, the DigiPen campus library houses a vast collection of print and digital materials, including books, periodicals, films, and a growing catalogue of over 500 video games and game console equipment—an exceptional resource both for study and amusement.

OFF-CAMPUS OPPORTUNITIES

DigiPen's close proximity to hundreds of game and technology companies doesn't just benefit students after they graduate. It allows them to tap into a deep well of industry experience and begin building their professional network even before they graduate, thanks to a wealth of local off-campus events and internship opportunities.

DigiPen's internship program is a carefully monitored work experience in which students learn about their discipline in a professional development studio under the supervision of an industry veteran. DigiPen interns have earned their names in the credits of published AAA game titles, taken part in Microsoft research projects, and even assisted in the development of the Nintendo Wii controller.

Outside of the classroom, students can take advantage of a mix of fun activities throughout Redmond and the greater Seattle area. At the annual PAX West, a gaming expo that draws tens of thousands of visitors each year, DigiPen students plan, set up, and operate a student game arcade booth where they demo their academic projects to attendees—in the same venue as some of the largest game publishers in the world. The region is also home to other annual events, such as the Emerald City Comicon, Bumbershoot, GeekGirlCon, and more.

ACADEMICS

DigiPen's degree programs give students a comprehensive understanding of the academic fundamentals of their field while preparing them with the skills that will allow them to thrive in a professional environment.

While many schools tout their programs as being "interdisciplinary," the concept of an integrated curriculum is more than a buzzword at DigiPen—it's a central component of what students experience every day on campus. Beginning with a strong focus on foundational theory, each program at DigiPen challenges students to apply what they learn in the classroom toward intensive, sometimes year-long projects. Whether working on games, animations, or computer hardware devices, students put their knowledge into practice in a results-driven studio environment where they quickly learn the value of teamwork and communications. By working alongside their peers from other degree programs, students begin to think beyond the boundaries of their individual areas of study and to "speak the language" of the other disciplines. This cooperative method allows them to achieve the kind of standout student work that would be impossible to accomplish alone and prepares them for the challenges and realities of working in the professional industries after they graduate.

By the time they complete their degrees, students are equipped with a portfolio of work that can help them stand out to prospective employers, as well as the industry connections needed to jump-start their job search. More importantly, they leave with a depth of knowledge and experience that allows them to meaningfully contribute to their team from day one on the job.

Faculty Expertise

DigiPen faculty instructors come from a wide range of academic and professional backgrounds. From Ph.D. professors who have worked on Nobel-prize winning physics projects to instructors who cut their teeth on classic video games and blockbuster films, these faculty members bring to the classroom a unique blend of both scholarly and commercial expertise. Instructors at DigiPen are dedicated teachers whose primary motivation is to impart their years of knowledge to a new generation of creators and innovators. And with an impressive student-to-faculty ratio of 10:1, DigiPen students are able to receive individual mentorship and guidance.

MAJORS AND DEGREES OFFERED

DigiPen offers eight bachelor's programs and two master's degree programs in fields relating to computer science and engineering, as well as art, music, and design.

Computer Science

BS in Computer Science in Real-Time Interactive Simulation

BS in Computer Science and Game Design

BS in Computer Science and Digital Audio

BS in Computer Science

MS in Computer Science

Art, Music, and Design

BFA in Digital Art and Animation

BA in Game Design

BA in Music and Sound Design

MFA in Digital Arts

Engineering

BS in Computer Engineering (an ABET-accredited program)

TUITION, ROOM, BOARD, FEES

Tuition for the 2018–19 academic year for undergraduate students is $31,140, which covers the cost of 32-44 course credits per year and access to all of DigiPen's on-campus facilities and support services. There is no additional tuition cost for out-of-state U.S citizens and residents. Housing and meals, for students living in a DigiPen Housing apartment, costs an estimated $11,750. Administrative fees are $200 per year.

FINANCIAL AID

There are several types of financial aid available for students who qualify. DigiPen's Office of Financial Aid is ready to help by connecting students with a range of financial resources, including:

- Scholarships
- Grants
- Loans
- Federal Work Study
- Veterans Benefits

For the 2016–17 academic year, approximately 62 percent of DigiPen students received financial assistance in the form of scholarships, state grants, and federal grants and loans. The average scholarship awarded that year was $9,331.

DigiPen is committed to helping all students make the most of their financial investment by providing the resources needed to succeed, including one-on-one financial aid counseling to help make the costs of attendance affordable.

On-Campus Employment

In addition to offering Federal Work Study for students who qualify, DigiPen also provides a number of on-campus employment opportunities. Students can earn income and work experience by applying to student job openings in several academic and administrative departments on campus. Each summer, DigiPen employs hundreds of current students to work as teachers and teaching assistants for DigiPen's ProjectFUN youth education programs for students in grades 1–12.

STUDENT ORGANIZATIONS AND ACTIVITIES

The student body at DigiPen is a tight-knit community of people who share a passion for games, art, and technology. Students thrive on teamwork, creativity, and a spirit of learning—both in and out of the classroom.

Despite being a small school, DigiPen has attracted an amazing community of students who have come to campus from more than 50 countries. DigiPen is committed to fostering a diverse campus culture that is welcoming and supportive to students of all backgrounds.

A Lasting Network

The shared experience among students doesn't end at graduation. It's not uncommon for DigiPen alumni to be working together as professionals as well, either at major technology companies or at small, entrepreneurial startups. Some DigiPen graduates have also continued to give back to their alma mater by participating in the DigiPen Alumni Mentorship Program, helping current students to effectively prepare for the transition from college to career.

Campus Support Systems

At any time during their education, DigiPen students do not have to look far to receive the support they need. Students have access to a wealth of on-campus services, such as:

- Professional mental health counseling
- Disability support services
- Peer tutors and advisors
- Academic and faculty advisors

While the demands of DigiPen's curriculum can be intense, students also have plenty of ways to relax, unwind, and explore new interests and activities. From organizing clubs and social events to participating in the Student Senate leadership group, students join together to create a vibrant and inclusive campus community.

Speaking of student clubs, there are several to choose from, with brand new groups springing up each year. For those drawn to the friendly competition of Pokémon Club or for anyone looking to become educated on LGBTQ issues through DigiPen's PRISM (People Respecting Individuals and Sexual Minorities) club, these and other campus groups provide a great way to connect with fellow students outside the classroom.

ADMISSIONS PROCESS

DigiPen works on a rolling-admissions basis. Applications for admission are accepted year-round, and those who apply can typically expect to be notified of the college's decision within two to four weeks of submitting their application. You can learn more about DigiPen's specific admissions requirements, which vary by degree program, on the college's website.

Because applicants must select their degree program prior to enrolling, DigiPen encourages all of its prospective students to do as much research as possible before applying. Prospective students can learn more by visiting the website, requesting information, or participating in an on-campus or online informational event.

DigiPen Pre-College Program

DigiPen's Pre-College Program is an intensive college preparatory experience for students who have completed their sophomore, junior, or senior year of high school. Designed for students with strong academic aspirations, this program provides a glimpse into the DigiPen college experience and is an ideal introduction for students who may be interested in attending the Institute. Taught by DigiPen faculty over a four-week period during the summer, the Pre-College Program not only exposes students to DigiPen's academic coursework but also requires students to work together on multidisciplinary project teams.

EARLHAM COLLEGE

AT A GLANCE

Established in 1847, Earlham College is a selective, private liberal arts college. With its emphasis on experiential learning and profound inquiry, an Earlham education is excellent preparation not just for a first job, but a career and a lifetime of rewarding involvement.

Earlham has shaped its curriculum through an initiative called EPIC (Earlham Plan for Integrative Collaboration) in order to help its students connect their academic and personal passions with career preparation and opportunities. EPIC offers students multidisciplinary experiences that combine guided research opportunities, international education, and internships as well as academic centers devoted to entrepreneurship, global health, and social justice.

Among its distinctions, Earlham is committed to funding an internship, research experience, or community-based project for every student. Called the EPIC Advantage, the program offers these funded experiences to help students connect high-impact experiences with their traditional course work and even extracurricular activities.

Founded by Quakers, Earlham College has prepared students to contribute to the social good since its inception. Earlham embraces cultural and individual differences alike and offers unparalleled opportunities for leadership, friendship, and community.

Earlham sponsors 20 NCAA Division III sports teams; most compete in the Heartland Collegiate Athletic Conference. The College also sponsors a hunt seat equestrian team, an Ultimate (Frisbee) team that competes on the club level, and numerous recreational sports.

Earlham is accredited by the Higher Learning Commission of the North Central Association of Colleges and Schools.

LOCATION AND ENVIRONMENT

The Earlham campus is located on 800 acres in the city of Richmond, Indiana. It is situated along the Indiana-Ohio border, about an hour's drive from Indianapolis, Cincinnati, or Dayton.

CAMPUS FACILITIES & EQUIPMENT

Earlham's academic facilities are state-of-the-art and designed to foster collaboration. In recent years the College has invested more than $70 million in its campus, including new and renovated student center, science facilities, and a center for visual and performing arts.

OFF-CAMPUS OPPORTUNITIES

Richmond, named the No. 1 small city in Indiana by Cities Journal, has a population of 36,000 and a rich heritage of music, culture, and architecture. Shopping opportunities are plentiful and numerous restaurants have become student favorites. With the cities of Cincinnati and Indianapolis nearby, students are also within reach of the largest music tours in the nation.

ACADEMIC PROGRAMS

Earlham is one of the only colleges in the United States to offer a funded summer internship, research experience, or community-based project to every student. Eligible experiences take place in the summer anytime between a student's first year and fourth year of enrollment. Earlham helps students create an opportunity to put their education into practice without having to worry about finances. Even if the opportunity is on another continent, EPIC Advantage will cover the travel expenses. Earlham's collaborative advising model, which includes a team of academic and career advisers, helps each student to consider the available opportunities and integrate their experiences into academic plans and career aspirations. There is also funding to support other high-impact learning experiences, including student-faculty research, so many Earlham students benefit from multiple opportunities.

Earlham's unique approach to academic life, high-impact experiences, teaching, and mentoring has been uncommonly effective:

Recent graduates have earned such prestigious awards as the Rhodes Scholarship, Fulbright Scholarship, the Watson Fellowship, the National Science Foundation Pre-Doctoral Fellowship, the Samuel Huntington Public Service Award, and a Fellowship at the Carnegie Endowment for International Peace.

Of all colleges and universities in the U.S., Earlham also ranks in the top 2 percent for its percentage of graduates who go on to earn research doctorates.

A team of Earlham students won the 2016 Hult Prize, beating out 25,000 entrants in the world's largest student competition for the social good. They are using $1 million in prize money to launch a business that is already revolutionizing public transportation in several cities in Kenya.

Earlham's off-campus study programs send students all over the globe to explore new places and experience new cultures.

Semester-long programs include: Border Studies (Tucson), Ecuador, England, France/Senegal, Germany/Austria, Greece, Japan, Middle East/Jordan, New Zealand, Spain, or Tibetan Studies (India).

May Term programs include: Bahamas, Benin, Berlin, Borneo, Canada, China, Costa Rica, Curaçao, England, Galápagos Islands, Greece, Hawaii, Iceland, Italy, Martinique, Spain, or Turkey.

Internship, research, and project locations funded by Earlham's EPIC Advantage include local, regional, U.S. and international sites.

MAJORS AND DEGREES OFFERED

Earlham offers programs of study leading to bachelor degrees, including: African and African American Studies; ancient and classical studies; Arabic language and literature°; archaeology°; art; biochemistry; biology; chemistry; Chinese languages°; comparative languages and linguistics; computer science; economics; English; environmental sustainability; film studies°; French and Francophone studies; geology; German language and literature; global management (with tracks in finance, international business, leadership and change, marketing, social entrepreneurship and social change, and supply chain and operations/management information technology); history; human development and social relations; international studies; Japanese language and linguistics°; Japanese studies; Jewish studies°; mathematics; museum studies°; music; neuroscience; peace and global studies; philosophy; physics and astronomy; politics; pre-engineering; pre-health; pre-law; psychology; public policy; Quaker studies°; religion; sociology/anthropology; Spanish and Hispanic studies; TESOL°; theatre arts; and women's, gender, sexuality studies. (°Indicates programs that are available as minors only.)

In addition to more than 40 undergraduate majors, Earlham offers two dual-degree programs: a 3+2 degree for engineering and a 3+1 degree programs that allows students to earn both a B.A. and a M.A.T. in just four years.

TUITION, ROOM, BOARD, FEES

Earlham College tuition, room and board, and fees for the 2018–19 academic year are $56,850.

FINANCIAL AID

Earlham believes that paying for college should not be a barrier to going to college and is committed to creating financial access to qualified students from all backgrounds. The College offers scholarships to high academic achievers (up to full tuition), to those who demonstrate a financial need and a commitment to volunteer service, to Quakers, and to highly qualified members of underrepresented racial and ethnic groups. Financial aid can also include loans and student employment.

STUDENT ORGANIZATIONS AND ACTIVITIES

With a long and varied list of active, student-led organizations to choose from, Earlham students have every chance to get involved outside of the classroom. Some of the more popular organizations include dance teams, Frisbee golf, Ultimate, cultural clubs, and political clubs. In addition, there are numerous co-ops on campus, including the Barn Co-op, home to Earlham's equestrian team horses and other horses boarded by students.

Besides the 20 varsity sports the College sponsors, there are numerous club teams and opportunities to participate in intramural sports. For those desiring a workout, Earlham has extensive wellness facilities, including a field house, swimming pool, weight room, climbing wall, exercise classes, and a walking track.

The activity calendar at Earlham is packed with speakers, theatre productions, art exhibits and much more. The campus also kicks off each school year with Sunsplash, an annual festival that includes live music from major bands, and wraps up each year with SpringFest, an outdoor event with inflatable games and other excuses to let loose.

STUDENT BODY

Earlham is a residential college of about 1,100 students. A global perspective comes naturally to the campus community. Earlham is ranked fifth by U.S. News & World Report among liberal arts colleges in the U.S. for the percentage of international students enrolled. With such a variety of students, campus life at Earlham is both lively and welcoming.

Besides traditional residence halls, Earlham has friendship and theme housing for those who share like interests. Yet one kind of housing isn't found at Earlham—sororities and fraternities. Earlham's inclusive community has never had them.

ADMISSIONS PROCESS

Earlham College offers application plans for early decision (application materials due Nov. 15), early action (application materials due Dec. 1), and regular decision (application materials due Feb. 15). More information about these plans is available online at Earlham.edu/apply.

Earlham is selective, with six applicants for every seat in the first-year class. The College seeks students who are academically prepared, intellectually curious, and who possess a variety of special talents and interests. Earlham also looks for students who are comfortable in their own skin and embrace differences.

Earlham takes a holistic approach in its review of students' applications for admission, giving consideration to academic achievement, writing ability (the essay is important), and letters of recommendation from teachers and guidance counselors. In determining academic ability and college readiness, the College gives particular weight to a student's performance in high school courses and the quality of their chosen college preparatory academic program. Earlham also recognizes applicants' commitments, accomplishments and contributions beyond the classroom.

Earlham uses the Common Application, which includes a guidance counselor recommendation and a teacher recommendation. Earlham expects high school applicants to have completed at least 15 academic high school units or the equivalent: 4 in English, 3 in mathematics, and 2 or more in a second language, science, and history or social studies. Experience in the area of studio or performing arts is very desirable. Earlham has a test-optional policy which means applicants are not required to submit any standardized test scores (Home-schooled and international students are required to submit standardized testing.)

EMBRY-RIDDLE AERONAUTICAL UNIVERSITY

AT A GLANCE

Embry-Riddle Aeronautical University was founded in 1925 as the Embry-Riddle Company by barnstormer John Paul Riddle and entrepreneur T. Higbee Embry in Cincinnati, Ohio. This early vision began by teaching the adventurous how to fly, but soon grew into a world-class University combining expert faculty and state-of-the-art technology. Embry-Riddle Aeronautical University has become a world leader in higher education—offering you the flexibility of learning a vast array of skills in aviation, aerospace, and beyond.

Since our founding, Embry-Riddle Aeronautical University has continually striven to educate professionals in every facet of aviation and beyond. From Applied Sciences to Business, Computers & Technology to Engineering, and Safety, Security & Intelligence to Space Physics—Embry-Riddle has continually challenged itself to become a comprehensive, STEM-focused university. As such, our graduates have gone on to become pilots, engineers, security and intelligence agents, astronauts, and more.

In 2015, Embry-Riddle celebrated the 50th anniversary of its move from Miami to Daytona Beach, Florida, and in 2016 it marked the 90th anniversary of the university's founding. Embry-Riddle enrolled 31,100 students that academic year, offering more than 80 degrees at the associate, bachelor's, master's, and Ph.D. level.

Whatever campus or program you choose, you are sure to meet lifelong friends in classes, dorms, and student organizations. Our graduates go on to work for some of the world's biggest companies, so the relationships you make on campus can continue throughout your career.

When you earn your degree from Embry-Riddle, you become part of a network of more than 125,000 alumni who will support you throughout your working life.

Embry-Riddle Aeronautical University is a world-class aviation and STEM-focused institution featuring two residential campuses in Daytona Beach, FL, and Prescott, AZ, in addition to Embry-Riddle Online and our Worldwide Campus.

LOCATION AND ENVIRONMENT

Established in 1965, the Daytona Beach, Florida, campus is a 185-acre campus with year-round mild temperatures and more than 230 days of sunshine a year. A top vacation destination and an ideal place to live, study, and fly, the Daytona Beach Campus serves a diverse student body of approximately 5,700 undergrads and 600 graduate students from 50 states and 95 countries.

Embry-Riddle's second residential campus was built in Prescott, Arizona, in 1978, on 539 acres and celebrates its 40th anniversary in 2018. Prescott is a mile-high city and its climate reflects seasonable weather excellent for flying, with more than 270 days of sunshine. The local mountains reflect the spirit of the West, where students enjoy skiing, hiking, mountain biking, kayaking, rock climbing, and tours of the Grand Canyon. Prescott enrolls more than 2,000 undergraduate students and more than 60 graduate students, hailing from 48 states and 34 countries.

Through Embry-Riddle Aeronautical University's Worldwide Campus you can earn your degree at more than 125 learning centers in the United States, Europe, Asia, and the Middle East, or online, or through a blend of classroom and online modalities—meaning you can achieve your degree virtually anywhere. Cutting-edge technology offers you numerous undergraduate, graduate, and professional programs that fit into any lifestyle. Ranked #2 in the nation for best Online Bachelor's Degree Program by U.S. News & World Report 2018, Worldwide gives you a world-class education right at your fingertips. Worldwide undergraduate enrollment is more than 16,000 students and graduate enrollment is more than 6,000.

OFF CAMPUS OPPORTUNITIES

Whether you enjoy a sunny day at the beach, hiking in the mountains, or staying in—the opportunities are endless at Embry-Riddle's campuses. Daytona Beach features NASCAR's Daytona 500 and "The World's Most Famous Beach." Prescott has "The World's Oldest Rodeo" and a historic downtown that harkens back to its wild west origins. A wealth of adventures await students enrolled in Worldwide Campus learning centers located in Italy, Germany, Japan, South Korea, Spain, the United Kingdom, and others. Whatever your preference, Embry-Riddle makes it possible.

ACADEMICS AND MAJORS

Becoming a Student

Choosing a university and a degree are the hard parts. If you've decided on Embry-Riddle, we thank you and look forward to making the application process as easy as possible.

Applications can be submitted electronically for all three of our campuses: Daytona Beach, FL, Prescott, AZ, and Worldwide.

Different supporting documents are required depending on whether you are a first-time, transfer, nontraditional, or international student, or if you are seeking a graduate or undergraduate degree.

Applications are evaluated on a rolling basis, and once all necessary documents are received, we will notify you of your admission status.

We look forward to meeting the next class of Eagles soon!

Honors Programs

The Honors Program at Embry-Riddle is highly selective, offering students an enriched educational experience focused on leadership, research, and ethics, while also giving them opportunities to enhance campus and community life for others. Honors Program students enroll in three Honors Seminars, complete Honors directed research, and participate in the Honors Student Association's service, community, and professional development events. Graduates of the Honors Program are models of academic excellence and student leadership.

Study Abroad

Embry-Riddle is deeply committed to helping you experience the world. Studying abroad offers innumerable possibilities. Not only will you visit other countries and cultures, you will grow as an individual, deepen and enhance your academics, as well as expand and diversify your professional opportunities. As technology makes the world smaller and brings cultures together, an essential skill in any professional field is understanding how to navigate the cross-cultural workplace. Spending time abroad you will give you a deeper understanding of culture, creativity, innovation, and multiple perspectives on your chosen field.

MAJORS AND DEGREES OFFERED

Embry-Riddle Aeronautical University offers 46 bachelor's degrees, 31 master's degrees, seven doctoral degrees, seven associate degrees, and four certifications across seven fields of study: Applied Science; Aviation; Business; Computers & Technology; Engineering; Security, Intelligence & Safety; and Space.

Bachelor's Degrees:

Aeronautical Science; Aeronautics; Aerospace & Occupational Safety; Aerospace Engineering; Aerospace Physiology; Air Traffic Management; Astronomy & Astrophysics; Aviation Business Administration; Aviation Maintenance; Aviation Maintenance Science; Aviation Security; Business Administration; Civil Engineering; Communication; Computational Mathematics; Computer Engineering; Computer Science; Cyber Intelligence & Security; Electrical Engineering; Emergency Services; Engineering; Engineering Physics; Engineering Technology; Forensic Accounting & Fraud Examination; Forensic Biology; Forensic Psychology; Global Business; Global Conflict Studies; Global Security & Intelligence Studies; Homeland Security; Human Factors Psychology; Industrial Psychology & Safety; Interdisciplinary Studies; Logistics & Supply Chain Management; Mechanical Engineering; Meteorology/Applied Meteorology; Project Management; Safety Management; Simulation Science, Gaming & Animation; Software Engineering; Space Physics; Spaceflight Operations; Technical Management; Unmanned Aircraft Systems Science; Unmanned Systems Applications; Wildlife Science

Master's Degrees:

Aeronautics; Aerospace Engineering; Aviation & Aerospace Sustainability; Aviation Finance; Aviation Maintenance; Business Administration; Business Administration in Aviation Management; Civil Engineering; Cyber Intelligence & Security; Cybersecurity Engineering; Cybersecurity Management & Policy; Electrical & Computer Engineering; Engineering Management; Engineering Physics; Entrepreneurship in Technology; Human Factors; Human Security

& Resilience; Information Security & Assurance; Leadership; Logistics & Supply Chain Management; Management; Management Information Systems; Mechanical Engineering; Occupational Safety Management; Project Management; Safety Science; Security & Intelligence Studies; Software Engineering; Systems Engineering; Unmanned & Autonomous Systems Engineering; Unmanned Systems

Ph.D.:

Aerospace Engineering; Aviation; Aviation Business Administration; Electrical Engineering & Computer Science; Engineering Physics; Human Factors Psychology; Mechanical Engineering

Associate Degrees:

Aeronautics; Aviation Business Administration; Aviation Maintenance; Aviation Maintenance Science; Engineering Fundamentals; Logistics & Supply Chain Management; Technical Management

Certificates:

Aircraft Dispatcher; Aviation Maintenance Tech. Part 65; International Society of Transport Aircraft Trading (ISTAT); Information Assurance

CAMPUS FACILITIES AND EQUIPMENT

Laboratories

Our campuses offer world-class labs that give you the expert training your future career requires. Whether it's engineering facilities that enable you to build jet engines from scratch, or forensics biology labs that allow you to deconstruct the scene of the crime, Embry-Riddle combines real-world application with experienced instruction to help you develop the skills and techniques to succeed. Here are just a few of our world-class facilities:

- Spacecraft Development Laboratory
- Ergonomics Laboratory
- Robertson Aircraft Accident Investigation Laboratory
- Propulsion Lab
- Enroute Air Traffic Control Center
- Aerial Robotics Lab
- Forensic Science Lab

Equipment

When you become a student at Embry-Riddle, you gain access to state-of-the-art equipment and technology from your first day of class to graduation—even as an undergraduate student. These include aircraft, simulators, wind tunnels, 3D printers, and unmanned aerial systems—Embry-Riddle has it all, and we put you in the driver's seat.

Observatories, Planetariums, and More

Embry-Riddle's Daytona Beach Observatory: Students taking an Astronomy Lab, completing a Minor in Astronomy, or a Minor in Astrophysics use the observatory to carry out projects in observational astronomy. The Observatory is part of the Department of Physical Sciences and has the largest university-owned research telescope in the state of Florida and possibly the largest optical telescope in the Southeast, providing real-time images to our students.

The Jim and Linda Lee Planetarium: The Jim and Linda Lee Planetarium is the only Arizona planetarium north of Phoenix, and is capable of seating 116 students and visitors, showing them the cosmos in 360-degree 4K resolution. Much more than just a planetarium, the facility contains multimedia learning software that can take viewers from the inner complexities of the human body to the farthest reaches of the known universe.

The STEM Education Center: To help students achieve their greatest potential, the STEM Education Center houses industry-grade laboratories, workshops, and studios worthy of the scholars who use them. Featuring the LIGO Optics Lab, the Raisbeck Engineering Design Studio, the Margaret Morris Foundation Wildlife Science Lab, and the Energy and Thermo-Fluids Lab, to name a few, the STEM Education Center is one of the leading facilities in higher education for all of Arizona.

John Mica Engineering & Aerospace Innovation Complex (MicaPlex): This cornerstone building of the Research Park at Embry-Riddle in Daytona Beach, Florida, presents a unique collaborative opportunity for business and the university community to develop, refine, and bring new products and technological services to market. As an incubator space, the facilities and occupants of the MicaPlex provide such a network, which extends to the entire university, not only at the Daytona Beach Campus, but to resources on the Prescott, Arizona, campus and the extensive network that is the Worldwide Campus.

TUITION, ROOM, BOARD, FEES

For the most up-to-date numbers, visit https://erau.edu/becoming-student/

FINANCIAL AID

Daytona Beach: http://daytonabeach.erau.edu/financial-aid/

Prescott: http://prescott.erau.edu/financial-aid/

Worldwide: https://worldwide.erau.edu/admissions/financial-aid/

STUDENT ORGANIZATIONS AND ACTIVITIES

Students come to Embry-Riddle from 50 U.S. states and 141 countries. Creating an environment across and throughout the university that promotes inclusion, equality, and diversity is of the utmost importance to us. By promoting campuses with dynamic and active student activity, we ensure everyone is heard and supported on their Embry-Riddle journey.

Embry-Riddle Aeronautical University provides a comprehensive support system for student organizations that promote student achievement. Joining one of these many groups is a great way for students to become active within the university and enhance personal growth.

Research has shown that extracurricular involvement is an important factor contributing to student success, and at Embry-Riddle, there is a student organization for nearly every interest.

To see Student Organizations available at our Florida campus, visit https://connection.erau.edu/Organizations

To see Student Organizations available at our Arizona campus, visit https://thecontroltower.erau.edu/Organizations

ADMISSIONS PROCESS

An Embry-Riddle Aeronautical University education is nontraditional, unrestricted, and never ordinary. If that's the kind of thrilling collegiate experience you want for yourself, it all starts here.

Applications can be submitted electronically for all three of our campuses: Daytona Beach, FL, Prescott, AZ, and Worldwide.

Different supporting documents are required depending on whether you are a first-time, transfer, nontraditional, or international student, or if you are seeking a graduate or undergraduate degree.

Applications are evaluated on a rolling basis, and once all necessary documents are received, we will notify you of your admission status.

We look forward to meeting the next class of Eagles soon!

APPLICATION FEES AND DEADLINES

Application fees and deadlines vary between Embry-Riddle Aeronautical University's three campuses. For more details regarding fees and deadlines, please visit the following websites:

Daytona Beach, FL: http://daytonabeach.erau.edu/admissions/apply/

Prescott, AZ: http://prescott.erau.edu/admissions/apply/

Worldwide: https://worldwide.erau.edu/admissions/apply/

EMERSON COLLEGE

AT A GLANCE

Emerson College in Boston has exceptional programs in communications, visual and media arts, performing arts, journalism, marketing, political communication, sports communication, creative writing and writing, literature and publishing.

Emerson College is the only college in America dedicated exclusively to communication and the arts in a liberal arts context. Established in 1880 as a small regional school of oratory, Emerson has evolved into a diverse, coeducational, and multifaceted institution that educates students to assume positions of leadership in communication and the arts. Emerson is forward thinking, grounded in academic excellence, and committed to advancing the scholarship and creative work that brings innovation, depth, and diversity to those disciplines. Emerson has always been at the forefront of instruction in communications and the arts. Students are taking classes taught by industry professionals while engaging in hands-on projects to put what they learn in the classroom into practice.

LOCATION AND ENVIRONMENT

Emerson's campus is located across from historic Boston Common in the heart of the city's thriving Theatre District, and offers multiple theaters, television and film studios, and cutting-edge technical facilities for students. Emerson's connection with Boston's media, theater, and arts industries, as well as government, hospitals, and businesses, provides many opportunities for student internships and professional growth.

Emerson is home to 14 varsity sport teams, and over 80 student organizations including performance groups, student publications, and honor societies. More than half of the students are housed on-campus, some in learning communities such as the Writers' Block, Film Immersion Community, and Digital Culture Floor.

CAMPUS FACILITIES & EQUIPMENT

Emerson has the highest quality equipment, including sound-treated television studios, digital editing labs, audio post-production suites, industry standard software, a professional marketing research suite, and an integrated digital newsroom for aspiring journalists. Additionally, an 11-story performance and production center houses a theatre design/technology center, makeup lab, and costume shop. The College's Paramount Center opened in 2010 and includes a 560-seat theater, black box, scene shop, film screening room, and sound stage. Emerson is also home to the Robbins Speech, Language and Hearing Center, which provides evaluation and treatment for children and adults with communication challenges and serves as the primary clinical training facility for the Department of Communication Sciences and Disorders.

OFF-CAMPUS OPPORTUNITIES

Internships are popular with Emerson students and hundreds of opportunities exist throughout Boston and in major cities across the country, including exclusive placements in Los Angeles, home to our residential study and internship program.

Emerson's relationship with Los Angeles is long-standing, but Emerson Los Angeles (ELA) is a state-of-the-art facility that houses classrooms, residential space, faculty offices, an auditorium, screening room, event spaces, studios and more. It solidifies Emerson's commitment to their Los Angeles program and to creating opportunities for students and alumni on the west coast. The internship program enrolls approximately 200 students, mostly seniors, during both the fall and spring semesters. Emerson students who participate in the ELA program gain the knowledge, skills, and confidence to pursue their chosen fields before launching their post-graduate lives on the west coast.

In addition to ELA, Emerson owns a restored 14th-century medieval castle, Kasteel Well, which is home to their semester abroad program in The Netherlands. The castle is a national historical monument that provides living accommodations, classrooms, a resource center, and related facilities. Emerson also sponsors a semester in Washington, D.C. and, Beijing (at Communication University of China University), along with our Global Pathways Summer Programs in more than 14 locations including London, Prague, and Greece.

ACADEMICS

Emerson offers a wide range of undergraduate, graduate, and professional studies programs in communications and the arts. All undergraduate students take part in a robust curriculum including general education and liberal arts courses with advanced, specialized classes that are specific to individual departments and academic programs. Internships for academic credit are available to juniors and seniors, and the College's Institute for Liberal Arts and Interdisciplinary Studies offers first-year seminars, independent study options, and innovative courses that cut across academic disciplines. In addition, students can cross-register for courses with the six-member ProArts Consortium (Berklee College of Music, Boston Architectural College, Boston Conservatory, Emerson, Massachusetts College of Art, and the School of the Museum of Fine Arts).

MAJORS AND DEGREES OFFERED

Undergraduate students can earn a Bachelor of Arts, Bachelor of Science, or Bachelor of Fine Arts degree, depending on which major they select. More than 20 majors are available throughout the departments of Communication Sciences & Disorders, Communication Studies, Journalism, Marketing Communication, Performing Arts, Visual & Media Arts, Writing, Literature & Publishing and Liberal Arts & Interdisciplinary Studies. Students can also minor in several areas, including business, comedy, dance, entrepreneurship, fiction, hearing and deafness, history, literature, music appreciation, philosophy, photography, poetry, political science, publishing, psychology, radio, sociology, and women's and gender studies.

Emerson is accredited by the New England Association of Schools and Colleges and operates on a two-semester calendar.

TUITION, ROOM, BOARD, FEES

Basic expenses related to attending Emerson for the 2018–2019 academic year are $46,016 (tuition), $17,690 (double room and board), and $836 (Student Services Fee).

FINANCIAL AID

Emerson is committed to offering its students an excellent education at an affordable price. They have consistently set their tuition below their nearest competitors and are seen as a superb value in higher education. Students have all of the benefits of living in a world-class city, working with state-of-the-art equipment and in beautiful facilities, and learning from faculty who are top in their fields. The Office of Financial Aid will make every effort to help students finance the cost of their education. Emerson offers several types of financial assistance programs: need-based grants, employment, low-interest loans, merit scholarships, and alternative payment plans to help make an Emerson education possible. Each year, approximately two-thirds of the students receive some form of financial assistance. The College makes every effort to help students finance their education and provides need-based support packaged in awards that typically combine grant and scholarship, loan, and college work-study aid.

To apply for financial aid, students must complete the Free Application for Federal Student Assistance (FAFSA) and CSS PROFILE forms. More information can be found online at http://www.emerson.edu/financial_services or by contacting the Office of Student Financial Services at 617-824-8655 or finaid@emerson.edu.

STUDENT ORGANIZATIONS AND ACTIVITIES

In addition to the myriad of activities and events in Boston, student life at Emerson revolves around the more than 80 student-run organizations. These include radio stations, TV networks, publications, performance groups, service clubs, spiritual and cultural organizations, non-residential fraternities and sororities, professional societies, and intercollegiate and recreational athletics. Information about the specific organizations on campus can be found at http://www.emerson.edu/student-life/activities-organizations.

ADMISSIONS PROCESS

Emerson College accepts the Common Application or our Emerson Application and requires an application supplement. Admission is competitive. The college looks for students who present academic promise in their secondary school record, recommendations, and writing competency, as well as personal qualities as seen in extracurricular activities, community involvement, and demonstrated leadership. Emerson is a test optional institution. Applicants may choose not to submit SAT and/or ACT scores unless they feel as though it assists in the review of their application.

Successful candidates typically have four years of English and three years each of mathematics, science, social science, and three years of a single foreign language. The application deadline for September admission is January 15 (Early Action, November 1), and for January admission it is November 1. Transfer applicants should apply by March 15 for September admission, or by November 1 for January admission.

Prospective students are encouraged to visit campus. Tours and information sessions may be scheduled online at www.emerson.edu/ugvisit or by contacting the Admission Office at 617-824-8600 or admission@emerson.edu.

FASHION INSTITUTE OF TECHNOLOGY

AT A GLANCE

The Fashion Institute of Technology (FIT), a leader in career-oriented education, is a college of art and design, business and technology and liberal arts of the State University of New York (SUNY).

Founded in 1944, FIT is a State University of New York (SUNY) college granting both undergraduate and graduate degrees. FIT's schools include Art and Design, the Jay and Patty Baker School of Business and Technology, Liberal Arts, and Graduate Studies. FIT is accredited by the Middle States Commission on Higher Education, the National Association of Schools of Art and Design, The Council for Interior Design Accreditation and the American Alliance of Museums.

FIT provides it's over 9,200 students with an unmatched combination of specialized curricula, an in-depth liberal arts education, affordable tuition, and an extraordinary campus located in the center of New York City, the world capital of the arts, business, and communications industries. Students may also study at FIT's locations in Florence, Milan and Songdo, South Korea or at select study abroad sites across the globe.

Undergraduates choose from among 29 distinctive majors and 26 minors leading to an AAS, BFA or, BS degree. Our seven graduate programs lead to either a MA, MFA or MPS degree. The Center for Continuing and Professional Studies offers non-credit courses and credit/noncredit certificates designed for the non-traditional learner. FIT offers two fully online degrees including an AAS in Fashion Business Management and a BS in International Trade and Marketing. Students in middle school and high school may enroll in FIT's Pre-College Program offering a diverse curriculum of courses and workshops.

One of New York City's premier public institutions, FIT is an internationally recognized college for design, fashion, art, communications, and business. We are known for our rigorous, unique, and adaptable academic programming, experiential learning opportunities, academic and industry partnerships, and commitment to research, innovation, and entrepreneurship.

LOCATION AND ENVIRONMENT

Occupying an entire tree-lined block in Manhattan's dynamic Chelsea neighborhood, FIT's campus places students at the heart of the fashion, advertising, visual arts, design, business, and communications industries. Approximately 2,300 undergraduate students live on campus, in accommodations ranging from traditional dorm-style rooms with meal plans to apartment-style suites with kitchens, and from single to quad occupancy. FIT students studying abroad for a semester, year or summer term will also find suitable accommodations in major global centers.

CAMPUS FACILITIES & EQUIPMENT

The FIT campus is home to a creative community with diverse interests, talents, and backgrounds. With four undergraduate residence halls, two fitness centers, an intercollegiate athletics program, more than 60 clubs, and hundreds of on-campus activities, students find a wide range of resources for study, exploration, and fun. The David Dubinsky Student Center houses lounges, a game room, a dining hall, Barnes and Noble, Starbucks, a student radio station, a student-run boutique, student government and club offices, health services, disability support services (FIT-ABLE), Educational Opportunity Program (EOP), gyms, a dance studio, a fitness center, a counseling center, studios, and laboratories. The FIT Career and Internship Center provides an array of services to current students, alumni and employers.

Students have access to state-of-the-art technology and equipment in FIT's studios and labs. Facilities include art, printmaking, display design, and photography studios, a model-making workshop, a graphics printing service bureau, a toy design lab, and a textile testing lab. A computer-aided design and communications facility allows students to explore the latest advancements in technology and their integration in design, photography, and computer graphics and animation. The Annette Green Fragrance Foundation Studio, a professionally equipped fragrance development lab, is the only one of its kind on a U.S. college campus. Cutting and sewing labs offer the most advanced apparel production machinery among educational facilities in the nation. Other facilities include a lighting laboratory, broadcast studio, knitting and weaving labs, and a multimedia foreign language lab.

The Museum at FIT is New York City's only museum dedicated to fashion. Students, designers, and historians use the museum for research and inspiration. The museum, which is accredited by the American Alliance of Museums, operates year-round, and its exhibitions are free and open to the public. The Gladys Marcus Library provides more than 300,000 volumes of print, non-print, and electronic materials. The newspaper and periodicals collection includes 500 current subscriptions. Online resources include more than 90 searchable databases. The library also offers specialized resources, such as clipping files, fashion and trend forecasting services, and sketch collections. Also on campus are three multimedia venues-the Katie Murphy Amphitheatre, the Morris W. and Fannie B. Haft Auditorium, and the John E. Reeves Great Hall-used for fashion shows, exhibitions, student presentations, industry panels, conferences, and special events.

OFF-CAMPUS OPPORTUNITIES

FIT draws on its New York City location to provide a vibrant, creative environment for our college community. Students enjoy a wealth of opportunities to learn, to play, and to explore the city's abundant resources. A wide range of cultural and entertainment options-from museums to dining to theater are available within walking distance of the campus, which also offers convenient access to subway and bus lines and major rail and bus transportation hubs. One of New York's most dynamic neighborhoods, Chelsea boasts a lively gallery scene, exotic restaurants, a wide variety of retail outlets, and historic landmarks. FIT students also benefit from the campuses close proximity to industries, corporations, and organizations that offer our students internships and jobs.

ACADEMIC PROGRAMS

FIT prepares students for professional excellence in design and business through rigorous and adaptable academic programs, experiential learning, and innovative partnerships. FIT fosters creativity, career focus, and a global perspective and educates its students to embrace inclusiveness, sustainability, and a sense of community. Our innovative approach to education-experiential learning through professional critiques, industry competitions, internships and case studies—is the key to our students' future success.

FIT's liberal arts courses are creatively adapted to the needs of particular majors, and liberal arts minors are designed to balance each major's specialty skill. Presidential Scholars, FIT's honors program, offers a select group of high-achieving students specially designed liberal arts courses to stimulate their intellectual curiosity and creativity. Scholars receive a stipend and participate in a monthly colloquia series, annual retreats, and extracurricular and community service activities.

MAJORS AND DEGREES OFFERED

School of Art and Design

Accessories Design, Advertising Design, Communication Design Foundation, Computer Animation and Interactive Media, Fabric Styling, Fashion Design, Fine Arts, Graphic Design, Illustration, Interior Design, Jewelry Design, Menswear, Packaging Design, Photography, Textile/Surface Design, Toy Design, and Visual Presentation and Exhibition Design.

Jay and Patty Baker School of Business and Technology

Advertising and Marketing Communications, Cosmetics and Fragrance Marketing, Direct and Interactive Marketing, Entrepreneurship for the Fashion and Design Industries, Fashion Business Management, Home Products Development, International Trade and Marketing for the Fashion Industries, Production Management: Fashion and Related Industries, Technical Design, and Textile Development and Marketing.

School of Liberal Arts

Art History and Museum Professions, Film and Media, and liberal arts minors including both subject-based and interdisciplinary.

School of Graduate Studies

Art Market, Cosmetics and Fragrance Marketing and Management, Fashion Design, Exhibition and Experience Design, Fashion and Textile Studies: History, Theory, Museum Practice, Global Fashion Management, and Illustration.

TUITION, ROOM, BOARD, FEES

Fall 2017-Spring 2018 Tuition per Semester

	NY State Residents	Non-NY State Residents
Associate-Level	$2,345	$7,035
Baccalaureate-Level	$3,335	$10,096
Graduate-Level	$5,603	$11,449

Undergraduate room and board rates vary based on the number of residents per traditional halls/apartment-style housing. Rates depending on the housing selection and with/without meal plans range from $6,972 to $9,029 per semester for double rooms or quads.

FINANCIAL AID

FIT attempts to remove financial barriers to college entrance by providing scholarships, grants, loans, and part-time employment based on available funds for students with financial need. FIT is committed to providing a superior education at an affordable cost and to helping students find a way to pay for it. Financial aid is available to citizens of the United States from a variety of sources including scholarships, grants, federal loans, and work-study. Endowed scholarships are donated to the FIT Foundation by many companies, organizations, and individuals to support our students. Students must file the Free Application for Federal Student Aid (FAFSA) to be considered for need-based financial aid. International students are not eligible to be considered for federal, state or need-based financial aid at FIT.

STUDENT ORGANIZATIONS AND ACTIVITIES

FIT's over 9,500 students hail from across the country and around the world. They join a dynamic student body that includes full and part-time undergraduates, graduate students, non-traditional and on-line learners. Thirty percent of our full-time undergraduates live on campus in one of FIT's four residence halls located on 27th Street across from all major campus facilities. Upperclassmen live on 33rd Street in an apartment-style residence hall just a few blocks from campus. Students also commute from home or live in off-campus housing in and around New York City.

ADMISSIONS PROCESS

Undergraduate Admission

Admission to FIT's undergraduate degree programs is based on a holistic review of the applicant's academic profile, essay and personal characteristics including extra-curricular activities and achievements. Applicants to the School of Art and Design must also submit a portfolio that demonstrates their artistic and creative ability. Detailed information on the portfolio requirements for each major offered in the School of Art and Design can be found at fitnyc.edu/admissions

First-year applicants must submit an official high school transcript and essay. Results of the SAT or ACT are not required for admission unless the applicant is interested in being considered for the Presidential Scholars honors program. FIT requires its first-year enrolled students to take English and math placement examinations unless they have submitted SAT or ACT scores. International applicants must submit the results of either the TOEFL, ILETS or PTE exam if English was not their primary language of instruction. Transfer applicants must also submit official transcripts of all post-secondary coursework.

First-year applicants are considered only for admission to the two-year, AAS degree and must indicate their intended major on the application. Upon successful completion of the AAS degree, students are considered for admission into a two-year, BFA or BS program. Transfer applicants may be admitted either to a one-year or two-year AAS program or directly into the BFA or BS program based on their post-secondary coursework.

Graduate Admission

Applicants to the School of Graduate Studies will be considered for admission based on their academic profile, essay, recommendations and an interview. In addition, there are major-specific criteria which may include a portfolio, work experience and standardized test scores. Prospective students interested in learning about the graduate programs and admission criteria should contact the admissions office at fitnyc.edu/graduate-studies.

Continuing and Professional Studies

Prospective students should visit fitnyc.edu/ccps for detailed information on available courses and registration.

Deadlines and Important Dates

Undergraduate Admission

Prospective undergraduate students must submit their application and $50 non-refundable fee to www.suny.edu/applysuny and indicate their interest in being considered for admission to FIT for either the spring or fall semesters.

	Fall Semester	Spring Semester
Application Deadlines	January 1	October 1
Application Complete Date	February 1	November 1
Notification Dates	April 1	December 1
Tuition Deposit Deadlines	May 1	Two weeks from notification date

Prospective undergraduate students are encouraged to visit the campus for an information session and student-led tour. The admissions office also hosts weekend information sessions, open houses and portfolio preview days during select times throughout the academic year. For more information and to make a reservation please visit fitnyc.edu/admissions.

Please visit fitnyc.edu/graduate-studies for graduate application deadlines and fitnyc.edu/ccps for detailed information on credit, non-credit, certificates and Pre-College programs.

FLORIDA SOUTHERN COLLEGE

AT A GLANCE

Founded in 1883, Florida Southern is the oldest private comprehensive college in Florida and a national leader in engaged learning, offering nearly 60 distinguished undergraduate and graduate degree programs. FSC is conveniently located within an hour's drive of both Orlando and Tampa and home to the world's largest collection of Frank Lloyd Wright architecture, designated a National Historic Landmark in 2012. Florida Southern is an internationally-recognized place of beauty and academic excellence.

LOCATION AND ENVIRONMENT

Florida Southern College occupies more than 100 acres of rolling hillside on the north shore of Lake Hollingsworth in suburban Lakeland, Florida. As home to the largest collection of Frank Lloyd Wright architecture in the world, the campus is a National Historic Landmark that welcomes tens of thousands of visitors from around the world each year. In addition to thirteen Wright-designed structures, the campus features lavish gardens, dazzling lake views from nearly every vantage point, and several state-of-the-art buildings designed by leading American architect Robert A.M. Stern. These elements, combined with Florida's natural beauty and trademark sunshine, have led many to name Florida Southern College among the most beautiful college campuses in the nation.

CAMPUS FACILITIES & EQUIPMENT

The Becker Business Building, dedicated in fall 2015, is one of the most technologically advanced business school buildings in the nation. Becker Business Building features a virtual trading floor with Bloomberg trading terminals, an LED stock ticker and video wall, high-tech classrooms with full distance learning capabilities, and a cutting-edge market observation room where students can perform focus groups and gather market research data for area corporations. The Chatlos Communication Building houses a newly renovated television studio where students can polish their broadcasting skills. Head over to the Christoverson Humanities Building for a film studies theatre and modern language lab. The Rinker Technology Center is a quiet and comfortable computer lab located steps from the heart of the residential community. The recently expanded Blanton Nursing Building has the latest in nursing simulation technology, including a full mother-and-child birthing simulation lab. The Wynee Warden Dance Studio, which opened in fall 2015, houses a professional-quality dance studio with amazing views of Lake Hollingsworth. The Berry Science Building features several recent renovations, including a collaborative learning space for the Department of Computer Science and a brand new tissue culture laboratory for the biology program. For education majors, the campus is home to an on-site Preschool Learning Lab, the Roberts Center for Learning and Literacy and The Roberts Academy, a transitional school for gifted elementary-age students with dyslexia. The campus is also home to a heritage rose garden that serves as an outdoor laboratory for horticulture students, as well as a greenhouse and citrus grove. The Robert A. Davis Performing Art Center has every type of performance space a musician or theatre major could hope for, including the 1,800-seat proscenium theatre Branscomb Memorial Auditorium and the intimate 336-seat thrust-stage Loca Lee Buckner Theatre. The newly built Sharon and Jim France Admissions Center will welcome prospective students and their families to campus. The France Admissions Center was designed to fit into the College's architectural legacy with its collection of Frank Lloyd Wright designs, which is the largest in the world.

OFF-CAMPUS OPPORTUNITIES

Located just an hour's drive from both the world-class resorts of Orlando and the stunning beaches of Clearwater-St. Pete, Lakeland is the perfect mid-sized haven for college living. The College is a short walk from Lakeland's lively downtown, home to an array of boutique shopping, vintage shops, and craft dining. Downtown Lakeland features live entertainment, a monthly food truck rally, and a Saturday morning farmer's market. If upscale shopping is on your agenda, catch the College shuttle to nearby Lakeside Village, where more restaurants, shops, and department stores await, as well as an IMAX multiplex movie theater. On the weekends, pick your road trip: head to the some of the best beaches in the country, grab dinner at Disney Springs, or catch some thrills at Busch Gardens Tampa or Universal Orlando Resort.

ACADEMIC PROGRAMS

FSC is a national leader in engaged learning, an approach that incorporates hands-on experience into each degree program and gives students a taste of daily life in their field and a deeper understanding of the curriculum through real-world application of knowledge. Science students conduct research in the field alongside professors and present papers at national conferences; theatre and music students take the stage alongside world-renowned guest performers; political science majors spend a semester interning at a senator's office in Washington, D.C.; and business students analyze problems and present real solutions to executives at major area corporations. Beyond these opportunities, which are an integral part of the engaged learning experience, each student is guaranteed an internship in his or her field, a crucial step in gathering resume-building experience prior to graduation.

We also guarantee each student a study abroad experience. Once a student has completed four full semesters in good standing, they qualify for Junior Journey, often at no additional cost beyond the usual FSC tuition! Junior Journey trips are hosted by faculty members and designed to take education far beyond the classroom—political science and history students travel to Germany to study the history of WWII and the Holocaust, marine biology students head to the Bahamas to study shark conservation and biology, and theatre students travel to New York City for behind-the-scenes tours of Broadway shows. Each semester offers a host of options to suit a multitude of interests and majors, and each trip is a once-in-a-lifetime experience!

The Honors Program at Florida Southern offers talented and motivated students the opportunity to work one-on-one with faculty mentors on a senior project of their own design. Honors students also enjoy collaborative, interdisciplinary seminars with exceptional faculty, a series of "supper seminars" that host expert speakers, and specially designated facilities—including classrooms, the Honors Lounge, and special housing—which foster an enriching living-learning environment. All honors students receive priority registration and are able to take course overloads without paying additional fees.

To ensure student success in their academic journeys, the Student Solutions Center launched Academic Fuel, a combination of group peer tutoring programs including the FSC Writing Center, Scholars Strengthening Scholars, and Peer Assisted Study Sessions (PASS). Academic Fuel is designed to help each student stay on top of their academic progress. The atmosphere is relaxed and friendly; students support each other and professional staff ensures that each student is matched with the best resources for their needs. Students are encouraged to use Academic Fuel programs early and often to stay ahead academically and realize the benefit of connecting with peers.

Florida Southern College courses are taught almost entirely by full-time faculty members, many of whom hold the highest credentials in their field. Our faculty members have chosen to teach at Florida Southern because they value the opportunity to work one-on-one with students. Here, your professor won't just know your name. They will know you and will take an active interest in helping you achieve your goals.

MAJORS AND DEGREES OFFERED

Florida Southern offers nearly 60 undergraduate degree programs, including highly successful pre-dental, pre-medical, pre-optometry, pre-physician assistant, pre-veterinary, pre-law, pre-physical therapy, pre-theological, pre-engineering, pre-occupational therapy, and pre-pharmacy professional programs.

Bachelor's degree programs are available in accounting, art education, art history, biochemistry and molecular biology, biology, biotechnology, business administration, business and free enterprise, chemistry, citrus and horticultural studies, communication, computer science, criminology, dance performance and choreography, dance studies, economics and finance, elementary education, English environmental studies, exercise science, graphic design, healthcare administration, history, humanities, marine biology, mathematics, medical laboratory sciences, music, music education, music management, music performance, musical theatre, nursing, philosophy, political communication, political economy, political science, psychology, religion, self-designed major, social sciences, Spanish, sport business management, sports communication and marketing, studio art, technical theatre/design, theatre arts, theatre performance, and youth ministry. Many areas are available as concentrations and interdisciplinary minors are available in advertising design, integrated marketing communications, Latin American studies, pre-law, and women and gender studies.

TUITION, ROOM, BOARD, FEES

Full-time (12–18 credits) tuition per semester is $17,824. The standard 20-meal plan, required for all first-year students, is $2,300 per semester. The average cost for housing in a double-occupancy room is $3,535 per semester. Total tuition, fees, and room and board per year for a first-year student averages $48,018.

FINANCIAL AID

Each year, Florida Southern College offers more than $28 million in institutional aid on the basis of academic merit, talent in athletics or fine arts, demonstrated leadership or service, need, and other factors. Combined with federal, state, and other private funding sources, FSC students average $52 million in overall assistance, and 100 percent of FSC students receive some form of aid. It all begins with our net price calculator, available on our website. Answer a few simple questions, and we'll give you an immediate assessment of some of the financial aid options available to you. Additionally, your admissions counselor will work with you to ensure that you are considered for every possible scholarship, grant, and source of aid available.

STUDENT ORGANIZATIONS AND ACTIVITIES

Florida Southern is home to over 100 student clubs and organizations, 14 Greek Life chapters (7 sororities and 7 fraternities) and 20 NCAA Division 11 men's and women's varsity sports teams.

ADMISSIONS PROCESS

Florida Southern currently has a traditional undergraduate class of about 2,411 students from nearly all 50 states and 47 countries around the world. The average GPA is 3.73 and the average SAT/ACT is 1190/26. For more application information please visit www.floridasouthern,edu.

THE GEORGE WASHINGTON UNIVERSITY

AT A GLANCE

The George Washington University, located in downtown Washington, D.C., provides students with invaluable learning experiences on campus, throughout the city and around the world.

Founded in 1821 by an Act of Congress, the George Washington University (GW) offers more than 70 majors and over 2,000 courses across seven undergraduate schools.

We go beyond the typical university experience with an education that is deeply connected to our location in the center of Washington, D.C. Our nearly 10,000 undergraduates actively engage the city and the world through hands-on learning experiences, where they study alongside faculty experts, policy leaders and extraordinary individuals in every discipline to shape global progress and define the issues that will shape the present and future.

LOCATION AND ENVIRONMENT

GW maintains two fully integrated campuses in Washington, D.C., with residence halls and classrooms located on both and free shuttle service provided. Through these two different learning environments, students have the ability to create a college experience that is uniquely their own.

Our Foggy Bottom campus is blocks from the major landmarks that make Washington one of the most recognizable cities in the world. Our students can study on the steps of the Lincoln Memorial, jog to the Washington Monument or take a stroll to the White House and Kennedy Center.

Our Mount Vernon campus, just a few miles from the hustle and bustle of downtown, offers a residential liberal arts campus experience while still providing all the opportunities of D.C. Our Women's Leadership Program and GW Athletic fields are located on this campus.

Explore both campuses in our virtual tour at http://virtualtour.gwu.edu.

CAMPUS FACILITIES & EQUIPMENT

GW is full of world-class facilities, such as Gelman Library, at the heart of campus, the Smith Center, home of GW Athletics, Lisner Auditorium, which hosts performances and lectures to enrich our community, and the Science and Engineering Hall, full of highly specialized lab facilities. Learn more about our facilities at http://virtualtour.gwu.edu.

OFF-CAMPUS OPPORTUNITIES

What distinguishes a GW education is the way we consistently put knowledge into action through research, internship and service opportunities for students in all academic areas.

Our students have access to innovative facilities and faculty to support their research in all subjects. Students and faculty have worked together on topics including food waste in D.C. public schools, cholesterol transport in HIV and Tangier disease, and how personality affects purchasing.

As a top school for internships, we excel at helping students land internships in the nation's capital and beyond. GW students gain invaluable professional experience and often even security clearance during internships at the White House, U.S. Department of State, Folger Shakespeare Library and NPR, just to name a few.

In addition, we encourage students to give back on the local, national and international levels through university-wide community service, including Freshman Day of Service and Alternative Spring Breaks. That dedication to service continues after graduation, as GW is the top-ranked Peace Corps feeder among medium-sized schools.

ACADEMICS

Learn more about these programs at https://undergraduate.admissions.gwu.edu/special-interest-programs.

Civic House

Politics & Values Program

Scholars in Quantitative and Natural Sciences

Seven-Year B.A./M.D. Program

University Honors Program

Women's Leadership Program

MAJORS AND DEGREES OFFERED

With more than 2,000 courses in over 70 majors for undergraduate students, GW offers a wide range of academic opportunities, including business, engineering, fine art, international affairs, journalism, liberal arts and public health. Our average class size is 28, and 70 percent of classes have fewer than 30 students. Browse all of our majors at http://go.gwu.edu/gwmajors.

Columbian College of Arts & Sciences

- Africana Studies
- American Studies
- Anthropology
- Arabic Studies
- Archaeology
- Astronomy and Astrophysics
- Biological Anthropology
- Biology
- Biophysics
- Chemistry
- Chinese Language and Literature
- Classical Studies
- Communication
- Criminal Justice
- Dramatic Literature
- Economics
- English
- English and Creative Writing
- Environmental Studies
- French Language and Literature
- Geography
- Geological Sciences
- German Language and Literature
- History
- Human Services and Social Justice
- Japanese Language and Literature
- Judaic Studies
- Mathematics
- Organizational Sciences
- Peace Studies
- Philosophy
- Physics
- Political Science

- Pre-law option
- Pre-medicine option
- Psychology
- Religion
- Russian Language and Literature
- Sociology
- Spanish and Latin American Languages, Literature and Culture
- Speech and Hearing Sciences
- Statistics
- Women's Studies

Corcoran School of the Arts & Design

- Art History
- Art History and Fine Arts
- Dance
- Fine Art
- Fine Art Photography
- Graphic Design
- Interaction Design
- Interior Architecture and Design
- Music
- Photojournalism
- Theatre

Elliott School of International Affairs

- Asian Studies
- International Affairs
- Latin American and Hemispheric Studies
- Middle East Studies

School of Media & Public Affairs

- Journalism and Mass Communication
- Political Communication

Milken Institute School of Public Health

- Exercise Science
- Nutrition Science
- Public Health

School of Business

- Accountancy
- Business Administration
- Finance

School of Engineering & Applied Science

- Applied Science and Technology
- Biomedical Engineering
- Civil Engineering
- Computer Engineering
- Computer Science
- Electrical Engineering
- Mechanical Engineering
- Systems Engineering

TUITION, ROOM, BOARD, FEES

Earning a GW degree is invaluable, but it takes an investment of time, effort and money. We believe that investment is within reach for every admitted student, and we leverage our resources to make it worthwhile.

GW guarantees students fixed tuition for up to five years of study, meaning the tuition you pay your first semester will be the tuition you pay for your final semester. No surprises here.

GW also invests more than $185 million in financial aid, which is awarded to 70 percent of the incoming freshman class.

We believe that your investment in GW will pay dividends for the rest of your life.

Tuition $55,140

Room and Board $13,850

Student Association Fee $75

FINANCIAL AID

All applicants for admission are automatically considered for scholarships (with the exception of special programs which may require a separate application). Need-based aid is determined by the Office of Student Financial Assistance. For more information, visit http://financialaid.gwu.edu.

STUDENT ORGANIZATIONS AND ACTIVITIES

Our nearly 10,000 undergraduate students come from all across the U.S. and more than 130 countries. While at GW, they participate in student organizations and community groups. GW's student body is regularly ranked as the most politically active, which should be no surprise given our close proximity to the White House and the nation's top policy makers. Students have an open dining plan, which offers options on and off campus, and are required to live on campus for their first 3 years.

450 student clubs and organizations

50 club sports and intramural teams

27 NCAA Division I sports teams

35 Greek life chapters

ADMISSIONS PROCESS

GW strives to recruit a diverse and inclusive class each and every year. We do this through our holistic review process, which takes into account not just overall grades, but also course rigor, essays, recommendation letters and extracurricular activities. This allows us to admit students who have the academic preparation, personal qualities and motivation to thrive in GW's dynamic environment.

GW is test-optional, allowing students to choose whether or not to submit SAT/ACT scores, because we believe that a student's performance throughout high school is the best indication of college readiness.

GEORGIAN COURT UNIVERSITY

AT A GLANCE

Georgian Court University is a coeducational, diverse, forward-thinking institution in New Jersey that encourages intellectual inquiry, moral analysis, and social dialogue. At GCU, you will experience a comprehensive liberal arts education in the Mercy Roman Catholic tradition. GCU students learn to expand possibility while fostering their unique gifts and becoming more engaged citizens of the world. The university, which maintains a historic special concern for women, welcomes students of all faiths and backgrounds and offers a curriculum that is broad enough to be truly liberal, yet specialized enough to prepare you for graduate study or an exceptional career.

Georgian Court University is a place where you will learn the Mercy core values of integrity, respect, compassion, justice and service. Upon graduation, you will leave armed with unimaginable knowledge, a powerful sense of purpose, and a determination to change our world.

Georgian Court University is set on a magnificent 156-acre estate, rich with an amazing history, which once belonged to financier George Jay Gould. We are conveniently located one hour from New York City and Philadelphia and only 15 minutes from the Jersey Shore. The campus borders Lake Carasaljo and is both a National Historic Landmark and a National Arboretum.

POINTS OF PRIDE

2018 US News & World Report

"Best Colleges & Universities"

2017 Washington Monthly

"Best Bang for the Buck"

2017 Strive for College Partner

First-Generation College Students

2017 Catholic College of Distinction

2017 College of Distinction

2017 New Jersey College of Distinction

2017 Military-Friendly School

2017 Champion of Good Works

LOCATION AND ENVIRONMENT

With over 2,300 students of diverse faiths and backgrounds and a 13:1 student/teacher ratio, Georgian Court University also offers seven lush garden spaces, including a Japanese Garden, a marble pool, a bowling alley, four residence halls and GCU is the only American University with a court tennis court.

Georgian Court University cares about its students and the environment. 1,639 solar panels help heat and cool Jeffries Hall; and, there are low-mow natural zones and recycling initiatives throughout campus.

CAMPUS FACILITIES & EQUIPMENT

GCU's 67,000-square-foot Wellness Center is a state-of-the-art centerpiece on a campus fully equipped for physical fitness, athletic excellence, and environmental awareness. The LEED Gold certified center features recycled materials, water and energy-saving design, and an Earth-friendly roof. The Wellness Center Complex features:

A 1,200-seat arena, five athletics fields (including new synthetic turf), a six-court outdoor tennis center, and an abundance of training space for GCU's conference-winning NCAA Division II student-athletes; An advanced exercise science lab and two professional dance studios; A state-of-the-art fitness center; and a rich, diverse range of fitness and wellness programs.

Jeffries Hall is Georgian Court's largest academic building, providing classrooms, seminar rooms, offices, art studios, and computer labs. The state-of-the-art Audrey Birish George Science Center offers the latest laboratory and instruction space for scientific study.

Other campus buildings include the Sister Mary Joseph Cunningham Library, the Raymond Hall Complex, which houses the School of Education, the Raymond Hall Computer Center, and the GCU Dining Hall. The School of Business and the Department of Psychology reside in Farley Center, which includes a computer lab, student lounge, and an International Collaboration Center.

OFF-CAMPUS OPPORTUNITIES

Georgian Court University is conveniently located one hour from the Big Apple (New York City) and historic Philadelphia, and only 15 minutes from the beautiful beaches at the Jersey Shore. GCU is conveniently accessible from Rte. 9, the garden state parkway and 195 allowing students to venture out and enjoy all the local amenities the Jersey Shore has to offer.

ACADEMICS

- Undergraduate Programs
- Graduate Programs
- Evening Programs
- Online / Off Campus Programs
- Nursing Program, including RN-BSN

GCU works to help students develop their academic skills in a supportive, caring environment. The Academic Development & Support Center (ADSC) offers tutoring and other academic support services so students can get the most out of their education. Disabilities Services, Peer Tutoring, and a fee-based support program for students with learning differences are also available.

Georgian Court University's Honors Program allows students to pursue academic honors and collaborate with faculty members in a variety of special courses. Honors students can benefit from courses that emphasize primary texts and sources, rigorous scholarly writing assignments and oral presentations, belonging to a committed community of scholars, preference in academic advisement and course registration, assistance with funding to present at regional and national conferences, and special advising regarding graduate and professional school applications and prestigious fellowship opportunities.

The Office of Career Services, Corporate Engagement and Continuing Education helps bridge the gap from being a student to becoming a professional and progressing through a career. The office has a wide array of tools and resources to help students find jobs and internships, identify and market their skill set, network, compile a resume, and prepare for interviews. These life-long, free services are available to both students and alumni.

MAJORS AND DEGREES OFFERED

The Schools of GCU

GCU is comprised of three schools that serve our undergraduate and graduate students:

- The School of Arts and Sciences
- The School of Business & Digital Media
- The School of Education

GCU boasts more than 30 undergraduate degrees, 10 graduate degrees, and a variety of certificate programs for existing professionals looking to advance their careers. In fact, GCU is ranked by U.S. News & World Report as one of the best regional universities—and one of the best colleges for veterans.

Degrees Offered

- Bachelor's Degree
- Master's Degree
- Certificate
- Post-Bachelor's certificate
- Post-Master's certificate

MAJORS

Georgian Court University offers degree programs in the following disciplines: Accounting; Applied Arts & Sciences; Art & Visual Studies; Biochemistry; Biology; Business Administration; Chemistry; Clinical Laboratory Sciences; Criminal Justice; Dance; Digital Communication; Digital Design; Education; English; Exercise Science, Wellness & Sports; Finance; Graphic Design & Multimedia; Health Information Management; Health Profession Studies; Health Sciences; History; Interdisciplinary Studies; Latino Business Studies; Management; Marketing; Mathematics; Medical Imaging Sciences; Natural Sciences; Nursing; Pre-Professional Career Preparation (preparation for medical careers); Psychiatric Rehabilitation & Psychology; Psychology; Religious Studies; Social Work; Spanish; and Visual Art. Minors are offered in: Accounting; American Studies; Anthropology; Biology; Business Administration; Chemistry; Coaching; Computer Information Systems; Dance; Dance Therapy; Digital Communication; Economics; English; Exercise Science, Wellness, & Sports; Finance; Gerontology; Global Justice & Society; Graphic Design; History; Homeland Security; Integrative Health; International Area Studies; Latino/a and Caribbean Studies; Law Enforcement & Corrections; Management; Marketing; Mathematics; Politics, Law and History; Psychology; Religious Studies; Social Media Marketing; Social Work; Sociology; Spanish; Sports Management; Studio Art; Sustainability; The USA and the World; Women's Studies; and Writing.

TUITION, ROOM, BOARD, FEES

For the 2017–18 academic year, tuition was $15,400 per semester for full-time students (12–18 credits); full-time nursing program tuition was $16,489; part-time (11 credits or less) was $704 per credit; nursing part time was $776 per credit; room and board with 7-day meal plan was $5,404 per semester, with a $1,293 single room supplement; comprehensive full-time fee was $730; comprehensive part-time fee was $365; full year parking fee was $193 (plus $13.27 New Jersey sales tax). A deposit of $250 is required for resident and commuter students. This is applied to the semester bill and is nonrefundable.

°All tuition charges are for full time and based on full-time attendance.

The charges listed are in effect for the 2017–2018 academic year. The university reserves the right to change its schedule of tuition, fees, and refunds policies at any time. For more information, see georgian.edu/tuition.

FINANCIAL AID

Being able to pay for attending college is no easy task. Located in the Lake House, the Office of Financial Aid offers assistance to you and your parents to ensure that you have the financial resources to focus on your education.

Whether you are an incoming freshman, a returning undergraduate, a transfer student or a graduate student, we offer a wide range of financial aid options such as loans, grants, and scholarships to make your education at GCU possible. We encourage all students to fill out their FAFSA with GCU's code: 002608.

Georgian Court University is proud to meet the financial aid needs of its students with an annual budget of $20,000,000 in institutional aid. The University believes that a good education is a right—not a privilege. Through internal scholarships and outside scholarships, Georgian Court strives to make education attainable for all students.

In addition, there are GCU institutional, Federal, and State grants available for students who meet specific criteria. Students can also take advantage of the loan programs that are explained in further detail in the student loan section of the University's website.

STUDENT ORGANIZATIONS AND ACTIVITIES

During 2017–18, GCU's diverse student body was made up of 25 students from 19 international countries, with over 2,200 coming from New Jersey, while students from 19 other states represented the out-of-state population. Over 40 percent of GCU's full-time undergraduates were first-generation college students; and, over 52 percent were full-time Pell recipients.

Georgian Court University is a proud member of the National Collegiate Athletic Association (NCAA) Division II. We also belong to the Central Atlantic Collegiate Conference (CACC). Division II reflects our own philosophy. It's an ideal balance between athletic excellence and academic achievement. GCU student-athletes maintain an above-average GPA, participate regularly in community service projects, and make their mark on college athletics. Many qualify for athletic scholarships.

The Student Government Association (SGA) of Georgian Court University is the official representative voice of the GCU student body. The SGA advocates on behalf of the students' interests and concerns. Through representation on University committees and other special meetings, the Student Government Association continues to play a vital role in fostering community and providing a direct link between students, faculty, and administration. The University also boasts several programs to help engage and develop students' leadership abilities, as well as a plethora of other clubs and organizations catering to a broad range of interests and lifestyles.

The Office of Campus Ministry at Georgian Court University exists to support the spiritual growth of all members of the GCU community. Campus ministry's mission includes: Gathering a vibrant community for worship, prayer, and reflection; Celebrating the Catholic Christian faith of our sponsors, the Sisters of Mercy; Cultivating faith-filled leaders who can have a positive impact on our world; and Animating the GCU community for compassionate service and advocacy for justice.

For a list of student organizations that are available or to learn how to start your own club, visit georgian.edu/clubs-organizations.

ADMISSIONS PROCESS

Georgian Court University welcomes applications from qualified students of all faiths and backgrounds who desire a liberal arts education. The University strives to enroll students who can benefit most from its academic program. In 2017, 43 percent of GCU's student population were first-generation college students. Entrance is based on individual merit. The high school record of achievement is of primary importance and must reflect solid performance. The majority of students at Georgian Court ranked in the upper half of their senior high school class. Transfer students are accepted into the freshman, sophomore, and junior classes for fall and spring semesters. All transfer applicants must be in good standing at their previous college. Applicants with fewer than 24 credits must fulfill all requirements for admission to the freshman class. Further consideration is given to the applicant's extracurricular activities and the letters of recommendation submitted by teachers, counselors, employers, or similarly qualified people.

Applicants must submit their completed application (online via the Common Application or print and complete a paper application), a $40 application fee, their official high school transcript, SAT (GCU code: 2274) or ACT (GCU code: 2562) scores, two letters of recommendation, and an optional essay. Georgian Court has rolling admissions for first-year students, so applications can be accepted throughout the year.

A campus interview is encouraged but not necessary. A guided tour of the campus is available at the interview.

Undergraduate Student Profile (update as of Fall 2017)

- 1613 undergraduate students (777 graduate students)
- 71 percent female, 29 percent male
- 19 states and 19 foreign countries represented
- 69 percent of first-year applicants are accepted

Faculty (update as of Fall 2017)

- 13:1 student-faculty ratio
- 87 full-time instructional faculty members
- 25 percent minority faculty
- 92 percent of full-time faculty members have doctoral degrees

GONZAGA UNIVERSITY

AT A GLANCE

Gonzaga University, founded in 1887, is an independent, comprehensive university with a distinguished background in the Catholic, Jesuit, and humanistic tradition. Gonzaga emphasizes the moral and ethical implications of learning, living, and working in today's global society. Through the University Core Curriculum, each student develops a strong liberal arts foundation, which many alumni cite as a most valuable asset. In addition, students specialize in any of more than 75 academic programs and majors. Gonzaga enrolls approximately 5,000 undergraduates and 2,500 graduate and law students.

Gonzaga's 131-acre campus combines the old and new: College Hall, the original administration building, and DeSmet Residence Hall with the modern architectural structures of the John J. Hemmingson Center, Foley Library, Hughes Life Sciences Building, Jundt Art Center and Museum, and the PACCAR Center for Applied Science. The campus is characterized by sprawling green lawns and majestic evergreen trees. Towering above the campus are the stately spires of St. Aloysius Church, the well-recognized landmark featured in the University logo.

Gonzaga encompasses five undergraduate schools: Arts and Sciences, Business Administration, Education, Engineering and Applied Science, and Nursing and Human Physiology. The University offers the BA, BBA, BEd, BS, BSCE, BSCpE, BSCS, BSEE, BSEM, BSME, and BSN degrees.

Gonzaga offers several unique options for students. The Honors Program provides a rigorous liberal arts curriculum for intellectually curious students who thrive in a competitive academic environment. Business leaders mentor the Hogan Entrepreneurial Leadership Program students, and internships are an integral part of the program. The award-winning Gonzaga Alumni Mentor Program (GAMP) connects current students and recent graduates with alumni in their professional areas of interest. Students in the Comprehensive Leadership Program take a leadership minor curriculum that may be combined with any major, and they participate in valuable, interactive leadership experiences. The Army ROTC unit prepares select women and men as leaders in service for their communities and their country. Gonzaga's nationally ranked debate team includes all skill levels. The Mock Trial Team competes nationally and involves students majoring in many different areas of study. Internships, research with faculty, and community service learning enhance class time while providing students first-hand experience.

LOCATION AND ENVIRONMENT

As the hub of the Inland Northwest, Spokane plays a vital role in shaping the University's character. While offering urban advantages such as museum exhibits, shopping, symphony, Broadway and ballet performances, Spokane still maintains an intimate, friendly, and community atmosphere. Used for running and cycling, part of the 37-mile Centennial Trail, runs through campus and to Coeur d' Alene, Idaho. Within a short distance of campus, students snow and water ski, hike, cycle, rock climb, swim, camp, and golf. With an average rainfall of only 16.7 inches per year, outdoor activities are easily accessible.

The 24 residence halls and apartments on campus, both single-sex and coed, house 40 to 360 students each. Freshmen and sophomores are required to live on campus. The Zagweb network provides students round-the-clock electronic access to email, Internet, campus intranet, and library holdings, all directly from residence hall rooms. Additionally, the whole campus is wireless. Resident Directors and Assistants, along with a Resident Chaplain, provide a fun, secure, and nurturing environment.

CAMPUS FACILITIES & EQUIPMENT

The Foley Library contains more than 800,000 volumes and microform titles, with two special collections of material especially rich in the areas of philosophy and classical civilization, as well as the nation's most extensive collection of works concerning the famous Jesuit poet Gerard Manley Hopkins. The historic College Hall houses the Harry & Colleen Magnuson Theatre, a Florentine-style University Chapel, and numerous classrooms and faculty offices including the Office of Admission. Jesuits living and working in the Spokane area reside on campus in the new Della Strada Jesuit Community. Gonzaga is also home to the Bing Crosby House Museum, which houses a large collection of material relating to singer and actor, Bing Crosby, in his original home.

Students are able to produce sophisticated multimedia presentations and research hundreds of libraries across the country from their own residence hall rooms, by accessing campus-wide wireless, or from one of many labs on campus. The Communications Building offers an arts lab for the Bulletin (the weekly student-published newspaper), KAGU, the University's radio station, and GUTV, a state-of-the-art TV production station where students learn all aspects of broadcast studies. The Herak Center for Engineering offers state-of-the-art CAD/CAM, electronic, digital, microwave, and calibration labs, and the PACCAR Center for Applied Science, which received a "Gold" certification rating from the Leadership in Energy and Environmental Design (LEED), adds more classroom space, a robotics lab, a computer science lab with a high-speed cluster computer array, and the rapidly growing Electric Utility Transmission & Distribution program.

The Martin Athletic Centre boasts a 13,000 sq. ft. state-of-the-art fitness center, and next door, the 6000-seat McCarthey Athletic Center houses the men's and women's basketball games as well as concerts and events throughout the year. Washington Trust Field at Patterson Baseball Complex hosts the Gonzaga baseball program. The new Volkar Center for Athletic Achievement is located south of the Martin Centre and is designated to help student-athletes succeed in competition, in the classroom, and in the community.

Gonzaga has committed that any new buildings on campus (including the recent addition of the 167,726 square-foot John J. Hemmingson Center which was certified "Gold") will seek at least "Silver" LEED certification. Additionally, as a signatory of the Presidents' Climate Commitment, Gonzaga has created a Climate Action Plan to reduce its carbon footprint by 20 percent by 2020 and 50 percent by 2035 (from 2009 levels).

OFF-CAMPUS OPPORTUNITIES

Recognizing the importance of an international perspective for learning, Gonzaga offers study abroad programs in over 35 countries including Argentina, Australia, Austria, Belgium, Bhutan, Cambodia, China, Colombia, Costa Rica, Ecuador, England, France, Ireland, Italy, Japan, Jordan, Mexico, Peru, Scotland (Honors Program students), South Africa, Spain, Tanzania, Turkey, Turks and Caicos, and Zambia. Gonzaga's campus in Florence, Italy is the most popular option.

ACADEMIC PROGRAMS

The core curriculum (an intentionally-designed set of courses bookended by the first-year and final year core integration seminars), encourages students to embrace an interdisciplinary mindset. All students take classes in writing, reasoning, scientific inquiry, mathematics, communication & speech, philosophy, religious studies, and English literature, and they further broaden their education with classes in the arts, humanities, social/behavior sciences, social justice, and global studies designated courses. The College of Arts & Sciences adds a requirement in modern or classical language proficiency that complements the core. Often, classes at Gonzaga require oral presentations or use of the written and discussion-based communication skills emphasized in the core curriculum.

MAJORS AND DEGREES OFFERED

Gonzaga offers the following areas of study in the five undergraduate schools. The College of Arts and Sciences offers art, biochemistry, biology (research), broadcast studies, chemistry, classical civilizations, communication studies, computer science and computational thinking, criminal justice, economics, English (writing concentration), environmental studies, French, history, international studies (including international relations and Asian, European, and Latin American studies), Italian studies, journalism, mathematics, mathematics/computer science, music (including emphases in composition, general studies, and performance), music education, philosophy (Kossel concentration option), physics, political science, psychology, public relations, religious studies (Christian theology and religious pluralism concentrations), sociology, Spanish, and theatre arts (performance and technical concentrations). Additionally, the School offers minors in art history, Catholic studies, conducting, dance, German, Italian, jazz performance, leadership studies, Native American studies, solidarity and social justice, women's & gender studies, and writing. Students interested in the following areas take tracks of classes respectively in pre-dentistry, pre-law, pre-medicine, pre-physical therapy, and pre-veterinary studies. The School of Business Administration offers majors in accounting or business administration (with concentrations in economics, entrepreneurship and innovation, finance, human resource management, individualized study, international business, law and public policy, management information systems, marketing, and operations and supply chain management). As well as granting teacher certification on both the elementary and secondary levels, the School of Education offers degrees in kinesiology and physical education, special education, and sport management. The School of Engineering and Applied Science offers computer science and civil, computer, electrical, and mechanical engineering degrees, as well as an engineering management degree and a 5-year BSEM/MBA option. Also, The School of Nursing and Human Physiology offers human physiology and nursing degrees at the undergraduate level. Advanced degrees in accounting, business, communication and leadership, education, educational leadership, engineering, law, leadership studies, nursing, organizational leadership, philosophy, teaching English as a second language, and theology and leadership are also offered.

TUITION, ROOM, BOARD, FEES

Tuition for the 2018–2019 academic year is $42,370; room and board is estimated at $11,944. Including tuition, room and board, books, fees, transportation, and living expenses, Gonzaga estimates $59,795 as the total cost of attendance for the 2018–2019 year.

FINANCIAL AID

Ninety-nine percent of admitted students earn scholarships and/or grants. The average package for 2017–2018 was $28,951 awarded in the form of grants, scholarships, loans, and campus employment. A number of merit-based, merit/need-based, athletic, music, debate, and other program scholarships are awarded to students each year. The Free Application for Federal Student Aid (FAFSA) is available on October 1, and Gonzaga encourages students to apply as close to October 1 as they can and up to February 1 to be eligible for Gonzaga's Priority Awarding Pool. Also, check the website for scholarship information and online applications. Gonzaga is committed to working with students and families to finance their investment in a quality education.

STUDENT ORGANIZATIONS AND ACTIVITIES

GU students enjoy a wide variety of activities on and off campus. The Gonzaga Student Body Association (GSBA) oversees over one hundred academic, social, and cultural clubs and provides the structure of student government. Some of the most popular clubs include the Outdoors Club, THIRST (a non-denominational worship group), GUTS (an improvisational comedy team), and the Hawaii Pacific Islanders Club. GSBA organizes service and conservation projects, dances, and countless other activities to channel and challenge the talents and passions of motivated men and women who seek to make a difference.

As the leading provider of service hours in the entire city of Spokane, Gonzaga University encourages students to engage with the community at any of the area nonprofit organizations. University Ministry, the Gonzaga Student Body Association, Unity Multicultural Education Center, and the Center for Community Engagement (CCE) provide organized projects through which students become involved in the greater Spokane community and other cities.

Division I, West Coast Conference sports include baseball (men), basketball, crew, cross-country/track, golf, soccer, tennis, and volleyball (women). Approximately 60 percent of students participate in intramural and club sports such as ultimate frisbee and rugby. The Harry & Colleen Magnuson Theatre hosts main-stage plays (including musicals), dance recitals, GUTS, sketch comedy, numerous one-acts and student directed scenes. Gonzaga's musical groups include a nationally recognized University Choir, a Chorale, the GU Symphony, the Jazz Ensemble, the Gonzaga Bulldog Band, The Big Bing Theory-an a cappella group, and numerous other ensembles. GU's students also host programs on Gonzaga's TV and radio stations. Additionally, many students participate in University Ministry events, such as retreats, the annual Pilgrimage hike, THIRST, Masses, Christian Life Communities, and interdenominational and/or interfaith services.

ADMISSION PROCESS

The University seeks diligent, inquisitive applicants with diverse backgrounds who will benefit from the rigorous Jesuit instruction at Gonzaga as well as enhance the University environment. A Common Application (www.commonapp.org) and the Gonzaga member page, SAT I (Essay Section not required) or ACT scores (Writing Section not required), a transcript, a teacher recommendation, a school report, an activities list or resume, and an essay are required. Transfer students and students with any college credit must submit official transcripts from all colleges. Transfer students must also complete the Common Application for Transfers, including the Transfer College Report and Academic Evaluation. International students must also submit official transcripts from all colleges attended. Additionally, international students must submit official results of their TOEFL examination. The Non-binding Early Action application deadline for freshmen is November 15, and decisions are mailed by January 15. The main advantages of the Early Action Program are early communication of admission and financial aid packages. Nursing and Engineering applicants are highly encouraged to apply under Early Action as those programs have direct entry admissions, and the limited spaces available make the majors the most competitive. The Regular Decision application date for freshmen is February 1. Students applying Regular Decision by this date will receive an admission decision by the beginning of April. After February 1, applications will be accepted only if space is available.

For more information on Gonzaga, please see: www.gonzaga.edu.

GRACELAND UNIVERSITY

AT A GLANCE

Founded in 1895 and sponsored by Community of Christ, Graceland University is much more than a school. Graceland is a community of passionate, caring and dedicated individuals who make up a worldwide community network that reaches far beyond the two campuses, located in Lamoni, Iowa, and Independence, Missouri.

Graceland University creates and maintains high academic standards of excellence by prioritizing a close student/faculty learning environment, providing nurturing communities that foster intellectual engagement and curiosity, and embracing the philosophy that learning is not confined to the classroom. Graceland integrates a strong tradition in the liberal arts with targeted professional learning.

LOCATION AND ENVIRONMENT

Situated on 170 acres of southern Iowa's rolling hills, our main campus in Lamoni, is home to just under 1,000 students and provides a beautiful, safe, residential campus where diversity of thought and culture are celebrated.

Graceland University integrates learning inside and outside of the classroom and provides limitless opportunities for involvement in educational service, leadership, and entertainment activities.

Graceland's Independence, Missouri Campus offers online learning opportunities—both graduate and undergraduate—in nursing, religion, and education.

Life at Graceland includes forums and guest speakers on the current issues of the day; community service projects; poetry readings at a downtown coffee house; new opportunities in an active Sustainability group or 40 other club organizations, as well as quiet time in a relaxed, countryside setting.

In 2012, Graceland's Lamoni campus finished construction of the $1.6 million Fitzgerald Fitness Center, a new student wellness center with a group exercise area and a variety of weight and cardio equipment.

Graceland also re-introduced the Shaw Center in the fall of 2012 after the $16 million expansion and renovation project. The Shaw Center features JR Theatre, a state-of-the-art black box facility; Carol Hall, an acoustically perfect recital hall; the Shaw Family Auditorium, with over 500 seating capacity; the outdoor Amphitheatre for spring jazz concerts and more. The Shaw Center is one of the most remarkable performing arts venues in Iowa.

The Resch Science and Technology Hall was dedicated in 2009. It provides state-of-the-art-sciences and math facilities. Nearly everything, including the computer science equipment, is new and industry-standard in Resch Hall. The Helene Center for the Visual Arts (2004) includes 29,000 square feet of classrooms, studios and exhibit space, and a large Mac lab with industry standard programs. It is regarded by artists as "the perfect place to be creative."

Campus computer facilities include three microcomputer labs and industry-standard equipment for desktop publishing and graphic design. Graceland's Internet Cafe provides 24-hour computer and printing access in a cozy atmosphere.

Our Closson Athletic Center boasts an indoor track and field facility with a beautiful hardwood basketball and volleyball court. We have a FieldTurf (an artificial turf football field), a wonderful outdoor track facility with a Rekortan track installed in 2016, and a top soccer complex with a new pitch in 2017 with multiple practice fields. The new Baughman Athletic Center boasts a large wrestling practice room, new locker facilities, and an indoor pitching practice area for the baseball and softball teams.

The Frederick Madison Smith Library uses the latest technologies to provide information services to accommodate student needs. Fully networked computer workstations offer access to the Internet and many research databases, including seven reference databases and more than 45 periodical databases, many providing access to full-text articles. Access to LIBBIE, the library's online catalog, and to the online reference sources, is available to all patrons. Articles and books may be ordered from a worldwide network of research libraries.

OFF-CAMPUS OPPORTUNITIES

Lamoni is a small, friendly town with a big heart. There's an old-fashioned pizza place, a bustling coffee house, and a university-owned movie theatre, called the Coliseum, all just a five-minute walk from campus. It's easy to venture into the Lamoni community. Hike around a beautiful nearby lake or use new, city bike trails by checking out one of the GU Sustainability bicycles available. Popular lakes at Slip Bluff County Park and Nine Eagles State Park offer swimming, boating, fishing, and camping, and both are only a few miles away. There are close bonds between Graceland and the small, but vibrant town of Lamoni, home to 2,500 residents. Des Moines is just a little over an hour north providing all the amenities of a large city.

ACADEMICS

Students learn in an individualized, challenging, yet supportive environment, with a 16:1 student/faculty ratio. Graceland helps students shape a new vision for their lives. It is a transformative education where each student can explore their interests and passions. The Graceland community will help them understand their strengths and values. And along the way, they will discover something invaluable: themselves. The University offers over 40 academic programs. Students will work closely with professors who are both teachers and scholars. Most of Graceland's professors hold a doctorate or the highest degree in their field. The Honors Program, highly acclaimed by participants, is designed for motivated students who want to expand their learning beyond the regular curriculum. The program takes annual cultural trips to Chicago and Minneapolis and gives students the opportunity to present at regional Honors conferences.

Graceland has a nationally competitive Enactus team with nearly 10 percent of all Lamoni campus students participating. Enactus is a worldwide program where students collaborate and compete on entrepreneurial-based projects that help develop the skills needed to become highly capable and socially responsible leaders. Graceland's Enactus team has won regional championships 13 out of the last 14 years. Our 80-strong Enactus team placed first in the U.S. and second in the world (at the competition in Paris) in 2006.

Graceland has a unique and strong sense of community that helps each student to succeed. It is The Power of Together. Graceland graduates go on to stellar careers in the sciences, the arts, nursing, education, business, athletics and human services. The GU alumni network is worldwide, and alumni state that their time at Graceland helped focus their passions and shape their futures. A new mentoring program, GU4U, infused with student energy, pairs successful alumni with current students for career tips, internship opportunities, and guidance.

In addition to traditional programs, Graceland offers many options for distance learners. Programs offered by our renowned School of Nursing include the Bachelor of Arts with a major in Healthcare Management, B.S.N. to R.N., R.N. to B.S.N., R.N. to M.S.N., M.S.N. and the Doctor of Nurse Practitioner program. The Master of Science in Nursing program has two tracks: Family Nurse Practitioner and Adult Gerontology Acute Care Nurse Practitioner. Post graduate Certificates include Family Nurse Practitioner, Nurse Educator, and Adult Gerontology Acute Care Nurse Practitioner. The nationally ranked Gleazer School of Education offers a Master of Education with five different emphases. The Master of Education program is offered online. The Community of Christ Seminary through Graceland offers a Master of Arts in Religion online.

MAJORS AND DEGREES OFFERED

Bachelor's Degrees

Accounting

Agricultural Business

Allied Health

Art: Studio°

Art: Graphic Design

Biology°

Business Administration

Chemistry°

Communications°

Computer Science and Information Technology

Criminal Justice

Economics

Elementary Education

English°

Health and Movement Science:

- Coaching
- Health
- Health Education°
- Physical Education°

Health Care Management

History°

International Studies

Liberal Studies

Mathematics°

Music°

Nursing

Organizational Leadership

Psychology

Social Media Marketing

Sociology:

- Criminology Concentration

Sport Management

Theatre°

Web Design

°Secondary teacher education program offered.

Pre-Professional Programs

Pre-Chiropractic

Pre-Dentistry

Pre-Forensic Science

Pre-Law

Pre-Medicine

Pre-Optometry

Pre-Pharmacy

Pre-Physical Therapy

Pre-Veterinary Medicine

Masters Programs

Master of Arts in Religion

Master of Education

Master of Science in Nursing

Doctorate Program

Doctor of Nursing Practice

TUITION, ROOM, BOARD, FEES

Graceland University has been named a "Best College in the Midwest" by The Princeton Review. We are committed to managing our costs, now and in the future, while maintaining the quality of education we provide every student. Costs for traditional students for the 2016–2017 academic year are listed below. Online program costs vary.

	Annual	Semester
Tuition	$28,600	$14,300
Room	$3,370	$1,685
Board	$5,390	$2,695
Activity Fee	$370	$185
Technology Fee	$270	$135
Total Direct Costs	$38,000	$19,000

FINANCIAL AID

Student Financial Aid is available for those students who qualify. All aid is based upon financial need, academic achievement, and/or meritorious performance. Financial aid is viewed as a supplement to the effort of the family to finance their student's college education. In order to receive federal or state financial aid, students must file a Free Application for Federal Student Aid (FAFSA) each year (add Graceland's code: 001866) and maintain satisfactory academic progress. Institutional Scholarships and Grants may be awarded to full-time students for academics, athletics, performing arts, and for Community of Christ students. When Graceland University receives all documents needed to complete a Financial Aid Package, an award notice will be sent to the student for review. More than 98 percent of Graceland residential students receive some form of financial aid.

STUDENT ORGANIZATIONS AND ACTIVITIES

Graceland sponsors more than 40 student clubs and organizations. GU boasts 20 varsity and numerous junior varsity teams and a variety of performing arts groups including a new drumline. Anyone who wants to play or perform at Graceland has ample opportunity to do so.

The basic residential and social unit of student life is known as a "House." The house system at Graceland on the Lamoni campus is a unique program that started in the 1960s and is based on the principle of inclusion. The importance of each student is recognized. Unlike fraternities and sororities, every student is involved in the house system. Members of each house elect a leadership council that plans social events and represents students in Student Government. By cooperative effort, the house organizes its own social, religious and intramural programs. Each student determines the extent of his/her participation in all house activities. Graceland students love this community approach to residential life with a built-in social system where all students are welcomed and made to feel at home.

Students on the Lamoni Campus hail from more than 48 states and 30 countries. Graceland's International Club is a hub of constant activity. GU is committed to providing an environment that is free of alcohol and tobacco. Graceland cares about spiritual life as well. Whatever faith tradition, GU students' spiritual lives will be nurtured through a wide range of worship experiences, service projects, and religion classes in an environment that is accepting with opportunities to learn and grow.

ADMISSIONS PROCESS

To be considered for acceptance at Graceland, students must meet two of the three following criteria: rank in the upper 50 percent of high school class, have a 2.5 grade point average (based on a 4.0 system) and a minimum composite ACT score of 21, or a minimum combined SAT score of 960. International students also need to score at or above 550 on TOEFL and prove ability to cover expenses while enrolled. Transfer students need a minimum 2.0 GPA on previous college coursework.

GROVE CITY COLLEGE

AT A GLANCE

Grove City College is a leading liberal arts and STEM college that integrates faith and learning in a tight-knit residential community an hour from Pittsburgh, Pennsylvania. Founded in 1876, Grove City College was modeled after the nation's fourth oldest institution of higher education, Princeton University. Thanks to the vision of its founder, Isaac Ketler, and the support of its benefactor and board chairman, Sunoco founder Joseph Newton Pew, Grove City College sought to provide an affordable education of the highest quality rooted in a rich Christian, moral, and ethical tradition with a firm commitment to promoting individual freedom, personal responsibility, and the common good. To this day, the College maintains its foundational purpose, equipping its 2,400 students to pursue their unique callings through an academically excellent and affordable education in a Christ-centered learning and living community.

As one of the nation's most rigorous Christian colleges, Grove City ranks in the top 12 percent of colleges and universities in the nation for alumni earnings, yet its tuition costs less than half that of peer institutions such as Wheaton College, the College of William & Mary, the University of Virginia, the University of Chicago, Emory University, and Williams College. Expense is not spared, however, when it comes to maintaining a dynamic community where students can fully engage on a stunning campus drafted by the venerable Olmsted landscape architecture firm. The Olmsteds designed New York's Central Park and quintessential college campuses such as Yale, Brown, Cornell, American University, Harvard Business School, Notre Dame, Stanford, and Johns Hopkins. Atypical for Christian colleges, Grove City excels in science, engineering, and computer science, with 42 percent of its students in the STEM disciplines.

Because of an institutional emphasis on human flourishing, Grove City students can reach their full potential in a vibrant social scene that is conducive to meeting the college's high academic standards. "As iron sharpens iron" (Proverbs 27:17), Grove City students push each other toward excellence, which is measurably reflected in the college's 96 percent job and graduate school placement rate (from a 98 percent knowledge rate for the Class of 2017 within six months of graduation). The financial future for Grove City graduates is bright, especially considering they typically make 9 percent more than competitor college alumni during their first five years of employment, and 21 percent more ten years after graduation.

Known for its 1984 U.S. Supreme Court case, Grove City College v. Bell, the College provides its students with private scholarships, loans, and need-based assistance while remaining free from federal government entanglement to safeguard freedom of conscience. In addition to operating nearly debt-free, the College practices transparent tuition pricing, abstaining from the common practice of artificial "discounting." As a result, the College does not transfer tuition dollars from some students to others as a recruiting tool. Thus, all students are charged the same price and enjoy equal opportunity to seek financial assistance and manage any remaining debt responsibly. In fact, 41 percent of graduates graduate debt free. Thanks to the College's high four-year graduation and job-placement rates, Grove City students typically repay their loans three years early.

So where does this college committed to the old Princeton ideal of faith-and-learning integration fit into the spectrum of higher education? At the intersection of academic excellence, human flourishing in a Christian context, personal and professional success, and true value—that's Grove City College. We invite you to come and see for yourself. To schedule a visit, click here or call 724.458.2100.

LOCATION AND ENVIRONMENT

Grove City College is located north of Pittsburgh in western Pennsylvania in a classic college town setting. Ranked nationally as the #2 Most Beautiful Christian College campus the picturesque 180-acre campus was designed by the same architects that designed the New York's Central Park and the U.S Capitol grounds. Neo-gothic buildings are set on wide lawns, surrounded by century-old trees. Students enjoy numerous activities in the culturally rich city of Pittsburgh (located one hour south of campus) and the historically significant western Pennsylvania/eastern Ohio region. Parks nearby afford students opportunities for outdoor activities such as white water rafting, hiking, caving, horseback riding, and water sports. The town of Grove City, also nationally ranked as one of the best small towns in America offers students community activities, restaurants, coffee shops, eclectic shopping experiences including premium outlet stores four miles from campus.

CAMPUS FACILITIES & EQUIPMENT

Campus encompasses academic buildings, including the state-of-the-art STEM Hall; 10 residence halls; the Henry Buhl Library; the Physical Learning Center, which features a competition pool, indoor track, basketball arena, fitness rooms, and a bowling alley; Breen Student Union, home to the GeDunk café and campus bookstore; the Pew Fine Arts Center, featuring three theaters, practice rooms, studio space, and an art gallery; a Christian activities building; varsity sports facilities, including Robert E. Thorne Field, soccer, baseball and softball fields, as well as expansive intramural playing fields; a technical learning center that is home to WSAJ studios; and Harbison Chapel, a beautiful neo-gothic cathedral that anchors the campus' central quad.

The College's Information Technology Program (ITP) ensures that each incoming freshman and transfer student is issued a lightweight tablet PC and printer/scanner/copier that provides direct access to campus-wide technology services, all as part of the College's continuing effort to integrate information literacy.

OFF-CAMPUS OPPORTUNITIES

The shops and movie theater of idyllic small-town Grove City, the cultural venues and professional sports teams of the City of Pittsburgh, missions trips throughout the world, international study, the Amish countryside, and exploring the Allegheny River and Moraine State Park are all easily available to Grove City students.

ACADEMIC PROGRAMS

Special programs

The Center for Entrepreneurship & Innovation at Grove City College is making its mark in the business world, fostering the startup ambitions of students through a variety of programs, including the VentureLab business incubator.

The College's Center for Vision & Values promotes faith and freedom in the public square, places students in premier think tanks in Washington, D.C. and state capitols, and holds an annual conference that draws leading thinkers and speakers.

The Trustee Scholar program supports some of the country's best students and future leaders.

Red Box and Inner-City Outreach missions provide students with opportunities to serve here and abroad, exercise leadership and expand their horizons.

CAREER SERVICES AND PLACEMENT

Grove City College's nationally-ranked Career Services Office works with students throughout their college career to help determine and pursue their professional calling. Along the way, students have access to exclusive internships and amazing opportunities through the office, which sponsors hundreds of on-campus job interviews and recruiting visits and coordinates an annual career fair that brings together students and recruiters from manufacturing, business, education, government agencies and ministry organizations. Within six months, 96 percent of Grove City College graduates are at work or continuing their education at the nation's leading graduate schools.

Faculty

Our extraordinary faculty are dedicated to educating hearts and minds. They are Christian scholars who understand their disciplines as deeply and as well as they understand humankind's place in God's creation. They are teachers, mentors and friends to students ready to be challenged and informed. Grove City College is a place where high academic standards produce outstanding outcomes for graduates well-prepared to pursue their life's calling. It's a transformational experience in more ways than you can imagine.

Additional information

Check www.gcc.edu for more on Grove City College, including detailed information on programs and majors, student success, faculty perspectives and the latest news.

MAJORS AND DEGREES OFFERED

Grove City College is dedicated to the liberal arts and sciences. Through courses that form the humanities core, all students are exposed to the leading thinkers, books and ideas in religion, philosophy, history, political science, economics, literature, art and music that represent our common heritage and encompass the wisdom of civilization. The College is known as a top undergraduate engineering and computer science school and one of the few Christian colleges to offer fully-accredited mechanical, electrical and computer engineering courses. Biology, business, education, the liberal arts, and communications studies are among the other strong programs that produce graduates prepared to enter the working world or continue their education at graduate or professional schools.

Accounting and Finance; Accounting; Accounting-Finance 150-hour Dual Major; Finance; Biblical and Religious Studies and Philosophy; Biblical and Religious Studies; Philosophy; Biology; Biology; Biology/Health; Conservation Biology; Molecular Biology; Exercise Science; Management and Marketing; Business Management; Industrial Management; International Business; Marketing Management; Chemistry; Biochemistry; Chemistry; Communication and Visual Arts; Communication Studies; Computer Science; Computer Information Systems; Computer Science; Economics and Sociology; Business/Economics; Economics; Sociology; Education; PreK-4 Elementary Education; PreK-8 Special Education with PreK-4 Elementary Education; Middle Level Math/English Education; Middle Level Math/History Education; Middle Level Science/English Education; Middle Level Science/History Education; Middle Level Science/Math Education; Grades K-12 Certification (Biology/General Science/Environmental, French, Music, Spanish); Grades 7-12 Certification (Biology/General Science, Chemistry, Chemistry/General Science, Englis, English/Communication, History, Mathematics, Physics, Physics/General Science, Social Studies); Electrical Engineering; Electrical Engineering with Computer Engineering Concentration; English; Entrepreneurship; History; Mathematics; Mathematics; Mathematics/ Actuarial Science; Mechanical Engineering; Mechanical Engineering; Modern Languages; French; Spanish; Music; Music; Music/Business; Music Education; Music/Performing Arts; Music/Religion; Neuroscience; Physical Education; Exercise Science; Physics; Physics; Physics/Computer Hardware; Physics/Computer Software; Political Science; Political Science; Psychology and Social Work; Psychology (B.A.); Psychology (B.S.); Neuroscience; Pre-Professional Programs; Pre-Health; Pre-Law

TUITION, ROOM, BOARD, FEES

Understanding how to pay for college shouldn't be difficult. We are confident our bottom line is financially comparable to or less than that of other private liberal arts institutions and even many public universities. Importantly what we do works for our students. Grove City's four-year graduation rate, job placement rate, alumni earnings, and time to pay off student loans is remarkable when compared to most of our competitors.

In fact, that's not just our opinion. Consumers Digest rated us as the #1 "Top Value" private liberal arts college in the nation. This ranking is based not only on the cost of education, but also on the academic achievement of our incoming freshmen and the quality of the education we provide our students throughout their time with us.

Besides affordability, the founders of Grove City College had another guiding principle: a commitment to maintaining our independence as an educational institution. That is why we operate without any federal assistance. Grove City College does not want to be held to the burdensome requirements that come with accepting federal aid. We continue to believe that our commitment to affordability, safeguarding freedom of conscience, and being able to act freely and independently justifies that decision.

Tuition and room and board for a year is less than $28,000 before scholarships and financial aid. That's about half the cost of competitive private colleges and the lowest cost among Pennsylvania's private schools. The College offers no discounts to attract students, since those discounts only result in higher costs for other students. Many students are able to graduate with little or no debt. In fact, 41 percent of the 2017 class graduated debt free.

FINANCIAL AID

For more about financial aid at Grove City College, visit this link.

STUDENT ORGANIZATIONS AND ACTIVITIES

Grove City College attracts students from a national pool, with the 2,400-member student body hailing from 46 states and a dozen foreign countries. Known as "Grovers," they reflect the institution's Christian character and commitment to faith and learning. They are very involved in campus organizations—of which there are more than 150 student-led, intramural sports, service-learning, campus and community service and entrepreneurship, along with their academic pursuits.

ADMISSIONS PROCESS

Average GPA: 3.7 (high school GPA)

Average ACT: 27 composite

Average SAT: 1232 (writing score not factored in)

Essay: Required

Interview: Not required, but strongly recommended

Application deadline: Early Decision I: November 1; Early Decision II: December 1; Regular Decision: January 20

Application fee: $50

Website: www.gcc.edu/futurestudents

HARDIN-SIMMONS UNIVERSITY

Private, Christian, liberal arts university located in Abilene, Texas with more than 85 versatile undergraduate and graduate degree programs.

AT A GLANCE

The founder of Hardin-Simmons University, James B. Simmons, had two questions that he asked himself and believed our students should ask themselves. 1. "What is the greatest thought that has ever occupied your mind? 2. What is your duty towards fulfilling it?" At HSU, we believe that everyone has a God-sized dream within them. The faculty and staff here will help you discover your dream and duty to fulfill it. We are passionate about breaking down barriers to truly change the world!

Hardin-Simmons University is a private, Christian, liberal arts university located in Abilene, Texas. Founded in 1891, HSU offers more than 85 versatile undergraduate and graduate degree programs. As a fully accredited university, we take pride in academic excellence, faith-inspired learning, affordability, family, global potential, and positive student outcomes.

LOCATION AND ENVIRONMENT

HSU embraces the old and the new throughout its growing campus. Familiar red brick buildings and shade-providing pecan trees express the heritage of our university, while groundbreaking ceremonies are becoming a frequent occurrence for new legacies.

Solitude can be found in the beautiful stained-glass chapel in the Logsdon Seminary, joy by befriending Gilbert the beloved campus goose with food, and heritage by taking a stroll through the acclaimed Alumni Circle.

HSU offers an environment where our more than 2,200 students can thrive. At HSU, you experience a culture of Western hospitality and authentic West Texas spirit that is second to none.

CAMPUS FACILITIES & EQUIPMENT

Students are watching the construction of a new fitness center that will house cardio and strength training areas, multi-sport courts, and outdoor training spaces that will give fresh opportunities for wellness and community. In fall 2018, two, new, on-campus apartment buildings will join the current apartment complexes and five residence halls.

We welcomed the new Physician Assistant program to campus during the fall 2017 semester and look forward to expanding our leading Physical Therapy department to a state of the art facility near HSU. Plans are evolving for a new Houston-Lantrip Center for Literacy and Learning that will provide training, research, and other resources for people with dyslexia, autism spectrum disorder, or other language learning difficulties.

Sid Richardson Library provides an array of options for studying, conducting research, or meeting with peers to grab some coffee in the lounge area. Whether you're studying, stocking up on books and HSU gear, grabbing a bite to eat in the dining hall, or taking a break with a game of bowling, our Moody Student Center is a great place to hang out. Behrens Auditorium hosts weekly chapel, graduation, concerts, and theatre performances.

OFF-CAMPUS OPPORTUNITIES

Just a few blocks away from campus is historic downtown Abilene where hip coffee shops, museums, and history can be found. There are endless opportunities to volunteer within the community of Abilene and connect with others.

- The Abilene Country Club
- Abilene Philharmonic Orchestra
- Abilene State Park
- Abilene Zoo and Discovery Center
- Buffalo Gap Historic Village
- Center for Contemporary Arts
- Century Theaters
- Dyess Linear Air Park
- Fort Phantom Hill
- Grace Museum Cultural Center
- Mall of Abilene
- Frontier Texas Museum
- National Center for Children's Illustrated Literature
- The Historic Paramount Theatre

ACADEMIC PROGRAMS

A diploma—most think it's the ultimate goal of attending college. And, they're not wrong. However, a diploma is only a representation of something far more important. A degree tells the world that you achieved knowledge…that you learned what you needed to learn.

Your degree from Hardin-Simmons won't be an empty promise. An HSU diploma will represent a rigorous, useful, and modern academic education, as well as the personal and spiritual development we provide all students. When you become part of the HSU family, we're committed to loving you, embracing you, and, of course, educating you.

When you hang your diploma, you'll know the Hardin-Simmons University seal represents an educational promise kept. And, you'll know you are a part of the HSU family forever.

MAJORS AND DEGREES OFFERED

Colleges & Schools

- College of Fine Arts
- Cynthia Ann Parker College of Liberal Arts
- Holland School of Sciences and Mathematics
- College of Human Sciences and Educational Studies
- Kelley College of Business
- Logsdon School of Theology
- Logsdon Seminary
- Patty Hanks Shelton School of Nursing

Distinctive Programs

- Honors Program
- International Studies (Study Abroad)
- Leadership Studies
- Literacy and Learning

Online Education

As a community of educators dedicated to providing excellence in education, enlightened by Christian faith and values, HSU Online allows the mission of our institution to extend beyond our physical campus to reach the entire world. Whether you are a student at home for the summer or a missionary in residence, our online delivery allows the HSU Difference to influence, educate, and transform.

TUITION, ROOM, BOARD, FEES

(Per Semester)

Full-Time Undergraduate Tuition: $13,645

General Fees: $850

Room: $2,040

Meals (average): $2,000

FINANCIAL AID

Investing in your future is crucial. Our staff are ready and equipped to best help you in your journey of investing in yourself. We take great care in discussing the various options available for your financial situation.

98 percent of students receive financial aid. Learn more at: https://www.hsutx.edu/offices/financial-aid/

Over $16.5 million in scholarships were awarded in the 2017–2018 year. View our net price calculator to estimate your financial aid options:

https://www.hsutx.edu/offices/financial-aid/financial-calculators/

STUDENT ORGANIZATIONS AND ACTIVITIES

With more than 50 student organizations, intramural and club sports, and 18 NCAA Division III men's and women's varsity sports, students can participate in a wide variety of activities. There are many distinctive undergraduate programs offered at HSU such as Honors, Leadership, and Study Abroad. Extracurricular activities give students leadership opportunities and experiences that they can take with them as they graduate from Hardin-Simmons University. The two biggest events at Hardin-Simmons are the campus-wide Christmas party and Gilbert's birthday party. HSU has frequent scheduled activities in the residence halls, Moody Student Center, and on Anderson Lawn.

ADMISSIONS PROCESS

Regular admission will be offered to students submitting:

- A minimum ACT score of 20 or
- A minimum SAT score of 1020 or
- A high school class rank of top 25 percent

Applicants not meeting these requirements may be evaluated on class rank, grade point average, and high school activities, as well as acceptable test scores. The writing portion of the ACT is optional. Conditional admission may be considered for students who do not meet these criteria.

Application Deadline: Rolling

Learn more about our admission process https://www.hsutx.edu/admission/.

HIGH POINT UNIVERSITY

AT A GLANCE

At High Point University, every student receives an extraordinary education in an inspiring environment with caring people. High Point University, founded in 1924, is a private, 4-year comprehensive institution that is rooted in the liberal arts. The environment of excellence transforms high school students into distinguished scholars who are prepared to tackle the challenges of the 21st century and thrive in an ever-changing global marketplace.

What makes High Point University distinctive are carefully crafted, holistic academic plans that merge classroom knowledge and experiences with the necessary life skills to make you competitive within the global marketplace. It begins right away with HPU President Nido Qubein's first-year Seminar on Life Skills and continues in more than 100 different ways throughout every student's four years at HPU.

LOCATION AND ENVIRONMENT

With 5,000 undergraduate students, High Point University is a small liberal arts school with big-school facilities. Its 16 varsity teams play at the NCAA Division I level. Students come to HPU from 50 states and 37 countries, providing the school with great diversity in student history and experience. High Point University offers its students a safe community that feels like home, where the average class size is 17, and professors don't just know students' names—they know who they are and who they want to become.

Nestled within the city of High Point, North Carolina, HPU sits in the center of the Piedmont Triad, North Carolina's largest metropolitan area with more than 1.9 million people. Both Greensboro and Winston-Salem are 20 minutes from campus. East of campus are Raleigh (1.5 hours away) and the Atlantic Ocean (4 hours away); south of campus are Charlotte (1.5 hours away) and Atlanta, GA (5 hours away); and west of campus are the Appalachian Mountains (2 hours away).

CAMPUS FACILITIES & EQUIPMENT

High Point University is committed to providing state-of-the-art facilities across disciplines that meet the needs of an Extraordinary student. Cottrell Hall, home to the Flanagan Center for Student Success, is a 40,000 square-foot facility that is the central hub of activity for students preparing for job interviews, seeking career development opportunities and looking for ways to diversify their career skills.

The state-of-the-art 220,000 square-foot Congdon Hall features a pharmacology research lab, a gross anatomy lab, a human biomechanics and physiology lab and more than a dozen simulation labs and spaces where real-world scenarios can come to life, including an operating room, emergency room, labor and delivery room, eight exam rooms, a pharmacy retail setting and pharmacy hospital setting.

The Nido R. Qubein School of Communication features two high-definition TV studios, audio recording studios, a screening theater, editing labs, a student-operated radio station, a nationally-cited survey and research center, an interactive media and game design facility and various computer labs. The school's Board of Advisers includes leaders in radio, television, newspaper and magazine companies across the nation.

HPU's School of Art and Design emphasizes the importance of hand skills combined with technological proficiency in profession-specific software. Students studying in the School of Art and Design have access to cutting-edge equipment including a technology lab and several design-specific computer labs.

The 31,000 square-foot, LEED-Certified Stout School of Education building houses the psychology department and the NCATE-accredited education school. It is equipped with simulated classrooms and clinical labs where psychology majors conduct hands-on testing and experiments.

The Plato S. Wilson School of Commerce houses the Center for Financial Research, which serves as a trading room and allows students to receive real-world, practical learning opportunities. The Center includes teaching and research technology, including financial databases, investment software, a stock ticker and more.

ACADEMIC PROGRAMS

High Point University has 50 majors and 57 undergraduate minors, 12 pre-professional programs and 13 graduate programs to choose from. Students may choose an area of study they've always been passionate about, a subject that they've recently become interested in or a major that they've never considered before. The opportunities are endless at HPU. Some of the most popular undergraduate majors include Business, Exercise Science, Communications, Education, Biology and Interior Design.

TUITION, ROOM, BOARD, FEES

For the 2018–19 academic year, High Point University's tuition and fees (including tuition, parking, laundry, entrance to athletic and cultural events, intramurals, Campus Concierge service, academic tutoring, library and media services, etc.) for full-time students is $35,118; room and board are $14,130.

FINANCIAL AID

The Office of Student Financial Planning works diligently to assist students in their pursuit of postsecondary education at High Point University. Although the financial aid process can be complex, HPU's Financial Planning staff are well trained and highly qualified to make students' experiences positive and rewarding.

Interested students should submit the Free Application for Federal Student Aid (FAFSA) electronically via www.fafsa.ed.gov. The earliest that students may begin filing the FAFSA is October 1 of the senior year prior to entrance to HPU. The HPU school code is 002933.

The results from filing the FAFSA will be electronically transmitted to HPU for review. This form will produce an expected family contribution based on the family's financial data and will determine students' eligibility for HPU's need-based programs.

HPU will not be able to estimate students' eligibility for need-based aid until the FAFSA is filed. While there is not a deadline date to the FAFSA, it is important to file as early as possible; HPU disperses financial aid package information for students by March 1.

All major High Point University academic scholarships are awarded through the Presidential and High Point Scholars programs. Each Early Decision or Early Action undergraduate admissions application also serves as an application for these scholarships.

STUDENT ORGANIZATIONS AND ACTIVITIES

High Point University's entire campus inspires students to perform at their highest levels both academically and socially. There are numerous opportunities for students to be involved, learn and grow, reinforcing HPU's call to action: Choose to Be Extraordinary! ®

HPU's Kester International Promenade is adorned with flags supporting the school's diversity, with students from 50 states and 37 countries. The residential communities are as diverse as the student population and even provide opportunities for honors housing and living and learning communities. All housing is new or recently renovated, with many dorms boasting high-end apartment-style living.

The campus is completely wireless, and students are able to check out complimentary iPads, Kindles or GPS units from the Campus Concierge. Students may also schedule academic tutoring, reserve a bicycle, and receive complimentary tickets to all athletic events, concerts, speakers and films.

HPU is committed to surrounding students with an environment that motivates and inspires learning. The university regularly hosts internationally acclaimed thought leaders who interact with the student body, helping students to discover their own path to personal growth and leadership. These leaders include people like Former U.S. Secretary of State, Condoleezza Rice; Broadcast News Legend and Best-selling author, Tom Brokaw; Apple Co-Founder and HPU's first Innovator-in-Residence, Steve Wozniak; and Former First Lady Laura Bush.

Opportunities for student fellowship run abound at High Point University. With 80 percent of students coming from out-of-state and 93 percent living on-campus, the student body has a distinct sense of family. From the Extraordinaire Cinema, the Arcade, the 14 dining locations (including a five-star fine-dining restaurant, Starbucks, and Jamba Juice), to the outdoor fire pits, pools, and group exercise classes, students have access to all that they need and more!

ADMISSIONS PROCESS

High Point University is an exclusive member of the Common Application. We are confident in the Common App and believe that our membership will help facilitate the application process for you. The Office of Undergraduate Admissions is here to help you throughout the entire application and decision process. If you have any questions about our university or application, we encourage you to reach out to us.

Complete and submit your application for admission and all required supporting documents online at http://www.commonapp.org/school/high-point-university.

Ask your guidance or college counselor to send your official high school transcript to the Office of Undergraduate Admissions or upload to the Common App.

Ask your guidance or college counselor to complete and submit the Common App's School Report Form.

Provide one letter of recommendation.

High Point University is test optional. If you would like to be considered for our Presidential Scholarship Program or Honors Scholar Program, an SAT or ACT score is required. Request that the official results of the SAT or ACT be sent to the Office of Undergraduate Admissions. High Point University's SAT code is 5293; the ACT code is 3108.

Application deadlines are as follows:

Early Decision (binding) application deadline: November 1

Admissions notification date: November 28

Early Action (nonbinding) application deadline: November 15

Admissions notification date: December 15

Early Decision II (binding) application deadline: February 1

Admissions notification is rolling

Regular Decision application deadline: March 15

Admissions notification is rolling past February 1

Over 85 percent of enrolled students each year apply using one of the two early November application plans.

HILLSDALE COLLEGE

AT A GLANCE

Convinced that it is the best preparation for meeting the challenges of modern life, Hillsdale offers a traditional, classically based, liberal arts education with teaching faculty and a strong core curriculum.

Hillsdale College is a private, independent, nonsectarian Christian institution of higher learning founded in 1844 by men and women who described themselves as "grateful to God for the inestimable blessings" resulting from civil and religious liberty and as "believing that the diffusion of learning is essential to the perpetuity of those blessings." The College has maintained institutional independence since its founding by refusing to accept aid from or control by federal authorities. Far-reaching private support from a national constituency has enabled Hillsdale to continue its trusteeship of the intellectual and spiritual inheritance tracing to Athens and Jerusalem. The undergraduate enrollment for Fall 2017 was 1,463, 51 percent men and 49 percent women, from 49 states, the District of Columbia, and 14 foreign countries. Approximately 34 percent of students are from Michigan. The entering freshman class in Fall 2017 had an average GPA of 3.87, ACT of 30, and SAT of 1347. All Hillsdale students sign an Honor Code challenging self-government and committing them to honesty, duty, and respect. Students are housed in dormitories, fraternity and sorority houses, and various off-campus dwellings. Single and double rooms are available on campus; there are no coed dormitories. Each College-owned residence hall is supervised by a resident director and resident advisers. All freshmen (except commuters) are required to live on campus; upperclass students seeking to live off campus must apply to the dean of men or dean of women for this privilege. Special student services provided by the College include career planning and placement counseling, academic advising and tutoring, and a health service staffed by a physician, a resident nurse, and counselors.

LOCATION AND ENVIRONMENT

Hillsdale College is located amidst the hills, dales, and lakes of south-central Michigan. The Indiana and Ohio turnpikes are each 30 minutes away, and the College is within close reach of such metropolitan areas as Detroit, Chicago, Cleveland, Toledo, Ft. Wayne, and Indianapolis. The town of Hillsdale is a county seat with a population of 10,000. Stores, churches, restaurants, and coffee shops are all within walking distance of the campus, and a movie theater within a 5-minute drive.

CAMPUS FACILITIES & EQUIPMENT

The Hillsdale College Mossey Library is a three-floor facility with a collection of more than 2,000,000 volumes. In addition to the main study and research collections, the library also contains a number of rare and special holdings, including the Ludwig von Mises, Russell Kirk, Richardson Heritage, and Richard Weaver collections. Connected to other Michigan libraries through MelCat, and with college libraries nationwide via interlibrary loan, students have access to almost any material necessary for on-campus research. Numerous individual study areas and group study rooms are available for students, as well as computer research terminals. Lane and Kendall Halls at the front of campus serve as the primary academic facilities in the humanities and social sciences and contain classroom space and faculty offices, as well as a special laboratory for experimental psychology. The Strosacker Science Center houses the departments of biology, chemistry, and physics. The Joseph H. Moss Family Laboratory Wing is a 17,000-square-foot addition that includes a microbiology/cell biology lab, anatomy/physiology lab with human cadaver access, conservation genetics lab, water lab, greenhouse, and organic/general chemistry labs. The 32,000-square-foot Herbert Henry Dow Science Building provides additional classrooms, research laboratories, animal rooms, and a computer lab. Slayton Arboretum is a 48-acre campus garden and bird sanctuary used by students to practice field exercises and conduct research. The Mary Randall Preschool is a circular laboratory school in which nursery school children are taught by students specializing in early childhood education and psychology. Experts in the field have called this building "a model for the nation." The Hillsdale Academy, a K–12 private model school, provides additional opportunities for classroom observation. The Roche Sports Complex is a facility available to varsity athletes and the general student body alike. The building houses the 60,000-square-foot Dawn Tibbetts Potter Arena, which features a student fitness center and basketball/volleyball courts. The building also houses the John "Jack" McAvoy Natatorium for swimming and diving, an exercise physiology and sports medicine facility, four racquetball courts,

extensive locker room space, and a weight/fitness room. Adjacent is the 7,000-seat capacity Frank "Muddy" Waters Stadium, which features an artificial surface football field; all-weather, Olympic-quality eight-lane running track; outdoor tennis courts; and fields for soccer, baseball, and women's softball. Located northwest of the Roche Sports Complex, the 76,000-square-foot Margot V. Biermann Athletic Center houses four acrylic tennis courts and a six-lane, 200-meter NCAA regulation Mondo surface track. The Sage Center for the Arts is home to the departments of art and theatre. This 47,000-square-foot facility contains studios, classroom space, an exhibition gallery, a prop and scene-construction shop, a sound studio, graphics lab, black box theatre, and the Markel Auditorium, a 353-seat performance hall (with orchestra pit). The 32,809-square-foot Howard Music Hall houses office, studio, classroom, rehearsal, and performance space for the John E. N. and Dede Howard Department of Music. Notable features include the McNamara Rehearsal Hall, Conrad Recital Hall, and studio space for percussion and jazz studies. Lower-level practice rooms are available to students during business hours without reservation. The 53,000-square-foot Grewcock Student Union is the center of student life. The two-story structure houses the cafeteria, bookstore, student mail center, offices for student activities and publications, a lounge with a 100-inch flat screen television, a formal lounge and conference room, AJ's Café, and a game area. Hayden Park sits at the northeastern perimeter of campus and encompasses 190 acres of rolling, partially wooded farmland. In addition to serving as a course for Hillsdale's cross-country teams, it provides a place for club and intramural sports, mountain biking, cross-country skiing, and general outdoor recreation. The 27,000-square-foot Christ Chapel is currently under construction and will be a center for spiritual life on campus and serve as a symbol of Hillsdale's Christian roots and identity.

OFF-CAMPUS OPPORTUNITIES

For forty years, the Washington Hillsdale Internship Program (WHIP) has provided students the opportunity to participate in full-time, academically intensive internships in the nation's capital. The program has been significantly bolstered with the 2008 establishment of the Hillsdale College Allan P. Kirby, Jr. Center for Constitutional Studies and Citizenship in Washington, D.C. Past interns and fellows have been placed in locations as challenging and rewarding as the U.S. House of Representatives, the U.S. Senate, the White House, various think tanks including the Heritage Foundation, news and media outlets, national security agencies, lobbying firms, international trade and relations organizations, and private sector companies. Through the College's affiliations with the Center for Medieval and Renaissance Studies and the Oxford Study Abroad Program, Hillsdale students are able to study abroad for a summer or a year at one of the more than thirty colleges of Oxford University. Hillsdale offers a summer business program in cooperation with Regent's College in London, England, and the opportunity to study at the University of St. Andrews in St. Andrews, Scotland. Science students benefit from Hillsdale's 685-acre field research laboratory in northern Michigan, as well as from a marine biology program in the Florida Keys, and internship opportunities with the Omaha Zoo. Foreign language students frequently study abroad in Argentina, France, Germany, and Spain. Qualified individual students who wish to study in another country for a semester or a year are assisted by their faculty adviser and the registrar in planning a program that enables them to gain academic credit as well as take full advantage of their experience.

ACADEMICS

Hillsdale operates on a two-semester schedule, with the fall term beginning in late August and ending in mid-December and the spring term beginning in mid-January and ending in mid-May. Two 3-week summer sessions are also offered. The College believes that a sound classical liberal arts education includes study in the humanities, natural sciences, and social sciences, and each student is required to complete a structured core of courses in these areas. Required courses include the Western and American Heritage, U.S. Constitution, Great Books in the Western and British/American Traditions, Classical Logic and Rhetoric, Western Philosophical Tradition, and Western Theological Tradition. All students declare a major by the end of the junior year. To graduate, students must complete a minimum 124 hours of course work and fulfill the requirements of at least one major field. The B.A. program includes a foreign language proficiency requirement. The B.S. program requires additional studies in mathematics and the natural sciences. The Collegiate Scholars Program enriches the academic experience of high-performing students by providing opportunities to become broadly and deeply versed in the contents and methods of inquiry of the liberal arts, preeminently of the Western intellectual tradition of humanistic and scientific learning in a manner consonant with the aims of the College's Core Curriculum. A combination of special seminars, campus lectures and discussions, retreats, subsidized foreign travel to a destination relevant to the Program's purpose, and the completion of an interdisciplinary senior thesis help to meet this goal. The Center for Constructive Alternatives conducts four weeklong symposia during the academic year and is one of the largest college lecture series in America. These programs, with themes ranging from historical to political, business, science, and the arts, bring to the campus distinguished scholars and public figures of national and international renown. All students are required to enroll in one seminar for credit.

MAJORS AND DEGREES OFFERED

Hillsdale awards Bachelor of Arts and Bachelor of Science degrees in accounting, applied mathematics, art, biochemistry, biology, chemistry, classics, economics, English, exercise science, financial management, French, German, Greek, history, Latin, marketing/management, mathematics, music, philosophy, philosophy and religion, physical education, physics, politics, psychology, religion, rhetoric, Spanish, sport management, sport psychology, and theatre. Interdisciplinary majors are also available in American studies, Christian studies, comparative literature, European studies, international studies in business and foreign language, political economy, and sociology and social thought. Pre-professional programs are offered in allied health sciences, chiropractic, dentistry, education, engineering, environmental sciences, journalism, law, medicine, ministry, optometry, pharmacy, physical therapy, and veterinary medicine. The Van Andel Graduate School of Statesmanship offers the Doctor of Philosophy in politics and the Master of Arts in politics.

TUITION, ROOM, BOARD, FEES

Annual tuition for the 2017–18 academic year was $25,540, room was $5,240, board was $5,370, and general fees were $1,202. Books, supplies, and personal expenses (including travel, recreation, and clothing) are estimated at $3,200 per year.

FINANCIAL AID

Financial aid at Hillsdale is available in many forms. Academic scholarships are awarded on a competitive basis, regardless of financial need. The priority application deadline for academic scholarship consideration is January 1. The application for admission also serves as the Hillsdale application for merit-based aid. Athletic scholarships are available on a competitive basis in men's baseball, football, and golf; men's and women's basketball, tennis, track, and cross-country; and women's swimming, softball, and volleyball. The departments of art and music also award a select number of scholarships based on strength of portfolio/audition. To apply for aid on the basis of financial need, students are required to file Hillsdale's Confidential Family Financial Statement (CFFS). Because Hillsdale does not accept government funds either directly for its operations or indirectly in the form of student aid, the FAFSA is not applicable; government funds are replaced with private dollars. Grants and loans are available from the College.

STUDENT ORGANIZATIONS AND ACTIVITIES

Four national fraternities, three national sororities, a newspaper and radio station, and more than 100 other social, academic, spiritual, and service organizations provide Hillsdale students with a diverse array of cocurricular opportunities. A resident drama troupe and dance company, a concert choir and chamber chorale, a jazz program with big band and combos, instrumental chamber ensembles from string quartets to percussion ensemble, and a symphony orchestra and band constitute the College's performing arts organizations. Hillsdale's Charger athletes compete in 14 intercollegiate NCAA Division II varsity sports as part of the Great Midwest Athletic Conference (GMAC). An active intramural program is also available. The Student Activities Board hosts campus-wide social functions throughout the year, including marquee events like Garden Party, Homecoming, President's Ball, and Centralhallapalooza.

ADMISSIONS PROCESS

Admission is a privilege extended to students who will benefit from, and contribute to, the academic, social, and spiritual environments of the College. Important determinants for admission are intellectual curiosity, ambition, leadership, and volunteerism. Accordingly, grade-point average, test scores, class rank, strength of curriculum, extracurricular activities, interviews, self-evaluations, writing samples in the form of two essays, and recommendations are all reviewed carefully and are important in the evaluation process. An admissions interview is strongly encouraged. A formal application includes a completed application form accompanied by a nonrefundable fee of $35 (free if submitted online) and all required credentials. Transfer students must submit the standard application, including the high school record, SAT or ACT scores, transcripts from all colleges previously attended, and a transfer form from the dean of students of the most recent college attended. Applications by transfers are evaluated similarly to non-transfers. Candidates for admission from other countries follow the regular entrance procedures. Students who come from a non-English-speaking country must complete the ACT or SAT to demonstrate proficiency in English as well as academic preparedness. The Test of English as a Foreign Language (TOEFL) or the Michigan Test of English Proficiency are recommended to help further demonstrate English proficiency. Students may apply to Hillsdale College any time after the completion of the junior year of high school. Hillsdale accepts The Common Application. Students may apply under one of three plans. Early Decision is a binding application deadline, where students are asked to withdraw applications from other institutions should their application be accepted by Hillsdale. The due date for Early Decision candidates is November 1. The deadline for Regular Decision is April 1, and students are notified of a decision within four weeks of finalizing their application (beginning December 15). Spring Admission candidates should submit application materials by December 1 and will receive notification in mid-December. Students wishing to be considered for priority scholarship should apply no later than January 1. Hillsdale College has been distinguished since its founding in 1844 by voluntarily adhering to a nondiscriminatory policy regarding race, religion, sex, and national or ethnic origin—long before the government began regulating such matters.

HOFSTRA UNIVERSITY

AT A GLANCE

Hofstra University is a diverse, dynamic community where you can pursue your passions, with a greater purpose. Our classes are small, and our programs are tailored to empower students to seek, shape, and discover their own educational and career path.

Live, work, and play on a suburban campus with landscaped quads and ivy-covered buildings that's less than an hour by train from New York City, with its countless cultural, recreational, and internship opportunities.

Build leadership skills through varied clubs, organizations, and service projects. Our students log 100,000 volunteer hours every year, and Hofstra has been recognized by the President's Higher Education Community Service Honor Roll for seven consecutive years.

Hofstra University is internationally recognized by U.S. News & World Report, The Princeton Review, and PayScale College ROI and Salary Reports. We are the only university to host three consecutive U.S. presidential debates (2008, 2012, and 2016), and one of only three universities in the New York metropolitan area with schools of engineering, medicine, and law.

Our more than 11,000 students come from 50 states and territories and 82 countries, but they share an entrepreneurial spirit, a curiosity about the world, and a desire to make a difference. At Hofstra, you will be challenged, you will be supported, you will discover your best self.

You will be a world changer.

LOCATION AND ENVIRONMENT

Hofstra is a global community just 25 miles east of Manhattan. Our 244-acre campus is a nationally registered arboretum with 75 outdoor sculptures that blooms with thousands of tulips every spring.

Students can choose to live in one of our 35 residence halls, each with a unique flair, community, and life of its own. We also offer 10 living-learning communities, in which students live with classmates in the same programs, or who share the same passion for leadership, health professions, or the arts.

CAMPUS FACILITIES AND EQUIPMENT

Connect with the real world through experiential learning in our cutting-edge facilities, including the Martin B. Greenberg Trading Room; WRHU-88.7 FM, Radio Hofstra University; a big data lab; a robotics and advanced manufacturing lab; and a cell and tissue engineering lab. Hofstra also boasts six theaters, as well as the most historically accurate replica of Shakespeare's original Globe stage in the U.S., which is used for the University's annual Shakespeare Festival.

The David S. Mack Sports and Exhibition Complex is a 5,023-seat arena that is home to the Hofstra Pride men's wrestling team and the men's and women's basketball teams.

Our nationally accredited museum has a permanent collection of more than 5,000 works of art.

OFF-CAMPUS OPPORTUNITIES

Hofstra extends learning beyond the classroom through internship programs, a Co-op program, and study abroad opportunities. Our internship programs capitalize on the University's proximity to New York City, allowing students to gain on-the-job experience in areas such as advertising, business, entertainment, finance, and media. The Co-op program at the Fred DeMatteis School of Engineering and Applied Science offers students paid work experience in a field related to their major.

Study abroad programs are offered in Europe, Asia, South America, and more. Students can explore the world while enhancing their college experience and earning course credits. Learn more at hofstra.edu/studyabroad.

ACADEMICS

Learn the art of filmmaking from an Emmy Award-winning director. Discuss economic policy with top business leaders and former Cabinet members. Debate political strategy with a former presidential candidate. Participate in faculty research projects sponsored by the National Science Foundation. Our professors are scholars, artists, and scientists who are passionate about their work and dedicated to teaching and training the next generation of leaders.

With an average undergraduate class size of 20 and a student-faculty ratio of 13-to-1, students are encouraged to debate, question, and think critically in an open, collaborative learning environment. Ninety-one percent of our full-time faculty hold the highest degree in their respective fields.

Requirements for graduation vary among schools and majors. A liberal arts core curriculum is integral to all areas of concentration. Hofstra's academic calendar is organized in a traditional fall and spring semester system, and offers an optional January session and three optional summer sessions (between May and August).

Hofstra offers innovative programs to meet the needs of its diverse student body. These include Hofstra University Honors College, Legal Education Accelerated Program (LEAP), Hofstra 4+4 Program (a highly selective BA-BS/MD program), and First-Year Connections.

Hofstra University Honors College students can study in any of the University's undergraduate programs and are involved in all fields of advanced study.

MAJORS AND DEGREES OFFERED

Hofstra holds 27 academic and 30 total accreditations. The University offers six undergraduate degrees—BA, BBA, BE, BFA, BS, and BSEd—and approximately 160 undergraduate program options. Hofstra also offers more than 100 dual-degree programs, which allow students to earn both an undergraduate and graduate degree in less time, and at lower cost, than if each degree was pursued separately.

The University comprises the following schools: Hofstra College of Liberal Arts and Sciences (Peter S. Kalikow School of Government, Public Policy and International Affairs; School of Education; School of Humanities, Fine and Performing Arts; School of Natural Sciences and Mathematics); Hofstra University Honors College; Frank G. Zarb School of Business; The Lawrence Herbert School of Communication; Fred DeMatteis School of Engineering and Applied Science; Academic Health Sciences Center (Donald and Barbara Zucker School of Medicine at Hofstra/Northwell; Hofstra Northwell School of Graduate Nursing and Physician Assistant Studies; School of Health Professions and Human Services); and Maurice A. Deane School of Law.

TUITION, ROOM, BOARD, AND FEES

The 2017–2018 annual tuition and fees for a full-time undergraduate student were $43,960. The cost of a housing and dining plan was approximately $14,930. Visit hofstra.edu/tuition for the full tuition and fees schedule.

FINANCIAL AID

Hofstra University works hard to make a private college education affordable for students and families, and offers several financial aid options for new undergraduates, including interest-free payment plans and a money-saving four-year locked-in rate for tuition and fees (hofstra.edu/lockedintuitionrate) to help students manage costs from admission through graduation. For details, students should visit hofstra.edu/financialaid.

STUDENT ORGANIZATIONS AND ACTIVITIES

Hofstra is home to 33 local/national fraternities and sororities, and more than 270 academic, media, multicultural, performance, pre-professional, religious, social/political, and sports clubs and organizations. Hofstra also offers 17 intercollegiate athletic programs competing at the NCAA Division I level.

The Student Government Association (SGA) is Hofstra's student-run governing body. Composed of full-time undergraduate students, the SGA is a liaison between students and the University's faculty, administration, and Board of Trustees. The SGA plans and executes multiple programs and initiatives throughout the academic year, and oversees the finances of over 180 clubs and organizations.

ADMISSION PROCESS

Hofstra University seeks to enroll students from diverse backgrounds and geographic locations, with varied interests. Applications are accepted for fall and spring admission. The Admission Committee reviews each application individually to assess academic achievement, curricular rigor, leadership potential, depth of extracurricular activities, standardized test scores, and overall interest in attending Hofstra. The application process provides an opportunity for the prospective student to share information that may not be apparent on a transcript or through a test score. Go to hofstra.edu/admission for information about the admission process, or go to hofstra.edu/visit to schedule a campus visit today!

JOHNS HOPKINS UNIVERSITY

AT A GLANCE

As America's first research institution, Johns Hopkins University has been tackling difficult questions and providing innovative solutions since 1876. Faculty and students work side-by-side in the pursuit of discovery, continuing the university's founding mission to bring knowledge to the world.

From day one, undergrads are given the freedom to chart their own academic paths and are encouraged to explore their interests both in and outside the classroom. Students across all majors learn how to think critically, analyze problems from different angles, and view the world from a wider lens. This prepares them to innovate in any subject they pursue and make new connections across disciplines. Collaboration—with peers, mentors, and professors—is built into the academic culture at Hopkins and the campus is designed to foster work across academic boundaries. Students get to know their professors and classmates the way they would at a small liberal arts college but have all of the opportunities of a major research institution with a global reach.

Living and learning at Hopkins is multi-dimensional. The Homewood campus brings together scholars with diverse interests and cultivates a dynamic, open-minded environment. Students are engaged beyond academics as leaders, creators, and performers. With over 300 student-run organizations, from fraternities and sororities to performing arts, they find opportunities to get involved on campus and beyond.

The university looks for students who will contribute to the campus community while taking advantage of all Johns Hopkins has to offer.

LOCATION AND ENVIRONMENT

The undergraduate Homewood campus has it all—green quads, brick pathways, and "The Beach," a grassy expanse used for sunbathing, studying, and socializing. Every week offers lectures, concerts, art and photography exhibitions, theater shows, film screenings, volunteer opportunities, and more. And just outside the campus gate waits the bustling, energetic city of Baltimore, Maryland. A short walk or a free shuttle ride leads to museums, concert halls, shops, historic movie-theaters, restaurants, and professional sports stadiums. With a traditional campus and big city amenities, it's where Johns Hopkins students live, research, learn, and play.

CAMPUS FACILITIES & EQUIPMENT

The Rare Books Collection, laboratory for Computational Sensing and Robotics, and other state-of-the-art resources on the Homewood campus allow undergraduates to follow their interests beyond papers and projects to make meaningful contributions across disciplines. From labs to libraries to film centers, groundbreaking discoveries happen everywhere at Hopkins.

Collaborative learning is fundamental to the academic environment and many buildings were designed to foster collaboration across disciplines. The Brody Learning Commons (BLC) is one of the most popular places for students to gather, study, and work together. Designed with student input, the building contains the latest learning technology to support collaborative work—like interactive projectors that allow students to write on walls and video teleconferencing capabilities. It's also directly connected to the Milton S. Eisenhower Library, part of the university's Sheridan Libraries, which provide one of the most comprehensive learning resources in the world.

The Undergraduate Teaching Labs (UTL) is a 105,000-square-foot facility equipped with the latest lab technology that enables synergistic, cross-disciplinary partnerships and research opportunities. Two on-campus creative centers provide resources for students in the arts: The Mattin Student Arts Center contains theaters, a dance studio, music practice rooms, film and digital labs, darkrooms, and art studios; the Brown Foundation Digital Media Center offers digital tools like high-end computers and cameras that enable digital and audio composition and editing, animation, virtual painting, and 3-D modeling and workshops for programs like Adobe After Effects. Off campus, just a short shuttle ride away, the Johns Hopkins-MICA Film Centre gives students access to professional-grade production facilities.

The Ralph S. O'Connor Recreation Center houses basketball and volleyball courts, a rock-climbing wall, a weight room, and fitness training and aerobics areas, as well as access to the Athletic Center's swimming facilities. Popular fitness classes include yoga, Pilates, kickboxing, step aerobics, spinning, and sports conditioning.

OFF-CAMPUS OPPORTUNITIES

Baltimore is a vibrant city—an entrepreneurial hub with a rapidly growing technology sector and dynamic arts scene. Students enjoy the fast-paced yet accessible nature of a city like Baltimore, which gives them access to coveted internships and careers. It's the perfect environment for real-world experiences like building professional networks or getting startups off the ground. It's an incubator for scientists, clinicians, artists, legal experts, venture capitalists, philanthropists—and students who want to change the world.

ACADEMICS

With over 50 majors, nearly 50 minors, and a unique interdisciplinary approach, thousands of different academic paths exist at Hopkins. The academic philosophy combines research with a liberal arts focus that offers students the freedom to create their own tracks—which is why over 60 percent of students have a double major or major and minor, and often find unique parallels between fields. This creates an undergraduate experience that teaches you how to think, create, and succeed, whatever your academic interests. Practical, hands-on learning adds depth to any course of study, making Hopkins students uniquely equipped for life after graduation. They're working with real companies to solve actual problems, testing their hypotheses out in the field, and working alongside professors to put what they learn in the classroom to the test.

Almost 75 percent of students across all disciplines participate in research, which takes place in labs, museums, and unconventional places throughout campus and the city of Baltimore. Several funded programs, such as the Provost's Undergraduate Research Awards and the Woodrow Wilson Undergraduate Research Fellowship, are available to give participants the chance to complete projects of their own design. Students also encounter real-world experiences—like implementing marketing plans for local companies and heading startup businesses on campus—through the Center for Leadership Education, which houses the popular entrepreneurship and management minor. Students can pursue their creative interests through the Center for Visual Arts, which offers an array of programs and almost 40 studio courses.

Several combined programs are available for undergraduates looking to broaden their educational experience. The Peabody Double Degree Program allows qualified students to simultaneously earn a Bachelor of Music from The Johns Hopkins Peabody Institute and a B.A or B.S. from Johns Hopkins University. The Direct Matriculation Program: Master's in International Studies allows qualified students displaying a strong interest in international studies to pursue a combined bachelor's/master's degree with the Johns Hopkins School of Advanced International Studies (SAIS) in Washington, DC. Similarly, the Direct Matriculation Program: Master's in Global Health Studies offers qualified students displaying a strong interest in public health to pursue a combined bachelor's/master's degree with the Johns Hopkins Bloomberg School of Public Health.

Hopkins students also have access to other facilities, classes, labs, and the endless opportunities provided by the university's many divisions and affiliates. Johns Hopkins has schools, centers, and affiliates all over the Baltimore area—and they are often linked by free shuttle bus—in Washington, D.C., across the country, and around the world. The larger Hopkins network offers opportunities for cross registration, independent projects, and internships.

MAJORS AND DEGREES OFFERED

Students define their own academic direction at Hopkins, often combining multiple majors, minors, and programs. They're active learners who pursue their interests across academic boundaries, discovering new ways to combine their passions as they find their own paths forward. The international studies major is one example of Hopkins' interdisciplinary curriculum that connects diversity of thought in the fields of political science, history, economics, anthropology, sociology, and languages. Students interested in pursuing law or medicine choose any major and minor—from philosophy to physics—but follow a pre-law or pre-med advising track offered through the Office of Pre-Professional Advising. The biomedical engineering (BME) program at Johns Hopkins is widely regarded as one of the best in the world.

TUITION, ROOM, BOARD, FEES

Costs for 2017–2018 are $52,170 for tuition and $15,410 for room and board, plus personal expenses like book and travel. (Expenses such as travel and room and board vary based on choices.)

FINANCIAL AID

Johns Hopkins is dedicated to enrolling the strongest students each year regardless of financial need and does so by offering a variety of financial support programs for all types of families as well as personalized guidance through the process of finding the right path for them. The university will meet 100 percent of calculated need and also offers a broad range of grants and support. Last year, students received over $100 million in Hopkins grant money towards their education, with an average need-based grant for first-year students of over $42,000.

STUDENT ORGANIZATIONS AND ACTIVITIES

Homewood is an active, engaged campus. All Johns Hopkins student groups are governed and managed by students, and there is something for everybody with organizations dedicated to theater and performing arts, politics, investments, service work, publications, student government, and even fire juggling. Athletics fuel school spirit, often found in full force at the Nest, a student seating section of Homewood Field. One out of six Johns Hopkins students participates in one of twenty Division III teams or club athletics, and more than half participate in the popular intramural program.

With the main undergraduate campus located in Baltimore, Johns Hopkins is dedicated to community engagement. Whether it's through the more than fifty volunteer student groups housed in the Center for Social Concern, each of which focuses on direct service to the city, or independent projects, research, or startups, Hopkins students put their unique skills to use while strengthening the city they call home.

ADMISSIONS PROCESS

The admissions committee conducts a well-rounded review of every applicant based on their accomplishments, goals, and potential impact within the Hopkins community. In addition to considering a student's academic achievement and intellectual curiosity, the university seeks students who are eager to contribute to the academic and campus community at Johns Hopkins. Academic character and extracurricular involvement also play a significant role in application review.

A student's intellectual interests and accomplishments are of primary importance, and the admissions committee considers each applicant's scholastic record, standardized test results, essays, and recommendations from secondary school officials. In addition to the application and the Hopkins supplemental essay, other required documents include: Two teacher recommendations, secondary school report, and the SAT Reasoning Test or the ACT. The university enrolls a first-year class of approximately 1,300 men and women from across the globe. In addition, transfer students from other colleges and universities are admitted to the sophomore and junior classes.

KETTERING UNIVERSITY

AT A GLANCE

Kettering University is a national leader in experiential STEM education, integrating an intense academic curriculum in science, technology, engineering, mathematics and business with applied professional and experiential learning opportunities. Through this proven approach, Kettering University inspires students to realize their potential and advance bold ideas.

During study terms, students learn in small classes taught by professors, not teaching assistants. During work terms, they gain professional experience at corporations related to their studies or in intensive full-time research experiences in labs alongside faculty. Students in all degree programs alternate between study terms and work terms throughout their undergraduate education.

Kettering students graduate with up to 2.5 years of real world experience and envy-worthy resumes—giving them a significant head start in their careers. Our students have worked on world-changing technologies ranging from the future of mobility and transportation technologies to designing biomedical tools, testing ballistic systems, re-engineering crowd management and designing rides at Disney World. Kettering University is one of the top universities in the nation at producing patent holders—Kettering produces more inventors per graduate than all but three universities in the U.S., ranking higher than Stanford University and Carnegie Melon University.

Research shows that students who participate in co-op and experiential learning programs are more mature, more creative problem solvers and more technically knowledgeable. Kettering students are in demand—98 percent of Kettering University students graduate with job offers within their fields or are attending graduate school within six months of graduating. The average yearly starting salary of a Kettering student is $64,000. Kettering ranks among the top 1 percent of private institutions in the U.S. in return on investment, offering more than $1 million in lifetime ROI to our graduates, according to Affordable Colleges Online. Kettering University ranks first in the Midwest in ROI and Alumni Earning Potential, according to Payscale.com.

LOCATION AND ENVIRONMENT

Kettering University is located in Flint, Michigan, approximately 60 miles north of Detroit and a short drive from Lake Huron. Flint has approximately 100,000 residents.

There are abundant opportunities for enrichment within the community. The Flint Cultural Center, located just one-and-a-half miles from campus, houses the Sloan Museum, Whiting Auditorium, Longway Planetarium, the Flint Institute of Music and the Flint Institute of Arts. Downtown Flint offers a growing number of dining and entertainment venues, a nationally recognized Farmer's Market and, as the home to four colleges and universities within the city limits, has more than 10,000 college students in the heart of the city on a daily basis.

While a sizable city, Flint also has 11,000 acres of woods, water and trails to offer as part of Michigan's largest country park system. Students can enjoy golfing, hiking, kayaking, hunting, disc golf, biking, skiing and snowmobiling and more, all within close proximity to campus. All freshmen live on campus while 36 percent of students live on campus the remainder of their college experience.

OFF-CAMPUS OPPORTUNITIES

More than half of a Kettering student's time is spent off campus, fulfilling professional co-op and experiential work requirements at a corporation that relates to their degree or interests. On average, students spend 11 academic semesters working for their employer and nine academic semesters in the classroom. Students work at one of Kettering's more than 550 employer partners located throughout North America and the world. On average, students earn up to $65,000 in co-op earnings over the course of their undergraduate experience.

Undergrads living on campus 36 percent

Registered Student Organizations: 50+

Number of Honor Societies: 13

ACADEMIC PROGRAMS

The unique structure of Kettering's program allows students to fulfill the academic requirements of 160 credit hours throughout a 4.5-year period. This is completed over nine academic semesters and up to 11 co-op work semesters. Students also complete a capstone thesis project on behalf of their co-op employer during their senior year for credit toward the 160 required hours. The academic year consists of two 11-week academic terms on-campus in Flint and two 12-week academic terms working for the corporate employer; students alternate their time between Flint and the employer's site. On average, a freshman student who spends 24 weeks during the academic year working for a professional co-op employer earns $11,000.

MAJORS AND DEGREES OFFERED

Kettering University's 4.5-year cooperative and experiential education program allows students to earn designated Bachelor of Science degrees in:

- applied biology
- applied mathematics
- applied physics
- biochemistry
- business administration
- chemical engineering
- chemistry
- computer engineering
- computer science
- electrical engineering
- engineering physics
- industrial engineering
- mechanical engineering

Kettering also offers more than 50 minors, concentrations, specialties, courses of study and dual degrees, in areas such as Applied Optics, Pre-Law, Computer Gaming, System and Data Security, and Pre-Med. Additionally, the school offers 12 master's degrees, including an accredited MBA program. Please visit kettering.edu for more information.

TUITION, ROOM, BOARD, FEES

Tuition for the 2017–18 academic year is $21,245° per term. Kettering is proud to offer students a Fixed Tuition Guarantee. Students making normal progress towards their degree will pay the same tuition rates for their entire college career. Kettering has also eliminated all academically-related fees in its all-inclusive tuition package.

Room and Board for the 2017–18 academic year is $4,020 per term.

°Please remember that tuition and fees are subject to change at any time.

FINANCIAL AID

Kettering University offers traditional need and merit-based financial aid, including a generous merit scholarship program. In fact, more than 99 percent of Kettering students receive some level of financial assistance. Factor in co-op earnings and our fixed-rate tuition guarantee, and students are investing in one of the best values in higher education today. Aid is given as grants, scholarships, loans and work-study awards. Students should fill out the Free Application for Federal Student Aid (FAFSA) and request a copy of the analysis be sent to Kettering University. The University works to create a financial package based on those results.

STUDENT ORGANIZATIONS AND ACTIVITIES

College life should offer students more than just learning opportunities. To this end, Kettering offers more than 50+ student organizations, such as Society of Automotive Engineers (SAE) competition teams, DECA, Student Association for Global Engineering, Society of Women Engineers (SWE) and National Society of Black Engineers (NSBE), and numerous social activities and intramural sports. Approximately a third of Kettering students join the 12 national fraternities and 7 sororities that are represented on campus. The University's active student government produces programs to develop peers' leadership skills, self-confidence, interpersonal relationships and organizational operations. Students at Kettering represent approximately 48 states and 18 countries, so they also benefit from learning and sharing with this diverse community.

ADMISSIONS PROCESS

Admission to Kettering University is competitive and based on scholastic achievement and extracurricular interests, activities and achievements. Applicants are required to have completed the following courses (one credit represents two semesters or one year of study): Two credits algebra, one credit geometry, a half credit trigonometry, two credits laboratory science (one of these credits must be from physics or chemistry, and both are strongly recommended), and three credits English. Applicants must submit SAT or ACT scores. Most Kettering University students rank at or near the top 10 percent of their high school class.

Kettering University also accepts transfer students. A minimum of 14 credits is required, but 16-20 credits are strongly encouraged. Admission decisions for transfer applicants are based on college records for those who have completed at least 30 credits.

Although applications are accepted all year long, prospective students are encouraged to file their application early in their senior year. Early application significantly improves students' chances for early co-op employment. Interested students can apply online at www.kettering.edu/apply.

KING'S COLLEGE (PA)

AT A GLANCE

King's is a Catholic, comprehensive college in the liberal arts tradition founded by the Congregation of Holy Cross offering 36 majors in business and 25 NCAA Division III athletic programs for men and women.

King's is a Catholic, comprehensive college in the liberal arts tradition founded in 1946 by the Congregation of Holy Cross from the University of Notre Dame. King's is located on a small urban campus in Wilkes-Barre, Pennsylvania. King's offers 36 majors in business, the humanities, engineering, social sciences, education, sciences and allied health programs, as well as seven pre-professional programs and 11 special concentrations. With over 50 clubs and activities and 25 NCAA Division III athletic programs for men and women, there is plenty to do outside the classroom.

Small classes and labs allow for meaningful interaction between professors and students. The average class size is 18 students, average lab size is 13 students, and the student/faculty ratio is 12:1. The favorable student-teacher ratio means more opportunities for personal attention, which in turn accounts for King's superior graduation rates.

King's academic programs are accredited by highly respected accrediting agencies, including the following:

- The Association to Advance Collegiate Schools of Business (AACSB) (The William G. McGowan School of Business is one of only 42 undergraduate schools of business nationwide accredited by the AACSB.)
- The National Council for the Accreditation of Teacher Education (King's is one of only 19 colleges in Pennsylvania with this accreditation.)
- The Accreditation Review Commission on Education for Physician Assistants
- The Commission on Accreditation of Athletic Training Education
- The American Chemical Society

LOCATION AND ENVIRONMENT

King's College is located in the City of Wilkes-Barre in northeastern Pennsylvania, within driving distance of New York City, Philadelphia, Washington, D.C. and other east coast attractions. The atmosphere is friendly and inviting, with a strong sense of community. The King's campus is easy to navigate and has impressive facilities, equal to those at much larger institutions. Located near to campus are malls, theatres and restaurants. The region hosts a busy schedule of cultural events, ethnic celebrations and festivals.

CAMPUS FACILITIES & EQUIPMENT

The new King's on the Square facility, located in the heart of Wilkes-Barre, is home to King's allied health programs. The College features a state-of-the-art sports medicine clinic for its athletic training program. New science labs and equipment enable students to conduct hands-on research. On campus radio and television studios offer audio and video editing equipment for students involved in communications or media. The D. Leonard Corgan Library offers a comprehensive collection of books, periodicals and catalogs, providing students with the informational resources they need to enhance their skills. The College's new food services partner maintains outstanding dining facilities, including a full-service Chick-Fil-A restaurant, located at King's on the Square.

Residence halls offer a variety of living arrangements from single rooms to apartments. Amenities include 24-hour computer labs in several residence halls; each room is equipped with cable TV access. These facilities are all secure, accessible either by student ID card or by the desk attendant on staff 24-hours a day. A state-of-the-art Wi-Fi network is accessible across the entire King's campus.

Athletics Facilities

The 33-acre Robert L. Betzler Fields at McCarthy Stadium is one of the finest facilities in the MAC for football, field hockey, baseball, softball, soccer, lacrosse and track and field. The William S. Scandlon Physical Education Center features the Robert McGrane Basketball Arena. The center also includes a sports medicine clinic, swimming pool, handball and racquetball courts, wrestling room, and new locker rooms. In addition, the recently completed gym expansion project has added a new facility to the Scandlon Center, including three multi-purpose courts as well as new offices, meeting rooms, and additional sports medicine facilities.

OFF-CAMPUS OPPORTUNITIES

It's not all limited to campus, we've got malls, theatres and restaurants minutes away as well as specialty shops, cultural events, ethnic celebrations and festivals. Our bookstore is located in a Barnes & Noble/Starbucks Cafe and is the centerpiece of a bustling downtown.

ACADEMICS

Special Concentrations

Chemistry of Materials

Ethics

Forensic Studies

Geography

International Studies

Latin American Studies

Physics

Political Economy

Statistics

Women's Studies

Core Curriculum

All King's College students, regardless of their majors, participate in the Core Curriculum. Core courses are broadly based so that fundamental aspects of human experience are approached from diverse viewpoints represented by a variety of disciplines. The Core Curriculum is designed to help students achieve competence in writing, speaking, critical reading and thinking, problem solving using mathematics, and making effective use of library and information resources. The Core also ensures students achieve a critical understanding of history, civilization, art, and literature, an awareness of global issues, an understanding of the scientific method and the ability to reason ethically.

MAJORS AND DEGREES OFFERED

Athletic Training; Biology; Biochemistry/Molecular Biology; Business (Accounting, Finance, Human Resources Management, International Business Management, Marketing); Chemistry; Clinical Laboratory Science (Medical Technology; Computers and Information Systems; Computer Science; Criminal Justice; Economics; Education (Preschool-Grade 4, Middle Level—Math/Science—Grade 4-8, Secondary Level, Foreign Language—Grades K-12, Special Education); Engineering

Civil; Mechanical; Engineering—dual degree with University of Notre Dame (Chemistry, Computer Science, Environmental Science, Physics); English—Literature; English—Professional Writing; Environmental Science; Environmental Studies; Exercise Science; French; General Science; History; Mass Communications; Mathematics; Neuroscience; Nursing (beginning Fall 2018); Philosophy; Physician Assistant (five-year master's); Physics; Political Science; Pre-Health (Pre-Chiropractic, Pre-Dental, Pre-Medical , Pre-Pharmaceutical, Pre-Veterinarian); Pre-Law; Pre-Theological; Psychology; Sociology; Spanish; Theatre; Theology

TUITION, ROOM, BOARD, FEES

2017–2018 Costs:

Cost	RESIDENT	COMMUTER
Tuition and Fees (full-time)	$35,830	$35,830
Average Room and Board	$12,408	N/A
Total	$48,238	$35,830

The College encourages every student to apply for financial aid no matter what their family circumstances are. Only after you have applied and been considered for all available assistance will you have a true idea of what your costs will be.

FINANCIAL AID

Ninety-nine percent of King's first-year students receive financial assistance. The College offers numerous scholarship, grant, loan and work-study programs, because we believe college is an investment in the future-both yours and ours. In 2016–2017, our average gift aid was $20,783, with average first year Financial Aid awards at $26,283. The King's College Office of Financial Aid takes the guesswork out of the application process. For more information, call 1-888-KINGS PA or email finaid@kings.edu.

STUDENT ORGANIZATIONS AND ACTIVITIES

At King's, we're proud of our diverse student body that includes individuals from many ethnic and religious traditions from across the country and around the world. Recognizing that involvement in student clubs and organizations is an important part of the educational experience, King's offers more than 50 student organizations to meet virtually any interest.

More than 82 percent of the King's College faculty has a Ph.D. or equivalent degrees. Faculty members have been entrepreneurs and practitioners, are authors, scientists, and researchers. They engage in scholarly research and ongoing professional development to support and strengthen their primary role of teaching.

The American Association of Colleges and Universities (AACU) Greater Expectations Initiative named King's as one of only 16 Leadership Institutions nationwide as part of an organized effort to influence the future of liberal arts higher education. The Center for Excellence in Learning and Teaching (CELT) gives King's faculty members a wealth of teaching resources. At King's, faculty members take the time to explain the lesson one more time, answer the question you just couldn't bring yourself to ask in class, and listen intently to your theories and opinions. Professors are interested in their students' success as individuals and therefore make themselves available whether it's during scheduled office hours, e-mail or even over coffee.

The Office of Career Planning offers a broad range of services from credit-bearing academic courses, individualized career counseling, and a variety of professional development activities, programs, and events. The Career Resource Center offers up-to date job search information by field and graduate school resources. The Center also sponsors and provides information about recruiting events, including company visits and information about job fairs and professional development seminars.

King's offer a number of special programs to enhance your learning experience. The First-Year Experience helps new students adjust to campus life. Special honors programs give exceptional students additional challenges. King's study abroad programs offer the chance to travel and study different cultures first hand. ROTC programs provide students an opportunity to serve their country. Other programs, such as the McGowan Center for Ethics and Social Responsibility, prepare you intellectually, morally, and spiritually for a satisfying and purposeful life. Guided internships enable you to experience and earn credit while working within your field of study, and the Experiencing the Arts program is designed to help you explore your artistic side.

ADMISSIONS PROCESS

Information about the King's College application process and downloadable (.pdf) versions of the application form can be found here: https://www.kings.edu/admissions/application-forms-and-links. Online versions of the King's application can be found here: https://www.kings.edu/admissions/applying_to_kings. (Note: The application fee is waived if you apply online.)

High school students must complete the application form in its entirety. You must also complete the top section of the school report form and submit it to your guidance counselor. Be sure to forward your SAT or ACT scores. (We accept either direct reports from the testing services or test scores included on an official high school transcript.) If you are choosing the Test Optional application decision, you must select that option on the application for it to be processed. If applicable, please submit any college/university transcript indicating course work completed.

Parents should complete the Free Application for Federal Student Aid (FAFSA) after October 1, 2016. The King's College Federal School Code is 003282 (this code must be entered correctly on the FAFSA in order for King's College to receive access to your federal record). Be sure to accurately report your social security number on the application for admission, financial aid application, and the FAFSA forms. To help, the College has assembled a number resources to help you navigate the application process, which can be downloaded here: https://www.kings.edu/admissions/application-forms-and-links.

transfer students may enroll at King's in the fall or spring semester after completing at least one semester or 12 transferable credits at another school. To apply, submit a completed application and the $30 fee. (Note: The application fee is waived if you apply online at www.kings.edu/admissions/applying_to_kings.) You must also submit official transcript(s) from all post-secondary institutions (including two and four-year colleges), an official transcript from a secondary school or a G.E.D., SAT or ACT scores (if available), and a personal essay.

International students must complete the International Application for Admission, available here:https://www.kings.edu/non_cms/pdf/international_application.pdf. Be sure to enclose the $50 non-refundable application fee when mailing. Checks should be made payable to King's College. (NOTE: There is no application fee if you apply online at https://www.kings.edu/admissions/applying_to_kings.) You must also submit your official high school transcript. Your official SAT, TOEFL or IELTS scores must also be submitted to the Office of Admission. If you have any questions about the application, please contact the Office of International Student Recruitment at 001-570-208-5834. In special cases we may choose to waive requirements and will process the application with available information.

For all students, we value the opportunity to meet our applicants in person and therefore strongly recommend scheduling a personal interview at your earliest convenience.

For more information, contact the Office of Admission at 1-888-KINGS PA or email admissions@kings.edu.

KNOX COLLEGE

AT A GLANCE

We're Knox College, a residential liberal arts college in the heart of the country that brings together an unusually diverse group of people to do uncommonly effective work.

We believe that beauty and sweat go together, that hard work is a beautiful thing, that every experience is an education, that every new venture, every fantastic idea, every great journey, is human-powered. We also believe you learn the most from the people least like you. Knox is one of the 50 most diverse campuses in America, with a campus community of 1,400 students from nearly every state and 51 countries, including a wide array of races, ethnicities, ages, cultures, backgrounds, genders and gender identities, sexual orientations, and beliefs.

A Knox education is not something you sit and watch—it's something you do. Our students test their knowledge by applying theory to practice both in and out of the classroom. That can take the form of advanced research and creative work, internships, off-campus (sometimes way off-campus) programs, community service, or some combination of your own devising. We help make these experiences possible with a $2,000 Power of Experience Grant available to all incoming students during their junior and senior years.

These experiences, combined with opportunities to live and learn with students from different backgrounds, empower students to find success after Knox. Our students become engaged, innovative, and productive global citizens, ready to lead lives of purpose. They run Fortune 500 companies and grassroots nonprofits, they conduct major research at sites around the world, they found startups and music festivals, they see a human need and they meet it.

Our future is also rooted in our past. The commitment to put learning to use to accomplish both personal and social goals dates back to the founding of the College in 1837. We take particular pride in the College's early commitment to increase access to all qualified students of varied backgrounds, races, and conditions, regardless of financial means.

Today, we continue to expand that historic mission and the tradition of active liberal arts learning. We provide an environment where students and dedicated faculty work closely together and where teaching is characterized by inviting and expecting students to pursue fundamental questions in order to reach their own reflective but independent judgments. Our aim is to foster a lifelong love of learning and a sense of competence, confidence, and proportion that will enable us to live with purpose and to contribute to the well-being of others.

LOCATION AND ENVIRONMENT

Knox is located in Galesburg, Illinois (pop. 33,000), full of enterprising, big-hearted people. Galesburg was founded alongside Knox, surrounded by prairie and farmland. We are at the heart of a national rail network; there's an Amtrak station a few blocks from campus; Chicago (home to many Knox alumni) is three hours away. And two regional airports are less than an hour away.

The Knox campus consists of 90 acres located in the heart of Galesburg. While our campus is home to academic and administrative buildings, both historic and modern, residence halls, and athletic facilities, it also features wide-open spaces that provide beautiful prairie vistas and provides plenty of room for our Ultimate Frisbee team to practice alongside students studying on the lawn. Our own 700-acre Green Oaks Biological Field Station—one of the country's oldest prairie restoration sites—is 20 miles from campus.

And one last slightly esoteric note about this exact place: The land around us is fairly flat. No one lives high on a mountaintop or deep in a valley. There's something deeply democratic about this. We all have power. We all have a voice. We all stand on equal ground.

CAMPUS FACILITIES & EQUIPMENT

Libraries: Knox College maintains two libraries: Seymour Library and the Science-Mathematics Library, housing more than 350,000 volumes, as well as Special Collections & Archives, which contains primary source materials used by students, faculty, and researchers from around the world.

Arts: The Ford Center for the Fine Arts houses theatre, dance, and music and features the 600-seat Harbach theatre (with a 360-degree rotating stage), the 325-seat Kresge Recital Hall, the Studio Theatre, as well as dance and music studios. Our newly constructed Whitcomb Art Center provides a state-of-the-art facility for students to study, create, and share their art.

Science: Knox continues to expand an equipment roster that includes electron microscopes, NMR, ESR, GC-MS, other spectrometers and chromatographs, X-ray, laser labs, 3-D printers, experimental psychology labs, four computer labs, a rooftop observatory, and a greenhouse. Green Oaks Biological Field Station, about 20 miles east of Knox, encompasses 700 acres of tallgrass prairie, old-growth oaks, second-growth oak-hickory forest, lakes, and streams.

Athletics: Fleming Fieldhouse provides an indoor six-lane 200-meter track and court space for numerous activities. Andrew Fitness Center offers separate cardio/weight machine and free-weight floors. Knosher Bowl, a true bowl stadium, features artificial turf and one of the best playing surfaces in Division III football. Blodgett Field is a pro-level baseball diamond, with special soil composition. Knox also maintains a main gym and basketball court, a six-lane outdoor track, softball and soccer fields, tennis courts, and natatorium. Golf is played at a nearby private 18-hole course.

OFF-CAMPUS OPPORTUNITIES

A few of the many reasons to like Galesburg:

It knows what it is: It is not Chicago; it is not a tiny farm town. It is a small city (pop. 33,000) that was founded alongside a great liberal arts college, surrounded by prairie and farmland, with 23 city parks, a public beach, and wooded biking/walking trails.

It runs on collective ingenuity: If you have a great idea, it's easy to bring people together to bring it to life. Example: A Knox alumnus wanted to turn Seminary Street into a classic independent shopping district. Now it's home to locally owned cafes, restaurants, a natural foods store, and an antique mall.

People make art here: At the Prairie Players Civic Theatre or in the Knox-Rootabaga Jazz Festival. Plus: The Galesburg Civic Art Center hosts exhibits by local artists. The Knox-Galesburg Symphony Orchestra—featuring many Knox students—performs at the historic Orpheum Theatre.

You can make a difference here: Our students contribute thousands of hours of service in Galesburg every year, through long-standing programs like the Knox Prairie Community Kitchen, our Days of Service, and the groundbreaking KnoxCorps program, which places current students and recent graduates in long-term positions with local organizations.

ACADEMIC PROGRAMS

We believe that every experience is a kind of education. Everything you learn gains value when you apply it. That's why every Knox student will participate in some form of experiential learning before they graduate. All students receive a $2,000 Power of Experience Grant during their junior or senior year to support a qualifying experiential learning opportunity, including research or creative work, an internship, community service, or study abroad.

Our immersive terms allow students to focus on one topic (entrepreneurship, studio art, Japanese language and history, clinical psychology, among others) for an entire term. They all provide hands-on experience—internships, research, travel, creative work. Two examples: In Green Oaks Term, students live at our biological field station, take interdisciplinary coursework in science, anthropology, and the arts, conduct research, and build a community. In Repertory Theatre Term, students research, design, produce, and perform two full-length plays—the most comprehensive undergraduate theatre experience in the country.

Knox has a longstanding (and pioneering) commitment to supporting advanced student research—intensive, long-term projects that go beyond coursework. The vast majority of our students (89 percent) produce research, independent studies, or creative work.

Half of our students study abroad, and our off-campus study programs—nearly 100 in total—are designed to work with the Knox experience. You take what you've studied at Knox out into the world; you gather new information, new ideas, new experiences; and you come back with a new way of seeing yourself, your education, and your future.

Our career center helps students find meaningful professional experience by making the most of their education, resources, and connections to secure internships and postgraduate opportunities across the country and around the world.

MAJORS AND DEGREES OFFERED

Knox offers more than 60 courses of study—in the arts, humanities, social sciences, and sciences. A Bachelor of Arts degree is available in all major fields of study, with the option to pursue a Bachelor of Science degree in the fields of biochemistry, biology, chemistry, computer science, mathematics, neuroscience, psychology, and physics.

Many students double major; you can also design your own major. Choosing a major and thinking broadly about the work you'll do in college and beyond, is in many ways a collaborative process, involving intensive conversations with peers, professors, counselors, and advisors (who are, in fact, professors). Our 3-3 academic calendar—three terms (fall, winter, and spring), three courses per term—allows students to fully explore course subject matter and fulfill research expectations.

TUITION, ROOM, BOARD, FEES

Expenses per academic year:

Tuition: $45,783

Room: $4,941

Board: $4,929

Fees: $771

Total: $56,424

Average cost for books and supplies: $900

FINANCIAL AID

Knox was founded on the idea that college should be accessible to people regardless of their financial means. We offer more than $40 million in financial aid every year. We're proud to offer a range of scholarships that recognize students' achievements in academics, arts, service and leadership.

For more information on scholarships or financial aid, visit knox.edu, or contact us at 800-678-KNOX.

STUDENT ORGANIZATIONS AND ACTIVITIES

Clubs and Organizations: The one quality that binds our 100+ student clubs and organizations is that they are all student-driven. Students create and run organizations in response to interests and needs. Some clubs focus on academic disciplines such as chemistry or physics. Others, such as Common Ground, Model United Nations, and Allied Blacks for Liberty and Equality focus on identity, culture, and politics. And, our successful club-level Ultimate Frisbee team and our music, dance, and performance ensembles provide an athletic and creative energy that characterizes Knox.

Intramural Clubs: More than half of our students participate in some kind of organized athletic activity, from club sports (water polo, fencing, women's lacrosse); to intramurals (basketball, indoor soccer, softball, volleyball); to fitness classes organized and taught by students (a few recent examples: Balinese dancing, yoga).

Student Governance: Our student government actually governs. The Student Senate helps determine how funds from student activity fees are spent, makes student appointments to faculty committees, and serves as a forum for the debate of important issues on campus. Our students shape the future of Knox; their work is a lasting legacy.

Civic Engagement: We pride ourselves on being deeply engaged in the life of a strong, sustainable community—whether that community is local or global. Our students contribute tens of thousands of hours of service every year through established partnerships, special programs, and our KnoxCorps program. Knox was the first college or university in the country to offer an official Peace Corps Preparatory Program; we rank among the top producers of Peace Corps volunteers.

ADMISSIONS PROCESS

Knox seeks students who are active, engaged learners. We value students who demonstrate their appreciation for a variety of educational experiences, both in and out of the classroom. Our admission counselors consider you as an individual when making our admission decisions.

You can apply to Knox online via the Common Application. Deadlines for first-year admission are November 1 for Early Decision and Early Action I, December 1 for Early Action II, and January 15 for Regular Decision. We also accept transfer applications for fall, winter, and spring terms.

For more information, please visit admission online or contact us directly.

Office of Admission

Knox College

2 East South Street

Galesburg, Illinois 61401-4999

United States

Phone: 800-678-KNOX or 309-341-7100

Fax: 309-341-7070

E-mail: admission@knox.edu

Web: knox.edu

LAKE FOREST COLLEGE

AT A GLANCE

Lake Forest offers students a rare combination: an exceptionally beautiful residential campus offering a rigorous curriculum, and the opportunity to tap into the many academic, cultural, and social resources of nearby Chicago.

Founded in 1857, Lake Forest College has a long tradition of academic excellence and is known for its innovative curriculum and focus on career preparation. In addition to majors in the humanities, social sciences, and natural sciences, the College features programs of study in pre-law, pre-health, communication, business, finance, computer science, and still other practical areas. Every first-year student and transfer student is assigned a career advisor, in addition to an academic advisor. Lake Forest prepares students to lead successful lives, and many go on to competitive graduate programs and top jobs. Abundant internships, research opportunities, personal guidance from professors, and connections to nearby Chicago also set Lake Forest apart. Students learn in a rigorous academic environment in small class settings where professors do all the teaching and also serve as advisors and mentors. Professors are accomplished scholars, published authors, and recipients of prestigious grants. Many have come from some of the top PhD programs in the country.

Students represent nearly every state and 70 countries around the world. Together they comprise a learning community that prepares them to succeed in a global society. More than eighty student groups provide a host of extracurricular opportunities that develop leadership skills and enhance students' campus experience and post-college prospects. Lake Forest College offers recreational music, art, and theater programs, as well as 23 varsity sports and intramural and club sports. It competes in NCAA Division III.

LOCATION AND ENVIRONMENT

Just an hour's train ride to Chicago, the College is located in the town of Lake Forest, Illinois, 30 miles north of the city along the shores of Lake Michigan. The 107-acre residential campus is a safe academic home in a beautiful wooded suburban setting within walking distance to the train to downtown Chicago, historic Lake Forest, and the beaches of Lake Michigan.

The College is only 25 miles from O'Hare International Airport and is also served by Midway Airport and Mitchell International Airport in Milwaukee.

The campus is surrounded by lush wooded neighborhoods, ravines, natural prairies, the beautiful beaches along Lake Michigan, and an extensive network of bike and running trails. Nearby Chicago boasts nearly 70 world-class museums, more than 200 theaters, seven major league sports teams, and one of the nation's top opera companies. Chicago is known for its cleanliness, abundant green space, good transportation system, and friendly people.

CAMPUS FACILITIES & EQUIPMENT

The new state-of-the-art Lillard Science Center, a $43 million renovation and expansion project, opened in January 2018.

The Sports and Recreation Center is a popular facility on campus and includes multipurpose courts, a suspended running track, an aerobic and dance studio, a batting/golf cage, strength, cardio, and fitness spaces, a pool, and an indoor ice rink just next door.

The Mohr Student Center is a student-centered social space that is the hub of social activity on campus. It features pool tables and other games, stage and performance space, large-screen TVs, lounges, deli/snack bar, grocery store, and an outdoor terrace with seating.

Center for Chicago Programs

Chicago provides a hands-on resource for student learning through research, internships, study, and fun. The Center is an on-campus hub for all Chicago-related programming. Students can plan visits to the city and professors can get help incorporating Chicago resources into their classrooms. The Center also brings well-known Chicagoans to the College for lectures and performances.

OFF-CAMPUS OPPORTUNITIES

Lake Forest encourages students to take advantage of study, internship, and research opportunities in Chicago, around the United States, and abroad. Internship opportunities are plentiful in the Chicago area and students have interned at places such as the Art Institute of Chicago, Chicago Blackhawks, Chicago Board of Trade, Chicago Council on Global Affairs, Edelman Public Relations Worldwide, Morgan Stanley, NBC Chicago, Second City, and the John G. Shedd Aquarium, among others. Students can choose to spend a semester living at our modern residential facility in Chicago and interning through the Lake Forest In The Loop program.

In addition to a well-established internship program, Lake Forest College students gain international experience through access to over 230 study abroad and internship options in more than 70 countries. There are international and/or domestic programs suited for every major, minor, or program, at Lake Forest. Students can choose a program based on major, minor, language ability, and desired semester. Most students' financial aid packages can be applied to the program of choice.

ACADEMIC PROGRAMS

The First-Year Studies Program (FIYS)

First-year studies classes are small in size to encourage interaction and discussion. The FIYS professors also serve as the students' primary academic advisors and help them navigate the College's academic offerings during their first year. With many topics to choose from, first-year studies courses cover a wide range of academic interests from music, art, and politics to neuroscience, terrorism and religion, many with a focus on Chicago or directly utilizing the resources available there. Chicago plays an integral role in the FIYS program. Students travel to the city with their class during orientation week, providing a first-hand introduction to how the educational, cultural, and social resources of Chicago will influence their coursework and experiences during their four years at Lake Forest.

The Richter Scholars Program

This program provides students, early in their academic careers, with the opportunity to conduct independent, individual research with Lake Forest faculty. In the summer after their first year, each student in the Richter Program is employed for a ten-week period and does independent research one-on-one with a faculty member.

Self-Designed Major

This program allowos students to develop an academic major of their own, working closely with a faculty advisor, culminating in a thesis or a creative project.

MAJORS AND DEGREES OFFERED

The academic calendar is based on two 15-week semesters, beginning in August and January. Students normally take four four-credit courses per semester (the equivalent of 16 credits).

There are no teaching assistants at the College. Courses are taught in small classroom settings by professors who are experts in their fields and who also serve students as one-on-one advisors. In addition to classroom studies, students are encouraged to complete an internship, conduct original research, and study abroad for a semester.

A Lake Forest graduate will have studied a broad range of ideas; developed real competence in writing, speaking, and quantitative skills; and gained significant experience in humanities, natural sciences and mathematics, and social sciences while completing requirements for a major in an academic department or interdisciplinary program. The College's General Education Curriculum, advising system, and major requirements are designed to support these educational ideals.

Lake Forest awards the Bachelor of Arts (BA) degree in both traditional academic departments and interdisciplinary programs. Areas of study include: African American studies, American studies, anthropology, area studies, studio art, art history, art education, Asian studies, biology, biochemistry and molecular biology, border studies, business (concentrations in accounting and marketing available), chemistry, cinema studies, classical studies, communication, computer science, digital media design, economics, education (elementary and secondary), engineering (dual degree), English (literature and writing), environmental studies, finance, history, international relations, Islamic world studies, journalism, Latin American studies, legal studies, mathematics, media design and technology, modern languages and literatures (Arabic, Chinese, French, German, Italian, Japanese, and Spanish), music, music education, neuroscience, philosophy, physics, politics, print and digital publishing, psychology, religion, social justice, sociology, theater, women's and gender studies. Lake Forest also offers pre-professional programs in law, medicine, dentistry, and veterinary medicine.

Accelerated and dual-degree programs are offered. Dual-degree programs are available in law, international studies, pharmacy, and engineering. Lake Forest is affiliated with several competitive law schools that allow students to complete a bachelor's degree and a law degree in a total of six years, rather than the usual seven. Qualified Lake Forest College students may be admitted to the Monterey Institute of International Studies with accelerated status and can complete their master's degrees with 48 credits as opposed to the 60 normally required. A dual-degree program has been arranged, leading to a Bachelor of Arts degree in biology from Lake Forest College and a Doctor of Pharmacy from the Rosalind Franklin University of Medicine and Science. The engineering program is in cooperation with the Sever Institute of Technology at Washington University (St. Louis).

TUITION, ROOM, BOARD, FEES

2017 -2018 Tuition: $44,824.00

Room: $4,800.00

Board: $5,252.00

Fees: $724.00

FINANCIAL AID

Lake Forest College provides an affordable, high-quality education through maintaining a strong commitment to supporting each student's demonstrated financial need.

The College offers academic scholarships up to $30,000 and talent-based scholarships in music, studio art, and theater.

STUDENT ORGANIZATIONS AND ACTIVITIES

Lake Forest College is a place to study, work, and live. With the diversity of the student body there is an eclectic mix of activities and opportunities outside the classroom.

Student organizations include student government, international interest groups, Greek Life, academic honor societies, community service, publications and media, music and performance, spiritual and religious groups, and many others.

Students have a voice in how the College is run and are actively involved in governance committees such as the College Council and have representation on the Board of Trustees. Student writers and performers can showcase their talents on stage with the Garrick Players, by hosting a show on "WMXM," the College's FM radio station, or through the student newspaper, literary magazines, chorus and instrumental ensembles. Academic honor societies enjoy active student participation as do the community service groups and many special-interest clubs. The College provides and maintains a comprehensive intramural and intercollegiate athletic program. There are two national fraternities and five national sororities, all housed within the residence halls. All students have equal opportunity to take advantage of the richness of the College's programs.

Lake Forest College competes in the NCAA Division III fielding eleven women's and ten men's intercollegiate varsity teams. Women's teams include basketball, cross-country, golf, handball, ice hockey, soccer, softball, swimming and diving, tennis, volleyball, track (indoor), and track (distance). Men's teams include basketball, cross-country, football, golf, handball, ice hockey, soccer, swimming and diving, tennis, track (indoor), and track (distance). The College also offers an extensive roster of intramural and club sports.

The College's Center for Chicago Programs facilitates engagement with the resources of Chicago which often complements programs for student organizations as well as provides students with information on cultural and social activities happening downtown. The train to Chicago is a short walk from campus and students enjoy traveling to the city for fun and entertainment as well as many class trips with professors. The College shuttle provides service seven days a week to popular shopping areas and destinations around campus.

ADMISSIONS PROCESS

The criteria used for selection include assessment of a student's program of study, academic achievement, aptitude, intellectual curiosity, qualities of character and personality, and activities.

Standardized test scores (ACT/SAT) are optional, except for international or home-schooled candidates, and those applying for some academic scholarships. A personal interview is required for students who do not submit scores.

Request More Information

https://www.lakeforest.edu/admissions/requestinformation.php

Apply Online

https://www.lakeforest.edu/admissions/apply/

Visit Campus

https://www.lakeforest.edu/admissions/visit/

Virtual Tour

https://www.lakeforest.edu/about/ourcampus/tour.php

Majors and Minors

https://www.lakeforest.edu/academics/

Scholarships and Financial Aid

https://www.lakeforest.edu/admissions/scholarships/

LAWRENCE TECHNOLOGICAL UNIVERSITY

AT A GLANCE

Lawrence Technological University is a private, personally focused university providing students a rigorous, high-quality education—an education that pays off. The Brookings Institution ranks Lawrence Technological University fifth among U.S. colleges and universities for boosting graduates' earning potential. Payscale. com reports that salaries of LTU bachelor's graduates are in the top 10 percent nationally. Some 88 percent of students are employed or registered for graduate school by the date of their graduation, greater than the national average.

The University, including its graduate programs, is accredited by the Higher Learning Commission and is a member of the North Central Association of Colleges and Schools. In addition to its ranking by the Princeton Review, LTU placed in the top tier of Best University-Masters-Midwest in the U.S. News and World Report's 2018 America's Best Colleges rankings. Other distinctions include designation as a Military Friendly School by G.I. Jobs.

Lawrence Tech's honors program is available for highly motivated and qualified students, as well as Quest, which encourages students to go above and beyond their studies and explore their interests on a deeper level. A scholars program is also available, designed to ease the transition from high school to college by providing support services. LTU's unique Leadership Program, integrated into all bachelor's degrees, helps students gain critical thinking, teamwork, and communication skills.

LTU's student-faculty ratio is 11:1. Most undergraduate classes have 19 or fewer students, and less than 1 percent of the classes enroll more than 50. Nearly 1000 students live in University Housing. Women make up 28 percent of the student body, and 33 states and 52 nations are represented on campus.

LOCATION AND ENVIRONMENT

The University is situated in Southfield, a dynamic suburb in Oakland County, Michigan. Hundreds of Fortune 500 and international companies are located nearby, and the region has one of the largest concentrations of engineering, architecture, and technology jobs in the world. Southeastern Michigan also offers a rich variety of recreational and cultural activities, with public transportation making most areas accessible to students. Hundreds of major research, manufacturing, scientific, and business enterprises are located nearby, aiding students who work full- or part-time while attending classes, as well as those in co-ops and internships, and participating in professional societies. The campus is close to major freeways and about a 30-minute drive north of downtown Detroit and Detroit Metro Airport.

CAMPUS FACILITIES & EQUIPMENT

Lawrence Tech's modern 107-acre campus includes a variety of academic, recreational, and housing facilities. Students use advanced, leading-edge facilities, including LTU's acclaimed Center for Innovative Materials Research; an environmental scanning microscope; architectural and design studios; a structural testing lab; a wind tunnel; wood, metal, and model shops; a 4 x 4 chassis dynamometer; labs for alternative energy, robotics, biomedical research, graphics; and the Taubman Engineering, Architecture, and Life Sciences Complex.

High-end personal laptops, customized with all the professional software students need, are provided through the LTuZone. This unique benefit, with an average retail value of $75,000, is the only one of its kind in the nation.

The University's four residence halls feature community living and one and two-bedroom apartment-style suites that accommodate two to four students. All utilities, wifi, basic cable TV, and parking are included.

LTU's library offers a wide selection of print and electronic materials, including numerous online databases, visual resources, digital images, and full-text periodical titles accessible on and off campus. Librarians provide research guidance and instruction. As a key part of the research community in Michigan, LTU's library participates in the reciprocal borrowing and sharing of resources with many other institutions.

The A. Alfred Taubman Student Services Center consolidates all student support services—from admissions through career services—into a convenient one-stop center. This innovative 42,000-square-foot building, which utilizes many energy-efficient and environmentally friendly features and technologies, serves as a "living laboratory" of sustainability, and is part of a regional stormwater management effort.

LTU's Johnson Controls Vehicle Engineering Systems Laboratory provides students opportunities to conduct sponsored research on a unique 4 x 4 vehicle chassis dynamometer.

OFF-CAMPUS OPPORTUNITIES

Students can participate in applied research partnerships that offer remarkable hands-on experience. Professional organizations provide additional opportunities to network with industry leaders.

Lawrence Tech's Detroit design programs are housed under one roof at the Detroit Center for Design + Technology, allowing students to explore community-based architectural, urban design, and community development projects. Architecture students regularly build homes for Habitat for Humanity.

LTU's Study-Abroad Program is open to all students. The University has partnerships with universities in China, India, Canada, Brazil, Mexico, Europe, and the Middle East. The Global Engineering Program arranges for engineering students to work and study abroad.

ACADEMIC PROGRAMS

Theory and Practice

LTU provides students the tools they need to compete and succeed within their chosen profession. Whether inside or outside of the classroom, the University's theory and practice approach to learning provides opportunities to combine practical knowledge with real-world applications.

Lawrence Tech is the recipient of numerous grants and awards for the development and implementation of innovative materials and practices that are expected to double the lifespan of concrete bridges and highways and provide armor protection for soldiers.

Student engineering teams design, build, and race hybrid, Supermileage, Baja, and Formula-style vehicles. Students also compete in bridge building and assembling and designing zero energy homes, airplanes, robots, and concrete canoes and toboggans.

MAJORS AND DEGREES OFFERED

LTU is a 4,500-student university offering over 100 undergraduate, master's, and doctoral programs in Colleges of Architecture and Design, Arts and Sciences, Engineering, and Business and Information Technology. Most programs are available days or evenings; many are offered on weekends and online. Dual majors and customized degree programs combining either associate and bachelor's programs or bachelor's and master's programs also are available. Pre-professional preparation includes pre-dental, pre-law, and pre-medical programs, as well as a post-baccalaureate certificate in premedical studies.

LTU's College of Architecture and Design offers bachelor's degrees in architecture, architectural studies, game art, graphic design, industrial design, interaction design, interior architecture, and transportation design. Lawrence Tech is one of the largest architecture schools in the nation.

LTU's College of Arts and Sciences offers bachelor's degrees in chemical biology, chemistry, computer science (business software development, game software development, scientific software development, and software engineering), English and communication arts, environmental chemistry, humanities, mathematical sciences, mathematics and computer science, media communication, molecular and cell biology, nursing, physics, physics and computer science, and psychology (clinical, general and applied, industrial/organizational, and pre-medical/biobehavioral).

Bachelor's degrees offered by LTU's College of Engineering are audio engineering technology, biomedical engineering, civil engineering, computer engineering, construction engineering technology and management, electrical engineering (computer engineering, electronics engineering, and power engineering), embedded software engineering, industrial engineering, mechanical and manufacturing engineering technology, mechanical engineering (aeronautical, alternative energy, automotive, manufacturing, nanoscience and nanotechnology, solid mechanics, and thermal fluids), and robotics engineering. A direct-entry master's degree in architectural engineering, combining bachelor's and master's programs, is also offered.

Accredited by AACSB International, LTU's College of Business and Information Technology offers undergraduate degrees in business administration (accounting, finance, general business, information technology, and marketing) and information technology.

Minors include aeronautical engineering, biology, business, chemistry, computer science, economics, energy engineering, English, general sciences, history, mathematics, media communication, military sciences and leadership (ROTC), nanoscience and nanotechnology, philosophy, physics, psychology, and technical and professional communication.

Associate degrees are offered in chemical technology, general studies, and radio and television broadcasting.

Undergraduate certificates can be earned in building information modeling and computer visualization, computer science, electrical power systems, embedded systems, entrepreneurial engineering, entrepreneurial skills, industrial/organizational psychology, technical and professional communication, and television and video production.

TUITION, ROOM, BOARD, FEES

Tuition for all undergrads includes being provided a laptop with all required software. The 2017–18 tuition for students majoring in arts and sciences is $840 per credit hour for basic studies courses. Sophomores, juniors, and seniors in arts and sciences, and business and information technology pay $1075 per credit hour. In architecture and design, tuition for freshmen and sophomores is $1010; for juniors and seniors, it is $1075 per credit hour. Tuition for engineering majors is $1075 per credit hour for all four years.

A normal course load is 12–17 credit hours per semester. The undergraduate registration fee is $135 each semester. International students on temporary visas must have sufficient funds to pay for an entire year of tuition, room and board, and books at the time of first registration. Additional fees for specific labs and studio courses vary.

Room costs vary, but average $6,700 per year. Meal plans are $2,800, per year, with a variety of options.

FINANCIAL AID

Over 85 percent of students receive financial assistance and the University awards more than $42 million in scholarships, grants, loans, and work-study funds each academic year. The average annual, need-based financial aid package is $27,588.54. Many privately funded scholarships are awarded to qualified students, based on need and/or scholastic performance. Part-time employment is available at the University on a first-come, first-served basis for full-time students. Student loans are also available from a variety of sources—state, federal, and private. Prospective students are urged to contact the Office of Financial Aid for information on deadlines and requirements for eligibility (www.ltu.edu/financial_aid).

STUDENT ORGANIZATIONS AND ACTIVITIES

More than 60 student clubs and organizations, including fraternities, sororities, honor societies, and student chapters of professional groups are active on campus and sponsor a variety of activities during the year. The Student Government sponsors and supports a variety of campus activities.

LTU features NAIA, ACHA, and USBC varsity and junior varsity athletics in men's and women's basketball, soccer, cross-country, lacrosse, bowling, ice hockey, golf, volleyball, and tennis; as well as women's softball, and men's baseball and football. Students can also show their Blue Devil spirit on LTU's marching band and dance team. Intramural leagues and tournaments are active in 18 sports. Club sports include lacrosse, mixed martial arts, and biking. LTU's Don Ridler Field House is open to all students and features a fitness track, gymnasium, racquetball courts, game room, saunas, and weight and conditioning room.

ADMISSIONS PROCESS

Admissions decisions are based on a student's recalculated GPA, ACT/SAT scores, essay, and letters of recommendation. Strong emphasis is placed on grade trends as well as the strength of the curriculum and rigor of a student's senior schedule. A portfolio is required for art and design majors.

Lawrence Tech's ACT code is 2020 and SAT is 1399. Required high school courses vary with the curriculum, and LTU offers a number of basic studies courses designed to augment incoming students' backgrounds if deficiencies exist.

Programs start in August and January, and an optional summer semester begins in May. Entry in the fall semester is advised but not required. Students must submit transcripts from all schools attended, along with a nonrefundable $30 application fee. Students may also fill out a brief survey and apply free at ltu.edu/applyfree. See our campus video at ltu.edu/StudentStories. To learn more, visit ltu.edu or contact:

Lawrence Technological University

Office of Admissions

21000 West Ten Mile Road

Southfield, MI 48075-1058

800.225.5588 or 248.204.3160

admissions@ltu.edu

ltu.edu

LE MOYNE COLLEGE

AT A GLANCE

Le Moyne College is a four-year, coeducational Jesuit college of approximately 2,800 full-time undergraduate students that uniquely balances a comprehensive liberal arts education with preparation for specific career paths or graduate study.

Founded in 1946, Le Moyne is the second youngest of the twenty-eight Jesuit colleges and universities in the United States. Its emphasis is on the education of the whole person and on the search for meaning and value as integral parts of an intellectual life. Learning, leadership and service are the hallmarks of a Le Moyne College education. Those values are evident in the College's undergraduate majors in more than 30 areas of study, as well as in its pre-professional studies and graduate programs in business administration, arts administration, education, nursing, occupational therapy, information systems and physician assistant studies.

Le Moyne's personal approach to education is reflected in the quality of contact between students and faculty members. With approximately 150 full-time faculty members, Le Moyne has a student-faculty ratio of 13:1 and an average class size of 20.

LOCATION AND ENVIRONMENT

Le Moyne's 160-plus acre, tree-lined campus is located in a residential setting 10 minutes from downtown Syracuse, the heart of New York state, whose metropolitan population is about 700,000. Just a few miles outside the city are the rolling hills, picturesque lakes, and miles of open country for which central New York is renowned.

CAMPUS FACILITIES & EQUIPMENT

Le Moyne students benefit from an ongoing commitment to technological excellence. The College's 42 buildings are equipped with accounting, biological sciences, chemistry, computer science, physics, psychology, and statistics laboratories. The W. Carroll Coyne Center for the Performing Arts houses generous production, performance, and classroom space; the latest light and sound technology; scene and costume shops; an aerobics and dance studio; and rehearsal rooms for instrumental and choral music. Academic facilities also include an extensively renovated color television studio; a radio/recording studio; a receiver-antenna satellite dish; transmission and scanning electron microscopes; a nuclear magnetic resonance spectrometer; a gas chromatograph/mass spectrophotometer; a 240,000-volume, open-stack library; and extensive on-site computer facilities. A wireless network allows students easy access to the campus network and Internet. All classrooms are smart classrooms, with multimedia capabilities that expand and enrich the learning process. Le Moyne students have access to other libraries through the Central New York Library Resources Council, and the campus Academic Support Center is available to students for instructional support. In addition, Le Moyne recently opened a 48,000 square foot addition to its existing science complex, as well as the new Madden School of Business featuring a state-of-the-art live trading floor and analytics lab. Athletic facilities include a new soccer and lacrosse turf field, a new softball field; baseball field, tennis, basketball, and wellness studios; a weight-training and fitness center; practice fields; and two gymnasiums. A recreation center houses an Olympic-size indoor swimming pool, jogging track, indoor tennis and volleyball courts, and additional basketball, racquetball, and fitness areas. The College also has a plaza, which houses its bookstore, a cafe, and a pizzeria. The Dolphin Den, which features a food court and a convenience store, is a popular space for students to meet, have a bite to eat, or just spend a quiet moment relaxing by the fireplace.

OFF-CAMPUS OPPORTUNITIES

Syracuse is convenient to most major cities throughout the Northeast, New England, and Canada and offers a wide array of shopping centers and restaurants, many near Le Moyne. Syracuse offers year-round entertainment in the form of rock concerts at the Landmark Theatre, professional baseball and hockey, the Bristol Omni-theatre, Syracuse Stage, the Everson Museum of Art, and the Armory Square district downtown, which offers one-of-a-kind eateries, pubs, and coffeehouses in addition to a wide variety of social and cultural events. Central New York is home to an extensive network of state and county parks, recreational areas, and other facilities that offer an abundance of recreational opportunities, including swimming, boating, hiking, downhill and cross-country skiing, snowboarding, and golf.

ACADEMICS

While each major department has its own sequence requirements for the minimum 120 credit hours needed for the Le Moyne degree, the College is convinced that there is a fundamental intellectual discipline that should characterize the graduate of a superior liberal arts college. Le Moyne's interdisciplinary core curriculum provides the foundation by including studies of English language and literature, mathematics, philosophy, history, theology and religion, natural science, and social science to reflect international trends within a liberal arts education. For exceptional students, Le Moyne offers an integral honors program that includes an interdisciplinary humanities sequence as well as departmental honors courses. The study-abroad program allows qualified students to spend a semester or year in numerous countries around the world. Le Moyne College has study-abroad programs or affiliations in Czech Republic, Dominican Republic, England, Germany, Ireland, Scotland, and Spain. Students can also use partner programs to study in locations such as Australia, Costa Rica, Egypt, France, Italy, Japan, and South Africa. Le Moyne is a participant in the sixty-member New York State Visiting Student Program. As part of the mission of preparing future leaders, Le Moyne College places a strong emphasis on career preparation through internships and other forms of experiential education. Academic departments and the Office of Career Advising and Development both provide programs and services for students interested in interning part time and full time, both locally and in major cities such as New York and Washington, D.C. The Offices of Service Learning and the Academic Deans are also involved in experiential education to promote learning outside the classroom. In the sciences, students take part in campus research with faculty mentors. Others receive assistance in pursuing outstanding opportunities off campus in leading research laboratories and health-care settings. Through the College's long-standing relationship with The Washington Center for Internships and Academic Seminars, students from all majors complete full-time semester-long internships in Washington, D.C., with government, business, or major nonprofit organizations. Faculty members in the Department of Political Science assist students interested in opportunities in Albany, N.Y., the state's seat of government, with either the State Senate or Assembly. Finally, the education programs at Le Moyne put students into school classrooms starting immediately as freshmen and continuing each year until graduation. Le Moyne students may enroll in Army and Air Force ROTC programs in conjunction with Syracuse University.

MAJORS AND DEGREES OFFERED

Le Moyne College awards the Bachelor of Arts degree in biological sciences, communication and film studies, computer science, criminology, cybersecurity, economics, English (creative writing, literature), French, history, mathematics (actuarial science, applied mathematics, pure mathematics, statistics), peace and global studies, philosophy, physics, political science, psychology, religious studies, sociology (anthropology, criminology, human services, research and theory), software application and system development, Spanish, and theatre arts. The Bachelor of Science degree is awarded in biochemistry, biological sciences (health professions, molecular biology, neurobiology), chemistry, economics, environmental science systems, environmental studies, physics, and psychology. The Bachelor of Science in business is awarded in accounting, business analytics, finance, human resource management, information systems, management and leadership, and marketing. A Bachelor of Science in nursing is also offered. Students may minor in advanced writing, arts administration, Catholic studies, classical humanities, film, gender and women's studies, health information systems, Irish literature, Italian, Latin, legal studies, medieval studies, music, or visual arts as well as most of the major fields of study offered. Pre-professional programs are offered in dentistry, law, medicine, optometry, physical therapy, direct entry physician assistant studies, podiatry, dental medicine, occupational therapy, and veterinary science. Students may prepare for teaching careers through certification programs in adolescent education, dual adolescent/special education, dual childhood/special education, and TESOL.

Le Moyne College and the L. C. Smith College of Engineering and Computer Science at Syracuse University have a dual-degree program in which students may earn a bachelor's degree from Le Moyne and a master's degree in engineering from Syracuse University in as few as five and a half years. Concentrations include aerospace, bioengineering, chemical, civil/structural, computer, electrical, environmental, geotechnical, and mechanical engineering.

Formal accelerated 3+3 and 3+4 programs are offered in physical therapy, dentistry, law, optometry, communication, public administration, forensic science, library science, and podiatry in cooperation with the State University of New York at Buffalo School of Dentistry, New York College of Podiatric Medicine, School of Information Studies at Syracuse University, Forensic and National Security Sciences Institute at Syracuse University, S.I. Newhouse School of Public Communication at Syracuse University, Maxwell School of Citizenship and Public Affairs at Syracuse University, and Syracuse University College of Law.

TUITION, ROOM, BOARD, FEES

For 2018–19, Le Moyne's tuition is $33,560. Room and board charges are $13,780. Additional fees amount to approximately $1,065.

FINANCIAL AID

Financial aid is offered to a large percentage of Le Moyne's students through scholarships, grants, loans, and work-study assignments. Le Moyne offers a generous program of merit-based academic and athletic scholarships as well as financial aid based on a student's need and academic promise. Federal funds are available through the Federal Pell Grant, Federal Work-Study, Federal Supplemental Educational Opportunity Grant, and Federal Perkins Loan programs. A student's eligibility for need-based financial aid is determined from both the Free Application for Federal Student Aid (FAFSA) and the Le Moyne Financial Aid Application Form. It is recommended that these forms be mailed by February 1.

STUDENT ORGANIZATIONS AND ACTIVITIES

A wide range of student-directed activities, athletics, clubs, and service organizations complement the academic experience. Intramural sports are very popular with Le Moyne students; nearly 85 percent of the students participate. Le Moyne also has twenty-one NCAA intercollegiate teams (ten for men and eleven for women). Between 80 and 85 percent of students live in residence halls, apartments, and town houses on campus. The Residence Hall Councils and the Le Moyne Student Programming Board organize a variety of campus activities, including concerts, dances, a weekly film series, student talent programs, and special lectures as well as off-campus trips and skiing excursions.

The College encourages student leadership in all activities with positions open to students in all class years. Students are represented by a Student Government Association and have formal representation through the senate on most College-wide committees involved in decision making and policy formation.

ADMISSIONS PROCESS

Le Moyne seeks qualified students who are well prepared for serious academic study. Secondary school preparation must have included at least 17 college-preparatory high school units, 4 of which must be in English, 4 in social studies, 3–4 in mathematics, 3–4 in foreign language, and 3–4 in science. It is also recommended that prospective science and mathematics majors complete 4 units of mathematics and science. Le Moyne is test optional, which means SAT and/or ACT scores are not required for admission. However, test scores must be submitted to be considered for top academic scholarships, for certain programs of study, for students who have been Home Schooled, and for international students for whom English is not a first language. SAT and/or ACT exams should be taken no later than December or January of the senior year in high school for test scores to be submitted as part of the application. Campus visits are strongly recommended, as the admission process is a personal one. As bases for selection, academic achievement and secondary school recommendations are of primary importance. Out-of-state students are encouraged to apply.

Le Moyne offers students the opportunity to apply in two ways: early action or regular admission. The early action program is nonbinding and provides high school students the opportunity to receive an admission decision starting December 15 of their senior year. The early action application deadline is November 15. Regular admission applications are reviewed and admission decisions are made on a rolling basis beginning January 1. The priority deadline for applications is February 1; all students who wish to be considered for academic merit scholarships should have a completed application on file in the Office of Admission before this date. Transfer students are encouraged to apply before August 1 for the fall semester and December 1 for the spring semester. Orientation programs for incoming freshmen take place in June and early July. Transfer student orientation programs are offered throughout the summer.

LEWIS & CLARK COLLEGE

AT A GLANCE

On a stunning campus in one of the most exciting and progressive cities anywhere, the next generation of global thinkers gathers to discard conventional thinking, civic complacency, and outmoded preconceptions. Leaders, visionaries, and problem-solvers, we come together to explore new ways of knowing through classic liberal learning and innovative collaboration.

At Lewis & Clark College in Portland, Oregon, we welcome all who are alive to inquiry, open to diversity, and eager to shape the new global century. Through our undergraduate programs in the arts, humanities, and sciences, and through our graduate and professional studies in education, counseling, and law, we undertake original research, interdisciplinary studies, and community service. We push beyond what is known in order to discover something new every day.

LOCATION AND ENVIRONMENT

Founded in 1867, Lewis & Clark College moved to its present location in Portland's southwest hills in 1942. The 137-acre campus sits on a wooded hilltop just six miles from Portland's dynamic downtown, offering stunning views of snow-covered Mount Hood.

Portland is a very livable city with an excellent public transportation system that includes buses, light-rail, and the Portland streetcar. In addition, a free Lewis & Clark shuttle runs frequently into the heart of the city and back to campus. The scenic Willamette River bisects metropolitan Portland, which is home to approximately 2.4 million people. There are endless things to do in Portland: 10,477 acres of parks; diverse galleries, museums, music groups, and theater and dance companies; and a nationally recognized food scene. The city also offers professional hockey, soccer, and the NBA's Portland Trail Blazers. Our students take advantage of the many internship and service opportunities available in the Portland metro area.

Just 50 miles east of campus rises Mount Hood with its 10-month-a-year skiing and snow-boarding. The rugged Oregon coastline is just 90 miles to the west. Throughout the state lie innumerable hiking, climbing, and backpacking opportunities.

CAMPUS FACILITIES & EQUIPMENT

Located on Palatine Hill on a former estate, Lewis & Clark offers students a campus of unmatched physical beauty, along with academic and residential buildings designed to support a rigorous academic environment and strong sense of community.

Academic buildings include the Aubrey R. Watzek library, which is open 24 hours on weekdays during the school year and houses over 770,000 items including books, documents, audiovisual materials, microforms, and periodicals. The library is a member of the Summit consortium, allowing access to approximately 28 million items from the 39 member institutions in the Pacific Northwest. Watzek library also houses the most extensive collection of printed materials known to exist on the Lewis and Clark Expedition. Evans Music Center includes a 410-seat recital hall equipped with an orchestra pit and stage elevator, 22 practice rooms, 43 pianos, 2 harpsichords, a Javanese gamelan, a Baroque organ, and an electronic music studio with digitally-based music production capability. An 85-rank Casavant organ is housed in the college chapel. Fir Acres Theatre houses a 225-seat Main Stage performance/teaching theatre and a black-box experimental theatre (also used as dance studio) along with a scene shop, costume room, green room and design lab. The Olin Center (physics and chemistry), the Biology-Psychology building, and BoDine (mathematical sciences) all house well-equipped classrooms and extensive laboratory spaces for our natural sciences. Our notable science facilities include a scanning electron microscope, a time-lapse deconvolution microscope, a gas chromatograph/mass spectrometer, a high-pressure liquid chromatograph, a 300 MHz nuclear magnetic resonance spectrometer, an observatory with Newtonian and solar telescopes, an astrophysics lab, an electrical instrumentation lab, a molecular modeling lab, a lab for studying the biomechanics of animal locomotion, and a lab for studying parallel computing. Nearby Tryon Creek State Park and the Columbia River Gorge are frequently used as laboratories for field courses in biology and geology.

Other academic buildings include the Fields Center, which houses studio facilities for drawing, painting, sculpture, ceramics, graphic design, and photography. The Miller Center and Howard Hall are home to the humanities and social sciences and offer state-of-the-art classrooms, small auditoriums, and the Keck Interactive Learning Center, a digital language lab.

Several computer labs for student use are available. These labs house more than 130 computers, along with peripherals such as scanners, laser printers, and digital video editing equipment. Other equipment including digital still and video cameras, digital audio recorders, and more are available for checkout. All residence halls have wireless capability. The institution has a 1000 Mbps connection to the internet.

OFF-CAMPUS OPPORTUNITIES

Overseas and off-campus study programs have been a big part of Lewis & Clark for more than 50 years. Each year, about 300 students participate in approximately 30 programs abroad and in selected areas of the United States. During the next few years, programs will be offered in the Arizona borderlands, Australia, Chile, China, Cuba, Dominican Republic, East Africa, Ecuador, England, France, Germany, Greece, India, Ireland, Italy, Japan, Morocco, New York City, New Zealand, Russia, Senegal, South Korea, Spain, Vietnam and Washington, D.C.

Whether their off-campus study is domestic or abroad, students earn credit (equivalent to a full semester or year) for their academic work. Depending on the specific program content, it is possible to earn General Education and/or major credit during these programs. 60 percent of students participate in one of these programs prior to graduating from Lewis & Clark. Students can use Lewis & Clark's financial aid and scholarships for assistance in these programs.

ACADEMIC PROGRAMS

A liberal arts education at Lewis & Clark connects classical learning with fresh inquiry and exciting research that pushes the frontiers of knowledge. Lewis & Clark considers the following elements essential to a liberal arts education:

1. Mastery of the fundamental techniques of intellectual inquiry: effective writing and speaking, active reading, and critical and imaginative thinking.

2. Exposure to the major assumptions, knowledge, and approaches in the fine arts, humanities, natural sciences and social sciences

3. Critical understanding of important contemporary and historical issues.

4. Awareness of international and cross-cultural issues and gender relations.

5. Application of theory and knowledge to the search for informed, thoughtful and responsible solutions to important human problems.

The curriculum combines structure and freedom. Depth and breadth of subject matter are highly valued, but equally important are creativity and critical thinking. There are many opportunities for students to take their learning to a higher level, such as honors projects within academic departments, independent research, and internships. Our fast-growing Bates Center for Entrepreneurship and Leadership offers academic and cocurricular opportunities to translate knowledge and experiences into skills for success beyond college.

Two 15-week semesters make up the academic year, and each semester students normally take four 4-semester-credit courses, and one or more activity courses. The average student course load is 16 credits per semester. The requirement for graduation is 128 semester credits, approximately eight classes each year.

MAJORS AND DEGREES OFFERED

Lewis & Clark offers one degree: the Bachelor of Arts. Students have a wide selection of majors from which to choose: art (studio), art history, Asian studies, biochemistry and molecular biology, biology, chemistry, classics, computer science, computer science and mathematics, economics, English, environmental studies, French, German, Hispanic studies, history, international affairs, mathematics, music, philosophy, physics, political science, psychology, religious studies, rhetoric and media studies, sociology/anthropology, theater, and world languages and literature. Students may also design their own major, pursue a double major, or select from 28 minors. Pre-professional preparation is available in the fields of law, business, education, entrepreneurship, and medicine. Dual degree (3-2 or 4-2) programs in engineering are offered in cooperation with Columbia University, Washington University in St. Louis, and the University of Southern California. Dual degree B.A/M.B.A. programs are available in conjunction with the Simon Graduate School of Business at the University of Rochester and the School of Business at Portland State University. A dual degree, 4-1 B.A/M.A.T program is offered through Lewis & Clark's Graduate School of Education and Counseling. In addition, there is a guaranteed admission agreement with Lewis & Clark's Law School for students meeting certain criteria.

TUITION, ROOM, BOARD, FEES

2018–19 tuition and fees are $50,934, and room and board are $12,490.

FINANCIAL AID

During the 2016–17 academic year, approximately 90 percent of Lewis & Clark students received some form of financial assistance. Institutional, state, and federal resources including grants, loans and work-study may be part of an aid package. Eligibility for need-based funds is based primarily on an analysis of the income and asset information submitted on the Free Application for Federal Student Aid (FAFSA) and the College Board's CSS/Financial Aid PROFILE. To receive priority consideration for all sources of need-based financial aid, students must meet appropriate deadlines for admission and should submit the FAFSA and PROFILE by the date appropriate for their admissions plan as noted at go.lclark.edu/fao.

STUDENT ORGANIZATIONS AND ACTIVITIES

Reflecting the college's national and global reach, approximately 90 percent of Lewis & Clark's 2,021 undergraduate students come from outside Oregon, representing 46 states plus the District of Columbia and 72 countries.

Over 120 student-run clubs and activity groups are offered, including social justice and service organizations; international, cultural, and diversity clubs; media groups, including a radio station and weekly newspaper; and religious and spiritual life organizations. Cultural events such as lectures, student-run symposia, art exhibits, theater productions, concerts, recitals, and dance performances occur on a regular basis. Currently, there are 19 NCAA Division III varsity athletic teams, 8 club teams, and numerous intramural sports. The renowned College Outdoors program offers adventures such as backpacking, rafting, snowshoeing, caving, sea kayaking, and environmental service projects in nearby wilderness areas. There are also plenty of opportunities for volunteering in and around the Portland area.

Lewis & Clark is committed to residential education, to creating a community dedicated to the exploration of ideas, values, beliefs and backgrounds, to the discovery of lifelong friendships; and to collaboration, both formal and informal, with peers, faculty, and staff. About 69 percent of undergraduates live on campus in residence halls; most of our residential space is co-ed. Along with personal living space (usually shared by two to four students), the residence halls host several community venues including coffee houses, convenience stores, art centers, outdoor basketball courts, recreation and fitness centers, lounges, and game rooms. Themed communities within the residence halls are also available, including those that focus on visual and performing arts, multicultural engagement, outdoor pursuits, environmental action, holistic wellness, and more. There is no Greek system at Lewis & Clark.

ADMISSIONS PROCESS

Commitment to academic excellence and personal and intellectual growth is imperative for successful Lewis & Clark applicants. Lewis & Clark is very selective, and every part of the application matters: academic records, essays, involvement in activities at school and in the community, leadership, and the strength of recommendations. Students are encouraged to visit our campus. Interviews are available but not required. The best-prepared applicants will have had four years of English, four years of mathematics, three to four years of history or social sciences, three years of laboratory sciences, two to three years of a foreign language, and one year of fine arts. Required credentials include the Common Application with essay and supplemental questions, an official transcript including first term grades from senior year, the school report form, and one academic teacher recommendation. Lewis & Clark requires the SAT or ACT, unless the student is applying via the Test-Optional Portfolio Path (see lclark.edu for details). Students apply using the online Common Application. There is no application fee. Keep in mind these deadlines for first-year applicants: November 1 for binding Early Decision (notification, December 15), November 1 for non-binding Early Action (notification, January 1) and January 15 for Regular Decision (notification, April 1). Transfer applicants are reviewed on a rolling basis beginning January 1.

LIM COLLEGE

AT A GLANCE

Founded in 1939, and located in New York City—the center of the fashion universe—LIM College educates students for success in the global business of fashion and its many related industries.

As a pioneer in experiential education, or "learning by doing," LIM fosters a unique connection between real-world experience and academic study.

LIM College's curriculum provides students with a foundation of core courses in liberal arts and business while offering diverse and intensive real-world preparation for the working world, particularly through required internships and interaction with faculty who are experts in the business of fashion.

Each year, LIM partners with more than 800 companies in the fashion and related industries to provide students with opportunities for internships, volunteering and employment, as well as guest speakers and special events.

LIM College boasts a highly personal learning environment. Classes are small and professors know students' names. Although most students come to LIM College directly from high school or transfer from other colleges, there are also those of nontraditional college age. LIM students hail from more than 40 U.S. states and approximately 30 countries. As of Fall 2017, undergraduate on-campus enrollment was approximately 1,400 students.

All LIM students receive extensive career advising, and, starting from day one, there are plentiful opportunities to participate in professional development activities, such as resume writing, interviewing, and job search strategy workshops. This contributes to a post-graduation employment rate of over 90 percent.

Alumni can be found pursuing successful careers in all facets of the fashion and related industries. In fact, a 2015 study measuring colleges' contributions to undergraduate student outcomes identified LIM as being among the top 10 percent of four-year colleges in the nation. And according to the College Scorecard, the median salary of LIM students 10 years after entering college is 42 percent higher than the national average.

LIM College also offers a range of valuable student support services. In addition to academic and career advising, personal counseling is available, as is tutoring in math and writing. Because classes are small, faculty members work closely with students and are readily accessible for help and advice.

Student life at LIM College is dynamic. Active clubs include the Fashion Show Production Club, the Student Life Activities Board, the Student Leadership Council, The Lexington Line student magazine (online and print), the Dance Team, the Philanthropy Club, and more.

LIM College's Open Houses offer students and their families the opportunity to tour the campus and learn about the College's unique academic programs, as well as the vast array of career options in the fashion industry. Open Houses also include presentations on financial aid, study abroad, and student activities. Current LIM students are always on hand at Open Houses to answer questions.

There are also many other opportunities to visit the LIM campus, including weekly information sessions, Transfer Services Days, mock classes for accepted students, and other special events.

LIM College is accredited by the Middle States Association of Colleges and Schools, and LIM's Bachelor of Business Administration, Bachelor of Professional Studies, and associate degree programs are also accredited by the Accreditation Council of Business Schools and Programs (ACBSP).

LOCATION AND ENVIRONMENT

LIM College is situated in three buildings: on East 53rd Street, East 45th Street, and on Fifth Avenue, one of the most fashionable locales in the world. Home to the headquarters of the garment, cosmetics, advertising, publishing, and textile industries, New York City offers unparalleled resources, many of which are directly incorporated into the LIM College curriculum in the form of guest speakers and field trips. The best the fashion world has to offer is right at the College's doorstep, including such famous names as Saks Fifth Avenue, Bergdorf Goodman, Cartier, Gucci, and Prada.

CAMPUS FACILITIES & EQUIPMENT

Academic facilities include the 5,000-square-foot Adrian G. Marcuse Library, with over 14,700 books, 1,118 librarian-selected e-books, 164 scholarly journals and print magazines, 855 bound volumes of magazine back issues, 1,161 DVDs, an archive of historic materials, and a large collection of fashion, business, and marketing books to assist students in their research. The library also has 42 CAD-enabled computers. The 60 subscription databases located on the library-run web page are available 24/7, on-or off-campus, and can be accessed by computer, tablet, smart phone, or any other Internet-ready device.

Student computer labs (Mac and PC) and lounges are found throughout LIM's buildings, and the Fifth Avenue location is equipped with two fashion merchandising studios, two 1,100-square-foot visual merchandising studios, as well as a Color and Materials Lab.

Located on the Upper East Side of Manhattan, LIM's residence hall offers a host of attractive amenities. All rooms have private bathrooms, complimentary wireless Internet access, phone service, and over 100 cable channels. Rooms are also equipped with refrigerators and 25-inch flat-screen televisions. In addition, the residence hall contains a private gym, game room, computer lab, and a modern communal kitchen.

OFF-CAMPUS OPPORTUNITIES (STUDY ABROAD)

From two-week immersion programs to semester-long study abroad experiences, LIM College offers students the opportunity to see the world and experience fashion on an international stage. With programs in Australia, Canada, China, England, France, Guatemala, Italy, the Netherlands, Spain, Vietnam, and Taiwan, students are given a global education for a global industry.

ACADEMIC PROGRAMS

LIM College offers bachelor's (four-year) degrees in: Fashion Media, Fashion Merchandising, International Business, Management, Marketing, and Visual Merchandising. Associate (two-year) degree programs are available in Fashion Merchandising and Fashion Merchandising & Management.

The Fashion Merchandising major offers a track in Retail Buying and Planning. Additionally, students may choose from a broad variety of concentrations, such as Cosmetics, Home Fashions, or Event Planning, which allow the pursuit of a focused area of study that complements the major. At the graduate level, LIM has several fashion-focused master's degree programs. A number of LIM's degree programs are available online as well as on campus.

LIM College features a combination of classroom education and supervised internships designed to prepare students for positions in all areas of the fashion and related industries. Experiential education, or "learning by doing," is an integral component of the LIM College curriculum. Students in four-year programs are required to complete three internships in order to earn their bachelor's degree. Each internship has a seminar attached to it that includes activities such as field trips, guest speakers, and portfolio-building activities that help students build their professional skills, network with industry executives, and find the specific fashion career path that's right for them. The experiential education program culminates with a nearly full-time, semester-long Senior Co-op internship.

LIM College's academic calendar runs on a traditional semester format. On-campus students may enroll in the both the fall and spring semesters. Summer and Saturday programs for high school students are also available. Blending academics with hands-on experience, these pre-college courses are a great way to explore the fashion industry.

MAJORS AND DEGREES OFFERED

Bachelor of Science

-Fashion Media

-International Business

Bachelor of Business Administration

-Fashion Merchandising°

-Management

-Marketing

-Visual Merchandising

Bachelor of Professional Studies

-Fashion Merchandising

Associate in Applied Science

-Fashion Merchandising & Management°

Associate in Occupational Studies

-Fashion Merchandising

Master of Professional Studies

-Business of Fashion°

-Fashion Marketing°

-Fashion Merchandising & Retail Management°

-Global Fashion Supply Chain Management

°Also offered online

TUITION, ROOM, BOARD, FEES

Undergraduate tuition and fees for the 2018–19 school year is $26,210. Housing charges for the 2018–19 year are $16,350. Books and supplies average approximately $900 per academic year and students living on campus may spend up to $4,000 a year on meal expenses. Students who commute spend from $1,200 to $2,000 for transportation, depending on distance, and personal expenses are approximately $1,500 per academic year. For students who do not have their own accident and health insurance, the mandatory insurance offered by LIM College is $1,700

FINANCIAL AID

LIM College believes that lack of funds should not keep students from attaining a degree. Therefore, admissions decisions and financial aid are totally separate, and a request for aid has no effect on admission. Approximately 81 percent of LIM College's students received some form of financial aid during the 2016-17 academic year. Institutional scholarships, Federal Pell Grants, Federal Supplemental Educational Opportunity Grants, and New York State TAP grants are all available for eligible students. In addition, the College participates in the Federal Stafford Loan program for students and Federal PLUS Loan program for parents. The College also works with several private lenders to offer alternative education loans for students to supplement their federal loans. International students are eligible to apply for alternative loans with a credit-worth U.S. based co-signer. The Free Application for Federal Student Aid (FAFSA) should be filed by all applicants by March 1 for priority consideration. Aid is granted on the basis of financial need and scholarships are merit-based, although some awards take need into consideration. Details of the financial aid programs are available on the LIM College website or are available directly from the Office of Student Financial Services.

LIM College offers a merit scholarship program for incoming freshmen and transfer students. These scholarship monies are awarded for academic achievement in high school or college. Students can remain eligible for their scholarship throughout their stay at the College by maintaining a GPA of 3.0 or above.

STUDENT ORGANIZATIONS AND ACTIVITIES

Student life at LIM College is dynamic, with the Office of Student Life at the center of student activities and clubs. Active clubs include the Fashion Show Production Club, the Student Life Activities Board, the Student Leadership Council, The Lexington Line, the Dance Team, the Philanthropy Club, and more.

The Fashion Show Production Club is extremely popular. It produces an annual fashion show at a major Manhattan venue that is attended by an audience of more than 1,000. Another popular activity is the student-run magazine, The Lexington Line magazine (online and print), which partners with The Daily Front Row to produce a special magazine for New York's Spring Fashion Week.

The College also offers diverse cultural celebrations, philanthropic service opportunities, and New York City sightseeing outings throughout the year.

ADMISSIONS PROCESS

LIM College's Admissions Committee recognizes that many intangibles go into the making of a successful student, and it evaluates each applicant individually and holistically. The College uses a rolling admission policy. Applicants are informed of the admission decision within approximately two to four weeks after all admission requirements have been fulfilled. An application may be obtained from the LIM College website or by contacting the Office of Admissions.

All undergraduate applicants are required to submit high school transcripts, one letter of recommendation, an essay, and the completed application with the application fee. LIM College has a test optional policy for admission, which means students can decide whether or not to submit their SAT or ACT scores. Transfer students must also submit all college transcripts, regardless of intent to receive credit for previous work. International students should review the LIM College website and contact the Office of Admissions for specific additional requirements. It is also strongly suggested that all applicants create an activity sheet or resume highlighting their experience, with an emphasis on business and fashion activities.

LIM College accepts qualified students as transfers throughout the four years. The maximum number of credits that LIM will accept towards a bachelor's degree is 65. Transfer students must complete the last consecutive 61 credits for BS degree students and 58 credits for BPS/BBA students at LIM College, including the Senior Co-op semester.

LOYOLA UNIVERSITY CHICAGO

AT A GLANCE

Ranked a Best Value university by U.S. News & World Report, Loyola University Chicago will help you prepare for a career with 80+ programs in business, sciences, and other disciplines.

Loyola is the largest Jesuit Catholic university in the United States, enrolling 16,673 students. Incoming freshmen come from 43 states and 57 countries. Loyola offers more than 80 undergraduate majors and more than 140 graduate, professional, and graduate-level certificate programs as well as three professional programs in law, medicine, and nursing.

Loyola helps students prepare for meaningful careers with top academic programs in business, the sciences, and numerous other disciplines, along with opportunities for internships throughout the city of Chicago and beyond. Loyola's well-rounded, transformative education will help students develop as a whole person-intellectually, socially, physically, and spiritually.

LOCATION AND ENVIRONMENT

Loyola gives students the best of campus and city life with diverse living and learning opportunities in the world-class city of Chicago. Located off North Michigan Avenue, Chicago's Magnificent Mile, Loyola's dynamic Water Tower Campus is home to the Quinlan School of Business as well as the Schools of Communication, Continuing and Professional Studies, Education, Law, and Social Work and connects students to myriad internship, job, and service opportunities. Loyola's Lake Shore Campus, home to the College of Arts and Sciences, the Graduate School, and the Marcella Niehoff School of Nursing, is located on the picturesque shore of Lake Michigan and offers students the comforts of a traditional residential campus. The Stritch School of Medicine is housed at the Medical Sciences Campus in west suburban Maywood, Illinois.

Exposure to Loyola's three Chicago campuses gives students three diverse experiences: a vibrant urban environment, the comfort of a more traditional collegiate setting, and the bustle of a professional medical environment. At each campus, students have access to computers, study areas, and dining halls, as well as a network of student groups and activities. A free intercampus shuttle is available between the Lake Shore and Water Tower Campuses.

CAMPUS FACILITIES & EQUIPMENT

The Schreiber Center is home to the Quinlan School of Business and offers students a 10-story business learning space designed to foster community, connectivity, and transparency. This sustainable, state-of-the-art building is a landmark on our Water Tower Campus and acts as a networking hub for students, faculty, and alumni. The recently completed, 100,000+ sq. ft. Damen Student Center is a LEED Silver certified building. Named after the founder of Loyola University Chicago, the Arnold J. Damen, S.J. Student Center provides students a dedicated space to build community and encourage co-curricular engagement. Damen is the place to relax, study, play pool, watch TV, grab a snack, or hang out with friends.

The Institute of Environmental Sustainability at Loyola is the latest way we are extending our commitment to responsible leadership. The Institute provides practical experiences that will translate to your future workplace, such as working on the student-run farm or in the ecosystem research labs, as well as through degree options in environmental studies and environmental science with concentrations in conservation and restoration, food systems and sustainable agriculture, and public health.

Our student-run biodiesel program is the first and only school operation licensed to sell reclaimed biodiesel fuel In the U.S.

Not only is Cuneo Hall a state-of-the-art building with a cutting-edge academic center—but it also uses sustainable technologies to reduce its ecological footprint. Cuneo is LEED Gold certified and will use approximately 60 percent less energy than comparable academic buildings.

The renovated Mundelein Center offers new options for fine arts programming. For plays and theatre are the new Newhart Family Theatre and the Underground Laboratory Theatre. Mundelein Music Hall has been completely renovated as well. These new spaces give students an opportunity to hone their craft in contemporary surroundings.

The School of Communication is in the heart of Chicago's creative and business communities. Located at the Water Tower Campus, the building features generously equipped computer labs, state-of-the-art classrooms and offices, and on-site production facilities, including street-side lab with a TV studio and radio interview sets.

The Information Commons is a four-story lakeside research facility that provides individual and group study space for students, as well as state-of-the-art technology with more than 200 computers, wireless internet connections, and a lakefront café.

Loyola's Michael R. and Marilyn C. Quinlan Life Sciences Education and Research Center provides numerous opportunities for undergraduates to engage in the latest scientific research alongside their professors in modern labs for biology, bioinformatics, chemistry, ecology, and other life sciences.

For information about campus facilities, visit http://www.luc.edu/campus_community.shtml.

OFF-CAMPUS OPPORTUNITIES

Students may study abroad at the John Felice Rome Center in Italy, our Vietnam location in Ho Chi Minh City, or choose from 150 other study abroad programs in 70 countries.

ACADEMIC PROGRAMS

The Core Curriculum is the foundation of Loyola's liberal arts education. Core courses are aimed at increasing students' understanding of themselves and the world while they explore diverse subjects and cultivate new interests. Courses provide a strong base of knowledge, skills, and values that will help students achieve academic, professional, and personal success throughout their lives.

Exceptionally well-qualified students may apply to the Interdisciplinary Honors Program.

Other special academic opportunities include pre-professional programs for law and health professions; 30+ five-year (bachelor's/master's) degree programs; 19 interdisciplinary programs; a six-year, early admission to Loyola's School of Law; early assurance to Loyola's Stritch School of Medicine; and the Loyola/Midwestern University Dual-Acceptance Pharmacy Program.

MAJORS AND DEGREES OFFERED

The College of Arts and Sciences offers undergraduate majors in African Studies and the African Diaspora, anthropology, art history, biochemistry, bioinformatics, biology, biophysics, chemistry, classical civilization, computer science, criminal justice and criminology, cybersecurity, dance, economics, engineering science, English, forensic science, French, global and international studies, Greek (ancient), history, human services, information technology, Italian, Latin, mathematics, mathematics and computer science, mathematics education, music, neuroscience, philosophy, physics, physics and computer science, physics and engineering, political science, psychology, religious studies, sociology, sociology and anthropology, software engineering, Spanish, statistics, studio art, theater, theology, theoretical physics and applied mathematics, visual communication, and women's studies and gender studies.

The Institute of Environmental Sustainability offers majors in Environmental Policy, Environmental Science, and Environmental Studies.

The Quinlan School of Business offers majors in accounting, economics, entrepreneurship, finance, human resource management, information systems, international business, management, marketing, supply chain management, sport management, and a US/Europe Business double degree.

The School of Communication offers majors in advertising creative, advertising and public relations, advocacy and social change, communication studies, film and digital media, and multimedia journalism.

The School of Education offers majors in bilingual/bicultural education, early childhood/special education, elementary education, foreign language education, middle grade education, secondary education and foreign language, and special education.

The Marcella Niehoff School of Nursing offers the Bachelor of Science in Exercise Science, Bachelor of Science in Nursing, a Bachelor of Science in Health Systems Management, an RN to BSN, and an Accelerated BSN program, which is available to students who have already completed a baccalaureate degree.

The School of Social Work offers an undergraduate major in social work and a combined bachelor's and master's degree in social work, which can be completed in five years.

Learn more at LUC.edu/majors.

TUITION, ROOM, BOARD, FEES

Tuition for 2018–2019 entering students (per year): $42,270

Room and board (per year): Room and board cost is dependent on students' selection of residence hall and meal plan (average is $14,280).

Tuition part-time (per credit hour): $788

FINANCIAL AID

At Loyola, we're committed to making a high-quality education affordable. Our Financial Aid Office works with students and families to address each student's specific situation and needs. Our expert staff evaluates financial aid eligibility for resources such as grants, scholarships, and loans to help make a Loyola education a possibility for students.

Approximately 97 percent of Loyola freshmen receive grants and/or scholarships. Students are encouraged to file the Free Application for Federal Student Aid (FAFSA) by February 15 in order to meet Loyola's March 1 priority processing date.

In addition to the many scholarships awarded with admission, students may also explore more than 75 types of additional scholarships. For more information, visit LUC.edu/scholarships.

STUDENT ORGANIZATIONS AND ACTIVITIES

Loyola's total enrollment is 16,673 students, both undergraduate and graduate. The 2017 incoming freshman class consisted of 2,658 students. These students came from 43 states, Puerto Rico, and 57 foreign countries. Of these students, 29 percent attended private/Catholic high school. Our diverse student population is comprised of 39 percent African American, Asian American, Latin American, Native American, and Multiracial/Other students. With 39 percent of our student body identifying as Buddhist, Easter Orthodox, Hindu, Jewish, Muslim, and Protestant, Loyola University Chicago is a home to all faiths.

Loyola offers students the chance to develop leadership and social skills by participating in any of its more than 250+ academic, athletic, cultural, hobby, media, political, social, and spiritual student-run organizations.

ADMISSIONS PROCESS

Students seeking admission to Loyola are evaluated on their overall academic record, including ACT or SAT scores. The freshman class entering in Fall 2017 had middle 50 percent ACT score ranges between 24 and 29, middle 50 percent range on the SAT Verbal between 570 and 660, middle 50 percent range on the SAT Math between 550 and 650, and an average GPA of 3.80. Most Loyola students rank in the upper quarter of their graduating class, but consideration is given to students in the upper half.

Transfer students with 20 credit hours or more are evaluated on the basis of their college work only. The minimum acceptable GPA varies from 2.0 to 2.5, depending upon academic interest. Candidates must also be in good standing at the last college attended.

Loyola notifies applicants four to six weeks after the application, supporting credentials, and secondary school counselor or teacher recommendation are received. The application is only available online and there is no application fee at LUC.edu/applyluc.

Prospective students are encouraged to visit campus by arranging individual appointments and campus tours up to two weeks in advance. Arrange a visit at LUC.edu/visit.

To learn more or arrange a visit, contact:

Undergraduate Admission Office

Loyola University Chicago

Sullivan Center

6339 N. Sheridan Road

Chicago, IL 60660

Telephone: 773.508.3075 or 800.262.2373 (toll-free)

E-mail: admission@luc.edu

Website: LUC.edu/undergrad

MANHATTAN COLLEGE

AT A GLANCE

Manhattan College is a Lasallian Catholic college in Riverdale, NY, which offers more than 100 majors and programs in business, education and health, engineering, liberal arts and science.

Manhattan College was founded in 1853 by the Brothers of the Christian Schools, a teaching order started by Saint John Baptist de La Salle, patron saint of teachers.

Students are guided by an internationally recognized faculty, sought-after leaders and real-world consultants in their fields, 93 percent of whom hold doctoral degrees. They have opportunities to study abroad in more than 30 countries.

Manhattan College participates in Division I sports as part of the MAAC, with 19 teams. The College is known for its student-athletes, with many ranking on the MAAC All-Academic teams, while also contributing to winning teams.

LOCATION AND ENVIRONMENT

At Manhattan College, we offer a truly unique location within the boundaries of New York City right next door to a subway stop. Unlike many other New York City schools, we have a true college campus—23 acres centered around a quad, where students play Frisbee, study under the sun and hang out with friends. Manhattan's professors use NYC as a classroom with field trips to Wall Street, museums and other world-famous locations.

The undergraduate student body of 3,444 hails from 44 states and 60 countries. With a four-year guarantee of resident housing, 82 percent of freshmen live on campus in both traditional style dorms and suite style living. Common interest communities bring students with a particular interest under one roof to live and learn throughout the year.

CAMPUS FACILITIES & EQUIPMENT

The Raymond W. Kelly ('63) Student Commons opened in fall 2014. The 70,000-square-foot building significantly enhances the College's ability to integrate academics and student life, and provides space for fitness and wellness programming, cultural and community events, dining, student activities, and student collaboration.

O'Malley Library is home to a number of new features and services, including more than 100 computer workstations, a round-the-clock Internet Café, a media center equipped with teleconferencing capabilities, and many group study rooms scattered throughout the five-story layout.

Both commuters and residents can take advantage of the Fitness Center and newly renovated cafeterias. There are a variety of dining options, as well as spaces to relax and study.

OFF-CAMPUS OPPORTUNITIES

Students actively define their commitment toward community around the city, country and world. Each year, Campus Ministry and Social Action (CMSA) runs several L.O.V.E. programs (Lasallian Outreach Volunteer Experience) giving students service experiences in areas such as New Orleans, Kenya, Ecuador, the Dominican Republic and West Virginia.

Many students also participate in local community service projects. These include Habitat for Humanity, working with the elderly in nearby nursing homes, volunteering in soup kitchens and tutoring at local schools.

Students are provided with internship opportunities in their field of study throughout the metropolitan area often networking with alumni.

ACADEMIC PROGRAMS

Manhattan College is one of the few American colleges to have chapters of all five of these distinguished national honor societies: Beta Gamma Sigma, Kappa Delta Pi, Phi Beta Kappa, Sigma Xi and Tau Beta Pi. Manhattan College is one of 286 institutions in the U.S. with a chapter of Phi Beta Kappa, the nation's oldest and most widely known academic honor society, which celebrates and advocates excellence in the liberal arts and sciences.

Other programs at Manhattan College:

1. The National Model United Nations: a unique opportunity to better understand the inner workings of the United Nations and other international organizations while building skills in diplomacy and compromise.

2. The Branigan Fellowships Program: undergraduate research in the humanities for student-initiated projects (grants over $3,000).

3. The Fellowships Committee: encourages graduate study and helps work through sometimes challenging application processes (students and alumni).

4. The Pre-Law Advisory Committee

5. Study Abroad Program: programs run for a semester, an academic year, a month-long summer program or a seven-week summer program.

6. Manhattan's Mentorship Program: opportunities to gain insight into intended careers by being paired with professionals, generally Manhattan alumni in those careers.

7. College Internship Program: complete at the minimum of one internship within their four years of study.

8. Manhattan's Finance and Economics Club: student preparation and participation in the Volunteer Income Tax Assistance Program (VITA) and other service activities.

9. Jasper Summer Research Scholars: a fellowship that will offer a stipend to scholars to pursue on campus summer research. It is managed though the Center for Graduate School and Fellowship Advisement and supports up to three students from each of the undergraduate schools.

MAJORS AND DEGREES OFFERED

Manhattan College offers more than 40 major fields of study on the undergraduate level and graduate degrees in continuing & professional studies, education, engineering and business. The College's professional schools are externally accredited by the following accrediting organizations: the O'Malley School of Business, Association to Advance Collegiate Schools of Business (AACSB); school of education, Teacher Education Accrediting Council (TEAC); and individual school of engineering programs are accredited by the Engineering Accreditation Commission (EAC) of ABET, Inc.

Programs include:

Liberal Arts: Art History, Communication, Economics, English, Environmental Studies, French, Government, History, International Studies, Labor Studies, Peace Studies, Philosophy, Psychology, Religious Studies, Sociology, Spanish, Urban Studies.

Business: Accounting, Business Analytics, Computer Information Systems, Economics, Finance, Global Business Studies, Management and Marketing. Graduate programs: Bachelor of Science in Professional Accounting / Master of Business Administration Program and the Bachelor of Science in Business / Master of Business Administration Program (five-year multiple award program) and a 36 credit stand-alone MBA program.

Education: Early Childhood Education, Childhood Education, Dual: Childhood/Special Education and Adolescent Education; and two undergraduate majors in the department of Physical Education and Human Performance in Physical Education Teaching (grades K-12) or Exercise Science. Graduate: Five-Year Childhood/Special Education Program, which combines baccalaureate and graduate work, allowing the student to receive a bachelor's and master's degree with eligibility to pursue certification for grades 1-6 in regular and special education; master's degrees and advanced certificates in school counseling, mental health counseling, marriage & family therapy, instructional design & delivery, special education, and school building leadership.

Radiological and Health Professions Program: Nuclear Medicine Technology, Radiation Therapy Technology, or Allied Health.

Engineering: Chemical Engineering, Civil Engineering, Computer Engineering, Electrical Engineering and Mechanical Engineering. Graduate: Chemical Engineering, Civil Engineering, Computer Engineering, Construction Management, Electrical Engineering, Environmental Engineering, and Mechanical Engineering.

Science: Biology, Biochemistry, Chemistry, Computer Science, Mathematics, and Physics. Graduate programs in Computer Science and Applied Mathematics/Data Analytics

Another option is the Five-Year Childhood/Special Education Program, which combines baccalaureate and graduate work, allowing the student to receive a bachelor's and master's degree with eligibility to pursue certification for grades 1–6 in regular and special education. The school of education also offers master's degrees and advanced certificates in school counseling, mental health counseling, special education and school building leadership.

The Radiological and Health Professions Program is also part of the school of education and health and is available to students pursuing a Bachelor of Science with three major selections: Nuclear Medicine Technology, Radiation Therapy Technology or Allied Health. The Engineering program offers programs leading to the baccalaureate degree in five disciplines: Chemical Engineering, Civil Engineering, Computer Engineering, Electrical Engineering, and Mechanical Engineering. Graduate study at the master's level is also available in: Chemical Engineering, Civil Engineering, Computer Engineering, Electrical Engineering, Environmental Engineering, and Mechanical Engineering.

The Science program offers students the chance to major in the following areas: Biology, Biochemistry, Chemistry, Computer Science, Mathematics and Physics.

TUITION, ROOM, BOARD, FEES

Undergraduate Tuition and Fees 2017–2018

A. Full Time Students, 2017–2018

Full time students register for 12 or more credits per semester.

Tuition Charges per Semester

New Students entering 2017–18

$19,100 (per semester)

Continuing students $18,450 (per semester)

Program Fees per Semester Arts, Education $720

Business $850

Science $910

Engineering $1,430

Over credit Charges° per credit hour

FINANCIAL AID

Manhattan College provides the maximum financial aid available to qualified students to make their attendance at Manhattan financially possible.

New Students: Students admitted to the College and demonstrating financial need will receive a financial aid assistance offer in the form of a financial aid award letter from the Office of Admissions and Financial Aid, which is based on an assessment of your financial need.

Continuing Eligibility: All financial aid is renewable on a yearly basis provided the student remains eligible.

Presidential Scholarships: Non-need-based scholarships awarded to extraordinary applicants. Eligibility is based on exceptional SAT or ACT scores, secondary school grade point average, and rank in class.

Dean's Award: Dean's Awards are offered to academically gifted students who fall slightly below Presidential Scholarship requirements.

Manhattan College Grant-in-Aid: Manhattan College awards grants-in-aid to accepted students who demonstrate financial need.

Manhattan College Campus Employment Program: Manhattan offers its own campus work program to students who need employment to meet college expenses but are not eligible for Federal Work Study

Athletic Grants: The Manhattan College Athletics department may fund athletic grants to students who, by the possession of certain athletic skills, can add to the community spirit and morale of the campus.

Resident Assistant Grants: These grants are awarded to students selected to serve as Resident Assistants in the dormitories.

Dollars for Scholars: As a collegiate partner, Manhattan College matches Scholarship of America awards up to $500 a year.

Other programs: Veterans Administration Educational Benefits, Post-9/11 GI Bill Participant, Tuition Remission, Tuition Exchange Scholarship

The school also awards endowed and special category scholarships as part of the existing financial aid package.

STUDENT ORGANIZATIONS AND ACTIVITIES

Manhattan College offers many events and activities for students to participate in with more than 60 clubs and organizations on campus.

Cultural Groups: Asian Culture Club, Association for Black Culture, Gaelic Society, International Student Association and the Multicultural Student Union

Special Interest Groups: Christ in Your Life, Lasallian Outreach Volunteer Experience (L.O.V.E.), Electronics Club, Fashion Student Association, Just Peace, LaSallian Collegians (service group), New York Water Environmental Association, Relay for Life and Student Government.

Club Sports: Cheerleading & Crew

Social Leisure Clubs: Games Club, Outdoors Club, Steppers

Performing Arts: Bagpipers, Jasper Dancers, Jasper Band, Jazz Band, Orchestra, Players, Scatterbomb and Singers.

Communication: Manhattanite (yearbook), MCTV, Quadrangle (college newspaper), WRCM radio station

Social Fraternities & Sororities: Alpha Sigma Beta, Fraternity; Alpha Upsilon Pi, Sorority; Gamma Alpha Sigma, Fraternity; Crimson & Cream Delta Sigma Theta Sorority

Co-curricular clubs: Accounting Society, American Advertising Federation, American Chemistry Society, American Institute of Biological Science, American Institute of Chemical Engineers, American Institute of Aeronautics and Astronautics, American Society of Mechanical Engineers, Amnesty International, Association for Supervision and Curriculum Development, Biology Club, Business Analytics Competition, Communications Club, Construction Management Association of America, Council for Exceptional Children, Economics and Finance Society, Emmersonian, Engineers Without Borders, Entrepreneurship Club, Feb Challenge, Government and Finance Club, Information Technology Club, Institute of Electronic and Electrical Engineers, International Genetically Engineered Machine, Investment Club, International Society for Pharmaceutical Engineering, The Institute of Transportation Engineers, Logos, Lotus Magazine, Management Club, Manhattan College Games, Manhattan Magazine, Manhattan Scientist Research Journal, Marketing Club, Mini Baja, Model U.N., National Society of Black Engineers, New York Water Environmental Association, Phi Delta Epsilon, Pre-Law Student Group, Public Relations Student Society of America, Psychology Club, The Quadrangle, Radiological Science Society, Society of Civil Engineers, Society of Hispanic Professional Engineers, Society of Mechanical Engineers, Society of Physics Students, Society of Women Engineers, Sociological Society, Spuyten Duyvil Undergraduate Mathematics Conference, St. Thomas More Law Society, Volunteer Income Tax Assistance, Women in Biology Club.

ADMISSIONS PROCESS

1. Course Selection and Performance: Most emphasis is placed upon student course selection on the secondary level and grades earned in those subjects.

2. SAT and/or ACT Scores

3. 1 Letter of Recommendation

4. Personal Statement

Students who are transferring without an associate degree or with an A.A.S. degree must submit:

High school transcript

Official college transcripts

List of courses presently being taken

College catalogs from all institutions previously attended

Financial aid transcripts from all collegiate institutions previously attended (even if you only took one or two courses while in high school)

MARLBORO COLLEGE

AT A GLANCE

Marlboro College is an intentionally small, intellectually demanding liberal arts school located in southern Vermont. Home to 300 students, Marlboro empowers students with the freedom and responsibility to create an individualized course of study in collaboration with faculty members and to participate in a self-governing community. Instead of traditional majors, students pursue a self-designed Plan of Concentration based on their academic interests, culminating in a major work of scholarship. Students graduate having completed a profound intellectual journey and go out into the world with greater self-reliance and the skills needed to forge their own career path or pursue graduate-level study.

LOCATION AND ENVIRONMENT

Marlboro College's setting in rural southern Vermont provides students with space for quiet contemplation as well as myriad opportunities for outdoor recreation. With 40 miles of trails on or near our 300-acre campus, and the Green Mountain National Forest nearby, students have easy access to hiking, mountain biking, skiing, caving, climbing and kayaking (among other activities). Each season includes Marlboro traditions such as Apple Days in the fall and the broomball tournament in winter.

Tucked on its own Potash Hill, the college is an integral part of the town of Marlboro, a community of less than 1,000 where many staff, faculty and students are active citizens. Some of the many benefits shared by both the college and the town include a volunteer fire company, a community newsletter called the Marlboro Mixer, cross-country ski trails, the Marlboro Historical Society, the Southern Vermont Natural History Museum, the Marlboro Community Fair and the January Book Swap. Marlboro is also the site of the world famous Marlboro Music Festival which occupies the campus during the summer.

CAMPUS FACILITIES & EQUIPMENT

The core of campus buildings is made up of historic farmhouses and barns, renovated into classrooms and dorms by the first students who attended Marlboro. These include Dalrymple Hall, the main classroom building; the dining hall; the admissions building; and Mather, the administrative building. Over many years the college has added more buildings, including residence halls, student cabins and cottages, Persons Auditorium/gymnasium, Whittemore Theater, Rice-Aron Library, the Campus Center and Total Health Center, and the Serkin Center for Performing Arts. The new Snyder Visual Arts Center adds exciting new gallery, studio and classroom space for the integration of visual arts with other disciplines. Other facilities include an integrated science lab, a DNA lab, a computer lab, and a digital media lab.

OFF-CAMPUS OPPORTUNITIES

With the vibrant town of Brattleboro just 10 miles away, Marlboro students have easy access to many resources and activities. Brattleboro is an eclectic community located in the Connecticut River Valley and a regional center for art, commerce and technology. It was listed as one of the "20 Best Small Towns in America" by Smithsonian magazine, one of the "10 Best Small Towns in America" by Fodor's, and in the top 10 in the book The 100 Best Art Towns in America, with many galleries, music venues, bookstores and performance spaces to experience. Among the blocks of historic red-brick buildings one can find cozy cafes and four-star restaurants featuring local fare and international cuisines including Thai, Korean, Greek and Italian. Mother Earth News named Brattleboro one of "Eight Great Places You've Never Heard Of," and its college-town feel was recently highlighted on Vermont Public Radio. Vans run from the college into Brattleboro multiple times a day and trips to Northeastern cities such as Northampton, Boston, New York and Montreal occur several weekends each semester.

ACADEMIC PROGRAMS

Rather than follow a prescribed academic program, Marlboro students work closely with faculty advisors to map out an individualized course of study based on their intellectual interests. This approach allows students to study broadly and creatively across disciplines before embarking on their self-designed Plan of Concentration, an in-depth examination of a focused academic area that culminates in a major work of scholarship. By taking ownership of and responsibility for the scope and topography of their intellectual exploration, Marlboro students learn how to define a set of goals, develop a comprehensive plan to meet them, and work through the obstacles that inevitably arise along the way. They employ initiative and grit throughout the process and emerge at the end with a joyful sense of accomplishment, heightened confidence, and invaluable experience.

Marlboro's faculty members bring an extraordinary degree of commitment, passion and academic mentoring to their teaching endeavors. Beyond the traditional classroom setting, faculty members interact with students through one-on-one tutorials, and plan advising sessions, service-learning trips and collaborative projects ranging from scholarly papers to films. Whether participating in Town Meeting or composing original music for a promotional video, faculty members make significant contributions to the vitality and spirit of Marlboro's learning community on a regular basis.

Whether their academic interests lean toward Russian literature or contemporary dance, students write prodigiously over the course of their time at Marlboro. Within their first three semesters, students must fulfill the Clear Writing Requirement, which involves submitting a portfolio of clear, concise and grammatically correct writing samples for approval by the faculty. Marlboro's focus on helping students develop their command of the written word speaks to the college's underlying focus on clear thinking, which is both a product and reflection of clear writing. Whatever career paths Marlboro students forge, they all benefit from the ability to process complex information and effectively communicate their ideas to others.

MAJORS AND DEGREES OFFERED

Marlboro College empowers undergraduate students to create an individualized course of study in collaboration with faculty members. Based on their personal academic interests and goals, students study broadly across disciplines before embarking on a self-designed Plan of Concentration that culminates in a major work of scholarship. This approach allows students to take ownership of and responsibility for the scope and structure of their intellectual exploration. Degrees offered include Bachelor of Arts, Bachelor of Science and, through the World Studies Program, Bachelor of Arts or Science in International Studies. Our degree fields are:

American Studies

Anthropology

Art History

Asian Studies

Astronomy

Biochemistry

Biology

Ceramics

Chemistry

Computer Science

Cultural History

Dance

Economics

Environmental Studies

Film/Video Studies

Gender Studies

History

Languages

Liberal Studies

Literature

Mathematics

Music

Painting, Drawing, and Mixed Media

Philosophy

Photography

Physics

Politics

Psychology

Religion

Sculpture

Sociology

Theater

Visual Arts

World Studies

Writing

TUITION, ROOM, BOARD, FEES

For the 2018–2019 academic year, the fees are as follows:

Tuition: $39,870

Fees: $970

Room: $7,142

Board: $5,206

Total: $53,188

Financial Aid

As a very small, private liberal arts college, Marlboro makes a conscious and continuous effort to keep tuition and fees as affordable as possible. In recent years, we've increased the amount of need-based grant aid provided to students and increased other awards for financial aid. Today more than 90 percent of full-time Marlboro students receive some form of financial assistance. Applicants should contact the Financial Aid Office directly to request a financial aid packet, which includes step-by-step instructions. The priority deadline for completing the Free Application for Federal Student Aid (FAFSA) is March 1. The financial aid office can be reached at 802-258-9312 or finaid@marlboro.edu.

STUDENT ORGANIZATIONS AND ACTIVITIES

Marlboro College operates based on a model of community governance. Students, faculty, and staff play an integral role in shaping campus life through their participation in Town Meeting, a monthly assembly during which college-wide issues are discussed and brought to vote. Students also serve on committees in areas ranging from curriculum development and faculty hiring to public art and food services.

Campus life at Marlboro College correlates directly with student interests. Extracurricular groups and activities evolve yearly with each incoming class. Through this ongoing collective creation of community, Marlboro students develop valuable skills in teamwork and community organizing as well as a strong sense of civic investment.

One of the most popular resources for student activities is the Outdoor Program, OP for short. The OP offers a variety of activities from week-long orientation trips for new students to weekend mini trips, to winter and spring-break trips in tropical climates. Some of the popular activities have been rock climbing, hiking, rafting, kayaking, camping, yoga, intramural soccer, broomball, and Ultimate Frisbee. The college also has an indoor climbing wall and regular intramural activities.

For a small campus, students enjoy a wide range of social, artistic, and cultural activities. A sampling of student activities in one semester would include performances by rock, folk, jazz, and ethnic bands; dances; lectures; poetry readings; recitals; plays; and concerts. Annual events that are considered traditions include midnight breakfast, Wendell-Judd Cup cross country ski event, Work Day, President's Fall Ball, Trails Day, broomball tournament, community and international dinners, Gender Bender Ball, and Apple Days.

ADMISSIONS PROCESS

If you are looking for an intentionally small, intellectually demanding liberal arts school where students are seen, heard, known and valued, Marlboro College would be a great college choice for you. Marlboro assesses student potential in the unique context of each applicant's experience, without the confines of GPAs or standardized test scores. There is no formula for what makes a student a "good fit" for Marlboro, but applicants are reviewed with an eye towards intellectual promise, self-motivation, self-discipline and ability to positively contribute to our community.

Students may apply to Marlboro under three different application plans.

Early Decision: Deadline-November 15; Notification-December 1

Early Action: Deadline-January 15; Notification-February 1

Regular Admission: Rolling

Please note that if you are applying for financial aid it is important to file the FAFSA by March 1.

In order to be considered for admission, please submit the following: a completed Common Application and Marlboro College Supplement with the "Why Marlboro?" personal statement (or the optional Marlboro College Application, if you are not already filling out the Common Application), the $50 nonrefundable application fee, all high school and college transcript(s), an expository writing sample, and two letters of recommendation (teacher and general). An interview is required for all students. Submission of SAT or ACT scores is optional.

MAYNOOTH UNIVERSITY

AT A GLANCE

Maynooth University is a modern and dynamic university with a tradition of academic excellence dating back to 1795. Our campus has both historic building and state-of-the-art research and teaching facilities. Located in the quaint town of Maynooth with a medieval castle at its gates, students are exposed to two worlds: the charm and tranquility of the student town and the vibrancy of Dublin, Ireland's capital city, located just 27km away.

The last two decades have seen Maynooth University grow rapidly in scale, strength and stature. Today, with more than 12,000 students and extensive research activities, we are Ireland's fastest-growing university. Ranked in the the top 50 under 50 globally, rated the top university in Ireland (out of the 7 participating institutions) in the 2016 International Student Barometer and listed among the 200 most international universities by the The World Rankings, Maynooth has a global reputation. Leading international researchers deliver small, friendly classes whilst our curriculum is designed to be flexible and maximize post-graduate success. We have a strong campus community with a student-centered and collegial ethos. These characteristics together create a student experience that is uniquely Maynooth.

The central elements of our new model of undergraduate education are deep engagement with a student's chosen disciplines; the ability to combine different subjects to create a more tailored educational experience and distinctive degree; time to broaden their perspective through electives, modern languages and multidisciplinary "Maynooth Modules"; and perhaps most fundamentally, the intellectual skills of analysis, reflection, critical thinking and clear communication that prepare students for today's world of work.

LOCATION AND ENVIRONMENT

Maynooth University has two campuses founded over 200 years apart! Our South Campus includes beautiful historic buildings, green fields, hidden walkways, and even a cemetery! Our North Campus is rapidly expanding and has seen a 250 million investment in recent years. A small road separates them and our modern, airy library marks the midway point. From one end of the South Campus to the other end of the North Campus students can expect to walk a maximum of fifteen minutes.

Maynooth is adjacent to Ireland's "Silicon Valley"; the university maintains strong links with Intel, HP, Google and over 50 other giants of industry and we have one of the best graduate employment records of any Irish university with a strong track record for commercialization of research. Bus and train routes make for easy connections into Dublin whilst coach routes connect Maynooth to the airport, Galway and the rest of Ireland!

Ireland, one of the few countries in the world boasting an unarmed police force, is a safe and beautiful historical country. You will have the opportunity to experience breath-taking land, sky and seascapes as well as an unparalleled cultural and archaeological heritage. All this surrounded by 'the world's friendliest people'!

CAMPUS FACILITIES & EQUIPMENT

Maynooth University provides a wide range of student supports and facilities. These include:

- 8 on-campus eateries
- Free access to our health and counselling service
- Budgeting advice
- A multi-faith worship room and a chaplaincy service
- Academic advisory office
- Math and writing learning centers
- Learning support services including career development, accessibility supports and an access program for mature learners
- We boast two libraries—one for rare books and manuscripts (we have bibles in over 1200 languages!) and one with over 45,000 items and 16 types of study spaces
- Library information and skills tutorials
- Critical skills classes for first years
- 24-7 campus security
- A fully equipped gym, several bookable sports halls, synthetic pitches, turf pitches and scholarships across six sports
- An on-campus shop, bank and bookstore
- Temporary housing for visiting friends and family

OFF-CAMPUS OPPORTUNITIES

Students can work up to 20 hours a week during term time and up to 40 hours a week during the holidays. More information can be found here: https://www.maynoothuniversity.ie/international/key-information/living-ireland

ACADEMICS

Maynooth University has an exceptional track record across many disciplines. From Anthropology to Celtic Studies, Robotics to Biomedical Devices, and Design Innovation to Ancient Classics we have a course to suit your interests.

We offer an education that is similar to liberal arts curriculum but a number of our departments focus on more vocational training. These include international development, performance music, digital humanities, equine management, experimental physics and media studies.

Our full range of academic undergraduate courses can be found here: https://www.maynoothuniversity.ie/study-maynooth/undergraduate-studies/courses

MAJORS AND DEGREES OFFERED

Maynooth has 34 academic departments across 3 faculties and 8 specialist research institutes. We offer flexible pathways, experiential learning, internships and electives at the undergraduate level and offer a full range of undergraduate and postgraduate programs.

TUITION, ROOM, BOARD, FEES

12,000- 13,500 p.a.

There is more information here: https://www.maynoothuniversity.ie/student-fees-grants/international

Room (including utilities): 4678- 6100 p.a.

Fees: N/A

Financial Aid

Maynooth University is certified to support a variety of financial aid, veteran's aid and scholarships. Find out more here: https://www.maynoothuniversity.ie/international/key-information/us-financial-aid

STUDENT ORGANIZATIONS AND ACTIVITIES

Maynooth has a diverse student body, representing many mature, commuter and first-in-the-family students. We cater to the fastest growing student body in Ireland but pride ourselves on our ability to provide a personal and intimate living-learning community. The MSU (Maynooth Students' Union): https://www.msu.ie is a body of over 9,000 students with the numbers rising every year. They answer solely to the Student body. Every year the student body elects officers to work on their behalf for the year ahead. MSU has four full time officers and eight part-time officers to work on your behalf for the year. They also provide support in education and welfare and organizes student-based events during the year to get students involved in social aspects of college life such as quizzes concerts and Clubs and Societies based activities.

MU has over 100 Clubs and Societies there is bound to be something that interests you. And if not, you can set one up! Further details here: https://www.msu.ie/clubs-socs/list-of-societies.html

ADMISSIONS PROCESS

Applications for undergraduate courses should be submitted online through PAC at http://www.pac.ie/ugrad/courses/courses.php?inst=mh&mode=u. Deadlines for applications is July 1st for incoming September cohorts.

Please read the below instructions carefully before completing the online application form.

1. Check the courses available using the Course Finder tool.

2. For the USA entry requirements are:

   o GPA plus SAT or ACT

Minimum High School GPA 3.0/4.0 (3.5/4.0 for certain degrees)

   o Minimum SAT Composite (reading, writing and math): 1000 / 1600 (1200 / 1600 for certain degrees)

   o Minimum ACT Composite: 22 / 36 (26 /36 for certain degrees (writing section not required)

   o Superscoring applies if tests are taken within two years of applying

   o Maynooth University's ACT code is 5483 and our SAT code is 7266.

3. Complete the PAC application, uploading all required documents:

   o All second level (high school) certificates or transcripts

   o Any third level (college) transcript(s)

   o Most recent English language qualifications (where relevant) clearly showing the level achieved (IELTS, TOEFL, or PTE)

   o Students wishing to transfer to Maynooth University from another degree programme should provide an official description of the courses they have taken to date as well as up-to-date transcripts, clearly showing all details of your current studies.

   o Any other documentation as specified in the country-specific entry requirements, or as requested by the International Office

MICHIGAN TECHNOLOGICAL UNIVERSITY

AT A GLANCE

Michigan Technological University (www.mtu.edu) is a leading public research university with a focus on STEM (Science, Technology, Engineering, Mathematics) fields.

Michigan Technological University (www.mtu.edu) is a leading public research university developing new technologies and preparing students to create the future for a prosperous and sustainable world.

Michigan Tech was established in 1885 as a school for mining engineers, to support the copper mines that flourished here. As the mines closed and the economy changed, Michigan Tech changed too, developing recognized expertise in automotive, civil, environmental and chemical engineering, as well as more recently, health sciences, biomedical engineering, environmental science, and computer science.

Michigan Tech faculty are known for their innovative concepts and entrepreneurial spirit. In fact, so many faculty and alumni have turned ideas developed at Michigan Tech into marketable products and thriving high-tech businesses that the north shore of Lake Superior is coming to be known as Innovation Shore.

Michigan Tech stresses learning by doing. Undergraduate participation in research is the norm. In our Enterprise Program and other special programs, students can try their hand at solving real-world problems, using the skills they've learned in class. They invest real money in the stock market; build satellites, snowboards, and video games; and journey to foreign nations to help the less-fortunate improve their access to clean water, sanitation, schools and other human needs.

Ninety-four percent of graduates find jobs in their field.

LOCATION AND ENVIRONMENT

Our rural setting in the Upper Peninsula of Michigan enables us to provide an excellent education in a spectacular location. Recreational opportunities abound, including a university-owned ski hill, a golf course, and 600 acres of on-campus recreational forest and trails for cross-country running, skiing, hiking, and biking.

The 925-acre campus is on the banks of the Keweenaw Waterway, just a few miles from Lake Superior. The air and water are clean, and the North Woods that surround us, pristine.

Ford Forest, in nearby Alberta, Michigan, is a 4,000-acre research forest managed by our School of Forest Resources and Environmental Science, with educational, recreational and conference facilities.

CAMPUS FACILITIES & EQUIPMENT

State-of-the-art laboratories and classrooms are found across campus, and wireless internet service is everywhere. On the waterfront, our Great Lakes Research Center (GLRC) is advancing knowledge in environmental studies, particularly winter-related research, across multiple academic fields. The GLRC houses a supercomputer called Superior, used by the entire campus.

Twenty research centers and institutes enable Michigan Tech faculty, staff, and students to focus on a broad range of inquiry, from climate change to transportation, from power and energy to computational science. The newest institute is doing pioneering work on pressing issues of cybersecurity. The Keweenaw Research Center hosts the annual Clean Snowmobile Challenge, and the Michigan Tech Research Institute in Ann Arbor focuses on remote sensing technologies, including the use of drones for road and bridge maintenance.

Michigan Tech offers 14 varsity sports including NCAA Division I Men's Ice Hockey. NCAA Division II sports include; football, women's soccer, women's volleyball and men's and women's basketball, tennis, track and field, cross country and Nordic Skiing.

Tech's 4,466-seart MacInnes Student Ice Arena features skyboxes, a lounge, and a high-tech video scoreboard.

OFF-CAMPUS OPPORTUNITIES

The entire local area is made for outdoor enthusiasts, with easy access to rivers, lakes, woods, downhill and cross-country skiing, and hiking/biking trails. There is an extensive system of snowmobile and ATV trails. Downtown Houghton and its sister city, Hancock (combined population 14,000) offer coffee shops, theaters, stores, and restaurants, as well as many kinds of specialty shops. Major retailers are a short drive or bus ride from campus. There is local bus service. Theatre, concerts, plays, ballet and other performances provide cultural experiences. Houghton and Hancock are safe communities with little traffic. It's said that in Houghton and Hancock, "rush hours" are "rush minutes." All in all, it's a great combination: a world-class education in a beautiful, livable location.

ACADEMICS

Our Physics Department awards one of the highest percentages nationally of PhDs to women. Our scientific and technical communication program is among the nation's largest. Recent academic program additions include a Bachelor of Science in Natural Resources Management, a Bachelor of Science in Statistics and a Master of Science in Applied Physics, as well as a graduate certificate in post-secondary STEM education. Many academic programs cross traditional disciplinary lines, as students and faculty work together on complex problems requiring input from diverse fields.

The Enterprise Program involves more than 1,000 students on 25 teams from all across campus, putting their classroom learning to work solving real problems for industry. Enterprise students are working on projects related to energy, the environment, robotics, video games, and homeland security, to name just a few.

The Pavlis Honors College draws together students and faculty from several honors programs throughout the university. The Honors College embraces any student with a sincere desire to become a scholar and a leader. There is no minimum GPA requirement.

The Applied Portfolio Management Program has won global investment competitions several years in a row. They control the investment of $1.5 million in actual money. The student investors also have their own "stock exchange," the LSGI Trading Room.

FACULTY

There are 477 faculty members at Michigan Tech, including all tenured, tenure-track, non-tenure-track, instructional and research faculty. The student-to-faculty ratio is 12:1 and the average class size is 24.

MAJORS AND DEGREES OFFERED

Michigan Tech offers more than 120 undergraduate and graduate degree and certificate programs in engineering; forest resources; computing; technology; business; economics; natural, physical and environmental sciences; arts; humanities; and social sciences. Degrees include Bachelor of Arts, Bachelor of Science, Master of Arts, Master of Science, Master of Business Administration, Master of Engineering, Master of Forestry, and 28 PhDs in a variety of fields.

TUITION, ROOM, BOARD, FEES

Undergraduate (in-state): $14,774 per academic year (2 semesters)

Room and Board: $10,416 to 14,669 per academic year (2 semesters)

Graduate Tuition: $950/credit hour (based on 9 credits per semester)

°Undergraduate tuition is based on 12–18 credit hours per semester. Out-of-state students pay $32,018 tuition per academic year (2 semesters).

FINANCIAL AID

Scholarships are the most familiar and sought-after type of financial aid. All admitted students are automatically considered for most merit-based scholarships. A special application form is not required, except for the Michigan Tech Leading Scholars Award and career-interest scholarships.

Grants are aid based on financial need and are available to US citizens and permanent residents. Accepted students are automatically considered for grants if their FAFSA results are released to Michigan Tech. Students must apply for grant renewal each year.

Loans consist of borrowed funds that must be repaid. They are available to most US citizens and permanent residents. Each loan program has certain maximum limits for borrowing. Students may not borrow more than the cost of attendance, less any other financial aid received. Accepted students are automatically considered for loans if their FAFSA results are released to Michigan Tech and they have indicated on the FAFSA an interest in receiving loans. Students must apply for loan renewal each year and make progress toward obtaining their degree according to the Satisfactory Progress Policy.

Part-time employment on campus is available through government-funded and university-funded programs. Students who complete the FAFSA and indicate they would like to work on campus are automatically considered for work-study employment.

Federal Work-Study

Federal Work-Study programs provide funds to employ students who are US citizens or permanent residents and who have financial need. Students must reapply for work-study each year and meet the Satisfactory Progress Policy requirements.

Specific departmental work-study assignments are made by the Financial Aid Office. Students normally work eight to ten hours per week. The hourly rate paid is equivalent to at least minimum wage.

University-Funded Student Employment

University-funded, on-campus employment is available to students regardless of need. Students may apply directly to the desired departments. On average, 2,000 to 2,500 students are employed on campus each year. Nearly every department employs students.

STUDENT ORGANIZATIONS AND ACTIVITIES

More than 230 registered student organizations offer individual and group activities and leadership opportunities in many categories, including Academic/Honors, Arts and Culture, Club Sports, Governance, Greeks, Programming/Social, Religious, and Service. There are active Undergraduate and Graduate Student Governments.

More than 27 percent of the student body is female, and 14 percent is international, coming to study at Michigan Tech from more than 60 countries. A majority of undergraduates live in campus residence halls. Many graduate students with families live in University-owned Daniell Heights Apartments.

Our traditions include Winter Carnival, featuring massive snow statues built by students, stage shows, and wacky winter competitions like snow volleyball, ice bowling, and broomball. The annual Parade of Nations and Multicultural Festival celebrates the international flavor and heritage of the Keweenaw and Michigan Tech. Other traditional events include K-Day on Lake Superior's shore and Spring Fling on campus.

ADMISSIONS PROCESS

Applying to college doesn't have to be stressful. In fact, Michigan Tech makes it pretty easy. You don't need to get teacher recommendations or even apply for scholarships with a separate form. Just submit your application for admission, official high school and/or college transcripts, and official ACT or SAT test scores.

Additional application materials are required for students applying for admission to the following degree programs: Audio Production and Technology, Sound Design, Theatre and Electronic Media Performance, and Theatre and Entertainment Technology.

Apply by January 15 of the year you plan to enroll for priority consideration for admission, financial aid, and scholarships.

We'll review your high school transcript (including your freshman year) and evaluate the courses you took in high school and the grades you received. The cumulative GPA provided by your high school is used in the admissions process. We do not recalculate your GPA.

MOLLOY COLLEGE

AT A GLANCE

Where can you get a great education with small classes, wonderful internships, community service projects and international trips, plus an amazing campus life program to round out your college experience? Welcome to Molloy College.

Molloy, an independent Catholic college based in Rockville Centre, was founded in 1955 by the Sisters of Saint Dominic in Amityville, NY. The College serves a student population of more than 4,900 undergraduate and graduate students. Molloy students can earn degrees in a variety of outstanding academic programs, including nursing, business, education, computer studies, social work, music therapy and many more.

Accolades and Recognition

Prospective students are always looking for an academic environment that offers the best fit for the student and the best value for their tuition dollar. Molloy was ranked a Top 3 Value Institution the last two years by Money magazine, the only college in the nation to claim that distinction. Molloy's top ranking was based on a variety of factors, including graduation rates and earnings of graduates.

Molloy continues to earn recognition in many areas. College Factual recently ranked Molloy the #1 college for health professions, as well as ranking Molloy's undergraduate nursing program the best in the nation. Molloy's Business students have the highest pass rate on Long Island for the CPA exam, and the College's Music Therapy program earned a #16 national ranking from thebestschools.org. Additionally, the College's residence halls were voted Best in New York by Niche. com, and these rankings also referenced Molloy's freshmen retention rate, which is among the highest in the country (85 percent). Also of note, Molloy graduates' starting salaries have ranked among the highest in the U.S. in surveys conducted by Georgetown University and PayScale.

LOCATION AND ENVIRONMENT

Molloy is located on the South Shore of Long Island in Rockville Centre. Its proximity to New York City, just a short train ride away from the 30-acre campus, enables students to benefit from the cultural and social opportunities that Manhattan has to offer. Molloy's location in the New York metro region provides its students with numerous opportunities for internships and clinical placements, critical for students in landing their first job upon graduation.

Molloy College also offers off campus locations for study at the Suffolk Center in East Farmingdale and at area hospitals and schools, all designed to provide convenience for our graduate and continuing education students. Molloy recently opened a new facility at 50 Broadway in Manhattan's downtown Oculus District. The new building houses the Molloy/CAP21 B.F.A. Musical Conservatory program, in addition to hosting a variety of lectures and other academic programs.

CAMPUS FACILITIES & EQUIPMENT
What's New

The College continues to find new ways to help its students grow. In recent years Molloy has added a number of new facilities, including two residence halls, a student center and a performing arts theatre, all of which enhance the student experience. Additionally, Molloy recently opened the Barbara H. Hagan School of Nursing to support its nationally ranked nursing programs. A new residence hall is scheduled to open in Fall 2019.

Molloy is a wireless campus and our computer labs house more than 325 PCs. Also, many departments have their own computer labs with state-of-the-art equipment.

The James E. Tobin (JET) Library is the center of academic research on the Molloy College campus. Beyond the library's physical collection of books, media and periodicals, it also provides 24x7 access to over 250,000 e-books as well as full text to over 170 million articles contained within its 80+ subscription databases. The facility itself contains reference computers, three classrooms, a media center and designated areas for both group and private study. The Information Commons, located in the Public Square, offers an additional 40 computers as well as four study rooms that can be reserved in advance. Reference services are available to both on campus and remote researchers in a variety of ways, including a chat service that is available all of the hours the library is open. Additionally, the Public Square provides numerous music studios, for both individual and group study.

The Wilbur Arts Center features art studios, a cable television studio, and the Lucille B. Hays Theatre. The school also has six science labs, a language lab, the education resource center, new state-of-the-art nursing labs, and a behavioral sciences research facility.

OFF-CAMPUS OPPORTUNITIES

Molloy students are also instilled with the belief that they can make a difference beyond the classroom. As part of Molloy's tradition of service, students become involved in projects that help underserved populations in New York City, New Orleans, Puerto Rico and Haiti, to name but a few locations. Through the College's international education program, students seek enrichment and greater understanding of the world by participating in trips to Europe, Japan, South America and other locales around the globe.

ACADEMIC PROGRAMS

At Molloy, small class size, engaging and experienced faculty and renowned academic programs will help ensure your success, both in the classroom and in your professional life. Our vibrant student life program will help you make a smooth transition to our campus.

We also make it easy for you to take classes when it is convenient for YOU. We offer evening and weekend classes, many in online and hybrid formats, with accelerated schedules designed to accommodate your busy schedule.

A minimum of 128 credit hours is required for a baccalaureate degree; these courses include a strong liberal arts general education curriculum for every major field of study. Students may choose a double major, and many minors are available. Molloy has a 4-1-4 academic calendar.

Students may earn CLEP and CPE credit, and advanced placement credit is granted for a score of 3 or better on the AP exam. Qualified full-time students may participate in the Army ROTC program at Hofstra University or St. John's University on a cross enrolled basis. Molloy students may also elect Air Force ROTC on a cross enrolled basis with New York Institute of Technology.

The vast majority of students at Molloy enjoy an internship at some point in their academic careers. These real-world experiences are a crucial part of the learning process and ensure that students enter their chosen field ready to make strong contributions. Molloy's location in the New York metro region provides its students with numerous opportunities for all-important internships and clinical placements that can lead to a full-time job upon graduation.

MAJORS AND DEGREES OFFERED

Molloy offers the AA degree in liberal arts; the AAS degree in cardiovascular technology and respiratory care; and the BA or BS degree in accounting, art, biology, business management, communications, computer science, computer information systems, criminal justice, education, English, earth and environmental studies, finance, history, interdisciplinary studies, marketing, mathematics, modern languages, music, music therapy, new media, nuclear medicine technology, nursing, philosophy, political science, psychology, respiratory care, sociology, speech language pathology/audiology, and theology; the BSW degree in Social Work; and the BFA in art, music and theatre arts. Teacher certification programs are available in childhood (1-6), adolescence (7¬–12), special education and birth—grade 2 childhood special education.

On the graduate level, Molloy offers a Master of Science degree as well as post-master's certification in nursing and education. M.B.A. programs are available in business, accounting, healthcare, marketing and personal financial planning; a master's program in clinical mental health counseling was recently launched as well. A master's in social work is offered through Molloy's partnership with Fordham University. Molloy also offers graduate degrees in criminal justice, music therapy, and speech-language pathology. The College offers three doctoral programs, a Ph.D. in nursing and a Doctor of Nursing Practice (D.N.P.), as well as an Ed.D. in Education.

Students interested in pre-dental, pre-law, pre-medical, or pre-veterinary programs are offered special advisement.

Experienced admissions counselors will evaluate your credits and put you on the path towards completing your degree. Articulation agreements with community colleges and established transfer credit policies ensure ease of transferability.

TUITION, ROOM, BOARD, FEES

For 2017–18, tuition was $29,100 and required fees were $1,190. Students can expect to spend about $1,400 on books.

FINANCIAL AID

Financial aid, which is based on academic achievement and financial need, is awarded to more than 85 percent of the student body. Aid is awarded in the form of scholarships, grants, loans, and Federal Work-Study Program employment. Merit-based scholarships and grants are also available.

Students are required to complete the FAFSA application every year. Full and partial tuition scholarships are available through the following: Molloy Scholars, Presidential Dominican Scholarships, Presidential Business Scholarships, Dean Scholarships, Academic Achievement, Fine Arts Scholarships, Community Service Awards, and other funded scholarships. The Transfer Scholarship Program awards partial tuition scholarships to students transferring into Molloy College with at least a 3.0 cumulative GPA. Nursing transfers are required to have a 3.3 GPA to be eligible for a transfer scholarship. Athletic grants (Division II only) are awarded to full-time students who show superior athletic ability in baseball, basketball, cross-country, equestrian, lacrosse, soccer, softball, tennis, bowling, indoor and outdoor track, field hockey or volleyball.

STUDENT ORGANIZATIONS AND ACTIVITIES

With more than 4,900 undergraduate and graduate students, Molloy has something for everyone. There are more than 50 academic programs, approximately 60 clubs and honor societies, various service opportunities and NCAA Division II athletics, providing abundant opportunities for each student to not only strive for academic excellence, but also explore new interests, pursue athletics and enrich our community.

ADMISSIONS PROCESS

While Molloy is a selective college, admissions counselors respect each individual applicant and consider the whole student—not just test scores—when making admissions decision. Prospective freshmen must submit their high school credentials, SAT or ACT scores, the Molloy application, and a $40 nonrefundable application fee. While not required, a personal interview is strongly suggested.

Entrance requirements include graduation from high school or equivalent with 20.5 units, including the following: 4 units of English, 3 units of a foreign language, 3 units of mathematics, 4 units of social studies, and 3 units of science. Those who plan to major in mathematics must have 4 units of high school mathematics and 2 units of science, including either chemistry or physics. Biology majors must have biology, chemistry, physics, and 4 units of mathematics. Nursing majors must have biology and chemistry. Cardio-respiratory science majors must have biology, chemistry, and mathematics. Nuclear medicine majors must have high school algebra and biology. Applicants lacking above requirements are reviewed on an individual basis.

A select group of freshmen are invited to participate in the Molloy College Honors Program. This program offers challenging coursework and encourages reflection and personal growth. Honors students are provided with several special participation incentives such as a laptop computer, and priority registration.

The HEOP and the Albertus Magnus programs may be options for students not normally eligible for admission.

Early admission is available. Molloy admits students on a rolling basis and students are advised of the admission decision within a few weeks of completion of the application filing process.

Prospective students should submit the following to the admissions office to be considered for enrollment: a completed application for admission (the Common Application is accepted), a nonrefundable $40 application fee, an official high school transcript or GED score report, official SAT I or ACT score, and official college transcripts (transfer students only).

MONMOUTH UNIVERSITY

AT A GLANCE

Monmouth University is a first-tier, private university that empowers students to reach their full potential as leaders who are able to make significant contributions to their community and society.

A comprehensive selection of baccalaureate and graduate degree programs in subject areas that are in demand in the workplace is offered. Small classes geared toward individual attention, and led by an innovative faculty, provide a transformative learning environment where students are active participants in their education.

Monmouth's academics, including majors like political science, communications, homeland security, business, and more, can easily be linked with world-class learning experiences in New York City and other nearby major urban areas. Students who are interested in coastal environmental studies can focus on biological, chemical, and physical sciences, together with environmental policy and natural resource conservation and management.

The University is also close to many technology firms, financial institutions, and a business-industrial sector that provides both employment possibilities for graduates and opportunities for undergraduates to gain experience.

Monmouth's location and network provide tremendous academic opportunities to students. For example, students in Monmouth's music industry program interface with industry professionals in and beyond the classroom, managing their own record label, Blue Hawk Records. There is a real spirit of entrepreneurship on campus that comes to life through student activities like the student-managed investment fund Hawk Capital. Marine and environmental biology and policy students benefit from the University's proximity to coastal waterways.

While preparing students for successful careers in leadership roles, Monmouth University believes that a major goal of higher education is to help students develop values. These include senses of citizenship and social responsibility that enable graduates to contribute actively to the societies in which they live. Academic programs and personal development opportunities at Monmouth prepare students to take the lead in an increasingly complex, multicultural world. These opportunities—combined with the myriad of art exhibits, concerts, lectures, and sightseeing trips planned each year—provide students with shared experiences outside the classroom to match the ones they receive inside.

LOCATION AND ENVIRONMENT

Located in the town of West Long Branch, New Jersey, Monmouth is situated on a beautiful, coastal campus that is one mile from the beaches of the Atlantic Ocean and also about one hour from New York City and Philadelphia. The 156-acre campus is home to a diverse student body comprising some 6,400 undergraduate and graduate students. Students come to Monmouth from 32 states and 34 countries to participate in the University's academic programs. A ratio of 14 students to each professor enables a personalized learning environment along with mentoring opportunities.

CAMPUS FACILITIES & EQUIPMENT

The Monmouth University Library holds approximately 360,000 print and electronic monographs, 74,000 print and electronic periodicals, 180 databases, and 1,200 media assets including CDs and DVDs. All academic programs are amply supported by state-of-the-art computer hardware and software and classroom/laboratory facilities. The major components supporting Monmouth academic programs include Windows, Mac OS, and Unix systems connected via an expansive wired and wireless network, which spans all campus buildings and encompasses more than 2,400 workstations in general and specialty labs and classrooms.

OFF-CAMPUS OPPORTUNITIES

Putting learning into action is what makes education come alive. Experiential education, which includes internships, study abroad, select service learning projects, dedicated experiential coursework, or cooperative learning experiences, is a required part of the undergraduate curriculum. By their senior year, 77 percent of Monmouth undergraduate students have completed a practicum, internship, co-op, or similar real-world experience; only 49 percent of graduating students at comparable institutions have done this according to the latest National Survey of Student Engagement.

At Monmouth, professional-quality experience comes in many forms, from collaborating on original research with faculty that can be presented at national and international conferences to traveling with the mock trial team and engaging in a wide-variety of academic field experiences. There are service learning and global study opportunities in Australia, England, Italy, Spain, Guatemala, Haiti, and more.

ACADEMIC PROGRAMS

Undergraduate students who are interested in the sciences, if qualified, can be involved in hands-on original research projects with faculty. Monmouth students present award-winning research at regional, national, and international conferences along with earning faculty co-authorship in peer-reviewed publications.

At Monmouth, about 10 percent of first-year students enroll in one of the University's five-year baccalaureate/master's programs. Subject areas for five-year programs are offered in computer science, business, criminal justice, education (select programs), English, history, social work, and software engineering.

Additionally, Graduate Studies at Monmouth University provides high-quality master's degree and certificate programs to students seeking to increase their professional skills and enhance their intellectual development. Monmouth also offers a Doctor of Nursing Practice (DNP) and Doctor of Education in Educational Leadership (EdD). Every program curriculum aims to improve students' leadership qualities and prepare them for career advancement, career changes, or further study.

Graduate students have chances to advance their knowledge and engage in scholarly research with faculty members who are not only impassioned teachers and mentors, but also leaders in their chosen fields. Those enrolled benefit from Monmouth's commitment to personalized attention and a strong bond between students and faculty members.

MAJORS AND DEGREES OFFERED

Anthropology°
Art°: optional concentration in Photography°
Biology°: optional concentration in Molecular Cell Physiology
Business Administration°: concentrations in Accounting°, Economics°, Economics and Finance, Finance°, Finance and Real Estate, International Business, Management and Decision Sciences, Marketing°, Marketing, Management, and Decision Sciences, or Real Estate
Chemistry°: optional concentrations in Advanced Chemistry, Biochemistry, or Chemical Physics
Clinical Laboratory Sciences: concentration in Medical Laboratory Science
Communication°: Communication Studies, Public Relations/Journalism, or Radio/TV
Computer Science°
Criminal Justice°
Education: Early Childhood, Elementary, Middle School, Secondary, English as a Second Language, Teacher of Students with Disabilities
English°: optional concentration in Creative Writing°
Fine Arts: concentrations in Animation or Graphic and Interactive Design
Foreign Language: concentrations in Spanish, Spanish and Communication/Journalism, or Spanish and Communication/Radio and TV
Health and Physical Education (teaching and non-teaching options)
Health Studies°
History°
History and Political Science
Homeland Security°
Marine and Environmental Biology and Policy
Mathematics°: optional concentration in Statistics°
Medical Laboratory Science
Music: optional concentration in Music Industry
Nursing (BSN) (direct admit program, freshmen only)
Nursing (RN to BSN) (transfer students with RN license only)
Political Science°: optional concentration in International Relations or Legal Studies°
Psychology°
Social Work

Sociology°
Software Engineering
Spanish and International Business

MINORS

Archaeology
Art History
Asian Studies
Business of Healthcare
Communication Sciences and Disorders
Forensic Investigation
Gender Studies
General Management
Geographic Information Systems
Geography
Global Sustainability
Graphic and Interactive Design
Information Technology
Interactive Media
Irish Studies
Italian
Journalism
Leadership Communication
Media Production
Musical Theatre
Philosophy
Philosophy and Religious Studies
Physics
Popular Music
Professional Writing
Public Policy
Public Relations
Religious Studies
Screen Studies
Social Justice
Social Services
Spanish
Spanish for Business
Sports Communication
Theatre

FIVE-YEAR BACCALAUREATE/ MASTER'S DEGREE PROGRAMS

Business Administration
Computer Science
Criminal Justice
Education (certain programs)
English
History
Social Work
Software Engineering

PRE-PROFESSIONAL ADVISING

Pre-Dentistry
Pre-Law
Pre-Medicine
Pre-Veterinary

°Major and minor available

TUITION, ROOM, BOARD, FEES

$38,100 (Commuter)

$52,100 (Resident)

FINANCIAL AID

Approximately 99 percent of Monmouth incoming students receive some form of financial aid. Those packages typically include scholarships, grants, student loans, and work-study that may be applied toward tuition and fees, room and board or living expenses, books, and other personal expenses.

Here are some facts to consider about the financial aid packages created for Monmouth's undergraduates last year:

About 96 percent received a scholarship or grant (federal, state, or University).

The average scholarship/grant package was $22,521.

The average financial aid package, including student loans and work-study, was approximately $26,900.

More than $59 million in University grants and scholarships was awarded; this places Monmouth among the more affordable private universities in New Jersey.

STUDENT ORGANIZATIONS AND ACTIVITIES

The University is proud to host a successful NCAA Division I intercollegiate athletics program that fields 23 teams for men and women. The University's basketball and track and field teams compete in the 153,200-square-foot OceanFirst Bank Center. All Monmouth students have access to the arena, which also houses a 200-meter, six-lane indoor track; fitness center; conference space; the University Store; and luxury suites. The University's football, men's/women's lacrosse and outdoor track and field programs opened their new home in Fall 2017, with the debut of Kessler Stadium. The new stadium, adjacent to the OceanFirst Bank Center, will accommodate 4,200 fans and feature state-of-the-art media facilities and end zone to end zone seating.

Beyond athletics, students have an assortment of extracurricular activities to choose from, including more than 110 student-run clubs and organizations, as well as sororities and fraternities that engage in service work on behalf of the University and the community. Students can also get involved with the Student Government Association, the campus newspaper (The Outlook), the student-run online news portal (The Verge), the FM radio station (WMCX), the television station (Hawk TV), the yearbook (Shadows), and the literary magazine (Monmouth Review).

ADMISSIONS PROCESS

The early action deadline for first-time, full-time students is December 1, and for regular decision it is March 1.

Students applying to the spring semester must do so by December 1.

If you're applying as a part-time student, applications for the fall semester are due by July 15, and for the spring semester they are due by December 1.

Applicants to the Bachelor of Science in Nursing (BSN) program must submit their applications by December 1 for the fall start term only.

An application includes the application form, a non-refundable $50 application fee, all official transcripts, standardized test scores, at least one letter of recommendation, and a personal essay of 250 to 500 words.

MOUNT ALOYSIUS COLLEGE

AT A GLANCE

Mount Aloysius College is a private and affordable Catholic liberal arts college sponsored by the Sisters of Mercy. The College welcomes people of all faith traditions. Established in 1853, Mount Aloysius College offers undergraduate and graduate education. Today, there are nearly 16,500 alumni world-wide. The College provides small class sizes, and students benefit from accessible faculty and staff. Mount Aloysius students come mostly from throughout Pennsylvania and the mid-Atlantic Region. There are over 2,500 students enrolled (unduplicated headcount).

Mount Aloysius College is one of 17 Mercy-sponsored colleges and universities in the United Sates and is a member of the Conference for Mercy Higher Education. Students are encouraged to synthesize faith with learning, to develop competence with compassion, to apply their talents and gifts to the service of others, and to assume leadership in their community. Student activities play a distinctive role in personal growth. At Mount Aloysius College, there are approximately 100 organized clubs, groups, honor societies, and an intramural sports program. Activities include a student newspaper, residence hall associations, student government, cheerleading, dance team, scholarship-funded theater and choir programs, and a student activities planning board. Mount Aloysius fun includes social events, intramural sports, athletic events, comedians, live music, theater, educational events, campus forums, and awesome guest lectures.

Mount Aloysius College is a member of NCAA Division III. Athletic programs involve both women and men and include basketball, cross-country, golf, soccer, and tennis. Men's baseball and women's bowling, lacrosse, softball and volleyball are also offered. Athletes benefit from the Ray S. and Louise S. Walker Athletic Field Complex, which includes a softball field, one of the finest soccer fields in the area, and the Calandra-Smith baseball complex. Recently the Mountie Stables were opened to the College and to the community. The Stables add dugouts, lockers, showers, storage, and concession facilities to the school's athletic infrastructure.

On the western edge of beautiful 193-acre campus sits the Athletic Convocation and Wellness Center, a spectacular 87,000-foot multi-purpose facility. This facility takes Mount Aloysius athletics to a new level and adds a welcomed special events venue to the southern Allegheny Mountains. Located within the Athletic Convocation and Wellness Center (ACWC) is a main gymnasium and events venue with seating for over 2500. Athletic offices, Intuitional Advancement, Student Affairs and Business faculty offices are located within the building. The ACWC also contains home and visitor lockers and trainer facilities. On the ground floor, a new state-of-the-art Wellness Center offers both cardio and resistance training in a spacious and modern environment.

The main campus building is a picturesque structure dating to 1897; it houses the admissions, financial aid, security, health, and academic offices, along with the Office of the President, classrooms, the Region's premiere nursing simulation center, and the Wolf-Kuhn Art Gallery. Cosgrave Center is the hub of campus life. The building contains the dining hall, snack bar, bookstore, child-care center (part of the elementary education/early childhood program at the College), lounges, recreational rooms, student affairs offices, and meeting rooms. The Sr. Virginia Bertschi Center and Technology Commons is situated in the center of campus. The Bertschi Center is a multi-purpose facility with student-centered space where commuter and resident students can relax, socialize, study, conduct meetings, enjoy games and manage the business of over 100 student clubs, teams and organizations on campus. The Digital Grotto—the video and social media hub—is also located in this building. Resident dorms include Saint Joseph and Saint Gertrude Halls, Ihmsen Hall, Misciagna Residence, a state-of-the-art dormitory with 25 suites and private bathrooms and McAuley Hall that features both double and single rooms and a large multipurpose room and study lounges on all three floors.

Alumni Hall is a historic, multipurpose facility used for College drama, musicals, lectures, and performing arts events. The College operates 12 months per year and opens its facilities to the Southern Allegheny community. The College is 100 percent wireless, and smart classrooms are located throughout the campus.

Mount Aloysius is fully accredited by the Middle States Association of Colleges and Schools and approved by the Pennsylvania Department of Education. All nursing and health studies programs are fully accredited by their professional accrediting bodies, including the National League for Nursing Accrediting Commission, the Commission on Accreditation for Programs of Diagnostic Medical Sonography, the Commission on Accreditation in Physical Therapy Education, the American Association of Medical Assistants, and the Joint Commission on Accreditation for Programs of Surgical Technology. In addition to its undergraduate programs, Mount Aloysius offers master's degrees in business administration, behavioral specialist consulting, community counseling, and psychology

LOCATION AND ENVIRONMENT

The College is located in the scenic Southern Allegheny Mountains of west-central Pennsylvania, in the town of Cresson. Convenient and accessible from U.S. Route 22, the College's setting is rural but mere minutes from State College, Altoona, Johnstown, State College and Pittsburgh Pennsylvania. The area has warm, beautiful summers; brisk, breathtaking autumns; invigorating winters; and cool, blooming springs. Well maintained and safe facilities are close and available for biking, golfing, swimming, horseback riding, waterskiing, women's bowling, boating, hiking, spelunking, cross-country and down-hill skiing, picnicking, and amusement and water parks. A well-kept system of State Parks is convenient to the College as are shopping malls, golf courses, and numerous historical sites.

CAMPUS FACILITIES & EQUIPMENT

In 1995, Mount Aloysius College opened both a new Library and a new era, signifying greater access to information for the College community. This state-of-the-art Library is the campus hub for technology and study. With a Buhl Electronic Classroom and more than 80,000 print and nonprint titles, the Library is an impressive, 31,000-square-foot facility with ample seating space, four group-study rooms, a reading lounge, a law library and classroom, an unparalleled 18,000-volume Ecumenical Collection donated by Pastor Gerald Myers, and ample room for expansion. This facility is completely automated, with an online catalog and access to remote libraries and the Internet through the more than 30 workstations. The Library also houses the Information Technology Center, home to 15 multimedia workstations and the latest educational software.

Pierce Hall, the College's science center is expanding. When completed in the fall of 2018, the building will be known as The Learning Center for Health Science and Technology. This state-of-the-art learning center will reflect the College's career-oriented advancements in the health sciences. Academic Hall is home to the College Honors Program. It houses classrooms, labs, seminar rooms, faculty offices, and electronic classrooms. The College is proud of its bridge to the past and its progress in providing 21st Century learning facilities.

ACADEMIC PROGRAMS

Whether preparing students for careers upon graduation or for graduate school, Mount Aloysius recognizes the importance of a broad and liberal education. Thus, in addition to receiving solid preparation for a chosen career, every student at the College receives a foundation in the arts, sciences, and humanities through an outstanding core curriculum. Strong emphasis is placed on the specialized courses within each program of study, and many academic programs combine classroom experience with internships and related training at area clinical sites, agencies, and institutions. In addition to its regular academic programs, Mount Aloysius offers independent and directed study with a commitment to service, a central component to a Mercy education. The College has an excellent honors program and academic services area. The academic calendar has two traditional semesters and optional summer sessions.

Off-Campus Programs

An important feature of many academic programs is off-campus training. The majority of the College's programs of study require credit-yielding practicums at partnering hospitals, public and private schools, or health or human service agencies. Students in all health programs benefit from required clinical training during their time at the College.

MAJORS AND DEGREES OFFERED
Division of Humanities

Accounting Accounting/MBA 4+1; Accounting: Digital Forensics Investigation Concentration; Accounting: Forensic Accounting in Criminal Investigations

Concentration; American Sign Language/English Interpreting ; Business Administration; Business Administration/MBA 4+1; Business Administration: Health Care Administration Specialization; Business Administration: Human Resources Specialization; Business Administration: Marketing Communication Media Specialization; Business Administration: Marketing and Entrepreneurship Specialization; Business Administration: Sports Management Specialization; Communications; Criminology; Criminology: Correctional Administration Certification; Criminology: Criminal Justice Addictions Certification; Criminology: Digital Forensics Investigation Concentration; Criminology: Forensic Accounting in Criminal Investigations Concentration; Criminology: Forensic Investigation Certification ; Education Early Level Pre-K–4 ; Education Early Level Pre-K–4 English Concentration; Education Early Level Pre-K–4 History/Political Science Concentration; Education Early Level Pre-K–4 Science Concentration; Education Middle Level 4–8 ; Education Middle Level 4–8 English Concentration; Education Middle Level 4–8 History/Political Science Concentration; Education Middle Level 4–8 Science Concentration; English; English: Secondary Education Certification; English: Theatre Concentration ; History/Political Science; History/Political Science: Social Studies Secondary Education Certification; Information Technology; Information Technology: Computer Security Concentration; Information Technology: Digital Forensics Investigation Concentration; Information Technology: Business Analyst Concentration; Interdisciplinary Studies ; Pre-Law; Pre-Law: Business/ Accounting Specialization ; Pre-Law: Criminology Specialization; Pre-Law: English Specialization; Pre-Law: History/Political Science Specialization ; Pre-Law: Paralegal Certificate; Psychology; Psychology: Counseling Specialization ; Psychology: Criminal Justice Addictions Certification; Psychology: Forensic Investigation Certification ; Psychology: General Specialization; Psychology: Human Resources Specialization; Undecided/Exploratory

Division of Health Studies and Sciences

Biology; Biology: Organismal and Evolutionary Biology ; Biology: Environmental Science Specialization ; Biology: Forensic Investigation Certificate ; Biology: Molecular Biotechnology Specialization ; Biology: Pre-Health Professional; Biology: Secondary Education Certification ; Chiropractic 3-1; Dental Medicine 4-4; General Science; General Science: Pre-Medical Lab Science; General Science: Secondary Education Certification; Medical Imaging/Radiography 2+2; Medical Imaging/ Ultrasonography Concentration 2+2; Nuclear Medicine 3-1; Occupational Therapy 3-2; Osteopathic Medicine 3-4; Pharmacy 3-3; Physician Assistant 3-2; Physical Therapy 4-3; Ultrasonography

School of Nursing

Nursing 2+2 ; Nursing (RN to BSN); Nursing (LPN to RN); Nursing (RN)

Associate Degrees

Applied Technology ; Business Administration; Business Administration: Accounting Specialization; Business Administration: Computer Applications Specialization; Business Administration: Management Specialization; Criminology; Early Childhood Education Information Technology ; Legal Studies; Liberal Arts; Liberal Arts: Humanities and Social Science Specialization; Liberal Arts: Health Studies and Science Specialization; Medical Assistant; Medical Assistant: Office Management Specialization; Medical Assistant: Phlebotomy Specialization; Medical Assistant: Professional Coding Specialization; Medical Imaging/ Radiography ; Medical Imaging/ Ultrasonography; Medical Imaging/ Vascular Sonography; Medical Laboratory Technician; Physical Therapist Assistant ; Surgical Technology

TUITION, ROOM, BOARD, FEES

Annual tuition, fees and room and board for the 2017–2018 academic year for full-time students are $31,350. Up-to-date cost information is available online at http://www.mtaloy.edu/tuition-fees/.

FINANCIAL AID

Mount Aloysius prides itself on affordability. Many MAC students hail from proud families of modest means and many are first-generation students. The College understands the expense involved in acquiring a quality education and encourages all students to apply for all available aid. Through the Office of Financial Aid, the College assists students in applying for state and federal grants, loans, work-study awards, merit scholar-ships and more. The College awards academic monies based on GPA and SAT or ACT scores. These awards are renewable over a four-year period and range from $2000 to $12,000 per year. Mount Aloysius College participates in all federal and state programs; fully 94 percent of Mount Aloysius College students receive some form of financial aid. U.S. News & World Report has ranked Mount Aloysius College as one of the best-priced private liberal arts colleges in the United States.

STUDENT ORGANIZATIONS AND ACTIVITIES
Faculty

The Mount Aloysius faculty consists of approximately 175 members, whose primary responsibility is teaching and advising students. Many faculty members hold advanced or terminal degrees and are expected to maintain close instructional ties with students. Many professors hold national professional certificates in such disciplines as criminology, education, law, and nursing. The Mount Aloysius student-faculty ratio of 13:1 allows close contact between students and faculty members, providing personal attention in a highly structured environment-a key ingredient in the College's academic philosophy.

Student Government

The Student Government Association (SGA) represents students on all issues that concern the College. The SGA appoints student representatives to all student-oriented College committees. The College encourages active student participation in the general governance structure and in other matters concerning the development and implementation of policies on residential student life.

ADMISSIONS PROCESS

The College enrolls a freshman class of approximately 350 students. The total class of 550 includes transfer students. Admission is selective and based on academic promise, as indicated by a student's secondary school performance and activities, standardized test scores, and special experience and talents. Applicants are required to have, or expect to earn, a diploma from an approved secondary school or a GED diploma. Submission of official transcripts and SAT or ACT scores is required. In addition to the general admission requirements, specific admission requirements exist for the health programs.

For further information, students should visit the College's Web site at http://www.mtaloy.edu. Prospective students are encouraged to visit the scenic 193-acre campus. The College is open Monday to Friday from 8:30 to 5 and on select Saturdays.

To apply for admission to Mount Aloysius College, candidates are encouraged to submit their application to the Office of Undergraduate and Graduate Admissions. In addition, students may apply online.

For further information, students should contact:

Office of Undergraduate and Graduate Admissions
Mount Aloysius College
7373 Admiral Peary Highway
Cresson, Pennsylvania 16630
Phone: 814-886-6383
888-823-2220 (toll-free)
Fax: 814-886-6441
E-mail: admissions@mtaloy.edu
Web site: http://www.mtaloy.edu

Mount Aloysius College, located on a beautiful 193-acre campus in Cresson, Pennsylvania provides a safe, vibrant learning community. Nestled in the southern Allegheny Mountains, Mount Aloysius College is one of 17 Mercy-sponsored colleges and universities in the United Sates and is a member of the Conference for Mercy Higher Education. Mount Aloysius offers year-round recreational and cultural opportunities. Students enjoy both the security of the campus and the proximity to State College to the east and Pittsburgh to the west. Mount Aloysius College is minutes away from all the amenities of Altoona and Johnstown, Pennsylvania. Interstate highways, the Pennsylvania Turnpike, AMTRAK train service, bus service, and several airports make Mount Aloysius College convenient from anywhere.

NAZARETH COLLEGE

AT A GLANCE

Nazareth provides a comprehensive education with a proactive approach to career and life readiness. Nazareth's Center for Life's Work pairs students with a personal career coach to guide experience-based learning and build skills, confidence, and career-launching connections. Nazareth students demonstrate readiness for academic rigor and eagerness to make their mark in the world. Admission is based primarily on academic achievement. The College seeks students with a high level of competency and recommends applicants complete a rigorous college-preparatory curriculum in high school that includes English, a foreign language, math, science, and social studies. Successful completion of Advanced Placement and International Baccalaureate courses are looked upon favorably. An audition or portfolio review is required for applications to art, dance, music, and theatre programs. Co-curricular activities, the essay, and letters of recommendation are also considered. A campus visit is highly recommended. Information sessions and campus tours are available Mondays through Saturdays.

Nursing applicants are required to submit standardized test scores (SAT, ACT, or both). For all other programs, test scores are helpful, but not required. Approximately 75 percent of applicants submit scores. For admissions details: naz.edu/admissions, email admissions@naz.edu, or call (585) 389-2860. Nazareth offers merit-based awards for excellence in academics, art, dance, music, and theatre, as well as need-based aid. Students seeking aid complete the Free Application for Federal Student Aid (FAFSA). For cost and financial aid details: go.naz.edu/tuition-aid

LOCATION AND ENVIRONMENT

Nazareth is situated on 150 acres in the charming town of Pittsford, seven miles from Rochester, New York state's third largest city. Classic and modern buildings are interspersed amongst expansive lawns, shady woodland groves, and landscaped gardens. Cultural, co-curricular, and entertainment opportunities include: music, dance, and theatrical presentations at the Nazareth College Arts Center and newly constructed Glazer Music Performance Center, 24 Golden Flyer athletic teams, 50+ clubs and organizations representing students' academic, cultural, interfaith, and athletic interests, and presentations from national and international scholars and performers.

CAMPUS FACILITIES & EQUIPMENT

In recent years, Nazareth College has invested nearly $47 million to provide enhanced learning and research facilities including: Peckham Hall Integrated Center for Math and Sciences, York Wellness and Rehabilitation Institute, renovated nursing labs and learning spaces, and the Glazer Music Performance Center. Construction recently began on The Golisano Athletic Training Center, which is scheduled to open in 2019.

OFF-CAMPUS OPPORTUNITIES

Nazareth is known for its civic engagement–locally, regionally, nationally, and globally, as detailed at naz.edu/civic-engagement.

ACADEMIC PROGRAMS

The College offers a broad spectrum of 60 undergraduate majors, including education, foreign languages, health and human services, pre-professional fields, sciences and math, business and management, and visual and performing arts. Nazareth's student-centered community includes small class sizes and an environment committed to providing students with research, hands-on learning, and professional skill-building opportunities that prepare them for their life's work. The College is nationally recognized for its Fulbright global student scholars and national recognition for commitment to civic engagement. Nazareth is coeducational and is an inclusive religiously independent comprehensive college. The Nazareth student experience includes a liberal arts education, as well as local, national, and global service learning opportunities to prepare students to live peacefully in a diverse world that's increasingly interconnected.

MAJORS AND DEGREES OFFERED

Degrees Offered: Bachelor of Science, Bachelor of Arts, Bachelor of Fine Arts, Masters, and Doctoral degrees

Biological and biomedical sciences: Biochemistry; Biology/Biological Sciences; Biomedical Sciences

Business, Management, Marketing and Related: Accounting; Business Management; Finance; Marketing; Music Business

Communication, Journalism: English; Communication and Media; Communication Sciences and Disorders

Education: Art Teacher Education; Biology Teacher Education; Business Teacher Education; Chemistry Teacher Education; Education, General; Elementary Education and Teaching; English/Language Arts Teacher Education; Environmental Science and Sustainability Education; Foreign Language Teacher Education; French Language Teacher Education; History Teacher Education; Junior High/Intermediate/Middle School (Adolescence) Education and Teaching; Mathematics Teacher Education; Music Teacher Education; Secondary Education and Teaching; Spanish Language Teacher Education; Special Education and Teaching, Other; Speech Teacher Education; Teacher Education, Multiple Levels; Theatre Arts Education

English languages, literatures, and linguistics: English Language and Literature

Foreign languages, literatures, and linguistics: Foreign Languages, Literatures, and Linguistics, Other; Chinese Language, Literature; French Language and Literature; Italian Language and Literature; Spanish Language and Literature

Health Professions and Related Clinical Sciences: Art Therapy/Therapist; Clinical Laboratory Sciences; Communication Disorders Sciences; Music Therapy/Therapist; Nursing/Registered Nurse (RN, ASN, BSN, MSN); Occupational Therapy (B.S./M.S.); Physical Therapy/Therapist (B.S./D.P.T.); Pre-Dentistry Studies; Pre-Medicine/Pre-Medical Studies; Pre-Veterinary Studies; Public Health; Social Work; Speech-Language Pathology/Pathologist

History: History, General; Museums, Archives, and Public History

Mathematics: Mathematics

Multi/interdisciplinary studies: Community Youth Development; International and Global Studies; 3 + 3 Law Degree with Syracuse University; Music Business; Women and Gender Studies

Natural Resource and Conservation: Environmental Science and Sustainability

Philosophy and Religious studies: Philosophy; Religious Studies

Physical Sciences: Chemistry; Toxicology

Psychology : Psychology

Public Administration and Social Service Professions: Community Youth Development; Social Work

Social Sciences: Anthropology; Economics, General; Legal Studies; Peace and Justice; Philosophy; Social Science

Political Science and Government, General: Political Science; Religious Studies; Sociology and Social Science

Visual and Performing Arts: Acting; Art History; Art Studio/ General; Dance Studies; Music Education; Music History, Literature, and Theory; Music Performance; Musical Theatre; Music Theory and Composition; Music, General; Technical Theatre/Theatre Design and Technology; Theatre Arts; Visual Communication Design

TUITION, ROOM, BOARD, FEES

The College offers merit-based awards for excellence in academics, art, music, and drama, as well as need-based aid.

Financial Aid

Students seeking aid complete the Free Application for Federal Student Aid (FAFSA). Full cost and financial aid details: go.naz.edu/tuition-aid

STUDENT ORGANIZATIONS AND ACTIVITIES

Under the guidance of faculty, students frequently find themselves working with peers (including students from other disciplines) in clinical and lab settings, and on projects and productions. As one student recently mentioned: "There's a community feeling on campus and the surrounding area of Rochester is welcoming to students. The school offers variety and diversity and I believe the school is dedicated to their students' wholeness, health, and overall well–being. It's not ALL about your academic success but your overall growth along with personal maturity and life preparation. The advisors are truly dedicated to insuring you are on the right path and advice instead of tell." Professors and advisors encourage students to link their studies with practical experiences, including study abroad, service-learning, research, and internships. Students can support or discover their varied interests through involvement in over 50 clubs and organizations ranging from academic clubs, athletics, culture and entertainment, and interfaith groups. It's common for a math major to be a member of the dance team, a physical therapy major to minor in music, or a biochemistry major to minor in legal studies.

All campus clubs are initiated and led by students. Current campus clubs and organizations include Art Club; Art Therapy Club; ASL Club; Association of Social Work Students; Badminton Club; Ballroom Club; Best Buddies Club; Black Student Union; Capoeira Club; Campus Activities Board; Center for Spirituality Council; Chinese Club; Communications, Sciences and Disorders Association; Club Italianissimo; Community Youth Development Collective; Dare2Dance; Diversity Council; French Club; German Club; Gerontology Club; Golden Creative Marketing Agency; Golden Gazette; Habitat for Humanity, Inc.; International Club; Lambda Association; LASMA-Spanish Club; Marketing Club, Math Club; Millennial Action Council; Mind Over Matter; Music Business Club; Music Therapy Club; National Association for Music Education; Nazareth Commuter Association; Nazareth Crew Club; Nazareth Dance Organization; Naz Ultimate; Nursing Club; Philosophy Club; Physical Therapy Club; Pre-Health Professionals Club; Psychology; Public Health Club; Quidditch Club; Racquetball Club; Residence Hall Council; Science Club; Student Athlete Mentors; Student Occupational Therapy Association; Student Veterans of America; Theatre League; Women and Gender Studies Student Association; and WNAZ The Beat Campus Radio Station. The Undergraduate Association provides student advocacy. For more: naz.edu/student-activities

ADMISSIONS PROCESS

Nazareth uses the Common Application. In addition, applicants must submit an official high school transcript, an essay, and a letter of recommendation. Test scores are optional except for nursing. An audition or portfolio review is required for applications to art, dance, music, and theatre programs: naz.edu/auditions. A campus visit is highly recommended: naz.edu/visit International students should consult the website for application guidelines: naz.edu/international

In addition to Regular Decision (RD), Nazareth offers two Early Decision (ED) application tracks. Application deadlines are: November 15 for ED 1, January 10 for ED 2, and February 1 for RD. The College seeks students with a high level of competency and recommends applicants complete a rigorous college-preparatory curriculum in high school that includes English, a foreign language, math, science, and social studies. Successful completion of Advanced Placement and International Baccalaureate courses are looked upon favorably. Co-curricular activities are also considered.

Nursing applicants are required to submit standardized test scores (SAT, ACT, or both). For all other programs, test scores are helpful, but not required. Approximately 75 percent of applicants submit scores. For admissions details: naz. edu/admissions, email admissions@naz.edu, or call (585) 389-2860 or (800) 462-3944. Nazareth offers merit-based awards for excellence in academics, art, dance, music, and theatre, as well as need-based aid. Students seeking aid complete the Free Application for Federal Student Aid (FAFSA). For cost and financial aid details: go.naz.edu/tuition-aid

NEW YORK UNIVERSITY

AT A GLANCE

New York University is the largest independent research university in the United States, and is unlike any other institution of higher education. NYU has degree-granting campuses in New York, Abu Dhabi, and Shanghai, and 11 global academic centers around the world.

NYU's more than 20,000 undergraduates come from all 50 states and over 130 countries. NYU is both the No. 1 sender and receiver of students studying internationally, and we believe our global network raises the level of discourse in the classroom and provides a modern education for our global society. NYU's global sites are fully owned, operated, and staffed by NYU, creating a seamless experience for students.

The energy and resources within New York City, Abu Dhabi, and Shanghai serve as extensions of our campuses which, by design, are in and of their cities, providing unique opportunities for research, internships, and job placement. Within our New York campus, NYU has 10 undergraduate schools and colleges nine of which surround Washington Square and one, our school of engineering, in downtown Brooklyn.

Students choose from thousands of courses in over 230 areas of study. Despite our size, we have a remarkably intimate academic environment on our campuses. In fact, our student to faculty ratio in New York is 10:1 and our average class size is fewer than 30 students.

A faculty of renowned scholars, researchers, and artists teach our students who take courses both inside and outside a chosen major, providing breadth across different disciplines and depth in a chosen area of concentration. NYU's urban locations enables us to attract stunning diversity in academia talent, with faculty who have won awards ranging from the Pulitzer Prize and Abel Prize in Mathematics to the Grammys and Tony's. Being in cities at the crossroads of the world enables us to offer students thousands of internship opportunities and comprehensive career preparation during their undergraduate studies. For the class of 2017, over 95 percent of our students were employed or enrolled in graduate school within six months of graduation. NYU is also ranked #1 for graduate employability by Times Higher Education.

LOCATION AND ENVIRONMENT

The energy and resources within New York City, Abu Dhabi, and Shanghai serve as extensions of our campuses which, by design, are in and of their cities, providing unique opportunities for research, internships, and job placement. Within our New York campus, NYU has 10 undergraduate schools and colleges nine of which surround Washington Square and one, our school of engineering, in downtown Brooklyn.

CAMPUS FACILITIES & EQUIPMENT

NYU offers an exceptional range of facilities and student services, including a range of residence halls, meal plans, and dining locations on each campus. Academic facilities include nine libraries and institutes renowned for their research in applied mathematics, physics, neural science, and fine arts. Foreign language and cultural centers offer lectures, films, and concerts. Students may also access NYU's Wasserman Center for Career Development, and student support offices addressing almost every student need, from health and wellness to academic support and enrichment. The Kimmel Center for Student Life houses dining facilities, student lounges, computers, club spaces, and the Skirball Center for the Performing Arts, lower Manhattan's largest performance space.

OFF-CAMPUS OPPORTUNITIES

Students have access to NYU's extensive global network, within which they can pursue their studies and explore new cultures and perspectives while remaining connected to all of the University's academic resources. They may choose from 11 global academic centers—in Accra, Ghana; Berlin, Germany; Buenos Aires, Argentina; Florence, Italy; London, England; Madrid, Spain; Paris, France; Prague, Czech Republic; Sydney, Australia; Tel Aviv, Israel; and Washington, DC—or in one of many exchange programs NYU has with outstanding research universities around the world. Each location provides a rich curriculum in which students—whose financial aid will travel with them—can complete some of their general degree requirements and, in many fields, take courses in their major. In fact, a number of NYU's schools, colleges, and programs (like the Global Liberal Studies program and the major in Business and Political Economy) offer specific curricula and majors with an international focus. With all of these opportunities, it's no surprise that NYU is #1 for the number of students who study abroad (per the most recent IIE Open Doors report).

ACADEMICS

At NYU in New York City, students enroll into one of the University's undergraduate schools, colleges, or programs: The College of Arts and Science; the Core Program in Liberal Studies; the Global Liberal Studies Program; the Leonard N. Stern School of Business; the Steinhardt School of Culture, Education, and Human Development; the Tisch School of the Arts; the Gallatin School of Individualized Study; the Silver School of Social Work; the Meyers College of Nursing; the School of Professional Studies; and the Tandon School of Engineering.

NYU Abu Dhabi is NYU's second degree-granting campus and a major research center. Located in the United Arab Emirates, it draws students from around the world, preparing them for the challenges and opportunities of our interconnected world. It offers degrees in the liberal arts and sciences as well as engineering, and is the first comprehensive liberal arts college in the Middle East to be operated by and integrated into an American private research university.

NYU Shanghai is NYU's third degree-granting campus in China. NYU Shanghai offers students an immensely cross-cultural, close-knit learning community, along with a strong foundation in the liberal arts and sciences with emphasis in science, technology, engineering, and mathematics, as well as Chinese language and culture. It supports world-class academic research and graduate and professional education.

NYU faculty are among the world's leading scholars, and have received Nobel, Crafoord, and Pulitzer Prizes; MacArthur, Guggenheim, and Fulbright Fellowships; and Oscar and Emmy Awards. Faculty members teach undergraduate and graduate courses, allowing undergraduate students to become directly involved in research projects with internationally renowned professors and experts in their fields.

MAJORS AND DEGREES OFFERED

NYU students begin their studies at one of NYU's three dynamic urban locations: in New York City; in Abu Dhabi, UAE; or in Shanghai, China. No matter where their home campus is, all students graduate with an NYU degree, and may travel throughout the NYU global network as they complete their majors.

In New York, students enroll directly into one of the aforementioned undergraduate schools, colleges, or programs, all of which have earned national recognition in their respective fields.

Among the more than 230 areas of study offered by NYU's three campuses are: Anthropology, Arab Crossroads Studies, Biochemistry, Economics, Dance, Education, Engineering, Environmental Science, Film and Television, Finance, Global Public Health, Hospitality and Tourism Management, Individualized Study, Integrated Digital Media, Marketing, Metropolitan Studies, Nursing, Real Estate, Social Work, Theatre, and Recorded Music.

TUITION, ROOM, BOARD, FEES

On average, tuition and fees are approximately $49,000 for two semesters; room and board cost approximately $24,000 per year. Most NYU students receive one or more forms of financial aid to support contributions made by them and their families. (Financial aid information is subject to change; please visit admissions. nyu.edu for the most up-to-date information.)

FINANCIAL AID

The vast majority of financial aid awarded at NYU is need-based. Low-interest education loans are available for both students and parents. NYU also offers or participates in a variety of payment plans, ranging from interest-free prepayment plans to extensive loan programs that allow families to finance the cost of a college education over many years. A financial aid package might include any combination of scholarships, loans, or work-study programs. The average scholarship/grant for incoming freshmen in New York is approximately $37,000.

Students wishing to be considered for financial aid must submit the Free Application for Federal Student Aid (FAFSA)° and the CSS/Financial Aid PROFILE (and CSS Noncustodial Parent PROFILE, if applicable), administered by the College Board.

Financial aid information is subject to change; visit admissions.nyu.edu for the latest deadlines and more specific details pertaining to financial aid for each NYU campus.

°NYU Abu Dhabi applicants, and any non-US citizens or US permanent residents are not required to complete the FAFSA.

STUDENT ORGANIZATIONS AND ACTIVITIES

NYU's more than 20,000 undergraduates come from all 50 states and over 130 countries.

With 21 varsity sports teams that compete at the NCAA Division III level, as well as intramural sports, club athletics, over 400 student clubs, and numerous volunteer activities, NYU students are actively involved both on and off campus.

Student-run clubs are as varied as the student body. Whether their interests lie in world languages, politics, ballroom dancing, writing for the Washington Square News or working at NYU's radio station, students will find something (or more likely, a dozen things!) they love to do.

Hundreds of students annually serve communities across the city, country and world through the Office of Student Activities' C-Team, Alternative Breaks Program, student OutReach Program, fraternities and sororities, and student grassroots organizations. Students deliver meals to the needy and homebound, tutor children, paint public schools, clean up parks, rebuild areas devastated by natural disasters, provide healthcare services in underdeveloped areas, and more.

NYU is anything but cookie-cutter—that's one of the best things about being a part of a larger, global university. The culture of openness, opportunity, and inclusion that is cultivated here allows NYU students to thrive. There are so many choices here about what to do that no two students make the same selection.

ADMISSIONS PROCESS

When choosing a new entering class, the Admissions Committee conducts a holistic review, carefully considering many significant factors, including a comprehensive review of the applicant's academic background, standardized test scores, extracurricular activities, an essay, personal statements, and recommendation letters. Several programs also require the applicant to audition or submit creative materials. Applicants who have successfully completed a broad range of challenging course work throughout high school are the most desirable candidates. Also considered are your unique talents, personal attributes, and future goals.

Applicants are expected to demonstrate their talents and mastery of subject matter to support their applications and to make their best case for admission. As a result, NYU accepts a wide range of national examinations in addition to the SAT, ACT, SAT Subject Tests, AP exams, and IB scores. International students may be required to submit TOEFL, iELTS, or PTE Academic results as proof of English language proficiency. More information about NYU's complete standardized testing requirements can be found online at admissions.nyu.edu

NYU accepts applications in three separate rounds: Early Decision I, Early Decision II, and Regular Decision.

Certain programs at NYU conduct interviews, which are by invitation only. Prospective students are strongly encouraged to visit campus and attend an information session. The admissions staff also visits high schools and hosts receptions worldwide. For dates and times, and for reserving a space at our information sessions and campus tours, go to admissions.nyu.edu/visit.

NIAGARA UNIVERSITY

AT A GLANCE

Founded by the Vincentian community in 1856, Niagara University is a comprehensive institution, blending the best of liberal arts and professional education, grounded in values-based, Catholic tradition. With more than 80 majors, 55 plus minors, six-preprofessional options, master's programs and a Ph.D. program, NU students are immersed in meaningful real-world opportunities from the moment they step foot on the university's beautiful campus.

Niagara's colleges of Arts and Sciences, Business Administration, Education and Hospitality and Tourism Management offer programs at the baccalaureate level, master's and doctoral. All four of the university's academic colleges have received the highest rankings from the top accreditation boards in their fields. In addition, the university offers an award-winning Academic Exploration program for students who are undecided about their major.

A student-to-faculty ration of 12:1 and an average class size of 20 allow for personal attention and classroom interaction. The faculty members at Niagara are internationally renowned for their abilities as researchers and teachers, helping students accomplish things they never thought possible. A recent survey indicated that 97 percent of Niagara's graduating class was employed or enrolled in graduate school within one year of graduation.

Niagara offers a wide variety of entertainment options on and off-campus, including trips to professional sporting events, local landmarks, concerts, malls, restaurants and cultural festivals in the U.S. and nearby Ontario, Canada. And with 18 Division 1 athletics programs, there are numerous chances for NU students to put their "Purple Pride" on display.

LOCATION AND ENVIRONMENT

Niagara University's picturesque 160-acre campus is located in the town of Lewiston, New York, two minutes off the I-190 on Route 104. The campus is situated on Monteagle Ridge overlooking the lower Niagara River, which connects the two Great Lakes of Erie and Ontario. The University's suburban campus setting is just a few miles from the world-famous Niagara Falls, 20 minutes from Buffalo, which offers a variety of cultural events, sports, and entertainment opportunities, and just 90 minutes from Rochester and Toronto, Canada's largest metropolitan area. In addition, the University is minutes away from the quaint village of Lewiston, New York, and the city of Niagara Falls, New York.

CAMPUS FACILITIES & EQUIPMENT

Niagara University's housing accommodations include five residence halls, a grouping of five small cottages, and a student apartment complex.

The university's library supports student learning and knowledge creation by providing assistance and access to online and print information resources, technology, and individual and collaborative work and study space. Assistance is available in person and via online chat, text, email, and phone. The library's main floor is open 24 hours a day during the school year.

The newly renovated and expanded Russell J. Salvatore Dining Commons is the newest structural addition to Niagara's campus. The B. Thomas Golisano Center for Integrated Sciences offers 50,000-square-feet of learning space and cutting-edge equipment that encourages collaboration among scientific disciplines. The Academic Complex, the home to the College of Education and the College of Business Administration (Bisgrove Hall), is a state-of-the-art learning facility, with a simulated trading floor in the Glynn Atrium. Dunleavy Hall, outstanding both educationally and architecturally, includes a computerized lecture hall and TV production rooms. The university's facilities also include the Computer Center; St. Vincent's Hall; the Kiernan Center, NU's athletic and recreation center; the Elizabeth Ann Clune Center for Theatre; the Castellani Art Museum; and the Dwyer Arena, a dual-rink ice hockey complex.

ACADEMICS

Niagara University's curricula enable students to pursue their academic preferences and to complete courses that lead to proficiency in other academic areas. Courses that have been considered upper-division courses are available to all students. This provides students with the opportunity to avoid introductory and survey courses and permits motivated students to take advantage of more challenging courses early in their collegiate career. The Niagara University honors program provides special academic opportunities that stimulate, encourage and challenge participants. In addition, an accelerated three-year degree program is offered to qualified students. Students pursuing a bachelor's degree must complete a total of 40 or 42 course units (120 or 126 credit hours) to meet graduation requirements. Niagara grants credit for successful scores on the Advanced Placement and the College-Level Examination Program and the International Baccalaureate tests. Internships, research, independent study, study abroad and cooperative education are available in many academic programs. An Army-ROTC program is also offered. NU is fully accredited by the Middle States Association of Colleges and Schools. Its programs in the respective areas are accredited by the Council for the Accreditation of Educator Preparation (CAEP), AACSB International–The Association to Advance Collegiate Schools of Business, and the Council on Social Work Education, and the chemistry department has the approval of the American Chemical Society. The travel, hotel and restaurant administration program is accredited by the Commission for Programs in Hospitality Administration.

MAJORS AND DEGREES OFFERED

The College of Arts and Sciences offers the Bachelor of Arts degree in art history with museum studies, chemistry, communication studies, English, environmental science, French, gerontology, history, international studies, liberal arts, life sciences, mathematics, philosophy, political science, psychology, religious studies, social sciences, sociology, and Spanish. The Bachelor of Science degree is awarded in actuarial science, biochemistry (with a concentration in bioinformatics), biology (with a concentration in biotechnology), chemistry, computer and information sciences, criminology and criminal justice, environmental science, mathematics, nursing, psychology and social work. This division also offers the Bachelor of Fine Arts degree in theatre studies (with concentrations in performance, design & production, and theatre specializations). Preprofessional programs are offered in dentistry, law, medicine, pharmacy, veterinary medicine, and Army ROTC. An associate of arts degree is available in general studies. Enrichment courses in fine arts and languages are also available. A combination five-year B.S./M.S. program is available to students in the criminal justice program; psychology majors can engage in a six-year B.A. or B.S./M.S. program in clinical mental health counseling; an accelerated nursing program, and an R.N.-to-B.S. program in nursing is offered for students who already have their R.N.

Preprofessional Partnerships: In addition to the programs listed above, NU offers a number of preprofessional partnerships. These include a 3+4 partnership in pharmacy with the State University of New York at Buffalo (SUNY), a 2+3 partnership in pharmacy with Lake Erie College of Osteopathic Medicine (LECOM), and 3+4 partnership in medicine with LECOM. Qualified premedical Niagara students are eligible to apply for the early assurance program sponsored by the SUNY at Buffalo.

Niagara University's College of Business Administration is accredited by AACSB International—The Association to Advance Collegiate Schools of Business and offers a B.B.A. and a combination B.B.A./M.B.A. degree (five-year program) in accounting. This division offers B.S. degrees in economics, finance, management (with concentrations in human resources, international business, and supply chain management), and marketing (with a concentration in food marketing), as well as a B.A. in economics. In addition, an A.A.S. degree can be earned in business. Students gain real-world experiences through internships, study abroad, and via cooperative education programs as well as research being conducted in several business-focused campus centers. These centers include the Family Business Center, the Center for Supply Chain Management, the Center for International Accounting and Research, and the Technology Transfer Center.

Holding the highest accreditations possible in both the United States and Canada— the United States Council for the Accreditation of Educator Preparation (CAEP) and Canada's Ontario College of Teachers—Niagara University's College of Education provides students with an option of earning dual certification to teach in both countries. The College of Education offers bachelor's degree programs leading to New York State initial certification in early childhood and childhood (birth–grade 6), childhood and middle childhood (grades 1–9), middle childhood and adolescence (grades 5–12), special education and childhood (grades 1-6), special education and adolescence (grades 7–12) and in Teaching English to Speakers of Other Languages (TESOL). All education majors pursue an academic concentration to establish expertise in one of the following subject areas: business & marketing, English language arts, French, liberal arts, mathematics, social studies, and Spanish. Business education is offered only for grades 5–12. The academic concentration in liberal arts can only be pursued in the early childhood and childhood (birth–grade 6), and special education and childhood (grades 1–6). Most other states, and Puerto Rico, have reciprocity agreements with New York, so an NU education would qualify education majors to teach in those states as well.

The College of Hospitality and Tourism Management provides a career-oriented curriculum leading to a B.S. degree in three specific areas: hotel and restaurant management (with concentrations in food and beverage management; luxury hospitality operations; and hotel planning, development, and operations), sport management (with concentrations in sport operations and revenue management), and tourism and recreation management (with concentrations in event and meeting management and tourism destination management). The College of Hospitality and Tourism Management offered the world's first bachelor's degree in tourism. NU's hotel and restaurant program, the second oldest in New York state, has the distinction of being the seventh program nationally to be accredited by the Accreditation Commission for Programs in Hospitality Administration by the Council of Hotel, Restaurant, and Institutional Education. The College introduces students to a comprehensive body of knowledge about the hotel, restaurant, tourism, and recreational areas and applies this knowledge to current industry challenges. The College requires that its students accumulate 800 hours of industry-related experience. These and other practical experiences offer NU students the knowledge necessary to advance in the field. Students work with industry leaders in classroom projects, join academic clubs and professional organizations, and participate in special trips to trade shows and conventions and specially designed study-abroad experiences, making NU a national leader in the area.

For students who are undecided about which major to choose, Niagara University offers its award-winning Academic Exploration Program (AEP). AEP provides a structured opportunity for students to participate in a thorough, organized process of selecting a major that meets their academic talents and career goals while fulfilling requirements to graduate with classmates on time.

TUITION, ROOM, BOARD, FEES

Tuition for 2017–18 was $30,500. Room and board (with a choice of meal plans) cost an additional $12,950 per year. Fees were estimated at $1,450 per year.

FINANCIAL AID

The highest in quality, Niagara is also an exceptional value—a prestigious private university education at a reasonable cost when financial aid packages are taken into account.

Ninety-nine percent of entering freshmen and transfers receive financial aid. This aid may come in the form of merit scholarships, loans, grants, or campus employment. Students seeking financial assistance should file the Free Application for Federal Student Aid (FAFSA). New York State residents should also file a Tuition Assistance Program (TAP) application.

Niagara University offers a program (NUOP) that provides institutional admittance as well as financial and intensive academic assistance to students who otherwise would not meet admission criteria.

Additionally, the Level Tuition Program allows first semester freshmen to "lock in" one tuition rate for four consecutive years. This makes it much easier for students and families to budget the cost of their education.

Finally, Niagara's NUSTEP program reduces the overall cost of attendance by providing high school students with opportunities to obtain college credits.

STUDENT ORGANIZATIONS AND ACTIVITIES

There are approximately 3,100 undergraduate and 850 graduate students enrolled at Niagara. A large percentage of these students take advantage of the more than 100 extracurricular and cocurricular activities offered, including student government, NU Honors, WNIA (student radio), Club Managers Association of America and Brothers and Sisters in Christ.

ADMISSIONS PROCESS

Niagara University welcomes students who have demonstrated aptitude and academic achievement at the high school level. The university has adopted a test optional admissions policy for most first-year undergraduate applicants, beginning with the fall 2018 entry year.

Niagara has joined a growing number of the nation's most competitive and well-respected institutions by giving students the option to submit or withhold standardized test scores (SAT/ACT) as part of their admissions application.

The Office of Undergraduate Admissions will continue to accept standardized test scores from students who believe their results are reflective of their academic abilities to succeed at the university. If they feel that it doesn't reflect their ability and academic skills, they have the option of not submitting.

The few exceptions to this test optional policy includes students who are seeking entrance into a nursing or biology major, those who wish to be considered for Trustees or Presidential Scholarships, students looking to apply for science-related scholarships such as NUSURF (Niagara University Science Undergraduate Research Fellowship), and homeschooled students

International students are required to submit the results of their TOEFL examination and, if transcripts are not in English, these transcripts must be sent to Niagara University visa the World Education Services (WES) for a "Course by Course Report" evaluation. Interviews are recommended.

Transfers are accepted in any semester. (Transfer credit is evaluated by the dean of each division.) Students who complete high school in less than four years are eligible for early admission. Students may also apply under an early action program. Economically and academically disadvantaged students from New York State are eligible to apply through the Higher Education Opportunity Program (HEOP).

Niagara operates on a rolling admission basis and adheres to the College Board Candidates Reply Date. Nursing and theatre applicants are encouraged to apply be mid-December of their senior year. A visit to the campus is recommended, and overnight accommodations in the residence hall are available through the Niagara Nights program.

NORTHEASTERN UNIVERSITY

AT A GLANCE

A world leader in experiential-learning education, Northeastern emphasizes educational programs that link course work with a variety of practical experiences, including global opportunities, service-learning, research and our signature co-op program.

There's a certain energy about Northeastern University. It comes from the bright, ambitious students, exhibiting a strong sense of purpose in the classroom and while working or studying abroad. In the city of Boston—the ultimate college town—and across the globe, Northeastern students challenge themselves intellectually, investigate career options, participate in community service, and graduate both personally and professionally prepared for their future careers and graduate school.

Founded in 1898, Northeastern is a leader in interdisciplinary research, urban engagement, and the seamless integration of classroom learning with real-world experiences. The academic curriculum is enhanced by experiential learning through research, professional, global, and service experiences. Anchored by the world's largest, most innovative cooperative education program, Northeastern prepares students for a lifetime of achievement, and allows them to make an impact on the world before they graduate.

The current undergraduate enrollment of 18,107 is made up of students of all backgrounds and interests, giving Northeastern its distinctive culture. Students can participate in any of Northeastern's more than 400 student organizations, join a cultural club, participate in cutting-edge research with faculty from various disciplines, or perform with an award-winning a cappella group. They can travel to nearby New Hampshire for a ski club trip, play varsity or club basketball, tutor local children, and more. Students have countless opportunities to make lifelong friendships, to try something brand new—a class, a sport, or a career path—to hone their leadership skills and have fun. Quiet corners of the campus feel far from city streets and give students a secluded haven to read, write, or relax. The 73-acre campus is dynamic and welcoming, a beautiful stretch of leafy green in the heart of Boston.

LOCATION AND ENVIRONMENT

Northeastern's residential campus is located in the heart of Boston, where the distinctive neighborhoods of the Back Bay, the South End, the Fenway, and Roxbury meet. Over half of the student body lives on campus and many of the residence halls have amazing views of the Boston skyline.

The Back Bay area, known for its many cultural and educational institutions, is just steps away from Symphony Hall, the New England Conservatory of Music, the Museum of Fine Arts, and the Isabella Stewart Gardner Museum. The South End is home to elegant Victorian row houses, a vibrant arts scene, hidden gardens, and some of the finest dining in Boston. The Fenway area, with its beautiful rose garden, bicycle and jogging paths, and Fenway Park (home of the Boston Red Sox) is also just a few blocks away.

CAMPUS FACILITIES & EQUIPMENT

Northeastern is home to more than fifty research centers and undergraduates have ample opportunities to work alongside their professors to aid and conduct research on a variety of topics. The university library system is comprised of Snell Library, a 240,000-square-foot central library on the Boston campus, the School of Law Library, and a small supplemental collection at the Nahant Marine Science Center. Snell Library houses 780,669 print volumes, 548,806 e-books, 1,163,735 microfilms, and access to 83,511 licensed electronic journals, as well as 23,437 audio, video, and computer software items, and 5,712 linear feet of archival material as of June 2014.

Northeastern University provides a broad range of academic and administrative computer resources to students, faculty, and staff members. Many computing resources are available, including an extensive wireless network, Internet connections for all offices and university-owned residence halls, technology-assisted classrooms, computer labs, and the MyNortheastern Admitted Student Portal, which allows students to access many administrative and academic functions online.

ACADEMICS

At the heart of a Northeastern education are award-winning faculty mentors, a rigorous and innovative curriculum, and undergraduate research and global experiences that challenge and transform. Northeastern's innovative programs encompass a wide range of majors, concentrations, and interdisciplinary studies along with honors, pre-professional, and study-abroad programs.

Northeastern's approach to educating its students integrates a challenging academic curriculum with a variety of experiential learning opportunities including research, global experiences, service learning, and the university's signature cooperative education program (co-op), enabling students to make deep connections between their field of study and the world around them. After completing their freshman year, Northeastern students integrate classroom learning with six-month periods of full-time, immersive professional work, global study, or research experiences related to their major or interests. Northeastern's flexibility enables students to choose a four or five-year path with up to eighteen months of experience, strengthening their professional network and giving them confidence-and a significant edge in the job market. Students learn what career is a good fit for them—and what careers are not—all before graduating. In addition, over half of the students are offered full-time jobs from co-op employers. Northeastern partners with over 3,350 co-op employers around the globe, including some of the world's largest and most reputable companies: Pfizer, John Hancock, Yahoo, Fidelity Investments, IBM, General Electric, Massachusetts General Hospital, Microsoft, and the Boston Globe, just to name a few.

Experiential learning opportunities—including U.S. and international professional co-op, service learning, research, and study abroad—are currently available in 134 countries around the world.

The University Honors Program allows students to participate in enriched educational experiences and offers opportunities that include honors sections of required academic courses, honors seminars, independent research, and specialized study abroad.

The university has more than 1,330 full and part-time faculty members with a wide variety of research and teaching interests and specialties. Academic counselors in each college work closely with students to assist them in developing programs suited to their interests and abilities. Co-op advisors assist students in resume-building, honing interview skills and tactics, and in developing contacts with businesses and employers to support networking and professional opportunities.

MAJORS AND DEGREES OFFERED

Northeastern's academic programs are divided among eight colleges. The College of Arts, Media and Design awards undergraduate degrees in architecture, art, media arts and design, communication studies, game design, journalism; media and screen studies, music/music industry, music composition and technology, studio art, and theater (including concentrations in performance and production).

The D'Amore-McKim School of Business offers two degree options: the Bachelor of Science in Business Administration (B.S.B.A.) and the Bachelor of Science in International Business (B.S.I.B.). The B.S.I.B. program includes language instruction and international study and work. The college offers concentrations in accounting, entrepreneurship and innovation, finance, management, management information systems, marketing, and supply chain management.

The College of Computer and Information Science awards degrees in computer science and information science and also offers combined majors that pair computer science with biology, business, cognitive psychology, communication studies, computer engineering, cyber operations, digital art, environmental science, game design, interactive media, journalism, mathematics, music, music composition and technology.

The College of Engineering offers degrees in bioengineering, chemical, civil, computer, electrical, industrial, and mechanical engineering.

The Bouvé College of Health Sciences awards degrees in health sciences, nursing, pharmacy and physical therapy. The college also offers a six-year Doctor of Pharmacy degree and a six-year program leading to a Doctor of Physical Therapy.

The College of Science awards undergraduate degrees in applied physics, behavioral neuroscience, biochemistry, biology, biomedical physics, chemistry, environmental science, environmental studies, linguistics, marine biology, mathematics, physics, and psychology.

The College of Social Sciences and Humanities awards undergraduate degrees in African American studies, American Sign Language, Asian studies, criminal justice, cultural anthropology, economics, English, history, human services, international affairs, Jewish studies (combined major only), philosophy, political science, religious studies, sociology, and Spanish.

The Explore Program for undeclared students offers a wide array of academic opportunities designed to help students who feel strongly about exploring their options before making a commitment to a major. The program provides the support and guidance students need to explore and eventually choose one of Northeastern's undergraduate programs.

TUITION, ROOM, BOARD, FEES

For the 2017–2018 academic year, the estimated tuition is $48,560 and room and board fees are estimated at $15,660. Regardless of time to degree, tuition is charged only while students are earning academic credit.

FINANCIAL AID

The university operates a substantial aid program designed to make attendance feasible for all qualified students. We are dedicated to meeting each incoming domestic financial aid applicant's full demonstrated need. By coordinating the resources of the university and various public and private scholarship programs, the Office of Student Financial Services was able to provide more than $264 million in grant and scholarship assistance. More than 75 percent of students receive some form of financial aid. Northeastern participates in all federal aid programs. Financial aid is based on need and academic merit and may consist of scholarships, grants, loans, work-study employment, or any combination of these funds. To apply, students must file the Free Application for Federal Student Aid (FAFSA) and a CSS PROFILE form with the College Scholarship Service by the priority filing date of February 15.

STUDENT ORGANIZATIONS AND ACTIVITIES

Students have access to over 400 clubs and organizations and an extensive network of advisement and counseling services. Approximately 16,500 students participate in student organizations. Programs and services sponsored by the African American Institute, the Latino/a Student Cultural Center, the Asian American Center, the International Student & Scholar Institute, and many other organizations enrich Northeastern's social life and cultural fabric. In athletics, Northeastern competes in NCAA Division I and maintains varsity teams in 8 men's and 10 women's sports.

ADMISSIONS PROCESS

Students may enter the university with advanced credit on the basis of test scores on Advanced Placement (AP) examinations, the International Baccalaureate (I.B.) examinations, or with successful completion of accredited college-level courses. In addition to the application for admission, prospective freshmen must submit official high school transcript(s) (or official GED score reports); official transcripts for any college-level course work taken while a secondary-school student; written recommendations from their secondary school counselor and a teacher; and scores on the SAT (Northeastern's College Board code is 3667) or ACT, including the writing section. Please visit the university's website for additional admission details for specific student populations and transfer admissions requirements (northeastern. edu/admissions).

Application and Information

Admission to Northeastern is selective and competitive. For the freshman class entering in Fall 2018, the university received more than 62,000 applications for 2,800 seats in the freshman class. Students are reviewed in the context of their environment, with attention paid to their academic course selections and rigor, academic achievement, extracurricular involvement and impact, and their potential fit with Northeastern, including the demonstration of personal traits like leadership, adaptability, a global perspective, or an entrepreneurial spirit.

November 1 is the deadline for the early action admission program. Northeastern also offers two binding early decision programs. The deadline for Early Decision I is November 1, and the deadline for Early Decision II is January 1. Students who have carefully explored their college options and have decided that Northeastern is where they want to enroll may choose to apply under the early decision program. The deadline for the regular admission program is January 1. Admitted early action and regular decision students are required to pay a deposit by May 1 to secure a place in the class. Early Decision I students are required to pay a deposit by January 15, and Early Decision II students are required to pay a deposit by February 20. For transfer students, the admissions deadlines are April 1 for fall and October 1 for spring admission. Fall transfer and spring admission decisions are made on a space-available, rolling basis.

Northeastern offers a variety of visit options including information sessions and campus tours. For more information, or to register, visit northeastern.edu/admissions/connect/visit. For more information, students should contact:

The Office of Undergraduate Admissions

240 West Village F

Northeastern University

360 Huntington Avenue

Boston, Massachusetts 02115

Phone: 617-373-2200

E-mail: admissions@northeastern.edu

Website: northeastern.edu/admissions

OCCIDENTAL COLLEGE

AT A GLANCE

Founded in 1887, Occidental College fully integrates the liberal arts and sciences with the cultural and intellectual resources of one of the world's great cities. Situated on a 120-acre residential campus in Los Angeles' Eagle Rock community, our location serves as a springboard for putting theory into practice and ideas into action. Here, you can expect to spend as much time in the lab, in the field, in the community, and in the studio as you do in the classroom. Students benefit from our small-classroom environment with stimulating faculty, who take their teaching as seriously as their research. Our distinctive interdisciplinary approach will give you the chance to explore new ideas and see the world from a new perspective. With more than 40 majors and minors; exemplary, one-of-a-kind programs such as the Kahane United Nations Program and Campaign Semester; and our emphasis on research through the Undergraduate Research Center and senior comprehensives, Occidental provides its students with a compelling intellectual adventure. Academic rigor is enhanced by internships and community partnerships across Los Angeles. Students graduate from Occidental as strategic thinkers and effective communicators. Uncommonly inclusive and consciously collaborative, our students seek to embrace difference and make a difference in the world. Occidental is reinventing the liberal arts and sciences for a new generation of problem solvers, creators, and thinkers. It's an education that is distinctly Oxy.

LOCATION AND ENVIRONMENT

Located in Los Angeles' Eagle Rock community, Occidental's 120-acre campus is studded with mature oak trees and eucalyptus. The beauty of our campus and its red tile-roofed, Beaux Arts-style buildings has made it a mecca for filmmakers since 1919. State-of-the-art science facilities and our uniquely designed solar array share the campus with historic residence halls and classroom buildings. The atmosphere is, in a word, idyllic—students from all over the world visit and never want to leave. Somehow the L.A. traffic seems miles away, though the city is just outside our door—and is an integral part of an interdisciplinary, multicultural Occidental education. Our location allows Occidental to offer students the best of both worlds—the intimacy of a close-knit campus located in a residential community and access to the educational, cultural and recreational resources of Los Angeles and Southern California. Our location provides students a wide range of opportunities, from internships at the Grammy Museum and the L.A. Zoo to community involvement in programs addressing the environment, housing, nutrition, and urban development. Faculty and students routinely use the city as a resource for field study and research, whether it involves an evening poetry reading or a semester diving off the Pacific coast and studying marine biology.

CAMPUS FACILITIES & EQUIPMENT

The European-style 400-seat Keck Theater and attached shop is the main venue for Theater Department productions. (All stage sets and costumes are produced in-house.) Art students have access to multiple studio spaces, including printmaking, printing and sculpture studios, and three galleries.

In addition to standard science labs, Oxy has a superconducting magnet, a world-class paleomagnetic laboratory, a complete geochemical/environmental lab with an inductively-coupled plasma spectrometer, and a fission track lab.

Occidental's internationally known natural history collections, including the Moore Bird Collection and the Cosman Shell Collection, provide cutting-edge opportunities for genomic research.

Special Collections in the Library is home to one of the world's leading collections of material relating to the poet Robinson Jeffers (Oxy Class of 1905), a World War II Japanese-American relocation archive, and the 16,000-volume Guymon collection of mysteries and detective fiction.

Los Angeles weather allows for year-round use of outdoor athletic facilities, including Kemp Stadium, a practice venue for the 1984 Olympics. The new 25-yard by 34-meter Townsend-Crosthwaite Pool is now under construction.

OFF-CAMPUS OPPORTUNITIES

Whether you hail from five miles away or 5,000, Oxy will challenge you to explore your academic interests in contexts beyond the classroom and Los Angeles. Three-quarters of our students pursue Oxy's multiple routes to global citizenship: traditional study abroad, and research, internships, and fellowships on six continents.

Oxy offers the country's only residential undergraduate United Nations program. Students of all disciplines can spend a semester in New York City, taking classes and working as interns at UN-related organizations. Every two years, students get the chance to participate in Campaign Semester, spending the term working on key elections all while earning course credit.

InternLA is a unique summer internship program that funds more than 35 students to intern in Los Angeles based organizations and companies in six broad sectors: business, policy, media, research, advocacy, and the arts. Students intern full-time for 10 weeks over the summer while also enrolling in a weekly on-campus educational component.

Occidental has a strong history of producing winners of national fellowships and scholarships, a reflection of our rigorous undergraduate preparation. These highly sought after and extremely competitive awards give Oxy students opportunities to pursue advanced study and research at home and abroad.

ACADEMIC PROGRAMS

The foundation of our commitment to a liberal arts and science education is embodied in the Core Program, which is designed to spur students to think critically and creatively. The Core Program exposes students to a broad range of cultural, geographical and historical issues while developing their writing and research skills and encouraging interdisciplinary inquiry.

Research opportunities are possible for students in every discipline. For more than 15 years, we've offered a full-time Summer Research Program, an experience that often results in co-authored publications and positions students to win prestigious awards and gain entrance to graduate programs. As scholars equally committed to teaching and research, our professors open doors and champion student work. They drive an approach to the liberal arts at Oxy that encourages students to venture outside of their comfort zones. With a class size averaging 19 students, and a 10:1 student-faculty ratio, students get to know their professors and their classmates, engage in critical discussion, and learn from and about one another.

Every Oxy student completes a Senior Comprehensive Project, a project reflecting Oxy's educational philosophy of learning deeply and independently. Comps take a variety of different forms: projects, fieldwork, theses, exams, presentations, or creative works. Each discipline defines its comps expectations differently, and they all challenge and inspire students in unexpected ways. Many of our students draw senior comps inspiration from their multicultural surroundings in Los Angeles as well as research and exploration abroad.

MAJORS AND DEGREES OFFERED

Occidental offers 34 majors across our departments, as well as countless opportunities for independent research and experiential learning.

Majors Offered:

American Studies
Art and Art History
Biochemistry
Biology
Chemistry
Chinese
Classical Studies°
Cognitive Science
Comparative Studies in Literature & Culture
Computer Science
Critical Theory & Social Justice
Diplomacy & World Affairs
East Asian Languages and Cultures
Economics
Education°

English
French
Gender, Women, & Sexuality Studies°
Geology
German°
Group Language
History
Interdisciplinary Writing°
Japanese
Kinesiology
Latino/a and Latin American Studies
Linguistics°
Mathematics
Media Arts & Culture
Music
Neuroscience°
Philosophy
Physics
Politics
Psychology
Public Health°
Religious Studies
Russian
Sociology
Spanish
Theater
Urban & Environmental Policy

° Minor only

TUITION, ROOM, BOARD, FEES

Estimated cost of attendance for 2017–18:

Tuition: $52,260

Room & Board: $14,968

Required Fees: $578

Total: $67,806

FINANCIAL AID

We extend financial aid through merit scholarships, need-based grants and scholarships, work-study and student loans to meet the various needs and circumstances of our students. Our aid programs often make Oxy's cost comparable to those of public institutions.

If you are interested in Oxy, we encourage you to apply for financial aid—regardless of your financial circumstances. The New York Times has consistently ranked Occidental as one of the country's most economically diverse colleges. The Financial Aid Office is committed to meeting the demonstrated need of every enrolled student.

STUDENT ORGANIZATIONS AND ACTIVITIES

Students come to our residential campus from all over the world, each contributing their unique perspective to our ongoing conversation. Oxy students come from 48 states and 56 countries; international students make up 7 percent of the student body. From academic initiatives to a thriving network of student clubs and multicultural living communities, Oxy is a place for nuanced, sophisticated discussions about our differences, our similarities and where we can go from here.

About 20 percent participate in the Greek system, more than 25 percent are varsity NCAA Division III athletes, and hundreds more compete in year-round club and intramural sports.

Residence life is the heart of the student experience at Oxy. More than three-quarters of all students live on campus in one of 13 coed residence halls, including four reserved for first-year students.

Students consistently give Oxy's on-campus dining high marks. Not only is the food delicious, but Oxy's Dining Services is also environmentally friendly, taking part in the Real Food Challenge by providing local, organic food in the dining facilities.

Oxy students don't just take classes. They take charge and create new opportunities for innovation and learning. Oxy students thrive in their extracurricular pursuits, having founded and run over 100 clubs and organizations.

Dance Production, which features the work of student choreographers and dancers, is the largest student club on campus and sells out each of its three annual performances. For the vocally inclined, Glee Club has been a central part of the Oxy community since 1906. With L.A. being the home to a large portion of world media, it's no surprise that our students show interest in these areas. The campus TV station, CatAList TV, leapt onto the campus scene a few years ago, while KOXY radio and the Occidental Weekly have much longer histories. (Weekly alumni include two Pulitzer Prize-winning journalists.)

As the hub for the arts at Occidental, Oxy Arts promotes a socially-conscious, interdisciplinary conversation about contemporary arts practices on campus and in the community. Oxy Arts also serves as a comprehensive source of information for arts events and cultural happenings, including music, theater, film, the visual arts, literature, and art history.

Oxy students are running small businesses and departments on campus every day. From the student-run Green Bean Coffee Lounge to Oxy Design Service and the Bengal Bus shuttle service, student initiatives provide essential services and job opportunities that have led to post-graduation jobs.

Reaching out and supporting other areas of L.A. is important to Oxy students. From tutoring and mentoring to preparing meals for those in need, Oxy has a rich tradition of students partnering with the local community.

Sustainability is a passion for many Oxy students, and food plays a big part in that. That's why the Oxy campus has a student-run organic garden and a student-managed bike-sharing and repairing program. The student government Renewable Energy & Sustainability Fund supports student sustainability projects that make Oxy a better place to study and live.

ADMISSIONS PROCESS

Occidental is committed to admitting and enrolling a highly qualified and diverse student body. To that end, the admission committee evaluates each applicant individually and holistically. Academic preparation is paramount, so we will closely examine your high school transcript, focusing on your performance and course rigor. We also give serious consideration to qualities such as motivation, intellectual curiosity, leadership ability, and distinctive talents. Your personal statement, short answer responses, extracurricular activities, and letters of recommendation offer us valuable insight into these areas.

Whether you are applying as a first-year or transfer student, the following materials must be submitted by the appropriate application deadline with a non-refundable application processing fee of $65 or a fee waiver:

- High school transcript
- Standardized test scores (SAT or ACT)
- Extracurricular activities
- Personal statement
- Short answer responses
- Letters of recommendation

To learn more about the application process, visit oxy.edu/admission-aid/apply.

QUEENS COLLEGE OF THE CITY UNIVERSITY OF NEW YORK

AT A GLANCE

A storied institution with a long history of graduating students who go on to serve our global community, Queens College (QC)—a senior college of the City University of New York (CUNY)—will challenge you and help you build your future.

Since its founding in 1937, Queens College has enjoyed a national reputation for its liberal arts and science programs, its world-class faculty, and its affordability. Less than 10 miles from Manhattan, Queens College offers exciting academics and an innovative program that no other college in New York City offers: QC in 4, which guarantees that you will graduate in four years.

Opportunities to study abroad and internships abound, some right on campus in our Tech Incubator, where students can learn from budding entrepreneurs. Phi Beta Kappa, the oldest and most respected undergraduate honors organization in the United States, has a chapter at Queens, a distinction shared with only 10 percent of the nation's liberal arts colleges. And all this happens on a beautiful 80-acre campus with a centrally located residence hall, top recreational facilities, and the only Division II athletics program in CUNY.

Thanks to our low tuition and generous financial aid, 90 percent of our students who graduate in four years receive their degrees without any student loan debt. What's more, Queens College ranks in the top 1 percent of institutions in the country that propel students from poverty to prosperity. And there's a reason why the Center for World University Rankings placed Queens College in the top 4 percent of all colleges in 2018: the quality of our curriculum and our faculty, and the accomplishments of our graduates.

QC is one of America's most diverse colleges, in every sense of the word. We educate students of all ages and interests. Three military guides recognize us for our support of veterans and members of the armed services. We make every effort to accommodate people with disabilities. Culturally, we reflect the population of our home borough: Our students come from all over the world and many speak a language other than English. As a result, this campus offers a unique learning environment that prepares our alums to enter the global economy and affect change, wherever their lives and careers may take them.

Queens College enjoys a national reputation for its liberal arts and science programs, its world-class faculty, and its affordability. Ninety percent of our students who graduate in four years receive their degrees without any student loan debt.

LOCATION AND ENVIRONMENT

Queens College is located on 80 tree-lined acres in a quiet, residential neighborhood of Queens, New York City's largest borough. The attractions of Manhattan aren't far away, and year-round events—from performances at the Kupferberg Center for the Arts to Division II games on our field and courts—make the campus a destination in its own right. The college is served by public bus lines, as well as college shuttles that bring riders to and from two major mass transit hubs. Drivers can get here via the I-495. Although most students commute to class, The Summit Apartments, QC's residence hall, has affordable housing for just over 500 in fully furnished, two- and four-person suites.

OFF-CAMPUS OPPORTUNITIES

Queens College knows that top students look for challenges beyond the classroom. Our Center for Career Engagement and Internships tracks more than 1,200 positions. Interns earn academic credit and often more: the average QC internship stipend is $1,200 to $1,500. Service learning and leadership opportunities abound: you can build houses with Habitat for Humanity during spring break, go on a Midnight Run to feed the homeless, or conduct geological research in one of our local waterways. QC is also part of the CUNY Service Corps, in which students spend 24 weeks in paid, part-time positions working on projects that address public health, education, the environment, and more. In addition, the college encourages students to take advantage of international academic programs with opportunities on every continent.

MAJORS AND DEGREES OFFERED

Queens College has 69 undergraduate majors, in programs leading to BA, BBA, BS, BFA, and BMus degrees, as well as BA/MA tracks that allow you to earn combined undergraduate and graduate degrees in just 5 years.

ACADEMIC PROGRAMS

QC's departments and programs are organized into four divisions: Arts and Humanities, Education, Math and Natural Sciences, and Social Sciences. In addition to participating in CUNY's Macaulay Honors College—which provides full tuition for in-state residents—the college offers its own honors programs, including one for transfer students. QC in 4, a program exclusive to Queens College, creates a path for entering freshmen to complete a bachelor's degree in four years, guaranteed.

FACILITIES AND EQUIPMENT

Faculty and students conduct research in fully equipped labs with cutting-edge tools. Business and science majors can intern for startup companies at the college's Tech Incubator or launch their own businesses. The renowned Aaron Copland School of Music has professional performance spaces and recording studios, as well as practice rooms equipped with Steinway pianos. Students can get in shape in our fitness center; swim laps in our Olympic-size pool; train on our track, soccer, softball or baseball fields; and play basketball and tennis year-round—we have courts indoors and out. Wi-Fi access around campus makes it easy to field email and catch up on work from a seat in a campus café or outside on the quad.

TUITION, ROOM, BOARD AND FEES

For New York State residents, yearly undergraduate tuition is $6,530; out-of-state and international students pay $580 per credit. Fees add from $142.10 to $303.85 a semester, depending on both the semester and the number of credits carried by the student. Some courses have material and transportation fees, from $9 to as much as $150.

A semester of on-campus housing at The Summit Apartments costs $6,190 for a shared bedroom, or $7,763 for a private bedroom.

FINANCIAL AID

More than 60 percent of the college's students receive some form of need-based financial aid. Possibilities include federal and state grants, federal loans, federal work-study programs, and scholarships, including the New York State Excelsior Scholarship program.

STUDENT BODY

Current undergraduate enrollment exceeds 16,000 students, two-thirds of whom attend full-time. Almost a third of our students are Hispanic, and nearly as many are Asian-Pacific Islanders. Ethnic breakdowns don't quite capture the diversity of Queens College. More than half of our students were born overseas; they come from nearly 170 countries and speak more than 100 languages and dialects.

STUDENT ORGANIZATIONS AND ACTIVITIES

You name it, Queens College has it—on a campus with more than 100 clubs and intramural sports, there is an outlet for every student. Greek life is well represented, as are cultural, professional, and service organizations. The only CUNY school in NCAA Division II, QC fields men's and women's teams.

ADMISSION PROCESSES AND REQUIREMENTS

All students apply to Queens College through CUNY (www.cuny.edu/prepare). In addition to completing the CUNY form, prospective freshmen must submit a high school transcript, GED, or proof of high school equivalency, as well as SAT, ACT, AP, IB, or New York Regents test scores. Selective programs, such as Macaulay Honors College and Freshman Honors, have supplemental applications.

Prospective transfers need to complete an application form and submit transcripts from high school and all previous colleges. Admission is automatic for anyone holding an AA or AS from a CUNY/SUNY school, or an AAS from CUNY. Other applicants have to meet entry requirements. Students with fewer than 30 credits need a 2.75 GPA for admission based on the freshman criteria. Students with 30 to 60 credits must have a 2.25 GPA calculated from all college transcripts.

The best preparation for Queens College is a high school program incorporating 4 years of English, 4 years of social studies, 3 years of math, 3 years of a foreign language, and at least 2 years of lab science. Applicants who are non-residents of the United States and non-native English speakers should submit a TOEFL (Test of English as a Foreign Language) score.

QUINNIPIAC UNIVERSITY

AT A GLANCE

A survey of recent graduates indicated that close to 95 percent were either employed or enrolled in graduate school within six months of graduation.

Quinnipiac, founded in 1929, is a private, co-educational, non-sectarian university located in a uniquely attractive New England setting in Hamden, Connecticut and nearby North Haven. Quinnipiac's mission is to provide a supportive and stimulating environment for the intellectual and personal growth of its approximately 7300 undergraduate and 3000 graduate, law and medical students.

The university offers broadly-based undergraduate programs together with graduate programs in selected professional fields. At the undergraduate level, through integrated liberal arts and professional curricula, programs in the Schools of Business, Engineering, Communications, Education, Health Sciences, Nursing, and the College of Arts and Sciences prepare students for career entry or advanced studies. Graduate programs are designed to provide professional qualifications for success in business, education, health sciences, nursing, communications, social work, medicine and law.

An education at Quinnipiac embodies the university's commitment to three important values: excellence in education, a student-centered campus, and a spirit of community. The entire university shares a service orientation toward students and their needs. Its collegial atmosphere fosters a strong sense of community, identity, and purpose among faculty, staff and students.

LOCATION AND ENVIRONMENT

Hamden, Connecticut: 8 miles north of New Haven, midway between Boston and New York City. Quinnipiac is a suburban campus with 600 acres on three sites. The Mount Carmel Campus is adjacent to Sleeping Giant State Park, with 1,700 acres of trails for hiking and walking. A picturesque setting provides an enjoyable academic and residential campus experience for students. Ninety-five percent of freshmen choose to live on campus. A campus shuttle system provides easy access to theaters, shopping, museums, sports, recreation and a variety of area dining and entertainment options. The nearby York Hill Campus is home to the TD Bank Sports Center with 3500-seat twin arenas for basketball and ice hockey, a lodge-like student/recreation center, plus suite-style residence halls with single and double rooms, kitchens and common living areas. The North Haven Campus, about five miles away, provides upper-level and graduate students in Health Sciences, Nursing, Education, Social Work, Medicine and Law with a state-of-the-art setting on 100 acres.

Driving time to Quinnipiac from Boston or New York City is about two hours. Metro-North and Amtrak provide train service to New Haven's Union Station, which is 15 minutes from campus. Airline service is available through Bradley International Airport, about 30 minutes from campus, and through John F. Kennedy, LaGuardia and Newark airports serving the New York City area. Ground transportation is available from all airports to New Haven.

CAMPUS FACILITIES & EQUIPMENT

Bernhard Library is the centerpiece of academic life and is open 24/7 during the fall and spring semesters. Automated library systems, wireless technology, and individual study carrels and team study rooms provide a great setting for studying and relaxing.

The Learning Commons offers academic support with free tutoring as well as sessions to improve study techniques, writing skills and research methods. Quinnipiac's Writing Across the Curriculum initiative is designed to help students develop strong critical thinking and communication skills through writing. Essential Learning Outcomes have been identified that broaden students' knowledge and engage them in the educational process.

The University Honors Program fosters the needs and interests of the most academically talented and committed students. Service Learning courses integrate meaningful community service with instruction and reflection to enrich the learning experience, teach civic responsibility and strengthen communities.

OFF-CAMPUS OPPORTUNITIES

Quinnipiac is a suburban campus with easy access to nearby shopping, restaurants and activities offered in Hamden, New Haven and North Haven. Students, faculty and staff are involved in community service through the "Big Event" held each April. Local community service opportunities also include Habitat for Humanity and tutoring in the elementary schools.

ACADEMIC PROGRAMS

School of Business majors: accounting, biomedical marketing, computer information systems, entrepreneurship and small business management, finance, international business, management and marketing. The Lender School of Business Center offers case method classrooms, a financial technology center, center for innovation and entrepreneurship, a software application development classroom and team study rooms for project work. An innovative 3+1 BS/MBA invites academically strong students to complete two degrees in four years. A five-year BA/MBA "fast track" option offers the MBA to students from all majors in the University. (AACSB accredited)

School of Engineering, with ABET accredited programs in civil, industrial, mechanical and software engineering, along with computer science, offers state-of-the-art labs including: a thermodynamics and heat workshop, environmental and hydraulics workshop, geotechnical lab, and an advanced automation and production lab.

School of Health Sciences and School of Nursing majors: athletic training, biomedical sciences, diagnostic medical sonography, health science studies, microbiology and immunology, nursing, occupational therapy (5½-year BS/MOT master's program), physician assistant (6-year BS/MHS master's program), physical therapy (6- or 7-year BS/DPT doctorate) and radiologic sciences (accelerated 3-year BS). Health Science Studies offers a 3+2 combined degree option with the MSW graduate degree. The North Haven facility offers state-of-the-art labs including a diagnostic imaging suite, orthopedics lab, adaptive model apartment, clinical skills labs, intensive care unit, clinical simulation labs, and biomechanics lab.

College of Arts and Sciences majors: behavioral neuroscience, biochemistry, biology, chemistry, criminal justice, economics, English, game design and development, gerontology, history, independent majors, interdisciplinary studies, law in society, mathematics, philosophy, political science, psychology, sociology, Spanish language and literature, and theater. Also offered is a combined 3+2 BA/MSW to academically strong students.

School of Communications majors: advertising and integrated communications, communications /media studies, film, television and media arts, graphic and interactive design, journalism, and public relations. The Ed McMahon Center for Mass Communications provides a professional-grade facility with a digital high-definition television production studio, media innovation classroom, audio production studio, 4k editing room, and more. An innovative 3+1 BA/MS degree offers academically talented students the opportunity to complete two degrees in four years. Students across all majors can experience a semester in Los Angeles, combining classes with an internship in the fall, spring or summer in the QU in LA program which provides cohort housing and an on-site director.

For those interested in teaching (K–6 or 7–12), completion of an undergraduate major in a liberal arts or natural sciences discipline, combined with courses in the School of Education plus, a fifth year as a full-time graduate education student, culminates in the Master of Arts in Teaching degree.

A pre-med program is designed to provide the undergraduate student interested in a career as a health professional the appropriate background necessary to meet the entrance requirements of a variety of medical schools. Students interested in Law are guided by a pre-law advisor. Academically talented students may consider the 3+3 BA or BS/JD combined degree with the Quinnipiac School of Law.

All programs at Quinnipiac offer an ideal combination of classroom learning with internships or clinical experiences. Students in business, engineering, communications, and liberal arts and sciences intern at nearby corporations, health care agencies, or media outlets. Students in health sciences and nursing are placed in a wide variety of clinical settings as part of their learning experience.

Students can take advantage of study abroad opportunities during the academic year or summer months (3.0 cumulative GPA required.) Program sites include: Ireland, Australia, Austria, Czech Republic, England, France, Spain, Italy, Netherlands and South Africa and through affiliates such as AIFS, API, and Semester at Sea.

Career Development services within each academic division provide students with assistance with résumé writing, interview skills and job placement. A survey of recent graduates indicated that close to 95 percent were either employed or in graduate school within six months of graduation. Each year about half of students in internships are offered permanent jobs as a result of their work.

Quinnipiac is where professors who want to know students by name come to teach, and where students who want a personal, challenging education come to learn. Quinnipiac's approximately 400 full-time faculty members are experts in their respective fields and include published authors, health care practitioners and researchers. Generous with their time and eager to share their knowledge with students, Quinnipiac faculty also lend their expertise to the public forum through op-ed pieces, newspaper articles and television discussions.

MAJORS AND DEGREES OFFERED

Undergraduate students can choose from almost 60 majors through the College of Arts and Sciences and the Schools of Business, Engineering, Education, Communications, Health Sciences and Nursing. About 30 percent of all entering freshmen remain at Quinnipiac through their graduate degree program. Several innovative combined undergraduate/graduate degree programs benefit students with fixed tuition and graduation at least a year ahead of their peers in Business, Communications, Law, Social Work and Biology/Molecular Cell Biology.

Graduate students specialize in law, medicine (Frank H. Netter MD, School of Medicine), business, organizational leadership, health management, computer information systems, journalism, interactive media and communications, sports journalism, public relations, education, social work, and health science programs for physician assistant, pathologists' assistant, medical laboratory sciences, molecular and cell biology, cardiovascular perfusion, radiologist assistant and nursing. Several programs are offered online.

TUITION, ROOM, BOARD, FEES

Costs for 2018–19: Tuition & Fees $47,260; Technology Fee $700, Room and Board $14,540.

FINANCIAL AID

The Office of Financial Aid works with all applicants to ensure they receive the maximum state and federal aid for which they are eligible. Families are encouraged to file the FAFSA for federal student aid (code: 001402) after Oct. 1. The university also offers merit-based scholarships to incoming freshmen (fall semester). No additional application is necessary for scholarship consideration; recipients are notified by the admissions office. If you have any questions, please contact the Office of Financial Aid at (203) 582-8750 or (800) 462-1944, or e-mail: finaid@qu.edu.

STUDENT ORGANIZATIONS AND ACTIVITIES

Quinnipiac University offers more than 140 student clubs and organizations including student government, newspaper, yearbook, radio station, service organizations, community activities, religious fellowships, diversity awareness (Black Student Union, Latino Cultural Society, Asian and Pacific Islander Association), dance and drama productions, and Greek life, along with numerous recreation activities, providing a balanced college experience. An active intramural program has team competition in more than 30 sports and activities.

Quinnipiac's 10,000 undergraduate, graduate, law and medical students hail from 46 states and 61 countries. Housing options include traditional residence halls, suites, and suites with kitchens. Freshmen and sophomores generally live on the Mt. Carmel campus; juniors and seniors live on the York Hill campus and in university-owned houses.

Quinnipiac Bobcats: www.quinnipiacbobcats.com

The NCAA Division I athletic program in 21 sports includes Men: basketball, baseball, cross-country, lacrosse, ice hockey, tennis, and soccer. Women: acrobatics & tumbling, basketball, softball, cross-country and track (indoor and outdoor), field hockey, golf, ice hockey, lacrosse, rugby, soccer, tennis and volleyball. Quinnipiac competes in the MAAC in most sports, the ECAC (ice hockey, acrobatics and tumbling), Rugby Northeast (rugby) and the Big East (field hockey.)

Athletic and recreation facilities include a gymnasium, two fully-equipped fitness centers, a Spinning® studio, dance/yoga studios, tennis courts, a 24,000-square-foot recreation center with an indoor track, and a sports center with twin 3500-seat arenas for ice hockey and basketball.

ADMISSIONS PROCESS

High school students should begin applying for admission early in the fall of their senior year. Visit www.qu.edu/apply for application information. Quinnipiac is a member of the Common Application. A completed application consists of the application form which includes an essay, followed by official high school transcript, first-quarter senior grades, and one letter of recommendation. Students applying to the Schools of Health Sciences or Nursing must submit official SAT (QU code—3712) and/or ACT (QU code—0582) test scores. International and homeschooled students, as well as athletes playing a Division I sport (per NCAA rules) also must submit official test scores. For all other majors, files will be reviewed for an admission decision as well as consideration for scholarships based on overall academic work. If test scores are received, the highest critical reading and math scores or the highest ACT composite score will be chosen.

Quinnipiac reviews applications on a 'rolling admissions' basis and also offers an Early Decision option for freshman applicants. Early Decision candidates must file their application by November 1. The admissions office begins reviewing applications as soon as they are complete and begins notifying candidates of admission decisions in November. Students applying for the 6-year BS/MHS Physician Assistant program should submit the application by Oct 15. Those applying for the BS/DPT in physical therapy, BS/MOT occupational therapy and BSN nursing programs should apply by November 15. For all other applicants, February 1 is the recommended final deadline.

All programs subscribe to the nationally recognized candidate reply date of May 1. Waitlisted students who indicate an interest in being considered for admission if spaces become available are notified as soon after May 1 as possible. In general, Quinnipiac admits between 65–69 percent of its applicants.

Transfer students who have or will receive an associate degree prior to entrance are not required to provide high school transcripts and SAT results. Official transcripts of all courses taken at other colleges must be provided to the admissions office. The entry-level physician assistant and physical therapy programs are not available to transfer students.

To schedule an interview, campus tour, group information session or register for a spring or fall open house, go to www.qu.edu/visit . For questions, email admissions@qu.edu or call 800-462-1944 or 203-582-8600. www.qu.edu.

RAMAPO COLLEGE OF NEW JERSEY

AT A GLANCE

Established in 1969, Ramapo College is New Jersey's Public Liberal Arts College, dedicated to providing students a strong foundation for a lifetime of achievement and preparing them to be successful leaders for a changing world.

Ramapo College offers bachelor's degrees in the arts, business, humanities, social sciences and the sciences, as well as in professional studies, which include nursing, social work, and teacher certification at the elementary and secondary levels. Ramapo College also offers seven graduate programs, as well as, articulated programs with other reputable institutions.

Ramapo College of New Jersey is sometimes mistaken for a private college. This is, in part, due to its unique interdisciplinary academic structure, its size of approximately 6,000 students and its pastoral setting in the foothills of the Ramapo Mountains on the New Jersey/New York border. Ramapo College students receive an elite education at the cost of a public college.

The College is committed to academic excellence through interdisciplinary and experiential learning, and international and intercultural understanding. The international mission is accomplished through a wide range of study abroad and student exchange links with institutions all over the world. Additional experiential programs include internships, co-op and service learning.

The College's interdisciplinary commitment helps students push intellectual boundaries; our commitment to experiential, hands-on learning allows them to push personal and professional boundaries as well. The commitment of our faculty to attentive teaching and mentoring empowers students to learn actively and attain the skills they will need to succeed professionally and become lifelong learners.

Ramapo College is committed to maintaining strength and opportunity through diversity of age, race, gender, sexual orientation, ethnicity, and economic background among faculty, staff, and students. Barrier-free, the College maintains a continuing commitment to persons with disabilities.

LOCATION AND ENVIRONMENT

Ramapo College is spread across 300 acres, resting within the foothills of the Ramapo mountains in Mahwah, New Jersey. Enhancing these tranquil surroundings is the knowledge that the campus is approximately 32 miles from the nation's cultural Mecca, New York City.

Campus is located just five minutes from major highways such as I-287, the New York State Thruway, and Route 17, making it very easy to bring you right to Ramapo's doorstep.

CAMPUS FACILITIES & EQUIPMENT

A campus-wide building program during recent years has resulted in the renovation of the G-wing building and completion of the Adler Center for Nursing Excellence, a central feature of the main entrance to the campus. The renovations include expanded classrooms, as well as, a research and simulation laboratory space. This 36,000 square-foot facility is connected by an overhead walkway to the College's science/social science building.

Within the Anisfield School of Business academic facility is a real-time Global Financial Markets Trading Laboratory, which features 32 workstations, ticker displays inside and outside the lab, and three LCD television screens.

The Bill Bradley Sports and Recreation Center features a 2,200-seat arena, fitness center, 24 ft. high Edelman climbing wall, as well as track and dance/aerobics studios.

The Angelica and Russ Berrie Center for Performing and Visual Arts houses performance theaters, art galleries and specialized spaces devoted to fine arts, computer art, photography, theater, dance and music.

The campus also boasts the Sharp Sustainability Education Center and the Salameno Spiritual Center.

Newer projects scheduled include the renovation of the George T. Potter Library, construction of a Learning Commons, and the construction of the Padovano Commons. A campus-wide photovoltaic installation project is underway.

Housing at Ramapo College offers students convenient, modern amenities within the eight residence halls on campus, including air conditioning, cable television, complimentary laundry, and semi-private bathrooms within each suite.

The campus features new and upgraded facilities that enhance all areas of campus life, including a library with electronic research facilities; a student life building with FM radio station, student offices, cafeteria, and entertainment and meeting rooms; housing for more than 3,000 students; and modern academic buildings with 24-hour computer labs.

OFF-CAMPUS OPPORTUNITIES

Ramapo College encourages students to take advantage of experiences outside of the classroom, such as internships, co-op, and study abroad opportunities.

Ramapo College has developed a diverse selection of more than 400 individual study-abroad program options in more than 60 countries. Opportunities exist for ALL majors and range from one week to a full year.

Being only 32 miles away from New York City makes it easy for Ramapo College students to take advantage of internship opportunities with over 200 NYC companies and even more in New Jersey. Students in the past have completed a co-op or internship at companies like Google, Madison Square Garden, Yahoo!, BMW of North America, Deloitte, and Sony.

Students are able to purchase discounted bus tickets from Roadrunner Central and take a bus service that leaves from campus and takes them to The Port Authority of NY & NJ station in Manhattan.

ACADEMIC PROGRAMS

Undergraduate students can choose from 36 different academic programs. Ramapo College boasts an average student/faculty ratio of 18:1 and average class size of 23, affording students the opportunity to develop close ties to the College's exceptional faculty.

95 percent of our faculty members hold terminal degrees in their field, allowing them to be excellent mentors to students inside and outside of the classroom.

Undergraduate students have the opportunity to engage in faculty-guided research, present papers at national conferences, and take advantage of over 200 different internship and co-op opportunities in nearby New York City companies.

To strengthen the student's college background before concentrating on major courses for a degree, students are required to complete an all-college general education program consisting of courses in English, Mathematics, the Humanities, Social Sciences, and Natural Sciences.

All students are assigned an academic advisor during their first semester, allowing the choice of major to be made by the end of the sophomore year (with the exception of Nursing and Biology). There is ample time to explore several fields of interest before selecting a major.

MAJORS AND DEGREES OFFERED

Ramapo College offers the following undergraduate degree programs, which are hosted within our five academic schools on campus:

ANISFIELD SCHOOL OF BUSINESS

Accounting (BS) | Business Administration/Finance (BS) | Business Administration/Management (BS) | Business Administration/Marketing (BS) | Economics (BS) | Information Technology Management (BS) | International Business (BS) |

SCHOOL OF CONTEMPORARY ARTS

Communication Arts/Digital Filmmaking (BA) | Communication Arts/Global Communication and Media (BA) | Communication Arts/Journalism (BA) | Communication Arts/Visual Communication Design (BA) | Communication Arts/Writing (BA) | Contemporary Arts (BA) | Music/Industry (BA) | Music/Production (BA) | Music/Performance (BA) | Music Studies (BA) | Theater/Acting (BA) | Theater/Design & Technical Theater (BA) | Theater/Directing & Stage Management (BA) | Theater Studies (BA) | Visual Arts/Art History (BA) | Visual Arts/Electronic Art & Animation (BA) | Visual Arts/Drawing & Painting (BA) | Visual Arts/Photography (BA) | Visual Arts/Sculpture | Visual Arts/Sculpture (BA) |

SALAMENO SCHOOL OF HUMANITIES AND GLOBAL STUDIES

Africana Studies (BA) | American Studies (BA) | History (BA) | International Studies (BA) | Liberal Studies (BA) | Literature (BA) | Literature/Creative Writing (BA) | Political Science (BA) | Spanish Language Studies (BA) |

SCHOOL OF SOCIAL SCIENCE AND HUMAN SERVICES

Elementary Education | Environmental Studies (BA) | Law and Society (BA) | Psychology (BA) | Social Science/Community Mental Health (BA) | Social Science/Cultural Studies (BA) | Social Science/Ethnic Relations (BA) | Social Science/Gender Studies (BA) | Social Science/Labor Studies (BA) | Social Work (BSW) | Sociology/Criminology (BA) | Sociology/Public Sociology (BA) |

SCHOOL OF THEORETICAL AND APPLIED SCIENCES

Biochemistry (BS) | Bioinformatics (BS) | Biology (BS) | Chemistry (BS) | Clinical Lab Science (BS) | Computer Science (BS) | Engineering Physics (BS) | Environmental Science (BS) | Integrated Science Studies (BS) | Mathematics (BS) | Medical Imaging Science (BS) | Nursing (BSN) |

TUITION, ROOM, BOARD, FEES

The approximate tuition and fees for undergraduates in the 2017–2018 academic year are as follows:

In-state tuition and fees: $14,080.00

Out-of-state tuition and fees: $23,214.40

Room and board (all students): $11,680.00

FINANCIAL AID

Because Ramapo College is a state institution, the cost of attending is affordable compared to many other institutions. About 82 percent of Ramapo's students receive some form of financial assistance. This aid includes grants—funds which the students are awarded but don't have to pay back—and loans, which must be repaid. Students also can receive a work-study job to earn money to help pay for school.

To apply for aid at Ramapo College, students should complete the Free Application for Federal Student Aid (FAFSA) by March 1. No other application forms are required. By complying with this priority deadline, students will be notified by April 1 about their expected aid package. The FAFSA is available after October 1 at www.fafsa.ed.gov. Applicants should use Ramapo's school code (009344) when filing.

Transfer students must initiate a school code change on the Student Aid Report (SAR) to ensure that their account will be appropriately credited. Students should begin this process at the time of application. Contact Ramapo's Financial Aid Office at (201)-684-7549 and finaid@ramapo.edu.

STUDENT ORGANIZATIONS AND ACTIVITIES

At Ramapo College, student clubs and organizations are recognized as important parts of the total learning experience. Students are urged to take advantage of the many opportunities available, since not all their time is spent in class.

There are more than 100 groups including cultural, academic, religious, recreational, entertainment, political, social and special interest groups. Clubs and organizations at Ramapo College are run by students under the general supervision of the Center for Student Involvement. Each group operates under its own constitution, according to the interests and enthusiasm of its membership. All welcome new members, new ideas and new directions. Many groups can provide valuable experience and connections to the job market.

Ramapo College offers 18 NCAA Division III sport teams, 30 honor societies, and 21 fraternities and sororities.

ADMISSIONS PROCESS

Every year, Ramapo College welcomes more than 900 freshmen primarily from New Jersey, the Mid-Atlantic and Northeast regions of the United States and from many foreign countries. In addition, Ramapo College receives over 6,000 applications from all 21 counties in New Jersey, 21 different states and 31 foreign countries.

A complete application to Ramapo College includes:

- Application (Apply at www.ramapo.edu/apply or at www.commonapp.org)
- $65 application fee
- Official high school transcripts
- One letter of recommendation (two preferred)
- Essay
- Official SAT or ACT scores

The Test of English as a Foreign Language (TOEFL) is required of all international students and is recommended for all students who have resided in the United States fewer than four years.

Ramapo College practices a holistic review process. Each application is evaluated individually with emphasis placed on academic achievement in high school and standardized test scores, however, successful applicants also present a record of extracurricular activities that reflect maturity, responsibility and commitment.

Ramapo College seeks the very best students for its Educational Opportunity Fund (EOF) Program. If you qualify, you will join a community of achievers who are supported by a partnership between the college and EOF that is outstanding not only in financial assistance to cover your college cost, but also in personal and academic counseling, career planning, and leadership training. Your admission to the Ramapo College EOF program depends upon meeting financial eligibility requirements and academic standards.

Fall Application Deadlines:

Ramapo College offers binding Early Decision for students who know Ramapo College is their number one choice. Early Decision applicants must apply by November 1 and will receive their decision by December 5.

Students who are applying to the Nursing or Biology program must apply by December 15. The priority deadline for merit scholarship consideration for all majors is also December 15. The supporting documents and credential deadline (date by which Ramapo College must receive your documents, including transcript, test scores, recommendation letters, and EOF questionnaire, if applicable) is January 15.

The final deadline for all other majors outside of the Nursing and Biology program is March 1. All decisions for completed applications will be sent by April 1.

Scholarships:

Ramapo College scholarships are merit-based opportunities, meaning they are offered to students based on their academic and personal achievements, not financial need. Students who apply by December 15 and submit all required credentials by January 15 and are in the top 10 percent of their high school class with SAT scores of at least a 1270 total or at least a 27 ACT score will be considered for a merit-based scholarship.

Unfortunately, due to an increase in applications and limited funding, the college may be unable to offer every student that fits the above criteria a merit-based scholarship.

Awards are continued for four years provided that students maintain the required number of credits and grade point average. No separate application is necessary.

If you have any questions, please email us admissions@ramapo.edu.

REED COLLEGE

AT A GLANCE

Intellectual. Free-thinking. Classical. Iconoclastic. Paradoxical. This constellation of features only begins to describe Reed: one of the most distinctive colleges in the nation.

Reed attracts serious scholars. Always engaged and often engrossed in a demanding, exhilarating educational adventure, "Reedies" thrive on a mix of classical study, critical analysis, and guided inquiry that rewards creativity, independence, and reflection. Classes are small, faculty members are highly accessible, and students adhere to an honor principle both inside and outside the classroom.

Reed recruits nationally, with strong representation from California, the Pacific Northwest, and the East Coast. The student body is also composed of 11 percent international students. Reed ranks second among U.S. liberal arts colleges in the percentage of graduates going on to earn doctoral degrees and fourth among all institutions of higher education. The breadth, depth, and rigor of the curriculum provide great preparation for nearly any career. Many Reed alumni found or lead companies and organizations, earn medical or law degrees, write books or create works of art, and work to make life on the planet better for all.

LOCATION AND ENVIRONMENT

Located in a quiet residential neighborhood is a 116-acre campus of verdant lawns, winding paths, statuesque trees, a wooded natural wetland preserve, and a spring-fed lake frequented by migratory birds and other wildlife. Reed is a short bicycle, bus, and light rail ride from the energy and excitement of downtown Portland, which is widely cited as the nation's most livable urban center. Portland boasts a wealth of diverse cultural, entertainment, shopping, and dining opportunities in an environment characterized by a combination of youthful exuberance and Pacific Northwest nonchalance. The Oregon Coast is 90 minutes to the west and Mt. Hood 90 minutes to the east where Reed has its own ski cabin.

On the campus itself, century-old brick Tudor gothic buildings are interspersed with newer traditionally designed and remodeled facilities. The library, classrooms, and laboratories resonate with the history of decades of inquiry and discovery, supported with modern technology.

CAMPUS FACILITIES & EQUIPMENT

The Reed College campus was established on a tract of land known in 1910 as Crystal Springs Farm. In a park-like setting near the heart of the city, the rolling lawns and open spaces of Reed's 116-acre campus include some of the largest and finest specimen trees in the Portland area.

The social center of the college is the Gray Campus Center. It includes a commons building, student union, kitchen, dining room, private meeting rooms, student activities offices, bookstore, and mail services.

At the physical center of campus is the canyon, a beautiful wooded upland surrounding a spring-fed lake and emergent marsh. A walking trail around the lake provides numerous opportunities to observe migratory birds and other woodland wildlife. The college recently built a fish passageway that creates a link from the upper Reed Lake area to the Crystal Springs stream below.

In fall 2013, Reed opened a new Performing Arts Building, representing a major step forward in the College's commitment to the important role the arts have played throughout Reed's first 100 years. For the first time in Reed's history, the departments of music, dance, and theatre are housed in one building that includes rehearsal and performance space, offices, scene and costume studios, collaborative spaces, and a multimedia lab.

Housing at Reed includes traditional residence halls, as well as theme dorms, co-ops, and language houses.

OFF-CAMPUS OPPORTUNITIES

Reed undergraduates may participate in a number of domestic exchange and study abroad opportunities. Domestic programs include: Howard University in Washington, D.C.; Sarah Lawrence College in New York; and Sea Education Association in Massachusetts. In addition, Reed provides study-abroad opportunities for students in Australia, Argentina, China, Costa Rica, Cuba, Ecuador, Egypt, France, Germany, Greece, Hungary, Ireland, Israel, Italy, Morocco, Kenya, Lebanon, Palestine, Russia, South Africa, Spain, Turks and Caicos, and the United Kingdom. Students may also arrange independent study plans in consultation with appropriate faculty members.

ACADEMIC PROGRAMS

The curriculum at Reed is both demanding and wide-ranging. Through required studies, Reed students receive a solid grounding in the liberal arts and sciences.

All freshmen must complete Humanities 110, which introduces students to academic life at Reed and gives rigorous instruction in research and writing. Distribution requirements set a substantial portion of a student's curriculum for the first two years at Reed. Students must complete two courses in each of the four major divisions of the college. Beyond Humanities 110, no specific courses are required; students are free to pursue their interests within the boundaries of the requirements.

Reed juniors take a comprehensive qualifying exam in their major to allow faculty members the chance to evaluate and assist in the student's readiness for his or her senior thesis project. The required senior thesis is the capstone experience of a Reed education. Every senior produces an original independent research project over the course of the final year.

Reed strongly believes that learning should be undertaken for its own sake, not for the sake of letter grades. Accordingly, students do not receive grade reports unless they wish to. A student's transcript does include letter grades for all courses taken, but students can better gauge their progress through professors' written evaluations of their work and one-on-one meetings with faculty. Most prefer this system, which greatly reduces competition among students and allows them to focus on the content of their academic work.

MAJORS AND DEGREES OFFERED

Reed confers the Bachelor of Arts degree in 40 traditional academic departments and interdisciplinary combinations across a wide selection of fields. Approval of an interdisciplinary program (linking two or more disciplines) is reviewed by the student's adviser and the departments concerned.

Reed offers a number of 3-2 (dual degree) programs; these allow undergraduates to earn a three-year bachelor's degree from Reed, then earn a professional degree in engineering, computer science, or forestry from a cooperating institution (Caltech, Columbia, Duke, RPI) in two additional years.

TUITION, ROOM, BOARD, FEES

Tuition for the 2017–2018 academic year is $53,900. A $300 student body fee is added. Room and board is an additional $13,670, bringing the yearly total cost to $67,870.

FINANCIAL AID

Reed College meets 100 percent of the demonstrated need for its incoming students and continuing students who maintain good academic standing and who meet all other requirements of the aid process (such as application deadlines). The college maintains a need-based assistance program that allows students of all economic backgrounds to attend the college. For the incoming class of 2021, the average financial aid package including grants, loans, and work opportunities was approximately $43,306. Reed students' average graduating loan debt for all four years is $19,528, well below the national average. The college is the primary source of grant money for its students. Reed also administers federal grants and a number of other awards. Campus employment and work-study programs also figure into many aid packages. Roughly 50 percent of Reed undergraduates receive financial aid.

STUDENT ORGANIZATIONS AND ACTIVITIES

Reed maintains inclusivity in all organizations and activities, so the college has no fraternities or sororities and no NCAA or NAIA athletic teams (more about sports below). All campus organizations are student-created and student-run. Student organizations must lobby the Student Senate for funding annually, after which the Senate oversees a vote in which the entire student body decides what organizations should be funded. Thus, the number and nature of campus organizations at Reed changes every year to meet current student interests. Instead of NCAA or NAIA competition, students participate in sports on an informal basis. Intramural sports and club sports proliferate in basketball, fencing, rugby, sailing, soccer, squash and ultimate Frisbee. A three-semester physical education requirement underscores the importance of physical fitness and the balance of healthy mind and body.

ADMISSIONS PROCESS

Reed seeks students who demonstrate a commitment to learning and to the ideals embodied by a rigorous and stimulating liberal arts education. Freshman and transfer applications are welcome. The ideal incoming class is diverse in its range of talents, interests, ethnic and socioeconomic backgrounds, and perspectives, and comprised of students who share a common passion for academic inquiry. Successful applicants have pursued a rigorous secondary school curriculum that includes honors and advanced courses and typically includes 4 years of English, at least 3 years of a foreign or classical language, 3 to 4 years of mathematics, 3 to 4 years of science, and 3 to 4 years of history or social studies. Because secondary school curricula vary widely in quality and content, Reed sets no fixed requirements in this area. With rare exceptions, incoming students have obtained a secondary school diploma prior to enrollment. The admissions committee sets no "cutoff points" for high school grades, college grades (for transfer students), or standardized test scores. Reed seeks candidates who demonstrate excellence of character, motivation, intellectual curiosity, individual responsibility, and social consciousness. The admission committee recognizes the importance of creating a diverse community in which individual differences contribute to the vitality of the campus. Reed recommends a personal interview but it is not required. Early Decision applications should arrive at Reed by November 15 (Option 1) or December 20 (Option 2). Early Decision at Reed is binding: students who are admitted under Early Decision are expected to matriculate. Early Action applications should arrive at Reed by November 15. The deadline for regular freshman admission applications is January 15. Transfer candidates should apply no later than March 1.

REGIS COLLEGE

AT A GLANCE

Regis is boldly empowering the next generation of leaders to impact the world around them and change lives.

A coed, Catholic university founded by the Sisters of Saint Joseph of Boston, Regis offers more than 40 academic programs across four schools which include arts and sciences, business and communication, health sciences, and nursing.

What sets Regis apart is our community—an open-minded environment that welcomes all without distinction. Professors both challenge and support their students; tradition is honored as much as scientific innovation. As you learn more about Regis, we're confident you'll see why #YouBelongHere.

LOCATION AND ENVIRONMENT

Located on a beautiful 132-acre classic New England campus in Weston, Massachusetts, Regis students enjoy being a part of our close-knit community. When they're ready to pursue an internship or explore a dynamic city, they are only 12 miles away from downtown Boston, America's premiere college city and the country's top spot for cutting edge innovation..

A complimentary shuttle transports students to surrounding areas and public transportation for easy access to work, internships, and social events and outings.

CAMPUS FACILITIES & EQUIPMENT

The Regis campus was recently updated with modern suite-style residential space, a beautiful new quad and renovated library. We have state-of-the-art medical imaging labs, nursing simulation centers and occupational therapy labs.

Regis guarantees four-year, on-campus housing for undergraduates, with approximately 90 percent of first-year students living on campus. Students are able to take classes at several other nearby universities as part of our cross-registration program.

Regis' 18 championship-winning athletic teams compete on the athletic facility's indoor and outdoor complex. Indoor facilities include three fitness rooms, a six-lane swimming pool, gymnasium, athletic training room, and team room. Outdoor facilities consist of a turf field surface for field hockey, lacrosse, and soccer; an eight-lane track around the field; six tennis courts; and a softball diamond with a dirt infield and grass outfield.

OFF-CAMPUS OPPORTUNITIES

Regis is located just 12 miles from Boston, America's greatest college city. Students have direct access to exciting events and attractions such as Fenway Park, home of the Boston Red Sox; the TD Garden, home of the Boston Bruins and Celtics; the Museum of Fine Arts; and Prudential and Copley shopping districts. The university's 2018 commencement ceremonies were held in the city's world-famous Seaport District. Regis is also located 4 miles from Waltham—minutes away from restaurants, shops, and businesses.

The Center for Internships and Career Placement provides a variety of career-development and job-search services for Regis students and alumni. Career Center staff assist students and graduates in planning careers, securing internships, developing resumes, implementing effective job-search strategies, identifying employers in various industries, and exploring graduate-school options. In addition, the office maintains listings of internship opportunities, as well as full-time, part-time, and summer jobs for both on and off-campus positions.

Internships are crucial and allow students to apply classroom learning to the career world and enable students to explore various opportunities while developing marketable skills. One hundred percent of Regis students participate in an internship, clinical or field work experience before graduating. Ninety-seven percent of the class of 2017 had secured professional employment and/or attended graduate school six months after graduation.

ACADEMIC PROGRAMS

Regis offers several special academic opportunities that allow students to explore subjects of interest and customize their learning experience. Students can extend their learning beyond the classroom through various methods, including seminars, off-campus study, global experiences, individualized study, pre-professional programs, special cooperative degree programs, and academic honors programs.

A Global Perspective

Whether students are interested in a semester-, academic year-, or week-long trips, the Office of Global Connections provides personalized support to ensure that students have an enriching global experience.

Regis is directly affiliated with Regent's University in London, England; University College Cork in Cork, Ireland; Assumption College Rome in Rome, Italy; and Kyoto Notre Dame University in Kyoto, Japan.

Students can also participate in faculty-led programs that supplement coursework. Trips range from one to three weeks and have taken place in Italy, England, Cuba, and Belize.

Our renowned faculty are actively engaged in their disciplines, conducting research, publishing books and articles, and serving as leaders in in their areas of expertise. One of the best aspects of a Regis education is the support and mentorship from faculty. With a 12:1 student-to-faculty ratio, faculty members get to know each student and are instrumental in advising them on everything from research and graduate school programs to internships and job opportunities.

A Classroom Without Walls

Regis is committed to providing an academic experience that is increasingly enriched by technological resources. Through the iPad initiative, all students are provided iPads to facilitate collaboration and enhance learning.

The campus network provides access to campus apps and the internet through 24/7 wireless and wired connectivity, spanning across campus in all classrooms, learning spaces, residential halls, and exterior spaces.

MAJORS AND DEGREES OFFERED

Regis offers innovative programs in the arts and sciences, business and communication, health sciences, and nursing. Majors include: Biology, Biomedical Engineering, Communication, Criminal Justice Studies, Cybersecurity, Diagnostic Medical Sonography, Education, English, Environmental Sustainability, Exercise Science, Global Business Management, Interdisciplinary Studies in the Humanities, Neuroscience, Nuclear Medicine, Nursing, Nutrition, Psychology, Public Health, Social Work, Sport Management, and Therapeutic Recreation.

Pre-professional and special programs include 3+3 Law Degree, Pre-Dental, Pre-Healthcare Advising with Occupational Therapy, Physical Therapy, and Physician Assistant Tracks, Pre-Law, Pre-Medical, and Pre-Veterinary.

Fast Track to Master's 4+1 Program

Regis offers a five-year combined bachelor's and master's track for certain areas of study, including Communication, Education, Health Administration, and Regulatory and Clinical Research Management.

° Some restrictions apply

Articulation Agreements

Regis has a variety of articulation agreements for undergraduate students wishing to transfer in for a bachelor's degree and for students wishing to earn a graduate degree after finishing a bachelor's degree at their home school.

Regis has agreements for direct entry into select graduate programs once a student completes the bachelor's degree at Regis. Graduate schools include Saint George's University in Grenada School of Medicine and School of Veterinary Medicine; Salve Regina University; and Western New England University School of Law.

Honors Program

The honors program at Regis provides qualified students with an intellectually stimulating and challenging academic experience that extends beyond the classroom, as leaders in both campus activities and community service. In addition to taking honors-level courses, students participate in a variety of service-learning projects, workshops, and discussions with renowned faculty and alumni. Admitted first-year applicants with a minimum high school GPA of 3.5 and combined SAT math and reading scores of at least 1100, or an ACT composite score of 24, are encouraged to join the Honors Program, as are Regis students who have maintained a GPA of 3.5 or higher during their first year.

The Learning Commons for Academic Student Support

Regis students are invited to participate in various opportunities offered through the Learning Commons. Students are encouraged to engage in tutoring services, academic coaching, learning strategy workshops, and various learning communities to promote their academic, personal, and professional growth. As a team, the staff helps students develop habits that will enable them to become resilient and curious life-long learners capable of reaching their academic and personal goals.

First-Year Seminar

First-Year Seminar (FYS) is an essential part of all incoming students' fall semester. FYS introduces new students to the Regis history and heritage, build their academic and social skills, engage in a variety of co-curricular experiences, and participate in a challenge-based learning project. FYS is taught by faculty members from across Regis who also serve as the student's academic advisor during his or her first year. During the spring semester, students stay with their FYS classmates and are enrolled in a linked course that meets one of the Regis Core Curriculum requirements.

TUITION, ROOM, BOARD, FEES

2017–2018 Academic Year:

Tuition: $39,820

Room and Board: $14,740

At Regis, we are committed to making an investment in every student's potential. More than 95 percent of our full-time, incoming first-year students receive some type of financial aid. The average award, not including federal and state funding, is $20,000.

We offer educational opportunities to students regardless of their ability to pay and only after acceptance are financial aid applications considered. Students are only required to complete the FAFSA.

FINANCIAL AID

Merit scholarships are awarded upon acceptance to the university and federal aid eligibility is evaluated using the FAFSA. Additional scholarship opportunities are available to students who graduate from select parochial schools, students with siblings at the university, and students who receive the Alumni Sponsor Award.

The Financial Aid team at Regis works with students on payment plan opportunities through Tuition Management Systems. Additionally, Regis students have the opportunity to use SALT program, a free and interactive money-management tool to help students with their financial planning.

STUDENT ORGANIZATIONS AND ACTIVITIES

Regis' undergraduate student body represents a diverse mixture of backgrounds and heritages. Thirty-three percent of students comes from diverse backgrounds, and 40 percent are first-generation college students.

Students have many different opportunities to become involved on campus, from joining one of the many active clubs and organizations to playing intramural sports such as volleyball, flag football, and dodgeball.

The Center for Student Engagement sponsors many events throughout the semester, including musical and comedy performances, cultural and sporting events, "Pizza with the President," and other social get-togethers. Additionally, the center coordinates a number of Regis's traditional events, including Welcome Week, Regis Fest Family Weekend, Halloweek, Senior Week, Spring Weekend, and the annual Christmas Tree Lighting.

Regis students are encouraged to be engaged citizens of the world. The Center for Ministry and Service coordinates service-learning and community engagement trips. Whether it's rebuilding homes in New Orleans, teaching health education to children in Haiti, or participating in one of the local service projects in honor of Regis' annual Founders' Day of Service, our student strive to make the world a better place.

Health and Wellness

Regis has a comprehensive Health Center on campus which provides students with medical care, including counseling services. Health Services also offers health education programs and events throughout the year.

Athletics

Regis is a Division III member of the National Collegiate Athletic Association (NCAA) and competes in the Great Northeast Athletics Conference (GNAC). Regis Athletics has 18 collegiate sports (10 women's: basketball, cross country, field hockey, lacrosse, soccer, softball, swimming & diving, tennis, track & field, volleyball. 8 men's: basketball, cross country, lacrosse, soccer, swimming & diving, tennis, track & field; and volleyball). Regis has won 32 championships since 2007.

ADMISSIONS PROCESS

Students seeking acceptance to Regis must submit the online Common Application. In addition to the application, first-year applicants are required to submit:

- Official secondary school transcript
- One signed letter of recommendation on official letterhead from a secondary school counselor/college counselor or teacher
- Application fee of $50
- Regis is a Test Optional institution and only requires SAT/ACT scores for those students seeking admission into the Nursing program, homeschooled students, and those interested in the St. George's University accelerated medical/veterinary school program. The SAT CEEB code is 3723; the ACT code is 1886.

RIPON COLLEGE

AT A GLANCE

Ripon College is a national leader in liberal arts and sciences education and Wisconsin's best-value private college, devoted to ensuring every student realizes their unique potential. Ninety-six percent of alumni are employed, in graduate school or student-teaching within six months.

Established in 1851, Ripon College is a national leader in liberal arts and sciences education and Wisconsin's best-value private college, devoted to ensuring every student realizes their unique potential. Students receive a top notch private education at a net price similar to a state school. Ripon's five-course Catalyst curriculum rigorously develops the 21st-century skills employers seek while streamlining the path to graduation. The core only requires 20 credits and upon completion each student earns a concentration in Applied Innovation. Students enjoy extensive freedom to pursue multiple majors and minors, study abroad and intern—all in just four years. Students are overwhelmingly satisfied with the amount of personalized attention they receive from devoted faculty and staff throughout their time on campus. Within six months of graduation, 96 percent of alumni are employed, in graduate school or student-teaching.

Ripon is a member of the prestigious Associated Colleges of the Midwest (ACM). We compete athletically as part of the Midwest Conference and offer 21 NCAA Division III varsity teams. Our brand new $23.5 million Willmore Center provides students with state-of-the-art facilities to train and workout and boasts the best NCAA indoor track in Wisconsin. To find out more, visit ripon.edu/willmore-center.

Ripon has a student to faculty ratio of 12 to 1, and the average class size is fewer than 20 students. As a matter of fact, 76 percent of classes at Ripon have fewer than 20 students, and 92 percent of classes have fewer than 30 students.

LOCATION AND ENVIRONMENT

The College is located in the historic city of Ripon, Wisconsin—a friendly, safe community of just under 8,000 people, 80 miles northwest of Milwaukee, 70 miles southwest of Green Bay, 73 miles northeast of Madison, 180 miles northwest of Chicago and 255 miles southeast of the Twin Cities in Minnesota. The nearest airport is 40 minutes away in Appleton, Wisconsin.

The campus spans 250 tree-lined acres and includes 27 buildings—10 of which are listed on the National Register of Historic Places. A sustainable campus, Ripon is home to the Ceresco Prairie Conservancy with 130 acres of native prairie, oak savanna and wetland habitat in the making.

CAMPUS FACILITIES & EQUIPMENT

The Ripon campus is adjacent to downtown Ripon and includes tree-lined walkways and 27 buildings—10 of which are listed on the National Register of Historic Places. Historic limestone buildings are complemented with more modern structures and continual updates, such as an apartment-style residence hall, a $23.5 million renovation and expansion of athletics, health and wellness facilities, and upgrades to the student union, dining facilities, and career and professional development.

The athletics, health and wellness facilities feature new high-tech classrooms, state-of-the-art fitness center, an NCAA indoor track, performance courts, fitness studios, athletic training center, and other enhancements.

Ripon College provides a secure, high-speed (802.11ac) WiFi network in every building on campus. In addition, a state of the art fiber optic network (10 Gb/s) connects all academic buildings, administrative buildings and residence halls. Connectivity to the Internet and Internet2 is provided by WiscNet at a speed of 1 Gb/s.

Student, faculty, and staff are issued a G Suite account that offers a variety of productivity tools (Gmail, Calendar, Drive, Docs, Hangouts…) to enhance campus collaboration and communication. Multi-functional devices (MFDs) are located in every academic and administrative building to service the campus printing, copying and scanning needs. The College also has new 3D printers that several faculty have incorporated into their course curricula.

Open-use computer labs are located across campus, offering both Windows and Mac OS devices, projectors, and MFDs.

Ripon College has partnered with Apogee to provide a cutting-edge cable TV/video solution. With the revolutionary IPTV service, Stream2, students can view HD content live, on-demand, or recorded (20 hours of DVR storage per user) on their laptops, tablets, and smartphones.

Library staff provide friendly, efficient circulation, reference, instruction and interlibrary loan services that aid in research. The library also houses the College archives, a computer lab, digital media stations and more than 25 online databases. Library holdings include access to over 300,000 physical and electronic books, and 55,000 periodicals.

C.J. Rodman Center for the Arts is home to a theater with a state-of-the-art computerized lighting system, a newly renovated recital hall with one of only 50 existing Bedient organs, an art gallery, a high-tech lab and a sculpture garden.

Bovay's Study Bar & Mercantile opened in March 2017 in a historic building in downtown Ripon. This unique venue features a 30-student collaborative study and event space, a study bar with barista coffee service, and a mercantile with official Ripon College apparel and gifts. Bovay's is open late into the evening and features barista coffee service during peak study hours. Student interns working in the space will benefit from hands-on experiential training in marketing, merchandising and small business management.

OFF-CAMPUS OPPORTUNITIES

U.S. or abroad? Three weeks, one semester, two semesters? Choose from more than 40 programs, each officially sanctioned by and affiliated with Ripon. Although most programs are connected with a major or minor program, all are open to every Ripon student, regardless of major. Scholarships are available to pursue off-campus study.

U.S. Programs: Chicago, Illinois Chicago: Arts (ACM), Chicago, Illinois Chicago: Business, Entrepreneurship and Society (ACM), Chicago, Illinois Chicago: Urban Studies (ACM), Chicago, Illinois Newberry Seminar in the Humanities (ACM), Chicago, Illinois Teach Chicago! Program, Chicago, Illinois Urban Education: Student Teaching (ACM), Knoxville, Tennessee Oak Ridge Science Semester (ACM), Nashville, Tennessee Fisk-Ripon Exchange Program, Southwest, USA American Indian Reservation Project, Washington, D.C. Washington Semester, Woods Hole, Massachusetts SEA: Sea Education Association, Woods Hole, Massachusetts SES: Semester in Environmental Science, Marine Biology Laboratory.

International Programs: Argentina Córdoba, Botswana Development in Southern Africa (ACM), Brazil Semester Exchange Program (ACM), Costa Rica Community Engagement in Public Health, Education & the Environment (ACM), Costa Rica Field Research in the Environment, Social Sciences & Humanities (ACM), England/Italy London & Florence: Arts in Context (ACM), France -Montpellier, France Paris, Germany Bonn Program, Hungary Budapest, India Pune: Culture, Traditions & Globalization (ACM), India Pune & Jaipur: Development Studies & Hindi Language (ACM), International Education Indiana University Global Gateway Program, Italy Coldigioco: Earth and Environment, Italy Florence: Arts, Humanities & Culture (ACM), Japan Tokyo (ACM), Jordan Amman (ACM-AMIDEAST), Russia St. Petersburg, Scotland University of St. Andrews, Spain Alicante, Spain Madrid, Spain Seville, Spain Toledo, Tanzania Ecology & Human Origins (ACM), Wales Bangor, Bangor University, Wales Swansea University Program.

Ripon College offers three-week Liberal Arts In Focus courses in May and August. Taught in short, intensive blocks, In Focus courses are designed as immersion experiences to provide a bridge between the theory and content of disciplines. Recent courses have included history lessons in Italy, intensive biology field studies in Costa Rica and the Wilderness Field Station near Ely, Minnesota, and a unique English course in Great Britain covering children's fantasy literature from Beatrix Potter to Harry Potter.

ACADEMICS

Our innovative new curriculum, Catalyst, began rolling out to the first-year class during the fall semester of 2016. The five-course curriculum rigorously develops the 21st-century skills that employers seek while streamlining the path to graduation. Catalyst ensures students have extensive freedom and are able to complete multiple majors and minors, study abroad and hold internships in four years.

Ripon's liberal arts curriculum introduces students to a wide variety of disciplines. About 40 percent of our students complete double or triple majors, while some create special self-designed majors. Hallmarks of a Ripon education are excellent communications skills, both written and oral; critical-thinking and problem-solving skills; and the opportunity to explore serious research pursuits alongside faculty as an undergraduate, no matter what your major.

A Ripon education will take you anywhere! You could study psychology and play basketball at Ripon, and then become a seven-time Grammy winner like jazz singer Al Jarreau (1962). You could become a Nobel Prize winner in economics like Oliver Williamson (1954). You could guide the space shuttle into orbit like Jeff Bantle (1980), a chief flight director with NASA, or become an international opera star like Gail Dobish (1976). Perhaps you'll set records in medical science like neonatologist Dr. John Muraskas (1978), who is on record for saving the world's smallest premature baby, or cover world events, like Richard Threlkeld (1959), former Moscow correspondent for CBS News. You could make your mark in the world of entertainment like Harrison Ford (1964), Spencer Tracy (1924) or Justin Neibank (1978). Or perhaps you'll end up studying at Oxford University as a Rhodes Scholar like Zach Morris (2002), who also found time to play touch football with former President Bill Clinton and spent an evening at Buckingham Palace with the Queen.

MAJORS AND DEGREES OFFERED

Ripon College offers a four-year graduation guarantee with 31 majors and 42 minors, including a variety of fast-track pre-professional programs. Every student graduates with a concentration in Applied Innovation upon completing the innovative five-course Catalyst curriculum.

Majors include Anthropology, Art History, Biology, Business Management, Chemistry, Chemistry-Biology, Communication, Economics, Educational Studies, English, Environmental Studies, Exercise Science/Athletic Training, Foreign Languages and Cultures, Global Studies, History, Mathematics, Music, Philosophy, Physical Education, Physical Science, Physics, Politics and Government, Psychobiology, Psychology, Recreation Physical Education, Religion, Sociology, Spanish, Sport Management, Studio Art, and Theatre.

Minors include American Studies, Anthropology, ARMS (Ancient, Renaissance & Medieval Studies), Art History, Biology, Business Management, Chemistry, Classical Studies, Coaching, Communication, Criminal Justice, Dramatic Literature, Economics, Educational Studies, Educational Studies-Early Childhood, Educational Studies-Middle School Childhood and Early Adult, English, Entrepreneurship, Environmental Biology, Francophone Studies, French, Health, History, Latin American and Caribbean Studies, Law and Society, Mathematics, Military Leadership, Music, National Security Studies, Nonprofit Management, Philosophy, Physics, Politics and Government, Psychology, Religion, Socially Responsible Leadership, Sociology, Spanish, Special Education, Studio Art, Theatre Production, Women's and Gender Studies.

Ripon College offers fast track programs that allow students to get professional degrees sooner in engineering, law and osteopathic medicine. We currently have a fast track program in engineering with Washington University; law with Marquette University, American University, Mitchell Hamline University and St. Thomas University; and osteopathic medicine with Lake Erie College of Osteopathic Medicine. Other pre-professional programs available include: Government Service, Journalism, Library and Information Science, Military Leadership, Ministry, Pre-Med & Health Sciences (medicine, dentistry, veterinary medicine, optometry, podiatry, physical therapy, pharmacy, nursing, chiropractic medicine, sports medicine), and Social Work.

Teacher certification is offered in Early Childhood, Elementary, Middle/Junior High, Secondary, and Bilingual/ESL. In addition, Ripon offers licensure in 21 subject areas. Teacher certification programs approved by the Wisconsin Department of Public Instruction prepare students for licensure at the early childhood/middle childhood level (grades PK through 5), the middle childhood/early adolescence level (grades 1 through 8), and the early adolescence/adolescence level (grades 6 through 12). The educational studies department also offers PK–12 certification programs in

art, foreign language (French and Spanish), music, physical education, physical education and health, and theatre (pending program approval).

TUITION, ROOM, BOARD, FEES

Pursuing a college degree is an important investment in your future. That's why at Ripon College your family's financial circumstances will never affect our admission decision. We provide 100 percent of our students with the financial assistance necessary to graduate and make it our mission to ensure a great economic value per every dollar spent. Tuition is $43,508, Room and Board is $8,401, and fees are $300, for a total cost of $52,209.

Average cost for books and supplies: $900

FINANCIAL AID

We are proud to offer our students competitive packages with funding from many sources: merit-based scholarships, need-based grants, educational loans, work study and scholarships from outside organizations. Academic scholarships range from $20,000 to $34,000 per year.

STUDENT ORGANIZATIONS AND ACTIVITIES

The faculty committee on academic standards establishes the criteria for admission. The school considers a variety of factors. An admission application and secondary school record are required for admission while standardized test scores (SAT or ACT), recommendations, a written essay, and extracurricular or community service activities may also be considered. Ripon's admission process reflects the personal attention students can expect to receive during their college careers, and applicants are encouraged to provide any additional information that they consider helpful.

From pre-professional programs to paintballing, Ripon College hosts more than 60 student-run clubs and organizations. Students at Ripon are encouraged to lead the programs, supported by the Student Senate's activity fee. This allows students to collaborate together in conceiving, organizing, marketing and developing unique activities.

In addition, Ripon offers a variety of intramural sports throughout the year, including: kickball, dodgeball, flag football, indoor soccer, inner tube water polo, basketball, bowling, volleyball and aerobics.

Ripon's NCAA Division III Intercollegiate Teams compete in the Midwest Conference:

Men's varsity sports: baseball, basketball, cross-country, cycling, football, soccer, swimming and diving, tennis, and indoor and outdoor track and field.

Women's varsity sports: basketball, dance, cross-country, cycling, soccer, softball, swimming and diving, tennis, indoor and outdoor track and field.

ADMISSIONS PROCESS

Ripon encourages applications from those students who are best prepared to benefit from and contribute to the academic and extracurricular programs that it offers. In evaluating applications, attention is paid to evidence of academic achievement, as indicated both by the distribution of courses taken in secondary school and by performance in those courses.

The faculty committee on academic standards establishes the criteria for admission. Ripon is test optional. We will consider test scores if you elect to submit them.

For more information contact:

Admission Office

Ripon College

300 Seward Street

PO Box 248

Ripon, WI 54971

Telephone: 800-947-4766

E-mail: adminfo@ripon.edu

ROCHESTER INSTITUTE OF TECHNOLOGY

AT A GLANCE

RIT is a place where brilliant minds assemble and collaborate, where they pool together their individual talents across disciplines in service of creative projects and innovative solutions. It is a vibrant community teeming with students collaborating with experts and specialists; a hub of innovation and creativity. As one of the nation's largest private universities, RIT has an unmatched array of specialized, career-oriented academic programs that attracts designers, artists, photographers, journalists, and filmmakers on the one hand, and scientists, engineers, computing scientists, social scientists, and entrepreneurs on the other. It is a launching pad for a brilliant career, and a highly unique state of mind.

LOCATION AND ENVIRONMENT

RIT's 1,300-acre campus is located in the suburbs, about six miles from downtown Rochester, NY. More than 7,100 diverse, creative, ambitious students live on campus in residence halls or apartments, and the self-contained, suburban location gives the campus a safe, residential atmosphere. RIT also maintains locations in China, Croatia, Dubai, and Kosovo.

CAMPUS FACILITIES & EQUIPMENT

RIT is comprised of nine colleges and two additional degree-granting units. The campus is filled with the latest equipment, software, laboratories, and conveniences to give students the tools they need to excel. RIT offers academic facilities that are rarely matched on other university campuses. A selected list of facilities includes: American Packaging Corporation Center for Packaging Innovation; Artificial Intelligence Lab; Center for Sustainable Packaging; Center for Accessibility and Inclusion Research; Entertainment Lab for 3D modeling, game, and interactive media development; Mobile Computing and Robotics Lab; William G. McGowan Center for Telecommunications, Innovation, and Collaborative Research; REDCOM Telecommunications Systems Laboratory; Integrated circuit design center; Computer labs with industry-standard CAD software packages; a Class-1000 clean-room laboratory space for the fabrication of integrated circuits; A machining and manufacturing center equipped with state-of-the-art CNC machinery; 3D printing equipment; Center for Applied Psychophysiology and Self-regulation; Center for Bioscience Exploration and Technology; 30 fully equipped photographic studios, 20 fully equipped b/w and color darkrooms; Image Permanence Institute.

OFF-CAMPUS OPPORTUNITIES

Rochester provides a perfect setting—it's large enough to provide the dining, shopping, and night life opportunities found in a bigger city, yet small and friendly enough to be inviting and accessible. In fact, Rochester was ranked 10th best among large cities in the Northeast in a recent Money magazine Best Places to Live in America survey. The greater Rochester area is home to more than 1 million people, making it the third-largest metropolitan area in New York State. Rochester's reputation as an active and inventive community is supported by extensive cultural and intellectual opportunities.

ACADEMIC PROGRAMS

At RIT, some of the world's most talented, ambitious, and creative students find a remarkable array of academic programs; diverse, talented and accessible faculty; sophisticated facilities; an unusual emphasis on experiential learning; and a vibrant, connected community that is home to students from more than 100 countries. Excelling in teaching and research, RIT's faculty are passionate about their role in the classroom and in their field. RIT's faculty are diverse, innovative and resourceful, and engage students in the process of personal and professional discovery. RIT's nine colleges offer more than 90 undergraduate programs. To complement their specialized field of study, students select from more than 80 minors available at RIT. Students can also complete a master's degree in five years through one of the university's accelerated BS/MS or 4+1 MBA programs.

Experiential Learning

Since 1912, the hallmark of an RIT has been experiential education. RIT was among the first universities in the world to offer cooperative education, and its co-op program is now one of the largest in the world. Last year more than 4,400 students completed nearly 6,000 co-op work assignments by alternating periods of study on campus with paid employment in more than 2,300 firms across the United States and overseas. Experiential learning also includes internships, study abroad, and undergraduate research.

Regardless of background or academic interest, students find that RIT offers a stimulating environment for intellectual and personal growth.

MAJORS AND DEGREES OFFERED

Art Design and Visual Communications

3D Digital Design; Advertising and Public Relations; Ceramics; Digital Humanities and Social Sciences; Film and Animation; Fine Arts Studio; Furniture Design; Glass; Graphic Design; Illustration; Industrial Design; Interior Design; Media Arts and Technology; Medical Illustration; Metals and Jewelry Design; Motion Picture Science; New Media Design; New Media Interactive Development; New Media Marketing; Photographic and Imaging Arts (options in Advertising Photography, Fine Art Photography, Photojournalism. Visual Media); Photographic Sciences (options in Biomedical Photographic Communications, Imaging and Photographic Technology); Studio Arts

Business and Management

Accounting; Applied Technical Leadership; Economics; Finance; Hospitality and Tourism Management; International Business; Management; Marketing; Management Information Systems' New Media Marketing' Supply Chain Management

Computing and Information Sciences:

3D Digital Design; Bioinformatics; Computational Mathematics; Computer Science; Computing and Information Technologies BS; Computing Security; Game Design and Development; Human-Centered Computing BS; Management Information Systems BS; New Media Interactive Development BS; Software Engineering; Web and Mobile Computing

Engineering and Engineering Technology

Biomedical Engineering; Chemical Engineering ; Civil Engineering Technology; Computer Engineering; Computer Engineering Technology; Electrical Engineering; Electrical Engineering Technology; Electrical Mechanical Engineering Technology; Industrial Engineering; Manufacturing Engineering Technology; Mechanical Engineering; Mechanical Engineering Technology; Microelectronic Engineering; Packaging Science

Software Engineering

Health Sciences and Technology

Biomedical Sciences; Diagnostic Medical Sonography (Ultrasound) BS; Dietetics and Nutrition; Exercise Science; Nutritional Sciences; Physician Assistant

Science, Mathematics, and Imaging Science

Applied Mathematics; Applied Statistics and Actuarial Science; Biochemistry; Bioinformatics; Biology; Biomedical Sciences; Biotechnology and Molecular Bioscience; Chemistry; Computational Mathematics; Diagnostic Medical Sonography (Ultrasound) ; Environmental Science BS; Environmental, Health and Safety Management; Imaging Science BS; Physics

Social Sciences and Humanities

Applied Modern Language and Culture; ASL-English Interpretation; Communication; Criminal Justice; Environmental Science; International and Global Studies; Journalism; Museum Studies; Philosophy; Political Science; Psychology; Public Policy; Sociology and Anthropology BS

TUITION, ROOM, BOARD, FEES

For 2017–18, tuition and fees cost $40,068; room and board averaged $12,666; and books, transportation, and other expenses averaged $2,026.

FINANCIAL AID

RIT's Office of Financial Aid and Scholarships assists students and their families in identifying sources of financial aid to help meet the cost of a quality education. Currently, more than 12,000 RIT undergraduate and graduate students receive over $320 million dollars in financial assistance from federal, state, and institutional resources, in the form of scholarships, grants, loans, and part-time employment.

STUDENT ORGANIZATIONS AND ACTIVITIES

The backgrounds and interests of RIT students contribute in many ways to the quality of campus life. With students from all 50 states and more than 100 countries, RIT is a living-learning environment rich in diversity in classrooms, residence halls, and everywhere else on campus. RIT attracts students from every state and approximately 2,700 international students from more than 100 countries. Embodying our commitment to diversity, nearly 3,200 students of color have elected to study at RIT. Adding a social and educational dynamic not found at any other university are more than 1,100 deaf and hard-of-hearing students supported by RIT's National Technical Institute for the Deaf.

Students take their academic pursuits seriously, but they'll be the first to tell you that they are passionate about life outside of the lectures, labs and studios. RIT is alive with energy and excitement-24/7. A number of campus organizations and student services focus on the unique needs and interests of minority, deaf, and international students at RIT. You'll have plenty of opportunity to interact with a mind-expanding mix of people. More than 7,100 full-time students live on campus in residence halls or apartments, and our self-contained, suburban location creates a safe and secure atmosphere. Clubs and organizations exist to bring students of similar interest together and provide them with opportunities to become effective leaders. These groups enhance the quality of student life by fostering social interaction, leadership development, school spirit and an affinity to RIT. Clubs and Organizations promote activities, diversity, service and learning outside of the classroom. Currently there are approximately 300 active clubs, 10 Major Student Organizations, and 30 Greek Organizations on campus. Last year, clubs and organizations held nearly 1,300 events on campus.

RIT's intercollegiate teams have a history of excellence, recording many impressive seasons and capturing a number of conference and national championships. The men's and women's hockey teams are Division I. The remainder of the intercollegiate teams competes at Division III. RIT teams are members of the National Collegiate Athletic Association (NCAA), the Eastern College Athletic Conference (ECAC), the Atlantic Hockey Association, the College Hockey America, the Liberty League, and the New York State Women's Collegiate Athletic Association.

ADMISSIONS PROCESS

RIT seeks a diverse and multicultural student body. Entering students come from a variety of geographic, social, cultural, economic, and ethnic backgrounds. Admission to RIT is competitive, but the admission process is a personal one. The university is interested in learning about students' interests, abilities, and goals in order to provide the best information and guidance as they select the college that is right for them. Factors considered in our admission decisions include, but are not limited to, past high school and/or college performance (particularly in required academic subjects), admission test scores, competitiveness of high school or previous college, and academic program selected.

Students applying for freshman admission for the fall semester (September) may apply through an Early Decision Plan or Regular Decision Plan. The Early Decision Plan is designed for students who consider RIT their first-choice college and wish to make an early commitment regarding admission. Early Decision requires that candidates file their applications and supporting documents by November 15. Regular Decision applicants should file the required application materials by January 15.

SACRED HEART UNIVERSITY

Sacred Heart University, the second-largest independent Catholic university in New England, offers more than 70 undergraduate, graduate, doctoral and certificate programs on its main campus in Fairfield, Conn., and satellites in Connecticut, Luxembourg and Ireland. More than 8,500 students attend the University's five colleges: Arts & Sciences; Health Professions; Nursing; the Jack Welch College of Business; and the Isabelle Farrington College of Education.

AT A GLANCE

Distinguished by the personal attention it provides its students, Sacred Heart University (SHU) is recognized for its commitment to academic excellence, award-winning advisement program, cutting-edge technology, championship Division I athletic teams, and nationally recognized community service programs. Situated in Fairfield, Connecticut, the main campus is ideally located one hour north of New York City and 2.5 hours south of Boston in proximity to world-class hospitals, nationally ranked elementary and secondary schools, a high concentration of Fortune 500 corporations and access to the employers in Connecticut's creative corridor. SHU also has international campuses in Dingle, Ireland and the European business center of Luxembourg, a partner campus in Rome, and study abroad options worldwide. Students may spend their freshman fall semester abroad program or participate in short-term and semester programs throughout their four years. Within the AACSB-accredited Jack Welch College of Business, College of Arts and Sciences, College of Health Professions, College of Nursing, Isabelle Farrington College of Education, School of Computing and School of Communication and Media Arts, students in all majors engage in hands-on education both in and outside of the classroom. Cutting-edge technology in the Frank and Marisa Martire Business & Communications Center allows students to apply their skills in real world settings such as the Finance Lab & Trading Floor, full-size television studios and a motion capture lab. The new Center for Healthcare Education features the latest technology available to health professions students. Students in the sciences utilize recently renovated laboratories and state-of-the-art computer labs. A hallmark of a SHU education is the strong connection between students and faculty beginning in the freshman year. Faculty connect with students in interactive, innovative spaces in our academic buildings; through online communities such as SHUSquare for freshmen; in joint research projects; in advising sessions and through many academic clubs, organizations and activities. Faculty lead students on study trips across the globe and on excursions to locations such as Washington, D.C. for political science students and the New York Stock Exchange for finance students. The University's commitment to experiential learning incorporates concrete, real-life study for students in all majors including research, internships, clinical placements, independent study, service learning and work-study. Drawing on the rich resources in New England and New York City, students are connected with research and internship opportunities ranging from full-time internships at sought-after sites such as Madison Square Garden to research with faculty on marine life in the Long Island Sound. These opportunities help pave the way for a 95 percent placement rate for graduating seniors in full-time jobs and graduate study. SHU's experiential learning opportunities are complemented by a rich student life program offering more than 160 student organizations, including Greek life; leadership programs, media organizations such as the TV station, radio station and newspaper; academic clubs and multicultural organizations. The University has a well-respected Division I athletic program and a robust club sports program with more than 1,500 athletes who compete in 32 varsity sports and 27 competitive club sports teams. The University's strong performing arts program, led by a Tony-and-Grammy-nominated producer, includes the theatre arts program (also available as an academic major), a choir program with various ensembles, an instrumental music program including marching band, pep band and concert band among other ensembles and a dance program with a variety of ensembles. The campus has a lively atmosphere with over 90 percent of freshmen living on campus and many school spirit, cultural and social events offered throughout the year.

LOCATION AND ENVIRONMENT

Sacred Heart University comprises more than 300 acres of land, including an 18-hole golf course and the former global headquarters of General Electric, now named West Campus. The main campus of the University sits on more than 100 acres in Fairfield, Conn.—less than 60 miles from Manhattan and approximately 150 miles from Boston.

The University-owned golf course is located in Milford/Orange, Conn. It is a signature Tommy Fazio-designed facility that has been ranked fourth-best in Connecticut by Golf.com. The recently acquired West Campus will be used as an innovation campus to expand the School of Computing and develop STEM field programs. Certain elements of the Jack Welch College of Business, including the new hospitality management program, the Isabelle Farrington College of Education, will be moved to the site.

The Center for Healthcare Education houses the College of Health Professions and College of Nursing. The Center is designed to offer students with aspirations in any health-care profession the best possible learning environment to ensure that they are prepared to succeed in the booming health-care industry.

SHU's newest dining hall, JP's Diner, is a '50s-style diner and the first on-campus diner in all of New England. Named for SHU President John J. Petillo, JP's is located on SHU's newly-constructed Upper Quad. Sacred Heart's newest residence Toussaint Hall is also part of the Upper Quad.

The University maintains satellite campuses for graduate students in the Physician Assistant Program in Stamford, CT and for Graduate education students in Griswold, CT.

CAMPUS FACILITIES & EQUIPMENT

The Edgerton Center for Performing Arts; Martire Business and Communications Center featuring an active trading floor with 30 work stations, 13 Bloomberg terminals, wallboard ticker tapes and real time data from NASDAQ and NYSE, screening venues, smart classrooms with multi-media technology, interactive labs, a motion capture lab, and two large television studios for TV, video and film production; The new Center for Healthcare Education containing an audiology suite, motion analysis and human performance labs, driving simulator, pediatrics clinic, medical gym, an immersive acute care simulation lab with video and data capture capability, a simulated outpatient suite, high-fidelity manikins, home-care suite, cadaver lab, and many more learning resources featuring the latest technology; School of Computing facilities including a Gaming Lab (which also supports the intercollegiate Gaming team), computing labs, a closed LAN laboratory, 3D printing lab and the motion lab; Fashion design studio; Art studios; Jandrisevits Learning Center includes spaces and technologies to provide academic support to students, including those with disabilities.

OFF-CAMPUS OPPORTUNITIES

SHU offers over 60 programs in 30 countries around the world, including two of our own global campuses in Ireland and Luxembourg. International experiences are available to SHU and visiting students— with study abroad programs that support a broad range of educational, professional, and personal goals. Looking at New England liberal arts colleges to study business? SHU has the only American-accredited MBA program in Luxembourg.

Through service abroad, students learn about a new culture, generosity, and the value of servicing others. With our Office of Volunteer Programs and Service Learning, opportunities to volunteer abroad in Latin America and the Caribbean include helping to build homes, schools or medical facilities for those in need.

SHU also offers undergraduate and graduate nursing and health professions students the opportunity to complete clinical service hours, capstone projects or service learning hours in Guatemala, Haiti, Jamaica, Uganda, India and the Cheyenne River Sioux Tribe Reservation in S. Dakota, as well as experience the local healthcare systems in each nation.

ACADEMIC PROGRAMS

The University comprises five distinct colleges and two schools: College of Arts & Sciences; School of Communication & Media Arts; School of Computing; College of Health Professions; College of Nursing; Isabelle Farrington College of Education; and the AACSB-accredited Jack Welch College of Business, committed to educating students in the leadership tradition and legacy of Jack Welch.

The University offers more than 70 undergraduate, graduates, doctoral and certificate programs including online degree programs.

Upon introducing the new undergraduate Core Curriculum in Fall 2007, the University was invited to become a member of the Association of American Colleges & Universities (AAC&U) Core Commitments Leadership Consortium, which includes just 23 institutions nationally. AAC&U has recognized SHU's Core Curriculum as a national model of values education. A newly revised core curriculum was launched in Fall 2015.

MAJORS AND DEGREES OFFERED

At the undergraduate level, Sacred Heart University offers two baccalaureate degrees: Bachelor of Arts or Bachelor of Science depending upon the nature of the discipline of the major. SHU also offers Associate in Arts and Associate in Science degrees. A central component of undergraduate study is the University's Core Curriculum, the Human Journey, which embodies the University's commitment to academic excellence, social responsibility, and ethical awareness. All candidates for the baccalaureate degree must complete at least 120 credits, with a minimum of 30 credits taken at Sacred Heart University. A minimum cumulative GPA 2.0 is required.

Majors include: Accounting Major, Art and Design Associate in Arts: General Studies, Art and Design, Biochemistry Biology Business Economics, Certificate Program in Home Healthcare Management for RNs—Online, Chemistry , Communication Studies , Computer Gaming Design and Development Certificate Program, Computer Science and Information Technology Certificate Program, Computer Science, Computer Science, Cybersecurity Concentration, Criminal Justice, Digital Communication, English , Exercise Science, Finance, Game Design and Development, General Studies, Global Studies, Health Science, History, Information Technology, Information Technology, Cybersecurity Concentration, Interdisciplinary Studies, Interdisciplinary Studies, Management, Marketing, Mathematics, Media Arts, Nursing Completion Programs (RN-to-BSN and Accelerated RN-to-BSN-to-MSN Program), Nursing, Philosophy, Political Science, Pre-Occupational Therapy, Pre-Physical Therapy, Pre-Physician Assistant Studies, Pre-Speech-Language Pathology, Psychology, Social Work, Sociology, Spanish, Sport Management, Theatre Arts, Theology and Religious Studies

TUITION, ROOM, BOARD, FEES

Tuition for the 2017–18 school year is $39,570. Room and board is $14,770.

FINANCIAL AID

Sacred Heart University works with all students throughout the financial aid process. There are a wide variety of aid types SHU including need-based scholarships and grants, loans and student and University employment.

STUDENT ORGANIZATIONS AND ACTIVITIES

The entire mood here is very upbeat, gushes one Sacred Heart student, and another adds that "door holding symbolizes us because we care about those around us and are very genuine people." When it comes to school spirit, Sacred Heart has it in spades. As one student puts it, "Sacred Heart University exemplifies school spirit and hospitality to every single student that walks [through] our campus." To sum it up, "The entire student body is one giant family." Much of the student body from the Tri-State area but students stress that Sacred Heart is "all about embracing diversity and cultivating a caring, safe, and academically prosperous environment." The school is a "tightly-knit community where people are excited to try new things and professors encourage students to branch out."

Campus Life

It's easy to keep busy at Sacred Heart, as "there's always something happening on campus and on the weekends thanks to [the] Student Life department." Students say that when their peers are not "studying or working, they are volunteering their time in the volunteer program." Fairfield is "a great college town so there is a ton to do off campus," and for those who want to venture a little farther, New York and Boston aren't too far away. Greek life plays a role on campus but students seem to consider it just one more thing in a long list of potential things to do at Sacred Heart, rather than the only activity available. According to one student, "If you're not the biggest partier, SHU is a great school for you." One popular watering hole on campus is Red's, "the on-campus pub," where "senior students enjoy nightlife in town" and which also has "all-age nights where no alcohol is served and it is open to students of any class year." When students want a break from campus, especially "when the weather is nice, students hang out at the beach, get some ice cream, and often are dining downtown." As the school continues to expand—something students praise—parking is a growing issue that students hope the administration will address.

ADMISSIONS PROCESS

Students heap praise on this small Catholic university located in Fairfield, Connecticut, a place where "academics meet real-world experiences." Sacred Heart University is a Catholic school, but students underscore that "we do not force religious teachings upon the student body; rather, we offer a helping hand in times of despair as well as times of fortune." One of Sacred Heart's points of pride is being known as a "door-holding" school: "We all hold doors for each other, help each other out, and look out for one another." With an undergraduate population of a little less than 5,500, students say, "The student body is one of the most tight-knit groups of people [they] have ever been a part of." The school's proximity to New York City, Hartford, and Stamford provide opportunities for real-world experiences outside the classroom, and students say the "internship and job opportunities we have here are unique and amazing." Specific programs of note for students include the "business, nursing, and health professions programs," with one student declaring that the choice to attend SHU was down to the school's "fantastic nursing program." Professors are "enthusiastic, encouraging, and helpful" on the whole, and students appreciate that some "also allow students to engage with their research which then will allow kids to get published." Beyond the coursework, one student says that professors at Sacred Heart have "opened my eyes to how the world works."

SAINT ANSELM COLLEGE

AT A GLANCE

Saint Anselm College encourages you not only to challenge yourself academically, but also to lead a life that is both creative and generous. Saint Anselm students are active both in and out of the classroom.

Saint Anselm College prepares students for life. With a liberal arts education, they're ready for real career experience, for the challenges that lie ahead. They take their Saint Anselm experience with them to think critically, communicate effectively, and solve problems creatively.

Saint Anselm graduates are CEOs, doctors, engineers, teachers, marketers, and researchers. They are humanitarians, healers, and philanthropists. They graduate Saint Anselm with the drive to achieve, empowered to make the world a better place.

In fact, 99 percent of the class of 2017 was employed, in graduate school, or engaged in service within 6 months of graduation.

The Princeton Review ranks Saint Anselm as one of the country's best institutions for an undergraduate education and number 8 out of 3,000 national colleges for its food.

LOCATION AND ENVIRONMENT

Saint Anselm College is located on 380 acres in Manchester, N.H., the largest city in the state. Just minutes from downtown Manchester, students can find great restaurants and coffee shops and all the venues a small city has to offer, a theatre, museum, minor league baseball and hockey teams, and the Verizon Arena to name a few. The Manchester-Boston Regional Airport is also just minutes from campus. The college is an hour drive from Boston, the seacoast, and the White Mountains.

CAMPUS FACILITIES & EQUIPMENT

There's much to see and do on campus from open skate nights at Sullivan Arena to spring concerts on the quad. Academic buildings including the Goulet Science Center and Gadbois Hall house innovative labs where remarkable research happens every day. There are cell culture labs, climate controlled environmental chambers, a green house, a sleep lab, SimMan labs in Nursing, and more. In the library, students have access to a range of workspaces for individuals and groups in addition to technological advances.

Recreational facilities include the Carr Center with basketball courts and the recently renovated 9,000-square-foot, three-level fitness center. Saint Anselm College boasts some of the top athletic facilities in the Northeast-10 Conference. The college's 20 intercollegiate athletic teams play all of their home contests on campus (with the exception of the golf and alpine ski teams) whether at Grappone Stadium, Sullivan Arena, or Melucci Field.

Ninety-one percent of Saint Anselm students live on campus in traditional residence halls, suites, townhouses, or apartments. A new 47,000-square-foot, 150-bed residence hall opened in August 2014 offering students an innovative, living-learning community. Whether students live on campus or commute, everyone has access to Saint Anselm College's amazing food, named 8th in the nation by the Princeton Review.

Saint Anselm is home to the New Hampshire Institute of Politics & Political Library (NHIOP), which offers unparalleled opportunities for students to be in the front row of the democratic process. Its auditorium, West Wing, TV-studio, and classrooms are where students meet today's most prominent political policy thinkers and researchers, journalists and authors, scientists, industry executives, global leaders and presidential candidates. Have we mentioned all the U.S. presidents in the last 50 years have visited Saint Anselm?

OFF-CAMPUS OPPORTUNITIES

At Saint Anselm College, a liberal arts education gives students a solid foundation for any career but opportunities out-of-the-classroom give students a competitive edge and real job experience.

Students find all kinds of experiential learning opportunities at Saint Anselm College including internships, research, study abroad, and volunteering. Students of all majors and interests can find opportunities for internships through the Career Development Center, which also brings employers to campus and advises students throughout their job search.

Internships are offered in Boston, M.A., New York City, N.Y., Washington, D.C. and Manchester, N.H. Recent internships opportunities include: The White House, The Boston Bruins, United States Secret Service, Fidelity Investments, The United States Senate, Fox News, and the American Cancer Society.

Many students work closely on research projects with faculty on campus to gain valuable lab skills but there are also opportunities at local hospitals and businesses.

Students interested in study abroad can travel the world visiting such places as Thailand, Morocco, and South Africa. In recent years, students have studied marine biology on Australia's Great Barrier Reef, art history in the museums of Florence, finance in London, language in Spain and France, the culture of peace in Peru, and political history in Ireland.

If studying abroad for an entire semester seems too long, Saint Anselm students have traveled with faculty members on week-long trips to places such as China, Panama, Vietnam, and Belize.

Saint Anselm students have gained essential leadership and organizational skills through volunteering. Last year, students volunteered more than 51,907 hours through the Meelia Center for Community Engagement doing everything from teaching English to new Americans to working the crisis hotline at the YWCA.

In addition, every winter and spring break, Saint Anselm students travel to organizations around the country to volunteer at service sites through Service & Solidarity Mission Trips. These service trips challenge students, giving them valuable perspectives and changing their views on the world.

ACADEMIC PROGRAMS

The core curriculum focuses on humanities, college writing, and learning outcomes. It is a balance between common courses that foster academic community and elective courses that allow for individual choice.

At Saint Anselm College's New Hampshire Institute of Politics & Political Library, students hear major policy speeches and meet today's most prominent political policy thinkers, journalists, scientists, industry executives, and global leaders. The Institute, nationally known to political scholars and strategists, is an essential campaign stop for presidential candidates offering unparalleled opportunities for students to be in the front row of the democratic process. In fact, every United States president in the last 50 years has visited Saint Anselm College.

MAJORS AND DEGREES OFFERED

At Saint Anselm College, students may pursue a Bachelor of Arts degree in the following academic programs and majors: accounting, American studies, archaeology, behavioral neuroscience, biochemistry, biology, business, chemistry, classics, communication, computer science, computer science with business, computer science with mathematics, criminal justice, economics, education (secondary and elementary), engineering (3-2 program), English, environmental studies, environmental science, finance, fine arts, forensic science, French, German studies, great books, history, international business, international relations, mathematics, mathematics with economics, marketing, natural science, peace and justice studies, philosophy, physics, politics, psychology, social work, sociology, Spanish, and theology. The college also offers a Bachelor of Science in Nursing (BSN) through a traditional, undergraduate nursing program and a hybrid RN to BSN Program.

Saint Anselm students may pursue pre-professional programs in dentistry, law, medicine, theology, veterinary medicine, and other allied health fields, such as pharmacy, physical therapy, and physician assistant.

The engineering (3-2 program) partners with the University of Notre Dame, University of Massachusetts-Lowell, Catholic University of America, and Manhattan College. Learn more at www.anselm.edu/engineering.

TUITION, ROOM, BOARD, FEES

The 2018–2019 school year tuition and fees is $41,200 and room and board costs are $14,500. Total cost is $55,700

FINANCIAL AID

Saint Anselm provides students with financial aid opportunities through both private and federal aid programs. The college provides financial aid to offset the reasonable monetary investment that the student and family are expected to contribute.

Ninety-seven percent of the college's undergraduates receive some degree of financial aid. Saint Anselm's financial aid opportunities include grants, loans, scholarships, and employment positions. Outstanding students may also be eligible for merit scholarships through the Office of Admission.

Merit awards are awarded to outstanding students. Two forms are required in applying for institutional need-based aid; the student must submit the CSS/Financial Aid PROFILE and the Free Application for Federal Student Aid (FAFSA) by February 15.

Average Freshman Total Need-Based Gift Aid= $22,000

STUDENT ORGANIZATIONS AND ACTIVITIES

With more than 60 clubs and organizations, 20 varsity athletic teams, a performing arts center, and an art gallery, Saint Anselm students have plenty of activities to explore. From the soccer club to the mock trial team to the Muslim Student Association, there is a club for every interest, cultural to academic.

Students interested in service will be right at home volunteering through the Meelia Center for Community Engagement or through Campus Ministry. Saint Anselm students volunteered more than 51,907 hours last year doing everything from teaching English to new Americans to working the crisis hotline at the YWCA. Every winter and spring break, Saint Anselm students travel to organizations around the country to volunteer at service sites through Service & Solidarity Mission Trips.

Saint Anselm College with 1,900 enrolled students, is part of the Division II Northeast-10 and ECAC Conferences with 20 varsity teams: men's intercollegiate sports in baseball, basketball, cross-country, football, golf, ice hockey, lacrosse, skiing, soccer, and tennis and women's sports in basketball, cross-country, field hockey, ice hockey, lacrosse, skiing, soccer, softball, tennis, and volleyball. For students interested in club or intramurals, Saint Anselm has a variety of club, recreational, and intramural sports teams.

ADMISSIONS PROCESS

In reviewing applicants for the first-year class, admission considers each prospective student carefully. Counselors assess each applicant's secondary school performance, SAT I or ACT scores (optional for non-nursing majors, nursing majors must submit scores and should apply Early Action or Early Decision), recommendation letters, extracurricular involvement, and the written essay. Of highest priority is the applicant's secondary school transcript, with a specific focus on both the rigor of course study and the marks received. Saint Anselm invites transfer and international students to apply.

Saint Anselm College has the following admission deadlines:

Early Action, November 15

Nursing Majors, November 15 or December 1

Early Decision, December 1

Regular Decision, February 1

Saint Anselm College invites students and families to visit campus for a tour, information session and/or interview.

For more information, students should contact:

Office of Admission

Saint Anselm College

100 Saint Anselm Drive

Manchester, NH 03102-1310 Telephone: 603-641-7500 or 888-426-7356 (toll-free)

Fax: 603-641-7550

Email: admission@anselm.edu

Website: www.anselm.edu

SAINT FRANCIS UNIVERSITY (PA)

AT A GLANCE

Saint Francis is a private, Catholic, co-educational liberal arts university. Established in 1847, the University is among America's first Franciscan institutions and is the nation's 12th-oldest Catholic institution of higher education. Saint Francis operates under the conventions of the Franciscan Friars of the Third Order Regular. The University is dedicated to providing each student with top-rated academics, a vibrant student life, opportunities for leadership, and unflagging attention from a distinguished faculty. For the past century and a half, Saint Francis University's commitment to academics and student life has embodied two important values: high-quality education and respecting students as individuals.

LOCATION AND ENVIRONMENT

Saint Francis University is located on a 600-acre mountaintop campus in the town of Loretto, Pennsylvania. Just 80 miles east of Pittsburgh and 60 miles west of State College, the campus has its own lake, nature trails, ski tubing park and championship golf course. Near to campus are three state parks, four biking/walking trails and four ski resorts. The beautiful campus has an impressive suite of academic and research facilities as well as 19 residence halls to offer students a comprehensive experience. Student recreational, athletic, eateries and a student union provide each student a robust campus living experience.

CAMPUS FACILITIES & EQUIPMENT

Saint Francis offers a totally wireless campus, computer labs, a Macintosh-based computer lab, and numerous Smart Classrooms. The cost of attendance at Saint Francis includes a laptop computer as well as technical support. Other facilities that complement student learning include well-equipped science labs, on-campus radio and television stations, and the Southern Alleghenies Museum of Art.

A recently completed state-of-the-art Science Center sits at the center of campus. The facility houses highly competitive science, technology, engineering and mathematics programs. The DiSepio Institute for Rural Health and Wellness education and research center features the DiSepio Center for Rehabilitation, Student Health Services, Fitness Center, Spiritual Wellness Center, Human Performance Laboratory, and Ernest J. Scharpf Family Conference Center. A complete renovation of Schwab Hall was recently completed in an effort to house the Shields School of Business.

OFF-CAMPUS OPPORTUNITIES

Saint Francis University's Office for Study Abroad offers a truly unique semester abroad program in the beautiful village of Ambialet, in southern France. Students can experience the adventure, beauty, and history of Europe in the halls of a centuries-old Franciscan monastery. Travel and research abroad are components of many academic programs at Saint Francis University. Students are encouraged to engage in the multitude of semester long or condensed travel abroad experiences facilitated by the Office for Study Abroad.

ACADEMIC PROGRAMS

Bachelor's degrees are typically earned within eight semesters. To graduate, each student is required to complete a course of study that meets with approval from the University Provost. The University operates on a two-semester academic calendar, with three sessions in the summer. The University offers students over 45 academic programs of study and a wide variety of minors and concentrations to choose. Among the most competitive academic offerings are two entry-level master's health science majors (Occupational Therapy and Physician Assistant Science) and an entry-level Doctoral program in Physical Therapy. The institution is well known for the cooperative student-faculty research that occurs within the School of Science. Petroleum & Natural Gas Engineering and Environmental Engineering are among the most recent program additions to the School of Science. In the School of Arts & Letters Early Childhood Education students may complete dual certification in Special Education in four years. Saint Francis University also has an extensive list of minors and concentrations available for students to complement their academic program of study.

MAJORS AND DEGREES OFFERED

Saint Francis University students may earn bachelor (BA, BS) degrees, master's degrees and doctoral degrees. The Division of Adult Degree & Continuing Studies offers certificate, associate and Bachelor's degree programs in a flexible, on-line learning environment.

SCHOOL OF ARTS & LETTERS

American Studies
Arts & Letters
Criminal Justice
Digital Media
Strategic Communications
Education
-Early Childhood (PreK-4)
-Education/Special Education Certification
-Middle Childhood (Grades 4-8)
-Education/Special Education Certification
-Secondary Education Certification
English
-Literature (C)
-Media Studies (C)
-Secondary Education (C)
Environmental Studies
Fermentation Arts
-Fermentation Administration (C)
-Fermentation Culture (C)
History
-Pre-Law (C)
-Secondary Education (C)
International Business French
International Business Spanish
International Studies
Philosophy
Philosophy and Religious Studies
Political Science
-Political Communications (C)
-Pre-Law (C)
Psychology
-Secondary Education (C)
Public Administration/Government Service
Religious Studies
Social Work
Sociology
Spanish
-Secondary Education (C)

SCHOOL OF BUSINESS

Accounting
Economics
Finance
Management
-Healthcare Management (C)
Management Information Systems
Marketing
-Entrepreneurship (C)

SCHOOL OF HEALTH SCIENCES

Exercise Physiology
-Fitness Professionals (C)
-Pre-Allied Health (C)
-Pre-Professional (C)
-Research/Graduate (C)
Health Care Studies
-Pre-Allied Health (C)

-Pre-Occupational Therapy (C)
-Pre-Physician Assistant (C)
Nursing
Occupational Therapy (MOT)
Physical Therapy (DPT)
-B.S. Health Science
-B.S. Exercise Physiology
Physician Assistant Sciences (MPAS)
Public Health
-Pre-Professional (C)

SCHOOL OF SCIENCES

Aquarium and Zoo Science
Biology
-Biochemistry (C)
-Environmental Science (C)
-Marine Biology (C)
-Molecular Biology (C)
-Pre-Pharmacy (C)
-Pre-Professional (C)
-Secondary Education (C)
Biochemistry
Chemistry
-Biochemistry (C)
-Environmental Chemistry (C)
-Forensic Science (C)
-Pre-Pharmacy (C)
-Pre-Professional (C)
-Secondary Education (C)
Computer Science
-Gaming/New Media Design and Production (C)
-Information Technology and Security (C)
-Software Development (C)
Cyber Security
Engineering (3-2)
Environmental Engineering
-Ecological Engineering (C)
-Renewable Energies (C)
General Engineering
Petroleum and Natural Gas Engineering
Medical Laboratory Science/Med Tech
Mathematics
-Actuarial Science (C)
-Applied Mathematics (C)
-Secondary Education (C)
Pharmacy
-Pharm.D. Affiliate Program with Lake Erie College of Osteopathic Medicine
-Pharm.D. Affiliate Program with Mylan School of Pharmacy at Duquesne University
(C) denotes concentration

TUITION, ROOM, BOARD, FEES

2017–18

Tuition: $33,856

Room: $5906

Board: $6022

Technology Program Fee: $1100

Financial Aid

Saint Francis University awards financial aid to greater than 90 percent of its student body. Need-based federal and state awards are awarded based on information obtained from the Free Application for Federal Student Aid (FAFSA). In order to qualify for financial aid students must apply for admission and complete a FAFSA. Saint Francis University has a generous merit-based scholarship program. Students who have been accepted for admission are awarded merit-based scholarships based upon their academic performance. Academic performance is measured by credentials submitted upon application including high school grade point average, SAT/ACT scores and class rank.

Saint Francis University participates in NCAA Division I athletics in the Northeast Conference. Athletic scholarships may be granted in all 23 athletic teams. Students may also receive scholarship money in Pep Band, Marching Band, Cheerleading, and Dance.

STUDENT ORGANIZATIONS AND ACTIVITIES

Saint Francis University is a diverse campus community with approximately 2,600 students. Our students arrive at Saint Francis University from over 30 states and 25 countries.

The University provides students many opportunities to exercise their interests and talents. Over 60 on-campus clubs and organizations representing a wide range of interests are available to students. These range from departmental clubs to volunteer organizations, and include social and service sororities and social, service, and business fraternities. Student-run activities on campus include theatre productions, SFU singers, Greek life opportunities for men and women as well as Club Baseball, Ice Hockey and Rugby. Each year, the Student Activities Organization brings a lively docket of comedians, concerts, films, and lectures to campus. The University is a NCAA Division I member institution and maintains a comprehensive program that consists of men's and women's teams. Students may also participate in cheerleading, pep band, and marching band.

ADMISSIONS PROCESS

Admission to Saint Francis University is granted on rolling basis. All applicants must submit a completed admissions application including essay, an official high-school transcript, ACT or SAT I (critical reading and math) scores, and a minimum of one recommendation letter from an academic source. Students may apply via an online Saint Francis University application or via the Common Application. A November 15 Priority Application deadline applies to the physician assistant program. The physical therapy and occupational therapy programs have a Priority Application deadline of January 15. To learn more about Saint Francis University, students and families are encouraged to call the Office of Admissions at 1-866-DIAL-SFU (toll free).

SAINT LOUIS UNIVERSITY

AT A GLANCE

Saint Louis University was founded in 1818 as the first university west of the Mississippi River. At the core of this diverse community of scholars is SLU's service-focused mission, which prepares students to make the world a better, more just place.

WORLD-CLASS: SLU is a Jesuit, Catholic research university, highly ranked by the Princeton Review and by U.S. News & World Report.

SLU boasts 18 academic programs in the top 50 in their fields and several in the top 10, along with accolades for campus sustainability efforts, military-friendliness and as a "best value" in private education. SLU is also the first Jesuit university to receive the Higher Education Excellence in Diversity Award.

URBAN AND INTERNATIONAL: With two dynamic, urban campuses—in St. Louis, Missouri, and Madrid, Spain—the university is home to nearly 13,000 students from 50 states and 75 countries. SLU's international focus and 45+ study abroad programs invite students to engage with and learn from the global community. The St. Louis campus is a welcoming residential oasis located steps from some of the region's top art and culture venues, while SLU-Madrid puts students in the heart of one of Europe's most vibrant, history-rich cities.

HANDS-ON: One of only nine Catholic universities with a "higher" or "highest" research activity designation, SLU empowers students to collaborate with faculty mentors on groundbreaking research and gain hands-on experience. From developing systems to filter arsenic pollution out of water to exploring innovative ways to get fresh produce into low-income neighborhoods, students don't just contemplate solutions to the day's most challenging problems—they actively work to make those solutions a reality.

SERVICE-MINDED: Jesuit tradition inspires the SLU community's commitment to service and social justice. Designated a "character-building college," SLU was also the first institution named to the President's Higher Education Community Service Honor Roll for nine consecutive years. Students cook meals in the Campus Kitchen, volunteer at student-run medical and law clinics, and work alongside dozens of community organizations to serve their neighbors.

A SLU education gives graduates not only the skills to succeed in their careers but also the wisdom to lead lives of meaning and purpose. SLU alumni have become mayors of major cities, helped put men on the moon, directed Hollywood blockbusters and worked side-by-side with Mother Theresa.

LOCATION AND ENVIRONMENT

At Saint Louis University, students are in the center of everything, whether studying at SLU's Midtown St. Louis campus or SLU's international campus in Madrid, Spain.

ST. LOUIS: SLU's beautiful urban campus in Midtown St. Louis stretches across more than 230 acres of lush greenery, flowers and fountains. Students and visitors alike appreciate the unique vibe of a close-knit community nestled in the middle of a dynamic city.

The St. Louis metro region boasts nearly 3 million people. The city's mix of Midwestern friendliness and large-city amenities has helped St. Louis garner its ranking as one of the best cities for young professionals. In 2015, St. Louis grabbed the No. 1 spot on Popular Mechanics' "Best Startup Cities in America" list. The city also is home to the iconic Gateway Arch and a variety of cultural, historical and sporting attractions.

Students love cheering on the SLU Billikens. The only NCAA Division I school in town, SLU fields teams in 11 different sports, and the Billikens have earned many accolades, including 10 NCAA men's soccer championships—more than any other team in the United States.

MADRID: In 1967, SLU became one of first American universities to establish a foreign campus. Each semester, 750 students from 40+ countries pursue their studies at SLU-Madrid. Southern Europe's greenest city, Madrid offers refreshing parks and a beautiful riverside promenade. The historic central district is easy to cross on foot, and the barrios popular among students are only a few metro stops away—Madrid's mass transit system is among the best in the world.

CAMPUS FACILITIES & EQUIPMENT

During the past three decades, Saint Louis University improvements and expansions have totaled approximately $850 million. In recent years, the University completed some of the most significant building projects in its history, including the $82 million Edward A. Doisy Research Center, which offers SLU's innovative researchers a world-class facility.

SLU's on-campus housing options include two brand-new residence halls, reflecting a nearly $115 million investment in student housing.

Also on campus is the 10,600-seat Chaifetz Arena, which is the home of Billiken basketball and also hosts many of the country's top entertainment acts, and SLU's 70,000-square-foot Center for Global Citizenship. Students can enjoy countless recreational activities at the university's 120,000-square-foot Simon Recreation Center, which features indoor basketball and handball courts, a bouldering wall and an indoor pool.

OFF-CAMPUS OPPORTUNITIES

ST. LOUIS: Midtown St. Louis offers access to affordable living as well as the excitement of the Grand Center arts district, the cultural heart of St. Louis. The booming performing arts neighborhood features opportunities to experience world-class art, theater, dance and music just steps away from SLU's campus.

Minutes away by car, bus or light rail train, students can explore Forest Park, the 1904 World's Fair site that's larger than even New York City's Central Park and home to the city's world-class art museum, zoo, science center and history museum—all free to the public. Check out the Delmar Loop, one of the "10 Great Streets in America," or head to "The Hill," a nationally noted neighborhood for authentic Italian cuisine, including St. Louis' famous toasted ravioli. Then go downtown to catch a game. St. Louis is noted for being one of the nation's best sports cities, and residents root for the St. Louis Cardinals baseball team, St. Louis Blues hockey team, and a bevy of independent sports teams.

MADRID: The city of Madrid is home to 230,000 university students. It's a cosmopolitan capital, a metropolis alive with learning and all that Spanish life has to offer, from flamenco shows to late-night tapas.

Madrid offers cultural experiences to rival any city in Europe, including a Royal Palace, a train station designed by Eiffel, countless theaters, museums and glorious churches. Gorgeous fountains with splashing waters can be found at the intersections of the city's grand, tree-lined avenues, and the city's beautiful parks are ideal for weekend picnics or morning runs.

ACADEMICS

High-achieving young men and women come from around the globe to pursue a world-class education at Saint Louis University. SLU offers nearly 90 undergraduate programs of study and more than 100 graduate and professional programs, with many ranked among the nation's top 50 programs in their respective disciplines.

For the most up-to-date selection of majors and programs offered, visit slu.edu/majors-and-programs.

UNDERGRADUATE PROGRAMS

Accounting °; Aeronautics ^; Aerospace Engineering; African American Studies; American Studies °; Analytics and Enterprise Systems; Anthropology; Art History; Athletic Training °; Aviation Management ^; Biochemistry; Biology ° ^; Biomedical Engineering; Biostatistics; Chemistry °; Civil Engineering; Classical Humanities; Communication ° ^; Communication Sciences and Disorders °; Computer Engineering; Computer Information Systems ^; Computer Science °; Criminology and Criminal Justice °; Economics; Education ^; Electrical Engineering ° ^; Engineering Physics; English ° ^; Entrepreneurship; Environmental Science ^; Environmental Studies ^; Finance; Forensic Science; French °; General Studies; Geology; Geophysics; German Studies; Greek and Latin Languages and Literature; Health Information Management; Health Management; Health Sciences; History °; Information Technology Management; Interdisciplinary Engineering; International Business °; International Studies; Investigative and Medical Sciences; Italian Studies; Latin American Studies; Leadership and Human Resource Management; Magnetic Resonance Imaging; Marketing; Mathematics °; Mechanical Engineering; Medical Laboratory Science; Medieval Studies; Meteorology °; Music ^; Neuroscience; Nuclear Medicine Technology; Nursing ° ^ »; Nutrition and Dietetics ° ^; Occupational Science; Organizational Studies; Organizational Leadership and Technology; Philosophy ° ^; Physics; Physical Therapy (direct-entry doctoral program); Political Science °; Project Management; Psychology °»; Public Health °; Radiation Therapy; Russian Studies; Security and Strategic Intelligence; Social Work °; Sociology ° ^; Spanish °; Sports Business; Studio Art ^; Theatre; Theological Studies ° ^; Women's and Gender Studies °

ADDITIONAL GRADUATE PROGRAMS

Anatomy
Applied Analytics
Applied Behavior Analysis
Applied Financial Economics
Aviation
Biochemistry and Molecular Biology
Bioinformatics and Computational Biology
Business Administration
Curriculum and Instruction
Dentistry »
Educational Foundations
Educational Leadership
Family Therapy
Geographic Information Sciences
Geoscience
Health Administration
Health Care Ethics
Health Data Science
Health Outcomes Research and Evaluation Science
Higher Education Administration
Integrated and Applied Sciences
International Business and Marketing
Law »
Leadership and Organizational Development
Medicine
Molecular Imaging and Therapeutics
Molecular Microbiology and Immunology
Occupational Therapy »
Pathology
Pharmacological and Physiological Science
Physician Assistant
Public Administration
Public and Social Policy
Public Health, Biosecurity and Disaster Preparedness
Public Health Studies
Software Engineering
Special Education
Supply Chain Management
Sustainability
Urban Planning and Development

° Indicates graduate program offered

^ Indicates undergraduate concentrations offered

» Indicates graduate concentrations offered

TUITION, ROOM, BOARD, FEES

Annual tuition for full-time undergraduate students is $41,540. Room and board amounts to approximately $10,874 per student (depending on specific residence hall and board plan). Fees average $626 per year.

FINANCIAL AID

Saint Louis University remains committed to keeping its one-of-a-kind education within reach and understands the sacrifices students and families make for quality education. SLU is dedicated to serving others, in part, by providing financial access to an unparalleled and life-changing educational experience.

In 2017, 96 percent of SLU's first-time freshmen received some sort of scholarship or financial assistance.

Scholarships are awarded based on academic merit, talents, service, leadership and financial need. In addition to SLU's financial aid programs, the state of Missouri and the federal government also provide assistance.

Contact SLU's office of student financial services at 314-977-2350, 800-SLU-FOR-U or sfs@slu.edu.

STUDENT ORGANIZATIONS AND ACTIVITIES

Students participate in about 200 clubs, honor societies and service organizations; 18 NCAA Division I teams; intramural sports; and community service efforts that see 80 percent of SLU students volunteering at least once during the academic year.

Talent and commitment matter at SLU, and high levels of energy and dedication exist in everything Saint Louis University students pursue: academic societies, athletics, performing arts and media groups, student government, cultural and political organizations, and fraternities and sororities. SLU's multicultural organizations highlight and celebrate the diversity of the University community, and a variety of faith-based organizations support and challenge students as they explore their own faith traditions.

ADMISSIONS PROCESS

For information about the admission process at Saint Louis University or to schedule a campus visit, call the office of admission at 800-SLU-FOR-U, email admission@slu.edu, or check out visit.slu.edu.

SAINT MICHAEL'S COLLEGE

AT A GLANCE

Founded in the great Catholic intellectual tradition and steeped in a history promoting social justice and compassion, Saint Michael's is a selective, fully residential college in Vermont's beautiful Green Mountains. Our closely connected community delivers internationally-respected liberal arts and graduate education near Burlington, ranked regularly among the country's best college towns. To prepare for fulfilling careers and meaningful lives, young adults here grow intellectually, socially, and morally, learning to be responsible for themselves, each other and their world.

Saint Michael's College enrolls approximately 1,800 undergraduates; 300 graduates, and more than 150 international students — 55 percent women; 45 percent male. Our students hail from 33 states and 32 countries. Our average class size is 19 students and the student to faculty ratio is 12:1.

A Saint Michael's education is a four-year experience that will change the way you see and care for the world. You'll know your professors—and they'll know you. Our faculty include acclaimed scientists, authors, musicians, historians and directors. And, they are here to teach you: every course is taught by a professor, not a teaching assistant. Our student-faculty ratio is 12:1, with 1:1 advising with a professor in your field of study and guidance not only with your coursework but your plans for the future. Service to the community and to all humankind is at the heart of St. Mike's..

LOCATION AND ENVIRONMENT

Place any town on the shores of Lake Champlain and surround it with mountains and you'd have a special place to go to college. Add the shops, businesses, restaurants and energy that you find in downtown Burlington and you have a place that Travel & Leisure Magazine just named the top college town in America. Burlington is known as one of the healthiest, happiest and most appealing cities in the whole country (one that draws 14,000 college students a year).

Live music, great food from around the world, the beaches of Lake Champlain, the Community Boathouse, the seven-mile bike path, internship-friendly companies like Global Foundries, GE Medical, Burton Snowboards, Dealer.com and Ben and Jerry's, and quick access to top ski areas like Smugglers' Notch, Stowe, and Sugarbush are just part of our location's appeal.

Vermont is green, in more ways than one. The Green Mountains surround campus, providing spectacular views of Camel's Hump and Vermont's highest peak, Mount Mansfield. The Adirondacks of New York are just across the lake. We also care deeply about the environment. On campus, we recycle, we compost, we refill our water bottles, we eat local and shop local. We're a Fair Trade institution and we have our own organic garden and farm stand during the growing season..

Right outside of campus are sites for hiking, rock climbing, river and lake kayaking, and fly fishing. Our Adventure Sports Center will get you into the great outdoors in ways you might never have imagined (ice climbing, perhaps?)

Vermont is not only a beautiful state and Burlington a city with a vibrant cultural scene, it is a place with a scale that offers more opportunities. As a small state with an approachable and welcoming culture, professors can introduce you to almost anyone you might want to meet. That means opportunities for internships, interviews, or important insights on a project are within easy reach.

People come from around the world to visit our part of Vermont. St. Mike's students are lucky enough to make this place their college home.

CAMPUS FACILITIES & EQUIPMENT

Our campus is a 24-hour living and learning community where our students not only eat, sleep and study, but socialize, get involved, develop lifelong friendships and become better citizens. All full-time undergraduates live on campus (unless you live with your family). With more than a dozen residence halls and student apartments, there are plenty of housing options at St. Mike's Dining options provide something for everyone, just about any hour of the day or evening. The Green Mountain Dining Room is open daily from early morning until night and serves three meals a day with unlimited servings. The menu changes daily and includes a variety of main dishes, pizza, a deli counter, burritos, grill specialties, chef's exhibitions, custom salads, soups and desserts. Vegetarian options are always available. The Durick Library supports research and scholarship by students, faculty, and staff. Collections include 460,000 books (including over 230,000 ebooks), 120,000 online journals and magazines, and 5000 DVDs, with 4000 items added each year. The library provides access to state of the art search technology, including 160 research databases and off-campus access to online resources.

Students can operate the telescopes at the Holcomb Observatory on campus. Advanced labs for science students, which includes a new scientific imaging lab and a Nuclear Magnetic Rosonance Spectormeter, are throughout the Cheray Science building with modern and advanced equipment to support the College's vibrant research culture. Other dedicated labs include a Media lab for journalism/digital arts; and for computer students, Canvas, Linux and Mac labs. We also have Learning Resource Center, multiple computer labs and public and teaching labs. Public Safety and Fire & Rescue share quarters in the modern and well-equipped Sutton Station across the street from main campus. Our Chapel of Saint Michael the Archangel is the largest Catholic worship space in Vermont and serves as a gathering space for speakers, music, and community discussions. It is a and welcoming place for students from all backgrounds to gather and contemplate.

OFF-CAMPUS OPPORTUNITIES

Over 70 percent of our students participate in service trips through our Mobilization of Volunteer Efforts (MOVE) office, traveling to sites like soup kitchens in New York City, reservations in South Dakota and animal shelters in Utah. Students at St. Mike's are deeply involved in community service projects and some have taken the initiative to start their own organizations to help the needy or raise awareness about important societal challenges.

Students also gain valuable hands-on experience through our Liberal Arts @ Work program, internships, or do student teaching in their fields. As for going even farther off campus, more than 1/3 of St. Mike's students study abroad, choosing from more than 100 programs based all over the world.

Members of our celebrated and long-established Fire and Rescue Squad serve campus and the surrounding communities 24 hours a day, 365 days a year; interacting closely and frequently with other first-responders and medical professionals.

MAJORS AND DEGREES OFFERED

Saint Michael's College offers 38 majors and 38 minors, all taught by professors (never by teaching assistants) who are highly regarded experts in their fields. The typical class size is 19 students, which means that everyone knows each other by name, and learning happens through conversation as well as through lectures.

As a selective liberal arts college, Saint Michael's fosters intellectual inquiry and challenges and rewards academic achievement. The College is one of only 280 institutions in the country, and one of only four Catholic colleges in the Northeast, to shelter a chapter of Phi Beta Kappa, the nation's oldest and most widely known academic honor society.

In addition to a grounded liberal arts curriculum and ample honors opportunities, St. Mike's Liberal Arts at Work and Life After College programs helps to prepare you for your professional life post-college — this includes introducing new perspectives, developing independent thinking skills, and promoting a greater understanding of the deeper meanings of life.

TUITION, ROOM, BOARD, FEES

Undergraduate Program Tuition and Fees for 2018–2019

Tuition:$45,050

Student Activity Fee: $325

Room and Meals: Traditional Residence Hall $12,220

Total: $57,595

FINANCIAL AID

At Saint Michael's, we will do everything we can to help make your education investment affordable.

°Over 90 percent of our students receive financial aid.

°All admitted students are automatically considered for merit-based scholarships.

°The FAFSA is the only application required to be considered for need-based aid, including grants, loans and work-study.

STUDENT ORGANIZATIONS AND ACTIVITIES

When our students aren't in class, studying or performing research with their professors, you'll find them lining up for concerts at Turtle Underground, rock climbing in Bolton, representing their fellow classmates in our active Student Government, playing lacrosse or field hockey, heading down to the Flynn Center to see a Broadway musical, and so much more.

Learn to be a leader with our Adventure Sports Center leadership training programs—many of our students graduate and become wilderness guides. Or join the family at Fire and Rescue; you'll learn to be a first responder, gain life-saving skills as an EMT and be prepared for a career in health or public service. Write for the Defender, our campus newspaper, and join the long history of student and alumni journalists.

More than 70 percent of our students participate in service, reflecting our passion for and history of social justice. You can explore spirituality through retreats and campus ministry programs, and put faith into action with extended service trips.

ADMISSIONS PROCESS

Saint Michael's has a highly personalized admission process; we will evaluate your application carefully, focusing on your individual strengths and achievements in academics and in your community. We want to get to know you and help you get to know us.

Application Deadlines

Early Action 1—November 1

Early Action 2—December 1

Regular Action—February 1

Notification Dates

Early Action 1—Mid-December

Early Action 2—Late January

Regular Action—Mid-March

Here are the steps you can take to apply to Saint Michael's College:

1. Complete the Common Application.

2. Submit the $50 application fee or a fee waiver.

3. Request that your official high school transcript be sent to the Admission Office, along with the School Report form.

o Applicants using the Common Application will find these forms on the Common App web site.

o Transfer applicants should also request a transcript from their current college.

4. Send us your test scores. St. Mike's is a test optional institution. That means it's your decision whether or not to include standardized test scores. If you choose to do so, you can submit your scores from the SAT 1 (code 3757) or ACT with Writing (code 4312).

5. For 2018 applicants, Saint Michael's College will accept both the new SAT and the old SAT. We will compare your scores using concordance tables to determine your highest scores on either the new SAT or the old SAT.

6. If you are a first-year applicant, you are required to submit one or two recommendations from teachers and/or counselors.

For more information, visit our Common Application information page.

SAN DIEGO STATE UNIVERSITY

AT A GLANCE

San Diego State University is a major public research institution providing transformative experiences and a rich campus life, both inside and outside of the classroom, for its 36,000 undergraduate, graduate and doctoral students.

SDSU is committed to student success and life-changing opportunities for students, such as study abroad, undergraduate research, internships and entrepreneurial experiences. SDSU is the oldest higher education institution in the San Diego region, and these deep community roots provide access to internships, mentoring relationships, and volunteer opportunities that complement and enhance the classroom experience.

LOCATION AND ENVIRONMENT

SDSU's campus is within a 15-minute drive of downtown San Diego and the Pacific Ocean and only two hours south of Los Angeles. The second largest city in California, San Diego is a thriving cultural, scientific and educational center. Bordering the Pacific Rim and Mexico, San Diego is recognized globally as a dynamic international hub. SDSU's mission revival architecture reflects the diversity and history of the region, with bell towers, beautiful arched walkways and ornamental ironwork.

CAMPUS FACILITIES & EQUIPMENT

SDSU's campus is a unique blend of old and new, classic and modern. The exterior of the Conrad Prebys Aztec Student Union, for example, draws inspiration from historic mission revival architecture. But its interior is an ultramodern double LEED Platinum certified hub for student organizations, events and activity. The recently opened Engineering and Interdisciplinary Sciences Complex also embraces the Spanish-style architecture with an interior that features state-of-the-art labs and collaborative teaching space necessary for transformative innovation and exploration.

ACADEMIC PROGRAMS

SDSU ranks in the top 10 universities nationwide in the number of students who study abroad to gain new perspectives and to grow personally and intellectually. More than 3,000 SDSU students study abroad each year in more than 70 countries, including the United Kingdom, China, Italy, Mexico and Spain.

Campus-based academic programs and centers reinforce this global perspective. They include the Center for International Business Education and Research; the Center for Latin American Studies; the International Security and Conflict Resolution degree program; and the International Business major, which ranks No. 12 in the nation.

Additionally, SDSU is dedicated to entrepreneurship and innovation and encourages students to turn their ideas into tangible products that will benefit their communities both locally and globally. Entrepreneurship at SDSU involves a unique blend of coursework and experiential learning opportunities. This combination enables students to adopt innovative thinking and develop the competencies they will need to succeed in today's society.

MAJORS AND DEGREES OFFERED

SDSU is an academically comprehensive university that provides endless possibilities for students: bachelor's degrees in 91 areas, master's degrees in 78 fields, and 22 doctoral degrees (Ph.D., Ed.D., Au.D., DNP, and DPT). SDSU is a place for the best and brightest to study disciplines from biology and viromics to international business, entrepreneurship, musical theatre and more.

TUITION, ROOM, BOARD, FEES

SDSU is consistently ranked among the best value universities in the nation and for the number of students graduating with the least amount of debt. California resident students are charged flat rate tuition and fees depending on enrollment. Full-time fees are charged for students who enroll in more than 6 units; part time fees are charged for students enrolling in 6 or fewer units. In addition to basic tuition and fees, nonresident and international students pay non-resident tuition. SDSU has a wide variety of on-campus housing and dining options. Costs vary depending on location, number of roommates, and meal plan chosen.

FINANCIAL AID

To apply for all federal, state, and institutional aid, file a Free Application for Federal Student Aid (FAFSA) as soon as possible after October 1st. Be sure to check AidLink, SDSU's online financial aid system, regularly to see if additional documentation is needed.

SDSU offers a large number of scholarships based on need, academic merit, and other criteria. Scholarship applications are submitted online, and the largest scholarship cycle runs from August through February.

STUDENT ORGANIZATIONS AND ACTIVITIES

Diversity is a hallmark of the SDSU community of 36,000 students. Upon becoming Aztecs, students embrace the more than 121-year history of SDSU and its mission of education, research and service. They are active in more than 300 different student clubs and organizations, many of which participate in community service and philanthropic projects. Our students are enthusiastic supporters of Aztec Athletics; in fact, The Show, a legion of men's basketball fans, has created a game-day atmosphere rivaled by few in the nation.

Faculty in SDSU's eight colleges are equally committed to ensuring student success and advancing research in their fields. Our faculty members author definitive textbooks in their fields, chair national academic organizations, publish research in peer-reviewed journals, and receive research funding from the National Institutes of Health and the National Science Foundation. At the same time, they are skilled teachers and mentors, drawing on knowledge of the latest developments in their fields to enrich the classroom experience.

Through partnerships, education and programming, SDSU's Career Services Department provides current Aztecs and Aztec alumni with many opportunities to define, develop and realize their career potential. We work closely with employers and community partners to fill important staffing and internship positions from within the diverse and talented student body. Career Services oversees two important programs—the Aztec Mentor Program, which pairs more than 1,200 students with alumni mentors in their chosen fields, and Aztecs Hiring Aztecs, which works with alumni-owned and -operated businesses to transition recent graduates into the workplace.

ADMISSIONS PROCESS

SDSU attracts highly qualified students each year. The average high school GPA for fall 2017 admitted freshmen was 3.88 with an average SAT Reasoning (critical reading and math) score of 1229 or ACT score of 27.

Students can apply online at https://www2.calstate.edu/apply between Oct. 1 and Nov. 30, 2018 for fall 2019 admission.

The following criteria is used to evaluate applications:

1. Eligibility Index (a calculation of GPA and SAT/ACT scores)

2. Completion of the "a-g" college prep curriculum

3. Intended major

For more information about applying to SDSU for fall 2019 admission, visit sdsu.edu/admissions.

SCHOOL OF VISUAL ARTS

AT A GLANCE

School of Visual Arts, located in the heart of New York City, has been a leader in the education of artists, designers and creative professionals for over seven decades. With a faculty of more than 1,000 distinguished working professionals, a dynamic curriculum and an emphasis on critical thinking, SVA is a catalyst for innovation and social responsibility. Comprising more than 6,000 students at its Manhattan campus and 35,000 alumni in 100 countries, SVA also represents one of the most influential artistic communities in the world.

Bachelor of Fine Arts degrees are offered in Advertising; Animation; Cartooning; Computer Art, Computer Animation and Visual Effects; Design, Film; Fine Arts; Illustration; Interior Design; Photography and Video; and Visual & Critical Studies.

Master of Arts degrees are offered in Critical Theory and the Arts; Curatorial Practice; and Design Research, Writing and Criticism.

Master of Fine Arts degrees are offered in Art Practice; Art Writing; Computer Arts; Design; Design for Social Innovation; Fine Arts; Illustration as Visual Essay; Interaction Design; Photography, Video and Related Media; Products of Design; Social Documentary Film; and Visual Narrative.

Master of Professional Studies degrees are offered in Art Therapy, Branding, Digital Photography, Directing, and Fashion Photography.

A Master of Arts in Teaching degree is offered in Art Education.

SVA also offers workshops, continuing education classes, studio residencies, international student programs, summer programs abroad, and a pre-college program for high school students.

For more information on the College and its offerings, visit sva.edu.

LOCATION AND ENVIRONMENT

SVA's urban-style campus comprises 15 buildings with state-of-the-art studio facilities, workshops, residence halls and gallery spaces. As the creative capital of the world, New York City is home to more artists than any other U.S. city, with a creative workforce of 300,000. It is also home to over 14,000 creative businesses and non-profits. Students come here to be immersed in real-world experience, not the insulated experience of other schools. Surrounded by a thriving and artistic urban environment during their years at SVA, students are able to transition to the working world with ease, finding unique opportunities for internships and mentorships.

MAJORS AND DEGREES OFFERED

Bachelor of Fine Arts degrees are offered in Advertising; Animation; Cartooning; Computer Art, Computer Animation & Visual Effects; Design; Illustration; Interior Design; Film; Fine Arts; Photography and Video; and Visual and Critical Studies.

A Master of Arts degrees is offered in Critical Theory and The Arts, and Design Research, Writing and Criticism.

Master of Fine Arts degrees are offered in Art Writing; Art Practice; Computer Arts; Design; Design for Social Innovation; Fine Arts; Illustration as Visual Essay; Interaction Design; Photography, Video and Related Media; Products of Design; Social Documentary Film; and Visual Narrative.

Master of Professional Studies degrees are offered in Art Therapy; Branding; Digital Photography; Directing; and Fashion Photography.

A Master of Arts in Teaching degree is offered in Art Education.

TUITION, ROOM, BOARD, FEES

Expenses for 2018–2019

Application fee: $50

Tuition: $39,900 per year for undergraduate programs; for Graduate program tuition, please visit http://www.sva.edu/students/student-accounts/tuition-and-fees

Departmental fees: $640 to $1,465 per semester depending on undergraduate major

Estimated Supplies: $1,050 to $3,150

Housing Charges: range from $15,000 to $18,500 per year

FINANCIAL AID

Currently, 43 percent of SVA first-time freshmen receive some form of financial aid. Undergraduate merit scholarships are also available through Admissions. A payment plan is available.

STUDENT ORGANIZATIONS AND ACTIVITIES

The Student Engagement and Leadership Office provides a diverse range of programming designed to enrich the SVA student's experience. Students are offered the opportunity to tap into a multitude of social, cultural, educational and recreational activities. Students are encouraged to take advantage of all New York City has to offer.

The Visual Arts Student Association (VASA), the student government, represents the students' point of view at SVA. Participating in VASA gives students the opportunity to develop leadership skills by coordinating events and activities. VASA funds and supports a number of clubs and activities that are organized by students.

ADMISSIONS PROCESS

Undergraduate Application Deadlines:

Deadline for freshman and transfers: rolling

Deadline for Early Action: December 1

Deadline for all application materials to be submitted for the Silas H. Rhodes Scholarship Program: February 1 for first-time freshman applicants and March 1 for transfer applicants. There is no separate application for the Silas H. Rhodes Scholarship Program.

Requirements:

-Application for Undergraduate Admission

-A nonrefundable $50 application fee

-Official transcripts from all high schools and colleges attended

-Results of the SAT or ACT

-Statement of intent

-Portfolio

-Interview (optional)

-Demonstration of English proficiency (required of all international applicants whose primary language is not English)

SEATTLE UNIVERSITY

AT A GLANCE

Students who are adventurous, forward-thinking, creative and have an interest in social justice are drawn to Seattle University, located in the heart of a city with unparalleled access to innovation and culture. With more than 65 academic programs across five schools and colleges, Seattle University offers students an education that is both contemporary and rooted in a nearly 500-year-old Jesuit Catholic tradition. Our curriculum and character stretch far beyond the classroom and into the world that surrounds us.

Our 4,600 undergraduate students have endless opportunities for career development and exploration. You can spend your summer interning for a Fortune 500 company in downtown Seattle and your evenings hanging out where music fans first discovered Nirvana. It all begins here at Seattle University. That first class. That first student club. That moment when you and your peers look around and realize that in a city so full of culture and history, you are one of the ones prepared to make a difference.

LOCATION AND ENVIRONMENT

Our 50-acre campus, in the vibrant Capitol Hill neighborhood, was designated an official Backyard Sanctuary by the Washington State Fish and Wildlife Department. While Seattle University is located in the heart of the Emerald City, our campus maintains a traditional feel; students are members of a vibrant university community with a NCAA Division I athletic program and more than 130 student clubs.

CAMPUS FACILITIES & EQUIPMENT

The university is considered an "urban oasis" between the First Hill and Capitol Hill neighborhoods in the center of Seattle. The campus has 28 buildings enhanced by $200 million in additions, renovations or new construction in the past 15 years.

A major expansion of the campus library, now the Lemieux Library and McGoldrick Learning Commons, provides state-of-the-art digital learning opportunities. The library's media production center features a recording studio, control room, audio/video editing facilities and a theater-style screening room.

The College of Nursing's 20,000-square-foot Clinical Performance Lab is among the most technically advanced in the nation, with two clinical practice rooms and a suite of laboratories. The state-of-the-art William F. Eisiminger Fitness Center, tennis courts, track and both natural and synthetic turf playing fields draw students in their off hours. School spirit gets a big boost from Division I athletics, and the university completed a renovation of the Connolly Complex in 2016 to improve the experience of athletes and spectators alike.

OFF-CAMPUS OPPORTUNITIES

The immersive city of Seattle makes learning second nature. On campus, our facilities are state-of-the-art, while off campus, art, culture and nightlife are in a constant state of reinvention—and all within walking distance. One minute you're studying in the acclaimed Lemieux Library and McGoldrick Learning Commons, the next you're feasting on world-class sushi then discovering a rock legend-in-the-making long before Spotify does.

ACADEMICS

At the center of Seattle University's Jesuit academic experience is the Core Curriculum. With an emphasis on rigorous, contemporary courses, the Core is comprised of 12 classes to be taken over four years. Classes have been designed by faculty members who have used their expertise to shape the content of each class, and the curriculum invites students into engaged learning about themselves, their communities and the world. A few interesting sample course titles include: "The Rhetoric of Sustainable Food," "Biotech: Problem or Solution?," "Cross Cultural Perspectives," and "Potions for Muggles."

Designed to help students develop intellectual abilities, there's a strong liberal arts focus with broad exposure to the humanities, social sciences, natural sciences and arts. Instead of broad survey courses, Core courses focus on specific questions. The study of those questions gives students a closer look at a discipline and how knowledge is pursued. There's also a focus on global engagement so students can examine their roles in local, regional, national and transnational cultures and communities.

Study abroad programs at Seattle University range in length from one week, one summer, an entire academic year abroad and everywhere in between. Seattle University students come to understand the motivations, ideologies and cultures of other people by simply living among them. Each year, some 550 students travel, learn and make positive impact through community service in more than 55 countries.

MAJORS AND DEGREES OFFERED

The university offers 65 majors and 31 minors in five colleges and schools: Albers School of Business and Economics, College of Arts and Sciences, College of Nursing, College of Science and Engineering and Matteo Ricci College. Undergraduate degrees include Bachelor of Arts, of Science, of Science in Nursing, of Social Work, of Criminal Justice and of Arts in Business Administration. For specifics on majors and minors, visit the Seattle University website at seattleu.edu.

TUITION, ROOM, BOARD, FEES

For the 2018–2019 academic year, full-time tuition is $43,785; room and meals are $12,288. The estimate for books, supplies, fees and personal expenses is an additional $5,535. Costs are subject to change. Seattle University operates on a quarter calendar with fall term beginning in late September. Students are required to live on campus for their first two years, and six on-campus residence halls house more than 2,000 students.

FINANCIAL AID

More than 87 percent of undergraduates in 2016–17 received financial aid; the average award was more than $28,000. These awards usually include scholarships, grants, loans and Federal Work-Study. Last year, Seattle University awarded more than $116 million in aid to undergraduates. Students are required to apply for financial aid by Feb. 1, as awards are made early each spring for the following fall quarter. Applications that are received after this deadline will be evaluated in the order received for any remaining aid. Students must submit the Free Application for Federal Student Aid (FAFSA) and be accepted for admission to be considered for financial assistance. A number of freshman scholarships are awarded on the basis of academic achievement, extracurricular involvement and community service. Transfer scholarships also are available.

STUDENT ORGANIZATIONS AND ACTIVITIES

Student Government of Seattle University promotes opportunities for student leadership and involvement and assists in the development of a cohesive undergraduate community. You also can take your pick from more than 130 extracurricular clubs and organizations.

Seattle University students accomplish just as much outside of the classroom as they do in it. Get steeped in the Seattle coffee scene with the Coffee Club. Dig for the truth with the student newspaper, The Spectator. Land an on-air role at KXSU 102.1 FM, the student-run radio station. Or roll up your sleeves to be an advocate and ally for LGBTQ with the Triangle Club. If you have a love for it, we probably have a club for it.

ADMISSIONS PROCESS

Seattle University is committed to qualitative decision making based on evaluations of students as a whole. Decisions are based primarily on individual course selection, performance and trends. The expected academic program comprises 16 units of coursework, including four years of English, three years of social studies or history, two years of a foreign language, three years of college-preparatory mathematics and two units of lab science (three are preferred). Laboratory physics and chemistry, as well as four units of college-preparatory mathematics are required for engineering; the university also requires laboratory chemistry and biology for admission to the nursing program. Also required for all programs are official scores from either the ACT or the SAT. The middle 50 percent of enrolling freshmen have secondary school averages of 3.4–3.9 (on a 4.0 scale).

Essays or personal statements are required for admission and are carefully considered during application review. College credit is awarded to those who have successfully earned minimum scores on Advanced Placement or International Baccalaureate examinations.

Applications and information can be obtained by contacting the Admissions Office. Secondary school students who have completed at least six semesters are encouraged to complete the application process no later than Jan. 15 of their senior year, the deadline for regular admission. For those who wish to apply via Early Action, the deadline is Nov. 15. Transfer students must submit official transcripts from all post-secondary institutions attended, regardless of whether course work was completed. The recommended financial aid/admission deadline for transfers is March 1, however transfer applications are welcomed until Aug. 15.

Campus visits are scheduled Monday through Friday and many Saturdays. Guests can attend a class, meet with faculty, participate in a campus tour and speak individually with representatives from admissions.

Students can apply directly or online at seattleu.edu. Seattle University is a member of The Common Application.

SETON HALL UNIVERSITY

AT A GLANCE

As one of the nation's leading Catholic universities, Seton Hall provides over 90 rigorous academic programs that are highly ranked by The Princeton Review, U.S. News & World Report and Bloomberg Businessweek. We offer all the advantages of a large research university national reputation; challenging academic programs; notable alumni; state-of-the-art facilities; renowned faculty; and extensive opportunities for internships, research and scholarship with all the benefits of a small, supportive and nurturing environment. Our 14:1 student-to-faculty ratio and average class size of 21 students means faculty know more than just your name.

Our accomplished faculty include Fulbright Scholars, prominent researchers, authors, artists, filmmakers, former school superintendents and principals, leaders in nursing, former ambassadors, analysts and lawmakers-all of whom are dedicated to their fields and their students. They have graduated from some of the nation's leading institutions, including Seton Hall, Harvard, Columbia, Yale, Princeton, and Dartmouth. Each day, our faculty members shine in the lecture halls and on the national stage. They meet regularly with students outside the classroom and help them develop great minds.

Seton Hall offers more than 17,000 internship opportunities, and over 80 percent of our students have an internship or two on their resume before graduation, this is just one of the reasons our students have a 90 percent employment rate after graduation and mid-career earnings 50 percent higher than the national average. In fact, Seton Hall was recently ranked top 5 in the nation for providing internship opportunities. Our national reputation and stellar academic programs draw over 550 employers to campus each year just to recruit our graduates. Seton Hall has also been rated as one of the best schools for a return on your investment and for having the highest paid graduates for the investment and Forbes has rated Seton Hall one of America's Best Value Colleges

Seton Hall is a Catholic university with over a 160-year tradition of educational excellence. A welcoming community, Seton Hall embraces students of all faiths and inspires students to become servant leaders who make a difference in the world. That's why our community performs over 40,000 hours of community service annually. You'll feel at home on our campus, where it's easy to make friends and get involved.

LOCATION AND ENVIRONMENT

Nestled in the suburban village of South Orange, New Jersey, Seton Hall provides small-town charm combined with big-city opportunities. The University's suburban, 58-acre park-like campus sits proudly within this picturesque town with tree-lined streets; historic, gracious homes; and quaint shops just 14 miles from New York City close to all the action, yet not engulfed by it.

Just a five-minute walk from campus lands you in the middle of a bustling town center where you'll find diners and pizzerias, banks, pharmacies, Starbucks, Cold Stone Creamery, a gourmet marketplace, South Orange Performing Arts Center, a movie Theatre, and so much more. You might not ever want to leave this quiet suburbia, but if you do, the train station, right in the center of town, is your direct link to NYC's Penn Station just 30 minutes away.

We take full advantage of all the Big Apple has to offer-where the worlds of entertainment, art, publishing, global finance, international diplomacy and fashion collide. NYC is also one of the world's largest job markets, brimming with internship and job placement opportunities in a variety of companies. Over 80 percent of Seton Hall students have an internship or two on their resume before graduation at leading companies like Goldman Sacs, American Express, CNN, the Secret Service, Merck, Lincoln Center, The New York Mets, the United Nations, The New York Times, NBC, Prudential, Sony Music, JP Morgan Chase and more.

And if all the advantage and opportunity of the Big Apple aren't enough, New Jersey's got you covered. One of the wealthiest states in the nation, New Jersey is brimming with opportunity. Seton Hall's backyard boasts a powerhouse corporate corridor of more than 50 Fortune 500 companies, pharmaceutical giants and major corporations. For you this means networking, internships and career opportunities.

CAMPUS FACILITIES & EQUIPMENT

Seton Hall places a strong emphasis on the use of state-of-the-art technology, facilities and support services to aid in its students' development. Many investments have been made to the campus infrastructure, including the recent construction of a new academic classroom building, new residence hall space, a new parking deck, a Dunkin Donuts and a new state of the art recreation and fitness center. In addition, the campus boasts a state-of-the-art research library complete with a computerized catalog and 200 computer terminals. The Science and Technology Center, is home to state-of-the-future biology and chemistry labs, an atrium and auditorium, as well as an observatory and greenhouse. The campus also offers man unique learning labs like our Mock Trading Room, Patient Simulation Laboratory, Market Research Center, Sport Polling Center and WSOU, the number 1 ranked college radio station in the nation.

ACADEMIC PROGRAMS

Seton Hall offers over 90 rigorous academic programs in seven undergraduate colleges. They have excellent programs in business, education, communication, diplomacy and International relations, nursing, humanities, social sciences, biology, chemistry, physics as well as direct admission joint degree programs in physical therapy, athletic training, occupational therapy, physician assistant and speech language pathology. In 2018 they are slated to open a new medical school in partnership with NJ's leading Hospital Hackensack University Medical center. The University plans to offer direct admission BS/MD programs in the near future. The New School of Medicine will be located in Clifton & Nutley, NJ on the former site of Roche Pharmaceuticals. The site will also house our School of Health and Medical Sciences as well as our College of Nursing which is ranked in the top 5 percent of Nursing programs nationwide.

Seton Hall's Stillman School of Business has the number one rated leadership program in the country and has AACSB accreditation, the most rigorous accreditation a business school can hold, putting them in the top 10 percent of business schools in the world and their accounting program in the top 1 percent in the world. Graduates of the business school, along with graduates of the College of Communication and the Arts, The College or Education and the School of Diplomacy and International Relations have 100 percent admit rates into graduate school and nearly a 100 percent employment rate for students within six months of graduation. Seton Hall also has a 93 percent admit rate into medical school for its pre-med students.

MAJORS AND DEGREES OFFERED

Accounting•
Accounting (5-year B.S./M.S. dual-degree∞)
Africana Studies•
American Humanics√
Ancient Greek†
Anthropology•
Applied Scientific Mathematics†
Arabic†
Archaeology†
Art (Art History•, Fine Arts•, Graphic Interactive and Advertising Design•)
Art (BA/MA in Museum Professions)§
Asian Studies•
Athletic Training (5-year B.S./M.S. or B.A./M.S. dual-degree)∞
Biochemistry
Biology (B.A. or B.S.)
Broadcasting and Visual Media•
Business Administration•‡
Catholic Studies•‡
Catholic Theology•
Chemistry•
Classical Culture†
Classical Languages†
Classical Studies•
Communication Studies (B.A./M.A. in Communication or Public Relations)∞
Computer Graphics√
Computer Science•
Creative Writing
Criminal Justice•
Cybersecurity√
Data Visualization and Analysis√
Digital Media and Video√

Digital Media Production for the Web√
Diplomacy and International Relations•
Early Childhood Education (integrated with elementary and special education)
Elementary Education (integrated with early childhood and special education)
Education with Speech Language Pathology (6-year B.S.E./M.S. dual degree)∞
Economics (B.A. or B.S.)
Engineering (Biomedical, Chemical, Civil, Computer, Electrical, Industrial, Mechanical)§
English•
Entrepreneurial Studies‡
Environmental Sciences†
Environmental Studies•
Ethics and Applied Ethics†
Finance
French•
Gerontology√
History•
Information Technologies√
Information Technology Management‡
International Business†
International Relations
Italian•
Italian Studies†
Journalism•
Latin†
Latin America and Latino/Latina Studies•
Law (3+3 with Seton Hall Law)∞
Legal Studies in Business†
Liberal Studies
Management
Marketing
Mathematical Finance
Mathematics•
M.B.A. (5-year B.S./M.B.A. or B.A./ M.B.A. dual-degree)∞
Modern Languages
Music (Comprehensive Music/Music Education, Music Performance•)
Musical Theatre†
Nonprofit Studies†
Nursing
Occupational Therapy (6-year B.A./M.S. dual-degree)∞
Online Course Development and Management√
Philosophical Theology√
Philosophy•
Physical Therapy (6-year B.S./D.P.T. dual-degree)∞
Physician Assistant (6-year B.S./M.S. dual-degree)∞
Physics (B.A. or B.S.)•
Political Science•
Pre-Dental°
Pre-Law°
Pre-Medical°
Pre-Optometry°
Pre-Veterinary°
Psychology (B.A. or B.S.)•
Religion•
Russian†
Russian and East European Studies†√
Secondary Education (optional integration with special education)
Social and Behavioral Sciences
Social Work•
Sociology•
Spanish•
Special Education (integrated with early childhood, elementary, and secondary education)
Speech Language Pathology (6-year B.S.E./M.S. dual degree)∞

School Says . . .

Sport Management•
Supply Chain Management√
Theatre•
Web Design√
Women and Gender Studies†
Writing†
Undecided

• Minor also available

† Minor only

√ Certificate program only

‡ Certificate program also available

§ Dual-degree Program with NJIT

∞ Seton Hall dual-degree program (please contact the Office of Admissions for details)

° Pre-professional programs (you must also select a major)

TUITION, ROOM, BOARD, FEES

Seton Hall offers a flat-tuition rate for students taking between 12–18 credit hours. The 2017–18 tuition and fees are $40,888. Room and Board fees range depending on meal plans; however, an average cost is $13,502.

FINANCIAL AID

Paying for college is a major investment. Seton Hall University is committed to providing students with the resources needed to make your dreams a reality. The University gives over $96 million in aid each year and 98 percent of our students receive some form of financial aid with 97 percent receiving scholarships or grants directly from the University. Seton Hall University has been rated as one of the best schools in the nation for a return on your investment. Most scholarships are automatically awarded upon admission and do not require a separate application. However there are also several special scholarships for which students can apply learn more at shu.edu/go/scholarships. Seton Hall also provides need-based aid to eligible students who complete the Free Application for Federal Student Aid (FAFSA) form by November 1.

STUDENT ORGANIZATIONS AND ACTIVITIES

On campus, Great minds learn to put their ideas into action; discover something new; become part of a community; and build trust, spirit and lasting friendships. Here, you'll find activities galore, over 130 clubs and organizations and 22 Greek societies. You can audition for one of the nearly dozen theatre performances cast each year or broadcast at the #1 ranked college radio station in the nation, WSOU-FM, which attracts more than 120,000 listeners a week from the NYC area. Join the Brownson Speech and Debate Team, ranked in the Top 20 college and university forensic teams for years or write for one of our three student newspapers. You'll not only make lots of new friends and have fun, you'll also learn about your leadership style. More than two-thirds of our students participate in clubs and organizations.

You don't have to be a superstar athlete to be part of the game at Seton Hall. Our athletic programs include competition on varsity, intramural and club levels. In fact, almost 50 percent of our students participate in club or intramural sports. Even if you don't know a handball from a handoff, you'll be decked out in blue and cheering your heart out when you attend any one of Seton Hall's 14 NCAA division I Big East athletic events. So grab your friends and catch some Pirate fever!

ADMISSIONS PROCESS

At Seton Hall, we take a holistic approach to reviewing your application. When we receive your application, we start by considering your academic performance in high school, your grades and the rigor of your curriculum, as well as your standardized SAT and/or ACT scores. These are essential indicators of your ability to succeed at Seton Hall. We also will consider your personal essay, recommendations and extracurricular activities.

For more information, contact the Office of Undergraduate Admission:
Website: admissions.shu.edu
Telephone: 1-800-THE-HALL (843-4255)
E-mail: thehall@shu.edu
#halladmissions
Text: 973-996-8181

SKIDMORE COLLEGE

AT A GLANCE

Founded in 1903, Skidmore College is an independent, coeducational, liberal arts college in Saratoga Springs, N.Y., that prides itself on its creative approaches to just about everything. Creativity is at our core. It powers the way we think, communicate, and do. We boldly declare that, here, at Skidmore, more than anything, Creative Thought Matters. With a diverse student body of 2,500 students from 44 states and 67 countries and a faculty of 304 dedicated teacher-scholars, Skidmore offers 43 majors in the arts, humanities, sciences, and social sciences, as well as in pre-professional fields.

Skidmore is known for its interdisciplinary approach to learning, faculty-student collaborative research, funded research opportunities, off-campus study, and the prominence of the performing and visual arts. The college's rigorous academic program begins with the foundational First-Year Experience, which integrates the curricular and cocurricular and gets students involved in the life of the community from day one. Students enjoy close relationships with faculty members who have earned recognition through Guggenheim, Pulitzer, and Emmy awards, and fellowships and grants from Fulbright, MacArthur, the National Science Foundation, and others. Half of our students carry two majors or add a related minor to their major, and nearly 60 percent are attending graduate or professional school or have completed advanced degrees within five years of graduation.

LOCATION AND ENVIRONMENT

Skidmore truly offers the best of both worlds—a beautiful, safe, and expansive campus and an active, thriving hometown in Saratoga Springs, one of the most interesting and vibrant small cities in the US. Famed for its "health, history, and horses," Saratoga Springs is a popular year-round cultural and tourist destination. The Saratoga Performing Arts Center is summer home to the New York City Ballet, Philadelphia Orchestra, and Opera Saratoga, and is a performing venue for top rock and jazz musicians. And downtown Saratoga is brimming with galleries, museums, shops, coffeehouses, bistros, and restaurants. No wonder Travel & Leisure named it the sixth-best college town in the nation. The city's location near the foothills of the Adirondack Mountains puts an abundance of outdoor recreational opportunities within an hour's drive, including great downhill and Nordic skiing. Boston, New York City, and Montreal are each approximately 180 miles from campus.

CAMPUS FACILITIES & EQUIPMENT

Skidmore's 1,000-acre campus offers buildings that are designed and arranged to blend with the natural surroundings and to foster intellectual and social interaction. The newest academic building, the Arthur Zankel Music Center, features a spectacular 600-seat recital hall and a state-of-the-art recording studio. The beautifully renovated Murray-Aikins Dining Hall boasts a variety of food stations and intimate seating arrangements. On the residential side, the Sussman Village Apartment project was completed in late 2013, enabling 94 percent of Skidmore's student body to reside on campus. And field hockey, lacrosse, soccer, and softball venues have all been recently outfitted with the latest turf fields.

In 2014, Skidmore installed a solar array that meets 12 percent of Skidmore's electricity needs. Also in 2014, Skidmore began receiving 18 percent of its electricity needs through the college's own hydro dam. Forty percent of Skidmore's heating and cooling needs come through geothermal energy, the most of any organization in the region. Soon more than half of campus building space will be heated and cooled through geothermal energy, with a goal of 60 percent by 2025.

ACADEMIC PROGRAMS

Skidmore offers numerous pre-professional and cooperative programs: prelaw advising; premedical/health professions advising; 4+1 M.B.A. programs (Clarkson, RIT); Whitman M.B.A. Advantage Program, 4+1 M.S.A., and 4+1 M.S.F. (Syracuse); dual-degree engineering programs (Clarkson, Dartmouth, RPI); B.S.N. (NYU School of Nursing); dual-degree programs in occupational therapy and physical therapy (Sage Graduate School); M.S. in Accountancy (Wake Forest); M.S. in Teaching (Clarkson); internships (academic credit, funded summer programs); applied civic-engagement courses; Periclean Honors Forum; faculty-student collaborative research (academic year and summer program); international and domestic off-campus study options; and the Moore Documentary Studies Collaborative.

Off-campus study: With more than 60 percent of students studying abroad at some point during their college years, Skidmore was recently ranked in the top ten on the list of top 40 baccalaureate institutions for number of students studying abroad for a semester. Students can choose from 120 approved programs in more than 45 countries, including Skidmore-run programs in England, France, New Zealand, and Spain.

MAJORS AND DEGREES OFFERED

Skidmore offers bachelor degrees in the following 43 majors: American studies, anthropology, art (studio), art history, Asian studies, biology, business (business-French, business-German, business-Spanish, and business-political science), chemistry, classics, computer science, dance, economics, education studies, English, environmental science, environmental studies, exercise science, French, gender studies, geosciences, German, history, international affairs, mathematics, music, neuroscience, philosophy, physics, political science (political science-French, political science-German, and political science-Spanish), psychology, religious studies, a self-determined major, social work, sociology, Spanish, and theater.

Most majors have minors. Others include arts administration, Chinese, intergroup relations, Italian, Japanese, Latin American studies, and media and film studies.

TUITION, ROOM, BOARD, FEES

Skidmore 2017–18 costs are as follows: tuition/fees: $52,446; room: $8,278 (dorm double); and board: $5,726.

FINANCIAL AID

Skidmore annually provides $45 million in financial aid on the basis of demonstrated financial need. The most recent first-year aid package was $42,000, ranging from $2,000 to $65,000; 42 percent of students received need-based grants; 50 percent received some form of financial aid; and 50 percent took advantage of the opportunity to work on campus. Average post-college student debt (just under $23,000) is well below the national average.

Aid is provided in the form of a student-aid package that usually includes a grant, campus job, and loan. We encourage any student interested in applying for admission to do so regardless of his or her intention to seek financial aid. A great place to start is our Skidmore student aid calculator, which will give you an idea for where you stand. A Free Application for Federal Student Aid (FAFSA), a copy of the federal income tax form, and the CSS Profile must be filed each year.

Skidmore also hosts an annual Filene Music Scholarship Competition to award four to six $60,000 ($15,000 per year) scholarships on the basis of musical ability without regard to financial need. Five to seven $15,000 Porter Presidential Scholarships in Science and Mathematics scholarships are also awarded annually ($60,000 over four years).

STUDENT ORGANIZATIONS AND ACTIVITIES

Students: Skidmore's 2,500 students come from 44 states and 67 countries; 41 percent are men, 59 percent women; 23 percent are domestic students of color and 11 percent international students; 6 percent of students carry dual passports; and 13 percent are first-generation college students.

Additional Information Varsity sports: A founding member of the highly competitive NCAA, Division III Liberty League, Skidmore offers 19 varsity sports: baseball, basketball (men and women), field hockey, golf, ice hockey, lacrosse (men and women), riding, rowing (men and women), soccer (men and women), softball, swimming/diving (men and women), tennis (men and women), and volleyball. Liberty League members are Bard, Clarkson, Hobart & William Smith, Ithaca, RPI, RIT, Rochester, St. Lawrence, Skidmore, Union, and Vassar.

Student clubs/organizations/leadership: Whether you engage in one of Skidmore's 120 student clubs or serve as a residential advisor, a varsity athlete or intramural participant, a student gardener, or a volunteer in a local school, you will find opportunities to use your creativity and round yourself out while giving back to the larger community.

Student Academic Services (SAS) serves all Skidmore students interested in strengthening their academic performance or skills by organizing peer tutoring, study groups, and drop-in tutoring and by offering professional one-on-one and small-group academic support. SAS collaborates with other campus offices and faculty to support Skidmore students with specific responsibility for international students, English Language Learners, students of color, student-athletes, and students with disabilities.

ADMISSIONS PROCESS

In 2017–18, Skidmore received more than 10,500 applications for a first-year class targeted at about 660 (including 35 students spending their first semester in London); 25 percent were offered admission; nearly half enrolled through Early Decision.

Those seeking admission to Skidmore's first-year class should complete a secondary-school curriculum that includes at least 16 credits in college-preparatory courses. The Admissions Committee also considers applications from qualified high school juniors who plan to accelerate and enter college early. Applicants typically have completed four years of English, a foreign language, mathematics, and social studies, and three to four years of laboratory science. Applicants must provide a secondary school transcript, letters of recommendation from two teachers of academic subjects, and a report from their guidance counselor. Skidmore encourages a campus visit and interview.

Skidmore is test-optional when it comes to standardized testing (SAT, ACT), though the college does require standardized test results from international students other than those who have attended an English language–based school for at least three years, homeschooled students, and students attending secondary schools offering written evaluations without accompanying grades. Applicants for the Porter Presidential Scholarships in Science and Mathematics are encouraged to submit SAT/ACT and any SAT subject tests in math and science. Of course, students may submit either the SAT or ACT if they feel their standardized testing results best represent their academic potential.

Through its participation in the Higher Education Opportunity Program (HEOP), Skidmore enrolls capable and ambitious New Yorkers who, because of their academic and financial situations, would not otherwise gain admission to the college under traditional requirements. Skidmore's Academic Opportunity Program (AOP) enrolls similar students who reside out of state and/or whose family income slightly exceeds HEOP guidelines. Together, HEOP and AOP are referred to as the Opportunity Program (OP). About 180 OP students are enrolled at Skidmore.

An applicant for admission must complete the Common Application and submit it with a $65 fee. All information for Regular Decision applicants should be postmarked by January 15. Applications from Early Decision applicants should be submitted by November 15 for the Round I Early Decision plan or by January 15 for the Round II Early Decision plan. Regular Decision applicants can convert their applications to Early Decision until February 1. Transfer applicants must submit their applications by November 15 for January admission or by April 1 for September admission.

International students are given special attention throughout the admissions process. Applicants whose first language is not English are encouraged to submit the results of the Test of English as a Foreign Language (TOEFL). There are a limited number of need-based financial-aid awards available for outstanding international students.

CAREER SERVICES AND PLACEMENT

Thanks in part to the college's strong internship, student-faculty summer research, and off-campus study programming, some 95 percent of Skidmore students report being employed or pursuing further education one year after graduating. Close to 60 percent complete or are enrolled in advanced-degree programs within five years of graduation. Career Development offers one-on-one career counseling (in person and virtual) for life; job fairs in NYC, Boston, Washington, D.C., and Los Angeles; off-campus job and internship interviewing fairs in New York, Boston, Washington, D.C., and Los Angeles; internship openings reserved for Skidmore students; graduate and professional school expo (nearly 50 institutions); several summer funded internship awards programs; and networking events such as Career Jam and Creative Thought (Net)Works.

FACULTY

277 full-time (304 FTE), 87 percent with doctoral or highest degree in their field. National and international recognitions include Guggenheim, MacArthur, Pulitzer, and Emmy awards and major fellowships and grants from Fulbright, Getty, NEH, NIH, NSF, and the Andy Warhol Foundation.

SOUTHERN ILLINOIS UNIVERSITY CARBONDALE

AT A GLANCE

Southern Illinois University Carbondale (SIU), chartered in 1869, is a comprehensive, state-supported institution with nationally and internationally recognized instructional, research and service programs. SIU is fully accredited by the North Central Association of Colleges and Schools. SIU offers more than 200 undergraduate majors, minors and specializations; three associate degree programs; 95 baccalaureate degree programs; 80 master's degree programs; 34 doctoral programs; and professional degrees in law and medicine. SIU is a multi-campus university that includes the Carbondale campus as well as the SIU School of Medicine at Springfield.

During the 2016 academic year, SIU's enrollment was 15,987, which included 12,182 undergraduate students, 3,183 graduate students and 622 professional students. The average age of undergraduates is 23.2. International students account for 8.5 percent of SIU's total enrollment. Of U.S. undergraduate students, 17.19 percent are African-American, 0.2 percent are American Indian/Alaskan, 1.8 percent are Asian or Pacific Islander and 8.8 percent are Hispanic.

Students who are ready to start college but not ready to commit to a specific major can enroll in SIU's Exploratory Student-Undeclared (EXPU) program. Advisers and career counselors help these students plan their education and careers.

LOCATION AND ENVIRONMENT

Carbondale is a city of 26,000 located six hours south of Chicago, two hours southeast of St. Louis and three hours north of Nashville, Tennessee. Four large recreational lakes, two great rivers (the Mississippi and the Ohio) and the 270,000-acre Shawnee National Forest are within reach of the campus. The mid-South climate is ideal for year-round outdoor activities.

CAMPUS FACILITIES & EQUIPMENT

In addition to the 2.6 million volumes, 3.6 million microfilms and more than 43,000 current periodicals and serials available in Morris Library, students and faculty members have access to more than 200,000 e-books. More details are available online at lib.siu.edu.

Students learn and practice in the Transportation Education Center based at the Southern Illinois Airport, outdoor laboratories, the student-run Daily Egyptian newspaper, WSIU-TV, WSIU-FM, art and natural history museums, a literary magazine, McLeod Theater, Memorial Hospital, a vivarium, plant biology greenhouses, University Farms and Touch of Nature Environmental Center.

All single students under the age of 21 not residing with their parents or legal guardians, and with fewer than 26 credit hours earned after high school, are required to live in university-owned and operated residence halls. SIU offers four on-campus residential areas for single students, each with a dining hall, post office and laundry facilities. Learning Resource Centers, available on both sides of campus, offer writing centers, computer labs and student lounges. University Housing Residence Hall Dining provides all-you-care-to-eat meals and late-night dining. Residence Hall Dining offers a variety of menus, vegetarian and light entrees, display cooking and a full-time dietitian to help students with special dietary needs. Apartment housing is available for sophomore-, junior and senior-level undergraduates, graduate students and students with families.

OFF-CAMPUS OPPORTUNITIES

Southern Illinois University Carbondale is committed to serving statewide, national and international needs. This commitment is reflected in SIU Extended Campus, which offers educational opportunities located off campus. SIU Extended Campus is present at 20 military installations and 17 nonmilitary locations across 14 states, offering 12 online degree programs, 12 off-campus programs and five military programs.

Off-campus credit programs are designed to meet the educational needs of adults wishing to pursue a degree but who are unable to travel to the Carbondale campus. Faculty members who teach off-campus courses travel to distant sites to teach SIU courses.

All credit courses offered through these programs carry full SIU academic credit and are taught by faculty members appointed by the academic departments of the university. Additional information can be found online at extendedcampus.siu.edu.

ACADEMICS

SIU's Continuing Education and Outreach auxiliary service provides nonacademic support services for SIU's Carbondale campus. Its noncredit classes, workshops and conference, as well as its contractual services program, offers the university's resources to a variety of groups and individuals both on and off campus. Continuing Education and Outreach provides specialized educational services to groups, organizations, governmental agencies and businesses on a cost-recovery basis. These services are provided regionally, nationally and internationally. Additional information can be found online at continuinged.siu.edu.

Faculty members are dedicated to excellence in teaching and to their advancement of knowledge in a wide variety of disciplines and professions. Many faculty members are well-known nationally and internationally for their varied research contributions. The student-faculty ratio is 14.52:1. There are 1,130 full-time and 224 part-time instructional faculty members.

MAJORS AND DEGREES OFFERED

The university offers two Associate in Applied Science degree programs—aviation flight and physical therapist assistant—at the College of Applied Sciences and Arts.

The College of Applied Sciences and Arts offers bachelor's degree programs in architectural studies; automotive technology; aviation management; aviation technologies; dental hygiene; electronic systems technologies; fashion design and merchandising; public safety management (off-campus only); health care management; information systems technologies; interior design; mortuary science and funeral service; radiologic sciences; and technical resource management.

The College of Agricultural Sciences offers bachelor's degree programs in agribusiness economics; agricultural systems; animal science; crop, soil and environmental management; forestry; horticulture; hospitality and tourism administration; and human nutrition and dietetics.

The College of Business offers bachelor's degree programs in accounting; business and administration; business economics; finance; management; and marketing.

The College of Education and Human Services offers bachelor's degree programs in almost two dozen undergraduate programs, many in conjunction with other colleges on campus. The programs include (° denotes educator licensure required through the university's Teacher Education Program): °agricultural education; °art education; behavior analysis and therapy; °biological science education; communication disorders and sciences; °early childhood; °elementary education; °English teacher education; exercise science; °foreign languages; °history teacher education; leisure services management; °mathematics education; °physical education teacher education; public health; organizational training and development; outdoor recreation leadership and management; rehabilitation services; social work; °special education; sport administration; and therapeutic recreation.

The College of Engineering offers bachelor's degree programs in civil engineering; computer engineering; electrical engineering; engineering technology; industrial management and applied engineering; mechanical engineering; and mining engineering.

The College of Liberal Arts offers bachelor's degrees in Africana studies; anthropology; art; classics; communication studies; criminology and criminal justice; design; economics; English; foreign language and international trade; French; geography and environmental resources; German; history; international studies; linguistics; music; musical theater; paralegal studies; philosophy; political science; psychology; sociology; Spanish; theater; and university studies.

The College of Mass Communication and Media Arts offers bachelor's degrees in cinema and photography; journalism; and radio, television and digital media.

The College of Science offers bachelor's degree programs in biological sciences; chemistry and biochemistry; computer science; geology; mathematics; microbiology; physics; physiology; plant biology; zoology; and pre-professional programs and advisement in the following areas: chiropractic; dental; medical; nursing; occupational therapy; optometry; osteopathic medicine; pharmacy; physical therapy; physician assistant; podiatry; public health; and veterinary medicine.

In addition to the many majors offered at SIU, specializations are offered in all colleges in many areas.

TUITION, ROOM, BOARD, FEES

Tuition and fee charges for the 2017–18 academic year (fall and spring) for students enrolled in 15 or more semester hours were $13,932 for Illinois residents and out-of-state domestic residents, and $28,107 international students. Room and board totaled $10,622. (All costs are subject to change.) The cost of books and school supplies varies among programs. The average cost is $1,100 per academic year.

FINANCIAL AID

More than $293 million in financial aid was distributed to 17,453 SIU students in fiscal year 2015–16 through federal, state and institutionally funded financial aid programs.

To apply for financial aid at SIU, students should complete the Free Application for Federal Student Aid (FAFSA). Applications that are filed before April 1 receive priority consideration for campus-based aid. The FAFSA can be completed electronically at the U.S. Department of Education's website (fafsa.ed.gov). When completing the FAFSA, students should list Southern Illinois University Carbondale (Federal School Code 001758) as a school of choice.

SIU has one of the largest student employment programs in the country, with about 4,000 students employed each year in a wide variety of job classifications.

STUDENT ORGANIZATIONS AND ACTIVITIES

SIU intercollegiate sports teams compete at the NCAA Division I level (football is Division I-FCS). Conference affiliations include the Missouri Valley Conference and the Missouri Valley Football Conference. Intercollegiate sports teams include men's and women's basketball, cross-country, diving, golf, swimming, and track and field; men's baseball and football; and women's softball and volleyball. The campus has various playing fields, several tennis courts, and a campus lake with a beach and boat dock. SIU's Student Recreation Center offers an Olympic-size pool; indoor tracks; handball/racquetball and squash courts; a climbing wall; weight rooms; basketball, volleyball and tennis courts; outdoor equipment rental; an aerobic area; wallyball; martial arts; and dance and cardio studios.

The Student Center is one of the largest in the United States without a hotel. It holds a bookstore, several restaurants, a craft shop, facilities for bowling and billiards, headquarters for more than 275 student organizations and the student government office, four ballrooms and an auditorium.

ADMISSIONS PROCESS

Freshman applicants whose ACT composite score is at or above 23 (SAT score at or above 1070) and whose high school grade point average at or above 2.0 (on a 4.0 scale) are admitted to the university. Applicants also can be admitted with an ACT composite score at or above 18 (SAT score at or above 870) and a high school GPA at or above 3.0 (on a 4.0 scale). All other applicants who meet the course subject pattern requirements will undergo a holistic review to determine potential admissibility. Admission of students who do not meet automatic admission requirements may be subject to conditions. Freshman applicants must meet course pattern requirements: four years of English, three years of mathematics, three years of laboratory science, three years of social science and two years of electives.

Transfer applicants must have an overall grade point average of at least 2.0 on a 4.0 scale, based on work attempted at all institutions and calculated by SIU grading policies. Transfer applicants must also be eligible to continue at the last institution attended. Some programs have higher admission requirements or require additional screening for admission. Undergraduates can apply online at admissions.siu.edu.

Admission is granted on a rolling basis. Application priority deadlines for freshmen and transfer students are May 1 for the summer term and fall semester, and Dec. 1 for the spring semester. The application fee is $40. For more information, prospective students should contact::

Undergraduate Admissions

Mail Code 4710

1263 Lincoln Drive

Southern Illinois University Carbondale

Carbondale, IL 62901

Phone: 618/536-4405

Email: admissions@siu.edu

Website: www.siu.edu

Facebook: http://www.facebook.com/SouthernIllinoisUniversityCarbondaleTwitter: twitter.com/siuc

SOUTHWESTERN UNIVERSITY

AT A GLANCE

Southwestern University provides a top-ranked integrated liberal arts and science education that prepares students to think critically, collaborate, adapt and solve problems. Our graduates leave ready to innovate and create positive change in their professional careers and in life.

Southwestern University, located in scenic Georgetown just 25 miles north of Austin, was the first institution of higher education in the state. It has a strong history of academic excellence. SU emphasizes an interdisciplinary approach to learning, where students develop the skills needed to create original ideas, adapt and innovate. Employers and top graduate programs recognize and seek these critical skills, proven by the fact that Southwestern's Career Services ranks #12 nationally.

Southwestern's curriculum incorporates humanities, fine arts, social sciences and natural sciences. It has 26 academic departments covering the core STEM disciplines, business, fine arts and more. In addition, SU offers seven pre-professional programs including pre-engineering, pre-law and pre-medicine, with acceptance levels into graduate programs significantly higher than the national average. °

During their time at Southwestern, students participate in high impact learning experiences such as studying abroad, collaborative research projects with faculty, community engaged learning and internships. With an average class size of 17, students are challenged and engaged, learning to collaborate and see things from multiple perspectives. SU students graduate with the skills to think, create, innovate and contribute solutions to real world problems.

The majority of SU students live on campus and are actively involved in one or more student organizations. Students are civic-minded and volunteer in the community at more than twice the national average. Athletically, the Pirates compete in 20 different varsity sports at the NCAA Division III level, with many more involved in club or intramural sports.

Recent SU graduate Taylor Lewis, class of 2018, explains the Southwestern experience as: "an exhilarating, rewarding and life-changing process of personal development and growth through experiential intercultural and interdisciplinary learning. Personally, my Southwestern experience has been one great big opportunity to discover my true passions, hone in on my strengths, and learn from my weaknesses—all while being a part of a community that not only supports me, but encourages me to be the best person I can be."

Office of Admissions
Southwestern University
1001 E. University Street
Georgetown, TX 78626
Telephone: 1-800-252-3166
E-mail: admissions@southwestern.edu
Website: www.southwestern.edu

CAMPUS FACILITIES & EQUIPMENT

As the first institute of higher learning in Texas, Southwestern's campus is filled with history and tradition. Located on 700 gorgeous acres in the heart of Georgetown, SU's towering oak trees, early 20th century buildings and lush lawns add to its picturesque feel. It has a strong commitment to sustainability, with two LEED-certified buildings on campus and an agreement with the City of Georgetown that allows for the use of wind power for electricity on campus, making SU the first university in the state and one of the first nationally to be 100 percent powered by wind.

Stroll through campus on any given day and you'll see students conversing on the lawn, lounging in a hammock or pedaling to class on one of the shared yellow Pirate bikes. There's a true feeling of community.

The majority of SU students live on campus, which adds to the camaraderie. All freshmen live in one of four residence halls (one female, one male and two coed dorms). The central dining hub on campus, Mabee Commons, features a variety of meal, snack and drink choices. The nearby Cove has a coffee bar and grill open late for playing pool or simply hanging out with friends.

Southwestern's location just 25 miles north of Austin provides the best of both worlds for its students. The city of Georgetown, with its historic downtown and the flowing San Gabriel River provides small-town charm with access to the capital city. Not only is Austin known for its live music, SXSW and world-famous BBQ, but it was recently dubbed the "Silicon Valley of the South" for its tech-focus and innovation.

ACADEMIC PROGRAMS

Southwestern provides students an integrated liberal arts and science program that incorporates humanities, fine arts, social sciences and natural sciences. All students take a First-Year Seminar that introduces them to the campus learning environment and sets the stage for critical thinking and innovative learning. Other requirements include social justice, foreign language proficiency and a capstone experience. SU's "Paideia" philosophy is woven throughout all courses, encouraging students to think outside a narrow focus, dig deeper and make connections. The curriculum allows for increased "student agency," where students have the freedom to pursue their passion and explore subjects outside their major. As a sociology and English double major explains, "It's nice to be able to get a taste of how others may see and understand the world in various other disciplines."

One of the unique advantages at SU is the opportunity for faculty-student research. While this type of work is often reserved for graduate-levels at other universities, it's not uncommon for a student to collaborate or co-author a paper with a professor. On campus, the Fondren-Jones Science Hall is currently undergoing a major renovation, with phase one complete and phase two scheduled to be open in Fall of 2019.

The Sarofim School of Fine Arts has a global reputation for providing a world-class arts education. Political science majors benefit from the school's proximity to Austin, the state capital. Additionally, the seven pre-professional programs, including pre-engineering, pre-law and pre-medicine, produce graduates accepted into top graduate programs at rates significantly higher than the national average.

SU provides many experiential opportunities such as community engaged learning, student-faculty research, study abroad, academic internships and innovative creative projects. The King Creativity Fund provides grants to support up to 20 "innovative and visionary projects" each academic year. The Research and Creative Works Symposium provides an annual opportunity for students to present original research and creative work in an academic conference setting. SU faculty lead programs in England, Spain, Peru and Argentina, as well as a service-learning program in Jamaica. The university also sponsors internships in Washington, D.C., arts apprenticeship programs in New York City and other countless other opportunities for hands-on learning.

MAJORS AND DEGREES OFFERED

Our curriculum allows for greater student agency, where students have the freedom to pursue their passion and explore subjects outside their chosen discipline, often resulting in a double major or minor. Even so, Southwestern's four-year graduation rate is nearly twice the national average. °

Brown College of Arts and Sciences

- Anthropology
- Applied Physics
- Biochemistry
- Biology
- Business
- Chemistry
- Classics
- Communication Studies
- Computational Mathematics
- Computer Science
- Economics
- Education
- English
- Environmental Studies
- Feminist Studies
- French
- German
- Greek
- History
- Independent Major
- International Studies

- Kinesiology
- Latin
- Latin American & Border Studies
- Mathematics
- Philosophy
- Physics
- Political Science
- Psychology
- Religion
- Sociology
- Spanish

Minors Only

- Animal Studies
- Chinese
- Data Science
- Exercise & Sports Studies
- Health Studies
- Race & Ethnicity Studies

Sarofim School of Fine Arts

- Art (Studio)
- Art History
- Music
- Theatre

Minor Only

- Architecture & Design Studies

Southwestern is known nationwide for our pre-professional pathways including:

- Pre-Medicine
- Pre-Dentistry
- Pre-Veterinary Medicine
- Pre-Law
- Pre-Engineering
- Pre-Ministry
- Pre-Physical Therapy

TUITION, ROOM, BOARD, FEES

Costs for 2017–18 Academic Year
Tuition (Full-time, 12-19 hours per semester): $40,560
Room and Board (approximate): $12,236
Other Fees:
  Part-Time Tuition-per credit: $1,690
  Fine Arts Music Fee/ Applied Music Lessons-per credit: $180
  Vehicle Registration Fee-per semester: $100
  Lab fee-per applicable class: $75

FINANCIAL AID

For a world-class liberal arts and science education at one of the best schools in the country, Southwestern provides an excellent return on investment. Tuition at public universities may seem lower at first glance, but when scholarships, financial aid and graduation rates are factored in the results can show quite a different story.

Southwestern awards over $30 million in merit scholarships and need-based grants. In addition, SU awards over $2.5 million in federal and state grants and over $4 million in student loans.

First-year merit scholarship amounts start at $17,000. Entering students are evaluated for merit scholarships on a holistic review basis using information from the admission application. Need-based financial aid is awarded annually and requires the submission of a FAFSA, which is available beginning October 1 prior to the year in which the student will enroll.

STUDENT ORGANIZATIONS AND ACTIVITIES

Southwestern's Career Services ranks #12 nationally by The Princeton Review. Career Services offers 50 programs per year, students gain skills they will need to obtain a job or continue their education upon graduation. They teach career-management skills needed throughout a lifetime including resume writing, interviewing, job search strategies. They provide opportunities to explore a variety of occupations and gain experience through internships. They also make connections to employers, graduate schools, and other resources.

With the help of Career Services, at least two-thirds of all students complete at least one internship program and 92 percent of graduates are employed or in graduate school within ten months.

This year, Southwestern introduced The Alumni Network Mentoring Program. This program provides Southwestern students the opportunity to be mentored by Southwestern alumni. Students are matched with alumni based on their professional interests and activities.

ADMISSIONS PROCESS

In looking for engaged learners, we consider academic performance, both grades earned and challenging courses in areas of interest, above all else. Additionally, strength and depth of writing samples, SAT and/or ACT score, participation and demonstrated leadership in extracurricular activities, cogency and content of recommendations, a visit to campus, legacy connections, United Methodist Church membership, and recognition/achievement in national programs allow us to determine how a student will fit within our community. We value the opportunity to get to know students better through an optional interview.

Our mission is to treat all applicants fairly and with respect. In all cases, our decisions are reached by multiple individuals reviewing the application and voting in a manner s/he believe is in the best interest of both the student and the University. We take this responsibility seriously and realize we are dealing with the lives and future directions of our applicants.

Beginning August 1, 2017, students may choose to apply Early Decision (binding), Early Action or Regular Decision, based on the time frame that works best for the student. Students may apply by submitting a Common Application, an Apply Texas application or by submitting Southwestern's own application.

Transfer students, students who have completed at least one semester (12 hours or more) following high school graduation, are welcomed during the Fall and Spring semesters and may apply using either the Common Application or Apply Texas. Students should submit an essay, an official high school transcript, official college transcripts from all schools attended, official SAT/ACT scores and a college official's report. An individual interview allows transfer students to ask question regarding course transferability.

To learn more, visit southwestern.edu/admission/

FACULTY

The Southwestern faculty truly sets the university apart. This diverse and dynamic group consists of innovative leaders and award-winning researchers in their respective fields. Professors often work side-by-side with students, conducting research and collaborating on research.

Ninety-nine percent of tenured or tenure-track faculty hold a doctorate or the highest degree in their respective field. As educators, Southwestern faculty excel at teaching in an intimate and engaged environment (student-to-faculty ratio is 12:1, with an average class size of 17 students). The university provides multiple development and training opportunities for its faculty, keeping them on the cutting edge of the latest research and ideas. As citizens of our community, the Southwestern faculty brings a collaborative and personal approach to their work. SU classes are taught by professors (not teaching assistants), and collaborative research and publication with students is common.

CAREER SERVICES AND PLACEMENT

Southwestern's Career Services ranks #12 nationally by the Princeton Review. Students begin utilizing the Career Services during their first year to develop the skills needed to obtain a job or continue their education after graduation. Career counselors stress important skills such resume writing, interviewing and job search strategies.

With the help of Career Services, at least two-thirds of all students compete in at least one internship program, and 92 percent of graduates are employed or in graduate school within ten months. They also make connections to employers, graduate schools, and other resources that benefit them throughout their career.

ST. JOSEPH'S COLLEGE, NEW YORK

AT A GLANCE
Ready. Set. Joe's

Inspire the next you at St. Joseph's College (SJC). Our innovative programs are developed by top industry leaders and will give you the competitive edge you're looking for.

Outside the classroom, campus life is rich and diverse, providing you with every opportunity to enjoy the full collegiate experience.

With more than 37,000 successful alumni now working at school districts, businesses, hospitals and start-ups, we're ready to help you reach your potential. It's no wonder Washington Monthly ranks SJC as the No. 9 "Best Bang for the Buck" college in the Northeast.

Since 1916, SJC has helped students achieve their highest personal and academic goals. Through our three campuses—SJC Long Island, SJC Brooklyn and SJC Online—the College offers degrees in more than 50 majors, special course offerings and certificates, and affiliated and pre-professional programs. A St. Joseph's education, regardless of major or field of study, is rooted in a liberal arts foundation—an essential component for success in any profession. As one of the most affordable private colleges in New York, SJC is the top choice for students seeking a quality return on their investment.

In small, hands-on classes with a 13:1 student-to-faculty ratio, students receive individual attention from dedicated professors. SJC's academic and career counselors will guide students through all aspects of their college career, from coursework preparation to job applications. Faculty and staff value commitment to personal growth and are mentors and valued advisers.

SJC is consistently recognized for its commitment to academic excellence and its status as an outstanding college. For more than a decade, SJC has been selected as one of the nation's top colleges by U.S. News & World Report. SJC is also one of the nation's most affordable private colleges, annually ranked by Washington Monthly as a "Best Bang for the Buck" college in the Northeast.

In recent years, SJC has developed programs in studio art, forensic computing, journalism and new media studies, hospitality and tourism management, and nursing to meet growing demands. The launch of SJC Online has also provided the best in education—all on your schedule.

CAMPUS FACILITIES & EQUIPMENT
SJC Brooklyn

Architecturally stunning halls in the historic Clinton Hill neighborhood of Brooklyn, an outdoor theater, The Hill Center and the nationally recognized Dillon Child Study Center combine to make SJC Brooklyn a unique community. The recently opened Hill Center is home to SJC Brooklyn's NCAA Division III athletic teams. It features a regulation-size gymnasium, a state-of-the-art fitness facility and many multipurpose areas. Career opportunities and extensive cultural attractions in Manhattan are within reach via public transportation.

SJC Long Island

SJC Long Island's 32-acre lakeside campus features the Business Technology Center, the John A. Danzi Athletic Center, the Clare Rose Playhouse, the Callahan Library and the state-of-the-art 24.8-acre outdoor athletic field complex for soccer, lacrosse, baseball, softball and tennis. SJC Long Island is located in Patchogue and is just minutes from the Great South Bay, L.I. MacArthur Airport, Brookhaven National Laboratory, Orient Point and many of Long Island's ocean beaches. New York City is just a short ride away.

Service

Service is at the heart of a St. Joseph's education. Students volunteer at numerous organizations throughout the year and often participate in service-based trips, where they help rebuild communities that have been affected by hurricanes, earthquakes and other natural disasters. Service-based destinations have included Colorado, South Carolina, Missouri, New Jersey and Nicaragua. SJC provides a strong academic and value-oriented education at the undergraduate and graduate levels, and prepares students for a life characterized by integrity, intellectual and spiritual values, social responsibility and service.

ACADEMICS
Undergraduate Majors

Accounting
Biology
Biology—Secondary Education
Business Administration
Chemistry
Chemistry—Secondary Education
Child Study
Criminal Justice
Computer Information Technology
Computer Science
English
English—Secondary Education
History
History, Social Studies—Secondary Education
Hospitality Tourism Management
Human Relations
Journalism and New Media Studies
Leisure Services Management
Marketing
Mathematics
Mathematics—Secondary Education
Medical Technology
Nursing
Philosophy and Religious Studies
Political Science
Psychology
Spanish
Spanish—Secondary Education
Speech
Social Sciences, Concentration in Economics
Sociology
Studio Art
Therapeutic Recreation

Minors

Accounting
American Studies
Art History
Fine Arts (LI)
Studio Art
Biology
Business Administration
Chemistry
Computer Information Technology

Computer Science
Criminal Justice
Economics
English
Environmental Studies
Film/Media
History
Human Relations
Human Resources
Journalism New Media Studies
Labor, Class, Ethics
Latino Studies
Marketing
Mathematics
Mindfulness and Contemplative Living
Music (LI)
Music History
Peace and Justice Studies
Philosophy
Political Science
Psychology
Religious Studies
Sociology
Speech
Spanish
Theatre
Therapeutic Recreation
Women's Studies

Graduate Programs

Accounting
Adult-Gerontology Primary Care Nurse Practitioner
Computer Information Technology
Criminal Justice
Forensic Computing
General Studies
Health Administration
Hospitality Tourism Management
Human Services
Marketing
Medical Technology
Nursing
Organizational Management

Certificate Programs

In addition to our undergraduate programs, SJC offers credit-bearing certificates that part-time students can complete in less than a year. These certificates may be earned individually or as part of an undergraduate degree. Certificate programs enable you to delve deeper into your specific interests, help you focus on your career goals and give you a head start when entering the work world.

We offer certificate programs in:

· Business Administration Marketing (Brooklyn and LI)

· Criminal Justice (Brooklyn and LI)

· Human Services (Brooklyn and LI)

· Industrial Organizational Psychology (Brooklyn and LI)

· Mathematics and Computer Science (Brooklyn and LI)

· Psychology (LI)

· Religious Studies (Brooklyn and LI)

· Social Sciences (LI)

A Service Members Opportunity College

As a core member of the Service members Opportunity College Degree Network System, SJC is committed to the transfer of relevant course credits, flexible academic residence requirements and credit learning from appropriate military training and work experience. SJC also offers online, on- and off-site class schedules for its military and veteran students, including class offerings at Fort Hamilton in Brooklyn and Fort Wadsworth in Staten Island, New York. In addition, SJC is an active participant in the Post-9/11 GI Bill® Yellow Ribbon Program, offering student veterans financial support, a monthly housing allowance and an annual stipend for books and school supplies.

GI Bill® is a registered trademark of the U.S. Department of Veterans Affairs (VA). More information about education benefits offered by VA is available at the official U.S. government Web site at www.benefits.va.gov/gibill..

TUITION, ROOM, BOARD, FEES

SJC is committed to providing quality education while maintaining the one of lowest private college tuition rates in New York. To supplement the cost of education, scholarships, loans and work-study programs are some of the financial aid options available. Currently, more than 80 percent of SJC students receive some form of financial aid.

FINANCIAL AID

SJC offers generous scholarships and financial aid packages to students who qualify. For a listing of scholarships available at SJC Long Island, visit http://www.sjcny.edu/long-island/admissions/financial-aid/sjc-scholarships. For a listing of scholarships available at SJC Brooklyn, visit http://www.sjcny.edu/brooklyn/admissions/financial/sjc-scholarships.

STUDENT ORGANIZATIONS AND ACTIVITIES

SJC students have an abundance of extracurricular opportunities within reach through the Office of Student Involvement and Leadership. Students can join clubs, athletic teams, organizations and committees that emphasize leadership, community service and effective communication.

ADMISSIONS PROCESS

What are the admissions requirements?

St. Joseph's College is a selective institution. Applicants are evaluated on an individual basis. The College enrolls students who are academically talented and diverse. Successful admissions candidates typically have:

• A high school diploma or its equivalent, or postsecondary transcripts.

• A personal statement or essay of recommendation.

• Standardized test scores that demonstrate the promise of success in college-level courses.

• Two letters of recommendation and a personal essay.

Students can obtain a copy of our application or also apply online, by visiting sjcny.edu/applynow.

When should I apply? When is the application deadline?

SJC admits students on a rolling basis, but there are scholarship priority dates. For the fall semester, the scholarship priority date is March 15 for freshmen and August 1 for transfer students. For the spring semester, the priority date is January 1 for both freshmen and transfer students.

What do I need to submit as a transfer student?

Applications can be submitted by mail or online. Transfer students should request that official transcripts from all former colleges, and a listing of courses in progress, be sent to our Office of Admissions. You are not required to submit a high school transcript if you have an A.A. degree or have successfully completed 24 or more credits from an accredited college. You may transfer a maximum of 64 credits if you have an A.A. degree; certain A.A.S. degrees are also transferable.

ST. LAWRENCE UNIVERSITY

AT A GLANCE

The mission of St. Lawrence University is to provide an inspiring and demanding undergraduate education in the liberal arts to students selected for their seriousness of purpose and intellectual promise.

Nestled in the small upstate New York town of Canton that's closer to Canada than it is to Manhattan, St. Lawrence is a liberal arts school with a strong sense of community and a dedication to academics. For one history major, St. Lawrence is "a university that pushes me to pursue my dreams," a place where "it felt like I was coming home, not leaving home." With roughly 2,400 students and a student to faculty ratio of 12:1, St. Lawrence prides itself on small classes and a tight knit environment where students and professors know their fellow Laurentians by name. With interdisciplinary studies encouraged, the most popular majors at St. Lawrence include economics, biology, government, psychology, and mathematics. Even though its location might be considered remote, the school's proximity to the Adirondacks is a huge draw and, as one anthropology major jokes, "St. Lawrence manages to be a place with countless opportunities and things going on despite being in the middle of nowhere."

LOCATION AND ENVIRONMENT

St. Lawrence University provides a distinctive learning environment, offering 63 majors, 40 minors, and three graduate programs in education. Its First-Year Program has become a national model as a living-learning environment that transitions students successfully out of high school and into college life. Just 80 miles from Ottawa, St. Lawrence is the closest American university to a foreign capital and is only 100 miles from Montréal. St. Lawrence celebrates diversity in the widest sense, welcoming students from more than 60 countries. It also boasts the Collegiate Science and Technology Entry Program, the Ronald E. McNair Scholars Program, and is a partner with the New York State Higher Education Opportunity Program.

CAMPUS FACILITIES & EQUIPMENT

St. Lawrence University has two libraries, the Owen D. Young Library and Launders Science Library, containing more than 630,000 print volumes as well as a number of electronic resources, a writing center, and ample space for reading and research.

Students also enjoy a performing arts center with recital hall and two theaters as well as an art gallery containing a 7,000-piece art collection and Newell Center for Arts Technology.

With a commitment to sustainability, St. Lawrence opened in 2007 the Johnson Hall of Science, which was the first LEED-gold certified science building in New York State. And in 2014, the University opened Kirk Douglas Hall, a 155-bed residence hall that features 24 geothermal heating/cooling wells and was built to LEED gold standards. There's also the 15,000-square-foot Sullivan Student Center, which is available for student activities and meetings, studying, staff offices, and a popular dining facility.

Recreational facilities include a network of trails available for running and cross-country skiing; a 133-station fitness center; a three-story climbing wall; indoor and outdoor tennis courts; and two gymnasium/fieldhouse complexes, one with a 9-lane/400-meter track and five tennis/basketball courts and the other with a 200-meter track, three tennis courts, and ten squash courts. There's also a pool, equestrian center, golf course, indoor golf facility, AstroTurf field, baseball, soccer and softball fields, and a boathouse for rowing teams located on the St. Lawrence River. Appleton Arena is home to St. Lawrence's only NCAA Division I sport teams, men's and women's hockey teams.

OFF-CAMPUS OPPORTUNITIES

St. Lawrence University offers 24 off-campus program sites in 19 countries, including Australia, Austria, Canada, China, Costa Rica, Czech Republic, Denmark, England, France, India, Italy, Japan, Kenya, New Zealand, Spain, Thailand, and Trinidad and Tobago. Students can also direct-enroll at foreign universities through the International Student Exchange Program (ISEP).

The University also offers four off-campus study programs within the United States at American University, Washington, D.C.; an exchange program with Fisk University, Nashville, Tennessee; the Liberal Arts in New York City, the Adirondack Semester, and a Sustainability Program located just 5 miles from campus.

ACADEMICS

The University offers the following degrees: Bachelor of Arts, Bachelor of Science, Master of Education, Master of Science in Mental Health Counseling, and a Certificate of Advanced Studies in Education.

There are 63 majors, which include a number of combined major programs in areas such as environmental studies, economics and biology. Students can even design their own major with faculty approval. The University also offers 40 minors and 53 interdisciplinary programs (see MAJORS AND DEGREES OFFERED.)

St. Lawrence has a number of affiliations, giving students the opportunity to pursue a five-year program in business administration (this program leads to the MBA) and engineering, combining coursework at St. Lawrence with work at other institutions.

Students can also enter a number of affiliate programs leading to degrees in pharmacy, nursing, physician assistant, and physical therapy. There are also tracks for pre-med and pre-law.

The St. Lawrence distribution requirements involve coursework in six areas. All students are expected to demonstrate writing competence before graduating. The University provides extensive opportunities for honors projects and independent work.

MAJORS AND DEGREES OFFERED

Students have the following major/minors to choose from:

African Studies, African-American Studies, Anthropology, Applied Statistics, Arabic Studies, Art & Art History, Asian Studies, Biochemistry, Biology, Biology-Physics, Business in the Liberal Arts, Canadian Studies, Caribbean and Latin American Studies, Chemistry, Chinese Studies, Communications, Computer Science, Conservation Biology, Creative Writing, Dance, Economics, Economics-Mathematics, Education Studies, English, Environmental Studies, Estudios Hispanicos (Spanish), European Studies, Exercise Science, Film and Representation Studies, Francophone Studies (French), Gender and Sexuality Studies, Geology, Geology-Physics, German Studies, Global Studies, Government, History, International Economics, International Studies, Italian Studies, Latin American Studies, Mathematics, Multi-Languages, Multifield (self-designed), Music, Native American Studies, Neuroscience, Outdoor Studies, Peace Studies, Performance and Communication Arts, Philosophy, Physics, Political Science, Psychology, Religious Studies, Sociology, Sports Studies and Exercise Science, Statistics.

TUITION, ROOM, BOARD, FEES

2017–2018

Tuition:	$ 52,610
Room:	$ 7,356
Board:	$ 6,300
Fees:	$ 380
Total:	$ 66,646

FINANCIAL AID

St. Lawrence University offers merit scholarships, as well as need-based financial assistance. The school grants aid in some form to more than 97 percent of its students. Aid packages typically consist of grants, student loans, and campus jobs.

Aid applicants must submit the Free Application for Federal Student Aid (FAFSA) between October 1 and February 1; the financial aid award will be included in the decision package if all required documentation is received by the deadline.

STUDENT ORGANIZATIONS AND ACTIVITIES

All first-year undergraduate students are enrolled in St. Lawrence University's nationally-recognized First-Year Program, which places approximately 30 first-year students in small communities that live and learn together.

Once they achieve upper-class status, students may choose to live in traditional residence halls, interest-based theme suites, theme cottages, Greek houses, or senior townhouses.

St. Lawrence provides a full range of services to students, including comprehensive career planning as well as graduate and professional school guidance.

Students seeking co-curricular activities can choose from over 100 organizations, including everything from student government to interest groups, to arts and culture.

St. Lawrence boasts 34 intercollegiate teams including NCAA Division I teams in men's and women's ice hockey. All other teams compete in the NCAA's Division III. Club sports are also available, as is participation in a broad range of popular intramural sports.

ADMISSIONS PROCESS

St. Lawrence seeks undergraduates with the capacity to manage a demanding academic regimen successfully. In addition, the ideal student contributes substantially to the quality of community life. The University strives to enroll students who represent the broadest possible range of economic, ethnic, geographic, and social backgrounds. The admissions committee values academic achievement, but ability in athletics, community service, leadership, or the creative arts is also considered a strong indicator of a student's capacity to benefit from her or his time at St. Lawrence. The University is test optional for all domestic students, so students may choose to submit the results of their SAT, ACT, both SAT and ACT, or none. Any submitted tests will be used during the evaluation process. Students are strongly encouraged to plan a campus visit; interviews may be scheduled to occur on campus. In certain areas, off-campus interviews are also an option.

The University makes no requirement of applicants' high school curricula; however, successful applicants generally demonstrate extensive preparation in the humanities, mathematics, the natural sciences, and the social sciences. Advanced Placement, IB and honors work are looked upon favorably, as they demonstrate the applicants' intellectual curiosity and maturity. These are qualities that are highly sought by the admissions committee.

St. Lawrence uses the Common Application exclusively. The application processing fee is $60, which is waived with an official campus visit. Applicants pursuing regular decision should submit all materials by February 1 and will be notified in mid-March of the University's decision. Students whose first choice is St. Lawrence may apply for early decision: the priority deadline for early decision applications begins on November 1 and goes until February 1. Notification of the early decision is sent approximately two weeks after the application folder is complete.

To request additional information, students should contact:

Office of Admissions and Financial Aid

St. Lawrence University

Canton, NY 13617

Visit www.stlawu.edu/admissions

ST. NORBERT COLLEGE

AT A GLANCE

St. Norbert College combines academic excellence with a deep commitment to the student experience in all respects. In small classes, faculty members provide individualized attention focused on student success. Outside the classroom, student life is rich with opportunities to participate in athletics, culture, artistic endeavors and a remarkable array of student organizations. All of it takes place on a quintessential college campus where historic buildings share a beautiful riverfront with state-of-the-art facilities.

St. Norbert is a private, coeducational liberal-arts institution with more than 40 fields of study, including several pre-professional programs. Academics are enhanced by an honors program, student-faculty collaborative research, professional internships and a popular study-abroad program. With an excellent four-year graduation rate and job and grad-school placement rates at better than 90 percent, St. Norbert provides exceptional return on educational investment.

Founded in 1898, St. Norbert is one of the top 10 Catholic liberal arts colleges in the nation. It welcomes students of all faiths who join an energetic and inclusive community, in keeping with the principles of the college's Norbertine founders. At St. Norbert, the goal is to help students pursue their passions and become engaged, informed global citizens.

LOCATION AND ENVIRONMENT

Located on the banks of the Fox River in De Pere (a residential community of 23,000) in northeastern Wisconsin, the St. Norbert campus comprises 40+ buildings on 112 scenic acres. Students also have easy access to the neighboring all-American city of Green Bay and its suburbs, with a metropolitan population of about 300,000. A safe, supportive atmosphere exists both on campus and in the surrounding community, which is frequently celebrated for its outstanding quality of life.

St. Norbert continues to experience great momentum with record-high enrollment in recent years, as well as outstanding academic achievements. And as the students come, so do the facilities and programs to support them. New is St. Norbert's $40 million Gehl-Mulva Science Center, also home to the Medical College of Wisconsin's northeast Wisconsin campus. Integrated facilities for hands-on learning, collaborative research and interdisciplinary study abound in this LEED-certified, state-of-the-art science center. Newer still is the $26 million Mulva Family Fitness & Sports Center, complete with competition-grade swimming pool, opened in 2016.

The past several years have also seen the opening of the Cassandra Voss Center that focuses on women's and gender studies and programming around issues of identity, and Dudley Birder Hall, a performing-arts space; both occupy renovated, historic buildings. The hub for meals and activities, the food at Michels Commons has been ranked the best among all colleges in Wisconsin and 15th best in the nation.

An outdoor athletics complex serves as the practice and competition venue for Green Knights football, soccer, and track and field. The Miriam B. and James J. Mulva library's lower level is home to a high-tech collaborative workspace for students.

Among other facilities, a campus center and marina located on the Fox River offer students a relaxing environment to grab a bite to eat, sit out on the deck or in the gazebo, or gather for a concert or movie. The campus coffee shop, Ed's, is another favorite student hangout.

Only a five-minute drive from campus, Green Bay and all its restaurants, shopping malls, museums and performing arts opportunities can be easily accessed by students when they've exhausted the shops and boutiques of charming De Pere.

ACADEMIC PROGRAMS

Experiential learning is the norm at St. Norbert. Research fellowships, as early as freshman year, give students hands-on opportunities to experience graduate-level research. Those collaborations with St. Norbert faculty continue throughout students' four years, and often include the opportunity to present work at local, regional or national conferences.

Students are also encouraged to participate in one of the more prolific study-abroad programs in the country, spanning six continents, 29 countries and more than 75 program sites. Approximately 30 percent of St. Norbert students study abroad each year—well above the national average.

International perspective is part of the fabric at St. Norbert on campus, as well. Our Center for Global Engagement on campus encourages a diverse student body, typically welcoming students, from more than 20 countries.

All students are assigned an advisor, who helps them chart their academic career and ensure they can graduate in four years. Students have the option of designing a personal major to help them achieve their academic objectives.

For high-achieving students, a challenging Honors Program provides plenty of opportunity for academic engagement. Honors students enjoy their own living-learning community of intellectually curious and creative students.

The metropolitan Green Bay area offers students nearly unlimited opportunities for internships. The region boasts Fortune 500 companies and numerous hospitals, schools and service organizations. Of course, students also regularly intern for the 13-time world champion Green Bay Packers, who hold their summer training camp on campus.

For those students more interested in volunteering, the Norbertine philosophy of self-emptying service is in abundant evidence. Local, national, and international service opportunities are hallmarks of a St. Norbert education, and the college has been recognized by both the John Templeton Foundation and the Carnegie Foundation for its exemplary civic-minded programs.

MAJORS AND DEGREES OFFERED

We offer Bachelor of Arts (BA), Bachelor of Science (BS), Bachelor of Music (BM) and Bachelor of Business Administration (BBA) undergraduate degrees.

Undergraduate Programs:

Accounting
American Studies
Art
Art Education
Biochemistry
Biology
Business Administration
Business Information Systems
Chemistry
Classical Studies
Communication and Media Studies
Computer Science
Economics
Education
English
Environmental Science
French
Geography
Geology
German
Graphic Design
Graphic Design and Implementation
History
Humanities and Fine Arts
Human Services
International Business and Language Area Studies
International Studies

Japanese
Leadership Studies
Mathematics
Military Science
Modern Languages and Literatures
Music
Music Education
Natural Sciences
Nursing
Peace and Justice
Philosophy
Physics
Political Science
Pre-Dental
Pre-Engineering
Pre-Law
Pre-Medical
Pre-Pharmacy
Pre-Veterinary
Psychology
Sociology
Spanish
Special Education
Theatre Studies
Theology and Religious Studies
Women's and Gender Studies

Graduate Programs:

Master of Business Administration
Master of Arts in Liberal Studies
Master of Theological Studies

TUITION, ROOM, BOARD, FEES

Full-time undergraduate students (3 or more full courses/12–18 credits):

$37,314 Tuition

$10,510 Average room and board

$815 Fees

FINANCIAL AID

More than 97 percent of St. Norbert students receive some form of financial aid. To achieve our goal of helping students obtain an affordable and quality college education, St. Norbert allocates funds each year for distribution to students with financial needs. Approximately $60 million in financial aid is available annually at St. Norbert College in the form of scholarships, grants, student employment and loans. We encourage students to submit the Free Application for Federal Student Aid (FAFSA) as early as possible, and preferably by January 1 of their senior year of high school. The St. Norbert FAFSA code is 003892. Financial aid awards typically go out in mid-to late-January.

STUDENT ORGANIZATIONS AND ACTIVITIES

Students quickly adjust to campus with a welcoming community of faculty, students and staff. First Year Experience (FYE) programming helps students acclimate to campus and to college life in general.

Students at St. Norbert tend to be very involved; because it's a residential campus, activities and opportunities are close at hand. The college offers more than 80 student organizations and clubs that provide a rich co-curricular campus environment. Students can find opportunities in academic, cultural, Greek, social, special interest, governing, media, recreation, service and faith organizations. And if students are looking for a particular interest that hasn't found its place on campus yet, they are encouraged to create a new student organization.

A Division III school, St. Norbert College offers 11 men's and 11 women's varsity sports, and our athletes have been named Academic All-Americans more times than any other school in the Midwest Conference. The Green Knights are frequent conference champions, averaging about four per year. Nearly one quarter of our students are involved in varsity sports, with many others participating in intramurals.

ADMISSIONS PROCESS

Students can apply using either the St. Norbert College online application or the Common Application.

Because St. Norbert reviews applications on a rolling basis and gives preference to students according to the date of admission and enrollment deposit, it benefits students to apply as early as possible during their senior year.

Notification of the admission decision is made on a rolling basis beginning in early September. After St. Norbert receives all of the required admission information, students receive notification via mail of their admission status within 2-4 weeks. A nonrefundable $350 deposit is required to confirm enrollment.

First-year domestic student important dates:

August 15 admission office begins reviewing applications

September 1 admission office begins notifying students of their application status

October 1 apply for financial aid at www.fafsa.ed.gov; St. Norbert's FAFSA school code is 003892

January 1 financial aid priority deadline

May 1 priority date for enrollment deposit

June summer orientation

For more information, prospective students are encouraged to contact:

St. Norbert College

Office of Admission

100 Grant Street

De Pere, WI 54115-2099

Phone: 920-403-3005 or 800-236-4878

Fax: 920-403-4072

Email: admit@snc.edu

Web: snc.edu

STATE UNIVERSITY OF NEW YORK COLLEGE OF ENVIRONMENTAL SCIENCE AND FORESTRY

AT A GLANCE

Founded in 1911, the College of Environmental Science and Forestry is a premier environmental college focused on building a sustainable future through research and degree programs in the environmental sciences, engineering, design and management fields.

ESF inspires tomorrow's environmental leaders through discovery and the development of innovative solutions. The college strives to actively inform and involve the greater society on the environmental challenges of our time.

As a small, doctoral granting institution, ESF attracts top-notch faculty who push the boundaries of knowledge in their academic fields. Working side by side with these highly acclaimed faculty on research ranging from restoring polluted lakes to developing new sources of biofuels, our students push those boundaries too. Unlike many research institutions, experience and outstanding teaching is our top priority. This close-knit community of faculty and students share interests and work together to improve the world around them. Together, they learn and work in labs, classrooms, forests and wetlands across ESF campuses and field stations. Other research and educational opportunities take place nationally, internationally, and through our study-abroad programs.

Every ESF major requires some type of experiential learning. Career-related internships provide invaluable work experience and often pave the way to a permanent position after graduation. The College has an extensive internship program to help students with those connections.

These connections include over 40 internships through the New York Department of Environmental Conservation (NYDEC) reserved specifically for ESF students. Alumni have had great success in the NYDEC, notably among them is the former commissioner, Joe Martens. In Martens' words, "ESF is poised like no other College to put people in positions of critical importance around the world." Alumnus, Ana Maria Menezes of the class of 2008, is a perfect example of that. Menezes works as an environmental consultant on adaption to climate change for the U.N. Alumni have been presidents of the Union of Concerned Scientists (UCS), chemists at Georgia-Pacific and Proctor & Gamble, engineers at Bristol Meyer Squibb and Kimberly-Clark, lawyers, forest rangers, hydrologists, podcasters, cartographers and countless other exciting positions.

Students at our main campus enjoy the benefits of a unique partnership with neighboring Syracuse University (SU). These benefits include the ability to take courses at SU, participate in academic and cultural events, the use of athletic and recreational facilities, dining and religious services, discounted tickets to SU NCAA Division 1 sports events and a club offering of over 350 student organizations between both campuses.

What makes ESF truly unique is the strong sense of community between students, faculty, and Alumni. It is a sense of pride, family, and belonging that travels far beyond graduation. "I experience this wherever I go. People are proud to tell me they went to ESF when I see them," says alumnus Joe Martens. Students arrive on campus as first-years and transfers, all eager to change the world for the better. They leave as skilled professionals ready to make a difference. Most start making that difference before they ever leave. It is a tradition of good will, positive energy, creativity and community that threads us together.

LOCATION AND ENVIRONMENT

ESF's main campus is in Syracuse, New York, immediately adjacent to the Syracuse University campus. This offers students a unique "small and large school" environment, where students benefit from small classes and personal attention from faculty on the ESF campus while also having access to the academic facilities, diverse student population, and active social life offered by Syracuse University.

CAMPUS FACILITIES & EQUIPMENT

ESF campuses include both the urban setting found on our main campus and more than 25,000 acres of forest and wetlands at seven regional campuses and field stations throughout the state. The College features a number of sustainability projects including a LEED platinum-rated Gateway Center housing the trailhead cafe and LEED gold-rated dorms. Computing, library, dining and sports facilities are available at ESF and neighboring Syracuse University.

OFF-CAMPUS OPPORTUNITIES

Syracuse is a medium-size city and a "college town" featuring many cultural and entertainment options. Students often attend NCAA Division I sports events at the Syracuse University Carrier Dome. The downtown area is a five-minute shuttle bus ride from campus, and the city culture is student-friendly. The largest shopping mall in the northeast (Destiny USA) is in Syracuse. Students with vehicles enjoy hiking in local and regional parks nature preserves and trail systems. Among these are Green Lakes State Park, Onondaga County Park and Clark Reservation. For those looking for winter sports recreation, there are several downhill and cross-country skiing locations within a 45-minute drive of campus. Trips are frequently scheduled to the Adirondack State Park through student organizations for camping, rock climbing, hiking, biking and canoeing excursions among others.

ACADEMICS

The faculty at ESF are leaders in their fields as both professors and accomplished researchers. A highly selective Honors Program is offered, focused on undergraduate research opportunities. Study-abroad programs take students to a variety of countries, providing opportunities to conduct research in a range of ecosystems. ESF's long-standing partnership with SU provides students with the opportunity to take classes there as part of their ESF degree program with access to hundreds of elective courses in the liberal arts and management fields among many others.

MAJORS AND DEGREES OFFERED

ESF offers more than 50 associate's, bachelor's, master's and doctoral degree programs focused on sustainability and the science, design, engineering and management of our environment and natural resources. All degree programs offer research and experiential learning opportunities. Popular programs include wildlife science, forestry and natural resources management, environmental science and conservation biology. Our engineering programs include environmental resource engineering, biochemistry, biotechnology, bioprocess engineering and paper engineering. Communication around the environment is also very important to us. Environmental studies, environmental interpretation and landscape architecture all focus on telling the story of our environment in different ways ranging from multimedia, to traditional interpreter positions to designing the sustainable parks and cities of the present and future. Our environmental health program prepares students to address challenges to human health from toxins, and pollution among other byproducts of modern society. We prepare students to address almost every issue related to the environment, its protection, the health of the plants, animals and humans living in it, and planning for a sustainable future.

TUITION, ROOM, BOARD, FEES

Tuition, room, board and fees for the 2018–19 academic year total $26,734 for New York state residents and $36,584 for out-of-state residents.

FINANCIAL AID

ESF has been ranked among the top 50 "Best Buy" colleges in the nation. ESF National Scholarships offset out-of-state costs up to $8,000 per year for qualified applicants. The College awards approximately half of its scholarships based on academic potential and half based on financial need. Last year, undergraduates received more than $18 million from all sources, including more than $7 million in scholarships and grants. Students file the Free Application for Federal Student Aid (FAFSA) for financial aid consideration, with a priority deadline of Feb. 1. Admissions applications must be submitted by Feb. 1 for academic (merit) scholarship consideration.

STUDENT ORGANIZATIONS AND ACTIVITIES

Students can participate in over 350 clubs and organizations jointly offered between ESF and SU. ESF offers intercollegiate athletics teams in basketball, soccer, golf, cross country, track, fishing and timber sports. Community service is an important part of the student culture at ESF. Many student activities focus on outdoor recreation and travel.

ADMISSIONS PROCESS

Admission is selective and the College attracts a diverse and academically qualified entering class. An Early Decision (first choice) application plan is offered. See www.esf.edu/admissions. Students apply to the specific major that interests them and most programs require strong grades in high school mathematics and science. SAT/ACT scores are also important, along with a demonstrated interest in sustainability and the environment.

ESF attracts a large number of transfer students (more than 250 per year) in addition to the entering first-year class, and a minimum college GPA of 2.80 or higher is generally required for transfer admission.

Students most often use the Common Application when applying, and a campus visit is strongly encouraged.

SWARTHMORE COLLEGE

AT A GLANCE

Swarthmore College is a highly selective college of liberal arts and engineering located half an hour outside of Philadelphia, in a charming suburban slice of Pennsylvania. The college is founded on the value of striving towards the greater good, and empowers students to intertwine their academic curiosity with social responsibility and a sense of purpose.

Swarthmore's staff are fully behind this mission, from the world-class professors who engage directly with students in meaningful ways, to the staff in the dining hall, coffee bars, and libraries, who can come to feel like friends. Close relationships with community members fuel life at Swarthmore. Many students collaborate with their professors on joint research projects, and the exchange of intellectual ideas between students and faculty is facilitated by small class sizes. The Honors Program extends the depth of free and critical discussion of ideas via small-group seminars.

One trademark of a "Swattie" is the desire to learn for the sake of knowledge, and the pursuit of interests inside and outside the classroom. Swatties can be astrophysicists who write poetry, economists who love to code and athletes with a passion for choreography. Almost half of the student body enjoys playing sports, whether it's at the competitive Division III level, or in more casual club and intramural sports teams.

The College's Quaker roots emphasize the concept of access regardless of income, this manifests itself in a cash-free campus; the annual activity fee covers everything from digital printing and sporting events to campus movie screenings and dance performances. Swarthmore's financial aid program ensures affordability—without loans. Almost 60 percent of the Class of 2021 received aid in 2016–17, with an average award of $51,111. Swarthmore makes admissions decisions for U.S. citizens and permanent residents without considering a family's ability to pay. International applicants are admitted on a need-aware basis, and are eligible for financial aid.

LOCATION AND ENVIRONMENT

The beauty of Swarthmore's 425-acre campus is immediately striking. Students draw inspiration from the meticulously-tended gardens, stunning arboretum specimen trees, and variety of woodsy trails. Each fall, The Graduate is screened on the lawn in front of Parrish Hall, allowing students to contemplate life beyond Swarthmore, and seniors to chant their class year with reckless abandon. With Philadelphia less than 30 minutes away, and New York City and Washington, D.C. within a 90-minute train ride, Swatties enjoy connecting to the wider world. The close-knit community allows each student to have access to the college's wide array of opportunities, such as the student who, partly on the strength of helping to build a database of Crum Woods ecological data, was offered a position at Google. The bottom line: Swarthmore's sense of place prepares you for anything and everything. Our alumni are equipped to make the most of where they've been—and make sense of what they haven't yet seen.

CAMPUS FACILITIES & EQUIPMENT

Swarthmore provides a dynamic array of arts spaces for students to enjoy or stage a performance—including professional theater facilities. Students explore their interests across campus, by learning a new dialect through immersion with Language Resource Center technology, making sense of the stars in the Peter Van de Kamp observatory, and working on social equity projects through the Lang Center for Civic & Social Responsibility. The forthcoming biology, engineering, psychology (BEP) building will feature cutting-edge labs and collaborative work spaces. The new Matchbox fitness facility offers a multifaceted, modern approach to wellness, recreation, and community. Whether students are snacking on a samosa while editing a project at the Media Center or chatting with friends about summer research over a meal at Sharples, the abundance of campus resources permeates life at Swarthmore.

OFF-CAMPUS OPPORTUNITIES

Swarthmore belongs to the Tri-College consortium, which links to nearby Bryn Mawr and Haverford Colleges both academically and socially. In addition, students can take courses at the University of Pennsylvania, a short train ride away. These extensions of the Swarthmore experience allow students to expand their intellectual and social capital, such as watching a play at Haverford, connecting with a Penn professor about an internship reference, or practicing with an a capella group at Bryn Mawr. The College offers shuttles to the other Tri-Co schools, community service sites, local restaurants and shops, and more. The train station at the edge of campus invites students to explore the rich cultural tapestry of center city Philadelphia (less than 30 minutes away).

ACADEMIC PROGRAMS

The interdisciplinary nature of the college's curriculum allows unique opportunities for academic discovery. For example, Swarthmore offers a wide array of courses in distinct and intersecting disciplines, with courses such as Race, Gender, Class and Environment which draws from multiple departments, including Black Studies, Sociology/Anthropology, Gender and Sexuality Studies, and Environmental Studies. Students have the chance to craft special majors, with recent examples including Medical Anthropology, Behavioral Economics, and Sustainable Development Studies. Swarthmore's program in education leads to Pennsylvania secondary school certification. All students have significant undergraduate research opportunities in the natural sciences, social sciences, humanities, and engineering.

One hallmark of the college's academic program is that first-year students take their fall semester courses pass-fail. Swarthmore encourages its students, many of whom spent their high school careers concerned about GPAs, to focus on learning for the sake of knowledge. The pass-fail semester provides a true sense of discovery for students, as they are empowered to experiment with new fields. Many students identify potentially life-changing passions, while knowing that they're free to make academic mistakes in the process. Swarthmore recognizes that adjusting to college is a learning process and achieving a balance between engaging in the campus community both inside and outside of the classroom is vital.

Some Swatties decide to take a deep dive into their area of interest. Those students find their intellectual home in Swarthmore's Honors Program. Modeled on the Oxford tutorial system, it features small groups of students working collaboratively with faculty to explore topics through spirited debate and thoughtful exploration of ideas. At the close of their senior year, Honors Program candidates are evaluated by visiting examiners, such as Federal Reserve economists and directors of world-class theater companies. You know you've truly mastered a topic when it's time to discuss your ideas with brilliant strangers.

MAJORS AND DEGREES OFFERED

Art and Art History

Asian Studies

Astronomy

Biology

Black Studies

Chemistry and Biochemistry

Classics

Cognitive Science

Comparative Literature

Computer Science

Dance

Design Your Own Major

Economics

Educational Studies

Engineering

English Literature

Environmental Studies

Film and Media Studies

Gender and Sexuality Studies

History

Interpretation Theory

Islamic Studies

Latin American and Latino Studies

Linguistics

Mathematics and Statistics

Medieval Studies

Modern Languages and Literatures (including Arabic, Chinese, French, German, Japanese, Russian, and Spanish)

Music

Peace and Conflict Studies

Philosophy

Physics

Political Science

Psychology

Religion

Sociology and Anthropology

Theater

TUITION, ROOM, BOARD, FEES

For 2017–2018, the College charges, including tuition, room, board, and student activity fee, amount to $65,774. The activity fee covers not only the usual student services—health, library, laboratory fees, for example—but admission to all social, cultural, and athletic events on campus. In addition, the College's Quaker roots manifest themselves in a cash-free campus, as the annual activity fee covers everything from digital printing and laundry to sporting events, campus movie screenings, and dance performances.

Tuition: $50,424

On-Campus Room and Board: $14,952

FINANCIAL AID

Swarthmore's commitment to financial aid and access is at the core of our educational mission. We understand that students are admitted from a variety of economic backgrounds. The College strives to make it possible for all admitted students to attend Swarthmore, regardless of their ability to pay, and meets 100 percent of determined need for all admitted students. If you are a U.S. citizen, permanent resident, or undocumented/DACA student graduating from a U.S. high school, the decisions about your admission to Swarthmore and your financial aid eligibility are made independently.

Nearly 60 percent of our entering class received need-based Swarthmore Scholarship aid from an overall financial aid budget of just under $40 million. Our aid awards consist of grants (which do not need to be repaid) and the expectation that students will work in a part-time campus-based job. Although Swarthmore financial aid awards are loan-free, your family might choose to borrow a loan to pay a portion of the educational expenses.

STUDENT ORGANIZATIONS AND ACTIVITIES

With more than 100 student clubs and organizations on campus, dozens of community service groups, 22 Division III varsity athletic teams, free lectures and performances occurring daily on campus, and full course loads, Swarthmore students are in perpetual motion.

ADMISSIONS PROCESS

First-year applicants may apply to Swarthmore via Common Application, Coalition Application, or QuestBridge Application. Swarthmore does not have a preference among any of our application options. Please submit only one application in an application year.

Required Materials

- Common Application, Coalition Application, or Questbridge Application
- Swarthmore College Short Answer
  - o As part of the Common or Coalition Application, you will be asked to submit no more than 250 words in response to the following short answer question (Questbridge applicants are asked this question on our Questbridge Conversion Form): "Please write about why you are interested in applying to and attending Swarthmore."
- $60 application fee or fee waiver
- School report
- Guidance counselor recommendation
- High school transcript
- Midyear grades: If your school does not have midyear grades, please provide a midyear progress report from your teachers.
- Self-reported or official standardized test scores
- Two academic-subject teacher evaluations

Optional Materials

- You may request an on-campus or off-campus interview. You may interview before submitting your application.
- You may submit a creative supplement with art, music, dance, theater, or creative writing materials. We accept supplements exclusively through SlideRoom, which provides instructions for submitting materials online, including a video tutorial. Please use the SlideRoom link that matches your choice of application. Submitting additional materials is strictly optional and is at no additional charge.
- Please review financial aid application instructions and deadlines for first-year applicants.

TEMPLE UNIVERSITY

AT A GLANCE

Temple University attracts some of the most diverse, driven and motivated minds from across the nation and around the world. These students and faculty bring the university to life and fuel its momentum in academics, athletics, research and the arts. Powering Temple's ascent are innovative approaches to admissions and affordability; a campus transformation; plentiful creative and research opportunities; rigorous academic programs; an indelible bond with the city of Philadelphia; and groundbreaking work in science, research and technology.

Temple is home to more than 40,000 students, is the thirty-first largest public, four-year institution in the United States and offers more than 570 academic programs in 17 schools and colleges, on eight campuses, including locations in Japan and Italy.

More than 3,800 distinguished faculty members; top art, business, dental, law and medical schools; five professional schools; and dozens of renowned programs make Temple an academic powerhouse. Students enjoy the advantages and atmosphere of a large urban, public research university with the individualized attention that comes from a 15:1 student-to-faculty ratio.

The majority of first-year students live on campus, where they are steps away from class; a state-of-the-art TECH Center; the library; fitness and recreation facilities; dining options such as cafés, dining halls and food trucks; and the many arts, cultural, sports and scholarly events that happen daily at Temple and throughout the city.

Temple's ongoing physical transformation ensures students have all that they need on campus. The newest living and learning residence, the 27-story Morgan Hall, offers unparalleled views of the Philadelphia skyline. The 247,000-square foot Science Education and Research Center supports student and faculty opportunities for discovery and innovation. And a new, modern library being built will feature a robotic book retrieval system and spaces devoted to traditional library activities and technology-enhanced activities, such as data visualization and 3-D printing.

Temple's influence also extends around the globe, with long-standing campuses in Tokyo and Rome; programs in London, Beijing and other locations; a worldwide alumni network of more than 320,000; and more than 3,700 international students at Temple's Main Campus hail from more than 127 countries.

No matter their background, Temple students—nicknamed Owls—are drawn to the university's vibrant location in the heart of Philadelphia. The professional world is a walk or subway trip away, and countless possibilities exist for hands-on learning and internships in business, healthcare, education, the arts and beyond.

By living and learning in an urban environment, Temple students are well prepared for the world. Employers laud Owls for their tenacity, teamwork and talent. Students also have access to an immense alumni network for guidance, job opportunities and mentoring.

LOCATION AND ENVIRONMENT

Temple students enjoy an electric campus in one of the country's liveliest urban centers. Philadelphia—recently named the first World Heritage City in the U.S.—is home to history, arts and culture, technology and innovation, healthcare, and many other fields and interests. Opportunities for learning, whether through a class, an internship or a research project, abound.

Nearly 80 percent of freshmen live on campus. They take walks to class, relax on the grass outside the library, meet friends at the skate park, get lunch at one of the many food trucks, and can work out at several different fitness facilities. Temple's campus has several residence halls and students can choose a living and learning community tailored to their major or interest.

CAMPUS FACILITIES & EQUIPMENT

Whether in the glass-blowing studio or the virtual balance lab, Temple students are immersed in world-class facilities. The Science Education and Research Center is one of the university's newest buildings and home to 68 research and teaching labs and leading-edge technologies such as clean rooms, powerful supercomputers and a scanning tunneling microscope that allows scientists to study matter on the nanoscale.

In the TECH Center—one of the largest student computing labs in the country—students can collaborate in breakout rooms, edit video in specialized labs, get assistance from the 24-hour help desk or work on one of 700 computers. There are also more than 100 other computer labs on campus, 3,600 student workstations and 450 technology-enabled classrooms.

Temple's libraries host intrepid, curious students and scholars. With the equivalent of more than four million bound volumes and an extensive special collection of rare books and archives, Temple's libraries are among the top research libraries in North America.

In addition, the university always has an eye toward building a premiere student life experience through facilities such as the new Aramark Student Training and Recreation Complex. The facility, which opened in fall 2017, includes recreation space, a 70-yard turf field and a juice bar, as well as classrooms and clinical training areas for the College of Public Health.

OFF-CAMPUS OPPORTUNITIES

Temple's Main Campus is located 1.5 miles from the center of Philadelphia. For Temple students, the city blends seamlessly with their studies. Those studying storm water management work hands-on with the water department, art students restore fading historical signs on older buildings, and political science majors learn from civic leaders.

As much as the city is a classroom, it's also a place of adventure. Students can explore more than 100 museums, a thriving restaurant scene, numerous professional sports teams and the largest landscaped urban park in the nation.

Owls interested in experiencing different languages and cultures by studying abroad have dozens of options. They can study at Temple campuses in Tokyo or Rome or join summer programs in Brazil, South Africa, Spain and beyond. Many of the programs tie in to areas of study, like business students studying real markets in hubs such as Paris and Mumbai, or art and architecture students studying among the masterpieces in Rome.

ACADEMICS

Temple has a long tradition of self-made success. The university started in 1884 as a night school so students who worked during the day could keep their jobs. Though a lot has changed, Temple's heritage still drives the work ethic of its students. Owls turn opportunities into accomplishments. World-class labs are the proving grounds for world-changing ideas. A classroom doubles as a tech startup's boardroom. Professors mentor students through graduate school and beyond. And it's all because of the uncommon drive Temple students and faculty share.

Students customize their college life in numerous ways: living and learning communities; an immersive Honors program; interdisciplinary majors; creative and research grants; internships; and career preparation and placement.

Temple encourages the spirit of entrepreneurship university-wide, so Owls know how to thrive no matter their course in life. To help foster such skills, annual innovation and business-idea competitions are open to the entire Temple community, and all students have access to mentors, resources and guidance to develop their business ideas and plans.

Temple also propels students into top graduate programs through challenging academic work, research opportunities and close partnerships with professors.

MAJORS AND DEGREES OFFERED

Students passionate about learning are attracted to Temple because of its variety of academic programs: More than 570 are offered, including more than 140 bachelor's degree programs. Students who need time to decide on a major work with advisors and professors to discover their strengths and options.

TUITION, ROOM, BOARD, FEES

Tuition and fees for the 2017–2018 academic year were approximately $16,658 for Pennsylvania residents and $28,418 for out-of-state residents (tuition rates vary by major). Room and board for the same period was about $10,810, on average.

FINANCIAL AID

Temple is known for its innovation in student-loan debt reduction and college affordability. Each year, the university awards more than $100 million in scholarships. A variety of programs are available and 71 percent of first-year students receive need-based financial aid. No separate application is necessary.

Applicants for need-based aid must file the Free Application for Federal Student Aid, also called FAFSA. Transfer students must file a financial aid transcript, even if they have received no aid from their previous school.

Each year, most incoming freshmen—93 percent—sign up for Temple's Fly in 4 program, which helps students limit their debt by graduating in four years. As a part of Fly in 4, Temple awards four-year grants to 500 eligible students to reduce their need to work for pay. Temple also helps Owls understand their finances through courses, workshops and a money-management website.

STUDENT ORGANIZATIONS AND ACTIVITIES

Temple's student body is known for its diversity: 127 countries are represented at the university. From all over the world and with different interests, students come to Temple and find corners all their own thanks to a wide range of programs and perspectives. It's with that experience that students gain a global understanding that prepares them for the world that awaits them after college.

With more than 300 student clubs and organizations on campus, students have no shortage of opportunities to explore their interests and champion their beliefs. The university also hosts 18 Division I sports teams and three dozen recreational clubs.

The Temple marching band's renditions of popular songs have earned the team national attention. Temple Student Government in 2017 was ranked among the "most active" student governments in the country. And if students seek an organization that doesn't exist, they're encouraged to create their own.

Throughout the year, students can attend academic talks and panels, art exhibits, cultural events, films, music and dance performances, theater productions and sports. There are several large venues for concerts and shows in the city and on campus, including the historic Temple Performing Arts Center and the university's 10,200-seat entertainment complex, which also hosts its NCAA Division I basketball games.

To keep students healthy and strong, Temple offers multiple indoor and outdoor sports, recreation and fitness facilities, including an outdoor volleyball court, a rock-climbing wall, running tracks, pools and several locations for weightlifting and classes.

ADMISSIONS PROCESS

Temple Option is an innovative admissions path for talented students who may not perform well on standardized tests. If students choose to apply though Temple Option, they answer brief essay questions instead of submitting SAT or ACT scores. Temple Option reflects the university's commitment to provide talented, motivated students of all backgrounds opportunities for high-quality college experiences.

Temple's admissions process is holistic: Every aspect of a student's academic history is considered. For freshman admissions, high-school grades, standardized test scores (sent directly from the appropriate testing agencies) or Temple Option responses, and other factors (such as a required essay, recommendations, extracurricular activities, work or leadership experience and other personal circumstances) are considered.

Typically, students with B+ averages or better in strong, college-preparatory curricula in grades 9 through 12 and in the top 30 percent of their graduating classes are accepted. For students submitting test scores, admitted students in 2017 averaged a 27 composite on the ACT, and a 1220 SAT score.

Temple has rolling admissions and early-action plans for the fall semester. The early-action deadline is November 1, with notifications scheduled for mid-January (or earlier). The rolling admissions deadline is February 1.

Students who apply as freshmen are automatically considered for merit-based scholarships and honors.

The application fee is $55, and most students apply online through Temple or the Common Application.

Temple University welcomes transfer applicants. Applicants are considered transfer students if they have attempted 15 or more college-level credits after high school.

Apply to Temple at nextstop.temple.edu/apply or via the Common Application. If you have questions, visit nextstop.temple.edu, email askanowl@temple.edu or find Temple Admissions on Twitter, Instagram or Snapchat: @admissionsTU

TROY UNIVERSITY

AT A GLANCE

Troy University, based in Alabama, is a public university founded in 1887. Through a network of locations and a robust online offering, TROY serves both traditional students and adult learners with a worldwide enrollment of more than 20,000. TROY operates four campuses in Alabama—Troy, Dothan, Montgomery and Phenix City -and locations in 7 states, in both Japan and Korea and partnerships with universities in China, Vietnam and Malaysia.

TROY is accredited by the Southern Association of Colleges and Schools Commission on Colleges, and offers degree programs at the Associate's, Bachelor's, Master's and Doctoral level.

Founded as a college to train teachers, Troy University has today grown into a thriving international university that enrolls more than 1,000 international students, representing more than 76 countries. Also highlighting the University's international focus, TROY is home to Alabama's only Confucius Institute that maintains a statewide mission of educating about the Chinese language, culture and history and forging economic development ties between the state and China.

Troy University offers degree programs in high-demand fields across its five colleges—the College of Arts and Sciences; the Sorrell College of Business; the College of Communication and Fine Arts; the College of Education; and, the College of Health and Human Services.

Troy University has more than 155,000 alumni worldwide and the University's Alumni Association has 64 local alumni chapters throughout the United States and international chapters in China, Russia and Vietnam.

LOCATION AND ENVIRONMENT

The complete university experience may be found at Troy University's beautiful, historic campus in Troy, Ala. The Troy, Ala. campus provides top-notch academic programs as well as experiences that shape careers and lives. Students on the Troy Campus enjoy more than 200 clubs, Greek organizations and philanthropic groups, as well study abroad programs, Division I athletics, an honors program and more.

The Troy Campus also offers a wide variety of residence halls, including apartment style units. The surrounding city of Troy is a charming Southern city with a picturesque town square featuring unique boutiques and food options.

Troy's Dothan Campus is located between Dothan and Fort Rucker and serves primarily adult learners through day, evening and weekend classes. The campus is home to R. Terry Everett Hall, named in honor of the longtime Alabama Congressman from the state's Wiregrass region, and includes in its library collection Everett's Congressional papers. The Wiregrass Archives, featuring historical photos and documents from the region, is also located at the campus.

The University's Montgomery Campus is located in the heart of the state's capital city, and has been a catalyst to revitalization within the downtown area. The campus' administrative offices are located in the former Whitley Hotel, which was renovated to include office and classroom space in what is now known as Whitley Hall. Another revitalization project that is a centerpiece of the campus is the Davis Theatre for the Performing Arts, a 1,200-seat theatre and performing arts venue which features performing groups from throughout the region. The campus is also home to the Rosa Parks Library and Museum, which is located on the site of Mrs. Parks' 1955 arrest that sparked the Montgomery Bus Boycott. The museum pays tribute to Mrs. Parks' legacy of courage and celebrates the people and events of the 381-day boycott, which led to the integration of the city's public transportation system.

The Phenix City Campus, includes a location on the banks of the Chattahoochee River, which has served as a catalyst for development along the East Alabama city's riverfront. The Phenix City campus serves primarily adult learners from East Alabama and neighboring Columbus, Georgia.

CAMPUS FACILITIES & EQUIPMENT

The Troy Campus offers a full complement of facilities for students, including numerous on-campus computer labs and study facilities, a dining hall complete with numerous dining options; the Trojan Student Center, which includes activity space for events, bookstore, food court, and fitness center; a comprehensive library; numerous residence halls that provide a variety of living options; fraternity and sorority houses; athletic facilities, including the 30,000-seat Veterans Memorial Stadium and Trojan Arena, which is home to men's and women's basketball.

Students also can take advantage of opportunities that will help them hone their skills and enhance their academic success. The John W. Schmidt Center for Student Success provides programs and services that enhance students' academic achievement, personal and social growth, campus and civic engagement and persistence to graduation.

ACADEMICS

Academic programs include a range of options in business, management and accounting, human resource management, criminal justice, education, psychology and counseling, social work, nursing, public administration and political science, athletic training, theatre and dance, art and design, and sport, tourism and hospitality management, among many others.

MAJORS AND DEGREES OFFERED

Troy University offers more than 225 undergraduate and graduate academic programs and concentrations. Accredited by the Southern Association of Colleges and Schools Commission on Colleges to award associate, baccalaureate, master's, education specialist and doctoral degrees.

With a student-first philosophy, Troy University continues to serve both traditional college-aged students and adult learners with quality academic programs, in high-demand fields, through its five colleges—the Sorrell College of Business, the College of Communication and Fine Arts, Arts and Sciences, Education and Health and Human Services.

TUITION, ROOM, BOARD, FEES

Undergraduate tuition for the 2017–2018 academic year is $316 per credit hour for in-state students, and $632 per credit hour for out-of-state students. Graduate tuition for the 2017–2018 academic year is $417 per credit hour for in-state students and $834 per credit hour for out-of-state students.

Fees charged each semester include:

- General University fee -$42 per credit hour
- Registration fee -$50 per semester
- Student Facility fee (Troy Campus only) -$100 per semester in fall and spring semesters and $50 in summer semester.

The Troy Campus features a variety of residential living options that vary in pricing. On campus residents are also required to purchase a meal plan that can be used in Trojan Dining or the food court located in the Trojan Student Center.

FINANCIAL AID

Troy University is committed to providing exceptional service to students and their families who apply for financial assistance. The Office of Financial Aid offers a variety of services and programs designed to help you find ways to meet the costs of education. Additional information on the various types of financial aid and their requirements can be found at www.troy.edu/financialaid.

A number of scholarship opportunities are also available through the University that can help students finance their education. For more information on available scholarships and their requirements, visit www.troy.edu/scholarships.

STUDENT ORGANIZATIONS AND ACTIVITIES

The University's Troy Campus is home to a diverse student population, including students from across the United States and more than 1,000 international students representing more than 76 countries.

Students on the Troy Campus have a variety of opportunities to enrich their college experience. Troy students have nearly 200 student organizations from which to choose, including fraternities and sororities, academic/professional clubs, honor societies, leadership and service groups, political and special interest organizations, religious groups, performing groups and campus publications.

One of the campus' largest student organizations is the Sound of the South Marching Band, which includes students from each of the University's five colleges. A variety of performing ensembles are also available through the John M. Long School of Music.

Leadership opportunities are available through participation in the Student Government Association, the Freshman Forum, Trojan Ambassadors, and IMPACT orientation leaders, among others.

In addition, the Office of Service Learning and Civic Engagement, a part of the John W. Schmidt Center for Student Success, connects Troy University students to applied learning opportunities where students can develop skills in leadership, project management and civic action, while making a difference in the local community. Current student Service Learning and Civic Engagement initiatives include: poverty and hunger, sustainability, healthy futures and community action and outreach.

ADMISSIONS PROCESS

Undergraduate Admission: High School graduates may be admitted as Freshmen to Troy University on the basis of acceptable high school records (a 2.0 Grade Point Average) and scores achieved on the American College Testing Program (minimum composite of 20 on the ACT) or the Scholastic Aptitude Test (minimum composite of 950 or 1030 if taken since March 2016). Applicants who are 25 years of age or older are not required to submit ACT/SAT scores for admission to the university. All applicants who are graduates of accredited high schools must submit an official transcript showing graduation and a minimum of fifteen Carnegie units, with three or more units in English. Of the units presented, eleven must be in academic courses. Applicants who are graduates of non-accredited secondary schools may be admitted provided they meet the same requirements as students from accredited schools. Pending judgment of the Admissions Committee, these students are expected to complete satisfactory academic work.

Undergraduate students applying to Troy University will be charged a $30 application fee.

Graduate Admission: Those students wishing to apply to Troy University to pursue graduate degrees must submit a letter of recommendation and final official transcripts from all colleges/universities attended, including the degree granted and award date. Graduate students must submit official test score results for the GRE, the MAT or the GMAT.

Graduate students applying to Troy University will be charged a $50 application fee.

Apply online today at troy.edu/admissions.

TRUMAN STATE UNIVERSITY

AT A GLANCE

Truman State University is Missouri's premier liberal arts and sciences university and the only highly selective public institution in the state. As one of the very few publicly funded liberal arts schools in the nation, Truman successfully combines affordability with the type of education and personal attention typically only offered at a private institution.

Truman has established an impeccable reputation in the Midwest and throughout the nation for the high-quality undergraduate programs offered. In fact, for more than two decades, U.S. News & World Report has ranked Truman State University as the number one master's level public institution in the Midwest. A commitment to student achievement and learning is the focus of the University.

LOCATION AND ENVIRONMENT

The Truman campus is beautifully situated on 180 acres in Kirksville, a town of approximately 17,000 located in the northeast corner of Missouri. The historic downtown area is within walking distance of the Truman campus and provides a connection to the Kirksville community with local restaurants, shops, and entertainment.

CAMPUS FACILITIES & EQUIPMENT

Students take advantage of numerous academic resources and facilities available to them. Improvements to campus facilities have included major renovations to Baldwin Hall—one of the most historic buildings on campus—housing classrooms, faculty offices, and Baldwin Auditorium, a 1400 seat performance space and home of the Lyceum Series. Barnett Hall has a modern Student Media Center encompassing facilities for the student-produced newspaper, Midwest travel magazine, radio station, and TV studio. Students also enjoy dining, socializing, and relaxing in the newly renovated Student Union Building.

The Health Sciences Building houses a speech and hearing clinic for Communication Disorders students, an independent learning center for Nursing students, a Human Performance lab, and the Fontaine C. Piper Movement Analysis lab. Additional facilities include a biofeedback laboratory, an organic chemistry lab, an observatory, a 400-acre university farm, a multicultural affairs center, student health center, and a career center. Athletic facilities include a 5,000-seat football stadium, a 3,000-seat arena with three basketball courts, an Olympic-size swimming pool, soccer and rugby fields, baseball and softball fields, tennis courts, a dance studio, and a Student Recreation Center.

Truman has been measuring its energy consumption and is implementing appropriate measures to lower it. Solar panels are located on five different buildings across campus. During the first year of implementation, Truman saw a reduction of 113.5 tons of CO_2 emissions producing 108 kW of useable energy from these panels. Efforts to manage the consumption of our natural resources are also a priority. We are proud of our beautiful campus, which has been named a Tree Campus USA site by the Arbor Day Foundation.

Residence halls also provide comfortable and enriching living environments for students. Most of the halls have been renovated within the last five years. All residence halls offer lounges, kitchenettes, laundry facilities, high-speed internet (including wireless), cable TV, and many other amenities. Students can eat in dining halls or in the food court style dining in the Student Union Building.

ACADEMICS

Truman also offers a challenging Honors Scholar Program. Students have the opportunity to select the most rigorous honors courses to satisfy the liberal arts component of their respective programs. Those who successfully complete this program benefit from an even richer academic experience at Truman and receive special recognition at graduation. Departmental honors are also available in several disciplines.

Students at Truman are active both inside and outside of the classroom. More than 400 Truman students participate in enriching and life-changing study abroad experiences each year. Students can participate in programs ranging from a couple weeks to a year in duration, and can choose from numerous destinations worldwide. The Chronicle for Higher Education recognized Truman as the top producer of Fulbright students for the 2017–18 school year among Master's institutions. This federal grant provides funds for studying or working abroad after graduation.

Truman offers a wide variety of experiential internships, a required component of some academic programs. The "Truman in Washington" program provides work-experience opportunities in the nation's capitol in such areas as foreign affairs/diplomacy, government affairs, criminal justice, international relations, health and human services, and communications as well as other areas. Truman also offers internship opportunities with the Missouri State Legislature. In recent years, students have completed internships with United States senators, the United States Supreme Court, the governor of Missouri, business and industry managers, advertising agencies, physical therapists, and artists. For the fall 2015 semester, Truman had three interns at the White House.

MAJORS AND DEGREES OFFERED

Undergraduate degrees offered by Truman include the Bachelor of Arts (B.A.), Bachelor of Science (B.S.), Bachelor of Music (B.M.), Bachelor of Fine Arts (B.F.A.), and Bachelor of Science in Nursing (B.S.N.). Truman offers more than forty areas of study in the following disciplines: Accounting, Agricultural Science, Art, Art History, Biochemistry and Molecular Biology, Biology, Business Administration, Chemistry, Classics, Communication, Communication Disorders, Computer Science, Creative Writing, Economics, English, Exercise Science, French, German, Health Science, History, Interdisciplinary Studies, Justice Systems, Linguistics, Mathematics, Music, Nursing, Philosophy and Religion, Physics, Political Science, Psychology, Romance Languages, Sociology/Anthropology, Spanish, Statistics, and Theatre.

Professional paths include but are not limited to dentistry, engineering, law, medicine, optometry, pharmacy, physical therapy, occupational therapy and veterinary medicine.

The teaching degree at Truman is the Master of Arts in Education. Students wishing to pursue a teaching career first complete a bachelor's degree in an academic discipline and then apply for admission into professional study at the master's level. Master's programs in special education, elementary education, middle school education, and secondary education are available.

Truman also offers Master's level degrees in Accountancy (MAc), Athletic Training (MAT), Communication Disorders (MA), Counseling (MA), English (MA), Leadership (MA) and Music (MA).

The Liberal Studies Program is the heart of Truman's curriculum and is intended to serve as a foundation for all major programs of study. The philosophy behind the Liberal Studies Program is based upon a commitment that Truman has made to provide students with essential skills needed for lifelong learning, breadth across the traditional liberal arts and sciences through exposure to various discipline-based modes of inquiry, and interconnecting perspectives that stress interdisciplinary thinking and integration as well as linkage to other cultures and experiences.

Students at Truman complete a "capstone," or culminating experience their senior year. This experience prompts seniors to reflect on the knowledge they have gained throughout their learning experience and to integrate the knowledge, skills, and attitudes of liberal learning with an in-depth understanding of the major.

TUITION, ROOM, BOARD, FEES

Tuition for Missouri residents for the 2017–18 academic year is $7,352; out-of-state tuition is $14,136. The average room and board rate for both Missouri residents and nonresidents is $8,638. Additional fees include a one-time freshman orientation fee, and annual fees including an activities fee, an athletic fee, a Student Health Center fee, a sustainability fee, a technology fee, and a parking fee for those with a vehicle, plus costs of books and personal expenses.

FINANCIAL AID

Truman offers automatic scholarships ranging from $500 to $5,000. Competitive scholarship awards vary from $500 up to full tuition, room and board, plus a $4,000 study-abroad stipend. The application for admission also serves as the application for the automatic and competitive scholarship programs.

A limited number of scholarships are awarded to students for excellence in fine arts, debate or foreign language. These scholarships are available for instrumental or vocal music; acting or dramatic production; studio art or art history; speech or debate; and foreign languages offered at Truman. Of special interest to piano students is the Truman Piano Fellowship Competition, a February competition offering scholarships to top pianists.

Truman, a National Collegiate Athletic Association Division II member, offers 20 men's and women's sports. The NCAA and the University authorize a limited number of grants to outstanding athletes. The value of this aid may vary with each individual recipient.

Truman accepts the Free Application for Federal Student Aid (FASFA) and participates in all Federal Title IV financial aid programs. Financial aid estimates are available upon request.

STUDENT ORGANIZATIONS AND ACTIVITIES

With approximately 250 student organizations to choose from, encompassing service, Greek, honorary, professional, religious, social, political and recreational influences, Truman students have tremendous opportunities to become involved on campus and in the Kirksville community. Truman student organizations sponsor a number of events throughout the year, such as Truman Live, International Idol, guest speakers, poetry slams, musical performances, dance recitals, volunteering events, and ever-popular food nights.

The Kohlenberg Lyceum Series also provides a variety of cultural programs that interest students throughout the year. Past programs have included brilliant performances by the Peking Acrobats, American Shakespeare Center, Vocalosity, and the Russian Festival Ballet.

Truman's Student Activities Board sponsors a variety of entertainment events. Recent SAB concerts include Andy Grammer and Sara Bareilles. Comedic acts and speakers like Donald Glover, Adam DeVine, and John Oliver have also come to Truman's campus in recent years.

ADMISSIONS PROCESS

Each applicant is evaluated for admission based upon academic and co-curricular record, ACT or SAT results, and the admission essay. Truman requires the following high school core: 4 units of English, 3 units of mathematics (4 recommended), 3 units of social studies/history, 3 units of natural science, 1 unit of fine arts and 2 units of the same foreign language.

Candidates are considered for admission on a rolling basis, although those interested in scholarship and financial aid programs are strongly encouraged to apply for admission and submit a resume/activity list by December 1. Students may apply online at the website listed below or through the Common Application. For further information or to schedule a campus visit, students should contact:

Office of Admission

Truman State University

100 East Normal

Kirksville, Missouri 63501

Telephone: 660.785.4114 or 800.892.7792

Fax: 660.785.7456

E-mail: admissions@truman.edu

http://admissions.truman.edu

UNION COLLEGE (NY)

AT A GLANCE

Union College is one of the nation's oldest and most distinguished liberal arts colleges. Chartered by the state of New York in 1795, Union is a leader in offering an integrated liberal arts education that fully embraces STEM while teaching students to be engaged, innovative and ethical contributors to a diverse, global and technologically complex society. The Union curriculum emphasizes collaboration with students and faculty through small classes and undergraduate research, interdisciplinary and international study, and service learning.

LOCATION AND ENVIRONMENT

The first planned campus in America, Union was designed by noted French architect Joseph-Jacques Ramée and includes the 16-sided Nott Memorial, a historic landmark, and Jackson's Garden, a certified natural wildlife habitat. Union is located on 130 acres in the revitalized city of Schenectady, part of New York's Capital Region. Steps from campus, the city features a lively mix of restaurants, cafés, shops, theaters and a popular weekly greenmarket. The region's rich cultural heritage, thriving high-tech industry and diverse economy offer opportunities for student/faculty research, internships and jobs. Union is a 20-minute drive from Albany International Airport and a short walk or drive from the Schenectady bus and train stations. It is within easy reach of New York City (a 3-hour drive), Boston (3 hours), Montreal (4 hours), and rural and wilderness areas.

CAMPUS FACILITIES & EQUIPMENT

Union is in the midst of the largest and most ambitious project in its history—a $100 million makeover and expansion of the Science and Engineering Center. A centerpiece of the revamped center, to be named the Integrated Science and Engineering Complex, will be an arc-shaped building featuring floor-to-ceiling glass walls and a four-story lightwell that allows individuals to glimpse the work of other disciplines. The reconstruction is designed to revolutionize teaching, learning and research across engineering, science and the liberal arts.

The Peter Irving Wold Center, an interdisciplinary hub, offers leading-edge programs in biochemistry, environmental studies, electrical engineering and music research. The Center for Neuroscience in Butterfield Hall brings together computer and research labs, classrooms and collaborative spaces. The F.W. Olin Center houses high-tech classrooms and laboratories.

The Nott Memorial is used for study, exhibits and special events, including the annual Study Abroad Fair, the Lothridge Festival of Dance, and guest lectures by such noted figures as U.S. Sen. Kirsten Gillibrand, architect Maya Lin, environmentalist Bill McKibben, activist Cornel West and journalist Bob Woodward.

Schaffer Library has over 1 million print and electronic volumes and more than 11,000 current print and electronic serial titles. Union also participates in the ConnectNY consortium, giving users access to the holdings of 14 other member libraries. The College Archives, Language Lab, Special Collections and Writing Center are also housed at Schaffer Library.

Karp Hall houses the departments of English, and Modern Languages and Literature. Lippman Hall is home to the Social Sciences, including Economics, History, Political Science and Sociology. Lamont House is home to Anthropology, Classics and Philosophy, and the Religious Studies program.

The Feigenbaum Center for Visual Arts includes studios for drawing, painting, sculpture, printmaking, 2D and 3D design, and metal-working, as well as a media lab, traditional dark room, public galleries and classrooms. Other arts facilities include the Mandeville Gallery and Wikoff Student Gallery, both in the Nott Memorial; the all-Steinway Taylor Music Center; the Yulman Theater, home to Mountebanks, the nation's oldest student performing group; and the Henle Dance Pavilion. Union's Kelly Adirondack Center in nearby Niskayuna houses one of the largest research collections on the Adirondack region.

Residential options for students include traditional dorms, apartment-style housing, theme houses, Minerva Houses, Greek houses, College Park Hall and Garnet Commons. Reamer Campus Center includes dining facilities, the bookstore and offices for student activities.

Among the athletic facilities are Alumni Gymnasium, which features the Breazzano Fitness Center, a swimming/diving pool, and exercise and yoga studios. Other recreational and sports facilities include the 3,000-seat Messa Rink at Achilles Center, home of Union's Div. I hockey teams, and the Travis J. Clark '00 Strength Training Facility for varsity athletes. The men's and women's crew teams train at the College's boathouse on the Mohawk River. The Wicker Wellness Center offers professional health, wellness and counseling services and is the home of Jenna, the campus therapy dog.

The Becker Career Center helps students align their personal passions with their academic and professional pursuits, and it works with employers and alumni to guide students in competing effectively in today's job market. Students can connect with alumni in all fields through the Union Career Advisory Network (UCAN). HireU, the center's internship and job database, contains opportunities from alumni and employers who are seeking Union students. Students regularly meet potential employers at campus career and internship fairs and other events. Ninety-eight percent of new Union graduates are employed or pursuing an advanced degree or fellowship.

OFF-CAMPUS OPPORTUNITIES

Union offers more than 40 terms and mini-term programs in 30 countries. Students can conduct anthropological research in Fiji, learn about Italian Renaissance architecture in Florence, study engineering in Turkey or visit alternative energy sites in New Zealand. There are also great opportunities for internships and service. Nearly 60 percent of Union students go on terms abroad, one of the highest percentages among colleges and universities. Most programs are led by Union faculty. Students also may design their own program of study abroad and participate in non-Union and exchange programs. In addition to full-term programs, three-week mini-terms are offered during winter and summer breaks in various U.S. cities and other countries. The unique Minerva Fellows program gives young alumni a chance to travel abroad their first year after leaving Union, instilling in them the power of an entrepreneurial approach in addressing poverty in developing countries.

ACADEMIC PROGRAMS

Union is committed to integrating the humanities and social sciences with science and engineering while emphasizing the practical application of ideas through experience. Students gain deep knowledge within their majors and also experience ideas and insights from multiple disciplines.

Students must complete a minimum of 36 courses (up to 40 for engineering degrees) and satisfy departmental and Common Curriculum requirements, including the First-Year Preceptorial and Sophomore Research Seminar, which promote reading, writing, research and critical thinking skills. Distribution requirements in the humanities, literature, social sciences, linguistic and cultural competency, quantitative mathematical reasoning and the sciences promote a breadth of knowledge about the social and natural world, and key skills in analysis, literacy and numeracy. Writing Across the Curriculum requires students to take five designated courses from at least two divisions and one Senior Writing Experience.

Union encourages student research in all disciplines. Three-quarters of students actively engage in research. They work one-on-one with professors and have access to sophisticated instrumentation often reserved for graduate students at large universities. At Steinmetz Symposium each spring, some 500 students present their research, scholarship and creative work. Approximately 140 students participate in summer research. Many students co-author publications with faculty and present at major conferences. Union consistently ranks among the top of its peer institutions in National Science Foundation awards.

Academic advisers help students select the right coursework, develop research topics, and pursue internships and service. Students participate in internships at more than 500 organizations worldwide, gaining real-world experience in such fields as businesses, health care, government, science, social service, technology and the arts. Union also sponsors IBM summer internships in China and Switzerland, as well as the Silicon Valley Internship on Innovation and Creativity, which combines internships in Bay Area startups and NGOs with courses in culture and entrepreneurship. There is faculty advising for business, law, medical and graduate school, and students also receive encouragement and support in applying for prestigious national and international scholarships and fellowships.

MAJORS AND DEGREES OFFERED

Union offers more than 40 majors and 58 minors. Students may choose double majors; combine majors and minors; or pursue interdepartmental and multidisciplinary programs, such as ethnic and cultural studies. Some students design their own Organizing Theme major. Most students take three courses in each of the three 10-week terms that comprise Union's academic calendar. The average introductory class has 21 students; the average upper level class, 14.

Union also offers numerous joint programs leading to advanced degrees. These include: a 3+3 accelerated law program (B.A. + J.D.); a 4+1 master of arts in teaching (B.A. or B.S. + MAT); a 4+1 master of science with degree with options in bioethics, energy systems and electrical or mechanical engineering (B.S. + M.S.); a 5-year business/management program (B.A. or B.S. + M.B.A.); and an 8-year leadership in medicine program (B.S. + M.S. or M.B.A. + M.D.)

TUITION, ROOM, BOARD, FEES

Union's comprehensive fee, which includes tuition, room, board, and mandatory fees, is $68,853 for the 2018–19 academic year. The estimated cost for books and personal expenses is $2,000.

FINANCIAL AID

Union is committed to admitting an economically diverse student body and to meeting the full demonstrated need of all admitted students. Its comprehensive financial aid program includes more than $65 million in aid from Union's own resources and from federal, state, institutional and other agencies. The College offers more than $45 million annually in the form of grants and scholarships that do not need to be repaid. Scholarship awards are based on academic performance and financial need. The average need-based Union scholarship is $35,000; need-based aid is evaluated annually. First-year applicants are automatically considered for merit scholarships. These scholarships are awarded to top applicants each year based on academic credentials. They range from $10,000 to $20,000 and are renewed annually

for four years. Students who demonstrate financial need are offered a financial aid package that generally consists of a grant, loan and work opportunity. More than 60 percent of students receive financial assistance from the College. Candidates for aid must file the Free Application for Federal Student Aid (FAFSA) and the College Scholarship Service's PROFILE form by Jan. 15; Early Decision (ED) candidates must file by the ED application deadline.

STUDENT ORGANIZATIONS AND ACTIVITIES

Union's approximately 2,200 full-time undergraduates come from 40 U.S. states and territories and 36 other countries, from Australia to Zimbabwe. International students make up 7 percent of the student body, and 20 percent of students identify themselves as members of a multicultural group.

Union has more than 100 campus clubs, including arts and cultural groups; the student newspaper, Concordiensis, and radio station, WRUC; sports clubs; academic societies; service and political interest groups; 9 residential fraternities and sororities; and 13 theme houses (devoted to arts, civil liberties, the LGBTQ community, sustainability, technology and more). Cultural events include concerts, theater, dance, film and exhibits. Union's comprehensive athletics program offers 26 varsity intercollegiate sports, organized intramurals, club sports, and recreational and fitness activities. Union is a member of the NCAA, Liberty League and ECAC Hockey. Men's and women's ice hockey compete in NCAA Division I programs; other teams are Division III. Union triumphed in the Frozen Four to capture the national men's hockey title in 2014.

The Minerva House system is a vibrant community and launch pad for an array of college experiences. All students and faculty members belong to one of seven on-campus houses, where they contribute in distinct ways to Union's social, cultural, academic and intellectual life. Student-run Minerva programs range from book clubs and barbecues to language tables, current events discussions and cooking dinner with professors. The longest running Minerva program, Green House jams, brings together students and faculty for musical jam sessions every Friday afternoon.

Union inspires and encourages students to engage with the local global community through meaningful volunteer work and charitable projects. Some 1,200 students each year are involved in more than 30 service programs and other opportunities for service and leadership. The Kenney Community Center is a hub that connects students with Big Brothers Big Sisters, Habitat for Humanity, tutoring programs and many civic projects. Many students groups, athletic teams, and Greek organizations also sponsor community service activities.

ADMISSIONS PROCESS

More than 6,500 applicants typically seek first-year class positions; roughly 70 percent are in the top 10 percent of their secondary school class. Admissions counselors look at grades, rigor of courses taken, class rank, teacher recommendations and extracurricular involvement. Typically, 16 units of secondary school preparation are required for admission. These should include credits in such fundamental subjects as English, foreign language, mathematics, social studies and science. It is strongly recommended that students visit Union for an interview and student-guided tour. Alumni interviews may be requested online. A student can choose not to submit his or her SAT or ACT scores for review, except for accelerated programs, which require applicants to submit the SAT and two SAT Subject Tests.

Early decision (ED) candidates have two options. The application deadline (including all supporting credentials) for Option I is Nov. 15, with notification by Dec. 15. Option II has a Jan. 15 deadline (including all supporting credentials) and Feb. 15 notification. Applications for regular decision (RD) admission must be filed by Jan.15; decisions are mailed by April 1. Applications to the Leadership in Medicine program are due no later than Dec. 15, and for Law and Public Policy, by Jan. 15. Those deferred under ED and all regular applicants are given a final decision by April 1. Accepted students have until May 1 to commit.

School Says . . .

THE UNIVERSITY OF CENTRAL FLORIDA

AT A GLANCE

The University of Central Florida is a comprehensive research university with over 66,000 students. As one of the nation's fastest growing and largest universities UCF enrolls a diverse student body representing all 50 states and over 120 countries. The University offers educational and research programs that complement the economy, with strong components in aerospace engineering, business, education, film, health, nursing, social sciences, and hospitality management. UCF's programs in communication and the fine arts help to meet the cultural and recreational needs of a growing metropolitan area. The University also offers many graduate programs leading to masters and doctoral degrees.

UCF has established extensive partnerships with businesses and industry in the central Florida area and beyond that provide students with exceptional research and learning experiences. These partnerships bring practical learning environments to UCF students through co-op and internship programs. Joint curriculum development strategies are used throughout the university.

The on-campus and campus-affiliated housing facilities include traditional residence halls, apartment-style options, and Greek housing that accommodates approximately 11,500 students. Several thousand students live in apartments located within walking distance of the campus.

LOCATION

The University of Central Florida: Competitive Advantages

A Focus on Undergraduate Education: We're committed to teaching and providing advising and academic support services for all students. Our undergraduates have access to state-of-the-art wireless buildings, high-tech classrooms and research labs, Web-based classes and an undergraduate Research and Mentoring program.

A Talented Student Body: As one of the fastest growing universities, total enrollment has reached over 66,000; 56,974 are undergraduates. Our emphasis on excellence in undergraduate education has produced many rewarding results: a Goldwater Scholarship awardee, a Rhodes Scholarship finalist, a Clarion awardee in Radio/Television, a Zonta International Amelia Earhart fellowship awardee, and internationally ranked Computer Science programming and Cyber Defense teams.

Career Opportunities: Our Career Services professionals help students gain practical experiences at NASA, schools, hospitals, high-tech companies, local municipalities, and the entertainment industry. UCF faculty sit on boards and planning committees, and our graduates make their mark in engineering, business, computer science, education, health care, science, tourism, film and public service.

An International Presence: With an international focus to our curricula and research programs, we currently enroll international students from over 120 nations. Our study abroad programs and other study and research opportunities include agreements with 98 institutions and 36 countries, including Australia, France, Germany, Holland, Italy, Russia, South Africa, Spain and Wales.

A Spacious, Modern Campus, plus Orlando: UCF's 1,415-acre campus provides a safe and serene setting for learning, with natural lakes and woodlands. The university provides housing for approximately 11,500 students on campus and through affiliated housing. The bustle of Orlando lies a short distance away: the Orlando Magic, the Orlando City Soccer Club, the Kennedy Space Center, major film studios, Walt Disney World, Universal Orlando, Sea World, and sandy beaches are all nearby.

CAMPUS FACILITIES & EQUIPMENT

In addition to the academic programs offered on the Orlando campus, upper division students can work toward a degree at 11 locations around the central Florida area. These regional campuses work cooperatively with local state colleges to provide all four years of course work in many academic areas. The library houses over 2 million print volumes and subscribes to more than 53,000 periodicals and journals (49,000 in electronic format). Students have access to an online computer catalog that provides information on the collections of the State University System libraries. An extensive online network of more than 600 computer terminals (both PC and Mac) cover the campus. The Institute for Simulation and Training gives students the opportunity to pursue undergraduate research. The College of Optics and Photonics allows faculty members and students to work directly with industrial personnel in conducting basic and applied research at the regional and national level. The Central Florida Research Park, located next to the UCF campus, houses more than 125 high-technology firms and agencies. This proximity fosters relationships between industry and the University, which strengthens the academic programs at UCF.

OFF-CAMPUS OPPORTUNITIES

Career Services and Experiential Learning provides comprehensive and coordinated career development, enhances academic study, and builds ongoing partnerships with employers and the community. The UCF Abroad Office offers study-abroad programs. UCF is also a participant in the National Student Exchange Consortium.

ACADEMICS

The University offers the degrees of Bachelor of Applied Science, Bachelor of Arts, Bachelor of Design, Bachelor of Fine Arts, Bachelor of Music, Bachelor of Music Education, Bachelor of Science, Bachelor of Science in Business Administration, Bachelor of Science in Education, Bachelor of Science in Engineering, Bachelor of Science in Nursing, Bachelor of Social Work, and Bachelor of Science in Social Sciences.

MAJORS AND DEGREES OFFERED

These degrees are available in the colleges listed below, with majors or areas of specialization as indicated. (for the most up-to-date list of colleges, departments, majors and minors visit www.ucf.edu)

The College of Arts and Humanities offers degrees in art, Architecture, digital media, English, film, French, history, humanities and cultural studies, Latin American Studies, music, Music Education, philosophy, Photography, Religion and Cultural Studies, Spanish, Theatre Studies, and Writing and Rhetoric.

The College of Business Administration offers degrees in accounting, Business Economics, economics, finance, Integrated Business, management, real estate and marketing.

The College of Education and Human Performance offers degrees in early childhood development and education, elementary education, exceptional student education, secondary education, sport and exercise science, teacher education, and technical education and industry training.

The College of Engineering and Computer Science offers degrees in aerospace engineering, civil engineering, computer engineering, computer science, construction engineering, electrical engineering, environmental engineering, industrial engineering, Information Technology and mechanical engineering.

The College of Health and Public Affairs offers degrees in athletic training, Communication Sciences and Disorders, criminal justice, Health Informatics and information management, health services administration, health sciences, legal studies, nonprofit management, public administration, and social work.

The College of Nursing offers degrees in nursing.

The College of Optics and Photonics offers degrees in Photonic Science and Engineering.

The College of Sciences offers degrees in actuarial science, advertising/public relations, anthropology, biology, chemistry, Communication and Conflict, forensic science, International and Global Studies, Human Communication, journalism, mathematics, physics, political science, psychology, radio/television, social sciences, sociology, and statistics.

The Rosen College of Hospitality Management offers degrees in Hospitality Management, Event Management, Entertainment Management, and Restaurant and Foodservice Management.

The College of Medicine and the Burnett School of Biomedical Sciences offers degrees in Biotechnology, Medical Laboratory Sciences, and biomedical sciences.

The College of Undergraduate Studies offers degrees in Environmental Studies and Interdisciplinary Studies.

Pre-professional programs are offered in chiropractic, medicine, occupational therapy, optometry, pharmacy, physical therapy, physician assistant, podiatry, public health, dentistry, veterinary medicine and law.

TUITION, ROOM, BOARD, FEES
Approximate Tuition, Health Fee, Room and Board Annual Rates 2017–18:

	Florida Resident	Florida Non-Resident
Tuition and Fees	$6,368	$22,466
Room and Board	$9,764	$9,764
Books (estimate)	1,152	$1,152
Approximate Total / Annual Cost.	$17,284	$33,382

Based on 15 credit hours per semester, double room and meal plan.

FINANCIAL AID
Financial aid is awarded according to each student's demonstrated need in relation to college costs and may include grants, loans, scholarships and part-time employment. Programs based on need include the Federal Perkins Loan, Federal Pell Grant, Florida Student Assistance Grant, Federal Work-Study, Florida College Career Work-Study Program, and Federal Stafford Student Loan. To qualify for these programs, students must complete the Free Application for Federal Student Aid (FAFSA). The priority application deadline is December 1. Approximately 76 percent of UCF students receive some form of financial aid.

STUDENT ORGANIZATIONS AND ACTIVITIES
Students participate in over 650 organizations, including special interest clubs, multicultural associations, fraternities and sororities, honor societies, and academic and pre-professional organizations. The Office of Student Involvement schedules a wide array of extracurricular programs, including concerts, movies, and guest speakers. The innovative LEAD Scholars Academy fosters leadership and service commitment through a comprehensive student development program for freshman. The Major Exploration Program (MEP) helps entering freshmen define their career goals and develop an academic strategy to reach their goals. UCF offers Air Force and Army ROTC programs.

The University of Central Florida is a member of the NCAA and the American Athletic Conference. All teams compete on the NCAA Division 1 Level. UCF's men's teams compete in intercollegiate baseball, basketball, football, golf, soccer, and tennis. Women's teams compete in basketball, cross-country, golf, rowing, soccer, softball, tennis, track and field, and volleyball. Intercollegiate coed club activities include championship cheerleading, crew, and waterskiing teams. The university offers an extensive intramural sports program.

ADMISSIONS PROCESS
A freshman applicant is a student with fewer than 12 hours of college coursework after high school graduation. The most important criteria in the admission decision for these applicants is the high school academic record, rigor of course work, grade point average, grade trends, and SAT I or ACT test scores. UCF operates on a rolling admission basis. Students are generally notified of their initial admission decision within two to three weeks after receipt of the application and all supporting documents. If the number of qualified applicants exceeds the number that the university is permitted to enroll, a waiting list will be established.

All applicants must have earned a minimum of 18 high school academic units (yearlong courses that are not remedial in nature). These include 4 units of English (3 must include substantial writing), 4 units of mathematics at or above algebra I, 3 units of natural science (2 must include a laboratory), 3 units of social science, 2 units of one world language, and 2 units of academic electives. Grades in honors courses, International Baccalaureate, Advanced Placement, AICE and dual enrollment courses are given additional weight in the GPA computation. Students must meet the Department of Education minimum eligibility to be considered for admission. Applicants should understand that the satisfaction of minimum requirements does not automatically guarantee admission to UCF.

Admission requirements for Transfer applicants vary by the number of college credit hours the student has successfully completed prior to enrolling at UCF. For complete details, go to http://admissions.ucf.edu/apply/transfer/. A transfer credit summary evaluation is provided to students once they are offered admission to UCF.

Students are encouraged to apply several months in advance. Transfers can apply online at http://admissions.ucf.edu/ and Freshmen can apply online at http://admissions.ucf.edu/ or through the Common Application. It is recommended that freshman students apply early during the fall semester of their senior year. Applications are accepted up to one year prior to the start of the term for which entry is desired. Priority application deadlines are May 1 for the fall term (July 1 for transfers), November 1 for the spring term, and March 1 for the summer term.

THE UNIVERSITY OF DELAWARE

AT A GLANCE

The University of Delaware was chartered in 1743 and is located in Newark, DE, a vibrant college town midway between New York City and Washington, D.C. For each of our 17,000 undergraduate students in each of our 150+ majors, our broad academic selections and our priority for hands-on research will stimulate a passion for learning and a curiosity for the larger world.

Our students come from nearly all 50 states and over 100 countries. Students choose UD for our Honors Program, Study Abroad opportunities and discovery learning experiences that ensure they will graduate with impressive resumes and meaningful degrees. Our distinguished faculty includes internationally known authors, scientists and artists. State-of-the-art facilities support UD's academic, research and service activities. Campus life is enriched by distinguished speakers, NCAA Division I intercollegiate athletics, 350+ engaged student organizations, concerts and other arts and cultural activities. The various opportunities and resources at UD lead to successful outcomes for our students. Learn more about student success at http://www.udel.edu/apply/career-outcomes/.

LOCATION AND ENVIRONMENT

The University of Delaware is located in the community of Newark, Delaware—a short drive from Wilmington, New York City, Washington, D.C., Baltimore and Philadelphia.

CAMPUS FACILITIES & EQUIPMENT

The University of Delaware's Science, Technology and Advanced Research (STAR) Campus provides educational and professional opportunities to students for research and collaboration. STAR campus is home to four cutting-edge, research-driven clinics as well as multiple laboratories providing undergraduates with opportunities to participate in research. Here you will find the Speech Language Hearing Clinic, Physical Therapy Clinic, Nurse-Managed Primary Health Care Center and Human Anatomy Lab.

The Patrick T. Harker Interdisciplinary Science and Engineering Laboratory (Harker ISE Lab) brings together students and faculty from various disciplines to teach, learn and conduct research in a collaborative environment. ISE Lab's four problem-based learning instructional laboratories feature lab spaces adjoining classrooms so students can discuss a problem and then immediately test a solution. UD faculty have designed curricula to optimally utilize these rooms.

The Venture Development Center (VDC) is home to the entrepreneurial community on campus and an applied learning laboratory for students that has meeting and co-working space, computer and printing resources, in-house media production, and an extensive network of community connections.

JP Morgan Chase Innovation Center engages faculty, students and JPMorgan Chase employees in joint applied research projects. The Innovation Center, built as part of a strategic JPMorgan Chase-University of Delaware collaboration, creates a pipeline of technology talent through University curriculum, enriching internships and joint research projects to drive innovation.

OFF-CAMPUS OPPORTUNITIES

Downtown Newark is located just blocks from the University of Delaware campus and features a multitude of restaurants, shops and businesses. A nearby Amtrak station offers easy access to Wilmington, Philadelphia, New York and Washington, D.C., good for exploring, internship opportunities and job hunting.

ACADEMICS

Students can apply to be considered for the UD Honors Program. They can also choose to supplement their major with over 100 minors or choose to enhance their degree as part of our Scholars and Fellows programs centered around cybersecurity, community engagement, global studies, engineering or entrepreneurship.

MAJORS AND DEGREES OFFERED

The University of Delaware offers more than 150 major fields of study across seven different colleges: Agriculture and Natural Resources; Arts and Sciences; Business and Economics; Earth, Ocean and Environment; Education and Human Development; Engineering; and Health Sciences.

Find your passion at www.udel.edu/majorfinder

- Accounting
- Actuarial Sciences
- Africana Studies
- Agriculture and Natural Resources
- Ancient Greek and Roman Studies
- Animal Science
- Anthropology
- Anthropology Education
- Apparel Design
- Applied Mathematics
- Applied Molecular Biology and Biotechnology Interest
- Applied Music - Instrumental
- Applied Music - Piano
- Applied Music - Voice
- Applied Nutrition
- Art (students interested in Fine Arts and Visual Communications)
- Art Conservation
- Art History
- Asian Studies
- Astronomy
- Athletic Training Interest
- Biochemistry
- Biological Sciences
- Biological Sciences Education
- Biomedical Engineering
- Business Undeclared
- Chemical Engineering
- Chemistry
- Chemistry Education
- Chinese Studies
- Civil Engineering
- Cognitive Science
- Communication Interest
- Comparative Literature
- Computer Engineering
- Computer Science
- Construction Engineering & Management
- Criminal Justice
- Early Childhood Education (includes Special Education)
- Earth Science Education
- Economics
- Economics Education
- Electrical Engineering
- Elementary Teacher Education
- Energy and Environmental Policy
- Engineering Undeclared
- English
- English Education
- Entrepreneurship & Technology Innovation
- Environmental and Resource Economics
- Environmental Engineering
- Environmental Science
- Environmental Studies
- European Studies
- Exercise Science
- Fashion Merchandising
- Finance

- Financial Planning & Wealth Management
- Food and Agribusiness Marketing and Management
- Food Science
- French Education Interest
- French Studies
- French/ Political Science
- Geography
- Geography Education
- Geological Sciences
- German Education Interest
- German Studies
- Health Sciences—Occupational Therapy
- History
- History Education
- History and Foreign Language
- Hospitality Industry Management
- Hotel, Restaurant and Institutional Management
- Human Relations Administration
- Human Services
- Information Systems
- Insect Ecology and Conservation
- International Business Studies
- International Relations
- Italian Education Interest
- Italian Studies
- Japanese Studies
- Landscape Architecture
- Latin American and Iberian Studies
- Latin Education Interest
- Linguistics
- Linguistics and French
- Management
- Management Information Systems
- Marine Science
- Marketing
- Mathematics
- Mathematics and Economics
- Mathematics Education
- Mechanical Engineering
- Medical Diagnostics Interest (optional Pre-Physician Assistant concentration)
- Medical Laboratory Science
- Meteorology and Climatology
- Music (includes Music Management)
- Music Composition
- Music Education—General/Choral/Instrumental
- Music History and Literature
- Music Theory
- Natural Resource Management
- Neuroscience
- Nursing
- Nutritional Science
- Operations Management
- Organizational and Community Leadership
- Pharmaceutical Sciences Interest
- Pharmacy Interest
- Philosophy
- Physics
- Physics Education
- Plant Science
- Political Science
- Political Science Education
- Pre-Veterinary Medicine and Animal Biosciences
- Psychology
- Psychology Education

- Public Policy
- Quantitative Biology
- Russian and History
- Russian Studies
- Sociology
- Sociology Education
- Spanish and History
- Spanish Education Interest
- Spanish/ Political Science
- Spanish Studies
- Sport Management
- Statistics
- Three Languages
- University Studies (Undeclared)
- Wildlife Ecology and Conservation
- Women and Gender Studies

TUITION, ROOM, BOARD, FEES

Resident Tuition & Fees:

- Tuition: $11,870
- Room: $7,462
- Board: $4,870
- Fees: $1,290
- Total: $25,492

Non-Resident:

- Tuition: $31,860
- Room: $7,462
- Board: $4,870
- Fees: $1,290
- Total: $45,482

°New rates are released every July. Optional Winter & Summer Sessions are charged separately. Actual rates for room vary for different housing arrangements. Amount shown is standard rate for first-year double room.

FINANCIAL AID

The University of Delaware awards more than 250 million dollars annually in financial aid, over 100 million dollars of this funding is in the form of grants and scholarships. To apply for need-based aid, complete the Free Application for Federal Student Aid (FAFSA) at www.fafsa.ed.gov as soon as possible after October 1. If you wish to be considered for merit scholarships, apply by January 15. No additional application is necessary for consideration.

STUDENT ORGANIZATIONS AND ACTIVITIES

UD attracts students from nearly all 50 states and over 100 countries, with approximately 70 percent of the student population coming from out of state. You'll feel right at home with our welcoming community and endless opportunities to get involved in social, cultural and co-curricular activities. Students have plenty of ways to explore their interests with more than 350 campus organizations ranging from community service, cultural and religious programming, leadership organizations, fraternity and sorority life and athletics.

ADMISSIONS PROCESS

Students applying to UD should have a strong background in core academic courses. High school honors, advanced placement, and International Baccalaureate coursework is encouraged. Applicants are required to have 18 core high school units including four years of English, 3 years of mathematics, three years of science (two with a lab) and two years of the same foreign language. The Admissions Committee takes a holistic approach to the admissions process and will consider academic performance, standardized test scores, letters of recommendation, extracurricular activities and essays when making a decision.

School Says . . .

THE UNIVERSITY OF MARYLAND, BALTIMORE COUNTY

AT A GLANCE

An Honors University with the teaching and student support traditions of a small liberal arts college. UMBC is also among the most rapidly developing and diverse research universities in the nation.

UMBC attracts creative and motivated students and rewards them with the resources and attention they need to succeed. We're a place where it's cool to be smart, and where students can be confident investing in their education.

UMBC is nationally recognized for professors who regularly involve students in research and creative collaboration. Cross-collaboration between fields of study (with both peers and faculty) results in active, interdisciplinary learning, which prepares students for multi-dimensional opportunities.

With an ideal proximity to Baltimore and Washington, D.C. students are interning, studying and working with industry leaders-and UMBC has built a reputation for getting students into jobs and graduate programs. In fact, 86 percent of UMBC class of 2017 is employed and/or in graduate school!

The on-campus climate is friendly and energetic; undergraduates have enough ideas and interests to support more than 250 groups, including Greek organizations, recreational sports clubs, community outreach efforts, and campus events. Students enthusiastically follow UMBC NCAA Division I athletic teams and attend games in the UMBC Stadium, Retriever Activities Center, and the new UMBC Event Center, where they cheer on the Retrievers, who made history this year in men's NCAA basketball.

UMBC President Freeman A. Hrabowski, III, has been named "one of the 10 best college presidents" and "one of the 100 most influential people in the world" by Time Magazine.

Theatre students rank third nationally in invitations to perform at the Kennedy Center American College Theatre Festival. A new Performing Arts and Humanities building opened in 2014, providing state-of-the-art facilities for several arts and humanities departments and programs.

Approximately 70 percent of freshman students live on campus, with 14 percent from out of state. The undergraduate student population is 44 percent female, 26 percent Asian American, 17 percent African American, 7 percent Hispanic American and Native American. UMBC houses 4,000 students in UMBC's residence suites and apartment communities. Residential communities feature ten living-learning programs, including the Center for Women in Technology; Intercultural Living Exchange; Shriver Living Learning Center.

LOCATION AND ENVIRONMENT

Located a few miles south of Baltimore, UMBC is 15 minutes from downtown Baltimore and 30 minutes from Washington, D.C. The Baltimore-Washington area is known for its music, sports, museums, restaurants, and historical traditions. UMBC's 530-acre campus features housing and dining facilities on one side and core facilities (classroom/lab buildings, performing arts center, a library, galleries, a student union, a bookstore, a gymnasium, an Olympic-size pool, and tennis courts) surrounding a central walkway. bwtech@UMBC Research and Technology Park, adjacent to the campus, attracts firms in the high-technology fields, including engineering, information technology, and the life sciences.

CAMPUS FACILITIES & EQUIPMENT

UMBC's landmark building, the Albin O. Kuhn Library and Gallery, contains over 1 million books and bound volumes of journals, an extensive reference collection, 4,200 journal and database subscriptions, more than 200 computers, wireless and wired connections for laptops, and more than 3 million other items, including slides, photographs, maps, musical scores, recordings, and microforms. The Commons, UMBC's state-of-the-art student center, the hub of campus life includes a food court, general lounges, the University bookstore, meeting spaces, a student recreation center, a full-service bank, student organization offices, retail-type spaces, wireless computer connectivity, and web-accessible kiosks. UMBC students have access to research opportunities and equipment such as conducting AIDS research on one of the world's largest nuclear magnetic resonance spectrometers in the only Howard Hughes Medical Institute lab at a public university in Maryland. Newer facilities include a Public Policy Building and a state-of-the-art Information Technology/Engineering Building. UMBC's a new Performing Arts and Humanities Building houses seven departments and new performance space that showcase the University's strong arts and humanities programs and creates a regional and national appreciation of UMBC as a cultural attraction. In January 2018 UMBC opened a new 172,000 square foot Event Center that seats up to 6,000 people and can host a variety of sports and entertainment events.

OFF-CAMPUS OPPORTUNITIES

Surrounded by business, government, and metropolitan centers, UMBC places students in over 1,200 co-ops and internships in more than 500 organizations each year in the Baltimore-Washington area. UMBC matches students with such employers as the federal Centers for Medicare and Medicaid, Bank of America, Silicon Graphics, MBNA, the Smithsonian Institution, NASA, and the National Aquarium. The university encourages students to participate in study abroad experiences during the semester or travel-study opportunities during winter and summer breaks. The Shriver Center links the resources of the campus to urgent social problems, places students in co-ops and internships at hundreds of businesses and organizations, organizes and manages community service projects that bring the resources of the university to people in need, and connects students to a wide range of social service projects.

ACADEMIC PROGRAMS

UMBC's academic calendar consists of fall and spring semesters, a four-week mini session in January, and summer sessions from six to eight weeks. To receive a UMBC degree, students complete 120 to 128 credits plus two physical education courses. In addition to the requirements for the chosen major, the general education program (GEP), provides a solid basis for a lifetime of learning. GEP courses encompass humanities and fine arts, mathematics and natural sciences, social sciences, and languages and culture. The Honors College at UMBC is a special option for students seeking a community of like-minded people for whom the quest for knowledge is its own reward. All Honors College students must take at least one honors course per semester. Students choose from honors versions of core courses, special honors seminars, and plenty of other honors courses.

MAJORS AND DEGREES OFFERED

Programs leading to Bachelor of Arts, Bachelor of Fine Arts, and Bachelor of Science degrees: acting, Africana studies, American studies, aging services, ancient studies, Asian studies, biochemistry and molecular biology, bioinformatics and computational biology, biological sciences, biological education, business technology administration, chemical engineering, chemistry, biochemistry and molecular biology, chemistry education, chemical engineering, computer engineering, computer science, cultural anthropology, dance, design, economics, financial economics, emergency health services, English, environmental science and geography, gender and women's studies, geography and environmental studies, health administration and policy, history, information systems, interdisciplinary studies, jazz studies, mathematics, mechanical engineering, media and communication studies, modern language and linguistics, music composition, music education, music performance, music technology, philosophy, physics education, physics, political science, psychology, social work, sociology, statistics, theater, translational life science technology, and visual arts. An interdisciplinary studies program allows students to design their own course of study according to their specific educational and career goals. UMBC offers pre-professional studies programs, including two-and four-year advisement programs to prepare students for clinical training in dental hygiene, medical and research technology, physician assistant, nursing, pharmacy, physical therapy, and veterinary medicine. Minors include Africana studies, American studies, ancient studies, Asian studies, astronomy, biological sciences, biomathematics, chemistry, computer science, critical sexuality studies, cultural anthropology, dance, East Asian history, economics, emergency health services, English, environmental science, entrepreneurship and innovation, French, gender and women's studies, geography, German, history, information systems, international affairs, Judaic studies, Korean, mathematics, medieval and early modern studies, modern languages and linguistics, music, philosophy, political science, psychology, quantitative biology, religious studies, social work, sociology, statistics, theater, and visual arts.

TUITION, ROOM, BOARD, FEES

Tuition and fees for 2017–2018 are $11,518 for Maryland residents and $25,654 for out-of-state students. Room and board averaged $11,836. Miscellaneous expenses, books, and transportation cost about $4200 for on-campus residents and $5200 for commuters.

FINANCIAL AID

More than 55 percent of undergraduates receive some financial aid. UMBC uses the Free Application for Federal Student Aid (FAFSA) to help determine a student's financial need. Aid is awarded to qualified applicants on a first-come, first-served basis. Since aid is awarded only to admitted students, early application for admission is also important. Well-qualified freshmen are automatically considered for general merit scholarships once they are admitted to the University. The Scholars Programs at UMBC provide special opportunities for outstanding entering freshmen who want to focus their education through intense study in their major. Scholars participate in a wide range of academic and cultural enrichment activities, extracurricular travel, or summer study. The selection process for specialty scholarships includes application, an interview, and, in some cases, nomination from a high school official.

STUDENT ORGANIZATIONS AND ACTIVITIES

The campus climate is friendly and energetic. UMBC's more than 11,234 undergraduates have enough ideas and interests to support more than 200 student groups, including Greek organizations and recreational sports clubs, such as fencing and sailing; community outreach efforts, such as Habitat for Humanity; and campus events, including lectures, films, concerts, and plays. Students enthusiastically follow UMBC NCAA Division I athletic teams, such as basketball, lacrosse, and soccer and attend games in the UMBC Stadium and Retriever Activities Center, which includes a multipurpose gym, auxiliary gym, weight room, and classrooms. The new Event Center also hosts sports events. Elections are held each year for officers in UMBC's Student Government Association (SGA). The SGA represents the student body on a number of administrative committees, including the Undergraduate Council, the Library Committee, and the Student Health Advisory Committee.

ADMISSIONS PROCESS

In fall 2017, the average incoming freshman had a 3.82 cumulative GPA, 53 percent ranked in the top quarter of his or her senior class and had a combined SAT score of 1251 (2 part). Approximately 59 percent of freshman applicants are admitted each year. Academic performance and curriculum strength play an important part in the decision. An essay is required, and a letter of recommendation is strongly encouraged. Transfer applicants are considered to be students who have completed a minimum of 24 college-level credits at an institution of higher education after receiving a high school diploma or a GED. The Admissions Committee evaluates transfer applicants on the basis of their academic record at previous institutions. Cumulative grade point average as calculated by UMBC, academic trends, strength of curriculum, and performance in courses related to the intended area of study are considered.

Prospective freshmen are encouraged to submit applications by the early action deadline of November 1. The Regular Decision deadline is February 1 for full consideration for admission, campus housing, financial aid, and scholarships. The priority deadline for transfer students is March 1 for fall admission and October 15 for spring.

THE UNIVERSITY OF NEW ENGLAND

AT A GLANCE

The University of New England is a private, top-ranked university offering flagship programs in the health and life sciences, as well as degrees in business, education, the social sciences and the liberal arts. UNE's three beautiful campuses in Biddeford and Portland, Maine, and Tangier, Morocco, are home to an active and close-knit student community engaged in rigorous academic experiences.

Innovation drives the University each day. In state-of-the-art facilities in Maine, Morocco and beyond, hands-on learning, interdisciplinary engagement and global awareness empower the next generation of leaders for New England and the world.

LOCATION AND ENVIRONMENT
BIDDEFORD CAMPUS

UNE's waterfront campus in Biddeford, Maine, offers more than 4,000 feet of scenic shoreline where the Saco River flows into the Atlantic Ocean. The local area has a long history as a coastal vacation destination. Within its 540 acres, the Biddeford Campus is the hub of undergraduate student life from its vibrant campus clubs and athletics teams, to its innovative study and living spaces.

PORTLAND CAMPUS

A rustic brick port sets the stage for a thriving buy-local economy and hip cultural scene —with outdoor adventure all around. UNE's Portland Campus, a classic, century-old New England quad just a short drive from the waterfront, anchors UNE's tight-knit, engaged community within this exciting city.

TANGIER CAMPUS

UNE set a new study abroad standard with its Tangier, Morocco campus, which features state-of-the-art labs and modern accommodations, as well as easy access to beaches, downtown and cultural attractions. Students can enjoy a semester abroad at our Tangier campus or with partner universities in Spain, France and Iceland for about the same cost as a semester in Maine.

CAMPUS FACILITIES & EQUIPMENT

Both the Biddeford and Portland Campuses feature buildings with a variety of uses to support the needs of the University community. On the Biddeford Campus, several research facilities are on campus, including the Arthur P. Girard Marine Science Center; the Harold Alfond Center for Health Sciences, with biology and chemistry labs as well as lecture halls, classrooms, a gross anatomy lab, and UNE's medical school facilities; the Pickus Center for Biomedical Research; and Peter and Cécile Morgane Hall, a science center providing additional classrooms and an undergraduate teaching laboratory. The Department of Creative and Fine Arts offers a dedicated building that provides faculty offices and studio space for drawing, painting, printmaking, sculpting and photography. The Biddeford Campus includes undergraduate student housing, graduate and undergraduate classrooms, labs and a makerspace; cafés and innovative study and gathering spaces in the new Danielle N. Ripich Commons; and various athletic facilities and fields, including an NHL-size hockey arena, blue turf field, basketball arena, and much more.

The Portland Campus houses Maine's only College of Dental Medicine, the College of Pharmacy, and the Westbrook College of Health Professions, which offers undergraduate and graduate programs in several allied health fields. The 41-acre campus also includes the Center for Global Humanities, Art Gallery and Maine Women Writers Collection. The Blewett Science Center, home to UNE's nursing program, consists of science labs and classrooms. UNE's Interprofessional Simulation and Innovation Center, which provides customized training and education for students and health professionals, is also on the Portland Campus.

OFF-CAMPUS OPPORTUNITIES

On any given weekend at UNE, thrilling adventures await. Students can ride countless miles of mountain bike trails and scenic rural roads, kayak and sail on Casco Bay, camp and hike at hundreds of great parks, or just take in some sun at UNE's own Freddy Beach. With more than 90 clubs and organizations on UNE's campuses, students discover many opportunities to get involved. Whether an academic club, an arts club, student government, a cultural organization or an outdoor recreation group, it's easy to find others who are ready to welcome new students aboard.

ACADEMICS

An education at UNE goes beyond training and beyond traditional. Professors include world-class researchers, authors and scholars who help students reach further, working side-by-side with them in the lab, in the field and across the globe.

UNE offers more than 40 undergraduate and 32 graduate/professional academic programs in needed, fascinating fields. UNE is home to Maine's only medical school and the only college of dental medicine in Northern New England. UNE is one of a handful of private universities with a comprehensive health education mission including medicine, pharmacy, dental medicine, nursing and an array of allied health professions. In addition to health sciences disciplines, the full range of liberal arts classes and majors makes UNE a unique participatory, educational environment.

MAJORS AND DEGREES OFFERED

Academic programs ensure that students have plenty of opportunities for extensive fieldwork, clinical experiences, research, internships and global experiences at both the undergraduate and graduate levels.

Undergraduate majors include animal behavior, applied exercise science, applied mathematics, applied social and cultural studies, aquaculture and aquarium science, art and design media, art education, athletic training, biochemistry, biological sciences, business, chemistry, communications, data science, dental hygiene, elementary/middle education, English, environmental science, environmental studies, global studies, health, wellness and occupational studies, history, interdisciplinary studies in the humanities (including pre-law), laboratory science, marine affairs, marine entrepreneurship, marine sciences, medical biology (pre-dental medicine, pre-medicine, pre-optometry, pre–physician assistant, and pre–veterinary medicine), neuroscience, nursing, nutrition, political science, pre-pharmacy, pre-physical therapy, psychology, public health, secondary education, social work, sociology, sport and recreation management, and sustainability and business.

Master's degrees are offered in applied nutrition, athletic training, biological sciences, education, health informatics, marine sciences, medical education leadership, nurse anesthesia, occupational therapy, physician assistant, public health, and social work.

Doctorates offered include dental medicine (D.M.D.), education leadership (Ed.D.), osteopathic medicine (D.O.), pharmacy (Pharm.D.), and physical therapy (D.P.T.).

TUITION, ROOM, BOARD, FEES

Tuition: $35,240

Required Fees: $1,290

On Campus Room & Board: $13,580

Total: $50,110

Financial Aid

98 percent of all full-time undergraduate students receive merit-based gift aid of up to $20,000.

STUDENT ORGANIZATIONS AND ACTIVITIES

UNE offers a variety of cultural and social events and encourages students to become involved in activities, clubs and sports. Popular interests include scuba diving, skiing, hiking, biking, varsity and intramural sports, swimming, surfing, music, theater, community service, and student leadership development programs.

UNE athletes—called Nor'easters after one of the nastiest storms in Mother Nature's arsenal—strive for success on and off the field. With 13 conference championships in the last five years, student athletes at UNE have a cumulative grade point average of 3.25. Our intercollegiate teams compete at the Division III level in men's basketball, cross country, golf, ice hockey, lacrosse and soccer. Football will see its first varsity action beginning in 2018. Varsity women's sports include basketball, cross country, field hockey, ice hockey, lacrosse, rugby, soccer, softball, swimming and volleyball.

The personal attention students receive from faculty both in and out of class, and the quality of faculty as experts in their fields are key strengths of the UNE experience. Students appreciate their faculty members as mentors and trust them as accomplished scholars who impact their fields. From designing coastal trails and restoring wetlands on campus to caring for patients in need, UNE faculty members work side-by-side with their students and are recognized by their peers and other leaders for their expertise. UNE faculty members are national award recipients, Fulbright scholars, authors and world-class researchers, and they share their knowledge unselfishly with their students.

ADMISSIONS PROCESS

Students applying for admission should submit a completed application, a $40 nonrefundable application fee, transcripts of all academic work (high school and college), and scores on either the ACT or SAT. Students who do not use English as their primary language must submit TOEFL scores. Students applying for admission should have completed a curriculum that includes English, mathematics, science, and social sciences. International students must also complete the International Student Supplemental Application.

The undergraduate admission application deadline is February 15. Applications received after that date are reviewed on a space-available basis. There is a nonbinding December 1 early action application deadline with a December 31 notification date. Applications for the spring term are accepted through December 1.

All prospective students are strongly encouraged to visit the University of New England at an open house or for an information session and tour. Information sessions and tours are held daily Monday through Friday; Saturday tours are also available on select weekends throughout the year. Prospective students can register for a tour at www.une.edu/visit.

UNIVERSITY OF NEW HAVEN

AT A GLANCE

The University of New Haven, founded on the Yale campus in 1920, is a private, coeducational university situated on the coast of southern New England. It's a diverse and vibrant community of more than 6,800 students with campuses around the country and around the world.

Within its five colleges, students immerse themselves in a transformative, career-focused education across the liberal arts and sciences, fine arts, business, engineering, public safety and public service. More than 100 academic programs are offered, all grounded in a long-standing commitment to collaborative, interdisciplinary, project-based learning.

At the University of New Haven, the experience of learning is both personal and pragmatic, guided by a distinguished faculty who care deeply about individual student success. As leaders in their fields, faculty provide the inspiration and recognition needed for students to fulfill their potential and succeed at whatever they choose to do.

LOCATION AND ENVIRONMENT

The University of New Haven is located in suburban West Haven, Connecticut. The campus is conveniently situated 75 miles from New York City and 135 miles from Boston. Only minutes away from the beautiful beaches along Long Island Sound, the university offers a shuttle to downtown New Haven and other local areas including two nearby train stations.

CAMPUS FACILITIES & EQUIPMENT

Over $200 million has been invested in facilities and academic programs at the University in just the past few years. Some of these include a freshman residence hall (Westside Hall) and new student dining area (Food on Demand), the 58,000 square-foot David A. Beckerman Recreation Center, the $48-million Celentano Residence Hall with apartment-style housing for upperclassmen, Ralph A. DellaCamera Stadium featuring our Blue & Gold turf field, and a STEM-based magnet high school on the University's campus. Standout academic facilities feature the Henry C. Lee Institute of Forensic Science, National Crime Scene Training & Technology Center, Cyber Forensics Research and Education Lab, Laurel Vlock Center for Convergent Media, Samuel Bergami Learning Center for Finance & Technology, TV and Film Production Studio, Digital and Analog Recording Studios, MIDI and Sound Synthesis Lab, Engineering Makerspace, Dental Center, and Hazel Nut Café (student-run coffee shop), Up-and-coming additions to campus include the Center for Marine Sciences right on the water in the greater New Haven area, a college village within walking distance to campus adding new commercial and residential properties, and a new academic building featuring state-of-the-art facilities for hands-on learning. Lyme Academy College, our fine arts campus, boasts 10 large studio spaces and dedicated studios for seniors.

ACADEMIC PROGRAMS

The University of New Haven mixes traditional degrees along with many unique programs across five academic colleges. The university also offers more than 60 graduate programs and certificates.

MAJORS AND DEGREES OFFERED

College of Arts and Sciences

The College of Arts and Sciences offers traditional majors such as Art, Biology, Communication, English, History, Mathematics, Psychology, and Political Science as well as unique majors in the areas of Dental Hygiene, Environmental Science, Genetics & Biotechnology, Forensic Psychology, Health Sciences, Global Studies, Graphic Design, Digital Art and Design, Interior Design, Interior Design—Pre-Architecture, Legal Studies, Marine Biology, Marine Affairs, Music, Music Industry, Music & Sound Recording, Nutrition & Dietetics, and Theater Arts. The university also offers minors in languages such as Arabic, Chinese, Italian, Russian, and Spanish.

College of Business

The College of Business offers degrees in Business Management, Accounting, Economics, Finance, International Business, Marketing, Sport Management, Health Sciences, and Hospitality and Tourism Management with concentrations in Hotel & Resort Management, Foodservice Management, and Event & Tourism Management. The College offers students an accelerated degree program making it possible to complete a three-year bachelor's degree and the option to tack on a one-year master's degree.

Tagliatela College of Engineering

The Tagliatela College of Engineering offers degrees in Chemistry, General Engineering, Chemical Engineering, Civil Engineering, Computer Engineering, Electrical Engineering, Industrial and Systems Engineering, Mechanical Engineering, Computer Science, and Cybersecurity and Networks.

Henry C. Lee College of Criminal Justice and Forensic Sciences

The Henry C. Lee College of Criminal Justice and Forensic Sciences offers degrees in Criminal Justice, Forensic Science, Fire Science, Paramedicine and National Security. The university offers separate Criminal Justice concentrations in Investigative Services, Crime Analysis, Police Science, Correctional Rehabilitation and Supervision, Crime Victim Services, and Juvenile Justice and Delinquency Prevention. The Henry C. Lee College of Criminal Justice and Forensic Sciences also contains two distinct degrees in the area of Fire Science - Arson Investigation and Fire Science Administration.

Lyme Academy College of Fine Arts

The Lyme Academy College of Fine Arts is located in Old Lyme, Connecticut. Lyme College offers four BFA degrees in Drawing, Illustration, Painting, and Sculpture, plus a minor in Art History.

Accreditations and Recognitions

Many of our academic programs have earned further distinction through high-level private accrediting bodies in the respective fields:

- AACSB (The Association to Advance Collegiate Schools of Business) accredits six of our undergraduate business degree programs: Accounting, Business Management, Finance, International Business, Marketing, and Sport Management.

- FEPAC (Forensic Science Education Programs Accreditation Commission) accredits our Forensic Science program.

- ABA (American Bar Association) approves our undergraduate degree in Legal Studies, one of only a few such programs at the undergraduate level in the entire country.

- ABET (Accreditation Board of Engineering and Technology) accredits six of our undergraduate academic degree programs in the Tagliatela College of Engineering: Civil Engineering, Chemical Engineering, Computer Engineering, Computer Science, Electrical Engineering, and Mechanical Engineering.

- ACEND (Accreditation Council for Education in Nutrition and Dietetics) of the American Academy of Nutrition and Dietetics accredits our very popular undergraduate degree in Nutrition and Dietetics, leading many of our students to become Registered Dietitians (R.D.). The university also has a dietetic internship program designed to fulfil ACEND-required competencies.

- ACS (American Chemical Society) accredits our Chemistry program. FEPAC (Forensic Science Education Programs Accreditation Commission) accredits our nationally renowned Forensic Science program. Only a select number of programs have earned this level of distinction through the American Academy of Forensic Science (A.A.F.S.).

- ADA (American Dental Association) accredits our Dental Hygiene program.

- NASAD (National Association of Schools of Art and Design) accredits our BFA programs in Drawing, Painting, Illustration, and Sculpture at the Lyme Academy College of Fine Arts as well as the University's BA program in Art and BFA programs in graphic design, digital art and design, and interior design.

Marvin K. Peterson Library

The Marvin K. Peterson Library offers over 240,000 volumes, 1,400 print journal and newspaper subscriptions, and electronic access to over 19,000 full-text journal and newspaper titles, approximately 550,000 pieces of microfiche, 12,000 volumes of microfilm, e-books, 33,000 e-journals and 162,000 paper U.S. Government documents. Students have 24/7 access to popular research databases, and can take a break from their studies in the library's lounge area and coffee shop.

TUITION, ROOM, BOARD, FEES

Cost for the 2018–2019 Academic year is: Tuition & Fees—$39,270 and Room & Board—$16,520.

FINANCIAL AID

Students are automatically considered for merit-based academic scholarships by simply applying for full-time admission to the University of New Haven. Merit-based scholarships range from $10,000 to $24,000 per academic year for students who qualify.

To file for need-based aid, students must fill out the Free Application for Federal Student Aid (FAFSA), which is available online at http://fafsa.gov. The priority deadline to file FAFSA is March 1 for the fall semester and December 1 for the spring semester.

STUDY ABROAD

The University of New Haven opened its satellite campus in Prato, Italy (Tuscany Region) in the fall of 2012. The course offerings at the Tuscany campus change from semester to semester. Students can take a total of 15 credits (5 courses) during the semester including one mandatory Italian language course. Each semester the university sends full-time faculty to teach courses alongside Italian faculty. Students can study abroad at our Prato, Italy campus as early as first-semester freshman year. The University of New Haven is also a leading provider of study abroad education, offering students over 300 options worldwide. We also offer an intensive study abroad program which offers 2-week abroad sessions with a University of New Haven faculty member during intersession for six credits at a number of locations such as London, Dubai, Rome and more.

ATHLETICS

As a member of the Northeast 10 Conference, the University of New Haven competes in 17 Division II varsity sports (7 men's and 10 women's) baseball, basketball, cross-country, field hockey, football, lacrosse, soccer, softball, tennis, track, and volleyball. The university also has a number of club sports, which compete at the intercollegiate level including: baseball, cheerleading, equestrian, field hockey, gymnastics, ice hockey, lacrosse (men's), rugby (men's and women's), soccer (men's), tennis, volleyball (men's) and wrestling. The 58,000-square-foot David A. Beckerman Recreation Center adds another dimension to athletic opportunities at the University of New Haven. It features a fitness center with aerobic equipment, weights, and televisions; multi-purpose rooms for yoga, aerobics, Pilates, spinning, and other wellness activities; two basketball/volleyball courts; a multi-sport court for in-line skating, floor hockey, indoor soccer, and other activities; an elevated indoor running track; and lounge areas including a juice bar/café.

RESIDENTIAL LIFE

The university has 13 on-campus and at least six off-campus housing options which offer a variety for students to choose from ranging from a traditional residence hall to apartment-style housing with suites of two or more bedrooms. In 2005, the university started a Living Learning Community (LLC) program where students enhance their overall living experience by combining academic and personal interests through field trips, guest lectures, unique and individualized academic support, and service-learning projects. A number of LLCs are offered each year. Some popular examples include Forensic Science, Engineering, Marine Biology, Honors, and ROTC.

STUDENT ORGANIZATIONS AND ACTIVITIES

The Undergraduate Student Government Association (USGA) oversees all aspects of undergraduate life, organizing campus social and cultural activities, supporting the student-run radio station and student-produced publications, and overseeing the budget for all undergraduate organizations. There are more than 170 campus clubs and organizations, including chapters of several professional societies, religious groups, social clubs, student councils, cultural clubs, and national fraternities and sororities.

ADMISSIONS PROCESS

The University of New Haven has an Early Decision and Early Action admissions policy; we begin to review applications on September 1st and continue until programs are filled. The university offers one binding and three non-binding admission programs for fall admission. To be considered for certain programs applicants must follow the established timelines and important dates. Early Decision Applications are due by December 1, Early Action applications are due by December 15, Early Action II applications are due by February 15, Regular Decision applications are due after December 15 with a priority deadline of March 1, and Spring Admission Applications are due no later than January 15.

Students may apply using the Common Application. To be considered for admission, candidates must complete the application and submit it along with a non-refundable $50 application fee. An application is considered complete once we receive the application, personal essay (250-600 words), transcript(s), standardized test scores (SAT or ACT), and one letter of recommendation (from an academic source).

Visiting Campus

We encourage all prospective students and their families to visit us and see what the University of New Haven has to offer. The university offers a variety of campus visits for students and their families to choose from seven days a week! Visits include daily information sessions and tours, Open Houses, major-specific Enhanced Visits, Accepted Student Days and much more! To view our campus visit calendar and register for an event, visit our website www.newhaven.edu/visit

For further information about the University of New Haven and to schedule a campus visit or personal interview, students may contact:

Office of Undergraduate Admissions

Phone: 203-932-7319

Fax: 203-931-6093

E-mail: admissions@newhaven.edu

Visit our website: www.newhaven.edu

THE UNIVERSITY OF PITTSBURGH AT BRADFORD

AT A GLANCE

The University of Pittsburgh at Bradford takes students beyond: beyond the classroom, by offering internships and research opportunities; beyond the degree, by providing a robust Career Services Office and an informal alumni network; beyond 9 to 5, by offering an active student life, a friendly residence life environment, excellent athletic and cultural facilities, and a wide range of recreational opportunities; beyond place, by providing a liberal arts education that exposes students to the world and offering students many study-abroad opportunities; and beyond students' expectations, by giving them a college experience that will transform them.

Students at Pitt-Bradford live and learn on a safe, intimate campus, where they receive individual and personalized attention from committed professors who work side by side with them. And, because Pitt-Bradford is a regional campus of the University of Pittsburgh, students earn a degree from the University of Pittsburgh, which commands respect around the world.

Learn more at http://www.upb.pitt.edu/About/

LOCATION AND ENVIRONMENT

Pitt-Bradford is located in Northwestern Pennsylvania. The 319-acre campus is nestled in the foothills of the Allegheny Mountains and is only steps away from the Allegheny National Forest.

Pitt-Bradford also is a short drive from larger cities such as Buffalo, N.Y., 80 miles to the north; Pittsburgh, 160 miles to the southwest; and Erie, PA, 90 miles to the west. Pitt-Bradford can also be reached easily by car and plane.

CAMPUS FACILITIES & EQUIPMENT

The CSI House enables criminal justice students to solve mock crime scenes in a realistic setting, using professional investigative tools. Nursing students can practice their skills in the simulation lab using electronic mannequins. Students studying computer information systems and technology have a lab where they can set up a server room, install and update software, and create virtual machines to back up and protect data; and a new virtual reality lab, which includes 13 new VR-ready, high-performance laptops and 13 sets of Oculus Rift viewers with touch-control bundles.

Students can work out in a state-of-the-art fitness center or swim in the six-lane swimming pool in the Richard E. and Ruth McDowell Sport and Fitness Center. The building also houses facilities for intercollegiate and intramural athletic events. Pitt-Bradford competes in Division III of the NCAA and fields seven men's (baseball, basketball, golf, soccer, swimming, tennis and wrestling) and seven women's teams (basketball, bowling, soccer, softball, swimming, tennis and volleyball).

The Frame-Westerberg Commons gives students a place to eat, gather and participate in campus life. The building houses the dining hall, where students can help themselves to a wide assortment of meals; a bookstore, which features an after-hours convenience store; offices for many student clubs and organizations; and areas for students to read or relax.

Blaisdell Hall, the university's fine arts and communication arts building, houses the communication arts, theater and music programs and features state-of-the-art equipment. The building also houses a multi-purpose theater, where students can participate in dramatic and musical performances. The building also serves as the cultural center for the region by housing plays, concerts, lectures and other arts-related events.

Hanley Library has more than 95,000 print books access to more than 700,000 ebooks. Since Pitt-Bradford is a regional campus of the University of Pittsburgh, you can also borrow materials from Pitt's other four campuses through interlibrary loan.

OFF-CAMPUS OPPORTUNITIES

Because of Pitt-Bradford's location, students have many opportunities to participate in unique academic and extra-curricular activities. Students may collect and examine specimens in the creek that runs through campus or set up easels along the edge of the surrounding woods. After class, they may cross-country or downhill ski, snowboard or snowshoe, ice skate, kayak, bike, fish, hike, and hunt.

ACADEMIC PROGRAMS

The academic programs stress critical-thinking skills and communication and encourage hands-on learning through field experience, internships, and faculty-student collaboration on research. A Pitt-Bradford bachelor's degree requires 120–128 credit hours (requirements differ slightly among programs). Students must complete between 60 and 70 credit hours to earn an associate degree.

The biology program prepares students for careers in health-related professions; education; research; field work; with companies that produce food, pharmaceuticals, chemicals, and biotechnology; and technical positions with governmental agencies. Most students interested in medicine, dentistry, optometry, pharmacy, osteopathy, optometry, physical therapy, occupational therapy, podiatry, chiropractic medicine, veterinary medicine, pre-clinical dietetics and nutrition, and a variety of careers in health and rehabilitation sciences are biology majors.

Students in the broadcast communications, English, public relations, and writing programs work on the student newspaper, The Source; broadcast over the college radio station, WDRQ: and publish original works in the award-winning student literary magazine, Baily's Beads. Students also have access to a state-of-the-art electronic newsroom, radio studio, television studio, and video editing room with analog and digital technology.

Students who choose to major in computer information systems and technology will get a broad IT background and gain hands-on lab experiences. Students will learn programming applications, network development, systems design and analysis, web technologies, multimedia applications, database development, and systems administration.

The criminal justice program provides opportunities for hands-on learning through the Crime Scene Investigation House, where students can solve mock crime scenes using many of the same tools as professional law enforcement agents; and internships with local and regional police departments, county courts and probation offices, and a federal prison.

The Early Level Education Pre-K–4 and secondary education majors prepare students for careers as teachers in a world of rapid political, economic, scientific and cultural change. The Education Department seeks to graduate students who have general knowledge and specific content knowledge, as well as sound theory and practice.

The nursing program at Pitt-Bradford offers an associate of science degree that can be completed in two years and the Bachelor of Science in nursing that requires two more years. Students may commence this program on completion of the ASN. Students may also pursue both degrees in a unique 1+2+1 program.

In psychology, students gain knowledge in the scientific and theoretical aspects of psychology as well as the application of this knowledge. The major prepares students for graduate work in psychology and related disciplines and for employment in social service agencies, mental health centers, industries, and not-for-profit and governmental agencies.

Students may relocate to another university campus to complete academic programs not offered at Pitt-Bradford. They may earn no more than 60 credits before transferring. All students in the arts and sciences may relocate provided they are students in good standing with a minimum GPA of 2.5. Engineering students may relocate if they maintain a GPA of at least 3.0.

Here is the University's relocation policy http://www.upb.pitt.edu/relocation/

MAJORS AND DEGREES OFFERED

Students at Pitt-Bradford may pursue four-year degrees in Accounting; Applied Mathematics; Athletic Training; Biology; Biology Education 7–12; Broadcast Communications; Business, Computer and Information Technology Education K–12; Business Management; Chemistry; Chemistry Education 7–12; Computer Information Systems and Technology; Criminal Justice; Early Level Education Pre-K–4; Economics; Energy Science and Technology; Engineering Science; English; English Education 7–12; Environmental Studies; Exercise Science; Forensic Science; General Studies; Health and Physical Education; History/Political Science; Hospitality Management; Interdisciplinary Arts; Information Sciences; International Affairs; Liberal Studies; Mathematics Education 7–12; Nursing; Petroleum Technology; Physical Sciences; Psychology; Public Relations; Radiological Science; Social Sciences; Social Studies Education 7–12; Sociology; Sport and Recreation Management; and Writing.

To learn more about our academic programs, visit http://www.upb.pitt.edu/academicprograms.

Students may pursue associate degrees in Engineering Science, Nursing (RN), Liberal Studies, Information Systems, and Petroleum Technology.

Students may study engineering for up to two years at Pitt-Bradford then complete a program at the Pittsburgh campus in bioengineering, chemical and petroleum engineering, civil and environmental engineering, electrical and computer engineering, industrial engineering, materials science and engineering, or mechanical engineering.

Students may pursue programs offered in conjunction with the University of Pittsburgh School of Dental Medicine and the Pennsylvania College of Optometry. Undergraduates begin their studies at Pitt-Bradford and, after three years, transfer to the appropriate graduate school to complete four more years of study.

Pitt-Bradford also offers the first two years of study leading to the doctorate in pharmacy. Students must complete the program at the Pittsburgh campus, where admission is competitive. The Pittsburgh School of Pharmacy pre-admits some qualified high school seniors, pending completion of the first two years of the pre-professional program at Pitt-Bradford.

TUITION, ROOM, BOARD, FEES

Full-time tuition for the two-term academic year in 2017–18 was $12,940 for Pennsylvania residents and $24,184 for out-of-state students. Tuition for students in the nursing program was $16,578 for Pennsylvania residents and $30,838 for nonresidents.

A double-occupancy room for the year was $5,490. A full meal plan per year was $3,568. Students must also pay yearly fees: $200 activity fee, $350 computer fee, $150 wellness fee, a $180 recreation fee, and an $80 parking and transportation fee. On average, students spend about $500 per term on books and supplies.

FINANCIAL AID

Our tuition and housing fees are competitive compared to other area institutions, and our room and board rates are among the top five most affordable for public colleges in Pennsylvania.

On top of that, we offer generous merit and need-based scholarships to qualified students. More than 98 percent of our students receive some form of financial aid through grants, loans, work study, or scholarships. For the 2017–18 academic year, the average financial aid award was $16,374 for Pennsylvania students and $23,000 for out-of-state students.

All aid applicants must submit the Free Application for Federal Student Aid (FAFSA) by March 1 to receive priority consideration. Pennsylvania residents who complete the FAFSA by March 1 are also eligible for Pennsylvania Higher Education Assistance Agency (PHEAA) grants. Non-Pennsylvania students should contact their state agency to learn more about the prerequisites for grants.

The university awards merit-based scholarships, which range from $1,000 to $13,000, to those who demonstrate exceptional academic achievement. The university ROTC program is another possible source of financial aid. The university encourages veterans to contact the VA about educational benefits.

Contact the Financial Aid Office or visit http://www.upb.pitt.edu/financialaid to learn more about financial assistance.

STUDENT ORGANIZATIONS AND ACTIVITIES

There are about 1,500 student enrolled Pitt-Bradford, who, along with the faculty and staff, form a diverse, friendly and caring campus community. Students come from 11 different countries, including Germany, Nigeria, Australia and Japan; 28 states, from California and Alaska to Massachusetts and Florida; and 62 of the 67 counties in Pennsylvania.

There are more than 60 clubs and organizations, ranging from the African-American Student Union and Gamers United, to academic clubs, honor societies, fraternities and sororities.

Because Pitt-Bradford is a personalized campus, opportunities for leadership abound. Many students become campus leaders as early as their sophomore year. Regardless of your background or interests, you will find many places to become involved as a student at Pitt-Bradford.

The Student Activities Council schedules many activities, including comedy performances, lectures, art exhibits, movies, and trips to such places as Toronto, Canada; Niagara Falls, N.Y.; and New York City. To learn more about clubs and organizations, visit http://www.upb.pitt.edu/clubs.

ADMISSIONS PROCESS

The Admissions committee primarily looks at three factors in evaluating applicants: high school achievement; standardized test results (SAT I or ACT), and letters of recommendation from teachers and/or a counselor at their high school. Class rank, extracurricular activities, personal qualifications, and potential role in the school community are also considered.

Pitt-Bradford accepts applicants on a rolling basis, which means applications are welcome at any time. The Admissions committee notifies candidates as soon as a decision has been made on their application.

Applicants must complete and submit the application online, which is free.

An official high school transcript and an official standardized test score report (SAT I or ACT) are also required. Transfer applicants must also submit official copies of all college transcripts, which must reflect a GPA of at least 2.0. Students and their families are welcome to visit our campus. The Office of Admissions schedules interviews and tours Monday through Friday, 9 a.m. to 4 p.m. all year long, as well as on selected Saturdays during the school year. Contact the Office of Admissions to arrange a visit.

Students seeking more information should contact:

The Office of Admissions

The University of Pittsburgh at Bradford

300 Campus Drive

Bradford, PA 16701-2898

Telephone: 814-362-7555

800-872-1787 (toll free)

Fax: 814-362-5150

http://www.upb.pitt.edu

Email: admissions@upb.pitt.edu

School Says . . .

UNIVERSITY OF SAINT JOSEPH

AT A GLANCE

At University of Saint Joseph, students thrive in a supportive, inspiring environment that focuses on their ultimate success. USJ graduates are leaders in their careers and communities.

Today, the University is a fully coed institution evolving from its origins in 1932, when the Sisters of Mercy of Connecticut set out to establish the first liberal arts college for women in the Hartford area. They were determined to develop a curriculum that balanced professional studies with the liberal arts; focused on service to others; and infused the Catholic intellectual tradition while welcoming students of all ages, races, religions, and cultures.

Throughout the history of the University of Saint Joseph, this inclusive mission has never been compromised. Guided by this vision, the University has flourished and is now recognized for outstanding programs that prepare graduates to serve their communities in dedicated and meaningful ways throughout their lives.

As the University of Saint Joseph has evolved into a vibrant educational complex, it has never strayed from its original vision: a steadfast commitment to preparing students for insightful leadership and service to others

LOCATION AND ENVIRONMENT

The University of Saint Joseph is an independent not-for-profit organization, founded by the Sisters of Mercy in 1932 in the Catholic tradition.

The beautiful 90-acre campus is one mile from West Hartford's thriving downtown, three miles from Hartford, and mid-way between Boston and New York City.

When you're on campus, you can be as involved in campus life as you would like, and there is always something happening here.

USJ students spend their time outside of the classroom participating in one of our 12 Division III athletic teams or intramural sport activities. They are involved in more than 20 clubs and organizations, from the Accounting and Business Society to the Dance Ensemble, or even the Student Government Association. Our Student Programming and Events Council (SPEC) is always planning something, whether it be a spring carnival on campus, a sports event, or a bus trip to a city with famous landmarks.

CAMPUS FACILITIES & EQUIPMENT

- Six residence halls—including suite-style housing for juniors and seniors
- NCAA Division III Athletics—12 teams
- The O'Connell Athletic Center—includes a six-lane pool, fitness center, indoor track, dance studio and more
- The Bruyette Athenaeum—includes the 365-seat Hoffman auditorium, the O'Connor Archives, an art studio, classrooms, and faculty offices
- The Art Museum—houses a distinguished collection of more than 2,000 works of art
- McGovern Student Center—the hub of student activity, which houses the Dining Hall, a snack bar, activities offices, a community lounge and the University Bookstore
- The Connor Chapel of Our Lady—the heart of the University's Roman Catholic tradition
- The Pope Pius XII Library—with 133,700 volumes and online resources
- Eight state-of-the-art science laboratories
- On-campus nursing lab
- Two laboratory schools:
  o The Gengras Center—private special education school, on campus
  o The School for Young Children—model lab preschool, one block from campus

OFF-CAMPUS OPPORTUNITIES

USJ also connects 95 percent of all students (undergraduate, graduate, and adult) to high-impact learning opportunities, including internships and experiential and clinical experiences in the laboratory schools, in Hartford, and Connecticut.

ACADEMIC PROGRAMS

USJ offers 30 undergraduate programs, as well as evening, weekend and graduate programs. These career-focused programs will help prepare you for a fulfilling future in your area of choice. Accelerated bachelor's-to-master's degree options, Online degree programs, and Yellow Ribbon GI Education Enhancement Program for veteran students, in collaboration with the U.S. Department of Veterans Affairs, are available.

MAJORS AND DEGREES OFFERED

Bachelor's, Master's, and Doctoral degrees are available from our:

Undergraduate College (B.A.; B.S.)

Graduate and Professional Studies Program (M.A.; M.S.; D.N.P.; MSPAS)

School of Pharmacy (Pharm.D.)

TUITION, ROOM, BOARD, FEES

Student payments are due August 1 for fall semester and December 21 for spring semester. School of Pharmacy student payments are due August 15 for fall semester, December 15 for spring semester and May 15 for summer session. Payment is due at time of registration if you register after semester due dates. Questions? Contact us at http://www.usj.edu/admissions-financial-aid/tuition-and-financial-aid/contact-us/ for more information or review our tuition payment options.

FINANCIAL AID

From merit scholarships, to University, state and federal grants, USJ offers a variety of University and external scholarships and grants.

Contact Student Financial Services at 860.231.5223 or financialaid@usj.edu, or visit the office on the second floor of Mercy Hall, Room 201 to find out more.

STUDENT ORGANIZATIONS AND ACTIVITIES

We are looking for applicants who display evidence of sufficient ability and potential in their academic record and standardized test scores, when applicable (see Test Optional Admission Policy below). It is expected that you will have completed 16 academic units in college preparatory courses distributed among English, mathematics, natural sciences, social sciences, and foreign languages. Special consideration may be given to selected applicants whose preparation varies from the recommended pattern, but whose record gives evidence of genuine intellectual ability and interest.

In the classroom:

- Faculty will inspire you to fulfill your potential
- Your average class size will include 14 students; student/faculty ratio is 11:1
- Your First-Year Seminar (FYS) course will help you transition to college-level learning and living

Join a club or create your own. There are more than 20 student organizations on campus, each led by students with guidance by a faculty or staff advisor.

Focused on academics, social and global concerns, diversity and cultural issues, community service and more, these clubs are created to enrich your academic and co-curricular interests.

Visit the Office of Student Affairs to find out more or inquire during your Orientation Program.

ADMISSIONS PROCESS
TAKE THE NEXT STEP: EASY ADMISSIONS PROCESS

- Submit your application online or through the Common App and we will waive the fee.
- Submit official Transcripts from your high school.
- Request your official test scores (SAT and/or ACT) be mailed to USJ.
- Submit an essay, 250 words or more in length.
- Have a teacher or high school counselor write a letter of recommendation and mail it to the University.
- Include a resume and/or schedule an interview with your personal admissions counselor (recommended, but not required).
- Include your ZeeMee link or unique profile page (optional) Learn more about ZeeMee.

Questions? Contact an Admissions Counselor at http://www.usj.edu/admissions-financial-aid/undergraduate-admissions/contact-us/.

THE UNIVERSITY OF SAN FRANCISCO

AT A GLANCE

The University of San Francisco—a private, Jesuit university—reflects the diversity, optimism, and opportunities of the city that surrounds it. USF provides students from all backgrounds an education that is intensely personalized, intellectually inspiring, and designed expressly to help them change the world for the better.

USF enrolls 6,745 undergraduate and 4,293 graduate students, offers over 100 undergraduate and graduate degree programs, and boasts a network of over 110,000 alumni who live in all 50 states, six US territories, and 129 countries. The school's hilltop campus, in the geographic center of the city, puts students in the middle of everything San Francisco has to offer.

CAMPUS AND LOCATION

USF's campus is a small and supportive community in the heart of a large city. The campus is just minutes from the Financial District, Golden Gate Park, and the Pacific Ocean. More than 90 percent of incoming first-year students live on campus, and all USF students take advantage of the city—music, museums, theater, dining, major sporting events—plus a wide range of research, internship, and employment opportunities.

DEGREES OFFERED

The College of Arts and Sciences offers both B.A. and B.S. degrees. The School of Management offers B.S. degrees. The School of Nursing and Health Professions offers a direct-entry, four-year B.S. in Nursing for qualified high school and transfer applicants. Major programs include accounting, advertising, architecture and community design, art history/arts management, Asian studies, biology, chemistry, communication studies, comparative literature and culture, computer science, critical diversity studies, data science, design, economics, English, entrepreneurship and innovation, environmental science, environmental studies, finance, fine arts, French studies, history, hospitality management, international business, international studies, Japanese studies, kinesiology, Latin American studies, marketing, management, mathematics, media studies, nursing, performing arts and social justice, philosophy, physics, politics, psychology, sociology, Spanish, theology and religious studies, and urban studies.

USF offers 71 minors and special programs, including astronomy; African studies; Asia Pacific studies; Catholic studies and social thought; ethnic studies; film studies; honors college; Jewish studies and social justice; Latin@/Chican@ studies; Middle Eastern studies; neuroscience; 4+3 dual degrees in law, premedical, and other pre-professional health studies; public relations; a five-year dual-degree teacher preparation program that results in teacher certification at the elementary or secondary level; and the School of Management honors cohort program.

PROGRAMS AND CURRICULUM

The University of San Francisco offers a well-rounded education that prepares students not only for successful careers but also for fulfilling lives. A baccalaureate degree is issued upon the successful completion of a 128-credit curriculum consisting of 44 credits in core requirements chosen from six specified categories, with the remainder of credits being taken as part of major requirements and electives. The academic year is based on two semesters, with summer sessions and a winter intersession also available. USF101, a 1-unit course available to first-semester undergraduates, helps students learn about USF's Jesuit mission, join the campus community, navigate the university's academic requirements and resources, and map their paths to graduation.

The USF Center for Global Education offers over 100 programs including exchange programs with universities in Argentina, Australia, Brazil, Chile, China, Colombia, Ecuador, England, France, Greece, Ireland, Japan, Korea, Mexico, New Zealand, Nicaragua, Peru, Philippines, Scotland, Spain, Taiwan, and Uruguay. The center also offers internship-specific programs in a broad range of fields including arts, business, hospitality, and international relations, plus field study programs focused on global issues such as sustainable development, public health, and climate change. USF helps students choose locations, apply to programs, make financial arrangements, register for academic credit, secure passports and visas, and make travel plans.

USF accepts Advanced Placement (AP) credits, as certified by the College Board's Advanced Placement Program exams, the International Baccalaureate program courses, and the College-Level Examination Program (CLEP). Students in the College of Arts and Sciences may earn a bachelor's degree in three years with a combination of Advanced Placement credits and an academically rigorous schedule.

The USF Pre-Professional Health Committee serves to guide and recommend students to medical and dental professional schools as well as to schools for pharmacy, optometry, veterinary medicine, and podiatry. A student may complete the premedical or other pre–health science requirements as part of, or in addition to, the requirements of an academic major. The Pre-Professional Health Committee assists students with the application process, collects and mails recommendations to professional schools, conducts interviews in preparation for application, and endorses approved candidates via a committee letter of recommendation sent to all professional schools selected by the student.

The St. Ignatius Institute offers a core curriculum based on the great books of Western civilization. Any undergraduate student, regardless of major, may take Institute courses to meet core curriculum requirements. The university also offers Army ROTC, which offers scholarships for qualified applicants and continuing students.

FACILITIES

At USF, the campus is small enough to walk across in ten minutes, but large enough to offer nearly everything. Students have access to Gleeson Library's 2.2 million holdings and to Lo Schiavo Center for Science and Innovation, which houses a digital lecture hall, spaces for collaborative learning, and labs for chemistry, toxicology, advanced biotechnology, and mathematics. Cowell Hall, the base for nursing classes and the Nursing Skills Laboratory, includes the Instructional Media Center. Malloy Hall, headquarters for the School of Management, houses a computer lab and special seminar rooms. Kalmanovitz Hall houses all programs in the humanities and social sciences and features state-of-the-art classrooms, a rooftop sculpture garden, and seventeen laboratories for language, writing, media, and psychology. The 281 Masonic building houses the Performing Arts and Social Justice department, the first program in the nation that trains young artists to create a humane and just society through their craft. The Presentation Theater and Lone Mountain Studio Theater offer space for theatrical productions and guest speakers.

University Center, in the heart of campus, is home to the USF bookstore, Center for Academic and Student Achievement, Career Services Center, and the Cultural Centers, which bring students together to increase their understanding, and embrace their roles, as members of a diverse local and global community.

The Koret Health and Recreation Center provides facilities for court games, weight training, massage, personal training, and various aquatic activities in an Olympic-size pool. Spin and yoga are just some of the free classes offered at Koret. Outdoor adventures include horseback riding, skiing/snowboarding, and sea kayaking. Intramural and club sports include basketball, soccer, flag football, sailing, table tennis, karate, lacrosse, rugby, water polo, Ultimate (Frisbee), and volleyball. NCAA Division I sports include baseball, basketball, cross-country, golf, soccer, tennis, track and field, and women's volleyball and sand volleyball.

EXPENSES AND FINANCIAL AID

Tuition and fees for the 2017–18 school year were $46,229. Room and board were $14,330 for the academic year.

A variety of financial aid programs are available at the university, including scholarships, grants, loans, and campus employment. Domestic students who wish to be considered for financial aid must file the Free Application for Federal Student Aid (FAFSA) and College Scholarship Service Profile (CSS) by February 15. More than two thirds of all USF students receive some type of financial aid. In addition to need-based financial aid, the university has a generous academic scholarship program based on the applicant's high school record and test scores. Eligible students are identified during the admission process and can apply as early action, early decision, or regular action applicants. Scholarship recipients are expected to maintain a competitive GPA while enrolled at USF.

FACULTY

The University has 1,239 full- and part-time faculty members; 95.6 percent of full-time faculty hold doctoral or terminal degrees in the fields they teach. USF fosters a close relationship between students and faculty members. This is reflected in the small classes (fewer than 25 students), the low student-to-faculty ratio (14:1), and the faculty members' availability for advising. The main focus of faculty is on classroom teaching and working with students on research. Classes are not taught by student teachers or teachers' assistants

STUDENTS

One of the most diverse universities in the United States, USF delivers the world on a campus. Students from 50 states and 96 countries create a rich environment, and in the best Jesuit tradition, USF welcomes students from all backgrounds—and from all religious faiths or no faith—and invites input from every perspective. The combination of academic rigor and open-minded inquiry creates an atmosphere in which students grow and thrive. USF has produced 270 U.S. judges (including four California Supreme Courts justices); a former United States senator; a California lieutenant governor; three Pulitzer Prize winners; three Olympic medalists; corporate CEOs and entrepreneurs; countless priests, nuns, and other religious leaders; educators; police chiefs; three NBA Hall of Famers; three NFL Hall of Famers; and Alejandro Toledo, the former president of Peru.

ADMISSIONS

The university seeks students who are sincerely interested in pursuing a well-rounded education and who hope to make a positive difference in the world. The admission process is selective, and each application is reviewed individually. To enhance the quality and diversity of its student body, USF welcomes students of all races, nationalities, and religious beliefs—or no religious belief—to apply. Eligibility is based on high school course work and GPA, the application essay, an academic recommendation, extracurricular involvement, and test scores. Domestic applicants are required to submit SAT or ACT test scores. International applicants are required to submit TOEFL or IELTS test scores; however, if an international applicant submits sufficient SAT or ACT test scores, the TOEFL or IELTS may be waived.

SPECIAL PROGRAMS

Because all USF students are encouraged to give back and to change the world in ways both small and large, the Leo T. McCarthy Center for Public Service and the Common Good forms partnerships between local communities and USF. Students take part in service-learning projects and volunteer projects that include habitat restoration, socially just urban design, and outreach to underserved children in local schools.

ADDITIONAL INFORMATION

Living and learning in a community that comprises students from 50 states and 96 countries is a unique opportunity. USF students participate in over 100 associations, including fraternities and sororities, honor societies, student media, performing arts groups, and culturally focused clubs. Annual events sponsored by student organizations range from Campus Movie Fest to theater productions and cultural events such as Black Cultural Dinner, Barrio Fiesta, Lu'au, Culturescape, and Dia de la Mujer. Students also participate in Campus Activities Board-sponsored events including Fright Night, Holiday Roller Rink, Donaroo Spring Concert, Spring Carnival, and Late Nights at Crossroads.

USF guarantees two semesters of housing to all first-time, first-year students who enroll for the fall semester. More than 90 percent of incoming first-years live on campus. Any new student who is not a first-time, first-year student may apply for housing and will be assigned housing based on space availability.

CAREER SERVICES AND PLACEMENT

USF uses its location, alumni base, and strong relationships with industry leaders to help connect students to internship and career opportunities in the Bay Area and beyond. Top employers regularly visit campus. Students visit the Career Services Center to research potential employers, get help with their resumes, and take part in practice interviews. USF alumni report an average mid-career salary of $92,400. They can be found working for organizations like Apple, Google, Deloitte, Tesla, and Teach for America. USF graduates rank among the top 3 percent in the U.S. for their earning potential. But they don't only do well in the world. They change it for the better.

THE UNIVERSITY OF TAMPA

AT A GLANCE

The University of Tampa is a private, medium-sized, comprehensive university in the heart of Tampa. UT offers students an exciting combination of challenging coursework and real-world learning experience in more than 200 areas of study. Situated on a beautiful 110-acre campus, the University is adjacent to the Hillsborough River and downtown Tampa. Students enjoy a traditional, self-contained campus only steps away from the professional and cultural opportunities of a bustling city. At the center of campus lies Plant Hall, once a luxurious hotel for the rich and famous. This historical landmark is complemented by modern surroundings and excellent facilities including a student union, art studios and gallery, theaters, computer resource centers, athletic facilities, science labs and new residence halls. Approximately 9,000 students (7,588 full-time undergraduates) are enrolled at UT. With students from all 50 states and 140 countries, UT provides diverse and dynamic environment. Students may choose from 260 clubs and organizations, including honor societies, student media, fraternities and sororities, community service groups and intramural sports. The University of Tampa has one of the top NCAA Division II sports programs in the nation, winning 15 national championships, including recent championships in baseball (2015, 2013, 2007, 2006), women's volleyball (2014, 2006) and women's soccer (2007). Women's beach volleyball is new for 2018 and competes at the NCAA Division I level.

LOCATION AND ENVIRONMENT

Located on the west central coast of Florida, Tampa has far more to offer than beautiful beaches and a pleasant climate. The Tampa Bay area is one of the fastest growing regions in the United States and is a leading center for the arts, international business, law, education, media and health and scientific research. Forbes and Newsweek consistently pick Tampa Bay as one of the nation's best places to live.

CAMPUS FACILITIES AND EQUIPMENT

UT has invested approximately $575 million in new academic facilities, technology and residence halls since 2000, making this national historic landmark the model of a modern university. 93 percent of residence halls are new within the past 15 years and most others have been renovated recently. (For residence hall video tours, visit www.ut.edu/residencelife/videos.) The Vaughn Center and residence hall complex serves as the hub of student life. Here students find food courts, recreational areas, a theater, student office space, the Barnes & Noble campus store and a ninth-floor conference center with incredible views of Tampa Bay. Morsani Hall offers state-of-the-art amenities and eight separate dining venues. Other outstanding facilities and resources include the Sykes College of Business, a waterfront Marine Science Field Station and research vessels, Ferman Music Center, Reeves Theater, the 1,000-seat Falk Theatre, Bailey Art Studios and Sykes Chapel and Center for Faith and Values. The Martinez Athletics Center, Naimoli Family Softball Complex and Naimoli Family Athletics and Intramural Complex represent some of the best athletic facilities in the country. Students also enjoy a new 21st-century fitness center, completed in fall 2016.

OFF-CAMPUS OPPORTUNITIES

Across the river in downtown is the Tampa Museum of Art, Straz Center for the Performing Arts, Florida Aquarium, Amalie Arena and an outstanding public library. Busch Gardens is several miles from campus, and Walt Disney World and Universal Studios are only 90 minutes away. Tampa International Airport is only 15 miles from campus.

ACADEMICS

The University of Tampa's undergraduate curriculum is designed to give students a broad academic and cultural background as well as a concentrated study in a major. Students complete a comprehensive core curriculum known as the Baccalaureate Experience, which is highlighted by the unique and innovative First-Year Experience—an extensive orientation program that encourages student development via exploration of global issues, career possibilities and critical thinking and communication skills. International experience is an important focus at The University of Tampa. Through globally oriented courses and study abroad opportunities, students are prepared to live and work internationally. In 2018 there are more than 20 faculty-led travel courses to countries such as Costa Rica, Ghana, China, Morocco and France. For qualifying students, UT offers a rigorous and rewarding Honors Program of expanded instruction, student research, internships and the opportunity to study at Oxford University.

MAJORS

The University of Tampa offers bachelor's degrees in accounting, advertising and public relations, allied health, applied dance, art, athletic training, biochemistry, biology, business information technology, chemistry, communication, criminology and criminal justice, cybersecurity, digital arts, economics, education (elementary and secondary certification), English, entrepreneurship, environmental science, film and media arts, finance, financial enterprise systems, forensic science, graphic design, history, human performance, international business, international studies, journalism, liberal studies, management, management information systems, marine science (biology and chemistry), marketing, mathematical programming, mathematics, music, music education, music performance, musical theatre, new media production, nursing, philosophy, physical education, physics, political science, psychology, public health, sociology, Spanish, sport management, theatre and writing. Minors and concentrations are offered in advertising, aerospace studies, applied sociology, art history, art therapy, Asian studies, biology/business, biology/molecular, biology/organismal and evolutionary, business administration, business analytics, criminal investigation, exercise physiology, French, international studies, law, justice and advocacy, leadership studies, military science, naval science, professional and technical writing, recreation, speech/theatre and women's and gender studies. Pre-professional programs offered include pre-dentistry, pre-law, pre-medicine, pre-veterinary science, allied health and chemistry. Certificate programs include Chinese, European studies, French, German, Italian, Japanese, Portuguese and Spanish. An undergraduate School of Continuing Studies offers 38 degree programs designed for adults who want to study part-time. Four summer sessions also offer excellent learning and professional advancement opportunities. At the graduate level, the business school offers an MBA (traditional, professional and executive options), 4+1 MBA and M.S. degrees in accounting, cybersecurity, entrepreneurship, finance and marketing. An M.S. in Nursing, Master of Physician Assistant Medicine, M.S. in Exercise and Nutrition Science, M.S. in Criminology and Criminal Justice, MFA in Creative Writing, M.Ed. in Curriculum and Instruction, M.Ed. in Educational Leadership, 4+1 M.Ed. and M.S. in Instructional Design and Technology are also offered. For a full list of programs, visit www.ut.edu/degrees.

TUITION, ROOM, BOARD, FEES

The average cost for the 2018–2019 academic year is $29,128 for tuition and fees and $10,802 for room and board. The average financial aid award for students in 2017 was $18,308, with 97 percent of students receiving financial assistance.

FINANCIAL AID

The high-quality, private education offered by The University of Tampa is not as difficult to finance as some students may think. Each family's situation is evaluated individually for need-based assistance. Academic achievements, leadership potential, athletic skills and other special talents are also recognized, regardless of need. Academic scholarships are awarded to most entering first-year students with a 3.0 unweighted GPA or above. Transfer, leadership, departmental, Phi Theta Kappa, International Baccalaureate and ROTC scholarships are also available. Learn more at www.ut.edu/financialaid.

STUDENT ORGANIZATIONS AND ACTIVITIES

UT offers 260 clubs, organizations and teams, making it easy for students to get involved in campus life. Options include academic and social clubs, leadership groups and student government, amongst many others. For a full list, visit www.ut.edu/studentorgs.

ADMISSIONS PROCESS

The University of Tampa is an academically competitive institution that offers several non-binding early action admission dates. Visit www.ut.edu/admissions for more details.

THE UNIVERSITY OF TULSA

AT A GLANCE

The University of Tulsa (TU) is a private, comprehensive doctoral-degree-granting university that provides education of the highest quality in the arts, humanities, sciences, engineering, business, education, applied health sciences and law. TU features four undergraduate colleges: the Kendall College of Arts and Sciences, the Collins College of Business, the College of Engineering and Natural Sciences and the Oxley College of Health Sciences, as well as the College of Law and Graduate School.

TU's 11:1 student/faculty ratio, average class size of 20, and emphasis on individual attention anchor an educational culture where students are rigorously challenged and comprehensively supported.

The university is fully accredited by the North Central Association of Colleges and Universities and is an NCAA Division IA participant in the American Athletic Conference. TU maintains a covenant relationship with the Presbyterian Church (USA).

Extracurricular opportunities include intramural sports, special-interest clubs, pre-professional organizations, national fraternities and sororities, community service organizations, an active student government, departmental honorary organizations and campus ministry groups.

Total fall 2017 enrollment was 4,433, with 3,343 undergraduates and 755 graduate and 335 law students. The ratio of men to women is 56:44 and 25 percent are multicultural students. Over half the students are from out of state and international students make up 20 percent of the student population, with 68 countries represented.

For the 15th consecutive year, the 2018 U.S. News & World Report includes the university among the top 100 Best Colleges, ranking TU #86.

LOCATION AND ENVIRONMENT

TU's 216-acre residential campus is in Tulsa, Oklahoma (961,561 MSA). The city's prominent industries include energy, telecommunications, high technology, manufacturing, health care, aerospace and education which present opportunities for internships and employment after graduation. Tulsans enjoy Broadway shows in the Performing Arts Center and pop concerts in the BOK Center (arena) as well as acclaimed ballet and opera companies, symphony, Philbrook Museum, Gilcrease Museum, Brady Arts District and cultural festivals. Local professional sports include minor league baseball, hockey and arena football. The popular River Parks area features jogging and bicycling trails, while Guthrie Green is a popular arts, music, and food truck destination.

CAMPUS FACILITIES & EQUIPMENT

Since 2002, The University of Tulsa has added one million square feet of building space and a stunning entrance.

Hardesty Hall, TU's newest building, houses 300 residents and houses the offices of Career Services, Center for Global Education, Multicultural Affairs, Greek Life and the English Institute for international students.

The Lorton Performance Center, which houses the School of Music and the Department of Film Studies, features a 700-seat concert hall, specialized rehearsal and practice rooms and a film production suite with post-production editing and scoring capabilities.

In 2012, the College of Engineering & Natural Sciences added two new buildings: J. Newton Rayzor Hall, which features 24 integrated classroom and state-of-the-art teaching/research laboratories. Razor houses the Tandy School of Computer Science and the Department of Electrical and Computer Engineering. Stephenson Hall is home to the McDougall School of Petroleum Engineering and the Department of Mechanical Engineering. Additional research facilities are located in Keplinger Hall and at TU's North Campus where government and industry-funded research consortia foster student learning while exploring innovations and solving petroleum industry problems.

The historic McFarlin Library and the Mabee Legal Information Center house more than 5 million items. McFarlin holdings include 991,000 volumes, more than 680,000 titles, 54,000 electronic journals, 450,000 electronic books, and more than 1,000 collections of electronic reference sources and databases as well as print resources. McFarlin's Department of Special Collections and University Archives' rare book holdings are internationally recognized, particularly in Native American history and law. The department includes one of the five largest collections in the world on James Joyce, the life archive of Nobel Laureate Sir V.S. Naipaul, and holdings in nineteenth and twentieth century Irish, British and American Literature. The library's Academic Technology Center annex includes computer labs, a coffee shop and reading rooms.

Helmerich Hall, which houses the Collins College of Business, was renovated to include innovative learning spaces such as the Williams Student Services Center and Studio Blue. Academic centers include the Schools of Accounting and CIS; Energy Economics, Policy and Commerce and Finance, Operations Management and International Business; as well as the Departments of Economics and Management and Marketing.

The Mary K. Chapman Center for Communicative Disorders, part of the university's new Oxley College of Health Sciences, serves the community in its clinical facility and is the learning center for the Department of Communication Disorders. The department has the latest equipment for research, diagnostic, and therapy activities.

Kendall Hall is home to the Departments of Theatre and Musical Theatre and features two fully equipped theatres, a scene shop, costume shop and computer design lab.

The Kendall College of Arts and Sciences features the Alexandre Hogue Gallery in the School of Art, Design and Art History, TUTV Media Lab, as well as psychology and anthropology labs.

Renovated in 2014, the Allen Chapman Student Union includes a food court with nine eateries and a convenience store. It also houses an ATM, offices for student organizations, lecture and meeting rooms, the Faculty Club, post office and the Hurricane Hut sports bar.

The Oxley College of Health Sciences, housed at 1215 S. Boulder Avenue in downtown Tulsa, occupies floors 1 through 5, encompassing 52,000 square feet of space remodeled for the college.

The TU College of Law received an "A" from National Jurist magazine for Best Law School Facility with more than 110,000 square feet.

The Oxley College of Health Sciences, housed at 1215 S. Boulder Avenue in downtown Tulsa, occupies floors 1 through 5 of remodeled space that encompasses 52,000 square feet. The college includes state-of-the-art classrooms and the Lawson Family Nursing Simulation Center and Skills Laboratory.

The Donald W. Reynolds Center is TU's arena and convocation center. This facility, home for the intercollegiate basketball and volleyball programs, has cutting-edge facilities for video editing and training.

The university's sports and recreation complex features the Collins Fitness Center, Michael Case Tennis Center (which has hosted NCAA Finals), track, intramural and NCAA-grade soccer fields, and softball fields.

In partnership with the city of Tulsa, the university manages Gilcrease Museum as well as the Zarrow Center for Art and Education, which provides gallery space, classes and studio space in the city's Brady Arts District.

TU students have the option of hundreds of attractive and convenient on-campus apartments and residence halls.

OFF-CAMPUS OPPORTUNITIES

The university strongly supports studying abroad, and the Office of Global Education helps students locate the perfect program, whether it is for TU credit or as an intern/volunteer. Students have hundreds of options through direct exchange with an international university, through an affiliate-sponsored program, or as part of a faculty-led course.

Many students take advantage of the of internship opportunities afforded by the city of Tulsa's business and industry community, as well as in the arts, social services and government agencies.

ACADEMICS

The Tulsa Curriculum links a broad, humanities-based core and writing for all students across all disciplines. TU students can receive a personalized education that is well-rounded. Candidates for graduation must complete at least 124 semester hours of course work.

The Honors Program engages students in a critical examination of the major epochs and ideas of Western thought and culture through careful study of primary texts. A separate application is required. The Tulsa Undergraduate Research Challenge (TURC) program combines advanced research, scholarship, and community service.

TU's Global Scholars Program engages students in global issues from the perspective of their particular major. Students take a set of classes that explore the big questions affecting the world today and participate in monthly programming on campus and an international study, research, or intern experience.

The two-year Presidential Leaders Fellowship program prepares students to maximize their college experience through various opportunities. Students accepted to the program are required to complete various

The TU Center for Information Security is developing defenses against cyber-terrorist attacks and information warfare. The center supports TU's National Security Agency (NSA)-accredited certificate program in information assurance and a curriculum that integrates information security with computer law and policy issues. TU has been designated a Center of Excellence in Information Assurance by the NSA and is one of six pioneer institutions selected by the National Science Foundation for the Federal Cyber Service Initiative (Cyber Corps).

Air Force ROTC is available through a satellite program.

Students may receive credit through Advanced Placement testing. Depending on their test scores, students who complete the International Baccalaureate diploma can receive up to 30 college credits.

The University of Tulsa operates on a semester calendar. The fall term begins in late August, the spring term in mid-January, and the summer session in late May.

TUITION, ROOM, BOARD, FEES

Estimated costs for the 2018–19 academic year are as follows: the typical cost for students living on campus is $52,625 including $40,484 for tuition, $11,116 for room and board, and $1,025 fees. Expenses for books average about $1,200 per year.

TU invested over $21,000,000 via scholarships to the freshman class of 2017. The average combined financial aid and scholarship package offered to Tulsa students in 2017 is approximately $29,300.

FINANCIAL AID

In 2017, 96 percent of entering students received some form of financial aid (including grants, scholarships, work-study, and loans). TU offers a limited number of highly competitive Presidential Scholarships that cover full tuition, room, and board. All applicants may be considered for a range of university scholarships based on academic merit. Performance scholarships are available in music and theater by audition. The University of Tulsa participates in National Merit and National Achievement Scholarship Corporation's Finalist program, and the National Hispanic Scholar Program. Applicants for aid should submit the Free Application for Federal Student Aid (FAFSA) as soon as possible after October 1 for priority consideration.

DATES—Notification Date—February 1

BOTTOM LINE Tuition at Tulsa is $40,484 annually, with an additional $11,116 approximately for room and board. Forty-two percent of Tulsa students have borrowed through one of the various loan programs, while the average need-based gift award for freshmen is roughly $8,400 (and $6,900 for other undergraduates). The average financial aid package offered to Tulsa students is approximately $24,900, and on average, Tulsa graduates leave school with around $29,161 of debt.

EXPENSES PER ACADEMIC YEAR—Tuition $40,484; Room and Board $11,116; Required Fees $1,025

STUDENT ORGANIZATIONS AND ACTIVITIES

TU hosts more than 200 student organizations and societies that appeal to a wide range of student interests—from professional to recreational. (For the complete listing, see https://utulsa.edu/campus-life/student-activities/student-organizations/.) Students can participate in a variety of activities on and off campus including intramural sports, special interest clubs, trips to Tulsa's museums, parks, shopping malls, cultural events, etc.

ADMISSIONS PROCESS

The University of Tulsa seeks students whose academic background indicates potential for success in the university's rigorous academic environment. Performance in high school college-preparatory subjects and scores on the SAT or ACT are key factors in the admission evaluation, but each applicant is reviewed holistically. The counselor recommendation, extracurricular activities, and indicators of leadership, creativity, and focus are all taken into consideration. Campus visits and interviews are highly recommended.

TU has a non-binding, Early Action freshman admission plan with an application deadline of November 1. Decisions are mailed within three weeks. Applications received after November 1 are reviewed under a Rolling Admission process with notifications made on an ongoing basis after mid-December.

An application with a $50 application fee, official high school transcript, ACT or SAT score results, and a guidance counselor recommendation are required of freshman applicants. TU accepts the Common Application or TU's application online, or paper application form. TU adheres to the national Candidate's Reply Date of May 1.

For additional information, students should contact:

The University of Tulsa

Office of Admission

800 South Tucker Drive

Tulsa, Oklahoma 74104-3189

Telephone: 918-631-2307 (in Tulsa), 800-331-3050 (toll-free)

Fax: 918-631-5008

E-mail: admission@utulsa.edu

Web: www.utulsa.edu/admission

THE UNIVERSITY OF VERMONT

AT A GLANCE

Since 1791, the University of Vermont has worked to move humankind forward. Today, UVM is a Public Ivy and top 100 research university of a perfect size, large enough to offer a breadth of ideas, resources, and opportunities, yet small enough to enable close faculty-student mentorship across all levels, from bachelor's to M.D. programs, and in nearly every field of study.

LOCATION AND ENVIRONMENT

Students' academic experiences and activities are enriched by UVM's location — from the energy and innovation of Burlington to the forests, farms, and independent spirit of Vermont. UVM provides students endless ways to explore the world, challenge ideas, and dig in on the most pressing issues of our time.

CAMPUS FACILITIES & EQUIPMENT

UVM's gracious campus overlooks the city of Burlington and Lake Champlain. Stunning historic architecture blends with state-of-the-art structures. Phase 1 of a $104M STEM facility and a brand-new first-year student residence hall in the heart of campus, featuring UVM's nationally recognized Wellness Environment, opened in 2017. Pre-med, nursing, and health sciences students benefit from clinical training at the university's expansive on-campus medical center, one of only 100 level one trauma centers in the United States. Other specialized facilities include an aquatic research vessel and laboratory located on Lake Champlain, one mile from the heart of campus; four research farms serving dairy, equine, and horticulture studies; nine managed natural areas for study ranging from wildlife management to effects of global warming.

OFF-CAMPUS OPPORTUNITIES

UVM's hometown, Burlington, perennially appears on national rankings that laud its livability, access to nature and recreation, thriving food and music scene, rising identity as a technology and innovation hub, and status as a top college town. Burlington's nickname, BTV, comes from the code for its airport, just 10 minutes from campus. With Montreal a 90-minute and Boston a 3.5- hour drive away, and daily flights available to NYC, international and metropolitan culture are easily accessible for weekend adventures.

ACADEMIC PROGRAMS

The University of Vermont offers study in disciplines spanning business, STEM, humanities, education, social services, food systems, health sciences, environmental studies, medicine and more (view all offerings at uvm.edu/academics).

Academics at UVM are supplemented and deepened by a world of hands-on learning opportunities, from travel-study to service learning, and a wide array of internships in locations ranging from Vermont to China. Undergraduate research opportunities are plentiful; students assist faculty with their groundbreaking research in state-of-the-art facilities across campus, including UVM's highly-ranked medical school in the heart of campus and in our brand new STEM facility.

The university's Honors College enrolls students from the full spectrum of academic programs at the university, providing a rigorous, multi-disciplinary academic challenge that complements and enriches the entire undergraduate experience.

MAJORS AND DEGREES OFFERED

UVM's 100+ undergraduate majors are offered through its seven undergraduate colleges: College of Agriculture & Life Sciences, College of Arts & Sciences, College of Education & Social Services, College of Engineering & Mathematical Sciences, College of Nursing & Health Sciences, Grossman School of Business, and Rubenstein School of Environment & Natural Resources.

UVM undergraduates have access to 29 accelerated master's degree programs. In total, the university offers 50 master's and 22 doctoral programs through its Graduate College, and an M.D. program through the Larner College of Medicine.

TUITION, ROOM, BOARD, FEES

UNDERGRADUATE 2017-18 COST OF ATTENDANCE
12-18 CREDIT HOURS FOR TWO SEMESTERS

	Vermont Residents	Out-of-State Resident
Tuition	$15,504	$39,120
Comprehensive Student Fee	$2,236	$2,236
Average Room and Board (VIEW ROOM AND BOARD RATES)		
	$12,052	$12,052
Estimated Books & Supplies	$1,200	$1,200
Est. Personal/Misc. Expenses	$1,882	$2,312
Total	$32,874	$56,920

FINANCIAL AID

83% of undergraduate students received scholarships or financial aid. Undergraduate scholarships are available for Vermont residents, out-of-state and international students and transfer students. Learn more at uvm.edu/sfs.

STUDENT ORGANIZATIONS AND ACTIVITIES

UVM students are known for being active in service and in sports and as social progress and environmental health defenders. They are national and international contenders in competitions ranging from debate to skiing to alternative race car design. There are countless ways for UVM students to get involved on campus, in the Burlington community, beyond borders – and they do.

Catamount pride swells for the university's 18 Division I sports programs. Enthusiastic crowds come out for soccer, hockey, and basketball games. Many of UVM's 50+ club sports also compete nationally and bring home trophies.

More than 70% of first-year students live in residential learning communities, where they engage in learning and projects with others who share their particular interests in art and creativity, wellness, leadership, outdoor experience, liberal arts, innovation and entrepreneurship, and global citizenry.

ADMISSIONS PROCESS

At the University of Vermont we look for talented students who share our passion for learning and living with purpose. We accept the Common Application or the Coalition Application. Through a holistic admissions review, we select students with strong potential for academic success who will contribute to our community. The rigor of an applicant's academic program; class standing and grades; standardized test results; and trends in performance are considered. Essays, recommendations, and other evidence of each student's life experience also assist our evaluation. Admission decisions are made without regard to family financial circumstances.

For detailed information about UVM's college/school requirements visit: uvm.edu/apply.

VANCOUVER FILM SCHOOL

AT A GLANCE

For over 30 years Vancouver Film School has been an innovative pioneer in education, being the first to offer a one-year production-based model to develop the most successful alumni across the industry. As Canada's Premier post-secondary arts institution, VFS offers students a connection to industry unlike any other school. First, through the industry experience provided across their faculty, and also through the innovative integration of outside industry partners that bring real work and expertise right into the classroom environment. No other school boasts more proudly an accredited alumni success track record throughout the industry. VFS offers a host of educational programs wherever you're looking to make your mark in the new creative economy. From 3D Animation & VFX, Digital Art & Design, Film & Television Production, Acting, Makeup to Writing for Film, Television & Games, Game Design and Programing, they see your creative potential differently than other schools.

LOCATION AND ENVIRONMENT

At the heart of Vancouver's Gastown district Vancouver Film School is an iconic part of Western Canada's most beautiful city. Nestled in among leading global tech and media companies, their 7 unique campus buildings house over 250,000 square feet of studio and learning facilities, connecting students to industry professionals and insightful instructors, as well as state of the art equipment in well-appointed learning spaces. A rich, deep connection to arts and culture comes naturally to Vancouver, with students immersed in a world bordered by the Rocky Mountains on one side and the Georgia Strait on the other. It's no surprise that some of the world's most creative talent has come from the VFS experience over the last 30 years.

CAMPUS FACILITIES & EQUIPMENT

The Vancouver Film School's commitment to cutting-edge and emerging technologies is apparent in each of their 7 well-equipped campus buildings. The facilities mirror those found in studios and production houses around the world, from the massive 180° green screen space to the best-in-class performance capture studio, used across a wide range of their programs.

OFF-CAMPUS OPPORTUNITIES

Vancouver provides the perfect blend of nature, arts and culture, and exposure to the fields that VFS alumni find so valuable. Students and grads can hit the slopes in the morning and ride the scenic seawall in the afternoon, taking in any of Vancouver's museums, theatres, and eclectic arts spaces in the evening–all in a single day. The creative economy in Vancouver is booming as well, helping students and grads connect to shoots, projects, and industry insiders in their field through a wide range of VFS-run and third-party events.

ACADEMIC PROGRAMS

- Game Design
- Programming for Games, Web + Mobile
- 3D Animation + Visual Effects
- Classical Animation Animation Concept Art
- Animation Concept Art
- Foundation Visual Art + Desig
- Digital Design
- Acting Essentials
- Acting for Film + Television
- Writing for Film, Television + Games
- Film Production
- Sound Design
- Makeup for Film + Television
- English for Creative Arts

MAJORS AND DEGREES OFFERED

Graduating students receive a Diploma

Upon completing Diploma programs, students can achieve accelerated Bachelor's Degree through pathway universities listed below:

- Wilfred Laurier University
- University of the Fraser Valley
- BCIT
- Regent's University in London

TUITION, ROOM, BOARD, FEES

VFS is an all-inclusive tuition, all school supplies, i.e. books, equipment and incidentals are included in your tuition fees. As a Canadian school the rates listed below are in CAD dollars.

Game Design:
- Tuition cost of $32,116 CAD (domestic tuition)
- Tuition cost of $49,250 CAD (international tuition)

Programming for Games, Web + Mobile:
- Tuition cost of $32,050 CAD (domestic tuition)
- Tuition cost of $49,050 CAD (international tuition)

3D Animation + Visual Effects:
- Tuition cost of $35,250 CAD (domestic tuition)
- Tuition cost of $53,250 CAD (international tuition)

Classical Animation:
- Tuition cost of $20,500 CAD (domestic tuition)
- Tuition cost of $30,500 CAD (international tuition)

Animation Concept Art:
- Tuition cost of $25,500 CAD (domestic tuition)
- Tuition cost of $30,500 CAD (international tuition)

Foundation Visual Art + Design:
- Tuition cost of $20,500 CAD (domestic tuition)
- Tuition cost of $30,500 CAD (international tuition)

Digital Design:
- Tuition cost of $27,250 CAD (domestic tuition,)
- Tuition cost of $42,250 CAD (international tuition.)

Acting Essentials:
- Tuition cost of $7,500 CAD (domestic tuition)
- Tuition cost of $10,500 CAD (international tuition)

Acting for Film + Television:
- Tuition cost of $20,500 CAD (domestic tuition)
- Tuition cost of $30,500 CAD (international tuition)

Writing for Film + Television:
- Tuition cost of $20,250 CAD (domestic tuition)
- Tuition cost of $28,250 CAD (international tuition)

Film Production:
- Tuition cost of $35,230 CAD (domestic tuition)
- Tuition cost of $53,230 CAD(international tuition)
- Program kit cost is $20

Sound Design:

- Tuition cost of $28,250 CAD (domestic tuition)
- Tuition cost of $43,250 CAD (international tuition)

Makeup for Film, Television + Games:

- Tuition cost of $32,250 CAD (domestic tuition)
- Tuition cost of $46,750 CAD (international tuition)

English for Creative Arts:

- Tuition cost of $6,600 CAD (domestic + international)

Room and Board:

VFS offers a robust housing and homestay placement service. Renting in Vancouver is expensive; however, VFS aims to provide convenient accommodation that makes it easier for students to focus on their academic and personal growth.

Their Housing Coordinator has well-established connections with landlords in Vancouver and will help you find accommodation that best meets students' individual and budgetary needs. Whether you want to rent your own apartment, share with roommates or live in a Homestay, they have excellent options for students to choose from.

FINANCIAL AID

Vancouver Film School's programs are recognized by all Federal and Provincial loan providers in Canada. Recently VFS offered The Search Scholarship where students could apply for a possible tuition reduction for their program. This campaign offered up to $500,000 in scholarships.

For students from outside of Canada VFS have a team that is dedicated to assisting students with payment plans and can work with a student's local loan providers to assist with tuition costs, etc.

STUDENT ORGANIZATIONS AND ACTIVITIES

The iconic Vancouver Film School backpack is a ubiquitous sign that the student body of VFS is everywhere in Vancouver. With a diverse mix of both Canadian and international students in every program, some are attending VFS as their first post-secondary stop to prepare for an immersive experience that connects them to real industry experience on their first day of class. For others, it's sometimes about changing directions and pursuing a longtime creative passion after already completing a different education somewhere else. What connects them all wherever they're from is that Vancouver is one of the most beautiful, safe and culturally rich cities to live and learn in.

VFS Students engage in a broad range of activities both inside and outside of the school. A passionate commitment to the arts means that most students are connected not only to their own projects, but to those of others as they work through intensive one-year programs together. A number of opportunities for activism, volunteerism, and other pursuits keep VFS students engaged every day.

ADMISSIONS PROCESS

Over the years, VFS Advisors have helped thousands of people through the application process. Advisors encourage applicants to be well-informed about their educational options and help ensure there is a strong fit between program choice and desired career outcomes. Advisors also assist prospective sutdents in putting together the components needed to satisfy specific program requirements (portfolios) where applicable. Once this has occurred, applicants are encouraged to apply.

Application Process + Criteria

1. Students can apply to VFS anytime, from grade 11 and up; however before attending classes, they must be either 19 or completed rade 12.

2. $50 Non-refundable Application Fee

3. Photo ID copy

4. 2 Reference Letters (Preferably these should be from someone who can knowledgeably comment on your passion and abilities in the area for which you are applying. Please note, family members are not eligible as references)

5. Transcript from High School or University

6. High School Diploma (if under 19 years old)

7. Online Application Form (https://vfs.edu/admissions)

8. Applicants are to submit program specific portfolios where applicable

VANDERBILT UNIVERSITY

AT A GLANCE

In 1873, on the heels of the Civil War, "Commodore" Cornelius Vanderbilt gave $1 million to the university that now bears his name, with the hope that it would "contribute to strengthening the ties which should exist between all sections of our common country." Since then, Vanderbilt has consistently enrolled intelligent and talented students and challenged them daily to expand their intellectual horizons in an inclusive environment based on open inquiry and respect. Vanderbilt's comprehensive interdisciplinary approach to education allows students to pursue a wide array of academic and curricular interests outside of their main focus of study, and the university's Opportunity Vanderbilt financial aid program ensures that it is often cited among the country's best values. Consistently ranked among the top 20 universities in the country by U.S. News & World Report, Vanderbilt is a private research university that features four undergraduate schools and six graduate and professional schools. Each year, 1,600 first-year students join the university, bringing the total undergraduate population to approximately 6,900 students, more than half of whom collaborate with professors on research across disciplines. The university's 7:1 student-faculty ratio gives students access to faculty members of prominence in every area of academic study. Faculty members provide a challenging, comprehensive education that encourages broad perspectives and critical thinking.

LOCATION AND ENVIRONMENT

Vanderbilt is located in the heart of Nashville, home to a diverse population of 1.7 million and marked by its unique blend of cosmopolitan flair and small-town charm. A thriving center of entertainment, publishing, health care, and technology, Nashville is consistently ranked as one of America's friendliest cities and was honored as one of the Best Places to Go in 2018 by Conde Nast Traveler. Nashville sits at the intersection of three major interstates, and Nashville International Airport provides nonstop service to more than 50 markets.

CAMPUS FACILITIES & EQUIPMENT

Vanderbilt University is located 1.5 miles southwest of downtown Nashville on a 330-acre, park-like campus that was designated an official arboretum in 1988. The university shares a name with and enjoys close collaboration with the separate, nonprofit Vanderbilt University Medical Center. The university comprises 177 buildings, including the Jean and Alexander Heard Library, home to over 8 million items. All first-year students live on The Martha Rivers Ingram Commons, a living-learning community for first-year students. Recent additions include Warren and Moore residential colleges, living-learning communities for upperclass students; a 230,000-square-foot state-of-the-art Engineering and Science Building; and a cross-disciplinary creative and makerspace called the Wond'ry, the new campus epicenter for innovation and entrepreneurship. The E. Bronson Ingram College, the newest residential college for upperclass students, is scheduled to open August 2018.

OFF-CAMPUS OPPORTUNITIES

Study abroad programs allow students to immerse themselves in languages and cultures around the world. More than 120 programs are offered in Argentina, Australia, Austria, Chile, China, Cuba, the Czech Republic, Denmark, the Dominican Republic, Egypt, England, France, Israel, India, Italy, Japan, Nepal, New Zealand, Russia, Singapore, South Africa, and Spain, among others. Students receive direct credit for courses, and the cost of tuition is usually the same as for study on campus in Nashville. In addition, any scholarships, grants, or loans a student has been awarded apply to Vanderbilt study abroad programs. Students may also participate in programs sponsored by other universities by working with an adviser.

Students also take advantage of internships in many industries located in Nashville, including entertainment, business, health care, government, publishing, and education.

ACADEMIC PROGRAMS

Students apply directly to one of Vanderbilt's four undergraduate schools: the College of Arts and Science, School of Engineering, Peabody College of Education and Human Development, or Blair School of Music. In all four schools, honors programs and opportunities for research, independent study, and internships are available. About 30 percent of undergraduate students pursue double majors within or across the four undergraduate schools, and about half add an optional minor. The College of Arts and Science (A&S) offers a wide spectrum of courses in the humanities, social sciences, and natural sciences along with majors in 49 departments and interdisciplinary areas. The core curriculum, AXLE (Achieving eXcellence in Liberal Education), fosters critical thinking, analytical expertise from diverse perspectives, and effective written and oral communication skills. The Blair School of Music offers the Bachelor of Music degree in composition, musical arts, musical arts/teacher education, and performance. Instruction is available in every instrument of the orchestra as well as piano, organ, euphonium, multiple woodwinds, saxophone, and voice. Unlike many schools of music, Blair has no graduate students. The curriculum combines intensive musical training with liberal arts studies. The Blair School also offers music minors and a wide variety of courses, private instruction, and performing organizations for non-majors.

For more than 125 years, the School of Engineering has educated engineers for careers in industry, government, consulting, teaching, and research. In addition to technical courses, each student's program includes a complement of course work in the humanities and social sciences, resulting in a balanced foundation for future achievement. All programs leading to a Bachelor of Engineering degree are ABET-accredited, and students can earn the Bachelor of Science degree while majoring in Computer Science or Engineering Science.

Ranked one of the top seven graduate school of education (according to U.S. News & World Report) for more than fifteen consecutive years, Peabody College offers degree programs leading to teacher certification and to careers in other areas of education and human development, including child development, child studies, cognitive studies, and human and organizational development. The degree reflects a strong liberal arts foundation combined with a solid program of pre-professional courses and a multitude of internship and practicum opportunities. All undergraduates must complete requirements in communications, the humanities, mathematics, the natural sciences, and the social sciences. Students gain an abundance of field experiences throughout their four years.

Across all four undergraduate schools, students engage in hands-on learning that complements and furthers their academic experience at Vanderbilt. Immersion Vanderbilt calls for each undergraduate student to participate in an intensive learning experience that takes place in and beyond the classroom and culminates in the creation of a final project. Students will engage in a civic and professional, creative expression, international, or research immersion experience.

MAJORS AND DEGREES OFFERED

Degrees are offered in African American and Diaspora studies; American studies; anthropology; art; Asian studies; biochemistry and chemical biology; biological sciences; biomedical engineering; chemical engineering; chemistry; child development; child studies; cinema and media arts; civil engineering; classical and Mediterranean studies; cognitive studies; communication of science and technology; communication studies; computer engineering; computer science; earth and environmental sciences; ecology, evolution, and organismal biology; economics; economics and history; education (early childhood and elementary, secondary, and special education); electrical engineering; engineering science; English; environmental sociology; European studies; French; French and European studies; German studies; German and European studies; history; history of art; human and organizational development; Italian and European studies; Jewish studies; Latin American studies; Latino and Latina studies; mathematics; mechanical engineering; medicine, health, and society; molecular and cellular biology; musical arts; musical arts and teacher education; music composition; music performance; neuroscience; philosophy; physics; political science; psychology; public policy studies; religious studies; Russian; Russian and European studies; sociology; Spanish, Spanish and European studies; Spanish and Portuguese; Spanish, Portuguese, and European studies; theatre; women's and gender studies.

TUITION, ROOM, BOARD, FEES

The estimated costs for 2018–2019 include: tuition, $48,592; housing, $10,550; meals, $5,614; books and supplies, $1,294; student activities and recreation fee, $1,216; personal expenses allowance, $2,802; travel allowance varies; first-year experience fee, $799; new student transcript fee, $100; engineering lab fee°, $800; and engineering laptop allowance°, $1,600 °The engineering laptop allowance and laboratory fee are for engineering students only. First-year engineering students are required to provide their own computer that meets published requirements.

FINANCIAL AID

Through Opportunity Vanderbilt, the university makes three important commitments to ensure that students from many different economic circumstances can enroll as undergraduates at Vanderbilt: the admissions process is need-blind for all U.S. citizens and eligible non-citizens; Vanderbilt meets 100 percent of demonstrated need for all admitted students; and Vanderbilt's financial aid packages do not include loans. This initiative does not involve income bands or income cutoffs that limit eligibility. Need-based aid is awarded according to the evaluation of the FAFSA and the CSS/Financial Aid PROFILE.

Vanderbilt also awards approximately 250 merit-based scholarships to select first-year applicants who demonstrate exceptional accomplishment and intellectual promise. Three signature scholarship programs comprise the majority of these merit scholarships: the Ingram Scholarship Program, the Cornelius Vanderbilt Scholarship, and the Chancellor's Scholarship. To be considered for the Cornelius Vanderbilt Scholarship, a separate application is required. To be considered for the Ingram or Chancellor's Scholarship, a separate application is strongly encouraged.

STUDENT ORGANIZATIONS AND ACTIVITIES

Vanderbilt undergraduates come from all 50 states and 48 countries, 51 percent are female, 49 percent are male, 39.3 percent are minority students and 7.7 percent are international students. Vanderbilt is recognized for an active campus life, where students balance their academic lives with enriching experiences outside the classroom. Students can select from among 430+ student-run organizations, including pre-professional, cultural, religious, political, recreational, and social clubs. Elected representatives of Vanderbilt Student Government work in conjunction with other student leaders and faculty to bring noted speakers, events, and musicians to campus. Vanderbilt also has a thriving college athletics program. A founding member of the SEC, Vanderbilt has 16 Division I teams that have won three national championships and 30 individual and team league championships since 2000.

ADMISSIONS PROCESS

Vanderbilt seeks students with high standards of scholarship and character. Admission is based on a holistic review of academic and personal credentials. The typical applicant will have completed 20 or more units in a challenging high school curriculum, including at least two years of a foreign language. School of Engineering applicants should complete at least four units of mathematics; calculus and physics are strongly recommended.

Generally, applicants who are admitted to Vanderbilt have exceptional academic credentials and are highly engaged in their communities, often serving in leadership roles. Admissions decisions are based on strength of high school transcript, standardized test results (either the SAT or ACT), personal essays, official recommendations, and extracurricular activities. SAT Subject Tests are not required.

Students may apply to Vanderbilt through Early Decision I or II, or Regular Decision. Early Decision I and II are binding decision plans and may be appropriate for students who are committed to attending Vanderbilt if they are admitted. The application deadline is November 1 for Early Decision I and January 1 for Early Decision II; admissions decisions are available by mid-December for Early Decision I and by mid-February for Early Decision II. Regular Decision applications are due January 1 and admissions decisions are available by April late-March.

To apply, applicants must submit official standardized test scores and all required parts of the Common Application, Coalition Application, QuestBridge Application, or Universal College Application, including two academic teacher letters of recommendation, a counselor letter of recommendation, an official high school transcript, and a $50 application fee, or fee waiver for qualified students. In addition to completing standard application materials, applicants to the Blair School of Music must submit a Blair Accept'd Application, which includes a prescreening video. Selected applicants will be invited to audition in person.

Campus visits are encouraged, although a student's demonstrated interest in Vanderbilt is not considered in admissions decisions. Students should visit vu.edu/visit to learn about group information sessions, campus tours, and half-and full-day visit programs. To visit Vanderbilt without traveling, take the virtual tour at vu.edu/virtualtour. Vanderbilt does not conduct on-campus interviews, but optional alumni interviews are available to first-year applicants in many locations.

WASHINGTON COLLEGE

AT A GLANCE

"Washington College is all about the student experience. Their happiness reflects our student-centric focus, which is the cornerstone of who we are and the positive impact we have on a student's personal and professional life."

-Kurt Landgraf, President of Washington College

A Washington College education affords students unmatched opportunities to work closely with an exceptional faculty on projects they are passionate about. We believe that a diverse liberal arts education is both academically rewarding and the most effective way to prepare for a future in anything you want to do. From studying on the Chesapeake Bay to interning at The White House, there's something for everyone at Washington College.

In their first two years on campus, WC students are encouraged to explore their interests, examine different perspectives, and challenge their old ways of thinking. There is no one-size-fits-all education at Washington College: from double-majoring to internships to study abroad and semester-long interdisciplinary programs, we encourage our students to think outside the box and shape a college experience that is right for them.

Founded in 1782, Washington College was the first college chartered in the sovereign United States of America. General George Washington lent us his name, donated 50 guineas to our founding, and served on our first Board of Visitors and Governors. Our goal back then was to cultivate responsible, educated citizen-leaders who could nurture the new democracy. That founding purpose still holds true today.

LOCATION AND ENVIRONMENT

Where we are is who we are. Our 120-acre campus in Chestertown, Md., is an integral part of Maryland's Eastern Shore, but still close enough to Washington, D.C., Baltimore, and Philadelphia that our students benefit from a wealth of distinguished speakers, internship opportunities, and institutional partnerships. Our newly-announced River and Field Campus grants students from all disciplines unprecedented access to 4,700 acres of waterfront, meadows, untouched hardwood forests, ponds, grasslands, marshes and riverine habitat.

Local life in Chestertown is deeply-rooted in community and tradition. The town dates back to 1706, when it was established as a major port town on the Chester River. Beloved for its historic homes, brick walkways, and close-knit feel, Chestertown warmly welcomes the students of Washington College each year. There's always room for students—take a walk down High Street on First Fridays or visit the Farmer's Market in Fountain Park on Saturday mornings!

CAMPUS FACILITIES & EQUIPMENT

With some buildings as old as the mid-nineteenth-century and others still under construction, Washington College seamlessly combines the old with the new. Our pathways might be red brick reminiscent of colonial times, but our Hodson Dining Hall is award-winning, our Cain Gymnasium received a new floor in 2017, and our Miller library contains a state-of-the-art Makerspace with a 3-D printer, one-button recording studio, and all the latest technology to bring your ideas to life.

We are committed to sustainability. Many buildings on campus incorporate alternative energy sources like solar and geothermal, and our Campus Garden is a growing experiment in permaculture, with plenty of edible plants and even our own beehives. Additionally, our River and Field Campus provides access to a diverse collection of Eastern Shore ecosystems, a bird banding laboratory, 2.5 miles of Chester River waterfront, and 4,700 acres of living laboratory for students of all majors to study.

We may be a small college, but we're not technologically-behind; our science centers provide majors with state-of-the art lab equipment, and our research vessels Callinectes and Lookdown give science students access to all the equipment they need to scan the bed of the Chester River and chemically test water and sediment samples.

The Chester River is an essential part of Chestertown, and our students have taken advantage of the unique opportunities it offers, from developing competitive varsity programs in rowing and sailing and club sport programs for waterskiing and wakeboarding, to learning to sail in class and enjoying recreational activities such as kayaking.

OFF-CAMPUS OPPORTUNITIES

There's something special about small-town life, and Chestertown delivers: grab a coffee at the local Play It Again Sam's or Evergrain Bakery, visit the shops on High Street, or head down to the water and rent a kayak for a day on the Chester River. For the more adventurous, campus is close enough to Baltimore, Philadelphia, Annapolis, and Washington, D.C. to make daytripping simple. The College offers a weekend shuttle to metro stations for those without individual transportation.

ACADEMIC PROGRAMS

Washington College celebrates the relationship between student and professor. Our diverse array of fellowships, internships, off-campus programs, and research opportunities provide chances for students to pursue their own interests and conduct research at a graduate level.

The Douglass Cater Society of Junior Fellows provides competitive grants to support self-directed undergraduate research and scholarship anywhere in the world. Additionally, our Presidential Fellows program puts high-achieving freshmen on the fast track to academic distinction, including the chance to work with full Cater Fellows as an apprentice, and provides multiple scholarships, including a chance for a full-tuition scholarship.

Other programs include: the Explore America Fellowships, which place students in paid summer internships at prestigious institutions including the Library of Congress, National Constitution Center, and the Smithsonian American Art Museum; the Alex. Brown Fund, which tasks students with managing an equities portfolio of $500,000; the Washington to Wall Street Program, which offers internships to students pursuing careers in business or financial sector; and the John S. Toll Science Fellows and Hodson Science Fellows programs, which enable students to conduct in-depth research with faculty while earning a stipend and a housing allowance.

Our three Signature Centers position students at a dynamic intersection of academics and hands-on learning in the "real world." Each Center provides programming, events, internships, and coursework in a singular area of focus: the environment (the Center for Environment & Society), literature and writing (the Rose O'Neill Literary House), and history (the Starr Center for the Study of the American Experience).

The Center for Environment & Society offers internships and fellowships in the great outdoors. The Center is also home to the Chester River Watershed Observatory and the Chester River Field Research Station. CES's interdisciplinary academic programs promote the integration of environmental issues, social values, and good old river mud.

The Starr Center for the Study of the American Experience is dedicated to fostering innovative approaches to the American past and present. Through educational programs, scholarship and public outreach, and a special focus on written history, the Starr Center seeks to bridge the divide between the academic world and the public at large.

The Rose O'Neill Literary House provides literary programming across disciplines, a diverse array of lecturers and writers each year, and training in new and antique printing technologies. Lit House students grow as artists under professional mentorship, and each year, one graduating senior is awarded the Sophie Kerr Prize, the largest undergraduate literary award in the world (the 2018 winner will take home $63,711).

Washington College also offers an extensive study abroad program with both short-term and long-term study opportunities. Our students have traveled to places like the Galapagos Islands, Ecuador, Germany, Israel, Japan, Peru, Turkey, and the United Kingdom.

MAJORS AND DEGREES OFFERED

American Studies
Anthropology
Art and Art History
Biology
Business Management
Chemistry

Communication and Media Studies
Computer Science
Economics
Education
English
Environmental Science and Studies
History
Human Development
Humanities
International Literature and Culture
International Studies
Mathematics
Modern Languages
Music
Philosophy and Religion
Physics
Political Science
Psychology
Sociology
Theatre

Minors and certifications

Accounting & Finance
African Studies
Archaeology
Art History
Asian Studies (Concentration)
Asian Studies (Minor)
Behavioral Neuroscience
Biochemistry
Biophysics and Biological Chemistry
Black Studies
Cell/Molecular Biology & Infectious Disease
Chesapeake Regional Studies
Clinical Counseling
Creative Writing
Dance
Earth & Planetary Sciences
Ecology and Evolution
Ethnomusicology
European Studies
Gender Studies
Global Business Studies
Greener Materials Science
Justice, Law and Society
Information Systems
Latin American Studies
Marketing
Near Eastern Studies
Organic and Medicinal Chemistry
Peace and Conflict Studies
Physical and Instrumental Chemistry
Physiology and Organismal Biology
Pre-Health
Secondary Education
Social Welfare
Studio Art

Interdisciplinary programs of study, advanced degree programs, partnerships:

Elementary and Secondary education certification
Engineering dual-degree program with Columbia University
Environmental management (MEM) program with Duke University
Forestry (MF) dual-degree program with Duke University
Environmental management (MEM) program with Duke University
Nursing dual-degree program with University of Maryland
Pharmacy dual-degree program with University of Maryland
Premedical and Pre-Law programs

TUITION, ROOM, BOARD, AND FEES

Basic educational fees for 2017–2018

Tuition (full-time) $45,888

Mandatory Student Fees $1,090

Standard Dormitory $6000

Standard Meal Plan $6414

Total $59,382

FINANCIAL AID

Washington College is committed to providing educational excellence and equity for all students; 90 percent of our students receive need-based financial aid and/or merit-based scholarships. We develop financial packages that include tuition scholarships, tuition grants, work/study, and low-interest loans, in addition to federal, state, and independent aid programs for eligible students. With the investment of funds for scholarships and grants from donors and benefactors, the College provides more than $20 million annually in scholarships and grants to help make it possible for students to get an education here. More than 50 percent of all Washington College students qualify for merit-based tuition scholarships averaging from $13,500 to $23,500 per year. In 2016, Washington College announced a fixed-rate tuition policy, FixedFor4, that will enable families to plan for college costs.

STUDENT ORGANIZATIONS AND ACTIVITIES

We may be a small campus, but Washington College supports more than 80 clubs, from the nationally recognized Habitat for Humanity Club to wakeboarding, sailing, and entrepreneurial activism through Enactus.

As a Division III member of the NCAA, our 18 intercollegiate teams compete in the Centennial Conference, the Middle Atlantic Intercollegiate Sailing Association, and the Mid-Atlantic Rowing Conference (MARC). Nearly a third of WC students are varsity athletes, and 60 percent participate in varsity, intramural, or club sports.

Our Student Events Board is always hard at work putting together amazing opportunities for students, from festivals and quiz nights to the semi-formal George Washington's Birthday Ball, which also welcomes back alumni.

ADMISSIONS PROCESS

Washington College is a selective institution. In order to assess an applicant's "fit" with the College, the Admission Committee requires the submission of all relevant academic records and test scores, an essay/personal statement, and a letter of recommendation. In some cases, an on-campus interview may also be required.

Prospective applicants are strongly encouraged to come to campus for an information session and tour. These visits should be scheduled in advance by calling 410-778-7700 or visiting washcoll.edu/visit.

Prospective students may apply online using the Common Application or via washcoll.edu/apply. Application deadlines are: November 15 for early decision; December 1 for early action; February 15 for regular decision. Admitted applicants must pay a $700.00 enrollment deposit by May 1. For details, visit www.washcoll.edu/admissions.

WELLS COLLEGE

AT A GLANCE

Wells College is a private, coeducational liberal arts college located in Aurora, New York. Our modern curriculum combines theory with real-world applications, resulting in graduates that are versatile, empathetic, and prepared to continue learning throughout their lives. The College boasts a highly collaborative learning environment with a 10:1 student-to-faculty ratio. Wells' professors are skilled and approachable teachers as well as respected scholars and professionals. Students come from diverse backgrounds to create a connected community in which openness, acceptance, and inclusion of all beliefs are appreciated and considered in their appropriate settings. The College's living-learning philosophy also means our students benefit from required internships and an array of study abroad opportunities that provide hands-on experiences. Wells students not only take a direct role in shaping their education, they are prepared to pursue advanced and professional studies as well as meaningful careers.

LOCATION AND ENVIRONMENT

The beautiful 300-acre lakeside campus is located in the historical village of Aurora on Cayuga Lake, in the heart of the Finger Lakes Region of New York State. Students enjoy phenomenal views and access to our campus boathouse. The campus is 30 minutes from Ithaca, one hour from Syracuse and Rochester, and approximately five hours from New York City.

CAMPUS FACILITIES & EQUIPMENT

Wells College provides state-of-the-art facilities for all students and student-athletes. Indoor facilities include a field house, fitness center, swimming pool, locker rooms, tennis courts, a renovated gymnasium, and athletic administration offices. Outdoor facilities include dedicated fields for men's and women's soccer, men's and women's lacrosse, and field hockey, along with four outdoor tennis courts. Completed in 2016, the new artificial turf field will serve as the primary site of competition for field hockey, baseball, softball, men's and women's soccer, and men's and women's lacrosse.

OFF-CAMPUS OPPORTUNITIES

During their four years at Wells, students may also participate in study abroad or affiliated programs in the following countries: Australia; Belize, Chile; China; Costa Rica; Germany; Ireland; Italy; Japan; New Zealand; South Africa; Spain; and the United Kingdom. Students may also pursue global study through the School for Field Studies in Australia, Cambodia, Costa Rica, Panama, Peru, Tanzania, and Turks and Caicos. The Albany Internship Experience at Marist University in Albany, N.Y. is another popular option. Wells students may also take courses at nearby Cornell University or Ithaca College through a unique exchange program.

ACADEMIC PROGRAMS

The Wells experience is deeply personal and intensely focused on superior academic achievement. Wells offers 27 majors and nearly 50 minors. With one professor for every ten students, professors really get to know each student. The average class size has thirteen students and is taught seminar-style, with discussions taking precedence over lectures. Fundamental to the Wells curriculum is an interdisciplinary approach to the liberal arts with the opportunity to experience hands-on work and innovative teaching methods. Through the Wells experiential learning program, students have opportunities to participate in quality internships, off-campus study programs around the world, and academic research projects tailored to individual interests and goals. Experiential learning enables students to apply principles learned in the classroom to real-life situations in professional environments.

MAJORS AND DEGREES OFFERED

Wells College offers a Bachelor's degree with majors in the following areas: Biochemistry and Molecular Biology, Biological and Chemical Sciences, Biology, Business, Chemistry, Computer Science, Criminal Justice, Economics and Management (Economics, Management), Inclusive Childhood Education, English (Literature, Creative Writing), Environmental Science, Film and Media Studies, Biological Sciences: Health Sciences, History, International Studies, Individualized Major, Mathematics, Philosophy, Physics, Political Science, Psychology, Sociology and Anthropology, Spanish, Sustainability, Theatre and Dance, Visual Arts (Art History, Studio Art, Book Arts), Women's and Gender Studies.

TUITION, ROOM, BOARD, FEES

For the 2017–2018 year: Tuition and fees: $39,600; Room and board: $13,730

FINANCIAL AID

Wells College offers both merit-based and need-based financial aid. Merit-based scholarships are awarded to students who demonstrate outstanding academic achievement, leadership skills, and have a strong record of service in their schools and communities. Nearly 100 percent of students at Wells College receive aid to fund their education. To receive need-based financial aid from Wells College, students must submit the Free Application for Federal Student Aid (FAFSA). Wells recommends families submit their completed FAFSA by December 1st. In addition to merit scholarships, students eligible to receive need-based financial aid may receive grants, scholarships, student loans, and campus work study opportunities.

STUDENT ORGANIZATIONS AND ACTIVITIES

Wells students enjoy all of the advantages of living in a closely-knit community. A well-respected Honor Code shapes the educational and social atmosphere of the campus. Wells supports more than 30 clubs and organizations including a literary journal and social issues magazine, music and drama groups, and political and cultural organizations, in addition to student-sponsored events, lectures, and performances. Wells is also a member of Division III NCAA. Wells women compete in nine intercollegiate sports: Cross country, field hockey, lacrosse, soccer, softball, basketball, volleyball and swimming. Wells men compete in seven intercollegiate sports: Baseball, basketball, cross country, lacrosse, soccer, volleyball and swimming. Wells campus also has a nine-hole golf course and canoes, kayaks, and sailboats available for seasonal student use.

ADMISSIONS PROCESS

Wells students are intellectually curious, open-minded, and creative. They are comfortable expressing themselves, listening to others and sharing ideas. They are caring citizens of the world, eager to travel beyond the campus. If you love learning, you will love the Wells experience.

Candidates for admission are expected to complete a solid college preparatory program throughout their four years in secondary school. For the best background for study at Wells, the College recommends: Four years of English grammar, composition, and literature; four years of history; three years of mathematics; two years of laboratory science; and coursework in a foreign language. Student records are enhanced by the addition of courses such as computer science, art, and music, when appropriate curricular choices are offered. To apply for admission to Wells College candidates must submit a completed application through the Wells application or Common Application by March 1 of the year of entrance.

In addition, the following credentials are required: A transcript of all secondary school work and at least one letter of recommendation from teachers in academic subject areas. A personal on-campus connection with your admissions counselor and a Creative Expression piece are recommended.

Wells College is committed to reviewing applications holistically and considering all facets of a student's potential. To honor that commitment, admission to Wells is now test-optional. As of Fall 2016, we no longer require SAT or ACT scores in the application evaluation process. International students must prove English language proficiency through the TOEFL, IELTS, SAT or ACT.

Admissions Deadline Options:

Early Decision. December 15: Students whose first choice is Wells College are encouraged to apply under the Early Decision option. This is a binding admissions option; if admitted, Early Decision applicants agree to accept Wells offer of admission and withdraw their applications from all other colleges.

Early Action. December 15: Students who would like to receive an early review of their application files are encouraged to apply under the Early Action option. This is a non-binding admissions option.

Regular Admission. March 1: All other applications to the College should be received by the regular admission deadline.

WENTWORTH INSTITUTE OF TECHNOLOGY

AT A GLANCE

Founded in 1904, Wentworth Institute of Technology is an independent, co-educational, nationally-ranked institution offering career-focused education through 17 bachelor's degree programs in areas such as applied mathematics, architecture, business management, computer science and networking, construction management, design, and engineering. The Institute also offers master's degrees in applied computer science, architecture, civil engineering, construction management, facility management, and technology management.

A leader in engineering, technology, design and management education, Wentworth's unique three-part experiential learning model combines class work, laboratory/studio work, and cooperative education (co-op) experience to provide students with a hands-on approach to learning. The co-op program, one of the largest and most comprehensive of its kind in the nation, has been active for 40 years and provides Wentworth students the ability to gain the professional work experience needed to succeed in their field. Wentworth is well-known for its academic excellence, community service, and support for the economic growth of the region.

Wentworth offers exciting opportunities for students looking to build a framework for success in the innovation economy. Wentworth's unique interdisciplinary curriculum combines technical studies, opportunities to collaborate and innovate, meaningful career training experiences, and an environment focused on developing practical solutions to real-world challenges. The result: Excellent preparation for a successful career. Additionally, Wentworth is a member of one of Boston's largest academic collaborations, the Colleges of the Fenway consortium, which is an association of five Fenway area institutions including Emmanuel College, Massachusetts College of Art and Design, Massachusetts College of Pharmacy and Health Sciences University, Simmons College and Wentworth.

For more information, please visit www.wit.edu.

LOCATION AND ENVIRONMENT
Small school benefits, big city resources.

This private, coeducational college is located on 31 acres in the heart of Boston. With over 4,000 students, it provides the friendliness of a small school, alongside the resources and excitement of the ultimate college town.

When it comes to college towns, there is no place more exciting or full of more opportunities than Boston. The original center of higher education in the U.S., it hosts 50 colleges and universities and draws a quarter of a million students every year, with nearly 20,000 of those students coming from outside the country. Boston is a city with exceptional character. In addition to its rich history, it's also a hub for technology, business and medicine giving Wentworth students access to educational and career opportunities they would not find elsewhere.

CAMPUS FACILITIES & EQUIPMENT
The Wentworth campus is well-appointed to deliver the top-notch education and living conditions demanded by today's students. Our modernized laboratories are at the vanguard of technology; the equipment mirrors that found in the leading employers in industry. The Institute has spent millions of dollars to upgrade its information technology infrastructure. And the facilities for sleeping are just as impressive as the ones for studying. The Institute operates seven residence halls: Evans Way/Tudbury Hall, Edwards/Rodgers Hall, Baker Hall, Louis Prang Apartments, 610 Huntington Avenue, 555 Huntington Avenue and the Apartments at 525 Huntington.

Whether you're looking for state-of-the-art computing resources, healthcare you can rely on, or one of several other services that make campus life better, you can rest assured that Wentworth is working hard to meet your needs.

The Flanagan Campus Center is the hub of student life at Wentworth. The campus center is home to the bookstore, the cafeteria, the Schuman Fitness Center. The Intercultural Center, Wentworth Internet Radio Experience (WIRE), a recreation room, study areas, and the Office of Campus Life.

The Learning Center and The Writing Center provide students with academic support services such as peer and faculty tutoring, computer-based tutorials, and subject study groups. We are dedicated to preparing students for academic success.

Wentworth is committed to helping you make the best use of computers. We offer a range of computing resources including: a wireless campus; labs equipped with the latest hardware and software; and a full-time Office of Information Technology. The result is a highly connected academic and social community where advanced computing is accessible and convenient.

Wentworth subscribes to the policies set forth in the Americans with Disabilities Act and in Section 504 of the Federal Rehabilitation Act of 1973, which mandate equal opportunity in educational programs and activities for students with disabilities.

At Wentworth, we work hard to provide the very best health services. In addition to expert primary medical care, we also offer specialized services including counseling, disability services and comprehensive health education.

In order to make the transition for international students as smooth as possible, Wentworth employs a full-time international student advisor who has extensive experience with international students, and assists them in their personal, social and academic adjustment to Wentworth and the U.S.

Conveniently located at the center of campus, the Douglas D. Schumann Library & Learning Commons is a valuable resource. The online catalogue includes the holdings of nine other libraries all available for use by Wentworth students. And, membership in the 14-institution Fenway Library Consortium provides access to more than 2,900,000 volumes and 13,000 periodical titles. Various services are also available through the Alumni Library.

OFF-CAMPUS OPPORTUNITIES
At Wentworth, building professional, paid work experience into the academic program is a priority. Cooperative Education (co-op) has been a fundamental part of our curriculum for 40 years, and ours is one of the largest and most comprehensive programs of its kind in the nation. All full-time day bachelor's degree candidates must complete two semesters of co-op, beginning after the first two years of study.

Wentworth's Office of Career Services assists students every step of the way, as they take advantage of opportunities in Boston, in other areas of the US, and abroad.

ACADEMIC PROGRAMS
A leader in technology education for over a century, Wentworth offers bachelor's degrees in 18 practical, career-oriented majors. All programs center on Wentworth's distinctive three-part experiential learning model, which incorporates classes, labs and studios, and co-op.

As Wentworth is a member of the Colleges of the Fenway, students can cross-register for one course each semester at the participating colleges (Emmanuel and Simmons Colleges and the Massachusetts College of Art and Design, and the Massachusetts College of Pharmacy and Health Sciences University).

MAJORS AND DEGREES OFFERED
Applied Mathematics (three-year program with a four-year option)
Applied Science (beginning Fall 2019)
Architecture
Biological Engineering
Biomedical Engineering
Business Management
Civil Engineering
Computer Engineering
Computer Information Systems
Computer Networking
Computer Science
Construction Management
Electrical Engineering
Electromechanical Engineering (five-year program)
Engineering-Interdisciplinary
Industrial Design
Interior Design
Mechanical Engineering

TUITION, ROOM, BOARD, FEES

Tuition for full-time students (12-20 credits) for 2018–2019 is $33,950 per year. Tuition includes the cost of a laptop computer. Laptops are provided to each student along with the specific software required for their major.

The per credit charge (less than 12 and over 20) is $1060 per credit.

Room and Board is approximately $14,158 per year.

Health Insurance, required by Commonwealth of Massachusetts is approximately $2000 per year (can be waived if student is covered by parent's health insurance).

Financial Aid

We are dedicated to helping you to create a financial plan that allows you and your family to afford a Wentworth education. In cooperation with financial aid specialists, financial services specialists can help discern how best to combine a student's financial aid package with alternative parent or student loans, as well as with Wentworth's monthly payment plan.

Approximately 85 percent of our students receive financial aid. For the fall of 2017, the average financial aid package for a first-time full-time student was $17,415. A typical package is made up of a combination of grants, loans, and work-study earnings. To be considered for financial aid you must complete the Free Application for Federal Student Aid (FAFSA) as early as possible after October 1. You do not have to be an applicant for admission to complete the FAFSA. However, you must be accepted to Wentworth to receive notification of your actual financial aid award.

STUDENT ORGANIZATIONS AND ACTIVITIES

Wentworth participates in 17 NCAA-sponsored varsity sports. More than twenty professional organizations operate on campus, offering unbeatable networking opportunities to students in every field. In addition, there are more than a forty-five clubs and organizations to help students make productive and fun use of their hours outside the classroom. And if students can't find what they're looking for on the Wentworth campus, they simply visit one of the five neighboring Colleges of the Fenway institutions with which the Institute is affiliated. In addition to Wentworth, the Colleges of the Fenway consist of the Massachusetts College of Art, Massachusetts College of Pharmacy, and Emmanuel, and Simmons Colleges.

Here's the makeup of the student body of Wentworth Institute of Technology during the 2017–2018 academic year:

4650 total students (3860 full time representing 38 states and 58 countries)

955 women (20 percent)

Mid-range SAT scores for Accepted Students: EBRW 530-620, Math 550-650

75 percent of new students live in on-campus housing

Students from Massachusetts 62 percent

Students from other New England states 21 percent

Students from New York, New Jersey, Pennsylvania 6 percent

Students from 29 other states and territories 3 percent

Students from 58 other countries 8 percent

NCAA Sports

Academic and Professional Organizations

American Institute of Architecture Students (AIAS)
American Society of Civil Engineers (ASCE)
American Society of Mechanical Engineers
American Society of Professional Estimators
Association of IT Professional Construction Management Association
Industrial Design Society of America Institute of Electrical and Electronics Engineers (IEEE)
Math Club
Mechanical Contractors Association (MCA)
National Society of Black Engineers Phi Sigma Pi (Honor Society)
Society of Automotive Engineers (SAE)
Society of Hispanic Professional Engineers

Society of Manufacturing Engineers
Society of Women Engineers
Solar-Powered Vehicle Club
Student Association of Facilities Management (SAFM)
Student Association of Interior Designers (SAID)
Wentworth Architecture Club (WAC)
Wentworth Robotics Association

Student Life Organizations (partial list)

Competitive Video Gaming Club
Dance Team
Game Design Club
Longboard Club
Louise Stokes Alliance for Minority Participation (LSAMP)
Mini Baja Club
Mountain Biking Club
Multicultural Student Association (MSA)
Note-oriety (A Cappella Club)
Outdoors Club
Parkour Club
PEAK (Peer Empowerment Advocacy Krew)
Real Life (Christian Organization)
Road Cycling Club
Rugby (M,F)
Self Defense Club
Ski & Adventure Club
The Green Team (Environmental Club)
Ultimate Frisbee Club
Wentworth Events Board (WEB)
Wentworth Improvisational Theater Club (WITC)
Wentworth International Students Club (WISC)
Wentworth Internet Radio Experience (WIRE)
Wentworth Student Government (WSG)
WIT Alliance (GBLT Organization)
And many more!

ADMISSIONS PROCESS

At Wentworth, we look for students who are qualified and motivated to succeed in engineering, design, technology, and management programs. We make our admissions decisions based on: Academic achievement measured by official transcripts

Performance on standardized tests (SAT I or ACT)

Personal qualities, such as leadership or creativity, indicated by information in the completed application form

At Wentworth, it's our goal to assist students and their parents as much as possible as they move through the admissions process. In fact, every applicant has a regional admissions counselor they can contact directly with questions.

To apply to Wentworth, you must submit the following materials: A completed Wentworth application ($50 application fee.) We accept the Common, Universal, and Wentworth applications.

Official high school transcripts

SAT I or ACT scores

A written personal statement

At least one letter of recommendation from a guidance counselor or teacher

TOEFL score, if your native language is not English

Wentworth practices rolling admissions, which means we review each completed application as soon as we receive it -so you can apply early and get a decision early.

WEST VIRGINIA WESLEYAN COLLEGE

AT A GLANCE

Here, you're home. West Virginia Wesleyan is a private four-year co-educational residential college that is affiliated with The United Methodist Church. West Virginia Wesleyan creates a unique learning environment enabling our students to develop the skills, values, relationships, and perspective needed for them to obtain employment, enhance their careers, and demonstrate leadership throughout their lives. Wesleyan graduates are well prepared to be successful and respected citizens in a rapidly changing world. Of those reporting, 95 percent of Wesleyan graduates either find employment in their respective field or attend graduate school within 6 months of graduation.

Over 80 percent of Wesleyan's faculty hold the highest degree in their respective teaching field and the student faculty ratio is 13:1. The College offers over 40 majors and over 40 minors of study, and several additional Master's programs spanning Athletic Training, Business Administration, English (Creative Writing), and Nursing.

West Virginia Wesleyan is accredited by the Commission on Institutions of Higher Education of the North Central Association of Colleges and Schools, and approved by the University Senate of The United Methodist Church. It is a member of the National Association of Schools of Music and is approved by the West Virginia Department of Education and the National Council for the Accreditation of Teacher Education. The College participates in the Interstate Certification Project whereby a number of states certify teachers graduating from Wesleyan's Department of Education. The athletic training program is accredited by the Commission on Accreditation of Allied Health Education Programs. Degree programs offered in business and economics, including the Master of Business Administration program, are accredited by the International Assembly for Collegiate Business Education.

All academic programs either require or strongly encourage the completion of an internship experience. Wesleyan's academic calendar is 4-4-1 that includes an optional May Term in which students pursue unique study abroad courses or intensive study curricular offerings. The Advising and Career Center assists students with course scheduling, academic advising, internships and study abroad, resume writing, job searches, and graduate and professional school placement. The Learning Center provides tutoring services as well as comprehensive services for students with diagnosed learning disabilities.

Of the more than 1,350 undergraduate students, 53 percent are from West Virginia, while the other 47 percent originate from 39 states and 19 countries. 16 percent of Wesleyan's American students are minority students. Over 90 percent of Wesleyan's students live on-campus and the College guarantees four years of on-campus housing for all undergraduate students. Housing options include double and single rooms, suites, and apartments. Campus dining is provided and prepared by a contracted professional catering service.

LOCATION AND ENVIRONMENT

Situated in the foothills of the Allegheny Mountains, Wesleyan's beautiful 100-acre campus is located in the quaint, residential town of Buckannon, West Virginia. Buckhannon has been included in Norman Crampton's book, The Top 100 Best Small Towns in America, a Random House Publication. Many students are drawn to this personal and picturesque setting and the numerous outdoor opportunities located in close proximity to campus. The local community offers movie theatres, coffee houses, department stores, and a wide selection of local and chain restaurants. Wesleyan is a short two-hour drive from Pittsburgh, Pennsylvania, and 90 minutes from Charleston, West Virginia, the state capital.

CAMPUS FACILITIES & EQUIPMENT

Wesleyan's 23 buildings include 10 modern residence hall units, including two suite style halls renovated or newly built in the last eight years. Located in the center of campus is Wesley Chapel, which chapel serves as a focal point of campus and houses many campus events, both religious and cultural. The hub of the campus, Benedum Campus and Community Center, houses a convenience store, bookstore, swimming pool, campus radio station, student development offices, study lounges, and a cabaret-style restaurant, The Cat's Claw. The Rockefeller Physical Education Center includes a main arena that seats 3,700 spectators, an intramural gymnasium, training rooms, and an indoor astro-turf training area. The multimillion dollar Reemsnyder Research Center was opened in 2009 and boasts state of the art laboratory space for the sciences. Other vital buildings on campus include Christopher Hall of Science; Middleton Hall, which houses the Nursing Department and region-renowned simulation facilities; and the Lynch-Raine Administration Building. In addition, the multimillion dollar Virginia Thomas Law Center for the Performing Arts, opened in 2009, offers the most advanced performing arts facility of its kind in the region. Most recently, a completely renovated student wellness center was opened in 2012 along with a new multi-sport stadium project in phase one in 2015. Since 2015 more than 30 classroom spaces have been completely updated and renovated with 10+ more planned for 2018–2019.

Wesleyan's Annie Merner Pfeiffer Library is committed to providing high quality resources and services that empower students for advanced learning. Currently, the number of print and electronic books is nearly equal at 150,000 each, and the nearly 20,000 electronic journal titles far exceed the 300 received in print. In addition to its collections and research services, the Library offers media viewing facilities, areas for group study, and a quiet place for reading and reflection.

The entire campus has been outfitted with a ubiquitous campus-wide wireless network ensuring access to all students, faculty, and staff from all major campus buildings and every residence hall room. Network speeds are improved yearly and rival any private college in the region.

OFF-CAMPUS OPPORTUNITIES

Wesleyan encourages all students to expand their education beyond the traditional classroom. Many students have studied abroad in such places as England, Ireland, Wales, Germany, Spain, Kenya, Scotland, and Australia. Professional internships are available in the Buckhannon area, Charleston, WV, Washington, D.C.; New York, NY; Pittsburgh, PA; and other states and countries.

ACADEMIC PROGRAMS

Wesleyan's liberal arts curriculum begins with a broad base view in a variety of core courses designed to enrich the student's whole view. The classes range from the humanities to contemporary issues and can be intermingled with the courses in the individual's major throughout the four-year program.

Wesleyan's Honors Program is offered for superior students who meet the specific requirements and demonstrate a high quality of academic excellence. Challenging, yet rewarding, classes, along with culturally enriching outings, offer Honors students a diverse and unique educational experience.

MAJORS AND DEGREES OFFERED

West Virginia Wesleyan offers four undergraduate degrees: the Bachelor of Arts; the Bachelor of Music Education; the Bachelor of Science; and the Bachelor of Science in Nursing. The most popular programs of study are in the sciences (biology, physics / engineering, pre-professional studies, etc.); education; business; athletic training; and nursing. Wesleyan also offers a number of master's degree programs.

TUITION, ROOM, BOARD, FEES

The 2017–2018 total direct costs at Wesleyan are $29,574 for tuition, $8,436 for standard room and board, and $1,178 for student fees, which includes a student activity fee, facilities fee, and a technology fee. These costs do not include books, travel, clothing, the laptop computer, medical insurance, or other personal expenses. Wesleyan offers an interest-free monthly payment plan during the academic year.

FINANCIAL AID

The College offers financial aid on the basis of a variety of criteria: scholastic achievements, special talents and abilities, and financial need. A number of scholarships are available including awards for academics, athletics, performing arts, leadership, community service, and visual arts. Student employment is available in most areas of the College community, financed through a blend of institutional and federal funds. Students may apply for low-cost federal loans. All students should file the Free Application for Federal Student Aid. Currently, more than 95 percent of all students receive grants or scholarships from Wesleyan.

STUDENT ORGANIZATIONS AND ACTIVITIES

Wesleyan has a balanced and diverse student life program that includes more than 70 campus organizations. Included among these are a campus radio station, newspaper, student government, departmental clubs, national fraternities and sororities, and religious organizations. Over 84 percent of Wesleyan students of those reporting in the NSSE survey participate in community service activities that include the complete administration of a youth basketball program to Special Olympics, to tutoring, mentoring, and educational activities to senior citizens programs to more global programs such as hurricane relief and international service trips.

Wesleyan features 21 varsity programs in NCAA Division II. Wesleyan competes in the Mountain East Conference. Our newest sports include Women's Lacrosse and Women's Acrobatics and Tumbling.

While Wesleyan is affiliated with The United Methodist Church, students of all faiths are welcome and active. The College holds an optional weekly ecumenical worship service every Tuesday morning and a Catholic Mass each Saturday evening.

ADMISSIONS PROCESS

Students are selected by the Office of Admission on the basis of ability, interests, academic preparation, character, and promise, as indicated by their own statements on the application, as well as by high school or college records, recommendations, and standardized test results. Open without discrimination to all qualified students, the College reserves the right to refuse to admit any applicant who, because of low scholarship or citizenship record, is deemed by the Admission and Academic Standing Council to be unlikely to succeed within the standards the College seeks to maintain.

Persons wishing to be admitted directly from high school should present an application for admission with $35 fee (waived for online applications); a transcript of record from an accredited high school; and a record of either SAT or ACT scores. Applicants from non-accredited high schools or completing General Educational Development may be considered for admission if satisfactory ability and achievement are demonstrated. Students are encouraged to apply for free online (www.wvwc.edu) or via the Common Application (www.commonapp.org). Neither of these applications require a fee.

Persons seeking to transfer from another accredited college or university may be admitted to advanced standing upon presentation of an application for admission; an official transcript showing all credits attempted at all post-secondary institutions previously attended; a high school transcript certifying graduation and showing courses pursued and grades earned and, if the cumulative grade point average is less than 2.5, either SAT I or ACT scores. Wesleyan will accept transfer credit courses compatible with its academic program. Grades and hours so earned shall count toward graduation. The College accepts no more than 60 semester hours of credit from a junior or community college.

Students who transfer to Wesleyan with an associate degree from a regionally accredited community or junior college may be admitted with the degree credited as fulfilling Wesleyan's general studies requirements when the total educational background, including high school record, shows compatibility with Wesleyan's general studies requirements. Deficiencies in general studies requirements, as determined by the Admission and Academic Standing Council, must be satisfied after enrollment at Wesleyan.

Wesleyan participates in the Advanced Placement Program of the College Entrance Examination Board and the International Baccalaureate Diploma Program. Students who have successfully completed AP or IB programs should contact the Office of Admission for credit transfer policies.

WESTERN STATE COLORADO UNIVERSITY

AT A GLANCE

Deep in the heart of the Rocky Mountains, Western State Colorado University delivers a full liberal arts curriculum to 2,900 undergraduate and graduate students at an affordable cost. The university's tight-knit community ensures students receive personalized attention and gain real-world experience before graduation. Set in the unique Gunnison Valley, Western offers students endless opportunities for adventure and hands-on learning, both inside and outside the classroom.

LOCATION AND ENVIRONMENT

Western is located in Gunnison, Colorado, a small town right in the Rocky Mountains. The campus is modern and intimate, surrounded by a vast landscape of mountains, streams and trails. Gunnison is just 30 miles from Crested Butte Mountain Resort and a 3.5-hour drive from Denver. Gunnison was named one of Outside Magazine's 16 Best Places to Live in the U.S. in 2016—due in no small part to a yearly average of 300 days of sunshine.

CAMPUS FACILITIES & EQUIPMENT

Western has state-of-the art facilities and equipment across all campus domains.

Notably, the Geology Department partners with software companies to use industry-standard technology in class and for independent projects. The High Altitude Exercise Physiology Lab enables Gunnison's rarefied air (7,700' elevation) to be used for research few other institutions can conduct. Kelly Hall houses biofeedback equipment that enables tremendous depth of research for psychology students. Within the newly renovated Quigley Hall, fully-equipped art studios and classrooms are each dedicated to a specific discipline, and music students have access to a recording studio, expansive rehearsal rooms and the Kincaid Concert Hall. With four additional theaters throughout campus, performing artists of all kinds have a platform to suit their needs.

The Leslie J. Savage Library offers modern study spaces for individual and collaborative work as well as a quiet study area in the historic West Wing. Beyond the library, students and community members can access the brand-new ICELab, a collaborative workspace dedicated to helping entrepreneurs. The lower level of the ICELab features a gourmet café and bar—a great place to host meetings, fill up or unwind.

The 65,000 square foot Mountaineer Field House has the space and facilities for NCAA athletes and the greater campus community to train, compete and play. Featuring a 200-meter indoor track, in-ground trampoline, foam pit and a 44-foot climbing wall, there is ample room to promote wellness.

OFF-CAMPUS OPPORTUNITIES

Western students embrace the vibrant culture of Gunnison and nearby Crested Butte. With local shops, art galleries, farmers markets and festivals, there are a multitude of opportunities for students to get involved with community members and organizations. Merely minutes beyond the streets of town, students can immerse themselves in the expansive mountain landscape of the West Elk and Elk Mountains, whether it be for a lab, research or recreation. With more than 400 miles of trail, countless mountain lakes, rivers and seas of sagebrush, there is an abundance of space for students to stretch their minds and legs.

ACADEMIC PROGRAMS

Western's academic programs promote intellectual maturity and personal growth in students, who graduate as citizens prepared to assume constructive roles in local, national and global communities. The University provides students with a solid foundation of skills in written and spoken communication, problem solving, critical thinking and creativity. Programs encourage a breadth and depth of knowledge, which serve as a foundation for a professional career or graduate study, and develop an appreciation of values appropriate to a liberally educated individual.

MAJORS AND DEGREES OFFERED

Undergraduate Programs

Bachelor of Arts

Accounting
• Financial Analysis
• Professional

Anthropology
Art
• Art History & Theory
• Graphic Design
• Studio Art
• K–12 Education
Business Administration
• Latin American Business
• Finance
• Management
• Marketing
• Resort Management
• Innovation + Creativity + Entrepreneurship
• Energy Management
Communication Arts
• Communication
• Film Studies
• Theatre & Performance Studies
• Strategic Communication
Economics
• Secondary Licensure
English
• Creative Licensure
• Secondary Licensure
Elementary Education
• Culturally & Linguistically Diverse Education
Environment & Sustainability
• Individualized Contract
• Water Studies
• Environmental Management^
Environmental Science (minor)
Geography and Geospatial Analysis (minor)
History
• Secondary Licensure
• Public History
Latin American Studies (minor)
Music
• Music (comprehensive)
• Music Business
• Music Technology (minor)
• K-12 Music Education
Philosophy (minor)
Physics (minor)
Politics & Government
• Pre-Law
• Global Studies
• Secondary Licensure
• Environmental Management^
Psychology
• Clinical, Counseling & School Psych
• Experimental
Recreation & Outdoor Education
• Outdoor Environmental Education^
• Outdoor Leadership
• Outdoor Education
• Recreation
Sociology
• Criminal Justice
• Environmental Management^
Spanish
• K-12 Education Licensure

Bachelor of Fine Arts

Art

- Painting
- Printmaking
- Photography
- Ceramics
- Sculpture
- Jewelry
- Graphic Design

Bachelor of Science

Biology
- Secondary Licensure
- Ecology/Environmental Management^
- Environmental Biology & Ecology
- General Biology
- Wildlife and Conservation
- Pre-Nursing
- Pre-Med/Cell & Molecular

Chemistry
- Biochemistry
- General Chemistry
- Secondary Licensure

Computer Science
- Computer Science (comprehensive)
- Information Security

Exercise & Sport Science
- Clinical Exercise Physiology^
- Exercise & Sport Science
- Exercise Science (Clinical or Health Fitness)
- Sport & Fitness Management
- Sport Psychology (minor)
- K-12 Physical Education

Geology
- Environmental Geology
- Geology
- Geoarchaeology
- Petroleum Geology
- Secondary Earth-Space Licensure

Mathematics
- Secondary Licensure
- Actuarial Science
- Data Analytics (minor)

^ For students planning to enroll in the corresponding 3+2 program only.

TUITION, ROOM, BOARD, FEES
2018–2019

	In-State	Out-of-State
Tuition		
	$6,624°	$18,096
Double Room	$5,030	$5,030
Board (15 meals/week)	$4,605	$4,605
Required Fees	$3,490.15	$3,490.15
Student Recreation Fee (optional)	$200	$200
Renewable Energy Fee (optional)	$30	$30
Scholarly Activity Fee (optional)	$20	$20
Total Annual Cost	$19.999.15	$31,471.15

°reflects that the College Opportunity Fund (COF) has been applied. Students can register for the COF at www.collegeincolorado.org.

FINANCIAL AID
Students are automatically considered for merit scholarships and discount programs. They are awarded whichever saves them more money.

Discount Programs
Under the Western Undergraduate Exchange (WUE) & Central Plains (CP) Programs, students from certain states pay just 150 percent of Western's total in-state tuition.

Students from neighboring states who demonstrate financial need are considered for an extra $1000 per year grant, totaling $4000 over four years.

Neighboring states: Wyoming, Utah, Arizona, New Mexico, Oklahoma, Kansas and Nebraska

WUE states: Alaska, Hawaii, Washington, Oregon, California, Nevada, Arizona, New Mexico, Utah, Wyoming, Idaho, Montana, North Dakota and South Dakota.

CP states: Minnesota, Iowa, Nebraska, Kansas, Oklahoma, Texas, Missouri, Illinois, Wisconsin, Michigan and Indiana.

Merit Scholarships
All merit scholarships are awarded upon acceptance. Freshmen may receive them for up to four years and transfer students may receive them for up to three years. Amounts awarded are determined by high school GPA and standardized test scores.

Early Action Discount°
If you are merit-aid eligible and are accepted for Fall 2019 by November 1, 2018, you will receive a $500 increase to your merit scholarship.

Additional Aid
Western also offers a multitude of program-specific scholarships,° work-study positions, grants and aid. For more information visit www.western.edu/aid.

°These scholarships are subject to Western's scholarship policy, rules and regulations.

ADMISSIONS PROCESS
Western carefully considers each application with the goal of adding dimension to a diverse and challenging community of scholars. The strongest applications are not always those with the greatest number of accomplishments, but those that resonate with authenticity and passion.

First-Time Freshman

1. Complete and submit Western's Online Application or the Common Application

2. Send your official high school transcript to Western

3. Send your official ACT and/or SAT test scores to Western

Submit the $30 application fee°

Western accepts Advanced Placement (AP), International Baccalaureate (IB), College Level Examination Program (CLEP) and concurrent/dual enrollment credits.

Transfer Students

1. Complete and Submit Western's online Application

2. Send all official college transcripts to Western

3. If you have less than 24 credit hours complete at the time of application, you must send your official high school transcript and your official ACT and/or SAT test scores to Western. Dual enrollment, concurrent enrollment and AP/IB credits taken during high school are not counted in the credit hour total.

4. Submit the $30 application fee°

°Access is central to Western. We accept fee waivers from the ACT, SAT and counselor statements as acceptable.

Application Deadlines Western is on a rolling admissions cycle. Applications are accepted throughout the year until a class is full. Typically, candidates will receive an admissions decision 2–3 weeks after receipt of all application materials.

Western recommends students apply before March 1st for the following fall semester for maximum scholarship consideration.

WORCESTER POLYTECHNIC INSTITUTE

AT A GLANCE

Here, you don't just learn—you do. Everything about WPI is designed to stimulate your curiosity, challenge you, and support you so that you can imagine anything and innovate everything.

Worcester Polytechnic Institute (WPI) is a nationally renowned, private research university college focused on science, technology, engineering, and math. WPI's founding motto of "Theory and Practice" provides a distinctive approach to education by balancing rigorous academics with hands-on learning. At WPI, students go above and beyond traditional classroom education.

WPI's unique project-based education converts classroom concepts into real-world impact. The WPI Plan (wpi.edu/wpi-plan) will set you apart in the world first as a student, then as a sought-after young professional, and ultimately across your career and life.

All WPI students complete two projects that allow them to tackle issues they feel passionate about and make a lasting difference on the world around us from improving access to clean water in rural communities to developing robots for underwater research. Through the Plan, you learn how to learn by applying your classroom experiences to projects that challenge you from a proficiency, social, and global perspective.

WPI was recently ranked No. 1 by the Wall Street Journal for "The Top Faculties; Schools that do the Best in Combining Scholarly Research with Classroom Instruction" and consistently receives high rankings as one of America's Best Colleges, according to the U.S. News & World Report. The university has earned praise and attention for its project-based curriculum, small class sizes, robust career services, study-abroad opportunities, return on investment, and ability to create futures. Find out more at wpi.edu/+formula.

LOCATION AND ENVIRONMENT

Founded in 1865, WPI's 95-acre campus is located in a residential area of Worcester (Wus-tah), Massachusetts, the second largest city in New England behind only Boston. With its beautiful architecture and green spaces, WPI has a classic New England feel. Ranked ninth on Forbes' "America's Most Livable Cities," the up-and-coming city offers the charm and ease of a college town with the convenience of urban living.

Worcester boasts over 38,000 college students attending nine universities. Along with a robust college population, Worcester offers world-class restaurants, cultural sights, concerts and sporting events, beautiful parks and affordable cost of living. The city also has easy access for area transportation to regional amenities such as skiing and hiking, plus quick travel to Boston, Cape Cod, and New York City.

CAMPUS FACILITIES & EQUIPMENT

With all of the amazing things WPI students and faculty do, our outstanding facilities should come as no surprise.

The new Foisie Innovation Studio serves as a hub for WPI's project-based curriculum. The 78,000-square-foot facility provides students with the physical space in which to immerse themselves in WPI's distinctive brand of learning. There are a variety of academic spaces ranging from high-tech classrooms to an innovation and entrepreneurship center and a global impact lab that will support the "hands-on" aspect of the WPI curriculum.

Our 125,000-square-foot WPI Life Sciences and Bioengineering Center at Gateway Park is a state-of-the-art research center housing faculty from four departments. The Fire Science Laboratory enables students and faculty to evaluate fire safety measures in actual fire simulations. Laser holography labs, computer music labs, medical imaging labs, a bioprocess lab—they're all here, and lots more.

WPI's Sports and Recreation Center is one of the greenest in the nation and includes a four-court gymnasium, indoor jogging track, 14,000 sq. ft. of fitness space, racquetball and squash courts, competition pool, workout studios, and rowing tanks.

ACADEMICS

WPI's academic program is built to be flexible. Students take the equivalent of three courses (as courses or project work) during each of four 7-week terms (two in the fall and two in the spring). As part of the WPI Plan, you have the freedom and the responsibility to choose the courses and experiences that best suit your goals and interests.

In addition, WPI does not have failing grades, in order for the focus to be on learning, teamwork, and collaboration, not on competing. You earn A, B, C, or NR (No Record). This unique grading system encourages you to branch out, experiment, and cross disciplines-that's where amazing things happen at WPI, and ultimately, in your career.

Ranked No. 1 as the best study abroad program by Princeton Review in 2016 and referred to as "life changing," the majority of WPI students travel to more than 40 off-campus locations, and every student receives a one-time scholarship of $5,000 towards the experience. Students make a difference to communities and organizations around the globe by bringing ingenious approaches to an astounding array of societal and technological challenges. Past projects have included the creation of an ambulance dispatch system for the city of Venice and improvements on earthquake mitigation and recovery efforts in Taipei.

MAJORS AND DEGREES OFFERED

WPI offers over 50 areas of study in engineering, science, management, and the liberal arts leading to the Bachelor of Science (B.S.) or Bachelor of Arts (B.A.) degree. Exciting interdisciplinary programs, driven by real-world demand, include interactive media and game development, environmental engineering, architectural engineering, and the nation's first undergraduate program in robotics engineering.

WPI offers pre-professional programs (law, medicine, dentistry, and veterinary) and a four and five-year BS/MS program. You can even create your own major or minor program and go out on co-op. A comprehensive academic advising program and a wide array of academic support services help students make the right choices and reach their goals.

TUITION, ROOM, BOARD, FEES

A great education costs a lot of money—so you should make sure to attend a university that delivers the return on your investment. WPI graduates have 32 percent higher starting salaries than the national average, and graduates are able to move quickly up the ranks to positions of influence as a result of WPI's real-world training.

Top-tier employers seek out WPI graduates for their real-world experience and ability to work collaboratively. With more than 92 percent of graduates in jobs or attending graduate school within several months of graduation, students are recruited by leading organizations such as Pfizer, General Electric, Fidelity Investments, Tesla, and Google. Each year, WPI graduates are accepted at many prestigious graduate schools, including MIT, Yale University, Princeton University, Johns Hopkins University and Tufts University Medical School.

FINANCIAL AID

All admitted applicants are considered for merit-based scholarships based upon academic performance, leadership, extracurricular involvement and community service—and there is no separate application required.

Students can also indicate they wish to be considered for need-based aid. Around 97 percent of WPI students receive merit or need-based aid to attend the university, not including federal aid. Most applicants will receive a financial aid package within two weeks of their acceptance.

Students are required to file the FAFSA and CSS Profile no later than February 1. It is best to file on or near the application deadline. By filing early, you will receive notification of your aid much sooner, allowing you to make informed decisions.

WPI boasts a 98.1 percent loan repayment rate, far above the national average of 88.7 percent—showing that WPI graduates earn strong salaries and are able to pay off their loans and live the life they want.

STUDENT ORGANIZATIONS AND ACTIVITIES

The WPI community is welcoming, close-knit, with a robust support system ready to help academically, emotionally, physically, and culturally. The university prioritizes inclusiveness and acceptance.

The student community of innovators and explorers that thrive here make their own decisions and set their own course, want to be leaders and not followers, are eager to tackle the issues that will make the world a better place, work in teams to get things done and love math and science but feel just as passionate about other subjects.

There's lots to do here at WPI and in the surrounding Worcester area to complement the skills you gain from the classroom with many different academic, professional, social, and athletic organizations. You can volunteer your time at a number of local nonprofit organizations, join a fraternity or sorority, offer your talents to over 200 student life groups, such as an a cappella group or theatre production, or channel your inner Saturday Night Live performer and participate in a sketch comedy group, and that's just the beginning.

Twenty varsity sports, and 44 club sports and intramural teams are sponsored by WPI, supporting a wide range of athletic interests and abilities. In addition, WPI's Sports & Recreation Center, opened in 2013, is one of the finest higher education athletic facilities in the Northeast, as well as one of the greenest sports centers in the nation.

ADMISSIONS PROCESS

WPI is a member of the Common Application, the exclusive method by which to apply to WPI. A $65 application fee is required for all applicants. (WPI endorses the fee waiver policy of the College Board, as well as accepts fee waivers from guidance or college counselors.) Seniors in high school should interview before December 15th of their senior year. Interviews are optional but are highly encouraged.

The regular decision deadline is Feb. 1, while the two early-action deadlines are Nov. 1 and Jan. 1, respectively. The deadline for transfer students to apply for fall admission is Apr. 15 on a rolling notification.

WPI is test-optional; SAT/ACT scores are accepted, but not required, and official scores do not need to be sent until deciding to enroll. Academic requirements include four years of math (including pre-calculus), four years of English, and two years of lab science.

Other requirements include:

- High school transcript including most recent senior grades
- Teacher recommendation (preferably in math or science)
- Guidance counselor recommendation
- Personal essay
- TOEFL, IELTS, or Pearson's Test of English (PTE) scores for international students whose first language is not English

INDEXES

ALPHABETICAL INDEX

The Princeton Review's Complete Book of Colleges

O

P

Q

R

INDEX BY LOCATION

University of San Francisco	773, 1070
University of Southern California	780
Westmont College	856
Whittier College	860
Woodbury University	873

COLORADO

Adams State College	11
Colorado Christian University	168
Colorado College	169
Colorado School of Mines	169
Colorado State University	170
Colorado State University—Pueblo	171
Colorado Technical University	172
Fort Lewis College	248
Johnson and Wales University—Denver	327
Jones International University	329
Naropa University	444
Regis University	526, 1008
Rocky Mountain College of Art + Design	540
United States Air Force Academy	667
University of Colorado at Colorado Springs	692
University of Colorado at Denver	693
University of Colorado—Boulder	694
University of Denver	698
University of Northern Colorado	754
Western State Colorado University	851, 1090

CONNECTICUT

Albertus Magnus College	17
Central Connecticut State University	127, 912
Charter Oak State College	133
Connecticut College	182
Eastern Connecticut State University	215
Fairfield University	233
Lyme Academy College of Fine Arts	378
Mitchell College	424
Quinnipiac University	521, 1002
Sacred Heart University	547, 1014
Southern Connecticut State University	590
Trinity College (CT)	658
United States Coast Guard Academy	668
University of Bridgeport	679
University of Connecticut	695
University of Hartford	703
University of New Haven	745, 1064
University of Saint Joseph	770, 1068
Wesleyan University	841
Western Connecticut State University	847
Yale University	877

DELAWARE

| University of Delaware | 697, 1058 |
| Wilmington College (DE) | 867 |

DISTRICT OF COLUMBIA

American University	25
Catholic University of America	122
Corcoran College of Art and Design	185
Gallaudet University	256
George Washington University	260, 938
Georgetown University	261
Howard University	302

FLORIDA

Baptist College of Florida	53
Barry University	55
Beacon College	59
Clearwater Christian College	150
Eckerd College	219
Embry-Riddle Aeronautical University (FL)	224, 930
Embry Riddle Aeronautical University—Worldwide	226
Flagler College	239
Florida A&M University	240
Florida Atlantic University	241
Florida College	241
Florida Gulf Coast University	242
Florida Institute of Technology	242
Florida International University	243
Florida Southern College	244, 936
Florida State University	245
Full Sail University	255
International College	318
Jacksonville University	322
Johnson & Wales University at North Miami	327
Lynn University	379
New College of Florida	448
Northwood University, Florida Campus	468
Nova Southeastern University	471
Palm Beach Atlantic University	492
Ringling School of Art & Design	532
Rollins College	541
Saint Leo University	552
Southeastern University	589
St. Thomas University	614
Stetson University	633
Trinity College of Florida	659
University of Central Florida	688, 1056
University of Florida	701
University of Miami	729

University of North Florida	753
University of South Florida	779
University of South Florida—St. Petersburg	780
University of Tampa	784, 1072
University of West Florida	799
Webber International University	837

GEORGIA

Agnes Scott College	13
Albany State University	16
The Art Institute of Atlanta	39
Augusta University	45
Berry College	69, 900
Brenau University	84
Clark Atlanta University	146
Clayton College & State University	149
Columbus State University	177
Covenant College	188
Emory University	228
Georgia College & State University	262
Georgia Institute of Technology	263
Georgia Southern University	264
Georgia Southwestern State University	264
Georgia State University	265
Kennesaw State University	335
LaGrange College	346
Life University	361
Mercer University	404
Morehouse College	432
North Georgia College and State University	458
Oglethorpe University	474
Piedmont College	506
Point University	510
Reinhardt College	527
Savannah College of Art and Design	568
Shorter College	578
Spelman College	599
Toccoa Falls College	654
University of Georgia	701
University of West Georgia	799
Valdosta State University	813
Wesleyan College	841

HAWAII

Brigham Young University—Hawaii	88
Chaminade University of Honolulu	131
Hawai'i Pacific University	289
University of Hawaii at Hilo	704
University of Hawaii—Manoa	705
University of Hawaii—West Oahu	705

IDAHO

ILLINOIS

INDIANA

IOWA

KANSAS

Southern Utah University	595
University of Utah	794
Utah State University	811
Weber State University	838
Westminster College of Salt Lake City	855

VERMONT

Bennington College	66
Burlington College	94
Castleton State College	121
Champlain College	132
College of St. Joseph in Vermont	166
Goddard College	267
Green Mountain College	275
Johnson State College	329
Landmark College	351
Marlboro College	388, 978
Middlebury College	413
Norwich University	469
Saint Michael's College	557, 1022
Sterling College (VT)	632
University of Vermont	794, 1076
Vermont Technical College	817

VIRGINIA

Averett University	48
Bridgewater College	86
Christendom College	135
Christopher Newport University	136, 914
College of William and Mary	167
Emory and Henry College	228
George Mason University	259
Hampden-Sydney College	281
Hampton University	282
Hollins University	298
James Madison University	322
Liberty University	361
Longwood University	369
Mary Baldwin College	390
Marymount University	393
Old Dominion University	483
Patrick Henry College	493
Radford University	521
Randolph College	523
Randolph-Macon College	524
Regent University	525
Roanoke College	534
Shenandoah University	576
Sweet Briar College	638
University of Lynchburg	718
University of Mary Washington	723
University of Richmond	767

University of Virginia	795
University of Virginia's College at Wise	796
Virginia Commonwealth University	819
Virginia Military Institute	819
Virginia State University	820
Virginia Tech	820
Virginia Wesleyan College	821
Washington and Lee University	830

WASHINGTON

Bastyr University	57
Central Washington University	129
Cornish College of the Arts	187
DigiPen Institute of Technology	201, 926
Eastern Washington University	219
Evergreen State College	232
Gonzaga University	268, 942
Pacific Lutheran University	489
Saint Martin's University	553
Seattle Pacific University	571
Seattle University	572, 1028
Trinity Lutheran College	660
University of Puget Sound	765
University of Washington	797
University of Washington—Bothell	797
University of Washington—Tacoma	798
Walla Walla University	825
Washington State University	832
Western Washington University	852
Whitman College	859
Whitworth University	860

WEST VIRGINIA

Alderson-Broaddus College	19
American Military University	25
American Public University System	25
Bethany College (WV)	70, 902
Concord University	178
Fairmont State University, including Pierpont Community & Technical College	235
Marshall University	389
Shepherd University	577
University of Charleston	690
West Virginia State University	844
West Virginia University	844
West Virginia University Institute of Technology	845
West Virginia Wesleyan College	846, 1088
Wheeling Jesuit University	858

WISCONSIN

Alverno College	23
Beloit College	63, 896
Carroll University (WI)	117
Carthage College	119
Concordia University Wisconsin	182
Edgewood College	220
Lawrence University	353
Marian University	386
Marquette University	389
Milwaukee School of Engineering	417
Mount Mary University	436
Northland College	464
Ripon College	533, 1010
St. Norbert College	612, 1042
University of Wisconsin—Eau Claire	801
University of Wisconsin—Green Bay	801
University of Wisconsin—La Crosse	802
University of Wisconsin—Madison	803
University of Wisconsin—Milwaukee	803
University of Wisconsin—Oshkosh	804
University of Wisconsin—Platteville	805
University of Wisconsin—River Falls	805
University of Wisconsin—Stevens Point	806
University of Wisconsin—Stout	807
University of Wisconsin—Superior	807
University of Wisconsin—Whitewater	808
Viterbo University	822
Wisconsin Lutheran College	871

\WYOMING

| Central Wyoming College | 130 |
| University of Wyoming | 809 |

INTERNATIONAL

INDEX BY SIZE

1,000 — 2,000 STUDENTS

Index by Size

Polytechnic Institute of New York University—Brooklyn	510	
Pomona College	512	
Queens University of Charlotte	519	
Quincy University	520	
Randolph-Macon College	524	
Reed College	524, 1006	
Regis College	526	
Rhodes College	529	
Ringling School of Art & Design	532	
Rivier College	533	
Roanoke College	534	
Roberts Wesleyan College	536	
Rockhurst University	539	
Rocky Mountain College of Art + Design	540	
Rollins College	541	
Saint Francis University (PA)	549, 1018	
Saint Martin's University	553	
Saint Mary-of-the-Woods College	554	
Saint Mary's College (IN)	555	
Saint Mary's University of Minnesota	556	
Saint Michael's College	557, 1022	
Saint Vincent College	558	
Sarah Lawrence College	567	
Schreiner University	570	
Scripps College	571	
Seton Hill University	573	
Sewanee—The University of the South	574	
Shaw University	575	
Shepherd University	577	
Shorter College	578	
Simmons College	581	
Southern New Hampshire University	593	
Southern Wesleyan University	596	
Southwestern College (KS)	598	
Southwestern University	598, 1036	
Spring Hill College	600	
St. Anselm College	602, 1016	
St. Bonaventure University	603	
St. Mary's College of Maryland	610	
St. Thomas Aquinas College	613	
St. Thomas University	614	
State University of New York— College of Environmental Science and Forestry	621, 1044	
State University of New York— Institute of Technology at Utica/Rome	624	
State University of New York— Maritime College	625	
Swarthmore College	638, 1046	
Taylor University	641	
Texas A&M University—Texarkana	646	
Texas Lutheran University	647	
Thiel College	650	
Thomas More College	652	
Trine University	656	

Trinity Christian College	657
Tusculum College	664
Union Institute & University	666
University of Advancing Technology (UAT)	671
University of the Arts	678
University of Charleston	690
University of Dallas	695
University of Dubuque	699
University of Hawaii—West Oahu	705
University of King's College	715
University of Lynchburg	718
University of Maine at Farmington	720
University of Maine—Fort Kent	721
University of Minnesota, Crookston	732
University of Minnesota, Morris	733
University of Mobile	738
The University of Montana—Western	739
University of Pikeville	761
University of Pittsburgh at Bradford	761, 1066
University of Pittsburgh at Greensburg	762
University of Rio Grande	768
The University of Saint Francis (IN)	769
University of South Carolina—Beaufort	777
University of St. Francis	783
University of St. Thomas	784
University of Virginia's College at Wise	796
Ursinus College	810
Vaughn College of Aeronautics and Technology	816
Vermont Technical College	817
Virginia Military Institute	819
Virginia Wesleyan College	821
Viterbo University	822
Wagner College	824
Walla Walla University	825
Wartburg College	828
Washington & Jefferson College	829
Washington and Lee University	830
Washington College	831, 1082
Waynesburg University	836
Western State Colorado University	851, 1090
Westminster College (PA)	854
Westmont College	856
West Virginia Wesleyan College	846, 1088
Wheaton College (MA)	857
Whitman College	859
Whittier College	860
Willamette University	863
William Peace University	865
William Penn University	866
Wilmington College (OH)	868
Wittenberg University	871
Wofford College	872
Woodbury University	873

2,000 — 5,000 STUDENTS

Abilene Christian University	10
Acadia University	11
Adams State College	11
Alabama A&M University	14
Albany State University	16
Alcorn State University	19
Anderson University (SC)	28
Arcadia University	33
Arizona State University at the West campus	35
Arizona State University Polytechnic campus	35
The Art Institute of Atlanta	39
Ashland University	40
Auburn University Montgomery	43
Augsburg College	44
Augustana College (IL)	44
Aurora University	46
Babson College	50, 888
Baldwin Wallace University	51
Barnard College	55, 890
Barry University	55
Belhaven College	60
Bellarmine University	61
Bemidji State University	63
Benedict College	64
Benedictine University	65
Bentley University	67, 898
Berkeley College	68
Berklee College of Music	69
Bethel University (MN)	72
Biola University	73
Bob Jones University	78
Bradley University	82
Brandeis University	83
Brigham Young University—Hawaii	88
Bryant University	91, 906
Bucknell University	93, 908
Butler University	95
California Lutheran University	100
Calvin College	111
Campbell University	112
Campbellsville University	113
Canisius College	113
Capital University	114
Carleton College	115
Carthage College	119
Catholic University of America	122
Cedarville University	124
Central Ohio Technical College	128
Champlain College	132
Christopher Newport University	136, 914
The Citadel, The Military College of South Carolina	137
Clark Atlanta University	146

Robert Morris University (IL)	536
Roger Williams University	540
Roosevelt University	542
Rose-Hulman Institute of Technology	542
Saint Leo University	552
Saint Mary's College (CA)	555
Saint Peter's University	558
Saint Xavier University	559
Salve Regina University	561
Samford University	563
School of the Art Institute of Chicago	568
School of Visual Arts	569, 1026
Seattle Pacific University	571
Seattle University	572, 1028
Shawnee State University	575
Shenandoah University	576
Siena College	579
Siena Heights University	580
Skidmore College	582, 1032
Smith College	583
South Dakota School of Mines & Technology	585
Southeastern Oklahoma State University	588
Southeastern University	589
Southern Adventist University	589
Southern Maine Community College	592
Southern Oregon University	594
Southwest Baptist University	596
Spelman College	599
Spring Arbor University	600
St. Ambrose University	601
St. Catherine University	604
St. Edward's University	605
St. John Fisher College	605
St. Joseph's College, New York (Patchogue)	609, 1038
St. Lawrence University	609, 1040
St. Mary's University	611
St. Norbert College	612, 1042
St. Olaf College	613
St. Thomas University	614
State University of New York— Alfred State College	618
State University of New York— Cobleskill	619
State University of New York— The College at Old Westbury	620
State University of New York—Fredonia	623
State University of New York—Potsdam	627
State University of New York— Purchase College	628
Stetson University	633
Stevens Institute of Technology	633
Stevenson University	634
Stonehill College	635
Susquehanna University	637

Tiffin University	653
Trevecca Nazarene University	656
Trinity College (CT)	658
Trinity University	660
Tuskegee University	664
Union College (NY)	666, 1054
Union University	667
United States Air Force Academy	667
United States Military Academy	669
United States Naval Academy	670
Université Laval—Faculté des sciences de l'administration	671
University of Arkansas at Pine Bluff	677
University of Baltimore	678
University of Bridgeport	679
University of Evansville	699
The University of Findlay	700
University of Hartford	703
University of Hawaii at Hilo	704
University of Houston—Clear Lake	707
University of Houston—Victoria	708
University of Illinois at Springfield	710
University of Indianapolis	712
University of La Verne	716
University of Maine—Augusta	721
University of Mary Hardin-Baylor	723
University of Mary Washington	723
University of Montevallo	740
University of Mount Union	741
University of New England	744, 1062
The University of North Carolina at Asheville	747
University of the Pacific	759
University of Pittsburgh at Johnstown	763
University of Portland	764
University of Puget Sound	765
University of Redlands	766
University of Richmond	767
University of the Sciences in Philadelphia	774
University of Scranton	775
University of South Carolina—Aiken	776
University of South Florida— St. Petersburg	780
University of Tulsa	793, 1074
University of Washington—Tacoma	798
University of West Alabama	798
University of Wisconsin—Superior	807
Upper Iowa University	809
Utica College	812
Valparaiso University	813
Vassar College	815
Virginia State University	820
Walsh University	826
Washburn University	829
Wayland Baptist University	834
Wayne State College	834

Webster University	838
Wellesley College	839
Wentworth Institute of Technology	840, 1086
Wesleyan University	841
Western Connecticut State University	847
Western New England University	850
Western Oregon University	850
Westminster College of Salt Lake City	855
West Virginia State University	844
West Virginia University Institute of Technology	845
Wheaton College (IL)	856
Whitworth University	860
Widener University	862
Wilkes University	863
Williams College	867
Wilmington College (DE)	867
Wingate University	869
Winthrop University	870
Worcester Polytechnic Institute	873, 1092
Worcester State University	874
Xavier University of Louisiana	875
Xavier University (OH)	876
Yeshiva University	878
York College of Pennsylvania	879

5,000 — 10,000 STUDENTS

Academy of Art University	10
Adelphi University	12
American University	25
American University in Cairo	26
Angelo State University	29
Arizona State University at the Downtown Phoenix campus	34
Arkansas State University	36, 884
Arkansas Tech University	36
Augusta University	45
Austin Peay State University	48
Azusa Pacific University	49
Belmont University	62, 894
Bloomsburg University of Pennsylvania	76
Boston College	79
Bridgewater State College	87
Brown University	90
California Baptist University	97
California State University, East Bay	103
California State University, Monterey Bay	106
California State University, Stanislaus	109
California University of Pennsylvania	110
Carnegie Mellon University	116
Case Western Reserve University	120
Central Connecticut State University	127, 912
Central Washington University	129

University of San Diego	772
University of San Francisco	773, 1070
The University of South Dakota	778
University of Southern Indiana	781
University of Southern Maine	782
University of Tampa	784, 1072
University of Tennessee at Martin	786
The University of Texas at Tyler	790
University of Washington—Bothell	797
University of West Florida	799
University of Wisconsin—Eau Claire	801
University of Wisconsin—Green Bay	801
University of Wisconsin—La Crosse	802
University of Wisconsin—Platteville	805
University of Wisconsin—River Falls	805
University of Wisconsin—Stevens Point	806
University of Wisconsin—Stout	807
University of Wisconsin—Whitewater	808
University of Wyoming	809
Vanderbilt University	814, 1080
Villanova University	818
Wake Forest University	824
Washington University in St. Louis	833
West Texas A&M University	843
Western Carolina University	846
Western Illinois University	848
Westfield State University	853
William Paterson University	865
Winona State University	869
Yale University	877

10,000 — 15,000 STUDENTS

Baylor University	58
Bowling Green State University	82
California State University, Dominguez Hills	103
California State University, San Marcos	109
City University of New York— Baruch College	138
City University of New York— Brooklyn College	138
City University of New York— City College	139
City University of New York— The College of Staten Island	140
City University of New York— Kingsborough Community College	141
Cleveland State University	151
Cornell University	186
DePaul University	198
East Tennessee State University	214
Eastern Kentucky University	216
Eastern Washington University	219

Embry Riddle Aeronautical University— Worldwide	226
Ferris State University	237
Florida Gulf Coast University	242
Fort Hays State University	247
George Washington University	260, 938
Georgia Institute of Technology	263
Indiana State University	311
Indiana University— Purdue Univ. Fort Wayne	315
Kean University	333
Liberty University	361
Loyola University Chicago	375, 974
Minnesota State University, Mankato	419
Montana State University	427
New Mexico State University	451
North Dakota State University	457
Northern Illinois University	462
Northern Kentucky University	462
Rochester Institute of Technology	537, 1012
Rowan University	544
Savannah College of Art and Design	568
Southeastern Louisiana University	587
Southern Illinois University— Carbondale	591, 1034
Southern Illinois University— Edwardsville	591
St. John's University (NY)	607
State University of New York at Binghamton	616
State University of New York— Empire State College	623
State University of New York— University at Albany	629
Syracuse University	639
Tarleton State University	641
Trinity College Dublin	658
Troy University—Troy (formerly Troy State University)	661, 1050
University of Alabama at Birmingham	672
University of Alaska Anchorage	675
University of Central Oklahoma	690
University of Houston—Downtown	707
University of Louisiana at Lafayette	717
University of Louisville	717
University of Maryland, Baltimore County	724, 1060
University of Massachusetts—Boston	727
University of Massachusetts—Lowell	728
University of Miami	729
University of Nebraska at Omaha	741
University of New Hampshire	744
University of North Carolina at Wilmington	751
University of North Dakota	752
University of North Florida	753

University of Pennsylvania	760
University of Rhode Island	766
University of South Alabama	776
University of Southern Mississippi	782
University of Tennessee at Chattanooga	785
University of Texas at Brownsville	788
University of Vermont	794, 1076
University of West Georgia	799
University of Windsor	800
University of Wisconsin—Oshkosh	804
Valdosta State University	813
West Chester University of Pennsylvania	842
Western Kentucky University	848
Western Washington University	852
Wichita State University	861
Wright State University	875
Youngstown State University	880

15,000 — 25,000 STUDENTS

Appalachian State University	31
Auburn University	42
Ball State University	52
Boise State University	78
Boston University	80, 904
California Polytechnic State University	101
California State Polytechnic University, Pomona	101
California State University, Chico	102
California State University, Fresno	104
California State University, Los Angeles	106
California State University, San Bernardino	108
Central Michigan University	127
City University of New York— Hunter College	140
City University of New York— New York City College of Technology	142
City University of New York— Queens College	143, 1000
Clemson University	150, 916
Colorado State University	170
Drexel University	208
East Carolina University	212
Eastern Michigan University	217
Florida Atlantic University	241
George Mason University	259
Georgia Southern University	264
Grand Valley State University	273
Illinois State University	309
Indiana University— Purdue University Indianapolis	316
James Madison University	322
Kansas State University	332
Kent State University—Kent Campus	336

INDEX BY TUITION

Webster University	838	Defiance College	196	Marian College	385
Wesleyan College	841	Delaware Valley University	197	Marietta College	386
West Virginia Wesleyan College	846, 1088	DePaul University	198	Marist College	387
Westminster College (MO)	854	Doane College	202	Marlboro College	388, 978
Wheeling Jesuit University	858	Dominican University	204	Mary Baldwin College	390
William Peace University	865	Drew University	207	Marywood University	395

Webster University 838
Wesleyan College 841
West Virginia Wesleyan College 846, 1088
Westminster College (MO) 854
Wheeling Jesuit University 858
William Peace University 865
William Penn University 866
Wilmington College (OH) 868
Wilson College 868
Wisconsin Lutheran College 871
Xavier University of Louisiana 875

$30,000-$39,999

Abilene Christian University 10
Adelphi University 12
American International College 23
Antioch College 30
Assumption College 41, 886
Augustana University 46
Austin College 47
Averett University 48
Azusa Pacific University 49
Baldwin Wallace University 51
Becker College 60, 892
Belmont University 62, 894
Berry College 69, 900
Bethel University (MN) 72
Birmingham-Southern College 74
Bradley University 82
Bridgewater College 86
Buena Vista University 94
California Baptist University 97
California Institute of the Arts 98
California Lutheran University 100
Calvin College 111
Capital University 114
Carthage College 119
Catawba College 121
Cazenovia College 123
Cedar Crest College 123
Cedarville University 124
Centenary College of Louisiana 125
Chestnut Hill College 134
Cleveland Institute of Art 151, 918
College of Mount Saint Vincent 160
The College of Saint Rose 164
The College of Saint Scholastica 165
Concordia College (Moorhead—MN) 178
Concordia University, Nebraska 180
Corcoran College of Art and Design 185
Cornish College of the Arts 187
Covenant College 188
Creighton University 189
Curry College 191

Defiance College 196
Delaware Valley University 197
DePaul University 198
Doane College 202
Dominican University 204
Drew University 207
Duquesne University 210
Elmhurst College 222
Elon University 224
Embry-Riddle Aeronautical University (FL) 224, 930
Embry Riddle Aeronautical University—Prescott 225
Emmanuel College 227
Endicott College 230
Fairleigh Dickinson University, College at Florham 234
Fairleigh Dickinson University, Metropolitan Campus 235
Florida Southern College 244, 936
Franklin Pierce College 252
George Fox University 258
Georgetown College 261
Georgian Court University 266, 940
Gordon College 269
Green Mountain College 275
Hamline University 280
Hanover College 283
Hiram College 295
Hollins University 298
Hood College 299
Hope College 300
Houghton College 301
Houston Baptist University 302
Hult International Business School 303
Illinois College 308
Iona College 319
John Carroll University 325
Johnson & Wales University at Charlotte 326
Johnson & Wales University at North Miami 327
Johnson and Wales University—Denver 327
Johnson and Wales University—Providence Campus 328
Lasell College 352
Lawrence Technological University 353, 966
Le Moyne College 354, 968
Lenoir-Rhyne University 357
Lewis University 359
Long Island University—C.W. Post 369
Loras College 370
Loyola University New Orleans 374
Lycoming College 377
Lynn University 379
Manchester University 382
Manhattanville College 384

Marian College 385
Marietta College 386
Marist College 387
Marlboro College 388, 978
Mary Baldwin College 390
Marywood University 395
Massachusetts College of Pharmacy and Health Science 396
Memphis College of Art 403
Mercer University 404
Meredith College 406
Messiah College 408
Milligan College 415
Millikin University 415
Millsaps College 417
Milwaukee School of Engineering 417
Minneapolis College of Art and Design 419
Misericordia University 420
Monmouth College 425
Moore College of Art and Design 430
Mount Ida College 436
Mount Saint Mary College 438
Mount Saint Mary's University 438
Mount St. Mary's University 440
New England College 448
New York School of Interior Design 452
Niagara University 453, 994
Nichols College 455
North Central College 457
Northland College 464
Northwestern College (IA) 466
Norwich University 469
Notre Dame de Namur University 470
Oglethorpe University 474
Ohio Dominican University 475
Ohio Northern University 475
Otis College of Art and Design 486
Palm Beach Atlantic University 492
The Pennsylvania Academy of the Fine Arts 494
Point Loma Nazarene University 509
Presbyterian College 515
Randolph College 523
Regis College 526
Regis University 526, 1008
Richmond, The American International University in London 531
Rider University 531
Rochester Institute of Technology 537, 1012
Rockhurst University 539
Roger Williams University 540
Sacred Heart University 547, 1014
Saint Francis University (PA) 549, 1018
Saint Martin's University 553
Saint Mary's University of Minnesota 556
Salve Regina University 561

Vanderbilt University	814, 1080
Wabash College	823
Wagner College	824
Wartburg College	828
Washington and Lee University	830
Washington College	831, 1082
Webb Institute	836
Whittier College	860
Whitworth University	860
Widener University	862
Willamette University	863
Wofford College	872
Worcester Polytechnic Institute	873, 1092
Yale University	877

OVER $50,000

Amherst College	27
Babson College	50, 888
Bard College	53
Bard College at Simon's Rock	54
Bates College	57
Bennington College	66
Boston College	79
Boston University	80, 904
Bowdoin College	81
Bucknell University	93, 908
Carnegie Mellon University	116
Chapman University	132
Colby College	155
Colgate University	156
Colorado College	169
Columbia University	175
Cornell University	186
Dartmouth College	194
Duke University	210
Emory University	228
Franklin & Marshall College	250
George Washington University	260, 938
Gettysburg College	266
Grinnell College	276
Hamilton College	280
Harvey Mudd College	287
Haverford College	289
Hobart and William Smith Colleges	296
Lafayette College	345
Lehigh University	356
Macalester College	380
Massachusetts Institute of Technology	397
Muhlenberg College	441
Northwestern University	467
Oberlin College	473
Occidental College	473, 998
Pomona College	512
Reed College	524, 1006

Rensselaer Polytechnic Institute	528
Scripps College	571
Stevens Institute of Technology	633
St. John's College (MD)	606
St. John's College (NM)	607
St. Lawrence University	609, 1040
Swarthmore College	638, 1046
Trinity College (CT)	658
Union College (NY)	666, 1054
University of Chicago	691
University of Notre Dame	756
University of Richmond	767
University of Rochester	769
University of Southern California	780
Ursinus College	810
Vassar College	815
Villanova University	818
Wake Forest University	824
Washington University in St. Louis	833
Wheaton College (MA)	857

*To view Index by Selectivity,
visit PrincetonReview.com/guidebooks.